THE HARPER ENCYCLOPEDIA
OF SCIENCE

THE HARPER ENCYCLOPEDIA OF SCIENCE

Edited by JAMES R. NEWMAN

Revised Edition

Managing Editor
JEROME WYCKOFF

Associate Editors
ROGER G. MENGES · EDMUND H. HARVEY, JR.

HARPER & ROW, PUBLISHERS · NEW YORK AND EVANSTON

SIGMA, INC. · WASHINGTON, D. C.

1967

Staff Editors

EDWIN M. RIPIN • PETER R. LIMBURG • BARBARA P. SHERIDAN
ALVIN LUKASHOK • CHARLES SPAIN VERRAL

Editorial Assistants

SARAH WORM • BARBARA VINSON
Judith Kelner • Rhoda Gluck
Winifred Courtney • Poldi Goetz-Wittels • Kathleen Barnes
Sara Hannum • Thomas Wyckoff • Patricia Cole • Lasky Associates

Special Editors

CHESTER JOHNSON • ELVIN ABELES
John Ferrone • Sybil Taylor

Bibliography

REGINALD R. HAWKINS

Design

WILLIAM SAYLES
Joseph Trautwein

Technical Adviser for Illustrations

EDWIN M. RIPIN

Photo Research

JANET CHENERY • KAREN NANGLE
Richard Eiger • Nancy Ford

Production

MARTIN CONNELL

Library of Congress Catalog Card Number: 67-22504

Second Edition

For information address Harper & Row, Publishers, 49 East 33rd Street, New York, N. Y. 10016
Created and Designed by Artists and Writers Press and Sigma, Inc.
Produced by Western Printing and Lithographing Company. Printed in U. S. A.
The text for this book was completely Fotoset by Graphic Services, Inc.

Contents

List of Color Plates

Using This Work

THE ARTICLES in this encyclopedia were prepared according to correlated entry lists covering the various branches of science. The articles are titled concisely, in scientific terms that are likely to be encountered by general readers. Considering the enormous scope of science, the reader will not expect to find here an article on every scientific topic; but after using this work for a time he will acquire a sense of how the material is organized—whether, for example, the topic he is seeking is likely to be found as a long article or a short one, or simply as part of an entry under a different title. If the topic sought is not found as a separate article, a cross reference may be found instead; and if there is no cross reference, the reader may refer to the General Index. The Index should be consulted, as a matter of course, for material that is relatively specialized.

The objective in each article has been a well-rounded, if brief, explanation. Close interdependence between different articles is indicated by the cross references, which are in small capitals and are in the form, or approximately the form, of the titles to which reference is made. The policy has been not to give cross references randomly but rather to send the reader only to articles bearing directly upon the material at hand. More extensive cross-referencing is provided by the General Index.

Only a limited number of abbreviations—those basic in scientific usage, and likely to be familiar to most readers—have been used in the text. All these, with some additional abbreviations considered standard in scientific usage, are listed on page ix.

At the end of each article is a set of initials identifying the author. In an article prepared by more than one author, the part prepared by each carries identifying initials. A complete list of the authors, with initials, begins on page 1275.

The General Index, beginning on page 1299, not only lists all substantial topics covered in the articles but also indicates the relationships between them. Overcomplication has been avoided, and trivial citations have been omitted.

The Bibliography, beginning on page 1282, represents at the same time a graded reading course in science and a list of books and other publications to which the reader can turn for further information on indexed topics. The introduction to the Bibliography explains its use.

—*J. W.*

Editor's Introduction

Felix qui potuit rerum cognoscere causas: Happy is he who has been able to learn the causes of things. Virgil's epigram was made in a happier time, a more innocent time, at any rate, when men supposed that while many causes were not known, yet in due course they could with diligence and ingenuity be found out. Of this we are no longer certain. The physical universe is a queer place—queerer, as it has been said, than we can even suppose. The more we know of it, the more we realize how little we know of it. The solid ground of Nature is a delusion; many of the comfortable, scientific truths we were raised on have been disproved and the rest will assuredly share this fate. Physics and astronomy, once so secure, are now in a marvelous chaos; biology and chemistry have in half a century been almost unrecognizably transformed; there has come into being in a few decades a veritable giant of a science, biochemistry, which promises to decode the intricate ciphers of living processes; and even mathematics has been drastically renovated and will never again be regarded as a temple of eternal verities. A scientific theory, as we now believe, has a major purpose: to be demolished. It can never be proved correct; it is useful to the extent that it suggests experiments which will help to disprove it.

This may be thought a strange introduction to an encyclopedia of science. But it is not my purpose either to discourage or bewilder the reader. Instead I want to impart some notion of the questions and difficulties which confronted those who planned this work and those who executed it. The main question was: In view of the complexity of modern science, is it possible to make an encyclopedia of science which will usefully serve the general reader? That such a work was needed did not admit of doubt. There are any number of primers and popularizations which deal with the several sciences; there are many excellent monographs and texts, of intermediate difficulty, which meet the requirements of the specialist reading outside his field. But a single reference work which covers the physical sciences as well as mathematics, logic, the history and philosophy of science, and the lives of the leading scientists is not available. This was the task we set ourselves.

What we had in mind was a compendium of moderate length, which would cover the whole field of science—the major facts and theories—from astronomy to zoology. What is radiation? What is metal fatigue? Why does a gas expand? How do animals communicate? When was the Jurassic Period? What is entropy? Is the North Pole shifting? What are the main principles of computers? Must all living organisms die? How do birds navigate? What is DNA? What is the principle of the transistor? Who wrote the first book on mathematics? What is the greenhouse effect? How does photosynthesis work? What is relativity? What is a standing wave? What is the parallel postulate? What is the twin paradox? How does a heat pump work? How are tunnels built? What are the different kinds of particle accelerators? What is animal camouflage? Is there life on Mars? What are supernovas? What did Gödel prove? What has modern physics done to the principle of causality? What is induction? What is information theory? How does a diesel engine work? What keeps a satellite up? How does a lightning rod work? What purpose is served by the hormones? What is the citric acid cycle? What is the principle of the spectroscope? Does light consist of waves or particles? What is electromagnetic theory? What are the principal minerals? Who has won the Nobel prizes since they were first given, and for what accomplishments in research? What is valence? What is parity? What are the principal scientific institutions and associations of the world? What are the major scientific works published since antiquity? What is standard deviation? What is the Doppler effect? What are Fourier series?

These are among the many thousands of questions—some sophisticated, some naive, some easily answered, some almost impossible to break down to an elementary level, some of the widest possible interest to persons of ordinary curiosity, some of concern only to the serious student or specialist—which the HARPER ENCYCLOPEDIA attempts to answer.

An encyclopedia, almost like an anthology, is a work of compromise, selection, preference, and taste. There are bound to be space limitations no matter how large the project. Centuries ago the Chinese compiled general encyclopedias running to a thousand or more volumes. The largest of modern encyclopedias may run to 50 or 60 volumes. A like number of volumes have been devoted to an encyclopedia which deals with a single subject, physics. But no one supposes that any of these compendia are, or were, in a true sense complete. The editors of this present work have of course labored under severe restrictions as to scope, as to depth and detail of treatment. Yet these, as we soon came to realize, could be as much an intellectual challenge as an editor's headache. We have been guided by one overriding principle: to answer questions well rather than to answer as many questions as possible. We have favored longish integrated articles rather than multitudinous dictionary entries; we have laid emphasis on explanation rather than on the cataloging of facts; we have asked our contributors to present science more as an approach than as a corpus of knowledge. We have insisted that articles be written with a minimum of jargon, with maximum clarity consistent with accuracy. The needs of the common reader—the student, the teacher, the non-specialist—have been our measuring rod. It is reference work made for use, not for proud display on one's shelves. This is not to say that every article will be understandable to everyone. A non-mathematician, for example, who is interested in understanding the concepts of tensor analysis will not find the article on this subject as accessible to his understanding as the article on bird navigation; and the biologist in search of an explanation of a complex chemical law may not be altogether satisfied that he grasps the meaning of the relevant article. Fortunately, however, different questions occur to different persons, and in every case the contributor of an article on a highly technical subject has devoted at least an initial paragraph to a simple layman's resumé so that no seeker after information, however abstruse, however removed from his educational background, will ever come away altogether empty-handed.

Two standard devices serve the reader's convenience and increase the value of the encyclopedia: cross referencing and indexing. Cross referencing, as everyone knows, is a mixed blessing and readily lends itself to abuse. The article with extensive cross references to topics only peripherally related to the main subject is confusing, not helpful. It makes the reader feel that the main article leaves out many essentials and it is therefore incumbent upon him to go on a treasure hunt in search of the missing pieces. We have tried to limit the cross references to topics which are closely related to the main subject and which are likely to broaden and deepen the reader's understanding of it. As regards the index we have not stinted; it is an essential part of the scheme, designed to guide the reader, to help him get the most out of the book whether he is engaged in serious research, hunting an elusive fact, or simply browsing. This policy fitted in particularly well with our favoring of longer articles and our encouragement of the reader to explore the many forms and shapes which scientific ideas have assumed.

A good deal of bibliographical material is included in the encyclopedia. Here again we have been most concerned with the needs of the average educated user. The bibliography can be used both as a graded reading list and as a source for further reading with respect to particular topics. The listings range from books and articles on the popular levels to basic texts and more advanced publications.

I have left to the last what is perhaps the most important point. More than 450 scientists and engineers have contributed the nearly 4,000 articles that appear in this work. The encyclopedia is of course their creation. They have brought to it energy, skill, and devotion. They have been friendly, patient, and admirably cooperative. They have not always approved of what we were trying to do and they have not always thought it feasible. Yet in good spirit they have set aside their doubts and, in more cases than not, have performed more ably than they suspected was possible when entering upon their task.

Special credit must go to the board of editorial consultants for their unwearying care. Each in his own department has had the task not only of preparing or editing the entry list and of finding authors, but also of reading, criticizing, and, in many instances, revising the manuscripts. That a distinguished group of men and women, already fully occupied with their professional duties, should have given so much of their time and energy to this enterprise is a tribute to their sense of social responsibility, to their awareness of the importance of opening the field of scientific knowledge to the understanding of the nonscientist.

As for our own editorial staff, it is no mere platitude to say that they have given the best that is in them—that, despite a variety of handicaps and limitations of time and space, they have carried out their work with unflagging energy, with good temper, and with the true craftsman's sense of dedication. The most fitting reward for what they have accomplished is their knowledge of the pleasure and enlightenment which I hope the reader of this book will derive from it.

In the last paragraph of his introduction to his great dictionary of the English language, Samuel Johnson used a phrase which I hope may here be permitted. "In this work," he said, "when it shall be found that much is omitted, let it not be forgotten that much likewise is performed. . . ."

—*J. R. N.*

Publisher's Note for the Second Edition

THE HARPER ENCYCLOPEDIA OF SCIENCE was conceived by James R. Newman as a work that would become standard, and that would grow in usefulness from edition to edition through the years. Even before the first edition went to press, Dr. Newman was looking forward to a second edition—and in fact to others in the more distant future—that would embody many improvements.

Dr. Newman's untimely death in 1966 occurred during the early preparations for this revised edition. Thereafter the work on the revision was carried forward in accordance with his views. The text was updated with reference to all major scientific developments, many of the articles were improved with the aid of the consultants and other authorities, all known errors of detail were corrected, the bibliography was completely revised and enlarged (with special attention to the hosts of excellent references now available in paperback form), and the index was corrected to take account of alterations in text and illustrations.

With the publication of this revised edition, the publishers are looking forward—as did James R. Newman—to a career of ever-increasing usefulness for THE HARPER ENCYCLOPEDIA OF SCIENCE.

Symbols and Abbreviations

FOLLOWING is a list of symbols and abbreviations commonly used in scientific publications and likely to be encountered in this encyclopedia. Abbreviations in everyday use among laymen (*e.g.* "ft" for "foot," "lb" for "pound") have been omitted. Compound abbreviations made up from simple standard forms also have been omitted (*e.g.* "amp-hr" for "ampere-hour"), but compound forms of less obvious construction have been included. Other abbreviations, signs, and symbols are given in various articles, particularly ELEMENT; MATHEMATICAL NOTATION; MINERAL; and PARTICLE, ELEMENTARY.

Symbols

° degree of temperature, *e.g.* 50°, fifty degrees; also, degree of arc in some angular measurements, *e.g.* 40°22′30″.

′ minute of arc in certain angular measurements, *e.g.* 40°22′30″.

″ second of arc in certain angular measurements, *e.g.* 40°22′30″.

^{2} square, *e.g.* 3 ft^2, three square feet.

^{3} cubic, *e.g.* 4 cm^3, four cubic centimeters.

/ per, *e.g.* mi/hr, miles per hour.

μ micron; also, micro-, *e.g.* μv, microvolt.

λ wavelength.

ν frequency.

Abbreviations

Å, Angstrom unit.
abs, absolute (temperature).
ac, a-c, alternating current (noun, adjective).
amp, ampere.
antilog, antilogarithm.
atm, atmosphere.
at. wt, atomic weight.
avdp, avoirdupois.
az, azimuth.
b, born.
bar., barometer.
Be, Baumé.
Bhn, Brinell hardness number.
bhp, brake horsepower.
bp, boiling point.
Btu, British thermal unit.
C, centigrade (Celsius).
c, curie.
c., circa.
ca, candle.
cal, calorie.
cemf, counter electromotive force.
cent., century.
cg, centigram.
cgs, centimeter-gram-second (system).
cl, centiliter.
cm, centimeter.
cn, cosine of the amplitude, an elliptic function.
colog, cologarithm.
conc, concentrate.
cos, cosine.
cosh, hyperbolic cosine.
cot, cotangent.
coul, coulomb.
cp, candlepower.
csc, cosecant.
c to c, center to center.
cy, cycle.
cy/sec, cycles per second.
db, decibel.
dc, d-c, direct current (noun, adjective).
deg, degree (of arc).
deg/sec, degrees per second (angular velocity).
dn, delta amplitude, an elliptic function.
dy, dyne.

e, electron (charge).
eff, efficiency.
emf, electromotive force.
ev, electron volt.
F, Fahrenheit.
fd, farad.
fl, fluid.
fnp, fusion point.
fp, freezing point.
fps, foot-pound-second (system).
ft-lb, foot-pound.
ft/min, feet per minute.
G.C.D., greatest common divisor.
gm, gram.
gm-awu, gram atomic weight.
gr, grain.
Gr., Greek.
h, henry, when used with prefixes; *e.g.* mh, millihenry.
^{h}, hour (in astronomical tables); *e.g.* 7^h.
hp, horsepower.
hr, hour.
hy, henry.
ID, inside diameter.
ihp, indicated horsepower.
j, joule.
K, Kelvin.
kc, kilocycle.
kcal, kilocalorie.
kg, kilogram.
kl, kiloliter.
km, kilometer.
kv, kilovolt.
kva, kilovolt-ampere.
kw, kilowatt.
l, liter, when used with prefixes; *e.g.* ml, milliliter.
lam, lambert.
Lat., Latin.
lat, latitude.
L.C.D., lowest common divisor.
L.C.M., least common multiple.
lin ft, linear foot.
liq, liquid.
lit, liter.
log, logarithm (common).
log. or ln, logarithm (natural).

long., longitude.
lt-yr, light year.
lu, lumen.
m, meter.
ma, milliampere.
max, maximum.
mb, millibar.
Mc, megacycle.
mg, milligram.
mh, millihenry.
min, minimum.
min, minute (of time).
ml, milliliter.
mm, millimeter.
mμ, millimicron.
mol. wt, molecular weight.
mp, melting point.
mv, millivolt.
new, newton.
OD, outside diameter.
oer, oersted.
pf, power factor.
r, roentgen.
rd, rutherford.
rev/min, revolutions per minute (rpm only in crowded tables).
rms, root mean square.
^{s}, second (of time, in astronomical tables); *e.g.* 10^s.
sec, secant.
sec, second (of time).
sin, sine.
sinh, hyperbolic sine.
sn, sine of the amplitude, an elliptic function.
sp gr, specific gravity.
sp ht, specific heat.
tan, tangent.
tanh, hyperbolic tangent.
temp, temperature.
ts, tensile strength.
v, volt.
va, volt-ampere.
v coul, volt-coulomb.
vib, vibration, *e.g.* vib/sec, vibrations per second.
wt, weight.

The scope of science: A cluster of nebulas in the constellation Coma Berenices, at a distance of about 40 million light years, appears on a photograph taken with the 200-in. Hale telescope. The inset is a field-ion microscope picture of the arrangement of atoms in the point of a tungsten needle. (*Mt Wilson* and *Palomar Observatories;* and *E. W. Müller/Penn. State Univ.*)

A

ABBE, CLEVELAND, 1838–1916, U. S. meteorologist and astronomer; b. New York. After working at Pulkowa Observatory, Russia, 1864–6, and at U. S. Naval Observatory, 1867, he became director, Cincinnati Observatory, 1868. As civilian assistant (meteorologist), Signal Corps Weather Bureau (U. S. Weather Bureau after 1891), 1871–1916, he was the first official weather forecaster in the U. S. A.—*D. H. D. R.*

ABDOMEN: in man and other vertebrates, the region of the body that lies between the thorax (chest region) and the pelvis. The body cavity containing the digestive organs is also referred to as the abdomen (or abdominal cavity). In insects and other arthropods, the abdomen is the rear region of the body and is usually segmented.—*A. P. E.*

ABEL, NIELS HENRIK, 1802–29, Norwegian mathematician; b. Kristiansand; largely self-taught in mathematics. In Berlin, Germany, he became associated with August Crelle, a civil engineer and mathematical amateur who established the first periodical devoted exclusively to mathematical research. In his memoirs Abel settled the hitherto-unanswered question as to the solvability of equations of higher degree than the 4th by proving that the general equation of the 5th degree cannot be solved by algebraic means. Abel's work, together with that of Evariste GALOIS, whom he never met, established the modern era of algebraic analysis. Abel also greatly broadened and deepened the knowledge of transcendental functions in his great work: *Memoir on a General Property of a Very General Class of Transcendental Functions* (1841).—*H. C.*

ABERRATION OF LIGHT: an apparent displacement in the position of a star or other heavenly body due to the combined effects of the motion of Earth and the finite velocity of light. It was discovered by James Bradley, 1725, when he was attempting to measure stellar parallax. Because of aberration, a telescope must be pointed slightly in advance of the object under observation (Fig. 1). In an analogous way, when one is carrying an umbrella in the rain, one points the umbrella

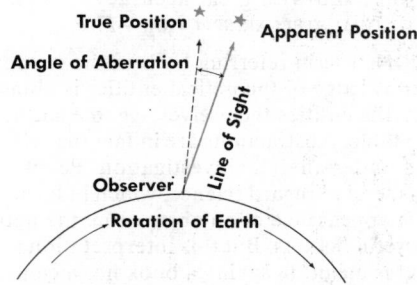

Aberration of starlight (Fig. 1): Apparent position of the star is in advance of true position, relative to direction of Earth's rotation.

slightly forward; the angle of tilt depends on one's speed and the speed of the rain. In the case of starlight, aberration shifts the apparent position of a star from its true direction toward the direction in which Earth is moving. As Earth revolves about the Sun, the direction of the star continually changes. In the course of one year, a star that is near the ecliptic pole appears to move in an almost circular ellipse; a star

further from the pole appears to move in a more flattened ellipse; and one that is on the ecliptic appears to move back and forth in a straight line (Fig. 2). This movement is called *annual aberration.* The maximum displacement is the

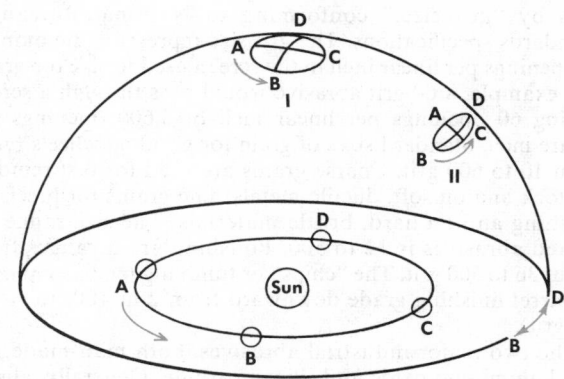

Aberration of starlight (Fig. 2): As Earth reaches positions A, B, C, D in its orbit, star appears at corresponding positions in small orbit it appears to trace in sky. Here Star I is near ecliptic pole. Star II, nearer to the plane of the ecliptic, traces narrower orbit.

same for all stars, 20″.49, and is called the *constant of aberration.* There is also a *diurnal aberration,* an eastward displacement of the apparent position of a star that results from the eastward rotation of Earth. This displacement has a maximum value of 0″.31 for an observer on Earth's equator, and decreases to zero for an observer at either pole.—*M. W. O.*

ABLATION: in aerotechnology, the process by which the outer parts of an object (*e.g.* space vehicle or meteorite) are wasted or cut away by melting or vaporization due to friction and compression of atmospheric air, which becomes extremely hot. Melting and vaporization take up the heat of the atmospheric air, keeping this heat from the object's interior. Thus excessive heating of the interior of a space vehicle can be prevented by coating its exterior with a material that will melt or vaporize during passage through the atmosphere. —*Wm. R.*

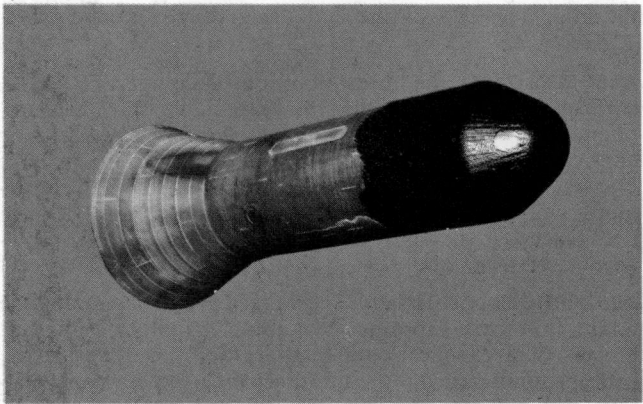

Ablated nose cone: Friction with atmosphere produced melting temperature of 6000°F on this nose cone of a ballistic missile. (Avco)

ABRASIVE: any substance used for grinding, belt-grinding, lapping, honing, polishing, buffing, pressure blasting, barrel finishing, etc. Abrasives act by means of their hard-edged particles, which cut and scrape away tiny portions of the material being worked. Besides loose abrasives, abrasive products include wheels (see GRINDING) and coated abrasives. The latter are made by coating a backing of paper or cloth with resin or glue, uniformly covering the surface with abrasive grain, and then sealing the surface with a second, or bonding, coat of adhesive. Abrasives are classified according to fineness by "grit size," conforming to National Bureau of Standards specifications. The grit size represents the number of openings per linear inch in the screen used to size the grain. For example, a 60-grit abrasive would pass through a screen having 60 openings per linear inch or 3,600 openings per square inch. Standard sizes of grain for grinding wheels range from 10 to 600 grit. Coarse grains are used for fast removal of stock and on soft, ductile metals; fine grains for precision finishing and on hard, brittle materials. The size range for coated abrasives is 12 to 500. Polishing grain ranges from about 36 to 500 grit. The "chips" or tumbling media employed in barrel finishing grade downward from 2 in. (00) to ¹⁄₁₆ in. (16 grit).

The two major industrial abrasives, both man-made, are fused aluminum oxide and silicon carbide. Generally, aluminum oxide is used for tumbling media and for grinding metals and alloys of high tensile strength such as carbon and alloy steels, malleable and wrought iron, and hard bronzes. Gray cast iron, chilled white cast iron, brass, copper, and aluminum are best ground with silicon carbide, also better adapted to grinding non-metallic materials like stone, glass, and ceramics. Diamond, the third most common industrial abrasive, ranks first in hardness, being close to three times harder than boron carbide, the next hardest on the Knoop scale for measuring microindentation hardness. Talc, chalk, and jeweler's rouge are extremely soft abrasives. ("Soft" abrasives crumble easily to their ultimate particles; "hard" abrasives resist this crumbling and tend to remain in larger aggregates.) Other abrasive substances include: cemented carbides, zirconium compounds, corundum ("natural" aluminum oxide), emery (corundum with iron-oxide impurities), garnet, quartz, quartzite, ground sandstone, sand, tripoli, feldspar, diatomite, rottenstone, pumice, flint, and chert.—*C. B. C.*

ABSCISSION: the process by which many plants, conspicuously some trees in the fall, drop their leaves, flowers, fruits, or other appendages. A special layer of cells, the *abscission layer,* develops crosswise of the stalks supporting the appendage, and under the right conditions shears off, allowing the appendage to drop. The end of the stalk is gradually sealed off.—*L. and M. M.*

ABSOLUTE ZERO: the lowest point on the temperature scale, corresponding to a condition of minimum, or so-called zero-point, internal energy. On the *absolute temperature scale* (KELVIN SCALE, or thermodynamic scale), the zero point is marked 0°K, which is equivalent to −273.16°C. Temperatures within a hundred-thousandth of a degree of 0°K have been reached in the course of cryogenic experiments. See CRYOGENICS; TEMPERATURE SCALES.—*A. E.*

ABSORPTION: in chemistry, an imprecise term suggesting the taking up of one substance by another by either a physical process or a chemical combination. (See the more specific concept SOLUBILITY.) If the substance taken up does not penetrate the surface, the process is ADSORPTION. For example, blood absorbs oxygen; a thin film of water may be adsorbed on a glass surface. In chemical engineering, absorption deals largely with gas absorption, *i.e.* removal of a soluble component of a gas mixture by a liquid, for purposes of purification or separation of gaseous mixtures. Absorption occurs in a variety of processes in animals and plants; thus the blood stream absorbs digested food from the intestine, roots absorb water and nutrients from soil, leaves absorb oxygen and carbon dioxide from air. In the physical sciences, absorption generally refers to the taking up of energy—*e.g.* heat, sound, electromagnetic radiation—by matter. Usually the energy is converted to some other form; thus, when light falls on an object, some is absorbed and may be changed into heat. For absorption of radiation by the earth's atmosphere, see ATMOSPHERIC RADIATION. See also BEER'S LAW.—*D. P. B.*

ABSORPTION SPECTRUM: the spectrum resulting from the passage of radiation through a substance, *e.g.* a liquid or a gas, that selectively absorbs certain wavelengths. The wavelengths absorbed are represented by dark lines or bands in the spectrum; the bright lines represent the transmitted radiation. Since every substance has its own characteristic absorption spectrum, these spectra provide a convenient, sensitive, and accurate means of identification. Quantitative analyses also can be made by measurement of absorption intensity.

Absorption lines: The violet region of the solar rainbow as recorded by a spectrograph. Each line indicates absorption by an element (*e.g.* iron) in Sun's atmosphere. Concentrated patch (*right*) is of wavelengths around 4,300 angstrom units. (*Mt Wilson*)

The most accurate absorption-spectrum analyses are made with the spectrophotometer, which measures light absorption electrically. Analyses may be made in the ultraviolet and infrared ranges as well as in the visible range; ultraviolet and visible spectra tend to be characteristic of the entire compound, while infrared spectra are characteristic of specific groups or sub-units of a complex molecule. Infrared spectrum analysis is particularly valuable in biochemistry, since many of the chemical constituents of living systems are colorless and also have weak ultraviolet absorption. Sharp differences in infrared absorption between various organic molecules, *e.g.* between ester and acidic linkages, make it possible to "fingerprint" a compound with great accuracy. See also SPECTROSCOPE; SPECTRUM; STELLAR SPECTRA.—*F. F.*

ABSTRACTION: a term referring both to the supposed process by which knowledge of theoretical entities is obtained, and to the product, the entities themselves, *e.g.* the surface of a table without the table. Abstractions are in fact the relevant aspects of anything under analytic investigation. People who dislike abstractions tend to regard science, which in its higher reaches takes on the appearance of an abstract mathematical system, as a set of useful fictions. But this interpretation is gratuitous: part of what is meant in saying a book has a center of gravity (an abstraction) is that you can balance it on your thumb.—*H. T.*

ACCELERATION: change in velocity per unit of time. Since velocity possesses both magnitude and direction, acceleration may involve either or both. If velocity changes by Δv during a time interval Δt, the *average* acceleration is $\Delta v/\Delta t$. Thus if a body accelerates from 10 ft/sec to 50 ft/sec during 10 sec, average acceleration is 40 ft/sec ÷ 10 sec, or 4 ft/sec/sec, often written as 4 ft/sec². The acceleration at any one instant, called *instantaneous* acceleration, equals average acceleration if acceleration is constant throughout the time interval. If acceleration is not constant, instantaneous acceleration is determined by the calculus as the limit which average acceleration approaches as the time interval approaches zero. The term acceleration alone is generally understood to mean *linear* acceleration, as defined above. *Angular* acceleration is a change in the rotational rate, or angular velocity, of a body spinning on a fixed axis (see ROTATION). It is equal to $\Delta\omega/\Delta t$, where $\Delta\omega$ is the total change in angular velocity over the period Δt. When a body moves in a circular path with a uniform angular velocity (hence with zero angular acceleration), it experiences a linear acceleration (owing to its change of direction) toward the center, known as *centripetal* or *radial* acceleration.—*R. G. M.*

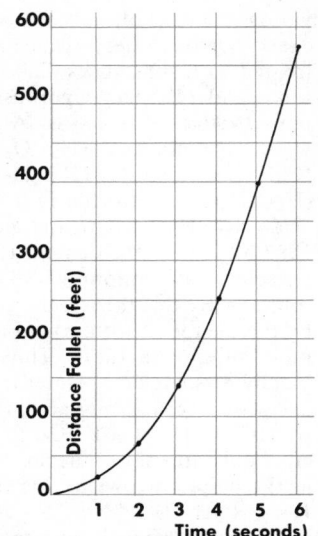

Acceleration due to gravity: A freely falling body falls according to formula $d = \frac{1}{2}gt^2$, where d = total distance fallen, g = acceleration due to gravity (32 ft/sec^2), t = time.

ACCELEROMETER: a device (based on Newton's law of motion) that measures the acceleration of the system with which it moves. It does this by registering the force involved in the changes of velocity of a given mass.—*W. P. C.*

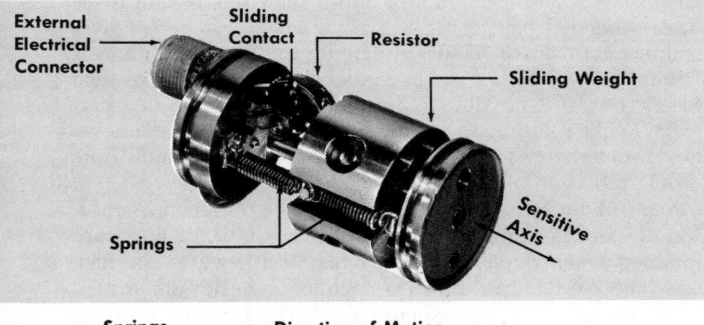

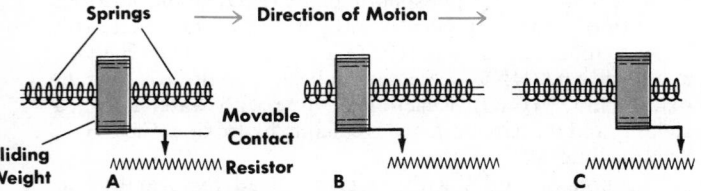

In this simple accelerometer, springs hold a sliding weight in an intermediate position at zero acceleration, when speed is zero or uniform (A). In this position, a sliding electrical contact attached to the weight gives an intermediate reading on a potentiometer. When the system accelerates, the sliding weight slips back (B) and a high voltage is registered; when the system decelerates, the sliding weight moves forward (C) and a low voltage is registered. In an aircraft or missile, a set of three accelerometers at right angles to one another can monitor acceleration in each direction. (*Giannini Controls Corp.*)

ACCLIMATIZATION: changes in the responses of an organism brought about by continued modifications in the surroundings. For example, if a goldfish is kept in water at 10°C for several weeks, it becomes acclimatized to that temperature and will die if exposed to temperatures below 0°C or above 30°C. A goldfish acclimatized to 25°C will die if exposed to temperatures below 5°C or above 36°C. The rapidity and degree of acclimatization varies from one species of fish to another. Acclimatization is distinguished from adaptation, which refers to structural, functional, or behavioral changes that take place over many generations and that have evolutionary significance. Adaptations are relatively permanent, whereas acclimatization is lost soon after the environmental stimulus ceases to act on the organism. For example, rats become fully acclimatized to cold in 4 to 6 weeks; brief exposures to heat reduce, or even erase, the cold acclimatization.

After exposure to hot environments, men become acclimatized, especially if they exercise in the heat. They show reduced amount of salt in the sweat; heart rate and body temperature increase more slowly during exercise; blood volume increases. Long periods of heat exposure, with exercise, condition men to perform strenuous duties in very hot weather. But scientific evidence that men become acclimatized to cold is meager. Such acclimatization is characterized chiefly by changes in perception of the cold: men in good physical condition remain comfortable, after acclimatization to cold, in surroundings intolerable to unacclimatized men.—*C. G. W.*

ACETALDEHYDE (CH_3CHO): a liquid of low boiling point made industrially by hydration of acetylene. Its polymers are paraldehyde (CH_3CHO)$_3$, a soporific, and metaldehyde (CH_3CHO)$_4$. In biochemistry, acetaldehyde is an intermediate bound to a form of the vitamin thiamin in the biological oxidation of carbohydrates. In the body, ingested alcohol is oxidized to free acetaldehyde, which is then oxidized further via acetic acid in the CITRIC ACID CYCLE. In fermentation of glucose by yeast, its reduction to alcohol can be blocked by bisulfite, leading to the production of glycerine instead of alcohol from the fermented sugar (see also GLYCOLYSIS). Since high concentrations of free acetaldehyde cause nausea, drugs which increase its concentration by inhibiting its further oxidation have been used to treat alcoholism.—*J. F. S.*

ACETATES: salts or esters of acetic acid, CH_3—$COOH$. When the terminal hydrogen atom, H, is replaced by a metal radical, the product is a metal acetate (a salt) and may be considered an inorganic chemical. When the same hydrogen atom is replaced by an organic radical, the product is an acetate ester. Commercially important metal acetates are aluminum acetate and lead acetate ("sugar of lead"), both used as mordants in dyeing. Important acetate esters are ethyl acetate, used in flavorings and as a solvent; and cellulose acetate, used in making film, acetate rayon, and plastics (see CELLULOSE).—*Ru. M.*

ACETIC ACID: the organic acid produced in largest quantity. It is the 2-carbon, carboxylic acid CH_3—$COOH$ (see ACETATES), made by bacterial fermentation of alcohol in fruit juices (vinegar), by dry distillation of wood, and by several synthetic processes. Acetic acid is commercially available at 99.5% purity. This pure product is corrosive to the skin, and is called *glacial acetic acid* because it solidifies at 62°F to ice-like crystals.—*Ru. M.*

ACETONE: CH_3—CO—CH_3, the simplest and most important of the KETONES. It is a product of wood distillation and of certain carbohydrate fermentations, and is also made synthetically. It is a volatile, fragrant liquid used chiefly as a solvent for polymers in the making of films, threads, fingernail polish, etc., and as a chemical intermediate.—*Ru. M.*

ACETYLCHOLINE: the choline ester of acetic acid. First isolated from adrenal glands, it was shown by Reid Hunt (1906) to exert a powerful dilator action on blood vessels, and it was identified by O. Loewi with "Vagusstoff" (1921). It is widely distributed in nature; through its breakdown by cholinesterase and resynthesis by choline acetylase, it is important in the functioning of the nervous system.—*B. J. J. and J. J. O'N.*

ACETYLENE: a colorless gas, H—C≡C—H, the first and only commercially important member of the family of aliphatic hydrocarbons which contain a triple bond. It is made cheaply by adding water to calcium carbide:

$$CaC_2 + 2H_2O \rightarrow HC≡CH + Ca(OH)_2$$

| Calcium carbide | Acetylene | Calcium hydroxide |

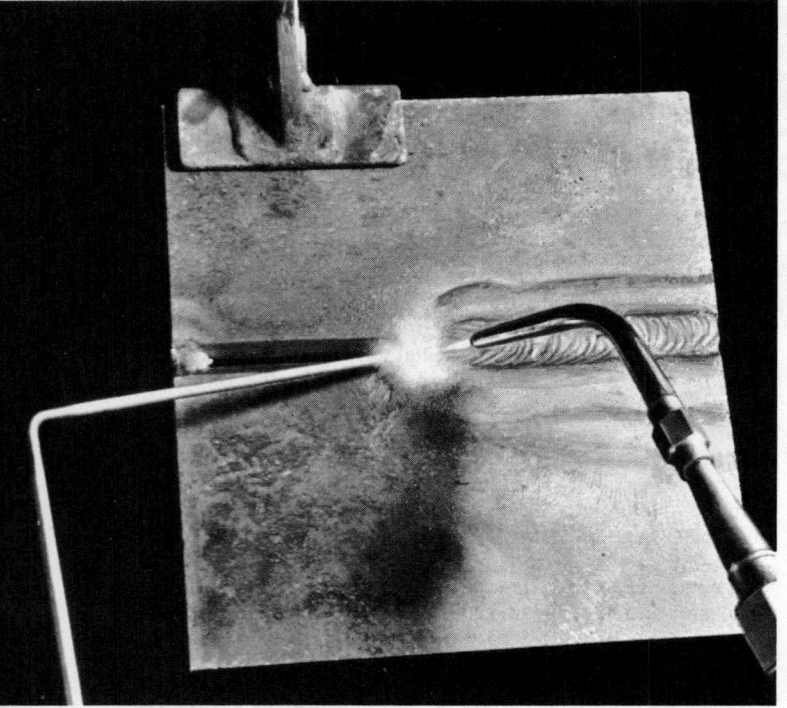

Acetylene at work: A flaming mixture of oxygen and acetylene issues from torch for a welding temperature of 6300°F. (*Union Carbide*)

Other methods are also used. Liquid acetylene is unstable to shock, but can be handled safely in tanks containing porous material saturated with acetone, one volume of which dissolves 300 volumes of acetylene at about 200 lb pressure. Acetylene is used mostly as a chemical intermediate and for oxyacetylene welding of metals. In a proper gas burner acetylene gives an intense, white flame.—*Ru. M.*

ACHESON, EDWARD GOODRICH, 1856–1931, U. S. inventor; b. Washington, Pa. As Thomas A. Edison's assistant he helped prepare Edison's exhibit at the Paris International Exhibition and installed the first Edison electric lights in Italy, Belgium, and Holland. He patented an electric furnace (1896), discovered the abrasive "carborundum," and devised a process for making a pure synthetic graphite. He also patented "Egyptianized" clay, a clay with increased plasticity, and such compounded lubricants as "oildag" and "gredag."—*R. J. F.*

ACID: any of a class of chemical compounds with the distinctive property of having a sour taste (Lat. *acidus,* "sour"). Early chemists also recognized other properties in these compounds, *e.g.* ability to (1) affect color of certain dyes, (2) corrode metals,

giving rise to evolution of a combustible gas (hydrogen), (3) cause copious effervescence (due to carbon dioxide) when treated with substances like chalk, baking soda, and washing soda, and (4) react vigorously with another class of compounds known as BASES. Among acids recognized earliest were carbonic acid (H_2CO_3), acetic ($HC_2H_3O_2$), carbolic (C_6H_5OH), lactic ($HC_3H_5O_3$), boric (H_3BO_3), oxalic ($H_2C_4H_4O_6$), hydrochloric (HCl), sulfuric (H_2SO_4), and citric acid ($H_3C_6H_5O_7$). The first modern theory was formulated in 1887 by the Swedish chemist Svante Arrhenius, who defined an acid as a compound which gives hydrogen ions in water solution. By this theory, the strength of an acid is determined by the degree of IONIZATION as measured by conductivity or other suitable methods. Thus hydrochloric acid, being completely dissociated in water into hydrogen and chloride ions, is considered a strong acid, its ionization being represented by $HCl \rightarrow H^+ + Cl^-$. On the other hand, acetic acid, principal constituent of vinegar, is only slightly ionized in water, as the paired arrows in this equation indicate: $HC_2H_3O_2 \rightleftarrows H^+ + C_2H_3O_2^-$.

Acids and Bases: Bases are a class of compounds related to acids. By the Arrhenius theory, their properties in water are due to hydroxyl OH^- ions. Ionization of a strong base such as sodium hydroxide, or "lye," can be represented by $NaOH \rightarrow Na^+ + OH^-$. Pure water itself is slightly ionized, giving equal numbers of hydrogen and hydroxyl ions as follows: $H_2O \rightleftarrows H^+ + OH^-$. It is therefore *neutral*. Acids and bases react with each other by a process called NEUTRALIZATION, which consists of union of hydrogen and hydroxyl ions to form water: $H^+ + OH^- \rightarrow H_2O$.

Acidity or *basicity* of a solution is determined by the concentration of hydrogen or hydroxyl ions. Since pure water, which is neutral, contains 60 million million hydrogen ions per cm^3, a solution containing more than this is said to be *acidic,* and one containing less is *basic*. A number of dyes assume characteristic colors at definite acidities; *e.g.* litmus is blue in basic solutions, red in acidic. By judicious use of such INDICATORS, it is possible to determine the strength of a particular acidic solution. In recent years, electrical devices known as pH meters (see pH VALUE) have been replacing indicators in determination of acidity.

Preparation: Most common acids can be obtained by reaction of oxides of non-metals with water; similarly, bases are obtained when oxides of metals react with water. In such cases the oxides are known as acidic or basic anhydrides. Sulfur trioxide (SO_3), phosphoric oxide (P_4O_{10}), and nitrogen pentoxide (N_2O_5) are acidic anhydrides which react with water to form sulfuric acid (H_2SO_4), phosphoric acid (H_3PO_4), and nitric acid (HNO_3). A common basic anhydride is calcium oxide, "lime" (CaO). Reaction of lime with water is called slaking, and the base obtained is calcium hydroxide ($Ca(OH)_2$), "slaked lime."

Reaction of oxides with water can lead to formation of either an acid or a base. Upon further investigation it appears that both acids and bases derived from oxides contain the hydroxy group (OH); *e.g.* the structural formulas of sulfuric acid and calcium hydroxide are represented by

$$H-O-\overset{\overset{O}{|}}{\underset{\underset{O}{|}}{S}}-O-H \qquad H-O-Ca-O-H.$$

Extensions of Acid-Base Concept: With sulfuric acid, ionization occurs by cleavage between hydrogen and oxygen, resulting in release of a hydrogen ion. In calcium hydroxide, it is a hydroxyl ion which is formed upon ionization, because the site of the cleavage is the bond between oxygen and calcium.

Linus Pauling and other contemporary chemists have been able to correlate this behavior with electrical properties of the central atom, *i.e.* sulfur in the case of sulfuric acid, and calcium with calcium hydroxide; hence a quantitative theory of acids and bases in which relative strengths can be determined from fundamental atomic structures and correlated with the position of the central atom in the periodic table.

Although the Arrhenius theory is very useful in explaining many acid-base phenomena, it is restricted to aqueous solutions. There are innumerable reactions in which another solvent may be involved and where chemists have found it useful to speak of "acid-base reactions" in which neither hydrogen nor hydroxyl ions participate. To encompass these reactions within the framework of the "acid-base language" a number of extensions of the acid-base concept have been developed. The two most widely used of these are the "proton-exchange" of J. N. Bronsted (1879–   ) and the electron-pair transfer of G. N. Lewis (1875–1946).—*M. K.*

ACKERET, JAKOB, 1898–   , Swiss engineer; b. Zürich. He introduced the concept of MACH NUMBER to express the ratio of aircraft speed to the speed of sound, and developed the theory of lift and drag for a two-dimensional linear wing moving at supersonic speed. This theory was of great importance in design of supersonic aircraft.—*D. H. D. R.*

ACOUSTICAL DEVICES: a class of instruments used for generation, transmission, detection, reproduction, and analysis of sounds. Devices for *generation* of sounds are many and varied. They include all musical instruments, LOUDSPEAKERS, sirens, and ULTRASONIC generators, as well as natural sources of sounds. All generators contain a means to set a relatively large amount of material vibrating. Many of them operate on a RESONANCE principle, most musical instruments being of this type. Thus we have resonant strings (violin), resonant air columns (pipe organ), resonant bars (marimba), and resonant shells (bell). All such devices have a predetermined pitch. In a loudspeaker or telephone receiver, where a definite pitch would be intolerable, an attempt is made to minimize resonances. *Transmission* systems can be roughly divided into two categories: those in which an attempt is made to transmit sounds without modification and those where modification is desirable. A speaking tube is an example of the first type, a muffler of the second. A transmission system may be purely mechanical or acoustical, as in normal conversation, or it may involve multiple energy-conversions, as in radio broadcasting. For sound *detection* one of the most sensitive devices is the normal human ear, which in a young person can almost detect the noise from the random motion of molecules in the air. Physical detectors of sound are of many types; some are general-purpose devices such as MICROPHONES, while others are designed for special purposes. The stethoscope is a detector coupled directly to a transmission system. Less well-known examples are the pressure probe, used to measure the sound pressure in the ear canal; the Rayleigh disk, which tends to orient itself at right angles to the direction of propagation of a sound; and the hot-wire microphone, which measures the square of the velocity of air particles set in motion by a sound wave. Devices for *analysis* of sounds include any device designed to measure one or more properties of a sound. A frequency meter is such a device, for the pitch of a sound is determined primarily by its frequency. Probably most important and most widely used is the sound-level meter, which gives a measure, in decibels, of the root mean square pressure in a complex sound. The next most important instrument is the spectrum-analyzer: it determines the amount of energy in a complex sound that is associated with a specified band of frequency. Some *special-purpose acoustical devices* are the interferometer, which measures velocity and absorption of sound in a medium; the audiometer, used to determine hearing acuity in a person; and the reflectoscope, employed to locate flaws in metals. Other special devices are the ultrasonic soldering iron, ultrasonic drill, and ultrasonic bath, for cleaning metal parts (*e.g.* in watches).—*H. M. T.*

ACOUSTICS: the science of sound, including its production, properties, and effects. (For properties and transmission of sound, see SOUND; ULTRASONICS; and NOISE. For applications, see ACOUSTICS, ARCHITECTURAL; ACOUSTICAL DEVICES; LOUDSPEAKER and MICROPHONE; and SOUND REPRODUCTION.) Acoustics is probably the oldest science after astronomy and medicine. The Greek philosophers Pythagoras, Aristotle, Aristoxenus, and Euclid discussed musical instruments, particularly stringed instruments, and the musical scales appropriate to them, with a precision and understanding not approached again for 2,000 yr. In the practical matter of effective acoustical design, the Greek open-air theater is still unrivaled in making the unaided human voice audible to large numbers of persons. After the long scientific holiday of the Roman Empire and the Dark Ages, Galileo in 1638 deduced the laws of vibrating strings quantitatively—the dependence of frequency on length, diameter, density, and tension—as well as explaining RESONANCE, sympathetic vibration, and CONSONANCE AND DISSONANCE. After him, many famous names appear: Robert Boyle, Isaac Newton, P. S. de Laplace, August Kundt (1839–94), J. A. Lissajous (1822–80), H. L. F. von Helmholtz, and John Tyndall. Their contributions culminate in the work of Lord Rayleigh, *The Theory of Sound* (1877). Most of the classical results and phenomena are treated in it; very little in the way of new theory or phenomena was added to the field until the 1930s, when D. V. O. Knudsen (1893–   ) and others detected anomalous absorption and dispersion of sound in air, the explanation of which required the quantum theory of specific heats. Since the 1920s the advent of electronics has made an enormous difference in the ease of production and measurement of sound, and the field has expanded.

Sources of Sound: It is a common observation that sound is associated with the vibration of something or other: a violin string, the metal of a bell, the vocal cords, a drumhead, or the air enclosed in a flute, organ pipe, or empty bottle. (The siren, invented by T. J. Seebeck [1770–1831] in 1822, is an exception, producing sound by a rapid series of puffs of air through holes in a perforated plate or cylinder.) The vibrations are transmitted to the air and radiate outward from the source with "the speed of sound." Acoustics is therefore a branch of the mechanics of vibrating bodies, and well-known mathematical results for such phenomena as resonance, forced vibration, and damping losses can be taken over directly.

The vibration of a violin string is a complex affair, which may be taken as representative of this class of musical instruments. As J. B. J. Fourier showed theoretically in 1822, the complex vibration may be considered as made up of a series of vibrations, each with a frequency that is a simple multiple of the lowest (or "fundamental") frequency, all of them coexisting, and each with its own energy. The balance between the vibrations depends strongly on the "bowing," *i.e.* on how the string is excited (among other things whether close to the bridge or nearer the middle of the string); the subjective tone heard by the auditor depends, of course, upon this balance.

Since a string is a very small object, whose coupling to the air around it is poor, some sort of sounding board is always added to the string to make a true musical instrument. This sounding board, of much greater area than the string itself, takes on the vibration of the string, but radiates the sound much more effectively. In the brass instruments, the vibrating air column, excited by the lip vibrations of the player, is coupled smoothly and efficiently to the atmosphere by the flare of the "bell." The human voice may be aided in the same way by use of the hands or a megaphone. The laboratory instrument giving the purest tone is the tuning fork (a U-shaped bar with a handle at the center), because it possesses only two weak overtones, not "harmonics," at 6.25 and 17.6 times the fundamental. When electrically excited, such a fork is an excellent frequency standard. Nowadays, however, a good electrical oscillator combined with a loudspeaker is more convenient.

There are numerous other musical sound sources, and noise sources are legion. Among musical instruments are the reeds (oboe, clarinet, bassoon) and the percussions (drum, xylophone), and since the 1930s a large number of unconventional ones, usually involving electronic production of the basic frequencies, have been invented. The most powerful of these is the Bell-Chrysler siren, used as an air-raid warning, which can produce a level of 150 decibels (db) at 10 yd (120 db is painful); this is in the same class of loudness as the jet airplane.

Sound Phenomena—*Echoes:* Like any other wave, sound waves may be reflected from any surface where there is a change in the medium carrying the wave. Classically, a rocky cliff face gives a perfect "mirror echo," as at Somes Sound in Maine or at many Alpine lakes. Not so familiar is the reflection of sound back down into the sea when a sound wave hits the surface from below. Multiple echoes produce the phenomenon of reverberation, a matter for serious consideration in the design of auditoriums. Echoes are used to measure the depth of the ocean and the ranges of hostile submarines or schools of fish (see SONAR). Whispering galleries owe their effectiveness to the focusing effect of curved walls and ceilings, overlapping the echoes so they reinforce one another, as in the Capitol in Washington or St. Paul's in London.

Doppler Effect: When a listener moves toward a source of sound, he passes through more waves per second than he would if he stood still; after he has passed the source—say a railroad grade-crossing bell—he passes through fewer waves. To him this sounds like a drop in pitch of the source as he goes by; it is the commonest example of the DOPPLER EFFECT, described by C. J. Doppler in 1842 (the description was first applied to the change in color of the spectrum of moving stars, not to sound). If the source is moving, not the listener, the effect is almost the same. If there is no wind, and motion is along the line between source and listener, then the frequency heard (F) will be $F = F^* (V \pm v_L)/(V \mp v_s)$, where F^* is the actual frequency of the source, and V, v_L, and v_s are the velocities of the sound, the listener, and the source, respectively. The upper signs are for approach, the lower for recession (*e.g.* if the listener is moving away from the source, the minus sign is used: $V - v_L$). At 70 mi/hr the total change of pitch is almost exactly a minor third, 6:5. A practical use of the Doppler effect is made in sound ranging in submarines: the pitch change in the echo received indicates whether the distance between the submarine and the other object is increasing or decreasing.

Refraction of Sound Waves: The velocity of sound depends strongly on the temperature; if the medium through which sound waves travel is not uniform, they will be refracted, just as light waves are refracted over a desert or black-top road in summer. Curious effects at long ranges are produced by this effect; *e.g.* explosions heard scores of miles away are inaudible quite nearby. This effect is at its most annoying in underwater sound ranging, because the ocean has a complex layered temperature structure that tends to make the sound plunge toward the bottom and miss targets near the surface.

Diffraction and Interference: Like other waves, sounds tend to curl around obstacles according to the laws of refraction and produce waves in every direction. These waves, and in fact any two or more wave trains, can interfere with one another in several ways. One is in the phenomenon of "beats," a more or less rapid pulsation, heard when two notes of nearly equal pitch are less than 5 or 10 cycles apart. This familiar phenomenon is used by all tuners of musical instruments; it is a type of interference in time. Constructive and destructive interference along lines in space, independent of time, also exists and can be easily demonstrated by holding a tuning fork close to the ear and rotating it slowly. Perpendicular and parallel to the line between the tines, the sound is loudest; at 45°, it is softest.

Directional sound sources (this also applies to microphones) can be built with almost any degree of directionality, but just as with radio antennas, the more directional they are, the bigger they must be. The antenna must be several times as big as the

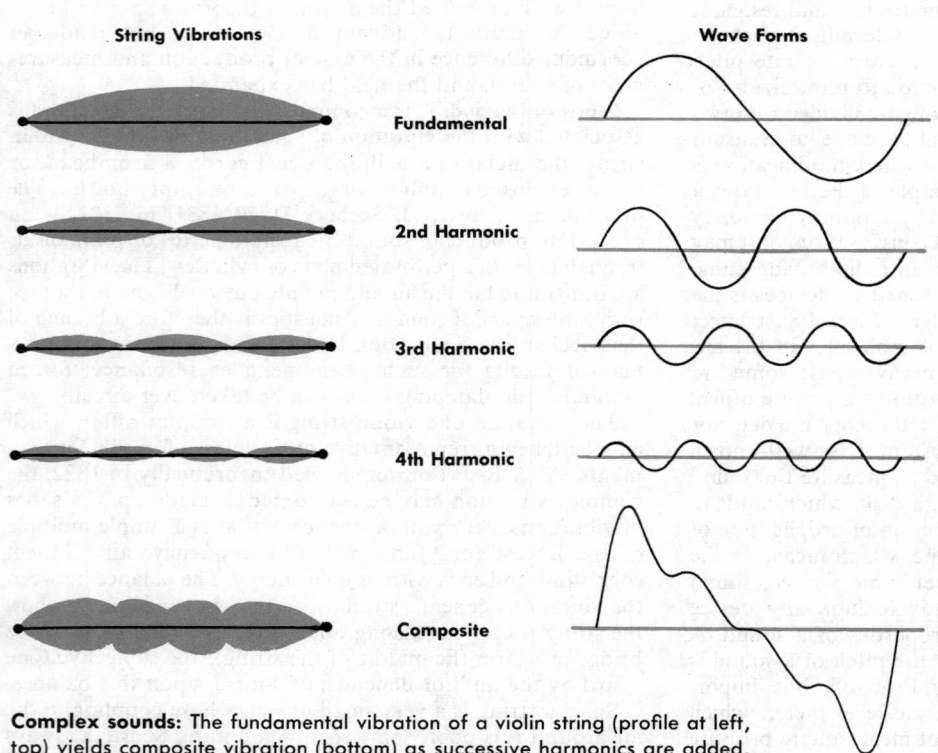

String Vibrations

Fundamental

2nd Harmonic

3rd Harmonic

4th Harmonic

Composite

Wave Forms

Complex sounds: The fundamental vibration of a violin string (profile at left, top) yields composite vibration (bottom) as successive harmonics are added. These vibrations would produce the oscilloscope traces shown at right. The heights of the string profiles are exaggerated.

Plate 1   ADAPTATIONS OF ANIMALS

When the ranks of the reptiles were thinned in the late Cretaceous, a great number of their habitats and ways of life became available to the mammals, which then developed the basic adaptations that would determine their ability to fly or swim, to eat meat or plants. In the 70 million yr that have elapsed since that time, more detailed adaptations have occurred. **1. The giraffe** branched off from the deer during Miocene times. It feeds today among the flat-topped trees of the African savanna, where its markings conceal its presence. The combined length of its forelegs and neck raises its mouth to some of the highest leaves of acacia trees and its eyes to an elevation from which it can spot prowling carnivores from a great distance (if it fails to spot them in time, it can defend itself with a memorable kick). *(H. Lanks/Shostal)* **2. The foxlike fennec** of the deserts of Arabia and N Africa is a small animal, head and body together measuring 15½ in., with enormous ears, which serve it in nocturnal hunting. *(Walter Dawn)* **3. The tamandua** has the prehensile tail of other tree-dwellers of S and Central America, but also a long muzzle and sticky worm-like tongue which it pokes into boles in search of termites; its muscular, clawed arms are as effective as crowbars in tearing apart termite nests. *(Robert C. Hermes/National Audubon Soc.)* **4. The nine-banded armadillo** of Texas and Central America belongs to the same mammalian order *(Edentata)* as the tamandua, but has very different adaptations and a much more varied diet. When attacked, it rolls into an armored ball or burrows into the ground at a furious speed. *(Walter Dawn)*

1

2

3

4

Plate 2 ADAPTATIONS OF PLANTS

Plants have developed a great variety of adaptations to environment, a few of which are shown. **1.** In a cypress lagoon the broad leaves of **water lilies,** buoyed up by gas-filled floats, blanket the surface, where they can capture plenty of light for the manufacture of food by photosynthesis. *(Walter Dawn)* **2. Cactus,** which grows in arid desert, has no leaves but carries on photosynthesis in spiny stems that store water. *(James M. Peterson/Shostal)* **3. The parasitic bracket fungus** feeds on the tissues of the host tree through special absorbing tips on the mycelium growing inside the bark. The visible bracket or shelf is the spore-producing body. *(Alfred O. Holz)*

1

3

4. Columbine, in contrast to fungus, reproduces by seeds. Pollination of the fertile stigma at the end of each pistil is carried out by insects attracted to its long-spurred nectar tubes. *(M. H. Berry / Shostal)*

2

4

Plate 3 ALGAE

Algae, the most ancient type of vegetation on Earth, have developed along widely different lines related to the dominant color of their pigment. Blue-green algae, the simplest and among the most primitive of plants, are among the few organisms that can tolerate temperatures as high as 185° F. They thrive in the hot waters of **Morning Glory Pool (1)** in Yellowstone Park. *(National Park Service)* Other types of green and brown algae, of both fresh and salt water, are shown in the three pictures below.

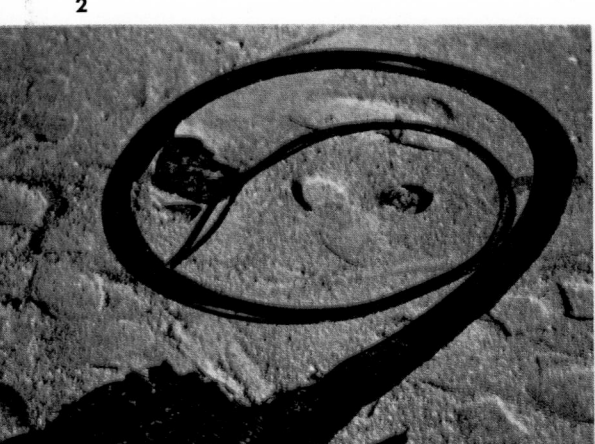

Three types of algae: Giant kelp (2) is a brown alga that lives along the California seacoast. It secretes a tough, elastic covering for its tubelike thallus that protects it against damage from rocks and waves, and also from desiccation when the receding tide leaves it exposed. *(Raymond McAllister)*

3. Spirogyra is a green fresh-water alga that fills the surface waters of ponds with a slippery growth of slender filaments. *(W. Hassler/Amer. Mus. of Nat. Hist.)* **Sargassum (4)** is a brown alga readily recognized by its berrylike bladders, which keep it afloat in great masses in the sea. *(Bruce Hunter/Amer. Mus. of Nat. Hist.)*

Plate 4 ALPINE FLOWERS

Alpine flowers grow at heights where the ground a few inches below the surface is permanently frozen. Brilliant color characterizes many of them, such as red heather and edelweiss.

1. Edelweiss has woolly bracts that envelop the terminal flowerheads and protect the plant against the brilliant sunlight of high altitudes. *(Hans W. Hannau/Shostal)* **2. Red heather** has needlelike leaves which lose little water by evaporation on the windy mountain slopes. *(Josef Muench)*

Plate 5 AMPHIBIANS

Ever since terrestrial insects became numerous in the Carboniferous period more than 300 million yr ago, vertebrate animals have found food waiting for them on land. First to take advantage of this bonanza were the amphibians, whose moist scaleless skins were suited only to regions of high humidity and dim light, and whose immature stages required water to live in. Today the principal amphibians are the tailed salamanders and the tail-less frogs and toads.

The salamander *Pseudotriton* returns from the woodland shade to the ponds in spring to lay its eggs. They hatch into gilled larvae with a broad mouth, two pairs of legs, good eyes, and a readiness to eat small insects. *(Charles M. Bogert / Shostal)*

Toads have a greater ability to withstand dry air than any other amphibians. Their warty glandular skin contains a poison that saves them from attack by many other animals. This toad, from central Chiapas province of Mexico, knows no winter and summer; it visits ponds to sing, mate, and lay eggs at the beginning of the rainy season after the annual drought. *(Walter Dawn)*

The tiger tree frog becomes active at night high above the ground in the tropical rain forest. Its tongue, used for catching insects, is almost as long as its long legs. In breeding season, the tree frog descends to mate and lay eggs in ponds at ground level. *(Axelrod / Shostal)*

wavelength of the radiation if a useful degree of directionality is to be achieved. (The microphone or speaker itself may, of course, be a small unit in the center of a large focusing dish: the dish's dimensions are controlling.) Under water, where the wavelength is five times that in air, the frequency must be in the ultrasonic range if the sound head is to be of reasonable size.

Detection and Measurement: In principle any of the oscillating properties of the medium carrying sound can be used in an instrument for detection and measurement: pressure, actual motion, density, or temperature. Most instruments nowadays are a form of electro-acoustical TRANSDUCER sensitive to pressure or to velocity, but THERMOCOUPLES have been used at sonic frequencies; also, changes in density of a medium resulting from sound transmission can produce bending of light rays passing through a sound field, and this bending can be measured. One of the oldest instruments is the Rayleigh disk, which detects actual particle motion and can be made into an instrument that measures sound directly. It consists of a very small, lightweight disk hung from a fine quartz fiber so that it stands when at rest 45° to the direction of the sound. The motion of the sound waves tends to swing it around more perpendicular to the sound path; the deflection is readily measured, being proportional to the sound intensity.

Resonance: Some musical instruments, *e.g.* the marimba and the xylophone, employ resonant chambers under the actual sound-producing element (see RESONANCE). These reinforce the sound in a manner somewhat different from the sounding board of the violin or piano, which is essentially non-resonant, since they can themselves vibrate only at one frequency. Lifting the pedal of the piano after a note is struck allows the higher strings to resonate to the harmonics of the struck note through "sympathetic vibration" and thus to produce a different artistic effect.—*M. C. H.*

Levels for Acoustical Quantities: It is becoming increasingly common for acoustical magnitudes to be given in terms of levels. The *level* of any quantity is 10 times the logarithm to the base 10 of the ratio of the value of the quantity to a reference value of the same quantity. The unit of level is the *decibel.* Thus to compute a level in decibels it is necessary to know both the value of the quantity under consideration and a reference value that in many instances is arrived at by national or international agreement. If, for example, the quantity under consideration is the square of an acoustic pressure and the reference value is 4×10^{-8} dynes^2/cm^4, then the result is a pressure squared level, a term usually shortened to *pressure level.* Some common reference values are: 10^{-12} watts for *power level,* 1 volt/dyne/cm^2 for *microphone sensitivity level,* and 1 dyne/cm^2/amp at 1 ft distance for *speaker sensitivity level.* Clearly such a list can be extended as desired.

Psychological responses such as *loudness levels* must be based upon statistical studies of groups of persons having normal hearing, and defined rather carefully. Thus the loudness level of an unknown sound or noise in *phons* is the pressure level of a 1,000 cycle/sec pure tone which a battery of listeners judges to be equally loud. The unit of loudness is the *sone,* which is the loudness associated with a 1,000 cycle/sec pure tone whose pressure level is 40 decibels above a listener's threshold of hearing.—*H. M. T.*

ACOUSTICS, ARCHITECTURAL: the science of producing favorable listening conditions in rooms and auditoriums. Listening difficulties all stem from the fact that walls tend to be good reflectors of sound waves. The percentage of the sound energy that is reflected from a wall when a wave strikes it (*reflection coefficient*) varies from one material to another. An excellent acoustical material may have a coefficient as low as 0.1 or 0.2;

Acoustical design: Convex surfaces on interior of Caspery Auditorium, N. Y. City, diffuse sound and prevent focusing at center of dome. (*Harrison and Abramovitz*)

a material such as concrete has a coefficient better than 0.98. Thus the walls of a room often are better reflectors of sound than the best Venetian mirror is of light. Since sound once generated in a room must stay there until it either is absorbed or leaks out through openings such as doors and windows, it is apparent that a sound wave will bounce from wall to wall, becoming less intense as time proceeds, until it finally disappears. Reverberation can be lowered in an enclosure by providing for more absorption. The reverberation time, which is defined as the time required for a sound to decay to one millionth of its initial intensity, should be less than 1 sec for speech, from 1 to 2 sec for chamber music, and 2 to 3.5 sec for a large concert orchestra. Certain wall contours, particularly curved surfaces, give rise to loud and soft spots in an auditorium. A good reflecting wall far removed from the stage can produce a loud and disagreeable ECHO. Two parallel reflecting walls can give rise to a sequence of echoes; this condition is called *acoustical flutter.*—*H. M. T.*

ACROLEIN: a volatile, lacrimatory liquid of highly irritating odor, CH_2=CH—CHO. It is commonly formed when grease is spilled on a hot stove. Acrolein is known for its extremely penetrating odor and is highly irritating even in low concentrations. It is used largely as an intermediate in the making of other chemicals. Made by dehydration of glycerine, it is the simplest compound that is both OLEFIN and ALDEHYDE.—*Ru. M.*

ACRYLIC COMPOUNDS: synthetic materials related to acrylic acid (CH_2:$CHCOOH$). Acrylic compounds are unsaturated and can be polymerized to yield a very important group of thermoplastic resinous products. Depending on initial reagents and polymerization conditions, these products range from hard, transparent, brilliant plastics (aircraft cockpit canopies, molded structural elements, costume jewelry) through resilient fibers (sweaters and fur-like pile fabrics) to adhesives and coating compositions.—*W. P. C.*

ACTH: see ADRENOCORTICOTROPHIC HORMONE.

ACTINIDES: the series of chemical elements that is introduced by actinium (at. no. 89) on the periodic table, and that includes thorium (90), protactinium (91), uranium (92), and the 11 man-made TRANSURANIUM ELEMENTS from neptunium (93) through lawrencium (103). These 11 transuranium elements were synthesized in nuclear reactions by Univ. of California scientists, 1940–1961. All actinides are radioactive. Only thorium and uranium occur in any quantity in nature. Because each actinide element has an analogous element among the lanthanides, or rare-earth elements (at. nos. 57–71), the actinides are sometimes called actinide rare earths or heavy rare earths. Like the lanthanides, the actinide elements are similar to one another in chemical properties, but may differ markedly in physical properties. Actinides are metallic; some show a strong metallurgical resemblance to their analogs in the lanthanide series, *i.e.* americium to europium.—*A. R. G.*

ACTINIUM: a metallic, radioactive element (Ac); at. no. 89; at. wt 227 (longest-lived isotope). One of the first radioactive elements to be discovered, actinium was identified in a sample of pitchblende (1899) by the Frenchman A. Debierne, working on the advice of M. and Mme. Curie. It is the proto-type element of the actinide series. Actinium²²⁷ has a half life of about 22 yr.—*E. H. H.*

ACTION AND REACTION: see NEWTON'S LAWS OF MOTION.

ACTION AT A DISTANCE: the idea in physics that one body can exert a force upon another without any direct mechanical link between them. Newton strongly denied the possibility of forces being operative in the absence of any medium capable of transmitting them, although the force of gravity would seem to be a perfect example of action at a distance. In order to account for the ability of gravitational, electric, and magnetic forces to operate through apparently empty space, 17th-, 18th-, and early 19th-cent. scientists postulated the existence of various hypothetical fluids (notably the luminiferous ether), which acted as the medium through which forces were transmitted in much the same way as in a hydraulic press or in the way sound is transmitted by the air.

When J. Clerk Maxwell worked out his differential equations for electromagnetic phenomena, they were essentially descriptive of the ether; however, he immediately realized that the equations would be equally valid even if the ether did not exist, and that the phenomena could be thought of in terms of fields that had no mechanical counterpart. The subsequent abandonment of the ether as a result of the MICHELSON-MORLEY EXPERIMENT, together with the demonstration of the equivalence of fields and particles by L. V. de Broglie, has removed the subject of action at a distance from serious controversy, present field theory accounting for such action in terms of non-mechanical interaction of fields that can exist in the absence of any material medium.—*E. M. R.*

ACTIVATION: excitation of a molecule to increase its internal energy so that it becomes reactive. Excitation may be effected by means of heating. Some substances, *e.g.* bromine, are activated by irradiation with ultraviolet light. Arrhenius suggested (1889) that there is an equilibrium of reactive and unreactive molecules in every system and only the reactive take part in a chemical reaction. Heat is usually required to induce more energy into the system so that most of the molecules will be activated. Heat absorption is coincident with energy consumption. The energy difference between an inactive and an active molecule can be determined by using the van't Hoff equation, in which the vapor pressure of a certain substance at a given temperature is shown to be equal to the rate at which the molecules of that substance are colliding with each other; rate-of-collision, in turn, is a measure of the molecules' activity.—*G. W. M.*

ACTIVE TRANSPORT: a biochemical process by which living cells are supplied with nutrients by selective passage across cell membranes. Cell membranes are able to admit molecules of certain substances while rejecting very similar ones. Active transport involves a specific chemical interaction between a substance and some membrane component or carrier, and requires energy. In some instances the process also involves a "pumping" mechanism which enables the cell to accumulate concentrations of substances higher than are present outside the cell. Active transport is thus a much more efficient method of supplying cells with specific nutrients than is random diffusion through the cell wall.—*E. S.*

ACTIVITY: popularly, the readiness with which a chemical element reacts with other elements; more technically, the effective concentration of a substance in a chemical system. By the law of MASS ACTION, the extent to which a chemical reaction proceeds is determined by the "active masses" or activities of the reacting components. In dilute (or "ideal") solutions the activity of the solute is substantially equal to its actual concentration. But in high concentrations the difference is substantial, and it is customary to multiply the concentration of each component by a correction factor called the *activity coefficient* to convert it to activity. From this viewpoint, activity is the *effective* concentration. Experimentally, it is possible to determine activity only on the basis of an arbitrarily selected standard state. Among techniques for determining activity of solutions are measurements of vapor pressure, freezing-point depression, osmotic pressure, emf of cells, equilibrium constant, and light scattering.—*M. K.*

ACYL MERCAPTIDES: acyl thiol esters, a class of compounds involved in metabolism. Metabolically, the important ones are those with the thiol or "SH" group supplied by coenzyme A. Fatty acids, for instance, are degraded in the organism after acyl coenzyme A formation.—*F. F.*

ADAMS, FRANK DAWSON, 1859–1942, Canadian geologist; b. Montreal. He classified the Laurentian rocks and wrote the classic *Geology of the Haliburton and Bancroft Areas, Province of Ontario* (1910). Owner of a great library of geology, he wrote one of the few scholarly general histories of that science: *The Birth and Development of the Geological Sciences* (1938). Adams was professor of geology at McGill Univ., a fellow of the Royal Society and an associate of the U. S. National Academy of Sciences.—*D. H. D. R.*

John Couch Adams
(Bettmann Archive)

ADAMS, JOHN COUCH, 1819–92, English astronomer; b. near Laneast, Cornwall. He shares with the Frenchman U. I. I. Leverrier the honor for an independent prediction leading to the discovery of the planet Neptune. Adams computed a predicted position of a new planet in 1845 (within 2° of the actual position of Neptune), but the search was not made until after Leverrier's prediction in 1846. Subsequent work on the Moon's parallax, 1852, and the secular acceleration of the Moon's motion, 1853, won him the gold medal of the Royal Astronomical Society, 1866. He also did research on the Leonid meteors and terrestrial magnetism. He was a fellow of the Royal Society, the recipient of its Copley medal, and an associate of the U. S. National Academy of Sciences.—*O. G.*

in redwood country, nor a redwood compete with grass where water is limited. Grass is adapted to a long annual dry season by its production of drought-resistant seeds. In strong winds it bends easily without breaking. It is scarcely harmed by fire or by its leaves' being eaten close to the ground several times in a season. The grass merely extends more leaf blade from growth centers at the leaf base, and takes advantage of abundant sunlight in a shadeless environment. Similarly, wings are an adaptation that usually aids an adult insect in reaching regions where its young will have suitable conditions. But on oceanic islands subjected to steady wind, shortness of wing and flightlessness are even more important adaptations. They reduce the likelihood that the insect will be blown out to sea and drowned. Plants, on the other hand, show remarkable adaptations in organs for storing food and water, in spines and gums and poisons that defend them from attack, in dissemination of spores, pollen, and seeds. Animals exhibit an even wider range of adaptations valuable in finding and capturing food, in winning mates and providing for the young, in concealment from enemies (ANIMAL CAMOUFLAGE) or in defense and escape. Some plants and animals show social adaptations ranging from mutualism (see SYMBIOSIS) to PARASITISM. (See also ECOLOGY.)—*L. and M. M.* (See Color Plates f.p. 6.)

Variety of adaptations: *Left*—Thick stems of desert-dwelling cacti store large amounts of water for use in drought; spines limit damage by animals. *Below*—Black skimmer uses protruding under part of bill to skim water for food. *Lower left*—Scaly anteater laps up ants with sticky tongue. For defense it has horny scales and a bad odor. *Lower right*—Large eyes of cloud forest snake gather relatively large amount of light, thus help when snake hunts in dim light. (*Photos at left, Ewing Galloway; at right, Walter Dawn*)

ADAPTATIONS IN ANIMALS AND PLANTS: all the features of structure and function that clearly improve an organism's chance of surviving and reproducing (see NATURAL SELECTION). Some adaptations, *e.g.* tanning of human skin, are reversible and individual, related to a way of life that may be temporary. Others are characteristic of species, having been produced by EVOLUTION over a long time. Usually they benefit the organism in one situation but not in others, for each adaptation relates to a specific aspect of the surrounding world. Where light is the chief limiting factor for a land plant, for example, a woody trunk that can be extended year after year becomes an adaptation holding the foliage high, out of reach of leaf-eating animals on the ground and beyond shading by competing plants. Giant redwood trees thousands of years old show the ultimate in this adaptation. But they can use it only where water is plentiful, the growing season long, deep freezing of the soil unlikely, and calamities such as floods, fires, and hurricanes rare. Grass cannot compete with a redwood

ADAPTIVE ENZYMES (inducible enzymes): ENZYMES produced by microorganisms in response to substances in the culture medium. The inducing substance in some unknown manner participates in enzyme formation, but need not be a substrate of the enzyme whose formation it induces.—*E. G.*

ADDITION: see ARITHMETIC and SET THEORY.

ADDITION REACTION: see HYDROCARBON.

ADHESION AND COHESION: forces of attraction between molecules, principally in solids. These forces are essentially electrical. Adhesion is the attractive force between unlike particles (molecules or atoms), cohesion the force between like particles. Thus fine dust and paint *adhere* to a smooth solid, but the particles of a steel cable *cohere* together. Both adhesion and cohesion depend on temperature, cleanliness of adjoining surfaces, intimacy of contact, degree of pressure, etc.

The constituent particles composing a body occupy positions determined by the principle of minimum potential energy (see ENERGY). If an attempt is made to bring these particles closer together, an elastic reaction is set up, resisting the compression. Conversely, if the particles are separated beyond their normal distance, forces of cohesion, opposing this separation, come into play. The same conditions govern the spacing of atoms or ions in the crystal lattice of a solid. (See CRYSTALLOGRAPHY.)

A clean, circularly shaped glass plate, suspended at its center by a spring, exhibits considerable adhesion when brought into contact with the surface of water. When finally separated from this surface, the plate emerges *wet,* indicating that the force of adhesion of water to glass is greater than the cohesion of water for itself. If the same experiment is tried with mercury, the glass plate, removable from the mercury surface only with considerable effort, is found to be *dry*; adhesion, now more marked than before, is nevertheless not as great as the cohesion between mercury particles.—*A. E.*

ADHESIVES: substances used for binding one object to another, generally with a very thin film. They are also called cements or adhesive cements. Many adhesives used today have a long history; *e.g.* flour-and-water mixtures for uniting paper surfaces, cements made with casein for household uses, balsams for lenses, ordinary GLUE, and the *mucilages* made from plant GUMS. Spectacular improvements have been made in adhesives in recent years through synthetic chemistry. The plies in plywood are bonded with waterproof urea-formaldehyde resins, and thin metal sections of airplanes are bonded more firmly with epoxy resins than by rivets. Although these synthetic resins (plastics) usually require a curing time, they are adaptable to household use (see RESIN).—*Ru. M.*

ADIABATIC PROCESS: a process in which matter undergoes a change without losing heat energy to, or gaining it from, an outside source. Imagine a gas confined in a piston-fitted cylinder that is thoroughly insulated to prevent exchange of

Adiabatic cooling: As air moves up a mountainside, it expands with increasing altitude and therefore cools. As it moves down the other side and is compressed, it warms again.

7000 ft	41.5°F
6000 ft	47°F
5000 ft	52.5°F
4000 ft	58°F
3000 ft	63.5°F
2000 ft	69°F
1000 ft	74.5°F

heat between the gas specimen and its surroundings. Any operation that proceeds without the entrance or escape of heat is called adiabatic. On removal of weights from the piston one at a time, the gas will expand very slowly, decreasing in pressure as the external pressure is diminished. Since work is performed in the raising of the load, there must be a loss of energy by the only source available, namely, the internal energy of the gas itself. In consequence, the temperature of the gas drops; the internal energy decreases by an amount equivalent to the work done. Adiabatic expansion of a substance results in cooling, whereas adiabatic compression warms it. Actually no process is 100% adiabatic; some heat is always gained or lost, though the amount may be negligible. Adiabatic processes may occur not only when they are insulated from the surroundings, but also when they happen so fast there is little time for heat exchange.—*J. E. W.*

Many applications of adiabatic processes are found in mechanical engineering. Such processes are important in the action of AIRFOILS and other elements in contact with air. In meteorology, adiabatic changes occur as air rises and falls. Air moving upward expands because atmospheric pressure decreases with altitude. As it rises, dry air cools adiabatically at a rate of 5.4°F for every 1,000 ft it is lifted. Sinking air warms at the same rate. Rising air with moisture condensing in it cools more slowly, because heat of condensation is added to the air as water vapor changes to liquid droplets. The rate at which this air cools is the "pseudo-adiabatic lapse rate"; it is about 3.2°F of cooling for every 1,000 ft of lift. (See CLOUD; INVERSION; LAPSE RATE; THERMODYNAMICS.)—*P. L.*

ADP: see NUCLEOTIDES.

ADRENAL GLAND: one of the pair of ENDOCRINE GLANDS located on the forward (or upper) end of each kidney. These small, caplike structures are richly supplied with blood vessels. Each is about the size of the end of a thumb and weighs less than ½ oz. An adrenal gland is composed of an outer shell-like layer (cortex) and an inner corelike center (medulla). These two parts are so different in origin, structure, and function that they may be considered different glands.

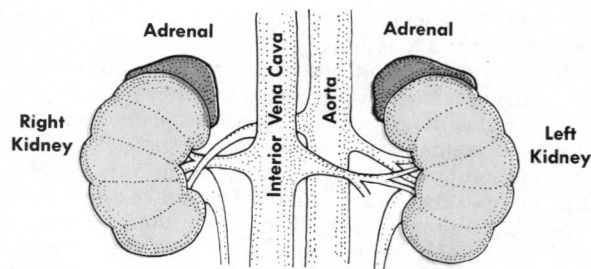

Adrenals: Endocrine glands, on upper ends of kidneys, secrete important hormones and discharge them directly into the bloodstream.

The *cortex* of the adrenal is essential to life. Destruction or removal of both right and left cortices is fatal. The cortex apparently secretes a number of hormones that have different functions (see ADRENOCORTICAL HORMONES). They are important in the metabolism of carbohydrates and proteins, regulate the development of sex organs, and control various chemical components of the blood. One of the most important cortical secretions is cortisone, which plays many significant roles in body activity. Malfunction of the cortex leads to the symptoms of Addison's disease, which results in a lowered concentration of sodium in the plasma and a loss of water from the blood. Tumors of the adrenal cortex, with consequent excess secretion of cortical hormones, have profound effects on sexual development. In young children, for example, such tumors lead prematurely to changes characteristic of puberty. The *medulla* is not essential to life and can be removed from both adrenals without noticeable symptoms. Unlike other endocrines, it is under nervous control; nerve impulses stimulate it to secrete ADRENALIN into the bloodstream. During an emergency, as in fear or rage, the medulla secretes large amounts of adrenalin, which speeds the flow of the blood, raises the blood-sugar level, decreases the clotting time of the blood, and delays fatigue—all changes that tend to increase the capacity for muscular exertion.—*A. P. E.*

ADRENALIN (or epinephrine): one of the two hormonal substances secreted by the adrenal medulla; norepinephrine is the other. Adrenalin increases the heartbeat, the systolic blood pressure, and the blood glucose and blood lactate levels. It prepares the body for emergency activities such as fight and flight. It was the first hormone to be isolated as crystals.—*F. F.*

ADRENOCORTICAL HORMONE: any of the biologically active steroids secreted by the adrenal cortex. Seven of them, sometimes referred to as corticosteroids, can be classed in two groups. Four steroids having a primary action on carbohydrate metabolism are called glucocorticoids. Three steroids having a primary action on electrolyte metabolism, particularly an effect to conserve body sodium, are called mineralocorticoids. In the human being, cortisol is the principal and most active glucocorticoid, and aldosterone is the most active mineralocorticoid. The remaining five steroids are produced in minor quantities. All these compounds have very similar structures, comparable to TESTOSTERONE or PROGESTERONE. The adrenal cortex also produces the sex hormones: progesterone, ESTROGEN, and ANDROGENS. The adrenal androgens are secreted in substantial amounts and are of considerable physiological importance, particularly in the female. The adrenal cortex and the secretions of its hormones are maintained and stimulated by the pituitary ADRENOCORTICOTROPHIC HORMONE (ACTH). The adrenal cortex is essential for life, because of the life-maintaining properties of the glucocorticoids and mineralocorticoids. Glucocorticoids in particular aid resistance to many forms of environmental stress and noxious stimuli, *e.g.* heat, cold, injury, toxins, burns; hence the use of these substances in medicine.—*F. U.*

ADRENOCORTICOTROPHIC HORMONE (ACTH): a protein secreted by the anterior lobe of the pituitary gland; it stimulates the growth and maintains the size and function of the adrenal cortex. ACTH stimulates the secretion of the adrenocortical hormones by the adrenal cortex. The human steroid hormone cortisol is produced in this manner. The major biological effects of ACTH are a result of adrenocortical stimulation. The pituitary secretion of ACTH is regulated, in part, by the circulating blood levels of cortisol. The inhibition of pituitary ACTH secretion by cortisol, a product of ACTH stimulation of the adrenal cortex, is a basic means of hormonal regulation, referred to as a negative feedback mechanism. ACTH secretion is also influenced by neurohumoral agents released from the hypothalamus. Purified forms of ACTH indicate the active substance to be polypeptide, containing 39 amino acids with a molecular weight of 5,000. The amino-acid sequence of ACTH obtained from several animal species shows only minor differences in structure, which do not affect biological activity. This molecule can be degraded further by partial digestion with a proteolytic enzyme, pepsin, leaving a residue with appreciable biological activity.—*F. U.*

ADRIAN, EDGAR DOUGLAS, 1889– , English physiologist; b. London. He developed electrical methods for investigation of the sense organs and engaged in research on the physiology of the nervous system. Adrian and Sir Charles Sherrington shared the Nobel prize, 1932, for their discoveries as to functions of neurons. Adrian wrote *The Basis of Sensation* (1928), *The Mechanism of Nervous Action* (1932), and *The Physical Background of Perception* (1947). He is a fellow of the Royal Society and an associate of the U. S. National Academy of Sciences.—*D. H. D. R.*

ADSORPTION: the process by which the surface of a solid or a liquid (the *adsorbent*) attracts and holds any atom, molecule, or ion (the *adsorbate*) from a solution or a gas with which it is in contact. Adsorption is thus a characteristic of the interfaces between two phases of matter; the total amount of material adsorbed depends upon the affinity between them and upon the total surface exposed to the mobile particles. Finely divided solids (clays, charcoal, powdered metals) or liquids (fine droplets, as in aerosols or sprays) have high adsorptive capacities because of the enormous amount of exposed surface relative to their mass. Adsorption is significant in certain biological phenomena (*e.g.* transport of dissolved nutrient material in soils), in several industrial processes (hydrogenation, air purification, petroleum cracking, sugar refining, desalting of sea water or other brackish waters), in laboratory separation of proteins and enzymes (*e.g.* by adsorption on earths or alumina), and in other laboratory techniques (*e.g.* CHROMATOGRAPHY). Adsorption may sometimes be a prelude to ABSORPTION (a penetration into the bulk of the solid or liquid), and is often, as in catalysis, a necessary prerequisite to chemical reaction.—*W. E. C.*

ADVANCEMENT OF LEARNING: see BACON, FRANCIS.

ADVECTION: the process of transfer, especially of heat and moisture, by mass horizontal motion of the atmosphere. Thus a very warm day can be caused not only by strong solar heating (radiation), but by winds carrying a mass of warm air into the area. (See AIR MASS; WEATHER SYSTEM.)—*P. L.*

AERODYNAMICS: the branch of fluid mechanics dealing with the action of air, or any other gas, with respect to forces being exerted upon it. It is generally considered to deal primarily with the principles governing flight through the atmosphere by heavier-than-air AIRCRAFT. An airplane or other heavier-than-air aircraft flies because it can obtain enough *lift* from its passage through the air to sustain it. When lift is augmented, as in the airplane, by *thrust* from a propeller or jet, the total force is more than enough to offset the downward effect of gravity and the static effect of *drag*, and the aircraft can fly forward and upward. Lift utilizes several aerodynamic forces. The concepts underlying these forces were recognized by Sir Isaac Newton and Daniel Bernoulli. According to Newton's first law, a body at rest or in motion will remain so until a force acts upon it to change its state of rest or motion; his third law states that for every action there must be an equal and opposite reaction. According to Bernoulli's theorem, an increase in the velocity of air will reduce its pressure.

An AIRFOIL (an aircraft surface such as wing, rudder, or propeller blade) makes use of all these concepts. The first step

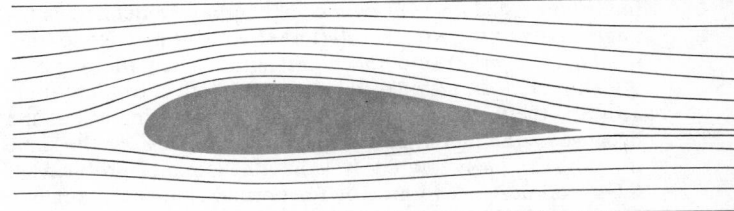

Air flow: Camber causes reduced pressure in air passing over airfoil, and increased pressure in air passing under it; hence lift.

in obtaining lift is to use a wing which will allow a stream-lined flow of air over and under it. Air striking its leading edge will divide, some going under the wing and some over. The air that goes under the wing produces a lifting effect similar to that which sustains a kite in the wind. This lifting effect due to positive pressure on the underside of a wing accounts for about 30% of the lift of a normal type of airfoil. The rest of the air, passing over the wing, produces lift by negative pressure. In most airfoils, the amount of camber (curvature) of the upper surface of the wing is greater than that of the under surface. Because of this, air passing over the top surface is deflected sharply upward, while that going under the bottom of the wing is deflected less. Thus a particle moving over the top of the wing has to travel in the same time a distance greater than that traveled by a similar particle moving under the wing. Its velocity is therefore greater, and since, according to Bernoulli's theorem, an increase in the velocity of air will reduce its pressure, the pressure on the top of the wing will be less than on the bottom surface. The pressure differential thus created between the top and bottom of the wing accounts for about 70% of the total lift which keeps an airplane in flight.

Drag: The total force of the air operating against and along an aircraft's path of flight is *drag*. It must be overcome to allow the wing (or other airfoil) to move through the air. In horizontal flight this is accomplished by the thrust of the propeller or jet. The type of drag caused by the deflection of air around a wing is known as *induced drag*. Since an increase in air deflection, up to a certain point, will cause increased lift, a short, wide wing such as that of the B-17 and most "trainers" gives these types a great deal of lift, but at the same time the greater drag caused by the increase in air deflection results in relatively low speeds. The type of drag caused by adverse pressures other than those due to lift is known as *profile drag*, and varies primarily with the cross-sectional area of the object; adverse pressures arise both from skin friction of air flowing along the surface and from the formation of turbulent wakes. In supersonic flight, additional drag caused by shock-wave configuration around the aircraft is called *wave drag*.

Airflow over wing: As angle of attack increases, so do lift and drag. Lift reaches maximum just before stalling point.

Factors Affecting Lift and Drag: A number of conditions affect the relationship between lift and drag. One of the most important is the *angle of attack*, which may be defined as the angle between the wing chord (line from leading edge to trailing edge of wing) and the flight path. When the angle of attack increases, as when the aircraft is put into a climbing attitude, the lifting force imposed on the wing increases, and because of the increased lift, the airplane rises. At the same time the drag is increased. It is one of the major problems of the airfoil designer to provide for normal changes in angle of attack, and still obtain maximum lift and minimum drag. As the angle of climb is increased further, the lift also increases

up to a certain point, known as the stalling point. Here, the smooth flow of air along the wing becomes broken, and the air itself, especially on the upper surface of the wing, becomes very turbulent and is said to "burble" (see TURBULENCE). Where burbling occurs, the motion of air above the wing is so disturbed that Bernoulli's theorem does not apply, and the air remains at atmospheric pressure. Consequently, there is a smaller pressure differential between the upper and lower surfaces of the airfoil, so that the airfoil's effectiveness is reduced sharply. At the same time the drag is greatly increased, because the burbling offers high resistance to the airflow. These conditions—a high angle of climb, with low lift and a large amount of drag—cause the airplane to "stall." At the actual stalling point the weight of the airplane more or less suddenly overcomes the remaining lift, the controls lose their effectiveness, and the airplane "falls off" sharply, either straight downward or into a spiral or spin.

An increase in air density will increase both lift and drag, as will a total increase in wing area. Lift and drag also vary with airspeed: at slow speeds there is less lift and less drag.

Aerodynamic Stability: A major problem of design is to offset any tendency of the aircraft to become so unstable in flight as to require excessive effort by the pilot in maintaining a normal path through the air and preventing any danger of stall. If the air always remained the same, this problem would be a negligible one; but air is usually in motion, and its density, movements, and turbulence change frequently, with consequent effects on the airfoil.

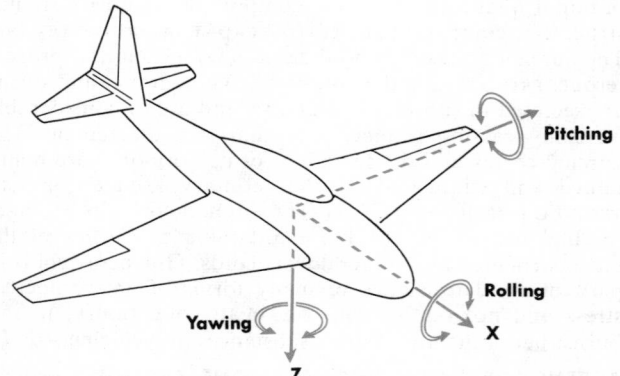

Variation from straight and level flight: Yaw, pitch, and roll are motions occurring on three mutually perpendicular axes.

Changes in *pitch,* which is motion of the airplane around its lateral axis, are usually compensated for by the horizontal stabilizer, the small "wing" which is part of the tail assembly. If, for example, the nose of the aircraft should go down, the lifting action of the tail becomes less because of its negative angle of attack. The tail assembly therefore goes down, so that the aircraft as a whole is level again.

Another variation from level flight is *roll* or "bank," which is movement of the airplane around its longitudinal axis, as one wing goes up and the other down. The tendency of an airplane to roll is usually compensated for by *dihedral,* a slight, built-in, upward slope of the wing from fuselage to tip. When one wing goes down, it therefore actually becomes parallel with the desired horizontal plane of flight, develops more lift, and tends to rise, so that the opposite wing, which is high, goes down. A wing with dihedral has slightly less lift than a straight wing, but its stability is much greater. Roll may also be corrected by the vertical fin of the tail assembly. Any roll is accompanied by a slight, sideward slip in the direction of the roll, and air striking the fin tends to return it to normal position and thus helps to level the wings.

The tendency of an aircraft, during normal, horizontal flight, to turn to one side or the other, is called *yaw*, and it is corrected by the vertical fin as well as by the rudder. Any yawing motion is accompanied by a slight slip, and as in the case of roll, air strikes the large surfaces presented by the fin and rudder, and straightens them in the original path of forward flight. Another aerodynamic feature which prevents yaw is sweepback, or taper of the leading edge of the wing from the fuselage to the tip. In normal flight no portion of a sweptback wing meets the airstream at a right angle. As the airplane yaws, however, turning around its vertical axis, the wing that is farther forward reaches a position where its leading edge is at right angles to the airflow. In this position it offers more resistance to the air, and thus has more drag than the other wing. The increased drag pulls the forward wing back, and the other wing moves forward to the position for normal, straight flight.

Torque: The turning moment caused by the rotation of a propeller is called *torque*. Its effect on the airplane in flight is a combination of roll and yaw. As the engine turns the propeller in a clockwise direction (facing forward from the cockpit), the airplane tends to rotate in a counter-clockwise direction around the fuselage. To offset torque the left wing is designed to have more lift than the right wing. It also has more drag, and as a result the airplane tends to turn to the left around the center of gravity. This yawing motion must be overcome by right rudder. To do away with the need for the pilot to carry right rudder for long periods, however, the vertical fin is offset an amount necessary to trim the airplane at cruising speed. In addition there may be rudder trim tabs, adjusted on the ground or controlled by the pilot, to compensate for the torque at any airspeed. Torque is, of course, most noticeable during the take-off run and climb, when the propeller is turning over at a high rate of speed. One of the great advantages of jet and rocket-propelled aircraft is the lack of torque that results from their having no propellers.

High-Lift Devices: The increased power and weight of modern airplanes tend to require high landing speeds. Not only is this more dangerous for the average pilot; it also requires longer and more substantial landing surfaces. Hence most modern airplanes are equipped with flaps and slots which enable the airplane to develop greater lift at lower speeds. Most types of *flaps* are built into the airplane as sections of the trailing edge of each wing. As they are lowered, the camber of the wing is thus changed to give more lift at the same angle of attack. As a result, with flaps down, an airplane can be flown slower at the same angle of attack than with flaps up. With flaps down, drag also is increased, but this is an advantage in landing. Acting as "air brakes," the flaps enable an airplane to be flown at a steeper negative angle in a glide or dive without appreciably increasing the airspeed. They thus aid a pilot landing in a small field or over obstructions surrounding a field. The simple flap is similar to an aileron, except that the flaps on both sides are lowered together. More efficient than the simple flap is the slotted flap, which has slots that allow the passage of air from the underside to the top of the flap. Air coming out of the slot tends to eliminate burbling over the top surface of the flap, and establishes a smooth flow of air that persists up to high flap angles. As a result, the airplane can be flown at even greater angles of attack, without increasing airspeed, than with the simple flap. *Slots,* the other major type of high-lift device, may be either fixed or controllable. Fixed slots are used in some light airplanes, especially near the wing tip, which has a tendency to stall first. Movable slots normally fit tightly

against the leading edge of the wing, but can be moved to a position in front of the wing to form a slot. Some are automatic in operation. The operation of both types of slotted wings is similar to that of slotted flaps. Air flowing through the slot tends to overcome the burble that collects on the upper surface of the wing as the stalling point is approached. Lift can therefore be maintained at high angles of attack, with the airplane in a very nose-high attitude. High-lift devices such as slots are especially important in transonic and supersonic aircraft because they help maintain laminar flow in the *boundary layer* (see below). They also lessen the tendency of wing tips and ailerons to stall out at high angles of attack and thus reduce landing and take-off runs. Furthermore, they allow take-off with heavier loads at the same speeds; and they may allow a reduction in the wing area and thus improve an aircraft's high-speed characteristics.

Transonic and Supersonic Flight: Until the advent of jet- and rocket-propulsion, aerodynamics was concerned principally with *subsonic* flight, *i.e.* flight at speeds below the speed of sound. New problems have arisen with the development of aircraft capable of flight in the upper SONIC REGIMES, *e.g.* *transonic* (at or near the speed of sound) and *supersonic* flight (above the speed of sound). The speed of sound varies with temperature. At sea level it is 761 mi/hr; it decreases with increased altitude up to about 35,000 ft, where it is about 660 mi/hr. Above that point, temperature—and therefore the speed of sound—remains relatively constant. So critical is the speed of sound in aerodynamics that the ratio of the velocity of an object to the velocity of sound has been given a name, the MACH NUMBER, after Ernst Mach (1838–1916), an Austrian scientist. Thus Mach 1.00 at sea level is 761 mi/hr; Mach 1.50, 1141.5 mi/hr; Mach 2, 1522 mi/hr; and so on. The speed of

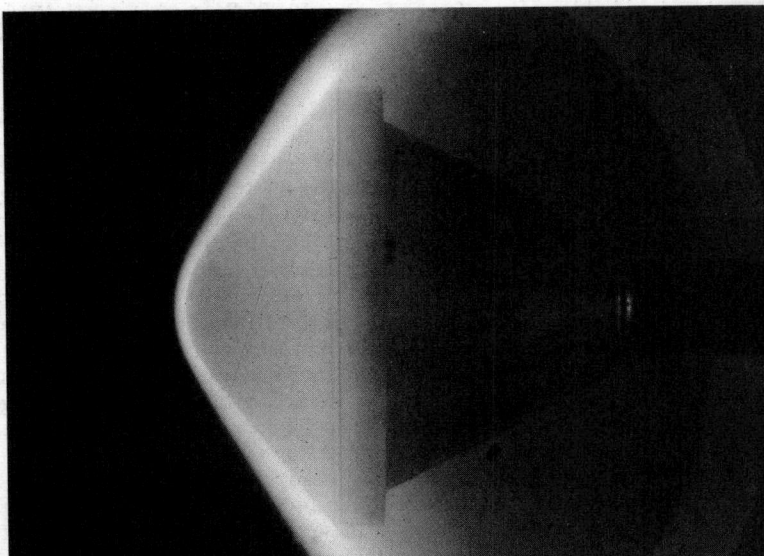

Air striking an experimental nose cone at 20 times the speed of sound is rendered luminous by the impact. (*USAF*)

sound was first exceeded in level flight on Oct. 14, 1947, when a U. S. rocket-propelled airplane, the Bell X-1, reached Mach 1.06. Speeds of Mach 5.00 and above have since been attained.

The basic new element at transonic and supersonic speeds is that the air flow is affected by the air's *compressibility:* this is directly related to the formation of shock waves over the airfoils as an aircraft approaches the speed of sound. In developing a condition of steady flight, an aircraft sends out a continuing series of sound waves or traveling pressure waves. As an aircraft approaches the speed of sound it begins to catch up to its advance pressure waves, which travel at the speed of sound. As the airplane reaches the speed of sound, these pressure (sound) waves bunch up to form a strong pressure wave or shock wave. Shock waves angle out from the airfoil much as the bow wave of a ship goes out sharply from the bow. A sudden jump in air density occurs as the aircraft passes through a shock wave; this distorts the air flow. Also associated with a shock wave are sudden pressure changes that give rise to high drag and sometimes, especially near Mach 1, violent buffeting that greatly reduces the effectiveness of the control surfaces. A SONIC BOOM may also result because of wave-focusing effects near the ground.

"Transonic" covers the range of speeds from where compressibility effects are first noticed up to about Mach 1.05. Since air traveling over the surface of an airfoil flows faster than the surrounding air, some of this air may reach the speed of sound while the aircraft is flying at only Mach 0.7 to 0.8. The effects of compressibility occur from this speed to the speed at which the entire aircraft is moving faster than the speed of sound. Transonic phenomena include severe changes in aircraft trim, severe vibrations, large shifts in load distribution, and large percentage variation in control forces. Buffeting—random oscillations of an aircraft—is common. Aeroelastic distortion of the fuselage and wings may cause momentary control reversal. The undesirable handling characteristics of modern jet aircraft at transonic speeds are combatted in a number of ways, *e.g.* by the use of completely power-operated control surfaces. The need for these is illustrated by the fact that a high-speed pull-out of a World War II fighter required the pilot to exert a force of 200 lb, while a similar pull-out of an F-86, without power assistance, would require a force of about 10,000 lb. Among other developments are flight- and fire-control systems; electronic engine controls; automatic fuel-tank selector systems; and many emergency devices.

In general, the sweptback wing and the delta arrowhead shape appear to be desirable for aircraft flying in the transonic range and up to about Mach 1.4. Sweepback delays the sharp rise in drag that takes place in aircraft approaching sonic speed and delays arrival at the critical Mach number (where compressibility effects first begin). Increased stability is achieved; although the aircraft may be flying faster than the speed of sound, the velocity of the air flow has dropped to subsonic by the time it reaches the wing tips. The delta wing is essentially a sweptback wing with the trailing edges filled in. The resultant increase in wing area decreases the wing loading (ratio of aircraft's gross weight to its wing area). Most of the advantages of the sweptback wing in the sonic area are retained in the delta shape. Although the sweptback wing and the delta shape appear to be desirable for aircraft flying in the transonic and low supersonic zones, at higher speeds the drag of these types increases so much that it becomes greater than that of the straight wing. In fact, the peak drag coefficient of the straight wing occurs at the speed of sound; then the drag coefficient decreases as the straight-wing aircraft moves further into the supersonic range. So, provided there is enough power to get it through its peak drag at the speed of sound, the straight-wing aircraft gives definite advantage for speeds above Mach 2.00. However, the wings must be very thin, and must have a small span compared with the chord.

The problem of maintaining lift at supersonic speeds has created much interest in the *boundary layer,* the thin layer of air adjacent to the wing. In this layer, the concept of which was first postulated by Ludwig Prandtl in 1904, the velocity of the air flow changes from a finite velocity at some small distance from the wing to zero at the wing surface itself. All the effects on the airflow of friction (or drag) between the wing and the air stream are generated in this thin layer. Flow in the boundary layer may be *laminar* (a regular and parallel flow, promoting lift) or *turbulent* (inhibiting lift and increasing drag). At a certain REYNOLDS NUMBER, the boundary layer changes from laminar to turbulent flow. One method of maintaining laminar flow, mentioned above, is the use of high-lift-type devices. Other methods under study include arrangements for blowing or sucking air over the wings, *e.g.* porous wing sections, exerting a suction effect.

After an aircraft passes through the transonic zone and begins to fly at truly supersonic speeds, it enters a realm of almost unbelievable smoothness. The control difficulties caused by shock-wave instabilities disappear, and a stable shock-wave configuration forms around the aircraft. However, as speeds push up past Mach 2, aerodynamic heating is severe. There are tremendous rises in temperature caused by friction with the air. At Mach 3, the temperature in the boundary layer rises as much as 600°F. Although time is required for this heat to flow onto the aircraft surface, cockpit refrigeration is a necessity; and much attention must be given to structural materials for supersonic aircraft. The phenomenon of CREEP results from aircraft structures being subjected to constant loads at high temperatures. In jet flight, aerodynamic heating is added to the heat of the engines; tail-pipe temperatures of jet engines may reach 2,000°F. Aluminum alloys lose much of their strength above 250°F. Other alloys, especially those utilizing titanium, are more satisfactory at high speeds. Above 400,000 ft, the air is so thin that friction effects die out (see THERMAL STRESS AND SHOCK).

Supersonic wings have sharp leading edges, and their general cross-sectional shape may be that of a double wedge, biconvex (a double circular arc), or a modified double wedge (see AIRFOIL). The main lifting surfaces of future supersonic aircraft will be generally smaller than those of today's aircraft because there will be larger lifting pressures for a given aircraft weight (see FLUID FLOW).—*A. P. E. and D. B.*

AEROELASTICITY: the deformation of a body such as a flying airplane in response to aerodynamic forces. Aeroelasticity thus draws together the study of aerodynamics and elasticity. With low-speed, stiff-structured aircraft, aeroelastic effects may be disregarded.—*K. K.*

AEROLOGY: the science of METEOROLOGY; or, more specifically, that branch of meteorology which deals with the phenomena of the upper atmosphere.

AERONAUTICS: a broad term covering design, construction, and operation of aircraft of all types, as well as design and operation of airports, air-traffic control, and design and manufacture of associated components such as communication equipment. The term is broader than AVIATION, which applies only to heavier-than-air aircraft. Aeronautics also covers those rocket-powered and ballistic vehicles which escape only briefly from the earth's atmosphere. By contrast, longer missions in outer space would fall into the category of *astronautics* (see SPACE TRAVEL). However, a sharp distinction between the two terms is not always made. Articles of general aeronautical interest are AERODYNAMICS (principles underlying heavier-than-air flight), AIRCRAFT (survey of types), AVIATION (historical development of heavier-than-air flight). Articles on specific phases of aeronautics include AIRCRAFT INSTRUMENTATION, AIRCRAFT PROPULSION, AIRFOIL, AIR NAVIGATION, and WIND TUNNEL. See also entries on individual aircraft types: AIRPLANE, AIRSHIP, BALLOON, GLIDER, HELICOPTER; also MISSILE and ROCKET.—*D. B.*

AEROSOL: a suspension of extremely fine particles of liquid or solid in gases, usually air (see COLLOID CHEMISTRY). Commercially, the term is applied to aerosol bombs, in which insecticides or other substances are dissolved and kept at pressures such that the propellant remains liquid—*i.e.,* about 35 lb/in.² When released, the solvent instantly vaporizes, leaving an aerosol of the solute.—*T. M.*

AFFINE GEOMETRY: the study of those properties of plane figures and relations between them that remain invariant under all cylindrical projections from one plane π to another plane π' (see figure). There is also an affine geometry for a space of greater than two dimensions; we limit ourselves, however, to the plane. A cylindrical projection is a transformation that establishes a one-to-one correspondence between the points of π and those of π' in a direction parallel to an arbitrarily given line *l*, which, however, must not be parallel to either π or π'. Such projections may be repeated any finite

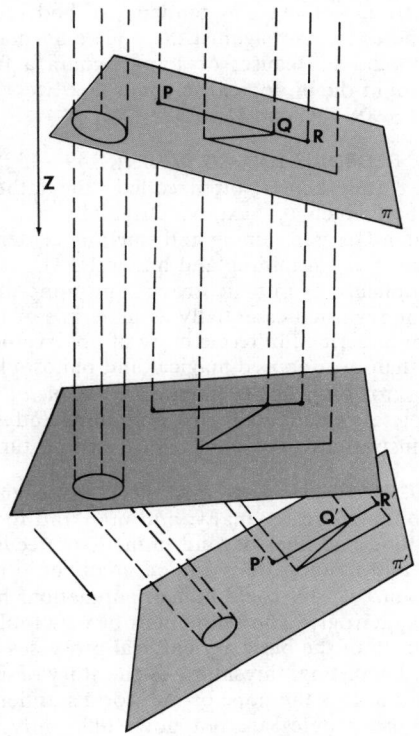

Projections: If a figure is projected from one plane to another, its shape may change. If the lines of projection are parallel, the change is an affine transformation.

number of times passing from plane to plane and terminating, possibly, on the initial plane π. A sequence of one or more cylindrical projections is called an *affine transformation.* The set of all affine transformations that transform the points of a plane into the points of the *same* plane is a closed set called a GROUP. By this we mean that the inverse of an affine transformation, which maps the image points on their pre-images, is an affine transformation and that the result of two such transformations successively is also an affine transformation.

Under cylindrical projection (and therefore also under the group of affine transformations in the plane), collinear points go into collinear points, parallel lines into parallel lines, concurrent lines into concurrent lines. If *P, Q,* and *R* are collinear points, and *P', Q', R'* are their affine images, the ratio $PQ:QR = P'Q':Q'R'$ is an invariant. However, the ratio of segments on intersecting lines is not an invariant. The ratio

of two areas remains invariant, but the shapes of their boundaries may change. For example, a circle may be transformed into an ellipse and a non-zero angle may be transformed into any other non-zero angle.

Affine geometry can also be treated analytically. In the case of the plane, let x_1, x_2 be the parallel coordinates of a point on the plane π, and let y_1, y_2 be the parallel coordinates of its image under an affine transformation in the same plane π; then the analytic expression of the transformation is given by the equations

$$y_1 = a_{10} + a_{11}x_1 + a_{12}x_2$$
$$y_2 = a_{20} + a_{21}x_1 + a_{22}x_2$$

where the a_{ij} are real numbers and $D = a_{11}a_{22} - a_{21}a_{12} \neq 0$. This analytic formulation of the group of planar affine transformations can be generalized to a space S_n of *n*-dimensions.

The planar affine group is a subgroup of the group of projective collineations (see PROJECTIVE GEOMETRY) which leave the "line at infinity" (the ideal line) of the projective plane invariant. Euclidean plane geometry, in turn, is concerned with such properties and relations of plane figures which remain invariant under the transformations of a subgroup of the affine group, namely, those which transform right angles into right angles. Affine geometry is from this point of view a halfway station between Euclidean and projective geometry. Affine geometry originated with Leonhard Euler (1707–83). In recent years interest in it has been renewed, and the subject has been considerably enlarged, particularly in the direction of affine differential geometry.—*J. M. F.*

AFFINITY: an attractive force assumed to exist between chemical elements. Under its action two or more atoms are drawn toward one another and held in proximity, forming a chemical compound. The attraction is greatest between very dissimilar elements such as metals and nonmetals; thus, table salt, a combination of metallic sodium with nonmetallic chlorine, is very stable. Nonmetals together may form stable compounds, as carbon and oxygen in carbon dioxide. Metals are only weakly attracted to one another; they may unite into alloys, like copper-zinc (bronze). Though stable, the alloys are not subject to the law of DEFINITE PROPORTIONS, and are not true chemical compounds. Affinity is measured as to the free energy of formation of a compound from its elements.—*C. S.*

AFTERIMAGE: the continued perception of an object by the eye, but in colors complementary to the originals, after the object has been withdrawn. Afterimages occur after prolonged and intense exposure to a fixed light stimulus and are attributed to fatigue of the retina of the eye. A long exposure to a strong yellow (red-green) light results in a complementary blue afterimage.—*A. E.*

Afterimage effect: Fix gaze on spot at center of drawing at left for a half minute or more. Then look at spot in center of drawing at right. Afterimage will fill out pattern of hand.

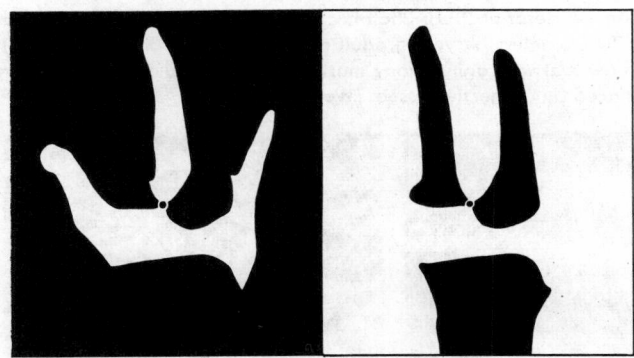

AGASSIZ, (JEAN) LOUIS (RODOLPHE), 1807–73, Swiss-American naturalist and educator; b. Motier, Switz. A pioneer in ichthyology, he published his first major work, *The Fishes of Brazil,* in 1829, and while professor of natural history at the Univ. of Neuchâtel (1832–45), produced the 5-vol. *Studies of Fossil Fishes* (1833–44). In 1836 Agassiz began his study of the glaciers of Switzerland, which led to *Studies of Glaciers* (1840) and *New Studies* (1847). He was the first in

Jean Louis Rodolphe Agassiz
(Harvard News Bureau)

Europe to recognize for what they were the scattered evidences of the recent GLACIAL AGES, and on going to the U. S. A. he found similar evidences in the northern states. Agassiz held the chair of natural history in the Lawrence Scientific School at Harvard (1848–73), founded the Museum of Comparative Zoology at Harvard (1858), and organized the first marine biological laboratory (1873), from which grew the present Marine Biological Laboratory at Woods Hole, Cape Cod. Popular and influential as teacher and lecturer, Agassiz also wrote the 4-vol. *Contributions to the Natural History of the U. S.* (1857–62). Although steadfastly opposed to Darwinism, which he felt improperly substituted biological for divine causes in the history of life, he was a major force in generating interest in careful observation as the basis for exact biological sciences. He was a fellow of the Royal Society and a member of the National Academy of Sciences.—*S. B.*

AGE: see AGING; GEOCHRONOLOGY; LIFE SPAN; RADIOACTIVE DATING.

AGGLOMERATION: (1) Aggregation of material into a compact, rounded mass. The aggregated fragments are relatively homogeneous, *i.e.* composed of more or less similar material. The cohesive force may be generated by heat, as with fragments of volcanic matter, or by pressure. (2) Flocculation of colloidal particles present in the sol (colloidal solution—see COLLOID CHEMISTRY). Thus, addition of alumina or other agglomerating agents to impure water containing very fine colloidal particles (organic and inorganic matter) produces a flocculent sediment of the impurities.—*C. S.*

AGING (or senescence): signs of change, between maturity and final death, shown by plants and animals. Most of these changes are evidences of deterioration. Even trees that continue to grow for centuries show signs of aging, both in old parts of the trunk and in the current crop of leaves, flowers, and fruits. As a person ages, the rate at which wounds repair themselves slows at a measurable pace. After age 40, our

Muscle deterioration: Photomicrographs of leg muscle, enlarged 570 diameters, in young adult rat (left) and old senile rat (right) show that with aging many muscle fibers have died and been replaced by connective tissue. (*Warren Andrew*)

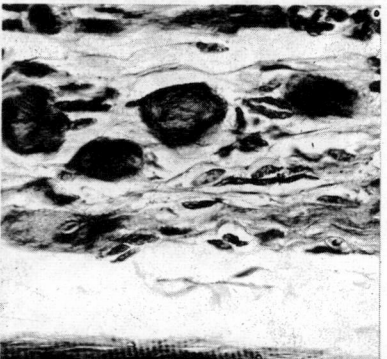

ability to hear high-pitched notes decreases about 50 vibrations/sec each 6 mo. The lens of the eye grows more yellowish, filtering out more of the violet end of the spectrum; it also becomes firmer and is less ready to adjust for focusing on near objects. Connective tissue replaces some muscular tissue, and the fibrous pads between bones of the vertebral column thin out, so that the body shortens. At the same time, fat tends to disappear from under the skin, and the skin wrinkles. These changes occur at different ages in different people, because of differences in heredity, health, and activity.

Degeneration of function and structure may be due to accumulation of products from metabolism in toxic concentrations. The whole aging process may be an inevitable price paid by an organism for adaptive specializations and extreme division of labor. Full expression of the genetic heritage, achieved at maturity, may carry with it the basis for changes leading to final death. Of interest is the possibility that aging represents loss of irreplaceable cells, *e.g.* due to radiation, or may result from an increasing tendency of body cells to produce antibodies that act against the body's normal constituents. The underlying causes of aging remain a frontier for investigation in the biological sciences. See ANNUAL RINGS; DEATH; LIFE SPAN.—*L. and M. M.*

AGRICOLA, GEORGIUS (GEORG BAUER), 1494–1555, German mineralogist and scholar, often called "the father of mineralogy"; b. Glauchau, Saxony. Originally a physician at Joachimstal, a German mining and smelting center, he began a systematic study of mining and minerals. The result was a series of publications in which rocks and minerals were for the first time regarded essentially as materials of the natural world, being described in terms more of observable, physical properties than of supposed magical and philosophical properties. His crowning achievement, *De re metallica* (1556), was a complete, systematic treatise on mining and metallurgy, with fine illustrations—the standard for two centuries.—*S. B.*

AGRICULTURAL TOOLS AND MACHINES have enabled one man to produce food for many, and mankind to produce a surplus of food and fiber beyond immediate needs. Without the leisure and freedom thus gained, man could never have become "civilized," nor could human populations have multiplied so staggeringly. The refinement of new tools and machines for each of the basic agricultural processes—planting, cultivating, harvesting, threshing—is the story of agricultural mechanization. It is the hope of the world's underdeveloped regions, whose peoples are not now sufficiently trained to build and use modern agricultural equipment, and are too poor to buy it.

Ancient Agricultural Tools: The first agricultural efforts were the gathering of berries, the digging up of edible roots, the hunting of game. First plantings probably were accidental; then primitive man began to scratch the earth with a stick before scattering seed, or to use a pointed stick to make a hole for the seeds. Cultivation came about when primitive man cleared away weeds which threatened his food plants, and first tools for cultivation were simply forked sticks—primitive hoes. The first harvesting tools were sticks, used to knock fruit from trees and grain heads from stalks; in fact man developed considerable skill in using sticks, as when lake-dwelling Indians harvested wild rice. Sticks were also probably the first tools used for threshing, *i.e.* separating the grain from its husk. In the Neolithic period, the digging stick was succeeded by the spade and hoe—little more than modified digging sticks. The plow came into use during the Bronze Age, when draft animals were domesticated. Although the first plows were little more than forked sticks, plows developed over the centuries into localized types suited to the regional

Colonial plow: Basic colonial tool was wooden, horse-drawn but was directed by hand. It wore out soon.

Metal plow: Modern plow, steered from tractor, plows several furrows faster and deeper than early models. (*Grant Heilman*)

Potato digger—1880: Chain-driven paddlewheel lifts dirt and potatoes. Grating separates them.

Potato harvester: Modern machine not only lifts and grades potatoes but loads them into wagon. (*Grant Heilman*)

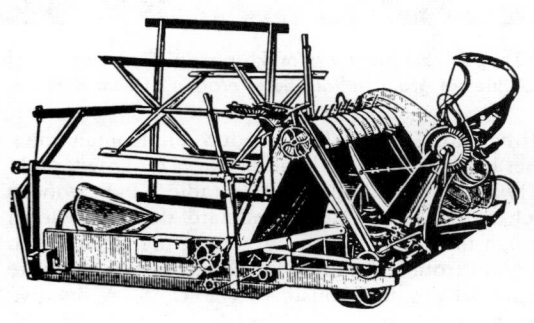

Early self binder: This device used wire to fasten bales, was used with harvesters. (Above engravings: *Farm Equipment Inst.*)

Field baler: Self-propelled machine picks up grain, ties it with string, and deposits it in attached wagon. (*Bert S. Gittins*)

soils and regional needs. Agriculture from classical times through the Renaissance was chiefly an extension and expansion of the Neolithic pattern: land cultivation and farming of all kinds increased, but this was principally because more people were engaged in farming, not because of any marked progress in agricultural methods or equipment. Farm production per man-hour did not significantly increase.

Beginnings of Modern Equipment: Interest in agricultural improvement in the 18th cent. led several theorists to consider mathematical principles upon which design of a plow's moldboard might be based in order to turn the soil with minimum resistance. The Rotherham plow, designed in Holland about 1730 and widely copied, may have been designed on such principles. Thomas Jefferson invented a scientifically designed moldboard in 1793. But the first American patent issued for a plow went to Charles Newbold, 1797. This plow, except for handles and beam, was of solid cast iron. Jethro Wood's cast-iron plow, patented 1814 and subsequently improved, was cast in three parts: moldboard, share, and landside. Its

interchangeability of parts was a major advance. When used in the American prairies, however, the cast-iron plow would not scour, *i.e.* soil would cling to its moldboard; hence in 1833 an Illinois blacksmith, John Lane, placed strips of saw steel over wooden moldboards, and such plows successfully turned furrows in the prairie. Four years later another Illinois blacksmith, John Deere, began making plows with highly polished steel shares and wrought-iron moldboards: these were widely used. John Lane's soft-center steel and John Oliver's chilled-iron process for hardening cast iron, both patented in 1868, proved very useful for plows. Sulky plows, upon which the plowman rode, were introduced commercially in 1864; gang plows, at about the same time. The former were first used with steam traction-engines, but are now used with internal-combustion tractors.

Harrows pulverize and smooth soil after it has been plowed. The simplest harrow, used in early American farming, was a bush or large tree limb dragged over the ground. This brush harrow was gradually superseded by a wooden drag, often

Spraying and dusting: Low-flying planes reduce time needed to treat large areas of crops. (*Grant Heilman*)

Irrigation: Water is pumped through pipes, which can be removed for cultivating or harvesting. (*Grant Heilman*)

Soil testing: Chemical and electrical tests determine soil makeup. (*Grant Heilman*)

Storage: Large grain elevators make possible the storage of large quantities of grain without deterioration. (*Grant Heilman*)

made with steel or wooden teeth set in timbers. During the 1870s the disc harrow, consisting of a series of revolving steel discs standing upright in a frame, became popular in the western U. S. A.

Most cereal grains were sown by hand scattering until very recent times. A horse-drawn grain drill was invented by Jethro Tull of England about 1731, but farmers were slow to use it. Not until 1841 were grain drills manufactured in the U. S. A. Since in corn planting the rather large seeds have to be planted in equally spaced hills to promote cross-cultivation, various devices for tripping a seed-planter at fixed distances had to be developed: most widely accepted was the check-rower, developed from a tripping device consisting of a cord knotted at regular intervals. When Tull reported on his grain drill in 1731, he also urged the use of horse-drawn hoes or cultivators, to stir the soil between rows of growing grain. This practice was followed by some in England, but never became popular in the U. S. A. for small grain. However, inter-row cultivation was essential for corn, cotton, and tobacco; and hoes and small horse-drawn plows were used in the U. S. A. for this purpose. After the first U. S. patent on a cultivator (1830), improvements were rapid, particularly for machines suitable for corn cultivation. Sulky machines, cultivating two rows at a time, came into wide use. Development of the small gasoline tractor about 1926 made the four-row corn-cultivator practical.

Harvesting was one of the first farm operations to be mechanized in America. Traditionally, the job required great expenditure of manpower, since ripened grain must be harvested with all possible speed to minimize risk of damage by wind, hail, or other mischance. The sickle, a curved iron or bronze blade attached to a wooden handle, had been the first important tool for cutting grain. The scythe, introduced in Roman times, had a heavier blade and longer handle. It was modified, probably in the 1700s, by the addition of the cradle, a light wooden frame which gathered the stems and laid the grain down evenly. Though the cradle speeded grain-cutting, it tended to shatter the grain from its heads. Mechanical harvesters were developed almost simultaneously in the U. S. A. by two inventors working independently, Obed Hussey and Cyrus H. McCormick. Hussey's machine (patented 1833) had a cutting knife consisting of a series of triangular plates riveted to a flat iron bar. One end of the bar was attached to a connecting rod, moved by a crank which received its motion from the main axle by means of cogs. McCormick's harvester (patented 1834) had a cutting knife given a reciprocating motion by a series of cogs. It vibrated between projecting wires (later spear-shaped iron guards) which held the grain while it was cut. McCormick made substantial improvements in his machine and eventually took over the Hussey business. The Marsh harvester (patented 1858) had a traveling apron which elevated the cut grain into a receiving box, from which it was taken and bound by two men riding on a platform. Mechanical wire binders were used in the 1870s, but were replaced by twine binders after John F. Appleby perfected a twine-knotter in 1878. A corn-picker, using rollers studded with iron pegs, was patented in 1850 by Edmund W. Quincy. In 1886, J. C. Patterson patented a corn-cutter, which was a sled with a deep V-notch in front, lined with sharp steel blades. A successful corn-binder was patented in 1892 by A. S. Peck. Since then, variations of these machines, as well as corn-shredders, have been widely used. Many cotton-harvesting devices have been patented: machines for stripping cotton from the stems are used in the southwest U. S. A.; spindle pickers are used in

Fertilizer: Tractor-operated automatic shovel lifts manure and then transfers it to spreader. (*Avco*)

Mechanical milkers: Machines draw off milk, which is piped to bulk cooling tank. One man milks several cows at once. (*Grant Heilman*)

Poultry: Hens are kept in rows of cages with slanted wire base. Eggs roll forward when laid, making collecting easy. (*Grant Heilman*)

Hog feeder: Food is mechanically shot from wagon into troughs. (*Grant Heilman*)

regions where the harvest is mechanized. Basically, these machines pass a series of rotating spindles through a cotton plant and twist the loose fiber from the bolls. The most successful of these machines was invented, 1927, by John D. Rust.

A harvested crop must often be further processed; thus cotton fiber must be separated from the seeds. In 1793, Eli Whitney revolutionized Southern agriculture by inventing the cotton gin, a cylinder fitted with wire teeth which drew the lint through a wire screen, leaving the seeds behind. Small grain, *e.g.* wheat, barley, rice, and rye, must be separated from its stems and heads by threshing. Early man beat his grain with sticks or drove his oxen over it; later he developed the flail, made by joining two sticks with thongs. The first successful threshing machine was invented (1786) by Andrew Meikle, a Scotsman. Thereafter the European machines improved rapidly, a few being shipped to the U. S. A. In 1837 the Pitts brothers of Maine were granted a patent on a threshing machine, and their machines along with those manufactured after 1844 by J. I. Case soon dominated the American scene.

In 1836, a *combine,* which simultaneously cut, threshed, and cleaned grain, was patented by Hiram Moore and J. Hascall of Michigan. In 1843 Hiram's son, A. Y. Moore, built a combine which he used for custom harvesting until 1853. He then sold the combine to a Californian, who strikingly demonstrated its effectiveness in harvesting his 600 acres of wheat. After 1880, many combines were in use in California, and by 1960 they were widely used throughout the U. S. A.

Many other specialized agricultural machines are used in the U. S. A., and the effect of mechanization can be judged by data on wheat production. In 1820, 50 to 60 man-hr. of labor were required to produce 20 bu. of wheat on 1 acre of land with a walking plow, brush harrow, hand broadcast of seed,

sickle, and flail. In 1960, 1½ to 3 man-hr. were required to produce the same amount of wheat on 1 acre with tractor, one-way disc plow, harrow, 14-ft.drill, 14-ft.self-propelled combine, and trucks.

Power for Agriculture: During most of history man himself has been the primary power source for operating agricultural tools and machines. Domestication of such animals as ox, horse, and water-buffalo provided new sources of power. The next step was the application of mechanical power to agriculture, and this is far older in theory than in practice. As early as 1618, two English inventors suggested an engine which would "ploughe grounde without horse or oxen." The early 1800s saw proposals for plowing with steam engines. After 1832, when John Heathcoat patented a plowing apparatus powered by a stationary steam engine, progress was rapid and a number of successful steam traction-engines and cable-drawing machines were placed in operation. Stationary steam engines were in use on American plantations and farms by the 1830s in competition with sweeps and treadmills powered by horses. The first portable steam engines for farming use were built in 1849; the first practical self-propelled engines followed in the 1870s. But even as the steam traction-engine was being perfected, American inventors were turning to the internal-combustion engine. The steam engine was too large and too heavy for the average farm. The internal-combustion engine had been invented in Europe, but its use as a farm traction-engine was an American development. John Froelich of Iowa built the first successful gasoline tractor of record in 1892. In 1903, C. W. Hart and C. H. Parr began commercial production of the Hart-Parr tractor. Though the change to mechanical power has come slowly, by 1950 tractors outnumbered horses on American farms.—*W. R.*

CLASSIFICATION OF AIRCRAFT

HEAVIER THAN AIR

POWERED

CONVENTIONAL TAKE-OFF

airplane

SHORT TAKE-OFF

Autogiro

STOL

VERTICAL TAKE-OFF

VTOL

helicopter

ground-effect machine

flying platform

NOT POWERED

glider

AIR: the colorless, odorless mixture of gases that envelops the earth and makes up its ATMOSPHERE. Its main constituents by volume are nitrogen (78.08%) and oxygen (20.95%), but it also contains small quantities of the so-called rare (or inert or noble) gases: argon (0.94%), neon (0.0015%), helium (0.0005%), krypton (0.00011%), xenon (0.000009%). A number of other gases are present in variable amounts, *e.g.* hydrogen and hydrocarbons. The most important variable constituents of air, however, are water, present in 0.01–0.02% concentration, and carbon dioxide, 0.03–0.07%. Nitrogen in the air is essential to the growth of plants and animals, though higher organisms are not able to utilize it directly. Some nitrogen is made available by the lightning-sparked reaction between nitrogen and oxygen to form nitric oxide, which unites with moisture in the air to produce nitric acid (HNO_3), whose nitrogen is available to plants. However, most nitrogen is made available to living things by the nitrogen-fixing bacteria, which convert nitrogen directly into compounds that can be utilized by higher plant life. The oxygen in air is necessary for respiration and many important industrial oxidations. Carbon dioxide is used by photosynthetic plants in the production of sugars, starches, and woody tissues, and is returned to the atmosphere by respiration and organic decay. Atmospheric carbon dioxide and water in combination with frost cause the weathering of rock particles into soil.

Air can be converted at low temperatures under pressure into a liquid that boils at −194°C. Liquid air can be separated into its components by fractional distillation. This is the basis for commercial air-separation plants in which nitrogen, oxygen, neon, krypton, and argon are produced. (Helium is normally produced in large quantities by extracting it from natural gas.) Nitrogen is used largely to make synthetic ammonia. Oxygen is used in steel production and in chemical processing as a substitute for air. Argon's inertness makes it useful as a shield in welding and in production of certain metals and other reactive compounds. All the inert gases glow when an electric current is passed through them and are used in gas-conductor-tube lamps ("neon lights") and fluorescent lamps, sometimes in conjunction with mercury.—*D. P. B.*

AIR CONDITIONING: increasing or reducing the moisture content of air and controlling its temperature, dust content, odor, and movement. Control of these qualities promotes human comfort and is essential in many manufacturing processes. Complete air conditioning may require mechanical ventilation, addition or removal of heat, and filtering. Since air conditioning involves specialized applications of basic thermodynamic, hydrodynamic, and fluid-flow principles, the development of suitable air-conditioning equipment for a particular location

requires careful observance of these principles. *Temperature* control is attained by thermostatically controlled heating or cooling units or by a combination heating-cooling unit (for thermodynamic principles, see HEAT PUMP). Heat is generated by either the combustion of fuels or the utilization of electrical-resistance elements. Refrigerative and evaporative units are used for cooling: refrigeration indirectly produces cooling through contact with another colder fluid; evaporation directly achieves both cooling and humidifying. Performance of the evaporative cooler depends on the vaporization of water by the sensible heat of the air. Increase or decrease of *humidity* (water-vapor content of air) is controlled by vaporization and dehumidification, respectively. Decrease of moisture in the air is accomplished either by condensation over a cold surface or by adsorption on a desiccant. *Air quality* is regulated by

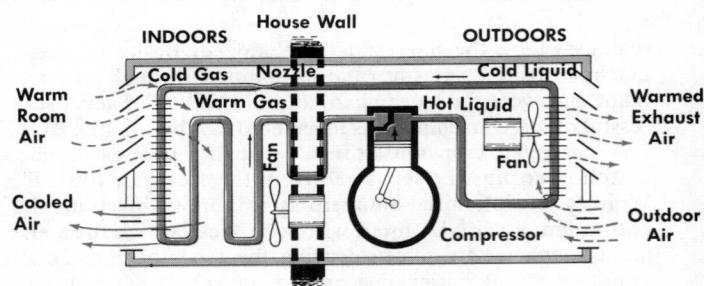

Refrigeration cycle: Indoor fan recirculates warm air continuously over liquid cooled by decompression nozzle; warmth transmitted to liquid is then dissipated outdoors.

forcing air through filters to remove suspended particles. Degree of purification depends on the filter type used. *Circulation* occurs naturally within any area, but must often be supplemented by mechanical means. This is achieved either by recirculation (*i.e.* air, replenished periodically with fresh air, is continuously recirculated through the area), or by ventilation, which circulates only fresh air on a once-through basis.—*K. T.*

AIRCRAFT: any structure, machine, or contrivance designed to travel through and be supported by the air. (The forces and phenomena enabling an aircraft to be thus supported are considered in AERODYNAMICS.) The term aircraft is generally restricted to airborne vehicles capable of carrying a burden of human beings, freight, instruments, or explosive weapons, and thus excludes model aircraft and kites. Some missiles and flying bombs (*e.g.* the World War II German V-1 and several current U. S. guided missiles) are supported by air and thus

LIGHTER THAN AIR

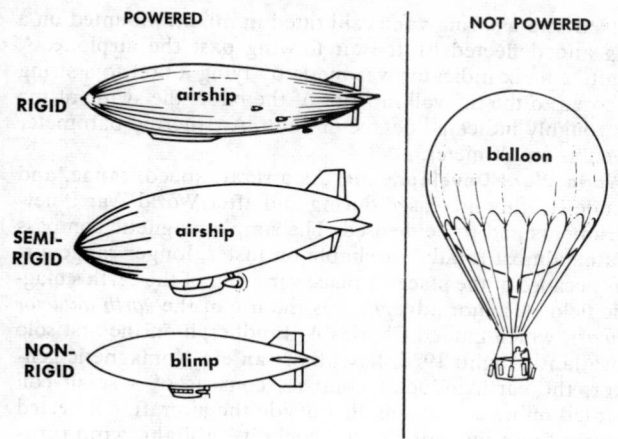

POWERED | **NOT POWERED**

RIGID — airship

SEMI-RIGID — airship

NON-RIGID — blimp

balloon

Varieties of airborne craft: The oldest types here shown are the lighter-than-air craft, of which the first spherical and directional forms were designed in the late 18th cent., the chief 20-cent. contributions being the addition of internal-combustion engines and the substitution of helium for hydrogen. The heavier-than-air craft (facing page) are based on the AIRFOIL, seen in its purest application in the glider. Of the powered craft, the oldest successful form is the conventional take-off plane, which adds to the airfoil a propulsive engine with a high power-to-weight ratio. As airplanes attained greater speeds, they required excessively long runways and were awkward to control at low speeds, such as at take-off and landing. Hence short take-off and vertical take-off craft have been designed.

are considered aircraft; others, like the U. S. Viking rocket, are not borne up by aerodynamic forces, and are the subject of BALLISTICS rather than aerodynamics. Aircraft are either "heavier-than-air" (airplane, Autogiro, helicopter, glider, ornithopter, VTOL-type) or "lighter-than-air" (airship, balloon).

All *heavier-than-air aircraft* make use of AIRFOILS to resist gravity (the force retarding upward motion) and drag (force retarding forward motion); these two forces are overcome by sufficient *lift* and *thrust,* respectively. The wings, fin (vertical tail surface), and the stabilizer (horizontal tail surface) of an airplane or glider are all airfoils. A GLIDER has no engine and relies solely on the dynamic action of air against its airfoil surfaces to remain aloft and make headway; to move forward, a glider utilizes the force of gravity, and thus, in general, must lose altitude to make headway. An AIRPLANE is no less dependent than a glider on the efficacy of its aerodynamic surfaces, but the addition of an engine to supply forward thrust (by means of propeller, jet, or rocket) greatly increases its versatility: it can take off under its own power, fly faster, climb higher, and perform effectively through a wider range of atmospheric conditions. These advantages have made it the dominant aircraft type of the mid-20th cent. While the fixed wings of airplane and glider serve only as airfoils, the engine-driven, rotary wings (rotor) of the HELICOPTER serve as both airfoils and propulsive device, capable of exerting both lift and, when tilted, thrust. A helicopter can change direction faster than an airplane, and can maneuver within a smaller space; it can take off and land vertically, and hover over a fixed point. In other areas of performance a helicopter is inferior to the airplane. An Autogiro combines features of both helicopter and airplane. It is essentially an engine-driven propeller airplane whose fixed wings have been replaced by free-turning rotary wings mounted over the fuselage. The rotary wings are moved during flight solely by the aerodynamic forces acting upon them (unlike those of a helicopter), and supply lift but not thrust. In principle, an Autogiro should have performance characteristics intermediate between helicopter and airplane, but this promise has never been fully realized; furthermore, the performance gap between helicopter and airplane is now being narrowed by other types of vertical-takeoff and -landing aircraft (see below). The ornithopter, whose power-driven wings beat like those of a bird, has been a persistent aircraft oddity, dating back to a design of the

Ornithopter: experimental post-World War II design had feathered wings that were moved by foot pedals, and handgrips that were operated like oars. Wing span was 36 ft. (*British Information Services*)

Greek philosopher and mathematician Archytas (fl. *c.* 400–350 B. C.). Ornithopter models have been flown successfully for over a century, and research is currently being conducted to determine the feasibility of their commercial or military use.

The term *vertical take-off and landing* (VTOL) is generally used to refer to heavier-than-air aircraft which, while having the speed and range of advanced airplanes, are also capable of helicopter-like flight, *i.e.* rising straight up from the ground, hovering, changing to and from forward flight, and landing straight down. Most VTOL designs can be considered modifications of the conventional fixed-wing airplane. Many such aircraft have been successfully test-flown in recent years, and proponents of the VTOL-type have suggested that it will ultimately make all other aircraft obsolete. VTOL designs include: (1) the "compound aircraft," which has both a propeller and a helicopter-type rotor, and which operates as a helicopter except in forward flight, when power is shifted to the propeller; (2) the "tail-sitter" airplane, which takes off and lands tail-down with the fuselage vertical, flying an arc path to and from level flight; (3) aircraft whose jet engines, ducted fans, or large propellers can be rotated through approximately 90° to provide either lift or forward propulsion (the wings

may rotate with the propulsion device, as in the "tilt-wing" type, or may be stable); (4) aircraft with partial wing-tilt which have either very large wing flaps behind the rotors or deflectors in the exhaust of their jet engine (the flaps or deflectors convert propulsive force, or thrust, to lifting force). If, in such aircraft, the lifting force is not sufficient for vertical or near-vertical take-off, but is nevertheless substantially more than that of a conventional airplane, the aircraft may be termed STOL (short take-off and landing). Control of VTOL aircraft in hovering and low-speed flight can be achieved in many ways: by helicopter-type rotors; by air jets at the wing tips or tail; by variations of propeller thrust; by vertical and horizontal surfaces behind the propellers or ducted fans, or in the jet exhaust; or by combinations of these. (See AERODYNAMICS, *high-lift devices.*)

VTOL: Wings of this experimental design (1960) are tilted through 90° to make transitions back and forth between vertical and horizontal flight. (*Boeing*)

Lighter-than-air aircraft rely on buoyancy to stay aloft; they are filled with a gas (*e.g.* helium, hydrogen, hot air) whose density is less than that of the air through which they rise. The BALLOON, the simplest lighter-than-air aircraft, is non-powered and non-steerable, and is used principally, either manned or unmanned, in meteorology and for high-altitude observation and research. The AIRSHIP is powered and steerable and, though widely built and flown 1910–35, is now a disappearing aircraft type.—*E. H. H.*

AIRCRAFT INSTRUMENTATION: the formulation, installation, and coordination of instruments that will receive information on an aircraft's position, environment, and performance, and relay this information (usually to a human pilot) so that it may be readily used for navigation, guidance, and control.

First Instruments: Early aircraft, flying for short distances at low altitude and slow speed, had little need for complex instrumentation. A pilot could roughly sense the attitude (position in flight) of his aircraft by the effects of gravity on his body—so-called seat-of-the-pants flying. Known landmarks served for orientation; a common magnetic compass, or simply railroad or trolley tracks, gave the pilot his bearings and heading; the position of cows in a pasture (tails to the wind) could provide wind direction; and the alignment of an airplane's nose and wings against the horizon served as a bank (roll) and pitch indicator. The first instruments to be airborne concerned engine-performance parameters only: oil pressure, fuel flow, rpm, and fuel-air ratio. Such instruments were taken over directly from ground-based internal combustion engines. The first instrument designed specifically for aircraft was a string pendulum suspended in the airstream near the pilot, indicating airspeed in a crude way. This shortly

evolved into a spring vane calibrated in mi/hr, mounted on a wing and deflected by the air flowing past the airplane. A primitive bank indicator was made by tying a bolt to a string anchored to the firewall in front of the pilot: the swing of the bolt roughly indicated degree of bank. An aneroid barometer served as an altimeter.

World War I Developments: As aircraft speed, range, and altitude steadily increased during and after World War I, new instruments had to be devised. The simple magnetic compass became almost totally unreliable on faster, longer-range aircraft because of the place-to-place variation of the earth's magnetic field. A major advance was the use of the *earth inductor compass,* which guided Charles A. Lindbergh on the first solo transatlantic flight, 1927. Essentially an electromagnetic generator, the earth inductor compass consists of a small coil mounted on a vertical spindle outside the aircraft, connected by wires to an indicator in the cockpit. In flight, wind turns the spindle, and the coil is thus made to rotate in the earth's magnetic field, cutting through the earth's magnetic lines of force. This generates a current, whose voltage is registered by a pointer on the dial indicator in the cockpit. The direction and strength of the current varies in accordance with the varying strength and direction of the magnetic field. In practice, the pilot sets the pointer of his compass dial on zero (the planned flight course) and during flight maintains this course. If the pointer wanders from the zero position (*i.e.* if more or less current is generated than should be on the aircraft's planned course), the pilot knows he is deviating from his desired course.

Although a marked improvement over magnetic compasses, the earth inductor compass was reliable only when the aircraft was flying a straight, pre-set course. On circuitous flights, pilots were beset by compass inaccuracies known as "north turning errors." These errors created a demand for some method of measuring an aircraft's rate of turn, to enable the pilot to correct his compass heading. The result was *rate-of-turn indicators,* followed by *rate-of-climb indicators.* Together with the compass, the altimeter, and the *airspeed indicator,* these instruments constituted the primary flight-instrument group at the end of World War I, when the first attempts to fly on instruments were made. The pilot, however, was still dependent upon ground observation, and his eyes still provided the only means to align the nose and wings of his aircraft with the horizon and thus assure level flight. Development of the *artificial horizon* released the pilot from these visual references. The artificial horizon is primarily a bank and pitch indicator. It is based on the principle of the stability of a freely mounted gyroscope. When the airplane rolls (banks) or changes pitch, the instrument case, which is fixed to the aircraft, moves with it. The gyroscope, mounted inside the case, continues to rotate in its original plane in space. In one type, a miniature aircraft is fastened to the instrument case. The little airplane moves with respect to an artificial horizon bar affixed to the gyroscope. Thus, all movements of the airplane in relation to the actual horizon are followed exactly and with no lag by the movements of the miniature airplane with respect to the horizon bar. In a climb, the little airplane appears above the horizon bar; in a descent, it is below. A bank scale shows the degree of bank, which is also depicted in the position of the wings on the horizon bar. Another type, called an attitude gyro, has a sphere attached to the gyroscope. Markings on the sphere supply the pilot with continuous indications for any position of the airplane. With the use of the artificial horizon, high altitudes, darkness, and massive cloud banks were no longer formidable obstacles; and immediately after World War I the first transatlantic flights were made (1919).

Jet airliner instruments: Fewer readings are required in this Boeing 707 cockpit than in smaller, older, propeller-driven airliners. The over-all trend is toward simpler instrument panels. (*Boeing*)

1	Autopilot disengage	22	Fuel flow
2	Navigation marker lights	23	Landing-gear control handle
3	Airspeed indicator	24	Static air temperature
4	Pilot directional indicator	25	Mach meter
5	Gyro-horizon	26	Navigation radio selection
6	Compass card	27	Glide-slope light
7	Altimeter	28	Autopilot disengage light
8	Clock	29	Oil-pressure warning lights
9	Rate of climb	30	Radio and radar controls
10	Emergency pneumatic brake	31	Air-brake handle
11	Autopilot axis indicator	32	Weather radar scope
12	Altimeter	33	Thrust levers
13	Ice-detector lights	34	Parking-brake latch
14	Engine pressure ratio	35	Engine-start levers
15	Low-spool engine RPM	36	Turn-and-bank indicator
16	Thrust reverser operating light	37	Hydraulic-system pressure
17	Tailpipe temperature	38	Brake-system pressure
18	High-spool engine RPM	39	Flap-control handle
19	Master warning light	40	Stabilizer-trim wheel
20	Flap-position indicators	41	Autopilot controls
21	Gear-down and locked lights	42	Rudder trim

Modern Instruments: In the 1920s and '30s the gyroscope principle was applied to other areas of instrumentation. The earth inductor compass was gradually superseded by the gyro flux-gate and gyrosyn types, whose gyro-stabilized detectors eliminated turning and acceleration errors, assuring correct readings at all times. Since World War II, gyro flux-gate systems have been installed on all large commercial and military aircraft, enabling them to fly unerringly over polar areas where other compasses are useless. An added advantage of these compass systems is the fact that they have no external rotating parts.

World War II accelerated development in all areas of aircraft instrumentation: guidance, navigation, flight control. In larger aircraft (*e.g.* a World War II heavy bomber) some sensing devices had to be far removed from the cockpit and pilot, and the problem thus arose of monitoring and adjusting these devices for varying flight conditions. Electromechanical components and servomechanisms were developed for this purpose; and electrical indicators became the rule on the instrument panel. War in the air placed a high premium on the precision of sensing instruments, as well as on the dependability and capacity of connecting circuits. Progress in these areas has continued unabated to the present day. Sensing devices have evolved far beyond their original forms (see ALTIMETER; AIRSPEED INDICATOR). Refinement of circuitry has continued, from the early mechanical, electrical, and electromechanical systems to electronic (vacuum-tube) systems, to

the solid-state (transistor) systems of the post-World War II period. Such advances have made feasible the complex control, navigation, and guidance systems which, today, practically enable an aircraft to fly itself. Automatic flight control systems and flight-director systems, for example, perform navigation functions automatically, display navigation and flight data, and compute and display visual flight commands for the pilot to execute manually. (See AUTOMATIC PILOT.)

Current Problems: As more and more precise instruments have been developed that give more and more detailed information about an aircraft's flight, aeronautical designers and engineers have been forced to consider the limitations of the human pilot. For example, in supersonic flight when a quick response is required to avert disaster, the human brain may not be capable, within the time allotted, of noting, interpreting, and acting on the information being received. This problem is being approached from two directions. One is the use of airborne computers to integrate a wide range of factors and, through instruments, provide the pilot with more easily interpretable data. Second, considerable effort is being made to consolidate and integrate cockpit displays for quick and accurate readability to minimize human error. One significant development is the use of vertical-scale instrumentation in integrated cockpit displays. Although vertical-scale concepts go back to the early days of flight (*i.e.* movable scales against fixed pointers and movable pointers against fixed scales,

New designs vs. old: Confusing array of instruments on obsolescent panel (*left*) can be regrouped and redesigned to make a panel (*right*) that pilot can read more rapidly with less chance of error. Note predominance of vertical scales on futuristic panel, making possible quick and continuous comparison of information relating to altitude, airspeed, and other flight-performance details. (*Douglas*)

operating either vertically or horizontally) modern vertical-scale techniques employ tapes and indices, either of which may be movable or fixed, integrated and consolidated to make for quick reading of individual parameters and quick comparison of all parameters along one vertical or horizontal reference. Current flight data, limits of operation, command information, power-plant parameters, and information from ground-based facilities are all displayed for pilot action or pilot monitoring.

Space exploration, manned and unmanned, has imposed new demands on instrumentation. Components must be at once smaller, lighter, tougher, and more reliable (*e.g.* the transistor replaces the vacuum tube). New kinds of sensing devices, new navigational techniques, improved methods of recording and relaying new kinds of information are needed. Engine and fuel-system performance must be monitored more precisely than ever before. Thus advances in the next few years (as in the past 15 yr) may be expected in the areas of miniaturization, integration, and consolidation of instruments, as well as in the minimizing of human error by pilot-direction, automatic control, and computer systems. See AIR NAVIGATION.
—*S. R.*

AIRCRAFT PROPULSION: All aircraft, except free-floating balloons and gliders, have power plants that convert the chemical energy of fuels to sufficient mechanical power (thrust) to overcome the forces of gravity and air resistance (drag). This power can be exerted in several ways: (1) through a simple air screw, a rotating propeller that pushes against the air in one direction and thus moves itself and all attached to it in the opposite direction; (2) by means of a reaction engine that accelerates a mass of gases in one direction, thereby producing a thrust that moves the engine and its aircraft in the opposite direction; (3) by a combination air screw–rotating wing, like the rotor blades of a helicopter; (4) by combinations of these three. Propeller engines are generally mounted in the nose of single-engine aircraft or along the leading edges of the wings of multiple-engine aircraft, pushing back on the air and pulling the aircraft with them. "Pusher" propeller engines, mounted singly over the fuselage or in multiples over the wings, face toward the tail of the aircraft, pushing against the air, but also pushing the aircraft. Heli-

copter rotors revolve in a plane parallel to the long axis of the fuselage, these rotors being tilted by the pilot whenever flight is desired in any direction other than vertical. In single-engine jet or rocket aircraft, the fuselage is literally built around the engine. In multiple-jet aircraft the engines are suspended from pods under the wings, and combination prop-jet engines are mounted more like conventional propeller engines. In a few cases jet engines are mounted externally near the tail.

Propeller Engines: In the 1850s, steam engines, generally fueled with coal, were used to drive the propellers of dirigibles. Heavier-than-air aircraft had to await development of the internal-combustion gasoline engine. In 1903, Charles H. Manley built a five-cylinder, water-cooled, 52.4-hp radial engine for an "Aerodrome" craft that failed to fly. The four-cylinder, 12-hp, straight-line engine that powered the first flight of the Wright brothers, Dec. 17, 1903, was built by them along the lines of contemporary automobile engines. Glenn H. Curtiss, 1904, built the first engine specifically intended for aircraft: a four-cylinder, 7-hp, straight-line type. A variety of cylinder arrangements followed, including "V," "H," "X," "double V," "W," "Y," horizontally opposed cylinders, and single- and double-row radial engines having cylinders arranged like the spokes of a wheel. Most of these were four-stroke cycle engines in which a mixture of gasoline vapor and air was taken in on the first downward stroke, compressed on an upward stroke, then ignited by a spark plug so that the exploding and expanding gases forced the piston down with power on the third stroke. The fourth stroke forced burned gases out of the cylinder, clearing the way for repetition of the cycle. Water cooling was later replaced by air cooling through thin metal fins around the cylinder heads. A few diesel engines, which depend on heating of the fuel-air mixture by high compression alone to ignite it, were also adapted to aircraft use. In these reciprocal internal-combustion engines power was transmitted from the piston through a connecting rod to the crankshaft, and through it to the propeller.

Jet Engines: Low efficiency halted development of piston-engine jets, which permitted the exploding gases to exhaust through a jet nozzle rather than against the piston. The turbojet introduced greater efficiency. The German Heinkel He 178 made the first successful *turbojet* flight in 1939. In the turbojet, a special fuel more like kerosene than regular gasoline is mixed with air and ignited in a combustion chamber. As the gases expand, they impinge upon, and turn, the blades of a turbine wheel. A shaft from the center of the wheel leads to the front opening of the engine to drive a compressor that continues to force more air into the engine. After the hot gases pass the turbine blades, they are again compressed through

Engines for aircraft: Basically, aircraft are propelled by accelerating a mass of gas toward the back of the craft. The speed at which this "jet" of accelerated gas is moving determines the efficiency of the propulsion system for different flight speeds. Low speed requires a low-speed jet, high speed a high-speed "jet." For given engine power the size of the jet varies inversely with its speed. Thus the large, slow-moving jet produced by a propeller is well suited to slow-speed flight, and the small, high-speed jet is well suited to very high-speed flight. At the intermediate speeds (up to the speed of sound) the compromise types (prop-jet and turbo-fan) are most efficient. In the latter, not all the air entering the engine is used to burn fuel; rather, some of the air sucked in by the fan (actually a compromise between the large-diameter propeller and the small-diameter turbine compressor) is bypassed around the engine and mixes with the high-speed exhaust gases from the turbine.

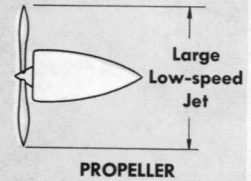

PROPELLER — Large Low-speed Jet

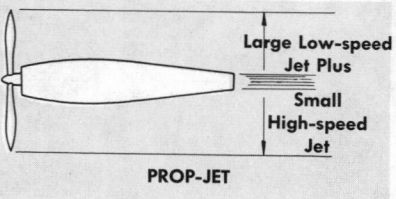

PROP-JET — Large Low-speed Jet Plus Small High-speed Jet

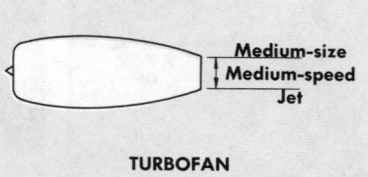

TURBOFAN — Medium-size Medium-speed Jet

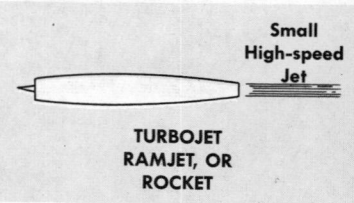

TURBOJET RAMJET, OR ROCKET — Small High-speed Jet

a constriction in the inner hollow tube of the engine that leads to the exhaust nozzle. Expanding through the nozzle, they increase in velocity and provide the thrust of the engine. To combine the advantages of propeller and jet propulsion, the jet-prop or *turbo-prop engine* interposes another turbine wheel just ahead of the exhaust nozzle. A shaft from this turbine leads to a propeller. After passing this stage, the gases pass out of the engine in jet fashion—their energy reduced, however, by the amount required to turn the propeller turbine. When aircraft were designed to fly at such high speeds that onrushing air provided sufficient pressure without a first-stage compressor, the *ramjet* engine was developed. The ramjet is little more than a long tube. Air, admitted at the front end, is compressed by being forced through a constriction, after which it is mixed with fuel; the mixture is ignited, and the expanding gases are discharged continuously through a nozzle at the rear. In an intermittent or *pulse jet,* the inflow of air is periodically stopped by flapping plates forced tight against the intake by the exploding gases. After the gases pass through the nozzle, the pressure drops for an instant, permitting the plates to swing open, and another cycle begins.

Rocket Engines: All the above are air-breathing engines. In 1928, rocket pioneer R. H. Goddard used a liquid-fueled rocket engine to propel a glider. Rocket engines generally use kerosene, alcohol, or hydrogen as fuel, and liquid oxygen, not air, as the oxidizing agent. They are much like a tube sealed at one end. Fuel and oxygen are piped in under pressure from separate storage tanks, ignited, and allowed to expand through a nozzle at the open end of the tube. In solid-fuel rockets, both fuel and oxidizing agents are packed directly into the chamber of the combustion tube, and burn either from the nozzle end back toward the closed end, or from the center outward to the walls of the tube. Nuclear aircraft engines, still under development, would use heat generated by a small atomic reaction to operate an air compressor and pre-heat the air in an engine similar to the turbojet. Controlled atomic explosions are thought unfeasible because of attendant radioactive contamination of the earth's atmosphere, but are being investigated for space use.—*K. A.*

AIR FLOW: see FLUID FLOW.

AIRFOIL: a structure, piece, or body designed to obtain a useful reaction—*lift*—upon itself in its motion through the air. An airfoil may be no more than a flat plate, but usually it has a cross section carefully contoured in accordance with its intended application or function. Airfoils are widely associated with AIRCRAFT, MISSILES, and other aerial vehicles or projectiles, and in application appear as wings, fins, stabilizers, and control surfaces (aileron, rudder, elevator); and also as propeller blades, and as blades in other aerodynamic fluid machinery such as turbines and compressors. An airfoil experiences, for purposes of normal flight, much more lift than drag: *lift* is the component of the total aerodynamic force acting on the airfoil perpendicular to the direction of flight; *drag* is the component of force parallel and opposed to the flight direction. The lift-to-drag ratio is an important parameter for evaluating airfoils. (See AERODYNAMICS.)

A number of terms and concepts are useful in discussing and evaluating the performance of airfoils (Fig. 1). The outline of the cross section of an airfoil is known as its *profile.* The *chord* is a straight line joining the airfoil's *leading edge* (the edge, normally the forward one, which meets the airflow first) with the airfoil's *trailing edge* (the edge over which the flow passes last). The chord may also be described as a line joining the extremities of the airfoil's *camber,* which is the mean line of the airfoil's profile. *Span* usually refers to the length of an airfoil from tip to tip, measured in a straight line. (Span in an airplane would be the straight-line distance from the right wing tip to the left wing tip.) *Aspect ratio* refers either to the ratio of the square of the span to the area of the airfoil, or to the ratio of the span to the mean chord. Larger aspect ratios (*i.e.* longer, narrower wings) give proportionately larger lifting effect, but with increasing speed they become less desirable because of structural weakness and instability. The aspect ratios for aircraft flying at subsonic speeds usually range from 6 to 8. Lower aspect ratios are used for high-speed aircraft; for supersonic aircraft, aspect ratios of 2 or less have been used. The short, stub wings of supersonic aircraft are a structural necessity: though they have less lift than longer wings, the amount of air flowing over them at supersonic

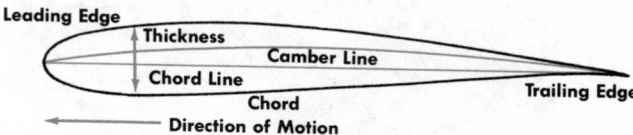

Fig. 1: Terms Used to Describe Airfoils

speeds gives them sufficient lift. An airfoil's *angle of attack* is the angle at which an airfoil meets the airflow, ordinarily measured between a reference line in the airfoil (*e.g.* its chord) and a line in the direction of flow or in the direction of movement of the airfoil (Fig. 2). A *negative angle of attack* occurs when an aircraft noses down, presenting the top surfaces of its airfoils to the airflow.

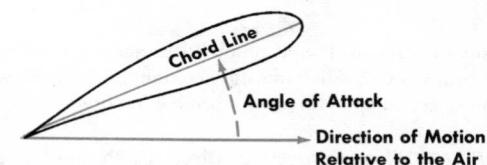

Fig. 2: Angle of attack: A critical factor in maintaining lift.

The design of a particular airfoil is influenced by many factors, one being the speed at which the airfoil is expected to perform. For low speeds, *i.e.* for subsonic flight, the optimum profile is usually a rounded leading edge and a sharp trailing edge (Figs. 3A and 3B). Though the rounded leading edge has good lifting qualities, it causes excessive drag at high speeds, and thus a thin, sharp leading edge is desirable for supersonic flight (Figs. 3C and 3D). Such an airfoil has less lift but also less drag. However, at hypersonic (very high supersonic) speeds, a rounded leading edge again becomes desirable because it reduces aerodynamic heating (large sweepback also helps). For supersonic flight it is also desirable to have a small *thickness ratio, i.e.* a small value for the ratio of the maximum thickness of the airfoil to its chord length; the result is thinner wings. See also SONIC REGIMES.—*K. K.*

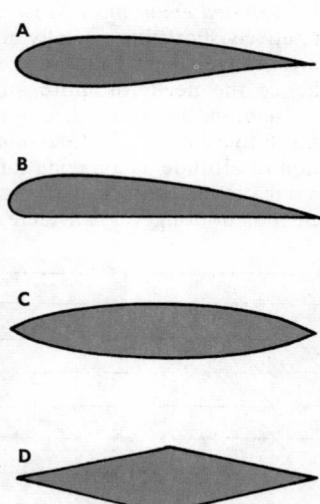

Fig. 3: Airfoil profiles: Different shapes are chosen for different speeds.

AIR MASS: in the earth's ATMOSPHERE, a body of air, covering a large area, in which temperature and moisture conditions are much the same throughout at any given altitude. An air mass is classified by the temperature and moisture characteristics it has acquired over its region of origin. Polar (P) air masses originate over cold regions, tropical (T) air masses over warm regions. Those that gain their moisture from ocean or sea areas are maritime (m); from land areas, continental (c). An air mass whose source region is the Mackenzie River Valley area, Canada, would be termed a cold, dry, continental polar (cP) air mass. (See FRONT.)—*P. L.*

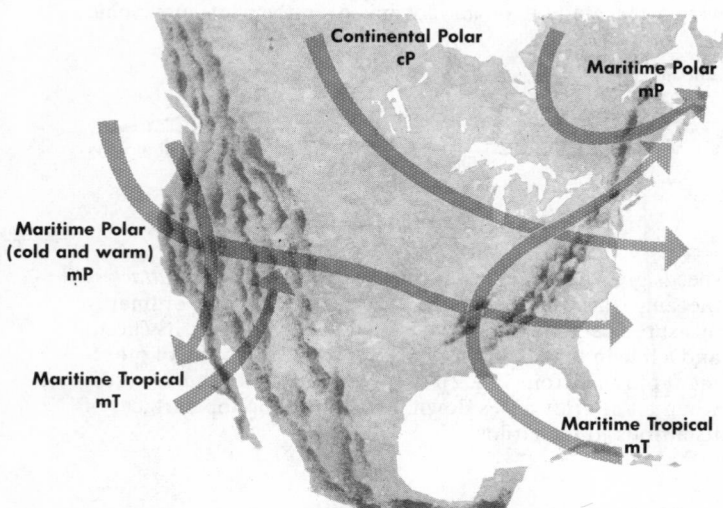

Air masses of tropical (T) and polar (P) origin are shown in typical paths over the U. S. Their moisture content depends on whether they formed over continental (c) or maritime (m) areas.

AIR NAVIGATION: the process of directing the movements of any type of aircraft, including airplanes, helicopters, dirigibles, blimps, balloons, guided missiles, satellites, and space vehicles. Its elements are basically the same as in marine or land navigation (see MARINE NAVIGATION), with differences resulting primarily from unique conditions encountered, notably: (1) *Need for continued motion:* Fixed-wing aircraft can not stop to await more favorable conditions, but must keep going. (2) *Limited endurance:* Most aircraft can remain aloft for a relatively short time, usually hours. (3) *Greater speeds:* Speeds may range up to thousands of times the speeds of ships; hence the need for more automatic, quicker methods of navigation. Some sacrifice of accuracy can be tolerated, but no serious errors. (4) *Three-dimensional situations:* The addition of altitude as a navigational dimension imposes greater navigational problems. For space craft the surface of the earth is no longer a satisfactory reference, and a greatly ex-

panded reference is required. Since the earth's geodetic properties are not well enough determined, future space craft will require complicated computational radio and radar aids. (5) *Effect of weather:* Visibility vitally affects ability to land and take off as well as ability to see landmarks or celestial bodies; hence the need for radio aids. Wind affects the position of an aircraft more than positions of ships or land vehicles, and changes of atmospheric pressure and temperature affect barometric altimeters used to indicate altitude.

Air navigation includes *pilotage* and *dead reckoning.* Pilotage involves frequent or continuous determination of position or line of position relative to known geographical points. Dead reckoning, or "deduced reckoning," is navigation in which position is determined on the basis of speed and direction from a known starting point. In its simplest form, pilotage is accomplished by observing the ground and identifying populated areas, railroads, lakes, and other features from appropriate charts. Light beacons on the ground assist the navigator at night.

Sextants have been used to obtain position information from celestial bodies (see CELESTIAL NAVIGATION), but since the computations are time-consuming and the aircraft is moving fast, automatic celestial navigators have been developed. Radio aids can furnish accurate, automatic position information for long distances and under adverse weather conditions. An automatic direction finder (ADF) or radio compass, for example, permits the aircraft to "home" or establish a line of position to special ground radio transmitters or commercial broadcasting stations. Radio ranges send out directional beams and more complex systems give fine-point position information. Airborne radar may be used to give a picture of the ground, and ground radar can "tell" an aircraft its position as seen from the ground. Other systems are under development.

When the navigator has no satisfactory geographical reference, or when radio navigation signals are not being received (as over ocean, polar areas, deserts, jungles), the navigator resorts to dead reckoning. Even in pilotage some dead reckoning must be performed to give continuity between individual positions. The navigator obtains heading (direction of movement) from his compass and air speed from his air-speed meter. Weather reports may give speed and direction of wind, which tends to blow the airplane off course and to slow it down or speed it up. Wind effects are combined with heading and air speed to compute actual speed and direction, from which, along with time of travel, progress can be estimated. Over the years, highly advanced dead-reckoning systems have been developed, including: gyroscopically stabilized magnetic compasses to give accurate heading; Doppler systems based on measurement of the shift of frequency of radio and radar beams from the aircraft to the ground to give accurate true ground speed; inertial navigation systems which measure aircraft acceleration; and automatic navigation computers.

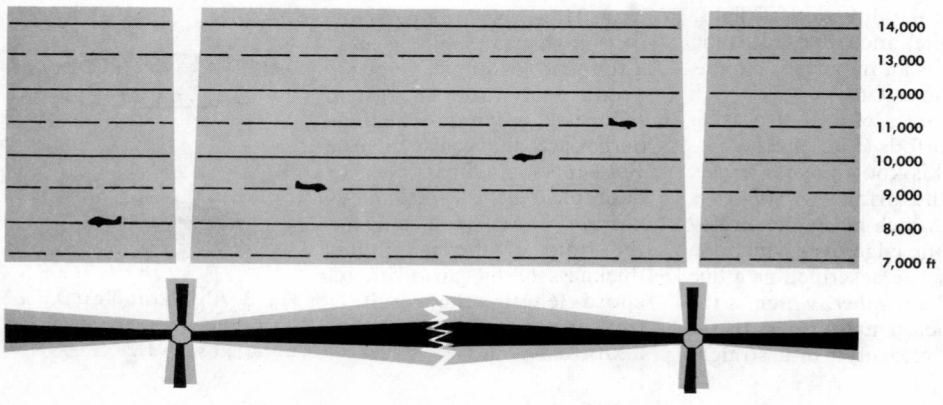

	14,000
	13,000
	12,000
	11,000
	10,000
	9,000
	8,000
	7,000 ft

Radio navigation: On transcontinental flights in the U. S. A., planes' instruments pick up and follow directional radio beams to minimize danger of collision (*top*); eastbound planes fly at odd altitudes, westbound at even altitudes, separated vertically by at least 1,000 ft. For the same reason (*bottom*) aircraft keep to right of "on course" radio beam (black bands). (*United Air Lines*)

Toward the modern airplane (*top to bottom*): John Stringfellow's steam-powered model (1848) had a 20-ft wing span; it was the first British model airplane to accomplish free flight. A later steam-powered model, Samuel P. Langley's "Aerodrome," made several short flights in the 1890s. Launched by catapult, it had two propellers, a wingspan of 17 ft, and flew as far as 4,200 ft, reaching speeds of 30 mi/hr. Some years later (Dec. 17, 1903) Orville and Wilbur Wright became the first to achieve free flight in a powered machine. Orville is shown (*bottom*) preparing to take off in a later Wright model, about 1909. (Top to bottom: *British Information Services; Inst. of Aerospace Sciences; last three—Wide World*)

These provide continuous, instantaneous, and accurate air navigation without use of ground-based radio systems or visual observation of the ground or stars. See INERTIAL GUIDANCE.—*H. J. R. and R. G.*

AIRPLANE: an engine-driven, heavier-than-air AIRCRAFT that obtains lifting force from the dynamic action of air against fixed wings. The basic airplane design has proved adaptable to a wide range of uses, conditions, and performance demands; and today the airplane is the most commonly observed and widely used type of aircraft.

Types: Airplanes are popularly classified by the surface from which they operate: as landplane, seaplane or floatplane, flying boat, or amphibian. However, they may also be distinguished by any one of several other criteria: number of engines; type of propulsion (propeller, jet, rocket); number of wings (monoplane, biplane, triplane); some special characteristic such as speed (subsonic, sonic, supersonic) or altitude (high-altitude) or configuration (swept-wing); purpose or use (agricultural, commercial, military, transport, reconnaissance); or compounds of these terms ("four-engined jet transport"). The *land monoplane* is now the most familiar type of airplane, and has come to be considered the conventional type. *Seaplanes* have floats in place of landing wheels; these floats must be buoyant enough to support the craft when it is anchored or moving slowly on the water. When the seaplane is taxiing fast, just before becoming airborne or immediately after landing, the floats *plane,* like the hull of a racing motorboat at high speed, and the seaplane is supported by hydrodynamic forces. To plane properly, the float's bottom surface must have a step and a sharp outer edge, and must be shaped in a shallow V. These desirable hydrodynamic characteristics are incorporated at the expense of aerodynamic "cleanness," and seaplane floats always have a considerable amount of drag. But many of the disadvantages of the float seaplane are eliminated in the *hydro-ski airplane.* Its skis provide a planing surface for water-taxiing at a wide range of speeds; and, because they are less bulky, the skis can be retracted: this reduces drag and thus the hydro-ski airplane can reach greater speeds than conventional seaplanes. The hull of a *flying boat* acts as a hydroplane; it is divided into watertight compartments. Wing-tip floats provide extra buoyancy for lateral stability. Flying boats were the first aircraft used in regular transoceanic service, but have now been almost completely replaced by land-based aircraft. The *amphibian* can take off and land on either ground or water. Because amphibians must carry a conventional landing gear as well as a flying-boat hull, they usually are slower than other aircraft with the same amount of power. Most early airplanes were *biplanes.* In 1927 Charles Lindbergh's spectacular flight across the Atlantic in the *Spirit of St. Louis* popularized the monoplane design, and later the Ford trimotor showed that this design could be adapted to heavy, multiengine aircraft. After 1930, the monoplane became much more common than the biplane. The two wings of a biplane give it more lift, but drag is increased by a relatively greater amount.

Pioneer monoplane: The airplanes of Louis Bleriot, first to fly the English Channel (1909), had far-reaching influence on later civil and military designs. (*Popular Mechanics*)

First to fly any ocean: An early chapter in military aviation was the transatlantic flight, U. S. A. to England, by the U. S. Navy Curtiss NC-4 with stops in Newfoundland, the Azores, and Portugal, May 8–31, 1919.

Supermarine "Spitfire": In the defense of Britain (1939–42), this fighter emphasized the airplane's new role as a major strategic weapon.

World War II bomber: Aircraft like the Boeing B-17 "Fortress," capable of dropping tons of high explosives from high altitudes, gave a new dimension to modern war. (*Photos: Smithsonian/National Air Museum*)

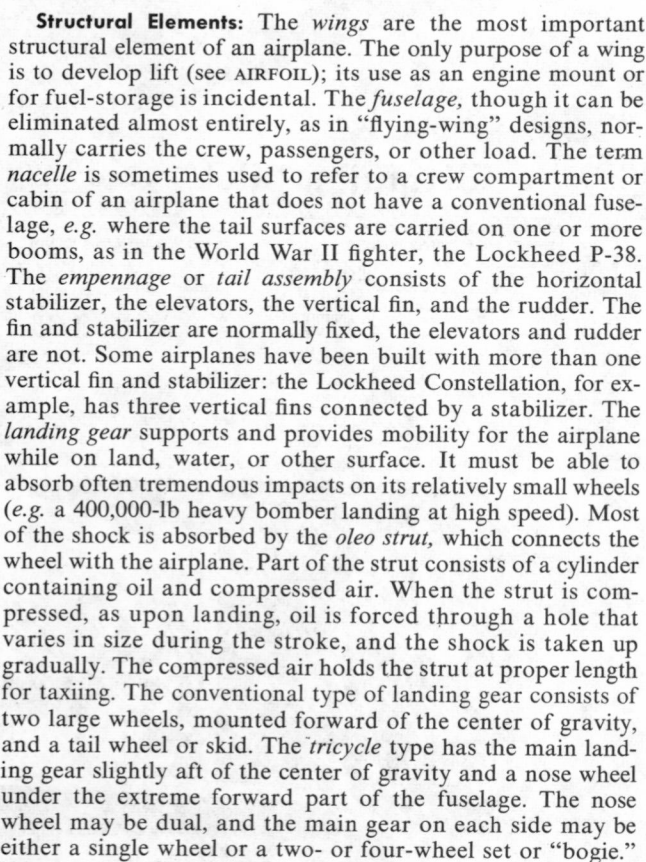

Structural Elements: The *wings* are the most important structural element of an airplane. The only purpose of a wing is to develop lift (see AIRFOIL); its use as an engine mount or for fuel-storage is incidental. The *fuselage,* though it can be eliminated almost entirely, as in "flying-wing" designs, normally carries the crew, passengers, or other load. The term *nacelle* is sometimes used to refer to a crew compartment or cabin of an airplane that does not have a conventional fuselage, *e.g.* where the tail surfaces are carried on one or more booms, as in the World War II fighter, the Lockheed P-38. The *empennage* or *tail assembly* consists of the horizontal stabilizer, the elevators, the vertical fin, and the rudder. The fin and stabilizer are normally fixed, the elevators and rudder are not. Some airplanes have been built with more than one vertical fin and stabilizer: the Lockheed Constellation, for example, has three vertical fins connected by a stabilizer. The *landing gear* supports and provides mobility for the airplane while on land, water, or other surface. It must be able to absorb often tremendous impacts on its relatively small wheels (*e.g.* a 400,000-lb heavy bomber landing at high speed). Most of the shock is absorbed by the *oleo strut,* which connects the wheel with the airplane. Part of the strut consists of a cylinder containing oil and compressed air. When the strut is compressed, as upon landing, oil is forced through a hole that varies in size during the stroke, and the shock is taken up gradually. The compressed air holds the strut at proper length for taxiing. The conventional type of landing gear consists of two large wheels, mounted forward of the center of gravity, and a tail wheel or skid. The *tricycle* type has the main landing gear slightly aft of the center of gravity and a nose wheel under the extreme forward part of the fuselage. The nose wheel may be dual, and the main gear on each side may be either a single wheel or a two- or four-wheel set or "bogie."

The *tandem* type has the main wheels in tandem under the fore and aft parts of the fuselage and has smaller "outrigger" wheels under each wing. This type can be retracted into the airplane's fuselage, and is one solution to the difficulty of getting wheels into the thin wings of high-speed aircraft. Airplanes can be equipped with special landing gear such as skis or pontoons. Large airplanes, and many small ones, are equipped with retractable landing gear. The retraction mechanism may be hydraulic, electric, pneumatic, or manual. The *engine* is also an important structural element of the airplane; types are discussed in AIRCRAFT PROPULSION.

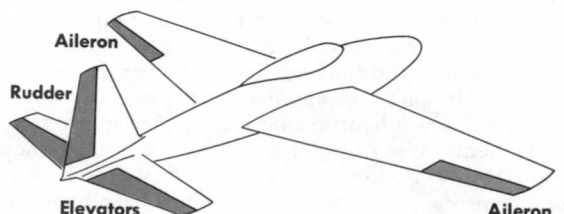

Fig. 1: Control Surfaces of an Airplane

Control Surfaces: These are movable surfaces (aileron, elevator, rudder) which control the attitude and motion of an airplane in flight (Fig. 1). There are two *ailerons,* one on each wing, located in the trailing edge near the wing tip. By deflecting the ailerons unequally or opposingly, unequal or opposing lifting forces can be created on opposite sides of the airplane and its motion in roll can be controlled. The *elevator* is located at the rear end of the horizontal stabilizer. It may be a single surface, extending from tip to tip of the stabilizer, or it may be broken by the vertical fin. The elevator (or elevators) can be deflected so as to obtain upward or downward lift (as compared to lift on the wing) on the stabilizer, and thus correct pitching motion. The *rudder* is located at the rear end of the vertical fin; deflection of the rudder causes yawing motion, principally. In addition, *flaps* are usually placed at the trailing edge of an airplane wing; these are high-lift devices, for use in take-off and landing. Deflecting or extending a flap increases the lift coefficient, by changing the camber, or profile, of the wing. Three types of flaps are shown in Fig. 2. (See AERODYNAMICS.)—*A. P. E.*

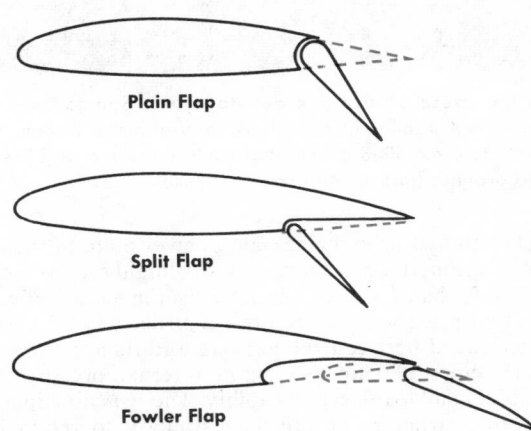

Plain Flap

Split Flap

Fowler Flap

Fig. 2: Three types of flaps: Flaps on trailing edge of wings are lowered to increase available lift during take-off and landing.

Airplane Construction: Early airplanes were essentially frameworks covered with fabric; the fabric was doped to tighten it and make it impervious to air flow. Today most airplanes are of all-metal construction, and the metal in most common use is aluminum. There are certain types of construction most frequently used for wings and stabilizers. Each of these types has its own distinct advantages, and the choice of a particular design depends largely upon the intended role of the airplane and the availability of tools. Generally speaking, the concentrated span-cap type of design is not suited to a high-speed machine, because the compression surface very rapidly buckles and this causes disturbance to the airflow and so gives an increase in drag. The distributed bending type of construction meets most common acceptance today.

In the earlier days of airplane design the fuselage was frequently a welded steel tubular structure covered by fabric. While this type of design has been retained in some very small craft, today's fuselages are normally *monocoques.* The first-generation monocoque fuselages were made of wood— an extremely satisfactory material for planes up to 20,000 lb. A. U. W. (all-up weight, or maximum gross weight) which are not subjected to use under tropical and desert conditions.

Today, notwithstanding, the metal monocoque finds almost universal acceptance. The principle of monocoque construction is that of a shell built around a matrix of transverse frames and longitudinal stringers. Generally speaking most constructions have four heavy members which stretch along the full length of the body at floor level and above window and door height; these members are termed longerons. It is common practice to attach stringers and longerons to skin by rivets and to leave frames free. A metal-to-metal ADHESIVE is now often used in place of the rivet.

When the design of an airplane is completed, a comprehensive series of static, dynamic, and fatigue tests must be made before the machine is put into active service. The purpose of these tests is to establish whether the completed structure will have the ability to carry the anticipated loads for the required lifetime. For this purpose most aircraft firms have very large and very well equipped test facilities. In their large machines complete components of an airplane can be placed and subjected to distributions and magnitudes of load representative of those anticipated in operation. Because of the great danger of explosive failure of a pressure cabin, particular attention is paid by all companies to the testing and establishment of a "fail-safe" fuselage.—*W. Ho.*

Through the sound barrier: Rocket-powered Bell X-1 (1945–47) was the first aircraft designed to reach sonic speeds.

The jet fighter: F-86 "Sabre Jets" (*bottom right*) were among the first operational military aircraft capable of supersonic flight. (*Photos: Smithsonian/National Air Museum*)

"A basic trainer for space flight": The Bell X-15 (*bottom left*) is used as a research vehicle near the edge of Earth's atmosphere. (*North American Aviation*)

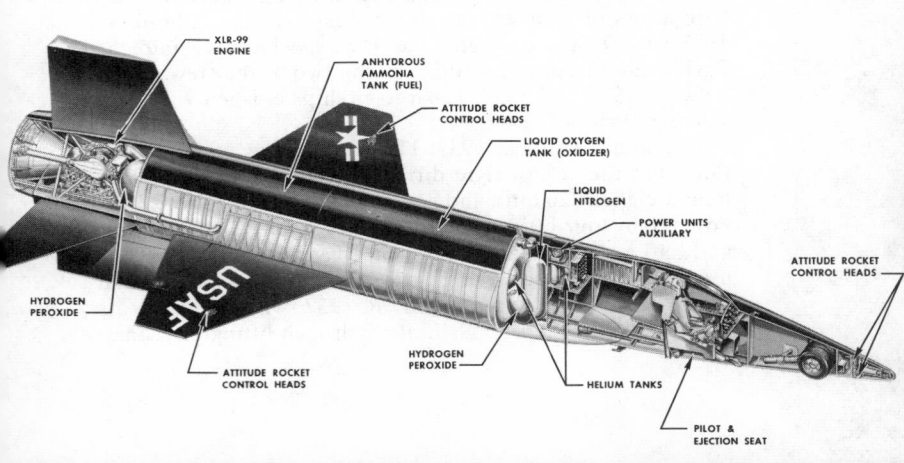

XLR-99 ENGINE
ANHYDROUS AMMONIA TANK (FUEL)
ATTITUDE ROCKET CONTROL HEADS
LIQUID OXYGEN TANK (OXIDIZER)
LIQUID NITROGEN
POWER UNITS AUXILIARY
ATTITUDE ROCKET CONTROL HEADS
HYDROGEN PEROXIDE
ATTITUDE ROCKET CONTROL HEADS
HYDROGEN PEROXIDE
HELIUM TANKS
PILOT & EJECTION SEAT

AIR POLLUTION: see ATMOSPHERIC POLLUTION.

AIRSHIP: a lighter-than-air aircraft capable of sustained and directed flight. Generally, an airship differs from a balloon in that it is steerable (dirigible) and powered; airships are thus sometimes called dirigible balloons, or simply dirigibles. After dramatic exploits during World War I and in the ensuing 20 yr, the airship has been much overshadowed by achievements of the airplane (see AVIATION), and since the mid-1930s has steadily declined in numbers and importance. A very few now remain in service. Airships are classed according to structure as non-rigid, semi-rigid, and rigid; these classifications are now largely historical.

The *non-rigid* airship or "blimp" is essentially a hydrogen- or helium-filled fabric envelope of streamlined shape to which a crew car and propulsive system are attached by cables.

In the cause of airplane development: Santos-Dumont (1906) tested the stability of one of his early airplane designs by attaching it to a modified airship that could be raised and lowered from the ground. (*Inst. of Aerospace Sciences*)

Early airship oddity: In 1863, a Professor Thitchie flew this pedal-driven machine over Hartford, Conn. (*N. Y. Public Library*)

Albert Santos-Dumont, airship daredevil (ca. 1909): The rich Brazilian's heroics inspired international interest in airship development. (*Inst. of Aerospace Sciences*)

(Though hydrogen, being lighter, gives more lifting effect per unit volume than helium, it is also highly flammable and is less safe than helium.) The *semi-rigid* machine differs only in that an integrating structure—a girder or keel member—is introduced between the gas bag and its appendages. Thus both types of ship rely upon internal pressure for their stability and load-carrying ability. The *rigid* airship is a fabric-covered structure of sufficient strength to retain its shape without the assistance of internal pressure. In this type of airship the filling gas is carried in light bags. Aerodynamic considerations are less important in airship than in airplane design, because the gross lift of the airship is essentially independent of the shape of the vessel and depends mainly on the specific gravity and bulk of the filling gas. Airships are steered by rudders horizontally and by elevators vertically.

A landmark in airship history was the round-trip transatlantic flight made by the British rigid airship R-34, July 2–13, 1919. Earlier (1917) the rigid German Zeppelin LZ-59 had made a nonstop military mission from Bulgaria to Khartoum, Africa, and return, traveling a distance of some 4,200 mi. Airships were used in World War I for various military purposes; the Germans used them for bombing. After the war Germany, France, Italy, Great Britain, and the U. S. A. built or purchased rigid airships for commercial and military use. Regular airship service was established between Germany, N America, and S America. The German *Graf Zeppelin* made 144 ocean crossings and logged over a million miles before being retired in 1937. Although many trips were without incident, a series of disasters demonstrated inherent shortcomings in large rigid airships. Among American airships lost were the Italian-built *Roma,* which crashed in 1922 killing 34 persons; the *Shenandoah,* wrecked over Ohio in a storm in 1925 with a loss of 14 lives; the *Akron,* lost over the Atlantic in 1933 with 73 persons; and the *Macon,* which fell into the Pacific during a storm in 1935, killing two of the crew. In all, between 1919 and 1937, 12 large airships crashed with considerable loss of life.

The climax came in 1937. The *Hindenburg,* completed in 1936, was the largest rigid dirigible ever built; it was 803 ft long, weighed 220 tons, and had a gas volume of 7,063,000 ft^3. Powered by four 1,050-hp diesel engines, it cruised at 78 mi/hr, and had a range of 8,750 mi. For a year the huge ship was used in transatlantic service, carrying up to 70 passengers and heavy loads of freight. On May 6, 1937, while it was at its moorings in Lakehurst, N. J., its hydrogen lifting gas some-

Most successful airship liner: German *Graf Zeppelin* was one of the few huge airships of the 1930s that did not meet disaster. It logged over a million miles before retirement, 1937. (*Wide World*)

how ignited, and it fell in flames. Of the 97 aboard, 35 were killed. Rigid airships were virtually abandoned after this disaster. Non-rigid airships, however, continued to be built and used, mainly for military service. In 1957, the U. S. Navy blimp *Snowbird* established new distance and endurance records for aircraft, remaining in air over 264 hr and traveling over 8,000 mi without refueling. Until 1961 the Navy kept a few blimps for submarine-detection and radar early-warning work; but in mid-1961 the remaining 15 blimps were scheduled to be deflated, dismantled, and stored, pending future need. It was thought that one or two might remain in service for experimental use as flying wind tunnels.—*W. Ho.*

AIRSPEED INDICATOR: an instrument that measures the speed of an aircraft relative to that of the air mass through which it flies. It contains a pressure-sensitive diaphragm, like that in an aneroid BAROMETER. Through a pitot-static tube projecting outside the aircraft in a forward direction, samples of incoming air are collected continuously. One stream of air is led directly against one side of the diaphragm, where it exerts a pressure proportional to its original velocity. A second stream of air, led to the other side of the diaphragm, is reduced to existing atmospheric pressure. The difference of pressure moves the diaphragm, and a pointer linked to it indicates airspeed on a scale calibrated in knots.—*K. A.*

U. S. Navy rigid airship: Ill-fated *Akron*, 785 ft long, was commissioned in 1931. It crashed in Atlantic, 1933, with a loss of 74 lives. (*Goodyear*)

Training "blimp": U. S. Navy used larger versions of this non-rigid ship in World War II for antisubmarine and rescue work. (*Goodyear*)

AL-BATTANI (Lat. **Albategnius** or **Albatenius;** Arabic, **Abu 'Abdallah Muhammad ibn Jabir ibn Sinan al-Battani, al-Harrani, al-Sabi**), *c.* 858–929, Islamic astronomer; b. Harran, Turkey. His most notable writing, *Concerning Knowledge of the Stars*, contains a star catalog for 880–81, reports an increase of nearly 17° in the Sun's apogee in the preceding 600 yr, and gives accurate values for the precession and inclination of the ecliptic. One chapter deals with trigonometry; Al-Battani used trigonometric sines, tangents, and cotangents in computations. He rejected the theory of trepidation of the equinoxes. His book, translated into Latin in the 12th cent., considerably influenced European astronomy.—*D. H. D. R.*

ALBEDO: a number used to describe the ability of a surface to reflect radiation, particularly light. The number represents the proportion of the incident light that is reflected or scattered diffusely by the surface (see REFLECTION OF LIGHT). Light that falls on an opaque object is either absorbed (thereby heating the object) or reflected. The reflection is rarely mirror-like; usually the reflected radiation is scattered in many directions. Upper surfaces of clouds have a high albedo, about 0.75. Other albedos are: dark forest, 0.05; dry sand, 0.30; Earth as a whole, 0.34 (with a high contribution from clouds); Moon, 0.07; Venus, 0.61; Jupiter, 0.41; Saturn, 0.42.—*M. W. O.*

In *nuclear reactor terminology*, albedo is the ratio of neutrons reflected from a medium to those entering it. Neutrons are necessary to a continuing nuclear reaction. To prevent their large-scale escape, the reactor is surrounded by a reflector designed for maximum albedo—*i.e.* for returning to the reactor core as large a fraction as possible of the neutrons escaping from the core.—*S. K.*

ALBERTI, LEONE BATTISTA, 1404–72, Italian painter, architect, organist, and writer; b. Venice. He was employed in architectural restorations in Rome by Pope Nicholas V. Creator of important church designs and author of *De re aedificatoria* ("Concerning Architecture or Building," 1485), Alberti is credited with being the first to investigate scientifically the laws of perspective, and with being the inventor of the *camera lucida.* He is said to have written on the art of representation, probably using some form of the *camera obscura.*—*S. B.*

ALBINISM AND MELANISM: conspicuous mutations in which skin, fur, or feathers of an animal lack normal pigment (albinism) or have an unusually black appearance (melanism). These conditions are inherited. Albinism consists of an inability to form the normal pigment, so that fur or feathers are left white and human skin pink (the latter because blood vessels become visible). The iris of the eye is pink, too, in albino birds and mammals. Albinos are often met among

Albinism: Tree squirrel owes its whiteness to a lack of pigmentation—a hereditary trait. (*W. Bryant Tyrrell, Nat. Audubon Soc.*)

Negroid peoples in the tropics. Occasionally robins, porcupines, and other animals show albinism. Melanism, due to a concentration of the dark pigment *melanin,* is more common among insects than in other animals. See MUTATION; COLORATION OF ANIMALS; HEREDITY.—*L. and M. M.*

AL-BIRUNI, 973–1048, Arab astronomer, geographer, mathematician; b. Khiva, Central Asia. He wrote an encyclopedia of astronomy; a general work on mathematics, astronomy, and astrology; a study of the history of calendars; and a description of India. Al-Biruni gave a clear account of Hindu numerals, studied those geometric problems that are nonsoluble with ruler and compass (Albirunic problems), wrote on precious stones and the hydrostatics of springs and artesian wells, and determined latitudes and longitudes.—*D. H. D. R.*

ALBUMIN: see BLOOD PROTEINS.

ALCHEMY: the chemistry and chemical theories of the Middle Ages. The widespread and erroneous view of alchemy as the pretended art of transmuting base metals into the noble metals, silver and gold, seems to have arisen largely from literary portrayals of alchemists, notably in Chaucer's *Canon's Yeoman's Tale* and Ben Jonson's play *The Alchemist.* Baron von Liebig in the 19th cent. regarded alchemy more truly as the chemistry of the Middle Ages. In its widest aspect, however, alchemy must be viewed as an extensive philosophical

system which sought to unify the microcosm of man with the macrocosm of the universe: "All that is without thee also is within," wrote a medieval alchemist. Close study shows alchemy to have consisted of a complicated web of rudimentary chemistry, philosophy, ASTROLOGY, mysticism, MAGIC, theosophy, and other ingredients, including conceptions of great interest in religion and psychology. Alchemy persisted from at least the early Christian era until the end of the 17th cent., and its ideas and imagery permeated the thought and art of the Middle Ages. Modern chemistry owes little to the alchemical visionaries; but the practical workers in alchemy, ranging from before Jabir, or Geber (9th cent.), to J. R. Glauber (17th cent.), made many contributions to the incipient science by discovering new substances and their properties and by inventing laboratory processes and equipment.

In broad outline, alchemical doctrine, as applied to the inanimate universe, held that all forms of matter have a common origin; that these forms are produced by evolutionary processes and that they possess a common and permanent soul confined in a variable and transitory body. Consequently, one form of matter might be transmuted into another. The deductive reasoning of alchemy was based mainly on two fundamental postulates: the unity of matter, and the existence of a potent transmuting agent known as the Philosopher's Stone. This agent, usually described as a red powder, was regarded as the medicine of base, or diseased, metals; therefore, because of the principle of unity, it became also (in a liquid or dissolved form) the medicine of man, or Elixir of Life.

Many alchemical conceptions were drawn from ancient Greece; the idea that metals can pass through a cycle of growth leading to the imagined perfection of gold is a reflection of Aristotle's dictum that Nature strives toward perfection. In the words of an alchemical writer: "Nature alwaies intendeth and striveth to the perfection of Gold: but many accidents coming between, change the mettalls." The exoteric, or uninformed, alchemists (sometimes called "puffers") devoted their energies entirely to arbitrary experiments in search of the Philosopher's Stone, with the aim of acquiring worldly wealth. The adepts, or informed "Sons of Hermes," valued such experiments in large measure as attempts to prove on an experimental plane the truth of their philosophical system. A further aspect of this "esoteric" alchemy was concerned with the spiritual regeneration of imperfect man. The doctrines and ideas of esoteric alchemy were usually expressed in cryptic language or concealed in emblematic representations.

The theory of materialistic alchemy was based essentially upon Aristotle's theory of the four elements (earth, air, fire, water) and the four qualities (wet, dry, hot, cold); it visualized a separation of the properties of matter from matter itself. The four qualities (also the elements fire and water) fall into pairs of contraries. It was probably in the 9th cent., during the passage of alchemy through Islam into W. Europe, that the opposed elements fire and water assumed a new guise in the sulfur-mercury theory of metals, in which sulfur was the principle of combustibility, and mercury that of metallicity.

In the 16th cent., Paracelsus added a third principle, known as salt. He brought about a parting of the ways in alchemy by insisting that its true goal should be to prepare healing drugs rather than to make gold. A period of medico-chemistry, or iatrochemistry, was thus inaugurated, and this lasted until about the opening of the 18th cent., during which period the old alchemy gradually faded away. The complex nature of alchemy has been well summarized by Albert Poisson (1891): "Scholasticism, with its infinitely subtle argumentation; theology, with its ambiguous phraseology; astrology, so vast and so complicated: these are but child's play in comparison with alchemy."—*J. R.*

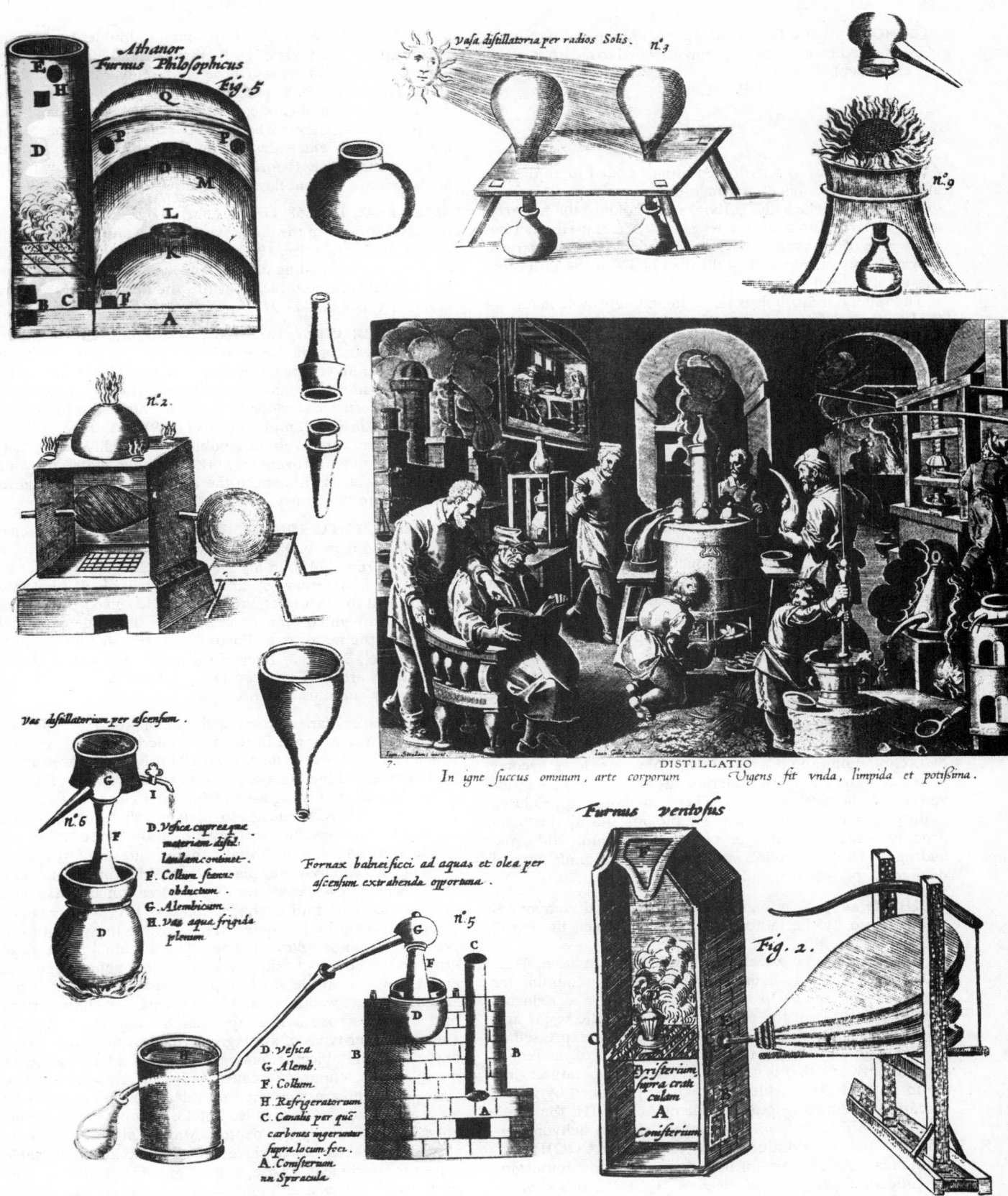

The stills and furnaces of the alchemists are represented in these illustrations from the Dutch edition of Athanasius Kircher's *Subterranean World* (1682). Some of the hardware used in the preparation of drugs appears in the scene of the alchemist's studio (*inset*), reproduced from Stradanus's *Mirror* (1580). (*Gossner Collection*)

ALCOHOL: any of a family of organic chemical compounds characterized by a hydroxyl group attached to a carbon atom, *e.g.* ethyl alcohol,

$$H-\underset{\underset{H}{|}}{\overset{\overset{H}{|}}{C}}-\underset{\underset{H}{|}}{\overset{\overset{H}{|}}{C}}-O-H$$

A hydroxyl group is a hydrogen atom bonded to an oxygen atom (OH). Alcohols do not include those compounds (such as phenols) in which the carbon atom holding the hydroxyl group is part of an aromatic ring. Aristotle and Hippocrates made note of the presence in wines of something they termed "spirits": this substance, first distilled in about the 11th cent., was ethyl alcohol.

The family of alcohols is large, including simple methanol (CH_3OH); alcohols composed of many carbon atoms; alcohols with more than one hydroxyl group (*e.g.* ethylene glycol with two hydroxyl groups); and very complex alcohols such as cholesterol. *Methyl alcohol* (methanol, CH_3OH) was originally produced by the destructive distillation of wood. Today it is synthetically produced by the reaction of carbon monoxide and hydrogen in the presence of a suitable catalyst. Methanol is used as a denaturant in ethyl alcohol, as a solvent, as an antifreeze in automobile engines, as a rocket fuel, and as an agent for the addition of the methyl group (CH_3) in the synthesis of other compounds. *Ethyl alcohol* (ethanol, C_2H_5OH) is produced by fermentation of sugars and grains (by action of appropriate enzymes) and synthetically from ethylene. Only a fraction of the total production of ethanol is used in alcoholic beverages. Larger uses are as a solvent and as an intermediate in preparation of other compounds. Of the two *propyl alcohols,* n-propyl ($CH_3CH_2CH_2OH$) and isopropyl ($CH_3CHOHCH_3$), the latter is more important. Synthesized from propylene, it is used as a solvent and as a chemical intermediate, and as "rubbing alcohol" (having replaced ethyl alcohol in this last application). *Ethylene glycol* is produced synthetically by a variety of processes including the hydrolysis of ethylene oxide. It is employed as solvent, antifreeze, and chemical intermediate. The so-called *higher alcohols,* containing about 8 to 20 carbon atoms, have become extremely important raw materials for preparation of a wide variety of chemical products. These alcohols are produced mainly by hydrogenation of vegetable oils and by the "oxo-process"—the reaction of an olefin, carbon monoxide, and hydrogen. Higher alcohols are used in the manufacture of detergents, plasticizers, and resins.—*R. W.*

ALDEHYDE: any of a group of organic chemical compounds characterized by the radical H—C=O, in which the fourth bond of the carbon is attached to another carbon atom. Aldehydes occur widely in living organisms, often accounting for their odor and flavor. In industry they find use as reducing agents, as well as in the production of synthetic resins and other chemicals. The aldehyde formula can be expressed as RCHO. FORMALDEHYDE, the simplest member of the family and the only one that is gaseous at room temperatures, has the formula HCHO. Aldehydes can be produced by gentle oxidation of the corresponding alcohol (RCOH); the name aldehyde, in fact, is a contraction of "alcohol dehydrogenatum." Further oxidation yields an acid (RCOOH), *e.g.* formic acid. Aside from formaldehyde, the most important *aliphatic* aldehyde is *acetaldehyde* (CH_3CHO): this is made commercially from ethanol, acetylene, or butane and is used, mostly in the same plant where produced, to make acetic acid ("anhydride") or butanol. Aldehydes owe their reactivity to the carbonyl group, although they can have additional functionality too; *e.g.* both acrolein (CH_2=CHCHO) and croton-

aldehyde (CH_3CH=CHCHO) contain double bonds and participate in reactions of both ethylenes and aldehydes. The lower aliphatic aldehydes (those containing 7 carbon atoms or less) have a strong, pungent odor, which becomes more pleasant as the number of carbon atoms increases, then all but disappears when the carbon atoms exceed 14. Some of the higher aliphatic aldehydes (citronella, citral) as well as some of the aromatic ones (benzaldehyde, cinnamaldehyde, vanillin) are important in food flavoring and perfumery.—*D. P. B.*

ALDER, KURT, 1902–58, German chemist; b. Königshütte. For the development of the diene synthesis, he and O. P. H. Diels shared the Nobel prize, 1950. Alder applied the results of this research to the building of large molecules for use in plastics. In 1940 he became director of the chemical institute of the Univ. of Cologne.—*D. H. D. R.*

ALDROVANDI, ULISSE, 1522–1605, Italian naturalist; b. Bologna. Professor of medicine at the Univ. of Bologna from 1560, he lectured on pharmacology and established one of the earliest botanical gardens (1567) connected with a university. Of his projected encyclopedic work on all living things, he completed three volumes on birds (1599) and one on insects (1602). Many other volumes, published after his death, contained some of Aldrovandi's work and much material by his pupils. This work influenced the development of zoological taxonomy for a century.—*D. H. D. R.*

ALEMBERT, JEAN LE ROND D', 1717–83, French mathematician and philosopher; b. Paris. A member of the Academy of Sciences (from 1741), in his *Treatise on Dynamics* (1743) he developed D'ALEMBERT'S PRINCIPLE and applied it to fluid motion and the theory of equilibrium. He solved the mathematical problem of the precession of the equinoxes and explained the nutation of Earth's axis. His writings include his memoirs, *Studies of Integral Calculus* (1746–48), scientific and literary articles for Diderot's encyclopedia, and books on philosophy and music.—*H. C.*

ALGAE: a large, varied group of simple plants. The 30,000 or so known species range in size from microscopic plants of a single cell to seaweeds more than 100 ft long. All are simple in structure, lacking the true roots, stems, and leaves of higher plants. Algae are distinguished from their close relatives, the fungi, by possessing the green pigment chlorophyll, which enables them to produce their own food by PHOTOSYNTHESIS. Algae and fungi are both thallophytes, the simplest plants.

Algae are chiefly water plants, flourishing in pools, lakes, and oceans; a few species live on soils, tree trunks, rocks, and other objects in moist, shaded places. Fresh-water algae usually develop best in quiet waters, where they often form dense, greenish or yellowish-green "pond scum." Some algae grow on the bodies of fish, turtles, and other aquatic animals, and a few live inside small animals such as Hydras. One-celled algae, as well as some larger forms, are an important part of PLANKTON, a floating mass of minute plants and animals. Other types of algae grow attached to stones, twigs, and other solid objects submerged in water. Many species of marine algae, commonly called seaweed, grow in shallow water or in the areas covered by tides, clinging to rocks by means of suckerlike disks called holdfasts. Other marine forms grow on rock at greater depths. Marine algae are usually absent from sandy shores, since shifting sands afford no stable place for attachment. Dense, tangled growths of marine algae form food sources and homes for crustaceans, fish, worms, polyps, and other marine animals. Many algae are first links in the FOOD CHAIN of the sea, for they serve as basic food for small marine animals, which in turn are eaten by larger animals. Of all marine life, algae alone are able to make food from water and carbon dioxide and minerals which they absorb from water. Thus, all sea life depends on algae for food. Algae are also an important food source in fresh water.

Algae reproduce by several means. Certain one-celled algae simply split in two, an asexual process. Many species reproduce asexually by spores, special cells that become detached from the parent and grow directly into a new plant. Other algae reproduce by various sexual processes, in which two sex cells unite and form a fertilized egg. (See REPRODUCTION.)

Algae produce gelatinous substances used as laxatives, as stiffening agents in ice creams and puddings, and as a culture medium (agar) for the laboratory growth of bacteria and other fungi. Marine algae yield iodine; often they are burned and their mineral-rich ashes used as fertilizer for soils. Especially in the Orient, algae form an important part of the human diet; in Europe and the United States, algae known as dulse and Irish moss (carrageen) are often eaten by people. Land is built up by carbonates secreted by algae, as in the travertine terraces of Yellowstone Park and in oceanic algal reefs, which rival those of coral. Fresh-water algae may contaminate water supplies. Algae growing on damp soils add organic matter and thus contribute to soil fertility.

Scientists throughout the world have conducted tests on algae as food and as fuel substitutes. Chlorella, a one-celled fresh-water alga, contains significant amounts of carbohydrates, proteins, and vitamin C. Upon fermentation, algae produce a mixture of methane and other gases that can be converted into liquid fuels such as kerosene and gasoline.

The following is a simplified classification of the major groups of algae:

Blue-green algae (*Cyanophyta*): Simplest algae and among the most primitive plants. They may be one-celled or many-celled; cells lack distinct nuclei. Size ranges from microscopic to large slimy masses seen floating in fresh water or covering soil, rocks, and other objects. The name blue-green algae is derived from the prevalence of certain pigments in the cell, but the color is not always blue-green; it may be blue, olive-green, yellowish, reddish, or violet. Certain blue-green algae grow in hot springs at Yellowstone National Park, which probably have the highest known temperature in which any living organism can survive. When present in great numbers in lakes or ponds, blue-green algae may cause pollution.

Flagellates (*Euglenophyta*): Microscopic, one-celled organisms that swim with whiplike extensions of the body wall known as flagella. Some flagellates are green, because of the presence of chlorophyll. Others lack chlorophyll and may be colorless, red, yellow, or brown. The classification of flagellates is a matter of dispute. Certain biologists consider green flagellates plants and place them with the algae. Other biologists put them with the one-celled animals (protozoa), because they move about as animals, react to stimuli as animals, lack the rigid cellulose cell wall representative of plant cells, and are unable in many cases to manufacture their own food as plants do.

Green algae (*Chlorophyta*): Chiefly fresh-water varieties. Many are shaped like filaments, and some are flat and leaflike (*e.g. Ulva,* or sea lettuce). A few are unicellular (*e.g. Protococcus,* found on tree trunks). Green algae have many characteristics found in higher plants: a distinct cell nucleus, chlorophyll localized within chloroplasts, a cellulose cell wall, and typical plant pigments. Many botanists think higher plants evolved from a similar form.

Yellow-green algae (*Chrysophyta*): Predominantly one-celled. Best known and most numerous are diatoms, with silicon shells in many shapes and with fine surface sculpturing. Shells are in two halves that fit together like the top and bottom of a pillbox. Abundant in marine and fresh-water plankton, diatoms are an important food source for animals. When diatoms die, their shells sink to the bottom and accumulate

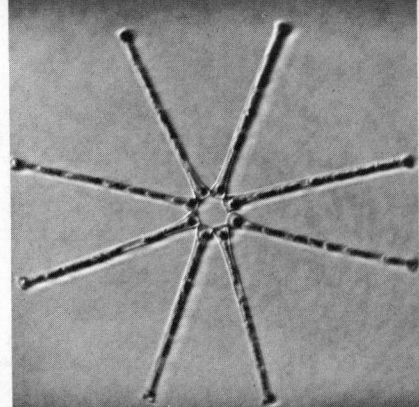

Variety of algal forms is seen in neat colony of eight diatoms (*left*) and in clumped strands of *Fucus,* a brown alga (*right*). Diatoms are one-celled algae that often live in groups. The strands of *Fucus* were photographed at ebb tide. At high tide they are buoyed up by their paired, bladderlike vesicles, which keep them within reach of sunlight, their primary source of energy. (*Left: Carl Struwe/Monkmeyer. Right: Douglas P. Wilson*)

in deposits of diatomaceous earth; this is mined and used in scouring powders and other products.

Brown algae (*Phaeophyta*): Largest and structurally the most complex of all algae. Most are salt-water plants, growing chiefly in cooler ocean waters of temperate zones; they are especially abundant in shallow water along rocky coasts. A few species are microscopic in size, but most forms are at least 6 in. long. Kelps, the largest brown algae, reach a length of several hundred feet. They have large holdfasts, long and branched stipes, and flattened blades, often with buoyant air bladders.

Red algae (*Rhodophyta*): Chiefly marine algae, found in the warmer parts of oceans, frequently at great depths. They are usually smaller and more delicate than brown algae, often appearing fernlike or feathery. In addition to chlorophyll, they contain a red pigment, which gives them their pink-to-purple color. Dulse and Irish moss are common.—*A. P. E.* (See also Color Plates f.p. 6.)

ALGEBRA: a generalization of arithmetic made possible by systematic use of symbols for unspecified, or unknown, numbers. These symbols are usually letters such as a, b, x, y, and greek letters α, β, etc. To solve a problem by purely arithmetic means, one must start with given numbers, discover the operations that will produce the solution, and apply them. The method of algebra permits one to express the required answer and other unknowns by letters, determine how the known and unknown quantities are related, and then find the values of the unknowns that fit the relation or relations. The algebraic method has greater range and power than arithmetic. The relations to be satisfied are usually equations. Hence the central problem of algebra is that of solving equations. The great advances in algebra have come out of efforts to solve more and more complex equations.

The algebraic operations are addition, subtraction, multiplication, division, raising to a power, and extracting a root. An algebraic process involves a finite number of these operations. A process transcends algebra if it requires operations other than these, such as differentiation in calculus; or if it requires an infinite number of algebraic operations such as summing an infinite series. Algebraic addition includes subtraction since subtracting a positive number is equivalent to adding a negative number; $5 - 3 = 5 + (-3)$. Addition and multiplication are called integral operations because, if they are applied to integers (whole numbers), the results are also integers. Raising to an integral power is really repeated multiplication, and hence is also an integral operation. If division is employed, the result may be a fraction, but it can always be expressed as a ratio of two integers. Hence, addition, multiplication, and division are rational operations. Root extraction may produce irrational results (*i.e.* numbers that cannot be expressed as ratios of integers), and so is called an irrational operation. Also, extracting the square root of a negative number requires the use of COMPLEX NUMBERS.

Although algebra uses letters to replace numbers, it does not use positional notation. Whereas 23 means two 10s plus 3, the symbol *ab* means *a* multiplied by *b* and is also written $a \times b$ or $a \cdot b$; and $2a$ means $a + a$, or $2 \times a$. However, numbers are used in the familiar way, so that $23ab$ means twenty-three times *a* times *b*. When letters are grouped by parentheses ( ), brackets [ ], braces { }, or a bar above the group, they are to be treated as a single symbol; thus $2(a + b)$ means that the sum of *a* and *b* is multiplied by 2. More complicated expressions may include parentheses within brackets, *e.g.*:

$$2[3(a + a) - 2a] = 2[3 \cdot 2a - 2a] = 2[6a - 2a] = 8a$$

The rules of operation with signed numbers are the following, where *a* and *b* are positive numbers:

$$(-a) + (-b) = -(a + b)$$
$$-a + b = b - a = -(a - b)$$
$$(-a) \cdot (-b) = ab$$
$$(-a) \cdot b = a(-b) = -ab$$

The last two inform us that the product of two quantities with *like* signs is positive; the product of two quantities with *unlike* signs is negative.

With the symbolism of algebra one can state the laws that govern the operations of addition and multiplication in both arithmetic and algebra. These are, for any numbers *a*, *b*, and *c*:

associative law—

$$(a + b) + c = a + (b + c), \quad (ab)c = a(bc)$$

commutative law— $a + b = b + a, \quad ab = ba$

distributive law— $a(b + c) = ab + ac$

These are fundamental laws of what may be called classical algebra, in contradistinction to other algebras which have a purely logical character not necessarily associated with the number system. In these other varieties of algebra, not all of the above postulates are assumed. One of the earliest of these was formulated by George Boole (1815–64). At the present time there is a good deal of interest in these new algebras, and they are often found to be useful in practical problems.

Exponents: A valuable contribution to the symbolism of algebra was made by the introduction of exponents, first used by Thomas Harriot (1560–1621). When a number is multiplied by itself, the product, $a \cdot a$, is written a^2 (*a* squared); similarly,

Rules of algebra can be demonstrated by cutting apart squares and rectangles. Below, the area of the largest rectangle is $a(b + c)$. This rectangle can be cut into two smaller ones of area ab and ac. Since their total area must still equal the original area, we have the distributive law: $a(b + c) = ab + ac$.

$a \cdot a \cdot a$ is a^3 (*a* cubed); $a \cdot a \cdot a \cdot a$ is a^4 (*a* to the fourth power); and so on. The quantity a^n is the *n*th power of *a*, and *n* is the exponent of the base *a*. If *n* and *m* are positive integers, the following rules and definitions apply:

$$a^n \cdot a^m = a^{n+m}$$
$$a^n \div a^m = a^{n-m}$$
$$a^{-n} = 1/a^n \text{ if } a \neq 0$$
$$(a^n)^m = a^{nm}$$
$$a^n b^n = (ab)^n$$
$$a^0 = 1$$

Algebraic Expressions: An expression in which letters, or letters and numbers, are multiplied together, *e.g.* $4a^2b$ or $-ab$, is called a term; in the term $4a^2b$, the number 4 is the coefficient of a^2b. The sum of the exponents of the unknowns is the degree of the term; the degree of $4a^2b$ is $2 + 1$, or 3. If terms are added together, the result is called a rational integral expression, or polynomial; if only two terms are added the result is a binomial, such as $x^2y + 2xy^2$; if three terms are added, the result is a trinomial.

The algebraic operations can be performed on polynomials, *e.g.* addition:

$$(4a + 2b - ab) + (a - b) - (3a - 3b + 2ab)$$
$$= (4a + a - 3a) + (2b - b + 3b) + (-ab - 2ab)$$
$$= 2a + 4b - 3ab$$

multiplication:

$$(4a + b)(a - 2b) = 4a(a - 2b) + b(a - 2b)$$
$$= 4a^2 - 8ab + ab - 2b^2$$
$$= 4a^2 - 7ab - 2b^2$$

The following products are particularly useful:

$$(a + b)(a + b) = (a + b)^2 = a^2 + 2ab + b^2$$
$$(a - b)(a - b) = (a - b)^2 = a^2 - 2ab + b^2$$
$$(a + b)(a - b) = a^2 - b^2$$
$$a^3 + b^3 = (a + b)(a^2 - ab + b^2)$$
$$a^3 - b^3 = (a - b)(a^2 + ab + b^2)$$

These relations state the product of two factors, or equally, the factors of a polynomial. The symbols *a* and *b* may represent any terms, *e.g.* $25x^2 - y^4 = (5x)^2 - (y^2)^2 = (5x + y^2)(5x - y^2)$. Many trinomials that are not perfect squares may also be factored, *e.g.* $x^2 - 7x + 12 = (x - 3)(x - 4)$.

Identities and Equations: The results of applying algebraic operations, including factoring, lead to algebraic identities.

The area of the large square is $(a + b)^2$. It can be cut apart to form a square of area a^2, two rectangles each of area ab, and a square of area b^2. This demonstrates the algebraic identity: $(a + b)^2 = a^2 + 2ab + b^2$.

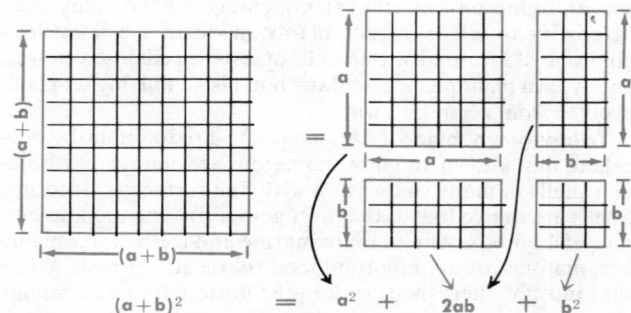

An *identity* is an equation which is valid for all values of the unknowns (with the exception of values which reduce both members to meaningless expressions). The relations above are identities. Identities are useful for changing an expression from one form to another. When two expressions are arbitrarily set equal to one another, a conditional equation is produced. The problem posed by a conditional equation is that of finding the value of the unknown, or values of the unknowns, which make it a true statement, or satisfy it. The term "equation" is usually interpreted as a conditional equation unless specified otherwise.

Equations are classified according to the kind of expressions which occur in them. The expressed equality of two polynomials, or of one polynomial set equal to zero, is a rational integral equation. Methods of solving other kinds of equations lead eventually to this type, and hence the emphasis upon it in the study of equations. Rational integral equations are classified by the number of unknowns and by degree. If only one unknown appears, a single equation is sufficient to determine its value. In general, as many equations are needed as the number of unknowns, forming a system of simultaneous equations. A rational integral equation in one unknown has as many solutions as the degree of the equation, if account is taken of possible repetitions.

Linear equations in one unknown are equations of the first degree. They are called linear because they are related to the functions $y = ax + b$, which in coordinate geometry are straight lines. Here the general equation is $ax + b = 0$, where a and b denote known numbers. Its solution is $x = -b/a$.

Quadratic equations in one unknown are a second type. The general quadratic equation is $ax^2 + bx + c = 0$, where a, b, and c are known numbers. The equation generally has two solutions,

$$x = (-b \pm \sqrt{b^2 - 4ac})/2a$$

which coincide only if $b^2 - 4ac = 0$. The quantity $b^2 - 4ac$ is called the *discriminant* of the quadratic. (See QUADRATIC EQUATION.)

Cubic and quartic equations in one unknown can always be solved. The general methods are considerably more complicated than for quadratic equations, and the reader is advised to consult a textbook.

Equations of degree higher than the fourth cannot be solved except in special cases. This was first proved by Niels Abel, about 1825. Special numerical equations can be solved exactly, and approximate methods can be applied to any numerical equation to obtain real roots as closely as required. Some equations can be reduced by factoring; others are irreducible. The theory of equations deals with these matters.

Non-integral and irrational equations are often reduced to rational integral equations by clearing the fractions, or by raising both members to a power. These processes may introduce roots into the rational integral equation which do not satisfy the original equation. They are called extraneous roots and must be discarded.

Simultaneous equations: A considerable body of theory has been developed on the subject of systems of linear equations, known as linear algebra. The most elementary methods suffice for simple systems. For example, the system $2x - y = 5$, $x + 2y = 10$ can be solved by multiplying the first equation by 2 and adding it to the second. The result is $5x = 20$, whence $x = 4$. We now find $y = 3$ by substituting $x = 4$ in either equation. The study of the theory of such equations leads to the consideration of matrices (see MATRIX) and DETERMINANTS. Systems of equations of degree higher than the first require special methods.

One equation in two unknowns is not sufficient to determine the values of the unknowns, and is *indeterminate*. The same may be said of a system of fewer equations than unknowns: this is an indeterminate system. If, however, a further condition is imposed, *e.g.* requiring the solutions to be integers, it is often possible to specify the solutions.

Inequalities: An inequality is a statement that one expression is less than ($<$) or more than ($>$) another. An absolute inequality is true for all values of the unknowns for which both members have meaning. An example is $x^2 + y^2 + 1 > 0$, where x and y are real numbers. A conditional inequality is true for some range of values only; to solve a conditional inequality is to determine this range of values. For example, consider $x^2 - 4x + 3 > 0$. Since $x^2 - 4x + 3 = (x-1)(x-3)$, we have $(x-1)(x-3) > 0$. This is true if both factors are positive or both negative. Both are positive if $x > 3$, and negative if $x < 1$. Hence the inequality is true in the range $x > 3$, and in the range $x < 1$. (See INEQUALITY.)

Progressions: Algebra deals with progressions of terms which proceed according to some rule. The three most important of these are *arithmetic, harmonic,* and *geometric* progressions. An arithmetic progression has each of its terms equal to the preceding one increased by a fixed amount. For example, 1, 3, 5, 7, 9 has each term equal to the preceding one increased by 2. In general, the arithmetic progression can be denoted by a, $a + d$, $a + 2d$, $a + 3d$, ..., $a + kd$. The nth term is $a + (n - 1)d$, and the sum of n terms can be shown to be $\frac{1}{2}[2a + (n - 1)d]$, or $\frac{1}{2}(a + l)$ where l is the last term.

A harmonic progression is one whose terms are the reciprocals of those of an arithmetic progression. For example, 1, ⅓, ⅕, ⅐, ⅑ is formed from the reciprocals of the terms of the above arithmetic progression. The nth term can be found from that of the corresponding arithmetic progression. There is no general formula for the sum of n terms.

A geometric progression has each of its terms equal to

A square of side $(a - b)$ can be obtained by cutting rectangles from a larger square of side a. If we were to take out the two rectangles that are each ab we would be taking out the square b^2 twice, so we must add that square back once. The area $(a - b)^2$ is therefore equal to $a^2 - ab - ab + b^2$, and we have the identity: $(a - b)^2 = a^2 - 2ab + b^2$.

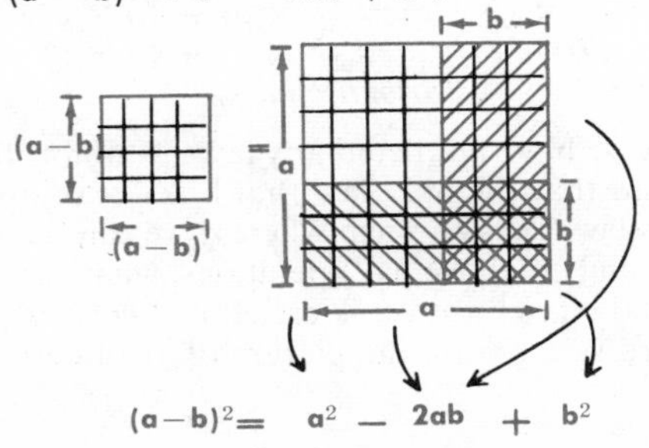

The square b^2 is cut from a larger square, a^2. What remains? Without altering the total remaining area, we can move the rectangle $b(a - b)$ next to the rectangle $a(a - b)$, to obtain a single rectangle with sides $(a + b)$ and $(a - b)$. We then have $a^2 - b^2 = (a + b)(a - b)$.

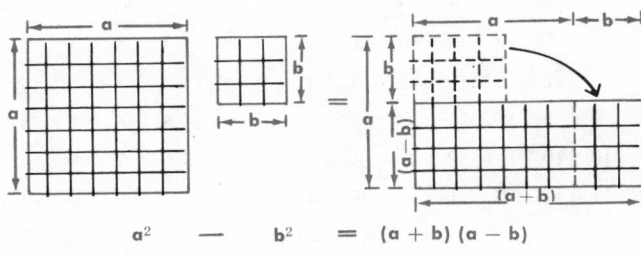

$(a-b)^2 = \quad a^2 \quad - \quad 2ab \quad + \quad b^2$

$a^2 \quad - \quad b^2 \quad = \quad (a + b)(a - b)$

the preceding term multiplied by a fixed number. An example is 1, 2, 4, 8, 16. In general, a geometric progression can be denoted by $a, ar, ar^2, \ldots, ar^k$. The nth term is ar^{n-1}, and the sum of n terms can be shown to be $a(r^n - 1)/(r - 1)$.—H. C.

ALGEBRA, ABSTRACT: the branch of mathematics that examines the methods of classical ALGEBRA in order to find the minimum number of algebraic properties which insure their success. The results of the examination are embodied in algebraic structures. The number system is an example of one type of structure; a more unusual one is that of arithmetic-around-the-clock.

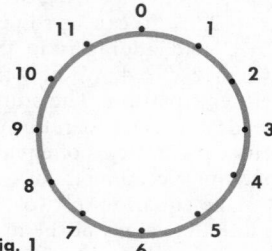

Fig. 1

When we tell time we start at 1 and count as usual, save that when we come to 12 we start all over—in other words, we equate 12 and 0. This state of affairs is easily visualized by the clock-diagram in Fig. 1. Let us limit our attention to the ciphers and the clock, thinking of them as the elements of a new mathematical system. It is natural to try to define what we mean by "addition" and "multiplication" for our new elements. The definitions should be such that the sum of 2 and 4 is 6, *i.e.* $2 + 4 = 6$, where $+$ denotes "addition" in our new world, and also $8 + 9 = 5$. Why? Simply because this·is the position we come to, when, along the rim of our clock, we first step off 8 units and then 9 more. Likewise 8 "times" 2, or 8×2, gives 4 as the product (not 16, which does not exist in our new structure).

The definitions of $+$ and $\times$ in our new system are: Let a and b denote any elements in our "world of twelve." Then, to find $a + b$, add a and b as if they were the usual numbers of our usual world. Once we get the usual sum, we reduce it by taking its remainder upon division by 12. And likewise for multiplication: first multiply as with ordinary numbers, then reduce the product obtained by taking in its place the remainder when it is divided by 12. By this rule we get, for example, $11 + 11 = 22 = 10$ and we call 10 the sum of 11 and 11 in our world "modulo 12." Likewise, $8 \times 9 = 72 = 0$, for 72 is exactly divisible by 12.

Addition and multiplication tables may be constructed for our new system. In Fig. 2 the sum $a + b$ should be read by finding the element lying at the intersection of row a and column b. Note that $a + b = b + a$ and also that $a + 0 = 0 + a = a$. Also note that the equation $a + x = 0$ always has a solution; *e.g.* the solution to $3 + x = 0$ is $x = 9$. We denote this x by the symbol (-3). In general, $a - b$ means $a + (-b)$.

$\times$	1	2	3	4	5	6	7	8	9	10	11
1	1	2	3	4	5	6	7	8	9	10	11
2	2	4	6	8	10	0	2	4	6	8	10
3	3	6	9	0	3	6	9	0	3	6	9
4	4	8	0	4	8	0	4	8	0	4	8
5	5	10	3	8	1	6	11	4	9	2	7
6	6	0	6	0	6	0	6	0	6	0	6
7	7	2	9	4	11	6	1	8	3	10	5
8	8	4	0	8	4	0	8	4	0	8	4
9	9	6	3	0	9	6	3	0	9	6	3
10	10	8	6	4	2	0	10	8	6	4	2
11	11	10	9	8	7	6	5	4	3	2	1

Fig. 3—Multiplication.

In Fig. 3, again $a \times b$ is read off at the intersection of row a and column b. Note that $a \times b = b \times a$, that $a \times 1 = 1 \times a$ for any a, and that it was not necessary to include 0 among the elements of our table, since $a \times 0 = 0 \times a = 0$ for all a. Note also that the equation $a \times x = 1$ does *not* always have a solution in our system for arbitrary a; for example, $2 \times x = 1$ has no solution.

Fig. 3 describes a mathematical system usually denoted by the symbol Z_{12} and called the "integers reduced modulo 12." Its elements obey the following laws:

(0) $a + b$ is a uniquely defined element of our system
(*law of closure*)

(0^1) $a \times b$ is a uniquely defined element of our system

(1) $a + (b + c) = (a + b) + c$
(*associativity of* $+$)

(1^1) $a \times (b \times c) = (a \times b) \times c$
(*associativity of* $\times$)

(2) there exists an element 0 such that $a + 0 = 0 + a = a$
(*neutral element for* $+$)

(2^1) there exists an element 1 such that $a \times 1 = 1 \times a = a$
(*neutral element for* $\times$)

(3) given any a, there exists x such that $a + x = 0$
(this x is denoted by $(-a)$)

(4) $a + b = b + a$
(*commutativity of addition*)

(5) $a \times (b + c) = (a \times b) + (a \times c)$
$(b + c) \times a = (b \times a) + (c \times a)$
(*distributive laws*)

Note that we have not listed any laws 3^1 nor 4^1 for multiplication, and that the only law that links both operations, $+$ and $\times$, is law 5. Any system wherein we can define operations like $+$ and $\times$ above, *i.e.* operations, whatever they may be, obeying the laws above, is called a *ring* (it is probable that the word stems from the picture of arithmetic-around-

$+$	0	1	2	3	4	5	6	7	8	9	10	11
0	0	1	2	3	4	5	6	7	8	9	10	11
1	1	2	3	4	5	6	7	8	9	10	11	0
2	2	3	4	5	6	7	8	9	10	11	0	1
3	3	4	5	6	7	8	9	10	11	0	1	2
4	4	5	6	7	8	9	10	11	0	1	2	3
5	5	6	7	8	9	10	11	0	1	2	3	4
6	6	7	8	9	10	11	0	1	2	3	4	5
7	7	8	9	10	11	0	1	2	3	4	5	6
8	8	9	10	11	0	1	2	3	4	5	6	7
9	9	10	11	0	1	2	3	4	5	6	7	8
10	10	11	0	1	2	3	4	5	6	7	8	9
11	11	0	1	2	3	4	5	6	7	8	9	10

Fig. 2—Addition.

the-clock). Mathematics affords many examples of rings. The system of polynomials with real coefficients studied in high school is a ring with $+$ and $\times$ the usual addition and multiplication of polynomials. The ordinary integers with the usual $+$ and $\times$ also form a ring. (We mention in passing that our definition of ring assumes the existence of a multiplicatively neutral element or unit, denoted by 1. This is the modern usage. A decade or so ago, our rings were called rings-with-unit.) For any integer n we can define the ring Z_n, by taking n units "around the clock," just as we did when $n = 12$. The tables for Z_3 are:

+	0	1	2		$\times$	1	2
0	0	1	2		1	1	2
1	1	2	0		2	2	1
2	2	0	1				

Multiplication in both examples above is commutative ($a \times b = b \times a$), but this need not be so. Rings of MATRICES and the ring of QUATERNIONS are ring structures where $a \times b \neq b \times a$. Rings where multiplication is always commutative are called *commutative rings*.

Note that Z_{12} does not allow for our always being able to solve $a \times x = 1$ for any a; in other words, not every $a \neq 0$ has a multiplicative "inverse." In Z_3, however, every $a \neq 0$ does have a multiplicative inverse; thus the inverse of 2 in Z_3 is 2 itself, for $2 \times 2 = 1$. A FIELD can be defined as a commutative ring such that every $a \neq 0$ has an inverse in the ring itself. Also note that the laws of addition numbered 0, 1, 2, and 3 tell us that a ring is a GROUP with respect to addition, while law 4 tells us that this group is commutative with respect to addition.

It may seem to the reader that we are belaboring the obvious, just giving names to new notions. This is so, and its importance is best perceived through counter examples.

Examples of non-commutative operations:
ordinary numbers under exponentiation: $2^3 \neq 3^2$;
multiplication of permutations (see GROUP and GALOIS THEORY);
coffee followed by whiskey $\neq$ whiskey followed by coffee.

Examples of non-associative operations:
ordinary numbers under exponentiation: $(2^3)^4 \neq 2^{(3^4)}$;
taking averages: $\frac{1}{2}[\frac{1}{2}(a + b) + c] \neq \frac{1}{2}[a + \frac{1}{2}(b + c)]$ except for special values. Formally, if we define $a \times b$ as $\frac{1}{2}(a + b)$, then necessarily $(a \times b) \times c \neq a \times (b \times c)$.

The great value, however, of isolating algebraic structures lies in the economy of thought and exposition afforded by studying rings, groups, fields, etc. apart from the special nature of their constituent elements. Note that in Z_{12} we have $3 \times 4 = 0$. Strange results like this can occur in certain rings, and it is therefore desirable to single out and study rings in which such results cannot occur. A commutative ring in which $ab = 0$ implies that $a = 0$ or else $b = 0$ is called an *integral domain,* the word "integral" reminding us of the ring of integers in which this condition always holds. We shall prove the following theorem as an example of how abstract algebra proceeds.

THEOREM: In any integral domain the *law of cancellation* is valid; that is, $ac = bc$ implies $a = b$ provided $c \neq 0$.

PROOF: If $ac = bc$, then $ac - bc = 0$. But $ac - bc = (a - b)c$ by the distributive law; hence, $(a - b)c = 0$ and either $a - b = 0$ or $c = 0$. But $c \neq 0$ by hypothesis. Hence, $a - b = 0$ and $a = b$. (Note that, as is usual, we have been writing $a - b$ to denote $a + (-b)$.)

Now that we have proved this theorem for integral domains, to assure ourselves that it applies equally well to polynomials with real coefficients we do not have to go through the steps of a similar proof for the ring of polynomials—all we need prove is that the ring of polynomials is an integral domain.

In studying the consequences of a suitably chosen set of laws which certain operations are assumed to obey, mathematicians are in fact examining all the properties that any example of such an algebraic structure must have; hence abstract algebra has been called the "skeleton key to mathematics."—*J. S.*

ALGEBRAIC GEOMETRY: the points of affine or cartesian n-space E_n are specified by n coordinates $(x_1, x_2, \ldots, x_n)$. An algebraic variety V in E_n is the set of points whose coordinates satisfy a number of polynomial equations. For example, an algebraic variety of dimension 1 (curve) in the plane is the set of points satisfying one polynomial equation in two variables (*e.g.* the parabola $y^2 = 4x$); a variety of dimension 2 (surface) in 3-space is the set of points satisfying one polynomial equation in three variables (*e.g.* the sphere $x^2 + y^2 + z^2 = 1$, or the cone $x^2 = y^2 + z^2$).

Algebraic geometry consists of the description of geometric properties of varieties as reflected in algebraic properties of the defining equations. For example, a variety V is called irreducible if it cannot be expressed as the union of two varieties both different from V. A curve in the plane or surface in 3-space will have this property if its defining equation cannot be factorized. This statement can be generalized to any varieties in any spaces by using a suitable generalization of factorization. If V is an irreducible variety, its dimension will be said to be k if k of the coordinates of points on V can be taken as independent variables, while the remainder are expressed (using the defining equations) as algebraic (in general many-valued) functions of these k. In this sense the curve and surface mentioned above have dimensions 1 and 2, respectively. The above ideas are frequently extended by replacing E_n with the spaces of projective geometry of two, three, and higher dimensions. In this case the defining polynomial equations must be homogeneous in the homogeneous coordinates. A more significant extension in the algebraic sense is the use as coordinates not only of numbers, real or complex, but also of elements taken from more general algebraic systems. This enables geometric methods and ideas to be used in the deeper study of certain algebraic concepts.

A central topic in algebraic geometry concerns the rational functions on a variety, *i.e.* functions defined on the variety and expressed as the quotient of two polynomials in the coordinates of points on the variety. For example, $(x^2 + y^2)/x = (x^2 + 4x)/x = x + 4$ is a rational function on the parabola $y^2 = 4x$. Consideration of integrals of such functions leads to the notion of abelian functions, of which the ELLIPTIC FUNCTIONS are a special case. If two varieties are so related that the coordinates on each can be expressed as rational functions on the other, then the set of rational functions on the one variety will be in one-one correspondence with those on the other. Such pairs of varieties are said to be birationally equivalent, and for many purposes in algebraic geometry can be regarded as essentially the same. For example, a circle and a line are equivalent in this sense (but not in the sense of projective geometry).

As well as being a highly developed subject in its own right, and one which has undergone spectacular advances in recent years, algebraic geometry is important for its applications. Many spaces which occur in other branches of mathematics (*e.g.* topology, theory of Lie groups, partial differential equations) turn out to be algebraic varieties.—*A. H. W.*

ALGEBRAIC NUMBER: a number that is the root of an equation whose coefficients are integers (positive or negative whole numbers, or zero). Specifically, algebraic numbers are the roots of all polynomial equations (of the form $a_0 + a_1x + a_2x^2 + \ldots + a_nx^n = 0$) whose coefficients $a_0, a_1, a_2, \ldots, a_n$ are integers. (The degree n of the equation may be any positive integer.) For example, $\sqrt{2}$ is an algebraic number because it is a root of $x^2 - 2 = 0$; this can be thought of as a polynomial equation with $n = 2$, $a_0 = -2$, $a_1 = 0$, and $a_2 = 1$. As a second example, $\sqrt[3]{5} - 1$ is an algebraic number because it is a root of $x^3 + 3x^2 + 3x - 4 = 0$. Every integer is algebraic; for example, 7 is a root of $x - 7 = 0$ and is thus an algebraic number. Also algebraic is every rational number, *i.e.* every number of the form b/c where b and c are integers, because such a number is a root of $cx - b = 0$.

An algebraic number can equally well be defined as one which is a root of an equation whose coefficients are rational numbers. The reason for this is that the roots, or solutions, of an equation are unchanged if the equation is multiplied by a constant: the roots of $x^2 - 2 = 0$ are $\sqrt{2}$ and $-\sqrt{2}$, and these are also the roots of $10x^2 - 20 = 0$. Thus we can convert any equation with rational coefficients, such as $\frac{2}{3}x^3 - \frac{1}{6}x^2 + \frac{1}{4}x - \frac{5}{3} = 0$, into an equation with integer coefficients, $8x^3 - 2x^2 + 3x - 20 = 0$, by multiplying by a suitable constant, in this case 12. Moreover, it can be proved that the roots of any polynomial equation whose coefficients are algebraic numbers are also algebraic numbers. This property is called the *algebraic closure* or completeness of the algebraic numbers.

Any specified algebraic number is the root of many algebraic equations; $\sqrt{2}$ is a root of $x^2 - 2 = 0$, $3x^3 - 6x = 0$, $x^3 - 3x^2 - 2x + 6 = 0$, and infinitely many other equations. Among all polynomial equations with integral coefficients that have a specified algebraic number as a root, the smallest degree n is called the degree of the algebraic number. The degree of $\sqrt{2}$ is 2 because it is a root of $x^2 - 2 = 0$, but not a root of any equation of degree 1 with integral coefficients. The algebraic number $\sqrt[3]{5}$, a root of $x^3 - 5 = 0$, is of degree 3. Rational numbers are precisely the algebraic numbers of degree 1. As an application of this theory to another part of mathematics, it can be proved that the lengths that can be constructed from a given unit length by the straight-edge and compass methods of Euclidean geometry are algebraic numbers of degree 1, 2, 4, 8, 16, and so on. From this it follows that the general angle cannot be trisected by these methods, because the trisection of an angle amounts, from an algebraic viewpoint, to constructing a length which is an algebraic number of degree 3. (See CONSTRUCTION PROBLEMS.)

Algebraic numbers are closed under addition, subtraction, multiplication, and division. This means that if β and γ are algebraic numbers, so are $\beta + \gamma$, $\beta - \gamma$, $\beta\gamma$, and β/γ, where $\gamma = 0$ is excluded in the last one, of course. Furthermore β^r is algebraic if r is rational (but not if r is irrational). Algebraic numbers form a subclass of the complex numbers. Complex numbers that are not algebraic are called TRANSCENDENTAL NUMBERS. See also COMPLEX NUMBER; IRRATIONAL NUMBER.— *I. N.*

ALGIN: one of the GUMS, used as a thickener in many commercial processes, *e.g.* in ice cream, in baking, in the paint and rubber industries. Algin is obtained by extraction from a brown seaweed (kelp) used in the Orient as a food. Structurally related to CELLULOSE, algin consists of salts of alginic acid. —*Ru. M.*

ALGOL (β Persei): a VARIABLE STAR in the constellation Perseus. Its brightness decreases from mag. 2.3 to 3.5 in about 6 hr, increases in another 6 hr to 2.3 again, and then remains almost constant until the next minimum. The minima occur at intervals of about 2 days, 21 hr. As early as 1783, this light variation was correctly interpreted as due to periodic eclipses of components of a double star (see BINARY STAR) too far away from Earth to be distinguished with a telescope. This explanation was confirmed in 1889 by observations of changing Doppler shifts in Algol's spectrum. Irregularities in the period of Algol, together with observations of the spectrum, show that there is a third component of the system that does not cause eclipses, as seen from Earth; this star moves around the eclipsing pair in a period of about 1.87 yr. Too faint to be seen in a telescope, this third star must nevertheless be very massive and is suspected to be a white dwarf. Algol is about 100 light-yr away, and its total luminosity is about 200 times the Sun's. It is on the meridian at midnight about Nov. 7.—*M. W. O.*

ALHAZEN (*Arab.* **AL-HAITHAM**), *c.*965–*c.*1039, Arab physicist; b. Basra. A physician, mathematician, astronomer, and commentator on Aristotle and Galen, he is chiefly known for his research in optics. His *Optics* strongly influenced later European science. He studied mirrors, spherical aberration, magnification with lenses, twilight and atmospheric refraction, vision, and the eye as a lens.—*D. H. D. R.*

ALICYCLIC COMPOUNDS: organic compounds which resemble AROMATIC COMPOUNDS in their cyclic structure, but resemble ALIPHATIC COMPOUNDS in chemical properties. (The name is a combination of "aliphatic" and "cyclic.") Because of their similarity to the chain compounds they are also known as *closed-chain* compounds. Such descriptive names differentiate these from aromatic compounds, *e.g.* benzene, in which the cyclic structure is based on an electronic arrangement that yields unique "aromatic" properties.

$$CH_3—CH_2—CH_2$$
$$CH_3—CH_2—CH_2$$

Hexane
An open-chain,
aliphatic hydrocarbon

$$CH_2—CH_2$$
$$CH_2 \qquad CH_2$$
$$CH_2—CH_2$$

Cyclohexane
An alicyclic
hydrocarbon

$$CH—CH$$
$$CH \qquad CH$$
$$CH=CH$$

Benzene
An aromatic
hydrocarbon

Ring compounds are generally said to be alicyclic if they are also homocyclic, like cyclohexane, as contrasted with the ring structures described in HETEROCYCLIC COMPOUNDS.—*Ru. M.*

ALIMENTARY CANAL (or **DIGESTIVE TRACT**): a long tube of tissue, extending through the body of an animal from mouth to anus, in which food is digested and absorbed, and from which waste is discharged. In a few animals (*e.g.* coelenterates) the tube has only one opening instead of two. Depending on the type of animal in which the tube occurs, it may show specializations such as a receiving area (MOUTH, buccal cavity); a conduction and storage area (esophagus, crop, STOMACH); a region in which food is broken up and mixed with digestive enzymes (stomach, GIZZARD, midgut or small INTESTINE); a region in which products of digestion are absorbed (midgut or small intestine); and, finally, an area in which the undigested residues are formed into feces before evacuation (hindgut or large intestine). See DIGESTION.—*B. T. S.*

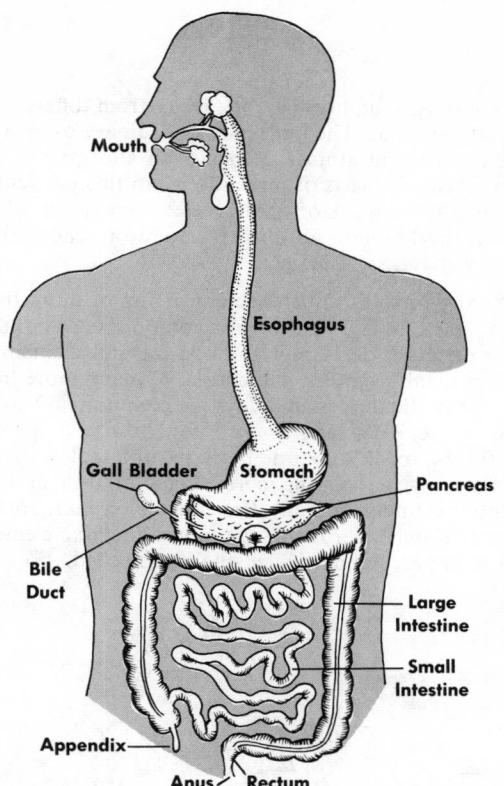

Alimentary canal in man begins with mouth and ends with anus. In between are the specialized structures that break up food, mix it with enzymes, digest and absorb it, and expel wastes.

ALIPHATIC COMPOUNDS: the open-chain carbon compounds in organic chemistry, constituting one of the four major groups of organic compounds, the others being *aromatic, alicyclic,* and *heterocyclic.* Aliphatic compounds include both straight-chain and branched-chain compounds, as well as those with double bonds and triple bonds. Some open-chain compounds were originally obtained from fats such as butter and lard, for which reason they were called aliphatic (Gr. *aleiphatos,* "fat"). The name is no longer exclusively associated with fatty characteristics. For descriptions of typical aliphatic compounds see: DIENE; FAT; GLYCERIN; OILS; TARTARIC ACID. For closed-chain compounds with open-chain characteristics see ALICYCLIC COMPOUNDS.—*Ru. M.*

ALKALI: an inexact term covering a broad range of important chemicals. It is frequently defined as a hydroxide or carbonate of either the ammonium radical (NH_4^+) or any metal in group 1A of the periodic table (ALKALI METALS). In common usage it includes any strong base, *i.e.* a substance that in aqueous solution produces a high concentration of hydroxyl ions. Thus, oxides and hydroxides of calcium, barium, and other metals of group II in the periodic table (ALKALINE EARTHS) are often classed as alkalies. In general, alkalies can neutralize acids, are soluble in water, and are "soapy" to the touch. The important alkalies are compounds of sodium, calcium, and to a lesser extent potassium; the term "alkali industry" refers to the well-integrated production of soda ash (sodium carbonate), caustic soda (sodium hydroxide), chlorine, baking soda (sodium bicarbonate), and sal (washing) soda. The alkalies' importance stems from their ability to neutralize acids or to contribute a group to another product. If neutralization is the only function, they can be used interchangeably, prime considerations being cost and ease of handling. In other cases, the choice of alkali affects the finished product; thus, in soap manufacture, sodium hydroxide will give a hard soap, while potassium hydroxide yields a liquid or soft soap.—*D. P. B.*

ALKALI METALS: the chemical elements lithium, sodium, potassium, rubidium, cesium, and francium (an artificial element), which fall into group I of the periodic table. They tend to form alkaline compounds, notably carbonates, of a similar nature. These metals have often been classed with, and confused with, the ALKALINE EARTHS, which are quite different chemically and fall into group II. In general, the alkali metals are soft, silvery, highly reactive elements, highly volatile and readily ionized, though with increasing atomic number they become less subject to explosive oxidation. Metallic sodium, manufactured by electrolyzing sodium salts, is a common commercial chemical, widely used in organic chemical technology for various reduction reactions, and also used in metallurgy. Metallic potassium is used on a much smaller scale, frequently in the form of an alloy with sodium. Recently the two heaviest naturally occurring members of the group, cesium and rubidium, have attracted attention because of their volatility and ease of ionization. In gaseous form they show considerable promise for use in such advanced energy-conversion systems as magnetohydrodynamic power generation and ion-propulsion engines for space flight. They are also used as "getters" in electron tubes—disposing of unwanted gases by reacting with them. They also show promise for use as nuclear fuel carriers and coolants, and for other high-temperature heat-transfer applications, since they melt at relatively low temperatures and have fairly good nuclear properties.—*A. R. G.*

ALKALINE EARTHS: elements of group IIA of the periodic table: beryllium, magnesium, calcium, strontium, barium, and radium. Like the ALKALI METALS, these elements form characteristic alkaline oxides and carbonates, and are frequently found in geological deposits that are highly alkaline ("lime" and "magnesia"); hence their name. Calcium, by far the commonest of the group, is generally considered the fifth most abundant metal in the earth's crust, but barium is also quite abundant, falling within the first 20. The lighter elements of the alkaline earths are soft and reactive (though not as reactive as sodium and potassium). Alkaline earths become less reactive with increasing atomic number. All are true metals, silvery-white, and can be formed and machined. However, their major commercial application is in compounds—oxides, chlorides, carbides, carbonates, and other salts—rather than in metallic form, though they are used in alloys for steel and nonferrous metals. Radium has special applications based on its radioactivity.—*A. R. G.*

ALKALOIDS: a group of heterocyclic bases containing nitrogen that are found in plants. They are extracted from plants by ether in alkaline conditions and by water in acidification. Many alkaloids have marked physiological effects and are therefore useful in medicine; the nervous system is peculiarly susceptible to their action. Among the better-known alkaloids are the following, classified according to ring system: (1) *pyridine ring:* nicotine (tobacco); (2) *quinoline ring:* quinine; (3) *isoquinoline ring:* codeine and morphine; (4) *tropane ring:* cocaine, atropine; (5) *purine ring:* caffeine. Others are strychnine and curare (muscle relaxant). The structures of many alkaloids are unknown.—*J. F. S.*

AL-KHWARIZMI, ABU 'ABDALLAH MUHAMMAD IBN MUSA, died c. 850, Islamic mathematician, astronomer, and geographer; b. Khiva, Central Asia. He synthesized Greek, Arabic, and Hindu knowledge. *Hisab al-jabr wa'l-muqabala,* his most important publication, contained analytic solutions of linear and quadratic equations; a corruption of the second word of its title became the word *algebra.* His book on arithmetic introduced the Hindu system of notation into the Islamic world;

his geographical writings represented a considerable improvement over Greek geography; and he prepared important astronomical and trigonometrical tables. All these works were translated into Latin, 12th cent., and exerted much influence in Europe. "Algorism" is a corruption of his name.—*D. H. D. R.*

ALKYD RESINS: substances made synthetically in large quantity for use in paints and enamels to provide unusually durable surfaces. They are the product of the reaction between polyhydroxy alcohols and polycarboxy acids (see POLYMERS: *Condensation Polymers*). The word alkyd is from *alc*/ohol + ac/*id*. This series of substances is known also as *glyptal resins,* because the alkyd resins made in largest quantity are the result of reaction between glycerin and phthalic acid.—*Ru. M.*

ALKYLATION: a chemical reaction by which an alkyl group (C_nH_{2n+H}) is attached to another compound. There are a number of alkylating agents; common ones include olefins, alkyl halides, and alcohols. Both organic and inorganic chemicals can be alkylated; for example, ethylene reacts with benzene to form ethyl benzene; ethyl chloride and an alloy of lead and sodium form tetraethyl lead. In petroleum refining, alkylation normally refers to the reaction of an isoparaffin (*e.g.* isobutane) with an olefin (*e.g.* propylene, butylenes, amylenes) to form a longer-chained, higher-molecular-weight isoparaffin. This product (alkylate) is a clean-burning compound used as a component of high-octane gasoline.—*D. P. B.*

ALLANTOIN: in biochemistry, an end product of PURINE metabolism. It is formed by action of the liver enzyme uricase on uric acid, which in turn is the product of the degradation of adenine, guanine, hypoxanthine, and xanthine. Animals possessing uricase excrete allantoin in the urine; man and other primates, lacking uricase, excrete uric acid.—*E. G.*

ALLEN, HORATIO, 1802–1890, U. S. engineer and inventor; b. Schenectady, N. Y. A pioneer in steam railroading in the U. S., he went to England, selected the first steam locomotives to be used in the U. S., and operated the first of these for the Delaware & Hudson Co. (1829). He was in charge of construction of the railroad from Charleston, S. C., to Augusta, Ga., and persuaded the South Carolina Railroad Co. to use steam locomotives rather than horses. An active businessman, Allen invented a number of valve mechanisms for steam engines. —*D. H. D. H.*

ALLOTROPY: existence of a chemical element or compound in more than one physical form (Gr. *allos tropos,* "other ways"). Many elements can exist pure in more than one physical modification. Allotropic forms of an element in the solid state consist of different crystalline species with widely differing physical properties. Since each allotrope is a pure element, consisting of one and the same kind of atoms, allotropy must be due to differences in crystalline structure. Carbon occurs in two spectacularly different allotropic forms: diamond and graphite. Each is pure elemental carbon, completely like the other chemically, as Lavoisier proved by burning both diamond and graphite to carbon dioxide and showing that the products of combustion were indistinguishable. Yet diamond is the hardest known naturally occurring substance, while graphite is sufficiently soft for use as a lubricant. In diamond, carbon atoms form a giant interlocking network in which each atom is joined by covalent bonds to four other atoms in highly symmetrical fashion. This symmetry with the special adaptiveness of the carbon atom for this tetrahedral arrangement results in a structure which is exceptionally strong. In graphite, there are planes of carbon atoms in which each atom is directly combined with only three others; these planes are only weakly bound to each other, and their slippage accounts for the softness of graphite. When allotropes exist in the gaseous state, *e.g.* oxygen and ozone, they result from different molecular configurations. The molecules of ordinary oxygen consist of pairs of oxygen atoms; in ozone, an allotrope of oxygen, each molecule consists of three atoms, in this particular case arranged in the form of an isosceles triangle in which the atoms at the base are not directly bound to each other. See also POLYMORPHISM.—*M. K.*

ALLOY: any metallic substance consisting of more than one element. An alloy is a mixture or a compound, or both, of two or more metals or of metallic and non-metallic elements; most alloys are highly complex and consist of many more than two components. Examples of alloys in common use are brass (copper 65 to 73%; zinc 27 to 35%); bronze (copper 88 to 96%; tin 14 to 12%); and, perhaps of greatest industrial importance, steel (varying percentages of iron and carbon with other elements added). Few metals, in fact, are used in their pure state; other metallic and non-metallic elements are added to impart the particular qualities needed.

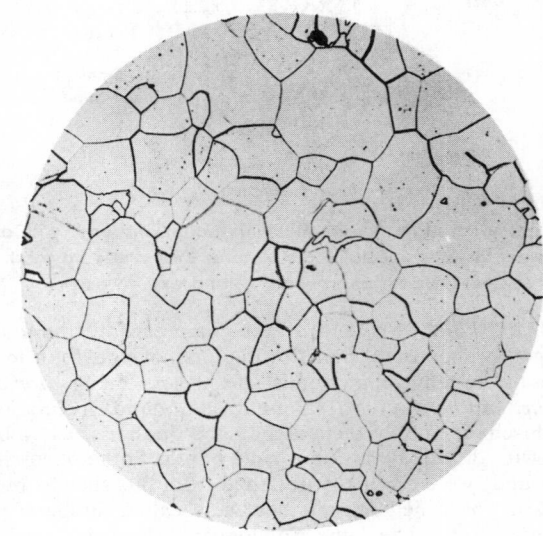

Alloy: microscopic view (500X) of low-carbon steel (less than 10% carbon), showing ferrite structure. (*U. S. Steel*)

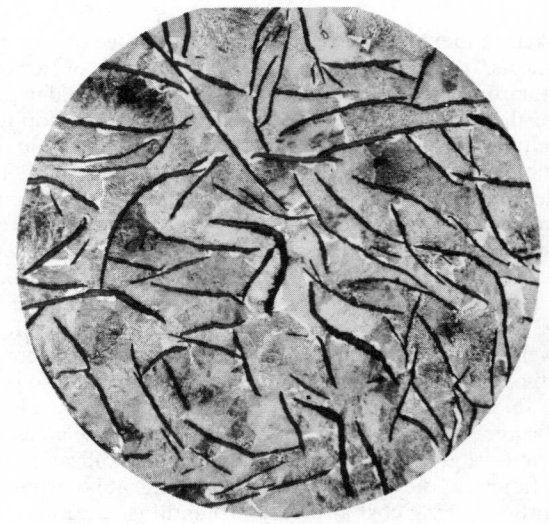

Alloy: Microscopic view (100X) of gray cast iron, showing graphite flakes. (*U. S. Steel*)

Alluvial fans: At foot of Panamint Mts (background) overlooking Death Valley, Calif., fan-shaped deposits of erosion debris have been built up by torrents of water produced by rare rainstorms. As stream slows on reaching valley, the coarser, heavier material is dropped first, near the apex of the fan, and the lighter material later, farther out toward the edges. *(Josef Muench)*

Alloys fall into three general categories: (1) *Alloys whose components are insoluble when the alloy is solid.* Each component exists independently in an intimate mixture and retains its own identity. The grain structure of each component can be clearly identified by microscope. In this group the most important are the lead-antimony alloys; they are used for storage-battery plates, acid-proofing coatings, type metal, and die castings. (2) *Alloys whose components are in complete or partial solution when solid.* Those in partial solution are by far the most important group of alloys. Typical commercial alloys which in solid state are partially soluble are lead-tin solders and those copper-silver alloys which are widely used for coinage. Of the alloys which are completely soluble when solid, cupronickels are of great industrial value. They are used in corrosion-resistant tubes for shipboard surface condensers. One of the better known alloys in the cupronickel group is monel metal (nickel 67%; copper 28%), which is characterized by its marked resistance to corrosion and by its ability to retain its strength at high temperatures. In this respect it is superior to ordinary steels. (3) *Alloys which when solid contain or consist of definite intermetallic compounds.* Although for the most part alloys in this group are brittle and lacking in strength and ductility, they are useful where hardness is needed. One such application is the use of copper-tin and antimony-tin compounds in babbitt metal, which is used for machine bearings. However, the widest use of this type of alloy is in steel; cementite, a compound of iron and carbon (Fe_3C), is found throughout the range of carbon and cast steels.

From antiquity, when man made his weapons of bronze alloys, to the present, when complex alloys are integral parts of space satellites, the use of metals has depended on the application of alloys. Often small percentages of less well-known elements can give to more familiar metals valuable specific qualities. The addition of 0.2% of manganese to ordinary brass increases its resistance to corrosion; such metal, known as *manganese bronze,* is used for ships' propellers and rudders. The addition of 2% of beryllium to copper gives that metal springiness and reduces corrosion from sparking. The alloying of steel is extensive: *e.g.* small percentage additions of chromium and vanadium increase its resistance to fatigue, the addition of tungsten imparts extreme hardness and cutting ability, the addition of lead gives machinability, and stainless steels are achieved through the addition of chromium. The applications of alloys are endless; a list of all their uses would be a catalog of modern technology.—*A. L.*

ALLUVIAL FAN (or **alluvial cone**): a deposit of sediment formed by a stream at the bottom of a steep descent. The loss of velocity in a stream reaching level terrain after flowing down a steep slope causes it to lose capacity to transport its load. The accumulated deposit soon diverts the terminal channel; a succession of such channel shifts results in a pattern of deposits radiating from an apex at the stream mouth, in the shape of a fan. Intermittent streams in arid regions often form alluvial fans in their flood stages. See RIVER AND RIVER VALLEY. —*E. A.*

ALLUVIUM: in geology, any earthy material deposited by running water, *e.g.* accumulations of mud, sand, gravel, and boulders, in river beds, on flood plains, or at the foot of mountain slopes. Flat lands along the lower courses of rivers, built up by such deposits, are called alluvial plains. Sloping, triangular deposits formed at the base of steep slopes are called *alluvial fans,* or *alluvial cones.* Deposits dropped by streams at their mouths, where they flow into other bodies of water, are termed DELTAS.—*A. P. E.*

ALMAGEST (or **"Mathematical Syntaxis"**) by Claudius Ptolemy, 2d cent. A. D. The last great product of Greek astronomy, the *Almagest* (its familiar Arabicized title) occupied a position of supreme authority for over 1,400 yr. Synthesizing all the Greeks had accomplished in observational and mathematical astronomy, Ptolemy invented little new himself. He firmly opposed those few predecessors who had suggested that Earth moves; placing it in the center of the universe, he worked out in detail the systems of combined circular motions (with eccentric, deferent, and epicycle) required for the Sun, Moon, and five planets (see PTOLEMAIC SYSTEM). This celestial geometry, in fair agreement with observational data, was translated and adopted first by Islamic astronomers, then by those of medieval Christendom. Ptolemy's Greek text was finally printed in the 16th cent.; Kepler was the first to emancipate himself wholly from its influence.—*A. R. H.*

ALMANAC: a term (probably from Arabic *al-manah,* "the sun-dial") originally applied by Roger Bacon, 1276, to permanent tables showing apparent movements of heavenly bodies. In general usage, an almanac is a year-book giving the calendar, rising and setting times of Sun and Moon, phases of Moon and tides, eclipses, positions of planets, dates of ecclesiastical feasts and fasts, and public holidays. Early almanacs frequently included astrological predictions, proverbs, and brief treatises on theology; a modern almanac may give information and statistics relating to the social and political life of the community. The traditional "farmers' almanacs" give advice on agriculture and also long-range weather forecasts (generally considered by meteorologists to be unscientific).

The oldest known copy of an almanac is preserved in the British Museum; it dates back to the time of Rameses the Great of Egypt (1200 B. C.), and is written in red ink on papyrus. The first known printed almanac is for the year 1448, and is believed to have come from the press of Gutenberg. The first almanac printed in England was Richard Pynson's *Kalendar of Shepardes* (1497), translated from the French. In the United States the first almanac printed was that of Capt. William Pierce, 1639, while the oldest of which there is a copy extant was Samuel Danforth's, printed by Matthew Day in 1646.

Nautical Almanacs: Of a more specifically scientific nature are the almanacs, published by government authority, which give precise predictions of positions and movements of Sun, Moon, and planets: essential information for celestial navigation and accurate time-keeping. These almanacs were started under pressure of necessity for the accurate determination of longitude at sea, and they had to appear several years in advance for the use of navigators on long journeys. In France the *Connaissance des Temps,* published by the Bureau des Longitudes, was begun in 1679. The first edition of *The Nautical Almanac and Astronomical Ephemeris* appeared in Great Britain for the year 1767, under the authority of the Commissioners of Longitude (who later became the Lords Commisioners of the Admiralty) and under the direction of the Astronomer Royal. *The American Ephemeris and Nautical Almanac* was launched in 1853 by the Navy Department.

The Nautical Almanac and Astronomical Ephemeris was originally considered "a Work which must greatly contribute to the Improvement of Astronomy, Geography and Navigation." Since the 18th cent., the needs of the astronomer and the navigator have diverged to some extent. While the full nautical almanacs remained the primary sources of astronomical information, the needs of the surface navigator were served by abridged versions in which the relevant information was extracted and presented in a form suited to the needs of the navigator. Further changes in presentation were demanded with the growth of air navigation, and separate air almanacs appeared.

To avoid unnecessary duplication of effort, reciprocal arrangements have existed between the various nautical almanac offices for the calculation of different parts of the almanacs. Since the issue for the year 1960, *The Nautical Almanac and Astronomical Ephemeris* and *The American Ephemeris and Nautical Almanac* have been appearing in unified editions (differing only in introductory matter). The unified edition of the abridged version for seamen appears under the title *The Nautical Almanac,* while *The Air Almanac* is now a joint publication of France, Great Britain, and the U. S. A. —*M. W. O.*

ALPHA, BETA, AND GAMMA RAYS: Natural radioactivity is essentially a process of spontaneous and uncontrolled emissions of radiations from the nucleus of an unstable atom. Such radiations differ from optical and x-ray emissions, which originate in the excited extranuclear structure of the atom. Radioactive materials emit *alpha* or *beta* particles, often accompanied by *gamma* rays. These particles, or rays, may be designated respectively by the symbols α, β, and γ.

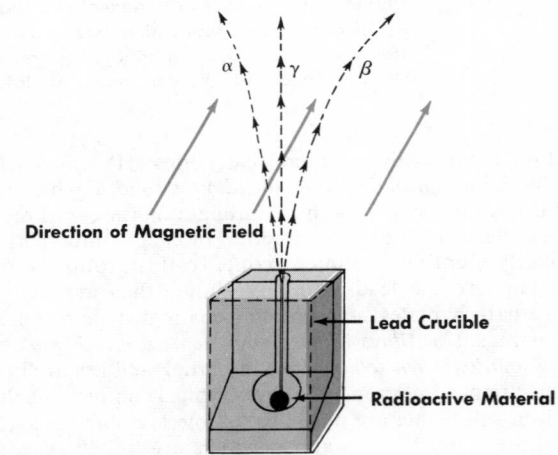

Alpha and beta rays consist of oppositely charged particles the paths of which are bent in opposite directions by a magnetic field. Gamma rays, unaffected, move in a straight line.

Alpha Particles were demonstrated by Lord Rutherford (1909) to be helium nuclei, each consisting of two protons and two neutrons. The nuclear symbol of an alpha particle is $_2\text{He}^4$, where the subscript 2 denotes the double positive charge carried by the two protons and the superscript 4 designates the atomic mass of the four constituent subparticles, or nucleons, on the atomic-weight scale. The "sphere" into which the separate nucleons are packed has a diameter of 3.22×10^{-13} cm; the mass is 6.65×10^{-24} gm. The charge carried by a single alpha particle is 3.19×10^{-19} coulombs, or exactly twice the magnitude of the negative charge carried by an electron. Alpha particles are emitted by such elements as actinium C′, polonium, radium, thorium C′, uranium I, and uranium II. The emission of an alpha particle causes the charge Z of an element $_ZX^A$ to be decreased by 2, and the atomic mass A to be reduced by 4. Thus an alpha emitter, such as $_ZX^A$, becomes $_{Z-2}Y^{A-4}$, with the very first alpha particle emitted. Alpha particles carry considerable energy (the amount depending on their source) and possess high ionizing power. They typically move with velocities of about 10,000 mi/sec, or some 5 to 7% of the velocity of light. They pass freely through the "empty" spaces of atoms, but are turned back or scattered by the atoms' positively charged nuclei. Alpha particles are stopped by a few centimeters of air, by about 1/1,000 in. of aluminum, or by a sheet of ordinary paper.

Beta Particles ($_{-1}e°$) are fast-moving electrons, each carrying an elementary negative charge of 1.602×10^{-19} coulombs and having a mass about 1/1,837 of the mass of a hydrogen atom. Beta rays may also be positrons ($_{+1}e°$), although no positron emitters are included in naturally occurring radioactive matter. Since there are no electrons in the atomic nucleus, W. Pauli (1931) and E. Fermi (1934) suggested that beta particles result from the spontaneous conversion of a neutron to a proton, with a *neutrino* (ν) constituting an additional product of the reaction ($_0n^1 \rightarrow {}_1p^1 + {}_{-1}e° + \nu$). The air path of a beta particle is usually several meters. Its penetrating power is about 100 times that of an alpha particle having the same energy. A beta particle penetrates several millimeters of aluminum or 1 mm of lead. The velocity of a beta particle may be nearly equal to that of light. Typical beta emitters are tritium ($_1H^3$), carbon 14, antimony 124, cobalt 60, sodium 24, calcium 45, and tantalum 73. The emission of a beta particle from a radioactive element $_ZX^A$ results in the formation of an element $_{Z+1}Y^A$.

Gamma Rays are photons, or quanta, of high-frequency radiation. The term *gamma* is now applied to high-frequency radiations whether or not they originate in the atomic nucleus. Wavelengths of gamma rays are considerably shorter than those of x-rays. The gamma component is the most penetrating of the three types of radioactive emission. Several centimeters of metal are required to reduce the intensity of gamma rays to one-half their original value. For complete shielding against gamma rays, thick layers of lead are needed.

It was discovered early that the radiations emitted by radioactive nuclei can be separated from one another. The figure shows the principle of *magnetic* separation. A sample of radioactive material, assumed to emit alpha, beta, and gamma rays, is placed at the bottom of a lead crucible, shaped so as to direct or *collimate* the emissions upward through an evacuated chamber carrying a photographic film at the top. The magnetic field, represented by inward-directed arrows, bends alpha particles to the left, beta particles to the right, but leaves the stream of gamma rays undeflected.—*A. E.*

ALPINE GLOW (or **alpenglow**): reappearance of sunset colors on mountains after the original sunset glow has faded. It is caused by scattering of white light by particles suspended high in the atmosphere during the few minutes the Sun is just below the horizon. Alpine glow also occurs less often before sunrise. Pre-sunrise glow is predominantly pink and purple; post-sunset glow, orange and red.—*P. L.*

ALPINE PLANTS: plants found at elevations approaching the limit of perpetual snow in the Alps and other mountainous regions. In the Andes, near the equator, at an elevation of 12,000 to 15,000 ft. above sea level, many kinds of alpine plants are found. Of humble growth, they resemble in general appearance plants that occur in Germany and Switzerland at

an elevation of 6,000 ft, plants that grow in Lapland on hills of low elevation, and plants found in northern Siberia at sea level. Alpine plants are distinguished by a low, diminutive habit, an extremely short growing period, and an inclination to form a thick turf—all adaptations to harsh climate. Some, *e.g.* the edelweiss of the mountains of Europe, Asia, and S.America, are covered with woolly hairs, which give protection against the powerful sunlight present at high elevations. Stems are often woody, and flowers are frequently very large, of brilliant colors, and quite fragrant.—*A. P. E.* (See Color Plates f.p. 6.)

ALTAZIMUTH: a mounting for a sighting instrument, *e.g.* a telescope or theodolite, that enables the instrument to swing vertically or horizontally, and thus be sighted on objects differing in altitude (angular distance above the horizon) or azimuth (angular distance around the horizon clockwise from the north or south point). To determine the position of an object, the mounting is equipped with two graduated circles, one vertical and one horizontal. The instrument is sighted on the object and its altitude and azimuth are read directly from the circles. Altazimuth mountings are suitable for all terrestrial work, but for astronomical TELESCOPES the equatorial mounting is usually preferred.—*B. P. S.*

ALTERNATING CURRENT (*abbr.* ac): electric current that reverses its direction of flow at regular intervals. In the simplest practical case, 60-cycle ac, the voltage reverses itself 120 times every second and 60 complete cycles occur every second. Such voltages (Fig. 1) are usually generated by machines called alternators, whose basic design is shown in Fig. 2. Coils

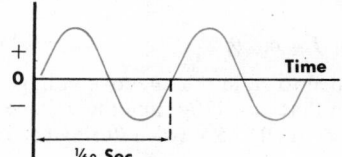

Fig. 1: Alternating sinusoidal voltage with a frequency of 60 cy/sec.

of wire, like *ABCD,* rotate in the strong magnetic field produced by electromagnets N and S. The currents induced in these coils as they sweep through the magnetic fields are conducted to the outside circuit through stationary graphite blocks E and F (*brushes*), which press against solid rotating *slip rings*. Since each wire moves alternately up and down across the magnetic field, the current must reverse itself twice during each revolution of the coil. In the U. S. A. a frequency of 60 cycles per second has been established for power transmission, but some other countries have adopted different frequencies.

The first a-c power plant in America, built at Great Barrington, Mass., was in operation by 1886. Today, alternating

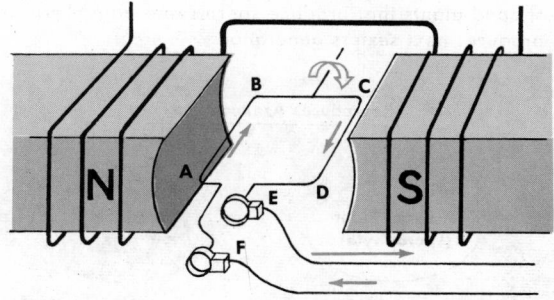

Fig. 2: Basic a-c generator: This type of generator consists of a single loop of wire that rotates in the magnetic field existing between the poles of an electromagnet.

current is used almost exclusively by the U. S. power industry, largely because alternating current can easily be increased or decreased in voltage by a TRANSFORMER, whereas direct current cannot. This enables the user to have alternating current of whatever voltage he needs, regardless of the voltage in the power lines. As a result the power company can transmit electricity at high voltages; efficiency is thus increased and transmission is feasible over far greater distances. See ELECTRIC POWER TRANSMISSION.

It is advantageous to have a *harmonic* a-c voltage, *i.e.* one as nearly as possible like a sine function, so that

$$V = V_o \sin 2\pi f t$$

where V is the voltage of any instant of time t, V_o is the maximum (peak) voltage during a cycle, and f is the frequency. If such a voltage were applied to a purely resistive circuit of resistance R, Ohm's law would be valid at any instant, the resulting current being $I = V/R = I_o \sin 2\pi f t$.

Since the voltages and currents fluctuate so rapidly in a-c circuits, the movable needles of meters cannot respond to the instantaneous values, but are usually made to indicate $V_o/\sqrt{2}$ or $I_o/\sqrt{2}$ (the root-mean-square values), called the *effective voltage*, or *effective current*. If an a-c voltmeter and an a-c ammeter are calibrated in this way and properly inserted in a purely resistive circuit, the product of their readings will give the average power expended in that circuit. However, if the circuit contains inductance and/or capacitance, the two sine curves representing the voltage and the current respectively will, in general, be out of step (out of *phase*) with each other by an angle θ. The current is said to *lead* or *lag* the voltage by a phase angle θ. The electric power is then given by the expression

$$P = V_{\text{eff.}} I_{\text{eff.}} \cos \theta.$$

It has become accepted practice to state the effective voltage in describing an a-c source, so that in a 110-v line the voltage rises to a peak of 110 $\sqrt{2}$, or about 155.5 v twice during each cycle.

In applications other than power transmission, the frequencies of alternating voltages and currents may vary from zero to billions of cycles per second. See GENERATORS.—*H. Sw.*

ALTERNATION OF GENERATIONS: the alternation of sexual and asexual processes of REPRODUCTION in the life history of an organism. The two generations may be alike or unlike in form. In almost all plants, a generation (the gametophyte) that reproduces sexually by the union of gametes (sex cells) alternates with a generation (the sporophyte) that reproduces asexually by spores. The relative size and degree of develop-

Reproductive cycle in ferns: Familiar mature fern (*left*) produces spores on underside of leaves. Successful spores grow into small lobe-shaped plants that produce sperms and eggs. Fertilization then produces next sexless generation.

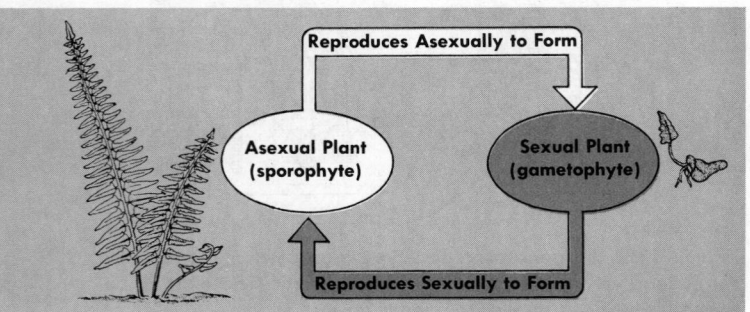

ment of sporophyte and gametophyte generations vary greatly in the various plant groups. A major trend in plant evolution has been the gradual reduction of the gametophyte and its consequent loss of independence from the sporophyte, contrasted with the progressive enlargement and independence of the sporophyte. For example, in some algae the sporophyte is represented only by the zygote (fertilized egg), whereas in many flowering plants the sporophyte consists of a tree and the gametophyte is reduced to an entirely dependent microscopic portion of the flower involved in seed formation.

Alternation of generations in animals (sometimes called *metagenesis*) differs slightly from that in plants. In animals there is the same alternation of asexual and sexual reproduction, but both generations are diploid—*i.e.* each possesses two sets of chromosomes in each cell. In plants the sporophyte is diploid, but the gametophyte is haploid (one set of chromosomes). The classical example of alternation of generations in animals is the succession of an asexual polyp generation and a sexual medusa (jellyfish) generation, as found in many coelenterates. Whenever both sexual and asexual reproduction occur in the same species, the two types tend to alternate, but the alternation may be irregular. Irregular alternation of generations occurs in certain protozoa, most coelenterates, some flatworms, annelid worms, rotifers, water fleas (Cladocera), sea squirts (tunicates), and a few insects. Some zoologists regard the complicated life histories of coelenterates and parasitic flatworms as a succession of highly modified larvae and sexually mature adult forms, rather than a true alternation of generations.—*C. F. L.*

ALTIMETER: an instrument that measures elevation above sea level. The conventional altimeter is basically an aneroid BAROMETER that measures the pressure of the surrounding air. It makes use of the general rule that atmospheric pressure decreases at a predictable rate as the elevation increases.

Older-type altimeter (*left*) is being replaced by faster-reading vertical-scale type (*right*). (*N. Y. Public Library*, below: *USAF*, right)

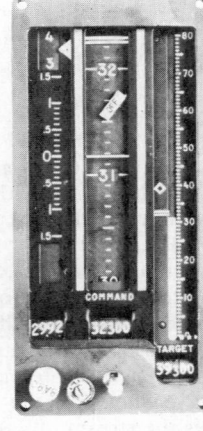

However, an altimeter must periodically be adjusted for regional fluctuations of temperature, humidity, and other weather factors which affect local atmospheric pressure. Thus an aircraft pilot before takeoff obtains an "altimeter setting," *i.e.* a reading of barometric pressure at the airfield, already corrected for prevailing weather conditions. He adjusts the setting scale of his altimeter accordingly. Also, he must adjust the altimeter's altitude scale to indicate the airfield's elevation above sea level. Altimeter setting and altitude scales are then locked together so that adjustment of the first will automatically correct the second. During flight the pilot obtains frequent reports from stations beneath him, and corrects his altimeter setting each time. Although an altimeter does not show actual height above ground, the pilot can compute this factor if he knows the elevation of the reporting station. The instrument may also give inaccurate readings if weather conditions at flying altitude differ greatly from those on the ground.

Aircraft required to fly through extreme fluctuations of weather or over mountainous terrain may be equipped with *absolute altimeters,* which use radio or radar-wave reflection from the ground. Typical is an FM system so arranged that altitude above ground level is read on a frequency meter. Because radar requires a good reflecting surface, such an instrument may be inaccurate over ground covered with a deep layer of soft snow. In the *capacitance altimeter,* height is indicated in terms of an aircraft's capacitance to the ground. The *sonic altimeter* measures absolute altitude by transmitting a distinctive sound, and timing the return of its echo from the surface.—*K. A. and D. B.*

ALTITUDE: in astronomy, the elevation of a celestial body above the horizon, *i.e.* the arc of the vertical circle between the celestial horizon and the body. It is stated in degrees, minutes, and seconds, and measured from 0° at horizon to 90° at zenith. With azimuth, it defines the location of a point in the horizon system (see CELESTIAL COORDINATES). Altitude can be computed for a known body when the observer's position and time are known; it can be measured with instruments, *e.g.* sextants, theodolites, astrolabes. The altitude of every celestial body is greatest when the body transits (crosses) the observer's celestial meridian.—*T. N.*

ALUM: a hydrated double salt of a trivalent metal (usually aluminum, chromium, or iron) with a monovalent metal or the ammonium (NH_4^+) radical. Principal alums are $K_2SO_4 \cdot Al_2(SO_4)_3 \cdot 24H_2O$ (potash alum); $(NH_4)_2SO_4 \cdot Al_2(SO_4)_3 \cdot 24H_2O$ (ammonium alum); and $K_2SO_4 \cdot Cr_2(SO_4)_3 \cdot 24H_2O$. Alums are used in papermaking, dyeing (as mordants), water purification, fire-extinguishing agents, baking powders, and astringents.—*D. P. B.*

ALUMINA: aluminum oxide (Al_2O_3; mp 2030°, sp gr 3.4–4.0), most important compound of ALUMINUM. It occurs in several forms including corundum, which is next to diamond in hardness. Ruby, sapphire, and emery are impure varieties of corundum. Activated alumina, a porous granular form, is used as a catalyst and to adsorb moisture from gases. Hydrated alumina ($Al_2O_3 \cdot 3H_2O$ or $Al(OH)_3$), used in commercial production of aluminum, is found in nature as the mineral BAUXITE.—*T. M.*

ALUMINUM (*Sym.* Al): a chemical element widely used in metallic form and as an ingredient in chemical compounds; at. no. 13, valence +3, at. wt 26.97. Composing 7 to 8% of the earth's crust, it there ranks third in abundance (behind oxygen and silicon) among the elements. Commonest aluminum-containing ores are the feldspars, micas, and kaolin, or clays which contain kaolinite; but BAUXITE is the most valuable source. In production of the metal, bauxite is purified to alumina (Al_2O_3), which is then reduced to aluminum by the HALL PROCESS. The metal has a great number of uses because of its unusual combination of properties: it is light (sp gr 2.7), has a tensile strength exceeded only by that of iron and copper, and can be formed or shaped readily by conventional metal-working methods. It is a good conductor of heat and electricity. On exposure to air, the surface of aluminum immediately oxidizes to aluminum oxide, forming a tight, invisible skin which protects it from further oxidation and provides good corrosion resistance. Aluminum melts at 660°C and is not suitable for high-temperature service, but it gains strength without loss of ductility at lowered temperatures and is a superior metal for service at sub-zero temperatures. Widely used aluminum chemicals include ALUMINA and the

ALUMS. Aluminum, alumina, and aluminum hydroxide are amphoteric, *i.e.* they neutralize either acids or bases to form aluminum salts or aluminates. Aluminum chloride ($AlCl_3$) is an important catalyst used in alkylations and in Friedel-Crafts reactions. Cryolite (Na_3AlF_6) is used in aluminum production to lower the temperature and increase conductivity of the electrolyte. Aluminum also reacts with organic compounds; aluminum trialkyls, *e.g.* triethyl aluminum, $Al(C_2H_5)_3$, is an ingredient of catalysts for the highly oriented polymerization of olefins, *e.g.* ethylene.—*D. P. B.*

AMALGAM: any mercury alloy, liquid or solid. Perhaps the most common use of amalgams today is in dental fillings (mercury, copper, zinc, silver, and tin). Formerly, their most important use was in the extraction of gold from its ore by dissolving the dispersed gold in mercury, later heating the amalgam of gold and mercury to evaporate the mercury and leave behind the gold. Most metals except iron and platinum form amalgams. This is accomplished in a variety of ways, such as direct contact, absorption, combining under the action of a mild acid, and electrolysis.—*A. L.*

AMBARTSUMIAN, VICTOR AMAZAPOVICH, 1908– , Soviet astrophysicist; b. Tiflis, Georgian S. S. R. He wrote the first Russian textbook in theoretical astrophysics, still useful after many years with its ideas and results from original investigations. His best-known work has been the description of STAR ASSOCIATIONS—complexes of gas, dust, and stars that play a key role in star creation. In 1946 he became director of a new observatory at Biurakan; since 1950 he has been a member of the Supreme Soviet of the U. S. S. R. His *Scientific Works* were published in Russian, 1960. He is an associate of the U. S. National Academy of Sciences.—*O. G.*

AMBER: see MINERAL (table).

AMERICIUM: (*abbr.* Am): a man-made, radioactive element of the actinide group; at. no. 95. The isotope Am^{241} was discovered (1944) when Seaborg *et al.* bombarded plutonium[241] with neutrons. It was the fourth transuranium element to be discovered. Am^{241} has a half life of approx. 470 yr; Am^{243}, approx. 7,800 yr.—*R. W.*

AMICI, GIOVANNI BATTISTA, 1786–1863, Italian astronomer, microscopist, and instrument-maker; b. Modena. He is best known for his achromatic lenses, the invention of which vastly improved the microscope. Using his own microscopes, Amici studied pollination: with orchids he showed (1846) the presence of the egg cell, its stimulation via the pollen tube, and the development of the embryo. He also engaged in astronomical observations, studying double stars and Jupiter's satellites.

Giovanni Battista Amici
(N. Y. Public Library)

He improved mirror designs for reflecting telescopes.—*D. H. D. R.*

AMIDES: a family of chemical compounds important principally as intermediates in chemical synthesis. Amides are regarded as substances in which H atoms of ammonia, NH_3, are replaced either by an inorganic metallic element or by an organic acid radical:

$K—NH_2$ Potassium amide (inorganic) $CH_3—\overset{\displaystyle}{\underset{\displaystyle O}{C}}—NH_2$ Acetamide (organic)

Most organic amides are crystalline solids with sharp melting points, and are thus used for identifying organic acids. For example, in the following reaction, where R represents an unknown hydrocarbon radical:

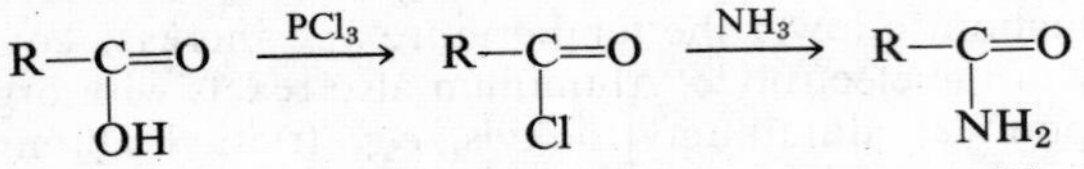

$$R-\underset{\underset{OH}{|}}{\overset{\overset{O}{\|}}{C}} \xrightarrow{PCl_3} R-\underset{\underset{Cl}{|}}{\overset{\overset{O}{\|}}{C}} \xrightarrow{NH_3} R-\underset{\underset{NH_2}{|}}{\overset{\overset{O}{\|}}{C}}$$

An unknown   An acid   An amide
acid   chloride

if the amide which results has a melting point of 82.0°C, it is *acetamide* (CH_3CONH_2), and the acid was *acetic acid.* Two H atoms of ammonia may be replaced by acid radicals, but not all three. Di-acid amides are called *imides:*

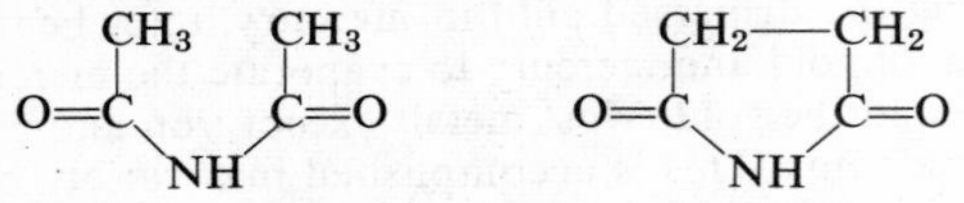

Acetimide   Succinimide

Succinic acid is representative of acids which have carboxyl groups at each end of a carbon chain, and thus can form a cyclic imide. *Simple amides* such as acetamide have little industrial importance except that some of their derivatives are excellent solvents. The amide of

carbonic acid, $HO-\underset{\underset{O}{\|}}{C}-OH$,   is urea, $NH_2-\underset{\underset{O}{\|}}{C}-NH_2$,

a metabolism product excreted in the urine of mammals. This crystalline compound is important as a fertilizer and as an intermediate, especially in the making of ureaformaldehyde plastics. Nylon polymers (TEXTILES) are *polyamides.—Ru. M.*

AMINES: a family of nitrogen compounds important mostly as intermediates in chemical synthesis. Amines are regarded as ammonia, NH_3, in which one or more H atoms have been replaced by alkyl radicals. Amines are called primary, secondary, or tertiary, depending on whether 1, 2, or 3 H atoms have been replaced:

CH_3NH_2 $(CH_3)_2NH$ $(CH_3)_3N$
Methylamine   Dimethylamine   Trimethylamine
(primary)   (secondary)   (tertiary)

These simple *aliphatic amines* are gases. They occur in herring brine, and smell like it. Their water solutions are alkaline, and with acids they form salts such as $[(CH_3)_3NH]^+ Cl^-$, trimethylammonium chloride. From a tertiary amine one can make a *quaternary ammonium salt,* in which four radicals are linked to nitrogen, *e.g.* $[CH_3(CH_2)_{15}N(CH_3)_3]^+Cl^-$, cetyltrimethylammonium chloride. The long 16-carbon chain in this positive ion gives the molecule detergent properties, analogous to those of a SOAP. It also has germicidal powers.

Aromatic amines are obtained when aromatic radicals replace the H atoms of ammonia. The simplest example is ANILINE, or phenylamine:

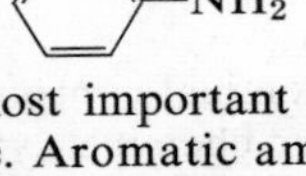

Aniline, a liquid, is most important of all the amines as a chemical intermediate. Aromatic amines are much weaker bases than aliphatic amines, and are far more toxic.—*Ru. M.*

AMINO ACIDS: chemical compounds that have both amino and acid groups. Most can be represented by the following general structure, in which a carboxyl group (COOH), an amino group (NH_2), a hydrogen atom (H), and another group

(R) are attached to a central carbon atom (C). The R group gives each amino acid its distinctive characteristics:

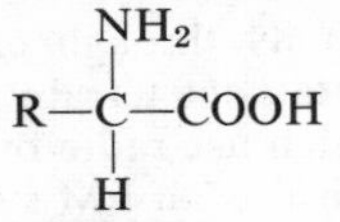

$$R-\underset{\underset{H}{|}}{\overset{\overset{NH_2}{|}}{C}}-COOH$$

Occurrence and Composition: More than 200 amino acids are now known to occur in nature. They may occur free, in linkage with other amino acids, or in combination with other compounds such as carbohydrates, lipids, and nucleic acids. Amino acids, free or combined, are found in all living cells and tissues. They are important as building blocks of proteins and as starting materials for synthesis of many key biological substances, including certain vitamins and hormones. They have a significant function in metabolism of ammonia and other nitrogen-containing compounds, *e.g.* nucleic acids.

About 23 amino acids are commonly found in PROTEINS. Amino acids are usually obtained by isolation from hydrolysates of proteins or by chemical synthesis. Of the many methods devised for separation of amino acids from natural sources and from hydrolysates of proteins, most currently used involve CHROMATOGRAPHY. Five of the amino acids which commonly occur in proteins possess hydroxyl (OH) groups (serine, threonine, tyrosine, hydroxyproline, hydroxylysine). Serine and threonine occur in some proteins as phosphorylated derivatives, in which a phosphate group is linked by an ester bond to the hydroxyl group of the amino acid. Two possess additional acid (carboxyl) groups (aspartic acid, glutamic acid), and there are two amino acids closely related to these in which the "extra" carboxyl group is replaced by an amide group (asparagine, glutamine). Four amino acids contain additional basic groups (arginine, lysine, hydroxylysine, histidine), and three amino acids contain sulfur (cysteine, cystine, methionine). Three amino acids (phenylalanine, tyrosine, tryptophan) contain a benzene ring. Tryptophan has a side chain containing the indole ring, and the R group of histidine has an imidazole ring. Two of the amino acids (hydroxyproline, hydroxylysine) are found only in the proteins collagen and elastin; the other amino acids are widely distributed among proteins.

Properties: All commonly occurring natural amino acids are white, crystalline solids which are stable at room temperature and decompose, usually over a range of several degrees, when heated to between 180 and 350°C. They are stable also in solution at room temperature. Most are soluble in water, although in varying degrees. Cystine and tyrosine are the least soluble of the common amino acids, and only proline is appreciably soluble in ethyl alcohol. Since amino acids possess both acidic and basic groups, they react as acids or bases according to conditions. In an electric field they may move as positively or negatively charged molecules depending upon the pH (see PH VALUE) of the solution (see ELECTROPHORESIS).

All amino acids (except glycine) commonly found in proteins have at least one asymmetric carbon atom and may therefore exist in at least two optically active forms (D and L). (See ASYMMETRIC CARBON ATOM; OPTICAL ACTIVITY.) Structures of these forms may be represented as mirror images:

L $R-\underset{\underset{H}{|}}{\overset{\overset{NH_2}{|}}{C}}-COOH$ $HOOC-\underset{\underset{H}{|}}{\overset{\overset{NH_2}{|}}{C}}-R$ D

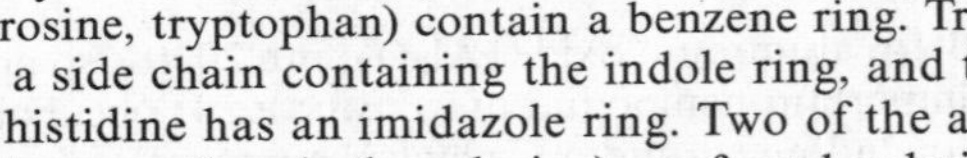

Four amino acids (threonine, isoleucine, hydroxyproline, hydroxylysine) have two asymmetric centers; there are therefore four stereoisomers of each of these acids—*i.e.* two pairs of optical isomers for each. Amino acids that occur in proteins are all of the L-configuration, and indeed, so are most of the

Photos by
Mario Marino; assemblages by
Dr. Herbert Jaffe,
The Rockefeller University

A1

A2

B1 B2 B3 B4 B5 B6 B7

C1 C2 C3

The structure of amino acids: The model at A1 is of a simple amino acid, cysteine; the large gray atom at bottom left is sulfur; the small white atom next to it is hydrogen (removing this hydrogen and doubling the remainder produces cystine, a double amino acid). The molecular grouping most characteristic of amino acids (occurring once in cysteine, twice in cystine) is shown at B1; it consists of the amine group NH₂ and the acidic carboxyl group COOH (bottom) joined by a carbon atom. It is to this carbon atom (at the free connection) that the various alternate "R groups" (see text) are attached. The simplest such chain is a single hydrogen atom (B2); adding it to the original group B1 produces glycine, the simplest amino acid. Adding the methyl group CH₃

(B3) to B1 produces alanine. More complex R groups include side chains: the groups at B4 and B5 go to make up valine and isoleucine; the group at B6, serine. The addition of CH₂SH, the B7 group, produces the sulfur alcohol cysteine, shown at A1. Cyclic amino acids also exist, featuring rings of carbon atoms with an atom of nitrogen strung in among them. One such ring is seen clearly in C1 (proline); the pentagonally arranged hydrogen atoms conceal the one nitrogen and four carbon atoms to which they are bonded. In C2 (hydroxyproline) the ring is seen edge-on. With the exception of glycine, every amino acid could exist in two mirror-image forms (C3); in fact, however, optical analysis of proteins reveals only the left-hand form.

optically active natural amino acids. Amino acids prepared by synthetic organic chemical methods are racemic mixtures containing equal amounts of D- and L-isomers. Such mixtures may be resolved to yield the individual isomers by various chemical and enzymatic procedures. There is now no evidence for occurrence of D-amino acids in proteins or in any form in higher animals. However, D-amino acids have been found in certain lower forms, chiefly in microorganisms and their products; *e.g.* cell walls of certain bacteria contain D-alanine, D-glutamic acid, and other D-amino acids, and a number of antibiotics yield D-amino acids when hydrolyzed. Configuration of an amino acid may be established by quantitative determination of the optical rotation of a solution of the acid (see OPTICAL ACTIVITY), and also by enzymatic procedures. Certain ENZYMES act specifically on L- or D-amino acids. It is interesting that in general a D-amino acid tastes sweeter than the corresponding L-amino acid, which may often be flat or even bitter. L-glutamic acid has a characteristic "meaty" taste and is widely used for seasoning of foods; D-glutamic acid is almost tasteless.

Chemical Structure: Amino acids of proteins are linked together by PEPTIDE bonds in which the amino group of one amino acid is bound to the carboxyl group of another amino acid (see PROTEIN). Thus, proteins consist of long chains of amino acids which may assume certain specific spatial configurations. The term *peptide* is employed for smaller molecules in which only a few amino acids are linked together in peptide linkage. Examples of such peptides are: oxytocin and vasopressin, which are hormones produced by the posterior lobe of the PITUITARY GLAND; glutathione, which consists of glutamic acid, glycine, and cysteine, and is found in many animal and plant tissues; carnosine and anserine, which are dipeptides found in skeletal muscle; and the hormone hypertensin, which increases blood pressure in man.

Biological Functions: It has long been recognized that proteins are required in the diet of higher animals and that certain proteins are more effective in promoting growth than others. The biological value of a protein depends upon its amino acid composition, the extent to which the protein is broken down to free amino acids in the digestive tract, and the extent to which the amino acids are absorbed from the intestine. It is therefore the amino-acid constituents of the protein which are required rather than the protein itself. Experiments in which mixtures of amino acids were fed to animals have shown that certain amino acids, the nutritionally "essential" amino acids, had to be supplied in the diet, while others, the nutritionally "dispensable" or "non-essential" amino acids, did not have to be included in the diet in order to promote growth or to maintain an adult animal in NITRO-GEN BALANCE. Thus, it is evident that "essential" amino acids cannot be synthesized by the body, or at least not rapidly enough to support growth, while "non-essential" amino acids can be effectively synthesized by the organism. Amino acids essential in the diet of man are isoleucine, leucine, lysine, methionine, phenylalanine, threonine, tryptophan, and valine. The dietary amino-acid requirements of other animals, *e.g.* rat, dog, chick, and mouse, differ in certain respects from man's; nevertheless these animals as well as certain insects and protozoa all require at least the same eight amino acids needed by man. Although mixtures of L-amino acids can effectively replace protein in the diet of these animals, all necessary amino acids must be available to the animal at the same time. Thus, if some are fed at one time and the remaining amino acids as much as a few hours later, the animal will fail to grow or, if an adult, will fail to remain in nitrogen balance. Even if only one essential amino acid is omitted, growth failure or negative nitrogen balance promptly occurs, often within one day. A similar effect may be observed when an amino-acid antagonist (ANTIMETABOLITE) is given to an animal.

Bacteria vary considerably in their amino-acid requirements; some require virtually all the protein amino acids for growth, while others, like most plants, are able to carry out synthesis of all amino acids and therefore can grow on media containing relatively simple inorganic compounds.

Amino acids are taken into cells of animals and plants by energy-requiring processes about which little is now known. However, it is clear that simple diffusion across the cell membrane is not a sufficiently rapid process to account for the considerable uptake of amino acids by some cells. The fate of amino acids within the cell varies widely, depending upon the particular amino acid and also the particular organism, tissue, and type of cell. A very important pathway of amino-acid metabolism leads to the formation of proteins. PROTEIN SYNTHESIS occurs in virtually all living cells. Although details of protein synthesis are incompletely understood, available evidence indicates that individual amino acids are prepared for peptide linkage by activation processes involving adenosine triphosphate and NUCLEIC ACIDS.

Metabolic Reactions: Protein molecules, once synthesized, may be broken down, often when the cell in which they are present is destroyed, by a variety of enzymes that specifically cleave peptide bonds (PROTEOLYTIC ENZYMES). The rate at which a given type of protein is degraded varies, depending upon the protein and often on other factors. Certain proteins, *e.g.* COLLAGEN, turn over relatively slowly; others, *e.g.* certain proteins of blood plasma, have relatively rapid turnover rates (see PROTEIN METABOLISM).

Besides being building blocks of proteins, amino acids participate in many other metabolic reactions. These reactions differ for each amino acid, and there is considerable variability in the type of amino-acid metabolism, depending upon the particular cell, tissue, and organism. Amino acids perform a key function in metabolism of nitrogen. In mammals, the major end-product of nitrogen metabolism is urea, and the cellular machinery responsible for synthesis of urea involves enzymatic transformation of four amino acids (aspartic acid, arginine, ornithine, and citrulline). See UREA CYCLE.

The metabolic breakdown of amino acids, in general, involves separation of the amino group from the carbon chain of the amino acid. This is usually accomplished by transamination, an enzymatic reaction, in which the amino group of an amino acid is transferred to another molecule. The enzymes that catalyze such amino group transfers are known as transaminases. Vitamin B_6 is the coenzyme necessary for the activity of these enzymes (see ENZYME; VITAMIN). The amino group is eventually converted to urea, or it may yield ammonia, which may be incorporated by enzymatically catalyzed reactions into glutamine and asparagine amide nitrogen. In mammals, the ammonia-utilizing mechanisms are extraordinarily efficient, so that relatively little free ammonia exists in blood and tissues. Carbon chains of amino acids are broken down by enzymatically catalyzed reactions, different for each amino acid. Ultimately, these carbon chains are converted to smaller molecules, which may be oxidized in the CITRIC ACID CYCLE to carbon dioxide and water.

Certain amino acids are transformed by specific enzymes to compounds of special biological importance. Thus, portions of molecules of aspartic acid, glutamine, and glycine are converted by a complex series of reactions to yield PURINES, a component of some nucleic-acid bases. Aspartic acid is also a precursor of the PYRIMIDINES, another nucleic-acid component. Glycine, although the simplest amino acid structurally, participates in many complex metabolic reactions, including those leading to formation of the porphyrin portion of the hemoglobin and cytochrome molecules, creatine, creatinine, hippuric acid, and choline. COENZYME A is synthesized from building blocks that include the amino acids glycine, glutamine, aspartic acid, valine, cysteine, and β-alanine.

The sulfur-containing amino acids cysteine, cystine, and methionine participate in a variety of metabolic "pathways." The methyl group of methionine serves as a precursor for the methyl groups of creatine, choline, adrenaline, and anserine. The sulfur atom of methionine may be converted to the sulfur of cystine, and the latter amino acid may serve as a precursor of taurine, an aminosulfonic acid which is condensed with cholic acid to yield taurocholic acid (see BILE ACIDS). Histidine is the precursor of the important vasodilating (blood-vessel dilating) agent HISTAMINE; this conversion involves loss of the carboxyl group of histidine by decarboxylation. Other amino acids are also decarboxylated by enzymes present in various animal and plant tissues and also found in microorganisms: lysine is decarboxylated to the amine cadaverine, and tryptophan (after oxidation to 5-hydroxytryptophan) is decarboxylated to SEROTONIN. Noradrenaline is derived from tyrosine by a series of reactions, one of which involves decarboxylation. The methyl group of methionine is transferred to noradrenaline to yield adrenaline. A reaction of particular significance is the decarboxylation of glutamic acid to yield γ-aminobutyric acid, an amino acid which seems important in transmission of nerve impulses. A number of other decarboxylation reactions are catalyzed by enzymes present in various microorganisms and plant cells. Metabolism of tryptophan leads to several products, including serotonin, indican, indigo, indole, and one of the B VITAMINS, nicotinamide. Tyrosine is a precursor of the more complex amino acid THYROXINE, a hormone of the thyroid gland, and it is also a precursor of the pigment melanin.

Certain bacteria and plants not only catalyze some of the reactions involving amino acids described above, but also are able to synthesize amino acids from relatively simple starting materials. Some bacteria synthesize amino acids (*e.g.* diaminopimelic acid) that are not found in animal tissues. Plants also frequently contain amino acids which do not exist in animals (*e.g.* γ-methyleneglutamic acid, azetidine carboxylic acid). Certain plants can utilize amino acids for synthesis of special compounds, *e.g.* alkaloids. In addition, some bacteria utilize amino acids (both L- and D-isomers) for synthesis of special cell wall structures and antibiotics.—*A. M.*

AMINOPTERIN: in biochemistry, a compound which is a metabolic antagonist to the vitamin folic acid. Folic acid is involved in the enzymatic synthesis of purines and pyrimidines, which are building-blocks of nucleic acids; aminopterin inhibits the synthesis of these compounds. It is of therapeutic value in treating certain types of tumors and leukemias.—*E. G.*

AMMETER: an instrument that measures electric current. D-c ammeters are usually permanent-magnet moving-coil instruments, in which the coil is fitted with a pointer that moves over a calibrated scale. Current enters the coil through flat-spiral or torsion springs, which serve to return the pointer to zero when the current ceases. The iron-vane and electrodynamomic a-c ammeters, whose operating force is independent of current direction, are used at power frequencies and at the lower audio frequencies, as is the rectifier ammeter. Hotwire thermocouple and expansion instruments are useful for measuring currents at audio and radio frequencies. Clip-on d-c and a-c ammeters utilize the magnetic fields about current-carrying conductors and can measure current without circuit interruption.—*J. G. B.*

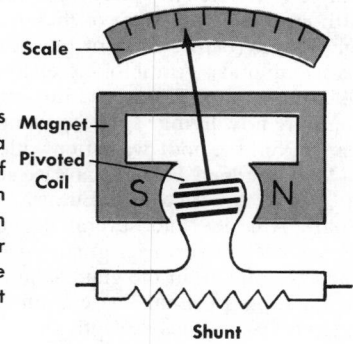

Moving-coil ammeter: This device is equipped with a shunt that bypasses most of the circuit current away from the coil, protecting it from damage and giving the meter a low enough total resistance to avoid affecting the current being measured.

Scale · Magnet · Pivoted Coil · Shunt

AMMONIA: a gaseous compound (NH_3) of nitrogen and hydrogen, melting point $-77°C$, boiling point $-33°C$, at. wt 17.03, density 0.677 at $-34°C$. It has a pungent odor, and is very soluble in water. An aqueous solution of ammonia is called ammonium hydroxide, containing the molecular species NH_3, NH_4OH, NH_4^+ and OH^-. Ammonia is prepared in the laboratory by heating an ammonium salt with a strong base; it may also be generated by heating concentrated aqueous ammonia. Ammonia is made commercially by the Haber process, which involves the combination of nitrogen and hydrogen gases at high pressure in the presence of an iron catalyst at $500°C$. Small amounts of ammonia are obtained by the cyanamide process and by the distillation of coal. The cyanamide process involves the passage of ammonia over hot calcium acetylide, and the resulting calcium cyanamide, $CaCN_2$, is treated under pressure with steam to give ammonia and calcium carbonate.

Liquid ammonia is a good solvent for salts. It can dissolve alkali and alkaline-earth metals without reacting with them. It also dissolves many metal salts by forming metal-ammonia complexes. Ammonia is used in the manufacture of ammonium sulfate and urea, which are good fertilizers. Pure ammonia is now being employed as a fertilizer by direct application to the soil on large farms. Because it is easily liquefied, ammonia is also used as a refrigerant.—*G. W. M.*

AMMONIUM HYDROXIDE: a chemical compound (NH_4OH) formed when ammonia (NH_3) is dissolved in water. A colorless liquid with a pungent, highly irritating odor, it can cause skin burns. Dilute solutions are sold as "household ammonia." Although a weak base, it does undergo typical basic reactions, as in neutralizing acids or saponifying fats. It is an important commercial chemical, used in the manufacture of ammonium salts and organic compounds.—*D. P. B.*

AMMONIUM SALTS: the product of the reaction of ammonia or ammonium hydroxide and an acid. Ammonium salts possess the same crystalline form as potassium salts. All ammonium salts are water-soluble and completely ionized. Ammonium chloride, formed from ammonia and hydrogen chloride, is used in soldering, galvanizing iron, textile dyeing, and in "dry" cell batteries. A large amount of ammonium sulfate is used in fertilizers. Ammonium nitrate is used as an explosive; mixed with TNT it is called amatol. Ammonium sulfide, prepared by bubbling hydrogen sulfide into ammonium hydroxide, is used in analytical chemistry to precipitate metal sulfides. Ammonium salts can be electrolyzed to hydrazine in the presence of glue or starch.—*G. W. M.*

AMONTONS, GUILLAUME, 1663–1705, French physicist; b. Paris. He studied frictional forces, which he considered proportional to load (1699), and concentrated on improving physical instruments, *e.g.* the air thermometer (1702–3), the hygrometer (1687), and various types of barometers, *e.g.* the baroscope (1695). His *Observations and Physical Experiments on the Construction of a New Clepsydra, on Barometers, Thermometers, and Hygrometers* appeared in 1695. The earliest careful investigation of the relation between the boiling point of water and air pressure was done by him.—*R. J. F.*

AMORPHOUS SUBSTANCES: substances that differ from crystalline substances in that their particles are not arranged to form geometric shapes. In nature, amorphous solids are rare; soot (amorphous carbon) is the best-known example. Amorphous solids have been made artificially by condensing slowly cooled vapors of solid substances on cold surfaces, so as to form films of solid particles; "flowers of sulfur" is prepared in this way from ordinary sulfur heated to its sublimation point. Another method is to cool viscous liquids by special procedures (undercooling) until they form truly amorphous solids known as *glasses;* ordinary GLASS is an example. Polymers in the solid state, *e.g.* commercial plastics, are usually amorphous.—*T. M.* ·

AMPÈRE, ANDRÉ MARIE, 1775–1836, French physicist; b. Lyons. He introduced the terms "electrostatics" and "electrodynamics" to distinguish between the forces between electrified objects, long known, and the new phenomena associated with electric currents. One of the first to conceive of *currents* of electricity, he distinguished between the cause of the current and the current itself, identified the electrochemical and electromagnetic effects as properties of current, dis-

André Marie Ampère
(Bettmann Archive)

covered that electric currents exert forces upon one another, and showed that Newton's third law applies to forces between currents. He invented the term "galvanometer" for current-measuring devices and did research in mathematics and on the application of mathematics to mechanics. Many of his writings appeared in the *Mémoires* of the French Academy of Sciences, and much of his electrical work was collected in his *Recueil d'observations électro-dynamiques* (*Collection of Electrodynamical Observations*), 1822. He was professor of physics at the Collège de France, Paris. He was a member of the Academy of Sciences and a fellow of the Royal Society.—*D. H. D. R.*

AMPERE: see ELECTRICAL AND MAGNETIC UNITS.

AMPÈRE'S LAW: a law of ELECTROMAGNETISM derived by André Marie Ampère from experiments conducted 1820–25. The law gives the magnetic flux density (the "magnetic induction" field) at a point near a current path due to the current in a small section (element) of the path in terms of the magnitude of the current, the angle between the current in the element and a straight line to the point in question, the distance between the element and the point, and the properties of the medium separating them. In algebraic terms:

$$\Delta B = k \frac{I \Delta l \sin \theta}{r^2}$$

where ΔB is the contribution to the total magnetic flux due to a current I flowing in a path element Δl at a point a distance r from Δl along a straight line that forms an angle θ with the direction of the current in Δl; k is a constant whose value depends on the characteristics of the medium and the units employed. The magnetic induction B, in turn, produces a force on a second current element $I'\Delta l'$ given by

$$\Delta F = B I' \Delta l' \sin \theta'$$

where θ' is the angle between the direction of B and that of the current element $\Delta l'$. Thus the law as a whole describes the magnetic force between two electrical currents.—*E. M. R.*

AMPHIBIAN: any cold-blooded vertebrate that breathes air with lungs and has thin, moist skin. The living types are *salamanders*, certain kinds of which are often called waterdogs and mudpuppies; *anurans*, usually called frogs and toads; and limbless tropical species known as *caecilians*. Salamanders differ from other living amphibians in having a long tail. They resemble and are often confused with lizards, but do not have claws and horny scales as lizards do; lizards are in fact reptiles. Anurans are unique among amphibians in that adults lack a tail; also, their four limbs are all well developed and the hind pair often much enlarged, whereas the limbs of salamanders are about equal in size, with some species lacking hind legs. Caecilians have rings around the body, and have such a short tail that in some species it seems to be absent.

The thin, moist skin of amphibians can soak up and also lose water readily; this is the chief reason why amphibians, even as adults, must live close to water or in a humid place. The skin lacks horny, water-resistant scales such as reptiles have. The thin skin is useful, however, as a respiratory organ; all respiration occurs through the skin while an amphibian is hibernating, and much of it while the animal is active.

Amphibia means "double-life," and refers to the existence, in many species, of two distinct developmental stages after

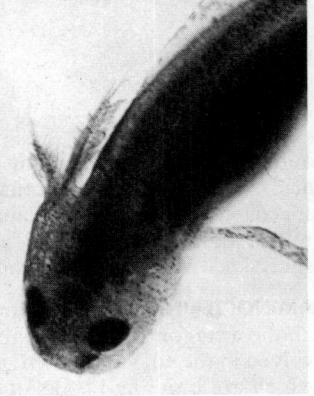

Swimming stage: Three weeks after hatching, this spotted salamander has limbs. It will retain gills throughout its larval life. (*George Porter from Nat. Audubon Soc.*)

hatching—a *larval* stage and a *transformed* stage. The larval stage is adapted to life in water and often lacks lungs; in that stage the amphibian has a thin skin, and jaws and teeth adapted to underwater foods. In anurans, the larva is a tadpole that lacks legs; it has a long intestine if, as is usual, the food consists of plant matter. In the transformed stage many changes occur in a short time, all adapting the animals to life on land: the gills are lost and, as a rule, lungs replace them in function; legs appear or strengthen, as befits a walking or crawling animal; the jaws and teeth change considerably in correlation with the completely carnivorous diet of all adult amphibians; and the intestine becomes short—even a tenth the length of the larval intestine.

The rather rapid transformation that takes place *after* hatching or birth, from a bodily structure adapted to life in water, like that of a fish, to a bodily structure adapted to life on land, like that of a reptile, is called METAMORPHOSIS. Amphibians are the only vertebrates that undergo metamorphosis, although the equivalent of metamorphosis occurs during the embryonic (before birth or hatching) stages of reptiles, birds, and mammals. Amphibians evolved from fishes some 250,-000,000 yr ago. Far more kinds existed and became extinct than are now living. The largest never exceeded about 8 ft in length, but the body was often wide and heavy, the head large.

Salamanders: These comprise some 250 species, restricted to North America and Eurasia, except for two species in South America and several dozen in Central America and Mexico. The size varies greatly, from ¾ in. in a tiny Mexican species to 69 in. in the giant salamander of mountain streams in Japan and China. These animals live chiefly in moist, cool regions. Numerous exceptions to the general rule of metamorphosis occur. Some kinds—*e.g.* the mudpuppy (*Necturus*), hellbender (*Cryptobranchus*), sirens (*Siren*), and congo-eel (*Amphiuma*)—fail to transform fully, or at all, and live in water throughout their lives. Others lay their eggs on land, and the young hatch as fully transformed animals. In most kinds, eggs are laid in water; a larva hatches and grows for a few months or years, transforming eventually to the adult, which often lives on land close to water, returning in the breeding season to mate and lay eggs. In newts, the larva transforms to an "eft" stage, which lives on land a year or two, but is not sexually mature; eventually the eft returns to water, becomes an adult, breeds, and never again leaves the water, although it continues to breathe air (the gills never reappear). A few primitive salamanders, like most fishes, practice external fertilization, the male swimming and scattering sperm over the eggs after they are laid. In most salamanders internal fertilization occurs by a curious, indirect procedure: in water the male stimulates the female in a more or less complex dancelike ritual, deposits one or more clumps of sperm in little masses of jelly, and the female walks behind him, picking up these "spermatophores" with her cloacal opening. The eggs are then fertilized as they are laid. In only one species of sala-

Terrestrial stage: With its four feet, this amphibian, an adult frog, is well adapted to life on land as long as moisture of some sort is nearby. (*Lynwood M. Chace from Nat. Audubon Soc.*)

mander is there a direct transfer of sperm to the female, accomplished by contact of cloaca to cloaca, as in birds, for there is no copulatory organ. Only two species of salamanders bear living young, one giving birth to larvae, the other to transformed young. All salamanders have four well-developed limbs, except for the congo-eel, which has tiny vestiges of limbs, and the sirens, which have no hind legs.

Anurans: About 2,000 species are widely distributed in temperate and tropical lands, a few species reaching the Arctic Circle. Extreme northern kinds survive winters by hibernating in deep lake waters that do not freeze. Some kinds, *e.g.* toads, have extremely poisonous skin secretions, as do some salamanders; the poison is dangerous only when it gets into the blood or is swallowed. There are no sharp or real distinctions between toads and frogs, but the word "toad" is commonly used for rough-skinned species, "frog" for smooth-skinned.

Most North American anurans lay their eggs in water, usually in spring, being stimulated by rains and warm temperatures. Males usually sing—the only vertebrates except birds, mammals, and a very few reptiles that do; they congregate in water and call others of both sexes to them. Males straddle the backs of females, embracing them with their forelegs, and as eggs are laid, the males strew sperm over them. In one or two species of frogs, internal fertilization occurs by cloacal contact; in the tailed frog, it occurs with the aid of a vestigial tail used as a copulatory organ. Eggs hatch in a few hours or weeks, depending upon species and temperature. The tadpoles are legless and live in water for a few days, weeks, or months, feeding chiefly upon algae with their specialized rasping set of mouth parts, and respiring by means of internal gills whose chambers open to the exterior by one or two small holes called spiracles. At transformation, hind legs develop, then forelegs; the tail disappears, the mouth parts change from a rasping to a biting apparatus, and the intestine shortens as the animals change their food exclusively to animals instead of plants. The transformed juvenile grows for several weeks, months, or years, depending upon species and temperature, before it reaches sexual maturity. Adults grow slowly, attaining ⅜-in. length in the smallest species, about 1 ft in the largest.

Many variations of this typical life history occur. Some anurans lay eggs on land, and transformed juveniles hatch from them. The eggs of the Surinam toad, as the toads swim, drop onto the female's back, where they sink into compartments formed in the thickened skin. Transformed juveniles hop from their separate compartments upon completion of development, skipping a free-living larval stage. In other anurans the eggs complete development in a large pouch on the back of the female or in the vocal pouch of the male.

Other variations occur in types, *e.g.* the obstetrical toad, that carry the eggs around, on land and in water, until they hatch during a visit to water. The poison frog carries its tadpoles around on its back as it hops back and forth from land to water. Some anurans lay their eggs in foamy nests hanging above water, the larvae dropping eventually into the water. Others lay the eggs in foamy nests on the ground above water line, where the larvae swim and eat the foam until high water releases them. Several kinds build protective shallow pools for the eggs and larvae, and some breed in small pools in hollow trees or water-holding plants of various sorts. All these variations are useful in protecting eggs and larvae from predators or in adapting to the absence of permanent streams or pools.

Caecilians: These amphibians look for all the world like earthworms, with their slick skin and numerous ringlike grooves around the body. The 100 or so species are restricted to tropical jungles all over the world. The smallest is 3½ in. in length, the largest about 4½ ft. Most burrow in the soil, but a few live always in water. They are blind or nearly so, have no external ears, and are thus deaf to air-borne sounds. They reproduce by copulation. Imbedded invisibly in the skin are numerous tiny, bony scales—remnants of prominent bony armor of ancient types of amphibians.—*H. M. S.* (See Color Plates f.p. 6.)

AMPHIBOLES: a very common and widespread group of silicate minerals which are major constituents of many IGNEOUS ROCKS and METAMORPHIC ROCKS. The amphiboles form several interlocking, partially to completely isomorphous series:

Orthorhombic

Anthophyllite series:

$(Mg > Fe)_7Si_8O_{22}(OH)_2$—Anthophyllite
$(Mg < Fe)_7Si_8O_{22}(OH)_2$—Amosite (asbestiform)
$(Mg,Fe,Al)_7Si_8O_{22}(OH)$—Gedrite

Monoclinic

Cummingtonite series:

$(Mg,Fe)_7Si_8O_{22}(OH)_2$—Cummingtonite
$(Mg, Fe, Mn)_7Si_8O_{22}(OH)_2$—Grünerite

Tremolite-Actinolite series:

$Ca_2Mg_5Si_8O_{22}(OH)_2$—Tremolite (includes Nephrite)
$Ca_2(Mg, Fe)_5Si_8O_{22}(OH)_2$—Actinolite

Hornblende series:

$Ca_2Na(Mg, Fe)_5AlSi_7O_{22}(OH, F)_2$—Edenite
$Ca_2Na(Mg, Fe)_4Al_3Si_6O_{22}(OH, F)_2$—Hastingsite
$Ca_2Na(Mg, Fe, Al)_5(Al, Si)_8O_{22}(O, OH, F)_2$—Hornblende
$Ca_2Na(Mg, Fe, Al, Ti)_5(Al, Si)_8O_{22}(O, OH, F)_2$—Basaltic Hornblende

Soda Amphiboles:

$Na_3Mg_4AlSi_8O_{22}(OH, F)_2$—Arfvedsonite
$Na_2Mg_3Al_2Si_8O_{22}(OH, F)_2$—Glaucophane
$Na_2Fe''_3Fe'''_2Si_8O_{22}(OH, F)_2$—Riebeckite

The amphibole structure is formed of double chains of SiO_4 tetrahedra (AlO_4 tetrahedra may substitute for some of the SiO_4 tetrahedra). In each chain every tetrahedron is linked to its neighbor through a shared oxygen ion. The two chains are cross-linked by the sharing of the free oxygen ions of every second tetrahedron in each chain. The resulting bands are elongate parallel to the *c*-axis of the crystal. The general structural formula, $X_{0-7}Y_{7-14}Z_{16}O_{44}(OH)_4$, permits a great range of possible compositions, with substitutions as follows: $X = Mg, Fe, Ca, Na, Li$; $Y = Fe, Mn, Al, Ti$; $Z = Al, Si$. The amphiboles are closely related to the pyroxenes in structure, composition, appearance, and occurrence. The most prominent distinction is in the prismatic cleavage planes, which meet at about 90° in the pyroxenes and at about 60° and 120° in the amphiboles. At lower temperatures, the amphibole structure is generally more stable than the pyroxene structure, and partial to complete replacement of pyroxene by amphibole (uralitization) is common. The use of amphiboles is limited almost entirely to the asbestiform varieties (see ASBESTOS), although some of the commercial talcs contain a large proportion of acicular tremolite. See MINERAL (table); PYROXENES.—*L. M.*

AMPHOTERIC COMPOUNDS: compounds that are able to neutralize both strong acids and strong bases. Thus tin hydroxide reacts with hydrochloric acid to form water and tin chloride: $Sn(OH)_2 + 2HCl \rightarrow SnCl_2 + 2H_2O$. Formation of water by combination of hydrogen ions from the hydrochloric acid and the hydroxide furnished by the tin hydroxide is a typical neutralization reaction, in which the latter substance behaves as a base. But when tin hydroxide reacts with sodium hydroxide, water is formed by combination of hydroxyl ions from sodium hydroxide and hydrogen ions from tin hydroxide: $Sn(OH)_2 + 2NaOH \rightarrow Na_2SnO_2 + 2H_2O$. In this case, since the tin hydroxide furnishes the hydrogen ions it is acting as an acid; the other material formed is the salt, sodium stannite.

How can amphoterism be explained? Consider the structural formulas of a strong acid, sulfuric acid, H_2SO_4; of an amphoteric substance, tin hydroxide, $Sn(OH)_2$; and of a strong base, calcium hydroxide, $Ca(OH)_2$:

$$H-O-\overset{\overset{\displaystyle O}{||}}{\underset{\underset{\displaystyle O}{||}}{S}}-O-H \quad H-O-Sn-O-H \quad H-O-Ca-O-H$$

These show that whether the substance behaves as acid or base depends on whether it is easier to cleave the oxygen-hydrogen bond, thus producing a hydrogen ion, or the oxygen-central atom bond, giving rise to a hydroxy ion. This course, in turn, is determined by the electrical nature of the central atom. Metals such as calcium give rise to bases, whereas non-metals such as sulfur form acids. In the case of elements intermediate between metallic and non-metallic nature, the metalloids—of which tin is one—the bond strengths in question are comparable and the molecule can cleave either way, depending upon whether it is an acidic or a basic medium.—*M. K.*

AMPLIFIER: a device for increasing the magnitude of electric current, voltage, or power. Although non-electrical amplifiers exist, in common usage the term generally applies to one or another of the basic three electrical types, and accordingly one can speak of a *current, voltage,* or *power* amplifier. Since electrical power is the product of current and voltage, amplification of either current or voltage may result in power amplification as well. In practice, amplifiers are constructed with the aid of electron tubes, transistors, and, in some more unusual cases, magnetic devices. (For a description of how amplification is accomplished in such devices, see ELECTRON TUBE and TRANSISTOR.) An ideal amplifier would alter only the signal amplitude, leaving the frequency and phase unaltered (see MODULATION for definition of these terms). Practically, it is impossible to construct an ideal amplifier which would operate on all frequencies; therefore, amplifiers are further classified by the frequency ranges in which they can operate. Thus the so-called audio amplifier, employed in a high-fidelity system, is designed only for frequencies audible to the human ear. "High fidelity" represents an attempt to approach, with practical circuitry, the ideal amplifier, which would amplify uniformly over a given frequency range. Amplifiers are perhaps the most common of electronic circuits. A radio receiver, for example, consists basically of three types of amplifiers: a radio-frequency amplifier, an intermediate frequency amplifier, and an audio amplifier, plus devices (see HETERODYNE CIRCUIT) which appropriately change the frequencies between the three. See also ELECTRONICS.—*G. S.*

AMPLITUDE: one half the difference between the extreme values (*i.e.* half the "swing" or range) of any variable quantity undergoing regular oscillation, *e.g.* voltage, pressure, or height of tide. The amplitude of a simple sinusoid (see TRIGONOMETRIC FUNCTIONS) is merely the largest value it attains. Use of the word amplitude implies that the quantity in question is vibrating about some position of equilibrium in a regular manner. In a complex vibration each component frequency will have its own amplitude. Mathematically, the amplitude of a generalized sinusoidal quantity at any value of x is the

Amplitude

Amplitude of a Sinusoidal Wave

value of the modifying function $f_0(x)$ at x_1; that is, if $y = f_0(x) \sin(wx + a)$, then the amplitude is $f_0(x_1)$.—*M. C. H.*

ANALOGY: proportion or likeness of relations. Analogy is not a reliable method of proof but in scientific inquiry it is useful in suggesting new ideas to be tested. When Poincaré defined mathematics as the art of calling new things by old names, he meant that mathematical discovery proceeds by analogy (thus, to see that the fourth dimension is an analogy, try putting four pencils each at right angles to all the others). But this is not distinctive of mathematics; *cf.* light "waves" and "bullets," or electric "currents." Since every analogy breaks down somewhere, its use is not probative, but may be suggestive. Judges sometimes decide novel cases by analogy: this is a form of judicial law-making. Argument by analogy may persuade the unwary, but because two things resemble each other in some respects, it does not necessarily follow that they will resemble each other in the further respects claimed. Useful questions to ask are: How close is the analogy? Are the resemblances relevant? What differences are there between the things being compared? Does the analogy break down in a relevant respect? What independent evidence can be offered for or against the underlying generalization? Can a counter-analogy be constructed, and what reasons are there for preferring the original analogy to it?—*H. T.*

ANALYSIS (in chemistry): see CHEMICAL ANALYSIS.

ANALYSIS (in mathematics): a relatively modern field that has grown out of differential and integral CALCULUS and rests on the fundamental concepts of that subject. It is today the most important area of mathematics. Calculus began as an organized subject with the work of Newton and Leibniz in the latter part of the 17th cent. The great power of the methods of the calculus enabled mathematicians to explore many areas by means of the new concepts. Thus, calculus of variations was developed by the Bernoullis, Leonhard Euler, Joseph Louis Lagrange, and others in the 18th cent. Newtonian mechanics and the great works of Lagrange and William Hamilton in this field were applications of mathematical analysis; the Einstein theory is a modern application.

Function theory is a comprehensive name for a large area of analysis. It is often subdivided into theory of functions of real variables and theory of functions of complex variables. In a sense, function theory comprises all analysis. But the term is generally reserved for the formulation of basic concepts, the general theory of large classes of functions, and the investigation of their properties as well as those of individual functions. The most important class of functions is analytic functions, such as $y = x^2$ and $y = e^x$, which have unique derivatives of all orders. Other classes of functions (which may also be analytic) are algebraic functions, and transcendental functions that include $\log x$, $\sin x$, etc. In the theory of functions of complex variables, such functions as $\log x$ and $\sin x$ are defined for imaginary and complex values of x, as well as for positive real numbers. (See FUNCTION THEORY.)

Another part of analysis is the study of DIFFERENTIAL EQUATIONS and INTEGRAL EQUATIONS. If a relation, in the form of an equation, contains a derivative of a function, it is a differential equation. It may be expected to contain an independent variable x, a dependent variable y, and the derivative dy/dx. If no derivative of higher order appears, it is an ordinary differential equation of the first order. To solve it is to find y as a function of x. Differential equations of higher order contain higher-ordered derivatives. If there are more than one independent variable, the derivatives are partial derivatives and the equation is a partial differential equation. Differential

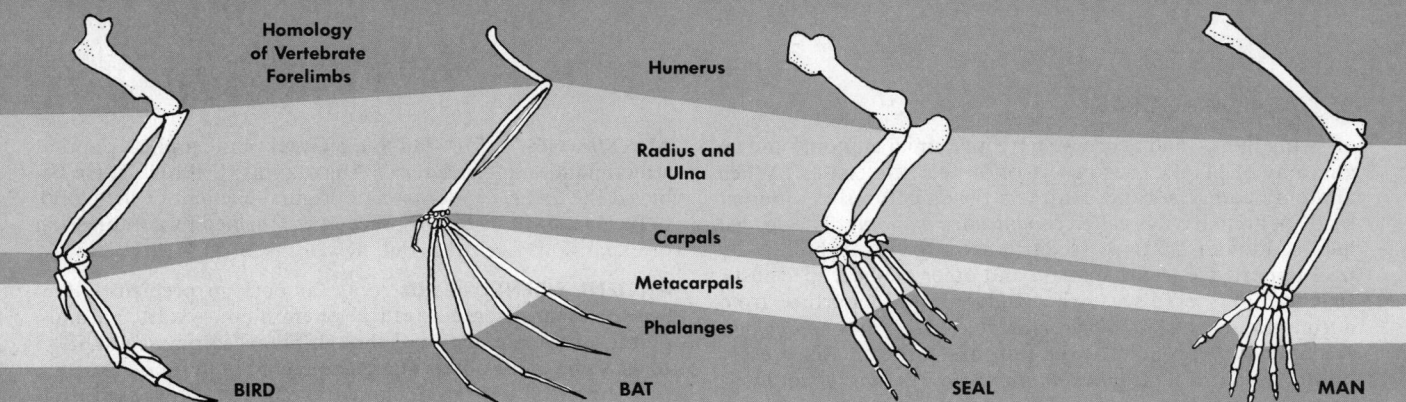

Homology
of Vertebrate
Forelimbs

Humerus

Radius and
Ulna

Carpals

Metacarpals

Phalanges

BIRD   BAT   SEAL   MAN

equations are of the highest importance in applied mathematics. The observed facts of a dynamical situation nearly always involve rates, such as velocities and accelerations, which are expressed by derivatives. Integral equations involve integrals rather than derivatives. An example is

$$y^2 \int_o^y s(x) \, [64 \, (y - x)] \, dx$$

where s denotes some unknown function; to solve it is to find this function. The subject of integral equations is considerably less vast than differential equations, and not as important.

One form of calculus—the CALCULUS OF VARIATIONS—was devised to solve maximum and minimum problems of a higher order of difficulty than those which yield to ordinary differential calculus. The minimum problem of differential calculus in its simplest form requires us to minimize a function of one variable. More complicated problems call for the maximizing or minimizing of functions of more variables, but always a finite number of them. An example of a problem in the calculus of variations, on the other hand, is that of determining the curve down which a ball will roll (without friction) from a fixed point to a lower one in the shortest time. The time required depends not upon one point or a few points of the curve, but upon all the points of the curve, which are infinite in number. Calculus of variations is a branch of analysis of great practical use as well as of theoretical interest.

The theory of infinite sequences and infinite series is included, to a large extent, in other branches of analysis. The limit of an infinite sequence is a concept that is fundamental to analysis. An analytic function is often defined as one that can be expressed by an infinite power series: $a_0 + a_1 x + a_2 x^2 + a_3 x^3 + \ldots$. Fourier analysis is a specialty under infinite series which has applications of the greatest importance in differential equations and elsewhere. It is one of the most powerful tools of analysis. Its central feature is the expressing of functions by infinite series of trigonometric terms. (See FOURIER SERIES.)

Analysis may also be applied to geometry in the form of DIFFERENTIAL GEOMETRY. It is concerned mainly with the properties of curves and surfaces in space. An important problem is that of determining the geodesics of a surface, *i.e.,* the curves of shortest distance on a surface.—*H. C.*

ANALYTICS, PRIOR AND POSTERIOR: two writings on logic by Aristotle, 4th cent. B. C. As the first treatise on formal logic, the *Prior Analytics* has a permanent place in the history of thought and is still capable of inspiring developments in modern logic. The *Posterior Analytics* deals with what we should today call SCIENTIFIC METHOD. It defines science as demonstrative knowledge of the causes of things by means of their necessary connections and goes on to consider syllogistic ways of resolving such questions as "Why is the angle in a semicircle a right angle," "Why did the Athenians become involved in the Persian War," "Why does one take a walk after supper?" Although much of this has a somewhat archaic air

Body structure: The wood engravings issued by Vesalius in 1543 (*below*) mark the Renaissance readiness to seek enlightenment in direct observation (*Burndy Library*). Comparative studies, as of vertebrate forelimbs (*above*), were begun by Pierre Belon in 1555.

SECVNDA
MVSCVLO.
RVMTA·
BVLA.

and would seem to be more applicable to mathematics, if even there, than to natural science, some of its insights are of lasting value, *e.g.* its insistence on the importance of economy of assumptions in scientific inference; its pointing out that scientific knowledge is not possible through perception alone; its definition of ignorance in its positive sense, as error produced by inference.—*H. T.*

ANATOMY: the study of form and structure of fully developed organisms. The literal meaning of the word anatomy is a "cutting apart," or dissection, but a realm of this science extends beyond the structures displayed by ordinary dissection with the unaided eye and into the territory revealed by the microscope. It is customary, therefore, to recognize two major subdivisions: gross anatomy (or macroscopic anatomy) and microscopic anatomy. In its broadest sense anatomy concerns all living things, and hence we have an animal anatomy and an anatomy of plants. (See PLANT ORGANS AND TISSUES.) When anatomy compares and contrasts the structures of different kinds of animals, it is called *comparative anatomy.* The special field of human anatomy (see HUMAN BODY) is of high practical importance to the surgeon and other medical specialists. In conditions of disease the study of the departure from normal constitutes *pathological* (morbid) *anatomy,* or *pathology.* A standard approach for the purposes of textbook presentation is that of *descriptive anatomy,* or *systematic anatomy,* through which the various structures are grouped and treated according to the natural systems into which they fall. Thus we have osteology (bones), arthrology (joints), myology (muscles), angiology (heart and blood vessels), splanchnology (visceral organs), and neurology (nervous system and sense organs). Similarly, under *microscopic anatomy* several progressive subgroups are recognized. Organology, sometimes also called microscopic anatomy, deals with the architectural plan and arrangements within the various organs of the body. Histology describes the building materials that enter into the composition of these organs; such aggregations of specialized cells are tissues, of which there are four types: epithelium, connective tissue, muscle, and nerve. Cytology is the study of the intimate structure of the actual cells, which are the ultimate building units of all tissues.

Anatomy is as old as the history of medicine, but its progress was greatly retarded by ancient prohibitions against the dissection of the dead human body. Aristotle (b. 384 B. C.) is commonly considered to be the founder of the science of human anatomy, but his conclusions were drawn from the study of lower animals; more accurately, he was the founder of comparative anatomy. Galen (*c.* A. D. 130–200) wrote a treatise on human anatomy, but it was based on the dissection of apes and still lower mammals. This remarkable work dominated medical thought and teaching until the 16th cent. Although his discussions of the systems of the body are astonishingly accurate in many respects, they contain serious errors. The renaissance of anatomy became possible when, at about the 14th cent., the dissection of human bodies began to be legalized. Modern descriptive anatomy stems from the studies of the Belgian anatomist Andreas Vesalius; in 1543 he published the first complete description of the human body based on actual, detailed observation. This book, which will ever remain one of the classics of science, led the attack that culminated in the overthrow of Galenic teachings. Anatomists remained largely concerned with the mere description of structure until about the beginning of the 20th cent., when greater emphasis was placed on experimental studies of the effects of removing and replacing structures. Today anatomists are using the techniques of the physicist, the chemist, and the electronics engineer to learn more about form and structure. —*A. P. E.*

ANAXAGORAS, 500–428 B. C., eminent Greek philosopher; b. Ionia. He held that all matter existed originally not in the form of the so-called elements of earth, air, fire, and water, but in the condition of atoms; that these atoms had existed from all eternity; and that order was first produced out of this chaos of minute particles through the operation of an eternal intelligence (Greek *Nous*).—*A. P. E.*

ANAXIMANDER, 611–547 B. C., Greek mathematician and philosopher, b. Miletus. He allegedly discovered that Earth's path around the Sun is not a perfect circle. His theory of the world's origin was based on eternal motion acting on an indeterminate substance to produce heat and cold, light and dark, and so forth. The conflict of these opposites caused the development of the world.—*A. P. E.*

ANAXIMENES, *c.* 570–480 B. C.; Greek philosopher, pupil of Anaximander and master of Anaxagoras; b. Miletus. He believed the *arche,* or eternal and original element of the world, to be air, of which all substances were formed by compression or expansion. Even the soul, he said, is of air.—*A. P. E.*

ANCIENT SCIENCE has its roots far back in prehistory. **Prehistoric man** observed natural phenomena—stars, animals, plants, and minerals—and though his reasoning is unknown to us, some of his observations are recorded in rock-drawings. In the earliest written documents (3,000 B. C.) we find rudiments of mathematics and astronomy being developed in the temple-schools of the Near East. (See ASTRONOMY and MATHEMATICS, HISTORY OF.) Because of Greek tradition, the contribution of **Egypt** to this development has been grossly overrated. A complicated system of symbols for both numerals and fractions restricted their mathematics to the simplest methods of multiplication and division, and calculations with fractions could be executed only by special techniques, which survived in classical times in treatises of surveying as the "Egyptian method of computation." Such mathematics served to solve simple problems of trade and engineering (*e.g.* earth-moving, volume of ramps) but reached no further. Egyptian astronomy never developed beyond the preliminary stage of observing and naming stars and planets until it came into contact with Babylonian astronomy, *c.* 300 B. C. The introduction of various CALENDARS started crude attempts at prediction of such phenomena as phases of the Moon, which led to the first attempts to find "cycles of years" as a link between the lunar, solar, and civil calendars. The 24-hr day is also an Egyptian contribution.

Cuneiform texts show that more progress was achieved in **Mesopotamia.** The Sumerians, by adopting well-chosen symbols for their sexagesimal system and a place-value system of numerals, carried mathematics beyond the stage of being a practical tool for the administration of temples, estates, and storehouses and beyond the "sums" required in commerce and engineering. Certain of their "problem texts" represent mathematical exercises which, by 800 B. C., allowed the Assyrians and Babylonians to apply their mathematics to complicated astronomical phenomena (*e.g.* predicting positions of certain planets in the sky in the near future) and thus started theoretical mathematical astronomy on its way. Be-

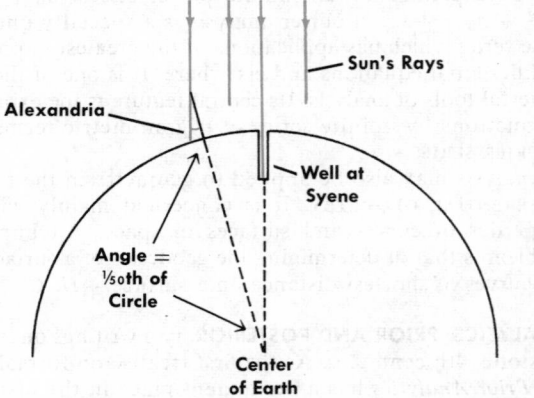

Triumph of ancient science: The measurement of Earth is credited to ERATOSTHENES, 3d cent. B. C. Seeing the noon sun reflected from the bottom of a deep well at Syene, at the summer solstice, he judged that it was directly overhead. Assuming its rays to be parallel, he deduced the value of the angle subtended by the arc from Syene to Alexandria (both almost on the same meridian). This angle was a fiftieth of a circle. The distance between the sites being 5,000 *stadia,* he derived for Earth's circumference a value of 250,000 stadia—about 24,660 mi.

tween 500 and 300 B. C. the Babylonians achieved great accuracy in predictions by applying mathematics to regular observations of the sky. About 380 B. C. they connected lunar and solar calendars by a 19-yr cycle (of 7 yr of 13 lunar months and 12 of 12 lunar months), also proposed by Meton of Athens (432 B. C.). The Metonic cycle later became important as a means of calculating the date of Easter Sunday.

By this time Near Eastern science began to feel the impact of science from **Greece**. Until then science had consisted of a series of computational rules and methods of calculation used in commerce and trade, engineering and taxation, prediction of astronomical phenomena, and determination of the calendar or religious festivals. The world of the senses as such was considered part of the world "as created by the gods in the beginning"; no ancient scientist dreamed of studying it for its own sake. Greek philosophers who, c. 600 B. C., started to explain natural phenomena without mythological dogmas, formulating certain hypotheses which could explain other phenomena causally, were the direct ancestors of the modern scientists. However, early Greek science was still an aspect of philosophy, from which it detached itself partly as the centuries went by; hence many of our modern concepts go back to one or more Greek schools of philosophy. Plato, inspired by Pythagoras, stressed the function of mathematics in science as a way "to save the phenomena." Plato held that the philosophers were able to disclose the structure of the unseen "true world of ideas," which observed phenomena revealed to our senses only in imperfect and distorted form. Science was to use mathematics to relate these observed events to the true structure of the world underlying these seemingly erratic and unorderly phenomena. From this stems our mathematically worded science, which is based on analysis of observations and is able to forecast the results of experiments to be conducted. Zeno of Elea and his school taught us to look for the unvarying in natural phenomena, a search which was to lead much later to the formulation of such principles as the conservation of energy and mass. From the atomism of Democritus (see ATOMIC THEORY) stem our views on the corpuscular structure of matter and all kinetic theories. Aristotle taught us to regard empirical data as the object of investigation; in general, a fundamentally empirical attitude toward nature, trying to discover general laws and to reduce the multitude of substances to compounds of a limited number of basic substances. Stoicism gave us the concept of nature as a great coherent entity subject to an all-embracing system of rationally comprehensible laws. Early Greek mathematicians may have borrowed from the Near East, but they developed their own typical mathematics as an abstract-logical edifice based on definitions and axioms. Thus Euclid's systematic exposition given at Alexandria (300 B. C.) could stand as a model for centuries. Archimedes of Syracuse, apart from his very original works on mechanics and hydrostatics (which were to inspire Galileo and his generation), developed rigorous methods for determining areas and volumes, heralding the rise of integral calculus in the 17th cent. Apollonius of Perga gave a theory of conic sections which stood equally long, and founded spherical geometry, so important to astronomy. In

mechanics and physics certain problems received mathematical treatment, e.g. the theory of the lever, hydrostatics, geometrical optics of mirrors, acoustics, and musical scales. Other questions, related to falling and projected bodies, sight, sound, and meteorology, are simply discussed. In astronomy Eudoxus, Apollonius, Hipparchus, and others, postulating Earth at rest in the center of the universe, created for the Sun, Moon, and each of the five known planets a set of revolving spheres fitting into one another, each sphere of a set entraining those inside it, the innermost of each set being a mathematical point representing the celestial body. The mathematical conclusions drawn from this kinematic picture of the actual motions of the celestial bodies conformed sufficiently well with what was observed to stand until the days of Copernicus.

Ancient science as a whole owed much to medicine. From this source stemmed many significant discoveries in anatomy, physiology, biology, and chemistry. The Greeks were preeminent in this field, but other societies also contributed. Among the most outstanding figures of ancient medicine were Hippocrates of Cos, Erasistratus and Herophilus of Alexandria, and Galen, who brought Greek medicine to Rome.

In the Hellenistic kingdoms formed in the Near East after the death of Alexander the Great, academies of science were founded in large towns such as Alexandria, Antiochia, and Pergamum. Here Greek science flourished in closer contact with earlier sciences, which often struck out on their own paths. Seleucid (Mesopotamian) astronomy used algebraic methods to interpret its observations and to construct tables. Seleucid and Hellenistic astronomy (with its new zero symbol) and mathematics traveled to **India** where, after 300 B. C., "Brahmi numbers" were in use as convenient symbols; these traveled to Europe much later as "Arabic numerals."

Contacts with **China** were few. Chinese arithmetic never developed into higher mathematics and was confined to the simplest practical calculations. It never became a tool of other branches of science. Chinese astronomy developed its own polar and equatorial system, star-catalogs (350 B. C.), and clock-driven sighting tubes (A. D. 125), but remained observational, collecting data on sunspots, eclipses, novas, and comets rather than establishing a mathematical discipline as did the Greeks. Only Chinese alchemy left its traces in early Hellenistic alchemy. This new art, born in late Babylonian times (600 B. C.), together with astrology flourished in Alexandria at the turn of the Christian era. Its object was to explain what happened when metals, dyes, and the like changed color as they reacted with other agents. Hellenistic alchemy later

Mechanical ingenuity: Indicator figure atop Chinese cart will remain pointing in whatever direction it is first set (traditionally, south). At the heart of the contraption is an assembly of pegged and toothed gears whose differential coupling assures that any turn of the cart produces an equal and opposite turn of the indicator. Casting aside a traditional estimate of its antiquity that strains credulity, the present reconstructor, G. H. Lanchester, has appealed to mechanisms thought to have been familiar to Chinese artificers of the first few centuries A. D. (*G. H. Lanchester, Science Museum, London*)

absorbed Far Eastern doctrines such as the search for the "universal medicine" (elixir), which also appealed to Arab alchemists. Astrology was very popular in imperial **Rome,** books by Manilius, Vettius Valens, Maternus, and Aratus being widely read because of the prevalent syncretic beliefs. Rome contributed nothing original to mathematics and natural science except encyclopedias like those of Pliny and Seneca, which together with the more scholarly textbooks by Boethius and Cassiodorus (A. D. 500) forged the first links between ancient science and early medieval Europe. The main body of Hellenistic and Greek science reached W **Europe** in the 12th cent. only through Arabic translations, often with commentaries and additions by Moslem scholars. The transmission of ancient science through Byzantium to Europe came much later (*c.* 1400), when at last the works by Archimedes and Apollonius edited by Eutocius (A. D. 500) reached the West.—*R. J. F.*

ANDERSON, CARL DAVID, 1905–   , U. S. physicist; b. New York City. With R. A. Millikan he began research in 1927 on cosmic rays, developing apparatus for the work. Anderson interpreted (1932) certain cloud-chamber tracks as having been made by a particle corresponding to the positron, whose existence had been predicted by P. A. M. Dirac. For his findings Anderson shared the Nobel prize (1936) with V. F. Hess. The mesotron, later known as "meson," whose existence was predicted by Yukawa, was discovered by Anderson. He is a member of the National Academy of Sciences.—*D. H. D. R.*

ANDESITE: an extrusive igneous rock and a type of lava, intermediate in composition between rhyolite and basalt. Its coarse-grained equivalent is diorite. Containing little or no quartz, andesite consists chiefly of plagioclase feldspar; up to a fourth of its content is ferromagnesian minerals. Numerous visible crystals occur in porphyritic andesite. The rock is associated with areas undergoing mountain-building (orogeny), particularly continental areas fringing the Pacific Ocean and notably the Andes Mts (whence the name).—*E. A.*

ANDRADE, EDWARD NEVILLE DA COSTA, 1887–   , English physicist; b. London. He has studied such topics as gamma-ray spectra, elongation of wires, and sound waves. His publications include *The Atom and Its Energy* (1947), *The Mechanism of Nature* (1930), *The Structure of the Atom* (1924), and *Approach to Modern Physics* (1957). He is a fellow of the Royal Society.—*D. H. D. R.*

ANDREWS, ROY CHAPMAN, 1884–1960, U. S. explorer, naturalist, and author; b. Beloit, Wis. Employed at the American Museum of Natural History, New York, from 1906 as a specialist on whales and other aquatic mammals, he directed the museum 1935–41. Numerous exploring expeditions took him to Alaska (1908), Dutch East Indies (1909–10), N Korea (1911–12), and Alaska (1913). Archeological and geological explorations in Tibet, SW China, Burma, and Mongolia, 1916–19, resulted in important discoveries of fossils and geological features. He wrote many popular books.—*S. B.*

ANDROGENS: biologically active substances which can stimulate development and activity of (1) spermatogenesis, (2) male accessory genital organs, and (3) secondary male sex characteristics. In addition to the primary sexual role, androgens influence growth and distribution of head and body hair, voice quality, texture of skin, libido, aggressive behavior, and weight and muscular build of the male. Androgens are used for promoting tissue repair and weight gain in debilitated and underweight individuals. The most potent natural androgen, TESTOSTERONE, is a steroid hormone produced by the testis. The adrenal cortex also produces androgenic steroids in male and female (see ADRENOCORTICAL HORMONE).—*F. U.*

Great Nebula in Andromeda (M31 or NGC 224): This is a vast spiral galaxy, a member of the Local Group, probably very like our own Milky Way system. It has two companion galaxies, M32 (*lower left*) and NGC 205 (*upper right*). (*Mt Wilson*)

ANDROMEDA NEBULA: an external GALAXY near·the star Beta in the constellation Andromeda. Visible to the naked eye as a very small, hazy patch of light, it was familiar to al Sûfi in the 10th cent., but was first seen in a telescope in 1612 by Simon Marius. On Charles Messier's list of celestial objects it was No. 31, and hence is known as "M31." A time-exposure telescopic photograph shows it as a vast spiral structure, containing about 100 billion stars. Individual stars in the nucleus were first resolved by Walter Baade with the 100-in. Mt. Wilson telescope in the early 1940s. This galaxy, one of the larger ones, is about 2 million lt-yr away. It is rotating, and has a velocity of approach to the solar system, although most galaxies are receding. More than 100 novas have been observed in this spiral. On photographs, bright blue stars can be seen in the spiral arms, together with dark lanes of interstellar matter and gaseous nebulas. The outer fringes contain globular star clusters similar to those of our galaxy. Red-sensitive photographic plates show that the nebula has an extended halo of red stars. The nebula is also a source of radio waves. There are two smaller galaxies, M32 and NGC 205, nearby. —*M. W. O.*

ANEMOMETER: an instrument for measuring wind speeds. The three main types are: (1) the *pressure-tube anemometer,* which uses the principle of the PITOT-STATIC TUBE to measure speed by the dynamic pressure of the wind; (2) the *mechanical type,* in which the rotation of cups mounted on a vertical shaft or of a small windmill is measured by counters or by means of a small electrical generator connected to the moving parts; and (3) the *hot-wire type,* which uses the principle that the cooling of a fine electrically heated wire by the wind changes its electrical resistance by an amount depending upon the wind speed. The hot-wire anemometer, very sensitive, is used mainly for research work.—*O. G. S.*

ANGIOTONIN (hypertensin or **angiotensin):** a peptide hormone produced in the kidneys when their blood supply is diminished. High blood pressure (hypertension) occurring in certain kidney diseases is believed due to the effect of angiotonin in bringing about contraction of the blood vessels of the entire body. See VASOMOTOR SYSTEM.—*J. Fl.*

ANGLE: A plane angle is a geometrical configuration formed by two straight line segments emanating from a common point. The line segments are the sides of the angle, and the common point is the vertex. The lengths of the sides are immaterial to the formation or measure of an angle. It is their difference of direction that determines the angle, and the amount of this difference is the measure of the angle. One may conceive of an angle as being generated by a line segment pivoting about one end. The initial position of the segment is the initial side of the angle, and the final position is its terminal side (see Fig. 1). Angles are at the foundation of TRIGONOMETRY. Values of the trigonometric ratios, or functions, of all angles are obtainable from tables and are used in a great variety of practical problems. Angles play a vital role in determining inaccessible distances, both terrestrial and astronomical. In surveying and navigation, angles are measured by means of a SEXTANT, a

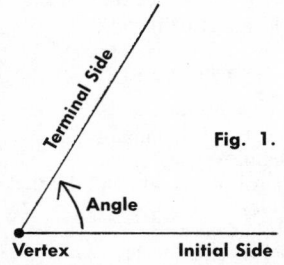

Fig. 1.

quadrant, or a TRANSIT; more refined instruments are needed for astronomical work. A protractor (Fig. 2) is useful for drawing angles of given sizes or measuring angles appearing in drawings.

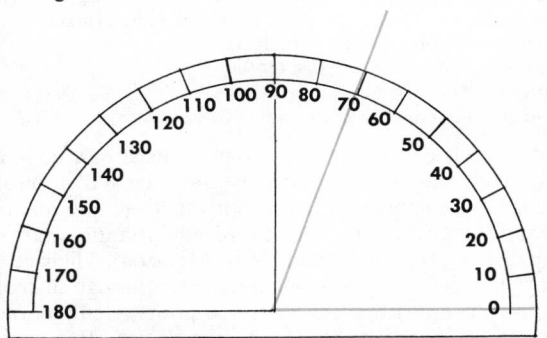

Fig. 2: The protractor here shows that the angle between the colored lines is 70°.

Many geometrical figures are named according to the angles they contain: triangle (three angles), hexagon (six angles), polygon (many angles). The angles in a figure determine its shape rather than its size. Thus all triangles having the same angles have the same shape, or are similar, although they may differ greatly in size. An angle of a triangle or other polygon is an interior angle unless explicitly stated otherwise. The sides of an interior angle are sides of the polygon; for an exterior angle, one side is a side of the polygon and the other is the extension of the adjacent side of the polygon through the vertex. An exterior angle and the interior angle at the same vertex are adjacent, having a common side. They are also supplementary, which means that together they make a straight angle, one-half of a revolution. If two supplementary angles are equal, each is a right angle. An angle less than a right angle is acute; one greater than a right angle is obtuse (see Fig. 3).

A natural unit of angular measure is a revolution, *i.e.* the amount of turning that brings the segment to its initial direction again, making the initial and terminal sides coincide. A degree is 1/360 of a revolution, a minute is 1/60 of a degree, and a second is 1/60 of a minute. The angle of 35 degrees, 22 minutes, and 40 seconds is denoted by 35° 22′ 40″. Degree

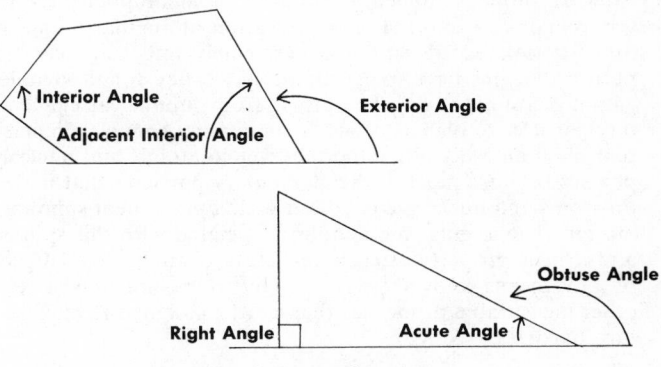

Fig. 3: Types of angles.

measure is commonly employed in practical work, *e.g.* engineering, surveying, and navigation. For some highly specialized purposes angles are measured in mils, a mil being 1/6,400 of a revolution. In theoretical work, especially if it involves calculus, the radian is the most convenient unit. With the vertex of the angle as center and any radius r, we describe an arc cutting both sides. The angle contains just one radian if the length of the arc is r. Since the complete circumference of the circle is $2\pi r$ units long, a complete revolution contains 2π radians. Since there are 360° in a revolution, 1 radian contains $360°/2\pi$, or 57.3° approximately, and 1° contains $2\pi/360$ radians, or approximately 0.01745 radians.

The angle of intersection of two curves—a curvilinear angle—is the plane angle whose sides are the tangents to the curves at the intersection point. (Either one of the two supplementary angles formed by the tangents may usually be used.) The concept of angle is extended to three dimensions through polyhedral angles. Two planes intersect in a line, or edge, and form a dihedral angle. Three adjacent faces of a cube form a trihedral angle. Their common point is the vertex; the line of intersection of any two faces is an edge.—*H. C.*

ÅNGSTRÖM, ANDERS JONAS, 1814–74, Swedish physicist; b. Lögdö. As professor of physics, Uppsala Univ., from 1858, he became one of the founders of spectroscopy. His studies of the solar spectrum led to the discovery (1862) of hydrogen in the Sun. He engaged also in studies of terrestrial magnetism. The Angstrom unit was named for him. He was a fellow of the Royal Society.—*D. H. D. R.*

ANGSTROM UNIT: see MEASUREMENT SYSTEMS (table).

ANGULAR ACCELERATION: See ACCELERATION.

ANGULAR MOMENTUM: a fundamental quantity characterizing the rotational motion of an object (see ROTATION). The angular momentum of a particle about an axis is the product of its linear momentum (mass times velocity) and the component of its distance from the axis perpendicular to the direction of its motion. This is equivalent to the product of the mass of the particle, the square of its distance from the axis, and its angular velocity about that axis. The angular momentum of any collection of particles is the sum of the angular momenta of all particles in the collection. It can be shown to follow from NEWTON'S LAWS OF MOTION that if an externally applied torque acts on a system (torque about a specified axis being the product of a force and the perpendicular distance from the axis to the line along which the force acts), the system's angular momentum changes at a rate that is proportional to the torque. This is analogous to the situation in linear motion, where change in linear momentum is proportional to the applied force. As a special case, if no external torque is applied, the angular momentum of the system remains constant. The conservation of angular momentum for isolated systems is an extremely important law of nature that has been experimentally verified for the whole gamut of rotating systems, ranging from subnuclear elementary particles to planets of our solar system. Angular momentum plays an especially important role in atomic and nuclear physics because most of the elementary particles that make up atoms and nuclei are endowed with a permanent spinning motion. The angular momentum associated with this spin is an intrinsic property of each particle—it cannot be changed by any means known today. In fact, there are only a few other measurable properties that can be assigned to elementary particles.—*S. K.*

ANHYDRIDE (or acid anhydride): any of the chemical compounds, either inorganic or organic, that form acids upon the addition of a molecule of water. As inorganic materials, they are non-metallic oxides such as phosphorus pentoxide and sulfur trioxide, which become phosphoric and sulfuric acid, respectively, when water is added. Organic anhydrides can be derived from CARBOXYLIC ACIDS, either (1) a monocarboxylic acid:

$$CH_3-\overset{O}{\underset{O}{C}}-O-\overset{O}{\underset{O}{C}}-CH_3 + H_2O \rightleftarrows 2CH_3\overset{O}{C}-OH$$

acetic anhydride   water   acetic acid
(one carboxyl group)

or (2) a dicarboxylic acid:

$$\begin{matrix} HC-C \\ \| \quad\quad O \\ HC-C \end{matrix} + H_2O \rightleftarrows \begin{matrix} HC-C-OH \\ \| \\ HC-C-OH \end{matrix}$$

maleic anhydride   water   maleic acid
(two carboxyl groups)   —*D. P. B.*

ANILINE (phenyl amine; aminobenzene): a partially water-soluble, oily liquid ($C_6H_5NH_2$) which is colorless when freshly prepared but on standing in air turns yellow and finally forms a brown resin. Originally obtained from indigo, a vegetable dye, it can be prepared by reduction of nitrobenzene or by amination of chlorobenzene. Aniline is an important industrial chemical; it is used in making synthetic dyes, as an intermediate for manufacturing drugs, perfumes, varnishes, and resins, and in the rubber industry in antioxidants and accelerators. Being toxic, it requires special handling.—*W. P. C.*

ANIMAL: any member of the animal kingdom, as distinguished from the plant kingdom. Animals range in size from 1/12,700 in. (diameter of malaria parasite) to 109 ft (length of the great blue whale, which weighs more than 150 tons). Animals large enough to be seen with the unaided eye usually can be told apart from plants by their ability to move about independently, at least in some stage of their life, and to react rapidly to changes in their environment. Also, unlike plants, animals cannot carry on PHOTOSYNTHESIS; unable to synthesize all the chemical building blocks needed for the manufacture of their own proteins, animals require food containing proteins manufactured by plants or by animals that eat plants. Among microscopic organisms, the distinction between animals and plants is often more difficult to draw. (See also ANIMAL-PLANT DIFFERENCES.)

More than 890,000 kinds (species) of animals have been discovered and given distinctive names. For convenience in identifying so many kinds of animals and in showing relationships between them, they are classified according to their body structure into 28 major groups (phyla), 12 of which (see table) include more than 99% of the animal kingdom as well as most familiar animals. (For a more complete list, see CLASSIFICATION OF LIVING THINGS.) Single-celled animals (phylum PROTOZOA) conduct all their life processes within a single cell. When the cell divides into two, each product of division is a new individual, and the parent cell has disappeared. As a result of these and other features, some biologists consider single-celled animals as a separate subkingdom of animals (subkingdom Protozoa) or group them with single-celled plants in a separate kingdom of life (kingdom Protista).

THE TWELVE PRINCIPAL PHYLA OF ANIMALS

Common Name	Phylum	No. of Species*
Single-celled animals	Protozoa	30,000
Sponges	Porifera	4,500
Jellyfishes, corals, and their relatives	Coelenterata	9,000
Flatworms	Platyhelminthes	9,000
Roundworms	Nematoda	10,500
Wheel animalcules	Rotifera	1,200
Moss animals	Bryozoa	6,000
Mollusks	Mollusca	40,000
Segmented worms	Annelida	6,000
Crustaceans, insects, spiders, and their relatives	Arthropoda	722,000
Echinoderms	Echinodermata	5,500
Chordates, including lancelets, tunicates, lampreys, fishes, amphibians, reptiles, birds, mammals	Chordata	45,000

* Estimates. Figures vary widely, depending on source.

All animals other than protozoans consist of a large number of cooperating cells. Usually only a small number of these cells are concerned with reproduction; the rest of the animal's body dies of old age. Multicellular animals are often grouped as a separate subkingdom (Metazoa). Their cells are arranged in definite layers called tissues, although in SPONGES (phylum Porifera) the tissues are so poorly defined and the structure so primitive that these animals are often regarded as belonging to another distinct subkingdom (Parazoa). In jellyfishes, corals, and related animals (phylum Coelenterata), the body consists of an outer layer of cells separated from an inner layer of cells by a layer of jelly, which is very thick in jellyfishes. The inner layer of cells is associated with a cavity connected to the outside world through the mouth; these cells are concerned with the digestion of food captured by the COELENTERATE animal. Jellyfishes and other members of phylum Coelenterata, as well as most ECHINODERMS, have the mouth located centrally in the body, either above (as in corals and sea lilies) or below (as in jellyfishes and starfishes). The body is symmetrical along various radii extending from the mouth and is said to be radially symmetrical. No right-hand or left-hand side can be distinguished. Animals with radial symmetry are usually ready to escape from danger approaching in any direction.

Most other multicellular animals show a distinct right-hand and left-hand side, being symmetrical in relation to a line drawn through the body from anterior to posterior; they are bilaterally symmetrical. Some single-celled animals, however, are spherical and are said to show universal (or spherical) symmetry, whereas some sponges are asymmetrical, showing no symmetry whatever.

From the flatworms to the chordates, animals of all phyla possess organs and generally show an increasing complexity of structure. Organs and organ systems present in man appear in simpler form in many of the lower animals. Flatworms have a true central nervous system, ROTIFERS a complete digestive tract, segmented WORMS a closed circulatory system with red blood. The ARTHROPODS, distinguished by jointed appendages and an external skeleton, are the most successful phylum, biologically, and INSECTS are the most successful arthropods. About three-fourths of all animal species are insects; more than 660,000 insect species have been identified, and new discoveries are made each year. The CHORDATES, named for their stiff rodlike notochord, represent the most complex group of animals. In this phylum are the familiar VERTEBRATES, supported internally by a vertebral column, or "backbone"; these include lampreys, fishes, amphibians, reptiles, birds, and mammals. All other animals are classed as INVERTEBRATES.

Each kind of animal is especially well fitted for the particular kind of environment in which it lives. Some members of every one of the phyla listed live in the sea; echinoderms, lancelets, and tunicates are found nowhere else. All but a very few kinds of sponges, coelenterates, and moss animals live in the sea; the rest live in fresh water. Many single-celled animals, flatworms, and roundworms live inside other animals, at their expense, as parasites. They show remarkable adaptations that aid them in getting inside new victims. (See ADAPTATIONS IN PLANTS AND ANIMALS; PARASITISM.)—*L. and M. M.*

THE ANIMAL KINGDOM

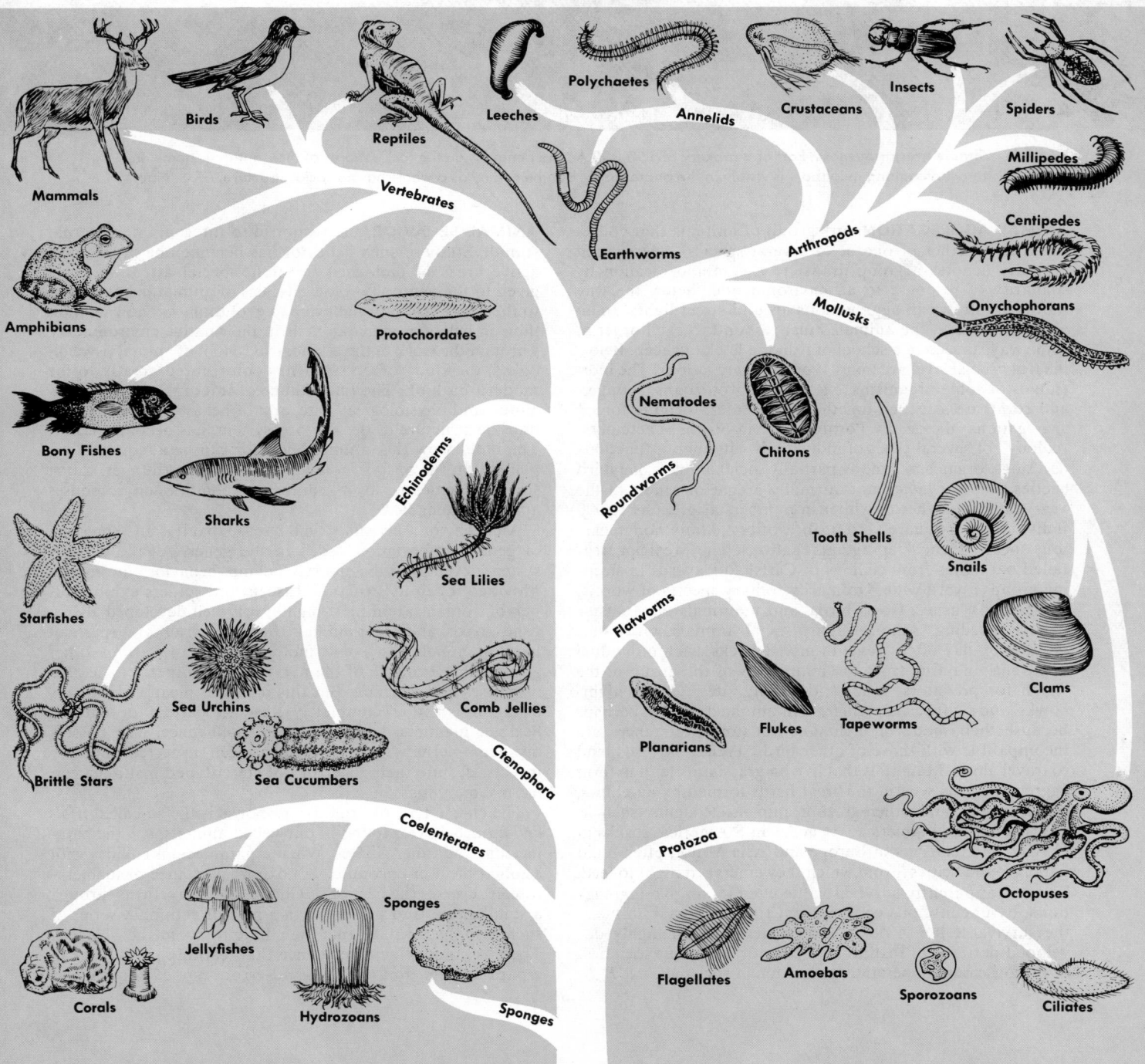

Simple gregariousness: Part of a rookery of 150,000 Adélie penguins on the rocky shores of their antarctic home. Interaction among neighbors is visible in the photograph, but the colony as a whole has no social structure. (*U. S. Navy*)

ANIMAL AGGREGATION: any group of animals that collect together, whether of one or of several species. Aggregation typically denotes a group drawn to a common location by similarity of response to an environmental factor, the way moths are drawn in aggregations around street lights. In an ANIMAL SOCIETY, the animals must respond to each other in some way, as seen in a school of fish or a flock of sheep. Below the truly social level are many types of aggregations. The individuals of some organisms, *e.g.* certain protozoans, sponges, and coral, are attached together in colonies, forming forced aggregations; the deadly Portuguese man-of-war is actually a "colony" of several types of individuals, although it functions as a single organism. Among partially social animals, ladybird beetles (*Coccinellidae*), not normally gregarious most of the year, gather together to winter in numbers as great as 10,000 individuals per square yard of forest floor. Many nongregarious species form sleeping aggregations. The Mexican free-tailed bat hangs from ceilings in Carlsbad Caverns in sleeping groups a yard wide. Ordinarily solitary species of worms, crustaceans, fishes, frogs, birds, and mammals may cluster during breeding. Among highly social animals, birds that migrate by day often travel in mixed flocks, each individual apparently gaining from the many eyes of the group in the watch for predators, food, and resting sites. Geese, nighthawks, and swifts usually migrate in unmixed groups, perhaps because their mode of flight and roosting preferences are incompatible with those of other birds. Predatory birds tend to travel alone. Mammals that live on grasslands tend to form aggregations, as seen in the great herds formed by antelopes, bison, zebras, and other grazing animals. Rodents, such as prairie dogs in N America, viscachas in S America, susliks in N Asia, and hamsters in Europe and Asia Minor, often build underground "cities" from which they emerge at night to feed. There is apparently survival value even in simple aggregations, by unconscious cooperation. In truly social animals, the survival value is obviously greater through highly developed patterns of instinctive behavior, as in ant societies, or by conscious cooperation, as in human societies.—*A. P. E.*

ANIMAL BEHAVIOR: the response to internal and external stimuli. Study of such behavior has become one of the most active areas of biological research, special attention being given to the neurophysiological basis of animal behavior and to the relationship of behavior to evolution (*i.e.* how adaptations in behavior affect animals in their native environment). Through the work of the ethological school of animal psychologists, the study of INSTINCT has contributed greatly to the modern outlook. The importance of internal stimuli, endocrines, and physiological state, and of behavior patterns built into the structure of the nervous system, has become clearer. The older view that animal behavior can be adequately explained on the basis of a few primary drives (hunger, thirst, sex) supplemented by a number of conditioned responses appears untenable.

All behavior is *hereditary* in the sense that it is an expression of genetic information coded in the genes. As the nervous system develops in the embryo, definite behavior patterns are provided for in its structure. Insects and spiders exhibit this nervous organization most highly; it is well developed also in fishes, birds, and other animals. In some vertebrates (particularly mammals), in some mollusks, and in various other groups, the structure of the nervous system permits flexible responses and learning. But this does not mean an animal's behavior is either completely fixed in pattern or entirely flexible: mammals, in addition to intelligence, also possess instincts—perhaps far more than has been suspected; similarly insects, despite their repertory of stereotyped instincts, can learn some things.

The classic type of primitive response is the so-called *trial-and-error* behavior found in one-celled animals, *e.g.* the paramecium and other ciliates. When a paramecium collides with a solid object or encounters a noxious substance or temperature, it reverses the beat of its cilia, backs away, turns through a small angle, and moves off in a new direction. A series of such responses will enable the ciliate to avoid the obstacle. There is no convincing evidence that learning takes place in a paramecium. But the trial-and-error response does occur in a host of different animals, and the successful trial may result in learning. A cat or a man attempting to escape from a confining puzzle box will resort to random trial and error by pulling, pushing, turning, squeezing, lifting, and depressing the door handle until the correct answer is stumbled on and the door opens: this is nothing less than pure empiricism.

Coelenterates, *e.g.* jellyfish and sea anemones, are regarded as having the most primitive type of nervous system, a mere network of nerve cells. The behavior of jellyfish is instructive because it illustrates how the behavior of animals is characteristic of the species and adapted to the type of environment in which the animals live. Jellyfish also illustrate the continual state of activity common in many kinds of creatures. *Cassiopea,* a jellyfish that lives in very shallow water around the Florida keys, spends its time lying on its "back," mouth up, while languid pulsations of its bell-shaped body keep a current of water passing over its tentacles. In this way it catches small fish and other animals. *Aurelia,* commonly studied in laboratories, and *Dactylometra,* the sea nettle, both live in coastal waters up to 30 ft or more in depth and act very differently from *Cassiopea.* These jellyfish swim slowly to the surface of the water, turn over, and then drift to the bottom, catching any small creatures that become ensnared in the tentacles. As soon as the animal hits bottom, muscular contractions begin; these send the jellyfish up to the surface again, and the pattern is repeated over and over. In marked contrast, jellyfish of the open sea (*e.g. Liriope*) never behave in this way, but swim rapidly at a fixed depth. If they allowed themselves to sink to the bottom, which in the open sea may be more than a mile from the surface, they would be in waters with very few living things of a size they could capture.

The kind of prefabricated answers to life's problems that *instincts* provide for their possessors can be profitably studied in the water flea *Daphnia,* the honeybee, and birds. Daphnias, which are small crustaceans living in ponds, instinctively swim to the surface whenever the concentration of carbon dioxide (CO_2) in the water increases appreciably. This is a very useful response, because close to the surface the concentration of CO_2 is low due to diffusion into the air, and the concentration of oxygen is relatively high. In the laboratory it is easy to show that this reaction is really a response to light, the response occurring whenever the water becomes sufficiently acid, which it does in nature when the CO_2 concentration rises. If the water in an aquarium is acidified, then, regardless of the amount of carbon dioxide, daphnias will rush toward a source of light. In a glass-bottomed aquarium illuminated from below, daphnias will swim to the bottom and remain there. As is often the case with instinctive behavior, no single stimulus is sufficient to elicit or release the response. In the example here, the acidity becomes the "releasing" stimulus, and the light the "directing" stimulus.

In their famous "language," honeybees exhibit a remarkable combination of learned and innate responses. When a worker bee returns to the hive ladened with nectar it performs a "waggle dance" on the comb. If the waggle part of the dance is vertical, the source of the food is directly toward the Sun. If the waggle is at an angle of 45° to the left of vertical, the food source is in a direction of 45° to the left of the direction of the Sun. The direction of the waggle in relation to the direction of the food source is not learned in any normal sense of the word, because bees do not have to be taught the correct signals to make on return to the hive. Nor do the bees in the hive have to be taught or have to learn by trial-and-error what these signals mean. But the color of the flowers yielding the nectar is something that bees do learn in the classical sense of conditioning. If a glass dish of sugar water and similar dishes of distilled water are placed on paper squares of different colors, bees quickly learn which color corresponds to sugar water and which to distilled water. Moreover, the color learned is the color seen just before the bee begins to drink the sugar solution. If the color is changed *after* the bee has begun to eat, the bee will return to the original, not the substituted, color; this is similar to what would occur in conditioning a dog.

The discovery of extensive and varied innate behavior patterns in birds has literally revolutionized our attitude toward bird behavior. For example, it is now recognized that hawks, gulls, ducks, and most of the familiar passerine birds will defend a certain area shortly before mating and while mated. This territory-defense behavior appears to be a trait inherited from the lizards, from whom birds descended. The characteristic bird song serves notice to others of the same species that a certain piece of real estate is claimed. This is the message conveyed when one male bird, whether wood thrush or barnyard cock, answers another. To a female the song may indicate a male and a possible mate. The actual song of some species is inherited, as has been demonstrated by rearing the birds by hand in the complete absence of others of the species. Male canaries so raised will sing a typical, although somewhat simple, canary song; for the development of the flourishes, apparently the example of other males is necessary. Female canaries never sing under normal conditions, but they possess the requisite neuromuscular apparatus; female canaries injected with male sex hormone will sing as long as the hormone lasts. (See BIRD CALLS.)

In defending their territories against intruding males of the same species, male birds respond to definite features that are characteristic of their rivals—even when these features are combined in some object only slightly resembling a rival bird. Thus male bluebirds will attack a ball of blue and reddish feathers. When male birds attack their own images in window panes or mirrors, they usually are trying to defend a breeding territory against intruding males. (See TERRITORIALITY.)

Nest building is also under the control of instinctive responses. Captive birds reared out of nests for several generations will construct the proper kind of nest, which they have never seen, when they mature and are provided with the necessary materials. This is not surprising when it is remembered that the nest of the common American robin, for instance, is built of three layers: an outer layer of relatively coarse twigs and rootlets, a middle layer of dried mud, and a lining of uniformly fine grass. The middle mud layer is invisible when the nest is complete. To suppose that baby robins examine and take mental notes on nest construction before flying off is ridiculous.

Dance language of bees: Worker bee performs circular "dance" on hive (*black square in each drawing*). Direction of dance along line dividing circle shows direction of food (*black circle*) relative to sun. Speed of dance indicates distance. (*After Moment*)

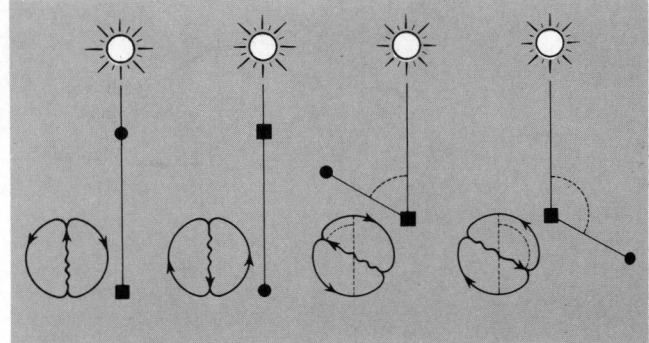

Learning is usually classified into four types, although it is by no means certain that these types are fundamentally different. The first type is *classical conditioning,* first extensively investigated by Pavlov. This has already been described in the case of honeybees and colors. A second type is usually referred to as *instrumental learning.* In this type of learning situation the animal is called upon to perform some act or series of acts more complicated than merely exhibiting some reflex such as salivation. Furthermore, the animal is usually motivated by hunger, thirst, or other strong drive. The animal is put in a Thorndike puzzle box, from which it has to escape to receive a reward, the so-called "reinforcement," or it is placed in a Skinner serve-yourself box, where the animal has to press the correct lever, or press it in the correct way, to receive a reward. It is worth observing that the initial behavior in these cases usually involves a period of trial-and-error random activity. A third type of learning, called *perceptual* or *insight learning,* is a scrap-basket category, but includes some very interesting phenomena. Many actions assigned to it appear to be based on mental trial-and-error and result in a sudden solution without overt random tries. Also included are such cases as the canaries and pigeons that learn to choose from a series of similar objects the one different object which covers a food pellet. For example, in a series of bottle corks and one nail, a canary will peck off the nail to get the food, but in a series of nails and one cork it will peck the cork. This appears to be almost an abstract generalization on the part of the canary. A fourth type of learning, *imprinting,* appears to be a rather special and extremely persistent type which takes place in certain species of birds within a few hours after hatching. Young ducklings normally follow the mother duck, but if they are raised in an incubator and the first large moving object they see is a football, they will henceforth follow a football, not a female duck, if the latter is presented later.

Much behavior in animals, from jellyfish to birds and mammals, falls into one of two general categories: *appetitive behavior* or *consummatory behavior.* Appetitive behavior is a more or less random series of actions, often an apparently aimless wandering, which may nevertheless serve to disseminate the species or bring a hungry animal into contact with food. Many caterpillars must spend a certain amount of energy in walking before they will settle down and spin a cocoon. A hungry hawk will fly in irregular lazy circles. A sexually mature male spider wanders at random until he comes into contact with the web of a female. Appetitive behavior is usually, and perhaps always, due to some motivation, drive, or "need." Consummatory behavior is the act or series of acts that end, or at least interrupt, the generalized appetitive phase and result in satisfaction of the drive. The spinning of the cocoon, the final swoop of the hawk that catches the prey, the

mating of the spider—all are examples of consummatory acts, either stereotyped instincts or complex learned responses.

Specific localized centers for a number of important drives have recently been discovered within the hypothalamus of the vertebrate brain. There are symmetrical groups of cell bodies, one group on either side of the hypothalamus, which control satiety. If the cells in these centers—or nuclei, as neurologists call them—are destroyed, an animal no longer knows when it has had enough to eat; it will eat and eat, becoming incredibly obese. Immediately lateral to each of the satiety centers is a smaller group of nerve cells having to do with appetite. If these cells are destroyed by an electric needle, an animal stops eating permanently. Such animals have to be force-fed to be kept alive. Other centers have been found for thirst, pleasure, and other drives. Centers representing specific consummatory acts have been harder to locate, but a specific part of the brain of the Cecropia caterpillar has been found to be essential for the spinning of a normal cocoon, whereas most parts of the caterpillar's brain can be removed without destroying this behavior. Much remains to be discovered. See also ANIMAL COMMUNICATION; ANIMAL INTELLIGENCE; ANIMAL SOCIETY; MATING AND COURTSHIP BEHAVIOR; MIGRATION.—*G. B. M.*

ANIMAL CAMOUFLAGE: Whenever the color and form of an animal aid it in blending with its customary background, we can recognize helpful adaptations serving as camouflage. Some are as simple as the white fur of a varying hare or of an ermine against winter snow. The spotted fawn is almost invisible in the dappled shade of open woodland. The striped tiger matches the tall grass in which it crouches. A few animals, *e.g.* flounders, actually alter their color pattern in ways that improve the match with surroundings. The illusion that no animal is present is often improved by black or colored markings that distract an enemy's attention from the outline of the body as a whole. The black mask of the raccoon and dark body stripes that extend on the eye itself in wood frogs and painted turtles are familiar features that interrupt the circular boundary of the eye, making it less conspicuous.

Many insects show a protective resemblance to leaves or to inedible objects such as pebbles, bird droppings, leafless twigs, and thorns. The leaf butterfly of India is world-famous for the perfection with which the exposed surfaces of its wings at rest match a dead leaf in outline, color, and markings. Stick insects resemble twigs; adult spittle bugs are often spine-like. So long as these creatures remain stationary they are almost impossible to detect.

Other insects possess adaptations giving them protection from enemies while moving about. They gain safety through resembling unrelated animals that are inedible or armed in

Characteristic webs of four different species of spiders illustrate instinctive behavior. Left to right: *Araneus* connects hideout to hub of web by "telegraph" lines that transmit vibrations caused by entangled insects. *Zygiella* builds hide-out tube as part of web, strings line along corridor. *Argiope's* web has distinctive stabilimentum. *Metepeira* weaves labyrinthian snare.

(After Moment)

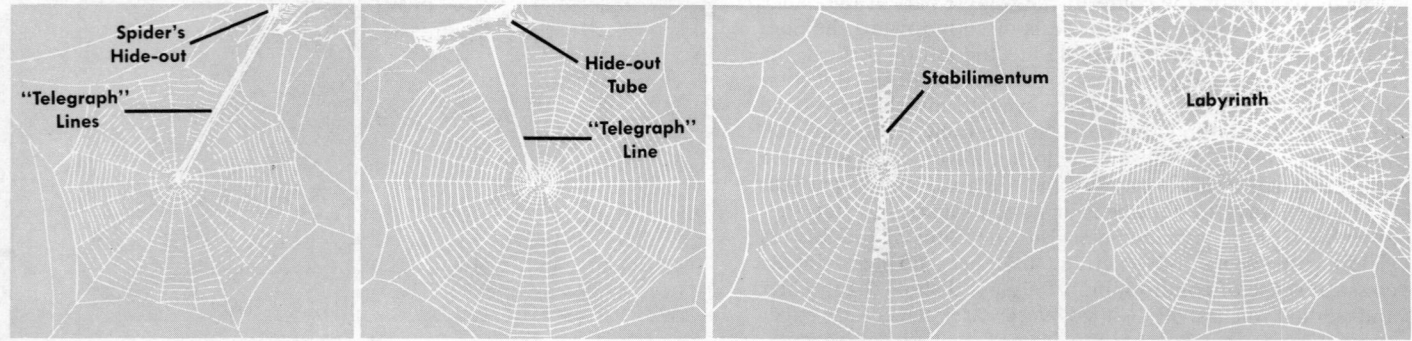

Art of concealment: Feathers pressed close to the body, head stretched skyward, this least bittern may well pass for a stump. Individual control of pupils even conceals eyes. (*Walter Dawn*)

some way: this is mimicry. A harmless dronefly, for example, is so similar in size, shape, color, and manner of movement to a honeybee that it is unlikely to be attacked while visiting flowers where sting-bearing honeybees are common. Mimicking insects resemble also stinging wasps and ants, hard-shelled beetles, biting spiders, and butterflies whose odor and flavor repel most insect-eating animals. Animal camouflage, particularly through protective resemblance and mimicry, is especially well developed in the creatures of the tropical rain forest. It was there that the naturalist-explorer Henry Walter Bates first recognized the import of these adaptations.—*L. and M. M.* (See Color Plates f.p. 70.)

ANIMAL COMMUNICATION: Among social animals information is conveyed in various ways. Contact may be employed, as when one animal pushes another away from a feed trough. Various chemical stimuli produced by an animal may indicate its location and physiological condition; for example, female moths emit an odor that signals their presence to males at distances up to ½ mi. Motor activities and displays convey visual information; such stimuli are important to animals with well-developed vision, *e.g.* birds, some fish, and jumping spiders. Sound is an important type of communication for land-living animals, ranging from the simple mating calls of grasshoppers and amphibians to the complex sounds of human speech. Sound communication is also important to many species of marine fish and some mammals. Bats and porpoises use sound to locate other objects by the process of echo-location. (See ANIMAL SOUNDS; ANIMAL SONAR.)

Most communication is directly related to the social behavior of the species involved, and one of the commonest types of communication concerns agonistic behavior, or responses to conflict. Alarm calls and signals occur widely in the animal kingdom. Thus goats and sheep snort and stamp their feet when alarmed, and catbirds give a loud "meow" at the approach of danger. Cries of pain and extreme fright are uttered by many birds and mammals; rabbits almost never vocalize except under these conditions. Recorded alarm cries of gulls and starlings have been used to repel these birds. (The songs of birds are in most cases territorial cries and serve to

warn away intruders.) Communication also plays a part in actual fighting: bulls bellow, wolves growl, and howling monkeys consistently substitute their calls for actual fights. (See BIRD CALLS; TERRITORIALITY.)

Sexual calls are particularly important to amphibians. The well-known, high-pitched call of the spring peeper, or tree frog, is made by the male and attracts females to him so that mating can take place. Mating behavior of male birds is often preceded by elaborate displays of plumage, of which the peacock shows an extreme example. (See MATING AND COURTSHIP BEHAVIOR.) Many mammals and birds make sounds in connection with the care of young. Sheep "baa" when separated from their lambs, and the clucking of chickens serves to attract the young. The young themselves signal to their parents when in pain and distress: chickens peep and puppies yelp. (See INFANCY.) Animals may also signal regarding the location of food: chickens have various food calls, and wolves howl when they have killed their prey. But the most elaborate system of this sort is the "dance language" of bees. On returning to the hive, foraging bees go through elaborate movements on the honeycomb which indicate the direction and distance where food has been found. A final social function of communication is coordination of behavior: the honking of geese in flight probably serves to keep the flock together and flying in order.

The kind and type of information communicated by animals is usually physiological, as in the state of receptivity of a female, or emotional, as in the danger and distress calls of birds and mammals; the "dance language" of bees is an exception. Most animal communication is involuntary and may evoke instinctive responses. However, in most mammals the responses to communication, as well as its meaning, are to a large extent learned. See also ANIMAL BEHAVIOR; ANIMAL SOCIETY.—*J. P. S.*

ANIMAL FLIGHT: Some animals are able to move through the air in a controlled manner, not merely to fall under the influence of gravity. Many different species make use of this type of locomotion, which is faster than swimming or running. Whether the purpose is to escape from a predator, to seek food over a wide area, or to move from one climate to another, flying animals have an advantage over their competitors.

The simplest form of animal flight is gliding from the branches of a tree to the ground, and there are flying frogs and flying lizards as well as the well-known flying squirrel. All these animals have webs of skin on their feet or bodies, which provide the flat aerodynamic surface needed. Some can control their direction of glide accurately and cover considerable distances. A different sort of glide is practiced by the flying fish, which swims rapidly through the surface of the sea and then uses its large pectoral fins to lift it clear of the waves; in a strong wind it may travel for more than 300 ft before falling again into the water, well clear of anything giving chase.

Gliding flight: Flying fish uses huge pectoral fins only for gliding; power comes from beating tail in water at takeoff. (*Harold E. Edgerton*)

Flapping flight: Extreme backward thrust at drake's takeoff.

Sustained flight: Upstroke ends in reduced backward flick.

Wing structure allows for bending of tip feather in upstroke. (*Joe Van Wormer from Nat. Audubon Soc.*)

Only four groups of animals have progressed beyond this gliding stage to true flapping flight, and one of these, the pterodactyls, has long been extinct. Birds, bats, and insects all fly by means of specially adapted WINGS, and the muscles that move these wings deliver their energy directly to the air, making the animal independent of gravity. The rhythmic cycle of movements in flapping flight comprises a forward and downward stroke with the wing inclined at an angle to its direction of motion, and an upward and backward stroke with the wing twisted so that its leading edge is raised. In the forward flight of birds, bats, and insects most of the propulsive thrust comes from the downstroke. The upstroke is a recovery stroke. In slow flight or hovering, practiced particularly by the hummingbirds and hoverflies, the wing turns completely over on the upstroke, so that this part of the cycle also contributes to the lifting force.

In level flight, geese and ducks can reach about 60 mi/hr, but small birds normally fly at 15 to 30 mi/hr; insects, although they appear to move very rapidly, cannot exceed 30 mi/hr and usually move at only 5 to 10 mi/hr. The most remarkable feature of insect flight is the high frequency of wing beat. More than 1,000 beats/sec have been recorded for a small gnat. Geese have been photographed at 29,000 ft, and the arctic tern is known to migrate 11,000 mi. (See BIRD MIGRATION.)

Full mastery of their environment is achieved by the soaring birds, which have learned to use the energy of moving air and so remain airborne for long periods without effort. Sea gulls use the rising air over cliffs, vultures the thermal up-currents produced by the heating of the ground by the Sun, and albatrosses the gradient of wind velocities near the surface of the sea. This is the ultimate triumph of flight in the bird world.—*J. W. S. P.*

ANIMAL INTELLIGENCE: the ability of animals to adapt to changes in environmental conditions through changes in behavior. In any species, intelligence reflects particular sensory, motor, and central nervous capacities, including the capacity for learning from previous experience, as well as the hereditary organization of these capacities. Thus broadly defined, some degree of intelligence is found in all animals that show behavior. The protozoan *Stentor*, a simple, one-celled animal, reacts to a flood of inedible carmine particles, first by avoiding them, next by blowing them away with its many hairlike cilia, and finally by contracting into its protective tube. If it is stimulated again when it emerges from the tube, it contracts immediately. This demonstrates the simplest process of adaptive or intelligent behavior: trying out a series of behavior patterns and finally choosing one that is successful. More highly organized animals have evolved in the direction of increasing variability of response patterns plus the ability to shorten or eliminate trial and error. (See ANIMAL BEHAVIOR.)

The simplest intellectual capacities are those of association, or conditioning (CONDITIONED RESPONSE). These can be measured by the number of trials it takes until a response is produced by the secondary or conditioned stimulus, plus the number of trials until the conditioned response reaches stability, being given consistently close to 100% of the time. This is essentially a test of simple memory. A maze test, on the other hand, tests complex memory. A rat is confronted with a number of alternate choices arranged in a series, and must remember the whole. Most rats can remember a single alternation pattern, but few can solve double alternation consisting of two right turns followed by two left turns, and so on.

Other tests measure the ability of an animal to discover a general abstract relationship in the arrangement of the environment. The multiple-choice apparatus permits an animal to search for a reward behind many closed doors or by uncovering a variety of objects. In one problem the animal must discover the general principle that the reward is never found consecutively in the same place. H. F. Harlow has used an "oddity test," where the clue to correctly choosing one of several objects is that only one is different from all the rest. The lever-pressing apparatus devised by B. F. Skinner can be set up as a problem in which an animal must discover the general scheme on which the machine pays off, in order to operate it most efficiently. Such tests provide problems to be solved by what is essentially an experimental approach by the animal. In contrast, tests devised by Wolfgang Köhler are such that the animal may solve the problem by insight, without trial and error, presumably by some sort of sensory symbolic process, *e.g.* visualization. Thus a chimpanzee, given two bamboo sticks each too short to reach a banana outside his cage, fits the sticks together and uses them to collect his reward.

In general, the lower animals such as flatworms are capable only of conditioning and may take hundreds of trials to reach stability. Short-lived animals such as insects show quite brief memory spans. In contrast, most of the vertebrates show long-lasting memory and the capacity to solve complex problems consistent with their behavioral capacities, mammals showing more adaptability than any other group. Recent experiments with octopuses show that these highly developed mollusks also are capable of solving many complex problems.

It is difficult to assess the relative intelligence of different animal species apart from differences in sensory and motor capacities, and to devise tests independent of these capacities. Animals are able to solve a variety of complex problems without using verbal symbols. In human beings, the capacity for LANGUAGE has been added to the capacity for nonverbal intelligence, and thus is created the possibility of conflict between the two. The primary function of language is communication of learned material, so that each generation does not have to solve problems anew. Language can also be used for the symbolic solution of problems, permitting a person to go through the process of trial and error in an abstract fashion. Measuring the capacities for symbolic solutions is the chief concern of human intelligence tests. In this recently evolved capacity there are wide individual differences produced by the combined effects of heredity and environment.—*J. P. S.*

Test: Young African elephant is invited to tell dark gray from light gray. Right answer wins apple. (*N. Y. Zoological Soc.*)

ANIMAL LOCOMOTION: Travel in search of food, mates, or places of concealment is customary among most animals. Sponges, corals, burrowing worms, oysters, barnacles, and sea squirts, however, become sedentary at an early age and thereafter live on food particles they can capture from water currents passing them. Single-celled animals move about by extending lobes of protoplasm in a flowing motion (as in amebas), by the traction of whiplash-like FLAGELLA (as in flagellates), or by the rhythmic beating of hairlike CILIA (as in ciliates). Most other animals move about by contraction of MUSCLES. Those of roundworms all run lengthwise, and the animal progresses by writhing movements. The body wall of segmented worms has encircling muscles as well as longitudinal ones, letting the worm advance or retreat in waves of controlled contraction. Further muscles operate bristles in earthworms or paddles in their marine relatives, giving these

worms better traction. Muscles used in locomotion are more efficient when they move fins or legs as levers, particularly if each muscle is attached firmly at its two ends to parts of the skeleton. This arrangement is found in arthropods such as lobsters, insects, and spiders (in which the hard nonliving skeleton forms an external covering), and in vertebrate animals (in which the "backbone," or vertebral column, and other bones provide an internal support of equal importance). See MIGRATION; ANIMAL FLIGHT.—*L. and M. M.*

ANIMAL NAVIGATION: Many animals are able to find their way over long distances, either in homing from unfamiliar territory or migrating to places they may never have visited before (see MIGRATION; BIRD MIGRATION); moreover, experiments performed with individually marked animals have revealed remarkable performances. Manx shearwaters, taken from their nests on a small island off the coast of Wales and transported in closed boxes by airplane, have flown home within days from the eastern part of the Mediterranean and from the Atlantic Coast of America, both of which regions are not normally visited. Young storks from the E German population, brought to W Germany and released there, did not take the route of the western population, which leaves in a southwesterly direction to reach South Africa via Gibraltar, but headed southeast as their parents do to reach the wintering quarters by circuiting the eastern end of the Mediterranean Sea. To navigate as well, man needs good maps, a reliable chronometer running on some standard time, a sextant, and a compass.

Recent investigations have thrown some light on how animals navigate. Birds, fish, and many insects and crustaceans can use the Sun at least to find their direction; during the migratory season even a caged bird tends to direct its activity in the compass direction the species usually migrates, provided the Sun is visible. Insects and crustaceans do not even need a direct view of the Sun; the pattern of polarized light on a patch of blue sky is enough to orient them. Under an overcast sky the animals are disoriented. To head in the right direction regardless of the time of day, animals have to compensate for the changing position of the Sun, which in our latitudes moves from east over south to west. They do so with the help of an internal "clock," which probably all organisms possess (see BIOLOGICAL RHYTHMS). Under natural conditions this clock runs on local time. In an experiment using artificial lighting, however, the "clock" can be reset by shifting the light-dark cycle in which the animals are kept. After such a treatment they will take a predictable "wrong" angle to the Sun, depending on the amount and direction of the reset.

Many animals migrate at night. Experiments have shown that warblers and shrikes can use the pattern of stars to find their way. The birds even have oriented correctly under the artificial sky of a planetarium. There is evidence that birds can use the Sun and stars not only as a compass to find direction, but also as an aid in performing true bicoordinate navigation, thereby determining their position relative to home, regardless of where they are. Here the birds have to compensate for daily movements of the celestial bodies and for the seasonal changes as well. For this they must be equipped not only with a very precise internal clock, but with the equivalent of a calendar and a sort of nautical almanac. However, bicoordinate celestial navigation has not yet been proved unequivocally, and its mechanism is still poorly understood.

Another type of navigation is used by salmon. After they have spent most of their life in the ocean, these fish return to their home river and migrate upstream to the very creek in which they were hatched years ago. Although they probably use some kind of celestial navigation in the ocean, experiments have shown that they find their home stream by remembering its odor and following this, however diluted it may be, as they retrace their course from ocean to river mouth to tributary to brook. If their nasal openings are plugged experimentally, they fail to orient and will distribute at random in the tributaries.

Although progress has been made in understanding the navigational faculties of some animals, in other instances virtually nothing is known. Many bats migrate regularly, some over hundreds of miles of open ocean, but no one knows how these animals navigate.—*K. Ho.*

ANIMAL PHYSIOLOGY: the science of normal living body functions in animals and in man. In contrast, *pathology* deals with malfunctions. Sometimes each makes use of the other in preparing its definitions; thus pathologists may show that a misfunctioning tissue is "diseased" by contrasting it with normal tissue. Physiology uses the techniques and principles of many other sciences in acquiring its own "body of knowledge." Statistics, in particular, has given physiology great impetus by helping to establish what is meant by "normal." The collection, tabulation, and analysis of vast quantities of data on functions in living organisms have provided knowledge of how a living body "works" and of the range of normal operation for each body part. Chemistry, engineering, physics, and mathematics also have contributed greatly to the understanding of body functions. To illustrate, consider the physiology of the hinge-like movement of an elbow. For this "hinge" to move, muscle contraction is required (fluid dynamics-engineering). An understanding of muscle movement requires a knowledge of enzymes (chemistry). Calculation of the optimal mechanical advantage requires knowledge of the bones that form this joint and their unique relation to each other (engineering). Also of interest are the tensions and compressions on various parts of the arm and the work limits within which the arm can move (physics). To discover how fast nutrients and oxygen can be delivered to muscles, thus making movement possible, the physiologist must calculate and derive equations (mathematics) for the blood flow into and out of the arm per unit of time. Study of such relationships clarifies the physiology of arm movement.

During the past century animal physiology gained from two concepts: *milieu intérieur* (proposed in 1878 by Claude Bernard) and *homeostasis* (proposed in 1929 by Walter B. Cannon). The concept of *milieu intérieur* (interior environment) points out that each internal part of the body is surrounded by its own environment and that this environment is perhaps as important to the proper normal function of the part as is the integrity of the part itself. Thus a muscle cannot be normal (cannot act physiologically) unless the blood that supplies it with food and oxygen is normal. The concept of homeostasis notes that every normally functioning body part is like a balance: when a part gets "out of balance," a mechanism in the body works to drive it back to normalcy. Thus, if a person topples, he rights himself; if a finger is cut, the body forms a healing scar; if one eats an unpalatable material, the body removes it. Similarly, all body parts that are "put out of sorts" are assisted back to normal by homeostatic mechanisms.

Plant cell: Electron micrograph (X8,200) shows section through cell from woody stem of locust tree. Dense cell wall, of cellulose and lignin, gives mechanical support. Conspicuous within the cell are the nucleus, the largest area; the mitochondria, which carry enzymes involved in respiration; the plastids (probably chloroplasts); and the vacuole, containing cell sap (water and reserve protein). (*Myron C. Ledbetter, Harvard Univ. Biol. Lab.*)

Important functions studied by physiologists include CIRCULATION, DIGESTION, EXCRETION, motion (see ANIMAL LOCOMOTION), RESPIRATION, REPRODUCTION, secretion (see GLAND), and sensitivity (see IRRITABILITY; NERVOUS SYSTEM). —*A. D.*

ANIMAL-PLANT DIFFERENCES: Animals characteristically possess muscles and a complex nervous system, whereas plants lack a neuromuscular system. But animals do not have the complex synthetic chemical machinery found in most plants. Except for many fungi, plants possess enzyme systems that enable them to manufacture carbohydrates, amino acids, vitamins, and other complex substances directly from simple organic molecules such as water, carbon dioxide, and mineral salts (see PHOTOSYNTHESIS). Plant and animal cells also differ. In plant cells the cell wall is virtually always present and composed of a carbohydrate derivative, cellulose. Some fungi are exceptions in that they secrete a polysaccharide, chitin, as a cell wall. The walls of animal cells, when present at all, are usually of chitin. But some animals secrete true cellulose, as in the case of the sea squirts (tunicates or ascidians), which are chordates closely related to the vertebrates. (See CELL.)

The major cleavage of the living world into animals and plants is now believed to have taken place very early in the history of life on this planet and to have been based on nutritional differences accentuated under the forced draft of NATURAL SELECTION. According to the most widely accepted theory of the origin of life (see LIFE, ORIGIN OF), the first living things were heterotrophs, *i.e.* dependent on outside sources for complex organic food molecules. There is good evidence that when life first appeared, complex food molecules were present in the primordial oceans. When these molecules began to become scarce, as more and more became incorporated into the protoplasm of living things, a nutritional crisis arose. As the famine increased, organisms bearing MUTATIONS of two very different kinds presumably were favored by natural selection. Any organism that possessed a mutation enabling it to get along with fewer kinds of complex molecules in its diet would have had an important advantage over those requiring the full complement. For example, if a given organism required substances A, B, C, D, and E, whereas a second could get along without E, the second organism would have had an advantage. A third organism that possessed an enzyme system allowing it to manufacture both D and E out of A, B, and C would have had a still greater advantage. Obviously such a line of selection leads to organisms with more and more complex enzyme systems able to subsist on simpler and simpler raw materials. In other words, this line of evolution leads to the plants.

The other possible line of selection, when the nutritional crisis stage was reached in the evolution of life, would have favored organisms that could move and that were able to

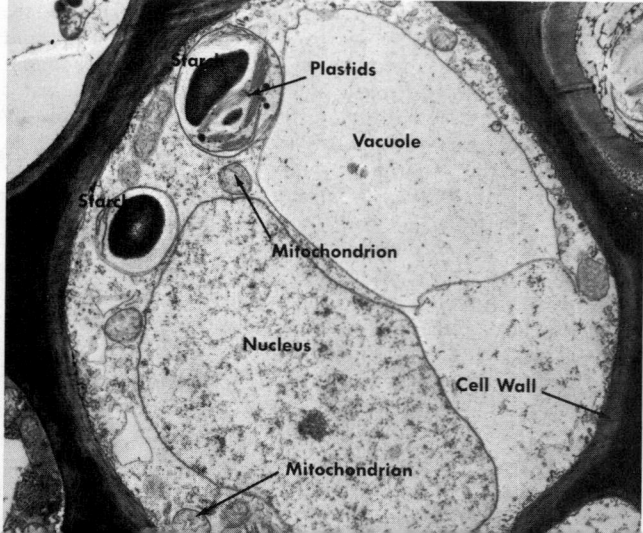

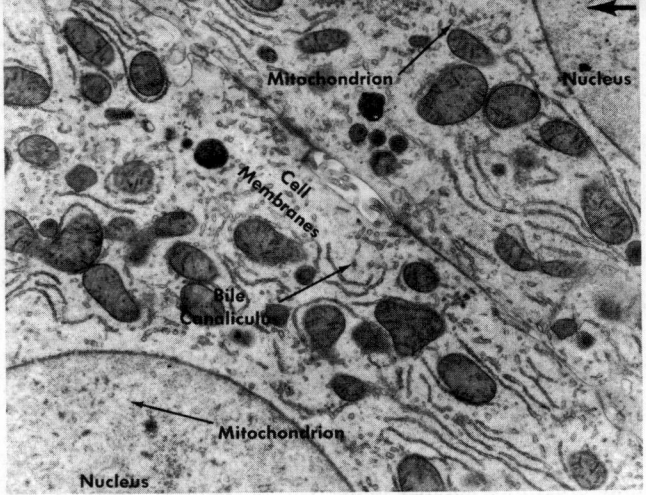

Animal cell: Electron micrograph (X8,200) of section showing part of two cells from liver of a rat. Animal cells have no vacuoles or chloroplasts, are separated only by thin membranes—here seen cutting micrograph diagonally, leaving a clearance for a minute bile canal. Material can pass from nucleus into surrounding cytoplasm through pore (*heavy arrow*). (*Keith Porter, Harvard Univ. Biol. Lab.*)

ingest other organisms. Even random movement would have tended to bring an organism into contact with more complex molecules. In a second stage, any mutation making it possible for an organism not only to move about but also to engulf other organisms would have conferred a selective advantage. This line of selection clearly leads to the animals. Thus the early populations of heterotrophs would have been pushed by the forces of mutation and natural selection in two divergent paths—into animals and plants.

But on both the cellular level and the biochemical level of energy liberation, animals and plants are basically alike. Chromosomes and chromosome behavior, and hence the laws of heredity, are the same. The major events of the sexual cycle, of meiosis, (*i.e.* reduction in the number of chromosomes from a double to a single set), and fertilization are essentially the same in animals and plants. Electron microscope studies reveal that the structure of the tail of the sperm of a mammal or of a fern is the same; so also is the structure of cilia, whether from protozoans or mollusks. The basic pathways of energy release in the glycolytic breakdown of glucose (see GLYCOLYSIS), the CITRIC ACID CYCLE, and the nucleotide and cytochrome transport system for hydrogen to free oxygen with the ultimate production of water are also basically the same. In both plants and animals energy is "packaged" in ATP (adenosine triphosphate) molecules. It used to be said that plants breathe in carbon dioxide and breathe out oxygen, whereas animals do the reverse. But only plants that possess chlorophyll or some other photosynthetic pigment take in carbon dioxide and give off oxygen, and they do this only in the light. At other times green plants respire as do animals (see RESPIRATION).—*G. B. M.*

ANIMAL SOCIETY: any group of animals that show some degree of mutual stimulation in behavior. Members of the group usually belong to the same species. The degree of social organization may vary from extremely simple to highly complex interactions within the group. Social organization depends on the social behavior of the species, which in turn depends on its hereditary capacities, including learning. Social behavior is organized into social relationships, defined as regular and consistent behavior between two individuals. Depending on the type of social behavior involved, such relationships result in DOMINANCE-SUBMISSION, mutual care, leader-follower relationships, etc. Relationships are also developed according to the biological types of individuals concerned. Thus in a society of howler monkeys relationships are developed between males, females, and young, in all possible combinations; however, such animals recognize individuals and develop specific

Social insects: Individuals in ant colonies work for benefit of whole community. Here, ants store pupa cases from which new adults will emerge. (*Lynwood Chace/Nat. Audubon Soc.*)

relationships with each member of the group. Successful study of an animal society thus depends on the investigator's ability to identify individual animals.

Animal societies may be divided into four types. In the lower invertebrates, social organization is usually restricted to *temporary aggregations* produced by shelter-seeking and sexual behavior (see ANIMAL AGGREGATION). Such are the aggregations of paramecia in reaction to the drying of a drop of water, and the mating swarms of marine annelid worms. Similar temporary social groups are found in many higher animals: the aggregations of water isopods in a swift current, and the mating swarms of mayflies. Temporary aggregations are probably the precursors of more permanent and complex societies.

The highly developed *insect societies* are based on caregiving behavior, involving both care of the young and mutual care such as is seen in the reciprocal feeding of ants (trophallaxis). Organization is based on division of labor between different biological types or castes. In termites there may be winged and wingless reproductive castes and two types of soldiers, as well as workers. Organization of insect societies is largely determined by heredity and other biological processes, so that the insect society may legitimately be called a supra-organism. All the complex insect societies are found in two orders: the Isoptera, or termites, and the Hymenoptera, including the ants, bees, and wasps. The most highly developed of these societies is that of the honeybee. This species maintains a continuing group year after year, integrated through a complex system of communication ("the dance language") and through a chemical compound ("queen substance") shared in the hive. The worker bees show a division of labor between age groups. As in many insects, the female or queen mates only at one brief period in her lifetime, so that sexual behavior is a rare and relatively unimportant part of social organization.

Vertebrate societies have only three kinds of individuals: males, females, and young, and they may or may not emphasize care-giving behavior. Many vertebrate societies are characterized by mutual imitation, or allelomimetic behavior, as in schools of fish, flocks of birds, and herds of mammals. Among many fish, *e.g.* common sunfish, the males build nests, guarding them as territories, and some species protect the young for a time after hatching. Birds have evolved many different types of societies. In song birds, *e.g.* blackbirds and

song sparrows, the breeding range is divided into territories, each with a resident pair. After the young are raised, both they and adults join migrating flocks, which are the social group for the rest of the year. Thus their social organization is highly seasonal in nature. Ducks and geese follow somewhat similar patterns, but often have more highly organized flocks, in which certain animals may be leaders.

Being less mobile, mammalian societies show somewhat fewer seasonal changes than birds. Prairie dogs (a variety of ground squirrel) have one of the most complex rodent societies. A colony is subdivided into territories, which include burrows and the surrounding land above ground. Here the young are reared, and the following year the adults move out to establish new territories on the edge of the colony. Thus the young are left with a cultural heritage in the form of the old burrows, and the experienced animals inhabit the area most exposed to danger from predators. Herd mammals such as deer and the domestic sheep and goats have societies that emphasize the mother-young relationship, which in sheep develops into a strong system of leadership. But not all mammals are highly social. Some, like house mice, may live in large populations, but show a low degree of social organization. Others, like woodchucks and weasels, are almost solitary except during the necessary processes of reproduction. Primate societies characteristically include adult males, females, and young, in long-lasting groups, but there is little indication that these groups are divided into distinct nuclear families, as in human societies. Finally, *human societies* are characterized by the development of language and communication, so that cultural heredity is developed to a higher degree than in any other sort of society.—*J. P. S.*

ANIMAL SONAR: a method of sound navigation used by a number of animals, comparable to man's military and industrial SONAR, and somewhat similar to RADAR (which depends upon radio waves rather than sound waves). BATS pursue and catch small insects one at a time, as they dodge through the night sky, by listening to the echoes from the insect's body as it reflects the sound of high-pitched chirps uttered in rapid succession by the bat. The chirps are all in the ultrasonic range, chiefly between 40,000 and 150,000 vibrations/sec, and hence inaudible to man's ears. The higher the vibration rate of a sound, the shorter is its wavelength, and the smaller an object can be while reflecting a good clear echo. Animal sonar (also called echo-location) also enables the bat to dodge small branches and even fine wires strung across its path. Cave swiftlets of the Far East and oilbirds of N South America use echo-location in finding their nest sites in dark caves. Porpoises, other toothed whales, seals, and sea lions use sonar in the ocean when pursuing prey, fishes and squids, and possibly also as a means of avoiding underwater obstacles and finding other members of their kind.—*L. and M. M.*

ANIMAL SOUNDS: Animals make noises incidental to various activities such as eating, drinking, and walking over dry leaves, but also they deliberately produce certain sounds that are useful in communication (see ANIMAL COMMUNICATION). Many crustaceans in the sea and insects on land stridulate by rubbing one hard body surface against another; they emit vibrations chiefly in the range of frequencies audible to our ears (30 to about 15,000/sec). Fishes produce sounds by rapid contraction of muscles attached to the air bladder (which acts as a resonator) or by rubbing their fins against their sides.

Usually we limit our use of the word "voice" to land animals that, as Aristotle pointed out, have "tongue and lung." Air passing over vocal cords in the LARYNX of amphibians, some reptiles, and mammals sets them vibrating and produces a call. Birds rely upon a syrinx located low in the neck, where the windpipe (trachea) divides to go to the two lungs. Muscles attached to the syrinx produce complex vibrations we hear as bird songs and chirps (see BIRD CALLS). The calls of bats, porpoises and whales, and many smaller mammals (*e.g.* mice and rats) are mostly too high-pitched for us to hear. They range from 40,000 to at least 150,000 vib/sec and are valuable to these animals both in communication and in echo-location. (See ANIMAL SONAR.)

Human speech and some animal calls are highly modified by movements in throat and lips. We make many sounds, in fact, for which no vibrations of the vocal cords are needed. Some African languages, in particular, include clicking sounds produced with the tongue and the glottis, as well as hissing and breathing sounds under careful control. Most of the energy in ordinary human speech is in frequencies below 1,000 vib/sec, much of it close to "middle C" (256) on the piano. Soprano voices seldom rise above 1,152 or bass voices drop below 83 vib/sec, whereas the lowest note on a bass viol is about 40 and the highest on a piccolo about 4,600. Strangely enough, our hearing is most sensitive around 2,000 vib/sec—higher than any human shriek for help. Yet we do not hear the special high-pitched whistles to which a dog can be trained to respond. (See SOUND.)—*L. and M. M.*

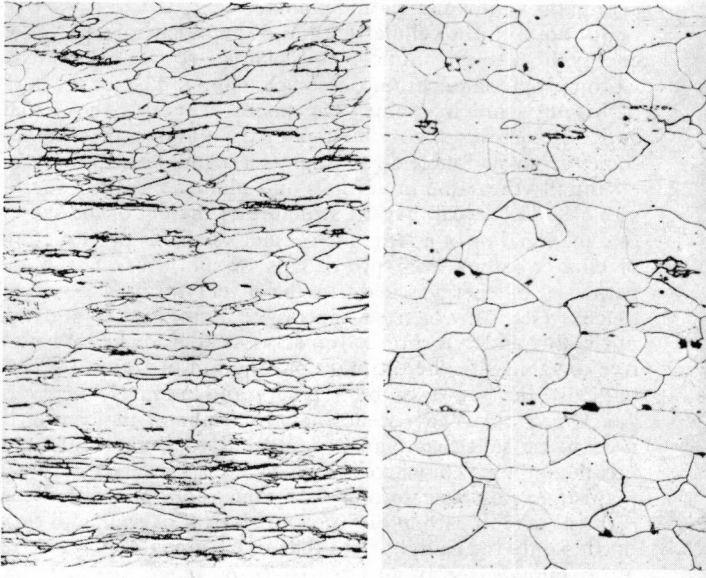

Stress relief: Photos (X100) show that more nearly round grains (*right*) have resulted from the annealing of the hot-rolled iron alloy at left. (*Research Center, Allegheny Ludlum Steel Corp.*)

ANNEALING: heat treatment of material, such as metal or glass, to remove strains resulting from previous operations and thus render it less brittle and tougher. The process commonly comprises holding a material at a predetermined temperature for a predetermined time, then cooling it at a rate and to a temperature that will produce the desired properties.—*R. W.*

ANNIHILATION OF MATTER: a violent disintegration that occurs when one of the sub-atomic elementary particles of matter collides with its ANTIPARTICLE. When isolated, an antiparticle is identical in all respects with the ordinary elementary particle to which it corresponds, except that it has an opposite electrical charge. But when the two collide they annihilate each other, producing electromagnetic radiation and, in the case of the heavier particles, other, more esoteric types of particles. The energy released in such annihilations is given by the famous Einstein formula $E = mc^2$.—*S. K.*

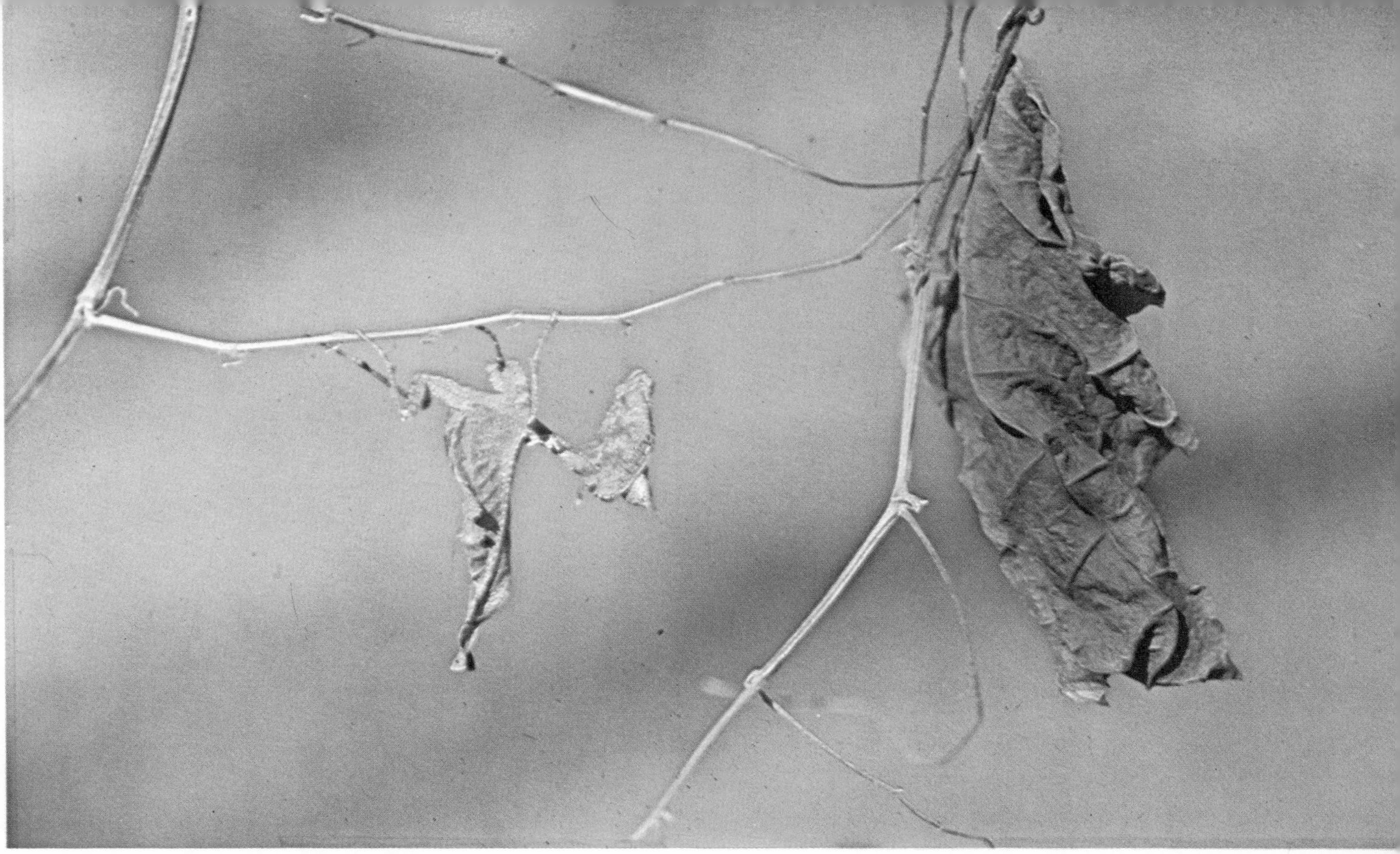

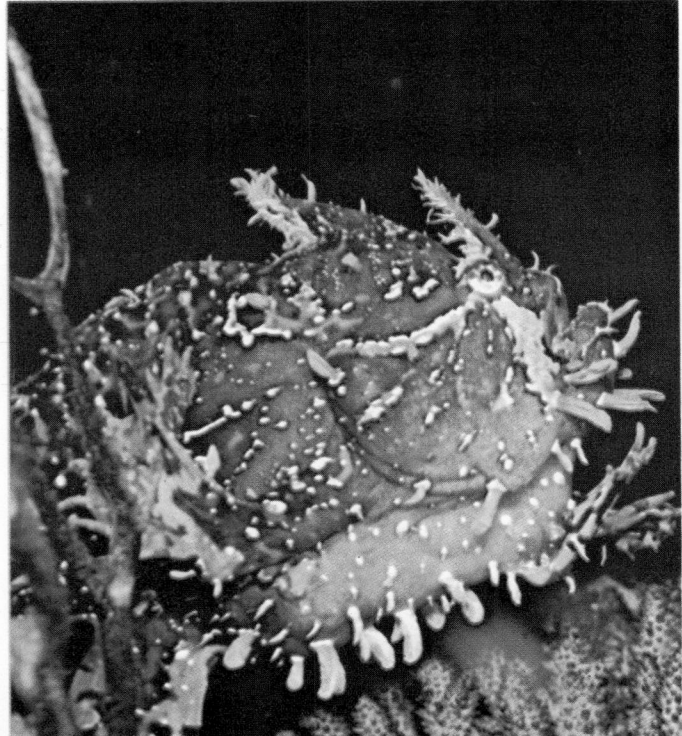

1

Plate 6   ANIMAL CAMOUFLAGE

Animals that remain motionless, either to escape a nearby predator or to wait for prey to come within reach, avoid detection more easily if they resemble their surroundings. Adaptations that camouflage an animal are many and varied.

1. Praying mantises of the tropics are often leaflike both in coloration and in shape. While swaying gently and looking about for insects to snatch and eat, a mantis blends so perfectly with its surroundings that human eyes have difficulty detecting it. *(Russ Kinne)* **2. The sargassum fish** *(Histrio)* swims slowly among sar-gasso weeds in search of food, effectively camouflaged by its white-dotted, brownish body as well as by fins with irregular margins that resemble the weeds. *(Walter Dawn)* **3. The varying hare** *(Lepus americanus)*, often called the snowshoe rabbit because of its big feet and rabbitlike form, is snow-white (except for black ear tips) in winter and matches its background. By the time the snow melts, the hare's color changes to red-brown above, light brown on the legs, and white below—still resembling its environment. *(Herbert Lanks/Shostal)*

2

3

Plate 7 AQUATIC ANIMALS

Aquatic animals include many inconspicuous invertebrates whose ancestors have always been aquatic, and a small number of larger animals whose ancestors re-invaded the seas and swamps. Some of the latter are shown on this page.

African crocodile (*Crocodylus niloticus*) can knock a person down with a blow of its heavy tail. It drags victims under water and drowns them. *(Alouise Boker/Amer. Mus. of Nat. Hist.)*

An old walrus (*Odobenus rosmarsu*) of arctic coasts may weigh a ton if a female, 3,000 lb if a male. Walruses use their strong tusks to grub shellfish from the bottom. Nails on the toes of front and rear flippers show that the ancestors of walruses were land animals which ran on legs, as most other mammals of the order Carnivora do today. *(Raymond E. Shaw/Shostal)*

Penguins are flightless birds of the Southern Hemisphere that swim under water, with their stiff flipperlike wings, in pursuit of fish and squid. *(Amer. Mus. of Nat. Hist.)*

Iguana lizards that live on islands off the west coast of S America are adept at swimming in the sea, where they feed on seaweeds. *(Robert C. Murphy/Amer. Mus. of Nat. Hist.)*

Plate 8 AQUATIC PLANTS

An abundance of water and light, together with access to the carbon dioxide in the atmosphere, provides green plants with the most important raw materials for growth. The combination is readily available to plants of swamp, pond, and ocean shore.

Bald cypress (*Taxodium distichum*) and cabbage palm (*Sabal palmetto*) fringe the Lettuce Lake (*left*) in the Corkscrew Swamp Sanctuary in Florida. Rosettes of water-lettuce leaves (*Pistia stratiotes*) float on the surface like a green carpet. (*Russ Kinne*)

Fragrant blossoms of water lily rise above floating lily pads. Both grow from horizontal stems embedded in muddy bottom. (*Josef Muench*)

Marine algae of many forms carry on photosynthesis in shallow water. Some are pale green, others darker. (*Bruce Hunter/Amer. Mus. of Nat. Hist.*)

Plate 9 ARACHNIDS

Spiders, scorpions, ticks, and mites are familiar arachnids. All walk on four pairs of legs, not on three pairs as do insects. They suck juices from their prey but have no real jaws. **1. A crab spider** (*Misumena*) sucks from a fly's body the once-solid contents that were liquefied by venom injected into the fly by the spider. (*Ken Middleham/Shostal*) **2.** Waiting for an insect to blunder into the sticky web, **the orb-weaver spider** (*Argiope*) hangs head downward, its eight legs clinging to the radial strands. (*Robert Holland/Shostal*)

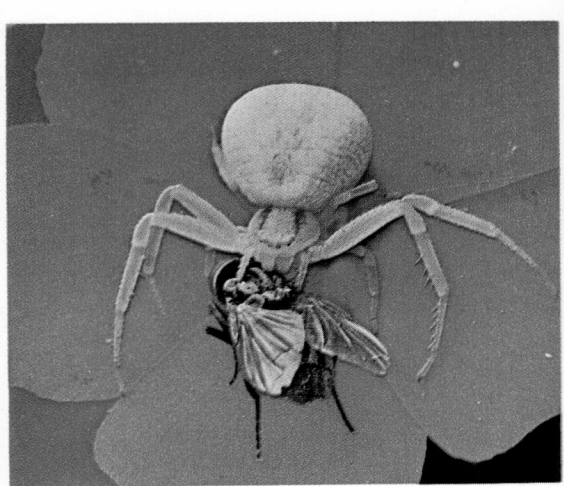

1

2

1

Plate 10   ARCHITECTURE

Climate, the character of the site, the availability of materials, social and economic forces, practical and aesthetic considerations —all these factors have had an influence on architecture, the art and science of building. The result has been a diversity of styles, varying from country to country and age to age, as exemplified in such structures as the ziggurats of Sumer, the tombs of Egypt, the temples of Greece, the cathedrals and palaces of Europe, and the towering skyscrapers of the U.S.A.

1. The temple of Athena Nike, on the Acropolis in Athens, reflects a technology of building with stone based on earlier timber construction. Made of Pentelic marble, it was erected circa 426 B.C. *(Pierre M. Martinot)* **2. The cathedral at Salisbury, England,** also was built of stone; construction was begun in 1220. *(The British Travel Association)* **3. Modern adaptation** of various stylistic elements, typical of much civic architecture in the U.S.A., is shown in the group of structures on Foley Square in New York City. Left to right are the New York County Courthouse, the U.S. District Courthouse, and the New York City Municipal Building. *(Dick Hanley/Photo Researchers)*

2

3

4

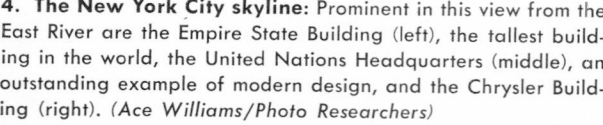

4. The New York City skyline: Prominent in this view from the East River are the Empire State Building (left), the tallest building in the world, the United Nations Headquarters (middle), an outstanding example of modern design, and the Chrysler Building (right). *(Ace Williams/Photo Researchers)*

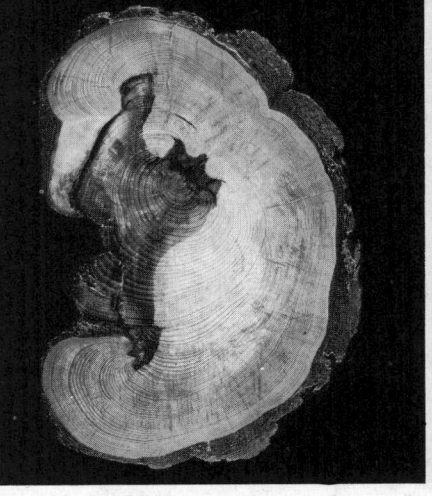

Rings of old-field loblolly pine tell of early crowded growing conditions and of open growth later.

Fire scars (experts detect nine) show in rings of 108-yr-old ponderosa pine.

Eccentric growth reveals red spruce was leaning in early years. (*Amer. Mus. of Nat. Hist.*)

ANNUAL: any plant that completes its life history during one growth year. The plant grows from seed, matures, produces seed, and dies before the end of the year. Familiar annuals include zinnia, marigold, corn, and pea. By preventing an annual from flowering, it may sometimes be induced to continue its growth for a second season. A plant that completes its life cycle in 2 yr is a BIENNIAL; one that continues to grow from year to year is a PERENNIAL.—*A. P. E.*

ANNUAL RINGS: the concentric layers of newly formed wood cells that represent the amount of a tree's growth during a growing season. In temperate countries growth occurs most rapidly in spring, when cells with large cavities are formed. As growth continues during early summer, cells with smaller and smaller cavities are formed. After a few weeks, growth ceases altogether until the following spring. The contrast between the cells formed in spring and the very compact tissue formed later makes a visible ring in the cross section of a trunk or stem. The width of the ring reflects the climatic conditions of the season in which it was formed. A wide ring indicates a year with sufficient water and sunlight, and a thinner ring a year of less favorable growth factors. In many countries, rings represent alternating wet and dry seasons instead of winter and summer; hence they are not truly "annual," but are more properly known as growth rings. All the wood laid down during one season, from one ring to the next, is often called a growth band. These bands give wood its grain. Growth rings in the giant redwoods and in trees in the Southwest have been used to reconstruct the climate of the distant past. The dating of past events by counting and analyzing growth rings is known as *dendrochronology*. This dating method, which can reach about 3,000 yr into the past, has proved particularly useful in dating American Indian ruins containing tree remains with readable rings.—*A. P. E.*

ANNUITY: any set of periodic payments, *e.g.* monthly mortgage payments, payments made on an installment buying contract, premiums paid on a life insurance policy, or retirement benefits received under social security. An "annuity certain" is one in which the number of payments is fixed, *e.g.* in an installment buying contract. A "contingent annuity" is one in which the number of payments is unknown and depends on some contingency, *e.g.* the premiums paid on a life insurance policy, because the number of premiums a person will pay depends on how long the person lives.

The periodic payment, called the *rent,* is usually invested, or assumed to be invested, at compound interest. The amount of money that is accumulated at the end of a fixed period of time from the payments and the interest earned on them is called the *sum* of the annuity. The amount of money that would have to be invested at compound interest so that all payments could be made from this account is called the *present value* of the annuity. The relationships between the rent, the sum, and the present value enable one to solve the practical problems that involve annuities. The periodic payments are often all equal, and the frequency with which the interest is compounded is the same as the frequency of the periodic payments. Under these conditions, the sum S and present value A of an annuity certain can be computed from the relations

$$S = R \cdot \frac{(1+i)^n - 1}{i} \qquad A = R \cdot \frac{1 - (1+i)^{-n}}{i}$$

where i is the interest rate per interest period, n the number of interest periods, and R the rent. The fractions

$$\frac{(1+i)^n - 1}{i} \quad \text{and} \quad \frac{1 - (1+i)^{-n}}{i}$$

are frequently denoted by the symbols $s_{\overline{n}|i}$ and $a_{\overline{n}|i}$. Since these fractions arise in all annuity problems, their values are computed and listed in tables for all practical values of i and n. The computation of S or A is thus merely a matter of looking up a number in the proper table and multiplying by R.

Mortgages, small loans, and installment buying contracts frequently provide that the principal and interest shall be repaid in equal periodic payments. Here the amount loaned, $A,$ is known, and it is necessary to determine the periodic payment, R. Such a problem is called an *amortization* problem. Another type is the *sinking fund* problem, in which the amount S is known, and it is necessary to find R. This problem arises when a fixed sum of money is invested periodically to pay off an indebtedness due in the future, *e.g.* the maturity value of a bond.

The value of a contingent annuity depends on the rate of interest and on the probability that the periodic payment will be made. Contingent annuities are commonly studied in conjunction with the mathematics of insurance.—*H. E. W.*

ANODIZING: production of a protective, corrosion-resistant oxide coating on a base metal, usually aluminum, by electrochemical means. The aluminum object to be coated is made the anode in an aqueous electrolyte containing sulfuric, chromic, or oxalic acid, depending on the process. As current passes through the cell, the oxide coating forms and becomes progressively thicker, usually being built to between 0.0001 and 0.001 in. This initially porous film can be "sealed" to render it denser by prolonged treatment with hot water; or it can be impregnated with various finishing materials such as dyes, oils, or corrosion inhibitors. By altering electrolyte, current density, and temperature, thinner non-porous coatings of high electrical resistance can be formed.—*A. M. S.*

ANOMALOUS SOUND PROPAGATION: the refraction of sound waves back to earth at a distance of about 100 mi from their origin. Fig. 1 shows the typical "zone of silence" which lies between the region in which the sound (*e.g.* from a large explosion) is heard *directly* and the region in which it is heard as a *sky wave*. This skip is caused by the bending of sound waves downward from the warm ozonosphere some 25 mi up (Fig. 2).—*D. H. L.*

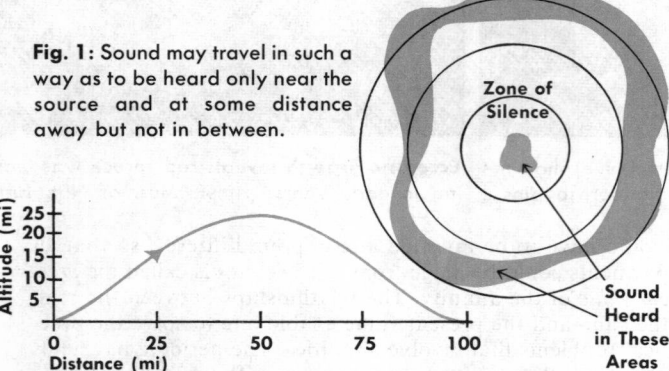

Fig. 1: Sound may travel in such a way as to be heard only near the source and at some distance away but not in between.

Zone of Silence

Sound Heard in These Areas

Altitude (mi)

25
20
15
10
5

0   25   50   75   100
Distance (mi)

Fig. 2: Skip is caused by the sound wave's being bent back toward the ground by a layer of warm air at a high altitude.

ANTENNA (radio and electronics): a mechanism for converting electrical energy into electromagnetic radiation, and vice versa; commonly, a structure designed to transmit and receive radio waves. At the transmitting station, the output signal in the form of an a-c current is sent to an antenna, from which it radiates into space in the form of electromagnetic radiation, *i.e.* radio waves which travel at the speed of light. At the receiver, the radio waves strike another antenna, which collects some of their energy as feeble electric currents. The construction of antennas depends largely on the frequency (wavelength) of the radio waves and also on the conflicting demands of antenna efficiency and directivity on the one hand and size, weight, and expense on the other. The majority of antennas, whose IMPEDANCES vary with frequency because of reflections or standing waves, are classed as *resonant* or *periodic*. The extensively used dipole or doublet consists of a straight conductor interrupted at the point where it is excited. Others are the folded-dipole, loop, turnstile, dielectric-rod, slot, and the resonant long-wire rhombic and vee antennas. Non-resonant, or aperiodic, antennas exhibit nearly constant impedance over a wide frequency range because of suppression of reflections. Examples are the terminated long-wire Beverage, echelon, rhombic, vee, horn, and helix antennas. Coupled antennas, called *arrays,* are used to achieve directivity; *i.e.* they radiate or receive more effectively in one direction than another. Directivity or gain is also obtained by use of parasitic elements called reflectors and directors, as in the Yagi antenna. The polarization of an antenna is the orientation of its electric field vector, which is often the same as that of the driven linear element.—*D. J. B.*

ANTENNAE: threadlike or feather-shaped organs found in insects and other ARTHROPODS. Antennae can have the dual functions of touch (they are covered with sensitive bristles) and chemical or odor sense (they have olfactory organs).—*L. and M. M.*

ANTHRACENE: a white, crystalline hydrocarbon obtained from coal tar. It fluoresces in varying colors depending on its state of purity. It is like naphthalene in structure, except that it has three fused rings instead of two. At one time it was an important intermediate in making dyes.—*Ru. M.*

ANTIBIOTICS: substances of natural origin having antibacterial properties. They have been derived from bacteria, molds, fungi, algae, and a number of substances including soy beans and garlic. Numerous antibiotics have been found, but most are toxic to man as well as to BACTERIA. In 1877 Louis Pasteur first observed a reduction in infectivity of anthrax bacillus in the presence of another bacterium. In 1929 Alexander Fleming observed the destruction of some bacteria in a culture by an accidental mold contamination. Fleming studied this mold, called *Penicillium notatum,* and discovered that it produced a substance which suppressed the growth of many bacterial organisms. Fleming called it penicillin. Selman Waksman discovered streptomycin, produced by *Streptomyces griseus,* in a like manner. Of the many antibiotics that have microbial specificity and low toxicity for man, only four groups have good therapeutic attributes. These are penicillins, streptomycins, tetracyclines, and chloramphenicol. They differ in structure and pharmacological action, each being more useful in certain infections than the others. Thus, different infections or diseases are treated with the antibiotic that will kill or inhibit the causative organism. The search for new antibiotics is a continuous process. Infectious organisms often develop forms resistant to a specific antibiotic, and hence newer antibiotics must be found.—*C. G.*

Symmetrical colony of mold: This is *Penicillium chrysogenum,* a mutant form of which produces most commercial penicillin. (Pfizer)

ANTIBODIES: proteins that develop in body fluids as a result of the introduction of "antigens," either foreign proteins or complex polysaccharides. Antibodies can combine specifically with the antigens that caused them to form; *e.g.* if a rabbit is injected with egg albumin at frequent intervals, its blood serum will become able to form a precipitate with minute amounts of egg albumin but not other proteins. Antibodies are mostly gamma-globulins, consisting of different combinations of polypeptide chains, which are synthesized under different genetic guidelines and are held together by disulfide bonds. These chains are: light (L) (molecular weight about 25,000) and heavy (H) (molecular weight about 50,000). H chains may really be two polypeptide chains instead of one. The antibody molecule has two sites at which antigens can become attached. Electron-microscope studies indicate that these are at the ends of the cylindrical antibody molecule.

There are two main theories of antibody formation. The *instructive theory* suggests that the antigen acts as template or as mutagen in a common cell capable of producing antibodies. Modified globulins are synthesized and the cell preserves a memory. According to the *selective theory,* either an extensive collection of inducible repressed genes is believed to exist in a common cell, or monospecific clones of mesenchymal cells are assumed to be individually induced to multiply and produce a specific antibody. See IMMUNIZATION.—*F. F.*

ANTICYCLONE (HIGH): in the atmosphere, a large-scale system of air rotating clockwise (in the northern hemisphere) or counterclockwise (in the southern hemisphere) around a center of relatively high pressure. Highs occur at all times of the year and are especially in evidence in winter over large continents (*e.g.* the great Siberian winter high). The weather of an anticyclone is quiet, with mainly clear skies in summer but with much low unbroken cloud and often fog in winter. See also WEATHER SYSTEMS.—*O. G. S.*

ANTIFREEZE: a substance which, when added to a liquid (commonly water), produces a solution with both a lower freezing point and an altered freezing process. When this solution is subjected to temperatures equal to or less than its freezing point, crystals of solvent (*e.g.* water-ice) form and a more concentrated liquid solution results. This "slushing process" proceeds until the remaining solution has a freezing point lower than the ambient temperature. Common antifreezes used in cooling systems of internal-combustion engines are methanol, ethanol, and ethylene glycol. For use in metallic or metal-containing systems, rust inhibitors must be added to the antifreeze solution. Typical inhibitors are borates, nitrates, thiazoles, and phosphates. Antifoam agents, *e.g.* silicones and organic phosphates, may also be added. Antifreezes are generally classified as to their volatility, the less expensive volatile substances (as methanol) being less efficient than the non-volatile (permanent) substances (as ethylene glycol). Included under the term "antifreeze" are snow-melting and de-icing agents, refrigeration brines, aqueous hydraulic fluids, and heat-transfer fluids.—*R. W.*

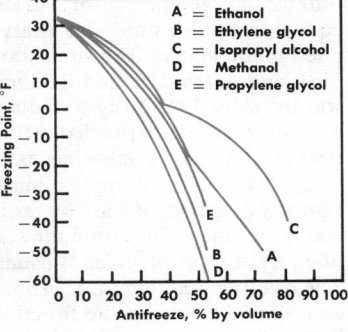

A = Ethanol
B = Ethylene glycol
C = Isopropyl alcohol
D = Methanol
E = Propylene glycol

Effectiveness of antifreezes: Graph shows relation of concentration of antifreeze base materials to freezing point of solution containing them. (*U. S. Bureau of Standards*)

ANTIGRAVITY: a force of mutual repulsion supposed to exist between two bodies; it is similar in nature to GRAVITATION, but opposite in effect. Antigravity would act between a body of positive mass and one of negative mass, driving them apart. Negative masses are possible theoretically, but there is as yet no evidence of them—*R. M.*

ANTIMETABOLITE: in biochemistry, a substance structurally related to a metabolite that inhibits utilization of the metabolite by blocking its normal enzymic reactions (see METABOLISM). Antibiotics function as antimetabolites for organisms like bacteria and fungi, inhibiting growth. Antimetabolites may inhibit metabolism of synthesized and ingested metabolites and help in study of metabolic pathways.—*E. G.*

ANTIMONY: a metalloid element (Sb) of the nitrogen family (group Va of the periodic table); at. no. 51, at. wt 121.76, density 6.68, melting point 630°C. Antimony metal is obtained by heating iron with the principal ore of antimony, *stibnite* (Sb_2S_3). It is brittle, silver-gray, expands on freezing (the rare phenomenon exhibited most familiarly by water), and is principally used in the manufacture of alloys. Because it expands on solidifying, antimony alloy is particularly useful in making good castings: the expanding alloy fills even the smallest crevices of the mold. Most available antimony comes from China; a common use in the U. S. A. is in lead-alloy plates of storage batteries. Its hardness also makes it suitable for type metal and metal bearings. Antimony metal reacts with nitric acid to form antimony pentoxide, but on reaction of aqua regia and antimony, the antimony hexachloride anion, $SbCl_6^-$, is formed. Antimony trioxide is formed by heating antimony metal in air at about 900°C. Because the trioxide is amphoteric, it dissolves in concentrated acids and bases. Antimony ion, Sb^{+++}, hydrolyzes readily to SbO^+, the antimonyl ion. Potassium antimonyl tartrate is used in medicine under the name of tartar emetic. Potassium antimonate, $KSb(OH)_6$, is very soluble in water, but the sodium salt is the least soluble of all sodium salts.—*G. W. M.*

ANTIOXIDANT: any of the substances used in rubber, surface coatings, food, and many other commercial products to prevent spoilage and corrosion due to atmospheric oxygen. The reaction with atmospheric oxygen molecules is self-propagated by a mechanism involving free radicals (see CHEMICAL BOND), which yield organic peroxides that in turn create free radicals. This chain reaction can be stopped for relatively long periods by small amounts of an antioxidant, but eventually any such inhibitor is used up and the free-radical reaction proceeds once more. Antioxidants may consist of aromatic amines and phenols, as well as many other types of compounds. Amines are employed in gasolines, and cresols (phenol-class compounds) in lubricating oils. In dried fruits, *e.g.* apricots, sulfur dioxide is used as an antioxidant; in meats and candies, ascorbic acid is used. See FOOD ADDITIVES.—*Ru. M.*

ANTIPARTICLES (or antimatter): According to fundamental laws of nature, as presently understood, each type of elementary PARTICLE of matter has a counterpart, called its antiparticle. A charged particle and its antiparticle have the same mass and share other properties, but they have opposite electrical charges. If brought sufficiently close together, they annihilate each other. When an electron and its antiparticle (called a positron) destroy each other, their combined mass is converted into electromagnetic radiation. The total energy carried off by the radiation is numerically equal to the annihilated mass multiplied by the square of the velocity of light, in accordance with Einstein's famous equation $E = mc^2$. When a proton and an antiproton annihilate each other, various subnuclear particles are produced in addition to radiation. The inverse reaction also occurs; namely, if a sufficient amount of energy can be concentrated in a small enough region of space, a particle and an anti-particle can be spontaneously created—the energy being converted into mass.

The existence of antiparticles was first suspected in 1928 when P. A. M. Dirac developed a theoretical description of the electron that was consistent with both quantum mechanics and the theory of relativity. Consideration of the full implications of the theory led him to postulate the existence of an antielectron. The prediction could not be verified immediately because—in our galaxy, at least—there is such a preponderance of ordinary matter that there can be no free antiparticles; any that might exist would be rapidly annihilated. However, high-energy cosmic-ray particles striking Earth's atmosphere have sufficient energy to produce all particle-antiparticle pairs. In 1932, C. D. Anderson discovered a positron so produced. Since then, nuclear physicists have constructed many PARTICLE ACCELERATORS that can impart enough energy to subatomic particles to enable them to produce positrons. A few accelerators can produce antiprotons and antineutrons, both first discovered in 1956. An intriguing problem in astrophysics is to determine whether any galaxies are constructed of antimatter—matter consisting of atoms constructed like ordinary atoms, but with antiparticles instead of particles.—*S. K.*

APHELION AND PERIHELION: the points in the elliptical orbit of a planet or comet at which the body is farthest from and closest to the Sun, respectively. The distances of the body from the Sun at these points (the apsides of the orbit) are the *aphelion* and *perihelion distances*; the ratio of the differences between these two distances to their sum defines the *eccentricity of the orbit, e.* For a circle, $e = 0$; for a parabola (the limiting ellipse of greatest possible eccentricity), $e = 1$. The parabola is, in fact, an open curve, with a definite perihelion distance but an infinite aphelion distance. Some comets have orbits that appear to be parabolas.—*M. W. O.*

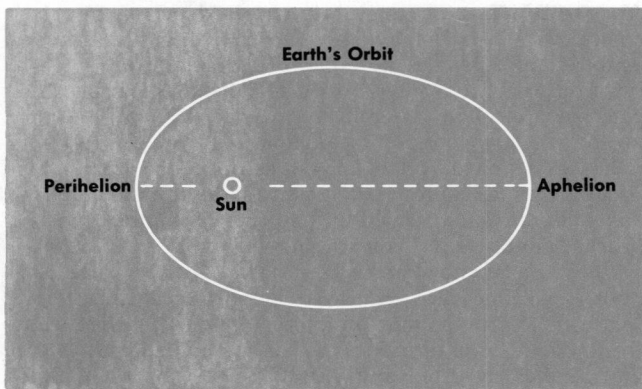

Aphelion and perihelion: These points in Earth's orbit farthest from and closest to the Sun are also called the apsides of Earth's orbit (whose eccentricity is much exaggerated here).

APIANUS, PETRUS (Peter Apian, Bienewitz, or Bennewitz), 1495–1552, German astronomer, cosmographer, and cartographer; b. Leisnig. He is said to have been the first to substitute mechanical operations (by means of plates and volvelles) for astronomical calculations, and the first to suggest the determination of longitude by lunar distances, while his contemporary Gemma Frisius was proposing the use of a chronometer. His principal works are *Cosmographicus Liber* (1524), containing some of the earliest known maps of America, and *Astronomicum Caesareum* (1540), illustrated with revolving planispheres and containing observations of the comet of 1531, later known as Halley's comet. His son **Philipp (Philippus) Apianus** (1531–89) was a distinguished mathematician.—*R. N. M.*

APOGEE AND PERIGEE: the points in the elliptical orbit of a celestial body about Earth at which the body is farthest from and nearest to the center of Earth, respectively. The flattening of Earth at its poles causes the perigee of a satellite orbit to move slowly round the orbit, and from observations of this motion (for artificial satellites) the flattening of Earth can be estimated.—*M. W. O.*

APOLLONIUS OF PERGA, *c.* 225 B. C., Greek geometer of the Alexandrian school. He carried geometry far beyond the state in which it was left by Euclid. He is principally known for a treatise on conic sections. As a pure geometer he was unequaled until the time of Jakob Steiner in the 19th cent.—*H. C.*

APPERT, NICOLAS FRANÇOIS, 1750–1841, French confectioner and inventor; b. Châlons-sur-Marne. He invented the method of preserving food by enclosing it in carefully stoppered bottles and then immersing it in boiling water for some time. In 1804 his food-bottling factory in Paris was set up. His *Art of Preserving Animal and Vegetable Substances for*

Several Years appeared in 1810. In 1815 he began using tinplate containers.—*R. J. F.*

APPLETON, EDWARD VICTOR, 1892–1965, English physicist; b. Bradford. Known for his studies of the ionosphere, he investigated the *Kennelly-Heaviside (E) Layer* and the higher *Appleton (F) Layer,* and showed that the amount of ionization in each depends on time of day, season of the year, and sunspot activity, and that it can be forecast. Since radio waves can be "bounced" off these layers, ionospheric forecasting is important for radio propagation studies. Winner of the 1947 Nobel prize, he was a fellow of the Royal Society.—*D. H. D. R.*

APPLIED MATHEMATICS: generally, those branches of mathematics created primarily to solve problems of the physical sciences, engineering, and, to some extent, the social sciences. Elementary ALGEBRA can be regarded as a branch of applied mathematics because the typical problem of elementary algebra, which is the solving of an equation to find the value or values of an unknown, is one which arises in scientific work. Plane GEOMETRY gives us information about lengths, areas, and volumes of figures used in science and engineering, and so is likewise a branch of applied mathematics. TRIGONOMETRY was created to calculate the sizes and distances of heavenly bodies. The CALCULUS was created and is still very much used to study problems of motion with variable speed and acceleration. Ordinary and partial differential equations, differential geometry, the calculus of variations, integral equations, and numerical analysis are also branches of applied mathematics. The subject of statistics, created to handle birth and death data and the incidence of diseases and crime, was developed seriously to reduce errors in astronomical data and was further expanded within the last century to solve problems of the social sciences.

Of all branches of applied mathematics, those treating DIFFERENTIAL EQUATIONS are by far the most important. The reason is that the information the scientist can obtain by analysis of a physical problem leads usually to a differential equation. The ensuing mathematical problem is to solve the differential equation; *i.e.* to find the function or functions which satisfy it. The basic laws of mechanics, hydrodynamics, electromagnetic theory, and atomic physics are most effectively formulated as differential equations, and the solutions of these equations give us information about the respective phenomena.

By contrast, the study of rigorous axiomatic foundations of the number system and of Euclidean geometry is generally considered pure mathematics. Such investigations are intended primarily to meet the objective of deducing the theorems of these branches from a minimum number of axioms. The developments are of interest to the pure mathematician, but hardly to the applied mathematician, because the theorems obtained ultimately from these investigations are the well-known properties of numbers and geometrical figures. For application it is the properties of numbers and figures that matter, and not so much what minimal axiomatic bases might yield these properties. Likewise, though functions are used enormously in applied mathematics, pure mathematicians would be interested in studying all kinds of functions, including some kinds that may never be used in science. In the field of differential equations the pure mathematician might investigate conditions under which these equations have a solution and, indeed, a unique solution. However, for purposes of application, the methods of finding the solutions are more important.

The interests of the pure mathematician differ further from those of the applied mathematician in that the former will often investigate themes already proved to be significant in application, but carry his investigations far beyond the immediate needs of science. He is satisfied to know that the theme is an important one, and trusts that further knowledge may also prove helpful. The pure mathematician also investigates subjects which have esthetic appeal. The most notable branch of mathematics developed for this reason is the theory of numbers, *i.e.* the study of the properties of whole numbers. The applied mathematician might well appreciate esthetic values, but he would be more concerned with mathematical concepts and methods that enable him to formulate and solve physical problems.

Another distinction between pure and applied mathematics lies in what is often called "rigor." The pure mathematician insists on precise definitions and strict proof in which each step is justified by an axiom or a previously established theorem. The applied mathematician is more concerned about getting an answer. He might be willing to accept as a justification for an argument a statement which is intuitively or physically very plausible, but not necessarily a theorem of mathematics. For example, the pure mathematician before solving a differential equation would assure himself by sound arguments that the equation has a solution, and only then proceed to find it. The applied mathematician, knowing the physical situation from which the equation arose, would be satisfied that a solution does exist, merely on the ground that physical problems must have answers, and he would proceed at once to find the solution. That the applied mathematician may sometimes be in error in presuming that there is a solution can be illustrated even in a simple problem of solving two simultaneous algebraic equations. The equations

$$x + y = 5$$
$$2x + 2y = 11$$

do not have a (common) solution. If, not knowing this, one should proceed to solve by the standard method, one would multiply the first equation by 2 and subtract the resulting equation from the second of the above two equations. One would then arrive at the conclusion that $1 = 0$. In the present case the fact that the two given equations do not have a common solution is almost obvious at the outset; even if this were not recognized, the apparent absurdity of the answer would show the mathematician that there was something wrong. However, the applied mathematician may, by assuming the existence of a solution, obtain an answer which is not patently absurd but actually erroneous. With respect to rigor, the applied mathematician works very much like a physicist. If the answers he obtains seem physically reasonable and if the use of his results in some construction, for example, leads to a mechanism or a structure which serves its purpose, he is satisfied with the mathematics he has produced.

Historically, practically all branches of mathematics arose from physical problems. Hence, one might say that in this respect at least almost all of mathematics is applied mathematics. However, as already indicated, not only does the mathematician often carry a theme, which first arose in applications, far beyond the needs of science, but the mathematician working on a mathematical difficulty may not personally care about the application. He may be excited by the challenge which the mathematical problem itself presents. Though he may be pleased to know that his results can be used by a scientist, and though the problem may have been set in the first place by a scientist who has come to the mathematician for help, the mathematician in this case is working as a pure mathematician. Such a mathematician may even be quite ignorant in the field of science and begin his work after the physical problem has been formulated for him in proper mathematical terms by someone else. Thus, the distinction

between pure and applied mathematics is not necessarily one of subject matter, but of the motivation of the mathematician working on the problem.

The distinction between pure and applied mathematics is not recognized by a number of mathematicians and, in fact, is of recent origin. They would assert that mathematics has always been concerned primarily with the investigation of the physical world, and since the language and theorems of mathematics are indispensable in science and are indeed the essence of many scientific theories, mathematics is a science in the same sense as physics, chemistry, biology, and so forth. They would grant the mathematicians' prerogative of pushing investigations beyond the immediate needs of science, because often such investigations prove to have new applications quite different from those which motivated the creation of the subject in the first place, but they would not defend the value of any branch of mathematics which did not have direct or indirect bearing on the study of the physical world or on some social science. This point of view does not ignore the search for esthetic satisfaction, but expects to derive this value from the development of themes significant for the sciences. However, many mathematicians today insist on pursuing concepts and axioms of their own creation which have no bearing on the physical world. This tendency in mathematics has been very noticeable in recent times.

Since science is expanding rapidly, the problems and ideas for research thrown into the laps of mathematicians have also expanded very rapidly. Hence the bearing of mathematics on science, whether or not the distinction between pure and applied mathematics is made, has become increasingly important. The high place of mathematics in our curricula and the increasing regard for and demand for the subject stem almost entirely from the values of mathematics in scientific investigations.—*M. Kl.*

APPLIED SCIENCE: The close cooperation between scientific research and technology and engineering is fairly recent. In antiquity the scientist, though sometimes using the craftsman's observations and experience, rarely deigned to apply his speculations to the harnessing of nature for the benefit of mankind. His "natural philosophy" left craftsmen groping and stumbling to improve their techniques, tools, and products. The practical engineers and architects of the later Roman Empire, likewise lacking scientific help, wrote in vain that thorough training in science was indispensable; the lack

Applied chemistry: This apparatus is used to separate and test organic chemicals in a program of medical research. (*Pfizer*)

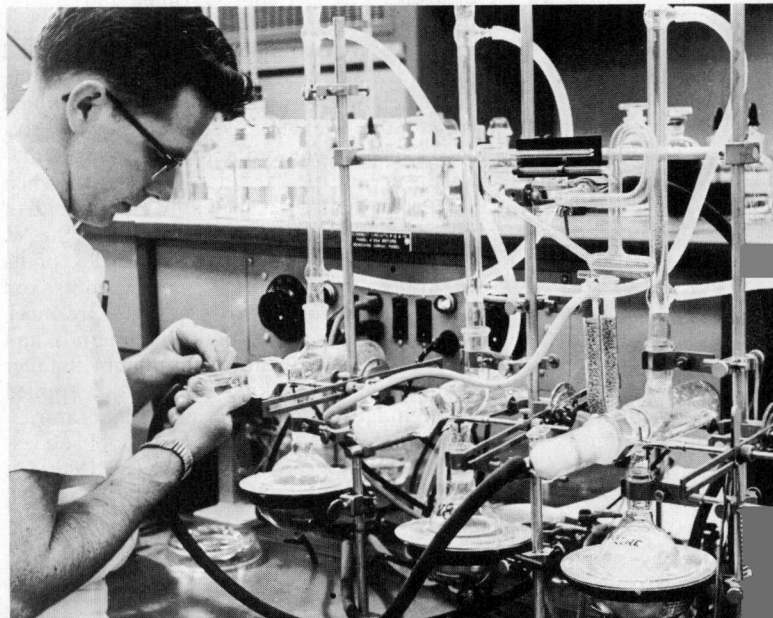

of such training encouraged the jealous guarding of both "trade secrets" and the hard-won lessons of experience. During the Middle Ages, master craftsmen clamored for help from the scientists without much result. The lofty Gothic churches were the result of daring and experience rather than of careful calculations based on the strength of materials and applied mechanics. Many such buildings collapsed during heavy storms or foundered because of insufficient foundations. Only gradually did master craftsmen like Leonardo da Vinci (1452–1519) and Simon Stevin (1548–1620) emerge, mastering scientific principles and applying them to construction of engines, windmills, waterwheels, dikes, and canals.

The invention of printing (c. 1450) started a stream of practical handbooks on metallurgy, mining, and other skills, which attracted the attention of several prominent scientists. Sir Francis Bacon, among others, perceived that "the mechanical arts give better insight into the secret places of nature. In mechanical operations the attention is concentrated, and the modes and processes of nature, not merely their effects, are seen." New learned societies, *e.g.* the Royal Society of London and the Académie des Sciences (Paris), studied practical problems like the drainage of mines and the design of better artillery, and advised their governments on industrial patents. They also started "histories of trades": proper descriptions of the various arts and crafts of the day. But the scientists were not yet able to cooperate effectively; they were still in the beginnings of controlled experimentation and the formulation of basic natural laws with the aid of recently developed mathematical methods. During the 18th cent. the laws of physics and mechanics began to be elaborated with the help of proper mathematical tools and scientific instruments, and the properties of common engineering materials were investigated. Certain sciences, including chemistry, lingered behind; not until about 1800 were basic chemical principles clearly formulated. However, the interest of government officials, bankers, and merchants led to scientific education of engineers in the French École des Ponts et Chaussées, the École Polytechnique, and similar schools. In Great Britain the traditional practical training as an assistant to famous engineers lingered on. But the 19th cent. saw the rise of professional training in practically every country and also the foundation of institutions such as the Royal Institution (London), Conservatoire des Arts et Métiers (Paris), and the Franklin Institute (Philadelphia) to promote research in science and technology.

Effective industrial research began about 1840 in certain university laboratories in France and Germany (*e.g.* von Liebig's application of chemistry to agriculture at Giessen) and in the laboratories of the rising German and British industries. The German government, quick to perceive the effects of this applied research, founded its Reichsanstalt and its Materialprüfungsamt shortly after 1870. At the turn of the century Great Britain followed suit and founded the National Physical Laboratory; this was followed by Washington's Bureau of Standards and by renewed activity and reorientation at the Paris Conservatoire. "The days were past, when an engineer could acquit himself respectably by the aid of mother wit alone or of his constructive instincts" (Sir W. Anderson, 1893). Modern industry spends up to 8% of its gross income on applying the latest scientific tools and methods to the improvement of its processes and products, the constant and systematic search for new materials and products, and the unraveling of technical problems. Smaller firms and the community as a whole profit from applied research by private foundations and government laboratories. From 1776 to 1954, research cost the American people no less than $40 billion, half of which was spent between 1948 and 1954. This indicates the acceleration of spending on applied

(and pure) research by both industry and government. A number of private concerns have specialized in applied research. Generally speaking, science and technology are now so interlocked that we can hardly imagine that such cooperation is only a century old.

Modern applied scientific research, it should be pointed out, is a matter of teamwork; the individual inventor, so prominent in the 19th cent., plays but a minor part. Equipment has become too costly, and specialization in every branch of science has turned practically every research problem into a cooperative effort of specialists in very different fields. For example, fundamental research in organic chemistry may reveal the basic mechanism of certain reactions and suggest how such reactions could give a high yield of a valuable chemical or turn a waste product into a useful one. This type of research takes place in industry or university laboratories. But the task of "translating" laboratory results into mass production requires many more experiments by teams of experts to establish the proper materials, equipment, control instruments, and routine procedures. See also SCIENCE; SCIENTIFIC RESEARCH; SCIENTIFIC RESEARCH CENTERS.—*R. J. F.*

APPROXIMATION: The role of approximation in science and mathematics is a major one. All measurements are approximate; even counting is at times approximate, as in census enumeration. Precision instruments are only more or less precise, and a human error in their use must always be expected. It is important to distinguish between precise and accurate measurements. Precise measurements of a quantity differ very slightly from some value which may not be the true value of the quantity; accurate measurements are precise, but differ only slightly from the true value. The target shown in Fig. 1 is the result of precise shooting; the one in Fig. 2 is the result of accurate shooting. There are therefore two kinds of errors in scientific measurements: errors in precision, which are minimized by taking averages; and errors in accuracy, which may often be compensated for by allowing for systematic deviations in the instruments, and for personal errors made by the observers.

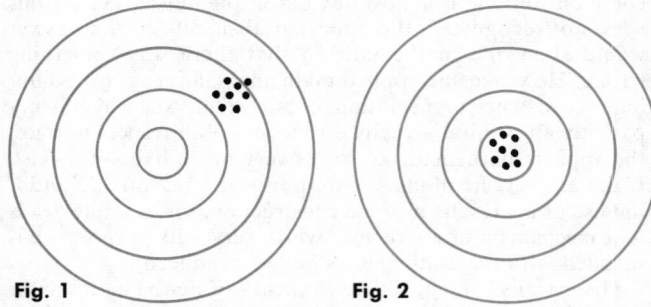

Fig. 1   **Fig. 2**

Precision and accuracy: When shooting is "precise," bullet holes are close together but off the center of target (Fig. 1). When shooting is "accurate," they are close together and dead center (Fig. 2).

An important aspect of measuring and calculating with measured quantities is the estimation of possible total error. It is sometimes possible to set bounds on the error and to express a result showing the range within which it must lie. If a weight is found to be 82 gm, with a maximum error of 0.2 gm, it would be written 82 ± 0.2 gm (the sign $\pm$ meaning "plus or minus"). When not specified otherwise, the accuracy of an approximate number is indicated by the significant digits, which are all the digits except zeros at either end. The specification of a distance as 532,000 mi is equivalent to expressing it as $532,000 \pm 500$ mi. The absolute error in approximate results is less important than the relative error, which is the ratio of the error to the correct value. In practice, since we do not know the correct value, we usually consider an acceptable approximation to the maximum relative error to be the ratio of the maximum error to the measurement found. Thus, for the weight of 82 ± 0.2 gm, the maximum relative error would be taken as $0.2/82 = 0.002$.

Many operations cannot be carried out to give accurate results. Approximations must be accepted, and it is important to have methods for obtaining them to any desired degree of accuracy. Horner's method and Newton's method (see EQUATIONS, THEORY OF) serve this purpose in solving numerical equations. Definite integrals are approximated by several methods, SIMPSON'S RULE being the best known. There are many ways of approximating solutions of differential equations. Even more important than approximate numbers are approximating expressions; many highly complex functions can be approximated to any desired degree of accuracy by polynomials. One of the most important theorems of calculus, TAYLOR'S THEOREM, provides one method of doing this. Other approximating expressions are finite sums of transcendental functions; the most important are the Fourier approximations, obtained from FOURIER SERIES of trigonometric terms. —H. C.

A PRIORI: as applied to knowledge about the world, the claim that it has been obtained from theoretical considerations alone, *e.g.* the statement of Eddington that the universe contains $\frac{3}{2} \times 136 \times 2^{256}$ elementary particles, and that this follows from "the principles of measurement." In the sense of Kant such knowledge is said to be both universal and necessary, and, although arising in the course of experience, not derivable from it. Although there have been spectacular anticipations of experience in scientific history, *e.g.* the prediction of the existence of the planet Neptune, an examination of the evidence on which the predictions were made will disclose an admixture of theoretical principles with material derived from empirical sources.—*H. T.*

APSIDES, LINE OF: an indefinite extension in both directions of the line of the major axis of an elliptical orbit. This line passes through the two foci of the ellipse, and the two apsides, the points of the orbit that are nearest and farthest from the primary body (Sun, planet, or star) that is at one of the foci. Perturbations by the other planets cause the line of apsides of the Moon's orbit, and those of the planets' orbits, to revolve slowly in an eastward direction. Because of this revolution, the time interval between successive passages of the Moon through perigee (this interval being the anomalistic month) is somewhat longer than the period of revolution of the Moon in its orbit (the sidereal month). Similarly, the revolution of the line of apsides of Earth's orbit makes the anomalistic year (from perihelion to perihelion) about 4½ min longer than the sidereal year.

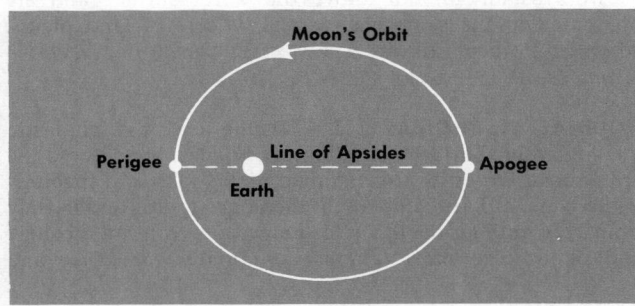

Line of apsides: The apsides of Moon's orbit—apogee and perigee—are points at which Moon is farthest from and closest to Earth. (Eccentricity of orbit is exaggerated here.)

In a close binary star, one star raises tides in the other, so that the two stars are no longer spherical, but ellipsoidal. This distortion also produces a slow revolution of the line of apsides of the orbit of one star about the other, and from observations of such motion in spectroscopic or eclipsing binaries, information can be obtained about the manner in which the mass of a star is distributed throughout its volume.—*M. W. O.*

AQUA REGIA: a mixture of nitric and hydrochloric acids. It can dissolve gold and platinum because the reduction potential of these metals increases in presence of chloride ions.— *G. W. M.*

AQUATIC ANIMALS: Originally, all animals were aquatic and inhabited ancient seas. Long ago, however, some ancestral types invaded fresh waters, and others took to life on land. Some, such as various insects, sea snakes and sea turtles, whales and porpoises are descendants of land animals that reinvaded aquatic habitats. Advantages of aquatic life for animals include buoyant support from the water, protection from desiccation, an environment whose temperature changes only slowly, and in the sea the availability of a great variety of chemical substances for the animal's requirements. Animals

Return to the sea: These marine turtles of Atlantic waters are descended from reptiles that lived on land some 200 million yr ago. The turtles live in offshore waters. (*N. Y. Zoological Soc.*)

that live in upper levels of fresh waters and oceans, where daylight penetrates and permits aquatic plants to carry on photosynthesis, can get their food by eating these plants or other animals. At greater depths, where no green plants can exist, animals must eat other animals (including the bodies of those sinking from lighted levels) or gain their nourishment from organic matter accumulating on the bottom. (See DEEP-SEA ANIMALS; PELAGIC ANIMALS; PLANKTON.) Dissolved materials brought by rivers improve living conditions for aquatic plants near shore and hence provide more food for animals than is to be found remote from coasts. As a result, particularly large numbers of animals live in aquatic situations near shore. Their chief hazard is being battered by wave action or cast up by storms. Various adaptations of many kinds aid these animals in resisting destruction. Some burrow in the bottom; others have means for clinging firmly to rocks. Many aquatic animals can wait from one high tide to the next, isolated in tidal pools; but these pools are subject to frost, the intense heat of the sun, drying up, and dilution by heavy rain.

The great majority of animals other than insects and parasites live in water. This is not surprising, because in area the oceans constitute about 70% of the earth's surface, and fresh water a fraction of 1%. But it is not in area that aquatic habitats surpass the terrestrial by the greatest margin; rather, it is in regard to volume of space. Terrestrial animals are restricted to a narrow vertical belt that extends from a few feet below the surface to less than 400 ft above it, whereas aquatic animals live from the water's surface to the greatest depth, which in the ocean is more than 7 mi. Among invertebrates, a number of whole phyla, *e.g.* sponges, coelenterates, ctenophores, and echinoderms, are almost exclusively aquatic, but not even one phylum is wholly terrestrial. The mollusks, with an estimated 40,000 species, are entirely aquatic in distribution, except for the snails. Aside from parasitic forms, protozoans and flatworms are mostly aquatic. Of the arthropods, crustaceans are largely aquatic, insects and arachnids mostly terrestrial, and the remaining classes exclusively terrestrial. Among vertebrates, the line that separates the typically aquatic and typically terrestrial forms passes through the amphibians, which may, as in the case of some frogs, be water animals in youth and land animals in adult life. Nevertheless, the crocodiles, turtles, and snakes among reptiles, many birds, and the sirenians, cetaceans, and seals among mammals, show that members of typically terrestrial groups may return to a purely aquatic life. The aquatic reptile, bird, or mammal retains its terrestrial habit of breathing air by lungs and shows no tendency to reacquire gills. But it reveals other adaptations to aquatic life. The whale, for example, as contrasted with an ordinary terrestrial mammal, shows striking modifications of structure. Its spindle-shaped form and lack of hair and hind limbs are adaptations to swift movement in water. Its use of the tail as the main organ of propulsion is a common practice among aquatic animals. Since the animal body in water loses a large proportion of its weight, limbs do not need to be as strong as in land animals.

A structure frequently found in the aquatic animals that are capable of rising and sinking in the water is some form of hydrostatic organ, or internal reservoir of gas. All air-breathing vertebrates have such organs in their lungs; fish usually have a swim-bladder; many cuttlefish have air spaces in their "bone," or float; the pearly nautilus has its chambered shell filled with gas; even some protozoans have bubbles of gas in their soft bodies.—*L. and M. M.* (See Color Plates f.p. 70.)

AQUATIC PLANTS: plants that live continuously in water. The distribution of green plants in fresh-water and marine habitats is limited by the depth to which daylight penetrates. Usually this depth is much greater in the sea than in fresh waters (because there is more suspended matter, chiefly organic, in fresh water) and is greater in the open ocean than in coastal waters (because of increased inorganic sediment and possibly more plankton near land). Below the lighted level, only fungi and bacteria thrive, living on organic matter that sifts down to them (see SAPROPHYTES). In both oceanic and fresh waters, microscopic drifting plants form an essential part of PLANKTON, which nourishes incredible numbers of AQUATIC ANIMALS.

Conspicuous plants in the sea are almost all ALGAE. They grow near coasts where their holdfasts can anchor them to the bottom in fairly shallow water. Many are left exposed to the air at low tide, but are prevented from drying entirely by a mucilaginous secretion over their surfaces; this makes them feel slimy. Some, *e.g.* sea lettuce (*Ulva*), are green algae. Most are brown algae, as bladder wrack (*Fucus*), ribbon weed (*Laminaria*), and the various giant kelps. Red algae grow mostly at greater depths than browns or greens; Irish moss (*Chondrus*) is an exception found in the intertidal zone, where people collect it to make into puddings.

In fresh waters, the larger aquatic plants produce flowers, as do water lilies and cat-tails. Their roots usually penetrate the bottom mud, but a few, *e.g.* duckweed (*Lemna*) and water soldier (*Stratiotes*), float or are at least free from the soil. The whole surface of a water plant in contact with the water absorbs liquid and gaseous food. Large air spaces occur in the cellular tissue of most water plants, and these become filled with gas, perhaps thus aiding in the respiration of the plant. Flowers usually bloom above the water surface and are pollinated in the same way as the flowers of land plants. Most aquatic plants are PERENNIAL. See BOG PLANTS.— *L. and M. M.* (See Color Plates f.p. 70.)

AQUINAS, ST. THOMAS (1225–74): the foremost scholastic theologian of the 13th cent., b. near Naples. He entered the Dominican Order in 1244, studied philosophy and theology at the Univ. of Paris, and taught theology at Paris and in Italy from 1256 until his death. Of his numerous works on theology and philosophy, most famous are *Summa theologiae* and

Aquatic life in a bog: A bald cypress rises among the water lilies in this Florida swamp. Invisible are algae clinging to underwater roots, and the drifting millions of microscopic diatoms that thicken the water of the lagoon. (*Walter Dawn*)

Summa contra Gentiles. He was canonized in 1323, and ranked with St. Augustine as one of the authoritative Doctors of the Catholic Church. Aquinas sought to harmonize the philosophy of Aristotle with Christian doctrine, using the philosophical language of Aristotle in reformulating and developing theology. Though he was well versed in the scientific knowledge of his time, and was an excellent expositor of Aristotle's scientific and philosophical writings, his more original work was in theology, metaphysics, and theory of knowledge. His influence on scholastic philosophy (see SCHOLASTICISM) was great during his lifetime and immediately thereafter, but it waned rapidly after the end of the 13th cent., when John Duns Scotus, and then William of Ockham, led scholastic thought in new directions. Since 1879, when Pope Leo XIII inaugurated a revival of the scholastic tradition with special emphasis on St. Thomas Aquinas, the Thomist doctrines have been taken as the norm of Catholic instruction in philosophy.—*E. A. M.*

ARACHNID: any animal of a class of ARTHROPODS, including spiders, scorpions, and ticks. Arachnids have six pairs of appendages, the first pair modified as chelicerae, or feeding organs; the second pair as pedipalps, or accessory feeding organs; the last four pairs as legs. There are nine modern orders (or types) of arachnids, and four orders known only as fossils. Best known are the spiders (order Araneida), scorpions (Scorpionida), mites and ticks (Acarina), and daddy longlegs (Phalangida). Less well known are the pseudoscorpions (Pseudoscorpionida), whip scorpions (Pedipalpida), micro whip scorpions (Microthelyphonida), sun-spiders (Solpugida), and podogonids (Ricinulei). Arachnids, which are primarily terrestrial, are closely related to two classes of marine arthropods: Merostomata (horseshoe crabs) and Pycnogonida (sea spiders).

Spiders, the most prevalent of large arachnids, are found in all terrestrial situations. They range from microscopic dwellers in the soil to tropical tarantulas with a body length of 3 in. and a leg span of 10 in. Perhaps their most distinctive characteristic is the engineering use they make of silk (finer and stronger than silkworm silk), produced from spinnerets near the posterior end of the abdomen. Not only do many spiders spin intricate webs for catching their prey (usually flying insects), but the silk may also be used for binding captured insects, building and furnishing homes, making egg cocoons, ballooning (to carry the spider through the air), and as a safety line and climbing rope. Spiders have poison glands that empty onto the tips of the chelicerae. The poison is effective in subduing insects, but only a few spiders have a poisonous bite dangerous to man. Black widows, whose bite can be fatal to man, are fairly common in most parts of the U. S. A. They can be recognized by their shiny jet-black bodies, on which a few red spots can be seen, and by the red hour-glass marking on the underside of the female. On the whole, spiders are economically valuable in that they destroy large numbers of harmful insects.

Scorpions are, in general, larger than spiders and are found chiefly in the tropics, though a few species invade the margins of the temperate zones. They possess a long, segmented tail that curves back and ends in a sting. The sting of most scorpions is no more harmful than that of a hornet, but a few species are deadly. Mating in scorpions is preceded by a complicated series of dances in which the male and female grasp each other's pedipalps and waltz about like ballroom dancers. *Mites* are the smallest and also the most economically important arachnids. Together with their larger relatives, the *ticks,* they are major pests of plants, domestic animals, and man. With the introduction of insecticides such as DDT, which kill insects that normally feed on mites, plant-eating

Wolf-spider: This long-legged arachnid, about an inch long, belongs to the easily recognized order of Araneida. (*Walter Dawn*)

Scorpion: Poisonous arachnid, with its four pairs of walking legs, was visualized in the ZODIAC. (*Bucky Reeves/Nat. Audubon Soc.*)

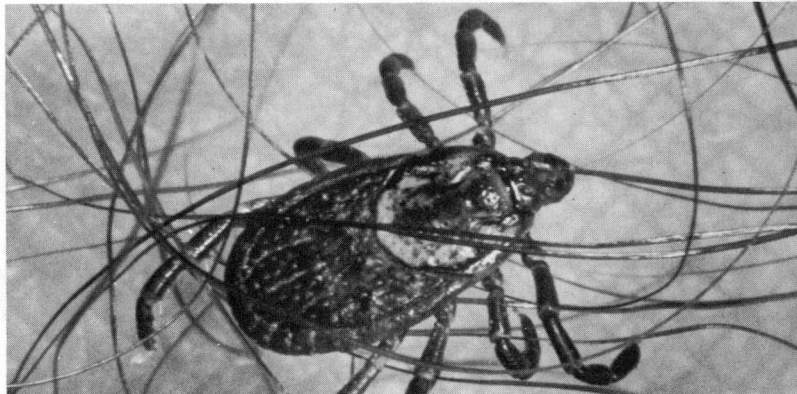
Tick: Small, bloodsucking arachnid, a major pest, carries disease to man and beast. (*John H. Gerard/Nat. Audubon Soc.*)

mites (especially those called red-spiders) have become major destroyers of orchards, cotton, and ornamental plants. Mites destroy much stored grain and other food each year. Mites that are major pests of man and animals are the mange mites, chiggers, and dermanyssids. Not only are their bites irritating, but some of them transmit rickettsial diseases. Two ticks in the U. S. A. carry Rocky Mt spotted fever, a human disease, and another tick is a carrier of Texas cattle fever, a disease once responsible for heavy losses to cattle raisers.

The *daddy longlegs,* or *harvestmen,* are fairly common arachnids; they have a compact body and extremely long slender legs, which break easily. These harmless animals use their first two pairs of legs in feeling their way about. They produce no silk and have no poison, but somehow capture as food many small mites, young spiders, and insects.—*G. W.* (See also Color Plates f.p. 70.)

ARAGO, DOMINIQUE FRANÇOIS JEAN, 1786–1853, French astronomer and physicist; b. Estagel, near Perpignan; self-educated. He made important contributions in astronomy, magnetism, electricity, meteorology, optics, and polarization of light. For his discovery (1820) of magnetism by rotation he received (1825) the Copley Medal of the Royal Society, of which he was a fellow. He worked 1806–08 with M. Biot on geodetic surveys in the Pyrenees and Balearic Is. His discovery of colors in crystallized bodies in polarized light led to a new method of analyzing light and to construction of a polariscope. In 1815 he observed the displacement of interference fringes. Because of blindness, he never completed his work (1832–50) on the velocity of light in media of varying density, but Fizeau and Foucault continued the experiments and established the wave theory.—*R. N. M.*

ARC: see ARCS AND DISCHARGES; CURVE.

ARCH: a structure designed to support loads over an open space. The arch is usually curved, though pointed arches have been used in architecture. Stone and brick were the chief materials for arch construction until the introduction of wrought iron in the 19th cent.; steel and reinforced concrete

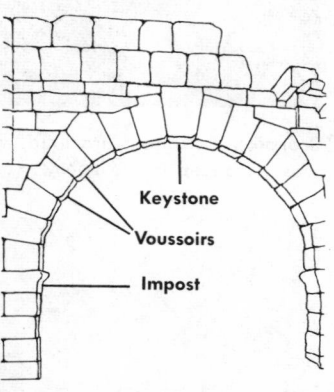

Round arch of "basilica" at Tyndaris, on northern coast of Sicily, shows perfection the form had reached by 1st cent. B. C. (*European Art Color Slide*)

are the principal materials used today. In theory the ideal arch carries its own weight and superimposed loads in simple direct compression. To function in this way the axis of the arch must follow a particular geometric curve determined by load distribution. If shape and loading are not thus related, flexural and shear stresses arise, as well as compression. In practice, the chief drawback of the arch is the horizontal thrust outward at its ends; this must be countered either by the resistance of

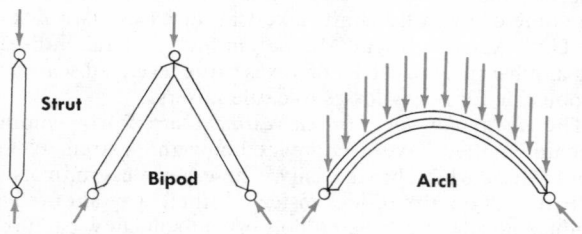

Structures That Carry Their Loads in Simple Compression

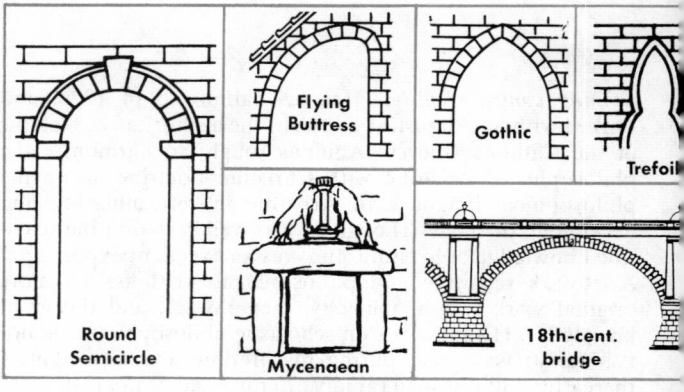

Forms of Arch

the arch supports or by a tie between the ends of the arch. An excellent site for an arch bridge is a deep gorge with solid rock slopes which can resist the lateral thrust. Arches may be advantageously used to achieve fairly large clear spans with materials which are weak in tension but strong in compression, *e.g.* masonry and cast iron. Where stresses other than simple compression exist, reinforced concrete, steel, aluminum, and timber are more suitable. Concrete is well adapted to spans up to about 100 ft; steel is generally used for spans over 400 ft. Between 100 and 400 ft, steel and concrete compete economically.—*W. W.*

ARCHEAN (ARCHEOZOIC) ERA: see PRECAMBRIAN TIME; GEOLOGICAL TIME CHART.

ARCHIMEDES, *c.* 287–212 B. C., Greek mathematician and physicist; son of the astronomer Pheidias; b. Syracuse, Sicily, where he spent most of his life. Although he was one of the greatest mechanical geniuses of all time, his work on applied mechanics was overshadowed by his contributions to pure mathematics. He is reported to have discovered the first law of hydrostatics (see ARCHIMEDES' PRINCIPLE) while lying in his bath, and to have leaped out and run naked through the streets of Syracuse shouting "Eureka!" (I have found it!). According to another story, to emphasize a law of levers, Archimedes once said, "Give me a place to stand, and I will move the world." Archimedes studied geometrical figures, which he traced on any surface available—sand, dust on a floor, even his own body, oiled after a bath. He made important contributions to astronomy and mechanics, and he is considered the greatest ancient mathematician. He devised methods of finding areas bounded by curves and volumes bounded by curved surfaces. Among the figures to which he applied these methods were circles, spheres, parabolic segments, cylinders, cones, and spheroids. He fixed the value of π, which is the ratio of the circumference to the diameter of a circle, as a number between $3\frac{1}{7}$ and $3\frac{10}{71}$. He invented a system of numeration applicable to numbers as large as desired, and he created the science of hydrostatics and laid down fundamental principles of mechanics.

In attacking mathematical problems, most Greeks worked by rules arbitrarily imposed. For example, only straightedges and compasses were permitted for geometrical constructions. Archimedes, however, used his imagination: his solutions of area and volume problems were suggested by applications of principles of the lever, and his determination of tangents to a spiral was based on consideration of the velocity of a moving point. Archimedes' work on tangents and areas anticipated the discovery of calculus 1,900 yr later, although he lacked the concept of a limit, which is fundamental in calculus. Archimedes also devised both a method of launching fully loaded ships singlehandedly and methods of repelling hostile ships from the shore. When the Roman general Marcellus attacked Syracuse, Archimedes was surprised by a Roman soldier while contemplating a diagram in the dust, and, according to one account, when the soldier stepped on the diagram, Archimedes protested and the soldier speared him.—*H. C.*

ARCHIMEDES' PRINCIPLE: a statement of the numerical equality of the buoyant force exerted on a body submerged in a fluid and the weight of the fluid displaced. The relationship was first formulated by ARCHIMEDES (3rd cent. B. C.). He is said to have discovered this principle while pondering the solution of the famous gold-crown problem presented to him by King Hiero of Syracuse. The king wanted to know whether the goldsmith who had made his crown (according to the king's strict size and weight specifications) had adulterated it with silver. Archimedes found that equal weights of gold and silver displaced different volumes of water. By comparing the volume of water displaced, first by a piece of pure gold equal in weight to the crown, then by the crown itself, he found each displaced a different volume of water: thus the crown was a fraud.

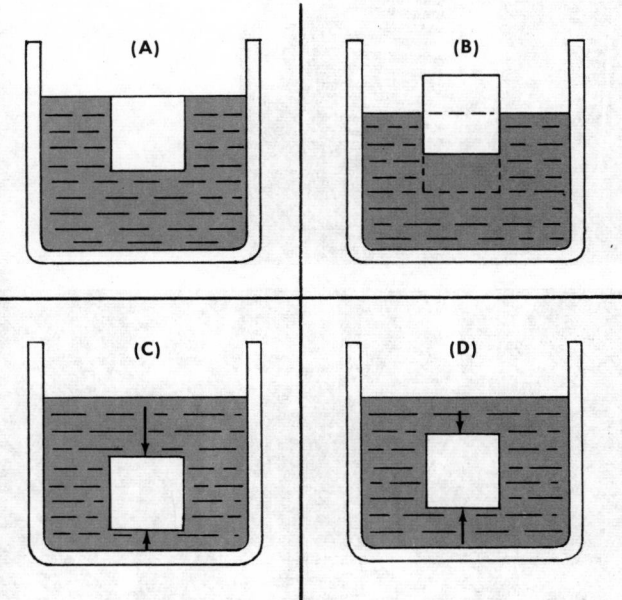

Archimedes' principle: If the weight of a body of given volume is exactly the same as the weight of an equal volume of water, the body will float in water with its top just at the surface (A). If the body weighs less than an equal volume of water, it will float higher, displacing just enough water to equal its own weight (B). If it weighs more than an equal volume of water, it will sink (C), since the net downward force on the water will be greater than the net upward force. The opposite is true for a body that will float (D).

The principle of buoyancy has its origin in the law of fluid pressure, which says that pressure varies directly with depth. Thus the upward pressure on the bottom of a submerged solid (assumed rectangular for the sake of simplicity) is greater than the downward pressure on the upper face. The *net* upward, or buoyant, force is equal to the difference in weight between two fluid columns whose bases are the upper and lower faces of the solid. Hence the buoyant force is equal to the weight of the portion of fluid displaced by the solid. For a floating body, the buoyant force also equals the weight of the floating body itself. If a body is denser than the fluid in which it is submerged, buoyancy proves insufficient to support the body, which thereupon sinks to the bottom.—*A. E.*

ARCHITECTURAL CRAFTS AND TOOLS: Architecture falls into two major divisions: (1) theoretical, which embraces planning, formal design, and stress calculations; (2) material, which includes actual processes and tools of construction. This article deals with the latter (see also ARCHITECTURE; STRUCTURAL DESIGN). Despite extensive mechanization of crafts and manufacturing processes, the building art is still largely a handicraft technique. Thus, although materials of modern building are either factory-made or prepared by power-driven machinery, and the individual members of large structures are often handled by mechanical devices, all techniques having to do with cutting, joining, and painting wood, laying masonry, riveting, bolting, and welding steelwork, installing utilities, plastering, and interior finishing are performed by hand. The proportion of handwork in a given structure usually varies according to its size: individual residences are built almost entirely by hand; large buildings can be constructed only by means of mechanical aids. The basic tools and machines of the building crafts are extremely old. HAND TOOLS such as the hammer, saw, axe, chisel, file, and trowel date from the prehistoric period. Devices for transporting, lifting, and placing members, *e.g.* wheelbarrows, cranes, pulleys, rollers, and levers, are of pre-classical origin. Large cranes, pile drivers, and other power-driven machines and tools have appeared mainly since the Industrial Revolution.

The architectural crafts and their appropriate tools are determined by the type of work and the material used, and these in turn by the type of structure. All building construction has certain common features, *e.g.* preparation of site, erection of superstructure, installation of protective covering and mechanical equipment, and interior finishing. Thus certain basic tools are likely to be used in all types of building.

First in the process of construction is preparation of the site, which usually involves excavation. This was done by hand until the invention of the power shovel in the 19th cent. Now, excavation for even a small residence is done by power machinery, chiefly the power shovel, the bulldozer, and the tractor-driven scoop. Foundations and footings were once stone and timber, but are now usually concrete. For ordinary dwellings, concrete is poured by hand or by chute from a mixer. Site preparation for a large building may consume half the total time of construction; an extreme case is excavation and underpinning for a skyscraper in a region of water-bearing soil, where bedrock lies at a great depth below grade. The first step is excavation of the whole building area to a depth of 25 to 30 ft as well as excavation of the area to be occupied by column footings. Pumps and underground piping must be installed to keep the opening free of ground water; and braced timber or steel walls are built around the periphery to hold back earth, prevent adjacent buildings from settling, and block excessive seepage through the sides of the excavation. If the footings rest on piling, a steam-driven pile driver is used to drive the piles to bedrock. If they rest on caissons, the caisson wells are dug by hand—a tedious and costly operation —or mechanically by a caisson drill. The caisson well is then filled with concrete. The footing is poured on top of the piling or the caisson.

Building a superstructure of stone or brick has changed little since antiquity. Bricklaying continues to be a pure handicraft technique, the mason laying the bricks with mortar and trowel. After laying a course, he checks the horizontal with a level, and after several courses, he may check the vertical with a plumb-line. Stone masonry, if the blocks are small, is laid in the same way. For large blocks, the mason first applies mortar to the footings, then places the block in position by means of a pulley or crane and a sling. Extremely large blocks are handled by a power-driven crane. Stone blocks may be

Skyscraper goes up: Ground is broken (1) to open pit for foundation, which is then laid. Reinforced concrete walls (2) are shorn up in some places and about to be poured in others. Prestressed steel girders are placed by workmen (3), while cables hold vertical members of framework (4) till horizontal beams can be locked properly in place. Framework distributes thrust, so that curtain walls need not be installed during early stages of construction. While derricks hoist girders into place on upper floors (5), the lower stories are being finished. The result: the 60-story Chase Manhatten Bank stands as a finished building (6). It took 4 yr from ground-breaking to occupancy.

partly held in place by means of metal pins inserted into centered openings of two contiguous blocks. When arches, vaults, and domes are built of brick or stone, the masonry must be supported by centering scaffolding until every unit is in place and the mortar has set. Plastering is a special masonry technique in which the material is applied by trowel, and sometimes smoothed with a flat metal plate. See MASONRY AND BRICKWORK.

Timber FRAMING, the most common type of construction for dwellings, is the last major stronghold of the skilled carpenter, who once built palaces and bridges. In addition to the frame, he installs flooring, interior partitions, detailed woodwork, and roof planking, and he builds the wooden forms for concrete work (see CARPENTRY). Most lumber comes from the mill in the size and shape needed for the job, so that cutting and shaping form a minor part of the work. The saw, plane, chisel, and sander are the chief tools for these operations, the traditional ax being little used now. The major task of the carpenter is joining. Before the invention of the nail-making machine and the *balloon frame* in the early 19th cent., heavy members of the frame were usually joined by wooden pegs, in combination with mortised or scarfed joints. For over a century, however, joining has been accomplished mainly by nailing, less often by bolting. Timber pieces are generally light enough to be lifted and placed by hand.

Steel framing, derived from construction in cast and wrought iron, is the most highly mechanized operation because of the weight of the members, the accuracy with which they must be placed, and the height at which they are sometimes located. Older cast-iron and wrought-iron frames were joined by bolting. In modern steel framing, the members are lifted to position by power-driven cranes, and usually fixed in place by riveting. The separate members are joined by a variety of gussets, angles, splice bars, and the like. The rivet hammer is held by hand but operated by compressed air. The alternative to riveting is arc-welding (see WELDING). The structural steelworker needs not only the manual skills of his craft, but the courage and cool head necessary to cope with the dangers of working at great heights on narrow footings. Most steel-framed buildings are sheathed in curtain walls, whose separate panels, now often prefabricated, are lifted by crane or hoist and fixed in place by hand.

Construction in CONCRETE, whether in mass for dams or in frames, shells, or arches for buildings and bridges, requires little skill in the mixing and placing of the material itself. Proportioning, mixing, and transportation are largely mechanical and power-driven operations; pouring is accomplished by gravity from buckets, hoppers, and chutes. Concrete is sometimes pumped into the forms, as in the case of tunnels. The major skill in concrete construction, the making of wooden forms, is chiefly the work of the carpenter. Form work may be extremely elaborate when concrete is poured in shells of double curvature, and may require detailed working drawings. Once completed, the forms must be supported by temporary posts and jacks until the concrete has set. Reinforcing is essential in concrete work, but the placing and joining of bars require patience more than skill. After the concrete has set, the forms are stripped and the individual pieces re-used until they wear out.

Associated with the architectural crafts are many activities involving the installation of mechanical and electrical equipment. These lie outside the structural process, but since utilities now represent as much as 40% of the total cost of a large building, they affect many details of construction.—*C. W. C.*

ARCHITECTURAL DRAWING: a geometric and diagrammatic technique for representing accurately, and to scale, the form of a building, disposition of its functional and decorative elements, and location of its mechanical and electrical utilities. The geometric principle of representation is orthographic projection, in which all features lying in or visibly behind a given horizontal or vertical plane are projected perpendicular to a hypothetical plane, parallel to the given. Perspective drawing is sometimes used to present the actual appearance of the building. Architectural drawings are classified (1) according to parts of the structure shown, *e.g.* plans, elevations, and sections of the building; and (2) according to structural details, *e.g.* reinforcing, mechanical, and electrical details. Conventional symbols are used to represent different materials and utilitarian elements. Architectural drawings include all dimensions and copious explanatory notes, features which have grown steadily in number and detail since the first architectural drawings of ancient Egypt.—*C. W. C.*

ARCHITECTURAL ELEMENTS: the distinguishable features of a building. These may be divided into structural, utilitarian, and esthetic elements, although the esthetic may contain little that is physically separable from the structural and utilitarian. Esthetic form has often determined structure, but a structure arising from functional need may itself provide the basis of esthetic character.

Structural elements include the foundation, superstructure, and protective covering. Earliest *foundations* were of split logs or sections of treetrunks laid on, or slightly below, the ground. Stone footings for walls and columns appeared in pre-classical antiquity and remained common until the end of the 19th cent., when stone was rapidly supplanted by concrete. Chief purpose of the foundation is to distribute the building load over the soil or underpinning, and to carry it below the frost line. The older form of *superstructure* consists primarily of bearing walls of brick, stone, wood, or concrete, which carry the floor and roof loads by means of beams and joists. The later type is the framed structure, a rectangular array of columns and beams through which the building load is transmitted to the individual column footings. Framing systems have usually been of wood, ferrous metals, or reinforced concrete, though Gothic architects succeeded in building framed structures in stone. The *protective covering* extends around and above the superstructure in the form of wall sheathing and roof. In bearing-wall construction, the load-carrying structure and the protective covering of the sides are one. In framed construction the side covering is called a curtain wall. There is a diversity of forms and materials available for wall sheathing and roofing. Traditional materials such as wood, slate, and tile have been largely superseded by concrete, sheet metals, fibrous and mineral insulating panels, glass, plastics, and asphalt products.

Utilitarian elements of a building are the most numerous of all. Those forming a part of the building proper are doors, windows, stairways, openings for the passage of air, screens and canopies for weather protection, porches, balconies, and all interior partitions and openings. Fixed elements added for the satisfaction of specific human needs embrace all plumbing equipment, devices for the heating, cooling, and circulation of air, and electrical installations for lighting, refrigeration, communications, and automatic controls. Such utilities now constitute the largest, most complex, and most expensive part of construction, and have grown to such a point that the chief problem of the architect is often one of containing them, while preserving the spatial and esthetic character of building. *Esthetic elements* separable from the structural and utilitarian are chiefly: decorative patterns on walls and structural members, either colored flat against surfaces or carved and molded in relief; broad areas of color laid on surfaces; sculpture; and ornamental work derived from functional elements of past or exotic styles of architecture. But esthetic character arises

Parthenon in Athens (*upper left*) is a refined version of simple post-and-lintel structure. Doric colonnade supports lintel, which holds roof and pediment. Marble was joined, not mortared. (*Pierre M. Martinot*) **Temple of Heaven,** Peking (*upper right*), was built in wood but uses same principle. Curved roof is trussed by stepped post-and-lintel system. (*Wide World Photos*) **Taj Mahal** (*right*) in Agra is elaborately domed and arched. Interior space is broken by ornate supporting posts. (*Trans World Airlines*) **Frank Lloyd Wright** designed the Kaufman House in Bear Run, Pa. (*left*), to suit site. Light-colored eaves and rough-hewn stones blend house with the falls. He kept space, inside and out, light and uncluttered. (*Bill Hedrich / Hedrich-Blessing*)

chiefly from space itself, from organized rhythms of such structural and utilitarian elements as openings and overhangs, and from the textures and colors of building materials.—*C. W. C.*

ARCHITECTURAL ENGINEERING: the science dealing with the STRUCTURAL DESIGN and choice and location of utilities of a building for which the architect has already determined the site and internal plans, the over-all form, and the esthetic features. The roles of engineer and architect often overlap and sometimes merge. The design program begins with an investigation of the site as to topography, bearing properties of the soil, and meteorological characteristics of the region. With the over-all shape, size, location, and purpose of the building known, the engineer works out the detailed form of the structure. He calculates loads and their distribution: the dead load, which is the weight of the structure, all the fixed elements within it, and the snow that might accumulate on the roof; and the live load, which consists of the occupants and the wheeled vehicles they may use, the wind load (which may include pressure changes occurring during severe storms), and possible earthquake forces. On the basis of these computations the engineer makes a stress analysis to determine the sizes of specific structural members; it includes a calculation of tension, compression, and shear forces in individual members arising from distribution of the load. Design of utilities depends on the number and activities of the occupants of the building and on weather conditions in the region.—*C. W. C.*

ARCHITECTURE: the theory and technique of any kind of building consciously designed for expressive and symbolic ends, as well as for practical utility. The creation of an architectural work thus involves planning, structural design, artistic or symbolic design, and construction. These are arbitrary divisions, however, which cannot be regarded as distinct steps in the process. Although discussion here is limited to the structural base, materials, and techniques of building, and to their historical evolution, it must be noted that the esthetic component is inseparable from structure, material, and utility. Materials and utilitarian requirements to a great extent determine structural form, and it is from this that esthetic form is largely developed. For the actual process of construction see ARCHITECTURAL CRAFTS AND TOOLS and CONSTRUCTION METHODS AND EQUIPMENT.

Relationship of Materials and Design: The primary structural materials of building are wood, clay, stone, ferrous metals, and concrete. The multitude of structural forms into which they can be arranged may be classified into the following: the solid bearing wall; the post and lintel, or column and beam; the arch and its derivatives, the vault and the dome; the frame, which is usually a repetitive column-and-beam or column-and-rib system; and suspended construction. Stone in its natural state, and clay baked into bricks, are best adapted to construction of bearing walls and arch-like forms, while wood and iron are virtually restricted to framed structures. The plasticity of concrete gives it an almost unlimited range of structural uses, but its most economical one is in continuous forms, *e.g.*

vaults, domes, and flat slabs. There are certain conspicuous exceptions to this classification: wood has been employed in solid bearing walls, as in the log cabin; and stone was adapted by highly skilled medieval masons to framed construction. Other common materials of building—glass, sheet metal, tile, slate, plastics—are used for protective and decorative, rather than structural, purposes.

The architectural achievement of a people depends on more factors than the skill and imagination of the builder. The forms of buildings are determined by social habits, economic means, and collective needs, and they are consciously shaped to give expression to dominant values, and to mythical, religious, and philosophic world-views. In addition, there are external factors which are sometimes beyond human control. Climate determines whether buildings must provide protection against rain, snow, storm, and extremes of temperature, or may be left open in great part to the weather. But local availability of materials is the decisive element, not only for the form of buildings, but also for their size and durability. The plentiful supply of good building stone in Europe and the Mediterranean region, for example, made possible the great architectural development of Western culture, from ancient Egypt to 19th-cent. Europe and America. The great majority of Japanese buildings, on the other hand, are wood, as are many of those in Russia and the United States built during the 19th cent., reflecting in all cases the presence of extensive forests. The growth of mechanized industry and transport has tended to nullify such natural restrictions but has not obliterated them. Large-scale building in Latin America, for example, depends heavily on concrete, whereas comparable structures in the U. S. A. are of steel.

History: *Prehistoric building* depended entirely on materials available at or near the surface of the earth which could be shaped, placed in position, and joined by the simplest hand techniques. The most primitive method was the piling up of turf on logs spanning a shallow depression. A step beyond it was wattle-and-daub, in which the walls of a hut were made of interwoven twigs and branches, and the interstices filled with mud or clay. This method offered better protection against the weather, and made possible the introduction of an opening for light and the passage of smoke. The development of a true framing technique came slowly, beginning perhaps with the tectiform (tent-shaped) frame, and eventually reaching the rectangular frame of posts and beams. In the earlier type, flexible branches were driven into the ground in a ring, and the ends bent inward and joined to form a tent-like enclosure. The developed timber frame consisted of three rows of posts supporting longitudinal beams at the top of the walls and the ridge line of the roof. Rafters from ridge to wall beams carried the thatch or turf of the roof. The prehistoric frame, elaborated and refined, is still the major structural technique of contemporary residential building.

Large-scale architectural building in durable materials was achieved by *Egypt and Mesopotamia* in the third millennium B. C. There are extensive outcroppings of high-quality building stone in Egypt, chiefly granite, limestone, and sandstone; and Egyptian artisans rapidly developed the skills and tools necessary to quarry, transport, dress, and lay it up in masonry walls and columns. They depended on weight and friction to keep the separate blocks in place; mortar was apparently unknown to them. The Pyramids, earliest of the great works of stone construction, are notable more for their size and stability than for technical ingenuity. The huge temples that came later, whether rock-cut enclosures or free-standing structures, were distinguished by rows of stout, closely spaced columns supporting deep roof beams in a rectangular grid. Evidence from wall inscriptions shows that the Egyptian builder drew

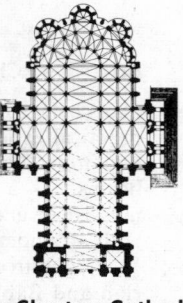

In Chartres Cathedral (*left; floor plan above*), spires show contrast of old and new: romanesque, conical and heavy; and Gothic, light and soaring. (*Giraudon*)

Amiens Cathedral in transverse section, showing its distinctive Gothic features: slenderness of vertical members and great height of nave in proportion to width—here 3:1—made possible by pointed arches and refined rib vaulting. Lateral thrust is absorbed by flying buttresses, making massive walls superfluous and thereby allowing openings for stained-glass windows. Protective roof is self-supporting, reducing the pressure on the vaulting.

Development of vaulting (*below*) is shown in three stages. Barrel vault is simply a prolonged arch. Groined vault combines two crossed barrel vaults, localizing the pressure at four points. Most efficient is the lighter, simpler rib vault.

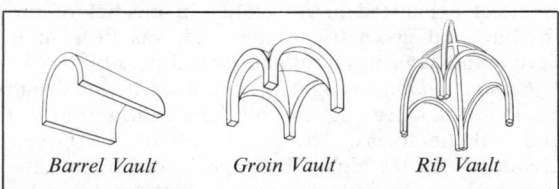

Barrel Vault *Groin Vault* *Rib Vault*

Flying buttresses (*below*) take huge thrust of vaults but have a light look. (*Giraudon*)

Nave and south transept at Chartres (*below*): Piers with attached shafts meet vaults. (*Giraudon*)

plans before undertaking construction. He recognized through practical experience that stone has negligible tensile strength and must be confined to very short spans when used for beams. As a consequence, Egyptian temples are extremely massive structures, somewhat crude by classical standards but with an undeniable power and dignity.

The relative scarcity of stone in Mesopotamia forced Sumerian and Babylonian builders to turn to clay as the primary material for large buildings. Rammed clay, known as *pisé*, the original form of the bearing wall, soon gave way to sun-dried and later baked, or kiln-dried, brick. Babylonian temples and palaces were generally constructed with brick bearing walls of extraordinary thickness. Columns were less frequent, but when used were of such great size that the diameter sometimes exceeded the space between adjacent members. Roofs were carried on timber beams spanning the columns. Distinguishing Mesopotamian features, continuing through the Assyrian and Persian periods, were relief sculpture cut into the brickwork of the wall, and brilliantly colored glazes applied to the external surface of the brick. The glaze had also the functional value of protection against weathering. The Babylonians built the first true vaults by laying wedge-shaped bricks radially around the arc of successive, contiguous rings. Asphaltic binding materials helped to keep the bricks in place, and provided a waterproof surface for canals and aqueducts.

Minoan and Hellenic building, although reaching unprecedented formal refinement, showed little technical advance over earlier work. The stone column-and-beam construction, nearly universal in Greek architecture, seems to have been derived from Mycenaean and hence Minoan prototypes of wood. Extensive outcroppings of marble and high-grade limestone on the Greek peninsula prompted a relatively early substitution of stone for timber. Main technical contributions of Greek builders of the Hellenic period were careful dressing of masonry blocks to insure tight, even joints, the introduction of wrought-iron beams to carry part of the load of long spans, and extensive use of metal dowels and cramps to keep the successive drums of the column shaft in line. The Greek architect exhausted his ingenuity in niceties of proportion, rhythm, and geometric shape, and was little interested in developing new structural and formal possibilities.

Roman building brought an enormous advance in the proliferation of new techniques, and the creation of new structural and esthetic forms. The great skill of the Greco-Roman architects and the highly developed social organization of the state were primary factors; beyond these were the Roman capacity for exploiting the achievements of every culture with which they came in contact, and the fact that they drew on the entire Mediterranean world for materials and talent. By the 2nd cent. A. D., the Romans had perfected the arch, vault, and dome as primary structural elements, and used them in spans not exceeded until the late 19th cent. They developed truss framing in metal as well as in wood. By discovering and exploiting natural deposits of hydraulic cement, they invented a true concrete which they often employed in mass for floors, vaults, and domes; it was also used as mortar for joints, as the infilling or core of double brick walls, and to increase the mass and rigidity of stone masonry. The vertical and horizontal thrusts of the dome and vault were sustained in Roman buildings by a solid bearing wall. The technique of carrying the dome to columns by means of small spherical triangles, known as pendentives, was the work of Byzantine architects, who also developed the method of sustaining the dome's outward thrust by peripheral semi-domes. The public and religious architecture of the Roman world was unparalleled, not only in its variety and scale but in its revelation of space as a dynamic entity shaped and defined by the individual

New materials have prompted new techniques and styles. Shown here is development from neo-gothic *Tribune Tower* (left), Chicago, to the more recent *Lever House* (right), New York, and the *Planalt Palace* (below), Brasilia (*shown in photo by M. Marino*).

building and by a number of buildings grouped in a civic plan. Roman achievement nourished centuries of architects, and some of the greatest buildings of our own age were derived directly from Roman precedents.

Medieval building developed from the more elemental Roman forms and techniques until the 12th cent., when a sudden outburst of creative activity produced the first system of framed construction in stone. The Gothic architect was primarily concerned with increasing the height of the cathedral, elongating vertical and horizontal perspectives, and admitting the maximum amount of light through immense stained-glass windows. To achieve these ends, he perfected a remarkable structure of slender, widely spaced columns, rib vaulting, and isolated buttresses, reducing all elements to a minimum cross-section consistent with safety. The entire complex, clearly visible inside and out, was structurally and esthetically unified by a rhythmic pattern of pointed arches running longitudinally between the columns and transversely and diagonally through the vault ribs. The outward thrust of the transverse ribs required a deepening of the narrow wall buttress, but to avoid this massive element, the architect separated part of the buttress from the wall, set it outside the main enclosure, and connected it to the inner structure by means of a shallow sloping arch. In such ways, the Gothic builder achieved an architecture of voids rather than solid masses.

Although the 16th and 17th cent. saw the establishment of modern empirico-mathematical science, little of this brilliant work was applied to the building art. The *Renaissance* architect was devoted to classical antiquity, but he was not a slavish idolater. By the end of the 15th cent., Italian builders had transformed the heavy, static Roman dome into the high ogival form of narrow ribs and pointed crown. In the 17th cent. the dome was developed into an ingenious arrangement of double and triple shells separated by truss framing, the outward thrust sustained by iron chains around the base of the dome. A further Baroque contribution was the construction of the solid bearing wall in an undulating form, often filled with niches, pilasters, and engaged columns to give the impression of intense rhythmic movement.

The *Industrial Revolution* at the end of the 18th cent. introduced two new factors, with radical consequences. Iron was substituted for traditional bearing materials, ending the long dominance of stone masonry. But even more decisive was the application of scientific method to the design and construction of buildings and to the investigation of the physical properties of their materials. By the close of the 19th cent., building art had been transformed from a pragmatic and empirical craft to an exact science. By 1885 architects and engineers had developed the internal steel frame of columns, beams, and shelf angles which carries the thin curtain wall of non-bearing materials—skyscraper construction, as it soon came to be called. Refinements such as wind-bracing, rigid framing, welding, and prefabricated wall panels made it possible to raise the height of a building to 1,000 ft or more, and to create the modern glass-walled skyscrapers that seem to float like weightless prisms above the ground.

The rediscovery of concrete as a structural material late in the 18th cent. offered an inexpensive substitute for the costly stonework of traditional building. The subsequent invention of reinforcing made it possible to use concrete in tension as well as compression, and by 1900 it began to appear in complete systems of internal framing. Since then it has been progressively applied to flat-slab construction (in which the beam no longer exists), to slender arch ribs, and to thin shells and plates. It has thus become possible to build vaults and domes of extremely wide clear spans with a shell only a few inches thick. The combination of folded concrete plates with steel suspension cables led to cantilever systems of unprecedented spans. Contemporary building is distinguished chiefly by an extraordinary lightness and buoyancy achieved by combining great linear dimensions with extreme delicacy of structural elements.—*C. W. C.*

ARCHYTAS OF TARENTUM, fl. *c.* 325 B. C., Greek mathematician and physicist. Founder of theoretical mechanics, and the first known to have applied mathematics to mechanics, he was the author of much of the mathematics of the Pythagorean School and the originator of a number of theorems. He duplicated the cube by means of intersecting cylindric sections and showed that there is no numerical geometrical mean between an integer and the next larger integer.— *D. H. D. R.*

ARCS AND DISCHARGES: Gases normally are poor electrical conductors. If a voltage difference is applied to plane parallel electrodes with gas between them, conduction sets in only when the voltage is made high. Under most circumstances, the gas then becomes ionized rapidly, probably in about 10^{-8} sec, and thus becomes an excellent conductor. If the voltage is supplied by a condenser, the condenser discharges rapidly. A violent phenomenon occurs in the gas with strong radiation of light (including ultraviolet) and a sharp noise: it is sometimes called a *spark*.

If the power supply is adequate to sustain some voltage difference between the electrodes, even with the heavy discharge current running, the current settles down to a steady-state value. In a sense, a *discharge* is still going on, as charge is flowing through the gas. There is emission of light but no noise except under special conditions. This state of affairs in the gas is now called an *arc* if the current is high, a *glow* if the current is low. The arc occurs when the cathode, or at least a spot on the cathode, is hot enough to yield appreciable THERMIONIC EMISSION, whereas the lower-current glow operates with cooler electrodes. The arc is therefore also a lower voltage phenomenon than the glow is. Arcs may operate with as little as 7 or 8 v potential difference, the typical carbon arc lamp usually running with about 50 v. Glows may occur at voltages as low as 75 v, but several hundred is more typical. Glow currents are usually under 25 milliamperes. Higher currents heat the cathode, and the glow changes to an arc.

The terms spark and arc are interchangeable in lay usage, but are sharply distinguished in scientific practice. The former refers to the high-voltage, short-duration, transient phenomenon; the latter refers to the low-voltage, high-current, steady-state process. Intermittent arcs are possible, but are normally started and stopped by external means. Sparks may be created only by applied voltages; arcs are often started by drawing apart two electrodes in contact—as when a switch is opened. The term *corona* refers to a variation of discharges characterized by non-uniform geometry of the electrodes. The term *gaseous discharges,* when used as a general title for a field of study, is today replaced by the term *gaseous electronics.* The field has been of great historical significance in the development of knowledge as to atomic structure, and has led to many practical uses, *e.g.* arc and fluorescent lighting.—*R. V.*

ARDUINO, GIOVANNI, 1714–95, Italian geologist; b. Caprino. He is known chiefly for his classification of N Italian rocks into: *primary rocks,* the cores of mountains, devoid of fossils; *secondary rocks,* stratified, containing many fossils; and *tertiary rocks,* made up of gravels, sand, clay, and other loose detritus. Arduino also wrote much on volcanoes.—*D. H. D. R.*

ARGAND, JEAN ROBERT, 1768–1822, French mathematician; b. Geneva. His *Essay on a Method of Representing Imaginary Quantities in Geometric Constructions* (1806) related to the development of complex numbers and their representation. It gave a geometrical representation of a complex number, $\sqrt{-1}$, and applied it to show that every algebraic equation has a root. This essay was published prior to the work of Gauss and Cauchy, but received little attention.—*S. B.*

ARGELANDER, FRIEDRICH WILHELM AUGUST, 1799–1875, German astronomer; b. Memel (then E Prussia). Noted for his research on the motion of the solar system, he was the first astronomer to solve the problem of PROPER MOTION (1837). He made observations on proper motions of stars, cataloging about 560 of them, and pioneered in research on variable stars. His *Durchmusterung* (1859–63) comprised a celestial atlas of positions and magnitudes (to the 9th) of 324,000 stars in the northern hemisphere (north celestial pole to declination $-2°$). Argelander's *Uranometria Nova* (1843) gave the then most accurate scale of magnitudes for all naked-eye stars in the northern hemisphere. He was a fellow of the Royal Society and an associate of the U. S. National Academy of Sciences.—*R. N. M.*

ARGON: an inert gaseous element (at. no. 18, at. wt 39.944, symbol A) found in the atmosphere (9.4 parts per 1,000). It is used to fill incandescent lamps and in certain phases of metalworking. See also INERT GASES.—*T. M.*

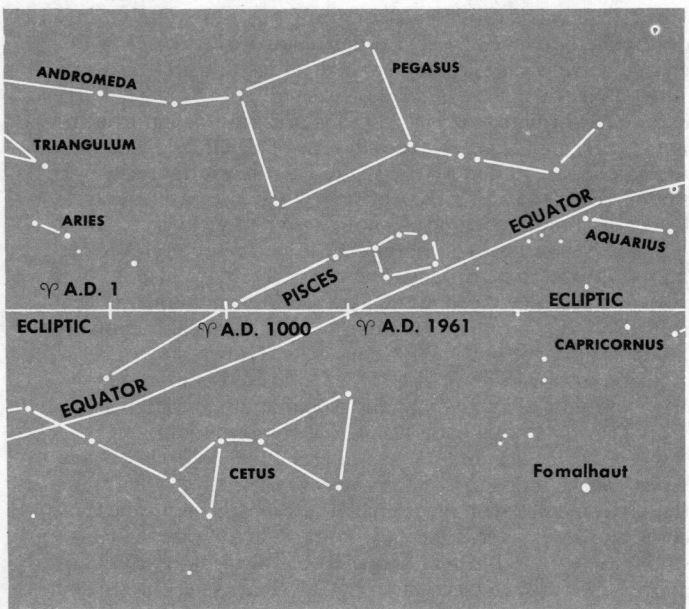

First point of Aries moves along ecliptic at rate of about 14° every 1,000 yr because of precession of the equinoxes. The point has moved from the constellation Aries into Pisces since 100 B. C.

ARIES, FIRST POINT OF: the vernal equinox, or point on the celestial equator crossed by the Sun from south to north about Mar. 21. The belt of sky that lies along the ecliptic (the Sun's path) is divided into 12 zones, or Signs of the ZODIAC. Their names are the same as the names of the zodiacal constellations, and at one time the signs and constellations corresponded. In ancient times when the Sun was at the vernal equinox, moving south to north, it was just entering the constellation Aries. However, owing to PRECESSION OF THE EQUINOXES (a slow westward motion of the equinoxes along the ecliptic), the signs of the Zodiac no longer correspond to the constellations of the same names. At present the first point of Aries lies in the constellation Pisces; it makes a complete circuit of the ecliptic in about 25,800 yr.—*M. W. O.*

ARISTARCHUS OF SAMOS, *c.* 310–230 B. C., Greek astronomer. He taught at Alexandria. Although not the first to suggest the Earth moves, Aristarchus maintained that Earth rotates on its own axis and revolves around the Sun. The first attempts to determine trigonometrically the distances of Sun and Moon from Earth and the relative sizes of these bodies were made by him. Aristarchus is credited with invention of the hemispherical sundial (scaphe) and with adding 1/1623 of a day to the estimate of 365¼ days for the length of a solar year proposed by Callippus.—*S. A. B.*

ARISTOTLE, 384–322/321 B. C., Greek philosopher and scientist; b. Stagira, Chalcidice. One of the most influential men who ever lived, he was the outstanding ancient figure in the history of science. His research in science, which extended through all areas, was probably most notable in observational zoology. He codified Greek knowledge in science and provided a comprehensive general theory of nature (the Aristotelian cosmology). His *Organon* (logical writings) introduced logic into science—probably the most significant scientific advance ever made, since logic enables scientists to organize theories and, since these are not directly verifiable, to test them by

observations. In contrast to the idealism of Plato, his teacher, Aristotle emphasized observation in science. When his works, particularly the *Organon,* became available in W Europe (12th cent.), they provided the foundation for modern science.—*D. H. D. R.*

ARITHMETIC: the oldest and most fundamental branch of mathematics, concerned with numbers, the operations by which numbers are combined, and their uses. There are two aspects of the mathematics of whole numbers, and "arithmetic" has been applied to both of them in different eras. The *arithmetica* of the Greeks was what is now called number theory. It was concerned with classes of whole numbers: odd and even, prime, composite, perfect, amicable, figurate. Mystical properties were sometimes attached to certain numbers. Modern number theory has often been termed a higher arithmetic. Arithmetic in common parlance is concerned with numerical calculation—the *logistics* of the Greeks and Romans. Some kind of arithmetic was developed by every primitive civilization, as a practical necessity. By modern standards the processes were often crude and inefficient, mainly because of the lack of a notation for numbers that was adapted to computation. Mechanical devices for rapid counting in groups, such as an abacus, were important instruments of arithmetic. With the development of POSITIONAL NOTATION and the use of a zero, the numbers of the Hindu-Arabic system became admirably adapted to computational needs. Consequently, modern arithmetic may be said to stem from the arithmetic of al-Khowarizmi (*c.* A. D. 825), which was based on this system. The term "algorism," or "algorithm," signifying a rule or process of calculation, is derived from his name.

Whole Numbers: What is a number? In particular, what is a whole number such as five? We use a definition given by Bertrand Russell. Imagine a set, or collection, of objects such as marbles, dogs, houses, that contains as many objects as there are fingers on one hand. Each object can be matched with one finger, and each finger with one object; the set of objects is said to be in one-to-one correspondence with the set of fingers, or with this set of crosses: X X X X X. The collection of all such sets is called the number 5. Every set in the collection contains 5 objects, and any set in the collection can be used as a representative of 5. Any whole number can be similarly defined as a collection of matched sets.

To determine the number of objects in a given set, one can search among the various collections until one finds a set to match the given set. The name of the collection to which the matching set belongs is the name of the number of objects in the given set. A shorter method of finding the number of objects in the set is known as counting. Counting implies that after the numbers have been defined as above, they are *ordered* with regard to size and placed in a sequence: 1, 2, 3, 4, 5, . . . Then to count a given set, we match the objects of the set with the words in the sequence in order until the set has been exhausted. The last word used in the matching process is the name of the number of objects in the set.

Operations with Whole Numbers: The arithmetic of whole numbers includes six operations: addition, multiplication, involution (raising to a power), and the inverses of these operations—namely, subtraction, division, and evolution (extracting a root). We shall define addition and multiplication using the set definitions of whole numbers given above. All of the other operations are then defined in terms of addition and multiplication.

Addition: What do we mean when we add two numbers, say 3 and 4? Recall that a whole number is a collection of matched sets. To add 3 and 4 (3 + 4 = ?), we select a representative (X X X) of 3 and a representative (X X X X) of 4 and place these two sets into a single set (X X X X X X X) called a *union*. The union is itself a representative set from some collection. By counting the objects in it, we find that the union contains 7 objects and therefore belongs to the collection called 7. We say that 7 is the sum of the addends 3 and 4. In general, to add whole numbers, pick representative sets for each addend and form the union of these representatives. The sum is the collection of which the union is the representative.

Multiplication: To multiply 3 and 4 ($3 \times 4 = ?$) we first pick a representative (X X X) of 3. Then we pair each object in this representative set with a representative (X X X X) of 4:

```
X            X            X
X X X X    X X X X    X X X X
```

We next form the union of these 3 representatives of 4. This union is a representative of the product of the factors 3 and 4; the product can be named, of course, by counting. The product of any two whole numbers can be obtained by this method.

Involution: This is the operation of raising to a power. To raise 3 to the 4th power ($3^4 = ?$), we use 3 as a factor four times and find the product; that is, 3^4 means $3 \times 3 \times 3 \times 3$, or 81. Here 3 is the base, 4 is the exponent, and the product 81 is the power. Involution can be defined in terms of collections of sets, but it is easier to define in terms of multiplication.

Subtraction: Here is the inverse of addition. An inverse operation is an "opposite" operation; it cancels the effect of a given operation. Thus, when 4 is added to 3 and then 4 is subtracted from the sum, we obtain the original 3. To subtract 3 from 4 ($4 - 3 = ?$), we must find that number (the difference) which, when added to 3 (the subtrahend), will give the sum 4 (the minuend).

Division: To divide 12 by 4 ($12 \div 4 = ?$), we find that number (the quotient), which, when multiplied by 4 (the divisor), will give 12 (the dividend) as the product. That is, $12 \div 4 = 3$ because $3 \times 4 = 12$. Note that division and multiplication are inverse operations, *e.g.* $(3 \times 4) \div 4 = 3$.

Evolution: Also called root extraction, evolution is the inverse of involution. To find the 4th root of 81 ($\sqrt[4]{81} = ?$), we find the number (the root) which, when raised to the 4th power (index 4), will give the power (the radicand) 81. Note the inverse relation $\sqrt[4]{3^4} = 3$.

The six operations above have been defined for whole numbers. When performed on whole numbers, the first three operations always lead to whole-number answers. But the inverse operations performed on whole numbers do not always yield whole-number answers; as, $6 - 8$, $2 \div 3$, and $\sqrt{4}$. To provide for these cases the system of whole numbers must be extended to include negative numbers, zero, fractions (rational numbers), and irrational numbers. (See NUMBER.)

Operations with Fractions: When a division (as $2 \div 3$) results in a fraction ($\frac{2}{3}$), the dividend (2) is called the *numerator,* and the divisor (3) the *denominator.* Many divisions produce the same quotient: $12 \div 4 = 6 \div 2 = 3 \div 1 = 3$. Written as fractions: $\frac{12}{4} = \frac{6}{2} = \frac{3}{1} = 3$. Thus removing, or canceling, a common factor from numerator and denominator does not affect the result, and it is often helpful to reduce a fraction to its lowest terms—*i.e.* to cancel all common factors.

Addition and *subtraction* of fractions is readily performed if the fractions have the same denominator: $\frac{3}{7} + \frac{2}{7} = \frac{5}{7}$. If not, they can be replaced by fractions with a common denominator: $\frac{2}{3} + \frac{1}{2} = \frac{4}{6} + \frac{3}{6} = \frac{7}{6}$. The least common denominator is the smallest number that contains each denominator as a factor. To find $\frac{3}{5} + \frac{2}{3} - \frac{1}{6}$, we observe that 30 contains each of 5, 3, and 6, since $\frac{3}{5} = \frac{18}{30}$, $\frac{2}{3} = \frac{20}{30}$, and $\frac{1}{6} = \frac{5}{30}$. Therefore

$$\frac{3}{5} + \frac{2}{3} - \frac{1}{6} = \frac{18 + 20 - 5}{30} = \frac{33}{30} = \frac{11}{10}$$

To *multiply* fractions, we simply multiply numerators and denominators; *e.g.*

$$\frac{4}{7} \times \frac{5}{6} = \frac{20}{42} = \frac{10}{21}, \quad \text{or} \quad \frac{4}{7} \times \frac{5}{6} = \frac{2 \times 5}{7 \times 3} = \frac{10}{21}$$

Division can be performed as multiplication with the use of reciprocals. The reciprocal of a number is 1 divided by the number: the reciprocal of 6 is $\frac{1}{6}$; the reciprocal of $\frac{2}{3}$ is $\frac{3}{2}$. To divide by a number, one multiplies by the reciprocal of the number, *e.g.*

$$\frac{5}{7} \div \frac{2}{3} = \frac{5}{7} \times \frac{3}{2} = \frac{15}{14}$$

Decimal Fractions: The decimal positional notation of whole numbers is extended to fractions. Thus, just as

$$324 = 3 \times 100 + 2 \times 10 + 4 = 3 \times 10^2 + 2 \times 10 + 4$$

so

$$0.528 = 5 \times \tfrac{1}{10} + 2 \times \tfrac{1}{100} + 8 \times \tfrac{1}{1000}$$
$$= 5 \times (\tfrac{1}{10}) + 2 \times (\tfrac{1}{10})^2 + 8 \times (\tfrac{1}{10})^3$$

The number 0.528 is called a decimal fraction. Every number of arithmetic can be expressed by a decimal, either exactly or to any desired degree of approximation. All operations utilizing positional notation can be extended to decimal fractions without change except for rules for placing the decimal point in the result. Consequently, decimal fractions have great utility.

Square Roots: Although roots are usually obtained by LOGARITHMS, square roots can be found by an algorithm. As an example, we will find the square root of 552.8. We first mark off pairs of numbers from the decimal point, 5,52.80, and examine the "pair" on the left, 5. The largest number whose square is less than 5 is 2, and $2^2 = 4$. We now subtract 4 from 5, and bring down the next pair:

```
2     5,52.80 ‖ 2
      4
      1 52
```

The 2 of the answer is doubled and multiplied by 10, resulting in 40. How many 40's are there in 152? The answer is 3, which is the next digit in the root. The 3 is multiplied by 43, and the product, 129, is subtracted from 152. The next pair is 0.80; the decimal point is placed in the answer, and the 80 brought down:

```
2     5,52.80 ‖ 23.
      4
43    1 52
      1 29
      23 80
```

Again the answer is doubled and multiplied by 10. How many 460's are there in 2,380? The answer is 5, which is the next digit in the root; 5×465 is 2,325, and this is subtracted from 2,380. Now a pair of zeros is brought down, the answer doubled, and the method repeated for as many decimal places as are required:

```
2     5,52.80 ‖ 23.51
      4
43    1 52
      1 29
465   23 80
      23 25
4701   5500
       4701
        799
```

—*B. P. S. and A. P. E.*

ARKWRIGHT, SIR RICHARD, 1732–92, English inventor and manufacturer; b. Preston, Lancashire. He learned the barber's trade and dealt in hair, but about 1767 devoted himself to the invention of a machine that could produce cotton thread of the firmness and hardness required in the warp. His spinning frame invention, patented 1769, accomplished all spinning operations simultaneously with a single power source. The hostility of spinners and weavers fearing unemployment forced Arkwright to move, and he went to Nottingham, where he built his first spinning mill, operated by horsepower. In 1771 he and his partners built a larger factory powered by a water wheel. In 1790 Arkwright introduced the use of a steam engine in his Nottingham mills.—*S. B.*

ARMSTRONG, EDWIN HOWARD, 1890–1954, U. S. inventor; b. New York City. One of the major contributors to the development of radio, he evolved the feed-back circuit (1914), greatly increasing the sensitivity of radio receivers; he also developed the superheterodyne circuit (1918) and invented frequency-modulation (FM) radio.—*D. H. D. R.*

AROMATIC COMPOUNDS: organic compounds the molecules of which have a benzene-ring or closely related cyclic structure (see diagrams below), and which exhibit chemical properties associated with BENZENE. They are so named because the first such compounds to be investigated were derived from substances with a penetrating, often fragrant odor, *e.g.* gum benzoin. Benzene itself is a hydrocarbon (C_6H_6), but its cyclic structure gives it properties markedly different from those of open-chain hydrocarbons (see ALIPHATIC COMPOUNDS). Also, though benzene has three double bonds in its molecular structure (see below), its double bonds are much more stable in the presence of chemical reagents than the double bonds of OLEFIN COMPOUNDS are. The cyclic structure of the aromatic compounds, however, does not alone explain their distinctive chemical properties; there are other cyclic compounds (*i.e.* ALICYCLIC COMPOUNDS) whose properties resemble those of aliphatic, not aromatic, compounds. Besides benzene, two other aromatic rings are thiophene and pyridine:

Benzene   Thiophene   Pyridine

According to current electron theory, each of the above molecules is perfectly flat and provides six electrons which have mobility in the ring structures (*i.e.* are not associated with any specific atom in the ring). Distinctive properties of the aromatic compounds are due to these mobile electrons.—*Ru. M.*

ARRHENIUS, SVANTE AUGUST, 1859–1927, Swedish physicist and chemist; b. castle of Wijk, near Uppsala. He won the Nobel prize in chemistry for his theory of electrolytic dissociation, presented in his *Researches on Galvanic Conductivity* (1903). Arrhenius also wrote *Textbook of Theoretical Electrochemistry* (1900) and works on biochemistry and planetary theory. His lectures at the Univ. of California, 1904, were published as the book *Immunochemistry* (1907). Arrhenius was director of the Nobel Institute for Physical Chemistry 1905–27. He was a fellow of the Royal Society and an associate of the U. S. National Academy of Sciences.—*D. H. D. R.*

ARS CONJECTANDI (The Art of Making Conjectures), by Jakob Bernoulli, 1713 (posthumously published): This early book on the theory of probability contains four parts. The first is an edition of the first book written on games of chance, the *De ratiociniis in ludo aleae* (*Reasonings on the Game of Chance*), by Christiaan Huygens (1657). The second part contains a theory of combinations, in which the so-called *Bernoulli numbers* are introduced as coefficients of the sums $1^k + 2^k + \ldots + n^k$, $k = 1, 2, 3$, *etc.* Here a form of induction is used. The third part deals with games of chance, and the fourth leads up to the so-called law of large numbers (or *Bernoulli's theorem*), expressing how the probability of an event can be obtained by studying its frequency in a large number of cases.—*D. J. S.*

ARSENIC: an element of the nitrogen family (group VA of the periodic table); symbol As, at. no. 33, at. wt 74.91. It has at least three allotropic forms, of which the best known and most common is a gray, crystalline form of density 5.73 and of metallic luster. This form sublimes without melting at atmospheric pressure, but melts at 814°C at 36 atm. This so-called "metallic" form of arsenic is a conductor of electricity and is relatively non-toxic in contrast to the other allotropic forms. It is prepared by reducing arsenious oxide with carbon. The element arsenic is widely distributed in the earth's crust, usually occurring in the form of metal arsenides, arsenious sulfide, or arsenious oxide. Arsenic forms two series of compounds, in which its valency is 3 and 5, respectively. Most arsenic compounds are produced from arsenious oxide, commonly called *white arsenic*. This is easily hydrated to arsenious acid, which forms salts with the usual metallic oxides. These salts, as well as the salts of arsenic acid, are highly toxic. Copper and lead arsenates are used as insecticides, and sodium arsenate as a weed killer. Arsenious oxide is also used in glass manufacture to counteract the coloring effect of iron and manganese impurities. Arsenic forms an extensive range of organic compounds, some of which have been used in chemotherapy, *e.g.* in treatment of syphilis and similar protozoan infections.—*G. W. M.* and *A. M. S.*

ARTERY: any of the vessels that conduct blood away from the heart. The artery into which blood is discharged directly from the heart *en route* to the tissues is called the aorta. Arteries that branch off from the aorta, in turn, branch repeatedly as they enter organs or tissues to which they supply blood. The diameter of each branch is smaller than that of the main artery, but the sum of the diameters, and hence the total cross-sectional area, of all branches is greater than the diameter or area of the main artery. From the smallest branches, called *arterioles,* the capillary network branches out.

Arteries are tubes, circular in cross section, with a wall that typically has three layers. The inner lining is endothelium, made up of thin, flat cells and continuous with the endothelial wall of the capillaries. The middle layer consists of alternating layers of elastic connective tissue and muscle cells whose fibers encircle the artery. The outer layer is thin connective tissue. In the aorta and larger arteries the middle layer is thick and mostly of elastic tissue. In smaller arteries and arterioles, the middle layer is thick and mostly of muscle. In the smallest arterioles the muscle layer becomes thin, with scattered cells. In larger arteries the outer layer has its own circulatory system of small arteries, capillaries, and veins—the *vasa vasorum,* or vessels of the vessels—which provide the middle layer with food and oxygen. In old age, in mammals at least, the elastic tissue of the middle layer becomes hardened by deposition of calcium salts, and the arteries lose their elasticity. Elasticity may also be lost, and the diameter of the arteries decreased, by deposition of cholesterol in the artery wall; this is atherosclerosis (a type of arteriosclerosis).

Arterioles, with their muscular walls, are important in regulation of blood pressure and blood flow. Resistance to flow of blood through any tube increases with decreasing diameter of the individual vessel, while volume of blood flow increases with total cross-sectional area of available channels. Arterioles, with a large total area and small individual diameter, account for most (about 55%) of the fall in blood pressure between the aorta and the great veins which return blood to the heart. This fall of pressure can be regulated by variations in diameter of arterioles. When muscle cells of the arteriole wall contract, the vessel is constricted; when these muscles relax, it dilates. General constriction of arterioles increases resistance to blood flow, hence increases blood pressure; dilation has the opposite effect. Constriction of arterioles in a local region diverts blood from that region to other regions where the cross-sectional area is greater; dilation increases flow through the dilated region.

The state of contraction of the arteriolar muscles is determined by three factors. Local products of tissue activity cause relaxation. Vasoconstrictor nerves, running in the sympathetic division of the autonomic nervous system, cause contraction. Vasodilator nerves from various sources cause relaxation. Vasodilators are of only local or intermittent importance. Vasoconstrictors are continuously active to varying degrees under the influence of the vasomotor nerve center in the brain and are the major factor in regulating blood pressure. The dilator effects of local tissue activity are the major factor in regulating blood flow through tissues. See BLOOD VESSELS; CIRCULATION IN LIVING THINGS; VASOMOTOR SYSTEM.— B. T. S.

ARTESIAN WELL: originally, a well in which GROUND WATER rises to the surface because of hydrostatic pressure; recently, any well in which the water level rises above the level of the water-bearing strata. The artesian well penetrates a permeable bed of rock, *e.g.* sandstone, which is sealed above and below by impermeable layers and which slopes so that the level at which the water enters is higher than the top of the well. The water-carrying bed is called an *aquifer*. If too many wells are dug into a specific aquifer, the water is taken out faster than it enters and pressure drops, rendering many of the wells useless. When the pressure is not great enough to cause the water to reach the surface, pumps are needed to draw out the water. Some wells are incorrectly called artesian simply because they are deep. True artesian wells are named for the province of Artois, France, where they were first drilled in the 12th cent. In North America, the Dakota sandstone layer, which underlies much of the western and central U. S. A. and Canada, is an important reservoir for artesian wells. This layer outcrops along the flanks of the Rocky Mountains, where it absorbs its water, and then dips downward beneath vast areas in Saskatchewan, Montana, the Dakotas, Wyoming, Nebraska, and Kansas. Argentina and Australia also depend largely upon artesian water.—*A. P. E.*

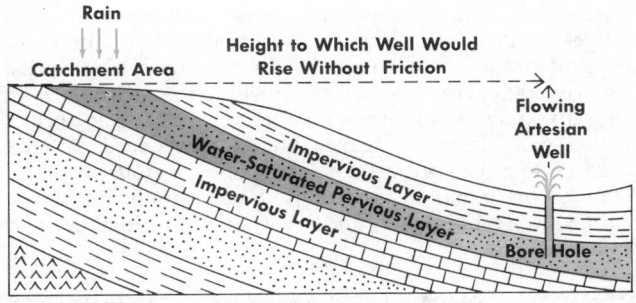

Artesian well: Surface water entering a sloping permeable bed at upper edge moves downward by gravity between layers of impervious rock. Water in well is under natural pressure.

700,000 species of arthropods populate Earth. This mandible-waving specimen—a crustacean—is a land crab. (*Walter Dawn*)

Crab's sturdy carapace is displayed in dorsal view. Impermeable material of exoskeleton helps retain body fluids. (*Walter Dawn*)

ARTHROPOD: any animal of the phylum Arthropoda, the largest division of the animal kingdom with its 700,000 described species. Insects, spiders, and crustaceans are familiar arthropods. Size ranges from microscopic mites to giant spider crabs with a leg span up to 20 ft. Arthropods are characterized by an exoskeleton, externally jointed appendages, and a body composed of more or less similar segments arranged in series. In all respects except development of a nervous system capable of intelligence, the arthropod plan of body organization is the most successful in every conceivable climate, geographic area, and habitat. Arthropods thrive from the arctic to the antarctic, from mountain top to ocean bottom.

Arthropods are most closely related to segmented worms (earthworms and the like); both probably evolved from a common wormlike ancestor in a remote geologic time. Another probable descendant from the same ancestor is the rare, caterpillar-like peripatus, a dweller in tropical forests. This "connecting link" between arthropods and segmented worms has some characteristics of each, in addition to some all its own. Although peripatus is usually put in a separate phylum (Onychophora), some zoologists think it belongs with the segmented worms, whereas others consider it an arthropod. The most primitive arthropods consisted of body segments that were nearly all alike, each segment bearing simple, flattened appendages. The extinct trilobites, oldest known arthropods, approached this form; modern fairy shrimp are only slightly different. But in the course of evolution the body and appendages of most arthropod groups became specialized in structure and function. Thus the body of insects and many other arthropods is divided into three regions: head, thorax, and abdomen. Similarly, appendages are modified for specific functions, *e.g.* feeding, locomotion, and nest-building.

The arthropod exoskeleton typically consists of a thin, waxy outer layer and two horny inner layers containing CHITIN. One inner layer is rigid, the other flexible. At joints, the rigid layer is lacking, and this permits articulated movement. Muscles are attached to the inside of the skeleton, in contrast to the skeletal muscles of man and other vertebrates, which are attached to the outer surfaces of bones. The exoskeleton not only serves as protective armor, but also helps keep watery tissues from drying out. Periodically the external skeleton is shed and replaced by a larger one in the process known as MOLTING, which permits the animal to grow. Exoskeletons may be thin and weak, as in flies and moths, or thick and strong, as in crabs and lobsters.

Typically, the external skeleton encloses a blood-filled cavity in which the internal organs are located. These consist of a dorsal brain and ventral ganglionic nerve cord, a digestive tube that runs from mouth to anus, reproductive organs, respiratory tubes (tracheae) in terrestrial forms (most aquatic forms breathe by means of gills), and in many cases a dorsal heart for pumping blood through the cavity containing the organs. Arthropods usually have two kinds of eyes, simple (ocelli) and compound. But they may have no eyes, ocelli alone, clusters of simple eyes, or only compound eyes. Simple eyes have but one cornea, which provides the eye with a single light-condensing structure. Compound eyes consist of many individual units known as ommatidia, each of which has a corneal covering known as a facet (see EYE). With relatively few exceptions, arthropods have separate sexes: species populations are represented by male and female individuals. Most arthropods lay eggs, but in some arachnids and insects the eggs are hatched within the mother and the young are born alive. PARTHENOGENESIS, or development of eggs without fertilization by the male, is found in some crustaceans and some insects. Complex mating behavior is often exhibited, especially by spiders and insects.

There are two major divisions of arthropods. The chelicerate branch, so named because the first pair of appendages are chelicerae (small pincers), includes horseshoe crabs, scorpions, spiders, ticks, mites, and their less well-known relatives (see ARACHNIDS). The mandibulate branch, characterized by mandibles that are usually in the form of strong biting jaws, is composed of CRUSTACEANS, INSECTS, millipedes, centipedes, and some lesser groups. Centipedes (about 1,700 described species) and millipedes (about 6,300 species) are wormlike, many-legged animals whose bodies are divided into two main regions: head and trunk. Depending on species, the trunk may consist of from less than 10 to more than 100 segments. Centipedes have one pair of legs per trunk segment; millipedes, two pairs. Centipedes are fast-moving and carnivorous; the legs of their first trunk segment are modified to form powerful pincer-like poison fangs that are used to seize and kill insects, worms, and other prey. Millipedes are slow-moving plant-eaters; along each side of the body are glands that emit a disagreeable odor. Whereas all millipedes are harmless to man, some giant tropical centipedes, which may reach a length of 10½ in., can inflict a painful bite.—*R. G. M.* (See Color Plates f.p. 70.)

ARTIFICIAL ELEMENTS: chemical elements which are found very rarely or not at all in nature, and must therefore be synthesized in the laboratory. They include technetium (element 43), promethium (element 61), astatine (element 85), francium (element 87), and the TRANSURANIUM ELEMENTS. None of these, apparently, has a stable form. If they existed at the time the earth was formed (and probably several did), they have long since decayed or disintegrated into lighter elements. Artificial elements are made in high-energy machines (*e.g.* cyclotrons) and nuclear reactors by bombarding nuclei of lighter or heavier elements with electrons, protons, neutrons, and larger nuclear particles, thus building up the lighter nuclei or breaking down the heavier ones to produce a nucleus of the desired weight. Thus technetium (element 43) is made by bombarding molybdenum (element 42) with deuterons ("heavy" hydrogen nuclei). Promethium is a uranium fission product but may also be made by irradiating neodymium, the next lighter element, with neutrons. Bombarding bismuth (element 83) with alpha particles (helium nuclei) produces astatine (element 85), while francium (element 87) can be made by bombardment of thorium and fission of uranium. Francium does have one "natural" isotope, resulting from alpha decay (emission of a nuclear particle corresponding to a helium nucleus) of actinium (element 89), but so little francium is produced this way that element 87 is not generally considered natural.

Aside from their instability and consequent radioactivity, the artificial elements do not differ from natural ones. They exhibit all of the chemical and physical properties of the natural elements, and are similar in these respects to the elements which surround them in the periodic table. Thus technetium is a metallic element, intermediate in properties between manganese and rhenium, and forms brightly colored pertechnates, corresponding to the familiar purple permanganates; while promethium fits neatly into the LANTHANIDES (rare earths) and is so similar chemically to the other lanthanides that it is difficult to distinguish it. Likewise, astatine fits with the halogen elements, being somewhat more electropositive than iodine, the halogen above it in the periodic table; and francium, one of the ALKALI METALS, is even more volatile and readily ionized than cesium, the highest "natural" element in the alkali metal series.—*A. R. G.*

ARTIFICIAL HORIZON: see AIRCRAFT INSTRUMENTATION.

ARTIFICIAL INSEMINATION: introduction of seminal fluid or a suspension of sperm into the reproductive tract of a female by artificial means. It has been useful in animal breeding. Because seminal fluid can be greatly diluted and then sent under refrigeration for long distances, the breeder can obtain many more offspring from a single male with a desirable heredity (*e.g.* resistance to disease) than would be possible with natural mating. Artificial insemination eliminates the need of smaller dairy farms to keep a bull and the need of horse breeders to transport valuable animals for stud purposes. Artificial insemination is also used successfully for sheep, poultry, honeybees, and, under certain conditions, human beings.—*G. B. M.*

ASBESTOS: any of several fibrous silicate minerals that exhibit resistance to heat and chemicals. The principal asbestos of commerce is chrysotile, a variety of serpentine. Less common are varieties of amphibole, including amosite and anthophyllite (both orthorhombic), and actinolite, tremolite, and crocidolite (all monoclinic); see MINERALS, table. Almost all the important deposits are of metamorphic origin, derived from ultrabasic igneous rocks or magnesian limestones. The three distinct forms of occurrence, each of which affects the beneficiation and ultimate use of the material, are (1) *Mass fiber:* irregular, unoriented aggregates disseminated through rock; (2) *Cross fiber:* Veinlets, in which the fibers are perpendicular to the walls; (3) *Slip fiber:* Bundles of fibers in fractured zones, the elongation of the fibers paralleling the direction of relative movements of the walls. Only slip-fiber asbestos and material from the widest cross-fiber veins are long enough to be used in fabrics and other products that require spinning and weaving. Mass-fiber deposits and most cross-fiber veinlets provide only "shorts," of considerably lower value, which are used principally in asbestos-cement construction materials. Fabrics made from asbestos are used for fire-fighters' garments, gloves, and shields, and for fireproof curtains and brake linings. The short fibers find use in insulating boards, shingles, papers, pipe coverings, molded products, electrical insulation, and filters for chemicals.—*L. M.*

ASCORBIC ACID: see VITAMINS.

ASPHALT: a black or brown semisolid or solid cementitious material derived from petroleum and consisting of a mixture of hydrocarbons. It gradually softens when heated. Found in natural deposits, asphalt also is obtained as the residue after distillation of certain crude petroleums or as the extract from selected petroleum oils. Mixed with mineral aggregate, fillers, or fibrous materials, it is used in road making, waterproofing, and coatings. In the United Kingdom the term "(asphaltic) bitumen" is used for "asphalt," and there "asphalt" refers to the mixture of "bitumen" and mineral aggregate.—*R. J. F.*

ASSAYING: analysis of an ore or an alloy for metal content. The term usually refers to precious metal ores and the older "fire assay" methods rather than to modern wet chemical or spectroscopic procedures. The first step in fire assaying for gold and silver is to heat a carefully selected sample with a suitable reducing flux and lead oxide to about 1200°C. The precious metal forms a lead alloy, which is readily separated from the flux after cooling. After further purification of this lead alloy "button" by fluxing and heating, the precious metal is separated from the lead by heating in a special bone-ash crucible called a cupel. The lead is oxidized to molten litharge, which is absorbed by capillarity into the walls of the cupel, leaving the pure gold-silver alloy. The silver is finally separated or "parted" from the gold by dissolving in nitric acid. (See CHEMICAL ANALYSIS.) The term "assay" is also applied to analysis of drugs for their active-ingredient content.—*A. M. S.*

ASSIMILATION: the process whereby food is taken into and made a part of a cell or organism. The food is first broken down by DIGESTION into its component parts, and then utilized to form new substances in anabolism or oxidized to provide energy in catabolism. See METABOLISM.—*B. T. S.*

ASSOCIATION: in chemistry, the connection or combination of simple molecules to form relatively complex ones of the same substance. This phenomenon is responsible for the unusually high boiling point and heat of vaporization of water,

Asteroid paths: Orbits of the minor planets lie chiefly between those of Mars and Jupiter, but many extend elsewhere in the solar system.

hydrogen fluoride, and acetic acid. Water or organic acid molecules associate by hydrogen bonding as

—*G. W. M.*

ASTATINE: a radioactive, very unstable element (At); at. no. 85; at. wt 210 (longest-lived isotope). It was first prepared in 1940 by E. Segrè *et al.* at the Univ. of California by bombarding bismuth with alpha particles in a cyclotron, but has since been found to occur naturally in very minute amounts. Though astatine is placed with the halogen elements in the periodic table (group 7A: fluorine, bromine, chlorine, iodine), it is more markedly metallic than the four principal halogens. At^{210} has a half-life of 8.3 hr.—*G. W. M.*

ASTEROID: any of a numerous group of small planets, also called *minor planets* or *planetoids,* located chiefly between the orbits of Mars and Jupiter. All are smaller than the nine principal planets: whereas the smallest principal planet (Mercury) is 3,000 mi in diameter, Ceres, the largest asteroid, is only about 480 mi in diameter. The smallest asteroids known are barely a mile or two in diameter, and these bodies probably grade into the yet smaller meteorites. Vesta is sometimes faintly visible to the unaided eye; no other asteroid is.

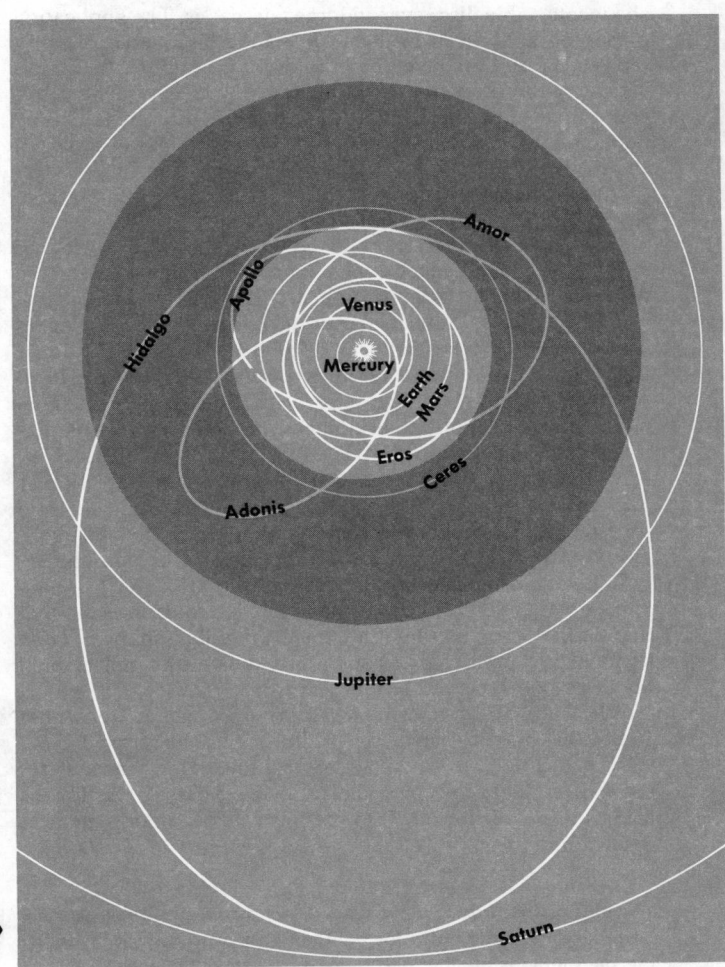

Asteroid's movement against background of stars shows up as trail on long-exposure photograph. Clock mechanism kept camera sighted relative to stars despite Earth's rotation. (*Yerkes*)

Discovery of a regular progression in planetary distances (BODE'S LAW) led to conjecture, in the late 18th cent., as to a "missing planet" between Mars and Jupiter. Piazzi discovered Ceres in 1801; and Pallas, Juno, and Vesta were also known by 1807. Visual discovery required the painstaking technique of recognizing a "star" that moved against the background of true stars, for only a few of the largest asteroids show detectable discs even in large telescopes. The application of photography from 1891 onward made discoveries of asteroids easier and inconveniently numerous. About 2,000 asteroids are now known well enough to have had their orbits computed; the total number must be much greater. Any adequate theory of the origin of the solar system must explain the swarm of asteroids, and they have been alternately interpreted as the fragments of a disrupted planet or as material which failed to form a single planet.

Most asteroids have orbits between those of Mars and Jupiter, but some exceptions occur. Icarus has a perihelion only 19,000,000 mi from the Sun, and Hidalgo has an aphelion near the orbit of Saturn. A few asteroids approach Earth's orbit very closely: Apollo, 3,000,000 mi, in 1932; Adonis, 1,000,000 mi, 1936; and Hermes, perhaps 400,000 mi, 1937. Asteroid orbits exhibit greater eccentricities and larger inclinations to the ecliptic than do orbits of the principal planets —(*e.g.* 0.66 and 43°, respectively, for the exceptional Hidalgo). All asteroids revolve around the Sun in the same direction as the principal planets. Kirkwood's Gaps in the main asteroid zone reveal the gravitational effects of Jupiter (see PERTURBATIONS) in positions where such action would be cumulative.

These small bodies lack the gravitational power to retain atmospheres. Light variations in some asteroids indicate that the bodies are rotating and have irregular shapes. Their surfaces are presumably rough and rocky, and reflect light about as poorly as the Moon (see ALBEDO).

When in 1931 the asteroid Eros approached to within 16,000,000 mi of Earth, it was intensively observed from various locations to get accurate positions. H. Spencer Jones reduced the data to secure the value of 93,010,000 mi for the mean distance from Earth to the Sun; this is among the best determinations so far of the *astronomical unit.*—*W. H.*

Astrolabe: This woodcut of 1585 shows astrolabes being used to determine the height of a tower. They were also used for measuring the altitudes of stars and planets. (*Gossner Collection*)

ASTON, FRANCIS WILLIAM, 1877–1945, English chemist; b. Harborne. In 1910 he joined J. J. Thomson at Cambridge in research on electrical discharges in vacuum tubes. From this he developed a method for separation of electrically charged gas particles, according to their atomic weights, by mass spectrometry. Thus he found that neon consists of two isotopes with at. wt 20 and 22. For his discovery, by means of his mass spectroscope, of the isotopes of a large number of non-radioactive elements, as well as for his discovery of the whole-number rule, he received the Nobel prize, 1922. He was a fellow of the Royal Society.—*E. F.*

ASTROBLEME: an impact scar left on the face of Earth by collision with a meteorite, asteroid, or comet head long ago. The term "astrobleme" is from the Greek for "star" and "wound by a thrown object." Initially, such hypervelocity impacts create METEOR CRATERS, *e.g.* Meteor (Barringer) Crater of Arizona, but eventually erosion reduces such depressions to a circular scar of deranged rock containing SHATTER CONES or COESITE. In recent years more than a dozen such astroblemes have been recognized by geologists. —*R. S. D.*

ASTROLABE: an ancient instrument for measuring the altitude of a celestial body, and for converting the observation into an hour angle; also, a modern instrument for determining latitudes. The ancient astrolabe was a metal disc with a sighting device (alidade) pivoted at its center. It was held suspended

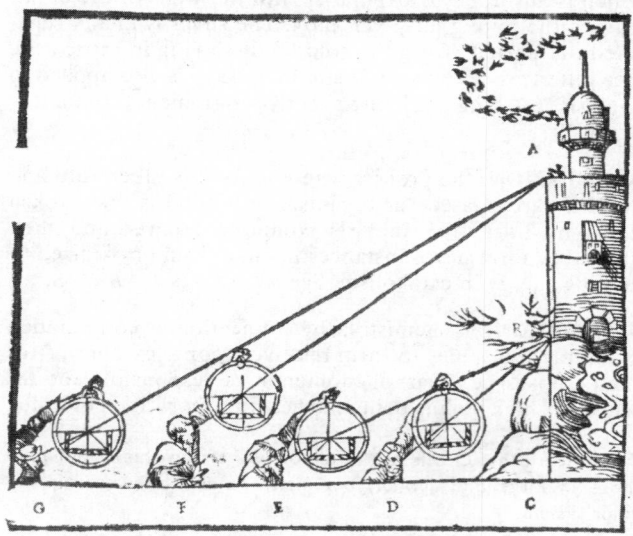

n. 1356.

by a ring from the observer's thumb, and the altitude of the body read directly from an engraved scale. The disc was engraved with star maps and a circle of the Zodiac showing the Sun's position throughout the year, with a scale of hour angles on the rim. The instrument also incorporated a series of tablets showing circles of equal altitude for given latitudes. Time could be determined directly from observations of the Sun. A primitive astrolabe was described by Ptolemy in the *Almagest* (c. A. D. 145), and the device was developed into an instrument of precision by the Arabs. It was much used in Europe in the Middle Ages, until replaced by the quadrant and the sextant. The modern, prismatic astrolabe consists essentially of a telescope with a 60° prism mounted in front of the object glass, and a basin of mercury placed so as to reflect light onto the lower face of the prism. On looking through the telescope at a star that is approaching and near to the altitude of 60°, the observer sees two images of the star moving toward each other. At the moment when the two images coalesce, the apparent altitude of the star is 60°. The time of this moment is taken and may be used to determine the observer's latitude.—*M. W. O.*

ASTROLOGY: formerly, the theory and practice of foretelling from stellar observations both astronomical and other natural events ("natural astrology"), and the course of human affairs as allegedly influenced by the stars ("judicial astrology"); in modern usage, only the latter form of divination. To primitives, astronomical and meteorological phenomena appear to be of the same nature or origin; their correlation in the seasonal cycle, and the different aspect of Sun and Moon in different atmospheric conditions, indicating weather changes, constitute an empirical nucleus for astrology, which originally views the world as dominated by divinities in the sky. First cultivated by Babylonian priests, who searched the sky for and interpreted signs of divine will affecting king and country, astrology penetrated Asia Minor and Greece, flourishing in late Hellenism. No longer concerned only with events of collective interest, but purporting also to divine an individual's fate from the configuration of planets and stars at his birth (horoscopy), and linked to alchemy and other lore, astrology spread throughout the Roman Empire, India, and China. Opposed by the early Church as incompatible with free will, astrology regained status in Europe with the revival of ancient learning through Arab influence, and acquired tremendous prestige at the royal courts and among the people in the 14th and 15th cent. Throughout history, statesmen and tyrants from Roman emperors to Hitler, men of letters (Chaucer, Francis Bacon, Milton), distinguished astronomers (Ptolemy, Brahe, Kepler), have held or professed belief in astrology. This fact appears less surprising if one notes that astrology, like any other doctrine, is "unscientific" only insofar as it lacks or contradicts evidence, or is inconsistent with an empirically supported scheme of things; it is not a priori illegitimate as an hypothesis. Astrology still has many devotees, though not in the scientific community.

No other single factor promoted astronomy more than astrology did. Through millennia of observation, the Babylonian priests disentangled the cycles in the apparent motions of stars and planets that make up the succession of seemingly ever-changing configurations, thus also making the intrinsic difference between meteorological and astronomical phenomena manifest. Though progressing only in the description of appearances, never questioning the primitive conceptions of the nature of the sky and its objects, astrologers accumulated a wealth of data that were to be the basis for Greek and subsequent astronomical speculation till the time of Brahe. See ASTRONOMY.—*G. G.*

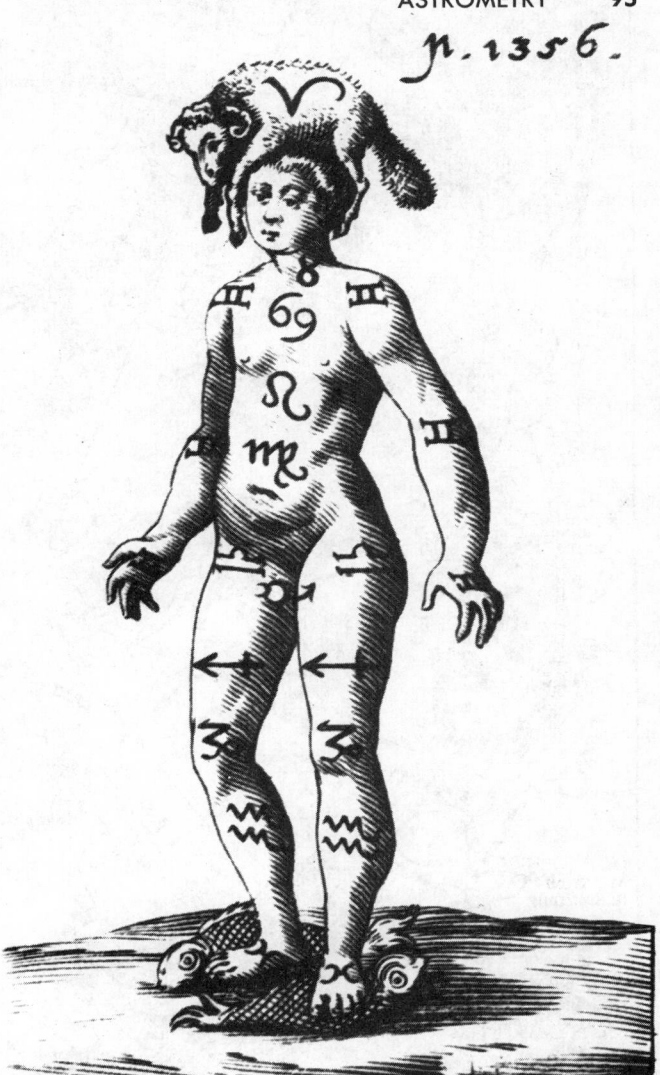

Zodiac man: Pseudo-medical lore was an integral part of medieval and Renaissance astrology. Health precepts based on the influence of zodiacal signs were usually included in popular almanacs—a practice which remained common to the end of the 17th cent. It was believed that each section of the human body was under the direct tutelage of a particular sign: Aries ruled the head; Taurus, the neck; Gemini, the shoulders and arms; Cancer, the chest and lungs; Leo, the heart and stomach; Virgo, the abdomen; Libra, the kidneys and hips; Scorpius, the lower abdomen; Sagittarius, the thighs; Capricornus, the knees; Aquarius, the legs; and Pisces, the feet. Users of astrological almanacs had, as a rule, a very poor knowledge of anatomy. Therefore, it was customary to include the picture of a zodiac man in which the appropriate zodiacal sign had been drawn on the corresponding limb. (*Gossner Collection*)

ASTROMETRY: positional astronomy; the branch of astronomy that deals with determination of the positions of celestial objects and of their movements perpendicular to the line of sight. Fundamental observations of position are made with a meridian transit instrument at the time a body is crossing, or near, the meridian. Positions and motions of fainter stars are measured photographically in relation to reference stars in the field. Observation of the northern sky has been much more thorough than for the southern sky, but increased astrometric observation of the southern sky is planned.—*R. N. M.*

Celestial map: Ornate maps of the heavens prepared by Renaissance artists included this woodcut, a polar projection, by Albrecht Dürer (1471–1528). According to the custom, mythological figures representing the constellations were portrayed in exquisite detail. The graduated circle gives ecliptic longitude. Portraits of famous astronomers adorn the corners. (*Nat. Gallery of Art*)

ASTRONAUTICS: see SPACE TRAVEL.

ASTRONOMIA NOVA ΑΙΤΙΟΛΟΓΗΤΟΣ **Seu Physica Coelestis Tradita Commentariis de Motibus Stellae Martis (A New Astronomy based on causes, or Celestial Physics, explained in commentaries on the motions of the Planet Mars),** by Johann Kepler, 1609: This most important of Kepler's books was made possible by his use of the careful astronomical observations of Tycho Brahe. Seeking the theory of the orbit of Mars among them, Kepler found (1) that the planes of all the planetary orbits pass through the Sun (a concept missed by Copernicus), and (2) that the planetary velocities must be such that a line from the planet to the eccentrically placed Sun sweeps over equal areas of the orbit in equal times (Kepler's 2d Law). At first he thought of this orbit as circular but, continuing his calculations, he could find no circle that accurately fitted Tycho's observations of Mars. After much

effort he hit the truth: the orbit is an ellipse with the Sun at one focus (Kepler's 1st Law). He explained this motion physically by the interaction of magnetic forces in the Sun and the planet. Thus the age-old problem of planetary motion was finally solved, and the empirical foundations of celestial mechanics laid.—*A. R. H.*

ASTRONOMICAL CATALOGS, MAPS, AND ATLASES: Astronomical catalogs list star positions and magnitudes, and may give also any of the following: proper motions, parallaxes, radial velocities, spectral classes, photometric magnitudes. Special catalogs list also variable stars, double stars, spectroscopic binaries, nebulas, or galaxies. Maps and atlases range from those showing a few hundred of the brighter stars, for visual use, to those showing millions of stars, clusters, and nebulas, visible only in large telescopes. Symbols are used to indicate stellar magnitudes and types of objects; other information, *e.g.* spectral classes and periods of variables, may also be recorded. Many large atlases are published together with a catalog.

Early maps showed only the naked-eye stars, grouped into CONSTELLATIONS defined by the distinct configurations of the brightest stars, *e.g.* Ursa Major. The constellations were given names mostly taken from Greek and Roman mythology, and were often depicted as mythological figures, sometimes hand-colored. The first star catalog recorded was made by Hipparchus (190–120 B. C.), and contained 1,080 stars. The oldest catalog extant was published by Ptolemy in his *Almagest* (A. D. *c.* 150); it grouped 1,028 stars into 48 constellations. The last catalog before the invention of the telescope was that published by Tycho Brahe in 1580, listing 1,005 stars.

No distinct sky boundaries were laid down by ancient peoples; hence there were many gaps in maps of the celestial sphere, especially for areas that never rose above the horizon of the observers in northern latitudes. It was not until after 1600 that new constellations were added to fill the vacancies —12 by Hevelius (1611–87), 8 by Halley (1656–1742), and 14 by Lacaille (1713–62). Important maps were those of Bayer (1572–1625), containing 1,709 stars; Bode (1747–1826), 17,240; and Lalande (1732–1807), 50,000.

Argelander (1799–1875) published catalogs and an atlas that indicated boundaries of constellations in the northern hemisphere; B. A. Gould (1824–1896) indicated boundaries in the southern hemisphere. Their boundaries were somewhat arbitrary and irregular, and in 1928 the International Astronomical Union adopted a new system. While following those of Argelander and Gould as closely as possible, the new system defines exactly the boundaries of the 88 constellations now recognized.

Modern atlases accompanied by catalogs include the *Bonner Durchmusterung* (BD), which catalogs 324,000 stars; the *Cordoba* (CD), about 580,000; and the *Cape Photographic* (CPD), which maps stars of the southern sky, cataloging 455,000. Catalogs that give positions with the greatest possible precision include the *Astronomische Gesellschaft Katalog* (AG or AGC) or improved observations of the (BD) stars, and the photographic *Astrographic Catalogue* (AC) of the *Carte Photographique Ciel,* a cooperative enterprise of 18 world observatories begun in 1887. Some of these charts are still to be published. The AC will list about 10 million stars.

The latest photographic map is the *Palomar-National Geographic Atlas,* which shows hundreds of millions of stars, down to 20th mag. The positions of stars in most catalogs are determined by comparison with a few stars whose positions are known with great accuracy. These accurate star positions are obtained from long series of observations of the heavens,

and are listed in fundamental catalogs such as the *Vierter Fundamental Katalog* (FK4). Among the best-known catalogs of star clusters, nebulas, and galaxies are Messier's *Catalog of Nebulas and Clusters* (M), published 1781 as a list of objects that observers should not confuse with comets; Dreyer's *New General Catalogue* (NGC); and the *Index Catalogue* (IC).

A celestial object may be designated by its number in any catalog. Thus the Andromeda Galaxy is M31 or NGC 224. Sirius, brightest star in the constellation Canis Major, is α Canis Majoris (Bayer), PGC 1732 (Boss), GC 8833 (Boss), BD − 16° 1591 (*Durchmusterung*), or HD 48915 (Henry Draper).—*R. N. M.*

ASTRONOMICAL DISTANCE UNITS: the unit of distance for objects within the solar system is the *astronomical unit,* the mean distance of Earth from Sun. It is determined, in miles, from observations of the distances of planets and minor planets by the method of parallax (see PARALLAX, SOLAR). Recent determinations give about 93,000,000 mi for this unit. For stars the unit of distance is the *parsec.* The distances of stars are determined fundamentally by the method of annual parallax (see PARALLAX, STELLAR). The distance of a star whose parallax is p'' is by definition $1/p$ parsecs. A star at a distance of 1 parsec would be 19.16 million million mi away. The nearest star (Proxima Centauri) really is at a distance of a little less than 1⅓ parsecs; the Sun is about 8,000 parsecs (8 *kiloparsecs*) from the center of the Galaxy; the diameter of the Galaxy is about 25 kiloparsecs. The nearest extragalactic nebulas (the Magellanic Clouds) are at a distance of about 45 kiloparsecs; the distances of remote galaxies are measured in millions of parsecs, or *megaparsecs.* An alternative unit of stellar distance, the *light-year,* is the distance that light travels in a vacuum in a year at 186,282 mi/sec. A light-year is 5.88 million million mi, or 0.3069 parsec. For methods of measuring astronomical distances, see PARALLAX (SOLAR, STELLAR, SPECTROSCOPIC).—*M. W. O.*

Star chart: Map used by observers of variable stars locates the variable R Leporis (circled, near center) in terms of right ascension and declination. Star field lies partly in the constellation Lepus, partly in Eridanus. Each white dot represents a star; dot size corresponds to visual magnitude (brightness); all stars in this sector of sky that are ordinarily of about mag. 11 or brighter appear on this map. Numbers next to certain stars are magnitudes, the decimal point being omitted before each final digit (thus "106" means 10.6 mag., and "59" means 5.9). Notations under the name R Leporis give position of the star as of 1950; the designation 045514 (upper left corner) was based on the slightly different position of 1900 (see STAR NAMES AND DESIGNATIONS). Star maps are available for varying astronomical purposes, ranging from the work of amateurs to the highly technical activities of astronomical observatories. (AAVSO)

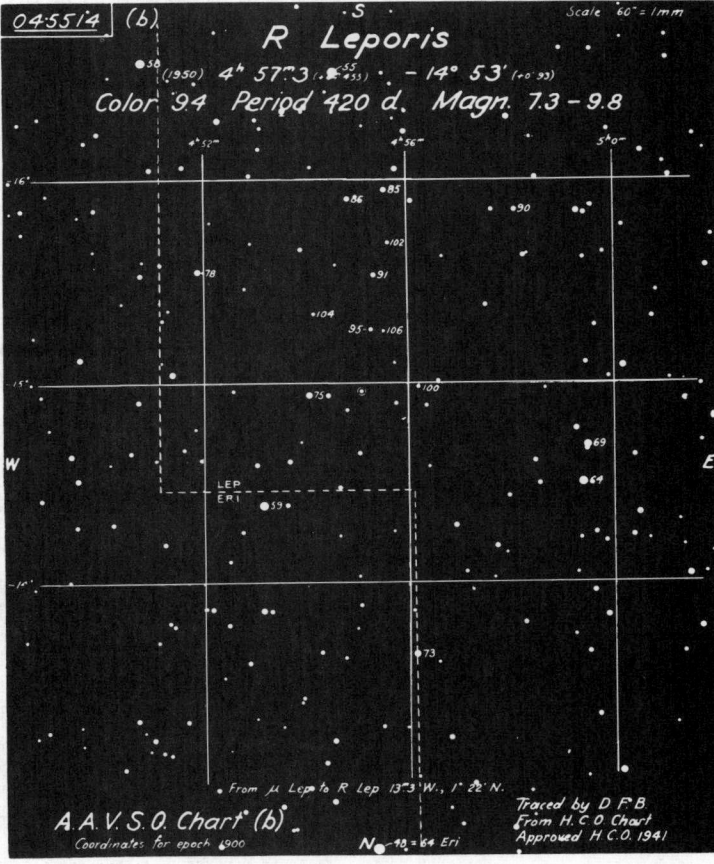

Schmidt telescopic camera: This instrument, with its 48-in. aperture and special design for wide-field photography, is much used for mapping the heavens. Very faint objects (*e.g.* farther galaxies), after detection by the Schmidt, can be studied in more detail with the giant telescopes of 100 to 200 in. aperture. (*Mt Wilson*)

Photography at a distance: First photos of Mars, taken by U.S. Mariner IV spacecraft beginning July 14, 1965, were translated into digital data, transmitted by radio to tracking station, then retranslated. The photo here, No. 11, showing Martian craters, was taken at a distance of about 7,800 mi. from Mars and covers an area 170 by 150 mi. (*NASA*)

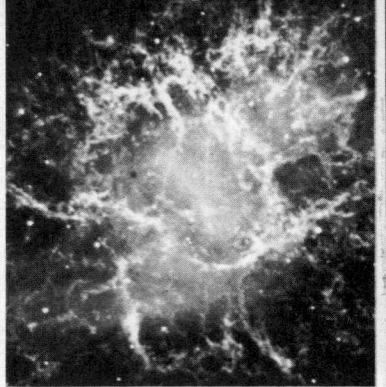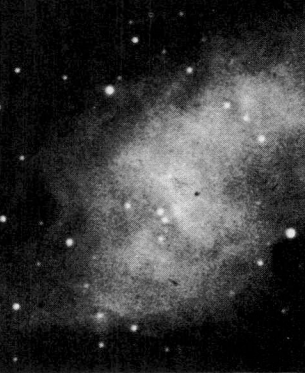

Crab Nebula in Taurus as photographed in red light (*left*) and in infrared. Different filters are used to bring out different kinds of physical features. (*Mt Wilson*)

ASTRONOMICAL PHOTOGRAPHY: the application of photographic techniques to the study of celestial objects. The discovery of the first photographic process (by Louis Daguerre, 1839) was publicly announced by the French astronomer François Arago, who had sensed at once its possibilities in astronomy. The original daguerreotype plate was not sensitive enough to photograph sky objects, but its improvement was rapid. In 1840, J. W. Draper obtained a photograph of the Moon, an inch in diameter, on which the principal lunar features could be identified. Two years later, the first photograph of a solar eclipse was taken at Milan. Other "firsts" followed promptly: the solar spectrum (1843), sunspots (1845), the star Vega (1850), the planet Jupiter (1851). Gradually, photography became the most powerful astronomical tool since the invention of the telescope. The advantage of the photographic process is twofold: its effects are *cumulative* and *durable*. Whereas the impression of a particle of light on the human retina is temporary, its impression on a photographic emulsion is permanent; as the light ray continually strikes the emulsion in the same spot, the resulting image gradually increases in size and density. Thus, with long exposures, one may photograph celestial objects too faint to be seen visually even with the largest telescopes. The durability of photographic records makes it possible to photograph the same star field at widely separated epochs and, by comparing the two sets of images, to measure distances and motions of stars in that field (see STARS, REAL MOTIONS OF). Besides the direct photography of celestial objects (planets, comets, meteors, stars, gaseous nebulae, star clusters, and galaxies) for determinations of brightness, position, motion, or appearance,

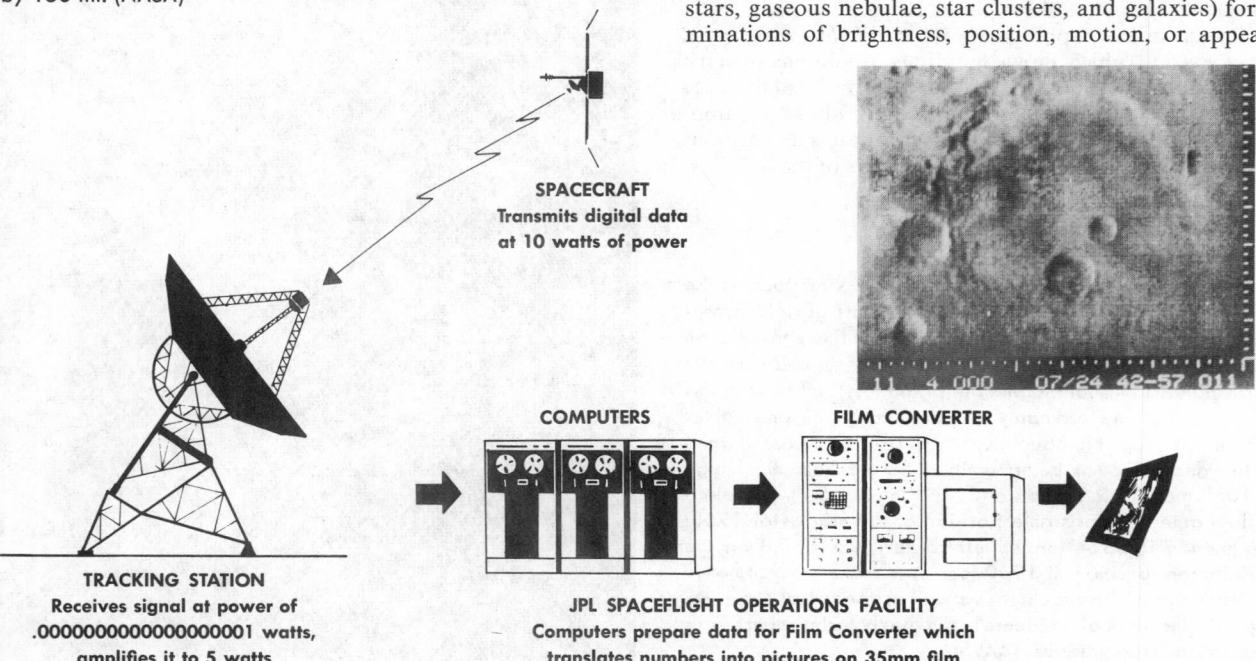

SPACECRAFT
Transmits digital data
at 10 watts of power

TRACKING STATION
Receives signal at power of
.0000000000000000001 watts,
amplifies it to 5 watts

COMPUTERS

FILM CONVERTER

JPL SPACEFLIGHT OPERATIONS FACILITY
Computers prepare data for Film Converter which
translates numbers into pictures on 35mm film

various techniques and instruments have been devised to assist astronomical research; *e.g.* the recording of a stellar or nebular spectrum on the same photographic plate as that of a comparison spectrum allows the detailed identification and analysis of its features (see SPECTROSCOPY; STAR SPECTRA). For objects too faint to be studied in this manner, similar, although less detailed, results are obtained from a series of exposures taken through various colored filters with appropriate color-sensitive emulsions. Any telescope can be used as a camera by attaching a plate-holder at the focus of the instrument. No optics are required other than those of the telescope itself, since this functions like the lens in an ordinary camera. Modern optical telescopes are designed almost exclusively for photographic use. They often incorporate special devices for use in specific areas of research; *e.g.* the CORONAGRAPH for studying the Sun's corona and prominences, the photoheliograph to record features of the solar surface, the SCHMIDT CAMERA for wide-angle photography of large sky areas, the Baker-Nunn camera for tracking artificial satellites. The effectiveness of astronomical photography has been augmented also by the use of PHOTOMULTIPLIERS.—*S. D. G.*

ASTRONOMY: the study of celestial bodies. Astronomy has been called "the mother of the sciences," and it is true not only that the study of astronomy can be traced back to prehistoric times, but also that it was investigation of the motion of the planets that led Newton to develop the application of mathematics to natural sciences, from which development modern science springs.

Early Astronomy: The earliest known astronomical activities were concerned with using the Sun and stars to mark the passage of the year, to regulate the sowing of seed and the reaping of harvest. In Europe, there are many sites of standing stones, artifacts of the megalithic period dating back to perhaps 2000 B. C., and some of these sites can be shown to be connected with observations of the direction on the horizon of the rising or setting Sun (which directions change throughout the year) and with the rising-points of bright stars. In Egypt and Mesopotamia there is evidence of orientations of temples in directions of astronomical significance, dating to even earlier times. In the tradition of the CONSTELLATION figures we have evidence of an early astronomical activity, since from the distribution of the ancient constellation figures over the celestial sphere (allowing for PRECESSION OF THE EQUINOXES) it can be shown that they were designed, essentially as we have inherited them, by 2500 B. C., and may have been used as aids to navigation. From prehistoric times there were attempts to understand the universe of stars in terms of analogy with human society, and with such practical concerns as the silting up or flooding of rivers. Crude as the ancient myths are, they represent the first attempts to understand, and not merely to observe, the universe.

Early man was much concerned with the apparent motions of the planets, or wanderers, which appeared to move against the background of stars. Originally, the planets included the Sun and Moon, as well as five bodies visible to the naked eye, namely Mercury, Venus, Mars, Jupiter, and Saturn. By the middle of the 4th cent. B. C., the Babylonian-Sumerian peoples had developed a complicated arithmetic that enabled them to predict with remarkable precision the motions of the planets.

Moon in different phases as drawn by Galileo, 1610: His 30-power telescope, very inferior by modern standards, revealed detail poorly. However, this astute pioneer observer did recognize that the Moon's surface is somewhat like Earth's, with its mountains, craters, and plains. This first discovery of an Earth-like body in the heavens had enormous philosophical and religious implications. (*Yerkes*)

Uraniburg, the observatory of Tycho Brahe, built on the island of Hven near Copenhagen, was the center of the great Danish observer's work during the period 1576–96. (*U. S. Navy*)

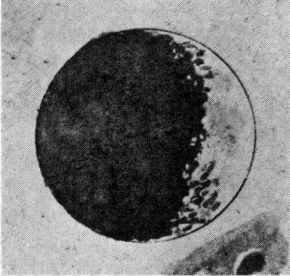

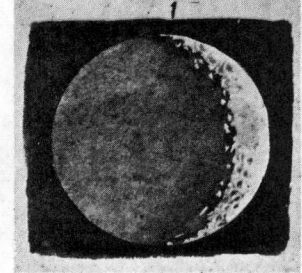

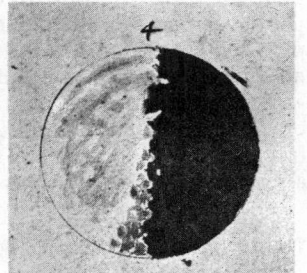

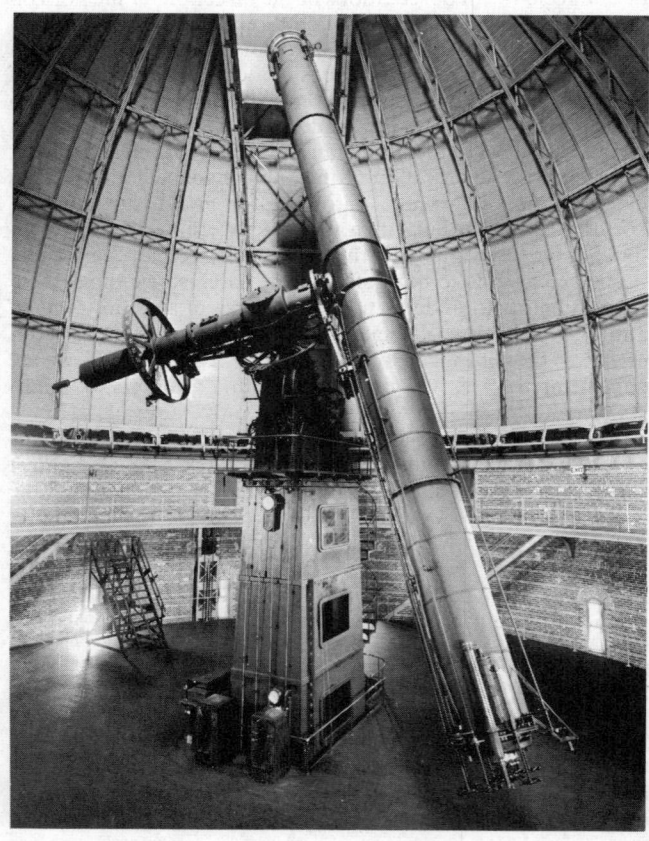

Observatory of Johann Hevelius, on roof of his house in Danzig, was an important center of astronomy in the 17th cent. Early astronomers had to develop their own equipment. (*U. S. Navy*)

the planetary theory of Ptolemy, who lived in Alexandria about A. D. 150 (see PTOLEMAIC SYSTEM). His picture of the traffic of the heavens, refined and improved by the Arabs, was accepted as true for 14 centuries, and it is a tribute to the efficiency of the system that it was capable of being adapted to account for later, more accurate observations.

The Heliocentric System: The year 1543 saw the publication of the important treatise *On the Revolutions of the Celestial Spheres* by Nikolaus Koppernigk (Copernicus). The Copernican system assumed the daily rotation of Earth and the revolution of planets around the Sun, but it retained the Ptolemaic principles of epicycles and deferents in its description of planetary motions. From the start, the new theory was the focus of heated controversy, on both philosophical and scientific grounds. One fact, in particular, made its acceptance difficult in its time: Earth's motion in its orbit should have been reflected in a small annual displacement of the stars; but sihce no such displacement could be observed with astronomical instruments of that epoch, it was necessary to assume that stars were enormously farther away than was earlier believed.

At the beginning of the 17th cent., two important advances were made. Copernicus, like his classical predecessors, had approached the problem of planetary motions by constructing a geometrical picture and then seeing if it worked. Johannes Kepler devised a method of working from astronomical observations to a geometrical model, and thus arrived at his laws of planetary motion (KEPLER'S LAWS). In Kepler's model, Earth and planets move around the Sun in orbits, but the orbits are ellipses, not circles. Thus at one stroke,

Classical Astronomers: Meanwhile, the Greeks had been developing geometrical pictures to describe the planetary motions. In the 4th cent. B. C., a member of the Pythagorean school, Philolaos, had a brilliant flash of insight: he supposed that the daily rotation of the CELESTIAL SPHERE is only apparent—in fact it is the observer who is moving. Philolaos thought of Earth as moving in a circle about the "center of the universe," the rotation of the celestial sphere being merely a reflection of this motion. At the center of the universe he placed the central fire, possibly to explain the phenomenon of EARTH-SHINE on the Moon, this central fire being invisible from the inhabited side of Earth, which was turned always outward. Another body, called "anti-Earth," was also assumed to move about the central fire, always invisible from Earth, possibly to account for eclipses of the Moon. The planets moved in circles about the center, but remained visible from Earth. This early picture, wrong as we now know it to be, was important, for it led first to the idea of a solid Earth rotating on its axis, and then, by 270 B. C., to the view of Aristarchus that Earth and planets move in circles about the Sun. However, the notion that our planet moves in an orbit, and rotates on an axis, affronted common sense, and the views of Aristarchus hence were not accepted. Instead the Greeks developed a number of geometrical pictures of planetary motion with a fixed central Earth and a rotating star sphere, with the planets orbiting around Earth. These models reached their culmination with

The 40-inch refracting telescope of Yerkes Observatory, located at Williams Bay, Wisc., has ranked since 1897 as one of the world's greatest astronomical instruments. (*Yerkes*)

he dispensed with the complex system of epicycles used by Ptolemy and Copernicus, and his picture was of commanding simplicity. Kepler had based his work on observations of the planets by Tycho Brahe, the last great pre-telescopic observer.

The Telescope: In 1610, a new era opened for astronomy when Galileo for the first time used a telescope for celestial observing. Although his instruments were crude and small by modern standards, they at once yielded a rich harvest of information. He found that the planet Venus sometimes showed more than half of its disc illuminated, whereas according to Ptolemaic theory Venus (and Mercury) could never appear as more than a crescent. Since the phases of these planets are not visible to the naked eye, a telescope was needed to show that the Ptolemaic theory was wrong. (In the Copernican and Keplerian systems, Venus and Mercury *can* show a gibbous phase.) Galileo also observed the four brightest satellites of Jupiter, and saw them revolving around this planet as it moved in its orbit. With his contemporaries Galileo observed sunspots, and he saw that the MILKY WAY was in reality composed of a vast number of faint stars.

As telescopes developed in quality and size, they revealed more and more detail of the surfaces of Sun, Moon, and planets. Saturn's rings were discovered (they had been glimpsed by Galileo), and the planets were found to be rotating. It became more reasonable to believe that Earth is but one among many planets. But the telescopes failed to show any stars as discs; these objects were indeed very remote. The idea gained acceptance that the stars are other Suns in space—that the Sun is but a typical star, and the reason it appears so much brighter than a star is that it is near us. With this concept in mind, Sir William Herschel, in the latter half of the 18th cent., began his monumental task of counting stars of different brightnesses in different areas of the sky, so building up the first picture of the structure of our Galaxy. The telescope also brought into view, in addition to double stars, faintly luminous, cloudlike objects called NEBULAS; it was suggested that these might be other, remote GALAXIES of stars. Some of the nebulas have proved to be of just this character.

At first, telescopes were used only as large magnifying glasses, to see enlarged images of the celestial bodies. But it became clear that another, and in certain ways more important, use of the telescope was to see fainter stars, to penetrate more deeply into space. A modern telescope is indeed used more often as a light gatherer than as a magnifying glass. Also, in the 17th cent. the telescope was used for making more accurate observations of the positions of stars and planets, and a number of national observatories were set up in Europe to make observations of Moon, stars, and planets, and to construct accurate tables for navigation purposes.

Celestial Mechanics: Astronomy is not only a description of the universe—it is also. an attempt to understand it. In the middle ages, the accepted COSMOLOGY was modeled on that of Aristotle. While terrestrial matter was subject to decay, the matter of which Moon, Sun, and stars were made was considered to be essentially different and eternal. Such a cosmology stood in the way of any attempt to understand the celestial bodies on the basis of experiments with physical objects on Earth. This barrier was broken down by Galileo and Newton in the 17th cent. They formulated the laws of dynamics that govern the motion of bodies on Earth, and Newton was able to show that the self-same laws of dynamics explain the motions of the planets according to Kepler's laws.

Newton's great unifying principle was the law of universal GRAVITATION: that every particle of matter attracts every other particle by a force that varies as the product of the masses of the particles, and inversely as the square of the distance between them. This single law comprehended the falling of an apple from a tree as well as the motions of the Moon and planets. The 18th cent. saw a great development of Newton's mathematical methods, applied to the science of Earth as well as that of the heavens. On the astronomical side, the theory of planetary motions was refined to take into account the perturbing effects of the gravitational attraction of one planet upon another (see PERTURBATIONS). The theories agreed with observation, except for the motion of Uranus (a planet beyond Saturn discovered by Herschel in 1781). The greatest triumph for the theory of gravitation came in 1845 when, independently, Le Verrier and Adams predicted correctly the position of yet another planet, Neptune, beyond Uranus; the perturbations of Uranus' orbit by Neptune accounted for the discrepancies between the computed and observed positions of Uranus. A smaller discrepancy in the motion of Mercury proved to be of even greater significance, however, for it showed that Newton's theory was not quite right, and this discrepancy was explained only by the theory of RELATIVITY formulated by Einstein in the early years of the 20th cent. It remains that, in almost every circumstance, the Newtonian theory gives the right answer within limits of observational accuracy, and it has been employed with success in discussing the motions of double stars, and the motions of stars in orbits in star clusters and the Galaxy.

Photography and Spectroscopy: Since 1860, the greatest observational advances have been made with the aid of photography and SPECTROSCOPY. ASTRONOMICAL PHOTOGRAPHY provides a permanent and reliable record of the images of stars, which can be measured accurately at leisure in the laboratory. This method has provided most of our present knowledge about the motions of stars and their distances (see ASTRONOMICAL DISTANCE UNITS). By splitting up the light of a star into its component colors, or SPECTRUM, and comparing the spectrum with the light emitted from terrestrial sources under various conditions of temperature and pressure, it has been possible to make a chemical and physical analysis of the outer layers of stars, and the nature of gaseous nebulas. The

DOPPLER EFFECT in star spectra has provided knowledge of the velocities of stars in the line of sight (radial velocities). It has revealed the presence of solar disturbances which have important effects on Earth's atmosphere; and it has revealed the most interesting phenomenon of the universe as a whole—its expansion, as revealed by the spectra of distant galaxies (see RED SHIFT).

Astronomy has also benefited enormously from developments of modern atomic and nuclear physics. We are now able to understand how STAR SPECTRA are formed, and to interpret the reasons for differences between the spectra of stars and terrestrial objects. The internal structures of SUN and stars can be investigated theoretically in terms of laboratory-tested theories, and the generation of energy by Sun and stars understood in terms of nuclear reactions taking place at high temperatures at the centers of these bodies. In the universe, we find matter under extremes of temperature and density that cannot be reproduced in the laboratory, so that ASTROPHYSICS has also provided a useful testing-ground for theories of physics. Indeed, modern astronomy is, in a real sense, a branch of modern physics.

Radio Astronomy: The modern astronomer uses his telescope as a light-gatherer, and he has developed a range of auxiliary equipment for recording and analyzing the light that it gathers. While photography is still of great importance because of the vast amount of information that can be recorded on one negative, for the most sensitive work the light (or spectrum) is recorded with photoelectric photometers, which use some of the most complex equipment of the modern electronic engineer. But the greatest contribution of the electronic engineer to astronomy is in the field of RADIO ASTRONOMY. Radiation from space falls on Earth, carrying with it information about the distant universe. This radiation is spread throughout the whole electromagnetic spectrum, from very short wavelength gamma radiations, through x-rays, ultra-violet light, visible light, and infra-red waves, to radio waves. Of all this spectrum, radiation in only two narrow bands can get through Earth's atmosphere. Until the end of World War II, our picture of the universe had been built up entirely from radiations of visible, or near-visible wavelength. Now, we can observe another band of radiations in the radio part of the spectrum, which can also pass through the atmosphere. To receive these radiations, and pin-point their directions in space, RADIO TELESCOPES are built which dwarf in size the largest optical telescopes. Stars, while they give out much light, give little radio radiation. The radio waves come rather from INTERSTELLAR MATTER, from tenuous nebulas, from the remains of exploded stars, and from remote pairs of colliding galaxies. We can observe radio waves from the Sun: they appear to come mostly from its extended outer atmosphere (the corona) and from regions of disturbance near sunspots. The interstellar gas in the Galaxy has been mapped by radio astronomers—they can detect neutral hydrogen gas, which is invisible to optical astronomers. Since radio waves pass through interstellar clouds, the whole galaxy is "visible" to the radio astronomer; and a picture of its spiral structure has been built up. Finally, radio waves can be detected from distant colliding galaxies far beyond the limits of penetration of optical telescopes, so that determinations as to the structure of the universe may depend upon the radio astronomers.

Another use of radio in astronomy has been in radar methods. A radio wave is transmitted from the ground, and its echo from a celestial object is received (see RADAR ASTRONOMY). By timing the delay between transmission and receipt of echo, the distance of the object can be found; e.g. the distance of the planet Venus has been redetermined in this way. Likewise, the train of ionized atoms in Earth's atmosphere left by the passage of a meteor can reflect radio waves, so that our present knowledge of the orbits and distribution of meteoritic matter is also augmented by radar observation.

Satellite Astronomy: To the astronomer, it is tantalizing to think that radiation that may have taken a billion years to reach Earth is absorbed, or distorted almost beyond recognition, in less than a thousandth of a second as it passes through Earth's atmosphere. For this reason, great promise attaches to the making of astronomical observations from above Earth's atmosphere, from satellites. Already, x-ray and ultra-violet observations have been made of the Sun, and far ultra-violet radiation from stars detected. Sizable telescopes are being placed in satellite orbits. There can be little doubt that such developments will shortly revolutionize our view of the universe. Finally, there is knowledge gained by sending cameras and other instruments to Moon and planets to make direct observations of conditions there. Already, space probes have radioed back to Earth much interesting information about conditions in interplanetary space. Perhaps at last astronomy will progress from being a science of observation toward one of experimentation. But it will still depend upon observational techniques for the investigation of the universe outside the solar system, and to the astronomer artificial satellites are most important as observatories above Earth's atmosphere. See SATELLITE, ARTIFICIAL.—*M. W. O.*

ASTRONOMY, PRACTICAL: application of the methods of spherical trigonometry to observations of the celestial bodies, leading to precise determination of the calendar, time, direction, latitude, and longitude. CELESTIAL NAVIGATION is a branch of practical astronomy.—*T. N.*

Mt Stromlo Observatory, near Canberra, Australia, is largest in southern hemisphere. Main dome (*center*) houses a 74-in. reflecting telescope. Other domes contain smaller reflectors, refractors, and other equipment, including Schmidt camera, transit instrument, and zenith tube. (*Mt Stromlo*)

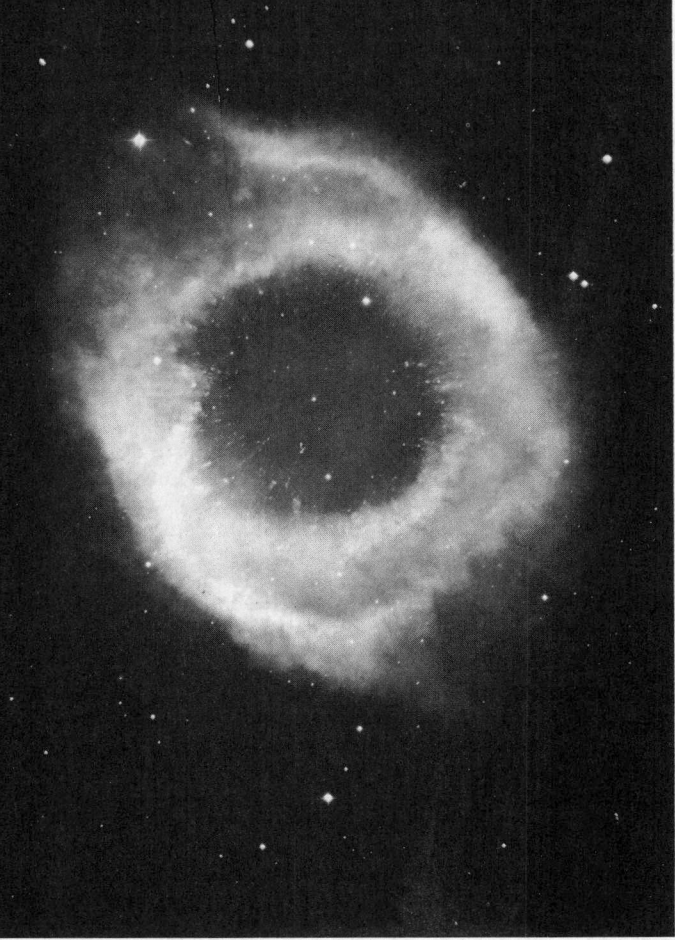

Important current problems in astrophysics include that of the origin of planetary nebulae such as this one (NGC 7293) in Aquarius. (Mt Wilson)

fields in and around the galaxy; these phenomena too are in the astrophysicist's sphere. This sphere, then, involves virtually all branches of modern physics—plasma physics, magneto-hydrodynamics, nuclear physics, atomic physics, even solid-state physics—as well as certain branches of classical physics: electricity and magnetism, optics, heat, thermodynamics, and statistical mechanics.—*L. H. A.*

ASYMMETRIC CARBON ATOM: in organic chemistry and biochemistry, a carbon atom to which four different atoms or radicals are linked, so that the molecule has an asymmetric configuration. Such compounds can exist in two opposite isomeric forms, or enantiomorphs, which are mirror images of each other and which cannot be superimposed (see OPTICAL ACTIVITY; STEREOCHEMISTRY). The four carbon bonds are visualized as passing through the corners of a tetrahedron with the carbon atom at its center. Enantiomorphs have identical chemical properties but opposite optical activity. The enantiomorphs of alanine are shown below. L-alanine is found in protein and D-alanine in bacterial cell walls. Amino acids occurring in proteins are all in the D-form. Simple sugars, *e.g.* tetroses, pentoses, and hexoses, all have asymmetric carbon atoms, but only one form is found naturally. Enzymes acting on amino acids and sugars react with only one of the forms, not both.

$$\begin{array}{cc} \text{COOH} & \text{COOH} \\ H_2N - \diamondsuit - H & H - \diamondsuit - NH_2 \\ \text{CH}_3 & \text{CH}_3 \\ \text{L-Alanine} & \text{D-Alanine} \end{array}$$

—*J. F. S.*

ATAVISM: reappearance of an inheritable characteristic in an individual after that characteristic has been absent in several preceding generations. Any recessive gene, *e.g.* that for long hair in dogs, may remain unexpressed for an indefinite number of generations as long as it is masked by its dominant allele, a gene for short hair. However, when two genes for long hair come together in the same individual, long hair will reappear even though it may not have been present for many generations.—*J. M. P.*

ASTROPHYSICS: the application of physics, particularly modern physics and excluding classical mechanics, to astronomy. Its basic data are obtained by detectors of electromagnetic radiation: radio receivers, photoconductive cells, thermocouples, photoelectric cells, photographic plates, and the eye. Optical and radio telescopes of different types are employed as radiation-collecting devices; instruments have been flown above Earth's atmosphere. Among the problems for the astrophysicist are interpretations of spectra of Sun and stars with respect to the structures of their atmospheres, and including their pressures and temperatures, chemical compositions, and surface gravities. Solar physics is concerned not only with the nature of the steady state of the Sun, but also with transient phenomena, *e.g.* sunspots, prominences, and changes in the outer envelopes of the Sun—chromosphere and corona. Studies of gaseous nebulas and of gas and dust between the stars deal with matter at extremely low densities and, often, extremely low temperatures, whereas investigations of stellar interiors, the generation of energy in stars by nuclear transformations, and element building in stars all involve properties of matter at extremely high temperatures and densities. The astrophysicist studies properties of matter ranging from temperatures of 50°K to thousands of millions of degrees, and densities ranging from a trillionth of a trillionth of that of water to 100,000 times that of water. Cosmic rays appear to be produced in atmospheres of the Sun and other stars and in certain objects such as the Crab Nebula; their subsequent motions and accelerations are all strongly affected by magnetic

The Sun as revealed by the camera is a prime subject for the astrophysicist. Varying photographic techniques record various solar features and processes. Here are photos of Sun in (A) ordinary light and (B) hydrogen α, and two spectroheliograms: (C) calcium and (D) hydrogen, enlarged. (Mt Wilson)

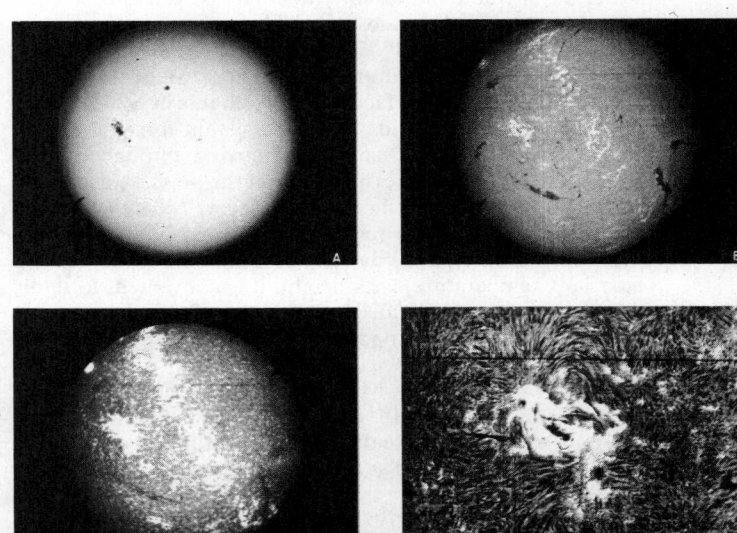

ATMOSPHERE: the mass of air surrounding Earth. In the lower layers it consists of dry air (a composite of many gases), water vapor, and microscopic particles such as dust, smoke, and various salts. The percentage composition of dry air by volume, for the principal gases, is: nitrogen, 78.08; oxygen, 20.95; argon (and other rare gases), 0.94; carbon dioxide, 0.03. This composition is practically constant up to 30 mi or more. Water vapor, a highly variable quantity in the atmosphere, ranges by volume from less than 0.001% in the arctic to more than 5% in the tropics. The forms of non-gaseous matter include domestic and industrial smoke, natural dust picked up from the earth by the wind, salt spray from the oceans and seas, and, within recent years, fission products of atomic tests and

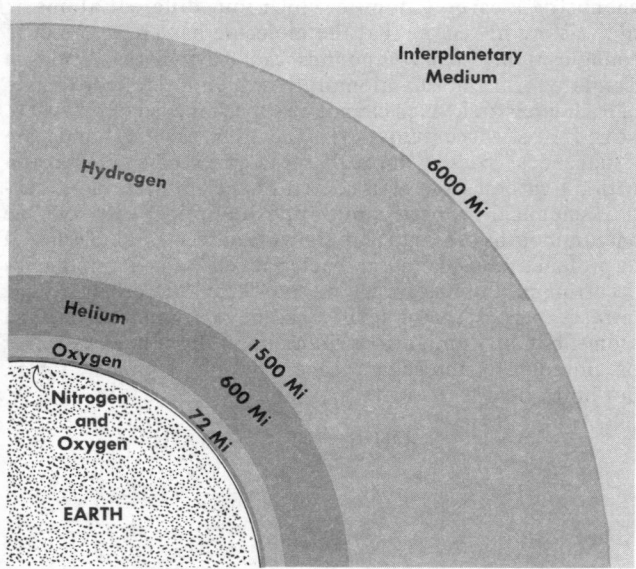

Composition of atmosphere: The air we breathe, composed mainly of nitrogen and oxygen, makes up only the thinnest layer of Earth's atmosphere. Above it, there are layers of oxygen, helium, hydrogen, and nitrogen in atomic and ionized forms. Our understanding of the atmosphere has been advanced in recent years by analysis of data collected by satellites in orbit around Earth.

nuclear reactors. These constituents make up an insignificant part of the total volume of the atmosphere, but are important; thus man-produced pollutants may cause serious community health problems (see ATMOSPHERIC POLLUTION), while salt particles contribute importantly to condensation and precipitation processes in the atmosphere. The atmosphere has mass, weighing 0.0764 lb/ft³ at 59°F and at an atmospheric pressure of 1013 mb (29.92 in. mercury). Because of its weight, air exerts pressure on surfaces with which it is in contact. Air, like water and other liquids, exerts a buoyant force on bodies immersed in it, and resists objects moving through it. The atmosphere is also compressible, so that the pressure decreases more rapidly with height in the lower layers, where density is high, than in the upper regions, where density is low. Because of the change in the physical properties of the air (especially temperature) with height, it is convenient to think of the atmosphere as divided into four layers which, proceeding upward, are called: troposphere, stratosphere, ionosphere, and exosphere.

Troposphere: This layer, lying next to and immediately above the earth's surface, contains about three fourths of the mass of the atmosphere, and more than nine tenths of its water vapor, cloud content, dust, and smoke. The troposphere is the tur-

bulent portion of the atmosphere, and within it occur a variety of atmospheric disturbances ranging in size from major storms, affecting hundreds of thousands of square miles, to showers and thunderstorms less than a mile in diameter. Almost all the rain, snow, hail, and other elements commonly associated with "weather" occur in the troposphere. But the outstanding characteristic of the troposphere is the steady decrease of temperature with altitude: on the average, about 19°F/mi, or 6.5°C/km. Occasionally, thin layers occur wherein temperature increases with height: these are called temperature INVERSIONS. Their existence at ground level is favorable for concentration of smoke, dust, and other atmospheric pollutants produced by domestic or industrial sources. Temperature inversions also affect transmission of sound through the atmosphere; *e.g.* certain noises may occasionally be heard over long distances beneath a temperature inversion (see ANOMALOUS SOUND PROPAGATION).

The principal wind systems of the troposphere are formed by warm air moving from the equator toward the poles, and cold air moving from poles to equator (see ATMOSPHERE, GENERAL CIRCULATION OF). Within the lower troposphere, winds due to unequal heating by the Sun are modified by Earth's rotation and surface friction, and the result is the primary wind belts: the *trade winds,* extending from near the equator to 30° N and S lat; the *westerlies,* between 30° and 60° lat; and the *polar easterlies,* from lat 60° to the poles. At higher levels, the principal feature of the mid-latitude wind pattern is the JET STREAM, a narrow ribbon of high-speed winds, blowing from the west, which may occasionally reach 250 to 300 mi/hr. The height of the troposphere varies from about 4 or 5 mi near the poles to about 10 mi at the equator. In the U. S. A. it is about 6 or 7 mi high—usually higher in summer, lower in winter. Its upper boundary, where the steady decrease in temperature with height ceases, is known as the *tropopause.*

Stratosphere: The layer lying immediately above the troposphere is the stratosphere. It was originally believed to be a region in which temperature remains constant with height; later it was found that temperature does vary significantly with height, and also that there exist stratified layers as a result of other phenomena. Thus an *ozone layer* has been identified between 12 and 30 mi above the earth, and a warm region near the top of the ozone layer. The stratosphere extends from the tropopause to a height of 35 to 40 mi above the ground.

Scientific knowledge of temperatures in the stratosphere above 20 mi or so has been derived from rocket observations, observations of meteors, ozone measurements, and computations based on the velocity of sound waves. Data indicate that temperature in the stratosphere increases, on the average, to about 50°F (10°C) in the layer 30 to 35 mi high, decreases again to about −105°F (−76°C) at about 50 mi, then increases again to values which exceed 1000°F (540°C) at altitudes of 150 mi or more. The lower warm layer is caused by absorption of certain solar ultraviolet radiation by the ozone present in the region (see OZONOSPHERE). The upper layer owes its high temperature to the heat released by the ionization of air at very high levels (see IONOSPHERE).

The major feature in the stratosphere is the mid-latitude *jet stream,* a strong west wind which penetrates through the tropopause and extends well into the stratosphere. In summer, however, because of the continuous sunlight and marked heating of the air over polar regions, winds above 10 mi at middle and high latitudes blow mostly from the east. Other characteristic winds in the stratosphere are the *polar-night jet,* a strong westerly wind existing at a height of 20 mi near the arctic circle; and the *krakatao wind,* which blows from the east above the 15-mi level in equatorial latitudes. Although very few clouds exist outside the troposphere, a few are found in the high stratosphere. An exceptionally beautiful group of water-droplet clouds are the *mother-of-pearl* (*nacreous*) *clouds* at altitudes of 12 to 18 mi. The highest and rarest formations, known as *noctilucent clouds,* occur at heights of 35 to 40 mi; they are believed to be composed of meteoritic dust. The extremely rarefied air of the stratosphere does not refract or scatter light rays as does the air of the lower levels; hence the

sky of the stratosphere appears dark blue or nearly black, instead of the light blue seen from nearer the ground (see ATMOSPHERIC REFRACTION). The ozone layer, in the region 12 to 30 mi above the earth, contains the rare form of oxygen O_3, a powerful absorber or filter of certain ultraviolet radiations from the Sun. Since portions of these radiations are harmful to living creatures, the ozone layer is very important as a protective shield.

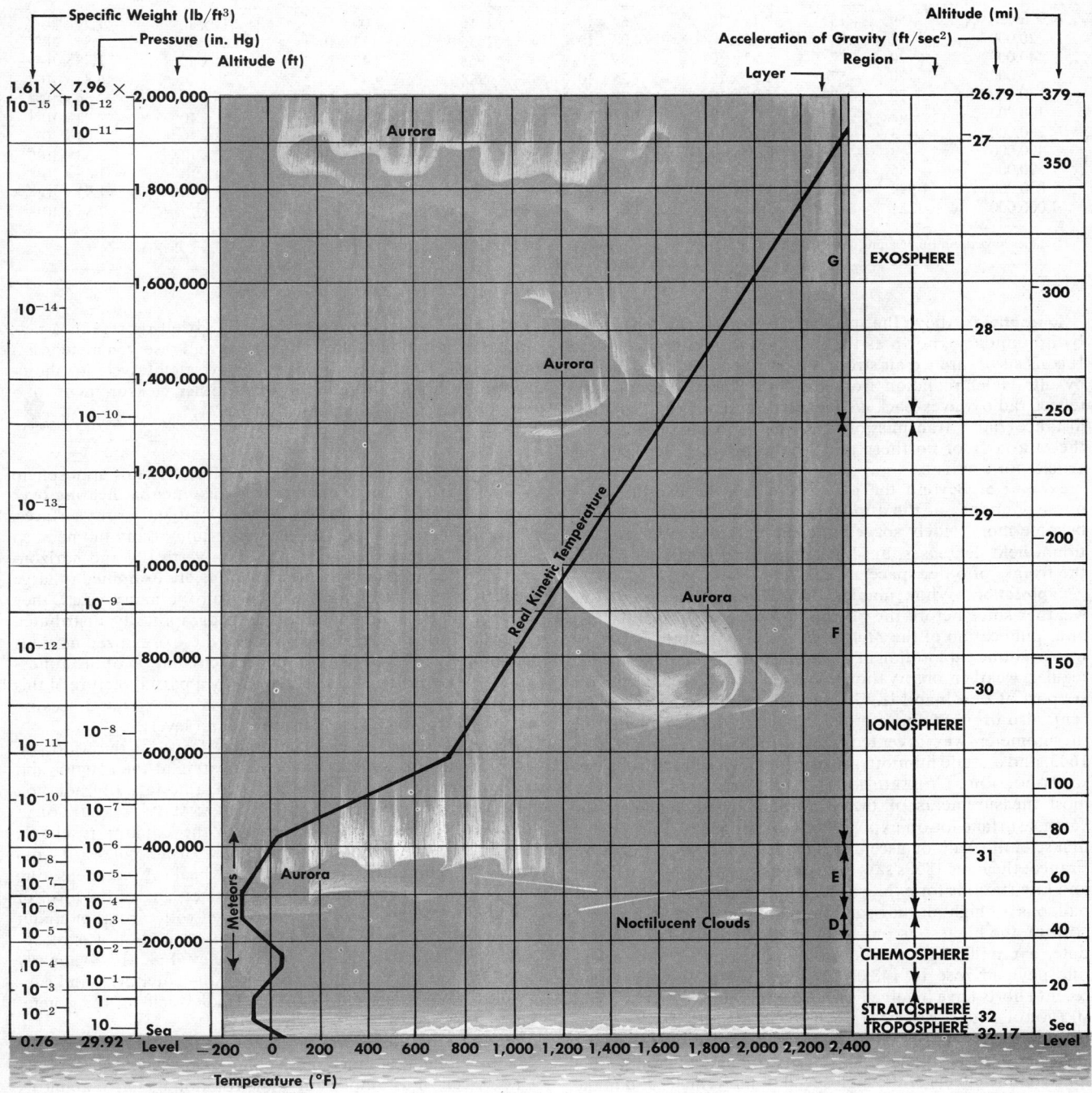

Cross-section of lower atmosphere: Chart gives calculated values for specific weight and pressure of atmosphere as well as gravitational acceleration to an altitude of 379 mi—well into the region composed principally of oxygen, which starts at the so-called F layer of the ionosphere. Graph in center shows variation with altitude of real kinetic temperature of the gas molecules. Real kinetic temperature is a measure of the molecule's average kinetic energy. Because atmosphere is so thin at high altitudes, its actual heat content is quite small; a thermometer carried to these altitudes would register a very low reading because such a small number of the fast-moving molecules would come into contact with it. (After *Garret Corp.*)

CHARACTERISTICS OF THE STANDARD ATMOSPHERE

(From "U. S. Extension to the ICAO Standard Atmosphere," U. S. Weather Bureau and Geophysics Research Directorate, 1958)

Altitude (ft)	Temperature °F	Temperature °C	Pressure (lb/ft²)	Weight (lb/ft³)	Speed of Sound (ft/sec)	Ratio of Density to Sea-level Density	Mean Free Path (ft)	Number of Molecules per ft³
(sea level)	+59	+15	2.12×10^3	7.64×10^{-2}	1116.4	1.00	2.17×10^{-7}	7.21×10^{23}
20,000	−12	−24	9.73×10^2	4.08×10^{-2}	1036.9	5.33×10^{-1}	4.08×10^{-7}	3.85×10^{23}
40,000	−70	−57	3.93×10^2	1.89×10^{-2}	968.1	2.47×10^{-1}	8.81×10^{-7}	1.78×10^{23}
60,000	−70	−57	1.51×10^2	7.26×10^{-3}	968.1	9.49×10^{-2}	2.29×10^{-6}	6.85×10^{22}
80,000	−70	−57	5.81×10	2.79×10^{-3}	968.1	3.65×10^{-2}	5.96×10^{-6}	2.64×10^{22}
100,000	−41	−41	2.31×10	1.03×10^{-3}	1003.2	1.35×10^{-2}	1.61×10^{-5}	9.98×10^{21}
200,000	−3	−19	4.75×10^{-1}	1.95×10^{-5}	1047.9	2.55×10^{-4}	8.53×10^{-4}	1.84×10^{20}
400,000	+3	−16	6.10×10^{-5}	2.11×10^{-9}	*	2.76×10^{-8}	6.73×10^0	2.33×10^{16}
600,000	+756	+402	1.15×10^{-6}	1.45×10^{-11}	*	1.89×10^{-10}	9.36×10^2	1.68×10^{14}
800,000	+999	+537	1.59×10^{-7}	1.43×10^{-12}	*	1.87×10^{-11}	8.13×10^3	1.93×10^{13}
1,000,000	+1251	+677	3.72×10^{-8}	2.61×10^{-13}	*	3.41×10^{-12}	4.08×10^4	3.84×10^{12}

* Values have doubtful meaning at very high altitudes, and are therefore not computed.

Ionosphere: Above the stratosphere, and separated from it by a boundary known as the *stratopause,* is the ionosphere. It consists of rarefied air strongly electrified or ionized, mostly by ultraviolet radiation from the Sun. These ionized layers reflect radio waves back to the earth and thus aid in long-distance radio transmissions. In the ionosphere exist also the AURORAS, or northern and southern lights. See separate article: IONOSPHERE.

Exosphere: Beyond the ionosphere lies the exosphere, or outer boundary of the atmosphere, where the air molecules become more widely spaced and the pull of Earth's gravitational field decreases, until at greater and greater distances the fringes of outer space are reached.

Exploration: While mankind has been interested in the weather since before the beginning of recorded history, not until publication of the *Meteorologica,* by Aristotle, 350 B. C., was scientific exploration of the atmosphere initiated. The first regular weather observations were begun in 1653 with the support of Ferdinand II, Grand Duke of Tuscany. The 17th cent. also brought about other important developments; the thermometer was invented about 1600, the barometer in 1643, and a crude humidity-measuring device about 1650 (see METEOROLOGICAL INSTRUMENTS). Until early in the 19th cent. most measurements of the atmosphere were made at the earth's surface, or on exposed mountain peaks. In 1804 the first scientific balloon ascent was made by J. L. Gay-Lussac in France; the later 1800s saw the establishment of both balloon and kite stations for exploring the upper atmosphere. Use of balloons for high-altitude soundings has continued (see RADIO-SONDE), the highest ascent being made Sep. 4, 1959. On that date, a 6-million-ft³ plastic balloon bearing a 96-lb scientific payload rose to 148,000 ft over South Dakota. Other recent efforts have involved the airplane, sounding rocket, and METEOROLOGICAL SATELLITE, which necessitate development of new observing techniques. Aircraft and rockets require specially designed meteorological instruments to compensate for dynamic effects of the high speed of the vehicle, and in the region 25 to 50 mi above ground, measurements of temperature are made by observing sound waves from grenades ejected intermittently from a rocket. Above 50 mi the shape of the shock wave following the nose cone of the rocket can be used to calculate the atmospheric temperature there. In the outer fringes of the atmosphere, temperatures can be deduced from density as measured by the effect of drag on man-made satellites. The meteorological satellite itself represents a new era in exploration of the atmosphere, and research meteorologists have been able to obtain from satellites cloud photographs, radiation observations, and other measurements of a kind never before available.—*J. C. T.*

ATMOSPHERE, GENERAL CIRCULATION OF: Earth's atmosphere is never at rest. Many factors, such as unequal heating over equatorial and polar regions, or over land and water surfaces, make it impossible to achieve equilibrium at any moment, so that air is forever being set in motion vertically and horizontally. Nevertheless, when these motions are examined in large scale, *e.g.* by averaging over a season for many years, they appear to have organized forms geographically distributed over the earth. The manifestations of these organized motions are broadly referred to as the general circulation of the atmosphere. Meteorologists as yet have only a partial picture of this circulation, incomplete because of its complexity and because of the lack of data over many areas and levels.

Solar Heating: The ultimate driving force for the wind systems of the atmosphere is unequal heating at the equator and poles, largely due to differences in amounts of radiation received from the Sun (see HEAT BALANCE OF EARTH; SOLAR RADIATION). The greater heating at the equator results in expanded air columns and an outflow of air poleward—nature's "attempt" to redistribute the heat. A compensating inflow toward the equatorial regions sets in, and a form of circulation thereby becomes established with a rotation about a horizontal axis. This simple type of circulation was recognized by the British scientist John Hadley (1682–1744) as early as 1735, and the motion of the air in the equatorial and subtropical zone is referred to as the "Hadley cell" of the general circulation.

Rotation of Earth: Many complicating factors make the general circulation much more complex than indicated by the Hadley cell: most important is the rotation of Earth about its axis. This imparts to the winds a deflection to the right in the northern hemisphere, to the left in the southern, as seen by a ground observer (see CORIOLIS ACCELERATION). The upper-level northbound currents of air from the heated tropics gradually turn to the right and become more and more westerly, while the lower air, feeding into the equator from the subtropics, becomes more and more northeasterly and easterly. In the northern hemisphere this motion is, at the surface, the well-known northeast TRADE WINDS.

In reference to the more complex average circulation of the temperate and polar latitudes, some experiments with a rotating pan of fluid cooled at its center (representing the pole) and heated at its rim (the equator) can be mentioned. In these experiments, pioneered by Dave Fultz, Univ. of Chicago, both the rate of differential heating and the rate of rotation could be varied at will. With differential heating and slow rates of rotation, motion pictures of the moving fluid (obtained through use of dyes) did indeed show the Hadley cell: water movement from the rim toward the center in the upper layers, and from the center toward the rim in the lower layers. However, when the rate of rotation of the pan was increased, the circulation broke up dramatically into some four to six long horizontal meanders or waves in the upper layer, and several whirls or vortices associated with these waves in the lower layer. These long waves are remarkably similar to the so-called planetary waves (see WEATHER SYSTEMS) of the atmosphere, and the whirls or eddies below to the cyclones and anticyclones (see illustrations in WEATHER FORECASTING and WEATHER SYSTEMS). The cyclonic eddies were observed to move toward the center of the pan; embedded in a general west-to-east drift (relative to the pan), but near the rim, the drift was from east to west. It appears, then, that the atmosphere is set in motion by the Sun's heat, but the net effect of Earth's rotation and the differential heating is to break up a simple system of circulation into big whirls or meanders which are fed by simpler whirls (cyclones and anticyclones).

Surface Friction: Another important modifying factor is friction between Earth's surface and the air currents flowing over it. This friction, operating on the northeast trade winds, creates westerly *momentum* which is carried upward by the rising currents, then poleward to temperate latitudes. The net effect of all these motions is to provide a means of transporting or siphoning off excesses of certain quantities like heat, energy, water vapor, and momentum from low to high latitudes, thereby tending to equalize things over the planet. Equalization is never completely established, because of the continual differential heating by the Sun. Thus the atmosphere near the surface is provided with a net east-to-west drift in subtropical latitudes and a net west-to-east drift in temperate latitudes. The latter is more chaotic than the former, because of the

constant formation and movement of eddies and long meandering waves. (In fact, the word "trade" refers to the steadiness of the northeast winds, and not to commerce.)

Bodies of Land and Water: The temperate-latitude belt of the westerlies is further modified by the continents and oceans, since these vary in the heat supplied to or extracted from the overlying air, as well as in their frictional influence. Thus there are preferred areas in certain seasons where the westerlies are distorted into meanders aloft and where cyclones tend to form and grow to maturity. For example, the effect of the Rocky Mt chain is to create a northward bulge or ridge in the westerlies and a southward bulge (trough) to the east. This wind pattern drives polar air masses southward over the Great Plains, and along the southern edge of the cold air (along the Gulf Coast) cyclonic storms are frequent. The temperature contrast between the air masses overlying cold land and the adjacent warmer waters often intensifies these storms as they move up the Atlantic seaboard.

These disturbances in the westerlies of temperate latitudes also produce modifications of the subtropical circulation. Instead of one globe-girdling band in the subtropics from which the trades and westerlies emanate, there are fractures or horizontal cells, thousands of miles across, around which the air appears to circulate. These are the so-called subtropical anticyclones or highs (like the well-known Bermuda High), which together form the high-pressure belt of light winds sometimes called the HORSE LATITUDES.

The westerlies, at least near the surface, do not extend to the poles, where a surrounding net drift of east winds is often observed. This drift is probably the result of geographical factors which favor cooling and hence piling up of air in polar regions, which in turn rebuffs cyclones in their northern sojourn. This is especially true of the high, cold Antarctic continent and areas of the Aleutian Islands where the effect of Alaskan-Asian land masses produces modifications in the wind systems.

Variations: The form of the general circulation varies considerably in the same season from year to year, giving rise to climatic fluctuations on many time scales. The reasons for these variations in general circulation are by no means understood, and until they are, long-range weather forecasting and studies of climatic fluctuations will be quite unsatisfactory. —*J. N.*

ATMOSPHERIC CONVERGENCE: in meteorology, a mainly horizontal flow of air into a region. Convergence is characteristic of winds in the lower levels of a cyclone (low) and is accompanied by a slow, widespread ascent of air which cools by expansion, causing clouds and precipitation. See DIVERGENCE; WEATHER SYSTEMS.—*O. G. S.*

ATMOSPHERIC DIFFRACTION: the bending of light rays by atmospheric cloud or dust particles, analogous to the slight bending of a light ray at the edge of an opaque disk. In the atmosphere small cloud or dust particles can act as diffracting disks. Most common of all atmospheric diffraction phenomena is the CORONA around the Sun or Moon; this is a set of one or more rainbow-colored concentric rings that appear when the Sun or Moon is covered by a thin cloud veil. Among other diffraction phenomena occasionally seen in the atmosphere are iridescent CLOUDS, BISHOP'S RING (diffraction by dust particles in the upper atmosphere), and GLORY, a system of colored rings surrounding the shadow of the observer's head on a patch of mist or fog.—*J. L.*

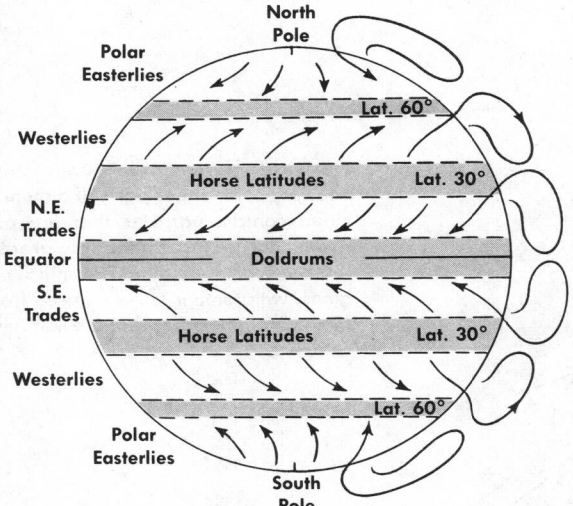

General air movements over Earth: Shown here is the general pattern of prevailing winds and regions of relative calm. In the northern hemisphere, winds are deflected to the right; in the southern, to the left.

ATMOSPHERIC DIFFUSION: the process by which matter, heat, and momentum are spread through the atmosphere by molecular agitation or by turbulence (eddy-diffusion). In meteorology, eddy-diffusion caused by the unsteadiness of the wind is far more effective than molecular diffusion. See ATMOSPHERIC POLLUTION; DIFFUSION; MICROCLIMATOLOGY; TURBULENCE.—*D. H. L.*

ATMOSPHERIC DIVERGENCE: see DIVERGENCE.

ATMOSPHERIC ELECTRICITY: free electrical charges in the atmosphere. The area of meteorology concerned with their formation, motion, and abstraction and their role in weather formation is usually divided into two sub-areas, depending on the origin and severity of the electrical effect: fair-weather conditions and thunderstorm-weather conditions. Under *fair-weather conditions,* for obscure reasons, the upper atmosphere, particularly the ionosphere, carries a positive charge of about 300,000 v with respect to the earth's surface. Except in the vicinity of thunderstorms, where local effects predominate, this potential difference between earth and atmosphere creates a vertically directed electric field which acts to drive positive charges downward. Near the earth's surface this field is approximately 100 v/meter during fair-weather conditions, although it varies widely from place to place because of air-pollution effects. At heights of 20,000 ft the fair-weather field seldom exceeds 10 v/meter. In the atmosphere, electric charges take the form of ions which are created by action of cosmic rays and radioactive minerals in the earth's crust: these two sources combined produce about 10 pairs of ions per cm³/sec at ground level. An ion pair consists of one positive and one negative ion. Because of these ions which are free to migrate in response to electrical forces, the atmosphere may be regarded as a high-resistance conductor. Ions are destroyed by recombination of positive and negative ions or as a result of being swept out by the electrical field. Clouds and fogs which develop during fair-weather conditions almost always exhibit electrical properties, since ions are always being created in the air in which the clouds form. In general, however, only thunderclouds develop charges capable of producing lightning and thunder.

Under THUNDERSTORM *weather conditions,* very intense electrical-charge centers arise. The electrical properties of a typical thunderstorm are shown schematically in the figure. In the upper parts of the cloud, where temperatures range between −10°C and −40°C, one or more regions of net positive charge appear; one or more negative charge centers occur near the freezing level. Secondary positive centers are frequently found in the rain areas near the base of thunderstorms. Inside a thunderstorm the electrical charges, positive and negative, are ions which are captured and concentrated upon the cloud particles, raindrops, and snowflakes. Differential motions resulting from differing falling speeds of the various-sized particles, in addition to the strong up and down air currents, are thought to provide the basic means by which the charges are separated, but there are many competing theories concerning details of the process.

The presence of intense charge centers within the thundercloud completely masks the normal fair-weather field condition. A few miles from the storm, the effect of the upper positive charge will predominate, and this causes an enhancement of the normal fair-weather field; near the thundercloud the lower negative charge center dominates and causes a reversal in sign of the field near the ground. Because of the intensity and relatively close separation of the two main charges, very strong electric fields may occur beneath and inside the thunderstorm. (Values over 100,000 v/meter have been measured immediately prior to a lightning discharge.) In these strong fields pointed objects such as tree branches, ships' masts, airplane propellers may develop a blue, firelike glow known as ST. ELMO'S FIRE or corona discharge. LIGHTNING, on the other hand, represents a complete electrical

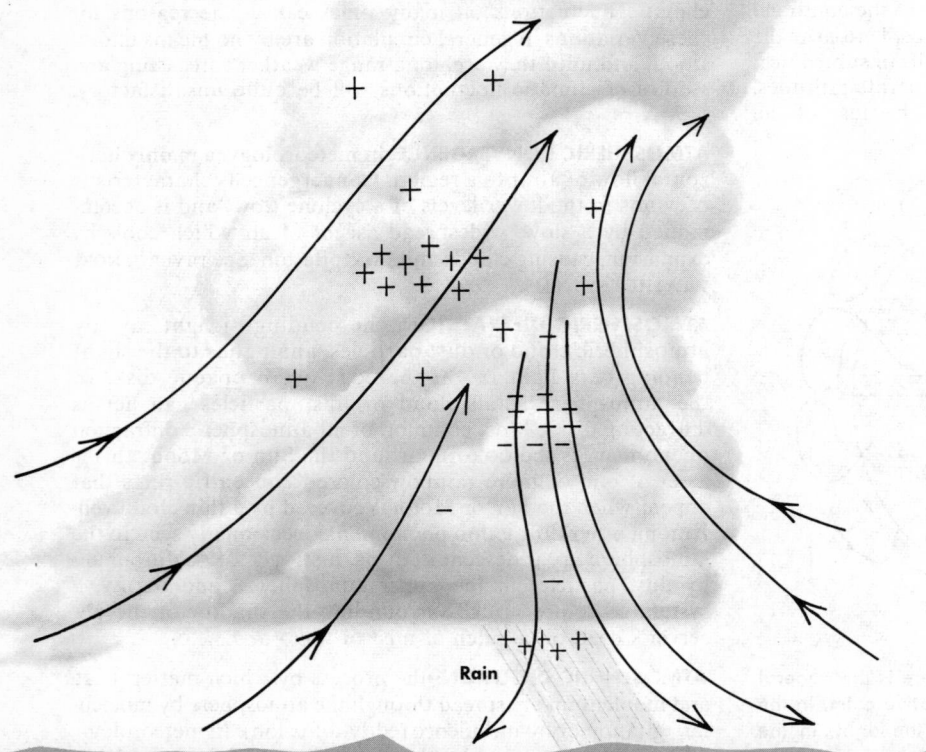

Electrical charges in a thundercloud: The very cold, upper parts of a thundercloud contain particles that are positively charged, as do the rain areas at the base of the cloud. The middle regions, with temperatures close to freezing, contain particles that are negatively charged.

Rain

Ground

breakdown of the air in response to the strong electric fields. Cloud-to-cloud lightning represents a spark discharge between the upper positive and lower negative charge centers. Cloud-to-ground lightning occurs when the lower negative center discharges to the ground below. Careful observers will also occasionally see lightning discharges between the upper positive center and the clear air regions outside the cloud.

Because the electric charges are carried on precipitation particles scattered randomly within the cloud, it frequently is not possible for a lightning flash to completely discharge a charged region in a single stroke; instead there will develop a series of closely spaced lightning strokes, following in the same channel at intervals of a few hundredths of a second, each draining small sub-areas of a charge center. To a human eye, which cannot resolve such closely spaced events, the several strokes will appear as a single flash. A typical lightning flash will consist actually of 5 to 10 separate strokes. As the current of the stroke passes along the lightning channel it heats the air, causing it to expand. Repeated expansions and contractions following the several strokes of a flash generate intense sound waves, which the ear hears as thunder. Since the sound of thunder has its origin in the lightning flash, one can estimate the distance to a thunderstorm by noting the time interval between flash and sound. At room temperature sound travels about ⅓ mi/sec. "Heat lightning" is simply the lightning of storms too far away for the thunder to be heard. —R. R. B.

ATMOSPHERIC POLLUTION: contamination of the atmosphere with artificially produced particles, gases, and vapors. Large dust particles are produced by grinding operations, road-building, plowing, and the transportation and handling of sand, gravel, concrete, and other construction materials; these tend to settle out of the air in a short time, and their polluting effect is therefore limited. Dusts resulting from industrial combustion are often carried high into the atmosphere by gases rising swiftly up smokestacks. Coal dust, coke dust, and fly ash are normal by-products of industrial furnaces. If the dust particles are sufficiently small, they tend to remain suspended in the air as AEROSOLS; typical suspensions are smokes and fumes formed by the condensation into very small particles of solids volatilized during combustion. Radioactive particles from nuclear explosions are often carried into the very high atmosphere; these tend to remain suspended for several years, during which time they are carried completely around the earth (see RADIATION HAZARDS).

Though usually not lethal, gases and other effluents from industrial processing often cause discomfort and annoyance even if carried miles from their source by the wind. Invisible gases and vapors are detectable by their smell, effects on materials and plants, and stinging or burning effects on the eyes or (in extreme cases) on the skin. Sulfur dioxide, a combustion product of most fuels, becomes sulfur trioxide on exposure to the ultraviolet portion of sunlight. The sulfur trioxide is hygroscopic and combines with water vapor in the air to become anhydrous sulfuric acid. Fortunately this sulfuric acid is very dilute, but on occasion the solution has been strong enough to cause holes to appear in nylon hose, to the surprise and vexation of the wearer.

Local catastrophes have been caused by industrial pollution of the atmosphere. An INVERSION under an anticyclone trapped smoke and fog in the Meuse Valley, Belgium, during the first five days of Dec. 1930. The concentration of smoke produced by the industrial city of Liége was so severe that hundreds suffered acute respiratory attacks, and in the final two days 63 persons died as a direct result. During a similar five-day period in Oct. 1948, 20 persons died and hundreds were made

Smoke pollution of Pittsburgh, "under study" since 1892, had reached above stage by the early 1940s. Sulfur dioxide and smoke from incomplete combustion of coal cast pall over city.

Intensive regulation of combustion brought visible improvement by late 1940s. Both views are from southern approach to Liberty Bridge over Monongahela. (*Pittsburgh Ch. of Comm.*)

ill by smoke pollution at Donora, Pa., a town in the deep, narrow valley of the Monongahela River near Pittsburgh. Industrial smoke pollution is rarely as severe as in these instances, but it is of great concern in urban areas all over the world. Los Angeles, situated on a coastal plain and bordered on three sides by mountains, has a perennial smog problem. Sea breezes, westerly winds, and the mountains serve to trap the smoke over Los Angeles. A prevailing inversion caused by subsidence on the eastern edge of the semi-permanent Pacific anticyclone forms a top to the box trapping the air in the Los Angeles basin. This city's problem is so acute that automobiles are required by law to be equipped with exhaust-pipe filters, hotels use special air-filtering equipment as well as the usual type of air-conditioning equipment, and the city itself spends hundreds of thousands of dollars per year on air-pollution research and control.

Control of industrially produced air pollution starts with properly designed smokestacks, which not only supply a natural draft to aid burning but also lift smoke high into the

Smog problem in Los Angeles: Top photograph shows the city on a clear day, when temperature inversion layer was at 4,000 ft. In next photograph, inversion layer is at only 200 ft, holding smog down upon the city, below the tops of tall

buildings. In bottom picture, inversion layer at 1,500 ft holds the smog at that level, well above tops of tall buildings. With an extensive program the city is attempting to solve the problem. (*Los Angeles Co. Air Pollution Control District*)

air. The height of the stack influences the concentration of smoke that reaches the ground; maximum concentration occurs about 10 stack-lengths away. Doubling stack height will reduce this concentration to a fourth, quadrupling to a 16th of that emanating from the original stack, since smoke concentration varies inversely as the square of the height of the stack. There are many ways to control waste gases, smoke, and fly ash. Large particles can be caught by passing the smoke through many-celled filters coated with sticky substances, through thick dry filters, and through specially treated cloth bags. Smoke can be scrubbed by passing it rapidly through high-pressure jets of water in the constricted part of a tube called a *venturi scrubber*. High-temperature smoke can be passed through catalysts which cause final burning of its particles. Waste gases can be recycled into combustion chambers or passed through afterburners for more complete burning. Smoke particles can be precipitated by passing the smoke between two electrodes, between which there is a unidirectional difference in electric potential. A high voltage passed through one electrode ionizes the gases near its surface; these ionized particles are then attracted to and deposited on the other electrode. Proper burning procedures in furnaces and incinerators—*e.g.* control of charging and of air flow, and the use of recombustion or afterburner chambers—reduces the output of harmful by-products. Some control procedures yield as by-products more than enough valuable chemicals to pay for the control.

Pittsburgh, Pa., and St. Louis, Mo., both once known as extremely smoky cities, are examples of how effective controls can be when laws exist to enforce their use. Careful consideration of climatic and geographical factors in the location of industrial plants, use of antipollution equipment, and voluntary or legal controls on operations during periods when natural dispersion factors are inoperative can all go far toward eliminating the annoyances and dangers of atmospheric pollution.

Atmospheric pollution has both widespread, long-term effects and local, short-term effects. In the past 100 yr, the burning of coal has probably increased the amount of carbon dioxide in the atmosphere. Since carbon dioxide helps prevent escape of heat from the earth, it is possible that if the present rate of increase of this gas continues, a general warming of the atmosphere, with changes in climate, migrations of plant and animal life, and a rise in sea level, could result.—*P. L.*

ATMOSPHERIC PRESSURE: pressure exerted by the weight of the air on the earth's surface and within the atmosphere itself. At sea level, average pressure on the surface is 1,013,250 dynes/cm² or 1013.25 mb (millibars), or 14.7 lb/in². Pressures decrease with increasing altitude; at 5,000 ft average pressure is 850 mb, and at 18,000 ft it is 500 mb, or approximately half the average sea-level pressure. The highest and lowest pressures ever recorded at the earth's surface are 1,078 mb and 887 mb. See also BAROMETER; CLIMATE.—*P. L.*

ATMOSPHERIC RADIATION: absorption and emission of electromagnetic energy by the atmosphere and the earth's surface. Generally it is an example of heat or thermal radiation, since the required energy is ultimately derived from the average kinetic energy (temperature) of the colliding molecules. In absorption, the energy raises the temperature of the absorbing body (or gas), whereas in radiative emission the energy is given off by the body and its temperature is consequently lowered. In the upper atmosphere, radiative processes also often involve various types of photochemical reactions.

Identity of Radiation: Application of PLANCK'S LAW shows that, for the observed range of atmospheric temperature, the major portion of the radiative energy originating at the earth's surface or in the atmosphere is confined to the wavelength interval 3μ to 100μ; hence atmospheric radiation is referred to as long-wave (infrared) to distinguish it from the short-wave (visible and ultraviolet) radiation which constitutes the bulk of the radiation from the Sun. One can deduce from Wien's Displacement Law that the wavelength of maximum radiative energy from the earth's surface (average temperature 15°C) is about 10μ: a fact that has important consequences for the radiative budget of the atmosphere.

In the infrared spectral region, the earth's surface and clouds more than about 50 m thick radiate nearly as black bodies; *i.e.* they absorb and emit almost perfectly at all infrared wavelengths. However, the absorption spectra of atmospheric gases are band spectra (involving discrete vibrational and rotational energy transitions of the gas molecules). The absorption within each band depends on the magnitude of the absorption coefficient and the amount of the absorbing gas present. The three gases most important in infrared atmospheric radiation are water vapor, carbon dioxide, and ozone. Although the major gas components of the atmosphere (nitrogen and oxygen) are responsible for absorption of solar ultraviolet radiation in the upper atmosphere, they play no role in the infrared radiative exchange process.

Atmospheric Absorption: Principal infrared absorption is due to water vapor, which has two strong absorption bands. One is centered at 6.3μ. The other, starting with very weak absorption just above 11μ, becomes intense beyond 24μ. Also water vapor has weak absorption bands through the visible spectrum and bands in the near infrared at 1.1μ, 1.4μ, 1.9μ, and 2.7μ. Large concentration and relatively strong absorption make water-vapor radiation most important in the lower atmosphere. Carbon dioxide shows absorption mostly in the spectral region 12.5μ to 18.1μ. Radiation leaving the earth's surface in this spectral interval is totally absorbed by carbon dioxide within the first few kilometers of the troposphere. Carbon dioxide also has absorption bands in the near infrared at 1.4μ, 2.0μ, 2.7μ (overlapping with water vapor), and a relatively strong band at 4.3μ. Primary ozone absorption occurs in the near-ultraviolet region—the Hartley (0.21μ–0.32μ) and Huggins (0.32μ–0.36μ) bands. Absorption by ozone of solar radiation in this interval is responsible for the high temperatures found in the upper stratosphere at about 50 km. There is also a weak band system in the visible called the Chappuis band (0.44μ–0.76μ). Infrared absorption by ozone takes place principally at 9.6μ, with two other absorption bands appearing at 4.75μ and 14.1μ. The 9.6μ band is by far the most important of the three, because it appears in the region of the spectrum close to the wavelength of maximum energy emission by the earth's surface and in the region of weak absorption by water vapor and carbon dioxide. As a result, ozone acts as a partial shield against radiation leaving the earth and tends to heat the lower stratosphere in areas where surface temperatures are high. Minor atmospheric gases showing infrared absorption include methane (3.3μ, 7.7μ), nitrous oxide (4.5μ, 7.8μ), carbon monoxide (4.7μ), and nitric oxide (5.35μ).

Little atmospheric absorption occurs in the wavelength interval 10 to 11μ. In this region the absorption follows BEER'S LAW, the exponential absorption coefficient being about 0.025 cm^{-1}, and being due mainly to absorption in the wings of distant water-vapor rotational lines. In the absence of clouds, about 90% of the surface radiation in this wavelength interval escapes to space without being absorbed by the atmosphere; this spectral region is sometimes referred to as the *atmospheric window*. In contrast to the transparency of the window region, the remaining infrared radiation leaving the

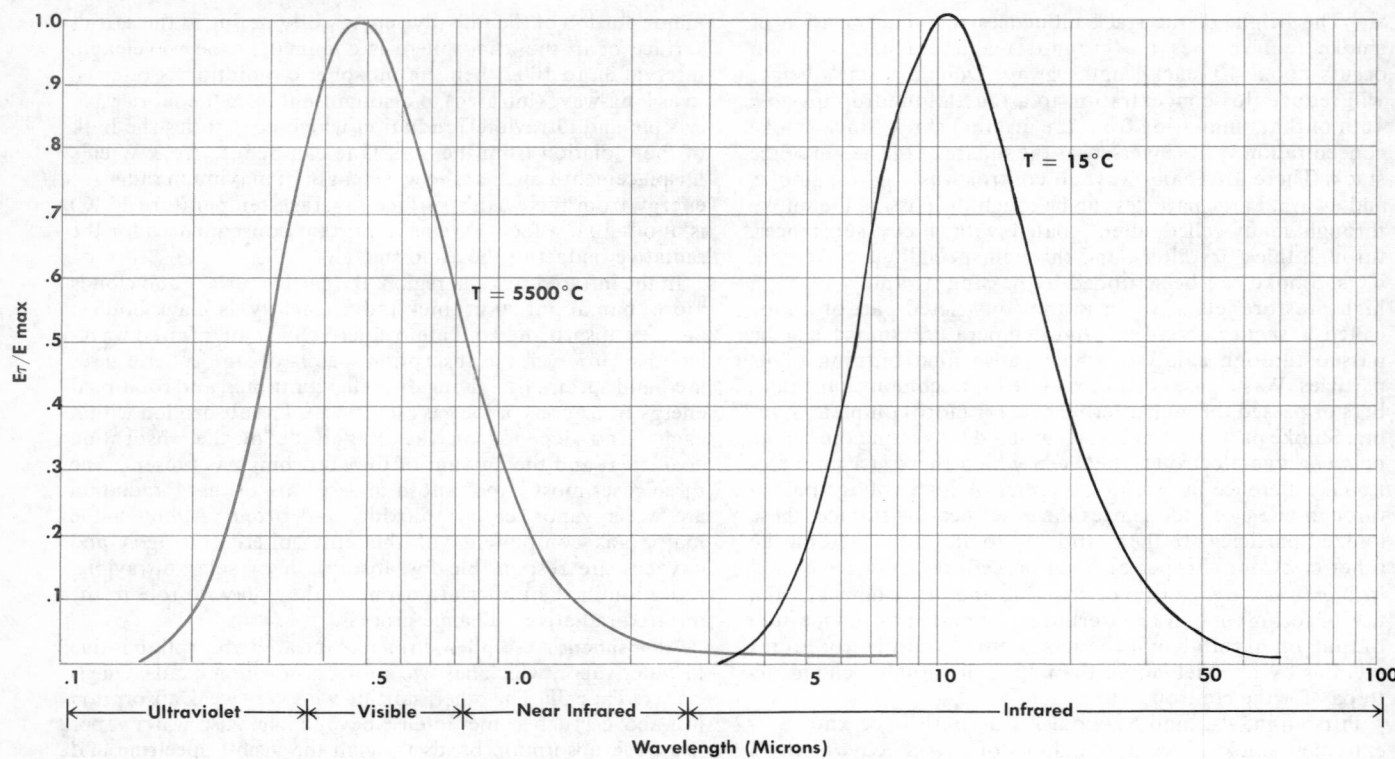

Wavelength (Microns)

Radiation from Sun and atmosphere: In these curves the radiative energy at a given wavelength (expressed as a fraction of the maximum value it could reach for a given temperature of the emitting source) is plotted against wavelengths from the ultraviolet to the far infrared. The curve at left joins values calculated for the temperature of the solar corona, with maximum energy at 0.48μ (yellow); the curve at right corresponds to temperature at Earth's surface, with maximum energy at 10μ (infrared).

ground is almost completely absorbed by atmospheric water vapor and carbon dioxide.

Radiation by Atmosphere: From the KIRCHHOFF LAWS it is known that within the same wavelength interval, radiating bodies absorb and emit radiation with equal efficiency. Thus the atmosphere, a good absorber of infrared radiation, also is a good infrared emitter. Much of the surface radiation absorbed by the atmosphere is emitted downward, at a temperature generally lower than that at the earth's surface. The difference between the upward surface radiation and the downward radiation from the atmosphere is called *effective (or nocturnal) radiation*. Except when there is a temperature inversion accompanied by a layer of low clouds, the effective radiation is always upward (that is, the earth's surface radiates more heat than it gains from the atmosphere). Effective radiation is largest when the surface temperature is high, the air dry, and the skies clear.

Greenhouse Effect: The atmosphere is semi-transparent to visible radiation. As a result, about 50% of the Sun's radiation reaches and is absorbed by the earth's surface. However, as noted above, because of its relatively low temperature, the earth radiates in the infrared region, where atmospheric water vapor and carbon dioxide absorb quite strongly. Thus, energy absorbed at the ground and reradiated by the earth's surface is trapped between the ground and a level a few kilometers above it. This trapped energy helps to raise the temperature of the surface and of the air in the lower atmosphere to the point where the surface and the lower air can eventually reradiate back to space sufficiently to balance the radiation received from the Sun. This process, which results in heating of the earth's surface and lower atmosphere somewhat as a greenhouse is heated, is called the atmospheric greenhouse effect.

As a result of atmospheric radiation involving water vapor,

the troposphere is constantly losing heat, at an average of about 1°C per day. This loss is compensated for by the transfer of latent and sensible heat from the ground to the atmosphere. Carbon-dioxide radiation contributes most to the infrared cooling in the stratosphere; however, the stratosphere is ultimately heated by the direct absorption by ozone of solar ultraviolet radiation (see also SOLAR RADIATION).—*J. L.*

ATMOSPHERIC REFRACTION: deflection or bending of a beam of light (or other wave ray) as it travels through layers of air of varied density. For two given layers, under given pressure and temperature conditions, the deflection (following Snell's law and Huygens' principle) is given by the relationship

$$\frac{\sin \phi_1}{\sin \phi_2} = \frac{v_1}{v_2} = n_{12} = \text{constant}$$

where n_{12} represents the index of refraction of layer 2 with reference to layer 1, ϕ_1 is the (acute) angle the incident ray in layer 1 makes with the normal to the interface, and ϕ_2 is the (acute) angle the refracted ray in layer 2 makes with the same normal. v_1 and v_2 refer to the phase velocity of the light wave in the first and second layer respectively. Refraction brings a light ray closer to the normal if n_{12} is larger than one. If the first layer is assumed to be a vacuum, the index of refraction of the second layer is simply $n = c/v$, where c is the velocity of light in a vacuum. For light corresponding to the D line of sodium (5893A), n is 1.0002926 for air at standard temperature and pressure, and is 1.333 for water at 20°C. For visible light, the index of refraction varies as the 6th root of the density; therefore under normal atmospheric conditions (density decreasing with height) the index of refraction decreases gradually with height. Thus, light from celestial sources follows slightly curved paths, concave downward, through the atmosphere. This effect is largest when the light ray traverses long atmospheric paths. With a setting or rising Sun or Moon, light from the lower limb undergoes larger refraction than light from the upper limb; hence an apparent flattening of the disc when it is close to the horizon.

Changes in the index of refraction near the earth's surface produce varied anomalous optical phenomena. In the case of a temperature INVERSION (temperature increasing with height), the density decreases rapidly above the surface and objects normally below the horizon come into sight (*looming*) when the inversion is at or near the surface. When the temperature inversion is above the surface, an object can appear above its surface position (*superior mirage*). The large increase of density above a strongly heated surface such as a concrete highway or desert sands causes rays near the ground to be refracted concave upward, and the object appears below its actual position (*inferior mirage*). In its most frequent appearance, the inferior mirage appears as "water" on a heated surface; it actually represents an image of the sky above. (See MIRAGE; SEEING.)

The refractive index for visible light increases with decreasing wavelength (dispersion); hence the oft-observed rainbow and the seldom-observed GREEN FLASH of the rising or setting Sun. Varied refraction effects occur also in the propagation of radio and acoustic waves in the atmosphere. (See ANOMALOUS SOUND PROPAGATION.)—*J. L.*

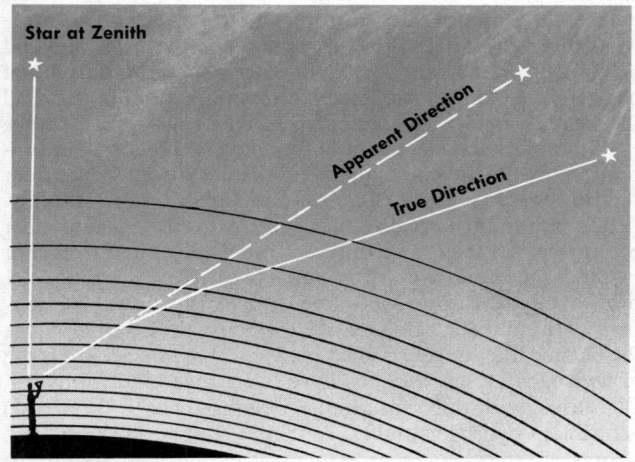

Atmospheric refraction: Layers of air in the atmosphere bend starlight so that the star appears higher in the sky than it is. The effect is greatest for an object at the horizon, least for one at the zenith. Effect is exaggerated here.

ATMOSPHERICS: electrical impulses causing noises in a radio receiver, especially during a thunderstorm. Lightning flashes are gigantic sparks which produce radio waves. They may be detected as far as 2,000 mi away. Very violent thunderstorms, such as those which sometimes develop into tornadoes, produce powerful bursts of radio energy, which have been used experimentally to trigger warning alarms. National WEATHER BUREAUS maintain networks of receiving stations (called *sferics nets*) to observe and to locate, by means of triangulation, the areas over which thunderstorms are active. These observations are valuable for preparing meteorological analyses as to oceans and other regions where regular observations are scarce. The audio-frequency part of the radio energy of a sferics burst travels along the lines of force of Earth's magnetic field. This signal is received at the ground in the opposite hemisphere as a low-frequency "whistler." Whistlers are studied not so much for meteorological purposes as for the information they carry about conditions in the outer atmosphere.—*D. H. L.*

ATMOSPHERIC TIDES: regular daily variations in atmospheric pressure, of a world-wide character. They are called atmospheric tides although they are due to solar heating as well as to the gravitational pull of Sun and Moon. Unlike oceanic tides, atmospheric tides have the Sun, not the Moon, as the main controlling agent. Daytime solar heating and nighttime cooling are responsible, respectively, for pressure minimums (low tides) at 4 a.m. and 4 p.m., and maximums (high tides) at 10 a.m. and 10 p.m., local standard time. The minimum at 4 p.m. is caused by the direct heat of the Sun and is more extreme than the minimum at 4 a.m. The maximum at 10 p.m. caused by nighttime cooling is more extreme than that at 10 a.m. This daily succession of barometric changes is called the *diurnal variation of pressure*. Variation from the normal pressure for the day ranges from 0.3 mb (millibars) near the poles to about 1.5 mb in the tropics. Other, less noticeable atmospheric tides, with periods of 8 and 24 hr, have also been observed.—*P. L.*

ATOM: a unit particle of a chemical element. The idea of atoms arose in early Greek philosophy (Gr. *atomos,* "indivisible") as a choice between the alternatives of infinitely divisible matter or division up to a point, and the atomistic concept is ascribed to the school of Democritus, which flourished about 400 B. C. Since experience showed, as far as the available tools permitted, that matter always could be subdivided, atoms were believed to be very small. Some attempts were made by ancient philosophers to explain the cohesion and other aspects of matter by appropriate features in the structure of atoms. Thus, liquids were thought to be composed of smooth atoms, whereas solids consisted of atoms hooking into each other. Aristotle, who largely influenced scientific thought in the Middle Ages, did not support the atomic theory but believed in four "elements."

Discovery: The work of the alchemists provided a large amount of factual information indicating that certain basic substances would combine to form compounds that had other properties than the basic substances, but that the basic substances themselves could not be split up. Such basic substances became known as chemical elements. The French chemist Joseph Louis Proust showed that these elements always combine with each other in certain definite proportions of weight, and early in the 19th cent. the English scientist John Dalton explained this behavior under the assumption that each element was made up of small identical units. These units, which were identified with the Greek atoms, had different weight and chemical properties for each chemical element. The researches of the Italian chemist Amedeo Avogadro and others strongly supported Dalton's atomistic hypothesis, which became widely accepted in the 19th cent., although some noted scientists refused to subscribe to it.

Structure: Originally the chemical atom was thought to be indivisible and immutable, and it was held that the transmutation of chemical elements was impossible. However, the discovery (1897) by J. J. Thomson of the electron, a particle with a mass almost 2,000 times smaller than the lightest atom, suggested that it might be a constituent part of atoms and thus that the chemical atom was a composite structure. That this is indeed the case was discovered in 1902 by the British physicist Ernest Rutherford, who demonstrated that electrons are emitted from radium atoms in radioactive decay. Further experiments by Rutherford and his school showed that all atoms consist of a central, positively charged nucleus, which is surrounded by a tenuous "cloud" of negatively charged electrons. The nucleus is itself a composite structure, made up of positive protons and uncharged neutrons, except for the nucleus of ordinary hydrogen, which consists merely of a single proton.

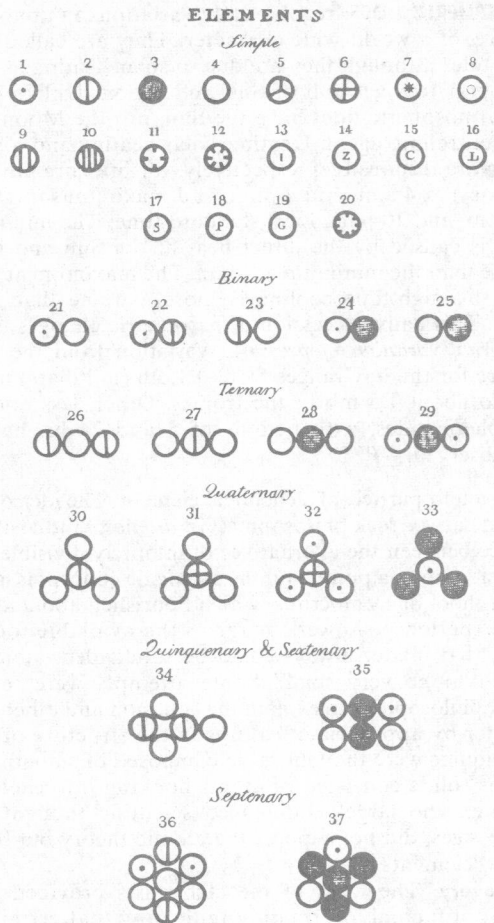

ELEMENTS

Simple

Binary

Ternary

Quaternary

Quinquenary & Sextenary

Septenary

Dalton's world: Dalton's symbols, though they did not suggest the names of the atoms (symbols 1 and 4 stand for hydrogen and oxygen), were easily grouped into molecular models. Symbol 21 shows water—to Dalton, the "binary" HO. (*Burndy Library*)

Because proton and electron each have unit, though opposite, charge, each proton in the nucleus will bind one electron, keeping the whole atom electrically neutral. The chemical properties by which the elements can be distinguished from each other are determined by the number of electrons in the "cloud." The weight, on the other hand, resides effectively in the atomic nucleus, since the mass of the electrons is negligibly small in comparison with that of the nuclear particles. The chemical elements have been numbered according to the weight of their atoms. Hydrogen, with its single proton, has the atomic number (Z) = 1. The next atom is that of helium (Z = 2), which has two protons and two neutrons in the nucleus and whose atomic weight (A) is therefore four times that of hydrogen. This is followed by lithium (Z = 3; A = 7), beryllium (Z = 4; A = 9), etc., up to uranium (Z = 92; A = 238), which is the heaviest atom found in nature. The uranium atom has 92 electrons, and a nucleus composed of 92 protons and 146 neutrons. The Russian chemist D. I. Mendeleyev discovered similarities in the chemical behavior of certain elements corresponding to a periodicity in Z, which have led to their arrangement into a "periodic system." These regularities have been explained by the arrangement of the electrons in concentric shells forming the "cloud" (see ELECTRON STRUCTURE OF ATOMS).

The average diameter of atoms is of the order of 10^{-8} cm (less than a hundred millionth of an inch), and that of the

nucleus, 10,000 times smaller. Thus the ratio of sizes is very roughly that of the whole solar system to the diameter of the sun; and since the electrons are in a state of rotation about the nucleus, this similarity has been much stressed in early models of the composite atom. However, atomic structure differs from the solar system in a number of important aspects. The force holding the electrons to the nucleus is not gravitational but electrical attraction. The electron orbits, unlike the planetary ones, do not lie in the same plane, but pass through all directions of space. The sizes and shapes of the electron orbits are, as was discovered by Niels Bohr, fixed to quite definite values in accordance with the QUANTUM THEORY, and upon the supply of energy an electron can "jump" into another of the quantized orbits, but not into an orbit of arbitrary size or shape. While it is possible to assign an electron to a definite quantized orbit, the UNCERTAINTY PRINCIPLE makes it impossible to state where in this orbit the electron can be found at any particular time.

Nucleus: Little is known about the structure of the atomic nucleus, which is very tightly packed, its density (mass/volume) being about a million million times that of ordinary matter. The electrostatic repulsion between the positively charged protons is counterbalanced by a nuclear binding force, which involves neutrons as well as protons. For light atoms the number of neutrons tends to equal the number of protons. It appears that, as the number of protons is increased, the number of neutrons has to be increased somewhat more rapidly in order to obtain stable nuclei. Beyond values of Z = 82 and A = 208, even a neutron surplus of over 50% becomes insufficient to maintain stability, and all the heavier nuclei are radioactive. This shows that, unlike gravitation or the electrostatic force, which decrease in proportion to the inverse square of the distance, the nuclear binding force (see NUCLEAR FORCES) falls off more rapidly.

It is important to realize that nuclei with the *same* number of protons (Z) may have different numbers of neutrons. For instance, the following three nuclei with Z = 1 exist: (a) 1 proton only; (b) 1 proton + 1 neutron; (c) 1 proton + 2 neutrons—(a) and (b) being stable, (c) being radioactive. Since the chemical atom is classified by Z, all three nuclei are those of hydrogen atoms. We thus have two stable kinds of hydrogen atoms with different atomic weights A. (Z = 1; A = 1) is ordinary hydrogen and (Z = 1; A = 2) is heavy hydrogen. Atoms of the same chemical element (equal Z) but with different atomic weights are called ISOTOPES. For instance, naturally occurring tin, with the average atomic weight of 118.70, is made up of the following stable isotopes whose percentage abundance is given in brackets: 112(1.02), 114(0.69), 115(0.38), 116(14.3), 117(7.6), 118(24.1), 119(8.5), 120(32.5), 122(4.8), and 124(6.1). In addition, unstable, radioactive tin isotopes with the following weights can be produced artificially: 108, 109, 110, 111, 113, 121, 123, 126, 127, 130, 131, 132.—*K. Me.*

ATOMIC BOMB (or atom bomb): an explosive weapon which derives its energy from a nuclear (atomic) reaction rather than from a chemical reaction, as in TNT. Although the term "atomic bomb" would cover explosions produced by either splitting (FISSION) or joining (FUSION) of atomic nuclei, this term is generally reserved for the former; HYDROGEN BOMB is reserved for the fusion type. Because the energy released by a fission reaction is so much greater than that available by chemical means, one small atomic bomb containing little more than 2 lb of fissionable uranium can match many thousands of pounds of chemical explosives. The atomic bomb, developed during World War II, was first demonstrated July 16, 1945, at Alamogordo, N. M., and was first used in warfare in the bombing of Hiroshima, Japan, Aug. 6, 1945.—*A. R. G.*

ATOMIC CLOCK: a device utilizing the vibrations of atoms or molecules to measure time. It produces the most accurate measurements of time intervals now available. The vibration may be a periodic inversion of one atom with respect to the others, as in the ammonia molecule, or a periodic change in the direction of magnetization of an electron in an atom such as hydrogen, cesium, or rubidium. In either case, the vibration is caused by a small change in energy, which produces an extremely precise microwave frequency. Atomic clocks are of two general types, functioning by absorption or emission. Older devices use absorption in either ammonia or cesium, the necessary energy being furnished by a microwave OSCIL- LATOR. High accuracy is achieved by automatically adjusting the frequency of the oscillator to that of the vibrating atom or molecule, which absorbs only the correct frequency. The oscillator is then arranged to drive a "clock." Newer clocks use the emission principle of the MASER. Ammonia molecules or hydrogen atoms pass through a focuser that allows only the most energetic to enter a microwave cavity. There they decay to a less energetic state (see ENERGY LEVELS) and, in so doing, emit their characteristic, stable frequency. The frequency is the time measurer, *i.e.* the clock. Ammonia clocks are accurate to one part in 10^{10}. The newest hydrogen type promises to have an accuracy of one part in 10^{15}, which means an error of 1 sec in 30 million yr! This high degree of precision will give improved methods of long-range navigation, will aid in timing atomic processes, and will be used to test the theories of gravitation and relativity, to check variations in the rate of rotation of the earth, and to accomplish many other important scientific tasks.—*I. R.*

Atomic bomb cloud: The first atomic bomb test explosion at Bikini Atoll, Marshall Is., 1946, produced this towering, characteristic mushroom cloud. (*Wide World*)

ATOMIC ENERGY (more properly, **nuclear energy**): energy released when the constituents of atomic nuclei are rearranged on a large scale, so that the nuclei lose some mass. This mass is converted into energy according to Einstein's relation, $E = mc^2$, where E is the energy, m the mass converted, and c the speed of light. Such nuclear transformations are responsible for the energy output of stars, of atomic and hydrogen bombs, and of nuclear power reactors.

Stellar Atomic Energy: In the fundamental stellar-energy process, four protons (hydrogen nuclei) fuse into a single helium nucleus, either directly (the proton-proton cycle) or by mediation of carbon as a catalyst (the carbon cycle). The proton-proton cycle is mainly responsible for the energy of our Sun, the carbon cycle for the energy of hotter stars. The nuclei involved in these FUSION processes are electrically charged and tend to repel each other by electrostatic repulsion. Only at temperatures such as are found in the interior of stars (about 20,000,000°C) are protons able to overcome their mutual repulsion often enough to cause an appreciable number of reactions.

In the proton-proton cycle, two protons combine, one decaying to a neutron and releasing a neutrino and a positron. The resulting deuterium nucleus reacts with another proton to form a helium³ nucleus. Two helium³ nuclei fuse into an ordinary helium⁴ nucleus, releasing two protons, which can start another cycle. The cycle as described releases 26 Mev of energy.

Eventually the hydrogen in a star is used up by the process of proton fusion; the star then collapses and its temperature rises. Equilibrium is arrived at when the star begins to "burn" heavier nuclei—particularly helium—and to produce neutrons as a by-product. Capture of these neutrons by nuclei is believed to be responsible for the formation of most of the heavier elements of the universe.

Terrestrial Atomic Energy—Fission: The large-scale release of nuclear energy on Earth became a possibility with the discovery of the FISSION of the uranium atom by O. Hahn and F. Strassman, 1938. Uranium²³³ and ²³⁵ as well as plutonium²³⁹ split into two fragments, or fission products, when they absorb a slow-moving neutron. Each fission releases about 200 million electron volts of energy, mostly in the form of kinetic energy of the fission fragments; in addition, an average of 2.5 fast neutrons is emitted in each reaction. Hahn's discovery opened the possibility of establishing a large-scale nuclear CHAIN REACTION, the general idea of which seems first to have been suggested by L. Szilard. In a chain reaction, a balance between the rate of production of neutrons and their rate of loss will exist only if a certain mass of chain-reacting material, called the CRITICAL MASS, is present. If the critical mass is exceeded, the reaction will increase in intensity. In a nuclear reactor, the increase is slow and the reaction is controllable; in an atomic bomb, the increase is very fast and the reaction uncontrollable.

Radioactivity measurement chamber: The cylinder contains a gaseous form of the deposits left in an auto engine from gasoline that had been treated with radioactive components. Measurement of the radioactivity of the deposits reveals which components are harmful. The chamber gives more accurate count than a Geiger counter. (*Esso-AEC*)

The first large-scale chain reaction was achieved by E. Fermi at the Univ. of Chicago, Dec. 2, 1942. The reaction took place in a "pile" of graphite in which were distributed 47 tons of ordinary uranium. The uranium was subdivided into roughly spherical lumps weighing a few pounds each, and the lumps were spaced about 8 in. apart. This general arrangement— discrete lumps of uranium distributed throughout a large mass of material of low atomic weight (the moderator)—is the fundamental scheme of most of the world's NUCLEAR REACTORS. The moderator slows down the neutrons emitted in fission. This is necessary in a chain reactor using natural uranium; otherwise too many neutrons will be captured in the very abundant uranium^{238}, and the chain reaction will be quenched. Chain reactions are easily controllable because about 0.7% of the neutrons emitted in fission of U^{235} come off after an average delay of about 15 sec. So long as the mass of the chain reactor is only a little above the critical mass, the time scale of the chain reaction will be determined by the relatively long time scale for the emission of these delayed neutrons.

In a mass of pure uranium^{235} or plutonium^{239} much larger than the critical mass, the chain reaction will no longer be paced by the delayed neutrons, but will build up in a few microseconds to a very high intensity. The ultimate intensity of the reaction can be further enhanced by forming the super-critical arrangement quickly. The resulting uncontrolled chain reaction constitutes an ATOMIC BOMB explosion. The first such explosion occurred June 1945, at Alamogordo, N. M. The bomb contained a few kilograms of plutonium and produced an explosion with energy equivalent to 20,000 tons of TNT. The great effectiveness of the atomic bomb comes not only from its huge energy release, but also from the extreme temperature reached in it, and from the associated radioactivity, both immediate and delayed.

Large-scale separation of the fissionable ISOTOPES for use in atomic bombs was accomplished during World War II by two main processes. In the *electromagnetic process,* the uranium isotopes are separated by allowing ionized uranium atoms to traverse a magnetic field. The heavier uranium^{238} has more momentum and is bent less by the magnetic field than is the lighter uranium^{235}. In the *gaseous-diffusion process,* a gaseous uranium compound (uranium hexafluoride, UF$_6$) is pumped through a permeable membrane or "barrier." The lighter isotope goes through the barrier a little more easily; this small effect is multiplied by cascading thousands of barriers in series. Large plants incorporating both separation methods were built in Oak Ridge, Tenn. Only the more efficient gaseous-diffusion method is now used.

In a nuclear reactor, much as in a very hot star, transmutations (changes from one element to another) occur as the result of neutron capture. The resulting isotopes are often radioactive, usually emitting beta particles (electrons) and gamma rays. Over 150 different radioisotopes are now produced and marketed commercially. The RADIOISOTOPES are used as tracers in scientific and production work, and as diagnostic or therapeutic agents in medicine. The most important isotope produced in a nuclear reactor is plutonium^{239}, which is formed when uranium^{238} absorbs a neutron. Plutonium^{239} can be used as the chain-reacting material in either an atomic bomb or a nuclear reactor. It was produced at Hanford, Wash., during World War II in the huge water-cooled reactors designed by E. Wigner.

Terrestrial Thermonuclear Energy—Fusion: The conditions of temperature and pressure in an atomic bomb momentarily approach those in the interior of a star, and light-element fusion can take place in this environment. The two heavy isotopes of hydrogen, deuterium and tritium, are most easily fused, and these materials, when disposed properly around an atomic bomb, convert the latter into a thermonuclear, or hydrogen, bomb. Because critical masses of hydrogen are not involved, there is no limit to the size of a thermonuclear explosion. The first HYDROGEN BOMB was exploded at Eniwetok, 1952; its yield was greater than the equivalent of 10 million tons of TNT.

Controlled FUSION on a large scale is profoundly more difficult for scientists to achieve than is uncontrolled fusion. In a controlled-fusion reactor, the reacting constituents, deuterium or tritium, must be a completely ionized, electrically neutral gas, or plasma, at a temperature of 10,000,000°C or more and at a pressure of about 100 atmospheres. Because of the very high temperature, this pressure must be contained by magnetic fields, not by material walls (which would melt). Although a world-wide scientific effort is being devoted to research in controlled thermonuclear energy, it is too early to say whether or not the necessary conditions of temperature and pressure will ever be achieved. If they are, controlled fusion will provide mankind with a limitless energy source relatively unencumbered by radioactive wastes.

Long-range Implications: Nuclear energy became competitive in the United States with energy from coal in 1964 when General Electric Co. contracted to construct a 600,000-kilowatt boiling-water reactor plant at Oyster Creek, N. J. Electricity from this plant is expected to be cheaper than electricity from a comparable coal-burning station. But though nuclear energy now seems economically competitive, its long-range significance lies in the essential inexhaustibility of its raw material: the residual uranium and thorium in Earth's granitic rocks. Tapping these resources requires a breeder reactor in which more fissionable material is produced than is consumed. With breeders, all natural uranium and thorium could theoretically be converted into fissionable materials for use as fuel in other reactors.

A seemingly very difficult long-range problem of atomic energy is the disposal of intensely radioactive fission-product wastes. Most radioactive wastes are now being stored as liquids in underground tanks. More permanent storage methods, *e.g.* reduction of the radioactive liquids to solids that are put away in unused salt mines, are sufficiently promising to suggest that nuclear energy will become mankind's primary energy source, without creating an intolerable radioactive hazard. See also NUCLEAR PROPULSION; NUCLEAR WEAPONS; NUCLEONICS.—*A. M. W.*

ATOMIC MASS: The masses of atoms, although extremely minute, can be measured to within a few parts per million (see MASS SPECTROMETRY). The simplest atom, hydrogen (one proton plus one electron), has a mass of $1.67335(10)^{-24}$ gm. Since the neutron mass is about equal to that of the proton, and the electron mass is only $\frac{1}{1840}$ of these, the approximate mass of any atom can be computed by multiplying the hydrogen mass by the number of neutrons and protons in its nucleus. Actually the precise mass of an atom is a shade less than the sum of the masses of all its neutrons, protons, and electrons. This difference, termed the binding energy, is a measure of the energy required to disrupt the atom. (See BINDING ENERGY; MASS.)—*S. K.*

ATOMIC NUCLEUS: the densely packed, positively charged core of the atom. Although the nucleus measures only about 10^{-12} cm in radius (some 10,000 to 100,000 times smaller than the radius of the atom as a whole), it accounts for about 99.95% of the mass of the entire atom. The nucleus of an element $_ZX^A$ is presumed to contain Z protons and $A - Z$ neutrons, where A denotes the atomic mass of the element as well as the total number of nuclear particles, or *nucleons*. Z also represents the number of extranuclear electrons. The net

charge of the atom is zero (Z positive and Z negative unit charges). The mass of the atom is the combined mass of $A - Z$ neutrons and Z protons, or a total of A mass units. The nucleus of $_{92}U^{235}$, for example, is composed of 92 protons and $235 - 92$, or 143, neutrons. A "cloud" of 92 electrons, occupying a number of shells and subshells, surrounds the nucleus.

If the number of neutrons for about 250 stable nuclei is plotted against the corresponding number of protons, it will be found that the neutron/proton ratio increases gradually from 1 to about 1.6. Nuclei with an excessive number of neutrons are unstable and decay by emission of negative beta particles ($_{-1}e^o$), causing neutrons to become protons (see ALPHA, BETA, AND GAMMA RAYS). A series of beta-decay steps may ensue, resulting in the final production of a stable nucleus. Nuclei with a marked excess of protons decay by the emission of positrons ($_{+1}e^o$), or by positive beta decay, causing protons to be converted to neutrons. Another adjustment may take place by the capture of additional electrons from the extranuclear part of the atom. In each case, a more stable nucleus is formed.

To account for the behavior of the nucleus, scientists have proposed various "models" of nuclear structure. The LIQUID-DROP MODEL OF THE NUCLEUS, proposed by Niels Bohr, pictures the nucleus as a drop of liquid held together by forces of surface tension. The theory accounts roughly for the instability of an extra-heavy nucleus and helps explain the process of nuclear FISSION. Another model assumes the existence

Studying effects of radiation on food: Potatoes (*left*) and milk (*center*) are lowered into water columns for irradiation by fuel elements in cadmium-lined boxes 17 ft below. (*National Reactor Testing Station—AEC*)

of nuclear shells of different energy levels, similar to the shells in the extranuclear space (see NUCLEAR SHELL MODEL). A compound nuclear model has now been proposed to account for the many-particle behavior of the more complicated nuclei. The forces that hold the nucleus together are as yet imperfectly understood. Gravitational attraction is definitely ruled out. At short range (about 10^{-13} cm), the nuclear attraction between two protons (or two neutrons, or a proton and a neutron) far exceeds the force of electrostatic repulsion. At greater distances, electrostatic repulsion outweighs any possible nuclear attraction. The MESON theory, advanced in 1935 by the Japanese physicist Hideki Yukawa, envisaged a hypothetical particle of an atomic mass close to 300 electron masses and carrying either a positive or negative charge. (Such particles have since been found to be constituents of cosmic rays and may be produced by high-energy accelerators.) Mesons interact strongly with nucleons and furnish a plausible explanation of the *exchange forces* that operate between nucleons. Thus, if a proton emits a positive meson, it loses its positive charge and becomes a neutron, whereas a neutron that gains this positive charge turns into a proton. The exchange of charges operates to hold the particles together. Neutral mesons account for the attraction of proton-to-proton and neutron-to-neutron. (See NUCLEAR EXCHANGE FORCE.)

The mass spectrometer reveals that the atomic mass of an atom is always less than the sum of its constituent particles. This is equivalent to saying that the total energy of the atom is always less than the sum of the energies of its individual parts. The resulting *mass defect* is known as the BINDING ENERGY of the atom. It is this energy that is released in the course of the formation of the atom from protons and neutrons. The same amount of energy must be supplied to break up the atom into its separate parts. See NUCLEAR PHYSICS.—*A. E.*

ATOMIC NUMBER: the number of protons in an atomic nucleus of an element. Since every ATOM, in its normal state, has as many electrons orbiting around the nucleus as there are protons inside it, the atomic number of an atom is also equal to the number of its electrons. All chemical reactions are interactions between the electrons of atoms; hence the atomic number of an atom determines its chemical behavior. Atomic nuclei do not play a direct role in chemical behavior, since they do not approach close enough to each other to interact. Thus, although the hydrogen nucleus (one proton) is quite different from the deuterium nucleus (one proton plus one neutron), their respective atoms have very nearly the same chemical properties, because they have the same atomic number.—*S. K.*

ATOMIC PHYSICS: the study of the atom, particularly its outer structure of electrons, which determines the atom's chemical properties, the interactions of atoms, and the emission of light and x-rays. The central nucleus and the phenomena associated with it are the province of NUCLEAR PHYSICS. Present theory of atomic structure stems from two major revolutionary concepts: (1) that light, classically considered a wave phenomenon, has particle properties; (2) that elementary particles, *e.g.* electrons, have wavelike properties.

The first idea was introduced by Max Planck in 1900 to explain the spectral distribution of BLACK-BODY RADIATION. He had to assume the existence of an indivisible unit of light energy, which has since been called a photon, or light quantum. Einstein explained the PHOTOELECTRIC EFFECT in terms of the collision of a photon and an electron in a metal and thereby established that the particle nature of light is manifest whenever it interacts with matter. To explain the temperature dependence of specific heats, he showed that acoustic waves in solids must also be quantized.

The wave nature of the electron was demonstrated experimentally by Davisson and Germer and G. P. Thomson (see DAVISSON-GERMER EXPERIMENT). The discovery that a wave equation for an electron could explain most atomic properties was due to Schrödinger (see SCHRÖDINGER EQUATION). This explanation was preceded by an approximate one by Niels Bohr, which emphasized that angular momenta of electrons occur in integral multiples of Planck's constant. This so-called quantization of angular momentum was demonstrated experimentally by Stern and Gerlach (see MOLECULAR BEAM). The final major contribution here was made in 1928 by P. A. M. Dirac, who combined the wave properties of electrons and the theory of relativity (see DIRAC ELECTRON THEORY). The resultant equation contained the spin properties of the electron and explained the finer details of atomic structure; it also predicted the existence of the positron. See also QUANTUM THEORY.—*S. Bo.*

ATOMIC SPECTRA: patterns of fine, sharply defined spectral lines corresponding to discrete electromagnetic radiations from excited atoms. Such emission lines, at first glance, appear to be jumbled in random order, but they are actually arranged in definite *spectral series*. Thus the spectrum of hydrogen consists of three principal series: the *Lyman series,* grouped at about 0.1μ wavelength (the ultraviolet region); the *Balmer series,* extending from 0.4μ to 0.7μ (the visible region); and the *Paschen series,* ranging from 0.8μ to 1.9μ (the infrared region).

Niels Bohr was the first to explain these series, doing so by postulating certain stationary states, or ENERGY LEVELS, in the hydrogen atom, in which no radiation whatever occurred. According to Bohr's theory, the emission of an energy quantum (a photon) takes place only when an electron descends from a high-energy level to one of lower energy. Because of the multiplicity of energy levels, different electron jumps are possible, with a spectral line signaling each jump. The theory of spectra of heavier atoms is more complicated than that for hydrogen, but is based on the same fundamental principles. See SPECTRUM; QUANTUM THEORY.—*A. E.*

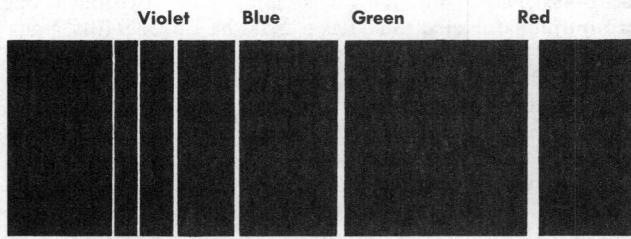

Atomic hydrogen spectrum shows positions of Balmer series lines.

ATOMIC THEORY: Originally the word "atom" meant an ultimate particle, incapable of subdivision into anything still more fundamental. An atomic theory is a scheme for explaining various phenomena in terms of these particles, their properties, and their interaction and combination. The earliest atomic theories were formulated by such Greek philosophers as Leucippus, Democritus, and Empedocles (all of the 5th cent. B. C.), and an atomic theory was integral in Epicurean philosophy. These early philosophical doctrines had little influence historically and are very inadequate from a contemporary point of view. Modern development of atomic theory began with John Dalton (1766–1844), who attempted to explain and correlate results of certain chemical experiments in terms of atoms and their properties. By the late 19th cent. the atomic theory had been greatly developed, in terms both of the number of elements known and of what could be accounted for by the use of the theory. At the same time, it became increasingly obvious that the atom was not indivisible and that there are still more fundamental particles. More recently, with the discovery of radioactivity and such developments as the quantum theory, atomic theory has been vastly extended. See ATOM.—*R. K.*

ATOMIC WEIGHT: the relative weight of an atom of a given element compared to the weight of an atom of the lightest ISOTOPE of carbon, arbitrarily assigned the value 12. Hydrogen, the lightest element, has an atomic weight of 1.008; that is, a hydrogen atom weighs about $\frac{1}{12}$ as much as an atom of carbon[12]. For many years, before refined isotope-separation techniques were available, oxygen with the assigned value 16.000 was the standard from which atomic weights of elements were calculated. Later, when O^{17} and O^{18} were discovered and their relative abundance in naturally occurring oxygen established, most chemists continued to assign the standard value of 16 to this natural isotopic mixture. Physicists, on the other hand, adopted a scale in which the standard value 16 was assigned to O^{16}. The two scales differed by about 275 parts per million—a difference of considerable significance in precise theoretical work. To eliminate this difficulty the present standard based on C^{12} was established in 1962.—*A. M. S.*

ATOMISM: the theory that all matter is reducible to ultimate "atoms," *i.e.* theoretically existent and irreducible particles. Related to this idea is the belief that these atoms are endlessly in motion and that their infinite combinations form the real structure of the universe. Democritus of Abdera, who first propounded the theory, held that spirit, itself, is composed of atoms.—*A. P. E.*

ATOM SMASHER: see PARTICLE ACCELERATOR.

ATP: see NUCLEOTIDES.

ATTENUATOR: a device which diminishes the magnitude of an electric signal. In a sense its operation is inverse to that of the AMPLIFIER. The volume control of the common household radio-phonograph is an example of an attenuator which, in actuality, is a variable resistor (see IMPEDANCE).—*G. S.*

ATWOOD, WALLACE WALTER, 1872–1949, U. S. geographer; b. Chicago. He strongly influenced the development of geography in the U. S. A. through his teaching and textbooks. As president (1920–46) of Clark Univ. he made it a center of geographic training. Atwood's scientific works include studies of the physiography of the San Juan Mts, the ancient glaciers of the Rocky Mts, and coal resources of Alaska.—*D. H. D. R.*

AUBISSON DE VOISINS, JEAN FRANÇOIS D', 1769–1841, French geologist; b. Toulouse. As a pupil of A. G. Werner, D'Aubisson was initially committed to Neptunism, the view that most rocks, including basalt and granite, formed from sediments in water. After seeing the ancient lava flows of the Auvergne, however, he became convinced that basalt was produced by volcanic action, and thenceforth he was an influential supporter of this viewpoint. His *Treatise on Geognosy* appeared in 1814.—*D. H. D. R.*

AUDIO AMPLIFIER: see AMPLIFIER; RADIO.

AUDIO FREQUENCY: see MODULATION.

AUDIOMETER: see ACOUSTICAL DEVICES; INSTRUMENTS, SCIENTIFIC.

AUDUBON, JOHN JAMES, 1785–1851, U. S. artist and ornithologist; b. Les Cayes, Santo Domingo (Haiti). Audubon's careful observation of birds, reflected in his detailed, artistic drawings and paintings, made his name almost synonymous with the study of bird life. In 1809 Audubon made the first experiments with the banding of wild birds in the U. S. A. The descriptive section of his great *The Birds of America* was published as *Ornithological Biography* (1831–39), with the assistance of

John James Audubon
(Nat. Audubon Society)

William Macgillivray, and as *A Synopsis of the Birds of America* (1839). Audubon produced an octavo edition of *The Birds of America* (1840–44) and subsequently published *The Viviparous Quadrupeds of North America* (1842–46) with Rev. John Bachman. He was a fellow of the Royal Society.—*S. B.*

AUER, KARL (BARON VON WELSBACH), 1858–1929, Austrian chemist, inventor, and industrialist; b. Vienna. By repeated fractional crystallization of didymium ammonium nitrate, he proved (1885) that Mosander's didymium does not exist but is a mixture of two elements which Auer named neodymium and praeseodymium. He invented the Welsbach gas mantle for converting heat into light, and pyrophoric alloys (cerium steels) for gas lighters. He also developed a method for preparing osmium filaments for use in electric light bulbs, the first successful bulbs with a metallic filament.—*R. E. O.*

AUGER EFFECT: the emission by a highly excited atom of one of its bound electrons. Ordinarily, when an electron is removed from its equilibrium orbit, the same electron or another one spontaneously falls back into the vacant orbit, simultaneously converting its potential energy into electromagnetic radiation (light or x-rays). However, if the vacant orbit is deep in the interior of the atom, the energy given off by an electron in filling the vacancy may be communicated to another bound electron, which is thus ejected from the atom. This mode of de-excitation becomes competitive with the usual radiative one. See ENERGY LEVELS.—*S. K.*

AURORA: a luminosity of the night sky occurring chiefly in near-polar regions, characterized by particular shapes or forms, by considerable changes in form, and by movement. The brightness of individual parts ranges from fainter than the Milky Way to over 250 times that of the region in Cygnus. In the largest displays the illumination on the ground can nearly equal that of the full Moon. The characteristic shapes or forms include a very diffuse glow, an arc across the sky, bands or distorted arcs with or without folds, rayed arcs and bands, isolated rays, narrow beams, patches or clouds that pulsate in brightness, and "flames" that are waves of light sweeping toward the zenith, each flame lasting a fraction of a second. When faint, the aurora is colorless. As it brightens, a yellow-green color first becomes evident, and then perhaps red glows, red tops to rays, and red at the lower borders of bands and arcs. Green, blue, yellow, and violet gray can also be seen on rare occasions. In the brightest bands there may be an ever-changing pattern of red, blue, and green rays. *Aurora borealis* (northern lights) is more frequent than *aurora australis* (southern lights). The former appears about 250 times a year, in a zone extending around the earth from central Alaska, through James Bay, S Greenland, Iceland, N Norway, and along the Siberian coast. North of this zone,

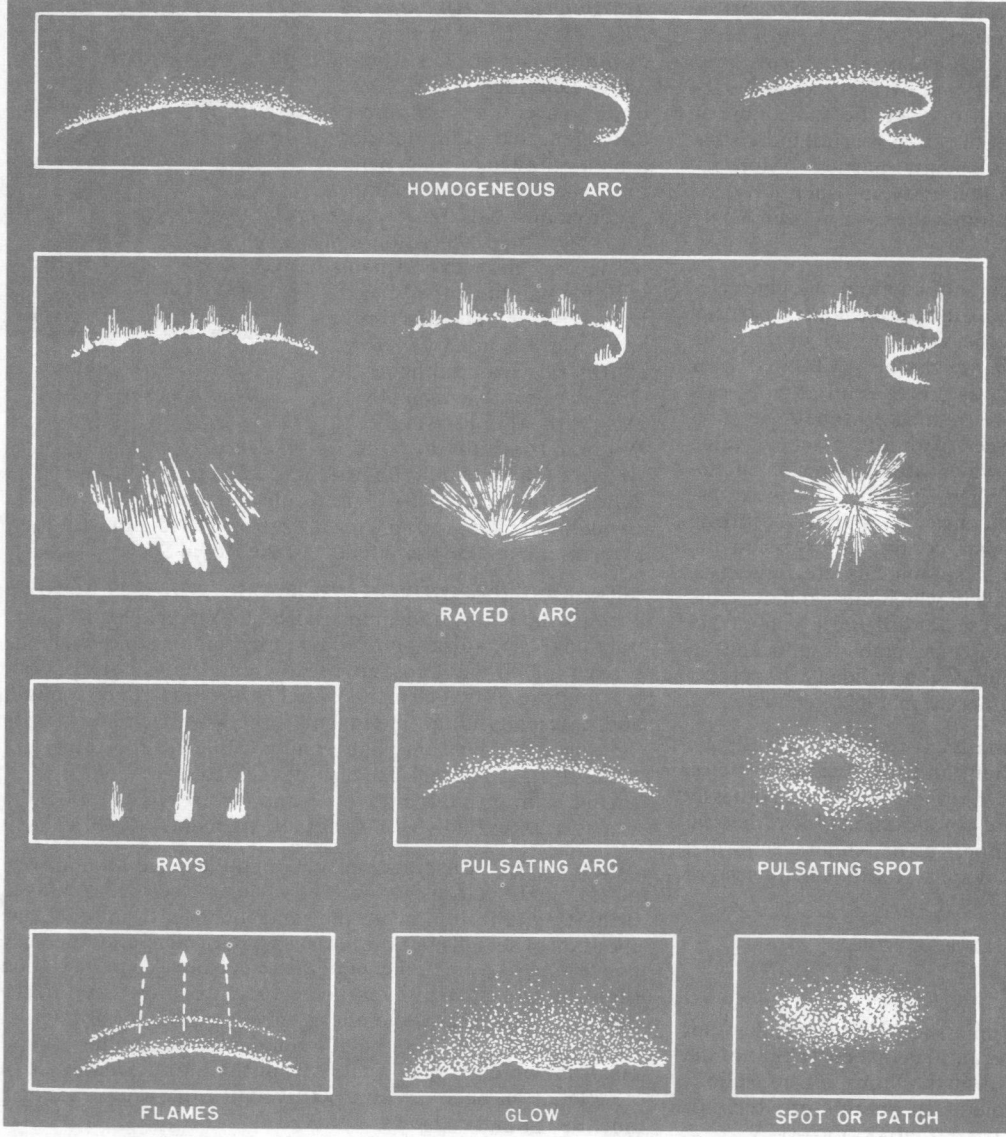

HOMOGENEOUS ARC

RAYED ARC

RAYS

PULSATING ARC

PULSATING SPOT

FLAMES

GLOW

SPOT OR PATCH

Forms of aurora: Auroras display a great variety of shapes, sometimes varying from one form to another in a few seconds. To aid in systematic study of the displays, observers use standard descriptions. (*IGY*)

auroras are less frequent and more diffuse. South of the zone, the frequency decreases, but an individual display tends to last for a longer time—several hours. About once in 10 yr the aurora can be seen from as far south as Cuba, Mexico, and S Europe. Auroras are also seen in regions near the south pole, but the zone for the aurora australis has not been well defined. There is evidence that displays occur simultaneously in the northern and southern zones, but further study is required.

The height of the aurora above the earth has been measured in North America, Norway, and New Zealand. The lower border is usually at an elevation of 60 to 80 mi, while red arcs and glows are at 100 to 200 mi. The isolated rays often begin much higher and may extend to 600 mi; at these elevations the aurora may be seen 15° south of the region where it is overhead. The lowest elevations may be from 40 to 60 mi.

The spectroscope reveals the auroral light as radiations from atoms and molecules of oxygen and nitrogen, with some radiation by hydrogen atoms. Thus we have the "forbidden" red and green lines of oxygen [OI], blue bands of ionized molecular nitrogen N_2^+, red bands of molecular nitrogen N_2; also some bands due to ionized oxygen molecules, lines from neutral nitrogen NI, and oxygen OI, ionized nitrogen NII and

oxygen OII, and three lines of neutral hydrogen HI, the Balmer lines. The H-radiations are broadened, showing the hydrogen to be in motion. The downward component may be nearly 2,000 mi/sec. Thus the hydrogen is an incoming particle (proton) and a partial cause of the aurora. Electrons are probably the principal exciting agent, though they cannot be directly observed.

Auroral displays are most frequent when a large and active group of sunspots is near the central meridian of the Sun's disk, particularly if a solar flare bursts out. This activity is most intense at times of sunspot maxima. Magnetic storms—erratic agitations of Earth's magnetic field—occur at the same time. An aurora visible in the equatorial limits of the zone is always accompanied by an increase in size of the simultaneous magnetic storm. The auroral zone described is approximately centered on the dipole axis of Earth's magnetic field. A principal purpose of aurora study in the IGY was the location of the zone of maximum overhead frequency. Tentative results indicate that this zone is located a little further south than the zone of maximum frequency of visibility or appearance. It is within a few degrees of geomagnetic latitude 60° and is definitely elliptical, with the long axis extending from eastern U. S. A. to Siberia. The fact that there is a zone and that it surrounds the dipole is proof that the primary cause of the aurora is charged particles which approach Earth at high speed and are deflected by the magnetic field into a ring. It may well be that the aurora-producing particles are a part of the outer Van Allen belt, since the aurora usually lies just outside (north of) the "horns" of the outer Van Allen belt. In one case, a bright aurora was just under a "spike" of intense Van Allen radiation. See Color Plate 14.—*C. W. G.*

AUTOCLAVES: steel reaction vessels, usually cylindrical in shape, capable of withstanding high pressure. They are used for chemical reactions requiring high pressures, and for confining in the reaction zone reactants and products, usually gaseous, that might otherwise escape.—*G. W. M.*

High-pressure process: The laboratory technician is removing tubes sterilized in the autoclave. (*American Cancer Society*)

AUTOLYSIS: self-breakdown or self-digestion of protoplasm catalyzed by enzymes present *within* the cell. This process is different from PUTREFACTION, in which the responsible enzymes are carried to the tissues by bacteria. Autolysis occurs when cells have been injured or when their oxygen supply is cut off. It probably occurs also after the natural death of cells, the breakdown products being used in the synthesis of new cells.—*F. F.*

AUTOMATIC PILOT: a device or apparatus that automatically controls, in some degree, the flight of an aircraft, missile, or ship. Usually, it is a device that maintains the attitude of an aircraft or missile and steers it in a desired path; such devices are also called *autopilots* or *automatic flight-control systems*. Automatic pilots are also used for steering ships, including submarines.

Early aircraft autopilots were simple pilot-relief devices, capable of maintaining straight and level flight with the desired heading. From these evolved the early guided missiles and the

remote-controlled aircraft (drones) used as targets in gunnery practice. Beginning with its first successful demonstration by E. A. Sperry in 1914, the automatic pilot has utilized the action of gyroscopes (gyros) as sensing devices, and the action of servosystems to operate the control surfaces. The gyros are mounted with their axes oriented so that any change in the aircraft's position about its three axes (*i.e.* pitch, yaw, or roll) can be measured. These measurements, as electrical signals, operate pneumatic or hydraulic actuators which move the control surfaces in the directions necessary to return the airplane to the desired heading and attitude. Once the airplane has returned to the desired path, the control surfaces are restored to their trim positions. The response of control surfaces to the sensed difference between desired and actual aircraft heading or attitude (gain) must be determined for each aircraft in each flight condition it may encounter; complicated gain-changing systems are necessary in autopilots for such aircraft as helicopters and supersonic jet fighters. In the case of relief autopilots, the pilot himself generally establishes reference heading and attitude, and corrects the autopilot's course setting and trim positions as necessary. Altitude sensing, through an altimeter, was an early addition to relief-type autopilots: desired altitude could thus be maintained while flying on autopilot.

Wiley Post's solo flight around the world in 1933 dramatically demonstrated autopilot capability, and autopilots subsequently became standard equipment on airline transports and large military aircraft. With the utilization of signals from an external reference, autopilot performance was both expanded and improved: it was realized, for example, that radio-signal inputs from a distant transmitter could be used to change an aircraft's heading. This gave greater flexibility than the autopilot systems used in drones and early guided missiles, which operated on a pre-set, programmed basis. During World War II, coupling of the autopilot to the bombsight allowed the bombardier to make precision course corrections during bomb runs by slightly altering the autopilot reference heading to conform to the bombsight heading. The autopilot would then keep the bomber dead on target, where an injured or distracted human pilot might not.

Currently, automatic pilots are complex systems employing a variety of different mechanisms and sensors to hold such parameters as Mach number (speed relative to speed of sound), altitude, attitude, and heading. Some, known as "stick-steering" autopilots, allow the pilot to maneuver the airplane with his regular flight controls, after which the autopilot "holds" the pilot's decisions. The versatility of automatic pilots has been further increased by utilizing inputs from external computing systems, such inputs generally being received through radio-signal links. *Automatic landing systems* have been developed, as well as *automatic intercept systems* in which an interceptor tracks a target by means of inputs received from a ground-based computer being fed radar data on the movements of both target and interceptor.—*H. A.*

AUTOMATION: an imprecise term popularly used to describe or suggest advanced mechanized performance of tasks, both mental and physical, that traditionally require the effort or attention of human beings. Although it is a new (post-World War II) word, automation does not signify a new trend: its current phase may be considered an extension of the mechanization inherent in the Industrial Revolution. As generally understood, automation implies the level of mechanization beginning with (1) automatic machine-performance of complex tasks, extending to (2) automatic machine-control of complex systems of machines, and culminating in (3) participation by machines in decision making.

Automation in steel industry: From a control booth, one operator oversees a continuous line of steel ingots passing through roughing rolls, preparatory to the ingots' being finished into final shapes. Manual control and human error are virtually eliminated. (*Westinghouse*)

History and Scope: Early in the Industrial Revolution, steam engines were fitted with automatically operating valves and with governors to control their speed; and textile machines of the 19th cent. made extensive use of mechanized controls. Jacquard looms (invented 1801) used punched cards to control their weaving action. Interchangeable machine parts and mass production, especially as developed in the early 20th-cent. automotive industry, were significant steps toward the advanced automation of production methods evident today: complex machines now perform a multiplicity of processing operations, including assembly of parts. Automation in chemical plants has been spurred by diversification of products, and by competitive factors such as increase in production rates, product quality improvement, and cost reduction. A general trend in industry is to impose production requirements that exceed human capabilities: machines often surpass human beings in their ability to observe with precision, maintain unwavering attention, process large amounts of information, and respond at speeds commensurate with competitive production rates. Corresponding trends are to be observed in information processing not directly associated with production. Increased volumes of data must be processed regarding raw-material resources, production, sales, and changes in technology and markets.

Machine systems are beginning to function as *intelligence amplifiers* in much the same way that microscopes and telescopes have extended the capabilities of human eyesight. Machines excel at reliable performance of complex routines (programs) at rates that may be as high as millions of operations per second. Reliability of machine memory, continually being extended by advances in technology, is a further advantage. However, machines can alter their programs only in accord with previously defined rules for responding to inter-

mediate results and input information. Aside from such program alterations, machines are incapable of exerting judgment and of thinking in any creative sense. But they already provide powerful aids to decision making and creative thinking.

In many applications, *e.g.* chemical production and automatic pilots, automation systems include devices for automatic monitoring of performance and for adjusting performance in accord with specified standards or purposes. Advances in this kind of automatic control, often referred to as "feed-back," include greater precision of the sensing devices, more versatile processing of their output signals, and improved stability of control (see AUTOMATIC PILOT). Feed-back control, utilizing the interaction of signals from sensing devices with previously acquired information stored in machine memory units, is being applied to simpler types of decision making.

Computer-type machines are rapidly finding use outside industry, in scientific, technical, and scholarly research. Increased speed of scientific computation continues to open up new opportunities for improved efficiency in scientific research and technological development. By extending the range of practically useful mathematical methods, research scientists and development engineers are able to broaden the spectrum of problems and assignments that they can attack with success. Automation to provide selective access to libraries and large files of documents was at about the same stage of development in 1960 as automation of numerical data-processing was 10 years before. The relatively simple automation procedures introduced into libraries since 1960 do no more than begin to exploit the potentialities. Continuing advances in methods for discerning patterns of relations among observational and experimental results give promise of ultimately providing powerful new tools for understanding of complex situations and for applying such understandings to decision making.

Social and Philosophical Implications: The tendency of machines to perform routine jobs faster, more reliably, and at lower cost often leads to organizational problems. Displaced personnel must be retrained for new job assignments. The question arises: Will increasing automation create intolerable social conditions, particularly widespread unemployment? Historically, the Industrial Revolution, lying behind Europe's and N America's present material prosperity, created new types of jobs, but virtually eliminated many well-established crafts. Social adaptation was not easy. Just so today, any routine manual job has to be regarded as a possibility for extinction by automation. Also, intellectual tasks may be automated in so far as they can be determined to be routine intellectual subtasks. Here the problem is one of definition: adding a column of numbers may be specifically defined as a routine subtask; but a general definition can be worked out, if at all, only by the formulations of symbolic logic, and by a reanalysis of operations, purposes, and objectives. *Systems engineering,* an important new discipline, is concerned with reaching agreement on what kinds of tasks, intellectual and manual, can profitably be automated. Precise definition of every step in a given operation is a prerequisite to successful machine performance; margins of uncertainty must be carefully controlled in any automated operation in order to justify its use. Somewhat less obviously, agreement must be reached as to which subtasks should not be performed by automation, but reserved for human performance, so that an agreeable division of labor between men and machines may be set up, and optimum machine-human teamwork realized. Thus two working principles emerge: (1) the potential limits of automation are set by human ability to define tasks to be performed by machines; (2) practical application of automation is limited by the usefulness of the results and by the cost incurred. It is assumed that if technological unemployment reached a critical point as a result of a lag in social adjustment to increasing automation, counter-measures (*e.g.* accelerated retraining of personnel) would be taken and the pace of automation adjusted accordingly. In the realm of philosophy, there is danger that the limits of human knowledge and understanding may be equated with what can be learned by the use of machines. On the other hand, a tremendous extension in our ability to correlate very large volumes of experimental and observational results seems certain to enhance greatly the effectiveness of the scientific method in both the physical and the social sciences. Politically, automation's capacity to process information and to control diverse types of operations could conceivably help tyranny maintain itself in power. But the possible dangers of automation are commensurate with its potentialities for technological and cultural progress; and, as with atomic energy, the responsibility of where and how to use it rests with human beings.—*J. W. P.*

AUTO-OXIDATION: the oxidation of a substance by oxygen (rather than by electron transfer) in the absence of a catalyst and at ordinary temperatures; an example is the rusting of iron. In the body, the major auto-oxidizable substance is the iron porphyrin protein cytochrome oxidase, an enzyme that takes part in the terminal step in the oxidation process called OXIDATIVE PHOSPHORYLATION. Some flavin coenzymes, *e.g.* the amino-acid oxidases, also are auto-oxidizable.—*J. F. S.*

AUTOTROPHIC ORGANISMS: those forms of life which, in terms of their energy requirements, are self-supporting—that is, do not depend on foods derived from other organisms. They require only inorganic substances such as salts, water, and carbon dioxide, and sunlight as a source of energy (see PHOTOSYNTHESIS). The ability to synthesize food from inorganic raw materials is limited to plants and a few bacteria; these are the ultimate energy source for all other forms of life. Organisms

Automation for safety: Uranium is recovered from nuclear reactors' used fuel elements in this U. S. test plant. (*Phillips Petroleum*)

such as animals, fungi, and most bacteria which depend on other organisms or their products for food are called *hetero-trophic*. See also ANIMAL-PLANT DIFFERENCES.—*P. R. L.*

AUXIN: a generic term for plant hormones which when used in very small amounts promote, by unknown means, the growth of plant cells. Such compounds are extensively used in higher concentrations to kill crab grass and weeds. Indole-acetic acid and "2,4-D" (2,4-dichlorophenoxy acetic acid) are well-known examples. Plant hormones are used also in orchards to control flowering and ripening of fruits.—*J. F. S.*

AVERAGE: see MEAN, MODE, AND MEDIAN; STATISTICS.

AVERROËS (or **AVERRHOËS**), known also as Abdul ibn Rushd', 1126–98, Arabian philosopher; b. Córdoba, Spain. The works of this tireless scholar and prolific writer deal with jurispru-dence, astronomy, grammar, and medicine. He is most famous for his commentaries on Aristotle, which were the scholastic philosophers' introduction to Aristotle, but his division of science from theology led to their opposition of him, notably by St. Thomas Aquinas, who wrote his *Summa contra Gentiles* to that end. There were Averroists among the scholastic philosophers, however—notably Roger Bacon.—*A. P. E.*

AVIATION: the technique or practice of flying or operating heavier-than-air aircraft. Although aviation in the mid-20th cent. has become almost synonymous with the technology surrounding the AIRPLANE, it is important to remember that the modern airplane evolved from experiments with the GLIDER, and that other heavier-than-air aircraft, *e.g.* the HELI-COPTER, may assume increasing significance in the future (see AIRCRAFT).

The legend of Daedalus and Icarus, the mythical magic car-pet of the *Arabian Nights,* and the winged gods of the early Egyptians, Greeks, and Romans are evidence of man's age-old desire to fly. The earliest attempts to produce heavier-than-air flying machines were based upon observations of birds, and designs were proposed for ornithopters or flapping-wing machines. According to a 12th-cent. English historian, Wil-liam of Malmesbury, about A. D. 1000 a Benedictine monk, Eilmer of Wiltshire Abbey, had two large wings strapped to his body and, "collecting the breeze on the summit of a

tower, he flew for more than the distance of a furlong." Reports of other such flights are recorded in medieval his-tories; none are entirely credible. In 1505, Leonardo da Vinci published a treatise on flight and gave detailed designs of several flying machines. Leonardo, like many of the early flight theorists through the 19th cent., was interested in vertical flight; thus many of his designs resemble helicopters more closely than airplanes. It is interesting that Robert Hooke (whose observations on the behavior of materials underlie modern structural analysis and design) observed that man's muscles are inadequate to produce artificial flight, and this conclusion was supported by Borelli (*de Motu Animalium,* 1680); but despite such opinions experiments have continued even to the present.

The evolution of the modern airplane can be said to begin with Sir George Cayley (1773–1857), in England. In 1809 he proposed the outstretched fixed wings, the horizontal and vertical tail surfaces, and the screw propeller driven by an internal-combustion engine. No such engine was available to Cayley, but in 1810 he built a glider in which his coachman is reputed to have flown across a valley. In 1842, W. S. Henson and J. Stringfellow constructed a steam-driven model, which was a failure. In 1848 Stringfellow achieved a flight of 120 ft; thus Stringfellow became the first man in history to construct a model capable of sustained and directed flight.

Significant technical developments were now taking place. F. H. Wenham (1824–1908) published a classic paper on arti-ficial flight; Alphonse Penaud (1850–1880) considered the problems of equilibrium involved in flight and built successful flying models. His design of 1876 is noteworthy for its novel features: dihedral, large aspect ratio, a movable trailing edge (the first semblance of an aileron), a glass windshield, rudder and elevator interconnected and controlled by a single lever, and an instrument system consisting of anemometer, compass, level, and aneroid barometer. In 1875 both Victor Tatin in France and Thomas Moy in England flew successful models, and these pioneers were followed by such experimenters as the Canadian Horatio Phillips (1845–1912) and the French-man Clement Ader, who was to claim he had achieved powered flight in 1897, six years before the Wrights. (Most aeronautical historians reject Ader's claim, since it was made only after the Wrights' success.) To Phillips goes the distinc-tion of having founded aerodynamics as an autonomous

New York to California, 1911: With breakdowns and bad weather, Cal Rodgers took 49 days to make this first coast-to-coast flight. (*Wide World*)

science; to Ader, of being the first aeronautical engineer to receive a government subsidy.

Otto Lilienthal in Germany in 1891 made and flew a glider. He experimented with such machines until his death in a crash, 1896. His outstanding work was contemporary with that of J. J. Montgomery and Octave Chanute, in the U. S. A., and Percy Pilcher, in Great Britain. Montgomery (1884) and Lilienthal (1891) are generally cited as the first to make successful flights in heavier-than-air aircraft. But in the same era Sir Hiram Maxim, British inventor, and Dr. Samuel Langley, American scientist, were experimenting with powered flight. Maxim, who began his investigations in 1872, after long experimenting completed a steam-driven, man-carrying machine in 1894. His machine was held down by a guard rail during trials, but developed so much lift that it ripped the rail away and crashed. A steam-powered model of Langley's construction made several flights in 1896. At this time the U. S. A. declared war against Spain, and the War Department commissioned Langley to build a full-scale device, but the project failed. The machine crashed in take-off, from aero-elastic effects, which caused bending and buckling of its framework. Some years later the plane was structurally modified and proved capable of flight.

The turn of the century brought success to two younger aeronauts, Orville and Wilbur Wright, who on Dec. 17, 1903, on the beach at Kitty Hawk, N. C., made the first powered flight. This epochal triumph, the result of much careful work, was based on two accomplishments not matched by Maxim and Langley. First, the Wright brothers had solved the problems of aerodynamic stability by long work with gliders before they tried powered flight. Second, they had a very much more stable structure. The Wrights credited the work of both Lilienthal and Chanute with having stimulated their interest in the problems of powered flight; and Chanute personally gave them encouragement in the years 1900–03, when they were testing the formulas and theories of their predecessors.

The success of the Wright brothers excited the world. By 1906, the first airplane flight had been made in Europe, by Alberto Santos-Dumont, a wealthy Brazilian. He was quickly followed by such outstanding persons as Louis Bleriot, Henri Farman, and Gabriel Voisin. (Bleriot is best known for his successful flight across the English Channel, 1909.) Although Frenchmen were the most energetic in the field, would-be fliers in England, Russia, Holland, and Germany were by no means idle. Names later known throughout the world for aircraft products were then just names of enthusiasts building their first planes: A. V. Roe (Avro), Geoffrey de Havilland, Igor Sikorsky, Anthony Fokker. In the U. S. A., too, the Wright brothers were challenged; Glen Curtiss was hard at their heels, and Martin, Boeing, and Vought soon followed. In 1910, Eugene Ely made history by flying off the deck of the *U.S.S. Birmingham* in Hampton Roads, and a few months later by landing on the *U.S.S. Pennsylvania* in San Francisco Bay. The principle of the aircraft carrier was thus established. In 1912 Curtiss built the world's first flying boat; the same year Lt. T. G. Ellyson, U.S.N., made the first catapult take-off.

European nations, particularly France and Germany, recognized the airplane's military potential. By 1914 France had some 600 planes, Germany more, and Great Britain 179, of which 82 were considered first-line. America lagged, and when she entered the war 3 yr later her air force stood at only 109 planes. But under pressure of war development everywhere was rapid. Speeds for fighters rose from 60 mi/hr in 1914 to 150 mi/hr in 1918; likewise payloads rose from a single passenger to 3,000 lb, while during the same decade service ceilings rose from 14,000 ft, in 1916, to 30,000 ft by 1918.

The next decade was one of exploration, of trying out the airplane as a means of mass transportation. Surplus World

New York to Paris, May 20, 1927: The high-wing monoplane *Spirit of St. Louis* was used by Lindbergh for his nonstop solo flight. (*Nat. Air Museum—Smithsonian*)

California to Hawaii, July 14, 1927: Ernie Smith and Emory Bronte flew this plane, similar to Lindbergh's, across the E Pacific. (*Wide World*)

Tokyo to the state of Washington, 1931: H. Herndon and C. Pangborn land at end of 4,600-mi nonstop flight. Landing gear was dropped after take-off to lighten plane. (*Wide World*)

Early air transportation: The Ford trimotor (*above, left*) was one of the first U. S. planes (1928) designed specifically for passenger, mail, and freight service. Durable, easy to fly, and able to get in and out of small fields with heavy loads, the "Tin Goose" inspired public confidence in air transportation. Among the most glamorous passenger planes were the Clipper flying boats, in service on transpacific and transatlantic routes in the 1930s. The Boeing 314 (*above, right*), one of the last Clipper types, appeared in 1938. It carried 89 people and had a range of 5,200 mi. Improvement of airport facilities made the Clippers obsolete. (*Ford,* left; *Boeing,* right)

Airliners come of age: The Douglas DC-3 (*left*), appearing in 1936, became the backbone of U. S. air transportation for over a decade. Versions of the DC-3 are still in use. As the C-47, it was the most commonly used transport in World War II. In the late 1950s, jet airliners such as the Boeing 707 (*right*) began service on transoceanic and transcontinental routes. (*Smithsonian,* left; *Boeing,* right)

War I bombers were converted into passenger and cargo carriers. In Britain, four airlines were formed, to be consolidated in 1924 into the British Overseas Airways Co., Ltd.; in France there were five; Germany, restrained by the Treaty of Versailles, had none till after the restrictions were removed, 1925. America was far behind. But by 1926 the transport airplane was no longer a converted bomber. The majority of the new transports came from three factories: Fokker in Holland, Handley-Page in England, Junkers in Germany. The largest airport in the U. S. A. was smaller than Croydon (London), Le Bourget (Paris), and Tempelhof (Berlin). However, Lindbergh's epic solo journey from New York to Paris, 1927, stirred America, and by 1934 the pendulum had swung the other way. The busiest airport in the world was now Newark, N. J.: traffic here exceeded the total for Croydon, Le Bourget, and Tempelhof, while Los Angeles, Chicago, and Camden (N. J.) airports were all busier than any one of these. The famous DC family, of which the DC-3 was to become one of the most remarkable planes yet produced, came into being. The large flying boat, *e.g.* the Clippers and the Empireboats, became synonymous with trans-oceanic luxury flying.

In 1931, Flight Lt. G. H. Stainforth of the Royal Air Force set a speed record of 415.2 mi/hr. The aircraft used sired the renowned Spitfire and the celebrated Rolls-Royce Merlin engine. Within a few years the British developed the heavy night bomber of the Lancaster type, the Germans their dive-bombing Stukas, the Americans the high-flying daylight bombers of the Boeing B-17 Flying Fortress class. Generally considered the most effective bomber in the early part of the

war, the Fortress cruised at about 200 mi/hr, could carry over 10,000 lb of bombs, had a range of over 2,000 mi, and was operational up to about 25,000 ft. All in all, World War II accelerated the development of aviation remarkably, and by its termination in 1945, there had been dramatic developments in propulsion and aerodynamic systems, among them the jet engine and the sweptback-wing configuration.

The story of the jet engine reaches back to 1920, when A. A. Griffith at the Royal Aircraft Establishment, England, made preliminary tests of a normal propeller driven by a gas-turbine engine. In 1929 Frank Whittle of the Royal Air Force started work on a pure jet system. After a promising start, the work lay dormant until 1935, when the Power Jets Co. was formed. An engine was tested by 1937, and an airplane powered by it flew in 1941. Concurrent with this British work were Hans von Ohain's activities in Germany: he commenced work on the same system in 1935; by 1937 an engine was tested, and by 1939 a prototype airplane flew. During the period of hostilities both sides brought jet aircraft into service: the Germans, the Me-262; the British, the Meteor I. In America the Bell XP-59, based on the original Whittle engine, was completed and flying, and the Lockheed 80 was in the advanced design stage. But the jet was not the only development in propulsive systems. Simultaneously the Germans brought the liquid rocket motor and the pulse jet to a stage of reliability and development which warranted their use in military aircraft. These systems of propulsion were used by them to power their Me-163 fighter and the V-1 weapon, respectively.

Substantial progress was also made in aircraft design in the decade preceding World War II and during the conflict itself. In 1940, Sikorsky built the first truly successful helicopter. Airplane construction and appearance in general underwent drastic modification. Early airplanes had been essentially framed structures covered with fabric, propelled by a rotating screw of fixed pitch directly driven by an internal-combustion engine, with a fixed undercarriage system for landing. Such designs disappeared one by one. The retractable undercarriage was invented, the variable-pitch propeller introduced, and the metal-skinned monoplane devoid of all external attachments became commonplace. Attention was directed toward improved structural performance; high-strength aluminum alloys were developed and stressed-skin construction evolved. Engines of 1,000 hp or more were produced, *e.g.* the 1,030-hp Rolls-Royce Merlin engine which powered the Spitfire and Hurricane fighters in the Battle of Britain. Armament no longer consisted of a single gun firing through the propeller hub; and, as in the Spitfire and other types of fighters, eight guns were fixed in the wings and arranged in such a manner that their lines of fire intersected progressively along the center line of the plane. Vertical, dorsal, and tail turrets were introduced; bomb loads increased to 10 tons and more, and bombing devices acquired almost incredible accuracy. Toward the close of the war, the Boeing B-29 Super Fortress became operational. Capable of bombing from above 30,000 ft, and with a range in excess of 3,000 mi and a top speed of around 350 mi/hr, it was a marked advance over earlier bombers. Also, rockets were added to the fighting power of aircraft. In Nov. 1945, a twin-jet British Meteor fighter set a new world's speed record of 606 mi/hr.

The decade following World War II was a remarkable one in aircraft development. The jet engine and the concept of the sweptback wing (developed over the previous decade) were blended to bring two outstanding achievements: flight at supersonic speeds, and the giant jet airliner. The aeronautical engineers of Germany laid the foundation for these developments with their pioneer work during the war, which ended with a world accustomed to flight, demanding rapid, comfortable, convenient transportation between all nations, with an atmosphere conducive to civil aviation development. The aircraft industry of America responded to this stimulus, and a generation of superb transport airplanes was developed. The super airliners—the DC-6, the Constellation, the Stratocruiser, the Martin 404—became the carriers of the world's air traffic. The British rapidly took advantage of the great advances made in propulsion. From Vickers came the world's first prop-jet airliner, opening an era of vibration-free flying, and from De Havilland the Comet Airliner—the first of the new generation of jet liners. These pioneer aircraft were followed by a number of equally outstanding airplanes of both American and Russian design—such as the American Lockheed Electra prop-jet and the Boeing 707, the Douglas DC-8, the Convair 880, and the Soviet's giant passenger plane, the largest in the world: Tu-114, a ship which rivals the pure jets in speed and has the phenomenal range of 9,000 mi. Likewise they operate the Tu-104, a jet airliner in the international class. By the 1960s all major powers had military airplanes that can fly at better than twice the speed of sound. Nuclear propulsion systems are under study. The carrying capacities and speeds of airplanes are being increased at a remarkable rate. Jumbo Jets will carry about 450 passengers; Super Jumbo Jets, which will evolve from the C-5A, an Air Force cargo airplane, will carry 850 passengers. The C-5A is designed for 250,000 lb of cargo. The Supersonic Transport (SST) under development will cruise at speeds up to Mach 3. Hypersonic air transports in the Mach 6–8 speed range will become feasible. In the first half of the 1960 decade air cargo nearly doubled. The rate of air-freight growth is so rapid that a tenfold increase from the mid 1960's to 1980 is predicted. V/STOL (Vertical/Short Take Off and Landing) technology will lead to commercial and military use of this class of aircraft. Research in supersonic combustion has paved the way for ramjets capable of reaching orbital velocity. (See AERODYNAMICS; AIRCRAFT INSTRUMENTATION; AIRCRAFT PROPULSION.)—*W. Ho.*

AVICENNA (Arabic, **Abu 'Ali al-Husain ibn 'Abdallah ibn Sina**), 980–1037, Islamic philosopher, mathematician, astronomer, and physician; b. Afshana, near Bukhara. One of the outstanding Islamic scientists, he is still known as "the prince of learning" in the Moslem world. His writings include the *Kitab al-shifa,* a philosophical encyclopedia concerned with all branches of knowledge, and the *Qanun,* a million-word medical encyclopedia. Avicenna's researches encompassed motion, the void, heat, light, harmony, and mineralogy.—*D. H. D. R.*

AVOGADRO, AMEDEO, CONTE DI QUAREGNA, 1776–1856, Italian physicist; b. Turin. He is best known for his paper "Essay on a Way of Determining the Relative Masses of Elementary Molecules of Bodies and the Proportions in Which They Enter into These Combinations" (1811). Avogadro provided a resolution of the conflict between Dalton's atomic theory and Gay-Lussac's researches by replacing Dalton's "rule of greatest simplicity" with AVOGADRO'S HYPOTHESIS. He did not originate this hypothesis, but extended its usefulness. It did not win acceptance by chemists until 1858, when S. Cannizzaro revived and clarified it.—*D. H. D. R.*

AVOGADRO'S HYPOTHESIS: "equal volumes of all gases at the same temperature and pressure contain the same number of molecules." Amedeo Avogadro developed this hypothesis (1811) to explain J. L. Gay-Lussac's observation that "gases, at the same temperature and pressure, which react chemically, have volume ratios which are simple integers to each other." An inference was that substances are normally molecular and not atomic (contrary to John Dalton's view) and that reactions take place between molecules, which could contain two or more atoms. Thus, in the reaction between nitrogen and hydrogen, which Gay-Lussac showed had the volume relationship 1 volume nitrogen + 3 volumes hydrogen → 2 volumes ammonia, if a volume is taken such that it contains a billion molecules, then the number of molecules of each species involved would be 1 billion molecules nitrogen + 3 billion molecules hydrogen → 2 billion molecules ammonia. The total numbers of atoms balance, since the nitrogen and hydrogen molecules each have two atoms and the ammonia molecule has one atom of nitrogen and three atoms of hydrogen. Thus, 2 billion atoms nitrogen + 6 billion atoms hydrogen → 2 billion molecules ammonia, which contain 2 billion atoms of nitrogen and 6 billion atoms of hydrogen. The hypothesis found little acceptance in Avogadro's lifetime but was used by Stanislao Cannizzaro (1858) to lay the framework for our understanding of molecular weights, gas behavior, and the interpretation of reactions between gases. See GAS; MOLECULE. —*L. Sc.*

AVOGADRO'S NUMBER: the number of molecules in 1 gram-molecular weight of a substance. Molecular weight is a relative quantity, and the oxygen molecule has been assigned a mol. wt of 32. One gm-mol. wt is the number of grams equal to the mol. wt, so 1 gm-mol. wt of oxygen is 32 gm. At standard conditions of temperature and pressure (0°C and 1 atm), 32 gm of oxygen has a volume of 22.4 liters. According to AVOGADRO'S HYPOTHESIS, equal volumes of all gases at the same conditions of temperature and pressure contain the same number of molecules. Therefore, the mol. wt of any gas can be determined by weighing 22.4 liters of it (at 0°C and 1 atm). For example, 22.4 liters of nitrogen weigh 28 gm; so 28 is the mol. wt of nitrogen. From the mol. wt, the atomic weight of elements in a gaseous compound can be determined. Since there is no absolute correlation between volume and number of molecules in a solid or liquid, the above method is not valid for solids and liquids; however, the number of molecules in a gm-mol. wt is again Avogadro's number, the presently accepted value of which is $(6.0248 \pm 0.0002) \times 10^{23}$. See ATOMIC WEIGHT.—*E. M. R.*

AXIOM: see EUCLIDEAN GEOMETRY; MATHEMATICS, LOGICAL STRUCTURE OF.

AXIOMATIZATION: the process of determining a set of propositions, called "axioms" or "postulates," from which all other propositions of a theory are derivable. The classic example, from which the process evolved, is the Greek work in geometry which culminated in the axioms and postulates given in Euclid's *Elements*. It is found in its most rigorous form in modern mathematics, where it forms an important tool for research, being no longer confined to geometric theories. The derivation of the other propositions ("theorems") of a theory from the axioms is usually done by logical deduction, but may be limited to certain stipulated rules (as is customary in the formal axiomatic systems of symbolic logic). It is gradually becoming a research tool in the natural and social sciences, especially in their theoretical aspects; but has not attained in these fields the perfection reached in mathematics. The choice of a set of axioms is influenced by the judgment of the particular investigator, since generally no unique choice is possible, *i.e.* the axioms for a given set of propositions can be selected in alternative ways. For example, many different axiom systems have been given for Euclidean geometry; the like holds for most other theories. Unless the theory to be axiomatized is completely formalized within a symbolic framework, the language used for stating the axioms is the natural language of the particular investigator; hence the choice of axioms involves a choice of basic technical terms to be left undefined, since the attempt to define all terms would lead to endless regression. Thus it is possible to axiomatize Euclidean geometry on the basis of the term "point" and a suitable ternary (three-termed) or quaternary (four-termed) relation between points (having to do with distance), all other geometric terms being ultimately defined in terms of these. In the application of an axiomatized theory, meanings are assigned to the undefined terms; the resulting interpretation yields a MODEL of the theory, to which the propositions derived from the axioms may be applied.—*R. L. W.*

AXIOM OF CHOICE: a mathematical principle (sometimes called the Zermelo Postulate) frequently invoked in the THEORY OF SETS. It may be stated in a number of equivalent forms, one of the simplest being: If G is a collection of nonempty sets or classes S_i, no two of which have common elements, then there exists a set C containing exactly one element of each set S_i. Thus, if we suppose G to be an *infinite* collection of sets or classes S_i, where each of these sets is a pair of socks such that no two of these sets have a sock in common, then the axiom of choice asserts that there is a set (or class) C, each member of which is a sock belonging to one of the pairs in G, and containing a sock from every pair in G (example of B. Russell). The need for the axiom arises from the fact that since the socks in each pair in G are entirely alike (*e.g.* the socks in each pair cannot be distinguished as "right" or "left," as would be the case if one were dealing with shoes), and since, because there are an infinite number of pairs in G, we cannot literally select a sock from each pair *seriatim*, we must postulate that nevertheless there will be a representative from each pair in the class C. Of course, if G were a *finite*

set of pairs of socks this difficulty would not arise. But in modern mathematics, classes (or sets) may not only be *not finite*, but also may be characterized as having *different orders of infinity*: they may be *denumerably* infinite (*i.e.* their members may be matched in a one-to-one fashion with the whole numbers or integers), or they may be *nondenumerably* infinite (*i.e.* it is impossible to establish a one-to-one correspondence between their members and the integers—*e.g.* the set of all real numbers in the interval from 1 to 2 is nondenumerably infinite).

Before the rigorous modern development of set theory, the principle was used without recognition that any special assumption was being made. In 1904, E. Zermelo used it to show that for every set S there exists a well-ordering; *i.e.* a simple ordering in which every nonempty subset of S has a first element. This result, intuitively unacceptable to many in case S is a nondenumerably infinite set, led to explicit formulation of the principle and to its rejection by some. Since many major theorems and methods of mathematics cannot be established without the principle, and in many instances are equivalent to it (*e.g.* Zorn's Lemma), it is generally conceded that it is necessary to the development of modern set theory. And since its rejection leads generally only to a serious delimitation of mathematics, it is not considered an axiom in the same sense as the parallel axiom, for instance, where denial of the axiom leads to important alternative theories.—*R. L. W.*

AZIMUTH: in astronomy, the arc of the horizon between the north point and the vertical circle passing through a celestial body, stated in degrees, minutes, and seconds, and measured from 0° at north clockwise through 90° at east, 180° at south, 270° at west, and 360° at north again. (In surveying it is often measured from the south point clockwise for 360°.) Together with altitude, azimuth defines the location of a point in the horizon system of CELESTIAL COORDINATES. The azimuth of a known celestial body can be computed for any instant of time when the observer's latitude and longitude are known, and can be measured with a theodolite, an engineer's transit, or, less accurately, with a compass.—*T. N.*

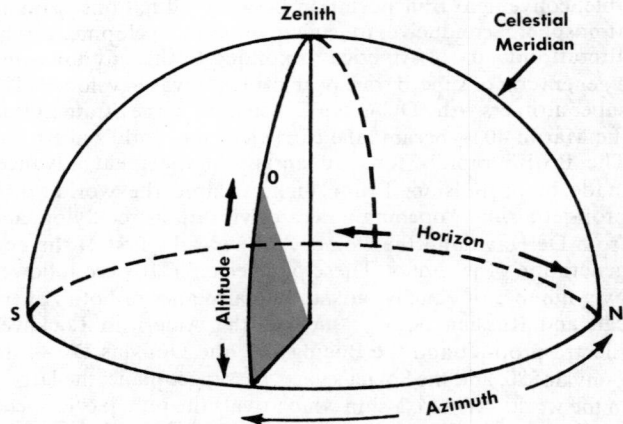

Azimuth and altitude: For a celestial object seen at point 0, azimuth is measured along the horizon from the north point clockwise (eastward). Altitude is measured from the horizon.

AZYR, FELIX VICQ D', 1748–94, French anatomist and physiologist; b. Valogne. In anatomical research he used the comparative method, particularly with regard to the extremities of mammals and the teeth of all vertebrates. In physiology he characterized organisms as to digestion, nutrition, circulation, respiration, secretion, ossification, generation, irritability, and sensibility, and he studied these functions comparatively in different life forms.—*D. H. D. R.*

B

BAADE, WALTER, 1893–1960, German-American astronomer; b. Schröttinghausen, Germany. He utilized the giant telescopes at Mt Wilson and Palomar Mt for observations relative to the evolution of stars and galaxies. From study of the Andromeda galaxy and its companions, he formulated the concept of star populations, 1944. Using this together with photometry of faint variable stars, he concluded that the distance scale for remote galaxies had been underestimated by at least a factor of two (1951). Baade discovered Hidalgo and Icarus, the asteroids farthest from and nearest to the Sun. —*O. G.*

BABBAGE, CHARLES, 1792–1871, English mathematician; b. Teignmouth, Devonshire. From 1828 to 1839 he was Lucasian professor of mathematics at Cambridge. He was instrumental in founding the Astronomical Society in 1820 and the Statistical Society in 1834. In collaboration with Sir John Herschel and George Peacock he tried to raise standards of mathematical instruction in England. Becoming interested in the construction of a calculating machine in 1822, he investigated calculators built on the Continent and started building his own (which was never completed). He was a fellow of the Royal Society.—*H. C.*

BABBITT, ISAAC, 1799–1862, U. S. inventor; b. Taunton, Mass. A trained goldsmith interested in the properties of metals in general, he produced the first britannia ware in the U. S. A., 1824. In 1839 he produced the first of the type of bearing metals named after him; it consisted of alloys of tin and small percentages of copper and antimony (see BABBITT METAL). Babbitt later made bearing metals and soap.—*R. J. F.*

BABBITT METAL: an alloy of tin, antimony, and copper (named for its inventor, ISAAC BABBITT). Anti-friction properties make it ideal as a lining for machine bearings. Grains of antimony-tin (SbSn) and copper-tin (CuSn) formed in the soft malleable alloy allow a hard surface to conform to the dimensions of the shaft. To reduce cost, lead is often substituted for tin.—*A. L.*

BACON, FRANCIS, 1561–1626, English political careerist, essayist, and philosopher; b. London; ed. Cambridge. He held a variety of high political posts, including that of Lord Chancellor. His *Essays* (1597) was an immediate literary success. Bacon conceived, but did not complete, an ambitious program for science, set forth mainly in *The Advancement of Learning* (1605) and *Novum organum* (1620): Science is to produce inventions for human welfare. But invention, heretofore haphazard, is to be systematically pursued; this requires understanding of the

Sir Francis Bacon
(British Information Services)

causes of things: "Knowledge is power." But Nature must be obeyed to be commanded: causes are to be revealed through observation and experiment guided by "true induction"—a form of induction, allegedly new, which "shall analyze experience and take it to pieces, and by a due process of exclusion and rejection, lead to an inevitable conclusion."

This method roughly consists in drawing up a table of instances which share a property F (*e.g.* heat) though otherwise dissimilar. A second table lists items similar to these instances in every respect except F. We then eliminate all properties present when F is absent and absent when F is present and (from a third table) which decrease when F increases. The remaining properties now are tentatively asserted as constituting the "Form" of F, *i.e.* the causes of F's presence. The required instances are to be collected without antecedent hypotheses regarding F's form; and the tabular method, ideally automatic, dispenses with individual genius and counteracts the pernicious influence of a variety of prejudices, termed "Idols of the Human Mind." These are: Idols of the Tribe (distorting tendencies inherent in human nature); Idols of the Cave (individual idiosyncrasies); Idols of the Market Place (looseness of language); and Idols of the Theater (uncriticized authorities and traditions). The ideal of cooperative and self-conscious inquiry, untainted by subjective preference and untested preconception, has been highly influential on scientific men and societies, though Bacon's method as such fails in theory and practice.—*Ar. D.*

BACON, ROGER, called **Doctor Mirabilis** (Wonderful Doctor), 1214?–92?, English monk, scholar, and scientist. Details of his life are obscure, but it is known that he made a great impression on the learned minds of his time, particularly with his activities in experimental science. His *Opus majus, Opus minus,* and *Opus tertium,* written at the request of Pope Clement IV, were an attempt at a systematic account of the state of learning. He quarreled with the Scholastic philosophers over his emphasis on a divine intelligence and a separation of science and theology which was probably derived from the Arabian commentators on Aristotle, such as Averroës. Certainly his knowledge of the science and pseudoscience of his day was great, including that of the manufacture of gunpowder and the manufacture and use of the magnifying glass. His writings include prophecies of the telescope and microscope, steam engines, the airplane, and circumnavigation of Earth. He detected errors in the Julian calendar through his knowledge of astronomy.—*A. P. E.*

BACTERIA: members of the class Schizomycetes (or phylum Schizomycophyta) of the plant kingdom. The types are numerous, including microorganisms that are larger than viruses and smaller than yeasts and molds, and that typically reproduce by simple cell division (fission). Bacteria are similar in structure to blue-green algae, but lack the pigment phycocyanin found in these algae, and differ in other ways. In addition to the unicellular bacteria familiarly known as germs, there are a variety of other forms of similar size (diameter). These organisms are widely distributed in soil and water, and in and on plants and animals. Most are free-living saprophytes, which use nonliving materials as foods, promote decay of organic matter, and maintain soil fertility. Some, however, are parasites (see PARASITISM), and many of these are pathogens, *i.e.* organisms that cause disease. Bacteria are regarded as plantlike because, as in higher plants, their cells have walls, and their food must be in soluble form. Unlike most higher plants, however, many in this class secrete extracellular enzymes that digest particulate matter (dead plant and animal materials) that can be used as their foods. Some of these organisms have a complex surface layer containing ribonucleic acid (see NUCLEIC ACIDS); such forms, when stained with crystal violet, a purple dye, and then with iodine, are not easily decolorized with ethyl alcohol and are described as *gram-positive*. Forms easily decolorized are described as *gram-negative*. These staining characteristics are used in the identification of bacteria.

Unicellular Bacteria: These are spherical, rod-shaped, or spiral forms that multiply by splitting into two cells of equal size. Rod-shaped and spiral organisms divide transversely. Spherical forms have one, two, or three planes of division. After this binary fission, cells may adhere to one another in characteristic masses or chains. Unicellular bacteria are separated into groups (*e.g.* orders, families; see CLASSIFICATION OF LIVING THINGS) on the basis of such characteristics as rigidity or flexibility of cell walls, motility with or without flagella, arrangement of flagella on the cell, formation of endospores, and formation of photosynthetic pigments (chlorophyll and carotenoids) similar to those of higher plants.

Unicellular Bacteria with Rigid Cell Walls: Of these there are two groups: those that form endospores and those that do not. The endospore (SPORE within a cell) is a resting body that survives conditions unfavorable to the cell which produces it. The resistance of endospores to killing by heat, *e.g.* boiling in water for 30 min, is not fully explained. Probably the low water content and some special forms of proteins in the spores render them less susceptible to heat damage than other forms of life are. Sterilization with steam heat in an autoclave is adjusted to a temperature (usually 121°C or 252°F) and time required to kill endospores. Their destruction is especially important in the canning of food and in the preparation of bandages and instruments for surgery. Most spore-forming bacteria are harmless saprophytes, some of which produce useful chemicals, *e.g.* acetone, butyl alcohol, riboflavin (a vitamin), and antibiotics (bacitracin, polymyxin, tyrocidin). Fortunately, only a few spore-formers cause diseases, *e.g.* tetanus, anthrax, gas gangrene, botulism, and foul brood of bees.

There are many species of the non-spore-forming organisms. Some oxidize inorganic materials in soil, *e.g.* ammonia and hydrogen sulfide, to minerals that higher plants utilize. The nitrogen-fixing bacteria (see NITROGEN CYCLE) use gaseous nitrogen from air to make their cell proteins; free-living forms are known. Also, the root nodule bacteria and leguminous plants (peas, clover, alfalfa) together form a symbiotic structure, the root nodule, which fixes gaseous nitrogen and enables the plant to grow in nitrogen-deficient soil. The photosynthetic bacteria absorb longer light waves than higher plants do and carry on PHOTOSYNTHESIS under anaerobic conditions (in the absence of air); these bacteria do not release oxygen during photosynthesis as higher plants do. The bacteria that ferment sugar to lactic acid ordinarily cause souring of milk; pure cultures of such organisms are used in the dairy industry (see BACTERIOLOGY). The bacteria that oxidize ethyl alcohol to acetic acid ordinarily cause souring of wine and are used in commercial production of vinegar. A few of the animal diseases caused by members of this group are typhoid fever, dysentery, diphtheria, plague, scarlet fever, whooping cough, undulant fever, gonorrhea, sore throat, boils, impetigo, and meningitis. Some of the plant diseases are blight, rot, wilt, leaf spot, and tumors.

Unicellular Bacteria with Flexible Cell Walls: Of the two groups that occur, the spirochetes are flagellated, spiral cells that exhibit wriggling motion. Most are free-living in soil or water; however, the organism that causes syphilis is a parasitic spirochete. The myxobacteria (slime bacteria) are flexible, nonflagellated rods that exhibit gliding motion. During a swarm stage in their life cycle, the rods secrete a bed of slime and glide forward over it in concert. A cyst stage follows

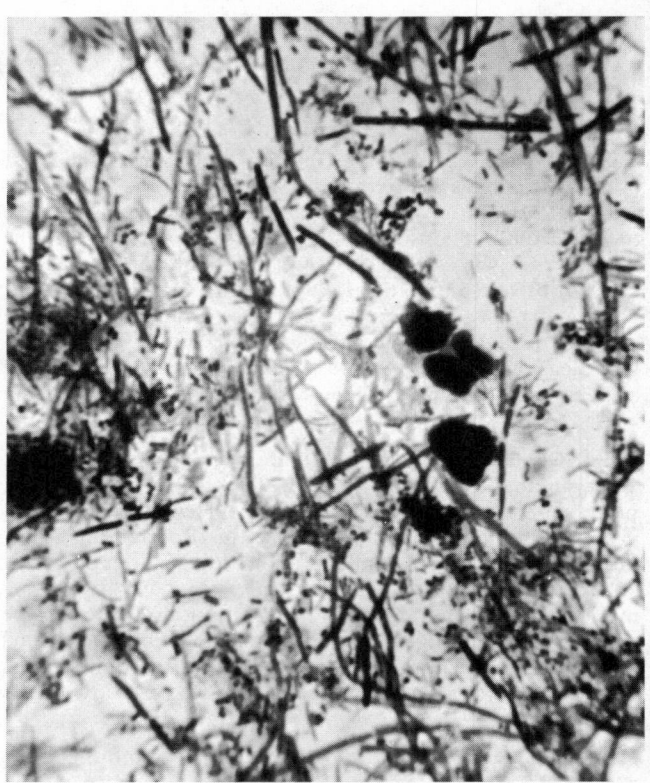

Assortment of bacteria: The rod-shaped organisms are Vincent's bacilli and spirilli, producers of Vincent's disease ("trench mouth"). The small, round objects are staphylococci. Large, dark objects (*right of center*) are pus cells. (*A. John Geraci from Nancy Palmer*)

swarming: the rods aggregate and heap themselves up into a fruiting body, in which the rods shorten and round up into resting cells called microcysts. The slime bacteria are active in natural decay, especially of old wood, dead leaves, and dung.

Higher Bacteria: The actinomycetes are examples of higher bacteria. They are often described as moldlike, because some form long filaments that branch and produce spores, called conidia; the filaments are not wider than 1.5 microns (about $^3/_{50,000}$ in.), a diameter characteristic of bacteria. These filamentous forms give a characteristic odor to rich garden and field soils; some produce medically useful antibiotics, *e.g.* streptomycin, aureomycin, and terramycin. The smallest actinomycetes form only short filaments, which break up into rods. The organisms that cause tuberculosis, leprosy, lumpy jaw in cattle, and potato scab are actinomycetes. The bacteria that form sheaths around their cells and those that form stalks which support the cells are aquatic types. They cause obstruction of water pipes and rot the hulls of ships, and are thought to play an active role in the formation of iron deposits.

Pathogenic Bacteria: Any departure from a state of health is described as disease, and any organism that causes disease is called a *pathogen*. Proof that a specific microorganism is the cause of a disease is based upon postulates developed by Robert Koch in 1876: (1) the organism must be present in all cases of the disease, (2) the organism must be isolated from the diseased host and grown in pure culture, (3) a pure culture of the organism must, when injected into a susceptible experimental host, cause the disease, and (4) the organism must be recoverable in pure culture from the experimental host.

The majority of pathogens enter a host through wounds or natural openings in the body, *e.g.* nose or mouth of an animal, stomates or lenticels of a plant. Virulent pathogens are organisms that easily overcome the host's defense mechanisms. A few species can invade tissues by digesting the cement that holds the host's cells together. Some, but not all, pathogenic bacteria have an external layer of slime that tends to protect them against ingestion by white blood cells. Pathogens that multiply in the host cause tissue damage (disease), which in many cases is due to toxins. Endotoxins are toxic constituents of the bacterial cells. Exotoxins are poisonous materials that the bacteria secrete into their environment. A few exotoxins are known to be destructive enzymes; however, the nature of the action of most toxins is not yet known. Staphylococcal food poisoning and botulism deserve special mention because neither is the result of infection (multiplication of a pathogen in a host): instead, both diseases are caused by exotoxins that the staphylococci and the botulism bacteria produce during their growth in food outside the body; when the food is eaten, the exotoxins cause illness. See Color Plate 15.—*H. B. F.*

BACTERIOLOGY: the science that deals with BACTERIA—their isolation, cultivation, and identification—and the description of their activities under natural conditions and in culture in the laboratory (see MICROBIOLOGY). Bacteria were first seen and described by Anton van Leeuwenhoek in the 17th cent. Systematic investigation of bacteria began during the mid-19th cent. under the leadership of Louis Pasteur, a French chemist, and Robert Koch, a German physician. Pasteur's interest in the issue of SPONTANEOUS GENERATION of life led him to devise methods for cultivating and handling bacteria in the laboratory; he helped resolve this issue with experimental evidence that living bacteria are not spontaneously generated by dead organic matter. Koch devised methods of obtaining pure cultures of bacteria (see below) and tested experimentally the germ theory of disease; he demonstrated that bacteria cause anthrax and tuberculosis, and thus defined the conditions for proof of a causal relation between a specific microorganism and a given disease. Following Edward Jenner, who developed the smallpox (virus) vaccine during the 18th cent.,

Growing a culture: Bacteria are grown in the laboratory for experimental purposes. A frequently used vessel for such cultures is the Petri dish, shown here. (A. *John Geraci from Nancy Palmer*)

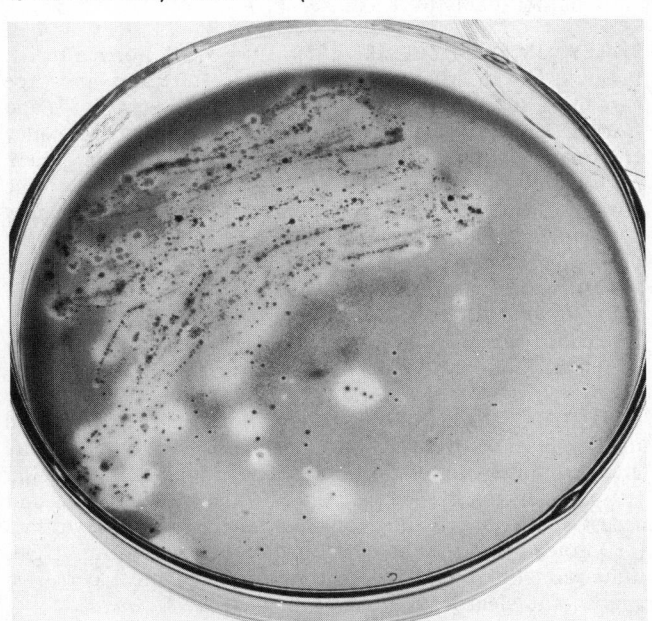

Pasteur found that bacterial vaccines (suspensions of dead bacteria) could be used to induce immunity to disease (see IMMUNIZATION). One of Pasteur's contributions to industry was his discovery that microorganisms which sour wine are destroyed by heating wine to temperatures below the boiling point, a process now called PASTEURIZATION. During the late 1800s, bacteriology developed rapidly. Sergius Winogradsky of Russia and M. W. Beijerinck of Holland initiated the study of soil bacteria and their relations to soil fertility. Joseph Lister, in England, introduced the use of antiseptics into surgery and laid the foundation for modern, aseptic surgery. Paul Ehrlich, a German chemist, established the principle of chemotherapy: he synthesized an arsenic compound that proved effective in treatment of syphilis. Two theories of immunity were developed: the humoral theory of Ehrlich, which led to the discovery of antibodies in blood, and the cellular theory of E. Metchnikoff, which emphasized the importance of phagocytes (body cells that eat bacteria) in defense mechanisms.

In the 20th cent., public health measures, *e.g.* treatment of drinking water and of sewage, pasteurization of milk, food inspection, control of food handlers, quarantine procedures, and the widespread use of vaccines, have drastically reduced the incidence of bacterial diseases. The discovery of ANTIBIOTICS (chemicals that microorganisms secrete into their environment) useful in treatment of disease and the development of methods for rapid diagnosis of disease have greatly reduced mortality due to bacterial infection. Today bacteria are grown on industrial scale for many purposes: the pathogens for preparation of vaccines; saprophytic (harmless) types to produce chemicals, ret flax, and prepare foods. Live preparations of root nodule bacteria are sold to farmers for use in cultivating leguminous plants. In research, bacteria are often used as tools for investigation of fundamental cell functions, *e.g.* protein synthesis and the action of genes.

A culture medium for a saprophytic bacterium is a watery solution of chemicals that supplies the foods needed for growth (multiplication) of the organism. A fluid medium is called *broth*. A solid medium can be made by adding 1.5% agar to broth. A culture medium together with its microbial population is called a *culture*. A pure culture consists of one kind (species) of microorganism. Procedures that are employed to exclude unwanted microorganisms (contaminants) from cultures are called aseptic techniques. Propagation of a saprophytic bacterium in test tubes involves: (1) preparation of the culture medium; (2) sterilization of the medium by heating or by filtering through a sterile unit with pores that retain bacteria; (3) inoculation of the medium, *i.e.* adding a small number of the bacteria; and (4) incubation of the new culture under conditions favorable to growth. Acidity or alkalinity of the medium, temperature, oxygen supply, and amount of light are incubation conditions that must be controlled. Large populations of bacteria make fluid media turbid; on solid media, they form colonies. Bacteria that are obligate parasites are grown in the host.—*H. B. F.*

BACTERIOPHAGE: a virus that attacks bacterial cells. Bacteriophage contains DNA, which it injects into the bacterium. The DNA possesses the information necessary for the production of complete virus particles. The cell's own DNA is degraded, and its activity comes under the control of the viral DNA. A bacterium may break open, sometimes within 20 minutes, and release perhaps 100 new particles of infectious virus. Sometimes the infective viruses carry pieces of genetic material away from their dead hosts, and if they now infect a genetically different host, they may recombine this material with the genes of the new host. A bacteriophage should be considered a genetic element enclosed in a protein coat.—*F. F.*

Millions of years of erosion produced these badlands at Bryce Canyon, Utah. Such terrain, found in several regions of western North America, result mainly from rapid cutting by temporary streams in weak rock. *(United Air Lines)*

BADLANDS: areas of barren terrain cut into deep, narrow valleys and ridges by running water. Such topography is common in semiarid regions but also occurs in humid areas where the natural vegetation cover has been destroyed. The conditions favoring development of badlands include soft, poorly consolidated surface rock, elevation above the surrounding terrain, and a dry climate. Because of the lack of vegetation, rainfall runs off very rapidly, producing vigorous erosion. Areas of this type in the Great Plains of North America were termed by the early French travelers as *mauvaises terres pour traverser* (bad lands to cross). They occur in the Dakotas, Wyoming, Nebraska, Colorado, Kansas, and the Southwest. Arid parts of China, the Near East, and Africa also exhibit extensive badlands.—*A. P. E.*

BAEKELAND, LEO HENDRIK, 1863–1944, Belgian-U. S. chemist and inventor; b. Ghent. Visiting the U. S. A. in 1889, he became research chemist for a manufacturer of photographic materials, then in 1891 established his own consulting office and laboratory. Baekeland perfected his Velox process and in 1899 sold it for a reported $1,000,000. His further research resulted in the invention of BAKELITE, or "synthetic resin" (oxybenzylmethylene-glycolanhydride),

Leo Hendrik Baekeland
(Union Carbide)

which formed the basis for an entirely new industry. He was a member of the National Academy of Sciences.—*S. B.*

BAER, KARL ERNST VON, 1792–1876, German biologist; b. Piep, Esthonia. His discovery of the mammalian egg was described in his *On the Mammalian Egg* (1827). His important *Development of Animals* was published in two parts (1828, 1837). He also discovered the *chorda dorsalis,* or notochord, the cylindrical stiffening rod found in the embryo stage of all

chordates, serving as the structural basis around which the vertebral column of vertebrates is formed. Baer was awarded the Copley medal of the Royal Society, of which he was a fellow. He was also an associate of the U. S. National Academy of Sciences.—*D. H. D. R.*

BAEYER, JOHANN FRIEDRICH WILHELM ADOLF VON, 1835–1917, German chemist; b. Berlin. His research on indigo enabled him to make it by synthesis, 1878. From van't Hoff's model of the carbon atom as the center of a tetrahedron, Baeyer calculated the angles between the valences and showed their relationship to the chemical reactivity when carbon chains are closed into "rings" (strain theory, 1885). In 1905 he received the Nobel prize in chemistry for his researches on organic dyestuffs and hydroaromatic compounds. He was a fellow of the Royal Society and an associate of the U. S. National Academy of Sciences.—*E. F.*

BAILEY, LIBERTY HYDE, JR., 1858–1954, U. S. horticulturist; b. South Haven, Mich. He taught horticulture and landscape gardening at Michigan State Agricultural Coll. (1885–87) and Cornell Univ. (from 1888), and was director of the Bailey Hortorium (from 1937). In addition to research on genera *Rubus* and *Cucurbita* and family Palmaceae, he was the author of such outstanding reference books as *The Standard Cyclopedia of Horticulture, Hortus Second,* and *A Manual of Cultivated Plants* (rev. 1949). In his honor, an important scientific publication is named *Baileya: A Quarterly Journal of Horticultural Taxonomy.* Bailey ranks as a leading U. S. horticulturist and explorer for useful plants. He was a member of the National Academy of Sciences.—*D. H. D. R.*

BAKELITE: a phenolic resin, or thermosetting plastic, produced in the presence of a catalyst by the combination of phenol and formaldehyde to form methylene bridges. Named after Leo H. Baekeland, its discoverer (1907), bakelite is the second oldest synthetic plastic, predated only by cellulose nitrate (celluloid). Molded bakelite products are strong, rigid, dimensionally stable, resistant to heat and most corrosive agents, and electrically nonconductive.—*T. M. and C. S.*

BAKER, SIR BENJAMIN, 1840–1907, British civil engineer; b. Keyford, Somerset. As assistant to Sir John Fowler, he helped construct the Metropolitan and District railways of London. Baker published many papers on bridge construction. Fowler and Baker built the famous Firth of Forth cantilever bridge, completed in 1890, and served as consultants to the Egyptian government on the Aswan dam, finished in 1902. Baker was largely responsible for the introduction of interurban underground railways in London. He was a fellow of the Royal Society.—*S. B.*

BAKING POWDER: an alternative to yeast as an agent for making breadstuffs rise. The leavening agent is sodium bicarbonate, $NaHCO_3$ (baking soda). An acidic substance (*e.g.* alum, or a primary phosphate, or sodium hydrogen tartrate "cream of tartar") is also present. Starch or flour is used to keep the powder dry in storage. When water is added, the baking soda and the acidic substance react, and carbon dioxide gas (CO_2) is generated; this gas causes rising as it passes up through the dough. By contrast, yeast produces CO_2 by fermenting sugars.—*L. Sc.*

BALANCE, CHEMICAL: an apparatus used to determine the weight of a chemical substance. It consists of a beam supported on a fulcrum with a pan hanging from each end. The material to be weighed is placed in one pan, and calibrated weights are added to the other pan until the two pans balance. Then, the weight of the substance equals the total of the calibrated weights. Refinements in balance construction include various devices to damp the swinging of the beam, chain-loading for the lighter weights, and automatic loading of the heavier weights. Errors in the use of the chemical balance include: inaccuracy of weights, buoyant air effects, and inequality of length of balance arms.—*G. W. M.*

BALANCE AND EQUILIBRIUM: the senses concerned with maintenance of normal posture and of orientation in space. A host of different sensory receptors commonly are involved. They signal the force of gravity and other acceleratory forces; the position of limbs and other body regions; the tension in muscles, joints, and tendons; and the regions of bodily contact with the substratum. Often the eyes, by fixing on the sky or horizon, help to indicate the direction of gravity. In man the membranous labyrinth of the inner EAR is an important organ of equilibrium. This organ is responsible for the dizziness and nausea associated with motion sickness and certain diseases (*e.g.* Meniere's). Two different structures of the labyrinth are involved: the semicircular canals and the otoliths of the utricle. The otoliths, movable calcareous masses, rest upon and stimulate hair cells, thereby indicating the direction of gravity. In addition, both the otoliths and the fluid in the canals, because of their inertial lag during acceleration of the head, stimulate the associated mechanoreceptors. The three semicircular canals in each labyrinth are oriented in three mutually perpendicular planes. A change in motion affects the fluid in one or more of the canals, and this indicates the direction of head displacement. Otoliths and hair cells also are found in the saccule of the ear, but their function here is not fully known. See SENSES.—*D. R. E.*

BALANCE OF NATURE: Unless disturbed by man or by the arrival of foreign kinds of life in unusual numbers, each community of plants and animals tends to reach a form that can reproduce itself without obvious change. This dynamic equilibrium represents the "balance of nature." It indicates that each species has reached an optimum population size in the community, one limited both by diseases and animals that attack it and by the availability of suitable soil and nutrients or

Rabbit population in Australia explodes repeatedly because of scarcity of predators there. Rabbits strip countryside of vegetation and drink waterholes dry until starvation and thirst deplete their numbers. (*Australian News & Information Bureau*)

of food, hiding places, and nesting sites. Any further reduction in population is likely to be corrected quickly by increased survival of offspring, because these will be less subject to diseases and attack and less limited by the availability of suitable food, hiding places, and nesting sites. Correspondingly, any major increase in the population is self-defeating, inviting attack, making epidemics more probable. The balance of nature is most stable in places where the fauna and flora are rich, with a food web offering a multiplicity of alternate connections. Normal fluctuations in the numbers of each species fail to disturb the community. In tundras and deserts, by contrast, the food web is much simpler, with comparatively few alternatives, because fauna and flora are poor. These are areas in which feast alternates with famine; hence the great increases in the lemming population, mass migrations of snowy owls, and spectacular changes in the numbers of snowshoe hares. Modern efforts in wildlife conservation are directed chiefly at restoring the balance of nature where man has upset it—*i.e.* restoring it either directly or through introduction of foreign plants and animals in unusual numbers. (See CONSERVATION; ECOLOGY.)—*L. and M. M.*

Rodent population is held in check by natural predators such as the barn owl, shown entering nest with rat. (*Ewing Galloway*)

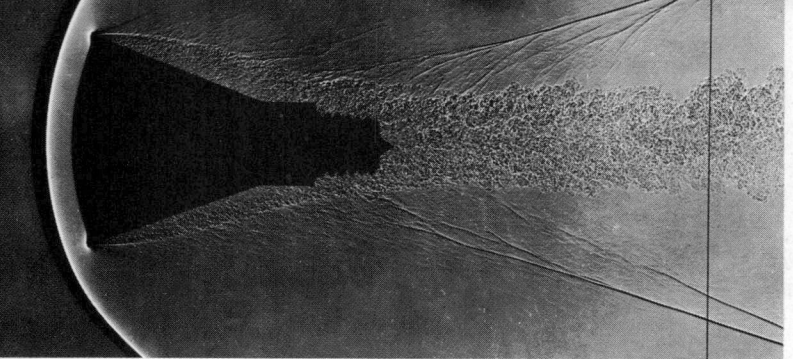

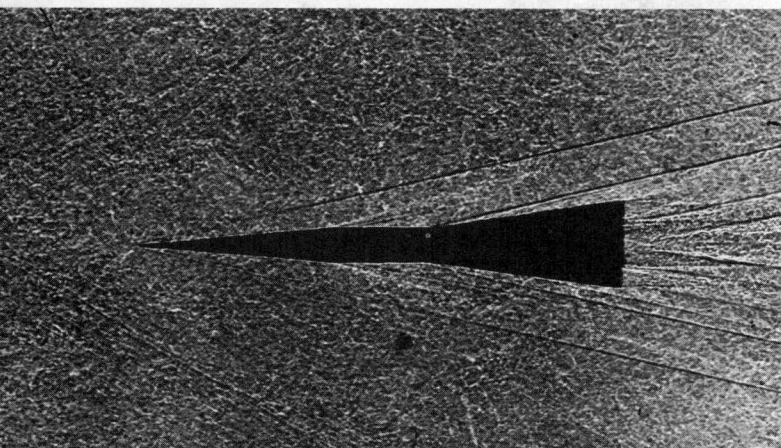

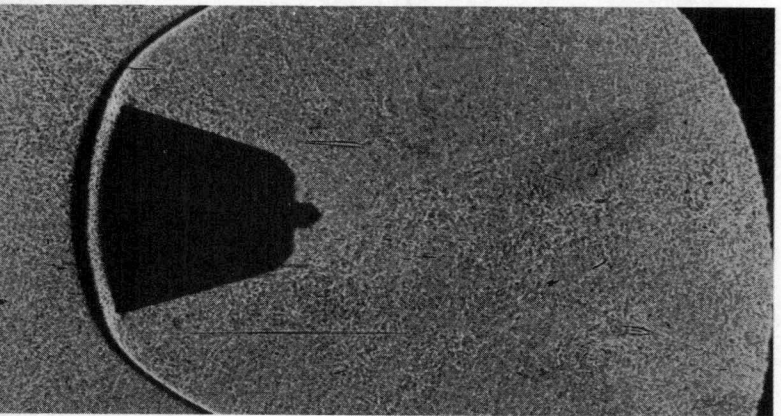

At supersonic velocities missiles move faster than the disturbances they produce; the resulting compression waves—here seen in schlieren photographs—reflect the shape and velocity of the missile and the density of the medium. Ratios of velocity of projectile to that of sound (MACH NUMBERS) in above photographs are 3 ("Mercury" capsule), 7, and 15. (NASA)

BALLISTICS: the science that deals with the motion, design, behavior, and effects of projectiles, especially bullets, aerial bombs, rockets, missiles, or the like. Ballistics has been divided into three major sub-areas: *interior ballistics* deals with the launch or propulsion phase, *i.e.* the behavior of projectiles in a gun barrel, or the pressures and temperatures developed in the barrel or in a rocket combustion chamber; *exterior ballistics* refers to the motion of projectiles in flight; and *terminal ballistics* concerns the behavior of projectiles at the end of their flight, including impact and penetration of targets. Historically, interest in ballistics has been associated with development of military armament, and the subject received only occasional scientific attention until the beginning of the 20th cent. Galileo, about 1600, made the first truly scientific observations of the behavior of projectiles; but the emergence of current concepts of ballistics dates from the work of the

German C. Cranz during the first three decades of this century. His student, H. Zornig (1888–   ) started the major U. S. ballistics research center at Aberdeen, Md. Today ballistics is concerned not only with ordnance but with the ballistics, aerodynamics, and thermodynamics of missiles and spacecraft; with atmospheric penetration of meteorites; and with other aerophysical phenomena resulting from the extreme projectile and vehicle velocities, *e.g.* optical radiation and ionization effects in both the atmosphere surrounding missiles and in their wakes.

A simple example of a ballistic trajectory is that of a rock after being thrown off a cliff. The rock traces a nearly parabolic path in accordance with the laws of motion of a body under the force of gravity. In practice, the path is somewhat more complicated because of air resistance, possible wind forces, and the Coriolis effect associated with the spin of Earth about its axis. In contrast to the motion of a compact body such as a rock or missile nose cone, the motion of a more extended body, especially one having lifting surfaces such as a glider, is said to be aerodynamic rather than ballistic in nature. There is no clear-cut boundary between the two.

Laboratory experiments in ballistics are performed in a ballistic range whose basic equipment includes a gun-type launcher, measuring stations, and a device for catching the projectile. Range-station instrumentation usually includes photoelectric timing devices and synchronized high-voltage, spark-type light sources providing less than one millionth of a second exposure for shadow photography of the flying projectile. The time-history of the motion down the range provides data for determining deceleration and therefore over-all drag. Shadow photography (see photos) emphasizes shock waves, wake turbulence, and other important features of the flow structure about the body. Launching of aerodynamic models in a ballistic range is possible by use of a *sabot,* or temporary casing which adapts the model to the shape of the barrel during the launching phase, and which drops away shortly thereafter. Among the most useful of such tests are those concerned with the stability of a projectile with respect to tumbling or oscillations during flight. Such unsteady motions can be stabilized by imparting spin to the projectile, either by rifling a gun barrel in the case of a bullet, or by properly oriented fins or auxiliary jets in the case of a rocket or missile. Tests of stability were made as early as 1920 by the use of the yaw card method. This involves shooting a model through a number of thin cards spaced along the range. From the holes made in the cards, the variation in orientation of the model with respect to the flight path can be determined.—*D. B.*

BALL LIGHTNING: a brightly glowing ball, about a foot in diameter, said to appear, rarely, just after LIGHTNING strikes nearby. The ball may enter a house through the chimney or a window, roll about on the floor with a hissing noise, then vanish with a loud detonation. No injury to persons results, and little damage is done. Although most authorities consider the ball an optical illusion caused by the lightning flash, some believe it is a small mass of very highly ionized gas produced by the lightning discharge.—*D. H. L.*

BALL MILL: a type of grinding device belonging to a group often referred to as tumbling mills, used to reduce the size of relatively coarse particles. It consists of a steel- or stone-lined horizontal cylinder or cone rotating around its horizontal axis. Into it are fed steel balls and the material to be ground. The tumbling action of the balls crushes the material. Other types of tumbling mills employ different grinding elements and are named accordingly: *e.g.* pebble mill, rod mill, and tube mill.—*D. P. B.*

1

2

Plate 11   ARTHROPODS

About three-quarters of the nearly 900,000 kinds of animals are arthropods. They are supported by a jointed external skeleton that is shed periodically and replaced by a larger one, permitting growth. By means of paired appendages, arthropods swim, burrow, creep, run, hop, and fly. They inhabit more different habitats than any other group of multicellular animals. Representatives of five different groups of arthropods are shown. **1. Horseshoe crabs** are "living fossils" related more closely to modern scorpions and spiders than to crabs; species shown is *Limulus polyphemus. (Walter Dawn)* **2. The wolf spider** *(Lycosa)* builds no web. Instead, it runs after and pounces upon its insect prey. *(Herbert Lanks/Monkmeyer Press Photo Service)* **3. Ghost crabs** *(Ocypode albicans)* are among the most terrestrial of crustaceans. If unable to run to their deep burrows in the beach, they stand and defend themselves with powerful pincers. *(Walter Dawn)* **4. The earwig,** of which there are more than 1,000 species, is an insect with a powerful pair of pincers at the rear of the body. These are used in defense and in the folding of the earwig's fan-shaped inner wings. *(Alexander B. Klotz/Monkmeyer Press Photo Service)* **5. The centipede** ("hundred-legged worm") subdues its prey and also defends itself with a pair of poison claws located close to the mouth. *(Alexander B. Klots/Monkmeyer Press Photo Service)*

3

4

5

Plate 12 ASTRONOMY

From ancient times, man has observed celestial bodies and tried to understand the universe. The need to have a calendar and predict seasonal changes was one spur to early observations; another was the superstition of astrology, which required — but misused — astronomical data. In recent centuries a great spur has been the development of new, powerful tools and techniques. Today, optical and radio telescopes have extended man's reach into the skies, at the same time increasing his knowledge and whetting his desire for more knowledge and understanding.

1

1. Ptolemaic conception of Earth at center of universe with Moon, Sun, and planets between Earth and stars is illustrated in this 15th-cent. French miniature. (*Bibliothèque Nationale*, [*Courtesy of Derek Price*])

3. Staff of Islamic observatory, 1575: Page from a Persian manuscript shows astronomers with instruments including astrolabes, quadrants, rules, an early clock, and geographical globe. (*Derek Price*)

3

2

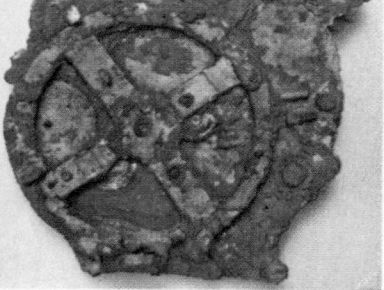

2. Fragment of Greek calculator, c. 82 B.C., found off Antikythera Island. Geared dials showed positions of Sun, Moon, and perhaps planets. Device was precursor of all clocks and calculating machines. (*Derek Price*)

4. Mayan observatory: Using observations made from this "Caracol" (observatory building) in Chichén Itzá, Yucatán, Mayans from the 5th cent. A.D. onward made tables of eclipses and formulated the most accurate calendar of pre-scientific times. (*Bruce Hunter/Amer. Mus. of Nat. Hist.*)

4

Plate 13   ASTRONOMY

5. Radio telescope at Jodrell Bank, England, has an antenna in the form of a paraboloidal dish, 250 ft in diameter; antenna can be steered about horizontal and vertical axes. *(Miss E. J. Cooke, Courtesy of the University of Manchester)*

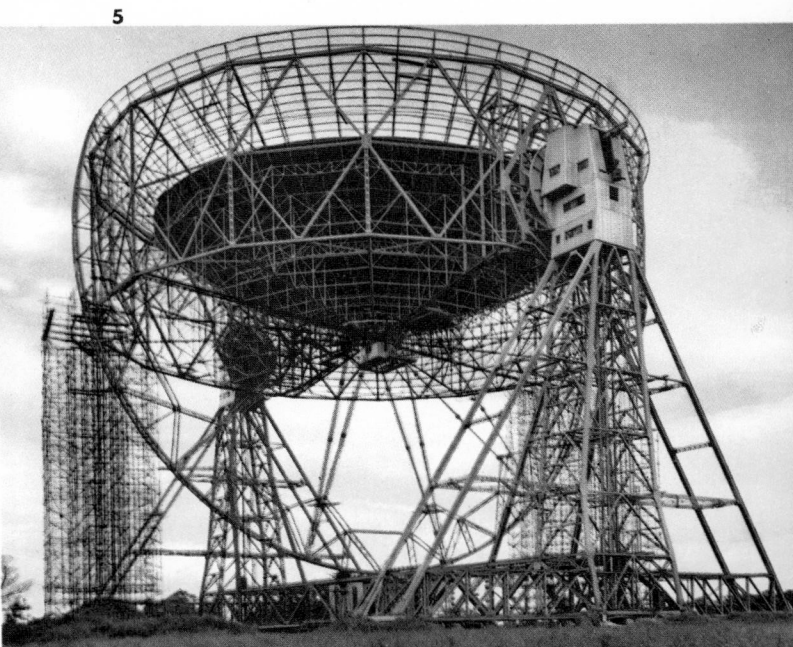

5

6. Uraniborg, Tycho Brahe's observatory, on the island of Hveen in the Danish sound, was built in 1576; it was the last major observatory of the pre-telescopic era. From data Tycho gathered here, Kepler developed the laws of planetary motion. *(Det Nationalhistoriske Museum på Frederiksborg)*

7. Hale telescope, Mt. Palomar, contains 200-in. diameter mirror at bottom of open-frame tube. Observer sits inside tube at top. Solid tube is part of telescope's mounting. *(Wilson Hole/Mt Wilson)*

Plate 14   AURORA

Auroral displays can be seen in the night sky mainly in near-polar regions; they are most frequent at times of sunspot maxima and are associated with magnetic storms. Their luminosity is the result of radiation from atoms of oxygen, nitrogen, and some hydrogen in Earth's atmosphere.

1. Aurora of rays, photographed in Alaska, was probably less than 100 mi high. Its red color is unusual, yellow-green and green being most common. *(C. J. Ott/National Audubon Soc.)*

1

2

2. Aurora in form of a rayed arc, also photographed in Alaska, was probably 100 to 200 mi high. *(Ernest Kaiser from Russ Kinne)*

Plate 15   BACTERIA

Of all microscopic life forms, bacteria are most familiar. Bacteria are simple, single-celled organisms that multiply rapidly. Many kinds can propel themselves by means of long whiplike flagella. A few bacteria contain chlorophyll, and are able to manufacture their food by photosynthesis; the vast majority rely upon processes of decay or a parasitic way of life for their nourishment. Although the shapes of bacteria are less distinctive than their manner of growth and their food requirements, three shapes are common: short straight rods (bacilli), small spheres (cocci), and spiral rods (spirilla). Two of these shapes are shown at right. **The section (1)** through human tissue is heavily infected with *Treponema pallidum,* the spiral bacterium that causes syphilis. **The sputum (2)** contains the spherical bacteria *(Diplococcus pneumoniae)* of human pneumonia. These bacteria reproduce within clear capsules of secretion, here contrasting against a solution of India ink. *(Both photographs © 1957 by Clay-Adams, Inc.)*

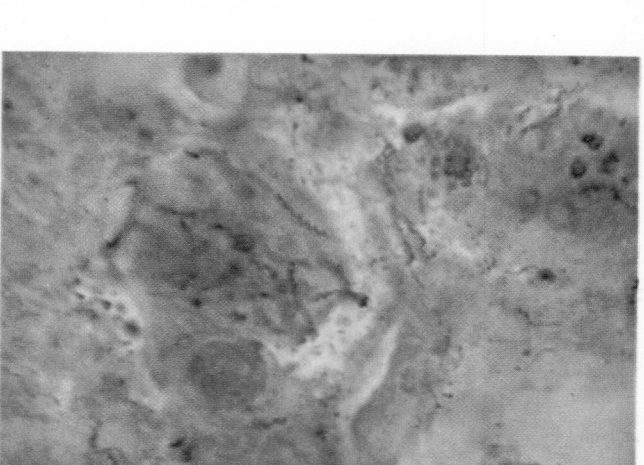

1

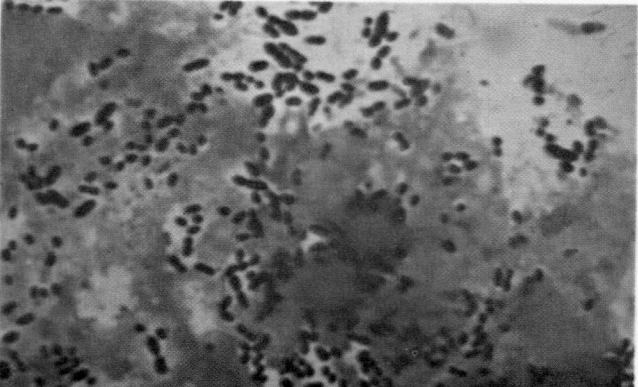

2

BALLOON: a nonpowered, nondirigible lighter-than-air aircraft incorporating, or consisting of, a spherical or elongated bag inflated with air or gas lighter than the surrounding air to give it buoyancy. It is generally distinguished from an AIRSHIP, which is powered and steerable. In flight, balloons may be manned or unmanned, captive (attached to the ground by rope or cable) or free. A basket (gondola) made of wicker or other light material may be attached under the gas bag for passengers, instruments, or other load. Free balloons have long been used for sport, for meteorological and upper-atmosphere investigations, for training, and for various military operations.

Balloons were the first successful AIRCRAFT and are the simplest. A free balloon is essentially a bag made of plastic (*e.g.* polyethylene), rubber (neoprene), or a coated fabric. Hydrogen, heated air, and coal gas were once widely used to inflate them, but now nonflammable helium is generally used. As a balloon rises, the pressure of the air outside it decreases continuously, and the contained gas expands under the reduced pressure. To prevent the expanding gas from bursting the gas bag, balloons are only partly filled at the beginning of an ascent; they also may have a sleeve providing an exit for excess gas volume. Free balloons that carry passengers have devices which give a certain amount of maneuverability. One of these is a valve at the top of the bag, controlled by a cord leading to the gondola. The balloonist opens the valve to reduce buoyancy, thus slowing his ascent or causing him to

Operation "Skyhook": 10-million-cu.-ft. Winzen research balloon is about to be launched from the Navy's aircraft carrier *Valley Forge*, Jan. 30, 1960. Balloons such as this have been increasingly important in high-altitude meteorological research. (*U. S. Navy*)

First man-carrying hydrogen balloon: On Dec. 1, 1783, in the Tuileries Gardens in Paris, a red-and-yellow balloon 27 ft in diameter rose in the air. Made of rubber-coated silk, it was filled with hydrogen generated by iron filings in sulfuric acid. In the basketwork "boat," waving flags to show that all was well, were the French physicist Alexandre Charles and one of the artisans who assembled the balloon. Two hours later they landed in a small village 27 mi away. (*Wide World*)

descend. Ballast, *i.e.* sand or shot, is carried so that the pilot can lighten the balloon's load at will. Another ballast device is a long, heavy rope carried in the gondola; when flying at low altitude, the rope is permitted to hang over the side and drag along the ground, thus lightening the weight of the gondola. When a free balloon lands in a wind, it must be deflated quickly to prevent its being dragged over the ground. For this purpose, a rip panel is installed in the upper surface of the bag: when the pilot pulls a rip cord attached to the upper end of this panel, the latter opens and allows the gas to escape rapidly.

An unsubstantiated story tells of a balloon being sent up in 1306, at the coronation of the Emperor Fo-Kien at Peking, China. However, the first undisputed success was that of the brothers Jacques and Joseph Montgolfier at Annonay, France. In a public demonstration, June 5, 1783, they sent up a large paper balloon inflated with hot air. Two months later another Frenchman, J. A. C. Charles, successfully flew a hydrogen-filled balloon of silk made gastight by a coating of rubber varnish. By the end of 1783, first animals, then men—Pilâtre de Rozier, the Marquis d'Arlandes, J. A. C. Charles—had made safe ascensions in both free and captive balloons. In Jan. 1785, the Frenchman Jean Blanchard and an American scientist, Dr. John Jeffries, succeeded in crossing the English Channel. Manned balloons have since established distance records approaching 2,000 mi, in-air records of over 80 hr, and altitude records in excess of 100,000 ft.

Almost from their first flight, balloons both manned and unmanned have made valuable contributions to knowledge of the atmosphere. In 1931, Auguste Piccard of Belgium ascended 9.81 mi into the stratosphere, and the following year, 10.07 mi. Both ascents were made in an airtight gondola, a device introduced by Piccard to prevent death by oxygen starvation—a fate that had befallen several earlier explorers. His gondola was fitted with meteorological instruments and apparatus for studying cosmic rays and other high-altitude phenomena. A notable recent ascent was that of Capt. Joseph Kittinger, Jr., who in Aug. 1960 rose to a new record of 102,800 ft, then parachuted to safety. Large numbers of unmanned balloons are launched daily by the U. S. A. and Canada for meteorological, cosmic-ray, and other upper-atmosphere research. Some carry no instruments, and are simply tracked from the ground to determine wind velocity and direction at different altitudes. Others carry a load of instruments, *e.g.* RADIOSONDES, that make observations automatically; readings are sent to the ground by a radio transmitter carried by the balloon. Navy "Skyhook" balloons have been used to carry rockets to about 70,000 ft, whence the rockets are launched into the higher atmosphere on research missions. Satellites of the "Echo" class are actually balloons. Echo I was an aluminum-coated sphere 100 ft in diameter. Deflated, it was fitted into a capsule of 30 in. diameter, and carried aloft by a rocket from Cape Canaveral, Aug. 12, 1960. Once the rocket was in orbit, the capsule was released and the balloon inflated.

Balloons were used for military observation beginning in the Napoleonic Wars, and continued to be used for this purpose in the U. S. Civil War, the Franco-Prussian War, and World War I. In World War II, captive barrage balloons proved effective in discouraging low-level bombing and strafing. During the latter part of the war, the Japanese released about 9,000 balloons carrying incendiary bombs, intending them to be carried by air currents to N. America. Most fell into the sea or in arctic regions, but about 1,000 reached their destination, causing slight damage and a few casualties. Somewhat similar were the balloons released by the Western powers after World War II to carry propaganda materials to Russian satellite nations in E Europe.—*W. Ho. and A. P. E.*

BALMER, JOHANN JAKOB, 1825–98, Swiss physicist; b. Lausen. Balmer's famous paper, "Notice Concerning the Spectral Lines of Hydrogen," contained the Balmer formula, an equation that yields the wavelengths of a whole series of spectral lines emitted by luminous hydrogen gas. It later had an important role in Bohr's theory as to the hydrogen atom.—*D. H. D. R.*

Sir Joseph Banks
(N. Y. Public Library)

BANKS, SIR JOSEPH, 1743–1820, British naturalist and patron of science; b. London. At an early age Banks became interested in botanical collecting. His inherited wealth enabled him to sail (1768) with Capt. Cook in HMS *Endeavour* on a 3-yr circumnavigation of the globe with a party of five assistants, making a large collection of plants from around the world. In 1778 Banks became president of the Royal Society, instituting a much-needed reform of that organization, which he ruled autocratically and successfully until his death. Bank's scientific publications were few and unimportant; his contribution was in making available to scientists his enormous natural-history collections and his remarkable library.—*D. H. D. R.*

BARCROFT, SIR JOSEPH, 1872–1947, British physiologist; b. Newry. He discovered the reservoir function of the spleen, which permits rapid addition of red blood cells to the circulation. His research on the dissociation curve of hemoglobin is described in his *Respiratory Function of the Blood* (1914). Barcroft pioneered in investigation of the respiratory and circulatory physiology of the fetus *in utero*. He was a fellow of the Royal Society and an associate of the U. S. National Academy of Sciences.—*D. H. D. R.*

BARDEEN, JOHN, 1908–   , U. S. physicist; b. Madison, Wis. His areas of research have been magnetic and gravitational methods in geophysical prospecting, the theory of the solid state, semiconductors, and superconductivity. Bardeen, W. H. Brattain, and W. B. Shockley shared the Nobel prize, 1956, for their investigations on semiconductors and the discovery of the transistor effect. Bardeen was at Bell Telephone Laboratories, 1945–51, then joined the faculty of the Univ. of Illinois. He is a member of the National Academy of Sciences. —*D. H. D. R.*

BARIUM: an alkaline earth element (Ba); at. no. 56; at. wt 137.36; density 3.75; mp 850°C. It has a gray luster and is slightly harder than lead. Barium is oxidized with water or acid to liberate hydrogen, and is also oxidized by the halogens, sulfur, and other, more electronegative elements with the aid of heat. Barium is found in the mineral *barite*, $BaSO_4$ (see MINERAL, table), and the pure metal is prepared by reduction of barium oxide with silicon at 1200°C. Barium is the only alkaline earth metal which forms the peroxide on heating in air. This metal is used as a thin film on the glass inside radio tubes to pick up any gases present in the tube, *e.g.* oxygen ($Ba + O_2 = BaO_2$). *Barium sulfate* is an important pigment, especially in mixtures with pigments of greater hiding power. It is extremely insoluble in water or dilute acid.

When x-ray photos of the intestinal tract are to be made, barium is taken internally, its heavy atom being opaque to x-rays. Since barium ion is very poisonous, the highly insoluble barium sulfate is the salt that is used. Barium nitrate and barium chlorite are used for producing green color in fireworks.—*G. W. M.*

BARK: the outer covering of old stems and roots of woody plants (*e.g.* trees). Technically the bark consists of all the outer tissue up to the phloem, although popularly it is considered to be everything outside of the wood. The outer bark consists of dead cells, *e.g.* epidermis, cortex, and cork, whereas the inner bark contains living cells of the cork cambium, phelloderm (thin-walled cells formed by the cork cambium), and phloem. See PLANT ORGANS AND TISSUES.—*F. L.*

BARKLA, CHARLES GLOVER, 1877–1944, British physicist; b. Widnes. After studying secondary radiation produced by x-rays in gases, he extended his research to solids and discovered that the secondary x-radiation produced from metals irradiated with x-rays was *characteristic* of the metal. For this discovery, which laid the foundations of the researches of H. G. J. Moseley and K. Siegbahn, Barkla received the Nobel prize, 1917. The prize-winning research was done at Liverpool Univ.; he held a professorship at the Univ. of London, 1909–13, and at Edinburgh Univ. from 1913. He was a fellow of the Royal Society.—*D. H. D. R.*

BARNARD, EDWARD EMERSON, 1857–1923, U. S. astronomer; b. Nashville, Tenn. From 1895 to 1923 he was professor of practical astronomy at the Univ. of Chicago and an astronomer at Yerkes Observatory. Known for his excellent photographs of planets and stars, he also discovered 16 comets, the fifth satellite of Jupiter, and "Barnard's star," the star with the most rapid proper motion known. He was a fellow of the Royal Society and a member of the National Academy of Sciences.—*G. H.*

BAROCLINITY: the state of a fluid in which surfaces of constant density intersect surfaces of constant pressure. A baroclinic state in Earth's atmosphere (here considered to be

Aneroid barograph: Diaphragm (middle), responding to changing atmospheric pressure, through appropriate linkage activates the stylus, which in turn records on the revolving cylinder. (*Smithsonian*)

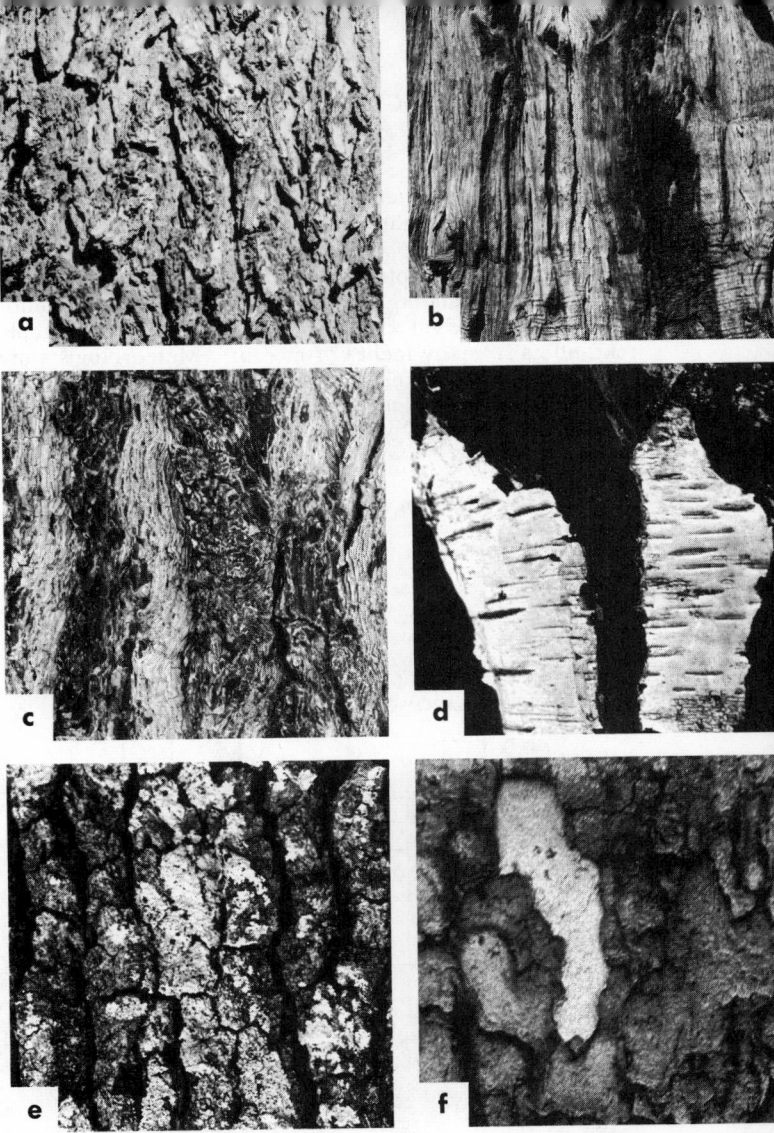

The outer layers of bark, which insulate and protect woody plants, are here seen on a variety of American gymnosperms (a, b, c) and angiosperms (d, e, f). The trees are (a) Coulter Pine, (b) Incense Cedar, (c) Mountain Hemlock (*Photos: Sumner/Monkmeyer*), and (d) Birch, (e) Live Oak, and (f) Buttonwood Sycamore (*Photos: William Hubbell, Watson/Monkmeyer, William Hubbell*).

a compressible fluid) is indicated when the temperature lines (isotherms) on a constant-pressure chart cut across the height lines (contours). Then ADVECTION takes place, causing changes in temperature and pressure, and in the intensity of highs and lows. See also BAROTROPY.—*P. L.*

BAROGRAPH: a recording BAROMETER. Ordinarily it is of the aneroid type. The recording is done on a revolving cylinder by a stylus which is linked to the pressure-sensitive element.

BAROMETER: an instrument for measuring atmospheric pressure. Three types are in common use: the mercury barometer, the aneroid (Greek "without liquid") barometer, and the hypsometer. The *mercury* instrument is standard for use in weather stations, laboratories, and generally when accuracy is the prime consideration.

The *aneroid* type is usually found in homes, aboard small craft, and wherever portability and ease of reading are a consideration. The *hypsometer,* in which the pressure is determined indirectly by measuring the boiling point of water, is rarely used in routine meteorological work; it is chiefly used in exploration and mountaineering (see HYPSOMETER).

The simplest form of mercury barometer is the J-tube *manometer* (Fig. 1), the longer leg of which is evacuated and sealed while the shorter leg is left open to the atmosphere. The difference in height h between the mercury levels in the two tubes depends upon the pressure p exerted on the free surface by the atmosphere. The pressure may be expressed in lb/in.² by calculating the weight of an inch-square column of mercury of height h. More often the pressure is simply read off as so many inches of mercury. Meteorologists use the metric absolute unit (millibar), which does not involve the value of gravity. One bar = 1,000 mb (millibars) = 29.53 in. of mercury at 0°C when gravity has the standard value (980.665 cm/sec²).

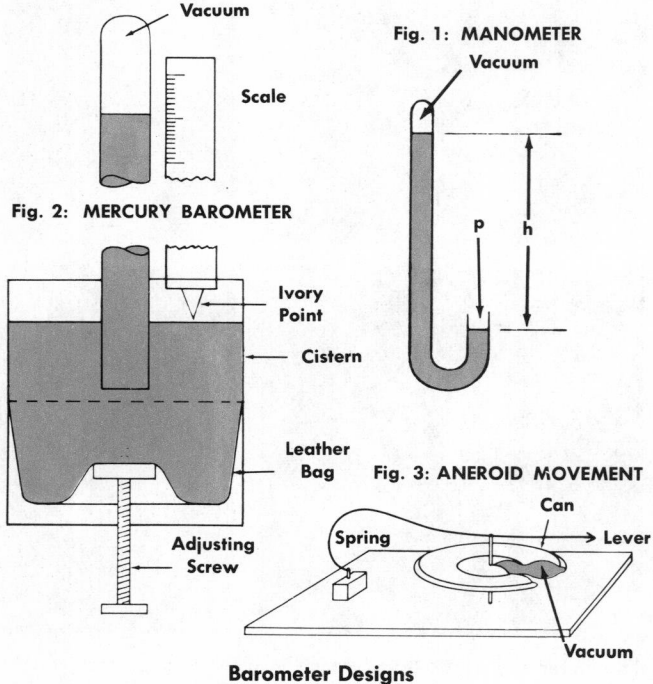

Barometer Designs

For practical reasons, barometers used in most weather stations are made in the form shown in Fig. 2. The short leg of the J-tube is replaced by a cistern of mercury in which the open end of the evacuated tube is immersed. The zero point of the height scale is the tip of a small ivory peg fixed to the top of the cistern. The mercury is held in a flexible leather bag, the bottom of which rests against an adjustable piston. In use, the piston is screwed up until the mercury in the cistern just makes contact with the ivory point. The level of the mercury in the upper tube is then read by means of the scale attached to the barometer frame. Some instruments compensate for the change in mercury level in the cistern, as barometric pressure changes, by compressing the scale by a factor equal to the ratio of the areas of the tube and the cistern. The aneroid barometer depends for its operation on the bending of the ends of an evacuated can made of thin steel. Fig. 3 shows a schematic diagram of a typical aneroid movement. The spring keeps the can from collapsing under the pressure of the atmosphere, but allows a small elastic response of the flexible ends of the can to changes in pressure. The lever transmits this motion to an indicating pointer.—*D. H. L.*

Columns of basalt forming "postpile" at Devil Postpile National Monument, Calif., have typical hexagonal cross section. Spectacular columnar basalts include those at Devils Tower, Wyo., and Giants Causeway, Ireland. (*National Park Service*)

BAROMETRIC TENDENCY: the change of atmospheric pressure (as measured by a barometer) in a given time. U. S. Weather Bureau stations report such changes every 3 hr. These values, recorded on the weather chart, are used in drawing ISALLO-BARS, an aid to forecasting.—*P. L.*

BAROTROPY: the state of a fluid in which surfaces of constant density coincide with surfaces of constant pressure. A constant-pressure chart with temperature lines (isotherms) and height lines (contours) paralleling each other indicates a barotropic condition in the earth's atmosphere. In such conditions, no large changes in the intensity of pressure systems will take place. See also BAROCLINITY.—*P. L.*

BARROW, ISAAC, 1630–77, English mathematician and classical scholar; b. London. He became first Lucasian professor of mathematics at Cambridge (1663), resigning 6 yr later to devote himself to theology. His mathematical writings include two works on geometrical optics and editions of the writings of Euclid, Archimedes, Apollonius, and Theodosius. His greatest work is his *Geometrical Lectures,* the most important work on the calculus before Newton's. His primary reputation is as an Anglican divine. He was a fellow of the Royal Society. —*D. H. D. R.*

BASALT: a glassy to microcrystalline extrusive basic IGNEOUS ROCK, generally dark gray to greenish gray. In crystallized varieties, the major constituents are labradorite feldspar and pyroxene, with minor amounts of olivine, titaniferous magnetite, ilmenite, epidote, and various deuteric minerals. Textures and structures vary greatly depending on the temperature and volatile-content of the initial lava, the mechanism of extrusion, and the terrane. The magmas which form basalt are believed to originate in a basaltic or peridotitic layer underlying the planet's crust. Basaltic magmas are generally quite fluid, so that LAVAS from these magmas may flow for great distances from vents and fissures. Basalts form most of the oceanic volcanoes and volcanic islands, as well as thick accumulations (plateau basalts) on the continents. GABBRO and DIABASE are, respectively, the plutonic and intrusive equivalents of basalt, formed from magmas of the same composition. Basalt is one of the rocks that commonly have a columnar structure, often with hexagonal cross-section, the joints assuming a pattern like that of mud cracks when an expanse of mud dries and shrinks.—*L. M.*

BASE: a substance which liberates the hydroxide ion (OH^-) in aqueous solution, neutralizes acids, or donates electrons by combining with an electron-deficient substance. Litmus paper is turned blue, dyes change their colors, and heat is liberated from acid solution when treated with an aqueous base. Bases usually have a bitter taste, and are slippery to the touch. *Inorganic bases* are formed by adding water to the oxide of a metal; their strength varies with degree of ionization. For example, sodium hydroxide is a stronger base than calcium hydroxide, because the former dissociates to a greater extent, liberating more hydroxide ions per equivalent of compound. Silver hydroxide is a very weak base, because there is no appreciable ionization in aqueous solution to yield hydroxide ions. *Organic bases* have the characteristics of either accepting protons or donating electrons in combining with electrophilic substances. Triethylamine, for example, can combine with a proton to form its acid salt, or it can react with boron trifluoride to form a triethylamine-boron trifluoride complex. The two available electrons of triethylamine's nitrogen atom combine with the electrophilic proton or the boron atom.—*G. W. M.*

BASE LEVEL: the lowest level to which a land surface may be worn by running water. At the margins of continents this is approximately sea level. Since the sea level itself changes over periods of time, base level also changes. The elevation of any river, pond, or lake may itself constitute a temporary base level for the streams flowing into it. EROSION, WEATHERING, MASS WASTING, and sometimes DIASTROPHISM are involved in the reduction of a land surface to base level.—*J. W.*

BASEMENT COMPLEX: the series of rocks, generally complex in structure, that are of pre-Cambrian origin and underlie the predominantly sedimentary rocks of later geological periods. Most of the basement rocks are igneous or metamorphic, and range in age from 1½ to over 3 billion yr, ages being determined by RADIOACTIVE DATING. In North America, the most extensive exposures of the Complex are in the Canadian Shield (see CONTINENTAL SHIELD), a vast area bordering Hudson Bay in Canada, but its formations extend under much of the rest of this and the other continents. In the Canadian Shield, the Complex is composed of two distinct series, separated by a marked break, or UNCONFORMITY. The older division, the base of which is nowhere known, is dominantly volcanic, with numerous sedimentary interbeds, while the later division consists of conglomerate and sandstone with minor quantities of volcanics. Both series were very intensely folded and faulted before later pre-Cambrian formations were deposited over them, indicating that great mountain ranges were built in which, at some depth below the surface, enormous quantities of granitic rock were developed. Very deep erosion has destroyed the mountains and has exposed immense areas of the granitic rock. The deformation and igneous action below the surface caused extreme METAMORPHISM of the sedimentary and volcanic rocks, so that they now bear little resemblance to the originals.—*N. E. A. H.*

BASIC SALTS: compounds intermediate in composition between hydroxides or oxides and normal salts. Their preparation usually involves the reaction of a normal salt with water (hydrolysis). An example is malachite, $Cu_2(OH)_2CO_3$.—*L. Sc.*

BAST: see PHLOEM.

BAT: a winged mammal of the order Chiroptera. Bats are the only mammals capable of actual flight (see ANIMAL FLIGHT). A bat's wings are modified forelimbs, with a membranous skin tightly stretched between the elongated digits. In the position occupied by the thumb in human beings, and inde-

Rafinesque bat from Tennessee is fitted for active flight by means of membranes stretched between second and fifth fingers. (G. Ronald Austing from Nat. Audubon Soc.)

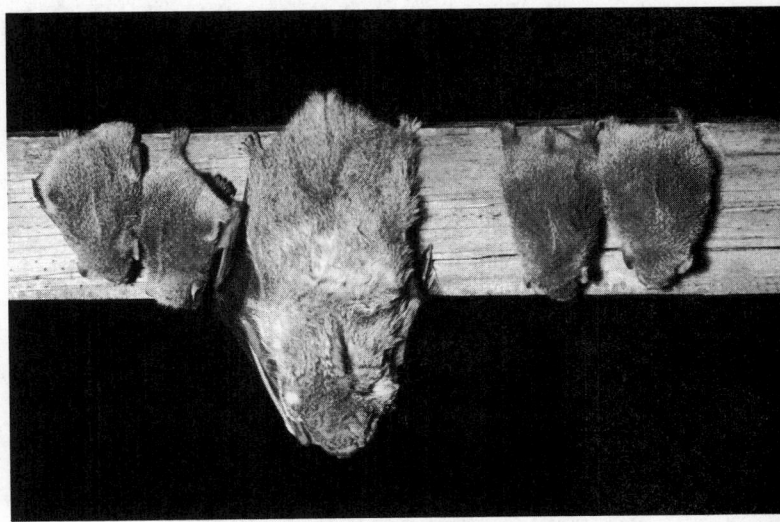

Young red bats, born in May or June, adopt mother's head-down posture as they cling to beam to roost. (*Leonard Lee Rue III from Nat. Audubon Soc.*)

pendent of the actual wing portion, is a claw. The claws, together with the hind feet, enable the bat to climb over cave walls, buildings, and trees with ease. A membrane that connects the tail and hind limbs in most species improves maneuverability in flight and occasionally entraps small insects. Bats can fly, avoid obstacles, and capture dodging insects in total darkness by an echo-location system employing the principle of sonar (see ANIMAL SONAR). While flying, bats emit extremely high-pitched sounds, undetectable by the human ear; the sound waves are reflected by any solid object, such as a tree branch or insect, and inform the flying bat of what is ahead. The sounds produced by each bat seem to be distinctive, for hundreds of bats can fly in a small area in total darkness without collision. Many bats have an outgrowth of skin or muscle, called a nose leaf, on the nose and lips; this structure appears to concentrate the sound waves into a beam ahead of the bat.

There are hundreds of species of bats widely distributed in the temperate and tropical regions of both hemispheres. The great "flying foxes" of Malaysia may have a wingspread of 5 ft and weigh 2 lb. They subsist primarily on fruits. Most smaller bats feed chiefly on insects, though some tropical species catch fish. The vampire of South and Central America is a blood drinker. Bats of many kinds are affected by rabies and may transmit the disease to livestock and even man. Contrary to popular belief, bats are not blind in daylight.—*A. P. E.*

BATESON, WILLIAM, 1861–1926, English biologist; b. Whitby. His study of *Balanoglossus* led to his recognition of the chordate affinities of this genus. He early recognized the importance of variation in the study of evolution and in 1894 published *Materials for the Study of Variation with Especial Regard to Discontinuity in the Origin of Species.* With the rediscovery of Mendel's work, he became an enthusiastic exponent of Mendelian genetics, and he later made important contributions in that field. A fellow of St. John's College, Cambridge, 1885–1926, he was elected to the Royal Society in 1894. He was also an associate of the U. S. National Academy of Sciences.—*D. H. D. R.*

BATHOLITH: an enormous mass of granite rock exposed by erosion. Some batholiths appear to have been formed by magma forcing its way toward the surface of the crust, arching and breaking overlying rock, melting such rock, or filling huge rents. Extending to unknown depths, batholiths are by definition at least 40 mi² in area, being larger than stocks. Some batholiths are related to the process of granitization (see GRANITE).—*J. Si.*

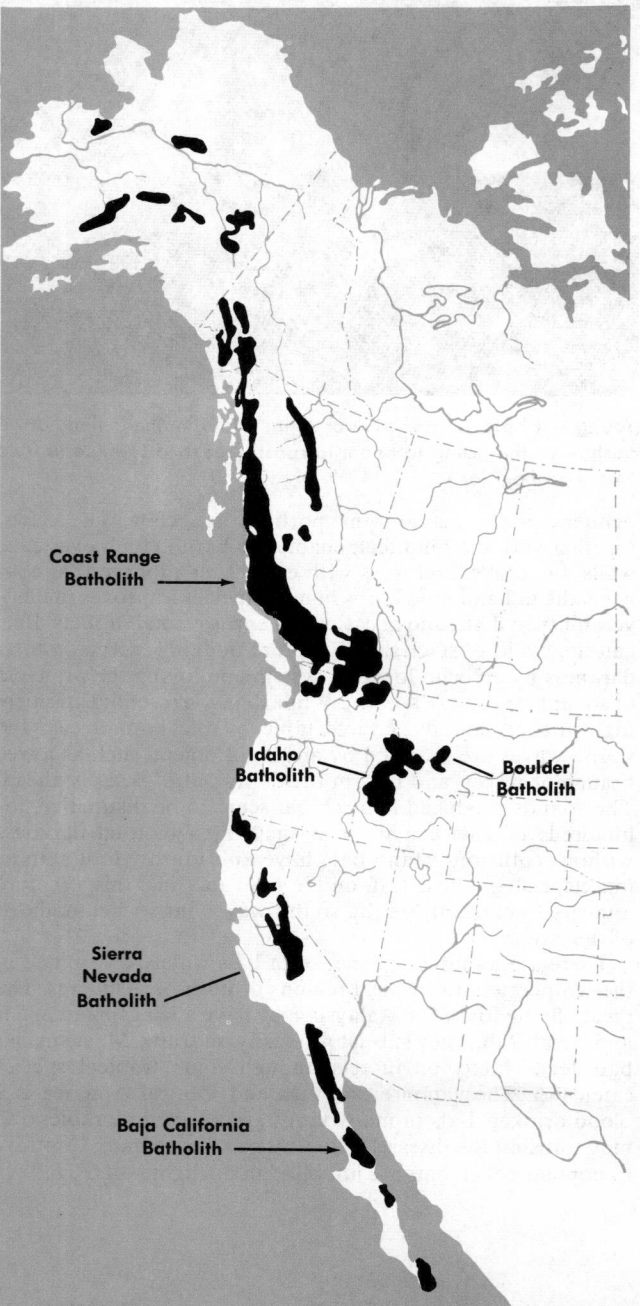

Coast Range Batholith

Idaho Batholith

Boulder Batholith

Sierra Nevada Batholith

Baja California Batholith

BATTERY: a structure (cell) designed to produce or store electricity by means of chemical activity. In the conventional design, it consists of two electrodes—the positively charged cathode and the negatively charged anode—and an electrolyte (a chemical compound that will dissociate into positively and negatively charged ions). The migration of the ions within the cell stimulates a flow of current in the circuit outside the cell.

Batteries generally are of two types: primary and secondary. The *primary cell,* of which the common flashlight battery is the classic example, is designed to deliver a specified amount of energy for a definite period, after which the cell is discarded; it cannot be recharged. The *secondary cell* is an electrical storage system, like the lead-acid battery in an automobile; it can be recharged a number of times during its useful life. Recent years have seen the development of rechargeable primary cells; but these are still costly and limited in application.

Primary cells are further divided into *wet* and *dry* types. The distinction is more theoretical than actual. The electrolyte is in fact always a liquid, but in dry cells it is incorporated in pastes and membranes so that, to all appearances, it is dry. However, sufficient moisture is present to allow the reaction to proceed. Primary cells combine a variety of electrode materials and electrolytes. The flashlight cell, for instance, is a zinc-ammonium chloride system, with manganese dioxide as the depolarizer. The depolarizer prevents accumulation at the electrodes of reaction products which would slow down and eventually stop the reaction. The zinc forms a container or cup, at the bottom of which is a layer of manganese dioxide. The electrolyte is in the form of a paste that fills the cup, and in its center is a carbon electrode. The reaction which takes place is:

$$Zn + 2NH_4Cl + 2MnO_2 \underset{\text{charge}}{\overset{\text{discharge}}{\rightleftharpoons}}$$

$$Zn(NH_3)_2Cl_2 + H_2O + Mn_2O_3$$

Other primary cells are the silver oxide-zinc-alkali, the magnesium-silver chloride, and the zinc-mercuric oxide types.

Many cells are named for the early pioneers of electricity who developed them. The *Leclanché cell* was the original zinc-ammonium chloride system from which the present-day flashlight battery developed. The *Daniell cell* is a zinc-copper sulfite system. The *Lalande cell* is a zinc-caustic soda unit. Others who gave their names to specific types of cells are Bunsen (zinc-acid), Grove (zinc-acid), and Poggendorf (bichromate).

Secondary, or *rechargeable,* cells are characterized by highly reversible reactions, as in the lead-acid batteries widely used in automobiles. These consist of a container for the electrolyte and a series of lead plates. Here, the reaction is:

$$PbO_2 + Pb + 2H_2SO_4 \rightleftharpoons 2PbSO_4 + 2H_2O$$

Another type of secondary cell in rather wide use is the nickel-iron alkaline battery, which uses potassium hydroxide as the electrolyte. Frequently known as the *Edison* battery, it is primarily for industrial use, in which its high efficiency is particularly desirable. There is also a nickel-cadmium secondary cell.

The above types of battery produce electrical energy by direct electrochemical oxidation of a metal (zinc, lead, iron, or cadmium). In recently developed batteries hydrogen, hydrocarbons, or other suitable organic compounds, such as alcohols, are oxidized electrochemically to produce electricity directly.

Batholiths: Long erosion has laid bare these once deep-lying bodies of granitic rock along the North American Cordillera. The Coast Range batholith is 1,200 mi long.

These units are called fuel cells because the materials they convert are conventionally used as fuels—*i.e.,* as sources of thermal energy via combustion.

The so-called "solar battery" (SOLAR CELL) is not a battery but a photoelectric energy-conversion system. The "atomic battery" uses a radioactive isotope to build up a charge. It can develop high voltages but little current. See CELL, VOLTAIC; and ELECTRICITY, *History.—A. R. G.*

BAUER, LOUIS AGRICOLA, 1865–1932, U. S. physicist; b. Cincinnati. Bauer founded the journal *Terrestrial Magnetism and Atmospheric Electricity* in 1896 and published more than 300 scientific papers concerning terrestrial magnetism and related subjects. Believing that large quantities of observational data would be necessary for improved knowledge of the earth's magnetism, he proposed the establishment of a department of terrestrial magnetism in the Carnegie Institution and became its first director (1904).—*D. H. D. R.*

BAUHIN, GASPARD (KASPAR), 1560–1624, Swiss botanist; b. Basel. One of the founders of plant classification, Bauhin emphasized "natural" classification, by grouping plant species on a basis of resemblance of structural details and life history. He attempted to compile all known descriptions and names of plants in his writings, which include *Preface to the Field of Botany* (1620), *Anatomy* (1591–92), and *Register of the Field of Botany* (1623).—*D. H. D. R.*

BAUMÉ, ANTOINE, 1728–1804, French chemist; b. Senlis. He improved processes for bleaching silk, dyeing, purifying saltpeter, gilding, and making sal ammoniac. Baumé is best known for his invention of the Baumé hydrometer and devising the two Baumé scales for graduating it: one measured liquids lighter than water, the other liquids heavier than water. His *Eléments de pharmacie théorique et pratique* (1762) went into nine editions.—*S. B.*

BAUXITE: the principal ore of ALUMINUM; a complex and varied mixture of a number of hydrated crystalline and colloidal aluminum and iron oxides, with various mechanically admixed impurities. The principal constituents include: gibbsite, $Al_2O_3 \cdot 3H_2O$, monoclinic; boehmite, $Al_2O_3 \cdot H_2O$, orthorhombic; and diaspore, $Al_2O_3 \cdot H_2O$, orthorhombic. Bauxite forms lateritic cappings in level areas subjected to tropical weathering with alternating wet and dry seasons and a fluctuating water table, and with consequent selective leaching of silica and alkalies. Most bauxite deposits are derived from ALUMINA-rich rocks, *e.g.* nepheline syenite, shales, schists, residual and alluvial clays from limestone. Detrital deposits form by erosion and redeposition of material from the original cappings. Bauxite is an ingredient in the alumina-rich, rapidly hardening, chemically resistant cement (*ciment fondu*) and in various aluminum chemicals. High-grade bauxite is calcined (or even melted in electric furnaces to form synthetic corundum) for use in refractories and abrasives. See also MINERAL (table).—*L. M.*

BAYER, JOHANN, 1572–1625, German lawyer and astronomer; b. Rain, Bavaria. His *Uranometria* (1603), the first convenient celestial atlas, designated the stars by Greek letters, thereby introducing the nomenclature still in use. Bayer formulated 12 new constellations in order to include the previously unmapped southern skies.—*O. G.*

BEACH: the deposit of sand and gravel which is in more or less active transit by waves and currents along a shore. Depending on the type and size of particles available and the magnitude of the waves and currents, the material of a beach may vary from very coarse gravel to fine sand and silt. Its motion along the shore is easily shown in the buildup of sand and gravel on one side of a groin or jetty and its removal from the lee side. At times of storm a beach may be cut away to some extent, then built out again during periods of low waves. Beach material shows very good sorting, and pebbles are apt to be well rounded from mutual abrasion during transport. Most beach sand is composed of fragments of quartz, although in places local concentrations of other minerals may be present, *e.g.* magnetite (black sand), zircon, rutile, coral, or gold. Along a rocky coast, beaches tend to be discontinuous and are found in protected bays away from the active erosion occurring at the headlands. Such bayhead beaches contrast markedly with the long, very extensive barrier beaches (offshore bars) characteristic of the South Atlantic and Gulf Coasts of the U. S. A., where the continent is fringed by a coastal plain. See also COASTLINE.—*J. Sh.*

Wave-built beach at Barnegat Lighthouse State Park, N. J., is a rapidly changing coastline. Transportation of sand by waves and currents is constantly changing the contours. The breakwater on the point prevents wave and current action from isolating the lighthouse. (*N. J. Dept. of Conservation and Development*)

BEADLE, GEORGE WELLS, 1903–   , U. S. geneticist; b. Wahoo, Nebr. His research has been on cytology and genetics of maize, physiological genetics of Drosophila, and chemical genetics of Neurospora. For their discovery, through experiments with bread mold, that genes transmit hereditary characters by controlling chemical reactions, Beadle and E. L. Tatum shared the Nobel prize for 1958 with J. Lederberg. He is a fellow of the Royal Society and a member of the National Academy of Sciences.—*D. H. D. R.*

BEARING: a device that reduces the amount of work wasted in overcoming the friction between moving parts of machinery; at the same time it supports the weight of moving machine parts and holds them in position. The oldest and simplest type is the *slider bearing.* This is little more than an expendable, replaceable liner around one or both surfaces of parts sliding past each other with uniform or periodic motion. Because of the large contact surfaces involved, these bearings, usually made of soft materials, were limited in their capacity to stand load and friction-produced heat, and were restricted to operating at relatively low speeds. In *roller bearings,* developed about 1900, the contact surface was confined either to a narrow strip along the surface of a cylinder or to a small area on the surface of a sphere. The location of the contact surface shifted continuously as the roller moved, reducing wear on the bearing and prolonging its useful life. Because rollers are required to move in a fixed direction, they are usually held in place by being set into grooves machined into the rings that contain

Typical deep-groove ball bearing: This type is widely used in all kinds of machinery for carrying thrust loads and also for loads to be transmitted radially. (*Marlin-Rockwell Corp.*)

them. In the case of thrust bearings, where the load is passed from the face of one ring to the face of another, the rollers are sandwiched between the rings. Where the load is transmitted radially, the rings are arranged concentrically, and the rollers are placed between the outside surface of the smaller ring and the inside surface of the larger one. The shape of the roller usually determines the name of the bearing, *e.g. ball, cylindrical, spherical* (barrel-shaped), or *needle.* In some cases the rings are tapered, like slices from a hollow cone; their rollers (*tapered roller bearings*) do not rotate about an axis parallel to the rotational axes of the rings. *Needle bearings,* really very thin cylinders, are usually held in place by small projections at their ends, or by small balls set into cavities at

the ends of the needles, forming a kind of sub-system of bearings for each needle. In recent years very thin films of lubricating liquids and even air have served as bearings between parts machined to extremely close fits. The entire bearing mechanism is sealed to prevent escape of the bearing fluid—a departure in principle from the customary use of lubricating oils in most roller bearings to reduce friction and remove heat. In steel bridge construction, the term bearing is applied to a part interposed between the trestle and a supporting column, to permit movement of the bridge in expansion or contraction with temperature changes.—*K. A.*

BEAUFORT SCALE: a system for estimating and reporting wind speeds from their effects on sails, developed in 1805 by Adm. Sir Francis Beaufort of the British Navy, and later modified for use on land, as shown in the table here. Wind speeds reported by use of this scale are given a Beaufort number; *e.g.* No. 4 is a moderate breeze of 11 to 16 knots (1 knot = 1.15 mph) that raises dust, blows loose paper about, and moves small branches on trees.

THE BEAUFORT SCALE

Beaufort Number	Mph/Knots	Description	Effects
0	0–1/0–1	Calm	Smoke rises vertically
1	1–3/1–3	Light air	Direction of wind shown by smoke drift, but not by wind vanes
2	4–7/4–6	Light breeze	Leaves rustle, wind vane moved by wind, wind felt on face
3	8–12/7–10	Gentle breeze	Leaves and small twigs in constant motion, wind extends light flag
4	13–18/11–16	Moderate breeze	Raises dust, blows dead leaves and loose paper, moves small branches
5	19–24/17–21	Fresh breeze	Small trees sway; small waves crest on lakes or streams
6	25–31/22–27	Strong breeze	Large-branches in constant motion, wind howls around eaves of house, wires on telephone poles hum
7	32–38/28–33	Moderate gale	Large trees sway; walking against wind inconvenient
8	39–46/34–40	Fresh gale	Twigs break off trees; walking against wind difficult
9	47–54/41–47	Strong gale	Branches break off trees, loose bricks blow off chimneys, shingles or roof tile loosened or blown off
10	55–63/48–55	Whole gale	Trees snap or are uprooted; can cause considerable damage to buildings
11	64–72/56–63	Storm	Widespread damage
12	73–82/64–71	Hurricane	See HURRICANE

After many years of use, the Beaufort Scale is now seldom employed. Today, by international agreement, all wind speeds for use by meteorologists, ship and aircraft navigators, etc., are reported in knots.—*P. L.*

BECHER, JOHANN JOACHIM, 1635–82, German scientist and adventurer; b. Speyer, Bavaria. After his plans to interest German princes in developing trade and colonization failed, he fled to Holland and then to England. His works on minerals and metals (*Physicae Subterranea,* 1669) discuss transmutation of metals and propose "terra pinguis," an element of combustibility liberated on combustion or oxidation. These ideas prompted G. E. Stahl, Becher's pupil, to announce the *phlogiston theory,* the last alchemical phase of chemistry (see ALCHEMY).—*R. J. F.*

BECQUEREL, ANTOINE HENRI, 1852–1908, French physicist; b. Paris. He discovered radioactivity when, in 1896, he noticed that wrapped photographic film had been affected by invisible radiation from a small crystal of a uranium salt left lying on the package. For research on this phenomenon of radiation, Becquerel and his associates Pierre and Marie Curie were awarded a Nobel prize, 1903. Becquerel also did research on various aspects of

Antoine Henri Becquerel
(N. Y. Public Library)

light, including polarization and absorption by crystals. He was professor of physics at the École Polytechnique from 1895. He was a fellow of the Royal Society and an associate of the U. S. National Academy of Sciences.—*D. H. D. R.*

BEDDING (or **stratification**): in geology, the occurrence of layers or strata in rocks. The term "bed" is used for layers more than ½ in. thick; thinner layers are called laminae (see also VARVE). The individual beds are separated by divisional surfaces called *bedding planes.* Each bed represents a single depositional episode, and the intervening planes reflect interruption of the process. Sedimentary rocks are termed "well bedded" when the individual layers can be traced over considerable distances and the stratification planes are smooth. The rocks are "unevenly bedded" when the layers wedge out within short distances. If the layers are tens of feet thick, the rock is called massive. Delta and dune deposits are typically cross-bedded; *i.e.* the laminations are inclined to the main stratification planes.—*W. Ha.*

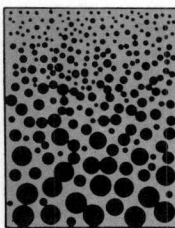 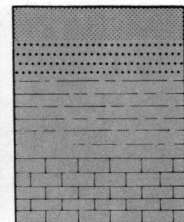

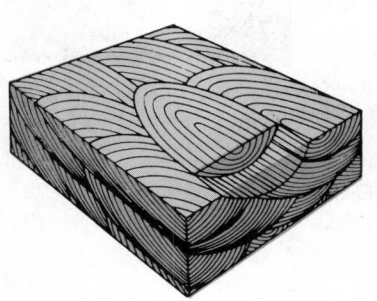

Conditions of deposition are reflected in bedding of sedimentary rocks. At left, homogeneous particles have settled out by size. At right, successive beds were formed by different kinds of sediments (sand, limy material, etc.) as environmental conditions changed. Cross-bedding (*left*) of sediments in dunes and deltas may occur as winds and water currents change speed or direction. Photo (*right*) shows cross-bedded sandstones in S New York. (*Jerome Wyckoff*)

BEEBE, CHARLES WILLIAM, 1877–1962, U. S. explorer, ornithologist, and naturalist; b. Brooklyn, N. Y. As head of numerous expeditions, he traveled to British Guinea, Mexico, the Himalayas, Borneo, and S America. He used the bathysphere for studying deep-sea life around Bermuda (after 1930) and observed marine life of the E Pacific in 1938 from the glass-bottomed schooner *Zaca.* Beebe's many books include *Galapagos, World's End* (1923), *Pheasants, Their Lives and Their Homes* (1926), and *Half Mile Down* (1934), describing bathysphere descents to over 3,000 ft.—*S. B.*

BEER'S LAW: a law governing the absorption of light passing through a medium; it was formulated in 1852 by August Beer. No substance is perfectly transparent: some of the light passing through it is always absorbed. A plane parallel light beam of any wavelength, of initial intensity I_o, traversing a "transparent" slab of thickness x, emerges with intensity I less than I_o; the energy lost by the beam is transferred to the medium. Beer's law states that in a homogeneous liquid the fractional decrease in intensity is the same in any equal interval of path, and also is proportional to the concentration of the liquid, because each molecule absorbs an equal fraction of the light falling on it. These relations are summed up in the equation $I = I_o\,e^{-bcx}$, where e is the natural logarithmic base (2.718), b the absorption coefficient for unit concentration of solute, and c the concentration. For solids a similar law, often wrongly attributed to Johann Lambert, was originally discovered by Pierre Bouguer (1698–1758).

Strong absorption is accompanied by strong reflection, as in metals. The amount of absorption may vary more or less sharply with wavelength. This *selective* absorption is responsible for color; it also causes *dichromatism,* in which a substance appears to have a different color depending on its thickness (*e.g.* thin layers of cyanine look blue, thick layers red). See ABSORPTION SPECTRUM.—*S. Br.*

BEHAVIOR: see ANIMAL BEHAVIOR.

BEILSTEIN, FRIEDRICH KONRAD, 1838–1906, Russo-German chemist; b. St. Petersburg. He studied the structure of chlorinated hydrocarbons and the properties of Russian petroleum, and developed the Beilstein test for halogens in organic compounds. The standard reference work on organic compounds is Beilstein's *Handbuch der organischen Chemie* (1880).—*A. I.*

BEKHTEREV, VLADIMIR MIKHAILOVICH, 1857–1927, Soviet physiologist and neuropathologist; b. Viatka province. He is known for studies of localization of brain functions and application of research on conditioned reflexes in dogs to man. Founder of the St. Petersburg Psycho-neurological Institute (1907), he wrote numerous works on the nervous system. His *General Principles of Human Reflexology* (1932) is a study of personality.—*D. H. D. R.*

BELL, ALEXANDER GRAHAM, 1847–1922, Scottish-U. S. technologist; b. Edinburgh. In 1876 he patented the telephone and demonstrated it at an exposition in Philadelphia and before the American Academy of Arts and Sciences in Boston. The telephone was in commercial use by the middle of the next year. He was a member of the National Academy of Sciences. —*D. H. D. R.*

BELL, SIR CHARLES, 1774–1842, Scottish physiologist; b. Edinburgh. He discovered the distinct functions of the nerves, and extended this discovery to the functional separation of sensory and motor nerves. His findings have been compared to those of Harvey on the circulation of the blood. He was a fellow of the Royal Society.—*D. H. D. R.*

BELON, PIERRE, 1517–64, French zoologist; b. near Le Mans. One of the earliest workers in comparative anatomy, he published a history of fishes, *L'histoire naturelle des estranges poissons marins* (1551), and of birds, *L'histoire de la nature des oyseaux* (1555). Belon traveled in the Near East and, in an account of these journeys, described many oriental species. He wrote the first monograph on a group of plants (coniferous trees), and illustrated all his works with clear, detailed drawings.—*D. H. D. R.*

BELTRAMI, EUGENIO, 1835–1900, Italian mathematician; b. Cremona; ed. Cremona and Pavia. He became professor of algebra and geometry at Bologna in 1862, and later professor at Pisa, again at Bologna, at Rome, and at Pavia. Beltrami contributed to non-Euclidean geometry, especially to the theory of hyperbolic space. He also published papers on differential parameters, on flexions of ruled surfaces, and on the general theory of surfaces. His papers in mathematical physics dealt with hydrodynamics, elasticity, physical optics, theory of potential, electricity, magnetism, and thermodynamics.—*H. C.*

Elevation of 19.121 ft above mean sea level is indicated by this brass bench mark near Connecticut shoreline. (*Russ Kinne*)

BENCH MARK: in surveying, a fixed point of known elevation above or below sea level. It is located accurately and placed so that its elevation will not change. The mark itself usually is a metal disk stamped with the necessary information. It may be set in a natural base, *e.g.* an outcropping of rock, or in an artificial base. Artificial bases include concrete posts, monuments, bridge abutments, masonry walls, and other permanent structures. Surveyors use bench marks as reference points. In maps the abbreviation B.M. is used with the elevation. See SURVEYING.—*A. P. E.*

BENEDETTI, GIOVANI BATTISTA, 1530–90; Italian physicist and mathematician; b. Venice. The six essays in his *Diversarum speculationum liber* (1585)—"Arithmetic Theorems," "Perspective," "Mechanics," "Proportion," "Disputations," and "Letters on Mathematics and Physics" contributed to the development of analytic geometry. In mechanics he attacked Aristotle's refusal to admit the possibility of a vacuum, formulated the concept of the lever arm, and applied the principle of inertia to circular motion. Benedetti was an important predecessor of Galileo.—*D. H. D. R.*

BENEDICT, FRANCIS GANO, 1870–1957, U. S. biochemist; b. Milwaukee, Wis. His most important work was on human metabolism during inanition (1907), work (1909–13), rest (1910), fasting (1915), and walking (1915), diabetes (1910–12), and infancy (1915). He was a member of the National Academy of Sciences.—*D. H. D. R.*

BENZENE: a volatile liquid, C_6H_6, until recently obtained only from the coal tar and coal gas resulting from dry distillation of coal. Although it is a cyclic aromatic hydrocarbon, it is now also made commercially by a catalytic process from saturated open-chain hydrocarbons in petroleum. Benzene is useful as a solvent for paints and varnishes and as an ingredient of liquid fuels for modern aircraft and automotive engines. It is most important as the raw material or intermediate for a vast array of chemical compounds used in practically every phase of modern technology. For benzene structure see AROMATIC COMPOUNDS. Benzene was once called "phene"; the radical C_6H_5 is called "phenyl."—*Ru. M.*

BERGERON, TOR HAROLD PERCIVAL, 1895–   , Swedish meteorologist; b. Gladstone, Surrey, Eng. He originated many of the international weather definitions, codes, and symbols. In his thesis *Über die dreidimensional verknüpfende Wetter-analyse* (1928), he systematized the Norwegian analysis method, introduced the concepts of air masses, provided the first explanation of kinematic frontogenesis, and foreshadowed an explanation of the release of precipitation from undercooled clouds. In another paper (1933) he elaborated on his precipitation mechanism (*Bergeron-Findeisen process*), which shows that precipitation from undercooled clouds results from colloidal instability caused by coexistence of cloud droplets and ice crystals. Bergeron coauthored (with J. A. B. Bjerknes) *Physikalische Hydrodynamik* (1933) and *Dynamic Meteorology and Weather Forecasting* (1958).—*S. P.*

BERGIUS, FRIEDRICH, 1884–1949, German chemist; b. Goldschmieden, near Breslau. He converted pastes of heavy residues of petroleum and tar with powdered peat, lignite, or coal into light motor fuels by treating them with hydrogen under pressures up to 200 atm at about 400°C (*Use of High Pressures in Chemical Actions,* 1913). His subsequent work resulted in a practical process for manufacture of synthetic gasoline, used on a large scale by the Germans in World War II. For

Friedrich Bergius
(*German Information Center*)

their contributions to the invention and development of chemical high-pressure techniques, Bergius and C. Bosch shared the 1931 Nobel prize.—*R. J. F.*

BERGMAN, TORBERN OLOF, 1735–84, Swedish chemist and mineralogist; b. Katrineberg. He learned to make artificial mineral waters, and did much to systematize chemical analysis and to further mineralogy. He worked on affinity, which he called "elective attraction," and issued extensive tables purporting to show the directions chemical reactions will take. Although based entirely on what was seen to occur and taking no account of what is now known as mass action, the tables were ranked with an importance comparable to that of modern atomic weight tables. His *Opuscula Physica et Chemica* (1779–84) was published (1785) as *A Dissertation on Elective Attractions* and as *Physical and Chemical Essays* (1784). He was a fellow of the Royal Society.—*R. E. O.*

BERKELEY, GEORGE, 1685–1753, British philosopher and clergyman; b. Thomastown, Ireland. At 26, he published his *Treatise Concerning the Principles of Human Knowledge,* a penetrating critical reaction to the Cartesian-Newtonian-Lockian conceptions of scientific knowledge, focusing on Locke's theory of knowledge. Though he was philosophically an empiricist, his motives were

George, Earl of Berkeley
(Scripta Mathematica)

religious: to refute the skepticism and atheism he saw inherent in Locke's position. The accepted view among most philosophers was that knowledge of the world consists of ideas as effects in us of objects acting upon us; it followed for Newton and Locke that *substance,* the cause of ideas, is never really known; all we can know is effects. Berkeley's main attack was against this idea of "unknown substance": if *matter* is unknowable, he said, it cannot be known to exist; all we can know is ideas. Berkeley's famous principle, *Esse est percipi* ("to be is to be perceived"), has these consequences: (1) statements about existence are verifiable only if they refer to perceptible data; (2) real objects are collections of observable qualities. Accordingly, critical of Newton, Berkeley construed *space, time,* and *motion* as relative (foreshadowing Mach and Einstein) and, in *The Analyst* (1734), advanced an acute and historically epochal criticism of the confused concept of "infinitesimals" in the newly born calculus. He was a fellow of the Royal Society.—*S. H. T.*

BERKELIUM: an actinide element (Bk); at. no. 97; at. wt 249 (stablest isotope). S. Thompson *et al.* at Univ. of California made berkelium (1949) by bombarding Americium^{241} with helium nuclei in a cyclotron. Berkelium's several isotopes have half-lives ranging from a few hours (Bk^{234}; Bk^{250}) to several thousand yr (Bk^{247}).—*G. W. M.*

BERNARD, CLAUDE, 1813–78, French physiologist; b. Saint-Julien. He interned at the Hotel-Dieu in Paris under François Magendie and succeeded him as professor (1855). Bernard became the first to occupy the chair of physiology at the Sorbonne and was elected to the Institute in 1868. A pioneer in the investigation of carbohydrate metabolism, he did his major work in the chemical phenomena of digestion and functions of the pancreas. Bernard discovered and named the polysaccharide glycogen, and in the course of investigating the glycogenic function of the liver, he performed the famous experiment of keeping rabbits on a diet of meat, thus showing that glycogen (a carbohydrate) can be formed from protein. His researches led to the discovery of the vasomotor system. He also studied the physiological action of poisons, particularly curare and carbon monoxide. His books include *Introduction à l'étude de la médecine expérimentale* (1865), *Physiologie générale* (1872), and 17 vols. of lectures. He was a fellow of the Royal Society.—*S. B.*

BERNOULLI: the name of a remarkable family of scientists and mathematicians. Of Belgian origin, the family settled in Basel, Switzerland, to escape religious persecution. Three generations were especially distinguished in mathematics. In the first, **Jakob,** 1654–1705, became professor of mathematics at Basel in 1687. He mastered calculus as formulated by Leibniz, developed it further, and applied it to important problems. He also made valuable contributions to analytic geometry, the theory of probability, and calculus of variations. "Bernoulli's numbers" are named for him. At Jakob's death, his brother **Johann,** 1667–1748, succeeded him as professor at Basel. Johann's work covered a wide range—astronomy, chemistry, and physics, in addition to mathematics. He did much to develop calculus and to popularize it, and he made significant contributions to calculus of variations. **Nikolaus,** 1662–1716, a third brother, taught mathematics at the Academy at St. Petersburg. Johann's three sons were all mathematicians: **Nikolaus,** 1695–1726, was professor of mathematics at St. Petersburg together with **Daniel,** 1700–82, and **Johann,** 1710–90, succeeded his father as professor at Basel. Best known is Daniel, who became a close friend and sometimes a rival of Euler. In 1732 he returned to Basel from St. Petersburg and became, in succession, professor of anatomy, of botany, and of physics. He made important contributions to calculus, differential equations, and the theory of probability in pure mathematics, and to many problems of applied mathematics. In the third generation, the two sons of the younger Johann were mathematicians. **Johann,** 1744–1807, became astronomer royal at Berlin. **Jakob,** 1759–89, became a member of the St. Petersburg Academy of mathematics and physics, but his career was cut short at 30 by accidental death.—*H. C.*

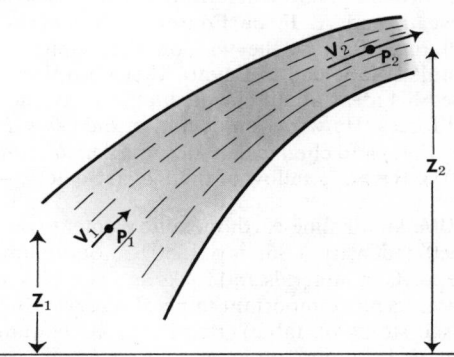

Steady flow: Bernoulli's principle states that the total energy at any point in the cross section of the pipe above is constant.

BERNOULLI'S PRINCIPLE OF HYDRODYNAMICS: Within a fluid either liquid or gaseous, under conditions of steady flow (*i.e.* pressure and velocity at any one point remaining constant) the sum of the energy of velocity, the energy of pressure, and the potential energy of elevation remains constant. Formulated by Daniel Bernoulli, Swiss mathematician, in 1738, this is a statement of the law of conservation of energy for fluids in steady flow. For convenience of application to problems of fluid flow through pipes, the terms of velocity and pressure energy are reduced to linear units:

$$\frac{V_1{}^2}{2g} + \frac{P_1}{W} + Z_1 = \frac{V_2{}^2}{2g} + \frac{P_1}{W} + Z_2 = \text{Constant}$$

where V is velocity, g is acceleration caused by gravity, P is pressure, W is fluid density, and Z is elevation above datum level. From this comes the usual statement that for steady flow the sum of the velocity-head, the pressure head, and the elevation-head remains constant. See FLUID FLOW.—*A. L.*

BERT, PAUL, 1833–86, French physiologist; b. Auxerre. His research included work in many areas of plant and vegetable as well as animal physiology; his best-known work (*Barometric Pressure,* 1878) was on the physiological effects of changes in air pressure; in it he showed the importance of the partial pressure of oxygen in maintenance of life. This research led to successful climbing, and later flight, to altitudes at which oxygen pressure is as low as one third of its sea-level pressure.—*D. H. D. R.*

BERTHELOT, MARCELLIN PIERRE EUGÈNE, 1827–1907, French chemist; b. Paris. Through work on production of acetylene from hydrogen and carbon in the electric arc he became a founder of synthesis in organic chemistry (*Organic Chemistry Founded upon Synthesis,* 1861). From studies of heat in chemical reactions he derived a "principle of maximum work" which, however, was in conflict with his own distinction between heat-developing, exothermic reactions and heat-absorbing, endothermic ones. Generally accepted was his law of distribution: "When two immiscible solvents are present, various amounts of a substance soluble in both are so distributed that the concentrations in the two solvents are in constant proportions." He organized an experiment station for his physiological work and published studies on the origins of alchemy (1885) and chemistry in the Middle Ages (1893), a biography of Lavoisier (1890), and many technical works, including *Essai de mécanique chimique* (1879), *Thermochimie* (1897), and *Chimie végétale et agricole* (1899).—*E. F.*

BERTHOLLET, CLAUDE LOUIS, 1748–1822, French chemist; b. Talloire, near Annecy, Savoy. A doctor of medicine, he discovered silver fulminate and chloric acid (1788), introduced chlorine bleaching, and collaborated with Lavoisier, Guyton de Morveau, and A. F. de Fourcroy on the new chemical nomenclature. In 1798 he was on the scientific staff that accompanied Napoleon to Egypt. After returning to Paris, he developed his ideas about chemical affinity as one among the physical forces. He wrote on dyeing in *Éléments de l'art de la teinture* (1791) and chemical statics in *Essai de statique chimique* (1803). He was a fellow of the Royal Society.—*E. F.*

BERYLLIUM: an alkaline-earth metallic element (Be); at. no. 4; at. wt 9.02; density 1.86; mp 1350°C. Beryllium occurs in small deposits in minerals and rocks as a complex silicate and aluminate. Its most important mineral is *beryl,* $3BeO \cdot Al_2O_3 \cdot 6SiO_2$ (see MINERAL, table). Beryl crystals containing trace amounts of chromium are green and are known as *emeralds;* blue-green beryl crystals are called *aquamarine.* The pure metal is prepared by electrolysis of a mixture of molten beryllium chloride and an alkali chloride (used to depress the melting point). Beryllium metal is used to prepare windows in x-ray tubes; it has the best mechanical properties of lighter elements, and light elements allow x-rays to penetrate them readily. Beryllium compounds are very poisonous.—*G. W. M.*

BERZELIUS, BARON JÖNS JAKOB, 1779–1848, Swedish chemist; b. Väfversunda Sörgård. Berzelius had wide scope, but his chief aim was the elucidation of the composition of chemical compounds through study of atomic theory and the law of multiple proportions. He improved the blowpipe method of chemical analysis; discovered cerium (1803), sele-

Baron Jöns Jakob Berzelius
(Smithsonian Institution)

nium (1817), and thorium (1828); determined the atomic and molecular weights of many substances, used oxygen as a standard or basis of reference for the atomic weights of other substances, developed Lavoisier's dualistic theory, and introduced the present notation for writing chemical symbols and formulas. He published much on mineralogy and chemistry, including his famous book on use of the blowpipe in chemical analysis.—*S. B.*

BESSEL, FRIEDRICH WILHELM, 1784–1846, German astronomer; b. Minden. In 1804 he calculated the orbit of Halley's comet from observations by Thomas Harriot in 1607. He supervised the construction of an observatory at Königsberg and directed it from its completion in 1813 until his death. His catalog of 3,222 stars was published in *Fundamenta Astronomiae* in 1818. His uniform system for reducing observations is still in use. He corrected the length of the seconds pendulum, measured an arc of the meridian in E Prussia and deduced an ellipticity of 1/299 for Earth, determined the first authentic parallax of a star—O".31 for 61 Cygni—and discovered the binary character of Sirius and Procyon. At the time of his death he was preparing to attack the problem later solved by the discovery of NEPTUNE. Modern astronomy as a precise science dates largely from Bessel, who also enlarged mathematical analysis by the introduction of Bessel functions. He was a fellow of the Royal Society.—*H. C.*

BESSEMER, SIR HENRY, 1813–98, English engineer and inventor; b. Charlton. He invented the BESSEMER PROCESS for manufacturing steel at greatly reduced cost, obtaining the first patent in 1855. In 1859 he erected in Sheffield steelworks which are still producing. Within five years the process was in use throughout the world. He patented 114 inventions in all, ranging from perforated dies for defacing used tax stamps to a ship containing an always-level room. His *Autobiography,* with a concluding chapter by his son, appeared in 1924. He was a fellow of the Royal Society.—*S. B.*

Sir Henry Bessemer
(N. Y. Public Library)

BESSEMER PROCESS: an industrial process by which pig iron is converted into steel. It was developed and introduced in 1858 by Henry Bessemer, an Englishman. Molten pig iron is charged to a tiltable, pear-shaped vessel called the converter, which is lined with a silica refractory, has a set of air inlets at the bottom, and ranges in capacity from 15 to 30 tons, approximately. Air is blown through the molten metal, burning the carbon, manganese, and silicon to the desired low levels in a period of about 15 min. The heat of combustion of these elements is sufficient to keep the charge molten. During the "blow," a spectacular plume of flame emerges from the mouth of the converter. When the conversion is completed, the converter is tilted downward to pour the steel into ladles or ingot molds.

The Bessemer process, run in this manner, does not reduce any phosphorus or sulfur that may be present in the pig iron. To eliminate these impurities further refining, usually in an open-hearth furnace, is necessary.

The Bessemer converter, fitted with a basic refractory lining instead of the acid silica, is used also in the Thomas-Gilchrist process for steelmaking (see STEEL). Although the Bessemer process is important as one of the first inexpensive methods of making steel in quantity, at present most steel in the U. S. A. is made in open-hearth furnaces.—*A. M. S.*

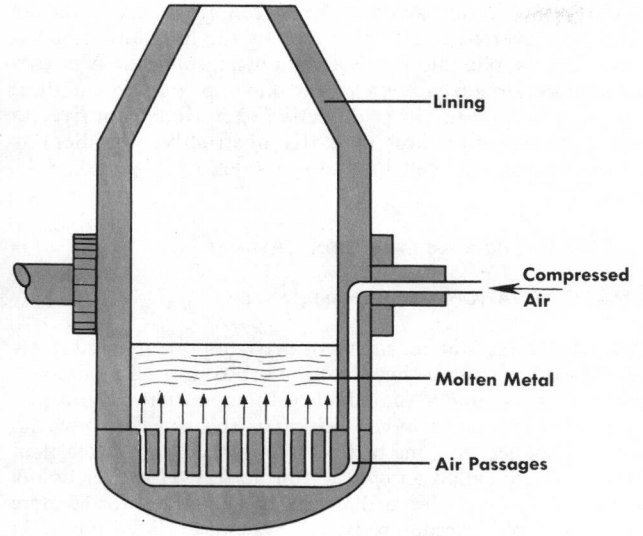

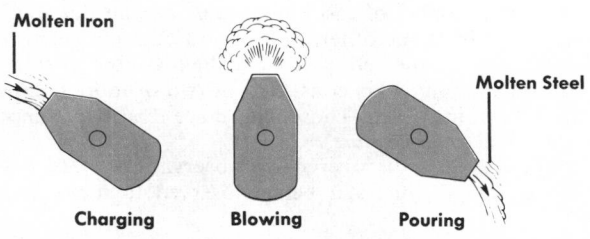

Bessemer converter: Air is forced into vessel through holes in bottom and passed through the charge of molten pig iron. Depending upon size of converter, 12 to 30 tons of steel can be made in a 12- to 20-minute blow. Diagrams show cross section of converter and positions for charging, blowing, and pouring. Photo shows blowing. (*Bethlehem Steel*)

BETA OXIDATION: a process described in a theory advanced by F. Knoop, in 1905, to explain the oxidation of fatty acids. It was supposed that an acid (*e.g.* hexanoic acid) is first oxidized at the carbon atom in the beta position (*i.e.* next but one to the carboxyl group), followed by cleavage of the carbon chain:

$$CH_3—CH_2—CH_2—\overset{\beta}{C}H_2—\overset{\alpha}{C}H_2—COOH$$

$$\downarrow$$

$$CH_3—CH_2—CH_2—CO—CH_2—COOH$$

$$\downarrow$$

$$CH_3—CH_2—CH_2—COOH + \text{oxidation products}$$

$$\downarrow$$

$$CH_3—CO—CH_2—COOH$$
(Aceto-acetic Acid)

In this way aceto-acetic acid could arise from fatty acids. In general, this is the way fatty acids are oxidized, although the details are different for each acid (see ENZYMES; FAT METABOLISM).—*K. H.*

BETA RAYS: see ALPHA, BETA, AND GAMMA RAYS.

BETATRON: see PARTICLE ACCELERATOR.

BETELGEUSE (α Orionis): the brightest star in the constellation Orion; its apparent visual magnitude varies from about 0.4 to 1.3, this variation being due to a pulsation of the star. The pulsation has been measured directly with the stellar interferometer; the radius of the star varies between 300 and 420 times the Sun's, so that at its greatest extension the star's radius is greater than the radius of the orbit of Mars about the Sun. The star is 500 lt-yr away, and is an intrinsically bright star, its luminosity being 17,000 times the Sun's. The surface temperature is low, about 5,400°F; the star is therefore a red supergiant, its spectrum showing bands due to simple molecules such as titanium oxide. Betelgeuse is on the meridian at midnight about Dec. 20.—*M. W. O.*

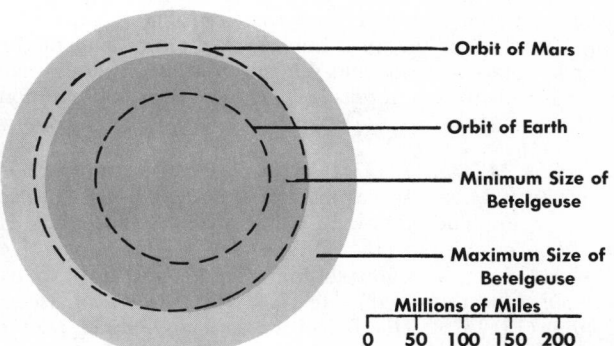

Red supergiant: Betelgeuse in its expanded phase has a radius greater than the distance of Mars from the Sun.

BETHE, HANS ALBRECHT, 1906–   , German-U. S. physicist; b. Strasbourg. He has done research in quantum electrodynamics, quantum theory of atoms and collisions, and theory of metals, atomic nuclei, and mesons. His work on energy production in stars led to discovery of the CARBON CYCLE, by which stars convert hydrogen into helium. He has been professor of physics at Cornell Univ. since 1937. He is a fellow of the Royal Society and a member of the National Academy of Sciences.—*D. H. D. R.*

BET THEORY: in physical chemistry, a theory proposed by Stephen Paul *B*runauer, Paul *E*mmet and Edward *T*eller, concerning the adsorption of gases, especially the relationship between the volume of gas adsorbed and the pressure of the gas above the adsorbent, at constant temperature. The BET equation expressing the above relationship can be used to compute surface areas of solids from the quantities of gas they are capable of adsorbing. The BET theory suggests that adsorption is similar to condensation of vapor to a liquid. The adsorbed layers of vapor are multimolecular rather than unimolecular.—*T. M. and C. S.*

BEVATRON: see PARTICLE ACCELERATOR.

BICHAT, MARIE FRANÇOIS XAVIER, 1771–1802, French anatomist; b. Jura. He introduced the concept of tissue and distinguished 21 kinds of tissue in the body. His major works were *Traité des membranes* (1800), *Sur la vie et la mort* (1800), and *Anatomie générale* (1801).—*D. H. D. R.*

BIENNIAL: a plant that flowers and fruits during its second year of life, then dies. It completes its life cycle in 2 yr, or less than 2 yr but more than one. Familiar biennial plants are carrots and beets. These and other biennials grow vegetatively for two seasons. During the second season reproduction occurs. A plant that completes its life cycle in one season is an ANNUAL; one that lives many years is a PERENNIAL.—*W. Ko.*

BIG-BANG HYPOTHESIS: the assumption that the universe started as a huge explosion from a highly condensed state. The motion of expansion inferred from the RED SHIFT OF GALAXIES suggests an early, very dense state of the universe in rapid expansion, slowed down since by gravitation. An explosion ("big bang") seems the only event that could have overcome the enormous gravitational force that held the original dense material together. Evidence of this explosion is sought in existing "fossil" remains. Elements heavier than helium were thought to be such remains until modern theory showed that their build-up is currently taking place in stars. Lemaître's model of the universe suggests that the heaviest cosmic rays were produced in the "big bang," and that the clusters of galaxies owe their origin to turbulence caused by the rapid expansion that followed the explosion. The STEADY-STATE THEORY, which is the most important alternative to the big-bang hypothesis, has serious difficulties in reconciling its consequences with the results of several recent observations. —*H. B.*

BIGELOW, JACOB, 1786/7–1879, U. S. physician and botanist; b. Sudbury, Mass. He was the first American botanist to collect New England plants and systematize his collections. His *Florula Bostoniensis* (1814), expanded to encompass New England flora, was the standard handbook until Gray's *Manual* appeared (1848). He also wrote *American Medical Botany* (1817–20). His *Discourse on Self-Limited Diseases* (1835), protesting excessive medical treatments, had a strong influence of U. S. medical practice.—*D. H. D. R.*

BILE ACIDS: a group of steroid acids derived from cholesterol; they are made by the liver and carried to the intestine through the bile ducts. They act as emulsifiers for fats and fat-soluble vitamins and thus aid in the absorption of these compounds; the acids are reabsorbed to a large extent. Typical bile acids are cholic acid, deoxycholic acid, and glycocholic acid and taurocholic acid; the latter two have the carboxyl groups conjugated to the amino groups of the amino acids glycine and taurine. Cholic acid is administered orally to stimulate production of bile by the liver. See FAT METABOLISM.—*J. F. S.*

BILE PIGMENTS: the excretory products of the heme portion of hemoglobin. They consist of a chain of four pyrrole rings linked by methylene bridges. The human red cell lives about 4 months, and on its death the hemoglobin content is split. The iron and amino acids of the globin are re-used, but the heme is converted to bile pigments by the liver and then excreted via the bile into the feces. An increase in bile pigments in the blood stream causes a yellow skin appearance (jaundice) and may be due to either defective excretion from liver to bile (cirrhosis, infectious hepatitis, obstructive jaundice) or an increase in red cell breakdown (hemolytic jaundice).—*J. F. S.*

BIMETALLIC STRIP: see EXPANSION, THERMAL.

BINARY NOTATION: see NUMBER SYSTEMS.

BINARY STAR: a star consisting of two components sufficiently close together so that they describe orbits around a common center of mass under the effect of their mutual gravitation. Two stars that appear very close in the sky but have no physical connection (one being much farther from Earth than the other) are called an *optical* double star. However, many more close pairs are seen than can be accounted for as mere optical doubles; some are true, physically related pairs. At the end of the 18th cent., Sir William Herschel discovered that, in a number of cases of close pairs, one star was in fact moving about the other, in a period of some years. Such a physically connected pair he called a binary star. Since Herschel, many stars consisting of two or more components have been identified. Those with more than two components are called *multiple stars.*

Binary stars discovered by observation as two distinct stellar images, one star being observed to move about the

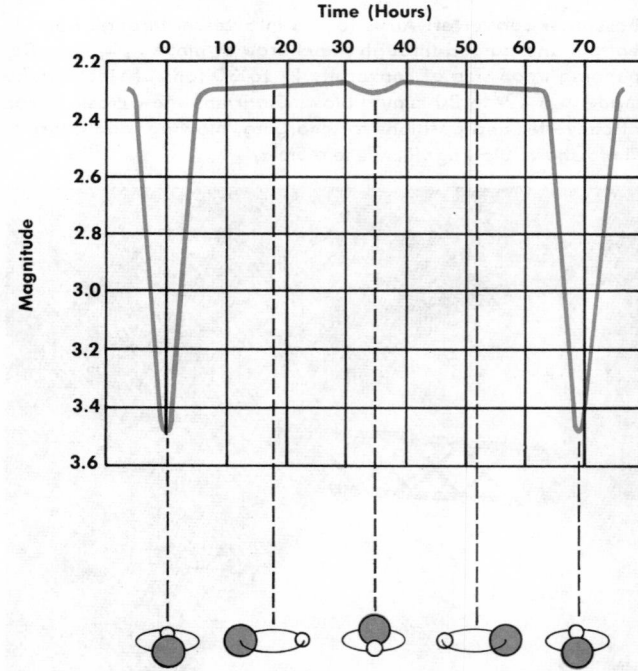

Light variations in binary star: When the less luminous component eclipses the brighter one, there is a sharp drop in amount of light noted by observer on Earth. When brighter component eclipses the fainter one, the drop is slight. The curve illustrated here is that of the star Algol (β Persei).

other, are called *visual double stars.* In such a system, both stars are moving about their common center of gravity. In practice, we cannot measure the motion of both stars of a pair, relative to the background of stars, but we can measure the motion of one about the other. This motion obeys Kepler's Laws, the relative orbit being an ellipse with the other star at one focus. From a series of observations, at different times, of the angular separation of the two stars in the sky, and the position angle of one with respect to the other, we can determine an apparent orbit. This may appear as an ellipse, or even a straight line if the orbit is tilted to the line of sight and seen in projection. The eccentricity and orientation of the true relative orbit can be found from the apparent orbit, and so can its semimajor axis in seconds of arc. The actual size, in miles, of the relative orbit can be found only if the parallax of the system is known. If the masses of the two stars are m_1 and m_2 (with the Sun's mass as unit), the period of the relative orbit P yr, the angular size of the semimajor axis a'', and the parallax of the system p'', then Kepler's third law tells us that $(m_1 + m_2) = a^3/P^2p^3$. If the value of p is known, the combined mass of the binary star can be found. On the average, the combined mass of binary systems is about 2 solar masses. For a star whose parallax is not known, we may assume that $(m_1 + m_2) = 2$, and calculate p. Such parallaxes are called dynamical parallaxes, and while individually unreliable, are of importance in statistical investigations of large numbers of double stars.

A close binary star that appears as single in the telescope may be revealed as a double by the spectroscope; it is a *spectroscopic binary star.* When the two stars are moving across the observer's line of sight, Doppler effect on the lines of their spectra is zero, and the two spectra exactly overlap. At some later time one star will be moving toward the observer, and the other star away from him; then the lines pertaining to the former are shifted to the blue, while those of the other star are shifted to the red. (These shifts are in addition to any common shift due to radial velocity of the system as a whole.) Thus, in the combined spectrum, the lines are sometimes single and sometimes double, indicating the duplicity of the apparently single star. In some cases, only one spectrum is visible (the other being too faint), but the periodic shift of the lines still reveals the duplicity. When both spectra are visible, the relative sizes of the orbits of the two stars about the center of gravity can be found, and hence the ratio of the masses of the two stars, but the inclination of the orbit to the line of sight (and hence the true sizes of the orbits, and the sum of the masses) cannot be found. The individual masses can be determined only if the inclination to the line of sight is known. This would be so if the star were also a visual double star, but in practice spectroscopic binaries are close, fast-moving pairs, while visual binaries are widely separated, slowly moving pairs. In only about a score of cases are the binaries observable both visually and spectroscopically.

The star Algol (Beta Persei) was observed by Montanari in 1670 to be variable. In 1783 John Goodricke suggested that the variation was due to the regular passage of a dark body in front of Algol. This suggestion was confirmed spectroscopically in 1889, when Vogel showed that it is a spectroscopic binary star whose orbit lies in the line of sight, so that the two stars periodically eclipse each other, as seen from Earth. Thus an *eclipsing binary star* (of which over 1,000 are now known) is physically the same as a spectroscopic binary star, but by geometric accident it can show mutual eclipses. The diagram at left shows the light curve of Beta Persei. The analysis of such a light curve, together with spectroscopic observations, can yield the individual masses of the component stars, as well as their physical dimensions.

Systems are known with more than two components. Algol itself has a third component. The star Zeta Cancri is a quadruplet system, consisting of a pair of stars about 5″ apart, the brighter one of which is a close visual double itself; regular variations of the position of the third star show that it has a faint companion. The star Epsilon Lyrae is called "the double double." To the naked eye, the star appears single, but with a pair of binoculars the star is seen double. With a telescope, each of the components appears again as a double: we see a system of four physically connected stars, in two pairs. One of the four is also a spectroscopic binary, so that the system is really a quintuplet. Castor (Alpha Geminorum) has three components, each of which is a spectroscopic binary: Castor is a sextuplet.—*M. W. O.*

About 40% of the stars in the Sun's neighborhood are double or multiple systems. The shortest known period is 0.2 day, in an eclipsing binary; the longest is of the order of 10 million yr, in a visual system. Separation of the components ranges from near contact to about 44,000 times the Earth-Sun distance. These double and multiple systems did not result from capture of a passing star by the gravitational attraction of another, nor by fission of an original star. Their components were born together, presumably by a condensation of gas and dust, and have been gravitationally bound since they were formed.—*S. D. G.*

BINARY SYSTEM: see COMPUTER; NUMBER SYSTEMS.

BINDING ENERGY: a concept that accounts for the stability of atomic nuclei or of atoms in general. In developing the special theory of RELATIVITY (1905), Einstein concluded that the mass of a single particle is not an invariable quantity, but increases as the velocity (or the kinetic energy) of the particle increases. From this arose the more general notion that mass may be transformed into energy in other forms; *e.g.* a system may lose mass and thereby gain kinetic energy. In such circumstances, if the amount of mass lost is represented by m, and the amount of kinetic energy gained by E, then $E = mc^2$, where c represents the velocity of light in vacuum. Loss of mass of only 1 mg, in these circumstances, involves gain of kinetic energy of 9×10^{17} ergs, or 9×10^{10} j, or about 2×10^7 kcal. A relatively minute disappearance of mass thus involves a relatively enormous release of energy.

An ATOM consists of a single nucleus, made up of protons and neutrons, surrounded by extranuclear electrons. Atomic nuclei can be classified as stable or unstable (radioactive). A stable nucleus will remain unchanged forever, if no energy is supplied to it. The mass of such a nucleus must be less than the sum of the masses of all the neutrons and protons that it contains, because energy must have been liberated when these particles coalesced to form the nucleus, in the first instance, and the mass equivalent of that energy must have disappeared. This energy, which is released when a nucleus is formed out of its constituent particles (or which must be supplied if the nucleus is to be broken down into its constituents), is referred to as the *total binding energy* of the nucleus. The amount of energy that must be supplied if a single neutron (or proton) is to be ejected from a nucleus is referred to as the binding energy of that neutron (or proton) in the nucleus. Similarly, the amount of energy that must be supplied if a single electron is to be ejected from an atom is referred to as the binding energy of that electron in the atom.

A radioactive (unstable) nucleus differs from a stable nucleus only in that the binding energy of the emitted particle is a negative quantity. If, for example, a nucleus of uranium[238] has energy available for the emission of an alpha particle (which is the case), then the binding energy of the alpha particle in the nucleus must be negative. But the total binding

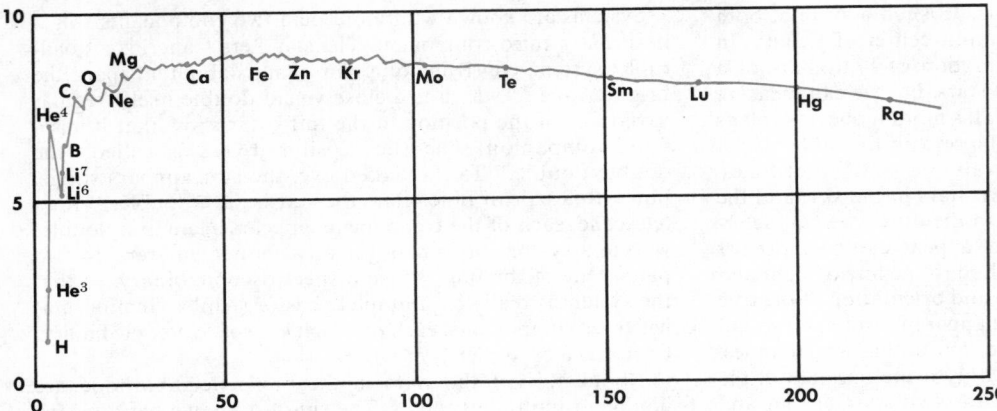

Nuclei, composed of nucleons (protons and neutrons), are difficult to break up. In these curves the binding energy per nucleon is plotted against the number of nucleons (the mass number) of the successive elements. Large jump at far left represents the alpha particle, He^4, a tight little package with a total binding energy of 28 Mev, or 7 Mev/nucleon.

energy of the radioactive nucleus is a positive quantity, as it is for a stable nucleus. See ATOMIC NUCLEUS; NUCLEAR PHYSICS; RADIOACTIVITY.

Binding energy is a useful concept for any "bound" system of objects, being the energy required to separate the constituents of the system. Our binding energy to the earth, for example, is the energy that would be required to enable us to escape from the earth's gravitational attraction into "outer space."—*N. F.*

BINOCULARS: in general, an optical instrument employing two low-power terrestrial TELESCOPES mounted on the same frame. As with the telescope, the purpose of binoculars is to gather more light than the eye can, and to magnify the object observed. In good binoculars each of the telescope units can be focused separately, and in many such instruments there is also a screw device for simultaneous changing of the focus of the units after the observer has adjusted each according to the peculiar requirements of his own vision. Because of the need for additional inverting and reversing lenses and for long-focus objectives (for higher instrument power), conven-

tional field glasses have been largely replaced by prism binoculars. The two internally reflecting right-angle prisms of the latter provide an erect image and, in addition, make possible a shorter tube length by "folding" the path of the light. The wider separation of the objective lenses in prism binoculars also serves to increase the binocular, or "stereo," effect, and thus permits more accurate judgment of distance by enhancing depth perception. See OPTICAL INSTRUMENTS.—*A. E.*

BINOMIAL THEOREM: A binomial is a mathematical expression containing two terms, as $(a + b)$ or $(x^2 + 1)$. The binomial theorem, which is proved in algebra, is of especial importance in probability and in statistics. It is the generalization of the expansion of integral powers of a binomial, such as $(a + b)^2 = a^2 + 2ab + b^2$; $(a + b)^3 = a^3 + 3a^2b + 3ab^2 + b^3$. A general statement of this theorem can be summarized in the formula

$$(a + b)^n = \sum_{r=0}^{n} \frac{n!}{r!\,(n-r)!}\, a^r b^{n-r}$$

The binomial coefficients $n!/[r!\,(n-r)!]$ are abbreviated

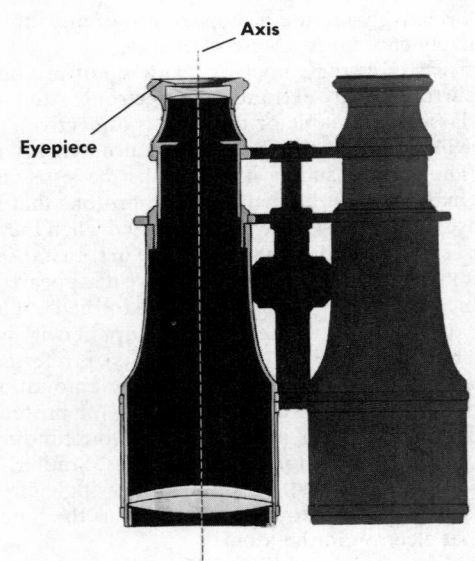

A simple field glass (*left*) consists of two small telescopes mounted with their axes parallel and about as far apart as the pupils of the user's eyes. Neither telescope has more than two compound

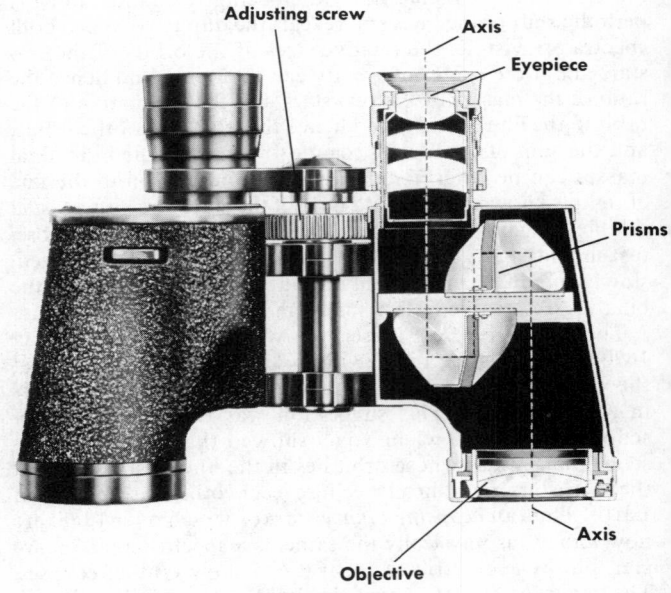

lenses. **Prism binoculars** (*right*) achieve long effective focal length by folding of light paths. Placing objectives farther apart than eyepieces enhances stereoscopic effect in viewing. (*Bausch & Lomb*)

by $_nC_r$, $\binom{n}{r}$, C (n, r), or C_r^n. They are the number of combinations of n things r at a time, and hence represent the number of samples of size r that can be selected from a population of size n. (The symbol $n!$ means $1 \cdot 2 \cdot 3 \cdots \cdots n$; for example, $3! = 3 \cdot 2 \cdot 1 = 6$.) The following is an example of the use of the formula:

$$(a + b)^4$$
$$= {_4C_0}a^4b^0 + {_4C_1}a^3b^1 + {_4C_2}a^2b^2 + {_4C_3}a^1b^3 + {_4C_4}a^0b^4$$

$${_4C_0} = \frac{4!}{0! \ 4!} = \frac{4!}{4!} = 1, \text{ since } 0! = 1, \text{ by definition}$$

$${_4C_1} = \frac{4!}{1! \ 3!} = \frac{4 \cdot 3 \cdot 2 \cdot 1}{1 \cdot 3 \cdot 2 \cdot 1} = 4$$

$${_4C_2} = \frac{4!}{2! \ 2!} = \frac{4 \cdot 3 \cdot 2 \cdot 1}{2 \cdot 1 \cdot 2 \cdot 1} = 6$$

$${_4C_3} = \frac{4!}{3! \ 1!} = {_4C_1} = 4$$

$${_4C_4} = \frac{4!}{4! \ 0!} = {_4C_0} = 1$$

Using these, and the fact that $b^0 = 1 = a^0$, we have

$$(a + b)^4 = a^4 + 4a^3b + 6a^2b^2 + 4ab^3 + b^4.$$

If p is the probability in favor of the occurrence of an event, and $q = 1 - p$ is the probability against the occurrence of an event, the terms of the binomial $(p + q)^n$ give all the probabilities associated with the repetition of the event n times. Thus, if three items are selected at random from a production line, where the probability of a defective item is p and the probability of a satisfactory item is q, the probabilities of 3, 2, 1, 0 defective items are the terms of the binomial $(p + q)^3$; that is, p^3, $3p^2q$, $3pq^2$; q^3. (See also STATISTICS.)

The coefficients of the successive powers of a binomial can be arranged in a table called *Pascal's triangle*. Each number in the table is the sum of the two adjacent numbers on the line above it. The binomial coefficients for, say, $n = 5$ are, in order, 1, 5, 10, 10, 5, 1.

$n = 0$						1						
$n = 1$					1		1					
$n = 2$					1	2	1					
$n = 3$				1		3	3		1			
$n = 4$			1		4	6	4		1			
$n = 5$		1		5	10	10	5		1			
$n = 6$	1		6	15	20	15	6		1			

—H. E. W.

BIOCHEMICAL GENETICS: a branch of science that applies the modern advances in knowledge of large molecules with biological function (*e.g.* DEOXYRIBONUCLEIC ACID, "DNA") to an elucidation of the classical laws of inheritance. This field of investigation comprises studies of the chemical nature and structure of DNA and the biological expressions of the gene action in terms of protein composition and enzyme activity. The basic unit of biochemical genetic research is the CHROMOSOME. Chromosomes, which contain thousands of genes in sequence, consist of DNA bound to protein. These macromolecules, which are long, paired strands containing a sequence of purine and pyrimidine bases attached to sugar and phosphate, are able to replicate themselves, so that when a chromosome yields two daughter chromosomes during cell division, each is identical with the parent in the nature and arrangement of its complement of genes. The deoxyribonucleic acids of the cell nucleus direct the biosynthesis of ribonucleic acids, which in turn control and guide the biosynthesis of the thousands of different protein molecules present in each cell. The genetic information contained in the specific patterns of arrangement of the components of the deoxyribonucleic acids in the chromosomes is thus expressed in the patterns of enzymes and other proteins the cell carries. When one of the genes on a chromosome in a cell is altered or destroyed by radiation or other influences, the enzyme and protein pattern of the cells derived from that cell changes accordingly. Research in the bread mold *Neurospora crassa* and in other biological systems has shown that each enzyme in a cell is controlled by one gene. A change in a single gene can cause the disappearance of an enzyme or an alteration in a protein molecule so that a normal metabolic reaction can no longer take place. An increasing number of hereditary diseases in man are being recognized and defined in terms of the biochemical defect caused by the genetic defect. See CHROMOSOMES AND GENES; HEREDITY; METABOLISM.—*E. H.*

BIOCHEMISTRY: that branch of science which deals with the chemical transformation of inorganic and organic compounds by living organisms—or, more specifically, with the interaction of a cell or an organism with its chemical environment and the transformation of the elements of this environment into its specific biological needs. Biochemistry thus forms a link between organic chemistry (dealing with the micro-world of

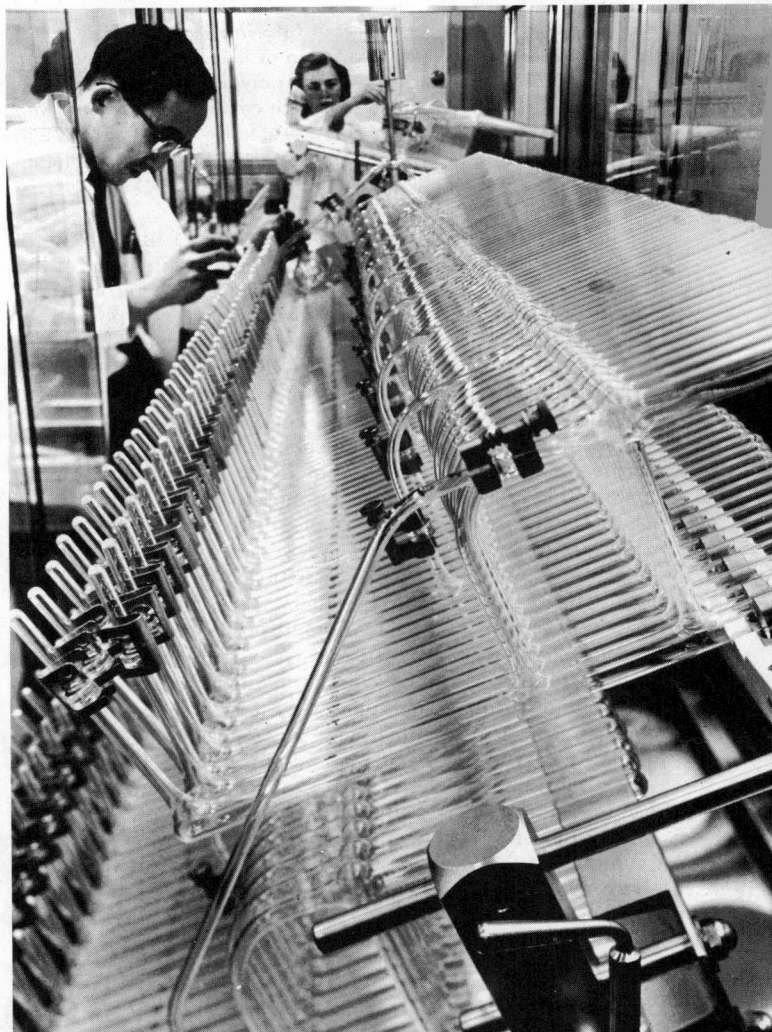

A counter current separator is prepared for tests in separations laboratory of a medical research center. Multitubular device is used to separate mixtures of antibiotics, steroids, and other medicinal compounds. (*Pfizer*)

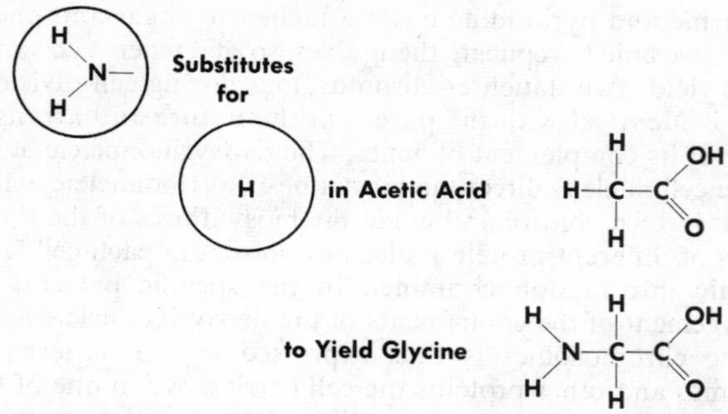

Substitutes for

H   in Acetic Acid

to Yield Glycine

Fundamental to living organisms are proteins. These, in turn, are made up of amino acids, which can be thought of as carboxylic acids in which one hydrogen atom has been replaced by an amino group, NH₂. In the above diagram, a hydrogen atom in acetic acid is displaced by an amino group to form glycine, the simplest of the amino acids.

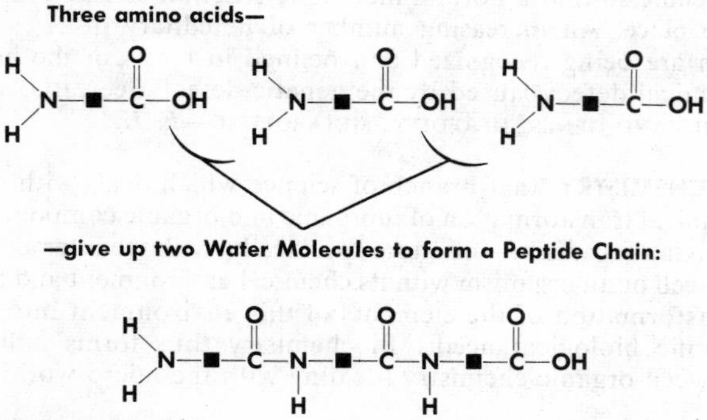

Three amino acids—

—give up two Water Molecules to form a Peptide Chain:

Investigations of Emil Fischer, in opening years of 20th cent., made it clear that the amino acids in proteins are combined into long strands. These are known as polypeptide chains. In the example above, three amino acids are condensed together, with elimination of water, to form a representative polypeptide chain. (Black squares represent groupings that would vary with the individual amino acids involved.)

molecules) and physiology (dealing with the functioning of the whole organism). Essentially, it is the measurement of the compounds that are taken in and given off by an organism and the tracing of what happens to these compounds in between. Among the most fundamental aspects of biochemistry is the study of the energy cycle of living systems. All organisms, from small, simple ones like bacteria to huge, complex ones like whales, require energy to exist, to grow, and to reproduce themselves. This energy is obtained in various forms: plants use the energy in light; bacteria use simple chemical compounds such as ammonia and carbon dioxide; and animals use complex substances which they obtain from plants or other animals. The processes of building up the compounds which constitute the tissues of plants and animals (anabolism) and of breaking them down to obtain energy (catabolism) are collectively termed METABOLISM.

With light as the source of energy, and with carbon dioxide and various compounds containing nitrogen, phosphorus, sulfur, and various metals as raw material, plants are able to synthesize their own constituent substances—carbohydrates, proteins, fats, nucleic acids, and so on. Some of these compounds are later broken down, or oxidized, to supply energy for the plant when sunlight is absent. Animals, by eating plants, obtain energy in the form of plant-synthesized compounds. But they are unable to utilize this energy, originally derived from sunlight, without an additional process of oxida-

tion. Animals are also unable to utilize plant compounds directly to build tissue; they must break down the larger, complex plant compounds (carbohydrates, fats, proteins, nucleic acids), which are specific for plants, into smaller molecules; these constituents are then re-formed into larger molecules which are specific for the particular animal. Thus, plant carbohydrates, *e.g.* starch, are broken down to simple sugars such as glucose; the simple sugar molecules are then synthesized by the animal to glycogen, or animal starch. The many different kinds of plant proteins are broken down to their constituent amino acids, from which animals synthesize their own individual, specific proteins. Fats and nucleic acids are treated similarly. All cells of all organisms, plant or animal, are alike in the way they handle the compounds listed above.

Hundreds of organic chemical compounds are thus transformed by organisms, and every such transformation is catalyzed by certain specialized proteins called ENZYMES. If there is a real distinction between the living and the non-living, it is the presence of these extremely efficient catalysts, which, in very small amounts, can cause the rapid transformation of one chemical compound to another without themselves being changed in the process, and without the need of an external source of energy, *e.g.* heat. Enzymes are specific; that is, a certain enzyme will catalyze only one type of chemical reaction—in most cases, only one particular reaction. They can split large molecules in two—or synthesize them from smaller ones; they can oxidize or reduce a compound; they can split off specific atoms or groups (*e.g.* phosphates, sulfates, water, carbon dioxide) from a molecule, or add them to it. The study of enzymatic reactions, their mechanism of operation, and the compounds affected is an important branch of biochemistry.

Also belonging to biochemistry is the study of how, chemically, cells reproduce themselves exactly. Cells obviously differ from one another in structure and function; chemically, the difference appears to lie not only in the particular enzymes present but in the way they are organized into the cell structure and made to produce specific larger molecules, *e.g.* proteins and nucleic acids. The heredity of a cell thus apparently

Antibiotic action: A characteristic zone of bacterial inhibition surrounds these colonies of *Penicillium notatum,* a variety of sac fungi. This action, noted by Alexander Fleming in the late 1920s, led to his discovery of Penicillin. (*Merck, Sharp & Dohme*)

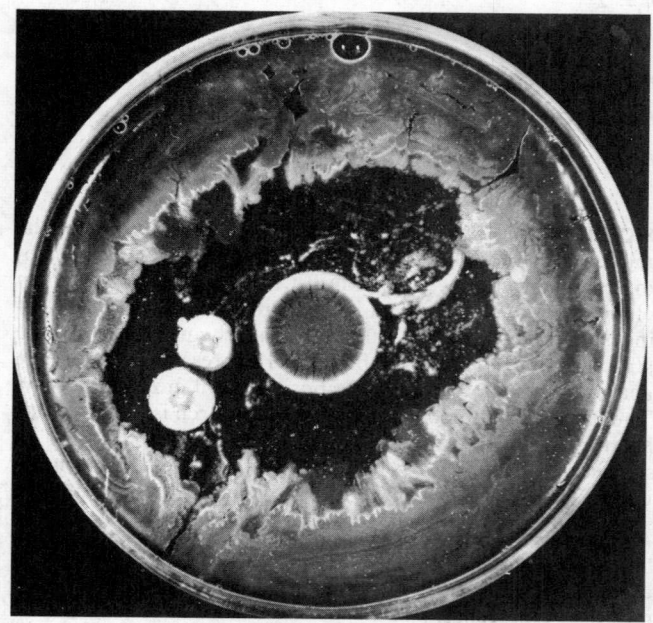

Microbiology: Freeze-dried bacterial cultures can be preserved in a dormant state indefinitely. (*Pfizer*)

Pharmacology: Vehicles and concentrations are determined for new drugs about to be tested. (*Nat. Institutes of Health*)

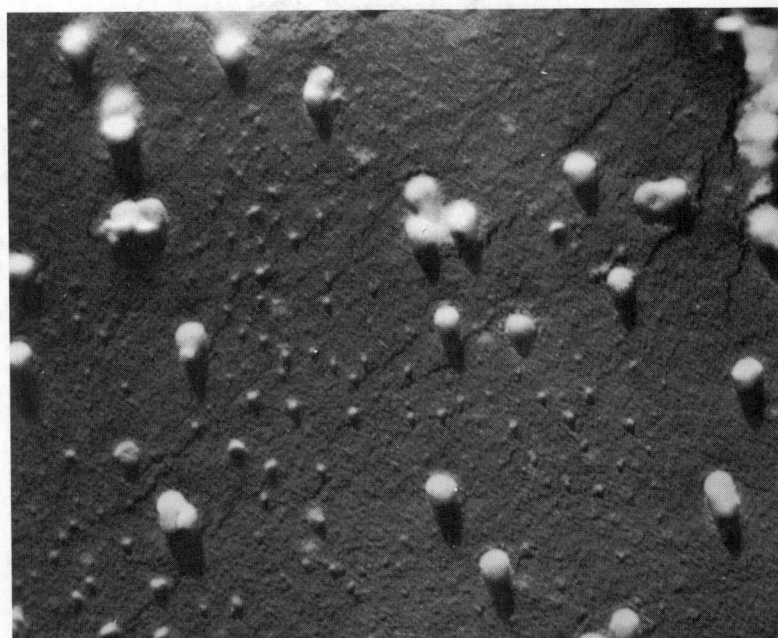

Virus particles: Individual balls of influenza virus can be studied under the electron microscope by allowing them to attach themselves to the surface membrane of red blood cells; they have a diameter of 100 millimicrons. (*Nat. Institutes of Health*)

lies in the genetic "information" which directs it to produce those enzymes which catalyze certain specific reactions. All but the simplest organisms are composed of many cells of differing structure and function, *e.g.* muscle, liver, and kidney cells. These diverse cells must be coordinated if the organism is to function as an integrated whole. Biochemistry includes the study of how the activities of the various cells of an organism are coordinated chemically, by means of hormones and other secretions.

The many other aspects of this science include study of the means by which specific chemical compounds get inside cells and of how certain chemicals are secreted by cells; the chemical and physical processes that take place when a muscle contracts; the transmission of nerve impulses; the mechanism of the storing of biological energy by cells; how many different kinds of cells may be produced from one cell in development; the causes of aging in cells; the way in which information for replication is transmitted from mother cell to daughter cell.

The history of biochemistry begins with the isolation from natural sources of many simple chemical compounds by C. W. Scheele (1742–86). J. J. Berzelius (1779–1848) and J. von Liebig (1803–73) extended this work, introducing quantitative elementary chemical analysis in their study of organic compounds. This *descriptive biochemistry* reached its high point in the work of Emil Fischer (1852–1919), who isolated, analyzed, and obtained the chemical formulas of hundreds of compounds, which he classified as fats, sugars, and amino acids. The basis of *dynamic biochemistry* was laid by the work of A. L. Lavoisier (1743–94), who formulated the present concept of oxidation, respiration, and the biological production of heat, 1780. E. F. W. Pflüger (1829–1910) extended this concept by showing that cells in tissues are responsible for this oxidation and heat; thus he started the branch of biochemistry known as *intermediary metabolism*. At the same time, T. Schwann (1810–82) and W. Kühne (1837–1900) began the study of the digestive enzymes. Since 1930, many investigators have elucidated distinct enzymatic steps involved in the breakdown of food into smaller molecules and the resynthesis of larger molecules from these. Many of these steps are now well known; the process of the biological production of energy is on the way to being solved. Still to be discovered are the means whereby all the enzymatic steps are integrated into the dynamic states of living cells; how the transformations of small molecules lead to changes in cell structure and function; and, finally, how biological information is chemically transferred to successive generations of cells.—*P. S.*

BIOCLIMATOLOGY: the study of the effects of climate on animal and plant life. It is closely related to MICROCLIMATOLOGY; by its concern with studies of relationships such as heat exchange between living organisms and the atmosphere, it is of value in medicine and agriculture.—*P. L.*

BIOELECTRICITY: electrical phenomena occurring in living things. Sensitive measuring devices can detect small differences of ELECTRIC POTENTIAL between different parts of any animal or plant. These small differences, amounting to only a few thousandths of a volt (*i.e.* a few millivolts, or mv), are often related to differences in metabolic rate or growth rate of the parts concerned. Larger potential differences, from 10

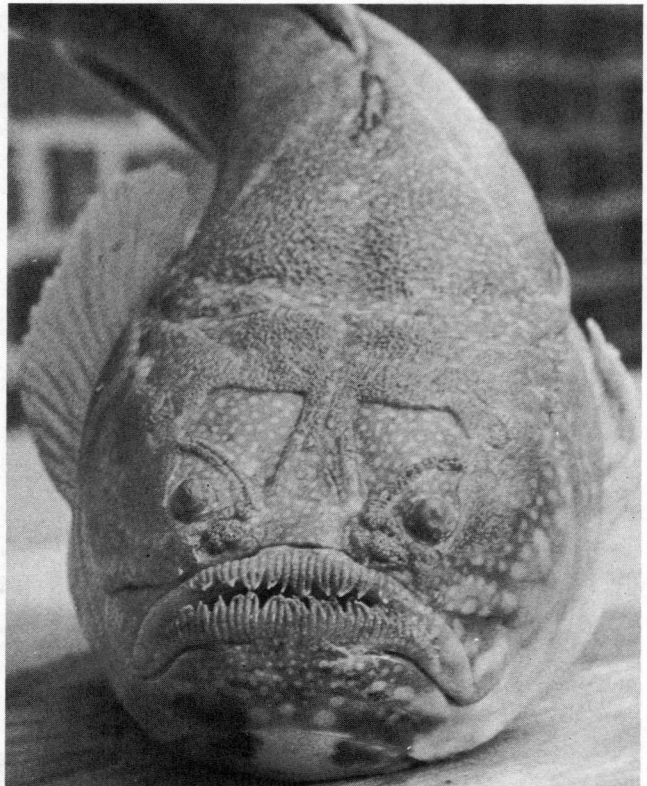

Stargazer, or Electric Toad (*Astroscopus guttatus*), which buries itself in sandy bottoms to ambush prey, can give a strong electric shock when touched in the area of its electric organs—the smooth, squarish areas behind the eyes. It is not known whether these organs are used for capture of food, self-defense, or both. (*Alice Mansueti*)

to 100 mv, can be measured across certain membranes in animals and plants: the wall of the stomach or intestine, the bladder wall of a toad or the skin of a frog, or the thin membrane which surrounds cells, especially nerve or muscle cells. These larger differences are associated with active transport, or "pumping," of electrically charged particles (ions) across the membrane; the ion most commonly pumped in animal membranes is sodium (Na$^+$), the positive ion or metallic constituent of common salt. When Na$^+$ is pumped across a membrane, it is separated from other ions such as chloride (Cl$^-$), and an unequal distribution of electric charge is produced; this leads to development of an electric potential. In nerve and muscle cells, the potential can be caused to change suddenly by an external stimulus. The potential change is called an "action potential," since it is associated with conduction of NERVOUS IMPULSES and leads to muscle contraction.

The largest electric potentials known in living things are found in the electric eel of South America. The eel's electric organs consist of some 6,000 units, each of which is a modified motor endplate (the structure across which a nerve impulse is transmitted to a muscle cell). The electric units are arranged in series, as one might arrange so many batteries. Each unit, when stimulated, develops a potential difference of about 100 mv; the whole organ may thus develop a potential of as much as 600 volts. When discharged, this amount of electricity can stun or kill fish and give a terrific shock to a man. Shocks of smaller voltage can be delivered by electric rays and certain African catfish.—*B. T. S.*

BIOGENESIS: the principle that all living matter must originate from other living matter and that, furthermore, an organism must have parents essentially similar to itself. The contrary theory (SPONTANEOUS GENERATION) that living matter can originate from inorganic material has been proved largely untrue, although the possibility of very simple organisms arising from nonliving material in early evolution has been supported in recent years by the biochemical experiments of H. Urey, S. L. Miller, and others. See LIFE, ORIGIN OF.—*J. M. P.*

BIOGEOGRAPHY: the study of the geographical distribution of animals and plants. There are distinctive Australasian, Paleotropical (African plus South Asian), Neotropical (Central and South American), and Holarctic (North Asian, European, and North American) realms. See PLANT GEOGRAPHY; ZOOGEOGRAPHY.—*L. and M. M.*

BIOLOGICAL ASSAY: the use of biological systems of various kinds for qualitative or quantitative determination of compounds. Biological assays are often more specific and sensitive than chemical assays; *e.g.* the presence of a few micrograms of an amino acid can be detected and determined, often without extensive purification, by using a bacterial strain which requires that substance for growth. The amount of growth is proportional to the amount of the amino acid.—*E. S.*

BIOLOGICAL NAME: the scientific name of an organism. It is made up of the name of the genus and the name of the species (see CLASSIFICATION OF LIVING THINGS). Both names are usually Latin or Greek or have classical endings. The genus name is always capitalized and given first, and both are either italicized or underlined. Since man belongs to a genus *Homo* and the species *sapiens* (meaning "wise"), he is called *Homo sapiens.* Other examples: *Canis familiaris,* dog; *Sternotherus odoratus,* musk turtle; *Felis leo,* lion; *Felis domestica,* common house cat; *Acer rubrum,* red maple. Occasionally a third name, referring to a subspecies or variety, is also used. The method of calling organisms by their generic and specific names is called "binomial nomenclature" and was first introduced systematically by Carolus Linnaeus (1707–78). It cleared up great confusion resulting from the use of a variety of common names for the same organism and has helped to point up the relationships among living things. Its usage is governed by an international commission.—*J. M. P.*

BIOLOGICAL RHYTHM: any regularly repeated pattern of activity in living things. Animals and plants are fundamentally rhythmic, and the rhythms are divisible into two groups. The first group contains such rhythms as brain waves, with many cycles per second, and heartbeat. These high-frequency rhythms are expressions of inherently periodic systems. The period lengths, timed by internal metabolic processes, are readily influenced by temperature and various chemical agents. The second group includes such relatively low-frequency rhythms as the daily rhythms of sleep and wakefulness in man and sleep movements of plant leaves; lunar tidal rhythms of activity of seashore-dwelling oysters and crabs; monthly, Moon phase-related reproductive rhythms of many marine organisms; and annual rhythms of growth and reproduction in numerous plants and animals. It is well known, for example, that the common fiddler crab regularly darkens its skin about sunrise and blanches near sunset; it runs most actively just before the time of low tide on its beach, and it rests, protected in its burrow, when the tide is high. This crab, therefore, displays simultaneously both solar-day and lunar-day rhythmic patterns. A small Pacific Coast fish, the grunion, swarms inshore to deposit eggs and sperm in the sand at water's edge at the exact time that monthly high tides are highest, indicating possession of extraordinarily timed Sun- and Moon-geared behavior patterns. Such rhythmic patterns clearly adapt the organisms to the rhythmic changes in their external physical environment. They parallel, or are simple multiples or fractions of, external geophysical rhythms such as daily light and temperature changes, lunar-day ocean tides, monthly change in nocturnal illumination, and seasonal changes in temperature and day-length. In fact, events in a daily biological rhythm are readily reset to any times of day by alteration of the time of light in the daily cycles, quite as normally would occur after a move to some different time zone. Tidal rhythms of feeding activity of seashore inhabitants are adaptively reset to local tidal times of a different beach. Such annual rhythms as plant flowering or bird migration may be reset to unnatural times of year by artificially altering the lengths of daily light periods, or photoperiods. (See PHOTOPERIODISM.)

Even when held in the laboratory in carefully controlled constancy of all known factors, organisms continue to display metabolic rhythmicity with all the earth's natural periods, ranging from day to year. Thus potato plants in unvarying light and temperature, and even under hermetic seal, have been shown to use oxygen more rapidly by day than by night, more rapidly at Moon's third quarter than at first quarter, and more rapidly in spring than in fall. In addition to metabolic rhythmicity, organisms often continue to repeat rhythmically, with close to natural periods, whatever specific daily or lunar behavioral patterns were impressed upon them by previous light, tidal, or "learning" experiences. The crabs' daily color and tidal running rhythms continue with accurate timing. Mice and rats may continue to exhibit their daily rhythm of nocturnal activity. Plants may continue to lower their leaves and close their flowers at night in their daily "sleep movements." Even long-stored dry seeds germinate more rapidly in late winter and spring than in late summer and fall. In brief, the organisms act as if they possessed resettable "clocks" with extraordinary properties for biological systems—*e.g.* accuracy uninfluenced by temperature and drugs. These clocks play an essential role in celestial navigation by such creatures as birds, fishes, insects and crustaceans (see ANIMAL NAVIGATION) and are perhaps also involved in the widespread response to photoperiod.

There are two hypotheses for the basic nature of these "clocks." One is that the timing is extrinsic, depending upon the same, as yet unidentified, physical forces responsible for the metabolic pulses geared to the earth's movements relative to Sun and Moon; the other is that timing is intrinsic, depending exclusively upon specialized metabolic oscillating systems. —*F. A. B.*

BIOLOGY: the study of living things. It first reached scientific form at the hands of Aristotle of Athens (384–322 B. C.),

"father of zoology," and his student Theophrastus of Eresus (*c.* 380–287 B. C.), "father of botany." Aristotle tried to organize the knowledge of his time and to add to it in relation to every kind of animal he examined. These, fortunately, include many he himself collected and others sent to him by his former student, Alexander the Great, from remote parts of the empire. Theophrastus began the earliest known botanic garden. The contribution of these two men was to regard knowledge of animals and plants as important for its own sake, rather than only in relation to uses as food and medicine.

Until the 16th cent., little new knowledge was added to what Aristotle and Theophrastus wrote, although their works were copied, translated, illustrated, misinterpreted, edited, and annotated throughout the Dark Ages until the originals, which had much accurate information, had become badly garbled. Then came the challenge of unfamiliar plants and animals as they were encountered by educated men from N Europe on Crusades to the Holy Land, and by explorers such as Christopher Columbus and Vasco da Gama. Through use of early MICROSCOPES, a whole new world in miniature was discovered, emphasizing anew the great breadth of biology. Many of the microbes had green coloring like plants, but moved about rapidly like animals. The plant and animal kingdoms were seen to be connected. Clearly a new summing-up was needed, particularly one in which some workable system would permit a clear and consistent international designation for each kind of creature. The Swedish naturalist-physician Carolus Linnaeus filled this great need with his books *Species Plantarum* (1753), on the plant kingdom, and *Systema Naturae,* 10th ed. (1758), on the animals. In these, for the first time, each kind of living thing known to Linnaeus received a two-part name, as well as a Latin description of its body structure. The name consisted of a generic and a specific term, *e.g. Pinus strobus,* the white pine; *Felis domestica,* the house cat; and *Homo sapiens,* modern man. Thereafter, with two words, a biologist anywhere could refer to a definite kind of living thing and feel confident that his discoveries concerning it would not be confused by biologists elsewhere, as had been true with earlier local methods of naming life forms. (See CLASSIFICATION OF LIVING THINGS; BIOLOGICAL NAME.)

In the century following, biologists all over the world busied themselves in collecting and classifying plants and animals. Museums grew important as storehouses of preserved specimens, and comparative anatomy became an important discipline as men searched for the differences by which species could be distinguished most reliably. Biology acquired a new dimension with the realization that FOSSILS offer a means for investigating the life of the past, including many kinds of extinct life (see PALEONTOLOGY).

A new idea which seemed dangerously heretical, presented during the 19th cent., turned biology into a battleground.

Like clockwork, when tides are highest, grunion spawn on California beaches. Riding ashore on wave, female burrows into sand tail first and lays eggs; male curls around female and releases sperms, which travel down her body and reach eggs. Fish are carried out by next big wave. Eggs hatch in time for young to enter water at following high tide in about two weeks. (*Moody Inst. of Science*)

First J. P. de Lamarck in Paris (1810), then A. R. Wallace in correspondence from the East Indies with Charles Darwin in London (1859), claimed that living things were changing slowly through EVOLUTION. Lamarck offered little real evidence and hazarded a poor explanation for the process causing the gradual change (see LAMARCKISM). Wallace presented only a limited collection of facts, mostly from memory, to support the same idea that Darwin held. Darwin, however, had spent 20 yr compiling an overwhelming array of evidence in support of his view that NATURAL SELECTION was constantly at work, weeding out the least well-adapted individuals in each population of living things, in a struggle for survival produced by chronic overproduction of new individuals by the regular processes of reproduction. Never before had so logical a theory been available to link together the fossil record, the anatomical findings, and the sequence of events in the development of embryo plants and animals, and to allow predictions about future discoveries—leading to countless new scientific investigations.

Not until the 20th cent. did virtually all biologists realize what a wonderfully unifying concept Darwin, Wallace, and Lamarck had provided. By then the hereditary mechanism that makes evolution possible had become known through the work of Gregor Mendel and others. All living things, from molds to men, follow the same basic principles in passing their inheritable characteristics from one generation to the next. Today, studies of the chemical basis for inheritance enable us to visualize a code concealed in a nucleic acid molecule at a specific site (the gene) within a chromosome of the nucleus in each living cell. This code, which is inheritable, serves as a blueprint for proteins that control the chemical reactions within the living substance. (See GENETICS; HEREDITY.) Other investigations of chemical processes in plants and animals have shed light on the way energy, which all life demands constantly, is passed along from molecule to molecule. These reaction pathways are known in considerable detail for complex activities such as photosynthesis, respiration, muscle contraction, nerve conduction, bioluminescence, and vision.

Along the borderline of life, viruses have been shown to simulate the reproduction process characteristic of living things by infecting living cells and inducing those cells to manufacture more virus molecules instead of substances important to the cells themselves. A virus is closely akin to a gene both in its chemical composition (being a nucleic acid) and in its blueprint-like ability to guide the chemical reactions of the living cell.

At the same time that some biologists have been probing into molecular dimensions, others have been placing new emphasis on plants and animals as communities living under measurable environmental conditions. The food relations between populations of animals and plants, and the dependence of terrestrial plants on soil and weather, have been receiving increased attention. Organisms living in the oceans, as well as many minute kinds that can be carried by air currents in the upper atmosphere, provide promising areas for investigation. Newer frontiers with entirely different organisms may appear as a result of space exploration. Meanwhile, on all levels—molecular, organismal, and ecological—discoveries are being sought and will undoubtedly be made. See BIOCHEMISTRY; BIOMETRY; BIOPHYSICS; BOTANY; ECOLOGY; LIFE; PLANT GEOGRAPHY; ZOOGEOGRAPHY; ZOOLOGY.—L. and M. M.

Firefly by day (*above*) is much like any other small beetle; by night (*below*), flashes from its abdomen help it find a mate. Five flashes made by a firefly over a reflector made this silhouette. (N. Y. Zoological Society)

BIOLUMINESCENCE: the production of almost heatless light by living things. A few representatives of almost every phylum of animals produce such light. Among plants, only certain bacteria and fungi are luminescent. Depending on species, color of the light may range from yellow to blue to green to red. Usually bioluminescence results from a slow oxidation, much slower than that in a flame, involving a special substance (luciferin) that combines with oxygen in the presence of a special enzyme (luciferase). In the firefly, the reaction also involves magnesium and ATP. (See LUMINESCENCE.) Light production does not necessarily depend upon life in the organism. The dried chemical compounds, mixed together, usually produce light when water is added.

Some organisms are not luminous in themselves, but contain light-producing bacteria or fungi. "Fox-fire," the light from rotten logs often seen in the woods at night, is the result of fungi living in the wood. Luminous bacteria account for the glow of a luminous organ under the eye of two kinds of East Indian fishes. These fishes can shut off their light, one by covering the light organ with an eyelid-like flap of skin, the other by turning the light organ so that its luminous side is against the body and not visible. Many animals, *e.g.* jellyfish and brittle stars, produce light only when stimulated. One species of squid, when disturbed, shoots out a luminous cloud. The light seen in a ship's wake at night is caused by *Noctiluca* and other protozoans that have been stimulated into light production by the ship's motion through the water.

Fireflies and Bermuda fireworms use luminous signals in the dark to bring mates together. In the black ocean depths, many small fishes, squids, and crustaceans have luminescent spots and supposedly rely upon them in recognizing one another. The angler fish has a lighted organ attached to its snout just above the mouth; this may serve as a lure. But many deep-sea crustaceans that are luminescent are also blind, and the function of the light is unknown. Similarly, no role has been shown for the light produced by bacteria, true fungi, and many feeble swimmers in the sea. Luminescence is found in such widely scattered groups that it is believed to have arisen independently in these groups, during the course of

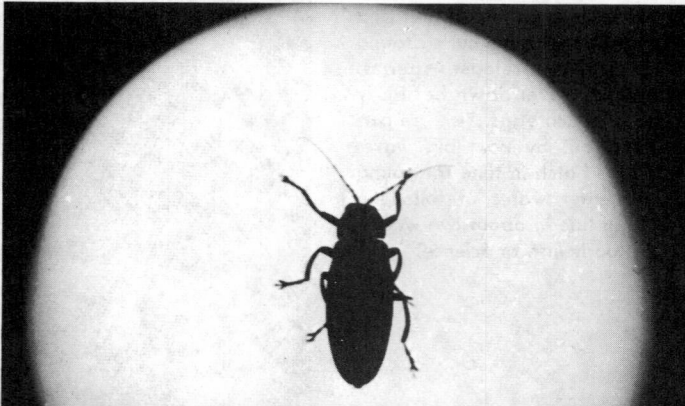

evolution, as a result of small changes in an organism's chemistry.—*L. and M. M.*

BIOME: the largest ecological unit, comprising all the many kinds of plants and animals occupying a broad region of the earth, *e.g.* an arctic tundra, a coniferous forest, a deciduous forest, a grassland, a desert, a tropical rain forest, or a marine environment. Each biome is kept distinct from the others by physical factors of temperature, rainfall, salinity, light intensity, and availability of nutrient materials. If left undisturbed, each biome comes to be occupied by a self-reproducing community that is essentially stable—a climax community. Many stages in a SUCCESSION of communities may precede arrival of the climax condition for the biome. See ADAPTATIONS IN ANIMALS AND PLANTS; ANIMAL AGGREGATION; BALANCE OF NATURE; ECOLOGY; LIFE ZONES.—*L. and M. M.*

BIOMETRY (or biometrics): the application of mathematics, especially STATISTICS, to the study of living things. It originated as a branch of biology in the work of Sir Francis Galton and Karl Pearson. Through the use of ratios, percentages, averages, frequency distributions, correlations, and other statistical devices, the research worker in biology can make quantitative descriptions of the variability of organisms and of the effects on them of various genetic and environmental factors (see HEREDITY; ECOLOGY). Such knowledge has helped in producing desirable traits and improving yield and fecundity in plants and animals, and has resulted in a better understanding of the relationships of living things to one another and to other features of their environment. Biometric methods are important in such fields as agronomy, animal husbandry, ecology, forestry, population genetics, public health, and medicine. The problem of the rise, spread, and control of epidemic diseases, for example, is partly a medical one and partly statistical. The premium rates set by life insurance companies are based on statistical tables of life expectancy at various ages. Statistical methods are particularly useful in the study of the GROWTH of living things. All correlations, including those derived from any kind of experiment, can be evaluated by statistical analysis.—*A. P. E.*

BIOPHYSICS: the study of living systems in terms of physical principles and by means of physical methods. Almost all inanimate matter can be understood on the basis of physical principles, including the laws of motion, electricity, and quantum mechanics. An equal understanding of living processes remains a major challenge of science. Early studies in biophysics included Julius Robert von Mayer's analysis of energy conservation in living systems and Herman von Helmholtz's studies on the mechanisms of vision and hearing, both during the 19th cent. With the development of atomic and nuclear physics and electronic engineering in the 20th cent., a huge array of new physical instruments and a much clearer understanding of the nature of atomic and molecular behavior became available for the analysis of biological actions. Thus, further analysis of the physics of vision has demonstrated that the human eye possesses the ultimate physical sensitivity to light, being able to respond to one or several light quanta. The ELECTRON MICROSCOPE, which permits detailed visualization of cellular structures only a ten-millionth inch long, has revealed the sizes and shapes of viruses and materials forming the walls of animal and bacterial cells. Improved electrical measuring instruments have been used to analyze precisely the tiny voltages generated by the brain, heart, and other organs, and are being used to clarify the nature of BIOELECTRICITY and the conduction of NERVOUS IMPULSES. The technique of X-RAY DIFFRACTION has clearly revealed the three-dimensional structure of protein molecules (of which all enzymes are composed) and of nucleic acids (which determine the hereditary constitution of every cell).

One important area of biophysical studies began in the 1920s with the demonstration by H. J. Muller that x-rays can change the heredity of living things by producing gene mutations. This opened up a tremendous area for physical investigation of genetic processes. Much data has since been obtained on the manner in which x-rays can produce either gross rupture of cell chromosomes or single gene mutations (see RADIATION GENETICS). Research with other high-energy radiations, *e.g.* alpha, beta, and neutron particles, has shown that these radiations, by randomly disorganizing the highly specific chemical bonds on which the integrity of living systems depends, can cause tremendously varied types of damage in cells, tissues, and organs (see RADIATION HAZARDS). Skin, gonads, blood-forming organs, and the lens of the eye are particularly sensitive to radiation. The molecular sequence of events between the initial absorption of radiation in living tissues and the ultimate physiologic or genetic damage that results is largely unknown.

Radioactive atoms are a particularly valuable research tool. With counters to detect their presence, radioactive atoms introduced into a living body act as markers, making it possible to follow the course of given molecules during metabolism within the body. This technique permits systematic identification of the steps in the chains of chemical events that take place in different types of cells in health and disease. The mechanism of action of drugs, the specific steps in the synthesis of proteins, and the dynamics of virus invasion of host cells are all actively illuminated by tracer studies with radioactive atoms (see RADIOISOTOPE).—*A. P. E.*

BIONICS: a field of science, described in 1959 by Jack Steele, in which living mechanisms are used as models for the design of hardware devices. Current research involves (1) classical use of biological prototypes and (2) analysis of biological mechanisms to learn their basic engineering features.

A biological mechanism that does a given job represents living proof to the engineer that a properly engineered hardware mechanism based on the same principle will actually work. The value of bionics to the engineer is further enhanced by the fact that living organisms are treasure-houses of new ideas which enrich the classical engineering approaches to hardware design.

The analysis of living organisms by engineering techniques is useful to the biologist because it acquaints him with the basic engineering principles that must be met even by living mechanisms. This approach has been most extensively used in relation to brain function. Since the brain normally performs control and information analysis functions, this area of bionics merges with the fields of CYBERNETICS and INFORMATION THEORY. However, the living organism contains many non-brain mechanisms which are not primarily concerned with cybernetic or information-theory functions, and the engineering analysis of these mechanisms falls solely within the field of bionics. Examples of these are: cardiac contraction, phagocytosis, transfer of lung gases, kidney clearance, and retinal conversion of light energy into electrical pulses.—*L. A. C.*

BIOSYNTHESIS: the formation of organic compounds in the cells of living organisms. The fundamental biosynthetic activity is PHOTOSYNTHESIS, through which green plants use carbon dioxide, water, and solar energy in the presence of chlorophyll to produce carbohydrates and other organic substances. Since this is an activity by means of which energy is stored and weight increased, it is regarded as an anabolic portion of METABOLISM. Cells of green plants in the dark, plant cells lacking chlorophyll, and animal cells all break down

Orders of birds arranged in "family tree" according to one classification scheme. Sequence of orders shown is not intended to portray a straight line of evolution. **1** ARCHAEOPTERYG-IFORMES (extinct, toothed)—*Archaeopteryx, Archaeornis;* **2** HESPERORNITHIFORMES (extinct, toothed)—water birds; **3** ICHTHY-ORNITHIFORMES (extinct, toothed)—water birds; **4** AEPYORNITHIFORMES (extinct)—*Aepyornis,* the elephant bird of Madagascar; **5** DINORNITH-IFORMES (extinct)—moas of New Zealand; **6** STRUTHIONIFORMES— ostriches; **7** RHEIFORMES—rheas; **8** CASUARIIFORMES—cassowaries, emus; **9** APTERYGIFORMES—kiwi; **10** SPHENISCIFORMES—penguins; **11** TINAMIFORMES—tinamous; **12** GAVIIFORMES—loons; **13** PODICIPEDI-FORMES—grebes; **14** PROCELLARIIFORMES—tube-nosed birds, e.g. albatrosses, shearwaters, petrels; **15** PELECANIFORMES—pelicans, tropic-birds, boobies, cormorants; **16** CICONIIFORMES—herons, storks, ibises, flamingos; **17** ANSERIFORMES—ducks; **18** FALCONI-FORMES—vultures, hawks, falcons, eagles; **19** GALLIFORMES—

the substances produced by photosynthesis. Through catabolic activities, they obtain the energy and raw materials needed for all other biosyntheses in plants and animals. This is the basis of maintenance, growth, and reproduction.

The growth of an organism depends upon the biosynthesis of new protein molecules from amino acids, an activity that occurs in submicroscopic cellular structures known as MICRO-SOMES. Hundreds of different proteins are produced in each CELL, where they serve both as structural materials and, in the form of enzymes, as catalysts for all other cellular chemistry. PROTEIN SYNTHESIS, in turn, is controlled by complex nitrogenous compounds, the nucleic acids, which determine the arrangement of amino acids in the protein molecule being synthesized. Currently it is believed that the amino acids first combine with the nucleic acids, in a sequence determined by the structure of the latter. This combination requires energy, which is derived from the oxidation of other organic substances. The amino acids become linked and then separate from the nucleic acids as a distinctive protein molecule. Thus the processes of biosynthesis are usually different from those used by chemists in synthesizing the same compounds in the laboratory. By supplying an organism with unusual food materials, however, it is often possible to induce the organism to synthesize unusual and highly useful products. Through this technique biochemists have been able to obtain several different kinds of penicillin from the mold *Penicillium,* each with its own peculiar ANTIBIOTIC characteristics.—*B. T. S.*

BIOT, JEAN BAPTISTE, 1774–1862, French physicist; b. Paris. In 1804, together with Gay-Lussac, he made the first balloon ascent for scientific purposes. In 1806, helped by Arago, he carried out research on the refractive properties of gases. Biot supported Newton's corpuscular theory of light, constantly amending it to fit newly discovered facts. His work on polarization of light made him the father of modern saccharimetry (1840), and his research in magnetism led to the "rule of Biot and Savart." He published a large number of books and papers on ancient Chinese and Hindu astronomy (1840, 1862); a study of Laplace's cosmology (1801); and the results of his many geodetical surveys (1821). He was a fellow of the Royal Society.—*R. J. F.*

BIOTIN: see VITAMIN.

BIRD: A covering of feathers distinguishes birds from all other animals. In possessing feathers, all birds are alike; in other respects they differ tremendously. Most can fly, but some have wings too small to support them, and one, the kiwi, has no visible wings at all. There are about 8,600 recognized species, grouped into 33 orders. They range in size from the

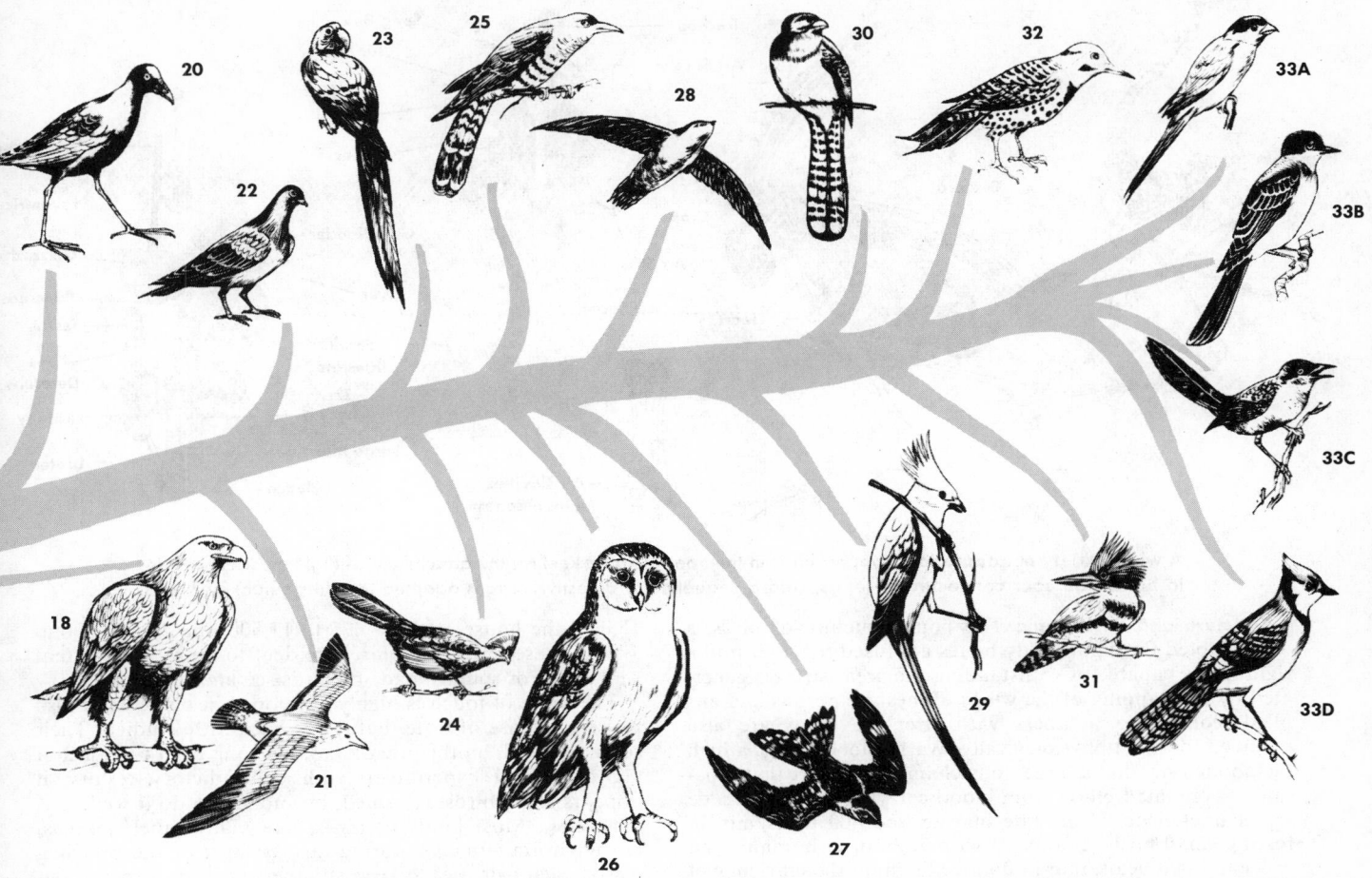

grouse, pheasant, turkey, hoatzin; **20** GRUIFORMES—cranes, rails; **21** CHARADRIIFORMES—plovers, sandpipers, gulls, auks; **22** COLUMBIFORMES—pigeons (including dodo); **23** PSITTACIFORMES—parrots; **24** MUSOPHAGIFORMES—touracos; **25** CUCULIFORMES—cuckoos; **26** STRIGIFORMES—owls; **27** CAPRIMULGIFORMES—oilbird, nighthawks, whippoorwill; **28** APODIFORMES—swifts, hummingbirds; **29** COLIIFORMES—colies; **30** TROGONIFORMES—trogons; **31** CORACIIFORMES—kingfishers, todies, motmots, bee-eaters, rollers, hoopoes, horn-

bills; **32** PICIFORMES—puffbirds, barbets, honeyguides, toucans, woodpeckers; **33** PASSERIFORMES—perching birds, in 4 suborders: **33A** broadbills; **33B** woodcreepers, antbirds, cotingas, manakins, flycatchers; **33C** lyrebirds, scrub-birds; **33D** larks, swallows, orioles, crows, bowerbirds, birds-of-paradise, titmice, nuthatches, creepers, babblers, dippers, wrens, thrushes, pipits, waxwings, shrikes, starlings, honeyeaters, sunbirds, flowerpeckers, vireos, warblers, tanagers, finches, weaverbirds, etc.

bee (or Helena's) hummingbird, which is about 2 in. long (more than half of that is bill and tail) to the ostrich, which reaches 8 ft in height and 300 lb, and the wandering albatross, which attains a wingspread of 12 ft. Most live on land, but some spend most of their lives at sea and visit land only to nest.

Earliest Birds: That birds evolved from reptiles is indicated by features of the skeleton, muscles, egg, and embryological development. The most ancient bird known is *Archaeopteryx,* fossils of which have been found in Bavarian rocks of the Jurassic geological period, about 150,000,000 yr ago. *Archaeopteryx* lived in trees and looked something like a large pigeon. The oldest American birds known are species of *Hesperornis* and *Ichthyornis,* fossils of which have been found in Kansas rocks of the Cretaceous period, perhaps 100,000,000 yr old. *Hesperornis* was a flightless, loon-like swimmer nearly 5 ft long, and *Ichthyornis* a small, gull-like flying bird.

Even larger birds than the ostrich and albatross once existed. Some of the moas that lived in New Zealand were about 13 ft tall and weighed nearly 500 lb. A vulture of which a fossil has been found in Nevada had a wingspread calculated at 16 to 17 ft; it was the largest known flying bird.

Flight: Birds are the most mobile of all animals, and many species annually migrate between nesting and wintering places great distances apart. One, the arctic tern, travels almost from pole to pole, nesting in the arctic and wintering in the antarc-

tic. (See BIRD MIGRATION.) Instead of migrating, one species, the poorwill of our West, is known to hibernate.

The ability of many species to "home" from unfamiliar places is astonishing. The homing of pigeons is well known, but even the best of their performances have been far outdone by some wild birds. A Manx shearwater, a bird resembling a gull, that was taken by plane from an island off Wales to Boston and there released, found its way home in 12½ days; the distance was 3,200 mi. A Laysan albatross that was taken by plane from Midway atoll to the Philippines flew home in 32 days—the distance was 4,120 mi. Both Boston and the Philippines are outside those species' natural ranges. (See ANIMAL NAVIGATION.)

Because it is hard to time flying birds accurately, reports of the speeds they can make vary considerably. Migrating geese have been reported flying at 42 to 55 mi/hr, ducks 29 to 59, herons 18 to 29, shorebirds 34 to 51, and small songbirds 20 to 37 mi/hr. When a bird is fleeing from danger or is in other exceptional circumstances, those speeds may be far exceeded; an aviator doing 90 mi/hr reported that he was passed by sandpipers which must have been doing at least 110. An osprey was timed at 80 mi/hr. Followed by a plane, a peregrine falcon (or duck hawk) is said to have flown at about 175 mi/hr, and one was also timed at that speed when swooping on prey. (See ANIMAL FLIGHT; WING.)

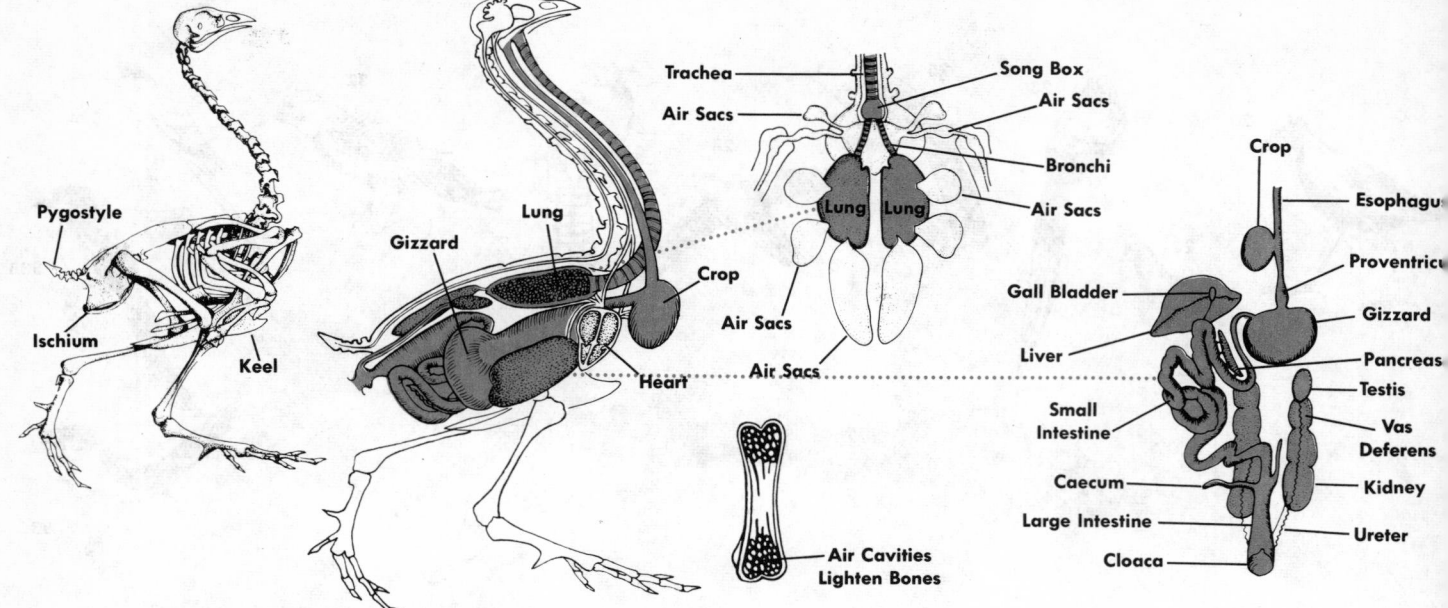

A wide variety of adaptations support birds in their aerial life: a keel for the attachment of flight muscles, cavities in bones, air sacs connected to lungs, and a sequence of digestive organs adapted to a large intake of food.

Structure and Physiology: The bone structure of birds is well adapted for flight. Body bones are fused together into a rigid frame capable of withstanding the great stresses generated by the flapping of the wings. Bones are porous and air-filled, combining lightness with strength. Birds are also modified for flight physiologically. Warm-bloodedness, a high metabolic rate, and a large, four-chambered heart that separates oxygenated blood from blood carrying carbon dioxide are characteristic. Heart rate may exceed 400 beats/min in resting small birds, compared with 70/min in humans, and exceeds 1,000 beats/min in flight. Matching the efficiency of this system, which may circulate the blood completely in less than a second, as compared to 8 sec in man, is the rate of food consumption. This may equal 80% of the body weight daily. A crop, or food sac, in some species serves as a storage bin, allowing a bird to eat a huge quantity of food at one time. A system of air sacs extending through the body increases the capacity of the lungs. Waste nitrogen is excreted as uric acid, a process requiring a minimum of water. (A urinary bladder is lacking.)

Senses: Birds' most acute sense is that of vision; as a class they have better sight than any other animals. The eyes of most species are somewhat movable—in a way that keeps the pupil centered—and can be moved separately; one may be turned in one direction while the other is turned in another. Many birds, when they want to examine an object very closely, turn the head sideways and focus a single eye on the object. Owls, however, have immovable eyes; in order to look around they must turn the whole head. A bird's eye is rather insensitive to blue but very sensitive to red light; both blue and green are believed to be seen as grayish colors. The eye has what is often called a "third eyelid," a nictitating membrane that can be drawn across the eyeball; it seems to have a protective function.

Birds' hearing is also very keen and, after vision, is their most important sense. Predatory species especially, and in particular night-hunting owls, have remarkable ability to locate sounds. The oilbird of South America, which is nocturnal, even finds its way about in the dark by the same means that a bat does—by uttering a succession of short, sharp clicks and by judging from the echoes the positions of nearby objects. (See ANIMAL SONAR.) However, studies of a few species indicate that the range of hearing is less than that of most mammals. Man hears sounds with frequencies of about 20 to 17,000 cycles/sec. The starling hears only those of 700 to

15,000, the house sparrow 675 to 11,500, the pigeon 200 to 7,500. These birds, therefore, are deaf to many sounds that we hear. (For sounds made by birds see BIRD CALLS.)

The sense of touch is highly developed in birds. They also possess a sense of taste, but it has been little studied. Their sense of smell, on the other hand, has long been a subject of argument and experiment, with contradictory results; it appears some birds can smell, but none can do it well.

Nesting: Most kinds of birds, like many other animals, are territorial; that is, during at least part of the breeding season each pair tries to keep all others of its own species out of its immediate vicinity. The area claimed is called a "territory." Birds that live in colonies may claim only a few inches around the NEST; hawks and eagles, several square miles; songbirds, anywhere from 1/10 acre to 17 acres. The bird that persistently flies against a windowpane is defending its territory; it has noticed its reflection in the glass, mistaken it for a trespasser, and is trying to drive it away. (See TERRITORIALITY.) The roles of the sexes in nest-building vary greatly from species to species; generalization is impossible. The cowbirds of America, cuckoos of the Old World, honey guides and some weaver finches of Africa, and one duck of South America make no nests; they lay their eggs in the nests of other birds and let those birds incubate them and raise the young.

Eggs are commonly laid on successive days, but certain species lay at longer intervals. Some species lay a fixed and some a variable number. The time at which INCUBATION is begun varies, sometimes even within the same species, from the first laying day to the last. The males of certain species help their mates incubate, but the males of other species do not; the males of a few do all the incubating—the phalaropes are the classic examples. The length of sittings varies greatly; songbirds commonly alternate sittings of about 15 to 45 min with feeding periods of about 10 min away from the nest; at the other extreme, a royal albatross is known to have sat for 14 days without relief and without food. The megapodes of Australia and neighboring areas do not incubate at all: they make mounds of sand or vegetation and bury their eggs in these, leaving the heat of the Sun or of fermentation to hatch out the chicks.

The incubation period is nowadays counted as the time between the laying and hatching of the last-laid egg of a nestful—because regular incubation may only have begun after the last was laid. The period ranges from a little over 11 days (brown-headed cowbird) to 80 days (royal albatross). For most songbirds it is about 12 to 14 days, for the pigeon 16½ days, for the chicken 21 days.

A species is called precocial (or nidifugous) if the young are able to run about and find their own food as soon as they hatch; chickens and ducks are examples. The species is altricial (or nidicolous) if the young, hatched naked (or practically so) and blind, require extended care in the nest. Although birds have the highest body temperature of all animals—102° to 112°F—altricial young at first possess no heat-regulating mechanism; until this develops they have to be brooded as well as fed. The period of nest life usually equals the period of incubation, and even when they take wing such young birds are still cared for by their parents for some time.

Many species raise one brood a year, but many others raise two, and some even more. Banding indicates that nonmigratory birds, once paired, stay paired for life; if one dies the survivor takes a new mate. Birds that migrate usually stay paired through the raising of all of one season's broods, but rather seldom succeed in coming together again in later years. Monogamy is the rule, but a number of species are regularly polygamous and a few others occasionally so.

Age: Elaborate studies of a few species suggest that the life span of songbirds averages only 2 to 3 yr; however, many individuals exceed the average. American robins have reached at least 8 yr, cardinals 13½. Various ducks have reached 6 to 9, a golden eagle 11½, a marsh hawk 13½. The greatest age known to have been reached by any wild bird is 28 yr; the bird was a herring gull. In captivity, a number of species have lived 30 to 38 yr; an eagle owl that attained 68 is believed to hold the record, with a greater sulphur-crested cockatoo next, at 56.—*H. Br.*

BIRD CALLS: sounds produced by birds, ranging from simple call notes to complex songs; also, devices by which man imitates bird sounds. Man's early appreciation of the calls of birds is shown by his use of such call-imitating names as whip-poor-will and cuckoo, but scientific study of these calls is relatively new, having been greatly aided by the invention of the tape recorder. Recorded calls can be analyzed in the laboratory and played back to birds to observe their reactions. Bird songs, because of their musical qualities, have received most attention. These are used to mark the territories that birds will defend. (See ANIMAL BEHAVIOR; TERRITORIALITY.) The simpler call notes have been less studied, but have wider communicative value. They are important as sexual recognition signals, in courtship displays, as food and danger signals, in relationships between parents and young, and as identification signals. Not all of a bird's call is necessary to convey information. A problem for future research is to identify the essential message-carrying features of each call.

The ability and tendency to produce specific calls seems to be mainly the result of heredity modified through learning. Thus the male songbird inherits the means to produce the outline of his song, but learns details by listening to other males. The relative influence of heredity and learning varies. Research on Baltimore orioles, for example, has shown that the song pattern is largely learned, whereas in certain finches it is mainly hereditary. Reactions of birds to calls are also partly inherited and partly learned. Some birds fail to understand "dialects" developed by members of the same species from distant parts. Thus herring gulls living on the W coast of Europe do not understand herring gulls living on the E coast of North America. Certain species respond to the calls of other species (*e.g.* gulls in Maine respond to calls of crows in the same region) or even to unnatural sounds. Devices for mimicking bird calls range in complexity from the unaided human voice to electronic devices using recordings. Research with these should throw light on the meanings of the calls to the birds and may suggest improved means to attract birds or to repel them when they become pests.—*H. W. F.*

BIRD MIGRATION: the annual movement of at least some individuals of a bird species from the breeding area to a specific non-breeding area and back to the breeding area. The evolution of migratory behavior is doubtless the result of advantages conferred on a species by the use of separate breeding and non-breeding areas. Thus migration allows many species of the north temperate zone to exploit the advantages of abundant food and long days for feeding young in the summers of more northern latitudes, and also the advantages of less severe winter conditions of more southern latitudes. The distribution of migratory and non-migratory species among the bird families and genera suggests that migratory behavior has developed many times in the evolution of birds.

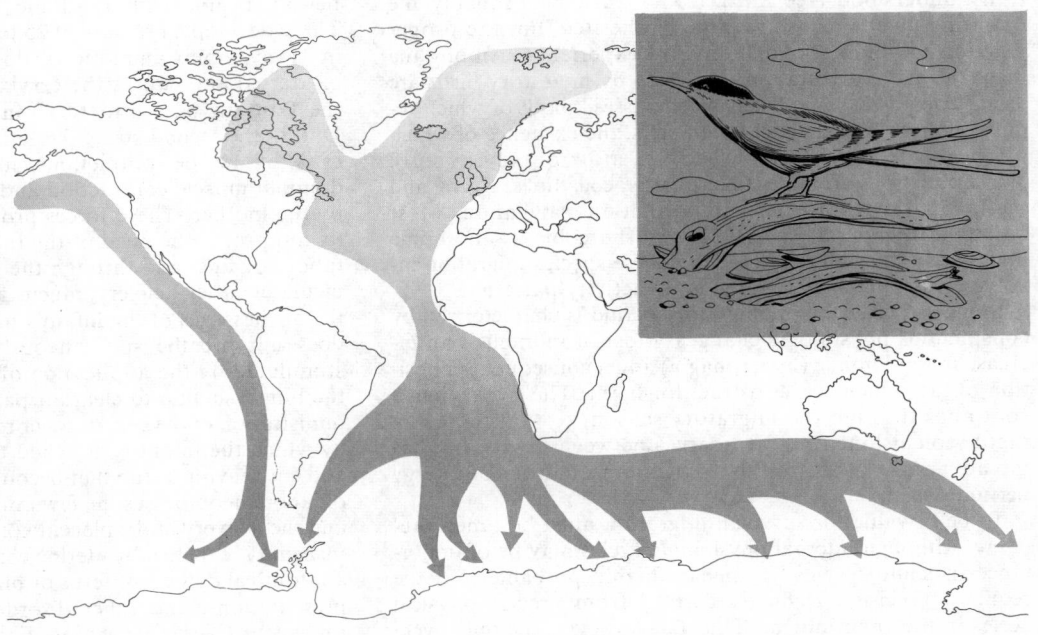

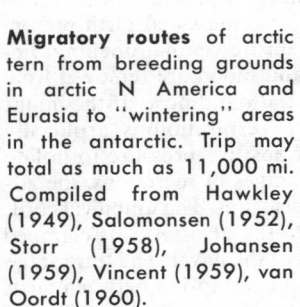

Migratory routes of arctic tern from breeding grounds in arctic N America and Eurasia to "wintering" areas in the antarctic. Trip may total as much as 11,000 mi. Compiled from Hawkley (1949), Salomonsen (1952), Storr (1958), Johansen (1959), Vincent (1959), van Oordt (1960).

administration of analgesics or anesthetics. See TWINS AND MULTIPLE BIRTHS.—*E. G.*

BISHOP'S RING: a dim, reddish-brown ring occasionally seen around the Sun in a clear sky. Bishop's ring is caused by diffraction of light by small particles. Dust clouds dense and high enough to cause Bishop's ring often result from volcanic eruptions.—*D. H. L.*

BISMUTH: a metallic element (Bi); at. no. 83, at. wt 209.00; density 9.8; mp 271°C. Bismuth occurs naturally as the sulfide, Bi_2S_3, and as *bismite*, $Bi_2O_3 \cdot H_2O$. Pure bismuth is obtained by reducing the oxide with carbon. It is hard, brittle, and a very poor conductor of heat. Bismuth alloys expand on cooling, and are useful in automatic fire extinguishers, in metal castings, and in boilers to guard against overheating. Bismuthyl nitrate, $BiONO_3$, and bismuthyl carbonate, $(BiO)_2CO_3$, are used for treating stomach disorders.—*G. W. M.*

BJERKNES, JACOB AALL BONNEVIE, 1897–   ; Norwegian– U. S. meteorologist; b. Stockholm, son of **Vilhelm Bjerknes** (1862–1951), Norwegian meteorologist. In his paper "On the Structure of Moving Cyclones" (1919), he proposed his cyclone model, which led to the development of the Bergen (later, Norwegian; still later, Scandinavian) School of Meteorology, headed by his father. Among the early contributions of the school were the discovery of the polar front and the life cycle of moving cyclones, the development of air-mass and frontal methods of weather analysis, the dynamics of the circumpolar vortex, and stability criteria of large-scale motion systems. The younger Bjerknes wrote on such subjects as the general circulation of the atmosphere, the dynamics of weather and motion systems, and the semidiurnal pressure wave. He coauthored (with T. H. P. Bergeron) *Physikalische Hydrodynamik* (1933) and *Dynamic Meteorology and Weather Forecasting* (1958).—*S. P.*

BLACK, JOSEPH, 1728–99, Scottish chemist and physicist; b. Bordeaux, France. His quantitative investigation of lime, magnesia, caustic, and fixed alkalis clarified the relation of limestone and lime (carbonates and oxides) and the setting of mortar and plaster. He lectured on heat (1761), introducing the terms caloric, specific heat, thermal capacity, heat of fusion, and latent heat. His *Lectures on the Elements of Chemistry* (1803) was published posthumously.—*R. J. F.*

Joseph Black
(N. Y. Public Library)

BLACK BODY: theoretically, a body that absorbs all the radiation that falls on it. In 1859 G. R. Kirchhoff showed that a good absorber of radiant heat is also a good emitter, and that the best possible emitter is a perfect black body. There is no known substance that actually absorbs all radiation falling on it, but in 1895 Otto Lummer and Wilhelm Wien devised an almost ideal black body. This is a small furnace with a single small opening; the furnace walls are maintained at a constant temperature. Radiation entering through the opening is absorbed by the walls; only a minute fraction finds its way back through the opening, which therefore behaves as a black body. When the enclosed space and the walls are in thermal equilibrium, the walls both absorb and emit radiation. The radiation seen through the opening (which is the

small fraction that escapes) is called BLACK-BODY RADIATION and has the characteristics of radiation from an ideal source; the frequencies involved are directly related to the temperature of the furnace, and all the frequencies predicted by theory are present in the expected relative intensities. This type of radiator is of the highest theoretical and practical importance, since it allows physicists to study the laws of radiation under ideal conditions.—*B. P. S.*

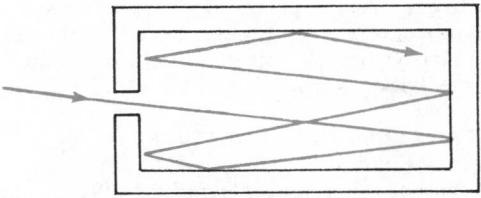

Black body: By trapping all incoming light, a box lined with a black mat surface offers at its orifice a laboratory approximation of black-body radiation.

BLACK-BODY RADIATION: the randomized electromagnetic radiation in an enclosed space that is in thermal equilibrium with the walls of its container. The radiation arises as follows: The atoms and molecules of every solid and liquid are continually vibrating about their equilibrium locations. These motions are random, in that the direction and speed of any atom are not correlated with those of any other atom. Although at any instant the kinetic energies associated with the oscillations have a wide range of values among the different atoms, the average energy is uniquely determined by the temperature of the material. The higher the temperature, the more violent the oscillations. Since atoms contain electrons, and since an oscillating electron radiates electromagnetic waves, it follows that every solid and liquid is continuously emitting electromagnetic radiations. This so-called thermal RADIATION consists of a superposition of trains of electromagnetic waves, random in direction, frequency, and phase, because of the disordered thermal motion of the electrons that generated them. The total energy—in the form of thermal radiation—emitted by an object increases with the object's temperature, as one would expect in view of the increased energies associated with the thermal motions of the electrons.

The inverse process also occurs; namely, when electromagnetic radiation strikes a chunk of matter, it forces the electrons of the matter into oscillation. Thus, when thermal radiation strikes the material, the intensity of the random oscillations of its electrons are increased, and the material becomes heated. We see, then, that matter is continually radiating and absorbing thermal radiation. If an object is at higher temperature than its surroundings, it radiates more energy than it absorbs until it is cooled down to the same temperatures as its surroundings. Thereafter, it absorbs energy at the same rate as it emits energy—the system is in thermal equilibrium. Black-body radiation, which is the thermal radiation bouncing back and forth in an enclosed space whose walls are all at the same temperature, is therefore in equilibrium with the walls.

Black-body radiation is historically famous, because it was the first of a sequence of phenomena that could be understood only by making some revolutionary assumptions about the laws of nature in the atomic domain—assumptions that form the basis for present-day QUANTUM THEORY. According to the laws of mechanics and electromagnetism, which we use for describing large-scale phenomena of everyday life, an oscillating electrical charge can have any energy and must continually emit electromagnetic energy while oscillating. Calculations based on these assumptions lead to the absurd prediction that the amount of energy appearing in the form of black-body radiation would be infinite! In 1901 Max Planck postulated that the oscillating electrons can have only a discrete set of possible energies and that they can emit or absorb radiation only in going from one ENERGY LEVEL to another. Calculations based on these assumptions gave complete agreement with the measured characteristics of black-body radiation. This was the first evidence that energy is *quantized* —*i.e.* can be transferred only in discrete packets, called quanta. In our macroscopic world we deal with astronomically large numbers of energy quanta; hence we do not observe this granularity; but to a single atom, a quantum of energy has a large "kick."—*S. K.*

BLACKETT, PATRICK MAYNARD STUART, 1897–   , English physicist; b. London. He obtained the first cloud-chamber photographs of nuclear disintegrations (1925) and thereby identified the particles produced. For his improvement of the Wilson cloud-chamber method and for the resulting discoveries in the field of nuclear physics and cosmic radiation, Blackett received the 1948 Nobel prize. He is a fellow of the Royal Society.—*D. H. D. R.*

BLAST FURNACE: see FURNACE.

BLEACHES AND BLEACHING: Bleaches are substances used for imparting or restoring whiteness to materials, and bleaching is the name of the process. Textiles, paper pulp, flour, oils, fats, and sugar are among materials which require bleaching. Bleaches function by reacting chemically with the discoloring components of the treated materials, oxidizing or reducing them to a colorless form or to a form which is soluble and can be removed by subsequent washing. Decolorizing agents which act by preferential adsorption of coloring matters, *e.g.* fuller's earth, used in vegetable oil and petroleum refining, are also generally referred to as "bleaching clays." The optical bleaches (or optical brighteners) are colorless fluorescent substances which absorb radiation in the invisible and fluoresce in the visible region and thus make fabrics appear whiter. The most widely used oxidizing bleaching agent is the common household laundry bleach, a water solution of sodium hypochlorite (NaOCl). Other popular oxidizing bleaching agents include salts of hypochlorous acid, chlorine, and such compounds as hydrogen peroxide and sodium perborate ($NaBO_3$). The peroxide bleaches are generally milder than those based on chlorine but are not as effective. The most widely used reducing bleaching agent is sulfur dioxide (SO_2), a pungent, irritating colorless gas, often stored and shipped in liquid form. Commercial bleaches often include fatty alcohols, sulfonated oils, salts, and other chemicals called bleaching assistants. Their function is to assure more uniform penetration of the bleach and more complete control of the process.—*W. P. C.*

BLIZZARD: a storm with low temperatures, high winds, and blowing snow. The snow in a blizzard is mostly fine, dry snow picked up from the ground by the strong winds, reducing visibility and tending to pile up in drifts. The U. S. Weather Bureau defines a blizzard as having winds of at least 32 mph, temperatures well below freezing, and visibilities reduced by snow to 500 ft or less.—*P. L.*

BLOCH, FELIX, 1905–   , Swiss–U. S. physicist; b. Zurich. Bloch discovered the nuclear-resonance method of studying atomic nuclei (discovered independently by E. M. Purcell) and has done important research in quantum theory, particularly of metals and ferromagnetism. For their discoveries and their development of new methods for nuclear magnetic pre-

cision measurements, Bloch and Purcell shared the Nobel prize, 1952. Bloch is a member of the National Academy of Sciences.—*D. H. D. R.*

BLOOD: the circulating body fluid of animals. Blood is an aqueous solution of proteins, salts, and small amounts of organic substances, containing various types of cells and cell products in suspension. Blood transports foodstuffs, wastes, hormones, respiratory gases, heat, and substances that help the organism resist infectious disease. Since its composition is kept nearly uniform by various regulatory mechanisms of the body, blood provides an almost constant internal environment for the activities of cells and tissues. The amount of blood in animals varies greatly, not only in relation to body size but also in relation to type of circulatory system. In general the blood of animals with closed circulatory systems makes up from 2 to 10% of body weight (8% in man, whose body normally contains 5 to 6 qt of blood). In animals with open circulatory systems, blood is 10 to 50% of body weight. Blood that is removed from the body may readily be separated by centrifugation into a fluid portion, the *plasma,* and a solid portion containing the "formed elements"—cells and cell products. Clotted blood that has been centrifuged separates into two parts: fluid, called *serum,* and solid, which contains the protein *fibrin,* a product of clotting.

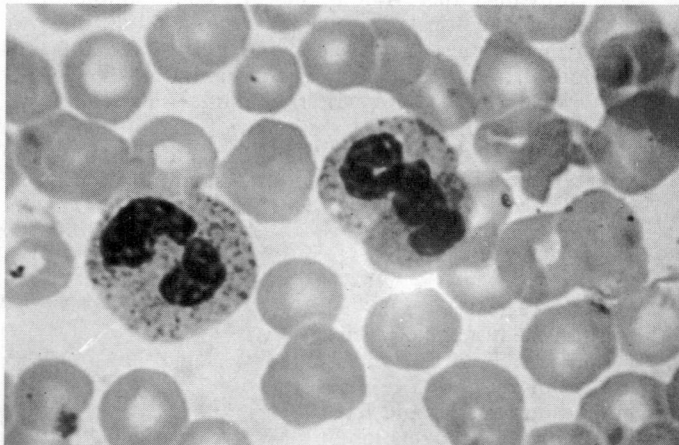

Cells carried by human blood: Three white cells are here seen surrounded by a host of red cells. The red cells, manufactured in the marrow of bones, carry oxygen from lung capillaries to cells throughout the body. The white cells, which look much like amebas, are active in combating bacteria. (*A. John Geraci from Nancy Palmer*)

The formed elements of blood differ somewhat in various animals, but generally include white blood cells (*leucocytes*) in all animals and red blood cells (*erythrocytes*) in vertebrates and a few others. In man, there may be between 2,500 and 12,000 leucocytes in a cubic millimeter (a mere speck) of blood. These leucocytes are of three major types: monocytes, granulocytes, and lymphocytes. Granulocytes and lymphocytes are the most numerous. Granulocytes are formed in the blood-forming tissue of the bone marrow of mammals, and lymphocytes are formed in the lymphoid tissue (see LYMPH SYSTEM). Leucocytes have a short life, usually 1 to 3 days, occasionally as long as 2 weeks. They are ameboid cells that can move freely from blood to tissues and back, forcing their way between the cells that form the walls of the capillaries. Monocytes and neutrophil granulocytes normally migrate to a site of injury or infection and feed on foreign materials, bacteria, and damaged tissue cells, removing these from the

The plasma, in which these formed elements are suspended, is made up of water (91%), protein (7%), inorganic salts (1%), and organic substances (1%). The major salt is sodium chloride, or table salt; small but physiologically important amounts of potassium and calcium ions, and a relatively large amount of bicarbonate ions, representing in part carbon dioxide in transport from tissues to lungs, are also present. Major organic constituents other than protein are the sugar glucose and the nitrogenous waste urea. The proteins in human blood can be separated into albumin (53%), four globulins (43%), and fibrinogen (4%). The blood of other species has somewhat different proportions, and bloods of some invertebrates contain in solution a respiratory pigment such as hemoglobin or hemocyanin. Fibrinogen is the major participant in BLOOD CLOTTING, and serum differs from plasma mainly in its lack of this component. One of the globulins appears to be involved in clotting as well, and another (gamma-globulin) contains antibodies that are important in immunity to disease and in the phenomenon of "blood groups." See CIRCULATION IN LIVING THINGS.—*B. T. S.*

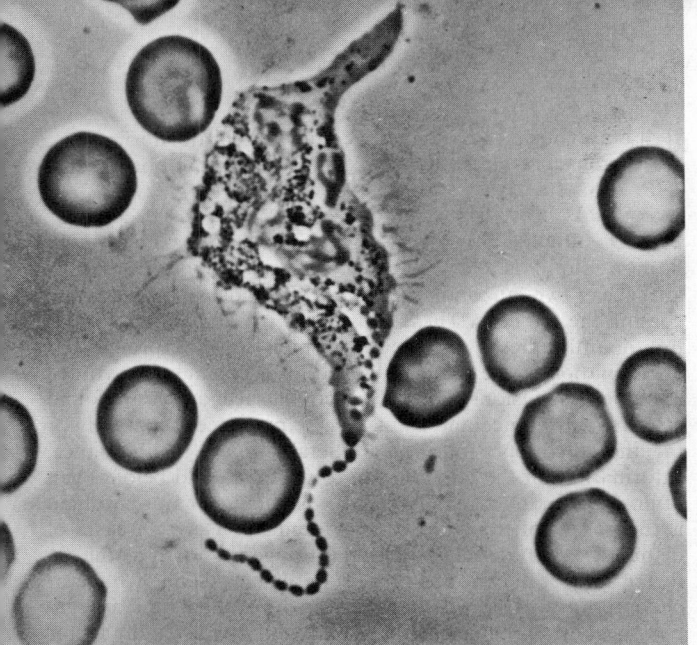

Attack on streptococci: Chain of beadlike streptococcus bacteria is being engulfed by a white blood cell. *(Pfizer)*

site. The pus formed in an infection is made up of living and dead bacteria plus leucocytes. Basophil granulocytes form heparin, which helps to prevent blood from clotting in the vessels, and monocytes may form antibodies, which are involved in development of immunity to disease (see IMMUNIZATION). Dead and dying leucocytes are removed from blood by reticulo-endothelial cells lining blood vessels in lungs, liver, and spleen, most of the action taking place in the latter two organs.

All vertebrates except larval eels and certain antarctic fishes have in their blood large numbers of erythrocytes. A cubic millimeter (mm^3) of human blood will normally have about 5,000,000; there are some 25 trillion in a human body. In man the red cells are disks, shaped somewhat like a doughnut with the hole partly filled in. They have no nuclei, although the erythrocytes of all lower vertebrates do. The cells are heavily loaded with the respiratory pigment hemoglobin, a protein that makes up over 30% of their weight. The cells serve in the transport of oxygen from lungs, where oxygen combines with hemoglobin, to tissues, where oxygen is liberated from hemoglobin (see OXYGEN TRANSPORT). This circuit from lungs to tissues and back takes on the average about 45 sec, and each red cell travels some 700 mi in its lifetime. About 1% of the red cells wear out each day, and all are renewed in about 4 mo. Worn-out erythrocytes are removed from blood and destroyed by the reticulo-endothelial or lymphoid system in the bone marrow, spleen, and liver. New red cells are formed in bone marrow of reptiles, birds, and mammals, or in the spleen of lower vertebrates. The rate of formation may increase 4 or 5 times after loss of blood. Formation of erythrocytes requires a supply of protein, iron, and the vitamins B_{12} and folic acid; deficiency of any of these in the diet may lead to anemia. The erythrocytes carry on their surfaces the special proteins (antigens or agglutinogens) responsible for the phenomenon of BLOOD GROUPS.

A third type of formed element in the blood of vertebrates is the blood *platelet.* Platelets are very small round structures with spike-like projections; when they come in contact with any surface wetted by blood, such as the edge of a wound, they tend to adhere to the surface, spread out, and disintegrate. This action initiates formation of a blood clot. Platelets are formed in bone marrow and appear to be fragments broken off from cells in that tissue; there are 250,000 to 500,000 in 1 mm^3 of normal blood.

BLOOD-BRAIN BARRIER: the layer of cells (glial cells) which surrounds the capillaries of the brain and spinal cord and acts as a barrier to the penetration of various types of molecules from the plasma. This barrier is thought to act as a device protecting the brain from noxious compounds in the blood. It prevents, for example, the transfer of amino acids and of various antibiotics from the blood stream to the brain cells. The permeability of this barrier is often changed as a result of brain tumors and hence has been made use of in diagnosis: radioactive tracer compounds, introduced into the blood, diffuse only into the tumor-damaged areas.—*J. F. S.*

BLOOD CHEMISTRY: the branch of physiological chemistry that deals with chemical analysis of blood. By means of such analysis many diseases can be diagnosed and treatments indicated. Blood consists of red and white cells and of plasma, a watery liquid in which proteins, sugars, hormones, and a large number of other substances are dissolved. Being the only tissue that is in contact with all parts of the body, blood serves as a system through which food and oxygen are transported to the cells and waste products are removed by passage to the kidneys and lungs. Illness is marked by the accumulation in the blood of materials that ordinarily would be transported through the system. Chemical analysis of the blood serves to detect interruptions of transport and possibly to identify the cause. Such analysis, a major function of hospital laboratories, is the province of the clinical chemist, and its practice can be illustrated by these blood conditions:

Disturbance in ionic composition: The ionic composition of the blood involves sodium, potassium, and bicarbonate content as well as acidity. It is closely regulated by the kidneys and lungs, and provides the cells of the body with a remarkably constant environment (thought to resemble that of the primordial oceans in which cellular life first originated). A disturbance in the ionic environment calls for corrective treatment.

Hormonal imbalances: Hormones are present in tiny quantities in blood, and can usually be assayed according to their effects. Thus, in diabetes, the lack of insulin results in an increase in blood sugar, and measurement of blood-sugar concentration indicates the dosage of insulin required to correct the situation. Again, since the thyroid hormone is the only iodine-containing compound in the body, the amount of protein-bound iodine in blood is a measure of the output of the thyroid gland.

Accumulation of enzymes: Enzymes normally stay inside the cells in which they are made, the only exception being those which are released into the intestinal tract to digest the food. The enzymes normally present in blood are concerned with the blood-clotting mechanism and are determined simply by measuring coagulation time. There are no other enzymes in blood plasma except as a result of cell breakdown. Since many tissues specialize in production of certain enzymes, the presence of these enzymes in plasma indicates tissue destruction. Thus acid phosphatase is found in plasma during the breakdown of cancerous prostate cells. Alkaline phosphatase is high in plasma in cases of bone cancer. In pancreatic disease, the digestive pancreatic enzymes (*e.g.* amylase, ribonuclease) are found in plasma. Transaminases increase as the result of heart, muscle, and liver damage, and the type of transaminase shows which tissue is affected.

Accumulation of metabolic intermediates: These intermediates are compounds that accumulate when the mechanisms utilizing them are defective; the cause may be an infectious disease. Thus, in viral hepatitis, the liver is unable to make excretable glucuronides out of bile pigments, and these pigments, accumulating in the blood, cause a yellow or jaundiced complexion. Metabolic intermediates may accumulate also because the enzyme needed to catalyze a certain process is absent; this happens in various hereditary diseases, as galactosemia, in which galactose accumulates in the blood after the ingestion of milk, which contains galactose. Plasma proteins are examined by separating them electrically (ELECTROPHORESIS). Changes from the normal pattern are characteristic of some diseases.—*J. F. S.*

BLOOD CLOTTING: the formation of a semi-solid gel (a clot) from components of whole blood that has come in contact with damaged tissues or with a surface that it wets (*e.g.* glass). This process is important in closing broken blood vessels; it stops loss of blood from small wounds. Clotting occurs in blood of vertebrates and some invertebrates, including arthropods. In vertebrates and certain arthropods the critical phenomenon in clotting is the conversion of soluble protein, fibrinogen, to an insoluble fibrous form known as fibrin. This change is brought about by the enzyme thrombin. Thrombin is not normally present in blood plasma, but is formed during the initiation of clotting from prothrombin, a plasma constituent. Conversion of prothrombin to thrombin requires calcium ions, and clotting can be prevented by adding to the blood such substances as citrate or oxalate, which combine with calcium ions. Formation of thrombin also requires a substance known as thromboplastin, which is formed when blood platelets break down, as they do when in contact with wettable surfaces or damaged tissues; such tissues may also liberate thromboplastin. Formation of thromboplastin may be prevented by the substance heparin, which is formed by the basophil granulocytes (one type of white blood cell) and which probably has a normal role in preventing clotting of blood while in the vessels. The steps in the clotting of vertebrate blood may be summarized as follows:

Stage 1:

Platelets + tissue and plasma components $\longrightarrow$

Thromboplastin

$$\text{Prothrombin} \xrightarrow{\frac{\text{Thromboplastin}}{\text{Ca}}} \text{Thrombin}$$

Stage 2:

$$\text{Fibrinogen} \xrightarrow{\text{Thrombin}} \text{Fibrin}$$

Clotting of invertebrate blood may also involve two stages or may occur in one stage: white blood cells break down on injury or contact and liberate a thrombin-like substance. Invertebrate thrombins do not act on vertebrate fibrinogens, nor do vertebrate thrombins act on invertebrate fibrinogens. —*B. T. S.*

BLOOD GROUP: any of the four major groups into which human blood is classified, according to the presence or absence of two mucopolysaccharide substances, "A" and "B," coating the red cells. These substances will induce the formation of antibodies in any blood to which they are foreign, and agglutination of the red cells will result. This must be avoided in blood transfusions. The two mucopolysaccharides are found also in gastric juice and saliva. Their presence (separately or together) or absence follows a predictable course in inheritance. Information on the blood group to which a child belongs can often exclude the possibility that a particular man or woman is the parent of the child; this evidence is useful in cases of disputed parentage. Another agglutinogen, known as the *Rh factor,* may or may not be present in the blood. The Rh factor becomes important when a woman who lacks it (is Rh-negative) becomes pregnant with a child who possesses the factor (is Rh-positive). If the woman previously received Rh-positive blood through a transfusion or through a defect in the placenta during an earlier pregnancy, she may have developed antibodies against the foreign blood. These antibodies may pass through the placenta into the child's bloodstream and destroy red cells, often causing the child's death.

BLOOD GROUPS

Red Cell Blood Group	Mucopoly-saccharide	SERUM BLOOD GROUP			
		O (anti-A and -B)	A (anti-B)	B (anti-A)	AB (no blood-group antibody)
O	None	−	−	−	−
A	A	+	−	+	−
B	B	+	+	−	−
AB	A and B	+	+	+	−

+ Agglutination   − No agglutination

Type O is a universal donor; type AB is a universal recipient, for transfusion.

—*J. F. S.*

BLOOD PROTEINS: Blood contains about 20% solids, mostly PROTEIN. Slightly less than half is in the liquid part (plasma), the rest in the formed-element part (red cells, white cells, and platelets). Not all the blood proteins have been identified; many "trace proteins" are present. Human plasma proteins can be separated electrophoretically into the following approximate amounts of four fractions: 57% albumins and 12% alpha, 13% beta, and 18% gamma globulins. Some important blood proteins are: (1) *hemoglobin,* the red protein in blood cells, whose major function is to carry oxygen from the lungs to the tissues; (2) *lipoproteins,* fatty proteins of the formed elements and plasma, which regulate permeability of the red cell wall and are released from platelets to hasten blood coagulation; in the plasma, alpha, and beta globulin lipoproteins carry dietary fat to fat depots; (3) *albumins,* which regulate exchange of fluids between blood and tissues, and serve as a reserve supply of protein; (4) *gamma globulins,* specific proteins of plasma called *antibodies,* which protect the animal by neutralizing viruses and bacteria; (5) *glycoproteins,* sugar proteins in the plasma fractions. An example of a specific blood protein is prothrombin, a beta globulin required for clot formation. Hemoglobin is synthesized by reticulocytes in the bone marrow; albumins and alpha and beta globulins and prothrombin are produced by the liver; gamma globulins are made by lymphoid tissue.—*E. M.*

BLOOD VESSELS: a system of tubes through which blood flows for part or all of its course through an animal body. Vessels that conduct blood away from the heart are called ARTERIES; those that conduct blood toward the heart are VEINS. Walls of arteries are generally thicker than those of veins and are often provided with muscle cells. If arteries and veins are followed away from the heart, they are found to branch extensively into smaller and smaller tubes. The smallest branches of the arteries are known as *arterioles;* the smallest branches of the veins, as *venules.* In animals with a closed circulatory system, blood flows from arterioles to venules through a network of very small vessels called CAPILLARIES. These vessels have very thin walls, and practically all exchanges of material between blood and tissues occurs through these walls. Other blood vessels serve merely to convey blood to and from capillary networks. See CIRCULATION IN LIVING THINGS. —*B. T. S.*

BLOOR, WALTER RAY, 1877–1966, Canadian–U. S. biochemist; b. Ingersoll, Ont. His research was concerned with carbohydrate esters, sugars in urine, fat in blood and milk, fat absorption, phosphatids in blood, phosphate distribution in blood, lipid metabolism, and lipids in cancer. He wrote *Biochemistry of the Fatty Acids and Their Compounds.* He was professor at the Univ. of Rochester, 1922–47.—*D. H. D. R.*

BLUSHING: reddening or flushing of the face that occurs briefly, usually as a result of timidity or embarrassment. Within reasonable limits it is normal. Confined to the face, it is due to temporary enlargement of blood vessels in that area. The impulse triggering this effect may arise in the higher centers of the brain, traveling through nerves of the vasomotor system. Blushing may also be affected by secretions of endocrine glands, particularly the adrenal and thyroid. Anger, which calls for activity by the adrenal gland, is a common cause. When the thyroid gland is overactive, blushing is likely to be extreme and to appear upon slight provocation.—*A. P. E.*

BODE, JOHANN ELERT, 1747–1826, German astronomer; b. Hamburg. Founder of *Astronomisches Jahrbuch,* 1774, which he edited for 51 yr, he is best known for the empirical rule known as BODE'S LAW, which instigated an international search for a planet predicted by it to have an orbit between those of Mars and Jupiter. The asteroid Ceres, fulfilling this requirement, was discovered by Giuseppe Piazzi, 1801.—*O. G.*

BODE'S LAW: an empirical rule that gives the approximate relative distances of the planets from the Sun. The numbers 0, 3, 6, 12,..., are written, each number after 3 being twice the previous one; 4 is added to each number, which is then divided by 10, giving the series 0.4, 0.7, 1.0, 1.6, 2.8, 5.2, 10.0, 19.6, 38.8,.... Taking the mean Earth-Sun distance as 1, actual mean distances of the planets from Sun are 0.39 (Mercury), 0.72 (Venus), 1.0 (Earth), 1.52 (Mars), 2.7 (mean of asteroids), 5.2 (Jupiter), 9.5 (Saturn), 19.2 (Uranus), 30.0 (Neptune), and 39.5 (Pluto). The series thus fails to give a number for Neptune. The law was discovered in 1772 by Bode, at which time the asteroids were not known. The discovery of Uranus, 1781, led to a search for a planet at distance 2.8, although the asteroid Ceres, at that distance, was found accidentally. It is not known whether the law has any physical significance.—*M. W. O.*

BODY CAVITY: In the simplest animals with tissues (*e.g.* coelenterates), the only body cavity is a blind sac opening at the mouth; it serves as a place where captured food can be digested. In higher animals, the body cavity separates a tubular digestive tract from the outer body wall. The body cavity of lobsters, insects, and other arthropods is actually a part of the circulatory system, and is filled with blood. In segmented worms and vertebrate animals, by contrast, the body cavity is a separate space, almost completely filled by organs bulging into it, and containing only a little fluid (lymph) as a lubricant between one part and another. The eggs of vertebrates burst from the ovaries into the bacteria-free body cavity, and are picked out of it by the open end of the oviduct (called a Fallopian tube in mammals) to be conveyed toward the outside world. Additional ducts from the body cavity of primitive vertebrates carry dissolved waste materials such as urea from the body. In higher vertebrates they become closed off and intimately associated with the blood stream as kidneys.—*L. and M. M.*

BODY SYMMETRY: the natural location of parts of an animal in such a way that the animal could be divided into equivalent halves, each the mirror image of the other. Most animals are fairly symmetrical, although many protozoans (*e.g.* ameba) lack symmetry. Other protozoans (*e.g.* volvox) reveal a *spherical symmetry:* like an orange, they can be divided into equivalent halves by any plane passing through their center. All sides of their bodies are equally affected by the surrounding medium. Coelenterates (*e.g.* jellyfish), ctenophores (*e.g.* sea walnuts), and echinoderms (*e.g.* sea stars) exhibit *radial symmetry,* much as a wheel does. They are symmetrical around a midline passing through their oral region. Through this type of symmetry the animal is well adapted for catching food or avoiding danger coming from any direction. Almost all active animals have *bilateral symmetry,* in which the body may be divided into corresponding left and right halves. The forward-moving part (usually containing the mouth) is *anterior,* the opposite end *posterior;* the upper surface (or back) is *dorsal,* the undersurface (or belly) *ventral.* In some instances it appears that animals evolved from asymmetrical forms through spherically and radially symmetrical forms to bilaterally symmetrical forms. Most plants do not show symmetry in the same strict sense that animals do, but their flowers, leaves, and stems are often truly symmetrical. A few of the lowest plants have spherical symmetry; a mushroom shows radial symmetry.—*E. G.*

Radial symmetry—around a single axis passing through the mouth —is characteristic of Porifera and Coelenterata and of adult echinoderms, such as this sea urchin. Bilateral symmetry (as in man) is the only symmetry apparent in most animal phyla, notably among chordates. (*Lorus and Margery Milne*)

BODY TEMPERATURE: Animals whose internal body temperature is regulated at a relatively constant level are called homoiothermal ("same heat"). Except on extremely hot days, their bodies are warmer than their surroundings, and they are often called warm-blooded. Only mammals and birds are warm-blooded. All other animals have body temperatures essentially identical with those of their surroundings: they are poikilothermal ("varying heat"), or cold-blooded. Actually, "warm-blooded" and "cold-blooded" are inaccurate terms, since a cold-blooded animal may have a higher body temperature than a warm-blooded animal on a very hot day or under direct sunlight. Average body temperatures in degrees Fahrenheit of various mammals and birds are:

Man	98.6	Rabbit	102.9
Horse	99.9	Elephant	97.1
Dog	101.5	Sparrow	106.7

In man, body temperature fluctuates over a range of about 1.8°F daily. In most women, there is a decrease of 1°F a few days before menstruation begins; temperature then rises and maintains a plateau until about the 14th day of the cycle, at which time there is a transitory fall of about 0.4°F, followed by a rise to approximately 0.5°F above the previous level. The 0.4°F drop followed by the rise occurs at the time of ovulation. The normal body temperature of any warm-blooded animal results from a balance of heat production against heat loss. If heat production surpasses heat loss, the result is fever; if vice versa, the result is a subnormal body temperature (hypothermia). Nerve centers for regulating body temperature are found in the part of the brain called the hypothalamus. When stimulated by a decrease in blood temperature, these centers stimulate skeletal muscles to increased activity (tonus) and the liver to greater expenditure of energy, adding heat to the blood. When stimulated by an increase in blood temperature, the nerve centers call for secretion of sweat, route more blood to skin areas, inhibit glandular activity of the liver, and lower the general tonus of skeletal muscles. These changes increase heat loss and reduce heat production.—*C. G. W.*

BOERHAAVE, HERMANN, 1668–1738, Dutch physician, anatomist, and chemist; b. Voorhout. His anatomical researches were based on the mechanism of G. A. Borelli, whose ideas he extended. A contributor to the development of chemical analysis, Boerhaave wrote *Elementa chemiae* (1724), which became a standard chemical textbook. He was professor at the Univ. of Leyden from 1709. *A Short-Title Catalogue of Books Written and Edited by Hermann Boerhaave* was published in 1927. He was a fellow of the Royal Society.—*D. H. D. R.*

Hermann Boerhaave
(N. Y. Public Library)

BOG: an aquatic habitat that develops in regions with poor drainage and a ground cover notable for retention of great quantities of water. The bog may vary in nature from areas of wet soil to expanses of open water. Usually bogs are located near slow streams or lakes and in the higher latitudes; cold climate, heavy precipitation, reduced evaporation, minimal drainage, and high atmospheric humidity are necessary factors for their formation and persistence. The water of a bog has

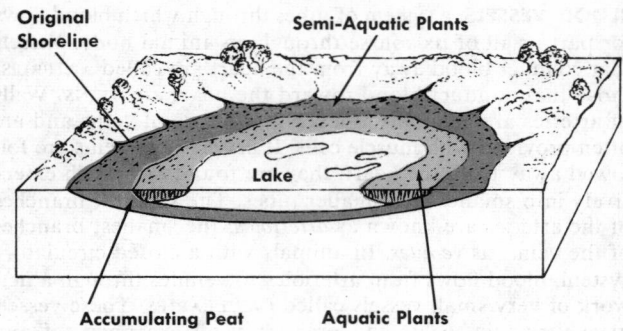

Bog formation: Model with cross-sectional cut shows peat being formed along margins of small lake. As peat accumulates, semi-aquatic plants replace aquatics; finally peat will fill lake.

so little opportunity to drain away that it becomes charged with acids and tannins from partial decay of plant debris. It remains cold through the summer because overlying vegetation, particularly peat moss (*Sphagnum*), insulates it from the Sun and warm air. Bacterial action is inhibited under these conditions, letting sunken plants accumulate faster than they decay, and gradually replace the water and become peat. The plants that can grow in bog water are almost all of kinds well adapted for survival without absorbing soluble nutrients through their roots. They conserve what moisture they have, absorb some from humid air, and take advantage of rain. Tamarack, Labrador tea, andromeda bush, and black spruce will grow with their roots surrounded by peat moss soaked with bog water. Pitcher plants and sundews thrive, supplying their needs for nitrogen by digesting insects they catch rather than absorbing nutrients through their roots (see CARNIVOROUS PLANTS).—*L. and M. M.*

BOHR, NIELS HENRIK DAVID, 1885–1962, Danish physicist; b. Copenhagen. Bohr worked with J. J. Thompson at the Cavendish Laboratory, Cambridge, Eng., 1911–12, and with E. Rutherford at Victoria Univ., Manchester, 1913. In 1920 he became head of the Institute of Theoretical Physics in Copenhagen. The 1922 Nobel prize was awarded to Bohr for his studies of the structure of atoms and the radiations from them. The Bohr model of the atom, with a modification

Niels Henrik David Bohr
(Mass. Inst. of Tech.)

by A. Sommerfeld, is the familiar atomic model in which electrons orbit about a nucleus. Bohr was a fellow of the Royal Society and an associate of the U. S. National Academy of Sciences.—*D. H. D. R.*

BOILERS: vessels which convert liquid into vapor, mainly water into steam. The basic elements of any boiler are: (1) a source of heat, usually derived from burning fuel—coal, oil, or gas; (2) a surface which transmits the heat to the water; (3) a space above the water where the steam can separate itself from water droplets. Industrial boilers were first extensively developed in the 18th cent. in conjunction with the steam engine. Wrought iron was used originally, and later, when higher pressures were needed, steel. In today's extremely high-temperature installations stainless steel is widely utilized. Although to resist pressure the ideal shape for a boiler is

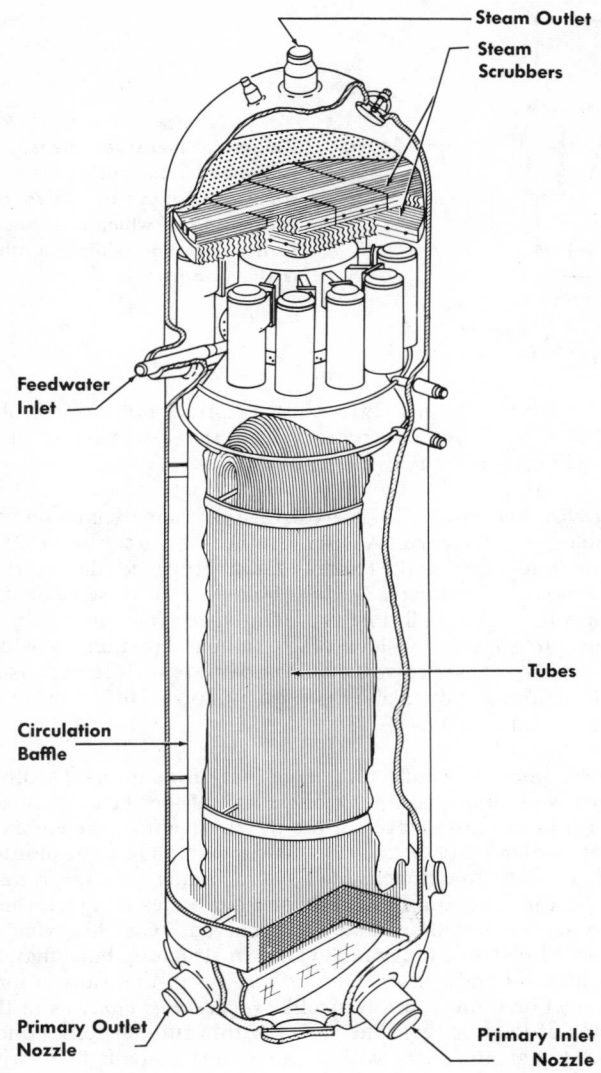

Steam Outlet

Steam Scrubbers

Feedwater Inlet

Tubes

Circulation Baffle

Primary Outlet Nozzle

Primary Inlet Nozzle

Vertical boiler (cylindrical design): Scrubbers clear the steam of water; baffle assists downflow in bent water tubes.

BOILING POINT: the temperature at which a liquid makes a transition to a gas throughout its volume. For water this temperature is 100°C when the pressure is one normal atmosphere (14.7 lb/in.²). When the boiling point of a liquid is reached, vaporization takes place, not only from the exposed surface as in EVAPORATION but also within the liquid itself. The resulting bubbling, which is ordinarily observed throughout a boiling liquid, is not an invariable accompaniment of this phenomenon, for boiling may occur quietly. A surer indication of boiling, at least for pure substances, is that the temperature remains constant during the vaporization (see CHANGE OF STATE). Boiling occurs when the vapor pressure of the liquid (the pressure exerted by molecules at the surface leaving the body of the liquid) exactly balances the atmospheric pressure. If the external pressure is low, boiling occurs at a low temperature; when water is heated at an elevation of 5,000 ft, for example, water boils at 87°C because of the diminished atmospheric pressure. If, however, the air and the vapor above the liquid are prevented from escaping because they are held in by a tight cover (as in a pressure cooker), the pressure will increase, and the liquid will be unable to boil until a much higher temperature than its normal boiling point is reached.—*J. E. W.*

BOISBAUDRAN, PAUL ÉMILE LECOQ DE, 1838–1912, French chemist; b. Cognac. Self-educated in science, he set up a private laboratory and began a study of the spectra of metals. He discovered gallium (1875), the first element to be discovered using a spark spectrum; samarium (1879); and dysprosium (1886).—*D. H. D. R.*

BOK, BART JAN, 1906–   , Dutch-U. S. astronomer; b. Hoorn, Netherlands. He is known for his researches on galactic dynamics, galactic structure, interstellar matter, and radio astronomy. In addition to numerous scientific papers, Bok wrote *The Distribution of Stars in Space* (1937) and *The Astronomer's Universe* (1958), and collaborated on *The Fundamental Properties of the Galactic System* (1941), *Basic Marine Navigation* (1952), and *The Milky Way* (1957). Director of the Mt. Stromlo Observatory, Australia, 1957–66, he became head of the Steward Observatory, Arizona, in 1966.—*D. H. D. R.*

BOLOMETER: an instrument that measures the intensity of radiant energy, usually in the infrared spectrum. In its simplest form, a bolometer consists of two thermistors, *i.e.* chips of semiconducting material whose electrical resistance varies

spherical, practical considerations of manufacture and manipulation of steam and water make the cylinder the most typical shape. Boilers generally fall into two groups: fire-tube and water-tube units. Fire-tube boilers have straight tubes, vertical or horizontal in position, surrounded by water. Hot gases from the furnace passing through the tubes heat the water. Boilers of this type have a large water storage capacity with a resulting stability of operation; they can reach efficiencies close to 75% and are in common operation in all types of small installations. Water-tube boilers, however, are far more extensively used; they are in all large installations from ships to utility power plants. Banks of water-filled tubes, either straight or bent and exposed to furnace gases, are placed between cylindrical drums. Convective currents (and pumps when necessary) carry the water-saturated steam to the drums where the steam and water droplets are separated. Because the drums of a water-tube boiler contain no heating surface, they are much smaller than the shells of fire-tube boilers and therefore much stronger and capable of standing higher pressures. Modern water-tube units can deliver over 1,750,000 lb of steam per hour at pressures up to 2,700 lb/in.² and operate at efficiencies close to 90%.—*A. L.*

Horizontal boiler: Integral brick-lined firebox receives fuel (oil) from sprayer at right. (*Babcock and Wilcox*)

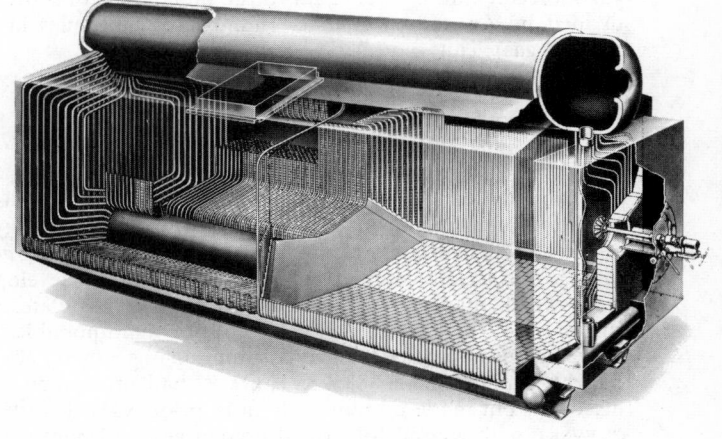

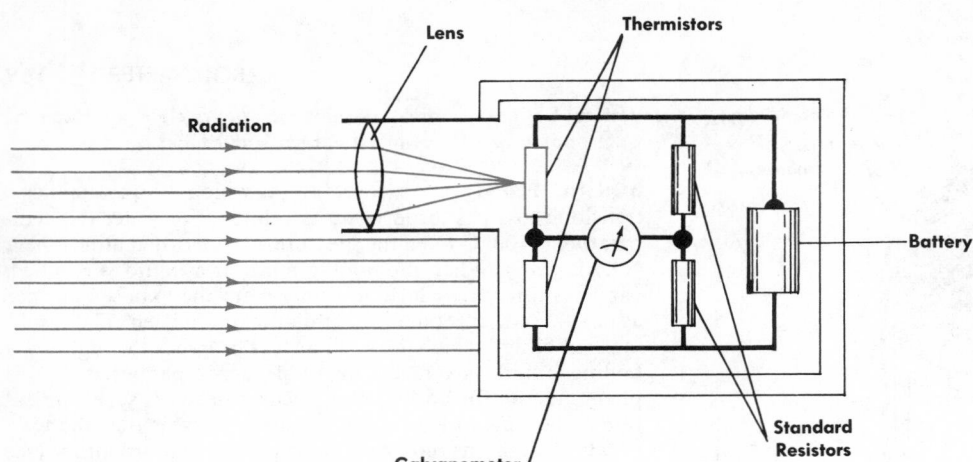

Bolometer measures intensity of radiation by comparing the electrical resistances of two thermistors, one of which is exposed to the radiation while the other is shielded from it.

Labels: Lens, Thermistors, Radiation, Battery, Galvanometer, Standard Resistors

with temperature. The resistance of a thermistor that is exposed to radiant energy is compared by means of a bridge circuit (see illus.) to the resistance of a shielded reference thermistor. See INFRARED RAYS.—*D. H. L.*

BOLTWOOD, BERTRAM BORDEN, 1870–1927, U. S. chemist; b. Amherst, Mass. He discovered ionium (discovered also by others, independently) and showed the relationship between uranium, ionium, and radium. An early worker in the field of dating minerals by radioactivity, he contributed to the understanding of isotopes. He was a member of the National Academy of Sciences.—*D. H. D. R.*

BOLTZMANN, LUDWIG, 1844–1906, Austrian physicist; b. Vienna. With J. C. Maxwell and J. W. Gibbs he developed statistical mechanics, particularly the theory of systems of particles subject to the laws of classical mechanics (the Boltzmann statistics). This theory is now applied also to systems of particles subject to the new mechanics. Boltzmann brought thermodynamics and molecular physics together with his H-Theorem, associating entropy with probability and identifying the flow of time with the increase of entropy. He demonstrated Josef Stefan's empirical law by the analysis of a Carnot engine operating on radiation (1884), and obtained the theorem of the equipartition of energy. His *Lectures on Gas Theory* (1896–98) contains his major work. He was a fellow of the Royal Society and an associate of the U. S. National Academy of Sciences.—*C. J. S.*

BOLTZMANN'S CONSTANT: a modification of the universal gas constant, *R,* occurring in the ideal-gas equation $pv = RT$ (see GAS). Based on a mole (gram-molecular weight) of any pure gas, *R* has a value of 8.314×10^7 ergs/mole = K°, or 8.314 j/mole-K°. Boltzmann's constant, *k,* is based on a single gas molecule and is thus equal to the molar gas constant *R* divided by Avogadro's number (number of molecules in a mole of gas). Thus

$$k = \frac{8.314 \times 10^7}{6.023 \times 10^{23}} = 1.38 \times 10^{-16} \text{ ergs/K°}.$$

—*A. E.*

BOLYAI, JÁNOS, 1802–60, Hungarian mathematician, co-discoverer of non-Euclidean geometry. He was a child prodigy, and by 1823 had completed a draft for his paper *Abstract Science of Space:* a complete, consistent, systematic development which made no use of Euclid's parallel postulate. It showed that the parallel postulate not only is impossible to prove but also is not a necessary assumption in geometry. This paper was published in 1831. K. F. GAUSS had anticipated the discovery but made no public claim to priority. N. I. LOBACHEVSKI, with whom Bolyai had no contact, had published a similar system in 1829. Because of prior publication, Lobachevski is generally credited with the discovery of non-Euclidean geometry.—*H. C.*

BONDI, HERMANN, 1919– , British mathematician and cosmologist, b. Vienna, Austria. Author of *Cosmology* (1952), Bondi together with Thomas Gold proposed the "perfect cosmological principle," which holds the universe to be uniform throughout all time as well as space. This principle led them to suggest the idea of continuous creation, in which material appears in space to compensate for the expansion of the universe of galaxies. See COSMOLOGY. He is a fellow of the Royal Society.—*G. H.*

BONE: the hard connecting tissue that forms the SKELETON of most vertebrates; also, any single unit of the skeleton. Bones form in the early stages of the development of the embryo, but hardening (OSSIFICATION) is not complete until months after birth, sometimes much later. General shape ranges from the long, tubular shafts of limb bones to short, thick masses of vertebrae, and from curved, band-like ribs to warped plates of the cranial vault. In structure, bone may be quite solid and dense (*compact bone,* as in the walls of long bones) or spongy and latticelike (*cancellous bone,* as in the ends of long bones). The cavity within tubular long bones, like the small spaces within cancellous bone, is filled with the soft tissue called marrow. Excluding marrow, bone is about 25% water, 30% organic materials (mainly protein), and 45% inorganic salts (chiefly tricalcium phosphate). The organic materials give bone elasticity, and the inorganic salts impart rigidity.

Since bone makes up the structural framework of the body and plays a purely mechanical part in movement, it often is mistakenly looked upon as an inert, lifeless material. Actually, bone contains living cells, richly supplied with nerves and blood vessels, and highly sensitive to changes in the organism. The outer layer of bone is a tough membrane, the *periosteum,* to which muscles are attached. Within the periosteum lies the hard (sometimes spongy) bony layer. Blood vessels, lymph vessels, and nerves enter the bony layer from the periosteum through a system of branching canals. These are called the *Haversian canals,* and they run lengthwise through the bony

STRENGTH OF BONE COMPARED TO OAK AND STEEL

	Tensile Strength (resistance to pull)	Compressive Strength (stress applied with grain)	Shear Strength (bending)
Bone	13,000–18,000 lb./in.²	18,000–24,000 lb./in.²	12,000 lb./in.²
White oak	12,500	7,000	4,000
Medium steel	65,000	60,000	40,000

layer. Bone cells are embedded in small cavities (*lacunae*) in the bony layer and are arranged in concentric rings around the Haversian canals. Extensions of the bone cells, passing through tiny tubes, connect one bone cell to another and to the Haversian canals. This system enables the bone cells to receive food and oxygen and to eliminate wastes. The marrow that fills the cavities of bones may be yellow (mostly fat) or red; red marrow, found only in mammals, produces red blood cells and certain white blood cells (see BLOOD).

In some animals bone may grow throughout life. Tubular bones increase in thickness through absorption of bone on the inside and deposition of bone on the ouside of the bony layer. Growth in length takes place only at the ends of the bone shaft, not at the ends of the bone itself. The shaft (*diaphysis*) is separated from the flared end parts (*epiphyses*) by a cartilage plate, which is the "growth apparatus." As one side of the plate grows, the other side calcifies, adding bone to the end of the shaft. As a hollow cylinder, bone is much stronger than it would be if the same amount of bone were in solid form. The strength of bone as compared with the strength of white oak and medium steel is indicated in the table.—*R. M. and A. P. E.*

BONNET, CHARLES, 1720–93, Swiss zoologist; b. Geneva. The discoverer of parthenogenesis in plant lice (aphids), he offered it as evidence in support of the theory of preformation (a female contains all of her descendants). He believed in a progression of the world toward perfection, a theory that contains some elements of Lamarckian evolution. His *Writings on Natural History and Philosophy* (1779–83) comprise 18 vols. His writings on natural history and philosophy were published in his *Oeuvres d'histoire naturelle et de philosophie* (1779–83). He was a fellow of the Royal Society.—*D. H. D. R.*

BOOLE, GEORGE, 1815–1864, logician and mathematician, b. Lincoln, England. He was professor of mathematics at Queens Coll., Ireland, and in 1857 was elected a Fellow of the Royal Society. He published important essays and texts on differential equations and the calculus of finite differences, but his best-known work, *An Investigation of the Laws of Thought* (1854), is devoted to mathematical logic and theory of probability. It contains one of the earliest attempts to discuss the logic of sentences and of sets using an artificial notation similar to notations employed in mathematics.—*I. L.*

BORA: a cold wind occurring on the Dalmatian coast of Yugoslavia. The air flowing downhill is so cold that adiabatic warming does not bring its temperature up to normal by the time it reaches level land or the sea coast. The bora is a katabatic, or fall, wind. (See WIND, LOCAL.)—*P. L.*

BORATES: inorganic salts or organic esters of boric acid, particularly of meta- and tetra-boric acid. The most common is borax (sodium tetraborate decahydrate). Borates react with strong acid solutions to form boric acid. Alkali metal borates normally react with soluble metal salts to precipitate heavy metal borates: a characteristic useful in water softening.—*D. P. B.*

BORAX: the mineral tincal, found in alkali lakes and deserts, or the commercial product of the same chemical composition: decahydrated sodium borate ($Na_2B_4O_7 \cdot 10H_2O$). The salt of a weak acid, borax hydrolyzes to produce a distinctly alkaline solution. When heated with metal oxides, it fuses and takes on a color distinctive of the metal; this is the basis for the borax bead test to determine the presence of certain metals. A white crystalline substance or powder, borax is used in enamels, heat-resistant glass, and glazing; as a scouring and cleansing agent, and as a softener for detergents.—*D. P. B.*

BORAZON: an extremely hard form of boron nitride prepared at very high temperature and pressure. It can substitute for the diamond in certain industrial grinding operations.—*W. P. C.*

Borazon (*left*), a hard synthetic crystal of boron nitride, is here shown with diamond as the two are being heated.

A minute and a half later, a temperature of approximately 1600°F causes the diamond (*right*) to oxidize.

In another minute, diamond vanishes. Borazon combines endurance at high temperatures with diamondlike hardness. (*General Electric*)

BORDET, JULES JEAN BAPTISTE VINCENT, 1870–1961, Belgian bacteriologist; b. Soignies. He studied the rupture of cells produced by bacteria and showed that two different substances were involved in the process. For this contribution to immunology and other discoveries concerned with immunity, he received the 1919 Nobel prize. After assisting Élie Metchnikoff at the Pasteur Institute in Paris, 1894–1901, he founded the Pasteur Institute in Brussels. The Univ. of Brussels appointed him professor of bacteriology in 1907. He was a member of the Royal Society of London.—*D. H. D. R.*

BOREL, ÉMILE FÉLIX ÉDOUARD JUSTIN, 1871–1956, French mathematician; b. Saint-Affrique, Aveyron. In 1927 he became director of l'Institut Henri-Poincaré. He was president of the Academy of Sciences. His most notable achievements were in function theory and theory of probability.—*H. C.*

BORELLI, GIOVANNI ALFONSO, 1608–79, Italian biologist; b. Naples. He did research in physics and astronomy, but most important was his study of the mechanical aspects of living things. His *Concerning the Motion of Animals* (1680–81) contains the first major application of mechanics to the movements of animals.—*D. H. D. R.*

BORIC ACID (or **ortho-boric acid**), H_3BO_3: a white solid which is an acid so weak that it barely affects litmus. On heating, it gives up water to form first metaboric acid (HBO_2), then tetraboric acid ($H_2B_4O_7$). Strenuous heating yields the anhydride, boric oxide (B_2O_3). The dehydrated forms all revert to boric acid when dissolved in water. Although toxic when taken internally, boric acid has wide use as an external medicine, particularly as an eye-wash, because of its bacteriostatic and fungistatic action.—*D. P. B.*

BORN, MAX, 1882–   , German physicist; b. Breslau. His research provided a reconciliation between the new quantum mechanics and the older classical mechanics. For this work—especially for his statistical interpretation of the wave function—he shared the 1954 Nobel prize with W. W. G. Bothe. Born is a fellow of the Royal Society and an associate of the National Academy of Sciences. Among his many publications are *The Restless Universe* (1936) and *The Natural Philosophy of Cause and Chance* (1949).—*D. H. D. R.*

BORON: a non-metallic element (B); at. no. 5, at. wt 10.82. It has at least two isotopes of at. wt 10 and 11. Though not a metal, boron is similar to aluminum in belonging to group III of the periodic table and in having valency 3. In chemical behavior it resembles silicon (and, to a lesser extent, carbon) more than it does aluminum. Elemental boron may be either dark (gray to black) crystals (sp gr 2.3) or a greenish-yellow amorphous mass (sp gr 1.73). It melts at 2300°C, boils at 2550°C, and is insoluble in water, alcohol, or caustic alkali solutions; it is soluble in sulfuric acid as well as in most molten metals. Boron reacts with all the halogens to form boron halides. At ordinary temperatures, it is not affected by air. At high temperatures (over 1,000°C) it reacts with air to form boric oxide and boron nitride. It is one of the few elements to combine directly with nitrogen. A white powder melting at approximately 3,000°C, boron nitride is similar to graphite in structure and lubricating properties and is sometimes referred to as "white graphite" (see also BORAZON). With carbon, boron forms boron carbide (B_4C), a refractory black solid that ranks next to diamond in hardness; it is probably not a true chemical compound but a solution of carbon in a boron lattice. Similarly the borides, produced by heating a powdered metal with boron, are probably lattice-like crystal structures. Another unusual characteristic of boron is

that although it is toxic to plant and animal life in certain concentrations, trace amounts of it are essential to plant growth. This element forms a series of compounds with hydrogen (boron hydrides) which are in some ways analogous to hydrocarbons: they have unusually high heats of combustion, approximately twice that of a hydrocarbon of the same weight on a calculated basis, and are used as high-energy fuels.—*D. P. B.*

BOSCH, CARL, 1874–1940, German chemist; b. Cologne. About 1910 he became interested in adapting to large-scale production the HABER PROCESS for synthesis of ammonia from nitrogen and hydrogen under high pressure. He invented and developed the equipment for industrial production of ammonia and for its oxidation to nitric acid, and also started the synthetic production of methanol on an industrial scale at the Badische Anilin-und-Soda-Fabrik. In 1931 he shared with Friedrich Bergius the Nobel prize in chemistry for contributions to chemical high-pressure methods.—*E. F.*

BOSE, SIR JAGADIS CHANDRA (CHUNDER), 1858–1937, Indian physicist and biologist; b. Mymensingh, Bengal. Most of his research was devoted to comparative studies of responses to stimuli of plant and animal tissues. He invented automatic recorders of high sensitivity and precision for his work, including an instrument for measuring plant growth. Bose also discovered that many inorganic substances react to stimuli somewhat as living tissue does. Founder of the Bose Research Institute, Calcutta, he was also the author of *Plant Response* (1936), *Comparative Electro-Physiology* (1907), *The Physiology of Photosynthesis* (1924), and many technical papers. He was a fellow of the Royal Society.—*D. H. D. R.*

BOTANY: the branch of BIOLOGY dealing with PLANTS. It began with the lore of the herb-gatherers, who collected specific plants for primitive medicines. No doubt these men came to know useless plants as well as useful ones. Yet Theophrastus, "father of botany," was the first to write an account of all the plants he knew, mentioning medicinal values only where these were clear to him. The economic side of botany continued to dominate after Theophrastus' time. Around A. D. 60, Dioscorides wrote the earliest *materia medica.* This manuscript, together with illustrations of economically important plants made by an earlier artist (Crateuas), was copied and translated as the principal information on the subject until the 16th cent. Then a new group of writers and illustrators busied themselves, particularly in the valley of the Rhine, as the "herbalists" who wrote "herbals" (books on herbs). The most famous of these and the dates of their works were Otto Brunfels (1530), Jerome Bock (1539), and Leonard Fuchs (1542). A century later, the English microscopist Nehemiah Grew began making consecutive studies of plant anatomy, but he regarded the drawings of sections he made through stems and roots as little more than intricate designs. His book *Anatomy of Plants* (1682) offers handsome illustrations, but no real information on function. Although Grew said that flowers might be involved in sexual reproduction, he did not pursue this experimentally; but his names for FLOWER parts have been used ever since. Details of flower function awaited the study of a self-taught botanist, Wilhelm Hofmeister of Leipzig, who worked out the embryology of flowering plants when he was 24 yr old (1849) and followed it by clarifying the reproductive cycles in liverworts, mosses, horsetails, and ferns. Our modern understanding of ALTERNATION OF GENERATIONS is merely an extension of Hofmeister's work, yet it provides one of the great unifying concepts, bringing the whole plant kingdom into one logical series.

During the past century, improved techniques and experiments have provided the basis for comprehensive theories on

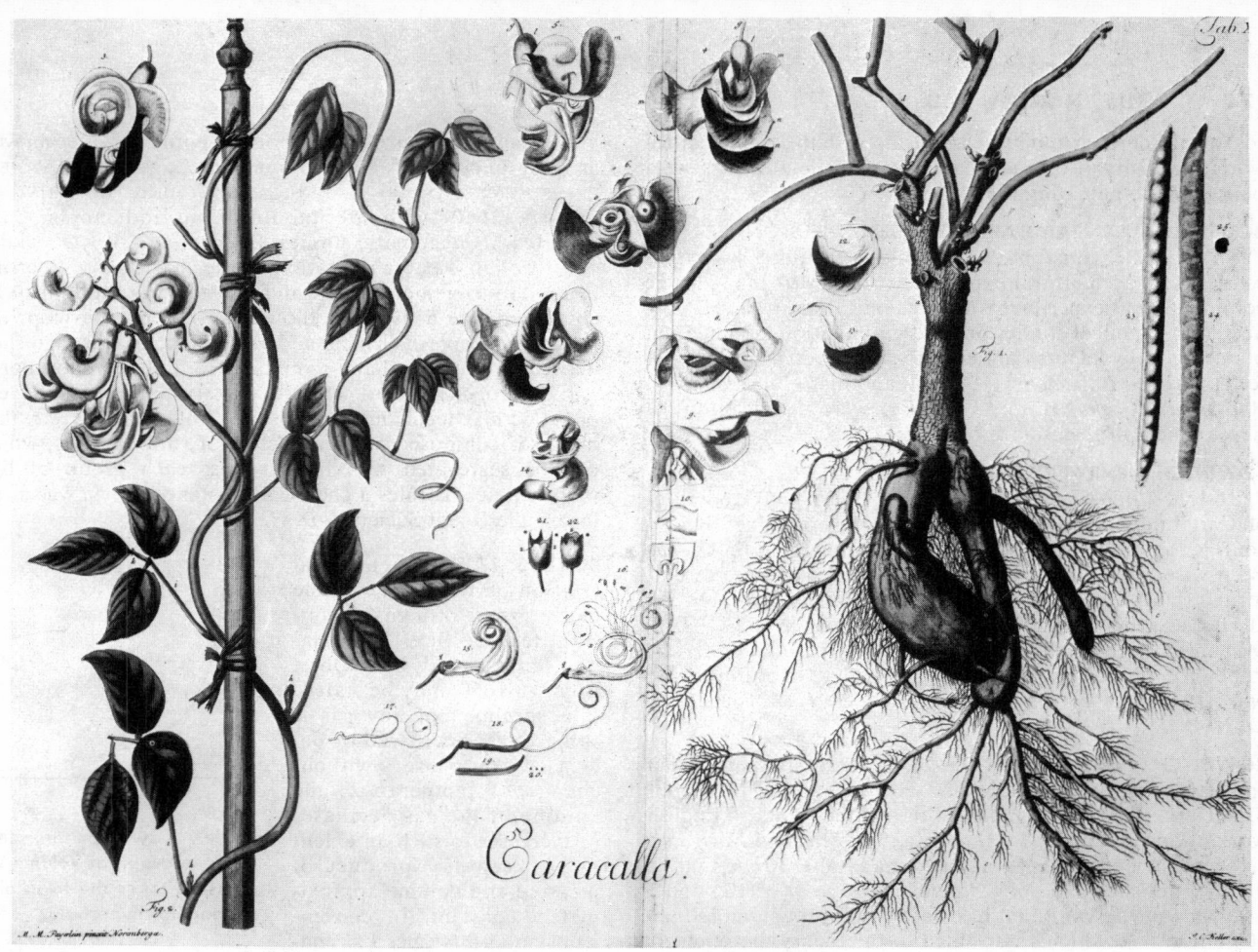

Old engraving of member of Pea Family, economically important and including 12,000 members, is one of the many closely observed renderings that put botany much in debt to artists. This engraving is from the posthumously published *Hortus nitidissimus,* or *Most Resplendent Garden (1779),* of the German scholar Christoph Jacob Trew.

the function of roots, stems, leaves, reproductive structures, and their parts. In recent decades, when radioactive chemical compounds became available as tracers in following pathways within a plant, many theoretical predictions were confirmed. Numerous complex reactions in PHOTOSYNTHESIS have been worked out. This vastly important chemical sequence is almost unique in converting solar energy into the energy of chemical bonds in substances used as food by plants and animals. Great human effort is going into devising machines to imitate photosynthetic chemistry.

The techniques of the microbiologist, which were introduced first by Robert Koch almost a century ago, have led to a better understanding of bacteria and inconspicuous fungi. Refinements of these techniques have allowed the investigation of filter-passing viruses and have led to the introduction of improved ways to combat or control the diseases caused by bacteria and viruses. Some bacteria have also been put to work producing chemical compounds, *e.g.* acetone and alcohols, valuable as solvents in industry. Botanical studies at the molecular level are helping biologists to understand inheritance in all forms of life and are providing a better idea of the nature of life itself. For example, work on the mold *Neurospora* has shown that genes in the chromosomes control enzymes, which in turn regulate chemical activities in the cells.

At the other extreme, botanists dealing with the whole plant in its natural environment have been able to account for the distribution of plants, habitat by habitat and biome by biome. Many of these men have investigated adaptations to environment, from both physiological and structural points of view. This is particularly fundamental information, since green plants usually provide the food for the animals in a biotic

province, and to a large extent influence the kinds that can thrive there. See ADAPTATIONS IN ANIMALS AND PLANTS; BACTERIOLOGY; BIOME; ECOLOGY; MICROBIOLOGY; PLANT GEOGRAPHY.—*L. and M. M.*

BOTHE, WALTHER WILHELM GEORG, 1891–1957, German physicist; b. Oranienburg. An experimental physicist, he developed important techniques in the study of cosmic rays and nuclear physics, and supervised the construction of Germany's first cyclotron (1944). He developed (with Hans Geiger) a coincidence method of counting subatomic particles and measuring very small time intervals. For his research in cosmic radiation—particularly the coincidence method and his use of it—he shared the 1954 Nobel prize with Max Born. He went to the Univ. of Heidelberg in 1932 and was director of the Institute of Physics there from 1934.—*D. H. D. R.*

BOURBAKI, NICOLAS: a pseudonym adopted by a group of French mathematicians. First appearing on the mathematical scene in the middle 1930s, the name was signed to notes, reviews, and other papers published in the *Comptes rendus* of the French Academy of Science and elsewhere. The group is engaged in writing a comprehensive treatise, entitled *Eléments de mathématique,* of which 25 vols. had appeared by 1960. This work is exerting great influence on the development of 20th-cent. mathematics. The membership of the group is not fixed, apparently varying between 10 and 20. All members have been French with the exception of Samuel Eilenberg, originally from Poland. André Weil and Jean Dieudonné, two of the founders, retired from the group upon reaching 50. Many stories have been promulgated concerning the imaginary corporeal Bourbaki and his relationship with the mathematical world. Far from discouraging such stories, the members seem bent upon perpetuating the hoax.—*H. C.*

BOUSSINGAULT, JEAN BAPTISTE JOSEPH DIEUDONNÉ, 1802–1887, French chemist; b. Paris. While operating his Alsatian estate as an agricultural experiment station (from 1834) he combined field experiments with chemical analysis. He pioneered in chemical studies on seed germination, assimilation of nitrogen by plants, soil fertility, and nutritive value of feeds. His *Rural Economy* (1843–44) and his 7-vol. *Agronomy, Agricultural Chemistry, and Physiology* were significant in the development of scientific agriculture.—*A. I.*

BOWDITCH, HENRY PICKERING, 1840–1911, U. S. physiologist; b. Boston. While working in the Leipzig (Germany) laboratory of Carl Ludwig, Bowditch stated the "all or none" law of contraction of the heart muscle and demonstrated the *Treppe* (step-wise) increase of its contraction under successive uniform stimuli. In the same year (1871) Bowditch established at Harvard the first physiological laboratory in the U. S. A. He continued research on heart physiology, vasomotor nerves, knee-jerk, physiology of vision, and growth of children. He was a member of the National Academy of Sciences.—*D. H. D. R.*

BOWDITCH, NATHANIEL, 1773–1838, U. S. mathematician and astronomer; b. Salem, Mass.; self-taught. In 1799 he published a revised and expanded edition of the standard English work on navigation by J. H. Moore, *The Practical Navigator.* In successive editions he made so many alterations that he finally published *The New Practical Navigator* (1802) under his own name, a work that has since gone through more than 60 editions. Bowditch contributed to the theory that meteors were of cosmic origin, and in 1815 he published the results of an 8-yr study of the New England meteor of 1807. A fellow of the American Academy of Arts and Sciences, he published 23 papers on varied astronomical and navigational subjects in the Academy's *Memoirs,* 1804–20. He translated and published 4 vols. of P. S. Laplace's *Celestial Mechanics* (1829–39), with elaborate additions that more than doubled the size of the work. He was a fellow of the Royal Society.—*S. B.*

BOWEN, NORMAN LEVI, 1887–1956, Canadian-U. S. petrologist; b. Kingston, Ont. From 1912 to his death he worked in experimental petrology at the Carnegie Institution, Washington, D. C. His success in crystallizing quartz from an anhydrous melt showed that water was unnecessary for quartz formation. He also put forth a theory of gravitative crystallization differentiation, and he worked on the order of crystallization of minerals in cooling magma. He was a fellow of the Royal Society and a member of the National Academy of Sciences.—*D. H. D. R.*

BOYLE, ROBERT, 1627–91, English physicist and chemist; b. Lismore Castle, Ireland. His interests were divided between pneumatics, chemistry, and theology. In pneumatics he conducted elaborate studies of reduced air pressure, evacuating containers by means of pumps built by D. Papin and R. Hooke; one consequence was BOYLE'S LAW. Boyle showed that air is a material substance possessing weight, and investigated the effect of

Robert Boyle
(N. Y. Public Library)

atmospheric pressure on the boiling-point of water as well as the function of air in sound propagation. His NEW EXPERIMENTS PHYSICO-MECHANICAL TOUCHING THE SPRING OF THE AIR (1660), with later modifications and supplements, reported his pneumatic studies. In chemistry, Boyle's major contribution was his refutation of the Aristotelian doctrine of the "four elements" of which matter was thought to be composed. He arrived at, though he did not develop, the modern concepts of element and compound, and distinguished between a compound and a mixture. He isolated phosphorus and hydrogen. In THE SCEPTICAL CHYMIST (1661) he expounded his "mechanical philosophy" of chemistry: *i.e.* that matter is composed of "corpuscles" of various types, which can be segregated into like groups; each group of like corpuscles constitutes a chemical substance. Boyle was a fellow of the Royal Society.—*D. H. D. R.*

BOYLE'S LAW: an empirical relation between the volume and pressure of a gas at constant temperature. This relation, first noted by Robert Boyle in 1660, may be stated: If a specimen of any gas is subjected to increased or decreased pressure without change of temperature, the volume of the gas decreases or increases to such an extent as to keep the product of pressure and volume approximately constant. In convenient symbols, P times $V \cong$ constant (T constant). When the temperature is high and the pressure low, most gases obey Boyle's law closely.—*J. E. W.*

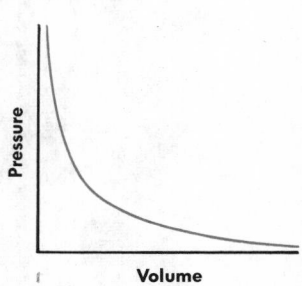

Boyle's Law: For an ideal gas, the graph of volume vs. pressure takes the form of a rectangular hyperbola.

BRADLEY, JAMES, 1693–1762, English astronomer; b. Sherbourn. He studied Jupiter's satellites and computed orbits of comets. In 1728 he discovered the ABERRATION OF LIGHT —an apparent shift in the positions of stars due to the orbital motion of Earth—and he announced it in a paper published in 1729. In another paper (1748) he announced his discovery of the nutation of Earth. Bradley became astronomer-royal of England in 1742. His *Miscellaneous Works and Correspondence* appeared in 1832. He was a fellow of the Royal Society. —*D. H. D. R.*

BRAGG, SIR WILLIAM HENRY, 1862–1942, English physicist; b. Cumberland. While professor of mathematics and physics at the Univ. of Adelaide, Australia, Bragg did research on the passage of α and β particles and γ rays through matter, and determined the range of α particles in various substances. These researches are described in his *Studies in Radioactivity* (1912). For his study of crystal structure by means of x-rays, he shared the 1915 Nobel prize with his son, W. L. Bragg, with whom he wrote *X-rays and Crystal Structure* (1915). He was a fellow of the Royal Society and received the Copley Medal for 1930. In 1923 he became director of the Royal Institution of Great Britain. He was an associate of the U. S. National Academy of Sciences.—*D. H. D. R.*

BRAGG, SIR WILLIAM LAWRENCE, 1890–   , Australian-English physicist; b. Adelaide. In 1912 he began research on crystal structure by means of x-rays—a method created by M. von Laue. His father, W. H. Bragg, worked with him, and their results were published in *X-rays and Crystal Structure* (1915). For this research they shared the Nobel prize, 1915. W. L. Bragg became a fellow of the Royal Society in 1921. —*D. H. D. R.*

BRAHE, TYCHO, 1546–1601, Danish astronomer; b. Knudstrup, Denmark (now in Sweden). His fame rests upon his design and construction of astronomical instruments of unprecedented accuracy, and his use of these to obtain positions of stars, planets, Sun, and Moon with notable precision. He also proposed a geostatic, heliocentric theory of the universe, the "Tychonic system." King Frederik II of Denmark gave Brahe the island of Hveen (1576) and ample funds to

Tycho Brahe
(U. S. Navy)

build there Uraniborg, a combined dwelling and observatory, and Stjerneborg, an observatory. Brahe did his most important work at Hveen during the next two decades, leaving Hveen when deprived of his royal pension. Kepler made extensive use of Brahe's observations in testing his theories of planetary motion. Brahe's own descriptions of his instruments appear in his *Astronomiae instauratae mechanica* (1598). (English trans., *Tycho Brahe's Description of His Instruments and Scientific Work,* 1946). His *Opera omnia* (15 vols., 1913–1929) were edited by J. L. E. Dreyer.—*D. H. D. R.*

BRAHMAGUPTA, b. 598, Hindu mathematician, birthplace unknown. *Brahma-sphuta-siddhanta* (628), his most important book (*siddhanta* means "astronomical book"), contains chapters on mathematics, including solutions of determinate and indeterminate equations of the first and second degree, a study of cyclic quadrilaterals, and rules concerning permutations. Many extracts from the mathematical parts are given in *History of Hindu Mathematics* (1935–38) by D. Datta and A. N. Singh. Brahmagupta's *Khandakhadyka* (665; English trans. by P. C. Sengupta, 1939) was an important treatise on mathematical astronomy. Brahmagupta's books exerted marked influence on Islamic mathematicians and astronomers and, through them, on Europeans. Little is known of his life other than that he worked at Ujjain.—*D. H. D. R.*

BRAIN: the principal center of nervous coordination in the body of a vertebrate animal. This enlarged anterior ("upper") portion of the central NERVOUS SYSTEM is continuous with the posterior ("lower") portion, the spinal cord. Analogous centers are found in the nervous systems of many invertebrate animals, *e.g.* worms, mollusks, and arthropods. Jawless vertebrates, such as lampreys, have only three major divisions of the brain: hindbrain, midbrain, and forebrain. Jaw-bearing fishes, amphibians, reptiles, birds, and mammals all show additional specialization, with the hindbrain and the forebrain both subdivided into anterior and posterior portions. These and other evolutionary changes in the brain parallel changes in the sensory, muscular, and peripheral nervous organization of the various vertebrates. The following description applies to the mammalian brain:

Hindbrain: Continuous with the spinal cord is the more posterior part of the hindbrain, the *medulla,* which has a thin roof but thick side walls and floor. The thick portions conduct excitation between the spinal cord and anterior regions of the brain. They also contain centers called nuclei, which are responsible for regulating breathing, blood pressure, and the rate of heartbeat. Anterior to the medulla, the hindbrain is enlarged dorsally into two small hemispheric masses constituting the *cerebellum.* These serve to coordinate the contraction of voluntary muscles, producing smooth movements of the body. Ventral to the cerebellum, the hindbrain provides

a continuation for the longitudinal nerve trunks linking the medulla and midbrain, and also contains relay nuclei for excitation going to and from the cerebellum. A prominent transverse swelling, the *pons* (Latin for bridge), contains fibers connecting the right and left sides of the brain.

Midbrain: In addition to conducting excitation between the hindbrain and the forebrain, the midbrain contains centers that project from the surface as the two pairs of *colliculi.* The anterior pair contain the control network for eye movements. The posterior pair are the centers of hearing.

Forebrain: The posterior of the two subdivisions of the forebrain has heavy side walls, the *thalami,* connecting the midbrain to the anterior subdivision of the forebrain. The floor of the posterior subdivision of the forebrain, the hypothalamus, contains nuclei regulating metabolic rate, body temperature, sleep, and many other functions—perhaps rage and fear as well. The hypothalamus appears to secrete into a ventral outgrowth, the posterior lobe of the pituitary gland, the hormones once credited to this lobe. The roof of the posterior subdivision of the forebrain projects dorsally as the pineal body, or epiphysis, and also continues forward as a finger-shaped extension into the cavity of the anterior subdivision of the forebrain. This extension, like the thin roof of the medulla, allows blood vessels to come close to the cerebrospinal fluid, which fills the cavities (ventricles) of the brain. In this way, food materials and oxygen can reach the brain from

The human brain: The visible divisions (here, of the left half) hardly begin to suggest the complexity of interconnection that enables the brain to serve as a central exchange of nervous impulses—correlating messages, representing the environment, storing impressions, thinking, and initiating action. An enlarged extremity of the central nervous system, it connects with the remainder through the medulla oblongata, a part of the hindbrain. Other hindbrain portions visible here are the cerebellum and the pons. Although, in man, some of the midbrain's functions have been transferred to the cerebrum, its reflex centers for eye adjustments and hearing—the colliculi—are still identifiable. On the posterior or "lower" forebrain, the thalamus, the hypothalamus, and the pineal gland can be discerned. The most distinctive feature of the human brain is the great development of the anterior, "upper" forebrain into the paired hemispheres of the cerebrum. Its thin outer layer, the cortex or "gray matter," lies on deep convolutions that extend its effective surface. Underlying the cortex is the "white matter," consisting of fibers connecting cortex cells to other parts of the brain, or interconnecting the two cerebral hemispheres by way of the prominent corpus callosum, which allows both sides of the brain to learn at once. (*Waldeck from FLO*)

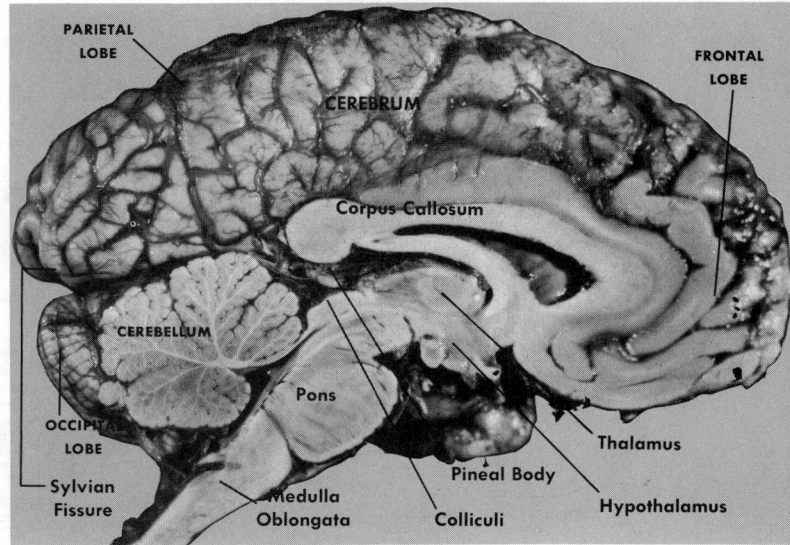

within, and wastes can be disposed of. The pineal gland secretes the hormone melitonin (which influences the development of the sex glands) and serves as a "biological clock," kept synchronized with daylight by nerves of the sympathetic part of the autonomic nervous system.

The anterior subdivision of the forebrain is the most highly developed part of a mammal's brain, usually equaling or exceeding in volume all other parts of the central nervous system. Its roof is organized into two massive swellings, a right and a left *cerebral hemisphere;* in mankind these hemispheres are so extensive that they completely cover all the rest of the brain. Most active cells are near the surface of the *cerebral cortex,* where they form a seven-layered gray zone of many millions of cells. Many different areas of the cortex can be distinguished, each concerned with a particular function. Sensory and motor activities of each body region have matching areas in the cortex. Other areas, known as association areas, seem responsible for thought and for memory. In their exposed position, the cells of the cerebral cortex can be bathed in additional amounts of cerebrospinal fluid, circulating between the sheaths (meninges) over the brain, and can be served, too, by fine blood vessels coursing over the surface of the brain. Connections from the cortex to other parts of the brain comprise the floor of this subdivision of the forebrain. Millions of additional fibers interconnect the two hemispheres, most of them in the *corpus callosum.* They allow the right side of the brain to learn from sensory experiences of the body's left side, and the left side of the brain to learn from the body's right side. Ordinarily one cerebral hemisphere excels in speed of learning and becomes the dominant hemisphere. Ability to speak and to understand speech then becomes limited to the motor and sensory areas in this hemisphere. Right- or left-handedness and the dominance of one eye correspond to the dominant hemisphere.— *L. and M. M.*

BRAKE: a device for controlling, reducing, and stopping movement. Although some brakes work by the direct application of an opposing force, most operate on the principle of gradually dissipating the kinetic energy of motion by converting it into heat of friction or by using it to wear away the brake mechanism. An example of direct-opposition braking is the injection of steam against the advancing face of a steam-engine piston: when steam pressure is equal on both sides, the piston stops. An electric motor is sometimes braked by cutting the current to it, so that the motor then acts as a generator, expending its kinetic energy in generating elec-

tricity. An early type of brake for a turning shaft or axle was a rope loosely coiled about the shaft; when tension tightened the rope coils, friction slowed the shaft. This friction-drag principle underlies most modern brakes, which consist primarily of a fixed brake drum and a movable brake shoe lined with material that has a high coefficient of friction and will wear uniformly. Different brake systems usually derive their names from the means used to activate them. The common automobile safety brake is an example of straight mechanical activation, through a cable or rod linkage system. As long as the brakes are not in operation, the brake shoes are kept off the drum by centrifugal force, gravity, or light springs. In *hydraulic brakes,* used in most automobiles and light trucks, a mechanical force on the brake pedal is converted by a master cylinder-piston into hydraulic pressure. This is transmitted through fluid brake lines and reconverted to mechanical force by individual wheel cylinder pistons that move the brake shoes. Westinghouse *power brakes* or *air brakes* utilize compressed air or other gases stored in a compressor-fed tank. Release of compressed gas against a pneumatic piston activates the brake shoes. *Vacuum brakes* using pneumatic pistons to activate brake shoes are of two types: in one, normal atmospheric pressure is maintained on both sides of the piston, and when a vacuum is created on one side, the piston moves in that direction; in the other type, a vacuum is maintained on both sides of the piston, and atmospheric pressure is admitted to one side to drive the piston through the vacuum side to activate the brake. In *electromagnetic brakes,* magnetic forces are used to draw drum and shoe together. Braking heat of friction is usually removed by conduction through metal parts, or by air-cooling the brake drum in such a way that dust or moisture does not intrude between drum and shoe.— *K. A.*

BRASS: an alloy of copper and zinc, often with various added components to impart special properties. It is the most important and widely used of copper alloys, being strong, ductile, and resistant to corrosion. Brasses generally fall into two groups: those with less than 15% zinc, called *low* or *red* brasses; and those with more than 20% zinc, called *high* or *yellow* brasses. Rich low brass, containing 15% zinc, has the best corrosion resistance of these alloys and is used for hardware, water pipes, and imitation gold jewelry. However, the most technically important brasses have 27 to 35% zinc, which imparts high tensile strength coupled with maximum ductility.— *A. L.*

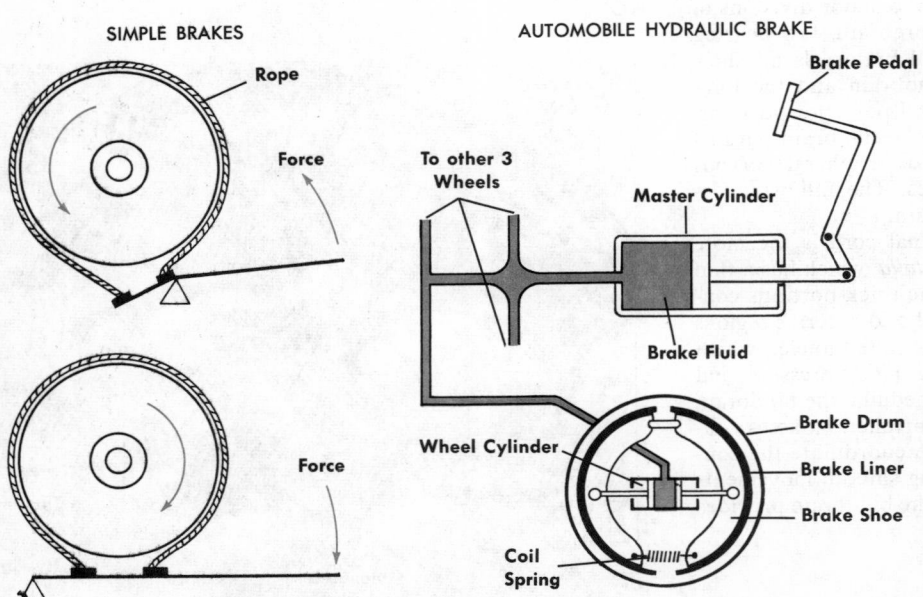

SIMPLE BRAKES

Rope

Force

Force

AUTOMOBILE HYDRAULIC BRAKE

Brake Pedal

To other 3 Wheels

Master Cylinder

Brake Fluid

Wheel Cylinder

Coil Spring

Brake Drum

Brake Liner

Brake Shoe

Friction-drag principle of braking is used in simple band brakes as well as automobile hydraulic brakes. At upper left: one end of the rope band is fixed to a stationary point and the other end to a lever; at lower left, ends of band are fixed to lever at different distances from fulcrum. Force is applied as shown and stops the wheel. In the automobile hydraulic brake, pressure on the brake pedal compresses fluid in the master (hydraulic) cylinder; this fluid pressure is then transmitted through tubing to each of the four wheel cylinders, which, in turn, press the brake shoes outward against the inner surface of a drum attached to the wheel. The coil spring keeps the shoes free of the drum when the brakes are not being applied.

Bird migration consists of a broad spectrum of routes, schedules, and behavior patterns characteristic of individual species. At one extreme are the relatively simple, but somewhat variable, movements of some populations; as unfavorable environmental conditions develop in fall or early winter, these birds move to lower latitudes, lower elevations, or both, returning in spring as conditions improve. The distance traveled usually varies with the extent of environmental change. Such *weather migrants* include populations of some species of ducks, finches, and woodpeckers. Many tropical and subtropical species whose movements coincide with the change between wet and dry seasons may also be termed weather migrants. At the other extreme of the migratory spectrum are the so-called *instinct migrants*. These species have developed timing mechanisms that cause them to leave breeding areas *before* adverse conditions appear and to begin their return migration so that they arrive at the breeding area at the time most favorable for reproduction. Instinct migrants include many species of petrels, sandpipers, plovers, swifts, warblers, vireos, tyrannid flycatchers, thrushes, and swallows. Two remarkable instinct migrants are the arctic tern, which breeds in arctic North America and Eurasia and "winters" in the summer of the Antarctic Ocean, and the American golden plover, which breeds in arctic America, with one population wintering in S South America and another in Polynesia. A less spectacular, but very typical, migrant is Harris's sparrow, which breeds in NW Canada and winters in south central U. S. A.

Migration is a more common phenomenon in the northern than in the southern hemisphere, probably because of the general increase in land area northward from the equator in contrast to the general decrease southward. Similarly, most trans-equatorial migrants are species that breed in the northern hemisphere. Among the exceptions is the short-tailed shearwater, which breeds in coastal islands of SE Australia and "winters" in the food-rich waters of the Bering Sea during the northern-hemisphere summer. In many species the individuals show a remarkable precision in returning each year to the same breeding and wintering sites. This precision is usually fixed for an individual bird after its first breeding season. Range extensions resulting from deviations from normal migratory pattern usually involve young birds.

Navigation and orientation in migration are still imperfectly understood (see ANIMAL NAVIGATION). Probably the orienting mechanisms are largely inherited, but the proper reaction to landmarks may involve experience. Among the mechanisms of orientation employed by migratory birds are "solar compasses" and "stellar compasses," both of which require internal biological chronometers, the existence of which has been adequately established (see BIOLOGICAL RHYTHM). Wind direction, prominent landmarks, coastlines, rivers, and mountain ranges are also important in navigation. Most passerine (perching) species, many shore birds, and some ducks are nocturnal migrants. For these species migration involves a drastic change in the daily activity pattern.

In most species the premigratory period is characterized by conspicuous physiologic changes. Most prominent is an increase in food intake (hyperphagia) and a consequent deposition of fat, which serves as fuel for flight. The hyperphagia continues through the migratory season, so that there is a rapid replenishment of fat reserves between flights. Fat has the advantage of storing the maximum quantity of energy per unit weight.

To be of value for survival, migration must be timed precisely. Although internal physiologic cycles may be of importance in some species, it appears highly probable that the required precision is finally derived from precise physical cycles in the environment. Thus far, however, the only cycle for which such a role has been demonstrated is that of the change in day length. There is ample evidence that increased day length, acting upon a system that includes the hypothalamus and anterior pituitary in the brain, causes directly the spring migration of some northern hemisphere species. To date, the effect of day length on the timing of migration has been established clearly only for some species whose migrations are confined to the northern hemisphere. Although day length probably also has a timing function in trans-equatorial migrants, no adequate experimental evidence of this has yet been found. Migration has often been regarded as one aspect of the annual reproductive cycle. The evidence does not support this interpretation, but suggests that migration and reproduction are related primarily by their dependence on timing systems that have important elements in common.—*D. S. F.*

BIRKHOFF, GEORGE DAVID, 1884–1944, U. S. mathematician; b. Overisel, Mich. His early researches were in linear differential equations and systems of difference equations. Influenced by Poincaré's work, he produced a notable memoir, *Dynamical Systems with Two Degrees of Freedom*. He investigated periodic orbits, the problem of three bodies, stability, and ergodic theory. Birkhoff's theorem on ergodic motion goes far toward supplying a foundation for statistical mechanics. His book *Aesthetic Measure* related mathematics to esthetics; he also wrote two books on relativity, and was professor of mathematics at Harvard 1919–44. He was a member of the National Academy of Sciences.—*H. C.*

BIRTH: In mammals, all but the most primitive give birth to living young. In most other animals, young are hatched from eggs. The condition of newborn mammals varies: most rodents and carnivores are born naked, blind, and helpless (a condition known as altricial), whereas deer and livestock at birth are haired, can see, and can move about (precocial). The birth process, called labor, normally begins when the fetus has completed its growth (see EMBRYONIC DEVELOPMENT; GESTATION). What actually sets off the birth process is unknown. The following description is of labor in mankind, although the general pattern is similar in other mammals.

Labor is divided into three stages. The first stage, which lasts 12 to 18 hr and accounts for about 9/10 of the total labor period, begins with rhythmic contractions of the uterus. These develop a pressure of 25 to 30 lb, which forces the fetus in its enveloping amniotic sac down toward the cervix (mouth of uterus) and causes the cervix to stretch enough to allow the fetus to pass into the 5-in.-long birth canal (vagina). During the second stage, the fetus is driven through the birth canal by uterine contractions, augmented by involuntary abdominal muscle contraction and straining ("bearing down") by the mother. These forces produce a pressure of about 60 lb and propel the head of the infant (the usual birth presentation) against and through the elastic vaginal opening. Immediately after delivery, mucus and blood are removed from the air passages of the infant's mouth and nose. If the infant does not breathe spontaneously, respiration is artificially stimulated by the application of positive pressure to inflate the lungs, suction to clear air passages of secretions, the administration of oxygen, or other measures. The umbilical cord, by which the infant is attached to the PLACENTA, is clamped and cut, leaving a stub that becomes the navel. The third stage of labor encompasses the few minutes elapsing between birth and the delivery of the placenta (afterbirth). Like the child, the placenta is expelled by uterine contractions. Labor difficulties, anatomical defects of fetus or birth passage, abnormal birth presentations, and other disorders may require the use of forceps or Caesarian section. Labor pain may be relieved by

Induction brazing: Tiny elements of klystron tube (top of column within bell jar) are brazed in hydrogen-gas atmosphere by heat from high-frequency current. (*Sperry Gyroscope*)

BRATTAIN, WALTER HOUSER, 1902–   , U. S. physicist; b. Amoy, China. His research has been on electron collisions in mercury vapor, thermionics, transistor physics, and surface properties of semiconductors. For their investigations of semiconductors and the discovery of the transistor effect, Brattain, W. B. Shockley, and John Bardeen shared the Nobel prize, 1956. Brattain, with Bell Telephone Laboratories since 1929, did war research on magnetic detection of submarines 1941–43. He is a member of the National Academy of Sciences. —*D. H. D. R.*

BRAUN, KARL FERDINAND, 1850–1918, German physicist; b. Fulda. Discovering that crystals of binary compounds possess the property of rectifying alternating currents, he suggested their use in radio ("crystal sets"). His introduction of coupled circuits into radio telegraphy vastly increased the output power of transmitters. For the development of wireless telegraphy, Braun and G. Marconi shared the Nobel prize for 1909.—*D. H. D. R.*

BRAZING AND SOLDERING: processes for joining metals by means of a non-ferrous brazing or soldering alloy having a melting point below that of the base metal. Brazing processes include: gas, arc, induction, resistance, furnace, metal-dip, and hot salt bath. Soldering is commonly done with an electric- or gas-heated iron. Brazing differs from soldering in that brazing alloys have melting points above 800°F. Principal brazing alloys contain silver, copper, and zinc with perhaps a very small percentage of cadmium; melting points range from 1,300 to 1,600°F. Phos-copper, an alloy of copper and phosphorus that melts at 1,382°F, also is used. Hard soldering employs alloys of silver, copper, and zinc and is thus merely another name for brazing. Soft soldering uses tin, lead, or, more commonly, alloys of tin and lead, with or without bismuth, antimony, silver, or arsenic. Melting points range from under 212°F (for bismuth solders) up to over 600°F. A popular solder is a 50-50 alloy of tin and lead (around 420°F). Jewelers' soldering compositions are made from gold, silver, copper, and zinc.—*C. B. C.*

BREATHING: the process in which air is drawn into the lungs (inspiration) and forced out of them (expiration). The lungs of mammals are contained in a closed cavity, the thorax; they open to the external air only through the bronchi, trachea, and respiratory passages of mouth and nose. When the volume of the thorax is changed, air enters or leaves the lungs through these passages. In inspiration, the thorax is actively enlarged either by contraction of the diaphragm or by contraction of the external intercostal muscles, or both. The diaphragm is a dome-shaped muscular disk separating the thoracic cavity from the abdominal cavity. When the diaphragm muscle contracts, the dome is flattened and the thoracic cavity is enlarged. When the external intercostal and other inspiratory muscles contract, the upper ribs are elevated, again enlarging the thoracic cavity. In normal quiet breathing, the thorax returns to its normal volume passively —*i.e.* by an elastic return of ribs and diaphragm to their resting positions. In active expiration, contraction of the internal intercostal and other expiratory muscles depresses the ribs, and contraction of the muscles of the abdominal wall forces the diaphragm upward; both movements decrease the volume of the thorax. The lungs themselves are passively inflated and deflated, as the thorax is enlarged and compressed.

Basic control of these movements resides in a nervous center located in the medulla oblongata of the brain. This center, through intrinsic nervous mechanisms not yet fully understood, produces regular rhythmic bursts of nervous impulses, alternating with periods of quiescence. Nervous impulses are conducted along the nerves to the inspiratory muscles and cause contraction. A second center, closely related to the first, sends impulses to the expiratory muscles. The activity of both centers is determined primarily by the concentration of carbon dioxide (CO_2) in the blood. If the CO_2 concentration is decreased, as in "overbreathing" (voluntary breathing at a rapid rate), breathing stops temporarily. If CO_2 concentration is increased, as in exercise or by rebreathing the same air, the rate and depth of breathing increase. Since the expiratory center is less sensitive to CO_2 than the inspiratory center, it is called into action only when the CO_2 concentration is high.

Breathing is also controlled by several reflexes and by centers in the higher parts of the brain. Sense organs located in the aorta and in the carotid artery leading to the head are stimulated when the oxygen content of the blood decreases, and send to the brain nerve impulses that excite the respiratory centers and increase breathing rate. Sense organs in the lungs are excited by the stretching of the lung wall and send to the brain impulses that inhibit the inspiratory center. Nervous centers in various parts of the brain modify the activity of the respiratory center in relation to swallowing, coughing, sneezing, speech, vomiting, emotional reactions, and other activities.

By bringing air into contact with lung surfaces that absorb oxygen and by carrying off carbon dioxide and other waste products, breathing plays an important role in the process of RESPIRATION.—*B. T. S.*

BRECCIA: rock consisting of many sharp, angular fragments of broken rock firmly cemented together by additional mineral matter. It is distinguished in many instances by strongly contrasting colors of fragments as compared to the cementing material. Breccias often form in fault fissures, in volcano throats, and in the rubble of talus slopes. Portions of ore veins often consist of brecciated country rock cemented together by economically valuable minerals such as sulfides. Colorful marble and limestone breccias are prized for ornamental building stones. The terrazzo flooring commonly used in public buildings is an artificial breccia.—*J. Si.*

BREEDER: a nuclear reactor that produces more fuel than it consumes. The fuel for any reactor is a material whose atomic nuclei are fissionable, *i.e* upon capturing a neutron the nucleus splits into two fragments which fly apart with considerable energy, and incidentally "boil off" several neutrons. To make a reactor breed new fuel, some of the surplus neutrons must be absorbed by non-fissionable nuclei, which thereupon are made fissionable. The two known materials convertible to fuel are thorium and the most prevalent form of uranium, U^{238}. A challenge to reactor technology is the problem of building a workable breeder, so that the world's supply of uranium and thorium can be fully utilized by the nuclear power industry.—*S. K.*

BREEDING OF PLANTS AND ANIMALS: the deliberate attempt to obtain improved genetic strains by careful selection of parent stock. Many domesticated plants and animals have been bred for thousands of years. In some cases, as with maize, wheat, cattle, sheep, dogs, and cats, the wild ancestors have become extinct or are so different that the relationship is no longer recognizable. Without understanding how inheritance operated, Charles Darwin in his book *Variation of Animals and Plants Under Domestication* (1868) drew attention to the spectacular successes achieved by plant and animal breeders. Until around 1900, when the principles of GENETICS discovered by Gregor Mendel were rediscovered, all breeding of plants and animals was based upon wise selection of individuals showing desirable features. Luther Burbank, the "plant wizard" of California, carried this method to its logical extreme by raising enormous numbers of seedlings and cuttings. From these he chose for further propagation any with interesting MUTATIONS. He developed seedless fruits, spineless cacti, huge flowers, and other valuable plants. Today, Burbank's methods are regarded as unnecessarily wasteful of space and time. By using the principles of genetics to make a smaller number of carefully planned crosses, the plant breeder now works on a less extensive, less expensive scale, with faster progress. He may select for hardiness, early ripening, high vitamin content, or size of fruit. The geneticist may refine his breeding stock for certain combinations of characteristics by consistently *inbreeding* through self-pollination of plants or brother-sister matings of animals. This technique in strains of laboratory rats and mice has produced animals of outstanding uniformity for use in medical and psychological research. Desirable results can often be achieved also by *outbreeding,* or crossing of parental strains that are unlike in a large number of particulars, with no recent common ancestors. Sometimes the hybrids show spectacular vigor ("hybrid vigor") even though they will not breed true and may be sterile. Tremendous crops of maize are now produced on hybrid plants from special parental strains, usually through a double cross: the pollen from hybrids between strains A and B used to pollinate hybrids between strains C and D. The special plants produced in this way not only yield amazing crops but show remarkable uniformity in rate of growth and final height, which are important where cultivation and harvesting are done by machine.

Through use of drugs such as colchicine, which causes faulty cell divisions during growth, plant breeders are often able to double the number of chromosomes in a few branches of a plant. Even crosses between species can sometimes be made in this way. Thus a cross between ordinary cabbage, with 20 chromosomes, and Chinese cabbage, with 18 chromosomes, yielded a hybrid with 19 chromosomes, which was sterile. When treated with colchicine to double the chromosome number to 38, it was still sterile. But when this strange plant was crossed with a rutabaga turnip with 38 chromosomes, an entirely new kind of cabbage emerged. It had 38 chromosomes, was fertile, and bred true.

Animal breeders cherish each new mutation they encounter, testing it in various combinations with different strains in an effort to gain advantages without introducing losses. They have developed turkeys of small size with enormous amounts of white breast meat to make these birds appeal to small families. They have greatly increased the quantity and quality of milk from some types of cattle, the quantity and quality of meat from others. Even a few new true-breeding types of cattle have been developed, such as the Santa Gertrudis strain, which combines the heat-tolerance of the Brahman bull (*Bos indicus*) with the meat-production of the shorthorn cow (*Bos taurus*). See HEREDITY.—*L. and M. M.*

BREWSTER, SIR DAVID, 1781–1868, Scottish physicist; b. Jedburgh. Brewster made important studies on diffraction of light, including polarization by reflection and refraction; discovered the polarizing structure induced by heat and pressure; and studied crystals with two axes of double refraction, the relation of optical structure and crystalline forms, metallic reflection, and the absorption of light. He rediscovered the kaleidoscope in 1816 and acquired much fame from it. He was a founder of the British Association for the Advancement of Science and a fellow of the Royal Society, which con-

Better wool is produced by breeding the smooth-coated merino ram (*left*) from the type having a wrinkled coat (*right*). Also, wool from the smooth-coated breed is much easier to shear. This is an outstanding example of the improvement of production through the scientific application of the principles of genetics as laid down by Gregor Mendel. (*U. S. D. A.*)

ferred on him the Copley medal, the Rumford medal, and a Royal medal, all for researches on polarized light. Among his many published works are *Treatise on Optics* (1831).—*S. B.*

BREWSTER'S LAW: the relationship discovered by Sir David Brewster in 1815 which states that for a light ray incident to a polished surface of an electrically nonconducting material at the *polarizing angle,* the reflected and refracted light rays are at right angles to each other. The polarizing angle is that angle of incidence of an unpolarized light ray for which the reflected light ray is wholly plane-polarized (see POLARIZED LIGHT).—*A. L.*

BRICK: a small rectangular building unit made of vitrified clay. Bricks were used from earliest antiquity to the fall of the Roman Empire; their use in Europe was revived in the 12th and 13th cent. Although bricks have been made in many ways and fired in a variety of kilns, most bricks in the U. S. A. today are made of mechanically kneaded clays and shales which are continuously extruded through a die and then cut to the desired length. After these "green" bricks are dried at controlled humidities and temperatures, they are sent through a tunnel kiln, where they remain 36 to 72 hr—until the clay is vitrified. "Common" brick is fired at temperatures of 900 to 1,000°C. There is a variety in size, content, and method of manufacture to suit specialized requirements; *e.g.* refractory brick is designed to resist extremely high temperatures. However, the most widely used brick in the United States is the "common" brick, with dimensions $2\frac{1}{4} \times 3\frac{3}{4} \times 8$ in.; when manufactured to engineering standards, it can resist pressures up to 10,000 lb/in.^{2}.—*A. L.*

BRIDGE: a structure built to carry a road, railway, or waterway over an obstacle, or to separate traffic arteries. Special forms, *e.g.* the transporter bridge, do not differ in structural character from the ordinary types. The primary supporting members are piers and abutments resting on rock or other suitable bearing material, often well below grade level. Above these is the superstructure that carries the deck, which in turn may be supported above the superstructure, within it, or suspended below it. The superstructure is the main feature which distinguishes one type of bridge from another, since a bridge of a given size or function may be built in any of the basic forms.

Bridge Types and Materials: The simplest and oldest structural type is the *pile-and-beam bridge.* It consists of a series of

John Rennie's Waterloo Bridge, with elliptical arches, utilized compressive strength of stone. Bridge is seen during erection (1809–17), with timber centering in place. (*N. Y. Public Library*)

longitudinal wooden beams supporting the deck, the ends of the beams resting on posts driven into the ground or into the bed of a stream. The manageable size of timber pieces and the strength limits of the material require that such bridges be built with short spans. They appeared early in all urban cultures and were well developed by Roman military engineers. They are still common in the U. S. A. for short spans on railways and secondary rural roads. The wooden-beam span was the direct ancestor of the *girder bridge* of iron and later steel, which was introduced simultaneously by William Fairbairn of England and James Milholland of the United States in 1846. In this form two or more longitudinal girders spanning between the piers or abutments carry closely spaced transverse beams underlying the deck. Because the depth of the girder must rapidly increase with the length of span, the girder bridge is rarely built with a clear span of more than 150 ft, although there are a few of much greater length. A girder supported at its ends is a *simple span;* one extending over three or more supports is a *continuous span.* A girder supported at only one end is a *cantilever.* A girder exerts only a vertical thrust on the piers or abutments. A special type of girder bridge, introduced in the early 20th cent., is the rigid

Preassembled steel truss being lowered into place for a railroad bridge over the Snake River in southern Idaho. (*Union Pacific Railroad*)

Stretching over 15 mi in Tampa Bay, the Sunshine Skyway (1954) joins St. Petersburg and Palmetto, Fla. (*Ewing Galloway*)

Arch span over Queen Creek gorge carries automobile traffic in mining country in central Arizona. (*Ewing Galloway*)

frame, in which the vertical supports form an integral and hence rigid unit with the horizontal girder.

The *arch bridge* of stone dates from classical antiquity and was brought to great size and exactitude by Roman engineers. Since stone has only a negligible tensile strength, any bridge of this material longer than a few feet must be built as an arch, which is subject chiefly to compression. An arch exerts both a vertical and a horizontal thrust at the ends and must therefore be sustained by deep abutments with sloping faces backed by earth or rock rather than by the simple abutment wall of the girder bridge. Although stone is a durable and beautiful material, it is costly and limited in use and has been superseded almost entirely by steel and concrete.

A plentiful supply of timber, the ease with which it can be shaped and joined, and its resistance to both tension and compression eventually led to the application of the wooden *truss* to the superstructure of large bridges. The ancestor of modern forms was invented by Andrea Palladio in the late 16th cent. The truss was not used in bridges until the end of the 18th cent., when it was rapidly developed into a diversity of forms by American builders. During the 1840s the truss was adapted to cast and wrought iron, and by 1880 to steel. After that date the length of the steel truss span steadily increased to the present maximum of 1,800 ft, in the St. Lawrence River bridge at Quebec (1911–17).

The truss can be used in a variety of ways. If the deck of the bridge is at the top chord, the structure is known as a *deck truss*; if at the bottom chord, as a *through truss*. The division into simple, continuous, and cantilever spans applies to the truss as well as the girder. The free length of a cantilever

Long spans (here 3,800 ft) are made possible by suspension principle. Mackinac Bridge, which was completed in 1958, connects upper and lower peninsulas of Michigan. (*Ewing Galloway*)

must be balanced or anchored by another truss extending from the pier in the opposite direction. The longest truss spans are composed of two cantilevers carrying a floating or suspended span between them.

Although a bridge truss behaves in its totality like a large beam, the actions of the different members are complex and cannot be described in general for all conditions of load. When the deflection of the truss is convex downward, the top chord is in compression and the bottom chord in tension, with both types of stress distributed throughout the verticals and diagonals of the web. Such a deflection is characteristic of a simple span. The stress distribution in the chords is reversed if the deflection is concave downward, which is the case with the cantilever. The double curvature occurs in the continuous span.

Most *movable bridges* are truss spans, but the construction does not differ in any essential way from that of the fixed type. The cantilever truss is used in *bascule bridges,* which open by rotating upward on a pin or circular segment, and for *pivoted swing bridges.* The simple truss is used in *vertical-lift bridges.*

Although the *suspension bridge* of iron chains was built in China as early as the 6th cent. A. D., it did not appear in the western world until 1741. The chain bridge with a rigid level deck was developed at the very beginning of the 19th cent. by James Finley of the U. S. A. Its popularity grew rapidly and it was soon used in bridges of comparatively large size. The introduction of the wire cable, primarily a French achievement, offered the advantages of reduction in weight and great increase in the tensile strength of the cable, with the result that the older form was superseded by 1850. The suspension principle has been used for the longest spans, but it is limited to highway and rapid-transit traffic. The maximum length is the 4,260-ft main span of the Verrazano Narrows Bridge across N. Y. Harbor. The suspension bridge is the simplest of long-span steel bridges in appearance, function, and structure. The deck is hung by cable suspenders from a

pair of main cables which stretch in a parabolic curve between the towers and downward from the towers to the anchorages. The flexible cable is wholly in tension. The rigidity of the deck is ordinarily maintained by longitudinal stiffening trusses.

The use of iron ribs in place of the stone vault for arch bridges came in 1779, with the completion of the River Severn bridge at Coalbrookdale, England. The subsequent development has been a direct evolution leading to the *long-span steel arches* of the present. But the substitution of iron ribs for solid masonry barrels gave rise to problems which required scientific solutions. Traffic loads on a narrow rib produce bending forces with attendant tensile stresses which must be taken into consideration in the design of the structure. Moreover, the traditional arch with fixed ends is an indeterminate form. To produce a form in which tensile and compressive stresses could be calculated more exactly, French engineers developed the *hinged arch* about 1850. The two-hinged arch has hinges or pins at the abutments, and the three-hinged at the abutments and the crown. For long-span bridges the arch rib is replaced by an arched truss or constructed as the bottom chord of a stiffening truss. The highway bridge over Kill van Kull at Bayonne, New Jersey (1929–31), is a spectacular example of the latter type.

The development of *concrete* as a structural material during the 19th cent. led to its substitution for stone in arch bridges. At first it was used in the traditional forms of stone masonry. The invention of *reinforcing* by French engineers, however, made possible the use of concrete in tension as well as compression. As a consequence, the stone arch with solid barrel and spandrel walls was eventually replaced by arches of narrow ribs and isolated spandrel posts. In 1901 the Swiss engineer Robert Maillart introduced thin slabs for deck supports and ribs. The invention of *prestressing,* chiefly the work of Eugène Freyssinet in France, quickly led to a marked increase in length of span combined with unusual lightness of structure. The Plougastel Bridge at Brest, France (1927–29), is the classic of prestressed concrete arches. Scientifically calculated reinforcing made possible the construction of simple, continuous, and rigid-frame girder bridges in which bending forces are very high compared to those in an arch. Prestressing again allowed great increase of span with economy and lightness of construction.

Bridge Planning: The major revolution in the history of bridge design followed the Industrial Revolution of the 18th cent. It has been distinguished chiefly by the progressive substitution of an exact science of stress analysis and the properties of materials for a pragmatic building craft. In 1800 the bridge builder relied mainly on a rule-of-thumb approach, following tradition and his own experience. A century later he had the resources of theoretical and experimental science at his command. The contemporary program of bridge design begins with a thorough investigation of the topographic, geological, and meteorological conditions of the site. With the purpose of the bridge established, the engineer then selects the most appropriate form for the site and for maximum safety and economy of construction. He calculates unit loadings on the basis of the dead weight of the structure, the live load of traffic and wind, and the weight of snow and ice. He finally makes an exact stress analysis to determine the tensile, compressive, and shearing stresses for each member of the structure. From these data the size of the individual member can be precisely calculated. For very large bridges he may conclude the program with load tests of a scale model. The steel fabricator must submit sample members to full load tests and metallurgical analysis. Only after this intricate procedure is completed will actual construction begin.—*C. W. C.*

World's longest lift span (544 ft) is that of vertical-lift railroad bridge over Cape Cod Canal. (*Ewing Galloway*)

Bascule bridge over Welland Canal, Southern Ontario, allows passage of Great Lakes shipping. (*Canadian National Film Board*)

Counterweighted leaf of bascule railroad bridge (New Jersey) works on horizontal pivot. (*Ewing Galloway*)

BRIDGMAN, PERCY WILLIAMS, 1882–1961, U. S. physicist; b. Cambridge, Mass. A member of the Harvard faculty from 1908, he was a lifelong investigator in the field of high-pressure physics. He received the 1946 Nobel prize for his invention of an apparatus for obtaining very high pressures and for discoveries he made with it. Among his works is *The Physics of High Pressure* (1931), a classic on the subject. In his *The Logic of Modern Physics* (1927) and *The Nature of Physical Theory* (1936), Bridgman codified earlier views on methodology in physics to produce "operational analysis" (see OPERATIONALISM), which has had a profound influence on thinking concerning physical theory. He was a fellow of the Royal Society and a member of the National Academy of Sciences.—*D. H. D. R.*

Percy Williams Bridgman
(Harvard News Bureau)

BRIGGS, HENRY, 1556?–1631, English mathematician. Professor of geometry at Gresham College, London, and later of astronomy at Oxford, he suggested to Napier that the logarithms invented by the latter would be more useful if reduced to the base 10, so that the logarithm of 10 would be 1. Napier agreed, and Briggs constructed a table based on the new plan. These Briggsian, or common, logarithms are the ones generally used in computation today. In 1624 Briggs published his *Arithmetica logarithmica,* which contained a 14-place table of common logarithms of the numbers from 1 to 20,000 and from 90,000 to 100,000. The logarithms of numbers between 20,000 and 90,000 were later filled in by Adrian Vlacq, a Dutch publisher.—*H. C.*

BRINE: a water solution of a salt or several salts such as sodium bromide, sodium chloride, sodium iodide, or calcium chloride. Brine may occur naturally beneath the surface of the earth or as sea water; or it may be formed merely by dissolving a salt or salts in water. Natural brines are sources of table salt, potash, calcium chloride, magnesium, bromine, and iodine. In the U. S. A., oil-well brine is an important source of iodine; the brine rises to the surface with oil in a ratio as high as 10 barrels of brine to one of oil. Also contained in oil-well brine may be bromine, chlorine, and salts of barium and calcium. Compared to sea water, oil-well brine contains less bromine, about the same amount of sodium chloride, and much more iodine.

Industrially, brine is used in food processing, meat packing, refrigeration, ice control, water softening, and dyeing. Sodium-chloride brine is used in the production of chlorine and caustic soda. Calcium-chloride and sodium-chloride brines, with practical freezing points below $-20°C$, are safe, cheap, and extremely efficient heat-transfer agents. The brine is cooled in a refrigerating plant, then circulated to the heat exchangers of the system. The brine picks up the heat, lowering the temperature of the item being frozen, *e.g.* water. (See REFRIGERATION.) Food items such as pickles and olives are packed in brine solutions, and turkeys and chickens are quickly frozen for market by spraying them with refrigerated brine solutions.—*A. P. E.*

BRITISH THERMAL UNIT (or **Btu**): see HEAT.

BROGLIE, LOUIS VICTOR, PRINCE DE, 1892–   , French physicist; b. Dieppe. His doctoral thesis (1924), on the quantum theory, was the starting point from which he developed the idea of "matter waves." His work, together with that of others such as E. Schrödinger and P. A. M. Dirac, established wave mechanics. For his prediction of the wave nature of the electron, de Broglie received the Nobel prize, 1929. He is a member of the Académie Française and a fellow of the Royal Society.—*D. H. D. R.*

**Louis Victor,
Prince de Broglie**
(French Cultural Service)

BROGLIE, MAURICE, DUC DE, 1875–1960, French physicist; b. Paris; elder brother of Prince Louis Victor de Broglie. He is best known for his studies of radioactivity, x-rays, and nuclear physics. He also did research on electricity and the ionization of gases. De Broglie was a member of the Academy of Sciences and the French Atomic Energy Commission. He was also a fellow of the Royal Society.—*P. R. L.*

BROMATE: a chemical compound that contains the negative ion BrO_3^-. Bromates are prepared by electrolyzing hot, concentrated bromide solutions and stirring so as to mix the two products liberated at the cathode and anode (*i.e.* the hydroxide, OH^-, ion and bromine, Br_2). The reaction is as follows: $3 Br_2 + 6 OH^- \rightarrow 5 Br^- + BrO_3^- + 3 H_2O$. Frequently, no attempt is made to separate the mixture of bromate and bromide salts recovered from solution, because they provide a simple, inexpensive, and readily transportable source of bromine upon acidification: $BrO_3^- + 5 Br^- + 6 H^+ \rightarrow Br_2 + 3H_2O$. Bromates are slightly better oxidizing agents than corresponding chlorates, being stronger and faster in action.—*L. Sc.*

BROMIDE: a chemical compound of bromine and a metal such as potassium or silver. Bromides are formed when a bromine atom accepts a single electron from a metal. Organic bromides contain bromine covalently bonded to a carbon atom. Silver bromide ($AgBr$) is the most important bromide commercially, because of its use in photographic emulsions. Potassium bromide (KBr) still finds some use as a sedative (hence the slang term "bromide"). The mixture of tetraethyl lead and ethylbromide in "leaded" gasolines forms lead bromide upon combustion of the GASOLINE; this reaction assists in preventing the deposition of lead in the engine.—*L. Sc.*

BROMINE: an element of the halogen family (Br); at. no. 35; at. wt 79.92. It is a dark brown, volatile liquid at room temperature, existing in the molecular form Br_2. Its vapor is intensely irritating (Gr. *bromos,* "stench") and is to be avoided even more than chlorine. Bromine occurs naturally as the stable isotopes Br^{79} (50.57%) and Br^{81} (47.43%). Its radioisotopes range from Br^{74} to Br^{89}. Br^{82}, the one most used in tracer work, has a density of about 3.2 g/ml; mp $-7.2°C$, and bp $58.8°C$. Compared to other halogen elements, bromine is more active than iodine but less so than chlorine. The oxidation state of chlorine and bromine in their compounds is analogous, except that bromine does not form compounds corresponding to Br^{+7} state, as with the perchlorates, ClO_4^-. Sea water contains about 0.2 lb of sodium bromide per ton; some salt-well brines give a higher yield.

Bromine is prepared by sweeping chlorine gas through slightly acidic bromide solutions or by acidification of bromate-bromide mixtures.—*L. Sc.*

BRONGNIART, ALEXANDRE, 1770–1847, French mineralogist; b. Paris. With G. L. Cuvier he wrote *Essai sur la géographie minéralogique des environs de Paris* (1811), the first French work to correlate rock strata by means of their fossil contents and to put forth the theory of successive invasions of the sea to account for the alternation of land and marine sediments. While director of the Sèvres porcelain factory (1800–47), Brongniart did important work in ceramic chemistry. He was a fellow of the Royal Society.—*D. H. D. R.*

BRONK, DETLEV WULF, 1897–   , U. S. physiologist and biophysicist; b. New York City. His research has been on the volume flow of blood, nervous control of the circulation, physiology of sense organs and of the nervous system, synaptic mechanisms, cellular oxidations, and aviation medicine. President of the National Academy of Sciences from 1950, he is also a fellow of the Royal Society of London, and director of Rockefeller University.—*D. H. D. R.*

Cast aluminum bronze: The combination of 7 parts copper and 1 part aluminum produces a corrosion-resistant alloy in which the needlelike dispersion of the aluminum contributes to the tensile strength (X100). (*Westinghouse*)

BRONZE: a copper-base alloy consisting essentially of copper and tin. It dates back to the Bronze Age, which began about 3000 B. C. It may contain between 2% and 4% zinc, small amounts of phosphorus, considerable amounts of aluminum, and small amounts of lead. Bronze is used for making bells and statuary, and modified bronzes are employed for various industrial purposes. Zinc bronzes (also known as government bronze, gunmetal, and admiralty gunmetal) are excellent structural and bearing materials. Phosphor bronzes are used for springs and bearings. Aluminum bronzes, being outstandingly corrosion-resistant, are favored for chemical ap-

paratus. Leaded bronzes are notably easy to tool and are favored for making intricately machined parts.—*R. W.*

BROOKS, CHARLES ERNEST PELHAM, 1888–1957, British climatologist; b. London. His research as a member of the staff of the Meteorological Office covered a wide field. He is remembered chiefly for his investigations into past climates, climatic change, and application of statistical theory to meteorology.—*O. G. S.*

BROOKS, WILLIAM ROBERT, 1844–1921, U. S. astronomer; b. Maidstone, England. By age 14 he had made his first telescope. Director of the William Smith Observatory, Geneva, N. Y., after 1888, he was a pioneer in the application of photography to astronomy and was the discoverer of 27 comets.—*D. H. D. R.*

BROUWER, LUITZEN EGBERTUS JAN, 1881–   , Dutch mathematician and originator of the intuitionist school of mathematics; b. Overschie. With his doctoral dissertation *Over de grondslagen der wiskunds* (1907), Brouwer undertook a severe criticism of several conceptions traditionally accepted among mathematicians. He rejected the universal validity of the law of the excluded middle, the nonconstructive existence proofs, and most of Cantor's theory of SETS, and affirmed the primacy of mathematics over logic and even over language. These ideas were not entirely new, but Brouwer gave them a most extreme expression. He also worked in topology, where he proved the invariance of the number of dimensions (1911) and the Jordan theorem for *n*-dimensional Euclidean space (1912). He is a fellow of the Royal Society.—*J. V. H.*

BROWN, ROBERT, 1773–1858, Scottish botanist; b. Montrose. A botanist on the Flinders Expedition to Australia (1801–05), he produced a pioneer work on the flora of that region. He was elected a fellow of the Royal Society, 1811, and was keeper of the botanical collections at the British Museum 1827–58. The first to describe exactly the BROWNIAN MOTION in protoplasm (1828), he also discovered the nucleus of the vegetable cell (1831) and did valuable work in fossil botany and plant geography. His observations were distinguished by accuracy and minuteness of detail.—*D. H. D. R.*

BROWNIAN MOTION: an unceasing zigzag movement of small particles suspended in a fluid. The motion is caused by the incessant bombardment of the particles by the fluid's molecules, which themselves are in continuous erratic movement. The English botanist Robert Brown, in 1828, first observed the phenomenon in a suspension of pollen grains in water; he later showed that any particles of microscopic size display the same motion. The full explanation of the effect was given in 1905 by Einstein. According to the modern KINETIC THEORY OF MATTER, the entire surface of an object immersed in a fluid is continually bombarded on all sides by billions of molecules.

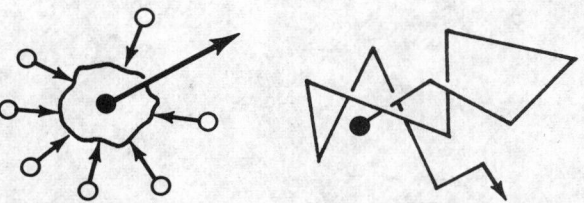

Brownian motion is illustrated by random movement of smoke particles in air. Particle (*left*) moves in one direction because of unbalanced collisions with air molecules. Constantly shifting pattern of collisions changes the direction of the particle's motion and results in completely random path (*right*).

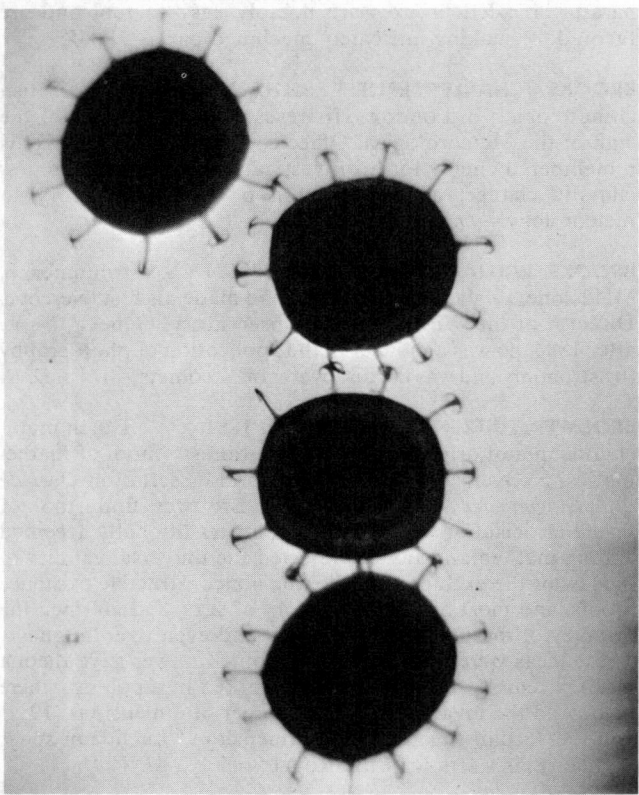

Fresh-water bryozoans: Individual animals live in gelatinous conglomerations (*below*); colony grows by asexual budding. Buds ("statoblasts") are hardy, anchor-studded little packages (*above*) about ½₅ in. in diameter. (*Hugh Spencer*)

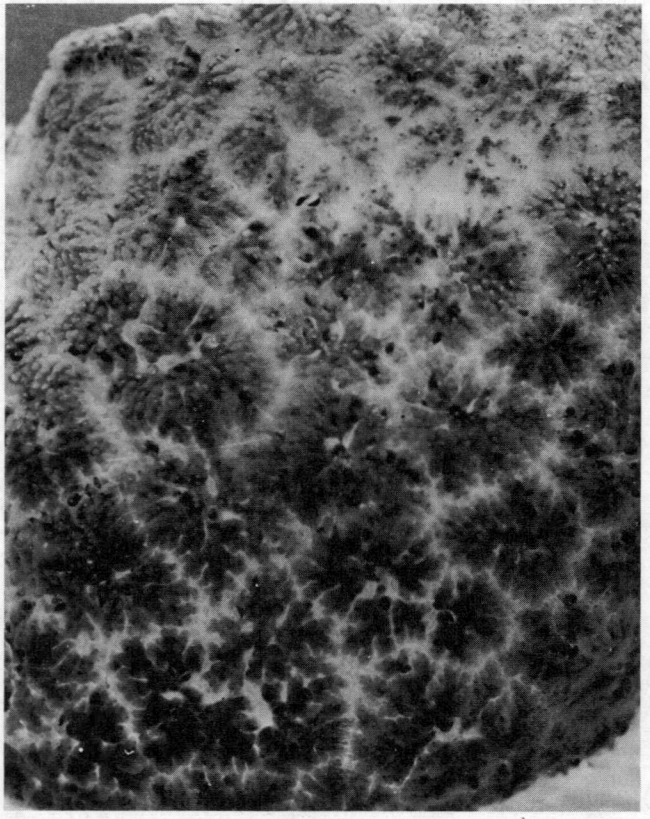

If the object were initially at rest, as many molecules would on average hit it on the left as on the right, so one might conclude that the net effect would be no motion. However, since the molecular motions are completely random, their net effects are subject to fluctuations. Occasionally, the object gets a larger jolt from one quarter than another and is accelerated in the direction of the larger force. While moving, it has more head-on collisions with molecules than collisions with molecules that overtake it. The net average effect is a resistive slowing-down force, called viscosity, which nevertheless does not change the direction of motion. But the next fluctuation in molecular velocities accelerates the object in another direction, and one observes a kink in its path. The larger the immersed particle, the larger is the fluctuation in molecular bombardment needed to produce a visible movement of the particle. Since it is also true that large fluctuations occur much less frequently than small ones, it is easy to understand why Brownian motion is unobservable for particles above microscopic size.—*S. K.*

BRÜCKNER CYCLE: a recurrence of periods of cold, wet weather alternating with warm, dry periods in Europe. An investigation by E. Brückner in 1890 suggested an average interval of 34.8 yr between successive maxima between 1691 and 1870. Individual cycles, however, were found to range from 25 to 50 yr. The existence of this cycle has been questioned in recent years; several investigators have produced evidence that the Brückner cycle is not real, but is simply a consequence of the mathematical methods employed.—*W. C. J.*

BRUNO, GIORDANO, 1548–1600, Italian philosopher and cosmologist; b. Nola. In 1566 he took vows in the Dominican order, which he left at 28 because of his unorthodox views. After a life of wandering and teaching in Europe and England, he returned to Italy (1591), then was seized by the Inquisition, tried and convicted of heresy, and burned (1600). In traveling, Bruno disseminated his ideas, chief among which was that the stars are other suns and that the universe is infinite, containing an infinite number of finite worlds like ours. His *De l' infinito, universo, et mondi* (1584) appears in English translation in D. W. Singer's *Giordano Bruno, His Life and Thought* (1950). He wrote more than 50 books.—*D. H. D. R.*

BRUNT, DAVID, 1886–   , British meteorologist; b. Montgomeryshire. His research has been on dynamics of the atmosphere and on heat-transfer processes, which led to an empirical formula for radiation from the earth's surface based solely on thermoscreen temperature and humidity observations. He also provided the nocturnal cooling formula associated with his name for predicting the decrease in the earth's surface temperature at night. His writings include many papers and the book *Physical and Dynamical Meteorology* (1934). He became professor of meteorology at Imperial Coll., London, in 1934. He is a fellow of the Royal Society.—*D. H. D. R.*

BRYOZOAN: a small, sessile, colonial animal found in lakes and oceans. Bryozoans form a major division (phylum Bryozoa) of the animal kingdom, consisting of 4,000 living and 15,000 fossil species. A colony of bryozoans may range from a few to millions of individuals, and usually appears as a mosslike growth on such objects as logs, piling, and rocks. Bryozoan bodies are embedded in a common gelatinous, chitinoid, or carbonate matrix, but each animal has a cluster of ciliated tentacles, which project out into the water and capture microscopic food particles. See CILIA; INVERTEBRATE.—*R. P.*

Gigantic structure at Brookhaven, N. Y., harbors bubble chamber 20 in. long in which tracks of nuclear particles are produced and recorded. The tracks are left by charged particles from the Cosmotron, also by uncharged particles that have collided with nuclei of dense liquid in chamber. (*Brookhaven National Laboratory*)

BUBBLE CHAMBER: a device used by nuclear physicists to record the trajectories of high-speed, electrically charged sub-atomic particles. When a charged particle passes through matter, the electrical field of force generated by the particle knocks electrons out of some of the atoms it encounters along its path. These released electrons transfer most of their acquired energy to neighboring atoms by means of collisions; the net result is a local heating of the medium along the trajectory of the particle. In a bubble chamber a liquid is kept at a temperature and pressure just below its boiling point.

When the pressure is released, the liquid goes into a so-called "superheated" state, in which it will begin to boil if excited. The local heating produced by any high-speed charged particles passing through at this time is sufficient to initiate boiling. If a photograph is taken a few thousandths of a second later, a string of bubbles is seen along the particle trajectories. (Still later the boiling spreads throughout the liquid.) The bubble chamber was invented in 1952 by Donald A. Glaser, and he was awarded the 1960 Nobel prize for his achievement.—*S. K.*

Evidence of neutral particles in 6-ft Univ. of Cal. bubble chamber is presented in photograph and accompanying key. An antiproton ($\bar{p}$) from the Bevatron enters at bottom. Its track comes to an end and after a brief hiatus is succeeded by two V formations—the tracks of a pi meson and a proton and of another pi meson and an antiproton. It is in this hiatus that the neutral lambda and antilambda hyperons are deduced to have existed. (*Courtesy of Lawrence Radiation Lab., Berkeley*)

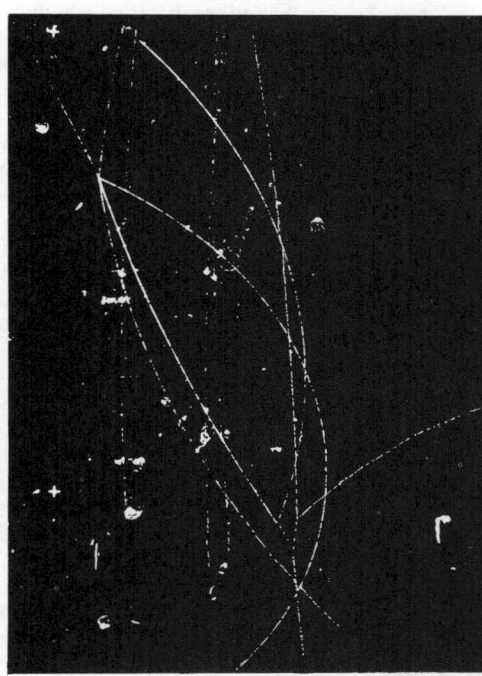

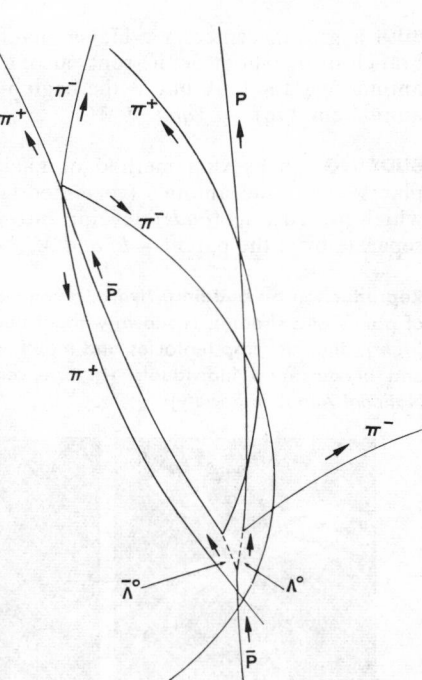

BUCH, BARON CHRISTIAN LEOPOLD VON, 1744–1852, German geologist; b. Stolpe, Pomerania. An outstanding observational geologist, he traveled widely and wrote extensively. He came to question the Neptunian doctrines of his famous teacher, A. G. Werner (see GEOLOGY), and became a highly influential supporter of the theory of the igneous origin of basalt and granite. Later he engaged in paleontological studies and edited a geological map of Germany. His collected works appeared 1867–85. He was a fellow of the Royal Society.—*D. H. D. R.*

BUCHNER, EDUARD, 1860–1917, German biochemist; b. Munich. From 1885 Buchner engaged in research on fermentation processes, and in 1896 he discovered that fermentation could occur in the absence of intact cells, but in the presence of extracts of cells. Before this, the presence of intact cells had been deemed essential for the occurrence of fermentation. For this research, which introduced the concept of fermentation as being caused by the action of enzymes, Buchner received the Nobel prize, 1907.—*W. P. C.*

BUCKLAND, REV. WILLIAM, 1784–1856, English geologist; b. Axminster, Devon. Professor of mineralogy and geology at Oxford, 1813–45, he was a leader of the school of catastrophism (see GEOLOGY) and became one of the first to accept the evidence of the recent glacial periods. He wrote *Geology and Mineralogy Considered with Reference to Natural Theology* (1836) and *Reliquiae Diluvianae* (1832). His *Life and Correspondence* appeared in 1894. He was a fellow of the Royal Society.—*D. H. D. R.*

BUCKLING (or **instability**): the action of a structural member due to a compressive loading, under which the member suddenly becomes unstable, with resulting excessive deflections and structural failure. This phenomenon is best visualized in terms of a slender column subjected to a compressive force along its axis; at a load called "critical" the column will suddenly deflect laterally. The value of critical load was first determined by Leonard Euler (1707–83). Buckling must be considered in the design of slender or thin-walled structures under compression stresses such as slender beams and columns, thin plates, and shells.—*K. G.*

BUD: a growth center in a higher plant that gives rise to a branch of the shoot or the root; also, a growth center in an animal (*e.g.* the limb bud is the beginning of the limb in an animal embryo).—*L. and M. M.*

BUDDING: an asexual method of REPRODUCTION, used by plants and some animals (coelenterates and ascidians), in which protrusions (*buds*) develop into new individuals and separate from the parent.—*L. and M. M.*

Reproduction by budding: Hydra, a common coelenterate animal of ponds and streams, is shown without buds (*left*) and with buds (*right*). Buds develop tentacles and mouth, separate from parent, and become new individuals. (*H. Spencer; G. T. Hillman; both National Audubon Society*)

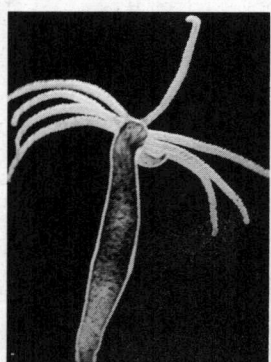 

BUFFON, COMTE GEORGES LOUIS LECLERC DE, 1707–88, French naturalist; b. Montbard. As keeper of the Jardin du Roi (Royal Botanical Garden) from 1739, he developed it into a major center of biological research. The outstanding theoretical biologist of his era, Buffon emphasized the unity of nature and life, minimized the division between plants and animals, and focused his attention on reproduction as the key characteristic of all life, modifying Leibniz's monad theory into a

Comte Georges Louis Leclerc de Buffon
(*N. Y. Public Library*)

particle theory of reproduction. His famous theory of the "epochs of nature," attempting to establish the chronology of Earth's history, correctly assumed a vastly greater age for Earth than was generally accepted, and his explanation of the origin of the solar system foreshadowed the much later TIDAL THEORY. He began publishing *Histoire naturelle* in 1749; it reached 36 vols. by his death, and 8 more were published posthumously. He was a member of the Académie Française and a fellow of the Royal Society.—*D. H. D. R.*

BUILDING MATERIALS: natural or prepared materials suitable for use as main supporting elements in construction (for other materials used in completed structures, see ARCHITECTURAL ELEMENTS). Four basic factors determine the building materials used by a civilization: availability, cost, ease of handling, and suitability for desired forms and functions. Thus ice and snow serve the Eskimo for making an igloo. In most primitive cultures, however, timber is the dominant material. Even the column, the basic element in Egyptian and Greek architecture, was first enunciated in wood; the ornamented capitals (like the lotus-bud) and the fluted shafts imitated, in stone, the timber column made of bundles of tree trunks with leafy tops. Construction in wood probably began with piling sticks and branches together to form a crude windbreak; this evolved into the wattle-and-daub hut, a framework of interwoven branches and twigs plastered with mud or turf; walls of close-set saplings or posts followed; construction with wood planks had to await the coming of woodworking tools and techniques. Where wood is not plentiful, the cheapest and most available material comes from the earth itself—clay, for sun-baked bricks. The Sumerians, who established the earliest known civilization in the Tigris-Euphrates Valley, based their building culture on brick. In northern climates, primitive societies found stone available and fitting for structures like clapper-bridges, built with stone piers and beams. Until Roman times, these three materials—wood, brick, and stone—were the only structural ones. The Romans discovered the first new material: concrete. *Pozzuolana,* a natural cement, was mixed with sand, water, and aggregate, and poured into wooden forms. However, with the fall of Rome the secret of natural cement was buried.

Two developments in the 18th cent. laid the groundwork for the modern use of building materials. One was the rediscovery of natural cement; the other was the production of iron suitable for construction. By 1713, in the town of Coalbrookdale, England, Abraham Darby (1677–1717) was producing cast iron by using coke to supplement charcoal; by 1745 the second Abraham Darby (1711–63) was using coke regularly to obtain a better cast iron. By 1800, Henry Cort (1740–1800), with his puddling process, was rolling structural members of wrought iron which were greatly superior to brittle cast-iron members. Meanwhile, towards the end of the century John Smeaton (1724–92), a British civil engineer, had found that the suitability of lime for underwater foundations lay not in the quality of the stone itself but in the presence of clay nodules; and in 1796 James Parker found in an estuary of the Thames small, hard lumps of clay which, after being burned and ground to a powder, hardened rapidly when water was added. He named this "Roman cement." Early in the 19th cent. in Leeds, England, Joseph Aspdin (1779–1855) invented and patented an artificial cement he called "Portland cement" because it resembled limestone from the Isle of Portland; this was first used largely for stucco. Although Aspdin is credited with first manufacturing artificial cement (1825), the best-known English experimenter and writer on artificial cements was Charles William Pasley (1780–1861), who published a treatise describing experiments leading to successful manufacture of an artificial hydraulic cement, 1829–30. The first American experiments in the manufacture of Portland cement were made at Coplay, Pennsylvania, by David O. Saylor, who patented his process in 1871.

French engineers were the first to appreciate the advantages of concrete; to this day they have remained leaders in handling it. The title "father of modern concrete construction" might be given to François Coignet (1814–88), who in 1861 wrote a book dealing extensively with the subject. It is likewise a Frenchman who is generally credited with the invention of reinforced concrete. Joseph Monier (1823–1906), owner of a garden establishment in Paris, took out a patent in 1867 for constructing basins and reservoirs of iron netting embedded in concrete. In the U. S. A. the pioneer builder in reinforced concrete was William E. Ward. a bolt manufacturer, who built (1871–72) a house of the new material at Port Chester, N. Y. Probably the first man to analyze correctly the stresses in a reinforced concrete beam was an American lawyer, Thaddeus Hyatt (1816–1901), who experimented with beams and slabs and in 1877 published his findings. But reinforced concrete really became an important building material only with the invention of steel. In 1856 Henry Bessemer announced a new, cheap method of converting molten iron into steel; a short time later, the Martin-Siemens process, now known as the open-hearth method, made mass-production of structural steel practical. By 1900, steel was the king of building materials; it has yet to be dethroned. See BESSEMER PROCESS.

During the 20th cent. metallurgists have produced progressively finer steel and steel alloys. Since the 1930s, concrete has found new expression both as "prestressed concrete" (in which the reinforcing rods are placed under tension before the concrete is poured) and as "pre-cast concrete" (in which the slab or beam becomes a structural member). The newest, most important building material is aluminum, about three times lighter than steel and rust-resistant. No doubt other metals and alloys will be found and manufactured to perform specific jobs in the buildings of tomorrow. See ARCHITECTURE; BRICK; BRIDGE; CEMENT; CONCRETE; STEEL; STRENGTH OF MATERIALS; WOOD.—*S. R. W.*

BULLARD, SIR EDWARD, 1907–   , English geophysicist; b. Norwich. He has studied the interior of the earth through research on gravity, seismology, Earth's magnetism, and heat flow. Most present models of the earth's interior show the influence of his synthesis. He is an associate of the U. S. National Academy of Sciences.—*R. W. D.*

The materials of 20th-cent. building include the mill-fabricated steel column (*right*), here being raised complete with connecting plates, and prestressed concrete (*below*) used as a structural element. In older tradition (*above*), masonry wall is shown being parged with cement. (*Mario Marino—Chase Manhattan Bank*)

BUNSEN, ROBERT WILHELM EBERHARD, 1811–99, German chemist; b. Göttingen. From 1837 he did research on organic

arsenic compounds, and from 1846 devised exact methods of gas analysis. Bunsen worked with Kirchhoff on the discovery of spectrum analysis (1859) and brought to light the two new elements cesium (1860) and rubidium (1861). Other areas of Bunsen's work were mineral analysis, production of cyanides by heating of alkalies with carbon in a current of nitrogen (1846), and investigations of the chemical action of light. Working with Henry Enfield Roscoe (1855), he formulated the reciprocity law. Bunsen produced numerous inventions for chemical

**Robert Wilhelm
Eberhard Bunsen**
(*Ewing Galloway*)

apparatus, *e.g.* the Bunsen battery (1840), grease-spot photometer (1844), Bunsen burner (1853), absorptiometer (1855), actinometer (with Roscoe, 1856), effusion apparatus (1857), filter pump (1868), and ice calorimeter (1870). *Gesammelte Abhandlungen* (1904) appeared after Bunsen's death. He was a fellow of the Royal Society and an associate of the U. S. National Academy of Sciences.—*S. B.*

BUOYANCY: see ARCHIMEDES' PRINCIPLE.

BURBANK, LUTHER, 1849–1926, American horticulturist; b. Lancaster, Mass. Becoming interested in plant breeding after reading the works of Charles Darwin, Burbank went into market gardening at Lunenberg, Mass. (1868), and in 1873 produced the first practical result of his experimentation, the Burbank potato. In 1875 he moved to Santa Rosa, Calif., where he continued his plant-breeding experiments for 50 yr. Burbank produced new types of plums, prunes, and berries; intro-

Luther Burbank
(*Ewing Galloway*)

duced numerous varieties of fruits, lilies, poppies, roses, tomatoes, corn, peas, asparagus, squash, and other vegetables; and succeeded in developing spineless cacti for feeding cattle in arid regions. He wrote *Luther Burbank, His Methods and Discoveries* (12 vol., 1914–15), *How Plants Are Trained to Work for Man* (1921), and *The Harvest of the Years* (1927), which he co-authored with Wilbur Hall.—*S. B.*

BURIDAN, JEAN, d. *c.* 1358, French philosopher and physicist; b. Béthune; ed. Univ. of Paris. His researches in mechanics established the impetus theory, from which Newtonian mechanics developed during the next 300 yr. Author of many commentaries on the works of Aristotle, he was philosophically a nominalist, attaching great importance to logic. His name is immortalized in "Buridan's ass," the donkey that stands midway between two identical piles of hay and starves because there is no more reason to go one way than to go the other.—*D. H. D. R.*

BURNER: a device for burning a fluid fuel under controlled conditions. The three types in use for fuel oils all atomize the oil to achieve efficient combustion. *Blast burners,* like scent-sprays, use a fast-moving blast of air or steam passing over the orifice of the oil-feed pipe to blow the issuing oil into a spray of fine droplets, the pressure varying from ⅓ to over 25 lb/in.^{2}. In *rotary cup burners* the fuel is fed into a cup rotating at high speed and is flung off the edge by centrifugal force in the form of a thin, flat disk. A low-pressure air blast moving

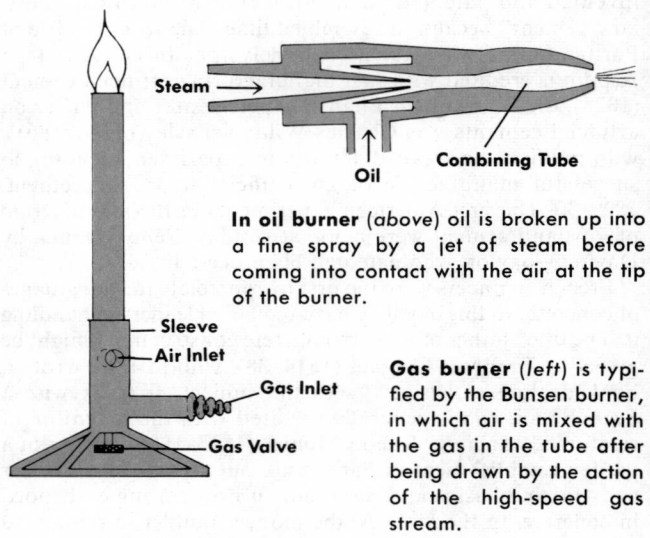

In oil burner (*above*) oil is broken up into a fine spray by a jet of steam before coming into contact with the air at the tip of the burner.

Gas burner (*left*) is typified by the Bunsen burner, in which air is mixed with the gas in the tube after being drawn by the action of the high-speed gas stream.

axially outside the cup then completes atomization. Such burners are particularly suitable for high-viscosity fuels. In *pressure jet burners* (for low-viscosity fuels) the oil is forced at high pressure through the atomizer; this is designed so that the issuing oil forms a conical film which then spreads and breaks into small droplets. The *Bunsen burner,* commonly used in laboratories, produces a hot, nonluminous flame by burning a mixture of gas and air. It is essentially a metal tube open at both ends. A current of flammable gas, drawing air in with it, enters the base of the tube. The gas and air mix and are ignited at the top of the tube, where they burn with a hot smokeless flame. An adjustable valve at the base of the tube controls the ratio of air in the mixture. *Meker* and *Fisher* burners utilize the Bunsen principle, but they have slight differences in the air-gas ratio control and emit a hotter flame. Ordinary gas-stove burners also operate on the principle of the Bunsen burner.—*R. J. F.*

BUSHNELL, DAVID, *c.* 1742–1824, U. S. inventor; b. Saybrook, Conn. Having demonstrated as a youth the feasibility of exploding gunpowder under water, in 1775 he completed a man-propelled submarine boat ("Bushnell's turtle"), bearing an underwater mine to be placed against a ship's hull and detonated by clockwork. Attempts (1776–77) to use the weapon against British ships at Boston, New York, and Philadelphia failed, but Bushnell's designs influenced the development of the submarine.—*D. H. D. R.*

BUTANE: see PARAFFINS.

BUTENANDT, ADOLPH, 1903–   , German biochemist; b. Wesermünde. In 1929 he obtained the female sex hormone in pure and crystallized form, and by 1931 had isolated a crystallized form of the male sex hormone. Later he found relationships in the chemical structure of sex hormones and carcinogenic substances. For his work on the sex hormones, he was awarded the 1939 Nobel prize (shared with Leopold Ruzicka), which the Nazi government forced him to decline. —*D. H. D. R.*

BUTTE: a steep-sided, isolated hill of rock. Often it is capped with an erosion-resistant rock stratum which protects underlying weaker strata. Common as an erosional remnant in arid and semiarid plateau regions, buttes differ from mesas in being less extensive and in having a high ratio of height to summit area. Many buttes are remnants of mesas.—*J. Sh.*

BUTYL: see RUBBER.

BUYS-BALLOT, CHRISTOPHORUS HENDRIK DIRK, 1817–90, Dutch meteorologist; b. Kloetinge. As chief of the Dutch meteorological services (1854–89), he introduced the barometric gradient and the aeroclinoscope (indicating center of depression). In 1857 the journal *Comptes rendus* published the law bearing his name (see BUYS-BALLOT'S LAW). Together with F. M. Klein, he wrote *The Foretelling of Weather* (1863).—*R. J. F.*

BUYS-BALLOT'S LAW: in meteorology, a principle that relates the direction of wind to atmospheric pressure distribution. The law: "If one stands with his back to the wind, the pressure to his left is lower than the pressure to his right." This is true for the northern hemisphere. In the southern hemisphere, low pressure will lie to the observer's right. The phenomenon underlying this law, formulated by BUYS-BALLOT

Buys-Ballot's law: This demonstration is for the northern hemisphere. For the southern hemisphere, the observer would be facing in the opposite direction.

(1857), results from rotation of the earth. (See ATMOSPHERIC PRESSURE; ANTICYCLONE; CYCLONE.)—*P. L.*

BYERS, HORACE ROBERT, 1906–   , U. S. meteorologist; b. Seattle, Wash. An associate of Carl-Gustaf Rossby, Byers endeavored to introduce the Norwegian methods of weather analysis into U. S. practices (1935–40). He did extensive research on thunderstorms (1945–48) in a project sponsored by the U. S. Weather Bureau. He is professor of meteorology at the Univ. of Chicago and since 1952 has directed large research projects on atmospheric electricity, physics of clouds, and precipitation processes. His textbook *General Meteorology* appeared in 1944.—*W. P. C.*

Rock masses isolated by erosion, buttes are the last stage in the life of a mesa. This series of buttes, known as the "Walls of Jericho," is in Cathedral Valley, Utah. (*Josef Muench*)

C

CABEO, NICCOLO, 1585–1650, Italian physicist; b. Ferrara. The discoverer of electrostatic repulsion, he also did research in magnetism and electricity, described in his *Philosophia magnetica* (1629). A Jesuit, and professor of mathematics at the Univ. of Parma, Cabeo was a stanch defender of the geocentric theory of the universe.—*D. H. D. R.*

CABLE, ELECTRICAL: an electrical conductor made up usually of a central wire surrounded by an insulating sheath. For protection and mechanical strength, the two are often housed in an exterior metal tube or wire-braid cover. The central conductor may also be braided, and there may be one or more separate conductors; cables are frequently made by winding together groups of individually insulated single wires. Power cables, such as are commonly employed for electrical high-tension lines, are designed to withstand high voltages and to conduct large currents. Communication cables are designed to operate at high frequencies but generally at low power levels. An example of a communication cable is the common so-called coaxial cable frequently employed to connect television and frequency-modulation radio antennas to their respective receivers. The coaxial cable is formed by two concentric conductors separated by a nonconductive insulator, *e.g.* a series of dielectric beads. The high-frequency signal is confined between and guided along the two coaxial conductors.—*G. S.*

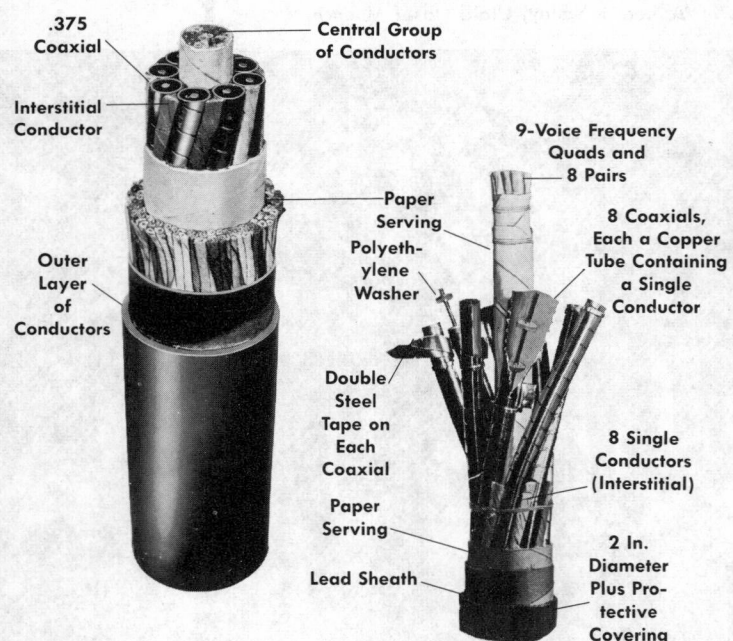

Two Types of Coaxial Communication Cables (*American Telephone and Telegraph Co.*)

CADMIUM: a metallic element (Cd); at. no. 48; at. wt 112.41; density 8.642; mp 321°C; bp 767°C. It occurs naturally as the yellow sulfide, greenockite, and in ores of zinc. Since cadmium is more readily reduced and more volatile than zinc, it comes off in the first distillate of zinc smelting. This distillate is fractionally distilled to yield pure cadmium. Cadmium metal is deposited electrolytically from a solution of its cyanide complex to form a protective coating for iron and steel. It is also used as an alloy in automatic fire extinguishers and in automobile bearings. Cadmium compounds form a series of valuable yellow-to-red pigments used in paints and printing inks. Cadmium metal and its compounds are toxic.—*G. W. M.*

Foundation for oil well off coast of Venezuela is built by joining already-sunk caissons (the column-like structures here) by means of metal frames. (*Amer. Petroleum Inst.*)

CAISSON: a vertical boxlike structure, with open ends, used in underwater construction, particularly for installing foundations and piers for bridges. A caisson is a shell of timber, steel, or concrete generally fabricated on land, launched, and then sunk into place at the foundation site, where it eventually becomes a permanent part of the structure being built. A cutting edge on the bottom allows the caisson to sink gradually as the bottom soil is dredged out by machinery; meanwhile the caisson sides are extended upward to keep the top above water. A diver is used to clean the bottom surface, and concrete is poured underwater to fix it in place. In more complicated construction jobs where the soil is soft or the foundation must go deep, a pneumatic or pressurized caisson is employed. A chamber at the bottom of the caisson with the river or harbor bed as its floor is kept free of water by maintaining the air at very high pressure. In this compartment workmen, commonly called "sandhogs," dig out the mud and sand as the caisson sinks until solid rock is reached. —*R. G.*

CALCINATION: a process in chemical industry in which a substance is subjected to heat, usually to effect a chemical change. For example, limestone (calcium carbonate, $CaCO_3$) is calcined in long rotating furnaces to quicklime (calcium oxide, CaO), carbon dioxide (CO_2) being driven off.—*Ru. M.*

CALCITE: a common mineral widespread in occurrence as the major constituent of marl, CHALK, LIMESTONE, and MARBLE; as a cement in sandstone; as a vein-filling; and in cave formations (flowstone and dripstone). (See SEDIMENTARY ROCK.) Calcite (trigonal) and aragonite (orthorhombic) are, respectively, the higher- and lower-temperature polymorphs of $CaCO_3$. Most shells, corals, and natural precipitates of $CaCO_3$ crystallize originally as aragonite, but accumulations of these materials, on burial and consolidation (diagenesis), invert to calcite. Calcite crystals may show an immense variety of faces, but the perfect rhombohedral cleavage, softness (hardness is 3), strong double refraction, and effervescence in cold dilute acids are distinctive. The simple CARBONATES form three distinct isomorphous series:

Calcite Series	$CaCO_3$	Calcite
(Trigonal, $\overline{3}$——)	$MnCO_3$	Rhodochrosite (ore of manganese)
	$FeCO_3$	Siderite (ore of iron)
	$(Fe, Mg)CO_3$	Breunnerite
	$MgCO_3$	Magnesite (ore of magnesium)
	$ZnCO_3$	Smithsonite (ore of zinc)
Dolomite Series	$CaMg(CO_3)_2$	Dolomite (ore of magnesium)
(Trigonal, $\overline{3}$)	$CaFe(CO_3)_2$	Ankerite
	$CaMn(CO_3)_2$	Kutnahorite
Aragonite Series	$CaCO_3$	Aragonite (pearls, coral)
(Orthorhombic)	$BaCO_3$	Witherite (ore of barium)
	$SrCO_3$	Strontianite (ore of strontium)
	$PbCO_3$	Cerussite (ore of lead)

The structures of these carbonates are based on the $(CO_3)^{-2}$ unit, an equilateral triangle formed by three oxygen ions linked to a carbon ion in the center. The independent CO_3 units are held together through shared divalent cations. The size of the cation is the determining factor in the symmetry of the molecular lattice and the resulting crystals. Calcium, in the high-temperature polymorph, and all cations with smaller ionic radii permit a denser packing, with orthorhombic symmetry.

In the calcite series, the CO_3 "triangles" are disposed in densely populated, flat layers, with alternating, sparsely populated layers of cations. This accounts for the strong anisotropism of the minerals of the calcite series, as shown by appreciable differences in index of refraction (double refraction = birefringence), hardness, and coefficient of thermal expansion between prismatic and basal directions.

Transparent calcite (*Iceland spar*) is used in optical instruments that produce polarized light, *e.g.* nicol prisms in microscopes and polarimeters, and optical gunsights. Calcite-rich rocks are used as sources of lime for cements, fertilizers, glass, ceramics, rock wool, metallurgical fluxes, and agents in many chemical processes. See MINERAL (table).—*L. M.*

CALCIUM: a chemical element, an alkaline earth metal (at. no. 20, at. wt 40). In metallic form it is a white, flammable solid, somewhat harder than lead; sp gr 1.55, mp 810°C, bp ap-

proximately 1200°C. On exposure to air, the metal tarnishes, assuming a thin, bluish-gray skin which helps prevent further oxidation. It reacts with water, releasing hydrogen and forming calcium hydroxide, which has only limited solubility in water and coats the metal to reduce the reaction rate. Calcium metal can be made by electrolysis of calcium chloride or by thermal dissociation of calcium chloride. It is used industrially as an alloying agent, deoxidizer, and reducing agent. The most common compound of calcium is CALCIUM CARBONATE ($CaCO_3$); when this is treated with hydrochloric acid calcium chloride (CaCl) is formed. Calcium carbonate is also a by-product of the ammonia-soda process for making soda ash and other industrial processes. Being deliquescent, the chloride is useful as a household dehumidifier and in reducing dust on unpaved roads. Since the saturated water solution freezes at −48°C, it is valuable as an anti-freeze and refrigerant. Calcium chloride is found in trace quantities in sea water and in some minerals. Calcium fluoride occurs naturally as the mineral fluorspar and is an important commercial source of fluorine. Calcium sulfate ($CaSO_4$) is found in nature as the mineral anhydrite; its hydrate, gypsum ($CaSO_4 \cdot 2H_2O$), occurs naturally and is a by-product in commercial processes. Gypsum is a necessary ingredient of Portland cement; and when heated, it gives up a molecule of water to form the hemi-hydrate ($2CaSO_4 \cdot H_2O$), plaster of Paris. This, when moistened with water, swells and resets in approximately half an hour to a solid mass of gypsum. Calcium carbide (CaC_2), produced in an electric arc by the action of coke on quicklime (CaO), is an important source of acetylene; when cold water is added, acetylene is produced and lime is regenerated. When calcium carbide is heated in an electric oven in the presence of nitrogen, it is converted to calcium cyanamid ($CaCN_2$), a fertilizer and a starting point for synthesis of other nitrogen compounds.—*D. P. B.*

CALCIUM CARBONATE ($CaCO_3$): a white or colorless crystalline material (sp gr 2.7–2.95). A stable compound widely found in nature, it is the main constituent of eggshells and, with calcium phosphate, of bones. LIMESTONE is essentially calcium carbonate. Although not soluble in water or alcohol, calcium carbonate is dissolved with decomposition by most acids. When heated, it evolves carbon dioxide, leaving quicklime (calcium oxide, CaO). See CALCITE.—*D. P. B.*

Dogtooth spar, a common crystalline form of calcite ($CaCO_3$), is represented by these crystals from Joplin, Mo. (*Amer. Mus. of Nat. Hist.*)

CALCIUM HYDROXIDE (CaOH), popularly known as hydrated, or slaked, lime: a soft, white, powdery material with sp gr 2.2. It is formed when water is added to quicklime (CaO). This heat-evolving reaction is reversible; the hydroxide when heated breaks down to quicklime and water. Hydrated lime is only sparingly soluble in water; solubility decreases with increasing temperatures. If calcium hydroxide is shaken with a sufficient excess of water, a suspension, "milk of lime," results. Calcium hydroxide is employed commercially as a cheap, readily available base and as whitewash. Its reaction with carbon dioxide in the air to form calcium carbonate is the basis of its use in mortar: a mixture of hydrated lime, sand, and water.—*D. P. B.*

CALCIUM OXIDE (quicklime): a compound of calcium and oxygen, CaO. It is prepared by decomposing limestone (CaCO₃) in chimney-like furnaces called lime kilns. The limestone is fed into the top, heated, and decomposed by a draft of hot gas, and the lime is collected at the bottom. A major use of lime is in the manufacture of cement. It is one of the least expensive bases, and as such is used in a wide variety of chemical processes.—*G. W. M.*

CALCULATING MACHINE: see COMPUTER.

CALCULUS, DIFFERENTIAL AND INTEGRAL: mathematics which introduces the operation of taking a limit—an operation not included in arithmetic, algebra, or geometry. Processes involving limits can be applied to problems involving changes in continually varying quantities, *e.g.* problems of velocity, acceleration, rate of flow of heat or fluids, rates of chemical reactions, and the slopes of curves. The methods of calculus are essential to modern physics and, indeed, to most branches of science. The word "calculus" alone is used for differential and integral calculus, although there are several other varieties, *e.g.* calculus of finite differences, calculus of probabilities, calculus of variations.

Although Isaac Newton (1642–1727) and Gottfried Leibniz (1646–1716) are credited with its discovery, calculus grew out of the efforts of many mathematicians to solve two geometric problems which interested the Greeks. These are the problem of finding the tangent to a curve at a given point, and the problem of determining the area bounded by a curve. Both were solved by Greek mathematicians for some special curves, but the methods of the Greeks were incapable of generalization.

Tangent, or Rate, Problem: The modern solution of the tangent problem employs the COORDINATE GEOMETRY, introduced by Descartes in 1637, less than half a century before Newton and Leibniz. A curve is considered to have an equation $y = f(x)$ in which $f(x)$ means "a function of x" (see FUNCTION). The equation $y = f(x)$ therefore symbolizes the equation of the curve. A simple example is $y = x^2$. To determine the slope of the tangent to the curve at a point P with coordinates $(1, 1)$ we proceed as follows: Consider a second point Q on the curve (Fig. 1) for which $x = (1 + h)$ and $y = (1 + h)^2$. The slope of the chord PQ is

$$\frac{(1 + h)^2 - 1}{h} = \frac{2h + h^2}{h} = 2 + h$$

This chord, of course, is not the tangent at P. But by taking h smaller and smaller, and thus bringing Q closer and closer to P, we obtain a sequence of chords which approach the desired tangent. As h tends to 0, the slope, which is always equal to $2 + h$, tends to 2. Hence the slope of the tangent is taken to be 2. More generally, if $y = f(x)$ the slope of the tangent at $P(x_1, y_1)$ is found as follows: At P we have $y_1 = f(x_1)$; at a nearby point Q we have $x = x_1 + h$, $y = f(x_1 + h)$. The

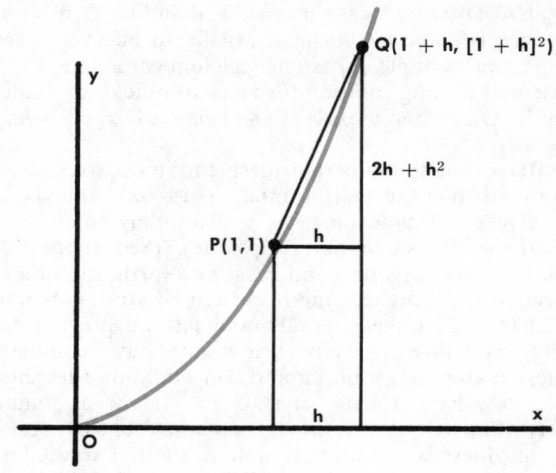

Fig. 1

slope of the chord PQ is $[f(x_1 + h) - f(x_1)]/h$ and the slope of the tangent is the quantity approached by this ratio as h tends to 0. In these statements, we refer to what we intuitively conceive the tangent to be. We make the definitions of the tangent and slope of the tangent conform to these intuitive ideas. Thus, the slope of the tangent at (x_1, y_1) is defined to be the limit of $[f(x_1 + h) - f(x_1)]/h$ as h tends to 0, and the tangent is defined to be the straight line through P which has this slope. This limit is symbolized by

$$\lim_{h \to 0} \frac{f(x_1 + h) - f(x_1)}{h}$$

The slope of the tangent is the rate of rise of the ordinate per unit change of the abscissa, or briefly, the rate of change of y with respect to x. This rate is uniform along the tangent line. The instantaneous rate of change of y with respect to x as a point moves through P along the curve is the rate which belongs to the tangent at P. Since any functional relation, $y = f(x)$, can be represented on a coordinate system, the slope of the tangent represents the rate of change of y with respect to x. Hence the solution of the tangent problem is very broad, giving the rate of change in a functional relation which may be interpreted in many ways. If distance s is a function of time t, this rate is the instantaneous velocity.

Differentiation: The calculation of

$$\lim_{h \to 0} \frac{f(x + h) - f(x)}{h}$$

is called differentiation, and the result is called a *derivative*. The process is facilitated by formulas for derivatives of all common functions. Several notations are in common use, the principal ones being the following. If $y = f(x)$ the expression for the derivative is denoted by Dy, $D_x y$, or $Df(x)$ (due to Cauchy); dy/dx, or $(d/dx)f(x)$ (due to Leibniz); y', or $F'(x)$ (due to Lagrange); or $\dot{x}$ (due to Newton).

The principal formulas are:

$Dc = 0$, where c is a constant

$D \ln x = 1/x$, if $x > 0$ $Dx^n = nx^{n-1}$
($\ln x$ means $\log_e x$)

$D \sin x = \cos x$ $De^x = e^x$

$D \tan x = \sec^2 x$ $D \cos x = -\sin x$

$D \sin^{-1} x = 1/\sqrt{1 - x^2}$, if $|x| < 1$ $D \tan^{-1} x = 1/(1 + x^2)$

In addition to these formulas (and others for less familiar functions), four rules make it possible to differentiate most elementary functions. These are the rules for differentiating a sum, product, or quotient of two functions and the chain rule for differentiating a function of a function, or compound function. They are

(1) $D[f(x) + g(x)] = Df(x) + Dg(x)$

(2) $D[f(x) \cdot g(x)] = g(x)\, Df(x) + f(x)\, Dg(x)$

(3) $D\left[\dfrac{f(x)}{g(x)}\right] = \dfrac{g(x)\, Df(x) - F(x)\, Dg(x)}{[g(x)]^2}$

(4) If $y = f(t)$ and $t = g(x)$, then $D_x y = D_t y \cdot D_x t$

In (2), if $f(x)$ is a constant c, we have (2a) $Dcg(x) = cDg(x)$, since $Dc = 0$. An example of the use of (1) and (2a) together with the first two formulas is the differentiation of a polynomial. For example, $D(x^3 + 4x^2 - 2x + 10) = 3x^2 + 8x - 2 + 0$. As an example of the chain rule, consider De^{x^2}. Here we can put $y = e^t$, $t = x^2$; then $D_x y = e^t \cdot 2x = 2xe^{x^2}$.

The slope of a curve at a point is a definite number, not a variable. The above formulas give these numbers for each x. The formulas themselves are functions, sometimes called *derived functions*. The word derivative is used both in the sense of a single value corresponding to one value of x and in the sense of a derived function. Each derived function can be differentiated again. The result is called a second derived function, or second derivative. Thus, if $y = x^4$, $Dy = 4x^3$, $D(Dy) = 4 \cdot 3x^2$. The notation for second derivatives is $D^2 y$, d^2y/dx^2, y'', $f''(x)$ or $\ddot{x}$. This process can be continued to obtain derivatives of still higher order: $D^3 y$, $D^4 y$, etc.

Rate Problems: There are two kinds of rate problems which can be solved by differentiation. One of these is illustrated by finding the velocity in a distance-time relation. For example, if a body falls s feet in t seconds, where $s = 16t^2$, what is its velocity at the end of 3 sec? Since velocity is rate of change of distance, the answer is given by the derivative, $v = Ds = 32t$. When $t = 3$, $v = 96$, or 96 ft/sec.

A second kind of problem is known as a related rate problem. Suppose we have a relation between two variables, both of which are functions of a third variable, *e.g.* time. If we know the rate of change of one of these variables, we can find the rate of change of the other. If a spherical balloon expands so that its radius increases at 2 ft/min, how fast is the volume increasing when the radius is 5 ft? We have $v = \frac{4}{3}\pi r^3$. Since r and v are functions of time, we can use the chain rule and write $D_t v = \frac{4}{3}\pi \cdot 3r^2\, D_t r$. Now $D_t r$ is given equal to 2. When $r = 5$, we have $D_t v = 4\pi \cdot 25 \cdot 2 = 200\pi$. Hence the volume is increasing at the rate of 200π ft³/min.

Maxima and Minima: Differential calculus furnishes a general method of solving the problem of finding the value of a variable which makes a function a maximum or a minimum. The method is easily grasped from a graphical illustration (Fig. 2). Let us find the maximum point of the graph of $y = 4x - x^2$. The derivative gives the rate of change of y with respect to x. If Dy is positive the curve is rising, if Dy is negative it is falling, and if $Dy = 0$ it is neither rising nor falling. If the curve passes through a maximum point, it rises toward this point and then falls. Hence we expect that $Dy = 0$ at the maximum point. In this example, $Dy = 2x - 4$. If $Dy = 0$, $2x - 4 = 0$, and $x = 2$. Hence, if there is a maximum point it must be at $x = 2$, $y = 4$. Similar reasoning leads to the conclusion that $Dy = 0$ at a minimum point. The maxima and minima we refer to are relative, a relative maximum being a maximum in the immediate vicinity although not necessarily the absolute maximum. In order to

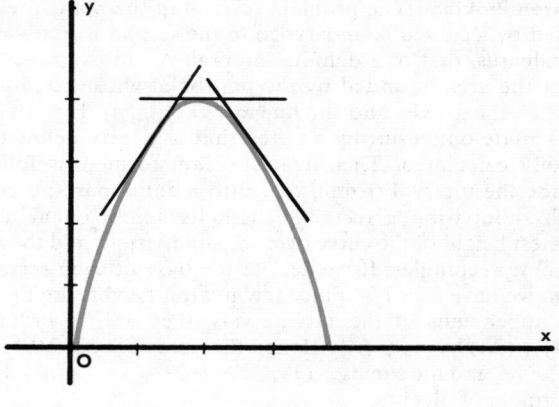

Fig. 2

find a value of x producing a relative maximum or minimum value of y, we set Dy, or $f'(x)$, equal to 0 and solve the resulting equation. This will determine values for which the slope of the curve is zero. These include such points as those shown in Fig. 3. Points A and D represent minima and point B a maximum, whereas C and E are neither, although $f'(x) = 0$ at these points. This suggests that a test is necessary to determine whether a value of x which satisfies the equation $f'(x) = 0$ corresponds to a maximum, a minimum, or a point of inflection like C or E. In practical problems such a test is seldom necessary. But we can see from the illustration that at a minimum point the derivative changes from negative to zero to positive values as x increases; at a maximum point it changes from positive to zero to negative values as x increases.

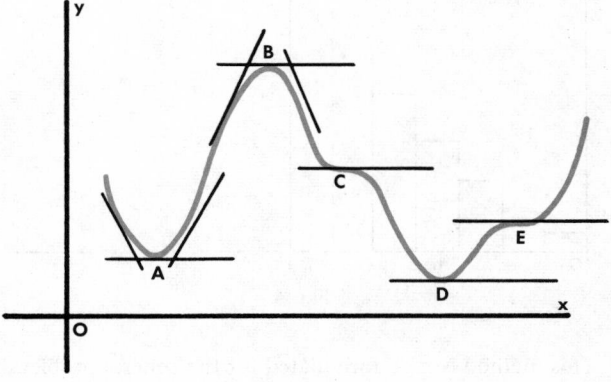

Fig. 3

Inverse Differentiation: The formulas for differentiation can be inverted so as to find a function having a given derivative. Thus, since $Dx^2 = 2x$, an inverse derivative of $2x$, denoted by $D^{-1}(2x)$, is x^2. There are, however, other functions having $2x$ as derivative, namely $x^2 + c$, where c is any constant. We write $D^{-1}(2x) = x^2 + c$. Each of the formulas for differentiation can be inverted to produce a formula for inverse differentiation. Actually, the symbol D^{-1} is usually replaced by the integral sign $\int$, and the process is often called indefinite integration. Instead of $D^{-1}x^{-1} = \ln x + c$, we write $\int x^{-1}\,dx = \ln x + c$, the symbol dx implying that the integration is with respect to x; that is, that we seek the inverse differential of the function of x. Similarly, $\int x^n\,dx = x^{n+1}/(n+1) + c$, if $n \neq -1$; and $\int \cos x\,dx = \sin x + c$.

Area Problem: The problem of finding the plane area enclosed by a curved boundary led to the second major concept of calculus, that of a definite integral. As an example, consider the area bounded by the parabola whose equation is $y = x^2$, the x axis, and the line $x = 1$ (Fig. 4). First, we approximate our result by an area that is clearly defined and readily calculated. This area is a sum formed as follows: divide the interval from 0 to 1 into n equal parts; erect on each subdivision a rectangle with its height equal to the greatest height of the curve over the subdivision; add the areas of these rectangles. If we denote the base of each rectangle by h, we have $h = 1/n$. Since the greatest heights are those at the upper ends of the subintervals, they are, in order, h^2, $(2h)^2$, $(3h)^2, \ldots, (nh)^2$. Hence the areas are h^3, 2^2h^3, 3^2h^3, $\ldots, n^2h^3$, and the sum is $h^3(1^2 + 2^2 + 3^2 + \cdots + n^2)$. From a formula of algebra,

$$1^2 + 2^2 + 3^2 + \cdots + n^2 = \tfrac{1}{6}n(n + 1)(2n + 1).$$

Therefore the sum is $\tfrac{1}{6}h^3n(n + 1)(2n + 1)$, which is equal to $2n^3h^3/6 + 3n^2h^3/6 + nh^3/6$. Now $nh = 1$, and therefore the sum is equal to $\tfrac{1}{3} + \tfrac{1}{2}h + \tfrac{1}{6}h^2$. This result is correct regardless of the size of n. As n increases more and more, the figure made up of all the rectangles approaches more and more closely the figure with the curve as its upper boundary. Hence we define the area to be the limit of the above sum as n increases beyond all bounds. This limit is easily found, since as n increases beyond all bounds h approaches 0. Therefore, $\tfrac{1}{3} + \tfrac{1}{2}h + \tfrac{1}{6}h^2$ approaches $\tfrac{1}{3}$, which is the required area.

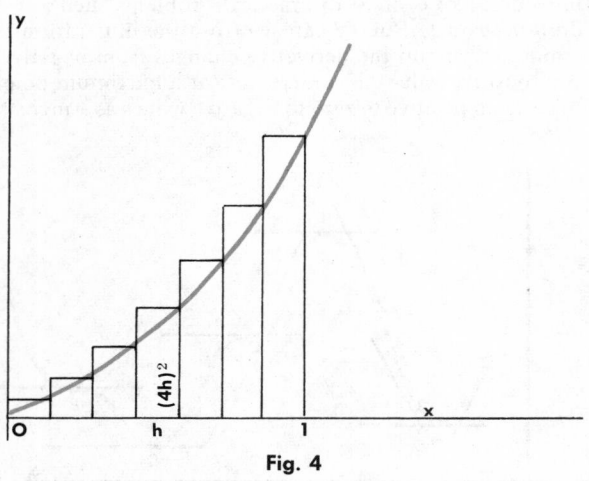

Fig. 4

This method can be formulated for the general problem as follows. Let the interval from a to b be subdivided into n subintervals, with widths $h_1, h_2, \ldots, h_n$ (not necessarily equal). Over each subinterval as base erect a rectangle with height equal to the height of the curve at some point in the subinterval (not necessarily the greatest height). These heights can be denoted by $f(x_1), f(x_2), \ldots, f(x_n)$. The sum of the rectangular areas is $f(x_1) h_1 + f(x_2) h_2 + \cdots + f(x_n) h_n$. If the subdivisions are formed so that every h tends to 0 as n increases beyond all bounds, it can be shown that the sum approaches a definite limit, independent of the mode of subdivision and of the choice of x in each subinterval. This limit is called the definite integral of the function $f(x)$ over the interval from a to b, and is denoted by the symbol $\int_a^b f(x)\, dx$. The definite integral is not a function of x; it is a number. The area in the example above is given by the integral, $\int_0^1 x^2\, dx = \tfrac{1}{3}$.

Except for the simplest functions the calculation of the integral by direct summation is difficult. Therefore the dis-covery of a practical general method of performing this calculation was exceedingly valuable. Among the contributions of Newton and Leibniz, this was one of the greatest. It is stated as follows. Let $Q(x)$ be an inverse derivative of $f(x)$. Then $\int_a^b f(x)\, dx = Q(b) - Q(a)$. Thus, since $x^3/3$ is an inverse derivative of x^2, then $\int_0^1 x^2\, dx = 1^3/3 - 0^3/3 = \tfrac{1}{3}$.

Applications of Definite Integrals: The definite integral has many applications depending upon the interpretations of the variables in the functional relation. Any quantity which can be formulated as the limit of a sum suggests an integral. The volume of a solid can be conceived as the limit of the sum of thin slices, the mass of a body as the limit of the sum of masses of small parts, the work done by a variable force as the limit of the sum of amounts of work done by constant forces each acting over a small distance, a total force as the limit of the sum of small forces. Many other applications can be found.

Partial Differentiation and Multiple Integration: The extension of differentiation and integration to functions of two or more variables leads to partial derivatives and multiple integrals. A function of x and y is differentiated partially with respect to x by considering y as temporarily constant. If $u = f(x, y)$, the partial derivatives of u with respect to x and y are denoted by $\partial u/\partial x$ and $\partial u/\partial y$, respectively. For example, if $u = 3x^2y + y^2 + 2x$, $\partial u/\partial x = 6xy + 2$ and $\partial u/\partial y = 3x^2 + 2y$. Such a derivative is interpreted as the rate of change of a function resulting from the change of one variable only.

Higher partial derivatives are illustrated by the above example as follows:

$$(\partial/\partial x)(\partial u/\partial x) = \partial^2 u/\partial x^2 = 6y$$
$$(\partial/\partial y)(\partial u/\partial x) = \partial^2 u/\partial y\, \partial x = 6x$$
$$(\partial/\partial y)(\partial u/\partial y) = \partial^2 u/\partial y^2 = 2$$

Functions of more than two variables may be partially differentiated in a similar way.

A double integral is the limit of a summation of a function of two variables over a two-dimensional domain of these variables. It provides a method of finding a volume under a surface, just as the single integral gives the area under a curve. For example, consider the volume bounded by the coordinate planes, the plane $x = 3$ parallel to the yz plane, the plane $y = 2$ parallel to the xz plane, and the surface $z = 10 - x^2 - y^2$ (Fig. 5). The volume is conceived as the limit of the

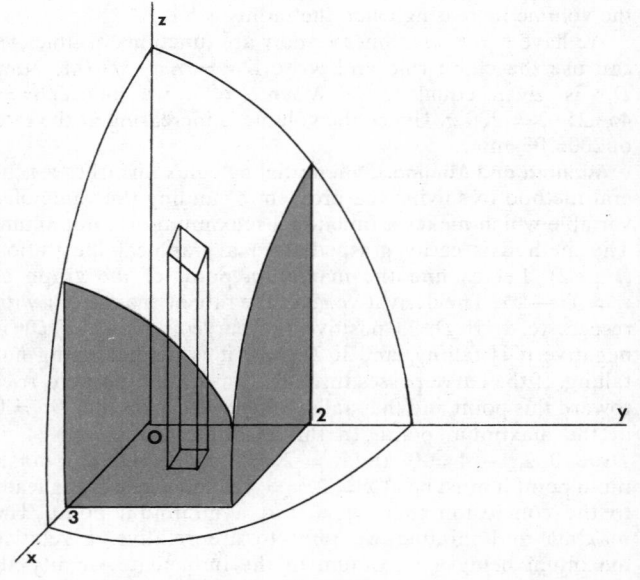

Fig. 5

sum of prisms based on the rectangular domain in the xy plane and bounded above by the surface, enough prisms being formed to cover the whole rectangle, and the limit being taken as their number increases beyond all bounds and the greatest distance across the base of each tends to 0. This limit is the double integral $\iint_A (10 - x^2 - y^2)\, dA$. It is calculated in a manner somewhat analogous to partial differentiation—by first integrating with one variable held fixed, after which integration with respect to the other variable completes the process. Thus, for the above example,

$$\iint_A (10 - x^2 - y^2)\, dA = \int_0^3 dx \int_0^2 (10 - x^2 - y^2)\, dy$$
$$= \int_0^3 (20 - 2x^2 - \tfrac{8}{3})\, dx = 34$$

Integration of functions of more than two variables may be carried out by an extension of this method. See also ANALYSIS; LIMIT; CALCULUS OF VARIATIONS.—*H. C.*

CALCULUS OF FINITE DIFFERENCES: a branch of mathematics somewhat analogous to differential and integral calculus except that it deals with discrete, rather than continuous, quantities. It deals with changes in functions for definite jumps in the values of the independent variable, *e.g.* the changes in $y = x^2$ as x takes the values 0, 1, 2, ... Its applications include statistical problems in which the values of the variables are integral (whole numbers), and actuarial problems. This calculus also provides an approach to continuous problems.

The principal tool of calculus of finite differences is a differences table. The simplest kind of table is constructed from values of a given function $f(x)$ associated with equally spaced values of x. First, the corresponding values of x and $f(x)$ are tabulated. Then we calculate a column of first differences $\Delta f(x)$, which are differences of consecutive values of $f(x)$; then a column of second differences $\Delta^2 f(x)$, which are differences of consecutive values of $\Delta f(x)$; and so on.

x	$f(x)$	$\Delta f(x)$	$\Delta^2 f(x)$	$\Delta^3 f(x)$
1	5			
		3		
2	8		1	
		4		0
3	12		1	
		5		0
4	17		1	
		6		0
5	23		1	
		7		
6	30			

In the example, $\Delta^2 f(x)$ is constant and $\Delta^3 f(x) = 0$. A situation like this does not always develop but if the elements of a column are all approximately zero, the table may be used in the same way as when they are exactly zero, with the understanding that the results are approximate. From the above table we can calculate values of $f(x)$ corresponding to further values of x, at will. For example, to obtain the value of $f(7)$, start with $\Delta^2 f(x) = 1$, adding $1 + 7 = 8$ for the next entry in the $\Delta f(x)$ column; then add $8 + 30$ for the required value of $f(7)$. In this way the table can be extended as far as necessary. A formula which produces any desired value is the Newton formula:

$$f(x + n) = f(x) + n\Delta f(x) + \frac{n(n-1)}{2} \Delta^2 f(x)$$
$$+ \frac{n(n-1)(n-2)}{2 \cdot 3} \Delta^3 f(x) + \cdots$$

In this formula, $f(x)$ is the known value corresponding to some value of x, the differences $\Delta f(x)$, $\Delta^2 f(x)$, etc. are those differences which go forward from $f(x)$, and the coefficients are those of the binomial expansion. For example, we can calculate $f(7)$ from the above table by starting with $f(1)$ and letting $n = 6$: $f(7) = 5 + 6 \cdot 3 + \tfrac{1}{2} 6 \cdot 5 \cdot 1$, the expression terminating because further differences are zero. The process of calculating values other than those in the table is called *interpolation,* and is one of the main problems of calculus of finite differences. It is possible to use the Newton formula to approximate values of $f(x)$ for values of x lying between those in the table by taking n fractional.

When the common difference in the values of x is h, not necessarily equal to 1, the Newton formula is essentially the same, but the differences correspond to differences of h in x, and we have

$$f(x + nh) = f(x) + n\Delta f(x) + \tfrac{1}{2} n(n-1) \Delta^2 f(x) + \cdots$$

There are many other interpolation formulas, adapted to special needs.

If the values of $f(x)$ are given for values of x at unevenly spaced intervals, the differences must reflect these unequal intervals. For this purpose divided differences are employed. A divided difference is the difference of values of $f(x)$ divided by the corresponding difference of values of x. The Newton divided difference formula accomplishes the same ends in this case as the above Newton formula for equal intervals.

Functions of a given form can be differenced. That is, formulas for their differences can be found, just as functions can be differentiated in differential calculus. For example, to find the first difference of the function $x(x - 1)$, we first substitute the next higher value, $x + 1$, for x, and obtain $(x + 1)x$. From this we subtract the original function. Thus $\Delta[x(x - 1)] = (x + 1)x - x(x - 1) = 2x$. This process can now be reversed. If $\Delta^{-1} f(x)$ denotes finding a function whose difference function is $f(x)$, we can write $\Delta^{-1} 2x = x(x - 1)$. These inverse operations have special significance for the second main problem of calculus of finite differences, which is the summation of a finite series of terms: $\Sigma_{i=1}^n u(i)$. If we can identify the terms of the series as the differences of some other series, we can write the sum immediately from the second series. For if $u(1) = f(2) - f(1)$, $u(2) = f(3) - f(2)$, etc, then $\Sigma_{i=1}^n u(i) = u(1) + u(2) + u(3) + \cdots + u(n) = -f(1) + f(2) - f(2) + f(3) + \cdots - f(n) + f(n + 1) = f(n + 1) - f(1)$. For example, $\Sigma_{i=1}^n 2i = (n + 1)n$. This follows from the fact that $\Delta x(x - 1) = 2x$. Here $u(x) = 2x$, and $f(x) = x(x - 1)$, so that $f(n + 1) = (n + 1)n$ and $f(1) = 0$. Thus operations denoted by Δ and Σ are related much as are integration and differentiation.—*H. C.*

CALCULUS OF VARIATIONS: a form of the calculus devised to solve maximum and minimum problems of a higher order of difficulty than those treated in ordinary differential calculus. Such problems arise in classical mechanics and in relativity theory. An example is finding the shortest path between two points on a surface. This is a minimum problem—but not of the kind of minimum (or maximum) problem treated in the ordinary calculus, such as finding the lowest (or highest) point on a given curve or surface. The difference is this. Any point A on a given curve (Fig. 1) may be characterized by a single number: its abscissa x; and if $g(x)$ denotes the height of A above the base line, the problem is to find a point A_0 such that $g(x_0) \leqq g(x)$ for any number x. A point on a surface may be similarly characterized by two numbers. But even if the surface S is a plane, the paths joining the two points P and Q are of such a variety (Fig. 2) that it is impossible to characterize each of them in a natural way by a number or by any finite group of numbers. Each path may, how-

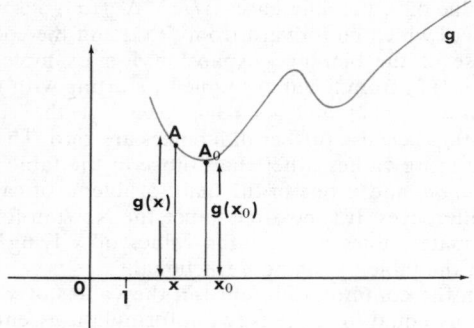

Fig. 1

ever, be characterized by a function, just as the curve in the first figure can be characterized by the function g associating the height $g(x)$ with any x. If one can somehow determine the length $L(f)$ of the curve characterized by the function f, then the problem of the shortest path amounts to finding a function f_0 such that $L(f_0) \leqq L(f)$ for any function f. If S is the plane, then $L(f) = \int_a^b [1 + (f'(x))^2]^{1/2} \, dx$; but even if S is more complicated, $L(f)$ is equal to an integral involving f and the derivative f' of f. Similarly, the time it takes a falling object to move in a vertical plane along the curve characterized by the function f is

$$T(f) = \int_a^b \{[1 + (f'(x))^2]/[f(x) - 1]\}^{1/2} \, dx$$

If by some integration process a number is associated with each differentiable function of a certain kind, then the theory of finding the functions with which the smallest (or largest) number is associated belongs to what is called the calculus of variations.

Historically, this branch of analysis began with the problem of the brachistochrone. The solution of this is a cycloid, since this curve is characterized by a function f_0 such that $T(f_0) \leqq T(f)$ for any function f. Leonhard Euler developed a condition (a 2nd order differential equation) that every minimizing or maximizing function must necessarily satisfy. In the case of the length problem (which is very important in relativity theory), that condition stipulates that the

shortest path is as little curved as possible: in the plane, straight; on a sphere, a great circle. W. R. Hamilton and K. G. J. Jacobi applied the calculus of variations to mechanics. In the 1870's, K. T. Weierstrass formulated sufficient conditions which, when satisfied by a function, guarantee that it actually minimizes (or maximizes). In this century, D. Hilbert and L. Tonelli proved existence theorems, which guarantee that certain problems have solutions. (An example of an *in*soluble problem is looking for the longest path between two points.) G. D. Birkhoff and M. Morse have also investigated minimaxes—curves by which an integral is minimized in comparison to some curves, and maximized in comparison to others, just as a mountain pass is the lowest point at which a mountain can be traversed and the highest point on the traversing road. At present, much attention is being paid to the determination of surfaces with given rims in space that minimize certain integrals, *e.g.* the area. Such so-called minimal surfaces can be materialized by soap films.—*K. M.*

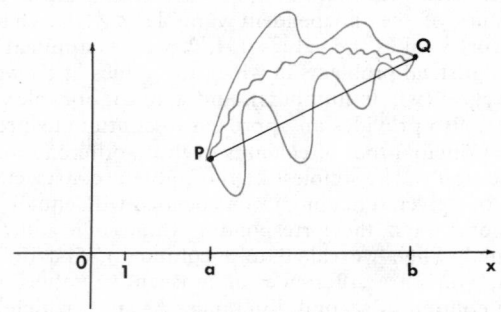

Fig. 2

CALDERA: a huge basin in the summit of a volcano, much larger than ordinary volcanic craters. Calderas are usually circular or oval in ground plan, with steep walls and relatively flat floors. They may be formed by an explosion so violent that it removes the entire top of a volcanic mountain; by the collapse of the mountain top after lava has withdrawn from

A **caldera**, 3,000 ft deep and 5 mi across, is all that is left of Mt Mazama, an Oregon volcano that blew its top off some 6,500 yr ago. Partly filled in by rain and snow, it appears on the map as Crater Lake. Little cone at far right is a younger volcano known as Wizard Island. (*Spence Air Photos*)

Primitive calendar: Erection of a durable marker fixing the Sun's most northerly point of rising, in midsummer, would give an annual reference point for the season-bound activities of a society dependent on cultivation of land. Only an incentive binding on their society as a whole could have motivated the builders of Stonehenge: 26-ton boulders had to be quarried, hauled, dressed, and erected before the monument could rise on the chalk plateau of Salisbury Plain. Thirty upright stones assembled in a circle 97 ft in diameter were surmounted by an equal number of lintels forming a closed circle 13½ ft above the ground. The photograph was taken along the sighting line of the monument. Visible through the space between the middle upright stones is an undressed boulder, the Heel Stone. An observer looking along the sighting line at sunrise at the summer solstice, 1500 B. C., would have seen the Sun's disk rising behind the Heel Stone. That it no longer rises there on June 22nd is due to Earth's precessional motion. (*Bettmann Archive*)

beneath it to lower depths; or by the combined effect of explosion and subsidence. Notable calderas are those of Crater Lake, Oreg.; Mauna Loa and Kilauea, in Hawaii; and Valle Grande, probably the world's largest (about 15 by 18 mi), northwest of Santa Fe, N. Mex.—*A. P. E.*

CALENDAR: a system of reckoning elapsed time for historical, civil, and religious purposes. From earliest antiquity, man has regulated his life by the alternation of days and nights, his religious observances by the return of the Moon's phases, and his farming activities by the recurrence of seasons. These periods are designated respectively by the terms solar day, lunar month, and tropical YEAR. On the average, a lunar month is equal to approximately 29½ days, whereas a tropical year contains slightly less than 365¼ days. Accordingly, these three fundamental periods are incommensurable.

Ancient Calendars: The most ancient calendars are based primarily on the lunar month, which is given alternatively 29 or 30 days, as required to keep in step with the lunar phases without introducing fractional days. The lunar months are reconciled with the tropical year by the use of intercalation, *i.e.* by insertion of an additional day or month to keep the calendar in accord with the cycle of seasons. (A modern counterpart of intercalation is the addition of Feb. 29 on leap years.) As civilizations become more complex, calendars depart gradually from strict adherence to lunar months; the tropical year emerges as the fundamental basis of their reckoning, and the month is retained only as a convenient subdivision.

The earliest known Egyptian calendar contained 12 months of 30 days each followed by 5 intercalary days, for a total of 365. The length of its months leaves little doubt that it had evolved from a prehistoric lunar calendar. The Egyptian year was divided into three seasons of four months each, called Flood time, Seed time, and Harvest time, corresponding to the agricultural tasks imposed by the annual rising of the Nile. Being shorter than the tropical year by about ¼ day, the Egyptian year shifted gradually with respect to the natural seasons. However, Egyptians had observed that the flooding of the Nile occurred at the time of year when Sirius rose in the east at sunrise (heliacal rising); therefore they were able to keep a record of the discrepancy between the calendar year and the natural seasons by observing the date of Sirius' heliacal rising. The Egyptian calendar, which was the only ancient one reckoned by fixed rule, rather than by observation or local ordinance, was particularly suitable for dating astronomical records. It was used by Ptolemy, *c.* A. D. 150, and favored by astronomers until the 16th cent.

By contrast, the Babylonian calendar was based entirely on the recurrence of lunar phases. The year contained 12 lunar months. The beginning of each month was the first day after new moon on which a lunar crescent was observed. An intercalary month was used at irregular intervals in order to keep the calendar attuned to the cycle of seasons. Prior to 480 B. C., such intercalations were wholly haphazard. After a transitional period, a set of fixed rules was introduced *c.* 380 B. C. whereby 7 intercalary months were distributed at specified intervals over each 19-yr period. It is always difficult, and in many cases impossible, to translate Babylonian dates into the present calendar: the visibility of the first crescent is affected by local weather conditions and other factors which do not lend themselves to astronomical reckoning; in addition, existing Babylonian texts offer a very incomplete record on the actual use of intercalation.

The Greek calendar followed essentially the same principles as the Babylonian. Years were comprised of 12 lunar months, with an intercalary month inserted as required to avoid too great a departure from the tropical year. Before the 6th cent. B. C. Greek calendar reckoning was in the hands of local authorities, who decreed not only the use of intercalation but the beginning of each month as well. These practices led to considerable variance among the different communities. More than 100 such calendars are known to have existed simultaneously.

A semblance of order was achieved, beginning in the 6th cent. B. C., as a number of astronomers devised various CYCLES for the use of intercalation. Instead of being left to the arbitrary decision of local authorities, the 13th month was inserted according to fixed rules designed to keep the average length of the year in closest possible agreement with its astronomical value. The Greek calendar retained its lunar character until the Roman period.

Lunar at first, the Roman calendar had already departed from strict adherence to the Moon's phases by the end of the 5th cent. B. C. From earliest historical times, the length of the Roman year was 12 months totaling 355 days, or almost exactly 12 lunations. An intercalary month was used whenever the pontifices deemed it necessary. This 13th month was inserted traditionally after Feb. 23 (which normally had 28 days). The last five days of February were omitted altogether, thus causing a shift of that many days in the position of the ensuing months with respect to the Moon's phases. Although intercalation should have been used every other year in order to achieve its intended purpose, the pontifices were often remiss in that respect. Julius Caesar, who became Pontifex Maximus in 63 B. C., followed this haphazard practice until the end of 47 B. C. In that 16-yr period alone, calendar months had receded by about 60 days from their customary position within the tropical year, not counting the normal intercalation which would have been required in the following February.

Julian Calendar: In preparation for a complete calendar reform, Caesar extended the length of 46 B. C. to 445 days to make up for past deficiencies. Thereafter, common years would have 365 days, and an intercalary day would be used at the end of February in every fourth year. Thus the average length of this reformed (or Julian) year was 365¼ days, a value which Caesar adopted on advice from the Alexandrian astronomer Sosigenes. As part of the reform, each month was assigned the length it has retained to this day.

Through misinterpretation of an ambiguous expression in Caesar's edict, the pontifices used an intercalary day every third year for a while, until their mistake was discovered during the reign of Augustus. To correct the cumulative effect of this error, all leap years were omitted between 8 B. C. and A. D. 7, inclusively, after which the normal sequence was resumed and remained unbroken until the Gregorian reform of 1582. Julian leap years of the Christian era are those divisible by 4.

Gregorian Calendar: The true length of the tropical year, as determined by astronomical means, is 365.2422 days, or slightly less than the value adopted in the Julian calendar. After a few hundred years, this difference resulted in a noticeable shift of calendar dates with respect to the seasons. At the beginning of the 16th cent., the spring equinox fell on Mar. 11 instead of Mar. 21, the date assumed in the ecclesiastical tables from which the date of Easter was computed. Thus Easter was celebrated too late in the year. To restore the agreement between the civil and ecclesiastical calendars, Pope Gregory XIII issued in 1582 a bull in which he ordained that the day after Thurs., Oct. 4, of that year be called Fri.,

Oct. 15. Furthermore, ensuing leap years were to be omitted when they fell on centurial years not divisible by 400. For example 1900, which was a Julian leap year, was a common year in the new Gregorian calendar; 2000 will be a leap year in both. The Gregorian reform was adopted for immediate use in all Catholic countries. Protestant countries opposed it at first but conformed gradually. The British Empire, including the American colonies, adopted it in 1752. By then, the difference between the two calendars had increased to 11 days because 1700 was not a Gregorian leap year; hence the British accomplished the change by calling Sept. 14 the day following Sept. 2. In the 20th cent., the Julian calendar is 13 days behind the Gregorian, because 1800 and 1900 were not leap years in the latter. At present, the Gregorian calendar is in official use for civilian purposes throughout most of the civilized world.

World Calendars: Current suggestions for calendar reform do not seek to alter the length of the Gregorian year or its astronomical basis; their principal purpose is to have the days of the month fall on the same weekday year after year. Numerous methods have been suggested.

Ecclesiastical Calendars: In addition to a change of dates, the Gregorian reform introduced new rules for the determination of the date of Easter. The intent of the Christian churches is to celebrate this festival on the first Sunday after the first full moon following the spring equinox. In practice, however, the full moon used in church reckoning is not obtained from astronomical determinations but from ecclesiastical tables based on the average recurrence of lunar phases. Originally, these tables were constructed by means of a 19-yr cycle of lunations first introduced in Alexandria. The *Golden Number,* which is the rank of a given year within the cycle, was then used to determine the dates of full moon for that year, and in particular that of the Easter, or Paschal, full moon. The papal bull which introduced the Gregorian calendar also revised the computation of Easter dates. Use of the Golden Number was replaced by that of the *Epact,* defined as the number of days elapsed on Jan. 1 of a given year since the preceding new moon. In addition, special rules were introduced to insure that Easter be celebrated no sooner than Mar. 22 and no later than Apr. 25. To this day, epacts are still obtained from cyclical tables rather than astronomical observation. Adoption of the Gregorian calendar for civilian purposes did not always imply acceptance of its ecclesiastical changes. Greek and Russian orthodox communities, in particular, still reckon their festivals by the Julian calendar and the Alexandrian cycle.

Differences of Style: The Julian and Gregorian calendars made no specific provision concerning the beginning of the civil year, which in most places was governed by local tradition. Both calendars have been in use with various initial dates, the most common being Dec. 25, Jan. 1, Mar. 1, and Mar. 25. These different methods of reckoning the year are called styles. In England, for example, Dec. 25 was used until the 14th cent., when it was replaced by Mar. 25; Jan. 1 was adopted concurrently with the introduction of the Gregorian calendar, in 1752. In the American colonies, where the change occurred at the same time, it became the custom, for a while, to show both the old and new styles whenever confusion might arise (*e.g.* Feb. 19, 1753/4). In some cases, the expressions "old" and "new" styles have been used to designate the Julian and Gregorian calendars respectively, but strictly speaking such usage is incorrect.

Hebrew Calendar: The ancient Hebrew calendar was similar in all respects to the old Babylonian described above, and presents the same problems concerning the correspondence of dates. Its modern form is based on a set of fixed rules believed to have been introduced in the 4th cent. A. D. by Rabbi

1

Plate 16　BRIDGES

From antiquity, bridge-building techniques have reflected changing needs and materials. Early bridges and aqueducts were of wood; but the Roman bridge builders used stone to make graceful, enduring arches. Busy pedestrian, vehicular, and shipping traffic in industrial England called for movable bridges such as the London Tower Bridge over the Thames. In the 20th cent., the use of steel and the advancement of engineering knowledge have made possible the construction of single arches of steel over wide expanses of water.

1. Pont Du Gard aqueduct bridge, 150 ft. high, with three tiers, was built by Roman engineers, A.D. 14, over the Gard River near Nîmes, France. Round stone arches were the trademark of the Roman builder. *(Ray Manley/ Shostal)*

2

2. Bascule bridge: London Tower Bridge was erected 1886-94. A double-leaf movable drawbridge, it consists of two 1,000-ton "leaves" working on horizontal trunnions anchored to massive piers. Spans rise rapidly to provide a 200-ft waterway for ships. *(G. Morris/Rapho-Guillumette)*

3. Steel arch bridge crosses Kill Van Kull from Bayonne, N. J., to Staten Island, N. Y. The arch span, longest in the world, is 1,652 ft; the entire structure covers 5,780 ft. Arch spans of 2,000 to 3,000 ft have been proposed. *(John Dunigan/Shostal)*

3

1

Plate 17 CARNIVORES

2

The carnivores form one of the largest orders of mammals, and a highly successful one. Primarily flesh-eaters, they spend much of their time in hunting. **1. Fur seals** in a sanctuary area along the Alaskan coast perch on rocks from which they can dive into the sea for fish. *(Ace Williams/ Shostal)* **2. Black-masked raccoon** takes time out from catching mice and frogs to scavenge for food in the dark of night; it handles everything with sensitive paws. *(Hal H. Harrison/Shostal)* **3.** In the desert **a gray fox** gets most of its water from its prey, which includes warmblooded animals such as mice and kangaroo rats, and also insects and lizards no warmer than the desert sands at night. *(Jack Novak/Shostal)* **4.** In the late afternoon **the bobcat** begins prowling over the desert in search of mice, jack rabbits, or other prey. *(L. and M. Milne)*

3

4

Plate 18   CAVE ANIMALS

Many animals of caverns, e.g. bats and cave birds, seek food on the outside. But smaller creatures usually subsist on the droppings on the cave floor or on food brought in by underground streams; most small cave dwellers are dark-seeking, but are related to species that roam outside the cave and that may represent the ancestral stock from which the cave forms evolved.

Oilbird (*Steatornis*) of northern S America and Trinidad finds way to daytime roosts in lightless caves by echo location, much as bats do. (*Russ Kinne*)

Cave salamander (*Eurycea lucifuga*) cannot see with its degenerate eyes, but has light-sensitive nerves in skin. (*Chas. Mohr/Nat. Audubon Soc.*)

Blind cave crayfish has longer and more sensitive antennae than does its nearest kin in the outdoor world. (*Chas. Mohr/Nat. Audubon Soc.*)

Plate 19   CELLS

All living things either are individual cells or are composed of cells in cooperating groups. Usually a cell contains a central body, the nucleus, which can be made distinct by "staining" the cell with suitable dyestuffs. The nucleus contains the heredity-controlling structures of the cell, whereas the surrounding cytoplasm is the site of the chemical reactions of life.

1. Cells of onion epidermis generally show two or three dark-staining nucleoli in each nucleus. A messenger material, ribonucleic acid (RNA), appears to originate in the nucleoli and carry to the cytoplasmic chemical centers the control information from the nucleus. (*J. P. Miksche/Brookhaven*)

1

Three types of cells: The ameba (**2**) is a one-celled animal that constantly changes shape. Flat cells from lining of human cheek (**3**) show small nucleus. *Paramecium* cells (**4**) show macronuclei stained purple. (© *1957 by Clay Adams, Inc.*)

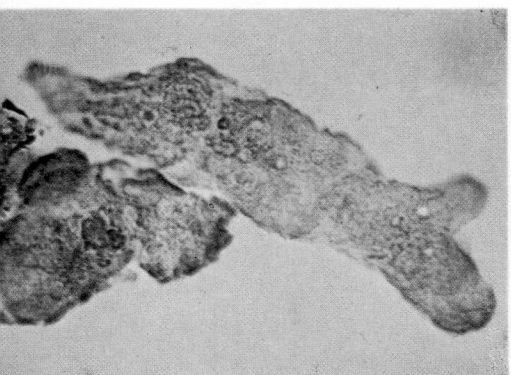

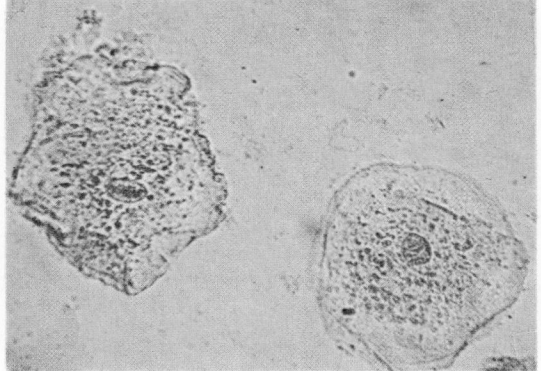

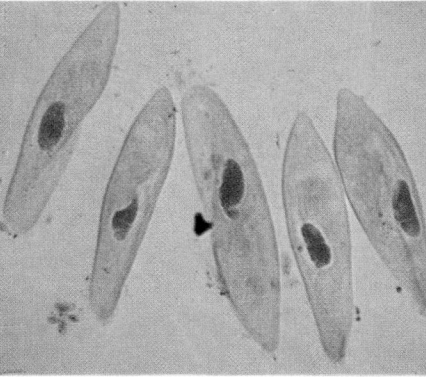

2   **3**   **4**

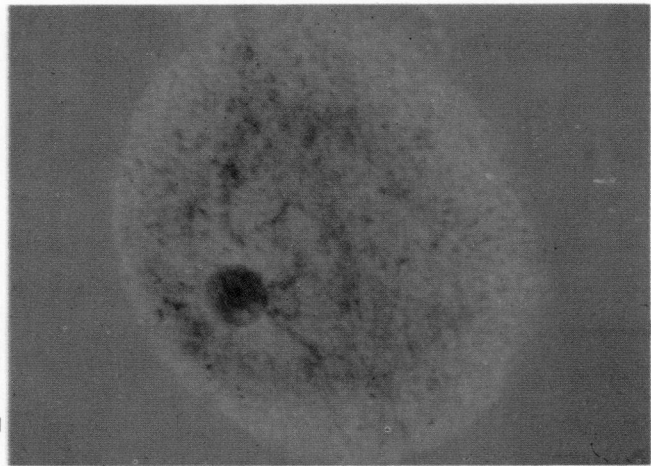

1

Prophase: (1) This cell of Indian corn (maize) is at an early stage of prophase. Nucleolus is solid blue; nucleus and threadlike chromosomes are pale blue against yellowish cytoplasm. At a later stage in a bread wheat cell **(2)** the nucleolus has largely disappeared, but chromosomes are shorter, denser, and visible as distinct paired bodies.

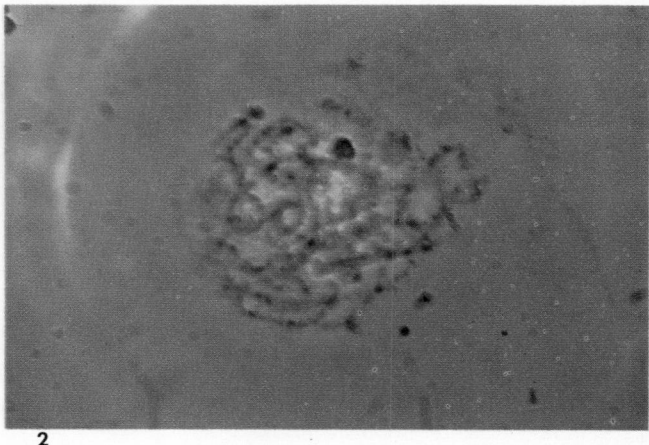

2

Plate 20   CHROMOSOMES AND GENES

Hereditary characteristics are transmitted by the genes, which are units of the chromosomes in the nucleus of a cell. These photographs, taken through an interference microscope, show what happens to the chromosomes during various stages of the special cell division known as meiosis. *(All by Arlene Longwell)*

Metaphase (3): In a dividing cell from the oyster plant *Rheo*, chromosomes line up in the equatorial plane.

3

Anaphase (4): In a cell of Indian corn, chromosomes separate and move to the two ends of a fibrous spindle.

4

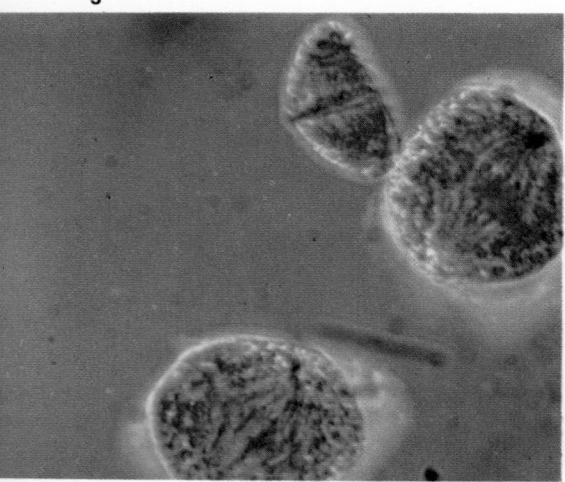

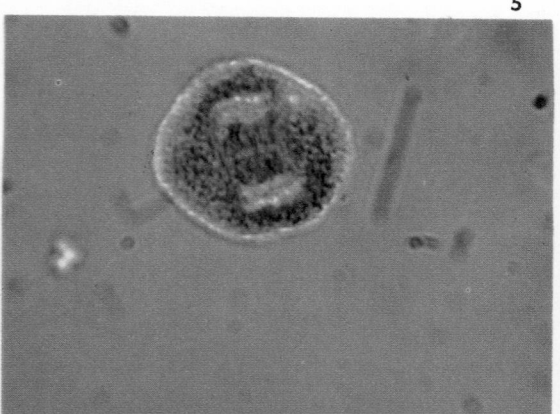

Telophase (5): In this final phase of the division of a wheat cell, two new daughter nuclei are visible.

5

Second division (6) produces four cells, each with half the original number of chromosomes. (Wheat cell is at late anaphase.)

6

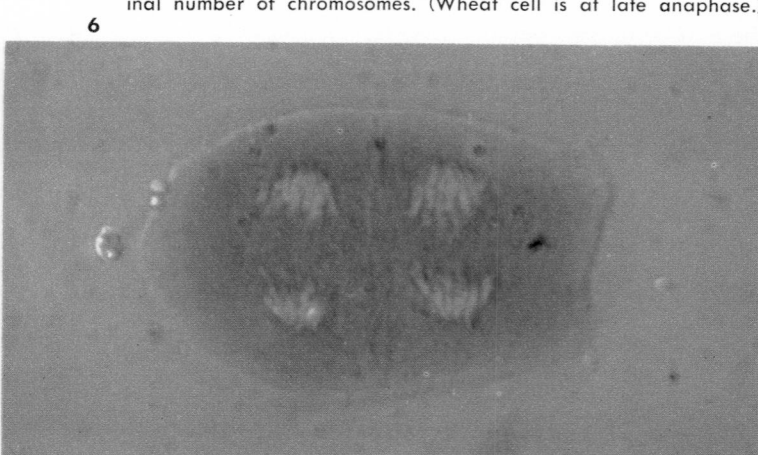

Stone calendar, derived from the Maya, enabled Aztecs to keep track of end-of-month festivals. The face of the sun god is in the center, surrounded by four square panels honoring previous avatars of solar divinity; in the circle immediately circumscribing these are the signs of the twenty days. Stone is 12 ft in diameter, was once buried as "evil" by Spanish conquerors. (*Philip Gendreau*)

Hillel II. The Hebrew year may be common or embolismic (leap year). The 12 months of a common year are, in succession, Tishri, Marheshvan, Kislev, Tebet, Shebat, Adar, Nisan, Iyar, Sivan, Tammuz, Ab, and Elul. In embolismic years, an intercalary month called Veadar follows Adar. The civil year begins in the fall on Tishri 1, but the religious year traditionally starts on Nisan 1. Tishri 1 is determined with respect to an ecclesiastical new moon, with the restriction that a year should not start on Sunday, Wednesday, or Friday, to prevent certain festivals from falling on inconvenient days of the week. For that reason, both common and embolismic years may be deficient (353 and 383 days, respectively), regular (354, 384), or abundant (355, 385). Years are reckoned from a traditional date of Creation taken as Oct. 7, 3761 B. C. (Julian). The festival of Passover, celebrated on Nisan 15, always occurs 163 days before Tishri 1.

Moslem Calendar: The calendar of Islam is reckoned from the date of the Hegira, July 15, A. D. 622. Its years are comprised of 12 lunar months each, and count variously 354 or 355 days. They begin with the month of Muharram, followed in order by Safar, First Rabia, Second Rabia, First Jumada, Second Jumada, Rajab, Shaban, Ramadan, Shawwal, Dhul-Kada and Dhul-Hijja. A cycle of 30 Moslem yr, totaling 10,631 days, is used to govern intercalation for the sole purpose of keeping the months in step with lunar phases. Therefore, the calendar pays no heed to the seasons, and 33 Moslem yr are roughly equivalent to 32 tropical yr. For religious purposes, the beginning of each month is determined by observation of the first lunar crescent after new moon.

Mayan and Aztec Calendars: The Mayas of Yucatan used an elaborate system by which they could reckon dates over extremely long periods. Their calendar combined a sacred year (tzolkin) of 260 days with a civilian year (haab) of 365 days. The tzolkin was subdivided into 13 periods of 20 days each, a tzolkin date being designated by a number from 1 to 13 followed by one of 20 different day names. The haab consisted of 18 months of 20 days and 1 month of 5 days. The complete dating of an event included both the tzolkin and haab designations. This, in effect, produced a 52-yr cycle, after which identical dates would be repeated. To avoid this ambiguity, the Mayas distinguished each 52-yr period from the next by the addition of other symbols, usually of astronomical significance. The Aztecs adopted the Mayan calendar essentially without change, but limited themselves to the use of the 52-yr cycle.

Julian Day: The reckoning by Julian Days should not be confused with the Julian calendar, from which it is entirely independent. The dating of ancient historical events often involves the use of chronological cycles of various lengths, the principal ones being: the solar cycle of 28 yr, after which the days of the week recur on the same days of the year in the Julian calendar; the cycle of 19 yr used in most lunar calendars; and the 15-yr cycle called Roman Indiction, which was used for purposes of taxation. To facilitate his handling of such problems, the French chronologist Josephus Justus Scaliger (1540–1609) invented a period of 28 × 19 × 15, or 7,980 yr, which he named in honor of his father Julius, a humanist and contemporary of Erasmus. Scaliger's Julian period was thus a common multiple of all three cycles. It was

taken to start on Jan. 1, 4713 B. C., or Julian Day 0, a date at which the beginning of those cycles would have coincided and which was sufficiently remote to encompass all historical events. Julian Days are numbered consecutively from that date. The first period will not end until A. D. 3268; therefore the numbering is continuous for all practical purposes. Julian Days have been adopted in astronomy as a convenient means of counting the number of days elapsed between widely separated observations.—*S. D. G.*

CALIFORNIUM: an artificial element (Cf) of the actinide group; at. no. 98. Californium^{245} was first synthesized in 1950 by S. G. Thompson *et al.* at the Univ. of California by bombardment of curium with helium ions in a 60-in. cyclotron. Other isotopes of californium (at. wt 244–254) have since been discovered; their half-lives range from a few minutes to about 500 yr.—*G. W. M.*

CALLIPPUS (CALLIPUS, or **CALIPPUS,** from Greek **KALLIPPOS),** 4th cent. B. C., Greek astronomer; b. Cyzicus, Asia Minor. He introduced a cycle of 76 yr that bears his name and is formed by 4 Metonic cycles diminished by 1 day. The cycle of METON had been in use about a century when Callippus detected an error of ¼ day and substituted a cycle of 76 yr, composed of 3 Metonic cycles of 6,940 days each and a 4th cycle of 6,939 days, thereby reducing the error to 1 day in 304 yr. He also modified the system of geocentric spheres of Eudoxus.—*R. N. M.*

CALORIC THEORY: a belief widely held in the 18th cent. that heat was an actual fluid substance that could flow spontaneously out of hot objects into nearby colder ones. This heat substance (the caloric) was believed to take up room, so that its passage into a cold body made the body swell as well as become warmer. This accounted for the expansion of materials with increasing temperature. But since the materials gained no weight, it was necessary to postulate that the caloric was weightless. Such hypothetical fluids, including phlogiston and the luminiferous ether, characterized the hypotheses of the earlier scientists. The description of phenomena in terms of fluids and flow has, in the present century, been largely replaced by atomistic conceptions. See ATOM; QUANTUM MECHANICS.—*J. E. W.*

CALORIE: see HEAT.

CALORIMETER: an instrument for measuring the evolution or absorption of heat in a chemical or physical process. In a *water calorimeter* the heat change is evaluated from the temperature change of the water. In an *ice calorimeter* it is calculated from the change in volume of the melting ice. Other calorimeter types have also been designed.—*Ru. M.*

CALORIMETRY: the measurement of heat transferred in chemical or physical changes. Usually the determination is made by the method of mixtures, which consists of adding a hot material of known mass m_1 and temperature T_1 to a quantity of colder liquid, whose mass m_2 and temperature T_2 are also known. The mixture is then stirred until it comes to a constant intermediate temperature T_3. Assuming adequate precautions to prevent loss of heat from the containing vessel (the calorimeter), the heat given up by the hot specimen equals the energy acquired by the cold liquid and the calorimeter. Since each of these energies is the product of a mass, a specific heat, and a temperature change, the equality may be represented symbolically by

$$m_1 \times s_1 \times (T_1 - T_3) = (m_2 + E) \times s_2 \times (T_3 - T_2)$$

where s_1 and s_2 are the specific heats of the hot specimen and of the cold liquid and E stands for the thermal equivalent of the calorimeter vessel, including stirrer and thermometer. E is easily computed if the mass and the identity of this equipment are known. For example, if the calorimeter is made of copper (specific heat 0.093), and its mass is 400 gm, the vessel is thermally equivalent to $0.093 \times 400 = 37.2$ gm of water. Supposing the liquid in the calorimeter to be 1,000 gm of water, the effect will be the same as if the heat exchange has occurred in 1,037.2 gm of water without any container.

It is clear that the foregoing equation permits the determination of any one of the eight quantities represented if the other seven are known. Frequently the desired quantity is the specific heat of the hot specimen or of the cold liquid. It may even be the initial temperature of a body whose specific heat is known. Thus, a strip of metal that has been heated in a flame may be dropped into the calorimeter and the temperature of the flame calculated from the final temperature attained by the liquid.

Calorimetry is effectively used for determination of the heat of combustion of fuels such as gas or coal and for determination of the energy content of foods. A common method is to place a weighed amount of the material in a steel bomb into which oxygen is also introduced. The bomb is locked and put into a weighed amount of water, after which the fuel is ignited electrically. The remaining steps are like those already described.—*J. E. W.*

CALVIN, MELVIN, 1911–   , U. S. chemist; b. St. Paul, Minn. For his use of carbon[14] to elucidate the chemical reactions taking place in photosynthesis, he received the 1961 Nobel prize. He is a fellow of the Royal Society and a member of the National Academy of Sciences.—*P. R. L.*

CAMBRIAN PERIOD: see GEOLOGICAL TIME CHART; PALEOZOIC ERA.

CAMERA: a lightproof container with a lens aperture and a means of holding a light-sensitive film or plate. The lens admits light and focuses it on the film in a reversed upside-down image. A simple camera can be constructed with a pinhole aperture and no lens. Standard cameras have a lens, an adjustable diaphragm, a shutter, a field viewer, often a rangefinder, and sometimes a light-meter. The lens, usually consist-

Camera of 1839: Samuel F. B. Morse built this box-type instrument from specifications provided by L. J. M. Daguerre, and used it in the first commercial studio in the U. S. A. (*N. Y. Public Library*)

ing of several elements, may be classified by f number, which is the ratio of its focal length (distance from lens center to point of focus) to its diameter. The diaphragm can be adjusted to vary the diameter of the aperture and thus the amount of light admitted. The shutter controls the length of time the film is exposed; shutter speed is usually adjustable. Lens-mounted shutters are placed behind or between lens elements; focal-plane shutters are mounted in front of the film. For comparable exposures under equal conditions, the smaller the aperture, the longer it must remain open. Also, the smaller the aperture, the greater is the depth of the field (or area) that is in focus.

Camera accessories for increasing flexibility and control include filters, used to alter a film's response to various colors; flash-bulb devices and electronic flash; and tripods, for steady support. Many cameras have a built-in rangefinder which uses the principle of triangulation; the proper distance of the lens from the film is set automatically when two images

Single-lens reflex camera, such as the 35mm model below, eliminates parallax, since view and lens image are identical. Labels show important elements, typical of refinements in today's cameras. (*Nikon*)

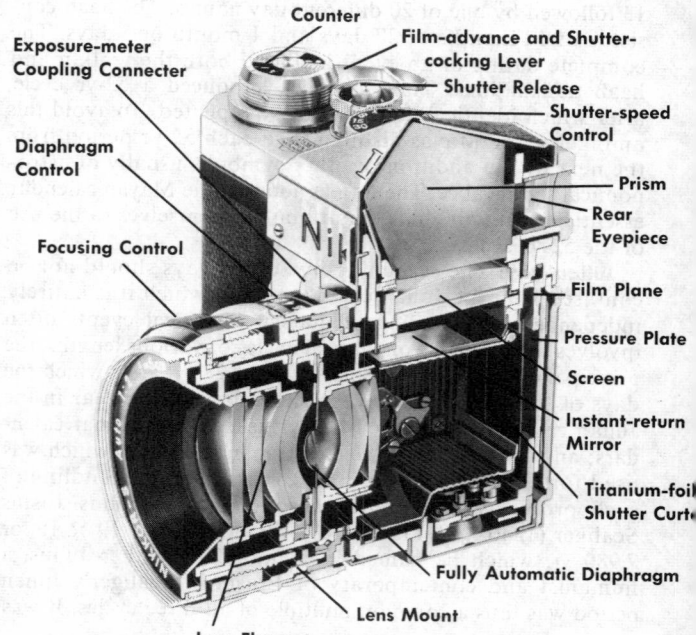

Counter
Exposure-meter Coupling Connecter
Film-advance and Shutter-cocking Lever
Shutter Release
Shutter-speed Control
Diaphragm Control
Prism
Rear Eyepiece
Focusing Control
Film Plane
Pressure Plate
Screen
Instant-return Mirror
Titanium-foil Shutter Curt
Fully Automatic Diaphragm
Lens Mount
Lens Elements

Polaroid Land camera utilizes special type of film (announced in 1947) to develop pictures inside the camera, giving a print by one-step process within 1 min; film roll allows 8 exposures. This "Electric Eye 900" contains a matchhead-size photocell to set both lens opening and shutter speed simultaneously; also incorporated is an automatic viewfinder-rangefinder system. (*Polaroid Corp.*)

of the subject are superimposed in the finder. In reflex cameras, focusing is done by means of a ground glass.

Many types of containers, lenses, and controls have been designed for general and specialized uses. *Box cameras* have a simple lens, fixed aperture, and fixed shutter speed, and take "average" pictures under average conditions. The roll film used ordinarily gives eight exposures. *Miniature cameras,* the most popular in general photography, are compact and have fast lenses (admitting much light) with considerable depth of field. A wide range of attachments, including various lenses, is available. Using 35-mm film, miniatures generally produce 20 or 36 negatives 1 x 1⅓ in. *Press cameras,* bulky

8mm motion-picture camera: This is the Model M6 Kodak Instamatic, for which drop-in film cartridges are available. The camera is of the zoom reflex design with f/1.8 lens, electric drive, automatic exposure control "through-the-lens," and a folding two-position pistol grip. (*Eastman Kodak*)

and versatile, produce large negatives (commonly 4 x 5 in.), allowing very sharp focusing and avoiding much of the loss of quality that occurs in enlargements from smaller negatives. The swinging lens minimizes foreshortening and distortions. Focusing is done on a ground-glass viewer. A sheet film or plate is inserted after focusing and may be developed immediately without wasting unexposed film. Ordinary viewers and rangefinders may also be used. Some press cameras take economical roll film. *View* and *stand cameras* resemble press cameras but are still bulkier.

Folding cameras, with extensible bellows between lens and body, permit fine adjustment of lens position and fold up compactly. The many models include press and view types. Many use roll film that produces negatives about 2¼ in. wide and 1⅝ to 2¼ in. long. Like box cameras, the folding types are giving way to the new, smaller, color-oriented, automated cameras.

In *reflex cameras,* a mirror reflects onto a ground-glass viewer the exact image "seen" by the lens. This permits precise focusing and composition. Cameras are usually light and compact, with fast lenses and considerable depth of field. In the single-lens type, a mirror reflects the lens image onto the viewer, and there is no parallax problem; this type

Loading a motion-picture camera: New camera designs permit use of the drop-in film cartridge for more rapid and more convenient picture taking. (*Eastman Kodak*)

usually takes 35-mm film. In the twin-lens reflex, the upper lens only is used for viewing, and a parallax problem thus occurs at close range. The negatives are usually 2¼ x 2¼ in. *Polaroid cameras* develop the picture inside the camera in about 10 sec, pictures being produced one at a time from a special 8-exposure roll. The basic process is exposure of the negative, followed by contact between negative and positive with transfer of the image by a reagent. *Stereo cameras,* with twin picture lenses spaced like human eyes, take two pictures of the subject that differ slightly in angle; thus a three-dimensional effect is achieved. Highly specialized still cameras include *high-speed* types, which "stop" motion in exposures of ten-thousandths of a second; *infrared* models, which take pictures by infrared rays only; and *aerial* cameras, for pictures from great heights.

Motion-picture cameras expose rolls of successive negatives, or "frames," at a rate of about 30 per sec. In most cases the frame is at rest during exposure. Because of persistence of vision, the positive film when projected at proper speed gives the illusion of motion. Theatrical film is mostly 35-mm, with negatives about 1 x ¾ in. Documentary films often use 16-mm; home movies, 8-mm. *Television cameras* convert the light image into electric impulses for transmission by broadcasting. In a basic type, the image is focused on a "mosaic" of microscopic-sized cells on a thin sheet of mica backed by a conductor. The electrical conductivity of the compound of which the cells are made varies according to the intensity of light, and the cells, caused by the image to emit varying quantities of electrons, are left with varying positive charges. As a beam of electrons scans the conductor, the charges are successively released as a current. Point by point, light values are converted into electric impulses of varying intensity for transmission to a receiver and reconversion to a picture. The camera scans about 30 pictures per sec. The impulses may be stored on magnetized tape for later use. See OPTICS; PHOTOGRAPHY.—*J. S. K.*

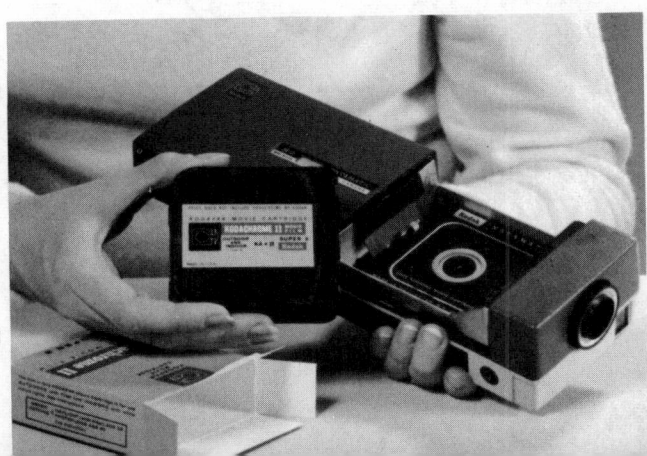

Lift locks of Welland Canal raise and lower ships over the 325-ft difference in level between Lake Ontario and Lake Erie. (*Canadian National Film Board*)

CAMERARIUS, RUDOLPH JACOB, 1665–1721, German botanist and physician; b. Tübingen. He proved the sexuality of plants by testing the hypothesis that separation of male and female plant organs would prevent the production of mature fruits. The results of his research appear in his "Letter on the Sex of Plants" (1694).—*D. H. D. R.*

CAMOUFLAGE, ANIMAL: see ANIMAL CAMOUFLAGE.

CAMPHOR: a crystalline but gummy substance that belongs to the terpene family of compounds (see TERPENES). Its natural source is the Japanese camphor tree, but it is also made from pinene, another terpene. Camphor is used chiefly as a PLASTICIZER in making celluloid and photo film.—*Ru. M.*

CANALS: man-made longitudinal cuts or channels in the earth to permit the flow of water into dry areas (see IRRIGATION) or to serve as artificial waterways enabling vessels to travel inland. A canal may connect two navigable rivers, two lakes (*e.g.* the Welland Canal joining Lake Erie and Lake Ontario in Canada), or two seas (Suez and Panama canals), or any combination of these. Canals also may connect a river port to the sea or serve as a detour around an impassable section of an otherwise navigable waterway. Canals in the ancient world were used primarily to water dry land or as a means of

Two-way traffic at 3.5 mi/hr navigates the 27.6-mi length of the Welland Canal. The water is 30 ft deep; its trapezoidal cross section measures 310 ft at the surface and 200 ft at the bottom. (*Canadian National Film Board*)

water control. A rare early example of a canal built specifically for shipping was a 23-mi canal built A. D. 45 between the Rhine and Meuse rivers, cutting through what is now The Hague and enabling ships to avoid the sea.

A canal must be constructed with slight decline from one end to the other so that water in it will flow fast enough to keep down the growth of weeds and carry away the accumulation of silt, but not so fast as to erode the banks. Concrete banks and brick-lined bottoms are sometimes used to prevent both erosion and leakage of water. Water for canals, which must be constantly replenished, may be supplied by adjacent lakes and streams or by artificial ponds. The most common canal traffic consists of barges; originally they were towed by horses but now are largely self-propelled by Diesel engines or towed by tugs or tractors on the towpath. Speed is no great advantage, since speeds in excess of 3 or 4 mi/hr may cause the banks to wash away.

Up through medieval times canals had to be built on level terrain in order to maintain the level of water. In the late 12th cent., however, the development of canal *locks,* rectangular chambers in which boat, barge, or ship could ascend or descend from one level to another, led to the widespread building of canals through variable terrain. A lock is basically a watertight chamber, wide enough for the largest vessel anticipated, and sometimes long enough to hold a train of barges. Gates at either end are mitered to make a watertight seal and point slightly outward toward the higher level to help resist water pressure. After the vessel enters, it is raised or lowered to the next level by water pouring in or draining out through sluice gates built into the lock. In cases requiring a high lift, two or more locks may be used together to provide a series of steps, although modern canals now tend to use one lock to provide a lift of 20 to 40 ft. Where an even higher rise is required, a lift lock or hydraulic elevator is used. In this case the lock with the ship in it is physically lifted or lowered to the desired level.—*R. G.*

CANDLE POWER: see PHOTOMETER AND PHOTOMETRY.

CANNIZZARO, STANISLAO, 1826–1910, Italian chemist; b. Palermo, Sicily. His great contribution was in pointing out the bearing of Avogadro's hypothesis on atomic theory and the distinction between atomic and molecular weights. In the Cannizzaro reaction, which he discovered, an aldehyde is converted into a mixture of the corresponding alcohol and acid. He was a fellow of the Royal Society.—*E. F.*

CANNON, ANNIE JUMP, 1863–1941, U. S. astronomer; b. Dover, Del. At Harvard (1896–1941) she helped devise the Harvard system of spectral types. She classified the spectra of nearly 400,000 stars, primarily for the *Henry Draper Catalogue* and its extensions (*Annals of Harvard College Observatory*, vols. 91–100, 112), and discovered more than 300 variable stars, detecting many by their spectral peculiarities.—*O. G.*

CANTILEVER: in construction, a flexural member which projects from a rigid support for the purpose of carrying a given force. The beam transmits the force to the support by means of internal flexural and shear stresses. In cantilever BRIDGES,

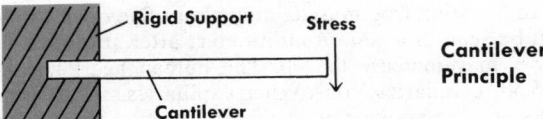

Cantilever
Principle

centrally located loads are carried by means of overhanging side-span cantilevers which pick up reactions from the central span.—*W. W.*

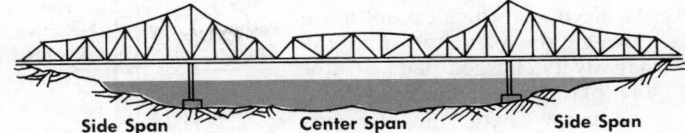

Simple Design for a Cantilever Bridge

CANTON, JOHN, 1718–72, English physicist; b. Stroud. He invented a number of electrical instruments, including an electroscope and an electrometer, and demonstrated that air could be electrified. The luminosity of sea water was attributed by him to decomposing animal matter. He was a fellow of the Royal Society and a recipient of the Copley medal.—*D. H. D. R.*

CANTOR, GEORG, 1845–1918, German mathematician; b. St. Petersburg, Russia. His professional career was spent at the Univ. of Halle. Cantor is known for his theories of aggregates and of infinite numbers. The revolutionary nature of his conclusions was one of the moving forces behind the overhauling of the foundations of mathematics in the 20th cent.—*H. C.*

CANYON: see SUBMARINE CANYON; VALLEY.

CAPACITANCE: the ratio of the charge on either conductor of a CAPACITOR to the difference of potential between the conductors; also, for an isolated conductor, the ratio of its charge to its potential. The greater the capacitance of a capacitor, the more charge it can store for a given expenditure of work, *i.e.* for a given voltage across its terminals.—*W. P. C.*

CAPACITOR (formerly called **condenser**): a device used in electrical circuits for the temporary storage of electrical charge. Although capacitors come in many sizes and shapes, they all consist essentially of two conductors separated by an insulator. (A conductor is a material through which electrons move freely, whereas an insulator offers very high resistance to electron flow.) The way a capacitor stores charge is illustrated in the figures. In Fig. 1 the capacitor is connected to a battery, which forces electrons through the wire to one of the plates while attracting electrons from the other plate. One of the plates thus acquires a net negative charge (a surplus of electrons), and the other acquires a net positive charge of equal magnitude (a deficiency of electrons). If the battery is

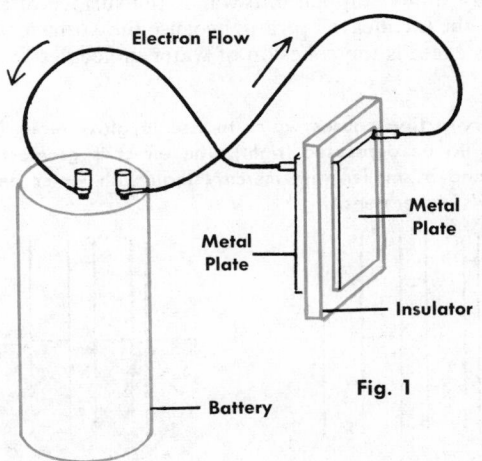

Electron Flow

Metal
Plate

Metal
Plate

Insulator

Battery

Fig. 1

disconnected (Fig. 2), the capacitor stores this separated electrical charge, since the positively charged plate exerts an attractive force on the electrons, which cannot move through the insulator from the negatively charged plate. If now the plates are connected by a conducting path, the electrons pass from one plate to the other. Thus, while the stored charge is being neutralized, there exists an electrical current capable of doing work, *e.g.* lighting a lamp (Fig. 3). The most important parameter

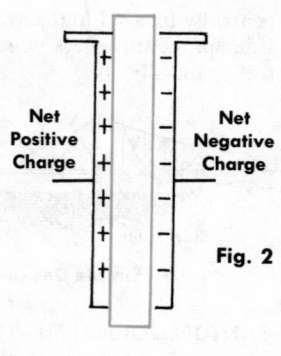

Net Positive Charge

Net Negative Charge

Fig. 2

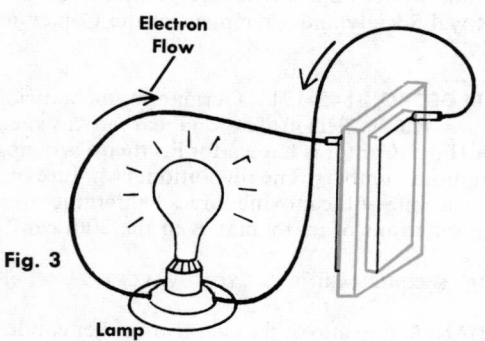

Electron Flow

Fig. 3

Lamp

of a capacitor is its CAPACITANCE—the quantity of charge that it can store for a given battery voltage. Capacitors find many applications in electrical circuits, *e.g.* in resonant circuits and filters (where they are used in connection with inductors) and in power-factor correction (where they are employed to offset the reactance of inductive loads to increase the efficiency of power transmission). See ELECTRIC CIRCUIT; ELECTRIC POWER.—*S. K.*

CAPILLARITY: the rise or fall in the level of a liquid in a capillary (minute-bore) tube, in relation to the level in the vessel in which the tube is immersed. The extent of this elevation or depression of level is directly proportional to the product of the surface tension of the liquid and the cosine of its contact angle, and inversely proportional to the product of the radius of the bore of the tube, the density of the liquid, and the value of the gravitational constant (*g*). When a glass capillary tube is dipped into water, the surface of the water in the tube is concave upward, because the ADHESION of water to glass exceeds the cohesion of water molecules for one an-

Capillary action causes water to rise in glass tubes (*left*) and mercury to be depressed (*right*). The effect is greatest in small tubes, and is smaller with mercury than with water because of mercury's higher density.

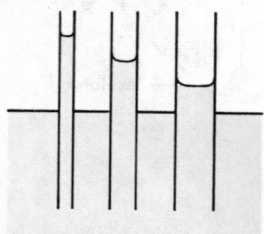
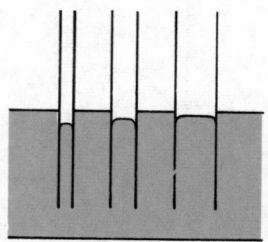

other. SURFACE TENSION now acts to flatten the curve, with the result that a creep upward results. The rise continues until the force of surface tension is balanced by the weight of the liquid in the capillary. With a glass capillary immersed in mercury, the surface of the mercury in the tube is convex upward (cohesion exceeds adhesion). Surface tension tends to flatten the surface and thus depresses the liquid to a level lower than that of the principal vessel. Once again the surface curves downward and is depressed still further. The process goes on until the upward force exerted on the "negative" column of mercury equals the surface tension.—*A. E.*

CAPILLARY: one of the blood vessels which are the smallest in the body of animals. In closed-type circulatory systems, capillaries form the connecting link through which blood flows from the smallest branches of arteries to the smallest branches of veins. Practically all exchanges of materials between blood and tissues, and between blood and air in lungs, or blood and water in gills, take place across the walls of capillaries. In man, capillaries are about 0.5 mm long and 5 to 15 microns (1 micron = 1/1000 mm) in diameter. They have very thin walls, made up of a single layer of endothelial cells surrounded by a basement membrane that protrudes between the cells. Capillaries are arranged in "beds" or networks, with many interconnections. In a typical bed a single large vessel, or thoroughfare channel, leads directly from arteriole to venule. Branching off from this vessel is the capil-

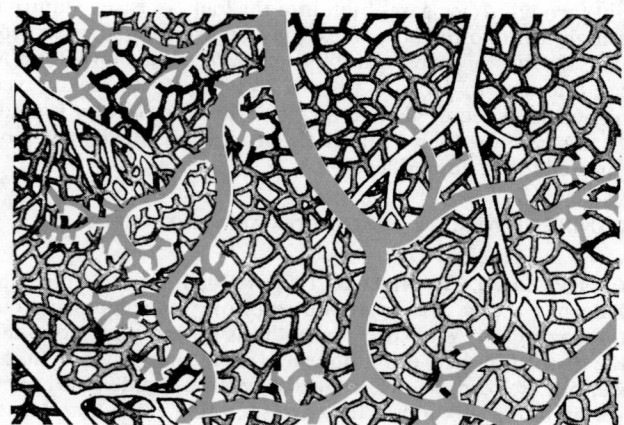

Capillary network in the web of a frog's foot: Blood flows from the arterioles (white vessels) to the capillaries (gray network) to the venules (blue vessels). Tissue cells lie in the meshes of the network, and materials are exchanged through the capillary walls between the tissue cells and the blood. (*From Young*)

lary network. The thoroughfare channel has some muscle cells in its wall, and at the beginning of each capillary is a circular ring of muscle, called the precapillary sphincter.

The flow of blood through the capillary bed is controlled by the sphincter as it contracts and closes the opening of the capillary or relaxes and allows blood to flow through. The major factors controlling these muscle contractions are products of local tissue activity or oxygen lack, which cause the muscles to relax, and the vasomotor nerves, which cause contraction. In a resting frog muscle, only about five open capillaries can be seen in a square millimeter; after stimulation, the number may increase to 200. The human heart has as many as 5,500 capillaries/mm². When capillaries are all open, their walls provide an enormous surface for exchanges with the tissues; the total area of capillary wall surface in the muscles of a man has been estimated at 6,000 m². Capillary muscles may also be relaxed by the substance histamine or by similar substances produced by injured tissues. Walls of capillaries generally permit all components of the blood except proteins and cells or formed elements to pass through freely. Just how this exchange between blood and tissues occurs is a subject of continuing research. White blood cells can force their way across the capillary wall, and red cells occasionally do so. When capillaries are stretched by a vigorous flow of blood, their walls become more porous and permit larger particles, *e.g.* protein molecules, to pass through. Injury or infections that damage tissues, even slightly, result in great increases in flow through the capillaries, and consequent reddening and swelling of the injured area. See BLOOD; BLOOD VESSELS.—*B. T. S.*

CARBIDE: a binary compound of carbon and another element, usually a metal, in which carbon has a negative valence. Best known is calcium carbide, CaC_2 (often called simply "*carbide*"), used to generate acetylene gas by addition of water. Other carbides are carborundum (silicon carbide), used as an abrasive; and Carboloy (tungsten carbide), used in tools for its hardness. See also ORGANOMETALLIC COMPOUNDS.—*Ru. M.*

CARBOHYDRATES: A large family of chemical compounds occurring in nature, including sugars, starch, and cellulose. The family name was applied by early chemists who regarded the sugars as hydrates of carbon: cane sugar is $C_{12}H_{22}O_{11}$, but it can be written $C_{12}(H_2O)_{11}$, which makes it look like carbon with water of hydration. Some sugars are known, however, in which the ratio of H to O is not the 2:1 ratio in water. Also, many compounds are known, *e.g.* formaldehyde (CH_2O), which have the atomic ratio of a carbohydrate but are definitely not carbohydrates. Carbohydrates are classified on the basis of the number of simple sugars (saccharides) to which they can be broken down by hydrolysis (see SUGAR): (1) The simple sugars such as xylose (a pentose) and glucose (a hexose) are called *monosaccharides*. (2) Complex sugars are in general called *polysaccharides*. Sucrose, lactose, and maltose can each be hydrolyzed to two simple sugars, and are therefore *disaccharides*. A sugar known as raffinose yields three simple sugars on hydrolysis, and is a *trisaccharide*. (3) Starch and cellulose are high-molecular-weight compounds called *colloidal polysaccharides*. Cellulose is the skeletal material in plants, whereas starch is the reserve food material. Substances related to starch and cellulose, and classified in this third group, are gums, pectins, chitin, etc., some of which have acidic (carboxy) or basic (nitrogen-containing) groups as side chains in the sugars from which they are built.—*Ru. M.*

CARBON: a non-metallic element (C) belonging to group IV of the periodic table, at. no. 6, at. wt 12; isotopes are known with at. wt 13 and 14 (radioactive carbon). Carbon¹² is the standard from which atomic weights of other elements are calculated. Carbon compounds are so numerous, complex, and important as to form a major chemical category. Carbon-containing compounds are the subject of ORGANIC CHEMISTRY; non-carbon-containing compounds, of INORGANIC CHEMISTRY. Normally, some of the simpler carbon chemicals (*e.g.* carbonates, carbon dioxide, cyanides) are considered inorganics. The three forms (allotropes) of elemental carbon are diamond, graphite, and amorphous carbon. Both diamond and graphite, the crystalline forms, occur naturally and can be prepared synthetically; both are chemically inert, although they will combine with oxygen at high temperatures; their difference in properties stems from their differing crystal-lattice structures. Diamond is the hardest natural substance known: sp

gr 3.5. Graphite is a soft black material, sp gr 2.2, with a number of applications because it is inert, is infusible at atmospheric pressures, is a good conductor of heat and electricity, and has a low coefficient of thermal expansion. Mixed with clay, it is made into pencil "leads" and derives its name from that property (Greek *grapho*, "I write"). Charcoal, lamp-black, coke, and anthracite coal are examples of amorphous carbon. Activated carbon is amorphous carbon treated with heat and steam to remove hydrocarbons and so greatly increase the surface area for adsorption purposes (see COLLOID CHEMISTRY). For the usefulness of carbon¹⁴ (radioactive carbon), see RADIOACTIVE DATING.—*D. P. B.*

CARBONATES: chemical compounds of a metal and the carbonate ion (CO_3^-). CALCIUM CARBONATE ($CaCO_3$) and magnesium-calcium carbonate, or dolomite ($MgCO_3 \cdot CaCO_3$), are abundant in nature. Sodium carbonate, or soda ash (Na_2CO_3), is an important product of the alkali industry. Metals whose hydroxides are weak bases (*e.g.* aluminum and chromium) do not form carbonates; most other metals do. Carbonates of alkali metals and of thallium are soluble in water. Ammonium sesquicarbonate, $(NH_4) HCO_3 \cdot (NH_4) (NH_2) CO_2$, is soluble in water but decomposes in hot water; other carbonates as a rule are only sparingly soluble.

Acids decompose carbonates, evolving carbon dioxide. Heat also drives off carbon dioxide from carbonates, leaving the metal oxide. (Alkali metal carbonates, however, melt before they are completely decomposed.) When an excess of carbon dioxide is bubbled through a carbonate solution, acid carbonates, or bicarbonates, are formed. (The bicarbonate radical is HCO_3^-.) As a rule, bicarbonates are more soluble than carbonates and may cause temporary hardness in water. Carbonates of calcium and iron dissolve as bicarbonates in water containing carbon dioxide. The reactions are reversible, however, and when heated, carbon dioxide is driven off and the insoluble carbonates precipitate.—*D. P. B.*

CARBON BISULFIDE (or disulfide): a colorless liquid (CS_2); sp gr 1.261, bp 46.3°C, mp −108.6°C. It is a highly flammable compound; its vapors, mixed with air, explode upon ignition. It is also toxic and is used as an insecticide and rodenticide. Principal methods for preparing it depend on direct action between carbon and sulfur at elevated temperatures. Carbon bisulfide reacts with chlorine to form carbon tetrachloride (CCl_4) and sulfur monochloride (S_2Cl_2). It is soluble in benzene and alcohol, and slightly soluble in water. A good solvent for many compounds, including sulfur, white phosphorus, rubber, and camphor, it also has important uses in manufacture of viscose rayon; it reacts with alkali cellulose to form cellulose xanthate, a key intermediate.—*D. P. B.*

CARBON CYCLE: *In biology,* the carbon cycle is a series of chemical reactions in which carbon is removed from the air, used by living organisms, and returned to the air. Although carbon is the most characteristic element in all organic compounds and essential to life, most of the world's carbon is in carbon dioxide (CO_2) in the atmosphere. Green plants in the light are almost unique in taking the carbon from CO_2 and building it into organic compounds (see PHOTOSYNTHESIS). Release of the carbon from these compounds (usually in the form of CO_2) is accomplished by green plants in darkness, by nongreen plants and animals at all times, and by fire as well as industrial processes. All living organisms participate in this cycle of carbon and maintain in their organic compounds the same minute proportion of radioactive carbon¹⁴ as occurs naturally in atmospheric CO_2. At death, however, participation in the cycle stops, and the proportion of radio-

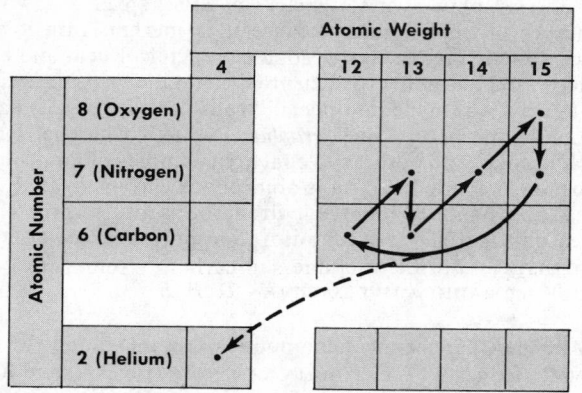

		Atomic Weight			
	4	**12**	**13**	**14**	**15**
8 (Oxygen)					
7 (Nitrogen)					
6 (Carbon)					
2 (Helium)					

(Atomic Number — vertical axis label)

Steps in carbon cycle are represented here by diagram in which atomic number is plotted against atomic weight. Adding a proton increases both quantities and causes a transition (first arrow) toward top right. Giving off of a positron, which causes a drop in atomic number but no change in atomic weight, is diagramed (second arrow) as a vertical downward transition. Further steps correspond to explanation in accompanying article.

active carbon in the organism slowly decreases at a definite rate over a period of thousands of years. Measurement of this change is the basis of so-called carbon dating (see RADIO-ACTIVE DATING).—*L. and M. M.*

In physics, the carbon cycle is a series of thermonuclear reactions in which hydrogen is converted to helium, with carbon[12] acting as a catalyst. First investigated by Hans Bethe (1939) and held to account in part for energy production in the Sun and other stars, the cycle is assumed to follow this series of steps: (1) A carbon[12] nucleus fuses with a proton (hydrogen nucleus), forming nitrogen[13] and a bundle of gamma rays ($C^{12} + H^1 \rightarrow N^{13} + \gamma$). (2) The resulting nitrogen[13] emits a positron ($_1e^0$) and a neutrino (ν), yielding carbon[13] ($N^{13} \rightarrow C^{13} + _1e^0 + \nu$). (3) The carbon[13] nucleus collides with another proton, forming nitrogen[14] and releasing additional gamma energy ($C^{13} + H^1 \rightarrow N^{14} + \gamma$). (4) Nitrogen[14] combines with still another proton, forming oxygen[15] ($N^{14} + H^1 \rightarrow O^{15} + \gamma$). (5) Oxygen[15] breaks down into nitrogen[15] by emitting a positron and a bundle of gamma rays ($O^{15} \rightarrow N^{15} + _1e^0 + \gamma$). (6) Finally, nitrogen[15] combines with an extra proton to form carbon[12] (regenerated at the end of the process) and helium ($N^{15} + H^1 \rightarrow C^{12} + He^4$). Thus the over-all effect is the conversion of four protons (hydrogen nuclei) into helium, with a release of a tremendous quantity of energy. Carbon[12] is recovered and may thus be regarded as a catalyst in the reaction. See ATOM; FUSION, NUCLEAR.—*A. E.*

CARBON DIOXIDE: at normal temperatures and pressures, a colorless, odorless gas (CO_2), mol. wt 44.01; it can be compressed and cooled to a colorless, heavy, highly volatile liquid which vaporizes, leaving a characteristic white "snow." In turn, this snow can be compressed to form solid carbon dioxide (dry ice), which sublimes (passes directly from the solid to the gaseous state) at $-78.5°C$. Carbon dioxide is present in air, about 0.03% by volume. It is produced industrially by burning carbon in an excess of air, by heating calcium carbonate (in lime kilns), and by fermentation processes. A stable compound, it does not support combustion or readily partake in chemical reactions. It does, however, dissolve readily in water, partially combining with water to form the weak, unstable compound carbonic acid (H_2CO_3). Carbon dioxide plays an important role in all forms of life. (See CARBON CYCLE; PHOTOSYNTHESIS; RESPIRATION.)—*D.P.B.*

CARBON DIOXIDE FIXATION: generally, the process, linked to photosynthesis, by which plants are able to extract gaseous carbon dioxide from the air and convert it into starch and sugars. This is part of the carbon cycle, for carbon dioxide is the end product of carbon metabolism in animals. The chemical reactions involved can be represented thus:

$$3C_1 + 3C_5 \rightarrow 6C_3$$
$$\uparrow$$
$$5C_3 \longleftarrow\!\!\!\longrightarrow 1C_3 \rightarrow starch$$

Three molecules of carbon dioxide, the 1-carbon compound, react with three molecules of a 5-carbon compound, ribulose diphosphate, which is formed by the action of adenosine triphosphate on ribulose phosphate. Three molecules of water enter into this enzyme-catalyzed process, the product of which is six molecules of phosphoglyceric acid (3 carbons). One of the phosphoglyceric acid molecules is converted to starch and sugars by a reversal of GLYCOLYSIS reactions. The others are used to regenerate the 5-carbon compounds. Other carbon-dioxide fixation reactions occur, also. In microorganisms, pyruvic acid reacts with carbon dioxide to form oxalacetic acid; in animal tissues, with the aid of $TPNH_2$, the "malic" enzyme catalyzes yet another reaction between these compounds to form malic acid. Both these processes are important in the supply of intermediates for the CITRIC-ACID CYCLE.—*K. H.*

CARBONIFEROUS PERIOD: see GEOLOGICAL TIME CHART; PALEOZOIC ERA.

CARBON MONOXIDE (CO): a colorless, odorless, highly poisonous gas. It reacts with hemoglobin in the blood to form carboxy-hemoglobin, a stable compound. Its affinity for hemoglobin is approximately 30 times that of oxygen, and since the carboxy compound does not absorb oxygen, the red corpuscles cannot transport oxygen to the body tissues. Although quite stable, carbon monoxide takes part in many important reactions at high temperatures or with the aid of catalysts. It burns with oxygen to form carbon dioxide, and with chlorine in the presence of sunlight it forms the poisonous gas phosgene (carbonyl chloride, $COCl_2$). Carbon monoxide results from burning of carbon in an insufficient quantity of air; it is produced on a large scale for use, mixed with hydrogen, as a reducing agent, as a source of hydrogen for ammonia, and for synthesis of methanol and other organic compounds. In most smelting operations carbon monoxide is the active reducing agent which converts the oxide ore to the metal.—*D. P. B.*

CARBON TETRACHLORIDE: a colorless liquid (CCl_4); sp gr 1.595; bp 76.8°C; molecular weight, 153.84. Not flammable, it is a good solvent for fats and oils, and has been used as a dry-cleaning agent. Its major use is as a solvent in the chemical processing industries. Being highly toxic, it should be used only when adequate ventilation is assured. Long-term exposure can lead to degenerative changes in the liver and kidneys and can be fatal. Carbon tetrachloride can be prepared by chlorination of methane or of carbon bisulfide.—*D. P. B.*

CARBONYL RADICAL: the group consisting of a carbon atom joined to an oxygen atom by a double bond, C=O, present in many classes of molecules. Examples follow.

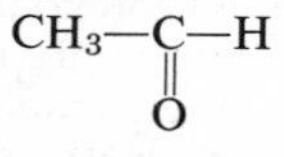

$$CH_3{-}\underset{\underset{O}{\|}}{C}{-}H \qquad \text{Acetaldehyde} \qquad \text{An ALDEHYDE}$$

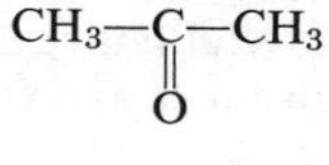

$$CH_3{-}\underset{\underset{O}{\|}}{C}{-}CH_3 \qquad \text{Acetone} \qquad \text{A KETONE}$$

$$CH_3-\underset{\underset{O}{\|}}{C}-OC_2H_5 \quad \text{Ethyl Acetate} \quad \text{An ESTER}$$

The chemical reactivity of the C=O group depends on the nature of the molecule in which it is contained. In simple aldehydes and ketones the C=O goes through addition reactions which open the double bond:

$$CH_3-\underset{\underset{O}{\|}}{C}-H + H_2 \longrightarrow CH_3-\underset{\underset{OH}{|}}{\overset{\overset{H}{|}}{C}}-H$$

Acetaldehyde Ethyl Alcohol

The C=O may also undergo condensation reactions, as in the formation of an *oxime:*

$$CH_3-\underset{\underset{O}{\|}}{C}-CH_3 + H_2NOH \longrightarrow CH_3-\underset{\underset{NOH}{\|}}{C}-CH_3 + H_2O$$

Acetone Acetoxime

—*Ru. M.*

CARBOXYLIC ACIDS: organic chemical compounds in which acidity is due to the H atom in the carboxyl group:

$$-\underset{\underset{OH}{|}}{\overset{\overset{\|}{C}=O}{}}$$

The first and simplest compound in this series is formic acid, H—COOH; the second is acetic acid, CH_3—COOH. The 18-carbon acid is stearic acid, $C_{17}H_{35}$—COOH. These are examples of aliphatic compounds. Among the aromatic compounds the typical example is benzoic acid, C_6H_5—COOH, where the carboxyl group is linked to the benzene ring. Carboxylic acids are generally weakly ionized in solution, but certain substituents in the chain or ring structures can raise the acidity to high levels.—*Ru. M.*

CARDANO, GERONIMO or GIROLAMO, 1501–76, Italian mathematician and physician; b. Pavia. Gifted and versatile, he held important chairs at the Univs. of Pavia and Bologna, and later became astrologer at the papal court. His best-known work, *Artis magnae* (1545), is a great treatise on algebra. In it appears Tartaglia's solution of the cubic equation, which had been revealed to the unscrupulous Cardano under pledge of secrecy. His autobiography has been published in English as *The Book of My Life* (1930). A translation of his work on games of chance appears in Oystein Ore's *Cardano, the Gambling Scholar* (1953).—*H. C.*

CARDIAC GLYCOSIDES: a large group of compounds consisting of a steroid nucleus to which several other groups, including some sugars, are attached. These compounds are mainly derived from plants but are known to occur also in sea urchins. They have a powerful action on the heart and are the active principles of such medicines as digitalis. Other cardiac glycosides, in small doses, cause heart stoppage; many of these have been used by South American and African aborigines as arrow poisons. See STEROLS.—*J. Fl.*

CARDINAL AND ORDINAL NUMBERS: positive whole numbers, the difference between which depends on their use. If the objects of a set (any collection) can be matched with the

fingers and thumb of one hand so that no objects or fingers are left over, then the cardinal number of the set is 5. The number of objects in any set can thus be found without counting, provided we have a collection of standard sets for comparison. In counting, we attach a number to each member of the counted set—1, 2, 3, *etc.*; these are ordinal numbers. With finite sets, the greatest ordinal number—the last one counted—is the cardinal number of the set. Infinite sets, however, can be assigned a transfinite cardinal number by matching but not by counting, although there are transfinite ordinal numbers. See TRANSFINITE NUMBERS.—*H. E. W.*

CARNAP, RUDOLPH, 1891–   , philosopher; b. Wuppertal, Germany. Currently professor of philosophy at the Univ. of California, Los Angeles, he was a member of the "Vienna Circle" (see LOGICAL EMPIRICISM). His many publications have profoundly influenced contemporary philosophical opinion in the U. S. A.—*I. L.*

CARNIVORE: in zoology, any member of an order (Carnivora) of MAMMALS that are primarily flesh-eaters. (In a broad sense, "carnivore" may refer to any flesh-eater.) Present-day members of this order are divided into two major groups, the suborders Fissipedia and Pinnipedia. Representatives of the Fissipedia are terrestrial and include dogs, wolves, foxes, and jackals (family Canidae); bears (Ursidae); raccoons and coatis (Procyonidae); skunks, weasels, mink, badger, marten, wolverine, and otter (Mustelidae); mongoose and palm civets (Viverridae); hyenas (Hyaenidae); lions, tigers, and other cats (Felidae). Members of the Pinnipedia are aquatic and include the eared seals and sea lions (Otariidae), hair seals (Phocidae), and walruses (Odobaenidae). Although carnivores have teeth modified for a diet of flesh, a number are omnivorous or insectivorous, some species (*e.g.* bear, fox, skunk) feeding on fruits, grasses, and insects. Incisor teeth are small, whereas canine teeth are usually large and dagger-like, being useful for stabbing or holding prey. Molar teeth are often sharp-

Aquatic carnivore: The flippered Pinnipedia are sharply differentiated from the other carnivores. The arctic walrus, shown here, breeds on land but otherwise lives in the sea, diving for shellfish and echinoderms. (*N. Y. Zoological Society*).

long distances each year. In the summer, great numbers of fur seals, for example, go to islands in the Bering Sea, where the young are born. See Color Plate 17.—*A. P. E.*

CARNIVOROUS PLANTS: plants that capture and digest animals, usually insects. Examples are rare. The delicate bladderworts (*Utricularia*) of fresh water have this habit. Modified leaves are the "bladders," each with a "door" hinged to swing sharply inward when touched on the outer surface; the swirl of water produced by the moving door draws small crustaceans and aquatic insects into the cavity of the leaf, where the plant digests them after closing the door again. All other carnivorous plants are terrestrial, bog-dwelling, or epiphytic (*i.e.* growing on other plants but not parasitically). Most spectacular is the Venus's-flytrap (*Dionaea*) of North Carolina, the leaves of which fold by a lengthwise hinge and capture insects that jostle trigger hairs on the upper surface. Sundews (*Drosera*) and butterworts (*Pinguicula*) secrete sticky tanglefoot from their leaves and digest insects that become trapped in it. Pitcher plants (*Sarracenia, Darlingtonia,* and *Heliamphora*) of American bogs and monkeycups (*Nepenthes*) of the Old World tropics have vase-shaped leaves in which rain collects and insects drown. The carnivorous habit appears to be a means for obtaining nitrogenous compounds where the environment does not furnish enough. See BOG PLANTS; EPIPHYTE.—*L. and M. M.*

edged, serving for cutting flesh. Toes are armed with claws; the sharp claws of cats can be retracted into sheaths, so that their sharpness is not blunted by contact with the ground. The mental alertness needed to capture other animals is reflected in a well-developed brain, a highly developed sense of smell, and legs that are capable of speed for short distances. The cheetah, fastest of land animals, can run up to 70 mi/hr for distances of 500 yd or less, and even some bears can travel at 25 or 30 mi/hr. Carnivores vary in size from the least weasel, which weighs 2 oz, to the great bears, which weigh more than 1,000 lb. Land carnivores are native to all continents except Australia, where several species, *e.g.* the fox, dingo, and stoat, have been introduced. Seals and walruses are represented in both Atlantic and Pacific oceans; they are adapted for an aquatic life by having the legs modified into flippers, on which toenails may still be present. These mammals migrate over

CARNOT, LAZARE NICOLAS MARGUERITE, 1753–1823, French military leader and mathematician; b. Molay, Burgundy. The military genius of the French Revolution, Carnot published a classic work on fortification, *De la défense des places fortes* (1812). Among his mathematical works were *Réflexions sur la métaphysique du calcul infinitésimal* (1797), *Géométrie de position* (1803), and an essay on transversals (1806); the latter two were important contributions to modern geometry. He invented a class of general theorems on projective properties of figures, later exploited by Poncelet, Chasles, and others. His son **Nicolas Léonard Sadi Carnot,** 1796–1832, b. Paris, was an engineer. In *Réflexions sur la puissance motrice du feu* (1824) he conceived of an ideal (Carnot) engine operating in a cycle. From the impossibility of perpetual motion he proved that the work obtained was limited solely by "the quantity of caloric . . . and the difference in temperature of the bodies between which the caloric is exchanged." His work, which led R. J. E. Clausius and W. T. Kelvin to the second law of thermodynamics and the absolute temperature scale, may be considered the origin of THERMODYNAMICS. Carnot also arrived at the law of CONSERVATION OF MASS-ENERGY.—*H. C. and C. J. S.*

CARNOT CYCLE: an idealized cycle of operations that establishes the ultimate limits on heat engines. All cyclic heat engines (*e.g.* steam engine and automobile motor) have three characteristics in common: during each cycle of operations they absorb energy from a hot reservoir by the transfer of heat; they perform work; and they discharge some energy by transfer of heat to a cold reservoir. For example, the boiler is the hot reservoir of a steam engine, and the condenser is its cold reservoir. The Carnot engine is a concept for determining the ultimate attainable efficiency for any heat energy as limited by the laws of THERMODYNAMICS. It is imagined to be an engine that goes through a particular cycle incorporating the three essential features of heat engines, but without any internal frictional losses. It can be shown that a Carnot engine has the highest possible efficiency (work accomplished divided by energy absorbed from hot reservoir). Its value equals one minus the ratio of the absolute temperature of the low reservoir to that of the hot reservoir. All real engines have an even smaller efficiency, of course, because of frictional losses. —*S. K.*

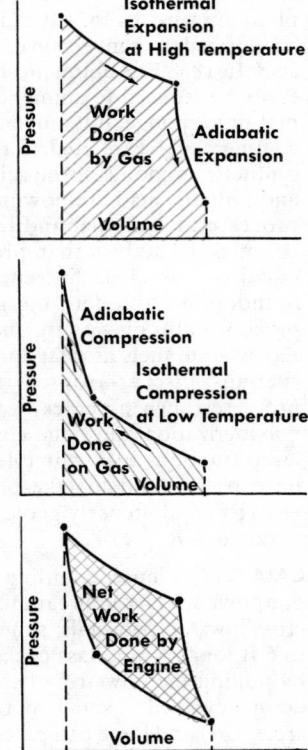

Carnot cycle for an ideal engine: A hot gas is introduced into the cylinder and allowed to expand and cool, so that it pushes on the piston and does work. This expansion takes place in two stages, the first at constant temperature, the second adiabatically. The area under the first curve represents the work done by the expansion. The gas is returned to its original pressure and temperature by compressing it in two stages; the work done on the gas is represented by the area under the second curve. The difference between the two areas represents the net mechanical energy converted from heat.

CARNOTITE: one of the two major ores of uranium in the U. S. A., the other being the related and similar mineral tyuyamunite. These minerals, $K_2(UO_2)_2(VO_4)_2 \cdot 3H_2O$ and $Ca(UO_2)_2(VO_4)_2 \cdot nH_2O$ respectively, occur mostly as bright yellow, earthy disseminations in sandstones, conglomerates, and limestones in deposits of the Colorado Plateau type. They result from the weathering and oxidation of primary uranium and vanadium ores, *e.g.* uraninite and roscoelite, which were precipitated from circulating waters by fossil plant debris in the rocks. The richest ore consists of fossil logs almost completely replaced by carnotite. See MINERAL (table); ORES AND ORE DEPOSITS.—*L. M.*

CAROTHERS, WALLACE HUME, 1896–1937, U. S. chemist; b. Burlington, Iowa. His most notable research was on linear polymers, and his work laid the foundation for the production of Neoprene and Nylon. He was a member of the National Academy of Sciences.—*D. H. D. R.*

CAROTID ARTERY: one of two arteries that carry blood to the brain of vertebrate animals. In mammals, these arteries are the first to branch from the aorta. Each, when some distance from its origin, branches into internal and external carotid arteries. At the branch point there is an enlargement, the *carotid sinus,* which contains important sense organs. By responding to the stretch of artery walls and to the concentration of carbon dioxide and oxygen in the blood, these sense organs provide the brain with important information about the pressure and composition of blood flowing to the brain.—*B. T. S.*

CARPENTRY: generally, woodworking techniques performed by hand. The rise of structural metals, concrete, and factory manufacture has narrowed the carpenter's domain to the woodwork of residences and other relatively small buildings. Even here, the lumber he uses is now usually cut and shaped by machine at the mill so that his work is confined primarily to joining. Traditionally, however, the carpenter's work has included timber-framing of ships, bridges, and buildings of all sizes; laying of floors and roof planking; erecting partitions; building stairways; installing doors, window sashes, and frames; making furniture and decorative woodwork; and building the forms for all cement work, arches, and vaults. Often, too, the carpenter has been a self-trained architect and engineer. Except for power-driven implements such as saws, drills, and sanders, the tools and techniques of the carpenter have changed little since prehistoric times. Shaping of the individual piece is accomplished by sawing, turning in the lathe, hewing with the ax, planing, and cutting in detail by means of a knife, chisel, gouge, or adze. Sanding is a technique for smoothing the shaped piece, or preparing the surface for painting. To make accurate shapes, and to join them properly, the carpenter uses a variety of tools to guide his eye and hand, chiefly the ruler, square, level, and plumb-line. Since individual pieces of lumber are generally light, they can easily be lifted and placed in position by hand. For heavy framing and formwork, however, the carpenter must use mechanical aids such as the crane and hoist; for very large structures these may be power-operated. Individual pieces are joined by accurately cutting the ends into matching shapes designed to prevent one piece from separating from the other. Most common shapes are parallel and diagonal scarfs, the tongue-and-groove, mortise-and-tenon, and dovetail. The principle in each case is known as keying, *i.e.* the insertion of one piece into a slot, groove, or angle of the other in such a way that they cannot be pulled directly apart without rupturing the wood. Simpler joints are the butt, lap, and splice. Fasteners, if used, were formerly wooden pegs and wedges. The 19th-cent. inventions of nail- and screw-making machinery and high-strength glues have simplified the techniques of joining, which are now chiefly nailing, bolting, screwing, and glueing.

In the tradition of building, the carpenter was designer as well as builder. By rule of thumb and accumulated experience, he selected lumber, determined the size and shape of the individual piece for the load it was to carry, and joined the pieces in such a way that they formed a rigid structure which observed the stress limits of the timber. With no scientific concepts of stress analysis to guide him, the American carpenter achieved extraordinary feats of truss-bridge construction in wood. But scientific building technology took the place of his skill and intuition before 1900.—*C. W. C.*

CARROLL, JAMES, 1854–1907, U. S. bacteriologist and pathologist; b. Woolwich, England. He worked with Aristide Agramonte (1869–1931), Jesse W. Lazear (1866–1900), and Walter Reed (1851–1902) to determine the cause and mode of transmission of yellow fever. Carroll, allowing himself to be bitten by an infected mosquito, developed yellow fever, thus demonstrating that mosquitoes transmit the disease (1900). The group also showed that the causative agent of yellow fever is a virus.—*D. H. D. R.*

CARTESIAN COORDINATES: see COORDINATE SYSTEM.

CARTILAGE (or **gristle**): a tough, rubbery CONNECTIVE TISSUE that serves as part of the body framework. In primitive vertebrates, *e.g.* sharks and rays, the entire skeleton is made of cartilage. Higher vertebrates—fish, amphibians, birds, mammals—begin life with skeletons of cartilage, but most of the cartilage is replaced by bone during the early development of the embryo. In man cartilage is found in the nose, outer ear, larynx, trachea, eustachian tube, and elsewhere.— *R. G. M.*

CARTOGRAPHY: see MAP.

CARVER, GEORGE WASHINGTON, 1864–1943, U. S. agricultural chemist; b. a slave, at Diamond Grove, Mo. As a member of the staff at Tuskegee Institute, Ala., from 1898, he began the study of crop rotation and urged the cultivation of peanuts, sweet potatoes, and pecans as a substitute for cotton. He developed 300 new uses for peanuts, 100 for the sweet potato, and 60 for pecans, thus making those crops economically feasible. Later he applied the same technique to develop uses for waste products such as wood shavings and cornstalks. A foundation bearing his name was established by him, 1940, to continue research on agricultural chemistry.—*D. H. D. R.*

CASEIN: a yellow-white powder derived from milk by precipitation with acid. A protein, it is used industrially as an adhesive; in making plastics, paint, and sizing for paper and textiles; and as an agent for producing suspensions. It is also a food for diabetics.—*H. W. F.*

CASSINI, GIOVANNI DOMENICO or **JEAN DOMINIQUE,** 1625–1712, Italian engineer and astronomer; b. Perinaldo. Famed as an astronomer, he discovered the rotations of the planets Mars and Jupiter (1667) and compiled tables of the motions of Jupiter's satellites. In 1669 he went to work at the new Paris Observatory, of which he became virtual director. In Paris he discovered four more satellites of Saturn (1671–84) and observed (1685) the division of Saturn's rings into two concentric portions ("Cassini Division"). Under his direction the parallax of Mars was observed; it yielded a value for the distance of Mars from Earth. Cassini studied and named the zodiacal light. In the field of mathematics he discovered the Cassinian oval. He was a fellow of the Royal Society. At the observatory he was succeeded by his son, **Jacques Cassini** (1677–1756).—*S. B.*

CATALYSIS: a term coined by Berzelius, 1835, to describe the influence of a substance (catalyst) which enters into and accelerates a chemical reaction at the molecular level, yet is reformed at the end of the reaction, able to accelerate a further series of like reactions between molecules of the reacting compounds. A catalyst may thus be said to serve as an expedient pathway, a short cut along which a reaction can be led again and again. The catalyst allows the reaction to take place at a temperature or pressure at which the uncatalyzed reaction would proceed too slowly for practical purposes. Reactions may be catalytically accelerated (*positive catalysis*) or retarded (*negative catalysis*). Catalysis may be brought about by one of the reagents or by one of the products formed (*auto-catalysis*). It may take place in homogeneous systems (gases, liquids) or heterogeneous systems (at the interface of gases and solids or liquids and solids). Since heterogeneous action takes place at the surface of the catalyst, the latter is frequently deposited on the outside of a neutral "carrier," *e.g.* silica. The reacting fluids are led through a bed of pellets of "catalyst." Since large quantities of heat are often evolved or absorbed during catalytic reactions, heat exchange poses an important problem, as does the inhibiting "poisoning" of the catalyst by minute traces of certain substances (*e.g.* sulfur compounds and metals). By appropriate heating processes the catalyst can, however, be regenerated. Catalytic processes now play an important role in technology.

In 1817 Sir Humphry Davy discovered that oxidation of alcohol by air was accelerated by the presence of a hot platinum wire. In 1831 P. Phillips found that red-hot platinum accelerated the conversion of sulfur dioxide and air into sulfuric acid. In 1838 F. Kuhlmann showed that nitrogen oxides could easily be reduced to ammonia by hydrogen in the presence of platinum sponge. But only in this century were such processes commercially exploited. Basic chemicals like sulfuric acid, synthetic ammonia, nitric acid, methyl alcohol, formaldehyde, and phthalic acid are now manufactured mainly by catalytic processes. P. Sabatier and J. B. Senderens (1897) discovered the nickel catalyst that promotes hydrogenation of such liquid oils as olive, linseed, or whale oil and thus laid the foundation of modern margarine manufacturing. Catalytic processes also play a large part in the hydrogenation of such second-rate fuels as peat and lignite to synthetic motor fuels (Bergius, Fischer-Tropsch), and in the oil industry catalytic processes such as cracking, alkylation, hydroforming, and polymerization allow the conversion of less desirable petroleum fractions into valuable chemicals. Catalytic processes have been found to take place in all living organisms (see ENZYME) and, in early geological periods, even in inorganic material.—*R. J. F.*

CATAPULT: a missile-hurling device used in warfare before gunpowder. The first catapults could be described as large crossbows on pedestals, shooting massive dart-like arrows, 2 to 6 ft long. A windlass cocked the engine; range was varied by pulling the bowstring back to different points. From this design evolved a small, portable catapult (the scorpion or crossbow) and large catapults that shot balls of stone or brick weighing 10 to 180 lb. In the 4th cent. B. C. designers substituted for the original bow a frame carrying a pair of skeins of hair, through which a pair of rigid throwing arms were thrust. The machine, cocked by twisting the hair, could send a dart 600 to 800 yd—twice the range of a longbow. In the Hellenistic period, catapults were used in large numbers in sieges, and small catapults were mounted on warships. Under the Roman Empire a new kind of stone thrower, the onager ("wild ass"), appeared. This had a single arm, worked by a torsion skein, with a spoon or sling at its upper end. When released, the arm flew up in a vertical plane against a padded

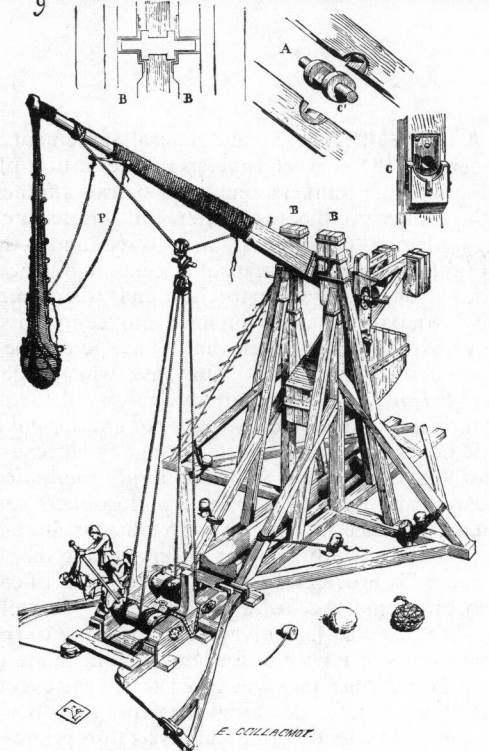

9

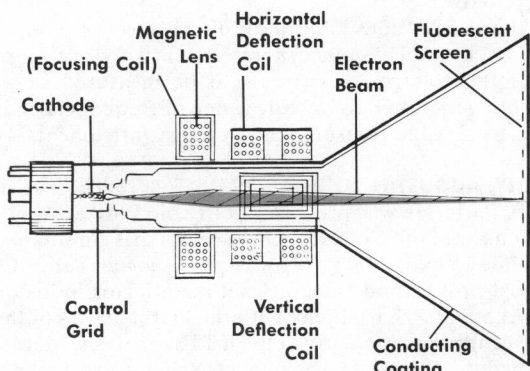

Medieval catapult: Instead of storing energy in a torsion skein as in catapults of classical times, this trebuchet of medieval design (here seen in a reconstruction) stores it in a counterpoise hung from the short arm of a lever; upon release, the long arm hurls its burden of stones. (*Bettmann Archive*)

stop. In the late Roman Empire, small catapults on wheels were used as field artillery. The two-armed torsion catapult disappeared with the downfall of the W Roman Empire, but all the other types continued in use. In the 11th cent. appeared the trebuchet, or counterweight stone thrower, with a sling at the long end of a pivoted throwing arm and a weight, adjustable in mass or position to vary the range, at the short end. Catapults of several types were employed until cannon made them obsolete in the 14th–15th cent. The term "catapult" is applied also to a naval-aircraft launching device. Aircraft catapults may be powered by gunpowder, compressed air, or steam; they may be either protruding struts moving

along a slot in the deck or carriages running on tracks. The force of a piston stroke, actuated directly or by hydraulic pressure, is transmitted to the aircraft directly or through cables and pulleys.—*L. S. de C.*

CATASTROPHISM: see GEOLOGY.

CATHODE RAYS: a form of radiation ultimately identified as a stream of electrons. If two metal electrodes are sealed through the walls of a glass tube and a pressure of about 0.0001 atm is maintained in the tube, when a voltage in the range of 4,000 to 10,000 v is applied a visible glow appears to emerge from the cathode (the negative electrode). The glow, which has the appearance of a beam, was first identified only as "cathode rays." Later, from the fact that the beam is deflected by magnetic fields, it became known that cathode rays are streams of electrons. The term cathode rays is used even if the rays are invisible, since the glow in the gas is a secondary effect produced by the rays. See CATHODE-RAY TUBE.—*R. V.*

CATHODE-RAY TUBE: a device for pictorial representation of variations of electric current or voltage. It employs for this purpose the deflection, by a magnetic or electric field, of a beam of ELECTRONS or cathode rays, so called because electrons, negatively charged particles which form part of all matter, are emitted by a negatively charged electrode, or cathode. The beam converges in a narrow cone on a fluorescent screen, where it forms a bright luminous spot—the scanning spot. In this manner changes in the currents or voltages which generate the deflection fields are rendered visible by displacements of the scanning spot on the screen. The cathode-ray tube differs from the familiar vacuum (or radio) tube in that the application of a voltage or current to it results in a change of direction of an electron current, and a consequent visible spot displacement, whereas in the vacuum tube it results simply in a change in output current amplitude. The cathode-ray tube was devised in 1897 by Karl Ferdinand Braun for the study of alternating currents. This use has made it an indispensable measuring and testing tool for the electrical engineer. Suitably modified, it has found much more extensive employment since 1930 as a TELEVISION viewing tube or kinescope. An outgrowth of this development is the use of the cathode-ray tube as a RADAR indicator during and since World War II.

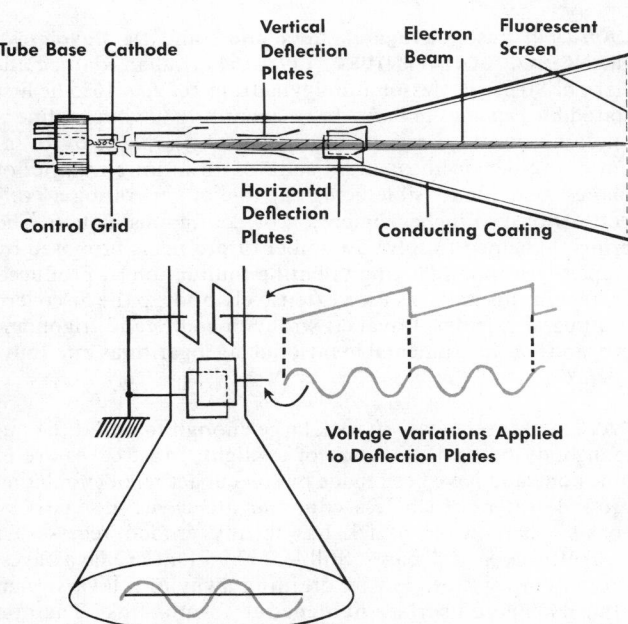

Voltage Variations Applied to Deflection Plates

Two ways of deflecting electron beams: In the electrostatic system (*left, top*), the beam passes first between deflection plates that govern the vertical component of the motion of the spot on the screen, then between the plates that govern its horizontal component. If a scanning voltage of appropriate frequency is applied to the vertical deflection plates, and the signal to be studied to the horizontal deflection plates (*left, bottom*), a stationary wave form appears on the screen. In the electromagnetic system (*above*), the beam is controlled by induction coils.

The essential elements of the cathode-ray tube consist, thus, of an electron beam source; an electron lens or focusing system which causes the emitted electrons to converge at the scanning spot on the screen; deflecting elements for the beam; and a fluorescent screen for rendering the scanning spot visible. In addition, the beam path must be enclosed in a highly evacuated vessel, commonly in the form of a conical glass bulb, since electrons are strongly scattered by even slight amounts of gas or air which may remain in the tube. In modern cathode-ray tubes, the electron beam is generally emitted from the end plate of a small nickel cylinder, indirectly heated by an insulated spiral filament traversed by electric current. The end plate, or cathode, is coated with oxides of barium and strontium to yield copious emission of electrons at moderate temperatures. The electron emission is accelerated and shaped into a convergent pencil by the electric fields surrounding a sequence of apertured electrodes; their focusing action may be supplemented by a magnetic lens, or a coil of current-traversed wire partly enclosed by an iron shield. The electrode adjoining the cathode is called the control grid. Its voltage, normally negative with respect to the cathode, controls the beam intensity.

The converged beam, finally, passes through the deflecting elements. These may be electrostatic, consisting of two successive pairs of plates, to which the voltages to be measured are applied; or they may be magnetic, consisting of two pairs of coils, traversed by the currents to be measured. Both electrostatic and magnetic deflection is employed in cathode-ray tubes for measurement purposes; in television viewing tubes, only magnetic deflection is used, since it permits deflection through larger angles and, hence, shorter tubes for a given picture area. One pair of deflection plates (or deflection coils) produces the horizontal deflection of the spot, the other the vertical deflection. In measurement applications, a continuously increasing current or voltage is usually applied to the horizontal deflection elements and the voltage or current to be measured, to the vertical deflection elements; thus the curve described by the scanning spot on the tube face shows directly the time variation of this voltage or current. If the process to be studied is periodic, a sawtooth voltage or current variation, with the periodicity of the phenomenon to be studied, is applied to the horizontal elements, so that the voltage or current variation in successive periods is superposed.

Cathode-ray tubes commonly form parts of cathode-ray OSCILLOSCOPES. These incorporate circuits for the amplification of the voltages or currents to be measured as well as sawtooth generators for a wide range of frequencies, making them very flexible measurement and test instruments.—*V. Z.*

CAUCHY, AUGUSTIN LOUIS, 1789–1857, French mathematician; b. Paris. He was professor at l'École Polytechnique, the Sorbonne, and the Collège de France in Paris simultaneously, and while in exile (1830–38) was professor at Turin. One of the most prolific and versatile mathematicians in history, he brought about a sharp break with the mathematics of the preceding century, particularly in the field of analysis. Mathematicians had developed the calculus of Newton and Leibniz and applied it to an amazingly large number of problems, but its fundamental concepts were not rigorously formulated until Cauchy's work. Cauchy revolutionized analysis and set the mood for proceeding with more rigor, which characterized mathematical research in the late 19th cent. He contributed to every branch of mathematics—especially calculus, theory of functions, and algebraic analysis—as well as to applied fields, notably astronomy, hydrodynamics, and optics. He was a fellow of the Royal Society.—*H. C.*

CAUSE AND EFFECT: There is no general agreement at present concerning the correct analysis of the notion of cause. According to some thinkers, one event causes another if and only if the former produces the latter. But this account leaves the crucial idea of "production" unanalyzed, and is therefore not helpful for interpreting causal statements in the natural and social sciences. The Aristotelian analysis of causation, especially with its emphasis upon final causes, presents similar difficulties. Aristotle suggested that a change can be caused or explained in four ways: we may ask what initiated the change (*efficient* cause), demand an analysis of the material and form of the changed entity (*material* and *formal* causes), and seek the goal or end of the change (*final* cause). The search for final causes has not, by and large, dominated scientific research, and according to some philosophers and scientists, science is concerned mainly with efficient causes.

Perhaps a more fruitful way of understanding the scientific use of "cause" is provided by the *regularity* view of causation defended by Hume. According to this view, a statement of the type "*a* caused *b*" is equivalent in meaning to the statement that events of type *A* and events of type *B* are lawfully connected in the sense that whenever an *A*-type event occurs a *B* one follows. Hume added that the cause must be spatially contiguous to the effect. Hume's analysis thus relates the notion of cause to that of law, and has occasionally been used to defend the questionable thesis that all laws of science are "causal" in the sense that they state the conditions for the occurrence of events in terms of simultaneously or previously existing events.

Many philosophers, basing themselves on the suggestion of Kant, have been inclined to equate "casual law" with "determinism" or "invariable concomitance," and throughout the 19th cent. many scientists believed science rests on the postulate that every event has a cause, *i.e.* every event must be shown to be an instance of a strictly universal regularity. This latter belief is challenged by recent developments in quantum mechanics. The analysis of "cause" offered by Hume and even Kant virtually identifies "cause" with "sufficient condition," or "necessary and sufficient condition," but scientists occasionally use the term "cause" more broadly, and sometimes understand by the cause of an event a contributory condition (*i.e.* a factor which is merely *part* of the sufficient condition) for the occurrence of the event.—*S. M.*

CAVALIERI (also **Cavaglieri, Cavalerius,** and **De Cavalerus**), **FRANCESCO BONAVENTURA,** 1598–1647, Italian mathematician; b. Milan. Professor at Bologna from 1629, in 1635 he first stated his *principle of indivisibles,* according to which a line is made up of an infinite number of points, a plane of an infinite number of lines, and a solid of an infinite number of planes—each indivisible being capable of generating a CONTINUUM of next higher dimension by continuous motion. The principle helped to solve a number of problems proposed by Kepler. Although lacking scientific foundation, it produced correct results and was used extensively prior to the discovery of integral calculus. Cavalieri wrote on conics and trigonometry and was instrumental in introducing logarithms into Italy. —*H. C.*

CAVE: a natural cavity in rock large enough to admit the human body beyond the reach of sunlight. Most caves are in limestone and have been made by solvent action of circulating ground water. Much less common are caves along rocky coasts where wave attack has locally eroded recesses in weaker rock at cliff bases. Still less abundant are lava caves, roofed empty tubes left by draining away of a lava stream after its exposed surface hardened to form a crust. The rare

Sandstone caves hollowed out by river action are numerous in western U. S. A. This one, in N Arizona, shelters the prehistoric Indian village Betatakin (barely visible here). *(Josef Muench)*

caves in glacial ice are made by meltwater descending through crevasses in the ice to the glacier bed.

In a geological sense, all caves are short-lived. Collapse of roofs makes sinkholes, and introduces fallen debris and wash from the surface. Water filtering down through limestone becomes saturated with lime carbonate and, on entering a cave, commonly deposits this as stalactites and stalagmites, flowstone on walls and floors, and rimstone damming cave streams. All these changes decrease the cave space.

Almost every enterable limestone cave is decadent. Few, even those with a stream on the floor, are increasing in size under present conditions. Cave-making, therefore, must have occurred when different conditions of ground-water flow prevailed. It seems clear that the entire cavity was completely full of water when solution began. Circulation in the formative period was pressure-directed, much as water is circulated in the mains of a city, and the cave originated much deeper than its present location. The land mass above subsequently was slowly worn thinner by surface wash and stream erosion, the level of completely saturated rock being lowered at the same time so that air finally entered and decadence began. Growing caves are indicated, but not enterable, in the great springs of Florida and the Ozarks. Almost every state in the U. S. A. offers caves as scenic attractions. Most extensive are Mammoth in Kentucky and Carlsbad in New Mexico. Luray, in Virginia, is probably the most lavishly decorated. At Cacahuamilpa, Mexico, is the longest known chamber in North America, 1.4 km long.

As natural shelters, caves where available were extensively used by prehistoric man, and thus became the protected repositories of his cultural records. Some caves, including many in Mediterranean countries, contain stratified, chronological evidence (bones and tools) of human occupation spanning tens of thousands of years. Among the most famous are those of Lascaux, France, and Altamira, Spain, with their particularly fine wall paintings by Cro-Magnon man.—*A. P. E.*

Carved out of limestone by the slow solvent action of ground water, the Big Room of Carlsbad Caverns, N. Mex., has since been partitioned by monumental stalagmites deposited by limestone drippings. *(Santa Fe Railway)*

Cave-visiting rodent (not a permanent cave dweller) is the paca, or spotted cavy, native to Central America. (*Walter Dawn*)

Twilight zone near entrances of North American Caves is home of orange cave salamander. The long tail is prehensile. (*C. E. Mohr/National Audubon Society*)

CAVE ANIMALS: In addition to bears, snakes, raccoons, and other animals that take refuge in caves near their openings, a considerable variety of animals penetrate more deeply or live their whole lives underground. Bats, cave swiftlets of the Far East, and oil birds of South America find their way to roosting areas in the complete darkness by echo-location (see ANIMAL SONAR). The permanent fauna, however, consist of creatures that rarely venture beyond the cave; these animals include crickets, beetles, spiders, centipedes, crayfishes, fishes, and salamanders. Most have degenerate eyes or are completely blind; they rely upon extreme sensitivity to vibrations and often possess tremendously long legs or antennae or body hairs that extend their sense of touch and improve their chances of escape when approached. The fishes and crayfishes usually rely upon food brought through the cave by underground streams. Cave crickets feed on mold that grows on the droppings of bats and cave birds. Beetles, centipedes, and spiders catch the crickets. The food web is extremely simple, and populations of cave animals fluctuate widely, particularly in relation to presence or absence of bats that migrate. See ADAPTATIONS IN ANIMALS AND PLANTS; BALANCE OF NATURE; FOOD CHAIN; and Color Plate 18.—*L. and M. M.*

CAVENDISH, HENRY, 1731–1810, English chemist and physicist; b. Nice, France. The first published paper of this extremely shy, eccentric person was "Facticious Airs" (1766). It reported experiments on "inflammable air" (hydrogen) and "fixed air" (carbon dioxide). He determined the densities of these gases relative to common air and investigated the extent to which they are absorbed by various liquids. His research on electricity remained largely unpublished in his lifetime, although he did publish, without evidence, the inverse-square law of electromagnetic attraction. In 1798 his paper "Experiments to Determine the Density of the Earth" reported experiments with the torsion balance, invented by J. Michell, on direct measurements of gravitational forces. Cavendish's papers were published in the *Philosophical Transactions* of the Royal Society, of which he was a member. *Electrical Researches* (1879) was edited from manuscripts and published by J. C. Maxwell; *Scientific Papers* appeared in 1921. —*D. H. D. R.*

CAVITATION: the phenomenon of bubble production in a liquid when the pressure on it is suddenly reduced. The effervescence of beer when the bottle cap is removed is a familiar example. Important in marine engineering and hydraulics is the sudden production and collapse of vapor-filled bubbles behind the blades of a fast-rotating ship's propeller or in high-speed pumps, turbines, and pipe lines. The violent collapse of bubbles actually erodes the propeller or other material surface. The two types of cavitation, gaseous and vaporous, are illustrated by the two examples just given. In gaseous cavitation the bubble formed contains permanent gas that does not immediately redissolve; in vaporous cavitation, while there may be a little gas, most of the content of the bubble is vapor of the liquid, and the bubble can collapse completely. Both types may be seen as a kettle of water is brought to boil, bubbles of air first rising, followed by bubbles of water vapor when the water boils. Cavitation sets an upper limit to the sound power (the rate of flow of sound energy) that can be radiated under water at sea from an acoustic transducer, an instrument used in SONAR devices that transforms electrical or other energy into sound energy. At low power the sound waves contain regions of pressure both higher and lower than the average static pressure of the water. When power is increased to the point where the lower swing of the pressure overcomes the static pressure, bubbles form in this part of the wave and strongly absorb its energy. Much higher powers can be radiated into de-gassed water in a laboratory.—*M. C. H.*

CAVITY RESONATOR: a hollow metallic cavity, of usually arbitrary shape, designed to respond to selected frequencies of electromagnetic radiation. Cavity resonators may be excited by means of probes or apertures in their walls, through which the electromagnetic radiation is fed; they sustain only those electromagnetic radiations capable of satisfying the electric and magnetic-field conditions imposed by the metallic boundaries of the cavity. With suitable cavity shapes, standing waves of electromagnetic energy can be sustained and excited with high amplitude and efficiency. Cavities are commonly used as tuned elements in centimeter wavelength oscillators or as accurate wave meters for frequency measurement.—*P. T. D. and F. J. E.*

CAYLEY, ARTHUR, 1821–95, English mathematician; b. Richmond, Surrey. Professor of mathematics at Cambridge from 1863, Cayley was one of the most prolific of all mathematicians, ranking with L. Euler and A. Cauchy. Early in his career he became acquainted with J. J. Sylvester, and their association remained mutually beneficial throughout their lives. Cayley is known for his work on algebraic invariants, the theory of MATRICES, and geometry of space of *n* DIMENSIONS. He was a fellow of the Royal Society and an associate of the U. S. Academy of Sciences.—*H. C.*

CELESTIAL COORDINATES: systems for describing the location of points on the CELESTIAL SPHERE. Each system, in general, defines a point called the pole, a great circle 90° from the pole, a point on the circle used as the origin, and the direction from the origin in which angles are measured. There are two coordinates in each system, one expressing the angular distance above or below the reference circle, the other the angular distance around the circle from the origin. Five systems are used: (1) *The horizon* or *altazimuth system* is a local system in which the observer is assumed to be on Earth's surface. The pole is the zenith, and the reference great circle is the celestial horizon. Altitude is measured from the horizon (positive if above, negative if below the horizon), and azimuth is measured around the horizon, usually from the north point eastward. (2) *The equatorial system* locates a celestial body with respect to the center of Earth. The reference great circle is the celestial equator, formed on the celestial sphere by the extension of the plane of the terrestrial equator. The poles are the celestial poles, formed by extending Earth's axis of rotation to the celestial sphere. Declination is angular distance north or south of the celestial equator. Right ascension is angular distance around the celestial equator, measured eastward from the vernal equinox. (3) *The semilocal system* facilitates conversion between the horizon and equatorial systems. Its coordinates are declination and local hour angle (distance around the celestial equator), which astronomers

count from 0° to 180° east and west of the local meridian. Navigators measure local hour angle through 360° westward from the local meridian; they also use Greenwich hour angle and sidereal hour angle, counted from 0° to 360° westward from the Greenwich meridian and the vernal equinox respectively. (4) *The ecliptic system* locates a body with respect to the plane of Earth's orbit. This plane intersects the celestial sphere in the great circle called the ecliptic. Celestial latitude is measured north and south from the ecliptic; celestial longitude is measured eastward around the ecliptic from the vernal equinox. Ecliptic coordinates can be geocentric (measured with Earth as center) or heliocentric (with Sun as center); in the latter case the coordinates are called heliocentric latitude and longitude. (5) *The galactic system* locates a celestial body with respect to the Milky Way. The reference great circle is the galactic equator, defined by a plane that nearly bisects the band of the Milky Way. Galactic latitude is measured north or south from the galactic equator; galactic longitude is measured eastward around the galactic equator from the assumed direction of the center of the galaxy (a point in the constellation Sagittarius).

The center of the equatorial system is Earth's center, and most celestial objects are so distant that the error in observations taken from Earth's surface is insignificant. A notable exception is the Moon, which is only 60 Earth radii away on the average. The greatest error occurs when the Moon is on the horizon. If it could then be viewed from Earth's center it would be nearly two lunar diameters (nearly 1°) higher than the position observed from Earth's surface (neglecting the effects of refraction). With very accurate instruments this error can also be measured for Sun and planets.—*B. P. S.*

CELESTIAL MECHANICS: the application of mathematical methods to the study of motions of heavenly bodies, principally those within the solar system. Its purpose is twofold: (1) from existing theories, to compute the ephemeris (table of predicted positions as a function of time) of a planet, comet,

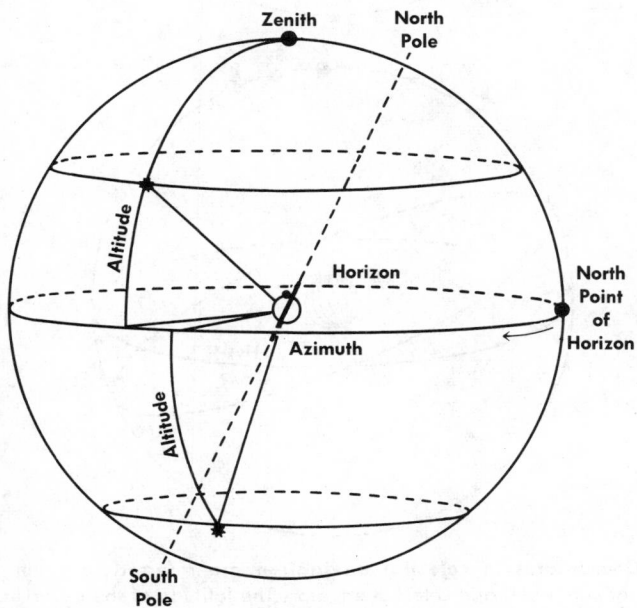

Horizon, or altazimuth, system: The coordinates of a celestial body are altitude, the angular distance above or below the horizon; and azimuth, the angular distance eastward around the horizon from the north point.

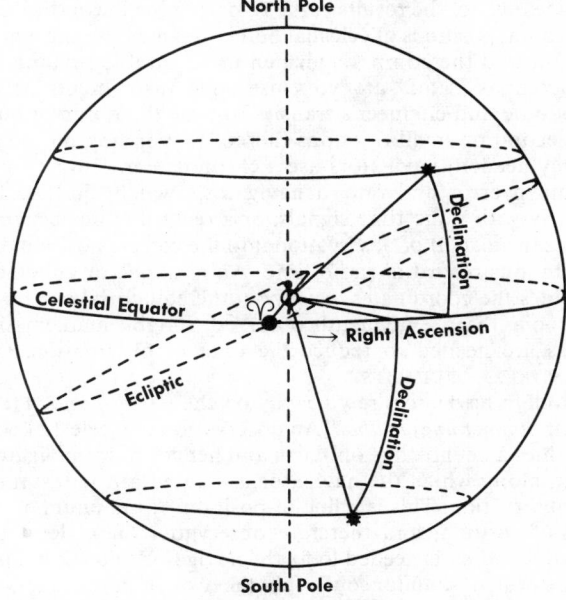

Equatorial system: In this system, the coordinates are declination, the angular distance above or below the celestial equator; and right ascension, the angular distance from the vernal equinox (♈) measured counterclockwise as viewed from the north pole.

or satellite; (2) from comparisons of observed and predicted positions, to improve the theories on which the ephemeris is based. The methods devised by the ancient Greeks culminated in the formulation of the PTOLEMAIC SYSTEM (*c.* A. D. 150), which remained in use until gradually supplanted by the COPERNICAN SYSTEM (1543). The publication of Newton's PRINCIPIA (1687) marked the birth of modern celestial mechanics. The author enunciated his three laws of motion and the law of gravitation; he also proved that KEPLER'S LAWS OF PLANETARY MOTION, which the latter had found empirically, could be derived mathematically from his new theory. In following centuries, Newton's principles were applied to develop the methods which are in use today. Their only fundamental modification has been the introduction of mathematical terms to account for certain effects predicted by the theory of RELATIVITY.

Practical problems in celestial mechanics usually lead to very complex solutions. Only in the case of two bodies revolving around each other and isolated in space, *e.g.* a double star, is the orbit an ellipse for which the equations of motion may be solved by a direct method. In all other cases, the orbit is not a true ellipse, and the gravitational attraction of the other bodies (*e.g.* the effect of the Sun and all planets on the Earth-Moon system) so complicates the equations that approximate solutions must be found. The most powerful means of achieving this goal is the method of PERTURBATIONS, which studies the distortion of the elliptical orbit caused by the other bodies (see also THREE-BODY PROBLEM). Modern electronic computers greatly facilitate the large number of calculations required.—*S. D. G.*

CELESTIAL NAVIGATION: navigation based on observations of celestial bodies. Such observations enable the navigator to determine where he is located and which way he must travel toward his destination: the two basic navigational problems. Celestial navigation is used on land, sea, and in the air, and will undoubtedly be used in space navigation, though somewhat differently. The principles are the same whether practiced by mariners, airmen, or surveyors, although for each the instruments and tables used, the details of solution, and the accuracy of the results vary. To determine the vertical and horizontal positions of celestial bodies, seamen use the marine sextant and the compass, airmen use a bubble sextant and gyrocompass, and surveyors use such instruments as the theodolite and engineer's transit. To time the observation to the second or small fractions thereof (depending on the accuracy needed) navigators use a chronometer or watch with a known error and rate, a navigator's watch checked frequently with radio time signals, or a recording device which places the instant of observation into the correct position on a continuous record of radio time. An almanac or ephemeris provides the coordinates, usually in the equatorial system, of the bodies that are frequently observed. Suitable mathematical tables are needed to reduce the data of observation. (See CELESTIAL COORDINATES.)

Modern navigators rely heavily on the *line-of-position* (also called *Sumner line*) *method*. An observation of a celestial body identifies a definite line on Earth and hence on the navigator's chart, along which the navigator is located at the instant of the observation. This is a line-of-position. A minimum of two lines-of-position, and therefore observation of at least two celestial bodies, is needed to fix the navigator's position. Since he is located simultaneously on the two or more lines, his position is at their intersection. His latitude and longitude are read from the chart.

One way of identifying a line-of-position is the distance-circle method. The navigator observes the ALTITUDE of a celestial body and notes the time of the observation. For that same instant, he obtains the declination and Greenwich hour angle of the observed body from an almanac or ephemeris. These two coordinates on the CELESTIAL SPHERE are measured from the plane of the equator and the meridian of Greenwich, as are the coordinates in the terrestrial system. Therefore the coordinates of the celestial body can be converted into the latitude and longitude of the point on Earth directly beneath the body at the instant of observation. This is the *substellar point* or *ground point* of the celestial body.

Subtracting the altitude of the celestial body from 90° yields the angular distance from the navigator's zenith to the body observed. This *zenith distance* is taken to be the same as that between the observer and the ground point, since the observer is directly beneath his own zenith and the ground point is directly beneath the celestial body. Angular distance along a great circle of Earth is the basis for the linear distance scale used by navigators: $1' = 1$ nautical mi, $1° = 60$ mi, $10° = 600$ mi. Thus, observation of a celestial body establishes the navigator's distance in nautical miles from the ground

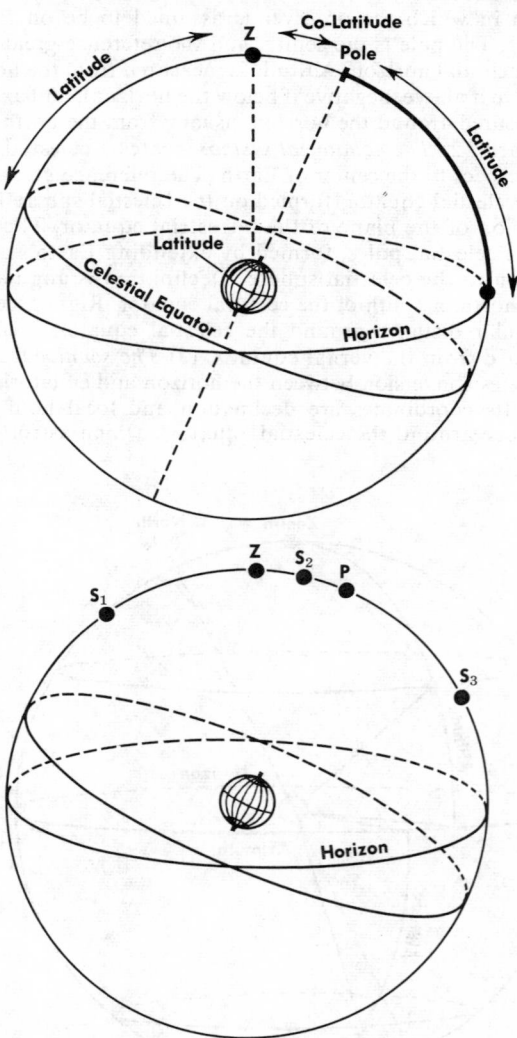

Coordinates in celestial navigation are referred to zenith, horizon, pole, and celestial equator. The latitude of the observer is equal to

declination + zenith distance of a body at S_1,
declination − zenith distance of a body at S_2,
180° − declination − zenith distance of a body at S_3.

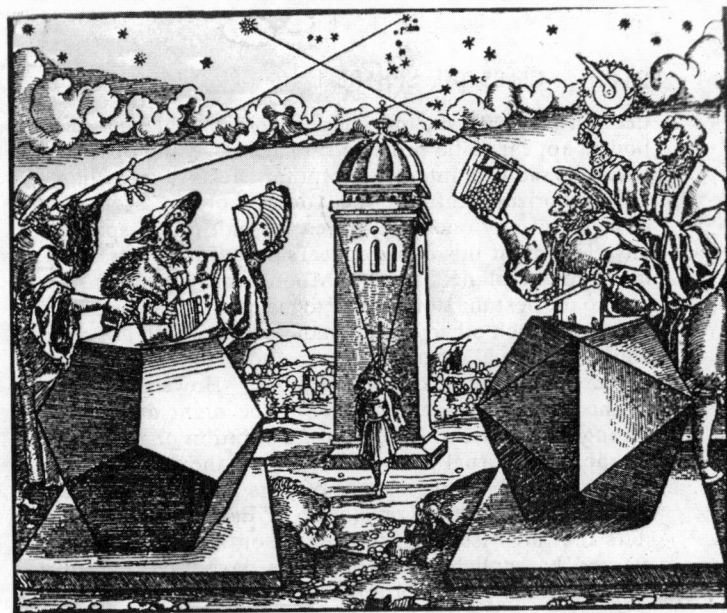

point; he must be located on the circumference of a circle with center at the ground point and radius equal to that distance. This distance circle, drawn on the chart, is the line-of-position on which the navigator was located at the instant of his observation.

This method is practical only if the altitude of the body is high; the zenith distance is then small and so is the radius of the distance circle. For lower-altitude bodies, the circle is too large to plot conveniently on ordinary charts. The procedure then used is the *intercept-azimuth method,* sometimes called the St. Hilaire method after its inventor, Marcq St. Hilaire. The navigator assumes a known position (dead-reckoning) and computes the altitude and azimuth that a celestial body would then have at a particular time. At that time he observes the altitude of the body. The difference in the observed and computed altitudes is called the intercept; with the azimuth, it can be used to identify the portion of the distance circle in the navigator's vicinity. This method is the one most widely used.

In special circumstances, several methods are useful for determining latitude. Latitude is the distance from the equator to the observer, and the distance from the observer to the pole is co-latitude. Since the celestial pole is directly above Earth's pole, the distance from the zenith to the celestial pole equals the co-latitude of the observer, and the altitude of the celestial pole therefore equals the observer's latitude. Any method of measuring the zenith distance or the altitude of the celestial pole readily gives the latitude of the observer. Observation of the pole star, Polaris, when suitably corrected, is one such method. Another is the observation of the two transits, above and below the pole, of the same circumpolar star. The average of the altitudes at the two transits is the altitude of the celestial pole and hence the latitude of the observer.

Another method of determining latitude is based on observation of the altitude of a celestial body at the moment it crosses the celestial meridian. At that time, the sum or difference of the body's declination (distance from the celestial equator) and zenith distance yields the observer's latitude. The zenith distance of the body is obtained by observation, and its declination from the almanac for the moment of transit. The method is widely used by marine navigators who observe the Sun at local apparent noon.

Longitude can be determined from celestial observations by any method which yields the local time, either solar or sidereal, at the meridian of the observer. The so-called *time sight* is such a method. From the observed altitude of a celestial body, the assumed latitude of the station, and the declination of the body given by almanac or ephemeris, several solutions by spherical trigonometry yield the local hour angle of the body observed; this, in turn, gives the local time by the body. The difference between the time at the prime meridian (Greenwich) and the local time so computed is the longitude of the station. The time at Greenwich can be obtained from an accurate clock or chronometer of known error and rate or from precise time signals that are broadcast continuously by various governments.

Another method involves the observation of the exact instant when a star of known right ascension crosses the local meridian. At that instant, the Greenwich sidereal time is computed for the universal time read from a chronometer that is accurately rated from radio time signals. The right ascension of the star in transit is the local sidereal time, and the longitude is simply its difference from the Greenwich sidereal time. Though simple in theory, this requires a very accurate determination of the local meridian, a very precise

pointing instrument, and an extremely stable platform. It is largely restricted to use by astronomical observatories.

The other important problem in navigation readily solved by celestial methods is the determination of the true meridian or the true direction of a given reference line, *e.g.* the north-south axis of a compass or a surveyed base line on land. The problem involves the measurement of the horizontal angular distance from the reference line to a celestial body, and the computation at the same time of the azimuth, or true bearing, of the same celestial body. At a given instant, the true direction of any celestial body can be computed from the equatorial coordinates of the body and the latitude and the longitude of the station from which the body is observed. The difference between the measured direction of the celestial body, from the reference line, and the computed true direction of the body will give the true direction of the reference line, and therefore the direction of the true meridian from the reference line. The accuracy of the method is limited primarily by the accuracy of the instrument used to measure the horizontal angle required. Several simple and rapid solutions are available in special cases, such as with the pole star, where a very simple correction to its observed direction gives the direction of true north, and with the Sun or any other body at the moment of rising or setting, where its true direction can be computed quickly from only its declination and the latitude of the station.

Theoretically, it has always been possible to determine a terrestrial position by simultaneously observing the vertical and horizontal coordinates of a celestial body. In practice, however, and in the absence of a sufficiently stable platform, the horizontal coordinate of the body could not be measured accurately enough. In recent years, devices known as automatic star trackers have been developed. Mounted on platforms accurately stabilized by gyros, these follow a bright celestial body, continuously measuring its zenith distance and true direction. Some trackers are sensitive to infrared radiation, and can track the brightest of celestial bodies—Sun, Moon, and bright planets—even when the sky is cloudy or the tracker is in a submerged submarine. These devices are also useful in high-speed aircraft for which ordinary methods are not sufficiently accurate or rapid. In recent years, the increased use of electronic aids to navigation, *e.g.* Loran, has greatly reduced the dependence of ships and aircraft on celestial navigation.—*T. N.*

CELESTIAL POLE: see CELESTIAL SPHERE.

CELESTIAL SPHERE: the imaginary sphere on which all celestial bodies appear to be projected; its center is the observer, to whom its radius is infinite. Except for effects of refraction and visible horizon features, the "dome" of sky seen by the observer at any one time represents half of the sphere. On any clear night this dome appears dotted with stars, and on many nights planets and the Moon can be seen. From one year to the next the stars appear to maintain the same positions relative to each other; their distances from Earth are so great and their actual angular motions so small that for many purposes they can be considered "fixed." However, the aspect of the sphere changes throughout the night and day, and throughout the year. The eastward rotation of Earth causes an apparent diurnal westward motion of the sphere: Sun and Moon rise and set, the pattern of stars moves across the sky. Because of the annual revolution of Earth around the Sun, stars that are visible on the sphere on a winter's night are masked by sunlight on a summer's day. Projected against these motions of stars are those of Moon, planets, comets, and meteors.

The diurnal motion of the celestial sphere looks different from different parts of Earth. At the north pole, the entire sky seems to rotate slowly about a vertical axis passing through the zenith, counterclockwise once per day. At the south pole, the apparent motion of the sphere takes place in the same manner, but clockwise. At Earth's equator, the celestial sphere appears to turn about an axis that passes through the north and south points, so that all celestial bodies rise vertically from the eastern horizon and set vertically to the western horizon.

At any latitude other than the poles or the equator, the celestial bodies follow diurnal paths that are oblique to the horizon. One or the other of the celestial poles will be above the horizon by a distance equal to the latitude of the position. Celestial bodies close to the pole, at least as close in angular measure as the latitude of the observer, will not rise or set, but will turn slowly around the pole. Such bodies are called *circumpolar.* In other parts of the sky at any of the mid-latitudes, the celestial bodies rise and set at an angle to the horizon which is equal to the co-latitude of the observer (see LATITUDE). The diurnal paths of all bodies are along circles parallel to the celestial equator.

Distances to the stars are so great that the revolution of Earth around the Sun produces no sensible change (*i.e.* to the unaided eye) in their positions relative to one another on the celestial sphere. Certain factors, *e.g.* PRECESSION and the PROPER MOTIONS of the stars themselves, cause the stars to shift on the sphere very slightly, but it requires hundreds and even thousands of years for these slight shifts to become noticeable to the unaided eye. Sun, Moon, and planets, however, are much closer to Earth, and undergo periodic and easily observed changes in their positions on the sphere.

The annual revolution of Earth causes the direction of our line of sight to the Sun to shift eastward, the direction of Earth's revolution, by about 1° per day, or entirely around the sphere in one year. The westward diurnal motion of the Sun, therefore, takes place at a slightly slower rate than that of the stars.

The effect of revolution on the Moon is even more apparent. Since the Moon revolves around Earth once in about 27⅓ days, it appears to shift eastward, the direction of its motion, completely around the sphere in this period. This amounts to a shift of about 13° per day. The rate of the Moon's westward diurnal motion, therefore, is considerably less than that of the stars: it requires on the average nearly 24 hr 50 min to move once around the sky. If the Moon is observed close to a certain bright star, it will be seen to move eastward with respect to that star by one diameter per hour, and can often be seen to cover and uncover a star within an hour.

There is a similar shift in the position of planets, because of their revolution around the Sun and Earth's revolution. Each planet constantly shifts its position on the celestial sphere; the closer it is to the Sun, the more rapid is its revolution and hence the greater is its apparent movement. The shift of the planets on the sphere is generally eastward, except for certain periods when the revolution of the Earth produces an apparent relative motion in a retrograde, or westward, manner.

The concept of the celestial sphere makes it possible to identify the locations of celestial bodies by means of several spherical coordinate systems, and to identify the motions of celestial bodies by changes in their spherical coordinates. Problems related to the relative positions and motions of points or bodies in the sky can then be treated by the methods of spherical trigonometry. The solution of such problems, which also occur in CELESTIAL NAVIGATION, is called spherical astronomy. Spherical astronomy provides a means of relating positions and distances on Earth to positions and angular measurements in the sky. The fundamental methods of measuring latitude and longitude and time on Earth are derived from the trigonometry of the celestial sphere, and hence the term *practical astronomy* is often used for this branch of the science. See CELESTIAL COORDINATES; TIME.— *T. N.*

CELL: in biology, the smallest unit of living matter capable of assimilation, respiration, growth, and reproduction. Many cells, *e.g.* protozoans, various simple algae, and bacteria, are individuals able to live independently and to reproduce their own kind. Others associate in colonies or well-organized multicellular plants or animals in which there is obvious division of labor among the many cells. Ordinarily each cell consists of a single nucleus, which contains chromosomes (see CHROMOSOMES AND GENES), and a surrounding layer of CYTOPLASM, in which most of the living activities take place. Exceptions are mature red blood cells of mammals, which lack a nucleus, and cells of bacteria and blue-green algae, in which the one or two chromosomes may be as much as 900 times as long as the cell, and are folded back and forth, occupying most of the space inside the cell wall. Also, in some kinds of life (*e.g.* the alga-like fungi) and in certain tissues (*e.g.* skeletal muscle cells) each cell contains several nuclei and is said to be multinucleate. If this condition arises due to the fusing together of several cells, as in the villi of the mammalian placenta, the tissue is known as a *syncytium.* Mature plant cells usually contain a large and conspicuous vacuole of cell sap and are surrounded by a nonliving wall of secreted cellulose. Both plant and animal cells commonly contain small vacuoles, fat droplets, starch or glycogen granules, and minute grains of pigment in the cytoplasm.

With an electron microscope, many minute structural features can be seen in the cytoplasm. Known collectively as *organelles,* these include: mitochondria (singular, mitochondrion), in which the aerobic steps of cellular respiration take place, producing adenosine triphosphate (ATP; see CITRIC-ACID CYCLE); ribosomes in small clusters, each a center for synthesis of proteins; lysosomes, in which the protein-splitting and fat-splitting enzymes are segregated, protecting the cell from digesting itself; and endoplasmic reticulum, as a complex series of folded membranes where enzymes are concentrated and much of the cytoplasmic chemical activity goes on. The endoplasmic reticulum appears to be connected to the plasma membrane that surrounds the cell and forms its outer living boundary, and also to the double nuclear membrane which envelops the nucleus. Secretory cells usually contain a Golgi

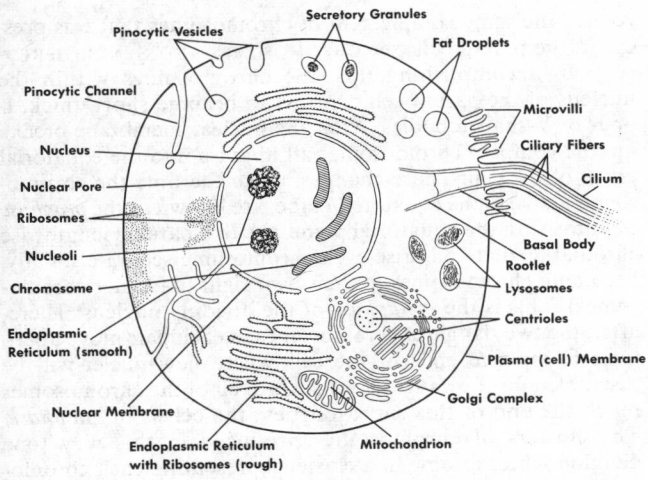

Pinocytic Vesicles
Secretory Granules
Fat Droplets
Pinocytic Channel
Microvilli
Nucleus
Ciliary Fibers
Nuclear Pore
Cilium
Ribosomes
Nucleoli
Basal Body
Chromosome
Rootlet
Lysosomes
Endoplasmic
Reticulum (smooth)
Centrioles
Plasma (cell) Membrane
Nuclear Membrane
Golgi Complex
Endoplasmic Reticulum
with Ribosomes (rough)
Mitochondrion

Composite cell shows structures from different types of cells. Every cell has some, not all, these structures. *(After Moment)*

apparatus as a specialized part of the endoplasmic reticulum; granules of secreted material can often be seen close to the Golgi apparatus. Other cell structures (see diagram) may include one or more nucleoli, which store RNA (see NUCLEIC ACIDS); nuclear pores, or minute openings in the nuclear membrane; centrioles, which are active during cell division; microvilli, fingerlike extensions of the cell surface; pinocytic vesicles and channels, which take in minute droplets of fluid; and hairlike structures called CILIA.

The evolution of plants and animals has come about only because cells were able to assume an enormous variety of forms and functions. Plant cells are modified in many ways. Some form leaves, which absorb energy; others form roots, which absorb solutions of salts; still others become pipes in the stem and bring all the food elements together. The success of the entire process depends largely upon the cells' walls of cellulose, which stiffen the whole organism so that leaves may rise into the sunlight and roots may dig deep into the soil.

Animal cells, which must hunt for their food, developed motility and, with it, methods of defense and offense. In organisms such as Hydra the cells for offense, defense, and movement became grouped on the outside, while those for eating captured prey were grouped inside. From this simple beginning came the complex structures of the modern mammal in which each of four or five thousand kinds of cells does its part in maintaining life in the whole animal. The word "cell" was first used by Robert Hooke who, in 1665, compared the little holes he saw in cork to the rooms in which monks lived.

For measuring the features of cells visible through the compound microscope, a special unit of length was established: the micron, which is 1/1000 mm. Human red blood cells, for example, are about 7 micra in diameter (about 3/10,000 in.). But nerve cells, which have long axons as a part of their structure, may be as much as 3 ft long. Details too small to see with the compound microscope are studied with the electron microscope, and their sizes given in millimicra (each 1/1000 micron or 1/1,000,000 mm) or in angstrom units (each 1/10,000 micron). See CYTOLOGY; CELL DIVISION; ANIMAL-PLANT DIFFERENCES; and Color Plate 19.—*L. and M. M.; A. P. E.*

CELL, ELECTROLYTIC: an apparatus or system in which chemical reactions are made to take place by passing an electric current through a liquid containing the reactants. It may be regarded in a sense as the opposite of a voltaic or galvanic cell, whose purpose is to generate electricity from suitably

controlled chemical reactions (see CELL, VOLTAIC). An electrolytic cell generally consists of a container for the liquid fitted with two electrodes connected to an outside source of direct current, and with means for collecting the reaction products. Materials used in constructing the container and electrodes vary widely, depending on the electrolytic reaction for which the cell is intended. The liquid, called the *electrolyte,* is usually an aqueous solution, although many important industrial materials are made by the electrolysis of fused salts at high temperatures. Electrolytic reactions are all of the oxidation-reduction type, oxidation (a loss of electrons) taking place at the anode or positive electrode, and reduction (a gain of electrons) at the cathode or negative electrode. To prevent the products from mixing, cells are sometimes compartmented by finely porous diaphragms that allow passage of the current-carrying ions but prevent gross convection of liquid. Most practical electrolytic reactions have a high current efficiency, *i.e.* the quantity of material converted per coulomb of electricity passed is close to the theoretical conversion expected on the basis of Faraday's law (see ELECTROCHEMISTRY).

Electrolytic reactions can be grouped broadly into two classes: those in which an electrode itself is a reactant or reaction product, *i.e.* is either consumed or augmented during electrolysis; and those in which the electrodes are inert, acting merely to transfer electrons to or from the electrolyte. The refining of copper is an example of the former. Copper is dissolved from an impure copper anode and deposited in pure form on the cathode. The preparation of caustic soda and chlorine by electrolysis of sodium chloride brine is an example of a process in which the electrodes are inert. Other important materials produced by electrolysis are hydrogen peroxide, fluorine, and a variety of organic chemicals. Electrolysis is most widely used in metallurgy. Copper, chromium, tin, nickel, zinc, gold, and silver are extracted, refined, and plated by electrolysis from aqueous solutions of their salts. Aluminum, magnesium, sodium are among the metals made by electrolyzing their fused salts.—*A. M. S.*

CELL, VOLTAIC: a device for transforming chemical energy into electrical energy. It is commonly called a BATTERY, but strictly speaking a battery is a group of cells connected electrically to act as a unit. Cells are of two basic types: the *primary cell,* which is usually irreversible in action and must be discarded after its elements have been consumed (*e.g.* flashlight dry cell), and the *secondary* or *storage cell,* which may be recharged a number of times from an external d-c source (*e.g.* automobile "battery"). Both types depend on the processes of OXIDATION AND REDUCTION for their energy-converting action.

In the simple single-fluid voltaic cell (named after Alessandro Volta, who first described it in 1800), two dissimilar metal strips (called electrodes), one of zinc and the other of copper, are immersed in an electrolyte consisting of a dilute solution of sulfuric acid. The action of the cell is shown schematically in the figure. The sulfuric acid dissociates, forming hydrogen and sulfate ions. Some of the zinc plate dissolves, delivering positively charged zinc ions (Zn^{++}) to the solution. Electrons are left behind and give the plate a negative charge. An ELECTRIC POTENTIAL of -0.76 v is thus established between the zinc plate and the solution. At the other electrode, hydrogen ions (H^+) in the solution deposit on the copper plate, and an electric potential of $+0.34$ v is established between the copper plate and the solution. If the two electrodes are now joined by a conducting wire, the excess electrons accumulated on the zinc plate are transferred to the copper plate, constituting a discharge current. A net electromotive force of $0.34 - (-0.76)$, or 1.10 v, is established

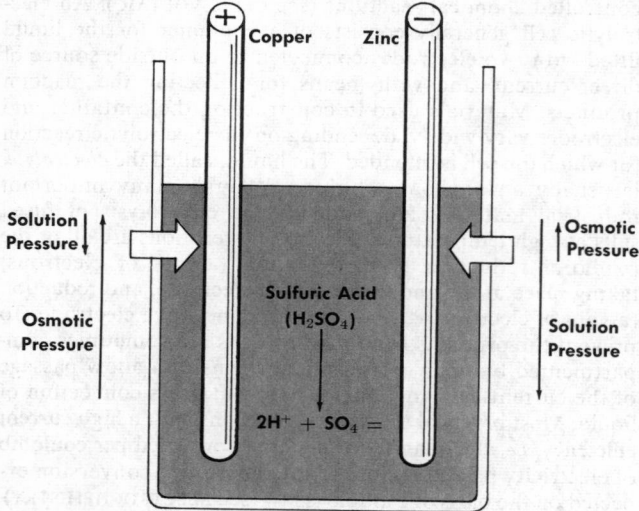

In voltaic cell, difference between osmotic pressure and solution pressures causes zinc to dissolve, leaving the electrode negatively charged, and causes hydrogen ions to be attracted to the copper electrode, leaving this positively charged.

across the terminals. A process of chemical oxidation takes place at the zinc plate, where neutral Zn^0 atoms lose electrons to become Zn^{++} ions, and a process of reduction takes place at the copper plate, where H^+ ions from the solution gain electrons to become H^0 atoms. The cell continues to function until the zinc plate is dissolved or until the electrolyte becomes too diluted with dissolved zinc. See ELECTROCHEMISTRY; ELECTROLYSIS.—A. E.

CELL DIVISION: the division of a living CELL into two or more daughter cells, which contain the same material that the parent cell did. Usually the daughter cells receive approximately equal amounts of cytoplasm. An unequal cell division occurs in yeasts; one daughter cell is so much smaller than the other that it is regarded as a "bud" from the parent cell; this particular asymmetrical cell division is called *budding*. Unequal distribution of cytoplasm is characteristic also during the two successive divisions in formation of an animal egg cell; almost all the cytoplasm goes to the daughter cell that will become the egg; the other daughter cell becomes a polar body, which dies or is absorbed. Animal cells complete the division process by a constriction of the flexible cell membrane, whereas plant cells ordinarily secrete a new transverse sheet of pectic material, upon which they lay down cellulose cell wall; the pectic material remains as an intercellular bonding substance between the daughter cells, each of which then is completely enclosed in its own cell wall.

Ordinarily, before a cell divides, its nucleus divides into two identical daughter nuclei by the process of *mitosis,* and only two cells are produced, each with one daughter nucleus. But some plant cells and animal cells undergo repeated mitotic division of the nucleus before the cell divides, and then apportion the cytoplasm of the multinucleated cell by multiple cell division. In this way, a large number of daughter cells are produced at once. Two successive cell divisions of a different sort occur during the formation of spores by plants that have ALTERNATION OF GENERATIONS, and also during the formation of gametes by animals. These two divisions follow the special process of nuclear division known as MEIOSIS; each parent cell gives rise to four daughter cells (spores or gametes).

The essential feature of mitosis is that the daughter cells receive the same complement of chromosomes that was present in the parent cell (see CHROMOSOMES AND GENES; HEREDITY). In accomplishing this, the chromosomes within the nucleus of the parent cell contract to become short, thick, I- or J- or V-shaped bodies. After the nuclear membrane breaks up, the compact chromosomes all migrate into the equatorial plane of the cell. These changes, up to the time the chromosomes arrive in the equatorial plane, are known as the *prophase* of mitosis. In the equatorial plane, the two parallel lengthwise chromatids that comprise each chromosome separate slightly, becoming chromosomes in their own right (daughter chromosomes). This is the *metaphase* of the dividing nucleus. Thereafter, the two daughter chromosomes in each pair move apart, toward opposite ends of the cell, where new nuclei will be assembled for the daughter cells. Until all of the chromosomes reach the end of this short journey, the cell is in *anaphase.* The clusters of chromosomes produced in this way (one daughter chromosome in a cluster representing each chromosome of the parent cell) become surrounded by nuclear membranes. Within these, the chromosomes elongate and expand, ready once more to function in controlling the normal chemical activities within the cell. After the period during which the daughter nuclei become organized (the *telophase*), the daughter cells usually separate and each cell is in the *interphase* condition.

During late prophase, when the nuclear membrane breaks up, as much as 10% of the cytoplasmic proteins in the parent cell may become organized into a special *division apparatus* in the form of a 3-dimensional *spindle*. The equator of the spindle lies in the plane where the chromosomes align themselves during metaphase. The poles of the spindle are located in the regions to which the daughter chromosomes move during anaphase. Radiating fibers around the poles of the spindle form a pattern known as an *aster.* In animal cells, the center of each aster is usually occupied by a *centriole,* which is a small cluster of short rods. Unlike the division apparatus and

Stages of mitosis, the usual process by which a cell divides in two. Before the division, each chromosome duplicates itself.

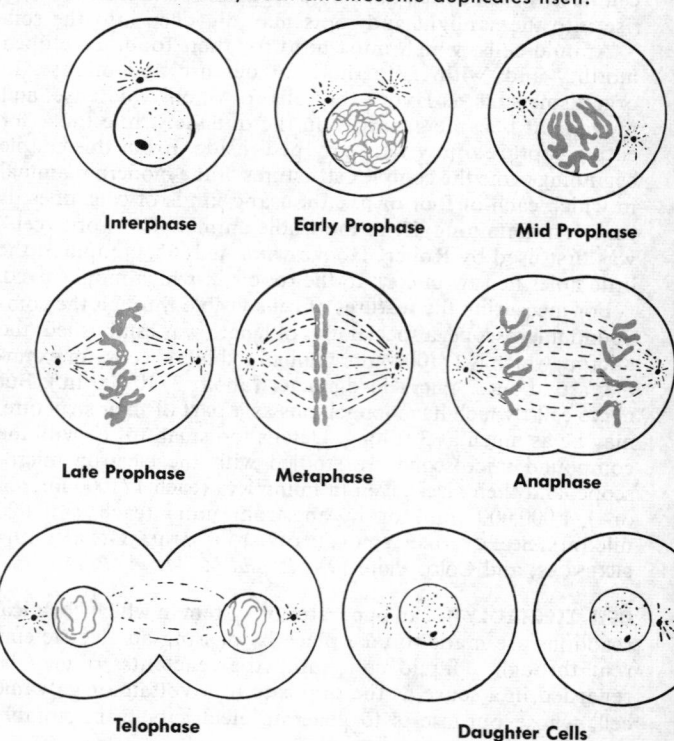

Interphase   Early Prophase   Mid Prophase

Late Prophase   Metaphase   Anaphase

Telophase   Daughter Cells

asters, which disappear in telophase, the centriole is a permanent part of the animal cell. Often the centriole duplicates itself late in telophase and shows that the plane of the next cell division is already established. In early prophase, the daughter centrioles separate, each moving a quarter of the way around the nuclear membranes to the pole positions of the spindle that is about to form.

Occasionally, the mitotic or meiotic division of chromosomal material is obviously unequal, providing one daughter cell with one or more extra chromosomes and the other with a correspondingly deficient complement. This abnormality (*non-disjunction*) gives rise to genetic differences between parts of the same organism or to new genetic races such as polyploids. Probably most cell divisions are qualitatively unequal to some extent in the distribution of nuclear and cytoplasmic materials to the daughter cells.

Cell division is most rapid in areas adjacent to a wound in an animal (where regeneration is in progress), in persistent meristems (growth areas) of plants, and during early stages of embryonic development. Ordinarily cell division ceases when regeneration is completed. It may cease altogether long before an embryonic tissue reaches full size or functional maturity, as happens in the brain cells of vertebrate animals. Further growth then depends entirely upon enlargement of cells already present. In the tissue from which blood cells arise, however, mitotic cell division occurs throughout the life of the individual animal.—*L. and M. M.*

CELLOPHANE: a transparent film of regenerated cellulose used in packaging. It is made from a cellulose solution by extrusion through a slit, and is usually coated with a supplementary layer to make it moisture-resistant. In many countries it is a trade-mark name, though no longer in the U. S. A.—*Ru. M.*

CELLULASES: see ENZYME.

CELLULOSE: a chain polymer of anhydroglucose, and the chief constituent of all plant wall tissue. Its chemical composition (basically the same as starch) is given by the formula $(C_6H_{10}O_5)_n$, where *n* stands for the number of anhydroglucose rings in the chain. Structure of the anhydroglucose ring can be represented thus:

$$
\left[
\begin{array}{c}
\text{H} \quad \text{OH} \qquad \text{CH}_2\text{OH} \\
\text{OH} \quad \text{H} \qquad \text{H} \quad \text{H} \qquad \text{O} \\
\text{O} \qquad \text{OH} \\
\text{H} \quad \text{H} \qquad \text{H} \\
\text{CH}_2\text{OH} \qquad \text{H} \quad \text{OH}
\end{array}
\right]_{n/2}
$$

The number of anhydroglucose units in a cellulose molecule varies widely, depending on the source, ranging from a high of 5,000 for native cotton to a few hundred for some regenerated fibers and films; also the arrangement of cellulose molecules within a given specimen of material varies widely. In many cellulosic materials the molecular arrangement is of such order that the atoms refract x-rays in the same manner as the atoms of the regularly spaced three-dimensional lattices of crystalline substances; thus cotton is said to be over 80% crystalline. However, the molecules in regenerated cellulosic fibers exhibit much less lateral order and are said to contain relatively more amorphous material. The mechanical properties of cellulosic materials depend largely on the degree of lateral order of the component molecules, highly crystalline materials being generally stronger but less flexible. The size,

distribution, and orientation of the crystallites, as well as other factors, also affect the mechanical properties of cellulose. Cellulose is insoluble in water and in organic solvents but soluble in cupric ammonium (Schweitzer's reagent). Acids hydrolyze it, yielding simple sugars.

Natural cellulosic fibers, *e.g.* cotton and linen, are widely used in textiles. Cellulose from wood, straw, grasses, cotton rags, and linters is used for making paper. Regenerated and chemically modified cellulose is used for making fibers, films, plastics, adhesives, explosives, protective coatings, and thickening agents.

Wood is the most important commercial source of cellulose. It contains 50% or more of noncellulosic materials, *e.g.* lignin, which are removed by the sulfite process (calcium or sodium bisulfite and sulfur dioxide), soda process (sodium hydroxide), or sulfate or Kraft (sodium hydroxide and sodium sulfide) process. The purest natural source is cotton.—*W. P. C.*

CELSIUS, ANDERS, 1701–44, Swedish astronomer; b. Uppsala. He is best known for suggesting in his paper *"Observationer om tvenne beständiga grader på en Thermometer"* (1742) a thermometric scale with 100 as the freezing point of water and 0 the boiling point. This suggestion of a 100° division was incorporated into the centigrade scale, although the order was inverted so that the boiling point was 100°. This centigrade scale has been renamed the *Celsius scale* in his honor. Celsius

Anders Celsius
(U. S. Navy)

studied the aurora borealis, supervised the building of the Uppsala Observatory (1740), and became its first director. He was professor at the Univ. of Uppsala from 1730. He was a fellow of the Royal Society.—*D. H. D. R.*

CELSIUS SCALE: a TEMPERATURE SCALE, more popularly called the *Centigrade scale,* universally used in scientific work and used for non-scientific purposes in Europe (except for the United Kingdom, Germany, and Scandinavia). On the Celsius scale the freezing point of water is designated as 0°C, boiling point 100°C, and absolute zero −273°C.—*E. M. R.*

CEMENT: any material, ranging from adhesive clay to bituminous asphalt, that causes adhesion between two surfaces or that combines particles into a solid whole. However, "cement" usually means portland cement, a pre-burned mixture of powdered limestone and clay which, after the addition of water, achieves a rock-like hardness. (For other cements, see ADHESIVES.) Portland cement is one of today's foremost BUILDING MATERIALS. Mixed with sand, it is used as mortar; when mixed with sand and gravel it is used as CONCRETE. The manufacture of cement consists of bringing together limestone and clay or shale, powdering them, mixing them intimately (usually by introducing water to produce a creamy slurry), and then burning them in a rotary kiln until clinkers are formed: the powdered clinker is portland cement. How cement hardens when water is added has been a controversial question since mid-18th cent. The four major components of cement are: (1) $4CaO \cdot Al_2O_3 \cdot Fe_2O_3$ (10%), (2) $3CaO \cdot Al_2O_3$ (7%), (3) $3CaO \cdot SiO_2$ (42%), and (4) $2CaO \cdot SiO_2$ (34%). It is believed that each of these compounds, when water is added, becomes crystals and that these crystals interlock to form the hardened cement. Chemists now propose there are other compounds in colloidal form which contribute to the hardening process. Many cements are made—*e.g.* high early-strength cement—which fulfill special requirements of the engineer and builder.—*A. L.*

CEMENTATION: the process whereby grains of minerals in rocks become bonded together by deposition of interstitial mineral matter (the cement). The term is usually applied to the cementing action by which unconsolidated sediments are converted to more indurated sedimentary rocks (see LITHIFICATION). Common cements include quartz, carbonates, and iron oxides.—*C. C.*

CENOZOIC ERA: the grand division of geologic time that follows the Mesozoic Era and extends to the present, spanning some 70 million yr. (For the subdivisions of the Cenozoic, see GEOLOGICAL TIME CHART.) The Cenozoic (from Gr.: ceno-, "recent," and -zoic, "life") is the period of Earth history which saw the development of the life forms that are dominant today, as well as the physical events—mountain building, subsidence and uplift, volcanic activity, and sculpturing by erosion—that have produced our modern landscapes. The mammals, which had made small beginnings in the preceding era, the Mesozoic (Age of Reptiles), proliferated during the Cenozoic, and some evolved into the modern types, including man; hence the Cenozoic is known as the Age of Mammals. Birds and insects also were abundant and varied. Simultaneously there occurred the further development of the flowering plants, including many modern genera of trees which had first appeared in the Mesozoic, and rich varieties of grasses not known before the Cenozoic. Throughout the era, marine life closely resembled that of the present (see LIFE, PREHISTORIC). The Cenozoic for most of its course has had milder climates than those of today, but in its latter phases a trend to colder climates culminated in the GLACIAL AGES (Pleistocene Epoch) which, incidentally, saw the rise of the human species, and which may not yet be concluded.

The opening of the Cenozoic Era found N America much as it is today in size and general outlines. The Appalachian landscape gradually assumed its present form after a complex and little-understood history of uplift and erosion in the Mesozoic. Some features indicate that extensive plains were cut across the folded rocks; others suggest that the present topography is representative of the entire era and that it evolved as the eastward-flowing streams ate headward into the divide between Atlantic and Gulf drainage. The eastern and southern borders of the continent were tilted down beneath the Atlantic and Gulf of Mexico and accumulated extensive deposits of sand, mud, and limestone, now partly exposed on the coastal plains. Florida emerged at times as a low island but was frequently entirely submerged. Two troughs, one along the Atlantic shelf, the other off the Texas-Louisiana coast, received great thicknesses of sediment and are apparently growing geosynclines. A long embayment which extended into the interior lowlands from the Gulf to Cairo, Ill., was filled gradually by sediment brought by the Mississippi and other streams. The Mississippi then swept enormous loads of sediment out into the Gulf to form a series of great deltas, of which the present is only the latest. Further west, the Rocky Mts, formed during the latter portion of the Mesozoic and the beginning of the Cenozoic, rose intermittently. Erosion carved away the softer rock to develop mountain forms, and, at times, cut steeply sloping, rock-floored plains (pediments) across large portions of the ranges. In the early Cenozoic, erosional debris from the mountains was deposited in basins between the ranges; later it was spread east-ward onto the Great Plains. These sediments contain an abundance of terrestrial fossils and provide a unique record of mammalian evolution.

Between the Sierra Nevada and the Middle Rockies, the modern Basin and Range Province was uplifted, with much faulting, and became desert as the mountains to the west (the Coast Range and the great fault block of the Sierra) rose up and cast their rain shadows eastward. The uplift of the Colorado Plateau during the late Cenozoic rejuvenated its rivers and produced the approximate drainage pattern—including the Grand Canyon—that is visible today. In the Northwest a long period of disturbance raised the Cascade Mts, and the Columbia Plateau, including areas of five states, was built up by outpourings of lava that occurred intermittently during the Cenozoic, reaching a climax in the Miocene. The Andes of South America had a history like that of the Rockies. In Europe the Alps, having originated in crustal folding of a great Mesozoic geosyncline, climaxed their complex growth late in the Cenozoic, and in the Pleistocene were, like the Rockies, deeply sculptured and much reduced by glacial action. The Himalayas were folded at the eastern end of the same geosyncline; they are still actively building today, and in the south have risen perhaps a mile in the geologically short span of a half million years. Cenozoic crustal disturbances resulted in the great system of rift valleys which extends from the Near East down through E Africa, and produced intense volcanic activity in Mexico and Central America, the Andes, the W Indies, the N Atlantic (Iceland, Scotland, Ireland) and the chain of Pacific islands known as the "Ring of Fire" (Aleutian Is, Japan, E Indies). This last area as well as portions of the W Indies contains troughs between the island ridges and apparently includes geosynclinal belts like the Appalachian system in the Paleozoic and the Alps in the Mesozoic. In contrast, Australia and S Africa have been stable throughout the era and have a history of very gradual uplift and erosion.

Forests predominated in the opening division of the Cenozoic: the Paleocene. Most mammals were small, short-legged, and small-brained. The herbivores had low, blunt molars fitted for succulent vegetation. The carnivores evolved cutting teeth but lacked agility and the intelligence of later forms. Arboreal forms, including primitive primates, abounded. Modern types evolved gradually—tiny horses and rhinos with four toes on each front foot and with simple teeth; rodents of squirrel-like form; rabbits; bats; small artiodactyls (even-toed hoofed animals); ancestors of the elephants; and, in the seas, archaic whales. These appeared during the Eocene Epoch, 55 to 35 million yr ago, and some of the early types became extinct. In the Oligocene Epoch nearly all the mammals belonged to recent orders, though most were smaller and more primitive in structure than their living relatives. Among the newcomers were cats, saber-tooth cats, and dogs, monkeys, and apes among the primates. Horses the size of collies, running rhinos, early camels, and extinct, rather sheep-like oreodonts, as well as giant pigs and various rodents, were common.

As the continents rose during the most recent phase of mountain building, in the Miocene and Pliocene epochs, the climate became cooler and drier over much of the earth. Wide areas became grassland, and the forests shrank. Some mammal groups remained in these refuges; others—the horses, the dogs and cats, rodents, rabbits, and camels and other artiodactyls—evolved types adapted to the new environment. The herbivores evolved high-crowned teeth with multiple grinding crests useful for crushing grass. The open environment placed a premium on speed, and horses, camels, and antelopes lost excess toes and developed long, slender legs. Elephants and rhinos found protection in size and with their tusks or horns.

Rodents took to burrows or to hopping habits. This phase of mammalian evolution was climaxed about 10 million yr ago (Pliocene Epoch), when mammals like those of the modern African veldt inhabited most of the continents. Marsupial mammals in Australia and primitive placentals in S America, isolated by seas, had evolved comparable adaptive types.

Climatic changes of the last million years (GLACIAL AGES) and man, fossil and modern, have contributed to the destruction of many mammals, particularly the larger ones. The human lineage itself diverged from the apes in the Miocene over 20 million yr ago. Miocene apes had shorter arms and longer legs than modern apes; by the glacial (Pleistocene) epoch the human lineage had evolved an upright, biped gait and apparently some social organization, along with tool-making and hunting techniques. Their brains, however, were still of ape size, and their jaws and teeth massive. Improved tools, the use of fire, larger brains, smaller jaws, and less massive skulls developed in the last 200,000 to 500,000 yr. Our own species appeared about 50,000 yr ago.

A million or more years ago, extensive icecaps developed on the northern continents and Antarctica, and Alpine glaciers appeared in high mountains even on the equator. As the ice advanced from the centers of accumulation, it stripped away the soil, removed parts of the bedrock, and then deposited this material along its margins, so that today much of central Europe and N America is veneered by glacial debris. Study of this debris indicates that there were four major ice advances, separated by relatively warm intervals. As water was frozen into ice on the continents, the oceans shrank, and sea level fluctuated perhaps as much as 450 ft between the glacial and interglacial stages. The portion of the Cenozoic Era in which we live today is notable as a time of comparatively cool (perhaps interglacial) climate, unusually active mountain building, widespread volcanism, high relief on the continental land masses, and rugged topography.—*J. B.*

CENTER OF GRAVITY AND MASS: The center of gravity of a body is that point of the body where its weight can be conceived as being concentrated regardless of the position of the body; the center of mass is the point where (for many purposes) its mass can similarly be regarded as concentrated. In a uniform gravitational field, these centers are at the same point. Archimedes (3rd cent. B. C.) defined center of gravity as that point where the body will balance no matter what its position, and this leads to an excellent method for locating the center of gravity or mass of simple objects. For instance, the center of gravity of a circle cut out of paper would be the center of the circle. When calculating the forces acting on a body, or the external effect of a body, the assumption of a center of gravity can simplify the problem considerably. The design of any mechanism, from the simplest pendulum to the largest drop-forge hammer, necessitates the location of the center of gravity of each part. And the determination of the center of gravity of bodies of irregular dimensions and variable densities calls on many of the talents of the mathematician and engineer.

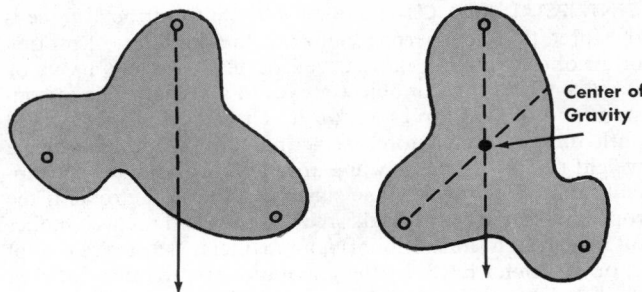

The center of gravity of an irregular object may be determined by suspending it from two different points and finding the intersection of the vertical lines dropped from these points.

For a system of two or more bodies, the center of mass is the point that moves as if the total mass of the system and all external forces were concentrated at that point. For example, the Earth-Moon system moves around the Sun as if the total mass of Earth and Moon were concentrated at one point, with the Sun's gravitational field acting solely at that point.—*A. L.*

CENTER OF MASS COORDINATES: a COORDINATE SYSTEM used by physicists in describing the motion of a collection of particles. The locations of all particles are specified by their distances from the center of mass of the collection. Certain simplifications in mathematics result from the use of this system.—*S. K.*

CENTIGRADE SCALE: now officially called the CELSIUS SCALE.

CENTRIFUGE: a spinning apparatus used to separate solids from liquids or, less commonly, to separate immiscible liquids. The principle is the same as that of FILTERS, except that the force acting upon the liquid instead of being restricted to gravity (or pressure) is increased enormously by centrifugal action, according to the equation $F = Wu^2/gr$, where F is the force developed (in lb), W the weight of the assembly, including load (in lb), u the peripheral velocity of the basket (in ft/sec), r the radius of the basket (in ft), and g the acceleration due to gravity (32.2 ft/sec^2). The centrifugal force is inversely proportional to the radius of the basket but directly proportional to the peripheral velocity squared. Thus, doubling the peripheral velocity (by doubling the drive speed in revolutions per minute) increases the force fourfold. On the other hand, if the radius is reduced by half while the peripheral velocity is maintained (which requires doubling of the drive speed in rev/min), the force is doubled. The simplest form of centrifuge is a vertical, rotating, perforated bowl or basket. It can be used to separate relatively fine particles from a liquid, to separate bulky articles as in the "spin-dry" of an agitator washing machine. There are numerous variations of the centrifuge. They are commonly classified by type of bowl (solid or perforated), and by operation (continuous or batch). See FILTRATION, CHEMICAL.—*D. P. B.*

In a tumbling wrench, thrown from left to right, center of gravity (indicated by black cross) describes parabolic arc. Arc made by crosses can be seen rising slightly above dashed white line, which is straight. (*Berenice Abbott*)

CENTRIPETAL AND CENTRIFUGAL FORCE: Centripetal force is the force that acts perpendicular to the direction of motion of an object moving in a curved path. NEWTON'S LAWS OF MOTION tell us that an object moves in a straight line at constant speed if no forces act on it. Thus motion in a curved path implies that a force *is* acting. For example, when a weight tied to a rope is swung around in a circle, the centripetal force is provided by the elastic tension in the rope. If the rope breaks, the centripetal force vanishes and the weight flies off in a straight line. Similarly, an artificial SATELLITE is kept in orbit around Earth by the gravitational attraction between the two; also, the centripetal force that keeps each electron in its orbit about the nucleus of an atom is the force of attraction between the opposite electrical charges of the electron and the nucleus (see ATOM).

The assertion that a force-free body moves in a straight line presupposes that the motion is not being observed in a rotating frame of reference. For example, when a person is in a car rounding a curve, it appears to him that all the loose contents of the car are being propelled outward by some kind of force; whereas to an observer outside the car they are merely continuing in a straight line in accordance with the laws of mechanics. The nonexistent outward "force," which seems to be needed to explain what is seen by an observer in a rotating frame of reference, is called centrifugal force. It is sometimes said that a satellite in orbit does not fall to earth because the pull of gravity is balanced by centrifugal force. Actually, the satellite tends to move in a straight line, but its path is bent by gravitational attraction. The concept of centrifugal force may be useful in problem-solving, but it must be remembered that there is no force involved.—*S. K.*

CERAMICS: an applied science dealing with the preparation and application of a diversified number of inorganic chemicals, usually earthy compounds themselves called *ceramics.* Until recently, ceramic materials were primarily silicate-bearing compounds, but now include oxides, graphite, carbides, borides, silicides, nitrides, and systems compounded of these groups. Typical ceramic products are pottery, whitewares, porcelain, enamels, refractories, glass, insulators, cement, bricks and fired building materials, and abrasives. For many centuries ceramic (Gr. *keramos,* "burnt stuff") referred to potter's clay or to pottery produced by the action of fire upon earthy materials such as clay. Clay is still the basis of most commercial ceramic products, despite recent developments of new types of ceramic materials. Fired clay products, such as pottery, are associated with the earliest days of man,

Special ceramic materials have been developed for extreme conditions to which nose cones are subjected. Here a technician is fitting a ceramic nose cone with metal band required for use of the cone on a missile. (*General Dynamics*)

and probably were first made soon after the discovery of fire. The use of ceramics predates that of metals, and the oldest relics of prehistoric ages contain fragments of crude ceramics (see PRIMITIVE TECHNOLOGY).

Ceramic products are usually man-made, although a number of ceramic products exist in a natural state, *e.g.* diamonds, graphite, mica, marble, and lava. Ceramic products can be classified by method of preparation into two groups: sintered and fused. For *sintered ceramics,* the starting materials are reduced to powder or granular form and are pressed or molded to a desired shape. The "green" body is then fired (or sintered) at high temperatures. *Fused ceramics, e.g.* glasses, glazes, and enamels, are produced by melting and do not require any pre-molding operation.

For sintered products, the initial powder is prepared from raw ceramic material by crushing, pulverizing, ball-milling, or other methods of comminution. The powder is sized (classified into particle sizes) by screening it through wire-mesh screens, then shaped into the desired forms by pressing it in dies, extrusion, molding, or slip-casting. The latter process is widely used in ceramic art as well as commercially. The casting slip is a suspension of ceramic materials in water, thin enough for pouring; deflocculants may be added to make the ceramic powder stay in suspension. The slip is poured into a dry plaster-of-Paris mold which absorbs water, leaving a finished shape. This "green" body has little mechanical strength, and must be dried carefully and baked or fired at high temperatures in kilns or furnaces. In ceramic art, kiln temperatures are measured through the use of "cones" which have characteristic sagging or softening temperatures.

Unlike most ceramic materials, which are crystalline (*i.e.* their atoms are arranged in definite geometrical patterns), *glasses* and other fused ceramics are amorphous in nature (their atoms are in disordered and haphazard arrangements, as in liquids). In fact, glass is considered an under-cooled liquid. However, by appropriate heat treatments, glass can be devitrified and a crystalline structure produced. Glass is formed while in the molten and viscous state, and glass products are made by pressing, blowing, drawing, and spinning. A *glaze* is a continuous adherent layer of glass or glassy material on the surface of a ceramic body. The glaze is usually applied as a suspension on the surface of a piece. During firing, the ingredients react or melt to form a thin glassy layer.

Silica (SiO_2) is the main ingredient of most ceramic products; its most common form is quartz. Kaolin or clay minerals are compounds of silica and other metal oxides, particularly aluminum and magnesium, and are used in pottery and whiteware manufacture. Mica minerals also consist of complex silicates in a layer-type structure, so that the material is easily split into sheets. Mica is used as an insulator in electrical and electronic equipment.

An extensive technology is now developing around the newer ceramics. Oxides have great potential because of their resistance to high temperatures and their electrical (insulation) properties; the oxides alumina, magnesia, zirconia, beryllia, and thoria are useful refractory materials. Graphite, because of its extremely high melting point and high temperature strength, is finding widespread use in rocket nozzles and related components of missile systems. Ferrites (mixed oxides of iron and other metals) have magnetic properties which are of interest for computer components. Titanates, sapphire, ruby, and garnets are finding applications in advanced communication equipment and energy- and power-conversion equipment. CERMETS (combinations of metals and ceramics) are becoming important ceramic systems. See also ABRASIVES; BRICK; BUILDING MATERIALS; CEMENT; ENAMEL; GLASS; REFRACTORY.—*J. J. H.*

CEREALS AND GRAIN PRODUCTS: Cereals are essentially those members of the grass family which bear edible starchy seeds used as human and animal food and for a number of other purposes outside the food industry. Grains, specifically, are the fruit of cereal plants. Most prominent among the cereals are wheat, rye, barley, oats, rice, corn or maize, sorghum, and some of the millets. Through genetic experimentation and hybridizing, many higher-yield, drought- or rust-resistant, summer- or winter-crop strains have been developed. Thus, hard or durum wheat yields harder edible products such as spaghetti and macaroni; soft wheat varieties, requiring different controls and equipment for milling, yield light flour for rolls, cakes, and refrigerated foods. Both types of wheat consist of starch (carbohydrate), gluten (protein), fiber, germ, bran, and oil in varying amounts. Historically, grain products have been needed to sustain concentrated populations. Excavations of grain storage ruins in Mesopotamia, Egypt, Greece, Italy, and in the Indian communities of the western hemisphere indicate the early civilization level in these countries. Today, cereals still provide more food with a smaller expenditure of effort than any other crops. Wheat, rice, and rye constitute the major crops for human food; maize, barley, oats, and sorghum are grown mainly for livestock feed.

Grain milling in Biblical times was accomplished by dry grinding between stones. This method was supplanted in the late 19th cent. by *roller mills,* and in the past few years by *turbo mills* which utilize high-velocity air streams in flour preparation. *Wet milling* is used extensively for corn to achieve maximum separation of corn oil from corn meal. In the case of wheat, the milling operation removes nearly 30% of the grain weight, mostly the germ, bran, and fat. Since germ and bran are the most nutritious portions of the grain, much of the vitamin and mineral content, except phosphorus and potassium, is milled out and goes into feed stock. Removal of fat permits extended storage of milled flour with a lessened threat of rancidity. The modern use of non-fat dry milk solids, synthetic vitamins, minerals, and other supplements returns the "enriched" flour to nearly the nutritive level of the unmilled grain.

Many industrial uses of grain products depend on fractionation of whole flour into its relatively pure components. Starches, for example, are important in the manufacture of sized paper, in laundry starch, and warp sizing in the textile industry. Different grains yield somewhat different starches, and chemical oxidation or modification greatly increases the number of specialty starches for specific uses; many types of adhesives can be made from starches and partially degraded starches (dextrins). Corn starch is a well-known cooking aid and confectionery ingredient; and other starches have specific uses, from dusts for rubber and surgical gloves to baby powders and slipping agents in the packaging industry. Several starches from grain and pulse sources are used in oil-well drilling muds; as fillers in resin or plastics encapsulation applicators; and in paper coatings. Edible packaging materials made of plant starches or protein films will allow the housewife to cook the package as part of her food. Grain fermentation to obtain industrial solvents such as ethyl and butyl alcohol and acetone has largely been replaced by chemical synthesis from petrochemicals. Beverage alcohol, however, is still obtained from grain by fermentation.—*R. W. F.*

CERIUM: a rare-earth (lanthanide) element (Ce); at. no. 58; at. wt 140.13; density 6.78. Its melting point has been variously reported between 620 and 815°C. Cerium compounds are used as decolorizing agents in glass manufacture, in pyrophoric compounds, and as de-oxidizers in the manufacture of steel.—*G. W. M.*

CERMETS: substances capable of withstanding extremes of temperature, corrosion, or abrasive wear. They are prepared from mixtures of CERAMICS and metals (whence their name) by a process of grinding, compacting, and sintering. Many different cermets can be made by varying the ceramic (*e.g.* metallic oxides, borides, carbides) and the metal (*e.g.* iron, chromium, aluminum).—*Ru. M.*

CESALPINO, ANDREA, 1519–1603, Italian biologist; b. Arezzo; ed. Univ. of Pisa. He was one of the first botanical taxonomists to classify plants on a basis of a comparative study of forms, using the nature of the flowers and fruit for this purpose. The results of his research were published in his *De Plantis* (1583). He was professor at the Univ. of Pisa and physician to Pope Clement VIII.—*D. H. D. R.*

CESIUM: an alkali metal element (Cs); at. no. 55; at. wt 132.91; density 1.90; mp 28.4°C; bp 670°C. Like other ALKALI METALS, cesium emits electrons when exposed to visible light; for this reason it is used (as cesium chloride) in photoelectric cells and in television cameras. Some use has been made of the isotope cesium[137] (half-life 33 yr) as a source of gamma rays for industrial and medical radiology; cesium may also find use in ION PROPULSION systems. The element was the first to be discovered with the spectroscope (1860, by Robert Bunsen and Gustav Robert Kirchhoff).—*G. W. M.*

CETACEAN: any member of the order (Cetacea) of marine mammals that includes whales, dolphins, and porpoises. A torpedo shape, smooth hairless skin, powerful horizontal tail flukes (used for swimming), and a thick blanket of blubber (which conserves body heat) all serve to adapt these animals to life in the sea. Cetaceans vary in size from the 5-ft porpoise to the great blue whale, which may be 100 ft long and weigh 125 tons. Whales are the largest animals that have ever lived, their great size being possible only because their body weight is borne by water. Even though cetaceans can remain under water for 15 min or more, they must surface to breathe. As a whale breaks the surface, it exhales air from its blowhole, and water vapor condensed from its breath forms the characteristic spout ("thar she blows"). Modifications of internal structures allow cetaceans to descend to great depths (more than 3,000 ft in the case of the sperm whale). For example, as a

Toothed cetaceans include the family Delphinidae, which itself includes killer whales and dolphins (but not porpoises). With its streamlined shape, front legs transformed into steering flippers, and powerful tail, the dolphin—whose ancestors were land mammals—represents an extreme form of specialization. (*Allan Cruickshank/Nat. Audubon Soc.*)

whale dives, its lungs collapse, forcing air into the air passages of the head, with the result that the rate at which nitrogen enters the blood is much reduced; this prevents formation of nitrogen bubbles in the blood, which would cause death.

Cetaceans are divided into two groups (suborders): whalebone whales and toothed whales. The former include the gray whale, humpback whale, blue whale, and right whales. All these have in the upper jaw an arrangement of horny plates, called baleen or whalebone, with hairlike bristles that serve as strainers to remove small fish and plankton from the water. The whale takes in a mouthful of water, presses its tongue against the bristles of the baleen plates, and forces the water out through them, leaving food in the mouth to be swallowed. Toothed whales, including the sperm whale, dolphins, porpoises, and killer whales, feed on larger fish, squids, and other marine animals. Most toothed whales have in both upper and lower jaws strong conical teeth that can grasp slippery prey. Porpoises and dolphins feed largely on fish, whereas the giant killer whales (close relatives of the dolphins) eat seals and often whalebone whales. The sperm whale, which has teeth only in the lower jaw, may consume a ton of food a day, consisting chiefly of squids. This great toothed whale is the chief source of ambergris, a fatty substance formed in the intestine and valued by man for the manufacture of perfume. Dolphins and porpoises are quite similar, but dolphins have elongated beaks, in contrast to the rounded muzzles of porpoises. Dolphins and some whales appear able to communicate with others of their kind by the sounds they make, and are thought to possess a high degree of intelligence. In pursuing prey, toothed whales and porpoises use ANIMAL SONAR. —*W. J. H.*

CHADWICK, SIR JAMES, 1891–   , English physicist; b. Manchester. For his discovery (1932) that the radiations from beryllium when bombarded by alpha particles are neutrons, he received the 1935 Nobel prize. He wrote the classic papers "Possible Existence of a Neutron" and "Existence of a Neutron" (both 1932). He is a fellow of the Royal Society and a recipient of the Copley medal.—*D. H. D. R.*

CHAIN, ERNST BORIS, 1906–   , German-British biochemist; b. Berlin. Chain and H. W. Florey undertook a systematic investigation of the antibacterial substances produced by microorganisms. One result of this work was the discovery of the chemotherapeutic action of penicillin, for which they shared the Nobel prize, 1945, with Alexander Fleming. Chain is a fellow of the Royal Society.—*D. H. D. R.*

CHAIN REACTION: a self-sustaining, neutron-induced nuclear reaction of a FISSION type, in which, for every impinging neutron, at least one neutron is set free to produce still another fission. A chain reaction progresses forward if the ratio of "daughter" to "parent" neutrons exceeds 1—in other words, if the multiplying factor (K) is greater than 1. A favorable neutron balance is achieved if the size of the reacting system (or, more exactly, its surface-to-volume ratio) is such as to minimize the escape of useful neutrons or their nonfission

capture by the materials of the reactor. If the system is small, its surface-to-volume ratio is correspondingly large; so the probability of neutron escape, which is a function of the surface area, is considerable. As the size of the reacting system increases, volume begins to gain over surface area, and the nonproductive loss of neutrons decreases. A chain reaction is made possible when the so-called *critical size* is attained. When this happens, the rate of production of neutrons by fission just equals the rate at which they are lost by nonfission capture or nonfission escape. Obviously, the reactor must be adjusted to a level beyond criticality (K made greater than 1) if the fission process is to become self-sustaining.

The figure shows in schematic form the chain-reaction process by which nucleus of the uranium[235] atom undergoes fission when struck by a neutron. The capture of the impinging neutron (n^1) by the U[235] nucleus results in the formation of an unstable compound nucleus, U[236]. Because of its instability, this nucleus splits, or undergoes fission, yielding a pair of light and heavy elements (*e.g.* krypton and barium), and one or more additional neutrons available for continuing the process. The energy released by the reaction, obtained at the expense of a loss of mass, includes the kinetic energy of fission fragments and fission neutrons, and the energy of gamma and beta radiation. See ATOMIC ENERGY.—*A. E.*

CHALK: a soft, whitish, fine-grained, porous LIMESTONE composed largely of tests of minute, floating, marine organisms (foraminifera) in a matrix of very fine CALCITE. Under high magnification the matrix appears to contain a myriad of extremely minute tests of organisms known as coccoliths. Hard parts of other organisms (mollusk, sponge, and radiolarian) may be present. Famous are the chalk beds (Cretaceous age) of Britain and W Europe, so well exposed in white cliffs along the shores of the English Channel. Within the chalk, which attains a thickness several hundred feet, are abundant small nodules and lens-shaped bodies of flint.—*C. C.*

CHAMBERLAIN, OWEN, 1920–   , U. S. physicist; b. San Francisco. He was a member of the Manhattan Project during World War II. Chamberlain and E. Segrè shared the Nobel prize, 1959, for their demonstration (1955) of the existence of the *antiproton*, a particle like the proton, except that its charge is negative, not positive. He is a member of the National Academy of Sciences.—*D. H. D. R.*

CHAMBERLIN, THOMAS CHROWDER, 1843–1928, U. S. geologist; b. Mattoon, Ill. His outstanding work was on glacial phenomena in the northern U. S. A., on climates of past ages, and on the origin of Earth. With F. R. Moulton he developed the PLANETESIMAL HYPOTHESIS of the origin of the solar system, described in the Carnegie Institution *Year Book* (1905) and in Chamberlin's *The Origin of the Earth* (1916). In 1893 Chamberlin founded the *Journal of Geology,* which he edited until his death. The leading U. S. geologist of his time, he was a member of the National Academy of Sciences.— *D. H. D. R.*

CHANGE OF LIFE (or **CLIMACTERIC**): the period in middle age when human reproductive organs cease to function. In women it usually occurs between ages 42 and 52, and becomes noticeable through gradual stopping of MENSTRUATION; hence change of life is called *menopause* in women. As the OVARIES gradually cease to function, both in producing eggs and as endocrine organs, the whole hormone system of the reproductive (menstrual) cycle is disturbed. The uterus is no longer stimulated to renew itself periodically, and it becomes smaller as it ceases to function. Other sex organs tend to decrease in size, too, in this natural process of aging. Many women pass through the period without discomfort,

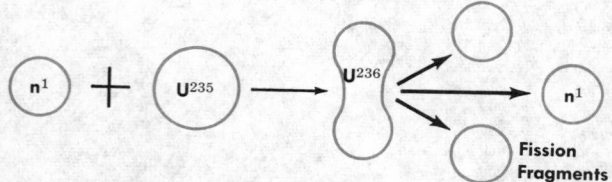

Chain reaction: A neutron striking a uranium[235] nucleus causes it to split into fission products that include a neutron which can cause another nucleus to split.

whereas others experience hot flashes, severe perspiration, stomach upset, and varying degrees of emotional disturbance.

A climacteric can be recognized in men; it usually occurs later than in women and with less obvious symptoms. Comparable changes can be noted in other primates; females of these also menstruate. Among other animals, individuals rarely live long after the end of their reproductive phase. Some, *e.g.* Pacific salmon, die soon after reproducing.—*A. P. E.*

CHANGE OF STATE: the transition between two PHASES (solid, liquid, or gaseous) of a crystalline substance. When a pure crystalline substance changes from one state into another, its temperature remains constant during the change. Thus ice at low temperature may be warmed by some steady source of heat until its temperature reaches 0°C. There it begins to melt, and, as melting proceeds, the temperature of the water-ice mixture remains constant until all the ice has melted, even though heat is being supplied continuously. Water, when boiling, likewise stays at a constant temperature of 100°C (at normal pressure) so long as any of the liquid remains. During the time the solid is melting or the liquid is boiling, the heat applied fails to raise the temperature of the water or ice (a measure of its internal kinetic energy), because the heat is being absorbed as an increase in the internal potential energy of the substance. This absorption of energy (see HEAT, LATENT) is required to break the bonds that hold the solid in its fixed shape or the liquid in its fixed volume, and is recovered if the gas condenses or the liquid refreezes. It is also possible for a solid to make the transition directly to the gaseous state: a process called *sublimation.* For example, dry ice (solid carbon dioxide) does not exist as a liquid under atmospheric pressure and hence evaporates entirely as a gas.

The temperature at which any change of state takes place is determined by the pressure under which the change takes place. Because an increase in pressure tends to strengthen the intermolecular bonds, it usually raises the boiling point, and a decrease in pressure lowers the boiling point. Thus one can make water boil at any temperature by evacuating the air in its container. Similarly, an increase in pressure normally raises the freezing point. Water is an important exception to this rule, because it expands on freezing; as a result, its freezing point is lowered by an increase in pressure. This explains why ice is "faster" for skating on mild days. The pressure of the skate blades lowers the freezing (melting) point of the ice enough so that it melts beneath the blades, providing a lubricating film of water between ice and blades.—*J. E. W.*

CHAPTAL, JEAN ANTOINE CLAUDE, COMTE DE CHANTELOUP, 1756–1832, French chemist and statesman; b. Nogaret. Interested in the promotion of chemical industries, he manufactured acids, soda, white lead, and other chemicals. He was made Councillor of State by Napoleon (1799), and later, as minister of the interior, he introduced the metric system of weights and measures in France and promoted the beet-sugar, alcohol, and chemical industries. Textbooks on chemistry, viticulture, and the manufacture of alcohol (1801), as well as *Chimie appliquée aux arts* (1807) and *Chimie appliquée à*

l'agriculture (1823), were among his achievements. He was a fellow of the Royal Society.—*R. J. F.*

CHARCOAL: an amorphous substance consisting almost entirely of carbon, formed by the thermal decomposition of wood or other vegetable material. Most wood charcoal is used for fuel or in the smelting of metallic ores. Some of the purer charcoals are used as adsorbents to remove impurities from gases or solutions. The adsorbing power is greatly increased by heating in steam, a process called "activation."—*A. M. S.*

CHARDONNET, LOUIS MARIE HILAIRE BERNIGAUD, COMTE DE, 1839–1924, French chemist; b. Besançon. The inventor of artificial silk (rayon), he obtained a patent (1884) on a process in which the thread was produced from nitrocellulose dissolved in alcohol and ether and pumped through small openings into a bath that removed the solvents.—*D. H. D. R.*

CHARGE, ELECTRIC: one of the fundamental attributes of the elementary particles of nature. Electric charges exert forces on one another. If the charges are of the same type (both positive or both negative), the force is one of repulsion; if the charges are opposite, the force is one of attraction. Equal and opposite charges in combination cancel each other and yield an electrically neutral or uncharged body. Electric charge is conserved in all physical and chemical processes; *i.e.* the net charge in any system always remains the same, and for any increase or decrease in negative charge, a corresponding increase or decrease in positive charge must occur. The smallest quantity of electric charge is that on an electron (negative) or proton (positive) and larger charges are multiples of the electronic charge. Charge is measured in terms of the force that it exerts; see COULOMB'S LAW.—*E. M. R.*

CHARGE-TO-MASS RATIO (e/m): a property of charged particles (ions, electrons, etc.), the measurement of which has been of great importance in the history of atomic and nuclear physics. In 1897, J. J. Thomson used a low-pressure gas discharge to obtain a narrow beam of electrons (cathode rays), which he then passed through crossed electric and magnetic fields. The beam subsequently struck a fluorescent screen so that its deflection by either field could be visibly observed. The deflection of the beam in the electric field alone, together with measurements of the intensity of the field and the distance between the plates, yielded a numerical value for e/mv^2, where v is the velocity of the electrons. The magnetic and electric fields were then both applied so that their forces on the electrons would cancel each other and not deflect the beam at all. In this case, the velocity v is equal to the intensity of the electric field divided by the magnetic induction. Thus v could be calculated, substituted into the value for e/mv^2, and e/m found. A few years later, Thomson undertook experimental determinations of e/m values for positive ions, again using a low-pressure gas discharge. He could not use crossed electric and magnetic fields to measure e/m, as for electrons, because the positive ions had a very wide distribution of velocities, and the earlier method demanded that the beam possess only a single velocity. He therefore devised a method

Thomson's procedure: A corpuscular beam produced in an auxiliary tube (*left*) is narrowed by slits. Subjected to the electric field, the pencil of electrons is deflected downward; in the magnetic field, it is deflected upward. The two fields can be applied simultaneously and adjusted to cancel each other.

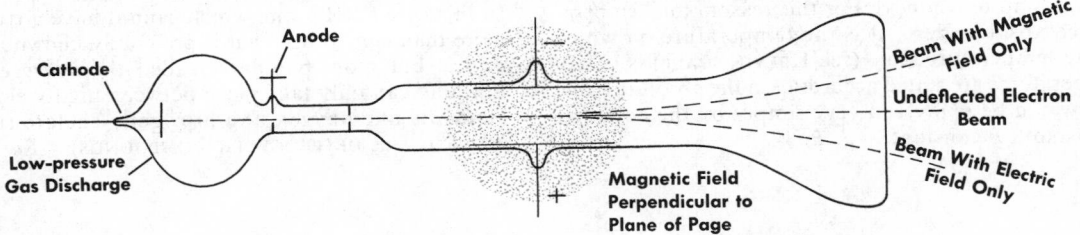

employing *parallel* electric and magnetic fields. An ion in such a field region experiences an electric force parallel to the field, and a magnetic force perpendicular to the field, and proportional to the ion's velocity. Ions of a given e/m then produce a parabolic trace on the fluorescent screen, with the extent of the line depending upon the velocity spread in the beam. Each e/m produces a different trace, so that various ionized elements and molecules can be identified. These experiments conclusively demonstrated that ions have discrete e/m values (that is, these values are not spread over a continuous range). In 1913, Thomson identified a trace that he attributed to a second isotope of neon. This was the first observation of the isotopic nature of the elements and definitely confirmed the hypothesis that elements whose atomic weights differed substantially from whole numbers consisted of several stable isotopes, each having a nearly whole-number atomic weight. Since then, determinations of e/m have aided substantially in the identification of stable and radioactive isotopes, and in precision determination of their masses.

More refined techniques, as worked out by F. W. Aston, A. J. Dempster, K. T. Bainbridge, and others, have resulted in the development of the modern mass spectrometer for e/m determinations. (See MASS SPECTROMETRY.)—*B. Be.*

CHARLES, JACQUES ALEXANDRE CÉSAR, 1746–1823, French physicist; b. Beaugency. About 1787, in connection with research on thermometry, he studied the expansivity of gases and discovered that for a gas under constant pressure the change in volume is proportional to the change in temperature. This relation, discovered independently by J. L. Gay-Lussac, is known as the *law of Charles and Gay-Lussac.* Charles made the first ascension in a hydrogen-filled balloon, and invented the valve at the top of balloons and the mode of attaching the basket to the gas bag with netting.—*D. H. D. R.*

CHARLES' LAW: an empirical relation between the temperature and volume of a gas at constant pressure. Toward the close of the 18th cent. the French physicists J. A. C. CHARLES

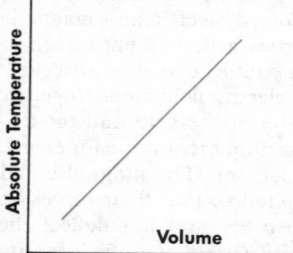

Charles' law: For an ideal gas, the graph of volume vs. absolute temperature is a straight line.

and J. L. GAY-LUSSAC established an approximate law, which states that the volume of a gas varies directly with its temperature at constant pressure. If a given volume of gas measured at 0°C is heated or cooled 1°C without allowing its pressure to change, the volume increases or decreases by 1/273 of its initial value. This suggests that if the temperature were decreased enough, the gas would vanish, having ultimately, at −273°C, a volume of zero. Actually all gases liquefy at temperatures higher than −273°C, and even before they do so they depart radically from the regular behavior indicated by Charles' law. Nevertheless, one can conceive of an ideal, incondensable gas capable of obeying Charles' law, which suggests that −273°C (more precisely −273.16°C) is the natural lower limit of coldness. For this reason, this temperature is called absolute zero; it is the temperature on which the absolute temperature scale (see KELVIN SCALE) is based. When temperatures are stated according to the absolute scale, Charles' law can be expressed very simply by the equation $V/T = $ constant (P constant).—*J. E. W.*

CHARNEY, JULE GREGORY, 1917–   , U. S. meteorologist; b. San Francisco. His research has been on the stability of atmospheric motions, general dynamical meteorology, and numerical weather prediction. Joining the staff of the Institute for Advanced Study, Princeton, in 1948, he became a long-term member in 1952. He has been professor of meteorology at the Mass. Inst. of Tech. since 1956.—*D. H. D. R.*

CHASE, PLINY EARLE, 1820–86, U. S. physicist and meteorologist; b. Worcester, Mass. Known primarily as a data collector in meteorology, he published more than 120 papers, including the important treatise "Numerical Relations Between Gravity and Magnetism" (1864). He reputedly could read 120 languages.—*D. H. D. R.*

CHASLES, MICHEL, 1793–1880, French mathematician; b. Épernon; ed. Paris. Professor of geodesy and mechanics at l' École Polytechnique and, later, professor of higher geometry at the Sorbonne, he elaborated modern projective geometry independently of Jakob Steiner, with whose work he was not acquainted. He solved many problems by his "method of characteristics" and "principle of correspondence." He calculated the attraction of an ellipsoid on an external point in 1846. In addition to his original memoirs, published in *Journal de l' École Polytechnique,* he wrote two textbooks: *Traité de géométrie supérieure* (1852) and *Traité des sections coniques* (1865). He was a fellow of the Royal Society and an associate of the U. S. National Academy of Sciences.—*H. C.*

CHELATES: ring compounds in organic chemistry which have been formed through dative bonds (see VALENCE). Thus compound I (below) is the beryllium salt of acetylacetone, but it does not behave like a SALT. The molecule has the structure II, called a coordination compound, in agreement with its behavior as an organic compound. Each molecule of acetylacetone is *bidentate;* that is, it has two "teeth," or coordinate bonds, one being the saltlike bond and the other the dative bond indicated by the arrow sign. The commercially important compound EDTA, used for removing metal ions from hard water, is *sexadentate.* The term chelation now covers similar structures in which no metal ions are present. An example is IV, ortho-hydroxybenzaldehyde, which does not have the properties associated with its "normal" structure shown in III.

In this case an H atom, which cannot have a true valence of more than *one,* forms what is preferably known as a *hydrogen bridge,* but more popularly called the *hydrogen bond.* The bridging can only take place between highly electronegative elements like oxygen and nitrogen. Chelate rings are heterocyclic (see HETEROCYCLIC COMPOUNDS).—*Ru. M.*

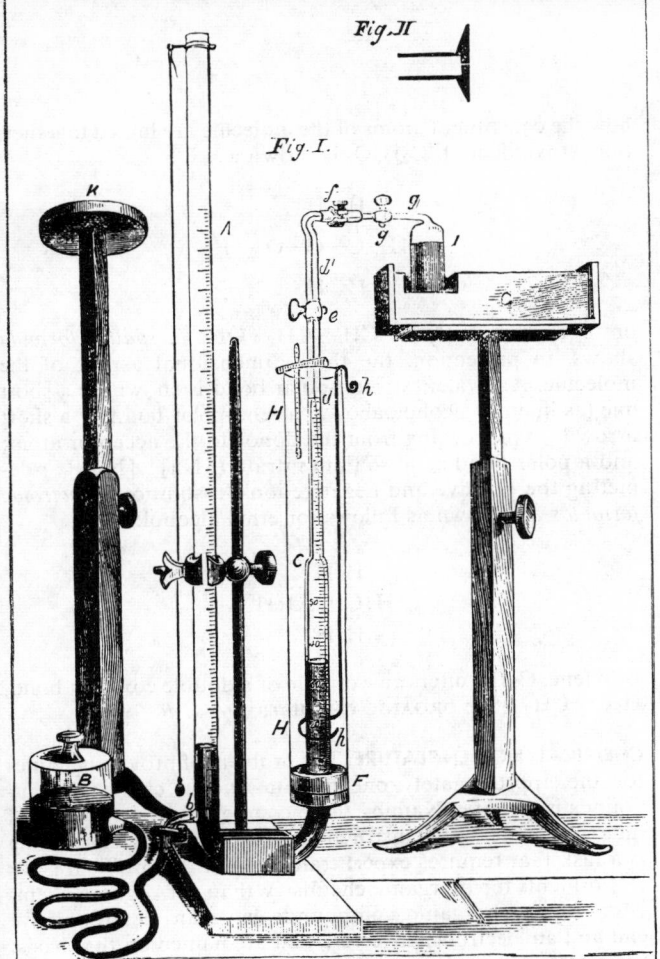

Fig.II

Fig.I

Accurate measurement of gas volume was achieved with this early apparatus designed by Sir Edward Frankland, 19th-cent. English chemist. The gas is trapped and measured in burette C between stopcock e and the leveling liquid (mercury or water). Pressure is adjusted by raising or lowering bulb B, and is measured by comparing liquid level in the two burettes. Temperature is measured in baffle H. (*N. Y. Public Library*)

CHEMICAL ANALYSIS: the use of chemical means to obtain information about the chemical composition of materials. *Qualitative analysis* is concerned simply with the detection and very rough measurement of the elements, compounds, or other identifiable constituents of a given sample; *quantitative analysis* is concerned with finding the exact percentage or concentration of any desired constituent, *e.g.* an element, a polyatomic group such as a radical, a functional group of an organic compound, a compound, or states of matter (phases) present. A qualitative analysis must always precede a quantitative one.

"Wet" qualitative analyses are those in which the desired constituent is recognized by a characteristic reaction it performs or undergoes in solution. This traditional, wet method has been supplemented by procedures such as spectrographic analysis, which makes use of the fact that metal elements emit a characteristic color when heated by flame or other means. The polarizing microscope, particularly one incorporating refractive index measurements, also provides a powerful tool for identifying materials, especially minerals, and for ascertaining whether the material is homogeneous or heterogeneous. Physical techniques, such as x-ray diffraction or fluorescence, and the determination of freezing points, boiling points, and densities, aid in qualitative examination and assist in quantitative determinations.

The selection of a quantitative technique depends upon the

size of the sample available, the percentage composition of the desired constituent, and the nature of the technique itself. A macro sample is one whose weight is greater than 0.1 gm; a semimicro (meso) sample will contain somewhere between 0.1 and 0.01 gm. A micro sample will contain from 0.01 to 0.001 gm while an ultramicro (submicro) sample will weigh less than 0.001 gm. Each of these concentration ranges may require a different analytical technique. In general, the classic gravimetric techniques, in which the desired constituent is transformed into a species that can be weighed, are desirable for macro determinations. Titrimetric methods are superior for somewhat smaller quantities (see TITRATION). Micro and ultramicro amounts are best determined through the use of an instrumental method such as spectrography, photometry, or one of the many electrometric methods. CHROMATOGRAPHY is used for a wide variety of analyses and separations of constituents.

There are four principal steps in a quantitative procedure: (1) sampling, *i.e.* choosing a representative sample of the material under study; (2) treatment of the sample so that the desired constituent is converted into a form which can be measured in some way, (3) measurement, (4) interpretation of the data. Generally step (2) is most critical and demands the most skill and knowledge, since serious problems may be encountered in solubilization of the sample, choice of a suitable procedure for converting the sample into a measurable form, control of the sample environment, isolation or separation of the desired constituent, and actual conversion to a form which can be measured. Step (3), measurement, can be based on a physical or chemical property which serves to make the desired constituent unique; it may entail weighing of an insoluble precipitate, measurement of a gas volume, or measurement of some physicochemical property such as color absorption, electrometric behavior, paramagnetism, or one of many titrimetric reactions.—*L. Sc.*

CHEMICAL BOND: strictly, the pair of electrons shared by two atoms or groups of atoms (see VALENCE). This is a *covalence* bond, and is illustrated here in the formula of chlorine. The formula of sodium chloride shows an *ionic* or *electrostatic* bond, in which the chlorine has sole possession of the electron pair:

Na^+ :Cl^-	Cl:Cl	$2\ Cl\cdot$
Sodium Chloride "Molecule"	Chlorine Molecule	Chlorine Free Radicals

There is no discrete molecule similar to that of chlorine; instead, there is a crystalline lattice of ions in which they are held in position by electric forces. This ionic union, however, is included in the category of chemical bonds. Under certain conditions of excitation, the two chlorine atoms in the chlorine molecule may be separated briefly as a unit, in which case they are the very reactive *free radicals,* characterized by the unpaired electron.

Certain substances, through hydrogen-bonding, form cage-like structures which can trap molecules of other substances, if they fit properly. When a solution of acetylene in quinol is cooled, the crystalline quinol traps in its cages the molecules of acetylene in a definite ratio. This is only a "pseudo" compound; there is no formation of a chemical bond, the molecules being held in the traps by *van der Waals forces.* These systems are called *clathrates,* or *inclusion compounds.*—*Ru. M.*

CHEMICAL COMPOSITION, LAWS OF: laws relating to the general make-up of chemical compounds, the two most important being the Law of Definite Proportions established by J. L. Proust, 1804–08, and the Law of Multiple Proportions established by Berzelius, 1810. A third, but derivative, law is the Law of Reciprocal Proportions. Implicit in these laws is the assumption of the validity of the Law of Conservation of

Mass, which states that in an ordinary chemical reaction (a nuclear reaction is not an ordinary chemical reaction) mass is neither created nor destroyed. From the chemical viewpoint this means that while atoms may be found in different chemical combinations at the beginning and at the end of a reaction, the numbers of atoms of like species at the beginning and end of a reaction must be identical. The *Law of Definite Proportions* is deducible from Dalton's atomic theory. It states that in a given compound the same atoms always must be found in the same proportions. Thus, in the compound water, there must be two hydrogen atoms to each oxygen atom; if this ratio is altered, the resulting compound cannot be water. The *Law of Multiple Proportions* shows that where two elements combine to form two or more compounds (hydrogen and oxygen, for example, can be made to combine to form either water or hydrogen peroxide), the ratio in which the atoms combine in their various compounds will bear a simple proportion to one another, *e.g.* $1:1, 1:2, 2:3$. The *Law of Reciprocal Proportions* states that if two elements, say A and B, are able to react individually with a third element, C, then A and B must react with each other in the same relative proportions as they each, separately, react with C. —*L. Sc.*

CHEMICAL ENGINEERING: see ENGINEERING.

CHEMICAL EQUATION: see EQUATION, CHEMICAL.

CHEMICAL EQUILIBRIUM: that point in a reversible chemical reaction at which reactions are proceeding with equal rapidity in both directions, so that no apparent change is taking place. Calcium carbonate will decompose completely into calcium oxide and carbon dioxide if heated in the open air, and calcium oxide will revert completely to calcium carbonate if kept in an atmosphere of carbon dioxide. Yet if calcium carbonate is heated in a closed vessel, the reaction proceeds only part of the way, until a state of balance or *kinetic equilibrium* is reached, the position of equilibrium depending upon the temperature and the consequent pressure. An important example in organic chemistry is esterification, as in the interaction of acetic acid and ethyl alcohol to form ethyl acetate: $CH_3 \cdot COOH + HO \cdot C_2H_5 \rightleftharpoons CH_3 \cdot COO \cdot C_2H_5 + H_2O$. The point of equilibrium depends upon the active masses (concentration in gram-molecules per liter), C_1, C_2, C_3, C_4, of the four reacting substances, the *equilibrium constant* (K) being expressed in terms of the law of MASS ACTION as follows: $K = C_1 \times C_2 / C_3 \times C_4$. In the above example about 67% of the acid is esterified under ordinary conditions; the same point would be reached by the interaction of ethyl acetate and water under similar conditions. Kinetic equilibria are also subject to Le Chatelier's principle: if a system in equilibrium be subjected to a restraint, a change occurs if possible of such a kind that the restraint is partially annulled. —*J. R.*

CHEMICAL FORMULAS: In chemical notation, Berzelius represented (1811) the atom of an element by its capital initial letter, sometimes followed by another characteristic letter from its name. Examples now in use are: O (oxygen), H (hydrogen), B (boron), Ba (barium), Bi (bismuth), I (iodine), Ir (iridium), Fe (iron, or *ferrum*). A molecule of hydrogen, consisting of two atoms, is written H_2. Formulas (formulae) for compounds are written similarly: H_2SO_4 (sulfuric acid), Na_2SO_4 (sodium sulfate), $CuSO_4$ (copper sulfate). An *empirical formula* is the simplest formula giving the ratio of the numbers of the constituent atoms of the molecule (CH_2O for glucose); a *molecular formula* gives their actual numbers ($C_6H_{12}O_6$ for glucose). A *structural* or *graphic formula* shows how the constituent atoms of the molecule are linked together; thus ethyl alcohol, C_2H_6O, is shown as

$$
\begin{array}{ccc}
\text{H} & \text{H} & \\
| & | & \\
\text{H}-\text{C}-\text{C}-\text{O}-\text{H} \\
| & | & \\
\text{H} & \text{H} &
\end{array}
$$

or more compactly as $CH_3 \cdot CH_2 \cdot OH$. A *spatial formula* shows, in projection, the three-dimensional aspect of the molecule. A covalent or non-polar bond is shown by a short line (as in ethyl alcohol, above); a semi-polar bond by a short arrow ($\rightarrow$) proceeding from the donor to the acceptor atom; and a polar bond as in sodium nitrate ($[Na]^+ [NO_3]^-$) depicting the positive and negative ions in solution. *Electronic formulas* are shown as follows for ethyl alcohol:

$$
\begin{array}{c}
\text{H} \quad \text{H} \\
\text{H}:\text{C}:\text{C}:\text{O}:\text{H} \\
\text{H} \quad \text{H}
\end{array}
$$

Ethylene, C_2H_4, offers an example of a double covalent bond, $H_2C{=}CH_2$. (See ORGANIC CHEMISTRY.)—*J. R.*

CHEMICAL NOMENCLATURE: The problem of providing names for the approximately one million known chemical compounds is gigantic. Naming these compounds for purposes of indexing, for textbook instruction, or for commercial handling is a task that requires expert training. But the problem is far less difficult for inorganic chemistry than for organic chemistry. Many inorganic compounds have an electropositive end and an electronegative end, and are named on that basis; these may be simple, as sodium chloride, but many are quite complex and indeed become most complex when organic radicals are introduced. Organic compounds considerably outnumber the inorganic. There is an almost endless possibility in the arrangements of carbon atoms to form the chain and ring structures of organic chemistry. At first, compounds were given common (trivial) names to indicate their nature or source; *e.g.* stearic acid from stearin. Such names are still needed because more systematic names are too clumsy for normal use. A systematic nomenclature was outlined in 1892 by an international congress at Geneva, and revised by the International Union of Chemistry in 1930 at Liége and in 1949 at Amsterdam; it is called the Geneva system, or I.U.C. system. The basic principles of the system are described in the college textbooks of organic chemistry, and complete details are obtainable in pamphlets issued by the American Chemical Society, Washington, D. C. Shorthand methods have also been invented for indexing purposes, making possible the use of modern high-speed business machines for searching an index for a particular type of compound or structural grouping.—*Ru. M.*

CHEMICAL REACTION: a chemical change that gives rise to one or more new substances. It can be promoted by physical or chemical agencies. The formation of new substances reflects one of four general types of change at the molecular level, among them: (1) *Decomposition*, in which one substance splits into two or more. Thus cane sugar under action of the enzyme invertase (sucrase) splits into the sugars glucose and fructose. (2) *Combination*, in which one substance unites with another to form a third (a chemical compound). In the combustion of coal, for example, the carbon in the coal combines with oxygen in the air to form the gas carbon dioxide. (3) *Exchange reaction*, in which substances exchange their respective components, so that new substances are formed. Thus when a solution of silver nitrate is mixed with a solution of sodium chloride, two new substances are formed: silver chloride, which is insoluble in water and precipitates out on the bottom of the glass; and sodium nitrate, which is soluble in water and remains in solution. (4) *Rearrangement* (of the atomic pattern), in which the substance is acted upon by a physical agent and is converted into a new substance. Thus fumaric acid on exposure to ultraviolet light changes into maleic acid, without anything having been added to or subtracted from it; the change consists solely in relocation of atoms, or groups of atoms, within the molecule of the substance.

A chemical reaction can be examined both qualitatively and quantitatively, and much of the resulting information can be summarized in chemical *equations* (see CHEMISTRY). Chemical reactions are accompanied by energy exchanges: thus, in the formation of water by the combination of hydrogen and oxygen, energy is disbursed in the form of heat in an exothermic reaction; in the decomposition of the resulting amount of water into hydrogen and oxygen, exactly the same amount of energy is absorbed in an endothermic reaction. Reactions can be described by the specific process involved, *e.g.* precipitation, oxidation-reduction, hydrolysis, equilibrium or reversible, and electrolysis (see articles under these titles). Neutralization reactions between acid and alkaline solutions are used in volumetric analysis, as are also certain oxidation-reduction and precipitation reactions, the last-named being also applied in gravimetric analysis. Further, reactions of many kinds enter into qualitative analysis. Reactions are often promoted by catalysts, either inorganic or organic (notably by natural enzymes). Organic chemistry, in particular, abounds in specialized reactions, *e.g.* polymerization and isomerization; addition, elimination, and substitution reactions; sulphonation, halogenation, nitration; esterification; hydration, dehydration, decarboxylation; and synthetic reactions wide in scope, such as the acetoacetic and malonic ester syntheses, the diazo reaction, and the Grignard reaction. Many of the reactions of organic chemistry have great biochemical importance, *e.g.* the alcoholic, lactic, and butyric fermentations, and many polymerization and condensation reactions.—*J. R.*

CHEMICAL RESEARCH: Until the second half of the 18th cent. chemical research was almost wholly a matter of haphazard experimentation; but with the advent of the atomic theory (1808) and other theories springing from it, an era of sys-

Priestley's classic 18th-cent. experiments with glass containers inverted in a mercury trough led to discovery of oxygen and carbon dioxide, and to the isolation of other important gases.

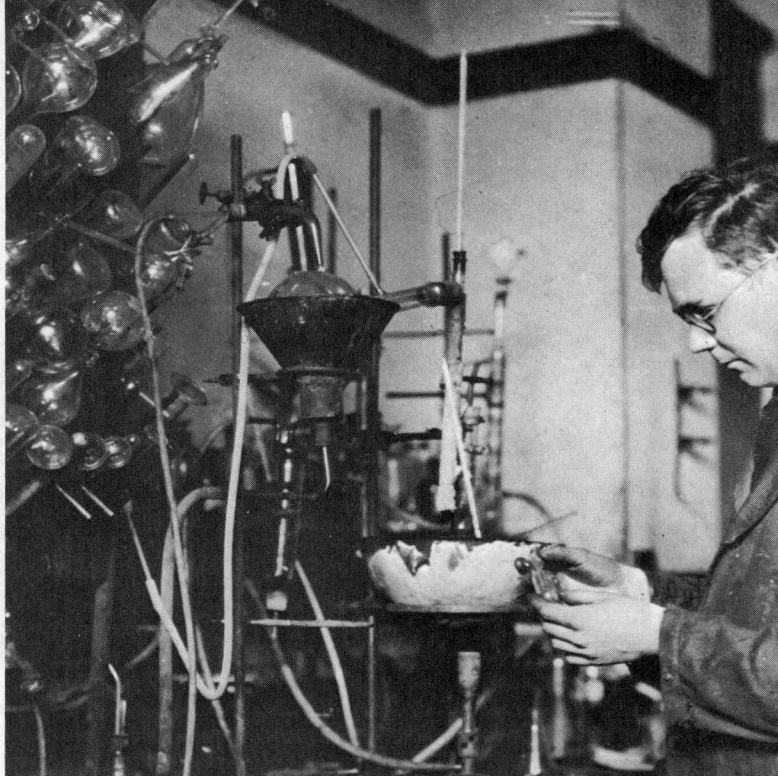

Dr. Wallace H. Carothers' seven years of research in long-chain polymers led to discovery of Nylon in 1934. (*Du Pont*)

tematic experimentation set in. Chemistry developed rapidly during the 19th cent., as one theory after another succeeded in coordinating known facts and pointing the way to further researches: a progression illustrating John Tyndall's dictum that imagination working upon accurate experiment and observation becomes the architect of physical theory. As a classical sequence in chemistry, Edward Frankland's theory of valency (1852) led to August Kekulé's theory of organic molecular structure (1858); this in due course expanded into the spatial theory of J. A. Le Bel and J. H. van't Hoff (1874); and this last theory acted as an indispensable guide to Emil Fischer in his brilliant experimental elucidation of the chemistry of the sugars, beginning in the next decade and leading on to ever-expanding researches on the constitution and synthesis of myriads of natural organic substances in the 20th cent. Ordered research directed toward a specific end sometimes leads to unexpected results. For instance, the youthful W. H. Perkin, seeking in 1856 to synthesize quinine, stumbled upon mauveine, the first synthetic coal-tar dye. This trigger-discovery touched off an unexampled sequence of researches, resulting in the synthesis of thousands of artificial dyes, besides expanding into many other fields of organic chemistry; but this expansion would not have been possible without Kekulé's further theory of the benzene ring (1865).

Directed chemical research had received a great stimulus from about 1840 onward in certain German university laboratories, particularly those led by Liebig, Wöhler, and Bunsen; and gradually academic research in all branches of chemistry spread to universities in general. Such research is often called "pure" research; but since results of technical importance accrue constantly from such work it is impracticable to draw a rigid distinction between "pure" and "applied" chemical research: the factory is apt to arise from the test tube, whether it is held by an academic or an industrial hand. No modern industrial firm of repute can dispense with an adequate staff of research chemists; also, since chemistry overlaps with many other branches of science (*e.g.* biochemistry and metallurgy), teamwork has developed to an increasing extent.

Eighteenth-century chemistry: Lavoisier's experiments in combustion were aided by Bernière's great burning glass. The whole clumsy apparatus, copied in part from Priestly, focused heat from the Sun through parallel lenses mounted on a multi-wheeled platform with controls permitting movement with the Sun.

The literature, in many languages, recording the prodigious output of chemical research is enormous and subject to rapid proliferation: thus, a search through this vast ocean of publications in order to survey previous work upon a specific topic is an arduous and time-consuming task, in spite of abstracts, chemical dictionaries, and other aids to the explorer. See also APPLIED SCIENCE; SCIENTIFIC RESEARCH.—*J. R.*

CHEMICAL SYMBOLS: letters used to represent chemical ELEMENTS, instituted by J. Berzelius (1811). The letters are usually abbreviations of elements' names, *i.e.* the first letter or letters of the element's name. Names of several elements are derived from Latin, *e.g.* Na for sodium (*natrium*), Au for gold (*aurum*). Chemical symbols signify either an atom of an element or the element itself. Thus sulfur (atom or element) is represented by the symbol S. However, molecular sulfur must be written S_8, because sulfur is an octatomic molecule. Symbols of compounds show (1) the elements the compound contains and (2) the numerical proportion of the atoms of these elements. For example, since four atoms of fluorine (F) and one of silicon (Si) make up a molecule of the compound silicon tetrafluoride, this is represented as SiF_4.—*G. W. M.*

CHEMISTRY: a branch of science dealing with the composition of the various kinds of matter and with the changes of composition that they undergo.

Character and Scope: Most natural materials are mixtures of individual homogeneous *substances*; chemistry is concerned with the separation in a pure state of each distinctive substance, and with the study of its properties. Since chemistry deals with material changes, it dominates the innumerable processes in the arts and manufactures in which raw materials are used as the basis of artificial products. A very important feature of chemistry lies in its character as an experimental science.

Elements and Compounds: Any particular substance is either an *element* or a *compound*. An element cannot be broken down by ordinary chemical means into other substances; but a compound can be broken down, or decomposed, into two or more new substances. Thus water when electrolyzed yields two gaseous substances, hydrogen and oxygen, always in the proportion 2:1 by volume, corresponding to the gravimetric (weight) proportion 1:8. (Water contains 11.1% of hydrogen and 88.9% of oxygen by weight.) This reaction is an example of a quantitative *analysis*. Conversely, a quantitative *synthesis* of water is effected by passing an electric spark through a mixture of two volumes of hydrogen with one volume of oxygen, whereby the two gases combine chemically, with liberation of heat, and are completely converted into water.

The combination of hydrogen and oxygen to form water is an example of a *chemical reaction* or *chemical change*. All such reactions are marked by the formation of a new substance or substances, whereas in a *physical change,* such as the conversion of ice into water, or water into steam, no new substance is produced.

Pure water, like all other pure substances, from whatever source it comes, always has the same chemical composition, both qualitatively and quantitatively. A so-called "law" embodying this experience has been formulated as the law of DEFINITE PROPORTIONS; it states that the same chemical compound always contains the same elements combined together in the same proportion by weight. Another fundamental law, following from the quantitative study of chemical changes, or reactions, known as the law of Conservation of Matter, states that in all ordinary chemical processes matter is neither created nor destroyed (see CONSERVATION OF MASS-ENERGY).

There are over 100 known elements, and these give rise to a vast number of compounds formed by combinations of two or more elements. Compounds found in, or produced from, lifeless mineral matter are called *inorganic*; those containing carbon as a constituent element are called *organic* because many of them are found in association with living or "organized" matter.

History: In the declining days of ALCHEMY, Robert Boyle (1661) advanced the modern conception of an element as a substance that cannot be broken down into simpler ones; but the progress of chemistry was halted for nearly a century by George Ernst Stahl's misleading theory of phlogiston (1697), according to which a burning body emitted an imaginary inflammable principle having that name. Joseph Black (1754 onward) showed that "magnesia alba" and chalk when heated lost weight and gave off a heavy gas, "fixed air" (carbon dioxide). He showed that gaseous "fixed air" could combine with solid quicklime to form solid chalk, and that this "air" could be weighed when "fixed" or brought into solid combination. This observation, conjoined with Joseph Priestley's discovery of oxygen (1774), led Antoine Lavoisier (1777) to put forward the modern view of combustion as combination of the burning body with atmospheric oxygen.

The Atomic Theory, published by John Dalton in 1808, was based upon experimental evidence summarized in various laws, notably the law of Definite Proportions and the law of MULTIPLE PROPORTIONS; the latter states that when two elements combine to form more than one compound, the different weights of one element which combine with a constant weight of the other bear a simple ratio to one another. Dalton postulated that every element had its own kind of atom, uncreatable and indestructible; all alike in weight and other attributes; and capable of uniting with atoms of other elements in small whole numbers to form "compound atoms" (later known as molecules), all of which were alike for a given compound. A physical change leaves the molecule intact; but a chemical change alters it.

In compiling his original list of atomic weights, Dalton adopted the atom of the lightest element, hydrogen, as a standard, with ATOMIC WEIGHT of 1. The relative weights of other kinds of atoms were determined solely from the percentage composition of compounds. Thus, water was found to contain 8 parts by weight of oxygen combined with 1 part by weight of hydrogen. Dalton assumed that the "compound atom" (molecule) of water contained 1 atom each of hydrogen and oxygen, corresponding to the molecular formula HO; he therefore assigned the atomic weight 8 to oxygen. Later, however, it was found that the molecular formula of water is H_2O, so that the correct atomic weight of oxygen is 16. The determination of molecular weights, and therefore of molecular formulas, was facilitated by AVOGADRO'S HYPOTHESIS (first put forward in 1811 but not recognized until 1858), which states that equal volumes of all gases at the same temperature and pressure contain equal numbers of molecules. Thus by comparing the weights of equal volumes of two gases, one is also comparing the weights of their single molecules. If one gas is hydrogen, the comparative weight of the other is called its *gaseous density.* Since from other evidence it is known that the hydrogen molecule contains 2 atoms (H_2), the molecular weight of a gaseous or vaporized substance is twice its gaseous density. For steam, this value is $9 \times 2 = 18$, corresponding to the molecular formula H_2O. Later, other methods of determining molecular weight were discovered. Also it was found that the molecular weight in grams, or *gram-molecular weight,* of any gas occupies 22.4 liters at $0°C$ and 760 mm pressure (standard temperature and pressure, or S.T.P.). This volume is called the *gram-molecular volume* (g.m.v.) of a gas. The actual number of molecules contained in 22.4 liters of a gas at S.T.P. has been calculated as 6.02×10^{23}, a value known as *Avogadro's number.* The absolute weight (or mass) of the hydrogen atom is 1.66×10^{-24} gm.

Equivalent and Valence: A conception of importance is that of the *equivalent* of an element or compound, which may be defined as the number of units of weight of it which will react either directly or indirectly with one of the same units of weight of hydrogen; *e.g.* the equivalent of oxygen is 8. *Valence* may be defined as the combining capacity of an atom. The univalent hydrogen atom has unit combining capacity, and the oxygen atom is usually bivalent, as in water, H_2O. The valence of an element may be expressed as the number of atoms of hydrogen with which one atom of the element will combine. If the element does not combine with hydrogen, its valence may be found by studying its combinations with other elements of known valence: For example, the zinc atom in zinc oxide (ZnO) is bivalent. Sometimes an element displays more than one valence, as phosphorus (3 and 5) in phosphorus trichloride (PCl_3) and phosphorus pentachloride (PCl_5). An important relationship may be expressed thus: Atomic weight = Valence × Equivalent. (See ELEMENT for atomic weights, atomic numbers, and symbols of elements.)

Atomic Structure, Atomic Number, and Isotopes: Ernest Rutherford and Niels Bohr (1913) pictured the atom as an assemblage of positive and negative electrical units, known as *protons* and *electrons,* with equal and opposite electrical charges. The consequent atomic model postulates a core consisting of protons and *neutrons.* A neutron includes both an electron and a proton. The mass of the atom lies almost entirely in the protons of its core or nucleus. The excess of protons over and above those of the neutrons imparts a positive charge to the nucleus. In the complete atom this positive charge is exactly matched by a negative charge carried by revolving "planetary" electrons equal in number to the excess of protons. The number of these electrons revolving in closed orbits about the core is identical with the number of protons over and above those of the neutrons. This number is called the *atomic number.*

The free planetary electrons are depicted in *shells* or layers, also known as *levels.* Those of the outermost shell are called valence electrons, and their number determines the chemical character of the atom. The maximum degree of stability is reached in a shell of 8 valence electrons, or *octet.* (See PERIODIC TABLE for number of valence electrons of each element.)

Atoms with the same number and arrangement of extranuclear electrons may have more than one kind of atomic nucleus. They have identical chemical properties and atomic numbers, but different atomic weights. Such varieties of an element are called *isotopes.* Most elements can exist in isotopic forms, and many such forms occur in nature. Even the lightest element, hydrogen, exists in three isotopic forms; and uranium, the heaviest natural element, has many, of which the three naturally occurring ones are shown diagrammatically below:

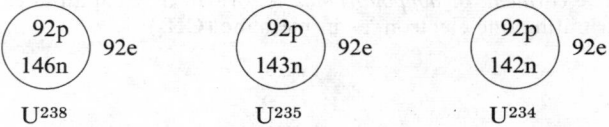

By adding the numbers of protons (p) and neutrons (n), in the nucleus, one arrives at the respective atomic weights 238, 235, and 234. The number of extranuclear electrons (e) corresponds to the constant atomic number 92. As another illustrative example, common chlorine is a mixture of Cl^{35} and Cl^{37} in a proportion that gives chlorine a mean atomic weight 35.457.

The vastly predominating, common form of hydrogen is called protium (at. wt 1); but deuterium (at. wt 2) and tritium (at. wt 3) also exist. In each case the atomic number is 1, and there is one planetary or valence electron (e):

By the loss of its solitary valence electron, the electrically neutral atom of protium becomes an electropositive univalent *ion.* This is identical with the proton, and is also called a hydrogen ion. It is often represented by $[H]^+$ or H^+.

Atoms are usually stable in ordinary chemical processes, but under special conditions some atoms undergo *transmutation* into other kinds. Indeed, certain atoms of high atomic weight, notably radium (226), break down spontaneously into others, with evolution of energy. In 1938 it was found that uranium[235] when bombarded with neutrons underwent a self-propagating process of atomic fission, accompanied by downward transmutation to lighter elements together with the release of energy on a tremendous scale. This discovery led to the fabrication of the atomic bomb (1945). Later researches have shown how to harness nuclear or atomic energy to useful ends. A notable example of upward transmutation, leading to a number of purely artificial *transuranium elements,* is *plutonium* (at. no. 94), manufactured in nuclear reactors from natural uranium; this element has great importance in the industrial utilization of nuclear energy.

Formulas, Valence Bonds, and Equations: The symbol for an element (see ELEMENT) represents one atom of the element. The *molecular formula* of a substance shows the nature and number of each kind of atom in the molecule; *e.g.* the hydrogen molecule (H_2) contains two atoms of hydrogen, and the water molecule (H_2O) contains two atoms of hydrogen combined with one of oxygen. A *structural formula* shows the arrangement of the constituent atoms of the molecule, the valence bonds being represented by short lines, as in H—O—H (water) and O=N—O—N=O (nitrogen trioxide, N_2O_3). Sometimes two atoms are linked by two or even three such bonds, known respectively as a double bond or triple bond. The *electronic theory of valence* gives an idea of the binding forces represented by the valence bonds. In writing electronic formulas only the valence electrons of the outermost shell are represented, and the number of them (shown as dots arranged arbitrarily about the atomic symbol) is related to the valence of the element:

$$H\cdot \quad \cdot\overset{\cdot}{\underset{\cdot}{C}}\cdot \quad \cdot\overset{\cdot\cdot}{\underset{\cdot}{N}}\cdot \quad \cdot\overset{\cdot\cdot}{\underset{\cdot\cdot}{O}}\cdot \quad Na\cdot \quad \cdot Mg\cdot \quad \cdot\overset{\cdot\cdot}{\underset{\cdot}{S}}\cdot \quad \cdot\overset{\cdot\cdot}{\underset{\cdot\cdot}{Cl}}{:}$$

The leading principle in the combination of two atoms is visualized in the formation of stable shells, or octets, of 8 valence atoms (or duplets of two valence atoms for hydrogen). The *covalent,* or *nonpolar bond,* is formed by each atom contributing one electron, as in methane (CH_4):

$$\begin{array}{c} H \\ H\!:\!\overset{\cdot\cdot}{\underset{\cdot\cdot}{C}}\!:\!H. \\ H \end{array}$$

The resulting molecule, in which the 4-valent carbon atom has completed its octet, is electrically neutral and does not split into ions. In the *electrovalent,* or *polar bond,* the combination of two atoms is brought about by the transference of one or more electrons from a "donor" atom to an "acceptor" atom. The resulting molecule is thus composed of positive and negative parts, with equal and opposite charges, and it readily separates, especially in aqueous solution, into positive and negative *ions.* This so-called *ionic dissociation* or *ionization* is shown particularly by acids, alkalis, and salts:

$$Na\cdot + \cdot\overset{\cdot\cdot}{\underset{\cdot\cdot}{Cl}}{:} \longrightarrow Na\!:\!\overset{\cdot\cdot}{\underset{\cdot\cdot}{Cl}}{:} \longrightarrow [Na]^+ + [:\overset{\cdot\cdot}{\underset{\cdot\cdot}{Cl}}{:}]^-$$

Un-ionized   Sodium Ion   Chloride Ion
Form of   (cation)   (anion)
Sodium Chloride

Equations: In an ordinary chemical equation the original reacting molecules are shown on the left-hand side and the products of the reaction on the right-hand side, *e.g.* in the formation of water from hydrogen and oxygen:

$$2H_2 + O_2 = 2H_2O, \text{ or alternatively, } 2H_2 + O_2 \rightarrow 2H_2O.$$

Qualitatively, the equation shows that, under certain unspecified conditions, hydrogen and oxygen are capable of reacting together to yield water and nothing else. Quantitatively it shows that 2 molecules of hydrogen react with 1 molecule of oxygen to yield 2 molecules of water; from this, by Avogadro's

hypothesis, 2 volumes of gaseous hydrogen react with 1 volume of gaseous oxygen to yield 2 volumes of water vapor (all these volumes being measured at the same temperature and pressure). If the atomic weights are known, the equation shows also that 4 parts by weight of hydrogen react with 32 parts by weight of oxygen to yield 36 parts by weight of water.

A more complete form of equation, showing the so-called heat of reaction, is termed a thermochemical equation. Such considerations belong to an important branch of chemistry known as *thermochemistry,* which in turn is a division of physical chemistry: a major branch of chemistry, ranking beside inorganic chemistry and organic chemistry and dealing with the study of physical properties and phenomena as related to chemical constitution and chemical change. Prominent in this field is the study of the behavior of gases, upon which the development of chemistry has always been closely dependent. (See ELEMENT; GAS; INORGANIC CHEMISTRY; KINETIC THEORY OF MATTER; ORGANIC CHEMISTRY; PHYSICAL CHEMISTRY.)—*J. R.*

CHERENKOV, PAVEL ALEKSEEVICH, 1904–   , Soviet physicist; birthplace unknown. In 1934 he announced the discovery of light emission by high-speed particles moving in liquids (CHERENKOV RADIATION). This radiation has been used as a detector of high-speed particles in research in physics. For the discovery and interpretation of the Cherenkov effect, Cherenkov, I. M. Frank and I. Y. Tamm shared the Nobel prize, 1958.—*D. H. D. R.*

CHERENKOV RADIATION: light emitted by an electrically charged particle when it moves through a medium at a speed faster than the speed of light in that medium. This phenomenon, first announced by PAVEL CHERENKOV, is the electromagnetic analogue of the "sonic boom" made by airplanes moving faster than the speed of sound in air, and of the V-shaped bow waves of ships whose speeds exceed that of surface waves on water. A most spectacular display can be seen in a "swimming pool reactor," the source of the light being the large number of electrons freed from water molecules and accelerated to high speeds by collisions with gamma rays escaping from the reactor.—*S. K.*

CHEVREUL, MICHEL EUGÈNE, 1786–1889, French chemist; b. Angers. As director of the Gobelin tapestry works (1824), he did classical research on color contrasts (*De la loi du contraste simultané des couleurs,* 1839), but he was more famous for his research on animal fats (*Recherches chimiques sur les corps gras d'origine animale,* 1823), describing how to separate the solid stearin from the fluid olein and isolate stearic and oleic acids. This work was the starting point of modern glycerin, soap, and candle manufacture. He directed the Paris natural history museum, 1860–79. He was a fellow of the Royal Society and an associate of the U. S. National Academy of Sciences.—*R. J. F.*

CHILDHOOD: see INFANCY.

CHITIN: a polysaccharide similar to cellulose that forms the hard shell of crustaceans and insects. It consists of N-acetyl glucosamine units linked together like the glucose units of cellulose. The material is resistant to acid and alkaline hydrolysis but is broken down by an enzyme, chitinase, found in micro-organisms and snails. See also SUGAR.—*J. F. S.*

CHLADNI, ERNST FLORENS FRIEDRICH, 1756–1827, German physicist; b. Wittenberg. Combining interests in physics and music, he invented two musical instruments, the euphonium (1790) and the clavicylinder (1800). The first of his many publications on sound was *Discoveries Concerning the Theory of Sound* (1787). He introduced sand figures (*Chladni figures*) for showing the modes of vibration of solid objects.—*D. H. D. R.*

CHLORATES: chemical compounds containing the chlorate (ClO_3^-) radical. Common chlorates are those of sodium, potassium, barium, and calcium. They are formed by reaction of an excess of chlorine with a concentrated alkali solution or by the electrolysis of chloride solutions. Because they decompose readily, liberating heat and forming the chloride and free oxygen, they are powerful oxidizing agents. Chlorates are toxic to plants and animals.—*D. P. B.*

CHLORIDES: chemical compounds of the general formula MCl, where M can be a metal atom or an organic or inorganic radical or complex, and Cl is chlorine. Metal chlorides can be prepared by direct combination of the metal and chlorine or by reaction of carbon and chlorine with the metallic oxide. Most inorganic chlorides are soluble in water, notable exceptions being silver chloride, mercurous chloride, cuprous chloride, and lead chloride, which is only partially soluble. Because chlorine is in its lowest oxidation state in chlorides, these normally react with strong oxidizing agents to generate free chlorine or higher oxidation products.—*D. P. B.*

CHLORINE: a chemical element (Cl), at. no. 17, at. wt 35.45, belonging to group VII of the periodic table. It is found in nature combined with other elements. At normal temperatures, chlorine is a diatomic gas (Cl_2), greenish-yellow in color and about 2½ times as heavy as air. It liquefies at atmospheric pressure at $-34.1°C$ to a yellowish liquid approximately 1½ times as heavy as water. The liquid freezes at $-100.98°C$. Chlorine was employed as a war gas during World War I; only 40 to 60 parts per million of chlorine in air inhaled for 30 minutes or more can cause serious injury. Chlorine is soluble in water and indirectly exerts bleaching and bactericidal action by reacting with the water to form hypochlorous acid:

$$Cl_2 + H_2O \rightleftharpoons HCl + HOCl \longrightarrow HCl + (O)$$

Chlorine Water   Hydrochloric Hypochlorous
                              Acid   Acid

The hypochlorous acid is unstable, giving up oxygen to form more HCl. The oxygen attacks and destroys bacteria; it also oxidizes colored organic substances, forming colorless or less-colored compounds; thus indigo (dark blue) is oxidized to isatin (orange):

$$C_{16}H_{10}N_2O_2 + 2HOCl \longrightarrow 2C_8H_5NO_2 + 2HCl$$

(Indigo)   (Isatin)

As one of the most active elements, chlorine ranks in reactivity about with oxygen. It combines directly and readily with hydrogen and most other non-metals except nitrogen, carbon, and oxygen; it also unites with all the familiar metals except gold and platinum. Participating in a number of important organic reactions, in some cases chlorine appears in the final product, as in insecticides (*e.g.* benzene hexachloride and DDT) or in the plastic, polyvinyl chloride; in other cases, it forms part of an important intermediate compound as in the classic Raschig synthesis of phenol:

$$C_6H_6 + HCl + O_2 \longrightarrow C_6H_5Cl + H_2O$$

Benzene Hydrochloric Acid (air)   Chlorobenzene Water

$$C_6H_5Cl + H_2O \longrightarrow C_6H_5OH + HCl$$

Phenol

Of the several methods for preparing chlorine, the most important commercially is the electrolysis of a sodium chloride solution.—*D. P. B.*

CHLOROFORM: trichloromethane, $CHCl_3$; a sweet-smelling, colorless, mobile liquid. It is an anesthetic, and also is used as an extractive solvent in the purification and extraction of penicillium and other antibiotics.—*R. W.*

CHLOROPHYLL: the green pigment in plants that acts as the light receptor for the process of PHOTOSYNTHESIS. Chemically, this pigment is related to cytochromes and the heme portion of hemoglobin. It is made up of four pyrrole groups hooked together by carbon bridges into a ring structure (tetrapyrrole nucleus). A long lipophilic tail (phytol) is attached to one of the pyrrole units of the ring. At the center of the tetrapyrrole ring is an atom of magnesium. The several forms of chlorophyll differ only in minor modifications of side groups attached to the tetrapyrrole nucleus. The predominant forms in higher plants are chlorophylls *a* and *b*. Chlorophylls *c* and *d* occur, in addition to *a* and *b*, in the algae. Bacteria contain yet another form: bacterio-chlorophyll. Each of the chlorophylls has its own characteristic absorption spectrum, certain colors of light being absorbed while others are transmitted. There is a close correspondence between wavelengths (or colors) of light absorbed by chlorophyll and the wavelengths that are most effective in photosynthesis.

In higher plants, chlorophyll is found in chloroplasts, tiny ellipsoid bodies suspended in the CYTOPLASM of the cells. Chlorophyll molecules are oriented in lamellae, or thin layers, within the chloroplasts; the chlorophyll-containing lipid layers alternate with layers of protein. When light strikes the chloroplast, chlorophyll is somehow "activated." This "activated" chlorophyll can split a molecule of water into oxygen and

Chlorophyll: The formation of organic matter requires energy, which in photosynthesis is supplied by sunlight. In vascular green plants the pigment that absorbs the light is usually chlorophyll *a*, of which the structure is shown below. It consists mostly of carbon (black) and hydrogen (white), along with a few atoms of oxygen and nitrogen and a single atom of magnesium. The molecule as a whole consists of two portions: a flat, squarish head, known as *chlorophyllin*, and a long tail, built much like a carotenoid, known as *phytol*. The single magnesium atom is at the center of the chlorophyllin head, bound to the four atoms of nitrogen (gray). One billion such molecules are normally found within each of the chloroplasts of a leaf cell. (*Harvard Univ. News Office*)

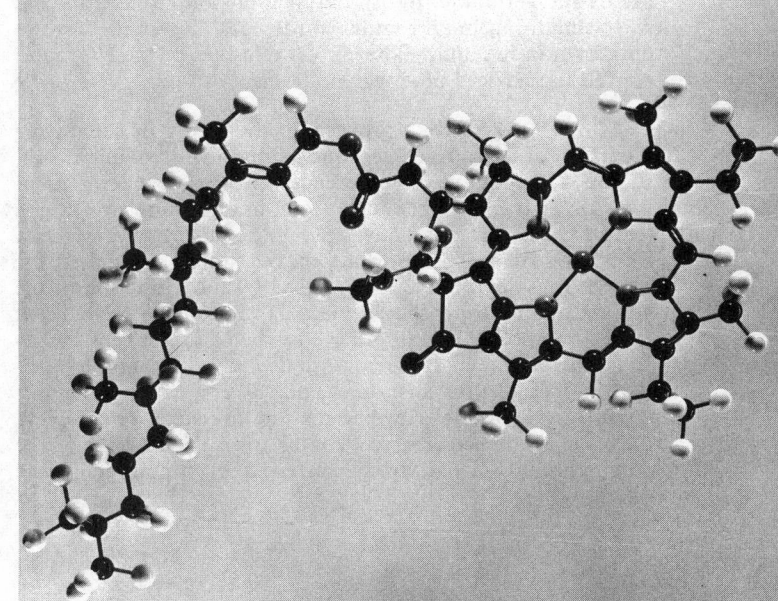

hydrogen ions. The hydrogen ion can cause a photochemical reduction of a suitable hydrogen acceptor, believed to be either DPN or TPN, yielding reduced DPN (DPNH) or reduced TPN (TPNH). This is the initial step in the process of photosynthesis. Chlorophyll *a* was synthesized in the laboratory for the first time by R. B. Woodward and coworkers in 1960. See also PYRIDINE NUCLEOTIDES.—*H. H.*

CHOLESTEROL: see STEROLS.

CHOLINE: a water-soluble base, $HO—CH_2—CH_2—N^+(CH_3)_3$, found in many phosphorus-containing fats (phospholipids), of which lecithin is the principal one. Choline is synthesized by animals on an adequate protein diet, but when the protein content of the diet is poor, choline must be added to the diet to prevent the development of "fatty liver." It is also involved in the metabolism of fat and of methyl groups. See also ACETYLCHOLINE; TRANSMETHYLATION.—*J. F. S.*

CHORD: a straight line segment that joins the end points of an arc of a curve. It is called the chord of the arc and is said to subtend the arc. The diameter of a circle is the chord of the semicircle. A chord of an arc of a closed curve is associated with two arcs; *e.g.* the diameter is associated with both semicircles into which it divides the circle. Any other chord of a circle has a greater arc and a lesser arc. Many theorems of plane geometry concern chords of circles. Chords played an important role in early trigonometry; subsequently half of the chord of an arc of a unit circle was taken to be the sine of half of the corresponding central angle.—*H. C.*

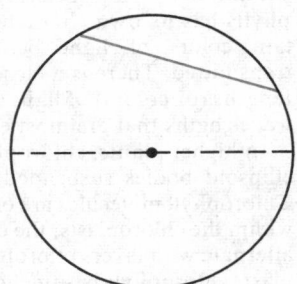

Chord: The blue line is the chord of an arc; the dotted line is the diameter, or chord of the semicircle.

CHORDATES: animals that possess at some stage of development a supporting rod of cells, the notochord, extending throughout the long axis of the body, a dorsal tubular nerve cord, and pharyngeal gill slits. In the lower chordates, namely the urochordates (tunicates), the hemichordates (enteropneusts), and the cephalochordates (amphioxus), the notochord and gill slits persist throughout life. In the vertebrates the notochord is more or less completely replaced in adult life by the vertebrae. In fishes and some amphibians the gill slits remain but in all reptiles, birds, and mammals they are outgrown in the adult. The closest relatives of the chordates are the starfish and other echinoderms.—*W. He.*

CHROMATOGRAPHY: a process for analyzing or separating members of a group of gaseous or dissolved chemical substances according to the differences in their adsorption affinities for a given adsorbent. Fluid containing the substances (called the adsorbates) moves along the adsorbent surface at a certain rate. Each adsorbate moves more slowly than the solvent to a degree that is increased by the attraction of the adsorbent and decreased by the attraction of the solvent and by the competition of all other adsorbates present for the reactive sites on the adsorbent. Practical chromatography consists in choosing the adsorbent and solvent, as well as maintaining a rate of flow slow enough to allow time for complete diffusion of the several adsorbates from the interior of the moving fluid to the adsorbing surface at each point along the

latter so that each is retarded only in accord with its over-all affinity. *Column chromatography* stems from the classical experiments of Michael Tswett in Warsaw, *c.* 1901–03, in which an extract of plant pigments (the adsorbates) in an appropriate solvent (light petroleum) is allowed to flow down a column of powdered limestone in a glass tube, leaving the pigments in a colored band at the top of the column. This band may be "developed" by washing with pure solvent ("eluent" or "elutrient"); the band now breaks up into several discrete colored bands, each of which progresses down the column at a different rate. This column "chromatogram" may be pushed from the tube and the individual bands cut apart with a knife; or they may be "eluted" ("elutriated") from the column serially by continuing the input of the same or different pure solvents, in which case they are collected at the bottom in the "eluate." An alternative process, *displacement chromatography,* consists in continuing the input of the mixture itself. Each adsorbate tends to replace those less strongly adsorbed and thus to push them ahead of it down the column, so that a series of adjacent or overlapping bands results. In *gas chromatography,* a gaseous mixture is separated by passage through a column of solid adsorbent, which may be wet with a non-volatile liquid solvent for one or more of the gaseous components. *Ion-exchange* (column) *chromatography* utilizes as adsorbent a substance that contains ionizing groups, and the adsorption process is an exchange of ions between solution and adsorbent. Originally a water-softening process utilizing the ion-exchanging properties of natural clays and zeolites (adsorbing calcium in exchange for sodium ion), ion-exchange has since 1935 received enormous impetus from the

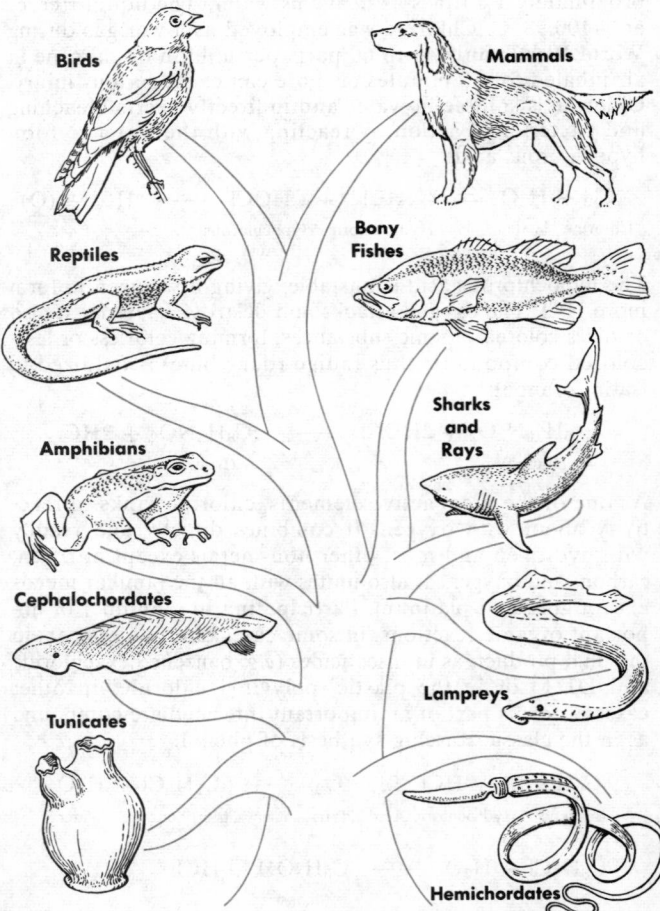

Family Tree of Chordates

Birds

Mammals

Reptiles

Bony Fishes

Sharks and Rays

Amphibians

Cephalochordates

Lampreys

Tunicates

Hemichordates

Fig. 1—Human cell with 46 chromosomes: Characteristic chromosome number can be clearly distinguished in the photomicrograph (about X 1100) of tissue culture made from biopsy of skin of a normal male. (*Ernest H. Y. Chu/Oak Ridge National Laboratory*)

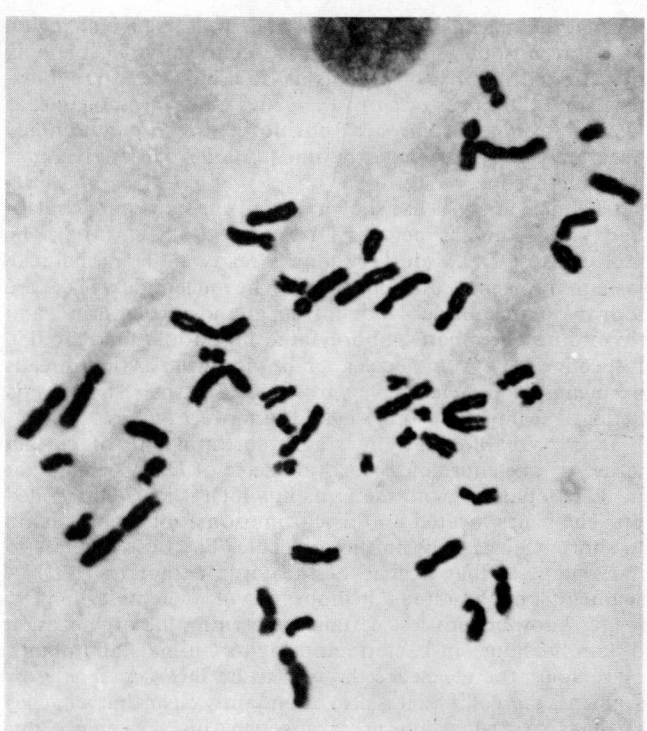

invention and production of chemically stable, very reactive synthetic exchangers, *e.g.* those based upon polystyrene and cellulose. Both these substances, either in small-bead or highly dispersed form, form a solid matrix or support for the attachment of the ionizing groups that do the actual exchanging. Although these materials were first used for displacement chromatography (in which each component pushes off the one ahead of it), their full potential was realized in the separation of rare earths and other fission products by "elution" chromatography at Oak Ridge, Tenn., 1943–47. Ion-exchange chromatography has been successfully adapted by biochemists for separating components of mixtures derived from materials of biological origin (*e.g.* components of nucleic acids and of proteins). *Paper (or partition) chromatography* utilizes a flow of solvent through paper or cloth-like material that has been impregnated at one end with the mixture to be separated. The basic principle is the same as when a mixture of dyes (*e.g.* ink) is slowly applied to a point on an absorbent paper or paper napkin, and is made to spread either by continuing the slow application of the dye-mixture itself or by adding a series of small drops of water or other solvent to the adsorbent surface. Concentric rings of different dyes appear, some being retarded more than others by a greater attraction to the stationary material. In "two-dimensional" paper chromatography, large sheets of paper are used. The starting mixture is applied as a spot at one corner: one solvent is allowed to flow uniformly from one adjacent edge toward a far edge; another solvent is allowed to flow at right angles to the direction of the first solvent, thus producing a second separation of the series of spots produced by the first solvent. Electric fields may be used to affect the relative mobilities of charged substances ("paper electrophoresis"). Various sprays or fluorescence methods are used for the detection of the substances separated, and the distance traveled by any one component is expressed as the ratio of its movement to that of the solvent front. (See ADSORPTION; CHEMICAL ANALYSIS.) —*W. E. C.*

CHROMIUM: a metallic element (Cr); at. no. 24; at. wt 52.01; density 7.1; mp about 1900°C. Discovered by N. L. Vauquelin (1797), chromium is now prepared by reducing chromic oxide with aluminum (Goldschmidt process). It is similar to platinum in luster, and, having high resistance to corrosion, is a major ingredient in stainless steel. Chromium has valence states of $+2$ (chromous), $+3$ (chromic), and $+6$ (chromate). Chromic oxide, the most widely used chromic compound, is formed by heating chromium in air. Chromic salts form coordination compounds (see CHELATES) with ammonia, cyanide, and thiocyanate. Potassium dichromate in acid solution is a very strong oxidizing agent. Chromates are used as corrosion inhibitors in cooling systems, as pigments, and as oxidizing agents in organic chemical technology.—*G. W. M.*

CHROMOSOMES AND GENES: Few generalizations of biology compare in scope with the chromosome theory of inheritance, according to which the control and transmission of hereditary characteristics are governed by the delicate, threadlike *chromosomes* of the cell nucleus. Chromosomes are microscopic in size, but can be easily demonstrated because of their affinity for certain dyes; hence the name, which means "color body." As a general rule each cell in the body of higher plants and animals possesses a group of chromosomes whose number is characteristic of the species. For instance, human cells contain 46 chromosomes (Fig. 1), whereas frog cells have 26 and corn cells 20. Bacteria and even viruses possess chromosomes, although considerably simpler than those of higher organisms.

Genetic analysis has shown that a large number of small units, the *genes*, are arranged in linear sequence along the length of each chromosome. The genes control the various hereditary characteristics of the organism, most probably by controlling the production of enzymes and other proteins. The exact number of genes on a chromosome is not known, but must reach hundreds or thousands. Much of our knowledge of genes came originally from studies of the small fruit fly, *Drosophila;* the most significant recent advances have involved work on molds, bacteria, and viruses.

Fig. 2 shows a chromosome segment of *Drosophila,* with the positions of some genes indicated. For instance, individuals possessing the gene *w* have white eyes instead of the

Fig. 2—Chromosome and genetic map of the salivary gland of drosophila: The various aspects of gene arrangement with their loci and crossing-over frequency are indicated in this significant portion of the chromosome. (*After C. B. Bridges*)

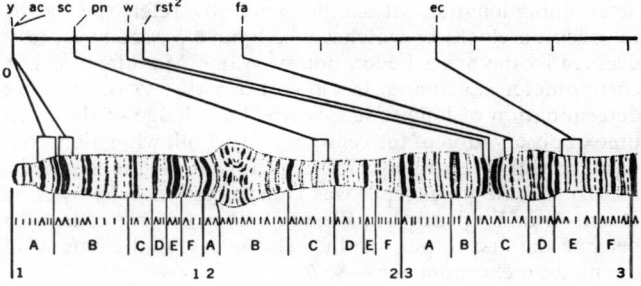

normal red. The assignment of a gene to a particular region of a chromosome is a difficult task, technically feasible only in a limited number of organisms. It should be noted, however, that the linear *order* of the genes on a chromosome, as distinct from their physical positions, may be determined accurately from breeding experiments alone, without recourse to a microscope.

Chemical analysis has shown that all chromosomes contain deoxyribose nucleic acid, or DNA (see NUCLEIC ACIDS). The molecules of DNA are very long threads, built in chainlike fashion from smaller chemical units, the nucleotides. There are four main nucleotides—adenosine, guanosine, cytosine, and thymidine phosphates, abbreviated here to A, G, C, and T respectively. DNA molecules can be visualized as thin threads by means of the electron microscope, but their structure is deduced from X-ray analysis and other techniques.

It is probable that the single chromosome of certain viruses is one enormously long molecule of DNA—long, that is, by comparison with the virus in which it is usually coiled up. The genes located on this chromosome must correspond to shorter lengths within the molecule. The best estimate to date suggests that a gene of the virus comprises a DNA segment some hundreds or thousands of nucleotides long.

Our knowledge is less certain concerning the organization of chromosomes in bacteria and higher animals and plants. Here again the genes are thought to be DNA molecules or segments thereof, and it is also abundantly clear that all genes on the same chromosome are arranged in a linear sequence. But how the genes are connected to one another, and what is their fine structure, are questions for the future.

As already mentioned, genes exert their influence by controlling the synthesis of proteins, and the individual gene consists of a long sequence of nucleotides in a DNA molecule. Just how the nucleotides control protein synthesis is perhaps the most fascinating question of modern genetics and biochemistry. It is now widely believed that the sequence of nucleotides in a given gene constitutes a "code" which specifies the sequence of amino acids in the protein controlled by that gene. There is, furthermore, reason to believe that nature uses a three-letter code. That is, three nucleotides in a row, such as UUU or UGC, would stand for one of the amino acids used in the construction of proteins. A protein chain consisting of 100 amino acids would therefore be coded by a DNA chain of 300 nucleotides. Progress is currently being made in determining the actual code and in discovering how the protein is assembled within the cell. See BREEDING; GENETICS; HEREDITY.—*J. G. G.*

CHRONOMETER: an instrument for precision time measurement; generally, a mechanical timekeeper designed for use on shipboard. Although resembling a large, well-made watch suspended in gimbals and poised to remain horizontal at all times, a chronometer differs in that it has a helical balance spring, a spring-detent escapement, and usually a fusee (see CLOCKS AND WATCHES). Formerly referring to any watch or portable clock having a detent escapement and intended for determining longitude at sea, the word now refers specifically to precision clocks or watches which have passed strict tests decreed by the Swiss Federation of Watch Manufacturers. A chronometer is essential in CELESTIAL NAVIGATION because determination of longitude involves knowledge of the exact time of observation of the celestial body. Following numerous unsuccessful attempts by 17th-cent. inventors, the first satisfactory marine timekeeper was constructed in 1761 by John Harrison in England; but Pierre Le Roy of France in 1765 became the first to put together all the essential elements of the modern chronometer.—*S. B.*

CHURCH, ALONZO, 1903–   , U. S. mathematical logician; b. Washington, D. C. Currently professor of mathematics at Princeton and editor of the *Journal of Symbolic Logic,* he is best known for his proof (1936) that the DECISION PROBLEM for the lower functional calculus is unsolvable, and for his contributions to the theory of effectively computable functions. —*I. L.*

CILIA: in certain PROTOZOANS, minute, hairlike living extensions of the cell. Typically, a protozoan has hundreds or thousands of cilia, beating movements of which propel the animal through its liquid environment and create currents that bring food particles to it. Cilia are also present in certain cells of higher animals, especially those cells that line the respiratory, reproductive, and digestive tracts. The electron microscope shows that a cilium consists of 11 distinct filaments fused inside an enveloping sheath.—*R. P.*

CIRCLE: a plane geometrical figure all points of whose boundary are equidistant from a fixed point. The fixed point is the center, and the common distance is the radius. The boundary is called the circumference. Frequently "circle" is used synonymously with "circumference," in the sense of a curve rather than the figure bounded by it. A straight line segment joining two points of the circumference is a chord; a chord passing through the center is a diameter. Clearly, the length of the diameter is twice that of the radius. The length of the circumference is equal to π (3.1416 approx.) multiplied by the diameter; and the area of the circle is π times the square of the radius. An arc of a circle is a part of the circumference lying between two fixed points. Each chord subtends two arcs; one arc is greater and the other lesser, unless the chord is the diameter, which subtends arcs of equal size. The part of a circle bounded by a chord and its subtended arc is called a segment. A sector is a part that is bounded by two radii and the intercepted arc. A secant is a straight line that cuts the circumference in two points. A tangent is a straight line that meets the circumference in one point only.

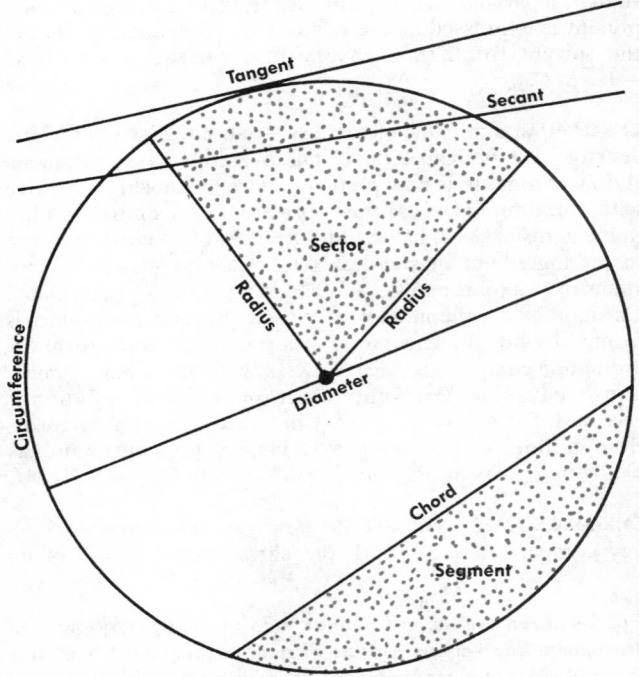

Terms Associated with Circles

Open circulation: Vessels from the heart of the crayfish pour blood into large irregular spaces called *sinuses*. Valves in the heart prevent backflow. Blood is colorless or blue (from hemocyanin pigment with which the oxygen combines); it moves slowly in peristaltic spurts.

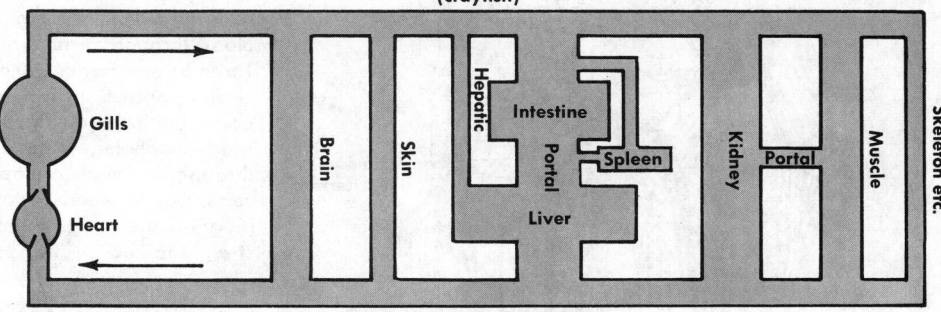

Open Circulation
(crayfish)

Single closed circulation: The blood flows in narrow vessels throughout its course, and a single heart pumps it through the gills for aeration. In this process, oxygen combines loosely and reversibly with the protein compound hemoglobin.

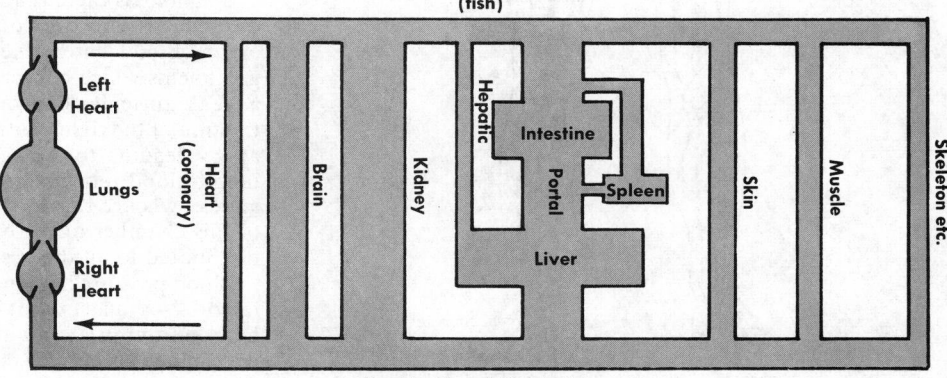

Single Closed Circulation
(fish)

Double closed circulation: From the right heart of a mammal, blood is sent to the lungs to be aerated. From the lungs it passes to the left heart, which pumps it to all parts of the body except the lungs. The blood is thus pumped first through the lungs and then through the body.

Double Closed Circulation
(mammal)

Circles play an important role in the subject of geometry. Book III of Euclid's *Elements* is devoted to them. They are studied effectively in coordinate geometry, where the definition of a circle leads to the equation $x^2 + y^2 = r^2$, representing the circumference of a circle with radius r and center at the origin. The intersections of a sphere by planes yield circular cross sections. Circles of latitude and longitude on the earth are boundaries of such sections.

The circle is found in innumerable places in nature. Its frequent and natural occurrence, together with the perfection of its form, led the Greeks to presume that the gods would require heavenly bodies to move in circular orbits. The Ptolemaic system is based on this assumption, which was relinquished reluctantly only within the last 400 years.—*H. C.*

CIRCULATION IN LIVING THINGS: the movement of blood in animals in a circuit from heart to tissues to heart; more generally, the transport of materials from one part of the body to another in any organism, whether this movement is essentially circular or not. In small organisms, DIFFUSION may be adequate to provide for the movement of oxygen and foodstuffs from surroundings into the interior of the cell or organism, or of carbon dioxide and other wastes in the opposite direction; but diffusion is slow, and in larger organisms the distance from the outer limits of the body to the center is so great that diffusion will not supply sufficiently rapid transport. Higher plants (seed plants) have a complex system of transport, involving specialized tissues. Phloem cells make up a distinct tissue in the stem which transports food materials between leaves and other parts of the plant. The living cytoplasm of adjacent phloem cells appears to be continuous through the stem, and food transport probably depends on movements of the cytoplasm itself. Xylem tissue is made up of long hollow cells and is concerned primarily with conducting water from roots to leaves.

In animals, the most primitive circulatory systems seem to be made up of tubes through which fluid is moved either by action of microscopic hair-like cilia or more often by contractions in muscular walls of tubes or BLOOD VESSELS, a process analogous to peristalsis in the alimentary tract. In higher animals, motive power for blood is provided by a specialized portion of the tube called a HEART, which is in effect a muscular blood pump. There are two basic types of circulatory systems involving hearts: closed systems, found in the vertebrates, annelid worms, and some mollusks; and open systems, in some mollusks and in arthropods. In the closed system, blood flows entirely within a system of tubes or blood vessels and never comes in direct contact with tissue cells; the latter are bathed in lymph (see LYMPH SYSTEMS), derived from the blood but somewhat different in composition. In the open

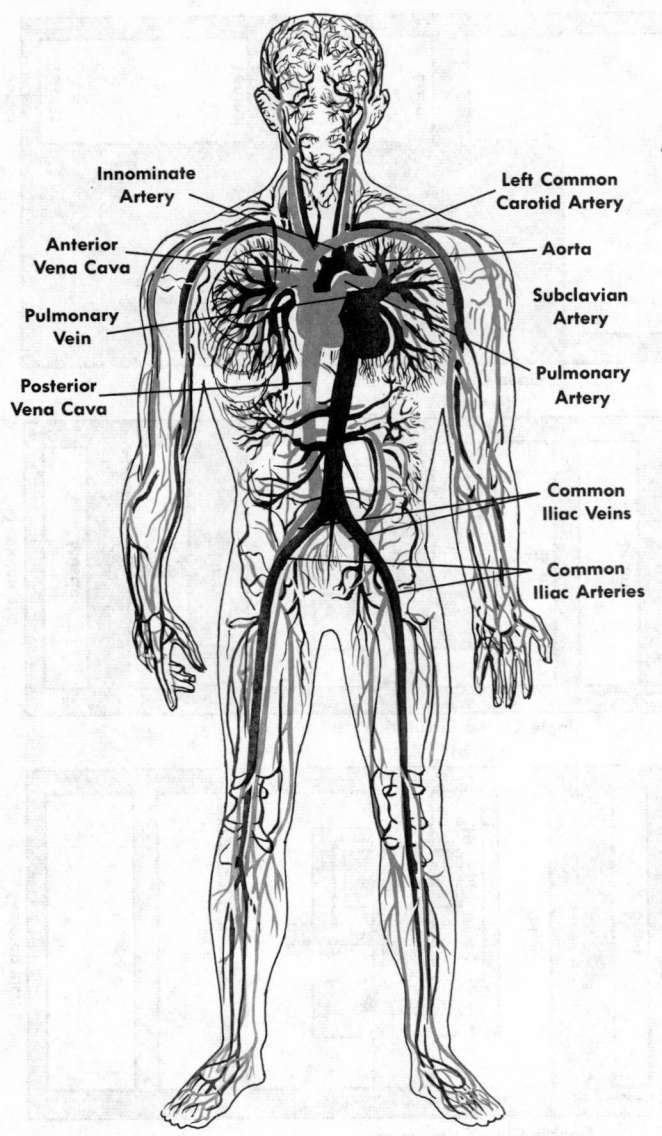

Innominate Artery

Left Common Carotid Artery

Anterior Vena Cava

Aorta

Pulmonary Vein

Subclavian Artery

Posterior Vena Cava

Pulmonary Artery

Common Iliac Veins

Common Iliac Arteries

Circulation in man: Flowing in closed system (only leak is lymphatic system, not shown), blood leaves heart by thick-walled arteries (seldom near surface, shown in black), returns by veins (thinner-walled, often just beneath skin, shown in blue); it passes from arterial to venous vessels by minute capillaries (invisible to naked eye, not shown). Pressure is maintained by contraction of heart, whose right and left halves share a common beat but do not exchange blood. Blood from all parts of body except lungs enters right side of heart, from which it is squeezed out through pulmonary artery and led to lungs, where its hemoglobin picks up oxygen. Aerated blood returns from lungs to left side of heart by pulmonary vein. Contraction of left side of heart propels blood through aorta, which leaves heart as arched elastic tube. Three large arteries (innominate, left common carotid, left subclavian) branch off from aorta to supply head, neck, and arms; aorta continues downward, divides into common iliac arteries, which supply legs. After exchanging substances with body tissues through thin walls of capillaries, blood returns to heart though veins, finally entering right side of heart by two venae cavae. (Sugar-rich blood from intestinal capillaries, instead of returning straight to heart, is first processed by liver.)

tion of lungs and aerial respiration. In higher reptiles, birds, and mammals there is a double circulation, involving division of the heart into two complete hearts functioning as a single organ. Blood enters the right atrium, or auricle, from the great veins which collect blood from tissues, and is forced by a weak auricular contraction into the right ventricle. Contraction of the right ventricle forces blood into the pulmonary artery, leading to the capillary beds of the lungs. From the lungs, blood returns through the pulmonary vein to the left auricle, whence it is forced into the left ventricle. Contraction of this chamber forces blood into the aorta, from which it is distributed to all the tissue capillary beds.

Blood pressure in man and other mammals depends on two factors—cardiac output (volume of blood pumped out of the heart per minute) and arterial resistance. Cardiac output is determined entirely by the amount of blood entering the heart from the veins, while frictional resistance depends mostly on the diameter of blood vessels, especially of the arterioles, smallest branches of the arteries. When arterioles are constricted, blood pressure tends to increase; when arterioles become larger, or are dilated, blood pressure tends to fall. During digestion of food, for example, products of tissue activity dilate intestinal arterioles; during muscular activity, products of this activity dilate arterioles of the muscles. Dilation results in an increased flow of blood into the tissues concerned; it also tends to decrease blood pressure, but in healthy individuals no marked decrease occurs because there are automatic regulating devices to prevent this.

The arterioles all over the body are under continuous control of a nerve center in the medulla oblongata of the brain, which constantly sends out nerve impulses causing constriction of the arterioles. The aorta and the carotid artery, which leads to the brain, contain in their walls sense organs which are stimulated when these vessels are stretched, as by an increase in blood pressure. These sense organs send impulses to the circulation nerve center in the brain, and the impulses inhibit the activity of this center, hence decreasing the dispatch of constricting impulses. If blood pressure falls, the activity of this reflex system decreases, and the number of constrictor impulses sent out increases. This feedback system keeps blood pressure constant within rather narrow limits, regardless of local dilation of arterioles in special tissues during activity; local effects of activity usually will predominate over the constrictor nerve impulses, and the automatic constriction occurs in inactive tissues, thus forcing

system, blood flows from the heart in arteries which, after some branching, have open ends through which blood flows directly into large tissue spaces, or sinuses, bathing the cells directly. In general, closed systems have small volumes of blood flowing at high velocity under high and constant pressure, while open systems have large volumes of blood flowing slowly under low and variable pressure.

Blood flows through at least part of either system in consequence of the force exerted by contraction of the heart. Hearts undergo a regular cycle of contraction (systole) followed by relaxation (diastole). During diastole, blood flows into the heart from the VEINS. In systole, the muscular walls of the heart contract, building up pressure on the blood within the heart, which is prevented from flowing back into the veins by valves. When pressure within the heart exceeds that in the artery (aorta) leading from the heart, the valve separating the heart from the aorta is forced open, and blood is ejected into the aorta. When relaxation of the heart muscle begins, the pressure in the aorta forces the valve shut again, so that the blood must flow away from the heart along the aorta into the system of arterial blood vessels.

The general course of blood flow is somewhat different in various kinds of animals. In fishes, blood flows from heart to gills in the ventral aorta, and from gills to tissues in the dorsal aorta and its many branches; veins return blood from tissue capillaries to the heart. In vertebrates, one can trace the evolution from fish to frog to reptile, bird, and mammal of a more complicated circulatory system, paralleling the evolu-

Plucking and abrasion of rock in mountainside by glacial ice of Pleistocene ice ages produced this great cirque in Canadian Rockies. Note rock debris on slopes. (*Canadian Govt. Travel Bureau*)

blood to flow through active tissues in increased amounts and diverting it from inactive tissues. Special regulatory mechanisms keep blood flow to the brain constant regardless of variations in other parts of the circulation. In diving animals, these mechanisms are so effective that the whole circulation, except that to the brain, can be shut down during a dive, thus conserving oxygen in the blood entirely for use by the brain.—*B. T. S.*

CIRQUE: a steep-walled niche, shaped like half a bowl, in a mountainside, excavated mainly by frost action. Cirques start to form beneath snowbanks, usually just above the lower limit of perennial snow. Excavation at first is the result chiefly of freezing meltwater that has penetrated openings in the rock beneath snowbanks; rock fragments are pried out and carried away downslope by trickling water. As a snowbank grows to become the head of a GLACIER, the cirque grows also; some cirques are more than 2,500 ft. wide. When occupied by a glacier the excavation of the cirque hollow by frost wedging is aided by ice which plucks out loosened blocks of rock, as well as by abrasion. Many glaciers have cirques at their sources, and adjacent cirques are widened until the area between them may be completely eroded away. Numerous cirques now visible, including those in mountain ranges now without glaciers, were made during glacial ages.—*R. F.*

CITRIC-ACID CYCLE (also **tricarboxylic-acid** or **Krebs cycle**): the principal oxidative mechanism for the production of energy from food (named after H. A. Krebs, who formulated it). It is called a cycle because one of the reactants, oxaloacetate, is regenerated after the oxidative steps and can therefore act catalytically in small amounts. The other reactant, acetyl coenzyme A, is oxidized in a turn of the cycle. This compound arises from the breakdown of protein, fat, and carbohydrate. In the catabolism or breakdown of carbohydrate, pyruvic acid is formed; this compound is decarboxylated, with the aid of coenzyme A, to give CO_2 and acetyl coenzyme A. In the breakdown of most amino acids, arising from the hydrolysis of protein, either pyruvate or acetate is formed, both giving acetyl coenzyme A. In catabolism of fats, acetyl coenzyme A is the end product. The citric-acid cycle starts with the acetyl coenzyme A derived from all these sources and is responsible for the oxidation of the two carbons of this compound to CO_2 and H_2O.

The individual enzymatic steps in the cycle are: (1) con-

densing enzyme catalyzes a combination of acetyl coenzyme A with oxaloacetate to form citrate and free coenzyme A; (2) aconitase establishes an equilibrium among citrate, isocitrate, and cis-aconitate, with isocitrate as the compound active in the cycle; (3) isocitrate dehydrogenase oxidizes isocitrate to α-ketoglutarate, CO_2 being split off; (4) α-ketoglutaric dehydrogenase catalyzes a reaction similar to the formation of acetyl coenzyme A from pyruvic acid; succinyl coenzyme A is formed and CO_2 is given off (this reaction is the only irreversible one in the entire cycle); (5) succinyl thiokinase catalyzes the reaction in which the energy of the succinyl coenzyme A bond is transferred to form the high-energy bond in ATP (adenosine triphosphate); (6) succinic dehydrogenase, a riboflavin enzyme, subtracts two hydrogen atoms from succinate to form fumarate; (7) fumarase adds a molecule of water to fumarate to form malate; (8) malic dehydrogenase oxidizes the alcohol group in malic acid to a keto group, thus forming oxaloacetate again. We return, then, to the beginning of the cycle, with oxaloacetate ready once more to condense with another molecule of acetyl coenzyme A. Since all reactants are regenerated except acetate and oxygen, the over-all net reaction is: $CH_3COOH + 2O_2 \rightarrow 2 CO_2 + 2 H_2O$. One CO_2 is produced in reaction step (3) and the other in step (4).

The oxidations in the cycle consist essentially of subtracting hydrogen and adding water. The carbon dioxide which is produced has, therefore, as one of its constituents the oxygen atoms from water. The oxygen consumed by respiration is used to convert hydrogen to water. This mechanism is typical of almost all biological oxidations, which only rarely add oxygen to carbon directly. Although oxaloacetate is regenerated by the cycle, some is lost through various side reactions. It can be supplied by all foods except fat. On a low-carbohydrate, low-protein diet, containing meager sources of oxaloacetate, the cycle cannot function properly, and acetate is inadequately oxidized; the result is an accumulation of keto acids, leading to ketosis. A lack of carbohydrate oxidation, as in diabetes, produces similar results, because again there is an insufficiency of oxaloacetate. The vital nature of the cycle is shown by the rapid death caused by giving an animal fluoroacetate: this poison combines with the enzyme aconitase (step 2), rendering it inactive and halting the cycle at step (2).

The citric-acid cycle plays an important role in cellular metabolism. It serves as a source of essential metabolic inter-

241

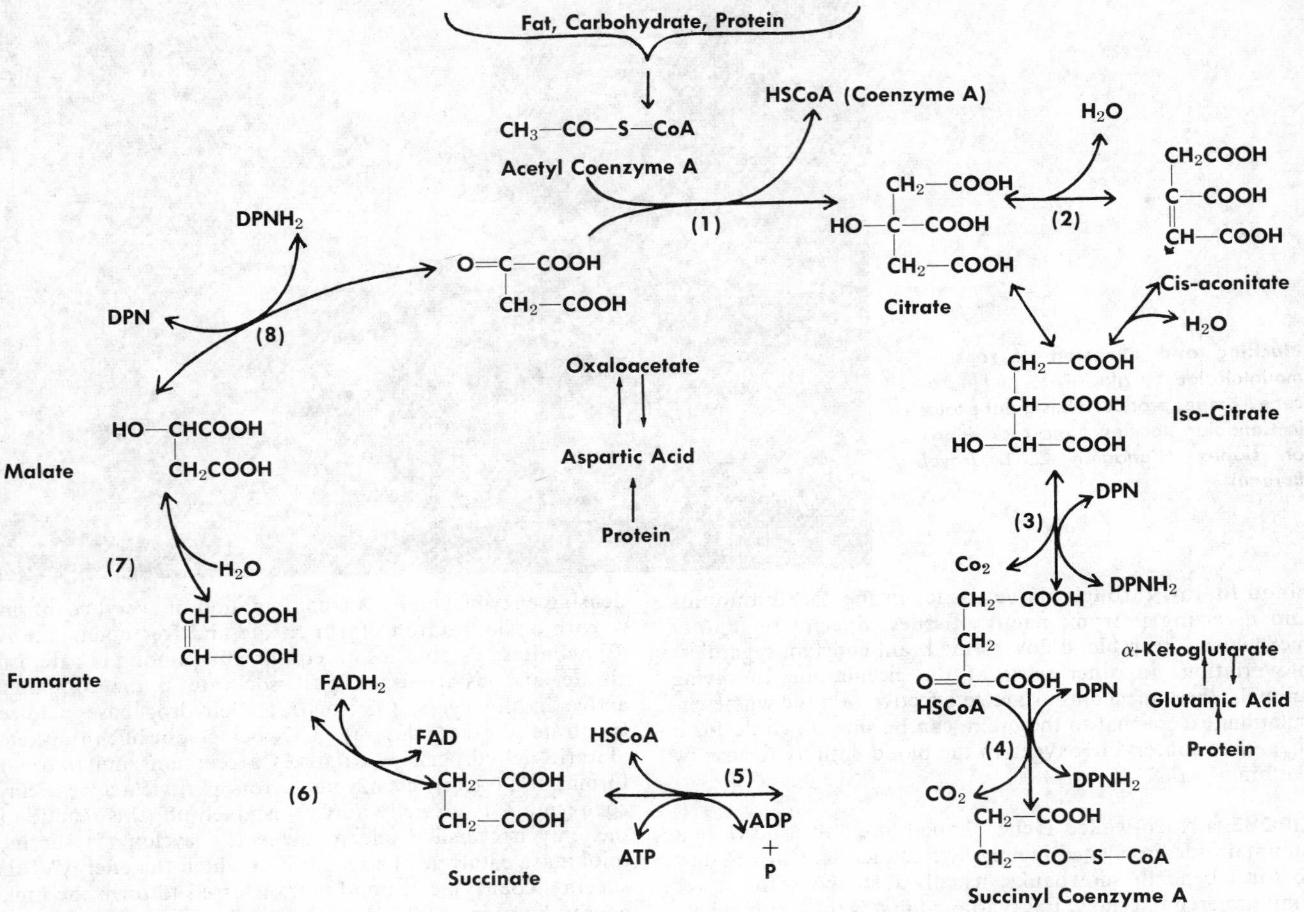

Fat, Carbohydrate, Protein

$CH_3-CO-S-CoA$
Acetyl Coenzyme A

HSCoA (Coenzyme A)

(1)

H_2O

CH_2-COOH
$HO-C-COOH$
CH_2-COOH
Citrate

(2)

CH_2COOH
$C-COOH$
$CH-COOH$

Cis-aconitate
H_2O

DPNH₂

DPN

(8)

$O=C-COOH$
CH_2-COOH

Oxaloacetate

Aspartic Acid

Protein

CH_2-COOH
$CH-COOH$
$HO-CH-COOH$
Iso-Citrate

$HO-CHCOOH$
CH_2COOH
Malate

(3)

DPN

Co_2

DPNH₂

(7)

H_2O

$CH-COOH$
$CH-COOH$
Fumarate

CH_2-COOH
CH_2
$O=C-COOH$
HSCoA

DPN

α-Ketoglutarate
Glutamic Acid

Protein

FADH₂

FAD

(4)

DPNH₂

CO_2

CH_2-COOH
$CH_2-CO-S-CoA$
Succinyl Coenzyme A

(6)

CH_2-COOH
CH_2-COOH
Succinate

HSCoA

(5)

ATP

ADP
+
P

Citric-acid cycle, pieced together by H. A. Krebs in 1937, offers a model of the pathway by which carbohydrates, fats, and proteins are converted into high-energy phosphate groups usable by living cells. (The numbers are keyed to the text.)

mediates, *e.g.* glutamic and aspartic acids, amination products of α-ketoglutaric and oxaloacetic acids which are constituents of proteins; and succinic acid, involved in heme formation. But its most important function is to provide energy from the catabolism of fat, carbohydrate, and protein. The energy is produced as follows: for every acetyl coenzyme A which is oxidized by one turn of the cycle, 12 high-energy phosphate bonds are produced in the form of 12 ATP molecules. This amount of energy is about 60% of that contained in the acetate molecule; the rest is lost as heat. The performance is more efficient than that of the best mechanical engine. One ATP is formed via substrate phosphorylation, as illustrated in step (5), while the other 11 are formed via a process called oxidative phosphorylation.

In the latter process, the oxidizing agent in the cycle is not oxygen directly, but consists of coenzymes which are reduced in the process. The coenzymes are vitamin-derived compounds: DPN (diphosphopyridine nucleotide), which contains the vitamin nicotinamide; and FAD (flavin adenosine dinucleotide), which contains the vitamin riboflavin. They can exist in the oxidized or reduced states, DPN and DPNH₂, and FAD and FADH₂, respectively. The oxidized forms of these coenzymes oxidize the reactant in the citric-acid cycle in steps (3), (4), (6), and (8), and in turn these coenzymes become reduced. The reduced coenzymes are reoxidized through a series of reactions in which inorganic phosphate is a participant: oxidative phosphorylation. In this process, there are two ATP molecules formed for every FADH₂ oxidized, while there are three ATP molecules formed for every DPNH₂ oxidized. The coenzymes are thus regenerated to the oxidized state and are able to serve again as oxidizing agents. This means that a small amount of coenzyme derived from vitamins acts catalytically to oxidize the much greater quantity of citric-acid cycle acids coming from catabolism of food.

Most of the energy produced by the cell takes place through the oxidations of the citric-acid cycle, these oxidations being coupled with phosphorylation to produce a uniquely biological energy unit, ATP. Both processes take place in structures called mitochondria, in the cytoplasm of cells. Mitochondria are found in all cells except red blood cells, bacteria, and some fungi; because of their function, mitochondria have been called the powerhouses of the cell.—*J. F. S.*

CLAIRAUT, ALEXIS CLAUDE, 1713–65, French mathematician and astronomer; b. Paris. His *Recherches sur les courbes à double courbure* (1731) gained him admission to the Academy of Sciences at 19. In 1736 he participated with P. L. de Maupertuis in the expedition to Lapland to measure a degree of meridian. *Théorie de la figure de la terre* (1743) and *Théorie de la lune* (1752) were among his works. In 1758 he computed the return of Halley's Comet. He is known also for his studies of the three-body problem, the development of potential theory, and applications of the calculus. He was a fellow of the Royal Society.—*D. J. S.*

CLARIFIERS: mechanical devices for the removal of solid particles suspended in liquids. Filters are used to remove crystalline solids. Very fine noncrystalline particles that will not settle under gravity are removed by CENTRIFUGES. Large amounts of crystalline or colloidal material are clarified in metal tanks, some of them more than 300 ft wide, by a continuous operation: the suspension is first introduced slowly at the top of the tank, to avoid turbulence, then the lower layers of the suspension are mechanically circulated in such a way that the sediment is drawn into a small central opening at the bottom of the tank; finally, the clarified, supernatant liquid is either decanted or allowed to overflow into collection channels built around the tank. Such tanks are used for clarification of water after the softening procedure, for purification of sewage-plant water, and for beet-sugar refining. The same type of equipment is used in the reverse process, where valuable suspended material is collected and the liquid discarded, *e.g.* coal and metal recovery, cement manufacture. See FILTRATION, CHEMICAL.—*T. M. and C. S.*

CLARK, ALVAN GRAHAM, 1832–97, U. S. astronomer, lens manufacturer, and telescope maker; b. Fall River, Mass. A self-educated scientist, Clark discovered 16 double stars in his lifetime. He also discovered a companion of Sirius (its existence had been predicted by others). Among the notable lenses on which he worked were those for the 40-in Yerkes telescope, the largest telescope of his time.—*D. H. D. R.*

CLARK, WILFRID E. LE GROS, 1895–   , English anatomist; b. Hemel Hempsted. A prolific contributor to research in human anatomy, he is even better known for his studies of fossil and living primates. Among his works are *Early Forerunners of Man* (1934), *History of the Primates* (1949), and *The Miocene Hominoidea of East Africa* (written with L. S. B. Leakey, 1951). He has held professorships at St. Bartholomew's Hospital and Oxford. He is a fellow of the Royal Society.—*D. H. D. R.*

CLARKE, WILLIAM BRANWHITE, 1798–1878, English-Australian geologist and clergyman; b. East Bergholt, Suffolk. He devoted much of his life to geological exploration, writing nearly 200 geological reports on more than 100,000 sq mi of world territory. In New South Wales, in the 1840s, he discovered gold and tin, and developed the coalfields. He was a fellow of the Royal Society.—*D. H. D. R.*

CLASSIFICATION OF LIVING THINGS: the description, naming, and grouping into categories of all animals and plants according to their similarities and relationships. This is the task of a special branch of biology known interchangeably as TAXONOMY or systematics. Some 350,000 different kinds of plants and more than a million kinds of animals have been classified. Without systematic classification, any attempt to deal with the seemingly endless array of organisms would result in complete chaos.

Taxonomic Characters: Classification involves the constant comparison of plants and animals with one another. At first, the differences among the plants or animals of a given area will stand out; *e.g.* a pine tree has certain definite characters that a dandelion lacks, and vice versa. By comparing the pine tree with other trees and plants, its important and distinguishing characters can be determined. If pines are then compared, certain additional diagnostic characters are found that differentiate one kind of pine tree from others. In identifying a plant or animal, then, one must first compare it to, and differentiate it from, other organisms. Finally, one must place it with the particular kinds with which it agrees in all essential characters. However, diagnostic characters, by which plants or animals are readily differentiated from others, may be of minor or no importance in classification. A sound classification system must be based on fundamental, inheritable characters and not on quantitatively variable or otherwise secondary characters. While diagnostic characters are essentially derived from the external appearance of an organism, the basic characters used in classification are derived from the external and internal structural details of an organism and its life history, distribution, mode of life, behavior, requirements, and chemical constitution.

As all information derived from various studies of a plant or animal is assembled and interpreted, the systematic position of an organism or a whole group of organisms may have to be changed. For example, many organisms undergo complex life histories involving various stages often drastically different from one another (see ALTERNATION OF GENERATIONS; METAMORPHOSIS). Before the life history of such an organism is worked out in all its details, several of these stages are likely to go under different scientific names. Such is the case in certain members of the fungi, whose life histories are incompletely known.

In comparison and evaluation of taxonomic characters, it is most important that those characters have the same origin and relationship; then they are regarded as being *homologous* (see HOMOLOGY AND ANALOGY). Classic examples of homologous organs are the reproductive organs of higher plants, or the arms of man, the front legs of horses, and the wings of birds. But the leaflike organs of moss and the leaves of flowering plants are not of similar origin, despite the similarity in function. The same is true of the wings of birds and the wings of butterflies. Organs of this kind are called *analogous*.

Species Concept: All animals and plants can be placed in different and serially graded groups, often called *taxa*. For all ordinary purposes of classification the lowest of the taxa is the *species,* the fundamental unit in taxonomy. One or several species, sometimes more than a thousand, are grouped together in a higher category, the *genus*. A species is normally given a two-part name (see BIOLOGICAL NAME), consisting of the generic name followed by the specific name. Thus the white pine is a member of the genus *Pinus* (pine), the species being *Pinus strobus*. Species and sometimes genera are not always so clearly separated that they can be readily distinguished one from another. Concepts of the nature of the species have undergone a drastic change over the last century, mainly under the influence of the theory of EVOLUTION and the newer knowledge in the field of GENETICS (see also HEREDITY; MUTATION). Whereas earlier biologists believed that species were fixed, modern biologists interpret species as a cross-section of an evolutionary line at a particular moment only. Today clearly defined taxonomic groups are interpreted as remnants of old stocks that have since become extinct and have given rise to the remaining groups. Connections between various existing groups indicate that evolution is still going on. In view of the multitude of life histories represented by known plant and animal species, no single definition of species can yet be given that applies to all known groups. But working biologists agree that species represent complex groups made up of greater or lesser numbers of breeding populations, each with its own characteristic genetic constitution and range of variability. The complex nature of species is indicated by the number of subspecies (also called races, breeds, or varieties) of cultivated plants and domesticated animals. Often three-part scientific names are used to designate subspecies of animals or varieties of plants (*e. g. Turdus migratorius propinquus,* western American robin).

Revolutionary changes in the species concept are reflected in modern systems of classification. Classifications based arbitrarily on a single set of characters (woody plants versus nonwoody ones) are called artificial. If a multitude of characters, mostly of a structural kind, are used, the system is called natural, since it brings together related forms. The full meaning of this relationship is made apparent by the theory of evolution, which provides the logical interpretation of the relationship among members of a group by considering them to be descendants of a common ancestor.

Higher Categories: For practical purposes a series of increasingly higher categories of classification has been worked out. According to it, every species belongs to a genus, one or more genera belong to a family, one or more families belong to an order, one or more orders belong to a class, one or more classes belong to a phylum or division, and phyla or divisions belong to a kingdom. When more categories are needed, subdivisions of the basic categories can be interpolated, *e.g.* suborder, superclass. Thus man (species *Homo sapiens*) is a member, with several extinct species, of the genus *Homo,* which belongs to the family Hominidae, the only family in superfamily Hominoidea (anthropoids lacking a tail and cheek pouches), which is one of three superfamilies in suborder Anthropoidea (primates having nails on all fingers and toes), in order Primates (mammals with nails on some fingers and toes), in subclass Eutheria (mammals with a placental connection between mother and unborn young), in class Mammalia (vertebrates with mammary glands and hair), in subphylum Vertebrata (animals with a skull and vertebral column), in phylum Chordata (animals with a notochord, hollow dorsal nerve cord, and other characteristics at some stage in development), in superphylum Coelomata (animals with a body cavity lined with peritoneum), in subkingdom Metazoa (multicellular animals with distinct tissues), in the kingdom Animalia. Similarly a dandelion is classified as follows (from higher to lower categories):

Kingdom Plantae
  Subkingdom Embryophyta
    Phylum Tracheophyta
      Subphylum Pteropsida
        Class Angiospermae
          Subclass Dicotyledoneae
            Superorder Sympetalae
              Order Campanulales
                Family Compositae
                  Subfamily Liguliflorae
                    Genus *Taraxacum*
                      Species *Taraxacum officinale*

The various categories are subject to change and expansion as a result of new discoveries. For instance, bacteria were at times separated as an entire kingdom, but are now known to possess genetic behavior similar to that of other organisms and are thus grouped with them. Depending on the system of classification preferred by the biologist, bacteria may be classified as a class (Schizomycetes) of fungi, a phylum (Schizomycophyta) of the plant kingdom, or occasionally as a phylum of a third kingdom (Protista) that includes all single-celled organisms. The subjective element in evaluating and defining higher categories as well as lower ones can never be completely eliminated, but the criteria for proposing changes in a system of classification can be constantly improved. The flexible nature of the current system may be annoying to those who look for so-called stability, but it permits extension or contraction at any point, without disturbing the basic structure.—*A. P. E.*

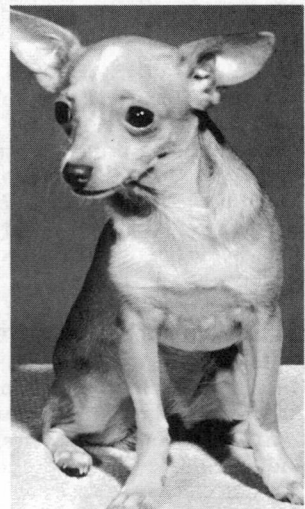

Appearances can be deceiving: In scientific classification basic characters are derived not from external appearance but from characteristics of internal structure of an organism. The two dogs, the tiny Mexican chihuahua (*middle*) and huge St. Bernard (*top*) do *not* resemble each other but are both members of the same species, *Canis familiaris.* The iguana, a reptile (*bottom*) and salamander, an amphibian (*immediately below*) look alike but are not even members of the same class. (*Jeanne White, Michael Pakeltis, Van Nostrand, Hal H. Harrison/Nat. Audubon Soc.*)

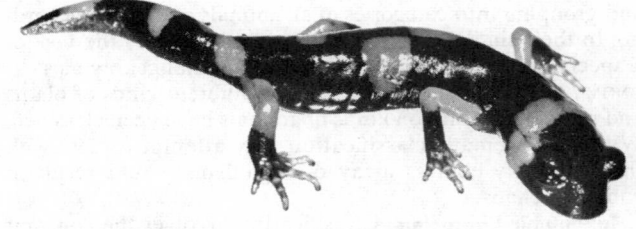

THE TWO-KINGDOM CLASSIFICATION

KINGDOM PLANTAE—PLANTS

SUBKINGDOM Thallophyta—Thallus Plants (Algae and Fungi)
  Phylum Cyanophyta—Blue-green Algae
  Phylum Euglenophyta—Euglenoid Flagellates*
  Phylum Chlorophyta—Green Algae
  Phylum Chrysophyta—Diatoms (Golden-green Algae)
  Phylum Pyrrophyta—Cryptomonads and Dinoflagellates*
  Phylum Phaeophyta—Brown Algae
  Phylum Rhodophyta—Red Algae
  Phylum Schizomycophyta—Bacteria
  Phylum Myxomycophyta—Slime Molds
  Phylum Eumycophyta—True Fungi
      Class Phycomycetes—Alga-like Fungi
      Class Ascomycetes—Sac Fungi
      Class Basidiomycetes—Club Fungi

SUBKINGDOM Embryophyta—Plants with Embryos
  Phylum Bryophyta—Bryophytes
      Class Hepaticae—Liverworts
      Class Musci—Mosses
  Phylum Tracheophyta—Vascular Plants
  Subphylum Psilopsida—Psilopsids
      Class Psilophytinae—Psilophytes
  Subphylum Lycopsida—Lycopsids
      Class Lycopodineae—Club Mosses
  Subphylum Sphenopsida—Sphenopsids
      Class Equisetineae—Horsetails (Scouring Rushes)
  Subphylum Pteropsida—Pteropsids
      Class Filicineae—Ferns
      Class Gymnospermae—Gymnosperms
      Class Angiospermae—Flowering Plants (Angiosperms)
          Subclass Dicotyledoneae—Dicots
          Subclass Monocotyledoneae—Monocots

KINGDOM ANIMALIA—ANIMALS

SUBKINGDOM Protozoa—Unicellular Animals
  Phylum Protozoa—Protozoans
      Class Mastigophora (Flagellata)—Flagellates*
      Class Rhizopoda (Sarcodina)—Pseudopodia for locomotion
      Class Sporozoa—Parasitic (no locomotion)
      Class Ciliata (Infusoria)—Ciliates
      Class Suctoria—Suctorians

SUBKINGDOM Parazoa—Body cavity a spongocoele
  Phylum Porifera—Sponges

SUBKINGDOM Metazoa—Animals with tissues
  Phylum Coelenterata (Cnidaria)—Coelenterates
      Class Hydrozoa—Hydroids
      Class Scyphozoa—Jellyfishes
      Class Anthozoa—Sea Anemones and Corals
  Phylum Ctenophora—Comb Jellies
  Phylum Platyhelminthes—Flatworms
      Class Turbellaria—Free-living Flatworms (Planarians)
      Class Trematoda—Flukes
      Class Cestoda—Tapeworms
  Phylum Nemertinea—Ribbon Worms
  Phylum Nematoda—Round Worms
  Phylum Rotifera—Wheel Animalcules
  Phylum Gastrotricha—Gastrotrichs
  Phylum Kinorhyncha (Echinodera)—Kinorhynchs
  Phylum Nematomorpha—Horsehair Worms
  Phylum Acanthocephala—Spiny-headed Worms
  Phylum Entoprocta—Entoprocts
  Phylum Sipunculoidea—Sipunculoids
  Phylum Priapuloidea—Priapuloids
  Phylum Echiuroidea—Echiuroids
  Phylum Mollusca—Mollusks
      Class Monoplacophora—*Neopilina*-like Mollusks
      Class Amphineura—Chitons
      Class Scaphopoda—Tooth Shells
      Class Gastropoda—Snails and Slugs
      Class Pelecypoda—Bivalves
      Class Cephalopoda—Cephalopods
  Phylum Annelida—Segmented Worms
      Class Polychaeta—Sandworms and Tubeworms

      Class Oligochaeta—Earthworms
      Class Hirudinea—Leeches
  Phylum Arthropoda—Arthropods
      Class Onychophora—Velvet Worms
      Class Tardigrada—Bear Animalcules
      Class Trilobita—Trilobites (extinct)
      Class Crustacea—Crustaceans
      Class Diplopoda—Millipedes
      Class Chilopoda—Centipedes
      Class Insecta—Insects
      Class Eurypterida—Sea Scorpions (extinct)
      Class Xiphosura—Horseshoe Crabs
      Class Arachnida—Spiders and Allies
      Class Pycnogonida—Sea Spiders
  Phylum Pogonophora—Beardworms
  Phylum Phoronida—Phoronids
  Phylum Bryozoa (Ectoprocta)—Moss Animals
  Phylum Brachiopoda—Lamp Shells
  Phylum Chaetognatha—Arrow Worms
  Phylum Hemichordata—Tongue Worms
  Phylum Echinodermata—Echinoderms
      Class Crinoidea—Sea Lilies
      Class Echinoidea—Sea Urchins
      Class Asteroidea—Sea Stars (Starfishes)
      Class Ophiuroidea—Brittle Stars (Serpent Stars)
      Class Holothuroidea—Sea Cucumbers
  Phylum Chordata—Chordates
  Subphylum Tunicata (Urochordata)—Tunicates
      Class Ascidiacea—Sea Squirts
      Class Thaliacea—Salps
  Subphylum Cephalochordata—Lancelets
  Subphylum Vertebrata—Vertebrates
      Class Agnatha—Jawless Vertebrates
          Subclass Ostracodermi—Ostracoderms (extinct)
          Subclass Cyclostomata—Lampreys and Hagfishes
      Class Placodermi—Armored Jawed Fishes (extinct)
      Class Chondrichthyes—Sharks and Rays
      Class Osteichthyes—Bony Fishes
      Class Amphibia—Amphibians
      Class Reptilia—Reptiles
      Class Aves—Birds
      Class Mammalia—Mammals

* Includes organisms showing features of both plants and animals.

CLAUSIUS, RUDOLF JULIUS EMANUEL, 1822–88, German physicist; b. Köslin. He introduced the second law of thermodynamics ("heat will not flow, of its own accord, from one object to a hotter one") in his paper "On the Moving Force of Heat, and the Laws Regarding the Nature of Heat Itself Which Are Deducible Therefrom" (1850; trans. 1851). His applications of thermodynamics to the steam engine contributed to the development of the concept of ENTROPY. His "Concerning the Kind of Movement Which We Call Heat" (1857) extended Daniel Bernoulli's work on the kinetic theory of gases. He was a fellow of the Royal Society and an associate of the U. S. National Academy of Sciences.—*D. H. D. R.*

CLAVIUS, CHRISTOPHER, 1538–1612, Jesuit astronomer; b. Bamberg, Bavaria. He undertook the calculations for Pope Gregory XIII's calendar reforms, verifying the scheme originally set by Aloysius Lilius of Naples. Clavius developed and explained the Gregorian calendar in an 800-page treatise published in Rome in 1603: *Romani Calendarii a Gregorio XIII P.M. restituti Explicatio.* Other works include his *Algebra* (1609) and *Astrolabium* (1593).—*O. G.*

CLAY: a soft, extremely fine-grained material or sedimentary rock composed predominantly of CLAY MINERALS (hydrous aluminum silicates). Additional constituents include variable amounts of quartz, feldspar, carbonate, and ferruginous and organic matter. Clays commonly become plastic when wet and highly indurated (stonelike) when heated or baked. Upon consolidation (lithification) clays convert to SHALE.—*C. C.*

CLAY MINERALS: a group of minutely crystallized, platy silicates produced by weathering of feldspars and other rock-forming minerals, and of volcanic glasses. Clay minerals are major constituents of residual soils and of mudstone and shales. Fine size makes clay minerals difficult to identify and classify; thus a variety of highly specialized techniques has been applied to their study, including optical and electron microscopy, selective staining, x-ray diffraction, and differential thermal analysis. Most clay minerals are apparently monoclinic. The major ones include:

Kaolinite Series (t-o)	$Al_4(Si_4O_{10})(OH)_8$	Kaolinite, Dickite, Nacrite, and Halloysite (all polymorphs)
Montmorillonite Series (t-o-t)	$Al_2(Si_4O_{10})(OH)_2 \cdot nH_2O$ $Fe_2(Si_4O_{10})(OH)_2 \cdot nH_2O$ $Mg_2(Si_4O_{10})(OH)_2 \cdot nH_2O$ $Zn_2(Si_4O_{10})(OH)_2 \cdot nH_2O$	Montmorillonite Nontronite Saponite Sauconite
Illite Series (t-o-t)	$K(Al,FeMg)_4[(Si\ Al)_9O_{20}](OH)_4$	(Generalized formula; illites are intermediate between clays and micas.)
Magnesian Clays (chain structures)	$Mg_5Si_8O_{20}(OH)_2(H_2O)_4 \cdot 4H_2O$ $Mg_4Si_6O_{15}(OH)_2 \cdot 6H_2O$	Attapulgite Sepiolite (meerschaum)

The structure of clay minerals is based on varied combinations of sheets, each having a specific or closely limited ionic composition. Layers may be bonded together as "sandwiches" through the sharing of anions; the "sandwiches" have only weak Van der Waals bonds between them, and this accounts for the platy shape and probably for the minuteness of the crystals. *Kaolinite* is a stack of "open sandwiches" each consisting of a silica layer (t=interlocked SiO_4 tetrahedra) and a gibbsite layer (o=interlocked $Al(OH)_3$ octahedra) linked together through the sharing of O and OH ions. *Montmorillonite* is basically a stack of three-layer sandwiches, with silica layers as the "bread" and the gibbsite layer as the "meat." The actual structure is complicated by loosely attached cations and water, which account for the swelling and ion-exchange properties of bentonite (altered volcanic ash) of which montmorillonite is the principal constituent. Physical properties based on the structures of the clay minerals account for their use as bleaching and purifying agents (fuller's earths), carriers for fertilizers and insecticides, binders in foundry molds, and drilling-muds. The high alumina content of the kaolinite group accounts for their use in ceramic wares, in cements, and as a potential source of metallic aluminum. The fine grain size of all makes them valuable as fillers of various types. See MINERAL (table).—*L. M.*

CLEAVAGE: the tendency of a rock such as slate, or of a mineral, to split along preferred planes. The well-known tendency of mica, for example, to split into very thin sheets is not accidental but is directly related to the way in which the atoms of this mineral are arranged within the crystal. In many crystals, but not all, atoms exercise a greater degree of mutual attraction in certain directions and less in others. If differences are sufficiently pronounced, it becomes possible to split or cleave the crystal along the planes across which the attractive forces are weakest. A crystal of mica can be compared to a pile of thin paper sheets: in both substances, greatest strength is found within each sheet, but very little attractive force holds them together. It is a simple matter to peel off sheets or to split the pile at any desired point. Some minerals do not cleave at all; others cleave with difficulty, and some very readily. Furthermore, some minerals cleave in only one direction, others in as many as six; however, in all cases the planes of cleavage are invariably related to the internal atomic structure of the minerals concerned and hence to the external forms of well-developed crystals. Such relationships provide valuable recognition features in identification.—*J. Si.*

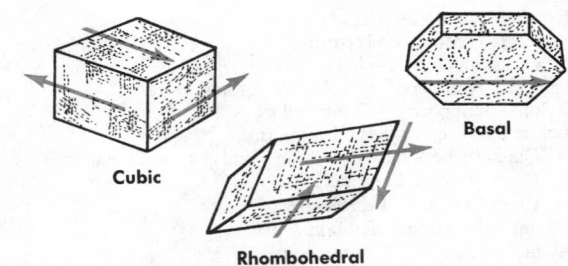

Cleavage characteristics of galena (*left*), calcite (*center*), and mica crystals (*right*) are shown above. Arrows indicate direction of splitting or cracking of each mineral.

CLIFFORD, WILLIAM KINGDON, 1845–79, English mathematician and philosopher; b. Exeter. He became professor of mathematics at University College, London, in 1871 and was made a fellow of the Royal Society in 1874. His mathematical work generalized Hamilton's quaternions by creating biquaternions, and recognized the implications of non-Euclidean geometry for Kant's theory of *a priori* propositions. Clifford studied topological structures of space and, in 1870, suggested a relationship between matter and curvature of space that foreshadowed Einstein's general theory. His views on space were further developed by Karl Pearson. Clifford also contributed to the study of Abelian functions, algebraic forms, and projective and algebraic geometry.—*H. C.*

CLIMATE: the sum total of weather over a long period, involving not only arithmetical averages taken by meteorological measurements, but also the deviations from the average as well as the frequencies of occurrence of special (sometimes rare) weather phenomena. The unique climate of any given locality is governed by (1) solar climate (corresponding to its latitude); (2) location relative to the continents and oceans or other major physiographic features; (3) location relative to the major features of the general atmospheric circulation; (4) effects of local geographic factors, *e.g.* altitude.

Planetary Climate: On a planet with an absolutely uniform surface, the climate of any place would be determined completely by the amount of solar energy received at that place during the course of the annual solar cycle. Under these conditions all points on a given parallel of latitude would possess identical climates, even though a meridional and zonal transport of heat and other properties would be provided for by an atmospheric circulation. Earth does not present such a uniform surface. Although regional climatic characteristics are influenced greatly by the location of the region with respect to general atmospheric circulation, meridional variations in atmospheric flow are determined by such factors as distribution of seas and continents, location of major ocean currents, and orientation of mountain chains.

Continental and Oceanic Effects: The interiors and eastern parts of large continents are said to possess a *continental climate.* Such climates are characterized by variable precipitation, low humidities, and great ranges in temperature, both between day and night and between winter and summer. At middle and high latitudes the solid land surfaces of the continents lose heat rapidly in winter and become very cold; in summer they rapidly absorb the increased solar energy and become heated. The result of these seasonal alternations in thermal balance is a climate that can best be described as a *climate of extremes.* But, on the other hand, the western portions of the continents, the oceans, and insular locations are said to possess a *maritime climate.* Because of the moderating effects of ocean surfaces, climates characterized by a predominance of maritime air masses are more humid, tend to have more consistent rainfall, and present a more uniform temperature. There are some exceptions, as on the western sides of the continents in the subtropics, where dry, desert-type climates may exist; but even here there is an absence of variability from day to day and between the seasons. In any event, whether moist or dry, a maritime climate is a *moderate climate.*

Climate and the Circulation: The distribution of heat, moisture, and other physical properties by the atmosphere is accomplished through a circulation that exhibits definite and persistent annual and seasonal patterns, and these features have a profound effect on the climate (see ATMOSPHERE, GENERAL CIRCULATION OF). For example, the region of convergence between the trade-wind systems of the two hemispheres (the intertropical or equatorial zone of convergence) constitutes one of the rainiest regions of the world. It includes the dense *equatorial rain forests* of Africa, Asia, and South America; here pressure gradients are small, winds are light, humidity is oppressive, and temperatures are high with very little diurnal or annual variation. This equatorial rainy belt (often referred to as the "doldrums") exists primarily north of the equator and is bounded on both sides by the relatively dry belts of the trade winds. The northeast trades extend from about 10°N to 30°N; the southeast trades extend from the equatorial zone of convergence near the equator to approximately 25°S. The trade-wind systems are best developed over the oceans, where they blow with exceptional regularity. The result is fair, dry weather, except where the winds are forced

to pass over mountain barriers; there the lifting may produce heavy rains along windward slopes (as in the Hawaiian Is.).

Poleward from the trade-wind belts the pressure-wind relationships which give rise to the trades require the existence of belts of high pressure in each hemisphere (near 30°N and 30°S). These belts, called the "horse latitudes," are regions of divergent air flow; this produces a climate quite different from that of the equatorial region with its convergent air flow. The climate of the "horse latitudes" is exceedingly dry, with clear skies, greater temperature extremes, and light variable winds. However, the horse-latitude high-pressure belt is not continuous but is broken up into individual cells (anticyclones). The continents also exert noticeable thermal effects. These anticyclonic regions, together with portions of the trade-wind belts, encompass the world's greatest deserts: the Sahara, the Arabian, the Kalahari, and those of South America, Australia, and SW North America.

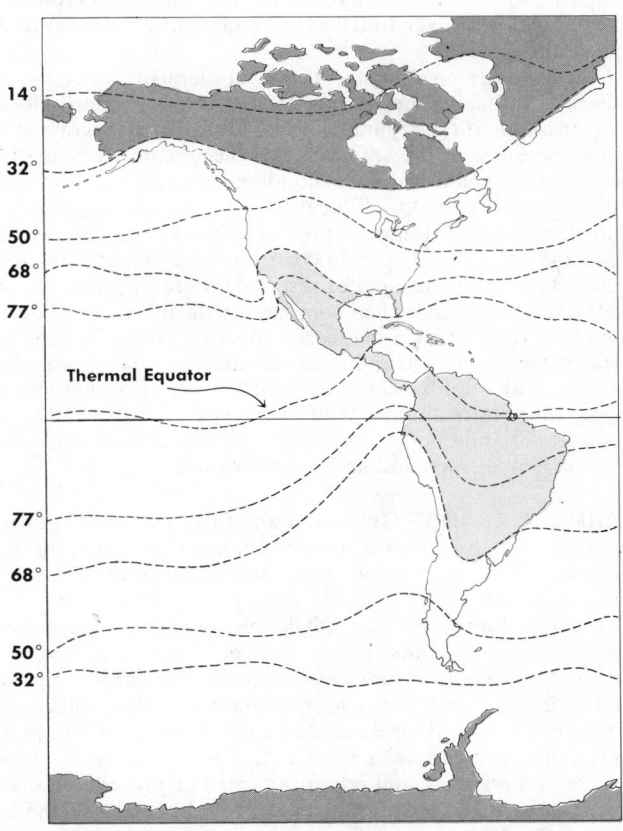

Climate is greatly influenced by distribution of land and water. If Earth were a uniform sphere (all land or all water), the isothermal (dashed) lines here would be more nearly horizontal.

The polar regions in each hemisphere also are characterized by divergent anticyclonic flow; the antarctic polar high is better developed than that over the arctic, because of additional intensification through continental cooling. Polar climate is marked principally by almost continuous cold and a snow cover which is continuous in most portions even though the annual amounts of snowfall are not excessive.

Broad regions of convergence occur between the westerly winds along the poleward peripheries of the "horse-latitude" anticyclones and the easterly winds which surround the polar anticyclones. In general, westerly winds prevail, but the weather is characterized by alternate passage of cyclones and anticyclones, with accompanying alternations in weather between wet and dry and between warm and cold. Here is the *temperate zone,* or the zone of the westerlies. The regional climates within the westerlies are highly variable and include regimes which range from those that are almost constantly cool and wet (as in Scandinavia) to those which are predominantly warm and relatively dry (as in S Europe). The latter type is commonly referred to as a *Mediterranean climate.*

Monsoon Climates: Over the largest continents a direct thermal circulation of a seasonal nature (MONSOON) develops. The ideal circulation is marked by flow inward toward a thermal low in summer, and outward from a cold continental anticyclone in winter. In summer this flow produces heavy rains as the moisture-laden maritime air converges either against a mountain barrier or against an opposing air stream. In winter the monsoon circulation brings dry continental air over the region and produces little if any rainfall, unless a significant overwater passage is involved (*e.g.* winter air masses reaching Japan from the Asian mainland). The monsoon climate is best developed over India and the maritime portions of SE Asia and China.

Local Effects on Climate: The final class of factors which directly influence the climate of a region is primarily local, *e.g.* location of the region with respect to local orographic air flow; nearness of lakes, forests, or other features which affect the thermal character of surrounding surfaces; and the elevation of the region. Of all local factors, elevation is probably most important. Temperature decreases with altitude at an average rate of 3°F per 1,000 ft, so that climates on lofty mountains near the equator resemble those of polar regions. Mountain climates, when compared with those of surrounding lowlands, show a decreased pressure, temperature, and specific humidity and an increased intensity in solar radiation, winds, and—up to moderate altitudes—increased precipitation. Mountain climates tend to resemble maritime climates in that variability of such elements as temperature and winds is less than in surrounding lowland areas.—*W. C. J.*

CLIMATIC CHANGE: Geological and fossil evidence indicates that climate in various regions has greatly fluctuated through history. Thus it is now well established that four great GLACIAL AGES have occurred during the past million years, the latest during the past 500,000 yr. Between these periods of glaciation the climate was relatively warm, and fossil evidence shows that at times semitropical and warm temperate climates extended to much higher latitudes than today. The last great ice age itself is believed to have included four major glaciation periods, each representing a progressively shorter stage of advancing and retreating ice. The present ice sheets of Greenland and Antarctica are probably relics of the last ice age, which is now apparently closing. Though the ice sheets at the time of their greatest extent never covered more than a fraction of Earth's surface, they undoubtedly exerted a marked influence on the world climate. Their existence would deflect storm tracks closer to the equator, with a resultant lowering of temperature and an increased precipitation at lower latitudes.

The evidence for more recent climatic changes (*e.g.* within the past 5,000 yr) is less conclusive. Our meteorological records cover a time interval short compared to the intervals covered by major climatic fluctuations, and many of these records are of doubtful quality. Nevertheless, certain evidence has some degree of acceptance among climatologists. Most notable were the dry period of the 16th cent., the increase in glaciation in the 17th cent., and the world-wide rise in temperature and recession of glaciers that began during the last century and is apparently continuing today. Warming since the start of our century has been particularly significant within the

arctic during winter months, exceeding 5°F in W Greenland and 3°F over a large part of the adjacent area. There is some evidence of significant trends in precipitation since about 1885, but these changes are not as consistent as the changes in temperature. Precipitation appears to have decreased over most of the U. S. A., Central America, N South America, Africa, and Australia, while an increase appears to have occurred over the Arctic, Mexico, S India, and SE Asia. H. Wexler has noted that these anomalies in temperature and precipitation are dynamically in agreement with correspond-

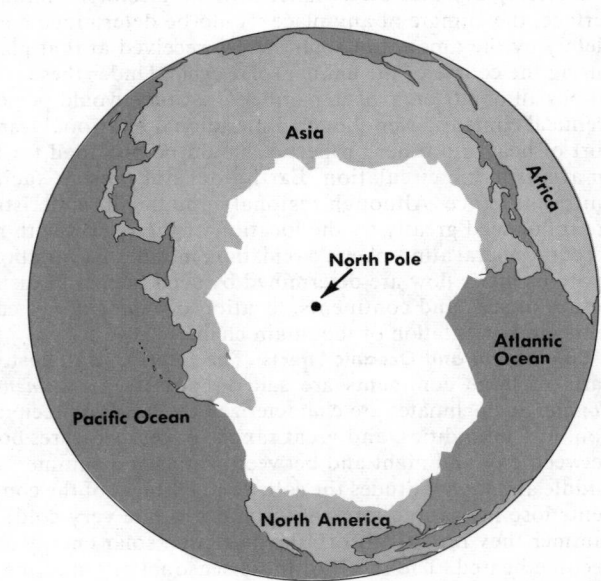

Farthest advance of Pleistocene arctic ice sheet—to 50°N in Europe and 38°N in N America—occurred some 20,000 yr ago.

ing pressure (wind) change patterns that occurred during the same period at middle and high latitudes; he has also noted a correlation between temperature and precipitation changes, on the one hand, and periods of sunspot maxima and sunspot minima on the other.

Meteorologists generally doubt the existence of any internal mechanism within the atmosphere that could account for a progressive or cyclical change in climate; hence the causes are sought in extra-terrestrial factors or the behavior of Earth itself. Plausible causes include (1) changes in the character of Earth's surface; (2) changes in the inclination of Earth's axis of rotation, changes in planetary tidal forces, or changes in orbit; (3) variations in intensity or spectral distribution of solar radiation; (4) variations in atmospheric transparency to solar and terrestrial radiation; (5) changes in amount of heat transported by ocean currents. The first groups of causes (1 and 2) can be neglected as to recent (historical) climatic change, but one or more of these factors may have been important during geologic time. The coincidence of major changes in Earth's surface and the occurrence of ice ages leads some investigators to believe that the former are principal causes of ice ages—a plausible line of reasoning because, obviously, any significant change in distributions of seas, continents, and mountains would profoundly influence world climates. With respect to group (2), one theory is that the stages of glacial advance which occurred within the glacial periods were concomitant with periods when Earth's axis was most nearly perpendicular to the plane of its orbit. This occurs about once in every 40,000 yr and is associated with the PRECESSION OF THE EQUINOXES. As to hypothesis (3), variations in the solar constant may have been of greater magnitude than is observable in the 11-yr sunspot cycle. In the short-term sense, some authors have tried to show that rather significant climatic variations have occurred in connection with variations in sunspot activity. In the longer-term sense, such climatic fluctuations would be cyclic in nature and would correspond in frequency to those observed for the sunspot cycle. With respect to cause (4), some evidence exists that the world-wide warming observed during the last half-century may be attributed to two secular (nonperiodic) trends—in-

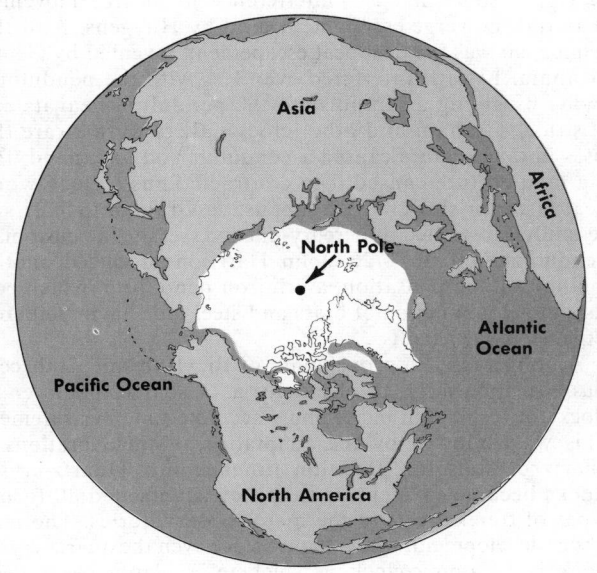

Today's arctic polar cap—including glaciers and floating pack ice—is smaller and thinner (max. 9,000 ft deep over Greenland).

creasing CO₂ content and decreasing atmospheric turbidity. The first results from increased output of products of combustion by our civilization, and the second from the decrease in explosive-type volcanic activity during the past 50 yr. Each of these factors could alter the radiative balance of the earth and hence its temperature, energy distribution, and in the final analysis, all other elements of its climate. As to (5), there is recent theoretical and empirical evidence that the amount of heat transported into high latitudes by ocean currents may fluctuate with a period of the order of a decade. The question is whether these account for important fluctuations in sea-surface temperatures and particularly in the extent of flow ice in polar seas. The latter has been considered in attempts to account for the alternations of glacial and interglacial climates which occurred during the Pleistocene (see GLACIAL AGES).—*W. C. J.*

CLIMATIC EXTREMES: In climatology, the extreme is the highest or lowest value of a meteorological element observed during a given period, *e.g.* an hour, month, season, or year. If this value is that which is recorded for the whole period for which observations are available, it is called the *absolute extreme.* Some of the absolute extremes are:
Temperature: highest, 136°F at Azizia, Tripolitania, Sep. 13, 1922; lowest, −125°F, Vostok, Antarctica, Aug. 25, 1958; highest in U. S. A., 134°F, Death Valley, Calif., Jul. 10, 1913; lowest in U. S. A., −70°F, Rogers Pass, Mont., Jan. 20, 1954.
Surface pressure: highest, 31.75 in., Irkutsk, Siberia, Jan. 14, 1893; lowest, 25.90 in. at 14°N, 137°E, Sep. 24, 1958; lowest for U. S. A., 26.35 in., Long Key, Fla., Sep. 2, 1935.

Highest surface wind speed (gust): 231 mph, Mt. Washington, N. H., Apr. 12, 1934.
Snowfall: greatest annual, 1,000 in., Paradise Ranger Station, Wash., 1955–56; greatest 24-hr, 76 in., Silver Lake, Colo., Apr. 14–15, 1921; greatest depth on ground, 454 in., Tamarack, Calif., Mar. 9, 1911. (These are U. S. records.)
Rainfall: greatest yearly, 1,042 in., Cherrapunji, India, Aug. 1860–Jul. 1861; greatest in calendar month, 366 in., Cherrapunji, India, Jul. 1861; greatest 24-hr, 46 in., Baguio, Philippines, Jul. 14–15, 1911; greatest 1-min, 0.69 in., Jefferson, Ia., Jul. 10, 1955.
Days with rain: maximum during year, 347, Bahia Felix, Chile.
Longest period without rainfall: 19 yr, Wadi Halfa, Sudan (entire period of record); in U. S. A., Bagdad, Calif., recorded no rain between Oct. 3, 1912, and Nov. 8, 1914, a period of 767 days.
Maximum average number of days per year with thunderstorms: 322, Buitenzorg, Java; in U. S. A., 86, Tampa, Fla.
Largest recorded hailstone: 1.5 lb, Potter, Neb., Jul. 6, 1928.
—*W. C. J.*

CLIMAX COMMUNITY: see SUCCESSION.

CLIMBING PLANTS: plants that attach themselves to and climb on supporting structures, often other plants. This adaptation enables a plant without a stem rigid enough to support it to reach heights where it receives more light. Climbing plants use various means for attachment. English ivy (*Hedera*) and creeping fig (*Ficus*) extend short aerial roots that are helpful in clinging to rough surfaces. Morning glory, bindweed, and *Philodendron* spiral around vertical supports. Grape, poison ivy, Virginia creeper, and *Clematis* hold on with modified branches, whereas climbing pea plants cling with leaves modified as tendrils. Woody vines in tropical rain forests, after climbing a tree trunk, often spread over the jungle canopy and link it to the ground as vertical lianas. See also LEAF; ROOT.—*L. and M. M.*

CLOACA: a common passage through which are discharged the residues of digestion (feces), the excretory products of the kidneys (urine), and the sexual products (eggs or sperms). A cloaca occurs in all vertebrate classes, but is rare among the mammals. Instead of a cloaca with its single opening to the outside of the body, most male mammals have a separate anus from the digestive tract and a urogenital passage for both urine and semen, and most female mammals have distinct openings from the urethra and the reproductive system. See also UROGENITAL SYSTEM.—*B. T. S.*

CLOCKS AND WATCHES: A clock mechanism consists of (1) a source of motive power in the form of a falling weight or uncoiling mainspring; (2) a train of geared wheels for transmission of the power; (3) an escapement controlling the mechanism's rate of speed by converting the circular force of the escape wheel into an oscillating motion of the regulating device—*i.e.* foliot, balance wheel, or pendulum (this regulator in turn governs the speed of rotation of the wheel train); and (4) an assembly of pinions and wheels, controlled from the train's center wheel, by means of which the index or hands indicate the time. A clock may also have alarm, striking, chiming, and other attachments. The word "clock" was derived from the Latin *clocca,* "bell." The identity of the inventor of the mechanical clock and the date of its first construction are unknown, but a clock may have existed in Europe by the 12th cent. Among important early examples are the great clock of the Strasbourg Cathedral (1358) and the astronomical masterpiece of Giovanni de Dondi (1348–1364). It was recently discovered that mechanical timepieces existed in China

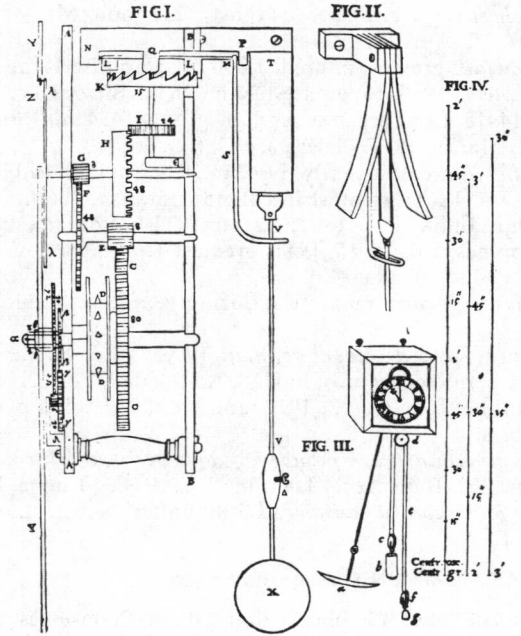

Seventeenth-century interest in time functions was reflected in Huygens' attempts to increase the accuracy of timepieces. The figure labeled FIG. II. shows the metallic cycloidal restraining cheeks Huygens developed to make the pendulum isochronous in large arcs. Plate is reproduced from his *Horologium oscillatorium* of 1673. (*Courtesy of the Burndy Library*)

prior to their known use in Europe. An elaborate water-powered astronomical clock was constructed in A. D. 1088 by Su Sung, and there is evidence that similar though probably less complicated clocks were built by the Chinese between the 7th and 9th cent. A. D.

The earliest regulating device was the foliot. This consisted of a pivoted rod with weighted arms, moved back and forth by a weight-driven, toothed escape wheel. At its pivot point, the foliot rod's tooth-like verges or pallets intermeshed with the teeth of the escape wheel. With each period or complete cycle, the foliot allowed the wheel to escape the width of a single tooth. This mechanism is termed a verge escapement; the foliot was eventually superseded by a bar balance and later by a weighted balance wheel. Of major importance was the invention of a coiled steel mainspring restrained within a barrel. The uncoiling spring provided motive power for the clock's operation. However, its driving power lessened as the spring uncoiled. This resulted in erratic performance until devices (the stackfreed and later the fusee) were developed to equalize the spring's pull. The latter device consists of a conical drum with a spiral groove. The mainspring's pull is equalized through a cord or chain unwinding from this groove.

The invention which probably contributed most to accurate time measurement was the application of the PENDULUM to control the rate of rotation of the clock's wheel train. As Galileo Galilei first observed, 1581, the period (time duration) of a pendulum's swing is dependent on the length of the pendulum, not on the distance the pendulum may swing. Within certain limits, no matter how far a pendulum of one given length may be made to swing, its period remains constant. Thus a pendulum's period is a reliable measurement of time. By increasing or decreasing a pendulum's length, its period can be lengthened or shortened, and made to correspond to a desired interval of time. Galileo saw the possibility of constructing pendulum clocks, and before his death instructed

both his son and a disciple, Viviani, on the application of a clock mechanism to keep a pendulum swinging; but the degree of their success remains controversial. At any rate, Christian Huygens of Holland first patented the application of a pendulum to clockwork, and produced the first known successful pendulum clocks, 1656–57. It was Huygens, too, who patented the spiral balance spring, which permitted clocks and watches to operate accurately in any position.

Another important 17th-cent. achievement was the anchor escapement, first found in clocks made by William Clement, 1671. It permitted a smaller arc of swing to the pendulum and gave somewhat less interference to its free movement than did the verge escapement used by Huygens. A further refinement was the deadbeat escapement, invented by George Graham, 1715. It interfered even less with the pendulum's swing by giving an impulse to the pendulum near its zero position. Graham and other clockmakers were aware that rises in temperature caused a pendulum rod to expand; falling temperature caused it to contract. Thus a clock would beat faster or slower. To compensate, Graham in 1721 successfully substituted a mercury-filled vessel for the customary pendulum bob. In 1726, John Harrison produced another method of compensation, a gridiron pendulum, which consists of a combination of brass and steel rods having different expansion coefficients.

Among many improvements of the 19th and 20th cent. was the application of electricity as a source of power for clocks; it resulted in increasingly accurate time measurement. This was followed by the adaptation of the vibrations of quartz crystals for precision timekeeping. Quartz-crystal clocks became so accurate that they superseded all former types of timekeepers in the major observatories. The most recent development, which may replace even the quartz-crystal clock, is the atomic clock, in which an oscillating electric current can be synchronized with the electric field of cesium atoms to achieve amazingly accurate timekeeping.

The watch (Anglo-Saxon *waeccan* or *wacian,* "to wake" or "the night watch") evolved gradually from portable clocks. Replacement of the falling weight by the coiled mainspring as the source of motive power by the early 16th cent. made possible considerable reduction in the size of timekeepers. Development of the first true watches is generally attributed to Peter Henlein (or Hele) of Nuremberg, who produced them between 1500 and 1510, but some scholars claim watches were worn in Italy in the 15th cent. Henlein's watches, shaped like spherical musk-balls or pomanders, were worn around the neck. Major steps in watch development were Huygens' spiral balance spring, patented 1675; the cylinder escapement, 1720; and the detached lever escapement produced by Thomas Mudge, 1755. The early spherical form of the watch changed to an oval drum shape and then to a thick, lens-like form which remained in general use until the abolition of the fusee, *c.* 1765, made possible the production of the first thin watches. See Color Plates 23–24.—*S. B.*

CLOUD: in meteorology, any visible mass of condensed water vapor suspended in the atmosphere. Clouds are formed when air containing water vapor rises, expands under the lower pressures which exist at higher levels in the atmosphere, and thereby cools, roughly adiabatically, until the temperature falls below the dew point. The vapor then condenses into a cloud, composed of myriads of tiny water droplets (see CONDENSATION). Until the dew point is reached, the cooling proceeds at the *dry adiabatic lapse rate* of 1°C for every 100 m of ascent; afterward, condensation of water vapor liberates latent heat and reduces the rate of cooling to the *saturated adiabatic lapse rate,* whose value depends upon the rate of condensation but is typically about half the dry adiabatic

A lenticular cloud is formed by ascent of air over a mountain barrier. (*B. J. Mason*)

lapse rate (see ADIABATIC PROCESS). Sometimes clouds form a vast sheet hundreds of miles across, indicating a steady ascent of air over large areas; at other times they are scattered over the sky in isolated puffs and heaps with clear spaces in between, revealing irregular local up-currents. These are respectively the *stratiform* or *layer clouds,* and the *cumuliform* or heap clouds. With either kind the prolonged ascent of air leads to successively deeper and denser clouds, and finally to rain: widespread continuous rain from the layer clouds, and showers from the heap clouds (see PRECIPITATION).

The widespread layer clouds that are associated with cyclonic depressions, fronts, and other bad-weather systems are often composed of several layers extending up to 30,000 ft (9 km) or more, separated by clear lanes which become filled in as rain or snow develops. The approach of the storm is heralded by the appearance, at heights of more than 20,000 ft (6 km) above the ground, of thin high clouds in the form of trails or streaks composed of delicate white filaments, or as tenuous white patches and narrow bands. Because of their fibrous or hair-like texture they are called *cirrus* (Latin "lock of hair") clouds. Cirrus streamers are often drawn out by the wind into long trails popularly known as *mares' tails.*

Gradually the clouds may thicken and the bands merge to form a great veil of silken cloud, covering the whole sky. In this sheet of cirrus cloud, now called *cirrostratus,* a halo is often seen around the Sun. The cirrus clouds are composed almost entirely of small ice crystals.

Some hours after the appearance of the first cirrus, the clouds overhead may thicken so that the Sun is almost obscured; this layer is called *altostratus.* As the storm center approaches, the cloud continues to thicken, becomes lower, and patches of cloud form beneath it, making dark, wavy patterns. Soon the first rain falls; it becomes heavier, and the cloud deck lowers close to the ground; this gray rain cloud is called *nimbostratus.* At a height of 2 to 3 km in this cloud, where the temperature falls below 0°C (the so-called *freezing level*), the rain gives way to snow, and higher still the snowflakes become smaller and are replaced by clouds of ice crystals which reach up to the cirrus levels. After some hours, the steady rain ends, and the upper cloud begins to break up, but the lower overcast of ragged, amorphous *stratus* clouds persists and gives intermittent drizzle.

Some time later, the wind may freshen, the lower clouds lift and break, and there appear widely scattered *cumulus* clouds,

Altocumulus clouds form in billows above stratocumulus clouds on fringe of a storm system. (*F. H. Ludlam*)

Fair-weather cumulus clouds drift across sky. Some are tending to form stratocumulus. (*Clarke Collection/Royal Meteorol. Soc.*)

which have fairly level bases and rounded tops like cauliflowers. Some of these clouds grow larger and taller and, within about 15 min, tower up to 20,000 ft or more. Before long we see beneath the largest clouds descending trails of rain; they have become *cumulonimbus,* the shower clouds. As the shower develops, the sharp, clear outlines of the cloud tops become smudged, ragged, and soft and take on the fibrous texture of cirrus. This indicates that the upper part of the cloud has become frozen and consists largely of ice crystals. Often this upper part is drawn sideways by the stronger winds aloft, projecting beyond the cloud base in the shape of an anvil. Large cumulonimbus of this variety generally produce heavy rain, sometimes hail, and often develop into THUNDERSTORMS. Near the base of cumulus clouds the speed of the rising air is usually about 1 m/sec, but may reach 5 m/sec, and similar values are measured inside the smaller clouds. The upcurrents in thunderclouds may reach 20 m/sec or more.

On the fringes of the large storm-cloud systems and in weaker storms, the layer clouds are usually thinner and broken up into dapples or parallel rows called *billows.* The dapple clouds which form among cirrus are called *cirrocumulus.* These are composed of small white "flakes" which may be arranged in lines or in ripples resembling those of sand on the seashore, or like the markings on a mackerel's skin— hence the term *mackerel sky.* The other dapple clouds are classified either as *altocumulus* or as *stratocumulus,* according to whether they are more or less than about 7,000 ft (2 km) above the ground. The dappled pattern is characteristic of all shallow layer clouds whose upper surfaces lose heat by radiation to a practically clear sky above and thereby set up slow convective motions within the cloud layer. In stratocumulus layers, which may be quite thick, the rolls are often so close together that their edges join to give the undersurface an undulating appearance without any clear chinks. Such clouds sometimes cover the sky for days on end in spells of quiet winter weather. All the dapple and billow clouds, except perhaps some of the high cirrocumulus, are composed of liquid water droplets even though their temperatures may be well below 0°C, the ordinary freezing point of water.

The rather special *orographic* clouds are produced by the ascent of air over hills and mountains. The air stream is set into oscillation in being forced over the hill, and the clouds form in the crests of the (almost) stationary waves. There may therefore be a succession of such clouds stretching downwind of the mountain which remain stationary relative to the ground although a strong wind may be blowing. They often have very smooth outlines and are called *lenticular* (lens-shaped) or *wave clouds.* Thin wave clouds may take form at great heights (up to 10 km, even over hills only a few hundred meters high) and are occasionally observed even in the stratosphere (at 20 to 30 km) over the mountains of Norway, Scotland, Iceland, and Alaska. These stratospheric wave clouds are known as MOTHER-OF-PEARL CLOUDS because of their brilliant iridescent colors. See Color Plates 28–29.— *B. J. M.*

CLOUDBURST: a sudden heavy fall of rain, usually during a thundershower. "Cloudburst" is a popular rather than an official meteorological term; standards of judgment for calling a particular shower a cloudburst vary widely from section to section. A rate of rainfall of 10 cm (about 4 in.) per hr has been proposed as a criterion.—*D. H. L.*

CLOUD CHAMBER: a device invented by the Scottish physicist C. T. R. Wilson and used by nuclear physicists to record the trajectories of high-speed, electrically charged sub-atomic particles. When such a particle passes through matter, the

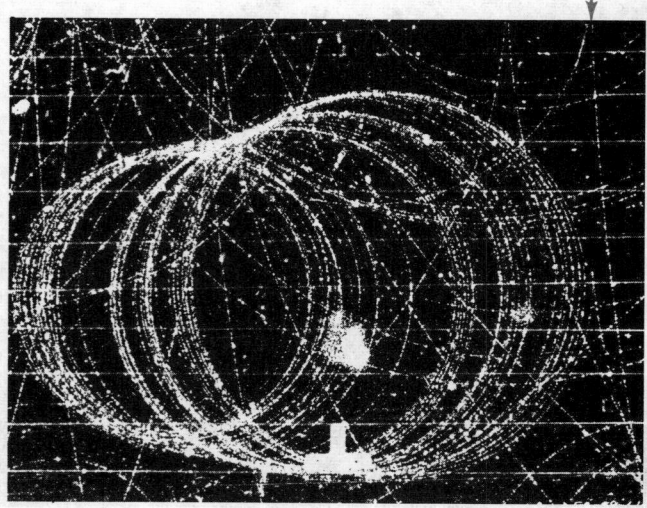

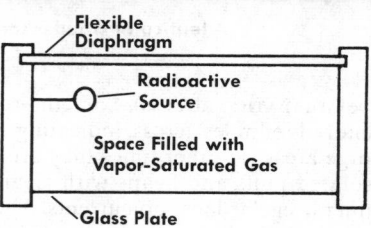

Course of ionizing radiation, made visible by condensation droplets, can be read in photograph (*top*) taken through glass plate of cloud chamber (*bottom*). Gamma radiation entering helium and argon atmosphere gives birth to electron-positron pair where colored arrows meet. Electron, tracing slightly curving path, exits at ×; positron, caught up in magnetic field of 10,000 gauss, registers family of clockwise whorls. (*Photo: Atomic Energy Comm.*)

electrical field generated by the particle knocks electrons out of some of the atoms it encounters along its path. The particle thus leaves a trail of charged atoms (ions) behind it. In a cloud chamber a gas saturated with the vapor of a liquid such as alcohol is cooled by suddenly expanding the volume available to the gas. The cooling causes the vapor molecules to collect on the ions and form droplets of liquid alcohol. Thus if one takes a photograph of the gas shortly after the expansion he observes a string of droplets along the trajectory of the particles that passed through. So-called "diffusion" cloud chambers act continuously, without the necessity of the expansion.—*S. K.*

CLOUD SEEDING: see WEATHER MODIFICATION.

COAGULATION: the process by which colloidal particles are removed from the liquid in which they are dispersed, forming a flocculent or gelatinous solid mass. Three methods are commonly used: (1) *Heating:* Proteins on heating either flocculate or form a hard coagulum, *e.g.* hard-boiled egg, in which case the yolk is flocculated and easily crumbles, while the white becomes a tough, solid mass. (2) *Addition of chemical inorganic agents*—salts, acids, and alkalies: "Salting out" proteins from their colloidal solution is a well-known procedure of this type. Nitric acid is used to detect minute quantities of proteins by flocculation. Because of its high sensitivity, this test is applied in medical laboratories. Bases are used to remove proteins (flocculation) from liquids; hence they are efficient purifiers of water. (3) *Addition of enzymes:* The milk enzyme, rennet, a well-known example, is used industrially in cheese making (curdling of milk).—*T. M. and C. S.*

COAL: a natural, black, fossilization or decay product of plant material, usually of forests. Coal consists mainly of carbon but also contains numerous other elements; it occurs in every continent and in the West Indies. Coals are classified as: (1) lignite, including brown coal and lignite; (2) bituminous (soft coal); (3) anthracite (hard coal), containing semi-anthracite, meta-anthracite, and anthracite. Coal is the result of carbonization of dead leaves and wood which have accumulated to create peat beds. Some deposits accumulate where the plants once grew; others accumulate elsewhere because of the action of water currents.

Plant material undergoes a biochemical change to peat, a dark brown soil. Conversion of peat to coal is caused by oxidation and by the action of aerobic bacteria and fungi in the presence of oxygen, or of anaerobic bacteria where no oxygen is available. The composition of the peat determines what type of coal will be formed; in the metamorphic formation of coal, changes in pressure affect the hardness, strength, and porosity of the coal. Temperature affects the chemical composition, an increase in temperature increasing the per cent of hydrogen and oxygen. Peat, lignite, and bituminous and anthracite coal are progressive stages in the metamorphosis of coal: with each successive stage, the carbon content increases.

Coal occurs in irregular strata of varying thicknesses. These deposits may be separated by layers of shale or clay or other mineral matter. Coal as it occurs in the bed possesses a rather complex morphological structure characterized by bands of identifiable form, although some coals such as *cannel* are unbanded, being distinguished by their blocky fracture and greasy luster. *Vitrain* is the name given to lustrous bands of coalified wood, such as occur in banded bituminous coal. *Clarain,* a structure in coal formed from wood and leaves, is rather lustrous in appearance. *Durain* is a dull variety of coal with a high ash yield. Associated with these types of coal is *fusain,* which is known as mineral charcoal. It is produced when the peat bed has been set afire by lightning or other agency, leaving a charcoal residue which eventually becomes a part of the coal bed.

Macerals, the mineral constituents of coal, are derived

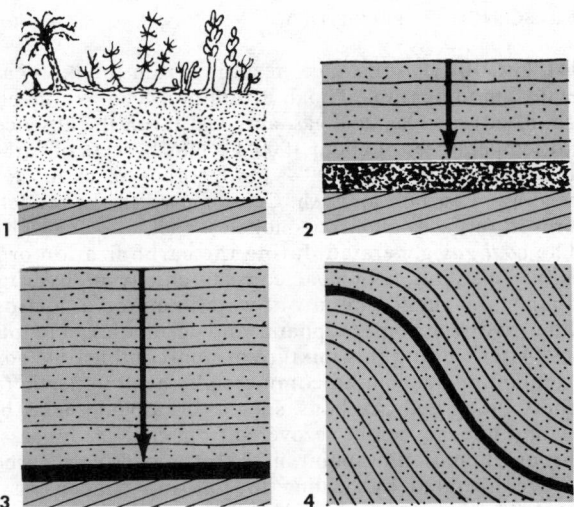

Formation of coal: Plant remains (1) accumulate in prehistoric swamps, (2) are buried by accumulating sediments above, (3) are gradually converted by pressure and heat into bituminous (soft) coal, and (4) are changed into anthracite by intensified heat and pressure due to folding of strata.

from substances such as wood resins and exines, and their presence provides a means of sub-classifying durains, vitrains, clarains, and fusains. Macerals can be divided into three groups: (1) vitrinites, (2) resinites, and (3) inertinites. Macerals are identified by examination of their forms and reflectivity, greater reflectivity indicating greater carbon content.

Coal is widely used as a fuel, as a source of gaseous products, and for carbonization. Its use for combustion includes domestic, industrial, and railroad facilities, anthracite being mainly used for domestic purposes. Special bituminous coals as well as mixtures of bituminous coal and anthracite are used in producing metallurgical coke (carbonization). Lignite is a source of industrial gases and carbon. (See COAL PRODUCTS; MINING.)—*G. W. M.*

High-ranking coal deposits: Laid down for the most part in formations of Pennsylvanian Period some 250 million yr ago, the world's economically recoverable coal deposits can be expected to be consumed in the course of the 20th and 21st cent.

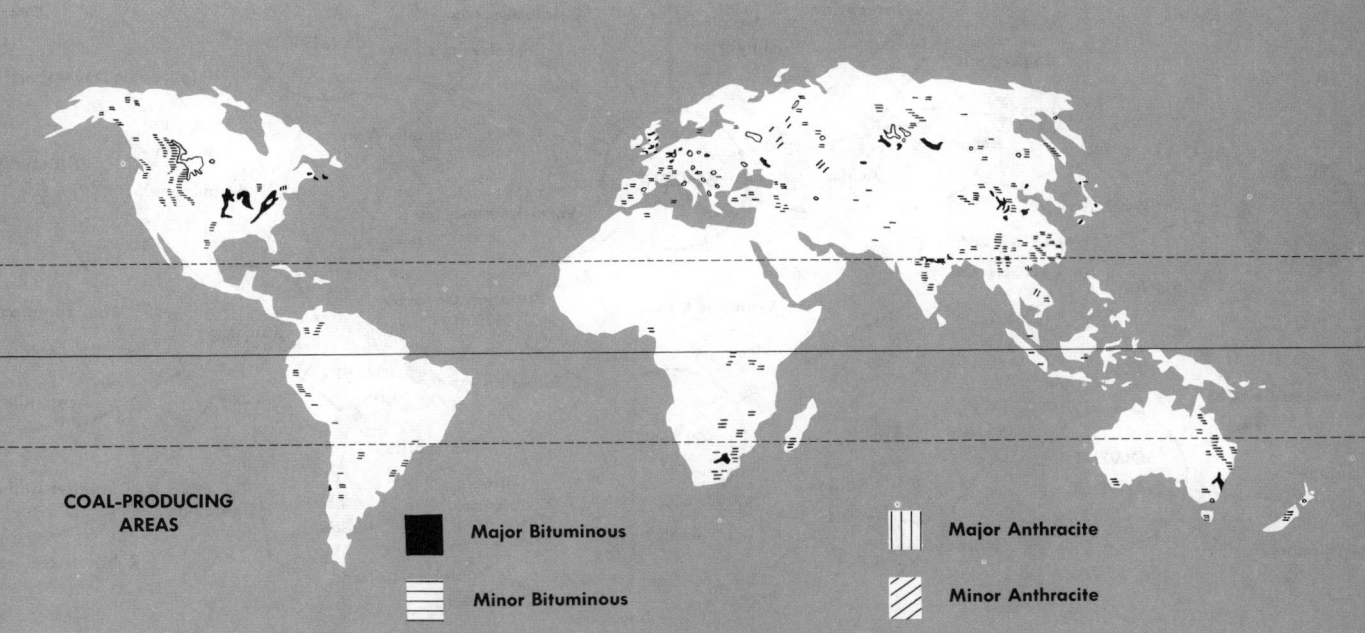

COAL-PRODUCING AREAS

■ Major Bituminous

▤ Minor Bituminous

▥ Major Anthracite

▨ Minor Anthracite

COALESCENCE: see PRECIPITATION.

COAL PRODUCTS: substances resulting from the physical or chemical modification of coal. Bituminous coal is converted (carbonized) to coke, coal gas, and coal tar in the absence of air at temperatures of about 1000°C. This process of carbonization yields primarily COKE—a hard, porous, black substance consisting of carbon and ash. Coke is used in the reduction of ores in furnaces and as a smokeless fuel.

The *coal gas* generated during the carbonization or destructive distillation of coal consists chiefly of hydrogen, methane, and small amounts of water, ammonia, hydrogen sulfide, hydrocarbons (aliphatic and aromatic), and other gases. After ridding this mixture of non-combustible gases, the remaining gas is used commercially as a domestic fuel. Higher-boiling hydrocarbons, such as cyclopentadiene, benzene, and toluene, can be recovered from coal gas by passing it through high-boiling-point oil. The trapped hydrocarbons are then liberated by heating the oil and condensing the vapors. This condensed liquid which saturated the coal-gas mixture is known as the light-oil fraction, accumulating 3 gal/ton of coal.

Coal tar is a black, viscous liquid resulting from the condensation of less volatile vapors. It varies in composition according to the method of carbonization. High-temperature distillation produces a tar rich in chemicals. The coal tar constitutes about 3% of the total weight of coal, and upon distillation of this coal-tar fraction, approximately a 40% yield of chemicals is obtained. These chemicals are fractionated into light oils (25–200°C), middle oils (200–250°C), heavy oils (250–300°C), anthracene oils (300–350°C), and pitch, a tarry residue. These fractions are further separated by chemical and physical means, the resulting chemicals being either neutral compounds (hydrocarbons), tar acids (compounds soluble in sodium hydroxide), or tar bases (compounds soluble in dilute sulfuric acid).

The light-oil fraction obtained from coal tar, consisting mainly of aromatic hydrocarbons and olefins, is much smaller than that derived from scrubbing coal gas. It is distilled, washed with dilute acid to remove the tar bases, and then washed with dilute sodium hydroxide to remove tar acids. The residual oil is treated with concentrated sulfuric acid to polymerize lower-molecular-weight olefins, producing upon distillation a mixture of benzene, toluene, and xylenes. Benzene from coal tar contains small amounts of thiophene, a cyclic olefin containing sulfur. It closely resembles benzene, since it can be nitrated and sulfonated. Thiophene is more inert and stable than other olefins. Its chemical similarity to benzene left it undetected in benzene from coal tar until Victor Meyer in 1883 found that a sample of benzene, prepared from the decarboxylation of benzoic acid, did not produce the characteristic benzene blue color when mixed with concentrated sulfuric acid and isatin.

The middle-oil fraction is combined with the residue from the light-oil fraction, and the mixture is cooled to precipitate naphthalene, which is removed by centrifuging. The naphthalene is purified by distilling, washing it with acid, alkali, and water, and again distilling. The remaining oil from the residual fraction is washed with sodium hydroxide to extract tar acids. Bubbling carbon dioxide through the sodium hydroxide solution precipitates the tar acids, and they are separated from the aqueous phase and distilled to produce mainly phenol,

Coal derivatives: Heating bituminous coal in chemical-recovery coke ovens yields coke, coke oven gas, and coal tar. From coke oven gas, coke oven light oil is obtained, and from it, several primary intermediates —benzene, phenol, toluene, solvent naphtha, nitrobenzene, and aniline. From each primary intermediate, many end products can then be synthesized. Similarly, several primary intermediates are obtained from coal tar.

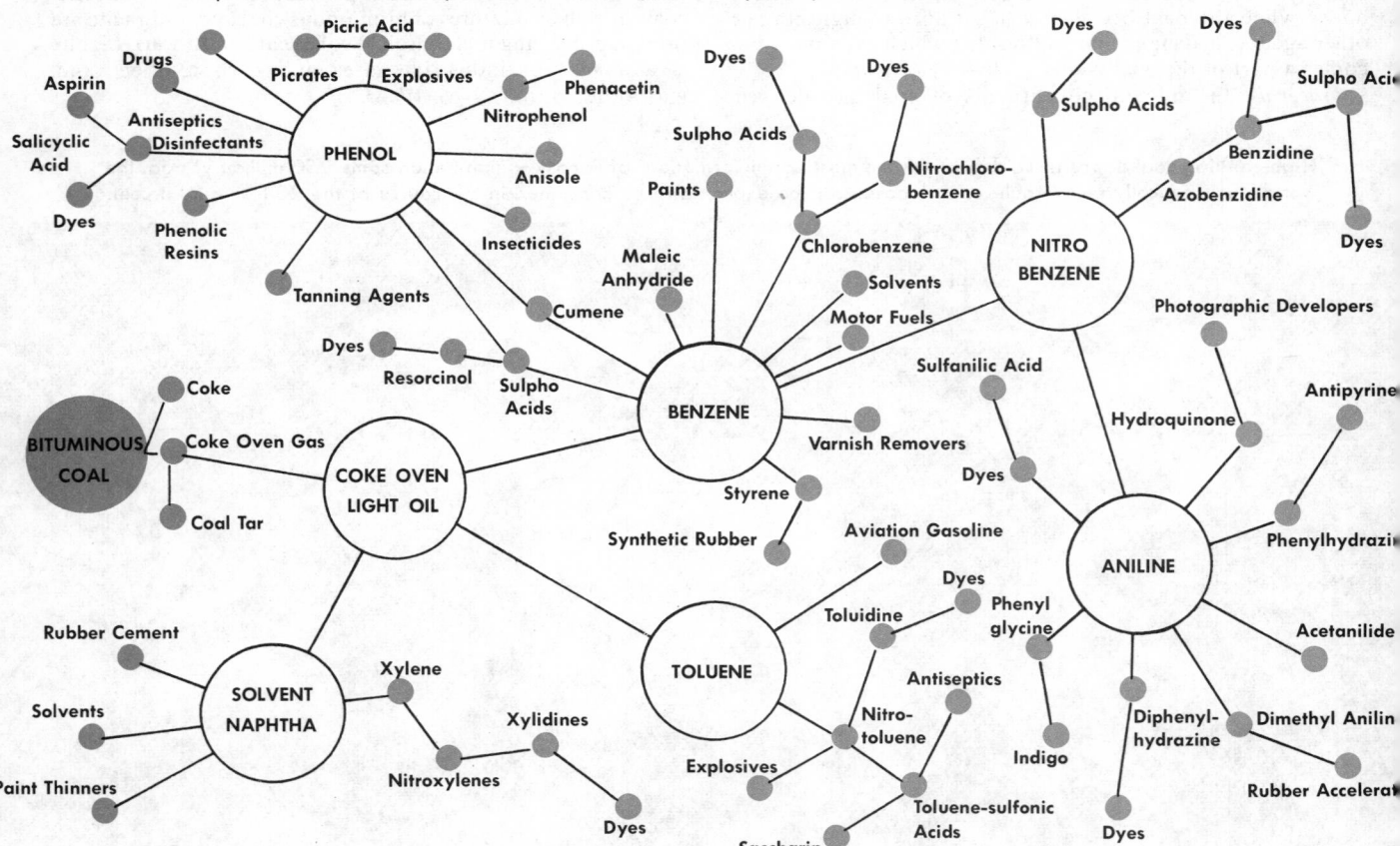

Coal Sack in southern Milky Way is seen at left and slightly below two bright stars near center in this photo. These stars, with two fainter ones diagonally above, to right, form the Southern Cross. (*Harvard Obs.*)

which is further purified by recrystallization. The oily residue from the extraction with alkali is treated with dilute sulfuric acid to solubilize the tar bases in an aqueous acid medium, leaving an organic residue. This aqueous acid medium is then treated with sodium hydroxide to produce tar bases, *e.g.* pyridine, and these are purified by distillation. The organic residue from this treatment gives both naphtha and cumar resin, a solid.

The heavy-oil fraction is also cooled to precipitate naphthalene; further, the higher-molecular-weight aromatic nitrogen compounds (*e.g.* quinoline) and substituted phenols (*e.g.* cresol oil) are separated by the acid-base technique used in recovering compounds from the middle-oil fraction. The fraction known as green oil or anthracene oil sets for several weeks until it crystallizes. The mass is filtered, and the solid is subjected to pressure to remove liquid impurities. The solid is washed with naphtha to remove the hydrocarbon phenanthrene. The residual mass is then washed with pyridine to remove nitrogenous heterocycles (*e.g.* carbazole) and sublimed to yield practically pure anthracene. Since it is commercially more economical to synthesize many of the chemicals contained in the high-boiling fractions, these fractions are used as wood preservatives. They are called creosote oils, because of their strong odor of cresol.

Over 200 chemical compounds have been isolated from coal tar, naphthalene (1820) being the first. Phenol, anthracene, quinoline, aniline, pyrrole, and chrysene were discovered during the following 20 yr. Several new compounds were isolated periodically up to the period 1931–46, when more than 100 new compounds were isolated because of rapid development of new separation techniques. Liquid fuels can be obtained from coal by destructive hydrogenation. Since coal is a great mesh of rings of carbon, they are cleaved and hydrogenated by destructive hydrogenation, forming alkyl and cycloalkyl hydrocarbons. The process is carried out under pressure with the use of a tin or lead catalyst. The gasoline and oil are separated by distillation. The usual gasoline fraction contains 75% paraffins, 20% aromatics, and 5% olefins. By treating coke with steam at high pressures, carbon monoxide and hydrogen are produced. Further catalytic hydrogenation of the carbon monoxide produces aliphatic hydrocarbons (Fischer-Tropsch process).

Many of the compounds isolated from coal tar are used in the synthesis and production of dyes. The oxidation of anthracene forms anthraquinone, an important intermediate in the preparation of fast vat dyes for cottons. Aniline is used in aniline black, in the synthesis of indigo, as a constituent of triarylmethane dyes (*e.g.* methyl violet), and in numerous other dyes. The benzpyrene, chrysene, naphthacene, and other polynuclear hydrocarbons present in small amounts in coal tar have been recently found to cause tissue malignancy. See also PETROCHEMICALS.—*G. W. M. and A. M. S.*

COAL SACK: a vast cloud of cosmic dust particles seen in the southern Milky Way as a dark marking, measuring 3 to 4° across, directly east of the Southern Cross. This mass of INTERSTELLAR MATTER, a so-called dark NEBULA, is readily seen with the naked eye on a moonless night. Star counts for this region of sky and neighboring fields, combined with data on reddening of light from stars seen through it, show it to be a cloud 40 lt-yr across, about 500 lt-yr from the Sun. A. W. Rodgers estimated its minimum mass—from cosmic dust particles of optimum dimensions alone—as equivalent to 14 solar masses. The most probable value is of the order of 50 solar masses, and the unknown gas content may raise this figure to over 1,000.—*B. J. B.*

COASTLINE: the line marking the inner margin of the shore zone; essentially, the line between land and sea. Shapes of coastlines vary widely from place to place. Whenever sea level either rises or falls with respect to the land, a new part of the earth's surface is subject to wave and current attack, and the shape of the new shoreline will depend initially on either the topography of the coastal region prior to flooding or that of the sea floor near the coast before its uncovering. If sea level rises, the ocean will invade pre-existing valleys to form estuaries, ridges between valleys will form promontories, and hilltops may protrude above water to form islands, thus producing a *drowned coast*. On such a coastline all the irregularities of an eroded land surface show up in the complexities of the new shoreline, as for instance that of Chesapeake Bay, where the ocean has flooded the seaward end of a whole river system. The principal channel of the drowned Susquehanna River follows roughly the central part of the Bay, and the seaward ends of former tributaries are now located where the offshoots of the Bay occur. In other regions, elevation of the land with respect to sea level is indicated by the presence of raised wave-cut cliffs and terraces and beach deposits, such as occur on the Pacific Coast of the U. S. A. In many places coasts give evidence of both drowning and elevation, and thus must at various times have stood alternately higher and lower.

Invading sea gradually cuts away the coastline of Oregon, in Ecola State Park. Similar topography occurs where sea level has risen with respect to the land, and waves and currents are attacking a rocky shore. (*Union Pacific Railroad*)

Any coastline is constantly being modified by wave action, with the production of various erosional features such as cliffs and terraces and offshore rocky islets (*sea stacks*), or the formation of depositional features such as sand and gravel bars and beaches, spits and tombolos. The direct action of waves cannot, however, ever result in the deep estuaries produced by the drowning of an irregular landscape. Wherever the land is composed of relatively weak material, the sea will modify the coastline quite rapidly; thus at Cape Cod sand bars and wave-cut cliffs are far more extensive than, for instance, on the Maine coast, where resistant rocks face the sea, although both of these areas were drowned at approximately the same time. See Color Plate 21.—*J. Sh.*

COATING: broadly, a layer of any substance used to cover or protect a surface; *e.g.* paint, lacquer, or enamel. More specifically, coatings are protective layers which basically change the properties or utility of materials they cover. When coatings are applied as thin layers, they add relatively little weight, bulk, or over-all cost in relation to performance improvements. Glass, for example, has long been used to coat the inside of hot-water heaters, markedly prolonging their life. Ceramic coatings are familiar on tiles, porcelain, and metal wall panels. A dramatic recent example is ablative coatings, used on space vehicles which must re-enter the atmosphere. Here multiple layers of glass, ceramic, or plastic absorb frictional energy and dissipate it by disintegration of outer coating layers rather than transmitting it as heat to the interior of the unit (see ABLATION).

Development of *synthetic rubbers,* as polymerized chlorobutadiene, chlorosulfonated polyethylene, and fluoroelastomers, has led to coated fabrics which are used in such diverse forms as firewalls in aircraft, inflated structures like radomes, and diaphragms in fuel pumps. In addition, elastomers are being used as fluid-applied roofs, particularly over free-form concrete or plywood structures, and as protective coatings for chemical processing equipment. *Urethanes* are used for durable, corrosion-resistant coatings and long-wear-

Drowned coastline at Plymouth, Mass., is mantled with glacial drift. The sand and gravel are worked by waves and currents into spits, bars, and other such forms, which contrast with the ruggedness of the Oregon coast above. (*Lawrence Lowry*)

ing floor finishes. *Plastic films* are used as laminates over metals, wood, and other materials. Polyvinyl fluoride, for instance, laminated to steel or aluminum for building use, is tougher and more durable than paint, with outstanding resistance to ultraviolet light and weathering. Metalized films, most familiar in decorative trim on automobiles, combine utility and decoration, while underprinted polyester films provide mar-resistant decorative surfacing for walls, room dividers, radiant screen panels, and industrial shapes. *Plastic resins* are widely used as special-purpose coatings. An example is tetrafluoroethylene resin, noted for chemical inertness, heat resistance, and anti-sticking properties. Used to coat industrial equipment, it prevents build-up of glues, sizes, or other sticky materials, and has been used in evaporator units to prevent scale build-up. In a domestic application, it lines frying pans, where its anti-sticking quality eliminates need for grease and fats in cooking.—*H. C. F.*

COBALT: a metallic element (Co); at. no. 27; at. wt 58.94; density 8.93; mp 1495°C. Cobalt occurs in the minerals cobaltite, $CoAsS$; smaltite, $CoAs_2$; and linnaeite, Co_3S_4. Extensive deposits of cobalt minerals are found in Ontario, Canada. Pure cobalt metal is obtained by reducing the oxide with aluminum or carbon. Cobalt is separated from nickel by the Mond process; it is used in special alloys, such as Alnico, a ferromagnetic alloy. Cobaltous chloride is used in invisible inks: if the ink is heated after drying, a blue coloration of anhydrous cobaltous chloride is produced on the paper surface. Cobaltous oxide is dissolved in molten glass to impart a blue color to the hardened glass.—*G. W. M.*

COCKCROFT, SIR JOHN DOUGLAS, 1897– , English physicist; b. Todmorden. With E. T. S. Walton he built the first high-energy particle accelerator (1932) and used it to bombard lithium atoms with protons, producing helium atoms from the lithium (see COCKCROFT–WALTON EXPERIMENT). This result gave experimental evidence for Einstein's theory of the equivalence of mass and energy. For their pioneer work on the transmutation of atomic nuclei by artificially accelerated atomic particles, Cockcroft and Walton shared the 1951 Nobel prize. In 1946 Cockcroft became director of the British Atomic Energy Establishment. He is a fellow of the Royal Society.—*D. H. D. R.*

COCKCROFT-WALTON EXPERIMENT: the first successful attempt to break up the nucleus of an atom by artificially produced, high-speed, charged particles. It was performed in 1932 in England by J. D. Cockcroft and E. T. S. Walton, using a machine they invented (see PARTICLE ACCELERATOR). They directed a beam of protons (hydrogen nuclei) of 150,000 electron volts energy at a target of lithium. They first detected the emission of alpha particles (helium nuclei) from the lithium target by observing the scintillations the particles produced on striking a phosphorescent screen. These results are explained by a proton penetrating the lithium nucleus, after which the product nucleus breaks into two alpha particles, each with 8.7 million electron volts energy. The greatly increased energy of the alpha particles over that of the incident proton is obtained from the conversion into energy of a very minute part of the mass of the lithium nucleus. This pioneering experiment illustrates both the transmutation of elements and the conversion of mass to energy. (See also CONSERVATION OF MASS-ENERGY; NUCLEAR PHYSICS; RELATIVITY.)—*E. E.*

Coelenterates, like this sea fan of European waters, are for the most part oceanic. Deceptively chicorylike in appearance, this specimen (magnified 1½ times) is in fact a colony of carnivorous animals. (*Douglas P. Wilson*)

COEFFICIENT: a multiplier, or factor, in a mathematical term. In the simple instance, a term such as $3x^2$ is composed of the square of the unknown, x^2, and its coefficient 3. It is usual to restrict the word to a fixed number, but, with a broader interpretation, we may include variable factors in a coefficient. Thus, in the term $3xy^2$, 3 is the coefficient of xy^2 and $3x$ is the coefficient of y^2. In general forms of polynomials, the constant coefficients are represented by letters; general solutions of equations are expressed in terms of the literal coefficients. For example, in the general quadratic equation $ax^2 + bx + c = 0$, the letters $a, b,$ and c denote known quantities and are called the coefficients; the formula for the solution of this equation gives the roots in terms of these coefficients. (See EQUATIONS, THEORY OF.) The coefficients in an expression may assume a special importance of their own. The coefficients in the binomial expansion have special interpretations and uses in problems in probability.

In physical science the term "coefficient" is applied to special multipliers, which are proportionality constants. For example, if the temperature of a solid bar is raised from 0° to 1°C, the ratio of the increase in length to the original length is the coefficient of linear expansion; a coefficient of absorption expresses the absorbing power of a substance; a coefficient of friction expresses the force of resistance of a material to an object sliding or rolling over it. See FRICTION; EXPANSION, THERMAL; VISCOSITY.—*H. C.*

COELENTERATE: any one of a large group of simple, invertebrate animals that have radial symmetry (see BODY SYMMETRY) and capture their prey by means of stinging cells (nematocysts). Stinging cells, unique among coelenterates, are spherical or ellipsoid capsules filled with fluid and containing a coiled thread, which is shot out in self-defense, in capture of prey, or in anchoring the body temporarily as an aid to locomotion. Most coelenterates are marine; some are common and familiar animals of the seashore. One group grows as bushy, plantlike colonies on rocks, shells, pilings, and other objects; a second group grows with individuals attached in large colonies having stony exoskeletons (outside coverings), which contribute to formation of CORAL REEFS. A few live in freshwater lakes, ponds, and streams. The body of a coelenterate,

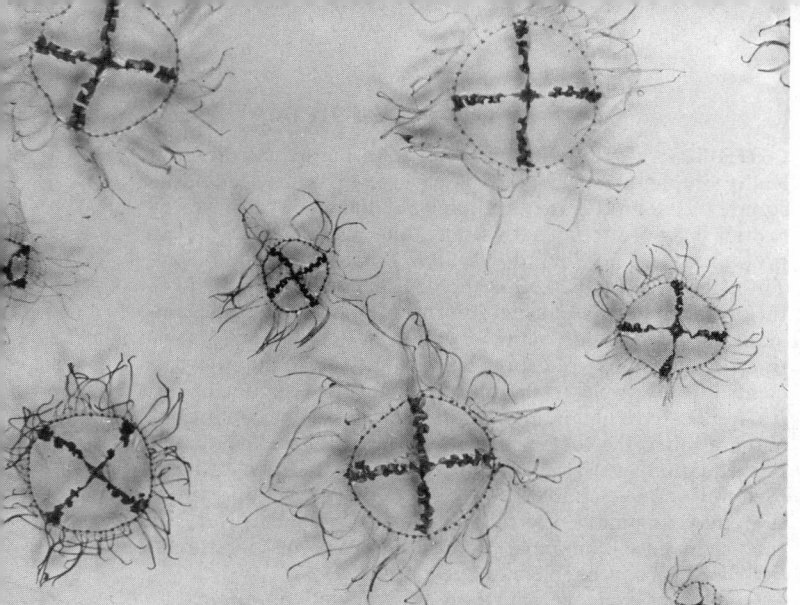

Ancestral form of coelenterates may well have resembled the little Gonionemus of our eastern coastal waters. Its perfunctory polyp stage alternates with the more conspicuous medusa stage shown above. Traversing the transparent bell of jelly are four radial canals bearing ovaries or testes; a nerve ring studded with sense organs coordinates the animal's behavior. (L. and M. Milne)

usually watery and jellylike, is composed of two tissue layers (an outer protective layer and an inner digestive layer) separated by an intervening layer of gelatinous material called mesoglea. There are two major body forms: the attached polyp and the free-swimming medusa, or jellyfish. The polyp has a tubular body with one end closed and attached to the substrate and the other end bearing a mouth, usually surrounded by several movable tentacles. The free-swimming medusa has an umbrella-shaped gelatinous body with tentacles around the margin and a mouth at the lower end of a central projection. The two body forms may occur within a single species of coelenterate (a phenomenon called POLYMORPHISM).

Coelenterates without medusa stage: The sea anemones (class Anthozoa), of which there are about 1,000 species, appear only as polyps. Basal disk by which solitary individual clings to tidepool rock has been cut away; exposed transverse section shows radial partitions that increase its digestive surface and enable it to digest entire fishes. (L. and M. Milne)

Often these two body forms alternate in the life cycle of a coelenterate as an asexual polyp stage and a sexual medusa stage. This is called metagenesis (see ALTERNATION OF GENERATIONS). Many coelenterates are notable for their luminescence (see BIOLUMINESCENCE) and their extensive ability to replace lost parts by REGENERATION. The phylum Coelenterata (Cnidaria) includes three classes: the Hydrozoa, represented by both polyps and medusae, e.g. the freshwater hydra, the colonial sea plumes, the stinging corals, and the Portuguese man-of-war; the Scyphozoa, or true jellyfishes, including the moon jelly, the sea wasps, and the giant sea blubber; and the Anthozoa, e.g. sea whips, sea fans, corals, and sea anemones, among which only the polyp stage occurs. See CTENOPHORE. See Color Plate 22.—C. F. L.

COELOSTAT: a device for reflecting a beam of light into a telescope that is fixed in position. It is essentially a plane mirror rotated by clockwork and so mounted that its axis of rotation is parallel to Earth's axis. The mirror rotates once in 48 hr, causing the reflected beam to rotate once in 24 hr, thus compensating for Earth's rotation. A second mirror sends the beam down the axis of the horizontal or vertical telescope, which, although fixed, can now "follow" one part of the sky. Coelostats are used in tower telescopes built for solar observation.—A. P. E.

COENZYME A: a NUCLEOTIDE consisting of residues of adenine—ribose phosphate—two phosphates—pantothenic acid—mercaptoethylamine. The last-named residue contains a mercapto group (—SH) which is the key to the activity of this compound; hence it can be written Co A · SH (or HS · Co A) for short. It participates in the degradation of fatty acids (see ENZYMES); its acetyl derivative (acetyl coenzyme A) is formed from fatty acids and from carbohydrates (see OXIDATIVE DECARBOXYLATION), and enters into the CITRIC ACID CYCLE and GLYOXYLIC ACID CYCLE and into acetylation reactions generally. Coenzyme A is thus of extraordinary importance in metabolism.—K. H.

COENZYME Q (Ubiquinone): in biochemistry, a quinone which acts as an electron carrier in the transfer of electrons during oxidation of the substrate (see HYDROGEN TRANSPORT). It enters the electron carrier system at the level of cytochrome b, but whether it is on a side path or on the main path of electron transfer is uncertain.—R. Wu

COESITE: a rare, superdense form of silica (SiO_2). It was first made in the laboratory by Loring Coes, Jr., in 1953, with an apparatus producing pressures exceeding 20,000 atm. Fragments of coesite have been discovered at several sites where large meteorites are known to have struck Earth in past times (see METEOR CRATER).—J. W.

COFFERDAM: a temporary dam used in simple underwater construction work where the water is shallow. It is an enclosure formed around the foundation site usually by sinking either wooden or sheet-steel piling and filling in between with clay. The enclosed space is then pumped dry, so that work can be done inside.—R. G.

COHESION: see ADHESION AND COHESION.

COINCIDENCE (ANTI-COINCIDENCE) COUNTING: an experimental technique of recording counts which occur in two or more counters simultaneously (coincidence counting), when one counter does not count (anti-coincidence counting), or within a given time interval (delayed coincidence counting)

(see COUNTER). A set of counters may include some in coincidence and others in anti- or delayed coincidence, permitting great flexibility in the detection of nuclear particles and radiation. For example, the direction in which a particle is traveling can be determined by using counters in coincidence and arranged in a line. Coincidence counting is widely used in nuclear and cosmic-ray research.—*E. E.*

COKE: a carbon residue from the pyrolysis or destructive heating of bituminous COAL in the absence of air. Coke can also be made from pitch or asphalt. The residual coke from the destructive distillation of soft coal is used in the reduction of ores in blast furnaces, and as a smokeless household and industrial fuel. The coke derived from a petroleum residue such as asphalt can be roasted to produce pure carbon for making carbon electrodes.—*G. W. M.*

COLD-BLOODEDNESS: see BODY TEMPERATURE.

COLD WAVE: a period of weather which is cold enough to interfere with normal activities and in which, according to official U. S. Weather Bureau usage, the fall in temperature has taken place within 24 hr. In most of North America, a cold wave follows the passage of a cold front which separates a merely cool air mass from an intensely cold mass of polar continental air, which typically originates over NW Canada. —*D. H. L.*

COLLAGEN: animal proteins, which are the main constituents of connective tissue. They occur in cartilage, bone, tendon, and also skin. Up to 40% of the protein in a human adult may be collagen. The amino-acid composition of these proteins is unusual in its relatively high hydroxyproline and hydroxylysine content. Collagen is converted to gelatin by boiling and is an important commercial source of gelatin and glue.—*F. F.*

COLLISIONS, ELASTIC AND INELASTIC: An elastic collision is one in which the internal states of the colliding objects are the same before and after the encounter. In an inelastic collision, the internal condition of one or more of the colliding objects is altered. The sketch shows two conceivable collisions between a pair of springs with billiard balls attached to their ends. The collision depicted in (*A*) is elastic, because the billiard balls rebound with essentially no deformation and the springs are unaffected. In the head-on collision depicted in (*B*), the springs are compressed during the instant of contact and are thereby set into oscillations that continue after the

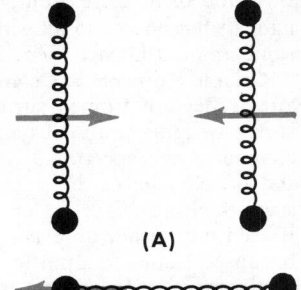

rebound, making this collision inelastic. In all inelastic collisions the speed of separation of the objects after the encounter is less than the speed with which they approached each other, because some of the kinetic ENERGY associated with the relative motion has been transformed into internal energy (the vibrational motion of the springs in the example). An extreme example of an inelastic collision is the firing of a bullet into a block of wood. In addition to the drastic change in structure of the wood along the path of the bullet, the block is heated by the collision; *i.e.* most of the kinetic energy of the bullet is expended in setting the wood molecules into more violent random motions. Study of collisions is important

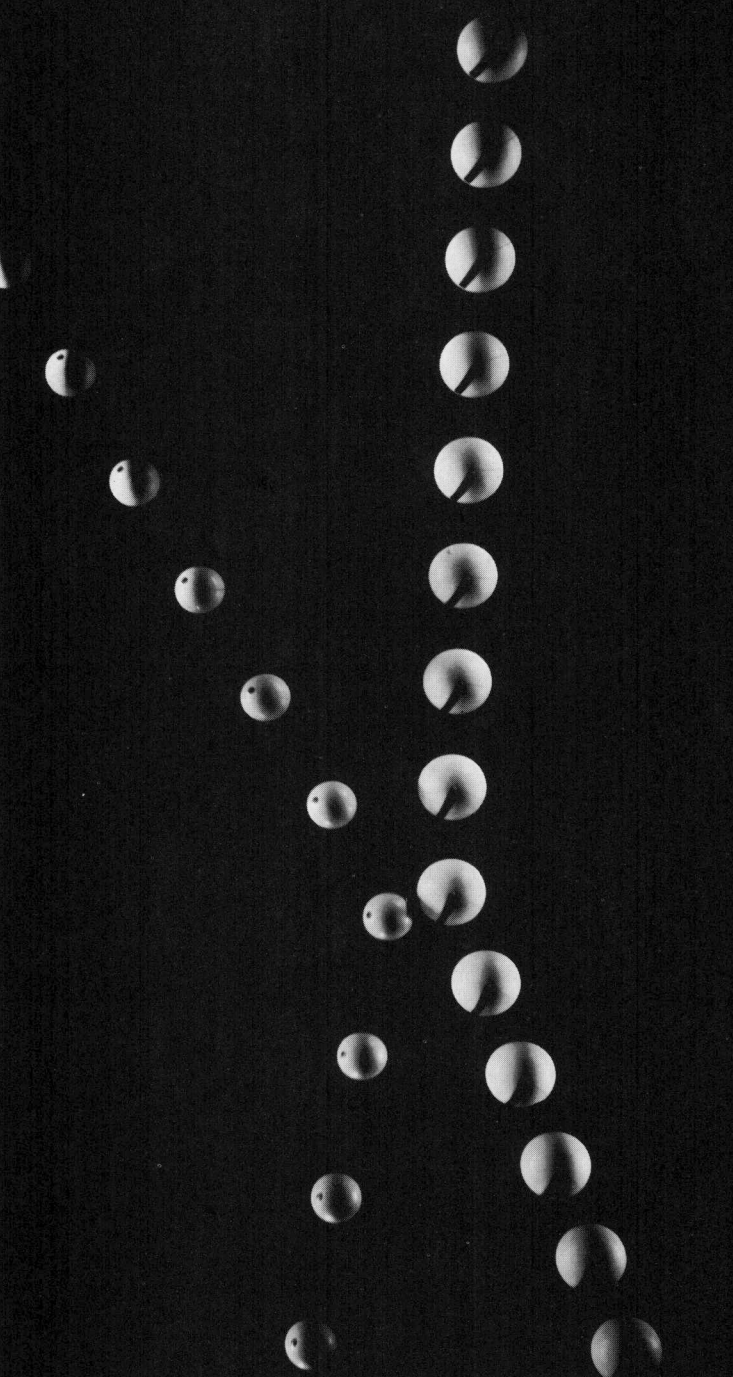

Elastic collision is shown in multiple-flash photograph. Note that the speeds of the two balls (indicated by the distances between positions) remain substantially unaltered by the collision but that the smaller ball is deflected far more than the larger ball, which is about 2⅓ times as massive. (*Berenice Abbott*)

in NUCLEAR PHYSICS, wherein the principal research technique is to bombard atomic nuclei with nuclear projectiles from PARTICLE ACCELERATORS and to analyze how the projectiles are scattered; elastic collisions provide information about the external forces exerted by nuclei, and inelastic collisions yield knowledge about the internal structure of nuclei.—*S. K.*

COLLODION: a solution of pyroxylin, usually in an alcohol-ether solution, from which films can be made, *e.g.* over wounds. Pyroxylin is a cellulose nitrate which is less highly nitrated than guncotton.—*Ru. M.*

Varieties of colloidal dispersion: gas in liquid, liquid in solid, liquid in liquid (oil and water), solid in gas (smoke). In each example, the particles of the dispersed phase are of colloidal dimension. (*Robert F. Waldeck/Frances Orkin*)

COLLOID CHEMISTRY: A colloidal system consists of finely divided particles dispersed in a gas, liquid, or solid. Dimensions of colloids are usually considered to be in the range from about 5×10^{-7} to 5×10^{-4} cm. The upper part of the range is just visible in the electron microscope, an important tool for studying colloidal systems. Other techniques for studying them utilize the TYNDALL EFFECT (see SCATTERING), BROWNIAN MOTION, OSMOSIS, and sedimentation in the centrifuge. The special properties of colloidal dispersions are due to the high ratio of surface area to volume of the colloids. Consider that a 1-cm cube has a surface area of 6 cm²: if this is pulverized to cubes with 0.000001-cm edges, the same amount of material will have 6,000,000 cm² of surface area. The properties that depend upon particle size and surface area are thus so greatly altered as to warrant setting up a separate branch of chemistry to study them.

If colloidal particles are suspended in a gas, the system is called an AEROSOL; fogs and smokes are examples. A suspension of solid particles in a liquid is a *sol*. Liquid droplets dispersed in a mutually insoluble liquid constitute an *emulsion*. Colloidal systems can be formed by either condensation or dispersion methods. Thus, a water aerosol can be formed by condensation by cooling humid air containing condensation nuclei below the dew point, so that liquid water will condense on the nuclei; under proper conditions of humidity and concentration of nuclei, the water droplets will be of colloidal dimensions. Or, a water aerosol can be formed by dispersion by spraying water at high speed through small orifices. Because of the large area of their surfaces, colloidal systems are very adsorptive, and many *solid colloids* such as charcoal strongly adsorb both gases and materials dissolved in liquids. This ability to adsorb gases renders certain solid colloids effective as catalysts in industrial processes, *e.g.* cracking of gasoline and synthesis of ammonia.

The colloid chemist has extended his domain to include disperse systems which have even a single dimension in the colloidal range. Thus, extremely fine fibers are colloidal, no matter what their length, and certain oils that have the property of spreading over the surface of water, forming thin films, also are considered colloidal. Indeed, W. D. Bancroft, who is one of the pioneers in the field, has termed colloid chemistry the "chemistry of bubbles, drops, grains, filaments, and films."—*M. K.*

COLOR: a sense perception induced by light entering the eye. Although we associate colors with objects we see rather than with the light by which we see them, the color of an object depends on the light that falls on the object as well as on the way in which the object absorbs or reflects that light. The physical characteristic of light that determines the color perceived is the distribution of its energy in the spectrum (see SPECTRUM and SPECTROSCOPE). Most light contains some energy at all visible wavelengths, but the amounts present in each wavelength region may vary widely. The color seen is affected also by the intensity of the light. For a given spectral distribution of light, the color seen depends upon many factors. For a given state or condition of the eyes when the color is seen, these statements are true:

1. If two beams of light have different colors, their spectral distributions are different.

2. If two beams of light exactly match for color, their spectral distributions may or may not be the same. Many different spectral distributions will match any given color, but different colors of the same brightness will not have identical spectral distributions.

If light from two sources falls on a white screen, the light from both sources is reflected toward the observer's eyes. The light he sees is an *additive mixture* because the two lights are added together before he sees them. The total amount of energy in each wavelength region is the sum of the energies in that region from each source of light. Any set of three light beams that will mix to give white are *primary* colors. Because red, green, and blue give the largest range of colors when mixed, they are known as the primary colors. They are primary in no sense except that they are the customary starting set for this kind of mixture. Sunlight is the usual example of white light. It has energy in all wavelength regions, and roughly the same amount in each. See LIGHT.

Colored Pigments or Colorants: Some light reaches the eyes after reflection from a surface. If this surface does not absorb any light, or absorbs all wavelengths equally, there is no change in the spectral distribution of the light as reflected and no change, except a change in brightness, in the color seen. Such a surface appears white if seen alone in sunlight. If seen with other objects it might appear gray or black, or, because of color adaptation of the eye, may appear to contain some hue. In general, nonwhite bodies do not reflect all wavelengths of light equally, but absorb some wavelengths more strongly than others. Such surfaces are selective absorbers or reflectors. They normally appear colored to the eye.

An enormous number of materials absorb light selectively, notably the pigments and dyes used in paints and colored fabrics. If white light falls on a surface coated or dyed with such materials, the selective absorption of the surface changes the spectral distribution of the light, and the surface is seen as some color other than white. If two selective absorbers that give rise to different colors are mixed together uniformly, they both continue to absorb selectively as before. Light reflected from the treated surface is then selectively absorbed by both of them and a new color results. Production of color by this means is known as *subtractive mixture* because each dye subtracts its quota of energy from the original light. Selectively absorbing materials are *colorants.*

Colors produced by subtractive mixtures of colorants are different, in general, from those produced by additive mixtures of color lights. In subtractive mixture we see what is left over after the absorptions; in additive mixture we see the sum of the lights. The colors produced by subtractive mixtures of colorants cannot be predicted without a knowledge of the spectral absorptions of the colorants, but the colors produced by additively mixing two lights can always be predicted from the colors of the lights. Blue and yellow lights can be found that produce white when mixed; pigments or dyes that match these lights may appear red or black when mixed, but usually produce green.

Complementary Colors: Any two lights that can be mixed to produce white light are called complementary colors. Similarly, two colorants that mix to give gray or black are complementary colorants. The colors of a pair of complementary colorants are not, however, necessarily the same as those of a pair of lights that mix to give white, even if one colorant matches one of the lights. In general, the remaining light and colorant will differ substantially from each other in color. This concept of complementary colors is used widely in color and colorant systems and in descriptions of the uses of color. In general, colorants whose colors in white light are complementary do not produce gray when mixed unless they have been specially selected to do so. Moreover, the addition of black paint to white seldom produces a gray, but usually either a blue or a yellow gray.

Color Designation: A color may be described by means of three properly chosen terms, representing variables. In the nomenclature of the Optical Society of America these variables are *hue; lightness* (for surfaces) or brightness (for light itself); and *saturation.* Using words in their common speech meanings, hue (or color) is the variable that gives rise to the simple color names such as red, blue, or green. Two colors may have the same hue but one may be lighter (or brighter) than the other. Two colors may have the same hue and lightness, but may differ in saturation—the percentage of hue they contain.

Color Sensitivity: The ability of the eye to change in color sensitivity accounts for the fact that colors do not change more than they do when taken from one illuminant to another, such as from daylight to incandescent light. (Color photographic film does not have this adaptability and therefore comes in different types designed for "daylight" or "artificial light.") In general, the eye tends to adapt itself so that the major illumination falling on a scene appears white. A white paper in this illumination tends to be seen as white; similarly, other colors tend toward their daylight colors. If the colors are strongly selective, however, they may change in different directions.

Arising from the phenomenon of color adaptation are the effects of color contrast and the related phenomenon of afterimages. If we look steadily at a color, the eyes partly adapt to it and tend to see it as white. If we then look at another color, the condition of the eyes is such that they tend to subtract the first color from the second. That is, they tend to move the second color toward the complementary of the first. This effect is local in the eye, so that if the first area has a strongly marked pattern, this pattern appears in the second area as an *afterimage.* In *simultaneous contrast,* two adjacent colors move away from each other in hue if the eye looks back and forth from one to the other. In *successive contrast,* the colors are presented to the eye one after the other. See Color Plate 25.—*R. M. E.*

COLORATION OF ANIMALS: A white rabbit, a black cat, a cardinal redbird, and an iridescent blue *Morpho* butterfly (such as is used in jewelry) differ markedly in coloration. Our eyes and brain detect these differences in terms of the reflected proportion of white light falling on them, and also in terms of any non-uniformity in the various parts of the solar spectrum. A white rabbit may reflect 95% of the light striking it, and a black cat only 5%; a cat reflecting 50% would be gray. All of these are neutral shades, but colored animals are non-neutral. The cardinal redbird is red because it reflects more of the longer wavelengths we see as red than of the shorter wavelengths we see as green or blue. The black cat and the cardinal alike owe their coloration to particular chemical compounds in hair and feathers. These substances are pigments that reflect some light and absorb the rest. The black, brown, and reddish pigments in hairs and feathers and on fish scales are melanins derived from the amino acid tyrosine. Pigments usually fade with time and can be dissolved out or bleached. Through heredity, some animals lack normal pigmentation of the skin, feathers, or fur, and the iris of the eyes; they are albinos (see ALBINISM AND MELANISM). The varying hare (snowshoe hare) in winter resembles an albino except for its dark eyes and black tips on the ears; its summer fur has yellow and black pigments, which together give the sensation of brown. (See ANIMAL CAMOUFLAGE.) The blue *Morpho* butterfly derives almost all of its brilliant metallic color through the interference of light waves reflected from the slightly brownish microscopic scales covering its wings. Each scale bears on its exposed surface a large number of parallel slanting ridges in which are thin films of alternating high and low refractive index, producing the iridescent effect. Its color has a structural basis and is permanent, but may disappear temporarily if the scales are wetted.

The coloration we see in animals depends upon our own eyes and brain, particularly upon our color vision. Some people and a great many kinds of animals are color-blind in various degrees. To a cat—one of the completely color-blind creatures—all other cats are white or gray or black, in a landscape as neutral as a black-and-white photograph. To a honeybee, other living and nonliving things are seen in yellow-green, green-blue, blue-violet, and ultraviolet, as well as in neutral shades. To an insect able to see ultraviolet (as we cannot), the luna moths we see only as pastel-green insects will be either blond ultraviolet-reflecting males or brunette ultraviolet-absorbing females. Hence the coloration of animals varies in significance according to the abilities of the eye seeing it. See COLOR VISION and Color Plate 26.—*L. and M. M.*

COLORATION OF PLANTS: Green is the most conspicuous color in plants: the color of leaves, twigs, and inner bark, and the predominant color of fresh-water and marine algae. Yellow and orange are more widely distributed than green, but less conspicuous. Certain yellow and orange pigments are always associated with the green ones and are masked by them. In autumn, when the green disintegrates and disappears, the yellow and orange colors are unmasked. Yellow and orange unconcealed by green are conspicuous in such specialized plant parts as roots, fruits, and flowers. Familiar examples are carrots, sweet potatoes, tomatoes, oranges, marigolds. Blue pigments accompany the green and yellow in blue-green algae, and unrelated blue and red pigments occur in flowers, in roots, and (as in red beets) in leaves. The green coloring matter of plants is CHLOROPHYLL—usually chlorophyll *a,* accompanied in many species by secondary chlorophylls such as those labeled *b, c,* or *d.* Most yellow and orange pigments and some orange-red ones are carotenoids. These fat-soluble, carotenoid pigments are of two principal types: carotenes, containing about a dozen pigments; and xanthophylls, containing six or seven dozen. One carotene, beta-carotene, and several xanthophylls always occur with the chlorophyll in green plants. The occurrence of particular pigments in various species has provided clues to evolutionary history; *e.g.* diatoms, dinoflagellates, and brown algae with the same minor chlorophyll (chlorophyll *c*) and with the same principal xanthophyll (fucoxanthin) have been found to have many other characteristics in common, thus indicating a common ancestry.

Most green and yellow pigments are formed in chloroplasts: highly specialized, microscopic organs. Pigments in these chloroplasts and associated pigments in blue-green and red algae utilize sunlight for production of oxygen and organic nutriments from water and carbon dioxide. This absorption and utilization of sunlight, known as PHOTOSYNTHESIS, is a vital function of the pigments. It provides the basic organic material required by virtually all living things, and provides the oxygen utilized by animals for their respiration of this organic matter.

Some carotenoid pigments of plants are absorbed selectively by animals. The xanthophyll lutein, for example, colors egg yolks yellow but plays no indispensable role in development of the chick. The alpha-carotene and beta-carotene absorbed by animals are converted into the indispensable vitamin A in the liver.

In addition to the chlorophylls and carotenoids, there are numerous other plant pigments of less common occurrence and less understood functions. The red, blue, and purple colors in certain flowers, in roots of red beets and radishes, and in fruits of apples, plums, and some grapes are caused by water-soluble pigments. These pigments, occurring in the cell sap apart from the chloroplasts, conceal the chlorophyll in leaves of purple cabbage, red beets, cockscomb, and coleus. The shade of color produced by some of the water-soluble pigments, such as the anthocyanins, depends upon the acidity of the cells in which the pigments develop. Litmus, another acid-sensitive pigment, occurs in certain lichens. See Color Plate 27.—*H. H. S.*

COLORIMETER: an instrument designed for the direct measurement of color. There are visual colorimeters and photoelectric colorimeters. In a visual colorimeter, one part of the field of vision is filled by an unknown color, while an adjacent part, the comparison field, is filled with an adjustable but known color—*e.g.* that of an additive mixture of three fixed colors (primaries). The operator compares the two fields and adjusts the color of the comparison field until he obtains a match between the two fields. The adjustments required for a match are taken as the specification of the unknown color. In a photoelectric colorimeter, the unknown color is viewed by a photosensitive device, the spectral responses of which are made to closely duplicate those of a human observer. The recorded photocurrents are taken as the specification of the unknown color. See COLOR; COLOR VISION.—*G. W.*

COLORIMETRY AND SPECTROPHOTOMETRY: All colored solutions absorb light of certain wavelengths, and many solutions which are not visibly colored absorb either ultraviolet or infrared light. Colorimetry is the technique of estimating the amounts of colored compound present in a solution by measuring the amount of light absorbed during passage of the light through the solution. The amount of absorption of incident light is proportional to the concentration of the colored compound. In spectrophotometry, the intensity of light absorption is determined electronically as a function of incident wavelength. Also, the pattern of the ABSORPTION SPECTRUM is

characteristic for the compound and is thus useful in the identification of unknown materials. If the material to be quantified is not itself colored, it can be treated with other chemicals yielding colored products which can then be estimated colorimetrically. Modern electronic spectrophotometers and colorimeters can identify and quantify as little as a millionth of an ounce of compound.—*Ph. F.*

COLOR VISION: the ability to distinguish between shades of neutral gray, ranging from black to white, and non-neutral (colored) shades, according to the distribution of wavelengths in the light coming from lights or objects. The ability to see colors is possessed solely by animals that have well-developed eyes and that are active principally by day. Among mammals, only some primates (including humans) have color vision. The bull and the cow, the horse, dog, cat, and rat are all color-blind. They see the world in shades of gray, much like those of a black-and-white photograph. All diurnal birds and reptiles seem able to see colors, but nocturnal birds (*e.g.* owls and whippoorwills) and reptiles (*e.g.* rattlesnakes and alligators) lack this ability. Some fishes with good eyes and with habits that keep them in well-lighted waters can respond to colors. So can many insects and crustaceans, as well as the octopus and squids among cephalopod mollusks. The rest of the animal world appears to be color-blind.

The most nearly satisfactory explanation for color vision was offered in 1801 by the English physicist and physician Thomas Young. Known as the three-component theory, it was made more specific by the German physiologist Hermann von Helmholtz and became known as the Young-Helmholtz theory. It held that the cone cells of the retina in color-sensitive vertebrate animals are of three different types, each with a pigment that absorbs light of a different wavelength: "R" cones, which are most sensitive to long wavelengths and hence report to the brain on the redness of light striking them; "B" cones, which are concerned particularly with short wavelengths, as in blue light; and "G" cones, which respond most to intermediate wavelengths of the solar spectrum, corresponding to the sensation green. When all three are stimulated by a mixture of wavelengths comparable to that in sunlight, the brain interprets the information from the cones as the sensation of "white" or gray—neutral shades. White is also induced by other mixtures—*e.g.* yellow and blue, which are therefore known as complementary colors. Yellow is another sensation that arises in the brain rather than in the eye; it can be induced by alternately flashing red and green light into one eye, stimulating the "R" and "G" cones in rapid succession.

The three-component theory of color vision is helpful also in explaining the color deficiencies in the vision of some people. Generally the term "color-blindness" is applied even to men and women who can distinguish parts of the solar spectrum, but not all of it. The commonest forms are an insensitivity to red light (red-blindness, or protanopia) or an inability to distinguish red from green (red-green blindness, or deuteranopia); these appear to be caused by a lack of the "R" cones or of the "G" cones, respectively; both are sex-linked inherited characteristics in mankind, affecting approximately one in each 100 men and one in each 400 women. Blue-blindness (tritanopia) is rarely congenital; sometimes it is acquired through inflammation of the retina or through retinal detachment; it seems to be the result of impairment of the "B" cones. A congenital lack of both "R" and "G" cones is characteristic of rare individuals suffering from achromasy—an inability to detect color of any hue as being distinct from some shade of gray; achromasy sometimes develops through degeneration of the retina. Far more people are "color-weak" than color-blind, and are described clinically

Plate 21   COASTS

The coastline along the eastern margin of the U.S.A. is characteristically an irregular one, formed of estuaries and promontories. There are many large islands off the coast of Maine, and extensive sand bars and beaches from New Jersey southward. The Pacific Coast, in contrast, is more precipitous, with many wave-cut cliffs, raised wave-cut terraces, and sea stacks.

1   2

1. Shoreline of Ecola State Park, Oreg.: An old wave-cut terrace above present beach, and the wave-cut cliff, indicate a relative rise of the land with respect to sea level. The small rocky islets are sea stacks; they represent former parts of the land now isolated by removal of the material from around them by wave and current action. *(Bob Ellis/FPG)* **2. Gay Head,** Martha's Vineyard, Mass., displays a cliff in which clays deposited during the recent glacial periods have been exposed by sea action. *(H. and M. Nielson/Shostal)*

Plate 22   COELENTERATES

2

Coelenterates are the simplest of animals with tissues. The sac-like body encloses a digestive cavity that opens to the outside only through the mouth. Coelenterates are distinguished by the possession of nettling capsules (nematocysts), used to anesthetize and capture small animals. **1. The organ-pipe coral** (*Tubipora musica*), a colonial coelenterate, secretes deck after deck of cylindrical tubes. It lives in the topmost deck and extends tentacles studded with nettling capsules to catch its food. *(Amer. Mus. of Nat. Hist.)* **2. Sea anemones,** the "flower animals" of tidal pools, can expand petal-like tentacles in a ring around the central mouth. *(Reeves-Franklin Photo)*

1

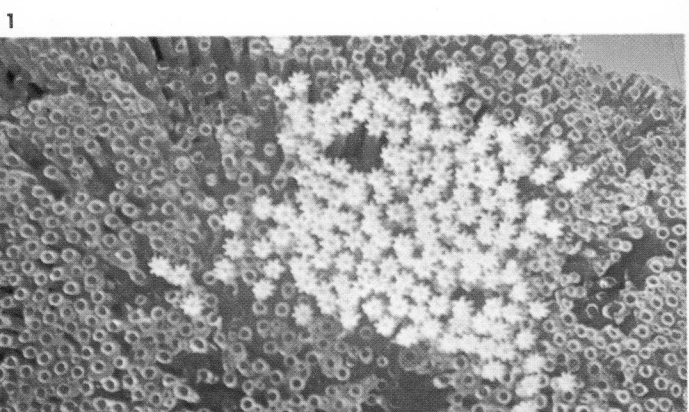

Plate 23   CLOCKS AND WATCHES

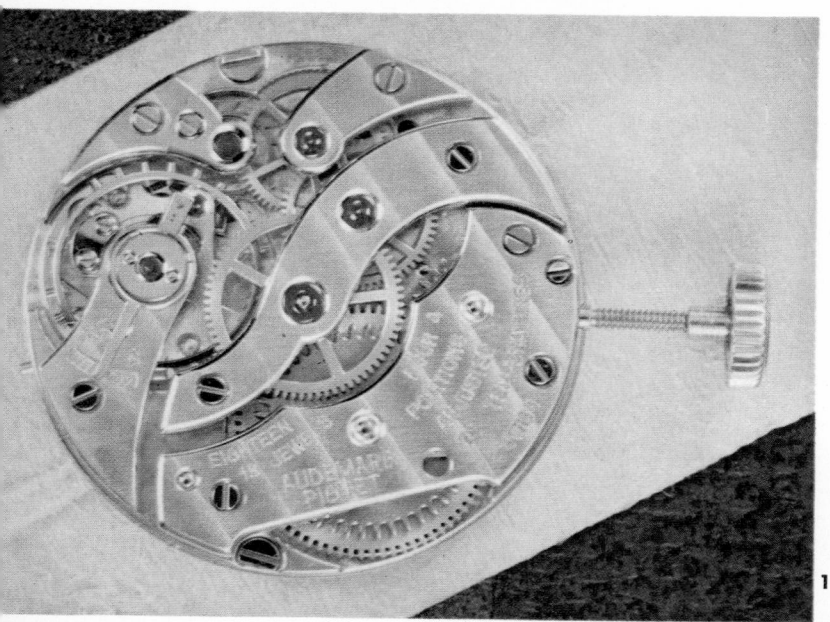

A clock or watch contains a source of power, a regulating device, and gears to transmit power and move the hands. The power source may be a falling weight, an uncoiling mainspring, electricity, or a power cell. Among regulators are the pendulum, the balance wheel, the constancy of alternating current, and the vibrations of a quartz crystal, a tuning fork, or (as in the atomic clock) cesium atoms.

1. Jewel bearings are harder than metal and resist shocks and friction. This watch has 18 jewels. **2. Stopwatch** with interchangeable slip-on disks calibrated for measuring speeds. *(Watchmakers of Switzerland)*

3. Automatic or self-winding watch has pivoting weights that wind mainspring as wrist moves. This version includes extra calibrations for accurate timings. **4. Braille watch** for the blind has raised dots replacing numerals and raised tip on hour hand. **5. Electronic watch** contains power cell regulated by tuning fork; it is accurate to 1 min per month. **6. Luminous dots** make this watch clearly readable in the dark. *(3, 4, 6 Watchmakers of Switzerland; 5 Bulova Watch Co.)*

7. Miniature secretary contains clock and music box. The gold case is set with agate stone and paste jewels. London, c. 1765. **8. Clock in form of bust** of African woman on bronze and marble, enameled music box. French, 18th cent. **9. Clock with ten different dials:** Gilt bronze case has relief and engraved decoration, below a pierced dome. Vienna, 1568. **10. American banjo clock** with painted glass panel set in partly gilded mahogany case. Boston, early 19th cent.

11. Gilded watch with enameled scenes. Paris, c. 1650.

12. Musical repeater: Napoleon on back. French, c. 1800.

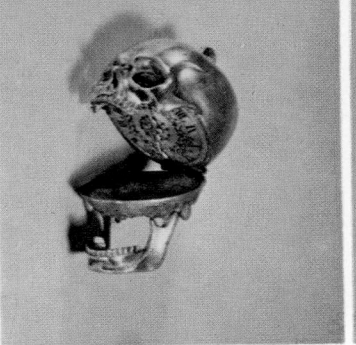

13. Skull-shaped silver case conceals dial. Geneva, 17th cent.

14. Gold watch with double case. English, early 18th cent.

15. Astronomical watch shows age of moon. German, c. 1580.

16. Plain silver watch with egg-shaped case. English, 1640.

17. Watch with crystal lid, enameled back. Swiss, 17th cent.

18. Repeater has kitchen scene. Swiss, 19th cent.

19. Mahogany tall clock with painting of sea battle between the *Constitution* and the *Guerriere*. Boston, c. 1812. *(Photos 7-19 Russ Kinne and The Met. Mus. of Art. See acknowledgment, p. 1298.)*

Plate 24   CLOCKS AND WATCHES

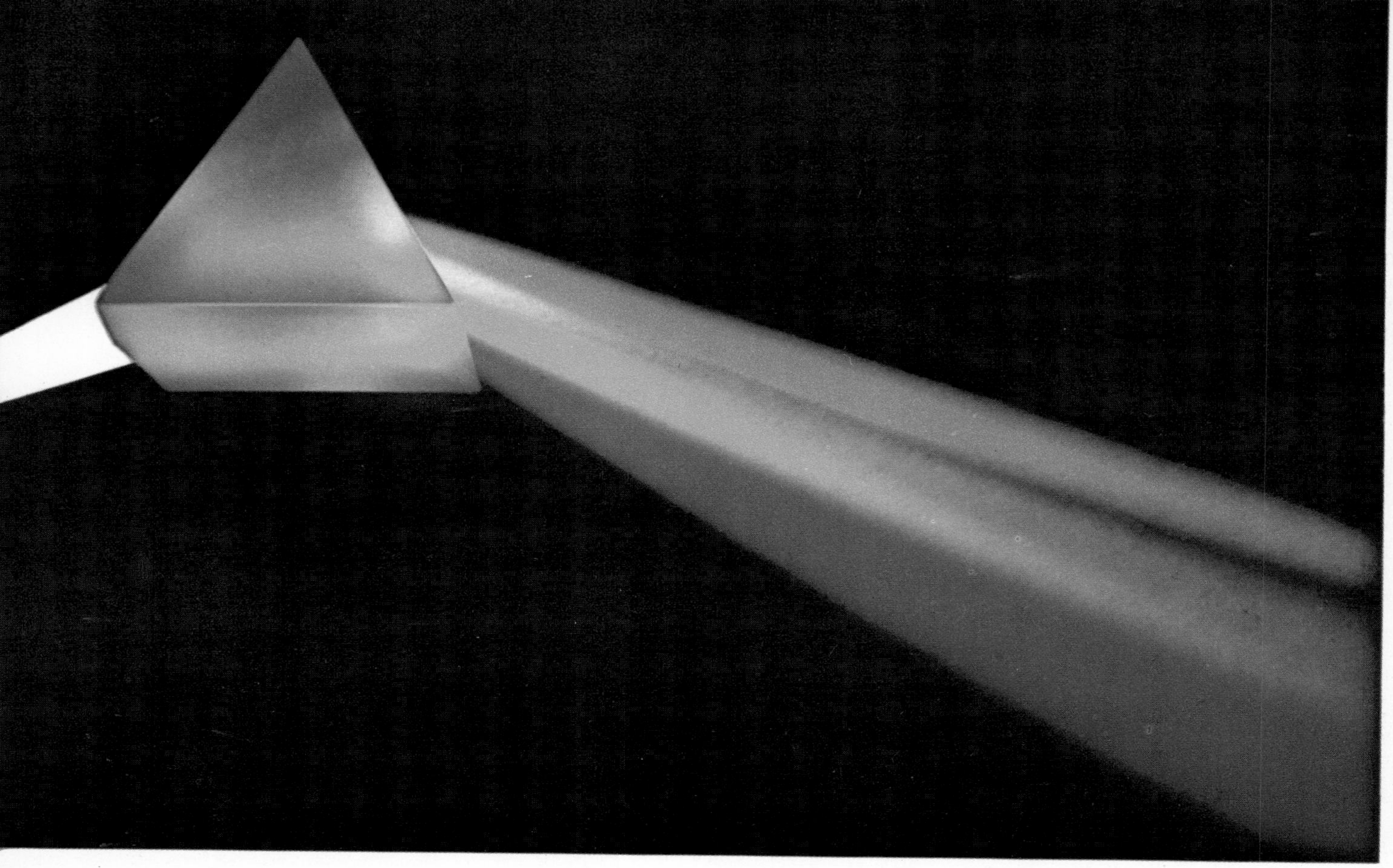

Plate 25 COLOR

Demonstration by means of prism that white sunlight is composed of all colors in the visible spectrum. *(Bausch and Lomb)*

Plate 26 COLORATION OF ANIMALS

The colors of animals are produced usually by pigments, which absorb some colors of white light and reflect or transmit the rest, and sometimes by diffraction and interference of light reflected from overlapping thin plates or fine parallel ridges. **1. Painted lady butterfly** *(Pyrameis huntera)* shows a completely different color pattern on the undersurface of its wings, because of pigments in the overlapping minute scales. *(Lynwood P. Chase/Nat. Audubon Soc.)* **2.** Few birds can rival **male bird-of-paradise** for bright colors, produced by pigments and by interference of light in feathers of bizarre forms. *(Amer. Mus. of Nat. Hist.)* **3. African chameleons** change their color rapidly by altering the size of star-shaped pigment cells in the skin. *(Walter Dawn)*

1

2

3

as protanomalous, deuteranomalous, or tritanomalous.

An alternative theory of color vision was suggested in 1920 by the German psychologist Ewald Hering. He believed that a fourth pigment must be involved to account for some apparent exceptions to the Young-Helmholtz theory, particularly in relation to shades of gray. In 1964 the conflict between these two theories was cleared up suddenly. At the Johns Hopkins University, Dr. Edward F. MacNichol and colleagues succeeded in recording electrically the excitation of individual cone cells, confirming the Young-Helmholtz theory at this level in the retina. At the same time, they were able to show that intensity of light, which is the subjective sensation of grayness, is interpreted by ganglion cells in the deeper layers of the retina. This provided for the features called for in the Hering theory. Later in the same year, Dr. George Wald and colleagues at Harvard University demonstrated that the three different types of cones called for by the Young-Helmholtz theory could be separately fatigued by red, blue, or green light, again proving that the cones are physiologically different. See COLOR; EYE; VISION.—*L. and M. M.*

COLT, SAMUEL, 1814–62, American inventor; b. Hartford, Conn.; self-educated. Colt invented the revolver, patented in England in 1835 and in the U. S. A. in 1836. The manufacture of interchangeable parts and the modern production line were developed by Colt to an unprecedented degree. Colt helped to develop the percussion cap and experimented with underwater mine explosions (1842–45), detonating submarine mines by electrical impulses sent from shore through an insulated cable. An associate of Samuel F. B. Morse in the telegraph enterprise, Colt also experimented with the first underwater electric cable.—*S. B.*

COLUMBIUM: see NIOBIUM.

COMBINATIONS: see PERMUTATIONS AND COMBINATIONS.

COMBUSTION: the reaction of oxygen with a substance to produce heat and, normally, light. Any substance that readily ignites upon contact with a flame is said to be combustible. A combustible substance will burst into flame in air or oxygen when it is heated to its *kindling temperature, i.e.* the characteristic temperature at which a given substance burns. For example, dialkyl zinc compounds burst into flame upon exposure to air. Red phosphorus has a kindling temperature of 260°C, whereas white phosphorus has a kindling temperature of 30°C. When a substance bursts into flame without application of heat, as in the case of zinc dialkyls, it is said to be *spontaneously combustible.* A substance is more likely to be spontaneously combustible if it has a low kindling temperature. Thus hay will sometimes ignite spontaneously. Fermentation in the green mown hay of a haystack evolves heat. The heat is not dissipated from the center of the hay stack, and the temperature there rises. When the temperature within reaches the kindling temperature of the dry hay, this catches fire. Turpentine or paint-soaked fabrics ignite spontaneously because of oxidation of the oil base in these substances. *Heat of combustion* is the heat generated when a combustible substance burns in air or oxygen. The oxidation of food in the body is sometimes referred to as combustion. Excess food which is not used up in this oxidation process can be metabolized and stored up in the body as fat. Hence, the calorie (heat energy) content is a measure of a food's tendency to add weight to the body (see RESPIRATION).—*G. W. M.*

Orbit of Halley's Comet extends from within Earth's orbit to outside Neptune's. The comet returns every 76 yr.

COMET: one of a group of relatively large, mostly solid bodies which are among the principal objects of the solar system, and which often develop a "tail" as they approach the Sun in their elliptical or nearly parabolic orbits. In medieval times, comets were widely regarded as forewarnings of disaster. Of the four to six comets discovered each year, the great majority remain too faint to be more than telescopic objects, but every two or three years one can be seen with the unaided eye, and a few each century are brilliant enough to be visible in daylight.

Appearance: When first becoming visible, a comet shows a hazy diffuse head, *coma,* or envelope, only vaguely luminous and transparent to stars lying beyond. The light of the coma appears to be sunlight reflected from small particles. The coma may have no definite boundary and seem of different size when viewed by different instruments; a few have exceeded the Sun in volume. The coma almost certainly consists of very widely spaced tiny, solid particles; most of the volume is unoccupied by matter. Within the coma, but not always central, there may develop a small, almost starlike area of intense light, the *nucleus.* The nucleus forms, if at all, as the comet approaches the Sun; some comets develop more than one nucleus. The nucleus may correspond to a small, central, compact body within the comet (possibly a conglomerate of ice and dust about 1 km in diameter). As the comet moves nearer the Sun, it becomes much brighter than decrease of distance would account for, and it also undergoes rapid internal changes and distortions; but there is a tendency for the size to decrease with distance from the Sun. In approaching the Sun the comet sometimes begins to emit gaseous material that yields additional light; in many cases a tail begins to form, streaming away from the Sun. Some tails are 200 million km long—apparently molecular gases and very fine dust driven out from the head. The driving force is most likely pressure exerted by solar radiation. Material in the tail eventually scatters away and is permanently lost to the comet.

Light: Light from a comet contains the spectrum of reflected solar light, indicating the presence of solid particles within the comet producing the reflection, and an emission spectrum consisting of bright lines and bands that are identifiable as originating from gas molecules within the head. These involve mainly carbon, hydrogen, nitrogen, and oxygen, and molecules combining these same elements. Comets passing extremely close to the Sun show the presence of sodium lines, and, for a few, possibly magnesium, nickel, and iron lines. A comet is not a self-luminous object, nor is its total brightness simply the result of reflection, but its freed gas molecules can absorb solar ultra-violet radiation and re-emit this energy as light of longer wavelength. In addition, the comet appears capable of producing finely divided dust within itself (as well as releasing gases) while near perihelion, and the combined result of these several effects can be an enormous increase in intrinsic luminosity.

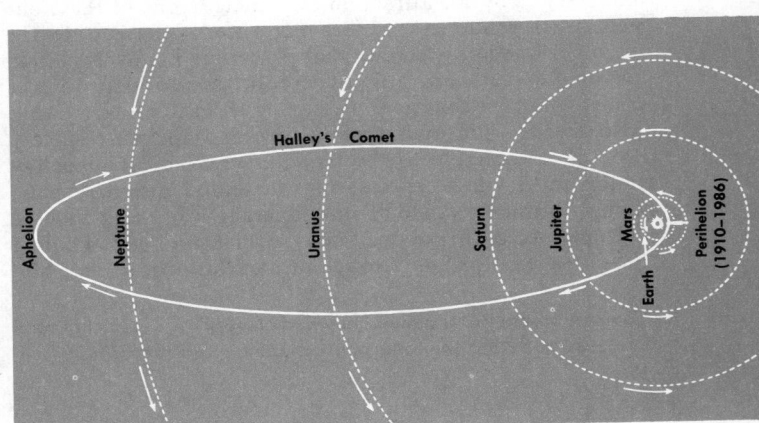

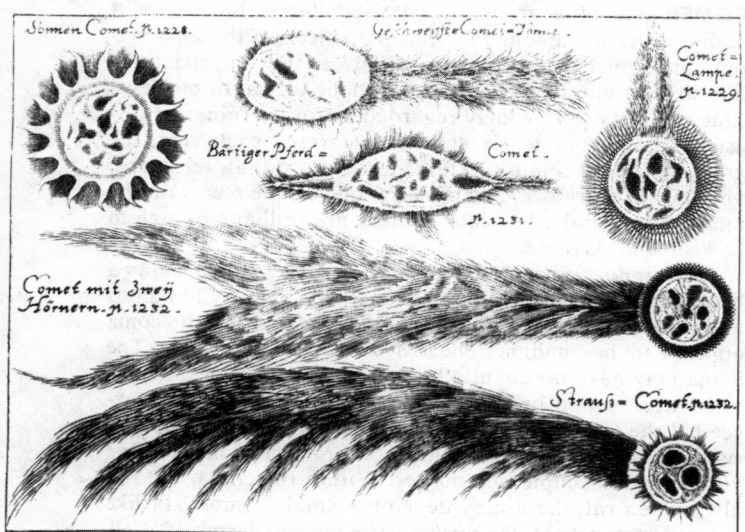

Drawings of comets published in 1676: Though somewhat fanciful these drawings show the heads, comas, and tails that are typical of comets. (*Gossner Collection*)

Orbits: *Short-period comets,* numbering about 100, are nearly all associated with the orbit of Jupiter. Their orbits are mainly direct (same sense as the planets), highly elongated, and at moderate inclinations (20 to 30°) to Earth's orbital plane. Intrinsically they are small, faint objects. The *long-period comets,* far more numerous, have paths reaching out to hundreds or even thousands of astronomical units from the Sun. All move in highly elongated, nearly parabolic orbits, and can become visible only in the relatively tiny portion of their paths near Earth and Sun. Most are intrinsically large and attain high luminosity when near the Sun. Short-period comets very likely are remains of former long-period comets that have been deflected by the planet Jupiter into short-period orbits, and in these they will probably decay (perhaps in a few thousand years) and, disappearing as comets, become meteor streams.

Orbital elements have been computed for nearly 500 long-period comets, and a similar number for the various returns of the short-period ones. Only two of the periodic comets move in almost circular orbits: most have orbits of high eccentricity (Encke 0.846, Halley 0.967); inclinations are moderate, averaging about 13°. A few, such as Halley's Comet, have retrograde motion.

The almost parabolic orbits of the long-period comets have inclinations of all values; as many move retrogradely as directly. The so-called "hyperbolic" comets, which appear from the small observed part of their path to have an eccentricity greater than unity, begin in fact with elliptic orbits that are changed by the attraction of planets. None of these objects has therefore entered the solar system from outside. On the other hand, it is certain that planets can convert elliptic orbits of comets into truly hyperbolic ones, and as a result comets must be continually escaping from the solar system. Also, there is little doubt that the present shape of a cometary orbit is due largely to the cumulative effect of planetary action rather than representing the initial primitive path, though this surely would be almost parabolic of long period.

Origin: According to one theory, comets are formed during the passage of the Sun through interstellar dust clouds. Ma-

Comet Cunningham: a multiple-tailed comet. Stars in background made trails during the long photographic exposure. (*Mt Wilson*) ▶

terial is focused, by solar attraction, into a narrow stream in the axial line behind the Sun as it moves through the cloud, and material loses energy by collisions as it enters the stream from the sides. In this way capture can occur for the inner part of the stream to great distances from the Sun. The density in the stream is far higher than in the original dust cloud and sufficient to enable self-gravitation to form loosely bound clumps of particles. These then fall in toward the Sun, but the action of the planets (and possibly of passing stars) deflects some of them slightly sideways and thereby permits them to escape falling directly into the body of the Sun at first approach. A number of Sun-grazing comets are actually observed. On this theory, a comet would consist of a gigantic swarm of widely separated dust particles. From the dynamical behavior of such a swarm, it follows that collisions of particles will occur within the comet during the perihelion part of the motion, with the consequent production of much finer particles and the release of volatile gases.

An entirely different theory, dating back a century or more, rests on the belief that the Sun and planets are surrounded by a gigantic cloud of comets extending to 150,000 astronomical units (halfway to the nearest star). This cloud would be an intrinsic part of the solar system, as evidenced by the fact that comet orbits are elliptical even before they approach the Sun. It is necessary to suppose that over 100 billion (10^{11}) comets populate this cloud; occasionally, perturbations from nearby stars deflect one of these comets into an orbit that brings it close enough to the Sun to become visible.

Comets of Special Interest: The first comet for which a return was successfully predicted was Halley's Comet, named after Edmund Halley. He established the similarity of orbit of the comets of 1531, 1607, and 1682, and concluded that these were different returns of the same comet having a period of about 76 yr; hence he predicted its return in about 1758, and it was seen at the end of that year. Records exist of observations of every apparition of Halley's Comet, save one, back to the year 240 B. C., and with less certainty even to 467 B. C. Comet Encke has the shortest-known period, 3.3 yr, and is one of some 40 that make up the Jupiter family of comets. Several instances have been observed of encounters of short-period comets with Jupiter. The orbit of Comet Pons-

Winecke, with a period of about 6 yr, roughly half that of Jupiter itself, undergoes rapid secular changes from óne revolution to the next because of the near commensurability of its period with Jupiter's (see PERTURBATIONS).—*R. A. L. et al.*

COMMENSALISM: a type of SYMBIOSIS in which two different kinds of animals habitually associate with one another to the detriment of neither and the gain of only one. Examples are the remora fish, which clings to sharks and sea turtles until close to food particles of small size; the small fish that hides between the tentacles of the Portuguese man-of-war; the pea crab that takes refuge in the mantle cavity of clams; and the pearl fish that spends most of its life in the breathing cavity of a large sea cucumber.—*L. and M. M.*

Commensal relationship unites two Polychaetes—worms with a pair of paddles on each body segment. *Lepidasthenia* (left) lives as a guest in a tube in the mud made and occupied by *Amphitrite* (shown coiled, out of tube). (*Douglas P. Wilson*)

COMMENSURABLE QUANTITIES: The concept of commensurability may be illustrated by two lines, one of which is a whole number of times the other. For example, lines 1 ft long and 1 in. long are commensurable, the first being 12 times the second. A line of 9 in. and one of 1 ft also are commensurable, since one is ¾ of the other. In general, the lengths l and L are commensurable if there are two whole numbers n and m such that $nl = mL$. From this it follows that the ratio of l to L is expressed by a rational fraction.

Early Greek mathematicians thought all lengths were commensurable. The discovery that they were not produced great consternation. They learned that the side and diagonal of a square are never commensurable, for the ratio of the diagonal to the side is $\sqrt{2}$, which is not a rational fraction. Since much of their early geometry was based on the presumption of commensurability, additional work was necessary to bring incommensurable quantities within its scope. The incommensurability of two lengths, for example, means that the ratio is an irrational number. Hence what was needed was a clarification of the concept and properties of irrational numbers. Book V of Euclid's *Elements* (actually the work of Eudoxus)

accomplishes this by a method which was improved by the work of Richard Dedekind in the late 19th cent. in his theory of irrationals.

Today many concepts and theories involving incommensurables are handled by the theory of limits applied to sequences of commensurables. For example, if the length and width of a rectangle is commensurable it is easy to derive the formula for the area by counting squares: $A = lw$. To establish this formula for a rectangle with l and w incommensurable, we consider a sequence of rectangles, all with the same width w, and with lengths $l_1, l_2, \ldots, l_n \ldots$ commensurable with w and tending to the limit l. The area of the rectangle is then defined to be the limit of the sequence $l_1w, l_2w, \ldots, l_nw, \ldots$, which is lw. The radius of a circle and its circumference are incommensurable, and the circumference and area are found by a similar use of the theory of limits.—*H. C.*

COMMON-ION EFFECT: Many chemical compounds on dissolving in water and other liquids decompose into ions (electrically charged atoms), whose behavior follows the law of MASS ACTION. When to such a solution another substance is added that has one kind of ion in common with the first substance, the total concentration of common ions increases. At the same time the concentration of the other ions decreases, to maintain the ionization constant (the law of mass action). This means that a portion of the non-common ions combine with a portion of the common ions to form a non-ionized molecule, which can be removed from the solution. An illustration is provided by hard water which contains minute amounts of the salt calcium carbonate, partly in the form of calcium and carbonate ions and partly non-ionized. When carbon-dioxide gas is introduced into the water, it forms carbonic acid, which ionizes into hydrogen ions and carbonate ions. The common carbonate ions repress the ionization of calcium carbonate. More of the non-ionized salt is formed, and being only slightly soluble it precipitates out, thus lowering the calcium content of the water.—*T. M. and C. S.*

COMMUNICATION THEORY: see INFORMATION THEORY.

COMMUNITY, ANIMAL AND PLANT: the sum of all the separate POPULATIONS of animals and plants habitually sharing the resources of a single HABITAT. The members of a community show definite interrelationships and interdependence, as parts of a food web. Certain kinds occupy the large *niche* of the food-producers. Other kinds fill smaller niches as herbivores (plant-eaters), first-level carnivores (herbivore-eaters), second-level carnivores (carnivore-eaters), parasites, scavengers, and decomposers. Food webs of complex communities comprised of many species are more stable than food webs in which fewer species participate. Nevertheless, even complex communities are dynamic and change slowly through regular steps of SUCCESSION.

Large niches in a community are ordinarily occupied by many species, one or two of which may be dominant and give the community its name, *e.g.* "spruce-fir community." This particular community is one with an enormous geographic extent in Canada and NE United States. Other communities may be severely restricted, *e.g.* fungus communities on rotting pine cones. The use of animals in the naming of communities (*e.g.* "spruce-moose association") is of less value because of the greater mobility of animals; yet many animals are remarkably faithful to definite habitats. When the ecologist considers a community of animals and plants in relation to nonliving features of their environment, he refers to the community plus environment as an *ecosystem*. See ECOLOGY.

Critics of the community concept have pointed out that sometimes the association of species is a coincidence without statistical significance; that in other cases the association occurs merely because of similar ecological requirements; that a shift of habitat factors gradually changes the composition of the association. Hence the alternative to discrete communities is the concept of continuous variation (*continuum concept*). —*L. and M. M.*

COMPASS: see MAGNETIC COMPASS; MATHEMATICAL INSTRUMENTS; RADIO COMPASS.

COMPLEMENTARITY PRINCIPLE: a philosophical principle enunciated by Niels Bohr, 1927, which states in qualitative terms the ultimate limits to which we can probe into the detailed structure of matter. Before the principle can be stated in a meaningful way, it is necessary to outline the developments leading to its formulation.

Before 1900 the science of mechanics was considered a closed subject. NEWTON'S LAWS OF MOTION seemed entirely adequate to describe the motions of all objects on Earth and in the skies; *e.g.* astronomers could calculate the times of eclipses with great precision. According to Newtonian mechanics, if the electric charges and masses of all component particles of a system were known, and if their positions and momenta (momentum = mass × velocity) were measured at any instant of time, then the positions and momenta of all of the particles for all times, past and future, could be calculated. The universe was pictured as a completely deterministic machine. Although it was suspected that there might be new kinds of forces (other than gravitational and electrical) holding the ultimate particles of matter together, there was no reason to suspect that Newtonian mechanics would not also describe the motions of particles, with as much detail and precision as obtained in describing the motions of planets.

However, when physicists began to probe into the structure of atoms, they found in a series of decisive experiments that Newtonian mechanics is not valid in the atomic domain. (See BLACK BODY RADIATION; PHOTOELECTRIC EFFECT; FRANCK-HERTZ EXPERIMENT; DAVISSON-GERMER EXPERIMENT; COMPTON EFFECT.) These experiments demonstrated that atomic systems are quantized and not completely deterministic; that is, all their interactions are characterized by transfers of energy and momentum in discrete, indivisible packets called quanta; furthermore, the time and place at which the quantum "jumps" (transfers) occur is not predictable with certainty, but only the probability of the occurrence can be calculated. Thus the future development of an atomic system whose state is known at one time cannot be predicted with complete certainty. And, it is not even possible to know the state of the system at one instant of time in as complete detail as had been previously supposed. Heisenberg demonstrated this in his famous UNCERTAINTY PRINCIPLE, which arose from the above-mentioned experimental results. This principle asserts that it is impossible to measure simultaneously the position and momentum of a particle with unlimited precision. Any experimental arrangement that increases the precision of the determination of one of the two variables introduces additional uncertainty in the value of the other. The reason is that any measurement involves an interaction with a measuring device, and all interactions involve indivisible, incompletely predictable quantum jumps. The effect is not observable with objects we encounter in everyday life, because the momentum involved in a single quantum transfer gives an immeasurably small "kick" to such objects. Not so, however, for a single atom. To the atom, a quantum represents a big kick.

These revolutionary discoveries led Bohr to recognize that in the atomic domain the system under observation and the measuring instrument constitute an inseparable whole; if one changes the experimental arrangement, one also changes the state of the atom. Therefore, evidence obtained under different experimental conditions provides different partial "views" of the atomic system, none of which can be as detailed as was expected before 1900, but which complement each other in giving as complete a picture as nature will allow. This, roughly, is the meaning of the complementarity principle.—*S. K.*

COMPLEX NUMBER: a number that has two components, one called real, the other imaginary. The positive and negative integers (whole numbers), fractions, and irrationals constitute the real numbers. The square of any one of them is a positive number, *e.g.* $-3 \times -3 = 9$. What, then, is the square root of a negative number, say -9? This question arises in the attempt to solve the quadratic equation $x^2 + 9 = 0$, or $x^2 = -9$. To complete the solution of such equations, the *imaginary unit i* was introduced, and defined as the square root of -1. Thus $i = \sqrt{-1}$, and $i^2 = -1$. Hence $(3i)^2 = 9i^2 = -9$, and $(-3i)^2 = 9i^2 = -9$, and the solutions of $x^2 + 9 = 0$ are $x = 3i$ and $x = -3i$. The expressed product of a real number multiplied by i is called an imaginary number. Complex numbers are formed by adding an imaginary number to a real number, *e.g.* $2 + 3i$, and $5 + (-2i) = 5 - 2i$. In general any number that can be written in the form $a + bi$, where a and b are real, is a complex number. This makes real and imaginary numbers also complex, since if $b = 0$, $a + bi$ is real, and if $a = 0$, $a + bi$ is imaginary. With the introduction of complex numbers, it can be stated that every quadratic equation has two roots (solutions), every cubic equation has three roots, and, in general, every nth-degree equation has n roots, some of which may be real, some complex.

Complex numbers can be added, subtracted, and multiplied much as these operations are performed on binomials. Thus $(2 + 5i) + (3 - 2i) = (2 + 3) + (5 - 2)i = 5 + 3i$; $(2 + 5i) - (3 - 2i) = (2 - 3) + [5 - (-2)]i = -1 + 7i$; $(2 + 5i)(3 - 2i) = 2 \cdot 3 - 2 \cdot 2i + 3 \cdot 5i - 2 \cdot 5i^2 = 6 - 4i + 15i - 10(-1) = 16 + 11i$. Division can be performed as in the following example of $(2 + 5i) \div (3 - 2i)$:

$$\frac{2 + 5i}{3 - 2i} = \frac{(2 + 5i)(3 + 2i)}{(3 - 2i)(3 + 2i)} = \frac{6 + 4i + 15i + 10i^2}{9 - 4i^2}$$

$$= (-4 + 19i)/13 = -4/13 + 19i/13.$$

The rule here is to multiply numerator and denominator by the conjugate of the denominator. The conjugate is the complex number formed by changing the sign of the imaginary

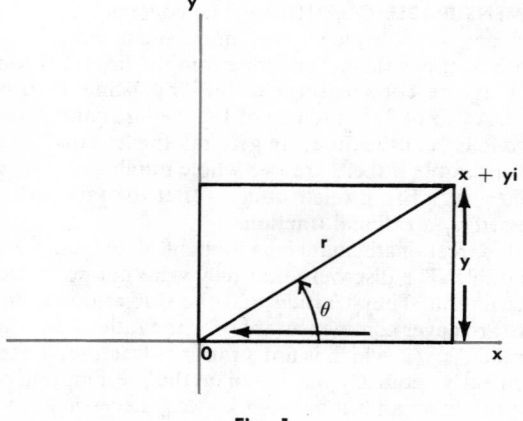

Fig. 1

part. The product of a complex number and its conjugate is always real.

A rectangular coordinate system provides a geometrical representation of complex numbers. The real and imaginary components are plotted on the horizontal and vertical axes, respectively. Thus, each complex number has a definite location and each point corresponds to a definite complex number. This system is credited to Jean Robert Argand (1763–1822), and the plot of the number is its Argand diagram, Fig. 1. The Argand diagram shows that a complex number $x + yi$ is determined by its distance r from the origin and the angle of inclination θ. In fact $x = r\cos\theta$, $y = r\sin\theta$, and $x + yi = r(\cos\theta + i\sin\theta)$. The quantity r is called the modulus, or absolute value, of the complex number, and the angle θ is its amplitude, or argument. The expression $r(\cos\theta + i\sin\theta)$ is the polar form of the number, since it utilizes the polar coordinates of the point. The modulus of the number $4 + 3i$ is $\sqrt{4^2 + 3^2} = 5$, and the amplitude is $\tan^{-1} \frac{3}{4} = 53° \, 8'$, approximately. The modulus of $a + bi$ is $\sqrt{a^2 + b^2}$ and the amplitude is $\tan^{-1} b/a$.

The polar form facilitates multiplication, division, raising to powers, and extracting roots. First, we have the following theorem, obtained by multiplication and use of the addition

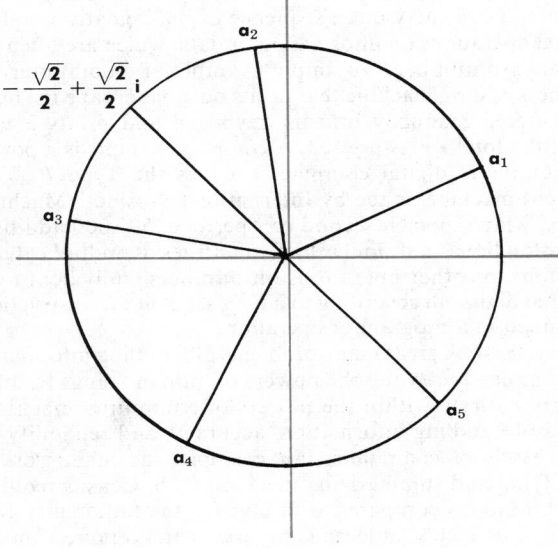

Fig. 2

formulas of trigonometry: $[r_1(\cos\theta_1 + i\sin\theta_1)] \cdot [r_2(\cos\theta_2 + i\sin\theta_2)] = r_1 r_2(\cos[\theta_1 + \theta_2] + i\sin[\theta_1 + \theta_2])$. This rule for multiplying complex numbers in polar form directs us to multiply moduli and add amplitudes. De Moivre's theorem for raising to powers follows from this: $[r(\cos\theta + i\sin\theta)]^n = r^n(\cos n\theta + i\sin n\theta)$.

In order to extract roots we express the root by a fractional power and apply this theorem. Thus, the square root of $4(\cos 60° + i\sin 60°)$ is $[4(\cos 60° + i\sin 60°)]^{1/2} = 4^{1/2}(\cos 60°/2 + i\sin 60°/2) = 2(\cos 30° + i\sin 30°)$. Since $(\cos 60° + i\sin 60°)$ can be replaced by $[\cos(60° + 360°) + i\sin(60° + 360°)]$, we also obtain the square root: $2[\cos(30° + 180°) + i\sin(30° + 180°)] = 2(\cos 210° + i\sin 210°)$. In this way we can always obtain n nth roots of each complex number. In Fig. 2 are shown the 5 fifth roots of $-\sqrt{2}/2 + \sqrt{2}i/2 = (\cos 135° + i\sin 135°)$. The first one is $a_1 = \sqrt[5]{1}(\cos 135°/5 + i\sin 135°/5) = (\cos 27° + i\sin 27°)$. The second is $a_2 = \sqrt[5]{1}[\cos(135° + 360°)/5 + i\sin(135° + 360°)/5] = [\cos(27° + 72°) + i\sin(27° + 72°)] = (\cos 99° + i\sin 99°)$. All five roots are obtained from $\sqrt[5]{1}[\cos(135° + n \cdot 360°) + i\sin(135° + n \cdot 360°)]$ where n can be 0, 1, 2, 3, or 4. If we let $n = 5, 6, 7, \ldots$, we merely obtain the same roots again, since $(135° + 5 \cdot 360°)/5 = 27° + 360°$, and so on for higher values of n.

Although complex numbers were originally introduced for the solution of equations, they can also be used to represent vectors. The magnitude of a vector is given by the absolute value of the number, and its direction by the argument (the angle θ) of the number. A large branch of mathematics—FUNCTION THEORY—deals with complex numbers and has many applications in science and engineering.—*H. C.*

COMPOUND: a substance consisting of atoms that are of more than one kind. The different atoms are present in a definite numerical ratio, because all compounds have a definite composition. Common examples of compounds are sugar, soap, and water. Sugar contains atoms of carbon, hydrogen, and oxygen; soap contains atoms of sodium, hydrogen, oxygen, and carbon. Water contains two atoms of hydrogen and one of oxygen.

Compounds are ionic, polar, and non-polar, according to the type of bonds formed between their atoms. An *ionic compound* is one in which the electron affinity of one atom is far greater than that of another, so that the outer electrons of the atom of less electron affinity will be lost to the other atom. There is then an ionic bond between the atoms, consisting of the electrostatic attraction of the positive atom for the negative one: sodium chloride is an example. When two atoms equally share electrons to form a bond between them, they are electrically neutral. This type of bond, as in methane, characterizes a *non-polar compound*. When the affinity of one atom for electrons is somewhat greater than that of another atom, the electrons forming the bond between them are attracted to one atom more than the other, and the bond becomes polarized, so that a *polar compound* such as iodine monochloride results. (See CHEMICAL COMPOSITION, LAWS OF; CHEMISTRY, *Formulas, Valence Bonds, and Equations*.)—*G. W. M.*

COMPRESSIBILITY: the property of materials that enables them to decrease in volume when subjected to pressure from all sides. When matter is deformed the fractional deformation is called *strain,* and the associated restoring force per unit area is called *stress*. Within the elastic limit, stress divided by strain is a constant called the *elastic modulus,* of which one type is the *bulk modulus*. Compressibility is the reciprocal of the bulk modulus.—*C. E. B.*

COMPRESSOR: a machine designed to increase the pressure of a gas. Increased pressure may be desired to overcome pipe friction developed in transporting the gas, to supply air to a blast furnace, to drive tools, or for other purposes. Compressors may be of the reciprocating, centrifugal, axial-flow, or rotary type. Compressors developing low pressures are known as *fans,* those developing intermediate pressures, as *blowers*.

A *reciprocating compressor* consists of a piston reciprocating in a cylinder with suitable valves. Such compressors are generally used for relatively small volumes per unit time and high pressures. They may be directly driven by the expansion of steam or connected to a relatively slow-speed, or geared, motor. The piston draws in a supply of gas during one stroke, a valve closes, and the gas is compressed and discharged. They are generally double-acting and may be water-cooled to increase efficiency. To develop higher pressures, several cylinders are used in series. *Centrifugal compressors* consist of a rotating impeller inside a stationary casing. The impeller imparts to the gas a velocity which is converted into pressure in the casing. These compressors are driven at a relatively high speed by a steam turbine or motor, and may be used in series (multi-staged), as in the case of reciprocating compressors. The action in an *axial-flow compressor* is similar to that occurring in a desk fan; in order to attain a desired pressure these compressors are almost invariably multi-staged. This type of compressor may be incorporated in jet engines, where the action is aerodynamic rather than centrifugal. *Rotary compressors,* similar in action to reciprocating compressors, trap the gas in a chamber and then discharge it against a higher pressure. However, no valves are required, since compression is achieved by use of close clearances. Many types of rotary compressors are available, with variously shaped lobed impellers or meshing screws or gear teeth. The gas is trapped in the space between the lobes or teeth and is then delivered in small "slugs" to the high-pressure side. (See FAN; FLUID MACHINERY; PUMP.)—*A. C.*

COMPTON, ARTHUR HOLLY, 1892–1962, U. S. physicist; b. Wooster, Ohio. In 1923 he showed that when a light quantum (whose existence Einstein had postulated in 1905) falls on an electron, the electron acquires kinetic energy from the photon and the photon's frequency accordingly decreases. He thus explained changes in frequency (also observed by C. G. Barkla) and further confirmed Einstein's theory of light quanta. Discovery of this COMPTON EFFECT brought Compton the Nobel prize, 1927. He was a member of the National Academy of Sciences.—*D. H. D. R.*

COMPTON EFFECT: an effect first observed by A. H. Compton, 1923, demonstrating that electromagnetic radiation, under certain conditions, behaves like a stream of particles. Compton bombarded a target with a beam of X-RAYS (very high-frequency electromagnetic radiation) and observed those rays scattered by the loosely bound electrons in the target atoms. He discovered that the scattered x-rays were of lower frequency than the incident ones and that the change in frequency depended upon the angle of scattering only.

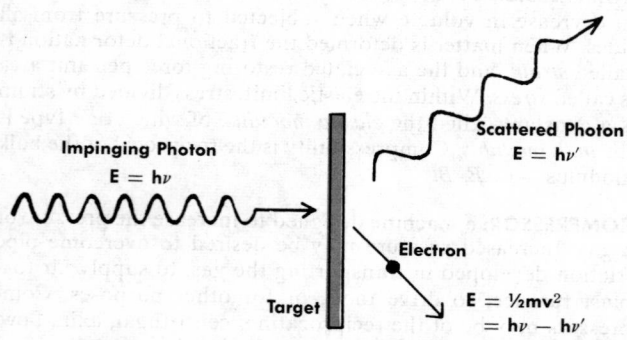

Compton effect: the impact between a high-energy photon and electron, in which momentum and kinetic energy are conserved.

This Compton effect, as it came to be known, is contrary to the predictions of classical electromagnetic theory. According to that theory, x-rays consist of traveling waves of electric and magnetic fields; the passing electric fields would force the electron to oscillate, and this oscillation of charge in turn would re-radiate new waves of the *same* frequency. If one took into account the smaller forces exerted by the magnetic fields, and assumed the electrons to be free enough of atomic binding to be accelerated forward, then a change in frequency of the scattered radiation at a given angle would be observed, but it would change with time. As shown in Compton's experiment and subsequent observations, the frequency change is determined by the angle of scattering. This effect can be explained by assuming that the energy and momentum of the radiation is carried by a stream of point particles

and that the energy of each of these particles—called photons —is proportional to the frequency of the radiation. The latter assumption had previously been used successfully by Max Planck and Albert Einstein to describe BLACK BODY RADIATION and the PHOTOELECTRIC EFFECT, respectively. Using both assumptions, and picturing the scattered photon as having collided with an electron in billiard-ball fashion, Compton was able to obtain quantitative agreement with experiment. Qualitatively it is possible to understand why the frequency of the photon decreases, because in colliding with a stationary electron the photon necessarily imparts some of its energy to the former in setting it into motion. According to the second assumption, then, the reduced energy of the photon reflects itself in a reduced frequency of the radiation.

The wave-particle duality of radiation and matter implied by the Compton effect and many other phenomena can now be understood in terms of modern QUANTUM THEORY.—*S. K.*

COMPUTER (also called computing machine, automatic computer, automatic data processor, or electronic brain): a machine that can carry out a sequence of mathematical and/or logical operations on information or data, which are often but not always numbers. A simple example of a computer is a business adding machine that prints on a paper tape the number entered manually into its keyboard and prints a total when the total key is pressed. A complex example is a powerful automatic digital computer such as the Type 7030 (or Stretch) machine, made by International Business Machines Corp., which in each second can perform 500,000 additions or subtractions, and similar high quantities of multiplications, divisions, or other operations on numbers equivalent to 16 decimal digits, all according to a long sequence of instructions contained in a program of operation.

Usefulness: A great many problems of handling information are completely beyond the powers of human beings to solve, but are entirely within the powers of computing machines. Speed of handling information, accuracy, and reliability are basic assets of computers. For example, the main work of classifying and summarizing the 1960 U. S. Census required about 8 mo, as compared with 6 yr for the far smaller 1890 census. The fastest modern computers can do more computing work in 3 min than a man can do in a lifetime. The cost of 10,000 calculating operations with the fastest modern computers is less than 2½ cents.

Computers have been applied in engineering, science, business, industry, and military and government operations; language translation, *e.g.* Russian to English; playing of games, *e.g.* checkers and "management games," in which two competing teams of managers try out business-planning strategies in model business situations; guidance of missiles and navigation of submarines. More than 400 fields of application of computers were inventoried in 1961. There is, in fact, no theoretical limit to the applications of computers to problems of handling information.

Information: Information, or *data,* for the purpose of a computing machine, is a set of arrangements of some physical equipment. This equipment may be counter wheels bearing along their edges the decimal digits 0,1,2,3,4,5,6,7,8,9; or it may be polarized spots on a magnetic surface, a north-south polarization standing for a 1, and a south-north polarization standing for a 0; or it may be the presence or absence of punched holes in a paper tape or a punch card of standard size and shape; or it may be the presence or absence of electrical pulses in certain channels at certain times; etc. The patterns of the arrangement express information for the purposes of the machine. The instructions for the machine are similar patterns of arrangement of physical equipment. This form of

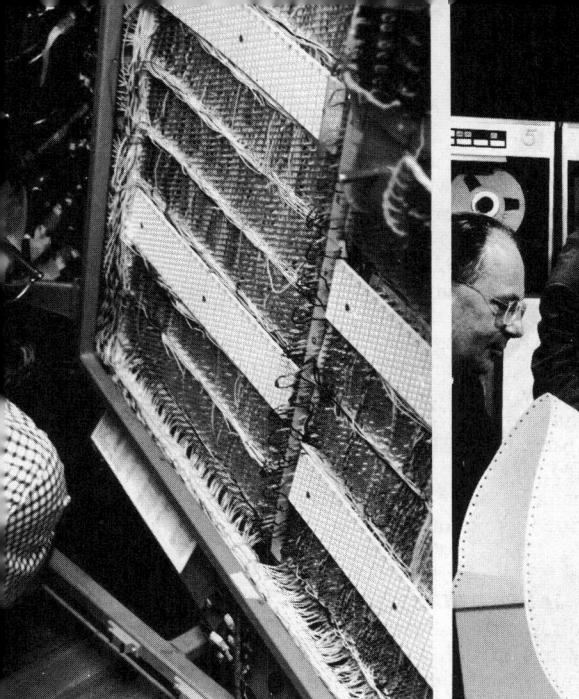

High-speed computers require miles of wiring to interconnect their input, operating, output, and memory circuits. The technician at left is checking the installation of a completed unit. Typical computer applications require the rapid solution of complex equations; the unit in the center here is used in the design of the Saturn space-vehicle engine. The strip of paper at right is the output of a computer designed to yield printed results; the type is carried on the loop of chain shown. *(IBM)*

representing information by separate, easily distinguishable states of the equipment is called *digital,* because the different patterns representing information are sharply distinguishable from each other. In the same way the fingers (digits, by another meaning of the word), when held up, may represent any number from 1 to 5. The other form of representing information in a computer is called *analog,* because the length of a distance on a slide or the amount of turning of a shaft, or the amount of an electrical voltage, etc., is *analogous* to the numerical magnitude that is to be represented. This is the principle used in the SLIDE RULE. Automatic analog computers, using swift electronic components instead of wooden slides, are useful for many scientific and engineering purposes.

Structure: It is remarkable that the principles of structure of an automatic digital computer are really simple. There are six essential parts. The *input unit* takes in numbers, other data, and instructions, prepared in acceptable machine language, *e.g.* holes in punch cards or polarized spots on magnetic tape. The *storage,* or *memory,* unit contains usually 1,000 to 50,000 or more registers in which units of information, as a number, word, or instruction, can be stored in machine language. The *arithmetic unit* can perform addition, subtraction, multiplication, division, and the other arithmetical and logical operations on numbers it receives from storage, and can send the result of the operation back to storage. The *output unit* takes computed answers in machine language and translates them into printed characters on paper or into some other language acceptable to human beings. The *buss,* or trunk, using wires, conveys information from one part of the machine to another in the form of electrical pulses. The *control unit* takes in each successive instruction from storage, and issues commands to the switches or gates inside the machine, controlling the connections of the buss with the registers. Basically, each instruction is of the form "Take the number in register . . . ; put it in register. . . ." For the machine to perform in this way, large numbers of electronic components such as diodes, transistors, pulse shapers, and amplifiers are needed. The demand of computer manufacturers for reliable, fast electronic components for computing has greatly influenced the electronics industry.

Arithmetical Operations: The arithmetic unit of a modern automatic digital computer receives information in the form of patterns of 1's and 0's. These patterns represent the digits 0 to 9, the letters A to Z, and certain other characters (*e.g.* \$, *). Each character is expressed as a code of six or seven 1's and 0's. The *binary scale* instead of the decimal scale may be used for the digits 0 to 9, with the result that these digits are coded as follows:

0	0000	5	0101
1	0001	6	0110
2	0010	7	0111
3	0011	8	1000
4	0100	9	1001

(If a six-digit code is being used for all characters, then the first two digits at the left may be 00.)

In the binary scale, or binary notation, each position of a 0 or 1 in the number designates a power of two, with units at the right, then twos, then fours, then eights, and so on. Thus 0 1 1 1 designates 0 eights, 1 four, 1 two, and 1 one, or adding the four, two, and one, we have seven. Addition in the binary scale can be expressed simply and executed rapidly in many different kinds of electronic circuits. For example, suppose we add in the binary scale seven and five. This is much like addition in the decimal scale except that 1 plus 1 is 10 (read "one-oh"), and we "put down oh and carry the one." Thus:

0111	four + two + one	7
0101	four + one	5
1100	eight + four	12

The operation in detail is as follows:

Right-most column: "One and one is one-oh; put down oh and carry the one."

Second column: "One and oh is one, and carried one, makes one-oh; put down oh and carry the one."

Third column: "One and one is one-oh, and carried one, is one-one; put down one and carry one."

Fourth column: "Oh and oh is oh, and carried one, is one; put down one, and carry nothing."

After adding two coded decimal digits, if the total is greater than ten (1010 in the binary scale), then 1010 must be subtracted by a second circuit, the result must be stored as the correct digit code for the right-hand decimal digit of the sum in this column, and a carry digit of 1 must be added into the code for the decimal digit next on the left.

In one second, more than 100,000 additions of binary numbers of more than 40 binary digits (or bits) can be performed. Other efficient binary codes for decimal digits may be used, instead of the pure binary scale.

History: The first computing machine was the *abacus,* a device used in ancient Greece and Rome for calculating, and even today widely used in China, Japan, and other countries. It represents numbers by the positions of beads strung on parallel rods. Frequently, each rod contains five beads in one section to represent by their positions 0, 1, 2, 3, 4 and another bead in a second section to represent by its position 0 or 5. The successive rods stand for the successive powers of 10. Thus the number 1,867 would be as shown in the figure.

An Abacus

The French mathematician Pascal is credited with the first invention (1642) of an adding machine with counter gears. To represent a digit, he made use of a ten-toothed geared counter wheel which had labels 0, 1, 2, 3, . . . , 9 around the circumference. When the counter wheel stood at 9, and one was added, the position of the counter wheel advanced from 9 to 0, and at the same time a small extra side tooth nudged the adjacent counter wheel on the left, causing it to advance one step, thus providing the carry. This machine has developed into the useful printed-tape adding machine common in most business offices today. A calculating machine that performed multiplication by rapidly repeated addition was built by Gottfried William Leibniz in 1694. The modern desk calculating machine, *e.g.* Friden, Marchant, or Monroe, is manually operated and has three registers: a keyboard, for taking in numbers; an accumulator, for showing the accumulated result of calculations; and a third register, for recording the multiplier as multiplication is carried out or the quotient arrived at in division. The machine may have a fourth register, to store the multiplier in advance of a multiplication. The time for multiplying one ten-decimal digit number by another is about 8 sec.

A digital computer much like those of today was proposed by Charles Babbage about 1835, but the building of such a machine awaited technological developments. The first automatic general-purpose digital computer was the Harvard IBM Automatic Sequence Controlled Calculator, completed in 1944. It handled numbers of 23 decimal digits, could store about 72 of them at one time, and could perform multiplication in about 4 sec, division in about 11 sec. This machine, constructed of mechanical parts, produced much useful calculation for the U. S. armed forces in World War II. The first electronic digital computer, ENIAC (for "electronic numerical integrator and calculator"), was built in 1946. In addition to computers proper, there are now more than 70 kinds of special-purpose computing machines—machines that automatically handle information in special situations. They range from the guidance mechanism in an observatory, which automatically keeps a large telescope following a star, to the automatically programmed vending machine, which permits a customer to choose any one of a dozen articles, takes in and verifies his money, and gives correct change. Teaching machines form a newly important class of special-purpose computers and data processors.—*E. C. B.*

COMTE, AUGUSTE, 1792–1857, French philosopher and founder of POSITIVISM; b. Montpellier. Sciences, he held, all develop through three stages: theological, metaphysical, and positive. In the first two stages, phenomena are explained as effects of hidden causes, respectively supernatural and natural. But positivistically, explanation is replaced with description, and phenomena are to be organized by means of laws which refer only to observables. His ideal that all of knowledge is to be scientific, and all of science positivistic, influenced Mach, Avenarius, and, more recently, logical positivism. Comte's major written works include *Cours de Philosophie Positive* (6 vols., 1830–42).—*Ar. D.*

CONANT, JAMES BRYANT, 1893–   , U. S. chemist, educator, and diplomat; b. Boston, Mass. His research in organic chemistry has included work on reduction and oxidation, hemoglobin, free radicals, the quantitative study of organic reactions, superacid solutions, and chlorophyll. His *On Understanding Science* (1947) suggested an historical approach in the teaching of science, as represented in his own teaching at Harvard. He was president of Harvard Univ. (1933–53) and ambassador to West Germany (1955–57). He is a fellow of the Royal Society and a member of the National Academy of Sciences.—*D. H. D. R.*

CONCRETE: a solid material made by mixing various portions of CEMENT, sand, water, and an aggregate consisting of broken stones or gravel. The strength of hardened concrete and its resistance to wear depend on the proportions of these materials used and their grades. *Reinforced concrete* has steel rods, usually in the form of a mesh, inserted in the concrete to add additional strength. Reinforced concrete is used in highways, bridges, and practically all other major concrete structures. The strength of concrete increases as the amount of water used in the mix decreases; however, since so-called dry concrete is harder to put into forms than a wet or soupy mix, manufacturers have developed concrete vibrators, which vibrate at speeds of about 10,000 vibrations/min, that are in-

Vibrating screed: Surface of a concrete bridge deck is simultaneously vibrated to consolidate it, and smoothed and finished by 40-ft sledlike device. (*Stow Mfg. Co.*)

Concrete in modern architecture: The potentialities of concrete as a medium of architectural expression became evident to many 20th-cent. architects, notably Pier Luigi Nervi, whose Big Sports Palace (Rome) appears here. While concrete alone is a poor structural material in tension (and good in compression), reinforcing with steel rods improves its tension-withstanding properties; thus the use of reinforced concrete (as here) strengthens supporting concrete arches. The Big Sports Palace, seating 55,000, also utilizes the "shell" construction, employing very thin concrete forms, that has enabled architects to achieve spacious interiors. (*Courtesy Museum of Modern Art*)

serted directly in the concrete. This vibration facilitates the working of the concrete, insuring a homogeneous mixture with no air pockets.

Certain concrete products are turned out on a factory production-line basis. Such *precast* products, made by using steel forms for casting, include concrete bird baths and similar ornaments, fence posts, and sets of steps. More important than precast concrete, however, is *prestressed concrete,* of which there are two types: pre-tensioned and post-tensioned. *Pre-tensioning,* the more widely used process, involves installing long strands of steel cable or wire in the forms, creating tensile stress in these cables by pulling on them, then pouring the concrete into the forms and over the cables. When the concrete has hardened and bonded itself to the cables, the tension on the cables is released, creating in the concrete a compressive stress designed to oppose the load stresses the concrete member will have to withstand in use. In *post-tensioning,* the cables are stretched and anchored after the concrete has hardened. Because of its high strength, low weight compared to steel, and low cost, prestressed concrete is now used in all types of buildings and bridges.—*C. F. H.*

CONCRETION: a nodular or irregular mineral concentration formed in place in sedimentary rocks by precipitation from percolating solutions. Concretions are composed of such minerals as quartz, carbonates, iron oxide, and iron sulfide. Concretions commonly exhibit a central nucleus, either mineral or fossil, about which concentric shells were successively deposited.—*C. C.*

CONDENSATION: in **physics,** the transition from the gaseous to the liquid PHASE of a substance, accomplished by cooling. A familiar example is the fogging or "sweating" of a cold glass in moist air. Here the temperature of the glass is below the point at which the relative humidity of the air would be 100%; this causes the water vapor to liquefy on the cold surface. Condensation is of great importance also in such processes as DISTILLATION and SEPARATION of gases. The vapor of a substance being boiled passes through a cold tube (the condenser, or "still") and condenses to a liquid. Careful control of the condenser and of the substance being heated helps to separate constituents of a mixture of vapors.—*E. M. R.*

In **meteorology,** condensation is the process by which atmospheric water vapor becomes liquid. When air containing water vapor is cooled, either by mixing with damper, colder air, or by expansion as it is lifted to higher levels and lower pressures in the atmosphere, the relative humidity increases. When the air temperature reaches the DEW POINT, some of the water vapor may condense upon the ground and the surfaces of vegetation as *dew*. In the free air, condensation occurs upon some of the myriads of small particles floating in the air to form CLOUD or FOG. These particles, which act as the centers of condensation, are called *condensation nuclei.* The relative humidity required for condensation to occur is determined by the size and nature of the nuclei. Because the equilibrium pressure of water vapor over a curved surface is greater than that over a plane surface, the relative humidity of the air must slightly exceed 100%—*i.e.* the air must be supersaturated—before condensation can occur on insoluble particles. But if the particles are soluble in water, the dissolved material reduces the equilibrium vapor pressure and condensation may occur on such *hygroscopic* particles at relative humidities of less than 100%. For example, condensation on insoluble particles 0.001 mm across would require a humidity of 100.1%, or a supersaturation of 0.1%; smaller particles require higher supersaturations. On the other hand, a soluble particle of sea salt would promote condensation at relative humidities of less than 80%.

The atmosphere contains a wide range of particles, some hygroscopic, some non-hygroscopic, and some of mixed nature containing an insoluble particle coated with a thin layer of hygroscopic substance. Sizes of the particles range from less than 0.000002 cm to more than 0.002 cm in diameter. Their concentrations, expressed as the number of particles in a cubic centimeter of air, also cover an enormous range—from only a few per cm³ in clean air over the oceans to more than a million per cm³ in the highly polluted air of industrial cities.

Condensation nuclei originate in three main ways: (1) by condensation of vapor during formation of smoke and in chemical reactions involving various gases in the atmosphere; (2) as particles of sea salt, soil, and mineral dusts carried up from the earth's surface by wind; (3) by coagulation of

Condensation of invisible water vapor into visible water takes place readily on a cool surface. The temperature of the air is lowered past the point of saturation, and excess water settles on the glass. (*Philip Gendreau*)

smaller nuclei to form larger ones of mixed composition. Substances formed in large quantities during combustion include ashes, soot, tar products, oil, sulfuric acid, and sulfates. Chemical reactions between the constituents of air, water vapor, and various trace gases such as sulfur dioxide, ammonia, and chlorine produce ammonium chloride, sulfuric acid, and ammonium sulfate, particles of the last two substances being a common source of condensation nuclei in industrially polluted air. Over the oceans, condensation nuclei are produced in the foam of breaking waves where air bubbles burst to produce small droplets of sea water. These evaporate to leave behind small particles of sea salt ranging from 0.00001 to 0.001 cm across. As the condensation nuclei are carried up into the atmosphere, water vapor condenses upon the largest and most efficient of them to form the tiny droplets of water which compose a cloud. Clouds formed over the oceans, far from land, have to depend largely upon sea-salt nuclei, but over the continents these contribute perhaps only 10% of the total numbers of nuclei involved in cloud formation; the rest are probably combustion nuclei produced in vast numbers by natural and man-made fires and particles originating from the land surface.

In a rising mass of cloudy air, the condensation nuclei have to compete for the water vapor being released by cooling of the air. Condensation occurs first on the larger hygroscopic nuclei; if these are unable to assimilate all the vapor, the supersaturation of the air increases and condensation then occurs on smaller nuclei. The cloud droplets grow at a rate determined by the temperature and rate of cooling of the air, the rate at which the cloudy air mixes with the drier surrounding air, and by the size, concentration, and nature of the condensation nuclei. A typical non-raining cloud contains a few hundred droplets in each cm^3 of air. The average size of the droplets varies with the type of cloud but droplet diameters of 0.002 cm are typical. See also PRECIPITATION: WEATHER MODIFICATION.—*B. J. M.*

CONDENSER, STEAM: a device for condensing steam into water. Modern condensers operate on the same general principle as the first condenser, built by James Watt, 1769. In Watt's condenser, steam was first made to lose heat by being directed into an externally cooled vessel. A partial vacuum created by the upward stroke of a piston caused the steam to expand rapidly and thus lose more heat, thus increasing the efficiency of the process. In *surface condensers* steam enters a cooling chamber (shell) that houses a system of tubes through which cold water is rapidly circulated. The steam condenses on contact with the outside surfaces of the tubes, and the water formed runs down, collecting on the bottom of the shell. It is removed by a water pump installed outside. An air pump is provided to increase the vacuum created by the condensate (water) pump. Surface condensers are installed where the water formed must be saved for subsequent use in the plant. *Direct contact (jet) condensers* have no separate cooling chamber. Water enters the steam chamber directly, through a system of nozzles. Flowing at high speed under pressure, it mingles with steam, condensing the latter on direct contact. The design does not provide for subsequent use of the condensate, which is discarded. The air pump is eliminated, since these condensers are used where the steam is practically free from air. In *evaporative condensers* steam flows through a system of tubes mounted on an open platform, with water running slowly down the outside of the tube walls. The heat of the steam escaping through the tubes raises the temperature of the water, causing it to evaporate slowly. The evaporation absorbs an enormous amount of heat from the steam, which undergoes rapid condensation.—*T. M. and C. S.*

CONDITIONED RESPONSE: a reaction that normally is shown by an organism in response to one stimulus, but that, because of earlier experience, follows detection of a different stimulus. This type of response was discovered by the Russian physiologist Pavlov (1849–1936), who found that dogs which salivated at the sight of food could be trained to salivate when a bell was rung. Repeatedly he sounded the bell at the same time the food was presented to the animal. After a number of trials, the dog would salivate to the sound of the bell alone, without the presentation of food. Here the response of salivation to the sound of the bell is a *conditioned response*. See ANIMAL BEHAVIOR.—*D. M. F.*

CONDUCTANCE: a measure of the ease with which electrical current can flow through a material. Quantitatively the electrical conductance of an object is defined to be the reciprocal of the numerical value of its RESISTANCE in OHMS. Appropriately, the unit of conductance is called the "mho."—*S. K.*

CONDUCTION: See CONDUCTIVITY.

CONDUCTIVITY (electrical): the measure of a material's ability to conduct electricity. The rate of conduction varies with the cross-section area of the conductor and the potential gradient (voltage difference per unit length) along it. Taking these conditions into account, the equation describing conduction of electricity contains a factor characteristic of the material through which conduction is taking place. This factor is the electrical conductivity of the material. When it is high, the material is said to be a good conductor; when it is low, the material is said to be a poor conductor and is called an insulator. A modification of Ohm's law for conduction of electricity in a metal is $J = \sigma E$, where J is the current density (current per unit cross-sectional area), E the electric field intensity (equal to the potential gradient), and σ the electrical conductivity. Metals are good electrical conductors, silver and copper being the best. Metals also are good heat conductors, silver and copper again ranking highest. Conduction in metals, whether electrical or thermal, involves the movement of free electrons; this is the basis of the Wiedemann-Franz-Lorenz law, which postulates that the ratio of electrical conductivity to thermal conductivity is constant for all metals and is proportional to the temperature. See CONDUCTOR AND SEMICONDUCTOR; ELECTRIC CURRENT; PHOTOCONDUCTIVE EFFECT; SUPERCONDUCTIVITY.—*A. E.*

CONDUCTIVITY (thermal): a measure of the rate at which heat travels through a unit distance of substance for a unit temperature difference. If a bar of metal is heated at one end, the adjacent parts increase rapidly in temperature and in turn cause the remoter parts to become warmer. The heat is said to be conducted along the bar. All substances, whether solid, liquid, or gaseous, can conduct heat to some extent, but the rate varies widely between such good conductors as metals and such insulators as porcelain or glass.

Experiment shows that for any given material the rate at which heat is conducted through it depends also on the cross-sectional area of the specimen—the greater this is, the faster the flow—and on the temperature gradient (rate of temperature change per unit of length). If the specimen chosen has unit cross-sectional area and the temperature gradient proves to be one degree per unit length, then the amount of heat conducted along the specimen in unit time is the thermal conductivity of the material. Symbolizing this property by k, we may write the equation for heat conduction as $\Delta Q/\Delta t = kA(\Delta T/\Delta l)$, where ΔQ represents the quantity of heat transferred in time Δt, while A is the cross-sectional area of the test piece and $\Delta T/\Delta l$ is the temperature gradient or difference in temperature between points Δl units apart. Taking copper as a typical good conductor, the thermal conductivity k is found to be 0.93 cal/sec between two points 1 cm apart if the two points differ in temperature by 1°C. Silica, a very poor conductor, has a conductivity less than 1/500 of the value. The conductivities of a few important materials are: silver, 1.01; iron, 0.15; water, 0.0014; and dry air, 0.00005.

When a substance changes its physical state, the thermal conductivity changes considerably. The conductivity of solids always decreases when they melt, and most liquids and gases are very poor thermal conductors. Even a good conductor, such as copper or silver, becomes a much poorer conductor if it is slightly impure. The effect of temperature on thermal conductivity is remarkable. Non-metals generally become more conductive as their temperature rises, whereas metals become less so. See HEAT TRANSFER.—*J. E. W.*

CONDUCTOR AND SEMICONDUCTOR: An element or compound that is a semiconductor is distinguished from one that is a good electrical conductor, or metal, by the following characteristics: (1) The room-temperature resistivity (resistance of a cube of the material 1 cm on each side) of the semiconductor is typically in the range from 10^{-2} to 10^9 ohm-cm, while that of the good conductor is about 10^{-5} ohm-cm. The resistivity of an insulator is generally in the range from 10^{14} to 10^{22} ohm-cm. Thus the resistivity of the semiconductor (and conversely its CONDUCTIVITY) is intermediate between that of the good conductor and that of the insulator. (2) The resistivity of the semiconductor varies much more with temperature than that of the good conductor. Typically, the resistivity of the semiconductor becomes extremely large at low temperatures, whereas the resistivity of the good conductor stays small. (3) The resistivity of the semiconductor varies greatly from one specimen to another, depending on the concentration of impurities and structural defects in the specimen, whereas the resistivity of a good conductor does not. It is possible to take advantage of this property of the semiconductor by deliberately incorporating impurities (called "doping") or defects to produce some desired value of resistivity. (4) In the metals with the lowest resistivity, conduction is by electrons. In a few metals with resistivity not quite so low, conduction is predominantly by holes (*i.e.* the absence of electrons from energy levels). In a specimen of a particular semiconducting element or compound, conduction may be by either electrons or holes or both. If the conduction is primarily by electrons (*n*egative charges), the specimen is called *n*-type; if primarily by holes (which act like *p*ositive charges), the specimen is called *p*-type. The conductivity-type of semiconductor, as well as the resistivity, may be controlled by doping or otherwise deliberately introducing defects. Important technologically is the property of a semiconductor whereby large temporary changes in the numbers of electrons and holes can be made by sending electric current through a specimen; by irradiating it with light, x-rays, gamma rays, or other nuclear radiation; and by various other means. This control over concentration of electrons and holes is not possible in a metal.

Some representative semiconductors are germanium, silicon, indium antimonide, gallium arsenide, bismuth telluride, and mercury telluride. Among the metals that are good conductors are gold, silver, copper, lithium, sodium, potassium, beryllium, zinc, aluminum, iron, and tungsten. The technological importance of metals is, of course, well known and dates back to ancient times. Semiconductors have acquired technological importance quite recently as a result of suitable exploitation of properties (2), (3), and (4) listed above. Some devices based on these properties are the TRANSISTOR, RECTIFIER, BOLOMETER, and SOLAR CELL.

An understanding of the origin of the differences between semiconductors and metals is provided by the *band theory of solids*. When a large group of atoms is assembled to form a solid body, the allowed ENERGY LEVELS for electrons in the atoms spread out to form allowed bands of energy levels. In a pure and perfect crystal, these allowed bands are separated from each other by forbidden bands. Electrons in the solid fill the allowed levels, two to a level, in accordance with the Pauli EXCLUSION PRINCIPLE. If the topmost allowed band that is at all occupied is completely filled, the material will be an insulator. Electrons cannot be accelerated by, or respond to, an electric field, because there are no empty levels nearby for them to enter. But if the topmost band that is occupied by electrons has vacant levels, the material will conduct electricity. The best conductors will have this band about half empty. The insulator described above can become a semiconductor by the introduction of the proper impurities or defects. These provide additional energy levels in the forbidden gap between the topmost filled band and the next empty band. When the temperature of the semiconductor is raised, electrons occupying the additional levels may be able to jump into the empty band, where they can conduct a current. This material would then be an *n*-type semiconductor. Another possibility is that the levels provided by the imperfections will be unoccupied, so that when the temperature is raised some electrons can jump from the filled band into such levels. This will leave behind holes in the previously filled band, making the material a *p*-type semiconductor. The band theory of solids thus explains why the semiconductor has higher resistivity than the metal, and why this resistivity is so dependent on the presence of impurities and defects, and on temperature.—*E. M. C.*

CONE: in ordinary usage, a right circular cone, which is a three-dimensional figure having a circular base and a lateral surface generated by a straight line that passes through a fixed point on the perpendicular drawn to the base at its center and that moves around the circumference of the base. The moving line in any of its positions is an element of the cone. The fixed point is called the vertex, and the perpendicular from the vertex to the base, the axis. The vertex angle is the angle between the axis and any element. Right circular cones have many uses, *e.g.* as containers and in architectural forms. The volume of a circular cone is derived from that of a PYRAMID and is $\pi r^2 h/3$, where r is the radius of the base and h the altitude.

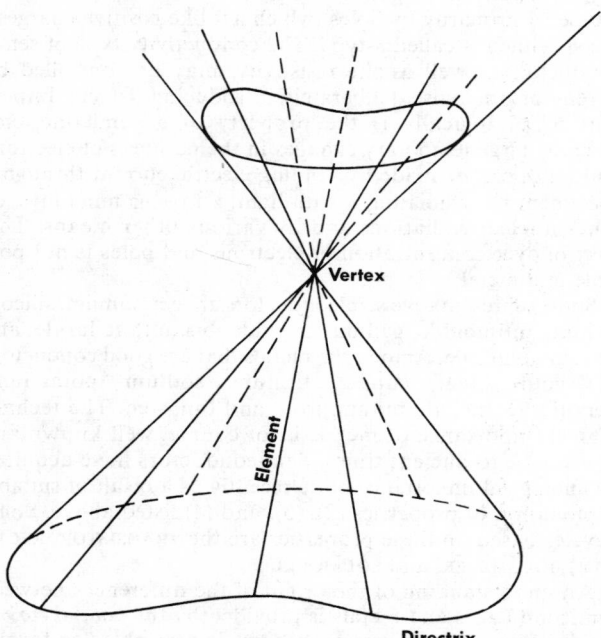

Conical surface is produced by a straight line passing through a fixed point (vertex) and moving along a fixed curve (directrix).

The more general concept of a cone is the following. A conical surface is generated by a straight line that passes through a fixed point and moves along a curve lying in a plane not containing the fixed point. The fixed point is the vertex. The various positions of the moving line are elements, or rulings, of the surface, which is called a ruled surface. A conical surface has two nappes lying opposite to one another and having the vertex as a point of symmetry. The curve along which the line moves is a directrix. It can have any shape and need not be closed. A cone is a solid bounded by a conical surface and a plane cutting across all its elements, but not passing through the vertex. (See CONIC SECTIONS.)—*H. C.*

CONE-BEARING PLANTS: see GYMNOSPERMS.

CONFORMITY: in geology, the mutual relation of beds lying one above the other in unbroken and parallel order. Conformity of beds indicates essentially continuous deposition. Parallelism of beds alone does not necessarily indicate conformity, for it is possible for part of the geologic record to be missing from an apparently conformable sequence (see STRATIGRAPHY; UNCONFORMITY).—*W. Ha.*

CONGLOMERATE: a SEDIMENTARY ROCK composed of pebbles, cobbles, or boulders in a finer-grained matrix. Conglomerates are lithified (cemented) gravels of many origins, *e.g.* alluvial deposits formed in river channels or along beaches, outwash fans in arid regions, glacial outwash, and submarine turbidity-current deposits. Their coarseness generally is evidence of transportation and deposition by powerful agencies. The composition and roundness of the coarse particles vary according to the sources of the constituents and the degree of weathering, reworking, and abrasion they have undergone prior to incorporation in the rock. Some conglomerates contain only very resistant particles, *e.g.* vein quartz and chert, whereas others may contain soft particles—limestone, sandstone, shale, weathered igneous rocks, etc. The degree of consolidation varies greatly, as shown by the range—from weakly cemented Pleistocene glacial gravels held together only by thin films of calcite, to Precambrian conglomerates strongly cemented through the interlocking of quartz grains recrystallized during regional metamorphism. "Intraformational conglomerates" in a sedimentary series consist of coarse particles derived from the immediately underlying formation in a matrix of the same composition as the next overlying formation. If the underlying formation broke into platy fragments, an *edgewise conglomerate* might have formed. Widespread *basal conglomerates* indicate a major rejuvenation of the sedimentary cycle as a result of uplift, which accelerates erosion. *Stretched-pebble conglomerates* result from dynamic metamorphism, the stress direction being indicated by the orientation of the deformed pebbles. Metamorphosed basal conglomerates are the host rocks of the gold and uranium of the Witwatersrand in South Africa and the uranium deposits of the Blind River district in Canada.—*L. M.*

"CONIC SECTIONS," by Apollonius of Perga, 3rd cent. B. C. This masterpiece of mathematical literature describes conic sections as plane curves of three types, called by Apollonius *ellipse, parabola,* and *hyperbola.* These new names are justified by his discovery that two areas, defined for any conic in terms of the tangent at any point and its conjugate diameter, are equivalent (parabola) or else one has an excess (hyperbola) or a deficit (ellipse) with regard to the other. A highly skillful theory of normals and of curvature also is presented. The theorems in this section were those on which Newton based his proof (in *Principia Mathematica*) that the inverse-square law of attraction implies elliptic trajectories for the planets, and conversely. Apollonius' theory of conics was not carried further for more than 1,800 yr.—*P. le C.*

CONIC SECTIONS (or **CONICS**): the curves—ellipses, parabolas, hyperbolas, and special cases of each—in which a plane intersects a right circular conical surface. Conics have been studied since the time of Plato, about 400 B. C. They represent the orbits of astronomical bodies and the trajectories of projectiles, and are used in the design of arches, bridges, and reflectors for sound and electromagnetic waves, including light. A right circular conical surface is generated by a straight line moving around a circle but always passing through a fixed point, the *vertex,* on the perpendicular to the plane through the center of the circle. The perpendicular is the *axis* of the conical surface. The two parts of the surface on opposite sides of the vertex are its *nappes.* Suppose first that the cutting plane does not pass through the vertex (Fig. 1). If it cuts completely through one nappe, an ellipse results; if the plane is perpendicular to the axis, the ellipse reduces to a circle. If the plane is parallel to any position of the generating line, then it can cut one nappe, but not completely through; the resulting curve is a parabola. If the plane is inclined still less to the axis, it cuts a figure through both nappes; this produces the two branches of a hyperbola. If the cutting plane moves parallel to itself into the vertex, these curves degenerate—the ellipse into a point, the parabola into a straight line or pair of parallel lines, the hyperbola into two intersecting lines.

Conics are commonly defined as loci. A conic is the locus of a point which moves in a plane so that the ratio of its distance from a fixed point to its distance from a fixed line is constant. This ratio is called the *eccentricity, e.* The curve is an ellipse, a parabola, or a hyperbola according to whether e is less than, equal to, or more than 1. If e approaches 0, the

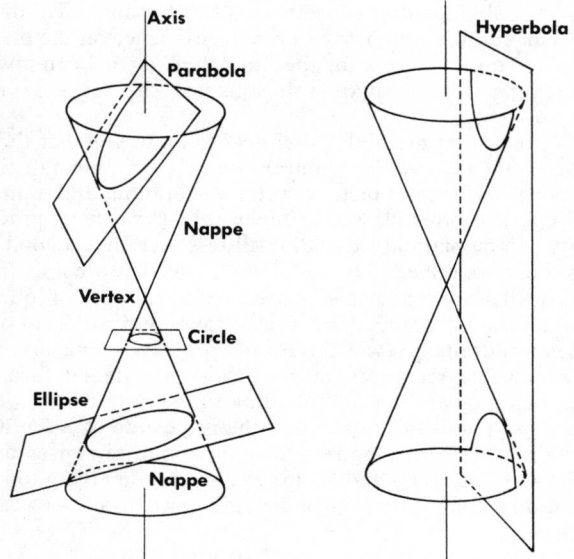

Fig. 1: Conic sections are the curves—ellipse, circle, parabola, hyperbola—in which a plane cuts a right circular conical surface.

ellipse approaches a circle; the circle thus becomes the limiting case, when $e = 0$. The fixed line is called the *directrix;* the fixed point, the *focus.* A parabola has one directrix and one focus; the ellipse and hyperbola have two directrices and two foci each (for the circle, the foci are coincident and the directrices "at infinity"). (See Fig. 2.)

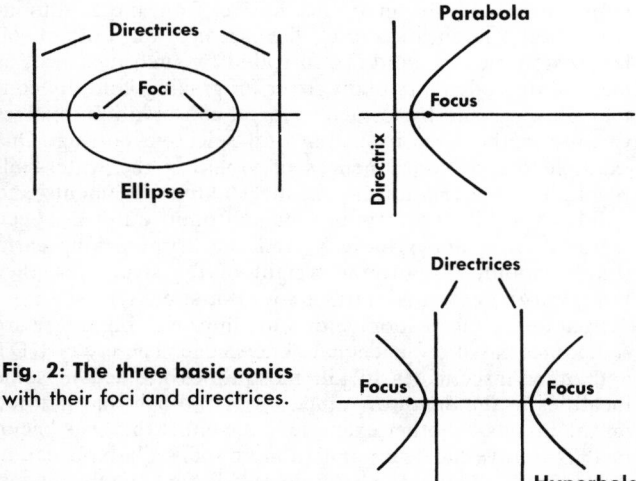

Fig. 2: The three basic conics with their foci and directrices.

The ellipse and the hyperbola are called *central conics* because they are symmetric about a central point. A chord through the center is a diameter. For the ellipse, the longest diameter passes through the foci and is called the major axis. The shortest diameter is perpendicular to this and is called

the minor axis. (If the major and minor axes are equal, the curve is a circle.) For any point on an ellipse, the sum of the distances from it to the two foci is a constant. For any point on a hyperbola, the difference between the distances from it to the two foci is a constant. These properties are often used to define the central conics.

Conics have been studied extensively by the methods of coordinate geometry. A conic may be represented by an equation of the second degree, and, conversely, any second-degree equation represents a conic. The general equation of the second degree is $Ax^2 + Bxy + Cy^2 + Dx + Ey + F = 0$, where the capital letters represent given numbers. If $B = 0$, the three kinds of conic can be distinguished as follows: parabola, either $A = 0$ or $C = 0$; ellipse, A and C have the same sign (circle, $A = C$); hyperbola, A and C have opposite signs. For any value of B, the conditions are: parabola, $B^2 - 4AC = 0$; ellipse, $B^2 - 4AC < 0$; hyperbola, $B^2 - 4AC > 0$.

To determine whether or not a conic is degenerate, one first calculates the *discriminant,* which is the determinant

$$\Delta = \begin{vmatrix} 2A & B & D \\ B & 2C & E \\ D & E & 2F \end{vmatrix}$$

If $\Delta = 0$, the conic is degenerate; if $\Delta \neq 0$, it is not. These conditions are summarized thus:

Condition	$\Delta \neq 0$	$\Delta = 0$
$B^2 - 4AC = 0$	Parabola	Straight line or two parallel lines
$B^2 - 4AC < 0$	Ellipse	One point
$B^2 - 4AC > 0$	Hyperbola	Two intersecting lines

See also ELLIPSE; HYPERBOLA; PARABOLA.—*B. P. S.*

CONJUGATION: a form of sexual reproduction found in some algae, *e.g.* the pond scum *Spirogyra,* and in many single-celled animals, as the slipper animalcule *Paramecium.* During conjugation, two cells become attached, and nuclear material from one is transferred to the other. In the ALGAE, a tubular connection is formed between mating cells from separate filaments; through it, all the contents of one cell move to fuse with the contents of the other; the product is a heavy-walled spore from which a new plant can grow. In PROTOZOANS, conjugation is reciprocal, with both cells of the mated pair giving and receiving nuclear material before separating again. —*L. and M. M.*

CONNECTIVE TISSUE: the binding and supporting tissue of the body, including bone, cartilage, tendons, ligaments, and other tissues. Adult connective tissue is made up of fibers, cells, and ground substance. Connective tissue other than BONE or CARTILAGE may be loose or dense in structure. Loose connective tissue covers, supports, and binds together most of the body structures. It acts as the framework for many organs, provides a pathway and protective padding for nerves and blood vessels, and serves as a filler in spaces between structures. Translucent and soft, it often contains fat cells and is then designated as adipose tissue.

In dense connective tissue the fibers are arranged in bands and sheets that form such structures as the dermis, the inner layer of the SKIN. When these fibers are irregularly arranged, they form the coarse, tough matting found in the capsules of body organs and in the periosteum, the thin tissue that covers bone. When the fibers are regularly arranged, they form cordlike structures and bands. Arranged in parallel fashion, these fibers lie close together to form structures of great tensile strength, *e.g.* tendons and ligaments.

Various types of cells can be found in connective tissue. Fibroblasts, which are responsible for forming fibers, are large and flat, with numerous processes projecting to join the processes of other fibroblasts. The ground substance varies from a fluid-like to a gel-like state. It seems to be important in stopping the spread of harmful agents in localized infections. —*A. P. E.*

CONSERVATION OF MASS-ENERGY: Energy is the capacity of a physical system for doing work. For a purely mechanical system, without friction, the Conservation of Energy Law states that the total ENERGY (kinetic plus potential) of an isolated system remains constant. If the system is a mass oscillating at the end of a spring, for example, there is a constant interchange during its motion between the potential energy of the spring and the kinetic energy of the mass, although the total energy of the oscillator is constant. In the presence of frictional forces the amplitude of oscillation gradually decreases, and the mechanical energy is dissipated. The loss of mechanical energy of the spring system is accompanied by the production of heat. Experiments performed by the English physicist James Prescott Joule in the 19th cent. showed that mechanical energy and heat are equivalent. One can think of heat as mechanical energy distributed among the atomic constituents of the body. If one enlarges the concept of energy to include heat, one can enunciate a conservation law stating that in an isolated mechanical system energy can neither be created nor destroyed but merely converted from mechanical energy to heat and vice versa.

The "law" stated in the previous paragraph is not completely valid. Mechanical energy and heat do disappear from isolated systems. To preserve the law, one must first include in its statement energies associated with all natural forces, such as electrical and nuclear energy. But even this is not enough. Einstein predicted in his theory of special relativity that MASS and energy would be found equivalent according to the formula $E = \Delta Mc^2$, where E is the energy, ΔM the mass created or destroyed, and c the velocity of light. This law has now been amply demonstrated experimentally. In any statement of the law of conservation of energy, the equivalence of mass and energy and their interconvertibility must be included. The final correct statement of the conservation theorem we have been discussing is: *The mass-energy content of an isolated system remains constant. The energy can be converted from one form to another or to mass, but can neither be created nor destroyed.*

The conservation of mass-energy, like all conservation theorems, is a useful physical principle because it limits the number of possible processes that a system can undergo, namely only those satisfying the conservation law. Like all physical principles it expresses no immutable truth; if strong evidence were presented to contradict it, scientists probably would abandon it. It is, however, so ingrained in physics that it would be relinquished only reluctantly. An example of how tenaciously physicists hold to this conservation law occurred in recent times. In the study of beta decay, the law of conservation of energy was apparently violated. To preserve it, the existence of a particle without mass or charge, called a neutrino, was postulated. Only many years after the prediction of the existence of a neutrino were reactions attributable to it directly observed and its existence established.—*S. Bo.*

CONSERVATION OF NATURAL RESOURCES: Efforts to safeguard Earth's resources of energy, minerals, animal and plant life, and natural beauty from wasteful exploitation date, in some respects, from very early times. Preservation of valuable timber and wildlife, improvement of agricultural practices, and wise use of water were concerns of the ancients. But only in the past 50 yr, with two great wars and the "population explosion," has the drain upon natural resources made conservation a matter of international concern. Actual shortages of materials (*e.g.* water, soil, certain minerals) have developed, causing economic dislocation and hardship in various regions. Underdeveloped countries are hurrying to industrialize and achieve the material wealth enjoyed by the U. S. A. and other Western nations—wealth achieved at a staggering expense of world resources. With the reserves of oil, coal, and certain key minerals—*e.g.* those of copper, lead, and zinc—going fast, and with population growth rates soaring, it is obvious that conservation has become a condition for man's future welfare and even his existence on the planet. There is no firm basis for the faith that science can always come up with adequate solutions for shortages as they develop.

Conservation methods differ according to whether the resource is renewable, nonrenewable, or inexhaustible. *Renewable resources* include water, vegetation, and animals. (SOIL is also often classed as renewable, because its productivity can be maintained with fertilizers; yet once a good soil has been removed from a locality, as by erosion, it is practically nonrenewable, since the formation of quality agricultural soil from bare rock, clays, and adjacent soils takes hundreds or even thousands of years.) Conservation of renewable resources ranges from enlightened farming, dam building, and forest replanting to the protection of local species of plants or animals and the protection of wilderness. In its most effective modern form, this kind of conservation deals with the cycles and chains of nature, attempting to keep them operating at full efficiency. (See BALANCE OF NATURE; ECOLOGY.)

The HYDROLOGIC CYCLE on Earth will last as long as the Sun shines, but to be useful, water has to seep slowly into and through the ground, preferably through a layer of good, root-laced soil, nourishing plants and trees. As ground water it is a source of water supply for man as well as plants and animals. If, however, the ground has become subject to rapid erosion because of poor farming or indiscriminate cutting of forests, it will not properly receive or hold water. The rain either collects in puddles, soon to be lost by evaporation, or becomes runoff that carries away topsoil, causes gullying, and—in some instances—produces flooding. At this late stage the building of a dam may become necessary, and long-range reforesting should begin at once upriver from the dam to increase water retention and to decrease erosion. Loss of soil by erosion on farmland is controlled by such measures as maintaining adequate plant cover on grazing land, by contour plowing, and by terracing; forest conservation involves various methods of reseeding and selective cutting. One example of the consequences of violating the water-soil-vegetation interrelationship is the sinking pavements and buildings of Mexico City: too much ground water has been removed from under the city, and the dry, cracking earth simply cannot support the weight of the structures. (See IRRIGATION; WATER POLLUTION; WATER SUPPLY.)

In animal conservation, efforts to "improve" on nature are sometimes based on inadequate knowledge. The use of DDT and other insecticides to kill mosquitoes has led in some localities to the death of valued birds and fish that had fed on the insects. Another example is the effort that was begun in 1907 to save the deer population on the Kaibab plateau in Arizona: the plan was to exterminate all the animals (pumas, wolves, and coyotes) that preyed on the Kaibab deer. But the 4,000 deer of 1907 became 100,000 in 1924; in the years 1925–26, 50,000 deer died from starvation, and by 1939 the deer population was down again to 10,000, with starvation (on the badly over-grazed Kaibab plateau range) still a greater cause of death than the predators had been. Thus

Good vs. poor land use: Adequate conservation has been practiced on north (*left*) side of the Samalá R. in Guatemala, while lack of conservation has caused heavy erosion on south side. Note (*left*) contour plowing, terracing, and heavy growth remaining on river bank. (*U. S. D. A.*)

animal conservation requires both informed planning and continuing management. Individual species can in many cases be preserved for future generations of sportsmen and nature lovers by hunting and fishing laws that serve to keep the species in balance with its environment, and by the restriction of building and other developments which harm the species' natural habitats. Certain organizations of duck hunters, for example, have bought large tracts of land in N Canada to protect the breeding grounds of wildfowl valued as game.

Nonrenewable resources include metals, coal, petroleum, natural gas, and most minerals. As high-grade deposits are used up, these resources will become so costly to extract and process that their utility to man may practically vanish. Conservation measures are limited to prevention of waste, improvement of extraction techniques, re-use of as much scrap as possible, and attempts to find substitutes (*e.g.* plastics). Prevention of waste is accomplished by improving methods of mining, recovery, and processing. Re-use of scrap has become especially important in the steel industry; many new steel-smelting plants have been designed to handle principally scrap rather than ore. Scrap copper and lead are also finding broader markets.

Inexhaustible resources include sunlight, rocks, and air. The Sun is the original source of all energy on Earth except atomic energy. It provides light and heat; it evaporates water and draws it up into the sky as water vapor, which later falls as rain; it enables plants to form organic matter by photosynthesis, without which there would be no life, no coal or oil. The amount of solar energy that reaches Earth is immense; in one day the land receives heat equivalent to that produced from burning 500 billion tons of coal—more energy than man has used up in all history. Experiments are being conducted for using the Sun's rays to heat houses, to cook food, and to generate electricity on a small scale. Eventually, direct SOLAR ENERGY may become an important source of commercial power. Energy from man-made nuclear reactions is also essentially inexhaustible, and may one day supply a large percentage of the world's energy needs. However, the efficiency of present nuclear reactors is low, their cost high, and the problem of disposal of radioactive waste largely unsolved. (See ATOMIC ENERGY; RADIATION HAZARDS.)

Although both air and rocks are theoretically finite in quantity, it is inconceivable that they will be exhausted before man himself dies out on Earth. Here and there man has replaced breathable air with smog, adding ATMOSPHERIC POLLUTION to other community problems. There is also the hazard from continued testing of nuclear weapons in the atmosphere. But the atmosphere as such is virtually inexhaustible. As for rocks, already used for their mineral content by the billions of tons, technology will render them increasingly useful without serious danger of depleting their abundance. The danger here lies in the damage that unrestricted quarrying does to natural scenery. Falling water as a source of mechanical energy may also be considered an inexhaustible resource, although the energy available is less than is generally imagined. If U. S. hydroelectric resources were now fully developed, they could provide only about 25% of the nation's energy needs. See HYDROELECTRIC DEVELOPMENT.—*S. W. B.*

CONSISTENCY: A system of statements from which it is impossible to derive a contradiction, (A) and not-(A), is said to be consistent. Consistency is a basic requirement for any scientific theory, since, from a contradiction, any statement whatsoever is provable. At the end of the 19th cent., the mathematical world was shaken by the discovery of several contradictions (the so-called paradoxes of Russell, Cantor, and Burali-Forti) in the theory of sets, at the very basis of modern mathematics. To avoid these contradictions, various rigorously formulated axiomatic systems (*e.g.* those of Russell and Zermelo) were proposed to serve as a foundation for all of mathematics. The symbols, meaningful sentences, axioms, and rules of inference were precisely described, and each system was designed so that the paradoxes would (apparently) not be provable. It was hoped that such a system was not only provably consistent but also complete in the sense that every sentence was either provable or disprovable. These hopes have been rudely shattered (by Kurt Gödel in 1931, with an extension by J. Barkley Rosser in 1936); if such a system is consistent, then it is incomplete; moreover, any proof of the consistency of the system would require methods not available within the system itself. In 1936, Gerhard Gentzen proved the consistency of a formal system for a small part of mathematics, elementary number theory, but, in conformity with Gödel's result, his proof used methods stronger than those of elementary number theory, namely, a portion of the theory of ordinal numbers. (See GÖDEL'S PROOF; METAMATHEMATICS; SYNTAX, LOGICAL.)—*El. M.*

CONSONANCE AND DISSONANCE: A consonance is said to exist between two musical sounds when they are pleasing together, dissonance when they are displeasing or harsh. It has been known since Pythagoras' time (*c.* 530 B. C.) that the frequencies of two consonant notes bear small whole-number ratios to each other: *e.g.* 2:1, an octave; 2:3, a fifth; 5:6, a minor third; etc. As the ratio goes to larger numbers (*e.g.* 15:16, a half tone) consonance changes to dissonance, and the larger the numbers, the greater the dissonance. Overtone structure and pitch are important also: complex tones are more dissonant with one another than are simple tones of the same frequencies, and low tones more than high. Modern ears, through musical sophistication, tolerate a much larger degree of dissonance than formerly. See SOUND.—*M. C. H.*

CONSTANT: see VARIABLE.

CONSTELLATIONS: areas of the sky set off by arbitrary boundary lines to include prominent and easily identified groupings of stars. They are useful in describing approximate positions of celestial objects. The stars in any particular constellation are, in most cases, not physically associated; they are at greatly varying distances from Earth, and the patterns depend simply upon the observer's line of sight. Many constellations, particularly those of the ZODIAC and the north polar region, originated with the ancients, who gave to these patterns names of heroes, animals, and other subjects associated with mythology. Others, the "modern" constellations, were

Major constellations are plotted on this map, based on a navigation chart. Right ascension is indicated horizontally near the margins; declination, vertically. As with geographic maps based on a similar projection, distortion increases with distance from the equator.

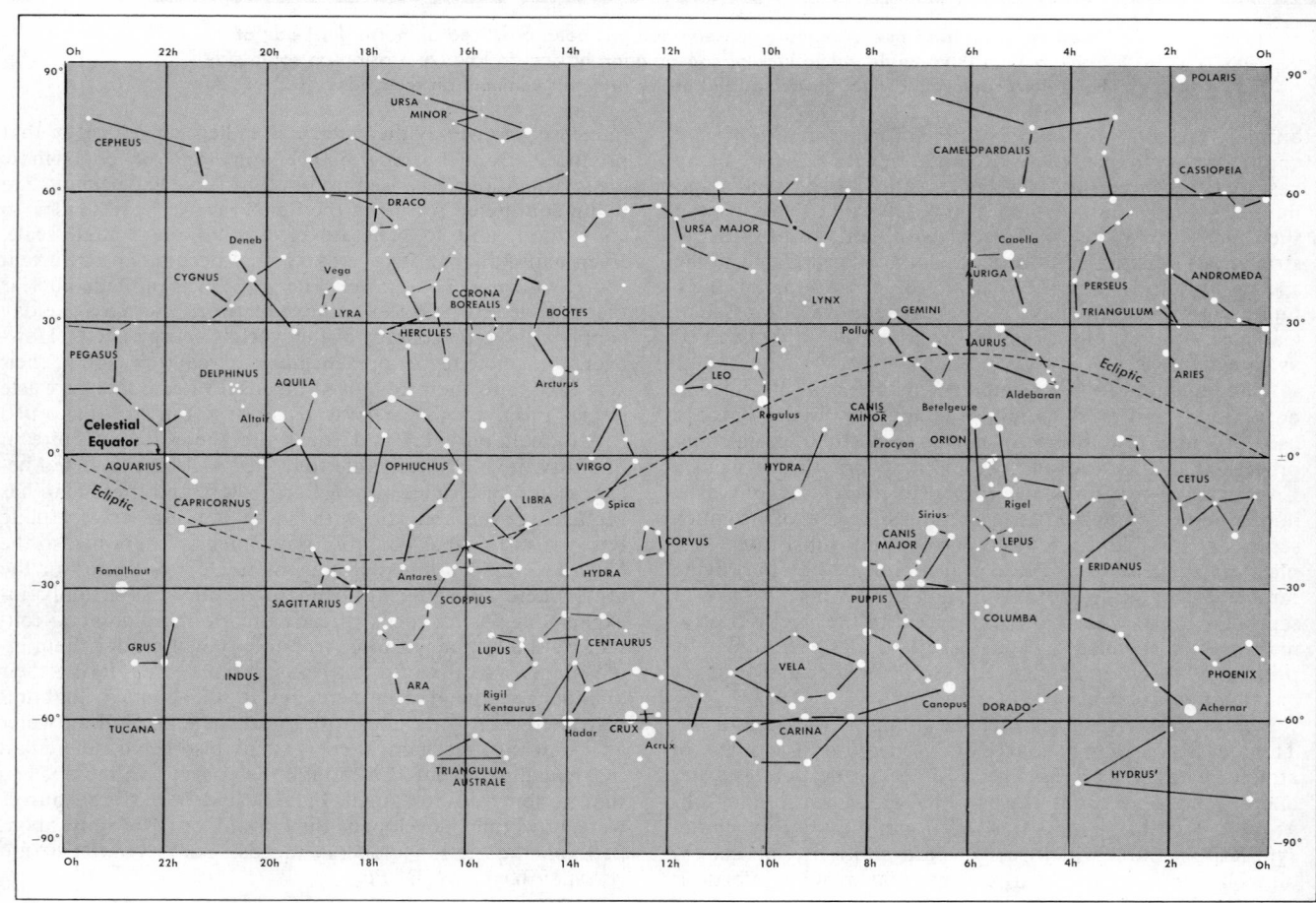

THE CONSTELLATIONS

The latitude given with each southern constellation is approximately the northernmost latitude at which the constellation is visible.

Constellation	On Meridian 9 p.m.	Constellation	On Meridian 9 p.m.	Constellation	On Meridian 9 p.m.	Constellation	On Meridian 9 p.m.
Andromeda	Nov. 10	Columba (The Dove) 50°N.	Jan. 30	Lepus (The Hare) 65°N.	Jan. 25	Sagitta (The Arrow)	Aug. 30
Antlia (The Pump) 50°N.	Apr. 5	Coma Berenices (Berenice's Hair)	May 15	Libra (The Scales) 70°N.	June 20	Sagittarius (The Archer) 60°N.	Aug. 20
Apus (The Bird of Paradise) 5°N.	June 30	Corona Australis (Southern Crown) 45°N.	Aug. 15	Lupus (The Wolf) 45°N.	June 20	Scorpius (The Scorpion) 55°N.	July 20
Aquarius (The Water-bearer) 75°N.	Oct. 10	Corona Borealis (Northern Crown)	June 30	Lynx (The Lynx)	Mar. 5	Sculptor 55°N.	Nov. 10
Aquila (The Eagle)	Aug. 30	Corvus (The Crow) 65°N.	May 10	Lyra (The Lyre)	Aug. 15	Scutum (The Shield) 75°N.	Aug. 15
Ara (The Altar) 30°N.	July 20	Crater (The Cup) 70°N.	Apr. 25	Mensa (The Table Mountain) 5°N.	Jan. 30	Serpens (The Serpent) 85°N.	
Aries (The Ram)	Dec. 10	Crux (The Cross) 25°N.	May 10	Microscopium (The Microscope) 50°N.	Sept. 20	Caput (Head)	June 30
Auriga (The Charioteer)	Jan. 30	Cygnus (The Swan)	Sept. 10	Monoceros (The Unicorn) 85°N.	Feb. 20	Cauda (Tail)	Aug. 5
Boötes (The Herdsman)	June 15	Delphinus (The Dolphin)	Sept. 15	Musca (The Fly) 15°N.	May 10	Sextans (The Sextant) 85°N.	Apr. 5
Caelum (The Burin) 45°N.	Jan. 15	Dorado (The Goldfish) 25°N.	Jan. 20	Norma (The Level) 35°N.	July 5	Taurus (The Bull)	Jan. 15
Camelopardalis (The Giraffe)	Feb. 1	Draco (The Dragon)	July 20	Octans (The Octant) 5°N.	Sept. 20	Telescopium (The Telescope) 35°N.	Aug. 25
Cancer (The Crab)	Mar. 15	Equuleus (The Colt)	Sept. 20	Ophiuchus (The Serpent Bearer) 85°N.	July 25	Triangulum (The Triangle)	Dec. 5
Canes Venatici (The Hunting Dogs)	May 20	Eridanus (The River) 70°N.	Jan. 5	Orion 85°N.	Jan. 25	Triangulum Australe (The Southern Triangle) 20°N.	July 5
Canis Major (The Great Dog) 65°N.	Feb. 15	Fornax (The Furnace) 55°N.	Dec. 15	Pavo (The Peacock) 20°N.	Aug. 25	Tucana (The Toucan) 20°N.	Nov. 5
Canis Minor (The Little Dog)	Mar. 1	Gemini (The Twins)	Feb. 20	Pegasus (The Flying Horse)	Oct. 20	Ursa Major (The Great Bear)	Apr. 20
Capricornus (The Goat, or the Sea Goat) 65°N.	Sept. 20	Grus (The Crane) 35°N.	Oct. 10	Perseus	Dec. 25	Ursa Minor (The Little Bear)	June 25
Carina (The Keel of the ship Argo, which is no longer a constellation) 25°N.	Mar. 15	Hercules	July 25	Phoenix (The Phoenix) 40°N.	Nov. 20	Vela (The Sails of the ship Argo) 35°N.	Mar. 25
		Horologium (The Clock) 25°N.	Dec. 25	Pictor (The Easel) 30°N.	Jan. 20	Virgo (The Virgin) 80°N.	May 25
Cassiopeia (The Queen)	Nov. 20	Hydra (The Sea Serpent) 70°N.	Apr. 20	Pisces (The Fishes)	Nov. 10	Volans (The Flying Fish) 15°N.	Mar. 1
Centaurus (The Centaur) 35°N.	May 20	Hydrus 15°N.	Dec. 10	Pisces Austrinus (The Southern Fish) 55°N.	Oct. 10	Vulpecula (The Fox)	Sept. 10
Cepheus (The King)	Oct. 15	Indus (The Indian) 35°N.	Sept. 25	Puppis (The Stern of the ship Argo)	Feb. 25		
Cetus (The Whale)	Nov. 30	Lacerta (The Lizard)	Oct. 10	Pyxis (The Compass) 55°N.	Mar. 15		
Chamaeleon 5°N.	Apr. 15	Leo (The Lion)	Apr. 10	Reticulum (The Net) 25°N.	Dec. 30		
Circinus (The Compasses) 25°N.	June 15	Leo Minor (The Little Lion)	Apr. 10				

given the names of scientific instruments. The star patterns recognized have varied from civilization to civilization; thus the Chinese used groupings and names different from those of the West. Through the centuries, the boundaries and numbers of constellations recognized have varied even in the West, though the shapes of many patterns have changed little. In 1928 the International Astronomical Union adopted a new method of bounding which followed closely the boundaries set up by Argelander and Gould at the end of the 17th cent. The new boundaries are parts of circles perpendicular and parallel to the celestial equator, and they may be described by right ascension and declination. Some small and insignificant groups were omitted, and some very large ones, *e.g.* Argo Navis in the southern sky, were broken up into smaller groups. Modern star maps show the new boundaries for 88 constellations.—*R. N. M.*

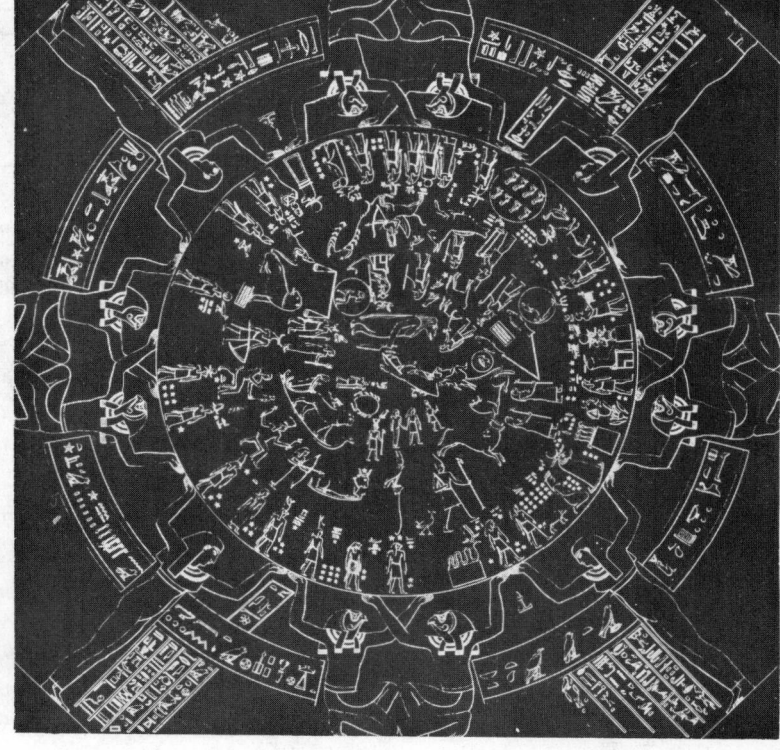

Ancient Egyptian constellations: The "Denderah stone," found in the Temple of Isis at Denderah in Egypt, represents constellations known to the Egyptians more than 2,000 yr ago. In these drawings, made from the original slab, a number of constellations familiar today are recognizable: Sagittarius the Archer, Cancer the Crab, Libra the Scales, Leo the Lion, and others—evidence that many basic star patterns have changed little in 20 centuries, and that some constellation identifications come down from remote antiquity. (*Sky and Telescope*)

CONSTITUTION OF ATOMS AND MOLECULES, by Niels Bohr, *Philosophical Magazine,* Vol. 26, 1913: In this paper Bohr showed that one could combine the Rutherford model of the atom (a small region of positive charge, the nucleus, surrounded by a diffuse region of negative charge) and the Einstein-Planck photon hypothesis to explain the light frequencies emitted by atoms. Bohr had to make an additional assumption, namely that the electronic orbits are determined by the circumstance that the angular momentum of an electron in its orbit is an integral multiple of Planck's constant. This successful explanation of atomic structure lent further credence to the photon hypothesis. See also ATOM.—*S. Bo.*

CONSTRUCTION PROBLEMS: A favorite activity in geometry, going back to antiquity, has been the construction of geometrical figures with the use only of a compass and a straightedge —*i.e.* a ruler used only for drawing straight lines, not for measuring distances. The restriction to these instruments limits the usable configurations to straight lines and circles. Bisecting a line, bisecting an angle, and inscribing a regular hexagon in a given circle are familiar construction problems that can be performed with them. Some other constructions, which appear innocent enough at the outset, are impossible with these instruments alone. The challenge of these unsolved, yet apparently approachable, problems has made them inviting brain-teasers for mathematicians for many centuries. Some amateurs, even now, continue to be tantalized by such problems either because they do not know that the solution has been conclusively proved impossible or because they do not understand the requirements of the problems. In addition to the limitation to straightedge and compass, it is required that the constructions be theoretically precise; that is, the method must be one which would produce the required result exactly if the instruments were perfect and there were no human error in applying them.

ume is x^3, and we must have $x^3 = 2s^3$. Therefore $x = s\sqrt[3]{2}$. If we could solve this problem when $s = 1$, we could solve it for any given s. But we cannot construct a line $\sqrt[3]{2}$ units long with straightedge and compass.

It can be proved conclusively that the limitation to instruments for drawing straight lines and circles is too restrictive to permit these constructions to be performed. The proofs are in the field of algebra. They show primarily that straightedge and compass suffice for the construction of any lengths expressible by rational numbers or by numbers that can be obtained from rational numbers by extracting square roots one or more times, but that lengths which cannot be so expressed cannot be constructed with these instruments. The problem of doubling a cube requires the construction of $\sqrt[3]{2}$; the angle trisection problem requires the construction of a root of a cubic equation that cannot be expressed by rational numbers or square roots; the circle squaring construction requires the construction of π, which is neither rational nor expressible by any algebraic operations applied to rational numbers. Proofs of these facts are often found in books on theory of equations.

Study of the problem of constructing regular polygons brought to notice a whole class of impossible constructions. It is easy to construct regular polygons of 3, 4, 6, or 8 sides. A regular pentagon can be constructed; a regular heptagon cannot. A regular polygon with 17 sides can be constructed; one with 19 cannot. At age 17, K. F. Gauss (1777–1855) investigated the possibility of constructing regular polygons having p sides where p is a prime number. He discovered that the regular polygon is constructible if p is a prime number that can be expressed in the form $p = 2^{2^n} + 1$, where $n = 0$ or any positive integer. If $n = 0$, $p = 3$; if $n = 1$, $p = 5$; if $n = 2$, $p = 17$; if $n = 3$, $p = 257$; etc. Hence regular polygons having 3, 5, 17, or 257 sides are constructible. But Gauss found that if p is a prime number which does not have this

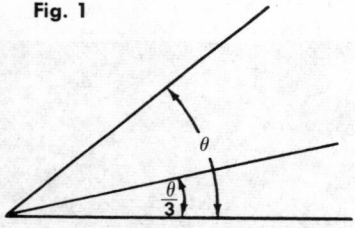

Fig. 1

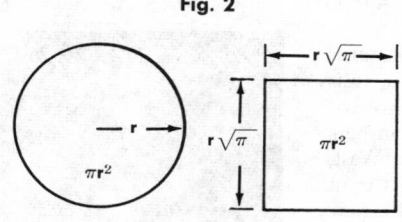

Fig. 2

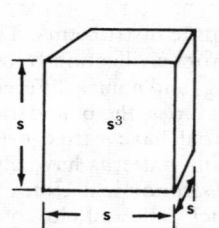

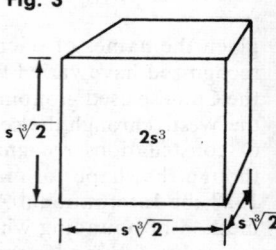

Fig. 3

Construction problems of antiquity included the construction of (Fig. 1) an angle equal to one-third of a given angle, (2) a square equal in area to a given circle, and (3) a cube with twice the volume of a given cube. The only tools allowed were straightedge and compass; it has been proved by algebra that with this restriction the constructions are impossible.

Probably the best known of these impossible constructions is the trisection of an angle (Fig. 1). A requirement of this problem is that the method must be applicable to any angle; to trisect some particular angle is no solution. (It is easy to trisect a right angle.) The problem known as "squaring a circle," or "quadrature of the circle," is that of constructing a square whose area is equal to that of a given circle (Fig. 2). If the radius is r, we must construct a side s so that $s^2 = \pi r^2$, or $s = r\sqrt{\pi}$. The difficulty lies, of course, in constructing a line $\sqrt{\pi}$ units long. If we could do this, we could construct one $r\sqrt{\pi}$ units long. Indeed, if we could construct a line π units long, we could construct one $r\sqrt{\pi}$ units long. But this cannot be done with straightedge and compass. A third problem, equally famous, is that of doubling a cube; *i.e.* constructing the side of a cube with a volume twice that of a given cube (Fig. 3). If the side of the given cube is s units long, its volume is s^3. If the side of the required cube is denoted by x, its vol-

form, such as 7, 11, 13, or 19, a regular polygon with this number of sides cannot be constructed. This great achievement by Gauss is reported to have been decisive in persuading him to devote his life to mathematics.

It should be realized that the impossibility of performing these constructions with straightedge and compass only has no disastrous implications in applied science. Results obtained by the use of good measuring instruments are quite as satisfactory in practical work as those obtained by geometrical construction. Moreover, other instruments make possible a great variety of constructions that cannot be performed by straightedge and compass.—*H. C.*

CONTACT AUREOLE: the contact metamorphic zone developed in the country rocks which surround an intrusive igneous body (see METAMORPHIC ROCK AND METAMORPHISM). Crystallization of magma releases heat and fluids which permeate and alter the host rocks. Intensity of alteration decreases gradationally away from the contact. Type of alteration depends on the initial composition, metamorphic grade, and temperature of the host rocks, and on the size, composition, and temperature of the intrusive. Vein and replacement ore-bodies of hydro-thermal origin may occur within contact aureoles.—*L. M.*

CONTACT DIFFERENCE IN POTENTIAL: the work required to take a unit charge from the interior of one substance to the interior of another in contact with it. For metals or semiconductors in contact, this is equal to the difference between the WORK FUNCTIONS.—*E. M. C.*

CONTINENT: any of the major connected land masses of Earth, of which there are generally held to be seven, unless Eurasia is regarded as a single unit. Together they form one of the two major divisions of the crust, of which the other is the ocean basins. The two are very different in topography, for at the continental slopes the continents rise nearly 3 mi above the ocean floors. The land masses are also more siliceous in composition and have different structures. Their study in three dimensions has been made possible by GEOPHYSICS. The continental crust (see EARTH) has an average thickness (down to the MOHOROVIČIČ DISCONTINUITY) of 20 mi, compared with 3 mi for the oceanic crust. ISOSTASY is considered to preserve these differences in level.

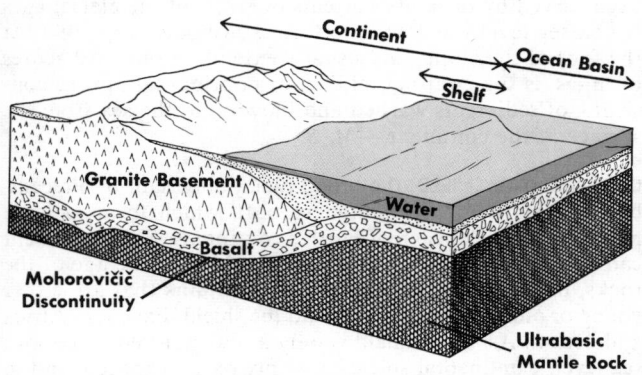

Model of Earth's crust: Continents, of relatively light granitic rock of 20-mi av. thickness, "float" on dense ultrabasic mantle; basalt carpet pressed between them continues out to sea. Iceberg-like buoyancy of continents leaves them floating partly above, partly below, basalt level of ocean beds.

The continents cover an area of 50 million mi^2; thus the volume of continental material is about 1 billion mi^3. The present rate of extrusion of lava from the depths would have produced approximately this volume since the formation of the oldest rocks 3 billion yr ago; thus it is possible that the continents, like the oceans and atmosphere, have accumulated on Earth's surface since its formation. Estimates by different authorities of the average composition of the continental rocks vary between 59 and 66% silica, and the composition of the commonest lavas lies in the same range. Thus continents

may have grown by the extrusion of volcanic rocks, their erosion to form sediments, and the metamorphism of the latter. The view that the continents have grown in this manner is supported by their division into provinces each of which appears to consist of the roots of former mountains, now eroded to a common plain forming a CONTINENTAL SHIELD, around which lie younger mountains and coastal plains. See also CONTINENTAL SHELF, SLOPE, AND RISE.—*J. T. W.*

CONTINENTAL DRIFT: the supposed process by which CONTINENTS and islands are moving relative to one another across the face of Earth. It was first proposed early in this century to explain similarities of outline observed between some coasts of adjacent continents, *e.g.* South America and Africa. Outstanding similarities were observed also in respect to some ancient faunas, floras, and aspects of glaciation which are the same in all the southern continents and the nearly parallel and matching opposite coasts of the Atlantic Ocean and the Red Sea. One or perhaps two primitive continents were considered to have broken up about 200 million yr ago, and to have drifted apart at a rate too slow to measure. The continents were regarded as slabs or rafts of siliceous rock drifting about in a viscous mantle of more basic rock. Mountains were considered to have been pushed up along the leading edges of continents or where the "rafts" collided.

Different versions of the theory, advanced by F. B. Taylor, A. Wegener, and A. L. du Toit, found some support in southern countries and in Europe, but little in North America. Chief objections were based on the absence of any known forces to cause the motion and the difficulty of propelling continental blocks through solid ocean floors. In the last two decades it has been found that some rocks preserve evidence of the direction of Earth's magnetic field at the time they were formed, and it has proved possible to measure these directions. Many recent measurements of such paleomagnetism (see TERRESTRIAL MAGNETISM) strongly suggest progressive relative movement of the continents. At the same time, studies of the ocean floor reveal that a smaller volume of sediments than might be expected, considering Earth's age, is preserved on the ocean floors, and volcanoes are fewer than expected. No sediments older than Cretaceous have been found. All this suggests that the ocean floors are indeed being renewed.

At the same time the CONVECTION THEORY has been advanced in a form which offers a possible cause of motion. Slow thermal currents may flow in the mantle and exert forces sufficient to move continents. The currents are considered to rise under the MID-OCEANIC RIDGE, there causing high GEO-THERMAL GRADIENTS. The rising currents may separate, exposing fresh ocean floor along the ridge, and then flow horizontally at a rate of perhaps an inch a year, bearing both continents and ocean floors away from the ridge. The currents could meet and sink under island arcs and mountain systems, piling up sediments and continental material into mountains on the surface, but dragging the crust of the ocean floors and the mantle downward. Presumably, if such convection occurs, the mantle has been churning extremely slowly with changing currents ever since it was formed, and the

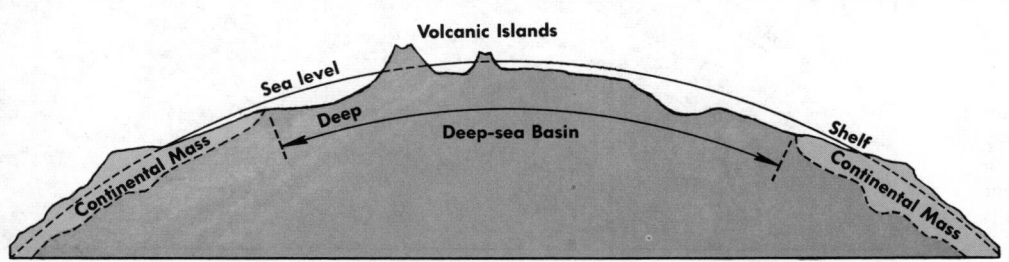

Relationship of continental masses to ocean basins is indicated in this profile of Earth's crust.

break-up of pre-existing continents and the slow coalition of the fragments into new ones has been repeated several times. The earlier view that continents were drifting like ships wafted across a sea is thus being replaced by a view of horizontal shifting of the whole crust and mantle so that the continents are now, as it were, caught in a current and are moving with it but not relative to it. This new hypothesis of continental drift is perhaps better termed horizontal mass motion.—*J. T. W.*

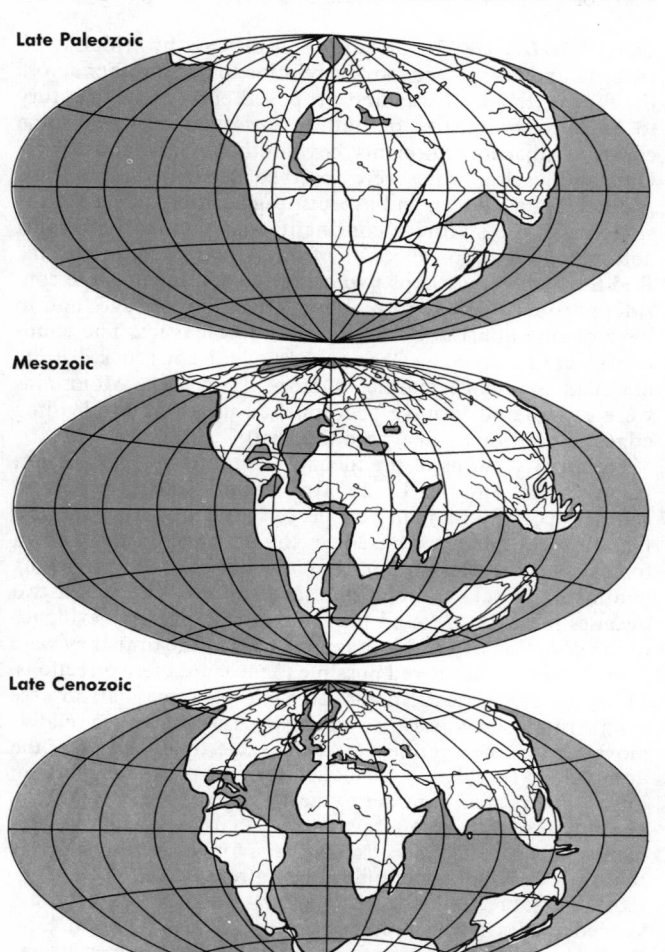

Late Paleozoic

Mesozoic

Late Cenozoic

Continental drift, suggested by the German geophysicist Alfred Wegener to account for the present distribution of the continents, is here shown in three stages. A single, massed protocontinent is assumed for the end of the Paleozoic Era (*top*); it breaks up during the Mesozoic (*middle*) and drifts into present configurations toward the end of the Cenozoic Era (*bottom*).

Continental shelf and slope off Atlantic Coast between New Jersey and Connecticut is cut by several submarine canyons; two appear here. Change from shelf to slope is notably abrupt.

CONTINENTAL SHELF, SLOPE, AND RISE: The zone around a continent extending from the low-water line to the deep-sea floor is divided into three major features: the continental shelf, slope, and rise. The *shelf* extends from the low-water line to the depth at which there is a marked increase in steepness toward the deep-sea floor; the steeper part of the zone is the continental *slope*. If there is more than one break in the slope, the most pronounced break may be considered as the lower margin of the shelf, provided it lies at a depth of less than 300 fathoms. The average width of continental shelves is about 40 mi, and the average depth of the first major break in slope is about 70 fathoms; however, both dimensions vary greatly. Although shelves may be relatively flat, sloping gradually and evenly from shore down to the break, commonly they have considerable relief. This is especially true off glaciated or mountainous coasts, where the topography of the shelf is much like that of the adjacent land. High points on a shelf are likely to be bare ledge or cobble heaps, while extensive flat areas are covered with finer sediments, including sand, silt, or clay, often mixed with shell fragments. The origin of shelves is obscure and probably complex, involving at least the cutting action of waves on a shore line and the gradual rise in sea level as the great glaciers of the recent glacial ages melted. Whereas the continental shelf slopes seaward at an average of 10 ft/mi, the corresponding figure for the slope is about 2,000 ft/mi. Many parts of the continental slopes have been carved by turbidity currents or rivers of the glacial ages (when sea level was lower) to form SUBMARINE CANYONS. At the foot of the slope, and usually extending outward scores of miles, is the continental *rise,* or continental apron, consisting of sediments washed and blown into the sea from the surface of the continent.—*M. S.*

CONTINENTAL SHIELD: the broad plain, underlain by Precambrian rocks (over 600 million yr old), which forms a large part of the mass of each of Earth's continents. Each continent can be divided, according to topography and the age of the rocks, into young coastal plains, mountains that are either young or only moderately old, and the shield. Except in Africa and central Asia, the shield is only a few hundred feet above sea level. Continental shields are only partly exposed, and in the exposed parts Precambrian rocks formerly called the BASEMENT COMPLEX lie at the surface. In covered parts the old metamorphosed rocks are hidden by a few hundred to a few thousand feet of younger, nearly flat-lying sedimentary strata. The term "shield" is sometimes used for the exposed part only, *e.g.* in references to the Canadian Shield. The term is still useful physiographically, but recent geological mapping

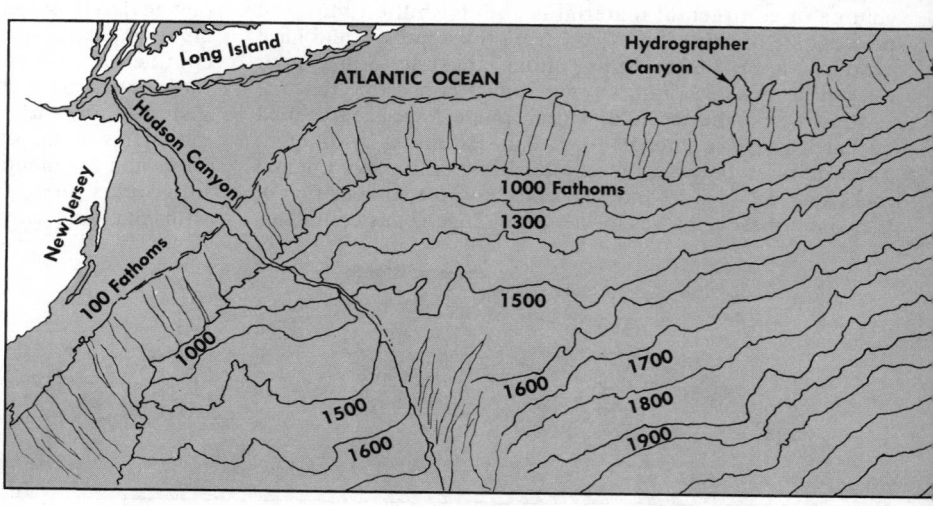

Long Island

Hudson Canyon

New Jersey

ATLANTIC OCEAN

Hydrographer Canyon

100 Fathoms

1000

1500

1600

1000 Fathoms

1300

1500

1600

1700

1800

1900

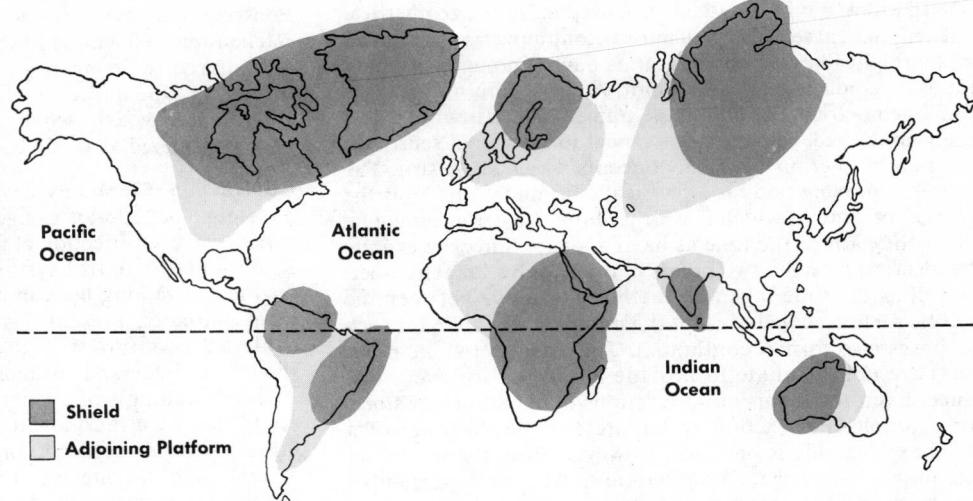

Continental shields: Heavy blue areas are exposed portions. Areas in light blue are portions of the shields that are covered with sedimentary rocks.

Pacific Ocean

Atlantic Ocean

Indian Ocean

■ Shield

□ Adjoining Platform

and especially the application of radioactive methods of age determination have shown that shields are divided into provinces having very different ages, and that these provinces are sharply separated from one another by great systems of faults near which ore deposits tend to be concentrated. The oldest provinces, over 2 billion yr in age, have a higher proportion of volcanic rocks and have been called *continental nuclei.* In the accompanying maps, the division of the exposed Canadian Shield is shown. Similar divisions exist in the covered shield under the interior plains of the U. S. A., but for lack of data the boundaries have not yet been precisely established. —*J. T. W.*

CONTINUED FRACTION: An expression of the form

$$a + \cfrac{b}{c + \cfrac{d}{e + \cfrac{f}{r + \cfrac{s}{t}}}}$$

in which the letters all denote integers, is a finite continued fraction. Each successive denominator except the last is an integer plus a fraction. If the process continues without ever reaching an integral denominator, the expression is an infinite continued fraction. If every numerator is 1, the expression is a simple continued fraction. Every finite continued fraction, simple or otherwise, represents a rational number, since it can be reduced to a quotient of two integers. By continued divisions, a rational number can always be written as a simple finite continued fraction. For example,

$$\frac{73}{29} = 2 + \frac{15}{29} = 2 + \cfrac{1}{\frac{29}{15}}$$

$$= 2 + \cfrac{1}{1 + \frac{14}{15}} = 2 + \cfrac{1}{1 + \cfrac{1}{\frac{15}{14}}}$$

$$= 2 + \cfrac{1}{1 + \cfrac{1}{1 + \frac{1}{14}}}$$

Each simple infinite continued fraction converges to an irrational number, and each positive irrational number has a unique expression in the form of a simple infinite continued fraction. Positive irrational roots of quadratic equations with

real coefficients can be put in the form of recurring continued fractions. The equation $x^2 - 2x - 1 = 0$, for example, has the positive root $1 + \sqrt{2}$. The continued fraction development can be formed as follows: divide the equation by x and write $x = 2 + 1/x$; in the fraction, replace x by $2 + 1/x$, and make the same replacement successively each time that $1/x$ appears. Putting $1 + \sqrt{2}$ for x on the left side, we have the recurring continued fraction for this irrational number. Upon subtracting 1 from both sides, we obtain a similar development of $\sqrt{2}$, namely,

$$\sqrt{2} = 1 + \cfrac{1}{2 + \cfrac{1}{2 + \cfrac{1}{2 + \cdots}}}$$

The fact that irrational roots of quadratic equations always have developments in the form of recurring continued fractions is analogous to the fact that all rational numbers can be expressed as recurring decimals.

The Wallis infinite product for $4/\pi$, which is

$$\frac{3}{2} \cdot \frac{3}{4} \cdot \frac{5}{4} \cdot \frac{5}{6} \cdot \frac{7}{6} \cdot \frac{7}{8} \cdots,$$

was transformed by William Brouncker (*c.* 1658) into the continued fraction

$$\frac{4}{\pi} = 1 + \cfrac{1^2}{2 + \cfrac{3^2}{2 + \cfrac{5^2}{2 + \cdots}}}$$

whence

$$\pi = \cfrac{4}{1 + \cfrac{1^2}{2 + \cfrac{3^2}{2 + \cfrac{5^2}{2 + \cdots}}}}$$

Leonhard Euler founded the modern theory of continued fractions in 1737. A development of the number e given by him is

$$e = 2 + \cfrac{1}{1 + \cfrac{1}{2 + \cfrac{1}{1 + \cfrac{1}{4 + \cfrac{1}{1 + \cdots}}}}}$$

—*H. C.*

CONTINUUM: a mathematical term used in both a geometrical and a numerical sense. A geometrical continuum is exemplified by a straight line. We conceive it as having no gaps or holes, not even as much as a single point. A curve with no breaks is also a geometrical continuum. A numerical continuum is less easily conceived, since it lacks appeal to the visual sense, yet there are numerous physical concepts which suggest it. The path of a moving body is a physical continuum and so is the interval of time in which it is in motion. We cannot imagine either the path or the time as having a gap. Since we express the distance between two points in the path by a real number, as well as the time taken by the body to move between the points, we must conclude that the numbers available for such purposes also form a continuum. The integers (whole numbers) are not adequate to provide a number for every distance. Even the inclusion of fractions is not sufficient since, for example, no fraction will represent the diagonal of a square whose side is one unit. However, from the totality of real numbers—integers, fractions, and irrationals—a number can be found for any distance, and therefore the system of real numbers is a continuum.—*H. C.*

CONTRACTION HYPOTHESIS: a hypothesis advanced to explain the origin of mountains. The realization that Earth is losing heat to space led to the assumption that it is cooling and getting smaller. The contraction hypothesis offered by James Dana and Elie de Beaumont in the mid-19th cent., and later developed particularly by Harold Jeffreys, appeared to give a reasonable explanation of the main features of continental mountains, but the theory has not been extended to explain the recently discovered MID-OCEANIC RIDGE. The discovery of heat-producing radioactivity opened the possibility that Earth may be warming, and this led to the rival CONVECTION THEORY.—*J. T. W.*

CONTRADICTION, LAW OF: in logic, one of the so-called Laws of Thought, a regulative principle. It may be seen functioning in ordinary discourse in the recognition, usually implicit, that one does not usually contradict oneself voluntarily; *e.g.* when a character in Dostoievski says, "Smoking was not allowed and was not prohibited either," we understand him to mean that the smoking regulations were not strictly enforced. Formally, the law derives its importance from the fact that any consequence whatever can be validly derived from a set of statements containing a contradiction, by the use of the usual rules of logic.—*H. T.*

CONTROL PROCESSES: operations designed to maintain a physical system in a desired mode of behavior in spite of disturbing forces acting on it. Such systems are found in engineering (as in satellites and space ships), in economics (automated factories), and in biology (the human body). A fundamental concept in carrying out monitoring operations is that of FEEDBACK control, in which the deviation of the system from the desired state is used as a restoring force. An application of this principle was made by James Watt in the construction of the governor for his steam engine.

A number of problems that arise in the mathematical theory of control processes can be cast in the mold of the calculus of variations. Typical is the question of choosing the vector function $y(t)$ so as to minimize the functional $J(y) = \int_0^T g(x,y)\,dt$, where x and y are connected by the equation $dx/dt = h(x,y)$, and $x(0) = c$. In general, the presence of constraints imposed by engineering realities, the novel features of modern technology, and the usual technical difficulties combine to force the development of new techniques if analytic and computational results are desired. Some of these are successive approximations, the "maximum principle" of Pontriagin and his school, and DYNAMIC PROGRAMMING.

The rapid refinement of the digital computer has expanded and altered the concept of a "solution" to problems of the foregoing type and even their formulation. Many effective algorithms now exist which 20 yr before would not even have been considered as feasible.—*R. B.*

CONTROL SYSTEM: any device or series of devices by which a system's performance, *e.g.* rate of fluid flow, frequency of a carrier wave, or direction of flight, is kept within desired limits. Rudimentary control systems, such as governors on steam engines, have long been in common use. Coupled with electronic circuits, present-day *feedback control systems* have achieved a versatility and sensitivity that particularly suit them to the demands of increasing AUTOMATION in industry. A simple example of a FEEDBACK system is a heating system controlled by a thermostat. If the heated air (the output) is either hotter or colder than the desired temperature, it will activate the thermostat (the input control). In turn, the thermostat regulates the fuel input to the furnace so that the air temperature is kept at the desired level. A SERVOMECHANISM is a special type of feedback control system. These are characterized by (1) a low-power input signal which when amplified allows the precise control of heavy loads, and (2) the mechanical positioning of the output, *e.g.* the movement of a lever or the rotation of a shaft. Servomechanisms are often used where rapid directional control of massive equipment is desired, *e.g.* with naval and anti-aircraft artillery, or rockets in flight.—*G. S. and A. L.*

CONVECTION: the motion of a fluid (liquid or gas) caused by a temperature difference. When a fluid expands on being heated, its density decreases, and the decrease causes it to rise above surrounding fluid that is cooler and therefore denser. Correspondingly, cooled fluid tends to sink below surrounding fluid that is less cool. Because most fluids are comparatively poor conductors of heat, convection is one of the most important means of HEAT TRANSFER in fluids; instead of the heat passing through the fluid itself, the warmer fluid moves from one point to another. Thus a steam radiator at floor level heats a room primarily by warming the air adjacent to it, which then rises to the ceiling, displacing cooler air, which, as it reaches the floor, is warmed by the radiator to create a continuous circulation. Conversely, air-conditioning ducts are placed near the ceiling to enhance convection.—*E. M. R.*

In meteorology, convection refers to the transfer of heat and other atmospheric properties from one location to another by mass motions within the atmosphere. The term is often restricted to upward vertical motion; downward vertical motion is termed *subsidence,* and horizontal mass motion, ADVECTION. Atmospheric convection may be either free or forced. Free convection results when the lowest layers of air become less dense (*e.g.* by heating) than the surrounding air, and rise. Forced convection currents are formed by mechanical lifting as air is pushed up slopes of the terrain (orographic lifting), by warm air flowing or pushed upward over cold air during the movement of fronts, or by low-level convergence, *e.g.* that existing in lows and cyclones, which also forces air upward. Convection causes the formation of cumulus clouds in moist air. Strong updrafts in both moist and dry air make flying dangerous at times and often are a cause of discomfort to aircraft passengers. Soaring birds and pilots flying motorless gliders often take advantage of convection currents to gain altitude. Tornadoes and thunderstorms are examples of extremely strong, localized convection penetrating to great heights. Dust devils are the result of very small-scale convection, while land-sea breezes result from broad-scale coastal convection. (See CLOUD.)—*P. L.*

CONVECTION THEORY: the theory that slow convection currents inside Earth carry to the surface the heat generated in the interior by radioactive elements, which have been found to be present in small quantities in all rocks. Although no direct observation of these currents has yet been possible, the only satisfactory explanation for the generation of Earth's main magnetic field (see TERRESTRIAL MAGNETISM) is that it is a consequence of dynamo action in the core, and the existence of such convection currents as explaining this action is now generally accepted. The view has been advocated by F. A. Vening-Meinesz and A. Holmes that slow convection currents exist also in the mantle; if so, the mantle must be a very viscous plastic solid. The currents probably rise under the MID-OCEANIC RIDGE and sink under island arcs and continental mountains, producing a form of CONTINENTAL DRIFT by their horizontal motion between. But the problems of explaining how convection currents flow through crust and mantle are great. At the base of the mantle the pressure is about 1,400,000 atm, and the temperature is perhaps 4000°C. These values are much greater than those at the surface; the currents must pass through horizontal layers having very different phases, densities, and viscosities.—*J. T. W.*

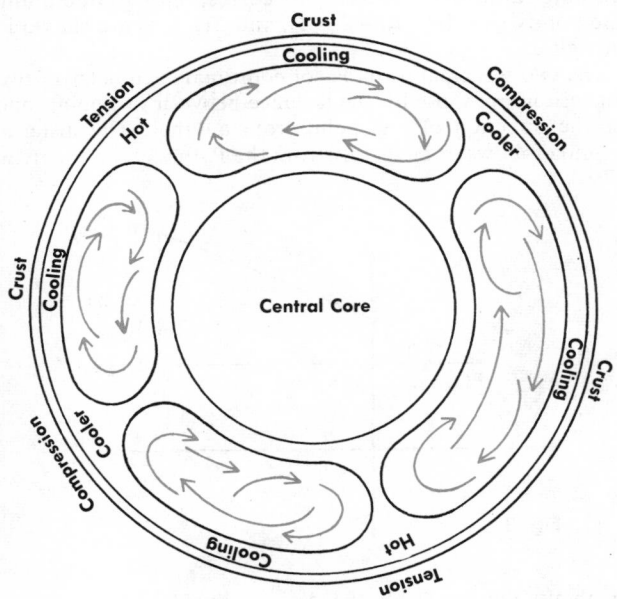

Slowly moving currents of nearly solid material in Earth's mantle, and perhaps in the core, have been postulated to explain the generation of the planet's magnetic field and the transfer of heat from the interior to the surface.

CONVENTIONALISM: a philosophical doctrine which in one version maintains that many statements in science apparently asserting empirical laws about matters of fact are actually definitional truths (or "conventions"), which merely stipulate the rules for using certain terms. In this form conventionalism is a mild doctrine, and becomes controversial only when various particular statements usually regarded as empirical truths are claimed to be covert rules. For example, it has been argued that Newton's First Law of Motion is simply a convention for defining equality of time, and that the law of conservation of energy is nothing but a disguised rule which tacitly defines energy as something which is conserved. Although conventionalists have been persuasive in pointing out conventional components in such scientific laws, they have not shown that the laws are merely conventional and have no empirical content.

In general, scientific theories contain both conventional and empirical components, but it is doubtful whether a sharp division can be made between statements whose truth is the result of convention alone and those which are based on empirical fact exclusively. Moreover, even though a statement functions as a convention in a given formulation of a theory, it may not have this status in another formulation of the theory. Some of these points were made forcefully by J. H. Poincaré when he discussed physical geometry as a theory purporting to describe the structure of physical space. He showed clearly that physicists must either introduce rules or conventions for measuring geometrical magnitudes (such as length) and then discover through observation which one of the alternate systems of pure geometry is true of the physical world, or they may adopt one such system of geometry as a matter of convention and in the light of the results obtained from using that system make suitable adjustments in the rules of measurement. While Poincaré was mistaken in predicting that scientists would always find it simpler to adjust the rules of measurement and other parts of physics in order to retain Euclidean geometry, his general observations about the role that conventions play in the test of a physical geometry are widely heeded.—*S. M.*

CONVERGENCE: see ATMOSPHERIC CONVERGENCE.

CONVEYOR: a device for transferring materials during production, packaging, or distribution. Appropriate supports or containers for solids or fluids are moved along fixed routes at controlled speeds. Materials may move by gravity down inclined slides, chutes, or banks of parallel rollers. Special operations or the nature of the material may require: a long belt circulating over a table, platform, or rollers, pulled by a turning friction roller at each end; or regularly spaced separators, platforms, pans, buckets, or hooks that are attached to cables moved by pulleys or to chains driven by toothed wheels, sometimes on tracks or rails. Homogeneous materials may be forced through a trough or pipe by long, rotating screws or under hydraulic or pneumatic pressure.—*K. A.*

CONYBEARE, REV. WILLIAM DANIEL, 1787–1857, English geologist; b. London. His *Outlines of the Geology of England and Wales* (1822), written with William Phillips, was the earliest comprehensive work on its subject. The authors used William Smith's principle of determining the relative ages of rocks by means of the fossils contained in them, and their book aroused increased interest in studies of fossils. Conybeare wrote on paleontology, hydrography, and vulcanology. He was a fellow of the Royal Society.—*D. H. D. R.*

COOLANT: a fluid whose purpose is to remove heat from a heat generating system. In the heat-treatment of steels, the term designates liquids, *e.g.* mineral oils, used for quenching (rapid cooling) of steel alloys. "Coolants" also refers to cutting oils, used in the machining of metals (see LUBRICATION). In NUCLEAR REACTORS, the coolant is a fluid that transfers heat from the fuel elements to the outside where it can be utilized. Usually the coolant fluid is made to flow through piping in thermal contact with a second fluid, and the latter is used to make steam or turn a turbine. Two separated coolants are used in order to minimize the danger of contamination of external machinery by any radioactive material that might leak into the primary coolant. Most operating power reactors in the U. S. A. today use water under high pressure as the coolant, but reactor types using other coolants have been proposed. The U. S. Atomic Energy Commission is sponsoring a long-range program in which prototypes of most of these reactors will be built and compared. The coolants in the other prototype reactors are: boiling water; heavy water (deuterium); molten sodium; molten bismuth; and helium gas under high pressure. (See HEAT TRANSFER.)—*S. K.*

COOLING, NEWTON'S LAW OF: the principle that a body exchanges heat with its surroundings at a rate proportional to their temperature difference. It follows that the *rate* of temperature change of the body is also proportional to the same temperature difference. Thus, if an object 30° warmer than room temperature is cooling off at a certain rate, it will cool off only about half as fast when its temperature has decreased to 15° above room temperature. When the temperatures of object and surroundings are nearly equal, the cooling rate is extremely slow. Newton's law, while not entirely accurate, is a good approximation if the temperature difference is not too great.—*J. E. W.*

COORDINATE or **ANALYTIC GEOMETRY:** a branch of mathematics in which geometrical and algebraic concepts are associated by means of a coordinate system. The invention of the subject is credited to Descartes (1637), although others, notably Fermat, knew the basic ideas at least as early as this. The fundamental objective of coordinate geometry is to represent curves and surfaces by algebraic equations. These equations can be investigated more readily to extract information about the curves and surfaces than purely geometric reasoning permits. Since curves are physically significant, *e.g.* the paths of projectiles, light rays, and celestial bodies, and surfaces are equally so, *e.g.* the shapes of ships' hulls and airplane wings, the ability to study relatively complex curves and surfaces by the powerful methods of algebra is vastly important.

To set up correspondences between geometrical and numerical entities, one starts with the most basic elements: geometrical points and real numbers. First, we make the real numbers correspond in a one-to-one way with the points of a straight line (Fig. 1). A zero point, or origin *O*, is designated,

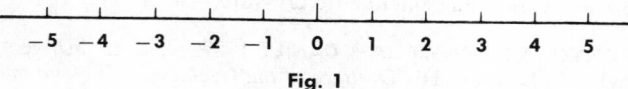

Fig. 1

and a unit of measure adopted. The end points of all segments measured from *O* are denoted by the numbers which represent the lengths of the segments, positive numbers in one direction from *O* and negative numbers in the opposite direction. Assuming that the real-number system provides a number for each distance, we have a number for each point and a point for each number. This number axis is a one-dimensional coordinate system, each number being the coordinate of the corresponding point. Letting x denote the coordinate of any point, x is greater than 0 on the positive part of the axis, and x is less than 0 on the negative part. Any interval of the line is described by an inequality. Thus $0 < x < 1$ for every point between *O* and 1. If x_1 and x_2 are coordinates of two points of the line, with the direction from x_1 to x_2 positive, then $x_2 - x_1$ is the distance between the points. This is true regardless of the signs of x_1 and x_2. Thus, if $x_1 = -2$ and $x_2 = 5$, the distance is $5 - (-2) = 7$.

A coordinate system in two dimensions is constructed by utilizing two number axes, intersecting perpendicularly at their zero points. This produces a two-dimensional rectangular cartesian coordinate system. In this system each point has two coordinates. It is customary to orient the axes as shown in Fig. 2. The horizontal x axis has its positive direction toward the right, and the vertical y axis has its positive direction upward, the point of intersection being the

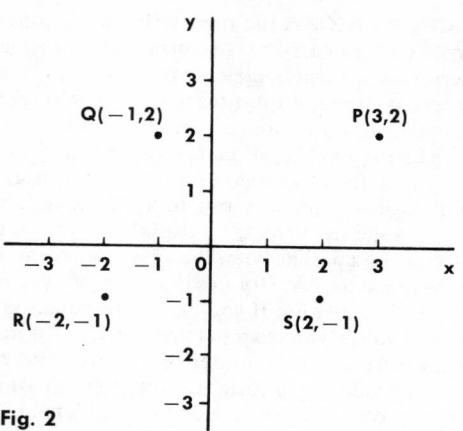

Fig. 2

origin. The point $P(3,2)$ has its x distance, or abscissa, equal to 3, and its y distance, or ordinate, equal to 2. Upon agreement to write these coordinates in the order of abscissa first, followed by ordinate, each point has one ordered pair of coordinates and each ordered pair corresponds to one point. The points $Q(-1,2)$, $R(-2,-1)$, and $S(2,-1)$ are shown in the figure.

The two principal formulas of coordinate geometry of two dimensions are those for the distance between two points and for the direction of one point from another. The distance formula follows immediately from the Pythagorean theorem.

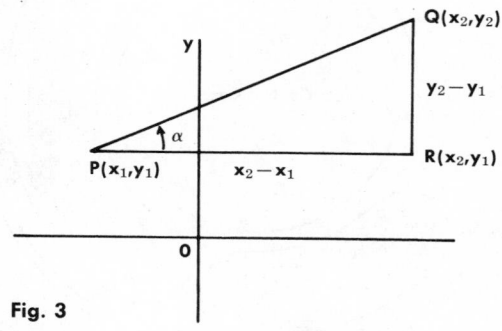

Fig. 3

To obtain the length of the oblique line from $P(x_1,y_1)$ to $Q(x_2,y_2)$, we can form a right triangle as in Fig. 3, with right angle at $R(x_2,y_1)$. Now the length of PR is $x_2 - x_1$, and that of RQ is $y_2 - y_1$. Hence $PQ^2 = (x_2 - x_1)^2 + (y_2 - y_1)^2$. If the points were differently located so that either $(x_2 - x_1)$ or $(y_2 - y_1)$ were negative, the formula would not be changed, since only the squares of these quantities appear. The direction from P to Q is given by the slope, usually denoted by m, which is the ratio $(y_2 - y_1)/(x_2 - x_1) = \tan \alpha$, where α is the angle of inclination. Here it is important that the differences appear in the same order, although it is immaterial whether we use $(y_2 - y_1)/(x_2 - x_1)$ or $(y_1 - y_2)/(x_1 - x_2)$. If the ratio is negative the angle α is obtuse. For the points $P(-1,1)$, $Q(3,4)$, we have $PQ^2 = [3 - (-1)]^2 + (4 - 1)^2 = 25$, whence $PQ = 5$, and $m = (4 - 1)/[3 - (-1)] = 3/4$. For the points $M(2,3)$, $N(-1,5)$, $MN^2 = [2 - (-1)]^2 + (5 - 3)^2 = 13$, whence $MN = \sqrt{13}$, and $m = (5 - 3)/(-1 - 2) = -2/3$. (See Fig. 4.)

The central concept in coordinate geometry is that of a geometrical locus and its algebraic description. In two dimensions we are interested in curves (including straight lines). One of the most familiar curves is a circle. Suppose a circle of radius 1 has its center at the origin. Let (x,y) be the coordinates of any point on the circle. Such a point must be 1 unit from the origin $O(0,0)$. Therefore $(x - 0)^2 + (y - 0)^2 = 1^2$, or $x^2 + y^2 = 1$. This is the equation of the circle. There are two main problems of coordinate geometry: given a curve, find its equation; and given an equation, find the geometrical locus. An equation E, in x and y, is said to be the equation of a curve C if every pair of values which satisfy E are coordinates of a point of C, and every point of C has coordinates which satisfy E. Because of this close identification we often denote the curve by its equation, $e.g.$, the circle, $x^2 + y^2 = 1$. The curve is also called the graph of the equation.

Coordinate geometry of two dimensions is concerned with a systematic study of plane curves and their equations—straight lines, circles, the conic sections, trigonometric curves, logarithmic and exponential curves. General methods for

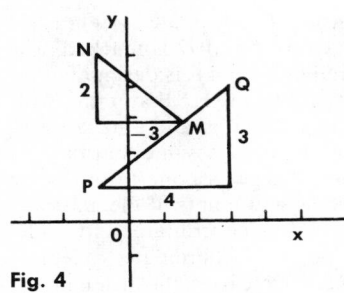

Fig. 4

finding the graphs of equations, and for finding the equations of loci defined geometrically, are developed. Among the important results are the facts that, in rectangular coordinates, all first-degree equations correspond to straight lines, and all second-degree equations to the CONIC SECTIONS—parabola, ellipse, circle, hyperbola. Some of the standard equations are the following:

Straight line, perpendicular to the x axis, through $(k,0)$:
$$x = k.$$

Straight line, perpendicular to the y axis, through $(0,k)$:
$$y = k.$$

Straight line through (x_1,y_1) with slope m:
$$y - y_1 = m(x - x_1).$$

Straight line through (x_1,y_1) and (x_2,y_2):
$$y - y_1 = [(y_2 - y_1)/(x_2 - x_1)] (x - x_1).$$

Straight line through $(0,b)$ with slope m: $y = mx + b$.

Straight line through $(a,0)$ and $(0,b)$: $x/a + y/b = 1$.

Circle with radius r and center at O: $x^2 + y^2 = r^2$.

Circle with radius r and center at (a,b):
$$(x - a)^2 + (y - b)^2 = r^2.$$

Parabola with vertex at O and focus at $(a,0)$: $y^2 = 4ax$.

Ellipse with center at O, foci at $(c,0)$ and $(-c,0)$, major axis, $2a$: $x^2/a^2 + y^2/(a^2 - c^2) = 1$.

Hyperbola with center at O, foci at $(c,0)$ and $(-c,0)$, transverse axis, $2a$: $x^2/a^2 - y^2/(c^2 - a^2) = 1$.

Starting with an equation, we can try to trace its graph by using a few general principles. Information as to intercepts upon the axes, lines or points of symmetry, regions from which the curve is excluded, and asymptotes is helpful. Methods of gaining this information are illustrated by the

following example, in which we find the graph of $x^2y - 4x + y = 0$. Solving for y, we have $y = 4x/(x^2 + 1)$. Solving for x by the quadratic formula gives $x = (4 \pm \sqrt{16 - 4y^2})/2y$. The y intercepts are found by putting $x = 0$, either in the original equation or in the second form, obtaining $y = 0$. This is the only intercept on either axis, namely the origin. A curve is symmetrical about the y axis if, for each point (x,y) on it, the symmetrical point $(-x,y)$ is on it. This will be true if replacing x by $-x$ leaves the equation unchanged. We find, however, that the equation is changed; as is the case, also, if $-y$ replaces y. Hence the curve is not symmetrical about either axis. But if $-x$ and $-y$ replace x and y, respectively, the equation is unchanged. Hence, for each point (x,y) of the curve, the point $(-x,-y)$, which is symmetrical with respect to the origin, is on the curve. No values of x make y imaginary, but, if $y < -2$ or $y > 2$, x is imaginary. Hence y is restricted to the interval $-2 \leqq y \leqq 2$. For each value of y in this interval except 0 there are two values of x. As y approaches 0, one of these values approaches 0, producing the crossing at the origin. The other value becomes very great, and we conclude that the line $y = 0$, which is the x axis, is an asymptote, $i.e.$ it is a straight line which the curve approximates indefinitely closely, both in position and direction, as it recedes infinitely

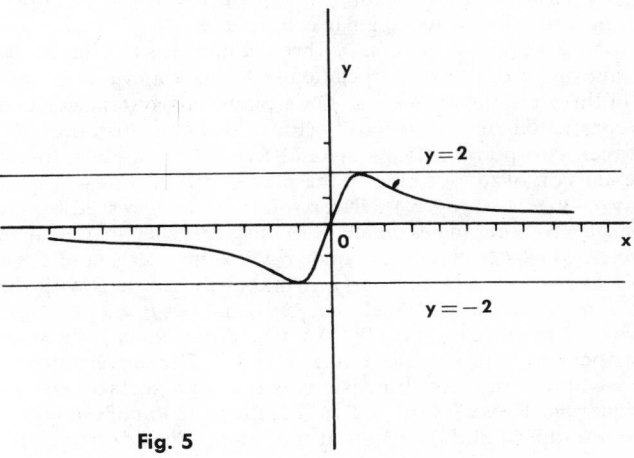

Fig. 5

far off. Finally, we can make a small table by substituting arbitrary positive values of x. Because of the symmetry, it is not necessary to substitute negative values. The curve is shown in Fig. 5.

x	0	1	2	3	4	5	10
y	0	2	8/5	6/5	16/17	10/13	40/101

A polar coordinate system is better adapted than the rectangular system for some curves. In this system a point is located by its distance from a fixed point and its direction from a fixed direction. It is analogous to a latitude and longitude chart in a polar area. The fixed point is the *pole O*, and the fixed direction is that of a polar axis. Positive angles are measured counterclockwise and negative angles clockwise. The angles are often measured in radians (π radians $= 180°$). Positive values of the distance, r, are measured from O along the terminal side of the angle; negative values in the opposite direction. A definite point corresponds to each distance r and angle θ, which are, by convention, written (r,θ). But the correspondence is not one-to-one, as in the rectangular system, for each point can have many sets of polar coordinates. Thus, $(2, \pi/4)$, $(2, 9\pi/4)$, $(2, -7\pi/4)$, $(-2, 5\pi/4)$, and many other pairs locate the same point (Fig. 6). This system is convenient for representing graphs of many trigonometric functions; and

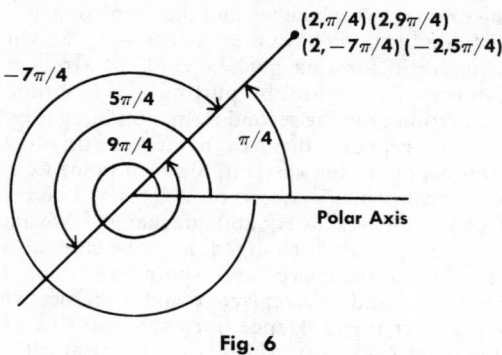

$(2,\pi/4)(2,9\pi/4)$
$(2,-7\pi/4)(-2,5\pi/4)$
$-7\pi/4$
$5\pi/4$
$9\pi/4$
$\pi/4$
Polar Axis

Fig. 6

equations of many curves are simpler in polar coordinates than in rectangular. For example, the equation $r^2 = \cos 2\theta$ has the polar graph shown in Fig. 7. The rectangular equation of this curve is derived below.

Relations between polar coordinates and rectangular coordinates can be found by superposing one system on the other, with the pole coinciding with the origin and the polar axis with the x axis. It is then easy to see that $r^2 = x^2 + y^2$, $\tan \theta = y/x$, $x = r \cos \theta$, $y = r \sin \theta$. The equation $r^2 = \cos 2\theta = \cos^2\theta - \sin^2\theta$ becomes $(x^2 + y^2)^2 = x^2 - y^2$, upon transformation to rectangular coordinates.

A rectangular system in three dimensions is made by annexing a third axis perpendicular to the x and y axes, with all three origins coinciding. On a plane this system must be represented in perspective (Fig. 8). The distance between two points $P(x_1,y_1,z_1)$ and $Q(x_2,y_2,z_2)$ is given by an extension of the formula in the plane: $PQ^2 = (x_2 - x_1)^2 + (y_2 - y_1)^2 + (z_2 - z_1)^2$. Direction is now expressed by the cosines of the angles made with lines parallel to the three axes. Thus PQ makes the angle α with the x axis, and $\cos \alpha = (x_2 - x_1)/PQ$. Similarly, it makes the angle β with the y axis, and the angle γ with the z axis, and $\cos \beta = (y_2 - y_1)/PQ$, $\cos \gamma = (z_2 - z_1)/PQ$. In two dimensions a curve is associated with its equation in x and y. The corresponding association in three dimensions is that of a surface with its equation. Thus $x^2 + y^2 + z^2 = 1$ is the equation of the sphere with radius 1 and its center at the origin. First-degree equations represent planes, and second-degree equations represent quadric surfaces—spheres, ellipsoids, paraboloids, and hyperboloids. A straight line is the intersection of two planes, and hence requires two equations of the first degree. Similarly, a curve is the intersection of two surfaces, and requires two equations.

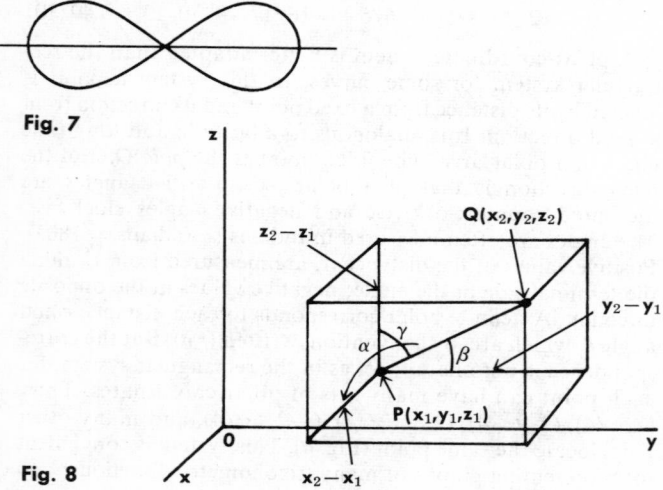

Fig. 7

z
$z_2 - z_1$
$Q(x_2,y_2,z_2)$
$y_2 - y_1$
γ
α
β
$P(x_1,y_1,z_1)$
O
y
Fig. 8
x
$x_2 - x_1$

Coordinate systems other than rectangular are often utilized in space, especially cylindrical coordinates and spherical coordinates. (See COORDINATE SYSTEM.) Coordinate geometry is extended to more than three dimensions in an abstract way, even to n dimensions, where n is unspecified except that it is a positive integer. Geometrical visualization is, of course, impossible beyond three dimensions.—*H. C.*

COORDINATES, CELESTIAL: see CELESTIAL COORDINATES.

COORDINATE SYSTEM: a method of designating positions by numbers. A familiar coordinate system is that in which two numbers, one giving the latitude and the other the longitude, exactly locate a position on Earth's surface. In the neighborhood of the equator the circles of latitude and longitude closely approximate a rectangular coordinate system. Coordinate systems are essential to mapping and are the basis of COORDINATE GEOMETRY.

A one-dimensional coordinate system is simply a number scale, or axis. A zero point O is marked, a unit of measure agreed upon, and every point is designated by the number of units in the distance from O to that point, with a positive sign if measured in one direction and a negative sign if measured in the other (Fig. 1). If we assume that there is a real number for each point, this gives a one-to-one correspondence between real numbers and points of the axis; *i.e.* each point has one number, called its coordinate, and each number corresponds to one point. A coordinate system for a plane was developed by René Descartes, the originator of coordinate, or analytic, geometry. This cartesian coordinate system is based on two intersecting number axes. These are called the x axis (horizontal) and the y axis (vertical). If the axes intersect perpendicularly, we have a rectangular coordinate system. Oblique coordinates (Fig. 2) are seldom used. The zero-points of the axes are made to coincide at point O, called the origin. Each point in the plane is determined by two real numbers denoting its distances parallel to the two axes. By convention, the distance parallel to the x axis is always written first. With this agreement it is clear that there is a one-to-one correspondence between the points of the plane and ordered pairs of real numbers. Fig. 3 distinguishes between the points $(2,3)$ and $(3,2)$. The points $(-2,3)$, $(-3,-2)$, and $(2,-3)$ are also shown. The first, or x, distance is called the abscissa of the point, the y distance its ordinate, and the two together its coordinates. In a rectangular system, lines along which the abscissa remains constant and those along which the ordinate remains constant form a rectangular network. Having established a correspondence between points and ordered number pairs, we can represent many geometrical facts and quantities by means of the numerical coordinates. These include the distance between two points, the direction of one point from another, the area of a triangle with known vertices, and, most important of all, the condition that a point shall be on a given locus, or curve.

A different coordinate system in a plane is similar to the system of latitude and longitude near the north or south pole. It is the system of polar coordinates, in which a point is located (Fig. 4) by its distance from a fixed point, called the pole, and its direction as compared with that of a fixed line through the pole, called the polar axis. The distance r is called the radius vector, and the angle θ the vectorial angle. Usually θ is measured in radians, π radians being equivalent to 180°. Lines along which r remains constant are concentric circles, and lines along which θ remains constant are radial lines. Positive values of θ are measured counterclockwise and negative values clockwise. Positive values of r are measured outward from O along the terminal side of the angle θ, and

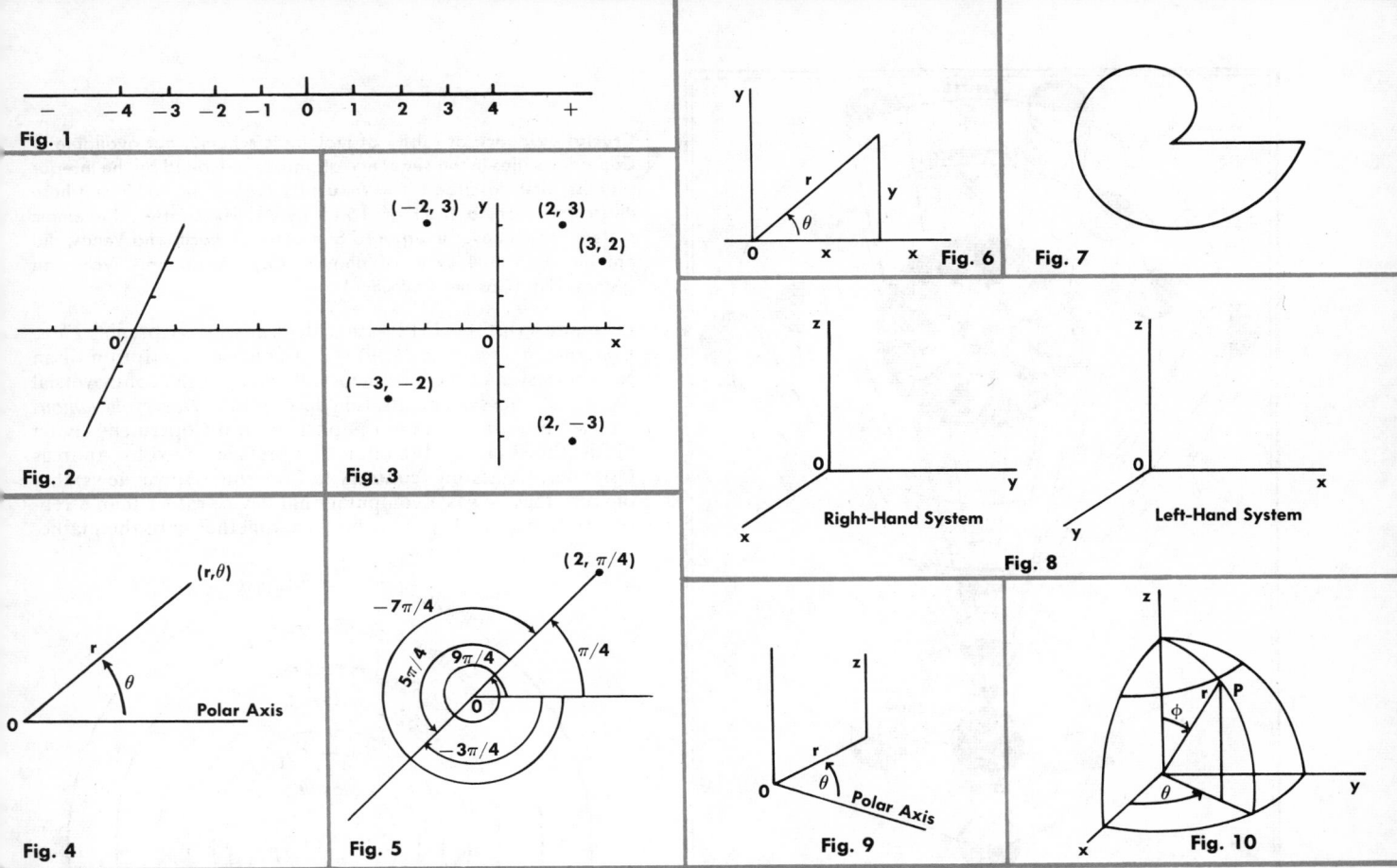

Fig. 1

Fig. 2

Fig. 3

$(-2, 3)$ y $(2, 3)$

$(3, 2)$

O x

$(-3, -2)$

$(2, -3)$

Fig. 4

(r, θ)

r

θ

Polar Axis

O

Fig. 5

$(2, \pi/4)$

$-7\pi/4$

$9\pi/4$

$\pi/4$

$5\pi/4$

O

$-3\pi/4$

Fig. 6

y

r

y

θ

O x x

Fig. 7

Fig. 8

z

O

y

x

Right-Hand System

z

O

x

y

Left-Hand System

Fig. 9

z

r

θ

O

Polar Axis

Fig. 10

z

r

P

ϕ

θ

y

x

negative values in the opposite direction along the backward extension of the terminal side. For each pair of values (r, θ), customarily written in this order, there is one point. But for each point there are many pairs of polar coordinates. Thus the point $(2, \pi/4)$ also has the coordinates $(2, 9\pi/4)$, $(2, -7\pi/4)$, $(-2, -3\pi/4)$, $(-2, 5\pi/4)$, and many others (Fig. 5).

Relations between polar and rectangular coordinates can be found by superposing one system on the other, with the origin coinciding with the pole, and the positive x axis with the polar axis. We see that $r = \sqrt{x^2 + y^2}$, $\tan \theta = y/x$, $x = r \cos \theta$, $y = r \sin \theta$ (Fig. 6). The same curve is represented in polar coordinates and in rectangular coordinates by different equations, e.g. the circle with center at O and radius 1 has the polar equation, $r = 1$, and the rectangular equation, $x^2 + y^2 = 1$. Also, equations of identical form represent different curves in the two systems. For example, the equation $y = x$ in rectangular coordinates represents the straight line through the origin, inclined at $45°$. In polar coordinates the equation $r = \theta$ represents the spiral shown in Fig. 7.

A rectangular coordinate system in three dimensions consists of three mutually perpendicular axes intersecting at a common zero point, or origin. Two orientations are possible. If we think of the axes as the x, y, and z axes, we have a right-hand system (Fig. 8) if turning from the positive x axis to the positive y axis would cause a right-hand screw to move in the direction of the positive z axis. It is a left-hand system if this rotation would cause a left-hand screw to move in the direction of the positive z axis. Each point has three coordinates, and each ordered triple of real numbers is the set of coordinates belonging to a point. As with two dimensions, many geometrical quantities and facts can be expressed numerically by means of coordinates. These include the distance between two points, the direction of one point from another, the volume of a tetrahedron with given vertices, and

the condition that a point lie on a given surface or curve.

Two useful systems of coordinates in space that are analogous to polar coordinates in the plane are cylindrical coordinates and spherical coordinates. Cylindrical coordinates consist of polar coordinates in a plane with an axis perpendicular to the plane at the pole. Thus a cylindrical coordinate system is a hybrid—part polar and part rectangular. Imagine a three-dimensional rectangular system, with the rectangular coordinates in the xy plane replaced by polar coordinates, but with z unchanged (Fig. 9). A point is located by r, θ, and z, usually given in that order. On the $r\theta$ plane, $z = 0$, and on the plane one unit above it, $z = 1$. The angle θ is constant in a plane which includes the z axis, and r is a constant on a cylindrical surface having the z axis as its axis. Spherical coordinates are based on a distance and two angles. Consider a point P on a three-dimensional rectangular system. Instead of describing it by its rectangular coordinates, we might give (1) its distance r from O; (2) the angle ϕ which OP makes with the z axis; and (3) the angle θ which the projection of OP on the xy plane makes with the x axis (Fig. 10). The three numbers (r, θ, ϕ) are the spherical coordinates of P. If these numbers are given, a definite point is determined as follows: (1) it is on the sphere with center at O and radius r; (2) it is on the cone with vertex at O, vertex angle ϕ, and axis agreeing with the z axis, and hence it is on the circle of intersection of the sphere and cone; (3) it is on the plane which includes the z axis and makes the angle θ with the xz plane, and hence at the intersection of this plane with the circle in (2).—H. C.

COPERNICAN SYSTEM: the Sun-centered description of the planetary system proposed by the Polish cleric Niklas Koppernigk (Copernicus), 1543. It explains the apparent rotation of the CELESTIAL SPHERE by a contrary rotation of Earth on its axis, carrying the observer with it. Earth is supposed to

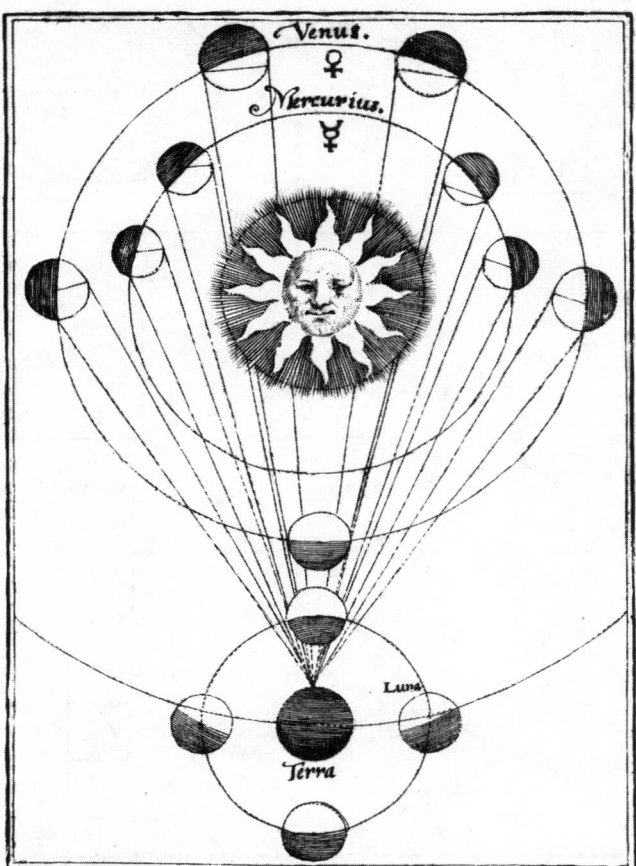

in manuscript *c.* 1512; English trans. E. Rosen's *Three Copernican Treatises,* 1959) was a concise description of an earlier version of the new theory. Because of the controversial nature of the system, its full description, *De revolutionibus orbium coelestium,* was not published until Copernicus lay on his deathbed (1543). It contained a preface added by Andreas Osiander, suggesting (contrary to Copernicus' own views) that the new theory was a computational device rather than a representation of reality. This preface, together with the mathe-

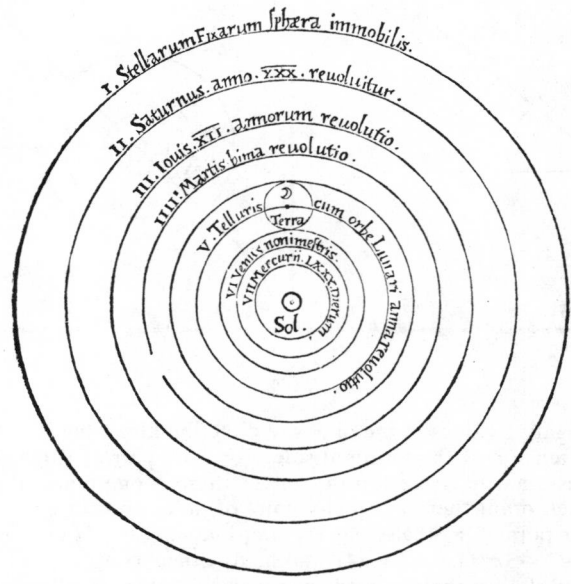

Historic diagram from Copernicus' *De revolutionibus* shows Earth clearly sharing its center of revolution with the other planets known at the time. The simplicity of this model is deceptive: a full setting out of the Copernican scheme would exhibit 34 circles. (*U. S. Navy*)

matical similarity of the Copernican to the Ptolemaic system, delayed serious controversy over the new theory for half a century. The Copernican system, providing a foundation for the work of KEPLER and NEWTON, materially changed our conception of the universe by displacing Man from his traditional place at its center.—*S. D. G.*

COPPER: a metallic element (Cu); at. no. 29; at. wt 63.54; density 8.92; mp 1083°C. It has two isotopes, of mass 63 and 65. Copper occurs naturally in elemental form, as well as in sulfide ores (chalcopyrite, $CuFeS_2$; chalcocite, Cu_2S) and oxide ores (cuprite, Cu_2O; malachite, $Cu_2(OH)_2CO_3$); see MINERAL (chart). Pure copper is obtained from sulfide ores by a succession of steps: (1) concentration of the ore, (2) roasting, (3) formation of cuprous sulfide, (4) reduction of cuprous sulfide to "blister copper," and (5) electrolytic refining of the blister copper. The principal use of copper is in electrical transmission, because of its good electrical conductivity and ductility. Because of its high thermal conductivity and inertness, it is also used in water heaters, boilers, and cooking utensils. Copper forms many alloys, *e.g.* brass (with zinc) and bronze (with zinc and tin).

move about the Sun in a circular orbit in a period of a year, and the other planets to move in circles about the Sun, in orbits of various periods and sizes. The system explains the apparent motion of a planet in the sky as the result of a combination of its orbital motion with the orbital motion of Earth. It failed to represent the observed planetary motions as accurately as the Ptolemaic system, so Copernicus "improved" his system by using off-centered circles, and adding epicycles, exactly as in the Ptolemaic system. His theory met with little support at the time of its publication, but strongly influenced Kepler and Galileo, who paved the way for modern planetary gravitation theory. See also COSMOLOGY.—*M. W. O.*

COPERNICUS, NICOLAUS (Lat. name of **Niklas Koppernigk**), 1473–1543, Polish astronomer; b. Torun, Poland. He studied the liberal arts, law, and medicine at the universities of Cracow (1491–*c.*1494), Bologna (1496–1500), and Padua (1501–*c.*1503) and received a doctorate in canon law from the Univ. of Ferrara (1503). Copernicus returned to Poland no later than 1506 and, having been elected in absentia (1497)

Nicolaus Copernicus
(*U. S. Navy*)

a canon of the cathedral at Frauenburg, he assumed these new duties in 1512. His interest in astronomy, probably awakened at Cracow, was spurred by his association at Bologna with the Italian astronomer Domenico Maria da Novara (1454–1504). He modified the Ptolemaic geocentric theory (PTOLEMAIC SYSTEM) to construct his COPERNICAN SYSTEM, which places the Sun at the center of the universe with a rotating Earth in orbit around it. *Commentariolus* (circulated

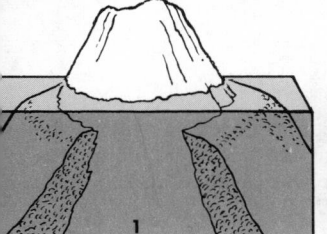 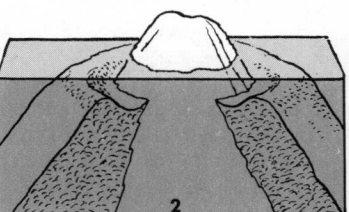 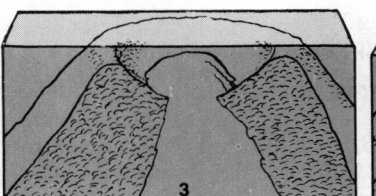 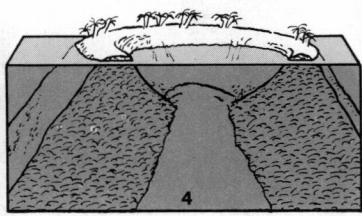

Development of a coral atoll: (1) Fringing reef grows on flanks of volcanic island. **(2)** Coral builds upward toward ocean surface as island subsides. **(3)** Island is now completely submerged; coral continues to build upward from it. **(4)** Storm waves shatter coral and throw up the debris to form an atoll.

Copper forms compounds in which it has +1 (cuprous), +2 (cupric), and +3 valences. Those with +3 valence are very unstable. Cuprous salts are prepared from cupric compounds by electrolysis, reaction with cyanide, decomposition of cupric oxide by heat, and reduction of cupric compounds in alkaline solution. Cuprous oxide, because of its red color, is used in making ruby glass and colored porcelain. Cuprous salts dissolve in hydrochloric acid, ammonia, and alkali cyanide in forming $CuCl_2^-$, $Cu(NH_3)_2^+$, and $Cu(CN)_3^=$, respectively.

The blue color of cupric compounds results from the hydrated cupric ion, $Cu(H_2O)_4^{++}$. Most cupric salts are prepared by reaction of an acid and an oxidizing agent upon copper metal or by the metathetical exchange of anions of other salts with cupric salts. Cupric ion forms complexes with many inorganic and organic compounds, the most notable being the cupric ammonium complex, $Cu(NH_3)_4^{++}$. It also forms complexes with proteins, amino acids, polycarboxylic acids, and a wide variety of other organic compounds. Cupric sulfate is the most important copper salt; its anhydrous salt is colorless. A mixture of copper sulfate and slaked lime is used as a fungicide under the name "Bordeaux mixture." Cupric sulfate is used as an electrolyte in a gravity battery, in electroplating and electrotyping, and in swimming pools and water works to prevent the growth of algae.—*G. W. M.*

CORAL: a minute marine animal that forms a hard, cuplike external skeleton of calcium carbonate. The true corals, including about 2,500 living species, are COELENTERATES of the class anthozoa. The term coral is often applied to other marine animals and plants that form limy skeletons, as well as to the skeletal material itself. Most corals live attached to one another in colonies in shallow tropical seas, where the combined bulk of their skeletons may form CORAL REEFS AND ATOLLS. A typical dried chunk of coral reef looks like a piece of porous limestone dotted with distinct holes. In life, an individual coral, or polyp, protrudes from each hole. The bodies of the polyps are connected to one another through the numerous pores, or *solenia*. Living corals are often brilliantly colored in tints of green, red, blue, pink, and yellow.

The typical coral's body is cylindrical. At one end a crown of short tentacles surrounds an oval disk containing a slitlike mouth. A gullet, or pharynx, connects the mouth to a gastrovascular cavity that serves as both a digestive and a circulatory organ. The coral animal feeds on plankton, which it captures with its tentacles. As a coral polyp grows, it reproduces asexually by budding, and becomes two connected individuals, which produce other individuals. Each secretes its skeleton from substances extracted from sea water. In this way a colony develops. From time to time, the polyps reproduce sexually. An egg released into the water develops into a free-swimming larva (*planula*) that eventually attaches itself to the substratum and grows into a polyp capable of forming a new colony. See Color Plate 30.—*A. P. E. and R. M.*

CORAL REEFS AND ATOLLS: Corals are small animals which customarily grow in large colonies, often shaped much like a shrub or small tree. In warm seas the stony corals secrete massive skeletons of lime and, together with lime-secreting algae, form reefs in shallow water. The corals and algae are firmly cemented together through processes of solution and precipitation occurring in the interstitial water. With the help of other shell-forming animals and of debris which fills up interstices, they form a nearly solid deposit with a flat, though rough, surface. The corals and algae grow upward until their tips are exposed to the Sun and to drying, so that the reefs are awash at low tide. When storms break pieces off the reef, these either tumble down the slope or pile up on the reef and become foundations for islands. Reefs whose surfaces run right to the beach are called *fringing reefs*. A reef separated from the land by a lagoon is called a *barrier reef*. A reef not related to any emergent land is called an *atoll*, and commonly encloses a shallow lagoon which communicates with the sea through channels in the reef. Charles Darwin explained these three forms by pointing out that if coral established a fringing reef around an island such as a conical volcano, and the island sank a short distance, when the reef grew up to the surface again it would have a lagoon between it and the beach and would be a barrier reef. If the island sank slowly, clear out of sight, the reef would grow into an atoll. Although not all the characteristics of coral structures are explained by this simple theory, no other theory explains so much.—*M. S.*

CORI, CARL FERDINAND, 1896– , Austrian-U. S. physiologist and biochemist; b. Prague. His research has been chiefly on enzymes and hormones, particularly relating to carbohydrate metabolism. For their discovery of how glycogen and starch are metabolized, he and his wife, **Gerty Theresa Cori** (1896–1957), shared the 1947 Nobel prize in physiology with Bernardo A. Houssay. He is a fellow of the Royal Society and a member of the National Academy of Sciences. —*D. H. D. R.*

CORING: the technique of drilling with a hollow drill and retrieving the material collected in the drill. It is a relatively rapid method of obtaining information on the succession of subsurface strata, and thereby the sequence of geological events, in a material that would not otherwise be exposed. In the simplest case the hollow drill is just a vertical length of pipe, but many corers have an outer barrel, a liner, an attachable cutting head, and means of keeping the core from falling out when the corer is raised. Cores are examined for grain size and distribution, chemical composition, micro-fossils, magnetism, and radioactivity. In petroleum exploration, 20-ft core barrels are commonly employed, but when diamond cutting heads are used they are often mounted on 100-ft lengths of barrel to obtain cores up to 90 ft long. In a hard substratum on land or in shallow water, a drilling rig rotates the corer, and with a diamond head can penetrate hard rock. In deep water, oceanographers have used corers driven into the bottom by their own weight or by various impelling devices. Such corers can be used only in soft material, but cores more than 65 ft long have been obtained. On land, successive cores taken in the same hole, end to end, may total thousands of feet. (See also MOHOROVIČIĆ DISCONTINUITY.)—*M. S.*

CORIOLIS, GASPARD GUSTAVE DE, 1792–1843, French physicist and engineer; b. Paris. A student of mechanics, he introduced the term "work" into physics, with the special meaning of force times distance, and assisted in the definition of kinetic energy. His name is preserved in the terms CORIOLIS FORCE and CORIOLIS ACCELERATION, used in theoretical mechanics. His published works include *Calcul de l'effet des machines* (1829) and *Théorie mathématique des effets du jeu de billard* (1835).—*D. H. D. R.*

CORIOLIS ACCELERATION: a dynamic effect, important in meteorology and oceanography, which arises because a particle fixed in a rotating system is accelerated with respect to a fixed (inertial) external coordinate system. Mathematically, the particle is subjected to a centrifugal and a tangential (Coriolis) force. Physically, the effect may be illustrated by attempting to draw a straight line from the center to the circumference of a rotating disk (figure); an observer fixed on the disk could regard the resulting curved line as evidence of a force acting at right angles to the motion. In meteorology such a fictitious force, called the CORIOLIS FORCE or *deviating force* of Earth's rotation, is used to simplify calculations. Because of the Coriolis acceleration, a particle of air outside the equatorial zone moves, not directly from regions of high to regions of low pressure, but along the ISOBARS as the geostrophic wind. In the Northern Hemisphere the Coriolis force, which is proportional to the product of the wind speed and the sine of the latitude, produces a deviation to the right, so that winds blow counterclockwise around a low. This rule is reversed in the Southern Hemisphere.—*D. H. L.*

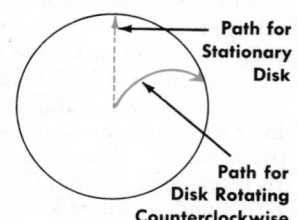

Coriolis effect: If one attempts to draw a straight line from center of rotating disk to circumference, result is a curved line.

CORIOLIS FORCE: a fictitious force invented as an aid in solving mechanics problems when the motion is referred to a rotating reference system. So long as the position of an object is measured in an inertial system (*i.e.* a coordinate system moving at constant velocity with respect to the fixed stars) the motion of the object is completely described by NEWTON'S LAWS OF MOTION. These tell us how to calculate the trajectory of any piece of matter when the forces acting on it are specified. Obviously, if that same trajectory is referred to a rotating coordinate system the trajectory will appear more complicated; if one wanted to continue to use the formula provided by Newton's laws he would have to pretend that additional forces were acting. The so-called Coriolis force and centrifugal force are just such artificial constructs. An example of the Coriolis force is the following: Suppose a rifle was fired from Earth's north pole. Neglecting air friction, once the bullet left the muzzle the only force acting upon it would be gravity, so it would fall to the ground at the end of its range without suffering any deflection east or west—in relation to an observer in space. But while the bullet was in flight, Earth would be rotating underneath it. An observer who followed the trajectory by referring to latitude and longitude lines fixed on Earth would say the bullet was deflected westward. If he insisted on using Newton's laws in his rotating reference system, he would need to invent a force to account for the westward deflection. This is the Coriolis force. See also CORIOLIS ACCELERATION.—*S. K.*

CORONA: a ring of faintly colored light which often surrounds the Sun or Moon as seen through thin clouds. The corona, usually steel-blue inside and pink outside with a narrow white zone between, is produced by diffraction of light by the small water droplets of the cloud. The word is used also to denote certain forms of AURORA.—*D. H. L.*

CORONA, SOLAR: see SUN.

CORONAGRAPH: a type of telescope especially designed for observing the solar corona (see SUN). The corona, being only about 1/100 the brightness of clear sky near the Sun, is visible without special equipment only during a total eclipse. A coronagraph (invented by B. Lyot, 1930) produces an "artificial eclipse" by interposing an occulting disk at the image of the Sun formed by the objective lens of the telescope. The much fainter light from the corona passes around the disk and is then collected by appropriate optical parts. Coronagraphs are operated at high altitudes, where the sky is clear and dust-free. Coronal light is further separated from sky light, and analyzed, by using the coronagraph in conjunction with a spectrograph, a monochromatic filter, or a polarimeter. —*D. E. B. and L. H.*

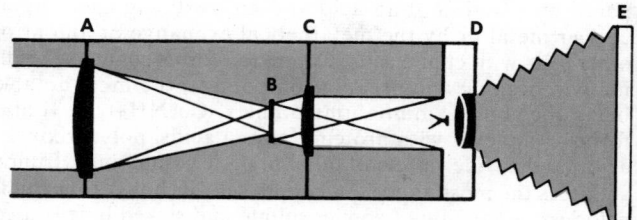

Design of coronagraph: Eclipse of Sun by Moon is simulated by interposing disk *B* (representing Moon) between objective *A* and field lens *C*. Camera lens *D* forms image of solar corona on photographic plate *E*. Additional specialized optical parts are required.

CORPUSCULAR THEORY: a theory of the nature of LIGHT, dating from the time of Democritus (5th cent. B. C.), the first "atomist" on record. Democritus assumed that luminous sources and visible objects emitted streams of particles, each a "replica" of the corresponding portion of the source. Later, Sir Isaac Newton revived what he then called the corpuscular theory of light and used it to explain REFLECTION and, with somewhat poorer success, REFRACTION. The corpuscular theory prevailed for some time in spite of attack by such men as Christian Huyghens (1629–95), who proposed the wave theory of light. It was not until the beginning of the 19th cent. that the wave theory became solidly established, because it was essential to an understanding of INTERFERENCE and DIFFRACTION of light, which had then been first observed. In a limited sense, the modern QUANTUM THEORY is slightly reminiscent of the corpuscular hypothesis, but, of course, a quantum is a packet of energy rather than matter.—*A. E.*

CORRELATION (geology): the determination of equivalence of strata (see STRATIGRAPHY). Two types of correlation are recognized. The first, lithostratigraphic correlation, is based on the lithology (composition) and stratigraphic position of a unit, and constitutes recognition of the same continuous unit at different places. Such a unit may or may not be of the same geologic age at all points, and cannot be traced beyond the limits of the local depositional basin. The second type, biostratigraphic correlation, is based on the use of index FOSSILS, and establishes equivalence of geologic age of separate and often dissimilar deposits. Biostratigraphic correlations are not limited areally, and are used to establish synchroneity of deposition between distant areas, or even between the various continents. (See diagram on next page.)—*W. Ha.*

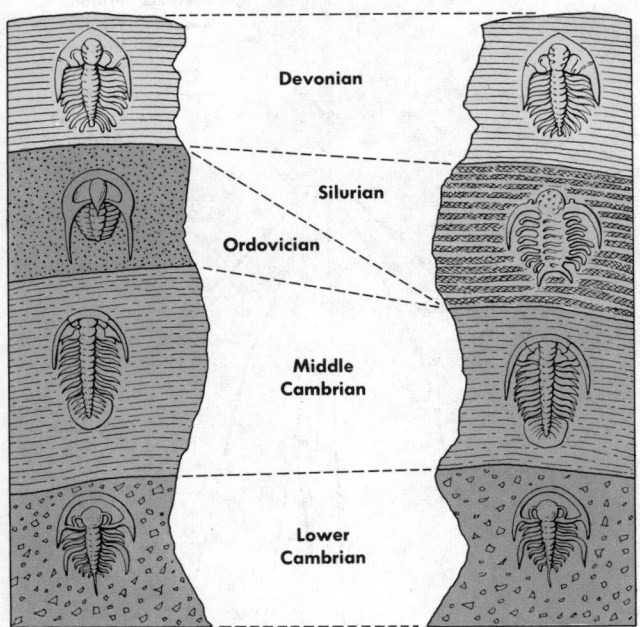

Use of index fossils in geological correlation: Equivalence of fossils establishes equivalence of strata in the face of seemingly disparate sequences or misleadingly similar lithology. Clue to missing strata—Silurian missing at left, Ordovician at right—is given here by series of fossil trilobites.

CORRELATION COEFFICIENT: see STATISTICS.

CORROSION: slow destruction of a substance by chemical action at its surface. This is distinguished from *erosion,* an analogous disintegration by mechanical action. The corrosion of metals, *e.g.* iron, may be regarded as a reversion to a more stable, compound form. Iron is rarely found free in nature, but is laboriously extracted from its compounds. Some metals rapidly form a protective surface film when their surfaces are exposed; *e.g.* aluminum develops an aluminum oxide coat which is tough and adherent. Iron's oxide coat, however, is friable and flakes off as rust. An electrochemical theory of metallic corrosion postulates that at a certain area of a metal's surface (due to impurity, strain, or other cause) metal atoms lose electrons and the area becomes an *anode.* The electrons flow in the metal to an area that accepts them, which becomes a *cathode.* Electrolytic cells are set up if the air contains moisture which can form an aqueous film on the metal surface. If the metal is iron, iron goes into solution at the anode as positive ions (Fe^{++}) which combine with oxygen to form iron oxides, or rust. Corrosion can be stopped by applying an organic coating such as paint, with which metals will not react electrically. In the process known as galvanizing, a coat of zinc is applied to iron or steel. Zinc gives up electrons more readily than iron (see ELECTROMOTIVE SERIES); hence, if corrosion conditions develop, the zinc becomes the anode of the resulting electrolytic cell, and zinc ions go into solution rather than iron ions. This is called *cathodic protection* because iron, forming the cathode of the system, is protected from corrosion at the expense of zinc. Magnesium or aluminum are sometimes used in place of zinc.—*Ru. M.*

CORTICOSTERONE: see HORMONES (chart).

CORTISONE: a steroid hormone secreted by the outer covering or cortex of the adrenal gland upon stimulation by adrenocorticotrophin (see HORMONES). Isolated in crystalline form from beef adrenal gland extracts in 1935, it was first

synthesized in 1944. Cortisone is used to treat many diseases involving inflammation of tissues, *e.g.* rheumatoid arthritis, acute gout, skin diseases, severe allergies. It is effective in treating conditions caused by adrenal cortical insufficiency, *i.e.* inability to maintain the proper body equilibrium of sugars, sodium, chloride, and water, and to make adjustments in blood circulation following stress. It is also useful in treatment of some forms of cancer, particularly acute leukemia. In man, administration of cortisone at higher than physiological levels may be accompanied by undesirable side effects. See also STEROLS.—*E. H.*

CORUNDUM: the mineral species which includes rubies, sapphires, and many other color variants of aluminum oxide, Al_2O_3. Some corundum occurs as a primary mineral in igneous rocks, but most natural corundum was formed by the metamorphism of ALUMINA-rich, silica-deficient rocks such as shales, or by reactions through which "normal" intrusive rocks were de-silicated by silica-poor host-rocks such as peridotites or limestones. The alumina that would ordinarily enter into feldspars and micas was thus freed. At high temperatures, titanium dioxide can enter into the corundum structure, but on cooling is released (exsolved) as needle-like crystals aligned in the hexagonal pattern of the enclosing corundum. Light reflected from these inclusions causes the asterism of star rubies and sapphires. The great hardness (9) of corundum and its resistance to heat and chemicals accounts for its uses in instrument bearings (as "jewels"), REFRACTORIES, and ABRASIVES. Most of the corundum in commercial use and many of the GEMSTONES, even the asteriated stones, are produced synthetically. Rods of synthetic ruby are used in optical MASERS. See MINERAL (table).—*L. M.*

COSMETICS: chemical substances which cleanse, color, or somehow change a person's external appearance to conform to a particular culture's standard of physical beauty. Cosmetics are primarily for the hair, skin, and nails. They appear as creams, powders, suspensions, emulsions, and aqueous or nonaqueous solutions. Cosmetology, the science of external human embellishment, has been practiced since the earliest recorded civilizations, where it was usually associated with medicine, physicians being the personal administrators of cosmetics. In the 15th cent., the French separated cosmetology from medicine, and it became the domain of barbers, pharmacists, hairdressers, and alchemists, who formulated, improved, and applied cosmetics. Around the time of World

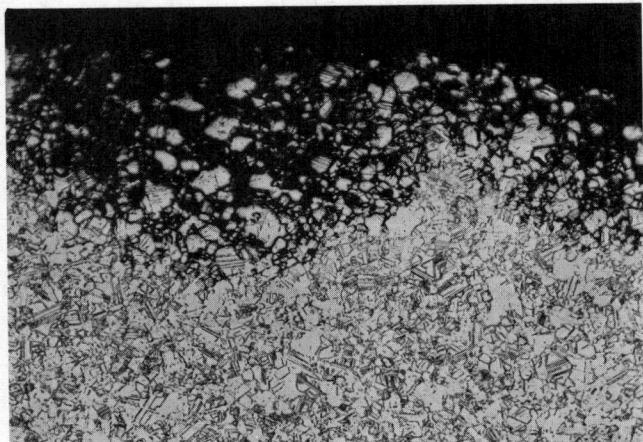

Intergranular corrosion: Microphoto reveals corrosion (dark areas) moving along grain boundaries in sample of alpha brass. (*Bridgeport Brass Co.*)

War I, substantial investments in cosmetic research were made by promoters and manufacturers, especially in the U. S. A., and cosmetics have since become a noticeable factor in the U. S. economy. Today, cosmetic preparation is often an exacting science, having taken over from chemistry advanced methods of purification, testing, and measurements. The ingredients of cosmetics are as varied as their uses. Inorganic salts and some minerals, in addition to a wide variety of organic substances, are formulated to produce a cosmetic preparation for a given purpose. The organic substituents include oils, fats, waxes, surface-active agents, soaps, paraffins, gums, resins, alcohols, esters, starches, dyes, and other substances, both natural and synthetic. Acids, alkalies, water, hydrogen peroxide, and metallic salts are some of the inorganic substituents. Colors are either inorganic pigments or synthetic organic dyes. Skin- and hair-coloring agents of various shades and stabilities are also available in various mediums determined by sales objectives. Mechanical devices used to impart cosmetic effects, *e.g.* hair curlers or razor blades, are also referred to as cosmetics. The ingredients of cosmetics have been strictly regulated by the Federal Food, Drug and Cosmetic Act of 1938.—*G. W. M.*

COSMIC DUST: see INTERSTELLAR MATTER.

COSMIC RAYS: high-energy RADIATION arriving on Earth from outer space. Primary cosmic rays, which penetrate the high atmosphere, contain mostly protons, with a mixture of a variety of atomic nuclei, and perhaps a few very-high-energy gamma rays, and electrons. They are quickly modified by collision with atomic nuclei in the atmosphere. The resulting radiations observed in the lower atmosphere (secondary cosmic rays) are composed of many fundamental particles, including electrons, neutrons, muons, and diverse kinds of mesons, some of which are very short-lived.

Discovery: It had been known for a long time that well-insulated, unevacuated electroscopes slowly lose their charges. This leakage was traced to a very weak conductivity on the part of the gas surrounding the electrically charged parts of the instruments. The conductivity was caused by the presence of mobile charged atomic particles called ions. Since ions were known to be produced by x-rays and by radiation from radioactive substances, it was reasonable to suppose that the leakage of electroscopes was due to ionizing radiation present naturally in the atmosphere. Experiments made by V. F. Hess in 1910 during balloon flights at high altitudes showed that the radiation increased considerably with altitude and could only originate from sources outside of the atmosphere. The name cosmic rays was coined by R. A. Millikan in 1927.

Instrumentation: Instruments used for the detection and study of cosmic rays are all based on the rays' ability to produce ions in the matter they traverse. In the ionization chamber, the current carried by these ions between two electrodes in a gas is measured; the size of the current depends upon the intensity of the radiation. The sensitivity of this instrument is too low for the detection of single particles, the detection of which is accomplished by the Geiger-Müller tube in which single ion pairs, created in the space between a cylindrical electrode and an axial wire, trigger a temporary discharge. By the simultaneous use of several COUNTERS it is possible to follow the trajectories of single cosmic-ray particles through great thicknesses of matter. CLOUD CHAMBERS, BUBBLE CHAMBERS, and spark chambers go even further in the analyses of the rays, whose tracks are visible through droplets, bubbles, or sparks formed along the lines of ions created in gases or liquids. Scintillators make use of light produced by the recombination of ions after the passage of the cosmic particles, or of the Cherenkov radiation created by charged particles of

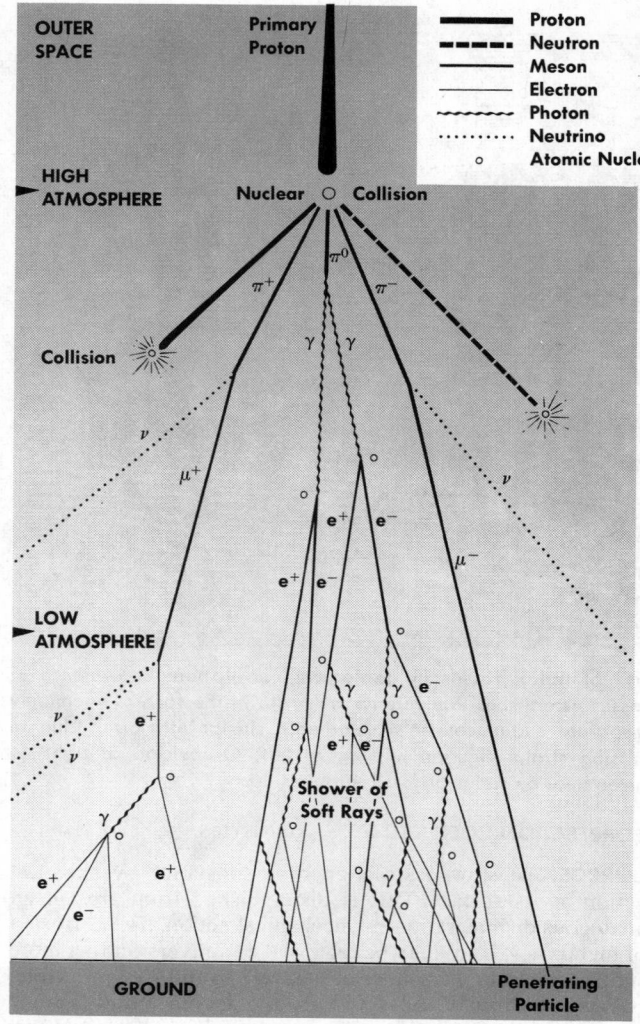

Primary cosmic particle from Sun or galactic space shatters the nucleus of a nitrogen or oxygen atom in the upper atmosphere, bringing forth a shower of secondary particles—notably charged pions, which disintegrate into muons. The lower atmosphere is traversed by a dense fallout of low-energy material—photons, electrons, and gamma radiation.

very high velocity. One of the most fruitful methods of studying cosmic rays uses photographic emulsion, where the tracks appear as lines of silver grains.

Nature of Rays: Cosmic rays were first supposed to be of the nature of very-short-wavelength gamma rays (electromagnetic waves), but they were shown by experiments with counters (Kolhörster) and with cloud chambers (D. Skobelzyn) to contain high-energy charged particles. The energy of these particles could then be measured by the simultaneous use of cloud chambers and magnetic fields, and was found to reach many millions of electron volts. Studies with emulsions and cloud chambers proved the presence, in addition to electrons and gamma rays, of protons, neutrons, and a number of new particles, which decay after a short lifetime and produce lighter particles. Such particles are necessarily of a secondary nature, produced when the primary particles incoming from outer space toward the high atmosphere collide with atomic nuclei in the air or in the matter surrounding the apparatus. Extensive work with emulsions and counters carried up in the high atmosphere by balloons or rockets have shown that the primaries consist essentially of bare nuclei of light elements, mostly hydrogen.

Among the numerous elementary particles found in addition to the protons and neutrons in the secondary radiation, the pi-mesons (pions), mu-mesons (muons), positive and negative electrons, and photons (gamma rays) play the principal role. In conversion of primaries to secondaries, the first event is generally a collision between a high-energy proton and the nucleus of an atom of the atmosphere. Protons, neutrons, and pions are produced and, much more rarely, some heavy elementary particles (heavy mesons, hyperons). The pions can be neutral or charged. The secondary protons and neutrons can produce new collisions and are finally slowed down. The charged pions mostly decay in flight (lifetime 2.5×10^{-8} sec), each producing one muon with the same charge and one neutrino. The muons show very little interaction with atomic nuclei, and penetrate great thicknesses of matter (some are still detectable underground in deep mines); they finally decay (lifetime 2.2×10^{-6} sec) into one electron and two neutrinos. The neutral pions decay immediately (lifetime 10^{-15} sec) into two photons. The photons and electrons resulting from the decay processes mentioned produce new electrons and new photons (B. Rossi, P. M. S. Blackett). The repetition of these two processes results in a more or less thick shower.

Energy; Intensity: Study of the secondary particles (mostly electrons and muons) and of the curvature of their tracks in magnetic fields has made it possible to measure their energies, which cover a large spectrum extending to very high values. The highest energies registered so far in any atomic process are those of the primaries responsible for very large showers, progressively built up through the atmosphere, containing many millions of particles and covering an area of several acres when they strike the ground. Some giant showers (Auger-showers, 1938) correspond to energies up to billions of billions of electron volts. But the energies of the bulk of the primary particles lie in the region of a few hundred million to ten billion volts. These particles are strongly deviated by the magnetic field of Earth before reaching the atmosphere, causing variations in the intensity of cosmic radiation with latitude; and since primary particles are mostly protons (positively charged), and the magnetic field points north, more particles are bent toward the east, and thus more come from the west than from the east. At sea level, the number of particles per square inch per minute is of the order of 10 to 20; this number increases rapidly with altitude.

Origin: Some primary cosmic rays in the lower energy range originate in the Sun, as shown by the coincidence of some changes in intensity of the radiation with solar phenomena such as flares. But the sources of the more energetic cosmic particles are still unknown. According to some theories these particles are accelerated by interaction with variable magnetic fields in space; other theories relate them to the violent star explosions creating supernovas. The fact that primary cosmic rays seem to arrive in equal numbers from the different parts of the sky can be explained, even in the hypothesis of discrete sources, by the strong deviation of their trajectories in the magnetic fields of the galaxy. It is even believed that the action of these fields can trap the particles inside the galaxy for millions of years, this making the cosmic radiation more intense and less directional.—*P. A.*

COSMOLOGY: the study of the astronomical universe as a whole and as a physical system. Man's efforts throughout history to understand the origin and structure of the universe began with the crude but highly imaginative efforts of cosmogonic myths, *e.g.* the Babylonian *Enuma Elish,* and culminate in the recent advances of scientific cosmology. While some significant strides in the scientific approach were made

centuries ago, by William Herschel, Immanuel Kant, Isaac Newton, H. Olbers, and others, it was not until the early decades of the present century that cosmology became a fully developed science, actively pursued by astronomers and physicists. Instrumental resources of the observational astronomer now include radio telescopes as well as the more conventional but powerful optical telescopes, *e.g.* the 200-in. Hale telescope on Palomar Mt. The use of artificial earth satellites or moon-stationed observatories will likely afford man an unprecedented view of the depths of the universe.

Beginning in 1924 with the epoch-making disclosures of Edwin Hubble, using the Mt Wilson 100-in. reflector, the current conception of the universe as constituted of galaxies and clusters of galaxies as its main units became firmly established. This conclusion was first made possible with the settlement of the fact that the galaxies (extragalactic nebulas) are vast systems of stars, gas, and dust that lie beyond our own Galaxy, the Milky Way system. Observation establishes the roughly homogeneous distribution of the galaxies: when large volumes of space are considered and local irregularities are "smoothed out," the galaxies are found to be uniformly distributed and thus do not give evidence of forming part of some supersystem. Furthermore, the galaxies show the remarkable property that the greater their distance, the greater the RED-SHIFT in their spectra. According to the Doppler principle, this means that the galaxies are receding from one

In early cosmology, phenomena were explained through relations among the divinities. In this cast of a 350 B. C. relief at Saqqara, Nut, benevolent goddess of the celestial vault, arches her back protectively over Earth; the solar disk, seen in three successive positions, crosses a field of barely legible stars along her flank. In the cosmological model of the priests of Heliopolis, a self-created author of the universe had produced the god of the air and his wife, the spirit of moisture. They, in turn, had given birth to Nut. (*Metropolitan Museum of Art*)

another with velocities proportional to their distances. This observationally established result (up to half the velocity of light) lends support to the idea of an expanding universe.

Meanwhile from the side of mathematical physics a variety of models of the universe have been developed to interpret the findings of the astronomer and to help guide him in the search for fresh data. Such models are conceptual tools devised by the physicist on the basis of the best available physical theory or ones specially constructed for such purpose, for understanding the distribution of matter and motion in the universe. The initial effort in this direction was made in 1917 by Einstein, who showed how one can use the field equations of the general theory of relativity for constructing a model of the universe that is spatially finite and unbounded. Since that early but now superseded proposal, other models have been developed both within the framework of general relativity theory and independently of it. The researches of A. Friedmann, W. DeSitter, G. Lemaître, A. S. Eddington, H. P. Robertson, R. C. Tolman, and G. C. McVittie were important in developing the resources of relativistic cosmology and particularly in the construction of various forms of expanding-universe models. E. A. Milne in the 1930's developed a kinematic model of the universe which dispensed with general relativity theory and stressed the use of an *a priori* deductive approach. In 1948 H. Bondi and T. Gold introduced the radically novel conception of a STEADY-STATE universe with a continuous creation of matter in an elemental form in an amount that compensates for the drifting apart of the galaxies. These ideas were subsequently developed by F. Hoyle and D. W. Sciama. According to the steady-state theory, the universe has an infinite time scale and consequently cannot be said to have developed from some singular state in the finite past. The idea on the other hand that the universe has evolved from an original state of highly superdense matter (the BIG BANG THEORY) is favored by such evolutionary models of relativistic cosmology as those of Lemaître and G. Gamow, who undertake thereby to determine the "age" of the universe. For many cosmologists, studies of QUASI-STELLAR RADIO SOURCES indicate that the big bang theory is sound.—*M. K. M.*

COTTON: the name given to various species of the Gossypium family of plants. Cotton was probably first grown in the Indus Valley, but it is now cultivated in many areas of the world between 47°N and 30°S lat. Production methods depend on climate, soil type, water supply, and topography; in the U. S. A., planting time varies from February in the South to June in the North. Cultivating and harvesting, which in the past required much manual labor, is now often done by machines. The mature cotton bolls, formed on the ovary of the flower, are harvested and brought to the gin, where the hairlike fibers on the seeds are removed. The removed cotton lint is graded on the basis of such characteristics as the length of fibers, their color, maturity, uniformity, strength, and fineness. The short linters left on the seeds are also removed; they are used in making batting, felts, and absorbent cotton, and in the manufacture of high-quality paper and rayon. The ginned seeds are dehulled and the meats crushed to produce oil and meal for foods and animal feed supplements. Of the world's 1960–61 crop of 46.9 million 500-lb bales, nearly one third—14.3 million bales—came from the U. S. A. The estimated value of 1960 cotton and cottonseed production in the U. S. A. was $2,395,000,000. Cotton fibers are manufactured into all types of apparel, household, and industrial textile products. The utility and esthetic qualities of cotton fabrics are often enhanced by special finishes which impart such properties as ease-of-care, wash-and-wear, water repellency, and flame, mildew, and rot resistance.—*W. P. C.*

COULOMB, CHARLES AUGUSTIN DE, 1736–1806; French engineer and physicist; b. Angouleme. He used the torsion balance (invented by J. Michell, improved by H. Cavendish) to measure very small forces. Among his memoirs on these researches, published in *Histoire et mémoires* of the French Academy of Sciences, the most famous are two on electrostatic forces (1785), verifying the inverse-square law for electrostatics (COULOMB'S LAW). This work made possible the definition of *quantity of electric charge.* One unit of charge, the *coulomb,* is named in his honor.—*D. H. D. R.*

Charles Augustin de Coulomb
(N. Y. Public Library)

COULOMB'S LAW: a fundamental principle of ELECTROSTATICS, formulated by Charles Augustin de Coulomb. He verified this law by varying the magnitudes of electric charges and the distance between them, and measuring the relative forces with a torsion balance. The law states that the force of attraction (between unlike charges) or repulsion (between like charges) is proportional to the product of the magnitudes of the charges and inversely proportional to the square of the distance between them. In algebraic terms,

$$F = K\frac{Q_1 Q_2}{D^2},$$

where F is the force between two small spherical bodies carrying charges Q_1 and Q_2 respectively, which are separated by distance D between their centers. The constant K depends on the choice of units for F, D, and Q. If F is in dynes, D in centimeters, and Q_1 and Q_2 are in electrostatic units, K is equal to 1; if F is in newtons, D in meters, and Q_1, Q_2 in coulombs, K is numerically equal to 9×10^9. To describe the net force between two charges immersed in a DIELECTRIC medium, the law is sometimes written with a factor κ (the dielectric constant) in the denominator.

Coulomb also verified the analogous law for the forces between two well-localized magnetic poles. It, too, is an inverse-square law: the force between two poles varies directly with the product of the pole strengths and inversely with the square of the distance separating them.—*H. Sw.*

COUNTER: any device that enumerates a sequence of similar events. An automobile speedometer (odometer) is a common example of a mechanical counter. Electronic counters are used to count signals too close together for mechanical counters to follow (see AUTOMATION; COMPUTER). Radiation counters, *e.g.* the Geiger-Müller counter, indicate the intensity of radioactivity by counting the number of subatomic particles (*e.g.* electrons) emitted by a specimen. Essentially, the Geiger-Müller counter is a positively charged wire surrounded by a negatively charged cylinder. An electron shooting through the cylinder will knock off another electron from one of the gas molecules surrounding it. This process continues until an "avalanche" of negatively charged electrons falls to the positively charged wire and, similarly, an avalanche of positively charged ions to the negatively charged cylinder, producing an electrical pulse. A more accurate device is the scintillation counter, in which each alpha particle, as it strikes a zinc-sulfide screen, produces a flash. Because of the great number of flashes per sec, electronic devices are needed to do the actual counting. See COINCIDENCE (ANTI-COINCIDENCE) COUNTING; SCINTILLATION.—*A. L.*

COUNTING: see ARITHMETIC.

COUNTRY ROCK: in geology, the pre-existing rock in a region that is penetrated by intrusions of igneous material.

COURTSHIP: see MATING AND COURTSHIP BEHAVIOR.

CRAB NEBULA: a faint, oval, gaseous nebula visible in small telescopes in the constellation Taurus. Photographs show its intricate filamentary structure, and polarization measurements demonstrate the presence of internal magnetic fields. The nebula is the third-strongest radio source, its radio emission resulting probably from radiation produced by electrons spiraling at high speed around the magnetic lines of force. The nebula itself appears to be the after-effect of a supernova explosion observed A. D. 1054 principally by Chinese scholars. It is at a distance from the Sun of about 4,000 lt-yr and appears to be expanding at a rate of 1,300 km/sec. Some astrophysicists consider this nebula to be the source of most cosmic rays observed on Earth.—*B. J. B.*

CRAFTS, JAMES MASON, 1839–1917, U. S. chemist and educator; b. Boston, Mass. He moved to Paris (1874) and devoted his time to research in chemistry, publishing more than 135 papers, many with C. Friedel. Together they studied the use of aluminum chloride in organic syntheses, discovering the FRIEDEL-CRAFTS REACTION (1877). Professor of organic chemistry at Mass. Inst. of Tech. from 1892, he was president 1898–1900, then engaged in research on catalysis and thermometry. He was a member of the National Academy of Sciences.—*D. H. D. R.*

CREATININE: an excretory product of human metabolism. Next to urea it is the major basic nitrogenous constituent of urine. It is derived from creatine phosphate by spontaneous ring formation (see TRANSMETHYLATION; ENOL PHOSPHATE):

$$H_2N—C=N—\overset{\overset{O}{\|}}{P}—OH \longrightarrow H_2N—C=N$$
$$CH_3—N—CH_2—COOH \qquad CH_3—N—CH_2$$
$$\longrightarrow \;\; C=O + H_3PO_4$$

Creatine phosphate   Creatinine

Creatine phosphate serves to store energy in muscle cells and is constant in concentration. It breaks down to creatinine at a constant rate; thus, excretion of creatinine is proportional to the muscle mass of an individual and is not affected by diet or urine volume.—*J. F. S.*

CREEP (physics): time-dependent deformation of a material under constant load or stress. First systematic studies were made, 1914, by E. N. daC. Andrade (1887–   ). In aeronautical engineering, creep is especially significant in materials at high temperatures. The phenomenon is not clearly understood, but three phases are generally recognized: the primary, or transient; the secondary, or steady; and the tertiary. The secondary phase, normally the significant one, is best described by an empirical law in which creep rate is proportional to the *n*th power of the stress. The exponent *n* depends on material and temperature. For aluminum at ordinary temperatures $n = 3$.—*W. Ho.*

CREOSOTE: a colorless or yellow-brown liquid with antiseptic properties, used to preserve wood and control putrefaction. It is a distillation product of wood tar, coal tar, and petroleum tar (see PHENOLS).—*Ru. M.*

CREPUSCULAR RAYS: the fan-shaped pattern of dark bands sometimes seen in the western sky a few minutes after sunset, or in the eastern sky before sunrise. The bands are the shadows cast upon hazy air by towering clouds beyond the horizon. The fan shape is an illusion due to perspective.—*D. H. L.*

CRETACEOUS PERIOD: see MESOZOIC ERA; GEOLOGICAL TIME CHART.

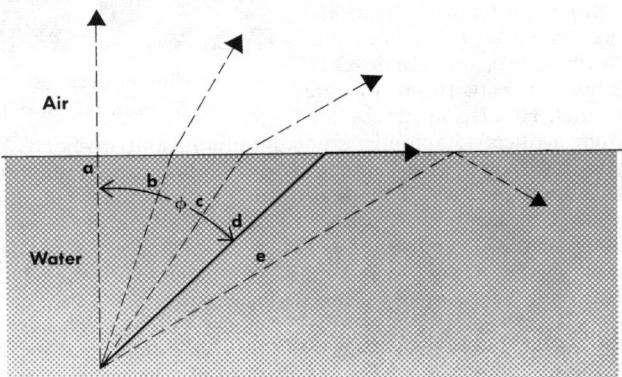

The angle ϕ here is the critical angle for rays of light passing from the optically dense to the optically rare medium.

CRITICAL ANGLE: the minimum or limiting angle at which a ray of light, proceeding from an optically dense to an optically rare medium, can be totally reflected from the boundary separating the two media. The figure shows light rays *a, b,* and *c* passing from water into air and bent toward the surface in accordance with Snell's law (see REFRACTION OF LIGHT). The limiting ray is one marked *d,* which strikes the interface at the *critical angle* ϕ and grazes the surface on its way out. A more oblique ray, such as *e,* does not emerge at all and is *totally reflected* as shown. The sine of the critical angle (measured from the normal, or perpendicular, to the surface) is equal to the reciprocal of the *index of refraction,* or $\sin \phi = 1/\mu$.—*S. Br.*

CRITICAL MASS: the mass of fissionable material (uranium or plutonium) that must be incorporated in a nuclear device to achieve a CHAIN REACTION. In the fission of a heavy element, two medium-weight nuclei and a number of neutrons are released in addition to a quantity of energy. Each of the neutrons is theoretically capable of causing the fission of another heavy nucleus; however, a number of them leak out of the reactor, others are absorbed in its shielding, and some are moving at velocities either too high or too low to achieve fission. If a chain reaction is to take place, enough fissionable material must be present so that (on the average) one of the neutrons yielded by each fission must cause another fission. If the design of the device is proper, and sufficient fissionable material is available, the fission reaction will be self-sustaining and will continue at a constant rate; if there is less fissionable material in the device than this critical amount, the reaction will die down exponentially; if there is more, the reaction will accelerate exponentially.—*E. M. R.*

CRITICAL TEMPERATURE AND PRESSURE: Experiment shows that if a gas at a sufficiently low temperature is compressed, it will ultimately liquefy. For every gas, however, there is a *critical temperature* above which it cannot be liquefied, regardless of the pressure exerted on it. The lowest pressure that will liquefy a gas at its critical temperature is called the *critical pressure.*—*J. E. W.*

CROOKES, SIR WILLIAM, 1832–1919, English physicist and chemist; b. London. He discovered and isolated thallium (1861), and a by-product of this research led to his invention of the radiometer. In studying electrical discharges through a rarefied gas he developed the CROOKES TUBE and elaborated his theory of "radiant matter." In 1883 he began investigations of rare earths. He also produced mi-

Sir William Crookes
(London Stereoscopic Society)

nute artificial diamonds, studied radium, and invented the spinthariscope (used in studying α-radiation) and a glass for shielding the eyes of workers from rays emitted by molten glass. Crookes was the author of *Select Methods in Chemical Analysis* (1871) and other works on chemistry. He was a fellow of the Royal Society and an associate of the U. S. National Academy of Sciences.—*S. B.*

CROOKES TUBE: a gaseous-discharge tube first used by Sir William Crookes (c. 1879). It consisted of a vessel of glass or other insulating material that had at least two metal electrodes sealed through the walls. When the tube was partially evacuated and an adequate voltage was applied to two of the electrodes, a glow discharge appeared in the tube (see ARCS AND DISCHARGES). The device is generally called a discharge tube today.—*R. V.*

CROSS SECTION (physics): If a beam of particles or radiation is incident on matter, one or more kinds of interaction may occur, *e.g.* scattering, absorption, ionization, or capture. The probability of such interaction per particle (atom, nucleus, electron, or molecule) of the "target" is expressed as an area, called the *cross section*. For example, if n_0 is the number of incident particles per unit area per unit time striking n_t target particles, and N is the number of reactions per unit time, the cross section is $N/n_0 n_t$. For nuclear processes, the accepted unit for expressing cross sections is 10^{-24} cm², commonly called the "barn." A knowledge of the cross section and consequently of the rate of reaction is of prime importance in the design of nuclear reactors, where fission is produced by the bombardment of uranium[235] by neutrons.—*P. T. D. and F. J. E.*

CRUCIAL EXPERIMENT: a term derived from the idea of Francis Bacon that when two conflicting hypotheses are about equally confirmed, an experiment can be devised that will decide between them. Thus in the 19th cent. it was believed that the experiments of Fizeau and Foucault, which showed by direct measurement that the velocity of light in water is less than in empty space, disposed of the corpuscular theory of light in favor of the wave theory. To avoid over-simplification in the use of this idea, one must remember both that an experiment, being a particular, can only confirm a general hypothesis, never prove it, and also that a disconfirmation only shows that there is something wrong, somewhere, with the material which has led to the mistaken prediction, but cannot actually pinpoint it down to the hypothesis which alone, supposedly, is being tested.—*H. T.*

CRUIKSHANK, WILLIAM CUMBERLAND, 1745–1800, British anatomist; b. Edinburgh. He is known principally for his research (with W. Hunter) on the lymphatic system, published in *The Anatomy of the Absorbing Vessels of the Human Body* (1786). He was a fellow of the Royal Society.—*D. H. D. R.*

CRUSTACEAN: any animal of the class Crustacea, a major group of ARTHROPODS. The group is divided into about 30 orders, with over 25,000 species. Most familiar are the shrimps, lobsters, and crabs, all in the order Decapoda. The other orders include fairy shrimps, water fleas, fishlice, barnacles, woodlice, sandhoppers, mantis shrimps, and many others, mostly without English names. Crustaceans occur in almost every type of aquatic habitat, from small puddles to ocean depths. There are species even in underground waters, hot springs, and brine pools. On land not so many species occur, but woodlice abound under logs, land crabs may climb mountains, and coconut crabs climb trees.

Anatomically, crustaceans are unique in having two pairs of antennae, the second pair biramous (forked). The head also bears a pair of mandibles and two pairs of maxillae, both being mouth parts used in eating. There are one to three eyes, the lateral ones with many facets and often on movable stalks. The trunk usually is segmented and typically is divided into thorax and abdomen. Often an integumental fold, or carapace, projects back from the head to enclose much or all of the thorax. There may be up to 60 pairs of trunk limbs, often biramous, of different form on the two parts of the body.

The eggs of crustaceans generally are carried by the female until they hatch, usually as free-swimming larvae. At hatching, the larva often has only three pairs of limbs and is then known as a nauplius. The crustacean cuticle, or exoskeleton, is tough and often calcified, so that growth requires a series of molts. Attainment of the adult form is by a gradual or sudden metamorphosis.

In size, crustaceans vary from some small enough to live between sand grains to others, such as the Japanese spider crab, with a leg span of about 10 ft. Most species are expert in one or more types of locomotion, *e.g.* swimming, creeping, walking, running, jumping, climbing, or burrowing. Many are filter-feeders, straining out tiny particles from the water. Others are herbivores, scavengers, or predators, consuming larger food. Many species, of various orders, have become parasites, sometimes so modified as to be recognizable as crustaceans only from their larvae.

The economic importance of crustaceans is not restricted to the fish market. Copepods and others are vital in the FOOD CHAIN that links minute aquatic plants to fish and to whales. Shells of fossil ostracods are used for dating rocks in oil prospecting. Destructive activities of Crustacea include the fouling of ships by barnacles, destruction of wooden boats and docks by certain isopods, extensive local damage to crops by crayfish and land crabs, undermining of European river banks by the mitten crab, infestation of fish by parasitic forms, and transmission of various parasitic worms to man and domestic animals. See Color Plate 31.—*J. H. L.*

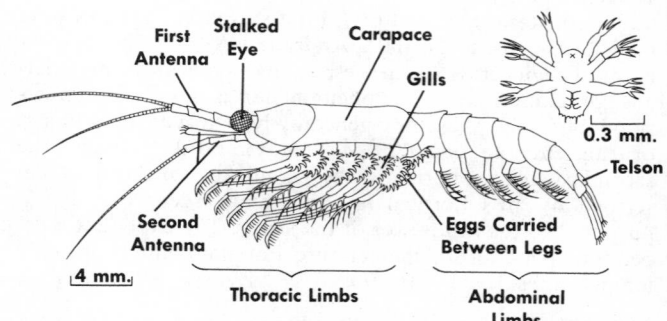

Euphausiid crustacean and its nauplius larva (*upper*). Euphausiids live in open ocean and are the chief food of baleen whales. All antennae and limbs are forked, except first antenna in nauplius.

CRYOGENICS: the techniques of producing very low temperatures. While in principle the term applies to refrigeration generally, it commonly denotes the attainment of the temperature of liquid air (about $-200°$C) and below. To produce such low temperatures, first a coolant is coerced in such a manner that its entropy, *i.e.* degree of statistical disorder, is reduced. This can be achieved, for instance, by the compression of a gas or by application of a magnetic field to certain salts. Heat produced during this coercion is conducted away and not allowed to return to the coolant. When the coercing parameter, *i.e.* the pressure or the magnetizing field, is subsequently reduced to a low value, cooling results. Gases can be used as coolants until the temperature is reached at which they liquefy, *i.e.* the boiling point. This is $20°$K (about $-253°$C) for hydrogen and $4.2°$K for helium. By reducing the vapor pressure over it, liquid helium can be cooled to $0.7°$K. About $0.3°$K can be reached with the rare isotope helium³, and temperatures of about $0.05°$K by changing the concentration in a liquid mixture of helium³ and helium⁴. Temperatures below $0.01°$K can be reached by demagnetization of paramagnetic salts, *e.g.* iron alum. Very recently efforts have been made at reducing the temperature to the order of $10^{-5}°$K $(0.00001°$K) by demagnetization of atomic nuclei.—*K. Me.*

CRYPTOGRAPHY: the art of secret writing, whether in cipher or code, or with invisible inks. *Cryptanalysis,* the solution and reading of cryptic messages, is the constant work of many experts in so-called intelligence agencies throughout the world. A *cryptogram* or *message* is any communication written in cipher or code. The communication that is to be transmitted is called the *clear.* Strictly speaking, cryptography distinguishes between ciphers and codes. In codes, a single word may be used for an entire phrase, and a code book or mechanical device is necessary both to encode and to decode the message. In a cipher, once the key is learned, any message transmitted can be read.

Essentially cryptography is concerned with ciphers, of which there are three major classifications. The *concealment cipher* has the true letters of the message hidden or disguised. Francis Bacon (1561–1626) used mixed fonts of type to conceal the fact that he was using a cipher. The *transposition cipher* takes the letters of the message out of their text order and rearranges them according to a pattern or *key* previously agreed upon by the correspondents. In the *substitution cipher* the original text letters are replaced by substitutes or cipher symbols (letters or numbers) arranged in the same order as the original message. In addition, there are combinations of each of these major types and several forms of each classification. In the substitution cipher, for example, there may be more than one substitution, the first encipherment being in turn enciphered; or, a message may be put in substitution cipher and then re-enciphered by transposition. Such multistep ciphers can be very complicated: a fact well-illustrated by a book attributed to Roger Bacon (1214?–1294), which has never been deciphered. Substitution ciphers are among the most commonly used. But, as Edgar Allan Poe showed in his story *The Gold Bug,* certain letters of the alphabet recur at a known frequency in any given number of words. Thus this form is the simplest to decipher. In ordinary literary English, letters occur in the order shown in this frequency table: e, t, a, o, i, n, s, h, r, d, l, u, c, f, m, p, y, g, w, b, v, k, j, q, x, z. All languages have their own frequency tables. These frequencies can be hidden by using more than one symbol for each letter in the alphabet. The simplest substitution ciphers were first used by the ancient Greeks. The Romans further developed substitution ciphers, and since the Renaissance cryptography has been constantly used by governments, armies, and navies.

The basis of many modern ciphers was originated in Paris by Blaise de Vigenère, about 1570. A method of double substitution, this cipher requires only that sender and receiver memorize an arrangement of letters and a keyword. The letters of the alphabet are arranged in a *tableau,* one form of which is the square array below:

```
A B C D E F G H I J K L M N O P Q R S T U V W X Y Z
B C D E F G H I J K L M N O P Q R S T U V W X Y Z A
C D E F G H I J K L M N O P Q R S T U V W X Y Z A B
D E F G H I J K L M N O P Q R S T U V W X Y Z A B C
E F G H I J K L M N O P Q R S T U V W X Y Z A B C D
F G H I J K L M N O P Q R S T U V W X Y Z A B C D E
G H I J K L M N O P Q R S T U V W X Y Z A B C D E F
H I J K L M N O P Q R S T U V W X Y Z A B C D E F G
I J K L M N O P Q R S T U V W X Y Z A B C D E F G H
J K L M N O P Q R S T U V W X Y Z A B C D E F G H I
K L M N O P Q R S T U V W X Y Z A B C D E F G H I J
L M N O P Q R S T U V W X Y Z A B C D E F G H I J K
M N O P Q R S T U V W X Y Z A B C D E F G H I J K L
N O P Q R S T U V W X Y Z A B C D E F G H I J K L M
O P Q R S T U V W X Y Z A B C D E F G H I J K L M N
P Q R S T U V W X Y Z A B C D E F G H I J K L M N O
Q R S T U V W X Y Z A B C D E F G H I J K L M N O P
R S T U V W X Y Z A B C D E F G H I J K L M N O P Q
S T U V W X Y Z A B C D E F G H I J K L M N O P Q R
T U V W X Y Z A B C D E F G H I J K L M N O P Q R S
U V W X Y Z A B C D E F G H I J K L M N O P Q R S T
V W X Y Z A B C D E F G H I J K L M N O P Q R S T U
W X Y Z A B C D E F G H I J K L M N O P Q R S T U V
X Y Z A B C D E F G H I J K L M N O P Q R S T U V W
Y Z A B C D E F G H I J K L M N O P Q R S T U V W X
Z A B C D E F G H I J K L M N O P Q R S T U V W X Y
```

The clear is written out with the keyword below it, repeated as many times as necessary; thus with the keyword EDGAR, the prepared clear might be:

> READ THE GOLD BUG
> EDGA RED GARE DGA

To encipher the first letter of the clear, the cryptographer finds it in the top row of the square, and follows down its column until he reaches the row commencing with the key letter E. The letter at the intersection of the R column and the E row is V, which is the first letter of the message. The next letter, H, is at the intersection of the E column and the D row. The final message is arranged in groups of five letters to disguise the individual word lengths: VHGDK LHMOC HEAG. The message may also contain *nulls,* meaningless symbols interspersed to confuse an interceptor; and *stops,* symbols to indicate the ends of sentences or words. To decipher the message, the recipient writes the keyword above it, finds the column in the tableau headed by the first key letter, and follows down it until he reaches the first message letter. The first letter of the clear is then read from the first column.

One of the simplest and best ciphers ever devised is the Playfair cipher, based on a keyword. This word is written in the first positions of a five-letter square containing the alphabet, from which "J" is dropped. If the key is SANDWICH, the square is arranged as shown below, with letters that

```
S A N D W
I C H B E
F G K L M
O P Q R T
U V X Y Z
```

are not in the key following those in it. For enciphering, the clear is divided into two-letter groups. When two letters appear in the same column, the letter below each is substituted. When two letters occur in the same line, the letters to the right of each are used, but if the last letter in the line or column appears in the clear, then the first letter of the line or column is used as that after the last. If letters are in neither the same line nor column, the pair at opposite corners of the rectangle for which they form a diagonal are used. Double letters are separated by inserting X or Z. The clear TUNA

SALAD ON RYE would be enciphered as OZDNA NGDSR QDBZ. Electronic means, *e.g.* radio, have also been used for enciphering messages. One such device is a four-channel transmitter which shuffles the message, either in the clear or ciphered, into an unintelligible garble. A rotating switch, synchronized with a similar switch on the transmitter, sorts out the message at the receiver, dividing it into its four previously scrambled parts.

In World War II some field radio messages were enciphered through the use of an ancient underworld method: jargon. Seemingly meaningless words were used in normal sentence structure to convey information or orders. Criminals have, for centuries, used this and other means of encipherment to conceal the meaning of their communications. Other simple methods of encipherment have included the translation of the clear into an obscure language before applying the cipher. In World War II, American Indians engaged in this on the field telephones in the Pacific. Diplomatic codes, no matter how complicated or cleverly conceived, are seldom used for more than six months, even in peacetime, since they are expected to be deciphered by other nations.—*A. P. E.*

CRYSTALLIZATION: spontaneous arrangement of the molecules of a substance into a repetitive orderly array (see CRYSTALLOGRAPHY). Almost all substances solidify in crystalline form whenever the attractive forces between the molecules are strong enough to overcome the disordering influence of their thermal agitation. Glasses and plastics are the principal exceptions, and even those solids show small orderly patches in their disordered structures. Crystallization can proceed directly from the vapor of a substance (*e.g.* snowflakes from moist air), from its liquid state (*e.g.* crystalline from molten metals), from its disordered rigid state (*e.g.* the "devitrification" of a glass), or from its solution in another substance (*e.g.* common salt from salty water). It is convenient to distinguish two stages in all these processes: *nucleation,* the spontaneous formation of submicroscopic nuclei of ordered molecules; and *crystal growth,* the progressive deposition of more molecules on the surfaces of the nuclei, extending the same form of orderliness outward. When a molten metal, for example, cools to its "melting point" (the temperature at which it melts when heated and solidifies when cooled), innumerable nuclei suddenly form, and grow until no metal remains molten (below, left). To say a metal breaks "because it has crystallized" is a mistake, since solid metals are always crystalline. Often, however, the rupture strength of a metal is reduced because it has *recrystallized:* a few of its crystals have slowly grown larger at the expense of many smaller crystals, and the metal can break along the "grain boundaries" between relatively large crystals. Many methods, appropriate to different materials, have been developed for producing large *single crystals,* under the spur of their increasing technological use; thus large single crystals of quartz (see below) are systematically grown from solutions of silica

in alkaline water at 400°C and a pressure of 25,000 lb/in.² for use in PIEZOELECTRIC devices.—*A H.*

CRYSTALLOGRAPHY: the science of precisely describing crystals: their external forms, arrangements of their atoms, the symmetries of their properties, and their manner of aggregation to form the world of solid matter. Strictly it is a branch of applied geometry, not of physics, since it inquires only into forms crystals take, ignoring the physical question of how the forces between atoms determine those forms and properties. But it paints the picture of solid matter which physics must explain (see SOLID STATE PHYSICS) and uses many physical principles and tools, such as X-RAY DIFFRACTION, to produce that picture.

Crystallography started about 1670 with Steno's observation that when crystals of any substance grow unobstructedly they exhibit "natural faces," and, whatever the relative sizes of those faces, the *angles* between corresponding faces are the same on all crystals of the same substance. A century later the abbé Haüy noticed that any crystal of calcite could be cleaved, parallel to some of its natural faces, into rhombohedral blocks, and that all the natural faces on calcite might be constructed if the crystal were made of submicroscopic building blocks shaped like a cleavage block and all of the same size. From measurements of the interfacial angles, appropriate building-block shapes have since been found for thousands of substances, whether or not their crystals exhibit cleavage. The fact that building blocks can always be chosen to possess one of six types of SYMMETRY led, about 1780, to the classification of crystals into *six crystal systems* (Fig. 1). Today the building-block picture of a crystal remains valid, provided a "block" is interpreted as representing a group of atoms. Thus the meaning of crystallinity in physics

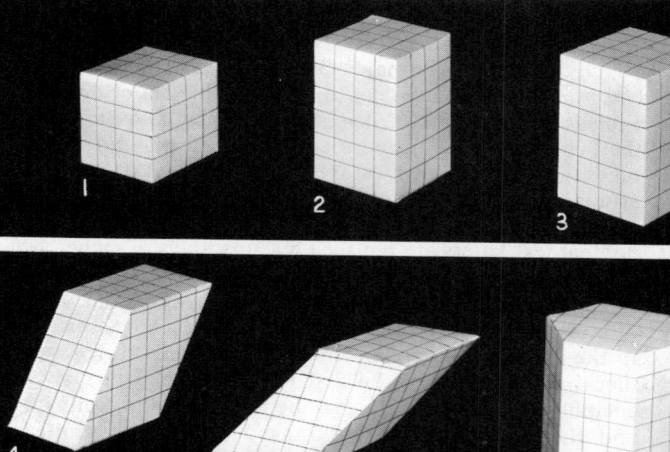

Fig. 1: Any crystal belongs to one of six crystal systems, corresponding with its most symmetrical building block. The blocks are: **(1) Cubic**—All angles are right angles, and all sides are equal. **(2) Tetragonal**—All angles are right angles, and there are two different lengths of sides. **(3) Orthorhombic**—All angles are right angles, and there are three different lengths of sides. **(4) Monoclinic**—Similar to the orthorhombic block but pushed so that eight of its angles are no longer right angles. **(5) Triclinic**—No right angles remain, and there are three different lengths of sides. **(6) Hexagonal**—The vertical sides make right angles with two regular hexagonal faces. (*Bell Telephone Laboratories*)

Nucleation

Quartz Crystals

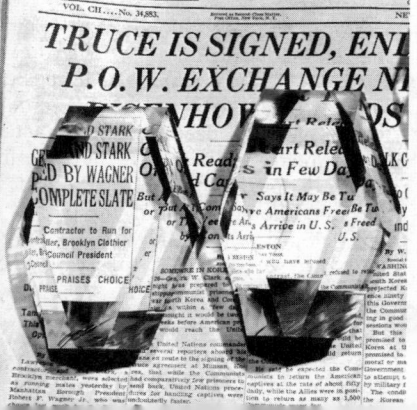

(*Bell Telephone Laboratories*)

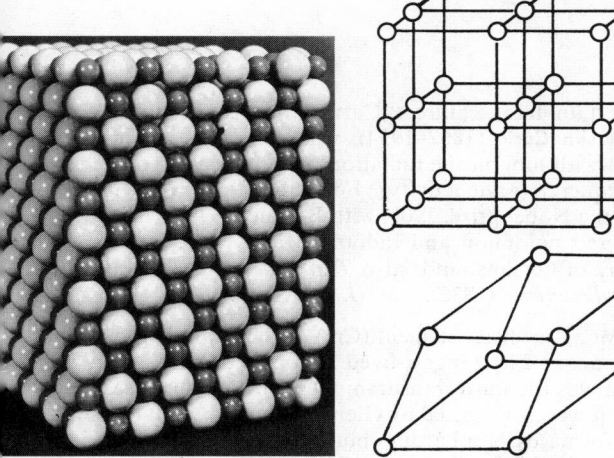

Fig. 2: The orderly array (*above*) of sodium and chloride ions in a crystal of common salt is constructible by repeating a cubic unit cell (*upper right*) or a smaller but less symmetrical rhombohedral unit cell (*lower right*). (*Bell Telephone Laboratories*)

becomes the *repetitive orderly arrangement* of an atomic grouping (Fig. 2). A building block, furnished with its group of atoms, is called a *unit cell*.

Often the natural shape of a crystal is less symmetrical than its appropriate building block, reflecting a less symmetrical arrangement of atoms within the block. For example, sodium bromate grows in regular tetrahedra, which can be built of cubic blocks but have less symmetry than a cube. By mathematical studies of these symmetries, Hessel in 1830 subclassified the six crystal systems into 32 crystal classes.

Since the symmetry of a crystal is determined by the symmetry of the atomic grouping in a unit cell, and since the atomic constitution is responsible for all the physical properties of the crystal, these properties may also reflect that symmetry or asymmetry. For example, the symmetry of quartz does not demand that heat be conducted at the same rate in all directions in the crystal. If a slab is cut from a single crystal of quartz, coated with wax on one side, and heated at one point, the wax will melt away from that point into a pool with an elliptical rather than a circular shape, with the long axis of the ellipse in the direction of greatest heat conduction (Fig. 3). In other words, a single crystal is homogeneous

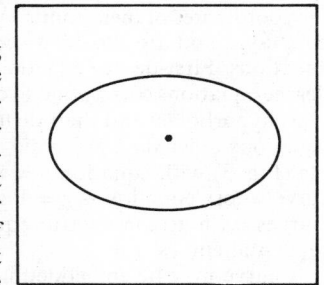

Fig. 3: In de Senarmont's experiment on heat conduction in a quartz crystalline plate, a surface coating of wax melts into an elliptical pool about the point at which heat is supplied.

(the same at all points) but not isotropic (not the same in all directions). Determining the symmetry class to which a crystal belongs thus becomes important for predicting its physical properties. Conversely, an experimental examination of those properties is necessary for determining its symmetry class. Fortunately, the natural growth shape of a crystal—resulting from a single property, the rate of its growth in different directions (Fig. 4)—is usually a reliable embodiment of its symmetry, but often its optical properties, or "etch figures" and "striations" on its surfaces, must also be studied. In 1912 the arrangement of atoms in crystals in repetitive orderliness, theretofore only suspected, was confirmed by the discovery of X-RAY DIFFRACTION, since developed into the principal tool of modern crystallography. With its aid, the size of the building block (usually about one ten-millionth of a centimeter) and the *crystal structure* (the detailed arrangement of the atoms) has been determined for crystals of many substances.

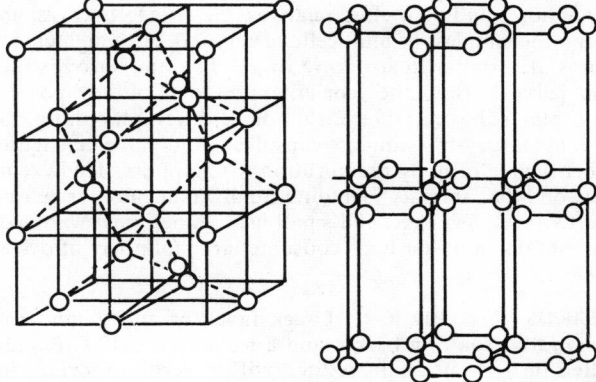

Fig. 5: Carbon adopts two different crystalline arrangements: diamond (*left*) and graphite (*right*).

Diamond and graphite, the two crystal structures adopted by carbon (Fig. 5), provide a simple example of the relation between crystallography, on the one hand, and physics and chemistry. In diamond structure each carbon atom is tightly connected with four others by bonds which stand rigidly toward the four corners of a regular tetrahedron. The three-dimensional network of those bonds assists in giving to diamonds their celebrated hardness. But since the planes perpendicular to those bonds are crossed by a smaller number of bonds per unit area than other planes, the gem-cutter can cleave diamonds into octahedra, by sharp blows on a properly directed chisel. This "tetrahedral bonding," characteristic of the bonds formed by carbon in the ALIPHATIC COMPOUNDS of organic chemistry, leads the chemist to think of a diamond as a single gigantic molecule. In graphite structure, carbon atoms are tightly bonded into plane hexagonal nets, and much weaker forces perpendicular to those planes hold them together. Extremely ready cleavage between those nets is partly responsible for the utility of graphite as a lubricant. The chemist finds carbon bonded in plane hexagonal rings in the AROMATIC COMPOUNDS of organic chemistry.

The picture of a crystal as a regular repetitive array of atoms is an idealized one in two respects. First, the thermal energy of the atoms makes them vibrate constantly in a disorderly way about their orderly positions. Studies by x-ray diffraction are yielding information about the magnitudes and directions of these thermal motions in crystals. Second, the regularity of arrangement in most crystals is marred by relatively stationary defects; *e.g.* unoccupied atomic sites and impurity atoms on or between the sites. Study of these and other defects is yielding an understanding of such properties as the plasticity of metals, and defects are being deliberately

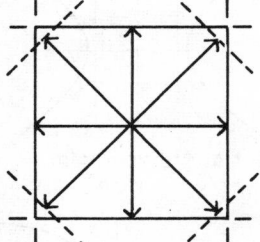 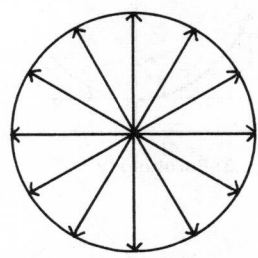

Fig. 4: When the growth rate of a crystal in any direction is represented by the length of an arrow in that direction, the symmetry of the shape of a crystal is seen to correspond with the symmetry of its growth rates. If those rates were the same in all directions, the crystal would grow into a sphere.

created and exploited for such devices as luminescent screens, transistors, and solar batteries.

Extensions of the methods of crystallography are revealing how widely and diversely crystallinity feathers out in nature. Partial crystallinity is evanescent in liquids and frozen in glasses. Natural fibers, and the protein structures of animals, exhibit repetitive atomic orderliness, and some viruses have been crystallized. Indeed crystallography has a role in the biophysical inquiry into genetics and the nature of life.—*A. H.*

CTENOPHORES: a small group (about 80 species) of invertebrate animals with transparent gelatinous bodies that bear eight longitudinal rows of characteristic comb-like plates consisting of fused CILIA. Ctenophores are often called "comb-jellies," "sea walnuts," or "sea gooseberries." They inhabit all oceans, but are found particularly in warm tropical seas. Most species swim in the surface waters, but some occur at depths to 10,000 ft. Many are luminescent (see BIOLUMINESCENCE). Ctenophores and their close relatives, the COELENTERATES, are among the simplest of multicellular animals. Although ctenophores are similar in structure to jellyfish, they are distinct from jellyfish and other coelenterates in that they possess comb plates, have a different mode of development, do not have nematocysts (stinging capsules), and have a slightly higher degree of body organization. Ctenophores feed exclusively on other animals, including small larvae of other marine invertebrates, fish eggs, and small fish. Sometimes swarms of ctenophores in oyster beds consume large numbers of oyster larvae.—*C. F. L.*

CTESIBIUS, fl. *c.* 100 B. C., Greek inventor and engineer of Alexandria; son of a barber and a barber himself. Ctesibius, skilled in hydraulics, is credited with several important inventions, including catapult machines for defensive warfare, the force pump as described in the treatise of Philo, the water organ, and the parastatic water clock. Since none of his treatises has survived, knowledge of his accomplishments has been derived chiefly from the works of his pupil, Philo of Byzantium.—*S. B.*

CUBE: a solid figure bounded by six plane faces that are equal squares. All angles of intersection of faces or edges are right angles. The cube is one of the five regular polyhedrons. Because of the ease of fitting cubes together, the cube provides a natural unit of measure of volume: a unit of volume could simply be an arbitrarily chosen cube. The volume of a solid is the number of replicas of this cube into which it can be subdivided. Even though the form of a solid may be such that not all its subdivisions can be cubical, indirect means are found for obtaining its volume in terms of a given cubical unit. Cubical space or cubical content always means volume. A cubical volume unit has each of its edges one unit long. Consequently, the volume of a cube with edge x units long is $x \times x \times x$, or x^3. The term cube is borrowed to designate the third power: x^3 is "cube of x," or "x cubed." Any polynomial of the third degree is called a cubic expression.

Cubical shapes are utilized for many practical purposes: architectural, artistic, and industrial. The word cubicle means an approximately cube-shaped room. Cubism is a form of modern art in which a variety of three-dimensional geometric forms are used, with the cube playing an important role.—*H. C.*

CULTURE: see BACTERIOLOGY.

CURIE: see RADIATION UNIT.

CURIE, PIERRE, 1859–1906, French physicist; b. Paris. His early researches were on piezoelectricity and magnetism. He discovered that ferromagnetic substances lose their magnetism at a certain temperature ("Curie point"). His wife, **Marie Sklodowska Curie** (1867–1934), whom he married in 1894, worked with him on the radiation phenomena discovered by H. Becquerel (radioactivity). For this research the Curies shared the Nobel prize, 1903, with Becquerel; later the Curies discovered polonium and radium. Marie Curie wrote a biography of her husband; also *Traité de radioactivité* (1910) and *Radioactivité* (1935).—*D. H. D. R.*

CURIUM: an artificial element (Cm) of the actinide group; at. no. 96; at. wt 248 (longest-lived isotope); density about 7.0. Curium was the third transuranium element to be discovered (1944); it was synthesized by Glenn Seaborg *et al.* at the Univ. of California by bombarding plutonium[239] with helium ions in the cyclotron at Berkeley. Curium[248] has a half life of about 500,000 yr; Cm[249], the shortest-lived, a half life of about 1 hr.—*G. W. M.*

CURVES: A plane curve is the boundary separating two parts of a plane, and can be visualized as a path traced by a moving point. A section of such a path is called an arc. From this point of view, a straight line, or a broken line made up of several straight line segments, is a curve. A path whose direction changes gradually is termed curvilinear.

A curve is often described by reference to a coordinate system (see COORDINATE GEOMETRY). A plane curve is a set of points satisfying a condition expressed by an equation in two variable coordinates. For example, the coordinates of the points of the circle with center at the origin and radius r satisfy the equation $x^2 + y^2 = r^2$ (Fig. 1). Curves may then be classified according to the equations which are satisfied by the coordinates of their points. Algebraic curves have algebraic equations, and are classified according to the degrees of their equations. First-degree equations yield straight lines; second-degree equations correspond to conics—circles, ellipses, parabolas, hyperbolas, and their degenerate forms. Curves having equations other than algebraic are *transcendental*. The parabola (Fig. 3) with equation $y = kx^2$ is an algebraic curve; the curve whose equation is $y = \log x$ is transcendental (Fig. 5c). Curves with trigonometric equations are important transcendental curves (Fig. 6).

A curve may be embedded in three dimensions and fail to

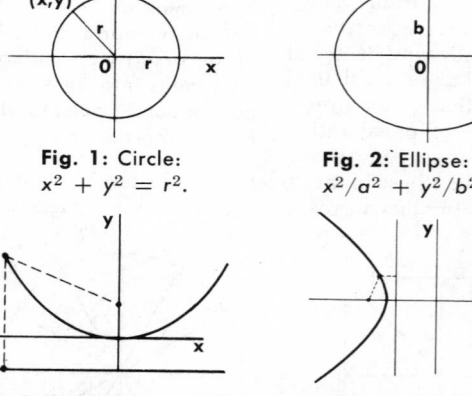

Fig. 1: Circle: $x^2 + y^2 = r^2$.

Fig. 2: Ellipse: $x^2/a^2 + y^2/b^2 = 1$.

Fig. 3: Parabola: $y = kx^2$.

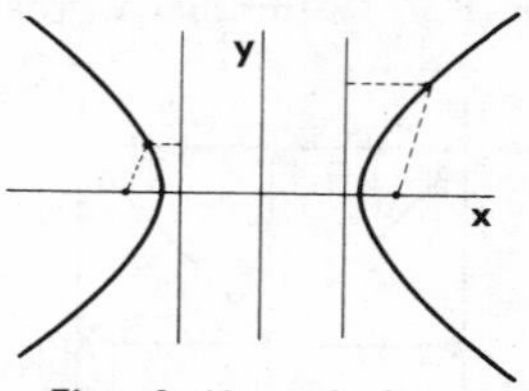

Fig. 4: Hyperbola: $x^2/a^2 - y^2/b^2 = 1$.

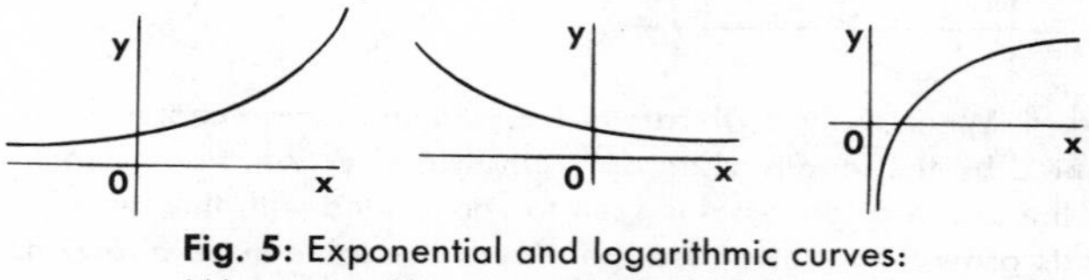

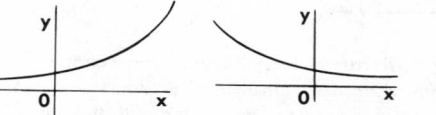

Fig. 5: Exponential and logarithmic curves: (A) $y = e^x$; (B) $y = e^{-x}$; (C) $y = \log_e x$.

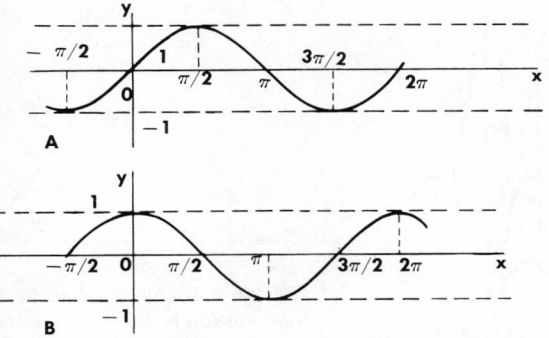

Fig. 7: A space curve—the intersection of two surfaces.

Fig. 6: Trigonometric curves: (A) $y = \sin x$; (B) $y = \cos x$; (C) $y = \tan x$.

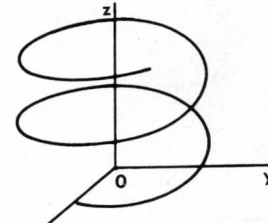

Fig. 8: Helix: a curve that lies on a cylinder or cone and cuts the elements at a constant angle: $x = \cos \theta$, $y = \sin \theta$, $z = \theta/4$.

Fig. 9: Curve with points of inflection.

Fig. 10: Folium of Descartes: $x^3 + y^3 = 3axy$.

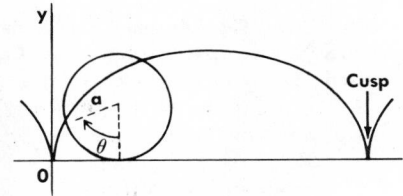

(A) Cycloid:
$x = a(\theta - \sin \theta)$
$y = a(1 - \cos \theta)$

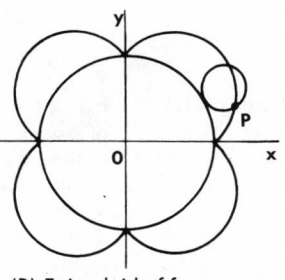

(B) Epicycloid of four cusps:
$x = 5 \cos \theta - \cos 5\theta$
$y = 5 \sin \theta - \sin 5\theta$

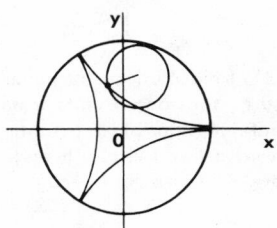

(C) Hypocycloid of three cusps:
$x = 2 \cos \theta + \cos 2\theta$
$y = 2 \sin \theta - \sin 2\theta$

Fig. 11: Cycloid: a curve generated by a fixed point on the circumference of a circle that rolls, without slipping, on a fixed path.

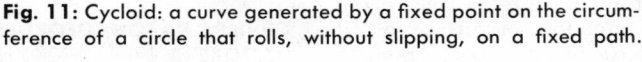

Fig. 12: Curve with an isolated point.

Fig. 13: Catenary: the curve in which a uniform, perfectly flexible, heavy cable hangs if it is supported only by its own weight:
$y = \tfrac{1}{2}a(e^{x/a} + e^{-x/a}) =$
$a \cosh (x/a)$.

Fig. 14: Spiral of Archimedes: $\rho = a\theta$.

Fig. 15: Logarithmic spiral: $\rho = e^{k\theta}$.

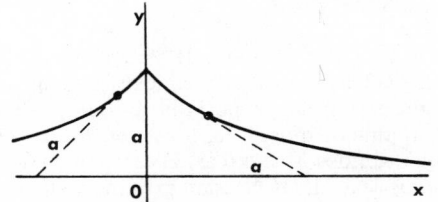

Fig. 16: Tratrix:
$x = \pm [a \log (a + \sqrt{a^2 - y^2})/y - \sqrt{a^2 - y^2}]$.

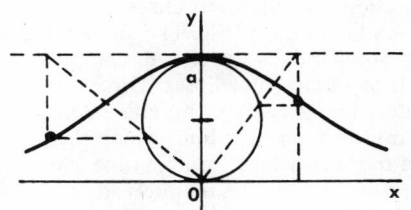

Fig. 17: Witch of Agnesi: $y(x^2 + 4a^2) = 8a^3$.

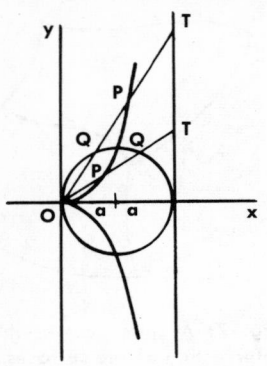

Fig. 18: Cissoid of Diocles: the locus of points P such that $QP = QT$: $2ay^2 = x(x^2 + y^2)$.

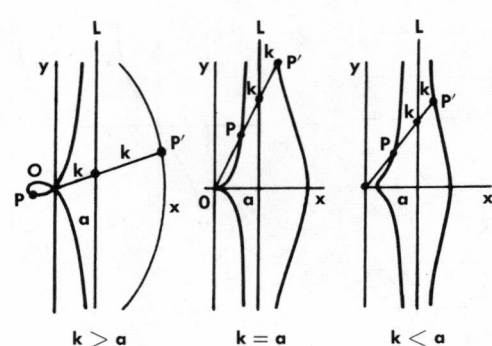

$k > a$ $k = a$ $k < a$

Fig. 19: Conchoid of Nicomedes: the locus of points P and P' that are always k units from a fixed line L, measured along the line through the origin O: $(x - a)^2 (x^2 + y^2) = k^2x^2$.

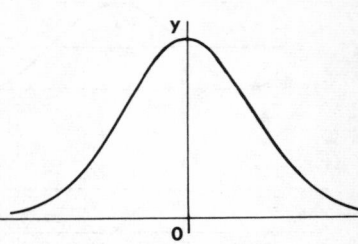

Fig. 20: Probability curve: the curve that represents the normal, or Gaussian, distribution: $y = e^{-kx^2}$.

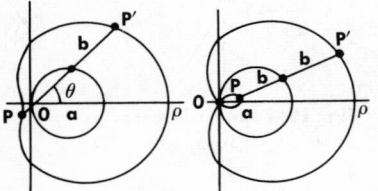

Fig. 21: Limacon: locus of points P and P' that are b units from the intersection of a rotating line and a fixed circle through the origin: $\rho = a \cos \theta + b$.

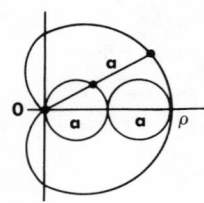

Fig. 22: Cardioid: a special limacon in which $b = a$: $\rho = a(\cos \theta + 1)$.

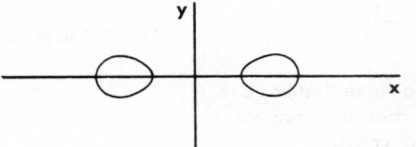

Fig. 23: Cassinian ovals: locus of points such that the product of their distances from two fixed points is constant: $(x^2 + y^2)^2 - 2a^2(x^2 - y^2) + a^4 = k^4, k^4 < a^4$.

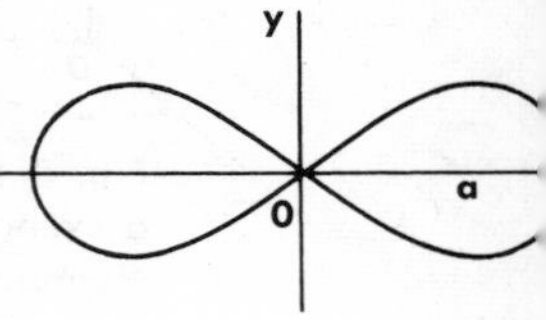

Fig. 24: Lemniscate of Bernouilli a special case of the Cassinia ovals in which $k^4 = a^4$: $(x^2 + y^2)^2 = 2a^2(x^2 - y^2)$.

lie wholly in a plane. Such curves are space, or twisted, curves. A space curve is a boundary separating two parts of a surface. It may also be conceived as the intersection of two surfaces (Fig. 7). In three-dimensional coordinate geometry, the locus of points satisfying an equation is a surface so that the two equations of the two intersecting surfaces represent a curve. Both in two dimensions and in three it is often convenient to express the coordinates of points of curves in terms of an auxiliary variable, or *parameter*. Thus, $x = 30t$, $y = 100t - 16t^2$ are parametric equations of a parabola; and $x = \cos \theta, y = \sin \theta, z = \theta/4$ are parametric equations of a space curve called a *helix* (Fig. 8).

Much of the study of curves is concerned with special properties. The curvature of a curve is a measure of the bending—how fast the direction of a moving point changes as it generates the curve. Except for the straight line whose curvature is everywhere zero, and the circle whose curvature is constant, the curvature of a curve varies from point to point. Its value is found by differential calculus. A point of a curve where the curvature is zero, but with the direction of concavity different on either side of it, is called a point of inflection (Fig. 9). Many curves have loops, or nodes (Fig. 10); others have cusps (Fig. 11); some have isolated points (Fig. 12). Some curves are closed, completely bounding a region, such as circles or ellipses. Others are open and extend infinitely far. A curve of infinite extent may have one or more asymptotes: straight lines which the curve approaches more and more closely, approximating them both in nearness and direction as it moves infinitely far away (Figs. 4 and 5).

Certain special problems related to curves had much to do with the development of calculus. These are the problems of finding the exact direction of a curve at any point, of finding the length of a curved arc, and of finding the area bounded by a curve. (See also CONIC SECTIONS; ELLIPSE; HYPERBOLA; PARABOLA.)—*H. C.*

CUVIER, BARON GEORGES LÉOPOLD CHRÉTIEN FRÉDÉRIC DAGOBERT, 1769–1832, French naturalist; b. Montbéliard; ed. at home and at Stuttgart Academy. His *Tableau elementaire de l'histoire naturelle des animaux* (1798) was the first statement of his famous classification of the animal kingdom. His major paleontological and geographical investigations were published in his *Recherches sur les ossemens fossiles de quadrupèdes* (1812), *Discours sur les révolutions de la surface du globe* (1825), and *Le règne animal distribué d'après son organization* (1817). In dividing the animal kingdom, Cuvier stressed the structure and relation of inner parts instead of external characteristics. A man of tremendous intellectual scope and influence, Cuvier was among the first to see in fossils the evidence of evolution, and he is regarded as the father of paleontology. His view of Earth's history as divided by cataclysmic events into separate eras was much modified, however, by his successors (see GEOLOGY). He was a fellow of the Royal Society.—*S. B.*

CYANIDE: any of the compounds that contain the cyanide $(CN)^-$ radical. This radical is chemically similar, in some respects, to the HALOGENS, especially to iodine. Cyanides can be either organic or inorganic; however, the preferred term for organic cyanides is NITRILES. Hydrogen cyanide (hydrocyanic or prussic acid, HCN) is an extremely poisonous liquid boiling at 26.5°C; the gas has the odor of bitter almonds. Like the halogen acids, it is soluble in water; unlike them it is a weak acid. Other important cyanides—those of potassium, sodium, barium, and calcium—liberate hydrogen cyanide and must be handled with extreme care. *Cyanogen* (C_2N_2) is a colorless, deadly poisonous gas. It can be considered as the polymerized free cyanide radical (*i.e.* it has neither a positive nor a negative charge). When heated to 400°C, it polymerizes to paracyanogen, a white solid. Cyanides also unite with metals to form complex ions.—*D. P. B.*

CYBERNETICS: a field of interest defined by Norbert Wiener in his book *Cybernetics* as: "the study of control and communication in the animal and the machine." The word cybernetics was originally coined in 1834 by André Ampère from the Greek for "the science of control." The subject has developed rapidly during the past decade, mainly in the U. S. A., Britain, and the U. S. S. R. It straddles a variety of disciplines, bringing together physiologists, engineers, mathematicians, behavioral psychologists, phoneticians, and others.

A concept of fundamental importance to cybernetics is that of *feedback*—the "feeding back" of part of the action of a mechanism to partly control the input. By means of feedback, corrective action can be taken on the basis of errors made. An example is the control of a gas heater by a thermostat. Some of the output—heat—causes a capsule in the thermostat to expand; when the temperature, and thereby the expansion, exceeds a pre-set amount, the capsule closes a valve, stopping the flow of gas and the production of heat. Without heat the capsule contracts until it opens the valve, allowing gas to flow and heat to be produced. An example of feedback being used to control a goal-seeking action occurs whenever a person reaches for an object. His hand movement is detected by eye and proprioceptive sense organs; if his hand moves too far to the left the detectors feed this information to the brain, which sends a signal to the muscles, causing a correcting movement to the right. Examples abound in electronic circuits and in SERVOMECHANISMS. Whatever the application, the essential parts of a feedback system are the detection of the output, comparison with predetermined requirements, communication with a controlling device, and control of the input.

Interest in cybernetics was originally restricted to problems of control and feedback. These problems included the possibility of learning many lessons from nature and imitating, functionally at least, various controls in the animal body. These interests have since expanded. The pattern of development over the past 10 yr suggests that those active in the field fall into two broad camps, but with much contact and exchange between them. The first is concerned with what may be the conceivable limits of machines: what essential biological functions can or cannot be imitated by machines? Under consideration are not only control processes and unconscious reflex actions, but also the question of whether machines can show "thought-like" behavior. Learning by trial and error and by association may be imitated, as well as recognition of visual shapes or of speech. Such studies may be regarded as part of the drive toward automation in industry and the rapid taking-over of many forms of clerical and mental tasks by COMPUTERS. The interests of those in the second camp are mainly biological. They use the methods of cybernetics as a discipline for making more precise mathematical descriptions of biological processes. For example, they isolate the essential properties of neurons and then analyze the behavior of vast masses of such abstracted elements when connected in nets; self-organizing properties of neurons are of special interest.

The inclusion in a machine of an element of randomness, for useful ends, represents one novel contribution. Sources of chance, or randomness, were once normally regarded as a

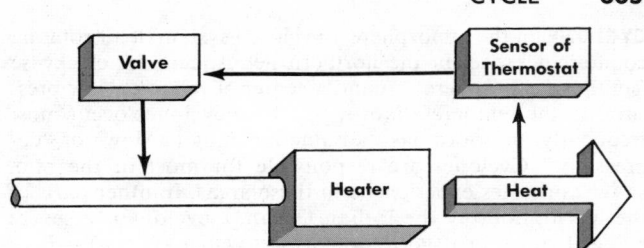

Feedback "loop" of a heater controlled by a thermostat.

nuisance, but Ross Ashby in Britain has studied experimentally how a mechanism can grope its way toward stable conditions by regularly making random (chance) changes in its internal organization. Goal-seeking actions, a hallmark of biological functioning, are being applied to the design of "goal-seeking" machines (see CONTROL SYSTEM). Cybernetics has called up the vision of a whole field of mechanisms that learn about their environment and adapt themselves to it, once they are given the general facilities for doing so.—*E. C. C.*

CYCLE: (1) a period of time associated with the recurrence of certain events or phenomena. For example, the *sunspot cycle* is the interval of approximately 11½ yr between minima of sunspot activity. Similarly, the SAROS *cycle* is a period of 223 lunations or 18 yr 11⅓ days after which Sun, Earth, and Moon return very nearly to the same relative positions.

(2) A device used in CALENDAR reckoning. For practical purposes, the calendar year must contain an integral number of days; but the astronomical period on which it is based includes a fractional day which, if neglected, causes a progressive shift of calendar dates with respect to the natural seasons. In the modern calendar, this fact is compensated for by using a 400-yr cycle, *i.e.* by introducing intercalary days according to an accepted leap-year pattern repeated every 400 yr. Most ancient and religious calendars are reckoned according to the lunar phases in addition to the recurrence of seasons. Therefore, these calendars are based, in general, on more elaborate *lunar cycles,* in which a number of years are made equal to an integral number of lunations and of days, and in which intercalation is governed by the rank of the month and year within the cycle. The oldest known lunar cycle is the *octaeteris,* or 8-yr cycle, dating from the 6th cent. B. C. Invented by the Greek astronomer Cleostratos, it made 8 yr equal to 99 lunations and to 2,922 days. A more accurate cycle was invented by the Athenian Meton, 432 B. C. The *Metonic cycle* makes 19 yr equal to 235 lunations and to 6,940 days. Variations of this 19-yr pattern are still in current use in religious calendars. For dating astronomical observations, the Athenian Callippos introduced further refinements in 330 B. C. by using a 76-yr cycle equal to four Metonic cycles minus one day. The *Callippic cycle* was used until the Middle Ages.—*S. D. G.*

(3) In physics and other branches of science, as well as in engineering, an orderly sequence of changes carried out by a system, ending in a return to the initial state of the system. A piston in an automobile engine moves down the cylinder to draw in gasoline vapor, back up the cylinder to compress the vapor, down as the engine fires, and back again to force out the exhaust fumes. The four strokes, which are repeated, constitute one cycle. When an alternating current flows in a wire, electrons move alternately backward and forward. Each complete to-and-fro movement is one cycle. The number of cycles in each second is the FREQUENCY. For convenience, a thousand cycles is called one kilocycle (kc); a million cycles, one megacycle (Mc). See CARBON CYCLE; CARNOT CYCLE; CITRIC-ACID CYCLE; HARMONIC MOTION; LIFE CYCLE; NITROGEN CYCLE.—*B. P. S.*

CYCLONE: in the atmosphere, the closed system of air rotating counterclockwise (in the northern hemisphere) or clockwise (southern hemisphere) around a center of relatively low pressure. In the temperate latitudes, where cyclones occur most frequently, the word has the same meaning as "low" or "depression." Cyclones are responsible for most of the rain, snow, and gales experienced in these areas. In other parts of the world, notably the Indian Ocean, a cyclone is a severe tropical storm or HURRICANE (see WEATHER SYSTEM).—*P. L.*

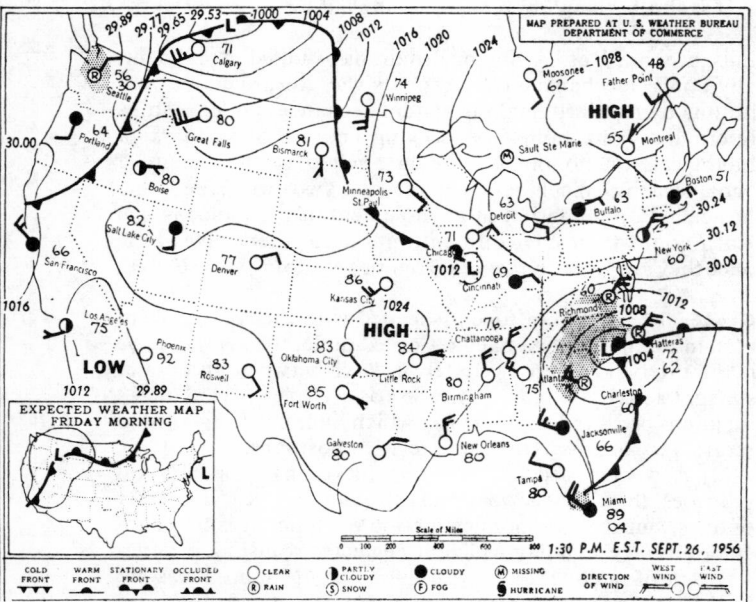

Cyclones ("lows") and anticyclones ("highs") appear on this U. S. Weather Bureau map. Solid lines are isobars, connecting points of equal pressure. Larger numbers at ends of isobars represent millibars of pressure; smaller numbers, inches.

CYCLOTRON: see PARTICLE ACCELERATOR.

CYLINDER: A right circular cylinder is a three-dimensional figure having two bases that are congruent circles in parallel planes, an axis that is a common perpendicular to the bases and joins their centers, and a lateral surface generated by a straight line that is always parallel to the axis and moves around the circumferences of the bases. Right circular cylinders have many practical uses; *e.g.* as containers, roller bearings, and parts in the interior of a piston engine.

The more general concept of a cylinder is the following: A cylindrical surface is generated by a straight line that remains parallel to a fixed line and moves along a curve lying in a plane that does not contain the fixed line. The various positions of the moving line are elements or rulings of the surface, which is called a ruled surface. The curve along which the line moves is a directrix of the surface. It can be any shape and need not be closed. A cylinder is a solid bounded by a cylindrical surface and by two parallel bases that cut all its elements. For a cylinder of finite extent the directrix must be closed.—*H. C.*

CYTOLOGY: the study of cells and their constituent parts, particularly in relation to structure, function, reproduction, and life history. Cell structures are commonly studied in killed, preserved, sectioned, stained specimens observed through the compound microscope. Through use of nontoxic "vital" dyes, living cells can be made to show some of their internal organization. With a phase-contrast microscope, distinctions between parts of cells with different refractive qualities become visible while the cells are still alive. Finer details of cells require

the electron microscope, limited to carefully prepared dead specimens. See CELL; CYTOPLASM; NUCLEUS.—*L. and M. M.*

CYTOPLASM: the living components of a plant or animal CELL outside its nucleus. The cytoplasm and nucleus together constitute the PROTOPLASM of the cell. On the outside the cytoplasm is bounded by a *plasma membrane,* or cell membrane, through which the cell obtains its raw materials and secretes or excretes its products. A *vacuole membrane,* similar to the plasma membrane, walls off the cytoplasm from any droplet of water or other vacuole of watery solution enclosed in the cell.

Except in purple bacteria and blue-green algae, where the nuclear material is distributed diffusely in the cytoplasm, photosynthesis takes place only within cytoplasmic organelles known as *chloroplastids;* the photosynthetic reactions proceed in close association with the green pigment CHLOROPHYLL, which is in thin layers within disk-shaped internal parts (grana) of each chloroplastid. Protein synthesis appears to be equally localized in minute bodies called *microsomes,* or ribosomes, which contain ribonucleic acid (RNA). Similarly, the stages of aerobic respiration utilizing pyruvic acid and oxygen seem to occur only in the "powerhouses of the cell"— the *mitochondria;* adenosine triphosphate (ATP), needed to give energy to biosyntheses elsewhere in the cell, and also carbon dioxide and water, all emerge from a living mitochondrion as it carries on these respiratory activities. It seems likely that the enzymes for the several reactions in the citric-acid ("Krebs") cycle are components of the inner wall of the double-walled mitochondrion, perhaps forming the shelf-like projections extending into the central cavity.

By subjecting cells to powerful forces in a centrifuge, it is possible to separate the many mitochondria from the rest of the cytoplasm and to identify a somewhat gelatinous *endoplasmic reticulum* as distinct from a more liquid *cytoplasmic ground substance.* In suitable preparations for the electron microscope, these components and the microsomes can be recognized in relation to one another. The endothelial reticulum takes the form of a large number of fine tubes, between which is the cytoplasmic ground substance. The mitochondria are suspended in the cytoplasmic ground substance between the tubules, and the microsomes are attached to or are part of the membrane of the tubules—projecting slightly into the cytoplasmic ground substance. In some cells prepared for study through the electron microscope, the membrane separating the cytoplasm from the nucleus (the *nuclear membrane*) appears to be double, and the space between the layers seems to be connected to the spaces within the slender tubules of the endothelial reticulum.

Prior to division of the nucleus in the process of mitosis, as much as 12% of the cytoplasm becomes organized into a special *cytoplasmic division apparatus,* or mitotic apparatus, composed primarily of proteins (at least 95%) and ribonucleic acid (at least 3%). These form the spindle fibers, chromosomal fibers, interchromosomal fibers, and, in animal cells, the astral rays evident during the mitotic sequence. How these structures arise, gain their orientation, and function during the separation of two complete sets of chromosomes, only to disappear again, remains to be discovered (see CELL DIVISION).

Many cells possess slender extensions of the cytoplasm that are able to beat with a whip-lash movement, propelling the cell within a liquid or a liquid past the cell. The shorter extensions of this kind, known as *cilia,* are usually numerous, whereas the longer extensions, called *flagella,* may be single. A flagellum differs, however, from the propulsive tail of a sperm cell, in its action; with it the cell reaches out into the water, and pulls water toward the cell, whereas a sperm tail is a sculling organelle.—*L. and M. M.*

D

DAGUERRE, LOUIS JACQUES MANDÉ, 1787–1851, French painter, inventor, and pioneer in photography; b. Cormeilles. At first a theatrical scene-designer, he invented (1822) the Diorama, a pictorial exhibit which anticipated the principles of the animated cartoon and three-dimensional projection. He became interested in fixing images obtained with the *camera obscura,* and in 1829 went into partnership with J. N. NIÉPCE, who had succeeded in fixing images on plates coated with light-sensitive varnishes. After Niépce's death (1833) Daguerre succeeded (1837) in obtaining a permanent image on a silver plate that had been treated with iodine vapor. After exposure, the plate was developed with mercury vapor, which condensed on the areas of the plate affected by the light and thus formed the lighter portions of the picture. The plate was "fixed" by dissolving off the unchanged silver iodide with a solution of sodium hyposulfite ("hypo"). The "daguerreotype," the first practical method of photography, remained in use until the mid-1860s. See also PHOTOGRAPHY.—*P. R. L.*

DALE, SIR HENRY HALLETT, 1875– , British physiologist and biochemist; b. London. His research on the pharmacology of ergot led him to studies of tyramine, histamine, and acetylcholine. He and Otto Loewi established the chemical transmission of nerve impulses, and they shared the Nobel prize, 1936, for this work. Dale was president of the Royal Society (1940–45), and has strongly influenced the development of the medical sciences, especially in England. He is also an associate of the U. S. National Academy of Sciences.—*D. H. D. R.*

D'ALEMBERT'S PRINCIPLE: the principle that the sum of all the external forces acting on a body plus the kinetic reaction ($-ma$, often called an inertial or fictitious force) is zero. The content of the principle, stated in 1742 by Jean le Rond D'Alembert, is the same as Newton's law of motion, $\mathbf{F} = m a$, but as a method for solving problems it is often useful, since the body may thus be considered to be in equilibrium, no matter what its acceleration.—*M. P.*

DALÉN, NILS GUSTAF, 1869–1937, Swedish inventor; b. Stenstorp. His numerous discoveries and inventions relative to acetylene gas accumulators and their use in lighting made lighthouses operating with this fuel safe and practicable. For his invention of automatic regulators to be used in conjunction with gas accumulators for lighting beacons and light buoys, Dalén received the 1912 Nobel prize a few weeks after he had been blinded by a research accident.—*D. H. D. R.*

DALTON, JOHN, 1766–1844, English chemist and physicist; b. Eaglesfield. He is best known for his ATOMIC THEORY, which grew out of his observations of the behavior of gases. He concluded that such phenomena as the differing solubilities of gases in water depended on differences in the weight and structure of the "ultimate particles" of which the gases are composed. He enunciated this theory in a paper, "The Absorp-

John Dalton
(N. Y. Public Library)

tion of Gases" (1803), in which he also furnished a rudimentary table of atomic weights. Hydrogen was assigned the value of 1. The same paper contained his law of partial pressures: in a mixture of gases, the molecules of each gas exert the same pressure as they would if present alone, and the total pressure is the sum of the partial pressures exerted by the different gases in the mixture. Attempts to explain atmospheric diffusion led him to the conclusion that atoms of different gases occupy different volumes. His theories were elaborated in his major work, *New Systems of Chemical Philosophy* (1808–27), in which he postulated that chemical combination was the result of the union of discrete particles with definite weights characteristic of each element. He believed that atoms are indivisible and indestructible, and that all atoms of a given element are identical. He also devised a system of classification for chemical compounds based on the number of atoms involved. A man of wide interests, Dalton kept a 57-yr diary of meteorological observations containing over 200,000 entries. In 1794 he published the first detailed description of "Daltonism," or color-blindness, from which he and his brother suffered. Dalton's observations were crude, and many of his conclusions were erroneous, but his atomic theory and concept of atomic weights were fundamental. He was a fellow of the Royal Society.—*D. H. D. R.*

DALTON, JOHN CALL, 1825–89, U. S. physiologist; b. Chelmsford, Mass. Influenced by Claude Bernard, from whom he acquired a belief in the value of the experimental approach, Dalton became the first U. S. physician to devote himself to experimental physiology. His published works include *Treatise on Human Physiology* (1859), *Experimentation on Animals as a Means of Knowledge in Physiology, Pathology, and Practical Medicine* (1875), *The Experimental Method in Medical Science* (1882), and *Topographical Anatomy of the Brain* (1885). He was a member of the National Academy of Sciences.—*D. H. D. R.*

DALY, REGINALD ALDWORTH, 1871–1957, U. S. geologist; b. Napanee, Ontario. He investigated the ways in which igneous rocks are emplaced; the implications of isostasy; the strength of Earth's crust and interior; the rise of sea level caused by melting glaciers, and how it controls growth of coral reefs; and the carving of submarine canyons by turbidity currents. Among his many scientific papers and books is *Strength and Structure of the Earth* (1940). He was a member of the National Academy of Sciences.—*R. W. D.*

DAM, CARL PETER HENRIK, 1895– , Danish biochemist; b. Copenhagen. For the discovery of vitamin K, Dam shared the 1943 Nobel prize with E. A. Doisy. Dam's research has been on the biochemistry of vitamins E and K and of sterols and fats.—*D. H. D. R.*

DAM: a structural barrier to contain or regulate the flow of a body of water. Dams have been used since earliest antiquity. Irrigation dams were necessary to the civilizations of ancient Mesopotamia. The ancient Egyptians built a dam on the Nile at the present site of Aswan. The Chinese and Indians built dams for water storage; in Ceylon there are traces of a reservoir contained by a dam over 11 mi long and 70 ft high. At present most dams are multipurpose, and functions may include: (1) production of electricity by running the stored waters through turbines, (2) distribution of water for irriga-

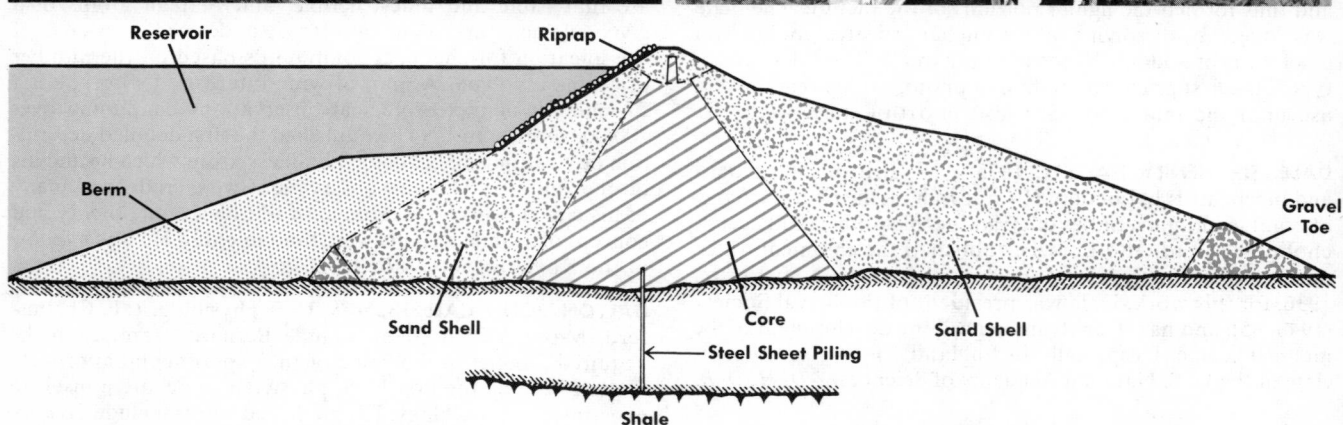

Dams: Preliminary arched dam at Dixence, Switzerland (*upper left*), is part of 935-ft-high complex on a tributary of the Rhone in Pennine Alps. (*Giegel/Swiss Nat. Tourist Off.*)—Hoover Dam (*upper right*) in Montana, also an arched dam, is highest in U. S. (726 ft), completed 1940. Harnessing Colorado River for 1,103,000 kw of electric power, it also irrigates seven states. (*Union Pacific Railroad*)—In Fort Peck Dam, Montana (*diagram*), an earth dam completed in 1940, a nearly impervious core is sandwiched between pervious zones, with gravel at downstream toe. Earth-fill totals 128 million yd^3. (*Data from U. S. Army Corps of Engineers*)

tion, (3) storage and gradual release of water for flood control, (4) increase of river depth for navigation. However, to utilize the many advantages of river control, a system of related dams is usually needed. The ten outstanding dams in the world by virtue of their size or importance are: (1) Grand Coulee, on the Columbia River; (2) Hoover, on the Colorado; (3) Fort Peck, on the Missouri; (4) Kariba, on the Zambesi in Rhodesia; (5) Grand Dixence, on the Dixence in Switzerland; (6) Mauvoisin in Drante, Switzerland; (7) the dams of the Tennessee Valley Authority; (8) Bratsk, on the Angara in Siberia; (9) Bhakra, on the Sutlej in India; (10) Aswan, on the Nile. When completed, two Soviet dams, the Inguri (988 ft high) and the Nurek (984 ft), will be the highest dams in the world. All major dams are built of masonry or earth, depending on the foundation available, the shape of the surrounding land, and the materials at hand. Masonry dams, which need a foundation of solid rock, are either *concrete-gravity, i.e.* dams which rely mainly on their weight for resistance to water pressure, or *concrete-arch, i.e.* dams in the shape of a horizontal upstream arch, which transmit the weight of the stored water to the steep river banks supporting the arch. Many important structures, *e.g.* Hoover Dam, are a combination of these two types. Earth dams are made of many layers of carefully chosen soils and gravels. Because of the flexibility and availability of the materials, this type is widely used; *e.g.* Fort Peck Dam, on the Missouri. To control the height of

water stored, most dams provide spillways, made of stone masonry to resist erosion. To discharge water below the height of the dam, interior siphons are provided: these help to solve a major problem of dam design—the eroding of the structure by debris, floating ice, and turbulent water at the downstream toe. Other major problems are leakage under the foundation, leakage through cracks caused by partial failure, and the filling of the reservoir by silt. See Color Plate 33.—*A. L.*

DAMPING: in a resonant system, the gradual decrease in amplitude (but not in frequency) of OSCILLATION that occurs unless additional energy is supplied. In a mechanical oscillator, *e.g.* a pendulum, damping is caused by friction. In an electrical oscillator, it is due to resistance losses.—*I. R.*

DANA, JAMES DWIGHT, 1813–95, U. S. geologist and zoologist; b. Utica, N. Y. Geologist and mineralogist on the Wilkes expedition to the South Seas (1838–42), he produced significant reports on the geology of the Pacific Ocean, volcanoes of the Hawaiian Is., and coral reefs, and comprehensive works on zoophytes and crustaceans. He succeeded Benjamin Silliman as editor of *American Journal of Science* (1840) and as professor of natural history at Yale Univ. (1849–94). His *Textbook of Geology* (1864) markedly influenced geological thought. He was a fellow of the Royal Society and a member of the National Academy of Sciences.—*D. H. D. R.*

DARCY, HENRI PHILIBERT GASPARD, 1803–58, French engineer and physicist; b. Dijon. A civil servant, Darcy supervised the construction of many public works. His particular interest was water: canals, wells, purification problems, and flow of water in pipes. *Darcy's law* states that the velocity of flow of a column of liquid is directly proportional to the difference in pressure at the ends of the column and inversely proportional to the length of the column. His most famous writing was *Les fontaines publiques de la ville de Dijon* (1851).—*D. H. D. R.*

DARWIN, CHARLES ROBERT, 1809–82, English naturalist; b. Shrewsbury. The son of a wealthy family, Darwin traveled as the unsalaried naturalist aboard HMS *Beagle* (1831–36) on an expedition around the world, returning to England with extensive collections and volumes of notes from field observations. Some of Darwin's most significant discoveries were incorporated into his *Journal of Researches* (1839–40), but his scientific reputation developed as the result of

Charles Robert Darwin
(George Eastman House)

a monograph on barnacles (1854). He became greatly interested in the problem of the origin of species, particularly because he had noted distinct differences among related birds on isolated islands, *e.g.* in the Galápagos. After reading T. R. Malthus' *Essay on Population* in an 1838 edition, he became convinced that the environment of living things provides a "natural selection" analogous to the techniques of the plant and animal breeder. He saw this as the explanation for the EVOLUTION of life, an idea put forth in 1809 by Lamarck. For 20 yr Darwin amassed factual evidence for evolution in the past, relating it to his theory of NATURAL SELECTION, but was reluctant to publish his work. In 1858, A. R. Wallace offered the same theory on the basis of far less evidence, and in 1859 Darwin's historic volume, *The Origin of Species by Means of Natural Selection,* appeared. Darwin considered this merely an abstract, hastily compiled, and followed it with additional volumes: *Variation of Animals and Plants under Domestication* (1868), *The Descent of Man and Selection in Relation to Sex* (1871), *Effects of Cross- and Self-Fertilization in the Vegetable Kingdom* (1876), and *Different Forms of Flowers on Plants of the Same Species* (1877). He contributed original and outstanding research work on the action of earthworms in the soil, the fertilization of orchids, and other topics, but withdrew as far as possible from the intense controversy provoked by *The Origin of Species,* leaving his theory for others to test. The great burst of investigation that it stimulated provided so much supporting evidence that the concept of evolution came to be regarded as the one great unifying feature in biological sciences. He was a fellow of the Royal Society.—*L. and M. M.*

DARWIN, ERASMUS, 1731–1802, English biologist; b. Elston. The grandfather of Charles Darwin, he was one of the early writers on evolution. He published *The Botanic Garden* (1789), in verse, and *Zoönomia, or the Laws of Organic Life* (1794–96), in which he proposed the theory of a gradual improvement of the species in the animal world through the inheritance of acquired characteristics—a view developed at the same time or a little later by Lamarck.—*H. I. S.*

DATA LINK: a communication channel between two points capable of relaying desired information. In simplest form a data link may be a telephone or telegraph line. More complex systems employ wireless radio waves; *e.g.* information collected by satellites and other space-probes are relayed back to Earth via radio-telemetry data links.—*G. S.*

DATING: see GEOCHRONOLOGY; RADIOACTIVE DATING.

DAVISSON, CLINTON JOSEPH, 1881–1958, U. S. physicist; b. Bloomington, Ill. He and L. H. Germer, working at the Bell Telephone Laboratories, discovered (1927) and investigated the diffraction of electrons by crystals—experimental research that supported the theoretical research of L. V. de Broglie. For this experimental discovery of the interference phenomena in crystals irradiated by electrons, Davisson and G. P. Thomson shared the Nobel prize, 1937. Davisson was a member of the National Academy of Sciences.—*D. H. D. R.*

DAVISSON-GERMER EXPERIMENT: a crucial experiment performed in 1927 which first demonstrated that the fundamental subatomic particles of matter, under certain conditions, appear to be spread out in space as if they were traveling waves. The experiment consisted in bombarding a nickel crystal with a beam of electrons and observing the angular distribution of the scattered electrons. The reflected electrons exhibited a DIFFRACTION pattern. This is a characteristic alternation in intensity exhibited by waves scattered by regularly spaced rows of obstacles, when the spacing between rows is comparable to the distance between successive crests (wavelength) of the waves. It happens that the atoms inside a crystal are arranged in an orderly repetitive pattern; also, diffraction of short-wavelength electromagnetic waves (x-rays) had already been demonstrated. The Davisson-Germer experiment thus clearly confirmed the earlier hypothesis of Louis de Broglie that matter has wavelike properties; indeed, the wavelength was exactly as theoretically predicted. Further experimental and theoretical discoveries culminated in the present-day QUANTUM THEORY, which adequately describes all atomic and many nuclear phenomena.—*S. K.*

DAVY, SIR HUMPHRY, 1778–1829, English chemist; b. Penzance, Cornwall. Inspired by Lavoisier's *Elements of Chemistry,* he experimented with gases and discovered the exhilarating effect and anesthetic qualities of nitrous oxide (1799). His investigations were reported in his *Researches Chemical and Philosophical, Chiefly Concerning Nitrous Oxide or Dephlogisticated Nitrous Air and Its Respiration* (1800); they included decomposition of alkalies by electricity and preparation of potassium, sodium, and calcium by electrolysis (1807–8); identification of the so-called oxymuriatic acid as one of the elements, which he named "chlorine"; research on iodine; identification of the diamond as carbon; and research on the rare earths. In 1812 he hired Michael Faraday as his laboratory assistant; this has been called by some "Davy's greatest discovery." His experimentation with flame and explosions in 1815 led to the invention, with Faraday, of the miner's safety lamp. Davy also invented the electric arc. His books include *On Some Chemical Agencies of Electricity* (1807), *Elements of Chemical Philosophy* (1812), and *Elements of Agricultural Chemistry* (1813). In 1820 he became president of the Royal Society.—*S. B.*

DAWSON, SIR JOHN WILLIAM, 1820–99, Canadian geologist; b. Pictou, Nova Scotia. He developed a technique of making thin sections of rock for microscopic study. A controversy was started by Dawson when he labeled certain objects discovered by Sir W. E. Logan in the Laurentian area as *Eozoön canadense* ("dawn-animal of Canada"). Later evidence indicated that the material was probably not organic but inorganic in origin.—*R. G.*

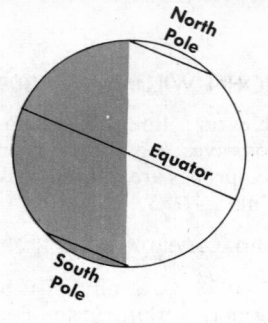

Summer

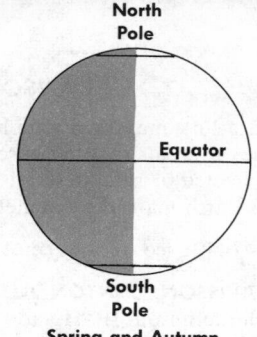

Spring and Autumn

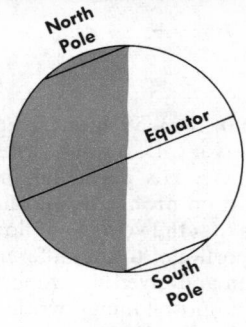

Winter

Fig. 1: Length of day at any place changes with season because Earth's axis is tilted with respect to plane of its orbit around Sun. In each drawing, Sun is assumed to be at far right. Seasons indicated are for northern hemisphere.

DAY AND NIGHT: the periods of light and dark that alternate as Earth's surface rotates before the rays of the Sun. Day begins at the moment the Sun's upper limb is on the eastward horizon, and ends when the upper limb is on the westward horizon. At day's end, twilight begins; by definition, civil twilight ends when the Sun is 6° below the horizon, and astronomical twilight ends when the Sun is 18° below the horizon. Night spans the interval between end of evening twilight and beginning of morning twilight.

Because the plane of the equator is tilted to the plane of the ecliptic (Earth's path around the Sun), the lengths of day and night at any place depend upon its latitude and the season of the year (Fig. 1). The refraction of light by the atmosphere is also a factor. Because of refraction the Sun is visible for a few minutes before it has actually risen and after it has set; at the equator the day lasts not 12 hr but about 12 hr 7 min. There are no seasons at the equator; so its day is the same length all year. All places on Earth have close to the same period of daylight at the equinoxes, about Mar. 21 and Sept. 23. (Day and night are not, as is commonly supposed, equal in length at this time, but day is some minutes longer because of refraction and the fact that the equinoxes are defined with respect to the Sun's center, whereas daylight depends on the position of the Sun's upper limb.) After Mar. 21, the Sun rises and sets further north each day, bringing the long days of summer to the northern hemisphere, and the short days of winter to the south. At any place in the north, the longest day occurs at the summer solstice (about June 21), and the shortest at the winter solstice (about Dec. 22).

The longest days and nights of all are those at the north and south poles, where summer is one continuous "day" and winter one continuous "night," relieved only by periods of twilight just before and after summer. The north pole's "day" lasts 189 days, from about the vernal to the autumnal equinox. Away from the pole, the long polar day and night gradually shorten, and are separated by spring and autumn days of alternating day and night. All places above a certain latitude have a 24-hr day at the summer solstice, when they experience the MIDNIGHT SUN. Theoretically this latitude should be that of the arctic and antarctic circles (66° 33′), but because of refraction it is about latitude 66°. The 24-hr night of the winter solstice occurs at all latitudes higher than 67°.

At the equator, the Sun rises and sets almost vertically, and twilight lasts for little over an hour (Fig. 2). At other latitudes the Sun's path is oblique, so that twilight is always longer, increasing with latitude, and being longest at the summer solstice. At that time, all regions nearer the pole than latitude 48.5° have no true night—the sun is never more than 18° below the horizon. (See also TIME.)—*B. P. S.*

DEAMINATION: in biochemistry, the enzymatic removal of amino groups with production of ammonia. Hydrolytic deaminases are known for some compounds, *e.g.* adenine and guanine, which substitute a hydroxyl group for the amino group. For amino acids this enzymatic reaction is an oxidative process catalyzed by amino-acid oxidases with keto acids as a product. L-amino acid oxidases, D-amino acid oxidases, and specific deaminases for certain amino acids are found. See also UREA CYCLE.—*E. S.*

DEATH: cessation of the essential processes of life. The death of higher animals is marked principally by the stopping of heartbeat and respiration, and the loss of muscle tone. Shortly after death, the body begins to cool (*algor mortis*), muscles stiffen (*rigor mortis*), and blood settles in and reddens certain tissues (*livor mortis*). Death comes one cell at a time, and many cells survive for minutes, hours, or even days after the individual as a whole has died. The cornea of the human eye, for example, may survive for hours and can be transplanted to a living individual to replace a defective cornea (see GRAFTING). During the lifetime of an individual, many cells die normally and are replaced by new ones, as in the skin and blood. This is known as *necrobiosis,* in contrast to *necrosis,* the abnormal death of cells or tissues. In certain diseases, *e.g.* gangrene, parts of the body may die without causing the death of the individual.

Death is inevitable in complex many-celled animals, but some organisms appear to be immortal. For example, when they grow old, most one-celled animals such as the paramecium simply divide into two new individuals, renewing life and leaving behind no dead body. This process goes on indefinitely unless the organism is destroyed by some accident. A similar phenomenon occurs in certain plants. (See REPRODUCTION.) Nor is death necessarily a property of individual cells of an organism: cells of mammals will grow for indefinite periods when removed from the body and grown in a suitable environment, a procedure called tissue culture. Thus the death of an organism is not the result of the inevitable death of its cells, but rather the result of a breakdown in the internal organization of the body and of the interrelations of various tissues and organs. Death may be caused by degenerative changes of aging, invasions by microorganisms, chemical poisoning, and countless other factors. Much data has been gathered about the physiology of death, but a real understanding is yet to be gained. See AGING; LIFE SPAN.—*A. P. E.*

DE BARY, HEINRICH ANTON, 1831–88, German botanist; b. Frankfurt am Main. Originator of mycology, the study of fungi, he discovered that plant diseases can be caused by the presence of parasitic organisms in plant tissues and also dis-

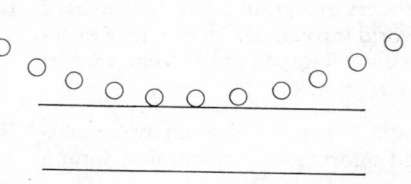

Horizon

18° Below

Sun's Path at the Equator

Sun's Path at Middle Latitudes

Sun's Path in Summer at the Arctic Circle

Fig. 2: Length of twilight depends on the angle Sun's path makes with the horizon. The more acute the angle, the longer the twilight. Twilight ends when Sun is 18° below horizon.

covered sexual reproduction of the fungi and the alternation of generations in the rust fungi. De Bary's research was on the morphology and physiology of fungi, on algae and ferns, and on plant pathology, and his most famous work was *Morphology and Physiology of Fungi, Lichens, and Slime Molds* (1866). He was a fellow of the Royal Society.—*D. H. D. R.*

DE BROGLIE WAVELENGTH: According to a hypothesis made by Louis V. de Broglie, 1924, a particle of mass *m* and velocity *v* has associated with it a wave whose wavelength is given by *h/mv,* where *h* is Planck's constant (see PLANCK'S LAW). Since waves produce interference effects (diffraction), the wave nature of particles can be directly verified, as first done by Davisson and Germer, and by G. P. Thomson, in 1927 (see DAVISSON-GERMER EXPERIMENT). Erwin Schrödinger, in 1926, incorporated L. V. de Broglie's hypothesis of the wavelike properties of elementary particles into a mathematical formalism called wave mechanics. After further generalization by other physicists the formalism has become known as QUANTUM MECHANICS.—*S. K.*

DEBYE, PETER JOSEPHUS WILHELMUS, 1884–1966, Dutch-U. S. physicist; b. Maastricht. He won the Nobel prize for chemistry, 1936, for his contributions to the study of molecular structure through his investigations on dipole moments and on the diffraction of x-rays and electrons in gases. His method of x-ray study of crystals (*Debye-Scherrer method*) is applicable to powders and important in the testing of materials. He has studied statistical theory of magnetism, abnormal behavior of concentrated solutions of strong electrolytes, and solid-state physics. He was a fellow of the Royal Society and an associate of the U. S. National Academy of Sciences.—*R. J. F.*

DECAY: see PUTREFACTION; RADIOACTIVITY.

DECIDUOUS PLANT: any tree or shrub that loses its leaves in autumn and remains leafless throughout the winter. In contrast, evergreens retain their leaves through the winter. Leaf fall normally follows the formation of a special layer of cells, the abscission layer, across the base of the leaf stalk. The walls of the abscission layer disintegrate and wind action ruptures the cells, causing the leaf to fall. After the leaf falls, the cells just below the abscission layer become corky and protect the leaf scar.—*A. P. E.*

DECISION PROBLEM AND DECISION PROCEDURE: A *decision procedure* is an effective way for solving any one of a given class of problems. For example, there is an effective process for finding the greatest common divisor of any two positive integers, and there is an effective way of testing a given integer to see whether or not it is a prime number. By an *effective process,* we mean one which follows a standard routine, not requiring any ingenuity. Such a process could be carried out by a suitable computing machine. Many interesting problems can be considered as questions as to whether or not a certain kind of decision procedure exists. It is easy, for instance, to describe a decision procedure to determine whether or not a polynomial in one variable with integral coefficients has an integral root. But it is an unsolved problem, Hilbert's Tenth Problem, whether or not there is a decision procedure to determine if a polynomial in arbitrarily many variables with integral coefficients has a solution in integers.

The *decision problem* of a formalized language is said to be solved affirmatively if there is a decision procedure to determine whether or not any given formula is a theorem. In order to prove that a certain type of decision procedure does not exist, it is necessary first to give a precise definition of the word "effective." It turns out to be sufficient to give a mathematical equivalent of the notion of effectively computable function of non-negative integers. This has led to the class of *recursive* functions, which has been defined in various equivalent forms by K. Gödel and others.

Roughly speaking, a recursive function $f(x_1, \ldots, x_n)$ is a function for which there is a finite list of equations involving only symbols for functions (including a symbol for f), variables, and non-negative integers, such that, for any non-negative integers $k_1, \ldots, k_n$, the correct value $f(k_1, \ldots, k_n)$ and only that value can be computed from the given equations by substituting non-negative integers for variables and replacing equals by equals. The hypothesis, known as Church's Thesis, that this precise notion corresponds to the imprecise intuitive notion can never be proved, just as the mathematical definition of continuous function can never be proved equivalent to the corresponding intuitive notion. However, it works well in all known cases, and the fact that many apparently different definitions (by Gödel, Kleene, Church, Turing, Post, Markov) have been shown to be equivalent further supports it.

Using this precise formulation, A. Church showed in 1936 that the decision problem for the first-order predicate calculus has a negative solution. (The first-order predicate calculus is the logical system built up from individual variables, predicate variables, propositional connectives [and, or, not, if . . . then - - -], and quantifiers "for all *x*" and "there is an *x*" over individual variables *x.*) In an equivalent formulation, this result tells us that there is no effective way of determining whether any given formula is logically valid. It has also been shown, by A. Tarski, that any sufficiently strong consistent mathematical system has a negative solution to its decision problem. Thus, there is no mechanical method of solving all mathematical problems.

Certain special mathematical problems have been solved with the aid of the notion of recursive function and Church's Thesis. In particular, P. S. Novikov proved the unsolvability of the word problem for groups. Among the few important decision problems which have received affirmative solutions are those of the theory of abelian groups (solved by W. Szmielew) and the theory of real-closed fields (solved by Tarski).—*El. M.*

DECLINATION: see CELESTIAL COORDINATES.

DEDEKIND, JULIUS WILHELM RICHARD, 1831–1916, German mathematician; b. Brunswick. Dedekind's work profoundly influenced current mathematical developments. In "Stetigkeit und Irrational Zahlen" (1872), he developed the idea of the "cut," later named the Dedekind cut. This cut is a means of defining all real numbers in terms of rational numbers. A partition of all rational numbers is made into set A and set B, with each number in B greater than any number in A. The partition, or cut, may either fall on a rational number and thus select, or define, it or not fall on a rational number, in which case it defines an irrational number. This concept has become basic in the study of the real number system on which all of analysis rests. Dedekind also created the modern theory of algebraic numbers and anticipated parts of the theory of lattices by his work on dual groups.—*H. C.*

DEDUCTION: see LOGIC.

DEEPS AND TRENCHES: For a century after methods of sounding to great ocean depths (more than 15,000 ft) were developed, about 1840, the deepest of any cluster of very deep soundings was often designated as a deep. Now, deeps are considered as not of great significance in the major topographic features among which they occur. Much more importance is attached to trenches, which are elongate depressions

Dwellers of the depths: *Left—*"Paper nautilus" *(Argonauta argo)* of tropical oceans. Not a true nautilus, it is more closely related to the octopus. Female's shell serves as egg case. *Right—*A decapod crustacean *(Oplophorus spinosus)* of the N Atlantic. *(Peter David)*

in the ocean floor along the convex sides of island arcs such as the Antilles, the Marianas, the Kurile, or along very mountainous coasts like that of Chile. The Challenger Deep of the Marianas Trench, with a depth of 35,800 ft, is the deepest known. Trenches commonly have depths greater than 25,000 ft; many are more than 1,000 mi long. In narrow places they may be no more than 10 mi wide, and the average slope of the sides (30%) may equal that of very steep walls in canyons on land. Deep-focus earthquakes nearly always originate in the neighborhood of trenches. Earth's crust is thin beneath trenches; the force of gravity here is less than elsewhere. Flow of heat from Earth's interior through the ocean bottom is low in trenches. The hypothesis has been advanced that trenches mark zones where slow-flowing hot material of the interior, cooled by contact with the crust, turns and starts to fall back toward the center. See CONVECTION THEORY.—*M. S.*

DEEP-SEA ANIMALS: Below the levels to which any light from the noonday sun can penetrate, representatives of almost every phylum inhabit the sea. These animals feed on one another or on the dead remains of creatures that have sunk from shallower levels. Some animals inhabit depths of more than 7 mi; there the water pressure exceeds $8\frac{1}{3}$ tons/in². They tolerate this pressure because it is the same inside and outside their bodies. Deep-sea animals possessing swim bladders full of gas usually explode if brought up to the ocean surface with its comparatively low pressures. In their native habitat, however, the chief hazards are other animals, starvation, the viscous nature of water under such great pressures, and cold. Deep water is often at a temperature below the freezing point; the pressure keeps it from freezing, but gives it an almost sirupy consistency, making movement difficult.

A considerable variety of worms, clams, heart urchins, and other creatures burrow in the bottom sediments, feeding on live bacteria and on nonliving organic matter that has been collecting there for millions of years. Sea stars and sea cucumbers creep over the ooze, grazing on debris that has fallen recently. Long-legged crabs move about slowly, scavenging for larger bits of food. Most deep-sea fishes have stretchable stomachs, and jaws that open very widely, enabling them to swallow creatures larger than themselves. Abyssal squids feel their way about, with long tentacles armed with suction cups, ready to grasp any fish or crab they touch. In the midwater depths, high above the bottom but still below any trace of daylight, many fishes, squids, and swimming crustaceans bear

distinctive luminous spots. Some produce their own light; others rely upon captive luminescent bacteria held in special pockets and often have a means for hiding the glow when trying to escape a pursuer (see BIOLUMINESCENCE). Although a few deep-sea animals are blind, many have exceptionally large eyes, apparently useful for finding luminous prey or locating mates bearing luminous spots. Less is known about the kinds of deep-sea animals and their ways than about any other creatures big enough to see with the unaided eye. Only a small proportion of deep-sea animals are too slow to escape from sampling nets towed by research ships on the ocean surface. New methods, particularly based upon deep-diving submarines, are needed to explore this last great frontier of Earth. See Color Plate 34.—*L. and M. M.*

DEFINITE PROPORTIONS, LAW OF: in chemistry, the principle that different samples of a given substance contain the same proportions of elements. It is also called the Law of Constant Composition or Definite Composition. For example, every molecule of sodium chloride has one atom of sodium and one of chlorine. (See CHEMICAL COMPOSITION, LAWS OF.) The discovery of isotopes at first seemed to challenge the applications of this law because it was realized that a random distribution of isotopes in a substance would not show two samples of that compound to have constant composition by weight. Subsequent experiments have shown that the natural distribution of isotopes is uniform in many elements.—*G. W. M.*

DEFINITION AND ITS KINDS: To define a term is to attempt to specify its meaning by reference to other terms. Frequently definition purports to present an expression which is synonymous with the defined term, but many scientific definitions merely give the necessary and sufficient conditions for the application of a term, and some only the sufficient one. Definitions are occasionally classified as either nominal or real. A *nominal definition* introduces a novel term into a language and assigns by stipulation a meaning to it; a *real definition* seeks to analyze and formulate accurately the meaning of a term that already has an established use. Many definitions in science are nominal, but even when scientists purport to be giving a real definition of a term they generally, and in the interest of precision and uniformity, slightly alter the tacit rules that previously governed its use.

Definitions play an essential role in the systemization of knowledge; if we discover that terms of type K can be defined by reference to terms of type L, we can use terms of type L as the basic vocabulary for all theories in which terms of type K appear. Moreover, if all scientific terms can be defined by reference to terms of a certain type, we can specify that type as the basic scientific one. Many empiricists hoped thus to define all theoretical terms in science by reference to observational ones, but such programs have not met with unqualified success.

In formalizing theories, scientists introduce certain terms as "primitive" ones and define others by reference to these. The hope in all these cases is that the defined terms are always eliminable in favor of the primitive ones, and that no inconsistencies arise within the system as a result of the introduction of definitions. Terms which are primitive within a system are not defined in that system, but are not necessarily inherently indefinable; they may be defined in another theory or system. Some scientists occasionally insist that all terms which are taken as primitive within a formalized scientific theory should be defined operationally, and that they must be shown to be synonymous with expressions describing certain overt operations that scientists can perform. But this program is both doubtful and vague.—*S. M.*

DE FOREST, LEE, 1873–1961, U. S. inventor; b. Council Bluffs, Iowa. He patented over 300 inventions, including the audion amplifier, which made long-distance telephony possible, and the oscillating audion, or three-electrode tube, making possible the electron's use as a radio detector, radio and telephone amplifier, and oscillator. De Forest also invented glow-lamp recording of sound on film for motion pictures and pioneered in the development of the radio: he broadcast Caruso's voice in 1910 and the first newscast in 1916, the year in which he established a radio station. His sound-on-film motion pictures were exhibited in New York in 1923.—*S. B.*

DE FORMATIONE PULLI IN OVO (On the Development of the Chick in the Egg), by Marcello Malpighi, 1672: Malpighi's was the pioneer work in microscopic embryology—he was the first to see more, with the aid of the new instrument, than the unaided eyes of a long line of observers from Aristotle to Harvey. Unfortunately, though his drawings of developing structures are excellent, Malpighi adhered to the then-fashionable view that all parts were "preformed" in the egg; there was enlargement but no development of new structures.—*A. R. H.*

DE GEER, BARON GERARD JACOB, 1858–1943, Swedish geologist; b. Stockholm. He is known principally for his geochronological work, based upon the identification of Baltic varved clays as annual deposits and upon their association with frontal moraines and gravel mounds. His dating system, which he extended to other continents, is explained in his *Swedish Geochronology: Principles* (1940). He was a fellow of the Royal Society.—*D. H. D. R.*

DEGREE-DAY UNIT: a difference of 1° between the mean temperature of a given day and a given standard temperature. In heating, the degree-day units for a given day are the number of degrees that the mean temperature for that day is below 65°F. Thus a day with a high of 60°F and a low of 40°F has a mean temperature of 50°F, which is 15°F below the standard reference temperature of 65°F; so this day registers 15 heating degree-day units. Agriculturists use a standard reference temperature of 41°F for growing degree-days, and construction engineers use 32°F for construction degree-days.—*P. L.*

DEGREES OF FREEDOM: In dynamics, a system has n degrees of freedom if n variables are needed to specify the position of every part of the system. A point on a fixed line has one degree of freedom, since its position can be specified by stating its distance from a zero point; a point on a surface requires two coordinates and therefore has two degrees of freedom. A rigid body has six degrees of freedom, three specifying its orientation and three locating one point on the body. In the PHASE RULE, if n variables can be changed without disturbing equilibrium, there are n degrees of freedom.—*Ba. H.*

DE HUMANI CORPORIS FABRICA (On the Fabric of the Human Body), by Andreas Vesalius, 1543: The *Fabrica* is the culmination and the unification of three trends in Renaissance anatomy: personal practice of human dissection by the anatomist; careful study of the Galenic books (far superior to the texts available in the Middle Ages); and use of woodcut illustrations to supplement verbal descriptions. While the last are superb and the best-known feature of the book, Vesalius was full, accurate, and often original in his text also. For the first time the topographical anatomy of the human body was accurately mapped in a systematic treatment of bones, muscles, veins, nerves, internal organs, brain, and so on. All subsequent anatomists leaned heavily on Vesalius' great work of scientific description—as they also did on hardly less eminent anatomists contemporary with him.—*A. R. H.*

DEHYDRATION: removal of molecules of water from a substance, causing a change in its chemical composition. This should be contrasted with DRYING, which results simply in reducing "wetness" of a substance. One illustration of dehydration is the action of heat on gypsum, $CaSO_4 \cdot 2H_2O$; the heat produces plaster of Paris, $CaSO_4 \cdot \frac{1}{2}H_2O$ by removing some of the water molecules from the crystal lattice of gypsum. Another example is the dehydration of ethyl alcohol, CH_3CH_2OH, to make ethylene, $CH_2{=}CH_2$, by the removal of a molecule of water, H—OH.—*Ru. M.*

DEHYDROGENASE: see ENZYME.

DELTA: a tract of land resulting from the deposition of sediment at the mouth of a stream. The Greeks so named the triangular area formed by the Nile River, because it resembled the shape of the fourth letter of their alphabet, delta (Δ). Deltas are formed wherever streams bearing sediment discharge into a quiet body of water, in the absence of strong shore currents or tides. The stream, on entering the lake or sea, abruptly loses velocity and with it capacity to transport its load. First the bedload, of coarser sediment, is dropped. Just beyond, the finer particles of the suspended load are dropped; deposition is hastened by coagulation caused by the salts in sea water.

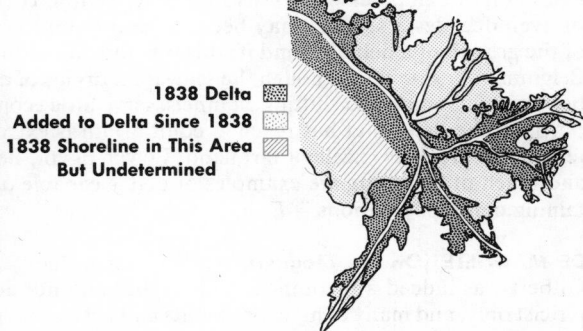

1838 Delta
Added to Delta Since 1838
1838 Shoreline in This Area But Undetermined

Mississippi Delta, looking southwest, as seen from the air near Venice, La., southernmost town on the delta. (*Frances Orkin*/Freeport Sulphur Co.) The map indicates the growth of the delta since 1838. (*Data from U. S. Coast and Geodetic Survey*)

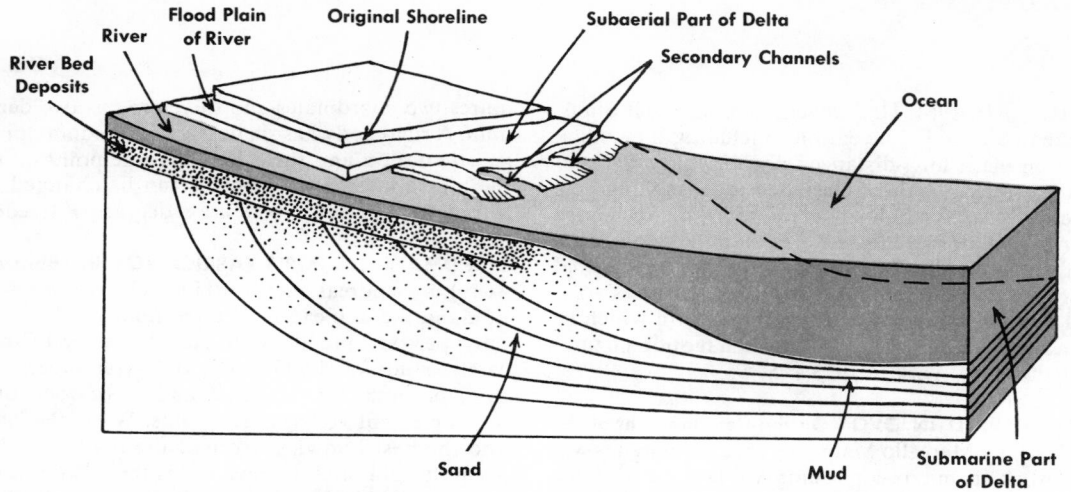

Structure of a delta: Essential features are the foreset beds, formed as the delta is built oceanward, the coarser sediments being dropped at or near the river mouth and the finer sediments farther out. Changes in sea level during formation of delta would complicate the simple, idealized pattern (with much vertical exaggeration) shown here.

The profile of an ideal delta would reflect this sorting-out process. The first layer of coarse material inclines from the channel bed at the stream mouth to the lake or marine floor; this layer is called a *foreset bed*. Successive deposition of foreset beds raises the advancing delta above water level. Simultaneously, layers of finer sediment are deposited horizontally on the lake or marine floor just beyond the foreset beds; these layers are called *bottomset beds*. As the delta advances, the bottomset beds are overlain, at a slight angle, by the foreset beds. The stream channel across the new land of the delta has virtually no grade, and numerous distributaries develop. Sediment is deposited in all these channels, forming another layer, the *topset beds*, which overlie the foreset beds. The radiation of the distributaries from the original stream channel, and the deposition around and within each subsidiary channel, account for the fan shape of the delta.

Few deltas conform in all or most respects to this ideal type; it is most likely to appear in small lake deltas. The type is important mainly as the pattern from which deviations may, for one reason or another, be traced. Great rivers, *e.g.* the Amazon, Mississippi, and Yangtze, have formed deltas over thousands of years that differ from one another and from all other deltas. Factors causing variation are the regimen of the stream, the composition of the load borne, the configuration of the marine (or lake) shoreline, and the effectiveness of shore currents. In all great deltas the mainstream flow shifts from one distributary to another. At least five successive main channels can be traced on the Mississippi delta, and the present channel is even now being abandoned by the river. The extension of deltas seaward is also variable. Within centuries or even decades a seaport may become land-bound because of the growth of a delta beyond it; this was the fate of Bruges, Belgium, for example. Although the seaward margins of deltas, because of flooding and shifting channels, serve little economic purpose, the delta that has reached equilibrium is extremely fertile and provides excellent farmland. Lower Egypt, Bengal, and much of Shantung are examples of deltas capable of sustaining dense populations.—*E. A.*

DE MAGNETE (On the Magnet), by William Gilbert, 1600: Gilbert was indeed a theoretical philosopher and not an empiricist only, and many of his experiments had been anticipated by others; but his great book remains the earliest large-scale attempt to investigate a natural phenomenon by making experiments and generalizing from them. Besides establishing the elementary properties of magnets, Gilbert showed that Earth itself is a magnetic body. Going rather beyond his evidence, he asserted also that magnetism is a universal and cosmically significant power of nature, linking it with gravity and with Earth's rotation. These notions had a major influence on subsequent astronomical theories, as Gilbert's example had on experimental science.—*A. R. H.*

DEMINERALIZATION OF SALINE WATER: conversion of brackish or sea water to fresh water needed for drinking, agriculture, and industry. Demineralization has been hailed as a solution to impending world-wide water shortages, and several national governments, as well as private interests, are currently sponsoring demineralization projects. The potential benefits of cheap, efficient, large-scale conversion of saline water are suggested by the fact that a great percentage of the world's arid lands lie close to the sea (average salinity 35,000 parts per million), and, furthermore, that large underground reservoirs of brackish or slightly saline water (1,000 to 10,000 ppm salinity) underlie many dry areas (*e.g.* the belt in N America extending from the plains of Alberta and Manitoba through the Dakotas to Texas and Mexico). Water up to 500 ppm salinity is generally considered fresh (potable) water. Many demineralization methods are in use or under study. None is yet capable of producing fresh water at a cost per gallon that the average individual consumer can pay, and most are therefore subsidized by government or industry. In the U. S. A. current costs of water from conventional sources range from 10¢ to $1/1,000 gal, but some segments of the economy pay less; *e.g.* many types of agriculture pay only 1 to 10¢/1,000 gal.

Sea water is currently demineralized most economically by various DISTILLATION processes, all of which are based on the principle that when salt water is heated to the evaporation point, the resulting water vapor is relatively salt-free; this "fresh" water vapor can then be condensed and channeled off for use. Certain areas of the Persian Gulf and the Caribbean use evaporators as their sole source of water. Costs of water from 500,000 gal/day plants are close to $1/1,000 gal. Many experiments using various evaporation and distillation methods are being carried out under the auspices of the Office of Saline Water of the U. S. Dept. of the Interior in efforts to obtain more economical conversion of saline water. These include the multiple-effect (12-evaporation unit) distillation plant at Freeport, Tex., which began operation June 1961, producing one million gal/day; the multistage flash-distillation plant being constructed at San Diego, Cal.; and the forced-circulation vapor-compression plant planned at Roswell, N. M. The use of sunlight alone for evaporation has been proposed as an ideal conversion method in arid regions with much sun. Although much testing and development work has been performed, it has not been possible to get more than 1 lb water/day/ft² of evaporator area. Thus, it would take over 4 million ft² of solar distillation units covering 100 acres of land to provide 500,000 gal water/day. Cost of water is $2 to $3/1,000 gal. The use of solar energy is therefore confined to very small units where it can serve effectively.

For conversion of brackish waters, ELECTRODIALYSIS is thought most practicable. Here the basic principle is that an electric current will separate the salts in brackish water into positive and negative ions; these ions can then be electrically "pulled" through special membranes, leaving fresh water behind. This method has been successfully tested in the Americas, the Middle East, Africa, and Asia. The U. S. Office of Saline Water is constructing an electrodialysis plant at Webster, S. Dak., to tap the underlying reservoir of brackish water. Present cost of conversion of brackish water by electrodialysis is about $1/1,000 gal. *Freezing methods* offer promise of economy because the latent heat requirement is many times less than the heat required for evaporation. When salt water freezes, salt-free ice crystals form. If the salt liquor could be readily separated from the ice crystals (which it now cannot be), fresh water might be made available in large quantities at 50¢/1000 gal.

One promising process involves forcing saline water under high pressure through semipermeable membranes. These are of the type suitable for osmosis, allowing water molecules to pass through but holding back salt molecules. Membrane composition must be carefully controlled, but this "reverse osmosis" process is potentially simple and inexpensive. For water softening, see WATER TREATMENT.—*R. E.*

Sea-water conversion: The 36-stage flash-distillation plant on San Diego, Calif., coastline is designed to test technical and economic aspects of demineralization. It produces 1,000,000 gal. of fresh water per day (*U. S. Office of Saline Water*)

DEMOCRITUS, *c.* 460 B. C.–*c.* 370 B. C., Greek philosopher; b. Abdera, Thrace. A disciple of Leucippus, Democritus systematized and elaborated Leucippus' work; thus, between them, they created the ATOMIC THEORY of matter. Democritus published works on ethics, physics, mathematics, astronomy, music, medicine, warfare, and agriculture, but only fragments of his writings have survived.—*D. H. D. R.*

DE MOIVRE, ABRAHAM, 1667–1754, French-English mathematician; b. Vitry, Champagne, but spent most of his life in England. His paper "Doctrine of Chances" contained much new material on the theory of probability. He is best known for *De Moivre's theorem,* which gives a formula for raising to a power a complex number in polar form: $[r (\cos \theta + i \sin \theta)]^n = r^n (\cos n\theta + i \sin n\theta)$. The formula $n! \approx (2\pi n)^{1/2} e^{-n} n^n$,

for approximating factorials, commonly known as Stirling's formula, was discovered by De Moivre. He was a fellow of the Royal Society.—*H. C.*

DE MORGAN, AUGUSTUS, 1808–71, British mathematician, a founder of modern formal logic, b. Madras, India. He contended that logic is about words rather than about ideas, as the prevailing view had it, and that the logician need not be concerned with what the symbols he analyzes denote. He developed a formal logic of relations, which, insofar as it suggested that classical syllogistic logic concerned itself with only a single relation (that of class inclusion), opened the way for development of a more comprehensive logic. De Morgan maintained a qualified subjectivist analysis of probability (*An Essay on Probabilities,* 1838), and insisted that the study of "partial belief" was as integral a part of logic as was deductive logic.—*F. Sc.*

DENDROCHRONOLOGY: see ANNUAL RINGS.

DENSITY: the mass per unit volume of a body. Since the volume of a body changes with temperature and pressure, density must be stated at a given temperature and pressure, although for solids the effect of pressure is negligible and is usually ignored. The densities of materials (at 4°C and pressure of 1 atm) encountered in everyday life range from 1/1,000 gm/cm³ for air through 1 gm/cm³ for water to 21.4 gm/cm³ for platinum. When the densities of materials are compared, the density of water is usually taken as a standard. The ratio of the density of a material to the density of water is known as the SPECIFIC GRAVITY of the material.—*S. K.*

DEODORIZER: a substance that nullifies the unpleasant effect of certain molecular dispersions upon the olfactory area of the upper nose. There are three methods of nullification: (1) chemical reaction, *i.e.* converting the compound to a less offensive chemical species, (2) elimination or removal of the dispersion, and (3) masking of the odor by use of other agents affecting the olfactory area. Chemical conversion may be accomplished by chlorination, treatment with high concentrations of ozone, photosynthesis, and by combustion. Offensive dispersions are removed by passage of the contaminated air through an absorbing medium, such as activated charcoal or silica gel. Masking is produced by the superimposition of a strong agreeable odor or by the reduction of olfactory area sensitivity to the disagreeable odor. The essential oils cinnamon, eucalyptus, lemon, lavender, pine, rosemary, sassafras, and thyme are common masking agents of the first type. Ozone, in low concentrations less than 0.1 ppm by volume, masks odors by decreasing olfactory sensitivity.

Personal deodorizers, usually called deodorants, may also act to inhibit perspiration, which becomes a source of body odor if left to dry or oxidize.—*R. W.*

DEOXYRIBONUCLEIC ACID POLYMERASES: enzymes which act to synthesize deoxyribonucleic acid (DNA). The reaction needs the triphosphates of the four nucleotides: deoxyadenylic, deoxyguanylic, deoxycytidylic, and thymidylic acids. Pyrophosphate is split off during the condensation; the remaining phosphate of the nucleotide is then covalently bound to the deoxyribose of the adjacent nucleotide, connecting the third carbon of one sugar to the fifth carbon of the other sugar. The reaction also needs the addition of small amounts of DNA to act as a "primer"; the DNA which is synthesized has the same arrangement of nucleotides as does the "primer" DNA. Each chain of DNA in the chromosomes is believed to act in this way during the enzymatic synthesis of another chain which is complementary to itself (see NUCLEIC ACIDS).—*P. S.*

DE RE METALLICA (On Metallurgy), by Georgius Agricola (Georg Bauer), 1556: Agricola's is not quite the first great printed book on technology, for it was preceded by Biringuccio's more limited, less elaborate *Pirotechnia* (1540), but *De re metallica* is a detailed and magnificently illustrated description of Central European mining and metallurgical techniques: it deals systematically with mineralogy; it treats the opening of mines, machinery employed for hoisting, pumping, and ventilating mines, methods of winning, assaying, and extracting metals from their ores, and many aspects of industrial chemistry. Agricola, a learned physician, showed that technology was a fit subject for scientific study; many later scientists paid tribute to his book by turning to it for information on geology, minerals, metals, and chemical processes. —*A. R. H.*

Agricola's empirical knowledge of mining and metallurgy, acquired in the course of a lifetime of observation in Bohemian and Saxon mining country, is reflected in the illustrations as well as in the text of his *De re metallica*, published posthumously in 1556. Among its 292 woodcuts is this view of an overshot water wheel of reversible design for use in raising ores. (*Burndy Library*)

DE RERUM NATURA (On the Nature of Things), by Lucretius, *c.* 60 B. C.: This finest scientific poem ever written was the final exposition of the atomic theory in antiquity. It follows the philosophy of Epicurus (341–270 B. C.); like his master an enemy of ignorance and superstition, Lucretius combined a moral purpose with scientific speculation. The true causes of things were not those commonly imagined, but were to be found in the mechanical coming together and separation of changeless atoms in the void. Little valued in classical times and almost unknown to the Middle Ages, *De rerum natura* aroused great interest when rediscovered in 1417, and stimulated the return to atomic, mechanistic concepts in science. —*A. R. H.*

DE REVOLUTIONIBUS ORBIUM COELESTIUM (On the Revolutions of the Celestial Orbs), by Nicolaus Copernicus, 1543: One of the most celebrated of scientific books, *De revolutionibus* is an attempt to express a totally new concept in the traditional forms of Greek and medieval astronomy. Convinced that true order could be restored to planetary theory only by making the Sun the pivot of the universe and by giving to Earth a triple motion (axial rotation, revolution about

the Sun, and a nutation of its axis), Copernicus retained the conventional spheres and epicycles. His book was thus the *Almagest* reconstructed upon a new principle; it did not effect a complete revolution in astronomy. During two generations it was ignored, rather than condemned, by all but a few mathematicians; it required the discoveries of Galileo and Kepler both to make the Copernican question critical and to complete the new theory of astronomy that Copernicus had begun. —*A. R. H.*

DESALTING: see DEMINERALIZATION OF SALINE WATER.

DESARGUES, GÉRARD, 1593–1662, French mathematician; b. Lyons. The most important work of this army officer, architect, and engineer was a treatise on the conic sections, *Brouillon Project* (1639). Little heeded at the time and virtually lost for two centuries, it was rediscovered by Chasles and has since been considered one of the classics of synthetic projective geometry. In it Desargues developed theorems on involution, harmonic ranges, homology, poles and polars, and perspective. Descartes and Pascal were much influenced by Desargues' thinking.—*H. C.*

DESCARTES, RENÉ, 1596–1650, French mathematician, physicist, and philosopher; b. near Tours. His chief contribution to science was his *Geometry* (published 1637 as an appendix to his influential *Discourse on Method*), in which he founded analytic geometry by showing how geometric configurations can be systematically studied by algebraic means. His views on physics were influential for a time but not permanently valuable. Descartes' philosophy was motivated by a passion for certainty, which he sought in mathematics because, he believed, it is independent of experience and proof against the errors of sense. All science might be securely based, he felt, if its method and structure could be made to conform to that of mathematics as he understood it: a system of propositions including a set of "simple principles" known intuitively, from which the remaining propositions followed deductively. In *Discourse on Method* (1637) Descartes formulated a highly influential program based upon uniformity of scientific method and universal mathematization of scientific thought. Dividing the world into two irreducibly different substances, roughly mind and matter (*res cogitans* and *res extensas*), he ascribed to these the defining traits respectively of thought and extension: "The nature of body consists not in weight, hardness, color . . . but in extension alone." All differences between bodies (*e.g.* organic and inorganic) are due to quantitative differences in extension; hence the entire material world yields to mechanical analysis and geometrical treatment. Descartes articulated and generalized the implicit views of many 17th-cent. scientists, and his own theory gained acceptance partly because of the immense prestige attaching to his positive scientific contributions in geometry, optics, and mechanics.—*Ar. D.*

DESCRIPTIVE GEOMETRY: a method of representing and solving three-dimensional, or space, problems by means of lines and points drawn on a plane, or two-dimensional, surface. The principles of descriptive geometry form the basic theory underlying the more common means of graphical expression used by engineers and architects to prepare drawings for the instruction of workmen. The principles also include those of design. Descriptive geometry is particularly applicable to the study of those curved surfaces which can be formed by bending a plane surface without tearing, crumpling, or stretching. Such surfaces are called developable surfaces. A cone or stove pipe is developable; a sphere is not.

Descriptive geometry is based on the idea that a point in space is completely specified by three mutually perpendicular

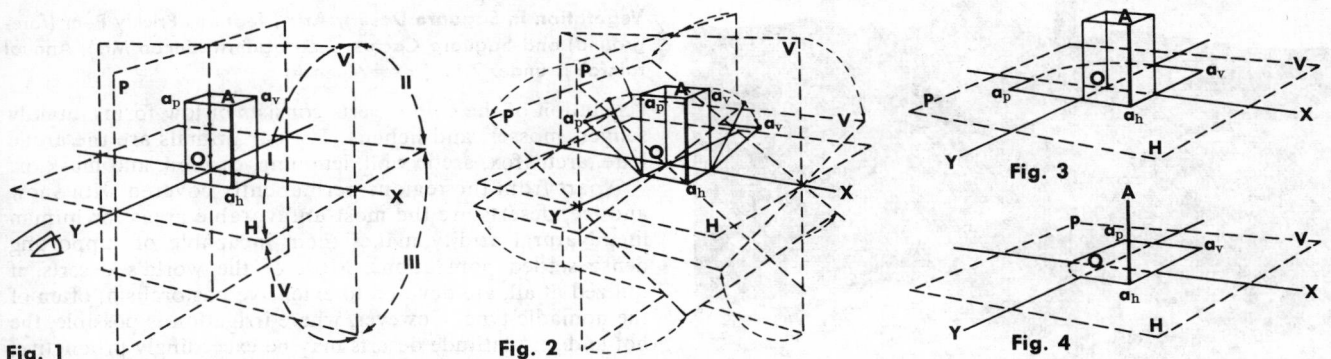

Fig. 1

Fig. 2

Fig. 3

Fig. 4

distances measured from three mutually perpendicular planes, and that if two of these planes are properly rotated into the plane of the third the three distances will appear in true length if drawn to a suitable scale. For example, Fig. 1 shows three mutually perpendicular planes marked *H, V,* and *P.* The horizontal plane is represented by *H,* the vertical plane by *V,* and the profile plane by *P.* The three planes intersect at a common point, or origin, *O,* and are considered to extend indefinitely. The horizontal and vertical planes divide space into four quadrants, marked I, II, III, and IV, when viewed by an eye in the position shown. Suppose a point, *A,* is placed in the first quadrant by moving it from the origin *O* three units to the right, two units forward, and five units vertically. If from point *A* perpendiculars are drawn to the vertical and profile planes, they will pierce the planes at a_v and a_p respectively. These points have the same vertical distance from the horizontal as point *A.* A perpendicular drawn from *A* will pierce the horizontal plane at a_h, which is as far forward from *V,* and as far to the right of *P,* as is point *A.* (To distinguish between *A* and *a,* the small letter refers to the projected view and the capital letter to the object itself.)

When the *V* plane is rotated on the *X* axis into the plane of *H,* as shown in Fig. 2, a_v will come to rest in the plane of *H* on a line perpendicular to the reference line *OX* and passing through a_h. (See COORDINATE GEOMETRY.) Likewise the *P* plane may be rotated into the plane of *H* about the reference line *OY,* and a_p ultimately will come to rest on a line passing through a_h and perpendicular to *OY.* Figure 3 is a plane drawing that shows the relationship between the three views resulting from completely rotating the profile and vertical planes into the horizontal. Proper interpretation of these views completely specifies the location of a point *A* in space with respect to the origin *O.* To locate a single point, it is necessary only to have any two of the projected views of that point, such as a_v, a_h, or a_p. A drawing such as Fig. 3, but with the profile plane rotated first into the vertical plane, and then with it into the horizontal plane (see Fig. 4), produces what the architect calls a plan view, a_h; a front elevation, a_v; and a left-side elevation, a_p. The plane drawing resulting in either case is a first-angle projection, when the point, or object, is placed in the first quadrant. Third-angle projection is universally used in the U. S. A. for conventional engineering drawings.

Descriptive geometry's methods for solving problems dealing with shapes are merely an extension of the basic ideas illustrated, using points and lines, since these are the elements of which shapes are constructed. Some of these problems consist of finding the lines of intersection of pipes and odd-shaped surfaces; the development of sheet-metal patterns that will form into desired shapes; the determination of the clearances between the members of a structure, or parts of a device, and the lines of intersection of plane surfaces; and determining what shadows are cast by architectural elements.—*A. P. E.*

DESERT: land rendered barren or semibarren because of meager precipitation. Deserts include not only areas where evaporation exceeds precipitation but cold regions with light precipitation and vegetation that is sparse because of low temperatures. In general, deserts receive less than 10 in. of precipitation in an average year. Three major types are commonly recognized: hot, mid-latitude, and cold deserts. Hot deserts, also known as tropical or low-latitude deserts, occur approximately between the latitudes 15° to 30° in both northern and southern hemispheres. Within these latitudes is a belt of descending, drying air that is unfavorable to the development of precipitation. Major hot deserts of the world are the Sahara and the Kalahari in Africa, the deserts of Arabia, the Thar Desert of Pakistan and NW India, the Australian Desert, the Atacama Desert of Chile, and the Sonoran Desert of NW Mexico and southwestern U. S. A. Mid-latitude deserts occur in the interiors of large continental land masses far distant from the oceans, which are the principal source of atmospheric moisture. Asia, the largest continent, has the most extensive mid-latitude deserts, including the Gobi. The interior of North America contains vast arid areas in the Great Basin and Colorado Plateau regions.

The aridity of deserts may be intensified by mountains, which act as a barrier to rain-bearing winds. Such dry areas are said to be in the rain shadow of the mountains. The hot deserts are generally the most arid of the desert types. Portions of the Atacama have had no rainfall for many years, and much of the Sahara receives less than 5 in. of rain in an average year. Desert precipitation, although very scanty and unreliable over a long period of time, may fall in torrential downpours. Runoff from desert highlands is usually rapid, because vegetation is sparse and dry soil repels water; hence downpours often cause local floods. Desert air generally has low humidity; consequently skies are apt to be clear and sunshine is abundant. Because of the lack of cloud cover, the land surface of deserts heats up rapidly in sunshine but cools quickly at night, causing a great daily range of temperature. Deserts tend to be windy and dusty, as there is little vegetation to reduce air movement over the ground or to secure loose surface material. Hot deserts frequently experience sandstorms or SIMOOMS. During the day intense heat causes a shimmering haze which when viewed at a distance may create a MIRAGE.

Desert land forms are characterized by angularity, resulting from relatively slow rock weathering, sparse vegetation cover, and lack of vegetation protection against erosion, including vigorous water erosion after the rare cloudbursts. Wind erosion and deposition are important in shaping the desert land surface, which is made up mainly of bare rock, rock fragments, and sand. Sandy deserts, called ergs, have sand piled in DUNES, which change their form and location under the influence of shifting winds. Desert stream valleys generally contain water only immediately after rainfall; they

Vegetation in Saguaro Desert, Ariz., features Prickly Pear (foreground) and Saguaro Cactus (seen against Rincon Mts). Annual rainfall is under 7 in. (*Josef Muench*)

are known as arroyos or wadis and are marked by steep-sided channels. Desert streams usually flow not to the sea but to basins of interior drainage where the excess water is lost by evaporation or seepage. The centers of such desert basins may contain salt deposits (playas or alkali flats) or saline lakes; such areas are completely sterile but may yield economically valuable salts. A few rivers with sources in humid regions possess enough volume to cross deserts and flow to the sea. Notable examples are the Nile, Tigris-Euphrates, Indus, and Colorado.

Deserts entirely without vegetation are rare; most desert regions support some vegetation adapted to the dry environment. Certain desert plants are able to withstand long periods of drought because their thick leaves and stems store water. Commonly the leaves are very small and protected so as to reduce moisture losses caused by transpiration. Plants growing in deserts are usually low and widely spaced, with well-developed root systems. Typical desert vegetation includes cacti, bunch grass, sagebrush, and creosote bush. Some desert plants are tolerant of ground containing a high proportion of alkali. The animals of deserts are generally small but surprisingly numerous. Reptiles are particularly common; true desert animals include the camel, gazelle, desert rabbit, kangaroo rat, and desert fox.

Cold deserts, or TUNDRAS, occur in the regions bordering the Arctic Ocean in North America, Europe, and Asia. Climatic conditions similar to those of the cold deserts may occur in any latitude at high elevations. The cold deserts differ in many respects from the hot and mid-latitude deserts. Strictly speaking, the cold deserts are humid regions for, although they receive only meager precipitation, the coldness keeps evaporation losses low. The moisture present in cold desert regions is generally unavailable, however, to plant and animal life because of the low prevailing temperatures. The sparse vegetation of the cold deserts consists of low forms, mainly sedges, mosses, and lichens. Typical animals are the arctic hare, arctic fox, arctic wolf, lemming, caribou, and musk ox.

Apart from the regions permanently covered with snow and ice, deserts are the most unfavorable areas for human life. Natural aridity makes them incapable of supporting dense settled populations. Most of the world's deserts, if utilized at all, are devoted to extensive pastoralism, often of the nomadic type. However, where irrigation is possible, the hot and mid-latitude deserts may be exceedingly productive, and some of the densest agricultural populations of the world occur in oases. See Color Plate 35.—*A. P. E.*

DESICCATION: in chemistry, a type of drying operation that employs a drying agent called a *desiccant.* A substance to be dried is placed in an apparatus called a desiccator, which can be tightly sealed and contains a quantity of the desiccant. There is a slow diffusion of water vapor from the substance being dried to the desiccant. Desiccants are compounds with great affinity for moisture, *e.g.* sulfuric acid, anhydrous calcium chloride, calcium oxide. The desiccant chosen depends on the chemical nature of the substance to be dried. (See DEHYDRATION; DRYING.)—*Ru. M.*

DE SITTER UNIVERSE: one of the simplest and most important uniform geometrical models of the universe, unique in combining the concept of expansion (see RED SHIFT OF GALAXIES) with that of changelessness in time. The distance between any two points of the system partaking of its motion increases exponentially in time. This universe is stationary but not static; it always shows the same motion; and hence it is the geometrical representation of the STEADY-STATE THEORY, according to which it contains matter of uniform and constant density. According to General Relativity, however, the model represents a universe which has expanded so much that the matter it contains is so sparsely distributed as to be negligible. Its "motion without matter" makes it an extreme FRIEDMANN MODEL. Its construction by William de Sitter, 1917, anticipated the observational discovery of the RED SHIFT OF GALAXIES and contrasted with Einstein's earlier "matter without motion" model.—*H. B.*

DESMAREST (or **DESMARETS**), **NICOLAS,** 1725–1815, French geologist; b. Soulaines (Aube). His observations (1763–64) in Auvergne, reported in *Mémoires* (1771–73), established that basalt is of igneous origin, and furnished evidence that valleys have originated by the erosive action of streams which flow through them—a doctrine not accepted by most geologists until the mid-19th cent.—*D. H. D. R.*

Dunes of Death Valley, Calif., almost totally barren, have an annual rainfall of less than 1.4 in. (*Union Pacific Railroad*)

DETERGENT: a material which when dissolved in water or another solvent in small amounts greatly enhances its ability to clean soiled objects. Non-aqueous detergents—those used in solvents other than water—are used in dry-cleaning systems and in engine oils to keep parts clean. Soap is the oldest and best-known aqueous detergent, but "detergent" in popular parlance does not include soap; it applies only to materials based on SURFACE-ACTIVE AGENTS.

Most aqueous detergents contain more than a single compound. Practically all those used for laundering, commercial textile processing, or personal use depend primarily on surface-active agents for their effectiveness; most contain auxiliary agents also. In the cleaning of cotton fabrics, soap though effective has been largely supplanted by the other household detergents. These contain a surface-active agent, a large proportion of a condensed alkaline inorganic phosphate (usually sodium tripolyphosphate), and minor proportions of special-purpose ingredients such as anti-corrosive agents, foam promoters, and optical brighteners.

Detergents for glass and ceramic surfaces, as in machine dishwashing systems, and for industrial cleaning of metals prior to painting or plating are based primarily on inorganic alkalis or alkaline-metal salts, but often contain surface-active agents to improve wetting power. A few inorganics, e.g. ammonia (for glass) and trisodium phosphate (for ceramics), are effective detergents in themselves, but most include the alkali-metal borates, phosphates, carbonates, silicates, or hydroxides.

Detergent action is complicated. Dissolved detergent molecules are strongly adsorbed by either the soil or the substrate, or both. Thus bonds that hold the soil to the substrate are loosened, and the water comes between them. Dislodged soil can then be flushed away easily.—*A. M. S.*

DETERMINANT: a square array of numbers (or functions) whose value is defined by a specific rule of combination of these quantities. The quantities are called elements. If there are four elements, they will be arranged in two rows and two columns, and the determinant will be of second *order*; a determinant of order n contains n^2 elements. Determinants are convenient notations for expressions that arise in solving simultaneous equations, in matrix theory, analytic geometry, and the calculus.

A second-order determinant may be denoted by the symbol

$$\begin{vmatrix} a_1 & b_1 \\ a_2 & b_2 \end{vmatrix}$$

and its value, or expansion, is defined as $a_1b_2 - a_2b_1$. The diagonal of the determinant from upper left to lower right is called the principal diagonal. Thus the expansion of the determinant is found by obtaining the products of the elements on the principal diagonal and subtracting the product of the elements on the other diagonal.

To make a general definition of a determinant, we make use of the idea of inversions in the natural order of the whole numbers 1,2,3,.... If the larger of two numbers precedes the smaller, this is called an inversion of the natural order. Thus the order 132 is said to contain one inversion (3,2) and two pair in natural order (1,3) and (1,2). The order 321 contains three inversions. The value of a determinant of the *n*th order may now be defined as the sum of all terms which can be formed by writing down the principal diagonal and all terms that can be formed from it by permuting the subscripts and prefixing a minus sign if the number of inversions of the subscripts is odd.

One useful method of evaluating higher-order determinants is by the use of minors. The minor of any element, *e,* in a deter-

minant is the determinant that consists of the elements that remain when the row and column containing *e* are omitted. Thus the minor of b_3 in the determinant

$$\begin{vmatrix} a_1 & b_1 & c_1 \\ a_2 & b_2 & c_2 \\ a_3 & b_3 & c_3 \end{vmatrix}$$

is the determinant

$$\begin{vmatrix} a_1 & c_1 \\ a_2 & c_2 \end{vmatrix}$$

The signed minor, or cofactor, is the minor of an element taken with a plus or minus sign according to the following rule: the number of the row containing the element is added to the number of the column; if the sum is even, the sign is plus; if the sum is odd, the sign is minus. In the above example, b_3 is in the third row, second column; $3 + 2 = 5$, which is odd, and therefore the cofactor of b_2 is *minus* its minor. To expand a determinant, any row or column is selected; the value of the determinant is the sum of the product of each element times its cofactor. For example, the following third-order determinant is expanded on its second row:

$$\begin{vmatrix} 2 & 1 & 0 \\ 1 & 4 & 1 \\ 6 & 3 & 2 \end{vmatrix}$$

$$= -1 \begin{vmatrix} 1 & 0 \\ 3 & 2 \end{vmatrix} + 4 \begin{vmatrix} 2 & 0 \\ 6 & 2 \end{vmatrix} - 1 \begin{vmatrix} 2 & 1 \\ 6 & 3 \end{vmatrix}$$

$$= -(2 - 0) + 4(4 - 0) - 1(6 - 6) = -2 + 16 = 14$$

This method is applicable to determinants of any order. The evaluation of a determinant of order n can thus be carried out by evaluating n determinants of order $(n - 1)$.

The evaluation of determinants can often be facilitated by means of various theorems about determinants. Some of the more important ones are: (*1*) The value of a determinant is unchanged if corresponding rows and columns are interchanged. (*2*) If all the elements of a row or column are multiplied by the same number, the value of the determinant is multiplied by that number. (*3*) If all the elements of a row or column are zero, the value of the determinant is zero. (*4*) The value of a determinant is not changed if to each element of any column (or row) we add k times the corresponding element of another column (or row).

The solution of simultaneous linear equations can be expressed by the use of determinants. Thus the solution of three equations in three letters

$$a_1x + b_1y + c_1z = d_1$$
$$a_2x + b_2y + c_2z = d_2$$
$$a_3x + b_3y + c_3z = d_3$$

may be given as

$$x = \begin{vmatrix} d_1 & b_1 & c_1 \\ d_2 & b_2 & c_2 \\ d_3 & b_3 & c_3 \end{vmatrix} \div D, \quad y = \begin{vmatrix} a_1 & d_1 & c_1 \\ a_2 & d_2 & c_2 \\ a_3 & d_3 & c_3 \end{vmatrix} \div D$$

$$z = \begin{vmatrix} a_1 & b_1 & d_1 \\ a_2 & b_2 & d_2 \\ a_3 & b_3 & d_3 \end{vmatrix} \div D, \quad \text{where } D = \begin{vmatrix} a_1 & b_1 & c_1 \\ a_2 & b_2 & c_2 \\ a_3 & b_3 & c_3 \end{vmatrix}$$

Determinants are also used in analytic geometry; for example, the area of a triangle whose vertices are (x_1,y_1), (x_2,y_2) and (x_3,y_3) is given by

$$\frac{1}{2} \begin{vmatrix} x_1 & y_1 & 1 \\ x_2 & y_2 & 1 \\ x_3 & y_3 & 1 \end{vmatrix}$$

—*H. E. W.*

DETERMINISM AND INDETERMINISM: two opposing philosophical concepts with far-reaching implications in science and other spheres of life. *Determinism* assumes that every event which occurs does so either in accordance with well-defined laws or as the result of the action of causes, or both. Lawless events or uncaused events do not exist. *Indeterminism* allows for the existence of such events, *i.e.* it admits that even a complete knowledge of all laws and causes may not enable us to explain or to predict everything that happens in the universe. Determinism was the dominant philosophy of the 18th and 19th cents. It was then also believed that all the laws which determine the course of events were already known and that they coincided with the laws of the mechanics of Newton. This does not mean that probabilistic assumptions were forbidden or frowned upon; on the contrary, rapid development of the kinetic theory led to tremendous extension of the use of probabilistic hypotheses; but such hypotheses were regarded as an expression of human *ignorance* rather than as an indication of a possible limitation of determinism. This position was criticized drastically by Ludwig Boltzmann and Franz Exner on the grounds that the empirical evidence in favor of determinism was not conclusive. Exner in particular pointed out that the existence of well-defined and stable probabilities is guaranteed even for events which are uncaused and which do not occur in accordance with deterministic laws. He also showed that the interplay of a great number of microscopic chance events can create, on the macroscopic level, exactly that impression of lawfulness and stability which had always been regarded as the main empirical argument in favor of determinism. The question as to whether determinism or indeterminism is the correct point of view can therefore be decided only by a more detailed study of the behavior of the ultimate constituents of matter. Such a study has been carried out by the QUANTUM THEORY, and for some time it seemed to decide the question in favor of indeterminism, the main reason being the dual character of these ultimate constituents—*i.e.* the fact that they can appear in two radically different forms, as particles and as waves, without there being any possibility of constructing a causal or deterministic transition from one form to the other. Thus indeterminism has become the dominant philosophy of the 20th cent. But it, too, can be criticized on the grounds that the empirical evidence in favor of it is not conclusive. David Bohm has pointed out that a very complicated deterministic mechanism whose details are beyond the limits of our experimental possibilities may well be able to create exactly those phenomena which are today regarded as very decisive empirical arguments in favor of indeterminism and chance. Combining this result of Bohm's with the above result of Exner, we are forced to conclude that neither determinism nor indeterminism can ever be established by experiment, yet both determinism and indeterminism may give a useful approximation of the behavior of physical systems of a certain size. A complete account of the behavior of physical systems will need a synthesis of determinism and indeterminism in which neither idea has absolute validity, although each one may be useful in restricted experimental domains.—*P. K. F.*

DE THIENDE (LA DISME, The Tenth), by Simon Stevin, 1585: Although Stevin did not invent decimal fractions, which had been used earlier by astronomers, in this small pamphlet he introduced them for the first time to the arithmetic of practical men. Through his teaching this elegant simplification passed into general use; moreover, Stevin was the first to realize the advantages of decimal systems of weights, measures, and currency. The modern notation for decimals (*e.g.* 3.142, which Stevin would have written 3⓪1①4②2③) was devised by John Napier (1550–1617).—*A. R. H.*

DETONATION: an explosion involving an exothermic reaction, which is extremely rapid (completed within a fraction of a second) and self-propagating, because of very high temperature and pressure developed by the reaction products. The reaction is triggered by a blow or friction, by heat, or by the impact of another detonation. It spreads in the form of a shock wave toward the still unreacted material at the rate of 3,500 meters/sec (for gaseous explosives) to 9,000 m/sec (for liquid and solid explosives). A characteristic feature is the sudden and discontinuous rise of pressure within the wave to between 10 and 100 times the initial value. The temperature and density of the reaction products also rise to a very high level. Behind the propagating wave the pressure decreases gradually to the point where a rarefaction wave finally succeeds the shock wave, damping the latter. The energy developed by the shock wave travels with the speed of sound, forcing the air in front to vibrate and propagate with the same velocity, producing the characteristic sound of detonation. See EXPLOSIVE; IGNITION.—*T. M. and C. S.*

DETOXICATION: the metabolic alteration by the body of toxic compounds to molecules which are less toxic and more readily excreted. Depending on the type of molecule to be detoxified, the body makes use of a variety of chemical reactions, including oxidation, reduction, hydroxylation, hydrolysis, and conjugation. The first detoxication mechanism, the synthesis by mammals of hippuric acid from ingested benzoic acid by conjugation with glycine, was discovered by W. Keller, 1842. Since then it has been found that conjugation may occur (1) with carbohydrates: ribose and glucose in plants and insects, glucuronic acid in animals and man; (2) with amino acids: glycine, ornithine, cysteine, and glutamine; (3) with sulfate; and (4) with acetyl and methyl groups. Thus, aromatic compounds are hydroxylated and the resulting phenols conjugated, generally with glucuronic acid or sulfate. Normal metabolites may be toxic when present in excess. Thus, epinephrine and norepinephrine are detoxified by methylation of their hydroxyl groups; bile acids are excreted as the glycine or taurine conjugates.—*E. S.*

DE USU PARTIUM (On the Use of the Parts), by Claudius Galen, 2nd cent. A. D.: This work, with *On the Natural Faculties* (a more general, speculative treatise), represents Galen's chief formulation of his physiological theories. It also reflects his anatomical investigations. Describing the functions of the organs and structures of the human and animal body, Galen dealt with digestion and assimilation, the uses of the heart, lungs, and vascular system, the excretory organs, muscles, and nervous system. Following earlier ideas, he employed the concept of the *four humors* (blood, phlegm, black bile, yellow bile) and attributed the material organization of the body to a *vital spirit* (in the arteries) and its nervous organization to a *psychic spirit* (in the brain and nerves). Like the *Almagest, The Use of the Parts* is a concluding synthesis of a major aspect of Greek science and it exerted an equally great authority for even longer, since some of Galen's ideas lingered into the 19th cent.—*A. R. H.*

DEUTERIUM: an isotope of hydrogen (H^2 or D); at. wt. 2.0147; mp 18.7°K; bp 23.5°K. Deuterium is known also as heavy hydrogen. A bond between deuterium and another atom generally differs in stability from a bond between hydrogen and the same atom. A deuterium atom has one electron circling a nucleus of one proton and one neutron; this nucleus, a *deuteron,* is used in nuclear-bombardment experiments.—*G. W. M.*

DEVILLE, HENRI ÉTIENNE SAINTE-CLAIRE, 1818–81, French chemist; b. St. Thomas, Virgin Is. One of the three independent discoverers of toluene (1841), he also prepared nitric anhydride (1849) and developed the first commercial process for obtaining metallic aluminum by action of sodium on aluminum chloride. Deville also greatly cheapened the production of sodium metal, prepared crystalline silicon (1854), and devised a means for obtaining high temperatures. With H. J. Debray he worked up immense amounts of demonetized platinum metal for the Russian government. In addition, he prepared the platinum-iridium alloy for the manufacture of the international standard meter and kilogram, developed methods for making artificial minerals, studied vapor densities, investigated thermal dissociations, and proposed the term "dissociation."—*R. E. O.*

DEVONIAN PERIOD: see GEOLOGICAL TIME CHART; PALEOZOIC ERA.

DEW: moisture which has condensed directly from the atmosphere onto vegetation or other objects near or on the ground. During a clear night the ground and objects near it lose heat by radiation, and if the adjacent air cools sufficiently to bring its temperature to the saturation point, some of the vapor condenses on these cold surfaces, just as moisture forms on a glass of ice water. See DEW POINT.—*P. L.*

DEWAR, SIR JAMES, 1842–1923, Scottish chemist and physicist; b. Kincardine-on-Forth. His early research was on chlorosulfuric acid, the oxidation products of picoline, the thermal equivalents of chlorine oxides, and the temperatures of electric sparks and of the Sun. In connection with work on specific heats he developed a vacuum jacket for insulating a calorimeter; this jacket or *Dewar flask* was the origin of the commercial Thermos flask. Much of his effort was devoted to low-temperature research; he was the first to liquefy hydrogen (1898), and he solidified it in 1899. Later researches included spectroscopic studies, studies of soap films, and safety of drinking water in London. He was a fellow of the Royal Society and an associate of the U. S. National Academy of Sciences.—*D. H. D. R.*

DEWEY, JOHN, 1859–1952, U. S. philosopher; b. Burlington, Vt. Ranked as the most influential U. S. philosopher in the first half of this century, he was a leading educational theorist and a distinguished liberal who participated widely in political and social affairs. In opposition to the view that modern physical theories reveal common-sense experience to be only the appearance of a superior reality, he maintained that scientific theories are actually powerful intellectual tools for controlling the course of events. Moreover, he was tireless in his efforts to show that the logic of inquiry (scientific method) used so effectively in the natural sciences can be employed in dealing with moral and social questions.—*S. M.*

DEW POINT: in meteorology, the temperature at which the air becomes saturated with water vapor and below which moisture is likely to condense in the form of DEW or airborne particles. The dew point varies according to the amount of moisture the air contains; for air containing 30.4 gm of water vapor per cubic meter it is 86°F; for air containing 7.27 gm/m³ it is 43°F. (See CONDENSATION.)—*P. L.*

DIABASE: a fine- to medium-grained basic intrusive IGNEOUS ROCK with a characteristic diabasic (ophitic) texture consisting of well-formed elongate crystals of labradorite feldspar in a matrix of coarse-grained anhedral pyroxene. Accessory minerals include olivine, titaniferous magnetite, ilmenite, biotite, and various deuteric minerals. Columnar jointing is well developed in many diabase bodies. Diabase generally occurs as dikes and sills, emplaced at moderate depths, and is the intrusive equivalent of BASALT and GABBRO, which are the extrusive and plutonic rocks formed from magmas of the same composition.—*L. M.*

DIABATIC FLOW: the flow of a fluid to which or from which heat is transferred. The transfer has interesting consequences. For instance, if a gas flowing in a tube is heated, the temperature of the gas can actually drop if the velocity is below, but close to, the speed of sound. By cooling a supersonic gas flow, the pressure which the fluid would have at low speeds can be increased. This phenomenon can in theory be employed to make a compressor with no moving parts called the aerothermopressor. Heating always tends to make the velocity closer to the speed of sound. With enough heating this point can be reached, and any additional heating will cause "diabatic choking"—a reduction of the flow through the tube. —*Wm. R.*

DIALOGO DI GALILEO GALILEI . . . SOPRA I DUE MASSIMI SISTEMI DEL MONDO (Dialogue on the Two Chief Systems of the World), by Galileo Galilei, 1632: This masterpiece of Galileo's long struggle to vindicate the Copernican system of the universe followed his descriptions of the first observations with the telescope (*e.g.* topography of the Moon, discovery of the satellites of Jupiter, phases of Venus, sunspots) and other works defending the freedom of scientific inquiry. It proved that the Ptolemaic system could not account for the new knowledge of the heavens with which the Copernican system was fully in accord; but Galileo recognized that this new knowledge did not definitely establish the motion of Earth. In the "Fourth Day," however, Galileo drew a proof of it from the tidal movements, mistakenly attributed by him to the combination of Earth's diurnal and solar revolutions. Important is Galileo's disproof of physical arguments against

On dedication page of Galileo's *Dialogo*, the engraver represented three arguing scholars: proponents of the Aristotelian, Ptolemaic, and Copernican systems. (*Burndy Library*)

Man-made diamonds: Once a dream, synthetic diamonds are now a reality. Other gems too, including rubies, sapphires, and emeralds of fine quality and large size, have been successfully synthesized. (Gen. Elec. Research Lab.)

the motion of Earth: by using the concept of inertia for the first time (though imperfectly) he showed that the relative displacements of a group of bodies are unaffected by a uniform motion in which all participate. The *Dialogo* was by far the finest exposition and defense of the Copernican system ever written; its publication led to Galileo's trial and condemnation at Rome (1633), and to the downfall of the Aristotelian-Ptolemaic cosmos.—*A. R. H.*

DIALYSIS: the process of separation of colloidal particles from molecular particles by diffusion of the latter through a membrane. Because dialysis is mainly dependent on the difference between the rate of diffusion of the dissolved substance and that of the colloidal particles, the dialyzing membrane does not act solely as a sieve or filter. Soluble substances, *e.g.* sugar or salt, diffuse more rapidly through the pores of the membrane than do the much larger insoluble colloidal substances, *e.g.* gelatin or glue. Dialysis is an important separation technique in the purification of colloidal systems. A mixture of colloidal and soluble substances is placed inside a membrane container, which is suspended in a solvent; most of the dissolved molecules pass through the membrane into the surrounding solvent, leaving the colloidal substance inside the membrane. Dialysis is an equilibrium phenomenon, and there exists, then, a distribution ratio of the molecules across the membrane.—*G. W. M.*

DIAMAGNETISM: a property of matter which causes it, when placed in a magnetic field, to become weakly magnetized in a direction opposite to the magnetization of the external field. As a result, purely diamagnetic substances are repelled by a magnetic field, *i.e.* tend to move into a magnetically weaker region. But this effect is overshadowed in substances that are paramagnetic (*i.e.* acquire weak magnetization in the same direction as that of the magnetizing field) or ferromagnetic (exhibit strong magnetization with no external field present): these substances are attracted into strong fields. Diamagnetism refers to the MAGNETIC MOMENT induced in the individual atoms and molecules by an applied field, the process being similar to that by which currents are induced in a conducting loop of wire when the flux linking the loop is changed. The induced moment is directly opposite to the applied field. See MAGNETISM; PARAMAGNETISM; FERROMAGNETISM.—*F. B.*

DIAMOND: a mineral consisting essentially of pure carbon (C). It is isometric, commonly in single octahedral crystals; sp gr 3.50–3.53, hardness 10, with perfect octahedral cleavage; brittle. The color is commonly faint yellow or brown; it may

be very pale blue, or colorless. Diamonds are, rarely, vivid yellow, green, pink, orange, mauve; also even black. Bort is diamond ranging from granular to cryptocrystalline; it has great toughness and hence is prized for many abrasive and drilling applications. The extraordinary brilliancy of a diamond, after faceting, is due to its very high refractive index, 2.417 for yellow sodium light, and the fire or play of colors results from the relatively large dispersion (index for blue light = 2.460 and for red light = 2.402). Diamonds crystallized in certain ultrabasic magmas at great depths, being brought to the surface upon intrusion and cooling of the ultrabasic material. The latter, known as kimberlite, commonly forms pipes, dikes, and sills. Important *in situ* deposits occur in Africa and India; small diamond-bearing kimberlite pipes are found near Murfreesboro, Ark. Alluvial diamonds are mined in Brazil, Africa, Siberia, and India. Crystals range in size from microscopic to as much as several pounds in weight (Cullinan diamond); the majority are of less than one carat (⅕ gm). Gems are cut on a rapidly revolving, soft cast-iron lap charged with diamond dust, cutting being possible only in certain directions of lesser softness in the stone; cutting and polishing are simultaneous. Industrial stones are mounted by peening or soldering into metal holders for use as abrasive wheel truers, dressers, large stone-cutting saws, and drills. Wire-drawing dies are prepared from selected, flat, distorted crystals which are pierced with tapered holes. Special tool points are cut by the same processes used for shaping gems. (See GEMSTONES.) Diamonds have been recently synthesized in the U. S. A. and abroad. Only very small crystals suitable for abrasive powder have so far been obtained, but experimentation is progressing toward growth of large single crystals.—*J. Si.*

DIASTROPHISM: the process by which the crust of the earth is deformed. It includes FAULTING and FOLDING, and is one of the three major geologic processes, the others being vulcanism (igneous activity) and gradation (weathering and erosion). Diastrophic forces acting at right angles to the earth's surface cause relative uplift or subsidence of parts of the crust and result, for instance, in the elevation of large plateau areas or in the subsidence of long, narrow oceanic DEEPS. Forces which act parallel to the earth's surface produce the folded and faulted structures characteristic of mountain areas. See also MOUNTAINS AND MOUNTAIN BUILDING; TECTONICS.—*J. Sh.*

DIATOM: see ALGAE.

DIATOMACEOUS EARTH: a fine-grained deposit formed on the ocean bottom by accumulation of the siliceous shells of diatoms. The compacted form is called *diatomite*. One very fine, porous form of diatomaceous earth obtained in Germany, called *kieselguhr*, is valuable as an absorbent and is used for absorbing liquid nitroglycerin to produce dynamite. Diatomaceous earth is also employed for decolorizing oils, as an insulating material, as a filler in such products as paints and fertilizers, and as a base for scouring and polishing powders. Deposits of diatomaceous earth are abundant in rocks of Cenozoic age.—*A. P. E.*

DIAZO COMPOUNDS: compounds highly prized by the chemist for their versatility in chemical synthesis. From an aromatic AMINE (I) can be obtained the diazo compounds (II) or (III).

(I) Aniline (II) Benzenediazonium chloride (III) Potassium benzenediazotate

The important product (II) can be "coupled" with other molecules to give azo dyes (see DYES AND DYEING), or it can be deprived of the diazo group to yield PHENOLS, ETHERS, and other compounds. The term diazo (Fr. *azote,* "nitrogen") suggests the ratio of two nitrogen atoms to one ring structure.—*Ru. M.*

DICHROISM: a property of certain materials, *e.g.* synthetic Polaroid and some natural crystals, whereby they transmit light vibrating only in a certain plane. Ordinary light vibrates in all directions perpendicular to its path. When light passes through a dichroic medium, only one component of each vibration is readily transmitted—the component that lies in a plane determined by the direction of propagation and a particular axis of the material; the other component is absorbed. The light emerging from the medium vibrates only in one plane and is called plane POLARIZED LIGHT.—*S. Br.*

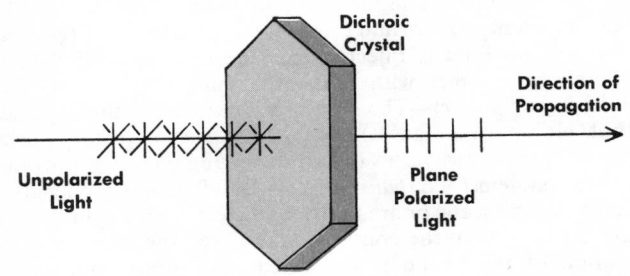

Unpolarized light, when passed through a dichroic crystal, emerges as plane-polarized light.

DICKSON, LEONARD EUGENE, 1874–1954, U. S. mathematician; b. Independence, Iowa. He was on the faculty of the Univ. of Chicago from 1900 until his retirement, 1939. He was a leading algebraist and wrote on invariants, groups, and theory of numbers. His principal book was *A History of Theory of Numbers* (3 vols., 1919–23). He was a member of the National Academy of Sciences.—*H. C.*

DICOT (or **dicotyledon**): any FLOWERING PLANT of the subclass Dicotyledoneae, including the broad-leaved trees, many ornamental plants, and crop plants such as tobacco, cotton, beans, peas, and tomatoes. Dicots are the most varied and numerous (about 200,000 species) flowering plants. They are distinguished from MONOCOTS, which comprise the other subclass of flowering plants, by having two cotyledons, or seed leaves (instead of one), in each seed. Other major features distinguish most dicots: the parts of the flower are in fours, as in cabbage, or in fives, as in cherry, or are multiples of these numbers; the leaves or leaflets have a network of smaller veins between the larger veins; the vascular bundles usually have a cambium that produces secondary tissues including xylem (water-conducting tissue) and phloem (food-conducting tissue). Concentric additions of secondary xylem surrounding the primary xylem (which is derived from the terminal growth center) may show obvious ANNUAL RINGS and provide the plant with a woody stem and root.—*W. Ko.*

DICUMAROL (**dicoumarol**): a white crystalline solid first isolated from spoiled sweet-clover hay. It is used in human medicine to prolong the blood-clotting time of patients with thrombosis, embolism, and phlebitis. Dicumarol depresses the formation by the liver of prothrombin, a protein required for blood clotting.—*E. M.*

DIDEROT, DENIS, 1713–84, French philosopher and man of letters; b. Langres. He was an intellectual leader of the French ENLIGHTENMENT and a prolific writer of drama, fiction, and criticism, as well as philosophy and science, but his main achievement was as editor of and chief contributor to the 28-vol. *Encyclopedia* (1752–80). The bulk of its entries were on science, technology, and mathematics; its philosophical viewpoint was materialistic; its purpose was in part to weaken authority by presenting reliable knowledge on every subject; and its influence was great despite censorship and intervention by the Church.—*Ar. D.*

DIE: a tool for shaping metals and plastics. Dies are usually made of hardened steel, with holes, projections, or contours that cut or deform materials by great pressure or impact. They are used to extrude wire and tubing, cut screw threads, punch holes, stamp impressions, and drop-forge cold or die-cast molten metals.—*K. A.*

DIELECTRIC: a substance that does not conduct electricity; an INSULATOR. Dielectrics are nonconductors because they lack the free electrons or holes required for conduction (see CONDUCTOR AND SEMICONDUCTOR). When a good conductor is placed in an electric field, the free electrons quickly redistribute themselves so that the field does not penetrate the conductor; but when a dielectric is placed in an electric field, there will be a field inside the dielectric. This field, however, is reduced by the presence of the dielectric because, although it is neutral over all, the dielectric is made up of positively charged atomic nuclei with negatively charged electrons held, more or less tightly, in some configuration about the nuclei. The electric field exerts oppositely directed forces on the nuclei and the electrons, causing change in the relative position of positive and negative charges; this change is called *polarization.* In the absence of the external field the electrons in a regular array of neutral atoms are arranged symmetrically around the nucleus, as indicated in A (see figures on next page). When the field is applied, the forces on the charges distort the atom, as shown in B. The "center" of the negative charges no longer coincides with the positive charge. Although the neutral atom does not give rise to a field outside itself, the polarized atom does. Some distance away, its field is the same as the field of a dipole, a pair of equal positive and negative charges separated by an appropriate distance. The polarized dielectric with its array of dipoles is shown in C. The field arising from the dipole is greater the greater its MOMENT, defined as the product of the magnitude of either charge and the distance between them. In calculating the field arising from a dielectric body, with its array of induced dipoles, it is useful to add the individual dipole moments to obtain a total dipole moment per unit volume, denoted by P. For most dielectrics, P is proportional to the applied electric field, the constant of proportionality being called the electric susceptibility of the material.

In dielectrics less simple than the one just described, the dielectric may consist of an array of separated positive and negative charges, even in the absence of an external field. If these are arranged with a high degree of symmetry, the net dipole moment in the absence of an applied electric field will be zero, and application of a field will create dipoles by causing relative motion of positive and negative charges, much as in the example discussed above. In crystals with less symmetry there may be a net dipole moment in the absence of an external field. See FERROELECTRIC.

From C it can be seen that the surface charges induced by the field give rise to an opposing field inside the dielectric. The resulting reduction in the field inside the dielectric is experimentally found to be approximately constant for any given dielectric. It is described by a quantity

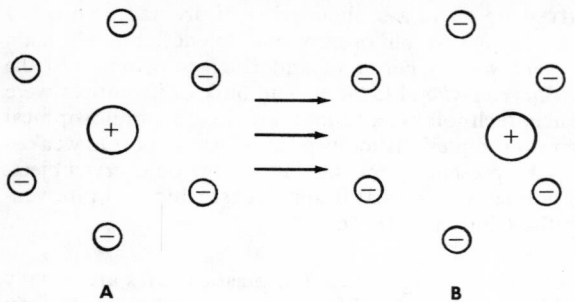

A   **B**

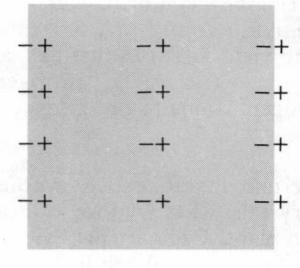

Atom in a dielectric substance has its electrons arranged in symmetrical orbits in the absence of an electric field (A). Applying an electric field distorts the orbits (B), producing an over-all polarization of a piece of the dielectric (C).

C

called the dielectric constant κ, operationally defined as follows: the dielectric constant, κ, of a substance is the ratio of the capacitance of a CAPACITOR with the substance filling the space between the plates to the capacitance with vacuum between the plates. Capacitance is the ratio of the charge on one plate to the potential difference between the plates. Since the field in the dielectric between the plates is reduced by a factor κ, the potential difference is reduced by κ, while the charge on the plates remains the same; hence the capacitance is κ times as great.—*E. M. C.*

DIELS, OTTO PAUL HERMANN, 1876–1954, German chemist; b. Hamburg. He discovered a new oxide of carbon, C_3O_2 (carbon suboxide, or malonic anhydride), and a method of removing hydrogen in a controllable fashion from organic compounds by the use of selenium, an important technique in determining the structure of certain complex organic substances. With Kurt Alder he discovered and investigated organic syntheses by means of dienes, and for that research they shared the 1950 Nobel prize.—*D. H. D. R.*

DIENE: an organic chemical compound with two double bonds; also called a *di-olefin.* An example is 1,3-butadiene, $CH_2{=}CH{-}CH{=}CH_2$, which is a building unit of some of the synthetic rubbers. The chemistry of a diene depends on whether the two double bonds in the chain are cumulative (on the same C atom), conjugated (as in 1,3-butadiene), or isolated (separated by at least two single bonds).—*Ru. M.*

DIESEL, RUDOLF, 1858–1913, German engineer; b. Paris, France. Diesel's fame rests upon his invention of an internal-combustion engine (DIESEL ENGINE) in which the fuel is ignited by the heat produced by compression, rather than by an outside source of heat, *e.g.* an electric spark, flame, or heated element. The engine was patented in 1893 but had to be redesigned more than once, and was not produced commercially until 1898. Diesel published a description of his engine, *Theorie und Konstruktion eines rationellen Wärmemotors,* in 1893.—*S. B.*

DIESEL ENGINE: an internal-combustion engine in which fuel, injected into a cylinder, is ignited by heat produced by the compression of air within the cylinder. This *compression-ignition* principle distinguishes the diesel from the common gasoline (Otto) engine conventionally used in automobiles, which relies upon an external spark source to ignite its fuel-air mixture. Thus the gasoline engine is frequently called a *spark-ignition* engine; it may also be called a *carbureted engine,* after the fuel-mixing device (carburetor) it employs. (For description of the gasoline engine, see MOTOR VEHICLE.) A diesel does not need a carburetor, since in a diesel the fuel does not need to be mixed with air before entering the cylinder. Both diesel and gasoline engines are internal-combustion engines, *i.e.* they both burn fuel within their cylinders. Both are heat engines in that they both convert heat released

in their cylinders into work (*e.g.* moving a piston); both are PRIME MOVERS. The diesel engine was patented in 1893 by the German Rudolf Diesel (see ENGINE).

The operation of a diesel engine may be described in five steps: (1) *Intake*—Air is drawn or forced into the cylinder. (2) *Compression*—The air in the cylinder is compressed to very high temperature and pressure by the piston. (3) *Ignition-combustion*—Fuel is injected into the cylinder and then is ignited on contact with the hot, compressed air. (4) *Expansion* (or *power*)—The resulting mixture of burning fuel (hot, high-pressure gases) expands against the piston, pushing the piston away and thus transferring energy out of the cylinder system. (5) *Exhaust*—The gases left in the cylinder after combustion escape or are blown out, clearing the cylinder for the next cycle. In the conventional diesel, the reciprocating motion of the piston is converted into rotary motion by means of a connecting rod and crank. Smaller diesels may be started by an electric motor connected to a storage battery; the motor actuates the pistons and fuel injectors. Larger engines are usually started by compressed air forced into the cylinders at a pressure of about 200 lb/in.²

A diesel has a higher *compression ratio* than a gasoline engine. This is the ratio between (*a*) the cylinder volume plus the volume of the connected combustion chamber, if any, at the stage of least piston intrusion into the cylinder and (*b*) the cylinder and combustion-chamber volume when the piston is at the peak of its compression stroke, at which time the piston fills most of the inside of the cylinder. An example of a compression ratio of 16:1 is a cylinder with a volume of 16 in.³ at the beginning of the piston's compression stroke, and a volume of 1 in.³ at peak compression. In such a cylinder at peak compression, air would have a temperature of 940°F and a pressure of 546 lb/in.² (assuming that at the beginning of the compression stroke, the air was at atmospheric pressure with a temperature of 100°F). These values are typical for all engines of 16:1 compression ratio, regardless of their gross dimensions. Diesel-engine compression ratios vary from about 12:1 to 22:1; gasoline engines ordinarily have compression ratios between 4:1 and 10:1. The lower compression ratios of the gasoline engine indicate only moderate temperature and pressure within the cylinder at the end of compression: thus the use of a spark to ignite the fuel-air mixture. The higher diesel compression makes the air within the cylinder hot enough to ignite the injected fuel oil, which has an ignition temperature ranging from about 600 to 800°F.

Partly because of its higher compression ratio (indicating a greater expansion of burning gases and thus a fuller use of the potential energy of the fuel with a consequently cooler exhaust) the diesel is more efficient than the gasoline engine. Another advantage of the diesel is that it is not plagued by the problem of *pre-ignition, i.e.* igniting of the fuel in the cylinder before the optimum time, the instant of peak compression. (Pre-ignition in the gasoline engine is caused by a temperature and pressure within the cylinder above the fuel's ignition point.) In the gasoline engine, especially one of relatively high compression ratio, the fuel may ignite spontaneously in the cylinder because of an overheated valve, spark plug, glowing carbon deposit, or improper fuel. Since pre-ignition causes burning before peak compression, the burning, expanding gases expand against the incoming piston; this causes reduction of power, "knocking," and overheating of the engine. In the smoothly operating diesel, fuel is not present in the cylinder until it is sprayed into the combustion space at or very near the instant of peak compression; thus pre-ignition does not occur in the diesel engine unless the injector is leaking fuel into the cylinder during compression.

In many particulars, the diesel engine closely resembles the more familiar gasoline engine. Both engines have crankshafts, connecting rods, timing gears, oil pumps, water pumps, camshafts, pistons, rings, cylinders, and valves. Many of the external accessories are also similar, especially on smaller diesels, *e.g.* cooling fans, generators, starters, and fuel-transfer pumps. The choice of the gasoline engine over the diesel for most automotive and aviation purposes is principally based on the former's better power-weight ratio. The diesel engine, because of its greater peak and higher average cylinder pressure, must have stronger, heavier parts than the gasoline engine.

One of the first diesel engines, now on display at the German Museum in Munich, was built in 1898 by Reisinger, Meier, and Diesel, the firm founded by Rudolf Diesel to manufacture his engine. Diesel, dissatisfied with the efficiencies of engines then in use, had patented the principle of the engine in 1893; but 5 yr were needed to develop a practicable cylinder and piston that would withstand the very high pressure (*i.e.* compression ratio) required to cause self-ignition of the fuel. Diesel also experimented with fuels: in the early models coal dust was injected into the cylinder by compressed air; later, oil was substituted for coal dust. Because of their great bulk and weight, early diesels were used mainly in large ships and stationary installations. Continued development has resulted in engines small enough to be used in locomotives and motor vehicles. (*Brown Bros.*)

The injection system of the diesel engine is designed to direct the right amount of fuel to the right cylinder at the right instant and at sufficient pressure to produce atomization of the fuel and to overcome the high cylinder pressure at the peak of compression. There may be a piston-type injection pump for each cylinder, or a single pump may be used with a distributor system. The high-pressure fuel opens the nozzle and is sprayed into the combustion space. Some of the problems in the design of a successful injection system are: (1) how to inject the fuel in carefully metered volumes from a trace amount to a cubic centimeter, depending on the engine load; (2) how to design the injection nozzle so that delivery of fuel begins and ends abruptly; (3) how to carry out the complete process of injection with timing to the nearest 1/10,000th sec; (4) how to atomize the fuel and produce penetration of the cylinder "charge" (*i.e.* the compressed air in the cylinder). Early diesels employed air injection; air pressure of nearly 1,000 lb/in.^{2} was used to force the fuel into the cylinders. Such pressures required heavy and inefficient air-compression equipment. Air injection has now been largely abandoned in favor of *solid injection, i.e.* direct mechanical injection of the fuel by fluid pressure. These later systems are capable of closer metering, faster operation for high-speed engines, and internal pressures of 30,000 lb/in.^{2}.

Diesel engines are 2-stroke or 4-stroke in operation. If the engine uses a stroke of the piston to induct the air (*i.e.* a charge stroke) and a stroke in the opposite direction after compression-combustion-expansion to scavenge (clear out) the exhaust gases, it is called a 4-stroke engine. A 2-stroke engine eliminates the separate charge and scavenge strokes by using a blower to scavenge the exhaust gases out through the exhaust port; this occurs when the piston is near the maximum-volume position. Most large diesels are 2-stroke. The 2-stroke engine completes the cycle and a power stroke in all the cylinders at every revolution, while the 4-stroke requires two revolutions to complete the cycle and execute a power stroke in all the cylinders. In theory, the 2-cycle engine requires only half as many pistons for a given power output, and thus half as many cylinders, liners, connecting rods, crankthrows, cam surfaces, valve mechanisms, injection pumps, and the like. In practice, a 30 to 40% reduction of moving parts is attained. The 2-stroke engine is thus much more compact. Its shorter crankshaft is stronger for a given power production. Less weight and bulk of metal are required for a given capacity; the valving is generally greatly simplified. The 2-stroke engine is easily reversible—an advantage in some large marine engines and other applications. *Supercharging* (forcing more air into the combustion space to promote fuller combustion) is possible by use of engine-driven scavenger blowers. In favor of the 4-stroke engine is slightly better efficiency, higher speeds, smoother engine performance, a cooler engine, generally easier starting, and the absence of a scavenging apparatus.

Diesels may also be classified by number of cylinders, by type of cylinder arrangement (in-line, radial, or vee), or by type of combustion chamber. Representative combustion-chamber types are the plain (open) chamber, which is merely the top space of the cylinder, the auxiliary-combustion type, the precombustion chamber, the air cell, and the energy cell. These modifications of the open chamber are designed to increase the turbulence of the fuel-air mixture within the cylinder during combustion. High turbulence generally improves engine performance and efficiency.

Diesel fuel is somewhat lower in cost and higher in energy content per gallon than gasoline; this further adds to the diesel's over-all efficiency and economy. In PETROLEUM REFINING, diesel fuel is usually taken from the residue remaining after the automotive and aviation gasolines, kerosene, and the lighter distillates have been removed from the crude oil. However, the hope of the early diesel developers that the engine would burn "practically any" fuel at high efficiency has not been borne out. A diesel fuel's *cetane number* is one measure of its *ignition quality,* and roughly corresponds to the octane number of gasolines. The ignition quality of a diesel fuel is its ability to ignite spontaneously in the cylinder. Fuel with poor ignition quality may cause a delay in ignition within the cylinder, and thus cause combustion "knock." Specifically, cetane number is the percentage of cetane ($C_{16}H_{34}$, a long, straight-chain hydrocarbon of the paraffin series) in a laboratory fuel which produces the same engine performance as the commercial fuel being tested. Other specifications affecting the ignition quality of a diesel fuel are its viscosity, flash point, and pour point, and its ash, sulfur, basic sediment, and water content.—*A. P. E. and E. H. H.*

DIET: see FOOD; VITAMIN.

DIFFERENTIAL CALCULUS: see CALCULUS, DIFFERENTIAL AND INTEGRAL.

DIFFERENTIAL EQUATION: an equation containing one or more derivatives of an unknown function. To solve it is to find the unknown function. Since a derivative symbolizes a rate of change, differential equations are used to solve problems involving such physical phenomena as velocity and acceleration, heat flow, electricity, wave motion; their importance in mathematical physics can hardly be overemphasized.

The simplest kind of differential equation is one in which a derivative is set equal to a function of the independent variable. An example is $dy/dx = x,$ whose solution is $y = \int x \, dx = \frac{1}{2}x^2 + c,$ where c is any constant. A solution of any differential equation of the form $dy/dx = f(x)$ is found by straightforward integration. A differential equation alone does not completely determine the unknown function, since one or more arbitrary constants of integration may appear. Subsidiary conditions, in addition to the differential equation, lead to unambiguous solutions in practical applications.

If a differential equation involves only one independent variable, a letter denoting an unknown function, and ordinary derivatives, the equation is an ordinary differential equation. If there are two or more independent variables, an unknown function of these variables, and partial derivatives, the equation is a partial differential equation. For example, $x \, dy/dx - y + 3x = 0$ is an ordinary differential equation, and $\partial z/\partial x = 2 \, \partial^2 z/\partial t^2$ is a partial differential equation. Ordinary differential equations are classified by order and degree. The order is that of the highest derivative in the equation: $dy/dx = y$ is of the first order, and $d^2y/dx^2 = y$ is of second order. The degree of an ordinary differential equation is the exponent of the highest derivative which appears in the equation: $(d^2y/dx^2)^2 + 4y^2(dy/dx)^3 = x$ is of the second degree. A linear differential equation is one of the first degree in the dependent variable and all its derivatives appearing in the equation. The general linear equation of second order has the form $\phi_1(x) \, d^2y/dx^2 + \phi_2(x) \, dy/dx + \phi_3(x) y = f(x).$

The geometrical interpretation of an ordinary differential equation is a family of curves in a plane. For example, the differential equation $dy/dx + x/y = 0$ states that the slope $= -$abscissa/ordinate. This is true of all circles having a common center at the origin (see Fig. 1). The equation of this family of circles is $x^2 + y^2 = r^2,$ which is the *general* solution of the equation. A particular circle of this family has an equation which is obtained from the general solution by

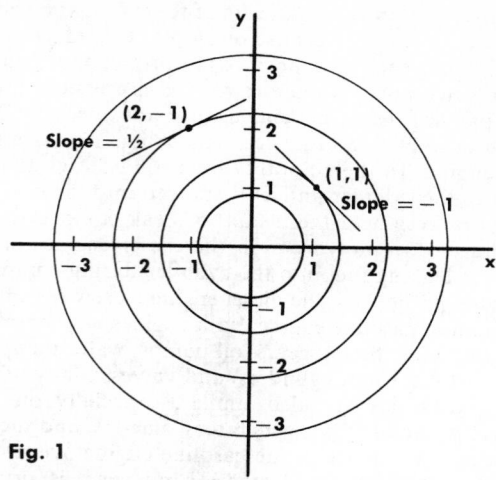

Fig. 1

giving the arbitrary constant r^2 a particular value; *e.g.* that which passes through the point (3,4) has the equation $x^2 + y^2 = 25.$ This is a *particular* solution of the differential equation. The general solution of a differential equation of the first order contains one arbitrary constant, or parameter. If the equation is of the first degree, the curves of this one-parameter family do not intersect. If it is of the second degree, two curves of the family may pass through a point; in fact, it is to be expected that two will pass through all or most of the points where there are any curves belonging to the solution. An equation whose degree is higher than the first may have a solution which does not belong to the general solution. Thus, the general solution of the equation

$$y^2(dy/dx)^2 + y^2 = 1 \quad \text{is} \quad (x - a)^2 + y^2 = 1,$$

representing the family of circles with radius 1 and centers on the x axis (see Fig. 2). The two lines $y = 1$ and $y = -1$ are tangent to all of these circles and form the *envelope* of the one-parameter family of circles of the general solution. On both of these lines, $dy/dx = 0,$ and the differential equation is satisfied; these two are *singular* solutions. They do not result from the general solution by giving the arbitrary constant a special value. In general, an envelope of a family of curves corresponding to the general solution is, itself, a solution. For at every point where one of the family is tangent to the envelope, its slope agrees with that of the envelope. Unless it happens, also, to be a particular solution, it is a singular solution. Differential equations of order higher than 1 correspond to much more complicated families of curves.

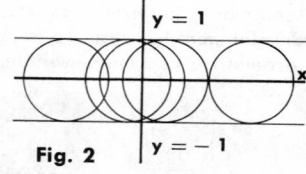

Fig. 2

An ordinary differential equation of order two contains two arbitrary constants. In fact, any solution of an equation of order n which contains n arbitrary constants is its general solution, provided there is no way of combining terms so as to reduce the number of arbitrary constants. A particular solution is obtained by assigning special values to these constants. It is easily verified that $y = a \sin 2x + b \cos 2x$ is the general solution of the second order equation $d^2y/dx^2 + 4y = 0.$ Particular solutions are often obtained to satisfy certain *initial* conditions, *i.e.* specified values of the solution function and its derivatives when $x = 0.$ Thus, in the example, if $y = 2$ and $dy/dx = 6$ when $x = 0,$ the general solution reduces to the particular solution $y = 3 \sin 2x + 2 \cos 2x.$ A particular solution can be obtained to satisfy *boundary* conditions—specified values of the solution function at given values of $x.$ In the example, if $y = 4$ when $x = \pi/4,$ and $y = 2$ when

$x = \pi/2$, the particular solution is $y = 4 \sin 2x - 2 \cos 2x$. Here the distinction between initial values and boundary values is trivial. In connection with partial differential equations it is much more important.

Methods of solving equations of the first order and first degree depend upon recognizing an exact derivative of a function of two variables, $(d/dx) f(x,y)$, and schemes for reducing the equation to an *exact* one, in which only such exact derivatives appear. For example, $(d/dx)(xy) = x \, dy/dx + y$. Hence the equation $x \, dy/dx + y = 0$ has the general solution, $xy = c$; and $x \, dy/dx + y = x^2$ has the general solution, $xy = x^3/3 + c$. The equation $dy/dx + x/y = 0$ is not exact, but multiplication by y makes it so, since $y \, dy/dx + x = (d/dx) \frac{1}{2}(y^2 + x^2)$. The general solution is $\frac{1}{2}(y^2 + x^2) = c$. In this instance y is an *integrating factor,* since multiplication by it makes the equation exact, and therefore integrable. If we write the equation in terms of differentials, we see that it is $ydy + xdx = 0$. Here the variables are *separated, dy* appearing only with y, and dx only with x. The use of integrating factors and methods of separating variables are extensive.

Linear differential equations are an exceptionally important variety. Methods of solution rest on the fundamental principle: if two or more solutions are found then any linear combination of these solutions is itself a solution. Thus, for the linear equation of second order, $d^2y/dx^2 + 4y = 0$, we observe that $y = \sin 2x$ and $y = \cos 2x$ are both solutions. Hence $y = a \sin 2x + b \cos 2x$ is a solution, and since it contains two arbitrary constants it is the general solution, provided there is no way of combining the terms so as to reduce the number of constants. The criterion for determining this is given by the *Wronskian* of the functions in the solution. The Wronskian of two functions, $f(x)$ and $g(x)$, is the determinant

$$\begin{vmatrix} f(x) & g(x) \\ f'(x) & g'(x) \end{vmatrix}$$

If this determinant is not identically 0, *i.e.* 0 for all values of x, the functions $f(x)$ and $g(x)$ are said to be *linearly independent* and no values of a and b exist which make $a \cdot f(x) + b \cdot g(x)$ identically 0. When this is the case the expression $a \cdot f(x) + b \cdot g(x)$ cannot be expressed with fewer than two arbitrary constants. The Wronskian of the functions $\sin 2x$ and $\cos 2x$ is

$$\begin{vmatrix} \sin 2x & \cos 2x \\ 2\cos 2x & -2\sin 2x \end{vmatrix} = -2 \sin^2 2x - 2 \cos^2 2x = -2$$

Methods of solving linear equations reduce to a search for enough linearly independent particular solutions (n of them for an equation of order n) in order to write the general solution by means of the principle stated.

Partial differential equations are essentially deeper and more difficult to solve than ordinary differential equations. Because a vast number of problems of science involve three or more variables, the basic scientific laws often take the form of partial differential equations. This lends great importance to this field of mathematics. Two examples are the following.

$$\text{Laplace's equation: } \frac{\partial^2 u}{\partial x^2} + \frac{\partial^2 u}{\partial y^2} + \frac{\partial^2 u}{\partial z^2} = 0$$

This equation is satisfied by potential functions which play an important role in many physical problems, particularly those arising in electromagnetic theory.

$$\text{Wave equation in one dimension: } \frac{\partial^2 u}{\partial x^2} = \frac{1}{a^2} \frac{\partial^2 u}{\partial t^2}$$

(a is a constant depending on the nature of the physical medium within which the wave is propagated.) In addition, it can be said that the whole field of electrodynamics is founded on Maxwell's equations, which are partial differential equations.

Much of the theory of differential equations is concerned with the existence of solutions satisfying specified conditions. To know under what conditions a unique solution exists is often as important as to know the solution. Moreover, such knowledge may provide an avenue of approach to the needed solution.—*H. C.*

DIFFERENTIAL GEOMETRY: the study of properties of curves and surfaces which vary from point to point. A circle curves at a constant rate, but the curvature of an ellipse actually changes from point to point. Likewise, the curvature of an ellipsoidal surface (*e.g.* the surface of a football) varies from point to point, whereas the curvature of the spherical surface is constant. Though the term "differential geometry" is rather recent, the beginnings of the subject go back to Newton and Leibniz, and there has been a steady development since 1700. The invention of the calculus enabled mathematicians to undertake the investigation of geometrical properties which vary from point to point, for the derivative is precisely the concept which enables one to calculate the rate of change of a varying quantity. This concept of rate of change applies to curvature, because the latter is the rate at which the direction of the tangent to the curve (the direction is given by angle ϕ in Fig. 1) changes with distance traversed along the curve.

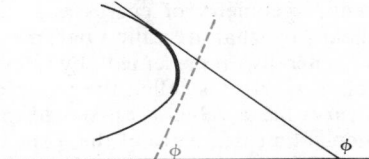

Fig. 1—The direction of a tangent to a curve is the angle between tangent and x-axis.

Elementary differential geometry may be regarded as an extension of Euclidean plane and solid geometry and of analytic, or COORDINATE, GEOMETRY. These latter branches are limited to establishing properties of figures that can be deduced directly from Euclid's geometric axioms, in the case of Euclidean geometry, and from Euclid's axioms and the algebraic equations of lines and curves, in the case of analytic geometry. With the help of the calculus, additional properties can be studied.

The most important property of plane curves (curves which lie entirely in one plane) is curvature. However, space curves, *e.g.* the helix (Fig. 2), which is exemplified physically by the wire of a coiled spring or the thread of a bolt, have an additional important property, namely, the rate, as one moves along the curve, at which the curve departs from a plane. This property is called torsion. Thus, the torsion of a helix, *i.e.* the rate at which the helix moves out of a plane or the rate at which it climbs, is constant. In the case of the thread of a bolt the torsion is what is known as the pitch, this being the rate at which the bolt as it turns moves into the nut. The thread of a screw is also a space curve. In this case the torsion is not quite the pitch but is mathematically related to it. The curvature of the thread increases with closeness to the point of the screw.

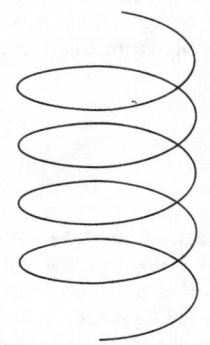

Fig. 2—Helix: An example of a space curve.

Given the curvature and torsion at each point of a curve, the curve is entirely determined. There are basic formulas, differential equations known as the Serret-Frenet formulas, by means of which the equation of the curve can be calculated. Conversely, given the equation, curvature and torsion at each point can be calculated.

The most important property of surfaces also is curvature. To express curvature mathematically, two concepts are required—mean curvature and Gauss curvature. The definitions of these are somewhat detailed, but, both together express what one means intuitively when one says that the curvature of a football is greater at either end than at some point near the middle of the surface. In the case of a circular cylinder, the Gauss curvature at each point is zero, but the mean curvature expresses the intuitive fact that the cross-section is a circle. Another noteworthy property of surfaces is the nature of the geodesic between any two given points on that surface, for, except in special cases, the geodesic is the shortest path on the surface between the two points. The commonest example is the sphere. If the two points are not on opposite ends of a diameter, then the geodesic and shortest path between them is the shorter arc of the unique great circle which passes through the points. To know the geodesics on a surface is useful in practice; thus the pilot of a ship or airplane, other conditions permitting, steers his craft along the shortest path between his point of departure and destination.

The differential geometry of curves and surfaces is best studied by means of what are called parametric equations. A curve is generally represented by three equations: $x(t)$, $y(t)$, $z(t)$, where t is called the parameter and each point on the curve has a value of t assigned to it. The parametric equations of a surface are of the form $x(u,v)$, $y(u,v)$, $z(u,v)$, where u and v are parameters. To each point on the surface there correspond a u- and a v-value, just as to each point in the plane there is an x- and a y-value as determined by a rectangular Cartesian coordinate system.

Elementary differential geometry begins as the study of special properties of curves and surfaces located in the ordinary space treated in Euclidean geometry. However, one soon discovers that it is the nature of the surface, and not the Euclidean space within which it lies, that determines its chief characteristics. For example, the defining characteristics of a spherical surface—namely, its curvature and its geodesics—are intrinsic and not affected by its lodgment in a three-dimensional space. But note that these intrinsic properties are not necessarily the same as those of the Euclidean plane. Thus the geodesics on a sphere are arcs of circles and not straight lines. The sum of the angles of a spherical triangle (a triangle formed by three arcs of three great circles) is not 180°, but may lie between 180° and 540°. Hence the geometry on a surface need not be two-dimensional Euclidean geometry. In fact the geometry is usually non-Euclidean and may be of a very general kind; *i.e.* it may differ far more radically from Euclidean geometry than the two famous non-Euclidean geometries, the one known as hyperbolic geometry, invented by Gauss, Lobachevsky, and Bolyai, the other known as elliptic geometry, invented by Riemann. The study of properties of very general surfaces is known as RIEMANNIAN GEOMETRY. The great significance of Riemannian geometry is that its concepts and techniques carry over to three- and four-dimensional space and so give us new geometries of the most varied sort to represent physical space or, as in the theory of relativity, space-time. See also NON-EUCLIDEAN GEOMETRY. —*M. Kl.*

DIFFERENTIATION: Most organisms begin life as a single cell, the fertilized EGG, which then divides into many daughter cells. The complex process whereby these cells take on progressively new characteristics and specialized functions is called *cellular differentiation*. The gradual formation of functional organs and organ systems from initially unorganized cells is similarly referred to as *organ differentiation*. Differentiation takes place to some extent throughout the lifetime of most organisms, but is spectacularly evident during EMBRYONIC DEVELOPMENT.—*R. L. D.*

DIFFRACTION: a common property of the interaction of any wave motion with matter, illustrated by the bending of waves into the region of the geometrical shadow of an obstacle. For example, light rays passing through an aperture do not travel in exactly straight lines, but spread out slightly from the path expected geometrically. The sharpness of images formed by lenses or mirrors is limited by diffraction, which gives even the sharpest line a fuzzy-edged image; this is usually a smaller-scale phenomenon than the aberrations caused by the fact that the lens or mirror is not a geometrically perfect image-forming device. Diffraction effects occur in sound and water waves, as well as in all types of electromagnetic radiation, including radio waves; microwaves; infrared, visible, and ultraviolet light; and x-rays. Diffraction effects in sound waves are more easily observed than in light because of the longer wavelength of sound and the fact that diffraction is observable only at distances comparable to a few wavelengths of the motion being studied.

DIFFRACTION GRATINGS are specially developed devices used in spectroscopes and spectrographs for the analysis of light beams into their constituent wavelengths, and they supplement the commonly employed prisms of glass, quartz, or perhaps other materials. X-RAY DIFFRACTION techniques have been most useful in determining the structure of crystals, while studies of diffraction at microwave frequencies have been important in the development of radar techniques. The theoretical study of diffraction is very complicated, mathematically. However, there are simple expressions that indicate the resolving-power limit of a microscope or a spectroscope as determined by diffraction. Diffraction effects can also be observed in fast-moving particles such as electrons (see ELECTRON DIFFRACTION). NEUTRON DIFFRACTION is an important phenomenon in nuclear physics.—*S. S. B.*

Diffraction of light produces fringes around the shadows of a fine wire (*left*) and a small circular disc (*right*). Note the light spot at the center of the disc caused by constructive interference of the light waves passing around it. (*R. S. Longhurst*)

DIFFRACTION GRATING: an optical device for dispersing light into a SPECTRUM. The simplest grating is a transparent plate covered with fine, parallel, opaque, equidistant bands. The behavior of a simple grating is shown in Fig. 1. Light, here assumed to be monochromatic, passes through the slit and collimator lens and arrives as parallel beams at the grating. Some of the light continues straight through the grating and

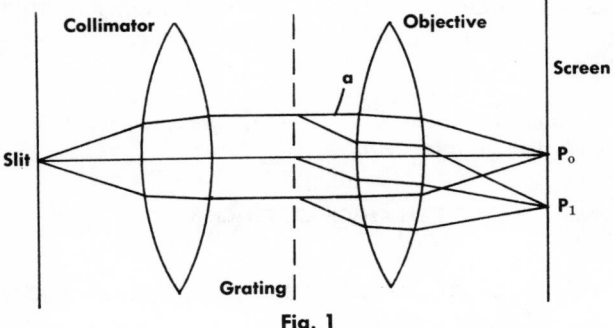

Fig. 1

is focused at P_0 by the objective lens. According to Huygens' principle (see WAVE AND WAVE MOTION), the transparent parts of the grating may be considered as secondary light sources, radiating in all directions. Light leaving the grating at an angle a, for example, will be focused at P_1. Fig. 2 shows a detailed view of rays diffracted (*i.e.* re-radiated) from two adjacent grating elements. Ray A travels farther than ray B by the distance AC. If waves are to reinforce each other (not interfere destructively) at the focus, distance AC must be an integral multiple of the wavelength. The position of P_1 on the screen relative to P_0 therefore depends upon the wavelength of the light illuminating the grating. If white light had been used instead of monochromatic in Fig. 1, P_1 would appear as a spectrum on the screen. (The rainbow colors seen in light reflected from an LP phonograph record prove that the same phenomenon appears when fine parallel grooves are inscribed on a shiny surface.)

The brightness and spread of the spectrum depend upon the fineness and uniformity of the grating. Gratings of 15,000 lines/in. are suitable for most spectrographic work, but gratings as fine as 100,000

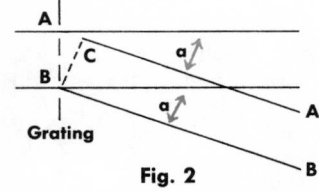

Fig. 2

lines/in. have been made. The ruling engines capable of working to these tolerances are among the most precise machines ever designed. The preparation of perfect gratings is so difficult that there are only a few really good ones in existence. Replica gratings made by pouring liquid collodion or plastic over a master grating, allowing it to dry, and then carefully peeling off the film are entirely satisfactory for most purposes.—*D. H. L.*

DIFFUSER: a flow passage that decelerates a stream of gas or liquid from a high to a low velocity. Diffusers are important elements in COMPRESSORS, PUMPS, WIND TUNNELS, and ramjets (see AIRCRAFT PROPULSION), the action of each of which involves deceleration of a fluid stream to increase fluid pressure. *Subsonic diffusers* decelerate gases or liquids traveling at subsonic velocities; *supersonic diffusers* decelerate a gas from a velocity higher than the speed of sound to a velocity less than sonic. In the latter, deceleration is accompanied by sharp pressure discontinuities, called SHOCK WAVES.—*F. K.*

DIFFUSION: The molecules of any substance, whether gaseous, liquid, or solid, are in continuous thermal motion and tend to penetrate the spaces between the molecules of other substances. Gases expand and diffuse easily into other gases, liquids, and solids. Liquids diffuse into other liquids only when miscible; they diffuse also through solids (see OSMOSIS). Solids generally diffuse through other solids only under pressure. Thus carbon diffuses through steel to form a uniform alloy, carbon steel. On a photographic plate, silver ions diffuse from places unaffected by light to places that have been exposed. Substances differ in their rate of diffusion, those with a higher rate of diffusion tending to diffuse through those having a lower rate. When diffusion rates are nearly alike, as between hydrogen and helium, the substances diffuse uniformly into each other. A rise in temperature increases a substance's rate of diffusion: a heated gas will diffuse through a colder one. Also, rate of diffusion increases with the concentration of a solid in solution. The movement will be from the stronger to the weaker solution (or from the solution to a pure liquid). Thus where a river meets the sea, sea salt diffuses into the fresh water, moving against the current, so that in slow-flowing rivers the river water may become nearly as salty as sea water before it reaches the sea.—*T. M.*

DIGESTION: the process whereby food is broken down mechanically and chemically into components that can be utilized in metabolism. In plants, food is formed in PHOTOSYNTHESIS and stored in the cells as starch or oil. Before the food can be transported or used, the plant must break down (digest) the starch to simple sugars, and the oils to fatty acids and glycerol. Animals consume as food the cells, tissues, or products of plants or other animals. Large particles of food must be broken down mechanically into small particles, and the carbohydrates, fats, and proteins that make up the food must be digested chemically into the smaller molecules of sugars, fatty acids, glycerol, and amino acids before they can be absorbed, transported, and used by cells. The basic process in digestion is *hydrolysis,* in which chemical bonds that hold together the components of large molecules are broken by the introduction of water, so that the large molecules are split into smaller component molecules. Each hydrolytic reaction in digestion is catalyzed by a specific ENZYME. Enzymes that hydrolyze starches (amylum) are called amylases; those that hydrolyze proteins are called proteases or peptidases (because they hydrolyze the peptide bond); those that hydrolyze fats (lipids) are called lipases.

In plants, the digestive processes take place in the cells where the food is stored. In many lower animals (protozoans and some others), digestion also takes place in the cell, often in special spherical vacuoles, which surround the food particles. In all higher animals, digestion takes place in a long, continuous, tubular digestive tract, or alimentary canal, extending from mouth to anus. In general, this tract consists of a mouth, which receives the food and may exert some mechanical action to break it up; a foregut or esophagus, which conducts the food to the midgut, where further mechanical action and the secretion of digestive enzymes is localized, and where absorption takes place; and a hindgut, which conducts undigested residues to the anus, forming them into feces for elimination. In a few animals (*e.g.* clams and mussels, which feed on very small particles, and some snails, which grind up the food into small particles before digestion) the food particles are not digested in the midgut, but are taken into the cells of a large digestive gland and digested there. In most animals, the enzymes are discharged into the midgut from separate glands or from small glands in the walls of the intestine, and perform their action on the food while it is in the gut. The foregut sometimes contains a storage sac, or crop, and the midgut may have a muscular gizzard or other device to grind the food into small particles

Fats and oils in the diet occur typically as triglycerides—compounds of three fatty-acid molecules combined with one molecule of glycerol, as at right:

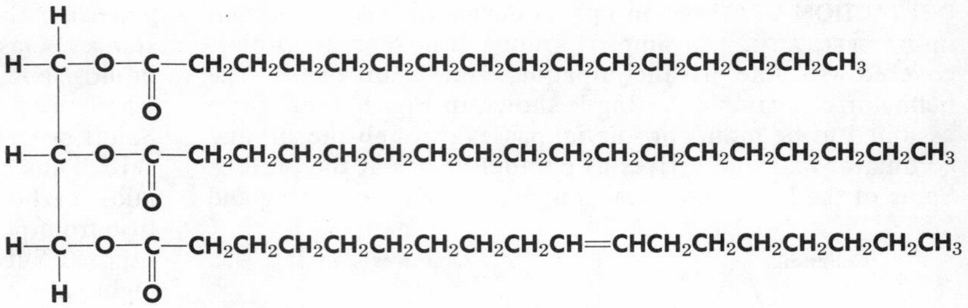

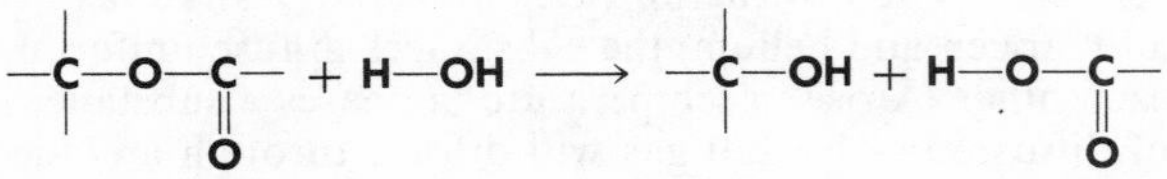

$$H-C-O-C-CH_2CH_2CH_2CH_2CH_2CH_2CH_2CH_2CH_2CH_2CH_2CH_2CH_2CH_3$$

$$H-C-O-C-CH_2CH_2CH_2CH_2CH_2CH_2CH_2CH_2CH_2CH_2CH_2CH_2CH_2CH_2CH_3$$

$$H-C-O-C-CH_2CH_2CH_2CH_2CH_2CH_2CH_2CH_2CH=CHCH_2CH_2CH_2CH_2CH_2CH_3$$

The enzyme lipase acts on the C—O—C bond, splitting it with the introduction of water (*left*).

$$-C-O-C- + H-OH \longrightarrow -C-OH + H-O-C-$$

The final products of lipase action are one molecule of glycerol for every three molecules of fatty acid:

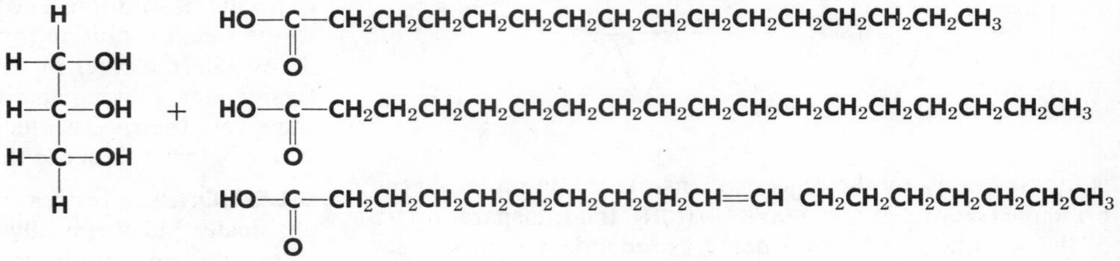

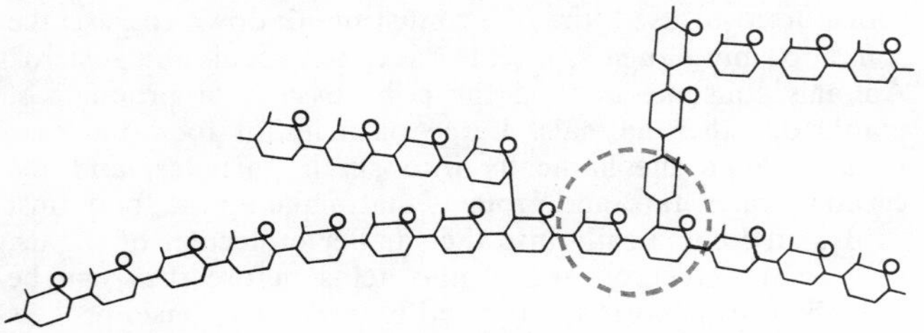

$$HO-C-CH_2CH_2CH_2CH_2CH_2CH_2CH_2CH_2CH_2CH_2CH_2CH_2CH_2CH_2CH_3$$

$$HO-C-CH_2CH_2CH_2CH_2CH_2CH_2CH_2CH_2CH_2CH_2CH_2CH_2CH_2CH_2CH_2CH_3$$

$$HO-C-CH_2CH_2CH_2CH_2CH_2CH_2CH_2CH_2CH=CH\ CH_2CH_2CH_2CH_2CH_2CH_3$$

Carbohydrates, such as starch, occur as granules made up of molecules of indefinite size; these are composed of long branched chains of glucose molecules (*above*). Magnified, the circled portion reveals the following structure:

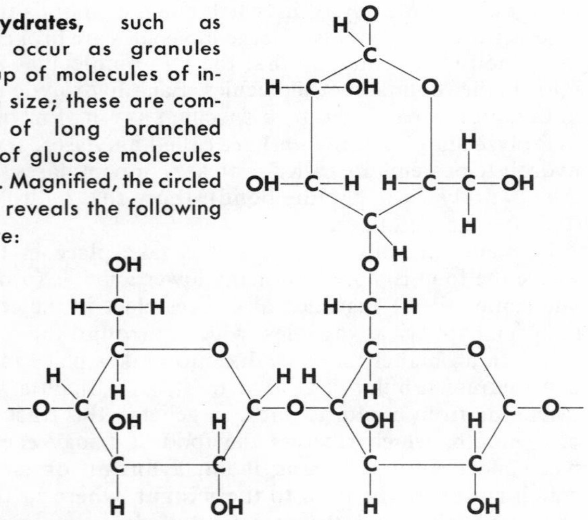

The enzyme amylase reacts with the C—O—C bond, splitting it with the introduction of water:

$$C-O-C + H-OH \longrightarrow O + C$$

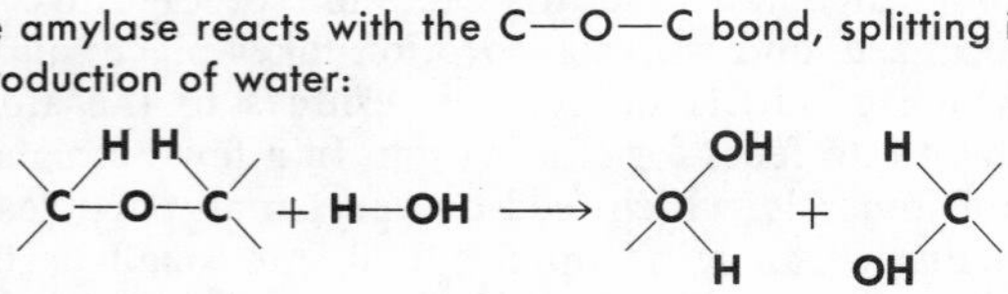

The final effect of amylase action is the splitting of the starch molecules into many molecules of glucose:

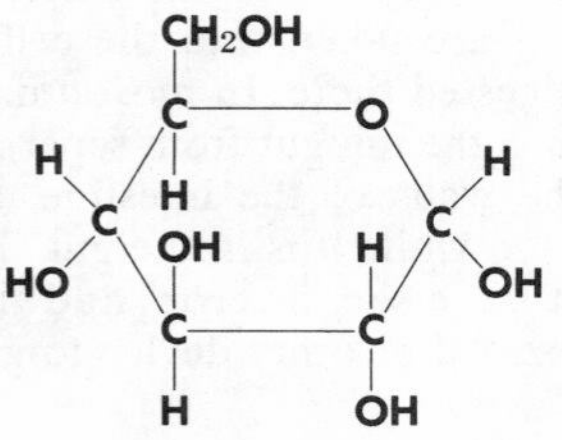

Proteins in food occur as large molecules of definite size composed of spiral chains of amino-acid molecules. A small portion of one of these chains could be diagramed thus:

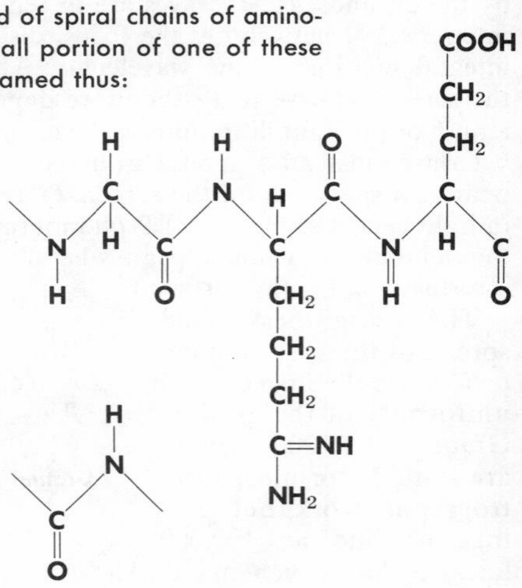

A proteolytic enzyme, such as pepsin or trypsin, reacts with the bond, shown at right, splitting it with introduction of water:

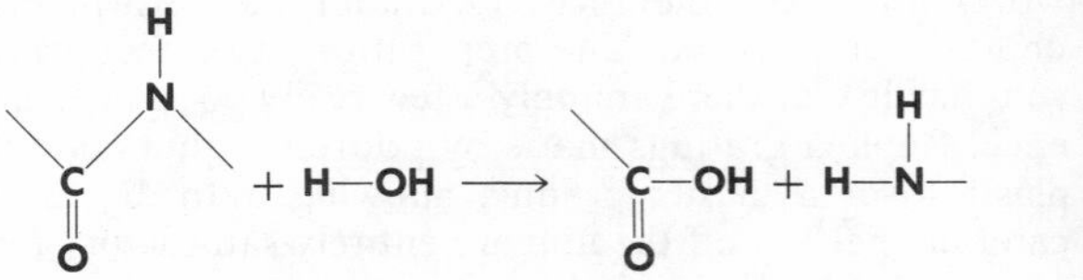

$$+ H-OH \longrightarrow C-OH + H-N-$$

The final effect of proteolytic enzyme action is the splitting of the protein molecule into many molecules of amino acids:

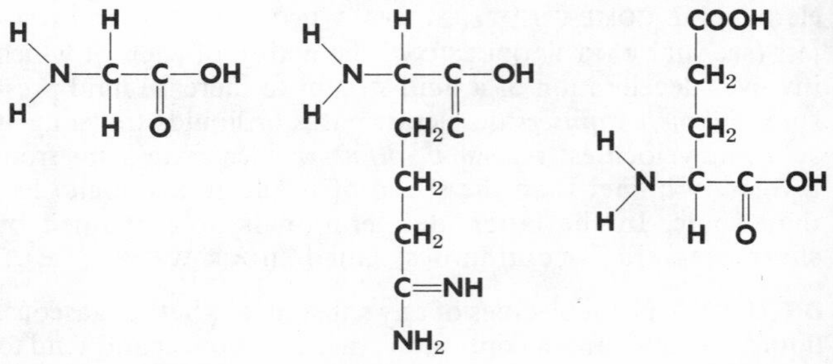

before it is digested. Earthworms, some snails, and birds have a gizzard filled with sand or gravel that aids the grinding; crabs and lobsters have a set of teeth in the stomach, with a sieve that permits only fine particles to pass on into the midgut.

In the vertebrates, food is often broken up mechanically in the mouth, with the aid of teeth, and is mixed with saliva, which serves to lubricate the passage along the esophagus; the saliva of man and a few other animals contains an amylase that initiates digestion of starch. The esophagus conducts the food to the STOMACH, where it is mixed with the acid gastric juice and where the digestion of protein begins under the action of the enzyme pepsin. When the stomach contents attain a semifluid state, the rhythmic peristaltic contractions of the stomach force the fluid out through the pyloric valve, or sphincter, into the duodenum, the first part of the small intestine. Here the alkaline secretion of the pancreas neutralizes the acid from the stomach and adds several enzymes: an amylase, the proteases trypsin and chymotrypsin, and a lipase. Bile from the liver is mixed with the intestinal contents; the bile salts have a detergent or emulsifying action on the fats, making them more susceptible to the action of lipases and also permitting their direct absorption without preliminary digestion. The glands of the walls of the small INTESTINE also discharge a fluid containing peptidases, lipase, and enzymes that hydrolyze such sugars as sucrose and lactose. As the food passes along the intestine, all of these enzymes act to reduce the material to forms in which it can be absorbed. Absorption takes place in the ileum and especially the jejunum, the more distal portions of the intestine. The undigested residues are passed into the colon, the first part of the large intestine, where they are subjected to bacterial action and formed into feces; in mammals, considerable amounts of water are absorbed from the residues in the colon. When the feces are formed, they pass into the rectum, from which they are evacuated at intervals.—*B. T. S.*

DIGGES, LEONARD, d. 1571?, English mathematician and surveyor; ed. University College, Oxford (no degree). He is credited with anticipating the invention of the telescope. His first book, entitled *A Geometricall Practise, named Pantametria,* was published by his son, Thomas Digges, in 1571. *An Arithmeticall Militare Treatise named Stratioticas; compendiously teaching the Science of Numbers* was completed and published by the son in 1579.—*H. C.*

DIGITONIN: a compound containing a steroid linked to sugar molecules; thus it is a saponin. It forms a soapy suspension in water. Digitonin is a constituent of digitalis, an extract of purple foxglove principally used as a heart stimulant in heart failure, but toxic in large amounts. Digitonin is used in biochemistry as a precipitating agent for steroids that have a hydroxyl group attached, as in cholesterol.—*J. F. S.*

DIKE: a wall-like body of rock cutting across the bedding or other structure of the country rock, usually in a vertical or nearly vertical plane. Most dikes form from injections of igneous material into cracks and fissures (see INTRUSIVE ROCK) and are therefore generally uniform in thickness and very narrow as compared to length and depth. Granitic pegmatite injections frequently form dikes, as do intrusions of diabase and basalt. If the rock enclosing a dike is less durable, it will erode faster than the dike, leaving the latter standing as a wall-like prominence. If the dike is less resistant than the enclosing rock, a cleft will be left in the latter after the dike has vanished.—*J. Si.*

DIMENSION: a measure of length, width, or depth. Although primarily associated with space, the idea is extended, by analogy to formulas involving geometrical dimensions, to equations and to many physical magnitudes; it also may refer to abstract mathematical space. In geometry, the concept is derived from that of extension. A point has no extension and hence no dimension; it is zero-dimensional, as is a set of isolated points. A straight line has extension, or length; it is one-dimensional, the magnitude of the length having no bearing on the dimensionality. A curve is also one-dimensional, although it is embedded in a space of more dimensions. A rectangle has two dimensions: length and width. An entire plane is also two-dimensional. A box has three dimensions: length, width, and depth. If each of the three dimensions were extended infinitely far in both directions, all of space as it is intuitively conceived would be included. This space is three-dimensional. A curved surface is, itself, two-dimensional, although it is embedded in three-dimensional space. While we cannot conceive intuitively of a physical space of more than three dimensions, we can construct abstract mathematical spaces with any number of dimensions, even infinitely many.

The dimensionality of a space can be defined as the number of coordinates necessary to specify its points. On a line or curve, one coordinate suffices; on a plane or curved surface, two are required; in solid geometry, three are needed. The space-time of modern physics is four-dimensional, since an event is specified by four coordinates, three of which are the usual space coordinates and the fourth is time. Just as three-dimensional space can be defined as the totality of ordered triples of numbers (x_1, x_2, x_3), which are the three coordinates of the points, so the totality of ordered n-tuples $(x_1, x_2, x_3, \ldots, x_n)$ defines an n-dimensional space.

In algebra, dimension is essentially the same as degree. Formulas for two-dimensional magnitudes are of the second degree in a letter representing length; *e.g.* the area of a square with side x is x^2. Hence equations of the second degree are called "quadratic"; this relates them to the basic unit of area, the square. Similarly, an equation of the third degree is called a "cubic." Equations of dimensions higher than three are easily grasped, although their geometric counterparts cannot be visualized.

Dimensional analysis treats physical magnitudes as dimensions. Mass, time, and length (distance) are the customary basic quantities in terms of which many others are expressed. Since, with suitable choice of units, velocity v is equal to distance L divided by time T, velocity is said to have the dimensions of L/T, or LT^{-1}, irrespective of the units employed. The table lists some common physical quantities and the dimensions ordinarily assigned to them. The choice of three basic dimensions, $M, L, T,$ is arbitrary but convenient, especially in classical mechanics. The problem is more complicated in describing electrical phenomena (see ELECTRICAL AND MAGNETIC UNITS).

DIMENSIONS OF PHYSICAL QUANTITIES

Mass	M	Momentum	MLT^{-1}
Time	T	Weight	MLT^{-2}
Length	L	Force	MLT^{-2}
Area	L^2	Work	ML^2T^{-2}
Volume	L^3	Energy	ML^2T^{-2}
Velocity	LT^{-1}	Power	ML^2T^{-3}
Acceleration	LT^{-2}	Density	ML^{-3}

—*H. C.*

DINES, WILLIAM HENRY, 1855–1927, English meteorologist; b. London. The leading exponent of experimental meteorology in early 20th-cent. England, he invented the pressure-tube anemometer. Dines was a fellow of the Royal Society. In 1905 he was appointed director of upper-air research for the British Meteorological Office.—*D. H. D. R.*

DIOPHANTUS OF ALEXANDRIA, 3rd cent., Greek algebraist. His fame rests on the great work *Arithmetica,* purportedly in 13 books, although none of the Greek manuscripts contains more than 6. The manuscripts include what is probably a separate work on polygonal numbers. Diophantus considered a great variety of problems, including both determinate equations of the first degree in 1, 2, 3, and 4 unknowns and equations of the second degree. The bulk of his problems, however, lead to indeterminate equations, called *Diophantine equations.* The Diophantine problem is that of finding all the whole number solutions of such an equation, though Diophantus accepted rational solutions. Several propositions in the theory of numbers are also included. For example, a number of the form $8n + 7$ cannot be the sum of three squares, and a number of the form $2n + 1$ can be the sum of two squares only if n is odd.—*H. C.*

DIORITE: a plutonic rock intermediate in composition between granite and gabbro. It is composed chiefly of andesine feldspar and ferromagnesian minerals (*e.g.* pyroxene, biotite, hornblende). Diorite is a coarse-grained rock, usually gray or dull green, formed at depth. It may crystallize from a magma that lacks sufficient silica to produce quartz, or form as a result of granitization. The fine-grained, extrusive equivalent of diorite is andesite.—*E. A.*

DIOSCORIDES, PEDANIUS, fl. mid-1st cent. A. D., Greek botanist, pharmacologist, and army doctor; b. Anazarbos, near Tarsus (Asia Minor). During the reign of Nero he wrote *De materia medica,* five books describing and illustrating about 600 plants and their medical properties. The encyclopedia, which describes such chemical and manufacturing processes as extraction of mercury from cinnabar, and tests such as detection of iron vitriol with gall-nut juice, was later printed (1478) and was regarded as the chief source of the science of pharmacy for 1,500 yr.—*R. J. F.*

DIP AND STRIKE define the attitude in space of any plane in a rock, *e.g.* bedding, foliation, or joints. The strike is the compass direction of the line formed by the intersection of this plane with an imaginary horizontal plane. The dip is the angle between the plane being measured and a horizontal plane in a direction perpendicular to the strike. Strike is measured with a compass, and dip with a clinometer, which employs the principle of the pendulum or spirit level.—*H. J.*

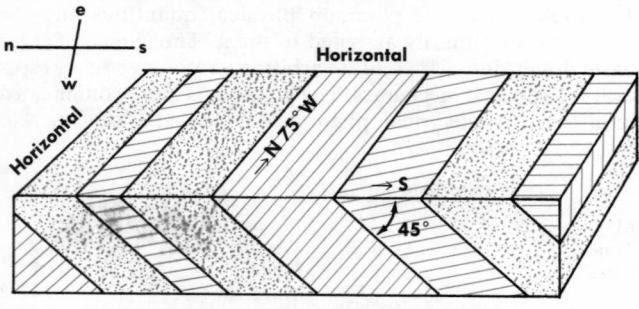

Orientation of rock strata: Here the dip is 45°SW and the strike is about N 75°W.

DIPOLE: a pair of equal and opposite charges whose centers are separated (*electric dipole*), or an ordinary magnet or compass needle (*magnetic dipole*). An oscillating electric dipole, the dipole ANTENNA, is widely used in radio transmission. In dipole antennas, a length of conductor acting between two plates of a capacitor, the earth being one plate, is charged by an a-c generator. The continuous alternating direction of the current produces the alternation of concentrations of both positive and negative charges at the terminals of the conductor; and this regular acceleration of the negative charges, or electrons, propagates ELECTROMAGNETIC WAVES. A receiving antenna whose circuit is properly resonant to the frequency of the waves being transmitted utilizes these waves to produce an alternating charge similar to, but much feebler than, the one produced by the transmitter.—*A. L.*

DIRAC, PAUL ADRIEN MAURICE, 1902–   , English physicist; b. Bristol. Building on the foundation of Louis de Broglie's ideas concerning the wave nature of matter, Dirac and Erwin Schrödinger developed wave mechanics. Dirac extended this theory to the study of high-speed particles by combining it with relativity theory. One consequence was the prediction of the existence of a new particle, the positron, later discovered by C. D. Anderson (1932). For the discovery of new and fruitful forms of atomic theory, Dirac and Schrödinger shared the 1933 Nobel prize. Dirac is a fellow of the Royal Society and an associate of the U. S. National Academy of Sciences. —*D. H. D. R.*

DIRAC ELECTRON THEORY: a theory describing the behavior of the ELECTRON, including spin, in terms of an equation. The British physicist Paul A. M. Dirac developed the equation in 1928; it combines relativity and quantum mechanics into one theory. H. A. Lorentz had tried unsuccessfully to consider the electron as a charged sphere. The Dirac theory, which is the basis for modern elementary-particle theory, assigns no "radius" to the electron, nor any simple model to replace Lorentz's sphere.—*A. M. B.*

DIRECT CURRENT: a flow of electricity whose direction is constant. Although the THERMOCOUPLE and the PHOTOELECTRIC CELL have the potentiality of being important producers of direct current in the future, at present the battery and the d-c generator are the major sources of direct current. In the battery, first built by Alessandro Volta in 1799 (see CELL, VOLTAIC), the reaction between two plates of different metals immersed in an electrolyte (a dilute acid in storage batteries) transforms chemical energy into electricity. Perhaps the widest application of the battery is in the automobile ignition system. Direct-current generators, like all generators, use the principle of induction, discovered by Joseph Henry in 1830. Coils of

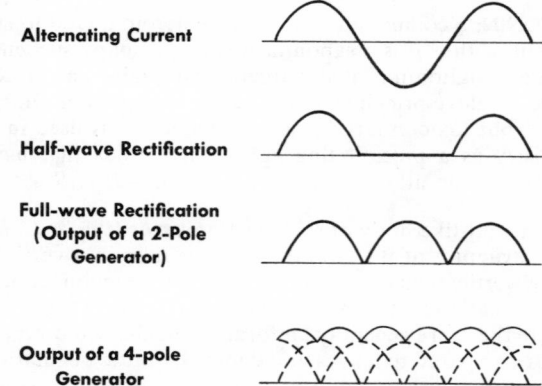

Direct current produced by rotating generators does not have a constant value. If the output of a simple a-c generator is rectified (as by a diode vacuum tube), a pulsating unidirectional current results and current flows only half the time. Full-wave rectification (achieved with two diodes) yields a continuous pulsating current, which is like that produced by a simple d-c generator. Adding extra poles to the generator yields a more steady current with only a slight ripple.

wire rotating in a magnetic field produce electric current, thus converting mechanical energy into electrical energy. The direction of current in a wire moving through a magnetic field depends on the direction in which the wire is moving; thus, as the coil of wire makes a complete rotation, the direction of current is reversed. In d-c generators, the periodic reversal of current flow resulting from rotation is corrected by commutating brushes, which redirect the current in a single direction only. The first d-c generating plant in America was Thomas Edison's Pearl St. Station, N. Y. C., put into operation Sept. 4, 1882. It consisted of six generators, each of which could light 1,750 50-watt lamps.

To be delivered efficiently over great distances, electric power must be transmitted at high voltages, which are then reduced to usable levels by transformers at the point of consumption. Since transformers cannot utilize direct current, at present alternating current is used almost exclusively for commercial distribution. Direct current, however, is still produced in quantity for the electrolytic refining of metals, especially aluminum. Direct-current motors have generally been used where high torque and good variable speed control is desired, *e.g.* hoists, cranes, elevators, and electric buses. For the same reason, d-c motors have been used on passenger and naval vessels, where ease of control is essential and long-line transmission is not a problem. But with the improvement of a-c machinery, direct current is rapidly being superseded except in the metal-refining industries. See also ELECTRIC CIRCUIT; ELECTRIC POWER.—*E. M. R.*

DIRICHLET, PETER G. L., 1805–59, German mathematician; b. Düren. He was professor at Breslau and Berlin, and in 1855 succeeded K. F. Gauss at Göttingen. Dirichlet's chief work was in the theory of numbers, and he was the first to lecture on that subject in German universities. His researches on complex numbers were published in 1841, 1842, and 1846. He also wrote on the theory of potential, equations of the fifth degree, and definite integrals, and he published a number of memoirs designed to make the work of Gauss more readable. He was a fellow of the Royal Society.—*H. C.*

DISCHARGE: see ARCS AND DISCHARGES.

DISCONFORMITY: see UNCONFORMITY.

DISCORSI E DIMOSTRAZIONI MATEMATICHE, INTORNO A DUE NUOVE SCIENZE (Discourses on Two New Sciences), by Galileo Galilei, 1638: Galileo had pondered the perennial problem of motion since his youth. After freeing himself from earlier errors, he regarded his own conceptions as constituting a new science (KINEMATICS). These conceptions arose from his definition of uniform acceleration ($v \propto t$: the velocity of a freely falling body is proportional to the time of its fall). He identified the free fall of bodies as a uniformly accelerated motion and brought forward experimental proof that such fall satisfies the law of distances ($s \propto t^2$: the distance traversed by a freely falling body is proportional to the square of the time of its fall). The latter law he had derived geometrically from the definition of acceleration. He did not attempt, like his predecessors, to explain *why* bodies fall or accelerate; yet Galileo's kinematics owed much to the tradition of mechanical theory going back to the 14th cent. In many applications (*e.g.* to the motions of pendulums and projectiles) Galileo illustrated his belief, also stressed in the *Dialogo* of 1632, that the truth of nature is learned through mathematical reasoning. The same belief is apparent in the other "new science," dealing with the strength of materials and extending to other problems of physics, *e.g.* the existence of the vacuum and the nature of sound. The *Discorsi* thus laid the foundations of modern mathematical physics.—*A. R. H.*

DISCOURS DE LA METHODE (Discourse on Method), by René Descartes, 1637: The foundation of Cartesian science was a specific metaphysics, described in the *Discours,* to which Descartes appended three treatises (*La Geométrie, L'Optique, Les Météores*) exemplifying the powers of the new method of reasoning his metaphysics brought him. All else (especially sense perception) being deceptive, the thinker is certain only of his own existence ("I think, therefore I am"), hence of the existence of God as the expression of the perfection that the thinker can only partially apprehend. God, as Truth, guarantees Descartes' most important postulate "that the things we conceive very clearly and distinctly are always true." The basic ideas of science are therefore *necessarily* true while its theory must be *formally* true if it is logically systematic; and Descartes recognized that formal truth is most readily attained in mathematical reasoning. He applied himself particularly to mathematics, developing in *La Geométrie* the method of analytical geometry. The other two treatises are examples of the use of mathematical reasoning in physics. Though some of his mathematical innovations had been anticipated, the 17th cent. learned them from *La Geométrie.*—*A. R. H.*

DISINFECTANT: a substance that either destroys or prevents the growth of microorganisms considered harmful to man or his possessions. The first compound specifically used for this purpose, by Joseph Lister in 1867, was PHENOL (carbolic acid). Activity of a substance as a disinfectant is still cited on the basis of a phenol-coefficient, *i.e.* efficiency compared to a 5% solution of phenol under standardized conditions. Synthetic disinfectants are now augmented by antibiotics, those made biosynthetically by microorganisms; an example is penicillin. Many of these can be used in the body of man. A disinfectant applied to living things is generally called an antiseptic. The first antiseptic used in the blood stream, by Paul Ehrlich in 1909, was salvarsan, which killed the organism causing syphilis. The common skin antiseptic is tincture of iodine, but many others are available. Air disinfection can be accomplished with formaldehyde or with ethylene oxide.—*Ru. M.*

DISME: see LA DISME.

DISPERSION: the analysis or resolution of a complex radiation into its single-frequency, or single-wavelength, components. Ordinarily, the term refers to the breaking up of white light into its "elementary," or spectral, colors—an experiment first performed under controlled conditions by Sir Isaac Newton (1666). Newton obtained his spectrum with the aid of a triangular glass prism. We now know that each constituent of white light exhibits a different index of refraction and is therefore retarded and deviated differently when passing through the prism. Thus in the visible spectrum, red light, associated with a relatively low index of refraction, is retarded and bent least of all colors, whereas violet light, with its high index, is retarded and bent the most. As a result, white light is separated into its spectral colors. See also REFRACTION; SPECTRUM.—*A. E.*

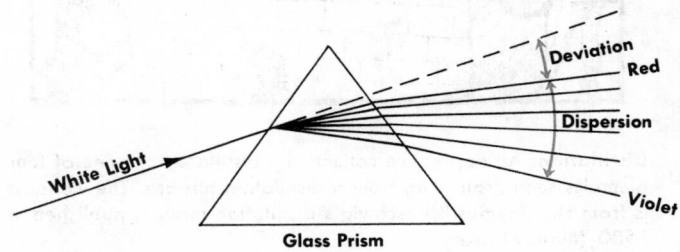

DISQUISITIONES ARITHMETICAE, by K. F. Gauss, 1801: This book, published when·Gauss was 24, opened a new period in the study of number theory. It contains a wealth of original discoveries. The first sections deal with congruences, and lead up to the theory of quadratic residues with the law of quadratic reciprocity ("theorema aureum"). The fifth section studies binary quadratic forms, hence studies the integral values taken by $am^2 + 2bmn + cn^2$ for integers m,n, when a,b,c are given integers. Also, ternary forms are discussed. The final (seventh) section investigates the cases in which the equation $x^n - 1 = 0$ (n positive integer) can be solved by square roots, and contains the construction of the regular polygon of 17 sides by means of compass and straightedge (discovered already by Gauss in 1796).—*D. J. S.*

DISQUISITIONES GENERALES CIRCA SUPERFICIES CURVAS (General Investigations Concerning Curved Surfaces), by Karl F. Gauss, 1828: Gauss's is the first systematic investigation of the geometry *on* curved surfaces, as contrasted with plane geometry. Basic therein are the concepts of the *geodesics,* or "straightest" lines on a surface, and of *Gauss's curvature.* The latter measures the divergence of the geometry on a surface in the proximity of any of its points from that on a (Euclidean) plane, not the bending of the surface in space (a "rolled-up" plane has zero curvature everywhere). This *intrinsic* geometry of a surface, or *two-dimensional manifold,* need make no assumptions concerning an enveloping space, and was later generalized for *n* dimensions by Riemann.—*G. G.*

DISSOCIATION: see ELECTROLYTIC DISSOCIATION THEORY.

DISSONANCE: see CONSONANCE AND DISSONANCE.

DISTILLATION: a 2,000-yr-old technique for separating various components of such mixtures as crude alcohol, tar, and petroleum by evaporation. When such mixtures are heated in a still, the more volatile, lighter components boil off first and are recovered by cooling and condensing the vapor. To effect good separation of the distillates, a still-head or fractionating column is inserted between still and condenser. In such a column there is a constant counter-current flow between ascend-

Distillation: An apprentice collects the distillate from one of four alembics seen protruding from a distillation furnace. The woodcut is from Hieronymus Brunschwig's distillation manual published in 1500. (*Burndy Library*)

ing vapor and descending liquid condensate; this flow promotes separation of fractions, each consisting of a pure component or a much simpler mixture of components, as the still temperature rises. Overheating of the residue in the still may result in decomposition ("cracking"); hence high-boiling mixtures or components are distilled in a vacuum. Modern distillation plants are capable of separating complex mixtures of narrow boiling range, and frequently are automatically controlled.—*R. J. F.*

DIVERGENCE: (1) In *mathematical physics,* a function formed from the components of a vector (*e.g.* velocity) which measures the spreading out of a vector field. The term also applies to the contraction of a field, or convergence, which is measured by the same function but with a change of sign. (2) In *meteorology,* a mainly horizontal flow of air out of a region. Divergence is found in the higher levels of a cyclone (low) and in the lower levels of an anticyclone (high). The characteristic quiet weather of a high is associated with the slow, widespread descent of air (subsidence) that accompanies the low-level divergence of the winds.—*D. H. L. and O. G. S.*

DIVIDE: see DRAINAGE BASIN.

DIVISION: see ARITHMETIC.

DNA: see NUCLEIC ACIDS.

DÖBEREINER, JOHANN WOLFGANG, 1780–1849, German chemist; b. Hof (Bayreuth); largely self-taught. He discovered the catalytic action of finely divided platinum on a mixture of air and hydrogen or such organic compounds as alcohol. His most important theoretical contribution was his theory of triads, in which he pointed out that in many groups of three similar chemical elements the atomic weight of the middle member is approximately the arithmetic mean of the other two. This may be regarded as a major step in the search for periodicity in the elements.—*R. E. O.*

DOG DAYS: the sultriest part of summer. The period it designates does not have a fixed beginning or end, although various dates have been assigned to it by different authors. In ancient Egypt, the return of summer and the annual rising of the Nile coincided with the time of year when the brilliant star Sirius was seen rising with the Sun; it was thought that the additional heat of the star caused the warm season. Greeks and Romans (who called Sirius the Great Dog Star) eventually inherited this belief. The superstition that dog days cause madness in dogs is modern and unrelated to ancient myths. —*S. D. G.*

DOISY, EDWARD ADELBERT, 1893–   , U. S. biochemist; b. Hume, Ill. For his discovery of the chemical nature of vitamin K, he shared the 1943 Nobel prize with C. P. H. Dam. He has also done research on a wide range of biochemical topics relating to hormone action. He is a member of the National Academy of Sciences.—*D. H. D. R.*

DOLDRUMS: the nautical term for the area near the equator marked by semipermanent low pressure, calms, and light surface winds, with occasional squalls and thunderstorms. In scientific meteorology, the region is known as the *intertropical convergence zone,* being bounded north and south by the belts of the NE and SE trade winds. Sailing ships venturing into the doldrums risked being becalmed for days or even weeks (see ATMOSPHERE, GENERAL CIRCULATION OF).—*P. L.*

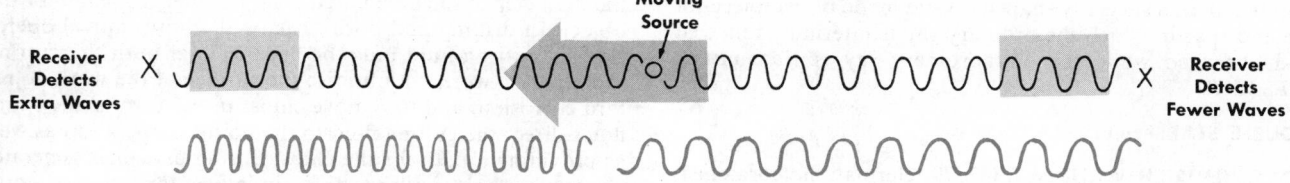

Doppler effect occurs when a source of waves (light, sound, etc.) and the receiver are in relative motion with respect to one another. When the distance between them is decreasing, extra waves are detected in a given time, so that there is an apparent increase in frequency. When the distance is increasing, fewer waves are detected, with an apparent decrease in frequency. The magnitude of the frequency difference depends on the velocity of motion.

DOLOMIEU, DÉODAT GUY SYLVAIN TANCRÈDE GRATET DE, 1750–1801, French geologist and mineralogist; b. Dolomieu, Isère. He traveled widely and wrote extensively on the volcanic regions of Sicily and the mineralogy of the Alps. The mineral dolomite was named after him. His theory of the earth included the Neptunian universal ocean (see GEOLOGY) but allowed for the production of basalt by submarine volcanic action.—*D. H. D. R.*

DOMINANCE-SUBORDINATION (or **dominance-submission**): in the strict sense, a social relationship between two animals, in which one animal controls the behavior of the other by force, fighting, or threats. It was originally described in flocks of domestic chickens and given the name "peck order," but occurs widely in the animal kingdom among animals having stable social groups and the motor capacities for fighting. The sum of all relationships in a group forms a dominance hierarchy, in which every animal has a definite rank in relation to the others. This may take the form of a straight-line hierarchy, as in a "peck order" in which each chicken pecks those ranking below it but not those above it. However, triangular relationships are also possible. Size, sex, and the genetic capacity for fighting all help to determine relative dominance. In naturally organized social groups, dominance relationships have the effect of minimizing destructive fighting, so that outright aggression is seldom seen. The effectiveness of these relationships as a means of social control is greatly reduced in artificially formed groups. Many other types of social control exist in ANIMAL SOCIETIES.—*J. P. S.*

DONATI, GIOVANNI BATTISTA, 1826–73, Italian astronomer; b. Pisa. He became director of the astronomical observatory at Florence in 1864. Donati discovered six comets, and one of them, which he first observed on June 2, 1858, was named for him. In 1864 he discovered the gaseous composition of comets by spectroscopic analysis of the light of a comet then visible.—*S. B.*

DOPPLER, CHRISTIAN JOHANN, 1803–53, Austrian physicist; b. Salzburg. His theory of the DOPPLER EFFECT (1842) states that a shift in the frequency is noted when a source of sound is approaching or receding from the observer. His hypothesis that the same effect should occur with light made possible the calculation of speeds of stars away from or toward Earth on the basis of the amount of the change in frequency of the light. See RED SHIFT.—*D. H. D. R.*

DOPPLER EFFECT: the effect of motion on the apparent frequency of light, sound, and other wave phenomena, as in the drop in pitch of a train whistle when the engine passes. It was explained by Christian Johann Doppler in 1842. Suppose a person *P* observes waves from a source *S*. If *P* and *S* are both stationary, the number of wave crests passing *P* per second (*i.e.* the *frequency* observed by *P*) equals the number per second emitted by *S*. The number of crests passing *P* per second will increase if he moves to meet the waves, and

diminish if he retreats; hence when he moves toward *S* he observes a higher frequency, and when he moves away he observes a lower frequency. With sound waves, higher and lower frequency correspond to higher and lower pitch of the sound heard (see ACOUSTICS). With light waves, higher and lower frequency correspond to changes of color toward the violet and red end of the spectrum, respectively.

If *P* is stationary and *S* moves, or both move, *P* observes a higher or lower frequency according to whether the distance *PS* is decreasing or increasing. The exact frequency change depends on how *P* and *S* move individually relative to the wave medium—except for light waves in empty space, the relativistic Doppler effect for which depends only on the *relative* motion of *P* and *S*.

Astronomers determine how rapidly stars and other celestial bodies are approaching us or receding from us by observing how much their spectra are shifted toward the violet or red by the Doppler effect (but see GRAVITATIONAL RED SHIFT). A BINARY STAR, which consists of two components revolving around a common center, can sometimes be identified spectroscopically, even if it appears single through a telescope; for one star can be approaching Earth while the other is receding, and vice versa, so that the spectra move rhythmically in opposite directions.—*Ba. H.*

DOUBLE REFRACTION (or **birefringence**): the splitting of a ray of unpolarized light into two equally intense rays which are polarized at right angles to each other and are refracted differently by the medium that causes the splitting. The effect is noted in such substances as quartz, calcite (Iceland spar), topaz, and certain stressed plastics; it arises from the fact that these materials have different optical characteristics for differently polarized light. Of the two rays, the "ordinary" ray obeys the usual laws of REFRACTION, whereas the "extraordinary" ray travels at a speed that depends on its direction. Since refraction is caused by the change in the speed of light that occurs when a beam enters a different medium, the rays are refracted through different angles and are separated on leaving the birefringent material. This fact is used to obtain POLARIZED LIGHT from unpolarized light, especially in the

Calcite crystal, placed over a sample of typewriting, demonstrates double refraction. (*Amer. Mus. of Nat. Hist.*)

Nicol prism, a specially shaped crystal made of two pieces of Iceland spar in which the ordinary ray is internally reflected and absorbed while the extraordinary ray is transmitted. —*E. M. R.*

DOUBLE STAR: see BINARY STAR.

DOVE, HEINRICH WILHELM, 1803–79, German meteorologist; b. Liegnitz. He mapped the distribution of temperatures and winds over the surface of the earth and was the first (1830) to introduce the concept of "meteorological fronts" moving in the atmosphere, a notion that remained unrecognized until reintroduced by V. F. K. Bjerknes about 1920. Among his books were *Meteorologische Untersuchungen* (1837) and *Klimatologische Beiträge* (1857–69). He was a fellow of the Royal Society and an associate of the U. S. National Academy of Sciences.—*R. J. F.*

DRAINAGE BASIN: the area from which runoff water gathers to feed a stream or stream system. Each permanent stream is fed by the runoff from rain or snow, collected from slopes by temporary rills and gullies or by sheet flow along more regular inclined surfaces. This drainage basin of the individual headwater stream is separated from that of the neighboring headwater stream by a line marking the highest elevation between the two streams: a divide. Each headwater stream erodes the land in the direction of its head, undermining the divide and eventually uniting the separate drainage basins. The combined drainage basins of the tributaries to a trunk river constitute the drainage basin of that river system. Such a drainage basin may comprise a significant portion of a continent. In those instances when all the streams on one side of a divide are tributary to rivers flowing into one ocean, while the streams on the other side of the divide contribute to a system reaching a different ocean, the watershed separating the drainage systems is called a "continental divide."—*E. A.*

DREYER, JOHN LOUIS EMIL, 1852–1926, Danish astronomer; b. Copenhagen. While serving in Ireland as director of the Armagh Observatory, he compiled the *New General Catalogue of Nebulae and Clusters of Stars* (1888) and the *Index Catalogues* (1894, 1908), still standard reference works for more than 12,000 objects. As a historian of science he wrote a *History of the Planetary Systems from Thales to Kepler* (1906), reprinted as *A History of Astronomy* (1953), and *Tycho Brahe, a Picture of Scientific Life and Work in the Sixteenth Century* (1890).—*O. G.*

DRIESCH, HANS ADOLF EDUARD, 1867–1941, German biologist and philosopher; b. Kreuznach. Although he began experimental embryology by work on developing eggs of sea urchins, he viewed his results as showing that the basis of life is a nonmechanistic vital agency, which he called "entelechy" (Aristotle's term). His work was highly philosophical. He wrote *Geschichte des Vitalismus* (1905), *Leib und Seele* (1916), and *Parapsychologie* (1932).—*D. H. D. R.*

DRILLING AND BORING: (1) the machining of holes in metal, wood, plastic, or other solid material; (2) penetration of Earth's surface to identify or recover underlying material. In metalworking and similar operations, drilling usually involves the creation of new holes (rather than enlargement of existing ones); this is done by such devices as a motor-turned twist drill or a drill press. In practice, drilling is confined to holes no larger than a few inches in diameter. (The surfaces of small-diameter holes are finished by reamers, either hand- or motor-turned.) Boring machines are used to enlarge existing holes or cut cylindrical surfaces of large diameter. In general, boring machines are used on large or bulky work where the diameter of the hole bored is larger than the length of the object. In drilling and boring, as in all chip-removal operations, a cutting fluid must be used to cool both the cutting tool and the work, to lubricate the surface of the work, to retard corrosion, and to remove chips; in twist drills, the spiral flutes direct the cutting fluid to the point of operation as well as providing a path for the chips. Boring machines generally use cutting tools similar to those in lathes: for ordinary work, carbon steel is widely used, and for high-speed work at relatively high temperatures (usually above 400°F) tungsten and molybdenum alloy steels are necessary (see MACHINE TOOLS).

Drilling beneath Earth's surface is done to locate mineral deposits, extract oil and gas, or add to geological knowledge (see GEOPHYSICAL PROSPECTING). The term *borings* is generally reserved for shallow drillings, down to about 1,000 ft, used to explore underground conditions or guide the design of buildings, bridges, and dams. By contrast, the average depth of oil-well drillings is about 3,000 ft; depths of 25,000 ft have been reached. Before the 20th cent., drilling through rock was accomplished by continuously raising and releasing a heavy steel point. The discovery of oil and the development of the steam engine prompted rapid improvement in drilling techniques. In 1901, rotary drilling—now the dominant method—was introduced. A steel-alloy bit, usually of fish-tail shape, is attached to the end of a sectionalized hollow steel pipe. This assembly is rotated by an engine at the well's surface. Simultaneously, mud is pumped down the pipe and up again between the pipe and the walls of the well to wash out the rock cuttings and to cool the bit. Whenever a new layer of material is reached, a hollow bit, often with diamond teeth, is introduced to drill out a sample core for examination by geologists. One of the most ambitious drilling operations ever attempted is "Project Mohole," an attempt to drill through Earth's crust to the mantle, a mass of high-density rock which forms most of Earth's volume. (See MOHOROVIČIĆ DISCONTINUITY.)—*A. L.*

DRIZZLE: in meteorology, a form of PRECIPITATION consisting of very fine water droplets of the order of 0.2 mm in diameter. Sometimes called *mist,* drizzle appears to float down, rather than fall, from low stratus clouds, at rates up to 0.05 in./hr. Fog, sometimes very dense, often accompanies drizzle. If the air temperature is slightly below freezing, drizzle may freeze on contact, forming a hard glaze of ice on roads, sidewalks, trees, and telephone wires.—*P. L.*

DROPSONDE: a type of RADIOSONDE which is parachuted to earth from a weather reconnaissance aircraft. The instrument measures the pressure, temperature, and humidity of the air below the aircraft, and radios the data to a receiver on board. Dropsondes often provide the only available data for WEATHER ANALYSIS over large regions of the ocean.—*D. H. L.*

DRUMLIN: a streamlined hill consisting of GLACIAL DRIFT—generally *till,* or unsorted sediments. The shape, suggesting the bowl of an inverted spoon, is due to the flowing movement of the ice sheet that made the drumlin.—*R. F.*

DRYDOCK: a basin-shaped structure in which ships are placed for building, repairing, cleaning, or painting. The ship is floated into the partially submerged dock, the gates or locks at one end are closed, and the water is pumped out, so that the entire hull is exposed. The sides of the dock are usually broad steps for the convenience of workmen. The largest drydocks in the U. S. A., located at naval shipyards on the E coast, are about 1,100 ft long and up to 150 ft wide. Fixed drydocks are commonly called *graving docks.* Another type is the floating drydock, a buoyant structure which lifts the ship out of the water when the water is pumped out. Predating the

Nuclear carrier being constructed in drydock: *U. S. S. Enterprise* as it appeared in late 1959. Note wooden platforms, which will follow ship's contour as construction proceeds. (*U. S. Navy*)

form of ice) is removed by sublimation in the evacuated apparatus; the original food substance is restored when it is warmed and water added. Similarly, biological cultures are preserved by rapidly chilling them, preferably to the temperature of dry ice at −110°F, and then drying them in a vacuum: this is often called *lyophilization,* because the dried product is lyophilic (liquid-loving) and readily takes water back again. Vacuum drying is more effective at temperatures at which ice (or water) has a higher volatility. In lyophilization the frozen material is sometimes warmed slightly to expedite the vacuum drying.—*Ru. M.*

DRYING OIL: any of the vegetable oils used in paints to produce a tough surface film. Drying oils are glycerides (see FATS AND OILS) in which the acid radicals have two or more double bonds per carbon chain. These unsaturated oils absorb atmospheric oxygen to form peroxides, which in turn catalyze development of solid POLYMERS.—*Ru. M.*

DUANE, WILLIAM, 1872–1935, U. S. physicist and biochemist; b. Philadelphia. One of the earliest U. S. students of radioactivity and x-rays, he made many technological improvements in the biological use of x-rays and established standards of measurement for their therapeutic use. He was a member of the National Academy of Sciences. See also DUANE AND HUNT LAW.—*D. H. D. R.*

DUANE AND HUNT LAW: a law expressing the wavelength of the hardest (shortest-wavelength) x-rays produced by an X-RAY TUBE running at a given voltage, as $\lambda = (1.24/V) \times 10^{-8}$ cm, where λ is wavelength and V voltage in kilovolts. This equation says that the most energetic x-ray, having the highest frequency and the shortest wavelength, is produced when the fastest electron gives up all its kinetic energy and comes to rest. The kinetic energy of the electron, in turn, was obtained by falling through the entire voltage (potential difference) of V kilovolts. The relation was pointed out by William Duane and F. L. Hunt in 1915.—*S. Br.*

DU BOIS-REYMOND, EMIL, 1818–96, German physiologist; b. Berlin. His life was devoted to research on the electrical phenomena of living beings, the results being published in his *Untersuchungen über tierische Elektrizität,* which appeared in parts, 1848–84. He was a fellow of the Royal Society and an associate of the U. S. National Academy of Sciences.—*D. H. D. R.*

DU FAY, CHARLES FRANÇOIS DE CISTERNAY, 1698–1739, French physicist; b. Paris. His research in electricity, described in eight memoirs in *Mémoires* of the French Academy of Sciences (1733–37), added considerably to knowledge of electrical phenomena. He discovered that there are two kinds of electrification, which he called "vitreous" and "resinous" (later named "plus" and "minus" by Benjamin Franklin). Du Fay's work led to the two-fluid theory of electricity (see ELECTRICITY). He was a fellow of the Royal Society.—*D. H. D. R.*

DUHAMEL DE MONCEAU, HENRI LOUIS, 1700–82, French chemist, botanist, and agriculturist; b. Paris. He wrote at least 20 of the studies in *Descriptions des arts et metiers.* Between 1755 and 1768 he wrote several books on the cultivation of crops and trees, including *Practical Treatise of Husbandry* and *Elements of Agriculture* (1762), which influenced the beginning of scientific agriculture.—*S. M. E.*

fixed drydock and first devised in 1700, the floating drydock has the advantage that it can be readily towed or transported anywhere. Its utility for emergency repairs led to its extensive use by the Navy in World War II. Two basic types of floating docks are the trough, which is a continuous structure from end to end (hence with great strength), and the sectional dock, which can be transported in sections and assembled at the dock site.—*R. G.*

DRY ICE: solidified CARBON DIOXIDE. Its temperature is about −110°F.—*Ru. M.*

DRYING: the process of reducing the water content of a substance by mechanical means such as decantation, filtration, or centrifugation; or by the use of heat, chemical reaction, or physical adsorption. The chemical engineer distinguishes drying from DEHYDRATION: drying does not bring about a chemical change of the material being dried. For example, the 5% water in ordinary alcohol can be removed on a laboratory scale by adding calcium oxide to react with the water, and then distilling from the resulting mixture; on a large scale the same result is obtained by a unique distillation operation, without chemical interaction. Moist solids are dried in open trays, rotating drums, or other apparatus by direct heat, radiant heat, or hot gases. Gases are dried by adsorption as they are passed through drying columns filled with agents that either react chemically with water (*e.g.* calcium oxide) or adsorb water physically (*e.g.* silica gel or activated carbon). Frozen foods can be processed by freezing them rapidly to low temperature and then drying them in a high vacuum: this is known as *vacuum-freeze drying.* In this process a food like peas largely retains its cell structure as the water (in the

DUHEM, PIERRE, 1861–1916, French physicist, and historian and philosopher of science; b. Paris. As professor at Bordeaux Univ. and as theoretical physicist, Duhem studied mainly energetics and thermodynamics. He sought strictly axiomatized theories, distrusting intuitive models of physical reality, which he felt not really to be part of science. In *Aim and Structure of Physical Theory* (1906, Eng. trans. 1954), theory is defined as "a set of mathematical propositions whose purpose is to represent as simply, completely, and exactly as possible a whole group of experimental laws." As between competing theories, no "crucial experiment" is decisive, for a theory may be saved by making suitable adjustments within the system, and at any rate a negative test fails to determine which sentence in the system is false.—*Ar. D.*

DUJARDIN, FÉLIX, 1801–60, French biologist; b. Tours. He distinguished protoplasm from other viscid substances, and was the first to recognize Infusoria as a special unicellular group. Among his publications are *Histoire naturelle des zoophytes infusoires* (1841), *Histoire naturelle des helminthes* (1844), and *Ouvrages et mémoires* (1844).—*D. H. D. R.*

DULONG, PIERRE LOUIS, 1785–1838, French chemist and physicist; b. Rouen. The discoverer of nitrogen trichloride (1811), he was severely injured twice by explosions of it. He also discovered hypophosphorous acid (1816), made extensive calorimetric studies of the origin of animal heat (1822), determined (with Berzelius) the gravimetric composition of water (1819), and verified (with François Arago) up to 27 atmospheres the validity of the Boyle-Mariotte law of the effect of pressure on the volume of a given mass of gas. With A. T. Petit he discovered (1819) the so-called DULONG AND PETIT LAW. He was an associate of the U. S. National Academy of Sciences and a fellow of the Royal Society.—*R. E. O.*

DULONG AND PETIT LAW: in physics, the principle that the atomic heats of nearly all solid elements are approximately the same. This discovery was made in 1819 by Pierre Dulong and Alexis Petit. The atomic heat of an element is its SPECIFIC HEAT multiplied by its atomic weight. This indicates that the differences in the specific heats of various substances are evidently due chiefly to the disparity in mass of their atomic constituents. For example, the specific heat of phosphorus is 0.17, whereas that of copper is 0.093—about half as much. On the other hand, the atomic weight of phosphorus is 31 and that of copper 63.6—about twice as much. It follows that a gram of phosphorus contains nearly twice as many atoms as a gram of copper, whence the heat required to raise its temperature one degree should be about twice the value needed for a gram of copper to warm up by one degree. The average atomic heat for most solid elements is 6.—*J. E. W.*

DUMAS, JEAN BAPTISTE ANDRÉ, 1800–84, French chemist; b. Alais. He criticized Berzelius' electrochemical theory (1826) and proposed instead a unitary theory (Type-Theory, 1839, based on the behavior of organic compounds), according to which certain types remain unchanged throughout substitution reactions. He discovered a method for determining vapor density, which he used to redetermine some 30 atomic weights (1858–60). Dumas also devised a direct method for the determination of nitrogen in organic bodies, and worked on alkaloids and nitriles. Founder of *Annales des sciences naturelles* (1824), he was also editor of *Annales de chimie et de physique* (1840). He wrote *Traité de chimie appliquée aux arts* (8 vols., 1828–48), *Leçons sur la philosophie chimique* (1836), and many other works. A member of the Académie des Sciences, he was also a fellow of the Royal Society and an associate of the U. S. National Academy of Sciences.—*R. J. F.*

DUNE: a hill or ridge of sand which has found lodgment against some obstacle and eventually overwhelmed it. Dunes develop mainly in great deserts, though they are found elsewhere also, as along coasts where the prevailing winds blow on shore and there is a moderate amount of available sand. In all great and small deserts, dunes occupy only a minor fraction of the area, since dunes can grow only where there is abundant sand. The chief mineral of dune sand is *quartz* (SiO_2), most resistant of all rock-making minerals.

The largest dunes are called longitudinal. They are ridges of moderate width but may exceed 100 mi in length and rise, in places, 700 to 1,000 ft. The ridges are roughly parallel and may cover vast areas. The largest example existing today, in the Libyan section of the African Sahara Desert, covers more than 250,000 mi². Another, much smaller dune type, also common in deserts, is the barchane, which is normally a beautifully formed crescentic hill, with the horns of the crescent extending outward from the lee side of the dune. A number of other dune forms also have been recognized.

Most dunes are unsymmetrical in cross section, the gentler side being in the direction from which the wind blows. After a dune reaches a certain height, the wind blows with maximum velocity over the windward slope, removing sand from that side and depositing it to the leeward. When the height of the dune is sufficient so that the wind does not carry sand to the bottom of the leeward side, the sand piles up below the crest, becomes unstable, and slides down, developing a quite steep "slip face."

Dunes commonly show a complex internal structure called *crossbedding*, with generally rather sharply defined intersecting layers. Crossbedding is a result of changes in directions and velocities of the winds, and of the constant paring down of the windward side of the dune by removal of sand during each storm.—*N. E. A. H.*

Rippled dunes of Death Valley, Calif., though much smaller in extent, are akin to some of the vast dune formations of the Sahara and S Arabia. The mountains in the distance are the Grapevine Mts of the Amargosa Range. (*Josef Muench*)

Dust storm approaching the farming community of Springfield, Colo., on June 21, 1937. The darkness observable on the left in the photograph hung over the town for some 30 min. (*U. S. D. A.*)

DUNS SCOTUS, JOHN, known as **"Doctor Subtilis,"** 1265?–1308?, Scottish scholastic theologian; b. Duns. A member of the Franciscan order, he founded the scholastic system called Scotism. He made a clear distinction between causal laws and empirical generalizations, claiming that the certainty of causal laws discovered in the course of investigating the physical world is guaranteed by the principle of the uniformity of nature, which he regarded as a self-evident assumption of inductive science. Duns Scotus claimed that motion is a fluent form, an incessant state in which it is impossible to isolate a state, and he asserted that the intensity of a quality such as heat is susceptible to expression in numerical degrees.—*S. B.*

DUST: small or microscopic particles of solid materials suspended in the atmosphere. Atmospheric dust causes reduced visibility; the Sun appears pale or colorless, and distant objects appear gray or tan. Dust includes soil blown into the air, volcanic ash, salt-spray particles from the sea, ashes and smoke from factories or forest fires, and other solid particles. (See ATMOSPHERIC POLLUTION.) Dust in the atmosphere eventually settles back to earth, though it may take years to do so. Volcanic ash from the explosion of Krakatoa in 1883 circled the earth for years, causing lurid sunsets everywhere. During drought, strong surface winds may cause dust storms, and thousands of tons of topsoil may be transported hundreds of miles, as in the central plains of the U. S. A. during the 1930s. (For cosmic dust, see INTERSTELLAR MATTER.)—*P. L.*

DUST-CLOUD THEORY: any of a number of theories which assume that planets and satellites have condensed from a cloud of dust and gas surrounding the Sun. Some of these theories ascribe the same mode of formation to the Sun itself. The earliest dust-cloud theory was proposed by Immanuel Kant (1755) and rediscussed by Pierre Laplace in 1796 (see NEBULAR HYPOTHESIS); its popularity waned by the end of the 19th cent. because it failed to account for the observed distribution of ANGULAR MOMENTUM within the solar system.

To be acceptable, such a theory must explain the observed similarity in the chemical composition of Sun and planets, as well as the fact that the Sun exhibits only 2% of the total angular momentum of the system whereas the Sun's mass exceeds 99% of the total mass. No presently available theory satisfies all these conditions, but the hypotheses first proposed by C. F. von Weizsäcker (1944) and modified by G. P. Kuiper (1951) seem to provide the soundest basis for further elaboration. According to von Weizsäcker, the Sun was originally surrounded by a rotating, disk-shaped dust cloud, extending outward to the present limits of the solar system, with a total mass about 1/10 the Sun's mass. The original cloud was composed mostly of hydrogen and helium, with 1% of heavier elements, but the lighter elements were driven out beyond the cloud's limits by radiation pressure, and its mass was reduced accordingly. The departing atoms, by colliding with the remaining molecules, increased the angular momentum of the cloud. Turbulence combined with the Keplerian orbits of the molecules to form a series of concentric rings, each containing a number of vortices (or eddies). Condensation into planets occurred where the vortices of two adjoining rings came in contact. Similar events in the atmospheres of the condensing planets gave rise to their satellites. The principal objection to von Weizsäcker's theory is that such condensation would not occur in a turbulent cloud. Kuiper attempted to overcome this objection by assuming that condensations (called *proto-planets*) in the cloud preceded the formation of the Sun. As the latter began radiating, the inner planets (Mercury, Venus, Earth, Mars) lost most of their lightest elements and became small solid masses. The outer planets (Jupiter, Saturn, Uranus, Neptune), being farther away, were less subject to radiation pressure and remained mostly gaseous. *Proto-satellites* formed in the atmospheres of the proto-planets. Asteroids formed in a region where greater gravitational stability precluded the formation of a large body.—*S. D. G.*

DUST COUNTER: an instrument used to measure the number, and often the sizes, of dust particles present in a sample of air. In the Aitken type, water vapor is made to condense on the particles to form sizable drops which can be counted; in another type, the particles are deposited on a microscope slide by the action of an electrically heated wire. In studies of industrial air pollution, air samples are drawn through filter paper moistened with chemical reagents. From colored spots which form around the dust particles, meteorologists can determine the composition of the dust and its probable origin. —D. H. L.

DUTROCHET, RENÉ JOACHIM HENRI, 1776–1847, French physiologist and natural philosopher, b. Néon. A contributor to the understanding of photosynthesis, he demonstrated (1832) that the stomata on the surface of leaves communicate with spaces within. It was already known that plants give off oxygen and absorb carbon dioxide, but Dutrochet showed (1837) that only those cells containing green matter, or chlorophyll, are capable of absorbing carbon dioxide. He also studied the eggs and feathers of birds.—S. B.

DUTTON, CLARENCE EDWARD, 1841–1912, U. S. geologist; b. Wallingford, Conn. Most of his life was spent in military service, but during 15 yr with the U. S. Geological Survey he studied the high plateaus of Utah and Arizona, and reported on the physical problems connected with uplift. Best known for his useful and important theory of ISOSTASY (1892), he also did research on earthquakes and volcanoes. He was a member of the National Academy of Sciences.—D. H. D. R.

DU VIGNEAUD, VINCENT, 1901–   , U. S. biochemist; b. Chicago. His research, mostly at Cornell Univ. Medical College, since 1938, has been concerned with the chemical structures of insulin and posterior pituitary hormones and biotin; the metabolism of choline and methionine, intermediary sulfur metabolism; amino acid, peptide, and protein chemistry; and penicillin. A member of the National Academy of Sciences, he won the Nobel prize in chemistry in 1955.—D. H. D. R.

DYES AND DYEING are problems with which man has been concerned since ancient times; the extensive empirical information collected has only recently been clarified by science. Dyes are substances which have color, and can be made fast to textiles by the process of dyeing. The dye problem is illustrated by this pair of azo($-N=N-$) compounds:

Azobenzene
(Orange color)

para-Aminoazobenzene
(Orange dye)

One of these is simply a compound with color, but the other is a colored compound with properties enabling it to form a reasonably stable union with a textile fiber. The general principles of COLOR are well understood. Benzene does not remove any of the radiation in the visible SPECTRUM; it is therefore a colorless substance. Quinone removes the darker colors, blue to violet, and transmits a mixture of colors which is yellow. Hydroquinone, which is reduced quinone, is colorless because its absorption is in the ultraviolet. Coal is black because it absorbs the complete visible spectrum when light falls on it.

Altering the structure of the benzene ring to that in quinone shifts absorption into the visible range and produces color. Quinone has an alternate system of single and double bonds, $O=C-C=C-C=O$, called a *conjugate system*. This arrangement is also present in azobenzene, thus,

Azo chromophore

The conjugate system of single and double bonds is said to be a *chromophore* (from Greek, "color-bearer"), and is the most important of the chromophores in dye chemistry. Some others are the nitro group, NO_2; the carbonyl group, $C=O$; the nitroso group, $N=O$; and to a small extent the arrangement of single and double bonds in benzene itself.

The reason for dye activity among dyes is found in their basic or acidic substituents. Azobenzene has no dye properties. With the basic amino, NH_2, group in the molecule there is dye activity (although of a low order) because it can react with acidic factors present in the fabric to be dyed. An acid grouping, *e.g.* the sulfonic acid radical, $-SO_2OH$, would have a corresponding reactive effect toward the basic factors of the textile.

The acidic and basic groups which help anchor a dye molecule have been called *auxochrome* groups (from Greek, "color-helper"), but it is now understood that they serve another important function with respect to the color itself. The electron conception of VALENCE has been extended by the resonance theory; one of the deductions from this theory is that electrons in the double bond of the unsaturated structure $C=C$ are more mobile, more easily displaced by an external source of energy, than are electrons in the single bond $C-C$. In other words, the single bond exposed to a beam of light may absorb some of the radiation, but only in the short wavelengths (high energy) of the ultra-violet; however, the double bond will absorb longer wavelengths (lower energy) which may affect the visible spectrum and produce color. The conjugate system of single and double bonds provides an unusually good path for the mobile electrons, and this facilitates absorption of energy from the visible spectrum.

With this brief explanation, it should be possible to follow the action of a chromophore and its associated auxochrome in the molecule of methyl orange, a dye much used in chemistry. Formula I (below) is its "normal" structure, with a basic group at one end and an acid group at the other. Actually, its structure is that of a zwitterion (dipolar ion) as in Formula II, but the positive charge may also be in the position shown in Formula III. According to the resonance theory, the molecule in acid solution will behave as if it were a hybrid of several possible structures; this hybrid has at least some characteristics of the conjugate system shown in III, which gives the red color in acid solution. When the solution is made basic, the positive charge (H^+) is removed by OH^- ions in solution, and the negative ion shown in Formula IV results. The conjugate system in IV gives the solution a yellow color. This behavior illustrates how the auxochrome, in this case $(CH_3)_2N-$, helps the azo chromophore develop color. Since the auxochrome is basic, it assists in the dyeing process, but methyl orange is not a good dye. Its different colors in acid and in base make it a useful acid-base indicator in chemistry.

IV $\left[O_3S - \langle \rangle - N = N - \langle \rangle - N - CH_3 \right]^{\ominus}$ with CH_3 below the N

Wool and silk are essentially proteins, and therefore have both acidic and basic properties; they are easily dyed. Cotton is cellulose and inert to most chemical reagents. It is difficult to dye cotton without the prior use of mordants, substances found to be capable of penetrating and adhering to the fibers. The dye then added forms an insoluble product (at one time called a lake) in the cotton fibers. For basic dyes an acid mordant like tannic acid is used; for acid dyes a basic mordant like an iron or aluminum salt is employed. Each type of synthetic fiber as it is invented introduces new dyeing problems depending on its chemistry. Nylon resembles proteins in composition; so its behavior to dyes resembles that of wool and silk.

Dyes may be found classified according to the method by which they are applied. *Direct* (or substantive) dyes are those which work without use of a mordant. There are relatively few direct dyes for cotton; some have an appropriate name, like Direct Blue. *Indirect* (or adjective) dyes require the use of a mordant to help precipitate the dyes in the fibers. *Ingrain* dyes are insoluble in water and cannot be applied from solution. They are synthesized on the fiber (usually cotton) by methods such as diazotization (see DIAZO COMPOUNDS). *Vat* dyes are likewise insoluble, but can be rendered water-soluble by reduction. Cotton treated in such a solution will be dyed when exposed to air or otherwise oxidized. The classic example of a vat dye is indigo.

Another method of classifying dyes is based on their chemical nature. Several dozen chemical classes are recognized; this structural classification is often based on the chromophores. Names of dyes are generally so confusing that the dye chemist relies on reference works in which dyes are cataloged and numbered. One such catalog is the *Color Index* (the C.I. numbers); another is Schultz's *Farbstofftabellen* (the S. numbers). The biggest single group of dyes in terms of commercial production are the *azo* dyes. Other classes are *nitro, nitroso, triphenylmethane, indigoid, anthraquinone,* etc. The first synthetic dye was accidentally discovered by William Perkin (1859)—aniline purple, or mauve.—*Ru. M.*

DYNAMIC PRESSURE: pressure of a moving fluid, equal to half the product of the fluid density times the square of its velocity. For a flying body, the magnitude of the dynamic pressure determines the magnitude of the lift and drag forces.—*D. B.*

DYNAMIC PROGRAMMING: a mathematical theory designed to study the formulation, analysis, and computational treatment of multistage decision processes. These are processes in which a sequence of decisions must be made, each of which affects the state of the underlying physical system and the choice of subsequent decisions. A *criterion function* is a mathematical statement of the utility, or value, of any particular set of decisions; a *policy* is a sequence of admissible decisions; and an *optimal policy* is a policy that maximizes a preassigned criterion function.

The mathematical formulation hinges upon the principle of optimality: "An optimal policy has the property that whatever the initial state and initial decision are, the remaining decisions must constitute an optimal policy with regard to the state resulting from the first decision."

In analytic terms, let p denote the state of the system at any stage; $T(p,q)$ denote the new state resulting from a decision q; $R(p,q)$ the return as a consequence of the decision q made in state p; and $f(p)$ the total return obtained when an optimal policy is used, starting in state p. Then the principle yields the functional equation

$$f(p) = \max_q \left[R(p,q) + f(T(p,q)) \right]$$

an equation which is typical of those arising throughout the theory of dynamic programming.

Three types of decision processes may be distinguished: deterministic, stochastic, and adaptive. In deterministic processes, a choice of the decision variable, q, uniquely determines the return and the transformed state. In stochastic processes, a choice of q determines the distribution functions for these quantities. In adaptive processes, some of the information required for the classical treatment of deterministic and stochastic processes is missing and must be obtained on the basis of observation and experimentation as the decision process continues. Particularly important processes of this nature occur throughout mathematical statistics.

In some cases, the conventional equations of mathematical physics can be written in the foregoing fashion. This alternative formulation allows two types of successive approximations to be employed: the usual approximation in function space and approximation in policy space, which always yields monotone convergence.

Applications of dynamic programming have been made to many areas of economics, industry, engineering, psychology, and mathematical physics. Particularly significant are the solutions it furnishes to many problems of feedback control, trajectory optimization, and satellite rendezvous.—*R. B.*

DYNAMICS: the branch of physics, and of applied mathematics, that deals with the motion of particles and rigid bodies. The subject is sometimes divided into two parts: kinetics, the study of the relation between motions and the forces that produce the motions; and kinematics, the analysis of the motions themselves. The principles and methods of dynamics apply to all problems of motion, whether of bodies as large as stars and planets or as small as the molecules of a gas. The problems arise in matters of ballistics (*e.g.* the range of a bullet and the force required to propel it), in mechanical engineering, in astronomy (*e.g.* the path of a planet or satellite), in other branches of physics, and indeed in any subject concerned with moving bodies.

Modern dynamics began with the work of Galileo. Before his time it was believed that a body would move only if some force were acting on it continuously. Although the nature of this force—a force that could propel an arrow while it was in midflight—could not be explained, the doctrine that had been propounded by Aristotle, was accepted until the end of the 16th cent. Galileo began his study by dropping bodies of different weights, sizes, and compositions to see how they fell. He concluded that "in a medium totally devoid of all resistance, all bodies would fall with the same speed." He then proposed that the speed of a freely falling body increases in proportion to the time, a motion he described as "uniformly accelerated." He tested, and established, this hypothesis by rolling balls down inclined planes. He discovered that any body falling freely along a frictionless plane will, on reaching the bottom, have the same speed as any other body falling freely down another frictionless plane provided the height involved is the same; that is, in free fall the speed is determined by the vertical distance traveled, not the horizontal distance traveled. Thus Galileo was able to state that for a body in free fall (and in the absence of air resistance), the horizontal motion, if any, is not affected and remains uniform.

Galileo applied this principle to the motion of a projectile. Although he correctly found that the projectile would describe a parabolic path, he did not develop the principle further, and it was left to Newton to draw conclusions that are fundamental

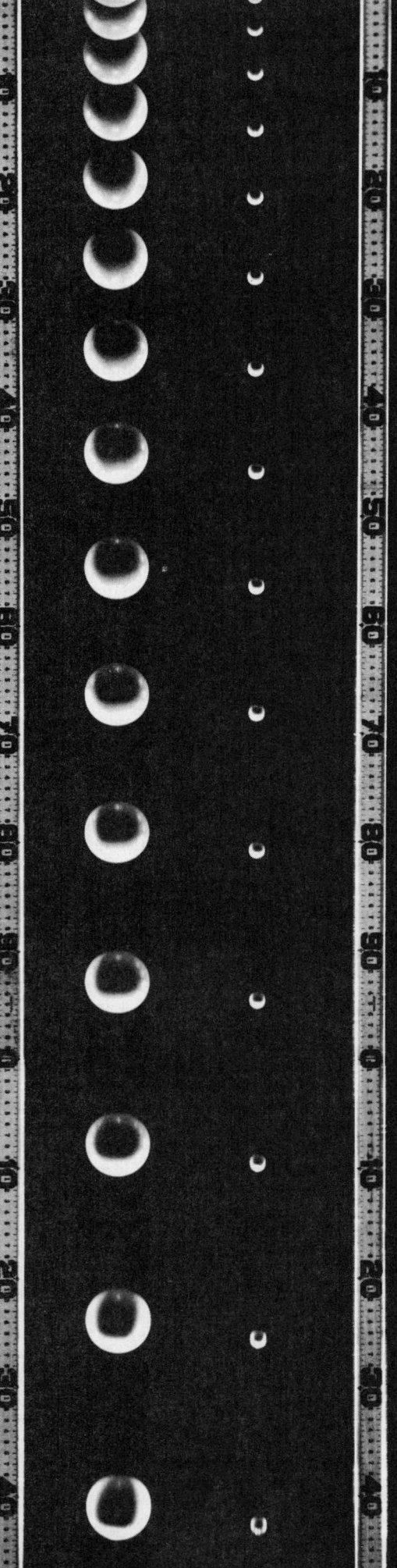

Galileo's notion that freely falling bodies of whatever weight would fall (ignoring air resistance) with the same acceleration is verifiable in a 20th-cent. laboratory. The lower edges of the two balls shown in this multiple-exposure photograph remain aligned as the balls fall after simultaneous release. The time interval between flashes is 1/30 sec; the vertical scale reads in centimeters. (*Berenice Abbott*)

to almost every aspect of physical science. In 1687 Newton published *Principia,* containing his laws of motion. His first law states, in effect, that a force is required to *change* the speed of a body or to make it deviate from a straight line. A small object resting on a rotating disc moves with constant speed, but since it is constantly departing from a straight-line path there must be a force acting on it. We say that its *velocity* is changing, velocity being speed in a stated direction. If either the speed or the direction changes, the velocity changes. The rate of change of velocity is called *acceleration.*

Newton's second law is an extension of the first. It says, in effect, that the force acting on a body is proportional to the mass of the body multiplied by the acceleration produced ($F = kma$); and that the direction of the force is that of the acceleration. The mass of a body is therefore a measure of its inertia—its resistance to a change in velocity. With a suitable choice of units, the constant of proportionality, k, can be made unity. For example, a *slug* is defined as that mass on which a force of 1 lb produces an acceleration of 1 ft/sec²; in another system a *newton* is defined as that force which produces an acceleration of 1 meter/sec² on a mass of 1 kg. With units such as these, one can state the famous formula $F = ma$.

In the case of a rotation, torque, τ, replaces force; moment of inertia, I, replaces mass; and angular acceleration, α, replaces acceleration. Thus instead of $F = ma$ we have $\tau = I\alpha$. The product of mass times velocity (mv) is called *momentum*; the product of moment of inertia times angular velocity ($I\omega$) is called *angular momentum*. In the absence of external force, the total momentum of a system is constant; in other words, momentum is conserved. (This is Newton's third law.) Similarly, angular momentum is conserved unless there is an external torque acting. See NEWTON'S LAWS OF MOTION; MEASUREMENT SYSTEMS; ROTATION.—*B. P. S.*

DYNAMITE: an explosive mixture used especially in mining and engineering for blasting. The first dynamite, invented by Alfred Nobel in 1866, was *nitroglycerin* absorbed on an inert material called *kieselguhr,* which reduced nitroglycerin's sensitivity to shock and made it safer to handle. In most U. S. dynamite formulations, ammonium nitrate replaces much of the nitroglycerin; and in place of inert kieselguhr an active absorbent is used, consisting of a carbonaceous material, *e.g.* wood meal (a fuel) mixed with an oxidizer such as sodium nitrate. In such a formulation the nitroglycerin is a sensitizer for the ammonium nitrate. See EXPLOSIVE.—*Ru. M.*

DYNAMO: see GENERATOR.

DYNAMOMETER: an instrument for measuring the power output of rotating machinery. There are two general types. One absorbs power directly and converts it to heat; the other transmits power to some other absorbing member. The Prony brake (band or rope varieties) is an example of an absorption dynamometer. A torsion device is of the transmission type. —*A. E.*

DYNAMO THEORY: see TERRESTRIAL MAGNETISM.

DYSPROSIUM: a lanthanide (rare-earth metal) element (Dy); at. no. 66; at. wt 162.51; density 8.56. It was discovered (1886) by the Frenchman Lecoq de Boisbaudran.—*G. W. M.*

Landforms on arid landscapes show effects of down-cutting by running water, sandblasting by wind, and deposit of erosion debris by streams and wind. **1. Mesas and buttes,** Monument Valley, Ariz. *(Santa Fe RR).* **2. Alluvial fans,** Mohave Desert, Calif. *(Balsley, U.S. Geol. Survey).* **3. Salt flats** (playas), Death Valley, Calif., with arid, bare Panamint Mts. in background *(Union Pacific RR).* **4. Pinnacles** sculptured by rainwash, Bryce Canyon, Utah *(Union Pacific RR).* **5. Wind-built sand dunes,** San Luis Valley, Colo. *(Siebenthal, U.S. Geol. Survey)*

EARTH AS SEEN FROM SPACE

1

2

3

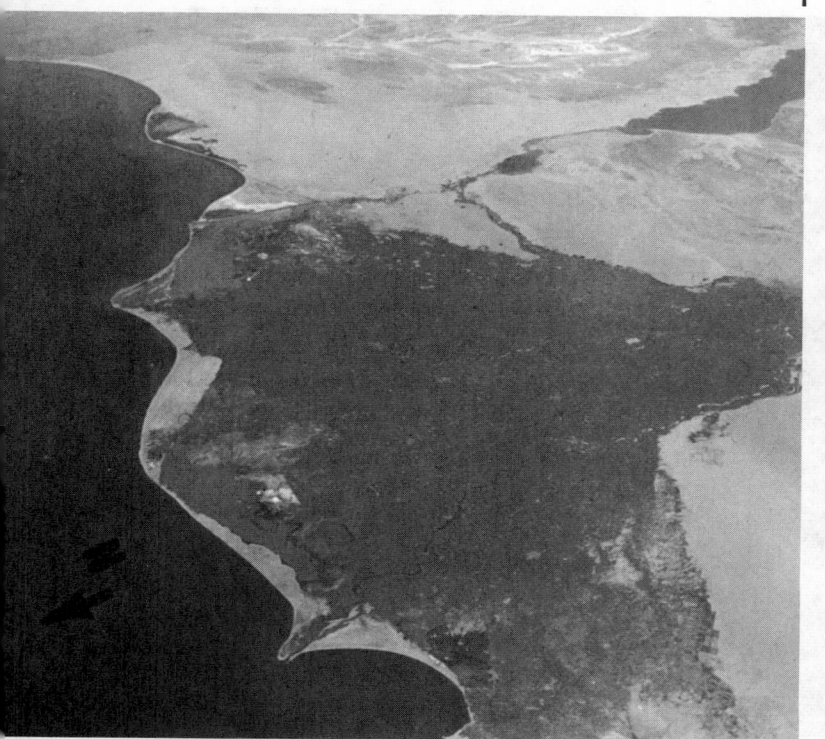

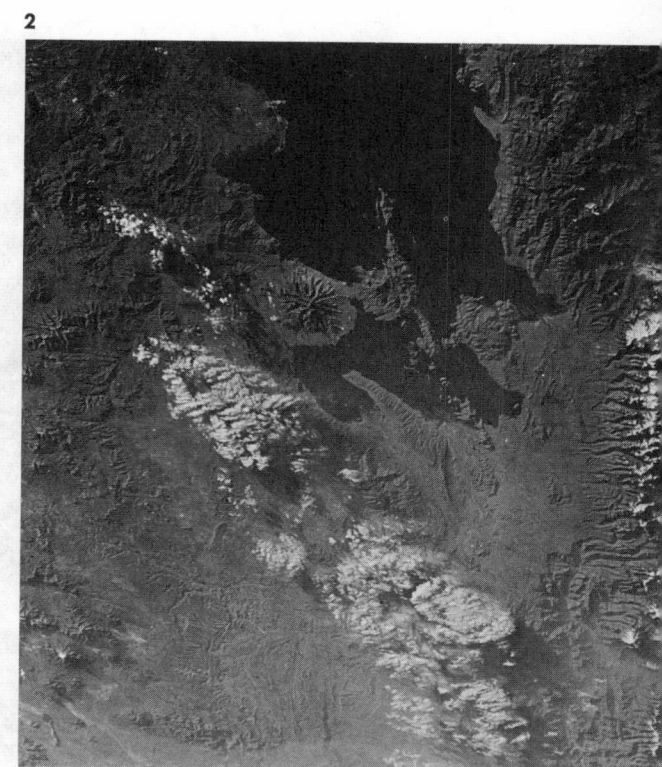

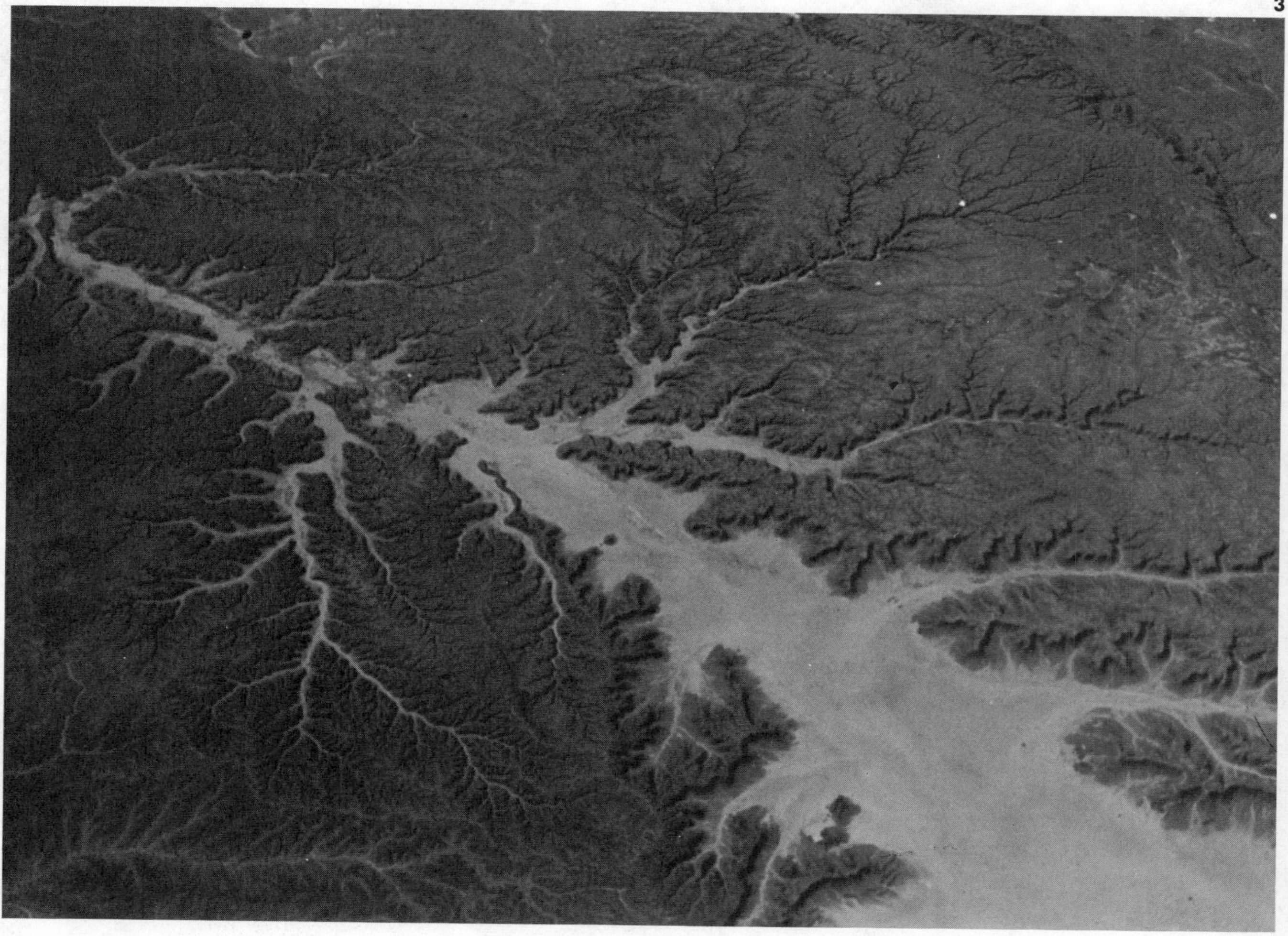

When viewed from altitudes of the order of a hundred miles, Earth's surface shows patterns which in the past could only be inferred by putting together large amounts of detail from short-range observations. The photographs on these pages were taken from orbiting artificial satellites. **1. The Nile Delta** is seen with Mediterranean Sea at left, Suez Canal and Red Sea in background. Dark areas are cultivated land; distance between prominent points on delta is about 90 mi. **2. A portion of Lake Titicaca**, Bolivia, appears with the Andes Mts. to the east (at right). The eroded core of an extinct volcano (with radial drainage) is visible at upper left center. **3. Dendritic drainage pattern** has been formed by temporary streams on Hadramaut Plateau, southern Arabia. Sand-floored Wadi Hadramaut dominates the 120-mi.-wide scene. **4. A 100-mi.-wide mountain landscape** is photographed about 400 mi. NW of Chungking, China. Streams have meticulously dissected the region. Adiabatic cooling has caused cumulus clouds to form over ridges. **5. The Namib Desert**, South-West Africa, displays longitudinal (seif) dunes over 100 mi. long. A series of large spits have built up where the desert meets the Atlantic Ocean. *(NASA)*

5

4

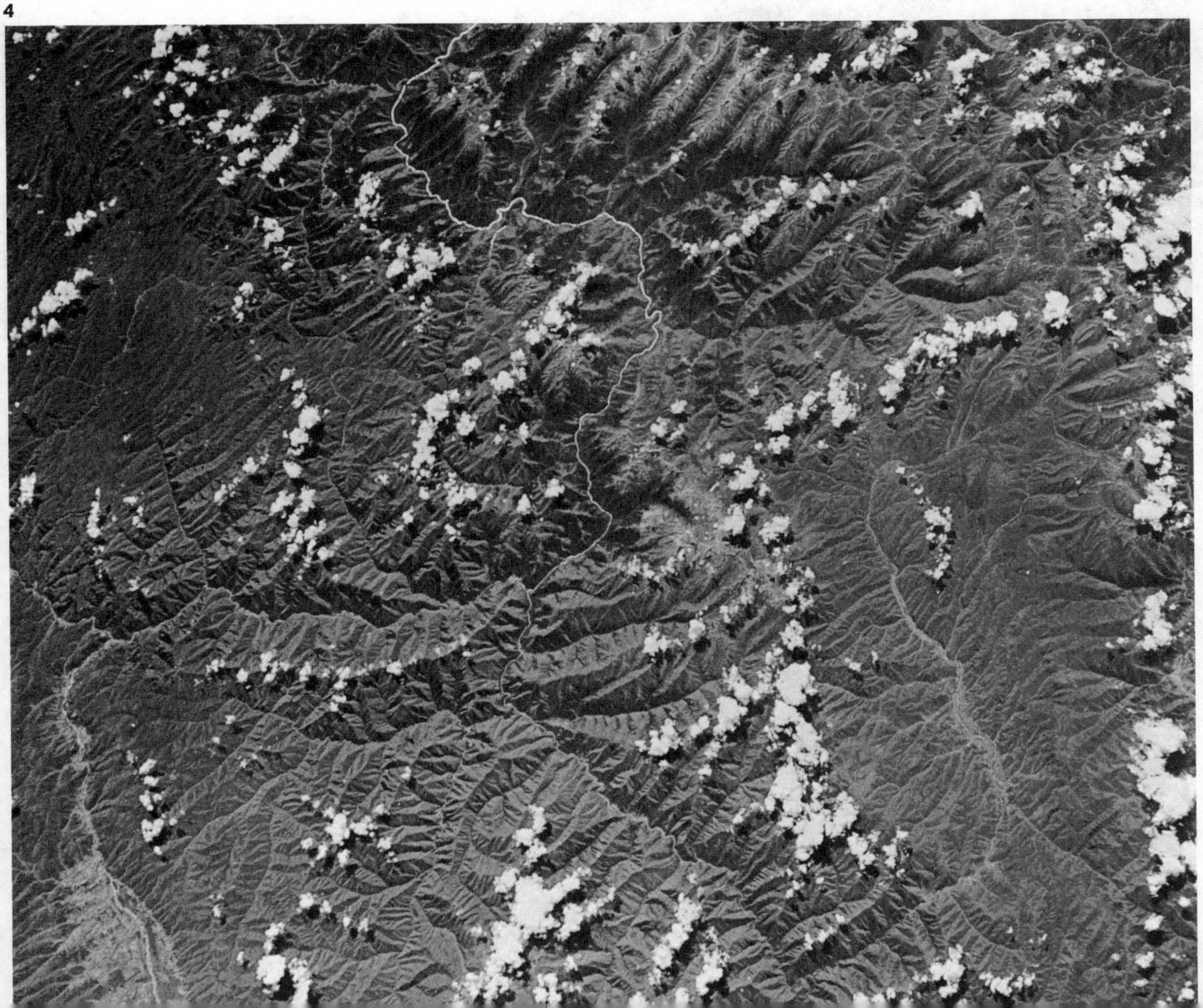

342 C

ELECTRONICS

Applications of electronics, still a relatively young technology, seem unlimited in modern life. **1. Electron tube** made possible the development of radio, television, and related industries *(RCA)*.

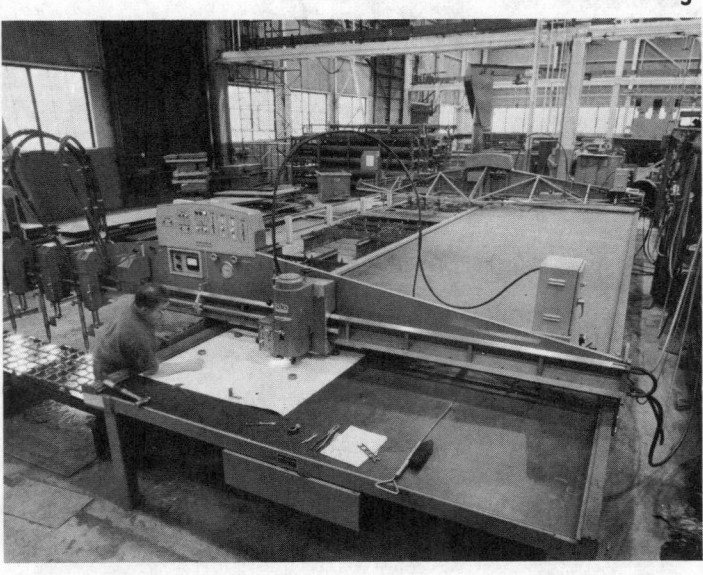

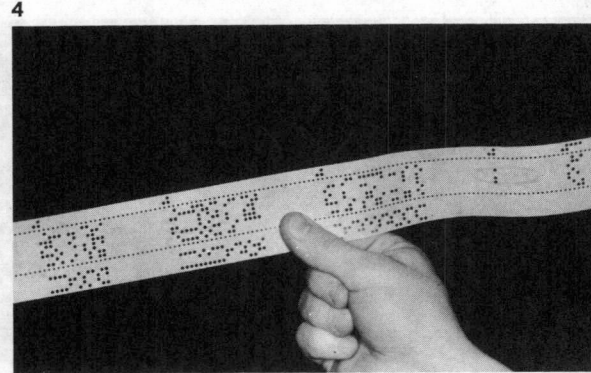

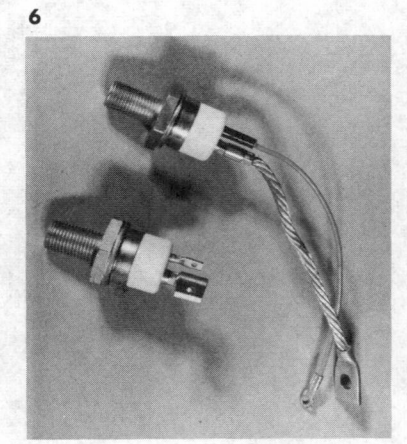

2. **Complex electronic computer** insures accuracy of Navy's 2,500-nautical-mi. Polaris missile (**Sperry Gyroscope Co.**). 3. **"Telephone terminal to outer space,"** Holmdel, N.J., in August 1960 relayed signals via artificial satellite Echo 1 to tracking center at Goldstone, Calif., inaugurating a new era in telephone communications. In foreground is "horn-reflector" antenna used as receiver; in background, the 60-ft. dish used as transmitter (*Bell Telephone Labs.*). 4. **Tape punched by keyboard operator** will guide a machine that sets type in the form of film (*Mergenthaler Linotype Co.*). 5. **Automatic gas burnout machines** are electronically guided to duplicate drawings made on drafting film. Drawings are scanned with oscillating optical head (*Westinghouse*).

6. **Transistors**—simple, small, economical—started revolution in electronics. These are 30-amp NPN silicon power transistors (*Westinghouse*). 7. **Two-way speaker system** connects home and classroom for child confined by illness (*American Tel. and Tel. Co.*). 8. **Technicians on U. S. Coast Guard cutter** use radar to chart course of aircraft in distress over open ocean (*United Nations*). 9. **Communications panel in control tower** enables railroad yardmaster to contact and direct all radio-equipped trains in yard (*Southern Pacific Lines*). 10. **Radar installation for small boats** provides protection in fog, storms, and darkness. Unit has range up to 5 mi. (*Sperry Gyroscope Co.*).

The shell of the nautilus, a cephalopod of Pacific waters between the Fiji Islands and the Philippines, grows by accretion into an equiangular spiral several inches wide. The animal itself—an older relative of the octopus and the squid—keeps moving outward as it grows, at any given time always occupying the outermost chamber; the previous chamber it seals off with a curved septum tangent to the inner and outer walls. The shell is in the form of a spiral (called logarithmic by Jakob Bernouilli the Elder, and equiangular by Roger Cotes) that has the property of remaining continuously self-similar in the course of time. This developing curve, which cuts each radius vector at an unvarying angle, was first described by Descartes in 1638 in a letter to Father Mersenne. The image of the nautilus shell is here seen as produced by 50-kv x-rays on a medical x-ray emulsion at a distance of 36 in. (*Eastman Kodak*)

E

e: an irrational number which plays a prominent role in mathematical analysis and its applications. It is defined to be the LIMIT of $(1 + h)^{1/h}$ as h tends to 0; or as the sum of the infinite series $1 + 1/1! + 1/2! + 1/3! + \cdots + 1/n! + \ldots$, in which $n!$ denotes the product $1 \cdot 2 \cdot 3 \cdots n$. Its approximate value is 2.7182818, correct to eight digits. Euler was the first to denote this number by the letter e. It is not only irrational (that is, a number which is not the ratio of two integers); it is also transcendental (it is not a root of any algebraic equation with whole-number coefficients and exponents. This was proved by Hermite in 1873.

The logarithms which come from the logarithmic function defined by $\log u = \int_1^u (1/t) \, dt$ have e as base. For if $x = \log u$, as given by this definition, then $u = e^x$. Such logarithms are called natural logarithms. They are closely related to the logarithms invented by Napier. (See also TRANSCENDENTAL NUMBER.)—*H. C.*

EAR: in vertebrate animals, one of a pair of sense organs that serve in equilibration and in detecting sound vibrations; in insects, analogous organs concerned with hearing. The vertebrate ear develops early in the embryo and can be distinguished before the head region is distinct. It soon becomes constricted into a dorsal lobe (the utricle) and a ventral one (the saccule). The former develops into delicate *semicircular canals* and an *otolith organ,* collectively referred to as the *vestibular* apparatus. Lampreys and other members of class Agnatha have only two semicircular canals in each ear—an anterior and a posterior; other vertebrates all have a third, horizontal canal. The canals lie in planes approximately at right angles to one another and serve to alert the animal to changes in its orientation. Movement of the head causes a swirling of the fluid in the canals, because of the inertia of the fluid; this swirling carries the fluid past hairlike extensions of sensory cells in local enlargements (ampullae) of the canals, initiating impulses along branches of the auditory nerve. Within the fluid-filled cavity of the otolith organ, one or more granules of lime roll about under the influence of gravity; they stimulate hair-cells lining the cavity and inform the animal about the static position of its head. Excessive growth of the lime granules is common in fishes, which are then said to have "ear stones." (See BALANCE AND EQUILIBRIUM.)

The ventral lobe (saccule) of the embryonic ear grows out into a slender projection (the lagena) in the cavity of which is fluid associated with further sensory hair-cells. These cells are sensitive to vibrations of the fluid in the frequency range we identify as sound—from as low as 15 to as high as 150,000 cycles/sec in some animals. In fishes, the vibrations from the surrounding water are transferred directly through the body to the lagena. In terrestrial amphibians, as in all reptiles, birds, and mammals, there is an additional mechanism that transforms feeble vibrations in air into more vigorous ones in the fluid of the lagena. Airborne sound energy is picked up by a thin membranous eardrum (tympanum), and transferred by a slender bone (the columella of amphibians, reptiles, and birds) or by a series of three minute bones (the hammer, anvil, and stirrup bones of mammals) across an air space of the *middle ear* to a small window in the bony wall of the skull. Here the cavity of the middle ear is separated from the fluid of the lagena by only a thin membrane. The ear bones are levers that translate comparatively coarse vibrations in the eardrum into exquisitely fine ones at the same frequencies, but as much as 60 times more powerful, in the fluid of the lagena. These vibrations may be detected even when the fluid shifts barely more than the diameter of a hydrogen atom!

In reptiles, birds, and mammals, the eardrum is protected within the head, being located at the end of an external auditory canal that comprises the *outer ear.* The lagena and the vestibular apparatus in these animals and in terrestrial amphib-

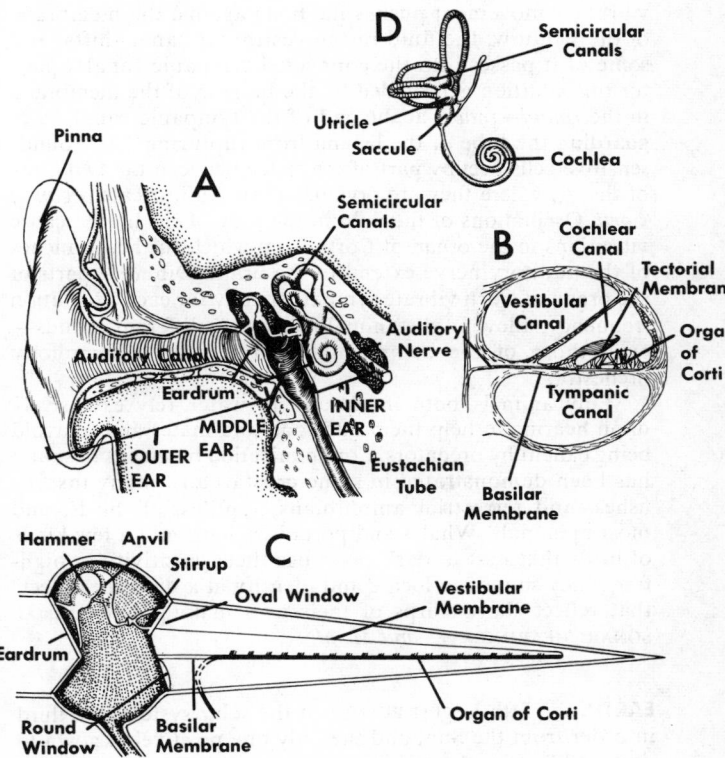

Human ear is a grouping of specialized mechanisms adapted to senses of hearing, accelerated motion, and balance. It is traditionally divided into three zones (A): outer ear (pinna and auditory canal); middle ear (chamber in which ossicles transmit sound from eardrum to oval window and which communicates with pharynx via Eustachian tube); and inner ear (cochlea and semicircular canals). All three zones mediate ear's functions in hearing: Sound vibrations, collected in cartilaginous pinna, are funneled through air in auditory canal; resultant vibration of eardrum is transmitted through minute articulated bones (hammer, anvil, stirrup) to oval window at base of cochlea. Compactly coiled cochlear canals are seen in cross section at (B); longitudinal section at (C) presents them uncoiled for clarity. Vibrations of cochlear fluids are converted to nervous impulses in organ of Corti, a complex of sensory cells on basilar membrane. Sense of accelerated motion is mediated by three semicircular canals (D) at right angles to one another; hairlike projections of their sensory cells register sloshing of canal fluid. Sense of balance in field of gravity is mediated by sensory cells in utricle. Function of sensory cells in saccule, apparently sensitive to low frequencies as well as to position, is ambiguous.

ians constitute the *inner ear*. Between inner and outer ears is the middle ear, which is connected to the pharynx by way of the Eustachian tube; this tube is dilated whenever the animal swallows, and serves to equalize pressure on the two sides of the eardrum.

In mammals, the lagena is a very long and slender tube, shaped like an inverted V that has been coiled compactly in the form of a snail shell; it is known as the *cochlea*, and varies in the number of its turns from about one in the sloth to five in the guinea pig. The ascending arm (the vestibular canal) begins at the membranous window against which the columella, or stirrup bone, of the middle ear presses. At the apex of the cochlea, the vestibular canal connects with the descending arm (the tympanic canal), which extends to a second membranous window in the wall of the middle ear. In man, the stirrup bone rests on the *oval window;* when vibratory movement pushes the bone against the membrane of the window, the fluid in the vestibular canal shifts, and some of it passes into the connected tympanic canal. Space for this addition is provided by the bulging of the membrane in the *round window* at the end of the tympanic canal, safeguarding the tube of the lagena from rupturing. The sound-sensitive cells occupy part of the space between the two arms of the ∧, where they are organized into an intricate *organ of Corti*. Oscillations of the fluid in the tube of the lagena cause vibrations in the organ of Corti, from which further branches of the auditory nerve extend to the brain. Different parts of the organ of Corti vibrate sympathetically for each oscillation frequency, allowing the animal to identify different sounds—even those of the complexity produced by a symphony orchestra.

Many animals, both in air and in water, rely extensively upon hearing to help them find food and mates and to avoid being caught by predators. Communication by means of sound has been demonstrated in some crustaceans, many insects, fishes, and terrestrial amphibians, reptiles, all birds, and most mammals. Whales and porpoises, bats, and a few kinds of birds that nest in dark caves use their sensitivity to high-frequency sounds to locate and identify at a distance objects that reflect short chirps of their own making. See ANIMAL SONAR; HEARING.—*L. and M. M.*

EARTH: the fifth-largest PLANET of the solar system, the third in order from the Sun, and the only one positively known to support life. Like the other terrestrial planets (Mercury, Venus, Mars), and unlike the mainly gaseous outer planets, Earth consists essentially of a nearly spherical mass of more or less solid rock. Unlike Mercury and Mars, it has sufficient gravitational attraction (because of its mass) to hold a substantial ATMOSPHERE; because of its distance from the Sun, its rotation, and the nature of the atmosphere, its temperatures are moderate, with relatively minor fluctuations. Solar heat, without which Earth would be a frozen and lifeless world, powers the HYDROLOGIC CYCLE, which makes water continuously available to living things over most of the planet's surface and, through the processes of EROSION, keeps working changes constantly on and in the crust. This crust, with its broad variety of topographical forms and chemical composition, is being altered further by thrusting, folding, faulting, and uplift or subsidence of its parts (see DIASTROPHISM), as well as by volcanic action resulting from the planet's internal heat. Although little is precisely known about Earth's interior, seismic evidence indicates that here, too, physical activity is continuous (see SEISMOLOGY). Altogether Earth seems unique among the planets in the variety of its characteristics and of the processes occurring over, on, and beneath its surface.

Movements: Like other planets, Earth revolves around the Sun and rotates on its axis; both motions apparently were imparted when the planet was formed. The gravitational attraction of the Sun, which prevents Earth from traveling into space beyond the solar system, is balanced by the centrifugal force of Earth's orbital motion. Earth swings in an ORBIT at an average distance from the Sun of about 93,000,000 mi, more distant than the orbits of the planets Mercury and Venus but less distant than that of Mars. In its circuit of almost 600 million mi, Earth moves at an average speed of 18½ mi/sec. The duration in time of the entire circuit defines the tropical year, 365 days 5 hr 49 min (see CALENDAR; TIME). The orbit is an ellipse of small eccentricity. In January, Earth is at perihelion (nearest the Sun), at a distance of 91,500,000 mi; in July it is at aphelion (farthest), 94,500,000 mi from the Sun. While the planet moves around the Sun, it spins upon its own axis, the ends of which are the north and south poles. The interval of rotation defines the time period known as a DAY, with its regular alternation of light and dark phases as the surface passes before the rays of the Sun. At the equator, the surface of Earth moves west to east around its axis at about 17.4 mi/min. This speed diminishes toward the poles, and has important meteorological results, since the atmosphere and the fluid hydrosphere (the larger bodies of water) are affected by the movement of rotation in relation to the rigid crust. (See ATMOSPHERE, GENERAL CIRCULATION OF; and TIDE.)

Earth's movement in its orbit and the 66°33′ tilt of Earth's axis to the plane of the orbit are responsible for the SEASONS: as Earth rounds its orbit during each year, first the northern hemisphere and then the southern hemisphere is inclined toward the Sun. Another movement of Earth, PRECESSION, is causing a gradual change in the direction in which Earth's axis points in space, but the motion is such that the angle of inclination of the axis to the plane of Earth's orbit does not change, and after about 26,000 yr the orientation of the axis in space will be the same as now.

Dimensions: The diameter of the solid sphere is 7,926.68 mi at the equator, and 7,899.98 mi between the poles, the difference being due to the centrifugal force of the planet's spin, which results in a slight bulge around the equator. There are,

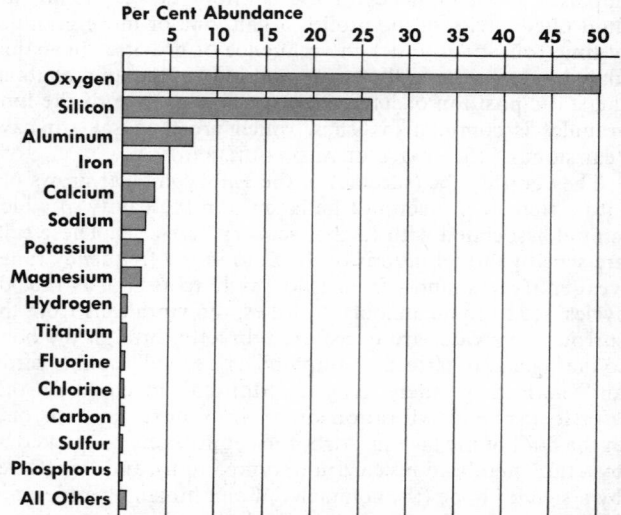

Relative abundances of elements, by weight, in Earth's crust, oceans, and atmosphere are expressed here as percentages of the total. Elements not listed here by name account for less than 0.1%. Nitrogen, being a gas, accounts for only 0.03%, although it forms about 78% of the atmosphere alone.

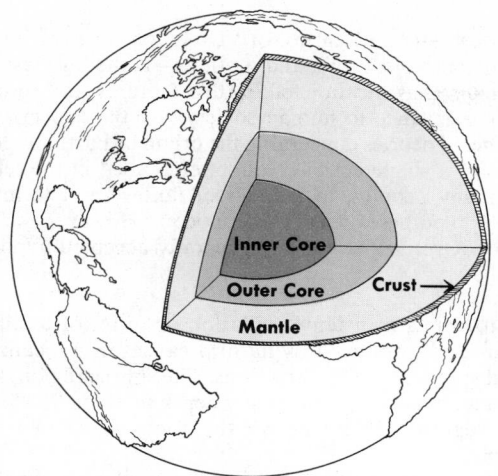

Anatomy of Earth's interior, below the crust, is inferred principally from seismic observations (see SEISMOLOGY).

in addition, minor deviations from regular spheroidal form, associated with changes in the distribution of materials on and beneath the planet's surface. The apparently rugged character of the surface—extremes of about 29,000 ft above sea level at the highest mountain peak, and ocean depths of about 36,000 ft—account for a maximum surface differential of only 65,000 ft, or less than 13 mi, approximately the same as that between the polar and equatorial radii. In both cases the departure from perfect sphericity is only about 0.33%.

The surface area is some 197 million mi², of which almost 70% is covered with water (see OCEAN). Most of the 56 million mi² of land belongs to the great continental masses (see CONTINENT), which have varied in outline and extent throughout the planet's history. Changes in climate affecting sea level, and tectonic movements in Earth's crust affecting coastline and land level, have caused great variations in the land-water ratio of Earth's surface. At present, the continents are more extensive than in most earlier periods.

Earth Zones: The planet's more or less solid, spherical mass is blanketed by the mixture of gases called the ATMOSPHERE, most of which is concentrated within a few miles of the ground; the outer limit of the atmosphere may be as far as 16,000 mi above the surface. The waters covering nearly 70% of the planet's surface are known as the *hydrosphere*. The term *lithosphere,* often applied specifically to the relatively rigid crust (rigid compared to the probably more plastic interior), may also be applied to the entire body of Earth except the atmosphere and hydrosphere, and is so used here. *Biosphere,* a term that sometimes designates the totality of living things, is more commonly applied to all the zones inhabited by living things.

The lithosphere is apparently composed of three well-defined zones which differ in the density and state of the material composing them. The core, the innermost zone, which has a diameter of about 4,320 mi, is believed to have a density of about 10 to 12 times that of water. It may be entirely fluid, or on the contrary, it may consist of a solid inner portion about 1,600 mi in diameter within a fluid shell. (This seems likely because secondary, or "S," seismic waves, which cannot penetrate fluids, do not pass through the core.) The mantle is some 1,782 mi thick, 3.3 times as dense as water, and rigid enough to allow passage of all seismic waves. It may, however, also possess qualities of plasticity, due to the enormous pressure at this depth, sufficient to allow its material to flow, perhaps in convection currents caused by heat (see CONVECTION THEORY). Most scientists believe there are a

number of discernible zones within the mantle, of which the outermost is composed of a rock similar to olivine (iron magnesium silicate). The percentage of iron is believed to increase, along with the density of the rock, in the direction of the core, and the structural constitution of the rock is believed to change with increasing pressure in the same direction. The comparatively thin *crust* is composed of less dense rock, grading outward from SIMA (with a high percentage of iron and magnesium in its essentially silicate composition) to SIAL (in which the proportion of iron and magnesium is less). The border between the crust and the mantle, called the MOHOROVIČIČ DISCONTINUITY (or "Moho") after its discoverer, is detected by the behavior of seismic waves, some of which are deflected here. The crust beneath the oceans is entirely, or almost entirely, simatic, and here the Moho is nearer the surface; for this reason, attempts to reach the Moho and penetrate the mantle by drilling are made on the ocean floor. The crust beneath the continents has a thinner layer of sima surmounted by a thicker layer of sial, with a maximum thickness at the sites of the great mountain ranges.

Mass: Earth's mass has been set at 6.59×10^{21} tons with a mean density approximately 5.5 times water. Since the density of all accessible solid matter near the surface averages only 2.7 times water, the core must have a density exceeding 5.5; it is calculated to be between 10 and 12, or approximately that of iron or nickel-iron.

Temperatures and Pressures at Depth: The temperatures in the several interior zones are unknown. Limited maximum penetration of the outer crust (some 4 mi) indicates a general temperature increase (GEOTHERMAL GRADIENT) of about 90°F for each mile of depth. At 20 mi, rock would presumably melt if the thermal gradient were maintained and the pressure were not too great; but seismic waves indicate that rock is solid at this depth. Pressure at Earth's center is calculated to be about 5 million atm. About ¹⁄₄₀ of this pressure, believed to prevail at a depth of 250 mi, is the maximum that can be simulated under laboratory conditions. Behavior of rock at further depths, and under greater pressure, is beyond present scientific determination.

No authoritative position can be taken concerning either the degree or the origin of whatever heat exists beneath the crust. Prevailing opinion is that most detectable subsurface heat originates from the radioactivity of the less dense rock (sial) found beneath the continents. If Earth's core is intensely hot, convection currents may slowly pervade the mantle, accounting for tectonic movements near and in the crust (CONVECTION THEORY). Igneous activity (volcanic eruptions, lava flows, geysers, hot springs) may be due to local concentrations of radioactive heat, local suspensions of pressure along fault lines, or both.

Gravitation and Magnetism: Earth, like all other bodies possessing mass, exercises a gravitational force. This force accounts for the subsurface pressure already mentioned. It draws water in or on the land irresistibly toward sea level—accounting for precipitation and stream actions of the hydrologic cycle. Gravity also retains the atmospheric envelope around the lithosphere, with the densest portion (the troposphere) nearest the surface. Finally, Earth's only natural satellite, the Moon, is kept in orbit by the force of gravity.

An object can be propelled from Earth with sufficient thrust to attain the balance between centrifugal force and gravity, thus becoming an artificial satellite. For this, a velocity of about 18,000 mi/hr must be attained in the upper atmosphere. If insufficient thrust is applied, gravity draws the object back toward Earth. With excessive thrust, the object attains escape velocity (7 mi/sec) and leaves the gravitational attraction of Earth to follow an orbit around the Sun.

Magnetism also is a property of Earth. TERRESTRIAL MAGNETISM is not entirely understood; but associated phenomena, including applications like the mariner's compass, suggest that Earth behaves magnetically somewhat like a giant bar magnet with poles near the planet's geographic poles. However, since bar magnets cannot retain magnetism at temperatures known to prevail within Earth, this comparison must be made with caution. Moreover, there is the fact that actual geomagnetic poles have changed, even reversed, throughout the planet's history. Modern theory holds that the planet's rotation may cause the more fluid part of the core to set up electric currents which are transformed into complex fields of magnetic force, generally aligned in the direction of the rotational axis. (See TERRESTRIAL MAGNETISM.)

Earth Science: Knowledge of the lithosphere is confined to rock at or near the surface, and to processes recorded in that rock or otherwise discernible by human techniques. Such processes have been extensive and profound throughout Earth's history; they are going on constantly despite the seeming changelessness of broad land and sea features. Even within the short span of a human life, significant changes are apparent. Volcanoes erupt and alter their size and shape, appear for the first time or virtually disappear; flood plains increase in area; fields are gullied; islands emerge or vanish; sandbars grow or are washed away; promontories are undercut and fall; shallow lakes evaporate; rivers alter their courses, or have them altered (for even man participates in this changing process).

Scientists of many disciplines are joining in the study of Earth, and their joint effort is becoming known as Earth Science. The present estimate of the planet's age, 4.7 billion yr, rests on findings of physicists who calculate the periods of radioactive disintegration (see RADIOACTIVE DATING). Composition of the outer crust, of seas and springs, and of the atmosphere is investigated by geologists, chemists, physicists, meteorologists, and oceanographers. Biologists and paleontologists reconstruct the story of life in a detailed chapter covering the most recent half-billion years. The planet's chronological history is read from rock strata by geologists specializing in STRATIGRAPHY and RADIOACTIVE DATING. The role of Earth in the universe—its origin and motions—is the business of the astronomer. Classification of Earth's features and resources, and their relevance to human society, are the concern of the geographer. Theories concerning the origin of Earth range from accounts of a single act of creation, embodied in the religious lore of many peoples, to marvels of fantasy and to intricate scientific hypotheses (see COSMOLOGY). However, scientific data do not yet suffice for any generally accepted hypothesis. —E. A.

EARTHQUAKE: a transient oscillation or series of oscillations of the ground, produced by natural causes in a localized region and spreading in all directions. The source region, known as the *focus,* may be located at any depth to about 700 km. The surface region directly above the focus is known as the *epicenter.*

Causes: Many earthquakes are believed to be caused by TECTONIC effects, especially the sudden release of accumulated elastic strain energy (see ELASTIC REBOUND THEORY). Among other possible causes are: sudden shearing accompanying plastic flow; volcanic activity, including explosive release of accumulated gas; abrupt volume changes produced by mineral crystallization and polymorphic phase transformations; and abrupt changes in circulation patterns of magma. Rock slides, meteor impacts, and collapse of subsurface caves are other, minor causes. Artificial explosions, under or above the surface, also produce ground motion which at large distances may be difficult (if not impossible) to distinguish from natural earthquakes.

Effects: Earthquakes can produce striking, often highly destructive effects. The intensity of an earthquake is a composite, qualitative measure of the damage to man-made structures and of changes in the surface features of the earth, *e.g.* visible faults and fissures. It is a measure of the stability of man's structures and of Earth's surface. The Mercalli Intensity Scale, presently in use, ranges from degree I, for an earthquake which is felt by a few persons and with no effects on structures, to degree XII, for an earthquake which produces

Earthquake and volcanic regions: Areas designated are those where earthquake and volcanic activity are most frequent or most severe. Both earthquake and volcanic areas are associated with lines of weakness in Earth's crust.

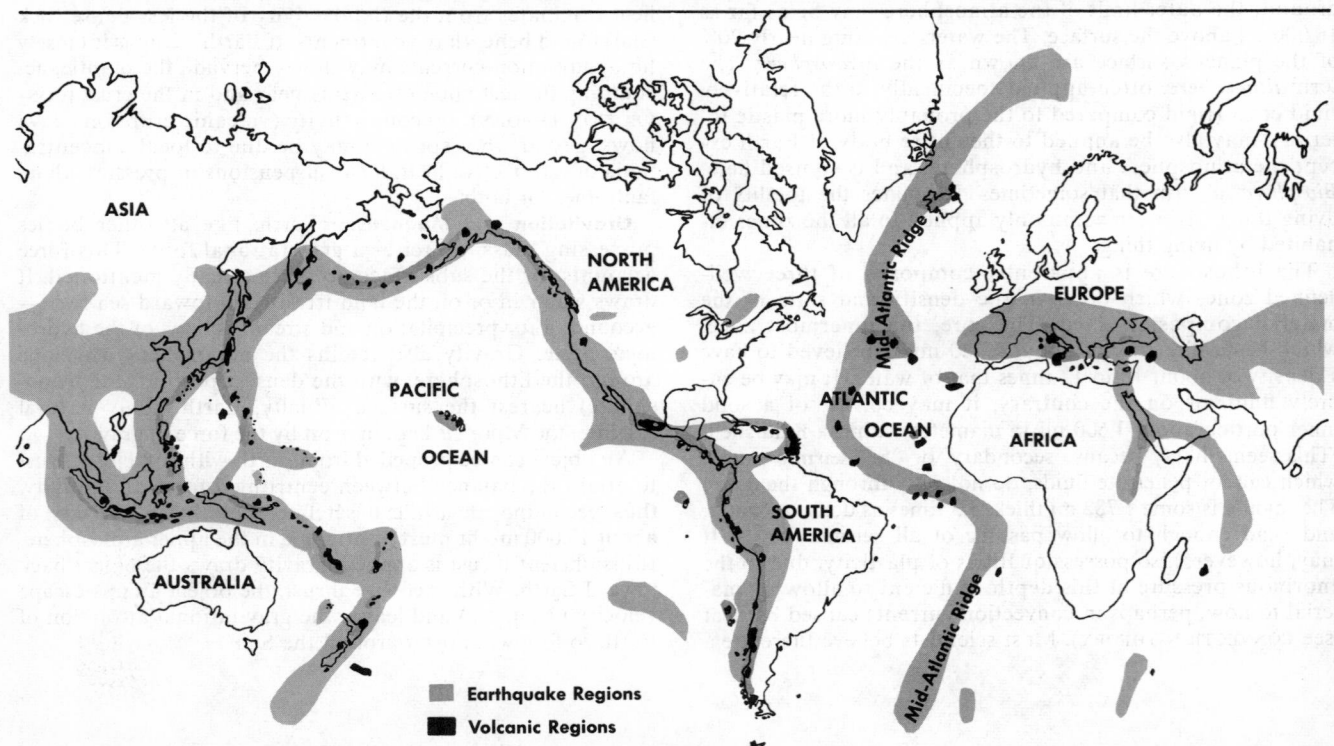

Earthquake Regions
Volcanic Regions

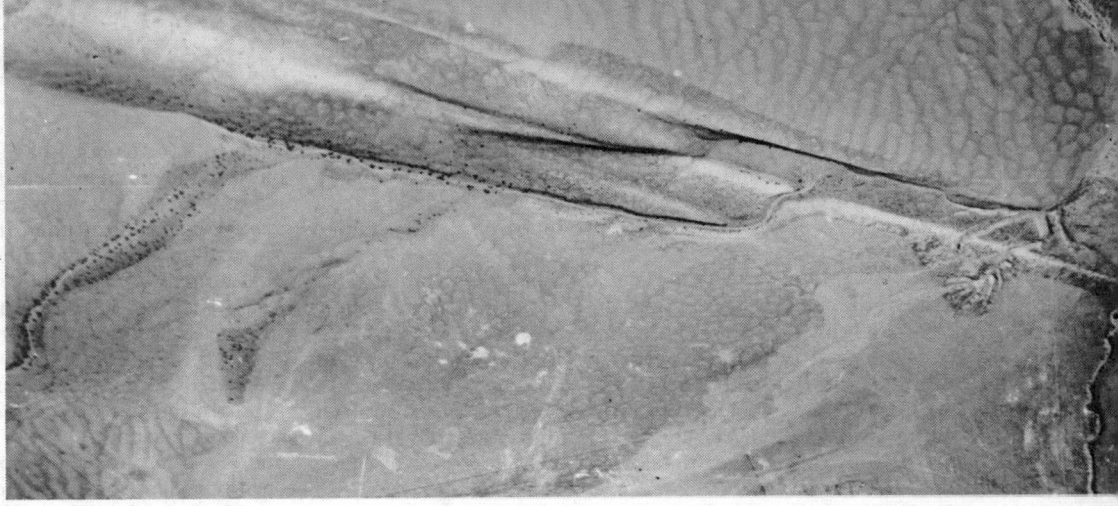

Air photo of San Andreas fault in California shows where offsets associated with earthquakes have altered course of river. Course is indicated by vegetation (black dots). (*U. S. Geological Survey*)

widespread panic, total destruction of buildings, ground accelerations exceeding that of gravity, visible ground motion, and permanent distortion of lines of sight and level. Among the visible effects on Earth's surface are continuous and discontinuous fault breaks at the surface (sometimes extending large distances), soil slumping, earth avalanches, and water and sand fountains. At sea, the elastic compressional and shear waves (see SEISMIC WAVES) are transformed into sound waves when they strike the ocean bottom from beneath. These sound waves are sometimes observed aboard a ship at sea by shaking of the masts and hull (seaquakes). Under special circumstances, an earthquake with focus near or under an ocean produces a seismic sea wave, known as TSUNAMI. The water in landlocked bays and lakes is sometimes excited by earthquakes, which produce an oscillating motion of the water surface, known as a *seismic seiche*. Frequently earthquakes, especially those occurring near areas of alluvial cover, are accompanied and preceded by audible sounds of low pitch. These are produced by compressional and shear waves in the alluvium, from which, under favorable circumstances, an appreciable sound wave may be transmitted into the air. Most large earthquakes are preceded and followed by a series of smaller shocks, known as foreshocks and aftershocks. A sequence of small earthquakes all occurring in the same region at small time intervals and of the same order of magnitude is known as an *earthquake swarm*.

Record Disturbances: The most severe recorded earthquake occurred in a sparsely settled region of central Assam, India, June 12, 1897. Some 1,500 persons lost their lives; all brick and stone buildings in an area of 30,000 mi² were destroyed; water in lakes and rivers almost 500 mi from the epicenter was set to oscillating. This region was the scene of another major quake Aug. 15, 1950. Other large earthquakes in Asia include the Mino-Owari earthquake near Tokyo, Japan, Sept. 1, 1923. In North America, the St. Maurice earthquake of Feb. 5, 1663, centered approximately halfway between Montreal and Quebec, produced great damage. Of the New Madrid earthquakes of 1811–12, in S Missouri, the one on Feb. 7, 1812, was the largest ever recorded on this continent. The topography of the Mississippi River region was considerably altered over an area of about 50,000 mi². On Aug. 31, 1886, a violent quake damaged Charleston, S. C., which had not experienced one since 1680. On Apr. 18, 1906, the San Andreas fault along the coast of central California broke for a distance of almost 300 mi, causing loss of life and extensive property damage in San Francisco. In Europe, the famous earthquakes of 1755 devastated much of Lisbon and caused great loss of life, the most destructive one occurring Nov. 1, 1755, All Saints' Day. Thousands of Lisbon's devout were congregated in the churches, nearly all of which were destroyed.

Farmer's fence near Woodville, Calif., was offset 8½ ft by California earthquake, April 18, 1906. (*U. S. Geological Survey*)

The most destructive earthquake in North America since 1906 and probably the most intense in the 20th century took place Mar. 27, 1964, at the head of Prince William Sound, Alaska. It resulted in the death of 115 and left 4,500 homeless, and caused extensive ground subsidence (as much as 40 ft) and property damage estimated at over $311 million. It generated a TSUNAMI which was felt over much of the Pacific Ocean; also many seiches, large fluctuations in ground-water level at least as far away as Florida, and pressure fluctuations in the atmosphere. Over 520 aftershocks followed it.

Seismic Belts: Earthquakes occur principally in two elongated regions. One passes around the Pacific Ocean (circum-Pacific belt), and includes New Zealand, New Guinea, Japan, the Aleutian Islands, Alaska, and the west coasts of North and South America. It has been estimated that energy released in earthquakes in this region account for 80% of the total earthquake energy release. The other region underlies the Mediterranean region eastward through Asia, passing under the Atlas, Alpine, Iranian, Himalayan, and Burmese Mountains, the island chains of Indonesia and New Guinea, the Solomon Islands, and the New Hebrides. The two regions meet at Celebes. A less active region consists of the MID-OCEANIC RIDGES, including the submarine mountains underlying the center of the Atlantic, Indian, and S Pacific Oceans.

Depths of Disturbances: Most earthquakes occur at depths of about 25 km; the frequency of occurrence diminishes with depth. The observed depth distribution permits classification into shallow-focus (0–70 km), intermediate-focus (70–300 km), and deep-focus earthquakes (300–700 km). The deepest-focus earthquake on record occurred at about 700 km. The deep-focus type are confined to the circum-Pacific belt.

Evidence from analysis of many quakes has suggested that the most common type of earthquake-producing fault movement is transcurrent—*i.e.* involving relative horizontal displacement of the two sides of a vertical fault (see ELASTIC RE-

BOUND THEORY). Such transcurrent faults may be the most important mechanism for shallow-focus disturbances throughout the circum-Pacific belt. Some earthquakes, especially the intermediate-depth ones, may be produced by normal fault movements.

Locating Epicenters: Any particular seismograph station can locate the epicenter and origin time of an earthquake approximately by determining the time interval separating the arrival times of various phases and by making use of particle motion in the Rayleigh surface waves (see SEISMIC WAVES). The U. S. Coast and Geodetic Survey locates the epicenter and the origin time precisely by combining the arrival-time data for the various earthquake phases as reported by stations all over the Earth.

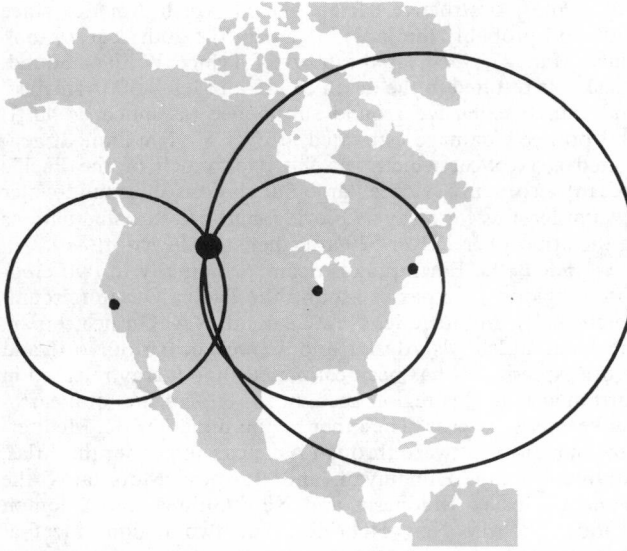

Locating an earthquake: Distance of epicenter from each of three seismic stations is determined by comparing arrival times of seismic waves. With this distance as radius, circle is drawn around location of each station on map or globe. Point of intersection of the three circles is location of epicenter.

Magnitudes and Frequency: The magnitude of a quake is determined by measuring the trace amplitude of a definite phase on a seismogram. This instrumental measure of earthquake magnitude has been empirically related to earthquake energy release. The magnitude scale was designed so that the smallest detectable disturbances, with an energy release of about 6.3×10^5 ergs, have a magnitude 0, while the largest ones, with an energy release of about 2×10^{25} ergs, have a magnitude of 8.5. The frequency of occurrence varies inversely with magnitude. From 1904 to 1957 there were only six earthquakes of magnitude 8.4 or greater. The average annual number of earthquakes ranges from 1 with magnitude 8 or more to over 300,000 with magnitude 2.9 or less. Altogether there are more than a million each year.—*Sa. K.*

EARTHSHINE: the phenomenon otherwise known as "the old Moon in the new Moon's arms." When the Moon is in a thin crescent phase, the part of the earthward side of the Moon that is not in direct sunlight may be seen by sunlight that has been reflected from Earth to the Moon, and then reflected by the Moon back to Earth. It is the counterpart of moonlight on Earth.—*M. W. O.*

EATON, AMOS, 1776–1842, U. S. botanist and geologist; b. Chatham, N. Y. His lectures on natural history before the N. Y. Legislature (1818) led to the establishment of the state geological survey (1836). He made geological and agricultural surveys of Albany and Rensselaer counties (1820–21) and the Erie Canal district (1824). Among his books on botany, geology, and chemistry was the long-standard *A Manual of Botany for the Northern States* (1817).—*D. H. D. R.*

ECHINODERMS: a group of marine invertebrate animals, of which four living classes are recognized: Crinoidea, including sea lilies and feather stars; Asteroidea, including starfish, brittle stars, basket fish; Echinoidea, including sand dollars, heart urchins, sea urchins; and Holothuroidea, the sea cucumbers. Eight other classes are extinct. Echinoderms typically have a bulbous or star-shaped body enclosing a true body cavity (coelom). The body is generally covered with a tough, leatherlike skin frequently studded with spines or spicules (small, hard spikes). The skeleton is formed by groups of distinct plates made of calcite, which are located within the body wall (mesodermal). The echinoderms are very closely related to the vertebrates, as shown by the superficial position of the nervous system and the character of the coelom, of the skeleton, of the embryo (in which the blastopore becomes the anus instead of the mouth), and of the bilaterally symmetrical larva. The adult organisms exhibit radial symmetry—*i.e.* similar parts are arranged symmetrically around a central axis. A network of canals (the water-vascular system) carries water through the body and terminates in closed tubes that project outside the body as the tube feet, each ending in a suction cup. By controlling the pressure of water in the system, some forms are able to extend and contract the tube feet and thus

Typical echinoderms (*left to right*): Purple sea urchin (*Arbacia punctulata*) has prominent spines that aid in locomotion as well as defense. Brittle stars (*Ophiothrix fragilis*) lose arms easily, but soon replace them. Spiny starfish (*Marthasterias glacialis*) feeds on shellfish, pulling shells open with its tube feet. (*Walter Dawn, left; Douglas P. Wilson, center, right*)

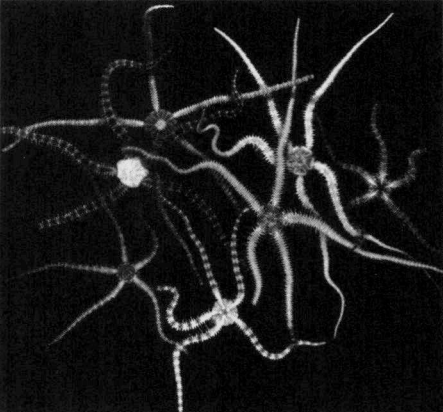

move about. Echinoderms frequently are able to regenerate parts of their body; if a starfish loses an arm it can grow another one.

All living echinoderms are bottom dwellers. Some (*e.g.* the crinoids) are attached to the bottom, at least during part of their life cycle, by a stem that raises the bulblike body above the sea floor. Others (*e.g.* the starfish) are able to move about the bottom freely. Since many echinoderms congregate in groups, or "gardens," great numbers are found in some places and none in others. They are important bottom scavengers, helping to keep the sea floor clear of dead organisms. Some extract organic material from bottom muds, which they pass through their body, whereas others (*e.g.* starfish) prey upon living animals, including mollusks, fish, and other echinoderms. Frequently, starfish destroy valuable oyster beds. The eggs of echinoderms have been much used in scientific experiments.—*J. M. P.*

ECHO AND ECHO RANGING: An echo occurs when radiant energy strikes a reflecting surface and bounces back, so that incident and reflected energy are detected separately. The many echoes from a shout in a large empty hall are common experience. Because of the time factor, echoes can be used to measure distance. If one knows the velocity of propagation of the energy, one can, by measuring the time between sending an energy pulse and receiving its echo, calculate the distance to the reflecting object by the simple relation $d = \frac{1}{2}t \times v$, which means distance equals one half the time of travel times the velocity of travel of the energy pulse.

Sound travels in air at about 1,100 ft/sec. The pilot of a coastal steamer opposite a cliff-lined shore toots his whistle and, 10 sec later, hears an echo from the cliff. He then knows the cliff is about 1 mi away. Sound travels in water, however, at about 5,000 ft/sec. Thus if an operator of a sonar instrument on a fishing vessel sends out a SONAR pulse, in 1/10 sec he gets a loud echo, and in 2 sec a longer, "mushy" echo. He knows then that the bottom is about 250 ft down, and a school of fish is about 1 mi away. Radio energy, finally, travels about 186,000 mi/sec. When an airport traffic controller sends out RADAR pulses, 1/1000 sec later he may get two echoes from the same direction only 50 millionths of a second apart. He then knows that about 100 mi away there are two airplanes only 5 mi apart, and he can warn the pilots of collision danger. See also ANIMAL SONAR.—*R. M. P.*

ECLIPSE: the passage of a celestial body into the shadow of another. If an opaque, non-luminous object is illuminated from the outside, it casts a shadow in a direction opposite that of the light source. The dense inner part of the shadow is called the umbra; the light outer part is the penumbra. In the solar system, all planets and satellites are opaque bodies receiving their illumination from the Sun; hence they cast enormous shadows into space. If, for example, Earth's shadow falls on the Moon, the latter is cut off from the Sun's rays and is said to be eclipsed.

Eclipses of the Moon (lunar eclipses) occur when the centers of Sun, Earth, and Moon, in that order, are in a straight line or nearly so. If all three bodies were to remain always in the same plane, there would be a lunar eclipse at each full moon. However, the Moon's path is tilted somewhat with respect to the ECLIPTIC and a lunar eclipse takes place only if the time

TOTAL LUNAR ECLIPSES, 1963–1970

Dec. 30, 1963	Apr. 24, 1967	Oct. 6, 1968
Jun. 24–25, 1964	Oct. 18, 1967	1969—none
Dec. 19, 1964	Apr. 13, 1968	1970—none

Total solar eclipse of June 30, 1954: Succession of exposures on one photographic plate shows progress of Moon across solar disk and sudden appearance of solar corona at the moment of totality. (*Roy E. Swan, Minneapolis Star*)

of full moon coincides very nearly with the time of the Moon's passage at one of the nodes of its orbit—*i.e.* at the points where its orbit intersects the ecliptic. Depending on how deeply the Moon is immersed in Earth's shadow, three kinds of lunar eclipses may occur: *total,* in which the Moon is entirely covered by the umbra; *partial,* in which a portion of the Moon's surface remains illuminated throughout; and *penumbral* (also called appulse), in which the Moon penetrates the penumbra but remains clear of the umbra. In appulses, only a slight dimming of the Moon's brightness is noticeable. Even in total eclipses the Moon does not become entirely dark: a small amount of the Sun's rays are refracted, or bent, by Earth's atmosphere into the cone of shadow and give the Moon a deep coppery glow. Because a lunar eclipse causes a true loss of illumination on the Moon, the phenomenon is observable from any point on Earth's surface from which the Moon is seen above the horizon at the time of the eclipse. Only a small amount of scientific data are obtainable from lunar eclipse observations, although an observed temperature

Lunar eclipse occurs when Sun, Earth, and Moon are in perfect alignment or nearly so. If Moon does not fully enter Earth's umbra, eclipse is only partial. Eclipse diagramed is total.

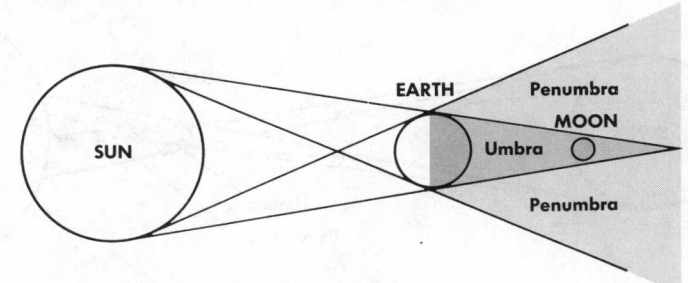

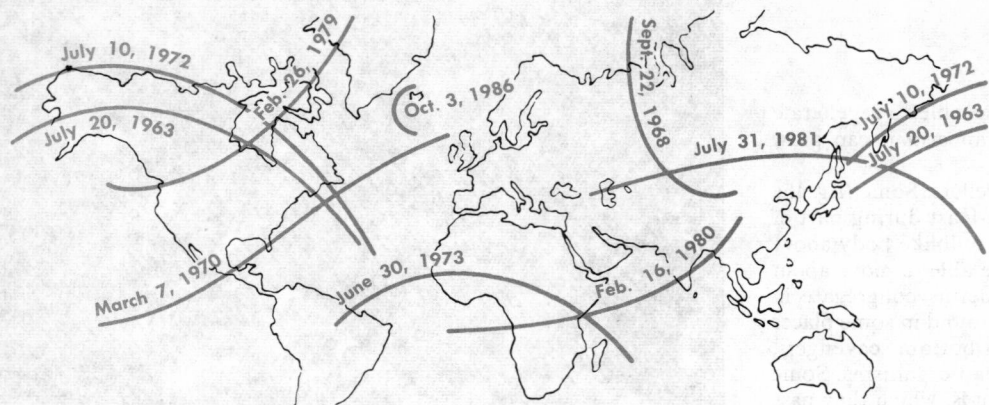

drop on the lunar surface, as the eclipse progresses, indicates that the outer layers conduct heat poorly, in a way comparable to crushed lava or volcanic residue. Historically, the circular shape of Earth's shadow seen advancing across the Moon's surface was one of the earliest proofs of Earth's sphericity.

Eclipses of the Sun (solar eclipses) take place when the Moon's shadow falls on Earth; *i.e.* when Sun, Moon, and Earth, in that order, are nearly in a straight line. According to the definition, it would be more appropriate to call them eclipses of Earth, a designation which purists have used occasionally in the past. Solar eclipses happen only at new moon, when the Moon is near one of the nodes of its orbit (see also SAROS). An observer on Earth's surface sees the apparent disk of the Moon projected against the Sun. The eclipse is *total* if the Sun is entirely hidden; it is *partial* if a portion of the Sun's disk remains visible. Owing to the variable distance of the Moon, its apparent size is sometimes too small to cover the Sun entirely; in such cases, it may be seen projected against the Sun's center while the Sun's edge remains visible as a ring of light; this type of eclipse is called *annular, i.e.* ring-shaped.

Partial eclipses are seen from all points on Earth's surface located within the Moon's penumbra. Total and annular eclipses are seen only from points within the umbra. As the relative positions of Earth, Sun, and Moon vary throughout the eclipse, and as Earth rotates on its axis, the umbra travels in a narrow path across Earth's surface at an average speed of about 3,500 mph. Although solar eclipses are more frequent than lunar ones, they are seen more rarely at a given place. This is particularly true of the total and annular phases, which are always confined to a very small area of Earth.

Total solar eclipses are among the most remarkable celestial events visible to the naked eye. Just before totality begins, the last few rays of sunlight seem to circle the Sun in a "diamond ring"; this breaks up into bright spots as the Sun shines briefly through the valleys at the edge of the lunar disk; this phenomenon is called *Baily's beads*. Once the entire solar surface is hidden, the sky is dark enough to allow stars to be seen; the Sun's corona and prominences, normally lost in the Sun's glare, become visible. The maximum duration of the total phase may attain 7 min, but it is much shorter in most eclipses. As the Sun begins to reappear, Baily's beads are seen again, followed by the diamond ring. The corona disappears and the crescent Sun marks the end of the total phase. Before the invention of the CORONAGRAPH, total eclipses provided the only available observations of the Sun's chromosphere, prominences, and corona. Even at present, they often yield greater accuracy of measurement than can be obtained by other types of observation. They are used in particular for studies of Earth's upper atmosphere, whose behavior is conditioned in part by the Sun's ultra-violet radiation; this radiation is cut off during eclipses, thereby causing measurable effects. *Great care must be taken to protect the eyes while observing solar eclipses*: use of heavily smoked glass or dark photographic film is essential. Direct viewing of the Sun through a telescope or binoculars, even for a brief moment, will cause permanent eye damage and possibly blindness.

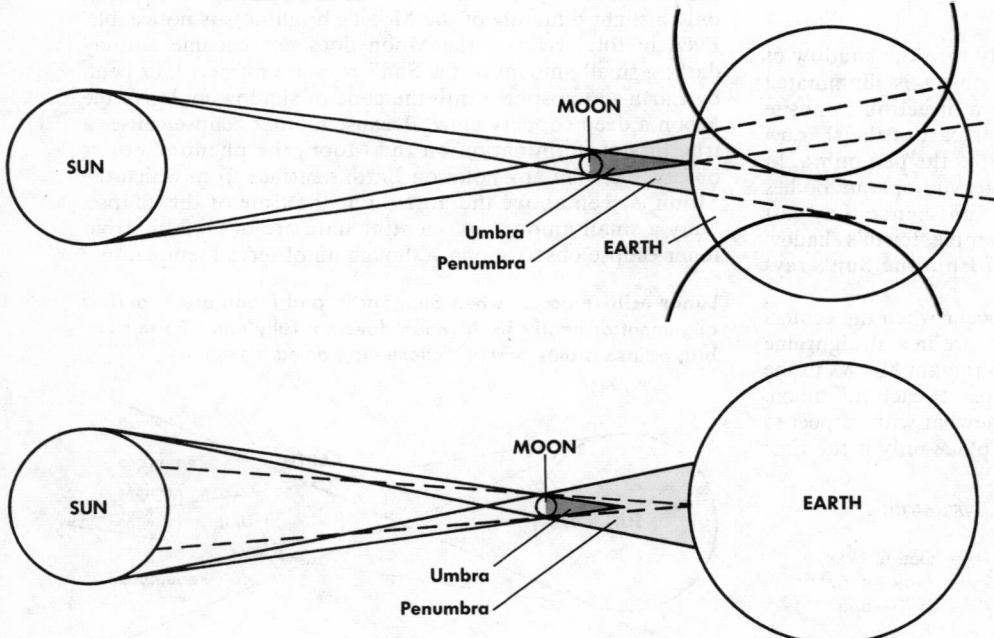

Total solar eclipse occurs when Sun, Moon, and Earth are in perfect or nearly perfect alignment, and Moon is near enough to Earth so that the umbra of its shadow reaches Earth. In the path traced by the umbra, eclipse is seen as total. In the lighter shadow (penumbra) beyond the umbra, a partial eclipse is observed. There can be no total eclipse when Earth is in a position such as that indicated by the colored circles.

Annular solar eclipse occurs when alignment is same as for total solar eclipse except that Moon is not near enough to Earth for the umbra of its shadow to reach Earth. Moon's disk is not large enough to eclipse Sun completely; observers see ring of light around Moon's disk.

Eclipses of Jupiter's Satellites: The four Galilean satellites of Jupiter (Io, Europa, Ganymede, Callisto) undergo eclipses similar in every way to lunar eclipses. Jupiter's shadow being many times as large as Earth's, the first three of these satellites are eclipsed at each revolution. Callisto occasionally passes clear of the shadow because its orbit is more inclined to the plane of the planet's orbit (in which the shadow also lies). In 1675, the Danish astronomer Ole Roemer noted a systematic lag between the predicted and observed times of these eclipses. He correctly interpreted this phenomenon as being caused by the finite speed of light, which, until then, had been thought to travel instantaneously. Satellite eclipses exhibit the same phases as lunar ones: partial while the satellite is in the course of entering or leaving the shadow, total when it is immersed in it. The time elapsed during the partial phase is a function of the satellite's diameter and of its orbital speed. The latter is known from Newton's theory of celestial motions; therefore the duration of partial phase may be used to estimate the other quantity from which it depends, namely the diameter. The satellites themselves cast a shadow into space which sometimes can be seen projected onto Jupiter's surface. This phenomenon, called a shadow-transit, is identical with a solar eclipse on Earth. An observer located within the shadow on Jupiter's surface would see the satellite passing in front of the Sun.

Eclipsing Binaries are star pairs, physically related, that move around a common center. When our line of sight to a binary is in the plane of its motion, the two component stars may be seen to eclipse each other (see BINARY STAR).—*S. D. G.*

ECLIPTIC: the great circle described by the Sun in its apparent annual motion on the CELESTIAL SPHERE. In the span of one year, Earth completes one revolution in its orbit; for a terrestrial observer, this causes the yearly displacement of the Sun against the background of stars. Therefore, the plane of the ecliptic is also that of Earth's orbit. Because Earth's polar axis—the line joining the north and south poles—is tilted with respect to the plane of the ecliptic, the latter is inclined to the celestial equator by about 23½°. The ecliptic bisects the ZODIAC.—*S. D. G.*

ECOLOGY: the study of plants and animals in relation to their natural environment, including both physical features and living things. Ecology is a summing up, an attempt to fit each living thing into its place in the world—as an individual, as a member of a constantly changing community, and as a possible ancestor of new generations that will evolve by becoming adapted to their environmental conditions. Ecology is a modernization of the old field of natural history; it is more functional, more quantitative. The term (originally spelled *Oekologie*) was devised in 1869 by the German zoologist Ernst Haeckel to emphasize the study of the home relationships of living things. Recognition that plants form distinct communities dates mostly from *Œcology of Plants* (1885 in Danish, 1909 in English), by the Danish botanist E. Warming. No single name stands out distinctly as the initiator of modern work in animal ecology. A British Ecological Society was formed in 1913, and the Ecological Society of America in 1916.

Essentially, each plant or animal develops individual adaptations that match common problems. It must get enough energy for life, whether from the Sun or from suitable chemical compounds. It must absorb nutrient substances needed in the synthesis of its own kind of cells. It must survive adverse climatic conditions, resist agents of disease, escape from being eaten, and reproduce—perhaps giving parental care to the next generation. The ecologist considers all of these adaptations and the environmental factors they match. To do so, he needs constantly to know the identity of each kind of animal and plant in the community he is studying and to keep up with the continual changes in numbers and activity of each kind.

Members of every community of plants and animals are related to one another in a complex food web. Green plants, whether microscopic ones drifting in surface waters or the green leaves of grasslands and forests, provide through PHOTOSYNTHESIS the energy link between the Sun and all other kinds of life in the region; they form the broad bottom tier of a "food pyramid." The surplus food produced by green plants (including fruits and seeds or other reproductive products beyond the number required to replace parent plants as they die) gives plant-eating animals and plant-disease organisms what they need to live. They are members of the second, smaller tier in the pyramid, and their numbers are regulated both by the food they can get without destroying the green plants (and their own future) and by attacks from members of the third tier. This tier is composed of animal-eating animals, and disease organisms and parasites of plant-eating animals and of plant-disease organisms. These members of the third tier are limited similarly to energy and nutrients from creatures of the second tier and can use only expendable members of the second tier if they are not to imperil their own future.

The more complex the interconnections between tiers, the more stable is the whole pyramid. The presence of alternate foods acts as a governor that prevents wide fluctuations in the populations of individual species. It is where the food web is simple that spectacular changes occur, as in the far north or in an area where man has changed the environment into one tailored for the production of some single crop. (See FOOD CHAIN; BALANCE OF NATURE.)

The nature of the soil available to land plants and the chemical nutrients in the water around water plants provide one group of limitations affecting the life of each area. At least as important are climatic conditions, including amount of daylight and water available. Together these determine what kinds of vegetation can grow, as the bottom tier in the food pyramid. Certain combinations of conditions match characteristic types of plants and animals in ecological units (BIOMES) that can be recognized easily. Examples are deserts, grasslands, tundras, and forests, with their associated types of life. Aquatic biomes are usually considered by specialized ecologists in the fields of oceanography and limnology.

These combinations of conditions usually follow a geographical pattern and produce a zonation of life. Which species of animals and plants will actually be found in each area of biome or life zone depends, of course, upon whether their ancestors had an opportunity to spread into the area. (See LIFE ZONES; PLANT GEOGRAPHY; ZOOGEOGRAPHY.)

Living things bring about alterations in their own environment, leading in each biome to a SUCCESSION of unlike communities in the same geographical area. Bare rocks, for example, may be colonized by lichens and capture enough dust to provide a place for mosses and ferns to grow. These plants can hold moisture that, when frozen, will cause chipping of the rock; crevices are produced and rock particles accumulate to provide sites for larger plants. Eventually an exposed rock surface can become covered by rock particles and humus materials from decay of plants, and serve as the bedrock upon which a forest grows. Conversely, the vegetation around a small lake, by holding sediments from water draining in, can gradually build out the margins, filling the lake. Eventually it too can vanish, to be replaced by a forest. Hurricanes, volcanic action, glaciation, and man's lumbering operations temporarily push back the succession. Reforestation programs advance the succession. But, with time, a new dynamic equilibrium is reached as the ecological climax typical of the particular biome.—*L. and M. M.*

EDDINGTON, SIR ARTHUR STANLEY, 1882–1944, English mathematician and astrophysicist; b. Kendal. His astrophysical researches, begun in 1916 and published in his *The Internal Constitution of the Stars* (1926), greatly clarified the mass-luminosity relation in stars and indicated the nature of the white dwarf stars. His interpretations (1921–22) of Einstein's theory of relativity led him to attempt computation of the "constants of nature" by theoretical means rather than direct measurements. His views on this mode of research were published in his *Fundamental Theory* (1946). Eddington was a fellow of the Royal Society and an associate of the U. S. National Academy of Sciences.—*D. H. D. R.*

EDDY CURRENTS: circulating electric currents induced in a conductor moving relative to a magnetic field or in a conductor placed in a changing magnetic field. Eddy currents usually cause a power loss due to heating of the medium, and result in mechanical coupling forces between the medium and the magnetic field. To eliminate eddy currents in the iron magnetic circuits of motors, generators, and transformers, the cores are built up of thin insulated sheets.—*H. Sw.*

EDISON, THOMAS ALVA, 1847–1931, U. S. inventor; b. Milan, Ohio; self-educated. Among his numerous inventions were quadruplex telegraphy (1874), the carbon telephone transmitter (1876), the phonograph (1877), and the practical form of the incandescent lamp (1879). He designed the equipment for the Pearl Street power plant in N. Y. City and had it in operation by 1882. His one theoretical discovery was the *Edison effect* (see THERMIONIC EMISSION), which he investigated no farther because he saw no practical value in it. He was a member of the National Academy of Sciences. —*D. H. D. R.*

Thomas Alva Edison
(*George Eastman House*)

EDLEN, BENGT, 1906–   , Swedish physicist; b. Ringarum. He is best known for his identification (1944) of hitherto-unexplained emission lines in the spectrum of the Sun's corona. Until then it was believed they might be caused by *coronium,* an element unknown on Earth; Edlén showed they are emitted in the Sun's rarefied atmosphere by iron atoms stripped of 13 electrons. For this important discovery he was awarded gold medals by the Stockholm Academy of Sciences, the Franklin Institute (Philadelphia), and the Royal Astronomical Society (London).—*S. D. G.*

EFFERVESCENCE: the bubbling of a solution caused by the escape of absorbed gas. Effervescent solutions contain gases, dissolved under pressure, which escape when the pressure is reduced, *e.g.* the escape of carbon dioxide from carbonated beverages when the bottle cap is removed.—*G. W. M.*

EFFICIENCY: see MECHANICAL EFFICIENCY.

EFFLORESCENCE: loss of water by a hydrated crystal. This phenomenon occurs when the vapor pressure of the hydrate system is greater than that of water vapor in the air. The crystal then loses water until the two vapor pressures become equal. Sodium sulfate decahydrate and sodium monohydrogen phosphate dodecahydrate are examples of efflorescent compounds.—*G. W. M.*

EGG: a female gamete, or ovum, which may unite with a male gamete (sperm) and develop into a new individual. In some animals an unfertilized egg may develop into a new organism (see PARTHENOGENESIS). Eggs are produced by the female gonads, called OVARIES. An egg usually reaches maturity and acquires most of its characteristics, *e.g.* the yolk, in the ovary. In some species maturation is completed only after FERTILIZATION. Mature eggs are generally expelled from the ovary and pass through a canal, the oviduct, where, in such forms as birds and reptiles, albumen (egg white) and a shell are added. In some animals, including humans, part of the oviduct is enlarged to form a uterus, within which a fertilized egg may develop. Females of birds and most invertebrate animals re-

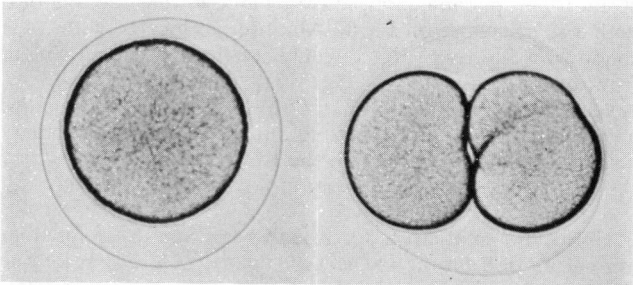

Egg of sea urchin is magnified here 130 times. Fertilized egg (*left*) divides into two cells (*right*). Beginning of division into four cells can be seen in right-hand cell. (*Douglas P. Wilson*)

lease eggs outside the body, where they hatch into young; these animals are called *oviparous.* In other animals (*e.g.* rattlesnake, garter snake, lizards, snails, and some insects) the fertilized egg with a very large yolk develops within the uterus of the female until the young is born, but is distinctly separated from the mother by an egg membrane; these animals are *ovoviviparous.* The embryo receives its nourishment from the egg yolk. In yet other forms, such as mammals, the egg, usually small, is also retained within the uterus, and the young is born alive, but the embryo receives nourishment from the mother during development; these animals are *viviparous.* In all animals the number of eggs produced by the female is considerably less than the number of sperms produced by the male. There appears to be a relationship between the number of eggs produced by a particular species and the chances of the offspring surviving to maturity; the smaller the chances of survival, the greater the number of eggs generally produced.—*J. M. P.*

EIFFEL, ALEXANDRE GUSTAVE, 1832–1923, French engineer; b. Dijon. Primarily a bridge designer and builder, he built the large sluices of the Panama Canal during the French period of its construction. The *Eiffel tower* was erected in the Champ de Mars, Paris, under his direction, for the exposition of 1889. It is made of 7,300 tons of wrought iron, is supported on 7-ft-thick underground concrete beds, and rises to a height of 984 ft.—*D. H. D. R.*

EIJKMAN, CHRISTIAAN, 1858–1930, Dutch bacteriologist; b. Nijberk. He participated in an unsuccessful search for a bacterial cause for beriberi in the Dutch E Indies, and later noted

1

2

3

Plate 27   COLORATION OF PLANTS

The pigments that give plants their distinctive colors are chiefly green chlorophylls, yellow and orange xanthophylls, red and blue and purple anthocyanins, and various shades of tan caused by tannins. The chlorophylls are usually in chloroplastids, the xanthophylls in chromoplastids, and the others dissolved in the watery sap within the cells. Plants without pigments are usually described as "colorless," although they may be various shades of gray and white.

Summertime colors: 1. On the forest floor, bright yellow spathes draw attention to a spiky flower cluster of an aroid plant related to skunk cabbage. *(Russ Kinne)* **2.** Anthocyanins give New England asters *(Aster novae-angliae)* their many shades of pink, blue, and purple, but the yellow in the center comes from xanthophylls and oils in pollen grains. *(Walter Dawn)* **3.** Indian pipe *(Monotropa uniflora)*, a parasitic plant, is a waxy white in color, but turns black on drying. *(Russ Kinne)* **4. Colorful date palm** *(Phoenix dactylifera)* of Asia, the fruits of which ripen in great pendant clusters, flourishes where hot weather is prolonged and winters do not chill below 10 degrees F. for more than a few hours at a time. *(M. de Longe/Shostal)*

4

Plate 28 CLOUDS

Clouds form when water vapor in the air condenses into tiny water droplets or ice crystals. The main types are stratus, a very low layer of droplets that indicates a horizontal rather than vertical airflow; cumulus, separate white clouds that may develop into cumulonimbus, the thundercloud; and cirrus, high-altitude ice-crystal clouds.

1. Cirrus uncinus (mares' tails). *(J. Wyckoff)*

2. Cirrostratus, with corona 20,000 ft. high. *(J. H. Conover)*

3. Cirrocumulus (mackerel) forms among cirrus. *(V. J. Schaefer)*

4. Altocumulus above 7,000 ft, below cirrus. *(J. H. Conover)*

5. Altocumulus lenticularis at evening. *(J. Wyckoff)*

6. Altostratus, a high foggy layer. *(V. J. Schaefer)*

Plate 29   CLOUDS

7. Cumulus humilis, typical fair-weather clouds. *(J. Wyckoff)*

8. Stratocumulus cloud; below 7,000 ft. *(J. H. Conover)*

9. Stratocumulus clouds, dark but not rainy. *(J. Wyckoff)*

10. Anvil cumulonimbus, the storm cloud. *(V. J. Schaefer)*

11. Stratus, amorphous layer, below 3,000 ft. *(V. J. Schaefer)*

12. Bad-weather cumulus, marking a cold front. *(V. J. Schaefer)*

Plate 30   CORAL

The soft sac-shaped body of a coral animal rests with mouth and tentacles uppermost, supported and protected by a floor and side walls of limy secretion, which is the "coral" with which everyone is familiar. Many corals form immense colonies that accumulate as reefs, as in the Great Barrier Reef of Australia. The crevices and irregularities of corals (1) provide crannies for many sea creatures. *(Amer. Mus. of Nat. Hist.)* Among unusual forms are (2) the branching skeletons of the horn corals (gorgonians) and (3) the convolutions of *Meandrina*, the brain coral. *(Russ Kinne)*

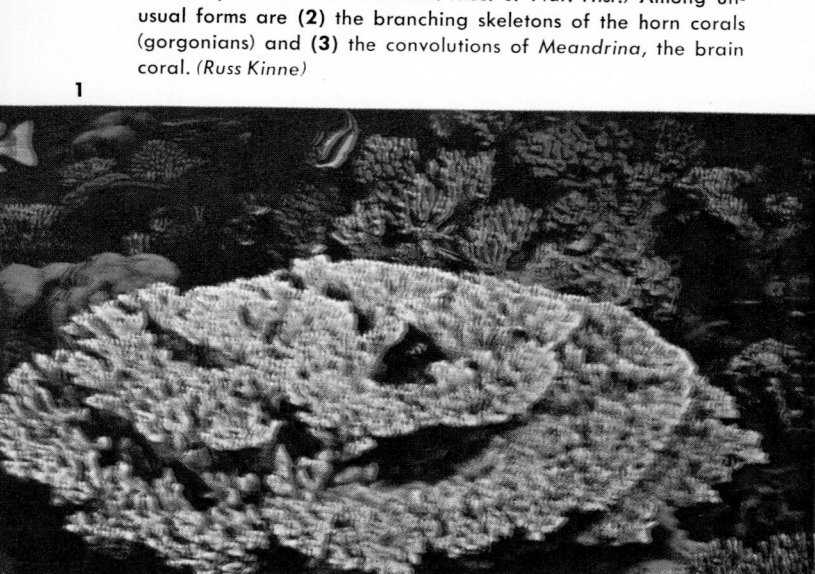

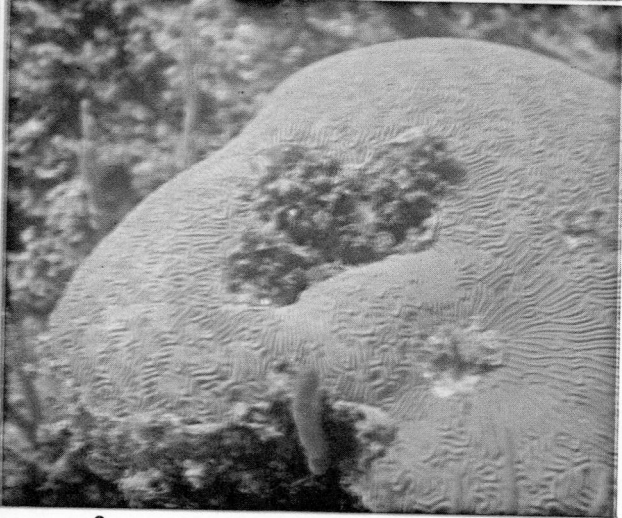

Plate 31   CRUSTACEANS

All but a few crustaceans are aquatic. The most distinctive feature of these many-legged arthropods is their two pairs of antennae. **1. The white shrimp** *(Penaeus setiferus)*, a scavenger of coastal waters, is of high commercial value. *(John H. Gerard/National Audubon Soc.)* **2. The common acorn barnacle** *(Balanus balanoides)* attaches itself to a solid support at an early age and produces a limy shell about its body. Through an opening protected by movable plates, it extends feathery feet to comb small plankton organisms from the sea water for food. *(Amer. Mus. of Nat. Hist.)* **3.** In tide pools, **the crab** prowls for live or dead animals that it can tear into edible chunks with its pincers. *(Reeves-Franklin Photo)*

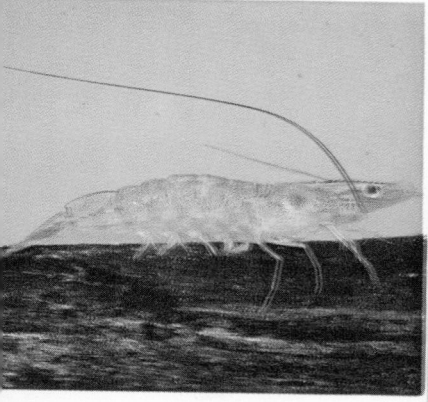

a polyneuritis resembling beriberi that appeared among laboratory chickens and then disappeared. After tracing the cause to the temporary use of polished rice as chicken food, he showed that the inner hull of the rice, removed by polishing, contained an extractable antineuritic substance. For his discovery of the antineuritic vitamin, he received the Nobel prize, 1929. He was an associate of the U. S. National Academy of Sciences.—*D. H. D. R.*

EINSTEIN, ALBERT, 1879–1955, German–U. S. physicist; b. Ulm; ed. Univ. of Zurich. The outstanding physicist of the 20th cent., he published more than 300 scientific papers and books. His paper "On a Heuristic Point of View Concerning the Generation and Transformation of Light" (1905), published while he was an engineer with the patent office in Bern, Switzerland, presents a theory of photoelectricity,

Albert Einstein
(*Trude Fleischmann*)

including the concept of photons of light. His "Electrodynamics of Moving Bodies" (also 1905) is the foundation of his RELATIVITY theory. While professor of physics (1914–33) at the Univ. of Berlin, he was also director of the Kaiser Wilhelm Inst. there. After being driven out of Germany by the Nazis in 1933, he joined the staff of the Institute for Advanced Study, Princeton, and there continued his research until his death. Having suggested to President F. D. Roosevelt (1939) the possibility of weapons using atomic energy, after World War II he was in the forefront of scientific leaders working for peace; he advocated world government. Among his books are *The Meaning of Relativity* (1921), *Investigations on the Theory of the Brownian Movement* (1926), *Unified Field Theory* (1929), and *On the Method of Theoretical Physics* (1933). He received the 1921 Nobel prize for both the photoelectric law and other work in theoretical physics. He was a fellow of the Royal Society and a member of the National Academy of Sciences.—*D. H. D. R.*

EINSTEINIUM: an artificial element (E) of the actinide group; at. no. 99; at. wt 254 (most stable isotope). It was the seventh transuranium element to be discovered. E^{253} was found in the debris of a hydrogen-bomb test explosion in the Pacific, Dec. 1952, by a group headed by Albert Ghiorso and including scientists from the Univ. of California Radiation Laboratory, the Argonne National Laboratory, and the Los Alamos Scientific Laboratory. Isotopes of at. wt 246 thru 256 have since been discovered. E^{253} has a half life of about 20 days; an isomeric form of E^{254} has a half life of 320 days.—*G. W. M.*

EINSTEIN SHIFT: displacement of spectral lines due to a difference in gravitational field between source and receiver. As a consequence of the principle of conservation of energy, the general theory of relativity predicts that the wavelength of a light source is increased under the action of a surrounding gravitational field; the stronger the field, the greater the increase in wavelength. If the spectrum of the source is observed with a receiver located in a different gravitational field, the measurements are, of necessity, referred to a comparison source within the receiver's field, and one of the following effects may be expected: (1) if the field of the observed source is stronger than that of the receiver, the spectrum of the source will exhibit a shift toward the red (longer wavelengths); (2) if the receiver's field is the stronger, the spectrum of the source will be shifted toward the ultraviolet (shorter wave-

lengths). The Einstein shift is very minute (0.01 Å for the Sun) but has been observed for the small but very massive (white dwarf) companion of Sirius. Terrestrially it has been tested by observing the shift of exceptionally sharp gamma rays (MÖSSBAUER EFFECT) between the top and the foot of a tower. —*S. D. G.*

EINTHOVEN, WILLEM, 1860–1927, Dutch physiologist; b. Semarang, now in Indonesia. He invented the string galvanometer, a device for measurement of amount and direction of electric currents (1903), and used it for obtaining electrocardiograms. His research into these made possible the identification of "normal" tracings and the association of abnormalities in the tracings with heart disease. For this work Einthoven received the 1924 Nobel prize. He was a fellow of the Royal Society.—*D. H. D. R.*

EISENSTEIN, FERDINAND GOTTFRIED MAX, 1823–52, German mathematician; b. Berlin. He was a favorite pupil of K. F. Gauss, who reportedly remarked that there had been three epoch-making mathematicians—Archimedes, Newton, and Eisenstein. His researches were mostly in the theory of numbers, in connection with which he studied quadratic forms and created the theory of cubic forms. He applied elliptic functions to the theory of numbers.—*H. C.*

EKMAN, VAGN WALFRID, 1874–1954, Swedish oceanographer; b. Stockholm. He is known for his explanation of "dead water" in relation to ship movement, his studies on compressibility of sea water, and his paper (1905) on ocean currents produced by wind friction. The *Ekman spiral* is the theoretical distribution of velocity downward from the ocean surface and upward from the ocean bottom. The *Ekman current meter* is widely used for measuring ocean currents.—*D. H. D. R.*

ELASTICITY: the property whereby a solid body that undergoes a change of shape and possibly size because of the action of applied forces will return fully to its original shape and size upon removal of these forces. For such a body, Robert Hooke discovered (1660) that there exists a linear relationship, presently known as HOOKE'S LAW, between the deformations and forces. Later, the work of Sir Isaac Newton on the fundamental laws of mechanics, of the Bernoulli family and Leonhard Euler on mathematical solutions, of C. A. Coulomb on mechanical properties of materials, and of Thomas Young on elastic and mechanical behavior properties all contributed considerably to the understanding of the reaction of elastic solid bodies subjected to applied loads. About 100 yr ago, C. L. M. H. Navier, A. L. Cauchy, and S. D. Poisson formulated basic equations of elasticity theory. Solutions to these equations have been difficult to achieve. A number of persons, *e.g.* G. Lamé, G. B. Airy, J. C. Maxwell, J. Boussinesq, J. H. Michell, P. F. Papkovitch, N. J. Muskhelishvili, R. D. Mindlin, and E. Sternberg, concerned themselves with these studies. Their successful mathematical investigations led to the development of a variety of methods suitable for solving many problems in the theory of elasticity, which is important today in structural and mechanical design in such fields as naval architecture and civil, aeronautical, and mechanical engineering. In classical elasticity theory, displacements and rotations are considered to be small; *i.e.* higher powers of displacements and rotations are neglected. Finite elasticity theory considers the second- and higher-order displacements and rotations, which are significant in treating problems concerned with rubberlike materials.

Isotropic and homogeneous materials are usually considered in the classical theory of elasticity. Isotropy implies that material properties are independent of the orientation of any axis fixed in the body, and homogeneity implies that material properties of a body with stress-strain relations remain the same from point to point. In elasticity theory it is assumed that materials are not stressed beyond the proportionality limit, the point where there is a change in the ratio of unit stress to unit deformation. Below this limit, which is different for most materials and which is a function of stress history, environment, and loading, the stress-strain relationships are given by linear functions. Hooke's Law for a tension member may be expressed by the following relations for small strain values:

$$e_x = \frac{S_x}{E}; \qquad e_y = -\frac{\nu}{E} S_x; \qquad e_z = -\frac{\nu}{E} S_x,$$

where E is a constant called the modulus of elasticity, or Young's modulus (E for steel is 3×10^7 lb/in.²), ν is a constant called Poisson's ratio (ν for steel is about 0.3), S_x is called the stress and may be expressed as force per unit area, and e_x, e_y, e_z are called the strains or elongations per unit length in the x, y, and z directions. Hooke's Law can be generalized:

$$e_x = \frac{1}{E}[S_x - \nu(S_y + S_z)]; \qquad e_y = \frac{1}{E}[S_y - \nu(S_x + S_z)];$$

$$e_z = \frac{1}{E}[S_z - \nu(S_x + S_y)],$$

where S_x, S_y, and S_z are the stresses in the x, y, and z directions, respectively. For isotropic materials, two elastic constants, ν and E, are sufficient to determine the stress-strain relations. The relations between shear stresses (S_{xy}, S_{yz}, S_{zx}) and shear strains (γ_{xy}, γ_{yz}, γ_{zx}), as shown in Fig. 1, for an isotropic material are

$$\gamma_{xy} = \frac{2(1+\nu)}{E} S_{xy} = \frac{1}{G} S_{xy};$$

$$\gamma_{yz} = \frac{2(1+\nu)}{E} S_{yz} = \frac{1}{G} S_{yz};$$

$$\gamma_{zx} = \frac{2(1+\nu)}{E} S_{zx} = \frac{1}{G} S_{zx},$$

where $G = E/2(1+\nu)$ is the shear modulus.

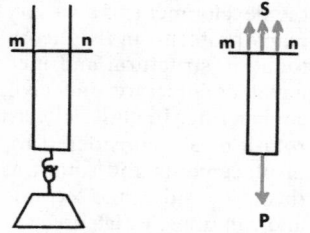

Fig. 1.

Rhombic crystals require 3 elastic constants, monoclinic crystals require 9, and anisotropic materials 21. In solving 3-dimensional elasticity problems, 24 equations are encountered, of which 3 are equations of equilibrium, 6 of stress-strain relationships (Hooke's law), 6 of strain-displacement relations, 6 compatibility equations, and 3 equations for the boundary conditions. When a great amount of accuracy is required in the design around a confined area, these complicated equations will be used. The plane- and axial-symmetric problems, however, require only some of these equations, and many engineering problems can be solved without using this highly elaborate and sophisticated mathematical approach. For example, the average stress in a tensile bar or the bending stress of a beam may be determined by such simple formulas as shown in Figs. 2 and 3.

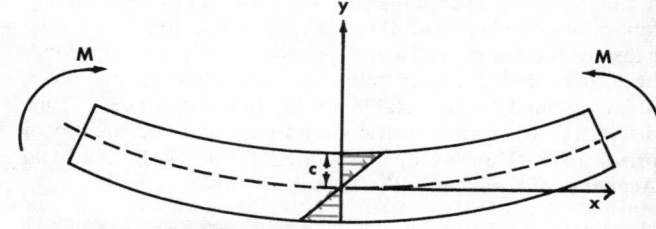

Fig. 3: $S = Mc/I$, where S is maximum tensile or compressive stress occurring in outermost fibers, c the distance to outside fiber, I the moment of inertia about the z-axis, and M the moment or couple applied.

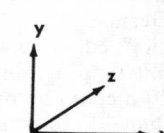

Present trends in elasticity theory are requiring that thermal stresses be considered. Consequently, a modification of Hooke's law is made by including the temperature terms. More difficult temperature problems require that strains be replaced by strain rates and that CREEP relations be included in the analysis. See STRENGTH OF MATERIALS.—*H. L.*

ELASTIC-REBOUND THEORY: a theory which attempts to explain the observation that many EARTHQUAKES involve a transcurrent (strike-slip) fault, *i.e.* relative horizontal displacement of the two sides of a nearly vertical FAULT. Under the action of tectonic forces, elastic shear strain slowly accumulates in certain regions. When the strain reaches a critical value, the crust fractures and rebounds elastically to a new position determined by the stress distribution. The fault pattern, length, and throw depend on the structural details of the region. Along the margins of the Pacific there are numerous such transcurrent faults, with the oceanic crustal blocks moving counter-clockwise with respect to the continental blocks. Examples include the Pacific Coastal area of California, where the 1906 San Francisco and the 1940 Imperial Valley earthquakes involved horizontal displacements along the San Andreas fault of up to 21 ft over a distance of 270 mi and 15 ft over a distance of 50 mi, respectively. Detailed geodetic measurements have demonstrated the slow, northwestward motion of the land on the westward side of the San Andreas fault, with respect to the eastern side, resulting periodically in an earthquake, with faulting to relieve the accumulated strain energy. An illustration of this shows the line AB immediately after an earthquake with all accumulated strain relieved. With the passage of time, the line is distorted into the new position CD by the force couple shown. When the mechanical strength of the crustal rocks is exceeded, fracture and an earthquake occur, bringing the line into position $EFGH$.—*Sa. K.*

(1) After Earthquake: Strain on Line AB Relieved

(2) Strain Accumulates, Distorting Line AB to CD

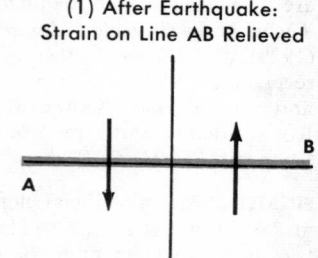

(3) Fracture Occurs, Bringing Line to Position EFGH

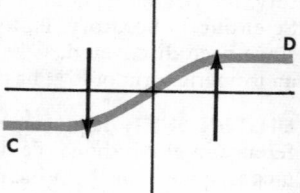

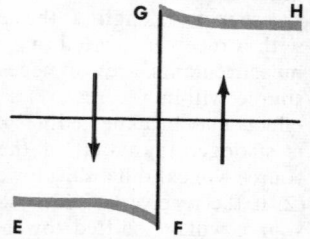

Elastic Rebound Theory

Fig. 2: $S = P/A$, where P is the force, A is the cross-sectional area, and S is the tensile stress or force per unit area.

E-LAYER: see IONOSPHERE.

ELECTRICAL AND MAGNETIC UNITS: standards for measuring electrical and magnetic quantities. The choice of units is complicated by the fact that a fundamental constant, the velocity of light in empty space, appears in the relation between electrical and magnetic phenomena, so that both cannot be simultaneously related to mechanical units by dimensionless constants. Thus in COULOMB'S LAW the force between two charges q_1 and q_2 separated by a distance r is written

$$F = K \frac{q_1 q_2}{r^2} \qquad (1)$$

The constant K can be taken as unity and dimensionless, and a unit of charge is thereby defined as that charge which will repel an exactly similar charge with a force of 1 dyne at a distance of 1 cm. This is the electrostatic unit (esu) of charge, and the corresponding unit of current is 1 esu of charge/sec. But currents can interact with each other magnetically; by Ampère's law, two long parallel wires of length l, carrying currents I_1 and I_2 and separated by a distance r, exert a force on each other given by

$$F = K' \frac{I_1 I_2 l}{r} \qquad (2)$$

where K' is another constant. If force and distance are again measured in dynes and centimeters, respectively, and the currents are measured in esu as defined above, K' is found empirically to be $1/c^2$, where $c = 3 \times 10^{10}$ cm/sec is the velocity of light.

On the other hand, K' in relation (2) may be taken as dimensionless and unity, thus defining a quite different electrical unit, namely, that current which will exert a force of 1 dyne/cm length at a distance of 1 cm on an equal and parallel current. This electromagnetic unit of current, commonly called the abampere (*absolute* ampere), corresponds to a unit of charge which is 3×10^{10} cm/sec times the esu of charge defined above, so that Coulomb's law would have to be written with $K = c^2$ if charge were measured in electromagnetic (emu or *absolute*) units. We note that the esu and emu of charge (or of current) differ not only in size but also in dimensions, since the conversion factor between them has the dimensions of velocity.

For atomic physics it has long been customary to use a mixed system of units, called the Gaussian system, in which charge and other electrical quantities are measured in esu,

CONVERSION FACTORS		
Multiply the number of mks units below	*by*	*to obtain the number of Gaussian (cgs) units of*
joule = watt sec = newton meter	10^7	energy in ergs
newton	10^5	force in dynes
ampere	1/10	current in abamperes
coulomb	3×10^9	charge in esu
volt = joule/coulomb	1/300	potential in esu
newton/coulomb = volt/meter	1/30,000	electric field intensity in esu
newton/ampere meter = weber/meter²	10^4	magnetic (flux) field in gauss
farad = coulomb/volt	9×10^{-11}	capacitance in cm
weber = volt sec	10^8	magnetic flux in maxwells
henry = volt sec/ampere	10^9	inductance in emu
ampere turns	$4\pi/10$	magnetomotive force in gilberts

while magnetic quantities (*e.g.* fields, magnetization) are measured in emu, and the velocity of light appears explicitly in equations relating magnetic to electrical quantities. There also came into general engineering use the *practical* system, based on the ampere = (1/10) abampere. The *coulomb* is a unit of charge, such that one coulomb/sec is one ampere, and one *volt* difference of potential exists between two points if one joule of work is required to transport one coulomb of charge from one point to the other. The ohm (volt/ampere) is a practical unit, as is the farad (coulomb/volt), which measures capacitance, but no practical units were defined for some quantities, such as magnetic field strength, which is usually measured in gauss, an absolute (emu) unit. More recently a complete set of units has come into fairly general use; it includes all the practical units and is called the mks (meter-kilogram-second) system, to denote the mechanical units of length, mass, and time involved (see MEASUREMENT), but the coulomb is also considered as a basic unit of charge, and dimensions include charge as well as length, mass, and time. For atomic processes energy is often measured in electron-volts (ev). One ev of energy is gained by one ELECTRONIC CHARGE in falling through a potential difference of one volt; 1 ev = 1.60×10^{-19} joules.—*M. P.*

ELECTRICAL DISCHARGES: see ARCS AND DISCHARGES.

ELECTRIC CELL: see BATTERY; CELL, ELECTROLYTIC; CELL, VOLTAIC.

ELECTRIC CHARGE: see CHARGE, ELECTRIC.

ELECTRIC CIRCUIT: a closed path that conveys an electric current. Conductors making up a circuit may be metals, ionized gases, or ionized liquids; however, metallic conductors are most often used.

In Fig. 1, a simple example of a d-c circuit (see DIRECT CURRENT), one wire is connected to the plus terminal of a battery and the terminal (a) of a light bulb, represented by resistor R_1 (see RESISTANCE); the other wire is connected from terminal (b) to switch S and from there back to the battery. If the switch is closed, the circuit is complete, and current will flow through R_1. If S is open, the circuit is broken and current ceases to flow. To calculate the current (I), the voltage (V) provided by the battery, or the resistance in ohms (R) of R_1, OHM'S LAW is used: $I = V/R$. If two (or more) resistors are connected as in Fig. 2, then the resistors are in *series*. Ignoring the resistance of the wire connectors, the total resistance R of the circuit equals $R_1 + R_2$. In Fig. 3, R_1 and R_2 are also connected in series, but their total resistance R_L, equal to their sum, is connected with R_3 in *parallel*.

In a parallel circuit, one branch of the circuit can be turned off, while the other branch or branches continue to carry current; in contrast, if one element in a series circuit is turned off, the circuit as a whole is broken and no devices in the circuit will receive current. In contrast to a series circuit, where the current is uniform throughout the circuit, current

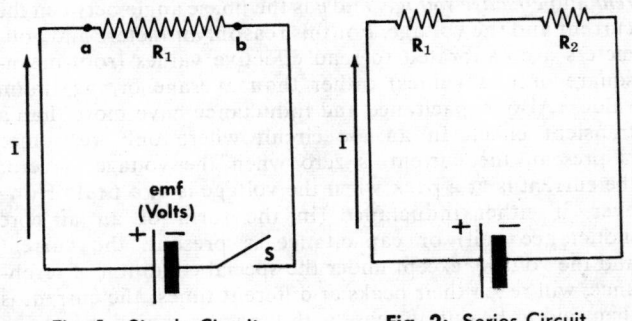

Fig. 1: Simple Circuit   **Fig. 2:** Series Circuit

passing through a parallel circuit divides between the two (or more) branches, but the total current entering at A (Fig. 3) must equal the total current emerging at B. The voltage drop for each branch is the same as the voltage drop for both branches. The current in each branch, however, is in inverse proportion to the resistance of that branch; thus in Fig. 3: $I_1/I_3 = R_3/(R_1 + R_2)$. If $R_L = R_1 + R_2$, the total resistance of the circuit (R_t) can be expressed by the equation $1/R_t = 1/R_L + 1/R_3$. When CAPACITANCE and INDUCTANCE are added to a d-c circuit, their effects on circuit performance last for an exceedingly short time and are termed transient effects. Naturally, most circuits are more complicated than the ones illustrated; circuits made up of many elements and many loops are called networks. Although Ohm's law remains the fundamental relationship underlying network analysis, additional laws and sets of theorems must also be used. KIRCHHOFF'S LAWS, which are primarily expressions of the law of conservation of charge and the law of conservation of energy in electrical terms, state that (1) the algebraic sum of the currents at any junction of an electric circuit is zero; and (2) the algebraic sum of the applied emf's and the potential drops due to resistances in any closed path of an electric circuit is zero. For example, in Fig. 3 the application of Kirchhoff's first law to

point A means that $I_t - I_1 - I_3 = 0$. Since I_t flows *into* the point, it is called positive, while I_1 and I_3 flow *out* from the point and are called negative. This is the same as saying that $I_t = I_1 + I_3$. The application of Kirchhoff's second law to the closed path, including the battery and R_1 and R_2, would be written: emf $- I_1R_1 - I_1R_3 = 0$. Around the closed path $R_1 - R_2 - R_3$ we write $I_3R_3 - I_1R_1 - I_1R_3 = 0$.

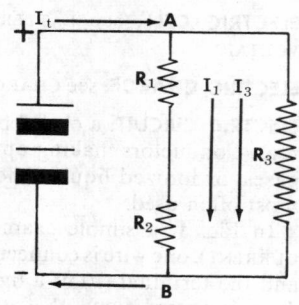

Fig. 3: Parallel Circuit

For circuits having more than one source of voltage (emf), the superposition theorem is of great value. It states that the total current in any element of a network resulting from several sources of emf is equal to the algebraic sum of all the currents which would be produced individually by each emf. A third method of network analysis is to construct a simple network which is the equivalent of the more complicated one and in which the value of particular elements can be calculated.

The analysis of a-c circuits (by far the most important industrially) is more difficult, because the instantaneous values of voltage and current are periodically varying in both magnitude and direction; and for one complete cycle both voltage and current take the form of a sine wave (see ALTERNATING CURRENT; HARMONIC MOTION). It can be shown that the power in an a-c circuit is given by $P = (I_{max}/\sqrt{2}) \times (E_{max}/\sqrt{2}) \times \cos \theta$, where $I_{max}/\sqrt{2}$ and $E_{max}/\sqrt{2}$ are called the *effective current* and *effective voltage*, and θ is the phase angle between the current and the voltage. For this reason, ammeters and voltmeters are calibrated to read effective values (root-mean-square or rms values) rather than average or maximum values. Also, capacitance and inductance have more than a transient effect. In an a-c circuit where only resistance is present, the current is zero when the voltage is zero; the current is at a peak when the voltage is at a peak. However, if either inductance (in the form of an air-core inductance coil) or capacitance is present, the current and the voltage, except under the special condition of resonance, will reach their peaks at different times; the current is then said to be out of phase with the voltage, and the cosine

of the phase angle is termed the circuit power factor (see ELECTRIC POWER). If inductance alone is present in a circuit, the current lags behind the voltage by a quarter of a cycle, or 90°; the opposition offered to the current by inductance is called the *inductive reactance* (X_L), and $X_L = 2\pi f L$, where f equals the frequency of the voltage, and L the inductance in henrys. If capacitance alone is present in a circuit, the current leads the voltage by a quarter of a cycle; the opposition offered to the current by capacitance is called the *capacitive reactance* (X_C), and $X_C = 1/2\pi f C$, where C equals the capacitance in farads. Both X_L and X_C are measured in ohms. When resistance, inductance, and capacitance are in series in a circuit, Ohm's law is modified: $I_{rms} = V_{rms}/\sqrt{R^2 + (X_L - X_C)^2}$. In this equation, $\sqrt{R^2 + (X_L - X_C)^2} = Z$; Z is called the circuit IMPEDANCE. It can be seen that when $X_L = X_C$, Z is at a minimum and I_{rms} at a maximum and equal to V_{rms}/R. Thus when $X_L = X_C$, the circuit is said to be resonant (see RESONANCE), and since $2\pi f L = 1/2\pi f C$, the frequency f equals $1/2\pi \sqrt{LC}$. Circuits where the current oscillates at the natural frequency of the circuit are said to be resonant circuits or tuned circuits, and they are widely used in radio and TV. In the analysis of a-c circuits, R, X_L, and X_C may be represented by vectors which, in turn, may be represented by COMPLEX NUMBERS. Kirchhoff's laws are applicable if the network elements are considered as vector quantities (see VECTOR ANALYSIS). The superposition theorem and many equivalent network theorems can only be applied (1) where the current varies directly as the voltage (linearly); and (2) where the current behaves similarly for voltage acting in either direction (bilaterally). Ordinary resistors, capacitors, and air-core inductors are linear in behavior, whereas ELECTRON TUBES and iron-core inductors are not. Resistors, inductors, and capacitors are bilateral, whereas rectifiers are not. Thus the use of the above theorems is limited in a-c networks, and direct measurement must be relied on to a great extent. See ALTERNATING CURRENT.—*A. L.*

ELECTRIC CURRENT: the passage of electric CHARGE caused by electromotive forces. In early theories of electricity the charging or discharging of a body was explained by assuming that one of two different fluids flowed into or out of the body. For example, it was supposed that when a glass rod was rubbed with silk, electric fluid flowed into the glass, and when the charged glass rod was touched to a piece of metal, the fluid flowed out of the glass and into the metal. The other electric fluid was the kind that flowed to resinous materials such as sealing wax when they were rubbed with fur or wool. Stephen Gray performed the first systematic experiments on the conduction of electricity in 1729, when he succeeded in transmitting electricity over damp packthread to distances of several hundred feet. The two-fluid theory persisted until the time of Benjamin Franklin (1706–90), who first thought of an electric current as consisting entirely of a flow of fluid, the absence of this fluid accounting for phenomena formerly attributed to a second fluid. By the end of the 19th cent., the contributions of H. A. Lorentz and J. J. Thomson had established the existence of electrons, and from then on an electric current in a metallic conductor has been thought of as a flow of negative charges (electrons) through the porous structure of the conductor.

Although the current in metals consists entirely of a flow of electrons, both positive and negative charges may move in liquids and gases. In ELECTROLYSIS and in an electrical discharge in a gas, positive ions move toward the cathode and negative ions move toward the anode. An electric current may also consist of a stream of electrons in a vacuum, as in an ELECTRON TUBE, or a stream of positive ions in a vacuum, as in a mass spectrometer (see MASS SPECTROMETRY). The custom has persisted in considering the direction of current flow in electric circuits as being from positive to negative, even though it is now known that, in metals, only electrons move, and they flow from negative to positive. A more subtle kind of current, called displacement current, was first understood by James Clerk Maxwell (1831–79), who recognized that a variable electric field in space produces the same magnetic effects as a current whose density is proportional to the time rate of change of the electric field. Such currents can exist in empty space, without any transfer of charge through that part of space, so long as the electric field intensity varies with time.

The current strength (usually called simply current) over a cross section of conductor is defined as the total amount of charge passing through that cross section per sec. The common unit of current strength is the ampere, defined as a current in which 1 coulomb of charge passes per sec. Since the charge on an electron is 1.6×10^{-19} coul, the ampere represents a flow of 6.2×10^{18} electrons/sec. Current strengths are measured by AMMETERS or GALVANOMETERS.

A current I that flows through a cross section A is said to have a current density equal to I/A. In direct current and even alternating current at low frequencies, the current density in a homogeneous conductor is uniform, but at high frequencies the current tends to flow near the surfaces of the conductor (skin effect), so that the current density decreases toward the interior. (See also ALTERNATING CURRENT; DIRECT CURRENT.)—*H. Sw.*

ELECTRIC DIPOLE MOMENT: the product of the magnitude of two equal but opposite electric charges (q) placed very close together and the distance between them (d). Thus $m = qd$, where m is the electric dipole moment; it is so named because the pair of charges is known as a dipole. The moment creates in the surrounding space an electric potential, the magnitude of which decreases with the square of the distance from the dipole. When the dipole is placed in a uniform electric field, a torque is exerted on the dipole, tending to align it with the direction of the field. Many molecules, *e.g.* those of water, contain separated electric charges and therefore possess an electric moment. DIELECTRICS are materials composed of molecules having either a permanent electric moment or a moment induced by an applied electric field. Forces due to the electric moment affect the structure, boiling point, and other properties of such materials. If the electric moment oscillates rapidly, due to a periodic change in either q or d, the dipole will emit ELECTROMAGNETIC WAVES. This explains the emission of radio waves by a simple antenna, since the motion of charge in the antenna constitutes an oscillating dipole.—*I. R.*

ELECTRIC FIELD: an excitation produced in space by an electric CHARGE. The nature of the excitation is unknown, but its existence is made known by its effect on another electric charge. The strength of the electric field at any point is defined as the magnitude of the force experienced by a test charge divided by the value of the test charge. It has been found experimentally that the strength of the electric field surrounding a point electric charge decreases inversely with the square of the distance from the source; this is known as COULOMB'S LAW.—*S. K.*

ELECTRIC FURNACE: a heating chamber in which electricity is used as the source of the heat. There are three general types: induction, arc, and resistance furnaces. First to be demonstrated was an arc furnace, with which Sir William Siemens, at the Paris Exposition, 1879, melted iron in crucibles. In the *induction furnace,* the crucible or chamber is surrounded by a coil carrying electric current with a frequency usually greater than 60 cycles but less than 3,000. EDDY CURRENTS are induced in the load of metal, known as the charge, and their circulation through the charge produces heat. This type of furnace is used for melting metal and for production of exact alloys. In the *arc, or Heroult, furnace,* electric arcs are produced from carbon or graphite electrodes positioned above a shallow bowl in which the charge is placed. The arc furnace is used in production of alloy STEELS and cast iron. In the *resistance furnace* the electrodes are buried in the charge, and the flow of electric current through the charge produces heat. The resistance furnace is used in production of silicon carbides.—*L. J. H.*

ELECTRIC INSULATORS: see INSULATOR, ELECTRICAL.

ELECTRICITY: the physical phenomena resulting ordinarily from (1) the accumulation of electrons, and (2) the orderly movement of electrons.

Fundamentals: The state of accumulation of electrons (arbitrarily termed *negative* charge) and the state of deficiency of electrons (arbitrarily termed *positive* charge) are both called *static electricity*. A simple way to build up a charge of static electricity is to rub a glass rod with silk; by this process the glass loses electrons, thus acquiring a positive charge, and the silk gains them, thus acquiring a negative charge. In dry weather, a person scuffing his feet on a rug may accumulate a charge of static electricity and will notice it with some discomfort when a spark jumps from his fingers to the doorknob he is attempting to grasp. At present, elaborate ELECTROSTATIC GENERATORS capable of accumulating considerable charges are used in the investigation of subatomic particles. The unit of charge is called the coulomb, after Charles Coulomb, who in 1784–5 first measured the force of repulsion between two charged bodies (see COULOMB'S LAW); one coulomb will repel an identical charge at a distance of one meter with the force of 9×10^9 newtons. (See ELECTROSTATICS.)

The orderly movement of electrons or electric charge, commonly called *current,* is the form in which electricity is most often encountered today (see ELECTRIC CURRENT). It differs from static electricity in that the charge moves, usually through a circuit, *i.e.* a closed path through which current is guided. In a circuit, electrical energy may be transformed by various devices into light, heat, sound, electromagnetic waves, chemical energy, and mechanical energy (*e.g.* the shaft rotation of a motor); and the energy of light or sound may be transformed into electrical energy. When the current has a constant direction, it is called DIRECT CURRENT; when its direction changes regularly, it is called ALTERNATING CURRENT. Alternating current that changes its direction at a high frequency produces ELECTROMAGNETIC WAVES capable of being picked up by receiving antennas. The modulation, transmission, and reception of electromagnetic waves constitute the field of wireless communication (see RADIO; RADIO BROADCASTING). The magnitude of the current in an electrical circuit is the *quantity* of charge per second flowing through the circuit. The unit of current is the ampere, named for André Marie Ampère; it is defined as the quantity of current that will transfer one coulomb in one sec. The work involved in moving a charge from one place to another is called ELECTRIC POTENTIAL difference. The volt, named for Alessandro Volta, is a unit of potential difference; it is defined as equal to one joule (10^7 ergs or 0.737 ft-lb) per coulomb. Thus the voltage is the energy available to carry electric charge through a circuit (see ELECTROMOTIVE FORCE).

How much current is carried through a given circuit depends on the voltage and on the opposition presented by the

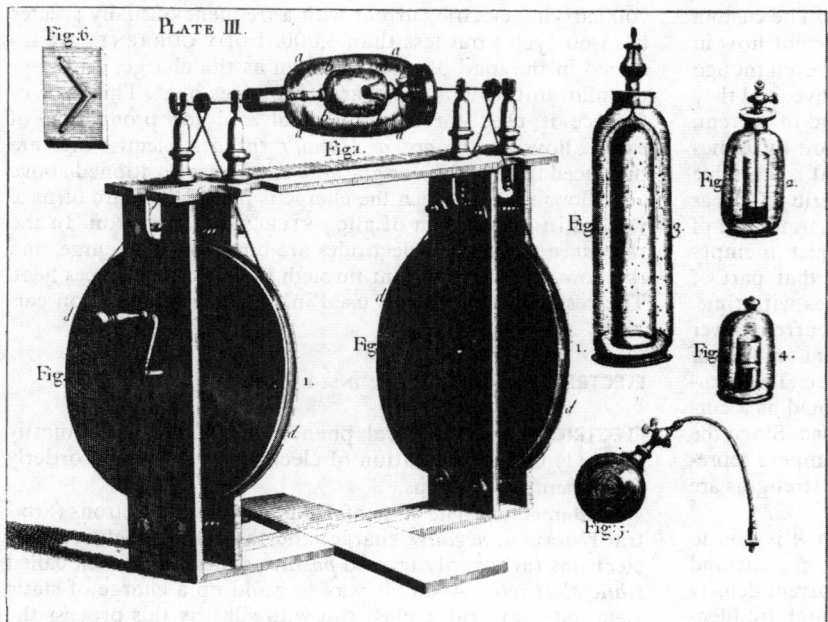

Fig. 1: Hauksbee's generator in which the two glass vessels rotated in opposite directions, producing a glow in the inner one when a dry hand was applied to the outer one. Detailed views of the parts of the apparatus are also shown. (*Burndy Library*)

circuit to current flow. A conductor made of copper offers less opposition than one of iron, and a wire of large diameter less opposition than one with a small diameter. The opposition to current is called RESISTANCE; its units are called ohms, after Georg Simon Ohm, who not only investigated the resistance of various materials but discovered the relationship (OHM'S LAW) between current, voltage, and resistance in metallic conductors; *i.e.* the current (I) is directly proportional to voltage (V) and inversely proportional to the resistance (R); or, $I = V/R$. However, the behavior and the quantity of current in a-c circuits is determined not only by the voltage and the resistance, but also by CAPACITANCE and INDUCTANCE. In a-c circuits containing only resistance, the voltage and the current increase and decrease, reach their peaks, and fall to zero simultaneously. But if a capacitor (often called a condenser) is added to an a-c circuit, it causes the current to lead the voltage. An inductor (often called an inductance coil or a choke coil) acts to delay the current, thus making it lag behind the voltage. The combination of both devices can cause the current to oscillate, and such circuits are often used to generate high-frequency carrier waves for radio transmission. But in all d-c and a-c circuits, Ohm's law (modified for the addition of capacitance and inductance in a-c circuits) still remains the basic relationship underlying the analysis of circuits composed of metallic conductors (see ELECTRIC CIRCUIT; REACTANCE; IMPEDANCE).

The widespread production of ELECTRIC POWER became practicable when in the early 19th cent. it was discovered that (1) an electric current invariably produces a surrounding magnetic field, and (2) the movement of a wire through a magnetic field produces current in the wire. Furthermore, a coil of wire excited by current acts like a magnet, and if a core of soft iron is inserted through the coil, the magnetic field is considerably intensified (see ELECTROMAGNETISM; ELECTROMAGNETIC INDUCTION). The consequences of these discoveries were that (1) electric current can be produced by rotating a coil through an electromagnetic field (the principle by which the GENERATOR transforms mechanical energy into electrical energy); and (2) magnetic fields excited by electric currents can rotate electromagnets mounted on a shaft (the principle by which the motor transforms electrical energy into mechanical energy). But although electrical energy could be

economically produced and transformed into mechanical energy, it could not be transmitted any great distance because of power losses in the transmission lines. Whenever current flows in a conductor, power is lost (in the form of heat) in an amount proportional to the resistance and the square of the current (power loss = I^2R). Thus transmission at high amperages entails high heat losses. However, if power (measured in watts and equal to the product of voltage and amperage) is transmitted at a high voltage and a correspondingly low amperage, the number of watts remains constant, but the heat loss is drastically reduced. The problem remained how to step down the high transmission voltage to commercially and domestically usable levels. This was solved by the TRANSFORMER. Since the relative movement of a magnetic field and a wire will induce a current in the wire, the transformer takes the *high-voltage*, low-amperage alternating current in one coil and uses the fluctuating magnetic field caused by the ac to induce in an adjacent coil *low-voltage*, high-amperage alternating current. As can be seen, the operation of the transformer depends on ac; and with the increasing use of electric power, often produced at great distances from the point of utilization, ac has virtually displaced dc for all but specialized applications. In fact, the development of the transformer and the consequent wide use of ac can be said to have finally ushered in the age of electricity (see ELECTRIC POWER TRANSMISSION).—*A. L.*

History: A dry glass rod, rubbed briskly with silk, will attract bits of paper and other small objects. This effect, now called *electrostatic attraction,* seems to have been observed first with amber, found in nature as fossilized resin from prehistoric pine trees and valued for its use in jewelry. The phenomenon was certainly known to Plato and other Greeks of the Athenian school, 4th cent. B. C., and probably known to the Greek philosopher Thales of Miletus as early as 600 B. C. However, through the Roman and Arabic periods, which followed, and through the Middle Ages—an interval of more than 2,000 yr after Thales—there was not enough experimentation to produce a definite demonstration of electrostatic repulsion. This was probably first recorded in 1629 by Niccolo Cabeo, an Italian Jesuit.

A small wad of crumpled aluminum foil suspended by a silk thread serves as a detector of electrification; the metal foil will be attracted to any object which, when rubbed with silk, wool, or fur, becomes electrified. William Gilbert, personal physician to Queen Elizabeth I, used a light metallic needle, supported as in a compass, to detect electrostatic attraction. With this simple device he classified objects into *electrics* and *nonelectrics*, observing that many substances besides amber became electrified when rubbed. These results, marking the beginning of systematic experimentation in electricity, were recorded in his book *De magnete* (1600), though this dealt primarily with magnetism. Gilbert visualized the electrical attraction as due to an *effluvium*, an emanation from the charged body which, like material tentacles, reached out and acted upon neighboring objects. Even Gilbert failed to observe electric repulsion; consequently his effluvium hypothesis was meant to explain attraction only. Though wrong, it helped to clear the air of primitive animistic explanations (in terms of the "soul" or "spirit" of amber) which had prevailed before his time. Gilbert also observed that the electric force decreased with increasing distances between the charged bodies, but the exact relation was not discovered until 1785, by Charles Coulomb.

Dry sulfur, which becomes strongly electrified when rubbed with fur or wool or with the dry hand, was used in the first practical electrostatic generator, built by Otto von Guericke (1602–1686), burgomaster of Magdeburg, whose inventive genius also produced the first vacuum pump and demonstrated the pressure of the atmosphere. The generator consisted of a sphere of sulfur (actually designed as a model of the earth) which could be rotated about a horizontal shaft. Holding his hand against this rotating sphere, von Guericke was able to produce audible and visible sparks and to confirm Cabeo's observation of electrostatic repulsion.

There was a persistent notion that electric forces could not act in a vacuum—a belief due, no doubt, to the vital part played by air in the Aristotelian explanation of any free motion of bodies through the atmosphere. An attempt to test this point had been made by members of the Accademia del Cimento in Florence in 1666, but their experimental skill, demanding manipulation in a vacuum, was not equal to the problem. Success was achieved, however, by Robert Boyle,

Irish chemist and philosopher and a member of the Invisible College, which later became the Royal Society of London. Boyle had greatly improved the air pump and, with advanced vacuum technique, was able in 1675 to publish researches showing that electrification and electric forces occurred in evacuated vessels as well as in air.

Francis Hauksbee (d.1713), an instrument maker in the employ of the Royal Society, improved two of the most important research tools of his day—the vacuum pump and the electrostatic generator. This was a fortunate combination, for it led to the first extended investigations of electrical discharges in rarefied gases. Hauksbee had become interested in a phenomenon reported in 1675 by Jean Picard, astronomer at the Paris Observatory. In carrying a mercury barometer from the observatory Picard had noticed a luminous glow in the vacuum at the top of the agitated mercury column. Hauksbee, using an improved vacuum pump and a new design of electrostatic generator, was able to demonstrate that such a glow could be produced in an evacuated vessel by agitating mercury in it or by electrifying it through rubbing or by placing it within another glass vessel which was electrified. Fig. 1 shows the advanced experimental technique achieved by Hauksbee. He thus established the electrical nature of the glow observed by Picard and, incidentally, confirmed Boyle's conclusion about the existence of electrical forces in a vacuum.

Up to this time no one had tested the possibility of transmitting the electrification from one body to another directly or through intermediate bodies. The experiments of Hauksbee and others had held the essential clues, but the discovery was not made until 1729, when Stephen Gray stumbled upon it by accident. Oddly enough, Gray used materials (first wood, later packthread) which we now consider to be very poor conductors but which, in the damp air of England, were able to "communicate the electric virtue" from his generator through increasing distances, finally reaching over 800 ft. He supported this world's first transmission line with silk thread, finding metal to be useless, thereby recognizing silk as a good nonconductor and metals as good conductors. However, he had been able to demonstrate that metals could be electrified by rubbing, like amber, provided they were suspended in

Fig. 2: One of Watson's spectacular demonstrations: The friction generator (*right*) charged both the boy and the girl, causing chaff on the table (*left*) to dance. Meanwhile charge carried from the suspended gunbarrel (*top right*) to one of two bells (*top left*) caused the clapper to swing between them, ringing them alternately. (*Burndy Library*)

nonconducting threads, a fact which Gilbert and others had failed to observe.

Speculation up to this time had been concerned mostly with what happened in the space between electrified bodies. The effluvium hypothesis, originated by Gilbert, was supported both in England and France in spite of the difficulty of explaining electrical repulsion. Then Charles Du Fay, superintendent of the Royal Gardens in Paris, focused attention on the nature of the electrified bodies themselves. In a letter to the Royal Society, 1733, he wrote, "... there are two kinds of electricity, very different from one another, one of which I call *vitreous* and the other *resinous* electricity. The first is that of glass, rock crystal, precious stones.... The second is that of amber, copal, silk.... The characteristics of these two electricities are that they repel themselves (similar electrifications) and attract each other (different electrifications)." Thus emerged the two-fluid theory of electricity; it explained all electrical charging and discharging in terms of movements of two fluids into or out of a body. A neutral, or uncharged, body was supposed to contain equal amounts of the two fluids. Later the vitreous electrification came to be called positive and the resinous negative.

By the mid-18th cent. popular interest in electrical experiments was strong in England, France, and Germany. The electrostatic generator (usually consisting of a rotating glass globe or cylinder against which the hand or a piece of fur was held) had been developed to the point where electric sparks were clearly visible and audible, and many designs were sold in large quantities to people who gave popular lectures on electricity or who used them for entertainment in their homes. People amused themselves by shocking their friends with the

new *Leyden jar,* a device for storing large quantities of electric charge and consisting of a glass jar or bottle coated inside and outside with metallic foil. Since these foils were insulated from each other, they could be highly charged with opposite electrifications and then connected to produce a spectacular spark. It was the prototype of the modern condenser, or CAPACITOR, and was invented (1745) independently by E. G. von Kleist of Pomerania and P. van Musschenbroek of Leyden. The popular appeal of electrical demonstrations is shown in Fig. 2, reproduced from an engraving published in a book of researches by William Watson (1748). The electrification is conducted through the body of a boy, suspended in silk ribbons, to a girl standing on an insulating tub of dried pitch. The hand of the girl is attracting bits of paper. The bells in the upper left corner rang when one of them was charged.

Popular lecturers even came to America to demonstrate the wonders of electricity. It was such a lecturer (a Dr. Spence or probably Spencer) whom Benjamin Franklin heard in Boston, 1743, and who inspired Franklin to buy the lecturer's equipment and begin experimenting seriously on his own. His experimental activity extended over less than 15 yr, years crowded with public responsibilities, and yet he made discoveries worthy of recognition by the scientific societies of Europe. He found that sharply pointed conductors were especially effective in discharging electrified bodies and applied this knowledge to the discharging of thunderclouds; this resulted in the invention of the lightning rod. He attached a pointed conductor to the top of a kite which he flew during a thunderstorm, obtaining a flow of electric charge down the wet string to a metallic key. The charged key behaved like any body electrically charged by friction—proof that the crackling and flashing of laboratory sparks were thunder and lightning on a small scale. Franklin also simplified the explanation of electrification by assuming that only one fluid, the vitreous (or positive) fluid, flowed into or out of bodies. This astute suggestion is still respected, except that we now call the fluid negative and know it to consist of charged particles called electrons.

Franklin had shown that the electric forces were zero inside a charged hollow sphere and had transmitted this information to Joseph Priestley without being able to explain the curious fact. Priestley, and later Henry Cavendish, explained the effect by making an ingenious comparison between electrical and gravitational forces. Many years before, Isaac Newton had proved mathematically that the gravitational force should be zero inside a hollow spherical mass if, and only if, the gravitational force between small masses varied inversely as the square of the distance between the masses. Why could not the same conclusion be drawn from the absence of electrical forces inside a charged hollow sphere? This conclusion, arrived at by analogy, was put to direct experimental test a few years later by Charles Coulomb. Using a simple but extremely sensitive torsion balance (Fig. 3), he measured the repulsions between similar charges of many different magnitudes and for varying distances. His results were in good agreement with the inverse square law (see COULOMB'S LAW).

Up to the end of the 18th cent., experimenters had been handicapped by lack of any device for producing a steady flow of electric current. The electrostatic machine had been greatly improved, but its discharge, though spectacular, was spasmodic and short-lived. Then in 1800 Alessandro Volta sent a paper to the Royal Society describing the "Voltaic Pile" and "Crown of Cups"—the first electric batteries. The pile consisted of stacks of silver and zinc disks separated by paper or cloth pads soaked in brine (Fig. 4). Volta's researches grew directly out of an observation by Luigi Galvani, pub-

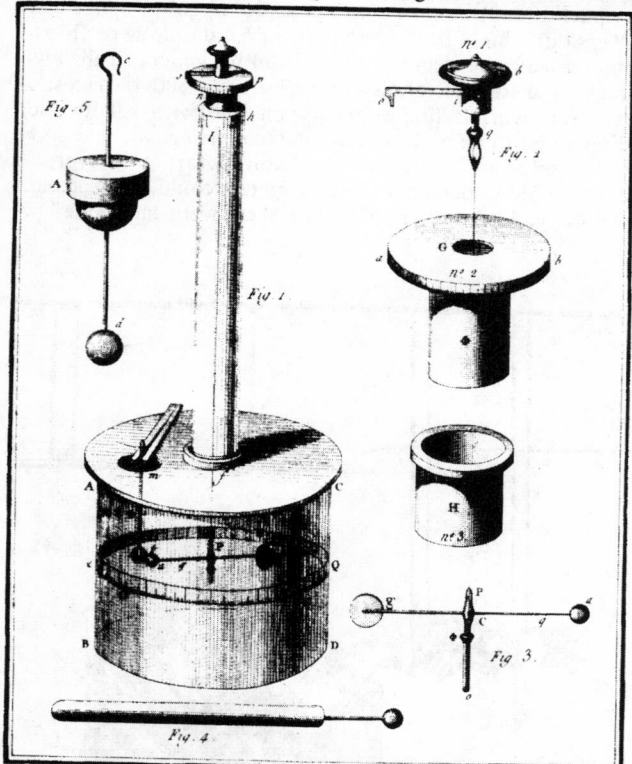

Fig. 3: Torsion balance with which Coulomb proved his law of electric charges. By applying different charges to the spheres within the cylindrical container and by varying the distances between the spheres, he showed that the forces between electric charges (measured by the twist imparted to the supporting fiber) obeyed an inverse-square law. (*Burndy Library*)

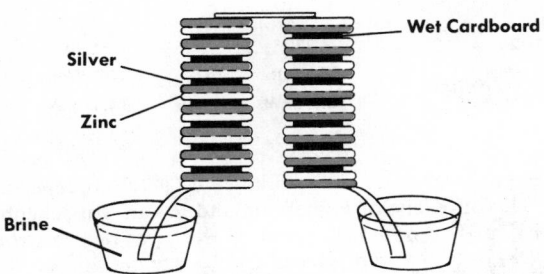

Fig. 4: The Voltaic pile: the first electric battery and the first source of a steady electric current.

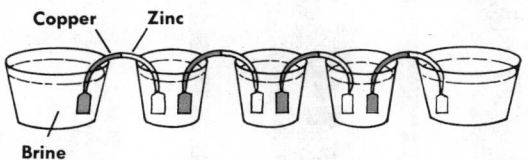

Fig. 5: Volta's crown of cups: an improvement over the pile shown in Fig. 4.

lished in 1791, that the muscle of a frog's leg twitched when an electric machine produced sparks nearby. Volta's crown of cups was an improved form of battery and consisted of cups, filled with brine, into which silver and zinc plates were dipped and connected externally (Fig. 5).

The possibility of producing steady sustained electric currents opened a new era in electrical experimentation. In 1820 H. C. Oersted, having built a large voltaic battery, discovered that in the region surrounding a wire carrying a current a compass needle turned at right angles to the wire (see ELECTROMAGNETISM). Thus, for the first time there was a direct experimental connection between electricity and magnetism, a connection which became all the more striking when Michael Faraday was able in 1831 to reverse the Oersted effect and cause an electric current to flow in a wire immersed in a variable magnetic field (see ELECTROMAGNETIC INDUCTION). It was this discovery, also independently made by an American, Joseph Henry, which made possible the electric generator, another device for producing a sustained electric current.

Electrical forces were now established as physical realities. Faraday had come to think of the space around electric charges as filled with *lines of force* which, though without mass, represented patterns of tension, or stress, in the medium. Unlike charges were attracted to each other by these elastic tentacles, while like charges repelled each other because lines of force in the same direction pushed each other aside laterally. But suppose a charge suddenly moved. How soon would neighboring charges "know" of this shift? This difficult problem was attacked and solved by James Clerk Maxwell and published in his *Electricity and Magnetism*, 1873. Maxwell was able to prove that when an electric charge is suddenly moved, kinks or pulses are set up in the lines of force, and these kinks travel with the velocity of light. If the medium were not a vacuum but some transparent substance, the velocity of the light could be calculated from electric and magnetic constants determined experimentally for that medium. This extraordinary synthesis proved that light, electricity, and magnetism were all related to each other; that light was, in fact, an ELECTROMAGNETIC WAVE. In 1887 Heinrich Hertz was able to demonstrate experimentally the generation of precisely the kind of wave which Maxwell had predicted, though of much longer wave lengths than those of visible light. These are now called radio waves.

There still remained the problem of the nature of the electric fluid. Franklin and his contemporaries and, in fact, Faraday and Maxwell thought of electricity as a continuous fluid, infinitely smooth and infinitely divisible. But by the end of the 19th cent., there were both theoretical and experimental reasons for believing that electric charges existed as extremely small particles. H. A. Lorentz found theoretical reasons for assuming that electricity was composed of tiny units, ELECTRONS, which had both mass and charge. J. J. Thomson furnished experimental evidence to support Lorentz by deflecting cathode rays (beams of negative charges) in electric and magnetic fields. However, the arguments of both Lorentz and Thomson were statistical in nature; they did not prove that all electrons were identical, but required only that the ratio of charge to mass be the same for all electrons. It was therefore vital that someone observe experimentally the effects of the charges of individual electrons. In 1911 R. A. Millikan did design such an experiment, extraordinarily sensitive, in which the effect of a single electronic charge on a tiny oil drop could be measured with great accuracy. As a result of this measurement both the charge and the mass of the electron could be calculated. It is now believed that an electric current in a metallic conductor consists of negative electrons which become detached from the atoms and move through the empty spaces in the structure.—*H. Sw.*

ELECTRIC LAMP: a device for producing artificial light by converting electrical energy into light energy. Electric lamps are of three general types: (1) incandescent, (2) electric-discharge or vapor, (3) electroluminescent. The incandescent lamp makes use of a filament that produces light by virtue of its high temperature. Current produces power in the form of heat in an amount proportional to the resistance of the conductor and to the square of the current. In the modern incandescent lamp a high-resistance filament, in the form of a fine-diameter tungsten wire, is enclosed in a glass bulb filled with an inert gas (*e.g.* nitrogen) to reduce the possibility of oxidation of the filament. Electric current is then passed through the filament; the resistive, or frictional, effect results in heating of the filament and the radiation of electromagnetic energy at all wavelengths, especially in the infrared and optical regions. This electromagnetic radiation is caused by excitation of the filament material to high energy levels (heat is temporarily stored as potential energy in the atoms of the filament) and subsequent radiation of electromagnetic energy when the filament atoms spontaneously drop their energies to lower levels. Most of the radiation is in the infrared region, and comes out as heat. About 5% of the total radiation of an incandescent lamp is in the visible (between 4,000 and 7,000 Å). Incandescent lamps are used in most household and industrial applications.

Electric-discharge, or vapor, lamps utilize the visible glow that results from the passage of electricity through an ionized gas. The mercury-vapor lamp consists of a tube containing some mercury and a small amount of argon. When the current is turned on, a starting circuit acts to vaporize the mercury; the mercury vapor then forms a low-resistance path through which the current can pass in an arc between the two main electrodes. This arc is the source of visible light as well as a quantity of invisible ultraviolet light. The fluorescent lamp uses the principle of the mercury-vapor lamp, but produces relatively more visible light by utilizing ultraviolet to activate a fluorescent powder lining the inside of the tube. It is made of a long, cylindrical glass bulb containing small amounts of argon and mercury, with filaments built into the ends of the tube. A fluorescent material such as zinc beryllium silicate is deposited on the inside of the cylindrical tube.

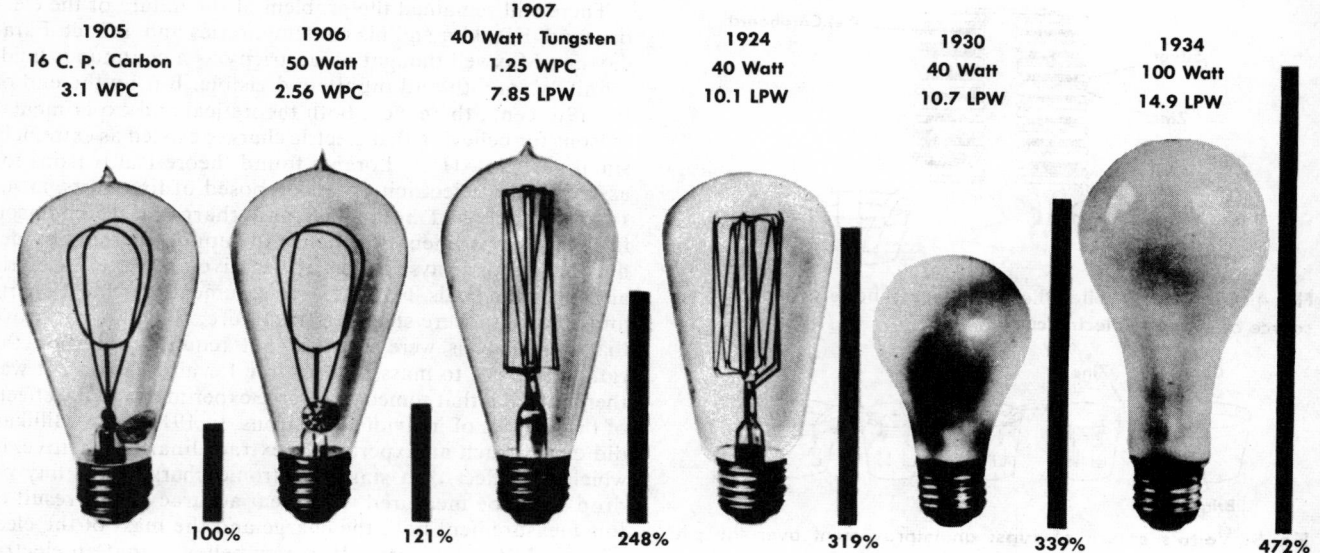

1905	1906	1907	1924	1930	1934
16 C. P. Carbon	50 Watt	40 Watt Tungsten	40 Watt	40 Watt	100 Watt
3.1 WPC	2.56 WPC	1.25 WPC	10.1 LPW	10.7 LPW	14.9 LPW
		7.85 LPW			

100%   121%   248%   319%   339%   472%

Lighting efficiency: Lumens per watt (LPW) has risen since 1905. Present 100-watt incandescent bulbs give about 16 LPW. (*General Electric*)

Ignition of the fluorescent lamp is accomplished by first heating the filaments to vaporize mercury in the tube. Thereafter, a wire which runs between the two filaments is opened automatically a few seconds after the filaments have become heated. Opening of this circuit creates a surge of high voltage across an INDUCTANCE in the supply line, which breaks down the argon gas and mercury. Ultraviolet from the mercury ionization illuminates the fluorescent material, creating a bright light. Advantages of the fluorescent lamp are that its efficiency is higher than that of the incandescent lamp, and that its bluish characteristic is desirable in certain industrial applications, as in drafting rooms. (See FLUORESCENCE.)

Electroluminescent lamps consist of several layers of phosphorus coatings that produce light by the direct application of electric current. Electroluminescent surfaces have the advantages of producing light uniformly over an entire area and of being cool to the touch.

Arc lamps and photoflash bulbs do not fall wholly into any of the above categories. The arc lamp consists of two carbon electrodes which carry a high-amperage current, often in the range of 125-150 amp. At the passage of current the carbon electrodes are separated by a fraction of a centimeter. The light is produced partly by the incandescence of the electrodes and partly by the electric arc between the two electrodes. The photoflash bulb consists of a glass bulb filled with oxygen and shredded aluminum or zirconium foil. The transient incandescence of the foil, when ignited by electric current, produces very intense light. (See LIGHTING.)—*A. L.; A. S.*

ELECTRIC MOTOR: a device for converting electric energy into mechanical energy. The motor works on the principle that a current-carrying conductor of electricity tends to move when in the presence of a magnetic field at right angles to the current. The conventional motor has a "rotor" and a "stator," on which are mounted the current-carrying conductors. The laminated steel rotor, shaped like a baker's rolling pin, is mounted in a steel stator or frame. The rotor is free to turn within the stator, the shaft or axle delivering the mechanical power. There is an "air gap" between rotor and stator surfaces. Imbedded in these surfaces are many electrical conductors, connected end to end to form continuous complete windings in which electric current is made to flow. One winding forms an electromagnet; this is called the field winding. The other winding (armature winding), when carrying current, moves in response to the magnetic field in the air gap; rotation of the rotor is thus accomplished.

In a modern d-c motor many coils of wire are completely packed into an *armature* made of soft iron. Each coil is connected to insulated copper segments of a *commutator* so that only one coil at a time has current flowing in it. This is achieved by stationary graphite blocks or *brushes* which press,

Force on current-carrying conductor: Electric current produces a magnetic field. Interaction between this field and the field of the magnets, as shown below, results in a force on the conductor. Electrical energy in the form of current becomes mechanical energy, *i.e.* force multiplied by the distance the conductor moves. This is principle of electric motor.

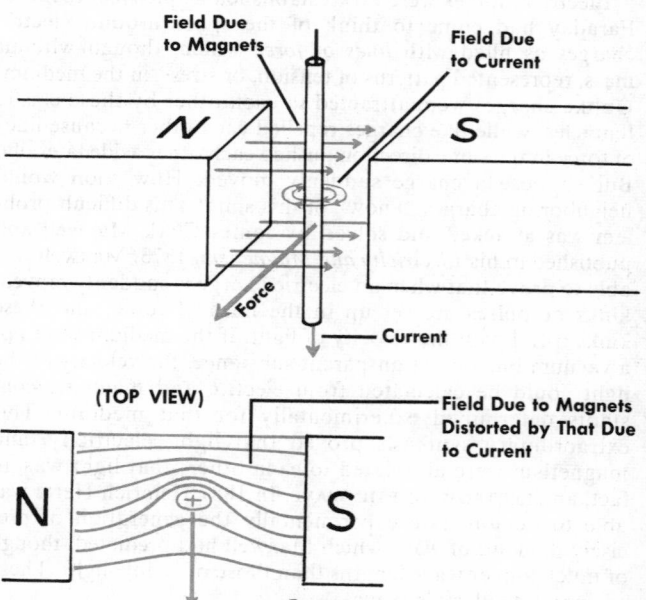

Field Due to Magnets

Field Due to Current

N   S

Force

Current

(TOP VIEW)

N   S

Force

Field Due to Magnets Distorted by That Due to Current

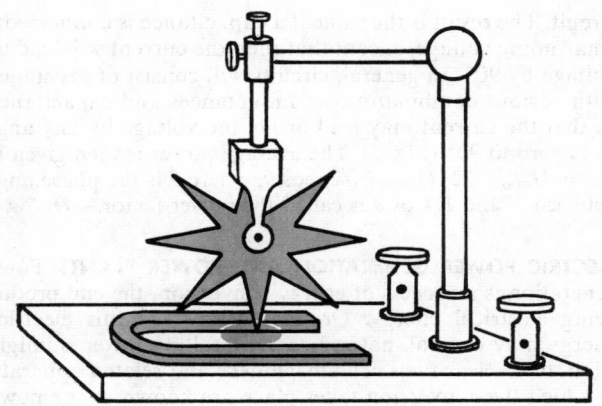

Stellate motor of 1823: Dipping into a mercury pool between the poles of the magnet, the star temporarily becomes a conductor and is pushed by the resulting force until the next point makes contact. Thus continuous rotation is established.

without much friction but with good electrical contact, on the rotating commutator segments. The brushes are so oriented that, as the armature rotates, current flows in the coils only when they are in the most favorable position for producing torque upon the armature. The strong magnetic field in which the armature rotates is usually produced by electromagnets. This standard d-c motor will not work on ac if the magnetic field is constant. However, if the coils of the electromagnet are also energized by the a-c source, the motor can be made to run successfully on either ac or dc. The small motors, called universal motors, are frequently constructed in this way.

In 1824 D. F. J. Arago demonstrated that a pivoted compass needle could be set into rotation by a copper disk spinning in a horizontal plane just above the needle. Arago did not understand the phenomenon involved but it is now known that the magnet induces eddy currents in the rotating copper disk and that these eddy currents set up magnetic fields of such polarity that they attract the poles of the magnet. If the magnet were rotated, instead of the disk, a similar *electromagnetic drag* would be produced on the disk. This phenomenon is the basis of another common type of motor, the *induction motor,* which was invented in 1888 when Nikola Tesla discovered how to produce rotating magnetic fields by means of

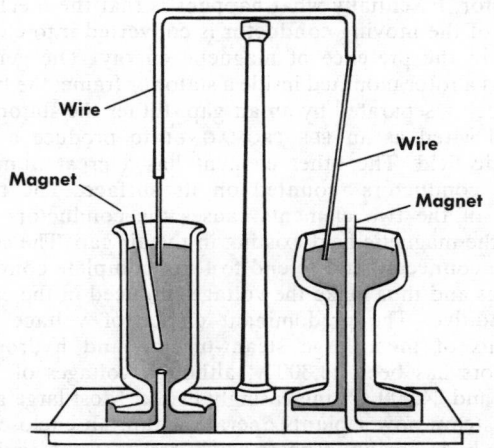

One of Faraday's early motor devices (1821): On the left, the stationary wire dipping in mercury makes a circuit, and the magnet rotates. On the right, the magnet is stationary, and it is the wire dipping in the mercury which rotates.

polyphase currents. In the same year, George Westinghouse purchased exclusive rights to Tesla's patents, and brought Tesla to Pittsburgh to direct construction of a number of polyphase induction motors. Because of their simplicity, these motors became "the workhorses of industry." In the *squirrel-cage* type of induction motor, the rotor has no commutator or wires but consists only of a number of conducting bars in which the eddy currents are induced. The *synchronous* motor is an a-c motor that has poles on the rotor which must be kept exactly in step with the changing field poles. Such a motor must be brought up to speed by some device, and if overloaded it gets out of step and stops.

Development of the electric motor could be said to date from 1819, when the Danish physicist Hans Christian Oersted discovered that the magnetic needle of a compass when in the vicinity of a current-carrying wire is deflected from its N-S position, and that the current-carrying wire itself experiences a force of reaction. Shortly thereafter, A. M. Ampère announced the dynamic action between conductors carrying electric currents. Of prime importance, however, was the discovery of the principles of electromagnetic induction by Michael Faraday, 1831. At the same time, without knowledge of the experiments of Faraday, Joseph Henry at the Albany Academy in New York constructed an electric motor which in reality was a rocking bar electromagnet pivoted at its center.

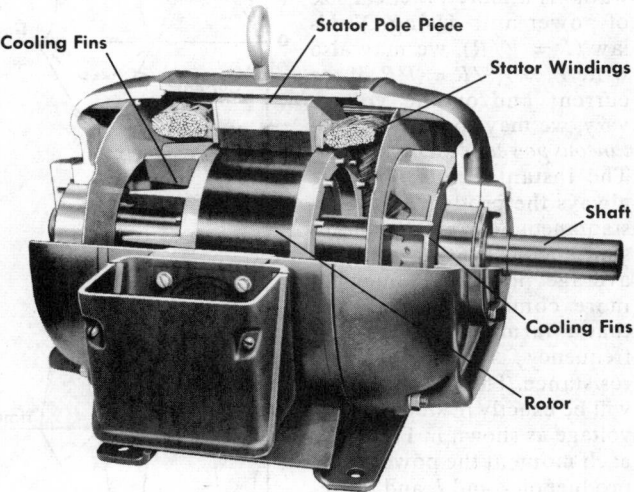

A-C induction-type motor: In this most widely used electric motor, the stator's magnetic field rotates, inducing current in the rotor. Force resulting from interaction of stator's field and induced field of the rotor turns the rotor. (*Robbins & Myers, Inc.*)

Electric motors are classified by size as "fractional horsepower" (less than 1 hp) and "integral horsepower" (1 hp and larger). A typical room air conditioner uses a 1-hp induction motor. There are also the three broad classifications according to type of electrical power required: alternating-current (a-c) motors, direct-current (d-c), and universal (a-c or d-c) motors. A-c motors have the advantage of being less expensive than d-c's, but because they operate at relatively fixed or constant speeds they are best used where variable speed control is either not important or not desired, *e.g.* in refrigerators, fans, phonographs, and air conditioners. Where variable speed control is desired, as in elevators and subway trains, d-c motors are used. Universal motors are similar in construction to d-c's and are used in small household appliances. —*H. Sw.; L. J. H.*

ELECTRIC OSCILLATION: see OSCILLATOR.

ELECTRIC POTENTIAL: If a positive electric charge is placed in an electric field, the charge will experience a force proportionate to the charge and the electric field strength, and in the same direction as the line of force passing through the point occupied by the charge. If the charge is moved at right angles to the lines of force, no work needs to be done, but if the motion is in any other direction, work will be involved. The work required to move a unit charge (*e.g.* one coulomb) from a very great distance up to a particular point is defined as the potential at that point. (In the same way a book lifted above a desk has potential energy, as does a stretched rubber band.) A more useful definition involves the difference of potential between two points, defined as one volt if one joule of work is required to move one coulomb of charge from one point to the other; the work required is independent of the path between the two points.—*H. Sw.*

ELECTRIC POWER: the energy dissipated in an electric circuit per unit time. The power P in a d-c circuit is equal to the voltage V times the current I, or $P = VI$. If V is in volts and I is in amperes, P will be in watts. The kilowatt (1,000 watts) is a more practical size of power unit. Using Ohm's law ($I = V/R$), we may also write $P = V^2/R = I^2R$. If the current and/or the voltage vary, we may speak of *instantaneous power* or *average power*. The instantaneous power is always the product of the instantaneous current and the instantaneous voltage, but the average power is somewhat more complicated. Suppose that a harmonic voltage V of frequency f is applied to a pure resistance. Then the current I will be exactly in step with the voltage as shown in Fig. 1. At each moment the power is the product of V and I, and the resulting power curve is also a harmonic but of twice the frequency of V or I. The power fluctuates between zero and a maximum value $V_{max} I_{max}$. The average value is therefore $V_{max} I_{max}/2$ or $(V_{max}/\sqrt{2})(I_{max}/\sqrt{2})$, or the *effective voltage* times the *effective current*.

If a harmonic voltage is applied to a pure inductance, the current will lag 90° behind the voltage as shown in Fig. 2. The instantaneous power is positive half the time and negative half the time, so that the average power is zero. Physically this means that power is alternately stored in the magnetic field of the inductance and then delivered back to the

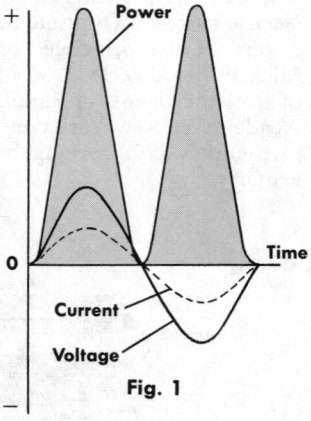

Fig. 1

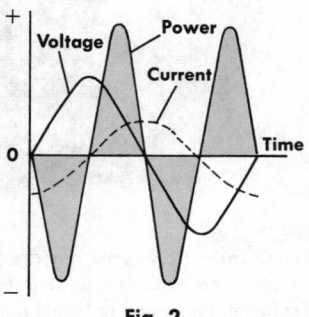

Fig. 2

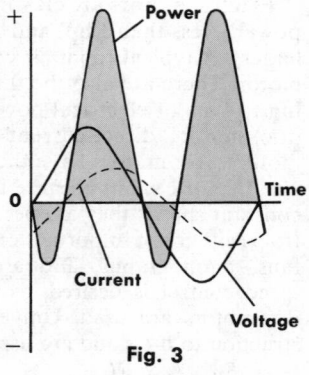

Fig. 3

circuit. The result is the same if a capacitance is connected to a harmonic voltage, except that then the current will lead the voltage by 90°. In general, circuits will consist of resistances with various combinations of inductances and capacitances so that the current may lead or lag the voltage by any angle from zero to 90° (Fig. 3). The average power is then given by $P_{av} = (I_{max}/\sqrt{2}) (V_{max}/\sqrt{2}) \cos \theta$, where θ is the phase angle between V and I. Cos θ is called the power factor.—*H. Sw.*

ELECTRIC POWER GENERATION AND POWER PLANTS: Power generation is a process of energy conversion, the end product being electrical energy. Original sources of this electrical energy may be coal, natural gas, oil, falling water, sunlight, wind, or nuclear fuels. The machinery and related apparatus in which the conversion takes place are known as the power plant. If the power plant is large, serving many consumers through transmission and distribution lines, it is known as a central station.

History: Probably the earliest central station in the U. S. A. was the one built in 1886 at Great Barrington, Mass., by William Stanley, a pioneer in electric power generation and transmission (see ELECTRIC POWER TRANSMISSION). Using a 25-hp boiler and engine to turn a Siemens generator rated at 500 v and 12 amp, Stanley supplied electricity for lighting "13 stores, 2 hotels, 2 doctors' offices, one barber shop, and the telephone and post offices." In 1900 the Hartford (Conn.) Electric Co. caused much excitement by installing a 2,000-kw steam-turbine generator unit. By 1920 a typical steam-turbine generator was rated at 30,000 kw, by 1959 the average rating was 90,000 kw, and today machines are built with ratings up to 1,000,000 kw. A single machine of 500,000 kw can produce electricity for a city of 500,000. Designers claim that a 2,000,000-kw unit can be built; two of these could supply all the electricity for a city the size of New York. The U. S. A. consumes nearly 40% of all the electrical energy generated in the world. In 1955 the total capacity of U. S. electric power plants was 116 million kw; in 1964, it was 221 million; and in 1970 capacity is expected to surpass 300 million kw.

Basic Designs: An important element of the power plant is the electric GENERATOR, a machine similar in construction to the ELECTRIC MOTOR. The operation of the generator is based on the principle of electromagnetic induction discovered by Michael Faraday, 1831. When an electric conductor is moved across a magnetic field so that the lines of force of the magnetic field are intercepted or "cut," a voltage is induced in the conductor. Essentially what happens is that the mechanical energy of the moving conductor is converted into electrical energy in the presence of magnetic energy. The generator contains a rotor mounted inside a stator or frame, the two elements being separated by an air gap. Either the stator or the rotor is wired as an ELECTROMAGNET to produce a strong magnetic field. The other element has a great number of electric conductors mounted on its surface. The relative motion of the two elements causes the conductors to cut across the magnetic field existing in the air gap. The conductors are connected end to end to form complete continuous windings and thus make the voltages induced in the conductors additive. The predominant choice of voltage at the terminals of most large steam-turbine and hydroelectric generators has been 13,800 v, although voltages of 18,000, 20,000, and 24,000 are increasingly in use. Most large generators in steam power plants operate within an enclosed low-pressure hydrogen atmosphere which assists in the dissipation of heat from the electrical conductors.

The generator receives its rotating (mechanical) energy from a turbine, a device similar to a pinwheel. The most common types are the steam turbine, driven by steam, and

Experimental methods of generating electric power: Recent advances in the technology of energy conversion have suggested new sources of electric power. The magnetohydrodynamic (MHD) generator (*left*) produces electric power by passing a highly ionized gas (a PLASMA) between the poles of a magnet. The gas is heated to about 5,000°F by ordinary furnace oil. The oblong plates in the trays (*right*) are thermoelectric couples (thermocouples), which are capable of changing heat directly into electricity. A technician tests a few of the thermocouple sets that form part of an experimental 5,000-watt generator under evaluation by the U. S. Navy. (*Westinghouse*)

the waterwheel or hydro turbine, driven by the force of falling water. Steam power plants, in which the boiler is fired by coal, gas, or oil, are the most important in the U. S. A. At the end of 1960, there were 1,057 steam power plants, producing approximately 80% of U. S. electric power, and 1,333 hydro power plants, producing approximately 20%. Only in the Northwest do hydro facilities provide the principal means of power generation. The 18 atomic power plants existing at the end of 1960 accounted for less than 1% of electric power production. By 1980, nuclear power is expected to represent over 20%.

Steam Plants: In a steam power plant water is heated in a boiler fueled with coal, gas, or oil, forming very dry steam of ultra-high temperature (up to 1100°F) and pressure (up to 3500 lb/in.²). Potential or stored energy in the fuel is released and transformed into the active energy of "live" steam. This active or kinetic energy is dissipated as the steam from a nozzle is forced against the blades or buckets of the turbine, causing it to turn in the same manner as wind turns a pinwheel. The kinetic energy of the steam is converted into mechanical energy of the rotating turbine, which in turn is converted into electrical energy in the generator.

Atomic power plants now in operation are similar to conventional steam power plants except that instead of burning coal, gas, or oil to generate steam, the heat is obtained from nuclear fuels. In a typical atomic power plant, atoms of uranium are split by bombarding them with neutrons. The heat developed is used to generate steam, which in turn drives a conventional turbine generator. Atomic power plants use only a few pounds of uranium fuel each year. In sharp contrast is even an efficient coal-burning steam power plant (1961), which consumes 0.88 lb of coal each hour that one kilowatt is generated (a kilowatt-hour). However, efficiencies of coal-burning power plants have improved markedly over the past 40 yr. In 1920, a kilowatt hour required the con-

sumption of 3 lb of coal, in 1925 the figure was 2 lb, and in 1948 it was 1.3 lb. Of the total electrical energy produced by coal, gas, and oil, coal represents about 66%, gas 26%, and oil 8%. The average cost of electrical energy produced in a steam power plant in the U. S. A. (1966) is 0.7¢/kw-hr. Considerable expenses are involved in the transmission and distribution of the electrical energy to the consumer. The average price of electricity to the consumer is 1.68¢/kw-hr. An average electric iron (500 w) used for 2 hr would consume 1 kw-hr of electrical energy.

Hydro Stations: These differ from steam stations in that the energy is derived from the force of falling water, which is funneled through a large-diameter pipe known as a "penstock" and then forced against the buckets of a waterwheel. The energy of the falling water is thus transferred to the wheel and thence to the electric generator, which is mounted on the same shaft or axle as the wheel; the generator converts the mechanical energy into electrical energy. Hydroelectric stations are, of course, feasible only at river sites where either a dam can be built or a natural waterfall exists. The largest hydroelectric power project in the western world was completed at Niagara Falls in 1961; it contains 13 waterwheel generators, each rated at 150,000 kw. In contrast, the first hydroelectric station at Niagara Falls, built in the 1890s, contained three waterwheel generators, each rated at approximately 3,000 kw.

Direct Conversion: Research is now being done in thermoelectricity (SEE THERMOELECTRIC EFFECT) toward generation of electricity directly from heat, without the intermediate steam cycle or the associated turbines and generators. One such direct-conversion process employs MAGNETOHYDRODYNAMICS (MHD). A superhot, electrically conducting gas (a plasma) is passed through a magnetic field, producing electricity.—*L. J. H.*

ELECTRIC POWER TRANSMISSION: the transfer of large quantities of electrical energy by means of high-voltage electric power lines from a central power plant or generating station to a low-voltage distribution system. The transmission system does not store electrical energy, but merely acts as a highway for electrical energy to leave the generating station. (See ELECTRIC POWER GENERATION AND POWER PLANTS.) Transmission lines are made of copper- or steel-reinforced aluminum, and are generally supported with porcelain insulators on steel-latticed towers spaced 650 to 900 ft apart. Most modern generating stations produce electricity at 13,800 v. By means of a transformer the voltage is raised ten to twenty times higher to reduce line losses, which are proportional to the square of the current (I^2). On the other hand, electric power is proportional to voltage times current; this is why high voltage and low current deliver maximum power over transmission lines. The line may be a few miles or a few hundred miles in length. At the receiving end of the line, the voltage is decreased to a subtransmission level, then to a distribution level, and finally to one of the common U. S. household voltages: 110, 115, 120, 208, or 240 v. Large consumers of electricity (*e.g.* factories or steel mills) generally receive the electrical energy at high voltage directly from the transmission line.

One of the first transmission lines (1886) was installed by William Stanley, an early associate of George Westinghouse, between his laboratory in Great Barrington, Mass., and the center of town—a distance of 4,000 ft. In 1890, a transmission line rated at 3,300 v was put into operation at Willamette Falls, Oreg., to carry electrical energy generated by water power to Portland, a distance of 13 mi. Early transmission lines were limited in voltage to 4,000 v, but improvements in technology permitted construction of lines rated at 60,000 v by 1900, 110,000 by 1908, 220,000 by 1923, and 287,000 v by 1937.

Transmission lines in the 1960s are being constructed at voltages as high as 330,000. Research stations are currently investigating extra-high-voltage (EHV) transmission. Such a project is in operation at Pittsfield, Mass., where transmission-line voltages up to 750,000 are being studied.—*L. J. H.*

ELECTROCHEMISTRY: the science of the relation between chemical changes and the passage of electricity. In primary electrical cells (also called galvanic, voltaic, or electromotive cells) chemical changes are used to produce electricity. Devices in which the opposite effect occurs and electricity is used to produce chemical changes are called electrolytic cells. Both types of cell consist essentially of a conducting liquid, called the electrolyte, in contact with two metallic-type conductors, called the electrodes, which can be connected through an external circuit. Current through the electrodes and external circuit is carried by free electrons; current through the electrolyte is carried by ions. It is at the surface of the electrodes that the primary chemical changes take place, being caused by the transfer of electrons between the electrodes and the ions. The electrode that takes electrons from the electrolyte into the external circuit of an electrolytic cell is termed the anode; the electrode that transfers electrons into the electrolyte is the cathode. Faraday was the first (1834) to recognize the fundamental quantitative law of electrochemistry, which may be stated as follows: "When a current passes across the junction between an electrode and an electrolyte, the quantity of chemical change produced, expressed in gram equivalents, is exactly proportional to the quantity of electricity passed." The quantity of electricity necessary to produce 1 gm equivalent of chemical change, *e.g.* the formation of 107.9 gm of metallic silver from an electrolyte containing silver ions, is called the faraday, and is equal to 96,500 coulombs. A wide range of chemical reactions, including some of great practical importance, are made to take place in electrolytic cells. (See CELL, ELECTROLYTIC; CELL, VOLTAIC; ELECTRODEPOSITION; ELECTROLYSIS.)

Another equally important branch of electrochemistry deals with the maximum voltage or emf that can be produced by an electromotive cell. The emf depends on the chemical reaction taking place in the cell, and is a thermo-

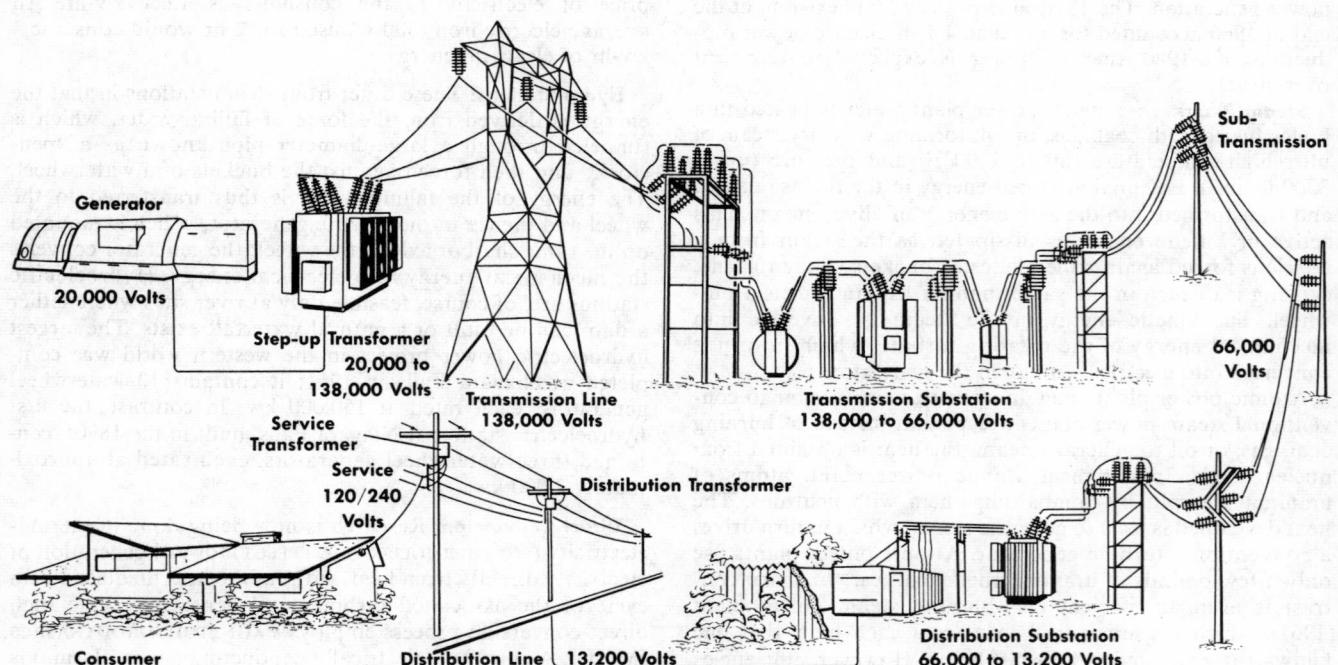

Typical Facilities Required to Supply Electric Service (*Long Island Lighting Co.*)

dynamic measure of the energy change accompanying the reaction.—*A. M. S.*

ELECTRODE: one of the terminals connecting a voltaic or electrolytic cell, a thermionic tube, a photocell, or an x-ray tube to the conductors constituting the rest of the circuit; the actual structures within the cell or tube are also sometimes called electrodes. The term *anode* is, by definition, the electrode through which the conventional (plus-to-minus) current enters the device. Thus, in a simple primary cell undergoing discharge, current leaves the copper electrode and enters the zinc electrode. Accordingly, the zinc plate is correctly described as an anode. By the same reasoning, the designation *cathode* properly applies to the copper electrode of the discharging cell. (This is often confused with the fact that the polarity of zinc with respect to copper is negative, the negative potential of the zinc terminal being erroneously assumed to denote the presence of a cathode.) In an acid-type secondary or storage cell, the anode is again the negative lead plate when the cell is being discharged, but shifts its position to the positive lead-peroxide plate when the direction of current is reversed during the charging process. The polarity of the cell, of course, remains fixed, but anode and cathode interchange positions depending on the direction of the current passing through the cell. In simple vacuum tubes (Crookes, Geissler, x-ray), as well as in thermionic tubes and photoemissive-type photocells, the term cathode designates an electron-emitter, and anode an electron-collector. This is not at variance with the procedure described above, although emphasis here is placed on electrons, rather than positive charges, as carriers of electric current.—*A. E.*

ELECTRODEPOSITION: the depositing of electrically charged particles of a substance in an electrolytic solution onto a desired surface or object. The process is simply a version of ELECTROLYSIS, and may involve either (1) the deposition of a metal from a solution of metal ions, called *electroplating*, or (2) the deposition of non-ionic electrically charged particles, sometimes called *electrophoretic deposition*. An example of the latter is the coating of rubber gloves utilizing electrically charged rubber particles in a latex suspension. (See CELL, ELECTROLYTIC; ELECTROLYTIC DISSOCIATION THEORY.) Most metals are deposited from solution near their reversible potential, *i.e.* a voltage which, if slightly increased or decreased, will cause a simultaneous increase or decrease in the formation of ions. The conditions of deposition of metals influence the physical appearance of the deposits. Since the deposited metals are crystalline, their physical appearance is particularly influenced by the rate of deposition and the rate of fresh nuclei formation. Rapid growth of crystal nuclei gives a fine-grained deposit; rapid growth of a single nucleus will cause a coarse-appearing crystal. (See CRYSTALLIZATION.) High metal-salt concentrations produce a rapid discharge of ions, and nuclei are formed faster than they can grow. Low temperature usually improves metal deposits; high temperature promotes coarse crystal formation. The addition of gelatin, agar, or camphor aids in uniform metal deposition. The metal on which the deposit is made also influences the appearance of the deposit. A variety of salts (*e.g.* sulfates, nitrates, chlorides, fluoborates, and cyanides) are used for the commercial deposition of heavy metals, as tin, copper, and nickel. Electroplating baths (*i.e.* electrolytes used in electrodeposition) may be either acid (pH less than 2), neutral (pH = 2 to 8), or alkaline (pH greater than 8). Thus silver electrodes are prepared by electroplating platinum wire in an *alkaline* silver cyanide bath; chromium metal is deposited on metal surfaces from a chromic *acid* bath with a suitable catalyst.—*G. W. M.*

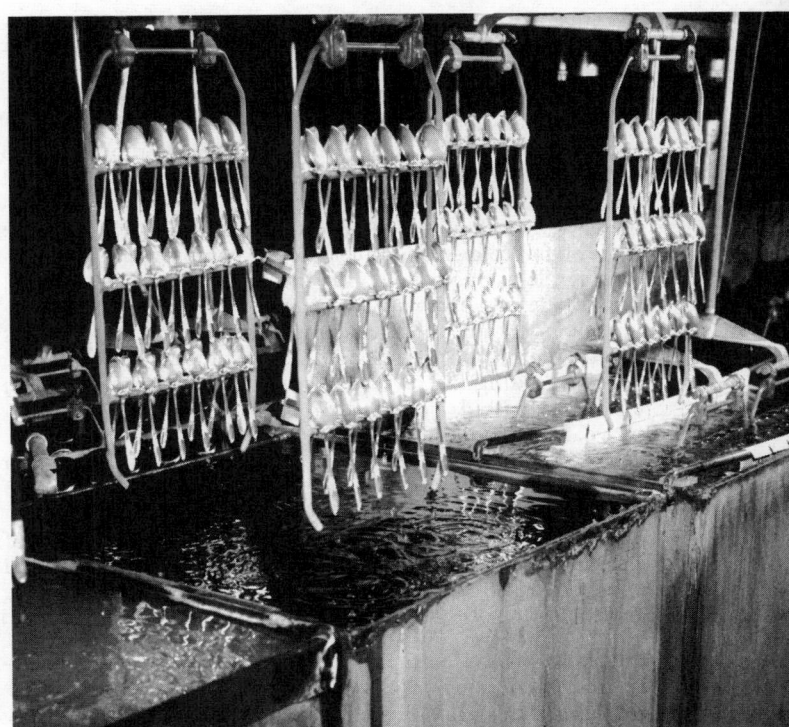

Electroplating of silver: Highly polished pieces to be plated are chemically cleaned, then hung in vats containing the electrolytic solution. Minute particles of silver from solid silver bars in the solution are deposited on the pieces. By a special process, more silver is deposited on back of each piece, because more wear occurs there. (*Oneida, Ltd.*)

ELECTRODIALYSIS: a process used primarily for demineralizing water. It employs an electric current to cause migration of the saline cations and anions through the solution, and a set of membranes each of which is permeable to the solvent (water), and to either the cations *or* the anions but not to both. These membranes are similar in composition to ion-exchange resins, containing permanently fixed, ionically charged sites. A cation-exchange membrane, which contains

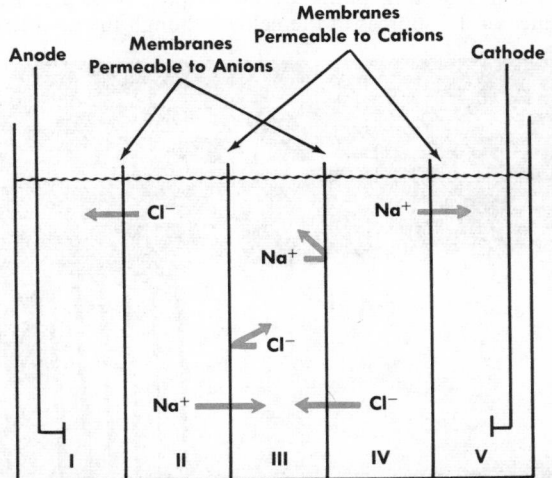

Desalination of salt water by electrodialysis: Sodium (Na^+) ions pass through a cation-permeable membrane, and chlorine (Cl^-) ions through an anion-permeable membrane, leaving salt-free water in compartments II and IV.

negatively charged sites, allows the passage of cations (positively charged ions) but retards the passage of anions (negatively charged ions). An anion-exchange membrane behaves in the reverse manner. The prototype of an electrodialysis cell is a three-compartment electrolytic cell acting on sodium chloride solution. The cathode compartment (into which the cathode or negatively charged electrode dips) is separated from the center compartment by a cation-exchange membrane which allows sodium ions to pass through from the center compartment into the cathode compartment while retarding the passage of chloride ions in the opposite direction. The anode compartment is separated from the center compartment by an anion-exchange membrane. This allows chloride ions to move through into the anode compartment, while retarding the reverse passage of sodium ions. When current is passed, both sodium ions and chloride ions can move freely out of the center compartment toward the cathode and the anode respectively, but neither type of ion can enter from the opposite side. Thus the salt concentration in the center compartment is continuously diminished. In practical operations the cells are multi-compartmented, and the partially desalinated solutions together with their enriched counterparts are circulated to give maximum efficiency. See DEMINERALIZATION OF SALINE WATER.—*A. M. S.*

ELECTRODYNAMICS: the branch of physics that seeks to describe those motions of electrically charged objects which are caused by the interactions between the charges of the objects. According to classical electrodynamics, every electric charge fills space with an excitation called an ELECTRIC FIELD, which evidences its presence by exerting a force on any other electric charge. When an electric charge moves with constant velocity, it also generates a MAGNETIC FIELD, which likewise exerts a force on any other moving electric charge. Finally, if a charged particle is accelerated, it radiates traveling, oscillating electric and magnetic fields called electromagnetic RADIATION.

In 1863 the great English physicist James Clerk Maxwell formulated a set of equations that permit the calculation of the electric and magnetic fields generated by any arbitrary collection of charged particles (see MAXWELL'S EQUATIONS). Having found the strengths of the fields at any point, one can calculate the force exerted on a test charge placed at the point. Then, using NEWTON'S LAWS OF MOTION, one can calculate the resulting motion of the sample charge under the influence of the sources of the field. Although the mathematical

difficulties become overwhelming for all but the simplest systems, it is nevertheless true that all problems in classical electrodynamics are, in principle, soluble. As the result of an overwhelming mass of experimental evidence accumulated since 1900, we now know that Maxwell's equations and Newton's laws are not adequate to describe phenomena on the atomic or subatomic scale. To describe these, QUANTUM MECHANICS has been developed. The part of quantum mechanics dealing specifically with the electromagnetic interactions is called QUANTUM ELECTRODYNAMICS. This is one of the most successful special fields of modern physics, in that the predictions of its theory are thus far in agreement with every relevant experimental measurement.—*S. K.*

ELECTROFORMING: the production of objects by the electrolytic deposition of metal on forms or molds. These forms are made of metal, graphite-coated wax, or plastic. The process differs from electroplating in that the metal is not actually joined to the base on which it is deposited. Electroforming is used in making medals, master phonograph records, and printing plates. (See ELECTRODEPOSITION; ELECTROTYPING.)— *E. E.*

ELECTROLYSIS: the process whereby electrical energy causes a chemical change in a conducting medium, which usually is a solution or a molten substance. The electrical energy enters and leaves the electrolytic medium (*e.g.* a salt solution) through electrodes, which ordinarily are pieces of metal. The electrode where electrons enter the solution is the *cathode;* the electrode where the electrons leave is the *anode.* Negatively charged ions (*anions*) are attracted to the anode; positively charged ions (*cations*) are attracted to the cathode. Passing an electric current through solutions of copper, zinc, nickel, lead, and silver, as well as others, causes deposition of pure metal at the cathode (see ELECTRODEPOSITION). Passing current through solutions of alkali and alkaline-earth salts results in liberation of hydrogen at the cathode. When the anode consists of a metal, metal ions pass from the anode into the solution as current flows. See METALLURGY.

An inert electrode, *e.g.* platinum, may allow liberation of an element: salt solutions other than those of HALOGENS liberate oxygen from an aqueous medium at the anode, whereas the halogen salts liberate free chlorine, bromine, or iodine. Fluorine is not liberated, because of its high oxidation potential.—*G. W. M.*

ELECTROLYTE: see ELECTROLYTIC DISSOCIATION THEORY.

ELECTROLYTE BALANCE: in biochemistry, that concentration of the various electrolytes of the blood plasma which is optimum for the functioning of the organism. The electrolyte composition of plasma is believed to be similar to that of the sea at the time when the first animals with circulatory systems developed. The principal ions involved are those of sodium, potassium, calcium, bicarbonate, chloride. If their respective concentrations are not kept stable within a narrow range, serious physiological disturbances result. Regulation of the electrolyte balance is accomplished mainly by filtration of the blood by the kidney. Most of the filtrate is reabsorbed; the waste surplus is discarded in the urine. Besides the kidney, sensory organs in the brain control acidity and salt (ion) concentration by stimulating the lungs to exhale carbon dioxide.

Refining by electrolysis: Cathodes on which pure copper has been deposited from electrolytic solution are being lifted from tank. Impurities have been removed. (Copper & Brass Research Assn.)

This system makes the cells independent of the external environment. Changes in electrolyte balance through ingestion of salts or vomiting of stomach acid are usually corrected by the body. When they are not, as in some diseases, they are treated by addition of electrolytes through venous infusion or by their removal by an artificial kidney (see BLOOD CHEMISTRY).—*J. F. S.*

ELECTROLYTIC DISSOCIATION THEORY: a theory dealing with behavior of compounds in solution. Svante Arrhenius proposed that certain compounds dissociate in solution, *e.g.* NaCl (common salt) into Na and Cl. These compounds, which he called *electrolytes,* divide so that the resulting atoms or groups of atoms are electrically charged due to the gain or loss of the shared valence electrons of the CHEMICAL BOND (see also CHEMISTRY—formula; valence bonds; equations). When the atom gives up its valence electron, it is termed a positive ion, or cation. When the valence electrons are retained, the atom assumes a negative charge and is called an anion. There are a great number of compounds which dissociate in this manner when placed in water or other polar solvents; the most common are the acids, bases, and salts. Thus hydrochloric acid forms hydrogen ions (H^+) and chloride ions (Cl^-); sodium hydroxide forms sodium ions (Na^+) and hydroxyl ions (OH^-); sodium chloride forms sodium and chloride ions when dissolved in water.

The electrolytes that dissociate almost completely are said to be "strong," and those that dissociate only partially are termed "weak." In the former group are to be found such compounds as sodium sulfate ($2Na^+SO_4^=$) and potassium nitrate ($K^+NO_3^-$); in the latter, such compounds as ammonium hydroxide ($NH_4^+OH^-$) and mercuric chloride ($Hg^{++}2Cl^-$). A measure of the strength of the electrolyte is its ability to conduct an electric current: the stronger the electrolyte, the less resistance it offers to the passage of electricity.

When an electric potential is applied between two electrodes immersed in an electrolyte, the anions in solution migrate to the anode, where they free electrons, and the cations migrate to the cathode, where they capture electrons. Thus the electric current is produced. The passage of the ions is retarded by three effects: (1) the physical friction of molecular contact, (2) the electrical attraction for ions migrating in the opposite direction, called the electrophoretic effect, and (3) the asymmetry effect, or the electrical drag created by the charged environment of the ion (see ELECTROMAGNETIC DRAG). —*R. W.*

ELECTROMAGNET: a device for producing a magnetic field by means of an electric current. It consists of an iron core around which is wound a coil of wire that will conduct electric current. In 1820, Hans Christian Oersted found that an electric current produced a magnetic field. William Sturgeon, 1825, made the first electromagnet by winding a bare copper wire around an iron core and running current through the wire from a voltaic battery. One of the most important uses of electromagnets is to provide the magnetic field needed in both the ELECTRIC MOTOR and the GENERATOR. Electromagnets are also used for opening and closing electrical contacts, *e.g.* in circuit breakers and automatic starters. As a solenoid (a spiral of wire wound in the form of a helix) the electromagnet can be used for exerting strong mechanical force, *e.g.* the braking of elevators.—*H. I. S.*

ELECTROMAGNETIC DRAG: a term that designates either of two electromagnetic phenomena: (1) The first of these phenomena is described by the Debye-Hückel theory (1923) of attraction forces between ions in a strong electrolyte. Because

Crane equipped with electromagnet is notably convenient for handling large masses of iron in irregular forms. (*U. S. Steel*)

of coulombic forces among ions in solution, positive ions are surrounded by an electron shield, negative ions by a positive ion shield. The resulting dipole moments of the ions' plus-minus and minus-plus charge distributions interact among themselves (as bar magnets would interact), thus influencing (exerting "drag" on) mobility, ionization, and diffusion rates in the solution. (See ELECTROLYTIC DISSOCIATION THEORY.) (2) The other, older use of the term "electromagnetic drag" refers to the dragging force exerted on a metal conductor by a moving magnetic field. This type of drag is exploited in the induction motor, in which the rotating magnetic field of the stator pulls the rotor around, thus transferring energy from the electromagnetic field into mechanical energy of rotation. (See ELECTRIC MOTOR.)—*A. S.*

ELECTROMAGNETIC INDUCTION: the creation of an electromotive force by the variation of a magnetic field. The diary of Michael Faraday records that on Aug. 29, 1831, he first produced an electric current by magnetic means. He wound two separate coils of insulated wire on an iron ring as shown in Fig. 1. One coil was connected to a galvanometer *G.* When the other coil was connected to a battery, the galvanometer deflected sharply, then fell back to zero and showed no deflection as long as the current remained steady. When the battery was disconnected, the galvanometer briefly deflected in the opposite direction. Since it was already known that a

Fig. 1: Faraday's device for producing electric current by magnetic means.

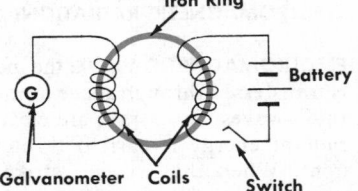

current flowing in a coil of wire would produce a magnetic field, it was clear to Faraday that the variation of the field produced by the coil when it was connected and disconnected caused current to flow momentarily in the other coil. Later Faraday produced the same effect by moving a permanent magnet in and out of a coil of wire connected to a galvanometer.

Quite independently, the American physicist Joseph Henry discovered the same effect about the same time. Henry wound a few turns of insulated wire around the iron keeper placed across the poles of a large electromagnet (Fig. 2). These turns were then connected to a galvanometer. Like Faraday, he observed a deflection of the galvanometer needle while the current in the large electromagnet was being turned on and off, but observed no effect while the current was steady. In addition, Henry observed one effect that Faraday had not recorded: the phenomenon we now call self-induction. A long piece of wire was found to produce a larger spark than a short wire when contact with a battery was broken. The spark was intensified if the long wire was wound up into a compact coil. Henry correctly concluded that an emf was induced in the coil because of the coil's own variable magnetic field.

From the work of Faraday and Henry it is evident that ELECTROMOTIVE FORCE is produced in a circuit whenever the total MAGNETIC FLUX linking the circuit is undergoing change, whether the change is produced by motion or by time variation of the MAGNETIC INDUCTION field. Faraday's law of electromagnetic induction states that the induced emf is given by the time rate of change of magnetic flux threading the circuit, *i.e.* passing through the area enclosed by the circuit. Important technological applications of electromagnetic induction are the GENERATOR, the TRANSFORMER, and the INDUCTION COIL.—*H. Sw.*

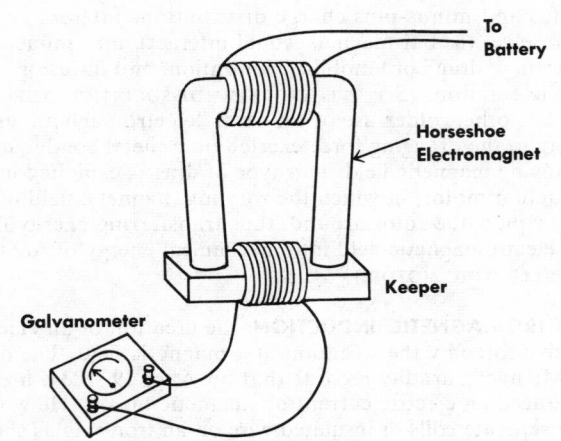

Fig. 2: Henry's demonstration of induction: Making or breaking of battery circuit produces current in galvanometer circuit.

ELECTROMAGNETIC PROPULSION: see PLASMA PROPULSION.

ELECTROMAGNETIC RADIATION: see ELECTROMAGNETIC WAVE.

ELECTROMAGNETIC WAVE: the means by which radiant energy is transferred through space or matter. Heat rays, light waves, radio waves, and x-rays are electromagnetic waves by which radiant energy is carried through space at the velocity of light. When these waves strike matter, they impart their energy to it. For example, a radio wave that encounters a conducting body such as an antenna produces a feeble electric current, which is then amplified and converted to sound by the radio receiver.

Electromagnetic waves are classified according to their length and frequency. Since they are transverse waves, they may be pictured as a series of crests and troughs recurring at a certain frequency. As a transverse wave passes through a medium, the displacement of the particles of the medium is perpendicular to the direction of propagation of the wave. For example, when one shakes a taut rope fastened to some solid object, the particles of the rope move up and down following the motion of the hand, but the resulting transverse wave travels along the length of the rope. In electromagnetic

waves the directions of the electric and magnetic fields are both at right angles to the direction of propagation. The wavelength (distance between successive crests, say, along the direction of propagation) varies considerably in electromagnetic waves. An ordinary radio wave may have a length of thousands of feet, in contrast to x-rays, which are only billionths of an inch long.

Scientists have always been confronted with the problem of how energy, mass, and momentum can travel across the vast interstellar space with no apparent medium to travel in. They know that some of the energy released from the Sun reaches Earth in amounts measurable in terms of intensity, wavelength, and frequency; they therefore assume that the rest of the energy speeds through space as so many ergs of radiant energy for every unit of cubic volume. Scientific calculations and experiments have further shown that this energy is in the form of electric and magnetic fields. Electricity and magnetism were long studied separately, and not until 1819 did the Danish scientist H. C. Oersted establish a connection between them; he showed that a magnetic field surrounds a wire carrying an electric current (see ELECTROMAGNETISM). In later years many scientists, notably the Englishman Michael Faraday, elaborated this relationship; Faraday introduced the concept FIELD. He showed that although there are no electrical phenomena associated with a stationary magnet or magnetic field, a change in the magnetic field produces electricity. Theoretical contributions of James Clerk Maxwell, published in 1864, showed that an oscillating electric charge is surrounded by an oscillating magnetic field, which in turn produces an oscillating electric field. Both these fields emanate in all directions from the charge, carrying with them the energy of the charge. Upon reaching matter this disturbance sets in motion electric charges in accordance with the oscillating pattern of the electric and magnetic field. Maxwell hypothesized that if electrical energy were propagated outward into space from an oscillating electrical disturbance, it might proceed in the form of a transverse wave. The crest of each wave would represent the maximum electric field, and the trough the minimum. He concluded that as the electric field travels it creates a magnetic field, and vice versa. He further stated that the two fields are always at right angles to one another and to the direction of propagation. Thus, if the wave were being propagated due north, the electric field might vibrate east and west and the magnetic field up and down.

These waves of energy are electromagnetic waves. Maxwell analyzed them and deduced many of their properties. One of the most important of these is the velocity of the wave. The velocity depends only on the magnetic and electric properties of the space through which the wave passes, *i.e.* its magnetic permeability and dielectric constant. These two constants cannot be determined individually, but their product, which determines the velocity of the electromagnetic wave, can be measured experimentally. This velocity is equal precisely to the ratio of the electrostatic unit of charge to the electromagnetic unit of charge (see ELECTRICAL AND MAGNETIC UNITS). From this information Maxwell deduced accurately the velocity through space of electromagnetic waves; the velocity proved to be the same as the speed of light.

In 1888 the German physicist Heinrich Hertz created electromagnetic waves by electrical means and showed that they have the properties which Maxwell had predicted. Hertz set up an electric charge in a CAPACITOR and allowed it to discharge through a spark gap. He thereby demonstrated that the flow of electricity in such a circuit accumulates so much momentum that it continues to flow after the condenser has been discharged and soon builds up an opposite charge; the

THE ELECTROMAGNETIC SPECTRUM

Wavelength (cm)	Name	Produced By	Effects	Uses
Above 10^{-11}	Cosmic photons	Majority of unknown origin; some from solar flares	Penetrate great thicknesses of matter; expose photographic film; ionize gas	Studies of interactions of nuclei; production of "strange" particles
10^{-11} to 10^{-8}	Gamma rays	Atomic disintegration; radioactivity	Penetrate all matter; expose photographic film; ionize gas	Atomic investigations; therapeutics
10^{-10} to 10^{-6}	X-rays	Stoppage of high-speed electrons by a metallic target	Less penetrating than gamma rays; expose photographic film; refracted by crystals	X-ray photography; medical diagnosis; therapeutics
10^{-6} to 10^{-5}	Ultraviolet rays	The sun; mercury arc; ionized gases	Expose photographic film; produce phosphorescence; induce chemical reactions	Photography; identification; medicine; disinfecting
10^{-5} to 10^{-4}	Visible light	The sun; hot bodies; ionized gases	Exposes photographic film; visible illumination; induces chemical reactions	Illumination; photography; optical instruments
10^{-4} to 10^{-1}	Infrared rays	Radiated heat	Expose special photographic film; produce sensation of heat	Special photography; heat lamps; industrial drying; identification of chemical compounds
10^{-1} to 10^3	Ultra-high-frequency radio waves	Ordinary and special types of electronic oscillators	Produce an electric current in a conductor; can be reflected and focused	Radar; television; FM radio; experimental
10^3 to 10^6	Radio waves	Radio transmitters; vacuum tube oscillators	Produce an electric current in a conductor; reflected from upper atmosphere	Communication; radio
Above 10^6	Alternating current	A coil rotating in a magnetic field	Electromagnetic induction; electrical heating; chemical and physiological changes	Transportation of electrical energy through conductors; source of alternating voltage

current then reverses, and an oscillation is produced. Further, the frequency of this oscillation is determined by the inductance and capacity of the associated ELECTRIC CIRCUIT. Under such conditions the oscillating electric discharge acts as a source of electromagnetic waves, whose frequency is the same as that of the oscillation. The waves are detected by another similar circuit, in which the passing waves create a spontaneous spark. Hertz was able to show that the waves are polarized and can be refracted and reflected, much like light; he was also able to measure their wavelengths. All his findings were in exact agreement with Maxwell's theory. Eight years later the Italian scientist G. Marconi made the first successful attempt to generate such waves and use them for long-distance communication. The modern development of the work of Maxwell, Hertz, and Marconi has given us radio, radar, and television.

It is now known that electromagnetic waves encompass not only light and the high-frequency radio waves of Hertz, but also low-frequency radio waves, such as those used in induction heating, all forms of radiant heat, x-rays, the gamma rays of radioactive substances, and some if not all cosmic rays. All these forms of RADIATION obey Maxwell's laws, although the highest-frequency waves, *e.g.* gamma rays, show few wavelike properties and are most easily interpreted by the QUANTUM THEORY. The different forms differ only in their frequency or wavelength. The product of the frequency of any electromagnetic wave and its wavelength is equal to the velocity of light, the same constant whose value was deduced experimentally by Maxwell. Electromagnetic waves exhibit such characteristics as REFLECTION OF LIGHT, REFRACTION OF LIGHT, DIFFRACTION, and DISPERSION.—*A. P. E.*

ELECTROMAGNETISM: the magnetic effect of an electric current; also, the branch of physics dealing with the relationship between electricity and magnetism. The principle of electromagnetism is used in solenoids and electromagnets, electric motors, electrical measuring instruments, television picture tubes, cyclotrons, and countless other devices. The discovery of the relation between electricity and magnetism dates from 1819, when H. C. Oersted showed that a current-carrying wire, placed close to and parallel to a compass needle, causes the needle to turn at right angles to the direction of the current. The deflection is the result of a magnetic field produced by the current. Later, it was found that the magnetic effect of a conductor can be intensified by winding the conductor in the form of a multi-turn helix or solenoid, energizing it with a strong current, and increasing the permeance (magnetic conductance) of the resulting electromagnet by inserting an iron core into the interior of the coil. Additional contributions to early electromagnetic theory and experimentation were made by A. M. Ampère, D. Arago, M. Faraday, and J. Henry (see MAGNETISM).

The traditional right-hand rule enables us to predict the direction of the magnetic field encircling a current-carrying wire (i.e. the direction the north-seeking pole of a compass needle would point): *If the conductor is grasped with the right hand so that the thumb points in the direction of the "Franklinian" (+ to −) current, the fingers will be found to curl in the direction of the field.* Another right-hand rule helps us determine the polarity of an electromagnet: *If the winding of the electromagnet is grasped with the right hand, with the fingers pointing in the direction of the current, the extended thumb will point in the direction of the north pole.* The magnetizing force (H) of an electromagnet may be expressed in ampere-turns/centimeter or ampere-turns/meter of winding length. The resulting magnetization (B), also known as flux density or magnetic induction, is conveniently expressed in lines of force/cm², or gauss. It may also be expressed in webers/m² (1 weber/m² = 10,000 gauss). An electric current may be defined as a movement of electric charges, and a current of 1 ampere as a rate of transfer of charge equal to 1 coulomb/sec. When a wire carrying current is placed at right angles to a magnetic field, the latter will exert a mechanical force on

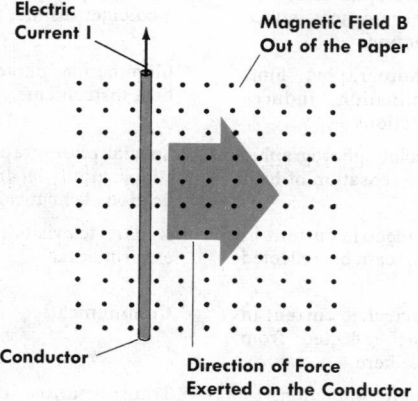

Fig. 1: Force on current-carrying conductor in magnetic field is perpendicular to directions of both current and field. It is the total of such forces on current-carrying wires embedded in the armature (rotor) that turns the rotor of an electric motor.

the electric charges and therefore on the wire itself, which will then move in a direction perpendicular to both the direction of the current and that of the field (Fig. 1). The force on the conductor is given by the equation $F = BIL/10$, where F is the force in dynes, B the flux density in gauss, I the current in amperes, and L the length of the conductor in centimeters. The direction of F can be predicted with the aid of the left-hand *motor* rule (the relationship that underlies the action of a motor). According to this rule: *If the thumb, index, and middle fingers are extended at right angles to one an-*

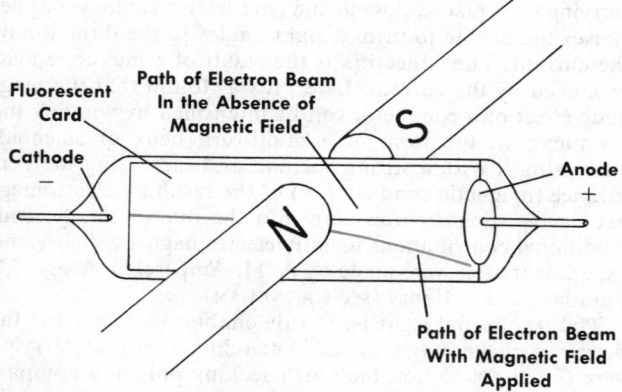

Fig. 2: An electron beam constitutes a current. In this vacuum tube it is deflected by the applied magnetic field. This principle is used in guiding beam in television picture tubes.

other, with the index finger pointing along the field and the middle finger following the direction of the current, the thumb will indicate the direction of the force exerted on the conductor. Application of this rule enables us to determine the direction along which electrons, traversing a partially evacuated tube, will be deflected if a magnetic field is established at right angles to the electron flow (Fig. 2). But it is important to bear in mind that the traditional or "Franklinian" current, for which the rule is designed, passes in a direction opposite to that followed by electrons.

Finally, it is interesting to note that two neighboring parallel wires carrying current in the same direction attract one another. If the wires are so arranged that currents pass through them in opposite directions, the force between them will be one of repulsion.—*A. E.*

ELECTROMETALLURGY: see ELECTRODEPOSITION; ELECTROLYSIS.

ELECTROMETER: a highly sensitive voltmeter capable of measuring electrostatic potentials because it draws almost no current in its operation. Among the earliest electrometers was the gold-leaf electroscope, essentially a sealed bottle containing a metal rod to which two small pieces of gold foil were attached. If electric charge is transferred to the rod, the gold leaves repel one another (see ELECTROSTATICS). The distance of their movement, measured by a microscope having a calibrated scale, gives the magnitude of the electrostatic potential. The electronic electrometer (essentially a vacuum-tube voltmeter) has gradually replaced the older forms of gold-leaf, quadrant, and vibrating-string electrometers. For precision work it has virtually superseded permanent-magnet, moving-coil galvanometers. The best portable moving-coil galvanometers have a sensitivity of the order of 10^4 ohms/v, whereas precision vacuum-tube electrometers achieve a sensitivity of close to 10^{12} ohms/v. The latter draw currents as low as 10^{-12} amp, as compared with 10^{-4} amp for the best moving-coil instruments.—*A. E.*

ELECTROMOTIVE FORCE (*emf*): the energy per unit charge supplied by a current source; this quantity is equal to the source's open-circuit voltage. In general, the voltage drop V between the terminals of a current source increases as the current I drawn from the source decreases. This occurs because every source has internal resistance R and therefore an internal voltage drop IR. Only when I approaches zero does V reach its maximum value E, called the electromotive force (emf). Therefore $V = E - IR$. Most voltmeters draw some current when connected to a current source and therefore measure not E but V.—*H. Sw.*

ELECTROMOTIVE SERIES: a group of elements arranged according to their tendency to become ions. Elements at the top of the series are more active reducing agents (*i.e.* substances that lose electrons) than are members lower in the series. Conversely, the ions of the elements low in the series are more active oxidizing agents, (*i.e.* substances that gain electrons) than are the ions of elements high in the series. (See ION; OXIDATION AND REDUCTION.)

The electromotive series is useful in predicting chemical reactions: in general any free element in the series will replace the ion of any of the elements below it. Thus the elements above hydrogen will replace the hydrogen ion in an acid solution, *e.g.* $2Al + 6HCl = 2AlCl_3 + 3H_2$ or $Pb + 2HCl = PbCl_2 + H_2$. However, no reaction will occur with elements below hydrogen in the series. For example, $Au + HCl$ = No Reaction. Since, according to the arrangement of the series, Zn has a greater tendency to become ionic than Cu, and Cu^{++} has a greater tendency to revert to the metallic state than Zn^{++}, a reaction of metallic zinc with copper sulfate could be predicted to take place in the following manner: $Zn + CuSO_4 = ZnSO_4 + Cu$.

The numerical values in the accompanying table are the approximate ELECTRIC POTENTIALS developed between an electrode of the element and a hydrogen electrode, when arranged as an electric cell by immersing the electrodes in a normal salt solution (see CELL, VOLTAIC). By taking the algebraic difference of their respective potentials, one can determine the theoretical voltage produced by a cell made up of any two electrodes in the series. If, for example, a zinc electrode and a copper electrode were immersed in a normal solution of copper sulfate (making a so-called Daniel cell), a voltmeter connected across the electrodes would show a potential equal to the algebraic difference of the individual potentials, or $+ .76 - (-.34) = + 1.10$ volts.—G. W. M.

Element	Electrode	Potential in Volts
Lithium	Li, Li+	+3.04
Potassium	K, K++	+2.92
Barium	Ba, Ba++	+2.90
Calcium	Ca, Ca++	+2.87
Sodium	Na, Na+	+2.71
Magnesium	Mg, Mg++	+2.37
Aluminum	Al, Al+++	+1.66
Manganese	Mn, Mn++	+1.18
Zinc	Zn, Zn++	+.76
Chromium	Cr, Cr+++	+.74
Iron	Fe, Fe++	+.44
Cadmium	Cd, Cd++	+.41
Cobalt	Co, Co++	+.27
Nickel	Ni, Ni++	+.25
Tin	Sn, Sn++	+.13
Lead	Pb, Pb++	+.12
Hydrogen	H, 2H+	+.00
Copper	Cu, Cu++	−.34
Mercury	Hg, Hg+	−.79
Silver	Ag, Ag+	−.80
Palladium	Pd, Pd++	−.83
Mercury	Hg, Hg++	−.85
Platinum	Pt, Pt++	−1.2
Gold	Au, Au+	−1.4

ELECTRON: one of the elementary, or "fundamental," particles of which the universe is constructed. It was the first to be discovered, is the best understood, and plays the most important role in our everyday lives. According to present knowledge, the electron has six intrinsic properties that completely determine its behavior:

1. Its mass, when measured at rest, of $9.11 (10)^{-28}$ gm.
2. Its single unit of negative electrical charge. Electric charge occurs in two kinds of discrete, indivisible units, distinguishable by the fact that like units repel each other and unlike units attract each other. The type of charge in the electron is arbitrarily called negative, while the other kind (which appears in some of the other elementary particles) is called positive. (See ELECTRONIC CHARGE.)
3. Its continuous spin about an axis passing through it—much like a top (see ELECTRON SPIN AND QUANTUM NUMBER). Unlike the spin of a top, however, the spin of an electron (or of any other elementary particle) cannot be changed by any known means. Spin is a unique property of all elementary particles and partly determines their behavior when in large crowds. (See QUANTUM STATISTICS.)
4. The steady magnetic field it produces, identical with one which would be produced by a tiny bar magnet lying on the electron's spin axis (see MAGNETIC MOMENT). This property can be understood in terms of the laws of ELECTROMAGNETISM, according to which any moving electrical charge produces a magnetic field.
5. The electron belongs to the class of elementary particles, leptons, that exert a peculiar kind of force called the "weak nuclear force." This force is much weaker than the electrical forces associated with the charge, but is stronger than the gravitational force between particles. The weak nuclear force plays an important role in nuclear physics, but not in atomic physics, where the electrical forces have the dominant role.
6. Finally, the electron does *not* interact by means of the other known force occurring in nature—namely, the "strong nuclear force." This is the force that holds the PROTONS and NEUTRONS (and perhaps some of the other elementary particles) together in very tightly bound packages, which constitute the atomic nuclei.

A cloud of electrons surrounds every nucleus. This phenomenon is an essential attribute of the structure of matter. The combination of the nucleus and its attendant electrons is called an atom, and each of the chemical elements is defined by the number of electrons surrounding its nucleus. An electron is bound to its nucleus by the attractive electrical force of a proton inside the nucleus, which has a unit positive electrical charge. The diameter of a typical nucleus is about 10^{-12} cm; the diameter of the orbit of a typical atomic electron is about 10,000 times larger—around 10^{-8} cm. Since the strong nuclear force has a very short range (it does not make itself felt much beyond the boundary of the nucleus), it plays no role in interactions between atoms under conditions encountered in everyday life. Only in stars, in nuclear particle accelerators, and in cosmic radiation do nuclei have sufficient energy to overcome their electrical repulsive forces and approach closely enough to interact via the strong nuclear force. Thus, most physical, all chemical, and all biological phenomena are determined by the interactions of the more loosely bound, outer electrons of the atoms. Furthermore, the fundamental laws governing the low-energy interactions between electrons by means of the electromagnetic forces are believed to be adequately described by present-day QUANTUM THEORY. In fact any such interaction is believed to be described by the SCHRÖDINGER EQUATION, with quantities representing the appropriate forces and properties (1), (2), (3), and (4) inserted. The vast complex of electrical and electronic devices in use today involves the process of separating large numbers of outer electrons from the atoms in various CONDUCTORS AND SEMICONDUCTORS, and causing the resulting streams of free electrons to act in various ways. See ELECTRON DIFFRACTION; ELECTRON EMISSION; ELECTRONICS; ELECTRON MICROSCOPE; ELECTRON MULTIPLIER; ELECTRON STRUCTURE OF ATOMS; ELECTRON TUBE. —S. K.

ELECTRON ACCELERATOR: a device designed to form a beam of high-energy electrons. In order of increasing energy, this beam may be used (1) to make electron diffraction studies of matter, (2) to create x-rays, (3) to create γ-rays, or (4) to probe the nuclei of atoms. In electron diffraction experiments, the relatively low-energy electron is scattered as a wave-packet and it preserves its identity in the scattering process. In x-ray as well as in γ-ray production, part or all of the electron's energy is converted into energetic electromagnetic radiation. In nuclear experiments, electrons up to several billion volts have been used to study interactions of such elementary particles as the proton and neutron with electrons moving with relativistic velocity (*i.e.* a velocity approaching that of light). Different kinds of electron accelerators are employed for the types of experiments described, but are similar in certain respects: each must have some source of electrons; each must have some system of electrodes to form the beam, which system is called the *accelerator electron optics*; and each accelerator will impart energy to the electrons by causing the beam to interact with one or another type of electromagnetic field. Commonly, the source of electrons is a hot filament which literally boils the electrons out of the metal composing the filament. The beam-forming electron-optic system employs magnets or is fabricated from metal electrodes which establish electrostatic fields; these fields in turn force the individual electrons into the desired beam shape.

The two most common accelerating fields are exemplified by the linear accelerator and the betatron. With the linear accelerator, the electron beam is caused to flow down the center of a wave guide. Running with the electron beam is a high-frequency electromagnetic wave which imparts a force to the electron in the direction of its longitudinal electric vector. The betatron operates on the principle that an alternating magnetic field creates a circumferential electric field in the plane at right angles to the magnetic field. The electron beam, bent by the magnetic field, will be accelerated by this induced electric field and thereby gain energy.—*G. S.*

ELECTRON CONFIGURATION: see ELECTRON STRUCTURE OF ATOMS.

ELECTRON DIFFRACTION: the bending of the path of an electron when it goes through an opening comparable in size to its wavelength (see QUANTUM MECHANICS), or passes near an obstacle (see also DIFFRACTION). Since diffraction is a wave phenomenon, the discovery of the diffraction of electrons by C. Davisson and L. H. Germer (and also independently by G. P. Thomson) in 1927 was important in establishing that electrons have a wave nature as well as a particle nature. Davisson and Germer made the discovery by shooting a beam of electrons at a crystal, which consists of a regular array of atoms (obstacles) with spacing comparable to the wavelength of the electrons in the beam. Instead of continuing through the crystal in its original direction, the electron beam was observed to come out at various angles to that direction, these angles being determined by the wavelength of the electrons and the spacing of the crystal atoms.—*E. M. C.*

ELECTRON EMISSION: the release of electrons from a material as a result of the supplying of energy to them. The energy required to free one electron is the work function. This energy may come from heat (THERMIONIC EMISSION), light (photoelectric emission; see PHOTOELECTRIC EFFECT), a high-energy electron beam (SECONDARY EMISSION), or a high electric field (field emission). For alkali metals, *e.g.* sodium, potassium, and cesium, the energy needed is quite small.—*E. M. C.*

ELECTRONIC CHARGE: the charge carried by an ELECTRON. Its magnitude was first measured with accuracy by R. A. Millikan, in 1909, in the famous oil-drop experiment. The American physicist studied the motions of tiny, electrically charged oil droplets under the action of gravity and of uniform electric fields. He calculated the charge on each drop from a knowledge of the fields, the velocity with which the drop fell, and the diameter and mass of the drop. Although the charges differed, they were all integral multiples of a basic charge, identified as that of a single electron. The electronic charge can also be measured by application of Faraday's law of ELECTROLYSIS, although the accuracy of this method is limited by the precision in our knowledge of AVOGADRO'S NUMBER. From refined experiments using these

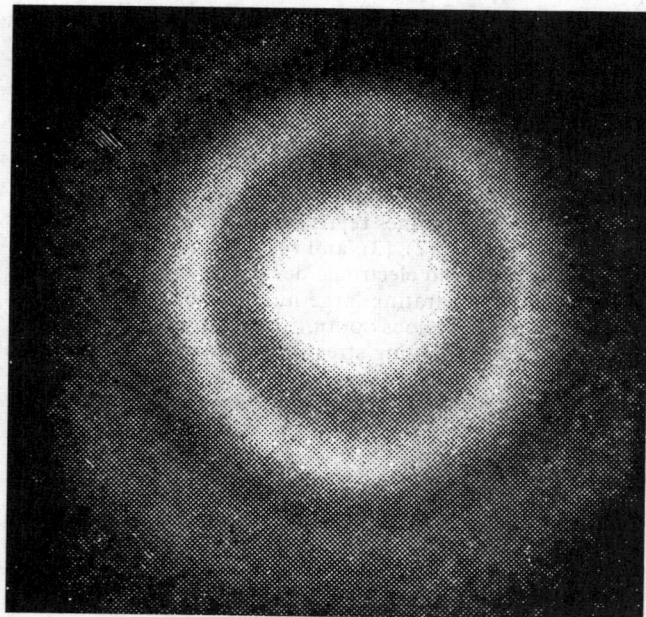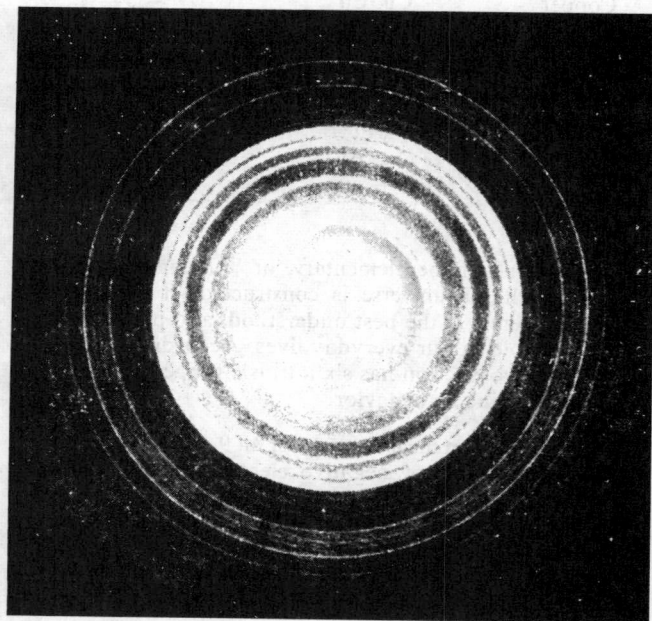

Electron-diffraction photographs: *Left:* an early photograph made by passing electrons accelerated by a potential of 40,000 volts through solid foil (K. Lonsdale). *Right:* a more recent photograph made by passing the electron beam through a crystal of zinc oxide (R. Bernard). Note the similarity of these patterns, with their alternating light and dark fringes, to those produced by light passing around an obstacle, shown in the article DIFFRACTION.

two independent methods, the magnitude of the electronic charge has been found to be $1.60207 \pm 0.00007 \times 10^{-19}$ coulomb.

A proton carries a charge equal in magnitude, but opposite in sign, to the charge of the electron. Since charge is an additive property of matter, the total charge of an electron and a proton combined is zero. By convention, the electron's charge is taken as negative, the proton's as positive. All electrical phenomena occurring in nature appear to be caused exclusively by positive and negative charges that are integral multiples of the electronic charge. Ordinary electric current, for example, is the result of the directed motion of electrons within conducting materials.—*B. Be.*

ELECTRONICS: a major subdivision of electrical science that deals with the principles governing emission of electrons from various solid and liquid materials, and the subsequent control of the freed electrons (by electrical or magnetic means) to perform desired functions, *e.g.* amplification, counting, modulation, oscillation, rectification, switching. (See ELECTRON EMISSION.)

Electronics as it is today cannot be considered as wholly an applied science or branch of electrical engineering, although any "science" of electronics can hardly be distinguished from applied electronics or electronic engineering, and the entire field is best described in terms of its applications (see RADAR; RADIO; TELEVISION) and its technology (ELECTRON TUBE; TRANSISTOR). This article discusses the general capabilities of electron devices, as well as the general scope and background of the field of electronics. Specific electron devices, principles, and theories are discussed in individual articles, as indicated.

Background and Development: Electronics is often said to have begun in 1907 with Lee De Forest's invention of the triode (or "Audion"), an extremely successful electronic amplification device. However, De Forest's triode was, from the standpoint of construction, only a slight modification of J. A. Fleming's diode (or "Fleming valve") which, besides being an effective rectifying device, Fleming used (1904) to receive wireless telegraph messages. Other pioneer achievements predating De Forest's should not be minimized. Among these were Thomas A. Edison's demonstration of electric current as moving negative charges (1883); J. J. Thomson's proof of the existence of the electron (1897); and H. Hertz's early observations (*c.* 1887) of the phenomenon of photoelectric emission, *i.e.* the liberation of negatively charged particles by light energy. (For working principles of diode, triode, and later modifications, see ELECTRON TUBE.)

Until the invention of the transistor (1948) and other solid-state devices, the term electronics was reserved for those electrical systems and circuits employing the electron tube. The term "electron devices" now includes both electron tubes and solid-state elements. The transistor, a so-called semiconductor, has served to bring together the fields of electronic engineering and SOLID-STATE PHYSICS since, from the first, development of transistor theory and application has been a joint effort of engineer and physicist (see CONDUCTOR AND SEMICONDUCTOR). For this reason, the term *"physical* electronics" is now used to emphasize the close connection between advanced electronic engineering and research in solid-state physics.

The transistor since its appearance has revolutionized electronic engineering. It is smaller than the electron (vacuum) tube and simpler, consumes less power, generates less heat, and lasts considerably longer. Before the invention of the transistor it was theoretically possible to perform any given electronic task using electron tubes—*if* size, weight,

Pioneers in electronics: Sir J. J. Thomson, Dr. Irving Langmuir, and Dr. W. D. Coolidge examine 250-watt pliotron, a World War I extension of De Forest's electron tube. (*General Electric*)

cost, and power-demand had not been considered. For example, a satellite *could* have been built that weighed hundreds of pounds more than a transistor-equipped satellite; or an advanced computer *could* have been built, but would have filled several rooms. Space-age requirements have spurred the development of micro-miniaturization techniques. These have materialized in the form of integrated circuits. The IC combines several transistor and diode elements along with their associated passive circuit elements on a single wafer or chip.

General Scope, Capabilities, and Limitations: The majority of individual electronic applications involve low power, the typical range of power-demand running from a few millionths of a watt to 1,000 w (about the power consumed by an electric toaster). Of course, if enough low-power electronic components are grouped together, as in a large computer, the total amount of power required may be substantial. Some relatively high-power, individual electronic applications are found in long-range radio astronomy and radar, but these are a small if important exception. In electronics, low power is almost always associated with low current, and thus electronics is sometimes referred to as "the low-current field."

The development of successful electronic *amplification* devices such as the triode and the transistor has been largely responsible for the great strides in the 20th cent. in the areas of communications, computers, and control systems. Amplification is the raising of the level of an electrical signal to a level where it can perform useful work. In a radio, for example, amplifiers raise the level of the feeble signal picked up by the antenna to a point where it is strong enough to operate the radio speaker. Since the signal picked up by the radio antenna is of the order of a few millionths of a volt, and the output signal to the speaker may be several volts, a voltage amplification of about one million times is involved. (An electrical signal is any form of intelligence carried in electrical impulses, *e.g.* speech, music, coded impulses in a computer, or disturbance signals from the stars.) As in a mechanical-advantage system like a pulley, which requires muscle power, all electronic amplification requires a source of power; this power supply may either be incorporated in the device itself, as in a portable battery radio, or may come from outside, as from conventional plug-in electrical outlets. There are limits to the amount of amplification that can be achieved, although such limits are continually being extended. There are also limits to the frequencies that can be amplified: the lower limit is d-c or zero frequency; the upper limit presently is moving into the optical region of the spectrum (approx. 10^{15} cy/sec). However, the upper frequency amplifiable by electron tubes is much lower, *i.e.* in the radio (or "electronic") range of the spectrum, or approx. 10^{10} cy/sec (see SPECTRUM).

In the field of communications, refinements in electronic amplification have made possible home-entertainment systems such as television, radio, phonographs, and tape recorders. The principle of electronic *switching* also figures prominently in communications, especially in more complex systems such as cross-country direct dialing, transoceanic voice-cabling, and satellite communication systems. Switching involves a complete shift from one circuit to another, or (as with electromechanical systems) the simple opening or closing of a circuit, as in turning off or on a light. (See ELECTRIC CIRCUIT.) This function of electron devices becomes extremely important in COMPUTERS, whose performance is limited by the *switching time* of its electron devices, *i.e.* the time it takes to alter an electrical signal from one discrete level to the next. Switching times are measured in *nanoseconds,* or thousandths of millionths of a second. In the field of CONTROL SYSTEMS, electronic amplification again plays a major role with switching playing a minor one. In most control systems, pneumatic, hydraulic, or electrical machinery is used for the "muscles"; electron devices are used for sensing and "muscle control." For example, electronic-control amplifiers are used on an ocean liner to control the actuators that move the fins which stabilize the ship in a rolling sea. In high-performance aircraft, automatic flight-control systems can completely fly the aircraft, and can be connected to electronic navigational computers for a completely "hands-off" cross-country flight. (See AIRCRAFT INSTRUMENTATION; AUTOMATIC PILOT.)—*H. J. P.*

ELECTRON MICROSCOPE: The human eye is unable to perceive objects which are below a certain limit of size unless aided by devices called MICROSCOPES. The usual optical microscope is a combination of refractive or reflective elements (lenses or mirrors) suitably shaped to provide a magnified image of the object. The magnification can be pushed beyond any prescribed limit by adding more and more imaging elements; but, beyond a certain limit, the magnification becomes "optically empty." The lack of detail in excessive magnifications is due to the fact that the wavelength of the light is setting the limit to the visibility of objects. An optical system can form an image of an object only if the object is commensurate with or larger than the wavelength of the light used for viewing it. Images of objects much smaller than the wavelength cannot be resolved. The smallest distance resolved by an optical system is approximately given by

$$\text{Resolved distance} = \frac{\text{Wavelength}}{\text{Numerical aperture}}$$

where numerical aperture means the product of the refractive index of the object space multiplied by the sine of the half angle used for viewing the object. The numerical aperture for the best optical systems using visible light is of the order of 1.6. Thus, the smallest resolved distance, using visible light, is about 0.0002 mm. No appreciable improvement in numerical aperture being in sight, the only way to image smaller dimensions appears to lie in the use of shorter wavelengths. The use of ultraviolet light improves the resolving power by a factor of two; but when it comes to much shorter wavelengths of electromagnetic radiation, proper optical elements such as lenses or mirrors are unavailable. The resolution of objects below 0.0001 mm thus appeared impossible until 1924, when Louis de Broglie made the discovery that elementary particles, such as electrons and others, can display a wave behavior. The wavelength of such particles can be described by the equation $\lambda = h/mv$, where h is a universal constant, m is the mass of the particle, and v is its velocity. For an electron accelerated by 50,000 v, the wavelength is 100,000 times shorter than the wavelength of green light. Moreover,

General view of an electron microscope installation (*Siemens & Halske, A. G., W Germany*)

the electron can be deflected by electric or magnetic fields, and thus such fields can be used as refractive media. By properly shaping electrostatic or magnetic fields, a lens-like action can be produced and the required high magnification together with very high resolution can be achieved.

At right is shown the arrangement of the essential elements of an electron microscope. The electrons are generated in the so-called electron gun, consisting of a tungsten filament heated to a very high temperature and of electrodes on which high potential differences can be applied to accelerate the electrons to a required high velocity. A good vacuum (about 1/10,000,000 atm) is necessary for the operation of the instrument. Lens action is provided by magnetic fields of axial symmetry, generated by means of circular coils through which a constant current flows. In the transmission-type observation, contrasts are produced through variations in the degree of scattering of electrons on different atoms of the specimen. The highly magnified image can be either observed on a fluorescent screen or recorded directly on a photographic plate. Instrumental magnifications varying between 200 and 200,000 are common, and photographic enlargements of micrographs in excess of 1,000,000 are often used.

The lenses used by electron microscopes have not achieved the same degree of correction as the lenses of optical instruments using visible light. The lens aberrations limit the numerical aperture of the system, and this is why the resolving power of the system is not 100,000 times better than the best light microscope, but somewhat less. At present, the smallest resolved distance achieved in a practical electron microscope is 5.6 Å (1 Å = 1×10^{-7} mm). If we take into account the lens aberrations, this is very close to the theoretically predicted value of the resolution of the system. Electron microscopes are widely applied now in different fields of science such as biology, bacteriology, chemistry, metallurgy, and crystallography, and daily contribute information hitherto inaccessible.—*L. L. M.*

ELECTRON MULTIPLIER: a device consisting of a number of electrodes the electron output of each of which is a multiple greater than one of the number of its incident electrons. Each of these electrodes, called *dynodes,* has as input the electron output of the previous stage. Thus if each dynode has an electron multiplication of n, the output of m such stages in series will be n^m. These dynodes, fabricated of appropriately formed metal plates, multiply the incident electrons as a consequence of the phenomenon known as secondary electron emission; when electrons of appropriate energy are caused to impinge upon a metal, other electrons, the "secondaries," are ejected. In a practical electron multiplier the succeeding dynode stages are frequently mounted in a circular array, together with other appropriate beam-forming (electron optic) electrodes to which are applied appropriate voltages chosen so as to insure that the secondary electron output of each stage becomes the input to the succeeding stage. The stages themselves must be housed in a vacuum tube for the electrons to pass from one dynode to the next. Perhaps the most common application of the electron multiplier is in the PHOTO-MULTIPLIER tube, in which electrons, initially ejected from a photosensitive surface by the incident light, are successively multiplied by the subsequent electron-multiplier dynode

Heart of the electron microscope is the tall column shown in a cut-away view. The electron beam generated at top is focused by magnetic lenses, passes through the specimen, and after additional focusing produces an image on the fluorescent screen at the bottom. (*Siemens & Halske, A. G., W Germany*)

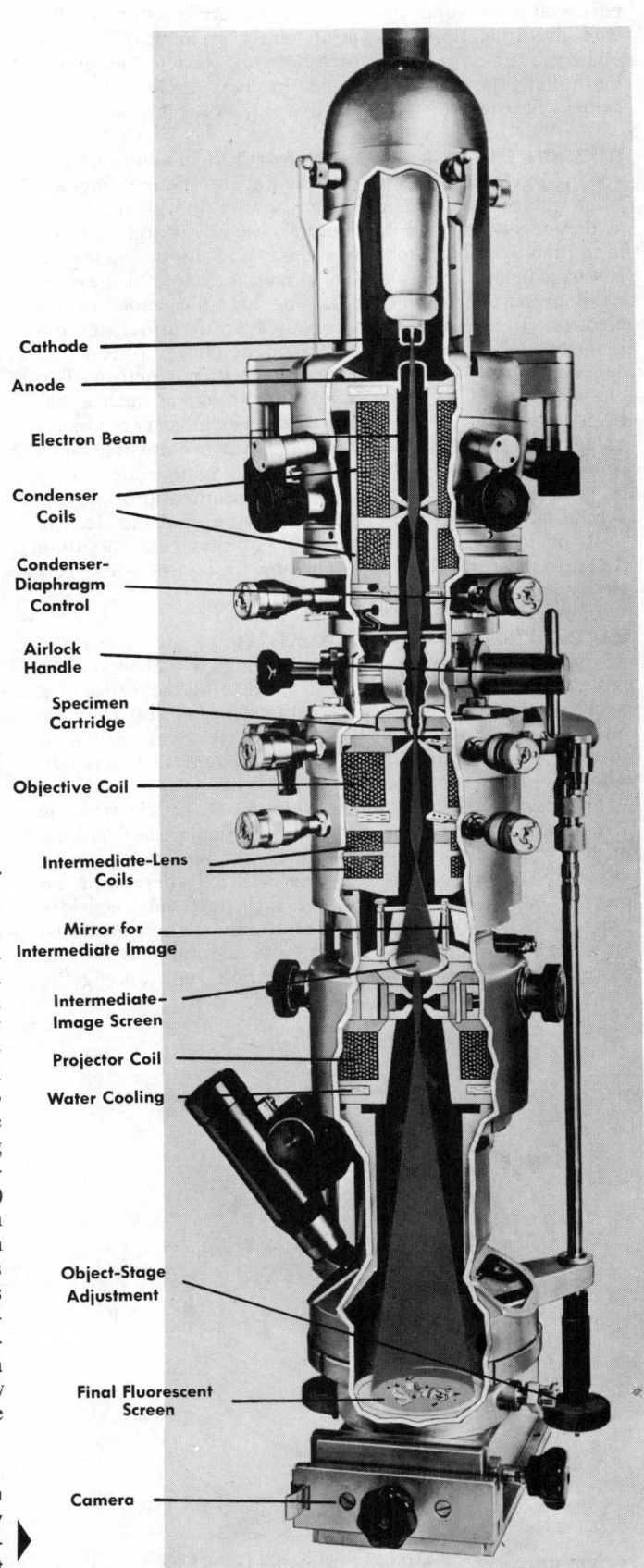

Cathode

Anode

Electron Beam

Condenser Coils

Condenser-Diaphragm Control

Airlock Handle

Specimen Cartridge

Objective Coil

Intermediate-Lens Coils

Mirror for Intermediate Image

Intermediate-Image Screen

Projector Coil

Water Cooling

Object-Stage Adjustment

Final Fluorescent Screen

Camera

stages. The output of the electron multiplier is directly proportional to the input light intensity but, because of the electron multiplication, is of sufficiently great amplitude to operate a meter or some other electrical device. The photomultiplier tube itself is employed in many applications such as the "electric-eye" type of switch.—*G. S.*

ELECTRON SPIN AND QUANTUM NUMBER: In addition to revolving in closed orbits around the nucleus of an atom, electrons spin on their axes rather in the way that planets rotate as they revolve around the Sun. Because any charged particle in motion is accompanied by a magnetic field, this spin gives rise to magnetic effects, and is, in fact, the cause of the magnetic properties of matter. If, for example, more of the electrons in an atom spin one way than the other, the uncompensated spin yields a net magnetic effect; if the atoms can be aligned, the effect causes over-all magnetism. This characteristic of an electron in orbit around a nucleus has been assigned a quantum number m_s, which has two possible values, $+\frac{1}{2}$ and $-\frac{1}{2}$, corresponding to the two possible directions of spin. Together with the quantum numbers describing the energy level, the orbital angular momentum, and the orbital magnetic moment (due to the motion of the electron in its orbit), this quantum number completes the quantum description of the electron's behavior. (See ATOM; QUANTUM MECHANICS.)—*E. M. R.*

ELECTRON STRUCTURE OF ATOMS: Atoms are electrically neutral combinations of positive and negative charges. The positive charge is localized at the center of the ATOM in a nucleus whose diameter is approximately 10^{-13} cm. The negative charge, consisting of ELECTRONS, is distributed in a structure of concentric "shells" about the nucleus in a region whose diameter is approximately 10^{-8} cm.

The basic shell structure is determined by electrostatic attraction between each electron in a particular shell and the nucleus, due allowance being made for the screening of some nuclear charge by electrons in inner shells. To determine the precise shape and position of the shell, one must consider other forces, *e.g.* the electrostatic repulsion between electrons. Of lesser importance are magnetic interactions between the currents and spins of the atomic particles and among the

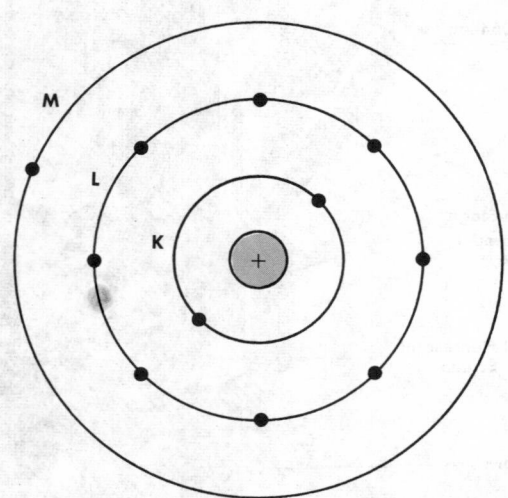

Sodium atom has 11 electrons arranged in 3 shells—2 in the K shell, 8 in the L shell, and 1 in the M shell.

spins themselves. Besides affecting the shell positions, the magnetic interactions cause a splitting of the basic shell structure into subshells whose separations are on the whole small compared to the separation between shells. Electronic shells are designated in order by the letters *K, L, M*, etc., starting with the shell closest to the nucleus; the subshells are designated by Roman numerals. The total number of electrons which can occupy any shell is restricted by the Pauli EXCLUSION PRINCIPLE. The order of occupation of the shells as one goes from one atom to the next in the periodic table is determined by the requirement that the energy of the resultant configuration be a minimum. This generally means that inner shells are completed before outer ones are started, but exceptions occur for heavier atoms.—*S. Bo.*

ELECTRON TUBE: a device designed to generate, detect, amplify, or control electrical signals; it consists of an envelope of glass, ceramic, or metal surrounding several electrodes (filaments), cathodes, grids, and plates (or collectors). Charged particles, as electrons and ions, flow from one electrode to another, creating currents whose variations produce the desired results. The envelope serves to maintain a vacuum or retain a gas, *e.g.* hydrogen, in the tube. The use of gas has the advantage of causing stronger currents within the tube, as the result of ionization of the gas when charges emitted from the electrodes hit neutral gas molecules; but a majority of modern tubes are vacuum-type, for ease of control of currents. Until recently, electron tubes were used in practically all radio, radar, television, and long-line telephone and telegraph circuits, as well as in many industrial control and processing operations, and in military weapons systems. Transistors, tunnel diodes, and other solid-state devices are now in use in many electronic systems, especially computers, data-processing apparatus, and home receivers. (See ELECTRONICS.) Nevertheless, electron tubes are still found in the majority of present-day electronic applications because of their special advantages of power-handling capability, versatility, and economy. Specific functions performed by electron tubes include oscillation, detection, modulation, amplification, rectification, voltage regulation, switching, counting, and automatic frequency control. Principal types of these tubes are diodes, triodes, tetrodes, pentodes, Klystrons, magnetrons, and traveling-wave tubes. Until World War II, the first four types were in general use; but the advent of radar and opening of the microwave and millimeter-wave regions of the electromagnetic SPECTRUM brought about development and widespread use of the magnetron, Klystron, and a series of traveling-wave tubes known as forward- and backward-wave oscillators and amplifiers.

Diodes: The electrodes of the diode (Fig. 1) include only a filament, cathode, and plate. The filament is a wire, frequently made of tungsten metal, which is heated by battery or transformer current. Heat from the filament is transferred via a nickel sleeve to the cathode, which is a cylinder wrapped directly around the nickel sleeve. The transferred heat increases the kinetic energy of electrons in the cathode, and those with sufficient velocity escape and are attracted over to the plate, which is maintained at positive voltage with respect to the cathode. Accordingly, a current flows from cathode to plate, thence through the high-voltage supply and the load resistance. If the high-voltage supply is alternating, current flows through the load only on positive polarity of the alternating voltage, so that intermittent direct current is produced. This is the *rectification* action of diode-type tubes.

Triodes: Insertion of an additional electrode in the form of a metallic mesh, termed the grid, transforms the diode to a *triode.* The grid is placed in close geometric proximity to the

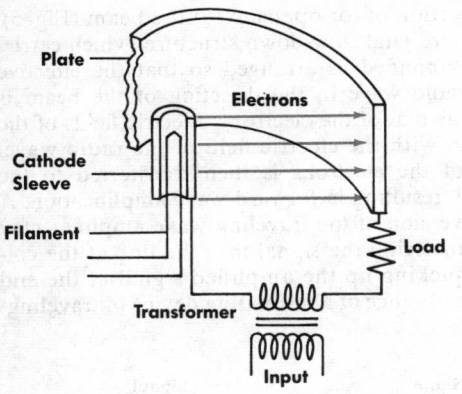

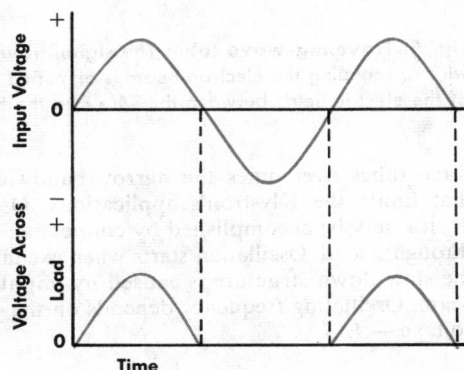

Fig. 1: Diode tube has two electrodes—the cathode, which emits electrons, and the anode (or plate), which collects them. Since electrons can travel only from cathode to anode, alternating current from the transformer is converted to pulsating direct current by the tube.

cathode, so that small changes in potential between grid and cathode (as might be caused by the weak signals picked up by a radio antenna) produce relatively large changes in cathode-to-plate current. The ratio of change in the plate-to-cathode voltage to change in grid-to-cathode voltage ($\Delta e_p/\Delta e_g$) is known as the amplification factor. For any increase in grid-to-cathode voltage (Δe_g) the amplification factor indicates the increase in plate-to-cathode voltage (Δe_p), and therefore the corresponding increase in plate current (I_p). Thus relatively small changes in signals applied from grid to cathode can cause large changes in plate current that can perform useful work, *e.g.* the production of audible frequencies in a radio loudspeaker. Figs. 2a and 2b show triode amplification.

Tetrodes and Pentodes: These are essentially refinements of, rather than departures from, the grid-type triode tube. *Tetrodes* are formed from triodes by introduction of a "screen-grid." Its purpose is to reduce the inter-electrode capacity between grid and plate elements, thus minimizing feedback currents from plate to grid, which would tend to cause oscillations in any amplifier circuit using the tetrode. The screen-grid is made slightly less positive than the plate, with respect to cathode, so that the space-charge cloud is attracted to the screen-grid, and is minimized. *Pentodes* are improvements on tetrodes in that, besides the grid and screen-grid, they have a third electrode (termed the "suppressor-grid") between screen-grid and plate, closer to the plate. The suppressor-grid is usually connected internally to the cathode.

Its purpose is to repel "secondary" electrons emitted when the plate is bombarded with electrons from the cathode. Repulsion of these "secondaries" helps prevent space-charge accumulation near the plate, and the resulting reduction of plate current. Tetrodes and pentodes are used in most current electron-tube applications, since their characteristics permit design of efficient circuits without imposing requirements of large physical size on the tubes and high-voltage capabilities on power supplies.

Magnetrons: Ordinary radio waves, the type received and amplified by triodes, tetrodes, and pentodes, are of the order of 100 m in wavelength. The possibility of using microwave beams for point-to-point communication with an accompanying reduction in power output stimulated the development of microwave (wavelengths ranging from 0.1 to 10 cm) transmission. The *magnetron,* for example, is a generator of microwave oscillations. Its operation depends on deflection of electrons emitted from a cathode, which electrons would normally go radially outward to a plate, concentric with the cathode. Deflection is caused by a magnetic field whose direction is parallel to the length of the cathode. Emitted electrons curve around in circular and cycloidal paths, inducing alternating voltages of microwave frequencies as they pass the vanes of the magnetron. The cavities between vanes resonate at the working wavelength of the oscillator. A pick-up loop is inserted into one of these cavities to transfer power out of the magnetron.

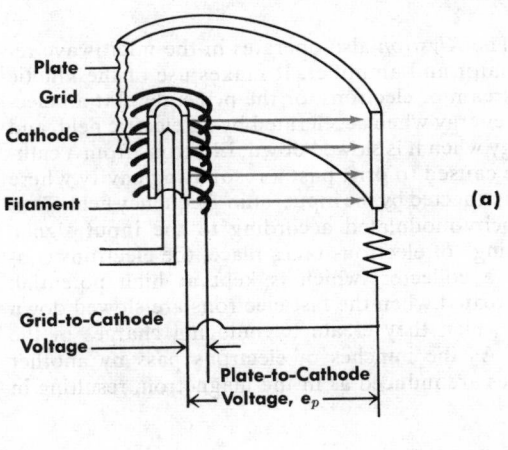

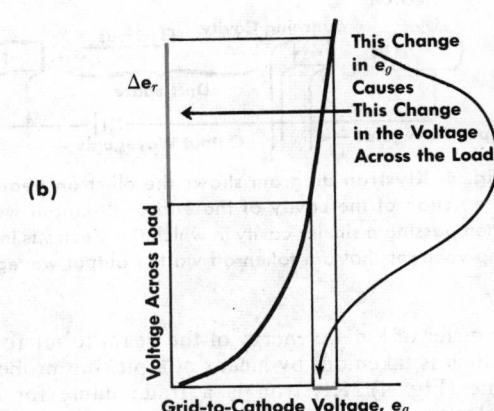

Fig. 2: Triode tube has three electrodes. The grid placed between the cathode and the plate controls the flow of electrons, and because of proximity of the cathode only a small change in grid voltage is required to cause a large change in the current through the tube and the voltage across the load.

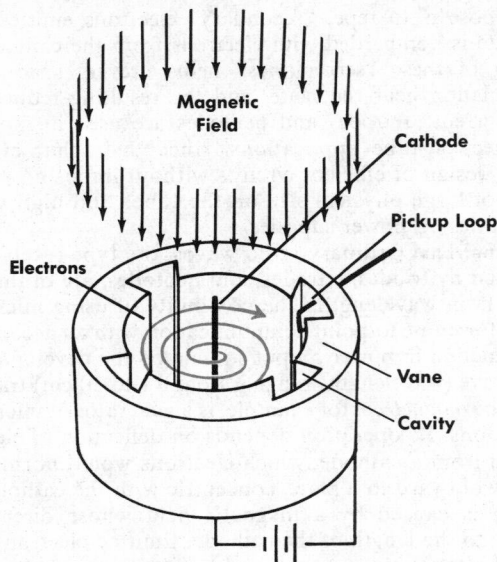

Fig. 3: Magnetron diagram shows the spiral path of an electron under the influence of the electric field between the vanes and the cathode and the magnetic field applied at right angles to it. The alternating voltages induced in the cavities between the vanes are taken off via the output loop.

Klystrons: The *Klystron* also operates in the microwave region, as oscillator and amplifier. It makes use of the kinetic energy of a stream of electrons, or the principle that an electron acquires energy when accelerated by an electric field, and gives up energy when it is slowed down. Electrons from a cathode (gun) are caused to drift past a resonating cavity where their velocity is affected by the input radio-frequency field. Thus they are velocity-modulated according to the input signal. After "bunching" of electrons takes place, the electrons continue toward a collector, which is kept at high potential. Bunching is created when the fast electrons are slowed down by the fields which they create by inducing charges in the cavity metal. As the bunches of electrons pass by another cavity, voltages are induced as in the magnetron, resulting in

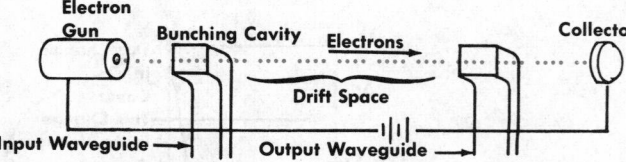

Fig. 4: Klystron diagram shows the electron beam bunched by the action of the cavity of the end of the input waveguide and then passing a similar cavity in which the electrons induce alternating voltages that are taken off via the output waveguide.

transfer of kinetic energy of the beam to microwave power, which is taken out by means of a pick-up probe and coaxial line (Fig. 4). Klystron is a trade name for one type of velocity-modulation tube. It is used mainly for amplification, although its utility is limited to narrow bandwidths.

The Traveling-wave Tube: This also is a velocity-modulated device but it has no resonating cavities. Traveling-wave tube action, as an oscillator or amplifier, depends upon interaction of a beam of electrons with a radio wave, which prop-

agates in the direction of (or opposite to) the beam (Fig. 5). The helical or interdigital slow-down structure, which carries the wave to be amplified, is arranged so that the effective velocity of the radio wave in the direction of the beam is almost the same as that of the electrons. Electric fields of the electrons interact with the electric field of the radio wave. Kinetic energy of the electrons is then transferred to the microwave signal, resulting in forward-wave amplification. A backward-wave version of the traveling-wave amplifier may be arranged by inserting the signal into the line at the collector end, and picking up the amplified signal at the end near the gun. The absence of a resonating device in traveling-

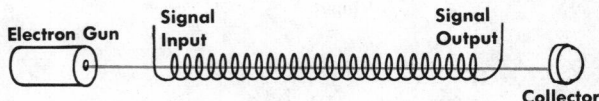

Fig. 5: Traveling-wave tube: The signal traveling in the spiral wire surrounding the electron beam is amplified by the interaction of the electric fields between the wire and the beam.

wave tubes overcomes the narrow-bandwidth requirement that limits the Klystron's applications. Oscillation of the device may be accomplished by connecting output to input through a load. Oscillation starts when excitation of waves in the slow-down structure is caused by impulse noises in the beam. Oscillating frequency depends on the gun-to-collector voltage.—*A. S.*

ELECTROPHORESIS: the migration of molecules in solution when placed in an electric field. Although the shape and size of the molecule influence the absolute rate of migration, the major factor is the net charge. Any molecule which is electrically charged can be separated from other molecules at the appropriate point. For example, electrophoretic analysis is used to characterize individual proteins in terms of mobility, to determine their purity, and to analyze protein mixtures quantitatively. Proteins possess both positive and negative charges which are equal at the isoelectric point of the protein; at this point electrophoretic mobility falls to zero, and the protein may readily be precipitated.—*F. F.*

ELECTROPLATING: see ELECTRODEPOSITION.

ELECTROSCOPE: see ELECTROMETER.

ELECTROSTATIC GENERATOR: a device for charging bodies electrostatically; it is usually used to produce a high electric potential. Electrostatic generators have their origin in the rotating sulfur sphere of Otto von Guericke and the spinning glass globes built by Francis Hauksbee (see ELECTROSTATICS). These depended on the generation of electric charge by friction. In modern electrostatic machines, electric charge is generated by induction, as in the *Wimshurst machine*. This was used as a high-voltage source for some of the first x-ray tubes built in the early 1900s and is still used for demonstration experiments in physics. The machine consists of two round glass plates that rotate very closely to each other and in opposite directions. Fastened along the rim of each plate are strips of metal. In the diagram, the inner ovals represent the metal strips on the front glass disk, which rotates counterclockwise, and the outer ovals represent strips on the back glass disk, which rotates clockwise. Assume a small positive charge on *A* at the start. *A,* very close to *B,* will attract electrons, causing them to flow through the stationary metal rod

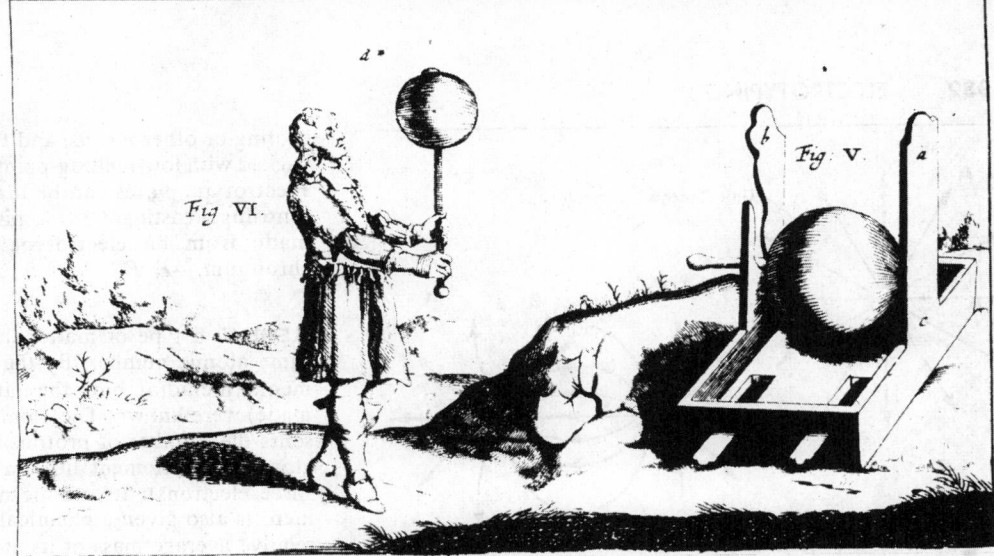

CB from *C* to *B*. This makes *B* negatively charged and *C* positively charged. Now *B* moves to *B′*, where its negative charge drives electrons from *A′* through the stationary connecting metal rod *A′D′* toward *D′*, making *D′* negative and *A′* positive. At the same time, *C*, which is positive, has moved to *C′*, where its positive charge tends to attract electrons into *D′*, thus aiding the effect of *B′* on *A′* and *D′*. Then *A′* moves to *A* while *D′* moves to *D*, and the inductive cycle is repeated. The net effect is that positive charge moves toward the collector at right and negative charge moves toward the collector at left. The collectors are usually connected to Leyden jars to increase the capacity of the system. The Leyden jars serve as CAPACITORS from which the useful electrical discharge occurs.

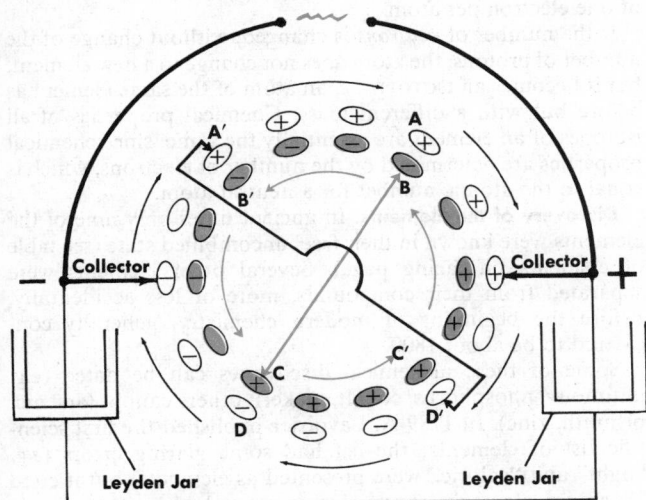

Wimshurst machine, shown in schematic diagram, employs two glass disks mounted on a single axle. The inner circle of ellipses indicates the charged metal strips on the front disk, which rotates counterclockwise; the outer circle indicates the metal strips on the back disk, which rotates clockwise. The charges are collected by brushes and accumulated in Leyden jars.

The most important electrostatic generator now in use is the VAN DE GRAAFF GENERATOR, invented by Robert Van de Graaff in 1931. In this device electric charges are sprayed upon an endless nonconducting belt, which carries the charges to a large hollow metallic conductor (frequently a hollow sphere), very well insulated, upon which a very high potential builds up. The effectiveness of this system lies chiefly in the fact that charges at relatively low potential are delivered to the *inside* of the hollow conductor, which is virtually free of electrical forces. The charges then spread to the *outside* of the conductor, where the electric potential may reach several million volts. Van de Graaff generators are used with almost all PARTICLE ACCELERATORS to provide the initial injection velocity.—*H. Sw.*

ELECTROSTATICS: the science concerned with those properties of electric charges not dependent on the motion of the charges. Since Charles François du Fay's letter to the Royal Society of London in 1733, it has been known that practically all solids except metals become electrically charged when rubbed with other substances. A dry piece of paper placed against a dry wall and rubbed briskly with the hand becomes electrified and sticks to the wall for some time. The first electrostatic machine to generate large charges by friction was made by Otto von Guericke, burgomaster of Magdeburg, in 1660. It consisted of a sulfur sphere that became electrified when rotated against the hand. With this machine von Guericke observed electrostatic repulsion and attraction.

It has become customary to call *positive* any electrification like that existing on a glass rod which has been rubbed with silk. Two such electrified glass rods will repel each other, but each will be attracted to a hard rubber rod or stick of sealing wax that has been rubbed with fur. The hard rubber is said to be *negatively* charged, and it will repel another charged hard rubber rod. To generalize, unlike electric charges attract each other, while like charges repel. The magnitude of the electric force *F* between two charges of magnitudes Q_1 and Q_2, separated by a distance *D* that is large in proportion to the dimensions of the charges, may be calculated from a law verified by Charles Coulomb, a French military engineer, in 1785:

$$F = K \frac{Q_1 Q_2}{D^2}$$

where *K* is a proportionality constant chosen to make the units in the equation compatible.

Electrification of solids is explained in terms of the movement of electrons into or out of bodies. Though matter is composed of both positive and negative charges, only a few of the negative charges (electrons) are sufficiently free to move through the structure. When glass is rubbed with silk, the silk, having a greater attraction for electrons than the glass, pulls electrons away from the glass, leaving it with an excess of positive charges.

The region of influence around electric charges is called the *electric field,* usually represented graphically by *lines of*

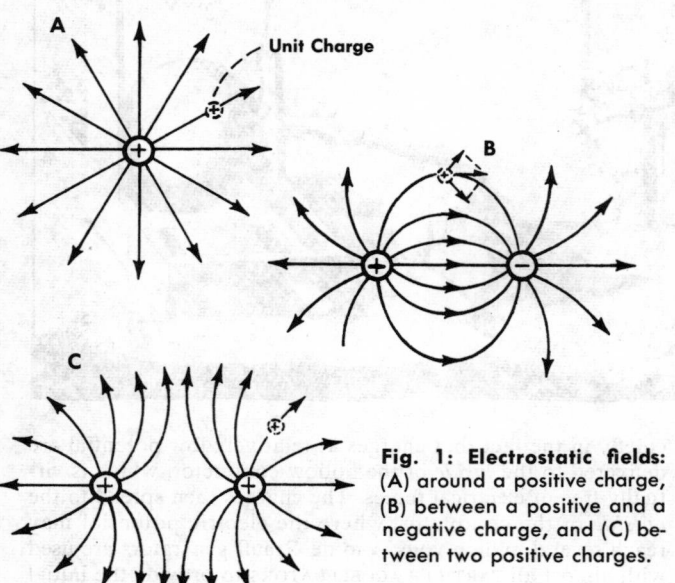

Fig. 1: Electrostatic fields:
(A) around a positive charge,
(B) between a positive and a
negative charge, and (C) between two positive charges.

force. Fig. 1 shows the maps of such lines of force for three simple cases. The directions of these lines are at all points the same as the directions of the electric forces which would act upon very small positive charges placed there.

A neutral body may be charged either by direct contact with a charged body or by induction. If a positively charged glass rod *B* is put near a neutral insulated metal sphere *A* (Fig. 2), free electrons in *A* will be attracted toward the side nearest *B*. Then as *B* is brought closer to *A*, a spark eventually passes between them; electrons jump directly from *A* to *B*. (Lightning is just such a spark between clouds or between clouds and ground.) If *B* now is withdrawn, *A* will have a deficiency of electrons; it will be positively charged. Suppose, however, that before the spark has passed, the sphere *A* is touched by the hand. Since the human body is a conductor in contact with the ground, and since the ground acts as a reservoir of electrons, there will be a flow of electrons into *A* as a result of the attraction of the positive charges on *B*. If the hand is now removed and then *B* is removed, *A* will be negatively charged. This procedure is called "charging by induction." See ELECTROSTATIC GENERATOR.—*H. Sw.*

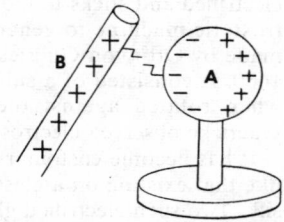

Fig. 2: Charging a neutral body (A) using a positively charged rod (B). The charge ultimately acquired by A may be positive, if the charging is accomplished directly, or negative, if the charging is by induction.

ELECTROTYPING: a process for making the metal plates, called *electrotypes,* used to print books and magazines. An electrotype is made by taking an impression in a thin sheet of wax, plastic material, or soft lead (for fine printing) of the original type and line cuts or halftones for illustrations all locked in position in a form. The wax or plastic mold is then coated with graphite to make its surface electrically conductive. A thin layer of copper, nickel, chromium, or similar metal is electrically deposited on the surface of the mold (see ELECTRODEPOSITION). The mold material is then removed by

heating or other means, and the remaining thin metal shell is backed with low-melting-point molten metal to give it rigidity. Electrotype plates can be made flat or curved by means of centrifugal casting. Over a million clear printed copies can be made from an electrotype plate coated with nickel or chromium.—*E. E.*

ELEMENT: a type of matter that possesses only atoms of the same atomic number. By the end of 1966, 104 different elements (including both the naturally occurring and the man-made) were known. The atomic number of an element represents the number of protons in one of its atoms; thus every atom of the element lithium has three protons (as well as three electrons): its atomic number is therefore 3. An element is also given a chemical ATOMIC WEIGHT, which is the relative average mass of its atoms compared to carbon[12], the average mass of which has been arbitrarily assigned the value of 12.00000.

The nature of an element is best discussed in terms of its individual atoms. Any given ATOM has a nucleus consisting of a certain number of protons and neutrons, surrounded by electrons. Any change in the number of these subatomic particles changes the properties of the atom in some way.

If the number of *protons* is changed, the atom is changed into an atom of another element. Thus the atoms of uranium (at. no. 92) emit alpha particles, each of which contains two protons, and become thorium atoms (at. no. 90) (see RADIO-ACTIVITY).

The loss or gain of *electrons* does not produce a new element, but does change the chemical properties. For example, the chemical behavior of neutral sodium atoms in sodium metal is different from that of sodium ions, which result from the loss of one electron per atom.

If the number of *neutrons* is changed, without change of the number of protons, the atom does not change to a new element, but it becomes an ISOTOPE, *i.e.* an atom of the same element as before but with a different mass. Chemical properties of all isotopes of an element are essentially the same, since chemical properties are determined by the number of electrons, which is equal to the atomic number for a neutral atom.

Discovery of the Elements: In ancient times only nine of the elements were known in their free, uncombined state (see table of elements on facing page). Several other elements were separated from their compounds, more or less accidentally, before the beginning of modern chemistry, generally considered to be about 1800.

Some of these alchemical discoveries can be dated (*e.g.* antimony, phosphorus, cobalt, nickel); others cannot (arsenic, bismuth, zinc). In 1789 A. Lavoisier published the first scientific list of elements; the list had some glaring errors (*e.g.* "light" and "caloric" were presented as elements) but it cited 23 actual elements. Lavoisier suggested chemical criteria (which he himself did not consistently follow) for proving that an element is not a compound or something else; and chemical reactions remained the sole means for proving a substance was indeed elemental until after 1860, when R. Bunsen and G. Kirchhoff pioneered the development of spectrochemical analysis. By that date, 63 of the presently verified elements had been discovered; by 1900, 82 had been discovered; and by 1925, all the now-known elements were on the list except the ARTIFICIAL ELEMENTS subsequently synthesized by nuclear bombardment. Scientific advances of general and far-reaching significance have tended to precede discovery of a number of new elements. Thus H. Davy's discovery, by means of electrolysis, of two alkali metals (sodium and potassium) and four alkaline earth metals (barium, calcium, magnesium, strontium) during 1807–08 followed a gen-

Faculty Me
Thursday, A
1:1!
McL R

Present: Robert Berg, Judy Berger,
Bruce Glassco, Alan Goldsmith, Jill Gra
Tom Lewis, Dr. Victor Macaruso, Ann
Viken Peltekian, David Peterson, Joe R
Richard Wagner, Jeanne Waits, Diane \

Absent: Vince Brautigam, Karl Fager
Jannusch, Mike Miller, Marlene Penf
Jonathan Stanley, Dr. Charles Stubbs.

CALL TO ORDER: 1:16 p.m. Academic D

OLD BUSINESS: None

NEW BUSINESS: None

UPDATES:

Copies of Mount Senario College's "Pla
Achievement" were distributed. The
special help in revising the document:
Saxild, Liz Sheridan. The Plan will be p
next faculty meeting

THE CHEMICAL ELEMENTS AND THEIR DISCOVERERS

Element and Symbol	Atomic Number	Atomic Weight	Discoverer and Date	Element and Symbol	Atomic Number	Atomic Weight	Discoverer and Date
Actinium (Ac)	89	227.0	A. Debierne (1899)	Mercury (Hg)	80	200.6	Prehistoric
Aluminum (Al)	13	27.0	F. Wöhler (1827)	Molybdenum (Mo)	42	96.0	K. Scheele (1778)
Americium (Am)	95	(243)*	G. Seaborg et al. (1944)	Neodymium (Nd)	60	144.3	C. von Welsbach (1885)
Antimony (Sb)	51	121.8	B. Valentine (1604)	Neon (Ne)	10	20.2	W. Ramsay and M. Travers (1898)
Argon (A)	18	39.9	W. Ramsay and J. Rayleigh (1894)	Neptunium (Np)	93	(237)	E. McMillan and P. Abelson (1940)
Arsenic (As)	33	74.9	Medieval	Nickel (Ni)	28	58.7	A. Cronstedt (1751)
Astatine (At)	85	(210)	E. Segrè et al. (1940)	Niobium (Columbium) (Nb)	41	92.9	C. Hatchett (1801)
Barium (Ba)	56	137.4	H. Davy (1808)	Nitrogen (N)	7	14.0	D. Rutherford (1772)
Berkelium (Bk)	97	(249)	S. Thompson et al. (1949)	Nobelium (No)	102	(254)	P. Fields et al. (disputed) (1957)
Beryllium (Be)	4	9.0	N. Vauquelin (1798)				A. Ghiorso et al. (1958)
Bismuth (Bi)	83	209.0	Medieval	Osmium (Os)	76	190.2	S. Tennant (1803)
Boron (B)	5	10.8	J. Gay-Lussac and L. Thenard (1808)	Oxygen (O)	8	16.0	J. Priestley (1774)
Bromine (Br)	35	79.9	A. Balard (1826)	Palladium (Pd)	46	106.7	W. Wollaston (1803)
Cadmium (Cd)	48	112.4	F. Stromeyer (1817)	Phosphorus (P)	15	31.0	H. Brand (1669)
Calcium (Ca)	20	40.1	H. Davy (1808)	Platinum (Pt)	78	195.1	D. de Ulloa (1735)
Californium (Cf)	98	(251)	S. Thompson et al. (1950)				C. Wood (independently) (1741)
Carbon (C)	6	12.0	Prehistoric	Plutonium (Pu)	94	(242)	G. Seaborg et al. (1940)
Cerium (Ce)	58	140.1	J. Berzelius and W. d'Hisinger (1803)	Polonium (Po)	84	210.0	P. and M. Curie (1898)
			M. Klaproth (independently) (1803)	Potassium (K)	19	39.1	H. Davy (1807)
Cesium (Cs)	55	132.9	R. Bunsen and G. Kirchhoff (1860)	Praseodymium (Pr)	59	140.9	C. von Welsbach (1885)
Chlorine (Cl)	17	35.5	K. Scheele (1774)	Promethium (Pm)	61	(147)	J. Marinsky et al. (1947)
Chromium (Cr)	24	52.0	N. Vauquelin (1797)	Protactinium (Pa)	91	231.0	F. Soddy and J. Cranston (1913); O. Hahn
Cobalt (Co)	27	58.9	G. Brandt (c.1735)				and L. Meitner (independently) (1917)
Copper (Cu)	29	63.5	Prehistoric	Radium (Ra)	88	226.1	P. and M. Curie (1898)
Curium (Cm)	96	(248)	G. Seaborg et al. (1944)	Radon (Rn)	86	222.0	E. Rutherford (*thoron* isotope) (1899)
Dysprosium (Dy)	66	162.5	L. de Boisbaudran (1886)				E. Dorn (*radon* isotope) (1900)
Einsteinium (E)	99	(254)	A. Ghiorso et al. (1952)	Rhenium (Re)	75	186.2	W. Noddack and I. Tacke (1925)
Erbium (Er)	68	167.2	C. Mosander (1843)	Rhodium (Rh)	45	102.9	W. Wollaston (1803)
Europium (Eu)	63	152.0	E. Demarçay (1896)	Rubidium (Rb)	37	85.5	R. Bunsen and G. Kirchhoff (1861)
Fermium (Fm)	100	(253)	A. Ghiorso et al. (1953)	Ruthenium (Ru)	44	101.1	K. Claus (or Klaus) (1844)
Fluorine (F)	9	19.0	H. Moissan (1886)	Samarium (Sm)	62	150.4	L. de Boisbaudran (1879)
Francium (Fr)	87	(223)	M. Perey (1939)	Scandium (Sc)	21	45.0	L. Nilson (1879)
Gadolinium (Gd)	64	156.9	J. C. de Marignac (1880)	Selenium (Se)	34	79.0	J. Berzelius (1818)
Gallium (Ga)	31	69.7	L. de Boisbaudran (1875)	Silicon (Si)	14	28.1	J. Berzelius (1823)
Germanium (Ge)	32	72.6	C. Winkler (1886)	Silver (Ag)	47	107.9	Prehistoric
Gold (Au)	79	197.0	Prehistoric	Sodium (Na)	11	23.0	H. Davy (1807)
Hafnium (Hf)	72	178.6	D. Coster and G. Hevesy (1923)	Strontium (Sr)	38	87.6	H. Davy (1808)
Helium (He)	2	4.0	W. Ramsay (1894)	Sulfur (S)	16	32.1	Prehistoric
Holmium (Ho)	67	164.9	J. Soret (1878)	Tantalum (Ta)	73	181.0	A. Ekeberg (1802)
			P. Cleve (independently) (1879)	Technetium (Tc)	43	(99)	E. Segrè and C. Perrier (1937)
Hydrogen (H)	1	1.0	H. Cavendish (1766)	Tellurium (Te)	52	127.6	M. von Reichenstein (1782)
Indium (In)	49	114.8	F. Reich and T. Richter (1863)	Terbium (Tb)	65	158.9	C. Mosander (1843)
Iodine (I)	53	126.9	B. Courtois (1811)	Thallium (Tl)	81	204.4	W. Crookes (1861)
Iridium (Ir)	77	192.2	S. Tennant (1803)	Thorium (Th)	90	232.0	J. Berzelius (1828)
Iron (Fe)	26	55.9	Prehistoric	Thulium (Tm)	69	168.9	P. Cleve (1879)
Krypton (Kr)	36	83.8	W. Ramsay and M. Travers (1898)	Tin (Sn)	50	118.7	Prehistoric
Lanthanum (La)	57	138.9	C. Mosander (1839)	Titanium (Ti)	22	47.9	W. Gregor (1791)
Lawrencium (Lw)	103	(257)	A. Ghiorso et al. (1961)	Tungsten (Wolfram) (W)	74	183.9	J. and F. d'Elhuyar (1783)
Lead (Pb)	82	207.2	Prehistoric	Uranium (U)	92	238.1	M. Klaproth (1789)
Lithium (Li)	3	6.9	A. Arfvedson (1817)	Vanadium (V)	23	51.0	N. Sefström (1830)
Lutetium (Lu)	71	175.0	G. Urbain (1906)	Xenon (Xe)	54	131.3	W. Ramsay and M. Travers (1898)
			C. von Welsbach (independently) (1907)	Ytterbium (Yb)	70	173.0	C. Marignac (1878)
Magnesium (Mg)	12	24.3	H. Davy (1808)	Yttrium (Y)	39	88.9	J. Gadolin (1794)
Manganese (Mn)	25	54.9	K. Scheele (1774)	Zinc (Zn)	30	65.4	Medieval
Mendelevium (Mv)	101	(256)	A. Ghiorso et al. (1955)	Zirconium (Zr)	40	91.2	M. Klaproth (1789)

* A number in parentheses under "Atomic Weight" is the mass number of the most stable isotope.

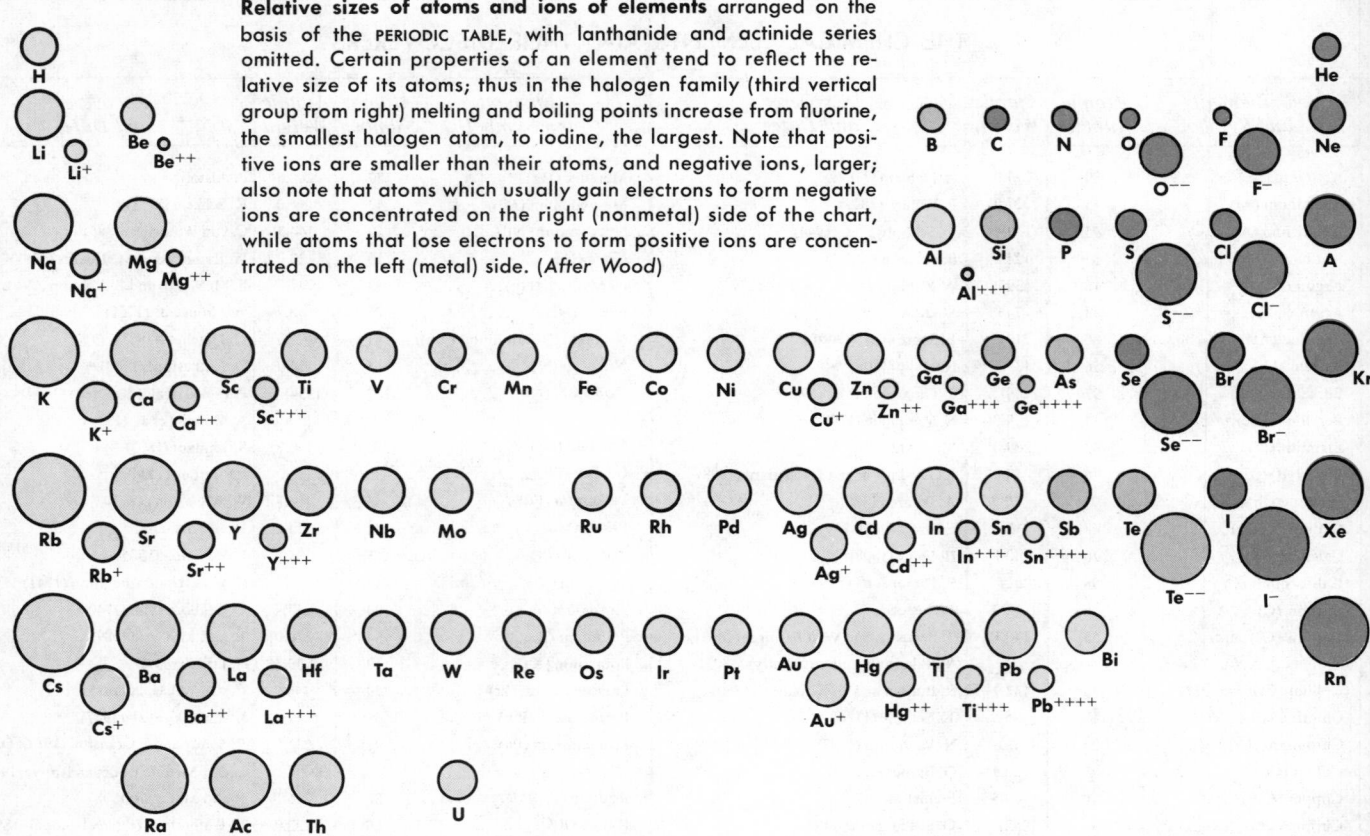

Relative sizes of atoms and ions of elements arranged on the basis of the PERIODIC TABLE, with lanthanide and actinide series omitted. Certain properties of an element tend to reflect the relative size of its atoms; thus in the halogen family (third vertical group from right) melting and boiling points increase from fluorine, the smallest halogen atom, to iodine, the largest. Note that positive ions are smaller than their atoms, and negative ions, larger; also note that atoms which usually gain electrons to form negative ions are concentrated on the right (nonmetal) side of the chart, while atoms that lose electrons to form positive ions are concentrated on the left (metal) side. (*After Wood*)

eral scientific awakening to the importance of electricity as a natural phenomenon and, particularly, of A. Volta's discovery (1800) of a method of producing continuous electric current. The joint development in the 1860s and '70s of the concept of the periodic table and the techniques of spectroscopy gave chemists revolutionary methods for detecting and predicting new elements, and in the period 1875–1905, no less than 25 new elements were discovered. Finally, the development of nuclear theory and technology in the 1930s led to the discovery of the four "missing" elements (technetium, at. no. 43; promethium, 61; astatine, 85; francium, 87) and, as of 1961, eleven transuranium elements up to lawrencium, 103.

Since the early 19th cent., attempts have been made to arrange the elements in a logical and meaningful order; these efforts led to the modern periodic table, based primarily on the work of D. Mendeleev.

Development of Theory of Elements: Present understanding of the nature of the elements stems from a series of epochal discoveries, mainly by English physicists, concerning the structure of the atom. In 1897 J. J. Thomson in England proved the existence of the electron, the first subatomic or elementary particle to be recognized; in 1898 the German W. Wein discovered the proton. These two discoveries spurred development of modern theories of the nature of atoms and elements, even though the third major subatomic particle, the neutron, was not discovered until 1932, by J. Chadwick in England. In 1908–09, H. Geiger and E. Marsden, working under the direction of the English physicist Ernest Rutherford, performed experiments that led to the view of the atom as a dense nucleus about which satellite-like electrons move; between nucleus and electrons is empty space. A little later another Englishman, H. G. J. Moseley, discovered how to determine the number of positive charges (protons) on the

nucleus of an atom, and found that the number of protons (beginning with 1 for hydrogen) increased as atomic weights increased. (Four exceptions exist among naturally occurring elements: potassium, nickel, iodine, and protactinium.) An element's number of protons became its atomic number. Moseley got his results by comparing the x-rays emitted by each known element when it was used as the anode in an x-ray tube. Each element, he found, emitted an x-ray of characteristic wavelength. Still another discovery in the same period forced eventual redefinition of the nature of an element. An element had been defined as a substance consisting of identical atoms, but the work of F. Soddy, J. J. Thomson, and others showed that some elements (Soddy worked mainly with thorium; Thomson with neon) were composed of atoms with different atomic weights. Thus all atoms of an element are not strictly identical. All, however, do have the same number of protons, *i.e.* the same atomic number. Soddy (1913) gave the name *isotopes* to these atoms of varying atomic weight representing the same element. It is now known that all elements have at least two isotopes.—*G. W. M.*

Abundance and Origin of Elements: Analyses of the strengths of the dark absorption lines in the spectra of the stars and of the Sun have shown that the two lightest elements, hydrogen and helium, are by far the most abundant in the universe. Normal stars contain about two-thirds by mass of hydrogen and one-third of helium. All the other elements together amount to about 2% by mass. The next three elements—lithium, beryllium, boron—are very rare. The following three —carbon, nitrogen, oxygen—account for most of the above 2%. The abundances of the heavier elements diminish rapidly as one continues to increase the atomic number, until about at. no. 30. Still heavier elements have abundances of a few parts per billion by mass relative to hydrogen.

RELATIVE ATOMIC ABUNDANCES OF ELEMENTS IN THE UNIVERSE

(Silicon = 10,000; values for extremely rare
or synthetic elements are omitted. *After Urey*)

1. H............	3.5×10^8		43. Tc..........	
2. He..........	3.5×10^7		44. Ru..........	0.019
3. Li..........	1.0		45. Rh..........	0.0067
4. Be..........	0.2		46. Pd..........	0.0091
5. B..........	0.24		47. Ag..........	0.023
6. C..........	80,000		48. Cd..........	0.055
7. N..........	160,000		49. In..........	0.0048
8. O..........	220,000		50. Sn..........	1.42
9. F..........	90		51. Sb..........	0.0097
10. Ne..........	9,000–240,000		52. Te..........	0.013
11. Na..........	462		53. I..........	0.014
12. Mg..........	8,870		54. Xe..........	
13. Al..........	882		55. Cs..........	0.001
14. Si..........	10,000		56. Ba..........	0.039
15. P..........	90		57. La..........	0.021
16. S..........	1,800		58. Ce..........	0.023
17. Cl..........	170		59. Pr..........	0.0096
18. A..........	130–2,200		60. Nd..........	0.033
19. K..........	69		61. Pm..........	
20. Ca..........	660		62. Sm..........	0.012
21. Sc..........	0.18		63. Eu..........	0.0028
22. Ti..........	27		64. Gd..........	0.017
23. V..........	2.4		65. Tb..........	0.0052
24. Cr..........	93		66. Dy..........	0.020
25. Mn..........	75		67. Ho..........	0.0057
26. Fe..........	7,250		68. Er..........	0.016
27. Co..........	22		69. Tm..........	0.0029
28. Ni..........	300		70. Yb..........	0.015
29. Cu..........	7.1		71. Lu..........	0.0048
30. Zn..........	2.6		72. Hf..........	0.007
31. Ga..........	0.11		73. Ta..........	0.0029
32. Ge..........	1.4		74. W..........	0.14
33. As..........	2.3		75. Re..........	0.00066
34. Se..........	0.35		76. Os..........	0.011
35. Br..........	0.43		77. Ir..........	0.0025
36. Kr..........			78. Pt..........	0.016
37. Rb..........	0.071		79. Au..........	0.0015
38. Sr..........	0.41		80. Hg..........	0.00016
39. Y..........	0.10		81. Tl..........	0.0011
40. Zr..........	1.5		82. Pb.......	<0.02
41. Cb..........	0.0077		83. Bi..........	0.0013
42. Mo..........	0.072		90. Th..........	0.0012
			92. U..........	0.0002

The spectral analyses of most of the heavier elements are rather inaccurate. Better relative abundances for nonvolatile elements can be obtained from chemical and radiochemical analyses of the common stone METEORITES, the chondrites. It has long been known that the elemental abundances, and particularly the abundances of individual isotopes, show striking regularities that appear to be related to the nuclear physical properties of the isotopes concerned. In 1956, H. E. Suess and H. C. Urey, assuming a regularity of nuclear properties, published an elemental abundance table in which the elemental abundances were interpolations of the best available chemical analyses. This table has been the key to the development of subsequent theories of the origin of the elements.

In previous years it had been assumed that the universe has in general a homogeneous chemical composition. This led to many suggestions that the elements had been formed during some very hot early phase in the development of the universe, when the temperature was high enough for nuclear reactions to take place. These ideas have not survived the discovery that there are large chemical inhomogeneities in the universe. In some stars the general level of heavy-element abundances is less than in the Sun by two or three powers of ten. In other stars certain elements are greatly overabundant because of nuclear reactions in their interiors.

It is now a widely accepted view that the heavy elements have been formed from hydrogen by nuclear reactions in star interiors. Stars condense from the gas and dust that lie between the stars. Thermonuclear reactions convert the large content of hydrogen into helium. As the stars age, their central temperature increases, and the helium is converted into carbon and oxygen. These are further transformed at still higher temperatures into progressively heavier elements, until iron is reached. Certain side reactions make neutrons, which are captured and build up the masses of the nuclei toward the heaviest elements observed in nature. The stars eject many of these products into space at the end of their active evolutionary period, often in spectacular NOVA and supernova explosions, thus increasing the heavy element content of the interstellar gas and dust.—*A. G. W. C.*

ELEMENTARY PARTICLE: see PARTICLE, ELEMENTARY.

ELEMENTS: by Euclid, *c.* 300 B. C. The work of the most modest of geometers, who claimed no discovery for himself, the *Elements* has become the best known of all mathematical books, remaining the basis for all teaching of geometry down to recent times. Euclid's contribution was to make an almost perfectly logical synthesis of the work of earlier Greek mathematicians, which he improved by new definitions (*e.g.* of "line" and "plane") and especially by the necessary Fifth Postulate (in its modern version: through a point outside a line one and only one parallel can be drawn to it). No doubt he also improved the arrangement and proofs of the propositions, but it is impossible to measure his originality precisely. It produced what has been, and indeed still is, the clearest demonstration of the power of mathematical reasoning.— *A. R. H.*

ELLIPSE: the shape of a circle seen in perspective. The ellipse is important in astronomy, since the orbits of planets, satellites, and many comets are elliptical. One of the CONIC SECTIONS, the ellipse is the locus of a point which moves in a plane so that the ratio of its distance from a fixed point to that from a fixed line, not through the point, is a constant less than 1. The value of this ratio is the eccentricity of the ellipse. The fixed line is called a directrix, and the fixed point a focus. One can show that the curve is symmetric (about the Y-axis in Fig. 1), so that if the focus is F and the directrix is the vertical line at the right, then there is another focus F' and another directrix (the vertical line at the left) which can be used to define the same ellipse. In Fig. 1 the point O, midway between the two foci F' and F, is the center

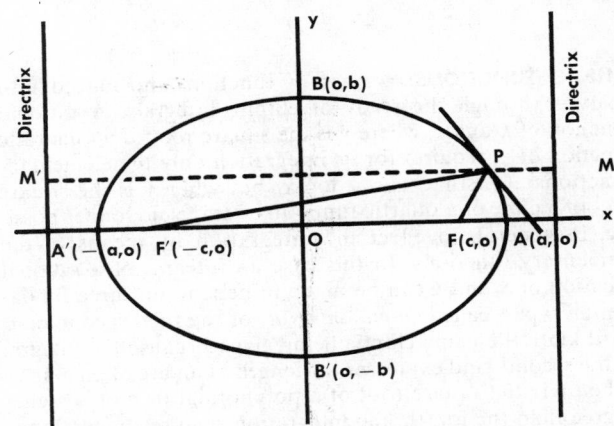

Fig. 1: Ellipse, showing foci, F' and F, and directrixes.

of the ellipse, and any chord through O is a diameter. The longest diameter, $A'A$, passes through F' and F, and is called the major axis. The shortest diameter, $B'B$, is perpendicular to this and is called the minor axis. The ends of the major axis are the vertices.

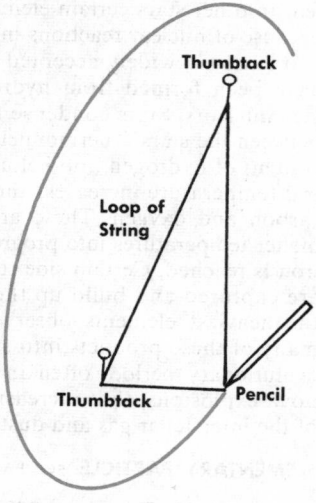

Loop of String

Thumbtack

Thumbtack   Pencil

Construction of ellipse with thumbtacks and string: Point of pencil sliding along string, while string is kept taut, traces an ellipse.

In the figure $PF'/PM' = PF/PM = $ a constant. From this can be derived a different property often used to define an ellipse. The above proportion can be transformed to $PF'/PF = PM'/PM$, whence $PF'/PF + 1 = PM'/PM + 1$, or $(PF' + PF)/PF = (PM' + PM)/PM$. Hence $PF' + PF = (PM' + PM) (PF/PM)$. Since PF/PM is constant and $PM' + PM$ is the constant distance between the directrices, it follows that $PF' + PF$ is a constant. Therefore, an ellipse is the locus of points such that the sum of the distances to two fixed points is constant.

The study of the ellipse is facilitated by the use of coordinates. For the greatest simplicity the origin is placed at the center, the coordinate axes coinciding with the axes of the ellipse. If the foci F and F' have coordinates $(c, 0)$ and $(-c, 0)$, and if the major axis is $2a$, the vertices A and A' have coordinates $(a, 0)$ and $(-a, 0)$. Now, $F'B + FB = 2BF$, and $F'A + FA = 2a$. Since $F'B + FB = F'A + FA$, it follows that $FB = a$. Hence $OB = \sqrt{a^2 - c^2}$. Denoting OB by b, the ends B and B' of the minor axis are $(0, b)$ and $(0, -b)$. The equation of the ellipse can be shown to be $x^2/a^2 + y^2/b^2 = 1$. The eccentricity e is equal to c/a. This quantity is small when the foci are close together, and is 0 for the circle, when the foci coincide. It approaches 1 as b decreases so that c becomes nearly equal to a.

The lines $F'P$ and FP make equal angles with the tangent at P. Because of this, if the curve were replaced by an elliptical mirror and a source of light were placed at one focus, all the rays would be reflected to the other focus. Similarly, in a room of elliptical shape, sound emanating from one focus is reflected to the other. Hence a weak sound at one focus can be heard at the other even though it is inaudible at nearby points.—*H. C.*

ELLIPTIC FUNCTIONS: a class of functions introduced into analysis through the study of elliptic integrals. A rational function of x and y, where y is the square root of a quadratic function of x, requires for its integration only the elementary functions, *e.g.* sin x, cos x, log x; but when y is the square root of a cube or a quartic function of x, it is no longer possible, in general, to effect the integration by means of the elementary functions. In this case an integral of a rational function of x and y can be made to depend on three fundamental types, called *elliptic integrals* of the first, second, and third kind, the name elliptic being given because the integral of the second kind expresses the length of an arc of an ellipse. When y is the square root of a polynomial in x of a higher degree than the fourth, the integration requires hyperelliptic integrals.

The elliptic integral u of the first kind is defined by the equation:

$$u \equiv \int_0^x (1 - t^2)^{-1/2} (1 - k^2 t^2)^{-1/2} \, dt$$
$$\equiv \int_0^\phi (1 - k^2 \sin^2 \theta)^{-1/2} \, d\theta$$

where $k < 1$, $x \equiv \sin \theta$. When ϕ is considered as function of u, the three functions sin ϕ, cos ϕ, $(1 - k^2\sin^2\phi)$ are *elliptic functions;* k is called the modulus; ϕ is called the amplitude of u, written am u; and the three symbols sin am u, cos am u, $(1 - k^2\sin^2$ am $u)$ are usually contracted into sn u, cn u, dn u. The passage from the elliptic integral to the elliptic function led to very extensive developments of the theory.

One of the most important properties of the elliptic functions is their *double periodicity*. Thus sn u has the real period $4K$ and the imaginary period $2K' i$, where K is the value of u when $\phi = \pi/2$, and K' the value of u when $\phi = \pi/2$ and k is replaced by the complementary modulus $k' = \sqrt{1 - k^2}$. The elliptic functions possess an algebraic addition theorem; *i.e.*, a theorem analogous to that which expresses sin $(A + B)$ in terms of sines and cosines of A and B.

Elliptic functions are functions not only of u but of the modulus k; the investigation of properties dependent on the modulus, and the expression of the functions in infinite series and in infinite products, have given rise to numerous important special theorems, and generally have led to some of the most characteristic features of modern mathematics. It has become customary to define elliptic functions without reference to elliptic integrals; in the hands especially of Weierstrass the subject thus acquired greater consistency, and its formulas greater flexibility, though the earlier methods of Jacobi are still of more than historical interest.—*A. P. E.*

ELUTRIATION: a separation process used in chemical industry, in which a solvent is employed to extract a desired component from a mixture or to purify a substance. Extraction may be accomplished by such means as LEACHING, or the mixture may be stirred with solvent and then separated by decantation or filtration. Variations of this procedure permit separation of finely divided solids according to particle size, because the solids have different settling rates; this is called *classification*. Elutriation is an essential step in CHROMATOGRAPHY, where it is called *elution*. (See SEPARATION.)—*Ru. M.*

EMBRYO AND FETUS: terms sometimes used interchangeably for the young of mammals before birth. Many embryologists prefer to use the term embryo for the early stages of development, fetus for the later ones. When used in this way for an unborn child, fetus refers to the child during the last five or six months before birth. See EMBRYONIC DEVELOPMENT.—*A. P. E.*

EMBRYOLOGY: the study of the development of organisms from the one-celled stage to the time they acquire features characteristic of adults of their species and attain independence through birth, hatching, or germination. All sexually reproducing animals and plants begin life as a single cell, the zygote, or fertilized egg. From this stage, the organism increases in size and complexity through the processes of cell division, growth, and differentiation, as the various parts of the embryo are formed and begin to function (see EMBRYONIC DEVELOPMENT). The science of embryology may be divided broadly into descriptive and experimental phases. *Descriptive embryology* seeks to trace the changing form and structure of the embryo at progressive stages of its development. Traditionally, emphasis has been placed upon microscopic study of dead tissues and organs from embryos, but recent work includes observations of living tissues and embryos, with the aid of artificial culture techniques. *Experimental embryology* seeks to understand causal relationships that guide complex processes of development—specifically, how the information carried in the nucleus and cytoplasm of the egg becomes translated into the adult organism. Techniques of biochemistry, genetics, immunology, microsurgery, tissue culture, and other fields are utilized. The experimental embryologist seeks to identify and understand the physical forces, cellular interrelationships, and chemical changes that initiate, control, and produce the particular structure and function seen at any given developmental stage.—*R. L. D.*

EMBRYONIC DEVELOPMENT: the pattern of processes by which a new organism arises from cells of a preceding parent generation. The pattern for any particular kind of animal is controlled by the hereditary information in the nuclei of its earliest embryonic cells. These, in turn, are the latest survivors of an unbroken chain of cells going back in time to the beginnings of life. Thus, modern developmental processes, evolved and modified through a long racial history, reveal in some measure the interrelationships of animals (see RECAPITULATION).

Origin of Earliest Embryonic Cells: In animals that have asexual methods of REPRODUCTION, aggregates of unspecialized cells within the connective tissue or, in some lower forms, tubular outgrowths from the digestive tract give rise to buds on the parent body which become new individuals by cellular rearrangement, transformation, and growth. The universal method of sexual reproduction consists of the union of hereditary material from two cells of different parental origin. Usually, these germ cells are different in size, chemical content, and physiology. The sperm, formed in the testis of the male parent, is a small, self-propelled, condensed nucleus, with only enough cytoplasm remaining to contain a chemical armament for entering the egg and a few particles which control respiration, synthesis, and the coordinated lashing of its tail. The egg, formed in the ovary of the female parent, is a large, whole cell with nucleus, cytoplasm, and a variable food reserve depending on the species. In the egg's long period of growth, nutritive substances from the ovary are converted within the cytoplasm of the egg into yolk, pigments, and specific compounds of other types such as enzymes. These substances are deposited or localized in a pattern—not randomly mixed. At the close of their formative period, both egg and sperm cast out half of their hereditary material during the process of maturation. Each is then an unbalanced system—the sperm because of loss of its cytoplasm, the egg because it has a disproportionately larger ratio of cytoplasmic/nuclear volumes than a normal cell.

Initiation of Development (see FERTILIZATION): The union of the mutually complementary sperm and egg sets off the train of events which leads to the new individual. Under the influence of a chemical emanating from the egg, the sperm ejects a filament which anchors it to the egg surface. An enzyme from the sperm head dissolves a hole in the membrane covering the egg. Far from remaining passive, the egg sends out protoplasmic protrusions which engulf the sperm and its filament (Fig. 1). The sperm head expands into a nucleus within the egg cytoplasm and unites with the egg nucleus to complete the fertilization. Fertilization in turn has three important results: it combines diverse heredity within a single cell, thus producing new combinations of hereditary traits which, through natural selection, form a basis for evolution; it affords the opportunity for hybrid vigor; finally, it stimulates the egg to start developing. The sperm can be dispensed with if the egg is activated by physical or chemical methods, as by pricking with a needle, chilling, or treating it

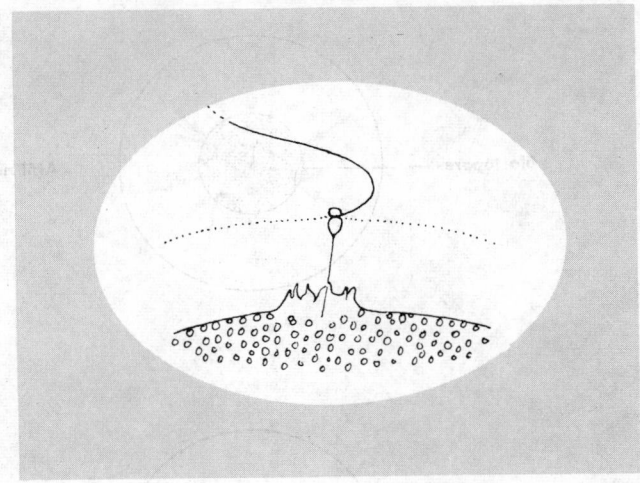

Fig. 1: Union of sperm and egg: Sperm, anchored by its filament to the egg, is about to be engulfed by protrusions from the egg.

briefly with butyric acid (see PARTHENOGENESIS). The embryologist knows the answer to the old riddle about which came first, the chicken or the egg: he knows that the egg is all-important, because within it is embodied all surviving heredity from the past and from it will come all future life. The body is simply a temporary house which has undergone much remodeling over the millennia.

Stages of Development: After the merger of the sperm with the egg to form the *zygote,* a series of successive cellular divisions ensues, with little growth between divisions at least in early stages. This process is called *cleavage* (Fig. 2). It has several important results: many cells of smaller size are formed which serve as building blocks for the construction of the embryonic body; the cytoplasm of each cell is reduced to that size which is most effectively controlled by its nucleus; and, most important of all, diversity arises among the cleaving cells.

Fig. 2: Cleavage: The process differs in eggs of different yolk content:

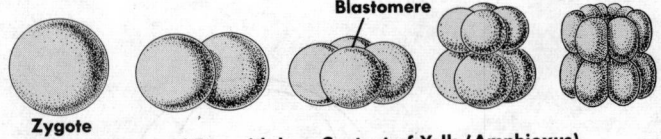

Cleavage of Egg with Low Content of Yolk (Amphioxus)

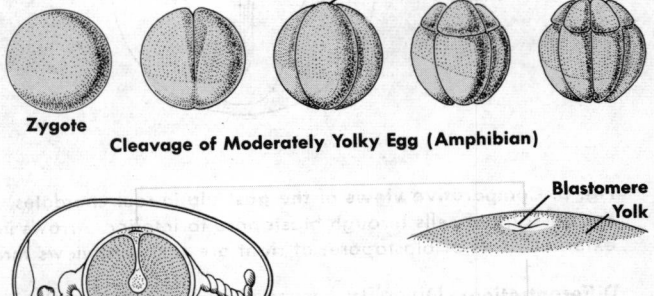

Cleavage of Moderately Yolky Egg (Amphibian)

Cleavage of Highly Yolky Egg (Sauropsidan)

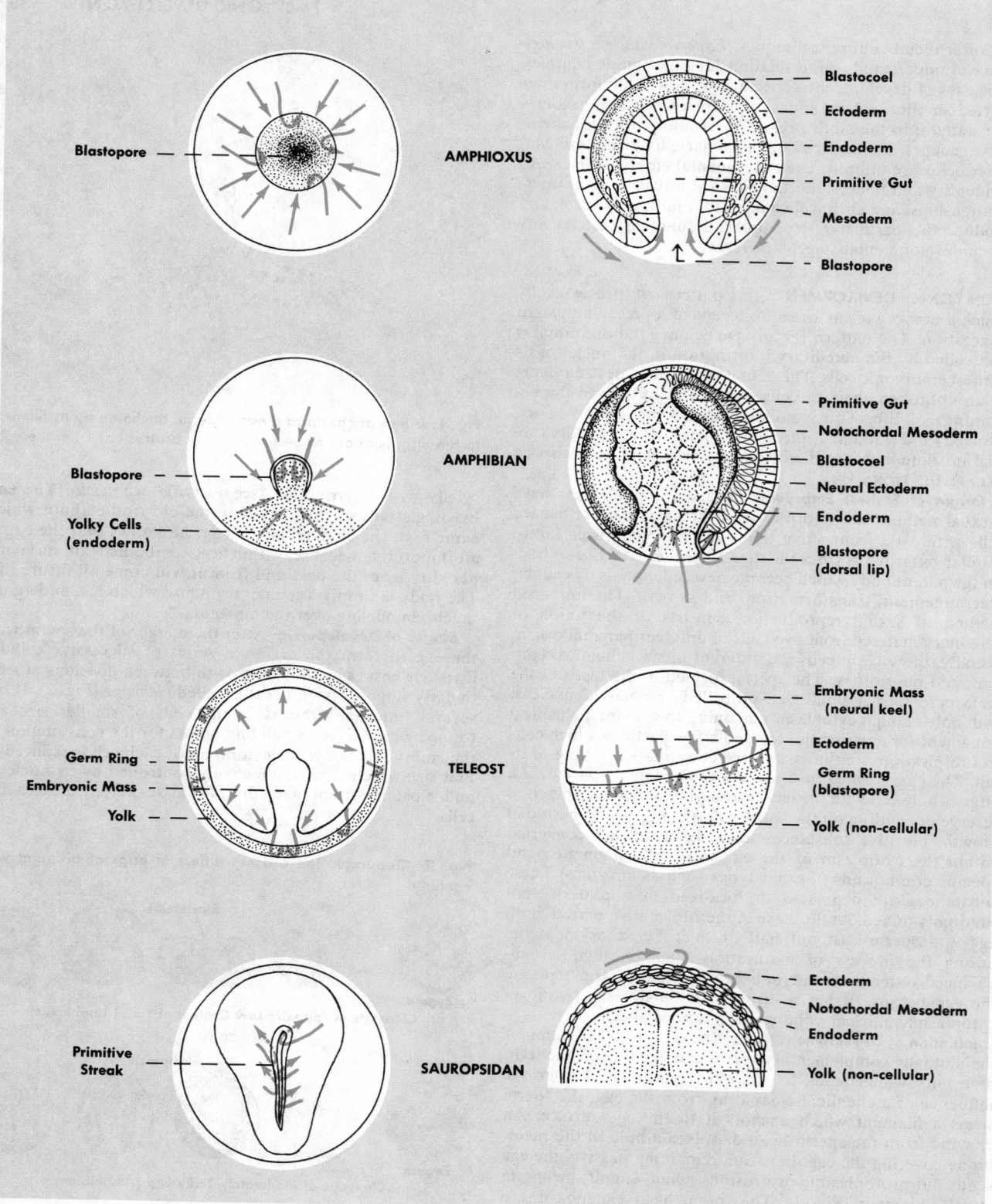

Fig. 3: Comparative views of the gastrula in four chordates. At this stage the embryo has developed three layers as a result of the passage of cells through blastopore to interior. Arrows indicate the amount and direction of cellular movement. At left are external views of blastopore; at right are sectional views through blastopore (except teleost, which is external view from side).

Differentiation: Diversity, or specialization, in cells is thought to have its basis in two other phenomena besides cleavage. Chemical substances arise within cells through synthetic activities controlled by genes in the nucleus. The genes act in sequence, some during the growth of the ovum in the ovary, others during fertilization and cleavage, others still later. Products of gene action are localized within certain areas of the cytoplasm. Cleavage segregates such localized substances into separate cells. Further gene actions may succeed in cells where a necessary substance is present, but fail where it is lacking. As a mechanical process, therefore, cleavage is important for compartmentalizing specific chemical substances. After five or six cleavages, the embryo consists of a solid cluster of cells, presenting a berry-like appearance, called the *morula* (Fig. 3). The cluster rearranges itself to form a single layer, either surrounding or surmounting a cavity, and is called a *blastula*. Although the cells may look alike and be similar in size at these stages, chemical differentiation has already progressed to a point such that in the surface cellular districts can be identified which are destined to form specific future organs. Cells then move in coordination toward one zone on the surface where certain of them pass inward and form two new layers, the *endoderm,* nearest the cavity, and the *mesoderm,* in intermediate position between surface and interior. The cells remaining at the outer surface become the *ectoderm.* The hole or groove through which the cells pass from surface to interior is called the *blastopore.* The three-layered embryo resulting from the movements of surface cells is called the *gastrula* (Fig. 3). By this time biochemical differences between cells are sufficiently marked so that certain districts are compatible with their neighbors, and others less so. The redistribution of the differentiating cells during gastrulation brings about a harmonious arrangement into three *germ layers* which constitute the primitive tissues.

Organogenesis: Interactions can now occur between the superimposed germ layers. The mesoderm of the midline of the embryo acts upon the overlying ectoderm presumably by a transfer of ribonucleoprotein, inducing the ectoderm to thicken and roll up into a tube which becomes the central nervous system. The mesoderm of the midline also influences the differentiation of the underlying endoderm into primitive gut and the adjoining mesoderm into segments. Tissue affinities and incompatibilities influence the details of cellular shape and orientation in neighboring tissues; for example, the neural tube is thick where touched by mesodermal segments, but thin where touched by ectoderm or by notochordal mesoderm. The neural tube, in turn, dilates at its front end to form the major divisions of the brain. The first of these, the forebrain, gives off a vesicle from either side which grows out toward the skin and becomes the retina of the eye. The skin ectoderm overlying these optic vesicles is induced by them to invaginate and form the lens. Later, the lens causes the overlying skin to thicken and become the transparent cornea. Thus, whole chains of inductions or tissue interactions may be involved in the formation of a single organ. Invaginations of the skin ectoderm form the nasal pits and the auditory sacs, or inner ear. Outpocketings of the primitive gut give rise to such internal organs as the thyroid gland, lungs, liver, pancreas, and bladder. In all vertebrate embryos, paired pockets from the foregut grow out to the skin and break

Fig. 4: Development of a chick in six stages after fertilization of egg: 2d, 5th, 10th, 15th, 20th, and 21st day. (*American Museum of Natural History*)

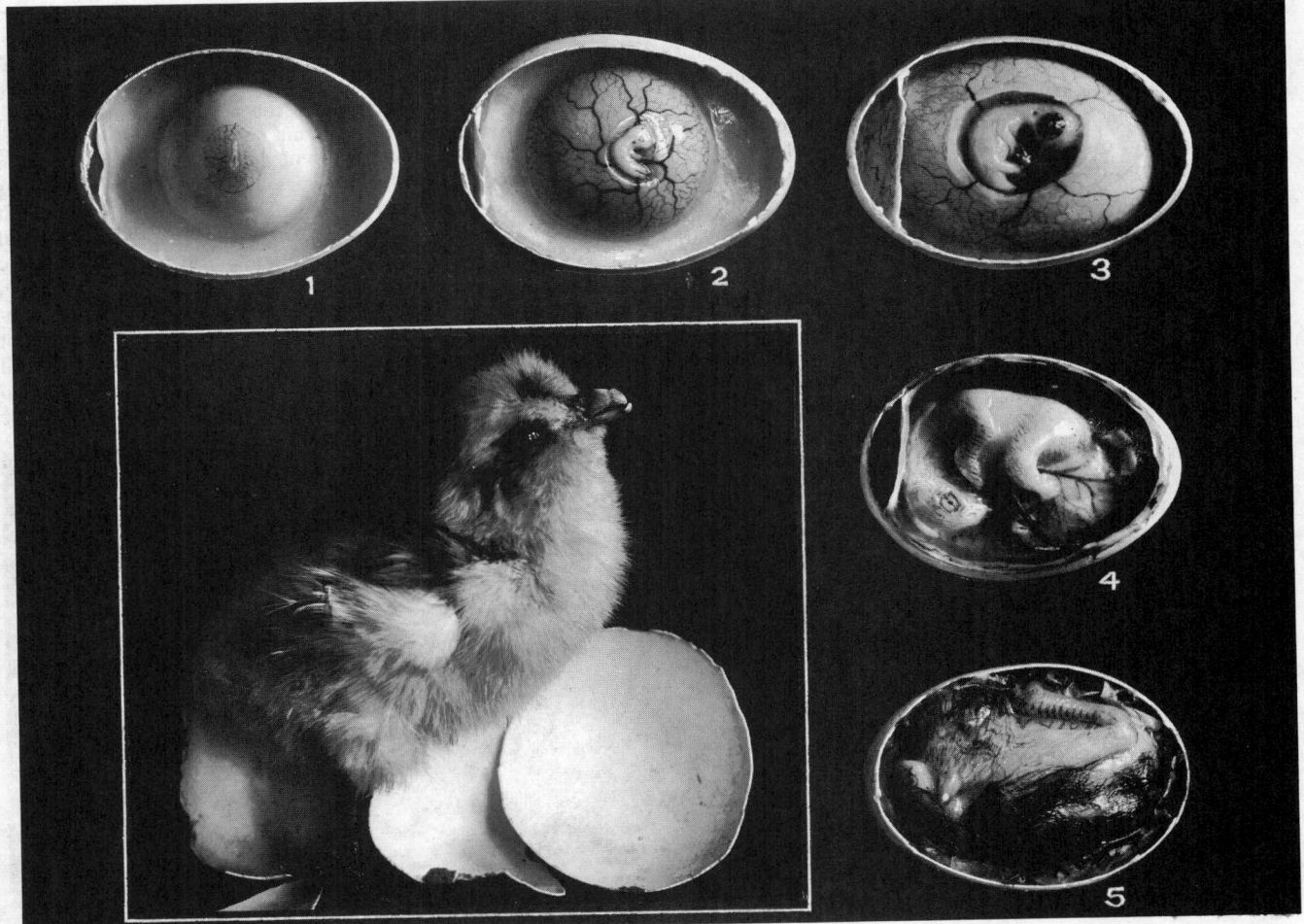

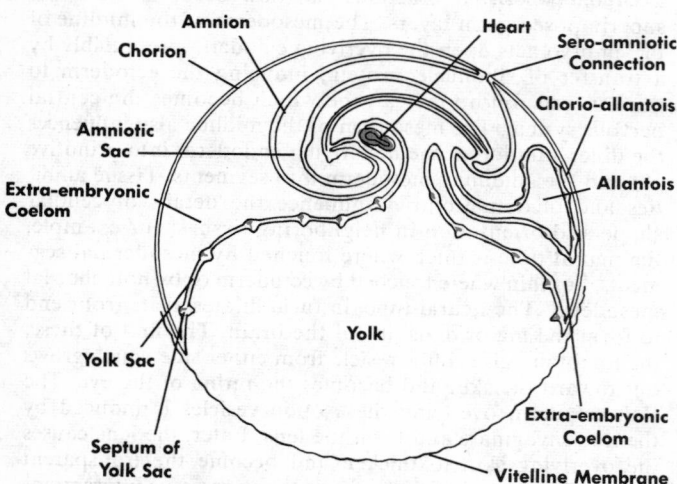

Fig. 5: Fetal membranes of chick: These show development typical in embryos of sauropsidans, the group including birds and reptiles. Heart and blood vessels are indicated in color.

through the surface to form the gill slits. By such mechanical processes as budding, invagination, evagination, and localized aggregation or thickening of cells, the various organs take shape.

Splitting of centers where organs are arising may lead to duplication of certain organs. If it occurs early, by a separation of the halves of the zygote at the two-cell stage or by a splitting of inductive centers in the blastopore during gastrulation, *identical twins* may be formed (see TWINS AND MULTIPLE BIRTHS). If the splitting of organizing centers occurs later, there may be partial twinning involving only part of the body or part of an organ. Normal development also requires a certain amount of twinning or fusion: the eye-forming area is single originally, but subdivides later. The heart-forming area is double at the time of gastrulation, but the two centers merge to form the single organ.

Differences in Development Among Animals: The general features of development, described above, are similar *functionally* in all vertebrates. The details of *structure* by which these functions are carried out may vary considerably. For example, the blastopore in protochordates (simple marine animals including Amphioxus) is an open hole. In amphibians it is open but partially occluded by yolky cells. In teleostean

fish it is a dilated ring (germ ring) surrounding noncellular yolk. In reptiles, birds, and mammals it is not an opening at all, but a groove ("primitive streak") in a shallow disc or clump of cells (Fig. 3). The function in each class is the same, namely the movement of surface cells to the interior to form germ layers, but the morphology is widely different mainly because of differences between the major groups in the amount of food stored within the egg. The amount of yolk is also related to differences in rates of development; in general, yolk retards rates of cleavage and gastrulation, but with a built-in food supply the embryo reaches a more advanced stage before having to fend for itself.

The emergence of animals from water to land has led to new mechanisms and structures for protecting the young during development. This has been accomplished in two ways: by enclosing the egg within a thick membrane or shell to prevent drying or by retaining the egg within the reproductive tract of the mother until a relatively advanced stage of development has been reached. In either case, special *fetal membranes* are developed to surround the embryo with an aqueous medium and to provide for respiration within the confines of the new environment. Starting with the reptiles (which were the first group to become wholly land-dwelling), double folds, composed of the outer two germ layers, grow over the back of the embryo from in front of its head and behind its tail, and fuse to form an outer *chorion* and an inner *amnion* (Fig. 5). The latter secretes a saline fluid which provides the embryo with the proper osmotic environment. A sac, the allantois, then pushes out from the hind-gut, carrying vascular mesoderm with it, and expands between the amnion and the chorion. Fusion with the latter establishes the *chorio-allantoic membrane,* which brings a network of embryonic blood vessels in close proximity to the environment. In reptiles, birds, and the primitive egg-laying mammals, the chorio-allantois lies next to the pores of the shell and is a respiratory organ. In higher mammals, the chorio-allantois is applied to the mother's uterine wall or fuses with it to form the PLACENTA. When this occurs, the chorio-allantois takes over the feeding function as well as respiration, because it can absorb nutrients as well as oxygen from the maternal tissues. It thus supplants the yolk sac and permits a drastic reduction in the amount of stored yolk and the size of the egg.

In mammals, the degree of fusion between the chorio-allantois and the mother's uterine lining is a measure of evolutionary progress with respect to conservation of eggs and care of the potential offspring (see INFANCY). There is no fusion in the pig, and its embryonic and fetal mortality are

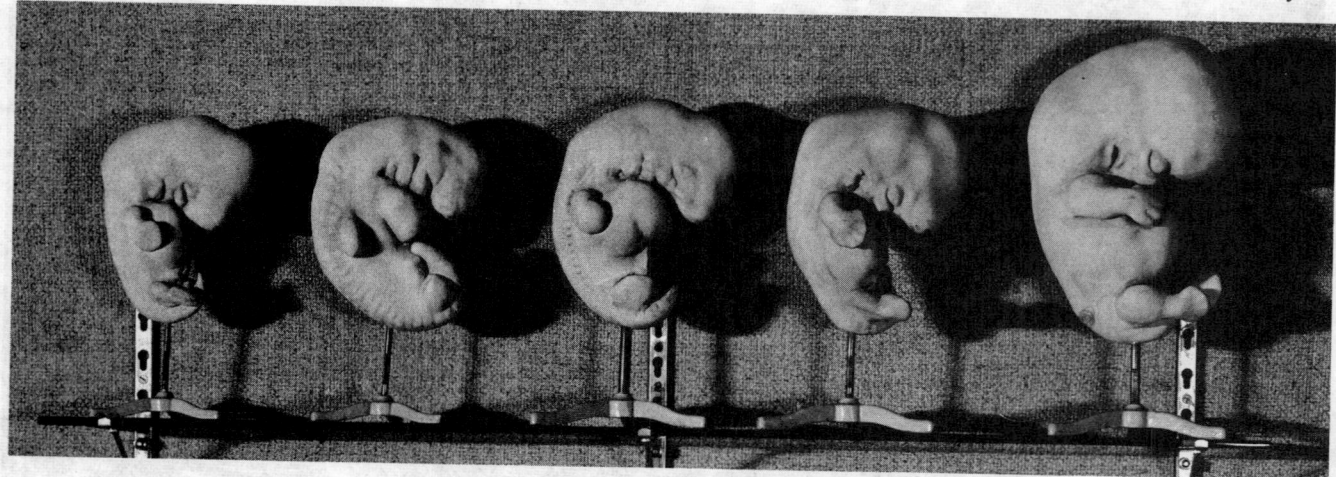

Fig. 6: Human embryo at (*left to right*) 3½, 4, 5, 6, and 6½ weeks. (*American Museum of Natural History*)

high. Other mammals have root-like villi on the chorio-allantois which invade the maternal uterus: in ungulates, only the epithelium is breached; in carnivores, both the uterine epithelium and connective tissue are penetrated; in rodents and primates, uterine blood vessels are also tapped, so that the villi are bathed by free-flowing maternal blood—the ultimate in efficiency for transfer of molecules across the chorio-allantois.

A *human embryo,* like those of other higher mammals, develops from a tiny ovum (0.13 mm, or 0.005 in., diameter), containing only a trace of yolk. Fertilized as it enters the oviduct, it cleaves while passing down the tube, and about 6 days after ovulation implants in the uterine lining, as a hollow ball, the *blastocyst.* This has a cluster of cells, the *inner cell mass,* at one side, from which the embryonic body will form. Two vesicles appear within the inner cell mass: an outer one which becomes the amnion, and an inner one which becomes the yolk sac. An outpocketing from one edge of the yolk sac becomes the allantois. The wall of the blastocyst becomes the chorion. These membranes arise before the end of the third week; such short cuts in their origin no doubt have evolved because of the loss of yolk. By the fifth week the embryo is about 5 mm (0.2 in.) long and has a tubular nervous system, gill slits, a four-chambered heart, many pairs of somites (body segments), and limb buds (Fig. 6). Rapid organogenesis occurs thereafter, and by 2 months the embryo is recognizably human. At 4 months the face is well formed; at 5 months fetal hair covers the body; at 6 months eyebrows and lashes appear; at 7 months the skin is red and wrinkled and the eyelids open; at 8 months fat is deposited to fill out the body contours; at 9 months (38 weeks) labor and birth occur. See EMBRYOLOGY; EPIGENESIS; NEOTENY; INCUBATION; METAMORPHOSIS.—*H. L. H.*

EMERGENCE: the philosophic doctrine that certain entities are hierarchically organized and exhibit modes of behavior which (1) are not exhibited by any of their parts and (2) are conditioned, but not completely determined, by their parts. Defenders of this doctrine hold that certain laws of behavior can be exhibited only at a certain level of complexity, and they doubt that such laws can be derived from those describing the behavior of entities at a lower level of organization. It has frequently been pointed out that this claim must be relativized, and that the concept of emergence can be defended only if it is shown that a given theory of the behavior of a complex entity is not reducible to a given theory of the parts of which it is composed. Biologists in sympathy with the doctrine of emergence frequently insist that this more complex and irreducible behavior allows the organism to achieve certain ends by acting as a unified or integrated whole. Essentially the same point has been made by some psychologists who oppose piecemeal analysis of human behavior and insist that the person must be studied as a whole. Critics of the doctrine insist that no investigation is possible unless certain selective features of behavior are attended to, and hence are dubious of the advice to study organisms as integrated wholes.—*S. M.*

EMERY: see CORUNDUM.

EMPEDOCLES: ancient Greek philosopher, 5th cent. B.C., a native of Agrigentum in Sicily. He is best known for his theory of the "four elements": earth, air, water, and fire, out of which the whole world has come into being, under the action of the forces of love and hate—i.e., attraction and repulsion. These and other doctrines he developed in his poems entitled *On Nature* and *Purifications,* of which only fragments remain.—*A. P. E.*

EMPIRICISM: in ordinary usage, procedures based on matters of fact or practical experience, in contradistinction to theoretical operations. The original Empiricists were Greek experimentalists in medicine, champions of practices based on "experience" (Greek *empeiria*); later, through the influence of Galen, who was critical, the term was used pejoratively to denote quackery, as late as the 17th cent. But the term has since acquired a special and established meaning as a philosophic doctrine that all knowledge is derived from experience and that nothing can be known to exist without experience. Accordingly, empiricists emphasize observation and experimentation in both acquisition of knowledge and testing of all claims to knowledge. Since this procedure of discovery and verification is most compellingly exhibited by the growth of science, empiricists have usually regarded scientific knowledge as the model *par excellence* of how knowledge is to be achieved; they have been correspondingly critical of metaphysical and mystical philosophies.

Modern empiricism, first given articulate expression by a line of British philosophers, notably Locke, Berkeley, Hume, and Mill, emerged primarily in opposition to the RATIONALISM of the 17th-cent. Continental philosophers, especially Descartes, Spinoza, and Leibniz. The basic issue of this historic controversy concerns the interpretation of knowledge. For rationalism, "knowledge" is understood in a sense of absolute, unimpeachable intellectual certainty about some subject matter. Consequently, because sense experience is fallible and often indeterminate, rationalists sought elsewhere for the ultimate principles of knowledge and were led to advocate "innate ideas," or purely conceptual notions originating in reason, as the crucial supplements to experience. Thus, although our idea of "green" is derived from experience of green objects, not all ideas are experientially derived; for example, our ideas of causality, substance, relations—even goodness and God—are held to be instances of knowledge grounded wholly in reason. Empiricists have either argued that all such knowledge is in fact compounded from experience, or denied the existence of purely conceptual ideas. In the spirit of the latter alternative, Berkeley denied that there is necessarily any idea (or meaning) attending the word "substance."

Fundamental for empiricism is the distinction between logically necessary statements (called "analytic") and contingent or factual statements (called "synthetic"). To illustrate: the truths of logic or arithmetic, *e.g.* "1 + 1 = 2," are necessarily true by definition, but no synthetic statement of fact, *e.g.* "Iron expands when heated," is a logically necessary truth. While rationalists claim that some synthetic propositions are also necessarily true, empiricists reject this claim. A famous example was HUME's analysis of causality, which was directed against the view that causes and effects possess a necessary connection. Some empiricists have even denied that mathematical truths are analytic, regarding them as synthetic generalizations from experience and conceivably to be disproved by further experience. While this has been debated, empiricists have appreciated the value of analytic propositions for systematizing knowledge and establishing the logical connections among propositions, but they continue to regard knowledge as the result of experience rather than logic.

For empiricism, then, our knowledge of the world never attains absolute certainty; it is always fallible, and subject to correction. Probability replaces certainty; but the loss of certainty on this score is viewed as a gain in our understanding of knowledge and of profound moral significance in its bearing upon human conduct. See SCIENCE; SCIENTIFIC METHOD.—*H. S. T.*

Emulsifier at work: When oil with an emulsifier is added to water, a spontaneous mixing action occurs, forming an emulsion "bloom." Oil and water are usually immiscible. *(Atlas Chemical Industries, Inc.)*

EMULSION: a dispersion of one liquid in another with which it is immiscible, the dispersion being in droplets generally smaller than 1 micron in diameter. Since one liquid is nearly always water, systems are classified as oil-in-water (O/W) and water-in-oil (W/O). The term *oil* represents any liquid immiscible with water. Simply shaking two immiscible liquids will produce a temporary emulsion, but to render the emulsification stable a third component, an emulsifier, is needed. This emulsifying agent lowers the surface tension at the interface so that the interface can be stretched to the large area which exists when one of the liquids is broken down to small drops. SOAPS and other DETERGENTS consisting of long hydrocarbon chains with polar groups at the ends are effective emulsifiers; sodium soaps favor O/W emulsions, but soaps of certain other metals (*e.g.* zinc or aluminum) yield W/O emulsions (see SURFACE-ACTIVE AGENTS). Hydrophilic (water-loving) colloids, *e.g.* gelatine and casein, are also effective emulsifiers; they form a protective film around oil droplets dispersed in water, preventing the oil droplets from drawing together (or *coalescing*) and thus destroying the emulsion. Milk is an O/W emulsion stabilized by casein, which (like gelatine) is preferentially "wet" by water. Emulsions can be broken by chemical treatment, or simply by heating, freezing, or agitating them. Emulsions appear commercially as cosmetics (shampoos, creams, ointments) and foods (mayonnaise, margarine); they also play an important role in many industries, *e.g.* dyeing, tanning, textiles, and paper. (See COLLOID CHEMISTRY.)—*Ru. M.*

ENAMEL: a type of fused ceramic applied as a coating to pottery, glass, or metals (commonly iron and steel) for protection or decoration, or both. Enamels are essentially a type of GLASS and, like glass, can be made from a wide variety of inorganic materials. Enamel coatings are hard, durable, and highly resistant to abrasion, heat, and most chemicals. (See CERAMICS; COATING.) Enameled products include household appliances and utensils, plumbing fixtures, signs, gasoline pumps, engine exhaust stacks, and jet-engine parts subject to high temperatures. Enameling as an art probably originated in Egypt. The term enamel is also applied to a water-resistant paint made by adding pigment to VARNISH, and used on a variety of familiar objects such as outdoor furniture, refrigerators, washing machines, and kitchen cabinets.—*W. P. C.*

ENCKE, JOHANN FRANZ, 1791–1865, German mathematician and astronomer; b. Hamburg. Director of the Berlin Observatory (1825–63), he worked on the motion and theory of comets and investigated a comet (later named after him) discovered in 1818 by J. L. Pons. Encke showed (1822) that the comet he rediscovered was moving in a nearly circular orbit and would complete its circuit in about 3⅓ yr. He also identified the comet as the one observed by P. F. A. Méchain (1786), Caroline Herschel (1795), and Pons, Huth, and Bouvard (1805). The comet has continued to appear regularly. Encke was a fellow of the Royal Society.—*R. N. M.*

ENDOCRINE GLANDS: special organs or parts of organs that produce hormones which regulate body activities of animals. Endocrinology is the study of these glands and their secretions. The endocrine glands in man and other mammals include the ADRENAL GLANDS, tissues of the PANCREAS and the intestinal wall, the THYROID GLAND, PARATHYROID GLANDS, PITUITARY GLAND, the sex glands (OVARIES and TESTES), the corpus luteum, the PLACENTA, the PINEAL GLAND, and the THYMUS GLAND. Endocrine glands are known also as ductless glands, since they do not have ducts for the transport of their secretions, as do exocrine glands (*e.g.* the liver, which secretes bile through the bile duct into the intestine). Endocrine glands secrete hormones directly into the blood, which carries the hormones to all parts of the body. Often the endocrine glands are remote from the "target organs" whose activities they influence.

Hormones, which are made from raw materials supplied by blood, differ widely in chemical composition. Those from the cortex part of the adrenal gland and from the sex glands, the corpus luteum, and the placenta are steroids. Those from the pancreas, the parathyroid glands, and the anterior part of the pituitary gland are either proteins or large polypeptides. Those from the posterior part of the pituitary gland, the medulla part of the adrenal gland, the thyroid, the pineal, and the thymus glands are simpler derivatives of proteins or amino acids.

Hormones may stimulate or inhibit growth, reproduction, assimilation of food, or other body processes, but the actual processes apparently do not depend on the presence of hormones. Each hormone has a specific effect, either by changing the permeability of cells in the target organ or by calling forth inherited mechanisms through activation of specific regions within chromosomes. Some hormones have similar effects, reinforcing one another, but others are antagonistic to each other. Hormones of different glands interact in such a way that a deficiency in one may lessen the activity of another. Thus a reduction in the amount of a hormone from the anterior pituitary leads to a decrease in the production of hormones by the sex glands. Some hormones seem to produce profound effects apart from their usual functions. Cortisone, for example, a constituent of the steroid complex produced by the adrenal cortex, is highly beneficial in treating arthritis, rheumatic fever, and poison ivy. The mechanism of these effects is unknown.

Information about the role of endocrine glands has been obtained by studying the effects of removing particular glands (or their parts) from animals, or by implantation of glands, or by injections of hormones extracted from glands. Hormones used in treating human patients with hormone deficiencies and in research are extracted from the glands of other mammals. Insulin, for example, is obtained from the beef pancreas; it is formed by special cells (the "islets of Langerhans") in the pancreas and is necessary for proper metabolism of sugar; an inadequate amount leads to the condition of diabetes mellitus. Several hormones, such as thyroxin, can be synthesized in the laboratory.

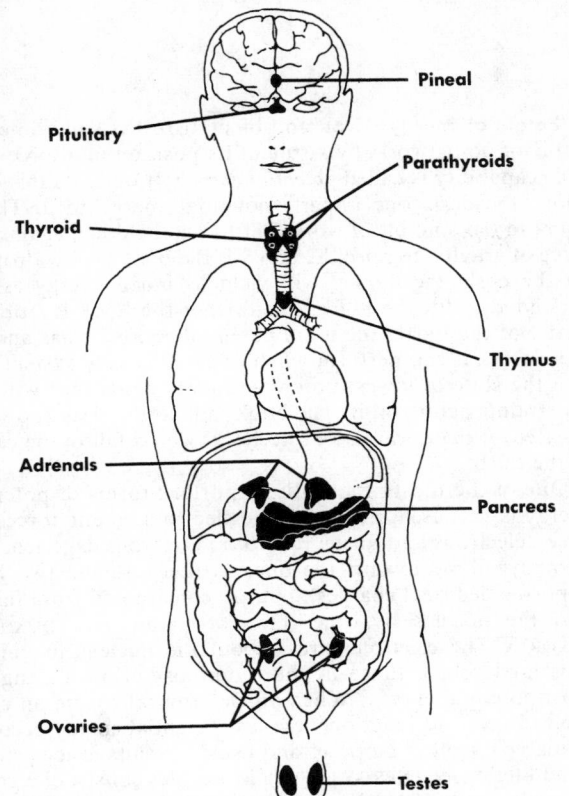

Human endocrine glands: For convenience, glands peculiar to males (testes) and to females (ovaries) are included in single figure. (*From Young*)

Pineal

Pituitary

Parathyroids

Thyroid

Thymus

Adrenals

Pancreas

Ovaries

Testes

Vertebrate animals other than mammals have comparable glands and hormones, although the effect of a specific hormone may differ from one kind of animal to another. For example, the pituitary hormone prolactin, which regulates milk production in mammals, stimulates hens to sit on their eggs and stimulates female frogs to ovulate. Thyroxin, from the thyroid, serves chiefly as a regulator of metabolic rate except in amphibians, in which it is involved in METAMORPHOSIS. Most studies of endocrine glands have been carried out on vertebrates rather than invertebrates, because the larger vertebrate glands are easier to study and because information concerning vertebrate hormones is more likely to be applicable to treatment of humans.

Among arthropod animals such as crustaceans and insects, endocrine glands have been discovered and something learned of the role of the hormones produced. In decapod crustaceans the eyestalks contain a special sinus gland, the hormone from which is part of the mechanism that controls pigment cells in the body surface, enabling the animal to change color. In insects such as grasshoppers and giant silkworm moths, a "juvenile hormone" is secreted by wing-shaped glands (corpora allata) close to the brain; this hormone inhibits another set of endocrine glands in the prothorax, which otherwise would produce the hormone ecdysone—inducing MOLTING and METAMORPHOSIS of the insect exoskeleton. At the end of normal development, the corpora allata becomes inactive, allowing ecdysone to form and act—ending the immature stage in the life history. Surgical removal of the corpora allata at an earlier age has the same effect, whereas implantation of active tissue from corpora allata can postpone metamorphosis even though the grasshopper nymph or caterpillar grows to giant size. In many insects that enter a dormant state (diapause) during development, a further hormone from brain tissue that has been chilled appears to be necessary, even after the corpora allata have degenerated, before the prothoracic glands will secrete ecdysone and start development again.

Moth pupae commonly require chilling for a few weeks before they can emerge—an experience that comes normally during the winter time and stimulates emergence in the spring.—*L. M. and M. M.*

ENERGY (in biochemistry): All energy utilized by organisms comes originally from nuclear reactions in the Sun. This energy is trapped by an organism in various ways. Green plants and some bacteria use the photosynthetic apparatus of the chloroplasts and chromophores to convert light energy into chemical energy (see PHOTOSYNTHESIS), thus creating many biochemical compounds and liberating oxygen; atmospheric oxygen, in turn, is used by these plants to release energy stored in the biochemical compounds. Many bacteria obtain their primary source of energy by using oxygen for oxidation of simple compounds in the soil, *e.g.* metallic iron and sulfur. Animals oxidize the chemicals found in plants, and this is their main source of energy.

Thus all forms of life use oxygen of the atmosphere and, either primarily or secondarily, the radiation from the Sun in synthesizing their chemical compounds. The compounds are built into living protoplasm, the energy for doing this being obtained by the breakdown and oxidation of some of the compounds. These events are collectively called metabolism; the breakdown is catabolism, the build-up is anabolism. Catabolism is conveniently divided into two parts: fermentation, in which oxygen is not used, and respiration, in which oxygen is used. In both cases, chemical compounds either are transferred into other compounds of lower energy levels, or are completely oxidized to carbon dioxide and water. In both cases, energy is produced, but more energy results from respiration than from fermentation.

For the cell to utilize this energy efficiently, it must be produced in a series of small steps, rather than in one large step, for in the latter event most of the energy would be lost as heat. The small steps take place in the various metabolic reactions in the cell, as in the glycolytic pathway (see GLYCOLYSIS) or the CITRIC-ACID CYCLE. The energy is released during oxidation of the various substrates of these metabolic cycles, and is in the form of a biologically usable compound, adenosine triphosphate (ATP). Most of the ATP in a cell is produced during a process called OXIDATIVE PHOSPHORYLATION, which occurs in the mitochondria. ATP is the biological energy coin of the cell, for it can be utilized to supply the energy necessary for synthesis of the great many different compounds of the cell. The energy can be supplied at one burst, at the chemical site of the synthetic reaction. When this occurs, an efficient reaction ensues, for up to 40% of the available energy entrapped in the ATP chemical structure can be used for synthesis. During the synthetic process the ATP is broken down, sometimes to adenylic acid and inorganic pyrophosphate, and sometimes to adenosine diphosphate (ADP) and inorganic phosphate; during both these processes there is an energy loss of 8,000 calories/mole. Some of these calories are used, as chemical energy, to bring about the synthetic reaction, while the rest are irretrievably lost to the cell as heat.

In simple thermodynamic terms, the chemically useful energy, called the free energy of the system, can be defined as that energy capable of doing work. Mathematically, the free energy $F = H - TS$, or change in F = change in H − T(change in S), where H is a heat constant, T is the absolute temperature, and S is the entropy. Since in cells the changes in temperature and in entropy are small, the change in free energy can be practically equated with the change in the heat constant. A process, or a chemical reaction, will proceed spontaneously when there is a loss in free energy. If ATP enters into such a reaction, with a great loss in free energy—the 8,000 calories/mole mentioned above—the reaction is practically irreversible, *i.e.* one compound will be completely changed to another. However, sometimes ATP enters a reaction in which another "high-energy" compound like itself is formed; then the free energy change is relatively small, and the reaction is easily reversible, resulting in formation of ATP.

The equation above is a form of the second law of thermodynamics, which states that systems in isolation, left to themselves, spontaneously tend toward states of greater disorganization. This means that eventually the free energy is reduced to zero, *i.e.* $H = TS$, and $H - TS = 0$. In other words as the system goes toward greater and greater disorganization, its entropy increases. But when free energy is added to such a system, the entropy decreases, and the state of organization increases. This seems to occur in living cells. If free energy is cut off, disorganization proceeds until the cell finally dies. Cell metabolism is maintained at a certain level of organization only by the continuous supply of free energy. This is described as a "steady-state" system: it is a state away from equilibrium and can only be made viable by a constant infusion of free energy from outside. The supply of free energy comes originally from the Sun, and animals obtain their energy secondarily through the oxidation of foodstuffs.—*P. S.*

ENERGY (in physics): the ability to do work. In physics, work has a precise, quantitative definition: When a force moves an object, the work done by the force is defined as the product of the average value of the force's component along the direction of motion, and the distance through which it moved the object. The energy, then, of any system is measured by the amount of work it can (in principle) perform. The energy of any particle of matter consists of the sum of three separate components: kinetic, potential, and rest-mass energy.

Kinetic Energy: A moving object exerts a force on anything with which it collides, and in so doing is slowed down. The work that a moving object is capable of performing in being brought to rest is its *kinetic energy*. The faster it moves and the more massive it is, the more kinetic energy it has. The kinetic energy of a body of mass *m*, moving with velocity *v*, is ½ *mv*².

Potential Energy: Even an object at rest is sometimes capable of doing work, by virtue of its position in a force field. This capability is called *potential energy*. If one lifts this book above the desk, one imparts potential energy to it. This is equal to the amount of work that had to be done, against the force of gravity, to raise the book. If the book is now dropped on the desk, the impact will yield as much energy as was expended to lift the book. The farther the book is from the center of the Earth, the more potential energy it has and the more work it can perform when released. Every system falls into the state of lowest potential energy consistent with the constraints acting on it. The book falls to the desk top when released; if there were no obstacles, it would fall to the center of the Earth.

One of the most practically important forms of potential energy is that associated with the electromagnetic forces between electrons and nuclei in ATOMS. Electrons experience an attractive force toward the nucleus (because the two have opposite electrical charges), but are constrained from falling into the nucleus by other laws of nature (see QUANTUM THEORY). The electrons circle about the nucleus in unique, separated orbits, those in the outermost orbits having the most potential energy. When an electron falls from an outer orbit to a vacant inner one, the lost potential energy becomes available for other purposes and usually results in the generation of light (see ENERGY LEVEL). Molecules consist of a group of nuclei surrounded by an appropriate number of orbiting electrons, the orbits being determined by a complicated interplay of electric and magnetic forces. When two molecules collide, the electrons and nuclei rearrange themselves into new configurations having the lowest potential energy consistent with the other constraints. If the potential energy of the new configuration is smaller than the old (*e.g.* if the average distance of electrons from nuclei is smaller), the lost potential energy is available for other purposes. This is what happens when an oxygen molecule interacts with a sugar molecule in the body: the body uses this freed energy to do work (lifting the book) or to keep itself warm.

Rest-Mass Energy: The third basic form in which energy appears in nature was discovered by Einstein as one of the consequences of his theory of RELATIVITY. The theory showed

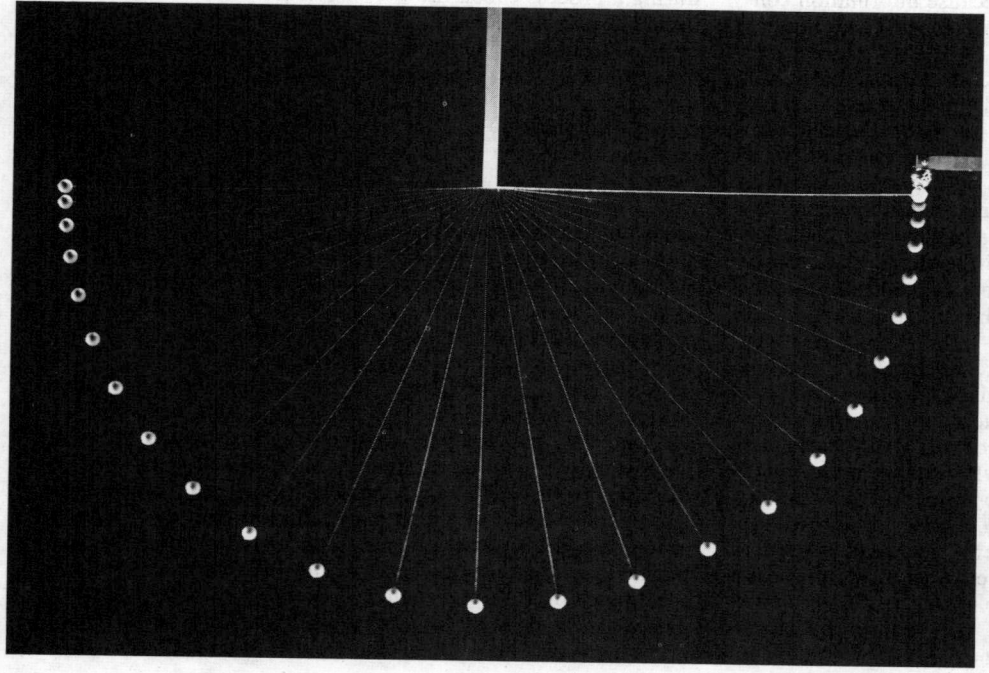

Swinging pendulum demonstrates a continuous exchange between potential energy (maximum at the ends of the swing and zero at the center) and kinetic energy (zero at the ends of the swing and maximum at the center).

that if matter could be annihilated, then an amount of energy would be freed that would be equal to the product of the mass of the annihilated matter and the square of the velocity of light ($E = mc^2$). Later, physicists discovered that the elementary particles of matter can be annihilated when they collide with their so-called ANTIPARTICLES, and that the released energy is given by Einstein's formula. The energy released upon annihilation of a particle of matter is called its *rest-mass energy.*

Internal Energy: Every chunk of matter has a kinetic energy associated with its motion as a whole, a potential energy associated with external force fields, and a rest-mass energy for all its constituent elementary particles. In addition, it has an internal energy. The latter is the sum of the potential energies of the electrons and nuclei within molecules of the matter, the potential energies of these molecules in the force fields of all the other molecules, and the kinetic energies associated with the so-called thermal motion of these molecules. It is a fact of nature that no molecules are ever at rest; they are forever vibrating about their equilibrium positions in solids and liquids, and flying through space in gases. Although these movements are completely random in direction and speed, the *average* energy associated with thermal motion is accurately measurable for ordinary-sized pieces of matter, which contain billions upon billions of molecules. This average is intimately associated with the temperature of the material. When two systems at different temperatures are placed in contact, the hotter system transfers internal energy to the cooler one until the temperatures of both are equal. The mode of transfer is collisions between the molecules: faster-moving molecules in the hotter system speed up slower-moving molecules in the cooler system. The transfer of internal energy—associated with thermal motion—from one body to another is called heat-energy flow.

Other Aspects: Energy is one of the most important concepts used by scientists in describing the observable universe, because (1) energy is universal (every speck of matter and radiation has energy) and (2) energy is one of the few conserved quantities in nature; it can be neither created nor destroyed—although it can be readily changed from one form to another or transferred from one system to another. The law of CONSERVATION OF MASS-ENERGY, which summarizes the results of innumerable experiments, holds that any collection of objects, if isolated from the rest of the universe, can neither gain nor lose in total energy regardless of how the objects interact among themselves. No exception to this rule has yet been found in the whole gamut of observable phenomena, inorganic and biological, ranging from the interactions of subnuclear particles in regions of space 10^{-13} cm in diameter to the processes occurring in stars, extending over distances measured in light-years.

A fundamental property of energy, discovered in 1900, is that it is quantized: the quantity of energy transferable from one system to another cannot be indefinitely divided, but rather there are indivisible "packets" of energy, called quanta. Electrons bound to atoms have only a discrete set of allowed energy levels, corresponding to a discrete set of allowed orbits. When an atom interacts with the outside world, the energy exchanges can occur only in the finite amounts equal to the differences in energy of the allowed levels. In such transitions an electron makes a discontinuous jump from one orbit to the other. In describing atomic and nuclear phenomena, physicists utilize an energy level diagram, in which the allowed energies are indicated by horizontal lines, the distance between lines being proportional to the energy difference. We do not observe the quantum nature of energy in our everyday life, because the amount of energy transfer involved in macroscopic processes involves astronomically large numbers of quanta, and the nondivisibility of a single quantum is unnoticeable. In a single atom, however, a single quantum is quite noticeable. Energy sources include the atom (see ATOMIC ENERGY), the Sun (see SOLAR ENERGY), FUELS, wind, and water (see HYDROELECTRIC DEVELOPMENT). See also ELECTRICITY; ENGINE; HEAT; PRIME MOVER; RADIATION.—*S. K.*

ENERGY LEVEL: the total energy of a system (*e.g.* atom, molecule, nucleus) when it is in one of its allowed configurations. The energy of a system cannot be just any value, because actual systems can exist only in particular states, each with a particular energy value. For example, associated with each atom there is a discrete set of allowed energy levels, each level corresponding to an allowed electron configuration. When an atom absorbs or radiates energy, the amount of energy transferred must be equal to the difference between that of the initial state and that of some other allowed state. In such a transition, the electron configuration changes to some other allowed configuration. The lowest possible energy level is called the *ground* state, and more energetic ones, *excited* states. A system can make a transition spontaneously from an excited state to a lower one by emitting the excess energy as some form of radiation, and it can make the transition to a higher state by absorbing radiation. In the case of an atom or molecule, the transition to a lower state is most often accompanied by the emission of light. For nuclei, one possible mechanism is the emission of radiation in the form of gamma rays, but other mechanisms, *e.g.* the emission of electrons, also occur. See ATOM; AUGER EFFECT; QUANTUM MECHANICS.—*S. Bo.*

ENGINE: a machine that receives energy and converts it to produce motion. Engines are prime movers; an electric motor is not an engine, since it operates on electrical energy previously produced by a PRIME MOVER. Common energy sources for engines are combustion, moving water, nuclear reactions, wind, and solar radiation. Classified by type of motion, engines are reciprocating (piston-driving) or rotary (*e.g.* turbines); classified by application, they may be either mobile or stationary. The major stationary engines are those in electric power plants. Large central generating stations use either steam or hydraulic turbines; smaller plants are more likely to have diesel engines. Nuclear power plants are slowly increasing in number. Mobile engines include gasoline types (passenger automobiles, light trucks, older aircraft), diesels (heavy trucks, tractors, earth-moving equipment, buses, locomotives, ships), steam engines (locomotives, ships), steam turbines (ships), jet engines (modern aircraft), and nuclear reactors (submarines and other naval vessels). Engines burning the so-called fossil fuels, coal and petroleum, are the most important; they are subdivided into the external- and internal-combustion types. The former includes reciprocating steam engines and steam turbines. The most familiar internal-combustion types are the gasoline (Otto) engine and the fuel-oil (diesel) engine. Steam and internal combustion still do the bulk of the world's work.

No type of engine is simpler, at least in theory, than the reciprocating STEAM ENGINE. A metal cylinder contains a movable piston which, though closely fitting, can slide freely within the cylinder. Steam, admitted through a valve at one end of the cylinder, forces the piston to slide. When the piston has reached the end of its stroke, a second valve admits steam to the other end of the cylinder; the piston is then forced in the opposite direction. Since it does work during both forward and return strokes, the piston and its engine are called double-acting. Through piston rod, crosshead, and connecting

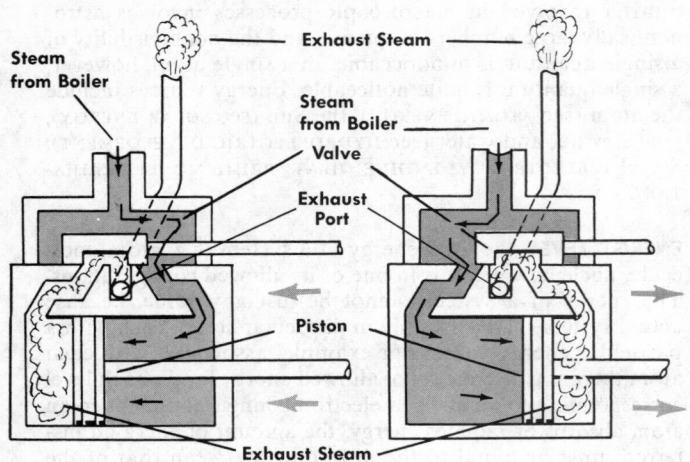

Reciprocating steam engine: The valve, synchronized with the movement of the piston, first allows steam to enter one side of the cylinder (*left*), pushing the piston one way, then permits entry of steam on cylinder's other side (*right*), pushing piston the other way. Used steam is forced out exhaust port by advancing piston.

rod, the push of the piston acts upon a crankshaft and a flywheel. The reciprocating motion is thus converted into rotary motion that will drive a railroad locomotive, turn a ship's propeller, or activate a factory's overhead shafts.

In contrast to a steam engine, which consumes fuel in a separate furnace or combustion chamber, the INTERNAL-

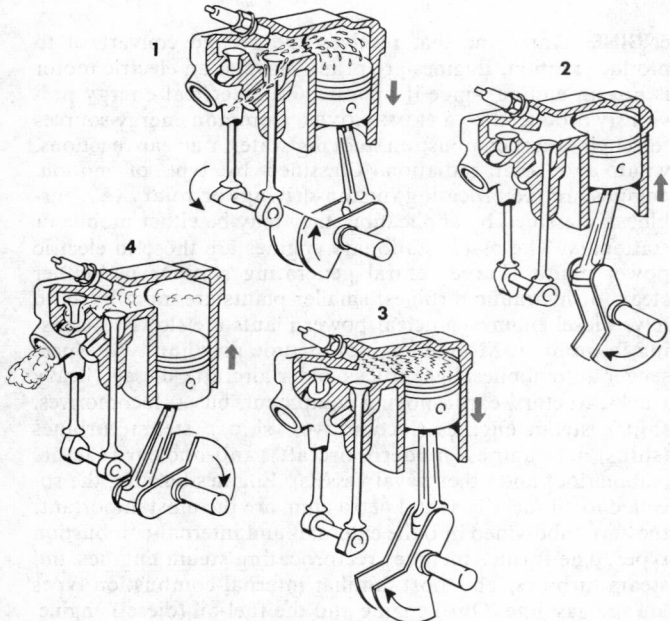

Otto (4-stroke-cycle) engine: A conventional gasoline, spark-ignition engine delivers power on only one stroke (3) of four; *i.e.* it has one power stroke for every two revolutions of its crankshaft. On stroke 1, a mixture of air and fuel is drawn through open valves by descending piston. On stroke 2, valves close and piston rises, compressing and raising the temperature of the air-fuel mixture. At this point, IGNITION timing produces spark from spark plug, air-fuel mixture burns and expands (3), pushing piston down in the power stroke. On stroke 4, the exhaust valve opens, the piston again is moving up, and the spent gases are forced out. The Otto engine is perhaps the most familiar internal-combustion engine because of its use in automobiles.

COMBUSTION engine operates by means of controlled explosions of fuel within its own cylinders. Most gasoline engines use the original four-stroke cycle devised by Nikolaus Otto in 1862 (see MOTOR VEHICLE). The Otto engine is single-acting; moreover, work is done only on its third stroke. A continuous output of work thus requires at least four cylinders, with explosions timed in proper sequence. Automobile and piston-type aircraft engines are chiefly of the Otto type. Automobile engines have their cylinders arranged in line or in a V. In aircraft engines the radial (circular)

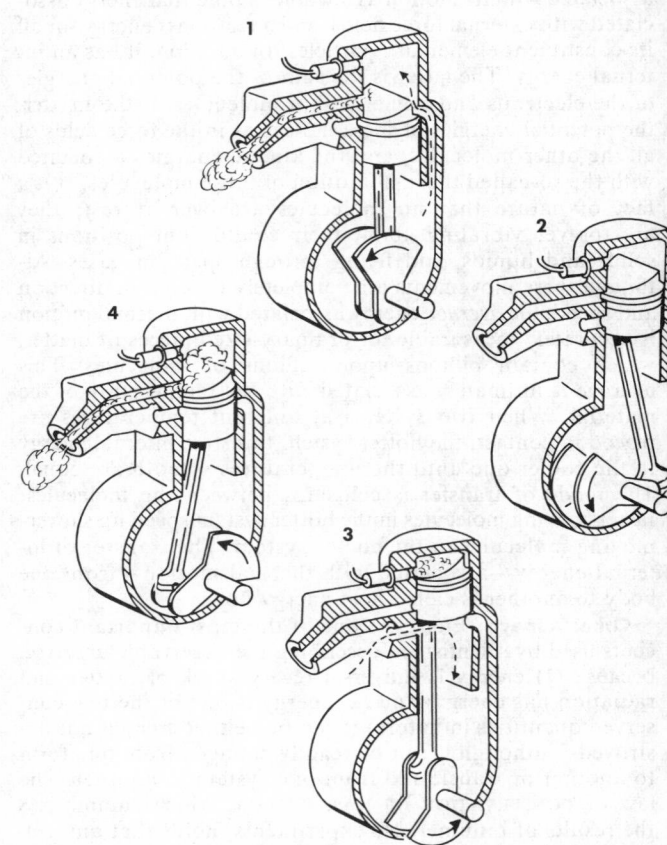

The 2-stroke-cycle engine delivers power on every full revolution of its crankshaft; *i.e.* with every two strokes (one up and one down) power is produced. Shown here is a two-stroke diesel, utilizing compression ignition rather than spark ignition. Air from crankcase enters through transfer port and fills cylinder (1) while at the same time the piston is falling to uncover the exhaust port, releasing spent gases. Rising piston covers all ports (2), compressing air in cylinder. Piston, still rising (3), uncovers inlet port, and fresh air is sucked into crankcase; then, almost simultaneously (3), injected fuel ignites in cylinder on contact with hot compressed air, and piston is pushed downward in power stroke. Descending piston (4) uncovers exhaust port and compresses air in crankcase, facilitating flow of air through transfer port into cylinder (1).

arrangement is probably the most common as well as the most satisfactory for air cooling. The Otto engine needs a carburetor to blend gasoline and air into a mixture neither too rich nor too lean; it also requires precisely timed electric ignition. Both are unnecessary with the DIESEL ENGINE, whose piston compresses the air trapped in the cylinder to a pressure of about $500\,lb/in.^2$ This raises the temperature to about $800°F$, at which oil ignites spontaneously. The diesel burns a low-cost fuel oil instead of gasoline, and its efficiency may be as high as 40%, compared to a maximum of 25% for the Otto

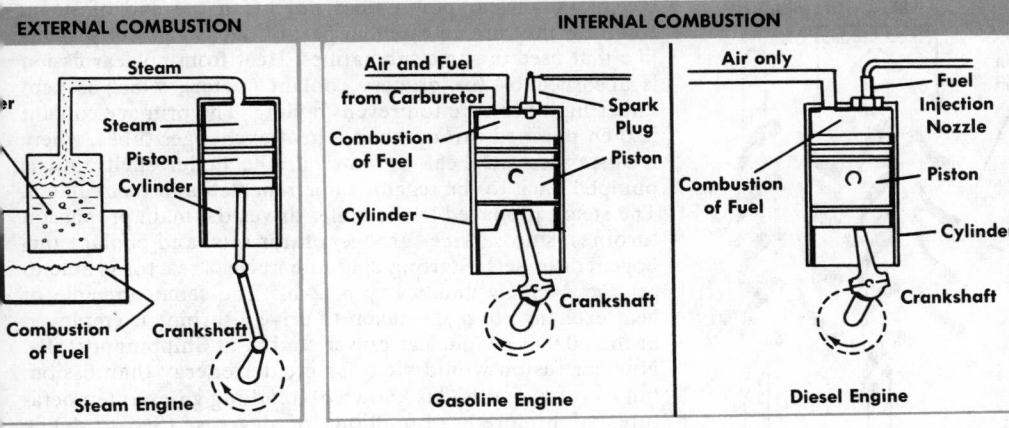

EXTERNAL COMBUSTION

Steam

Steam

Piston

Cylinder

Combustion of Fuel

Crankshaft

Steam Engine

INTERNAL COMBUSTION

Air and Fuel from Carburetor

Spark Plug

Combustion of Fuel

Piston

Cylinder

Crankshaft

Gasoline Engine

Air only

Fuel Injection Nozzle

Combustion of Fuel

Piston

Cylinder

Crankshaft

Diesel Engine

External vs. internal combustion: Principal difference is that in internal combustion the fuel substances (fuel and air) are also the substances that directly produce work, while in external combustion the combustible substances (e.g. coal and air) are used to heat water and turn it to steam, and it is the expanding steam that does the work.

engine. But the diesel may present problems in starting and in fuel injection.

Rocket and jet engines employ the principle of reaction propulsion, described in Newton's Third Law of Motion: "For every action there is an equal and opposite reaction." The gases of combustion are expelled from the rear at high velocity, imparting a forward thrust to the aircraft or space vehicle. The liquid-fuel rocket engine is a combustion chamber into which a propellant and an oxidizer are fed from separate tanks—a typical combination is gasoline and liquid oxygen. Since a rocket carries its own oxidizer, it can operate beyond Earth's atmosphere. Pulsejet, ramjet, turbojet, turboprop, and turbofan engines depend upon atmospheric air to support combustion. The intermittently firing pulsejet engine propelled the V-1 "buzz bombs" of World War II; today it is of minor importance. Ramjet and turbojet engines are used to power modern aircraft and air-breathing missiles. But the ramjet performs poorly below the speed of sound, since it depends entirely upon the "ram effect" of its forward speed to supply air to the combustion chamber. In the turbojet engine, a portion of the energy of the exhaust gases is diverted to the blading of a gas turbine, spinning it at several thousand rev/min. The turbojet provides a cruising speed of 550 to 600 mi/hr. The turboprop engine is used for aircraft in the medium-speed range, 400 to 450 mi/hr. Its turbine powers both an air compressor and a propeller. In the newer turbofan

engine, the propeller is replaced by a duct-enclosed, multiple-bladed fan. (See AIRCRAFT PROPULSION.)

TURBINES are powered by the forced passage of a fluid or gas; they are classified as impulse and reaction. (Actually, all turbines operate to some extent on both principles.) The Francis turbine, used in power generation, is a hydraulic reaction turbine. A large volume of water flows downward through a penstock and then horizontally through scroll case, speed ring, and inlet gates to the curved vanes of the turbine runner, which revolves on a vertical shaft. The principle of operation is basically the same as that of a revolving lawn sprinkler. The Pelton wheel is an impulse turbine; its shaft is usually horizontal. Water, forced through a nozzle by gravity, strikes as a pressure jet against "buckets" on the outside of the wheel. The vertical distance from intake at the top of the dam to discharge at the bottom of the wheel is known as "head." High head is more important than large water flow to the operation of the Pelton wheel. The higher the head, the greater the nozzle pressure and hence the more powerful the turbine. The steam turbine utilizes the pressure of expanding steam to turn a rotor, made up of a series of bladed disks (see STEAM ENGINE). Steam turbines may be of the impulse or reaction type, or a combination of the two.

In the aircraft industry and elsewhere, GAS TURBINES are strongly competing with piston engines. In the form of turbojet or turboprop engines they power many aircraft. Gas turbines

Hydraulic turbines: Three general types are the Francis, or reaction-type (*above*); the Pelton, or impulse-type (*right, top*); and the Kaplan, or propeller-type (*right, bottom*). Each is best suited to a different pressure and volume of water flow.

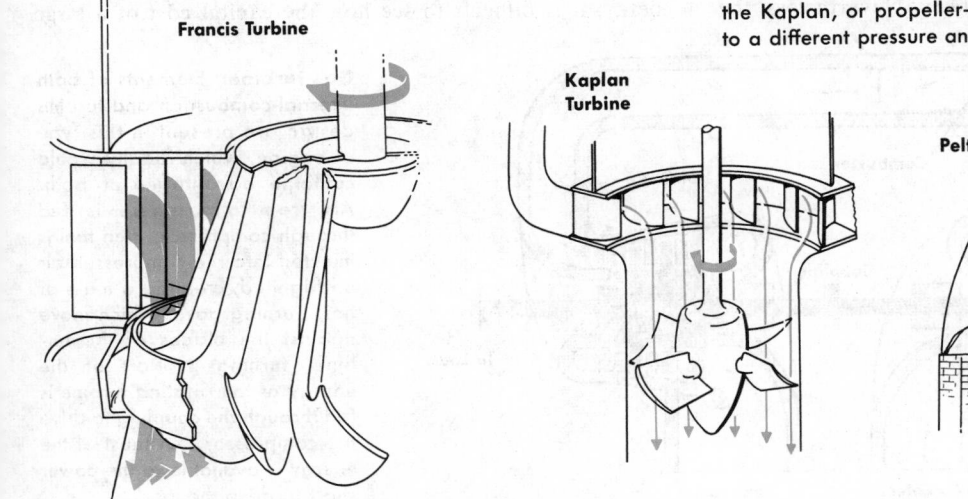

Francis Turbine

Kaplan Turbine

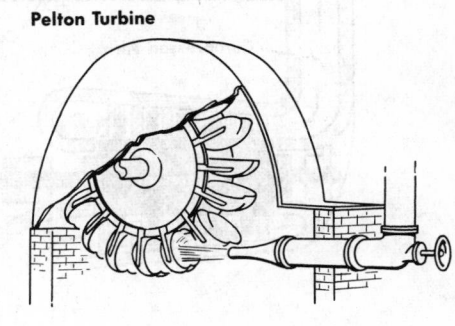

Pelton Turbine

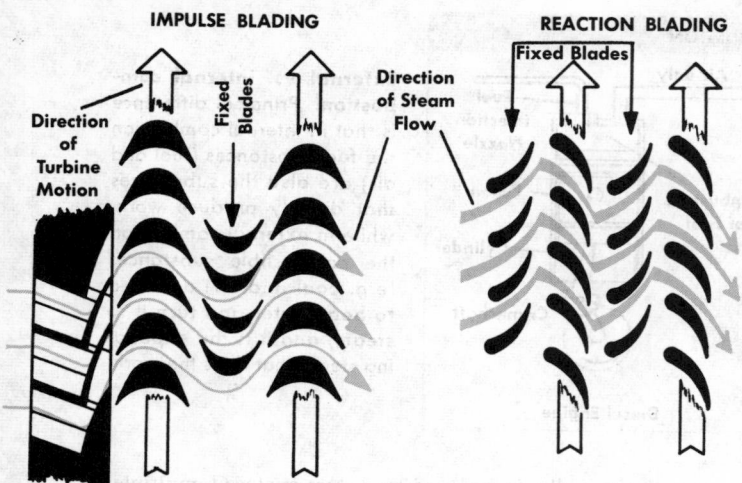

IMPULSE BLADING

Direction of Turbine Motion

Fixed Blades

Direction of Steam Flow

REACTION BLADING

Fixed Blades

Steam turbines can be described by type of blading as *impulse* (De Laval type) or *reaction* (Parsons type). Impulse blading causes change in steam's velocity because blading reverses direction of steam; this produces force against movable blades connected to power shaft. Reaction blading exerts a nozzle-like effect on steam; steam expands, with a resulting increase in its velocity relative to the blading. Thus a force of reaction, opposite in direction to that of the steam flow, is produced against the movable blades. In application, a turbine power plant has many more rows of blading than indicated above, and may be a combination of impulse and reaction types.

are used also, in a more limited way, in railroad locomotives, ships, electric generators, gas-line compressors, and water pumps. They may some day be used to power automobiles. Gas turbines can run on a broad range of fuels and develop more power for their weight and size than most other engines, but are expensive to build and use much fuel.

Steam and hydraulic turbines generate practically all our electricity. Steam-electric stations, mostly equipped with steam turbines, account for about 80% of the kilowatt capacity of the U. S. A. Hydraulic turbines, largely limited to the Northwest where water power is plentiful, produce almost all of the remaining 20%.

Nuclear reactors are also heat engines but on a vastly more powerful scale than coal-burning boilers. The chemical combination of one carbon and two oxygen atoms in combustion releases 1½ ev (electron volts) of energy. Each fissioning atom of uranium 236 (produced when an atom of U 235 absorbs a neutron) releases 200,000,000 ev. Nevertheless, the

advent of nuclear power does not mean the end of steam turbines; they are an essential part of nuclear power systems like that used in some submarines. Heat from nuclear fission is absorbed by the primary coolant (water), which is kept under high pressure to prevent boiling. The primary coolant is then pumped through boiler heat-exchanger tubes, where it surrenders its heat to water in the boiler shell, and is pumped back to the reactor to be reheated and recirculated. The steam produced in the boiler drives the main propulsion turbines, ship-service turbogenerator sets, and coolant turbogenerator sets. Starting cold, the nuclear reactor is able to get the *Nautilus* under way in 2 hr. The same principle of heat exchange to make steam to drive a turbine is employed at the 60,000-kw nuclear power station at Shippingport, Pa. Nuclear fusion would yield far greater energy than fission, but as yet no method is known of handling gases at temperatures of hundreds of millions of degrees. (See NUCLEAR REACTOR.)

Engines can be made to run from energy sources other than fossil fuels, flowing water, or nuclear fission. The windmill is a familiar example. But the Bible truism, "The wind blows where it wills," aptly describes the limitations of the wind engine. The picturesque Dutch windmill with its four giant sails, the American type with a balancing tail to keep its multibladed turbine wheel in the wind, the high-speed propellers that drive battery chargers—none of these or other possible wind engines can be expected to supply more than a small fraction of the energy the world is now consuming.

Tides are regular but have proved less easy to harness than the wind; little has been accomplished so far with tidal engines. But use of Earth's internal heat is already more than a dream. Wells drilled at various locations bring up "natural" steam to run engines.

Direct utilization of sunlight is another dream with aspects of reality. Small solar engines of 3 to 5 hp are being used in arid regions—*e.g.* in N Africa and New Zealand—at sites where conventional fuels are either too expensive or not available. These small engines are "steam" engines using liquid sulfur dioxide instead of water. The liquid is evaporated in a trough-shaped concentrator of solar rays. The vapor drives the engine and is then condensed by cold water for return to the evaporator. Many schemes have been proposed by which solar energy could be used on a bigger scale, *e.g.* heating a mercury boiler by large paraboloid reflectors on mountings geared to follow the daily course of the Sun. The mercury vapor could drive a turbine—while the Sun was shining. But a solar plant would never work at night and would lose heat every time a cloud passed across the Sun. Even with free energy, it is difficult to see how the capital cost of a large

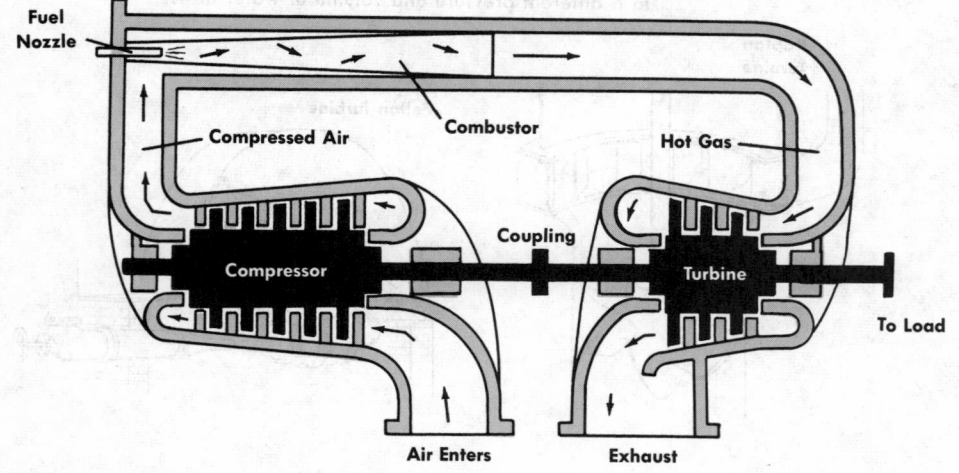

Fuel Nozzle

Compressed Air   Combustor   Hot Gas

Compressor   Coupling   Turbine

To Load

Air Enters   Exhaust

Gas turbine: Elements of both internal-combustion and turbine design are present in this type of engine, which ideally would combine advantages of both. Air from atmosphere is fed through compressor, then fuel is injected into the compressed air and ignited, creating a mass of hot, burning gases which move against the blades of the turbine, turning it. Part of the energy of the rotating turbine is fed through the coupling to drive the compressor, but most of the energy is available to the power shaft to drive the load.

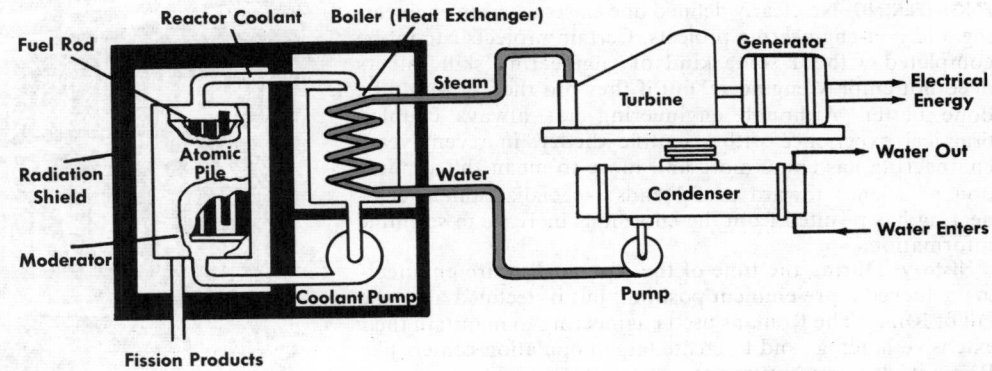

Nuclear power plant: Its principle is similar to that of an external-combustion, steam-turbine, electrical generating plant, except for the fact that atomic energy, rather than energy of a burning fuel, heats water to steam. Heat is produced by fission and collisions of atomic particles; rate and impact of collisions are controlled by nature of fuel material (e.g. uranium) and moderator material (e.g. graphite). The coolant (water, gas, or molten metal) leaves the pile section at a temperature of several hundred degrees, then in the boiler gives its heat to water. The water turns to steam, and the coolant, now much cooler, re-enters the atomic-pile section to pick up more heat.

solar installation could be economically justified. Out in space the limitations of solar power no longer prevail, and it is possible to get continuous energy from sunlight for satellite power plants, though as yet on a small scale. In 1960 silicon cells were used in two U. S. space satellites to recharge batteries and to power TV cameras and transmitters. These direct converters of radiant energy to electricity can already operate at an efficiency of 16%. Unfortunately, the silicon cell requires pure silicon, which is very expensive.

History: Sails, windmills, and primitive water wheels were the first useful engines. Windmills, known in Europe since at least the 12th cent., pumped water and ground grain. During the 17th and 18th cent. the overshot water wheel furnished power for grinding grain, sawing logs, and running textile machinery. It was turned by the weight of water flowing from above the wheel into buckets around its rim. Primitive water turbines also began to appear in the 18th cent.

The steam engine's long history begins in antiquity with Hero of Alexandria (1st cent. A. D.), who described a metal sphere that was rotated on its axle by steam escaping from backward-bent tubes. Hero's "aeolipile" was a true steam turbine of the reaction type. The first reciprocating steam engine was made around 1690 by Denis Papin, a French Protestant refugee in Germany, who heated water in a cylinder to create steam, which drove a piston forward. He then quenched his fire and waited for the cylinder to cool. When the steam had condensed, atmospheric pressure returned the piston to the original position. By using a separate boiler and squirting cold water into the cylinder at every cycle, Thomas Newcomen made a workable though inefficient "atmospheric" engine in 1711. In 1769 James Watt patented the use of an air pump to exhaust the used steam. Condensation outside the cylinder saved three quarters of the coal devoured by the Newcomen engine. Much more efficient was Watt's invention in 1782 of a double-acting engine which worked by steam pressure rather than atmospheric pressure. The practical Watt engine made it possible for Robert Fulton to build a paddle-wheel steamboat (1807) and Richard Trevithick the first steam locomotive (1804). The 19th cent. brought remarkable advances in water engines. The inward-flow reaction turbine was perfected by James B. Francis at Lowell, Mass., around 1855; the Pelton wheel was invented in California in 1880 by Lester A. Pelton.

The first internal-combustion engine, now long obsolete, burned illuminating gas. Nikolaus August Otto, a German engineer, devised a successful four-cycle gas engine in 1876 and patented a system of electric ignition 2 yr later. The four-cycle gasoline engine, also an achievement of Otto, was delayed until 1885. Other Germans, Gottlieb Daimler and Karl

Benz, working respectively in Cannstatt and in Mannheim, independently invented the automobile. By an odd coincidence, Daimler's motorized coach and Benz's three-wheeler were road-tested in the same year, 1886. Each had a single-cylinder engine of around 1 hp. In 1893 a patent was granted to Rudolf Diesel for the engine that now bears his name. Diesel had studied engines then in use and was dissatisfied with their efficiencies. (Simple steam engines, then the principal prime movers, converted only 6 to 8% of the potential energy of their fuels into useful work.) Diesel's design achieved far greater efficiency: it gets more work out of its fuel than gasoline (Otto) engines do, and much more than steam engines do. Diesel efficiencies commonly exceed 30%. The first fuel Diesel tested was a tarlike crude oil, too thick to flow through pipes. His hope was to develop an engine that would operate on an injection of coal dust, thereby freeing German industry from dependence on imported oil. Although Diesel's effort to build a successful solid-injection engine failed (as have all subsequent efforts), he himself did build several successful oil-injection engines. Diesel engines did not prove as suitable for aircraft and passenger autos as Otto engines, although diesel autos are built. An ocean-going ship was equipped with diesel engines in 1912, the first diesel truck engine appeared in 1923, and the first diesel locomotive, 1934. The compound steam turbine was invented by Sir Charles Algernon Parsons, of Newcastle-upon-Tyne, England, c. 1884, in response to the need for better engines to drive electric generators. The next major engine development was the jet-propulsion gas turbine, invented in 1930 by Air Commodore Sir Frank Whittle (Great Britain), but not perfected until 1946. The first jet passenger service, London to Johannesburg, was inaugurated May 1952.

Calder Hall, the first civilian nuclear power station, began operation Oct. 17, 1956, in Cumberland, England. Its American counterpart at Shippingport, Pa., started up Dec. 2, 1957. Since then, many nuclear power plants have been built in the U. S. A. and in Britain. Other countries involved in major nuclear projects include France, West Germany, U. S. S. R., Spain, Belgium, Sweden, Finland, Italy, Switzerland, Japan, and Canada. Both the U. S. A. and U. S. S. R. are building nuclear power plants combined with sea-water distillation plants scheduled for completion about 1970. The world's first nuclear submarine, the *USS Nautilus*, began her maiden voyage Jan. 17, 1955. Since then, about five nuclear submarines a year have been built in the U. S. A. The *NS Savannah*, the world's first atomic-powered merchant ship, was launched in 1959. The first nuclear-powered aircraft carrier, the *USS Enterprise,* with eight atomic reactors, was launched in 1960. Other nuclear naval vessels have followed.—*C. B. C.*

ENGINEERING: No clearly defined line exists between engineering and non-engineering projects. Certain projects cannot be completed without some kind of engineering skill; others need not employ engineers, but if they did the job would be done better. Although engineering has always coupled practical experience with scientific theory, in recent years engineering has come more and more to mean the application of science toward useful ends: specialization in engineering has resulted from the enormous increase in scientific information.

History: During the time of the Roman Empire engineering achieved a pre-eminent position, but it declined after the fall of Rome. The Romans used engineering to maintain their extensive holdings and to create large population centers like Rome itself (see ENGINEERING IN ANTIQUITY). The invention of gunpowder and the design of larger cannon created the need for a new type of military engineering: the building of fortifications, which reached a high point in the 17th cent. Many of the techniques developed by these great military engineers were valuable to the civil engineers of the 18th cent. Civil (non-military) engineering during the Middle Ages was limited to towns; there were none of the grand highways, harbors, and aqueducts of Roman times. Town water systems supplied by pumping stations were a major achievement: systems were installed in Toledo, 1526, and London, 1582. The increase in trade between towns, then between countries and continents, brought a demand for improved land and water transport. State-financed engineering projects came into being. France led the renaissance of engineering in the 17th and 18th cent. with such projects as the Languedoc Canal, 1666–81, which completed the connection between the Atlantic and the Mediterranean across France. Its system of locks, aqueducts, culverts, and tunnels was the engineering marvel of the age. In 1716 the office of Director-General of Bridges and Highways was established in France. The School of Bridges and Highways was founded, 1747, to train young men entering the engineering profession. Some lectures on engineering were given in English universities, but the apprenticeship system was maintained in all countries until well into the 19th cent. In the U. S. A. the first engineering schools were West Point and Rensselaer. Professional societies of engineers were not started until the 19th cent.: the British Institution of Civil Engineers was founded in 1818, and the American Society of Civil Engineers in 1852.

Engineering gradually grew from a craft and art to a profession requiring formal college training. Instead of being project overseers as they had been in ancient times, engineers became specialists who were expected to apply scientific knowledge to the design and construction of structures. With the invention of the steam engine and the growth of the factory, a group interested in the application of the sciences of mechanics and thermodynamics separated themselves from civil engineering and called themselves mechanical engineers. As the science of electricity grew in the 19th cent. and its application became more widespread, electrical engineering appeared. The ancient science of chemistry became the foundation for chemical engineering when the discovery of synthetics and the need for quantity production of chemicals established the chemical industry on a large scale. Such divisions continued until, at present, there are hundreds of subdivisions of engineering. All, however, have branched out from five major groups: chemical, civil, electrical, mechanical, and mineral. (See APPLIED SCIENCE.)

Chemical Engineering: Whenever a product is produced in the chemical laboratory that can be used in large quantities, it is the job of the chemical engineer to design a plant for large-scale production of the substance. Chemical manu-

Electrical engineer operates experimental computer. Its main "memory," recorded on magnetic film, enables it to perform computations much faster than is possible with earlier general-purpose computers. (*Lincoln Lab., M. I. T.*)

facturing processes consist of a relatively few basic chemical and physical transformations called *unit operations*. These unit operations are either physical (*e.g.* crushing, shredding, mixing, filtering, settling) or chemical (oxidation, reduction, chlorination, polymerization). Chemical engineering is the newest of the major branches of engineering. (The American Institute of Chemical Engineers was founded in 1908.) Chemical engineers supervise the design, construction, and operation of plants that produce heavy chemicals, fine chemicals, or foods. *Heavy chemicals* consist of acids, alkalies, salts, and other chemicals used in great quantities in manufacturing. *Fine chemicals* include pharmaceuticals, cosmetics, insecticides, and photographic materials.

Civil Engineering: Civil engineers are needed on all major construction projects: bridges, dams, tunnels, and commercial buildings usually require engineers for design and other engineers to supervise the construction. The design of the rights-of-way for highways and railroads is another area for civil engineering (see HIGHWAY and RAILWAY ENGINEERING). Like the overseers of old, civil engineers are also responsible for seeing that a structure is made according to the design specifications.

A major area of civil engineering is HYDRAULICS. Projects in this field include IRRIGATION, drainage, city WATER-SUPPLY systems, sewage-disposal plants (see SANITARY ENGINEERING), and pipelines for petroleum products. Civil engineers collaborate with mechanical and electrical engineers in designing construction machinery. They must work closely with electrical engineers in HYDROELECTRIC DEVELOPMENT. Chemical and mechanical engineers join civil engineers in the development of new construction materials.

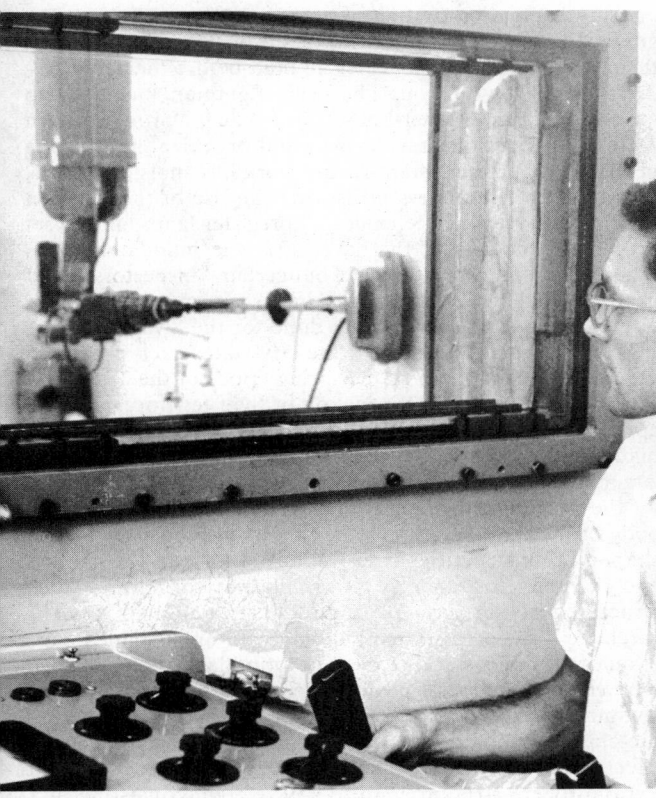

Nuclear engineers at Vallecito, N. M., Atomic Laboratory designed this remotely controlled floor polisher for increased safety and economy in the cleaning of experimental cells contaminated with radioactive materials. (*General Electric*)

Civil engineer tests navigation conditions prior to construction of Belleville, Ohio, dam and locks. Remote-control maneuver of miniature tow in this scale model of dam, locks, and approaches gives information that will guide design of dam. (*U. S. Army*)

Electrical Engineering: Two main divisions, communications and power, constitute electrical engineering. Communications makes use of minute quantities of electricity and deals with the design and manufacture of devices made from electron tubes and transistors (see ELECTRONICS). The tubes and transistors are located in circuits which convert sound and light into electrical impulses for transmission over considerable distances to receivers where the electrical energy is reconverted into sound and light. The electrical engineer designs and supervises the manufacture of radios, television, and telephone equipment. The versatility of electronic control makes it indispensable in industrial processes where accuracy beyond the capability of human senses is needed. Steel sheet within an accuracy of 1/1,000 in. can be made by using electronic controls. The electrical engineer worked with the chemical engineer in designing the completely automatic oil refinery. The mechanical engineer and the electrical engineer are cooperating in the introduction of AUTOMATION in an increasing number of industries. The computer is another product of the electrical engineer.

Electrical energy in large quantities is the field of power engineers. They design and supervise the manufacture of generators, switches, circuit breakers, transformers, and distribution systems. Besides the many home appliances, electrical power is almost the sole mover of industrial machinery. Being convenient, clean, and efficient, electrical energy is more widely used than any other form of energy. The electric-power engineer devises better methods of producing electrical energy whether by steam, water power, or atomic energy. Electricity's power to produce light has resulted in the field of illumination engineering, involving installations for office, factory, street, and airport. (See ELECTRIC POWER; ELECTRIC POWER GENERATION AND POWER PLANTS.)

Mechanical Engineering: Mechanical engineering is the use ful application of the sciences of MECHANICS and THERMODYNAMICS. The mechanical engineer deals with steam engines, turbines, air conditioning, and refrigeration, as well as with all power that comes from heat, whether produced in gasoline, diesel, or rocket engines. He designs MACHINE TOOLS for such operations as grinding, milling, and boring. Once these machines are as designed, a mechanical engineer supervises their construction and designs plants which can use these machines most efficiently in assembly lines. The ultimate in these efforts was the automated assembly line. All machines for handling materials, both raw and finished, are designed by mechanical engineers. Some examples are fork-lift trucks and conveyor belts, and escalators and elevators for human freight. Mechanical engineering naturally moved also into the field of aeronautics, which is concerned basically with the mechanics of moving bodies in a fluid, air (see AERODYNAMICS). Aeronautical engineering is one of the most important branches of mechanical engineering, but the problems in this new field have become so special that aeronautical engineering is fast becoming a branch of engineering on its own. A further subdivision, aerospace engineering, is increasingly recognized.

Mechanical engineers collaborate with electrical engineers in many fields, *e.g.* the design of steam-turbine and electrical generator units, or the design of diesel-electric systems. The mechanical engineer looks to metallurgical and chemical engineers for development of materials suitable for specific applications, as in rocket engines and nose cones.

Mineral Engineering: The materials for engineering construction are provided by the mineral engineer. The most ancient of man's crafts are mining, metallurgy, and ceramics, yet the field of mineral engineering is relatively new. (The American Institute of Mining, Metallurgical and Petroleum Engineers was founded in 1871.) The mining engineer explores by means of surveying, seismograph, aerial photography, and Geiger counter for deposits of minerals such as iron, copper, aluminum, and uranium (see GEOCHEMICAL PROSPECTING; GEOPHYSICAL PROSPECTING). Once a deposit large enough for exploitation is found, the engineer takes responsibility for extracting the ores safely and efficiently (see MINING). Mining engineers cooperate with civil engineers on the construction of mine shafts, and with mechanical and electrical engineers on the design of mining machinery. PETROLEUM engineering is closely related to mining engineering, although the petroleum engineer's knowledge must specifically include enough geology for extracting the maximum amount of petroleum from a given field. The metallurgical engineer is particularly active in the iron and steel industry, where he designs furnaces, oversees the operation of the plant, and constantly searches for methods to improve the end product (see METALLURGY). The metallurgical engineer works closely with the electrical engineer in the refining of aluminum and copper by electrolytic processes. Ceramic engineering deals with the manufacture of products made from nonferrous minerals. A ceramic engineer designs a variety of shapes from clay and glass, such as kitchen ware, sanitary ware, and electrical insulators. He also improves the techniques for manufacturing these products in quantity. (See CERAMICS.)

Nuclear Engineering: Nuclear engineering is unique in that it does not fall within any of the major branches of engineering yet depends on them all. The field is based on atomic physics, which is perhaps the fastest developing area in science. The nuclear engineer designs, supervises the construction of, and operates nuclear reactors for producing radio-isotopes, weapons, and fuel. His most serious problem is safety: radioactive materials must be stored, used, and disposed of without danger to the workers or nearby communities. See Color Plate 36.—*H. I. S.*

ENGINEERING IN ANTIQUITY: Ancient engineering was based not on technical education (undeveloped until the 18th cent.) but on the efforts and skills of craftsmen, supported by large numbers of unskilled workmen. Prehistoric farmers and hunters were able to build such remarkable structures as Stonehenge, whose bluestone uprights (4 tons each) were taken from quarries in Pembrokeshire some 150 mi by sea and land; the larger sarsens (30 tons) came from the Marlborough downs, 25 mi away. The tooling and erecting of these stone circles must have involved the organizing and feeding of several hundreds of workmen. Similar feats are still carried out by primitive tribes like the Nagas of Assam. In the early empires of the Nile, Euphrates, Tigris, and Indus valleys (*c.* 3000 B. C.) there was already a separate class of craftsmen, mainly concentrated in the cities, the seats of government, temples, and trade, where raw materials and products were readily available. Though many such things as pottery and textiles continued to be made in households, these craftsmen were specialists, concentrating on such skills as metallurgy and the working of natural stone and wood, leather, or glass. Such crafts were usually plied on a workshop scale, seldom in government or temple workshops with a larger output. But larger engineering projects were fostered by governments or temple authorities. The very basis of these early empires was the cooperative efforts of the prehistoric

farming population to drain the swampy river valleys and to guide the annual rise of the waters onto the fields to make them deposit their precious fertile mud before the water was drained off downstream. The early Egyptian kings set up government-run "water-houses" in each "province" (in reality an irrigation unit) to plan and organize the "cutting of the dikes," the constant repair-work of canals and dikes, to watch the Nilometers measuring the rise of the Nile (on which the harvest tax depended), to register lands, and to set up new boundaries of the fields after the inundation. This was partly administrative work, but certain "inspectors" must have had technical skill; in certain cases competent farmers were appointed to survey work done for the "water-house." In Mesopotamia we find that the city-states each organized the storing of the water of the spring floods of the Tigris and Euphrates rivers and the irrigation of their territory, and also appointed such temple-schooled officials as the "gurgallu" or made use of the experience of farm supervisors. In fact, all larger engineering works were state ventures. This holds good for the pyramids, the later forms of royal tomb, in which the body of the dead king was to be preserved. The early bench-shaped brick structures over the burial pit and the chapels and chambers for funerary gifts made way for natural-stone structures in the days of King Djozer (2700 B. C.). His "architect" Imhotep started building with brick-shaped units of quarried stone, stacking them to form blank walls in which were chiseled niches, or pillars which were then cut to imitate columns of bundles of reeds, until he discovered how to use pre-cut larger blocks of natural stone to achieve the desired effect. Later royal tombs like King Khufu's (Cheops') Great Pyramid were structures up to 450 ft high, consisting of a core of carefully chiseled 4-ton limestone blocks, in which a series of chambers and corridors were constructed to con-

Engineers of Caesar's army, employing sound principles of bridge construction, enabled the Romans to cross the Rhine. Old print is from Fra Gioconda's edition of Caesar's *Commentaries* (Venice, 1513). (*Harvard College Library*)

nect with similar corridors below the base of the pyramid, which was finished off with slabs of polished granite, quarried and brought from Aswan. The limestone blocks, quarried on the other bank of the Nile, were hauled onto the pyramid plateau and then up earthen ramps (which finally had as large a volume as the entire pyramid) to the construction level. Up to 100,000 workmen were employed at peak periods. They accomplished their tasks with such simple equipment as wooden mallets and wedges, copper saws and chisels, ropes, and wooden sledges. To furnish housing, food, and equipment for the workmen, and to remove debris, required a highly effective social organization. The building of the pyramids shows what careful planning could accomplish with relatively unskilled manpower and primitive equipment. The Egyptian state also conducted periodic expeditions to the copper mines of the Sinai Peninsula, worked by criminals and captives under the supervision of skilled mining and smelting experts, and protected by soldiers against marauding tribes. See MINING.

The city-states and empires of Mesopotamia built their brick temple-towers (ziggurat), which were often as high as 300 ft, interconnected by well-paved, wide procession avenues. Having invented the vault, the Mesopotamians bridged even large rivers like the Euphrates. They too conducted expeditions—to mountains to the east and north—to quarry building materials or to obtain ores and metals. In Greece and Rome, state-organized public works led to impressive engineering feats. Ancient hill-towns like Jerusalem often sank wells to be connected by subterranean water tunnels with a well or pool at the foot of the town wall to guarantee water supply even in wartime. King Sennacherib of Assyria (700 B. C.) was the first to attempt long-distance water-supply; damming the Khosr River near Bavian, he conducted its waters through a 55-km masonry channel to his palace gardens at Nineveh. The Greeks, imitating this first aqueduct, built public water-supply systems for the city of Samos (530 B. C.) and many other centers, using wood- or stone-encased lead siphons or bridges to support the ducts carrying the water over valleys. Public water-supply developments culminated in the aqueduct system of ancient Rome, where a total length of 351.6 km of ducts supplied over 1,000,000 m³ of water a day to its 11 public baths, 856 smaller baths, 1,352 fountains and cisterns, and private houses. The Roman water commissioner and his staff kept this system in repair, checking settling tanks, ducts, mains, and lead home-delivery pipes—the first standardized parts in the world. The Romans also laid out an imposing network of well-designed and well-drained four-layered highways, and also built harbor facilities in main ports to ensure the supply of wine and grain to the Imperial City. This involved construction of quays, storehouses, docks, and lighthouses, as well as precautions against silting. After lighthouse towers with open fires had proved a success at Ostia (A. D. 42) and Boulogne (A. D. 46) the famous Pharos of Alexandria, an 85-ft tower at the entrance of its harbor, built by Sostratos of Knidos about 280 B. C. as a daytime landmark for mariners, was converted into a lighthouse about A. D. 50. In mining, the Roman state took important steps to develop the ores of Spain, Carinthia, and other districts. In these mining districts we find large-scale application of the water-raising machinery invented by Hellenistic engineers (c. 300–0 B. C.)—e.g. the compartmented wheel, the wheel of pots, and the Archimedean screw—in order to lower the water level in the mines. The use of pozzolana, a volcanic earth, led to the use of concrete in architecture and road-building; the design of various types of cranes was furthered by their use on the public buildings of Greece and Rome.

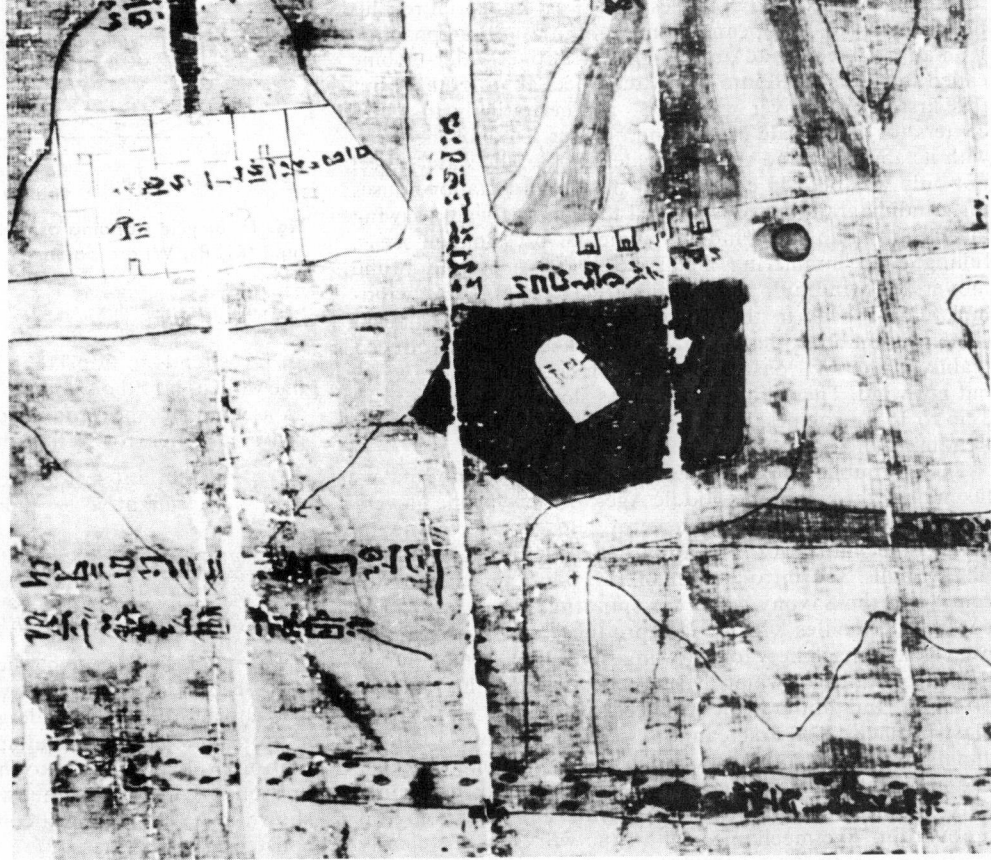

Papyrus map showing the site of ancient Egyptian gold mines at Wadi Hammamat in the Eastern Desert near Thebes, then (about 1300 B.C.) the capital. Hieroglyphs indicate mining sites in hills (shown in profile). Big building drawn at base of hill is a shrine; smaller ones are houses. Object set off on dark field is a commemorative stele, scaled to its importance rather than size. Map was used to move large statue through the mines, possibly to appease gods upset by the taking of ore. (*Turin Museo Egizio*)

If not sponsored and assisted by the state, the superior craftsmen, who often fully deserved the title of engineer, had little scope for their inventions and dreams. Most workshops were small and produced for the local market only. Only a few goods like wine, olive oil, and grain, produced on a large scale and shipped all over the ancient world, offered the ancient engineer an opening for his talents; from the ancient Egyptian bag-press were developed the beam-press, screw-press, and wedge-press. Out of the very old rubbing-stones grew the rotary grain-mill, consisting of two flat millstones, and later the Roman donkey-mill with its hourglass-shaped upper stone and conical lower stone. The roller-mill was improved and finally became the efficient Roman "trapetum."

Another incentive to engineering stemmed from the wars between the various tyrants and the Hellenistic kings. They prompted their "technitai" to try their skill at perfecting the war-engines and arms. Hence in the period 400–1 B. C. the bow was mechanized to become the catapult; the sling engendered the ballista. The torsion of bundles of tendons projected the missiles from the ancient "artillery," which was very effective and lasted until about two centuries after the first firearms appeared. The Roman armies had large groups of mobile carriage-drawn "carro-ballistae." But the fall of the Roman Empire, mainly the crumbling of central government, ended most progress. Some inventions like the hypocaust, a central-heating device using the combustion gases of a wood fire to heat the hollow floor and walls of larger buildings and private villas in the northern regions, were lost for centuries. Other engineering skills lingered on, scarcely financed by the younger struggling new kingdoms of W Europe.

New possibilities like the large-domed Byzantine churches, curved weirs, and Chinese inventions such as gunpowder, paper, and printing were temporarily in the hands of Arabic engineers. After political conditions became more stable, c. A. D. 900, the next two centuries saw a real industrial revolution, which put European engineering in a unique position. Roman engineers had turned the primitive water-turbine called the Norse mill into the water-wheel about 50 B. C. but this first prime mover was used only hesitatingly in a few centers for large-scale production of flour. Now in the West, with its abundant and constant water supply, the water-wheel not only was built in cities, monasteries, and manor houses for grinding grain, but was applied to pumping water, sawing marble and timber, grinding pigments, pressing oil-seeds, fulling, and hammering metals. By 1200 a second prime mover, the windmill, perhaps inspired by the Arabic windmill (dating back to the 7th cent.), but with a mechanism closely resembling that of the water-wheel, was introduced mainly in the low coastal plains which lacked running water but not wind. These timber structures slowly developed from 3-hp to 15-hp engines, moving medieval machinery alongside treadmills and horse-mills.

Though public works on the Roman scale were not undertaken until the end of the Middle Ages, the new prime movers promoted mechanization in several fields. In the textile industry, mechanization was apparent in the introduction of fulling mills, the introduction of the bobbing wheel (13th cent.) and the Saxony wheel for spinning, looms with foot-controlled heddles which could produce complicated fancy weaves, and machinery for throwing silk (1272). In metallurgy, the introduction of water-driven bellows led to the building of larger and hotter iron furnaces—ancestors of the true blast-furnace. The first cannon were cast about 1330. In mining, water-driven bellows, pumps, and hoists made deeper and more elaborate tunneling possible. Private capitalists took the lead in promoting industry and technological innovation. The mechanization of the workshops is clearly revealed in the first handbooks on engineering (c. 1500–1550). On the other hand, we also read there about the unbroken classical tradition. This also plays a part in the draining and recovery of marshy and coastal districts by planting and endiking (800–1100). In the Low Countries and in N Italy, where rivers had to be made navigable, the art of building canals and pound-locks or sluices occupied many engineers, including Leonardo da Vinci, the inventor of the mitered gates and the wicket of the lock doors. Dredgers were first built about 1435. But even the architect who built the lofty medieval cathedrals was only an "artifex" or "caementarius" (bricklayer)—a master craftsman, perhaps a man of wide experience and genius, but lacking a technical education. Even Simon Stevin and Leonardo were highly gifted but untrained technicians, whose influence amongst their fellow-craftsmen must not be overrated. See Color Plate 37.—R. J. F.

ENGINEERING MECHANICS: the branch of mechanics dealing with the effect of forces acting upon rigid bodies. If a body is constrained so that it cannot move, it is said to be in *static equilibrium* under the combined action of applied forces and the existing constraints. If a body is not constrained, it will move under the influence of the applied forces, and the body is said to be in *dynamic equilibrium* under the combined action of the applied forces and the inertial forces arising from its motion. In cases of static equilibrium both the resultant force and the resultant "moment" must equal zero.

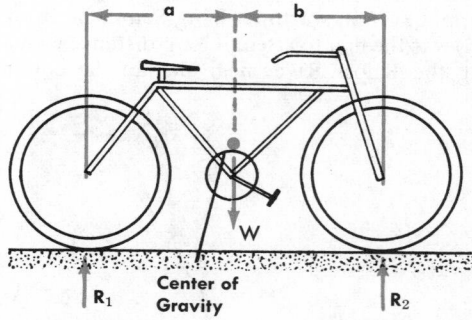

Fig. 1: Bicycle standing at rest is in static equilibrium. All forces on it (R_1, R_2, W) are balanced, so that no net force exists.

(A force tends to translate a body, *i.e.* move all parts of it in one direction at the same time and at the same speed, whereas a moment, the product of force and distance, tends to rotate it.) Thus, for static equilibrium

Resultant vector force $\overline{F} = 0$
Resultant vector moment $\overline{M} = \overline{l} \times \overline{F} = 0$

For example, with a bicycle standing at rest (Fig. 1):

$$R_1 + R_2 - W = 0$$
$$aR_1 - bR_2 \quad = 0$$

The conditions for dynamic equilibrium derive from Newton's second law of motion, which states that an object subjected to a force system undergoes a translational acceleration, a, proportional to the resultant force, and a rotational acceleration, α, proportional to the resultant moment. The proportionality factors for the two types of acceleration may be shown to be two physical constants for a given body. These constants are the mass, M, and the mass moment of inertia,

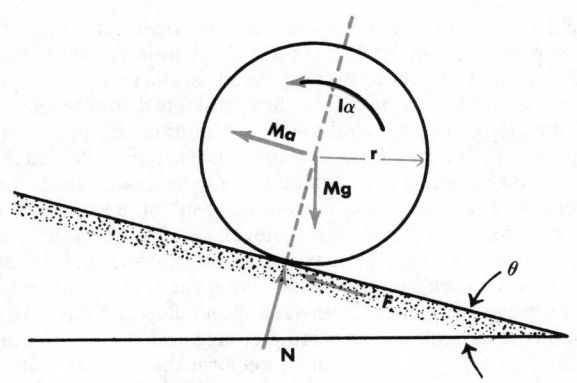

Fig. 2: Solid cylinder of radius r rolling down an incline is in dynamic equilibrium. It is subjected to a constant force, and this force produces a constant acceleration.

I, with respect to the center of gravity. Thus the two vector equations of motion involved are

$$\overline{F} = M\overline{a} \text{ and } \overline{M} = I\overline{\alpha}$$

These equations of motion may be rearranged slightly to take the form of equations of dynamic equilibrium (D'Alembert's principle):

$$\overline{F} - M\overline{a} = 0 \text{ and } \overline{M} - I\overline{\alpha} = 0$$

The motion of a solid cylinder rolling down an incline without slipping (Fig. 2) is denoted, for example, by the equations:

$$Mg \sin \theta - F - Ma = 0$$
$$rF - I\alpha = 0$$

Any determinate statics or dynamics problem in engineering mechanics may be analyzed through extensions of these basic concepts.—*W. W.*

ENLIGHTENMENT: a term applied by various 18th-cent. philosophers and scientists, especially in France and Germany, to their own era. Their ideals were, roughly, that knowledge is of absolute value, that it can be achieved by man in every area of experience and action, that evil results from ignorance alone, that society will progress as knowledge increases, and that knowledge will inevitably increase if free inquiry is tolerated. Science was regarded as the model of human knowledge, and Newtonian mechanics as the model of science. Characteristically, the thinkers of the Enlightenment regarded themselves as members of an international community of rational inquirers. Believing that nature is everywhere uniform and subject to natural laws, and every class of phenomena susceptible to scientific treatment, they optimistically extended the methods of science to psychological and social behavior. —*Ar. D.*

ENOL PHOSPHATES: high-energy phosphate esters, *e.g.* phosphoenol pyruvic acid,

$$\text{HO}-\overset{\displaystyle\overset{O}{\|}}{P}-O-\overset{\displaystyle\overset{CH_2}{\|}}{C}$$
$$\underset{OH}{\big|} \qquad \underset{COOH}{\big|}$$

whose hydrolysis liberates 8,000 to 11,000 cal per mole (see GLYCOLYSIS). They are of biological importance because they can transfer their phosphate groups to ADP to form ATP (adenosine triphosphate), which serves as energy source for all biological processes. No energy is lost in this transphosphorylation reaction.—*J. F. S.*

ENTHALPY: the thermodynamic state of a substance, representing its *total thermal energy* with respect to an arbitrary reference level. This energy, designated by the symbol H, is the sum of the internal energy U and the product of pressure P and volume V, which is a measure of the mechanical energy involved in a volume change. Enthalpy is a so-called *point function,* its magnitude being determined only by the physical state attained by a substance, not by the particular path connecting this state with a previous one. Absolute enthalpy cannot be measured, since its principal component, internal energy, cannot be measured in absolute terms. We are therefore concerned mainly with *changes* in enthalpy; the usual practice in steam engineering stresses the increase in enthalpy as the working substance, namely water, is carried from 32°F to a state of superheated steam. The arbitrary reference level for computing the change of enthalpy of a refrigerant is usually taken as −40°F. Enthalpy tables enable the engineer to estimate the maximum energy that may be released if the working substance in question returns to its original reference level. Enthalpy is a useful concept in fluid mechanics because the total energy of a moving gas can be expressed as the sum of its enthalpy and kinetic energy. In the compression and heating of air at the nose of a fast-moving airplane or missile, kinetic energy of the air relative to the moving body is traded for enthalpy. The enthalpy thus becomes a key quantity in the theory of aerodynamic heating.—*D. B.; A. E.*

ENTOMOLOGY: the study of INSECTS, which number over 660,000 species—about three quarters of all animal species. The vast majority of insects only indirectly affect man. These so-called noneconomic insects attract the attention chiefly of taxonomists, who are interested in classifying them, and ecologists, who study roles of insects in food webs. These noneconomic species actually are important as contributors to the chemical cycles that produce soil; as food for fishes, amphibians, birds, and mammals; and as pollinators of flowering plants. *Economic entomologists* are usually concerned primarily with insects that do damage to crop plants, stored products, or domestic animals, including insects that carry diseases to plants and animals. *Medical entomologists* specialize in insects that affect man's own health. In control of undesirable insects, chemical methods have become popular; but in many instances, insects have mutated to genetic strains showing outstanding immunity to chemical insecticides. Economic entomology relies also upon biological control—the use of organisms such as bacteria to reduce insect populations. In turn, insects may be used to control weeds or even other insects. Of greatest economic significance in biological control are the predatory insects (*e.g.* dragonflies, damselflies, aphis lions, ground beetles, ladybird beetles, and syrphid flies) and the parasitic insects (*e.g.* bristly tachina flies, ichneumon flies, and various parasitic wasps). Often the 9,000 species of ticks and mites, which are actually ARACHNIDS and not insects, are included among the animals considered by the entomologist.—*L. and M. M.*

ENTROPY: a thermodynamic property of a substance related to its absolute temperature, pressure, and volume, all of which serve to define the state of the substance. Entropy increases whenever a body's store of free or available energy decreases or whenever its internal disorder increases. Conversely, whenever there is a gain in available energy or a decrease in internal disorder, entropy diminishes. Thus, in such an irreversible process as the loss of heat by conduction, entropy increases. But in the course of the reversible process of solidification, or freezing, there is an increase in internal order and a consequent drop in entropy. Since loss of available energy and increasing disorder are the rule, rather than the exception, the total entropy of the universe tends to increase as time goes on.

We define entropy S as the ratio of Q/T, where Q is the quantity of heat energy transferred and T the absolute temperature at which this transfer takes place. Actually, absolute entropy cannot be determined; only *change* in entropy, ΔS, which is equal to $\Delta Q/T$, has any significance. The value of ΔS depends only on the initial and final states of the system under consideration; it is independent of the particular path connecting the two states. The dimensions of entropy are those of energy/temperature. Thus entropy may be expressed in calories per Kelvin (K) degree, or Btu per Rankine degree.

Assume a body undergoing a thermodynamic change at a constant temperature, so that an increased internal order results, and hence a lower entropy. In accordance with the equation $\Delta S = \Delta Q/T$, it follows that a drop in S must be accompanied by a drop in Q. The body will therefore lose heat to its surroundings and will assume a lower final temperature. This is what occurs in the course of liquefaction of a gas under high pressure. The heat generated in the process of compression is removed to cooler surroundings, after which the gas is cooled by expansion through a nozzle and ultimately attains a low enough temperature to liquefy. Evaporation of liquid helium may be used for further cooling, to roughly 1°K. To obtain still lower temperatures we resort to another ordering influence, namely that of adiabatic demagnetization of a paramagnetic substance. The switching on of the magnetizing field causes a production of heat, which is removed by a cooler material in thermal contact with the substance undergoing magnetization. When the magnetizing field is removed and the substance insulated from further loss of heat, a final temperature of nearly 0.001°K is attained.—*A. E.*

ENZYME: any of the substances in living organisms which catalyze their biochemical reactions, and thus guide essentially all the dynamic events of the life process. They are, for example, directly responsible for digestion of food, conduction of nerve impulses, contraction of muscles, use of sunlight energy for synthesis of carbohydrates, and clotting of blood. Without enzymes, most of the chemical reactions that occur in living organisms would take place very slowly, if at all. The rate and direction of the living process of any organism are thus controlled by the amount and efficiency of the various enzymes present. Each living system synthesizes its own distinctive enzymes, but enzymes that perform similar functions are usually very similar, though they may come from quite different organisms. The enzymes which burn glucose to give energy in yeast cells, for example, are very similar to those which burn glucose to give energy in the muscle cells of man. Each enzyme apparently carries out a single step in a sequence of reactions leading to the over-all physiological result: thus, over 20 reactions are involved when glucose is converted to carbon dioxide and alcohol in yeast cells (see GLYCOLYSIS), and each of these steps is catalyzed by a different enzyme. To illustrate: if a cell is to convert compound A to compound Z, this is accomplished in a series of small steps in which compound A is converted to compound B, compound B to compound C, and so on. The enzyme which converts A to B cannot convert B to C; a new enzyme capable of converting B to C takes over after A has been converted to B. The sequence of reactions yields the final product in much the same way that an assembly line produces an automobile.

Most enzymes can be extracted from the cell and their action duplicated in the test tube. Over 700 enzymes have been isolated and characterized so far. From the fact that many processes are still unexplored, it appears that many other enzymes are yet to be discovered. See accompanying list of representative enzymes and their biological functions.

Since many enzymes and many compounds are present together in the living cell, the system must be controlled so that the desired products are obtained from the available starting materials. The enzyme can exercise control because of its high specificity—a key property never yet duplicated in man-made catalysts. This property allows the enzyme to discriminate between closely similar chemical compounds much as a lock can discriminate between many closely similar keys. An enzyme capable of converting compound A to compound B will not react with D, E, or F, because they do not "fit" in the appropriate spot on the enzyme surface. Thus only A but not D, E, or F will be converted to B, and side reactions are controlled. The compound which is transformed (A in the above example) is called the "substrate" for the enzyme, and the compound produced is called the "product."

A second property of enzymes is their great efficiency as catalysts. One molecule of certain enzymes can transform hundreds of thousands of molecules of substrate to product in a minute, and this is achieved under the mild conditions of temperature, pressure, and concentration common to living systems. Minute concentrations of these catalysts in a cell provide it with energy and chemicals at the speed necessary to maintain life.

The fact that each enzyme catalyzes a key reaction explains the effect of some poisons and some hereditary diseases. Some poisons act by blocking the action of a specific enzyme, without whose action a certain physiological process cannot occur. For example, the nerve gas diisopropylfluorophosphate attacks the enzyme acetylcholinesterase and inactivates it; since this enzyme plays a key role in nerve conduction, the gas paralyzes the nerves. In some hereditary diseases, it is believed, a particular enzyme is missing because the apparatus to synthesize it is defective; thus, certain types of mental disease may be caused by a hereditary deficiency which prevents conversion of phenylalanine to tyrosine.

Enzymes are complex chemical compounds which can be isolated in pure crystalline form. All the enzymes so far isolated are proteins. They are made up of AMINO ACIDS connected together chemically like a string of beads (see PROTEIN). The smallest enzyme isolated so far contains 124 amino acids; the largest, more than 10,000. The complete amino-acid sequences of approximately 20 enzymes have been worked out, and it has been found that each position in the chain is occupied by a single specific amino acid. The string of amino acids occurs in nature in a three-dimensional form which resembles a tangled coil of rope. It is believed that the shape of the enzyme is specifically adapted to effect contact between amino acids from different parts of the chain. Although the mechanism by which enzymes convert one compound into another is unknown, a small area of the enzyme, called its "active site," is thought responsible for the unusual properties of these biological catalysts. Presumably the substrate in the cell diffuses toward the enzyme and is strongly attracted to this active site. When it is absorbed there, the active amino-acid residues cause a chemical change which converts the substrate into products. The products then diffuse away from the enzyme surface, allowing another molecule of substrate to approach. In some enzymes prosthetic groups (or coenzymes)—chemical structures which are not amino acids—are attached to the protein and aid the enzyme action. Even in these cases the amino-acid residues play a key role in the specificity and efficiency of the enzyme. See also ADAPTIVE ENZYMES; PROTEOLYTIC ENZYMES.—*D. Ko.*

REPRESENTATIVE ENZYMES

(Terms in SMALL CAPITALS are titles of articles elsewhere in this encyclopedia; terms in *italics* are names of enzymes listed separately in this table.)

Name	Biological Function	Occurrence	Notable Properties	Chemical Reactions
Aconitase	Catalyzes dehydration reactions in aerobic breakdown of carbohydrates in CITRIC-ACID CYCLE.	Found in many plants and animals.	Activated by ferrous ions and reducing agents, *e.g.* cysteine.	Catalyzes equilibrium between citric, cisaconitic, and isocitric acids
Adenosine Triphosphatase (ATPase)	Hydrolyzes adenosine triphosphate (ATP). Several different ATPases exist; one is related to the contractile muscle protein, myosin; others exist in the mitochondria and cytoplasm of many types of cells.	Widely distributed in animals and plants.	Activated by magnesium or calcium ions. Serves to maintain optimal concentration of ADP for fermentation and respiration.	Adenosine triphosphate $\rightarrow$ adenosine diphosphate (ADP) plus inorganic phosphates
Alcohol Dehydrogenase	Catalyzes oxidation-reduction reactions involving alcohols and the corresponding aldehydes or ketones, important in alcoholic fermentation.	Abundant in liver and yeast, also found in other animal, plant, or bacterial sources.	May react with either diphosphopyridine nucleotide (DPN) or triphosphopyridine nucleotide (TPN).	$CH_3CH_2OH + DPN^+ \rightleftharpoons$ $CH_3CHO + DPNH + H^+$
Aldolases	Catalyze aldol condensation to form new carbon-carbon bond, important in GLYCOLYSIS.	Widely distributed in animals and plants.	The enzyme molecule is composed of three subunits.	3-phosphoglyceraldehyde + dihydroxyacetone phosphate $\rightleftharpoons$ fructose-1,6-diphosphate
Amidases	Enzymes which break down amides, thus serve to salvage waste products of protein breakdown or to detoxify toxic materials.	Animals, plants, molds, and bacteria.	Certain amidases are activated by metal ions.	*Example:* Nicotinamide $\rightarrow$ nicotinic acid + NH_3
Amino-acid Oxidases	Oxidize amino acids to keto acids; the animal enzyme also oxidizes α-hydroxy-acids.	Liver and kidney tissues of animals; molds and bacteria.	Flavoprotein-containing enzymes; there are specific D-amino-acid oxidases and L-amino-acid oxidases.	$CH_3-\underset{NH_2}{CH}-COOH + \frac{1}{2}O_2$ $\rightarrow CH_3-\underset{O}{C}-COOH + NH_3$
Amino-acid Transaminases	Catalyze the interchange of amino groups between amino acids and alpha keto acids; responsible for the formation of many amino acids in the organism.	Various tissues and microorganisms.	Contain pyridoxal phosphate as a coenzyme.	Glutamic acid + pyruvic acid $\rightleftharpoons$ α-ketoglutaric acid + alanine
Amylases	Catalyze the digestion of starch and glycogen, hence important in digestion and utilization of polysaccharides (see SUGAR).	In many plant tissues, in saliva, and in pancreas of animals.	May be divided into α-amylase and β-amylase.	Starch or glycogen to maltose
Carbonic Anhydrase	Catalyzes the reversible decarboxylation of carbonic acid to water and carbon dioxide; important in gas exchange and acid-base equilibrium in the body.	In red blood cells, gastric mucosa, and kidney.	A zinc-containing enzyme.	$H_2CO_3 \rightleftharpoons H_2O + CO_2$
Carboxylase (also Pyruvate Decarboxylase)	Decarboxylates pyruvic acid to acetaldehyde and carbon dioxide; important in alcoholic fermentation in microorganisms.	In plants and microorganisms, but not in animals.	Requires thiamine pyrophosphate (derived from vitamin B_1) for activity.	$CH_3COCOOH \rightarrow CH_3CHO + CO_2$
Catalase	Catalyzes the decomposition of hydrogen peroxide —a toxic material formed during some biological oxidation reactions.	Widely distributed in animals and plants.	An iron-containing enzyme.	$2H_2O_2 \rightarrow 2H_2O + O_2$

Name	Biological Function	Occurrence	Notable Properties	Chemical Reactions
Cellulases	Catalyze the digestion of cellulose, a major constituent of cell walls of higher plants and some microorganisms.	In many wood-eating insects, anaerobic microorganisms, and the digestive tract of herbivorous animals.		Cellulose to cellobiose
Cholesterol Esterase	Catalyzes the hydrolysis and synthesis of fatty acid esters of cholesterol.	Pancreatic juice, liver, and dog serum.	Requires phosphate ion.	Cholesterol + long-chain fatty acids $\rightleftharpoons$ cholesterol esters
Choline Acetylase (also Choline Acetyltransferase)	Catalyzes the resynthesis of acetylcholine, which is hydrolyzed during transmission of nerve impulse.	Primarily in nerve fibers.		Choline + acetylcoenzyme A $\rightarrow$ acetylcholine + CoA
Cholinesterases (also Acetylcholine Esterases)	Hydrolyze acetylcholine at nerve endings during neuromuscular transmission; also act on other esters.	In nervous tissues and blood cells of mammals.	Irreversibly inhibited by diisopropylfluorophosphate (nerve gas) and certain insecticides.	Acetylcholine $\rightarrow$ choline + acetic acid
Deacylases	Catalyze the hydrolytic cleavage of carboxylic acids from their esters or amides. Thiol esterases are most important deacylases.	In liver, heart, and some bacteria.	Specific thiol esterases are: acetyl-CoA deacylase, succinyl-CoA deacylase, S-acyl-glutathione deacylase, etc.	Acetyl-CoA + H_2O $\rightarrow$ acetic acid + CoA
Debranching Glucosidase (also Amylo-1,6-Glucosidase)	Hydrolyzes limit dextrin to glucose by acting at the branch points of phosphorylase-degraded glycogen (limit dextrin).	In liver and muscle.		Hydrolyzes 1 $\rightarrow$ 6 bonds of limit dextrin to form glucose
Decarboxylases	Catalyze the removal of carbon dioxide from carboxylic acids and amino acids. A large number of nonoxidative decarboxylases are known.	In animal tissues and various microorganisms.	Dependent on pyridoxal phosphate for activity.	Oxaloacetic acid $\rightarrow$ pyruvic acid + CO_2; also: L-histidine $\rightarrow$ histamine + CO_2
Dehydrogenases	Catalyze the transfer of hydrogen atoms from a large number of compounds containing carbon-hydrogen bonds to respiratory carriers and eventually to oxygen.	In almost all living cells.	The respiratory carrier for most dehydrogenases is pyridine nucleotide (DPN or TPN).	$AH_2 + B \rightarrow A + BH_2$ where A is a carbonaceous compound, e.g. lactic acid, and B is a respiratory carrier, e.g. DPN
Deoxyribonuclease	Splits deoxyribonucleic acids at their phosphate diester linkages to yield small nucleotide units, important in NUCLEIC-ACID metabolism.	Animal tissues such as thymus and spleen; plants and microorganisms.	Requires magnesium or manganese ions for activity.	Exonuclease removes mononucleotides successively from the termini of DNA. Endonuclease hydrolyzes phosphodiester bands at many points within the DNA chain.
Deoxyribonucleic-acid Polymerases	Involved in synthesis of deoxyribonucleic acid (DNA) in living cells (see NUCLEIC ACIDS).	In nuclei of all cells.	Need small amount of DNA as a "primer."	Condense nucleotides into DNA by splitting off pyrophosphate; the remaining phosphate is bound covalently to the deoxyribose of the next nucleotide
Enolase	Catalyzes the conversion of 2-phosphoglyceric acid to phosphoenolpyruvate in GLYCOLYSIS.	Widely distributed in animals, plants, and microorganisms.	Activated by divalent metals.	2-phosphoglyceric acid $\rightarrow$ phosphoenolpyruvate + H_2O
Epimerases (also Waldenase)	Convert a compound to its epimer, i.e. isomer with different configuration about one carbon; conversion of galactose to glucose allows organism to utilize the former.	Animal tissues, yeast, and bacteria.	Some reactions take place at the level of sugar nucleotide derivatives.	Uridine diphosphogalactose $\rightleftharpoons$ uridine diphosphoglucose; also: ribulose-5-phosphate $\rightleftharpoons$ xylulose-5-phosphate
Esterases	Hydrolyze esters to yield their component acids and alcohols; some esterases also catalyze transesterification between different esters and alcohols.	Animal tissues, particularly liver; plants and bacteria.	Esterases hydrolyze simple esters; those that hydrolyze triglycerides are grouped under Lipases.	See Cholinesterases, Cholesterol Esterase

Name	Biological Function	Occurrence	Notable Properties	Chemical Reactions
Fatty-acid Dehydrogenases	Remove two hydrogen atoms from coenzyme A derivatives of fatty acids, important in FAT METABOLISM.	Mainly in animal tissues.	They are flavoproteins; reaction involves cytochrome c as hydrogen and electron carrier.	$CH_3-CH_2-CH_2-CO \sim S\ CoA \rightarrow$ $CH_3-CH=CH-CO \sim CoA$
Fumarase	Reversibly catalyzes the hydration of fumaric acid to malic acid in CITRIC-ACID CYCLE.	Animals, higher plants, bacteria, and yeasts.	Activity greatly influenced by anions.	Fumaric acid + water $\rightleftharpoons$ L-malic acid
Galacto-sidases	Hydrolyze various galactosides; α-galactosidases split melibiose, β-galactosidases split lactose and other β-galactosides.	Animal tissues, especially intestinal juices; also in yeasts, bacteria, and molds.		Lactose $\rightarrow$ glucose + galactose
Glucose Dehydrogenase	Oxidizes glucose to form gluconolactone, which is then hydrolyzed to gluconic acid.	Liver and certain microorganisms.	Diphosphopyridine nucleotide (DPN) is the coenzyme.	Glucose + DPN$^+$ $\rightarrow$ gluconolactone + DPNH + H$^+$
Glucose Oxidase (also Notatin)	Oxidizes glucose to form gluconolactone and hydrogen peroxide; the latter is an antibacterial agent.	From the mold *Penicillium notatum*.	Possesses flavin adenine dinucleotide as prosthetic group; reaction by-passes pyridine nucleotide.	Glucose + O$_2$ $\rightarrow$ gluconolactone + H$_2$O$_2$
Glucose-6-Phos-phatase	Hydrolyzes glucose-6-phosphate to glucose and phosphoric acid, important in the hepatic conversion of glycogen to glucose and in the maintenance of blood-sugar level.	Mainly in liver; smaller amounts in kidney and small intestine.	Activity is influenced by diet and by dietary state of the animal.	Glucose-6-phosphate $\rightarrow$ glucose + phosphoric acid
Glucose-6-Phosphate Dehydrogenase (also Phospho-glucose Dehydro-genase)	Converts glucose-6-phosphate to 6-phosphogluconolactone; the latter is then hydrolyzed to 6-phosphogluconic acid before entering the PENTOSE PHOSPHATE PATHWAY.	Animal tissues, plants, yeast, and bacteria.		Glucose-6-phosphate + TPN$^+$ $\rightarrow$ 6-phosphogluconolactone + TPNH + H$^+$
Glucosidases	Catalyze hydrolysis of various α- and β-glucosides by specific glucosidases, *e.g.* maltase, invertase, cellobiase.	Widely distributed in seeds, molds, bacteria, and digestive tracts of animals.	A subgroup of glycosidases. That from yeast acts on α-glucosides; that from almonds acts on β-glucosides.	See *Invertase* and *Glycosidases*
Glutamic Dehydrogenase	Oxidizes glutamic acid to form α-ketoglutaric acid and ammonia.	Animal tissues, particularly liver; plants and bacteria.	Specificity to diphosphopyridine nucleotides (DPN) or triphosphopyridine nucleotide (TPN) depends on the source of enzyme.	L-glutamic acid + DPN$^+$ + H$_2$O $\rightarrow$ α-ketoglutaric acid + NH$_3$ + DPNH + H$^+$
Glutaminase	Splits glutamine into glutamic acid and ammonia in the kidney, so that the toxic ammonia can be excreted.	Chiefly in kidney.		Glutamine $\rightarrow$ glutamic acid + ammonia
Glutathione Reductase	Reduces oxidized glutathione to reduced glutathione; the latter sulfhydryl compound is important physiologically, for it protects many enzymes from oxidative destruction.	Animal tissues, plants, yeast, and bacteria.	Triphosphopyridine nucleotide (TPN) reacts preferentially.	Oxidized glutathione + TPNH + H$^+$ $\rightarrow$ reduced glutathione + TPN$^+$
Glyceraldehyde-3-Phosphate De-hydrogenase (also Triosephosphate Dehydrogenase)	Oxidizes glyceraldehyde-3-phosphate to form 1,3-diphosphoglyceric acid in GLYCOLYSIS.	Widely distributed in animals, plants, and microorganisms.	That from animal source reacts with diphosphopyridine nucleotide (DPN); that from green leaves reacts with TPN.	Glyceraldehyde-3-phosphate + DPN$^+$ + Pi $\rightarrow$ glyceric acid-1,3-diphosphate + DPNH + H$^+$

Name	Biological Function	Occurrence	Notable Properties	Chemical Reactions
Glycerophosphate Dehydrogenase	Catalyzes the reversible conversion of glycerophosphate to dihydroxyacetone phosphate; the latter is an intermediate in GLYCOLYSIS.	Various animal tissues, especially skeletal muscles; also present in yeast.	The enzyme activity is found generally to be lower in tumor cells than in normal cells.	L-α-glycerophosphate + DPN$^+$ $\rightleftharpoons$ dihydroxyacetone phosphate + DPNH + H$^+$
Glycine Oxidase	Oxidizes glycine to glyoxylic acid.	In liver and kidney of mammals, and in bacteria.	Possesses a flavin prosthetic group; the flavin reacts directly with oxygen to form hydrogen peroxide.	Glycine + oxygen + H$_2$O $\rightarrow$ glyoxylic acid + ammonia + hydrogen peroxide
Glycosidases (also Carbohydrases)	Hydrolyze glycosidic bonds, *i.e.* bonds which link a simple sugar (monosaccharide) to some other mono- or polysaccharide.	In digestive juices of mammals, and in microorganisms.	There are several large subgroups of glycosidases, *e.g.* glucosidases, galactosidases, and amylase.	Starch to maltose
Hexokinase	Catalyzes the phosphorylation of hexoses (6-carbon sugars), especially glucose, to form glucose-6-phosphate; first step in cellular utilization of glucose.	Animal tissues; yeasts and other microorganisms.	Requires magnesium ions; specific hexokinases exist, *e.g.* glucokinase, fructokinase, galactokinase.	D-glucose + ATP $\rightarrow$ glucose-6-phosphate + ADP
Histaminase (also Diamine Oxidase)	Oxidizes histamine and other diamines, *e.g.* putrescine and cadaverine.	Mammals, birds, higher plants, and bacteria.	Possesses pyridoxal phosphate as prosthetic group.	Histamine + O$_2$ + H$_2$O $\rightarrow$ β-imidazole acetaldehyde + NH$_3$ + H$_2$O$_2$
Hyaluronidase (also Hyaluronate Glycanohydrolase)	Hydrolyzes hyaluronic acid (a mucopolysaccharide), chondroitin and mucoitin sulfates.	Bacteria, snake venom, and certain tissues of vertebrates, *e.g.* testes.	Acts as a "spreading factor," *i.e.* increases diffusion of drugs as well as toxins under skin.	Hyaluronic acid to smaller constituents
Hydroperoxidases (common name for Peroxidases and Catalases)	Catalyze breakdown of hydrogen peroxide; serve as detoxification agents in destroying peroxides.	Widely distributed in higher plants, bacteria; found in certain animal tissues.	Contain a heme prosthetic group. Complex with hydrogen peroxide gives characteristic absorption spectrum.	2 H$_2$O$_2$ $\rightarrow$ 2 H$_2$O + O$_2$
Hydroxyacyl Dehydrogenases (also β-Keto-reductase)	Remove two atoms of hydrogen from hydroxy fatty acids to form the corresponding keto acids, in fatty-acid oxidation (beta oxidation).	Mainly in animal tissues, particularly in liver and heart.	Act on coenzyme A derivatives of β-hydroxy acids of 4 to 12 carbon atoms.	CH$_3$—CHOH—CH$_2$—CO $\sim$ S CoA + DPN$^+$ $\rightarrow$ DPNH + H$^+$ + CH$_3$—CO—CH$_2$—CO $\sim$ S CoA
Hydroxybutyrate Dehydrogenase	Oxidizes β-hydroxybutyrate to acetoacetate, important in fatty acid oxidation, especially in ketone body formation.	Mainly in liver.	Acts on free β-hydroxybutyric acid, specific to the D-isomer.	CH$_3$—CHOH—CH$_2$COOH + DPN$^+$ $\rightarrow$ DPNH + H$^+$ + CH$_3$COCH$_2$COOH
Invertase (also Sucrase; Saccharase)	Hydrolyzes sucrose (cane sugar) to glucose and fructose; the simple sugars can then be utilized for energy or building blocks through GLYCOLYSIS.	Intestinal mucosa of animals; plants and microorganisms.	Also acts on other oligosaccharides such as raffinose.	Sucrose + water $\rightarrow$ glucose + fructose
Isocitric Dehydrogenase	Oxidizes isocitric acid to oxalosuccinic acid and decarboxylates (removes carbon dioxide from) the latter to form α-ketoglutaric acid, in CITRIC-ACID CYCLE.	Widely distributed in animal tissues, yeast, and molds.	Requires manganese ion for the decarboxylation step.	Isocitric acid + TPN$^+$ $\rightarrow$ TPNH + H$^+$ + oxalosuccinic acid; then oxalosuccinic acid $\rightarrow$ α-ketoglutaric acid + CO$_2$
Isomerases	Catalyze the conversion of a compound to its isomer (identical composition but different molecular structure); important in many biological transformation reactions.	Present in almost all forms of life.	Some act on free sugars, others act on phosphorylated sugars or sugar derivatives such as N-acetylglucosamine-6-phosphate.	Glucose-6-phosphate to fructose-6-phosphate; also: glyceraldehyde-3-phosphate to dihydroxyacetone phosphate

Name	Biological Function	Occurrence	Notable Properties	Chemical Reactions
Ketothiolase	Acts on coenzyme A derivatives of β-keto fatty acids to shorten the carbon chain by two carbons, in fatty-acid oxidation.	Mainly in liver.	Together with thiokinase, acyl—CoA dehydrogenase, enoyl hydrase, and β-hydroxy acyl dehydrogenase, completes the pathway of fatty-acid oxidation.	β-keto octanoyl—CoA + CoA $\rightarrow$ hexanoyl—CoA + acetyl—CoA
Lactic Dehydrogenase	In animal tissues this enzyme converts pyruvic acid to lactic acid, important in anaerobic GLYCOLYSIS.	Widely distributed in animals, plants, and microorganisms.	From certain microorganisms this enzyme converts lactic acid to acetic acid, CO_2, and peroxide.	Pyruvic acid + DPNH + H^+ $\rightleftharpoons$ lactic acid + DPN^+
Lecithinase (also Phospholipase)	Hydrolyzes lecithin, a fat containing two fatty acids and phosphoryl choline linked to glycerol, to form lysolecithin; the latter is strongly hemolytic.	Venoms of snakes, scorpions, wasps; also in plant and animal tissues.	Requires calcium ion for activity of lecithinase A and C.	Lecithin $\rightarrow$ lysolecithin + an unsaturated fatty acid
Lipases	Hydrolyze fats to fatty acids and glycerol or to monoglycerides; important in DIGESTION of fats.	Animal tissues, especially pancreas; plants, molds, and bacteria.	Lipase action is facilitated by the bile acids and activated by calcium ions.	
Malic Dehydrogenase	Catalyzes oxidation of malic acid to oxaloacetic acid, in CITRIC-ACID CYCLE.	Animal tissues, plants, and bacteria.	Specific to diphosphopyridine nucleotide (DPN).	L-malic acid + DPN^+ $\rightleftharpoons$ oxaloacetic acid + DPNH + H^+
"Malic" Enzyme (also Malate Dehydrogenase)	Catalyzes the reversible decarboxylation of malic acid to pyruvic acid and carbon dioxide, important in producing TPNH and in CO_2 fixation.	Animal and plant tissues (TPN specific); bacteria and *Ascaris* (DPN specific).	Specificity to DPN or triphosphopyridine nucleotide (TPN) depends on source of enzyme.	L-malic acid + TPN^+ $\rightleftharpoons$ pyruvic acid + CO_2 + TPNH + H^+
Malic Synthetase	Catalyzes condensation of glyoxylic acid and acetyl coenzyme A to form malic acid, important in synthesis of dicarboxylic acids.	In certain microorganisms, including molds.		Glyoxylic acid + acetyl CoA + H_2O $\rightarrow$ malic acid + CoA
Maltase	Hydrolyzes maltose to two glucose units, important in digestion of starch to utilizable sugar (glucose).	Pancreas and intestine.	This is an α-glucosidase.	Maltose + H_2O $\rightarrow$ 2 glucose
Myokinase (also Adenylic-acid Kinase)	Catalyzes phosphate transfer among adenine nucleotides; important in formation of ADP from AMP.	Muscle, brain, liver and kidney; also found in yeast, plants, and bacteria.	Requires magnesium ions.	ATP + AMP $\rightleftharpoons$ 2 ADP
Oxidases	Catalyze oxidation of various substrates or reduced electron carriers, *e.g.* cytochrome oxidase, laccase, xanthine oxidase, glucose oxidase, polyphenol oxidases.	Widely distributed in a great many plants and animal tissues.	Most oxidases contain either iron or copper as prosthetic groups.	In cytochrome c oxidase reaction: 4 cytochrome c (Fe^{++}) + 4 e + 4 H^+ + O_2 $\rightarrow$ 4 cytochrome c (Fe^{+++}) + 2 H_2O
Peroxidases	Catalyze oxidation of certain reduced substances, *e.g.* polyphenols, by hydrogen peroxide.	Widely distributed in higher plants, rarely found in animals.	Possess a heme prosthetic group; see HYDROPEROXIDASES.	AH_2 + H_2O_2 $\rightarrow$ A + 2 H_2O, where A is a phenol, ascorbic acid, etc.
Phosphatases	Hydrolyze esters of phosphoric acid, *e.g.* glucose-6-phosphate, adenylic acid, fructose diphosphate.	Widely distributed in animal tissues, *e.g.* blood plasma, milk, intestinal mucosa, and bone; also found in plants and bacteria.	Non-specific phosphatases are acid and alkaline phosphatases; specific phosphatases are glucose-6-phosphatase, 5-nucleotidase, etc.	See *Glucose-6-Phosphate; Phosphomonoesterases; Phosphodiesterases*

Name	Biological Function	Occurrence	Notable Properties	Chemical Reactions
Phosphodiesterases	Catalyze hydrolysis of one of the ester linkage in a phosphoric-acid ester containing two such linkages (a phosphodiester) to produce an alcohol and a phosphomonoester.	Snake venom, plants, and animal tissues, particularly spleen and pancreas.	Acts on ribo- and deoxyribo-oligonucleotides; acts on RNA and DNA.	Oligonucleotides or nucleic acids → mononucleotides, etc.
Phosphoglucoisomerase (also Phosphohexoisomerase)	Catalyzes conversion of glucose-6-phosphate to fructose-6-phosphate, in GLYCOLYSIS.	Animal tissues, plants, and yeast.		Glucose-6-phosphate $\rightleftharpoons$ fructose-6-phosphate
Phosphoglucomutase	Catalyzes conversion of glucose-1-phosphate to glucose-6-phosphate; the former is formed from glycogen or starch, important in sugar metabolism.	In animal and plant tissues.	Requires divalent metal ions; glucose-1,6-diphosphate is the cofactor.	Glucose-1-phosphate $\rightleftharpoons$ glucose-6-phosphate
Phosphogluconic Dehydrogenase	Oxidizes 6-phosphogluconic acid to form ribulose-5-phosphate and carbon dioxide in PENTOSE PHOSPHATE PATHWAY.	Animal tissues, plants, yeast, and bacteria.	Triphosphopyridine nucleotide (TPN) is the coenzyme.	6-phosphogluconic acid + TPN⁺ → ribulose-5-phosphate + CO_2 + TPNH + H⁺
Phosphoglycerate Kinase	Transfers phosphate from 1,3-diphosphoglyceric acid to adenosine diphosphate (ADP) to form adenosine triphosphate (ATP); important in GLYCOLYSIS.	Animal tissues, yeast, and plants.	Requires magnesium ions.	1,3-diphosphoglyceric acid + ADP → 3-phosphoglyceric acid + ATP
Phosphoglyceromutase	Catalyzes the conversion of 3-phosphoglyceric acid to 2-phosphoglyceric acid, in GLYCOLYSIS.	Animal tissues, yeast, and plants.	2,3-diphosphoglyceric acid is the cofactor.	3-phosphoglyceric acid → 2-phosphoglyceric acid
Phosphokinases	Catalyze the transfer of phosphate groups from adenosine triphosphate (ATP) to a substrate, e.g. glucose, creatine, glycerol, and many others.	Widely distributed in animal tissues, especially muscle and liver; yeast, bacteria, and plants.	Require magnesium ions.	See Hexokinase
Phosphomonoesterases	Hydrolyze phosphomonoesters (phosphoric acid esters containing one ester linkage) to form phosphoric acid and an alcohol; important in bone formation; metabolism of nucleotides, carbohydrates, and phospholipids.	Especially widely distributed in animal kingdom; also found in plants and bacteria.	Require magnesium ions.	Glycerol phosphate → glycerol + phosphoric acid; also: adenosine monophosphate → adenosine + phosphoric acid
Phosphorylases	Catalyze the breakdown of glycogen and starch to glucose-1-phosphate; important in mobilizing stored carbohydrates for various uses.	Animal and plant sources.	Other types of phosphorylases exist, e.g. nucleoside phosphorylase, maltose phosphorylase, sucrose phosphorylase.	Glycogen + phosphoric acid → glucose-1-phosphate + limit dextrin (see Debranching Glucosidase)
Prolidase (also Imidodipeptidase)	A peptidase which specifically splits the dipeptides of the type glycyl-proline; important in hydrolysis of proteins to amino acids.	Intestinal mucosa.	Requires manganous ions.	Amino-acyl-L-proline + H_2O → an amino acid + proline.
Pyrophosphatases	Hydrolyze energy-rich pyrophosphate bonds, liberating phosphoric acid and releasing energy to drive many energy-requiring reactions in the body.	Widely distributed in animals, yeast, plants, and molds.	Some enzymes split dinucleotides (e.g. DPN) to mononucleotides.	Pyrophosphate → 2 phosphoric acid (see Adenosine Triphosphatase)

Name	Biological Function	Occurrence	Notable Properties	Chemical Reactions
Pyruvic Kinase	Transfers phosphate from phosphoenolpyruvic acid to adenosine diphosphate (ADP) to form pyruvic acid and ATP, in GLYCOLYSIS.	Animal tissues, yeast, and plants.	Requires magnesium ions.	Phosphoenolpyruvic acid + ADP → pyruvic acid + ATP
Rennin (also Rennet)	Catalyzes coagulation of casein in milk, thus aiding digestion of milk.	In fourth stomach of calf; not in human stomach.	Requires calcium ions.	
Ribonuclease	Catalyzes hydrolytic cleavage of ribonucleic acids to form pyrimidine 3′-nucleotides and other products; important in nucleic-acid metabolism.	Many animal tissues; in seeds, microorganisms, and leaves of higher plants.	Also acts on 2′,3′-cyclic nucleoside phosphates.	
Ribonucleic-acid Polymerases	Involved in synthesis of ribonucleic acid (RNA) in living cells (see NUCLEIC ACIDS).	Widely distributed.	Catalyze the synthesis of RNA with nucleotide composition similar to that of whatever DNA is present.	Condenses nucleotides into RNA molecules by splitting off pyrophosphate; the remaining phosphate is bound covalently to the ribose of the next nucleotide
Succinic Dehydrogenase	Catalyzes oxidation of succinic acid to fumaric acid; see HYDROGEN TRANSPORT and CITRIC-ACID CYCLE.	Animal tissues, bacteria, and yeast.	Contains flavin prosthetic group and iron.	Succinic acid + flavin → fumaric acid + flavin H_2
Thiokinase (also Acyl-CoA Synthetase, or Fatty Acid Thiokinase)	Catalyzes conversion of a fatty acid to its coenzyme A derivative; the latter can then be oxidized; see *Ketothiolase*. Important in fatty-acid oxidation.	Heart, liver, higher plants, and some bacteria.	Acts on a number of fatty acids.	Butyric acid + CoA + ATP → butyryl CoA + AMP + PP
Triosephosphate Isomerase	Catalyzes intramolecular hydrogen transfer between the triosephosphates; important in GLYCOLYSIS.	Animal tissues, yeast, and plants.		Dihydroxyacetonephosphate → glyceraldehyde-3-phosphate
Transglycosidases	Transfer glycosidic bonds from one molecule to another; important in synthesizing polysaccharides and in interconversion of sugar compounds.	Mainly in bacteria and molds.	Various transglycosidases exist which are specific to sucrose, maltose, dextrin, and uridine diphospho-sugar compounds.	n sucrose → n fructose + (glucose)$_n$, where (glucose)$_n$ = starch or dextran
Urease	Hydrolyzes urea to ammonia and carbon dioxide, important in nitrogen cycle in nature.	Microorganisms and plants.	This was first enzyme to be crystallized (in 1926).	Urea → NH_3 + CO_2
Xanthine Oxidase	Oxidizes hypoxanthine to xanthine and further converts xanthine to uric acid; the latter is excreted as end product of purine metabolism.	Animal tissues, milk, and bacteria.	Contains flavin, iron, and molybdenum.	Hypoxanthine → xanthine → uric acid

—*Prepared by R. Wu.*

EOCENE EPOCH: see CENOZOIC ERA; GEOLOGICAL TIME CHART.

EPHEMERIS: a table of computed positions of a celestial body as a function of time. For example, a list of the predicted positions of Mars for every day of a given year constitutes an ephemeris of Mars for that year. Such tables are used by astronomers and navigators in the planning and utilization of their observations. The name "ephemeris" is also applied to the book in which such ephemerides are published together with other astronomical data; in this case the word is synonymous with ALMANAC.—*S. D. G.*

EPICENTER: see EARTHQUAKE.

EPICYCLE: a circle along which, according to old planetary theories, a heavenly body was supposed to move. The center of the epicycle was assumed to move along another circle, called a *deferent,* about a central body. The description by epicycles was an integral part of the PTOLEMAIC SYSTEM of planetary motions, the deferents of the planets being somewhat off center with respect to Earth. Epicycles were used also by Copernicus in the Sun-centered system he introduced in 1543. They were superseded by the introduction of elliptic

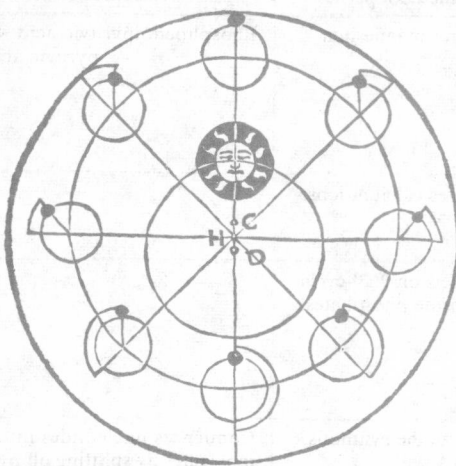

Theorica motus trium superiorum in epiciclo.

Stages of epicycle of planet are shown in 16th-cent. woodcut after the Ptolemaic scheme. Epicycle's center travels path around center of universe—the Earth. (*Gossner Collection*)

orbits in the theories later proposed by Kepler and Newton. See COPERNICAN SYSTEM; KEPLER'S LAWS; PTOLEMAIC SYSTEM. —*S. D. G.*

EPIGENESIS: a theory suggested by Aristotle and adopted by the English physician William Harvey in the 17th cent. It holds that the egg cell (ovum) is at first a relatively structureless mass of homogeneous material that, through progressive changes, develops into the embryo. Opposed to this is the theory of preformation, which was generally accepted by leading biologists during the 17th and early 18th cent. This discredited theory held that the embryo is fully formed in the ovum as a miniature adult and that the existing adult structures "unfold" through a period of development. See EMBRYONIC DEVELOPMENT.—*A. P. E.*

EPIGLOTTIS: see SWALLOWING.

EPIPHYTE: a plant that grows on the bark or branches of a larger plant (usually a tree), without obtaining any nourishment from its support. The epiphyte usually gains by living high above the ground, closer to sunlight and farther from foliage-eating animals of the forest floor. Yet it does not need to expend energy in producing a woody trunk. Lichens, leafy liverworts, mosses, ferns, Spanish "moss" and other members

of the pineapple family (Bromeliadaceae), and orchids are among the commonest epiphytic plants. Many have leaves adapted in shape and structure for capture and storage of rainwater. Most can tolerate long periods of drought; they revive and reproduce as soon as a rainy period arrives. In tropical rain forests, the horizontal branches of big trees are often weighted down by tons of epiphytic plants. These crash to the ground if the branch breaks, and die there— being unable to make use of the soil as a growing site. This is a catastrophe also for thousands of tadpoles and immature aquatic insects that have been developing in the water-storage organs of the plants high up in the rain forest. Many epiphytes, *e.g.* orchids and bromeliads ("air plants"), will grow and flower indoors if the air is humid—even while pinned to a window curtain or resting with no soil on a dimly lighted shelf. Indoors or out, epiphytes rely upon dust for their inorganic nutrients, and are self-sufficient—not parasites. Usually they grow where their seeds or spores fall, and thus are not climbing plants.—*L. and M. M.*

EQUATION, CHEMICAL: a representation in chemical symbols of a chemical reaction. A complete or balanced chemical equation shows on the left-hand side of its equality sign the formula of each of the reacting molecules and the number of each species entering into the reaction. The formula and number of each of the product molecules are shown on the right-hand side. Arrows indicating the direction in which the reaction proceeds are frequently used instead of the equality sign, particularly in reversible reactions. The typical chemical equation below represents the reversible formation of water gas (carbon monoxide and hydrogen) from coke (carbon) and steam (water vapor):

$$C + H_2O \rightleftarrows CO + H_2$$

—*A. M. S.*

EQUATION OF TIME: see TIME, SOLAR AND SIDEREAL.

EQUATIONS, THEORY OF: mathematical theory concerned with solving equations; for example, finding the values of x for which $5x^4 + 2x^3 + x^2 + 7 = 0$, or finding the values of x and y for which $3x + y = 0$ and $x^2 - 2y = 3$. On each side of an equation there is a sum of terms, which may be positive, negative, or zero. In each term of the examples above, the unknown is raised to a positive whole-number power (which may be 1) and multiplied by a number; these are rational integral equations. The theory of equations is concerned mainly with these, since other algebraic equations are solved by being first reduced to a rational integral form.

The degree of a term is the sum of the exponents of the unknowns: the term $4x^3y^2$ is of degree 5, the term $3x$ is of degree 1. The degree of an equation is the highest degree of any single term in it. The theory of equations has two main branches, one dealing with equations of any degree in one unknown, the other dealing with first-degree, or linear, equations in two or more unknowns.

Equations in One Unknown: The theory of the second-degree, or quadratic, equation is simple and complete. The general quadratic is $ax^2 + bx + c = 0$, and its solutions, or roots, are given by the formula $x = (-b \pm \sqrt{b^2 - 4ac})/2a$.

Common epiphyte of southern U.S.A. is Spanish moss, here hanging beardlike from live oaks in Louisiana. Not a true moss, it is a member of the pineapple family. (*U. S. Forest Service*)

Equations of the third degree (cubics) and fourth degree (quartics, or biquadratics) can be completely solved in all cases. Although the theory is more extensive than that of the quadratic, it has been complete for many years. The best-known solution of the general cubic was published by Cardan in his *Ars Magna* in 1545. It is called Cardan's solution, although he took parts of it from Tartaglia under promise of secrecy. Starting with the general cubic, $x^3 + bx^2 + cx + d = 0$, x is replaced by $y - b/3$, transforming the equation to $y^3 + py + q = 0$, where $p = c - b^2/3$, $q = d - bc/3 + 2b^3/27$. We now put $y = z - p/3z$, transforming the equation to $z^6 + qz^3 - p^3/27 = 0$, which is a quadratic in z^3. Thus z^3 is found, and hence z, y, and x. The details are tedious, and methods of approximating the roots are often preferred. The general quartic can also be solved by methods not essentially

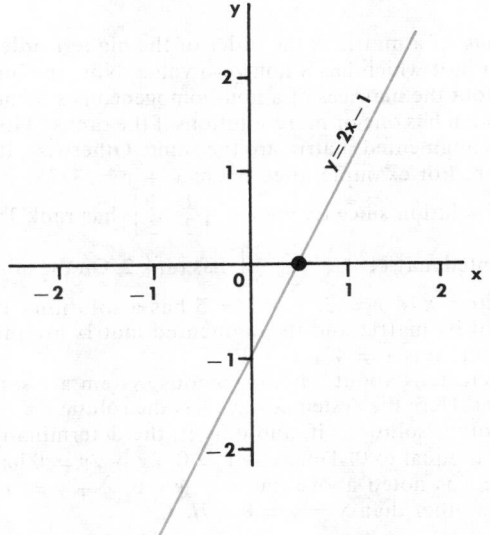

Root of linear equation: When line $y = 2x - 1$ passes through x-axis, $y = 0$. This occurs at $x = \frac{1}{2}$. Hence, root of $2x - 1 = 0$ is $x = \frac{1}{2}$.

more difficult than those needed for the cubic. Equations of degree above four cannot, in general, be solved exactly. This has been known since about 1825, when N. H. Abel proved that the general fifth-degree equation cannot be solved. A considerable body of theory has been developed, however, concerned with conditions under which equations of higher degree than the fourth can be solved, and practical methods of solving them.

General Theory: The fundamental theorem of algebra establishes the fact that a rational integral equation of degree n, with $n \geqq 1$, has a root. With this as a basis it is then proved that such an equation has precisely n roots, taking into account that some may coincide. Consider an equation written in the form $a_0 x^n + a_1 x^{n-1} + \cdots + a_n = 0$, with the coefficients all real numbers. The following facts are helpful in finding the roots:

(*1*) Possible complex imaginary roots occur in conjugate pairs.

(*2*) The possible distribution of positive and negative roots is given by Descartes' rule of signs: count the changes in signs of the terms, reading from left to right, and if there are k changes, the number of positive roots is either k or k diminished by an even number; reverse the signs of the odd-powered terms and again count the changes, and if there are h changes, the number of negative roots is either h or h diminished by an even number.

(*3*) Possible integral roots are factors of a_n; and possible fractional roots have their numerators factors of a_n and their denominators factors of a_0.

(*4*) If an exact root r_1 is found, the factor theorem states that $x - r_1$ is a factor and may be divided out, thus leaving an equation of lower degree which contains the remaining roots.

(*5*) Horner's method of approximating irrational roots is a process of iteration in which we find one digit at a time, and with some refinements may be able to find several decimal digits in one step. First, we locate a root by careful substitution in the polynomial. If, for example, the polynomial is negative for $x = 2$ and positive for $x = 3$, we know there is a root between 2 and 3; that is $r = 2.\text{---}$. We now substitute more carefully, and if we find the polynomial to change sign between 2.4 and 2.5, we know the root to be 2.4---. In this way substituting more and more closely packed numbers in narrower and narrower intervals, we can obtain the root as closely as we wish. The substitutions are facilitated by successive transformations of the equation, first reducing the roots by 2 so that we need substitute decimals of only one digit, then reducing the roots further by 0.4 so that again we substitute decimals of one digit; and so on.

(*6*) Newton's method of approximating a real root calls for the use of differentiation, and can be visualized graphically. The real roots of the equation $a_0 x^n + a_1 x^{n-1} + \cdots + a_n = 0$ are the abscissas of the intersections of the graph of $y = a_0 x^n + a_1 x^{n-1} + \cdots + a_n$ with the x-axis. Suppose, as above, we have located a root between the numbers 2 and 3. By calculus we can determine the tangent at any point, say at $x = 3$ and at $x = 2$. If the curve is concave upward between 2 and 3, we take the tangent at $x = 3$ and find its intersection with the x-axis, say 2.8. We can now determine the tangent at $x = 2.8$ and find its intersection with the x-axis. Repetition of the process produces better and better approximations to the root. A modification is necessary if the curve changes from an upward concavity to a downward concavity within the interval in use. Some refinements make it possible to estimate a root quite accurately with a minimum of labor. This method is not limited to rational integral equations.

(*7*) An equation may have repeated roots. This, of course, depends upon the coefficients. The relationship among them which produces repeated roots is expressed by putting the *discriminant* equal to 0. The discriminant is defined as the product of the squares of the differences of the roots. In the case of the quadratic $ax^2 + bx + c = 0$, it is $b^2 - 4ac$. For the cubic $ax^3 + bx^2 + cx + d = 0$, it is $18abcd - 4b^3d + b^2c^2 - 4ac^3 - 27a^2d^2$.

(*8*) Two equations may have a root in common. Again, this depends upon their coefficients. The process of finding the relation among them which exists when a common root is present is called elimination of x between the equations. When this relation is given by setting an expression in the coefficients equal to 0, the expression is called the eliminant, or resultant of the two equations. For example, the equations $ax^2 + 2x + a = 0$ and $a^2 x^2 + ax + a^2 - 1 = 0$ have a common root if $a^2 - 1 = 0$. The quantity $a^2 - 1$ is the resultant. If $a = 1$, the common root is $x = -1$; if $a = -1$, it is 1.

Linear Systems: By a *system* of equations we mean two or more equations which are satisfied by the same values of the unknowns; often they are called simultaneous equations. An example is $x + y = 5$, $x - y = 1$. Since both equations hold for the same values of x and y, the equation formed by adding them must hold, *i.e.* $2x = 6$. Hence $x = 3$, and by sub-

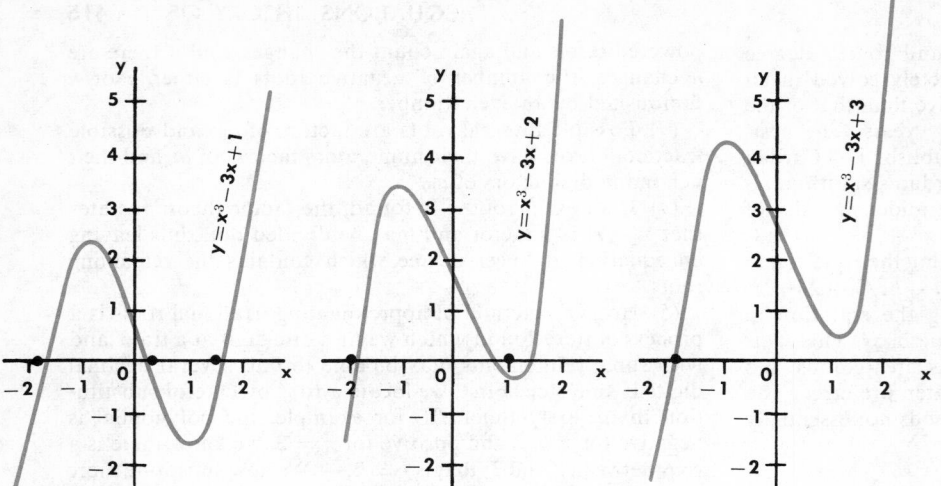

$y = x^3 - 3x + 1$

$y = x^3 - 3x + 2$

$y = x^3 - 3x + 3$

Roots of cubic equations: The first curve crosses the x-axis at three points. Its equation thus has three real roots: $x \approx -1.87$, $x \approx +0.34$, and $x \approx +1.54$. The second curve crosses the x-axis at one point and touches it at another. Its equation therefore has one root at $x = -2$ and two coincident roots at $x = +1$. The third curve crosses the x-axis once, giving a root for its equation at $x \approx 2.10$. The other two roots are imaginary, as shown by the fact that the curve makes no other contact with the x-axis.

stitution in either equation we find $y = 2$. Systems with three or more unknowns can be solved by elaborations of this method. In general, it is necessary to have the same number of equations as unknowns in order to determine a unique solution, *i.e.* a unique set of values satisfying all equations. But this condition does not guarantee a solution, and it is possible for many solutions to exist.

There are two distinct kinds of linear systems, with further classifications under each. An equation is said to be *homogeneous* if all its terms have the same degree. Hence a system of linear homogeneous equations has no terms free of unknowns. The illustrative example above is a non-homogeneous system, since the terms 5 and 1 are free of x and y. A homogeneous system is illustrated by $x + y = 0$, $x - 2y = 0$. This system has the solution $x = y = 0$, and no other, for, from the second equation, $x = 2y$, and substitution in the first equation gives $3y = 0$, and therefore $y = 0$. On the other hand, the system $x + y = 0$, $2x + 2y = 0$ has infinitely many solutions, for, from either equation, $x = -y$, and any value may be taken for y, with x equal to its negative.

The study of linear systems leads to the consideration of MATRICES and DETERMINANTS. Consider the non-homogeneous system of two equations in two unknowns: $a_1x + b_1y = c_1$, $a_2x + b_2y = c_2$. The *matrix* of this system is the array of coefficients of the left-hand members; the augmented matrix of the system is the array of coefficients of all members. A matrix is denoted by curved bars or brackets, so that for this system we have:

$$\text{matrix} \begin{bmatrix} a_1 & b_1 \\ a_2 & b_2 \end{bmatrix}, \quad \text{augmented matrix} \begin{bmatrix} a_1 & b_1 & c_1 \\ a_2 & b_2 & c_2 \end{bmatrix}.$$

A matrix is simply a formal array; it does not have a numerical value. The *determinant* of the matrix of the system is

$$\begin{vmatrix} a_1 & b_1 \\ a_2 & b_2 \end{vmatrix}$$

the straight bars being the symbol of a determinant. A determinant is a square array with a numerical value determined by a special rule. In the case of the second-order determinant above, the value is $a_1b_2 - a_2b_1$. For determinants of higher order, *i.e.* with more rows and columns, the rule for evaluation is more complicated. A single number can be regarded as a determinant of order 1. The augmented matrix of a system has several determinants. The second-order determinants of the above augmented matrix are

$$\begin{vmatrix} a_1 & b_1 \\ a_2 & b_2 \end{vmatrix} \quad \begin{vmatrix} a_1 & c_1 \\ a_2 & c_2 \end{vmatrix}, \quad \text{and} \quad \begin{vmatrix} b_1 & c_1 \\ b_2 & c_2 \end{vmatrix}.$$

The *rank* of a matrix is the order of the highest-order determinant in it which has a non-zero value. Now the important fact about the matrices of a non-homogeneous system is this: the system has one or more solutions if the ranks of its matrix and its augmented matrix are the same. Otherwise, it has no solution. For example, the system $x + y = 3$, $2x + 2y = 5$ has no solution since its matrix $\begin{bmatrix} 1 & 1 \\ 2 & 2 \end{bmatrix}$ has rank 1, and its augmented matrix $\begin{bmatrix} 1 & 1 & 3 \\ 2 & 2 & 5 \end{bmatrix}$ has rank 2. On the other hand the system $x + y = 3$, $x - y = 5$ has a solution, since the ranks of its matrix and its augmented matrix are the same. The solution is $x = 4$, $y = -1$.

Conclusions about a homogeneous system are somewhat different. Here the system always has the solution $x = y = 0$. It has other solutions if, and only if, the determinant of the system is equal to 0. Thus $x + y = 0$, $2x + 2y = 0$ has many solutions as noted above, but $x - y = 0$, $x + y = 0$ has no solution other than $x = y = 0$.—*H. C.*

EQUATOR, CELESTIAL: the fundamental circle in the equatorial system of coordinates. It serves the same function with respect to the sky as the terrestrial equator serves with respect to Earth, and is formed by extension of Earth's equatorial plane into the celestial sphere. Every point on the celestial equator is exactly above some point on the terrestrial equator. At Earth's poles, the celestial equator coincides with the

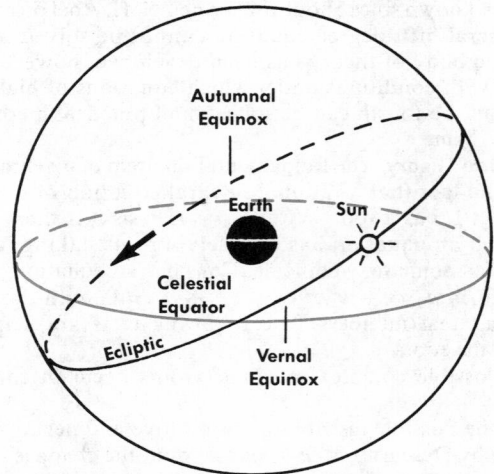

Autumnal Equinox

Earth

Sun

Celestial Equator

Ecliptic

Vernal Equinox

Celestial equator is shown here in relationship to Earth's equator and reference points of the celestial sphere.

416

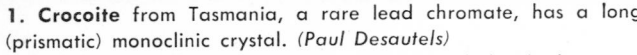

Plate 32   CRYSTALLOGRAPHY

All crystals, both natural and man-made, are solid geometric objects and can be divided into groups based on their symmetry. This symmetry may be displayed, for example, by the repetition of faces, edges, and corners as the crystal is rotated about some axis. The mineral crystals pictured represent the six symmetry groups: isometric, tetragonal, orthorhombic, monoclinic, triclinic, and hexagonal. Distortion of natural crystals sometimes obscures their symmetry.

1. Crocoite from Tasmania, a rare lead chromate, has a long (prismatic) monoclinic crystal. *(Paul Desautels)*

2. Paulingite from Oregon occurs only as the dodecahedron, one of the symmetrical forms in the isometric system. *(Paul Desautels)*

3. Wulfenite from Mexico is a highly colored tetragonal species. It contains both lead and molybdenum. *(Paul Desautels)*

4. Microcline from Colorado, a "feldspar," looks monoclinic, but is actually triclinic. This variety is amazonite. *(Amer. Mus. Nat. Hist.)*

5. Barite from Colorado, a very heavy mineral, often occurs in large orthorhombic crystals. *(Reo N. Pickens, Jr.)*

6. Pyromorphite from Pennsylvania always forms tiny, barrel-shaped, hexagonal crystals (15x). *(Paul Desautels)*

7. Celestite from Texas, a strontium ore, gets its name from sometimes celestial-blue orthorhombic crystals. *(Reo N. Pickens, Jr.)*

8. Copper from England appears in branching clusters of well-formed isometric crystals (10x). *(Paul Desautels)*

1

Plate 33   DAMS

One of man's earliest engineering projects, dams today serve many purposes: flood control, water storage, irrigation, river regulation, and the production of electric power.

1. Grand Coulee Dam, Columbia River, is a very large gravity-type masonry dam. The stability of such dams depends on their weight and shape. *(Jack Zehrt/Shostal)*

2. Roosevelt Dam, Salt River, Ariz.: In this curved, gravity-type dam, a small part of the water load is transmitted to the abutments by the curved shape. *(Chuck Abbott/Rapho-Guillumette)*

2

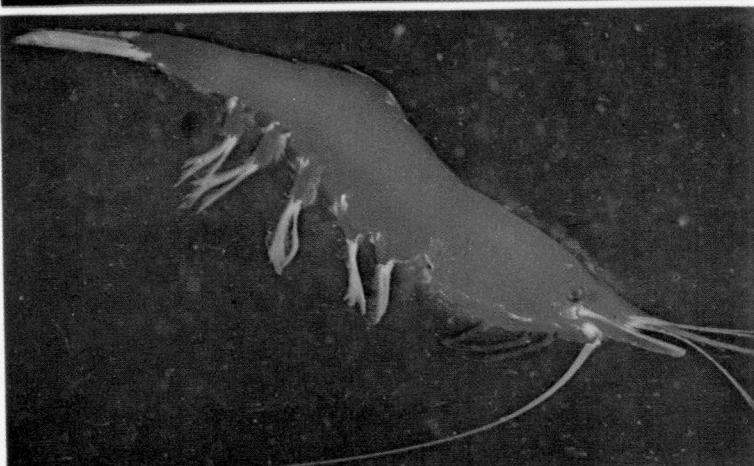

2

1

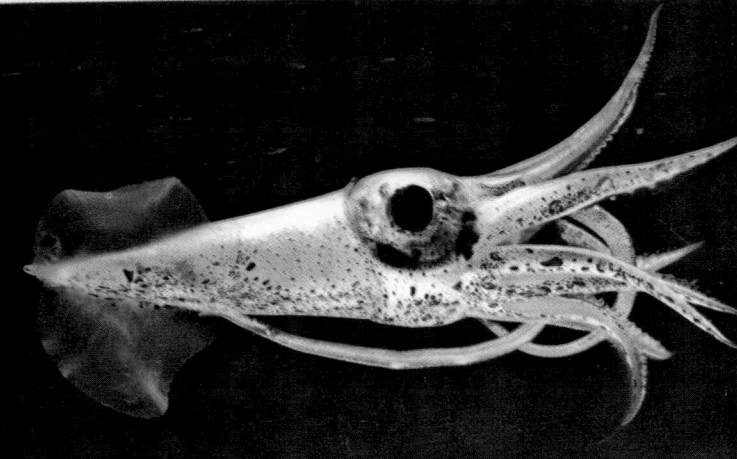

3

4

Plate 34   DEEP-SEA ANIMALS

The least-known animals of our planet are those that live in the parts of the oceans beyond the continental shelves. Many of these deep-sea animals have a broad depth range, living at or near the surface at night and dwelling in the depths by day. **(1) The deep-sea copepod crustacean** *Megacalanus* is not much larger than a grain of wheat. Yet it makes tremendous vertical migrations each day, rising to feed at night, and sinking down beyond the reach of daylight during sunny hours. Copepods form an essential link in the sea's food chain; they transform minute green plants of the upper levels of the sea into animal matter which appeals to small fishes of the depths. **2. The squid** *Ommastrephes pteropus* grows to a length of 6 ft in the depths of the N Atlantic, particularly in the cold waters underlying tropical regions. **3. The long antennae and legs** of the deep-sea crustacean *Systellaspis* are adaptations for detecting danger before it is so close as to be fatal. **4. Huge eyes and efficient light-producing organs** mark the pelagic deep-sea squid *Pyroteuthis margaritifera*. The lights may be a means for keeping a school of these squid together and for recognizing mates in the dark. **5.** The scientific name of this **common deep-sea fish**, *Chauliodus*, is derived from the Greek word for a person with buck teeth. Only a few inches long, the fish is jet black with a double row of light-producing organs along its sides. **6. Strange little snails** called heteropods undulate their flattened feet and swim through the water on their backs. A diminutive shell hangs below the body, and the foot or part of it forms a median fin. Snail shown is of the genus *Carinaria*. *(All photos from Peter David)*

6

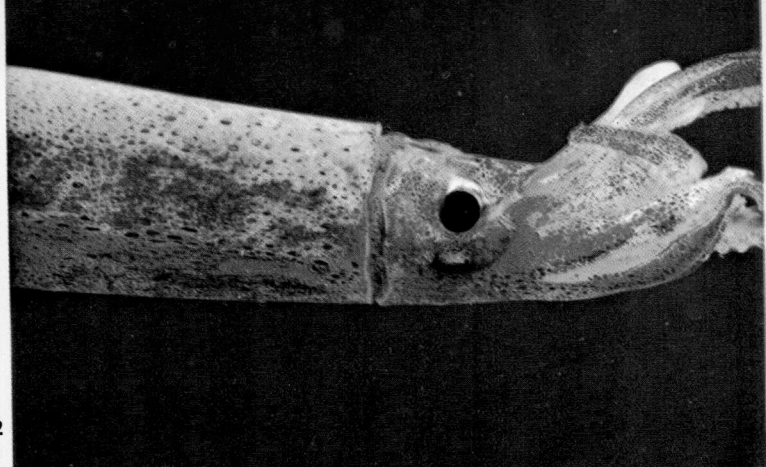

5

Plate 35 DESERTS

Being characterized by low rainfall, deserts have sparse vegetation, with relatively large temperature changes between day and night. These factors strongly influence the topography. Many deserts are sandy; but others display largely bare rock.

1

2

3

1. Arid landscape near Barstow, Calif., shows water-worn slopes and gullies typical where vegetation is sparse. (Brooks-Franklin Photo)

2. Monument Valley, Ariz., an arid part of the Colorado Plateau area, displays erosional remnants of a once-continuous rock layer. (Esther Henderson/Rapho-Guillumette)

3. Sahara dunes in the Great Western Erg, northern Algeria, represent part of a large sand-dune area where the dominant land forms are wind-produced. (George Rodger/Magnum)

celestial horizon; at Earth's equator, it passes through the zenith; and at any other point on Earth it passes across the sky from the east point of the horizon to the west point and crosses the celestial meridian at a height above the horizon equal to the observer's co-latitude. On the dates of the equinoxes, the Sun's daily path across the sky follows the celestial equator.—*T. N.*

EQUILIBRIUM (in physics): a condition of balance attained in situations involving translation (straight-line motion) or rotation (movement in a circle). For *translational equilibrium,* the vector sum (magnitude and direction) of all forces acting on a body must be zero; otherwise, the body would accelerate in the direction of the resultant force. With the sum-total of all forces (ΣF) equal to zero, or the sum of the separate x and y components (representing magnitude and direction) equal

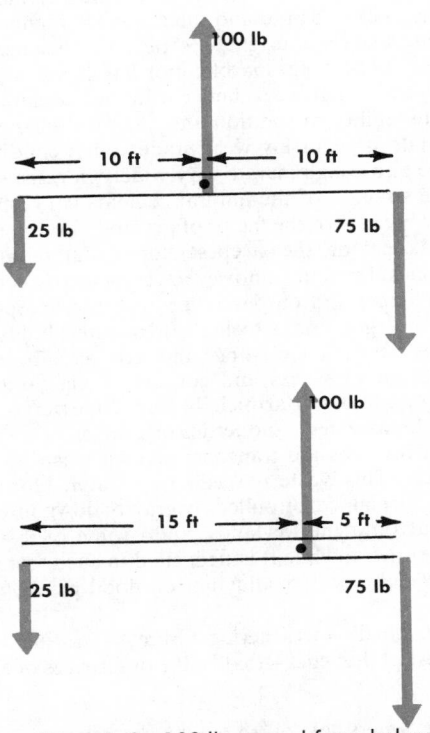

Equilibrium: Although the 100-lb upward force balances the two downward forces in the upper diagram, thereby providing translational equilibrium, the bar would tend to rotate around the point of the upward force's application because the clockwise downward torque is greater than the counter-clockwise downward torque. In the lower drawing, shifting the point of application of the upward force provides both rotational and translational equilibrium.

to zero, the body remains in a state of rest or maintains a condition of uniform motion in a straight line. If the forces acting on a body are not all in the same plane, translational equilibrium requires that ΣF_x, ΣF_y, and ΣF_z be each equal to zero. *Rotational equilibrium* is achieved when the sum-total of all torques ($\Sigma \tau$) is made equal to zero. A simple pivoted lever remains rotationally balanced if the algebraic sum of all the clockwise ($+$) and counterclockwise ($-$) moments or torques is zero. Such a lever is also in a state of translational equilibrium, since the sum-total of all upward and downward forces acting upon it is also zero. See MOTION; FORCE; ROTATION.—*A. E.*

EQUILIBRIUM, CHEMICAL: see CHEMICAL EQUILIBRIUM.

EQUINOCTIAL STORM: a storm occurring near the first days of spring and fall, popularly believed to be unusually severe and extensive, and to be caused by the equinox. Such beliefs are not confirmed by meteorological records, which do, however, confirm that weather tends to be more changeable in spring and fall than during other seasons.—*P. L.*

EQUINOX: either of two points on the CELESTIAL SPHERE where ecliptic and celestial equator intersect. The ecliptic is the great circle traced on the celestial sphere annually by the Sun; its inclination to the celestial equator is about 23½°. The *vernal equinox* is the point where the Sun crosses the equator from south to north on or about Mar. 21, bringing spring to the northern hemisphere. At the *autumnal equinox,* the Sun crosses the equator from north to south on or about Sept. 23, at which time autumn begins for the northern hemisphere. When the Sun is at either point, the day is only slightly longer than night (see DAY AND NIGHT). Hipparchus, *c.* 125 B. C., discovered that the equinoxes are not fixed in space, but move slowly westward along the ecliptic. This PRECESSION OF EQUINOXES amounts to only about 50″ per yr (30° in 2,000 yr). The vernal equinox is also called the First Point of ARIES.—*R. N. M.*

EQUIPARTITION OF ENERGY: a hypothesis put forward by James Clerk Maxwell, which he derived from the classical (Newtonian) theory of statistical mechanics. According to this theory, the molecular energy of a gas, consisting as it does of translational, rotational, and vibrational components, is divided equally among the various "degrees of freedom," or modes of energy absorption. Since a monatomic gas has only translational energy, with total heat energy U equal to ³⁄₂ RT per mole of the gas, the energy transmitted by equipartition to motion along each of the three axes (X, Y, and Z) is ⅓ of ³⁄₂ RT, or ½ RT. For a rigid polyatomic molecule, rotational energy is possible, and each additional degree of freedom, representing a possible axis of rotation, accounts for another ½ RT per mole of internal energy.—*A. E.*

EQUIVALENCE PRINCIPLE: see RELATIVITY.

ERASISTRATUS, fl. 3rd cent. B. C., Alexandrian-Greek anatomist and physiologist; b. Iulis, Ceos. The founder of physiology as a separate field of study, he made discoveries mainly in the physiology of the nervous system, brain, heart, and vascular system.—*D. H. D. R.*

ERATOSTHENES, *c.* 273 B. C.–*c.* 192 B. C., Greek mathematician, geographer, historian, philologist, and poet (hence nicknamed *Pentathlos*—"five-sports athlete"); b. Cyrene. He was the first to calculate the circumference of Earth. He found that the angular distance of the Sun from the zenith at Alexandria was, at noon on the summer solstice, about 7°, or approximately ¹⁄₅₀ of a complete circumference. At Syene, believed to be due south of Alexandria, the Sun was known to be at the zenith at that time. Hence he inferred that the distance from Syene to Alexandria was ¹⁄₅₀ of the circumference of Earth. This distance being known, he then calculated Earth's circumference—obtaining a figure within 50 mi of the present value. Eratosthenes devised an instrument to solve the problem of "duplication of the cube" and discovered the "sieve of Eratosthenes," a method for sorting out the prime numbers among the odd numbers. He wrote a *Geography* giving historical, mathematical, physical, and descriptive data, and also wrote a scientific chronology of Greece, *Chronographiae.*—*R. J. F.*

ERBIUM: a lanthanide (rare-earth metal) element (Er); at. no. 68; at. wt 167.2; density 9.16. Erbium was first recognized as an element by the Swedish chemist Carl Gustav Mosander, 1843. In his investigation of a sample of what was believed to be pure yttria (yttrium oxide, Y_2O_3), Mosander detected the oxides of two other elements, which he named erbium and terbium. As with most rare-earth elements, erbium and its compounds are extremely difficult to separate in pure form from other rare earths and rare-earth compounds with which they are found. Erbium occurs with other rare earths in the minerals polycrase (approx. 7.5% erbium oxide, Er_2O_3), euxenite, and gadolinite, among others. With the development in the last 20 yr of ion-exchange CHROMATOGRAPHY, it has become possible to produce larger amounts of pure erbium compounds than by formerly used fractional distillation methods. No large-scale use for erbium has yet been found.—*G. W. M.*

ERLANGER, JOSEPH, 1874–1965, U. S. physiologist; b. San Francisco. His research with one of his former students, H. S. Gasser, led to discoveries concerning the highly differentiated functions of single nerve fibers. For that work, Erlanger and Gasser shared the 1944 Nobel prize. Erlanger was a member of National Academy of Sciences—*D. H. D. R.*

EROSION: the wearing down of Earth's crust by natural agents that are in motion: running water, waves and currents, glacial ice, and wind. Of these agents, running water is by far the most effective. As permanent or temporary streams, and also as sheetwash, it destroys bedrock both at the surface and underground (see RIVERS AND GROUND WATER) through the abrasive and hammering action of the sediments it carries, and also through the removal of minerals by solution. Waves and currents attack shores by simple impact, hydraulic ramming, and solution, and by the abrasive and hammering action of waterborne rock fragments (see COASTLINES.) Submarine valleys have been in some instances cut by turbidity currents (see SUBMARINE CANYON). Glacial ice creeping overland destroys bedrock by ramming, wedging, and plucking, while rock fragments embedded in the ice exert a powerful gouging and abrasive action (see GLACIERS AND GLACIATION). Especially in DESERTS, rock surfaces are "sandblasted" by wind-blown sediments. All in all, erosion is generally a very slow process by

human standards, but it is—thanks to the enormous span of geologic time—the major factor in the shaping of Earth's crust.

The term erosion is often used to include WEATHERING AND MASS WASTING. Weathering refers to the static processes by which rock is destroyed: solution, chemical attack, breakup by the action of plants and animals, and expansion or contraction due to such causes as chemical change, temperature variations, and the freezing of water between rock grains or within crevices. Mass wasting designates the downslope movement of rock debris under the pull of gravity, as in LANDSLIDES, rockfalls, earthflow, and creep. Weathering and mass wasting occur simultaneously with erosion, hastening it and being hastened by it. The lowering of land elevation by erosion, weathering, and mass wasting working together is called degradation.

Erosion tends to be most rapid in humid regions, because of the abundance of water in the air and in streams. In humid and arid regions alike, erosion is faster on rock masses that are more fractured, mechanically weaker, or chemically more unstable than other rock. Granite and quartzite are highly resistant in any climate, and rhyolite, gneiss, slate, and schist may be almost as durable. Limestone, marble, and basalt are usually strong on arid terrains but weak under a humid climate because of their vulnerability to solution and chemical change involving water. Shale is relatively weak under most conditions, while sandstone and conglomerate vary widely in resistance according to the strength of the natural cements contained in them.

Mainly because of the factor of gravity, rates of erosion tend to be maximal on the steepest slopes and minimal on the gentlest ones. Erosion is, however, restricted by certain conditions. On slopes and on desert terrains it is hampered by the presence of vegetation, which absorbs water, holds soil, slows runoff, restricts mass wasting, and acts as a barrier against wind. Erosion by waves and currents along sandy shores is limited by naturally or artificially placed barriers such as spits and bars, breakwaters, and jetties or groins.

Erosion involves the transport of rock waste to lower and lower levels. This waste is washed by water, blown by wind, carried by glacial ice, or pulled by gravity down into mountain valleys, out onto the lowlands, and—some of it—eventually into the sea. Meanwhile it is deposited in such forms as valley fillings, glacial moraine, alluvium on flood plains, dunes, and deltas.

Erosion, aided by weathering and mass wasting, is responsible for most of the relief—that is, the differences of elevation—

Erosion by running water: Cumulative erosion by sediment-laden waters has carved out the characteristic profiles of the Colorado River's canyon, here seen in its Utah stretch. Cliffs have developed on resistant strata, gentler slopes on weaker ones. The La Sal range is seen in the distance. (Josef Muench)

Coastal erosion: Rock disintegrated by the unceasing attack of the sea has been deposited as sand along the Oregon Coast, as here at Bandon Beach. Sea stacks, the isolated remnants of a retreating coastline, stand not far from the shore. (*Oregon State Highway Department*)

on Earth's crust. The gullies, ravines, and valleys on most landscapes have been created by a process in which streams did the downcutting while slopewash, weathering, and mass wasting did the widening. Valleys usually originate along relatively weak zones, stronger zones surviving as highlands. Rugged terrains such as the Rockies, the South Dakota Badlands, the Maine Coast, and the eastern edges of the Appalachian Plateau owe their major features to streamwork guided by variations in rock resistance. Minor landforms such as mesas and buttes, caves and sinkholes, and oddly shaped pillars in deserts originate from the joint action of small streams (often temporary ones), weathering, and wind. Broad, low terrains such as the Great Plains and the Atlantic and Gulf coastal plains owe their topography to deposits of erosional debris and—in the case of the Coastal Plains—to the planing action of waves and currents as well. The rocky, cliffy shores of Maine, Oregon, and other such coasts represent mainly the work of waves and currents on a terrain originally sculptured by streams, then exposed to the action of waves and currents following a relative rise of sea level. Erosion by glaciers in middle and higher latitudes accounts for the horns, cirques, arêtes, and U-shaped valleys in the mountains, and also for many of the lake basins and the variously shaped deposits of glacial drift on the lowlands (see GLACIAL AGES).

Here and there on Earth's crust, relief has been produced directly by volcanism or crustal distortion. The Cascade Mountains of the Northwest, for example, were built up by volcanic eruptions over a period of some millions of years. The Teton Range of Wyoming consists of a rock mass gradually raised above the surrounding terrain by faulting—the fracturing and dislocation of the crust. But even such terrains are subject to erosion as they are being built or raised up, and after the volcanic or crustal activity ceases, the relief is increasingly determined by erosion.

As land elevation is reduced, the process of erosion grows slower and slower. It continues in some degree, however, as long as the land is above the sea—that is, above BASE LEVEL. Thus all lands are subject to the possibility of leveling (see PENEPLAIN). Actually, vast areas of continents have probably been reduced to elevations near sea level many times during the billions of years of Earth history. But the land has been renewed again and again by uplifts due to crustal unrest (see DIASTROPHISM; ISOSTASY), and also by periodic outpourings of lava from the planet's interior (VOLCANISM). As lowlands are uplifted or built up, their streams are rejuvenated, or reinvigorated, by the increase in gradient, and a new cycle of erosion begins.—*J. W.*

ESCAPE VELOCITY: the least velocity required by a body to escape completely from the gravitational attraction of a massive object such as a planet or star, without the use of any propulsive machinery. While the escape velocity depends on position (and becomes smaller as the distance from the massive object becomes greater), it is independent of the direction of flight, provided only that the subsequent orbit does not lead to collision with the massive object or to frictional retardation in its atmosphere. In the absence of propulsive machinery or an atmosphere, the orbit of a particle in the gravitational field of a spherical body is a CONIC SECTION with one focus at the center of the body. If this is an ellipse, then the distance from the body is limited, and the velocity at any point of such an orbit is less than the escape velocity there. If the orbit is a parabola or hyperbola, the particle will escape to infinity provided the path does not reenter the body's atmosphere. In a parabola the velocity always equals the escape velocity (which is also called parabolic velocity); in a hyperbola it exceeds it everywhere. Escape velocity, V, outside a spherical body is given by the formula $V^2 = 2GM/r$, where G is the universal constant of gravitation (6.67×10^{-8} in CGS units), M is the mass, and r the distance from the center of the body. By this formula the velocity of escape from Earth's surface is about 7 mi/sec, without allowance for resistance by the atmosphere. The velocity required to keep a satellite in a circular orbit is 0.71 times the escape velocity corresponding to the satellite's altitude.—*H. B.*

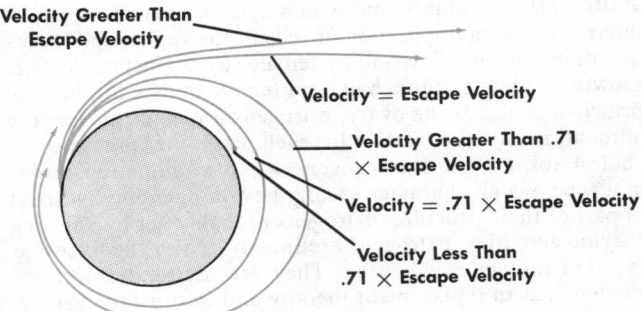

Velocity Greater Than Escape Velocity

Velocity = Escape Velocity

Velocity Greater Than .71 × Escape Velocity

Velocity = .71 × Escape Velocity

Velocity Less Than .71 × Escape Velocity

Orbits and velocities: At less than .71 × escape velocity, no stable orbit is achieved. At .71 × escape velocity, a circular orbit results. Higher speeds yield elliptical, parabolic (for exactly escape velocity), and hyperbolic orbits.

ESOPHAGUS: see DIGESTION.

ESPY, JAMES POLLARD, 1785–1860, U. S. meteorologist; b. Washington Co., Pa. His *Philosophy of Storms* (1841) was a milestone in meteorology. While serving as meteorologist to the War Dept. (from 1842) and the Navy Dept. (from 1848) he instituted the practice of sending out telegraphic bulletins on weather.—*D. H. D. R.*

ESSAY ON THE PRINCIPLE OF POPULATION, as It Affects the Future Improvement of Society, with Remarks on the Speculations of Mr. Godwin, M. Condorcet, and Other Writers, by Thomas Robert Malthus, 1798: This was not the first study of population problems (Benjamin Franklin and others had made earlier suggestions of the effect of population pressures) but Malthus' simplicity of statement aroused immediate attention. His many-sided argument was reduced to the simple formula: "Population, when unchecked, increases in a geometrical ratio. Subsistence increases only in an arithmetic ratio." The effect of this "law" was to provide a strong, constant check upon population, owing to the difficulty of obtaining food for subsistence. The concept of restraint upon population expansion was cited by Charles Darwin as having been helpful in the formation of the theory of NATURAL SELECTION.—*E. M.*

ESSENTIAL OIL: a volatile liquid obtained from plant sources, generally by distillation but occasionally by solvent extraction or other special methods. The name "essential oil" implies that the oily product possesses the characteristics of the plant source; for example, oil of rose is said to be the essence of the rose. Essential oils have a wide use in perfumes and flavorings based on their odoriferous properties. From some, however, substances are extracted for purely industrial purposes. Thus oil of camphor supplies camphor for medicine and for celluloid manufacture, and oil of turpentine yields products important to the paint industry.—*Ru. M.*

ESTER: a chemical compound formed by replacing the acidic H atom of an acid with an organic radical. In the following examples the ethyl radical, C_2H_5, replaces the acidic H atom in acetic acid (organic) and in hydrochloric acid (inorganic):

$$\overset{\displaystyle O}{\underset{\text{Ethyl acetate}}{CH_3\overset{\|}{C}\!-\!OC_2H_5}} \qquad \underset{\text{Ethyl chloride}}{C_2H_5\!-\!Cl}$$

Although resembling salts superficially, esters differ from them in being incapable of ionization.—*Ru. M.*

ESTIVATION: see HIBERNATION AND ESTIVATION.

ESTROGEN: any compound which acts as a female sex hormone, causing multiplication of cells of the vagina and uterus and development of secondary female sex characteristics, *e.g.* growth of breasts, pubic hair, and female body contour. The principal source is the ovary; estrogens are made also by the adrenal gland and testis. In each case the precursor is cholesterol. All natural estrogens, *e.g.* estradiol, are steroids of a type, which characteristically have a phenolic hydroxyl as part of their structure. Estrogens probably act by affecting enzyme activities. Estrogens are inactivated in the liver and excreted into bile and urine. They are used extensively in medicine, as in replacement therapy and in prostatic cancer. —*J. F. S.*

ESTRUS CYCLE (also **estrous, oestrus,** or **oestrous cycle**): the sequence of periodic changes that occurs in the reproductive organs of female mammals and culminates in OVULATION. In man, higher monkeys, and anthropoid apes, the estrus cycle corresponds to the menstrual cycle (see MENSTRUATION). In monestrus animals such as the dog, a single estrus cycle extends through the breeding season. In polyestrus animals such as the cow, mare, and sow, two or more estrus cycles occur during the breeding season and are separated by short periods of sexual quiescence. The typical estrus cycle begins with proestrus, a period during which there is an increased blood supply to the external genitalia and the uterus, and enlargement of the mammary glands. During this time the Graafian follicle is maturing (see OVARY), and in some animals (*e.g.* dog and cow) there is vaginal bleeding. This period is followed by estrus, during which ovulation occurs. The proestrus and estrus periods are sometimes referred to as "heat." Next, a period of pregnancy or pseudopregnancy ensues. At the beginning of this period certain uterine changes, *e.g.* those occurring in preparation for the implantation of the fertilized ovum, continue, and the growth of the mammary glands is further stimulated. If the ovum has been fertilized, these changes persist and merge into those of pregnancy (see GESTATION). If fertilization has not occurred, the uterus returns to its resting state, and there is a sloughing off of uterine debris. Following either pregnancy or pseudopregnancy, a period of sexual quiescence occurs. In some animals, *e.g.* the cat, rabbit, and ferret, ovulation and the accompanying uterine changes occur only after mating.—*A. P. E.*

ESTUARY: the lower course of a river as it approaches a sea, where its current is affected by tides; or an arm of the sea receiving a river. The water of estuaries is saline and tidal; certain estuaries with wide mouths are subject to a TIDAL BORE, a flow of water for many miles upstream at speeds up to 20 mi/hr and with crests up to 20 ft high. Estuaries are often the result of the drowning of river mouths by subsidence of the coast or rise of sea level.—*E. A.*

ETHANE: see PARAFFINS.

ETHER (in chemistry): an organic compound in which hydrocarbon radicals are linked through an oxygen atom:

$$\underset{\text{Ethyl ether}}{CH_3CH_2\!-\!O\!-\!CH_2CH_3} \qquad \underset{\text{Methyl phenyl ether}}{CH_3\!-\!O\!-\!\hexagon}$$

Ethyl ether, known simply as "ether," is a volatile liquid, used as a solvent and as an anesthetic.—*Ru. M.*

ETHER (in physics): a medium whose existence was postulated by James Clerk Maxwell and other 19th-cent. physicists to help them visualize how light is transmitted through space. For centuries a debate had raged over whether a light beam is a stream of particles or a train of waves (see LIGHT). Experiments demonstrating that light exhibits diffraction (bending around corners) and interference (mutual cancellation of two parts of a light beam, one of which has been made to travel a slightly longer distance), together with other effects, indicated the wave model was correct. Yet this model left physicists dissatisfied because it permitted light to pass through empty space without a carrying medium. The known wave phenomena of that day were all mechanical excitations. Since each elementary volume of the medium is mechanically coupled to its neighbors, the transmittal of the wave consists of nothing more than the successive motion of contiguous elements.

The troubling question was: How could there be a traveling wave of excitation without a medium to be excited? The way out was to assume the existence of the ether. A light beam was imagined to be a traveling elastic oscillation—like the shimmering of a gelatin mold. Even after Maxwell and

Heinrich Hertz had demonstrated that light consists of transverse oscillating electric and magnetic fields, the concept of the ether was maintained, though its properties were changed. The mechanical ether concept was doomed when the famous MICHELSON-MORLEY EXPERIMENT demonstrated that the velocity of light is independent of the velocity of the observer. This directly contradicted any model in which light is imagined to be a traveling wave in a stationary medium. In modern theory, electric and magnetic fields are independent *entities* generated by electric charges; they are not mere distortions of any medium. They travel through vacuum at a speed of $3(10)^{10}$ cm/sec independently of the velocity of the source from which they were emitted.—*S. K.*

ETHOLOGY: the study of the behavior of animals other than man; it is a counterpart of human psychology. Ethologists seek to describe accurately the responses of animals to events in their surroundings, and to relate these responses to definite stimuli received by sense organs. Studies include the behavior of the animal in finding and eating food, discovering and courting mates, caring for young, detecting and escaping from predatory animals, and communicating with one another. See ANIMAL BEHAVIOR.—*L. and M. M.*

ETHYL ALCOHOL: CH_3CH_2OH, a chemical compound in which the ethyl radical, C_2H_5, is linked to the hydroxyl (alcohol) radical, OH. This member of a series of ALCOHOLS is called simply "alcohol." It is made by fermentation of sugars through enzyme action, the sugars being obtained from various starches (mostly corn in the U. S., potatoes in Europe), and from the molasses by-product of sugar refining. Alcohol is also made on a large scale by synthetic processes. It can be concentrated by distillation to 95.6% by weight in water; the remaining water can be removed chemically to yield *absolute alcohol,* another name for anhydrous alcohol, which has special uses in chemistry. To prevent illegal use of alcohol which has not been taxed as a beverage, a poisonous or unpalatable denaturant is added.—*Ru. M.*

ETHYLENE (also **ethene**): in chemistry, an unsaturated hydrocarbon, $CH_2{=}CH_2$, and the simplest member of the OLEFINS. Ethylene is a gas with physical properties similar to those of ethane, the corresponding saturated hydrocarbon of the PARAFFINS. It is a product of catalytic cracking of petroleum; also catalytic dehydrogenation of ethyl alcohol. Ethylene is far more reactive than ethane, because of the ability of the double bond to undergo *addition* reactions. Thus, it will add a molecule of chlorine (Cl_2) or of hydrogen (H_2) (see UN-SATURATED COMPOUNDS). Ethylene, an important intermediate in chemical manufacture, also has anesthetic properties and is used to speed ripening of fruits.—*Ru. M.*

EUCLID, fl. *c.* 365 B. C., ancient mathematician, probably Greek. Little is known about his life. Probably founder of the school of mathematics at Alexandria, he is famous as author of the *Elements,* in which he collected and organized practically all of geometry that was known at the time. D. E. Smith states: "He was the most successful textbook writer that the world has ever known." The *Elements,* much altered by translations and reconstructions, has provided the source material for geometry courses for 2,000 yr. Not only does it include much basic knowledge of geometry, but it attempts to organize mathematical knowledge in a completely logical way (see EUCLIDEAN GEOMETRY). There is reason to think that in stating his famous assumption about possible parallel lines as a distinct postulate, he believed that the assumption cannot be demonstrated from his remaining postulates; and the repeated but vain attempts to demonstrate it during the next two millennia, culminating in the development of NON-

EUCLIDEAN GEOMETRY based on contrary assumptions, show that Euclid was right in this belief. Other works attributed to Euclid include a book on conics, which served as a basis for Apollonius' work on the same subject; the *Phenomena;* the *Data;* the *Optics;* and *On Divisions.*—*H. C.*

EUCLIDEAN GEOMETRY: the oldest and best-known part of one of the main fields of mathematics. Euclidean geometry stems from the axioms adopted by Euclid, and much of it was contained in his *Elements.* Prior to the Greek period, geometry, like other parts of mathematics, was indistinguishable from physical science, the word geometry meaning "earth measurement." As a physical science it was in part empirical, and the emphasis was upon practical results. In the hands of Greek geometers it became an abstract science, although some unconscious reliance upon physical concepts remained. It was made purely deductive, being based upon assumptions, or postulates. This it has remained, and all pure mathematics has adopted the same standard. Each conclusion is deduced logically from the basic postulates and is called a theorem. Euclidean geometry continues to have many practical values and is of constant use in science, technology, and everyday life.

Basic Elements: Because of the deductive nature of geometry, the most basic elements are undefined. These are point, straight line, and plane. Other elements are defined in terms of these. Euclid attempted to define all elements, but this necessarily leads to circularity. The defined elements are geometrical configurations, or simply figures, made up of combinations of the undefined elements. Two-dimensional figures lie in a plane, are called plane figures, and are discussed in plane geometry. Some of the most important defined elements are the following:

A *line segment* is the part of a line that joins two fixed points; it is terminated at both ends. An *angle* is the inclination of one straight line to another that it intersects; it is the difference in direction of the two lines. An angle may also be defined as the figure formed by two line segments emanating from one point. Instead of segments, *half-lines* may be employed, a half-line being a straight line drawn from a point in one direction. A figure is rectilinear if it contains only straight lines (no curves). Chief among the rectilinear figures are the POLYGONS, TRIANGLE, quadrilateral, pentagon, and so on. A regular polygon has all its sides equal and all its angles equal; it is equilateral and equiangular, or isogonal. Similar polygons have the same shape; the angles of one are each equal to those of the other, taken in the same order. A CIRCLE is a plane figure all points of whose boundary are at the same distance from a fixed point. The fixed point is the center, the common distance the radius, and the boundary the circumference.

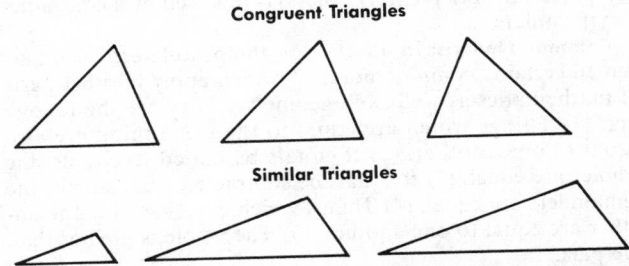

Congruent Triangles

Similar Triangles

Euclid's *Elements,* an Alexandrian assortment of propositions and methods, has been carried over bodily into the curriculum of recent centuries. In the familiar figures exhibited here, Euclid allows a triangle to be lifted out of the plane to show congruence (*top*), and reaffirms the nature of the plane in assuming that figures of different sizes can be similar (*bottom*).

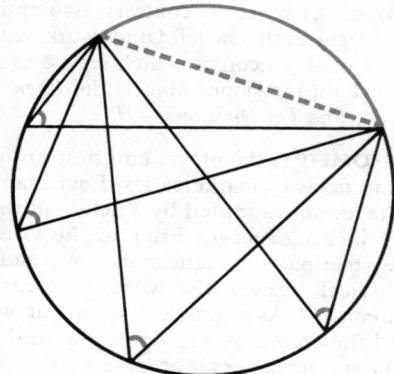

One of Euclid's theorems: Angles inscribed in a circle are equal if they subtend the same arc of the circle.

In more advanced parts of Euclidean geometry, other figures are studied, notably the CONIC SECTIONS—ellipses, parabolas, and hyperbolas. Euclid wrote a treatise on these curves, although Apollonius' work on the subject is better known. Today they are studied by methods of analytic geometry (see COORDINATE GEOMETRY), which was invented in the 17th cent. The analytic method associates points with numbers so that algebraic processes can be used. The synthetic method of Euclid applies reasoning directly to the geometric features of a figure.

Postulates: We usually conceive the elements of geometry as belonging to space and are guided in the adoption of abstract postulates by observations of physical space. This is not a logical necessity, and a mathematician who is habituated to purely abstract thinking may disengage geometry from physical concepts altogether. Proofs must depend only upon the postulates and are not affected by observations. The postulates of Euclidean plane geometry are as follows (from the T. L. Heath translation of the *Elements*): (1) A straight line can be drawn from any point to any point. (2) A finite straight line can be produced continuously in a straight line. (3) A circle may be described with any center and distance (radius). (4) All right angles are equal to one another. (5) If a straight line falling on two straight lines makes the interior angles on the same side together less than two right angles, the two straight lines, if produced indefinitely, meet on that side in which the angles are together less than two right angles. This is called the PARALLEL POSTULATE. It leads to the conclusion that through any point not on a straight line there exists just one parallel to the line. This fifth postulate is crucial in the distinction between Euclidean and non-Euclidean geometries. In NON-EUCLIDEAN GEOMETRY this postulate (and possibly others) is replaced by a contradictory postulate.

Common Notions: In addition to the postulates, Euclid assumed certain "common notions" which apply in other parts of mathematics as well as in geometry. They are the following: (1) Things which are equal to the same thing are also equal to one another. (2) If equals be added to equals, the wholes are equal. (3) If equals be subtracted from equals, the remainders are equal. (4) Things which coincide with one another are equal to one another. (5) The whole is greater than the part.

Theorems: The theorems of geometry are of two varieties: those which establish the properties of geometrical figures, and those which show how configurations can be constructed with a minimum of given parts. The first variety is illustrated by the PYTHAGOREAN THEOREM, which concerns a property of any right triangle. The theorem states that the area of a square having its side equal to the hypotenuse (the longest side of the triangle) is equal to the sum of the areas of two squares having as sides the other two sides of the triangle. Many of these theorems establish congruence, which is equality in every detail. A basic method of proving congruence of plane figures is that of superposition, in which we think of one figure as being moved so as to fit on another. Other theorems have to do with similarity: two triangles are similar if the angles of one are equal, respectively, to those of the other.

Many theorems concern measurement; thus numerical concepts are brought into geometry. Units of length, area, and angle are adopted. A unit of length is an arbitrary line segment. The length of another segment, in terms of this unit, is the number of times the unit must be used to cover the whole segment. The perimeter of a figure is the total length of the boundary. The unit of area is a square having an arbitrary line segment for a side: a square inch is the area of a square one inch on a side. Theorems establish means for determining the perimeters and area of many figures. For example, the perimeter of a square is four times a side; the area of a triangle is one-half the product of one side, taken as the base, and the *altitude* upon it, which is the perpendicular distance of the base from the opposite vertex; the area of a circle is the product of the number π (3.1416 approx.) multiplied by the square of the radius. The unit of angular measure is an arbitrary angle. The most common unit in practical work is the degree, which is 1/360 of the rotation which carries a segment around one end point so as to coincide with its original position.

Three-dimensional Euclidean geometry utilizes the five postulates given above. In addition, it is assumed that a plane can be passed through any three points. That is, three points are always coplanar. If the three points lie on one line, *i.e.* are collinear, many planes contain them. If the points are not collinear, they determine one plane. Postulates 3 and 5 must be understood to refer to elements in the same plane. Thus, in postulate 5, the two lines that are cut by a third must lie in the same plane. And in postulate 3, we observe that only one circle can be described with a given center and given radius in one plane, but many circles are possible if other planes may be utilized.

The theorems of solid geometry establish properties of solid figures, *e.g.* the SPHERE, CONE, CYLINDER, PYRAMID, and POLYHEDRON. Among them are included MENSURATION formulas. There are also construction theorems, although they do not play as prominent a role as in plane geometry.—*H. C.*

EUDOXUS OF CNIDUS, 408–355 B. C., Greek astronomer, mathematician, and physician. After studying with Plato in Athens, Eudoxus journeyed to Egypt. He later settled at Cyzicus, where he established a school, and his last years were spent at Cnidus, where he had an observatory. In scientific outlook Eudoxus was centuries ahead of his contemporaries. He made discoveries in geometry that were taken over by Euclid. Notable among them were his solutions of the problems of the area of a rectangle with incommensurable sides and of the area bounded by a curve by the "method of exhaustion." His theory of proportion, an achievement of the highest order, is the starting point for a modern theory of irrational numbers. His four books on astronomy were *The Mirror, The Phaenomena, Speeds,* and *Sphaerics.* He made an attempt to account for irregular motions of Sun, Moon, and planets by his system of homocentric (concentric) spheres, with Earth at their center. Research in acoustics and mechanics was ascribed to him, and he may have been the inventor of the astrolabe.—*H. C. and R. J. F.*

EUGENICS: a word coined in 1885 by Francis Galton, an English student of heredity, from the Greek *eugenia* (well-born), and defined by him as "the study of the agencies under social control which may improve or impair the racial qualities of future generations physically or mentally." An interest in improving the human race is at least as old as the ancient Greeks. Citizens of Sparta, that bleak model of the garrison state, exposed weak or deformed infants to die. Plato discusses eugenics favorably in his *Republic*. The desire that children should be born into the world sound in mind and body and, in fact, gifted is universal.

Two major types of problems arise when the ideals of eugenics come to be applied. The first concerns what is scientifically possible. Deleterious genes could be eliminated from a population in a single generation if such genes are dominant, *i.e.* always show their effects when present. This could be done merely by preventing afflicted individuals from reproducing. But most bad genes are recessive and only manifest themselves when inherited from both parents. Such genes are extremely difficult to weed out. The gene for albinism is an example. There are about five albinos in every 100,000 persons. On the basis of random marriages, this means that in every 100,000 persons there are, in addition to five albinos, 1,420 carriers in whom the albinism gene is masked by a normal gene. Sterilization of the five albinos would reduce the total number of carriers of genes for albinism by an insignificant amount. When more is learned about the linkage of genes on human chromosomes, it may be possible to make useful predictions about the probable results of specific marriages and thus avoid certain frightful hereditary diseases, such as Huntington's chorea.

When desirable intellectual traits are the objective, a second scientific difficulty arises: the difficulty of distinguishing between the effects of heredity and those of environment. This is far greater than the early enthusiasts imagined. An egg develops into a man or a mouse or a starfish because of its heredity, yet at every point in that development, environment plays a greater or lesser part. The organism is the resultant of these two forces, and only in one-egg or so-called identical twins can we begin to unravel the respective roles of what Galton called nature and nurture.

The second major problem is one of values far transcending everyday science. Who is to decide what are the desirable traits? A world without Beethovens, da Vincis, or Ted Williamses would be a far poorer place. But who would want to live on a planet entirely populated by Einsteins and Tolstoys? Nor would many persons advocate peopling our planet with standardized men, each as like the other as ants in a hill. Clearly a rich diversity of types, perhaps not far different from what we now are, is preferable. It would be scientifically possible for a ruthless dictator or a group of powerful philosopher-kings to produce as diverse and fantastic breeds of men as we already have of dogs and pigeons. The methods are well known and in common use among plant and animal breeders —inbreeding and selection followed by crossbreeding, and then more inbreeding and selection, keeping a sharp lookout for interesting mutations. Although there is no doubt that this is scientifically possible, it would require a very different standard of social values from our present one. It is not at all what Galton and his followers had in mind.—*G. B. M.*

EULER, LEONHARD, 1707–83, Swiss mathematician; b. Basel; ed. Univ. of Basel, where he was associated with the Bernoullis. He was attached to the St. Petersburg Academy from 1727–40, to the Berlin Academy from 1740–66, and again to the St. Petersburg Academy from 1766 until his death. Euler was one of the most prolific mathematicians of all time and a scholar of universal range, equally at home in all branches of mathematics of his time. His great treatises on calculus and calculus of variations are classics. His work on analytic mechanics was a contribution of the highest order. He was probably the greatest of all algorists (those who devise practical formulas for calculating). He also systematized and unified vast areas in which only partial and isolated results existed. Much of the material of college courses in mathematics today is essentially as Euler left it. Numerous expressions, formulas, and theorems bear his name. He was a fellow of the Royal Society. —*H. C.*

Leonhard Euler
(*N. Y. Public Library*)

EULER-CHELPIN, HANS VON, 1873–1964, German-Swedish chemist; b. Augsburg. He brought the chemistry of fermentation and enzymes into a systematic connection with the rest of chemistry in his *Chemie der Enzyme* (1910). For their investigations on the fermentation of sugar and of fermentative enzymes, he and A. Harden shared the Nobel prize for 1929. —*D. H. D. R.*

EUROPIUM: a lanthanide (rare-earth metal) element (Eu); at. no. 63; at. wt 152.0; density 5.24. Its discovery (by spectroscopic analysis) is credited to the French chemist Eugène Demarçay, 1896, although two discoverers of other elements, William Crookes and Lecoq de Boisbaudran, had previously reported experimental indications of the existence of a substance like europium. Owing mainly to the work (1936–41) of the Englishman H. N. McCoy, europium became available in sufficient quantities for thorough investigation; and its properties are therefore better known than those of most other rare earths, although it is among the scarcest. Europium is found naturally in the mineral monazite, as well as in the fission products of thorium, plutonium, and uranium. It is one of few rare earths that possess a +2 valence state.— *G. W. M.*

EUSTACHIAN TUBE: see EAR.

EUSTACHIO, BARTOLOMMEO, 1500–74, Italian anatomist; b. San Severino (?). He discovered the thoracic duct, the adrenal glands, the Eustachian tube, and the dental sac of the second teeth, and contributed to the study of comparative anatomy. His *Libellus dentibus,* a book on teeth, appeared in 1563, but the famous *Tabulae anatomicae* ("Anatomical Plates") was published posthumously, in 1714.—*D. H. D. R.*

EUTECTIC: When a melt or solution consisting of two components is cooled, the initial freezing point, *i.e.* the temperature at which a solid first forms, depends upon the relative proportions of the components as well as on their individual freezing points. The lowest freezing point attainable by varying the proportions is called the *eutectic point,* and the mixture having those proportions is the *eutectic mixture* or composition. The eutectic mixture also has the property of freezing completely at constant temperature, and depositing throughout the freezing process crystals that have the same composition as the liquid. Thus it freezes or melts completely at a single sharply defined temperature in the same manner as a pure substance. Non-eutectic mixtures melt and freeze over a temperature range. The eutectic point is always lower than the freezing point of either pure component. Eutectic mixtures of metals are called eutectic alloys; they are widely used as solders, electrical fuses, and fusible seals in sprinkler systems. Ternary and multicomponent eutectics also are known, and have even lower melting points than the corresponding binary or two-component eutectics. See FREEZING. —*A. M. S.*

EVANS, OLIVER, 1755–1819, U. S. inventor; b. near Newport, Del., often called "the Watt of America." In 1777 he invented a machine for making carding combs for wool and cotton, and in 1780 developed the first automatic grain mill. Utilizing ingenious adaptations of such familiar devices as the endless belt and the Archimedean screw, the mill could be operated by one person. In 1804 he constructed for Philadelphia an amphibious steam dredge which was the first wheeled vehicle in the U. S. A. to move under its own power and to employ a high-pressure steam engine successfully.—*S. B.*

EVAPORATION: the transition from liquid to gaseous phase occurring at the free surface of a liquid. Evaporation is the result of the motion of the molecules of the liquid. These molecules are held together by forces of mutual attraction, and inside the body of the liquid they experience, on the average, no resultant force tending to drive them either to the surface or deeper into the interior. Individual molecules approaching or near the surface may be "caught" and then "pulled back" into the liquid by the intermolecular forces. But the velocity distribution of these molecules is such that some of the more energetic ones will break through the surface and evaporate into the surrounding space. If the temperature of the liquid rises, more molecules acquire the critical kinetic energy needed for their escape. The rate of evaporation, per second and per unit area of the exposed surface, varies for different liquids; for a particular liquid, the rate depends solely on the temperature of the liquid.

Evaporation is accompanied by a reverse process, CONDENSATION, which is the return of vapor molecules back to the liquid phase. The rate of this return (per second and per unit area of the surface) is a function of the pressure exerted by the vapor, which depends on the vapor temperature. In a closed vessel, a condition of equilibrium for a given temperature is reached when the rate of evaporation is exactly equal to the rate of condensation. Obviously, in an open vessel, equilibrium cannot be attained; ultimately, all the liquid evaporates.

Since the more energetic molecules are the first to escape by evaporation, the average kinetic energy of the molecules remaining behind decreases, with the result that the process of net evaporation is always accompanied by cooling. Additional heat energy must therefore be supplied to the evaporating liquid to continue the process. See HEAT, LATENT; KINETIC THEORY OF MATTER.—*A. E.*

EVAPORITES: sedimentary rocks deposited by the evaporation of land-locked saline waters. Evaporites accumulate in interior basins (playas) or in bar- or reef-blocked arms of the sea in arid regions. Cyclic inundations over a long period may result in deposits up to several thousand feet thick. Anhydrite, gypsum, and halite (rock salt) are major evaporite minerals, but borates, nitrates, carbonates, and various salts of potassium, magnesium, strontium, lithium, iodine, and bromine also are obtained from evaporite deposits. In playas, the salines are derived through the weathering of the rocks of the drainage basin, possibly with some volcanic exhalations added; thus the compositions of these deposits may be varied and complex. The marine deposits are more regular in com-

position, but the sequence of crystallization and the proportions of constituents may vary greatly, indicating interruption or overlapping of cycles, tilting of the basin, or later leaching with removal of some of the more soluble constituents or reactions between constituents.—*L. M.*

EVENING STAR: SEE MORNING STAR AND EVENING STAR.

EVERGREEN: a plant that retains its green foliage throughout the year. An evergreen remains green because its leaves or stems have special structures that enable them to retain the green pigment chlorophyll or because it exists in a climate favorable to continuous vegetative growth. Evergreens shed their leaves, but not all at one time, as do DECIDUOUS PLANTS. In temperate areas (*e.g.* most of U. S. and Europe) only a few plants such as conifers and members of the heath, holly, barberry, fern, and grass families retain green leaves during winter. In temperate desert regions with little rainfall, most plants are deciduous, forming new leaves only in the wet season. But a few, *e.g.* the creosote bush (*Larrea divaricata*) and the pepper tree (*Schinus molle*), are evergreen. In wet tropical and subtropical regions, especially in the hot lowland rain forests and cooler cloud forests of the mountains, palms, mango trees, and many other families of tropical plants consist largely of evergreen species.

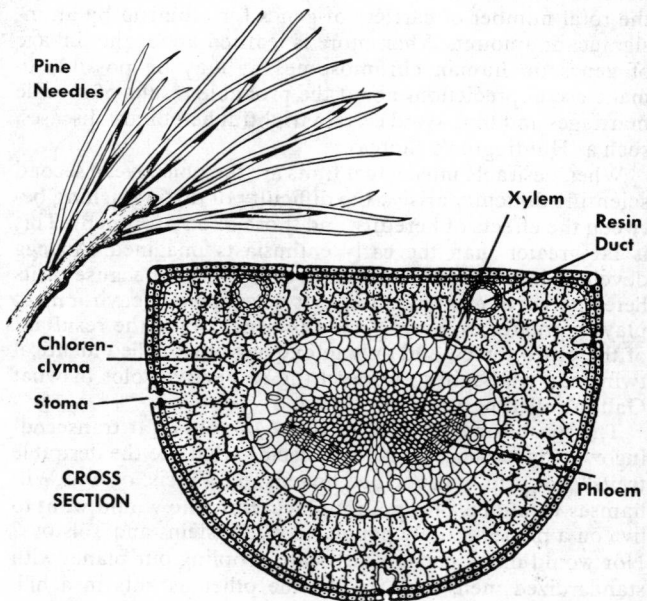

Pine needles are well adapted for conserving water in winter, when tree's roots absorb little water from soil. Evaporation is limited by reduced surface of needles, their thick, waxy outer wall, and their few, sunken stomata. (*After Kenoyer*)

In general two main types of evergreens may be distinguished in temperate and frigid regions of the eastern and western hemispheres: (1) the familiar type with fine, stiff, needle-like or scale-like foliage, mostly found among conifers, *e.g.* pine (*Pinus*), hemlock (*Tsuga*), and redwood (*Sequoia*); and (2) broad-leaved types with flat or plate-like, usually leathery or stiff foliage that exposes a relatively large surface, such as mountain laurel (*Kalmia*), boxwood (*Buxus*), bearberry (*Arctostaphylos*). Leaves of many evergreens are leathery, reduced in surface area (as compared with deciduous leaves), hairy, or otherwise adapted to resist cold and drought (see GYMNOSPERMS). In addition to the two main types, there are several minor types. Leafless evergreens include various cacti, euphorbias, and thorny shrubs such as *Glossopetalum*.

In most cacti the green leaflike parts are really stems, while the true leaves are represented merely by spiny hairs. Some thorny green shrubs, *e.g. Cercidium,* produce small leaves for a brief period during the rainy season, but these soon fall, and the stems continue to carry on PHOTOSYNTHESIS. Evergreens with fleshy and succulent leaves adapted for storing water are often found in hot deserts or alpine regions (see DESERT; ALPINE PLANTS). The familiar stonecrops (*Sedum*) and orpines (*Crassula*) exhibit this succulence. Many plants of tropical climates are tender-leaved evergreens, *e.g.* the bromeliads, many orchids, ferns, and various pitcher plants (*Nepenthes* and *Heliamphora*). Adequate moisture and warm temperatures enable them to retain their leaves, which often are either membranaceous or leathery in texture and have a prolonged tip known as the "rain tip." A sixth type of evergreen is represented by certain aquatic plants, which continue vegetative growth indefinitely in fresh or salt water. These include eelgrass (*Vallisneria*), species of pondweed (*Potamogeton*), and many others.—A. P. E.

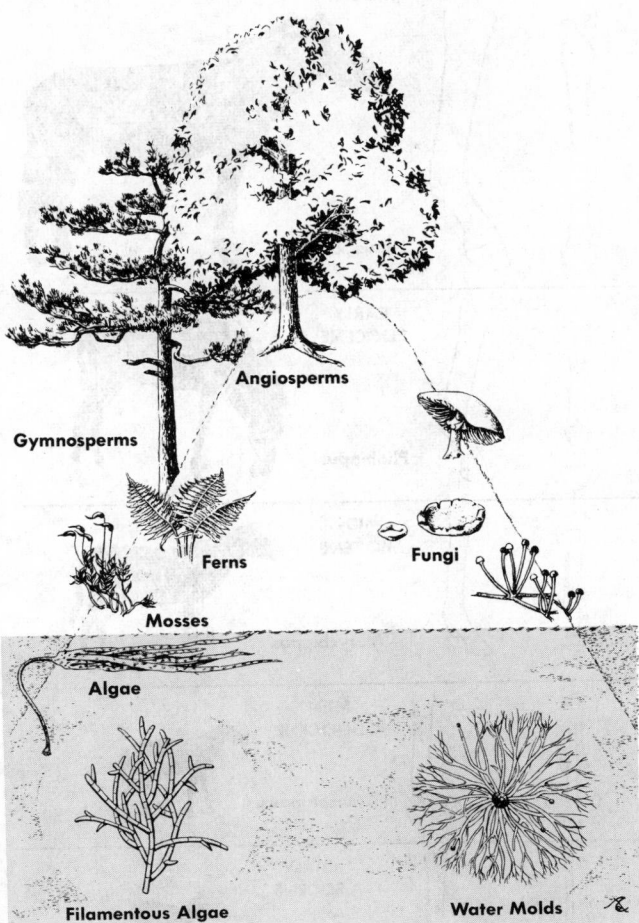

Evolution of plants resulted in the major groups shown above. Algae and molds, which developed in an aquatic environment, are relatively simple plants. The conquest of land, a major event in plant evolution, was achieved independently by green plants (*left*) and fungi. Among green plants, some (*e.g.* mosses) remained small and stayed in moist places, whereas others achieved great size and became the dominant land plants of today. (*From Bonner*)

EVOLUTION: the change of plant and animal forms in time; in current theory, the secular change of hereditary material in a population. This prevalent theory has its roots in the work of Darwin, but the concept of evolution is much older, for Lucretius wrote two millennia ago of perpetual change in nature and of the extinction of species. The literal acceptance of Hebraic cosmography and of Platonic realism through the first sixteen centuries of the Christian era dictated the repression of evolutionary ideas. During the latter part of this period, naturalists recognized an order among plants and animals, expressed in the classifications of John Ray and Linnaeus; they discerned the "great chain of being." In the 18th cent. they began to seek a naturalistic explanation of biological order; the discovery and interpretation of fossils shook the concept of permanent, immutable species. Lamarck, at the end of the century, offered a complete theory of evolution according to which change is directed by the inherent needs of organisms as modified by environment, and characters acquired in this interaction are inherited (see LAMARCKISM).

Charles Darwin and Alfred Wallace published simultaneous papers in 1858 outlining a theory of evolution by NATURAL SELECTION; Darwin's book *The Origin of Species* followed (1859). In essence, Darwin and Wallace suggested that reproduction would produce more individuals than could survive within the limits of any natural environment. Since every individual is different, some would have a greater chance of survival. To the extent that the superior characteristics were *hereditary,* they would be transmitted at an increased frequency. Darwin accumulated sufficient biologic and paleontologic evidence to convince most scientists, and intellectual selection diminished the numbers of his opponents, biological and theological. Unfortunately, Darwin had no adequate theory of inheritance, and natural selection could not change the "blending inheritance" he envisaged. Consequently Darwinism passed under a cloud in the late 1800s as biologists sought other explanations. GENETICS (the science of hereditary mechanisms) developed, however, a theory of particulate inheritance, and finally, a modified Darwinism arose from the ashes of the 19th cent. (see HEREDITY). Most biologists now recognize natural selection (differential survival and reproduction) as the directive force in evolution. MUTATION (modification) of the hereditary material supplies the raw material for change, but the general stability of this material restrains innovation and conserves information vital to development, growth, and survival. These deductions derive from knowledge of the processes in inheritance, of the effects of mutation, and of the relation between organisms and their environment. They are also supported by some experimental studies and by historical, *i.e.* fossil, evidence.

The basic unit of evolution is an interbreeding population (forming part or all of a *species*). The deer-mouse population in a woodlot would represent the smallest unit of this kind; presumably each male mouse would have an equal chance of mating with any female in the woodlot. Each mouse carries a packet of hereditary material part of which will be passed to its progeny. This material provides information for growth, development, form, physiology, and behavior of its bearer, although the environment may modify these characteristics within limits. One of the pieces of hereditary material controls coat color, and any mouse with this particular information has a dark gray coat. On very rare occasions this information is modified, or *mutates,* in an egg or sperm so that the new individual has a light gray coat. Since reproduction involves the combination of hereditary material from two parents, a wide variety of coat colors and an even wider variety of potential colors arise from a few such changes. If coat color has little effect on survival, the variety of hereditary material and coat colors will approach an equilibrium. In the shadowed forest, however, a darker coat conceals, and more individuals with a dark coat survive to reproduce, to transmit their bit of "dark" to succeeding generations. The population shows some variety, conceals much, and bears a potential for still more. If the environment changes so that

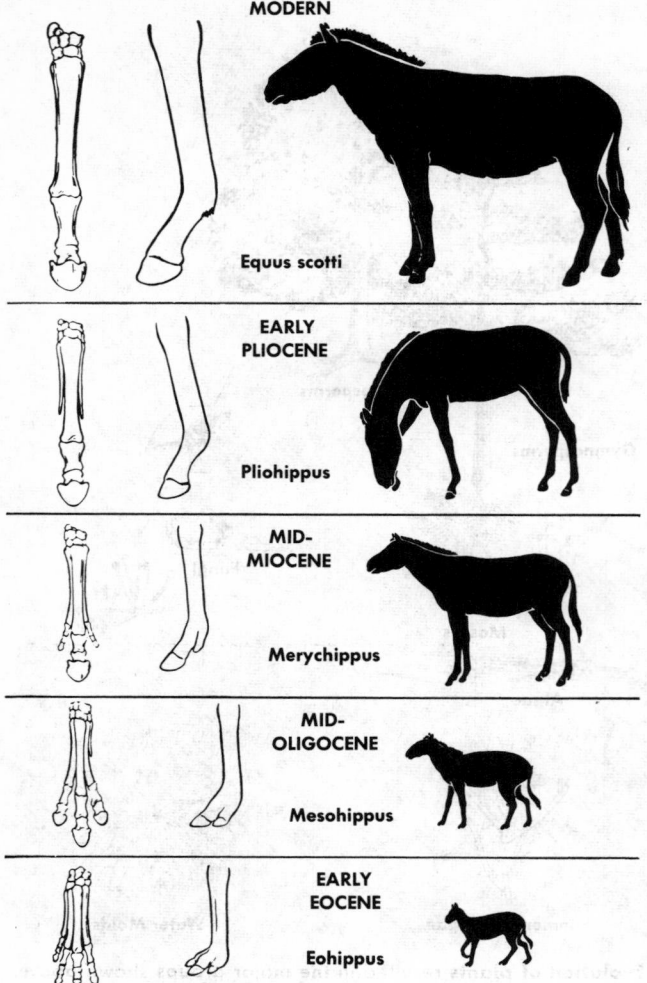

MODERN

Equus scotti

EARLY PLIOCENE

Pliohippus

MID-MIOCENE

Merychippus

MID-OLIGOCENE

Mesohippus

EARLY EOCENE

Eohippus

Evolution of horse during past 60 million yr was traced by fossil studies. Drawings at left show changes in bone structure of forefoot; silhouettes show the increase in relative size. (*From Young*)

the forest dies and grass and brush take over, survival values change. Light coats become advantageous; the dark are eliminated; and the deer-mouse population evolves. Other mouse populations survive in different environments with different hereditary combinations. Breeding between local populations blurs these differences, but the total is rather like a mosaic. In time, with changing environments, some bits of the mosaic expand; others diminish. Some shift in shape and color, and new colors and shapes appear. The mosaic, once "deer mouse," becomes "cotton mouse."

Environmental change can separate some populations from the total. Freed by ISOLATION, these evolve independently to form new mosaics. Thus, deer mice on the isolated desert mountain ranges of Mexico and the southwestern U. S. A. have diverged—have, among other things, become thirst-resistant. So one kind, one species, may split into numerous lines. Brought into contact, the mice fail to recognize kinship, do not interbreed, and form new, separate species.

Other factors and processes modify the pattern of evolution. If the bits of the mosaic, the local populations, are very small and sharply isolated from one another, chance destruction obscures natural selection, and the population "drifts" randomly. Selection, acting on several populations that diverged by drift, results in a variety of evolutionary paths—most into extinction. On the other hand, if the populations are not separated at all, the mixing of hereditary material swamps advantageous combinations and slows evolution. Organisms that reproduce asexually (see REPRODUCTION) must have somewhat different evolutionary mechanisms.

Hybridization between species may produce offspring with new and valuable features. In spite of these complications, natural selection, acting on variants produced by recombinations of mutant hereditary material, seems the keystone of evolution.

Among mammals, birds, and possibly insects, transmission of behavior patterns by imitation or teaching supplements physical inheritance. These patterns are stable ordinarily, but environmental changes sometimes evoke related modification in behavior unlike the random variation of hereditary material. Since behavior patterns influence individual and population survival, these also evolve by natural selection. In human populations, behavioral (or cultural) evolution predominates over changes in form and physiology.

Interaction of factors and processes leads to different rates and modes of evolution. These appear through the study of FOSSILS, the traces of ancient organisms, and of their succession in time (see PALEONTOLOGY and LIFE, PREHISTORIC). Some organisms, like the bivalve *Lingula,* have changed very little over 400 million yr. Others evolve at moderate rates: each step in horse evolution, the change from one *genus* to another, required around 10 million yr. Some forms emerge suddenly, in geologic terms; thus the human lineage has evolved over the past million years. The moderate rates conform well to current evolutionary theory, but the fast and slow pose problems. Lack of change might imply little variation, but all living populations appear to have an abundance of hereditary differences. Only a stable environment plus adaptability to minor changes accounts for such evolutionary stability, and, perhaps, such coincidences are inevitable, given enough kinds of organisms. Some biologists have suggested special mechanisms to account for very rapid evolution such as high rates of mutation or very large mutations. The majority, however, hold that strong selection of small variants produced at a low rate is adequate.

The consequence of evolutionary change is adjustment to environment. This adjustment, best called ADAPTATION, is a striking phenomenon in both recent and fossil plants and animals. As evolution continues, most populations become more and more closely adapted to a less and less diverse environment; in other words, they show specialization. So the ancestral, omnivorous opossum gave rise to koalas that eat only eucalyptus leaves. Divergent specialization by related species leads to adaptive radiation. As the deer mouse population of Mexico gave rise to several distinct species by isolation, so the ancestral flowering plants fragmented into species each in different environments. Initial divergence led into different habitats and habits. When the species were brought back together, competition forced further divergence of similar species. Through this process the various adaptive modes of flowering plants developed from a single root stock.

Related populations evolve in similar directions to meet similar adaptive needs. Desert rodents include many bipedal hoppers that developed independently from quadrupedal ancestors. This phenomenon, called *parallelism,* is similar to another, *convergence,* in which distantly related or unrelated groups evolve to resemble one another. Modern porpoises resemble the long-extinct "fish-reptiles," ichthyosaurs, more closely than their mammalian ancestors resembled their ichthyosaurian contemporaries. Specialization carries some to extremes of form, such as the immense antlers of the extinct Irish elk and the bizarre shapes of ancient cephalopods.

A few organisms resist part of this push to specialization. They retain or redevelop an omnivorous diet or a generalized mode of locomotion. The opossum is a current example; in fact, it represents one of the ancestral mammalian stocks preserved from the age of dinosaurs, 80 million yr ago. Such

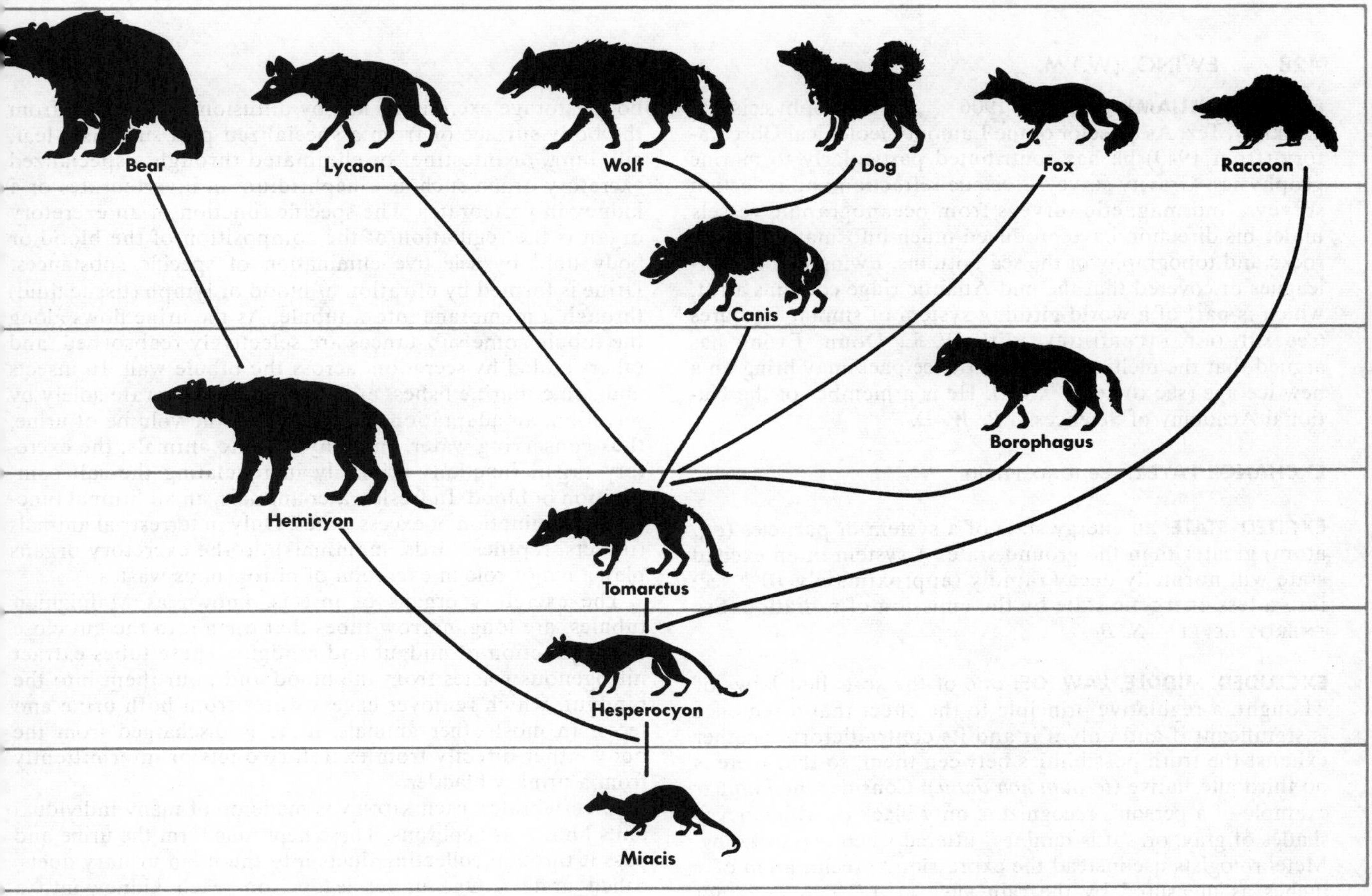

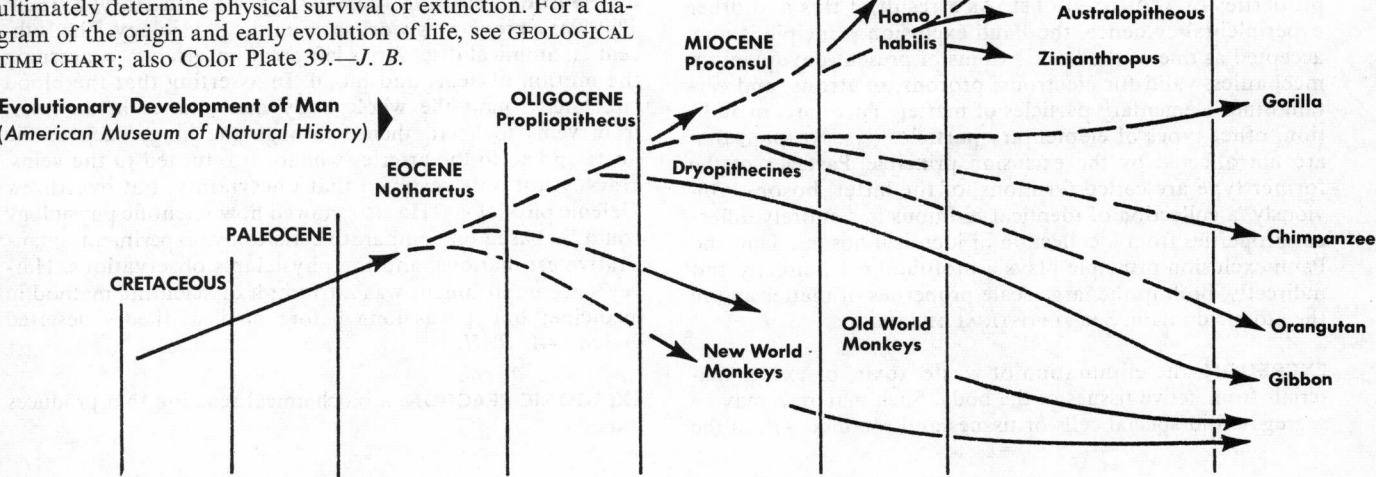

Bear **Lycaon** **Wolf** **Dog** **Fox** **Raccoon**

Canis

Borophagus

Hemicyon

Tomarctus

Hesperocyon

Miacis

populations provide new evolutionary potential when the need arises and form the initial stock for new adaptive radiations. On the other hand, most specialized groups appear foredoomed to extinction. As they disappear, the structure of the communities is disrupted and others follow them into extinction. The general evolutionary pattern seems a cyclic one of rapid adaptive radiation, followed by progressive specialization at moderate rates in stable communities, and concluded by almost catastrophic extinction.

Human evolution varied from this pattern with the introduction of social units integrated by culture and supported by technology. Since selection acts on social units and on culture and technology within units, the needs of social evolution directed changes in brain size and character, in teeth and alimentary system, and in the physiological factors underlying behavior. The processes of specialization, adaptive radiation, and extinction are confined largely to culture; they occur rapidly in contrast to physical evolution; and they will ultimately determine physical survival or extinction. For a diagram of the origin and early evolution of life, see GEOLOGICAL TIME CHART; also Color Plate 39.—*J. B.*

Ancestry of certain carnivores is traced in this simplified family "tree."
(*After Lois Darling, "Natural History," Feb. 1958*)

Evolutionary Development of Man
(*American Museum of Natural History*) ▶

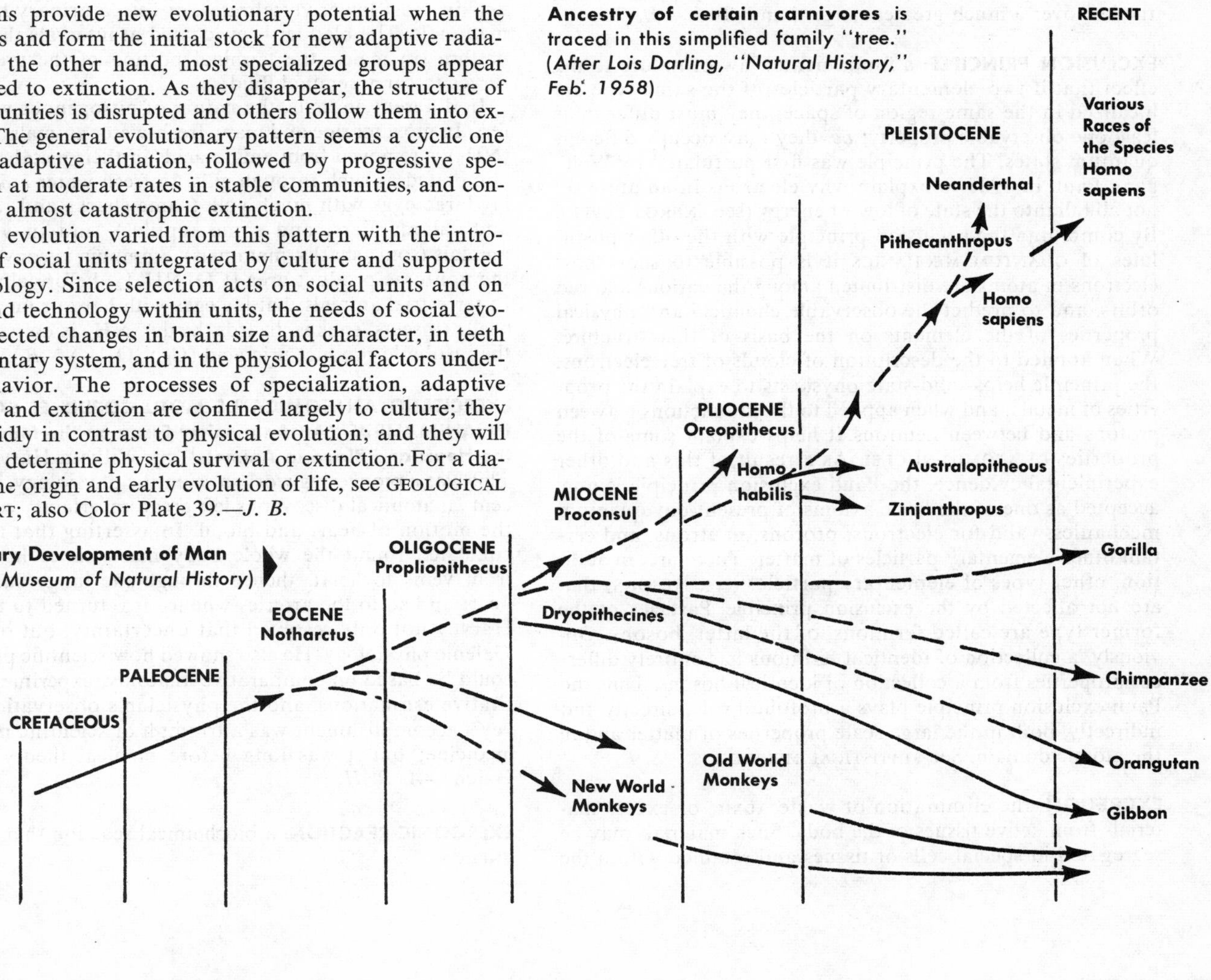

RECENT

Various Races of the Species Homo sapiens

PLEISTOCENE

Neanderthal

Pithecanthropus

Homo sapiens

PLIOCENE
Oreopithecus

Homo habilis

Australopitheous

Zinjanthropus

MIOCENE
Proconsul

Gorilla

OLIGOCENE
Propliopithecus

Dryopithecines

EOCENE
Notharctus

Chimpanzee

PALEOCENE

Orangutan

CRETACEOUS

New World Monkeys

Old World Monkeys

Gibbon

EWING, (WILLIAM) MAURICE, 1906–   , U. S. geophysicist; b. Lockney, Tex. As director of the Lamont Geological Observatory (from 1949) he has contributed particularly to marine geophysics. Gravity surveys, seismic refraction and reflection surveys, and magnetic surveys from oceanographic vessels under his direction have produced much information on the rocks and topography of the sea bottoms. Ewing and his colleagues discovered that the mid-Atlantic ridge contains a rift, which is part of a world-girdling system of similar fractures (see MID-OCEANIC RIDGE). With W. L. Donn, Ewing has argued that the melting of the arctic ice pack may bring on a new ice age (see GLACIAL AGES). He is a member of the National Academy of Sciences.—*R. W. D.*

EXCHANGE LAYER: see IONOSPHERE.

EXCITED STATE: an energy state of a system of particles (*e.g.* atom) greater than the ground state. A system in an excited state will normally decay rapidly (approximately 10^{-8} sec) into a less energetic state by the emission of radiation. See ENERGY LEVEL.—*S. Bo.*

EXCLUDED MIDDLE, LAW OF: one of the so-called Laws of Thought, a regulative principle to the effect that a sentence is significant if and only if it and its contradictory together exhaust the truth possibilities between them, so that there is no third alternative (*tertium non datur*). Consider the familiar example of a person's recognizing only black or white, never shades of gray, or, "It is raining," uttered when it is drizzling. Meteorologists use instead the expression "precipitation of x inches as measured by the rain gage at Y." This does not eliminate vagueness altogether, but it enables application of the law over a much greater range than before.—*H. T.*

EXCLUSION PRINCIPLE: a fundamental law of nature to the effect that if two elementary particles of the same type are localized in the same region of space, they must differ in at least one observable property; *i.e.* they must occupy different quantum states. The principle was first postulated by Wolfgang Pauli in 1925 to explain why electrons in an atom do not all fall into the state of lowest energy (see ENERGY LEVEL). By combining the exclusion principle with the other postulates of QUANTUM MECHANICS it is possible to show how electrons in atoms are distributed among the various allowed orbits, and to predict the observable chemical and physical properties of the elements on the basis of this structure. When applied to the description of clouds of free electrons, the principle helps solid-state physicists to explain the properties of metals; and when applied to the interactions between protons and between neutrons, it helps explain some of the properties of ATOMIC NUCLEI. As a result of this and other experimental evidence, the Pauli exclusion principle is now accepted as one of the basic axioms of present-day quantum mechanics, valid for electrons, protons, neutrons, and certain other elementary particles of matter. There are, in addition, other types of elementary particles (*e.g.* MESONS) that are not affected by the exclusion principle. Particles of the former type are called fermions, of the latter, bosons. Obviously, a collection of identical fermions has entirely different properties from a collection of identical bosons. Thus the Pauli exclusion principle plays a profound role, directly and indirectly, both in the large-scale properties of matter and in the atomic domain. See STATISTICAL MECHANICS.—*S. K.*

EXCRETION: the elimination of waste, toxic, or excess materials from active tissues of the body. Such materials may be segregated in special cells or tissues and retained within the body (storage excretion); lost by diffusion or secretion from the body surface or from a specialized part such as a leaf, gill, lung, or intestine; or eliminated through a specialized excretory organ such as a nephridium in invertebrates or a kidney in vertebrates. The specific function of an excretory organ is the regulation of the composition of the blood or body fluid by selective elimination of specific substances. Urine is formed by filtration of blood or lymph (tissue fluid) through a membrane into a tubule. As the urine flows along the tubule some substances are selectively reabsorbed, and others added by secretion, across the tubule wall. In insects and some marine fishes, excretory organs operate solely by secretion, an adaptation that decreases the volume of urine, thus conserving water. In many aquatic animals, the excretory organ functions primarily in regulating the salt composition of blood. In fresh-water animals, an additional function is elimination of excess water. Only in terrestrial animals (insects, reptiles, birds, mammals) do the excretory organs play a major role in excretion of nitrogenous wastes.

The excretory organs of insects, known as Malpighian tubules, are long, narrow tubes that open into the gut close to the junction of midgut and hindgut. These tubes extract nitrogenous wastes from the blood and pour them into the hindgut, which removes excess water from both urine and feces. In most other animals, urine is discharged from the body either directly from excretory ducts or intermittently from a urinary bladder.

In vertebrates, each KIDNEY is made up of many individual units known as nephrons. These nephrons form the urine and pass it through collecting ducts into the main urinary ducts, called ureters. One ureter leads from each kidney into a cloaca, a common passage for urine, feces, and sexual products in most lower vertebrates, or into a urinary bladder in mammals. The bladder is evacuated at intervals through the urethra (in males, the terminal portion of the urethra also serves to carry seminal fluid).

In different animals, the nature of nitrogenous wastes differs. In most marine and many fresh-water animals, ammonia (NH_3) is removed from amino acids in their metabolism, and eliminated as such through gills. In fresh-water animals that lay large eggs with much yolk (some sharks and rays, frogs and salamanders, and some reptiles), and in viviparous animals (some sharks, mammals), ammonia is converted into the nontoxic product urea ($CO[NH_2]_2$) before elimination. In terrestrial animals that lay eggs with hard or impermeable shells (insects, snakes, lizards, birds), NH_3 is converted into the insoluble product uric acid ($C_5N_4O_3H_4$).—*B. T. S.*

EXERCITATIO ANATOMICA DE MOTU CORDIS ET SANGUINIS IN ANIMALIBUS (An Anatomical Essay on the Movement of the Heart and Blood in Animals), by William Harvey, 1628: This was a pioneering work in scientific physiology. The 16th-cent. anatomical discoveries left great uncertainty concerning the motion of heart and blood. In asserting that the blood circulated round the whole body many times in an hour, from veins to heart, thence through the lungs back to the heart and so to the arteries whence it returned to the veins, Harvey not only resolved that uncertainty, but overthrew Galenic physiology. He also showed how scientific physiology could be based on comparative anatomy, experiment, quantitative estimations, and the physician's observations. Harvey's accomplishment was a triumph of scientific method in medicine; but it was long before medical theory deserted Galen.—*A. R. H.*

EXERGONIC REACTION: a biochemical reaction that produces ENERGY.

EXFOLIATION: the peeling of a thin "rind" of weakened material from even-textured rocks exposed to the atmosphere or buried in soil. Sharp edges are most readily destroyed; hence there is progressive rounding until masses are reduced to crudely spherical forms, *e.g.* Half Dome in Yosemite National Park, Calif., or Stone Mt near Atlanta, Ga.—*J. Si.*

EXOCRINE GLAND: any GLAND that releases its secretion, directly or by way of ducts, to the outside of the body or to the cavity of the alimentary canal.—*W. P. C.*

EXOSPHERE: see ATMOSPHERE.

EXPANSION, THERMAL: increase in size due to increase in temperature. All gases and most liquids and solids (water near freezing is an exception) expand when made hotter; conversely, they contract when their temperature drops. Heat agitates the atoms and molecules composing a body, causing them to enlarge their sphere of activity and thereby increasing the dimensions of the body as a whole. When a metal rod is heated, it increases in length by small increments, which are approximately proportional to the change in temperature as well as to the original length. The regularity of thermal expansion is very useful, for, having determined the expansivity for a unit change in temperature, we can then compute what the ultimate length will be at some considerably higher or lower temperature. The factor that expresses the relative change in length per degree change in temperature is called the *linear coefficient of thermal expansion* for the material being described. For liquids and gases it is the change in volume with temperature that is most useful. Since the *volume coefficient of expansion* for solids is almost exactly three times the linear coefficient, it is usually unnecessary to measure the former factor directly. A hollow vessel expands with temperature to the same extent as if it were solid, and the same is true of a perforated plate.

When identical strips of two different metals are welded together, face to face, the combination bends on being heated. Suppose, for example, that one layer of the strip is steel and the other brass. Since brass has a larger coefficient of expansion than steel, the brass layer must elongate more than the steel layer does. This is possible only if the combination bends into an arc with the brass layer on the outside. Bimetallic strips are useful in thermostatic devices where the strip, clamped at one end, can bend at the other end whenever the room temperature changes to make electrical contact with a relay, which starts the furnace.—*J. E. W.*

EXPANSION WAVE: a wave by which a supersonic air stream expands to lower pressure, temperature, and density with a simultaneous acceleration of the stream's motion. In supersonic flow, all flow changes are effected by waves in the stream; but in contrast to shock waves, expansion waves provide for continuous rather than step-like changes.—*D. B.*

EXPERIMENT: see CRUCIAL EXPERIMENT.

EXPERIMENTAL METHOD: see EMPIRICISM; SCIENTIFIC METHOD.

EXPERIMENTAL RESEARCHES IN ELECTRICITY AND MAGNETISM, by Michael Faraday, 1844–55: This important work contains the account of the author's experiments leading to his formulation of the laws (among others) of electromagnetic induction, electrolysis, and magnetic action on polarized light; it also presents his fruitful conception of the field as the carrier of proximate action, rather than as the mathematical representation of ACTION AT A DISTANCE. J. Clerk Maxwell's mathematical formulation of electromagnetic theory grew out of Faraday's work.—*G. G.*

EXPERIMENTS AND OBSERVATIONS ON ELECTRICITY, by Benjamin Franklin, 1751: The first great scientific book by an American, this was also the first great book in the history of electricity. Many phenomena of static electricity had been discovered before, but Franklin greatly enlarged their number and furnished the first comprehensive theory of electrification to explain them. Franklin's lightning-conductor experiment aroused admiration everywhere; equally, his single-fluid flow concept satisfied most experimenters. With the application of this concept, electrical science passed from chaos to order.—*A. R. H.*

Thermal expansion: A slash fire swept over this logging railway in the Pacific Northwest. The intense heat caused the iron rails to expand, with these grotesque results. (*U. S. Forest Service*)

2,750,000 lb of special water-resistant high explosive blasts out Ripple Rock, 120 mi northwest of Vancouver, B. C. Explosion created a safe channel, 50 ft deep, through once-dangerous Seymour Narrows, on inland waterway to Alaska. *(DuPont)*

EXPLOSIVE: a substance, or mixture of substances, capable of undergoing sudden decomposition with formation of heat and gas. Nearly all explosive actions are combustions similar to the burning of wood (*i.e.* the outer electrons of the atoms of the substance undergoing combustion are affected, with release of energy) but take place far more rapidly. (An exception is the ATOMIC BOMB, in which the central nucleus of the atom is involved in the explosion.) Explosives may be solid, liquid, or gas; the loud noise accompanying their combustion is caused by the vibratory movement imparted to the surrounding air. *Low explosives* (or *propellants*) are capable, when exposed to a spark or flame, of a comparatively slow chemical transformation into hot gases, pushing or propelling an object rather than shattering it. Black powder, or blasting powder, is the oldest low explosive known. It is used for fuses and also in mining to break rock and ore into large fragments without shattering; it has been replaced to a large extent by gelatinous smokeless powder for use as a propellant in firearms and in ordnance to impart velocity to projectiles.

The chemical transformation of both black and smokeless powder is known as *deflagration,* or "slow explosion," to distinguish it from *detonation,* or "fast explosion." Deflagration is accelerated, particularly when the powder is confined, by the hot gases evolved, which ignite adjacent powder grains. The rate of deflagration thus depends in part on the size and shape of the grains and the pressure and temperature developed. Black powder always behaves as a low explosive regardless of the conditions and the nature of the stimulus, but smokeless powder, even when unconfined, and particularly when in fine grains, can be detonated by a sufficiently powerful stimulus. Gasoline and many other combustible vapors, gases, and dusts in admixture with air normally function as low explosives but may detonate under certain conditions, particularly when highly compressed.

Primary explosives (*primers* or *initiators*) are very sensitive to detonation by heat, flame, friction, impact (blows), and shock. They detonate without burning. Examples are copper acetylide, silver acetylide, fulminating gold, nitrogen sulfide, nitrogen chloride, tetracene, lead azide, lead styphnate, diazodinitrophenol, and mixtures of chlorates with red phosphorus or sulfur. Some of the primary explosives, particularly fulminate of mercury, are used extensively as constituents of detonators or blasting caps to initiate the detonation of less sensitive high explosives. For this purpose the primary

explosive, together with an ignition charge and usually a base charge of tetryl or other high explosive, is loaded into small cylindrical capsules, usually of copper, which can be inserted in the high explosive to be detonated. Plain blasting caps are detonated by the sparks from a time fuse; electric blasting caps are provided with a connecting wire for detonation by an electric current. Percussion or primer caps, as the name implies, are detonated by an impact or blow.

High explosives have low sensitivity, and are detonated by the shock of detonation of a suitable primary or high explosive. They differ from primary explosives in being comparatively insensitive to explosion or detonation by heat, flame, friction, impact, and shock, and are in general more powerful. Unlike primary explosives, most high explosives when exposed to flame will burn, and if in small quantity, no explosion is likely to occur. In order to obtain the maximum detonation velocity of high explosives, a suitable quantity of a powerful but somewhat more sensitive high explosive known as a "booster" is used in addition to the charge of primary explosive. For example, tetryl (trinitrophenylmethylnitramine) is commonly used as a booster to reinforce the primary explosive in initiating the detonation of TNT. When a booster is employed, it is necessary to use only a small amount of the more sensitive and dangerous primary explosive. High explosives when detonated, whether confined or not, have a shattering or disruptive effect, known as "brisance." While brisance is believed to be due mainly to the tremendous velocity of detonation, the specific or volumetric density of the gaseous products of transformation is an important factor. High explosives include TNT, tetryl, picric acid, nitroglycerin, blasting gelatin, dynamite, PETN, guncotton, ammonium nitrate, ammonal, and liquid oxygen with wood pulp or carbon black. See also COMBUSTION; DETONATION; DYNAMITE; GUNPOWDER.—*A. P. E.*

EXPONENT: a numerical superscript attached to a mathematical symbol, such as the 2 in x^2, used to denote a power. Whole-number exponents were invented to provide a concise symbol for repeated multiplications, so that x^2 means x times x, and x^n denotes $x \cdot x \cdot x \cdots$ to n factors. This assumes n to be a positive whole number. From this definition four theorems are derived:

$x^n \cdot x^m = x^{n+m}$; for example, $2^3 \cdot 2^4 = 2^7$.

$x^n \div x^m = x^{n-m}$, if $n > m$; for example, $2^5 \div 2^3 = 2^2$.

$x^n \div x^m = 1/x^{m-n}$, if $n < m$; for example, $2^3 \div 2^5 = 1/2^2$.

$(x^n)^m = x^{nm}$; for example, $(2^3)^2 = 2^6$.

$x^n \cdot y^n = (xy)^n$; for example, $2^3 \cdot 5^3 = 10^3$.

If $n = m$, the second theorem can be used only if a zero exponent is defined, for $x^{n-n} = x^0$. In this case, $x^n \div x^n = 1$, and hence, x^0 is defined to be 1, this definition applying for all values of x except 0. Thus $2^0 = 3^0 = 10^0 = (-1)^0 = 1$. If $n < m$, then the exponent $(n - m)$ is negative and no meaning is given to a negative exponent by the basic definition. Instead, we use the alternative, in which $(m - n)$ is positive. The necessity of distinguishing between these situations is eliminated by adopting a definition of a negative exponent. Hence we define x^{-n} to be equal to $1/x^n$, provided x is not equal to 0; *e.g.* $2^{-3} = 1/2^3 = 1/8$. With this definition and that of the zero exponent, the rule $x^n \div x^m = x^{n-m}$ can be applied if n and m are any integers. Fractional exponents are brought into the system by defining $x^{n/m}$ to be $\sqrt[m]{x^n}$, or $(\sqrt[m]{x})^n$; for example, $2^{3/5} = \sqrt[5]{2^3} = \sqrt[5]{8}$. The definitions of negative, zero, and fractional exponents are consistent with the four theorems derived for positive integral exponents.

Hence these theorems can be applied freely for all rational exponents; for example, $2^{1/2} \cdot 2^{1/3} = 2^{1/2+1/3} = 2^{5/6} = \sqrt[6]{2^5} = \sqrt[6]{32}$; and $2^{1/3} \cdot 2^{1/3} = (2 \cdot 3)^{1/3} = 6^{1/3} = \sqrt[3]{6}$. The necessity of extending the range of exponents to include irrational numbers does not arise in algebra, but only in more general studies of continuous functions, where an irrational exponent is defined by means of a limit.

The use of exponents greatly facilitates the writing of algebraic expressions. A valuable elementary application is found in scientific notation. In this form, a number is expressed as a product of a number between 1 and 10 and a power of 10. For example, the number 3,200,000,000 is written 3.2×10^9; and 0.000,000,7 is written 7×10^{-7}.

The word "exponent" is also used to denote the irrational number e, the base of natural logarithms (see e).—H. C.

EXTENSIONAL LOGIC: a system in which the substitution of any other true sentence for a true sentence or any other false sentence for a false sentence does not change the truth value of the expression in which the substitution occurs; or, a system in which two classes are regarded as identical if they have the same membership no matter how different the properties are which the members of the classes must satisfy. Such a logic is peculiarly suited to the needs of mathematics; thus, although "Commander in Chief" and "President of the United States" are two different concepts, they represent the same individual, and we would hardly want to count him twice.—H. T.

EXTINCTION: see CONSERVATION; EVOLUTION; NATURAL SELECTION.

EXTRACTION: in chemistry, a method for selectively removing one or more components from a *mixture* by means of a solvent. The solvent is so chosen that the component to be removed (usually called the "extract" after separation) is more soluble in it than are the other components of the mixture (called the "residue" or "raffinate" after separation). Mixtures from which a component is extracted may be gaseous, liquid, or solid. In all cases it is advantageous to have intimate contact over a large interfacial area between the solvent and the mixture. Well-designed extraction apparatus therefore provides for thorough mixing and fine subdivision of the two phases. Extractions may involve chemical action between the solvent and components of the mixture, as well as the purely physical action of dissolving. For example, aqueous caustic-soda solutions are used in extracting the acidic components from petroleum and from acidic or "sour" gases. Extraction is very extensively used in the petroleum and chemical industries and in metallurgy. The term "extraction" also sometimes refers to the simple separation of liquid from solid by centrifugation or wringing. This meaning is common in the textile and laundry industries, where it is applied to the centrifugation of wet fabric.—A. M. S.

EXTRAPOLATION: see STATISTICS.

EXTRUSION: a process whereby materials such as metals, alloys, glass, clays, plastics, or rubber are made to pass through a restricted orifice in order to impart to them a desired shape. The materials, either hot or cold, are usually subjected to pressure by mechanical or hydraulic presses

A great basalt plateau, consisting of lava poured out intermittently by volcanoes in the Miocene Period, covers about 250,000 mi² of Washington, Idaho, Oregon, California, and Nevada. Palouse Canyon, eastern Washington, has been cut into this mass of extrusive rock by the Palouse River. (*Bob and Ira Spring*)

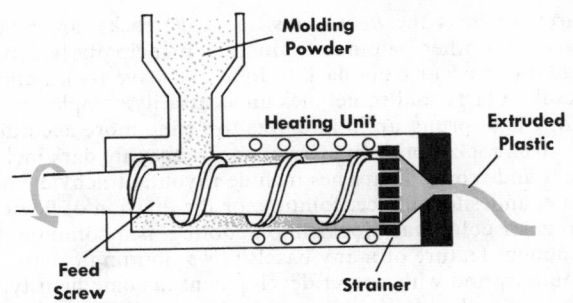

Hot extrusion, producing a molded plastic strip from powdered plastic. The rotation of the feed screw forces the powder past the heating unit and through a die at right.

(*e.g.* a screw or a plunger) to form such products as steel, brass, and lead cables and tubular products; filament yarn; brick and tile. In cold extrusion, a distinction is made between *forward extrusion* (*e.g.* Hooker process), in which the material being extruded is pushed ahead of a plunger (or "punch") out through a shaped orifice; and *backward extrusion,* in which the material, blocked from moving ahead of the punch, backs up along the sides of the punch, between the punch and the walls of the surrounding die. Hot extrusion is somewhat similar to forward-type cold extrusion, except that the material is preheated and forced through a relatively smaller orifice. Artificial fibers are made by extruding hot plastic through spinnerets under gravity or externally applied pressure (see RAYON) into a continuous filament, which is then wound on take-up drums. Many types of foods—cereals, macaroni, butter, cheeses, hard candy—are molded by extrusion, as are soap cakes and lipstick.—E. H. H.

EXTRUSIVE ROCK: igneous rock that has formed on Earth's surface from lava which poured out through fissures or which was ejected by volcanoes as flows or as PYROCLASTICS. Extrusive materials cool rapidly on exposure and thus they develop fine-grained textures, the individual mineral crystals often being indistinguishable to the naked eye. Obsidians and pitchstones are natural glasses; often they are devoid of discernible crystals and resemble ordinary pitch in color and fracture; some types are translucent to transparent, with or without bandings and flow marks. Most extrusive rocks, however, are granular, with fracture surfaces like fine sandpaper or broken earthenware. If certain constituents crystallize while much of the extruded material is still fluid, the result may be relatively large crystals, or phenocrysts, embedded in glassy or finer-grained material in the varieties collectively known as porphyries. Extrusive rocks are conveniently classified on the basis of general coloration: the *dark* kinds, or *basic* extrusives, contain much of the dark ferromagnesian minerals, commonly hornblende, augite, biotite, etc., with little or no

quartz, whereas the *light* kinds, or *acidic* rocks, are rich in quartz and other pale-hued minerals, principally feldspars. Gradations occur from dark to light extrusive rocks, and as a result, a large and sometimes unnecessarily complex terminology has sprung up in attempts to define more accurately any given rock. Common extrusive rocks that are dark include basalt and scoria; light ones include rhyolite, trachyte, latite, dacite, andesite, pumice. Jointing, or the division of flows into regular columnar blocks upon cooling, is a common and prominent feature of many basalt flows; jointing occurs less commonly and with poorer development in some light types. Extrusive rocks are abundant and widespread in the western U. S. A.; 250,000 mi² of Washington, Idaho, and Oregon are covered by basalt flows, some thousands of feet thick. Light extrusive rocks are less extensive, and occur in certain mountainous regions of the western U. S. A. and in Mexico. —*J. Si.*

EYE: a multicellular organ in which the fundamental sensitivity of protoplasm to light energy is exploited and made more meaningful to the central nervous system through accessory parts that are not themselves sensitive to light. These accessories may be simple, as in the pinhole-camera-type eyes of the MOLLUSK known as a nautilus. Here, opaque-pigment cells restrict to a small hole the region where light can enter the eye; light passing through this hole falls on light-sensitive cells (the retina) arranged in a cup-shaped cluster. In the ocelli ("simple eyes") of segmented WORMS and ARTHROPODS, there is also an opaque shield, but light passes through a thickening of the cuticle that forms a lens, which concentrates the light on the sensitive cells. In some animals many ocellus-type eyes form a convex cluster, each unit having a elongate conical form with the cuticular lens at the outer and larger end of the cone.

Compound eye of praying mantis consists of many simple eyes, each of which forms a separate image. (*Robert C. Hermes*)

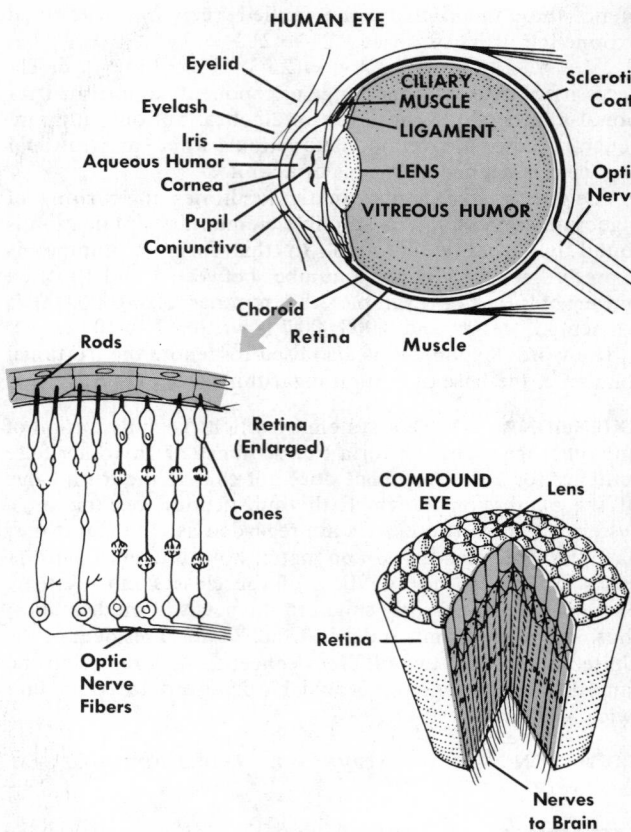

Two types of eye, shown diagrammatically. Compound eye probably produces fuzzier image, but is superior in detecting motion.

In this "compound eye" each unit keeps the animal informed of changes in light intensity from a small portion of the total visual field.

Compound eyes with a hard, convex outer surface are characteristic of crustaceans and insects, comprising more than three-quarters of the species in the animal kingdom. The single eyes of squids and octopus are soft, and resemble a camera with a lens, as do also the eyes of vertebrates.

The human eye, like that of other vertebrates, admits light through a thin, transparent covering of skin (the conjunctiva, which continues also as the lining of the eyelids), through a transparent outer portion (cornea) of the supporting globe (the remainder is the white, opaque sclera), through an anterior chamber filled with transparent fluid (the aqueous humor), through an opening in an adjustable curtain (the pupil in the iris—usually the colored part of the eye), through a posterior chamber filled with a transparent gelatinous material (the vitreous humor), through several layers of blood vessels and nerve cells, and finally to the light-sensitive rods and cone cells of the retina. Energy absorbed by rods and cones can be used to trigger messages by way of the nerve cells and the optic nerve to the visual centers in the brain, giving a sensation of sight. Light not absorbed by the rods and cones continues to the next layer of the eye (the choroid), where it is absorbed in the black pigment. Cone cells are responsible for COLOR VISION and for detailed vision at the center of the visual field; they are sensitive only to daylight (or full moonlight). Rod cells give us black-and-white vision and less detailed information, but are sensitive at intensities as low as the light reflected from soil and foliage under starlight with no moon. See VISION; Color Plate 40.—*L. and M. M.*

F

FABRE, JEAN HENRI CASIMIR, 1823–1915, French entomologist; b. Saint-Léons. As an amateur, Fabre worked in isolation, avoiding books and confining himself to personal observations and experiments on insects, spiders, and scorpions. He opposed the Darwinian theory of evolution. Fabre produced an enormous number of popular works, including many for children, on natural history. His most important publication is the *Souvenirs entomologiques* (10 vols., 1879–1907).—*D. H. D. R.*

FABRIC: see TEXTILES.

FABRICIUS AB AQUAPENDENTE, HIERONYMUS (Ital. GIROLAMO FABRIZIO), *c.* 1533–1619, Italian anatomist and embryologist; b. Aquapendente. He was a pupil and the successor of Fallopius at Padua. Fabricius described in his writings the embryonic development in mammals, birds, reptiles, and sharks, using in all his research the comparative method. His anatomical studies of the larynx, eye, and ear were important. Fabricius' discovery of the valves in the veins, published in his *De venarum ostiolis* (1603), influenced William Harvey.—*D. H. D. R.*

FACIES: in geology, the total aspect of a stratigraphic unit, including lithologic type (lithofacies), fossil content (biofacies), and tectonic position (tectofacies). The term was originally used in a discussion of different kinds of synchronous deposits in the Jura Mts in Europe. Now the term facies is used in a narrow sense to refer to different deposits of equivalent geologic age and, in a broad sense, to refer to the lithologic-paleontologic characteristics of sedimentary deposits. In paleontology, fossils found in only one sort of deposit, and presumed to have lived only in a specific environment, are referred to as "facies fossils." In petrology, "facies" are parts of igneous or metamorphic rock bodies distinguishable from other parts by appearance or composition. See STRATIGRAPHY. —*W. Ha.*

FAHRENHEIT, GABRIEL DANIEL, 1686–1736, German instrument-maker; b. Danzig. Although not first to use mercury instead of alcohol for a thermometric liquid, he saw its vast superiority. He used a number of different scales, the FAHRENHEIT SCALE being one that divides the thermometer into 180 parts from the freezing point of water (32°) to the boiling point (212°). His papers on thermometry were published in the *Philosophical Transactions* (1724) of the Royal Society, of which he was a fellow. He also invented a hygrometer and a hypsometer.—*S. B.*

FAHRENHEIT SCALE: a TEMPERATURE SCALE devised by the German physicist GABRIEL FAHRENHEIT and used in the English-speaking countries. On this scale the freezing point of water is designated as 32°F and the boiling point as 212°F; 0°F represents the lowest temperature Fahrenheit could obtain, using a mixture of salt and ice. Absolute zero on the Fahrenheit scale is −460°F.—*E. M. R.*

FALLACIES AND PARADOXES (in mathematics): A fallacy is an argument that appears genuine but actually involves illogical reasoning or the breaking of pre-established rules. A paradox is a conclusion that seems absurd but may in fact be true. (See LOGIC.)

Consider the following argument, where a and b represent real numbers: Let $a = b$; then $a^2 = ab$, and $a^2 - b^2 = ab - b^2$. Factoring, $(a - b)(a + b) = b(a - b)$. Dividing by $(a - b)$ we have $a + b = b$. But $a = b$, and therefore $2b = b$, whence $2 = 1$. This argument purports to be infallible, but leads to a result that is nonsense. The result forces us to re-analyze the argument and thus we uncover an illegitimate step in the reasoning, namely in dividing by $(a - b)$, which is zero. The result, that $2 = 1$, appears paradoxical—yet we shall not call the above argument a paradox, but rather a fallacy.

Fallacies can be fruitful. One such is the "proof" that all triangles are isosceles: Let *abc* be any triangle. Bisect the

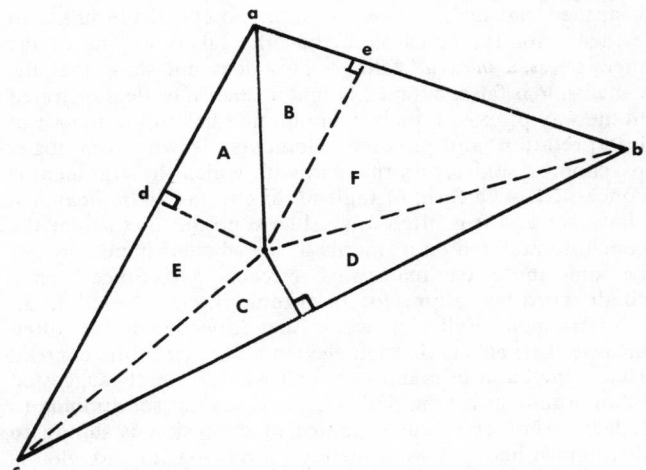

Fallacious "proof": that all triangles are isosceles.

angle *a*; from the middle of *bc* draw a perpendicular to *bc*; the bisector and the perpendicular meet at a point. From this point draw lines to *b* and *c* and perpendiculars to the sides *ab* and *ac*. The triangles *C* and *D* of the accompanying figure are then congruent; also the triangles *A* and *B* are congruent, whence *ad* = *ae*. Accordingly, the third pair of triangles *E* and *F* must be congruent, whence *cd* = *be*. Hence *ad* + *cd* = *ae* + *eb*, or *ab* = *ac*; Q.E.D. Fallacies like this impelled men to take a closer look at the assumptions underlying Euclid's *Elements,* to examine notions like "betweenness" and "inside and outside of a triangle." In this way the fallacies contributed to the necessity for axiomatizing geometry, a task accomplished toward the end of the 19th cent. by M. Pasch, Max Dehn, and David Hilbert.

If "fruitful" is an adjective for fallacies, then the word with which to qualify paradoxes must be "dramatic" or "tragic." In the paradoxes that follow we make no attempt to distinguish between "true" paradox and "pseudo" paradox. These paradoxes will all be characterized by the fact that an assumption "*P* is true" leads to the assertion of its contradictory "*P* is false," while the assumption "*P* is false" leads to the assertion "*P* is true."

The Paradox of the Liar: Epimenides was a Cretan who, one day, to plague logicians, said, "All Cretans are liars," and then wanted to know whether what he said was true or false. If true, then Epimenides is a liar. But if his statement is a lie, it is false. If false, then some Cretans are not liars, and Epimenides might be one of them and therefore might be telling the truth.

Bertrand Russell's Paradox: All classes may be divided into classes that contain themselves as elements and classes that do not contain themselves as elements. For example, the class of abstractions is itself an abstraction and therefore is a member of itself; but the class of apples is not itself an apple and is therefore not a member of itself. Consider the class X of all classes that do *not* contain themselves as elements. Is X a member of itself or not? Suppose X is a member of itself. Then X satisfies the property characterizing all elements of X; that is, they do not contain themselves as elements. Hence X is not a member of itself, contradicting our first hypothesis. Suppose then that X is not an element of itself. Then it satisfies the property characterizing all elements of X and is therefore a member of itself.—*J. S.*

FALLACY: in logic, a defect in argument. The nature of the fallacy depends on the claims, explicit or implicit, made for the argument in the context in which it is offered. Thus if it is argued that the premises are true and constitute sufficient evidence for the conclusion, then the falsity of any of the premises is a *material* fallacy. This does not show that the conclusion is false, but merely that it can not be demonstrated in the way proposed. Fallacy imputation belongs to the art of interpretation and involves elements drawn from logic, psychology, ethics, and the field with which the argument is concerned. As a form of fault-finding it has an *ad hominem* character and it is often advisable to go on to consider the conclusion offered on its merits to see whether there may not be some more legitimate way of reaching it. Since even a single word may represent an argument, *e.g.* "New!" in an advertisement, fallacies when they are persuasive often achieve their effects through elements implicit in the context. Hence the habit of making explicit what is merely suggested in an argument is a helpful safeguard against succumbing to fallacy. Another frequent source of confusion is failure to distinguish between what merely sounds logical and what is so; *e.g.* "Simple logic says if it is against the law to sell sweepstakes tickets it must be against the law to buy them" —a *non sequitur* ("it does not follow"). It is also necessary not to allow oneself to be distracted by charges which may

be true but are actually irrelevant, *e.g.* an attack on the character of a person making a statement (*ad hominem* argument); thus, if a witness is proved to have been previously convicted of perjury, this does not prove his present testimony is false. Other helpful questions to ask are: Does the argument claim that a statement is true because it has true consequences (it may also have false consequences); or that a statement is false because it is the consequence of a false statement (it may also be the consequence of a true statement). Does the argument confuse "all" with "only"?; note the difference between "Only Communists believe that and he believes that" and "All Communists believe that and he believes that" (Undistributed Middle). Does it confuse "all" with "most," as in applying to a particular case a principle that is true only for the most part and not necessarily always (Fallacy of Accident)? Does it generalize from quite possibly exceptional cases, *e.g.* almost any specimen of a chemical may be typical of it (however, the existence of isotopes should teach us caution even here), but it takes considerable investigation indeed to determine how typical of his people a particular member of a racial or religious group is (Converse Fallacy of Accident). Does it use the same word in two senses when the argument requires it to have the same sense?; *e.g.* a trade association accused of conspiring to fix prices asserted that its members were actually "competing in the old-fashioned sense of 'striving together for common interests'" (Equivocation). Does it assume that which in the context requires proof?; *e.g.* "Let us be realistic about this," *i.e.* the speaker is being "realistic" and his opponent is not (Question-Begging). Does it confuse the collective with the distributive senses of class terms (note: what belongs to everyone collectively, public property, belongs to no one distributively); *e.g.* "If everyone looks after his own welfare, then the general welfare will be provided for." But will it? (Fallacies of Composition and Division.)—*H. T.*

FALLOPIUS or FALLOPIO, GABRIELLO, 1523–62, Italian anatomist; b. Modena. His research covered a wide range, including the structure of bone, the hearing organs, and the nervous system. Fallopius' most notable research was on the sexual organs, and his name was given to the Fallopian tube. *Observationes anatomicae* (1561) is the only one of his works published during his lifetime.—*D. H. D. R.*

FALL-OUT: see RADIATION HAZARDS.

FAMILY: see CLASSIFICATION OF LIVING THINGS.

FAMOUS PROBLEMS: see CONSTRUCTION PROBLEMS.

FAN: a device for moving air and other gases, sometimes used to move solid materials temporarily suspended in air, as in a vacuum cleaner. A fan designed to move air from a space so that the required work is done upstream of the air flow is called an *exhauster.* A fan that forces air into a space so that the work is done downstream from the air flow is a *blower.* Fans operate on one of two principles, axial-flow or radial-flow. The axial-flow type moves air perpendicularly to the plane in which the blades rotate and parallel to the axis of rotation of the blades. The blades may be flat or slightly curved, and are set into the center hub at an angle so that they act like moving inclined planes that push the air downstream while more air takes its place from upstream. In some large industrial applications these blades are given air-screw shapes, like airplane propellers, for greater efficiency. In general they move large volumes at relatively low pressures

Industrial fan: An axial-flow, propeller-type, multibladed fan is used in this roof ventilator. Hinged top facilitates lubrication and repair of the moving parts. (*DeBothezat Fans*)

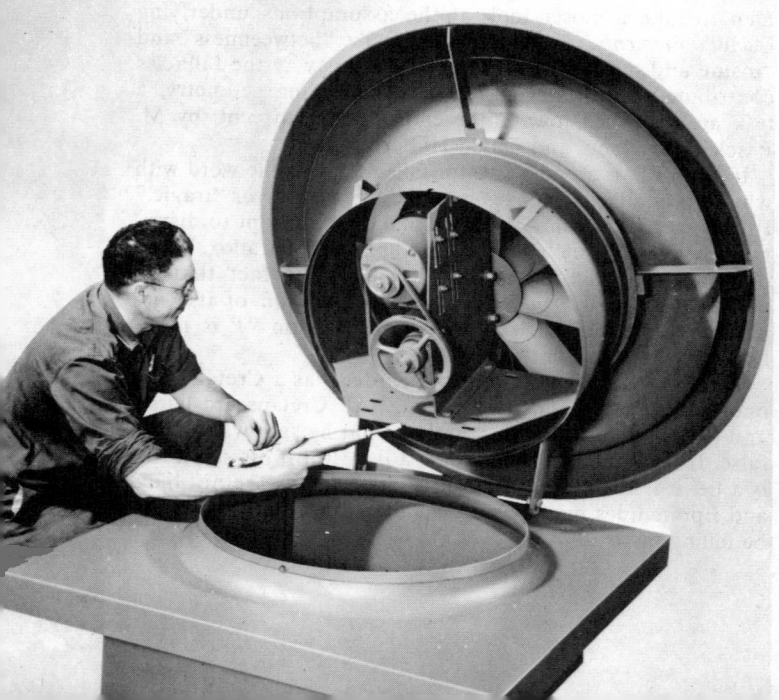

and are used primarily for domestic circulation and ventilation. The radial-flow or centrifugal fan is more of an air compressor. It consists of a cylindrical drum with blades mounted parallel to the axis of rotation, along the surface of the cylinder. As the cylinder of blades rotates in its housing, air enters an open end of the cylinder and is set into circular motion; the air thus subjected to centrifugal force is driven out through the blades, compressed between blades and housing. The air eventually escapes through a duct set radially into the housing. This type is used typically in ventilating mine shafts, moving sawdust in lumber mills, and as the blower on oil burners.—*K. A.*

FARADAY, MICHAEL, 1791–1867, English physicist and chemist; b. Newington Butts. Self-educated, Faraday became an assistant to Humphry Davy in 1812 and published his first scientific paper in 1816, beginning a career of productive research surpassed by few men in all history. He succeeded in liquefying chlorine (1823), and discovered benzol (1825). Perhaps his most far-reaching discovery from an economic viewpoint was his discovery of ELECTROMAGNETIC INDUCTION (1831). His work with ELECTROLYSIS established the intimate relationship between fixed quantities of electricity and matter. After a period of enforced rest, 1841–45, he returned to his research and discovered the so-called FARADAY EFFECT (1845). His most influential contribution to scientific theory was his invention of the concept of FIELD to replace the ACTION-AT-A-DISTANCE view that had dominated scientific thinking for over a century. Davy and Faraday between them made the Royal Institution famous. A fellow of the Royal Society, Faraday contributed massively to its journal, the *Philosophical Transactions.* His *Experimental Researches in Electricity* (3 vols., 1839–55) and his *Researches in Chemistry and Physics* (1859) are notable books in the history of science; his *Diary* was published in 1932–36. He was an associate of the U. S. National Academy of Sciences.—*D. H. D. R.*

Michael Faraday
(New York Public Library)

FARADAY EFFECT: the rotation of the plane of polarization that occurs when a beam of POLARIZED LIGHT passes through a material in a direction parallel to that of an applied magnetic field. The effect is named for Michael Faraday, who discovered it in 1845. The degree of rotation depends upon the strength of the magnetic field, the length of the light path, the frequency of the light, and the nature and temperature of the material through which the polarized light is passing.—*E. M. R.*

FATIGUE (in biology): a decrease in ability to perform muscular or mental tasks during the performance of such tasks. Fatigue is in part a physiological phenomenon, caused by accumulation of lactic acid in muscle cells that are stimulated repeatedly to contract. Lactic acid, which tends to block further excitation from reaching a muscle cell through the associated motor nerve, is a by-product of the anaerobic ("without oxygen") step in muscle contraction. Glycogen, stored in the muscle cell, is converted to lactic acid in releasing the energy used in contraction. If the muscle cell is allowed to recover fully before being called upon to contract again, the lactic acid disappears by three routes: (1) some diffuses

into the blood stream, where it stimulates the body centers concerned with increasing the rate and vigor of heartbeat and the depth of breathing; (2) some is oxidized to carbon dioxide and water, with oxygen diffusing into the muscle cell from the blood stream, thereby making energy available; (3) with this energy, the remaining lactic acid is reconstituted into glycogen. But during violent exercise, lactic acid may accumulate faster than it can be oxidized, because oxygen is not supplied in sufficient quantity quickly enough. As a result, the muscles do not contract any more under normal stimulation and are said to be fatigued. Even in fatigued muscles, however, there is still enough glycogen in the muscle cells for further contraction, as can be demonstrated by stimulating the muscles directly with electricity. After a rest, fatigued muscles not only dispose of the lactic acid blocking them from the normal avenue of stimulation, but also absorb blood sugar and build up glycogen reserves to normal maximum.

Synaptic junctions within the nervous system appear subject to fatigue of an analogous type, but nerve cells themselves seem immune to such symptoms of weariness. Perhaps comparable accumulations of chemical substances within nervous pathways of the brain account for some instances of psychological fatigue, *e.g.* those developing from long continuation of a routine task. The person who is "tired" when doing one thing may recover abruptly when given more interesting work. High motivation often seems to reduce fatigue accompanying an otherwise exhausting activity.—*L. M. and M. M.*

FATIGUE (in materials): structural weakening of a nonbrittle material such as steel or other hard metals when subjected to repeated strains (*e.g.* bending, torsion, vibrations). Every material has an endurance limit—the highest strain it is able to withstand without injury. If this limit is at any time exceeded, the crystalline structure undergoes local distortion, *i.e.* rupture of interatomic bonds, with formation of amorphous spots. The result is imperceptible cracks which, with repeated stress, gradually open up and lead to fracture.—*T. M.*

FAT METABOLISM: in biochemistry, the breakdown and synthesis of the naturally occurring compounds that are soluble in various organic solvents, *e.g.* alcohols, ethers, acetone, hydrocarbons, chloroform. These compounds, called "fats" or "lipids" (lipoid, lipine, lipin), can be classified into several groups which often appear unrelated. Most prominent are triglycerides, phospholipids, sterols, complex lipids, and carotenoids. Enzyme-catalyzed hydrolysis of triglycerides by lipases, phospholipids by phospholipases, and cholesterol esters by esterases yields fatty acids and the corresponding alcohols. Fat as fuel is one of the two basic energy substances used by living things; the other is sugar. Fatty acids and derivatives thereof constitute a major component of these compounds, and their metabolism is of great importance. Biological combustion of fatty acids (fatty acid oxidation) takes place in the mitochondria, the cell's "powerhouse." Enzymes necessary for the oxidation of fatty acids are positioned within the mitochondria so as to allow complete oxidation of fatty acids without accumulation of intermediates. The fatty acids are carried across the mitochondrial membrane as carnitine $((CH_3)_3\overset{+}{N}CH_2CHOHCH_2COO^-)$ derivatives. For reactions during oxidation of fatty acids see Scheme I.

A fatty acid $(CH_3(CH_2)_nCOOH)$ is first activated by the fatty acid-activating enzyme thiokinase, on the outer membrane of the mitochondria. Adenosine triphosphate (ATP), COENZYME A (CoA), and magnesium ion (Mg^{++}) are required; the final active product is the fatty-acid derivative acyl coen-

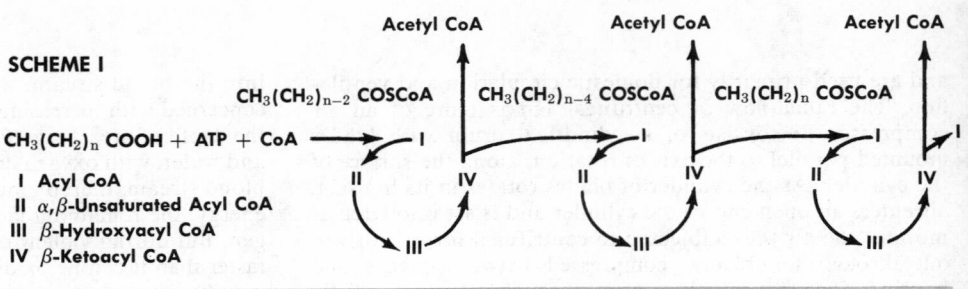

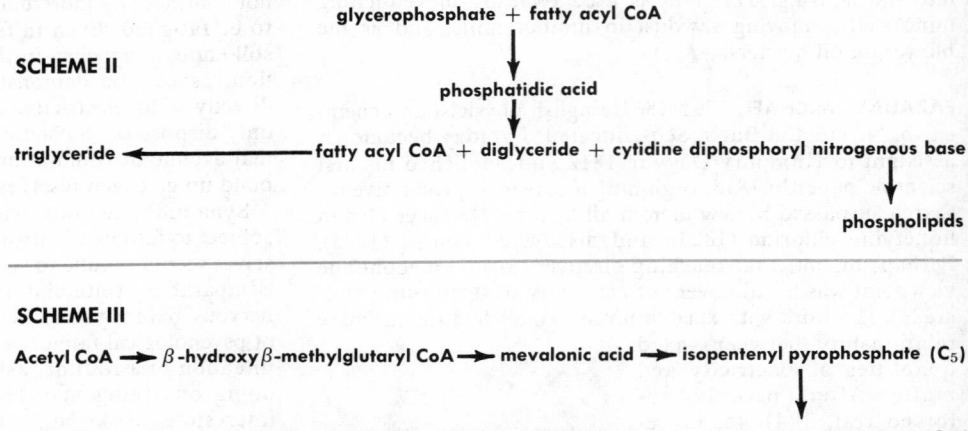

SCHEME I

$$CH_3(CH_2)_n\ COOH + ATP + CoA \longrightarrow$$

I Acyl CoA
II α,β-Unsaturated Acyl CoA
III β-Hydroxyacyl CoA
IV β-Ketoacyl CoA

Acetyl CoA   Acetyl CoA   Acetyl CoA

$$CH_3(CH_2)_{n-2}\ COSCoA \quad CH_3(CH_2)_{n-4}\ COSCoA \quad CH_3(CH_2)_n\ COSCoA$$

Fat metabolism: Formulas show oxidation of fatty acids (Scheme I); formation of triglycerides and/or phospholipids (Scheme II); and formation of cholesterol (Scheme III).

SCHEME II

glycerophosphate + fatty acyl CoA

↓

phosphatidic acid

↓

triglyceride ◄——— fatty acyl CoA + diglyceride + cytidine diphosphoryl nitrogenous base

↓

phospholipids

SCHEME III

Acetyl CoA ➞ β-hydroxyβ-methylglutaryl CoA ➞ mevalonic acid ➞ isopentenyl pyrophosphate (C_5)

↓

Cholesterol ◄——— squalene(C_{30}) ◄——— farnesyl pyrophosphate (C_{15}) ◄——— Geraniyl pyrophosphate (C_{10})

zyme A (I). This is transferred to carnitine by a specific enzyme (palmityl CoA-carnitine transacylase) yielding palmityl carnitine, which passes across the mitochondrial inner membrane. Inside the mitochondria the palmityl group is transferred back to CoA by action of the same enzyme. The fatty acyl CoA (I) is then acted upon by various enzymes of the BETA-OXIDATION sequence. It is first oxidized by the enzyme fatty acyl coenzyme A dehydrogenase, which removes two electrons from the α and β carbon atoms of the acyl CoA and yields the corresponding α-β unsaturated acyl CoA (II). This compound (II) is then hydrated by the enzyme enoylhydrase. The product, β-hydroxyacyl CoA (III), is then oxidized further in the presence of the enzyme β-hydroxyacyl dehydrogenase to form β-ketoacyl CoA (IV), which is then cleaved in the presence of coenzyme A by the enzyme thiolase to form acetyl CoA and acyl CoA with 2 carbon atoms less than the original acyl CoA ($CH_3(CH_2)_{n-2}$ COSCoA). Acetyl CoA is oxidized by the CITRIC ACID CYCLE to CO_2, H_2O, and energy. The resulting acyl CoA undergoes the same sequence of reactions to yield another acetyl CoA and an acyl CoA shorter than the original acyl CoA by four carbon atoms ($CH_3(CH_2)_{n-4}$COSCoA). Thus with each cycle two carbon atoms in the form of acetyl CoA are cleaved off from the fatty acids, so that ultimately there is complete conversion of the fatty acid to acetyl CoA. Since the naturally occurring fatty acids contain even-numbered carbon atoms, acetyl CoA is the final product of β-oxidation. However, if an odd-number fatty acid were oxidized, then the final step would yield acetyl CoA plus a three-carbon acyl CoA (propionyl CoA). The latter compound is then converted by a specific sequence of reactions to succinic acid, a member of the citric-acid cycle.

The body's method of converting foodstuffs into fatty acid prior to combustion appears to take place by an entirely different pathway. Until recently it was widely assumed that synthesis of fatty acids was simply the reversal of the above-described oxidation process. But present information indicates that the enzymes involved in the synthesis are located in the non-mitochondrial portion of the cytoplasm, that palmitic acid is the main product of this system, and that all of

the carbon atoms arise from acetyl CoA. Since acetyl CoA is formed by decarboxylation of pyruvic acid, which is the main product of glycolysis, this is the way the body converts excess carbohydrate into stored fat. Acetyl CoA is first converted to malonyl CoA, a three-carbon acyl derivative of CoA, by the addition of a CO_2 molecule in the presence of ATP and a biotin-containing enzyme, acetyl CoA carboxylase. This enzyme is markedly stimulated by citrate, isocitrate, and other dicarboxylic acids of the citric-acid cycle. This positive allosteric effect is physiologically important in diverting acetyl CoA into fatty acids at a time when concentrations of di- and tri-carboxylic acids are high. Seven molecules of the malonyl CoA produced join with acetyl CoA—the building block—to release CO_2 and form intermediate compounds, which are reduced completely to palmitic acid. This conversion is catalyzed by a complex enzyme system composed of at least eight different proteins. One of these, Acyl carrier protein (ACP), contains as a prosthetic group 4'-phosphopantitheine, which is the active site found in CoA. Thus ACP functions as a coenzyme like that of CoA in fatty-acid oxidation sequence. Acetyl and malonyl groups are transferred from CoA to ACP to form acetyl ACP and malonyl ACP, respectively. Acetyl ACP and malonyl ACP condense to form acetoacetyl ACP, CO_2, and ACP. Acetoacetyl ACP is reduced to D($-$) β-hydroxyacyl ACP, which is dehydrated to α-β unsaturated acyl ACP and consequently reduced to butyryl ACP. This sequence of condensation, reduction, dehydration, and reduction is repeated six more times until palmityl ACP is formed; this is then hydrolyzed to palmitic acid. Palmitic-acid synthesis from acetyl CoA and malonyl CoA is stimulated by phosphorylated sugars such as fructose 1, 6-diphosphate and glucose 6-phosphate. This stimulation appears physiologically significant, for it is manifested when there is ample supply of glucose to the cell, thereby facilitating conversion of acetyl CoA to fatty acids.

The triglycerides are composed of two main components, fatty acids and glycerol. The glycerol is derived from dihydroxyacetone phosphate, itself a product of glucose catabolism. The glycerol is phosphorylated to glycerophosphate, which is condensed with two molecules of fatty acyl CoA to form phosphatidic acid (cf. Scheme II). This compound is dephosphorylated by the enzyme phosphatidic acid phosphatase to form a diglyceride, which may then either condense with another molecule of fatty acyl CoA to form the triglyceride or be used in phospholipid synthesis.

Phospholipids, *e.g.* lecithin and cephaline, are insoluble in acetone and are composed of glycerol, fatty acids, phosphate, and nitrogenous bases such as choline in the case of lecithin, ethanolamine in the case of cephaline, the amino acid serine in phosphatidyl serine. The introduction of the nitrogenous base into the phospholipid involves the use of cytidine triphosphate. The phosphate derivative of nitrogenous base reacts with the cytidine triphosphate to form a cytidine diphosphate derivative, which reacts with the diglyceride to form the phospholipids (see Scheme II).

Another class of phospholipids are the sphingosine derivatives. These are complex lipids found mainly in lipids of brain and nerves. Sphingosine is a long-chain alcohol ($CH_3(CH_2)_{12}$ $CH=CHCH(OH)CH(NH_2)CH_2OH$) deriving its carbon chain from palmitic acid and the amino acid L-serine. A fatty acid reacts with sphingosine through the amino group to form an amide derivative, ceramide, which then reacts with cytidine diphosphate choline to form sphingomyelin. Sphingosine also reacts with uridine diphosphate galactose to form psychosine, which is then acylated by fatty acyl CoA to form cerebrosides. More than one sugar can be attached to the ceramide, forming more complex lipids: gangliosides.

Steroids and terpenes are biologically important substances which bear no structural relationship to fatty acids but are classed as lipids merely because of their solubility in organic solvents. Many of these compounds contain multiples of five carbon atoms related structurally to isoprene.

$$CH_2=\overset{\overset{\textstyle CH_3}{|}}{C}-CH=CH_2$$

Isoprene

This class of compounds includes essential oils such as citral, pinene, geraniol; resin acids and rubber; carotenes, vitamin A, and squalene; steroids; cholesterol (main animal sterol) and ergosterol (main plant sterol). The general biosynthesis of these compounds involves two main steps: (1) formation of an activated isoprene unit from acetyl CoA; (2) multiple condensation of isoprene units to form terpenes and the cyclization of the latter compounds to form steroids.

Three molecules of acetyl CoA condense together in two distinct steps to form β-hydroxy β-methylglutaryl CoA, which is then reduced to mevalonic acid. This is phosphorylated to the pyrophosphate derivative, which is then decarboxylated in the presence of specific enzymes and cofactors to yield an active isoprene compound, isopentenyl pyrophosphate (Scheme III). Two molecules of this are condensed together to form a C_{10} compound known as geraniyl pyrophosphate, which adds another molecule of isopentenyl pyrophosphate to form farnesyl pyrophosphate (C_{15} compound). Two

molecules of the C_{15} compound are coupled together to form a C_{30} compound, squalene. This, abundant in shark liver, is readily converted to cholesterol by undergoing cyclization and several oxidation-reduction steps to yield cholesterol (C_{27} compound) and CO_2 (see Scheme III). Reduced triphosphopyridine nucleotide is used in some of these steps. Not much is known about oxidation of cholesterol except that it can be readily oxidized by animal liver to bile salts, which are excreted through bile.—*S. J. W.*

FATS AND OILS: organic chemical compounds found widely distributed in plants (especially in seeds) and animals. They are substances built from glycerol (GLYCERIN), an alcohol with three OH groups, which can form ESTERS with three molecules of straight-chain CARBOXYLIC ACIDS. These esters are called *glycerides*. In the representative compound shown here (bottom of page), the first acid used to build the molecule is STEARIC ACID, the 18-carbon acid. The second is oleic acid; like stearic acid it has an 18-carbon chain, but it also has an OLEFIN double bond right in the middle of the chain and is therefore an unsaturated acid, as contrasted with stearic acid, which is saturated. The third acid in this typical molecule is any carboxylic acid, where R represents a saturated or unsaturated hydrocarbon chain. In nature, glycerides are usually "mixed"; that is, several different acid radicals will be present in the molecule combined with glycerol, as in the illustration.

Glycerides that are liquid at room temperature are called *oils,* and those that are solid at room temperature, *fats.* In general, glycerides containing a larger proportion of *saturated* long-chain acids tend to be fats, while those with a larger proportion of *unsaturated* long-chain acids are oils. Saturated acids with a short chain, *e.g.* butyric acid (a 4-carbon acid), also tend to form oils or fats with relatively low melting points, such as butter. Vegetable fats and oils are recovered from seeds and fruits by various pressing methods or by solvent extraction. Animal fats are processed by dry-heating (known as *rendering*), by steam treatment, or by cooking in hot water, as in the kitchen. When fats and oils are cooked with water containing an alkali (sodium hydroxide, NaOH) the glycerides are hydrolyzed to glycerol and to the sodium salts of the acids. These salts of the long-chain acids, *e.g.* sodium stearate, are the commercially important SOAPS, and the glycerol is a commercially important by-product. The alkaline hydrolysis of glycerides is called *saponification.*

The glyceride oils can be converted into fats by simply passing hydrogen through the oils, with finely divided nickel as CATALYST. Hydrogen atoms add across the double bonds of the unsaturated acid radicals in the glycerides. This HYDROGENATION process is commercially important because fats are generally in greater demand than oils and bring a higher price. However, in the early 1960s a consumer demand was developing for less saturated fats and oils ("*polyunsaturates*") because of tentative evidence indicating that they offer certain health and dietary advantages.—*Ru. M.*

Typical glyceride (fat or oil) breaks down, on hydrolysis, to glycerol, stearic acid, oleic acid, and an acid in which R is either a saturated or an unsaturated hydrocarbon chain.

A fat or oil
A glyceride

Glycerol

Stearic acid

Oleic acid

FATS IN BIOCHEMISTRY: Fats, also called lipids, may be viewed as tissue constituents (they constitute the fatty, or oily, part of the tissue) and as foodstuffs (*e.g.* butter, lard, coconut oil) or articles of commerce. All these are ESTERS of the alcohol glycerol with two or three acids, known as fatty acids. The most abundant fats contain three fatty acids, and in general differ one from the other according to the particular fatty acids they contain. The fatty acids present in fats are likely to be among the following:

acetic acid (vinegar)	CH_3COOH
butyric acid	C_3H_7COOH
caproic acid (hexanoic acid)	$C_6H_{12}O_2$
caprylic acid (octanoic acid)	$C_8H_{16}O_2$
capric acid (decanoic acid)	$C_{10}H_{20}O_2$
lauric acid	$C_{12}H_{24}O_2$
myristic acid	$C_{14}H_{28}O_2$
palmitic acid	$C_{16}H_{32}O_2$
stearic acid	$C_{18}H_{36}O_2$
oleic acid	$C_{18}H_{33}O_2$
linoleic acid	$C_{18}H_{32}O_2$
linolenic acid	$C_{18}H_{30}O_2$

The last three members of the above list are unsaturated acids; *i.e.* they do not contain as much hydrogen per carbon atom as do the others. Such unsaturated acids, when they combine with glycerol, form unsaturated fats, or oils. They are thought by some scientists to be important in maintaining another fatty substance, cholesterol, at low levels in the blood stream, and thus perhaps to aid in preventing atherosclerosis (hardening of arteries). The other acids in the foregoing table (acetic through stearic) are classified as members of the fatty-acid series. When combined with glycerol they normally give rise to hard fats, *e.g.* beef tallow (stearin).

Fats are useful in diet as lubricants and are excellent sources of energy, furnishing approximately twice as many calories per unit of weight as carbohydrate or protein. Organisms store extra energy as fat rather than as protein or carbohydrate.

Another important class of fatty substances is the PHOSPHOLIPIDS, with two fatty acids in combination with glycerol plus a molecule of phosphate plus a nitrogenous base plus occasionally one or more sugars. These complex substances, slightly soluble in water, are also soluble in fatty media; hence they seem important as emulsifying agents, assisting in digestion of fats by the blood stream and also in building brain and nerve tissue, which is fatty yet must coexist with a watery (blood) system. Although phospholipids have been known over half a century, their importance is just being fully recognized, as new information is being brought to light. A third class of fatty substances, the STEROLS, is related to Vitamin D, sex hormones, and cholesterol.—*V. H. C.*

FAUJAS DE SAINT-FOND, BARTHELMY, 1741–1819, French geologist, b. Montélimart. His studies on the extinct volcanoes of France and the basalts of Scotland gave important support to the view that basalts are igneous in origin (see GEOLOGY). His many publications include *Recherches sur les volcans éteints du Vivarais et du Velay* (1778) and *Voyage en Angleterre, en Ecosse, et Iles Hébrides* (1797).—*D. H. D. R.*

FAULT: a fracture in the Earth's crust along which adjacent blocks have shifted with respect to each other. A joint, by contrast, is a crack along which there is no evidence of relative motion between the adjacent blocks. Faults occur in all types of rock but are most obvious when they cut across and displace identifiable layers in sedimentary or metamorphic rocks. As a result of the mutual abrasion of one moving block

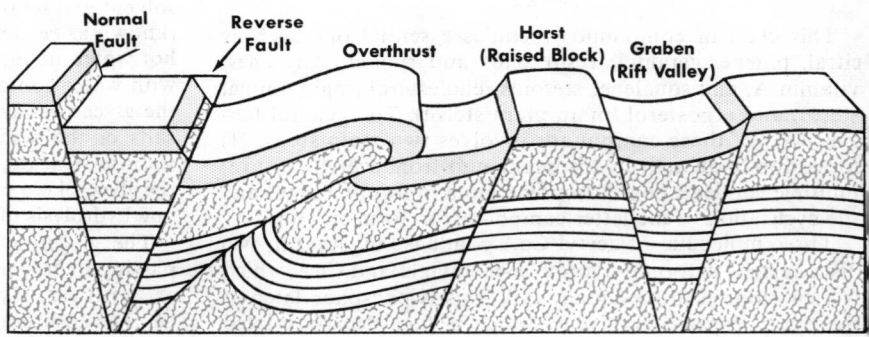

Types of faults: Only simple examples appear in diagram. In many instances several types of faults are involved in a fault zone, and relationships are complex.

Along great fault scarp on E side of Sierra Nevada near Mt Whitney, fault line shows clearly. Block that forms the Sierra dips westward, its western side being covered with sediments. (*U. S. Geological Survey*)

on the other during faulting, grooves called slickensides may be produced. The surface of a fault plane is rarely flat for any great distance, and all faults if followed to their extremities will be found to either die out or intersect other fault planes. Commonly, diastrophic motion will not be confined to a single fault surface but to a number of parallel fractures, thus giving rise to a *fault zone*, and if such faults occur in an overlapping arrangement, they are said to be *en echelon*. The relative motion of the neighboring blocks may consist essentially of horizontal shifting, thus giving a *strike-slip* or *lateral fault*, or the motion may be essentially vertical, for a *dip-slip fault*. If the motion has both a strike-slip and a dip-slip component, the term *oblique-slip* is applicable. Most fault planes are inclined at some angle to the vertical, the rock above the fault plane being called the *hanging wall* and that below the fault the *footwall*; this terminology was introduced from the mining industry. Ore veins frequently follow faults, and in digging out such an ore deposit the miner stands on the foot wall, with the hanging wall over his head. Under compressive forces in the crust, the motion along a dip-slip fault will be such that the hanging wall is pushed up with respect to the footwall, thus producing a *reverse fault*. If the fault plane is nearly horizontal or has at most a low angle to the horizontal, it is called a *thrust fault*. On the other hand, under tension rocks will yield in such a manner that the hanging wall moves relatively down with respect to the footwall, and a *normal fault* is produced.

The motion along a fault may be a fraction of an inch or a number of miles, and in some of the major faults the fracture may extend for hundreds of miles. The San Andreas Fault in California is 600 mi long and extends from a point south of the Mojave Desert to the coast north of San Francisco. This is a strike-slip fault, and in 1906 a horizontal motion of 21 ft was measured in one place and a vertical shift of only 3 ft. Motion along a fault is rarely over a few feet at any one time, and where motion of a number of miles is noted, faulting, with accompanying earthquakes, undoubtedly has occurred many times over probably thousands of years before the total displacement was attained. The east side of the Sierra Nevada Mts is marked by a normal fault along which motion of more than 2 mi occurred during the uplift of the mountains. In the Lewis Thrust Fault of the N Rockies, Pre-Cambrian rocks have been pushed as much as 20 mi over younger Cretaceous rocks. Chief Mt, Montana, is an erosional remnant of this thrust sheet. For a discussion of valleys formed by faulting, see GRABEN; for fault mountains, see MOUNTAINS AND MOUNTAIN BUILDING.—*J. Sh.*

FAUNA, FLORA, and BIOTA: the animal population (fauna), plant population (flora), or both (biota) of a particular region, geologic period, or environment. Subdivisions are commonly designated by a prefix or modifier, *e.g.* avifauna (bird species only) or marine flora.—*H. M. S.*

FEATHERS: outgrowths of the skin that form the characteristic external covering of BIRDS. Feathers are composed of KERATIN, the same substance that forms animals' horns and claws and human nails. A typical quill feather, which grows in the wings and tail, consists of the shaft, or rachis, bearing on each side a vane made of parallel barbs. From the sides of the barbs, barbules arise, and from the sides of these, barbicels. On the side of the barbicels toward the tip of the feather are hooks called hamuli, and on the side toward the base of the feather are ridges. The hamuli of one barbicel catch on the ridges of the next and so hold the vane together. Feathers grow practically all over the body of ostriches, penguins, and a few other birds, but on most species grow only

Interlocking structure of the vane of a covert feather of a hummingbird is shown in this microphotograph. (*Carl Struwe/ Monkmeyer*)

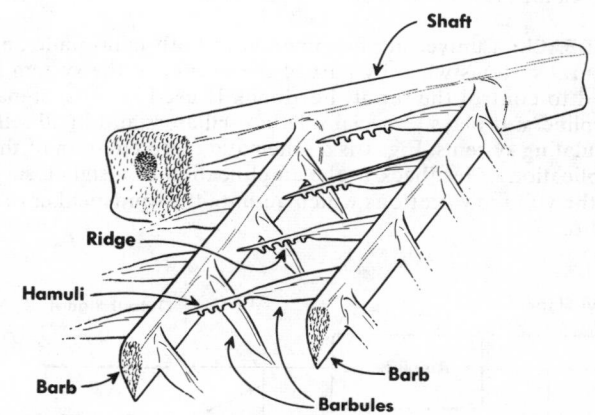

Detail of structure: Magnified view of small section of quill feather's central shaft, showing two barbs and their barbules. Hooked hamuli and notched ridges interlock. (*After Pettingill*)

Feather filament, as seen through microscope. This is a single barb, with barbules, of a down feather. (*Leonard Lee Rue III / Monkmeyer*)

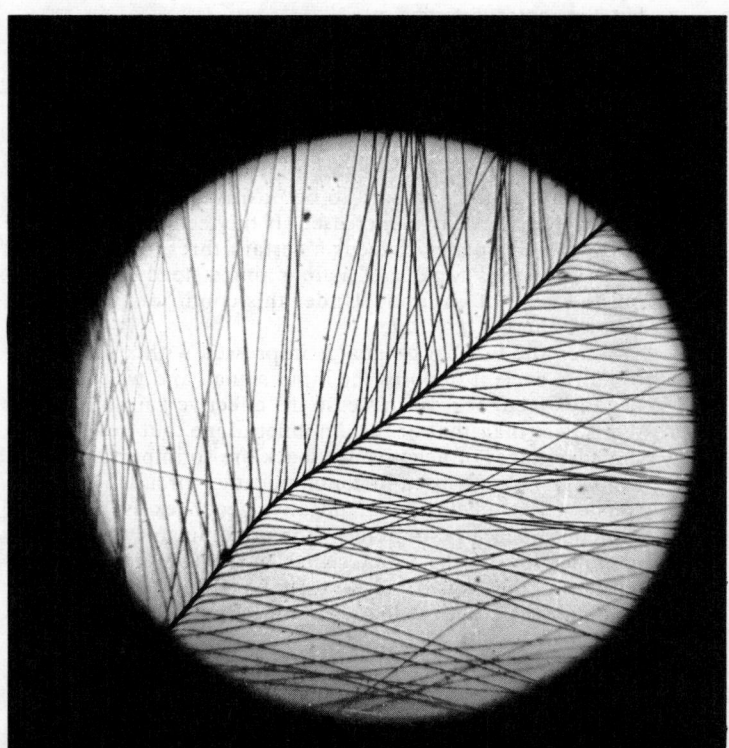

in certain areas, called feather tracts, and overlap to cover the rest of the body.

There are various types of feathers, some peculiarly formed for use in courtship, as the egret's plumes, and some for making sounds, as the manakin's wing feathers. Birds that spend the whole year in regions of great temperature change have more feathers in winter than in summer. Oil on the feathers of waterbirds provides a waterproof, "buoyant," insulated covering. Red, orange, yellow, black, brown, and some green feathers get their color from pigments; white ones from their structure; blue and some green ones from a combination of pigment and structure (see COLORATION OF ANIMALS). Birds shed their feathers and grow new ones at least once a year (see MOLTING). The difference in feathers between males and females is controlled in some species, such as the brown leghorn chicken, by sex hormones. In such cases castrates of both sexes possess similar plumage. In other species, such as the English sparrow, castration does not affect the characteristic sexual difference in feathers. See Color Plate 41.—*H. Br.*

FEEDBACK: a universal phenomenon in both man-made and natural systems whereby part of the output of the system is used to control the input. Feedback is used in most signal amplifiers; it plays a crucial role in oscillators and in all self-regulating systems. Fig. 1 is a schematic representation of the application of feedback to the amplification of a signal, such as the voltage variations which actuate the loudspeaker of a radio.

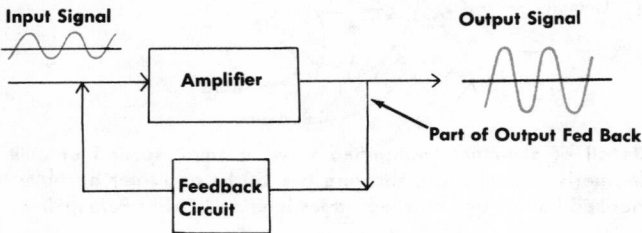

Fig. 1: Feedback in an amplifier circuit: Negative feedback reduces over-all amplification but, on the other hand, improves signal quality. Positive feedback increases over-all amplification, but it increases distortion as well.

The feedback circuit impresses a fraction of the output voltage back onto the input side of the amplifier, as indicated by the arrows. If the circuit is designed so that this additional input signal rises and falls simultaneously with the original input, the feedback is said to be positive, and the effective gain of the amplifier is increased. If the feedback signal at a particular frequency exceeds a certain threshold value, the system becomes capable of maintaining a steady signal without the need of an input. Under this condition, the system becomes an OSCILLATOR.

When the feedback signal is impressed with a time delay of half a cycle it opposes the input signal, and we then have negative feedback. In this case the effective gain of the system is less than that of the amplifier alone, but nevertheless the advantages of negative feedback are so important that it is now universally used in communication circuits.

The basic advantage of negative feedback is that, with proper choice of parameters, it is possible still to get some amplification of the input signal, while simultaneously attenuating the noise and distortions generated inside the amplifier. (Positive feedback amplifies both.) Because of this

effect the output of a negative feedback amplifier is a more faithful reproduction of the input signal. The fact that the signal has been amplified less than it would have been otherwise can be easily compensated for by introducing another stage of amplification.

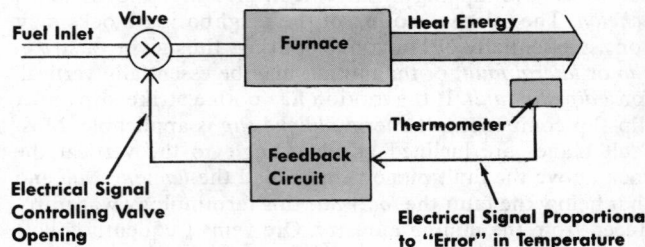

Fig. 2: Thermostat-controlled heating system: This system employs feedback to turn heater on and off in response to changes in temperature, which are indicated by the thermometer.

The role of feedback in self-regulating systems is illustrated in Fig. 2, which is a schematic sketch of one type of home heating system. In this case, the feedback circuit compares the temperature reading on the thermometer with the desired value, and sends to the inlet valve an electrical signal whose intensity is directly proportional to the difference between the desired temperature and measured temperature. If the room temperature is too low, the sense of the signal is such as to open the inlet valve further, thus allowing more fuel to enter the furnace. Automatic control by feedback finds innumerable applications in industry, and is becoming increasingly important as industrial processes become more complicated. Oil refineries are already almost completely automated, and the trend will probably continue (see AUTOMATION). Feedback is also an essential principle in biological phenomena; thus the human body regulates its temperature, heart rate, blood pressure, and its concentration of various materials in the blood by means of feedback mechanisms. See FEEDBACK CONTROL.—*S. K.*

FEEDBACK CONTROL: in biochemistry, a method of regulating the activity of enzymes in living cells. A handy example of a simple mechanical feedback system is the governor of an engine, which maintains a constant running speed under variable loads. It has been suggested that energy production in cells may be partly regulated by similar means. Thus, in the following reversible reaction in GLYCOLYSIS:

Phosphoglyceraldehyde + ADP + H_3PO_4 + DPN $\rightleftharpoons$
    Phosphoglyceric acid + ATP + $DPNH_2$

When adequate concentrations of phosphoglyceraldehyde and DPN are present, the rate of the forward reaction is controlled by the concentration of ADP (adenosine diphosphate) and H_3PO_4. This rate will slow down as ADP and H_3PO_4 are converted to ATP (adenosine triphosphate). When ATP is broken down in synthetic (energy-consuming) reactions, ADP and H_3PO_4 are formed. Thus a fall in the concentration of ATP creates the conditions needed for its synthesis. In bacterial metabolism it has been shown that, in some cases, the end product of a whole series of enzymatic reactions will inhibit the enzyme responsible for the first step in the enzymatic series; thus the product, when it reaches a certain concentration, will shut off its own synthesis by this sort of feedback process.—*K. H.*

FELDSPAR: any of a group of closely related aluminosilicates, and the most abundant of all minerals. In most igneous rocks the composition of the contained feldspar or feldspars is a major factor in the classification of the rock and furnishes information about its origin and history. The feldspars show a considerable range of isomorphism, the end members being:

Alkali Feldspars	$KAlSi_3O_8$	Sanidine	Monoclinic
		Orthoclase	Monoclinic
		Microcline	Triclinic
	$(K, Na)AlSi_3O_8$	Anorthoclase	Triclinic
Plagioclase Feldspars	$NaAlSi_3O_8$	Albite *	Triclinic
	$CaAl_2Si_2O_8$	Anorthite	Triclinic
	$BaAl_2Si_2O_8$	Celsian	Monoclinic

* Complete range in composition.

The feldspar structure is a three-dimensional network of SiO_4 and Al_2O_3 tetrahedra, continuously linked by sharing all oxygen ions. The cations fill the interstices and balance the charges.

Isomorphism in feldspars is much more extensive at higher temperatures than at low ones. On cooling, crystals break down into two intergrown phases showing typical exsolution patterns. The exsolution lamellae in perthite and antiperthite are usually readily visible ribbons or plates. The opalescence and colorplay of moonstone, peristerite, and labradorite are caused by submicroscopic exsolution plates. The metallic flash (*Schiller*) of sunstone (aventurine) is caused by minute oriented flecks of hematite. The potash feldspars are polymorphous. Orthoclase, the higher-temperature phase, is the common potash feldspar of the finer-grained, relatively quickly cooled igneous rocks, whereas microcline, the lower-temperature form, occurs in pegmatites and veins which crystallized more slowly and at lower temperatures. The crystal structures of all feldspars are similar. Although some show monoclinic symmetry and others are triclinic, the actual differences in axial ratios, interfacial angles, and cleavage angles are very small.

Compositions and Approximate Stabilities of Feldspars

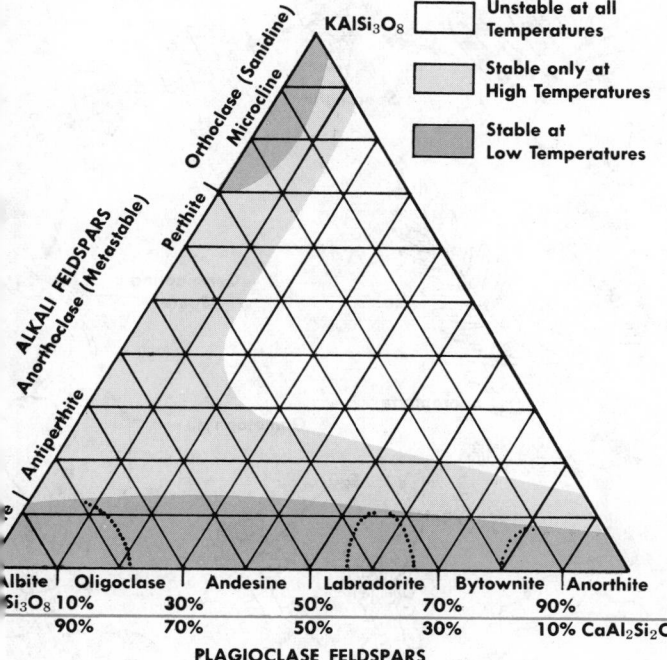

PLAGIOCLASE FELDSPARS

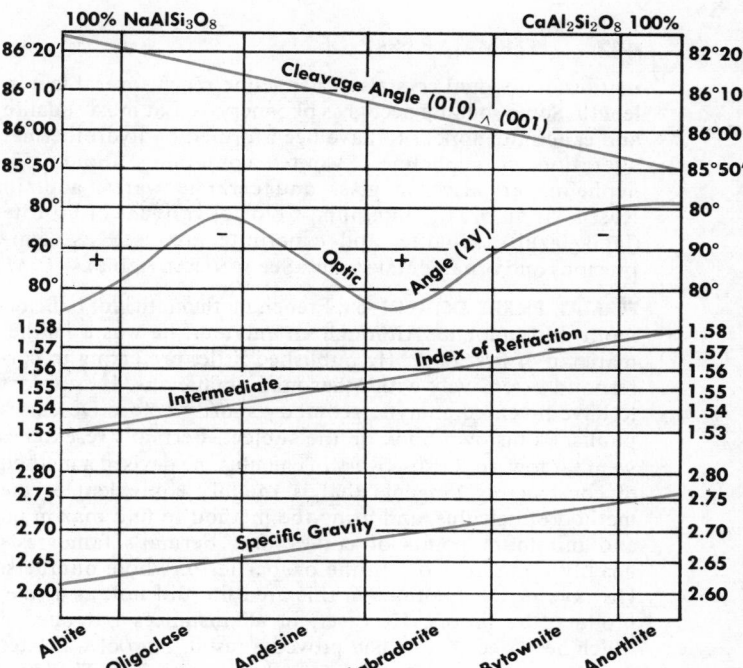

Compositions and Some Properties of Plagioclase Feldspars

The diagnostic properties of the isomorphous plagioclase series vary directly with composition. Polysynthetic (repeated) albite-law twinning, which appears as parallel, closely spaced striations on the basal cleavage planes is characteristic of the plagioclase series but is absent from the potash feldspars. The alkali feldspars are major ingredients of glass and various ceramic wares. They are used as the abrasive agents in "non-scratching" scouring powders because their hardness is very close to that of glass and porcelain enamels. See MINERAL (table).—*L. M.*

FELDSPATHOIDS: a group of alkali alumino-silicate minerals chemically related to the FELDSPARS but containing less silica. In silica-deficient igneous or metamorphic rocks, feldspathoids crystallize in place of the analogous feldspars. The feldspathoids include several different structural groups, with very limited solid solution between them:

Isometric	$KAlSi_2O_6$	Leucite
	$Na_4(AlSiO_4)_3Cl$	Sodalite ⎱ Iso-
	$Na_5(AlSiO_4)_3S$	Lazurite ⎰ morphous
	$(Na > Ca)_4(AlSiO_4)_3(SO_4)$	Haüynite
	$Na_8(AlSiO_4)_6(SO_4)$	Noselite
Hexagonal	$NaAlSiO_4$	Nepheline ⎱ Iso-
	$KAlSiO_4$	Kalsilite ⎰ morphous
	$KAlSiO_4$	Kaliophilite
	$(Na > Ca)_2(AlSiO_4)_3(HCO_3)$	Cancrinite

The feldspathoid structures are three-dimensional (tectosilicate) networks of SiO_4 and Al_2O_3 tetrahedra, continuously linked by sharing of all oxygen ions. Large cations and, in some cases, anions or anionic groups fill the interstices and balance the charges.

Nepheline and leucite are the principal rock-forming feldspathoids. Leucite occurs almost entirely as phenocrysts in porphyries. Nepheline occurs both as phenocrysts in porphyries and in even-grained igneous rocks, also as a metamorphic mineral in gneisses. In some silica-deficient pegmatites, individual crystals of nepheline reach several feet in length. Some sodalite occurs as phenocrysts, but most sodalite and cancrinite appear to have been formed by hydrothermal alteration of nepheline. Syenites containing about 25% nepheline are used in glass and ceramic wares, and, in Russia, as an ore of aluminum. Colorful varieties of lazurite (lapis lazuli), sodalite, and cancrinite are used as semiprecious and ornamental stones. See MINERAL (table).—*L. M.*

FERMAT, PIERRE DE, 1601–65, French mathematician; b. Beaumont-de-Lomogne. Although an amateur, he was a mathematician of first rank. He published little, preferring to correspond extensively with other mathematicians. He appears to have invented analytic geometry shortly before Descartes published his own book on the subject. Fermat's researches went far toward the discovery of calculus; he devised a method of constructing tangents that is roughly equivalent to the method of calculus, and using the method to find maximum and minimum points of curves. But Fermat's fame rests heavily upon his work in the properties of whole numbers. He gave many theorems in this area but did not, as a rule, produce the proofs. However, in all instances but one, in which he stated that he had proved a result, a proof was later found. The one exception is known as Fermat's Last Theorem, which states that there are no whole numbers or fractions that can be substituted for x, y, and z to satisfy the equation $x^n + y^n = z^n$, if n is a whole number greater than 2. Fermat commented on the margin of a book that he had a marvelous proof of this theorem, but that the margin was too narrow to contain it. No one has been able to prove or disprove this theorem in the 300 yr since Fermat's death, although the greatest mathematicians of the world have worked on it. Fermat is known in physics for *Fermat's principle,* which states that the path actually traversed by light in going from one point to another is that which takes the least time.—*H. C.*

FERMENTATION: see GLYCOLYSIS.

FERMI, ENRICO, 1901–54, Italian-U. S. scientist; b. Rome. In 1934 he began bombarding the complete range of known chemical elements with neutrons, succeeding in obtaining a new element (element 93, now called neptunium) by adding a neutron to the nucleus of uranium. In so doing, he also became the first to split the uranium atom, but failed to recognize the significance of his achievement. In 1934 he also discovered that interposing certain substances, *e.g.* paraffin, water, or graphite, between the neutron source and the target slows the velocity of the neutrons and thus greatly increases the nuclear effect produced. This was of great significance in the production of artificial elements and radioactive isotopes. In 1938 Fermi left Italy because of his opposition to Fascism and came to America, where he became professor of physics at Columbia Univ. (1939). As one of the principal figures in the development of the atomic bomb, he assisted in the design and construction of the first atomic pile at the Univ. of Chicago and directed the first controlled nuclear chain reaction (Dec. 2, 1942); he also participated in the work at Los Alamos, where the first atomic bomb was developed. For his identification of new radioactive elements produced by neutron bombardment and his discovery of nuclear reactions effected by slow neutrons, Fermi received the 1938 Nobel prize. The artificial element fermium (no. 100) is named for him.—*R. G.*

FERMIUM: an artificial element (symbol Fm) of the actinide group; at. no. 100; at. wt 253 (most stable isotope); the eighth transuranium element to be discovered. It was found, 1953, in the debris of a hydrogen-bomb explosion by the same group that had discovered EINSTEINIUM a few weeks be-

fore in debris from another thermonuclear explosion. No fermium isotope appears to have a half life much longer than a day; thus weighable amounts of the element fermium are extremely difficult to obtain.—*G. W. M.*

FERN: a flowerless VASCULAR PLANT with roots, stems, and leaves. Ferns exhibit an obvious ALTERNATION OF GENERATIONS, the two generations being plants of distinctly different forms. The conspicuous fern is the sporophyte stage, which reproduces by means of spores blown by wind. Each of its cells contains a nucleus with the double (diploid) number of chromosomes, and spores are formed by MEIOSIS. Usually the leaves arise from a horizontal underground stem (rhizome) as curled buds called "fiddleheads." They unroll and expand, typically as pinnately compound leaves, on the underside of which are clusters (sori) of spore cases (sporangia). When the mature sporangia become dry, they suddenly crack open and act as slingshots, throwing the spores into the wind. In favorable situations, usually on moist soil, a spore will germinate into a flat, thin, heart-shaped gametophyte plant, which is commonly only ⅛ to ¼ in. long; it bears multicellular sex organs. On the short stalks are small bags called antheridia, in which antherozoids (male gametes) are produced, ready for discharge into dew or rain water. In each of the flask-shaped organs called archegonia is a single egg cell, which an antherozoid can reach by swimming down the tubular neck of the "flask." The fertilized egg (zygote), with a nucleus containing one set of chromosomes from the antherozoid nucleus and a second set from the egg nucleus, divides by mitosis during embryonic development, so that a new sporophyte fern results.

Life cycle of fern: Familiar sporophyte plant bears spores in sporangia on bottom sides of leaves. When a sporangium bursts, spores are released. A spore germinates on moist soil and develops into a gametophyte plant. The gametophyte produces egg cells in archegonia and sperm cells in antheridia. Union of a sperm with an egg results in a zygote that develops into a sporophyte, and the cycle begins anew. (*After Cronquist*)

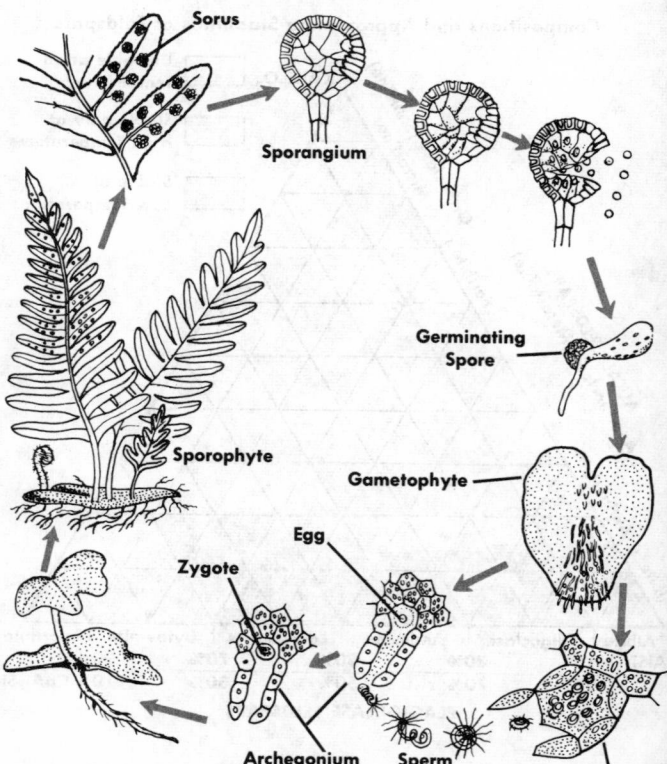

About 10,000 species of ferns have been named. They range in size from tropical tree ferns 40 or 50 ft high to small floating water ferns ¼ in. across. One living genus, *Botrychium,* is composed of land ferns showing affinities to the extinct *Protopteridium,* a close relative of *Rhynia,* the simplest known vascular plant. See Color Plate 44.—*L. B.*

FERNALD, MERRITT LYNDON, 1873–1950, U. S. botanist; b. Orono, Maine. He was known internationally for his research on the systematic and geographic botany of North American plants, their relation to Old World plants, and the distribution of higher plants in North America, particularly with regard to NE plants. He directed the Gray Herbarium, Harvard Univ., from 1937. He was a member of the National Academy of Sciences.—*D. H. D. R.*

FERREL, WILLIAM, 1817–91, U. S. meteorologist; b. Fulton County, Pa. His "Essay on the Winds and the Currents of the Ocean" (1856) made him famous. Ferrel held positions in the Coast and Geodetic Survey, invented a tide-predicting machine, and published numerous works in meteorology. He was a member of the National Academy of Sciences.—*D. H. D. R.*

FERROALLOYS: see ALLOY.

FERROCYANIDE: a salt of ferrocyanic acid, $H_4[Fe(CN)_6]$. In this complex acid, iron is divalent (ferrous). Soluble ferrocyanides are used to detect the presence of trivalent iron, *e.g.* ferric chloride, $FeCl_3$.—*Ru. M.*

FERROELECTRIC: a crystalline DIELECTRIC that is naturally polarized (*i.e.* contains oriented dipoles), the direction of polarization being reversible by application of an electric field. When measurements of the dipole moment per unit volume P as a function of applied electric field E are made on a ferroelectric, it is found that P does not increase linearly with E, as with simple dielectrics; rather, their relation is given by a HYSTERESIS loop, just as is the relation between the analogous quantities, magnetization and magnetic field intensity, for a ferromagnet. Barium titanate is a well-known ferroelectric.—*E. M. C.*

FERROMAGNETISM: the magnetic properties of certain substances, notably iron. Ferromagnetic substances are characterized by being very strongly attracted by magnets. They are important commercially not only because of the strong magnetic forces they experience, but also because of their ability to carry very large MAGNETIC INDUCTION fields.

Magnetic substances contain permanent magnetic dipoles of atomic or electronic dimensions. (A magnetic dipole is two opposite magnetic poles of equal magnitude.) In the presence of a magnetic field there is a tendency for these dipoles to be aligned, but this tendency is opposed by thermal agitation, the heat motion of particles of the substance. In substances in which the sole aligning force is the result of the external field, only a very slight degree of magnetization is achieved. Ferromagnetic materials owe their very marked degree of magnetization to internal forces that neighboring magnetic dipoles exert on each other. These forces are not primarily magnetic; they are quantum mechanical forces primarily of electrical origin, as are the binding forces in molecules or in solids.

These short-range interatomic forces tend to produce local alignment that does not necessarily extend throughout a sample. As a result, ferromagnetic materials are magnetized in domains or regions of varying sizes and shapes. The magnetization process consists either in the rotation of the magnetization of these domains under the action of an externally applied field, or in the movement of domain boundaries in such a way that domains whose magnetization is essentially parallel to an applied field grow at the expense of others whose magnetization is less favorably oriented.

Ferromagnetic materials are characterized by hysteresis; that is, the state of magnetization depends not only on the field applied, but on the previous history of the sample. The degree of magnetization in the absence of an applied field is called the *remanence.* The strength of the reverse field required to demagnetize a sample is called the *coercive force.* For permanent magnets, materials having a high coercive force and a high remanence are wanted, whereas for transformers or other pieces of apparatus in which the magnetization is to follow an applied field, materials with little hysteresis (low remanence and coercive force) are wanted.

In addition to ferromagnetic materials in which there is a tendency for neighboring magnetic moments to line up parallel to each other under the influence of local forces, other substances are made up of strongly interacting dipoles. In some substances, atomic magnetic moments line up antiparallel to each other in pairs, the paired moments being parallel but opposite in direction. This results in zero spontaneous magnetization. These substances are called antiferromagnetic. An antiferromagnetic crystal may be thought of as consisting of two interpenetrating ferromagnetic lattices with oppositely directed magnetization. In some cases of this kind the two lattices are not of equal magnetization; hence a pseudo-ferromagnetism called *ferrimagnetism* results. See MAGNETISM; MAGNETIC MATERIALS.—*F. B.*

FERROUS METALS: see IRON; STEEL.

FERTILIZATION: the union of a male sex cell (sperm) with a female sex cell (egg), and the fusion of the hereditary lines in the fertilized egg (zygote). Fertilization is the central event in sexual REPRODUCTION; two parental lines combine their inheritable features in producing each offspring. In asexual reproduction, by contrast, a new individual originates from a single parent without fertilization. Among multicellular animals, it is usual for part of the sperm cell actually to enter the cytoplasm of the egg cell; generally this is the stimulus needed to induce the egg nucleus to ready itself for the CELL DIVISIONS leading to the formation of a multicellular embryo. Fusion of nuclear materials (chromosomes) usually occurs at the metaphase stage of the first mitotic cell division. Experimentally it is sometimes possible to stimulate an unfertilized egg by mechanical, chemical, or thermal means so that the egg develops into an embryo; this is the technique of artificial PARTHENOGENESIS.

Many animals and plants that reproduce by sexual means have accessory structures that aid in bringing the sex cells (gametes) together. Internal fertilization is common in insects and many vertebrate animals, particularly those living on land. Usually the male has a penis with which to transfer sperm to the female, who receives it in a special chamber (vagina) connected by tubes to the vicinity of the ovary, from which eggs emerge. In vascular plants with pollen (GYMNOSPERMS and FLOWERING PLANTS), it is wind, insects, birds, or water that serves to carry pollen to the part of the cone or flower nearest the egg. A pollen tube grows from the pollen grain, conveying sperm cells to the ovule in which an egg is readied for fertilization. Other parts of a flower or cone serve in making this event more probable, sometimes by attracting insects that transfer pollen from one flower to another. See EMBRYONIC DEVELOPMENT; POLLEN.—*L. and M. M.*

FERTILIZER: a substance which improves plant growth by supplying essential nutrients. The term may be restricted to products of chemical technology, but natural fertilizers, *e.g.* horse and cow manure, also modify soil favorably and aid crops. The importance of certain elements to plants was recognized by early 19th-cent. organic chemists. The three predominant elements in fertilizers are nitrogen (N), phosphorus (P), and potassium (K). Calcium, magnesium, and sulfur, needed by plants in generally smaller quantities, may be included. Other elements, needed only in trace quantities, may be present in special fertilizers; these elements include boron, copper, iron, manganese, molybdenum, and zinc. The body of a plant is cellulosic, consisting of carbon, hydrogen, and oxygen; these three elements are obtained from water and carbon dioxide. See NUTRITION.

Synthetic AMMONIA is the source of most nitrogen-providing fertilizers. It may be used directly as gas or in water solution, or converted commercially into fertilizer salts, *e.g.* ammonium sulfate, ammonium nitrate, and ammonium phosphate. Also, by reaction with carbon dioxide, ammonia is made into the important fertilizer urea. Another nitrogen fertilizer is made from calcium carbide (see ORGANOMETALLIC COMPOUNDS), which is capable of absorbing nitrogen from air at high temperature to yield cyanamide (actually, calcium cyanamide). The chief source of fertilizer phosphorus is phosphate rock, used on some soils in raw, crushed form. By reaction with sulfuric acid, phosphate rock is converted into superphosphate, or by treatment with phosphoric acid into triple superphosphate; these are more soluble than raw phosphate rock. Basic slag, a by-product of steel manufacture, can be used as a source of fertilizer phosphorus if the original iron ore had a high phosphorus content. Another phosphate fertilizer is bone meal, obtained from the meat-packing industry. Potassium salts for use as fertilizers are mined from extensive underground POTASH deposits or extracted by suitable processing from brine lakes or seas. The common potassium salts are the chloride and sulfate, sometimes applied in mixture with salts of magnesium.

Use of fertilizers requires care, because of their diverse effects. Phosphates, for example, form insoluble compounds quickly at the top of the soil; they do not penetrate with water, and are said to be "fixed" by the soil. Phosphorus compounds stimulate root formation and growth of seeds. Nitrogen fertilizers prevent leaf-yellowing and promote tissue growth. Ammonium sulfate often produces higher soil acidity; sodium nitrate does not, but is more easily washed away. Potassium salts promote synthesis of carbohydrates in plants and tend to lengthen the growing season. Mixed fertilizers give a "balanced" effect; *e.g.* a fertilizer labeled 5-10-10 contains 5% available nitrogen, 10% available phosphorus calculated as P_2O_5, and 10% potassium calculated as K_2O.—*Ru. M.*

FICK, ADOLPH, 1829–1901, German physiologist; b. Kassel. Although his main field was physiology, Fick is primarily remembered for his work in gaseous diffusion. *Fick's law* states that the rate of flow of particles per unit area is proportional to the negative gradient of the concentration.—*D. H. D. R.*

FICTIONS (in science): In the formulation or application of scientific theories, reference is sometimes made to objects which are definitely known not to exist in the form described by the theory and which yet make successful prediction possible. Such objects are called fictitious objects, or fictions. Obvious examples are point masses, incompressible fluids, perfectly rigid bodies, perfectly reflecting mirrors, the black body of the theory of radiation, the Carnot machine, the harmonic oscillator. Fictions make possible the formulation of relatively simple laws to describe the behavior of the entities represented by the fictions. A fiction also may be a good starting point for successive approximations. Fictions are, on the other hand, useful because the fictitious objects *do* possess certain similarities to the real objects they are supposed to represent, *i.e.* because the differences are either not of interest or else so small that they do not lead to any observational discrepancies. Thus the apparent diameter of a fixed star for a terrestrial observer is so small that its replacement, in the calculation of the effects the star has upon Earth, by a mass supposedly located at a point cannot possibly lead to predictions that disagree with experimental results. The use of a fiction is therefore nothing but a picturesque way of expressing the fact that certain approximations or idealizations have been made and that one is aware of them. This remark at once refutes the claim which has sometimes been advanced that *all* the objects described by scientific theories (*e.g.* atoms, electrons, genes, electromagnetic fields, the space-time continuum of the general theory of relativity) are nothing but convenient fictions (*fictionalism*). For this claim cannot be applied to those theories whose approximate and idealized character has not yet been revealed by the discovery of their partial empirical inadequacy.—*P. K. F.*

FIELD (in mathematics): a generalization of a number system, studied in abstract algebra. A field is an algebraic structure wherein, between any two elements *a* and *b*, are defined two operations, $\oplus$ and $\otimes$, such that:

(1) $a \oplus b = b \oplus a$ (1′) $a \otimes b = b \otimes a$

(2) $a \oplus (b \oplus c)$ (2′) $a \otimes (b \otimes c) =$
$\quad = (a \oplus b) \oplus c$ $(a \otimes b) \otimes c$

(3) there exists a "zero" with respect to $\oplus$; that is, an element 0 such that $a \oplus 0 = a$

(3′) there exists a "unit" with respect to $\otimes$; that is, an element 1 such that $a \otimes 1 = a$

(4) for every *a*, there exists a "negative"; that is, an element which we denote by $(-a)$ and such that $a \oplus (-a) = 0$

(4′) If $a \neq 0$, then there exists an "inverse" a^{-1} such that $a \otimes (a^{-1}) = 1$

(5) The operations $\oplus$ and $\otimes$ are linked by the distributive law, $a \otimes (b \oplus c) = (a \otimes b) \oplus (a \otimes c)$.

The above axioms imply certain conclusions which we might anticipate; *e.g.* the "zero with respect to addition" and the "unit with respect to multiplication" are both unique. Moreover, if $a \otimes b = 0$, then either $a = 0$ or $b = 0$. However, we give "addition" and "multiplication" tables for a finite field of only three elements.

$\oplus$	0	1	2
0	0	1	2
1	1	2	0
2	2	0	1

$\otimes$	0	1	2
0	0	0	0
1	0	1	2
2	0	2	1

The operations $\oplus$ and $\otimes$ are *completely* defined by the above tables, and formally we need give no meaning nor interpretation to these operations. It suffices to check that the above system of symbols and operations verifies the necessary axioms to know that they constitute a field. In reality, however, this field arises when we take any two ordinary integers *a* and *b*, multiply or add them together in the usual sense of arithmetic, and then replace the result by the remainder obtained upon division by 3. For example, $2 \times 2 = 4$ in ordinary arithmetic, but when divided by 3 gives a remainder of 1. Hence $2 \times 2 = 1$ in our field of three elements, known usually as Z_3, or the "field of integers modulo three." See ALGEBRA, ABSTRACT.—*J. S.*

FIELD (in physics): a useful concept for describing forces or interactions between particles. Its development started with Newton. To explain the motion of the planets, he postulated a gravitational force between them and the Sun. The correctness of his explanation showed that it was possible to have forces between bodies not in contact with each other. In the subsequent development of mechanics and electricity, two competing ideas of forces acting at a distance were used. One considered the force as a direct interaction between the bodies involved. According to the other concept, the existence of one of the bodies alters all of space in such a way that other bodies in space will experience a force acting on them. This property of space, namely that bodies in it will experience a force, is called a *field*. These concepts, ACTION AT A DISTANCE and "field," were used interchangeably for a while, although in electricity and magnetism the field concept was simpler to apply.

The field idea was strengthened by the theory of relativity. The limitation that signals could not propagate faster than the speed of light meant that if two particles (*e.g.* a positron and an electron) were suddenly created, there could not be a force between them until some signal could traverse the distance between them. For action at a distance, one would expect the force between the bodies to appear immediately. One could, however, easily conceive that the field created by one particle propagates with the speed of light and that no force is felt by the second until the field reaches it. The use of the field concept becomes a virtual necessity whenever relativistic effects are of importance.

Further application of quantum theory to fields led to the following picture: There are many fields in nature, each characterized by a mass, a charge, and a spin. Associated with each field is a particle. Thus the photon is associated with the electromagnetic field, electrons and positrons with the electron field, protons and neutrons with the nucleon field, various mesons with mesic fields, and so on. These fields interact with one another. Forces between like particles are due to their interaction with another field. The electrostatic force between electrons is due to the interaction of each with the electromagnetic field, forces between nucleons are due to their interaction with the mesic fields, etc. The mechanism of the interaction in the case of electrons, as an example, is the following: Because of its interaction with the electromagnetic field, an electron emits a photon, which upon reabsorption by a second electron, produces a force between the particles. The self-absorption of a photon by the electron emitting it alters the electron's mass and charge. Since the interactions are always present, the charge and mass of any particle we measure is the one that incorporates the effects of all its interactions.

Although the field concept is undoubtedly correct, at present there are grave difficulties in a consistent mathematical description of relativistic quantum mechanical fields in interaction with others. See UNIFIED FIELD THEORY; ELECTRIC FIELD.—*S. Bo.*

FIELD EMISSION: the ejection of electrons by a metal in a strong electric field (of a gradient of the order of 10^9 volts/cm or higher). Since the metal emitting the electrons need not be heated, the process is also known as cold emission. Field emission cannot be explained in terms of classical physics, because the electrons do not have enough energy to surmount the POTENTIAL BARRIER at the surface of the metal. However, the phenomenon becomes intelligible in terms of quantum theory: because of the wave nature of electrons, they can "burrow" through the potential barrier in what is known as the TUNNEL EFFECT. As contrasted to THERMIONIC EMISSION, which is caused by heat, field emission is not commonly employed as a source of electrons, but is used in the study of catalysis, corrosion, and the adsorption of gases on the surface of metals. Field emission from the point of a fine metal needle produces a greatly enlarged image of the needle tip on a fluorescent screen. A device employing this technique is known as a field-emission microscope. A modification of this instrument, the field-ion microscope, uses a gas such as helium around the needle tip and has a reversed electric field, so that positive ions are emitted instead of electrons. These instruments, invented by E. W. Müller in 1937, magnify up to 1,000,000 diameters (see illustration facing page 1).

FIELD THEORY: a concept of theoretical physics. If with every point in space there is associated a certain physical quantity, then the whole set of quantities is said to be a field. The quantity may vary from point to point, like the decrease in air pressure related to an increase in altitude; and it may vary from instant to instant, like the variations in air pressure (waves) that constitute sound. Fields may be defined for a wide variety of quantities, *e.g.* for pressure, temperature, velocity of a fluid, and stress in an elastic solid. Field theory proper, however, refers to the use of fields in the study of special kinds of physical quantities. Examples of such quantities are magnetic force and electric force, both of which may extend not only over matter but also over empty space. Variation in intensity from point to point in a magnetic field may be shown by the familiar experiment of sprinkling iron filings on a sheet of paper held over a magnet. Variation from

Electric field surrounding two wires with currents that are flowing in opposite directions is mapped by grass-seed floating on the surface of a dish of water. (*Berenice Abbott*)

instant to instant in the magnetic field is related in a specific way to such variation in the electric field, and the two fields together are called the electromagnetic field. Field theory in the 19th cent. was concerned primarily with study of the electromagnetic field, including the variations in electric and magnetic field intensities (electromagnetic waves) that, depending on wavelength, constitute light, radio waves, and certain other kinds of radiation. Field theory in the mid-20th cent., however, is used primarily in the study of a related but different physical system: namely, photons, electrons, protons, and other elementary particles. In this use the field is *quantized.* By limiting the values that the amplitude of a wave may assume and by certain other maneuvers, the field is made to lose some characteristics usually associated with fields and to acquire other characteristics usually associated with particles. (See PARTICLE, ELEMENTARY; QUANTUM ELECTRODYNAMICS.)—*J. Tu.*

FIGURATE NUMBERS: numbers connected with certain geometric forms or figures. They were first studied by the Pythagoreans. Polygonal numbers are related to various regular polygons. They are the numbers of uniformly spaced dots that can be arranged in equilateral triangles, squares, and other regular polygons. Fig. 1 shows that the triangular num-

Fig. 1

bers are sums of arithmetical progressions. If there are n dots on a side of the exterior triangle, the total number of dots is $\frac{1}{2} n(n + 1)$. The square numbers have the form n^2, as shown by Fig. 2. Pentagonal numbers come from such arrangements as appear in Fig. 3. It can be shown that if the exterior pentagon has n dots on a side, the total number of dots is the

Fig. 2

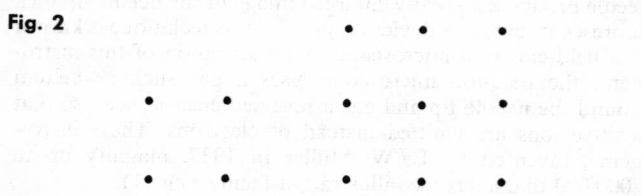

same as that in a square surmounted by an equilateral triangle, as in Fig. 4, the square having n dots on a side and the triangle $n - 1$. The total number of dots is therefore $n^2 +$

Fig. 3   **Fig. 4**

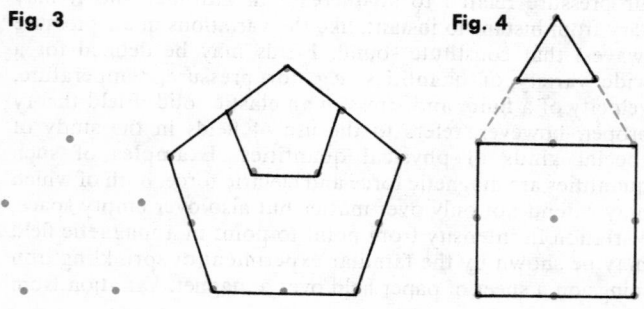

$\frac{1}{2} n(n - 1)$. Many theorems concerning polygonal numbers can be established by geometrical means.

Solid figurate numbers are associated with arrangements in polyhedral form. Among them are the pyramidal numbers, which relate to piling of round shot in pyramids.—*H. C.*

FILM, PHOTOGRAPHIC: a material with a sensitized coating used for making pictures. It consists structurally of two major parts: the support, which serves the purely mechanical function that its name implies, and the emulsion, which is spread evenly over the support and contains the photosensitive components. The use of glass for support has been giving way to the use of film, even in x-ray photography. Most support is now made of flexible plastic, usually cellulose acetate or acetate-propionate. This has largely replaced the once widely used but dangerously flammable cellulose nitrate. Film support is made in thicknesses ranging from 0.003 to 0.008 in. It must be clear and uniformly flat, and closely controlled with regard to flexibility.

The emulsion consists essentially of a very fine suspension of silver halide (*i.e.* compounds of silver with a HALOGEN), predominantly silver bromide, in gelatin. It also contains a variety of other materials added to control the working and processing properties of the film. Films differ primarily with regard to their speed (sensitivity to light) and color response (region of the spectrum to which they are sensitive). High-sensitivity or high-speed emulsions contain silver bromide together with a small amount of silver iodide. Silver chloride tends to make a slower emulsion. Size of the silver-halide grains in the emulsion also affects speed, larger grains tending to be faster.

Emulsion and film manufacture takes place in several stages, each requiring scrupulous cleanliness, care, and control. First the emulsion is formed, by reacting silver nitrate in dilute gelatin solution with the selected mixture of sodium halides. It is then ripened, or aged, at elevated temperature to modify the grain size; it is chilled, washed, remelted, and reripened. Additives for controlling film performance are usually introduced at this stage. Sulfur compounds such as alkylthiourea increase the film speed. Also added are hardeners such as chrome alum or formaldehyde to increase the mechanical strength of the gelatin, plasticizers such as glycerol, and spreading agents to facilitate spreading of the finished emulsion on the support. Anti-foggants (materials that prevent "fog," or development of grains that have not been exposed to light) and sensitizing dyes (which increase the sensitivity of the emulsion to varying regions of the spectrum) may also be introduced. The most common type of black-and-white film, panchromatic, is sensitized to respond to the full visible range of the spectrum, including the red end. Special sensitizers are used for infrared, ultraviolet, and x-ray film, and for nuclear-tracking emulsion film. Before receiving the emulsion, the support is coated with a very thin layer of fugitive dye which prevents back-reflection of light and blurring of the image. This anti-halation layer is removed by the developing solutions during processing of the exposed film. Finally, the emulsion coating is applied to the support, forming a layer about 5 to 50 microns thick; the finished film is then dried and packaged.

Special types of film, both color and black-and-white, of varying speeds and of varying sensitivity to different colors, are manufactured for special purposes. In one of the most widely used color-film processes the support is coated successively with a red-sensitive emulsion, a green-sensitive emulsion, a yellow filter layer, and finally a blue-sensitive emulsion. During development after exposure the color is formed in each layer by treatment with "couplers"—chemicals that react in the exposed areas to form the dye. See PHOTOGRAPHY.—*A. M. S.*

FILM, SHEETING, AND FOIL: In plastics, film and sheeting are terms used for any material that is cast or extruded into a thin, usually transparent or translucent, flexible membrane. The difference between the two terms depends primarily upon thickness; membranes under 10 mil (0.01 in.) thick are classed as film, while those over that gage are sheeting.

Packaging applications account for most of the use of film and sheeting, consuming nearly 700 million lb in 1960. Other industrial uses, primarily electrical insulation, fabric replacement, and surfacing applications, raised the total to close to a billion pounds. Plastic film and sheeting are now commercially produced from at least 11 classes of chemical compounds: cellulosics, polyesters, polyolefins, polyfluoro- and polychlorocarbons, polycarbonates, polyacrilates, polystyrenes, polyvinyl alcohols, polyamides, and rubber hydrochlorides.—*P. R. Le.*

Metal foils are metal sheets of 0.005-in. thickness or less, made by precision rolling mills, *e.g.* the Rohn mill, Steckel mill, and Sendzimir mill. Historically, foils have been made only from metals of the highest malleability and ductility; but new rolling methods have made possible the production of foil from even very hard metals and alloys. Most metal foil today is made from aluminum and aluminum alloys. Aluminum foil is moisture- and gas-proof, greaseproof, tasteless, odorless, and corrosion-resistant; it reflects heat, and is impervious to light. These qualities make aluminum foil useful in all kinds of food and tobacco packaging. Tin foil is also an excellent packaging material, but because it is more expensive has been replaced by aluminum foil in most applications. Lead foil is used for electrical condensers and general soldering; it is not used for food packaging, because in contact with water lead may dissolve and give off poisonous ions. Gold foil is used in dentistry, gilding, and decoration of dinnerware.—*E. H. H.*

FILTER, ELECTRIC: an electric circuit or device that acts selectively to permit or block the transmission of an electric signal, usually a current at a particular frequency. For example where an a-c circuit's INDUCTANCE (L), CAPACITANCE (C), and RESISTANCE (R) are connected in series, and the inductance and capacitance are each of a magnitude such that they cancel each other out, the circuit will be equivalent to one in which only resistance is present. In this circuit, the current is in phase with the voltage, and the current is at a maximum. Such a circuit is said to be resonant: its inductive reactance X_L ($= 2\pi f L$, where f equals frequency) is equal to its capacitive reactance X_C ($= \frac{1}{2}\pi fC$). (This can be seen from the equation $I = V/\sqrt{R^2 + (X_L - X_C)^2}$, where I is current and V is voltage.) Thus a circuit's inductance and capacitance can be chosen so that for a particular *frequency* there will be resonance. For a-c circuits where the inductance, capacitance, and resistance are connected in parallel, the circuit is resonant when the impedance Z (equal to $\sqrt{R^2 + (X_L - X_C)^2}$) is at a maximum value; thus the current is low. Filter circuits can be designed so that at one frequency the circuit acts as if certain of its elements were connected in *series* and resonant at that frequency; at another chosen frequency the circuit acts as if the elements were connected in *parallel* and resonant at that frequency. Thus at one frequency (when the circuit is series-resonant) the current is large and the signal passes; at another frequency (when the same circuit is parallel-resonant) the current is low and the signal is blocked. Filters are used in all types of electronic equipment. A familiar application is in radio circuits: the desired incoming signal is usually in a restricted frequency (*i.e.* the frequency of a particular radio

station) and a filter is designed to transmit that frequency and block all others. Filter circuits can be specifically designed to eliminate known sources of interference, *e.g.* frequencies produced by a nearby power-transmission line. —*A. L.*

FILTER, PHOTOGRAPHIC: a device used to modify the light falling on a subject or the light passing through the lens of a camera, its purpose being to achieve compatibility between the light source and film sensitivity, or to obtain a particular effect in the final result. Filters are commonly made of dyed gelatin, colored plastics, and glass. Thus a filter used over a light source to alter the spectral characteristics of the output may be a sheet of dyed gelatin or colored glass; a filter used over a camera lens may consist of one or more pieces of dyed gelatin inserted between two disks of clear glass which are mounted in a ring. Filters for specialized applications may be made of these materials or they may consist of containers of colored liquid. Classified according to usage, the most common types of filters are those for color correction, contrast, color-conversion or compensation, polarization, color-separation, and reduction of light intensity. *Correction filters* change the light reaching the film and thus change the film response so that recorded brightness values are approximately those seen by the eye. For example, orthochromatic and panchromatic materials have an excess blue sensitivity, but a yellow filter tends to correct this factor; or a yellowish-green filter, used with panchromatic materials, will give a better rendition of multicolored subjects such as flowers photographed in daylight or outdoor portraits against the sky. *Contrast filters* are used to lighten or darken a color of a subject, *i.e.* to obtain a difference in the brightness values of two colors which otherwise would appear the same in a black-and-white photograph. Either the tone contrasts can be rendered correctly or the color contrasts can be subdued or emphasized. For example, unfiltered red and green can appear to be the same tones of gray, but a filter can change one or the other so that contrasting gray tones are recorded;

Yellow filter, used for second photo of skyline, absorbed sunlight that had washed contrasts and natural textures out of first photo. (*Pierre Martinot*)

a red filter will lighten red and darken green. A filter will lighten objects of its own or neighboring colors and darken those farthest from it in the spectrum. Thus, a blue sky can be darkened, to contrast with clouds, by using a yellow filter, or a red filter if still greater contrast is desired. Atmospheric haze may be reduced with a very pale yellow or colorless ultraviolet-absorbing filter. *Color-conversion filters* are used with color films, especially when the film is being exposed with illumination for which it is not balanced, *e.g.* when exposing a daylight-type color film with artificial light. Yellow filters lower, and blue filters raise, the color temperature. Film manufacturers suggest filters necessary for making compensations for all combinations of films and light sources. Color-conversion filters are used to change the over-all color balance of a scene, *e.g.* to make the colors warmer or colder. *Polarizing filters,* made of glass or plastic, reduce light vibrating at one plane and are used chiefly to eliminate reflection, or, in some cases, to alter the tone of a blue sky, *e.g.* when the camera is aimed at right angles to the sun's rays. *Color-separation filters* are used in making color photographic prints and in several phases of photomechanical reproduction. Customarily a set of three filters—red, green, and blue—is used both to make color-separation negatives or positives for graphic processes and in certain color photofinishing operations. The exact colors reproduced depend on such factors as the type of film and color of printing light. A *neutral-density filter* transmits all colors and reduces the intensity of lighting without changing color values. Typical uses are to prevent over-exposure when using a large-aperture lens or when exposing high-speed film in open-sunlight locations such as a beach or desert. There are also a number of filters for specialized applications in photography and related fields, *e.g.* infrared filters for aerial and night photography and in several types of medical diagnosis and criminal investigation, and ultraviolet and narrow-band filters for research, as in chemical analysis by photolytic methods.—*M. B. K.*

FILTRATION, CHEMICAL: removal of solids from fluids by means of a porous medium which retains the solid but allows the fluid to pass through. Efforts have been made to develop a mathematical basis for filtration, but translating this theory into practice is difficult because of wide variation in the properties of particles to be filtered and variations in batches of

the same material. The almost limitless array of filter types cannot be broken down into broad categories that will include all known types. The simplest filter type, however, is a sand filter that consists of a sand-filled wooden box with a perforated bottom. Refinements include the use of pressure (or vacuum) to speed passage of the liquid, and use of paper or cloth (rather than sand) as the filter medium. Filtering rates can also be improved by the use of coagulants (ferrous or aluminum sulfate) which hydrolyze and form a precipitate to absorb finely suspended particles. Filter aids (*e.g.* diatomaceous earths) are frequently employed to improve filter efficiency. Still another standard device is the filter press, with two principal versions: the chamber press and the plate-and-frame filter, each consisting of a series of vertically suspended filter plates through which the solution to be filtered is forced horizontally. A third type is the rotary filter, consisting of a drum rotating in a trough of the material being filtered. The outside of the drum is divided into several individual filtering sections: a filtering section entering the trough comes under vacuum as it is submerged and accumulates a cake of the solid particles; this cake is removed after the filter section emerges. The filtrate is sent to receiving tanks. This rotary device has the advantage of permitting continuous operation.—*D. P. B.*

FINDEISEN, THEODOR ROBERT WALTER, 1909–   , German meteorologist; b. Hamburg. His research included studies of atmospheric ice-particle formation, supersaturated water vapor in clouds and condensation nuclei, size and number of water drops in fog, humidity measurements, and electrical phenomena associated with clouds. He vanished, May 1945, in Prague.—*D. H. D. R.*

FIORD: the lower part of a valley or mountain canyon which was eroded to a depth below present sea level by a glacier which followed this course to the sea. In canyon fiords, walls rise abruptly a few hundred or even a few thousand feet from the water's edge. Along the magnificently glaciated Norwegian coast, some fiords are more than 100 mi long. Other splendid examples may be seen along the coasts of NE Labrador, British Columbia and Alaska, Chile and Patagonia, and New Zealand. When glaciers were at their last major climax, about 20,000 or 25,000 yr ago, sea level was about 250 ft lower than now. Its rise since accounts for some of the coastline embayments, but many of these were eroded by ice action considerably below this minimum sea level. At the lower end of fiords, and below sea level, there is commonly a lip beyond which and behind which the water deepens. Lips may be in part deposits left by receding glaciers. Most are believed to have resulted from up-valley erosion, which is more intensive than erosion at the terminus, where the glacier is relatively thin.—*N. E. A. H.*

FIRE: Fire results from the rapid combination of oxygen with combustible materials, releasing energy as heat and light. The first use of fire was a discovery; the contriving of devices for producing it were inventions. Proto-humans may have discovered the potentialities of naturally caused fires. The oldest known association of charcoal with remains of man (Peking man, Middle Pleistocene epoch) is not conclusive evidence that fires were intentionally kindled. Somewhat later the hearths of Neanderthal man indicate effective control, which

Singlefiord, on northern Norwegian coast, is one of many river valleys that were gouged deeply by ice during recent glacial periods, then flooded by rising sea waters as great ice sheets melted. (*Swedish National Travel Office*)

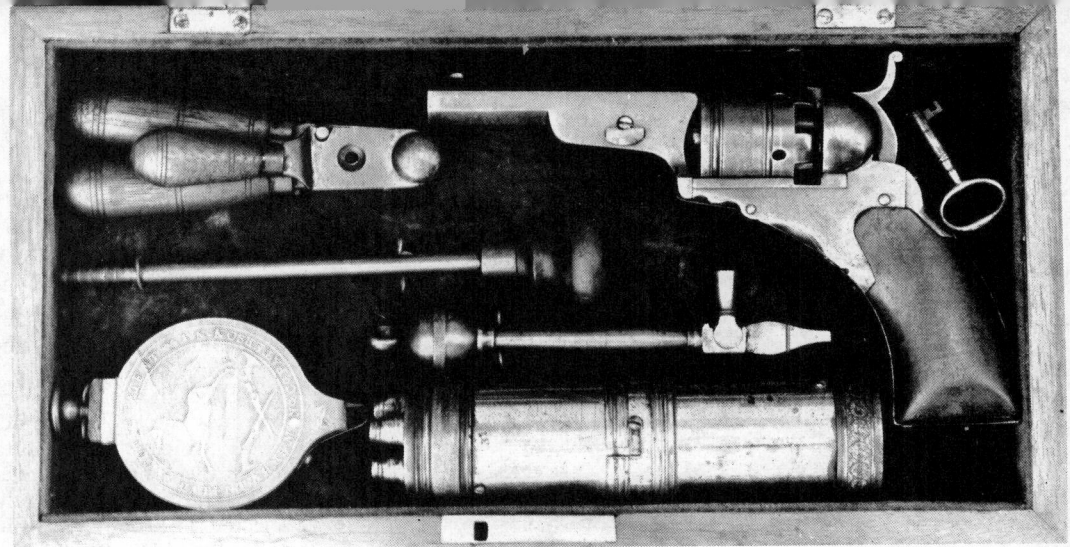

Small arm: 28-cal. "Baby Paterson" pocket revolver was produced at Samuel Colt's factory, founded 1836, at Paterson, N. J. Case contains bullet mold, cleaning rod, and percussion-cap magazine or dispenser (left, top to bottom), as well as a combination loading lever, nipple wrench, screw driver, and nipple-cleaning wire, and a combination powder and bullet flask (middle, under barrel). Concealed folding trigger snapped out when pistol was fully cocked. (*Harry C. Knode & Co.*)

was certainly established in Upper Paleolithic (Late Pleistocene) times. Use of fire led to a more complex life. Fire furnished warmth and light, permitted migration into inhospitable regions, gave protection against beasts, increased the range of usable foodstuffs, and provided means of felling trees, hollowing vessels, and shaping materials. Heat, originally furnished by fire alone, became basic to many technical processes. Methods of making fire by friction, known to recent primitive peoples, were probably those of antiquity. The fire-drill is most common (a wooden rod twirled between the palms on a wooden base to form glowing wood dust); less common are the fire-plough (a stick rubbed in a groove in the base) and the fire-saw (a rattan strip sawed across the base). Striking sparks with steel and flint dates from the Iron Age—3,000 to 4,000 years ago in the Near East. The chemical MATCH was invented about 1805.

The first naturalistic explanations of fire were attempted by Greek philosophers. Heraclitus (6th cent. B. C.) considered fire the primal element; Empedocles (5th cent. B. C.) named it one of the four constituents of matter, with earth, air, and water. The phlogiston theory of the late 17th cent. held that heat is an invisible fluid or principle of all matter. A century later Antoine Lavoisier and others showed that burning is oxidation.—*L. S.*

FIREARM: any weapon consisting of a cylinder from which a projectile is discharged by means of an explosive. The sudden expansion of gases from the explosion drives the projectile out of the cylinder.

Heavy Arms: Firearms followed the invention of GUNPOWDER, attributed to the Chinese (*c.* 600 B. C.). The first cannon was a deep iron bucket into which a powder charge was poured; a round stone was put on top of this and the charge was fired by inserting a red-hot wire into the powder through a small touch-hole in the bottom. The explosion hurled the stone in a high arc for some distance. By the early 14th cent., firearms were being used in Europe, and cannon played a part during sieges in the Hundred Years' War. By now the cannon had become a long tube, usually cast of iron or brass (although wooden barrels reinforced by metal hoops or by rope wound around them were sometimes used). At first the barrel was fastened to a wooden platform by metal straps; later it was fastened to a wheeled carriage. Deflection was obtained by traversing the carriage, elevation by raising or depressing the barrel with quoins or wedges under the breech. Early cannon were used chiefly to batter the walls of castles or fortresses, and when the great lords were thus no longer impregnable in their moated keeps, feudalism disappeared.

Modern artillery dates from the time when the rifled barrel superseded the smooth-bore cannon; this was in the era of

the U. S. Civil War. The spiral grooves gave the projectile a gyroscopic spinning motion for greater accuracy and effective range. The modern cannon, instead of being loaded from the muzzle, is a breech-loader, which makes for quicker, handier loading, and permits the use of fixed (preassembled) ammunition, like the rifle cartridge, in the smaller calibers. The modern fixed-carriage gun is used on warships, forts, and aircraft, and for antiaircraft defense. The mobile cannon may be a pack-gun, carried dismantled on mule-back, or a field gun, on a wheeled carriage drawn by horses, trucks, or tractors; it may also be mounted in a tank or be self-propelled on a truck or tractor chassis. The recoilless cannon has no carriage and may be carried by men. The caliber of the modern cannon runs from the 40-mm rapid-fire gun to the huge 16-in. rifle of the battleship. There are long-barreled, long-range guns, howitzers with shorter barrels for shorter ranges, mortars with very short barrels for high-arc plunging fire, and guided missiles fired from launchers.

A great improvement in cannon was the invention of the recoil mechanism, which takes up the shock of the discharge by means of plungers in oil-filled cylinders. Still another improvement was the automatic aiming device; fire-control stations could figure ranges by means of elaborate calculating machines. With the invention of RADAR in World War II, cannon could be aimed and fired at targets invisible because of distance, bad weather, or darkness.

Light Arms: The hand gun, light enough to be carried by the unarmored foot soldier, put him on equal terms with the mailed knight, and made knighthood and armor obsolete. The first hand gun was simply a tiny cannon mounted on the end of a stick. Probably the first true musket was the hackbut, which had a metal barrel fitted to a wooden stock; it was about 3 ft long and weighed 10 lb, and it fired a ¾-in. ball about 100 yd. Around 1540 the harquebus (a corruption of "hackbut") became the most popular weapon. From 6 to 7 ft long, weighing 40 to 50 lb, with a range of 200 yd, it had to be rested on a forked stick for aiming.

Until modern times, ignition of the explosive was the great problem. A hot wire had always to be red-hot—an awkward requirement on the battlefield. The matchlock was an improvement; its fuse, made of hemp soaked in saltpeter, would smolder for hours while fastened to one end of an arm or trigger called a serpentine. When the trigger was pulled, the smoldering fuse touched the powder in the priming pan and (through a small hole in the barrel) set off the main charge. Rain, of course, put the matchlock out of business. But then came the wheel lock, on which a small steel wheel (its rim entered the priming pan) was caused to rotate by a spring and, when touched by flint or pyrites held in the jaws of the hammer, made sparks to ignite the primer charge. Next came

Artillery of 17th cent.: Print from *La pratique de la guerre* (1636) showed "how mortars must be fired." Gunner was required to light both shell fuse and propelling charge simultaneously, using a different hand for each. (*N. Y. Public Library*)

the flintlock, the standard for centuries: in this a piece of flint held between the jaws of the hammer struck a steel L-shaped hinged cover over the priming charge and made sparks, at the same time driving back the cover to let the sparks ignite the powder. But priming a gun was slow, and by 1835 the flintlock had given way to the percussion cap, which fitted over a nipple on the barrel. When the hammer struck the copper cap, the detonating compound in the cap exploded. This sent a flame down the nipple hole to set off the charge in the barrel. The next important improvements were the rifled barrel and breech loading. By the end of the Civil War only shotguns, which were designed to fire a scattered charge of small shot, were smooth-bored. Breech loading had been tried for centuries, even with cannon, but until the early 19th cent. every breechblock that was built leaked so much gas that the gun lost power and range. Then the makers of the Sharp's rifle (1848) and others solved the problem, and the breechloader at once became popular. Various types of repeating firearms had been tried for centuries but they were expensive and not very reliable. In the late 1840s the metallic cartridge was invented, with a brass casing to hold the pointed bullet, the powder charge, and the percussion cap all in one package. The metal cartridge in turn made possible the repeating rifle, in which the bullets were stored in a tube in the butt, or under the barrel, and loaded by a lever action; later they were held in clips in a chamber under the breech.

In the U. S. A. the repeating rifle tamed the West. The Plains Indians might for years have defied troops armed only with single-shot rifles, but they could not stand up to the 7- or 8-shot Sharp's and Spencer repeaters, or the Henry (later Winchester) 15-shot repeater. Next came the machine gun, operated by recoil or gas and fed by bullets in clips or belts; it was followed by automatic rifles, pistols, and small cannon. The machine gun doomed the cavalry saber charge and made obsolete the close-order infantry bayonet charge.

For centuries the pistol was used mostly by cavalrymen, who needed one hand for their reins. It was heavy, clumsy, and hard to load. Then in 1836 Samuel Colt invented the first practical revolver; this had a single barrel in front of a revolving cylinder which contained the percussion caps, powder, and bullets. Colt's pistols were later produced by machine tools; therefore, they could be supplied in large numbers at comparatively cheap prices, and with interchangeable parts requiring a minimum of hand fitting. The revolver made the sword obsolete as a weapon for personal protec-

tion; then after many years the revolver was superseded, for some purposes, by the automatic pistol, in which the bullets were not loaded separately into the chambers of a cylinder, but rather were stored in a clip fitted into the grip of the pistol and were brought up as needed by a spring underneath. See also BALLISTICS; EXPLOSIVE.—*W. B.*

FIRE EXTINGUISHER: a device operated either manually or mechanically to project chemical agents capable of smothering a fire. Most large city fires are extinguished by the cooling effect of plain water propelled through a hose by a fire engine. The most common portable extinguisher contains sodium bicarbonate solution and sulfuric acid, which react when the container is inverted: carbon-dioxide gas is generated and an aqueous solution of the reaction products is ejected. Carbon tetrachloride sprayed from a portable cylinder is also effective, providing a heavy vapor blanket, but it should not be used in confined spaces because it is decomposed by heat to *phosgene,* which is toxic. Electrical fires are preferably extinguished by means of carbon-dioxide gas from a suitable pressure cylinder, since carbon dioxide, unlike water, does not conduct electricity. Numerous chemical systems are commercially available which propel foamy mixtures to smother fires, especially oil fires, which are not easily extinguished by water alone.—*Ru. M.*

FISCHER, EMIL, 1852–1919, German chemist; b. Euskirchen. Phenylhydrazine, which he discovered in 1875, became a valuable reagent in his later studies of carbohydrates. For his syntheses in the groups of sugars and purines he received the Nobel prize, 1902. By analysis and synthesis he showed that proteins are composed of amino acids in characteristic patterns and that the hydrolyzable tannins are carbohydrate compounds (glycosides). From his excursions into physiology came the sedative veronal, a barbiturate. His autobiography appeared posthumously (1922). He wrote on the preparation of organic materials in his *Anleitung zur Darstellung organischer Präparate* (1901). A collection of his papers, *Untersuchungen über Kohlenhydrate und Fermente,* was published 1909. Other collections appeared posthumously. He was a fellow of the Royal Society.—*E. F.*

FISCHER, HANS, 1881–1945, German chemist; b. Höchst, near Frankfurt-am-Main. The pigments of the green leaf (chlorophyll) and of blood (hemin) were the main subjects of his work. For his researches into the constitution of hemin and chlorophyll, especially for his synthesis of hemin, he received the 1930 Nobel prize. In certain pigments of feathers he discovered analogous chemical structures, with copper in place of the iron of hemin.—*E. F.*

FISCHER-TROPSCH PROCESS: any one of several processes for producing liquid hydrocarbons or their oxygenated derivatives from water gas or other mixtures of carbon monoxide and hydrogen. The desulfurized gas mixture is catalytically converted (typically at 200°C and 20 atm) into a synthetic oil which is a base material for the manufacture of gasoline, diesel fuel, fatty acids, waxes, and detergents. Catalyst, temperature, and pressure of the conversion depend on the main end-product desired. The process was originated in Germany by Franz Fischer (1877–1947) and Hans Tropsch (1889–1935), in 1923, when experiments were started to supply motor fuel from native base materials such as coal, coke, peat, and lignite.—*R. J. F.*

FISH: a cold-blooded vertebrate animal that lives in water, has a two-chambered heart, breathes by means of gills, and propels itself by muscular movements of the tail or by the action of paired fins. The 15,000 different kinds (species) of modern fishes and 10,000 kinds of fossil fishes represent the lowest group of vertebrates on the evolutionary scale. All depths in oceans and fresh water throughout the world are home to fishes. The study of fishes is called ichthyology (Greek *ichthys,* "fish"). Fishes are divided into three broad groups.

Jawless Fishes (class Cyclostomata): These lack jaws, paired fins, and scales. They are the round-mouthed hagfishes, slime eels, and lampreys. Hagfishes and slime eels live only in the sea, where they scavenge for sick or dead fishes. Often they damage fish caught on lines or in nets before fishermen arrive to collect their catch. These scavengers rasp their way into the bodies of victims and feed on the blood or whatever flesh they can liquefy with their strongly digestive saliva.

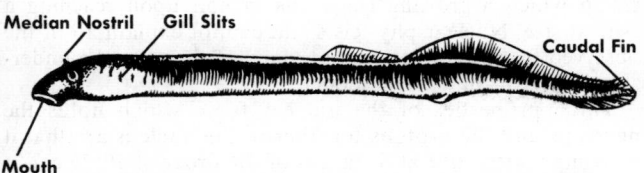

Lamprey has a poorly defined head, a suction-disk mouth, and seven circular gill slits. In the adult fish, vertebrae made up of cartilage develop around the notochord. (*After Kenoyer*)

Lampreys develop in fresh water for a long time—three to seven years. All through larval life they are blind, living in U-shaped burrows in sandy or muddy bottoms and filtering from the water food particles of minute size. When they become adult, acquiring eyes, horny teeth in the mouth, and reproductive organs, some kinds of lampreys feed no more; they die soon after mating. Other lampreys, as adults, become destructive parasites on fishes. Holding to a victim with the mouth as a suction cup, the lamprey rasps through the skin with its teeth and floods the wound with a digestive saliva, meanwhile breathing through its many pairs of gill openings. Sea lampreys usually migrate to the ocean when ready to attack fishes, returning to fresh water in mating season, but some sea lampreys are landlocked in the Great Lakes and have become adapted to feeding on fishes there; recently they spread through ship canals into the upper Great Lakes and ruined the fisheries industry by destroying all fishes of commercial importance.

Sharks and Rays (class Chondrichthyes): These are almost all predatory fishes; they have a ventral mouth, strong jaws, a series of gill openings, and paired fins. Their skeleton remains completely cartilaginous, with no true bone. Usually their skin is rough, with sharp-pointed scales that resemble teeth in having a pulp cavity within. Except for a few sharks in fresh water (most notably in Lake Nicaragua and the Ganges River), all of these fishes are marine.

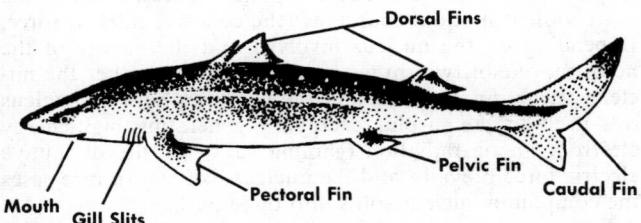

Dogfish is a small shark up to 3 ft in length. Like other sharks, it has a ventral mouth with jaws and a cartilaginous skeleton. Skin is covered with scales. (*After Kenoyer*)

Sharks have a spindle-shaped body and swim by vigorous movements of the tail. The largest sharks, measuring as much as 40 ft long and weighing 2,500 lb, include the harmless whale shark and basking shark, which swim close to the ocean surface and filter out small plankton plants and animals as food, and the dreaded man-eater ("white shark"), which normally relies on catching large fishes but sometimes attacks humans. Smaller sharks may attack swimmers, too, but usually eat only fishes, squids, and crabs.

Rays and skates have a flattened body, extended greatly to the sides by a front pair of fins, with which they propel themselves by graceful movements as though flying through the water. The tail, long and slender, in some species is armed near the base with one or more special spines, which account for the name "sting ray." Most of these creatures glide along the bottom, grinding up in their jaws whatever shellfish they can get. A few, such as the giant devil ray, which reaches a width of 22 ft and a weight of 3,500 lb, swim near the surface of warmer seas, catching small pelagic animals.

Bony Fishes (class Osteichthyes): These fishes have at least some bony plates covering the skull and usually possess a completely bony skeleton. Most bony fishes are covered with solid bony scales, which may be rhomboidal plates with an enamel covering, fitting together like armor, or they may lack the enamel and overlap like shingles. The rhomboidal plates are characteristic of "ganoid fishes" such as the sturgeon and the gar. Most fishes possess overlapping scales. Scales of tarpons can be as much as 2 in. in diameter. Often the age of a fish can be learned from examining the pattern of concentric growth rings in its scales.

Most bony fishes live in the ocean and stay there. A smaller number of kinds are equally restricted to fresh water. But some fishes habitually migrate from one habitat to the other as mating season approaches. Eels, which achieve most of their growth in fresh water, swim downstream and travel thousands of miles to breeding places deep in the sea. Salmon, shad, smelt, and alewives go in the opposite direction—away from salt water into brackish estuaries or flowing rivers —to mate and lay their eggs. The giant tarpon, as much as 8 ft long and 315 lb in weight, seeks out nursery shallows along tropical coasts. Trout, which live entirely in fresh water, go from lakes into rapid rivers to lay their eggs. Sometimes they choose sites close to spawning grounds of salmon that have come from thousands of miles out at sea. Knowledge gained from recovery of individual fish that were tagged when young makes it clear that many of these creatures return from great distances to the same tributary of the identical river in which they hatched (see MIGRATION).

The large group to which minnows belong is well represented in both oceanic and fresh waters. Both habitats are home to catfishes, which have sensory feelers around the mouth, but no scales in the skin. Carp, of which goldfishes are special varieties, tolerate considerable salinity and find food in the bottom of very turbid water. Suckers feed in the same way. Electric eels in the Amazon River, however, use their internal batteries to produce shocking currents in adjacent water, stunning small fishes upon which they prey (see BIOELECTRICITY). Guppies and many tropical fishes are members of this same group. The bass, the freshwater perch, and the tropical angelfish belong to a group represented in the oceans by the handsomely marked mackerel, the meaty tuna, and the predatory barracuda. Fishes of this type include many of great value as food, as well as species that provide entertainment for sports fishermen.

Variety in the form and habits of fishes is almost endless. Some, such as the 2-in. lanternfishes of the ocean depths, carry rows of luminous spots on their sides. Others, such as

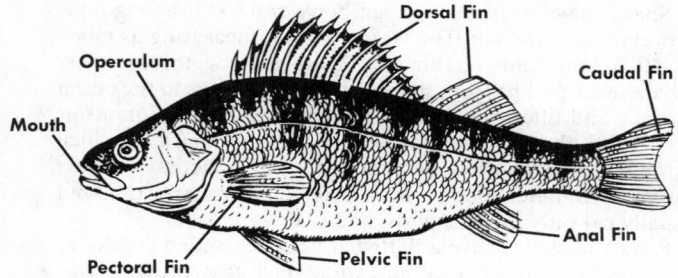

External structures of a bony fish (perch). (*After Kenoyer*)

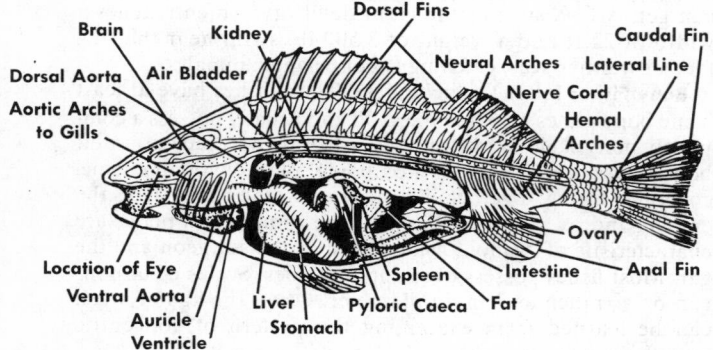

Internal structures of a bony fish (perch). (*After Kenoyer*)

the flounders and angler fishes, lie on the bottom and wait for small fishes to come within reach; flounders adjust their color pattern to match the bottom and thus gain security through camouflage; angler fishes dangle above their mouths a wriggling lure at the end of a long flexible spine projecting from the head, and snap up any minnow that comes to investigate. The shark-sucker (remora) uses its modified dorsal fin as a suction cup with which to cling to the underside of a shark or a sea turtle; it rides along as a passenger until it comes close to a school of small fishes, then darts away from its carrier to get a meal. Flying fishes leap from the water and glide on outstretched front fins while trying to escape from pursuers. Pipefishes and sea horses balance themselves vertically by rapid movements of their fins while sucking in minute crustaceans among the seaweed beds where they live. Lungfishes, in rivers of the southern hemisphere, wall themselves up in mud cells during the annual dry season and breathe air by means of lunglike air bladders connected to the mouth. Probably many equally remarkable fishes remain to be discovered in the deep sea. A few years ago a 5-ft lobe-fin fish was captured off the east coast of South Africa and found to represent an order (the coelacanths) that had been regarded as extinct for 75 million yr. See Color Plates 42 and 43.—*L. and M. M.*

FISSION: in biology, division of a single-celled organism into two equal daughter cells (binary fission) or into many cells (multiple fission). It occurs in asexual REPRODUCTION of bacteria, protozoans, and some algae and fungi.—*L. and M. M.*

FISSION, NUCLEAR: the property, exhibited by nuclei of a few heavy metals, of splitting in half under certain conditions. The phenomenon was discovered unexpectedly in 1938 by Otto Hahn and F. Strassmann in Germany. At that time, it

was known that all atomic nuclei consist of protons and neutrons (collectively called nucleons) in varying numbers, and that the element uranium is the heaviest of all. It was also known that neutrons can be ejected from some nuclei by artificial means, and that these neutrons, in turn, make excellent projectiles for penetrating other nuclei. Nuclear scientists of that time expected that by adding another neutron to uranium, they could produce still heavier nuclei; and, indeed, these so-called transuranic elements were produced. But Hahn and Strassmann demonstrated that nuclei approximately half the size of uranium nuclei also were produced! Immediately thereafter, Lise Meitner and O. R. Frisch correctly attributed the lighter nuclei to the splitting of the bombarded uranium nuclei. They named the phenomenon "fission" because of its analogy to the biological fission process in which a growing cell splits in half upon reaching a critical size. Nuclear physicists still cannot explain all of the observed features of fission, but many of these can be understood in terms of a crude model.

Three properties of the nuclear force which holds the neutrons and the protons together in the nucleus are that it is strongly attractive at distances of the order of 10^{-13} cm, it vanishes for larger separations, and it becomes repulsive for smaller ones. Thus, each nucleon is held at a fixed distance from its closest neighbors, just as a group of balls might be held in a pattern by a system of stiff rods. But the number of "balls," or nucleons, that can be held in the system is limited. Protons are electrically charged; each has one unit of positive charge, and since like charges repel, they tend to disrupt the nucleus. Furthermore, since electrical force is not limited in range, each proton feels a repulsive force from every other proton. Thus, a proton at the surface of a nucleus is attracted toward the interior by a force proportional to the number of its neighboring nucleons (which number would be the same for a medium or heavy nucleus), but it is repelled by a force which is proportional to the *total* number of protons in the entire nucleus. Obviously, then, the electrical force sets an upper limit to the number of protons that can be packed into a nucleus.

The maximum allowable number of neutrons is set by a fourth property of the nuclear force, called the symmetry effect. Nuclei containing an excess of either protons or neutrons become unstable as the imbalance increases. If the neutron excess becomes too large, a neutron spontaneously decays into a proton plus other particles. The largest, completely stable nucleus is an isotope of lead, lead^{208}. It has 82 protons and 126 neutrons. Since uranium nuclei have too many protons for complete stability, they eject tightly bound nuclear sub-assemblies called alpha particles, each consisting of two protons and two neutrons. If a neutron enters a uranium nucleus, it rapidly shares its energy with all the nucleons, and thus the instability of the nucleus is increased. The additional energy imparted to the surface protons makes their equilibrium still more precarious, and the surface undergoes oscillatory distortions as the electrical repulsive forces, aided by the more violent motion, counteract the cohesive nuclear force. Depending on the nucleus involved and the energy of the neutron, one of two things usually happens: either the nuclear attraction prevails, and the resulting heavier nucleus rids itself of the surplus energy by generating high-energy electromagnetic radiation (gamma rays); or the disruptive electric force prevails, and the nucleus fissions. In rare cases the compound nucleus splits into three parts.

Fission can be triggered by bombarding the nucleus with gamma rays or high-energy charged particles or neutrons. Some elements lighter than uranium can be made to fission by bombardment with very high-energy particles. At the other extreme, certain of the transuranic nuclei are so unstable that they readily fission spontaneously. Once the nucleus breaks up, the fragments are repelled by a strong repulsive electrical force arising from their large positive charges. As a result, the fragments fly apart with tremendous speed, but the energy supplied by a bombarding neutron only triggers the fission. The main source of the kinetic energy of the fragments is the electric potential energy associated with the packing of the protons into the small volume of the nucleus (see ELECTRIC POTENTIAL). This is analogous to the potential energy residing on a condenser plate when electrical charges of the same sign are brought together on it. The large kinetic energy of the fission fragments is what makes nuclear fission of so much practicable interest. The fragments collide with neighboring atoms, speeding them up, thereby heating the environment. This is how heat is produced in a reactor.

Besides their energy of motion, the fission fragments are also in a highly excited state internally. In each fragment the neutrons and protons rearrange themselves into the configurations appropriate to medium-weight nuclei. By the time the reshuffling has been completed, the fragments have generated more electromagnetic radiation (gamma rays); some of the excess neutrons have decayed into protons and a few have been ejected from the fragments. From a practical point of view, the last is the most important result of the reshuffling, because these ejected neutrons are then available to induce fissions in other uranium nuclei and support a CHAIN REACTION. Without the chain reaction, nuclear fission would today be only a laboratory curiosity, and we should not be confronted with the problems and opportunities of our atomic age.—S. K.

FISSION PRODUCTS: the atomic "fragments" that result when atoms are split in a CHAIN REACTION. The splitting of a large or heavy atomic nucleus, e.g. that of uranium, results in the liberation of free neutrons and gamma radiation, and leaves shattered nuclear "by-products," which are the nuclei of smaller atoms. Generally, in the case of uranium^{235} fission, these smaller atoms are in the 85-95 and 130-150 nucleon ranges. Among them are krypton^{85}, strontium^{90}, barium^{140}, and promethium^{147}. Almost all of these fragments are themselves radioactive. See FISSION, NUCLEAR.—A. R. G.

FITTIG, RUDOLF, 1835-1910, German chemist; b. Hamburg. An editor of *Annalen der Chemie,* 1895-1910, he published with his students about 400 papers that greatly influenced organic chemistry. Best known for the general method (which bears his name) by which aryl halides react in ether with sodium to produce hydrocarbons, he also reported the discovery of the pinacone reaction, diphenyl, and isophthalic acid, and produced cumerone, diacetyl, and phenanthrene. Fittig clarified the relationships and structure of many organic compounds.—V. B.

FJORD: see FIORD.

FJØRTOFT, RAGNAR, 1913-   , Norwegian meteorologist; b. Olso. Director of the Norwegian Meteorological Institute from 1955 and former Professor of Meteorology, Univ. of Copenhagen, he has also worked for extended periods at the Institute for Advanced Studies, Princeton, N. J., at the Univ. of Chicago, and at the Univ. of California, Los Angeles. He has written a number of highly original papers on theoretical meteorology, fluid motion, stability criteria, and numerical weather prediction. In his paper "On the Use of Space-Smoothing in Physical Weather Prediction" (1955) an important method of graphical integration of the equations of fluid motion is developed.—S. P.

FLAGELLUM: a long, whiplike, living cellular extension found in certain PROTOZOANS. Commonly only one or a few are present on a single protozoan, but some species have abundant flagella. Flailing or lashing movements of the flagella produce locomotion.—R. P.

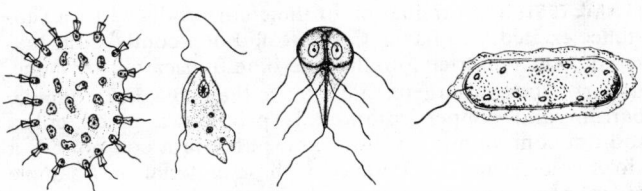

Various types of flagella on protozoans are diagramed above. Flagella may be used for locomotion or for obtaining food.

FLAME: a luminous mass of burning gas or vapor. A typical flame in which the gas or volatilizing fuel issues from a narrow source before igniting, e.g. a candle flame or Bunsen-burner flame, consists of three zones: (1) an inner, relatively cool, nonluminous zone; (2) a middle zone in which the vapor is actively combining with oxygen; (3) an outer zone in which combustion is essentially complete. The yellow or white luminosity of ordinary flames formed by burning hydrocarbons results from thermal decomposition or cracking of the vapor before combustion is complete. This cracking forms solid soot particles, which become hot enough to glow brightly before they are transformed into the much less luminous gaseous combustion products. Burners designed to feed an excess of air into the flame, e.g. kitchen gas burners or gasoline blowtorches, produce blue flames of very low luminosity. Flames used as a medium for carrying out high-temperature chemical reactions are regulated to promote oxidation or reduction, as desired, by adjusting the relative amounts of fuel gas (reducing agent) and air or oxygen (oxidizing agent) entering the BURNER.—A. M. S.

FLAMEPROOFING: the treatment of textile fabrics, paper, or other normally flammable fibrous materials to make them resistant to burning. Usually applied to cellulosic material such as cotton, flameproofing treatments cannot prevent the material's eventual destruction when exposed to continuous fire. An effectively flameproofed material, however, will tend to char in a fire rather than to be consumed, and will not continue to burn after the igniting fire has been removed. Most of the standard tests for flame resistance are based on measurements of these two effects.

All flameproofing processes involve the addition of a relatively large amount (about 10 to 50%) of the effective flameproofing ingredient to the fabric. The so-called *non-durable treatments* are used on indoor non-apparel fabrics, e.g. theater, hotel, and restaurant draperies and decorations. These neither need nor exhibit resistance to weathering or water-leaching. They employ a very limited group of water-soluble inorganic salts, particularly borates and borax, ammonium phosphates, and sulfamates. The most effective *durable treatments,* for use on outdoor non-apparel fabrics such as tentage, are based on antimony oxide suspended in highly chlorinated paraffin wax. Much progress has been made recently in the development of *durable wash-resistant* flameproofing agents for apparel, certain phosphonium compounds and phosphine oxides having proved to be very effective.

Flameproofing agents exert their effect by both physical and chemical mechanisms. Some agents decompose to form a glassy coating over the fabric, and emit clouds of non-combustible flame-smothering gas. The more effective agents catalyze breakdown of the heated cellulose into carbon and water vapor, thereby minimizing the formation of volatile tarry material, which is the major flame-propagating product of the combustion.—*A. M. S.*

FLAME TEST: an examination of the color produced by a substance excited by a flame. Certain solid non-combustible materials, when inserted into the pale-blue Bunsen burner flame, impart a strong characteristic color to the flame. For example, barium and copper compounds produce a green color, sodium compounds a yellow, and potassium compounds a violet color. Thus the presence of these materials in a sample of unknown composition can be detected by inserting the sample in the flame and noting the color. See Color Plate 46.—*A. M. S.*

FLAMSTEED, JOHN, 1646–1719, English astronomer; b. Denby, near Derby. His essay on the true and apparent diameters of the planets (1673) furnished data for Newton's third book of the *Principia*. Flamsteed began systematic observations in 1689, and these observations as well as the Greenwich star catalog were published posthumously (1725) as *Historia coelestis britannica*. He was the first Astronomer Royal of the Greenwich Observatory, established by Charles II in 1675, and was a fellow of the Royal Society.—*S. Bo.*

John Flamsteed
(U. S. Navy)

FLASH POINT: the temperature at which an inflammable material first gives off a flash of flame in air. By contrast, *fire point* is the temperature at which an inflammable material will give off sufficient vapor to burn continuously. Several different devices have been standardized for determining both flash and fire points, and are used for specification purposes on inflammable substances.—*R. J. F.*

FLAVIN NUCLEOTIDES: in biochemistry, a class of compounds involved in cellular oxidation reactions. Combined with certain enzymes to form *flavoproteins,* they function as oxidizers by accepting hydrogen ions. The flavin nucleotide serves as a coenzyme. Two flavin nucleotides are known: flavin mononucleotide (FMN) and flavin adenine dinucleotide (FAD). FMN consists of phosphate, ribitol, and dimethylisoalloxazine; it conforms to the general pattern of nucleotides, although its carbohydrate group is a sugar alcohol, not a true sugar. Minus its phosphate group, FMN becomes riboflavin (vitamin B_2). FAD consists of adenine, ribose, two phosphates, ribitol, and dimethylisoalloxazine. In both FMN and FAD it is the dimethylisoalloxazine group that is active in hydrogen-ion transfer. Certain flavoproteins (FP) can react with the reduced form of Coenzymes I or II, which they reoxidize as follows:

$$DPNH_2 \text{ (or } TPNH_2) + FP \rightleftharpoons DPN \text{ (or } TPN) + FPH_2$$

| (reduced coenzyme) | (oxidized coenzyme) | (reduced flavoprotein) |

The further reaction of FPH_2 is discussed under HYDROGEN TRANSPORT. Other flavoproteins, *e.g.* succinic dehydrogenase, can react directly with substrates rather than with DPN or TPN. See also NUCLEOTIDES; PYRIDINE NUCLEOTIDES.

FLAVOR: see TASTE AND SMELL.

FLEMING, SIR ALEXANDER, 1881–1955, British bacteriologist; b. Lochfield, Scotland. His research was concerned with the study of human blood and of antiseptics. In 1922 he discovered lysozyme, a substance in human tears "which is capable of rapidly dissolving certain bacteria." In 1928 he discovered penicillin in a mold contaminating a bacteria culture. For the discovery of penicillin and its therapeutic effect in the cure of different infectious maladies, Fleming, E. B. Chain, and H. W. Florey shared the Nobel prize, 1945. He was a fellow of the Royal Society.—*D. H. D. R.*

FLEMING, SIR JOHN AMBROSE, 1849–1945, English electrical engineer; b. Lancaster. His research included work on transformers, high-voltage transmission, low-temperature research on electric and magnetic properties (with J. Dewar), and radio. Fleming's paper "On the Conversion of Electric Oscillations into Continuous Currents by Means of a Vacuum Valve," read to the Royal Society in 1905, describes the radio tube, which he invented. He was a fellow of the Royal Society and professor at University College, London. His *Memories of a Scientific Life* was published in 1934.—*D. H. R.*

FLEXIBLE SHAFT: a shaft for transmitting rotary motion from a power source over a curved path to drive some device. It consists of an inner rotating core assembly covered by a non-rotating flexible housing or cover, called a casing assembly, which acts as the bearing surface for the core. The core is made up of layers of steel wire, with the successive layers wound in opposite directions. Fittings to connect to the drive and driven elements are attached to the core. The casing is made of a variety of materials to suit the particular application; *e.g.* the casing for a speedometer drive shaft such as used on a car is a low-cost flexible metal hose, while for concrete vibrators, where the casing must resist the abrasion of wet concrete and yet be very flexible, a rubber and neoprene abrasion-resistant casing is used. Flexible shafts are available in sizes from ⅛ in. to 1⅝ in. core diameter and will transmit as much as 10 hp. They have found wide application in design of mechanical equipment because of their inherent advantage over other methods of transmitting rotary motion. Such a shaft allows engineers freedom in locating components; it can connect two shafts having relative motion; it eliminates dangerously exposed rotating parts; it does not require accurate alignment; and it is little affected by vibration. The two main types of flexible shafting are remote-control and power-drive. Remote-control flexible shafting is used for low-speed application, where only torque is a factor; *e.g.* for remotely controlling valves on ships and for sewer cleaners. Power-drive flexible shafting is made more flexible than the remote-control type to insure long life under continuous flexing; it is used to drive grinding wheels and other tools, farm implements, and accessories on cars, trucks, and aircraft.—*C. F. H.*

FLIGHT: see AERODYNAMICS; ANIMAL FLIGHT.

FLINT: see QUARTZ.

FLOOD CONTROL: mitigation or prevention of flood damage by engineering works. Throughout history extensive damage and loss of life have occurred when streams swollen by excessive runoff have overflown their channels and inundated adjacent lands. The flood, common to most streams, ranges from the desert cloudburst on an ephemeral stream to the disastrous inundations of the plains of great rivers such as the Hwang-ho, Indus, Ganges, and Mississippi. Devastation

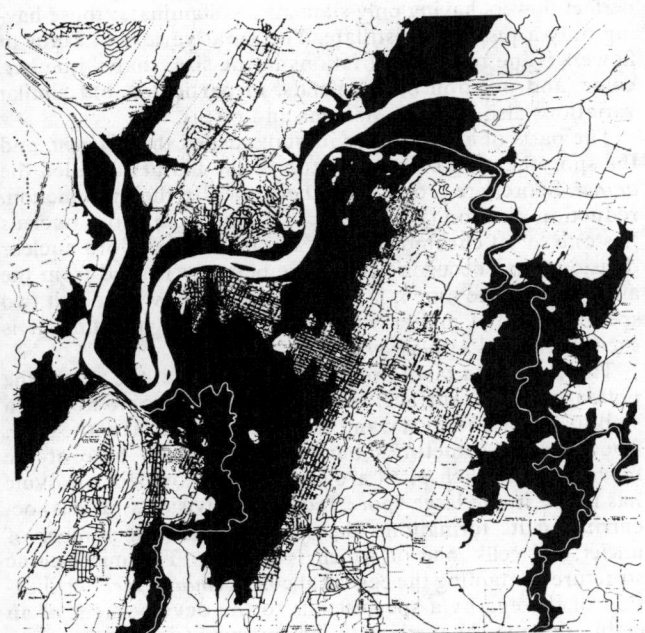

The flood that might have been: But for the city's reservoir system, the flood of Jan.–Feb. 1957 in Chattanooga, Tenn., would have covered 8,000 acres within city limits, as shown here in black. Ordinary coverage by river and local creeks is shown by white areas within the black. (*TVA*)

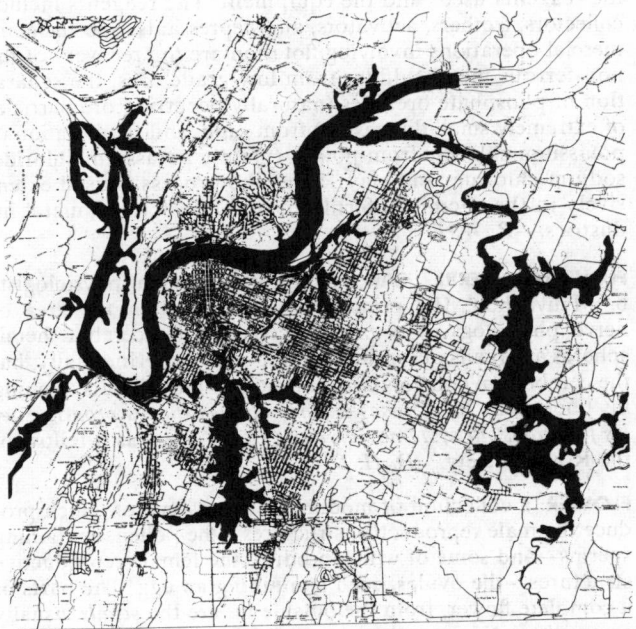

The flood that was: Multiple-purpose reservoir system reduced crest of flood by almost 22 ft. Flooding at right side of map resulted mostly from overflow of Chickamauga Creek, not from the Tennessee River. Floodwaters were confined to low-lying, sparsely occupied areas. (*TVA*)

on the N China plain by the flooding Hwang-ho led this river to be called "China's Sorrow."

Intense flooding is caused by concurrence of extreme meteorological events. Heavy rains falling on watersheds already previously soaked, or on snow, cause extreme and rapid runoff. Peak discharges from several tributaries at once rapidly swell the main-stem river. Engineering measures for control include deepening of the channel near the mouth, confining of the river by levees, providing reservoir storage on the main river, and watershed treatment to retard runoff and increase soil infiltration. While effective, as on the Tyne of Scotland, channel deepening is usually too expensive. Use of levees is more common, and is exemplified on the lower Mississippi, where 2,780 mi of embankment averaging 24 ft in height protect the riparian plain below Cape Girardeau. During extreme floods levees may spill the overflow to areas of relatively low value. Rivers naturally wander and spill their flood-borne sediments over their plains, and thus their confinement often leads to continued aggradation of their beds, so that levees must be periodically raised. Reservoir storage may be used to reduce peak flows, as on the Missouri above Sioux City, Iowa, but flood-control reservoir operation conflicts with use for irrigation and power and, furthermore, reservoirs often inundate large areas of valuable land. Watershed treatment consists of improving vegetable cover, contouring, and construction of reservoirs on smaller tributaries. Such measures are effective on the smaller watersheds but cannot alone control great floods caused by the disastrous concurrence of extreme conditions.—*D. F. P.*

FLOOD PLAIN: that part of a river valley which is submerged during flooding. Each flood results in deposition of sediment (alluvium), accumulations of which raise the plain above the normal level of the channel. Flood plains are characteristic of "old" landscapes (see VALLEY). They are likely to be

extremely fertile. Those built up as described provide excellent farmland.—*E. A.*

FLORA: see FAUNA, FLORA, AND BIOTA.

FLOREY, SIR HOWARD WALTER, 1898–   , British biochemist; b. Adelaide, Australia. In 1939 Florey and Ernst Boris Chain began the study of penicillin, discovered by Sir Alexander Fleming in 1929 but never investigated for its therapeutic possibilities. They later produced purified penicillin and successfully tested it clinically. Florey came to the U. S. A. and helped to develop methods of purifying penicillin on a large-scale production basis. In 1945 he shared the Nobel prize with Fleming and Chain for the discovery of penicillin and its use in infectious maladies. He is a fellow of the Royal Society.—*R. G.*

FLOTATION: a process for the separation of finely pulverized particles of a mineral ore according to their relative affinities for various phases (water, oil, gas bubbles) in aqueous media, instead of according to the particles' specific gravities. Flotation has proved increasingly valuable as an economical method of recovering metals from low-grade ores. After pulverizing, the mineral ore may be treated by one of three processes: (1) *Froth flotation,* used almost exclusively today, is applicable when certain minerals in water attach to gas bubbles (*e.g.* air) in the water and rise with the bubbles to the surface, where the froth can be separated. (2) The *bulk-oil process* depends on the selective surface-wetting characteristics of a particular mineral when shaken in an oil-water, two-layer system. One type of material passes into the oil phase and others into the aqueous phase. (3) In the *film* or *skin process,* dry minerals are deposited on water, and the non-wetted material floats because of surface tension and hydraulic forces. Factors influencing flotation include: nature of the minerals; type of solid phase, liquid phase, or gaseous phase; the reagents used; and the equipment. The reagents include collectors, frothers, activators, and depressants. Specific commercial operations involving flotation are the recovery of the non-ferrous metal sulfides from low-grade ores, the separation of phosphate ore fines (naturally occurring ore particles of extremely small dimension) from sand, and the isolation of potassium chloride from potash (mainly potassium chloride, sodium chloride, and clay). Thus the process is used extensively in the chemical, fertilizer, and non-ferrous metal industries.—*R. W. F.*

FLOURENS, PIERRE JEAN, 1794–1867, French physiologist; b. Mauveilhon. His principal research was in the area of nerve physiology. The first to consider the cerebral hemispheres as organs of sensation, he showed experimentally that the cerebellum controls coordination of movements. Among his books was *Recherches expérimentales sur les propriétés et les fonctions du système nerveux* (1824). He was a fellow of the Royal Society.—*D. H. D. R.*

FLOWER: a collection of modified leaves, some of which produce the male reproductive structures—the pollen, containing sperms—and some of which produce the female reproductive structures—the ovules, each containing an egg. The parts of a complete flower, from the outside in, are the *sepals,* usually green; the *petals,* usually colored; the *stamens,* which produce pollen; and the *pistil* or *pistils,* which produce ovules. If either sepals (collectively, the *calyx*) or petals (collectively, the *corolla*), or both, are lacking, the flower is incomplete. If either stamens or pistil is lacking, the flower is imperfect. Imperfect flowers having only stamens are staminate; those having only a pistil are pistillate. The great variety in kinds of flowers is the result of variations in the size, shape, number, color, and position of the petals, in particular, but similar variations also occur in stamens and pistils.

The parts of a stamen are its stalk, called the *filament,* and the spore-bearing case at the top of the filament, called the *anther.* Spores are produced in the anther. In their production, reduction division (MEIOSIS) occurs, and each spore nucleus has one set of chromosomes in it. One or two more nuclear divisions may occur in each spore before it is shed from the anther; so at the time it is shed, the spore may have in it two sperm cells. No matter what its contents, at the time it is shed it is called a *pollen grain.*

The parts of a pistil are the enlarged base, the *ovary,* the pollen-receptive surface, the *stigma,* and in some flowers a stalk between the ovary and the stigmatic surface, the *style.* The ovary is sometimes buried in the fleshy base of the flower. Inside each pistil are one or more ovules. An ovule has inside it one large spore, reduction division (meiosis) occurring in its formation. The spore produces a number of nuclei and cells, one of which is the egg. The microscopic structure containing the egg is called the *embryo sac.* Fertilization of the egg by a sperm leads to the development of an embryo plant. The ovule with the embryo inside matures into a SEED. The ovary, and in some plants other parts of the flower, mature into a FRUIT. See FLOWERING PLANTS; POLLEN; REPRODUCTION. See Color Plate 45.—*H. Cr.*

FLOWERING PLANT (or angiosperm): any VASCULAR PLANT in which the organ of sexual reproduction is a FLOWER. A flower may produce POLLEN or OVULES, or both. After pollination of a flower and fertilization of the egg cell in each of its ovules by sperms from the pollen grains, embryo flowering plants begin developing. Each is a SEED enclosed by structures of the parent plant that constitute a FRUIT. About two thirds of the known species of vascular plants produce flowers and fruits; they are taxonomically in the class Angiospermae, distinct from the classes Gymnospermae (GYMNOSPERMS) and Filicinae (FERNS). Flowering plants range in size from the minute duckweeds, which float on ponds and are less than ¼ in. across, to giant trees such as eucalyptus, with a trunk 6 to 8 ft in diameter. A few, *e.g.* eelgrass, live submerged in fresh or salt water as AQUATIC PLANTS. Others, *e.g.* cacti, are highly adapted to surviving long periods of drought (see XEROPHYTE). But most flowering plants live on land where a moderate amount of water is available. They are primary sources of food and oxygen for man and other animals, and supply us also with building material, textile fibers, cooking oils, spices, perfumes, and drugs.

Approximately 200,000 species of flowering plants are DICOTS—their seeds each have two seed leaves (cotyledons). Usually their flower parts are in fours or fives or multiples of these; the veins in the leaves form a network; the conducting tissue in stems and roots is arranged in a circle or cylinder; and secondary growth can be extensive through the activity of a cambium. About 50,000 species of flowering plants are MONOCOTS, their seeds each having a single cotyledon. Usually their flower parts are in threes or multiples of three; the veins in the leaves usually run parallel from base to apex; the conducting tissue in stems and roots takes the form of scattered bundles, and a cambium is rare. Modern classification of these two great subclasses of flowering plants is based principally upon features of the flower, although these features often are accompanied by distinctive characteristics in roots, stems, leaves, seeds, and fruits.

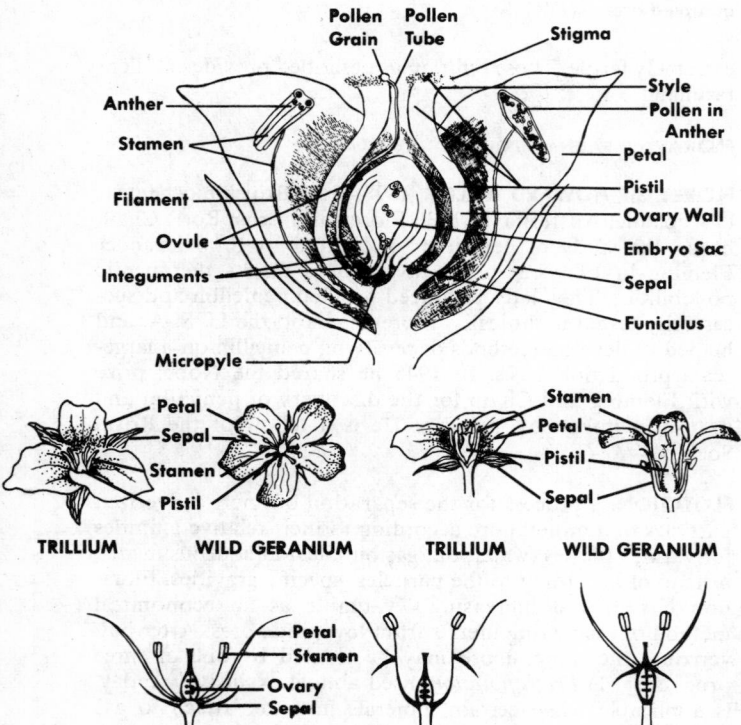

Flower structure: *Top*—Longitudinal section shows pollen tube through which sperm travels to reach and fertilize egg in ovule. Ovule then develops into seed, and surrounding ovary ripens into a fruit. *Middle*—Parts of a typical monocot (trillium) and a typical dicot (wild geranium). *Bottom*—Three types of flowers, characterized by position of ovary, are (*from left*) hypogynous, perigynous, and epigynous. (*Top drawing from Whaley; bottom drawing after Cronquist*)

Life cycle of flowering plant: Familiar sporophyte plant produces flowers. Within the pollen sacs of the anthers of each flower, pollen grains develop by meiosis. In the ovary of each flower, ovules develop. In pollination, a pollen grain (male gametophyte) reaches the stigma of a flower and forms a pollen tube, which grows through the style into an ovule. Meanwhile, in the ovule, a spore produced by meiosis has grown into an embryo sac (female gametophyte). Now a sperm nucleus from the pollen grain passes through the pollen tube and fuses with an egg nucleus in the embryo sac. Both sperm and egg nucleus are haploid (contain a single set of unpaired chromosomes each), and they form a diploid zygote (which has a paired set of chromosomes). The zygote develops into an embryo plant within the hard covering of a seed, and the ovary enclosing such seeds ripens into a fruit. Eventually a seed reaches the soil, sprouts, and grows into an adult plant of the next generation. (*After Young*)

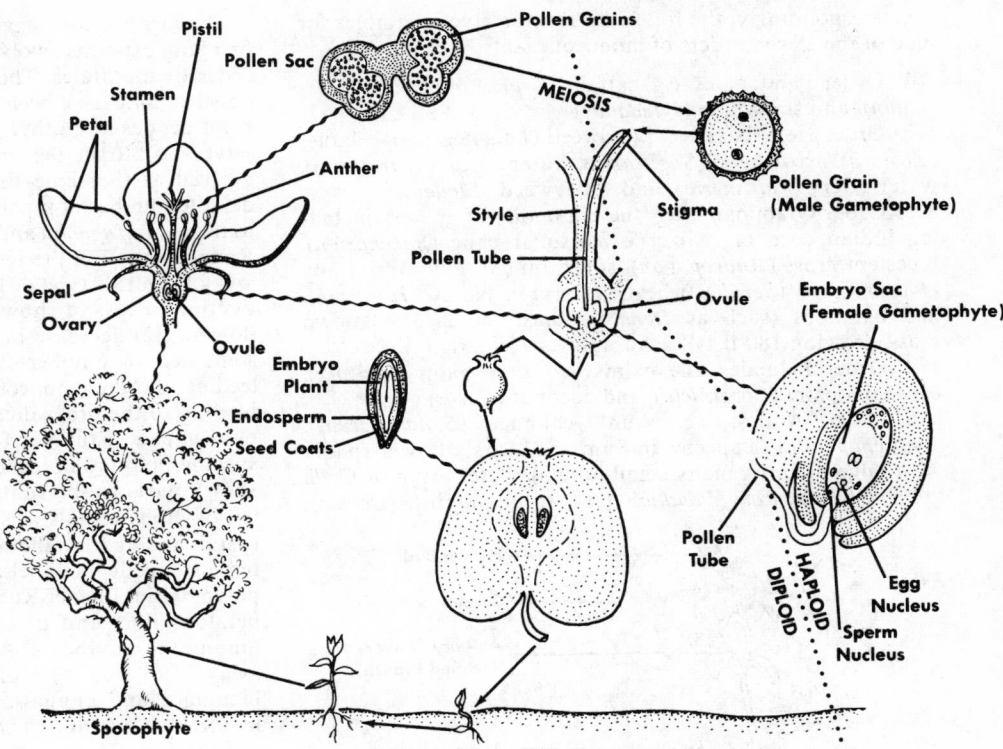

The following resumé of dicot plants gives examples for 23 of the 34 orders; the first 18 of the numbered orders have flower petals separate from one another (polypetalous) or lack petals (apetalous), whereas the remaining five orders have petals joined to form a cup or tube (sympetalous). Familiar genera are shown in italics.

1. Order Salicales, *e.g.* willows (*Salix*) and poplars (*Populus*).
2. Order Juglandales, *e.g.* walnut (*Juglans*), hickory and pecan (both *Carya*).
3. Order Fagales, *e.g.* hazelnut and filbert (*Corylus*), birch (*Betula*), alder (*Alnus*), beech (*Fagus*), chestnut (*Castanea*), and oak (*Quercus*).
4. Order Urticales, *e.g.* elm (*Ulmus*), mulberry (*Morus*), breadfruit and jackfruit (both *Artocarpus*), fig and banyan (both *Ficus*), stinging nettle (*Urtica*), and hemp (*Cannabis*).
5. Order Aristolochiales, *e.g.* Dutchman's pipe (*Aristolochia*) and *Rafflesia*, a parasitic plant of the East Indies producing the largest flowers known (to 36 in. across and 20 lb).
6. Order Centrospermales, *e.g.* four-o'clock (*Mirabilis*), ice plant (*Mesembryanthemum*), chickweed (*Stellaria*), carnation (*Dianthus*), and other pinks.
7. Order Ranales, *e.g.* waterlily and lotus (*Nelumbo* and *Nymphaea*), buttercup (*Ranunculus*), columbine (*Aquilegia*), *Magnolia*, barberry (*Berberis*), and avocado (*Persea*).
8. Order Papaverales, *e.g.* opium poppy and Iceland poppy (both *Papaver*), mustard and cabbage (both *Brassica*).
9. Order Sarraceniales, *e.g.* pitcher plants (*Sarracenia*, *Nepenthes*) and sundews (*Drosera*).
10. Order Rosales, *e.g.* sycamore (*Platanus*), *Spiraea*, pear and apple (both *Pyrus*), raspberry (*Rubus*), strawberry (*Fragaria*), roses (*Rosa*), apricots and plums (both *Prunus*), *Acacia*, lupine (*Lupinus*), sweet pea (*Lathyrus*), peas (*Pisum*), and beans (*Phaseolus*).
11. Order Geraniales, *e.g.* flax (*Linum*), cranesbill (*Geranium*) and storksbill "geranium" (*Pelargonium*), nasturtium (*Tropaeolum*), lignum vitae (*Guaiacum*), orange and lemon (*Citrus*), mahogany (*Swietenia*), *Croton,* and *Euphorbia,* as well as other spurges.
12. Order Sapindales, *e.g.* pistachio (*Pistacia*), poison ivy and staghorn sumac (both *Rhus*), holly (*Ilex*), maples (*Acer*), and horsechestnut (*Aesculus*).
13. Order Rhamnales, *e.g.* grape (*Vitis*), Cascara (*Rhamnus*).
14. Order Malvales, *e.g.* basswood or linden (*Tilia*), cotton (*Gossypium*), *Hibiscus*, cacao (*Theobroma*—source of cocoa and chocolate), *Cola*, baobab (*Adansonia*), and kapok (*Ceiba*).
15. Order Parietales, *e.g.* tea (*Thea*), violets (*Viola*), passionflower (*Passiflora*), papaya (*Carica*), and *Begonia.*
16. Order Opuntiales, *e.g.* various cacti, including saguaro and night-blooming cereus (both *Cereus*), and prickly pear (*Opuntia*).
17. Order Myrtales, *e.g.* pomegranate (*Punica*), Brazilnut (*Bertholletia*), mangrove (*Rhizophora*), and myrtle (*Myrtus*).
18. Order Umbellales, *e.g.* English ivy (*Hedera*), ginseng (*Panax*) and poison hemlock (*Conium*), carrot (*Daucus*), and dogwood (*Cornus*).
19. Order Ericales, *e.g.* wintergreen (*Pyrola*), *Rhododendron*, blueberry (*Vaccinium*), and the various heaths.
20. Order Gentianales, *e.g.* ash (*Fraxinus*), olive (*Olea*), privet (*Ligustrum*), *Strychnos* (source of strychnine and curare), gentians (*Gentiana*), and milkweed (*Asclepias*).
21. Order Tubiflorales, *e.g.* morning-glory (*Convolvulus*), *Phlox, Verbena, Salvia,* mint (*Mentha*), potato (*Solanum*), tomato (*Lycopersicon*), and tobacco (*Nicotiana*).
22. Order Rubiales, *e.g.* *Cinchona* (source of quinine), coffee (*Coffea*), honeysuckle (*Lonicera* and *Diervilla*), and elder (*Sambucus*).
23. Order Campanulales, *e.g.* muskmelon and cucumber (both *Cucumis*), pumpkin and squash (both *Cucurbita*), *Lobelia,* and all of the big family Compositae, including goldenrod (*Solidago*), *Aster,. Zinnia, Dahlia,* dandelion (*Taraxacum*), chicory and endive (both *Cichorium*), and lettuce (*Lactuca*).

Correspondingly, the following resumé gives examples for nine of the eleven orders of monocot plants.

1. Order Pandanales, *e.g.* cattails (*Typha*), burreeds (*Sparganum*), and screwpine (*Pandanus*).

2. Order Helobiales, *e.g.* pondweed (*Potamogeton*), eelgrass (*Zostera*), arrowhead (*Sagittaria*), water-soldier (*Stratiotes*), water-celery (*Vallisneria*), and waterweed (*Elodea*).

3. Order Graminales, *e.g.* the big family of grasses, including Indian corn or maize (*Zea*), sugar cane (*Saccharum*), bluestem grass (*Andropogon*), sorghum (*Sorghum*), timothy (*Phleum*), rye (*Secale*), wheat (*Triticum*), barley (*Hordeum*), and bamboos (such as *Dendrocalanus,* the largest known grass, growing 180 ft tall as rapidly as 15 in. daily).

4. Order Palmales, the palms, *e.g.* date palm (*Phoenix*), carnauba palm (*Copernicia*), and coconut (*Cocos*).

5. Order Arales, *e.g.* skunk cabbage (*Symplocarpus*), *Amorphophallus* (a species in Sumatra bears a flower spadix 15 ft tall, enclosing many small florets), water arum or *Calla* "lily," *Philodendron, Caladium,* jack-in-the-pulpit (*Arisaema*),

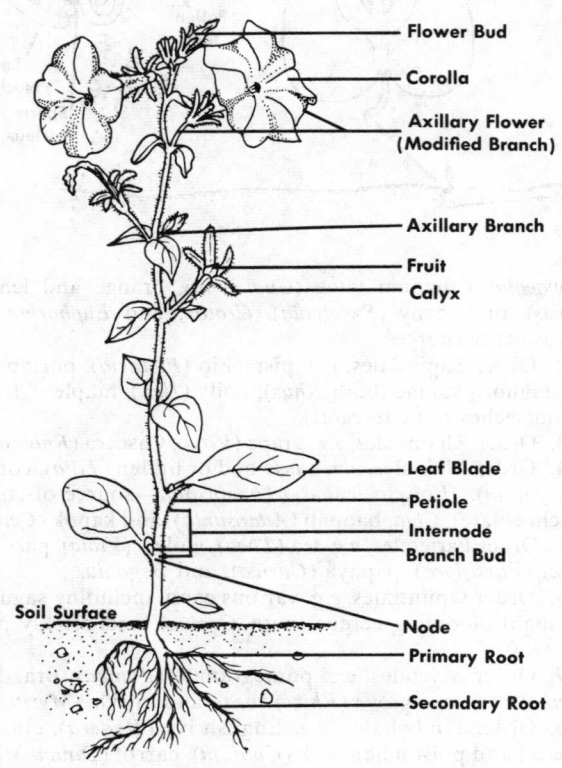

Flower Bud

Corolla

Axillary Flower
(Modified Branch)

Axillary Branch

Fruit

Calyx

Leaf Blade

Petiole

Internode

Branch Bud

Soil Surface

Node

Primary Root

Secondary Root

Characteristic Structures of Flowering Plant (*After Kenoyer*)

and also floating duckweed (*Lemna*), and watermeal (*Wolffia*) —the smallest known flowering plant.

6. Order Farinales, *e.g.* spiderwort (*Tradescantia*), pineapple (*Ananas*), Spanish moss (*Tillandsia*), and pickerel-weed (*Pontederia*).

7. Order Liliales, *e.g.* rushes (*Juncus*), and the big lily family (Liliaceae), including tulip (*Tulipa*), Easter lily (*Lilium*), hyacinth (*Hyacinthus*), Spanish bayonet and Joshua tree (both *Yucca*), lily-of-the-valley (*Convallaria*), *Trillium, Asparagus,* the yams (*Dioscorea*), the aloes (*Agave*), the irises and crocuses.

8. Order Scitaminales, *e.g.* banana (*Musa*), traveler's tree (*Ravenala*), bird-of-paradise flower (*Strelitzia*), ginger (*Zingiber*), *Canna,* and arrowroot (*Maranta*).

9. Order Orchidales, the orchids, *e.g. Vanilla,* lady's slipper (*Cypripedium*), showy orchis (*Orchis*), *Cattleya,* and *Cymbidium.*

The fossil record suggests that during the Mesozoic Era the first angiosperms evolved, perhaps from the gymnosperm order Bennettitales. The enclosed ovule, which made a fruit possible, may have been an adaptation safeguarding the seeds from beetles and other insects; the showy sepals and petals served to attract the first moths and bees, as these insects evolved at the same time. The earliest flowers had an indefinite number of sepals, petals, stamens, and pistils, similar to those of *Magnolia* and other members of the modern order Ranales (no. 7 in the resumé of dicots). Evolutionary trends away from this type of flower can be traced, through (1) reduction or loss of showy parts, to develop wind-pollinated flowers; (2) decrease in the number of sepals and petals to some definite number of each—multiples of three in the line leading into the monocots, multiples of four or five in the line leading to the other dicots; (3) fusion of showy parts into a cup-shaped or tubular flower, often limiting access to a few specific pollinating insects or birds; and (4) adhesion of the showy parts to the central pistil, changing the flower from hypogynous (petals arising below the ovary) to epigynous (petals arising from the sides of the ovary). Epigyny is characteristic of orders Umbellales, Myrtales, and Opuntiales in the polypetalous line, of Rubiales and Campanulales in the sympetalous line, and of orders Scitaminales and Orchidales among the monocots. A further trend can be seen, leading away from tree style of growth to herbaceous perennials, biennials, and annuals. See also ALPINE PLANTS; ANNUAL; BIENNIAL; PERENNIAL; PLANT; POISONOUS PLANTS; SEED PLANT. —*L. and M. M.*

FLOWERLESS PLANTS: Until the middle of the 19th cent., when Wilhelm Hofmeister of Leipzig traced out the reproduction of seed plants, ferns, horsetails, mosses, and liverworts, it was customary to distinguish between flowerless plants, whose reproductive parts are hidden, and FLOWERING PLANTS, which produce flowers, fruits, and seeds. The flowerless plants were called Cryptogams ("hidden marriage"); the flowering plants, Phanerogams ("visible marriage"). Flowerless plants reproduce by means of spores, and might be called spore plants in contrast to seed plants. They include the FERNS, horsetails, clubmosses (now grouped with the SEED PLANTS because they possess conducting tissues), MOSSES AND LIVERWORTS (now grouped separately because they lack conducting tissues but develop like the vascular plants from an embryo), FUNGI, ALGAE, and LICHENS. The concept "flowerless plants" no longer appeals to botanists, because it fails to show the heterogeneous nature of the plants included. Modern terminology, although related to features that are less obvious, corresponds to the separation of lines of descent in the evolution of the plant kingdom. See BOTANY; PLANT.—*L. and M. M.*

FLOW METER: see FLUID METERING.

FLUID: a general term denoting both liquids and gases. Fluids have no elasticity of shape, can flow through openings, produce pressures on containing vessels, and exert buoyant forces on bodies suspended in them. Unlike liquids, gases are readily compressible and can fill completely any closed vessel in which they are placed. Unlike solids, the structure of liquids exhibits only a long-range order; that of gases shows no order at all.—*A. E.*

FLUID FLOW: The behavior of a flowing fluid is a result of physical and geometrical conditions, and also of the intrinsic physical properties of the fluid. The study of these properties and conditions has a wide relevance to current problems of aerodynamics (where the fluid is air), hydraulics, and meteorology; and special relevance to design problems associated with supersonic and hypersonic flight.

Turbulent-wake flow: Shadowgraph of F-84 model at Mach 1.04 shows downstream turbulence caused by deceleration and separation of fluid as it flows past model's surfaces. Shock waves are clearly delineated, one just ahead of model and the others trailing from wings and tail surfaces. (*U. S. Army*)

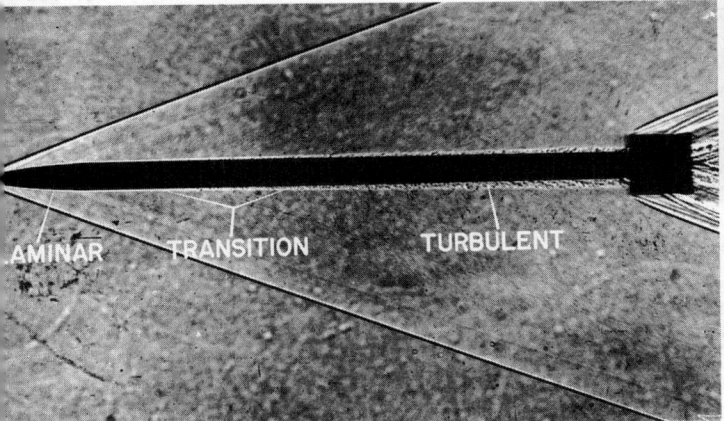

LAMINAR   TRANSITION   TURBULENT

Boundary-layer flow: Shadowgraph of missile model at Mach 3 in free-flight wind tunnel shows the gradual transition from laminar to turbulent flow in the boundary layer. Turbulence increases drag and aerodynamic heating. (*NASA*)

In steady water flow through a pipe, the magnitude of the driving pressure and the shape and size of the pipe constitute the principal conditions. However, the speed of honey flowing through the pipe under the same conditions would be considerably less than that of water, which is a less viscous fluid. Exact analysis of any fluid-flow system requires use of equations dealing with conservation of matter, momentum, and energy. When heating effects take place, thermodynamic laws have to be used as well.

There are several categories of fluid flows. The first deals with the *incompressible* flow of an *ideal* fluid. "Incompressible" means that the density remains constant; "ideal" means that the fluid is frictionless, *i.e.* its viscosity is zero. Many examples of both liquid flow and gas flow at slow to moderate speeds are covered by this category; *e.g.* the efflux of liquid from a vessel under the influence of gravity, or flow through ducts. Such flows are governed by Bernoulli's law, which states that the sum of the pressure, the square of the speed, and the fluid height or elevation is constant along the path of any fluid element, *i.e.* along a streamline. Thus when a horizontal pipe necks down to a smaller diameter, the increase of fluid velocity which takes place is accompanied by a drop in the fluid pressure.

But the more complex types of fluid flow cannot be described by Bernoulli's law as stated above. In the case of very viscous fluids such as honey, viscous or frictional shearing forces act against the flow everywhere. For slightly viscous fluids moving at appreciable speeds, the frictional effects are concentrated at or near solid surfaces, or at the

boundaries of jets or wakes. The friction layer near a wall is called a *boundary layer*. When the viscous effects in a boundary layer are sufficiently strong, the boundary layer fluid flow has the form of sheets of fluid sliding over each other. This is called *laminar* flow. The alternative to this is a flow containing random eddying motions, called *turbulent* flow. In many applications of hydraulics, aerodynamics, and meteorology, turbulent flow is the more important of the two.

The assumption of incompressible behavior must be abandoned when the fluid velocity approaches or exceeds the velocity of sound. Appreciable changes in both density and temperature may occur in the fluid, and the flow is referred to as *compressible*. When the fluid speed is greater than sound speed, the flow is said to be *supersonic*. Such flows differ from slower-speed (subsonic) flows in that they may contain strong stationary or moving waves which produce sudden jumps in pressure, density, and temperature. The jumps are called *shock waves*. When a very-high-speed flow is abruptly decelerated, its temperature may rise to the point where the molecules dissociate and the atoms become ionized. A flow of this kind develops chemical reactions and displays electrical conductivity.

A large class of flows are nearly uniform except for the presence of a small disturbance, *e.g.* that produced by a thin airfoil. For these flows, the complex and largely insoluble complete equations can be simplified into a linearized form. Physically, this means that the motion of such *linearized flow* can be described by a superposition of very small disturbance motions. Mathematically, the linearized equations are generally well understood and can be solved. Linearized flow has had extensive application to slender-airplane theory and to wing theory.

Investigators have been able to develop a more unified treatment of the many possible types of flow; it takes into

Critical Velocity

←——— LAMINAR FLOW ———→ ←— TURBULENT FLOW —→

Velocity Distribution — Thick Boundary Layer — Velocity Increases as Pipe Narrows — Thinned Boundary Layer — Velocity Distribution

Fluid flow in a tapered pipe: As pipe narrows, velocity of flow increases and, in pipe shown, breaks from laminar to turbulent flow. The boundary layer adhering to the pipe walls thins, and the straight lines of the laminar flow pattern break up into eddies characteristic of turbulent flow. As velocity distribution curves would show, average velocity under turbulent flow conditions is more nearly the maximum velocity achieved along the pipe's axis than it is under conditions of laminar flow.

account the variation of physical properties among different fluids. This is done by making use of numerical ratios which act as scaling factors to relate different flows. The most important of these are REYNOLDS NUMBER and MACH NUMBER. As an example, it is found that transition from laminar to turbulent flow in a pipe takes place at the same Reynolds number whether one uses air or water. See MODELS AND MODELING.

ENTROPY provides a useful basis for distinguishing ideal streamline fluid flows without heat addition, whether incompressible or compressible, from flow with viscous stresses, turbulence, or shock waves. Ideal streamline flows are characterized by the constancy of entropy along streamlines and are referred to as *isentropic*. An isentropic flow will recover its full head of pressure when brought to rest; a non-isentropic flow will not. This is an important consideration in the design of high-speed wind tunnels and turbines.—*D. B.*

FLUIDIZATION: a procedure in chemical engineering in which a solid-state catalyst is prepared as a fine powder and introduced into a stream of gas to promote a desired reaction. The powder is set into turbulent motion by the gas stream, and as a result of the intimate contact the catalyst exerts its maximum effect on the reaction. When the gas stream consists of petroleum hydrocarbons at high temperature, the process is called *fluidized catalytic cracking*. If the operation is designed to permit the catalyst to move with the gas stream, the catalyst can be separated later by a device such as a cyclone separator, and recovered. (See CATALYSIS.)—*Ru. M.*

FLUID MACHINERY: in a narrow sense, machinery used to transport liquids and gases, as in chemical engineering and petroleum refining. Such machinery consists primarily of conveying pipes with appropriately placed vacuum or pressure PUMPS, VALVES, and control instruments to keep the desired amount of fluid moving in the right direction at the desired rate. The machines may be very small, like those used to remove air from tiny perfume bottles before pumping perfume in. In a broader sense, fluid machinery includes all machines which take advantage of mechanical, dynamic, or thermodynamic properties of liquids or gases, *e.g.* a FAN or PROPELLER, to accomplish some objective other than mere fluid transportation. The earliest type of such fluid machinery probably was the water wheel, which got its energy from an under- or over-shooting stream of water and had buckets to lift the water. Because both liquids and gases can be placed under uniform pressure, they can be used as transmitters of force in pneumatic and hydraulic jacks or lifts. The fact that fluids can rather efficiently convey momentum imparted to them has made them of use in gas, steam, and hydraulic TURBINES. The ability of liquids to absorb substantial quantities of heat from solid surfaces underlies their use in heat-exchange machinery, for heating or refrigeration and air-conditioning systems. Because atoms of molecules move relatively freely in fluids, a mixture of liquids or a mixture of gases can sometimes be separated (by centrifuging) according to the respective specific gravities of the fluid components. Liquids can also be separated by vaporization because of differences in boiling points. In the broadest sense, devices for these separations are fluid machinery.—*K. A.*

FLUID METERING: measurement of fluid-flow (liquid, gas, or vapor) rates in weight or volume per unit time. The simplest method is to determine the time a fluid takes to fill a known volume or to build up to a given amount. More common is measurement by differential-pressure devices, *e.g.* orifices, venturis, or nozzles in a flow line, which utilize pressure dif-

ference developed by a fluid flowing through a constricted area (see illus.). In these devices the flow rate is proportional to the square root of the differential pressure across the constriction. For engineering calculations, flow rate may be expressed in lb/sec or in ft^3/min. For consumer billing of domestic-gas flow meters, the flow rate is given in ft^3 between successive readings.

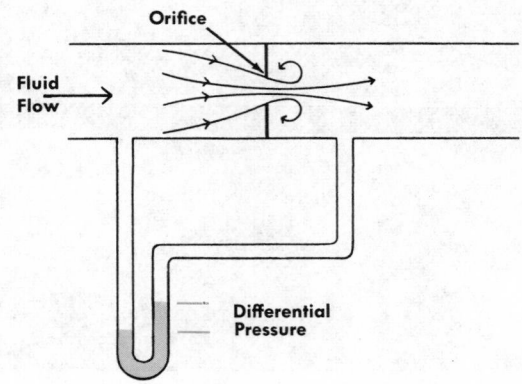

Differential-type orifice flow meter measures rate of flow from difference in fluid pressure due to passage through orifice.

Current or velocity-type meters are basically propellers placed in the stream. The speed of rotation is a function of velocity and can be obtained by mechanical or electronic means. Anemometer and screw and turbine instruments are examples. The rotameter is a variable-area flow meter. A moving float in a slightly tapered pipe is actuated by the flow forces so that it is lifted upward by increased flow, thus increasing the cross-sectional flow area. The rise of the float is a measure of the flow rate. In the case of conducting fluids, *e.g.* liquid metals or blood, the flow can be metered electromagnetically by measuring the voltage generated as the fluid flows through a magnetic field.—*F. K.*

FLUORESCENCE: the glow emitted by some substances when irradiated by violet or ultraviolet light. In its commonest form, fluorescence occurs when violet or ultraviolet light falls onto a fluorescent substance, causing it to radiate visible light during the period of irradiation. If the emission continues after the radiation is cut off, the term PHOSPHORESCENCE is used. Many substances exhibit both fluorescence and phosphorescence, the best known being natural zinc sulfides. Strongly fluorescing substances are called *phosphors*. In general, any electromagnetic radiation, visible or not, may be used for irradiation; and the emitted radiation invariably has a *longer* wavelength than the incident radiation. Fluorescence is responsible for the glow of fluorescent lamps (see ELECTRIC LAMP), CATHODE-RAY TUBES (used in oscilloscopes and television sets), and gaseous NEBULAS. The phenomenon is useful in GEOPHYSICAL PROSPECTING. See Color Plate 47.—*R. N. V.*

FLUORINATION: introduction of one or more fluorine atoms into a compound, sometimes by direct action of fluorine (F_2), but more often indirectly through another fluorine compound, *e.g.* cobalt fluoride (CoF_3). (See FLUOROCARBONS; HALOGEN.) Fluorination is a key process in producing Freon (CCl_2F_2), used both as a solvent in Aerosol insecticide bombs and as a refrigerant; it is also the basic process in the making of tetrafluoroethylene resin (Teflon), a high polymer that is chemically inert, *i.e.* extremely resistant to heat and acid attack, and thus valuable as a COATING. The term *fluoridation* is used to designate the adding of fluoride ions to water supplies to promote dental health (see WATER TREATMENT). —*Ru. M.*

FLUORINE: an element of the halogen family (F); at. no. 9; at. wt 19.00; sp gr 1.108; mp $-217.8°C$; bp $-188°C$; the most reactive of NONMETALS. At ordinary temperatures, it is a pale-yellow, flammable gas, 1.695 times as heavy as air. Because of its reactivity, fluorine is not found in nature uncombined. It is, however, widely distributed in Earth's crust—in fluor-spar (CaF_2), cryolite (Na_3AlF_6), and phosphate rocks. It can be prepared by the electrolytic decomposition of hydrogen fluoride and was in fact discovered by this method in 1886 by Moissan. The only element that is able to form simple binary compounds with any of the inert gases (it can do so with xenon), fluorine reacts directly—often violently—with oxidizable materials. Although normally this gas does not react with oxygen and nitrogen, compounds of fluorine and these two elements can be formed. With other HALOGENS, it reacts to form compounds such as chlorine monofluoride (ClF) and chlorine trifluoride (ClF_3). Fluorine can partially or completely replace hydrogen in some organic compounds to form the commercially important FLUOROCARBONS.—*D. P. B.*

FLUOROCARBONS: chemical compounds containing the elements carbon and fluorine, and sometimes hydrogen. They may be thought of as hydrocarbons (*i.e.* compounds of hydrogen and carbon) in which fluorine atoms have replaced either *most* of the hydrogen atoms (highly fluorinated or polyfluorinated hydrocarbons) or *all* the hydrogen atoms (completely fluorinated hydrocarbons); thus a given fluorocarbon has a corresponding hydrocarbon analog. The so-called *fluorocarbon derivatives* contain other elements in addition to fluorine, carbon, and hydrogen. Since fluorine is a halogen element, fluorocarbons are members of the broader class of HALOGEN compounds. Fluorocarbons are chemically very stable, their chemical inactivity being surpassed only by their inert gases. For example, a given fluorocarbon has lower freezing and boiling points than almost any other substance of equal molecular weight, except the inert gases. Such properties make the fluorocarbons useful as starting materials for a great many kinds of plastics, resins, waxes, oils, fibers, and elastomers. Commercial polyfluorinated hydrocarbon polymers, *e.g.* Teflon, Fluorothene, and Polyfluoron, are extremely unreactive, and are finding increasing use where resistance to heat and chemicals is important, *e.g.* in coatings, gaskets, molds, insulators, high-temperature lubricants, tube sockets, and laboratory ware. The commercial Freons (compounds of carbon, fluorine, and usually chlorine or bromine) are used widely as refrigerants because of their low boiling points, and because they are non-toxic.

Interest in the preparation and utilization of fluorocarbons has developed mainly since World War II, when great advances were made in methods of handling fluorine and in controlling FLUORINATION reactions. It was found that fluorocarbons were the only materials capable of resisting the corrosive attack of the fluorine-containing compound uranium hexafluoride, UF_6, uniquely useful in separating the desired fissionable uranium isotope, U^{235}, from the nonfissionable U^{238}. Fluorocarbon sealants and diluents were thus developed. Since this discovery, the study and application of fluorocarbons and their remarkable properties has become almost a field in itself.—*G. W. M.*

FLUOROSCOPE: a device employed for making a preliminary x-ray examination of the human body or other objects. A patient undergoing fluoroscopic examination is placed be-tween the X-RAY TUBE and the fluoroscope. The latter is simply a light-tight box carrying a fluorescent screen at one end and open for visual observation at the other. Using this device, the doctor may examine the patient's heart or stomach in continuous action. The fluorescent screen is usually coated with barium platinocyanide. The impinging x-rays excite the atoms composing this fluorescent material, causing their electrons to move to more distant orbits. When the electrons return to lower orbits, they re-radiate the absorbed energy, but at a lower frequency, in the form of light (see ENERGY LEVEL). Thus an invisible radiation, namely the x-rays, is translated into visible light on the screen.—*A. E.*

FOAM: see EMULSION.

FOCUS (in mathematics): see CONIC SECTIONS.

FOCUS (in optics): the point in space at which an optical image is formed. In a camera, for example, the lens focuses an image of the object to be photographed on the surface of the film. In general, an optical instrument is said to be in focus when all the rays of light that pass through the instrument's aperture from a point on the object-side of the lens are brought together at a single point on the image-side. For a simple thin lens, the image distance D_i, the object distance D_o, and the focal length f of the lens are related through the following formula: $1/D_i + 1/D_o = 1/f$. In practice, the

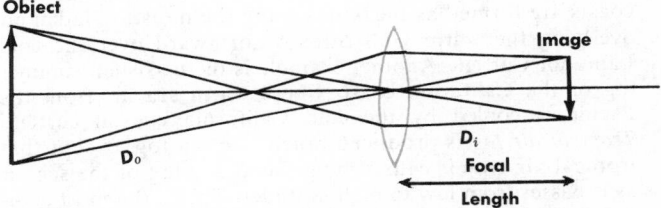

Focal length f of lens, object distance D_o, and image distance D_i have relationship expressed by $1/D_i + 1/D_o = 1/f$.

effects of DIFFRACTION and lens aberrations limit the sharpness with which any optical system can be focused. Instead of a point, the light rays at the image form a tiny circle—for a good camera lens, less than 0.002 in. (0.05 mm) in diameter. If the object does not lie all in one plane, its entire image cannot be in focus at once. In photography, an acceptably sharp image can be obtained over a certain distance on either side of the object plane; this distance, called the *depth of field*, varies with the focal length and aperture of the lens, with the object's distance, and with the required sharpness of the photograph. In inexpensive fixed-focus cameras, the depth of field runs from about 6 ft to infinity, with the sharpest focus set for about 12 ft. More complicated cameras are fitted with a scale that allows the photographer to estimate the depth of field for any lens setting.—*D. H. L.*

FOG: a cloud that forms on or near the ground, reducing horizontal visibility to the point where flying, driving, or even walking becomes hazardous. Fog is most common along seacoasts in temperate zones, and near large inland bodies of water. A cloud capping a mountain may also be called fog. Fog is widespread in areas where the prevailing winds carry moist air inland over gradually rising terrain. Such an area is the Mississippi Valley basin, where the prevalent air flow from the Gulf of Mexico spreads fog far inland during fall and winter months. Fog may form in one area and be blown into another. The most common physical process that results in fog is the cooling of the air to its saturation temperature. The addition of water vapor to the air until saturation results is another means by which fog may be formed. Fog and the low-lying stratus clouds often associated with it reduce visibility and ceilings so greatly that all flying into affected areas is hazardous, and take-offs must be restricted. Attempts have been made, with varying success, to dissipate fog by artificial means (see WEATHER MODIFICATION).

Fogs are generally divided into two main classes: air-mass fogs and frontal fogs.

Air-mass Fogs: These are fogs that occur *within* air masses, entirely uninfluenced by events along frontal zones. There are four basic types: (1) *advection fogs,* which include those caused by the movement of warm air over a cooler surface, and by the flow of cold air over a warm surface; (2) *radiation fogs,* the most prevalent of which is ground fog; (3) *advection-radiation fogs,* in which cooling is accomplished by the combined effects of advection and radiation; (4) *upslope fogs,* in which cooling is produced by adiabatic expansion. The most prevalent type of advection fog is caused by the cooling of warm, moist air by an underlying cold surface. The *land-sea breeze fogs* of the New England coast are caused by the flow of warm, moist air from the land to the cold coastal waters. These fogs are found on the east coasts of continents and over large bodies of inland water such as the Great Lakes. *Sea fogs* are another example of the cooling of warm, moist air by an underlying cold surface; they form as warm, moist sea air passes abruptly from warm to cold waters. The dense sea fogs of the Grand Banks off the Newfoundland-Labrador coasts are formed as the winds bring the moisture-laden air overlying the warm Gulf Stream northward over the cold Labrador Current. Another example is the persistent summer fog of the California coast, where warm sea air from the Pacific is cooled by the cold California coastal current. *Tropical-air fog* is produced much like sea fog, except that tropical-air type is caused by gradual cooling of the sea air as it passes from low to high latitudes. This is the most common variety found over the open sea. *Steam fogs* are advection fogs formed by movement of cold air over warm water. They can be reproduced by placing a pan of water outdoors in very cold air, the fog being caused by evaporation of water vapor from the water surface into the cold air, where it condenses rapidly into visible droplets. Steam fog is seen over unfrozen lakes and streams during very cold weather; it can occur with air temperature as high as 41°F, provided the water temperature is 9 to 12°F warmer than the air temperature. These fogs sometimes extend as high as 50 to 100 ft above the water surface. Steam fogs formed in polar regions, where both ice and open water are present, were named "arctic sea smoke" by early explorers. *Radiation fog* is caused by nighttime radiative cooling of moist air to its saturation temperature. On a night with clear skies and very light winds, the air will cool sufficiently for the formation of ground fog, a dense fog on the ground, through which the sky, however, can be seen during daylight hours, or the stars at night. Light

winds are essential for the formation of ground fog; if the air is calm, dew instead of ground fog is most likely to form. The ground type formed in areas where smoke is present tends to become denser when the sun comes up. Sunlight promotes the combination of fog and smoke into particles that attract more water vapor, thus increasing its density until considerable warming takes place. *Advection-radiation fog* is produced by a combination of the above two processes: the nighttime radiation cooling of warm, moist air that was advected inland from over the sea during the preceding daylight hours. This type of fog is a frequent late-summer and autumn phenomenon in the Gulf Coast areas of the southeastern U. S. A. It causes very low ceilings and visibilities over widespread areas during the last hours of darkness and the early daylight hours. *Upslope fog* forms as a result of cooling by adiabatic expansion. As air is forced gradually upslope by the prevailing wind, it expands and cools adiabatically (see ADIABATIC PROCESS). The Great Plains of the U. S. A. and Canada, which slope gradually upward from south to north, are subject to widespread fogs when winds blow steadily northward from the Gulf of Mexico. The great Atlantic coastal peneplain also affords the sloping terrain necessary for upslope fog formation. With strong easterly winds, upslope fog forms in the foothills on the eastern slopes of the Appalachians.

Frontal Fogs: These fogs are caused by the addition of moisture to cool air from falling rain. Since warm rain falls into cold air ahead of warm fronts and behind cold fronts, frontal fog is either pre-warm frontal or post-cold frontal. —*P. L.*

FOLD: in geology, a curvature in layered rocks. Folds are generally associated with sedimentary rocks or their metamorphic equivalents, *i.e.* with rocks which, with few exceptions, were originally horizontal. Stresses built up in the crust of the earth (see TECTONICS) are relieved by either fracturing (FAULTING) or folding. The degree of deformation by folding varies from barely noticeable curvature to highly contorted and crumpled forms, and folds may vary from the microscopic in size to those many miles across. It is only the small-scale folds that can be seen in their entirety in rock samples or on cliff faces; the presence and the type of the large-scale folds become evident after the strike and dip of outcrops over a wide area are plotted on a map.

Fig. 1 illustrates the basic types of folds. A *syncline* is a downfold, and an *anticline* an upfold. Each has two limbs, and a syncline and an anticline that are adjacent have a limb in common. The crest is the top of an anticline, and the trough the bottom of a syncline. A *monocline,* or one-limbed flexure in otherwise horizontal layers, is commonly found in plateau areas where uplift has not been uniform; a monocline may, if traced along its length, change gradually to a normal fault. The *axial plane* divides a fold (anticline or syncline) into two equal halves, and the intersection of this plane with any bed forms a line, the *axis* of the fold, whose orientation

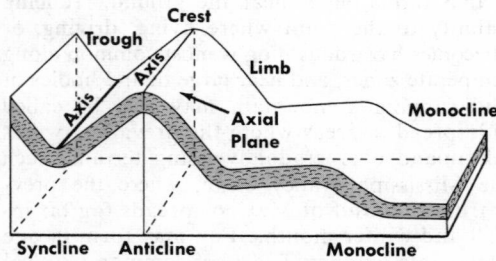

Fig. 1: Basic Types of Folds.

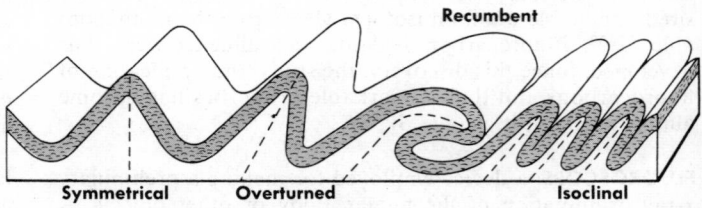

Fig. 2: Variety of Synclines and Anticlines.

Small syncline (human figure gives scale) is apparent in this highly folded formation in sandstones and shales of Washington County, Md.

Anticline in same region of Maryland is revealed through exposure of upfolded strata. (Both photographs U. S. Geological Survey)

defines the direction of folding. The axial plane in a simple symmetrical fold is vertical. In all other folds, however, it is inclined, and in some folds may be a curved surface rather than plane. Fig. 2 illustrates a variety of anticlines and synclines from simple *symmetrical,* to *overturned* (one of the limbs overturned), *recumbent* (a fold which if traced along its length may merge into a thrust fault), and *isoclinal* (a series of folds whose axial planes are equally inclined). The traces of the axial planes of the anticlines are shown dotted.

A *dome* is an anticlinal uplift in which the limbs dip away from a central point. A *basin* is a symmetrical downwarp in which the limbs dip toward a central point. Both of these structures have no trend and thus no axis. An *anticlinorium* is a major anticline composed of a number of smaller-scale folds, and a *synclinorium* is a major syncline composed of a number of smaller-scale folds.

Highly folded rocks are found in limited, narrow belts where the crust has been subject to great compression, *e.g.* the Alps, Rockies, Appalachians, and Himalayas. Elsewhere, the layered rocks have in general only slight dips, commonly associated with large basin and dome structures. Folded rocks resemble to some extent a crumpled tablecloth. In both, a fold if traced along its length will be found to die out, and where the fold disappears it plunges. The *angle of plunge* is the angle which the fold axis makes with the horizontal. In the process of folding there must be some differential motion between the various layers. In a sequence of sediments such as alternating sandstone and shale layers, the shale is far less competent to carry stresses, and most of the relative shifting and adjustments will take place here. An individual shale

layer may noticeably thicken at the crests and troughs of a fold, and thin along the flanks.

On erosion, a sequence of folded rocks gives rise to roughly parallel ridges and valleys. The ridges are located where resistant layers are exposed and the valleys where there are weaker layers. In the case of a plunging fold, ridges will not be parallel but will converge. Both parallel and converging ridges and valleys are well developed in the Appalachian Mts.—*J. Sh.*

FOLIATION: a kind of layering in metamorphic rock due to segregation or replacement of constituents on recrystallization. It is particularly conspicuous if constituents differ in color. Foliation may develop along inherited planar structures, *e.g.* the flowage of igneous rocks or the bedding of sedimentary rocks, or even along earlier secondary structures, *e.g.* axial-plane cleavages. Recrystallization under directed stresses may result in foliation that transects earlier structures. Platy or elongate minerals that crystallize under stress tend to parallel the foliation planes and cause ready cleavage (= fissility or schistosity) along these planes. Foliation is the characteristic feature of all GNEISSES AND SCHISTS.—*L. M.*

FOLIC ACID: see VITAMIN.

FOOD: the materials taken into the body of an animal and used as a source of chemical energy as well as a source of materials needed for maintenance and growth. Food may be derived from the bodies or products of plants, animals, or both. All foods are made up largely of three basic foodstuffs:

PROTEINS, CARBOHYDRATES, and FATS (or lipids). These foodstuffs are used in METABOLISM as sources of energy and as raw materials for the synthesis of tissue constituents. The word *diet* is used to describe the quantity and nature of foods eaten. The science of *nutrition* is concerned with the characteristics of diets adequate to support life, health, and growth, and with the composition of foods and the mechanisms of action of food components in the body. An adequate diet must contain certain quantities and proportions of the basic foodstuffs, and of accessory substances such as vitamins and minerals. See also ENERGY (in biochemistry).—*B. T. S.*

FOOD ADDITIVE: a substance, usually a chemical or combination of chemicals, added in the production, processing, packaging, or cooking of food to preserve, protect, or enhance flavor or nutritive content. Each of these substances, whether natural or synthetic, is used for a specific end; many of the over 2,000 additives recognized by the U. S. Food and Drug Administration are common chemicals such as sugar, salt, vinegar, and vitamins. General types of additives are: preservatives to minimize spoilage (*e.g.* salt, benzoic acid, sorbic acid); antibiotics (used in poultry dips and feed for medication and growth stimulation); ANTIOXIDANTS to delay oxidative deterioration (ascorbic acid and butylated hydroxyanisole); food sequesterants for chelating trace metals and food texturizers and physical stabilizers (citric acid, sodium phosphate, and calcium chloride); surfactants (SURFACE-ACTIVE AGENTS) and emulsifiers (see EMULSION) to stabilize oil-water combinations (lecithin, sorbitan stearate); stabilizers, thickeners, and gelling agents (pectin, plant gums, and cellulose derivatives); bleaches such as hydrogen peroxide or benzoyl peroxide; food buffers to control the acid-alkaline balance for flavor, texture, or cooking response (cream of tartar, citric acid, and sodium bicarbonate); food colors to enhance appearance (colors for butter, margarine, oranges, candy, and ice cream); non-nutritive sweeteners such as the saccharines and cyclamates; nutritive supplements such as minerals and vitamins. Flavoring agents include synthetic flavor components, salt, monosodium glutamate, essential oils, and vanilla; other additives serve as humectants, wax texturizers, anti-sticking agents, and rising agents.—*R. W. F.*

FOOD CHAIN: a group of organisms constituting a "chain" (rarely including more than six kinds) each member of which is eaten by the next. Charles Darwin pointed out that in Britain the success of bumblebees was related to the availability of nectar from red clover flowers and to the rarity of attacks by mice on bumblebee nests in clover fields. If house cats eat enough mice, bumblebees tend to increase to the limit of their nectar supply. The energy in nectar is passed along from clover plant to bee to mouse to cat, making this a food chain. Actually, the food-chain concept is an oversimplification. Each ecological situation is linked together into a food web with alternative pathways. (See BALANCE OF NATURE; ECOLOGY.)—*L. and M. M.*

FOOT: a general non-technical term for the part of an animal that rests against the surface on which it moves. In a man or bear, it consists of the portion of the leg beyond the ankle joint. In a cow or horse, the foot is only the end of one or two toes, since the heel is high above the ground and regarded as part of the shank. In an ARTHROPOD such as an insect, the foot is the tarsus—the outermost few segments beyond the tibia. Clams have on the midline a single foot with which they reach into the mud and pull themselves along. Snails and slugs are regarded as gliding on a single flat foot, whereas a squid or octopus is "head-footed" (hence "cephalopod") in that the part of the body corresponding to the foot of a snail bears the elaborate eyes and extends into a number of sucker-studded tentacles or arms. (See MOLLUSK.) ECHINODERMS bear tube-feet as part of their unique water-vascular system. Starfishes, sea cucumbers, and sea urchins use tube-feet in locomotion, whereas sea lilies employ them only in capturing food. See SKELETON.—*L. and M. M.*

FOOT-POUND-SECOND SYSTEM: the units of length, force, and time, respectively, used as a system in English-speaking countries. Since the dominant tendency in modern science is quantitative—*i.e.* to draw conclusions by measuring the results of experiments—a consistent system of measurement is necessary. In 1799 the METRIC SYSTEM, based on the meter as a unit of length, was adopted by France; it has since been accepted

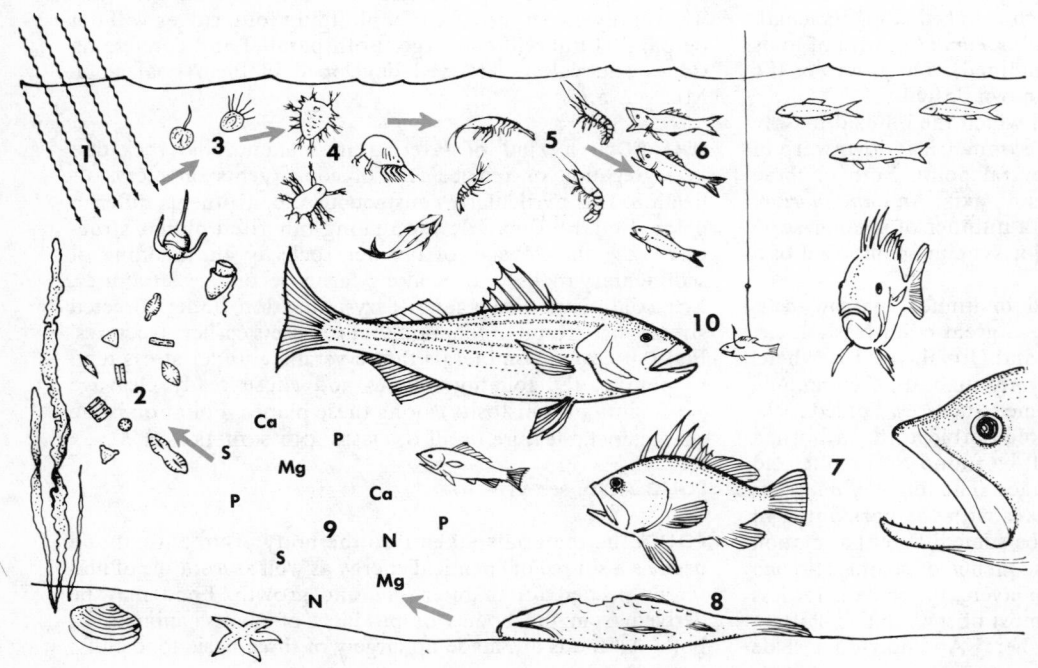

Marine food chain: Sunlight (1) furnishes energy used by plants (2) and certain protozoa (3) to make their food by photosynthesis. These organisms are eaten by larvae and crustaceans (4, 5), which are food for small fish (6) that are eaten by larger fish (7). Fish die and decay (8), providing water with nitrogenous and mineral matter (9) that is absorbed by plants and animals (2, 3), completing the chain. Sometimes man becomes a link of the chain (10). Organisms are not drawn to same scale. (*After Manter*)

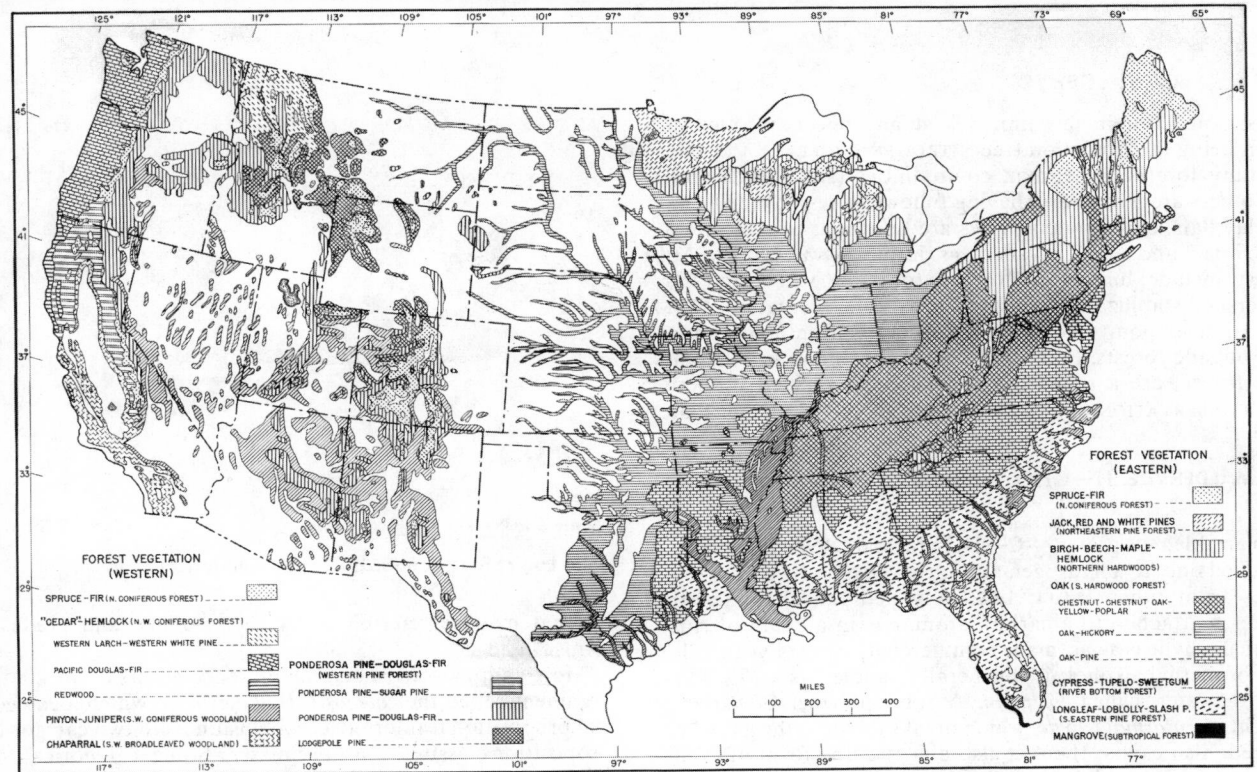

Distribution of Forest Vegetation in the United States (*U. S. Forest Service*)

FOREST VEGETATION
(WESTERN)

SPRUCE–FIR (N. CONIFEROUS FOREST)

"CEDAR"–HEMLOCK (N. W. CONIFEROUS FOREST)

WESTERN LARCH–WESTERN WHITE PINE

PACIFIC DOUGLAS–FIR

REDWOOD

PINYON–JUNIPER (S.W. CONIFEROUS WOODLAND)

CHAPARRAL (S.W. BROADLEAVED WOODLAND)

PONDEROSA PINE–DOUGLAS–FIR
(WESTERN PINE FOREST)

PONDEROSA PINE–SUGAR PINE

PONDEROSA PINE–DOUGLAS–FIR

LODGEPOLE PINE

FOREST VEGETATION
(EASTERN)

SPRUCE–FIR
(N. CONIFEROUS FOREST)

JACK, RED AND WHITE PINES
(NORTHEASTERN PINE FOREST)

BIRCH–BEECH–MAPLE–
HEMLOCK
(NORTHERN HARDWOODS)

OAK (S. HARDWOOD FOREST)

CHESTNUT–CHESTNUT OAK–
YELLOW–POPLAR

OAK–HICKORY

OAK–PINE

CYPRESS–TUPELO–SWEETGUM
(RIVER BOTTOM FOREST)

LONGLEAF–LOBLOLLY–SLASH P.
(S.EASTERN PINE FOREST)

MANGROVE (SUBTROPICAL FOREST)

MILES
0   100   200   300   400

by scientists everywhere. But in English-speaking countries, the traditional weights and measures based on the foot and the pound are used commercially and in engineering practice. The unit used universally for measuring time is the second, defined as 9,192,631,770 oscillations of a cesium atom in an atomic clock.—*A. L.*

"FORBIDDEN" LINES: spectral lines produced by quanta emitted during the transition of an excited atom from a nearly stable state to a lower ENERGY LEVEL. Collisions between atoms reduce the probability of such a transition to near-impossibility at normal gas densities because they provide energy for the atom to get into a less stable state; from this it can make an "allowed" transition rather than the "forbidden" one. At low densities, however, such as are found at the fringes of Earth's atmosphere and the Sun's corona, as well as in nebulas, collisions are so rare, relatively, that "forbidden" transitions do occur. The green color of the aurora is the result of a forbidden line produced only when an excited oxygen atom lasts for half a second or more between collisions.—*D. H. L.*

FORCE: the physical agent that brings about a change in the momentum, or "quantity of motion," of a body. In accordance with Newton's second law of motion, force is directly proportional to the product of the mass of the body (*m*) and the time rate of change of the body's velocity, or its acceleration (*a*). Since $F = kma$ (where k is a factor of proportionality), it is desirable to set k equal to 1 by defining a unit force as that which is required to impart to a unit mass a unit acceleration. Accordingly, a force of 1 dyne is that which accelerates a mass of 1 gm at a rate of 1 cm/sec² in the direction of the force applied. Similarly, a force of 1 newton will accelerate a mass of 1 kg at a rate of 1 m/sec². Finally, an acceleration of 1 ft/sec² is imparted to a mass of 1 lb by a force of 1 poundal, and to a mass of 1 slug (about 32 lb) by a force of 1 lb. The above are units of force in the cgs, mks, and fps (engineering) systems of measurement, respectively. (See MEASUREMENT SYSTEMS.) A force that displaces an object

does WORK, and the time rate at which the work is done is known as POWER.—*A. E.*

FOREL, FRANÇOIS ALPHONSE, 1841–1912, Swiss geographer and geologist; b. Morges. He investigated seismology, Alpine glaciers, and the geology of Lake Geneva, on whose shores he was born and lived. The results of his researches on the lake are summed up in his *Le Léman* (3 vols., 1892–1902). He also wrote *Handbook of Limnology* (1901).—*D. H. D. R.*

FOREST: any assemblage of vegetation dominated by trees in a more or less continuous canopy. Woody vegetation that is more open is distinguished as woodland; isolated trees and small clumps in grassy plains are called savannas. According to structure and dominant tree types, forests of the world are generally divided as follows: *tropical rain forest*—evergreen and broad-leaved trees, many lianas, epiphytes (*e.g.* in Amazon basin); *temperate rain forest*—evergreen and broad-leaved trees, but with a less complex structure (*e.g.* in Formosa); *monsoon forest*—large-leaved deciduous trees in tropical areas with dry season (*e.g.* India); *deciduous forest* (*e.g.* maple forests in eastern U. S.); *dry evergreen hardwood forest*—small-leaved trees (*e.g.* live oak hammocks in southeastern U. S.); *evergreen conifer forests,* with undergrowth of lichens and mosses (*e.g.* Canadian spruce forests). The distribution of these forest types is limited by climatic factors.

Forests can be thought of as highly stratified vegetation. A tall tree layer, a lower tree layer, a shrub layer, an herb layer with spring flowers, and a moss layer form the integrated biological unit called the forest "stand" (see COMMUNITY, ANIMAL AND PLANT). The component tree species of a forest vary with HABITAT and geographic location (see PLANT GEOGRAPHY). Each continent has its own flora; thus a European deciduous forest is composed of different species than its American counterpart. Habitats such as flood plains support cottonwood and sycamore; valleys and coves often contain species like hemlock and tulip tree, while dry SOILS favor pines and oaks. Most forest soils are characterized by deep weathering and leaching. Compared to agricultural soils, forest soils contain few minerals at any one time, most of them being in circulation (see NITROGEN CYCLE).

Many forests are climax communities (see SUCCESSION), but others are temporary, having followed fires, invaded sand or clay flats, etc. Climax species are known as tolerant trees, subclimax and early invaders as intolerant trees. Uses of forests include: lumber supply, pulp for paper, wood products, watershed stabilization, shelter for wildlife, recreation. Conservationists point out that many species of animals cannot live outside forests, that flood control begins in forests, and that forests are a renewable resource if managed properly (see CONSERVATION OF NATURAL RESOURCES). See Color Plate 48.—*K. L.*

FORMALDEHYDE: H—CHO, the simplest chemical compound

$$\overset{O}{\underset{\|}{}}$$

with an aldehyde group, —C—H. In formaldehyde the group is attached only to a hydrogen atom; this gives it different properties from other ALDEHYDES, in which the characteristic group is attached to a carbon atom, *e.g.* in a chain or ring. Formaldehyde is a gas, made commercially by catalytic oxidation of methyl alcohol; it is generally handled as a 37% solution in water, called *formalin.* A solid polymer of variable weight, *paraformaldehyde,* which breaks down to the gas when heated, also exists; there is also a crystalline form of cyclic structure. Formaldehyde is used as a disinfectant and as a preservative for biological specimens. It is an important intermediate for chemicals, medicinals, and explosives. Formaldehyde ties up amino groups of proteins, thus rendering toxic proteins harmless, but does not change their immunological properties. This is the basis for production of Salk polio vaccine and of tetanus and diphtheria toxoids. In the cell, formaldehyde serves as a precursor of methyl groups.—*Ru. M.; E. S.*

FORMAL LOGIC (classical and mathematical): Formal logic is the systematic study of demonstrative reasoning, the process in which one proposition (the conclusion) is affirmed to follow necessarily from one or more other propositions (the premises) which are accepted as the starting point of the process. The goal of formal logic is to develop methods and principles for distinguishing correct from incorrect reasoning. It approaches this goal by abstracting from the content or subject matter of the reasoning and focusing attention on the *form* of the argument in which the reasoning is expressed. This formal approach to the study of reasoning is not new. It was used by Aristotle, the ancient founder of logic, in his investigations of fairly simple kinds of reasoning or inference.

The bulk of classical formal logic derives directly from Aristotle, who was concerned almost exclusively with so-called categorical propositions and inferences involving them. A categorical proposition is one containing a single subject term and a single predicate term. The four standard forms of categorical propositions may be illustrated by the following: (1) All men are mortal; (2) No men are mortal; (3) Some men are mortal; (4) Some men are not mortal. An *immediate* inference is one in which a conclusion is drawn from a single premiss. Fairly obvious immediate inferences involving categorical propositions are: *conversion,* in which "No *P* is *S*" is validly inferred from "No *S* is *P*," and "Some *P* is *S*" is validly inferred from "Some *S* is *P*"; *obversion,* in which "No *S* is non-*P*" is validly inferred from "All *S* is *P*," and "Some *S* is non-*P*" is validly inferred from "Some *S* is not *P*"; and *contraposition,* in which "All non-*P* is non-*S*" is validly inferred from "All *S* is *P*." It is clear that these immediate inferences are formally valid in the sense that any arguments of these forms are valid regardless of the particular subject mat-

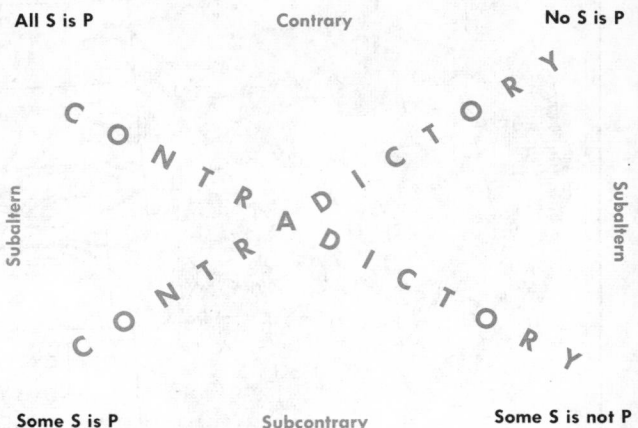

Logic: four standard forms of categorical propositions.

ter that may be referred to by their subject and predicate terms *S* and *P*.

More complicated (mediate) inference occurs in the kind of argument called the *categorical syllogism,* in which a categorical proposition is inferred as conclusion from two categorical propositions assumed as premises. Some categorical syllogisms are obviously valid, *e.g.* "All *M* is *P*, all *S* is *M*, therefore all *S* is *P*"; whereas others are clearly invalid, *e.g.* "Some *M* is *P*, some *M* is *S*, therefore some *S* is *P*." Every possible form of categorical syllogism was classified as valid or invalid by Aristotle. Medieval followers of Aristotle elaborated his logical results without extending them significantly from the point of view of formal logic.

Other ancient formal logicians, of the Stoic School, developed a formal logic of compound statements, where a *compound* statement is a proposition that contains one or more categorical propositions as component parts. Typical valid arguments considered by the Stoics were: "If *p* then *q, q* is false, therefore *p* is false," and "If *p* then *q,* if *q* then *r,* therefore if *p* then *r,*" in which the letters *p, q, r* represent propositions rather than terms. The formal logic of the Stoics was rediscovered only recently, having been without influence during the medieval and early modern periods.

Mathematical formal logic is a comparatively recent development, although it was previsioned long ago by the philosopher-mathematician Leibniz (1646–1716) as a *calculus ratiocinator* which would reduce all reasoning to exact calculation. One of the earliest modern formal logicians, George Boole (1815–64), developed a theory and symbolism for categorical propositions that permitted algebraic manipula-

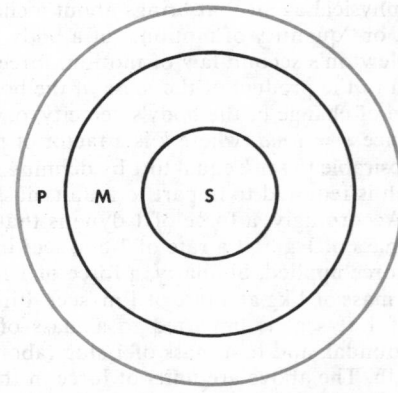

Logic: If all S is M and all M is P, then all S must also be P.

tions to be performed on them. The essence of his treatment was to interpret both subject and predicate terms as designating classes: thus the categorical proposition "All soldiers are patriotic" is construed as asserting that the class of all soldiers is entirely contained in, or is a subclass of, the class of all patriots. To permit such propositions to be expressed in the form of equations certain abstract notions were introduced and certain symbolic notations were utilized. Perhaps the central abstract notion was that of the *empty class,* the class containing no members whatsoever, for which the numerical zero symbol *0* is often used. Now to say that there are no things of a certain kind (say, centaurs) is to say that the class of all things of that kind is empty. Using the letter *C* to designate the class of all centaurs, the proposition denying that there are any centaurs can be expressed by the equation $C = 0$. And using the letter *H* to designate the class of all horses, the proposition affirming that there are horses can be expressed by the inequality $H \neq 0$. Two other notions must be introduced for two-termed categorical propositions to be expressed as equations. One is the notion of the *complement* of a class, which is another class containing all those things and only those things that are not members of the given class. For example, the complement of the class *H* of all horses contains everything in the universe that is not a horse, and is symbolized as H'. The other notion required is that of the *product* of two classes, which is another class containing all and only those things that belong to both of the given classes. For example, the product of the class *S* of all soldiers and the class *P* of all patriots is the class *SP* of all patriotic soldiers. With these notions and notations the four standard forms of categorical propositions previously mentioned can be written as equations: "All *S* is *P*" as $SP' = 0$, "No *S* is *P*" as $SP = 0$, "Some *S* is *P*" as $SP \neq 0$, and "Some *S* is not *P*" as $SP' \neq 0$.

The equations expressing categorical propositions can be manipulated algebraically in ways very similar to the ways in which numerical algebraic equations are solved. There are significant differences, however, and the logical system devised by Boole is called "Boolean algebra." It can be used to classify a large range of arguments into the valid and the invalid, and also to deduce conclusions from premises by algebraic processes of combination and cancellation. Interpreted as dealing with classes, as originally intended by Boole, Boolean algebra is commonly referred to as the "Algebra of Classes." Boolean algebra is an abstract formal system, however, and can be given other interpretations and put to other uses. One of the most fruitful of these alternative interpretations is in terms of voltage states of electrical systems, in which Boolean algebra has direct and important application to general switching theory and to the logical design of electronic digital computers.

Not all arguments, however, can be adequately expressed in the notations of Boolean algebra. Arguments involving *relations* are of too high an order of logical complexity to be treated by these traditional or elementary methods. For example, the argument "All horses are animals, therefore the head of a horse is the head of an animal," is a non-syllogistic inference that all the logic of Aristotle and Boole combined will not permit one to draw. Studies in the logic of relations were begun by the American logician Charles S. Peirce and the English mathematician Augustus De Morgan and have occupied a central place in all subsequent logical investigations.

Newer and more advanced systems of formal mathematical logic were developed and applied to the growing body of mathematics proper in two ways. In one way the notions of logic were used to give *definitions* of strictly mathematical concepts, *e.g. number* and *function.* Gottlob Frege and Bert-

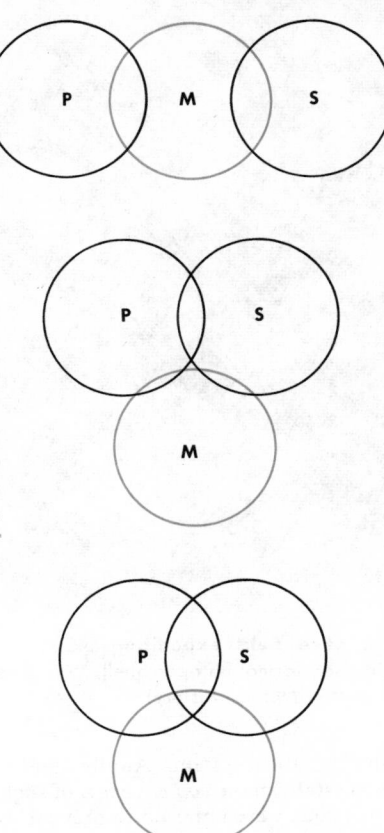

Logic: If some M is P and some M is S, some S may or may not be P. As shown in bottom diagram, it is possible also that some of the P that is M is some of the P that is S.

rand Russell discovered independently that *all* mathematical concepts could be defined in terms of the notions of pure logic. Another application of logic to mathematics proper was the deduction of *mathematical truths* as *theorems* from truths of formal logic accepted as *axioms.* The most impressive result of this line of investigation was the monumental 3-vol. *Principia Mathematica* of Alfred North Whitehead and Bertrand Russell, intended to provide a deductive system in which all truths of mathematics could be deduced from a small set of purely logical axioms.

Meanwhile contradictions had begun to appear within both mathematics and logic itself. Of these the simplest and easiest to explain was discovered by Bertrand Russell, and is generally called "Russell's paradox." Most classes do not seem to contain themselves as members. For example, the class *H* of all horses is not itself a horse and therefore is not a member of *H*. But now consider the class of all classes-which-do-not-contain-themselves-as-members, which we can represent by the letter *C*. If *C* is a member of *C* then it must be a class-which-does-not-contain-itself-as-member, whence *C* is *not* a member of *C*. But if *C* is not a member of *C,* then *C is* a class-which-does-not-contain-itself-as-member, whence *C is* a member of *C*. Here is the contradiction made explicit: *C* both is and is not a member of itself. Alternative resolutions of this type of contradiction are available—Russell himself provided one of the most satisfactory of them in his Theory of Types. But there remained the danger that other kinds of contradictions might arise within logico-mathematical systems. A new task had presented itself: that of proving the *consistency* of

Paleontologist of a field expedition excavates a dinosaur skeleton in Morrison formation near Shell, Wyo. (*Barnum Brown/ American Museum of Natural History*)

such logico-mathematical systems. Another and clearly related problem was to establish the *completeness* of such systems, for if enough restrictions were imposed to prevent the emergence of contradictions, perhaps this would prevent the derivation of some desired mathematical truths as well.

In 1931 a bold attempt was made by Kurt Gödel to prove the completeness and consistency of a logico-mathematical system within that system itself. In his investigation he made use of a symbolic device that had been suggested centuries earlier by Leibniz. But the result Gödel obtained was just the reverse of that which he had been seeking. Gödel's result can be informally stated as follows: If any logico-mathematical system of the general type of *Principia Mathematica* is consistent, then it is necessarily incomplete—incomplete in the sense that there is a purely mathematical formula expressible in the system such that neither the formula nor its denial is provable in that system. Of course larger and more comprehensive systems can be constructed, adequate to the derivation of larger numbers of mathematical truths, and adequate to deciding the validity of more and more complicated arguments. But no such system can ever be complete so long as it is self-consistent. From one point of view Gödel's result can be regarded as setting a limit on the results attainable in the field of formal logic. But from another point of view he can be said to have proved that there is no limit to the development of more and more nearly complete consistent systems of logic.—*I. C.*

FORMIC ACID: a carboxylic acid with the simplest structure,

$$H-\overset{\overset{\displaystyle O}{\|}}{C}-OH,$$ and with the properties of an aldehyde ($H\overset{\overset{\displaystyle O}{\|}}{C}$). It is a metabolite of one-carbon fragments in the body which arise in nucleic-acid synthesis and breakdown and in the metabolism of the amino acids glycine and serine. A derivative of the vitamin folic acid is involved in the transfer of formyl groups from glycine to form serine and also the PURINE and PYRIMIDINE bases of the nucleic acids and nucleotides. —*J. F. S.*

FOSSIL: in geology, any evidence of plant or animal remains deposited prior to the close of the last glacial period. The word is from Latin *fossilis,* "something dug up." Fossils may consist of preserved bones, shells, or wood; or impressions on rock of any part of an organism, as a foot, skin, leaf; or natural casts of complete organisms, as sea shells; or of some part of an organism, as a brain cast from which the bone covering has been removed. Eggs and excreta of extinct animals, too, are fossils. The study of fossils is called PALEONTOLOGY. Organisms in which the hard parts are preserved may become altered through petrifaction or remain in their original state. Usually the degree of alteration increases with the specimen's age; thus bones of Paleozoic and Mesozoic animals (at least 60 million years old) are nearly always well altered and composed principally of a replacing mineral. When a vertebrate, for example, is buried in sediment, the soft parts may decompose and disappear rapidly, leaving only the hard parts. Through the millions of years that follow burial, minerals in solution are carried by ground water to the bone, where they crystallize out of solution and fill all of the minute pores of the bone. Much of the original bone material may be dissolved and by a complex process replaced with mineral matter. Such replacement may preserve even the most minute detail of the cellular structure of the specimen. Wood is usually preserved in this manner.

Many small organisms, particularly insects, have been preserved in their entirety by being covered alive with resin exuded by pines. The hardened resin is known as amber. Extinct mammoths that have lain frozen in the ice of Alaska and Siberia for thousands of years are occasionally preserved without alteration; in some cases the meat is so perfectly preserved that wolves have been known to eat it. Often showers of volcanic ash have buried and preserved organic material in essentially natural form. In Los Angeles, Calif., fossils exist that have been preserved in an asphalt seep known as Rancho La Brea; here the tarlike substance has acted as an excellent preservative and the bones have survived in their original state. There is every gradation between this type of fossil and those that are completely altered.

Design of fossil fern was preserved in exquisite detail in rock for millions of years. (*American Museum of Natural History*)

Many plant fossils have been preserved by coalification (carbonization), which occurred when plants fell into water, became waterlogged, and sank to the bottom, where, in the absence of air, the process of decay was delayed. When such specimens were covered with sediment they lost hydrogen, oxygen, and volatile organic substances, leaving a residue composed chiefly of carbon. But only rarely has this process achieved perfect preservation; most coal contains little intact tissue.

In fossils that consist of impressions, molds, or casts, no original part of the organism is preserved. Often the shell of a shellfish, for instance, was completely dissolved after burial, leaving a cavity or mold. This space then became filled with mineral matter, which made a natural cast showing all details of the original. Many invertebrate and plant fossils are impressions only, because there were no hard parts to survive.

Tracks of animals ranging from insects to the largest of dinosaurs are frequently found as fossils. Footprints were left in soft mud or sand which subsequently became covered with more mud or sand while the tracks were still present. Much later, the overlying deposits were eroded away and the footprints exposed. Leaves, rodent burrows, and holes bored by worms or other invertebrates are frequently found as casts or impressions. Very rarely such soft animals as jellyfish have been preserved or have left their impressions in rock. The skin of certain dinosaurs is well known from preserved impressions.

Sea-shell fossils of many ages are commonly found in ancient marine deposits, which are widely distributed because in different stages of the geologic past most parts of the continent have been submerged. Deposits containing remains of land animals are not so widely distributed nor so abundant as marine fossil beds. A series of Permian deposits in Texas (the Texas Red Beds) has produced numerous skeletons of primitive reptiles and amphibians. Fossil-bearing Triassic beds occur in New Mexico, Arizona, Colorado, Wyoming, and along the East Coast; the most fruitful Triassic bone deposits occur in South Africa. Jurassic and Cretaceous beds exposed in a long strip through the Rocky Mt states from Canada to Mexico are highly fossiliferous. Cenozoic fossils, consisting chiefly of mammal bones, are abundant in Wyoming, Nebraska, South Dakota, Montana, and Texas. Deposits of the last glacial period, the Pleistocene, are scattered widely over Canada and northern U. S. A., and almost any excavation in loose mantle rock may yield fossils.

Many impressions and petrifactions are found on surfaces of weathered rock or exposed in quarries. Vertebrate fossils are frequently found partially or wholly exposed along river banks, steep slopes, and canyon walls, where erosion has removed the overlying rock. Fossil bones, being very often brittle, are carefully exposed, hardened with shellac, and covered with paper and then plaster of paris. When the plaster is hard, the specimen is undermined, turned over, and given the same treatment on the underside. It can then be transported safely.

Many fossils, especially plant remains, are not easily accessible and are sought in mines and deep quarries. Much of the knowledge of Carboniferous plant life comes from plants preserved in clay concretions that are exposed in coal mines.

That fossils are the remains of ancient life was suspected by some of the ancient Greeks, and known by pioneers of geology in the 18th cent.; yet not until about 1796 was a practical scientific use for them discovered. William Smith, English founder of the technique of STRATIGRAPHY, was the first to show the usefulness of certain fossils as indicators of the relative ages of sedimentary rocks in which they occur. Since then "index fossils" have been the key to the reconstruction of the earth's history during the past 600 million yr. The occurrence of such fossils in any sedimentary formation is an immediate clue to its age. Knowledge of index fossils is of advantage in oil prospecting, which involves consideration of both ages and relative positions of hidden strata.

The relative ages of fossils are indicated by the relative ages of the strata in which the fossils are found. Absolute ages (in years) of fossils can often be approximately determined by RADIOACTIVE DATING.

Fossils provide proof of evolution, enabling zoologists and botanists to trace the history of living things. They also aid in biological classification. See LIFE, PREHISTORIC; PALEONTOLOGY; and Color Plate 49.—*P. McG.*

FOUCAULT, JEAN BERNARD LÉON, 1819–68, French physicist; b. Paris. His researches include work on light, electricity, and magnetism. However, he is most famous for the FOUCAULT PENDULUM (first demonstrated 1851), which continues to swing in one plane as Earth turns, giving the illusion of slowly changing its plane of rotation. Foucault also invented the gyroscope (1852). His scientific writings were published as *Collection of Scientific Works* (1878). He was a fellow of the Royal Society.—*D. H. D. R.*

FOUCAULT PENDULUM: a demonstration of the earth's rotation first displayed by J. B. L. Foucault in Paris, 1852. The pendulum consists of a massive weight suspended on a long, fine steel wire. If the pendulum is allowed to swing for a

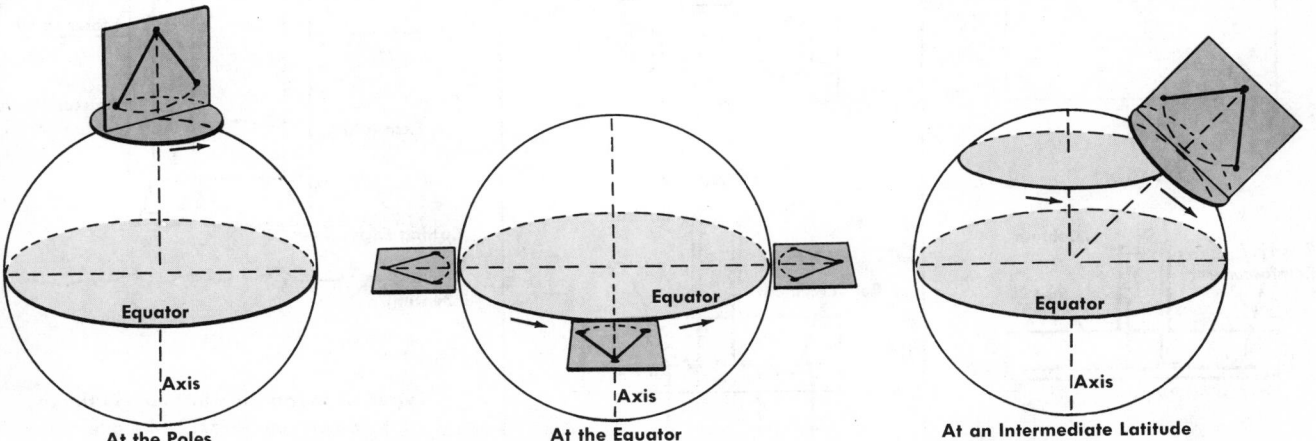

Foucault pendulum appears to rotate once in 24 hr if set up at the pole (*left*), and not at all if set up at the equator (*center*). At intermediate latitudes the period of rotation is greater than 24 hr. (After *Larousse*)

period of several hours, its plane of oscillation rotates with respect to the earth beneath it. This effect may be explained by considering the circle swept out by the plane of oscillation during a complete rotation. Assuming that the pendulum is set up in the northern hemisphere, the earth's rotation causes the southern edge of this circle to move from west to east at a slightly higher rate of speed than the northern edge, because the southern edge is farther from the earth's axis. The difference in the two rates, and hence the rate of apparent rotation of the plane of oscillation, depends on the latitude at which the pendulum is set up. At the equator the plane does not rotate at all, since both edges of the circle are equidistant from the axis; at the poles the plane rotates once in 24 hours, since the edges of the circle are on opposite sides of the axis. For intermediate latitudes, the rate is given by the formula $R = 15° \sin L$, where R is the rate of rotation in degree/hr and L is the latitude. The rate of rotation of the pendulum at the United Nations in N. Y. City (latitude about 40°43′) is about 9.78°/hr, and a complete rotation takes about 36 hr 49 min.—*E. M. R.*

FOUNDATION: commonly, the underlying portion of a structure which bears its weight. A structural foundation must be considered in two parts: (1) the ultimate foundation, or earth material on which the structure rests, and (2) the substructure, which serves to distribute the weight of the superstructure over the relatively weak (except for rock) foundation material. Most structures rest on soil, and the foundations engineer must deal with the behavior of soils under loads. Through theoretical soil mechanics, experimental investigations, and practical experience the engineer can with reasonable accuracy predict the bearing strength and the amount of settlement to be expected for a given structure at a known location: this is essential to total foundation design. (See SOIL PHYSICS AND MECHANICS.) Design of the substructure depends not only upon the magnitude and distribution of loads imposed by the superstructure above but also upon the nature of the foundation material below. Substructures for heavy buildings and bridges may be either (1) shallow or spread footings, (2) pile foundations, or (3) caissons. For *spread footings,* masonry or nonreinforced concrete piers in the form of truncated pyramids are the simplest designs. Timber grillages, consisting of two or more layers of heavy timbers set at right angles to each other, are suitable for temporary structures. Steel I-beam grillages support many of the permanent buildings in our large cities. The most important type of spread footing is the reinforced-concrete pad, which may support a single isolated column (column footing), two or more columns (combined footing), a bearing wall (wall footing), or a whole building (mat footing). *Pile foundations* consist of a series of long load-carrying elements driven or drilled into soft ground in order to reach good bearing material at depth (these are bearing piles) or to develop resistance through skin friction between the surface of the pile and the soil (friction piles). Piles are made of timber, concrete, steel, or combinations of these. They are usually driven with steam hammers, but some types of concrete piles are poured into previously drilled or driven holes. Their bearing strengths are determined by loading tests, pull-out tests, or rational pile-driving formulas. CAISSON *foundations* involve large, deep excavations to reach firm bearing material. The caisson is a permanent shell which is sunk into position as the excavation proceeds and which remains in place as an integral part of the foundation. An open caisson is a simple box open at top and bottom. A pneumatic caisson is closed at the top, and compressed air is used to keep mud and water from flowing in at the bottom during excavation.—*W. W.*

FOUNDATIONS OF MATHEMATICS: the clarification and justification of basic mathematical concepts and procedures. One of its tasks is to organize mathematical subjects into *formal systems* in which theorems are obtained from axioms by explicit rules of inference. Another is that of reducing complex mathematical notions to simpler ones by means of suitable definitions. Axiomatization and definition have always been important in mathematical research. The "foundations" are reached when the constructed axioms and concepts are basic or ultimate, *i.e.* are not further reducible within mathematics itself. Then the task of criticizing and

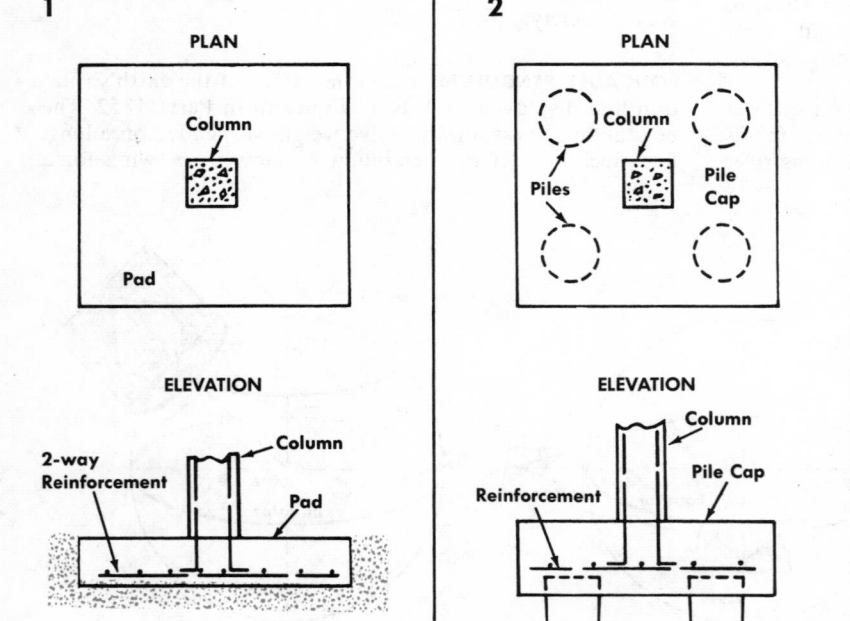

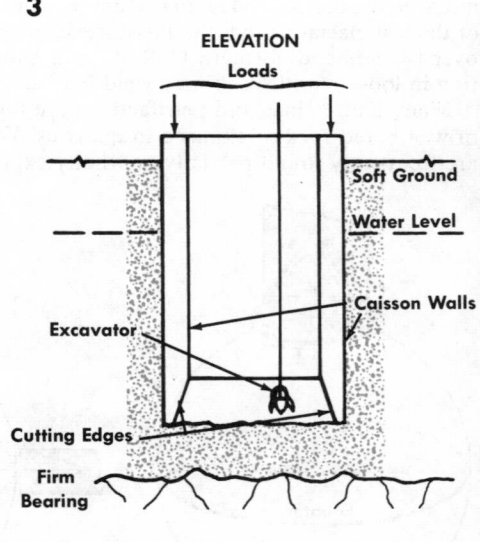

Types of foundation include (1) the reinforced-concrete pad, (2) the pile foundation, and (3) the caisson foundation.

justifying choices of basic terms and axioms is inescapable.

The following are typical questions: What is the nature of mathematical truth? Is mathematics a natural science resting, like physics, upon observation? What is meant by the existence of mathematical objects? Are mathematical results absolutely certain? Can the notion of a valid proof be completely defined? Such questions about the scope, source, and authority of mathematical

Bertrand Russell
(N. Y. Public Library)

knowledge are of great importance to philosophy and have been repeatedly discussed by its masters (*e.g.* Plato, Aristotle, Descartes, G. W. von Leibniz, Immanuel Kant). Not until the second half of the 19th cent. did the use of precise logical and mathematical methods begin to produce substantial progress. The 20th cent. has seen more advances in the subject than in all its previous history.

A powerful stimulus was the discovery of NON-EUCLIDEAN GEOMETRY by N. I. Lobachevsky, 1826, and by Karl Friedrich Gauss and János Bolyai. This showed the futility of· the ancient hope of proving the parallel axiom (that through a given point in a plane exactly one line runs parallel to a given line) and enforced a reluctant recognition of the relativity of geometrical truth. In the second half of the 19th cent., the foundations of geometry were intensively studied. David Hilbert's *Foundations of Geometry* (1902) corrected the deficiencies of Euclid's *Elements* and placed geometry for the first time on a satisfactory footing. With geometry fully axiomatized, its objects were henceforward regarded as unspecified individuals, limited in their properties only by stipulated axioms. In this way geometry could be treated as a branch of applied logic. That is to say, every geometrical theorem could be treated as the second clause of an if-then statement whose first clause is the conjunction of all the axioms needed to prove the theorem; such if-then statements are logical truths. Another way of understanding geometry, equally important, is to convert its propositions into arithmetical statements, by the introduction of suitable coordinate systems. Questions about the nature of arithmetic have always been central for the foundations of mathematics. (Its other main technical problem turns upon the nature of set theory.)

The program of "arithmetizing" mathematics, by reducing its concepts to those of arithmetic, was strenuously advocated by Leopold Kronecker, who said, "God made the integers; all the rest is man's doing." By the end of the 19th cent., this program had been very successful. Richard Dedekind, for instance, had produced a method (the Dedekind cut) still valuable for defining IRRATIONAL NUMBERS as classes of fractions. Other arithmetical reductions proved possible for most higher-level mathematical concepts. Renewed attention to the concept of class or set (a modified version of the notion of a group or collection of things arbitrarily assembled) was induced by Georg Cantor's remarkable investigations concerning TRANSFINITE NUMBERS. Although he created a fairyland of infinite numbers, subjected for the first time to strict definition and exact algebraic computation, the status of his work remains a controversial topic in the foundations of mathematics.

Meanwhile, a great flowering of logic in the second half of the 19th cent. provided sharp-edged tools for investigating foundational questions. The preparatory work of George Boole, C. S. Peirce, E. Schröder, and others, by showing how to apply mathematics to logic, extended the province of the first and introduced exact method into the second. Gottlob Frege, a genius at first sadly neglected, provided the subject with its first great synthesis in his *Principles of Arithmetic* (1893). In this book, equally remarkable for its philosophical insight and its forbidding symbolism, Frege tried to prove that the whole of mathematics could be reduced to logic. On this view, later known as *logicism,* mathematics is logic writ small, and the distinction between the two subjects is merely one of practical convenience. This view was also defended by Bertrand Russell in his important book *The Principles of Mathematics* (1903). A decade of intensive collaboration with Alfred North Whitehead yielded the second great classic of logicism, *Principia Mathematica* (1910–13). Using a symbolism more practicable than Frege's, its authors performed the herculean task of actually constructing the basic mathematical concepts and axioms from logical materials. A definite arithmetical statement such as "There are two poles" can be analyzed relatively easily into "There is a pole and another pole" (where the ideas used, *there is a* and *another,* can be shown to belong to logic) but the definition of number in general demands logical virtuosity. In the end, it still seemed doubtful whether the claims of logicism were sound. The emergence of logical paradoxes (see PARADOXES, LOGICAL) threatened for a time to jeopardize the foundations of logic as well as those of mathematics. Russell's cure for the disorder (the "theory of types") lacked sufficient philosophical justification. Worse still, the need for an axiom of infinity, to guarantee the existence of enough individuals to construct infinitely many different integers, was an intrusion of an inappropriate appeal to experience. Use of the notion of "set," or the roughly equivalent notion of "property," seems to some critics to involve an extra-logical notion. Logicism has still to make its claims good.

Moved by dislike of the complexity thus introduced and a desire to preserve the autonomy of mathematics while safeguarding it from the threat of internal contradiction, the great mathematician David Hilbert founded the movement since known as *formalism.* His guiding idea was to view mathematics as composed of symbols handled without regard for their meanings, according to definite rules for combination and transformation. Formalism treats mathematics as if it were an exact but meaningless game played with marks on paper. So conceived, mathematics itself becomes a proper subject for mathematical investigation under the title of *metamathematics* (mathematics about mathematics, also known as proof theory). A chief task of metamathematics is to prove that arithmetic cannot yield a result of the form "*P* and not-*P,*" *i.e.* to prove its freedom from contradiction. The formalist program envisaged a series of consistency proofs of ever-increasing scope, to culminate in a comprehensive proof of consistency of the whole of mathematics. Metamathematics itself is not "formal" (though it can be formalized) and uses a meaningful vocabulary and well-understood principles. The formalists limited their non-formal methods to very simple procedures (called "finitary") whose validity could hardly be questioned. In this way they hoped to avoid circularity in using mathematics to demonstrate the consistency of mathematics. In spite of initial successes, the formalist program suffered a crippling setback in the famous theorems proved by Kurt Gödel in 1931. Similar results were established by Alfred Tarski in 1930 by a different method, and important refinements were later added by Alonzo Church, J. B. Rosser, and others. Gödel showed conclusively that any formal system adequate to express elementary arithmetic must necessarily be incomplete. That is to say: If the system is consistent, there are propositions which should belong to the system but which cannot be proved inside it, although they can be shown to be true by non-formal considerations *about* the system. Gödel showed how to produce such true but unprovable formulas at will; given a formal system, the "Gödel sentences" can be actually written down. Each such unprovable formula is readily demonstrable in another system, but that in its turn must contain unprovable true results. (An interesting by-product is the fact that there cannot be a universal computing machine capable of doing arithmetic, *i.e.* one able to answer *every* question for which it can be programed.) Thus the ancient ideal of formalizing the whole of mathematics in a single unified system was finally proved illusory. Gödel also proved the important corollary that Hilbert's comprehensive consistency proof must be a will o' the wisp. To avoid complete bankruptcy, the formalists were therefore compelled to relax their finitary standards. Gerhard Gentzen succeeded in 1936 in giving an allegedly formalist proof of the consistency of arithmetic, but the method he used (transfinite induction) was, as Gödel foresaw, more complex than any method he was examining. The value of such a proof is dubious.

The influential movement known as *intuitionism,* founded by L. E. J. Brouwer, has always held that logicism and formalism are on the wrong tracks. Mathematics cannot be reduced to logic, nor is it reducible to the blind manipulation of meaningless formulas. Logic is too narrow for mathematical purposes and consistency is not enough. Mathematical method is constantly guided by unique intuitions that generate the series of integers by free acts of the human imagination; and more complex creative acts produce evolving sequences ("choice sequences") as a basis for the theory of functions. Most famous of all was Brouwer's provocative rejection of the ancient "law of the excluded middle" that every proposition is either true or false. His objection turned upon the concept of mathematical existence: intuitionists reject indirect proofs of the existence of mathematical entities that rely upon the absurdity of the contrary assumption. They insist that every admissible mathematical entity shall be constructed, or at least that the feasibility of a construction in a given finite number of steps shall have been proved. This restricts the mathematical armory and substantially complicates the proof of fundamental mathematical principles. It is questionable whether such complexity is inescapable, given the obscurity that shadows the basic intuitionistic tenets.

The most recent period, dating from Gödel's results, has seen relative neglect of philosophical foundations and increasing sophistication of techniques. Interest in recursive functions, for instance, fostered by applications to the theory of computing machines, engages the full time of specialists. Important work on "non-standard" models (unwanted interpretations of formal systems) has cast further doubt on the prospects of logicism. As cross-connections between the three approaches accumulate, the old conflicts begin to look oversimplified. A wealth of alternative constructions of the foundations has been brought to light (*e.g.* in the modified formalism of R. L. Goodstein and Paul Lorenzen), and the prospects of further discovery have never been brighter. —*M. B.*

FOURCROY, COUNT ANTOINE FRANÇOIS DE, 1755–1809, French chemist; b. Paris. As a member of the Convention in 1792 he promoted the adoption of the metric system of weights and measures, and in 1801 he became director of public instruc-tion. He was a co-editor of the *Annales de Chymie* from its foundation in 1789, and his great work was *Système des Connaissances Chimiques* (10 vols., 1801).—*E. F.*

FOURIER, BARON JEAN BAPTISTE JOSEPH, 1768–1830, French mathematician; b. Auxerre. Largely self-educated at the local military college he took part in the Revolution and later became a friend and follower of Napoleon. He was professor of mathematics at l'École Normale and later at l'École Polytechnique. Fourier's fame rests mainly upon his *Theorie Analytic de la Chaleur,* in which he developed the FOURIER SERIES. This is an infinite series of terms involving sines and cosines that can be so constructed as to represent any one of a wide class of functions. It is of the highest importance in mathematical physics. He was a fellow of the Royal Society. —*H. C.*

FOURIER SERIES: Many physical phenomena are periodic, *i.e.* recur regularly in a fixed order; examples are sound waves, the vibration of strings, light waves, a-c electricity, and the motions of planets. Joseph Fourier (1768–1830) applied trigonometric series to the study of such problems. Although the basic ideas were known to other mathematicians before him, notably Jean Le Rond d'Alembert and Leonhard Euler, Fourier's work stimulated the growth of the subject which bears his name. The principal theorems justifying the applications of the series were established by Peter G. L. Dirichlet (1805–59).

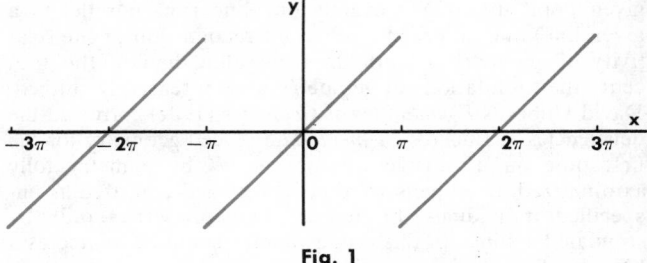

Fig. 1

Roughly stated, a Fourier series is a sum of an infinite number of sine and cosine functions. The surprising fact about such series is that they can approximate rather arbitrary functions. As an example, the function $y = x$ is represented in the interval $-\pi < x < \pi$ by the infinite series $2(\sin x - \frac{1}{2} \sin 2x + \frac{1}{3} \sin 3x - \ldots)$; and this series represents the periodic extension of the function outside the given interval, shown graphically in Fig. 1. That is, the series converges to the function represented graphically by the set of diagonal lines. At $-\pi, \pi, 3\pi$, etc., which are points of discontinuity, it converges to 0. The advantage of representing a function such as $y = x$ as a sum of sine functions is that it tells us that the physical behavior represented by the function $y = x$ is equivalent to the sum of an infinite number of periodic "behaviors." (In practice, a finite number is used to approximate the function as closely as required.) Thus, an arbitrary musical sound is no more than a sum of simple periodic sounds, the harmonics of the original sound.

In general, the series has the form

$$a_0 + \sum_{n=1}^{\infty} (a_n \cos nx + b_n \sin nx).$$

Since the period of this sum is 2π, the series can represent only a periodic function with period 2π. Other restrictions must be placed on the function to be represented. It is sufficient to require both the function and its derivative to have no infinite discontinuities and no more than a finite number of finite dis-

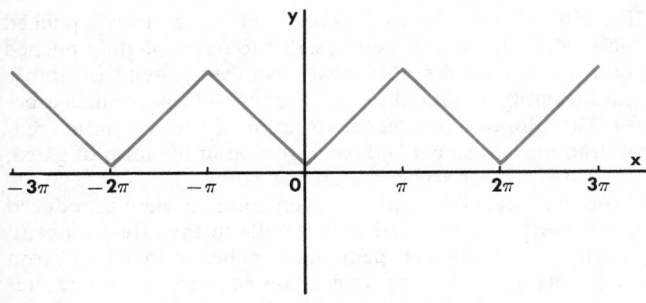

Fig. 2

continuities in the interval $-\pi \leqq x \leqq \pi$. In addition, at each discontinuity we make the function equal to the average of the two limits approached by the function on opposite sides of the discontinuity. Under these conditions the Fourier series converges to the given function in the interval $-\pi < x < \pi$ and to the periodic extension of this function outside this interval. The coefficients are found in the following way: Suppose $f(x) = a_0 + a_1 \cos x + b_1 \sin x + a_2 \cos 2x + b_2 \sin 2x + \ldots$. Integrate both sides over the interval $-\pi \leqq x \leqq \pi$. We get $\int_{-\pi}^{\pi} f(x)\, dx = 2\pi a_0$, all other terms yielding zero results, since $\int_{-\pi}^{\pi} \sin nx\, dx = 0$ and $\int_{-\pi}^{\pi} \cos nx\, dx = 0$. Hence $a_0 = (1/2\pi) \int_{-\pi}^{\pi} f(x)\, dx$. Any coefficient after the first can be obtained as follows. To determine b_n, multiply the equation by $\sin nx$ and then integrate as before. All terms on the right are zeros except $\int_{-\pi}^{\pi} b_n \sin^2 nx\, dx$, which is equal to πb_n. Consequently $b_n = (1/\pi) \int_{-\pi}^{\pi} f(x) \sin nx\, dx$. In a similar way a_n is found by multiplying through by $\cos nx$ and integrating, and is equal to $(1/\pi) \int_{-\pi}^{\pi} f(x) \cos nx\, dx$. By replacing the term a_0 in the original form of the series by $a_0/2$, general formulas for the coefficients can be expressed:

$$a_n = \frac{1}{\pi} \int_{-\pi}^{\pi} f(x) \cos nx\, dx, \quad \text{for } n = 0, 1, 2, \ldots$$

$$b_n = \frac{1}{\pi} \int_{-\pi}^{\pi} f(x) \sin nx\, dx, \quad \text{for } n = 1, 2, \ldots$$

If $f(x)$ is known to be an odd function, that is, $f(-x) = -f(x)$, the Fourier series can be obtained as a series of sines; and if it is an even function, $f(-x) = f(x)$, as a series of cosines. The coefficients are now equal to integrals over the interval $0 \leqq x \leqq \pi$:

$$a_n = \frac{2}{\pi} \int_0^{\pi} f(x) \cos nx\, dx$$

for an even function, and

$$b_n = \frac{2}{\pi} \int_0^{\pi} f(x) \sin nx\, dx$$

for an odd function. Thus the sine series given in the above example can be found from

$$a_n = \frac{2}{\pi} \int_0^{\pi} x \sin nx\, dx = (-1)^{n+1} \frac{\pi}{n} \cdot \frac{2}{\pi} = (-1)^{n+1} \cdot \frac{2}{n},$$

giving the series

$$2(\sin x - \tfrac{1}{2} \sin 2x + \tfrac{1}{3} \sin 3x - \ldots)$$

The function $f(x) = |x|$, which is identical with x when $x > 0$ and with $-x$ when $x < 0$, is an even function and can be represented by a cosine series. We have $a_0 = \pi/2$, $a_n = 2/\pi \int_0^{\pi} x \cos nx\, dx = 0$ if n is even, and $= -4/\pi n^2$ if n is odd. Therefore

$$|x| = \frac{\pi}{2} - \frac{4}{\pi}\left(\cos x + \frac{\cos 3x}{3^2} + \frac{\cos 5x}{5^2} + \ldots\right)$$

for $-\pi \leqq x \leqq \pi$. The series converges to the periodic function, shown graphically in Fig. 2, for all real values of x.

The period of the Fourier series can be made any finite positive quantity by a change of variable. Thus, if we put $x = (\pi/h)t$, the period becomes $2h$. In this way a Fourier series can be found to represent a periodic function with any period if it meets the conditions mentioned above.

The calculation of the Fourier coefficients depends upon the facts that $\int_{-\pi}^{\pi} \cos nx \cos mx\, dx$ and $\int_{-\pi}^{\pi} \sin nx \sin mx\, dx$ are equal to 0 if $n \neq m$, and $\int_{-\pi}^{\pi} \cos nx \sin mx\, dx = 0$ for all values of n and m. These functions are special instances of orthogonal functions. The set of functions, $\phi_n(x)$ is termed orthogonal on an interval (a, b) if $\int_a^b \phi_n(x)\, \phi_m(x)\, dx = 0$ when $n \neq m$. Although Fourier series are usually understood to be the series described above, formed from the trigonometric functions, such series are special examples of the generalized Fourier series whose terms may be formed from any set of orthogonal functions.—*H. C.*

FOURTH DIMENSION: see N-DIMENSIONAL GEOMETRY.

FRACTION: see ARITHMETIC.

FRACTURE: the ordinary open break produced in a rock or mineral by application of force. Fracture directions and the nature of fracture surfaces are influenced by internal structure. Thus a skilled stonemason causes fractures in even-grained rocks such as granite to develop in any desired direction, but even his skill is unable to prevent the natural easy splitting of a strongly layered rock such as slate. Fracture surfaces vary considerably in smoothness depending on the size of constituent grains in rocks and, in minerals, upon the atomic structure. Special plane fractures in minerals due to atomic structure are discussed under CLEAVAGE.—*J. Si.*

Conchoidal fracture in the volcanic rock obsidian (*upper photo*) contrasts with earthy fracture on surface of a boulder of the mineral bauxite (*lower*). Boulder, behind hammer, is embedded in sand. (*Upper, Amer. Mus. of Nat. Hist.; lower, U. S. Geological Survey*)

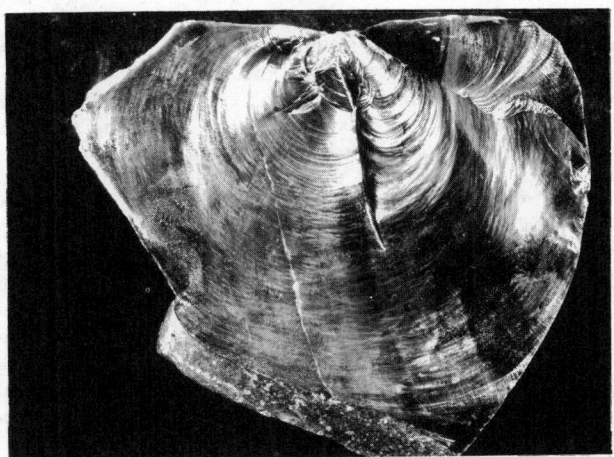

Upstairs window openings are framed while outside walls on ground floor are being sheathed during construction of multiple-dwelling housing project. Studs and joists are in place; floors and roofing will follow. (*Ewing Galloway*)

FRAMING: a structural system composed of separate columns and beams or ribs which support the floors, wall covering, roof, and internal contents of a building.

Timber Framing: Simple framing of posts and short roof rafters was developed by a variety of prehistoric cultures wherever wood was plentiful. The technique was elaborated and highly refined by medieval European carpenters, and carried to America by the earliest colonists. The standard *braced frame* used for most timber building prior to the mid-19th cent. consisted of the following elements: *sill,* a stout beam laid on the stone foundation; *posts,* framed into the sill; *girts,* heavy beams mortised into the posts and carrying the smaller floor beams, or *joists; plates,* extending horizontally along the top of the posts; *roof rafters,* spanning from the ridge beam to the plate; *purlins,* extending horizontally across the rafters and carrying the roof planking; and *diagonal bracing,* which was located either at the corners, as in the New England frame, or in every bay between posts, as in medieval French framing. Joints were usually mortise-and-tenon until iron bolts became common in the 19th cent. The *balloon frame,* invented in Chicago in 1833, represented a marked advance. Its superiority lay in ease of erection, made possible by the use of a large number of light, closely spaced *studs* and joists, which were framed into the sills and plates at the edges of the floor and roof. The studs replaced the heavier posts, and the multiplicity of joists made it possible to abandon the heavy floor girts. A balloon frame can be erected by a carpenter with hammer, nails, and saw. The system was adopted in the American West for nearly every building of the new frontier, and it is used in the structure of most residential building today, with variations to meet the changing requirements of domestic living arrangements. Framing systems for structures with large open interiors, *e.g.* churches and other public buildings, differ from the basic forms mainly in the use of ribs or trusses for roof supports.

The rib is employed to support vaulted or steeply pitched roofs, while the truss is best adapted to flat or slightly pitched roofs and low vaults. The most advanced systems of timber truss framing appeared in the railroad station trainshed before the adoption of iron construction. Once common, arch-rib framing is seeing a 20th-cent. revival in the form of glued, laminated timber arches (see WOOD).

Iron and Steel Framing: Cast-iron columns were introduced to support the floors of English mills in the late 18th cent. Shortly after 1800, European builders began to use cast iron for beams as well as columns, thus securing complete fire-proofing of the primary structure. Cast iron, however, has a relatively low tensile strength and is not well suited to use for beams, which are subject to deflection. Wrought iron began to replace cast iron in beams about 1845. Little was known about the physical properties of either metal at the time, and the frequent collapse of large mill buildings forced builders to undertake extensive scientific investigations of the new materials. Chief pioneers in this extremely important building innovation were William Fairbairn (1789–1874) and Eaton Hodgkinson (1769–1861) in England. The need for greater strength in structural members, and the development of low-cost steel, led to the progressive substitution of steel for iron by the end of the 19th cent. The first building to use steel framing elements was the Home Insurance Building (1884–85) in Chicago, designed by William Le Baron Jenney (1832–1907). This celebrated structure was also the first modern skyscraper, in the sense that the floor and roof loads were carried almost entirely by the internal frame of iron and steel. The fully developed, riveted-steel frame consists essentially of the following elements: *columns; girders,* the primary horizontal members between the columns; *beams,* lighter horizontal members carrying the concrete floor slab and spanning the space between girders; *spandrel beams,* which carry the curtain wall or external envelope; and *diagonal bracing* to sustain wind loads. Arc-welded joints, first substituted for riveted ones in 1920, are now often used to frame fairly tall buildings. The great advantage of welded joints over riveted construction is the weight reduction achieved through elimination of rivets, gussets, angles, and splice plates. Welding transforms a building's internal structure into a series of rigid frames, *i.e.* frames in which the horizontal and vertical members form a rigid, continuous unit. Refinements in rigid framing, growing out of investigation of its stress patterns, have made it the most efficient type of steel construction yet developed. In arched forms rigid frames are especially suited to wide-span enclosures.—*C. W. C.*

FRANCIUM: an alkali-metal element (Symbol Fr); at. no. 87; at. wt 223 (most stable isotope). Francium is extremely rare, occurring as the result of radioactive disintegration of actinium; and it is very short-lived, Fr^{223} having a half-life of 21 min. Though discovered in 1939 (by Marguerite Perey in France), francium has not been isolated in weighable amounts, because of its extreme instability.—*G. W. M.*

FRANCK, JAMES, 1882–1964, German-U. S. physicist; b. Hamburg. For their discovery of the laws governing the impact between an electron and an atom, Franck and Gustav Hertz shared the Nobel prize, 1925. Their research gave experimental support to Niels Bohr's atomic theory and provided a method for determining the value of Planck's constant. Franck was a fellow of the Royal Society and a member of the National Academy of Sciences.—*D. H. D. R.*

FRANCK-CONDON PRINCIPLE: a principle of physics, proposed in 1925 by J. Franck and generalized in 1926 by E. U. Condon, who also worked out the quantum theory of the principle in 1928. It governs the intensity of certain lines in the electronic band spectra of molecules. A molecule consisting of two atomic nuclei, say, and a number of electrons, can exist only in definite allowed energy states, or levels. When the ENERGY LEVEL changes, light is emitted or absorbed. The energy involved is the result partly of electron configuration (arrangement) and partly of the vibrational motion of the nuclei. The central idea of the F-C principle is that an electron jump from one energy level to another takes place so rapidly in comparison to the vibrational motion that immediately after an electronic transition the nuclei have very nearly the same position and velocity as just before it. In other words, electronic transitions of this kind are more probable than any others, and therefore the corresponding light (and spectral lines) is most intense.—*S. Br.*

FRANCK-HERTZ EXPERIMENT: a classic experiment, devised in 1913 by James Franck and Gustav Hertz, which gave early independent evidence of discrete ENERGY LEVELS in atoms, confirming Bohr's theory of ATOMIC SPECTRA. It won a Nobel prize. In the experiment, atoms of a gas (originally mercury vapor) are bombarded with electrons, whose energy is controlled by an accelerating voltage. As this voltage is raised slowly, a point is reached where resonance occurs: the electrons begin to transfer energy to the atoms and the gas glows. The explanation of the experiment is as follows: An atom needs an *exact amount of energy,* or quantum, to change its energy state, and it must get it all from one collision, so no energy at all is picked up from the bombarding electrons until their energy is high enough. The energized excited atom returns almost at once to its ground state, emitting, in the form of light, the exact amount of energy it took from the electron. For common gases the excitation voltage is only a few volts. Such gases are used in ordinary vacuum tubes, the luminosity of which is a familiar illustration of this effect. —*S. Br.*

FRANK, ILYA MIKHAILOVICH, 1908–   , Soviet physicist. He is known for his studies of neutrons and of the production of electron-positron pairs from gamma rays ("pair production"). With I. Y. Tamm, Frank developed a theory based on classical electrodynamics (1937) to account for CHERENKOV RADIATION. For the discovery and interpretation of the Cherenkov effect, Frank, Tamm, and P. A. Cherenkov shared the Nobel prize, 1958. Frank is a professor at the Univ. of Moscow. —*D. H. D. R.*

FRANKLIN, BENJAMIN, 1706– 90, American statesman, scientist, man of letters; b. Boston; self-educated. Called "the first American scientist," Franklin devoted his early life largely to business and letters, his later life to statesmanship and diplomacy, but throughout he was by interest a scientist and inventor. His most important scientific work was in electrostatics. He studied electrical charge, induction, grounding, and insulation; he established experimentally the electrical nature of lightning, and formulated the influential "one-fluid" theory of electricity. Among his inventions were the bifocal lens, the Franklin stove, and the lightning rod. In 1743 he founded the American Philosophical Society.—*R. K.*

Benjamin Franklin
(Science Service)

FRASCH, HERMAN, 1851–1914, U. S. chemical engineer; b. Gaildorf, Württemberg, Germany. A petroleum chemist, he invented a process for desulfurizing Canadian and Ohio crude oils. Later he developed the *Frasch process* for mining sulfur from the deep-lying Gulf Coast deposits; the sulfur is melted by superheated water and pumped to the surface. —*A. I.*

FRAUNHOFER, JOSEPH VON, 1787–1826, German physicist; b. Straubing. This expert lens and mirror maker, who constructed many fine optical instruments, observed and mapped 576 dark lines ("Fraunhofer lines") in the solar SPECTRUM. These lines also appear in light reflected from Moon and planets, but Fraunhofer observed different lines in the spectrum of starlight. He concluded that such

Joseph von Fraunhofer
(New York Public Library)

lines originate in the light source. He was the first to use diffraction gratings extensively. His collected writings were published in 1888.—*D. H. D. R.*

FREE FALL: the unimpeded motion of a body in a gravitational field. The gravitational field of a body, such as Earth, causes nearby bodies to fall toward it with an acceleration that varies inversely with the square of the distance from the center of the attracting body. Near Earth's surface the average value of this acceleration is 32.2 ft/sec². Because of air resistance, which slows falling bodies, true free fall is not encountered within Earth's atmosphere; however, it is the condition under which space satellites orbit Earth. A passenger inside an orbiting satellite is undergoing free fall and therefore feels weightless. See GRAVITATION; WEIGHTLESSNESS. —*E. M. R.*

FREEZE DRYING: see DRYING; LYOPHILIZATION.

FREEZING: the transformation of a liquid to a solid that takes place when the temperature is sufficiently lowered; it is the opposite of MELTING. Pure chemical substances that are crystalline in the solid state freeze under constant pressure at a constant sharply defined temperature called the freezing (or melting) point, which is a characteristic physical property of the substance. The freezing of a unit weight of substance is accompanied by a loss to the surroundings of a definite quantity of heat called the *latent heat of fusion.* Freezing is, with the notable exception of water (see ICE) and very few other substances, accompanied by an increase in density or volumetric shrinking of the substance. Homogeneous liquid mixtures (*e.g.* alcohol-water solutions) freeze over a temperature range throughout which liquid and solid coexist in equilibrium. The initial freezing point of such mixtures is always lower than the freezing point of the pure higher-melting component. Thus mixtures of alcohol and water in any proportions start to freeze at a temperature below the freezing point of water. The final freezing point of the mixture, provided a sufficient quantity of each component remains in the liquid, is the EUTECTIC point, which is below the melting point of the lower-melting component.

It is normal scientific usage to refer to the *melting point* of a pure substance rather than to the *freezing point* even though they are identical for pure substances. There are many reasons for this, one being that the melting point is always reproducible and can always be found *experimentally* at the true solid-liquid equilibrium temperature. When a substance is frozen, *i.e.* when it passes from the liquid to the solid state, it is easy to *supercool* it and make it pass through the true solid-liquid equilibrium temperature (true freezing or melting point) before crystallization starts to take place. On the other hand, it is impossible, theoretically as well as practically, to *superheat* in going from the solid to the liquid state. Therefore, the experimentally determined melting point is the true melting or freezing point.—*A. M. S.*

FREGE, GOTTLOB, 1848–1925, German logician and mathematician; b. Wismar. He made important contributions to symbolic logic, semantics, and foundations of mathematics. Before B. Russell and A. N. Whitehead formulated and elaborated the same view, Frege argued that mathematics is a branch of deductive logic (see PRINCIPIA MATHEMATICA); he also presented the first clear account of the notion of a propositional function and of a truth function and made a fundamental contribution to the logic of indirect discourse. His principal writings include: *Begriffschrift* (1879); *Die Grundlagen der Arithmetik* (1884); *"Über Sinn und Bedeutung," Zeitschr. f. Philos. u. Philos. Kritik* (1892), pp. 25–50; and *Grundgesetze der Arithmetik* (1893, 1903).—*I. L.*

FREON: a member of a group of volatile organic compounds derived from methane and ethane by replacing hydrogen atoms with fluorine and, in most cases, chlorine or bromine. Being non-flammable, non-irritating, and almost odorless, Freons are widely used as refrigerants, aerosol propellants, and fire-extinguishing agents. Typical formulas are: CCl_3F (Freon-11), $CBrF_3$ (Freon-13B1).—*T. M.*

FREQUENCY: the number of times that any phenomenon repeats itself in a given time. Usually the phenomenon is understood to be a more or less regularly cyclic one, like Earth's rotation or the vibrations of sound in a musical note (440/sec for middle A), but some cyclic phenomena are quite irregular, like the beating of a dog's heart or the solar sunspot cycle, and the frequency is merely an average of the number of occurrences of the event over some interval of time.

The frequency of an alternating electric current is the number of times per second the wave form repeats itself exactly, which for a simple sinusoidal wave is the same as the number of times per second it reaches its maximum positive value. The range of electromagnetic frequencies that can be accurately measured is enormous. Its span embraces 25- and 60-cycle house currents, many thousands or millions of cycles for radio waves, 100,000 million million (10^{17}) cycles for visible light, and cycles at least a million million times greater still for high-energy cosmic rays. Radio frequencies are commonly stated in kilocycles (thousands of cycles), megacycles (millions of cycles), or kilomegacycles. For convenience, wavelengths rather than frequencies are used for light and other electromagnetic radiation of very high frequency. Mechanical frequencies range from those of the tides, once or twice a day, up to at least thousands of megacycles. The internationally accepted unit of frequency, not yet in common use, is the hertz (hz), equal to 1 cy/sec.

The measurement of frequency in the last few years has become one of the most accurate of all experimental techniques, since all that is required is a count of "events" and an accurate measure of time. Time, in turn, is determined by the crystal clock or the newer atomic clocks, in which the controlling element is some system—a crystal or an atom—known to maintain a constant frequency of vibration. Direct measurement of time to a few parts in 10,000 million or better is now possible, and differences in frequency of a few parts in 10^{17} have been detected, using the MÖSSBAUER EFFECT.

The relation of frequency *f*, wavelength λ, and wave velocity *v* is given by the equation $v = f\lambda$. See ACOUSTICS; ELECTROMAGNETIC WAVE; WAVE AND WAVE MOTION.—*M. C. H.*

FREQUENCY MODULATION: see MODULATION.

FRESNEL, AUGUSTIN JEAN, 1788–1827, French physicist; b. Broglie. His studies of the diffraction of light through a slit were published in his "Memoir on the Diffraction of Light" (1816), in *Annales de chimie.* His extensive investigations confirmed the wave theory of light of T. Young (see LIGHT). Fresnel's other research included work on double refraction. His complete works were published 1866–70. He was a member of the U. S. Academy of Sciences and a fellow of the Royal Society.—*D. H. D. R.*

Jean Augustin Fresnel
(The Bettmann Archive)

FRICTION: the force opposing the movement of one body over another or through a medium. The precise mechanism of friction is not fully known, but the forces involved are thought to be electrical in their fundamental nature. Work done in overcoming friction is converted to heat; this accounts for the diminished output and efficiency of machines. Friction, however, is not without certain advantages. Without it, the act of walking and the propulsion of vehicles over the earth's surface would be impossible.

The classical laws of friction, formulated by the French physicist C. A. de Coulomb in the late 18th cent., are at best only approximations, valid within certain prescribed limits. One law states that friction is proportional to the normal force, or the force pressing the rubbing surfaces together. Thus the *coefficient of friction* (μ), defined as the ratio of the force of friction (*fr*) to the normal force *N*, is fairly constant in value, depending only on the nature of the surfaces in contact. Two other laws state that friction is independent of the area of contact and that friction is independent of speed. The last statement is being particularly questioned today.

Friction is always slightly greater at the start of motion than it is once motion has been established. Accordingly, we distinguish between the coefficient of static friction (μ_s) and the coefficient of kinetic friction (μ_k). The first serves as a measure of so-called *limiting* friction, which prevails just before motion starts. The second or smaller coefficient applies to the condition when uniform motion is in progress. To determine μ_s, a block is placed on an inclined plane and the plane is tilted until the block just slides down. The tangent of the angle of tilt may be shown to be equal to the coefficient of friction between the block and the plane.

Rolling friction is considerably less than sliding friction; hence the use of roller and ball bearings in machinery. Lubrication also reduces friction by substituting for the contact of metal against metal the contact between metal and a film of lubricant.—*A. E.*

FRIEDEL, CHARLES, 1832–99, French chemist and mineralogist; b. Strasbourg. With James Mason Crafts he discovered the FRIEDEL-CRAFTS REACTION for synthesizing alkyl and aromatic compounds, an important group of chemicals.—*S. M. E.*

FRIEDEL-CRAFTS REACTION: in organic chemistry, an important reaction in which anhydrous aluminum chloride as a catalyst brings about substitution of an alkyl radical or an acyl radical into an aromatic hydrocarbon. Thus, reaction of benzene with methyl chloride yields toluene; and with acetyl chloride, acetophenone. In the first case, a hydrogen atom in the aromatic ring structure is replaced by a methyl radical, and in the second it is replaced by the acetyl radical. Since its discovery in 1877 by Charles Friedel and James M. Crafts, this reaction (and its extensions) has proved among the most valuable and far-reaching in organic chemistry. It is extremely important in petroleum refining, in the production of high-quality rubber, and as a method of producing iso-octane, the hydrocarbon against which gasoline is rated to determine its octane number.—*Ru. M.*

FRIEDMANN'S MODELS: geometrical structures representing uniform models of the universe, proposed by A. Friedmann (1921). These bridge the gap between Einstein's model of "matter without motion" and the DE SITTER UNIVERSE of "motion without matter." Assuming uniformity (see COSMOLOGY) and the laws of light propagation, the possible space-time geometries are limited. Time separates naturally from space, which must be of uniform curvature. This may be positive (elliptic, finite volume), zero (Euclidean), or negative (hyperbolic). Variation in time is arbitrary, involving universal scaling up of distances (expansion) or scaling down (contraction). General RELATIVITY theory allows the deduction of the material content (pressure and density) from the geometry. If the pressure is negligible, as in our universe, only certain Friedmann models survive, among them: (1) *Einstein universe:* "matter without motion," no expansion, finite volume unstable (see No. 3). (2) *De Sitter universe:* "motion without matter," permanent expansion, empty, infinite volume. (3) *Eddington-Lemaître model:* finite volume (an Einstein universe that eventually begins to expand, first slowly, then faster; with consequent diminution of density, it finally approaches de Sitter's universe). (4) *Einstein-de Sitter model:* Euclidean space, infinite volume (starts with extremely high density, expansion at first very rapid (BIG BANG), slowing down gradually; very simple geometry). (5) *Lemaître's universe:* finite volume (big bang start, as in No. 4, slowing down almost to standstill, then as in No. 3; very important model; details worked out—origin of elements, of cosmic rays, of clusters of galaxies). (6) *Milne's universe:* infinite space, flat space-time, big bang, unaccelerated motion of all particles; basis of kinematic relativity.—*H. B.*

FRISCH, KARL VON, 1886–   , Austrian-German zoologist; b. Vienna, Austria. He is known for his research on bees, his most famous discovery being the way bees determine directions from the polarization of light and communicate information to each other concerning direction. He also demonstrated color vision in bees. His publications include *Bees: Their Vision, Chemical Senses, and Language* (1950), *The Dancing Bees; an Account of the Life and Senses of the Honey Bee* (1954), and *The Language of Bees* (1939). Frisch is a fellow of the Royal Society and an associate of the U. S. National Academy of Sciences.—*D. H. D. R.*

FRONT: in meteorology, the sharp boundary zone between AIR MASSES of substantially different temperatures and humidities. If the colder of two air masses is moving into the warmer one, a cold front forms between them. A warm front forms when the warmer mass is replacing the colder one. The process of front formation is called *frontogenesis*. The colder, denser air mass tends to push under the warmer, lighter one, so that as visualized in cross section the warm air slopes up and over the colder air. Rain showers and thunderstorms usually develop along the line of a cold front, while warm fronts have wide bands of clouds and steady rain extending over the colder air from the line of the front to a distance of

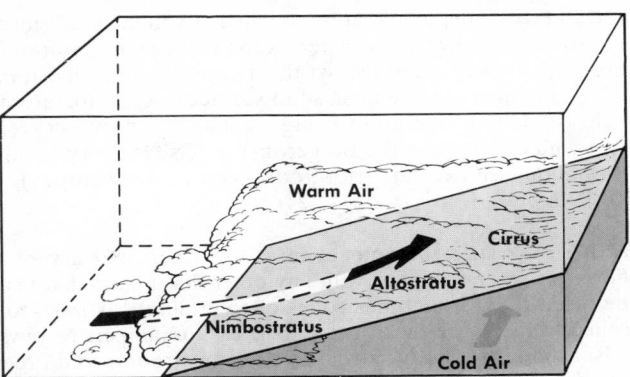

Warm front: A warm air mass rides smoothly over a wedge of cold air. Ground friction has drawn retreating cold air into a thin wedge. (Vertical dimension greatly exaggerated.)

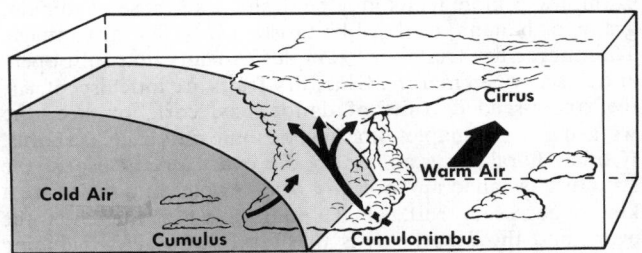

Cold front: A rapidly moving cold front pushes its stubby wedge under warm air as it advances. Abrupt lifting of warm air may produce thunderstorm. (*After Lehr et al.*)

as much as 1,500 mi ahead of the front. *Frontolysis*, or dissipation of a front, occurs when the air masses that originally came together to form the front flow away from each other. See also OCCLUSION.—*P. L.*

FRONTINUS, SEXTUS JULIUS, c. A. D. 35–A. D. 103, Roman official. He wrote books on the art of surveying and on war. In A. D. 97, while water commissioner of Rome, he wrote two books on its water supply—a history and a description of the aqueducts, including data on their construction and the treating, measuring, and distribution of water.—*R. J. F.*

FROST: in general, the weather condition which exists when the ground and objects near it cool to 32°F (0°C) or colder. If the surface cools to the FROST POINT, the water vapor of the air will be deposited as hoar frost, a layer of needle-like ice crystals formed by sublimation, *i.e.* transition to the solid phase directly from gaseous water vapor without an intermediate liquid phase. Frost is economically important because of its effects upon plants, damage to which usually occurs as the surface of the ground loses its heat through radiation under clear night skies. As the ground cools, the moisture of the air condenses on the surface first as dew, and then, as the surface temperature reaches 32°F (0°C), as hoar frost. Since the water's latent heat of condensation is given up to the surface upon which the dew or hoar frost forms, the fall of temperature is somewhat retarded. Radiation frost damage can be lessened by screening back the loss of radiated heat and supplying extra heat to compensate for the radiation loss. In one popular method, oil-burning smudge pots spread a dense layer of smoke to serve as a radiation screen between the ground and space, while the warm pots themselves radiate some heat to the plants. The discovery that air above tree-top level remains relatively warm (see INVERSION) has led to the practice of blowing this warm air down to the plants by means of tower-mounted propellers.—*D. H. L.*

FROST POINT: the temperature to which a volume of air must be lowered to bring its water-vapor content to saturation over a plane surface of ice. At this temperature a deposition of frost is likely to occur on solid surfaces. At temperatures below 0°C the frost point is higher than the DEW POINT: a fact which is basic in the Bergeron-Findeisen theory of rain formation (see PRECIPITATION; CONDENSATION; HUMIDITY).—D. H. L.

FRUIT: in a strict botanical sense, the ripened ovary of a flower or several flowers, with any other floral parts that may be fused to it. Sometimes cones of such plants as pines are called fruits, as are the arils, or "berries," of junipers or yews. Also, the reproductive structures of mushrooms and other fungi, of algae, or of other kinds of plants are often called fruiting bodies. True fruits can be classified as *simple,* if they consist only of a single ovary and its contained ovules, now ripened and called seeds. Tomatoes, grapes, and pea pods are examples. Simple fruits may be fleshy, like those of tomato, grape, or banana, or dry, like those of pea, lily, or cabbage. These three dry fruits are examples of fruits that split open, or dehisce, when mature. Other dry fruits are indehiscent, *e.g.* the single-seeded fruits of dandelions, corn, or rice; the winged fruits of maples or ashes; or some nuts such as acorns. If other floral parts adhere to the ovary or enclose it, the structure is called an *accessory fruit.* Apples and pears are a kind of accessory fruit, called a pome, in which the core is the ovary and the fleshy part is the floral receptacle, including bases of sepals, petals, and stamens. Another accessory fruit is the strawberry; the fleshy part that is eaten is the receptacle, and the true fruits are the small, hard, one-seeded, and ripened ovaries that it bears. If a fruit is a cluster of ripened ovaries produced by a single flower, it is called an *aggregate fruit.* Raspberries are an example. If a cluster of several ovaries is

Types of fruit: Simple fruits include those that are fleshy (tomato), dry and dehiscent (pea), and dry and indehiscent (maple, acorn). Accessory fruits include apple and strawberry. Blackberry is an aggregate fruit, mulberry a multiple fruit. Bottom line shows diagrammatically how two different fruits, an aggregate fruit (raspberry) and a simple, fleshy fruit (blueberry), develop from flowers. Note that the raspberry consists of a cluster of ovaries, the blueberry of a single ovary. (After Transeau and others)

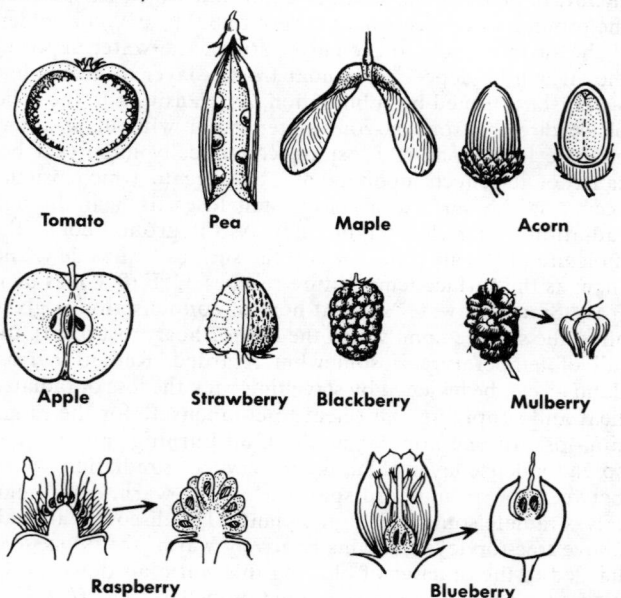

Tomato **Pea** **Maple** **Acorn**

Apple **Strawberry** **Blackberry** **Mulberry**

Raspberry **Blueberry**

produced by several flowers, the fruit is said to be a *multiple,* or *compound, fruit.* Pineapples, figs, osage oranges, and mulberries are examples.—*H. Cr.*

FUEL: any material used as a source of heat energy. The carbon-containing materials that are burned with air or with oxygen derived from air are the most important fuels: coal, petroleum, and natural gas. For heat-energy production in modern space vehicles, many noncarbon fuels are employed, *i.e.* metal-base and synthetic chemical fuels of high propellent performance. Nuclear fuel, not yet in large-scale use, may soon be an important source of heat energy, and thus fissionable material should be classified as fuel (see ATOMIC ENERGY).

Carbon-Containing Fuels: The heat energy released by combustion of carbonaceous fuels may be employed directly as a heat supply, as in a FURNACE, or may be converted into mechanical energy, as in an ENGINE. The use of the combustion heat of gasoline to raise the temperature, and thus the pressure, of the working fluid (combustion gases and air) in an INTERNAL-COMBUSTION engine is an example of the conversion of heat energy into mechanical energy. Fuels are generally classified by their physical state (solid, liquid, gas) under normal conditions of pressure and temperature, release of heat on combustion, and combustion characteristics. *Solid fuels* include the various ranks of COAL (anthracite, bituminous, sub-bituminous, and lignite) and the coke and char derived from coal. Wood, charcoal, and peat, while still employed (mostly for special uses), make up only a small fraction of the solid-fuels market. Solid fuels are classified as to (1) size of solid particles, (2) amount of smoke produced by combustion, and (3) moisture and ash content. *Liquid fuels* are mainly petroleum products, *e.g.* gasoline, fuel oil, kerosene, benzol, coal tar, and tar oil. These fuels are generally classified according to their flash point, pour point (lowest temperature at which a fuel will pour), per cent water and sediment, carbon residue, ash, distillation temperature, and viscosity. *Gaseous fuels* include natural gas, which provides about one seventh of all the energy produced in this country, and petroleum-derived gaseous products. Also of great importance are manufactured gases; thus coke-oven gas or water gas, produced from steam and incandescent coke, finds important usage as a heating gas for coke ovens and as a diluent for natural, oil, or coal gas. Propane and butane are burned in gaseous form but marketed under pressure as liquids and called LPG (liquefied petroleum gas). Heating values below represent heat released during combustion as measured in a calorimeter (see CALORIMETRY).

Fuel	Heating Value
Anthracite coal	13,500 Btu/lb
Bituminous coal	14,000 Btu/lb
Gasoline	19,000 Btu/lb
Fuel oil	19,000 Btu/lb
Wood	5,000 Btu/lb
Natural gas (Pa.)	1,100 Btu/ft³
Coke-oven gas	580 Btu/ft³

Chemical Fuels: High heats of combustion per unit mass are obtained from metals in the first three series (horizontal sequences) of the first three groups of the periodic table, *e.g.* lithium, beryllium, boron, magnesium, aluminum. Fuels in which these metallic elements are principal constituents are called metal-base fuels. Their combustion results in high flame temperatures and combustion gases of low molecular weight—the two main requirements for high-performance propellants. The metal component may be incorporated in liquid or solid fuels and may be present in a pure state or as

Coke, produced by heating bituminous coal in the absence of air, is used predominantly as a fuel for the blast furnace. Above, 11.5 tons of coke (produced from 16 tons of coal) fall from a coke oven into a quencher car for transportation to the blast furnace. Coke-oven gas also is recovered in the process. (*U. S. Steel*)

a compound. Metallic-base fuels are generally costly, limited in supply, and smoky. Some also produce engine deposits that create severe operational difficulties. Other highly propellent chemical-fuel combinations are: liquid hydrogen as the fuel with liquid fluorine as the oxidant; liquid-hydrogen fuel with liquid-oxygen oxidant; liquid oxygen as oxidant and a mixture of 75% ethyl alcohol and 25% water as fuel.—*R. W.*

FULLER'S EARTH: a mineral clay possessing high natural adsorption properties. Other adsorptive clays must be activated by some process, *e.g.* acid treatment of bentonite clays. Fuller's earth consists chiefly of magnesium aluminum silicate, montmorillonite, and attapulgite; it is used in the decolorization and purification of fatty oils, the cleaning of solid surfaces, and the clarification of water.—*G. W. M.*

FULTON, ROBERT, 1765–1815, U. S. engineer and inventor; b. Lancaster Co., Pa. His inventions included a system for replacing canal locks with inclined planes (1794), an improved saw for marble, a rope-making machine, a ditchdigger, a flax-spinning machine, and a submarine, the *Nautilus.* Like other inventors of the time Fulton began experimenting with the idea of the steamboat, and with Robert R. Livingston, in France, he made experiments on the Seine. Fulton's *Clermont,* powered by an English-built steam engine, made its historic first cruise from New York to Albany on Aug. 17, 1807; it was the first commercially successful American steamboat.—*S. B.*

FUMAROLE: a natural opening in the ground in a volcanic region through which steam and other gases escape under pressure. (The term is from Latin *fumare,* "to smoke.") The steam is usually far in excess of other gases, but amounts of carbon dioxide, hydrogen sulfide, and even hydrochloric acid are sometimes noted. As gases escape at the surface, they cool and may leave coatings of minerals on the ground, including metallic ores and sulfur in commercially valuable amounts. Fumaroles are especially common in the famous Valley of Ten Thousand Smokes in S Alaska.—*R. E. M.*

FUNCTION: The modern concept of a function in mathematics is quite abstract, although it developed gradually from observations in physical science. In the late 16th cent., Galileo observed relations between varying physical quantities, *e.g.* time, distance, and speed. The physical quantities were the forerunners of mathematical *variables,* and a relation among them was later called a *functional relation.* For example, the formula for the number of feet (s) a body falls in any number of seconds, $s = 16t^2$, is a functional relation between s and t. Conceived physically, it describes a kind of variation—the way s varies with t. The study of such relations has become a dominant aspect of science. The COORDINATE GEOMETRY of René Descartes expressed relations between the two coordinates of a point. The notion of a path (or locus) generated by a moving point leads to the concept of variable coordinates, and the equation of a locus expresses a functional relation between such variables. A functional relation was therefore conceived essentially as a formula or equation, and such mathematicians as Leonhard Euler in the 18th cent. so viewed it.

The concept of a function as formulated by P. G. L. Dirichlet (1805–59) has dominated the study of functions. This definition is substantially the following. We start with a set of numbers, which might be all the real numbers in an interval, say from 0 to 1, or all numbers of some other class, *e.g.* the integers, and we let a letter x denote any one of these numbers. In this usage x is a mathematical variable. Now, if y is another variable such that to each value of x there corresponds a definite value of y, then y is a function of x. If a single value of y corresponds to each value of x, then the function is single valued; if more than one value of y corresponds to each individual value of x, the function is multiple valued. Thus $y = x^2$ expresses y as a single-valued function of x, whereas $y^2 = x$, or $y = \pm \sqrt{x}$, expresses y as a double-valued function of x. Multiple-valued functions are often studied by breaking them into separate single-valued ones. In this definition the variable x is the *independent* variable and y is the *dependent* variable, because we start with x, choosing any value in the domain at will, the corresponding value of y depending upon the choice. This definition of a function has proved adequate to the needs of mathematical analysis. Some more modern definitions phrase it in more abstract terms without essentially altering its meaning. The definition is easily extended so as to make a variable a function of two or more independent variables.

The manner of setting up the correspondence is not specified by this definition. It may be done by an equation, as the 18th-cent. mathematicians presumed, but it can equally well be done by a graph such as the temperature chart of a fever patient, by a tabulation such as the logarithm table, or by some other form of description. The fact that the correspondence exists is expressed by the symbolic equation $y = f(x)$, read "y equals eff of x," which may refer to a graphical or tabular function as well as one defined by an equation. The fact that z is a function of two variables, u and v, is symbolized by $z = f(u, v)$. Other letters than f can be used, such as $g(x)$ or $\phi(u, v)$. Most of the functions studied in mathematics do, in fact, have equations, although the equations may be complicated and may contain symbols created to denote new functions. For example, the equation $y = \text{sn } x$ involves the elliptic function denoted by sn x.

Some ways of classifying functions depend upon the kind of equation used. An equation which puts y equal to an expression containing only x and fixed numbers gives y as an *explicit* function of x. An example is $y = x^2 - 1/x$. If, on the other hand, the two variables are intermingled, as in the equation $y^2 - xy - x^2 + 10 = 0$, the functional relation is *implicit.* A symbol $f(x)$ denoting an explicit function can be interpreted as a shorthand symbol for the explicit expression which defines the rule of correspondence. Thus, we might identify $f(x)$ with $x^2 - 1/x$ in the first example given. Functions expressed by equations are commonly classified as algebraic and transcendental.

The most important algebraic functions are rational integral functions, expressing y as a polynomial in x, e.g. $y = x^3 + 2x^2 + 3$; the rational functions, expressing y as a quotient of polynomials in x, e.g. $y = 1/(x^2 + 2)$; and irrational functions which involve root-taking as well as the other algebraic operations. The equation $y = \log x$ is not algebraic; and y is a transcendental function of x. The elementary transcendental functions are those expressed by exponentials such as e^x, logarithmic functions, the circular functions (e.g. $\sin x$ and $\cos x$), and the hyperbolic functions (e.g. $\sinh x$ and $\cosh x$). Higher transcendental functions are generated by such operations as summing infinite series and the calculus operation of integration. The integral

$$x = \int_a^y (1/\sqrt{P(t)})\, dt,$$

where $P(t)$ denotes a polynomial of 3rd or 4th degree, is called an elliptic integral, and the function defined by inverting the relation so as to give y as a function of x is *elliptic.* If $P(t)$ denotes a polynomial of 5th or higher degree, the integral is Abelian and y is an Abelian function of x. These functions have been of the utmost importance in the development of modern analysis.

A different classification of functions is based upon intrinsic properties rather than the form of representation: (*1*) Suppose the domain of the independent variable is an interval of the real numbers, which is a continuum. A function may be continuous or discontinuous at a point in this domain. The function $f(x)$ is continuous at $x = x_1$ if x_1 is a value for which the function $f(x)$ exists, and if, for any number $\varepsilon > 0$, there exists a $\delta > 0$ such that $|f(x) - f(x_1)| < \varepsilon$ if $|x - x_1| < \delta$. Otherwise the function is discontinuous at $x = x_1$. Discontinuity can result because $f(x)$ increases in magnitude beyond all bounds as x tends to x_1, because there is a sudden change in the value of $f(x)$ as x reaches x_1, or because, as x approaches x_1, the values of $f(x)$ fluctuate in some way so that the function does not converge to a limit. A function is continuous throughout an interval if it is continuous at every point in the interval. (*2*) A function is monotonic increasing if $f(x)$ always increases as x increases, e.g. $\log x$, and monotonic decreasing if $f(x)$ always decreases as x increases, e.g. $-x^3$. (*3*) A periodic function repeats its value at regular intervals, e.g. $\sin x$, which repeats its values at intervals of 2π. (*4*) In the study of functions of a complex variable, a class of functions designated as *analytic* is of basic importance. See FUNCTION THEORY.

The study of functions is one of the most basic and extensive fields of mathematical study. It consists of investigating the properties of functions and applying them to mathematical and scientific problems, and of constructing functions possessing specified properties (see SPECIAL FUNCTIONS).—*H. C.*

FUNCTION THEORY: a branch of mathematics divided into two parts, one concerned with functions of real variables and the other with functions of complex variables. The theory of functions of real variables is the basic theory underlying calculus and its extensions. It is concerned with the nature of a variable and of a numerical function, classifications of functions, the construction of functions, the study of special properties, and detailed study of special functions. (See FUNCTION.) The theory of functions of complex variables rests on this theory in many fundamental ways, but much of its develop-

ment is specialized, because of the nature of a complex variable. This article is concerned with functions of a single complex variable.

A complex variable z has a real part x and an imaginary part yi: $z = x + yi$. If a function of z is set equal to w, $w = f(z)$, w also has a real part and an imaginary part: $w = u + vi$, where u and v are real functions of the real variables x and y. Since each pair of real values of x and y determines u and v, it would seem that the theory of functions of a complex variable is identical with that of two real variables, and this would be so if no limitations were placed upon this broad interpretation of function. The restriction which has proved most fruitful focuses attention upon what are called *analytic* functions. The study of analytic functions has proceeded from two different standpoints. One, guided to a considerable extent by geometrical concepts, starts with a definition of an analytic function by the partial differential equations of Augustin Cauchy (1789–1857) and Bernhard Riemann (1826–66). The other is based on the definition of an analytic function by a power series. This was the program followed by Karl Weierstrass (1815–97). The two developments are equivalent, although proceeding in quite different ways.

The geometric interpretation of a complex variable requires a plane, rather than an axis as in the case of a real variable. Complex numbers are plotted on a coordinate system made up of two perpendicular axes, one for the real parts and the other for the imaginary parts, as in Fig. 1, which shows four

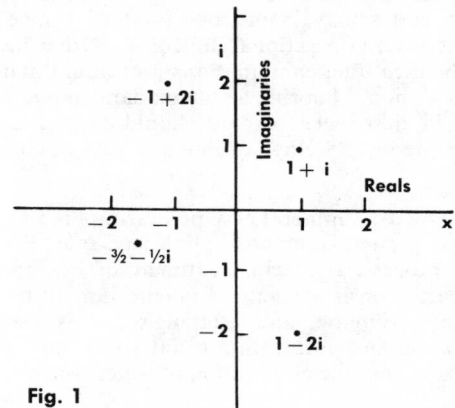

Fig. 1

complex numbers. Now if $w = f(z)$, where $z = x + yi$, the *domain* of z is a set of points on this two-dimensional system, which is called the *z*-plane. It might be a region bounded by one or more curves, such as the unit semicircle R in Fig. 2a. To each z in domain R there corresponds a $w = u + vi$, which can be plotted in a w-plane, Fig. 2b. Which point of the w-plane corresponds to a given z in domain R of the z-plane depends, of course, upon the function $f(z)$. If $w = z^2$, any z in R leads to a w in the unit circle R'. This follows from the

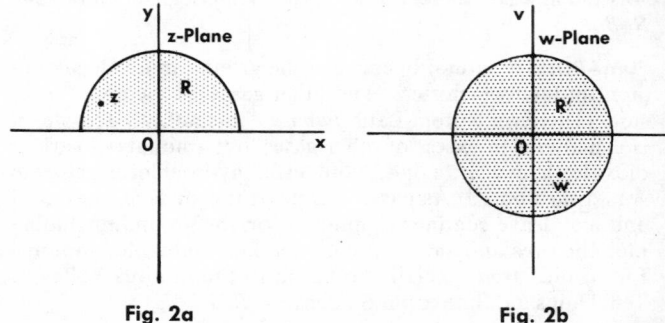

Fig. 2a   **Fig. 2b**

1

Plate 36   ENGINEERING

Each of the many divisions and subdivisions of engineering demands some special competence, based on firm scientific ground. **1.** The efforts of both structural and hydraulic engineers were required in construction of the 768-ft **Eisenhower lock** in the St. Lawrence Seaway. *(G. Hunter/Shostal)* **2. Dynamos in power house of Hoover Dam** bear the stamp of electrical and mechanical engineers. *(John Beranek/Shostal)* **3.** With mass production of the automobile in the 20th cent., highway engineering, a branch of civil engineering, has been called upon to design super-highway systems such as the **interwoven "freeways"** of Los Angeles, Cal. *(Union Pacific Railroad Co.)* **4.** Sanitary engineering, also a branch of civil engineering, is typified by **settling basins** which convert sewage into irrigation water and fertilizer. *(Dorr-Oliver, Inc.)* **5.** The engineer at the controls of an **electronic computer** represents a new major branch of engineering. *(International Business Machines)*

3

2

4

5

Plate 37 ENGINEERING IN ANTIQUITY

Engineering has grown out of man's desire to make something useful and lasting out of the materials in his environment. In pre-industrial cultures, the most dramatic expressions of this desire have been massive structures and buildings such as those shown on this page.

1. Roman aqueduct in Segovia, Spain, built circa A.D. 100, still brings water from river 10 mi away. Bridge portion, built of granite blocks, is 2,440 ft long. *(J. Barnell/Shostal)*

2. Incan fortress: Ruined wall of Sacsaihuaman dominates the ancient city of Cuzco, Peru. Founded in the 11th cent. A.D., Cuzco may have been Incan capital. *(J. Barnell/Shostal)*

3. Mayan pyramidal structure, El Castillo, rises above site of Chichén Itzá, Yucatán, first founded A.D. 432. Pyramid is 84 ft high, 184 ft along each of four sides, and is topped by two-chamber temple of Kukulkan. *(Pierre M. Martinot)*

Plate 38   EROSION

Most erosion is accomplished by water running off the land. However, glaciers, the wind, underground water, and ocean waves and currents may be locally effective agents in carving the land.

1. Hudson Highlands, southern New York, were carved from crystalline rocks by streams and smoothed by ice sheets of glacial ages. *(Jerome Wyckoff)*

2. Monument Valley area, southern Utah and northern Arizona, shows erosional remnants of a once continuous, resistant sedimentary layer. A small sand dune, showing wind ripple marks, appears in foreground. *(Santa Fe Railway)*

3. Eroded McNairy clays near Metropolis, Ill. Such fine gullying produces a badland type of topography. *(Harold Wanless)*

4. A small gully near Bacchus Marsh, Victoria, Australia, was eroded into relatively weak rock. *(Harold Wanless)*

5. Portage Glacier, Alaska, gouged out valley when glacier was larger. Glaciers are powerful agents of erosion, being able to carry as "grinders" large quantities of broken rock. *(Alaska RR)*

6. Double Arch, Arches National Monument, Utah, was carved from colorful sandstone by rain and weather. *(Harold Wanless)*

Plate 39 EVOLUTION

Living things evolve by gradual accumulation of small changes—changes that help them survive and reproduce, and that adapt them to special living conditions. Some of the results and mechanisms of evolution appear in these charts, *both from Chicago Natural History Museum.*

Evolution from extinct types of reptiles resulted in ancestral mammals, from which the various modern mammals developed. Beginning at lower left and proceeding clockwise, the main mammalian branches are: egg-laying mammals; pouched mammals; insectivores; man and his relatives; flying lemurs; bats; carnivores and whales; rodents; even-toed hoofed animals; tapirs, rhinoceroses, and horses; hyraxes, elephants, and sea cows; aardvarks; pangolins, sloths, and anteaters.

FAMILY TREE OF LIVING MAMMALS

Evolution of species is illustrated by birds of Galápagos Islands, 600 mi off coast of Ecuador. Charles Darwin's observations on these islands greatly influenced his thoughts on evolution. Two stages in evolution of three hypothetical species are shown at top. First, ancestral population from another land area invades three islands. Then, three island populations gradually change, each adapting to its particular habitat. Because three populations are separated, they do not interbreed and develop along different lines, finally becoming three distinct species. On Galápagos Islands, mockingbirds have developed into separate species or subspecies, one to an island. Darwin's finches, whose ancestors arrived from the mainland long before those of the mockingbirds, have gone beyond this stage. First they evolved into different species on different islands; later, these species invaded neighboring islands. This, along with further development of species, resulted in several species of finch on each island. Birds shown are: mockingbirds—(A) Abingdon (*Nesomimus parvulus personatus*), (B) Bindloe (*N. parvulus bindloei*), (C) Tower (*N. parvulus bauri*), (D) Albemarle (*N. parvulus parvulus*), (E) Barrington (*N. parvulus barringtoni*), (F) Chapham (*N. melanotis*), (G) Three-banded (*N. trifasciatus*), (H) Hood (*N. macdonaldi*); finches—(I) Black-headed tree-finch (*Camarhynchus parvulus*), (J) Large ground-finch (*Geospiza magnirostris*), (K) Medium ground-finch (*G. fortis*), (L) Small ground-finch (*G. fulitinosa*), (M) Sharp-billed ground-finch (*G. difficilis*), (N) Warbler-finch (*Certhidea olivacea*).

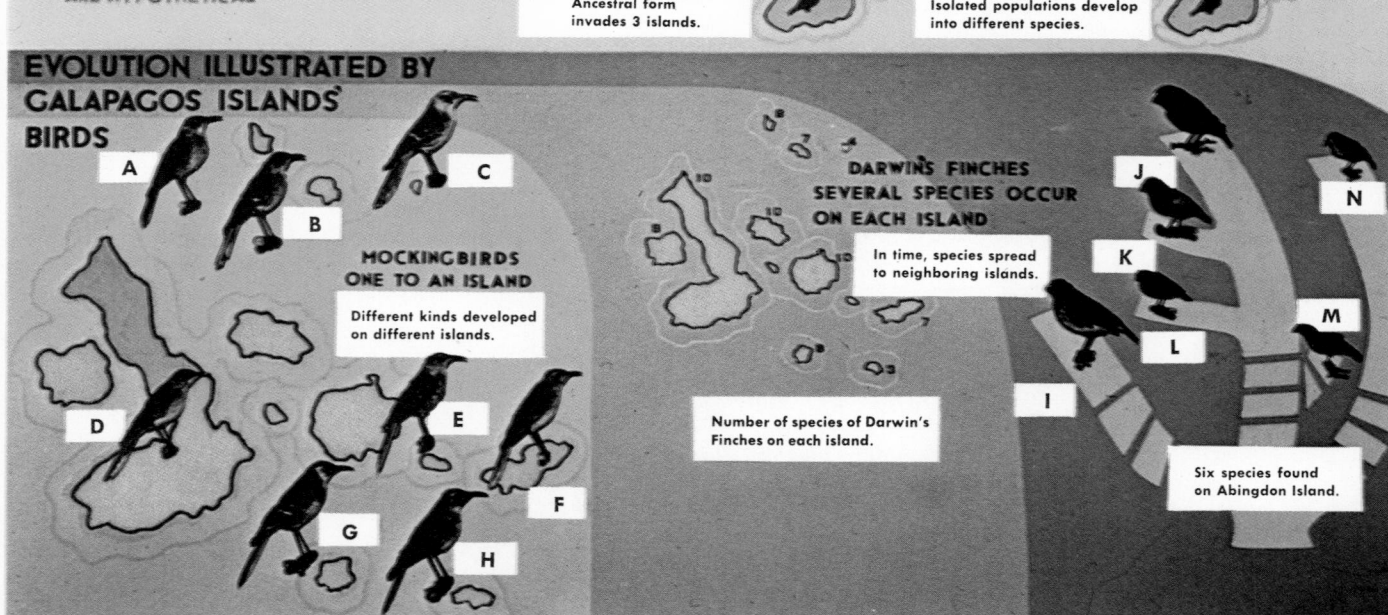

SPECIES EVOLVE ONLY IN ISOLATION
ISLAND POPULATIONS ILLUSTRATE THIS

DIAGRAMMATICAL EVOLUTION OF THREE SPECIES
BOTH BIRDS AND ISLANDS ARE HYPOTHETICAL

STAGE I
Ancestral form invades 3 islands.

STAGE II
Isolated populations develop into different species.

EVOLUTION ILLUSTRATED BY GALAPAGOS ISLANDS BIRDS

MOCKINGBIRDS ONE TO AN ISLAND
Different kinds developed on different islands.

DARWIN'S FINCHES SEVERAL SPECIES OCCUR ON EACH ISLAND

In time, species spread to neighboring islands.

Number of species of Darwin's Finches on each island.

Six species found on Abingdon Island.

fact that the polar form of any number in R is $r(\cos\theta + i\sin\theta)$, where $0 \leq r < 1$ and $0 \leq \theta \leq \pi$. The square of this number is $r^2(\cos 2\theta + i\sin 2\theta)$, where $0 \leq r^2 < 1$, $0 \leq 2\theta \leq 2\pi$. The way in which a region of the z-plane maps on the w-plane is a characteristic of the function $f(z)$.

A limit of a function of a complex variable is defined: The complex number α is the limit of $w = f(z)$ as z tends to z_0, if, for any choice of a positive real number ε, there is a second positive real number δ such that w lies inside the circle of

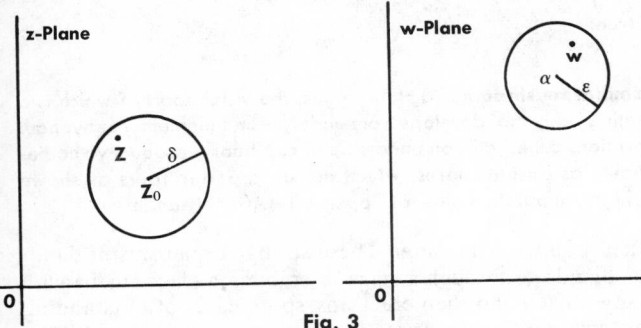

Fig. 3

radius ε about α whenever z is inside the circle of radius δ about z_0 but not equal to z_0, Fig. 3. That is $|w - \alpha| < \varepsilon$ if $0 < |z - z_0| < \delta$. If, in addition, $w = \alpha$ when $z = z_0$, the function is *continuous* at z_0. It is important to note that the same number α must be approached by w, regardless of the way in which z approaches z_0.

A derivative is defined, just as in ordinary calculus:

$$\frac{dw}{dz} = f'(z) = \lim_{\Delta z \to 0} \frac{f(z + \Delta z) - f(z)}{\Delta z}.$$

Since $\Delta z \ (= \Delta x + i\,\Delta y)$ can approach 0 in any way, we can put $\Delta y = 0$, making $\Delta z = \Delta x$, and then let Δx tend to 0. This gives us $dw/dz = \partial u/\partial x + i\,\partial v/\partial x$. We can, equally well, put $\Delta x = 0$, making $\Delta z = i\,\Delta y$, and then let $i\,\Delta y$ tend to 0 to obtain $dw/dz = (1/i)\,\partial u/\partial y + \partial v/\partial y = \partial v/\partial y - i\,\partial u/\partial y$. Since these two expressions for dw/dz must be equal, $\partial u/\partial x = \partial v/\partial y$ and $\partial v/\partial x = -\partial u/\partial y$. These are the Cauchy-Riemann equations, and they can be proved sufficient as well as necessary for the existence of a unique derivative. A function is *analytic* (or holomorphic) in a region if it has a unique derivative at every point in the region. A point at which the derivative fails to exist, so that the function ceases to be analytic there, is a *singular* point. The origin is a singular point of the function $1/z$. Many results concerning analytic functions follow from the Cauchy-Riemann equations. Not only does the first derivative exist, but so do derivatives of all orders. Consequently, the function can be expressed by a Taylor's series, valid in a neighborhood in which the function is analytic. This identifies functions that are analytic from this standpoint with analytic functions as defined by power series. The mapping determined by an analytic function is *conformal*: if two curves, in a domain in the z-plane in which the function is analytic, meet at an angle θ, their images in the w-plane meet at the same angle.

An integral of an analytic function is a line, or curvilinear, integral. Consider a curve C extending from a fixed point t_0 to any point z. Subdivide the curve by points $t_1, t_2, \ldots, t_n = z$, and form the sum $S = \sum_{v=1}^{v=n} f(t_v')\,(t_v - t_{v-1})$, where t_v' denotes any value of z lying on the arc C between t_{v-1} and t_v. Fig. 4. It can be proved that if the number of subdivisions increases indefinitely in such a way that all differences $|t_v - t_{v-1}|$ tend to 0, S_n tends to a limit independent of the choice of t_v'. The limit is called the definite integral of $f(t)$ along the curve C. The Cauchy theorem on integrals of analyt-

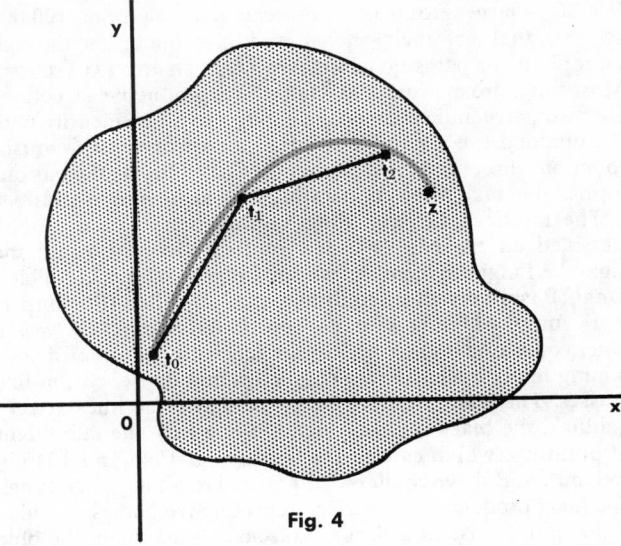

Fig. 4

ic functions states that the integral is independent of the path from t_0 to z, as long as it lies within a *simply connected* domain. Hence the integral is a function of z: $\int_{t_0}^{z} f(t)\,dt = F(z)$. Moreover, $(d/dz)\,F(z) = f(z)$. In order that a domain be simply connected it is necessary that it be bounded by a single connected closed curve which does not cut itself.

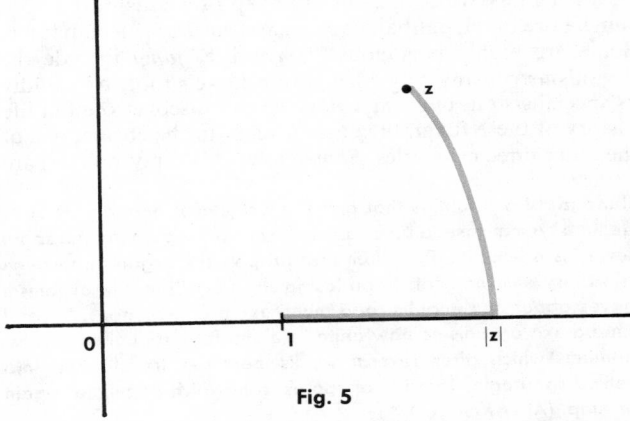

Fig. 5

This theorem can be applied to evaluate functions defined by integrals. For example, $\log z$ is defined as $\int_1^z (1/t)\,dt$. The integral can be evaluated along the path consisting of the real axis from 1 to $|z|$ and the arc of the circle $r = |z|$, Fig. 5. This gives

$$\log z = \log |z| + \int_0^\theta i\,d\theta = \log |z| + i\theta.$$

Thus, if $z = -1$, $\log z = \log(-1) = \log 1 + i\pi = i\pi$. This example illustrates how the theory of functions of a complex variable extends the scope of elementary functions. It also clarifies anomalies which arise in functions of a real variable, and which are otherwise inexplicable.

As an immediate consequence of the Cauchy theorem it follows that the integral of $f(z)$ around the complete boundary of a domain within which $f(z)$ is analytic is equal to zero. If, on the other hand, $f(z)$ is analytic at all points in the domain except $z = z_0$, the integral around the boundary is not in general zero, and, when divided by $2\pi i$, is called the *residue* of the function at $z = z_0$.

Practical applications of the theory of functions of a complex variable abound throughout physical science.—*H. C.*

FUNGI: a large group of non-green plants (about 100,000 species) that get their energy and raw materials through saprophytic or parasitic habits (see SAPROPHYTE; PARASITISM). Most fungi are microscopic. Only the reproductive structures are distinctive and conspicuous enough to let us identify with the unaided eye a mold, a mildew, a rust or smut, a mushroom or a bracket fungus, a morel or a truffle, or the various forms fungi take when cooperating with algal cells in LICHENS.

The multicellular true fungi (Eumycophyta) are usually classified on the basis of their reproductive parts into the alga-like fungi (Phycomycetes), sac fungi (Ascomycetes), club fungi (Basidiomycetes), and the catch-all called the "imperfect" fungi, which lack sexual reproductive parts. *Alga-like fungi* consist of branching tubes filled with protoplasm containing many nuclei. These plants develop dense, cotton-like masses. The water mold *Saprolegnia* that sometimes attacks goldfish, the black mold of bread (*Rhizopus*), the late blight of potatoes (which caused the famines of 1845 and 1846 in Ireland), and downy mildew of grapes are all alga-like fungi. *Sac fungi* produce characteristic reproductive bodies in which eight spores arise in a slim sac (ascus). *Penicillium,* the blue or green mold common on citrus fruits and the source of the drug penicillin, is a sac fungus. So are morels, truffles, cup fungi, powdery mildews, and the causative agents of apple scab, chestnut blight, Dutch elm disease, and ergot of rye. Yeasts appear to be degenerate sac fungi that rarely produce sacs. *Club fungi* produce spores on short blunt clubs (basidia), often on the surface of gill-like plates or vertical pores such as are seen under the cap of a mushroom. Gill fungi, pore fungi, puffballs, smuts, and rusts are all club fungi. Some are highly poisonous. *"Imperfect" fungi* include the organisms causing ringworm and athlete's foot. As rapidly as specialists on fungi (mycologists) can discover the full life history of these fungi, they assign them to the correct one of the other three categories. *Slime molds* (Myxomycophyta) are

Slime mold is a fungus that acts like an animal during part of its life. In a typical case, a bit of protoplasm from a germinating spore develops a whiplike flagellum that propels the organism through its watery environment. Soon losing the flagellum, the organism moves about and engulfs food much as an ameba does. Several ameba-like organisms now unite in a single mass called a plasmodium, which after several weeks becomes transformed into stalked sporangia. These bear spores from which flagellates again develop. (*After Kenoyer*)

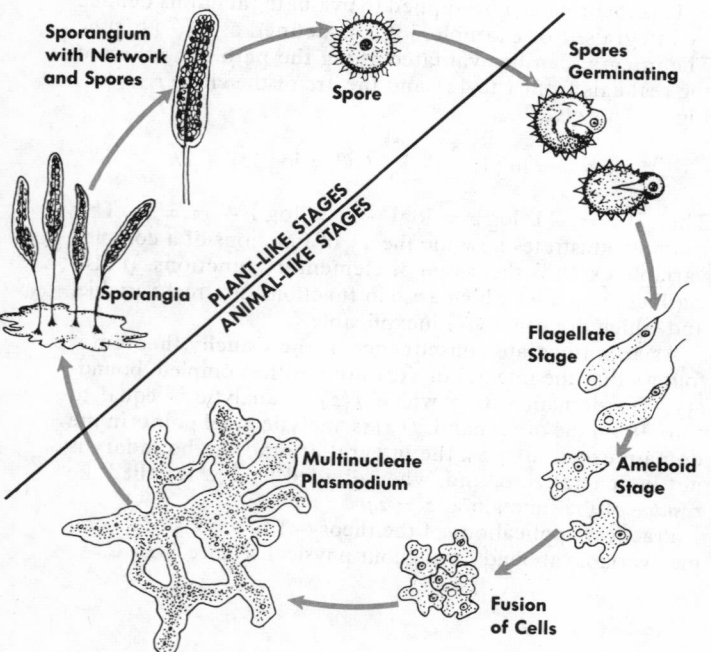

Sporangium with Network and Spores

Spore

Spores Germinating

PLANT-LIKE STAGES

ANIMAL-LIKE STAGES

Sporangia

Flagellate Stage

Ameboid Stage

Multinucleate Plasmodium

Fusion of Cells

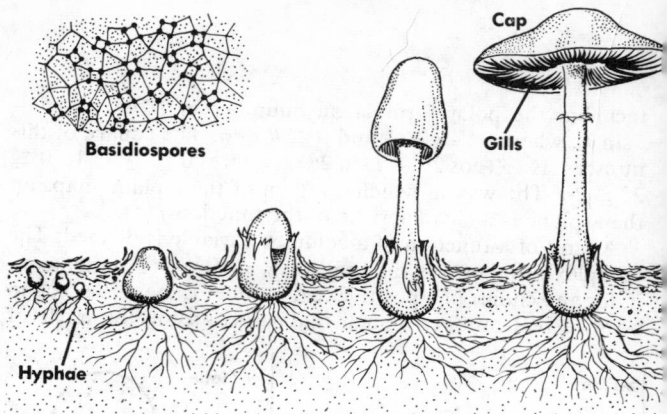

Basidiospores

Cap

Gills

Hyphae

Familiar mushroom is a club fungus, the visible part of which is a fruiting body that develops from underground filaments, or hyphae. Partitions called gills on underside of cap bear reproductive bodies known as basidiospores, which are arranged in fours as shown in highly magnified view at upper left. (*After Hylander*)

often grouped with fungi. These strange organisms of damp woodlands go through a stage resembling a giant ameba with many nuclei, and then erect tiny spore cases of outstanding delicacy and beauty. Some are large enough to see with the unaided eye. *Bacteria* (Schizomycophyta) can be grouped with fungi, although their cell structure is far simpler. The reason for linking BACTERIA and true fungi is that actinomycetes (which produce antibiotics such as streptomycin) are intermediate in their structure and complexity. See Color Plate 50.—*L. and M. M.*

FUR: the soft silky covering of many mammals, particularly of those indigenous to cold countries. Since the usual function of fur is to give warmth, the winter coat is often denser than the summer one. But the dense, close fur of the mole is related less to the necessity for warmth than to the protection of the skin from the irritating effects of particles of soil during burrowing. The somewhat similar fur of the beaver has partly, no doubt, a similar function; but more important is its power of throwing off water so as to prevent the chilling of the surface of the skin. The same type of fur, with the same double function, occurs in the Australian duckbill.—*A. P. E.*

FURANS: a series of organic compounds related to furan (furfuran), a 5-membered heterocyclic compound containing one oxygen atom. Furan itself is a colorless liquid with the smell of ether. Furfural, the best-known and most commercially important furan, is obtained from corncobs, oat hulls, rice hulls, and similar sources, and plays a role in the production of nylon, synthetic rubber, and certain bactericides. As a solvent, furfural is used in the refinement of lubricating oils, and to improve the quality of diesel fuels.—*Ru. M.*

FURNACE: a closed or partially closed chamber, insulated and usually lined with refractory material, which in use is maintained hotter than red heat. Furnaces can be used simply as heat generators in which fuel is burned; *e.g.* boiler furnaces. They can be used for achieving high-temperature chemical reactions; *e.g.* metallurgical furnaces.

Furnaces vary greatly in design, the two general types being (1) fuel furnaces, in which heat is generated by burning fuel within the chamber; and (2) furnaces in which the heat is generated externally. The latter, often called muffle furnaces, are much used in chemical laboratory work. The so-called ELECTRIC FURNACE is based on the heating effect obtainable from the passage of electricity, and is used mainly for the heat treatment of metals and alloys; basic types are the arc, induction, resistance, and resistor varieties. Fuel furnaces differ in type of fuel used, *i.e.* solid (coke and other types of coal), liquid (fuel oil), or gas (natural gas, propane, butane); small-scale furnaces are used for heating of domestic and industrial buildings. See HEATING SYSTEMS.

Of great importance industrially is the coke-fueled *blast furnace,* used to convert iron ore to pig iron and for the production of copper (see SMELTING). The main unit, a tall steel tower lined with brick, consists of the *stack* (upper section), *bosh* or air chamber (middle), and *hearth* (lower section). The ore, charged at the top of the stack, is mixed with limestone (*flux*) for slag formation. While the hearth is charged with coke, a stream of hot air at 1800°F (*air blast*) is injected into the bosh through a system of tube conduits (*tuyeres*) to facilitate the burning of the coke and thus maintain a high temperature (3400°F) sufficient for melting the iron and slag. The essential operation is the reduction of iron oxide ore to pig iron with carbon monoxide gas, a combustion product formed by interaction of carbon dioxide with coke. Another important combustion product is hydrogen liberated from the water contained in the ore. The mixture of carbon monoxide, hydrogen, and nitrogen (left over after the oxygen of the air has been consumed in combustion) forms a current of hot blast gases, which has strong reducing properties. The current, rising from the hearth and bosh to the stack, mixes with the descending stream of iron oxide ore and flux. The iron oxide is reduced to pig iron (91% pure), which contains carbon, manganese, sulfur, phosphorus, and silicon as impurities. The silica present in the ore is converted to calcium silicate (slag) by the action of lime liberated from the limestone by heat. Alumina and magnesia, if present, also collect in the slag. The fine particles of pig iron and the slag descend slowly from the stack to the bosh, where the temperature is high enough to melt both. The melt flows down to the lower section of the hearth (the *well*). The pig iron (heavier layer) and

From blast furnace to open-hearth furnace: Huge ladle empties molten pig iron, still high in undesirable impurities (e.g. 3 to 5% carbon) after primary reduction in a blast furnace, into an open-hearth furnace. Open-hearth furnace will further reduce impurities to produce high-quality steel. (*U. S. Steel*)

slag (lighter layer) separate under gravity. The remainder of the blast gas now contains the gaseous reaction products carbon dioxide and steam. This mixture (waste gas), still an efficient fuel, is washed for further use. In *open-hearth furnaces* carbon and other impurities left in the pig iron are oxidized by air blasts and removed as slag; this is a step in the production of STEEL (see OPEN-HEARTH PROCESS). In the *reverberatory furnace* the charge is heated by the flame only; there is no direct contact with the burning fuel. The flame rises over a brick ridge built high up in the firing chamber and is deflected (*reverberated*) toward a lower ridge placed over the hearth. This furnace is used in CALCINATION and

Modern blast furnace converts over 1,000 tons of iron ore daily. In 5 yr over 2,000,000 tons of pig iron may be made by a single furnace. Skip cars are used to load raw materials automatically. (*Bethlehem Steel Corp.*)

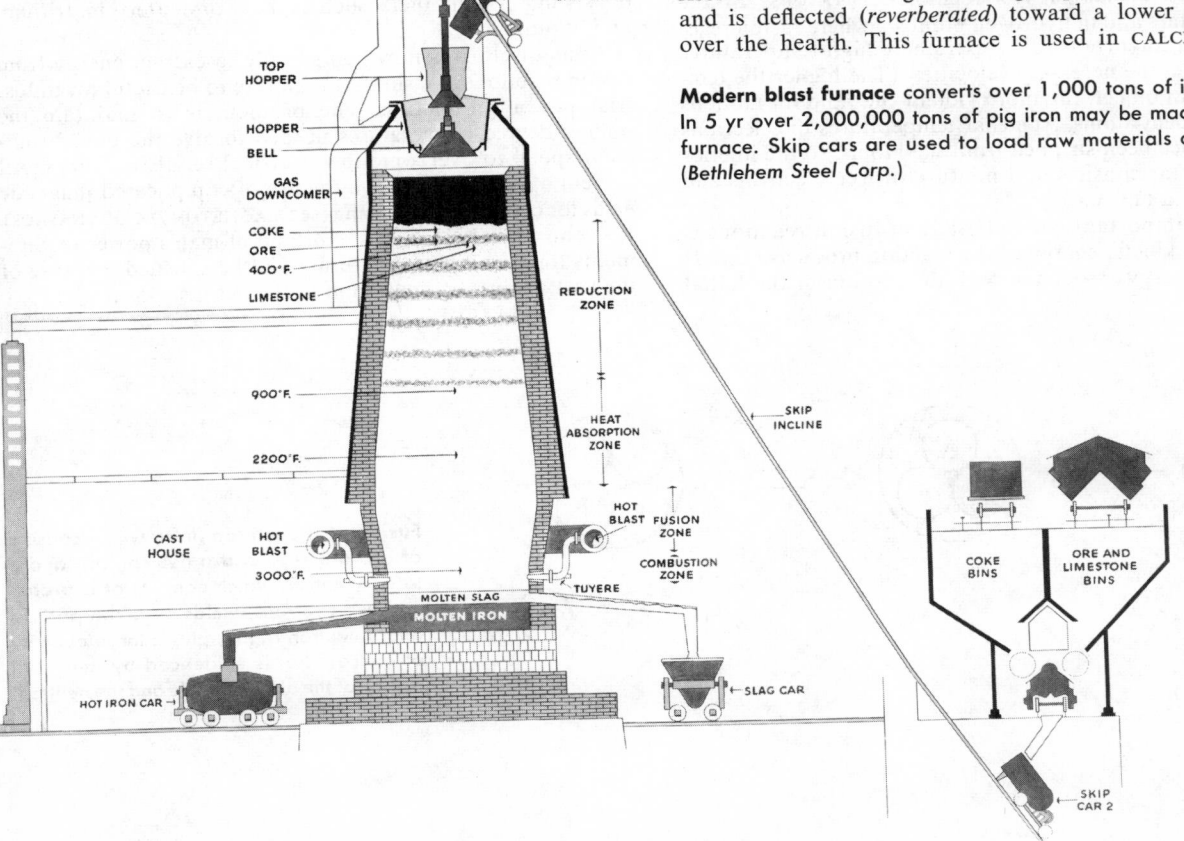

also in puddling of iron (*i.e.* conversion of pig iron to wrought iron or steel). The *puddling furnace* for refining pig iron is a reverberatory type in which the hearth is lined with iron oxide. The latter oxidizes to carbon dioxide nearly all the carbon present in pig iron. In the *muffle furnace* the charge is placed in a closed vessel (crucible). The flame heats the bottom of the crucible, but in some cases the heat is also circulated around its walls. The muffle furnace is used in making crucible steel (steel low in sulfur and phosphorus). The *retort furnace* is similar, but its closed vessel is shaped like a retort. It is used for distilling or subliming (vaporizing) metals such as mercury and zinc. In *roasting furnaces* the impurities are removed (volatilized) by subjecting the charge to a prolonged action of intense heat (see KILN). *Annealing furnaces* are used to temper (harden) metals by heating which is followed by sudden cooling (see ANNEALING).

FUSION: the change of state from solid to liquid, *i.e.* melting. Fusion occurs when a solid absorbs enough heat to overcome the attractive forces between its molecules. The heat required per unit mass is called the *heat of fusion.* The same amount of heat is released by a substance when it freezes. See CHANGE OF STATE; FREEZING; HEAT, LATENT.—*A. L.*

FUSION, NUCLEAR: a type of nuclear reaction in which two light atomic nuclei combine to form a heavier, more stable nucleus. In a typical fusion reaction (see diagram) the nucleus of a deuterium atom (consisting of one proton and one neutron) collides with a tritium nucleus (one proton and two neutrons). They coalesce momentarily to form a highly excited compound nucleus. Though these five particles cannot form a stable nucleus, two neutrons plus two protons form an extremely tightly bound combination (helium). The extra neutron is ejected, and the two products fly off at high speed. For this reaction to occur, the two original nuclei must approach each other at a speed high enough to overcome the repulsive force that exists between them as a result of the similar charges of their constituent protons. Nuclear physicists impart the required initial velocity to one of the reacting nuclei by means of PARTICLE ACCELERATORS. In the interiors of stars and in hydrogen bombs—where fusion reactions play an important role—extremely high temperatures give the nuclei the necessary velocities. (The higher the temperature of an object, the more violent the random motions of its constituent atoms. At stellar temperatures the electrons have long since been stripped from the atoms, so the interior matter of a star consists of a mixture of free electrons and nuclei, called a PLASMA.)

The most important characteristic of fusion reactions is that the total kinetic energy of the reaction products exceeds the kinetic energy associated with the motion of the initial nuclei. The source for this additional kinetic energy is the extra internal energy of the original nuclei over and above that of the helium nucleus. Since the force that exists between and holds together protons and neutrons (collectively called nucleons) is an attractive force, the most stable configuration of a collection of nucleons is one in which they are packed as closely together as their structure allows; this is the state of least internal energy. Any other configuration represents a state of higher internal energy. When such a configuration is rearranged so that the nucleons are brought closer together, a certain amount of internal energy is liberated as kinetic energy that can be used to do work—*e.g.* move mountains or destroy cities. The helium nucleus has less internal energy than the sum of that contained in the tritium and deuterium nuclei, because of a peculiarity of the nuclear force that enables nucleons to pack together more closely if the number of neutrons equals the number of protons.

Nuclear fusion reactions occurring in stars are the source of much of the energy radiated by stars and are the mechanism by which most of the nuclei in nature were synthesized. At high pressures and temperatures characteristic of stellar interiors, hydrogen nuclei have sufficiently high speeds to overcome their mutual electrical repulsion and thereby to initiate nuclear fusion. There follows a chain of fusion reactions, in which the net effect is that for every four hydrogen nuclei consumed, one helium nucleus is created together with other particles and electromagnetic radiation. This may take place as a CARBON CYCLE, or more directly without the utilization of the carbon nucleus as a catalyst for the reaction. The resultant helium nuclei may combine with each other and with hydrogen to produce more complicated nuclei.

The scientists at Los Alamos, N. M., who built the first atomic bomb, utilizing nuclear FISSION of uranium as the energy source, realized that the temperatures reached in the interior of such bombs are high enough to maintain fusion reactions for a brief interval of time. Thus, it was not long before hydrogen bombs were developed. A HYDROGEN BOMB consists of a uranium bomb core surrounded by a material consisting of light nuclei such as those of deuterium, tritium, and lithium.

A major effort is now being made to extract energy from fusion reactions at a slow enough rate to be useful for industrial power production. The problem is to maintain the million-degree temperatures needed to give the nuclei sufficient speed to overcome the electrical repulsive forces. All current approaches involve the use of complicated magnetic fields for confining the plasma (see MAGNETOHYDRODYNAMICS). If scientists succeed in this effort, all of man's power requirements for the foreseeable future will be satisfied, because of the vast amount of deuterium in the oceans.—*S. K.*

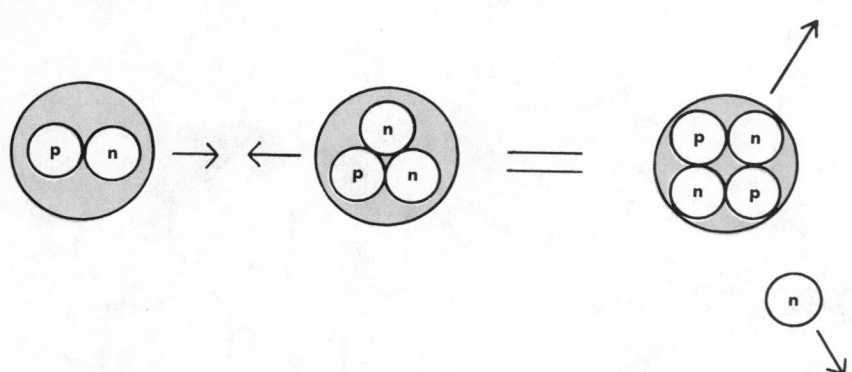

Fusion of a deuteron (*left*), which consists of a proton (*p*) and a neutron (*n*), and a triton (*center*), which consists of a proton and two neutrons, yields an alpha particle and a neutron (*right*), plus a large quantity of energy that is evidenced by the rapid motion of the alpha particle and the neutron.

G

GABBRO: a plutonic basic IGNEOUS ROCK consisting principally of labradorite feldspar and one or more varieties of pyroxene, with minor amounts of olivine, amphiboles, biotite, titaniferous magnetite, ilmenite, copper and iron sulfides, etc. Norites are gabbros in which the predominant pyroxene is orthorhombic. Gabbro grades into anorthosite with increase in plagioclase feldspar, and into pyroxenite with increase in pyroxene. Many large bodies of gabbro consist of alternating anorthositic and pyroxenitic layers, resulting from the rhythmic settling-out of the crystal phases during slow cooling. Gabbro is the plutonic equivalent of the extrusive rock BASALT and the intrusive DIABASE, all being formed from magmas of the same composition. *Traprock,* a catch-all term for most commercially used dark-colored igneous rocks, covers these three rocks as well as some similar-looking diorites and gneisses. Deposits of titaniferous magnetite and ilmenite are commonly associated with gabbro and gabbroic anorthosite. —*L. M.*

GADOLINIUM: a lanthanide (rare-earth metal) element (Gd); at. no. 64; at. wt 156.9; density 7.95. It was discovered in impure form (1880) by the Swiss chemist Jean Charles G. de Marignac in the mineral samarskite, and provisionally named by him Yα. By 1886 Marignac was convinced that Yα was indeed a new element, and he gave to it its present name. Gadolinium is found in many minerals other than samarskite, among them gadolinite, monazite, and Norwegian ytterspar. Since 1945 it has been possible to separate gadolinium in appreciable amounts from other lanthanides by means of an ion-exchange column (see CHROMATOGRAPHY). Gadolinium sulfate octahydrate (a salt) is used in the magnetic method of obtaining extremely low temperatures. The gadolinium isotopes, Gd^{155} and Gd^{157}, can be used to halt chain reaction in atomic fission, because they present exceptionally large CROSS SECTIONS for the capture of neutrons.—*G. W. M.*

GAGE: one of a group of measuring instruments of two basic types: fixed and indicating. Fixed gages—ring, plug, or snap —afford quick checking of a particular dimension that varies between tolerated limits among many interchangeable parts. The gage has two fittings; acceptable parts must fit the one set within the limits and not fit the other, which is set outside the limits. Indicator gages show fluctuating measurements on a scale calibrated appropriately for pressure or weight, size, temperature, etc. A spring, plunger, or other activating device sensitive to changes of what is being measured responds by exerting a proportional force to move a pointer over the scale.—*K. A.*

GALAXY: the basic unit star systems of which the universe is composed. The Milky Way system of stars and interstellar matter, of which the Sun with its planets is a member, is a galaxy. There are three broad types:

Spiral Galaxies: About 1900, these were called spiral nebulas, but this was found to be a misnomer when the basically stellar nature of these objects was recognized. There are two spiral galaxies in the so-called Local Group (within 2 million lt-yr from the Sun) in addition to our own MILKY WAY system. The more conspicuous is our nearest external galaxy, the Great Spiral in Andromeda, which measures more than 100,000 lt-yr across and is bigger and more massive than our own galaxy. It can be observed with the naked eye, but its stellar composition is shown clearly only in photographs made with large telescopes. The second, barely visible to the naked eye under good night conditions, is the spiral M33 (its number in Messier's catalog of clusters and nebulas) in the constellation Triangulum. All spiral galaxies are highly flattened, lens-shaped star systems, with an amorphous central nuclear region and with spiral arms emerging from the nuclear rim into the outer portions of the system. The spiral arms are composed principally of interstellar gas and dust and superluminous stars that are relatively young. All spirals are flattened because of rapid rotation around an axis perpendicular to the central plane; the arms seem to be winding up like the springs of a watch.

Barred Spirals: These are spiral galaxies in which the spiral arms emanate from a bar-like feature, passing through the

Spiral galaxies. (*Left-hand column:*) NGC 4594, with plane split by conspicuous dust lane; NGC 2841, displaying multiple arms around an amorphous lens; and NGC 5457 (M101), with clearly differentiated spiral arms branching from a small, amorphous nucleus. (*Right-hand column:*) NGC 2859, a galaxy of a type intermediate between elliptical galaxies and true barred spirals, and NGC 5850 and 7479, barred spirals. (*Mt Wilson*)

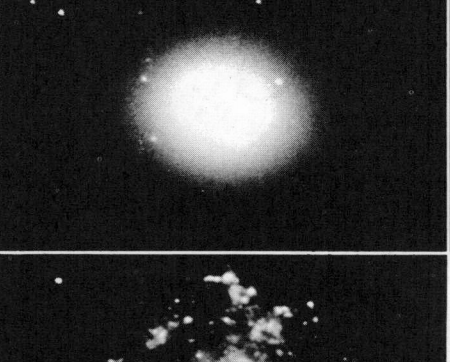
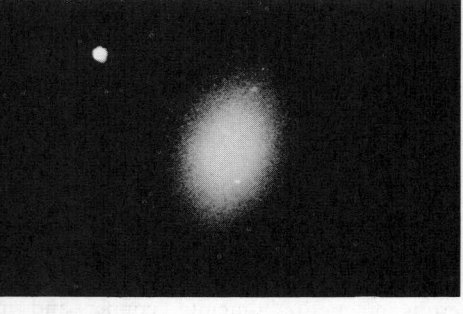
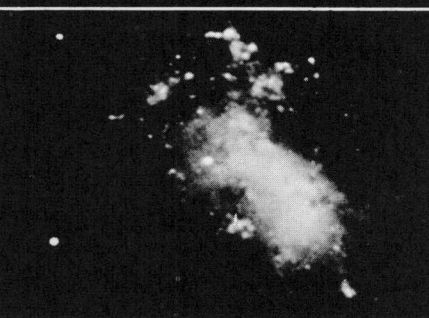

Elliptical and irregular galaxies: In the top row are NGC 3379, NGC 221 (M32), and NGC 4621 (M59)—all elliptical galaxies, shown in order of increasing apparent ellipticity. To the left are NGC 3034 (M82) and NGC 4449, both irregular galaxies. (Mt Wilson)

nucleus. The nature of these bars is not clearly understood. There is no barred spiral in the Local Group.

Ellipsoidal or Elliptical Galaxies: Elliptical galaxies appear generally as amorphous, nebulous masses. They show the typical absorption spectra of groups of stars, and it has indeed proved possible with the aid of large reflectors to resolve the nearer ones into stars. There are several of these galaxies in the Local Group; two of them are companions to the Andromeda spiral. The nearest of these, about 2 million lt-yr away, are inconspicuous because they are small (their diameters rarely exceed 7,500 lt-yr), because they possess no brilliant supergiant stars, and because they have little or no nebulosity (gas or dust) associated with them. The greatest observed flattening corresponds to an ellipticity of 0.7; none are as flattened as the normal spiral.

Irregular Galaxies: The Large and Small Magellanic Clouds are the closest irregular galaxies (about 200,000 lt-yr). There are two more irregulars in the Local Group, but both are more distant and smaller in diameter than the Magellanic Clouds. The Large Magellanic Cloud is extremely rich in interstellar gas and in supergiant stars belonging to the young star Population I, but it does possess some varieties of stars and star clusters of Population II. The Small Magellanic Cloud possesses stars of both populations; little interstellar matter is detected by optical techniques, but radio studies in Australia have revealed surprising amounts of interstellar hydrogen in the neutral atomic state.

Much uncertainty remains with regard to the probable distances of the galaxies. The estimates of the late 1920s were based on comparisons between cepheid VARIABLE STARS in the Milky Way system and in the nearest galaxies, but in the early 1950s it was discovered that these were not strictly comparable varieties of stars. This led to a doubling of the accepted distance scale; a further upward revision (to a factor 3 over original scale) is now generally accepted.

The accepted distances for most of the 17 galaxies in the Local Group are probably fixed to within 20%, but the percentage error becomes greater for more distant galaxies, which are little more than slightly elongated dots on our photographs. There are by now approximately one billion galaxies photographically within reach of our biggest telescopes. Some of these galaxies have distances as great as 20,000 to 30,000 million lt-yr—we see these objects not as they are now, but as they were 20,000 to 30,000 million yr ago. The spectra of galaxies show a shift of the spectral lines toward the red end. The most common interpretation of this fact is that galaxies are receding, with a velocity of recession proportional to their distance. This RED-SHIFT is of utmost significance in studies of the origin of the universe and in other aspects of COSMOLOGY.

Some of the strongest radio sources have been identified with remote galaxies. At first, these were thought to be a by-product of collision between galaxies, but this hypothesis has not stood up to close scrutiny. It is now thought that many of the radio sources represent after-effects of supernova explosions. Characteristically, the area of the sky from which the radio reaction comes is many times larger than that covered by the optical image of the responsible galaxy. The radio radiation presumably originates in gaseous shells or spheres of very low density, far beyond the main body of the galaxy, in which shells the electrically charged atomic nuclei and free electrons are accelerated in their movement in large-scale magnetic fields.

The category of galaxies may include also the puzzling objects called "quasars." See QUASI-STELLAR RADIO SOURCE.

Galaxies have a marked tendency to cluster. Between 2,000 and 3,000 clusters of galaxies have been found on survey photographs with large, wide-angle telescopes. The best-known cluster of galaxies within 50 million lt-yr of the Sun is the Virgo cluster, which covers an area of more than 10° in diameter in the sky in the constellation Virgo; it is rich in elliptical galaxies.—*B. J. B.*

GALEN, CLAUDIUS, *c.* 129–70 B. C., Roman anatomist, physiologist, and physician; b. Pergamum. He systematized Greek anatomical, physiological, and medical knowledge and added a great deal of factual knowledge in these fields. His voluminous works formed the principal foundations from which modern scientific work in zoological anatomy and physiology began. His own research was teleological in nature. He is known particularly for his study of the vascular system.—*D. H. D. R.*

GALILEO (GALILEO GALILEI), 1564–1642, Italian scientist and philosopher; b. Pisa; ed. Univ. of Pisa. One of the greatest of the founders of modern science, he contributed significantly to astronomy, physics, and development of scientific methodology. He made the first astronomically useful telescope (1609) and discovered Jupiter's four large moons and the phases of Venus (1609–10). These discoveries and his talent in mathematics and critical analysis made him the most influential exponent of the Copernican system and the most powerful critic of Aristotelian and Ptolemaic physics and astronomy. Important in physics were his investigations of the motion of falling bodies or, in general, the study of kinematics. Equally important were his contributions to the methodology of science, for it was in his work that observation, experiment, mathematics, and theory were for the first time combined in a fashion typical of much modern science. He was professor of mathematics at the Univ. of Pisa (1589–92), professor of mathematics at the Univ. of Padua (1592–1610), and after 1610 Chief Mathematician and Philosopher to the Grand Duke of Tuscany. His most important works include the *Sidereus Nuncius* (1610), *Letters on the Solar Spots* (1613), *Il Saggiatore* (1623), *Dialogo dei due massimi sistemi del mondo*

Galileo Galilei
(*New York Public Library*)

(1632), and *Dialoghi delle nuove scienzi* (1638). While he professed loyalty to the Catholic Church, beginning in 1610 his ideas came into conflict with those of certain churchmen and Aristotelian philosophers. In 1616 Copernicus' theory was condemned and Galileo ordered to abandon it. After publication of *Dialogo dei due massimi sistemi del mondo* he was again called to Rome, examined by the Inquisition, and compelled to abjure his belief in Copernicus. Sentenced to indefinite imprisonment, in 1633 he returned to his home near Florence to permanent house arrest.—*R. K.*

GALL BLADDER: in vertebrates, a hollow sac, arising from the bile duct, that serves for temporary storage of bile before it is discharged into the intestine. Bile is important in the digestion of fats. When digestion is not in progress, bile flows steadily from the LIVER and accumulates in the gall bladder, where it is concentrated by removal of some of its water. When food mixed with acid enters the duodenum from the stomach, the acid stimulates cells in the wall of the duodenum to liberate a hormone (cholecystokinin) into the blood. When this hormone circulates back to the gall bladder, the latter contracts and discharges its contents into the intestine. Occasionally, the cholesterol (a normal constituent of bile) is

deposited in the gall bladder and forms gallstones, which can obstruct the flow of bile. Surgical removal of the gall bladder in such cases does not interfere with the flow of bile, but the flow now becomes continuous instead of intermittent.—*B. T. S.*

GALLIUM: a metallic element (Ga); at. no. 31; at. wt 69.72; density 5.927; mp 29.78°C, bp 2070°C. Gallium is one of the few substances that expand, rather than contract, on freezing (two others being water and bismuth). Gallium's existence was predicted by D. Mendeleev (1871) on the basis of a "blank space" in his periodic table: "In this group [III]," Mendeleev wrote, "the element in the third series following zinc is lacking. Its atomic weight must be close to 68. We will call this element Ekaluminium, El = 68, because it follows directly after aluminum in the third group." In 1875 Lecoq de Boisbaudran first glimpsed gallium's distinctive spectral lines in a sample of zinc ore, and subsequently isolated sufficient amounts to investigate its chemical properties. Because gallium remains a liquid through a wide range of temperature, it is useful for high-temperature thermometers.—*G. W. M.*

GALOIS, ÉVARISTE, 1811–32, French mathematician; b. Paris. He was a mathematical genius. His papers, done entirely by his own efforts with little encouragement from, or contact with, other scholars, provided material for generations of mathematicians. His most important work was an investigation of the solvability of equations, to which he applied group theory. The body of theory that resulted, called GALOIS THEORY, is of great significance in modern mathematics. Galois became embroiled in the revolution of 1830 and was imprisoned. Soon after his release, he ran afoul of his political enemies, was drawn into a duel in an affair of "honor," and was killed.—*H. C.*

GALOIS THEORY: the application of GROUPS to the solution of equations. An algebraic equation of degree *n*, with real or imaginary coefficients, has exactly *n* real or complex roots. The key problem in the theory of equations is the determination of these roots. Equations of degree less than 5 can always be solved, but, in general, equations of higher degree cannot be solved by ordinary algebraic processes. About 1770, Joseph Louis Lagrange studied the special reasons for success in solving equations of degrees 1, 2, 3, and 4. Following him, Évariste Galois associated with each equation a group of permutations, and he showed how certain fundamental properties of the equation were mirrored in this group. In what follows, we shall attempt to make his ideas clear.

Consider on the one hand the general equation of degree 4:

$$(1) \qquad x^4 + a_1 x^3 + a_2 x^2 + a_3 x + a_4 = 0$$

where a_1, a_2, a_3, and a_4 are arbitrary constants; and on the other hand the biquadratic:

$$(2) \qquad x^4 + p x^2 + q = 0$$

Equation (2) is easier to solve than (1). Why? Because, even though we do not know the roots of (2), we know more about them than about those of (1).

Although we do not know the roots $\xi_1, \xi_2, \xi_3, \xi_4$ of (1) in all their individuality, we can nevertheless write down certain relations between these roots and the coefficients of equation (1), namely:

$$\xi_1 + \xi_2 + \xi_3 + \xi_4 = -a_1$$

$$\xi_1\xi_2 + \xi_1\xi_3 + \xi_1\xi_4 + \xi_2\xi_3 + \xi_2\xi_4 + \xi_3\xi_4 = a_2$$

$$\xi_1\xi_2\xi_3 + \xi_1\xi_2\xi_4 + \xi_1\xi_3\xi_4 + \xi_2\xi_3\xi_4 = -a_3$$

$$\xi_1\xi_2\xi_3\xi_4 = a_4$$

as well as any relations obtainable by combining these fundamental relations among themselves. It has been demonstrated that there exist no possible other relations.

Note that these relations are symmetric in $\xi_1, \xi_2, \xi_3, \xi_4$; *i.e.* they remain unchanged or *invariant*, hence exact, if we permute any of the ξ's among themselves. Of course, the above fundamental symmetric relations hold true for the biquadratic, but in the case of this equation we can also write down certain other relations, namely *non*-symmetric ones:

$$\xi_1 + \xi_2 = 0, \qquad \xi_3 + \xi_4 = 0.$$

These nonsymmetrical relations allow us to *discriminate* between the roots, so that now the four roots are not completely indiscernible among themselves. What we can say of ξ_1 and ξ_2, *e.g.* $\xi_1 + \xi_2 = 0$, cannot be said of ξ_1 and ξ_3, say. Furthermore, $\xi_1 + \xi_2 = 0$ does not remain valid when we replace ξ_2 by ξ_3, *i.e.* when we permute the roots by either of the following substitutions:

$$\begin{pmatrix} \xi_1 & \xi_2 & \xi_3 & \xi_4 \\ \xi_1 & \xi_3 & \xi_2 & \xi_4 \end{pmatrix} \quad \text{or} \quad \begin{pmatrix} \xi_1 & \xi_2 & \xi_3 & \xi_4 \\ \xi_1 & \xi_3 & \xi_4 & \xi_2 \end{pmatrix}$$

That certain relations between the roots of the biquadratic become inexact under some permutations is due to the fact that we can say specific things about some roots that we cannot say about others—we can, in short, make distinctions between the roots. This means that our lack of knowledge of the exact roots of this equation is not as great as in the case of the general equation of degree 4, where all substitutions are permitted in the relations among the roots, without destroying the relations.

In the case of the general equation of degree 4, we can carry out $4! = 24$ substitutions, without destroying any fundamental symmetric relation between the roots. What are the possible substitutions that can be carried out in the case of the biquadratic? We can interchange ξ_1 and ξ_2, for $\xi_1 + \xi_2 = 0$ then becomes $\xi_2 + \xi_1 = 0$ and the relation $\xi_3 + \xi_4 = 0$ remains unchanged. This is equivalent to carrying out the permutation

$$\begin{pmatrix} \xi_1 & \xi_2 & \xi_3 & \xi_4 \\ \xi_2 & \xi_1 & \xi_3 & \xi_4 \end{pmatrix}$$

Also possible are:

$$\begin{pmatrix} \xi_1 & \xi_2 & \xi_3 & \xi_4 \\ \xi_1 & \xi_2 & \xi_4 & \xi_3 \end{pmatrix}, \quad \begin{pmatrix} \xi_1 & \xi_2 & \xi_3 & \xi_4 \\ \xi_2 & \xi_1 & \xi_4 & \xi_3 \end{pmatrix}, \quad \begin{pmatrix} \xi_1 & \xi_2 & \xi_3 & \xi_4 \\ \xi_3 & \xi_4 & \xi_1 & \xi_2 \end{pmatrix},$$

$$\begin{pmatrix} \xi_1 & \xi_2 & \xi_3 & \xi_4 \\ \xi_3 & \xi_4 & \xi_2 & \xi_1 \end{pmatrix}, \quad \begin{pmatrix} \xi_1 & \xi_2 & \xi_3 & \xi_4 \\ \xi_4 & \xi_3 & \xi_1 & \xi_2 \end{pmatrix}, \quad \begin{pmatrix} \xi_1 & \xi_2 & \xi_3 & \xi_4 \\ \xi_4 & \xi_3 & \xi_2 & \xi_1 \end{pmatrix},$$

for they transform each of the given relations into the other. These seven permutations, plus the identity permutation, are the *only* admissible substitutions, *i.e.* those that leave invariant the relations between the roots. Because of the two described special relations between the roots, 16 substitutions become inadmissible. The more we know about the roots of an equation, the less numerous are the admissible permutations, and conversely, the more numerous are the admissible permutations, the greater our ignorance of the individuality of the roots.

Speaking with "less than full precision," we can say that the set of all the admissible substitutions for a given equation is a group—the Galois group of the equation. It is possible, without solving an equation and without knowing a single relation between the roots, solely with the help of the coefficients of the equation, to construct its Galois group and then use it as a guide in solving the equation. How this is done depends on the composition of the group and its order. The composition allows us to recognize, in certain cases, the important properties of an equation, without solving it.— *J. S.*

GALTON, SIR FRANCIS, 1822–1911, English meteorologist, statistician, and biologist; b. Birmingham. Galton coined the word "anticyclones" and called attention to their importance in his *Meteorographica, or Methods of Mapping the Weather* (1863). He began the collection of measurements of large numbers of people for statistical studies, one result being his demonstration of the value of fingerprints for identification. His numerous works on that subject include *Finger Prints* (1893). The first person to work out the method of *statistical correlation,* he also developed the questionnaire technique of eliciting data and made important contributions to psychology. His firm adherence to the Darwinian theory of natural selection led him to an extensive study of heredity (on which he published a number of works) and a particular interest in the heritability of genius. He became convinced that an indefinite improvement in the human race could be achieved if the "best" were to breed and the "worst" were not to breed, and he coined the term *eugenics* for such a policy. Galton was a fellow of the Royal Society and received its Royal, Darwin, and Copley medals.— *D. H. D. R.*

GALVANI, LUIGI, 1737–98, Italian physiologist; b. Bologna; ed. Univ. of Bologna. He did research on the hearing organs and genito-urinary tract of birds and on the irritability of tissue, and wrote *De viribus electricitatis in motu musculari commentarius* (*Commentary on the Force of Electricity in Muscular Motion*), 1791, which put forward a theory of production of electricity by animals that quickly became known as "galvanism." His work led to Volta's discovery of the voltaic cell and focused attention on the role of electricity in physiology, although Volta's work showed Galvani's theory to be incorrect. Galvani's works were published in 1841.— *D. H. D. R.*

GALVANIZING: a process of coating iron or steel with zinc for protection against corrosion. The word "galvanizing" originated in the idea of *galvanic* protection from the electrolytic causes of corrosion (see ELECTROMOTIVE SERIES). To be galvanized, an article must be thoroughly cleaned; it is then dipped in a bath of molten zinc. Three distinct layers comprise the coating: a layer of $FeZn_3$ adjacent to the iron, then a middle layer of $FeZn_7$, and finally a layer of pure zinc. The alloy layers are the thickest part of the coating. Galvanizing is the most popular of corrosion-resistant metal-coating processes and is used for a wide range of articles, from electrical transformer parts to water pipe and ash cans. Galvanizing is done also by electrodeposition or by covering the article with zinc dust and heating it.— *A. L.*

GALVANOMETER: an electromechanical device for detecting or measuring weak electric currents. Shortly after the publication in 1820 of Oersted's discovery that an electric current causes a compass needle to deflect, J. S. C. Schweigger greatly improved the sensitivity of response by winding many turns of wire in a coil placed around the magnetic needle. Each turn of wire contributed to the strength of the magnetic field. This was the first galvanometer. The galvanometer now in common use is the d'Arsonval design; it consists of many turns of fine wire formed into a rigid coil C, which is suspended by an elastic conducting fiber or ribbon F. The coil hangs symmetrically between the poles N and S of a permanent magnet. Frequently an iron cylinder I is fixed in the center of the coil, but not attached to it, to make the magnetic field in which the coil turns more nearly radial. The current to be measured flows in a circuit composed of F in series with the coil C and a conducting ribbon R that usually offers negligible resistance to the rotation of C. The current in C sets up a mag-

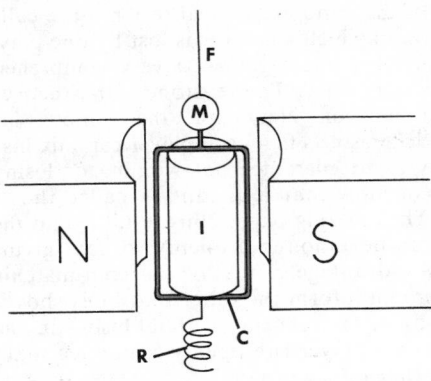

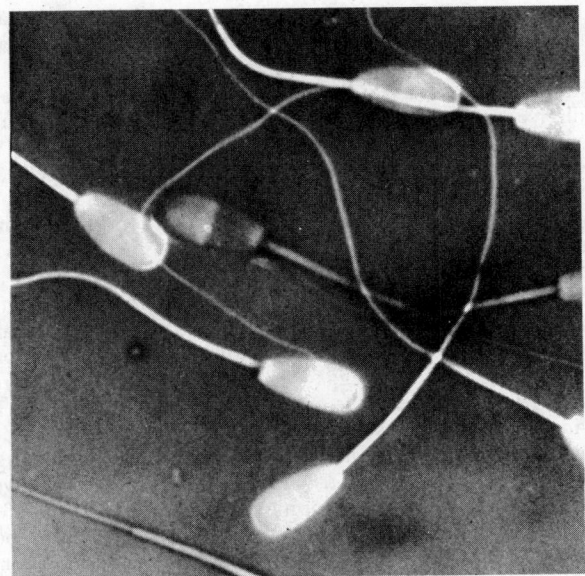

Galvanometer movement consists of a coil of wire (C) suspended by a filament (F) between magnet poles (N and S). The current to be measured passes through F and ribbon (R). Coil has mirror (M).

netic field which interacts with the field of the permanent magnet, causing the coil to turn against the restoring force of the elastic suspension *F*. To observe most easily the deflection of the coil, a mirror *M* is usually attached to the coil for viewing a distant scale or to form an optical lever for projecting a spot of light on a scale. The sensitivity of such a galvanometer is directly proportional to the number of turns and the area of the coil and to the strength of the magnetic field *N-S*; it is inversely proportional to the restoring torque per unit angle of twist of the suspension.—*H. Sw.*

GAMETE (or **germ cell**): a sex cell, as contrasted with a body cell. A male gamete is called a sperm; a female gamete is an egg or ovum. In plants, gametes arise by mitosis (see CELL DIVISION) from cells of the gametophyte generation, as one step in the cyclic ALTERNATION OF GENERATIONS. In animals, gametes arise by MEIOSIS from primary spermatocytes or

Gametes: Normal sperms of bull (*above*) and unfertilized egg of cow (*below*) are shown here, both magnified. (*J. O. Almquist*)

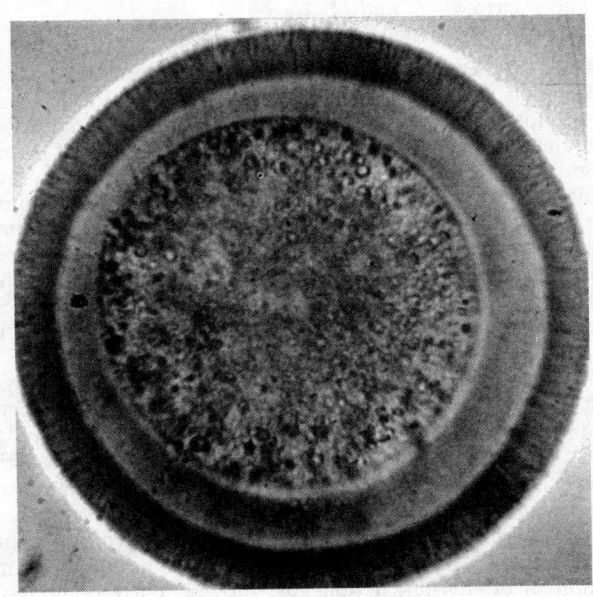

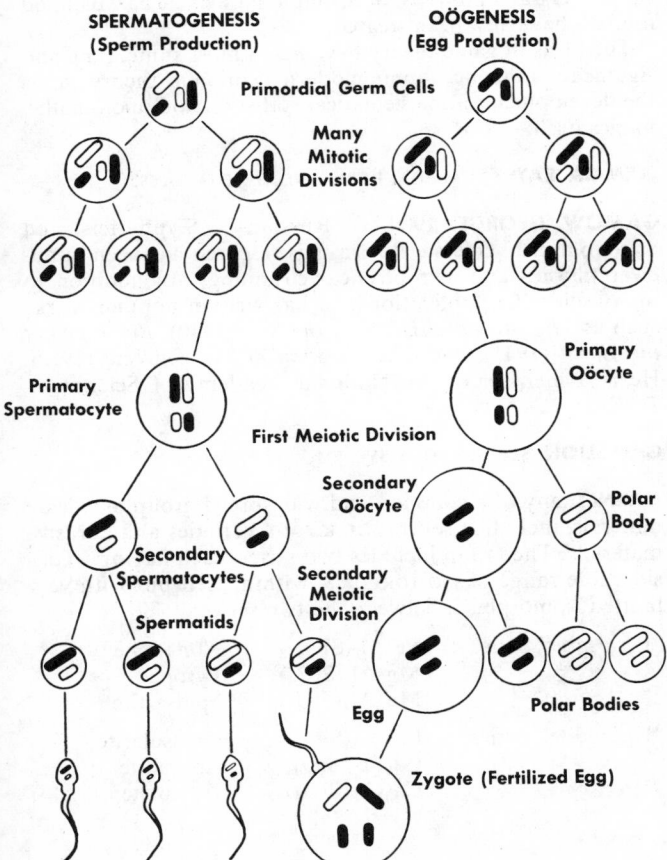

SPERMATOGENESIS
(Sperm Production)

OÖGENESIS
(Egg Production)

Primordial Germ Cells

Many Mitotic Divisions

Primary Spermatocyte

Primary Oöcyte

First Meiotic Division

Secondary Oöcyte

Polar Body

Secondary Spermatocytes

Secondary Meiotic Division

Spermatids

Polar Bodies

Egg

Zygote (Fertilized Egg)

Sperms

primary oöcytes, usually in a special layer of cells (the germinal epithelium) in the TESTIS or the OVARY, respectively. Usually a gamete contains a nucleus with the haploid (1*N*) number of chromosomes, which represents a single set. In FERTILIZATION, a sperm unites with an egg, the union providing the nucleus of the fertilized egg (zygote) with the diploid (2*N*) number of chromosomes, a paired set.

Male and female gametes arise through the steps outlined on the left and right sides, respectively, of the diagram at left, meiosis proper beginning in the diploid spermatocyte and oöcyte. In spermatogenesis (*left*), all four of the products of meiosis yield viable sperms; in oögenesis (*right*), three of the products ("polar bodies") are almost devoid of cytoplasm and disintegrate; the fourth, the egg, retains the food materials accumulated in the course of previous stages. (The number of pairs of chromosomes, which varies with the species, is here taken as two—as in the scale insect Icerya.)

In most nonflowering plants, and in vertebrate and many invertebrate animals, sperm cells are highly motile, the "head" of the cell (containing the nucleus) being driven along by lashing action of a whiplike "tail." In flowering plants and conifers, sperm cells are carried passively in the cytoplasm of the pollen tube. In arthropods and some other animals, sperms reach the egg by ameboid movements. Egg cells, by contrast, are rarely motile. Usually they are much larger and less numerous than sperm cells, and contain food upon which the embryo will depend during at least its early stages of growth.

Land snails, slugs, and earthworms are among the animals that combine both sexes in one individual; these animals are bisexual (hermaphroditic, or monoecious) and thus produce sperms as well as eggs. Most other animals are monosexual (dioecious); that is, sperms are produced by one individual (a male), eggs by a different one (a female). Among plants, both types of gametes may be produced by a single gametophyte plant; this is true of ferns. Commonly, however, the male and female gametophytes are separate. In conifers and flowering plants, male gametophytes develop within pollen grains, which are spores produced in the staminate cones or in the anthers of stamens. The female gametophytes of these plants are concealed in ovules, which are actually spores the plant does not shed. See FLOWER; HERMAPHRODITE; REPRODUCTION.—*L. and M. M.*

GAME THEORY: a mathematical theory devoted to the study of conflicts and interactions between two or more individuals or groups. It has numerous applications to the analysis of economic and industrial processes, *e.g.* the setting of prices, competitive bidding, allocation of advertising and research budgets, and the organization of companies, and to a number of military operations of tactical and strategic nature. Since many experiments and tests may be regarded as "games against nature" in which the scientist is attempting to gain information that the physical world is "trying to conceal," there are many uses of the concepts of game theory in the theory of statistics.

A number of card games, *e.g.* blackjack, poker, and bridge, can be partially analyzed within this framework of competitive processes. Familiar activities of this type serve well to illustrate the fundamental ideas and have therefore been extensively studied by both E. Borel and J. von Neumann, the two independent founders of the theory.

Consider the particularly important case of two opponents or players. Let each one possess at any stage of the game a number of alternate actions, or "moves," corresponding to the situation in a two-handed poker game where each player can draw cards or not, bet or fold. If either player knows in advance what the other player is going to do, he has no difficulty in making his optimal move. The basic problem is that of playing in some sense optimally with incomplete information concerning the present state and future behavior of the opponent, *e.g.* the opponent's hand and drawing and betting. To balance the lack of information, each player mixes his moves, sometimes behaving in one way in a given situation, sometimes in another way. Bluffing in poker is one example of this; other examples occur in the way a quarterback calls plays in football and the way a coach or catcher signals for pitches in baseball. Perhaps the simplest example occurs in the matching of coins, where one player wins if the coins match and the other wins if they do not. The optimal policy for each player is to display heads or tails with equal frequency, but in a random pattern. One can insure this random pattern by tossing the coin, or by choosing a coin blindly from a number of coins, and so on.

Games of this kind are typical of what are called "zero-sum" games, in which whatever is lost by one player is won by the other. For these games, a very comprehensive and satisfying theory exists. The keystone of this theory is a result established by von Neumann, the famous "min-max" theorem, which asserts that each player can mix his moves in such a way as to guarantee not winning or losing, respectively, less or more than a quantity v, called the "value" of the game. The amazing part of this result is that the mixture of moves can be announced openly without giving the opponent any advantage. Thus, in the coin-matching game, each player can inform the other that he is showing heads and tails with equal frequency without losing any advantage, and in poker, a player can openly announce that he bluffs 10% of the time on a pat hand.

The numerical evaluation of v and the determination of the optimal mixtures or "strategies" are usually matters of some difficulty. LINEAR PROGRAMMING can be used, and there are several iterative techniques available, notably one due to Brown-von Neumann-Robinson, which mimics the play of an actual game.

If the gain to one player is not the loss of the other player, the game is called *non-zero-sum.* No definitive theory exists for games of this nature, which correspond more closely to economic, industrial, and military operations than do zero-sum games; the same is true for games involving three or more players. A number of particular theories, fitting classes of games of greater or lesser generality, have been constructed by von Neumann-Morgenstern, and by J. Nash, Shapley, and others.

Further developments in game theory have been in the direction of games with a continuous range of choices, games of pursuit as studied by Isaacs, and multistage games, such as "games of survival," studied by Bellman-Blackwell-LaSalle, and Milnor-Shapley. Particular card games such as poker and blackjack have been considered under various simplifying assumptions, and simple models of baseball and football have also been treated.

The ideas of game theory have had a most stimulating and significant influence upon modern economic theory, upon the development of mathematical statistics, and upon mathematics itself.—*R. B.*

GAMMA RAY: see ALPHA, BETA, AND GAMMA RAYS.

GAMOW, GEORGE, 1904– , Russian-U. S. physicist and astronomer; b. Odessa, Russia. His research has been in nuclear physics and astrophysical cosmology. In addition to many scientific publications, he has written popular works such as *The Birth and Death of the Sun* (1940), *Biography of the Earth* (1941), and *The Creation of the Universe* (1952). He is a member of the National Academy of Sciences.—*D. H. D. R.*

GANGLION: see NERVOUS SYSTEM.

GARNET: any of a common and widespread group of silicate minerals, including several GEMSTONE varieties and abrasive materials. The group includes two series, each having a considerable range of ISOMORPHISM within itself but with very limited isomorphism between the two series:

"Pyralspite" Series	$Fe_3Al_2(SiO_4)_3$	Almandite
	$Mg_3Al_2(SiO_4)_3$	Pyrope
	$Mn_3Al_2(SiO_4)_3$	Spessartite
"Ugrandite" Series	$Ca_3Al_2(SiO_4)_3$	Grossularite
	$Ca_3Fe_2(SiO_4)_3$	Andradite
	$Ca_3Cr_2(SiO_4)_3$	Uvarovite

All garnets are isometric, and crystal forms are almost entirely limited to a range between simple dodecahedron and simple trapezohedron, rarely with hexoctahedral modification. Zoning is common, particularly in crystals of contact-metamorphic origin. The garnet structure is based on a dense packing of independent SiO_4^{-4} tetrahedra, linked through shared cations. Ti may substitute for some Si at high temperature (*e.g.* schorlomite).

Garnet compositions are closely related to occurrence. *Spessartite* and *almandite* are associated with acid to intermediate IGNEOUS ROCKS, *pyrope* with basic to ultrabasic igneous rocks. Almandite is most common as a metamorphic mineral, forming metacrysts in host rocks ranging from phyllites to basic amphibolites. *Grossularite* is characteristic of contact-metamorphosed limestones in an iron-poor environment, whereas *andradite* is common in the iron-rich skarns. *Uvarovite* is rare and is generally limited to contact-metamorphosed ultrabasic rocks. Garnets resist mechanical weathering, hence are common in the "black sand" concentrations of stream beds and beaches. Chemical weathering of spessartite may give rise to secondary deposits of the hydrous manganese oxide ores. Gem garnets include spessartite, almandite, and pyrope (various shades of red to purple), grossularite (usually pink), andradite (var. demantoid) (green), and uvarovite (emerald green). Almandite, the principal abrasive garnet, is used for sand-blasting, coated abrasive papers, dental wheels, etc. See MINERAL (table).—*L. M.*

Garnet crystals in isometric form with 12 to 24 sides (as here) are most common. Some occur with 36 or 48 faces. These, in schist, are from Alaska. (*Amer. Mus. of Nat. Hist.*)

GAS: one of the PHASES in which a substance can exist. The gaseous phase is the one in which the molecules of the substance are most loosely bound to one another. It is this looseness of binding that gives gases their familiar physical properties—they expand to fill any container, are easily compressed, diffuse through porous barriers, and intermix in all proportions. The study of gases has been of enormous importance in the history of science, especially in the development of atomic theory. John Dalton's development of the law of DEFINITE PROPORTIONS, AVOGADRO'S HYPOTHESIS (which forms the basis for calculating atomic weights and dimensions), and the development of the KINETIC THEORY OF MATTER all spring from investigations of the behavior of gases. Two fundamental gas laws date from the 18th cent. The first is BOYLE'S LAW, which states that at a constant temperature the volume of a gas varies inversely with its pressure. The second, CHARLES' LAW, states that at a constant pressure the volume of a gas varies directly with its absolute temperature. It follows that at a constant volume the pressure of a gas varies directly with its absolute temperature. These laws were later combined in a single relation known as the general gas law: $PV = NRT$, where P is the pressure of the gas, V its volume, T its temperature, N the number of moles (grammolecular weights) of gas being considered, and R a universal constant—*E. M. R.*

GASKELL, SIR WALTER HOLBROOK, 1847–1914, English physiologist; b. Naples, Italy. Holding that the vertebrates evolved from an arthropod stock, he explained that the gut of the arthropod, surrounded by its chain of ganglia, evolved into the spinal cord's central canal. This theory was published in numerous papers and in his *The Origin of the Vertebrates* (1908). He is best known for his research on the action of the heart and the involuntary nervous system. He was a fellow of the Royal Society.—*D. H. D. R.*

GASOLINE: an inflammable, liquid mixture of volatile, low-molecular-weight hydrocarbons obtained from PETROLEUM, and used mainly as a fuel for automobiles, aircraft, and other machines utilizing spark-ignition internal-combustion ENGINES. Gasoline also finds some use as a solvent and in incendiary mixtures. Its suitability as an engine fuel rests, first, on the heat of combustion of its hydrocarbon molecules and, second, on the fact that all its hydrocarbons have low enough boiling points (*i.e.* they are volatile enough) to be drawn as vapor into the cylinder of a gasoline engine on the downstroke of the piston; the gasoline vapor, mixed with air, is then compressed by the upstroke of the piston, and ignited by a spark across the spark-plug gap (see IGNITION). There are hundreds of different types of hydrocarbons in a typical gasoline mixture, ranging in molecular size from a 5- or 6-carbon molecule (*e.g.* C_6H_{14}) to a 10- or 12-carbon molecule (*e.g.* $C_{10}H_{22}$); these have a boiling range of approx. 20 to 200°C. Gasoline mixtures intended for automobile use are generally adjusted for the season or climate. In cold weather, a higher proportion of the lower-molecular-weight, more volatile hydrocarbons aids quick starting and warm-up. In hot weather, the same highly volatile components may cause vapor lock; also, too high a proportion of the more volatile components would preclude safe and efficient storage and handling. The heavier (higher-molecular-weight) hydrocarbons have a proportionately higher energy content (Btu), but may cause uneven fuel distribution and engine deposits if too plentiful. Complete combustion of gasoline may be typically represented thus:

$$C_7H_{16} + 11O_2 \rightarrow 7CO_2 + 8H_2O + heat$$

Heptane,   Oxygen   Carbon   Water
a hydrocarbon   (in air)   dioxide
component of
gasoline

Incomplete combustion also occurs, producing small amounts of pure carbon (causing harmful carbon deposits) and carbon monoxide (a poisonous gas).

Gasoline was first obtained from petroleum in England, 1792. This was "straight-run" gasoline, *i.e.* produced by fractional distillation, which separates crude petroleum according to the boiling ranges of its components. The *gasoline fraction*, with its low average boiling point, "boils out" early, and its vapors can be condensed and collected. (See PETROLEUM REFINING.) Today straight-run gasoline accounts for only a very small percentage of marketed gasoline. There are two reasons: (1) demand has outstripped the quantity available by straight-run methods; (2) straight-run gasoline contains a large proportion of unbranched-chain hydrocarbon molecules, and these tend to cause "knocking." A great many processes have thus been developed with the twin purpose of converting other petroleum fractions into hydrocarbons of the gasoline boiling range, and reducing the adverse effects of unbranched-chain hydrocarbons either by increasing the proportion of the anti-knock, branched-chain type or by the use of anti-knock additives.

Knocking is caused by a non-uniform burning rate of the gasoline, and tends to increase as the compression ratio in the cylinder (see DIESEL ENGINE) goes up. Straight-run gasoline does not burn uniformly; its rate of burning within the cylinder remains relatively constant (about 25–250 ft/sec) until it is about three-fourths consumed, then the rate suddenly jumps to about 4 times as much (to as high as 1,000 ft/sec). This increases wear on the engine, is said to decrease power, and causes shock waves of a frequency detectable by the human ear (thus the "knocking" sound). A gasoline's *octane number* is simply a measure of the fuel's tendency to knock; the higher the number, the less knocking. One pure, *unbranched-chain* hydrocarbon, n-heptane, has been assigned an octane number of 0; another pure, but *branched-chain* hydrocarbon, iso-octane (2,2,4 trimethylpentane), has been assigned a value of 100:

$$CH_3CH_2CH_2CH_2CH_2CH_2CH_3 \qquad CH_3\overset{\overset{\displaystyle CH_3}{|}}{\underset{\underset{\displaystyle CH_3}{|}}{C}}CH_2\overset{\overset{\displaystyle }{}}{\underset{\underset{\displaystyle CH_3}{|}}{C}}HCH_3$$

n-Heptane 　　　　2,2,4 Trimethylpentane (iso-octane)

A given gasoline's octane number is determined by comparing its knocking characteristics in a test engine with those of given mixtures of iso-octane and n-heptane. If, for example, the gasoline being tested has the same knocking characteristics as a mixture of 80% iso-octane and 20% n-heptane, the gasoline's octane number would be 80. Whether the test gasoline actually contains any iso-octane or n-heptane is not relevant in arriving at its octane number.

High-octane Gasolines: The octane number of straight-run gasoline is about 50. By contrast, the "regular" grades of automotive gasolines have an average octane number a little

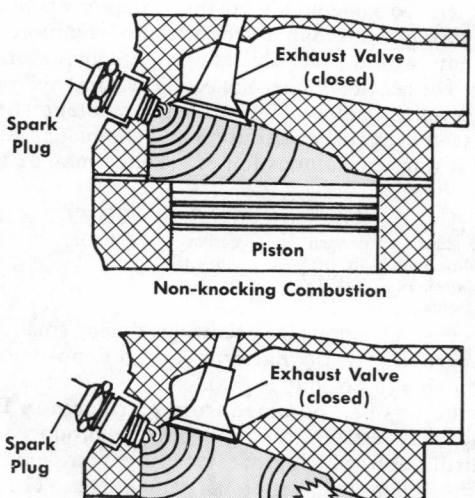

Knock vs. anti-knock gasoline: Non-knocking combustion results from regular progression of flame fronts (curved lines) after ignition of fuel by spark plug. Knocking is result of spontaneous ignition of gasoline at other points in cylinder, disrupting steady progression of flame fronts. Spontaneous ignition may occur when unsuitable hydrocarbons are present in gasoline. (*Gen. Motors*)

below 90, while "premium" grades average about 95. These high-octane gasolines contain a large proportion of aliphatic branched-chain hydrocarbons or of aromatic hydrocarbons, both of which have good anti-knock characteristics. The high-octane gasoline can be blended with straight-run gasoline to raise the latter's octane number, and the octane number of such a blend can be raised further by adding anti-knock compounds (see below). All high-octane gasolines are at least partially synthetic in the sense that many of the molecules composing them, although of a naturally occurring type, have been formed as the result of "cracking" or other chemical treatment. Cracking of petroleum means converting its high-molecular-weight, higher-boiling hydrocarbons into lower-weight molecules of the gasoline range; simultaneously, cracking increases the proportion of branched-chain hydrocarbons, and thus raises the octane number of the gasoline. James Young in 1865 first observed partial cracking or pyrolysis of crude oil by distilling it under pressure. William M. Burton was the first to develop a large-scale cracking process (1912) for a U. S. oil company. Many processes have been developed and improved since that time. *Thermal cracking* (heat and pressure treatment) yields gasoline of 55 to 80 octane number, indicating the formation of a larger proportion of the desirable branched-chain molecules than by straight-run methods. High-weight hydrocarbons, fed through cracking chambers, are subjected to temperatures of 400 to 600°C and pressure of 10 to 250 lb/in.². *Catalytic cracking* is basically the same as thermal cracking, but employs a catalyst in the form of a fine powder that is sprayed in a jet through the cracking chamber. More of the desirable branched-chain molecules are formed because of the catalyst. Commonly used catalysts are natural clays or alumina-silica mixtures. In large refineries, catalytic cracking is a continuous operation with a daily output of hundreds of thousands of gallons. An economic advantage of the catalytic process is the fact that residual coke can be used as a heating fuel, rather than the more expensive, quicker-heating gaseous fuel needed in thermal cracking. Catalytic cracking yields some very low-weight hydrocarbons not suitable as such for gasoline stock because of their extremely low boiling points; they include methane (CH_4), ethene (ethylene, C_2H_4), ethane (C_2H_6), propene (C_3H_7), propane (C_3H_8), butane (C_4H_{10}), and butene (C_4H_8). These compounds may be used in a variety of chemical syntheses (*e.g.* production of alcohol or synthetic rubber) or may be used as starting materials for production of gasoline by polymerization or alkylation (see below). A special type of catalytic cracking is *isomerization* (or *re-forming*). With aluminum chloride or aluminum bromide as a catalyst, unbranched-chain hydrocarbons are converted into isomeric branched-chain hydrocarbons. The branched isomeric form, though containing the same number and proportion of atoms as the un-branched forms, will have a considerably higher octane number, *e.g.* 100 or more:

$$CH_3CH_2CH_2CH_2CH_2CH_3 \xrightarrow[\text{high temp.}]{AlCl_3} CH_3\overset{\overset{\displaystyle CH_3}{|}}{\underset{\underset{\displaystyle CH_3}{|}}{C}}CH_2-CH_3$$

n-Hexane 　　　　　2,2-Dimethylbutane
(an unbranched hydrocarbon) 　(a branched hydrocarbon)

Polymerization is the process by which similar, low-boiling hydrocarbons are made to combine and form higher-molecular-weight, higher-boiling hydrocarbons suitable for gasoline stock. For example, propene (C_3H_7) is polymerized to 4-methyl-1-pentane (C_6H_{12}) with sulfuric acid as a catalyst. (See POLYMER.) *Alkylation* also involves the building up of gasoline-type hydrocarbons from the low-molecular-weight molecules. However, in alkylation the starting molecules are of different types. For example, a molecule of propene may be made to combine with a molecule of propane. Aviation gasolines are generally produced by either polymerization or alkylation, since these two processes yield uniform-weight mixtures with very high proportions of branched-chain molecules. *Aromatization* (or dehydrogenation), as the name implies, is the conversion of straight-chain hydrocarbons into AROMATIC COMPOUNDS such as benzene and toluene which are valuable in gasoline because of their high energy and their excellent anti-knock properties; platinum is used as a catalyst.

Many anti-knock additives are available which promote uniform burning and thus raise octane number. The most successful has been lead tetraethyl, $Pb(C_2H_5)_4$, now used in concentrations up to 0.01% in about 85% of all gasolines sold in the U.S.A.; in this concentration lead tetraethyl raises octane number as much as 15 points. Lead tetraethyl has been found to be most effective when mixed with ethylene bromide and ethylene chloride to make so-called "ethyl gasoline." Lead tetraethyl is the active ingredient that reduces knocking; ethylene bromide and ethylene chloride reduce the formation of lead deposits (formed by combustion of lead tetraethyl) around the spark plugs. They do so by forming compounds with lead (lead salts) that are relatively volatile and thus escape with the exhaust gases. Other types of gasoline additives are antioxidants, to inhibit the formation of gummy resins, and metal deactivators, which prevent the metal of the gas tank from catalyzing deterioration of the fuel.—*E. H. H.*

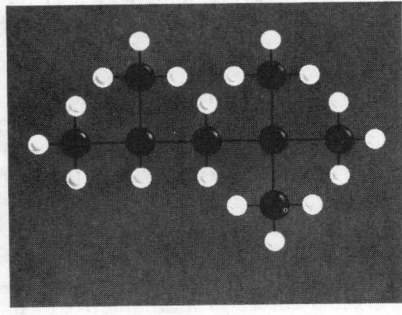

In model of iso-octane, the branched-chain hydrocarbon assigned an octane number of 100, the dark balls are carbon atoms, the light balls hydrogen atoms. (*Standard Oil Co., N. J.*)

GASSENDI, PIERRE, 1592–1655, French priest, philosopher, mathematician; b. Champtercier. While adding little directly to science, he aided the anti-Aristotelian movement in France, helped spread the work of Galileo and Kepler, and attempted a revival of the physical atomism of the ancient Epicureans. His work on logic and method was a prime achievement. Gassendi was professor of mathematics at College Royal, Paris.—*R. K.*

Pierre Gassendi
(*U. S. Navy*)

GASSER HERBERT SPENCER, 1888–1963, U. S. physiologist; b. Platteville, Wis. For their research leading to discoveries concerning the highly differentiated functions of single nerve fibers, Gasser and Joseph Erlanger shared the 1944 Nobel prize. Gasser was a fellow of the Royal Society and a member of the National Academy of Sciences. He was director of the Rockefeller Institute for Medical Research, 1935–53.—*D. H. D. R.*

Gas-turbine engine designed for military and commercial helicopter service is less than 5 ft long, 16 in. in diameter, and weighs about 280 lb. It delivers 1,050 hp. (*General Electric*)

GAS TURBINE: an air-breathing internal-combustion ENGINE that utilizes turbomachines, rather than the conventional cylinders and pistons, for compression and expansion of the gases. In theory, though not yet in practice, the gas turbine has the advantages of internal combustion without the disadvantages of reciprocating motion. It is a light, smooth-running and relatively simple machine, without the cranks, pistons, and connecting rods of the reciprocating engine, and thus it avoids some of the problems of vibration. Fuel is burned in a combustor located between the compressor and the expander. Compressed air from a turbomachine (turbocompressor) enters one end of the combustor; fuel is sprayed into the other end. The fuel-air mixture burns, creating hot gases which can be directed against the surfaces of another turbomachine (turboexpander), so as to turn it; the turboexpander's mechanical energy can then be transferred to a rotating shaft by which useful work is performed (though a portion of the mechanical energy is channeled back to drive the compressor). Slightly different use is made of the energy of the hot gases in the aircraft turbojet, a form of gas turbine. Here the hot gases leaving the combustor give up only a portion of their energy to a turbomachine, which is connected to and drives the turbocompressor. The hot gases then issue from the jet aircraft's tailpipe, providing a reaction thrust that propels the aircraft forward.

By far the most important application of the gas turbine has been in the form of the turbojet engine; but the gas turbine finds limited application as a drive for ships, locomotives, electric GENERATORS, gas-line compressors, water pumps, and propeller and turboprop aircraft. Its particular advantages are high ratio of power (or thrust) to weight, simple rotational motion, and ability to take a broad range of fuels. Principal disadvantages are high fuel consumption, high cost of manufacture, and high noise level. Gas-turbine power plants operate on a modified Brayton cycle, in which the efficiency potential is high if the maximum temperature of the working gases is high. Yet because of the steady-flow nature of gas-turbine processes there is a gas-temperature limit of 1500–1800°F. Somewhat higher temperatures are possible if turbine-blade cooling is used. By contrast, gases undergoing combustion in a reciprocating internal-combustion engine may reach temperatures of 4500°F; this is possible because

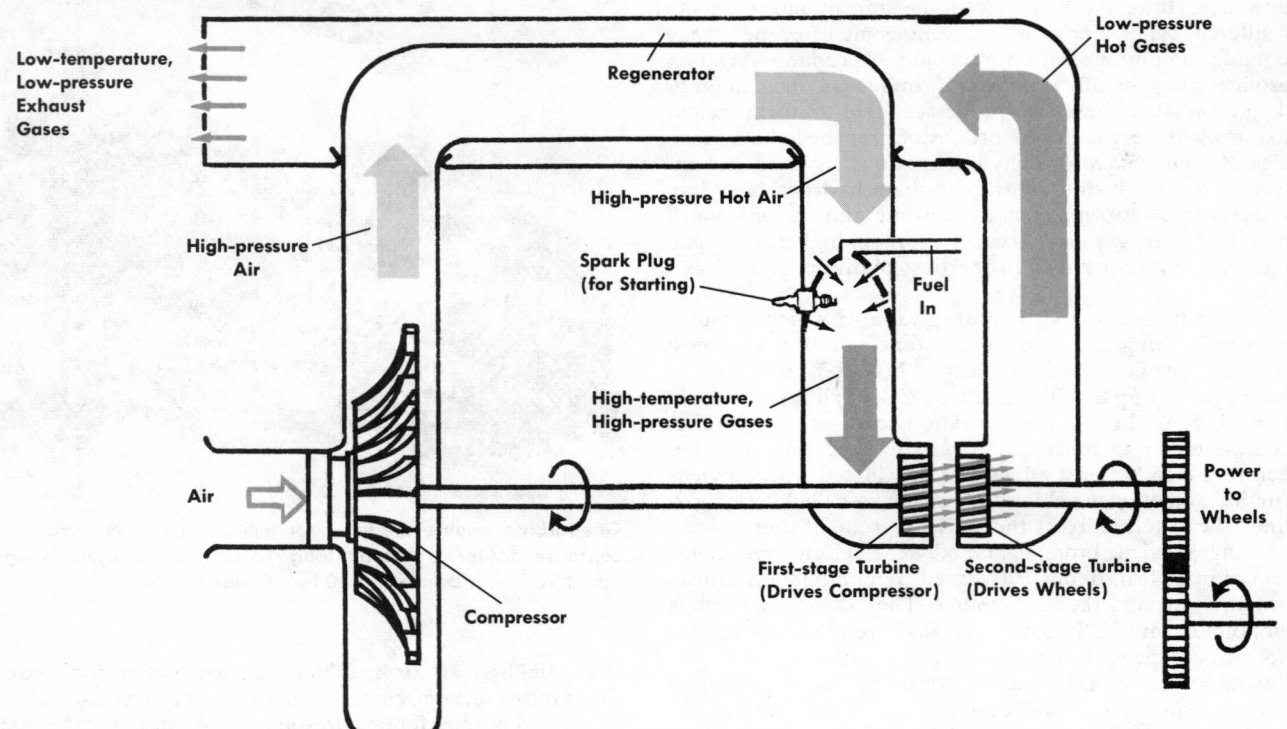

Gas turbine for automobiles: Development of an effective regenerating unit (*top*) was an important step in adapting the gas turbine to automotive use. The regenerator serves to transfer heat from the exhaust gas to incoming fresh air, thus raising the air's temperature before it enters the combustion chamber; also, the temperature of the exhaust gases is reduced. The total effect is increased fuel economy, since the heat of fuel combustion is more efficiently used. (*Chrysler*)

of the intermittent nature of the reciprocating process. However, the steady flow of the working substance in a gas turbine is a distinct advantage from the standpoints of smooth operation and regeneration potential. Regeneration uses the hot gases leaving the turbine expander to heat the relatively cool air leaving the compressor. Less fuel is then required to reach a given gas temperature, and fuel consumption is reduced. Effective regeneration can remove a serious objection to the gas turbine—high fuel consumption—and be a step toward the engine's more extensive application.

Although the gas-turbine principle dates from 1791 (if not earlier), when the Englishman John Barber obtained a patent on a design exhibiting many modern elements, engineering and mechanical problems prevented commercial consideration until around the first decade of the 20th cent. Three successful, though inefficient, gas turbines were then developed independently: first by the Frenchmen R. Armengaud and C. Lemale (1903–06), then by M. Karavodine, also in France (1908), and finally by the German H. Holtzwarth (1911). One of the first to grasp the gas turbine's applicability to aircraft propulsion was the Englishman Frank Whittle, about 1930. See AIRCRAFT PROPULSION; AVIATION; INTERNAL COMBUSTION; TURBINE.—*H. E. J.*

GAUGE INVARIANCE: The forces on a charged particle are caused by the electric and magnetic fields through which it passes. These fields can be expressed in terms of mathematical functions called potentials, which have no direct physical significance in classical physics, and which can be chosen in many possible ways to specify a given set of fields. Formally, the principle of gauge invariance, a fundamental principle of physics, states that every physical theory must be independent of the particular choice of potentials that specify the fields. See POTENTIAL.—*G. M. S. and L. S.*

GAUSS, KARL FRIEDRICH, 1777–1855, German mathematician; b. Brunswick. He is generally regarded as one of the greatest mathematicians of all time and as a peer of Archimedes and Newton. The son of middle-class parents, he was extremely precocious as a child. His education was made possible by the Duke of Brunswick, who remained a generous supporter until his death in 1806. Gauss attended Collegium Carolinum in Brunswick and entered the Univ. of Göttingen in 1795, undecided whether to pursue a career in mathematics or in philology. His brilliant success in mathematics decided the issue, and the years 1795–98 were the most prolific of his life. He also devoted much time to astronomical work, calculating the orbits of minor planets. Gauss published only papers of great significance, which he had worked over thoroughly; many other papers were discovered and published after his death, when it was found that his work had foreshadowed much of the mathematics of the 19th cent. Contributions of the highest order came from Gauss in arithmetic, algebra, analysis, geometry, astronomy, geodesy, and mathematical physics. His name is attached to many important results, *e.g.* the fundamental theorem of algebra, theorems in analysis and in electromagnetics, and numerous expressions and conclusions in differential geometry. Gauss as one of the founders of non-Euclidean geometry set the tone of modern requirements of rigor in analysis and established by strict proof many results that his predecessors had accepted uncritically.

Karl Friedrich Gauss
(*Yerkes Observatory*)

Among his best-known works are Disquisitiones arith-meticae (1801), *Theoria motus corporum coelestium* (1809), and *Atlas des Erdmagnetismus* (1840). He was a fellow of the Royal Society.—*H. C.*

GAY-LUSSAC, JOSEPH LOUIS, 1778–1850, French chemist and physicist; b. St. Léonard. In 1802 he extended the work of J. A. C. Charles on gases to demonstrate the relationship be-tween volume and temperature at constant pressure (see Charles' Law), and he proceeded to establish the coefficient of expansion for gases as ½₇₃ per degree C. In 1809 he pro-posed his *law of combining volumes* (sometimes called Gay-Lussac's law): gases combine in a simple numerical ratio by volume, and the volume of the compound formed bears a simple ratio to that of the constituents. This law provided the foundation for Avogadro's hypothesis. In 1808, with L. J. Thénard, he prepared elemental potassium from fused potash, later using it to obtain boron from boric acid (1809). Gay-Lussac also investigated chlorine (1809), fermentation (1810), hydrocyanic acid (1811), and iodine (1814). He described cyanogen and its compounds (1815) and investigated the nature of compound radicals and of acids. He is credited with being the first to prove that acids need not contain oxygen. Among his contributions to chemical technology were im-proved processes for manufacturing sulfuric acid (1818, 1827) and oxalic acid (1829). Of historical interest is his balloon ascent with J. B. Biot, 1804, to a height of 4,000 m, to ob-serve the force of terrestrial magnetism at varying elevations; this was the first aeronautical ascent to collect scientific data. His works include a paper on physico-chemical researches (with Thénard, 1811), *Recherches physiques et chimiques,* be-sides numerous other scientific papers. He was a fellow of the Royal Society.—*S. B.*

GEAR: a tooth-edged wheel, cylinder, or cone used in ma-chinery to transmit motion. Two or more gears form a con-nection through which rotational motion can be altered in direction, speed, or force. Gears are locked or keyed to the shafts or axles they must turn or be turned by. Gears turn-ing freely on bearings usually function as intermediaries, or "idler" connections, between other gears. The driving gear moves the driven gear through the lever action of their inter-locking or meshed teeth. Externally meshed gears always ro-tate in opposite directions; internally meshed gears turn in the same direction. The difference in number of rotations per minute of meshed gears of different sizes varies inversely with the ratio of their respective number of teeth: the smaller gear will turn more rapidly under a smaller force, while the larger gear turns more slowly, exerting a larger force. By varying

Model of sun-and-planet gearing. (*Watt Collection, Science Museum, London*)

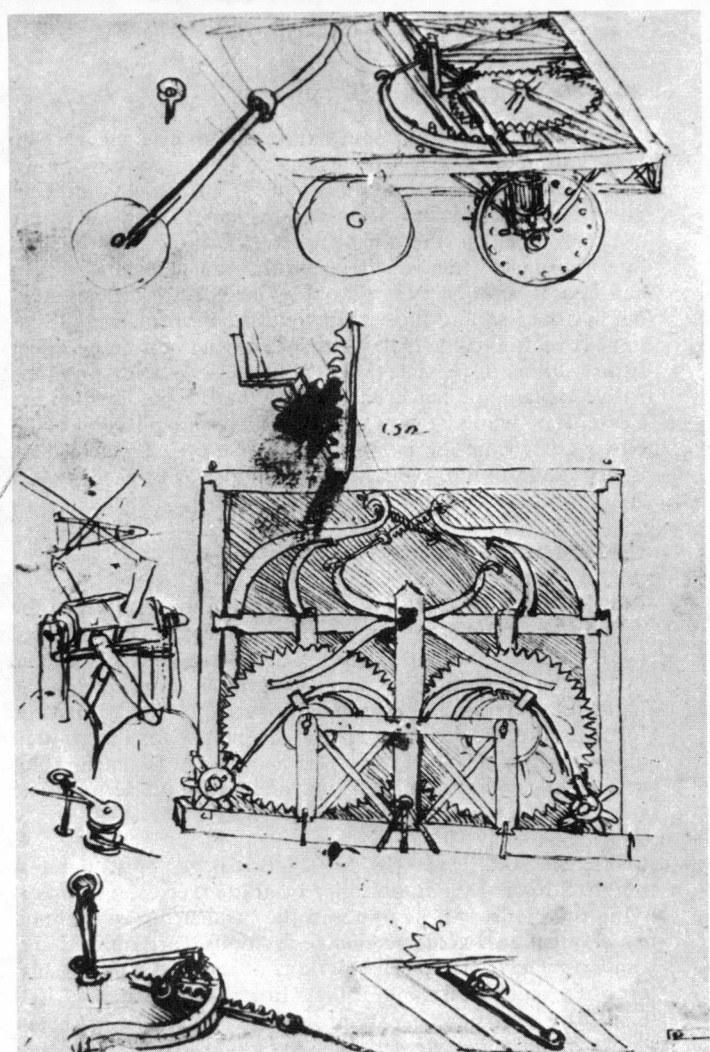

Gearing system designed by Leonardo da Vinci: Motive power for a spring-driven vehicle was supplied in this Da Vinci sketch by two systems of springs and gears, one for each rear wheel. Wheels operated independently, providing for the different rota-tional speed of each wheel as vehicle turned a curve. (*IBM*)

the shape of gear teeth and the angle at which they are cut with respect to their axis of rotation, motion can be diverted in almost any direction. Spur gears connect parallel shafts, and internal spur gears take motion from the inside of a rotating hollow cylinder. A small gear or pinion meshed with a rack transforms rotary to linear motion. Spiral gears link shafts askew to each other, while bevel gears connect shafts whose axes would intersect. Herringbone and helical gears, and those with double or multiple rows of teeth, provide longer lines of contact to transmit greater loads. A worm gear is actually a long inclined plane wrapped around a cylinder, rotating continuously, with the worm wheel sliding up the plane. It is used to link shafts not in the same plane, but usually perpendicular to each other.—*K. A.*

GEBER: see Jabir.

GEGENBAUR, KARL, 1826–1903, German anatomist; b. Würz-burg. He showed that the vertebrate ovum is a single cell. His textbooks on comparative anatomy and human anatomy were highly influential in both Germany and America. —*D. H. D. R.*

GEGENSCHEIN (or counterglow): a faint glow in the night sky opposite the Sun. It is about 5° in diameter at the point on the ecliptic which is due south at midnight. The gegenschein is very difficult to see; good eyesight, a clear dark moonless night, and rural location are required. The glow is indistinguishable if near bright stars, bright planets, and the Milky Way. From the northern hemisphere the glow is best seen in late February, when it is between the constellations Cancer and Leo. It is probably produced by meteoritic particles moving in orbits around the Sun beyond the orbit of Earth. Sunlight is scattered by each particle, and the combined effect from billions of particles causes the gegenschein. An alternative explanation has been given by the Russian astronomer Fessenkov, who suggests that Earth's atmosphere is being blown away from the Sun by light pressure. The gegenschein is, according to him, a scattering of light by this gaseous tail. See ZODIACAL LIGHT.—*G. S. H.*

GEIGER-MÜLLER COUNTER: see COUNTER.

GEIGER-NUTTALL LAW: an empirical rule, in relation to the properties of alpha-emitting RADIOISOTOPES, first formulated by H. Geiger and J. M. Nuttall in 1911. They discovered that if the logarithm of the disintegration constant (or the half-life) of an alpha-emitting isotope is plotted against the logarithm of the range-in-air (or the energy) of the emitted alpha particle, a straight-line plot is obtained for each radioactive series (uranium, thorium, and actinium series). The rule is only approximately valid.—*N. F.*

GEIKIE, SIR ARCHIBALD, 1835–1924, British geologist; b. Edinburgh. Stressing the importance of gradual erosion in modifying the landscape, he opposed the "catastrophist" school, which attributed geologic change to floods, earthquakes, and similar cataclysms. His elucidations of the past volcanic history of Great Britain and of the stratigraphy of the Old Red Sandstone were significant contributions to geology. His many books include *The Scenery of Scotland* (1865), *The Ancient Volcanoes of Great Britain* (1897), *Text-book of Geology* (1882), *The Founders of Geology* (1897), *Landscape in History and Other Essays* (1905), biographies of scientists, and the autobiographical *A Long Life's Work* (1924). Director-general of the British Geological Survey (1882–1901), he was a fellow of the Royal Society and an associate of the U. S. National Academy of Sciences. See also GEOLOGY.—*D. H. D. R.*

GEL: a system in colloid chemistry in which a small concentration of solid (the disperse phase) has combined with its liquid vehicle (the dispersion medium) to form a jelly-like mass that retains a characteristic shape. Only 2% of GELATIN in water is required to form such a gel. Most jellies and jams are gel systems.—*Ru. M.*

GELATIN: a protein substance that forms a gel with water. It has many well-known uses, *e.g.* as a photographic film base, ingredient of glues, thickener for ice cream, blender for meats, and ingredient of gelatin desserts, jellied meats, and soups, marshmallows, and other foods. It is obtained by prolonged action of boiling water on those animal proteins (principally *collagen*) in bones, skin, and connective tissue which serve as body framework. The dried product is generally sold in sheets or as a powder.—*Ru. M.*

GEMSTONES: minerals and organic substances possessing beauty, durability, and rarity, and prized for ornamental purposes. Traditionally, only diamond, emerald, ruby, sapphire, and pearl were considered "precious" stones; all the rest were "semiprecious." Today both terms are discarded as meaningless in view of wide quality variations in any specific gem-

stone. Beauty is most important; durability, including properties of hardness and toughness, ranks next, while rarity is significant because over-abundant gemstones do not enjoy great esteem. Durability is frequently sacrificed for beauty and rarity; thus pearls and opals are soft and fragile compared to many gemstones, yet fine specimens are extremely costly.

Transparent gemstones are customarily cut into prism-like or "faceted" forms to take advantage of repeated light reflections which produce the sparkling brilliant effect; non-transparent gemstones are ordinarily cut into rounded shapes known as cabochons. There are many styles of cutting within each of these categories, and some styles combine features of both; thus a cabochon may be cut with facets around its girdle. Faceted gems are generally cut in *brilliant* style or in *step-cut* style. The standard brilliant cut consists of numerous triangular facets completely covering the bottom of the stone and partly covering the top in a band around the girdle; the major portion of the top is truncated by a single large table facet. The step-cut style is also known as the emerald cut because this gemstone is customarily cut this way, and consists of a series of rectangular facets or "steps" covering the bottom of the gem, and again partly covering the top. In all faceted gems, light enters the top, most of it through the table facet; it strikes the bottom facets, which are carefully inclined at angles proper for the material being cut, and is then reflected upward toward the eye. If errors are made in cutting the bottom facets, much light escapes and the stone appears lifeless and dull. In very large gems, however, the bottom facets are often deliberately undercut to make the gems shallower and hence better suited for wear in rings. The brilliant cut, round, oval, marquise, or pendeloque, is used predominantly for diamond and other colorless or light-hued gemstones, while the step cut is favored for gemstones of rich coloration as emerald, ruby, sapphire, amethyst, etc. Cabochon styles are used exclusively for cat's-eye and star stones, since the characteristic shimmering lines of light which distinguish such gems would be distorted in facet-style cuts. Moonstones, opals, agates, and many other gemstones lacking full transparency are also cut cabochon.

The following *mineral* gemstones are commonly used in jewelry: diamond, corundum (ruby, sapphire, star stones), beryl (emerald, aquamarine), chrysoberyl (cat's-eyes, alexandrite), spinel, garnet, tourmaline, olivine (peridot), zircon, quartz (amethyst, citrine, smoky quartz, agate, carnelian, bloodstone, onyx), feldspar (moonstone), jade (nephrite, jadeite), opal. Commonly used in carvings are jade, quartz, malachite, lapis lazuli, serpentine. The following *organic* materials are used in all classes of work: pearl, shell, coral, jet, amber, tortoise-shell, ivory. Synthetic and imitative substances are very commonly substituted for natural gemstone materials; *e.g.* glasses, plastics, and in modern times, synthetic gemstones, either duplicating known minerals or creating mineral-like materials unknown in nature.

Synthetic corundum is the most common duplicate of a natural gemstone. It is prepared in large quantities by the Verneuil oven process as follows: powdered aluminum oxide is dropped through an intensely hot flame in a vertical oven to fall as molten droplets upon a clay pedestal; the latter is lowered by clockwork as the viscous mass cools and crystallizes; in a number of hours a cylindrical boule is formed. Boules are split longitudinally to relieve internal stresses and the halves cut into the gems so commonly seen in "birthstone" and "class" rings; watch and instrument bearings are prepared from thin boule slices, or more lately, from slender single-crystal boules whose thicknesses are carefully controlled during growth. Synthetic star stones are made by adding

titanium dioxide to the original powder: this results in the crystallization of myriads of exceedingly slender crystals when the boules are subjected to later heat treatment. Synthetic spinel, rutile, and the non-natural strontium titanate are prepared by the Verneuil process; synthetic emerald is grown in hydrothermal pressure vessels using ordinary beryl as nutrient with chromium added to cause deep-green coloration. Much cryptocrystalline quartz in the form of chalcedony is dyed in various colors imitative of such stones as natural black onyx, carnelian, and chrysoprase. Turquoise is often impregnated with oils or waxes to enhance color; porous types are sometimes impregnated with plastic resins which enhance color and provide a brilliant superficial polish. See Color Plate 51. —*J. Si.*

GENE: see CHROMOSOMES AND GENES; GENETICS; HEREDITY.

GENERATOR: a device for producing electrical energy from some other form of energy. The great bulk of the world's electrical energy is provided by electromagnetic generators, ELECTROSTATIC GENERATORS being excluded because of size. Generator structure is based on the principle of generating electricity by moving a conductor through a magnetic field, and it consists of two parts: the armature and the field (see ELECTRIC MOTOR, *illus.*). The armature contains the power-delivering conductors, while the field contains alternating north and south magnetic poles. The armature and field structures rotate with respect to each other, thus moving the conductors through the magnetic fields. In small machines permanent magnets may constitute the poles, but in large machines the poles are produced by d-c electricity flowing in conductors adjacent to iron or steel structures. The armature consists of stacked laminated steel sheets, with slots for holding the armature conductors. Laminations are used to reduce eddy-current power losses in the iron due to the alternating components of magnetic flux in this region. The field and armature steel provide low-reluctance paths for the magnetic flux that flows across an air gap between the field and the armature. One part of the machine, the stator, is fixed to a foundation, while the other part, the rotor, receives mechanical power from the PRIME MOVER. In a d-c generator the armature rotates, the generated ALTERNATING CURRENT (ac) being changed to DIRECT CURRENT by means of a segmented commutator, with brushes riding on the commutator providing the external connections. For reasons related to mechanical strength and electrical insulation, the conductor (armature) of an a-c machine is kept stationary, while the electromagnetic fields are mechanically rotated (by the rotor). The direct current for the field is provided by another machine, called the exciter, and brought to the rotor by brushes riding on slip rings. See ELECTRICITY.

In the U. S. A. the great majority of generators are of the a-c type, with direct current usually being provided by conversion apparatus. The standard alternating frequency (cyclic variation of the current with time) is 60 hertz (cycles/sec.) in the U. S. A.; in Europe 50 Hz is common. Lower frequencies are used for applications such as railway electrification, while higher frequencies are used in aircraft. Because the current goes through a complete alternating cycle each time a conductor passes two poles, the speed n, frequency f, and number of poles P are related by the formula $f = \frac{P}{2}\frac{n}{60}$, with n in rev/min. Generators obeying this relation are called "synchronous." For 60 cy, the highest possible speed is therefore 3,600 rev/min; it is used extensively when the prime mover is a steam turbine. Very low speeds are used for low-head hydroelectric plants. Such machines have a large number of poles, and consequently a large diameter. Since the distribution of electrical power is normally carried out by means of three-phase a-c systems, practically all a-c generators are three-phase (see PHASE ANGLE), so that three time-varying voltages are brought out through three armature terminals. The installed generating capacity in the U. S. A. is over 240 million kw, of which about ¾ is in steam plants; hence high-speed, steam-turbine-driven generators predominate in the

U. S. A. Units of 250,000 kw each are common. Generated voltages in such machines are of the order of 20,000 v per phase.

Small generators are self-cooled, while large machines have a forced-air system or hydrogen cooling. The armatures of some very large machines now have liquid-cooled windings. For equal powerhouse space, hydrogen and liquid cooling allow much greater power capacities. Recent advances have also been made in eliminating slip rings and d-c-exciter commutators, which are troublesome features on large steam-turbine generators: this is accomplished by means of an a-c exciter, the output of which is rectified electronically to direct current, the exciter and rectifiers being mounted directly on the generator shaft. Space-craft and aircraft electrical systems, originally d-c, now increasingly use alternating current with frequencies of 400 cy or greater. Here the problem is one of producing a fixed frequency from a generator with varying speed. This has been solved by using asynchronous generators (generators without field poles, but with a field supplied by a polyphase a-c source) or by converting a high variable-frequency current to a lower fixed-frequency current by electronic switching. Direct current may also be produced by a different form of the electromagnetic generator called the homo-polar generator, in which the prime mover spins a disk rapidly between north and south magnetic field poles. The current is taken from two brushes, one on the axle and one on the edge of the disk. For a disk of permissible size, the generated voltage is low; thus a number of disks must be placed in series to obtain a practical output voltage. The advantage of this generator consists of eliminating the voltage ripple (small voltage variations) found in a machine using a commutator. Devices to convert mechanical, chemical, and thermal forms of energy directly to electrical energy may eventually supplant the electromagnetic generator. Such devices have already been invented, but to date their energy output is small. Atomic fusion offers other possibilities. At present, however, large-scale power sources, including atomic reactors, rely on the conventional generator for energy conversion. See ELECTRIC-POWER GENERATION AND POWER PLANTS; ELECTROMAGNETIC INDUCTION.—B. O. W.

GENETICS: the study of the ways in which offspring inherit inborn characteristics from their parents, and of the variation among offspring of the same parents. This study begins with the development of the reproductive cells, continues through their union, and finally seeks to account for the interaction of inheritance and environment during the growth and maturation of each new individual. In almost all kinds of living things, the processes of growth and maturation are controlled by genes located at specific sites along the length of definite chromosomes in the nucleus of each cell (see CHROMOSOMES AND GENES). Genetics is concerned with tracing the replication of these genes in normal CELL DIVISION (mitosis), with the apportioning of sets of chromosomes to reproductive cells during reduction division (MEIOSIS), and with the random mating that occurs when large numbers of sperm cells approach each egg. It is concerned also with the natural and artificial ways in which genes are changed, as they undergo sudden MUTATION, and with the gradual spread of mutated genes through a population of plants or animals.

The inherited features, which tend to make each individual unique and different from all others, depend for their full expression upon factors of the environment during development. For example, a plant with the hereditary constitution for tallness may be stunted if the soil is poor. The geneticist attempts to separate variations due to differences in heredity from those due to features of the environment. Only the

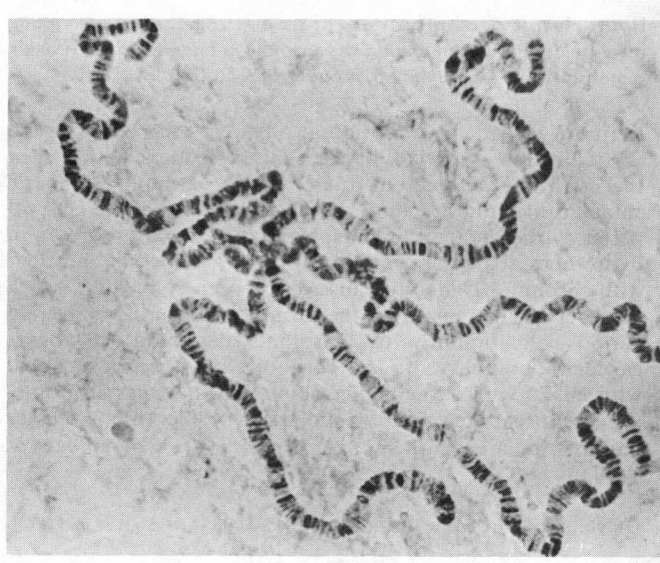

Electron photomicrograph of fruit-fly chromosomes: The chromosomes carry genes which determine heredity. (*Dr. B. P. Kaufmann*)

former are properly his concern. Each environment, however, acts as a filter. It permits individuals with certain inherited features to survive and reproduce more frequently than individuals with other inherited features. In this way it directs changes in the genetic constitution of the survivors until the population shows the combination of variations best suited to that environment. Another environment would filter out some other combination and stabilize it as most suitable. In studying these changes and differences, the geneticist is examining the process of NATURAL SELECTION in the gradual EVOLUTION of new races, new subspecies, and new species. See HEREDITY; RADIATION GENETICS; BREEDING OF PLANTS AND ANIMALS.—L. and M. M.

GENUS: see CLASSIFICATION OF LIVING THINGS.

GEOBOTANICAL PROSPECTING: in the search for mineral deposits, a rapidly expanding technique based on the close relationship between the occurrence of certain species of plants and the concentrations of specific metals in the underlying soils and rocks. Some associations were recognized long ago, *e.g.* mustards and pinks on the dumps of zinc mines, and various pinks, mints, and mosses near copper deposits. Detailed investigations on the Colorado Plateau proved that several species of vetch indicated concentrations of uranium and selenium in the underlying rocks. See GEOCHEMICAL PROSPECTING; ORES AND ORE DEPOSITS.—L. M.

GEOCHEMICAL PROSPECTING: application of the principles of geochemistry to the search for mineral deposits. It ranges from use of the gold pan (its most elementary form) to use of ion-exchange, colorimetry, spectrography, spectrometry, photospectrometry, x-ray fluorescence, polarography, chromatography, radio-activation and many advances in the basic field of geochemistry. Geochemical surveys involve sampling, analyses, plotting and contouring of results, and correlation of anomalies with geological information. The type of sampling depends on the materials being sought, and particularly on the geochemical cycle of the elements involved. Materials that are sampled include rock outcrops, drill cores and cuttings, soils, and stream waters; also the fine-grained sediments of stream beds (which tend to adsorb the heavy metals), the heavy mineral concentrates from stream beds, and twigs, leaves, and other parts of plants which may collect and concentrate various elements. The grid spacing of geochemical surveys is closely related to the scale of the program, with wide spacing for reconnaissance, close spacing for detailed investigations. See GEOPHYSICAL PROSPECTING; ORES AND ORE DEPOSITS.

Geochemical anomalies related to ore deposits are of two types:

(1) *Primary dispersion haloes,* in which the host rocks adjacent to ore bodies were weakly impregnated with some of the ore minerals during the original period of mineralization. Such impregnations may extend from a fraction of an inch to hundreds of feet from an ore body. On a larger scale, widespread but trace amounts of a particular element disseminated through the country rocks may indicate a region or "metallogenetic province" favorable for the occurrence of deposits of that element, *e.g.* traces of beryllium throughout the granitic plutons that are associated with beryl-bearing pegmatites and veins.

Coring devices are used by oceanographers to bring up sediments from ocean bottom for geochemical analysis. Sediments yield important evidence regarding Earth's history. (*Francis P. Shepard*)

(2) *Secondary dispersion haloes,* caused by the mechanical and chemical breakdown of ore deposits through weathering and soil formation. In some cases the anomalies may be caused by minute particles of the actual ore minerals, particularly in environments where mechanical disintegration outpaces chemical dissolution, or where the ore mineral itself is resistant to solution, *e.g.* gold, rutile, cassiterite. Most of the common ore minerals, however, are not resistant to attack by ground water. Some metals are relatively insoluble under soil-forming conditions and are retained in the soils overlying ore deposits, whereas others are more mobile and may be leached away by ground waters. Zinc anomalies tend to be erratic and may extend for considerable distances, whereas copper remains much closer to the source, and lead shows very little tendency to migrate in solution. Thus, an ore body containing all three metals might be represented by a zinc anomaly of wide diameter, a considerably narrower copper anomaly, and a very small lead anomaly. The shapes of secondary anomalies are affected by surface-slopes, which induce soil creep, and by surface and sub-surface drainage patterns, resulting in dispersion haloes, dispersion fans, and dispersion trains.

Soil horizons vary considerably in composition, pH, and oxidation or reduction power, and the metal contents may be affected accordingly. Thus, anomalies might be absent from an upper horizon but be strong in an intermediate or lower horizon in the same soil profile, whereas in a different soil-forming environment the relative positions of the anomalies might be reversed.

Streams flowing across mineralized areas may contain anomalously high contents of some of the metals. However, the proportions may show great seasonal variations, depending on climate. It has been found that the fine-grained sediments in stream beds tend to adsorb heavy metals from the waters and are thus more dependable indicators of mineralization in the upstream drainage areas. Organic materials tend to fix some of the metals, giving rise to strong anomalies in swamp and bog deposits.—*L. M.*

GEOCHEMISTRY: the study of the chemistry of Earth—or, more precisely, of its chemical evolution. This branch of science began roughly 100 yr ago, but modern geochemistry may be considered to date from the early 1930s. Its development has been greatly enhanced by many new and more refined methods of analytical chemistry. Extensively employed are colorimetric, radioactivity, and spectrochemical methods. At first, geochemists were particularly interested in relative abundance of the terrestrial elements. Later they attempted to account for the element distribution in different parts of Earth. Laws governing these distributions were then formulated in an attempt to investigate Earth's chemical evolution.

An early and relatively crude geochemical attempt to determine the age of the oceans was based on knowledge of the sodium content of sea water. More precise and reliable age determinations were made possible after the discovery of radioactivity. Within the last few decades considerable effort has been directed, by means of a wide variety of geochemical methods, to determining the absolute age of rocks and minerals (see GEOCHRONOLOGY; RADIOACTIVE DATING).

Knowledge gained from meteorites greatly influenced opinion as to Earth's internal make-up and led early to the concentric-shell Earth model, which consisted of a nickel-iron core, an intermediate shell or mantle, and a silicate crust. Compositional studies of igneous rocks have supplied the essential data regarding distribution of elements in the crust.

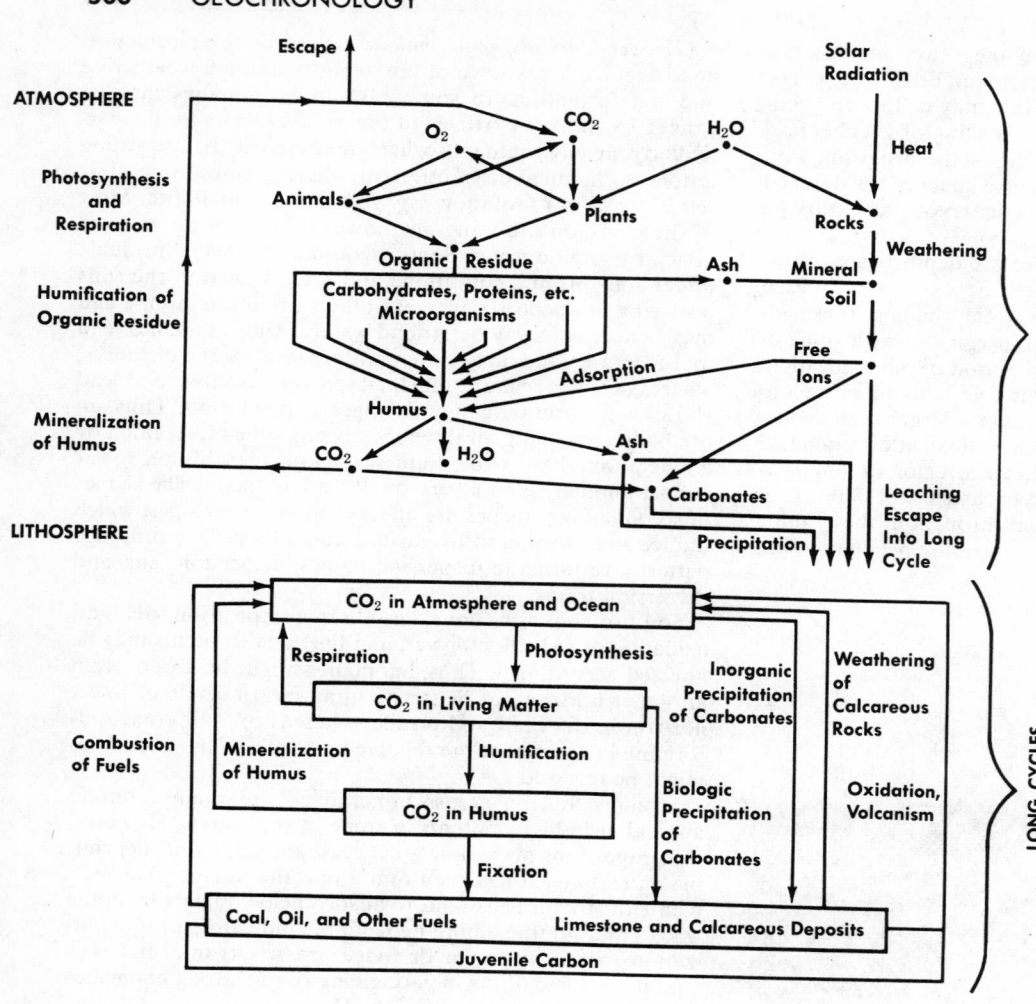

Geochemical cycles of carbon: While carbon compounds are constantly being reassembled, atom for atom, molecule for molecule, in their migration from atmosphere to lithosphere, the carbon content of the entire system is unvarying.

Phase equilibria investigations of numerous petrologic systems have contributed greatly to our knowledge of the composition and course of crystallization of magmas and their residual fluids. Compositional studies of rocks and of surface and underground waters have aided in disclosing the chemical processes and changes involved in weathering, erosion, and the formation of sedimentary rocks.

Very useful is knowledge of the distribution of elements in the various mineral phases of rocks. Such studies have been greatly aided by and have contributed to the newly developed field of crystal chemistry. The distribution of elements between co-existing mineral phases in rocks has perhaps been most valuable in advancing our knowledge of chemical reactions in the crust. By this means it is also possible to determine the temperature and/or pressure of mineral formation.

Chemical analyses of the air and of organic material when combined with studies of Earth's waters and rock material have made possible an understanding of the complicated interplay between atmosphere, hydrosphere, lithosphere, and biosphere. Recognition of the cyclic nature of many elements within and between these spheres has been a fundamental contribution of geochemistry. This concept of geochemical cycles is involved in certain phases of GEOCHEMICAL PROSPECTING. A variety of ore deposits may be located by determining the trace-element distribution in the soil, surface water, or in plants.—*C. C.*

GEOCHRONOLOGY: the branch of geology that deals with the dating, in both relative and absolute terms, of earth materials

and events. Relative ages of different rock units can be determined by the recognition of two basic relationships. The law of superposition states that in a sequence of SEDIMENTARY ROCK layers the youngest are on top, and the law of intrusion states that an igneous intrusion (*e.g.* sill or dike) is younger than the intruded rock. The development of a third law, that of faunal and floral succession, is associated with William Smith, who, in the latter part of the 18th and first part of the 19th cent., while working in the Jurassic rocks of England, discovered that fossil fauna succeed one another in a definite order, and that fossils could be used as indices to give relative ages of sedimentary rock units.

As soon as the principle of uniformitarianism (constancy of geologic processes) was generally accepted in the early part of the 19th cent., it became apparent that the age of many earth features and materials had to be measured in hundreds of thousands if not in millions of years. For example, it has been estimated that 6,500,000 yr were required for the seasonally banded Eocene Green River shales to be deposited to a depth of somewhat over 2,000 ft. And judging by the annual addition made by the Mississippi River to its delta, millions of years must have been required for the delta to form. About 1900, John Joly estimated the age of the oceans as about 1,000,000 yr by dividing the total amount of salt therein by the yearly addition carried by all the rivers. His assumptions, of course, were that the yearly addition of salt has been uniform throughout geologic time, that no salt has been lost by precipitation, and that the sea was fresh to start with. The first two assumptions are manifestly open to large errors.

Somewhat earlier, Lord Kelvin figured the age of Earth as perhaps 20 to 40 million yr, assuming it had cooled from a molten state and no more heat had been added since its formation. However, after the discovery of natural radioactivity in 1896 by Becquerel, it became clear that such a method of age determination is obviously unsound. Now, in the 20th cent., there have been developed a number of methods of determining rock ages by radioactivity itself. These methods (see RADIOACTIVE DATING) are all based on the general principle that a radioactive variety (isotope) of an element decays at a known rate to produce a stable isotope of another element. For instance, uranium[238] decays to produce helium and lead[206], and a determination of the age of a rock containing such uranium is obtainable by comparing the amount of helium or lead[206] present with the amount of uranium[238] remaining. The rate of breakdown must be known (the half-life of uranium[238] is 4½ billion years), and the assumption is made that no radiogenic lead or helium was present at the beginning (or, if present, the amount is known), that no lead or helium has been removed, and that no addition or subtraction of the uranium has been made in the long time span elapsing since it was first incorporated in the rock or mineral whose age is to be measured. Radioactive carbon, C[14], with a half-life of 5,568 yr, is useful for the dating of much more recent materials which had an organic origin, and can be used with decreasing reliability up to about 70,000 yr, beyond which time there is too little of this radioactive form of carbon left to be measured with accuracy. Other parent-daughter radioactive pairs which have been used in age determination include Rb[87]-Sr[87] and K[40]-A[40].

At the beginning of the 20th cent. the standard geology textbooks gave the age of Earth as *c.* 1,000,000 yr. By 1924 the age was being given as well over 500,000,000 (reflecting the early work on radioactive age determinations). Now the oldest rocks have been dated at somewhat over 3 billion yr, and the age of Earth itself is obviously still greater.—*J. Sh.*

GEODE: in general, any hollow, crystal-lined aggregate of minerals, easily separated from the rock which encloses it. This term is most used to describe the ball-like aggregates of quartz crystals commonly found in limestone and shale beds, but may include similar formations in igneous rocks.—*J. Si.*

GEODESIC: the shortest path between two points on a curved surface. The geodesic thus generalizes the properties of a straight line on a plane: namely, that it is the shortest and straightest path between any two of its points. A string stretched on a smooth convex surface between two of its points will lie on a geodesic. On a sphere the geodesics are the great circles. A straight line that lies entirely on a surface, *e.g.* a cylinder, is a geodesic. A curved line is a geodesic if and only if its osculating plane at every point is normal to the surface.—*J. M. F.*

GEODESY: the study of the size and shape of Earth. It arose from the needs of surveyors, and in the 18th cent. was one of the first scientific activities to develop a high degree of precision. Geodetic work proceeds by methods of successive approximations. As a result of earlier studies, a regular shape is chosen which is thought to be close to the shape or figure of Earth. At present, an international convention states that Earth is an oblate spheroid having an equatorial radius of 6378.388 km and a polar radius of 6356.912 km. The difference divided by the equatorial radius is known as the oblateness of the spheroid and, for these figures, has a value of 1/297. Surveys are then conducted over great arcs of the globe, and at many points observations of the stars are made

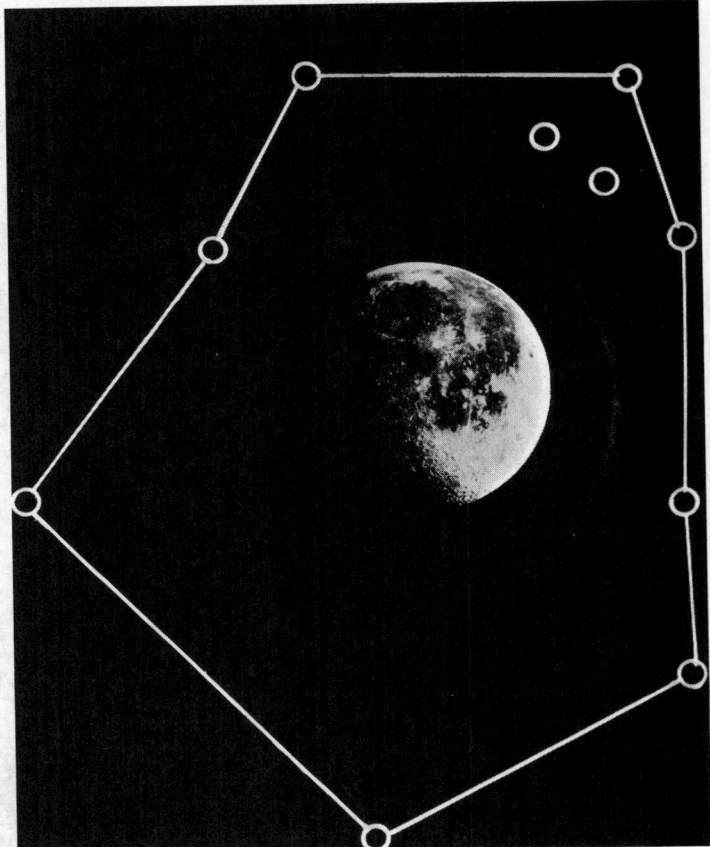

Moon's positions with respect to surrounding stars (in circles) provide new data for geodetic use in program begun in 1957 as part of International Geophysical Year. Simultaneous observation of Moon, as well as of artificial satellites, from different points on Earth's surface provides data for accurate measurement of distances between those points. (*U. S. Navy*)

to determine latitude and longitude. These observed values are compared with values calculated by assuming that the measurements had been made on the conventional spheroid. Systematic differences can be used to define a better conventional spheroid, while local differences can be used to find the shape of a second idealized body called the geoid.

The geoid may be thought of as a body corresponding to the sea-level surface of Earth extended by imaginary canals under the land surface. Because of the differing gravitational attraction of mountains and ocean basins, the geoid irregularly departs from the spheroid by distances of a few tens of feet. Finally, the geoid (which is the surface to which spirit levels respond) is used as a base from which to survey elevations and depressions in the land surface and ocean floor, and thus to prepare contoured maps and bathymetric charts.

If the shape of Earth and the distribution of density within it are known, the gravitational attraction at any point can be calculated. Departures of observed gravity from calculated values are called anomalies, and these indicate where, within Earth, there are excesses or deficiencies in mass, and these in turn bear on the extent to which ISOSTASY prevails, and show whether topographic irregularities are compensated by variations in density beneath them.

Since 1957, observations of satellites have provided a powerful new method for surveying Earth. Better measurements of its shape have been made, and it appears that the equator may be slightly elliptical, that longitudinal profiles may be very slightly pear-shaped, and that the oblateness is about 1/298. As a result of recent geodetic work culminating during the International Geophysical Year, it is probable that the spheroid will soon be redefined.—*J. T. W.*

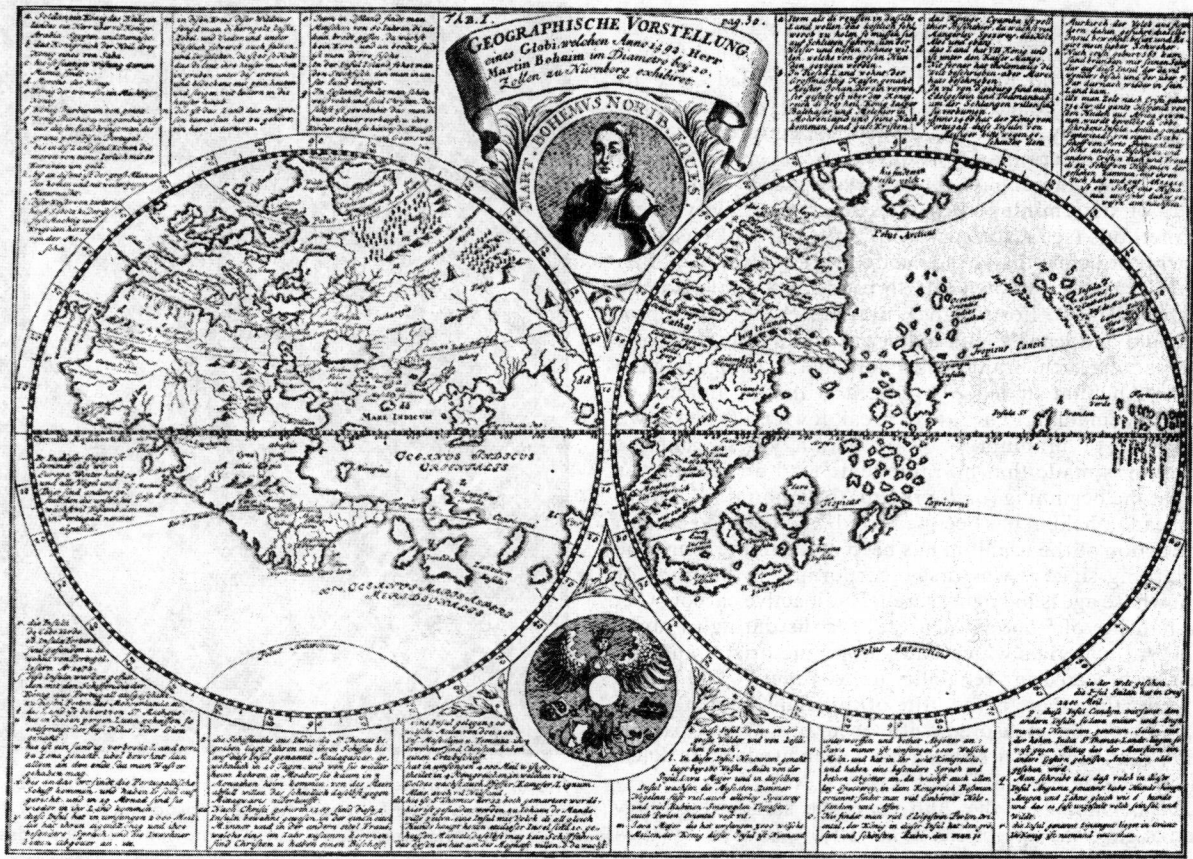

Geographic landmark: When Columbus stepped ashore in the Bahamas in 1492, Nürnberg-born cosmographer Martin Behaim was at work on this map of the two hemispheres. An employee of the Portuguese chart service, Behaim worked out this summary of pre-Columbian knowledge while visiting home, 1490–93. Since then the progress of geography—the exploration of land, sea, and air, as well as our deepened understanding of the planet—has depended heavily upon the progress of science and technology. (*Map Dept., N. Y. Public Library*)

GEOFFROY SAINT-HILAIRE, ÉTIENNE (1772–1844), French naturalist; b. Étampes. He is known for his theory of the unity of organic composition, which regards nature as having but a single plan of construction. From this point of view animals are regarded as all having the same parts interrelated in the same ways, differing only in details. Among his many writings are his *Philosophie anatomique* (2 vols., 1818–22) and *Sur le principe de l'unité de composition organique* (1828). —*D. H. D. R.*

GEOGRAPHY: the study of Earth as man's environment. As the subject matter of geography, Earth may be considered as the totality of its physical features, its biotic features (the product of plant and animal life), and the works of man. Yet each of these groups is of particular concern to other scientists. The geologist studies the physical features of Earth; biologists are specialists in flora and fauna; whatever man does concerns the social scientist. Obviously, then, this subject matter, insofar as it relates to geography, must be studied in a special way. To the geographer, it is the interrelationship of all these elements—physical, biotic, human—that is significant. Since this interrelationship is not studied abstractly, but as part of the human environment, geography is more closely allied to the social than to the physical or biological sciences.

The particular emphasis of the geographer, as contrasted with that of other scientists, may best be understood by describing the approach of each to a given field of study. A city, with its transportation system, industrial plant, agri-

cultural and mineral hinterland, cultural and educational facilities, and residential quarters, is a complex which, to a historian, results from a sequence of events. To an economist, it is a unit (or nexus of units) to be evaluated in terms of its efficiency in providing for human material needs. The geographer—in this case, the urban geographer—is likely to analyze a given city in comparison with others of the same population range elsewhere, to ascertain how significant differences may be attributed to specific factors, such as terrain, elevation, climate, access to navigable water, culture patterns, and political status. This systematic study of the city as city, a place on Earth's surface important to man, distinguishes the geographer from other scientists, interested in some particular aspect of the city. Similarly, the Great Plains is a flat region underlain with sedimentary bedrock, the result of the deposition of rock particles in shallow inland seas over long periods of time; this is the geologist's view. A historian identifies the Great Plains as the haunt of simple cultures, Indians classified as sedentary farmers and as foot nomads, succeeded by horse nomads; in the mid-19th cent. it became chiefly significant as a barrier separating the overflow population of the civilized East Coast from the mineral-rich West, a region to be crossed before it became a region to be ranched and then, with the help of irrigation, to be plowed. The geographer thinks of the Great Plains as an example of a specific type of grassland (a generic classification of vegetation type). It is characterized by short rather than long grass, thus resembling the steppes rather than the pampas; located in a middle latitude, like the steppes and pampas but unlike the savannas or llanos; used primarily for ranching, like the pampas but unlike the (Asiatic) steppes. All these considerations require explanation, which the geographer seeks to supply. He will discover from the social scientist why varying cultural patterns dictate different kinds of occupancy for apparently similar regions; he will learn from the botanist and geologist the reasons for variations in soil in seemingly similar locales. But his approach, insofar as it is systematic, is that of the geographer.

Specialization affects the study of geography, since the subject is extensive, complex, and related to many other sciences. A geographer may concentrate on natural features, to become a physiographer; on communities, to become an urban geographer; on the manner in which existing geographical phenomena developed, to become a historical geographer; on techniques of communicating geographical information through maps, to become a cartographer; or on precise measurements of Earth's surface and gravity, to become a geodesist. Branches of geography are as numerous as the significant patterns of phenomena: the study of the incidence of disease throughout the world is medical geography; the characteristics of mountains and their influence on man is the subject matter of orography; hydrology concentrates on the waters of the planet: the list can be extended indefinitely. Many geographers devote their attention to a single area, which they study in depth.

Two principal approaches are distinguished: the topical and the regional. Topical geography is based on the systematic study of a given phenomenon or group of interrelated phenomena on a world-wide scale. This might be termed a horizontal approach, as distinguished from the vertical approach of the regionalist, who concentrates on all aspects of a restricted segment of Earth's surface. Topical geography would appear to be of wider scope, regional more profound, in emphasis. But the distinction is largely illusory. Any region selected for study must be defined because it is homogeneous in one or more respects significant to a geographer. It may be dominated by a single crop, as is the Corn Belt; by a distinctive economic base, as are the Black Country of England or the Soviet Donbas; by the character of its drainage system, as is the Basin-and-Range Province of the American West. But a valid study of any such region requires a minimum of comparison with similar but not identical regions elsewhere, and thus is not merely "regional." Conversely, at least a sampling of regional analysis would seem essential for a sound "topical" approach, if only for purposes of exposition.

It is equally difficult to distinguish between so-called "human" geography and some other category, although such a distinction has been a matter of controversy within the profession. Perhaps "human" geography has more prominently the characteristics of an applied science, whereas the more abstract study of geographical subjects is comparable to the pure science of the physicist or mathematician. But such fields of study as climates, physical features, vegetation types, and ecology are within the realm of geography only to the extent that they are relevant to human society. Once this orientation is abandoned, they must be reassigned to some other science. Climatology becomes meteorology, a branch of physics; physiography becomes the geomorphology of the geologist; the geographer surrenders the forests to the botanist and the zoologist.

Perhaps because of the literally earth-bound aspect of the science, the problems facing the geographer are more capable of solution than those facing many other scientists, who are likely to receive the assignments beyond the pale of geography. Indeed, geography is sometimes considered merely a descriptive science, with the task of arranging the data of a variegated environment into meaningful patterns. But geography is not the listing of the hundred largest cities in the United States or the cataloging of the wheat-producing regions of the world; it is this plus the interpretation of such data, so that the student may understand which of these cities or granaries is likely to flourish, and why. Thus, with the approach, techniques, and functions of a science, geography serves humanity.—*E. A.*

GEOLOGICAL TIME CHART: a chart that gives the era, period, and epoch divisions of earth history (see following pages). It is arranged so that the oldest divisions are at the bottom of the chart, thus emphasizing the Law of Superposition: that younger sedimentary layers lie on top of older layers. The chart was developed in the 19th cent. (see GEOLOGY and GEOCHRONOLOGY), and the divisions were based on the types of life, shown by FOSSILS, existing during each interval. Thus the Paleozoic was the time of ancient life, the Mesozoic that of middle life, and the Cenozoic the time of recent life. The fossil content of rocks older than the Paleozoic is far too scattered and deteriorated to be used for purposes of correlation or relative dating. Period and epoch subdivisions were made on the basis of fossil evidence as well as breaks in the sedimentary record.

As first applied, the era and period names referred to sequences of rock, not to divisions of time. Now the Cambrian Period, for instance, refers to a time interval and the Cambrian System to the sequence of rocks deposited therein. In much the same manner the Paleocene Epoch refers to a time interval and the Paleocene series to the sequence of rocks. The *formation* is a stratigraphic unit. Thus the Lockport dolomite of New York State is a *formation* belonging to the Niagaran *series* of the Silurian *system*.

The dates have been added in the 20th cent. with data supplied from radioactive age determinations (see RADIOACTIVE DATING). In the future, as refinements of dating techniques are made, there will undoubtedly be at least some minor changes in the accepted values.

A number of chronological terms found in geological literature do not appear on the chart. In the simple 18th- and 19th-cent. time scale, the term "Primary" was applied to rocks of the era now called Precambrian, "Transition" to rocks of the Paleozoic, "Secondary" to the Mesozoic, and "Tertiary" and "Quaternary" to the Cenozoic. Some authors now divide the Cenozoic Era into periods called "Paleogene" and "Neogene."

The use of Precambrian time divisions on a world-wide basis is not valid at present, only divisions of local geographic extent being trustworthy. For a discussion of life forms characteristic of the various geological periods, see LIFE, PREHISTORIC. —*J. Sh.*

GEOLOGY: the study of Earth's crust. It includes such diverse, more or less overlapping subject matter as the crust's chemical composition (GEOCHEMISTRY), the origin and nature of minerals (MINERALOGY), the composition and physical forms of rocks (PETROLOGY), the origin of land forms (GEOMORPHOLOGY), volcanic phenomena (igneous geology), physical relationships between rock structures (structural geology), chronological sequence of rock strata (STRATIGRAPHY), forces at work in the crust (dynamic geology), ice sheets and glaciers (glaciology), ocean waters, continental shelves and slopes, and sea bottoms (OCEANOGRAPHY), the work of water in and on the crust (hydrology), sedimentation (sedimentology), the nature and behavior of soils (SOIL PHYSICS), and the relationships of geology to industry and commerce (economic geology). Historical geology, as the study of Earth's history

GEOLOGICAL TIME CHART

Age in Years	Era	Period or Epoch	Important Physical Events
1.0 ±.5 ►	CENOZOIC	PLEISTOCENE	Repeated extensions of ice caps in arctic and north temperate areas
			Continents generally elevated, mountains high, deserts widespread
13 ±1 ►		PLIOCENE	Mountain building in NW North America
			Deformation of Tethys geosyncline; Alps and Himalayas rise
25 ±1 ►		MIOCENE	Extensive erosion surfaces cut on Appalachians and Rockies
			Trend to cool, dry climates over much of the world
36 ±2 ►		OLIGOCENE	Initiation of mountain building in Tethys geosyncline
			River and flood-plain deposits begin on Great Plains
58 ±2 ►		EOCENE	Climates warm and uniform; widespread jungles and forests
65 ±2 ►		PALEOCENE	Development of basins between ranges along Pacific Coast and Rocky Mts
	MESOZOIC	CRETACEOUS	Mountain building in Rockies
			Seas invade much of W North America and cover Atlantic and Gulf coastal plains
135 ±5 ►		JURASSIC	Widespread mild, uniform climates
			Mountain building along Pacific Coast of North America
180 ±5 ►			Extensive marine invasions of southern and central Europe
		TRIASSIC	Fault basins in E North America
230 ±10 ►			Extensive deserts and dead seas in North America and Eurasia
	PALEOZOIC	PERMIAN	Continents generally elevated
			Appalachian and Ural Mts complete their development
280 ±10 ►			Tethys geosyncline from Spain to India
		PENNSYLVANIAN	Mountain building in S Appalachians and SW United States
			Ice age in southern continents
310 ±10 ►			Coal swamps in many parts of the world
		MISSISSIPPIAN	Beginning of mountain building in S North America and central Europe
345 ±10 ►			Extensive seas over much of interior North America
		DEVONIAN	Catskill delta built from New England mountains into New York and Pennsylvania
			Mountain building in NE North America
405 ±10 ►			Extensive submergence of geosynclines and interior of North America
		SILURIAN	Formation of Caledonian Mts in NW Europe
			Dead seas in Michigan, New York, Ohio, SE Canada
425 ±10 ►			Deltas and gravel beaches along eastern edge of Appalachian geosyncline
		ORDOVICIAN	Mountain building in NE North America
500 ±10 ►			Over 60% of North American continent covered by seas
		CAMBRIAN	Climates generally mild and uniform
			Seas invade North American continent
?600 ►			Development of geosynclines around edge of North America
1,000 ►		PRECAMBRIAN	Fault basins in Lake Superior region
			Deformation and mountain building through central North America
2,000 ►			Development of geosynclines throughout central North America
			Extensive mountain building in Lake Superior region
3,000 ►			Oldest dated rocks
4,500 ►			Probable origin of Earth from solar dust cloud

MILLIONS OF YEARS BEFORE THE PRESENT (ESTIMATES REVISED IN 1961)

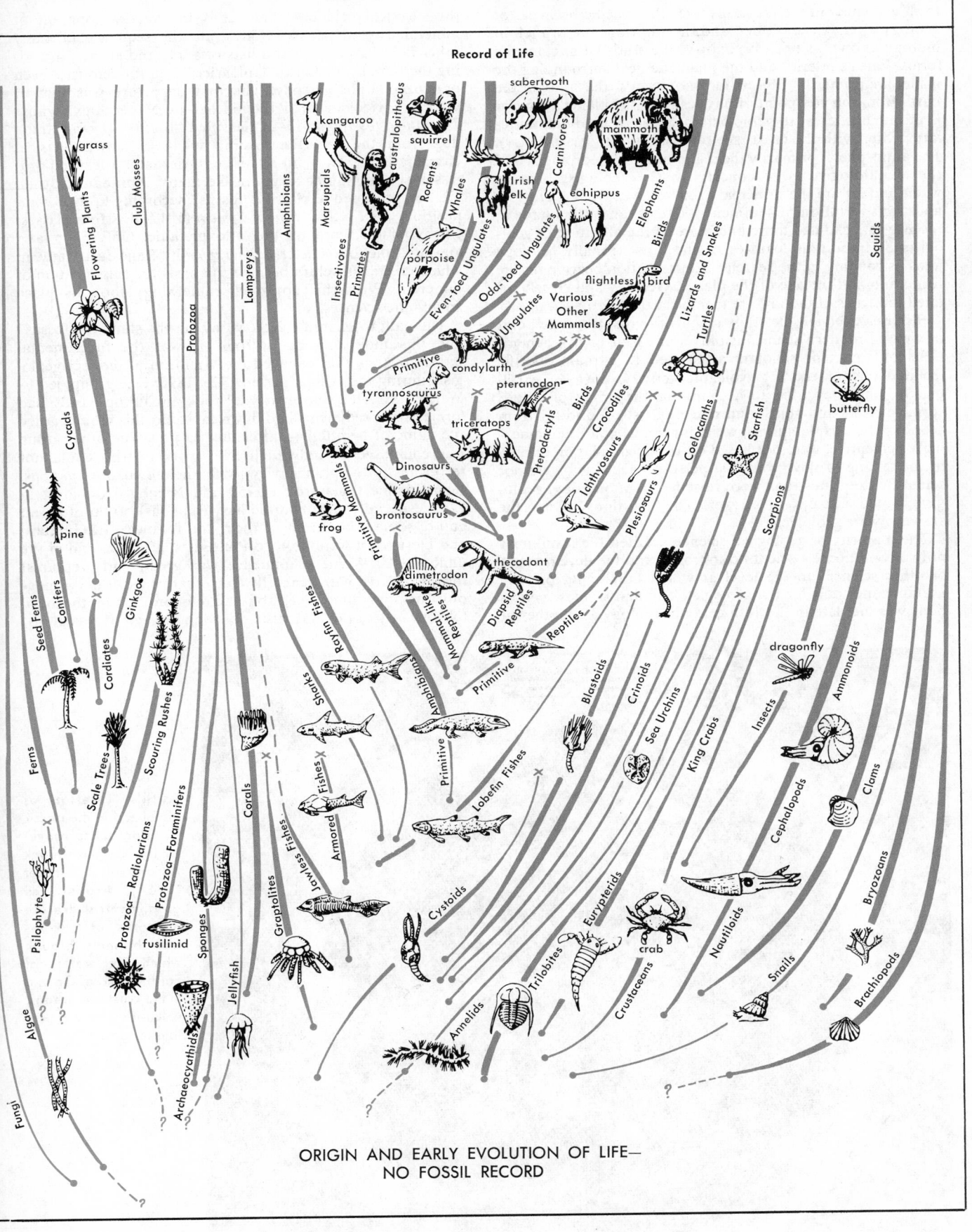

ORIGIN AND EARLY EVOLUTION OF LIFE—
NO FOSSIL RECORD

from evidences in the crust, involves the specific branches of geology already mentioned and, in addition, the branch of biology known as PALEONTOLOGY, the study of ancient life forms. Earth's interior and the magnetic field surrounding the planet are primarily subjects for GEOPHYSICS (the study of the Earth from the viewpoint of physics), but the planet's interior is of much interest to geologists because of its dynamic relationships with the crust (see DIASTROPHISM; SEISMOLOGY). The atmosphere, primarily the realm of the meteorologist and the climatologist, is of concern to the geologist because water and air are the principal agents in weathering, erosion, and transportation of sediments. The ocean basins have in recent years claimed more and more of the attention of geologists as important features of the crust. Finally, geology joins astronomy in the search for information bearing on the formation and the age of the planet. Geology and closely related branches of inquiry are together called *earth sciences.*

History: Although the study of Earth's crust from the point of view of modern science is only some four or five generations old, ancient scholars attempted to explain specific isolated phenomena, *e.g.* volcanic activity, tides, or earthquakes, and they tried to account for the origin of deltas, springs, rocks and gems, and marine fossils found far from the sea. Their explanations, while ingenious and often amazingly perceptive, were not based on the accumulation of data or the testing of theory against performance; they were not scientific. Yet questions were raised which, one day, geologists would attempt to answer. The questions, if not the answers, were geological.

The maturity of geological science awaited the fulfillment of two conditions: a scientific approach and the development of other sciences to the level at which they could provide example and tools for the geologist. The first of these conditions was met late in the 18th cent., in geology as in other of the physical sciences. The steps in the development of mineralogy and petrology illustrate the sequence in many other fields. Accounts and lists of gems and stones, including the famous medieval "lapidaries," had for centuries been organized alphabetically. The first departure was that of Georg Agricola, called the Father of Mineralogy, whose *De natura fossilium* (1546) classified "fossils" (*i.e.* anything dug from the earth) according to then known physical characteristics. Two and a half centuries later a learned professor at a mining academy in Germany, Abraham Gottlob Werner, proposed to classify "fossils" according to their composition; his *Letztes Mineral System* (1817) lists four classes: earthy, saline, combustible, and metallic. Only 5 yr later appeared the *Traité de cristallographie* by René-Just Haüy, in which crystal structure became the basis for classification of minerals. With this approach mineralogy took its place among the sciences.

The path to scientific geology lay via the study of "fossils" and the understanding of rock. It was the fundamental nature of rock that engaged the attention of pioneer geologists during the critical period 1775–1825. One group, led by Werner, asserted that nearly all rock, including basalt, had formed from sediments laid down in water; this group earned the name of Neptunists, after the sea-god. The other group was composed of individual field workers who could not reconcile the Neptunist view with their own observations. Jean-Etienne Guettard in 1752 and Nicolas Desmarest in 1765, especially, affirmed the fiery (igneous) origin of basalt and of some other kinds of rock, and followers of Guettard and Desmarest were dubbed Plutonists, after the god of the underworld. Werner's influence was great, and Neptunist theory squared with generally conservative views of cosmogony (including those of established religion), so that the inevitable victory of the Plutonists was long delayed. It was at last

Earth's interior as visualized in the classic *Mundus subterraneus* by the German monk Athanasius Kircher (1664). Around the great central fire are networks of caverns and channels through which the waters of Earth circulate. On and in the crust are oceans, volcanoes, and mountain ranges.

Drawing of pterodactyl skeleton, with visualization of winged reptiles in flight, suggests care and imagination of some paleontologists as early as first third of 19th cent. (*from* Geology and Mineralogy Considered with Reference to Natural Theology, *by Rev. William Buckland, Philadelphia, 1837*)

PTERODACTYLUS BREVIROSTRIS. Sömmer. *Nat. Size.*

formalized by the conversion of Werner's brilliant disciple, Christian Leopold von Buch, to the Plutonist camp. While Werner stayed home and reiterated his arguments, Von Buch traveled about Europe, inspecting volcanic regions such as the Auvergne in France, and came to believe what he saw.

Both Neptunists and Plutonists alike assumed that the processes by which Earth's crust had reached its present condition were sporadic and often violent—"catastrophic." This point of view, since called Catastrophism, favored tradition and religion; it accorded, for example, with the biblical Deluge and with such experienced phenomena as eruptions and earthquakes. But a head-on challenge to Catastrophism came from James Hutton in his THEORY OF THE EARTH (1795), which advanced the theory of Uniformitarianism. The obscure style of this work delayed the understanding of its thesis until John Playfair published *Illustrations of the Huttonian Theory of the Earth* in 1802. Thereafter this viewpoint gained in acceptance, finally becoming firmly established when Sir Charles Lyell's PRINCIPLES OF GEOLOGY appeared (1820–33). Lyell as well as Hutton, in fact, is credited with the theory of Uniformitarianism, which may be considered the watershed between early and modern geological science. It holds that processes still operating in nature, and capable of being observed and tested, account for the existing condition of Earth and everything in it. It necessitated drastic revisions in the concept of Earth's age, for some processes, notably the destruction of mountains by erosion, are obviously quite slow. Minds had to be prepared for this and other revolutionary attacks by geology on time-honored teachings and on what appeared to be common sense. Defense of Uniformitarianism required field work, the assembling of data, the aid of other sciences, and brilliant theorizing; and it required courage. Using the sound approach of Hutton and Lyell, geologists of the 19th cent. were able to develop their field of knowledge at a rapid pace, having emerged from the morass of false assumptions. Only a few landmarks need be cited.

One such landmark was the contribution of an English civil engineer, William Smith (1769–1839), founder of the science of stratigraphy. He grasped the fact that fossils are indicators of the relative ages of sedimentary rock strata, and thus he may be credited with laying the basis for historical geology. He also published the first geological map of England in 1815; 6 yr earlier William Maclure (1763–1840) had published a geological map of the U. S. A. The brilliant and versatile Georges Cuvier (1769–1832), in France, during the same period published studies of fossils from the biologist's point of view; these became foundation stones of pale-

ontology. But Cuvier was a staunch defender of Catastrophism; the further development of paleontology as a science had to await the principle of evolution as defined by Lyell's friend Charles Darwin (1809–82).

A major puzzle facing geologists was—and still is—the question of how mountains and continents originated. One of the first Huttonians to investigate this problem was James Hall (1811–98), who traced the Appalachian system. His field work resulted in the theory of GEOSYNCLINES, propounded in 1856; and this in turn raised the question of how a geosyncline could become a mountain range. As an answer, Clarence J. Dutton (1841–1912) proposed the theory of ISOSTASY in 1889. As to the question of how continents originate, Alfred Wegener published his classic statement in 1915 (appearing in English translation, *The Origin of Continents and Oceans,* 1924) that a process of CONTINENTAL DRIFT accounts for the present distribution of continents, all derived from a single supercontinent; this hypothesis continues to win support. Another theory, proposed by J. Tuzo Wilson in a symposium, *The Earth as a Planet* (1954), has depicted the continents as growing from stable nuclei, centered in the continental shields, by the acquisition of fringe arcs through a combination of tectonic and gradational processes.

Outlook: In the 20th cent. geology has matured as a science, yet finds itself still struggling with basic problems. Not only are the origins of continents and mountains still in question, but the concept of isostasy, which seems to explain so much, is still not completely accepted. The mantle, lying between Earth's crust and the outer core, has been investigated by seismological means but is still largely an unknown quantity; the Mohole project may provide solid data. The significance of the great ocean trenches, the tectonically active island arcs, and the mid-oceanic ridge is still little understood. There is the puzzle of the origin of Earth's heat, which seems inadequately accounted for by such factors as radioactivity in the crust, solar heating, and an original molten state of the planet. It is still not positively known what has caused the glacial ages and whether we are now in an interglacial period to be followed soon by a new ice age. The origin of certain granites remains a major problem in petrology. The lack of well-preserved fossils in rocks older than about a billion years—only a fifth of the age of the planet—leaves the origin of life in almost complete obscurity. Although radioactive dating has offered a probably reliable estimate of the age of Earth, the processes by which the planet formed—including the question of whether the primordial planetary mass was hot or cold—are still matters of speculation. On many fronts geology still faces tremendous unknowns.—*E. A. and J. W.*

GEOMAGNETISM: see TERRESTRIAL MAGNETISM.

GEOMETRY: according to one of the definitions in Webster's dictionary, the theory of space and of figures in space. It began with the discovery of facts about natural planes such as the flat banks of the river Nile: that a rectangular field whose length and width are 4 and 3 units can be decomposed into 4×3 (*i.e.* 12) nonoverlapping unit squares, and that a diagonal which divides such a rectangle into two triangles is 5 units long; that a looped rope divided into 12 equal parts can be formed into a right triangle whose sides are in the ratios $3:4:5$ (see Fig. 1). These and similar observations, which were of great importance for the surveyors and architects in ancient Egypt, are the foundation of one of the most imposing edifices of the human intellect.

Fig. 1

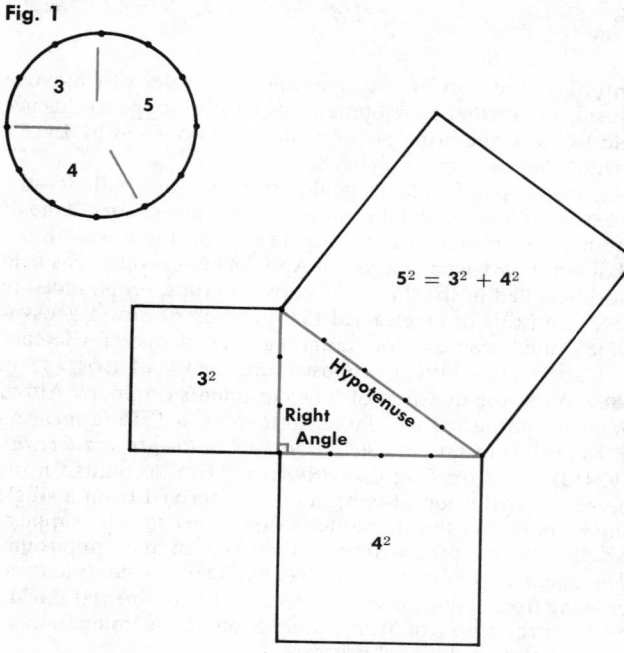

Early Developments: The first Greek geometers discovered that geometric facts are logically interrelated. Some of them are consequences of others; *i.e.* assuming certain geometric statements, one is sure of the validity of many others. The most celebrated of the Greek geometric proofs is the deduction from simple assumptions of Pythagoras' theorem that in each right triangle the area of the square on the hypotenuse (the side opposite the right angle) is equal to the sum of the areas of the squares on the two other sides. An even more profound theory of ratios was developed by Eudoxus. About 300 B. C., Euclid systematically developed plane and solid geometry from a few simple postulates, *e.g.* that through two points there is one and only one straight line. One assumption was somewhat more complicated—his PARALLEL POSTULATE: in a plane, for any line *l* and any point *P* not on *l*, there is exactly one line passing through *P* and not intersecting *l* (*i.e.* there is only one line through *P* parallel to *l*). Strictly speaking, Euclid's postulates, which he listed at the outset of his *Elements,* do not express observations; rather they idealize observations by extrapolating them in the large and by interpolating them in the small. The remainder of Euclid's book, the edifice of theorems following the initial postulates, passed for 2,000 yr as a model of rigor, in that all theorems were considered to have been derived from those postulates by

purely logical reasoning. Although since the 1880s this view has become untenable, the *Elements* remains one of the great books of all time because it established, even if it did not live up to, the ideal of logical rigor.

The universe of geometric objects studied in antiquity was very restricted. The *Elements* deals mainly with points, lines, and circles (which can all be drawn by means of straightedge and compass) and with planes, polyhedrons, and spheres. Apollonius later added a systematic theory of CONIC SECTIONS (ellipses, parabolas, and hyperbolas). But only very few other curves were studied: some, in Archimedes' work on area and tangents; others, in various attempts to double cubes, trisect angles, and square the circle—the so-called three classical problems, which the Greeks solved only by the use of instruments other than straightedge and compass, whereas these tools were sufficient to double squares and bisect angles.

Results of medieval Oriental geometers are hidden in the arabesques that cover floors and walls of mosques. Only the 19th-cent. study of groups in algebra has revealed the laws of those intricate patterns and symmetries. The geometers of the Renaissance were inspired (1) by the attempts of painters to represent solid objects by shapes on a flat painting, and this study of perspective gave rise to various investigations of projections, which later were systematized in *projective geometry*; (2) by the drawing of geographical maps—plane representations of regions on the curved surface of Earth.

Analytic or Coordinate Geometry: The idea of characterizing each point on the surface of Earth by two numbers (its *longitude,* or distance from an arbitrarily chosen meridian, and its *latitude,* or distance from the equator) was introduced into plane geometry by René Descartes and Pierre de Fermat. After choosing two perpendicular lines (*axes*) and a linear unit, one can describe every point in the plane by two numbers (*coordinates*), its distances from the axes, which are usually vertical and horizontal. The point at which the axes intersect is called the origin. If a straight line passes through the origin and makes an angle of 45° with each axis, then the two coordinates x and y of any point on it must be equal (see Fig. 2). This line can thus be represented by the equation $x = y$. In this way, the curves studied by the ancients appear as classes (or loci) of points whose coordinates are connected by simple numerical relations. Generally, equations of the form $ax + by = c$, where a, b, and c are given numbers, represent straight lines and are called *linear* equations. Equations containing a squared term, such as $y = x^2$, or $x^2 + y^2 = 4$, represent circles or other conic sections. Similarly, each point in space can be described by three numbers; the sphere of radius 1 about the origin is the class of all points (x, y, z) such that $x^2 + y^2 + z^2 = 1$. To every theorem of plane and solid geometry of the ancients, there corresponds an algebraic theorem about pairs and triples of numbers in analytic geometry. For example, one can prove that the three medians of a triangle meet in one point by algebraically computing the coordinates of the intersection of two medians of a triangle and demonstrating that these two numbers also satisfy the equation representing the third median.

An even more important achievement of analytic geometry than its new treatment of the known geometric objects and laws, was that it opened up a whole world of objects and facts undreamed of in antiquity. Besides lines, parabolas, and circles, Descartes studied the curves whose points are described by numbers (x, y) such that $y = x^3$, or $y = x^4$, or $x^3 + y^3 = 1$, or $x^4 + y^4 = 1$, and the like. Soon, in spite of initial opposition, curves described by equations such as $y = \log x$, or $y = \sin x$ were adopted in the realm of geometric objects. This universe was found to include objects with properties until then unheard of: curves having many

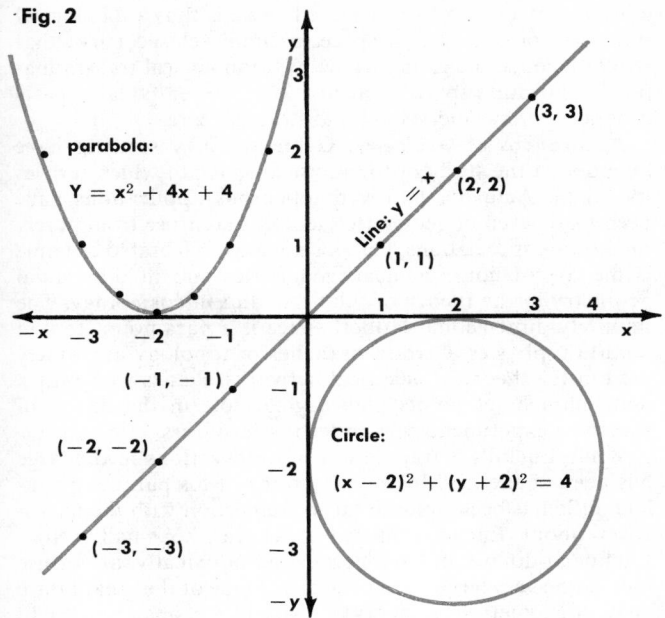

Fig. 2

parabola:

$Y = x^2 + 4x + 4$

Line: $y = x$

(3, 3)

(2, 2)

(1, 1)

(−1, −1)

(−2, −2)

(−3, −3)

Circle:

$(x − 2)^2 + (y + 2)^2 = 4$

branches, loops, isolated points; yet it lent itself to the establishment of order. For example, the algebraic curves and surfaces (*i.e.* those having equations that include only powers of *x* and *y* and not their logarithms or sines) could be classified according to the highest power occurring in their equation. If this power is 1 or 2 then, as has been mentioned, the curve is a straight line or a conic section; if it is 3, as in the case of the equation $y = x^3$, then the curve is said to be of degree 3 or cubic; and so on. From algebra, general laws could be established that were valid in this enormous new universe of objects; hence this study is called *algebraic geometry*. For example, any curve of degree *n* (a whole number) intersects any straight line in at most *n* points. In a later phase of the extremely fertile interaction of algebra and geometry, in the 19th cent., the three classical problems were proved to be insoluble by the mere use of straightedge and compass.

Differential Geometry: In the second half of the 17th cent., partly under the influence of analytic geometry, the differential calculus developed and, in turn, greatly influenced geometry. The calculus enabled geometers to study curves and surfaces locally—to find their tangents and curvatures at particular points—and to define and to classify strange singularities such as cusps and nodes. This *differential geometry* culminated in the theory of surfaces developed by L. Euler, G. Monge, and especially, K. F. Gauss, who considered surfaces intrinsically, *i.e.* without reference to the points of the surrounding space. In particular, he studied their curvature and the shortest (geodesic) paths joining two points on a surface.

Non-Euclidean Geometries: After Euclid, the "synthetic" geometry based on his postulates mainly aimed at proving the parallel postulate from Euclid's other assumptions. In the early 1800s, F. Bolyai and N. I. Lobachevsky conceived the idea of replacing Euclid's parallel postulate by a different assumption: that there is more than one line through *P* that does not intersect *l*. From this non-Euclidean parallel postulate in conjunction with Euclid's other assumptions they derived a geometry in which Pythagoras' theorem is not valid and the sum of the angles in each triangle is less than two right angles. For over 50 yr this theory was menaced by the danger that it

might lead to some contradiction. But about 1870, E. Beltrami and F. Klein discovered Euclidean models of the non-Euclidean geometry; that is to say, they found that certain points and curves in the Euclidean space satisfy all the assumptions made about points and lines by Bolyai and Lobachevsky. Hence if their geometry ever should lead to a contradiction, so would the theory of certain points and curves in the Euclidean space. Later, other non-Euclidean geometries were founded on other variations of the parallel postulate and on modifications of other Euclidean assumptions.

Analytic geometry also lent itself to modifications, *e.g.* to the replacement of the formula for the distance based on Pythagoras' law by formulas corresponding to non-Euclidean geometries—to those that had been developed from postulates and to still other ones. In fact, so many geometries arose that a clear survey was achieved only after Klein discovered a classifying principle: the nature of the transformations of the space that carry any object into another one that is considered its equivalent; and the kind of properties that remain unchanged (invariant) under these transformations. In Euclid's geometry these transformations are the motions that carry any object into a congruent object and leave the distance between any two points invariant. Analytic geometry was further modified by the introduction of coordinates that were not ordinary real numbers—in particular, by the study of spaces whose points have complex numbers as coordinates. Such spaces are, so to speak, much richer than the ordinary ones, a complex line (in which each point has one complex coordinate) being the equivalent of an ordinary plane. On the other hand, in this century, planes and spaces have been introduced which contain only a finite number of points, *e.g.* a plane consisting of only nine points and twelve lines (exactly one line through any two points) and satisfying Euclid's parallel postulate. The coordinates in this case are only the numbers 1, 0, and − 1, with proper addition and multiplication.

Of great importance was the introduction of higher-dimensional spaces. Just as a point in the plane (or in space) is described by 2 (or by 3) numbers, each point in spaces of 4 (and higher) dimensions, studied by H. Grassmann, is described by 4 (and more) numbers. Although such spaces cannot be visualized, they can be studied algebraically as readily as the earlier ones, and D. Hilbert introduced an extension of Euclid's space having infinitely many dimensions.

The Clarification of Geometry: In the 1880s, Pasch discovered and filled serious gaps in the *Elements*. Euclid had failed to formulate postulates concerning the order of points on a line as well as assumptions about the arrangement of the points in a plane. Yet, in the course of his developments, he made use of facts such as that a straight line divides the plane into two parts. Apart from perfecting geometry in a technical sense, the work of Pasch and the later writings of others, especially Hilbert, changed the entire outlook on geometry. Postulates had been considered as statements so simple that they are not capable of a proof and so obvious that they are not in need of proof. Pasch made it clear that every deductive theory, being nothing but the derivation of propositions from other propositions, *must* start with unproven statements—simple or not simple, obvious or not obvious—for the mere reason that proving cannot go on *ad infinitum*. The same is true for defining, wherefore every theory must start with undefined concepts. While the undefined and unproved foundations of a theory may well be defined and proven in another theory, this other theory must begin with concepts and statements that remain undefined and unproven *in it*.

In the early 1900s, in the course of the "arithmetization" of mathematics, analytic geometry also underwent a clarification. While Descartes and Fermat had associated two numbers with each point of a physical plane or a plane satisfying certain assumptions, now a pure analytic geometry was developed in which a point of the plane (or the space) was *defined* as a pair (or a triple) of numbers; in which curves and surfaces were *defined* as classes of such points satisfying certain relations; and so on. No underlying physical or postulational space was presupposed. This point of view eliminated what, at first, appeared mysterious about complex coordinates and higher dimensions. Complex three-dimensional geometry is simply an algebra of triples of complex numbers, called points. Pure four-dimensional geometry is an algebra of quadruples of real numbers, called points. Whether there is anything in the physical space that corresponds to such higher-dimensional geometries—whether there exist, for example, two planes having exactly one point in common—are questions of observation rather than of pure geometry, and according to all indications the answer is negative.

The Ultimate Extension of the Universe of Geometric Objects: During the 19th cent., the concept of a numerical relation, which formed the basis for the definition of geometrical objects, was slowly but steadily generalized. Even after non-algebraic curves, such as that given by $y = \sin x$, had been recognized as legitimate geometric objects, conservatives still required of a curve that it be smooth, *i.e.* have tangents everywhere except possibly at a few points. But Karl Weierstrass showed that even curves that have no tangent *anywhere* can be defined by generally recognized numerical expressions, and the same is true even for some objects that defy all graphical representation, such as the plane set consisting of all points on the line $y = 0$ that have an irrational abscissa, and of all points on the line $y = 1$ whose abscissa is rational.

Georg Cantor, in the last quarter of the 19th cent., took the final step in this program of liberalization by opening the domain of geometry to all sets of points, not only to those defined by numerical relations in the widest sense, but those defined in any other way—say, by joining or intersecting simpler sets, by omitting parts or by selecting one point from each member of a family of sets and uniting the selected points into one set. The variety of new objects thus introduced into geometry by point set theory dwarfed even the additions introduced by coordinate geometry 250 yr earlier. Some of these new objects exhibited such unexpected properties and deviated so radically from traditional patterns that they were said to defy intuition. The plane contains *arcs* (sets into which a segment can be transformed in a one-to-one bicontinuous way) whose area is greater than 0; three domains that have the same boundary; totally disconnected sets which, upon the adjunction of one single point, become connected. But the tremendous new world disclosed by point set theory was found to be governed by general laws: partly extensions and generalizations of classic results obtained in algebraic geometry, partly new laws of the most unexpected kind dealing with radically new patterns, where smoothness, instead of being the general rule, turned out to be a rare and not overly important exception.

Topology: The intrinsic study of subsets of coordinate spaces has led to an enormous generalization of the concept of space. *Topological* and *metric* spaces were introduced by Fréchet and Hausdorff as classes of any elements for which a limit or a system of neighborhoods or mutual distances are somehow defined. Klein's principle of classification was applied in studying properties that remain invariant under certain transformations. Topology, or "rubber-sheet geometry," deals with properties invariant under one-to-one bicontinuous transformations, in which a curve may be deformed provided that it is not cut and no two points are joined together. Any simple closed curve is thus a topological transform of a circle. In space, a simple closed curve that cannot be obtained from a circle by a topological transformation of the entire space is called a knot. Recently, large parts of topology have merged with abstract algebra.

Applications of Geometry: Geometry may seem to have abandoned the study of the physical space to which it owes its origin. Actually, however, numerous applications have been made even of geometric theories that arose from purely intellectual speculations. Perhaps the most celebrated example is the use of non-Euclidean geometries and of differential geometry in the theory of relativity and in cosmology. The infinitely-dimensional Hilbert space is a paramount tool in quantum physics. Certain branches of topology are widely used in the theory of electrical networks. Planes with only a finite number of points play a great role in the design of statistical experiments, *e.g.* in testing fertilizers.

While Euclid's extrapolation of observations in the large has been challenged by modifications of his parallel postulate, little has been done so far in connection with the microcosm about Euclid's interpolations in the small. (Non-Euclidean differential geometries, paradoxically, are of use only in the very large—in cosmology.) One of the great future tasks of geometry is a theory of space in the small that could be applied to microphysics. Since in the microcosm individual observations are affected by uncertainties, and only averages are significant, such a geometry in all likelihood will operate with statistical and probabilistic concepts and methods.

What Is Geometry? From an outline of the development of geometry it is clear that the often-heard question "What is Geometry?" does not admit of a sweeping answer describing in one sentence objects and methods. No such definition would do justice to all the already existing branches of geometry, not to speak of future developments. The only answer to the question is by a historical description of all the ramifications of endeavors that ultimately can be traced to the simple original observations concerning natural planes. See COORDINATE GEOMETRY; DIFFERENTIAL GEOMETRY; EUCLIDEAN GEOMETRY; INVERSIVE GEOMETRY; NON-EUCLIDEAN GEOMETRY; TOPOLOGY.—*K. M.*

GEOMORPHOLOGY: the study of the surface features of Earth, primarily their origin and development. Physiography covers much the same subject matter, but according to some authors also includes oceanography and climatology. The geomorphological explanation of topographic features rests on an appreciation of the part played by each of the three major geologic processes: gradation (weathering and erosion), diastrophism (folding, faulting, uplift, and subsidence of Earth's crust), and igneous activity (volcanism). Generally speaking, large-scale relief features result from the last two processes: igneous activity is responsible for the production of volcanoes and extensive lava flows, and diastrophism for mountain ranges and uplifted plateau areas. The forces of gradation working with the five agents of erosion—streams, underground water, glaciers, wind, and waves and currents—lead to the wearing down of the large relief features and, in the process, the production of many smaller-scale relief features both of erosion and deposition, *e.g.* valleys, deltas, sand bars, and dunes.—*J. Sh.*

GEOPHYSICAL EXPLORATION: the investigation of characteristics of Earth by means of the techniques of physics. It includes the study of phenomena and features such as terrestrial magnetism, rotation and shape of Earth, seismic events, the GEOTHERMAL GRADIENT, radioactivity of rock formations, gravity variations, and electrical conductivity. Events or fea-

Seismograph is tossed overboard by "shooter" in offshore oil prospecting. Suspended in water by the attached balloon, seismograph will record vibrations from bottom when underwater charge is set off. Vibrations will be interpreted to see if oil-bearing rock formations may exist in the area. (*Standard Oil*)

and as contoured plans and are then correlated with all available geologic information. In most cases, the geophysical results being sought are relative rather than absolute; they differ from the average (or "background") for a given area and are thus characterized as "anomalies." Some types of anomalies offer direct evidence of the presence of valuable minerals, whereas in other cases the minerals being sought do not in themselves produce any significant geophysical anomalies but are frequently associated with minerals that do. Ordinarily, however, geophysical anomalies afford only indirect information, and usually this pertains to geological structures. Thus depth of overburden or of unconsolidated materials (of great importance in engineering and water-

tures investigated may be naturally occurring, *e.g.* earthquakes, or artificially created, *e.g.* magnetic fluctuations due to the presence of electric power systems. Geophysical exploration is an important aspect of GEOPHYSICS.—*J. W.*

GEOPHYSICAL PROSPECTING: measurement and interpretation of physical properties of rocks in the detection and delineation of mineral deposits, reservoirs of oil and gas, and water-bearing formations, and in the evaluation of civil-engineering sites. Physical properties observed include density, magnetic susceptibility, magnetic polarity, propagation rate of sonic and seismic waves, electrical conductivity, dielectric constants, electrochemical activity, fluorescence, phosphorescence, thermoluminescence, natural and artificially induced radioactivity, and neutron absorption. Methods utilizing other physical properties, *e.g.* nuclear resonance and infrared fluorescence, are being tried. The techniques and instruments are as varied as the properties being measured, many being simple and others being of great complexity and sensitivity, since minute variations may be of major significance. Geophysical surveys are conducted at Earth's surface, on or beneath bodies of water, from the air, and underground by means of instruments lowered into boreholes. In many surveys only naturally existing phenomena are measured, but in others the rocks are subjected to some externally produced force or impulse and the resulting effects are measured. Also, combinations of geophysical techniques are common. The spacings (or "grid") at which measurements are made depend in part on the type of survey and in part on the scale of the program. Survey results are plotted in the form of profiles

Records made by seismograph are used to plot depth points in continuous profile. This is transferred to sub-surface contour map of local rock structures. On this map potential oil-bearing formations may then be located. (*Standard Oil*)

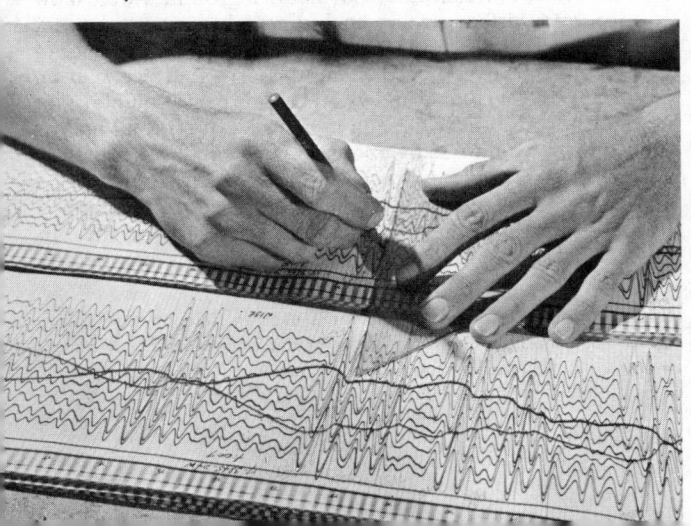

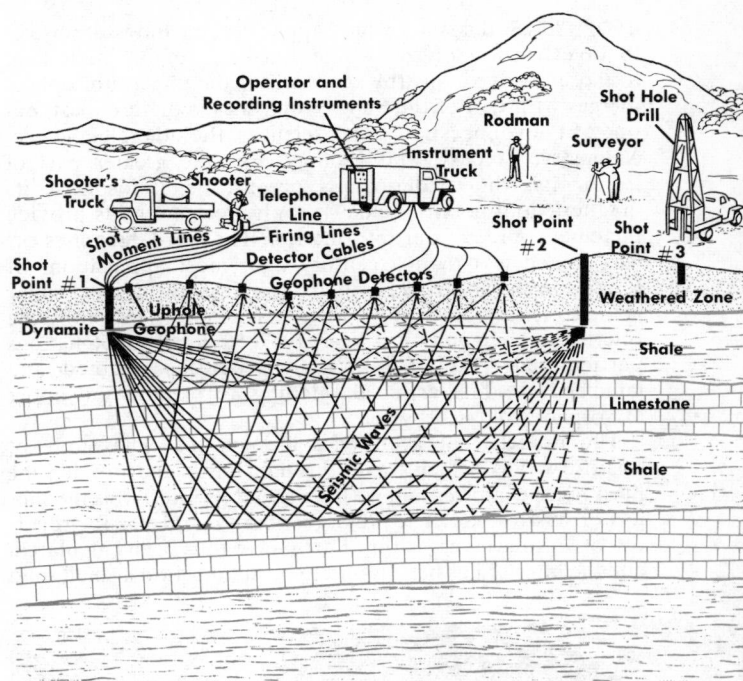

Oil prospecting: Blast set off at each shot point creates seismic waves, which are reflected differently from different strata. Reflected waves received by detectors are recorded electrically in truck. Comparison of records indicates whether strata are likely to have oil deposits. Similar techniques yield data on other geological matters such as correlation of strata and determination of rock composition beneath land surfaces and sea bottoms.

resource evaluations) may be indicated by resistivity and by reflection of sonic or seismic waves. Concentrations of heavy ore minerals may be indicated by positive gravity anomalies, whereas negative gravity anomalies may indicate salt domes, with possibilities of sulfur deposits in the cap rocks and oil and gas accumulations on the flanks. Sulfide deposits of the heavy metals may be indicated by strong conductivity and strong dielectric properties, and if the deposits are being attacked and oxidized by ground-waters, they may give rise to natural electrical currents. Weak radioactivity may outline an igneous intrusive, the contact zone of which might be favorable for the occurrence of ore bodies of hydrothermal origin.

As yet, except for actual oil-seeps, oil and gas occurrences are indicated only by indirect means, generally by geologically favorable structures. Such structures usually involve several kinds of rock, each having distinctive physical properties. Almost all oil- and gas-bearing reservoir rocks are very weakly magnetic sediments, but magnetic surveys may be of great value in delineating such deposits. The underlying, more strongly magnetic crystalline basement rocks may, on magnetic survey, show evidence of folding, doming, or faulting, which could have formed "traps" in the overlying sediments. Gravity surveys may also indicate similar dispositions of the basement rocks. Favorable structures may be delineated by determining the disposition and attitude of readily identifiable "marker beds" within the sedimentary series itself; this is done by seismic surveys using refraction and/or reflection techniques, coupled with resistivity, radioactivity, and neutron-absorption surveys in widely spaced "wildcat" boreholes. See also GEOCHEMICAL PROSPECTING; ORES AND ORE DEPOSITS.—*L. M.*

GEOPHYSICS: the study which applies the methods of physics to investigation of the whole Earth, from its inner core to those regions in nearby space where the upper atmosphere merges with that of the Sun. Geophysics is the broadest, but one of the youngest, of Earth sciences, the others being geochemistry, geodesy, and geology. For the greater part of Earth—its whole interior, its oceans, its atmosphere, its magnetic and gravity fields—geophysical methods provide the chief source of our information. The word "geophysics" was coined less than a century ago; most applications of physics to the study of Earth are recent, and the spectacular achievements were first brought to general attention by the International Geophysical Year, 1957–58, in which 66 nations participated. One of IGY's 14 programs planned and launched the first artificial satellites to explore the upper atmosphere and nearby space.

The branches of geophysics are various. The study of SEISMIC WAVES, which travel through Earth and provide the most precise information we have about its interior, is the subject of SEISMOLOGY. The pressure, density, and elastic properties of various layers within Earth have thus been calculated, and the interior has been found to be divided into a small solid

inner core, a liquid core having properties which fit those of molten iron, a mantle possibly of eclogite or other basic silicate rock, and a thin crust. (See EARTH.) In the last decade, information obtained from body waves has been supplemented and refined by studies of the natural oscillations of the planet. A few large earthquakes, notably the Chilean disturbances of May 1960, have been observed to set Earth ringing like a bell for several days, with vibrations each having a period measured in minutes. Information about the near-surface layers under continents and ocean basins has been obtained by the study of Love and Rayleigh surface seismic waves and by detonation of explosives.

The distribution of earthquakes in space and time is known as the seismicity of Earth. Knowledge of this distribution, combined with studies of the direction of movement observed in earthquakes and with theories of faults (see TECTONICS), constitutes *tectonophysics,* which may be thought of as the science of the study of mountain building (see MOUNTAINS AND MOUNTAIN BUILDING). Some important theories are the CONTRACTION HYPOTHESIS, CONTINENTAL DRIFT, and CONVECTION THEORY. Other information about the interior is obtained by measuring Earth's gravitational field; this is so closely related to the planet's shape that it is considered under GEODESY and ISOSTASY.

Geophysics also includes volcanology and geothermometry. Information about temperatures within Earth, which rise to perhaps 4000°C at the center, are obtained from VOLCANOES, from measurements of the GEOTHERMAL GRADIENT, from studies of radioactivity in rocks, and indirectly from seismic studies. Much of the interior is not far below the melting point, but it is kept solid by pressure except for local melting, which occurs at depths of a few tens of miles, giving rise to volcanism.

Earth's core is generally considered to consist of white-hot liquid in which convection currents circulate, rotating once every few hundred years. These currents carry off heat and are considered by the dynamo theory of geomagnetism (see TERRESTRIAL MAGNETISM) to be the cause of the planet's main magnetic field. Evidence for fluid mobility can also be seen in the slow westward drift of anomalies or variations in the magnetic field shown on world magnetic charts, and in the secular change in the rate of the rotation of Earth (amounting to a few thousandths of a second in a day, faster or slower). The main internal magnetic field creates a secondary field in the upper atmosphere, where the air is so thin as to be ionized and conducting. That part of the atmosphere above about 25 mi, called the IONOSPHERE, and its magnetic field are the subject of the science of aeronomy. METEOROLOGY deals with the lower atmosphere and its weather and climates. Physical OCEANOGRAPHY involves submarine geology (study of the ocean floors) as well as investigations of the currents, waves, tides, and work of the seas themselves. This study was greatly advanced during the International Geophysical Year. Hydrology, the study of fresh waters, deals with ground water, snow and ice, and surface waters, including lakes, rivers, run-off, and floods. GLACIERS and ice sheets, which are the province of glaciology, and cover 5,000,000 mi² of Earth's surface, play an important role in climate and weather. The exact volume of ice in Antarctica has not yet been measured, but if it all melted the sea level would rise by about 200 ft. Sea ice permanently covers the Arctic sea and much of the southern ocean.

Many of the geophysical studies mentioned can be applied to prospecting and the investigation of engineering sites. In seismic prospecting, near-surface strata can be mapped by

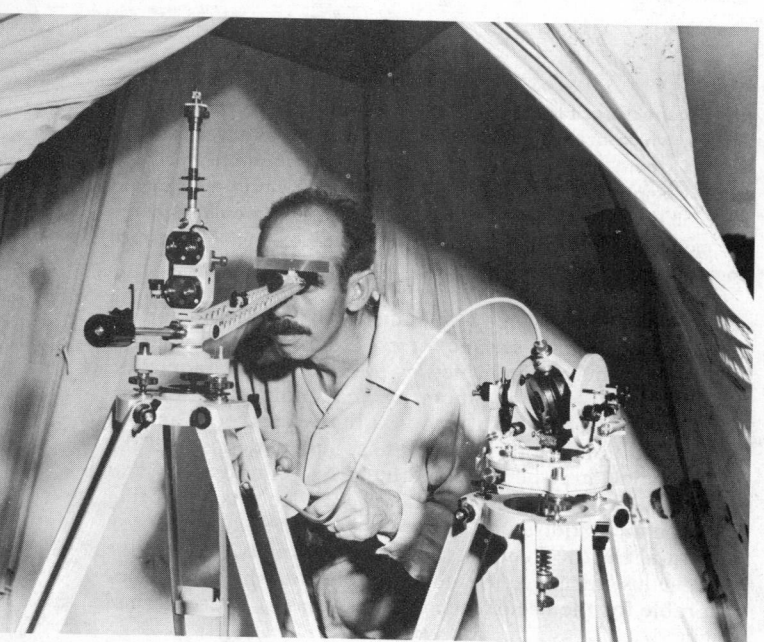

Ruska inductor and galvanometer is used in field or observatory for precise measurements of angle of dip or inclination of Earth's magnetic field. (*National Academy of Sciences IGY Photo*)

observing the echoes reflected from small explosions, and structures favorable for the accumulation of petroleum are thus located. Also, physical measurements are now made of the walls of oil wells: probes lowered into the holes measure such properties as electrical conductivity, porosity, and radioactivity. This procedure is known as *well-logging*. The logs from adjacent holes can be compared, and thus make possible a standard method of tracing strata and elucidating underground structure. (See GEOCHEMICAL PROSPECTING and GEOPHYSICAL PROSPECTING.) In prospecting for ores, advantage is taken of the fact that many ore minerals are denser, more magnetic, or better conductors of electricity than surrounding rocks. Measurements of these properties can reveal ore deposits. Such investigations are often started from the air; millions of square miles have in recent years been covered by aeromagnetic surveys (see SURVEY). If promising indications are found, geophysical ground surveys, geological mapping, and drilling follow.—*J. T. W.*

GEOSYNCLINE: an extensive trough-like area in the earth's crust which has slowly subsided throughout long periods of geologic time and in which thick layers of sediments have accumulated to a depth of thousands of feet. The term was

STAGE 1

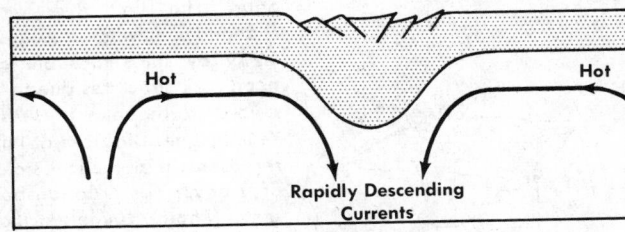

STAGE 2

STAGE 3

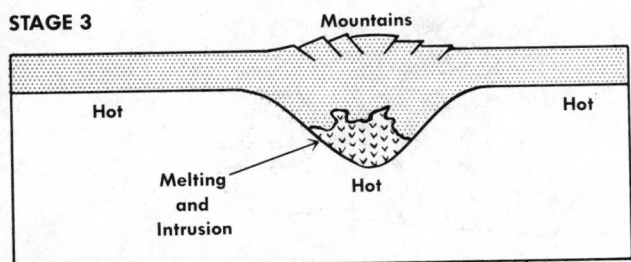

Geosynclinal mountain-building: Possible role of a geosyncline in mountain-building is suggested above in three stages: (1) Low-density sediments accumulate in crustal depression, which gradually deepens—perhaps from action of convection currents in mantle. (2) As sediments sink deeper, high compressive forces fold them and break them. (3) With end of convection process, low-density sediments, being lighter than surrounding crustal rock, gradually float upward, forming mountain range, while melting and intrusion occur at mountain's roots. See CONVECTION THEORY.

first introduced by J. D. Dana, 1873, in his discussion of the origin of the Appalachian Mts, which like many other major mountain ranges are composed of a thick sequence of folded and faulted sedimentary rocks. See MOUNTAINS AND MOUNTAIN BUILDING.—*J. Sh.*

GEOTHERMAL GRADIENT: the steady rise, with depth, of the temperature within Earth. It can be observed and measured in mines and drill holes, or in probes lowered into the ocean floor. The value varies between 10 and 50°C per kilometer of depth, but the heat flow, which is the product of gradient and conductivity, is more consistent, and in general close to 1 microcalorie/cm²/sec. The observation of this heat loss gave rise to the CONTRACTION HYPOTHESIS.—*J. T. W.*

GERARD OF CREMONA, 1114?–87, famous medieval translator; b. Cremona. He spent most of his life at Toledo in the college of translators established by Archbishop Raymond. He translated many classic works into Latin from the Arabic in which they had been preserved. These include the *Physics,* the *De caelo,* and the *Meteorologica,* Books 1–3, of Aristotle, Ptolemy's *Almagest,* the *Algebra* of Al-Khowarizini, the *Elements* and the *Data* of Euclid, and works of Galen and Hippocrates.—*H. C.*

GERGONNE, JOSEPH DIEZ, 1771–1859, French mathematician; b. Nancy. He was editor of a mathematical journal, *Annales de mathématiques* (1810–31), which carried his name and was for a time the only journal in the world devoted exclusively to mathematical research. In geometry he advanced the superiority of analytic methods over synthetic.—*H. C.*

GERMANIUM: a metalloid element (Ge); at. no. 32; at. wt 72.60; density 5.36; mp 958.5°C; bp 2700°C. The term "metalloid" refers to the fact that germanium (like a few other elements, *e.g.* boron, silicon, and tellurium) has some properties that suggest METALS and other properties characteristic of NONMETALS. Germanium is solid at room temperature, quite brittle, but unlike true metals is a poor conductor of electricity. Germanium ("ekasilicon") was predicted by Mendeleev with astonishing accuracy on the basis of his periodic table 15 yr before its actual discovery by Clemens Winkler in 1886. Wrote Mendeleev: "Ekasilicon will have properties intermediate between silicon and tin. . . ." The element is most abundant in residues of sulfide ores, especially those of zinc, and is separated by reduction with potassium cyanide and heat. When alloyed with small amounts of other elements, germanium permits current to pass through its surface in only one direction when in contact with a metal wire; this property enables germanium crystals to serve as a RECTIFIER. Since it is a semiconductor, germanium is used in TRANSISTORS for amplification of small currents of electricity. (See CONDUCTOR AND SEMICONDUCTOR.) Although expensive and rare, germanium is sometimes used to give hardness and strength to certain alloys.—*G. W. M.*

GERM CELL: see GAMETE.

GERMINATION: see SEED.

GESNER, KONRAD VON, 1516–65, Swiss physician, humanist, polyhistor, and bibliographer; b. Zurich. He wrote the 5-vol. *Historia animalium* (1551–58, 1587), in which he described almost all the higher animals known in his day; it is considered the basis of modern zoology. *Opera botanica* (1754), his work on plants, had influence despite its late publication. Gesner also wrote a number of mineralogical works.—*D. J. S.*

GESTALT THEORY AND SCIENTIFIC METHOD: The classical Gestalt theorists are Max Wertheimer (1880–1943), Kurt Koffka (1886–1941), and Wolfgang Köhler (1887–   ). They formulated their ideas first in psychology as a protest against introspective analysis but soon generalized them into a philosophy of scientific method. *Gestalt* means "structured whole"; a tune is Wertheimer's classic example. A tune is unchanged when played in different keys. Since the individual elements (notes) are different, the tune obviously is not merely a sum of its parts; rather, the whole (the tune) determines the status of the parts. According to Wertheimer, most philosophers of science ignore this fact and follow the model of Newton's classical mechanics, which is *analytical* or *additive*. Newton discovered a law—let us call it a "composition rule"—which allows one to derive deductively the mechanical laws governing the behavior of any number of bodies. But if the laws for any number of bodies can be derived deductively, this means that the addition of new bodies makes no fundamental difference—the nature of the new whole can be known beforehand, so to speak—and hence, according to Wertheimer, Newtonian mechanics is analytical or additive. Gestalt theorists admit that the Newtonian model adequately represents the logical structure of much of modern science, but they think it not adequate to all areas as its proponents believe. Köhler supplements it with what he calls the "model of dynamic interaction." Suppose, he says, there is a vessel with one opening for the entrance and one for the exit of water: how will the current be distributed in the continuous volume and how will alteration in the positions of the opening affect the distribution? The important thing is that the current at each point depends directly on the current at all points because the system is not restricted in its points of interaction. In this situation an equation for the steady distribution *as a whole* must be found if the equation for the steady flow at a point is to be found. If such problems as these were more familiar, Köhler says, "the belief would not be so general that physics is under all circumstances an 'analytical' science in which the properties of more complex extended facts are deduced from the properties of independent local elements."—*E. H. M.*

GESTATION (or **pregnancy**): the period during which an embryo develops in the uterus, from the time of conception to birth. In general, animals that produce litters (*e.g.* dog, rabbit) have a shorter period than do species that normally bear a single offspring. Length of gestation is roughly correlated with size of species: rat, 21 days; rabbit (various species), 30 to 36 days; cat, 60 days; dog and wolf, 63 days; man, 275 days; horse, 335 days; elephant, 665 days. Some mammals exhibit interrupted gestation: the developing embryo undergoes a long quiescent period during which growth ceases. As a result, some members of the weasel family may have a gestation of eight months to a year. Marsupials, in contrast, have a very short gestation. Opossum young are born in an undeveloped state after a gestation period of 11 to 12 days. Such undeveloped young remain in the pouch of the parent for two or more months. See EMBRYONIC DEVELOPMENT. —*A. P. E.*

GEYSER: a natural fountain of hot water which intermittently gushes up to a height varying from a few feet to over 100 ft. The name comes from a spring called Geysir about 55 mi west of Reykjavik, Iceland. That country, New Zealand, and Yellowstone Park in the U. S. A. have most of the world's geysers. Essentially, a geyser is a thermal spring with a crooked natural tube leading from the surface to a source of heat underground. The heat source may be molten rock (magma) or hot gases from such rock. Ground water deep in

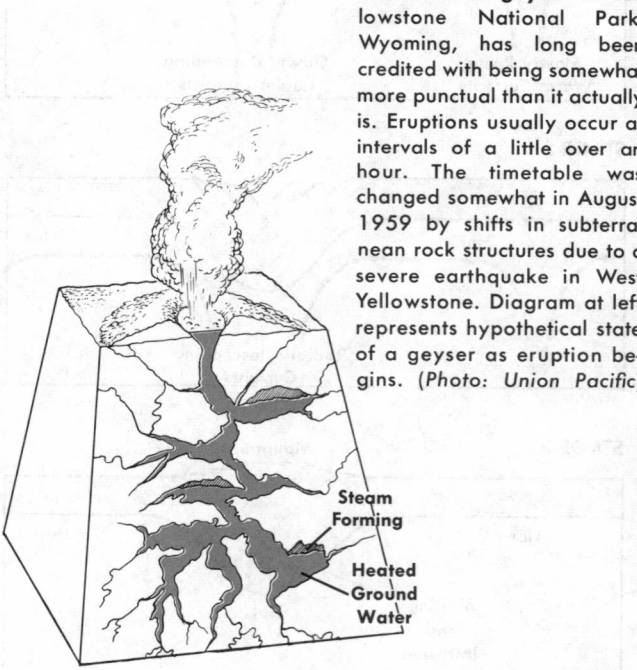

Old Faithful geyser in Yellowstone National Park, Wyoming, has long been credited with being somewhat more punctual than it actually is. Eruptions usually occur at intervals of a little over an hour. The timetable was changed somewhat in August 1959 by shifts in subterranean rock structures due to a severe earthquake in West Yellowstone. Diagram at left represents hypothetical state of a geyser as eruption begins. (*Photo: Union Pacific*)

Steam Forming

Heated Ground Water

the tube gradually becomes heated until it reaches the normal boiling point; but the pressure of the water above prevents boiling, and heating continues. Distribution of the heat by convection is prevented by the shape of the tube. Eventually the water at the bottom reaches a temperature at which it will boil. As steam forms, it raises the entire column of water, and the upper part spurts from the mouth of the tube. This spurt reduces the pressure on—and therefore the boiling point of—the remaining water in the tube, and that water quickly turns to steam and emerges explosively. The empty tube is then ready to receive more cool water and resume the cycle. As much as 10,000 gal. may be erupted consecutively. The regularity of the eruption intervals depends on a constant supply of ground water and an unfailing source of heat. Old Faithful in Yellowstone Park has an interval varying from 30 to 90 min.

The water ejected from a geyser deposits the chemicals it had previously dissolved. This deposit, mostly silica (geyserite), accumulates near the outlet of the tube, forming a cone. The activity of geysers and thermal springs reveals the presence of heat sources underground and is considered evidence of fairly recent volcanic activity in the area. Cones of geyserite in sites now quiet indicate past periods of volcanism.—*E. A.*

GIAUQUE, WILLIAM FRANCIS, 1895– , Canadian-U. S. chemist; b. Niagara Falls, Canada. A specialist in the production of extremely low temperatures and the study of physical phenomena at these temperatures, he developed the magnetic method for producing and maintaining temperatures less than 1° absolute. For his work in chemical thermodynamics, particularly in the behavior of substances at extremely low temperatures, he received the Nobel prize, 1949. He is a member of the National Academy of Sciences.—*D. H. D. R.*

GIBBS, JOSIAH WILLARD, 1839–1903, U. S. mathematician and physicist; b. New Haven, Conn. Regarded by many as the most notable U. S. scientist of all time, Gibbs spent all his years from 1871 as professor of mathematical physics at Yale. A memoir, "On the Equilibrium of Heterogeneous Substances" (1876, 1878), applied the first and second laws of thermodynamics to heterogeneous substances and established the theoretical basis for

Josiah Willard Gibbs
(*Yale University*)

physical chemistry. The memoir was translated into both French and German and was of enormous influence. It contains "Gibbs' Phase Rule." From about 1880 Gibbs worked to develop geometric algebra into a system of vector algebra suitable for the needs of mathematical physicists. This work was first fully published in E. B. Wilson's *Vector Analysis* (1901). Gibbs also did research on optics and statistical mechanics. *The Collected Works of J. Willard Gibbs* (1928) contains all his published writings. He was a fellow of the Royal Society and a member of the National Academy of Sciences.—*D. H. D. R.*

GILBERT, GROVE KARL, 1843–1918, U. S. geologist; b. Rochester, N. Y. He worked for various government surveys (1871–79) and for the U. S. Geological Survey (1879–1918). Under J. W. Powell, he studied the structure of the Henry Mts in Utah (1877), showing that they were formed by laccolithic intrusions. This work also clarified the fundamental principles of river action in the erosion of valleys. Among his other studies were those on ancient Lake Bonneville, on the life history of the Niagara River, and on recent earth movements in the Great Lakes region. He was a fellow of the Royal Society and a member of the National Academy of Sciences. —*D. H. D. R.*

GILBERT, WILLIAM, 1544–1603, English physicist; b. Colchester. His theory that Earth is a magnet opened the field of terrestrial magnetism. He distinguished between electric attraction and magnetic attraction, and his ideas on mass and the force exerted on the Moon by Earth influenced the development of gravitational theory. His books include *De magnete* (1600) and a cosmological work based upon manuscripts left at his death and edited by a younger brother: *De mundo nostro sublunari* (*Concerning Our World beneath the Moon*), 1651.—*D. H. D. R.*

William Gilbert
(*New York Public Library*)

GILLS: respiratory organs of aquatic animals. Gills are thin-walled projections of the body surface that can serve for exchange of oxygen and carbon dioxide between blood and the surrounding medium. Gills may be considered to form as outward foldings of the body surface, whereas lungs form as inpocketings. In general, gills serve for respiration in water, but in numerous instances they are modified for air breathing. Most gills have a highly branched or feathery structure, which greatly increases the surface area through which gaseous exchange can take place (see RESPIRATION). Generally there is good circulation of blood within the gill, and some provision for ventilation—the circulation of water over the outside surface of the gill. Ventilation is accomplished in clams and marine tubeworms by the beating of microscopic hairlike cilia, which sets up a gentle current of water; crabs, lobsters, and other animals move special appendages that sweep water over the gills; the octopus, the squid, and fishes achieve the same result by muscular movements of other body parts. Gills of fishes are probably the most efficient mechanisms for aquatic respiration. Water is forced over them by a combination of swallowing movements in the mouth and pharynx, and movements of the opercula (gill covers), which draw water out past the gills.—*B. T. S.*

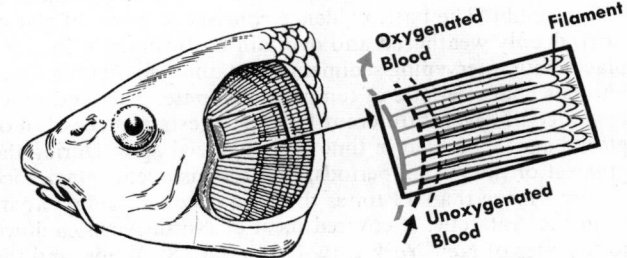

Gills of a fish whose gill cover has been removed. Ribbonlike gill filaments contain miles of capillaries through which blood flows. Path of blood entering and leaving filaments is shown in enlarged section. Blood absorbs oxygen from water flowing over gills, and discharges carbon dioxide into water.

GIMBAL: a type of suspension which permits rotation about a single axis through use of a hollow frame with external stub axles. It has been widely used for mounting air and marine navigation instruments, *i.e.* chronometers, compasses, gyroscopes. A series of gimbals one within another with rotational freedom on crossed axes will permit a platform to maintain a fixed position even though the supporting structure tilts or rotates. The gimbal, or Cardon suspension, probably originated in the 13th cent. "Gimbal" is loosely applied to engine mountings to mean "swivel."—*W. K.*

Heaps of sand and gravel, such as this kame in northern New Jersey, were left here and there by glacial ice as it melted at close of last glacial period. (*Jerome Wyckoff*)

Glacial striations on bedrock, with polishing, were produced by rock debris embedded in moving glacial ice. Compare this close-up with view from air on next page. (*U. S. Forest Service*)

GIZZARD: a thickened, highly muscular portion of the STOMACH of crocodiles and birds. The gizzard is derived from the stomach region known as the pylorus and it is lined with a tough secretion of the pyloric glands. Small stones ingested by the animal lodge in the gizzard; when rubbed together by contractions of the muscular wall, the stones serve to grind food. Some mollusks and earthworms have structures similar to the gizzard.—*B. T. S.*

GLACIAL AGES: the group of cold periods which, together with intervening warmer intervals, constitute the Pleistocene epoch of geologic history. The concept of a glacial age with widespread effects was first set forth in 1837 by Louis Agassiz in Switzerland. Evidence consisted of features obviously produced by glaciation (see GLACIERS AND GLACIATION) yet occurring far beyond the limits of existing glacier ice. The glacial theory, as it was called, gradually displaced the belief that GLACIAL DRIFT and erratics had been deposited by a universal, catastrophic flood, which some identified with the Biblical Deluge. Gradually it became clear that there had been not one but several glacial ages; the exact number is still in doubt. The basic evidence consists of layers of glacial drift, deeply weathered and overlain by fresh drift, in some places with intervening sediments containing fossil plants and animals characteristic of temperate climate. This and other evidence of several different kinds suggests a succession of glacial ages separated in time by nonglacial ages. During the greatest of the glacial periods, in the Pleistocene, glacier ice covered more than 13 times the area it covers today, apart from the Antarctic. It covered most of North America down to the sites of New York City, Cincinnati, St. Louis, and the Missouri River. Europe was blanketed by ice down to the vicinities of London, the Carpathians, and southern European Russia. In addition, high mountains throughout much of the world developed glaciers that spread downward to low altitudes; the snowline was lowered in places by more than 4,000 ft below its present altitude. Glaciers pushed out into tidewater and formed broad, floating ice shelves that broke off and formed innumerable icebergs. The Arctic Ocean froze over, and pack ice extended southward as far as the Grand Banks off Newfoundland, Iceland, and the Norwegian Sea. Much less is known about the thicknesses of these glaciers than about their areas; but there is some evidence that the Scandinavian Ice Sheet, which covered much of Europe, was as much as 10,000 ft thick over the Gulf of Bothnia, and that the great Laurentide Ice Sheet in North America was at least 5,500 ft thick over central New England, and perhaps much thicker.

This large volume of temporary ice did not necessarily require greater precipitation than is measured today in the areas formerly glaciated. Lowering of temperature by a few degrees —sufficient to produce an excess of accumulation of snow over melting of snow—plus time enough to allow the growing glaciers to spread to their fullest extent, could account for the ice that formed. Temporary storage, on the lands, of the unusual volume of moisture in the solid state caused lowering of sea level by at least as much as 300 ft, perhaps much more. Sediments and other features created during the latest glacial age and now submerged testify to the temporarily lowered sea level (see CORAL REEFS AND ATOLLS). The weight of the larger glaciers caused parts of Earth's crust on which they stood to subside—as much as 3,000 ft. As these glaciers melted and their substance ran back to the oceans as water, the depressed areas slowly rebounded. Localities that stood at sea level early in the last period of melting have risen as much as 1,000 ft since that time, and the movement is still continuing at a measurable rate.

Radiocarbon dating indicates that the last major expansion of glaciers began around 25,000 yr ago. Through the dating of a series of trees from groves that were successively destroyed and buried beneath glacial drift as the margin of the ice sheet crossed Ohio, the average rate of advance of that glacier has been calculated at 100 to 200 ft per yr. The glaciers reached their greatest extent 18,000 to 16,000 yr ago and then began to shrink. After various re-expansions, one of which reblanketed much of the Great Lakes region less than 11,000 yr ago, the shrinking ice had disappeared from most areas by 5,000 yr ago, although small bodies of ice have remained on highlands in middle latitudes up to today. Radiocarbon dates show that other, lesser glacial expansions occurred, in both Europe and America, around 60,000 and 40,000 yr ago. The intervening climates were cool and rather unlike the present climate. The last really nonglacial time, with climates comparable to or slightly warmer than today's, seems to have ended around 70,000 yr ago. The earlier glacial ages are beyond the reach of radiocarbon dating, and little is known about their chronology. The estimate, made long ago, that the Pleistocene epoch lasted about one million yr, is still widely quoted and has not been replaced by exact measurement.

The Pleistocene glacial ages followed a long period of relatively mild climate. Much earlier than that, other glacial ages occurred. Two such times occurred around 200 million and 600 million yr ago, and there were probably others.

A number of lines of evidence, mostly from fossils, suggest that the lowering of world temperature which brought on the latest glacial age was around 6°C. Regional changes were much larger or smaller, depending on latitude, altitude, and other factors. Smaller fluctuations, with time, have been superposed on this major one. The last change has been a general rise of temperature, amounting to as much as 1°C, since about A. D. 1850. The main causes of the fluctuation of climate responsible for the glacial ages are not known, but are believed by many to lie outside the Earth, possibly in variations of solar-energy output.—*R. F.*

GLACIAL DRIFT: sediments, *e.g.* gravel, sand, and mud, deposited directly by a glacier to form "till," or indirectly in glacial streams, lakes, and the sea. Drift is common in areas glaciated during the recent GLACIAL AGES. The name arose from an early 19th-cent. belief that all such deposits had been "drifted" into place by a vast flood. Drift that has not been sorted as to size by running water is *till*; it consists of sediments deposited directly from a glacier, without intermediate transportation in water. Glacial till that has been converted by cementation into sedimentary rock is called *tillite*. Some tillites are over 500 million yr old and indicate the existence of ancient glaciers in such areas as Central Africa and Australia.—*R. F.*

GLACIERS AND GLACIATION: A glacier is a body of ice, consisting mainly of recrystallized snow, moving on a land surface. Glaciers are closely related to the snowline, or lower limit of perennial snow, which varies from sea level in polar regions to 20,000 ft or more in some low-latitude areas. Glaciers have their origin above the snowline but spread downward from it in a flow-like movement. The length and volume of a glacier depend on (1) rate of accumulation of

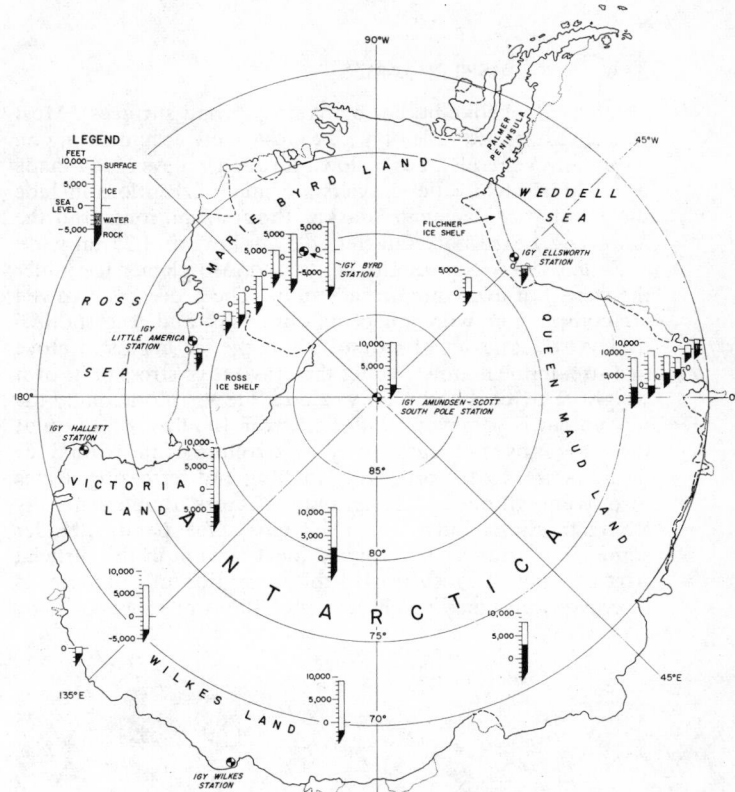

Geologic columnar sections show present estimated thickness of ice over portions of Antarctica. Estimates are made primarily by means of seismic sounding. Gravity and magnetic anomalies, as well as topography, also yield clues. (*IGY Bulletin/National Academy of Sciences*)

snow (mainly above the snowline), (2) amount of ice lost by melting and evaporation (mainly below the snowline), and (3) rapidity of transfer of ice by movement downward across the snowline. Glaciers can exist for a long period only in environments where the amount of snowfall is not exceeded by melting, which occurs chiefly in summer; hence glaciers are confined to high latitudes or high altitudes. Also, glaciers respond sensitively to changes in climate. The nearly worldwide shrinkage of glaciers during the last few decades reflects a general warming of climates. Today more than 95% of the aggregate area of the world's glaciers is on the Antarctic Continent and Greenland; the other 5% is distributed among thousands of glaciers, mostly very small, elsewhere, including high points in the equatorial regions. There are about 1,200 glaciers in the Alps alone, and about 1,000 in the U. S. A. exclusive of Alaska. As part of the world's hydrologic cycle, glaciers represent the temporary storage of moisture, in the solid state, on the lands. With sufficiently warmer climates, glaciers would melt, returning the moisture to the oceans; fallen snow would melt in summer, and the level of the sea would rise by perhaps as much as 200 ft. With colder climates, glaciers would expand and sea level would fall, as occurred under the cold-climate regimens of the GLACIAL AGES.

Glaciers have many shapes, which depend mainly on the thickness of the ice and on the configuration of the land beneath. Three major types are recognized: valley glaciers (long, narrow tongues), piedmont glaciers (lobate bodies on a lowland, fed by valley glaciers descending mountain slopes), and

Grooved, gouged, and polished landscape, dotted with lakes, resulted from glacial action in northern Canada during recent glacial ages. Grooving indicates direction taken by ice spreading outward from center of accumulation. (*Canadian Air Force*)

ice sheets (cakelike bodies blanketing broad surfaces). Most glaciers are of the valley type, because snow accumulating on mountains generally moves down through valleys ready-made by streams. Most valley glaciers are small; exceptions include the Hubbard Glacier in Alaska, about 75 mi long, and the Antarctic Beardmore Glacier, 125 mi long and 25 mi wide.

Fallen snow is gradually converted into glacier ice under the weight of overlying, fresher snow. The processes involved are compaction, with squeezing out of air, and recrystallization. At thicknesses of around 200 ft the ice begins to move in a streamline manner, under the gravitative stress of its own weight. The ice is commonly said to "flow," but actually the movement is somewhat different from the flow of a liquid; the mass moves at least partly by a rolling of individual ice particles and by the process of melting and refreezing. Rates of movement, depending on many factors, range generally from a fraction of an inch to a few tens of feet per day. Under some circumstances flow causes local tension in the surficial part of a glacier, resulting in the formation of open cracks (*crevasses*) that may reach depths of 100 ft or more. In some

Glacier which gouged this Alaskan valley into typical U-shape during recent glacial ages has now shrunk far back. In left foreground is the tongue of South Sawyer Glacier. Entire region shows effects of glacial scouring. (*U. S. Forest Service*)

areas crevasses are so numerous that travel on the glacier is impossible. The bergschrund, at the head of a valley glacier, is the gap left between the ice and the mountain side as the ice withdraws in its downward movement. Withdrawing ice keeps plucking out rock to which it has been frozen and thus helps to form a CIRQUE.

Erosion by glaciers consists partly of abrasion (essentially "sandpapering") and partly of plucking. Although some plucked blocks are enormous, the grinding, breaking, and crushing that occur in a glacier eventually reduce most rock fragments to very small size. A valley glacier, confined between high steep walls, erodes more effectively than does an ice sheet free to spread in all directions. Some glaciated valleys have been deepened by hundreds of feet, and have been converted into U-shaped, smooth-sided troughs by the planing off of side spurs. The tributary valleys to such major glacial troughs in many instances have not been eroded as deeply, and remain as *hanging valleys* after the glaciers have vanished. Hanging valleys are often the sites of impressive waterfalls. Fiords are glacially eroded valleys that have been partly flooded by the rising sea.

In broad lowland areas, glacial erosion rarely removes an average of more than a few tens of feet of rock material. In such areas, as in mountain valleys, the rock particles with which the flowing ice is armed abrade the bedrock to a smooth surface, which commonly bears characteristic grooves, scratches (striations), and polish. The predominantly bare-rock surface of much of NE Canada and large areas of Scandinavia is the result of glacial erosion. At and near their outer or lower margins, glaciers deposit their loads of rock particles as melting thins the ice and reduces its rate of motion. Sheetlike blankets of GLACIAL DRIFT are thus plastered over the ground, and characteristic forms such as drumlins, moraines, kames, kettles, and eskers are created. Much of the first-class agricultural soil from New York State westward through the Dakotas is developed in glacial deposits. Beyond the limits of the glacier ice itself, streams of meltwater carry away rock particles and deposit them on their beds, creating bodies of *outwash* sediments. The thick outwash body in the valley of the Mississippi River is the largest in the world, extending down the valley to the delta in the area of the river mouth. The average thickness of drift deposited by glaciers during the GLACIAL AGES, over the belt of country south of the Great Lakes, has been estimated at about 40 ft; it varies abruptly from place to place. In New England the thickness of drift is much less because there the bedrock is exceptionally resistant and less of it was eroded by the ice. See Color Plate 52.—*R. F.*

GLAISHER, JAMES, 1809–1903, English astronomer and meteorologist; b. London. As head of the new magnetic and meteorological department of the Greenwich Observatory (1838–74) he contributed to the improvement of meteorological instruments and to the organization of observations. He published many tables of meteorological data and made a large number of balloon ascents for meteorological observation. He was a fellow of the Royal Society.—*D. H. D. R.*

GLAND: a cell or group of similar cells that produce and secrete chemical substances of special use to the organism in which the gland occurs. If a gland pours its secretion directly into the blood stream, which delivers the secretion to where it is to be used, the gland is an ENDOCRINE GLAND. If the secretion passes directly from the gland, or through ducts, to the outside of the body or to the cavity of the digestive tract, the gland is an *exocrine* gland. Exocrine glands may be classified further according to how the secretion is released. Prob-

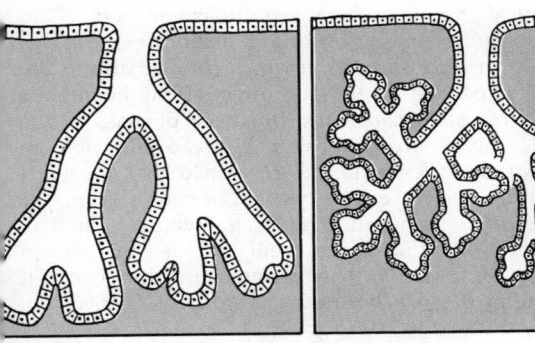

Glands are formed by inward folding of the epithelial surface. Two of a variety of possible patterns are shown. (*After Young*)

ably the most primitive of exocrine glands is the *apocrine* type, in which secretion material accumulates in the tips of the secretory cells; these tips are shed, freeing the secretion and leaving a concave extremity such as is characteristic of the "goblet" cells in the lining layer of the intestine. Each apocrine gland cell regenerates a new tip as it secretes more of its product. Other apocrine glands are those secreting wax in the external auditory canal of the ear, the MAMMARY GLANDS, PROSTATE GLAND, and glands around the anus, including SCENT GLANDS of skunks and certain other animals. The *eccrine* type of exocrine gland discharges a watery secretion without obvious change in the gland's shape; SWEAT GLANDS, TEAR GLANDS, and SALIVA GLANDS operate in this way. Sebaceous glands (see HAIR) are of a third type, called *holocrine* glands; in these glands the entire cell is discharged with the secretion, which is usually a waxy or oily material. The meibomian glands, located at the edge of each human eyelid, are holocrine glands. They release an oily film that lessens the likelihood of tears spilling over and down the cheeks.

Sometimes the word "gland" is applied to structures that are not true glands, *e.g.* lymph nodes and the SPLEEN.— *L. and M. M.*

GLASER, DONALD ARTHUR, 1926–   ; U. S. physicist; b. Cleveland, Ohio. In 1952 he began research on detection of nuclear particles with a BUBBLE CHAMBER, an instrument he invented. An improved chamber is now a major research tool in nuclear physics. For his invention he received the Nobel prize, 1960.—*D. H. D. R.*

GLASS: a class of materials which, on cooling from the molten state, gradually become more and more viscous until finally they become quite rigid while retaining the amorphous structure characteristic of the liquid state. This is in contrast to the tendency of most liquids when cooled to separate out crystalline phases, *i.e.* to solidify by progressive crystallization of each component at a definite temperature (melting point). In solutions comprising several components the separating out of some crystals generally alters the composition of the remaining liquid, which in turn alters the temperature at

Making of fine glassware has changed little since 18th cent. when D. Diderot illustrated making of a goblet in his famous *Encyclopédie*. The 18th-cent. glassmaker (*above*) tools base of goblet (still soft from heating) preliminary to final shaping. Modern craftsman (*below*) adds molten bits of glass to goblet to form decorative features. Ingredients of glass used by modern glassmaker are silica sand, potash (*i.e.* potassium compounds), and lead oxide. Fused at temperatures as high as 2500°C, the end-product is a clear, colorless, transparent crystal. (*Corning Glass Works*)

which further crystal growth occurs in the liquid; the curve of liquid-solid temperature equilibrium (*i.e.* a line on a graph connecting the melting points of each component) plotted against any parameter or parameters specifying the liquid composition is called the liquidus. The formation of glass seems to be entirely a question of time rate: if the material is highly viscous just above the liquidus temperature, crystal growth will occur very slowly so that such a material can be cooled down fast enough to prevent crystal growth; this is what is done in glass manufacture. (Since thermodynamic equilibrium below the liquidus temperature would correspond to the formation of crystals, glasses are in a metastable state rather than in thermodynamic equilibrium.) However, if any molten glass is cooled too slowly it will grow crystals, or devitrify—"devitrification" being the term used for undesirable crystallization.

Compositions: All commercial glasses are based on compositions in which silica (SiO_2) from sand is a major constituent. This material, as well as boric oxide (B_2O_3), aluminum oxide (Al_2O_3), and phosphorus pentoxide (P_2O_5), are the principal glass-formers. Other constituents in ordinary glass are the alkaline oxides, mainly sodium oxide (Na_2O), but also potassium oxide (K_2O), lithium oxide (Li_2O), and the alkaline earth oxides, lime (CaO) and magnesia (MgO). In addition, lead oxide (PbO), is an important constituent of dense flint glasses of high refractive index, used for certain optical purposes and also for glass art objects. Still other constituents such as oxides of iron may be added for deliberate gaining of color; or color may be obtained simply by not re-

moving certain constituents from the original raw material. Fused silica, obtained by melting sand, is a good glass for many purposes, but production is limited because its melting requires very high temperatures (1723°C) and it is extremely viscous even when melted. To lower the melting point, soda is added, usually in the form of sodium carbonate (Na_2CO_3), which decomposes to leave merely Na_2O in the glass. But this results in a glass of low durability that is easily attacked by water, so lime and/or magnesia, often in equal proportions from the natural mineral dolomite, is added. Approximately 1% of Al_2O_3 greatly improves the durability of such soda-lime glasses and is usually included in the formula. Since sand is the cheapest constituent, its proportion in glass is kept as high as possible.

Glasses containing considerable amounts of B_2O_3 are called *borosilicates*. Pyrex-type glass is a well-known example. It has a relatively low thermal-expansion coefficient, about one-third that of common soda-lime glass, and this gives it much greater resistance to breakage by the stresses of sudden temperature change. Glasses containing Al_2O_3, called *aluminosilicates*, also have this property and are capable of withstanding higher temperatures. Glass for oven baking ware is made of borosilicate, but that for cooking on an open flame on top of a stove is made of the harder aluminosilicates.

Manufacture: In industrial practice, glass is melted in large tanks, holding upward of 100 tons and made of refractory blocks. The melting process releases much gas, so the molten glass is usually held in the tank for an average time of 5 days (in a continuous-flow process) in order to give time for the gas bubbles to rise from the viscous mass; this is called *fining*. The molten product is drawn off in a refractory trough called a forehearth from which it passes through a feeder, where portions are cut with shears into gobs which are fed to automatic pressing or blowing machinery for making bottles or dishes. A similar process is used for fine optical glass, but here the tanks are platinum-lined to achieve better quality and composition control. A great variety of rolling, pressing, drawing, and other processes are used to make flat window glass, plate glass, tubing, electric-lamp bulbs, and other articles. In all these it is necessary to control carefully the rate at which the glass cools down to room temperature from the temperature at which it first becomes essentially rigid. If the cooling takes place rapidly and irregularly, stresses due to different cooling rates develop in different parts of the object and weaken it. The process of controlling the cooling so as to avoid such weakening effects is called ANNEALING. Even when there is essentially no internal stress, glasses will go on showing small drifts in their dimensions and in their refractive index for long periods of time; such small defects do not matter in window glass or bottles, but are very important in glass for optical instruments or for thermometers and other devices in which optical and dimensional stability is important. Thus optical glass requires more careful and elaborate annealing. Processes have been developed in which cooling stresses are deliberately introduced for the purpose of strengthening the glass; these are called *tempering*. Breakage of glass occurs where surface layers are in tension. If the cooling is controlled so that the internal stresses developed have the effect of putting the surface layers everywhere in compression, the glass is greatly strengthened. The strengthening is limited, however, by the fact that the internal stresses can result in violent disruption of the parts when breakage does occur, if the tempering process has been carried too far.—*E. U. C.*

GLAUBER, JOHANN RUDOLF, 1604–68, German chemist; b. Karlstadt; self-educated. He gave his name to *Glauber's salt* (sodium sulfate), which he discovered in an Austrian mineral spring and later prepared from sulfuric acid and common salt. He described it in his *De natura salium* (1658), ascribing many medicinal virtues to it. Later he prepared many new chemical substances, particularly salts of metals.—*D. H. D. R.*

GLAUBER'S SALT: the decahydrate salt of sodium sulfate, $Na_2SO \cdot 10H_2O$ ("decahydrate" = 10 water molecules). It is used as a cathartic and in chemical manufacturing. Its largest use is in the manufacture of sulfate-process wood pulp, which is, in turn, used to make kraft paper—the heavy, brown, high-strength wrapping paper.—*G. W. M.*

GLAZE: the smooth, clear covering of ice deposited on exposed objects by the freezing of supercooled rain. Glaze may reach a thickness of ½ in. during a severe ice storm, causing widespread damage to trees and electric lines. Glaze forms also on wings of aircraft flying through supercooled clouds. —*D. H. L.*

GLIDER: a lightly built, fixed-wing, heavier-than-air aircraft having no power plant; "an airplane without an engine." The absence of an engine imposes two basic restrictions on glider flight: (1) once launched, the glider must rely solely on its aerodynamic surfaces and on natural updrafts to obtain lift and thus prolong its flight (see AERODYNAMICS); (2) in calm air, a glider must lose altitude to make headway. Before the development of suitable airplane power plants in the 20th cent., the first heavier-than-air flights were made in gliders; and early aerodynamicists, *e.g.* Otto Lilienthal (1848–96), Octave Chanute (1832–1910), and J. J. Montgomery (1858–1911), used gliders experimentally to develop better lifting surfaces and control techniques (see AIRFOIL; AIRPLANE). The Wright brothers used gliders, at first tethered, later manned, for the same purposes, and Orville set the first modern in-air record, 9 min, 49 sec, on Oct. 24, 1911.

Wright brothers' glider, 1902: Using gliders, Wrights worked out aerodynamic, structural, and control problems before they attempted powered flight. (*Inst. of Aerospace Sciences*)

Sailplane, 1960: A graceful, streamlined aircraft, able to stay aloft for hours, this Schweizer 1-23H15 competed in 1960 international glider championship in Germany. (*Flying Magazine*)

Gliders are classed by performance and construction as primary or utility; the most advanced type, the *sailplane*, is often considered a class by itself. They may be single or multiplace. All make headway by either gliding or soaring. In gliding (which implies loss of altitude) gravity supplies the motive power; soaring (which implies a temporary gain or sustaining of altitude) makes use of air flows and currents for motive power. Primary and utility gliders are principally gliding machines. The simplicity of the wood or metal-tubing structure of the primary glider precludes streamlining; this type is used for elementary training. Utility gliders, with a greater performance potential, good stability, low flying speed, and integrated controls, are used for advanced pilot-training and routine flying. Their aerodynamic and control surfaces permit limited soaring under favorable conditions. The highest refinement of glider flight, however, is found in the sailplane, whose ultra-clean lines and high aspect-ratio wings, among other aerodynamic refinements, enable it to take maximum advantage of any air movements that may contribute to lift. In calm air, sailplanes have attained a sinking speed as low as 1.6 ft/sec, and a glide ratio as high as 42:1 (*i.e.* 42 ft of forward motion while losing only 1 ft of altitude). In soaring, the sailplane makes full use of rising convection currents ("thermals") as well as cloud and standing-wave phenomena which can produce upward components of velocity in excess of the glider's sinking speed. The variometer, a sensitive rate-of-climb indicator, helps the sailplane pilot locate and utilize these favorable atmospheric conditions. Sailplanes have soared as high as 44,000 ft above sea level, stayed aloft after launching for over 56 hr, and established distance records in excess of 500 mi.

The very early gliders were often launched at the top of a long slope, with the intent of giving the glider an angle of flight greater than the angle of the slope and thus keeping the glider airborne beyond the end of the slope. This is called "slope soaring." Methods of launching have ranged from teams of running men, to towing by water and land vehicles, to catapults. In the early days of glider flight, the operator, sitting in stirrups, ran till the glider rose. Now, gliders are usually launched either by being towed by powered aircraft to altitude and released, or by catapult-and-runway facilities which literally jump the glider into the air. The basic problem in launching (as in soaring) is to develop sufficient lift on the glider's aerodynamic surfaces to overcome gravity.

After World War I gliding became popular as a sport in Europe, especially in Germany, where powered aircraft were forbidden by the Treaty of Versailles. Competitions are now held regularly all over the world. During World War II, troop- and cargo-carrying gliders were widely used for airborne assaults. Attacks were usually made well to the rear of enemy lines. These aircraft, generally considered expendable, were usually built of wood covered with fabric.—*H. A.*; *E. H. H.*

GLISSON, FRANCIS, 1597–1677, English anatomist and physician; b. Rampisham; ed. Cambridge and Oxford universities. He is known for anatomical researches on liver, stomach, and intestines, described in his *Anatomia hepatis* (1654) and *Tractatus de ventriculo et intestinis* (1677). "Glisson's capsule" is the fibrous covering of the liver. He was one of the founding fellows of the Royal Society.—*D. H. D. R.*

GLOBULIN: see BLOOD PROTEINS.

GLORY: the disc of white light, sometimes surrounded by rainbow-colored rings, which encircles an observer's shadow seen on a cloud or fog bank. The glory is produced by the diffraction of light coming from behind the observer by water droplets. The observer must be at a higher altitude than the cloud or fog bank on which the phenomenon appears, as on a mountain or in an airplane.—*D. H. L.*

GLUCAGON: a hormone produced in the Islands of Langerhans in the pancreas; it has an action in many (but not all) respects opposite to that of insulin. Whereas insulin promotes conversion of blood sugar into glycogen in liver and muscle, thus tending to keep blood sugar at moderate levels and preventing hyperglycemia, glucagon promotes conversion of liver glycogen into sugar, which then passes into the blood, causing hyperglycemia. Glucagon is sometimes a contaminant of insulin preparations. See GLYCOLYSIS.—*J. Fl.*

GLUCOSE: see SUGAR.

GLUE: the crude product obtained by boiling animal *collagen* (see GELATIN) and drying the extract. Softened with hot water and allowed to swell, the extract yields an adhesive useful for bonding paper and wood, since it dries to a strong film. Pure gelatin in water is not a good adhesive. See also ADHESIVE. —*Ru. M.*

GLYCERALDEHYDE: in biochemistry, a 3-carbon intermediate in the breakdown of the common 6-carbon sugars, glucose and fructose. Glucose, eaten or formed by the breakdown of starch or glycogen, is transformed (in a series of enzyme-catalyzed reactions) into fructose-1, 6-diphosphate, which is then split by the enzyme aldolase into two 3-carbon compounds: D-glyceraldehyde phosphate and dihydroxyacetone phosphate. Dihydroxyacetone phosphate and D-glyceraldehyde phosphate are interconvertible, the transformation being catalyzed by the enzyme triosephosphate isomerase. Glyceraldehyde phosphate may also be formed from, and give rise to, a 7-carbon sugar (sedoheptulose) and a 4-carbon sugar (erythrose). In fact, glyceraldehyde phosphate is the central compound of a series of converging metabolic pathways by which 7-carbon, 6-carbon, 4-carbon, and 3-carbon compounds may be converted into one another. See GLYCOLYSIS; PENTOSE PHOSPHATE PATHWAY.—*J. Fl.*

GLYCERIN (preferably **glycerol**): a viscous liquid used as a sweetening agent for foods, as a humectant for foods and tobacco, in toilet preparations, in antifreeze, and as an intermediate in the manufacture of nitroglycerin. It is a by-product of soap manufacture (for its structure see FATS AND OILS), and is made synthetically.—*Ru. M.*

GLYCOGEN: see SUGAR.

GLYCOL: ethylene glycol ($CH_2OH—CH_2OH$), a liquid important as an intermediate in the manufacture of other chemicals, and widely used as a coolant for airplane motors and antifreeze for automobile radiators. Open-chain compounds with two OH groups are in general called glycols.—*Ru. M.*

GLYCOLYSIS: the biochemical conversion of simple sugars (glucose, fructose) and complex plant and animal sugars (starches, glycogen) to lactic acid with the release of chemical energy. This process occurs in a large number of bacteria, protozoa, algae, insects, and higher plants and animals. Glycolysis is sometimes referred to as "animal fermentation," since the chemical changes which the sugar molecule undergoes during glycolysis are identical, up to a point, with those by which yeast cells ferment sugars to ethyl alcohol. The energy released in glycolysis is derived from a rearrangement of the atoms of carbon and hydrogen to an energy-poorer

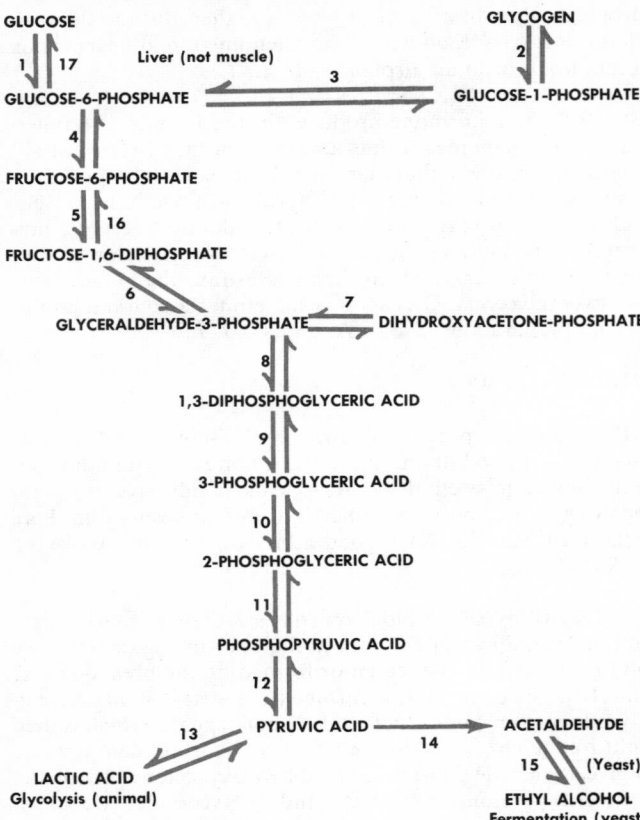

GLUCOSE

1 | 17   Liver (not muscle)

GLUCOSE-6-PHOSPHATE

GLYCOGEN

2

3

GLUCOSE-1-PHOSPHATE

4

FRUCTOSE-6-PHOSPHATE

5 | 16

FRUCTOSE-1,6-DIPHOSPHATE

6

GLYCERALDEHYDE-3-PHOSPHATE   7   DIHYDROXYACETONE-PHOSPHATE

8

1,3-DIPHOSPHOGLYCERIC ACID

9

3-PHOSPHOGLYCERIC ACID

10

2-PHOSPHOGLYCERIC ACID

11

PHOSPHOPYRUVIC ACID

12

13   PYRUVIC ACID   14   ACETALDEHYDE

LACTIC ACID
Glycolysis (animal)

15   (Yeast)

ETHYL ALCOHOL
Fermentation (yeast)

Summary of steps leading from carbohydrates to lactic acid (by glycolysis) or to ethyl alcohol (by fermentation). Numbers in diagram represent the following corresponding enzymes:

1. **Hexokinase**
2. **Phosphorylase**
3. **Phosphoglucomutase**
4. **Phosphohexose isomerase**
5. **Phosphofructokinase**
6. **Aldolase**
7. **Phosphotriose isomerase**
8. **Phosphoglyceraldehyde dehydrogenase**
9. **Phosphoglyceric kinase**
10. **Phosphoglyceromutase**
11. **Enolase**
12. **Pyruvic kinase**
13. **Lactic dehydrogenase**
14. **Carboxylase**
15. **Alcohol dehydrogenase**
16. **Diphosphofructose phosphatase**
17. **Glucose-6-phosphatase**

form, without an actual "burning" (oxidation) of glucose molecules to carbon dioxide and water. Glycolysis is therefore a means of deriving energy for bodily processes, *e.g.* muscular contraction, under conditions of oxygen lack, as during exercise. Though this is a quick way for tissues to produce necessary energy, it is also an inefficient one: of the total energy obtainable by complete combustion of glucose, only 8% is released on glycolysis (see also OXIDATIVE PHOSPHORYLATION).

The process of glycolysis consists of a sequence of intermediary reactions, each catalyzed by a specific enzyme and some requiring the presence of inorganic phosphate, adenine nucleotides, and NAD (see PYRIDINE NUCLEOTIDES). These reactions, elucidated by Meyerhof, Embden, Neuberg, Warburg, Cori, and Parnas, are shown schematically in the diagram. Glycogen initially is converted to molecules of glucose-1-phosphate by phosphorolysis through the action of phosphorylases. The reaction can also be initiated by the phosphorylation of glucose or fructose by the transfer of phosphate from adenosine triphosphate (ATP), catalyzed by hexokinases. Glucose-1-phosphate, glucose-6-phosphate, and fructose-6-phosphate are further phosphorylated to fructose-1,6-diphosphate, which is then cleaved to form two molecules of triosephosphate: namely, glyceraldehyde-3-phosphate and dihydroxyacetone phosphate. Triosephosphate is subsequently phosphorylated, oxidized (Step 8), dephosphorylated, rearranged and dehydrated (Steps 9–11), and finally dephosphorylated again (Step 12) to yield pyruvic acid. The hydrogen removed in the oxidation of triosephosphate to 1,3-diphosphoglyceric acid (Step 8) reduces the coenzyme nicotinamide adenine dinucleotide (NAD). Reduced coenzyme (NAD.H^+) is reoxidized in Step 13, in which simultaneously pyruvic acid is reduced to lactic acid, the end product of glycolysis. The diagram also

shows the essential similarity between glycolysis and alcoholic fermentation. In the latter process, pyruvic acid is first acted on by specific yeast carboxylase, resulting in liberation of CO_2. The acetaldehyde which is also produced is reduced by NAD.H^+ to yield ethyl alcohol, the other end product of fermentation.

The chemical energy which is released during glycolysis is contained in high-energy bonds (see ENERGY) of ATP molecules which are formed by transfer of phosphate from 1,3-diphosphoglyceric acid and phosphopyruvic acid to ADP (Steps 9 and 12). In the absence of oxygen (anaerobiosis), therefore, glycolysis is the only means of deriving energy from the metabolism of carbohydrate ("anaerobic glycolysis"). Aerobically, almost all of the carbohydrate undergoing breakdown passes through the steps of glycolysis up to the formation of pyruvic acid, which is then oxidized completely via the CITRIC-ACID CYCLE; carbohydrate may also be oxidized by way of the PENTOSE-PHOSPHATE PATHWAY. Only a small amount of lactic acid is formed ("aerobic glycolysis") in most tissues under these conditions. With the exception of a very few highly specialized tissues (*e.g.* the retina), significant aerobic glycolysis is encountered only in certain neoplastic tissues. This represents one of the very few known differences in the metabolism of normal and tumor tissue (see PASTEUR EFFECT).

Carbohydrate can be produced from lactic acid, or any other intermediate of glycolysis, by a reversal of the glycolytic process; this reverse process is referred to as glucogenesis. Liver is able to convert the end-product of muscle glycolysis (lactic acid) to glucose-6-phosphate, which may then be stored as glycogen or hydrolyzed by glucose-6-phosphatase to glucose, which is released to the blood and then becomes available to other cells and tissues. Muscle tissue can also form glucose-6-phosphate from lactic acid but, since it lacks the necessary enzyme, cannot liberate free glucose; instead glucose-6-phosphate is converted to, and stored as, muscle glycogen (reverse reaction of Steps 2 and 3). Brain tissue, which appears to be deficient in glycogen, depends for its principal source of energy on glucose supplied to it from other sources by way of the blood stream.

Glucose may be formed from a variety of chemical substances in addition to glycogen and intermediates of glycolysis. This formation of carbohydrate from non-carbohydrate sources is termed gluconeogenesis. Gluconeogenic materials include most of the amino acids (approximately 18), glycerol, and a variety of quantitatively less important substances. In plants, especially in germinating seeds, fatty acids are gluconeogenic. Possibly because of the lack of certain enzymes there is no good evidence of gluconeogenesis from fatty acids in humans and other non-ruminant animals.—*B. J. J. and J. J. O'N.*

GLYOXYLIC-ACID CYCLE: in biochemistry, a series of reactions akin to the CITRIC-ACID CYCLE, found in plants and micro-organisms; it converts fatty acids into carbohydrates. Isocitric acid is broken down to succinic and glyoxylic acids, under the influence of malic synthetase. The latter then condenses with acetyl coenzyme A to form malic acid. The complete cycle may be written:

Fats → acetyl coenzyme A
     +
oxalacetic acid —————————→ isocitric acid
     ↑
malic ←——— glyoxylic ←——————————┐ succinic
acid   acid + acetyl coenzyme A └→ acid
                    ↑
                   Fats

Since succinic acid is readily converted to carbohydrate via pyruvic acid, a net synthesis of carbohydrate can be achieved from fatty acids. This cycle is absent from animal tissues; hence animals cannot make a net conversion of fat to carbohydrate. See also FAT METABOLISM.—*K. H.*

GMELIN, LEOPOLD, 1788–1853, German chemist; b. Göttingen. He taught medicine and chemistry at Heidelberg, 1813–51, where his most famous pupil was F. Wöhler. Gmelin discovered potassium ferricyanide (*Gmelin's salt*) and a number of organic compounds, and introduced the terms "ester" and "ketone." Gmelin's reagent produces characteristic layers of colors with liquids containing bilirubin (bile pigment). Gmelin published *Handbuch der theoretischen Chemie* (from 1817), a textbook of chemical knowledge. From the 5th ed. (c. 1850) it dealt only with inorganic chemistry; since his death it has been issued under similar titles by various editors. The present (8th) ed. of Gmelin's *Handbuch der anorganischen Chemie* is edited by the Gmelin Institut staff.—*R. E. O.*

GNEISS: a coarsely crystalline rock showing distinct alignment of elongated minerals, a foliation, or a banded structure due to alternation of layers that have different mineralogies. Gneisses lack the prominent fissility of slates and schists, but break into thick blocks parallel to the foliation. Some gneisses

Hornblende granite gneiss, one of the common types of metamorphic rock, shows banding typical of some gneisses. Darker material here is hornblende. (*Amer. Mus. of Nat. Hist.*)

are formed by complete recrystallization of a layered or bedded rock such as a conglomerate, impure sandstone, shale, or volcanic flow under conditions of high temperature and pressure. Some banded gneisses, called *migmatites,* are formed by the injection of granitic material or quartz veins along the foliation planes of a schist. Many streaked *granite gneisses* are formed by the forced intrusion of granite masses while in a solid or near-solid condition, exhibiting the effects of shearing and brecciation. All these varieties are formed in the depths of geosynclines or mobile belts undergoing diastrophism. Many gneisses have about the same mineralogy as GRANITES, but those derived from other antecedents may contain garnet, andalusite, kyanite, sillimanite, scapolite, cordierite, and other silicates that do not normally result from crystallization of a magma.—*W. G. V.*

GODDARD, ROBERT HUTCHINGS, 1882–1945, U. S. physicist and rocket pioneer; b. Worcester, Mass. He became interested in the theory of rocket flight as early as 1906 and was the first man to build and launch a liquid-fuel rocket (1926). Continuing his rocket research at Roswell, N. Mex., he had his greatest success when one of his liquid-fuel rockets reached an altitude of 7,500 ft. Goddard has been

Robert Hutchings Goddard
(*Mrs. R. H. Goddard*)

called the first rocket engineer. His great contribution to high-altitude flight and space travel was belatedly recognized by the U. S. Government. Goddard's paper "A Method of Reaching Extreme Altitudes" was published by the Smithsonian Institution (1919).—*C. S. V.*

GÖDEL, KURT, 1906– , Czech mathematical logician; b. Brünn, Czechoslovakia. A member of the Institute for Advanced Study, Princeton, in 1933, 1935, and 1938–53, since 1953 he has been a professor there. He has made outstanding contributions to the study of foundations of mathematics (see GÖDEL'S PROOF), for which he was corecipient of the first Einstein Award, 1951. In "Die Vollständigkeit der Axiome des logischen Funktionenkalküls" (*Monatshefte für Math. und Phys.,* 1930) he showed that every logically valid formula of the first-order predicate calculus is provable, so that this calculus is complete. Other writings include "Über formal unentscheidbare Sätze der Principia Mathematica und verwandter Systeme I" (*Ibid.,* 1931) (see GÖDEL'S PROOF) and *The Consistency of the Axiom of Choice and of the Generalized Continuum Hypothesis with the Axioms of Set Theory* (1940), proving that if axiomatic set theory is consistent, then it remains consistent upon addition of the axiom of choice and the generalized continuum hypothesis. He is a member of the National Academy of Sciences.—*El. M.*

GÖDEL'S PROOF: The hope of finding a consistent and complete formal axiomatic system for mathematics was thoroughly shattered by a paper published by Kurt Gödel in 1931. Gödel showed that, under a certain consistency assumption, any "sufficiently strong" formal axiomatic system for mathematics must contain an undecidable proposition, that is, a sentence such that neither it nor its negation is provable. Moreover, any consistency proof for the system must use ideas and methods which go beyond the resources of the system itself.

Suppose we are given a formal axiomatic system L (cf. SYNTAX, LOGICAL). It was Gödel's idea to associate with each expression (or sequence of expressions) in L an integer, called the Gödel number of the expression or sequence of expressions. The following examples illustrate how this is done. Suppose L contains the symbols $'='$, $'x'$, and $'y'$, and that their Gödel numbers are 3, 11, and 13, respectively. The Gödel number of the formula $'x=y'$, constructed out of these three symbols, is then $2^{11} \cdot 3^3 \cdot 5^{13}$, which is the product of the first three primes each raised to a power equal to the Gödel number of the corresponding symbol; and analogously, the Gödel number of the formula $'y = x'$ is $2^{13} \cdot 3^3 \cdot 5^{11}$. Similarly, the Gödel number of the sequence of formulas $'x = y'$, $'y = x'$ is $2^a \cdot 3^b$, where a is the Gödel number of the first formula in the sequence and b the Gödel number of the second formula. The rules for assigning Gödel numbers can be stated in general form, and they guarantee that different expressions have different Gödel numbers. Moreover, an important consequence of associating numbers with expressions in L is that concepts and operations concerning the system L have corresponding numerical concepts and operations. For example, to the notion of formula of L corresponds the class of Gödel numbers of formulas of L; to the operation of substituting some constant for a variable in a formula of L corresponds the function which associates with the Gödel numbers of the constant, the variable, and the formula, respectively, the Gödel number of the formula resulting from the substitution; to the notion of proof corresponds the class of Gödel numbers of proofs (since a proof is a certain kind of sequence of expressions).

A number-theoretic predicate $R(x_1, \ldots, x_n)$ (e.g. $x_1 > x_2 + x_3 + \ldots + x_n$) is said to be representable in L if there is some formula $C(y_1, \ldots, y_n)$ of L such that, for any non-negative integers $k_1, \ldots, k_n$, if $R(k_1, \ldots, k_n)$ is true then $C(k_1, \ldots, k_n)$ is provable in L; and if $R(k_1, \ldots, k_n)$ is false, then the negation of $C(k_1, \ldots, k_n)$ is provable in L. (We assume that there is a way to "substitute" any numeral m for any variable y in any formula of L. This is true for any system L which, in some sense, contains elementary number theory, and certainly any system aiming to formalize mathematics must contain at least that much.) A numerical function $f(x_1, \ldots, x_n)$ is said to be representable in L if there is some formula $D(y_1, \ldots, y_n, u)$ in L such that, for any non-negative integers $k_1, \ldots, k_n, m$, if $f(k_1, \ldots, k_n) = m$ then the formula $(\forall u) (D(k_1, \ldots, k_n, u) \longleftrightarrow u = m)$ (i.e. for all u, $D(k_1, \ldots, k_n, u)$ if and only if $u = m$)) is provable in L. Now, if L contains a small fragment of number theory (e.g. Peano's postulates are more than enough), then it turns out that many of the numerical concepts and functions corresponding to syntactical concepts concerning the system L are representable in L. (This is proved by means of the theory of recursive functions; see DECISION PROBLEM AND DECISION PROCEDURE.) In this way, certain statements about L can be formulated within L itself. In particular, the following complicated predicate $B(u, v)$ is representable in L. $B(u, v)$: v is the Gödel number of a formula of L obtained from a formula with Gödel number u by substituting the number u for the variable "x_1." Let $\mathcal{B}(x_1, x_2)$ be the representing formula in L of the predicate $B(u, v)$. Consider the formula $(*)$ $(\forall x_2) \sim B(x_1, x_2)$ (where "$\sim$" stands for "not" and "$\forall x$" for "for all x"). Let this formula have Gödel number n. Then the formula $(**)$ $(\forall x_2) \sim \mathcal{B}(n, x_2)$ is the formula obtained from $(*)$ by substituting the Gödel number of $(*)$ for the variable "x_1." Thus, $(**)$ expresses, under the standard interpretation of the symbols, its own unprovability. (It is analogous to the Liar Paradox: "I am lying.") It is easy to prove that: (I) If L is consistent, then $(**)$ is not provable in L. (II) If L is

ω-consistent, then the negation of $(**)$ is not provable in L. (A system is ω-consistent if, whenever a formula $H(n)$ is provable for each numeral n, the formula $\sim(\forall x) H(x)$ [i.e. it is not the case that, for all x, $H(x)$] is not provable.) By a modification of Gödel's argument, Rosser in 1936 reduced the assumption of ω-consistency to ordinary consistency, constructing a sentence A such that if L is consistent, then neither A nor its negation $\sim A$ is provable in L. Thus, if L is consistent and contains a small fragment of elementary number theory, it contains undecidable propositions. In addition, by using Gödel numbers, the result (I) was formalized by Gödel into a proof within L of a formula $\text{Con}(L) \rightarrow (**)$, where $\text{Con}(L)$ is a formal counterpart of the assertion that L is consistent. (For example, $\text{Con}(L)$ may be the arithmetic formalization of: "There is no formula A of L such that both A and $\sim A$ are theorems of L.") Thus, if L is consistent, then $\text{Con}(L)$ is not provable within L; for, otherwise, $(**)$ would be provable, contradicting (I). Thus, in addition to proving that any attempt to set up a complete axiomatic formalization of mathematics is futile, Gödel's theorem also shows that any proof of the consistency of the formal system L must use methods and notions not contained within L itself.—*El. M.*

GOLD: a metallic element (Au); at. no. 79; at. wt 197.0; density 19.42; mp 1063°C.; bp 2600°C. Gold occurs naturally as the free metal and as the mixed telluride $AuAgTe_4$. It was one of the first elements to be discovered and has always been highly valued. Since antiquity it has been used for ornamental objects and as a medium of exchange. Because it is quite soft, gold is usually hardened by alloying with small amounts of copper or nickel; the gold content of the alloy is specified in terms of carats, or 24th parts. Pure gold is accordingly designated 24 carats; 14-carat gold is $^{14}\!/_{24}$ gold and the rest alloying metal. Chemically, gold is noted for its resistance to oxidation. It can be dissolved in aqua regia to form the complex ion $AuCl_4^-$, and can also be dissolved by aqueous potassium cyanide—a process used in winning gold from its ores.—*A. M. S.*

GOLDEN NUMBER: see CALENDAR.

GOLDEN SECTION (or **golden ratio**): numerically, the ratio 1 to $\frac{1}{2} (\sqrt{5} - 1)$, or approximately 1.618 to 1, or, more roughly, 8 to 5. This ratio was called "golden" by the Greeks because they considered the rectangle having its sides in this ratio to be esthetically more pleasing than any other. It was used in

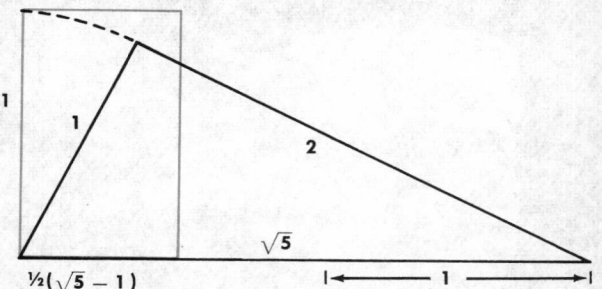

Geometrical construction of a rectangle the lengths of whose sides are in the golden ratio $1 : \frac{1}{2} (\sqrt{5} - 1)$.

determining not only rectangular shapes but also the ratios of dimensions of many other artistic creations. The golden section may be defined as the ratio of a line segment to one part of it such that the whole is to the part as that part is to the other. If the line is 1 unit long, divided into s and $1 - s$, then

$$\frac{1}{s} = \frac{s}{1 - s}$$

from which $s^2 + s - 1 = 0$. The positive solution of this equation is $s = \frac{1}{2}(\sqrt{5} - 1)$. The ratio of 1 to s is therefore $2/(\sqrt{5} - 1)$, or 1.618 approximately. Geometrically, this ratio is that of the radius of a regular decagon to its side. The golden section is fundamental in a modern theory of art known as dynamic symmetry. The ratio also appears in many natural phenomena; *e.g.* the spiral shells of some mollusks and the structures of certain plants.—*H. C.*

GOLDSCHMIDT, VIKTOR MORITZ, 1888–1947, Norwegian geochemist; b. Zurich, Switz. His research on the crystal structure of ionic compounds laid the foundation of the science of crystal chemistry, and his work on trace elements revolutionized knowledge of the distribution of the minor constituents of Earth's crust. He also investigated the composition of rocks altered by contact and zonal metamorphism.—*D. H. D. R.*

GOLGI, CAMILLO, 1844–1936, Italian anatomist; b. Corteno. His early research was on the lymphatics of the brain and on the nature of the neuroglia. Golgi developed his silver-impregnation method of staining nervous tissues (1873) and applied it to the central nervous system, discovering the two types of *Golgi cells* and obtaining evidence for the neuron theory. He also made many contributions to nerve pathology. In recognition of their work on the structure of the nervous system, Golgi and S. Ramón y Cajal shared the Nobel prize for 1906.—*D. H. D. R.*

GONAD: an animal organ that produces sex cells (GAMETES). The female gonad, called an OVARY, produces eggs; the male gonad, called a TESTIS, produces sperms. The ovotestis of HERMAPHRODITES (*e.g.* snails) produces both.—*R. G. M.*

GONADOTROPHINS: in physiology, a group of hormones which act as growth-promoting agents on the gonads (testis and ovary). The pituitary gland produces two types: follicle-stimulating hormone (FSH), which directs production of spermatozoa and ova; and luteinizing hormone (LH), which promotes secretion of the sex hormones testosterone and progesterone. During pregnancy the placenta produces a similarly acting hormone, chorionic gonadotrophin, the presence of which in the urine is the basis of the usual pregnancy tests. See HORMONES.—*J. F. S.*

GOODYEAR, CHARLES, 1800–60, U. S. inventor; b. New Haven, Conn. In 1834 he began work on a method for treating India rubber so that it could withstand temperature changes and abrasion. Combining a nitric-acid treatment with a sulfurizing process, 1839, he was successful. Part of a sample of his rubberized fabric which had dropped accidentally on a hot stove was found to be perfectly cured. Goodyear patented his new rubber "vulcanization" process in 1844. He described his discovery in *Gum Elastic and Its Varieties* (1853).—*S. B.*

GOUDSMIT, SAMUEL ABRAHAM, 1902– , Dutch-U. S. physicist; b. The Hague. His research has been on statistical problems in physics, the atomic-structure theory of spectra, and nuclear spin. He and G. E. Uhlenbeck used the hypothesis of electron spin effectively in a classical model of the atom (1925). During World War II, Goudsmit headed the Alsos Mission to evaluate Germany's progress in atomic weapons. In 1948 he joined the Brookhaven National Laboratory as senior scientist. He is a member of the National Academy of Sciences.—*D. H. D. R.*

GRAAF, REGNIER DE, 1641–73, Dutch anatomist; b. Schoonhoven. He investigated digestion and the anatomy of the sex organs, conducting (1663) experiments with the pancreas, and discovering (1672) the ovarian follicles that bear his name. Graaf reported on the functions of the juice of the pancreas in *De natura et usu succi pancreatici* (1663) and described female organs of generation in his *De mulierum organis generationi inservientibus* (1672).—*D. H. D. R.*

GRABEN: in geology, a term (German for "ditch" or "grave") referring to a block of Earth's crust which, as a result of FAULTING, has sunk relative to surrounding blocks; the term is considered by many geologists as essentially synonymous with rift valley. Grabens usually occur in groups, each member being separated from the others by minor faults, and the group being defined by great faults. Grabens are generally long in comparison with their width, and the bedrock of the sunken area is more or less completely covered with sediments and volcanics, which may be hundreds or even thousands of feet thick. A graben may be open at one or both ends (thus being a *fault trough*) or completely enclosed (*fault basin*). The grabens occupied in part by Great Salt Lake, Utah, are connected and hence are fault troughs. The Imperial Valley in SE California is a fault trough closed at its

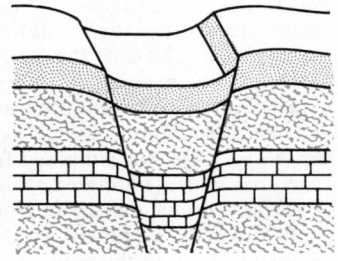

Fault-trough variety of graben (highly simplified here) is open at one or both ends. Fault basins are closed.

northern end. Death Valley, E California, and the Jordan-Dead Sea depression in Asia Minor are fault basins. In the last two, there is abundant evidence of recent faulting; in many others, erosion and deposition have so obscured the faults that the origin of the troughs or basins must be determined by indirect evidence, chiefly topographic.—*J. Sh.*

GRADATION: in geology, the wearing down (degradation) of higher eminences of Earth's crust and the building up (aggradation) of lower portions by the force of gravity and various agents of EROSION. These agents are running water (the most important), underground water, glaciers, winds, waves, and currents. Rock debris transported from higher parts of Earth is deposited in lower regions, most of it eventually being carried into the ocean.—*J. Sh.*

GRAFTING: the process of removing some part of an organism (this part being called the *graft*) and relocating it under conditions that allow it to unite with the tissue at the new site and continue to grow. Grafting is important in surgery, experimental biology, and horticulture. A graft from one location on an individual to another location on the same individual is an *autograft*; if the graft is from one individual to another of the same species, it is a *homograft*; and if it is to an individual of a different species, it is a *heterograft*. An extreme example of grafting is *parabiosis,* the surgical union of two animals to produce artificial Siamese twins.

In man, extensive loss of skin is made good by grafting thin sheets of skin obtained from the patient's own body. If the cornea of the eye becomes opaque or is damaged, sight

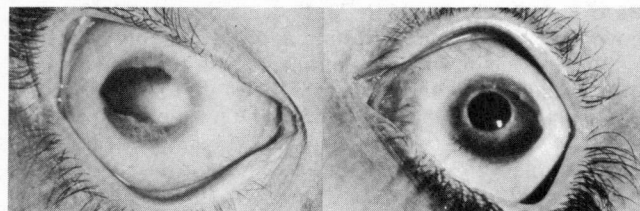

Before and after: eye with damaged cornea (*left*), and same eye with corneal transplant. (*Eye-Bank for Sight Restoration, Inc.*)

may be restored by replacing it with a corneal homograft obtained from a cadaver. Blood transfusions are really transplantations of blood cells. Unfortunately, with one or two exceptions (including that of the cornea) homografts do not usually survive for more than a week or two. The cells of different individuals differ with respect to the presence or absence of genetically determined biochemical ingredients known as *iso-antigens*; thus, like invading microorganisms, tissue homografts confront their hosts with substances that are "foreign" to them, they evoke an immunological response, and they are destroyed. If there is no genetic difference between donor and host, as in the case of identical twins, then tissues and organs as complex as kidneys can be grafted between them with permanent success. Blood transfusions are successful because the iso-antigens of donor red cells can be matched with those of the recipient.

In embryos amazing graft/host combinations can be made experimentally because the transplantation of tissues is not restricted by immunological considerations at this stage of life. Tissues can be combined from embryos of two *different* species as widely unrelated as mice and chickens. Our knowledge of the mechanism of embryonic differentiation—the progressive development of distinctive components in an embryo leading to the complexity of functional and morphological diversification of the adult—derives from grafting experiments. These have shown how one embryonic tissue influences another, affecting its differentiation. For example,

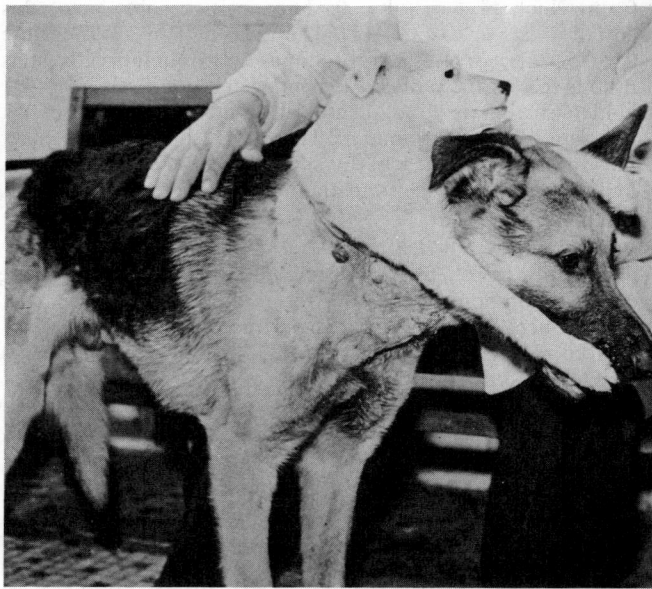

Puppy's head was grafted onto mature dog at First Moscow Medical Institute. For a month (until death) puppy's head remained mobile and alert, indicating retention of nerve connections and brain activities. (*Sovfoto*)

the lens of the eye develops from the epidermis of the skin as a consequence of a stimulus received from a component of the embryonic brain lying below it.

In plants, the purpose of grafting is to perpetuate, by propagation on established root systems, forms that are either infertile or will not breed true from seed. If a small bud or portion of a twig (the scion) from one plant is inserted into an incision in another (the stock) so that living cells of both components are juxtaposed, permanent union may occur. Grafting is possible only between related types of plants, and compatibility depends upon relative growth rates of stock and scion and the strength of the union.—*R. E. B.*

GRAHAM, THOMAS, 1805–69, Scottish chemist; b. Glasgow. In 1934 he formulated *Graham's law*: Relative diffusion rates of gases are inversely proportional to the square root of their density. His studies of the three forms of phosphoric acid (1833) led to the concept of polybasic acids. He established the study of colloid chemistry and developed the process of dialysis for separation of crystalloids from colloids. Graham's *Elements of Chemistry* appeared in 1841, and *Chemical and Physical Researches* in 1876. He was a fellow of the Royal Society.—*A. I.*

GRANITE: a common rock, generally classed as igneous (*i.e.* formed from magma), but in some cases resulting from metamorphism. It is invariably formed at depth, and may appear as an outcrop of colossal dimensions (batholith) or as a thin band interfingering within other rock. Granite is coarse-grained, light in color, and composed almost entirely of silicates. The most numerous of its crystals are potash feldspar; the remainder are plagioclase feldspar (sodium or calcium aluminum silicate) and quartz (silica); small amounts of mica, hornblende, and other ferromagnesian minerals may also be present. Granite is the type rock of SIAL. The proportion of the minerals in sialic magma that produces a granite

Granite quarry: Granites that are exposed cores of ancient mountain ranges occur in large masses. Granites of even texture and durability are prized. (*Rock of Ages Corp.*)

is confined to a certain compositional range; any alteration of this proportion will produce a rock similar to but not identical with granite. Thus, a substitution of plagioclase for much of the potash feldspar and quartz would produce diorite; a common rock intermediate between granite and diorite is granodiorite. The coarse grain which gives granite its name is likely to be the result of slow cooling, possible only at depth. A magma capable of forming granite would, if cooled quickly, become the fine-grained rock rhyolite or, if very suddenly cooled, glassy obsidian: these rocks are the common extrusive equivalents of granite. Because of its hardness and resistance to weathering, granite is an important building material.

A process called **granitization** accounts for some granites. For example, certain formations of sedimentary rock grade into the metamorphic rock schist, and in some instances the schist is penetrated by layers or interfingering of a mixed rock (migmatite) which in turn grades into granite. This phenomenon, which could not be produced by igneous intrusion, is explained as a process of metamorphism, during which material passes through the rock while the rock remains solid and in place, causing the substitution of elements found in granite (the sodium and potassium of feldspar) for the elements already existing in the rock (*e.g.* iron or magnesium). The previous rock is thus transformed into granite metamorphically; granite formed in this way must be considered a metamorphic rock. This may explain how plutons take shape amidst pre-existing sedimentary rock formations, leaving no evidence that these formations were displaced or that they even existed. The extent to which granitization may account for granites generally remains, however, controversial. —E. A.

GRAPH: a chart or diagram used to represent data pictorially. Common types are the circular percentage (or pie) chart, bar graphs, pictographs, and broken-line and curved-line graphs. The basic ideas of graphical representation were discovered by René Descartes, who recognized that it was possible to develop a correspondence between the basic geometric element, a point, and the basic algebraic element, a number. For example, on a straight line mark two points and assign the numbers 0 and 1 to them. Then use the distance between them as a unit distance and measure off distances of 2, 3, 4, etc. Assign to every point a number which represents its distance to the point 0. Thus we have a correspondence between all real numbers and the points on a line. A line on which such a correspondence has been set up is called a one-dimensional coordinate system. Now, if two one-dimensional coordinate systems are set up so that one line (or axis) is perpendicular to the other, we get a two-dimensional rectangular coordinate system. In this system, we now have a correspondence between a point in the plane and a pair of real numbers, called the coordinates of the point. Fig. 1 is a graph of the industrial production in the U. S. from 1948 through 1958. The index of industrial production in each month was plotted, and the successive points were joined by straight line segments. Here the data are discrete and, in such cases, only the plotted points have meaning, the broken lines serving only to carry the eye from point to point. Such data could also have been represented by a vertical bar graph, the bar being drawn to show the height of each point.

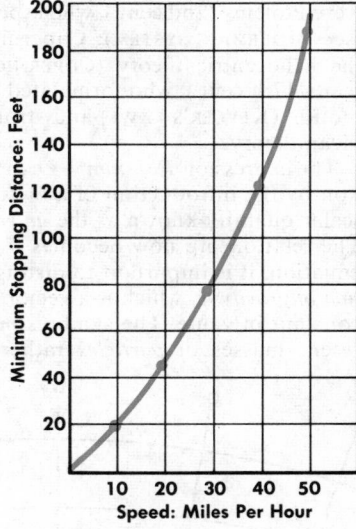

Fig. 2: Graph of minimum stopping distance vs. speed, based on the following data:

Mi/hr	10	20	30	40	50
Min. Stopping Distance (ft)	20	45	78	125	188

A smooth curve is drawn to connect the points on a graph when the data are continuous. For example, the minimum distance for stopping an automobile traveling at various speeds is shown in the table and graphed in Fig. 2. Here the independent variable (speed) can be any real positive number, and so the table only represents a partial selection of these. The smooth curve suggests approximately all of the possible pairs of values for this functional relation. If a relation contains more than two variables, we need more than two dimensions to draw its graph. Three-dimensional graphs can be constructed but we are unable to visualize graphs in more than three dimensions.—H. E. W.

GRAPHITE: a crystalline form of carbon. The carbon atoms in graphite are positioned as sheets of hexagons. These layers, held together by weak forces, slide easily over one another, making graphite an excellent lubricant, in contrast to diamond, which has a tetrahedral carbon structure rather than the layer structure, and is therefore very hard. Naturally occurring impure amorphous graphite, mixed with clay and fired, is used for lead pencils: the higher the proportion of clay, the harder the pencil lead. Since graphite is chemically quite inert, except toward oxygen at high temperatures, it is widely used for making metallurgical crucibles and electrodes. —G. W. M.

GRASSMANN, HERMANN GÜNTHER, 1809–77, German mathematician and Sanskrit scholar; b. Stettin. His mathematical researches led him to write of calculus of extension in his *Lineale Ausdehnungslehre* (1844), in which he developed an *n*-dimensional vector analysis. This was a milestone in 19th-cent. mathematics.—H. C.

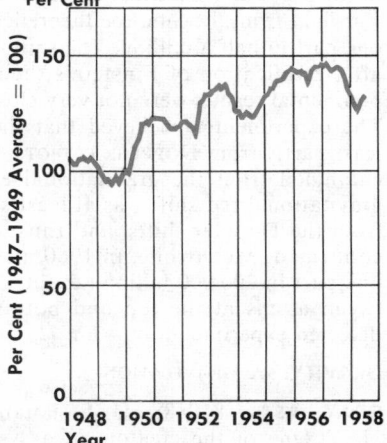

Fig. 1: Graph of U. S. industrial production.

GRAVITATION: the force of attraction between two masses. Isaac Newton was the first to conceive of weight as gravitational attraction between a body and Earth, and to assume correctly that the same force of gravity, combined with inertial force, explains the movements of astronomical bodies. Newton stated that every particle in the universe attracts every other particle with a force directly proportional to the product of their masses and inversely proportional to the square of the distance between them ($F \propto mm'/r^2$). It was natural for him to turn his attention to celestial bodies since, on Earth, the distance between a body and Earth could not be varied greatly, and the force of attraction between two different bodies on Earth was too feeble to be detected by methods then available. Newton's predecessors in astronomy were Ptolemy (2nd cent.), who espoused the geocentric theory (see PTOLEMAIC SYSTEM); Copernicus (16th cent.), who held the heliocentric theory (COPERNICAN SYSTEM); and Kepler (early 17th cent.), who formulated his three laws of planetary motion (KEPLER'S LAWS) and strongly supported the Copernican theory.

The expression $F \propto mm'/r^2$ can be converted into an equation by the introduction of a factor of proportionality G—a scalar quantity known as the *universal gravitational constant.* The relationship now becomes $F = Gmm'/r^2$. In using this equation, it is important to distinguish G from the *acceleration of gravity, g,* which is a vector quantity and by no means constant in value. The symbols m and m' theoretically represent masses of *particles* rather than those of extended

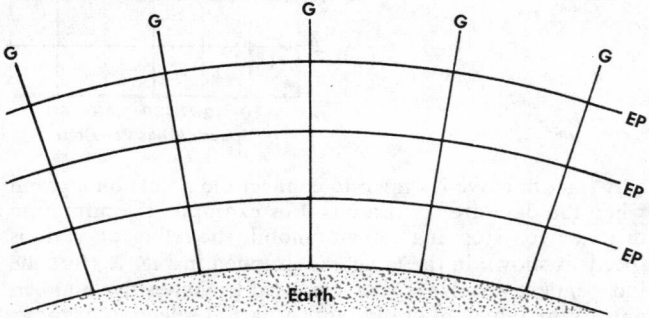

Equipotential lines in gravitational field around Earth form concentric circles perpendicular to the gradient lines.

bodies, but if spheres of uniform density are considered, their total masses may be substituted for the $m's$ without error. The distance between such spheres, r, is then the distance between their centers of mass.

The value of G was first determined experimentally by Lord Cavendish in 1798, using a torsional balance. He placed two small metal balls at the ends of a light rod suspended horizontally from a vertical, stretched quartz fiber. When two larger spheres were brought near the small ones, the transverse rod was rotated and the supporting quartz fiber was twisted through a small but measurable angle. Knowing the angle of twist, the torsion constant of the fiber, the masses of the attracting spheres, and their separation, Cavendish was able to compute the value of G, essentially a measure of the force between unit masses at unit distance. Today's highly accurate figure of G (6.673×10^{-11} newton-meter^2/kg^2) was determined by P. R. Heyl of the National Bureau of Standards.

The *gravitational field* is a vector field of force surrounding every material body. Newton did not use the concept of field, but relied instead on action-at-a-distance. It was Michael Faraday who, on the basis of his magnetic experiments, introduced the idea of the field, conceiving it as a sort of stressed medium filled with lines or "tubes" of force. The

intensity of the gravitational field, E, is the force exerted on a unit of mass placed in the field. This may be expressed symbolically as $E = F/m$. The definition is identical with that given for magnetic and electrostatic intensity.

The *gravitational potential, V,* as distinguished from gravitational intensity, is the potential energy, with reference to a datum line, acquired by a unit mass placed in a gravitational field. If we displace a particle of mass m from infinity (where the gravitational potential energy is zero) to some point nearer the reference plane, work will be done *by* the attractive forces acting on m, and a negative potential, equal to W/m, will be established at the point reached. Conversely, potential energy per unit mass may be regarded as positive if the body is moved away from the reference plane to some point farther from it. In the second case, work will have to be performed on the body *against* the force of gravitational attraction. It is important to note that the exact path covered by the body, as it changes its elevation, does not alter the value of the gravitational potential acquired.

The diagram shows a number of lines, marked *EP*, drawn above the surface of Earth and joining points of equal gravitational potential. Such lines (actually, surfaces) are called *equipotentials.* No work whatever is done on or by the body if it moves along an equipotential. Work is involved, however, if the motion takes place at right angles to the equipotentials, along gravitational *gradients* (marked G in the diagram). Gradients may also be considered lines of gravitational force and represent directions along which Newton's traditional apples fell from the tree under which he is supposed to have sat. As noted above, there is a striking similarity here to magnetic and electrical equipotentials and gradients.

Einstein's theory of gravity assumes space—a Riemannian manifold in four dimensions—to be so "warped" by the presence of material bodies as to cause a particle projected into space to travel along a *geodesic* line, which is the shortest and most direct path between any two points in the space-time continuum. Einstein's theory also predicted the deflection of light as it passed close to the rim of the Sun, as well as the red shift of spectral lines in strong gravitational fields. Astronomical observations have sustained these predictions. See GRAVITATIONAL RED SHIFT; RELATIVITY.—*A. E.*

GRAVITATIONAL RED SHIFT: According to Einstein's general theory of RELATIVITY, gravitation affects time: in a sense, time processes go more slowly the more deeply negative the gravitational potential is. Light reaching Earth from atoms on a star thus has lower frequency than light emitted by similar atoms on the much less massive Earth. Because lower frequency causes a shift of spectral lines toward the red end of the spectrum, the effect is called the gravitational red shift. For light from the Sun, the theoretical change in frequency is one part in half a million. The shift was first detected shortly after publication of Einstein's theory, but some of the experimental results were not very close to the predicted value. The experimenters believed that the discrepancies arose at least partly from DOPPLER EFFECTS, which are not easily disentangled from the gravitational effect. In 1961 the solar gravitational red shift was at least successfully disentangled from the Doppler shifts, and Einstein's prediction was well confirmed. Meanwhile, in 1960, the theoretical red shift of one part in 200,000 billion (about 1 sec in 10 million yr) between atoms at the top and bottom of a 76-ft tower was detected experimentally.—*Ba. H.*

GRAVITY: see GRAVITATION.

GRAY, ASA, 1810–88, U. S. botanist; b. Oneida County, N. Y. One of the creators of a systematic classification of

North American flora, he wrote *Manual of Botany of the Northern U. S.* (1848), *How Plants Grow* (1858), and *Statistics of the Flora of the Northern U. S.* (1856). In *Darwiniana* (1876), a collection of essays on evolution, he supported Darwin against Agassiz. His *Scientific Papers* were published in 1889. He was a fellow of the Royal Society.—*D. J. S.*

GRAY, STEPHEN, *c.* 1667–1736, English physicist; birthplace unknown. He studied electrical phenomena and discovered (1729) electrical conduction, the transference of electrical charge from one object to another. His discovery is described in "A Letter . . . Containing Several Experiments Concerning Electricity" (1731). Gray and his colleagues transmitted electrical charges over hundreds of feet of string from one object to another. He was a fellow of the Royal Society.—*D. H. D. R.*

GREASE: a class of lubricants, originally thick crude oils or semisolid fats, now specially prepared solid or semisolid dispersions of metallic soaps or inorganic thickeners in lubricating oils, to which chemical products like esters or silicones are sometimes added. Calcium, lithium, sodium, aluminum, and sometimes barium soaps as well as treated clays are used as thickeners. The fatty material, alkali, and a portion of the oil are heated in a closed pressure vessel or open kettle until the formation of soap is complete. The rest of the oil and thickeners are added, and the mixture is homogenized by stirring; small quantities of water, alkali, acid, or oil are later added to achieve the correct stiffness. Cheap, semisolid sett greases are made from rosin oil, alkali, and mineral oil. Greases are generally used when parts to be lubricated are difficult to get at, or when there is danger that a liquid lubricant will contaminate a product being processed. Greases are classified by the nature of the thickening agent and by their hardness and melting point. See LUBRICATION.—*R. J. F.*

GREEN FLASH: a brilliant blue-green coloration of the last bit of the Sun's disc to disappear at sunset. When the Sun sets behind a distant horizon in very clear air, the atmosphere acts as a weak prism, dispersing the sunlight into a spectrum. Green and blue are refracted slightly more than red and yellow, and so remain above the horizon for a few seconds longer.—*D. H. L.*

GREGORY, JAMES, 1638–1675, Scottish mathematician; b. near Aberdeen. In his *Vera quadratura* (1667), *Exercitationes geometricae* (1668), *Geometriae pars universalis* (1668), and correspondence he contributed in an original way to the invention of the calculus, anticipating Newton in the announcement of the BINOMIAL THEOREM (1670) and Taylor in the discovery of "Taylor's series" (1671). He was a fellow of the Royal Society.—*D. J. S.*

GREW, NEHEMIAH, 1641–1712, English physician and naturalist; b. Mancetter. He introduced the expression "comparative anatomy" in his *Comparative Anatomy of Trunks* (1675) and *Comparative Anatomy of the Stomach and Guts* (1681). Using an early compound microscope, he studied the anatomy of plant stems and roots from thin sections, and published handsome illustrations of these in his great *Anatomy of Plants* (1682). He guessed that the flowers of plants include reproductive parts related to two sexes, and he named the parts, but did not follow up his important idea with any experimental proof. He was a fellow of the Royal Society.—*L. and M. M.*

GRIGNARD, FRANÇOIS AUGUSTE VICTOR, 1871–1935, French chemist; b. Cherbourg. He described the method by which organic compounds of magnesium are prepared in the presence of ether. For the discovery of the *Grignard reagents*, used in synthesis of organic compounds, he shared the 1912 Nobel prize in chemistry with P. Sabatier. Grignard also worked on the production of toluene from heavy oils by cracking.—*E. F.*

GRIMALDI, FRANCESCO MARIA, 1618–63, Italian physicist; b. Bologna. In his *Physico-mathesis de lumine, coloribus, et iride* (*Physicomathematical Studies of Light, Colors, and the Rainbow*), 1665, he described a new optical phenomenon: that a beam of white light passing through two successive small apertures and falling on a screen produces a white spot larger than would be expected, and with colored edges. He named this phenomenon DIFFRACTION.—*D. H. D. R.*

GRINDING: removal of excess stock, usually metal, by the rotary action of abrasive-bonded wheels or the travel of abrasive-coated, machine-driven belts. (Manual use of coated abrasives, oilstones, whetstones, or hones is not considered grinding.) Most grinding is done by abrasive wheels in the shape of straight wheels, cylinders, cups, and cones. In the manufacturing of grinding wheels, ABRASIVE grains of selected grit size are mixed with the bonding material, and the bond is fused by heat. The most common bonding materials are clays, kiln-fired to form vitrified wheels. Next most common is the resinoid bond, cured in ovens. Others are rubber, shellac, silicate of soda, and oxychloride of magnesium.

Ratio of bond to abrasive determines a wheel's grade or "hardness." A grinding wheel properly selected for hardness tends to be self-sharpening, since the dull grains will break away as the work progresses to expose fresh, sharp grains. Harder grades release grains more slowly.

Rough grinding is done for fast removal of material, *i.e.* to clean metal castings, remove burrs or other imperfections, grind down welds, condition steel billets, etc. Abrasive sawing, by means of a thin cut-off wheel, is a specialized form. Precision grinders have mechanisms that control the infeed of the wheel to the work within close limits of accuracy, often within ten-thousandths of an inch or finer. Other mechanisms vary work speed, wheel speed, or both. Principal types of precision grinders are cylindrical (external), centerless, internal, surface, and universal. "Cylindrical," "centerless," and "internal" refer to cylindrical surfaces; "surface" to flat surfaces. Cylindrical grinders hold the work between "centers";

Polishing a diamond after cutting: Porous iron wheel, covered with diamond dust mixed with olive oil, and rotating at 2,500 rev/min, does polishing. (*South African Information Service*)

i.e., conical steel pins that fit into center holes in the work-piece. Centerless grinders use guides to direct the work between grinding and work-regulating wheels. Universal grinders are capable of doing both external and internal cylindrical grinding.

Precision grinders accomplish the same objective as machine tools such as lathes and milling machines; namely, the removal of metal to specified tolerances. Where the grinder does it by abrasive action, the machine tool does it by cutting off tiny metal chips. This is more likely to leave deeper scratches on the work than grinding. Hence grinding is the preferred process where very close tolerances and extremely smooth surfaces are desired.

Lapping, polishing, and buffing are refined finishing processes related to grinding. Lapping employs either very fine abrasive wheels operating at low speed or else a lapping compound (fine abrasive) used in conjunction with leather, wood, or soft-metal laps. Little stock is removed, but the surface finish, concentricity (in round work) or flatness, and parallelism are greatly improved. Polishing is done by soft abrasive wheels, often made of sewed canvas, or by coated-abrasive belts. It is an intermediate step between grinding and buffing. Buffing uses soft cloth wheels and a buffing compound. The amount of stock removed is negligible, but a mirror finish is produced on the work. Polishing and buffing are often done to prepare parts for plating.—*C. B. C.*

GROPIUS, WALTER ADOLF GEORG, 1883–   , German-U. S. architect; b. Berlin. Known for his functional designs, he is the author of such books as *The New Architecture and the Bauhaus* (1935), *Rebuilding Our Communities* (1945), and *Scope of Total Architecture* (1955). Founder and director (1919–28) of the Bauhaus at Weimar (later at Dessau), he left Nazi Germany in 1934 and taught at Harvard (1938–52). —*D. H. D. R.*

GROUND, ELECTRIC: an electrical connection deliberately made between the earth and a part of an electrical system Grounding is required to protect persons from electric shocks and equipment from damage, both of which may result from large currents being diverted by a short circuit to an unforeseen path, *e.g.* through a machine operator or the chassis of equipment. Protection is accomplished by grounding one terminal of the supplying generator, grounding the return conductor to this terminal, and grounding any part of the equipment with which a person may come in contact. If there is a short circuit, the current, instead of building up to a dangerous potential, takes the path through the ground wire, through the earth, returning to the grounded generator terminal and thus completing the circuit. The "fault current" resulting from the short circuit is just enough to operate protective devices (*e.g.* blow a fuse), but not enough to damage equipment or injure persons (if normal precautions are observed). Wind blowing over miles of transmission line, or the rotating parts of a machine, can build up a dangerous charge of static electricity, which a ground connection can safely discharge, again eliminating the danger of electric shock and also avoiding the possibility of an explosion caused by sparking in an atmosphere containing flammable gases. In addition to its safety function, grounding has been used in single-wire telegraphy circuits (which have been largely discontinued) to enable the earth to be used as a return conductor. Similarly, the steel structure of an automobile, also called a ground, completes the ignition circuit as well as providing an alternative return circuit to preserve the safety of the car's occupants should any fault arise in the ignition system. In general, the potential of ground or of a ground connection is taken to be zero.—*A. L.*

GROUND STATE: the lowest possible energy state of a system of particles (*e.g.* atom). Unless energy is supplied, the system will persist in this state indefinitely. See ENERGY LEVEL. —*S. Bo.*

GROUND WATER: water contained underground in the interstices of soil and rock. When rain falls on the earth, some evaporates, some is absorbed by plants, some runs off in streams, and the remainder sinks into the earth to become ground water. The amount that enters the ground depends on various factors: rain falling on loose soil sinks immediately; rain falling on clay either lies on the surface and evaporates or runs off; on steep slopes runoff will exceed absorption. The ratio of surface to ground water, moreover, varies considerably. Ground water exists everywhere in the earth's crust, generally not much deeper than about a mile; in desert the water table (upper level) may be hundreds of feet below the surface.

The quantity of water held in rock depends on the porosity of the rock: 1 to 50%, depending on the type. The size and number of pore spaces determine the permeability of a rock,

Profile of a water table: Top level of saturated zone approximately follows contour of landscape. Where it reaches surface there is a spring, lake or river, or swamp. Water table fluctuates with changes of season. Water-holding capacity of rocks in saturated zone varies considerably according to type of rock.

as do its jointing planes, fractures, and other openings. A coarse sandstone and a shale may each hold 10% of their volume in water, but the sandstone with its larger pore spaces will drain quickly, while the shale with its tiny spaces may not drain at all. A rock that holds and passes water is an *aquifer*; one that will not allow free flow forms a *barrier*, or *trap*.

The zone in the earth's crust in which ground water is held is called the *saturated zone*. Its upper level is the *water table*, which rises or falls with wet or dry seasons. Above this is the *zone of aeration*, through which rain water percolates to the saturated zone; this water in transit is *vadose* water. Underground, the water is generally in motion, seeking ever lower levels. Ground water emerges on the surface through openings called *springs*; most spring water is gravity-flow, but some is ARTESIAN-flow. The source of most surface flow is springs. Spring water is normally cold, but there are many instances of thermal springs. Geysers are eruptive hot SPRINGS.

Ground water dissolves certain rocks with ease; hence 90% of the world's CAVES are in limestone. Such water contains many minerals in solution, *e.g.* iron, calcium, silica, sulfur, and magnesium compounds. Sometimes the minerals in ground water give it therapeutic value. Minerals are often deposited from ground water to form veins in fissures of the rock through which it is circulated. Cave-type formations such as stalactites and stalagmites also are deposited from circulating ground water.

Ground water as a natural resource is a matter for concern to everyone. Where more water is taken from the ground than is replaced by nature, water resources become a problem. Ground-water supplies are decreasing in many areas, and considerable geological work is being done by both federal and state geological surveys to correct the situation.—*R. E. M.*

GROUP: one of the central concepts of abstract algebra. The notion was first discovered by Évariste Galois while studying algebraic equations, but has since been applied to more and more branches of mathematics. The nature of a group may be illustrated by the symmetric group of order 3. Consider any three objects numbered 1, 2, and 3. If we replace these numbers by 3, 1, 2, we have made a substitution or *permutation* of the original numbers. This permutation is represented by

$$\begin{pmatrix} 1 & 2 & 3 \\ 3 & 1 & 2 \end{pmatrix}$$

There are six possible permutations of 1, 2, 3:

$$\begin{pmatrix} 1\,2\,3 \\ 1\,2\,3 \end{pmatrix}, \begin{pmatrix} 1\,2\,3 \\ 2\,3\,1 \end{pmatrix}, \begin{pmatrix} 1\,2\,3 \\ 3\,1\,2 \end{pmatrix}, \begin{pmatrix} 1\,2\,3 \\ 1\,3\,2 \end{pmatrix}, \begin{pmatrix} 1\,2\,3 \\ 3\,2\,1 \end{pmatrix}, \begin{pmatrix} 1\,2\,3 \\ 2\,1\,3 \end{pmatrix}$$

The first substitution is called the *identity*; it does not change the order of the numbers. We can define a "product" of two substitutions as the new order obtained by carrying them out in succession:

$$\begin{pmatrix} 1 & 2 & 3 \\ 2 & 1 & 3 \end{pmatrix} \begin{pmatrix} 1 & 2 & 3 \\ 1 & 3 & 2 \end{pmatrix} = \begin{pmatrix} 1 & 2 & 3 \\ 2 & 3 & 1 \end{pmatrix}$$

The right-hand factor of the product is thought of as having been performed first: it sends 1 into 1, and then the left-hand factor sends 1 into 2; thus 1 becomes 2, as the final product shows. Similarly, 3 is sent into 2, then 2 into 1, so that in the final product 3 is sent into 1. Since the product of any two substitutions is itself a substitution, and since the six substitutions exhaust all possible substitutions, each product must be one of the six. This is the first requirement of a group: that the product of any two *elements* (in this case, the substitutions) is itself an element of the group.

We may denote the six substitutions by the letters *a, b, c, d, e, f*; and the operation of forming the product by the symbol $\otimes$. Then it can be readily verified that the associative law holds, *i.e.* that $(a \otimes b) \otimes c = a \otimes (b \otimes c)$. Finally, each substitution has an *inverse*, a^{-1}, found by inverting the rows: if

$$a = \begin{pmatrix} 1 & 2 & 3 \\ 2 & 3 & 1 \end{pmatrix} \text{ then } a^{-1} = \begin{pmatrix} 2 & 3 & 1 \\ 1 & 2 & 3 \end{pmatrix} = \begin{pmatrix} 1 & 2 & 3 \\ 3 & 1 & 2 \end{pmatrix}$$

so that

$$a \otimes a^{-1} = \begin{pmatrix} 1\,2\,3 \\ 2\,3\,1 \end{pmatrix} \begin{pmatrix} 1\,2\,3 \\ 3\,1\,2 \end{pmatrix} = \begin{pmatrix} 1\,2\,3 \\ 1\,2\,3 \end{pmatrix} = \text{the identity.}$$

In general, a set *G* of elements *a,b,c, . . .* is said to form a group with respect to an operation $\otimes$ if for every *a,b,c,* of *G*

(1) the product $a \otimes b$ is in *G*;
(2) the associative law $(a \otimes b) \otimes c = a \otimes (b \otimes c)$ holds;
(3) there is a unique element *I*, called the identity, such that, for every *a* in *G*, $a \otimes I = I \otimes a = a$;
(4) every element *a* has a unique inverse in *G*, denoted by a^{-1}, such that $a \otimes a^{-1} = a^{-1} \otimes a = I$.

Axiom (4) ensures the existence of solutions *x* and *y* in *G* of the equations $a \otimes x = b$, and $y \otimes a = b$; the solutions are the unique elements $x = a^{-1} \otimes b$, and $y = b \otimes a^{-1}$.

It should be noted that the operation $\otimes$ is unspecified and is an essential part of the definition of a specific group. The nonzero real numbers are a group with respect to the operation of multiplication; all the reals are a group with respect to addition. The identity of the nonzero reals with respect to multiplication is the number 1; the identity of the reals with respect to addition is 0. Furthermore, the inverse of the real number 3 in the group of the reals is the negative of 3, or -3. These two groups are commutative, *i.e.* $a \times b = b \times a$, for the one, and $a + b = b + a$, for the other. However, many groups, *e.g.* the above substitution group, are noncommutative, and $a \otimes b \neq b \otimes a$.

A set *H* of elements of a group *G* is called a *subgroup* of *G* if the product of any two elements of *H* is in *H*; and if *H* contains the identity element of *G* and also the inverse element h^{-1} of every *h* of *H*. Then *H* forms a group with respect to the same operation as does *G*. The integers form a subgroup of the reals under addition; the nonzero integers do not form a subgroup of the nonzero reals under multiplication.

The notions of group and subgroup are intimately connected with those of *invariance* and *equivalence*. Consider a one-to-one correspondence between the points of two regions of space. Among all of these correspondences we can study those which preserve (or leave invariant), say, the parallelism of lines, or the distances between any two points, or the collinearity of points, or any combination of these relations. Usually the set of all operations (or correspondences) of a given kind which leave invariant certain properties of the objects to which they are applied (or certain relations among these objects) constitutes a group. This viewpoint is at the heart of Felix Klein's *Erlangen Program*, a manifesto in which the author defined geometry as being the totality of properties of a space invariant under a group of transformations.

The number of elements in a group *G* is called its *order*. This number is either infinity, and we call *G* an infinite group; or it is a finite number *n*, and we call *G* a finite group of order *n*. A simple example of a finite group is the set of all *n*th roots of 1, under multiplication of complex numbers. A prototype for all finite groups is the group of permutations of *n* symbols, $a_1, a_2, . . . , a_n$, usually called S_n or the symmetric group of order *n*. We have illustrated its nature by examining S_3, the symmetric group of order 3. The theory of permutation groups plays a key role in the GALOIS THEORY of equations.—*J. S.*

GROUP VELOCITY OF WAVES: It is often mathematically convenient to analyze wave motion in terms of several waves, each having a single wavelength. A wave with a single wavelength has no real physical significance, however. An actual wave consists of a superposition of such ideal waves. The velocity of the peak of the superposition is known as the group velocity. See WAVE AND WAVE MOTION.—*G. M. S; L. S.*

GROWTH: usually, a progressive increase in volume, weight, number, or other measurable attribute. Growth is considered a fundamental, although by no means exclusive, property of living systems. Biological growth lends itself well to graphic description, hence to statistical treatment. The significance of such mathematical manipulations must always depend on the validity of the original measurements and on the soundness of the assumptions on which interpretation is based.

Growth Curve: A typical graph of growth, characteristic of a wide variety of living systems, is the logistic or sigmoid curve, formed when units of quantity are plotted on the vertical axis of a grid against time units on the horizontal axis. The curve (Fig. 1) will, with properly selected coordinates, describe progressive change in many cases: increase in height or weight of many animals (including man) during certain phases of the life cycle; increases in material of a plant during its growing season; increase in number of microorganisms introduced into a limited amount of nutrient fluid.

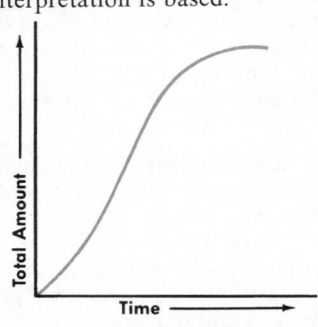

Fig. 1: General Logistic Curve

Common in these systems is the fact that, after a variably slow start, growth proceeds at a constant rate for a time. Since newly produced material also grows at the same rate, increments are progressively larger, and the curve rises logarithmically, as does a sum of money placed at compound interest. The growth described by the logistic curve is, however, self-limiting. At a certain point, marked by the inflection of the S, the rate begins progressively to decrease, and the curve levels off to a plateau or drops. For example, populations of organisms growing in a favorable environment gradually make that environment less favorable for continued increase. In the case of individuals, there are inherited as well as environmental limitations on bodily increase.

The logistic curve has been a useful model in many fields of biological inquiry. Microbial populations growing under defined conditions conform very closely to the model, which may be used as a standard for tests of nutritional requirements, internal biochemistry, or biochemical genetics of these unicellular organisms. Natural POPULATIONS seldom occur under comparably controlled conditions. Many statistical devices have been evoked to evaluate hereditary and environmental factors in population growth outside the laboratory, in order to predict future growth or to achieve its control.

The S-shaped curve is less useful as a model for growth of individuals. Measurement of a single ameba, between cell divisions, gives a slowly rising curve that is not sigmoid. Within a single cell, between divisions, nucleus and cytoplasm give different growth curves, neither being sigmoid. Growth of multicellular plants and animals, followed through the whole lifetime, presents cyclic increases and decreases of rate characteristic of individual species. The cycles are influenced strongly by environmental factors, but are also controlled by internal physiology, especially by hormonal mechanisms.

Over-all growth curves of complex individuals, animal or plant, are in fact rough summaries, not useful either in the analysis of factors involved or in suggesting mechanisms by which these factors operate. Much more fruitful has been the *comparison* of growth rates between different species or between different parts or organs of an individual. The concept of *differential growth* makes possible a mathematical treatment of morphology itself.

Growth Patterns in Unicellular Organisms: Single-celled plants and animals—bacteria, algae, molds, protozoa—display a wide diversity of geometric forms resulting from specific patterns of cellular growth. Any departure from spherical form must be ascribed to localized growth that produces deformation of some relatively rigid component of the cell. This component is frequently external: stiff "ectoplasm," cellulose wall, pellicle, mineral shell, or the like. Enlargement of external coverings, when investigated, is found to occur not uniformly over the surface, but in sharply localized areas of growth.

Growth Patterns in Vascular Plants: In the higher plants, growth is likewise restricted to very limited regions. Apical meristems, as well as pericycle and cambium layers, continually produce new cells of small size. These young cells subsequently differentiate into specialized tissues; in so doing they enlarge in a pattern that results in directed growth—longitudinal or radial—typical of the plant root or shoot. Interstitial addition of material to the existing cell wall seems the main mechanism of cell enlargement. Expansion of cell walls and increase of protoplasm depend on adequate external supply of raw materials and on physical factors, particularly light and temperature, which may impose cyclic growth. Immediate agents of cell-wall enlargement are the plant growth hormones, chiefly the AUXINS. The active growth of fruits can also be traced to the appearance of new sites of growth-hormone production and diffusion.

Animal Growth Patterns: The approximation of logistic growth found during EMBRYONIC DEVELOPMENT in animals can be interpreted by the following considerations: the individual begins as a single cell that proceeds to divide rapidly, giving a period of exponential growth. Soon, however, processes of cell differentiation set in. Differentiated cells usually are incapable of division, thus the growing material comes to constitute a smaller and smaller proportion of the whole, and the net growth rate soon decreases. In contrast to the situation in plants, attainment of mature form in animals usually is accompanied by cessation of net growth. In adult animals, some cells continue to divide, but this gain is compensated by loss or death of other cells. In higher animals the continuation or resumption of growth is exceptional, leading to regeneration, wound healing, or, pathologically, to tumor formation.

A wide variety of growth patterns in time and space is found, corresponding to distinctive patterns of body form characteristic of the various animal phyla and subgroups. Some invertebrates possess growing regions superficially comparable to plant meristems; the budding zone in some worms is an example. Even in the simplest multicellular animals, growth is typically localized, as it is in PROTOZOA; the size, shape, and displacement of the growing region control bodily form. In many mollusks (*e.g.* the chambered nautilus), the shell remains as a tangible self-written curve recording the growth of the mantle edge. Differentiated structures themselves may impose temporal as well as spatial restrictions; *e.g.* growth curves of arthropods consist of discontinuous cycles between hormone-controlled molts of the exoskeleton (see MOLTING).

As a simple example of differential growth in vertebrates, Fig. 2 shows human body outlines at different stages in the life history, drawn to the same absolute size. The differential progression of growth from anterior to posterior levels is

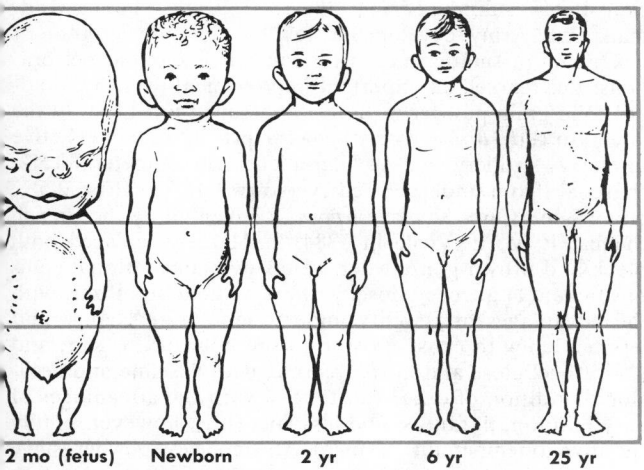

Fig. 2: Differential Growth of Human Body

| 2 mo (fetus) | Newborn | 2 yr | 6 yr | 25 yr |

growth and gain in body weight. The hormone has been crystallized; it has a molecular weight of 49,000. Animals resembling human acromegalic subjects can be produced by administration of this hormone. Deficiency of the hormone results in retarded growth or a form of dwarfism.—*F. F.*

GUANIDINE GROUPS AND PHOSPHATES: The compound guanidine, $HN = C(NH_2)_2$, does not occur in nature in the free state. But two of its derivatives, creatine and arginine, are important in MUSCLE CONTRACTION. In vertebrate muscle, creatine can react with ATP under the influence of creatine phosphokinase, to yield creatine phosphate, which contains an energy-rich bond (see ENERGY); the reaction is easily reversible, and hence creatine phosphate serves as an energy reserve. The muscle of invertebrates often contains arginine phosphate, with the same function. See also AMINO ACID and UREA CYCLE.—*K. H.*

GUANIDO ACETIC ACID: a biological intermediate in the synthesis of creatine from glycine. It is made by transfer of an amidine group ($-C\overset{NH}{\underset{}{=}}NH_2$) from arginine to glycine by an enzyme in the kidney. From there the blood carries it to the liver, where transfer of a methyl group ($-CH_3$) from methionine converts it to creatine, which in turn is utilized by muscle cells as a store of chemical energy. See TRANSMETHYLATION.—*J. F. S.*

GUDERLEY, KARL GOTTFRIED, 1910– , German-U. S. engineer; b. Bräunsdorf, Freiberg, Ger. A mathematical aerodynamicist, he did research in theoretical aerodynamics and on the problems of air flow over surfaces at supersonic speeds. He was an aeronautical engineer at the German Air Research Center, Braunschweig (1933–45); on the staff of the Wright Air Development Center, Dayton, Ohio (from 1946); and chief of the applied mathematics branch of the Aeronautical Research Laboratory (from 1955).—*D. H. D. R.*

GUERICKE, OTTO VON, 1602–86, German engineer and physicist; b. Magdeburg. As mayor of Magdeburg, Von Guericke studied all sorts of natural phenomena as a sideline. He is

characteristic of the vertebrate growth pattern, and is not unknown among invertebrates. Each organ of the body also has its own gradient of growth patterns, integrated in and under control of the whole. Many cases of periodic change in differential growth rate in vertebrate organs can, like molting in arthropods, be traced to cyclic endocrine mechanisms (see ENDOCRINE GLANDS; HORMONES).

Biochemical Growth Patterns: As the intimate biochemistry of protoplasm becomes more comprehensible, chemical growth—the accumulation of designated molecules—has become a useful measure of development in living systems. Many biologists now prefer to express over-all growth in terms of increases in protein, protein-nitrogen, or nucleic acid. Differential accumulation of special molecules, *e.g.* enzymes, can then be related to these standard increases. The chemical growth patterns of individuals or populations can thus be correlated with the morphogenetic patterns discussed above.—*D. Ru.*

GROWTH HORMONE: a protein hormone, secreted by the anterior pituitary gland, that affects the rate of skeletal

Test of vacuum: Sixteen horses, under the whips of grooms, are shown pulling on bronze hemispheres held together after evacuation by an air pump. This demonstration, staged by Von Guericke at the 1654 Diet of Regensburg, is shown in an engraving from his *Experimenta nova* of 1672. (*Burndy Library*)

most famous for his work in pneumatics, which led to the first air pump, 1650. This research, as well as work on a variety of other topics, is described in his *Experimenta nova (ut vocantur) magdeburgica de vacuo spatio* (1672). The book contains a famous drawing of the "Magdeburg experiment," in which two hemispheres held together by air pressure alone could not be pulled apart by teams of horses. His air pump was a direct precursor of Robert Boyle's.—*D. H. D. R.*

GUETTARD, JEAN-ÉTIENNE, 1715–86, French botanist and mineralogist; b. Étampes. He collected and classified fossils, and produced the first mineralogical maps of France (1752). As the first observer to recognize and describe the volcanic nature of the Auvergne region, he figured importantly in the controversy between the Neptunists and the Plutonists as to the origin of basalt and other rocks (see GEOLOGY). Guettard was also among the first to grasp the importance of erosion in the shaping of landscapes. He helped produce the *Atlas and Mineralogical Description of France* (1780).—*J. W.*

GUILLAUME, CHARLES ÉDOUARD, 1861–1938, Swiss-French physicist and metrologist; b. Fleurier, Switzerland. He entered the International Bureau of Weights and Measures at Sèvres, 1883, and became director in 1915. In 1891 he began the search for a suitable alloy from which to make the national standards of length and mass (provided by the Bureau), in order to re-place the extremely expensive platinum-iridium alloy then in use. His study of the anomalies in nickel-steel alloys led to the development of inexpensive Invar ("invariant") alloys, im-portant in metrology with their low coefficients of expansion. For this he was awarded the Nobel prize, 1920.—*D. H. D. R.*

GULLSTRAND, ALLVAR, 1862–1930; Swedish ophthalmologist; b. Landskrona. For his research on the dioptrics of the eye he received the Nobel prize, 1911. Gullstrand discovered intracapsular accommodation of the eye, showing that ac-commodation is accomplished largely by rearrangement of the internal parts of the eye and only partially by changes in shape of the lens of the eye. The slit lamp used by ophthal-mologists is his invention.—*D. H. D. R.*

GUMS, VEGETABLE: natural colloidal substances, gluey when moist but hard when dry, produced by a wide variety of plant life, particularly plant life in arid lands. Chemically, gums are highly complex carbohydrates. They are used as major components or as minor additives in adhesives, paints, cloth sizings, and confectioneries; they also find use in medicinals. Gums may be divided into those obtained from marine plants, as agar-agar, Irish moss, Iceland moss, and algin; and those derived from terrestrial plants and trees, as from acacia (gum Arabic), ghatti (British India gum), karaja (Stercula India gum), and tragacanth (Bassorin gum). The seed extracts—quince seed, locust bean, locust kernel, and guar—comprise still another group of gums. Two groups complete the list: the fruit extracts (pectins) and the processed starches, such as British gum, and dextrines.—*R. W.*

GUNPOWDER: historically, an explosive mixture of saltpeter (potassium or sodium nitrate), sulfur, and charcoal, known as *black powder.* It is a low explosive (*i.e.* has a low rate of re-action), detonating at a rate of about 1,215 ft/sec. This slow action gives it a heaving, rather than a shattering, effect, making it extremely effective in blasting out large chunks of stone. Other uses are as a propellant in FIREARMS, a noise-maker for military salutes, and a primer for artillery shells. Typical formulas for firearms are KNO_3, 74%; charcoal, 15.6%; sulfur, 10.4%; and, for blasting, $NaNO_3$, 71%; char-

coal, 16.5%; sulfur, 12.5%. In the 1850s, Capt. Thomas Rod-man, U. S. Army, developed a slow-burning powder grain of hexagonal prismatic shape with concentric circular perfora-tions; this marked an important improvement over the stand-ard solid-grain powder, with its dangerous short blast. In the late 19th cent. *brown (cocoa) powder* proved highly effective for heavy artillery fire: its ingredients are saltpeter, 80.5%; charcoal (from undercharred rye straw), 16%; sulfur, 2.5%; plus 1% moisture. *Smokeless powder,* invented by the French chemist P. M. E. Vielle in 1884, has largely replaced both black and brown gunpowder. It has two conventional com-positions: (1) nitrocellulose, with or without stabilizer, with the advantages of stability under temperature change and less tendency to cause erosion in the bore of the gun; and (2) nitrocellulose and nitroglycerine, with vaseline and occa-sional addition of other substances, with the advantages of easy ignition, lightness, and less cost (it is, however, highly sensitive to temperature change). All smokeless powders have a low burning rate and are stable to moisture. Another formula—2 parts potassium chlorate, 1 part potassium ferro-cyanide, and 1 part sugar—is known as *white powder*; it is extremely sensitive and explodes violently, and is used mainly for fireworks and percussion caps.

The modern manufacture of gunpowder is a nine-step pro-cedure: (1) Saltpeter is ground in a ball mill; (2) charcoal and sulfur are ground in a separate ball mill (to prevent explo-sion); (3) all ingredients are mixed and screened; (4) the mix-ture is ground in a wheel mill by two freely rotating wheels traveling a partly overlapping path to improve the milling; (5) the wheel cake is further broken up and then compressed into small cakes; (6) the small cakes are ground in a corning mill (graining); (7) the grains are polished by rotating in hardwood drums, then (8) dried and glazed with graphite and (9) packed into kegs, special fiber containers, or tin cans.

Little is known about the early history of gunpowder. The Chinese may have used some such explosive in fireworks. An incendiary composition used by the ancient Greeks ("Greek fire") probably consisted of niter (saltpeter) and shale oil. Berthold Schwarz (14th cent.), the "powder monk," is some-times erroneously credited with the invention of gunpowder, which he was the first to use in firearms. Albert Magnus in Germany and, before him, Roger Bacon in England (13th cent.) described the explosive properties of the saltpeter-sul-fur-charcoal mixture. See EXPLOSIVE.—*T. M. and C. S.*

GUST: a sudden and rapid increase in wind speed, often ac-companied by an equally sudden change in wind direction. Unlike a squall, gusts rarely last more than a few seconds. They are evidence of the turbulence of the wind and are most frequent and intense over rough, hot ground and, in the upper air, near jet streams.—*P. L.*

GUTENBERG, BENO, 1889–1960, German-U. S. geophysicist; b. Darmstadt. Director of the Seismological Laboratory at Calif. Inst. of Technology (from 1947), he specialized in re-search on the internal constitution of Earth, and was a leader in determining the depth and nature of the internal layers (see SEISMOLOGY). He wrote *Internal Constitution of the Earth* (1939) and, with C. F. Richter, *Seismicity of the Earth and Associated Phenomena* (1949).—*R. W. D.*

GUTENBERG, JOHANN, c. 1398–1468, German printer; b. Mainz (?). He was one of the earliest European printers to use movable type. The *Gutenberg Bible* (also called the *Mazarin Bible* or the *Bible of 42 Lines*), printed in 1456 or earlier, contains 1,282 printed pages. It is often incorrectly called the first example of printing with movable type.

Actually, fragments of a poem and an astronomical calendar printed by Gutenberg's firm before 1448 exist, and the Chinese used movable type of earthenware as early as the 11th cent. See also PRINTING.—*D. H. D. R.*

gitur pfecti sunt celi et terra·7 omis or
natus eorj.Compleuitqz de9 die septi
mo op9 suū qd fecerat·7 requieuit die
septimo ab uniūso ope qd patrarat.
Et benedixit die septimo·et sāficauit

Gutenberg's movable type, along with concomitant developments in paper manufacture, press design, and ink chemistry, was part of application of interchangeable-parts techniques to communication that occurred in mid-15th cent. These opening lines from 2nd chapter of Genesis are from the 42-line Bible; alternate letter forms and hand-painted initial are among devices used to disguise revolutionary technical innovation.

GUYOT, ARNOLD HENRY, 1807–84, Swiss-U. S. geographer and geologist; b. Boudevilliers, near Neuchâtel. He tested the theories of Louis Agassiz in glaciology and made important contributions to the knowledge of the laws of glacial motion, structure of glaciers, and movement of morainic materials (1838–48). Professor of physical geography and geology at Princeton (1854–84), he also worked with the Smithsonian Institution and established the first weather stations in the present system. His emphasis on field studies and the use of topographic maps strongly influenced the teaching of geography in the U. S. A. The flat-topped undersea mountains called guyots are named after him. He was a member of the National Academy of Sciences.—*D. H. D. R.*

GUYTON DE MORVEAU, BARON LOUIS BERNARD, 1737–1816, French chemist; b. Dijon. His views on crystallization and "phlogiston" were presented in his *Digressions académiques* (1772). He later abandoned his support of phlogiston for Lavoisier's views, attacked the archaic nomenclature of chemistry, and with Lavoisier, Berthollet, and Fourcroy wrote *Méthode d'une nomenclature chimique* (1787), which laid the foundations of modern chemical terminology. In addition, he studied the use of hydrogen chloride and chlorine as disinfectants. He was a fellow of the Royal Society.—*A. I.*

GYMNOSPERM: any SEED PLANT that produces its ovules in exposed sites, rather than enclosed by an ovary wall (as occurs in angiosperms, or FLOWERING PLANTS). After fertilization, the ovules develop into seeds. Often gymnosperms are loosely referred to as evergreens or as conifers, because most of them—but not all—retain their leaves more than a year and bear seeds in cones. All the 600-odd modern gymnosperms are woody; some form dense forests of valuable trees.

Gymnosperms were the earliest plants to develop the seed habit, this being a group of interrelated adaptations important to vegetation that is colonizing land areas where water in liquid form might not be available at the season of reproduction. Fossil gymnosperms are known from as far back as the Devonian Period, some 400 million yr ago. Members of two orders, the Cycadofilicales (seed ferns or pteridosperms) and Cordaitales, are well represented among Paleozoic sedimentary rocks, in which they occur as the remains of the first true forests. Seed ferns were long assumed to be true ferns rather than seed plants, for their leaves had the form of fern fronds. The oldest known seed fern reached a height of some 30 ft, a trunk diameter of 3 ft. Members of the Cordaitales bore leaves of varying forms on spreading branches arranged around the trunk in a spiral. In some types, the leaves were long and grasslike; in others, broad with dichotomous venation (*i.e.* each vein dividing at intervals into two smaller veins of equal size). Both orders survived into the Mesozoic Era and then became extinct.

Cycads: From the seed ferns two further orders appear to have evolved into dominant trees of worldwide distribution during the Mesozoic. One, the Bennettitales (known as cycadophytes), became extinct at the end of that era. The other, the Cycadales (known as cycads), is still represented by about 100 species in tropical and subtropical lands of the New World and the Old. Like the cycadophytes, the cycads are typically palmlike trees, bearing a handsome whorl of coarse compound leaves as a crown atop a thick, barrel-like woody stem. Members of the genus *Cycas* are often raised as greenhouse plants in temperate regions. *Zamia*, a very different cycad, occurs in Florida, where it is known as the coontie or the Seminole-bread plant. Its thick horizontal or vertical underground stem was formerly dug up by Seminole Indians and ground to make a substitute for flour in bread-baking. Cycads bear upright cones, one plant producing pollen, another ovules. The seeds are fleshy, with a stony center around the embryo plant. An ovulate cycad cone at maturity may weigh as much as 92 lb.

Gymnosperm life cycle (pine): Familiar tree is sporophyte. Reproductive organs are cones—staminate, or "male," cones (small) and ovulate, or "female," cones (large), both on same plant. Scales of staminate cones (1) bear pollen sacs (2), within which microspores are formed after meiosis. Microspores constitute first cells of gametophyte generation. Outer wall of each spore enlarges on each side (3) to form "wing." After nuclear divisions, mature pollen grain is formed; at maturity pollen grains are liberated and carried away by wind. Ovulate cone (4) carries two ovules (5) on each scale, each with large megaspore mother cell. This, following meiosis, gives rise to four megaspores, of which one survives. After its nucleus has divided a great number of times, resulting multicellular body is female gametophyte (6). After pollen grain has germinated, it forms pollen tube that penetrates egg and discharges contents into it (7). One sperm fuses with egg; from fertilized egg, with its diploid chromosome number, embryo of new pine sporophyte is formed (8). When seed has developed (9), it has (in many species) a membranous wing that facilitates dispersal. If seed germinates, embryo develops into seedling (10). (*After Young*)

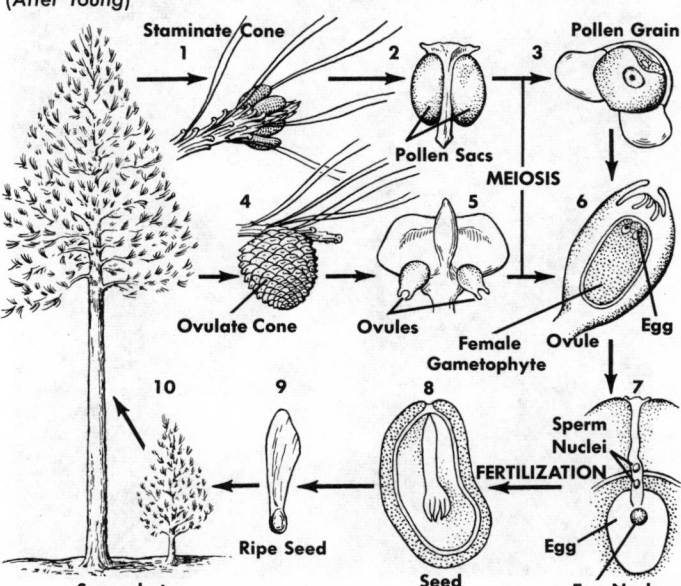

Staminate Cone · Pollen Grain · Pollen Sacs · MEIOSIS · Ovulate Cone · Ovules · Female Gametophyte · Ovule · Egg · Sperm Nuclei · FERTILIZATION · Egg · Egg Nucleus · Sporophyte · Ripe Seed · Seed

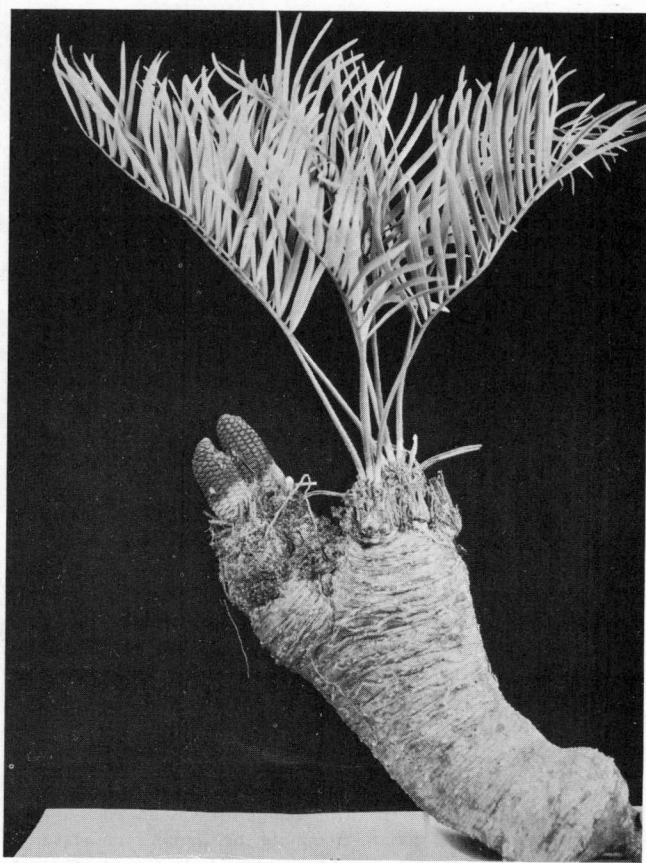

The Cordaitales may have been ancestral to two other orders of gymnosperms, the Ginkgoales and the Coniferales. The order Ginkgoales is represented today by only one species, the domesticated and deciduous maidenhair tree (*Ginkgo biloba*), which is planted as an ornamental shade tree in cities of America and Europe. Its unusual fan-shaped leaves, which are dichotomously veined, may be the reason for the domestication of the tree in the Orient before the dawn of history. The maidenhair tree seems adapted to a remarkable degree for life close to man. It is extremely tolerant of drought, smoke, adverse temperatures, and other environmental hardships. Sometimes the tree reaches a height of 90 ft, with all its roots spreading below paved streets and sidewalks. In spring, before the leaves reach full size, the maidenhair tree puts out little catkin-like groups of stamens or paired ovules on short, spurlike branches. Ordinarily, only pollen-producing maidenhair trees are planted, for the ripe seeds from an ovule-producing tree release an obnoxious odor, caused by slow decomposition of the fleshy outer layer that surrounds a stony covering for the embryo plant within.

The order Coniferales numbers about 520 species, including all the conspicuous and economically important gymnosperms of the temperate zones. Leaves are mostly needle-like, often waxy, and well adapted to shed snow and to reduce evaporative loss of water into dry air. In the northern hemisphere, the coniferous forest trees include the pines, spruces, hemlocks, firs, cedars, larches, and cypresses. Many of these grow tall and straight, yielding valuable lumber. So much of it is easier to work than are boards made from angiosperm trees that coniferous wood is commonly referred to as "softwood" in comparison to angiosperm "hardwoods." In the southern hemisphere, the less-famous conifers include many kinds of podocarps, phylloclads, and araucarias such as the monkey-puzzle tree of Chile, the bunya-bunya "pine" of Australia, the kauri "pine" of New Zealand, and the Norfolk Island "pine" of this island (north of New Zealand). The resin from many of these trees is valuable. The order Coniferales includes the largest and probably the oldest living organisms. The coastal redwood of California reaches a height of about 360 ft, a diameter of about 27 ft at the base; dwarf bristlecone pines in the California mountains show by their annual rings an age in excess of 4,000 yr.

The fourth living order, the Gnetales, consists of plants differing from all other gymnosperms in that they lack resin canals and possess vessels in the wood. The few species are grouped in three highly distinctive genera: *Ephedra, Welwitschia,* and *Gnetum.* Species of *Ephedra* are small shrubby plants, chiefly of desert or arid lands in both the Old World and the New. An Oriental *Ephedra* was long the source of the alkaloid ephedrine, used to reduce nasal congestion by stimulating the contraction of small blood vessels in the lining membranes. In the southwestern U. S. A., *Ephedra* shrubs are called jointfir or Mormon tea; a brew from the green, almost leafless stems was used for treating ills in pioneer days.

Welwitschia mirabilis is an amazing denizen of hot dry deserts of SW Africa. Each plant consists of an enormous parsnip-shaped root embedded in the soil and two opposite leaves that continue to grow from the base as leathery, strap-shaped extensions, year after year. Usually the leaves become torn by the wind by the time they are 6 ft long. If rain comes, which may occur once or twice in a decade, the *Welwitschia* raises either a few staminate branches or a tubular structure surrounding all but the end of the single ovule. The seeds are distributed by the wind and may germinate at the time of the next rain.

Gnetum plants are shrubs or woody vines found in tropical and subtropical forests of America and the Old World. Both

Gymnosperms: *Zamia floridana* (above) is one of the four species of cycad native to the continental U. S. A.; Florida Seminoles once valued its starchy stem (*Lorus and Margery Milne*). Longleaf pine (blossom, *below*) is a conifer, one of the Southern hard pines; its needles may extend to 18 in. (*Watson/Monkmeyer*)

the paired stamens (on one plant) and the solitary ovules (on another plant) develop at the bottom of a tubular structure, which suggests a perianth. In some species, *e.g.* the one grown for fiber in Indomalaysia, the tube around the ovule becomes fleshy at maturity and is edible, like the soft parts of a plum or peach.—*L. and M. M.*

GYPSUM: a common and widespread EVAPORITE mineral, closely related in occurrence and composition ($CaSO_4 \cdot 2H_2O$) to anhydrite ($CaSO_4$). Most gypsum occurs in granular form (*rock gypsum*) in bedded deposits which may be interlayered with limestones, shales, and salt beds (see SEDIMENTARY ROCK). *Anhydrite* is one of the least soluble and therefore the earliest of the precipitates produced by the evaporation of sea water. Beds of anhydrite up to 2,000 ft thick were formed by evaporation of sea water in shallow basins connected to the open seas only by narrow "passes." A cyclic pattern may have developed whereby anhydrite precipitated out and the dense, salt-enriched water returned to the main body by flowing out along the bottom of the connecting channels, while new sea water, of ordinary density, replaced it by flowing inward along the top of the channels. The thin regular layering (VARVING) of anhydrite beds indicates a cyclic mode of origin.

Gypsum is more stable than anhydrite under near-surface conditions, and most gypsum appears to have been derived from anhydrite. Outcropping beds of rock gypsum grade into anhydrite at depth. Very pure, microcrystalline rock gypsum, called *alabaster,* is used for carvings. Clear crystals and coarsely crystalline masses of gypsum (*selenite*) form veins in various rocks, and also occur in weathered sulfide deposits and as replacements in clays and shales. Fibrous gypsum (*satin spar*) occurs as veinlets in rock and is cut into ornamental objects showing the cat's-eye effect (chatoyance). Gypsum grains accumulate as sands in desert areas; the dunes of the White Sands National Monument, New Mexico, are formed of gypsum. On moderate heating (about 320°F), gypsum loses ¾ of its water, becoming "plaster-of-paris," which will "set"—*i.e.* revert to gypsum—on wetting. Plaster is a major ingredient in wallboard, wall plaster, and other construction materials. Crushed gypsum is used directly as a fertilizer, as a filler, and as a strengthening and set-retarding agent in portland cement. See MINERAL (table).—*L. M.*

GYROMAGNETIC RATIO: the ratio of magnetic moment to angular momentum of an atomic or nuclear system. The precessional frequency (see LARMOR PRECESSION) of an atom or nucleus in a magnetic field is equal to the gyromagnetic ratio times the field strength. Because of the large difference in mass between electrons and nuclei, atomic gyromagnetic ratios are characteristically about 2,000 times larger than nuclear ones.—*B. Be.*

GYROSCOPE: a massive wheel which is universally mounted and spins on smooth bearings. It has many technical applications, among them the directional gyro, the gyrocompass, and the gyrostabilizer. Gyroscopes also serve as controls in various types of modern guidance systems, such as those in rockets. The usefulness of the gyroscope derives from its tendency to undergo precessional motion (see PRECESSION) under the action of an external torque. If, for example, a gyroscope is mounted as in the figure, the angular velocity ω of the wheel around axis *A-A,* combined with the torque T produced by the wheel's tendency to fall, causes the wheel itself to precess, *i.e.* rotate around the *Y-Y* axis at a velocity ω'. This tendency for a spinning wheel to precess is expressed in the relationship $T = I\omega\omega'$, where I equals the wheel's

MOMENT OF INERTIA. If we have a wheel of large diameter, and therefore large I, and set it spinning at a high value of ω, it takes a large value of torque to give the wheel any considerable precession. Thus the spinning wheel tends to preserve its direction despite any small torques. A directional gyro uses this property to maintain an approximately constant direction even though it is mounted in an airplane that

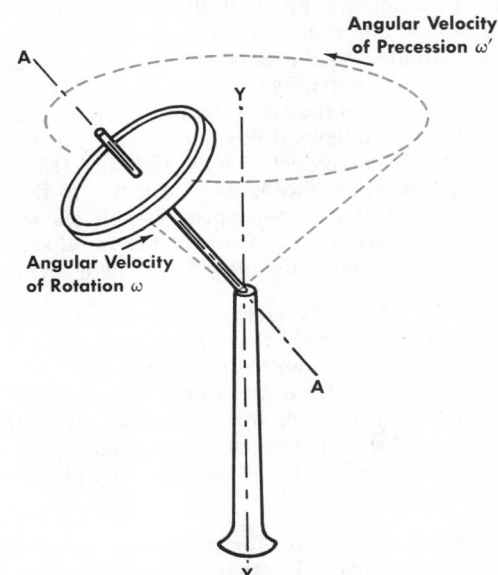

Angular Velocity of Precession ω'

Angular Velocity of Rotation ω

Spinning gyroscope precesses around a vertical axis (Y — Y) when its axis of rotation (A — A) is displaced from the vertical.

is rapidly changing direction. The torques produced by bearing friction are too small to produce significant precession. The direction of the gyro axis must be set, however, with respect to the plane's magnetic compass. A gyrocompass is a more complicated device designed to make use of Earth's rotational motion to produce a torque and consequently a precession of the compass axis until it points in a north-south direction. Frictional damping prevents the axis from overshooting. Thereafter, no torque exists unless the axis is displaced from the north-south direction, whereupon it precesses back into line. Guidance gyros all either rely upon the precessional velocity produced by an external torque, or, conversely, force the precessional motion and thereby generate a torque to produce the desired action. A gyrostabilizer operates in this latter fashion by creating a torque to counterbalance a disturbance of the ship produced by turbulence or wave motion. See AIRCRAFT INSTRUMENTATION; AUTOMATIC PILOT; GYROSTATIC COMPASS; INERTIAL GUIDANCE; MARINE NAVIGATION.—*B. Be.*

GYROSTATIC COMPASS: a nonmagnetic device for determining direction. It consists of an axially symmetrical body kept in rapid rotation (usually by a small electric motor) and mounted in GIMBALS so that it is free to rotate in any direction on its supporting frame. Its operation depends on the law of conservation of angular momentum. The axis of rotation is initially aligned to be parallel to Earth's axis of rotation. If the spin is maintained, the direction of the axis of rotation is fixed and continues to lie along the north-south line, irrespective of any movements of the supporting frame. Its value in navigation is that, unlike the MAGNETIC COMPASS, it is unaffected by the presence of nearby magnetic material and by the variable magnetic declination. See GYROSCOPE.—*O. M. P.*

H

H II REGION: a zone of ionized hydrogen gas surrounding hot stars, particularly those of spectral types O and B. Near a hot star, the overwhelming supply of ultraviolet radiation causes the ionization of interstellar hydrogen. Farther out, where the radiation is diluted by the distance, there is an appreciable abundance of neutral hydrogen; the absorption rises abruptly, and so little ultraviolet radiation is transmitted that the hydrogen remains neutral beyond this limit. Bengt Strömgren has shown that the boundary between the H II and H I regions is very sharp. Hence, on photographs sensitive to the light of hydrogen, the H II regions appear as spheres with well-defined edges. These regions delineate the spiral arms in the Andromeda galaxy and our Milky Way system.—*O. G.*

HABER, FRITZ, 1868–1934, German chemist; b. Breslau. He invented (with Karl Bosch) the Haber process for catalytic synthesis of ammonia from hydrogen and nitrogen at high pressures. Haber, director of the Kaiser Wilhelm Institute of Physical Chemistry, received the 1918 Nobel prize for chemistry for the synthesis of ammonia from its elements. He was an associate of the U. S. National Academy of Sciences.—*S. M. E.*

HABER PROCESS: a method for producing ammonia from nitrogen and hydrogen, originated by Fritz Haber (in collaboration with Karl Bosch) in Germany, 1914. The forerunner of large-scale ammonia processing methods, the Haber process was also one of the early successes in fixing atmospheric nitrogen, *i.e.* making usually unreactive nitrogen enter into a usable compound. The Haber-Bosch method consists of passing nitrogen and hydrogen over a catalyst at approximately 500° C. Some of the gases are converted to ammonia; the remaining gases are recycled. Since the volume of the ammonia is less than that of the nitrogen and hydrogen necessary to form it, the reaction (according to Le Chatelier's principle) is helped by pressure. Haber himself employed pressures of 200 atm and higher; recently, pressures up to 1,000 atm have been used.—*D. P. B.*

HABITAT: the place where a species of plant or animal lives. It is characterized by climate, substrate, and biological factors, the most important of these being temperature, moisture, wind, light, soil texture, acidity or alkalinity of soil, minerals, density of vegetation, diversity of food (see ECOLOGY; FOOD CHAIN). Major habitat classifications are: terrestrial, marine, fresh-water.—*K. L.*

HADAMARD, JACQUES SALOMON, 1865–1963, French mathematician; b. Versailles. He formulated much of the theory of functionals and made notable contributions to the theory of numbers, calculus of variations, the study of hydrodynamics and wave propagation, and the study of series. Author of *An Essay on the Psychology of Invention in the Mathematical Field* (1949) he was ranked among the most distinguished mathematicians of this century, his work being marked by its depth and the variety of mathematical branches to which he has contributed. He was a member of the Académie des Sciences, a fellow of the Royal Society, and an associate of the U. S. National Academy of Sciences.—*H. C.*

HAECKEL, ERNST HEINRICH, 1834–1919, German biologist; b. Potsdam. After publication of Darwin's *Origin of Species* (1859), Haeckel became the principal exponent of Darwin's views in Germany, and his monumental monograph on the radiolaria (3 vols., 1862, 1887–1888) clearly reveals Darwin's influence. His biogenetic principle states that the individual organism in its development repeats the stages through which its ancestors passed in the course of evolution ("ontogeny recapitulates phylogeny"). This idea was not original with him, but he applied it in many of his studies and is probably responsible for its influence in late 19th- and early 20th-cent. biology. He published many papers and books, including an outstanding treatise on calcareous sponges (1872) and another on jellyfishes (1879).—*D. H. D. R.*

HAFNIUM: a metallic element (Hf); at. no. 72; at. wt 178.6; density 11.4. In physical properties hafnium is similar to ZIRCONIUM; and hafnium forms the same types of compounds, although hafnium dioxide and hydroxide are more basic than the corresponding zirconium compounds. Practically all zirconium minerals contain about 1 to 2% hafnium. Pure hafnium metal is obtained by first forming an aluminum-hafnium alloy, then distilling off the aluminum. Hafnium was not discovered until 1923, when Dirk Coster and Georg von Hevesy in Copenhagen found its characteristic x-ray spectrum while conducting an x-ray spectrochemical analysis of zirconium minerals. Before this discovery, many scientists had searched for experimental verification of an element occupying hafnium's place (element 72) in the periodic table; and discovery of such an element had actually been claimed before 1923. These prior claims were rejected on the basis of either inadequate experimental evidence or faulty conclusions drawn from experiments. Two factors contributed to the late discovery of hafnium: (1) many researchers believed element 72 should show characteristics of the LANTHANIDE series (elements 58–71) rather than characteristics of the titanium-zirconium group (IVB) of the periodic table; (2) hafnium so closely resembles zirconium that its presence in zirconium minerals can hardly be detected by any means other than x-ray spectrochemical analysis, which was not fully developed until the 20th cent. Industrially, hafnium has found some use as an electric-lamp filament and also in the manufacture of vacuum tubes, where it has been used (as a so-called getter) to rid the sealed vacuum tube of any remaining gases by reacting with those gases to form solid compounds. The cost of hafnium is high, and it is commercially available only in very small quantities. Like GALLIUM, hafnium has a large CROSS SECTION for absorption of neutrons.—*G. W. M.*

HAHN, OTTO, 1879–   , German chemist; b. Frankfurt-am-Main. He discovered many of the early radioactive isotopes and (with Lise Meitner, 1917) the element protoactinium, discovered independently by Frederick Soddy and J. A. Cranston. In 1939 he and F. Strassmann published experimental results which Meitner and O. R. Frisch interpreted as meaning that nuclear fission had occurred. Hahn was awarded the 1944 Nobel prize for "his discovery of the fission of heavy nuclei." He is a fellow of the Royal Society.—*D. H. D. R.*

HAIR: an outgrowth of the skin of mammals, the only animals having true hair. In some marine mammals, hair is reduced to a few facial bristles; at the other extreme, hair may cover the whole body except palms and soles. Each hair grows from a tiny pocket, or *follicle,* in the skin. The follicle is lined with epidermis (outer skin), which folds inward from the skin

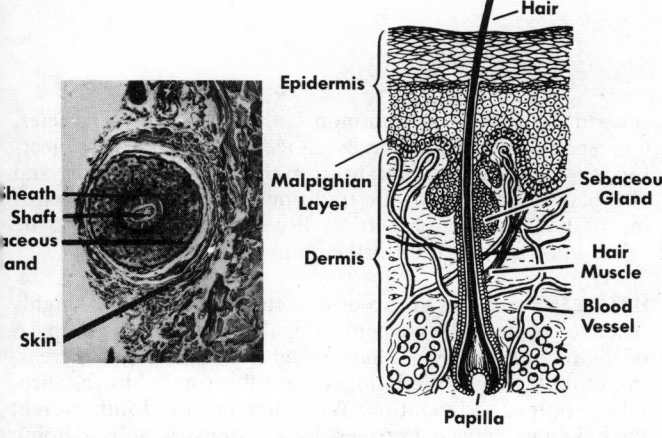

Human hair: Photomicrograph (*left*) shows cross section of hair (magnified about 500X). Transverse section (*right*) shows how Malpighian layer surrounds hair. (*Waldeck/F. L. O.; after Kenoyer*)

surface, dipping deeply into or through the compact dermis (inner skin). At the bottom of the follicle the epidermis is pushed up into a small mound by a projection of connective tissue, the *papilla,* which houses nerves and nutritive vessels. Here, cells multiply and form the hair root. The hair shaft is formed of dead cells, in which a tough protein, keratin, has replaced the cells' living protoplasm. Hard and horny, hair is given flexibility by oil poured into the sides of each follicle by *sebaceous glands.* These provide the natural oils of the skin.

Hair helps mammals maintain their body temperature; the air trapped between hairs acts as a blanket of insulation that diminishes loss of heat. In cold weather, the contraction of tiny muscles attached to the follicles serves to erect the hair of some mammals, increasing the thickness of the insulation; in man, the contraction produces "goose pimples." In whales, dolphins, and porpoises, blubber substitutes for hair as insulation. Certain hairs (the whiskers) in many mammals serve as organs of touch.

Hair is shed and replaced periodically, some mammals having their thick winter coat replaced by a lighter coat in spring, and growing a new winter coat in fall. The hair on the head of man is shed and replaced over a period of about 4 yr. The surface of individual hairs is sculptured distinctively in different species of mammals. Curliness is the result of asymmetrical flattening along the length of the hair. Common baldness in man is thought to be inherited and related to the secretion of sex glands; temporary baldness and other types are caused by diseases and nervous disturbances.—*R. G. M.*

HALDANE, JOHN SCOTT, 1860–1936, English physiologist; b. Edinburgh, Scot. A student of respiration, he showed (with John Gillies Priestly) the role of carbon dioxide in the regulation of lung ventilation (1905). Haldane also investigated the physiological effects of working in deep mines and of deep-sea diving. He wrote *Respiration* (1922), *The Philosophical Basis of Biology* (1931), and *The Philosophy of a Biologist* (1935). He was a fellow of the Royal Society and a member of the U. S. National Academy of Sciences. His son, **John Burdon Sanderson Haldane** (1892–1964), was known for his work in genetics and biometry. His publications include *Science and Ethics* (1928), *The Causes of Evolution* (1933), and *New Paths in Genetics* (1949). He was a fellow of the Royal Society. —*D. H. D. R.*

HALE, GEORGE ELLERY, 1868–1938, U. S. astrophysicist; b. Chicago, Ill. His research was concerned mainly with solar and stellar spectroscopy. Author of several hundred scientific papers, Hale was director of the Kenmore, Yerkes, and Mt Wilson observatories. The 200-in. telescope on Mt Palomar is named for him. He was a fellow of the Royal Society and a member of the National Academy of Sciences.—*D. H. D. R.*

HALES, STEPHEN, 1677–1761, English biologist; b. Bekesbourne. A vicar, he devoted much time to measuring biological quantities. His research included quantitative studies of animal blood systems (in which he sought to relate such quantities as blood pressure, blood velocity, pulse rate, blood-vessel size, and animal weight), the flow of sap in plants, the rates of water intake and loss by plants and the mode of loss (which he showed to be through the leaves), rates and mode of growth of leaves, and countless other detailed studies of plant and animal physiology. His two chief works, *Vegetable Staticks* (1727) and *Haemastaticks* (1733), were widely read. He was a fellow of the Royal Society.—*D. H. D. R.*

HALF-LIFE: the length of time it takes one half the atoms in any given sample of radioactive material to decay, each atom emitting a decay particle. Every radioactive material has a characteristic half-life. Depending on the material, this period may vary from a fraction of a second to many millions of years. The half-life of uranium[235], for instance, is 713,000,000 yr, whereas that of polonium[212] is less than a millionth of a sec. This means that a sample of uranium[235] after 713,000,000 yr will contain only half the original number of uranium atoms, and after the next 713,000,000 yr, only a quarter of that number. For applications such as RADIOACTIVE DATING, the term "ten half-lives" is coming into use, since this period represents the point at which 99.9% of the original atoms have decayed. See RADIOACTIVITY.—*A. R. G.*

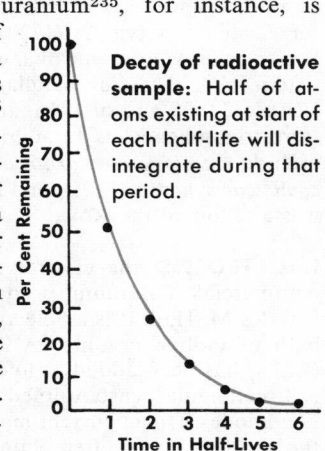

Decay of radioactive sample: Half of atoms existing at start of each half-life will disintegrate during that period.

HALL, CHARLES MARTIN, 1864–1914, U. S. chemist; b. Thompson, Ohio. In 1886 he invented (independently of Paul Héroult in France) a practical process for electrolytic reduction of aluminum from alumina dissolved in cryolite.—*A. I.*

HALL, EDWIN HERBERT, 1855–1938, U. S. physicist; b. Great Falls (now North Gorham), Me. In 1879 he discovered the HALL EFFECT. His later research was concerned largely with that effect and with closely related phenomena. He published many scientific papers and textbooks and summarized much of his research in *A Dual Theory of Conduction in Metals* (1938). He was a member of the National Academy of Sciences.—*D. H. D. R.*

HALL, JAMES, 1811–98, U. S. geologist and paleontologist; b. Hingham, Mass. He spent his life with the N. Y. State Geological Survey, training many outstanding geologists and becoming the leading U. S. paleontologist. He is credited with originating the science of stratigraphy in the U. S. A., and with developing the concept of sinking basins slowly filling with sediment (see GEOSYNCLINE). Hall was the first president of the Geological Society of America and was a member of the National Academy of Sciences.—*D. H. D. R.*

HALL EFFECT: the development of a voltage across a material carrying an electric current when a magnetic field is applied perpendicular to the current. This voltage, called the *Hall voltage,* is of interest because its sign indicates whether the current is carried by electrons (negative) or holes (positive); its magnitude is related to the number of these current carriers. —*E. M. C.*

HALLER, ALBRECHT VON, 1708–77, Swiss physiologist; b. Bern. He contributed to methods in modern experimental physiology. Showing that irritability (ability to contract when touched) is an attribute of many tissues, he distinguished it from normal muscular action. He also showed that all sensation is channeled through the nerves. His *Elementa Physiologiae* (8 vols., 1757–66) is the first modern work on physiology. He was a fellow of the Royal Society.—*D. H. D. R.*

HALLEY, EDMUND or **EDMOND,** 1656–1742, English astronomer, b. London. In St. Helena he catalogued 341 stars of the southern celestial hemisphere in 18 months. He made the first complete observation of a transit of Mercury, improved the seconds pendulum, and published the first map of the winds of the globe (1686). He assisted Isaac Newton in the publication of the *Principia*. Halley began a study of the orbits of comets in 1680 and made observations of the comet of 1682 **(Halley's comet),** calculating its orbit and predicting its return. Successor to Flamsteed as Astronomer Royal at Greenwich Observatory (1720), Halley detected the acceleration of the Moon's mean motion, indicated a method for determining the solar parallax by means of the transits of Venus of 1679 and of 1716, and contributed to the study of terrestrial magnetism. In addition to many papers, his works include *Catalogus stellarum australium* (1679), *Astronomiae cometicae synopsis* (1705), and *Astronomical Tables* (1752). He was a fellow of the Royal Society.—*S. B.*

HALL PROCESS: the electrolytic reduction process used in commercial aluminum production, invented in 1886 by Charles M. Hall. It is an electrolysis of alumina (Al_2O_3) in a bath of molten cryolite ($AlF_3 \cdot 3NaF$) to which fluorspar (CaF_2) has been added to lower the melting point. The cell is a rectangular, carbon-lined steel tank, or "pot," with carbon anodes. Direct current melts the charge and decomposes the alumina into molten aluminum, which sinks to the bottom and is periodically withdrawn, and oxygen, which attacks the anode, forming carbon dioxide and carbon monoxide. Alumina is added as needed to keep the process running continuously.—*D. P. B.*

HALO: in meteorology, a luminous ring around Sun and Moon, caused mainly by refraction of light by ice-crystals in the atmosphere. Most common is the ring of 22° diameter, corresponding to refraction by an ice crystal with faces meeting at 60°. Reflection of light from the surfaces of the crystal also plays a part. Halos are traditionally regarded as a warning of bad weather, but in reality are too common to be relied upon as a sign of forthcoming storms.—*O. G. S.*

HALOGEN: any of a group of five chemically related, highly reactive, nonmetallic elements, together making up group 7A of the periodic table; all have valence 1. In order of increasing atomic weight the halogens are fluorine, chlorine, bromine, iodine, and astatine. With increase in atomic weight the halogens' physical properties, *e.g.* density, boiling point, and melting point, show a corresponding increase: fluorine and chlorine are gases, bromine is liquid, and iodine and astatine are solids. As atomic weight increases, the halogens' chemical reactivity decreases; in many chemical reactions it is possible to replace a halogen with another halogen of lower atomic weight. In general, the halogens are so similar in chemical properties they are often represented in a chemical compound by the symbol X, *e.g.* a sodium halide by NaX. It is not unusual for the first member of a chemical series to exhibit certain peculiarities; this is the case with fluorine. Thus, while the other halogens form soluble salts with calcium, fluorine forms the insoluble calcium fluoride (CaF_2). Astatine, the heaviest member of the series, is present only in trace quantities in nature, but is made synthetically by nuclear reactions. It is radioactive, its most stable isotope having a half-life of only 8.3 hr. (See articles on individual halogen elements: ASTATINE; BROMINE; CHLORINE; FLUORINE; IODINE.)

Halogen Compounds: Inorganic chemistry is represented by compounds of the halogen elements as diverse as the crystalline sodium chloride (NaCl—common table salt) and the gaseous uranium fluoride, UF_6, used in A-bomb manufacture to separate fissionable uranium[235] from nonfissionable uranium[238]. Organic halogen compounds offer an even greater variety: chloroform, $CHCl_3$, is an anesthetic; carbon tetrachloride, CCl_4, a solvent; Freon-12, CCl_2F_2, a refrigerant.

Halogen compounds are of great importance in chemistry because they enable syntheses to take place with otherwise inert molecules. For example, methane, CH_4, is unreactive except to a halogen; and when a chlorine atom replaces one of methane's H (hydrogen) atoms by chlorination, as in chloromethane, CH_3Cl, a reactive molecule is obtained. Such halogenations are often made simply to obtain an INTERMEDIATE for further synthesis. Fluorine compounds are generally too stable for such use. See FLUORINATION; FLUOROCARBONS.—*Ru. M.*

HAMILTON, SIR WILLIAM ROWAN, 1805–65, Irish mathematician; b. Dublin. After mastering a phenomenal number of languages, Hamilton learned calculus, read Newton and Lagrange, and made discoveries of his own. He was appointed professor of astronomy at Trinity College upon his graduation there at 22. His reputation rests mainly on his development of quaternions, which he erroneously thought held the key to the mathematical explanation of the universe, and on his *Theory of Systems of Rays,* which did for optics what Lagrange's *Mécanique Analytique* did for mechanics. He also brought dynamics to a high degree of perfection. Basic to dynamics theory is *Hamilton's principle,* which generalizes the principle of least time (*i.e.* a light ray passes from one point to another by the path that requires the least time).—*H. C.*

Aluminum by the Hall process: Molten aluminum has been siphoned out of massive electrolytic cell (background) into ladle. From this it is being poured into pig molds. (*Alcoa*)

HAMILTONIAN FUNCTION: Sir William Rowan Hamilton formulated Newton's equations of motion for dynamical systems in terms of a mathematical function which today is called the Hamiltonian. Under many circumstances this function is the total energy of a system expressed in terms of the momenta and coordinates of the system considered as independent variables. The advantages of this formulation lie in the fact that it constitutes a systematic procedure for solving problems in dynamics, and for finding approximate solutions when no exact answer is possible. It also shows the intimate connection between optics and dynamics, and it is the most convenient starting point in making the transition from classical mechanics to wave mechanics.—*S. Bo.*

HANDBUCH DER PHYSIOLOGIE DES MENSCHEN (Handbook of Human Physiology), by Johannes Müller, 2 vol., 1834–38: The most important physiological text published since the *Elementa physiologiae* of Albrecht von Haller, 100 yr earlier, the *Handbuch* contains a remarkably complete survey of the knowledge of the forms and processes of animal and human life. It has a modern arrangement, moving from system to system within the body, including a section on the mind, a topic now relegated to psychology. Müller supplemented the reports of other physiologists with analytic comments and additional experimental and observational data. An important feature of the book is the almost complete absence of the influence of the speculative "nature-philosophy" which had been so prevalent in German science of the late 18th cent. Although clearly not a materialist, Müller was well acquainted with the contributions that physics and chemistry were making to the study of living systems. Characteristic of his approach in this text and in his teaching was his remark: "Whatever is not demonstrated by the scalpel does not exist."—*E. Me.*

HANDEDNESS: the preference for using one hand and arm rather than the other. Partly this preference has a hereditary basis; partly it arises through habit. Often, in a pair of identical twins, one is right-handed, the other left-handed, one being a mirror image of the other. Commonly handedness corresponds to a preference for using one foot and leg, *e.g.* drying one foot first after a bath or dipping one foot into water to judge temperature before entering a swimming pool. Handedness represents a functional difference in the two cerebral hemispheres of the brain, which seldom share their role equally. In right-handed persons, the left hemisphere is dominant; in left-handed persons, the right hemisphere is dominant. With practice, a person can become equally skilled in using the two hands and is then said to be *ambidextrous.* However, when a left-handed person is forced to neglect his left hand in favor of his right, effects of frustration may spread to the speech centers of the brain, which ordinarily are located in the dominant hemisphere. There is evidence that some speech defects, *e.g.* stuttering, have arisen in this way. Various animals, too, show "handedness." Of 20 parrots belonging to 15 species in the National Zoological Park, Washington, D. C., almost three-fourths used their left foot to pick up food, and three of one species were exclusively left-footed.—*L. and M. M.*

HAND TOOLS: implements used by man to perform hand work upon objects that would otherwise be inaccessible or less manageable with his bare hands. These tools increase the capacity of man's hands to grasp, push, pull, squeeze, twist, cut, tear, or gouge materials, because the tools are harder, tougher, stronger, or less subject to fatigue than human flesh, fingernails, sinews, muscle, and bone. Primitive man first adopted objects found in nature as tools with which to apply

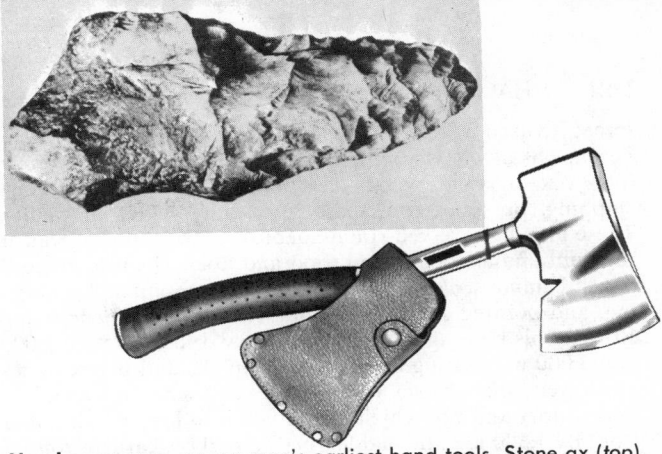

Hand axes were among man's earliest hand tools. Stone ax (*top*), found near St. Acheul, France, is around 200,000 yr old. About 6 in. long, it was laboriously chipped to desired form. Modern camper's ax is made of drop-forged steel, formed by repeated blows of drophammer. (*Amer. Mus. of Nat. Hist.,* top; *Fuller Tool Co.,* bottom)

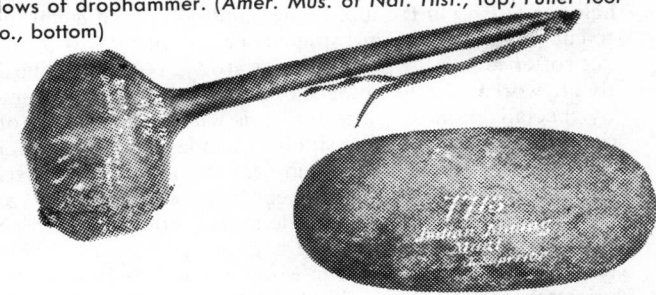

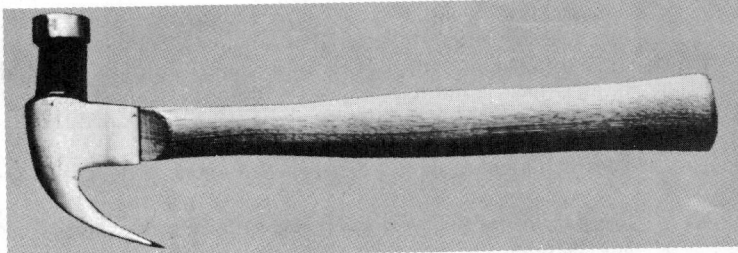

Hammers: 20-in. long, general-purpose stone maul (*top*) was fashioned by Dakota Sioux Indians. The 14-in. mining maul (*middle*) was used by Indians of NE American woodlands around Lake Superior. Shape of today's claw hammer (*bottom*) reflects modern carpenter's need for an effective nail-driving tool. (*Smithsonian Inst.,* top and middle; *N. Y. Public Library,* bottom)

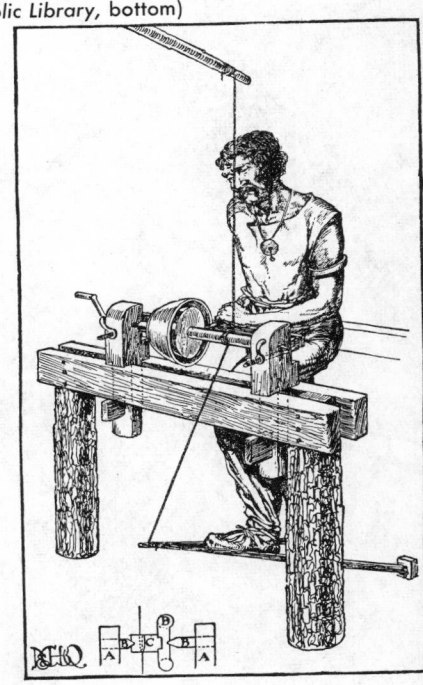

Toward the machine tool: Pole lathe (*right*), driven by workman's muscle power, belongs in category of hand tools; but when engine power became available in the 19th cent., such designs were readily adaptable for MACHINE TOOLS. (*Amer. Mus. of Nat. Hist.*)

force; he used a stone for a hammer and a stick for a lever. Perhaps as much as a million years ago he began fashioning tools out of stone, wood, and bone or ivory by breaking, chipping, or splintering these into sharp edges or points. These may have served simultaneously as weapons of war or the hunt and as tools to cut food and fiber. His tool kit contained hammers, cleavers, scrapers, cutters, pointers for piercing, and pointed shafts that when twirled by the encircling string of his hunting bow served as bow drills. Between 4,000 and 3,000 B. C., using deer antlers as picks and pelvic bones as shovels, man began mining ores and smelting metals—first copper and tin, which he alloyed into bronze, and later iron. By 1,300 B. C. he had learned to carbon-harden iron into crude steel. With these metals he made better tools. To gain mechanical advantage and to protect his hands from sharp-edged tools, he attached handles, first by hafting sticks to the tools with leather or fiber thongs, and later by cutting holes or slots to fit the tool to the handle. He used metal saws to cut wood, and set hard stone chips into metal saw teeth to cut softer metals. A new material always required a harder tool to work it. Growing social organization was accompanied by specialization of crafts, and this was the beginning of a cross-classification of tools still in use today. Under the broad grouping of hammers, for example, hammer heads of special shape are named for the carpenter (claw); machinist (ball peen or cross peen); mason, boilermaker, bricklayer, prospector, blacksmith, etc. Until the beginning of the mechanical revolution, at the end of the Middle Ages, tools were used primarily to shape household goods or in mining, farming, construction, weapon-making, or ornamental work. Some, like the carpenter's plane, fell into disuse and did not reappear until as late as the 13th cent. With the building of machinery a new class of tools, those of the mechanic who assembled or adjusted the machine, was developed. Essentially handles, *e.g.* wrenches or screwdrivers, these tools became highly standardized when mass-production (1)

caused standardization of ancient fastening devices (screws, pins, bolts) and (2) created standard, interchangeable parts for machines. To grind or polish, primitive man used sand or other abrasives, and hand grinding wheels survive today. As technology advanced, man was able to use mechanical energy to drive his cutting and drilling tools, and portable drills, milling cutters, and tool bits and holders used in lathes are still classed as hand tools. The lathe evolved from the ancient potter's wheel. Primitive man used his fingers, hands, and forearm (cubit) as standards of measurement, and today such things as scales, calipers, micrometers, and other indicators or gages are also called hand tools. Nor does the use of heat rather than force exclude soldering irons and blowtorches from being called hand tools. The preferred terminology in some arts or crafts, *e.g.* in medicine, is that the doctor's or surgeon's tools be called instruments, and, in fact, some of the mechanical measuring devices are frequently called instruments rather than tools.—*K. A.*

HARBOR ENGINEERING: the design and construction of a calm anchorage for large ships to enable repairs and overhauls, refueling, and the loading and unloading of cargo and passengers. Design of a safe harbor usually requires the planning and building of such structures as breakwaters and jetties, as well as the excavation and dredging of the bottom. Harbor engineering did not become a major branch of civil engineering (see ENGINEERING) until the late 18th cent., when the pioneering work of John Smeaton (1724–92) followed by John Rennie (1761–1821) and Thomas Telford (1757–1834) of Great Britain led to the design and construction of massive harbor works for British seaports. Harbor engineering requires a knowledge of the types of storms likely to strike the area, and their frequency; the expected height and force of waves, including tidal waves; the height and direction of tides; the velocity and direction of currents and winds; the type of bottom, including the amount of silt regularly accumulated; the

Using scale models, a hydraulic engineer by remote control maneuvers U. S. S. *Forrestal* through proposed Castle Hill Barrier, Narragansett Bay. Purpose is to determine whether this enormous aircraft carrier can cope with barrier proposed for reducing wave action in the bay. Models can simulate extreme natural conditions. (*U. S. Army Engineer Waterways Experiment Station*)

location of reefs and shoals; and the depth at various points around the harbor site. Structures must be built to provide the most efficient means of protecting ships in the harbor from the force of high winds and high waves. The need of maintaining and repairing these structures must also be considered.

Where the harbor site is exposed to the open sea, one or more breakwaters or long barricades must be built to break the force of the waves. Breakwaters may be designed to project from the shore and converge toward each other; they may project from one or both arms of a bay; or they may be unattached to land and constructed across the harbor parallel to the shore. If no severe waves or storms are expected, an effective breakwater can be built simply by continued dumping of loose rubble, primarily large stones, on the site, so that a mound is piled up above the water. The line of stones is advanced by using the gradually extending top of the breakwater as a roadway for trucks or as the bed for a railroad trestle. For greater strength, heavy concrete blocks can be used with the rubble. Stronger breakwaters requiring less maintenance are built by prefabricating CAISSONS of reinforced concrete, floating them to the site and sinking them in position by filling with stones or sand. Another method is to construct COFFERDAMS at the site and fill them with loose rock. Cofferdams are also used to build the vertical-face or solid breakwater, where the sea bed is rocky or firm. Concrete or masonry is poured into the dry interior of the cofferdam.

Where a harbor is located at the mouth of a river, jetties are generally constructed partially across the mouth to narrow the ship channel and thereby increase the force of the current. This produces a scouring effect which keeps down the accumulation of sand and silt on the bottom. Dredging of the harbor or the channel, however, is usually still required. Piers built straight out into the water from shore also provide additional protection to ships docking on the leeward side. Dredging the harbor is frequently necessary to deepen its bottom or to provide a channel to accommodate large ships; a depth of about 40 ft at low water is usually considered satisfactory. Periodic dredging is generally necessary to remove accumulated sand and silt, the type of dredge used being dependent on the type of bottom material (called spoil) to be removed. The ladder dredge, a continuous chain of small buckets moving around a rigid frame called a ladder, can excavate a bottom varying from mud to small boulders. Since it is a bulky and expensive piece of equipment, economical operation of the ladder dredge can best be achieved where it can be run continuously. The dipper dredge, essentially a crane that operates off the end of a barge, also can remove a variety of materials and has a harder bite and a larger capacity than the ladder dredge. A suction or hydraulic dredge is very effective when a large amount of soft material must be removed. The spoil is sucked up through a long pipe by pumping, after the material is first loosened, if necessary, by revolving knives. The special advantage of the suction method is that the spoil can be conveyed directly to the shore by pipes. Harbor engineering also includes the planning and marking of ship channels as well as the placement of lighthouses, buoys, radio beacons, and other navigational aids to insure the safe passage of ships into and out of the harbor.—*R. G.*

HARDEN, SIR ARTHUR, 1865–1940, British biochemist; b. Manchester. For investigations of the fermentation of sugar and of fermentative enzymes, Harden and H. von Euler-Chelpin shared the Nobel prize, 1929. Harden's work with autolyzed (self-digested) yeast led to the discovery of the involvement of sugar phosphates in fermentation. He was a fellow of the Royal Society.—*D. H. D. R.*

HARDY, GODFREY HAROLD, 1877–1947, English mathematician; b. Surrey. Hardy worked in pure mathematics and made notable original contributions in the study of series, inequalities, and analytical number theory. His text, *A Course in Pure Mathematics* (1908), raised the standard of English mathematical education. He influenced many 20th-cent. mathematicians beneficially, notably the Indian S. Ramanujan (1887–1920). Hardy was a fellow of the Royal Society. —*H. C.*

HARGREAVES, JAMES, d. 1778, English inventor and mechanic; b. near Blackburn. He was the inventor of the spinning jenny, which greatly speeded the production of thread for weaving. The first model had seven bobbins rotating on an axis driven by a single belt. Eventually the Hargreaves machine included 80 spindles. Harassed by working people fearful of unemployment, and later involved in legal actions against patent infringers, Hargreaves died a poor man.—*S. B.*

HARMONIC MOTION: a vibratory motion that repeats itself in equal time intervals. Thus a light object floating on water will bob up and down with very nearly harmonic motion when waves pass; and the strings of musical instruments usually vibrate so that their parts move at right angles to the string and with several harmonic motions at the same time. Harmonic motion is strictly defined as the projection of a uniform circular motion upon any straight line in the same plane. In the diagram, particle *P* moves with uniform speed around the circle whose radius is *R* and whose center is at *C*. The projection of *P* upon the straight line *AB* is *P′*, which moves up and down with harmonic motion and completes a *cycle* in a time *T*, called the *period,* while *P* makes a 360° revolution around *C*. Such a motion is much like that of a mass *M* hanging at the end of an elastic spring *S* (see HOOKE'S LAW). If *M*, from its position of rest at *O*, is pulled down to the point *B* and suddenly released, *M* and *P′* will oscillate up and down in step with each other, provided they start in step and provided they have the same period. *OP′*, the *displacement* of the particle, is equal to $R \sin\alpha$. The maximum value of the displacement, *OA* or *R*, is called the *amplitude.* The velocity of *P′* is a maximum at *O* and zero at *A* and *B*, while the acceleration of *P′* is zero at *O* and a maximum at *A* and *B*. The acceleration is always directed toward the center *O* and is proportional to the displacement.—*H. Sw.*

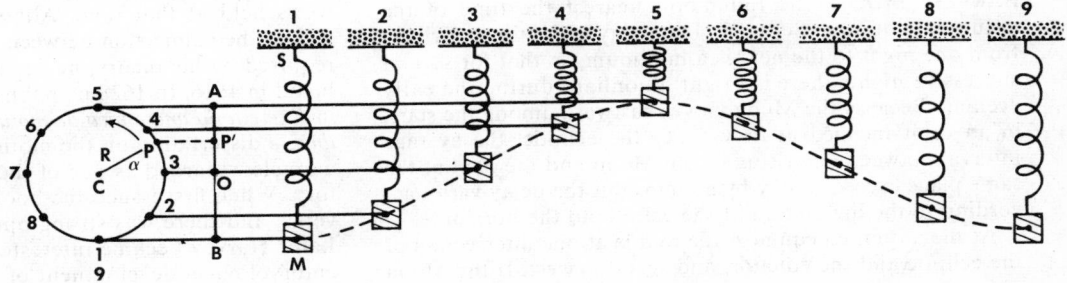

Motion of a mass suspended from a spring is the same as the projection of a point moving around a circle at uniform speed. A graph of displacement vs. time is a sine curve for both.

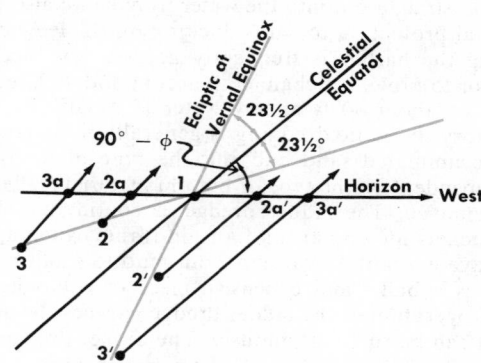

Wave form of a tone combined with its third harmonic is altered by relative phases. (*Left:* in phase. *Right:* 180° out of phase.)

— sin T	— sin T
— sin 3T	— −sin 3T
— Composite	**—** Composite

HARMONICS: whole-number multiples of a single frequency that are present in any wave whose form is not a pure sine wave. Any sustained sound carries energy to the ear at many frequencies in addition to the one that determines its apparent pitch (see SOUND). In most musical sounds, these frequencies, called *partials* or *overtones,* are whole-number multiples of a frequency, called *fundamental,* that may or may not actually be present, but that nonetheless determines the apparent pitch of the sound. All harmonics are partials, but not all partials are harmonics; the tympani and bells, for example, have "inharmonic" partials, whose frequencies are not whole-number multiples of any one frequency. The kind and intensity of the various partials largely determine the musical quality, or *timbre,* of a sound. In stringed instruments the harmonics arise very naturally, because any string can vibrate in one, two, three, or more sections at the same time, giving rise to corresponding frequencies heard together as a complex tone.

Any generator or amplifier of alternating energy is liable to produce harmonics of a pure fundamental frequency being generated or amplified, and when examined on an oscilloscope the wave will show a nonsinusoidal form. The illustration above shows a wave combined with its third harmonic in two ways: $\sin T - \frac{1}{2}\sin 3T$ and $\sin T + \frac{1}{2}\sin 3T$. The exact form of the wave is evidently dependent on the relative phase of the two waves.—*M. C. H.*

HARRIOT, THOMAS, 1560–1621, English mathematician and astronomer; b. Oxford. He became a tutor to Sir Walter Raleigh, who in 1585 appointed him geographer and surveyor for the expedition to Virginia with Sir Richard Grenville. Later Harriot wrote *A Brief and True Report of the New Found Land of Virginia,* which was later reprinted in Hakluyt's *Voiages.* He is considered the founder of the English school of algebraists. Among his contributions to algebra was the introduction of new symbols and notation, *e.g.* $<$ and $>$ for "is less than" and "is greater than," respectively, and exponential expressions, *e.g.* x^3 for $x\,x\,x$.—*H. C.*

HARRISON, JOHN, 1693–1776, English carpenter, mechanic, and inventor; b. Foulby, Yorkshire; self-educated. His interest in clocks and watches led him to invent the gridiron compensating pendulum (1726). He later developed a recoiling escapement to avoid the necessity of lubrication; also the going fusee and the chronometer, which made possible the determination of longitude at sea. The chronometer is described in Harrison's *A Description Concerning Such Mechanism as Will Afford a Nice or True Mensuration of Time* (1767).—*R. N. M.*

HARVEST MOON: the full moon nearest the time of the autumnal equinox, Sept. 23. The delay in its time of rising from one night to the next is a minimum, so that for several successive nights there is bright moonlight during the early evening. Because the Moon moves eastward among the stars, in an orbit inclined at only 5° to the ecliptic, the average interval between one rising of the Moon and the next at the same place exceeds a day by 50 min. But the delay varies according to the inclination of the ecliptic to the horizon.

At the autumnal equinox, the Sun is at one intersection of the ecliptic and the equator, and sets due west. If the Moon is at full phase at this time (and in the plane of the ecliptic), as the Sun sets due west the Moon will rise due east at the other intersection of ecliptic and equator, being then at position (1) in the figure. By the same time on the next night, the Moon will have moved to (2), and will be still below the horizon. The daily apparent rotation of the celestial sphere will carry the Moon from (2) to its rising point (2a). The distance (2) − (2a) thus represents the delay in the time of rising from one night to the next. At the vernal equinox, the ecliptic makes a large angle to the horizon, and the corresponding delay time is represented by the distance (2′) − (2a′), which is clearly greater. The full moon nearest the time of the autumnal equinox has the least delay from night to night, while that occurring nearest the vernal equinox (Mar. 21) has the greatest. The actual delay in time of rising at the harvest moon depends upon the inclination of the celestial equator to the horizon, which, in latitude ϕ, is 90° − ϕ. The delay is smaller the greater the latitude, and even in latitudes as low as 40° it may be as little as 13 min. The delay in successive rising for the full moon following the harvest moon is still small, and this full moon is called the hunter's moon. For southern latitudes, the least delay occurs for the full moon nearest the time of vernal equinox (which, however, takes place during autumn in the southern hemisphere).—*M. W. O.*

Demonstration of Harvest Moon Phenomenon

HARVEY, WILLIAM, 1578–1657, English physician and physiologist; b. Folkestone, Kent. He was the discoverer of the circulation of blood. By observing the action of the heart in living animals, he demonstrated that the blood flows in a continuous stream from the heart through the arteries into the veins and back to the heart. This theory was contrary to views held at that time. Although Harvey was never able to find the connection between the arteries and the veins, as required by his theory, he began to teach the circulation of blood in 1616. In 1628 he published his revolutionary theory in *Exercitatio anatomica de motu cordis et sanguinis in animalibus,* a dissertation on the motion of the heart and blood in animals, regarded as one of the great books in medical history. When first issued the book created a storm of controversy, and there was strong opposition to Harvey's theory. Later Harvey became interested in natural history and the embryological development of animals. He was among the

Plate 40 EYE

Some eyes are highly adapted to daytime activities, others for nocturnal habits. **1. The compound eyes of a land crab,** like those of lobster and crayfish, are borne on movable stalks that can be lowered into grooves for protection. *(Walter Dawn)* **2.** By day the pupils in a **cat's eyes** narrow to vertical slits, limiting the amount of light reaching the sensitive cells of the retina. By night the pupils open widely and let the cat see in very dim illumination. *(Oswald Roberts/Shostal)* **3.** In snakes, such as the **Indian python,** a scale of the skin covers the eye. Gradually the scale becomes cloudy, impairing the snake's vision. Then the reptile sheds its skin and once more can see well. *(Walter Dawn)* **4.** Thousands of visual organs are fitted together in **the compound eyes of a housefly.** The fly's eyes are fixed in its head, not movable as in crabs and lobsters. *(Amer. Mus. of Nat. Hist.)*

Plate 41 FEATHERS

1. So eager were milliners to decorate hats with the nuptial plumes of **the American egret** that this bird was threatened with extinction early this century. *(C. Sibley/Amer. Mus. of Nat. Hist.)* **2.** Aside from beauty **feathers are highly functional,** consisting of fine parallel branches hooked together to form a lightweight aerodynamic surface. *(© 1957 Clay-Adams, Inc.)* **3.** Some birds use feathers in courtship, as does **the peacock** when it raises its striking fan of feathers. *(Frank Puza/Amer. Mus. of Nat. Hist.)*

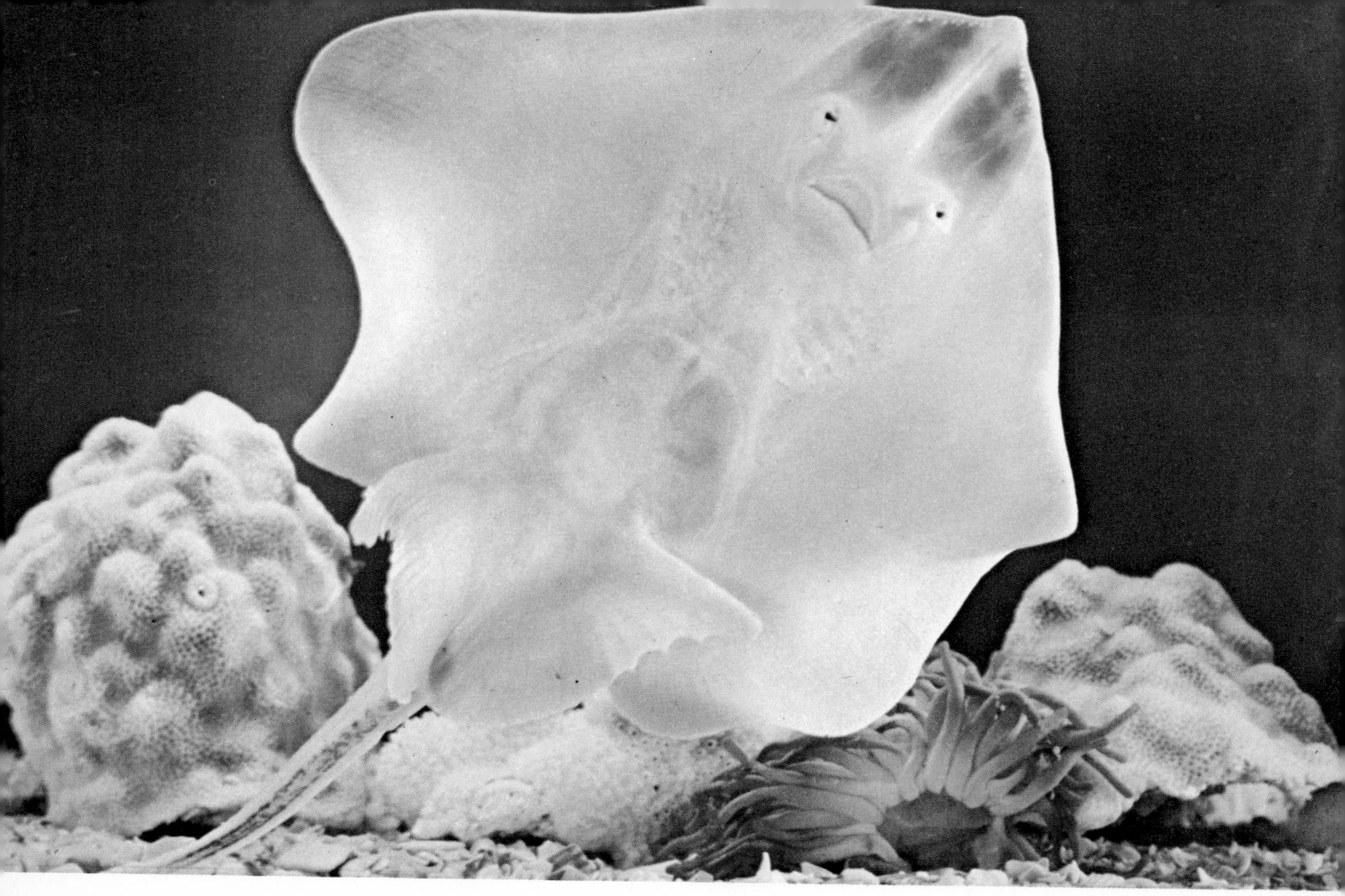

The flat-bodied skate, here seen from the underside, where nostrils, mouth, and gill openings are located, rests quietly on the bottom or swims with lazy winglike movements of its greatly enlarged pectoral fins; its long slender tail trails behind. Many species of skate are found in temperate seas. *(Stan Wayman/Rapho-Guillumette)*

Plate 42　FISHES

The colorful queen triggerfish *(Balistes vetula)* is widely distributed in shoal waters of the tropical Atlantic and Indian Oceans. It is like other members of its family in that so long as the second spine in front of its dorsal fin is raised, the whole fin is locked in the spread position. *(Walter Dawn)*

Plate 43 FISHES

More than 15,000 different kinds of fishes propel themselves through the world's salt and fresh waters, making the most of their fins but showing a host of different adaptations to special ways of life. Now that SCUBA (self-contained underwater breathing apparatus) is available, more and more persons are entering the world of the fishes; increased observations, along with eavesdropping on fish communications by hydrophones lowered into the water, are leading to a new understanding of fishes.

Tropical fish *(right),* in their infinite variety of bright colors and shapes, attract thousands of visitors to aquariums. The hobby of raising such exotic fishes in home aquariums has become increasingly popular. *(Harry Goodman/Shostal)*

Puffer fish *(below)* inflates itself into a globular shape when disturbed. Only a large fish could swallow a puffed-up puffer— and then the fish might be poisoned, for the internal organs of the puffer fishes contain toxic substances. *(Robert C. Hermes)*

Red and albino sea horses *(left)* are unusual varieties of the common brown sea horse *(Hippocampus),* which is found among seaweed in warm oceans. The male incubates the eggs in a special pouch. Both sexes cling to the seaweed with a prehensile tail, while feeding on minute plankton organisms. *(Stan Wayman/Rapho-Guillumette)*

Plate 44 FERNS

Ferns are perennial plants whose leaves are characteristically large and conspicuous. Unlike the leaves of flowering plants, which unfold, the leaves of ferns unroll from the bud. Usually fern leaves have a strong stemlike portion bearing leaflets on both sides—a form of leaf known as a frond. The leaflets may be divided so that the frond has a filmy or lacy appearance.

1

2

1. **Typical habitat** of ferns is moist, shaded glade, but some kinds of ferns grow in dry, sunny places. Few parts of U.S.A., even desert regions, lack ferns. *(Russ Kinne)*

2. **Leaves of the sensitive fern,** a denizen of wet places, die with the first frost of fall. *(Helen Cruickshank/National Audubon Soc.)*

3. **Groups of spore cases** called sori develop on underside of the mature fronds of many ferns. From these cases, spores are cast out into the wind. *(Maurice Broun/Shostal)* 4. **Unfolding fronds** are often called fiddleheads. Those shown are of the cinnamon fern. *(W. A. Pluemer/Amer. Mus. of Nat. Hist.)*

3   4

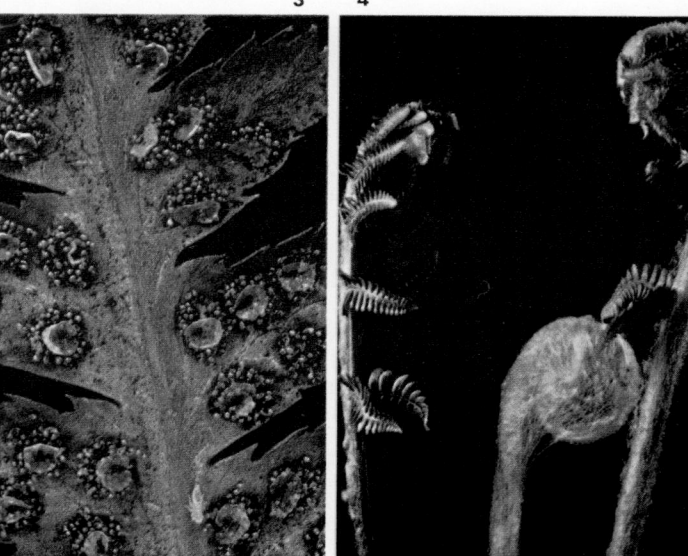

5

6

5. **Identification of ferns** is based on the shape of the fronds and also on the form of the sori that develop on the fronds. *(C. E. Mohr/National Audubon Soc.)* 6. **Leaflets of the Christmas fern** remain green all winter, often hidden under the snow. *(Helen Cruickshank/National Audubon Soc.)*

first to observe and describe the stages in the development of the chick. In 1651 he published a book on generation, *Exercitationes de generatione animalium,* now believed by many to mark the beginning of modern embryology. Harvey was made president of the Royal College of Physicians and during his lifetime was physician extraordinary to James I of England and also physician to Charles I.— *C. S. V.*

William Harvey
(New York Public Library)

HAUKSBEE, FRANCIS, 16??–1713, English instrument maker and physicist; birthplace unknown. He improved upon Robert Boyle's air pump and investigated the production of light from objects rubbed together in a partial vacuum. This work led him to the study of electrical phenomena, and he constructed (*c.* 1706) one of the earliest machines for generating electrical charges, based on discoveries by O. von Guericke. He also determined the relative weights of air and water. He was a fellow of the Royal Society. His research papers were collected in his *Physico-mechanical Experiments on Various Subjects* (1709). Hauksbee's nephew, **Francis Hauksbee** (1687–1763), constructed vacuum pumps and wrote on scientific subjects. He also was a fellow of the Royal Society. —*D. H. D. R.*

HAURWITZ, BERNHARD, 1905–   , German-U. S. meteorologist; b. Glogau. He is known for his work in dynamic meteorology, including a standard textbook. His research is characterized not only by deep physical insight but also by the elegance of the mathematical treatment, and the topics dealt with cover a large field. He is a member of the National Academy of Sciences.—*O. G. S.*

HAÜY, RENÉ JUST, ABBÉ, 1743–1822, French mineralogist; b. Saint-Just. After noticing the cleavages resulting when a cluster of calcite crystals was dropped and shattered, Haüy theorized in his *Essay on the Theory of Crystal Structures* (1784) that every mineral must be constructed of a basic nucleus or molecule of a shape characteristic of the mineral. Formulating this theory as the Law of Rational Intercepts, Haüy in his further work became a founder of the science of crystallography.—*C. J. S.*

HAVERS, CLOPTON, 1657?–1702, English anatomist and physician; birthplace unknown; ed. Cambridge Univ. and Univ. of Utrecht. Havers was the first to give a detailed and minute account of the structure of bone, and his name is given to the Haversian canals, the channels of bone in which the blood vessels run. His most important publication is *Osteologia nova, or Some New Observations of the Bones and the Parts Belonging to Them* (1691). He was a fellow of the Royal Society.—*D. H. D. R.*

HAWORTH, SIR WALTER NORMAN, 1883–1950, English chemist; b. Chorley, Lancashire. For his researches into the constitution of carbohydrates and vitamin C, he shared the 1937 Nobel prize in chemistry with Paul Karrer. Haworth clarified the constitution of maltose, cellobiose, lactose, gentiobiose, raffinose, and the ring structure of glucosides of normal sugars; he established the fundamental structure of starch, cellulose, inulin, and xylan molecules and the chain length in methylated polysaccharides. In 1934 he announced the synthesis of ascorbic acid. He wrote *The Constitution of Sugar* (1929) and was an editor of *Advances in Carbohydrate Chemistry.* He was a fellow of the Royal Society.—*V. B.*

HAYDEN, FERDINAND VANDIVEER, 1829–87, U. S. geologist; b. Westfield, Mass. Leader of the U. S. Geological Survey of the Territories (1867–79), the first large federal survey into the western U. S. A. to be devoted exclusively to scientific exploration, he was a pioneer contributor to stratigraphic and paleontologic knowledge of the Great Plains and Rocky Mts. His reports on the Yellowstone region (1870–1) helped to establish it as a national park. He was a member of the National Academy of Sciences.—*A. L. McA.*

HEARING: the sensation produced when the brain of an animal receives nerve impulses from the EARS. Normally these impulses arise when the ears are stimulated by sound vibrations from the environment. To an animal, the important characteristics of a SOUND are its *loudness* (which often indicates the distance to the source of the sound), its *pitch* or combination of pitches (which frequently permits identification of the producer of the sound), and the *direction* from which the sound comes. Loudness depends upon the sense organ as well as the amount of energy in the vibrations from the environmental medium (*e.g.* air or water). Human ears can detect sounds ranging in frequency from about 20 to about 15,000 cycles/sec, if the sounds are of sufficient intensity, but the ears are most sensitive to sounds in the range from 2,000 to 4,000 cycles/sec. At 10,000 cycles, a sound must be about 100 times as intense as at 2,000 cycles for a human ear to detect it. A dog's ears are sensitive to sounds at 20,000 cycles/sec; the animal can be taught to return home when it hears a special "Galton whistle," which cannot be heard by the person who blows it. Rats communicate with one another at a still higher frequency, hearing one another's calls at about 24,000 cycles/sec. Bats make use of echo-location, an animal equivalent of sonar, at frequencies as high as 150,000 cycles/sec, to which their organs of hearing are highly sensitive (see ANIMAL SONAR).

The pitch of a musical note is said to be low when it corresponds to only a few hundred cycles/sec, and to be high when it is at frequencies above those to which the human ear is most sensitive. The piano keyboard corresponds to a frequency range from 27.4 (lowest) to 4,214 (highest) cycles/sec; "middle C" is 256 cycles/sec.

Deafness of man and other vertebrate animals arises both from defects of the middle ear and from injury to the sensory cells or the nervous pathways to the brain. Defects of the middle ear cause *conductive deafness,* which usually affects sensitivity to all frequencies, causing a general loss of hearing. *Nerve deafness,* by contrast, is usually selective, shown by loss of sensitivity to specific ranges of frequency. Human ears show aging by progressive loss of sensitivity to the high end of the hearing range, while retaining most of their sensitivity to the low end.

The direction from which a sound comes is usually identified by turning the head until the sound is received by both ears simultaneously—within the same ten-thousandth of a sec—and with equal intensity. Even though the outer flap of the human ear cannot be turned significantly to gather sound efficiently from various directions, most people can identify the direction from which a sound comes within about 20 degrees. Upon this ability depends some of our listening pleasure while attending a musical concert. Stereophonic reproduction of music in the home is an attempt to duplicate by electronic devices this sensation of hearing.—*L. and M. M.*

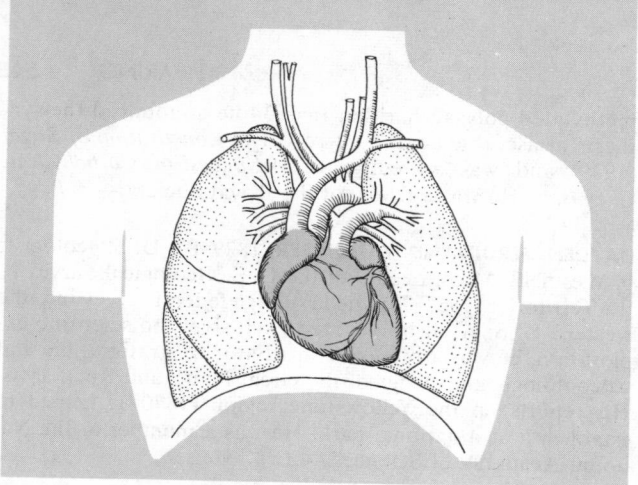

Heart is located in chest cavity just above diaphragm along midline of body. People often think heart is on left side, because strongest beat comes from lower tip, which extends leftward. Lungs partly cover heart. (*After Young*)

HEART: the muscular organ that provides the pumping action to propel the blood through the circulatory system (see CIRCULATION IN LIVING THINGS). In man and the higher vertebrates, the right and left halves of the heart function as separate, two-chambered pumps. Each half consists of a thin-walled *atrium* and a powerful *ventricle,* with one-way valves between the two chambers to keep the blood flowing in the proper direction. Fresh, oxygenated blood coming to the heart from the lungs enters the left atrium. Contraction of that chamber pumps the blood into the left ventricle. From there, blood is forcibly ejected through the aorta into the arteries. After delivering its content of oxygen and other nutrients to the organs and tissues of the body, the blood returns to the right side of the heart via the veins. This venous blood, oxygen-depleted and carbon-dioxide-laden, is pumped through the right atrium and ventricle back to the lungs.

The human heart normally contracts 60 to 70 times/min throughout the lifetime of an individual. Each beat consists of a contraction phase, called *systole,* and a period of relaxation, called *diastole.* These rhythmic contractions are stimulated by electrical impulses arising in a group of specialized muscle cells that form the *pacemaker* of the heart. As a result, a heart removed from an animal will continue to beat for many hours if proper culture conditions are provided. Under normal circumstances, the heart pumps about 4 qt of

blood/min, or approximately 2 oz with each beat. The rhythmic spurts of blood may be felt in superficial arteries (*e.g.* in the wrist) as the PULSE. The heart is nourished by blood vessels in its muscular walls. Occlusion or rupture of one of these crucial *coronary arteries* may lead to sudden death by heart stoppage, commonly known as a "heart attack."

In mammals, birds, and crocodilians the heart is four-chambered, but in other reptiles and amphibians both atria empty into a single ventricle. Fish have a two-chambered heart which pumps venous blood from atrium to ventricle and then to the gills, from which it is distributed throughout the body. This two-chambered condition indicates the persistence of the type of heart seen in early embryonic stages of all vertebrates, where it consists of a simple tube with bulges representing the primitive undivided atrium and ventricle. In crustaceans, insects, clams, and many other invertebrates, a single muscular sac serves as a heart, circulating the blood freely in spaces within the body cavity; these animals have few, if any, capillaries and veins.—*R. L. D.*

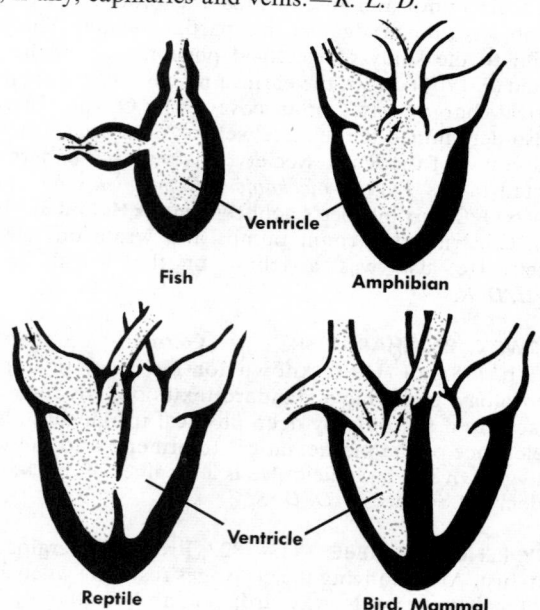

Evolution of heart in vertebrates parallels evolution of respiratory system. In fish, blood flows from heart to gills (where it is oxygenated), to all parts of the body, and back to heart. Only deoxygenated blood (shown by stippling) passes through heart. In amphibians, reptiles, birds, and mammals, blood flows from one side of heart to lungs, to other side of heart, to body tissues, and back to heart. Oxygenated and deoxygenated blood mix to some extent in single ventricle of amphibians, mix only slightly in almost completely divided ventricle of reptiles, and do not mix at all in completely divided, four-chambered heart of birds and mammals. As a result, blood reaching body tissues in birds and mammals is richer in oxygen and better able to support warmbloodedness. (*After Kenoyer*)

HEAT: the form of energy that passes from a body of higher temperature to a body of lower temperature. That heat is energy follows from the criterion for any energy form: Can it do physical work? The various heat engines, such as the steam engine, gasoline engine, diesel engine, and jet engine, all testify to the ability of heat to do work. One sees a simpler example when the loose cover on a pot of boiling water rises in the air as steam forms under it. Indeed, careful measurements would show that some steam condenses when this work is performed, and the heat lost is just equivalent to the work done in lifting the cover.

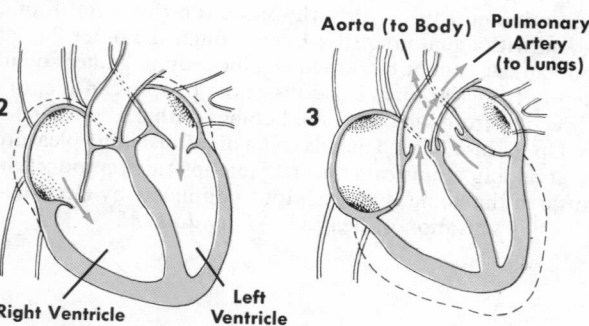

Heart cycle: (1) Blood enters left and right atria. (2) Atria contract, forcing blood into ventricles. (3) Ventricles contract, closing valve between atria and ventricles, opening valve to arteries, and forcing blood into arteries. Cycle starts again.

The amount of heat involved in any thermal, or heat, transaction depends upon the amount of material; the difference in temperature between source and receiver; and the SPECIFIC HEAT, which differs for different substances. It is obvious that the heat energy obtainable from a hot body depends on the amount of matter in the body. Burning matches or candles would scarcely be expected to warm a room appreciably, although the flame temperature is very high. When two bodies are in thermal contact, the amount of heat that passes from the hotter to the cooler body is proportional to the temperature difference between them. Given two identical bodies, a temperature difference of 20° will result in about twice as much heat transferred in the same time as a difference of 10°. Specific heat indicates the amount of heat a substance must absorb for a consequent temperature rise. Given equal amounts of two different substances, the substance with the higher specific heat will absorb more heat in reaching any particular higher temperature. Whereas relative hotness, or level of heat, is measured as temperature, quantity of heat is expressed in heat units. The older heat units, the calorie and the British thermal unit (Btu), are the most extensively used. They are defined by simple thermal effects: as the amount of heat required to raise the temperature of 1 gm of water 1°C (calorie) or of 1 lb of water 1°F (Btu). The modern trend, however, is to express heat energy in the same unit as mechanical and electrical energy: the joule, which is the work done when a force of 1 newton causes a displacement of 1 m in the direction of the force. (One joule equals 0.239 calories or 9.478×10^{-4} Btu.)

Earth's six most important sources of heat energy are the Sun, which supplies most of our heat, either directly or indirectly; the hot interior of Earth; chemical action, as in ordinary burning or in the oxidation of food in our bodies; mechanical energy, as in the rubbing of two materials together; electric energy, from which heat is produced when an electric current encounters resistance in a conductor; and nuclear energy, which is converted into heat energy by an atomic reactor.

Heat was once believed to be an actual fluid that flowed from one body to another, but this CALORIC THEORY was discredited early in the 19th cent. The work of Count Rumford, J. R. von Mayer, James Prescott Joule, H. L. F. von Helmholtz, and others led to the current theory that heat is the energy of motion of the tiny molecules that make up matter. The labor and imagination of these men produced in the middle of the 19th cent. the great physical doctrine known as CONSERVATION OF MASS-ENERGY, which states that energy cannot be created or destroyed, only changed in form (as from chemical energy to heat energy). Joule in particular performed many experiments that not only proved that energy is conserved in its transition from one form to another, but also established the numerical relation between the different units in which these forms of energy are measured.

The heat transferred in chemical or physical changes is measured by CALORIMETRY. Heat is transmitted by any of three methods: conduction (see CONDUCTIVITY), convection, and RADIATION. When heat is added to a body, the body expands as temperature increases (see EXPANSION, THERMAL).— *J. E. W.*

HEAT, LATENT: heat energy absorbed or liberated by a unit mass of a substance during a CHANGE OF STATE, the process taking place at a constant temperature. Ice, at its melting point, absorbs about 80 cal/gm (or 144 Btu/lb) as it passes into its liquid state. If the water is frozen again, the same 80 cal (or 144 Btu) is liberated for every gram (or pound) of ice formed. This quantity of energy constitutes the *heat of fusion* or, traditionally, the *latent* heat of fusion. Similarly, boiling water at 100°C (or 212°F) absorbs about 540 cal/gm (or 972 Btu/lb), the same amount being given off when steam condenses at this temperature. The energy per unit mass, absorbed or liberated as the case may be, is referred to as the *latent heat of vaporization* or, more simply, as the *heat of vaporization*. The large amount of heat required to convert boiling water to steam is explained by the fact that extra energy must be supplied to break up molecular cohesion and, to a lesser extent, be used to expand the resulting vapor against atmospheric pressure. The heat of vaporization of water at a temperature below its standard boiling point exceeds the 540 cal/gm figure because of the relatively greater molecular cohesion to be overcome. Another form of latent heat involved in changing a unit mass of a solid *directly* into its gaseous form, and vice versa, is known as the *heat of sublimation.—A. E.*

HEAT BALANCE OF EARTH: the equilibrium between the average solar radiation received and the average radiation reflected and emitted back to space by Earth and its atmosphere. (The amount of energy flowing up through Earth's crust, or reaching Earth from all stellar sources other than the Sun, is negligible in comparison with solar radiation.) On the average, Earth receives 2 cal/cm²/min of solar radiation at the top of the atmosphere on a surface *perpendicular* to the Sun's rays. This is called the SOLAR CONSTANT. Earth's surface area is equal to four times its cross-sectional area; hence the average amount of solar radiation received on a unit *horizontal* surface at the top of the atmosphere is 0.5 cal/cm²/min.

Because the effective radiative temperature of the Sun is approximately 6000°K, the solar energy intercepted by Earth is largely confined to the ultraviolet, visible, and near-infrared portions of the spectrum. This energy is in part absorbed in Earth's atmosphere, in part reflected back to space, and the remainder absorbed at the ground. That fraction of the incoming solar radiation (insolation) at the top of the atmosphere which is reflected back to space by Earth and its atmosphere is called Earth's *planetary albedo*. Its value according to the most recent estimates is approximately 35%. The remaining 65% of the received solar energy warms Earth and its atmosphere and drives the circulations of the ocean and atmosphere. This energy is ultimately radiated back to space.

Of the radiation received at the top of the atmosphere, on the average approximately 0.02% is absorbed by oxygen in the atmosphere above the 60-km level, about 3% is absorbed by ozone in the stratosphere, and about 15% is absorbed by water vapor, carbon dioxide, dust, and clouds in the troposphere. Thus only 18% of the solar energy is directly absorbed by the atmosphere.

Solar radiation is reflected back to space chiefly by clouds, but also by air, water vapor, and dust particles, and by Earth's surface. The reflectivity of clouds varies with their type and depth; thus cirrus clouds reflect as little as 10 to 15% of incident solar radiation, whereas the average reflectivity of altostratus clouds is about 50%, and of thick cumulonimbus, as high as about 80%. The average albedo of all clouds is very close to 50%. Since, in the mean, about half of the sky is covered by clouds, cloudiness accounts for 25% of the insolation being directly returned to space. Average cloud types and amounts vary with latitude, with resulting latitudinal variation of the reflection due to clouds. A part of the solar beam is scattered back to space by air molecules, water vapor, and atmospheric dust particles, which together contribute about 6% of the insolation to Earth's planetary albedo.

Ground reflection of solar radiation varies markedly depending on the nature of the underlying surface. Green forests reflect only 3 to 10% of the incident solar radiation, whereas reflectivity is about 35% for concrete roads and can be as high as 90% for fresh snow. Much of the reflection from Earth's surface is intercepted by the atmosphere and by clouds, and thus represents a relatively small component of the planetary albedo except at polar latitudes where the snow cover is extensive.

Solar energy reaches Earth's surface partly as direct radiation from the Sun and partly as diffuse radiation transmitted through clouds and scattered downward by the atmosphere. This energy is absorbed at Earth's surface and is largely used to evaporate water, principally from the surface of the oceans. On the average about 80 cm³ of water per cm² of Earth's surface (a total of approximately 4×10^{20} gm of water) is evaporated annually. In addition to evaporating water, the absorbed energy heats the top layers of the ground and oceans, which in turn heat the lower atmosphere.

Since Earth's mean temperature changes very little from year to year, the planet must radiate back to space the unreflected portion of incoming solar radiation. This re-radiation is confined to the infrared (long-wave) spectrum. In this spectral interval, the ground and almost all clouds absorb and emit radiation almost perfectly. Also, atmospheric gases such as water vapor and carbon dioxide, while they do not strongly absorb visible (solar) radiation, are reasonably effective infrared absorbers. As a result, incoming solar radiation penetrates through the atmosphere, but long-wave radiation leaving Earth's surface is largely absorbed and then re-radiated upward and downward from the atmosphere. If there were no atmosphere, and if Earth's planetary albedo remained at 35%, the average temperature would fall to $-23°C$! The downward radiation from the atmosphere, however, helps to keep Earth's temperature at an average of about 15°C. This increased temperature, due to the presence of water vapor and carbon dioxide in the atmosphere, is the result of the so-called "greenhouse effect" described above. At the ground the difference between the surface radiation and back radiation from the atmosphere is called effective (nocturnal) radiation. A part of the surface radiation and of the upward-directed radiation from each layer in the atmosphere is eventually lost to space. The combined outgoing infrared radiation amounts to 65% of the incoming solar radiation. A schematic picture of the average heat budget of Earth is given below.

The effective insolation, defined as the incoming solar radiation minus the insolation reflected back to space, is equal to the total outgoing radiation when both are averaged over all latitudes for long time intervals. Of primary importance to the general circulation of the atmosphere, however, is the latitudinal distribution of the difference between effective insolation and total outgoing radiation (radiation excess). On the average, the radiation excess is positive (*i.e.* more effective incoming than outgoing radiation) equatorward of 35° latitude, and negative poleward of 35°. This requires that heat energy be continuously transported poleward with a maximum of transport at about latitude 35°; hence the vigorous weather patterns found in middle latitudes.—*J. L.*

HEAT DETECTOR: a device for detecting and measuring heat energy. Many effects of heat on matter are used as basic operating principles for heat detectors. Since the application of heat usually causes an increase in an object's temperature, any detector of temperature change—*e.g.* the THERMOMETER and the PYROMETER—is a heat detector. Common thermometers, *e.g.* the mercury and bimetallic types, utilize the change of size in their materials due to heating or cooling. Changes of state, pressure, and electrical resistance are used, respectively, in the vapor-pressure, constant-volume gas, and resistance (bolometer and thermistor) low-temperature thermometers. The generation of an electric potential (emf) by unequal heating of junctions of dissimilar metals is used in the THERMOCOUPLE. Detectors for temperatures above about 500°C generally are called *pyrometers;* they measure the energy radiated from hot objects. Total-radiation pyrometers measure all wavelengths, including infrared, whereas optical pyrometers utilize only the optical spectrum, *i.e.* change of brightness and spectral color with temperature. The operation of a pyrometer requires some kind of TRANSDUCER—*e.g.* a photoemissive, photoconductive, thermoelectric, or photographic type—or simply the human eye.

Devices for the measurement of heat quantities are called CALORIMETERS. The conventional method is to measure the change in temperature of a calorimetric substance of known mass and specific heat; integrating thermometers and pyrometers may also be used. Other properties of matter that change with heat and so can be used as bases for heat detection are chemical structure, density, strength, viscosity, surface tension, velocity of sound, index of refraction, absorption, reflection, capacitance, inductance, and work function. —*D. J. B.*

AVERAGE HEAT BUDGET OF EARTH

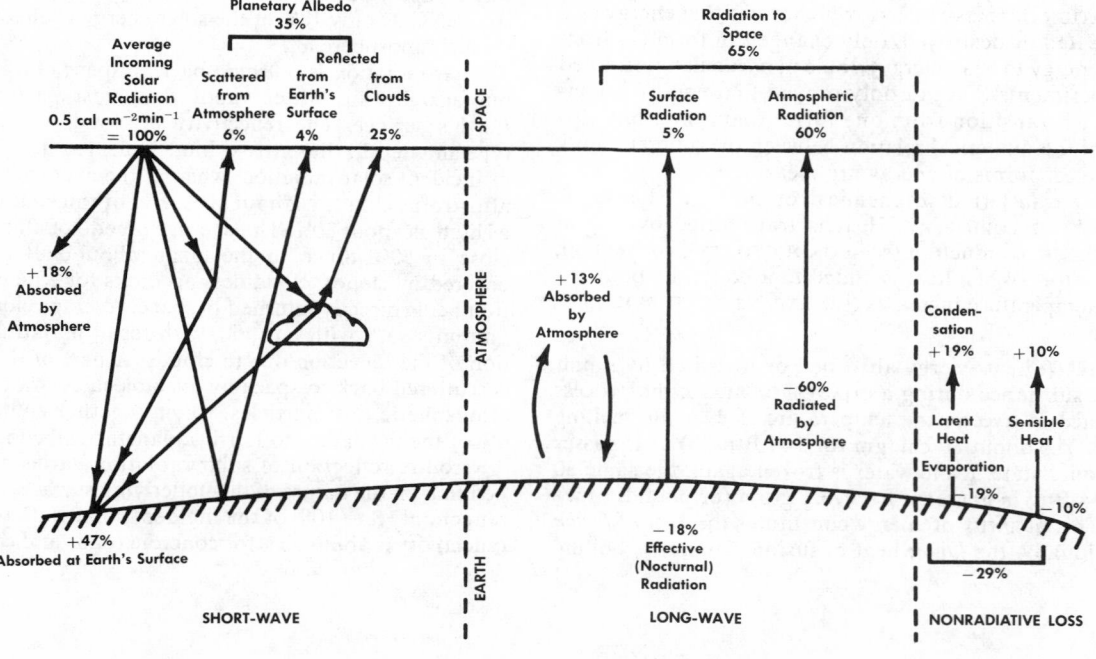

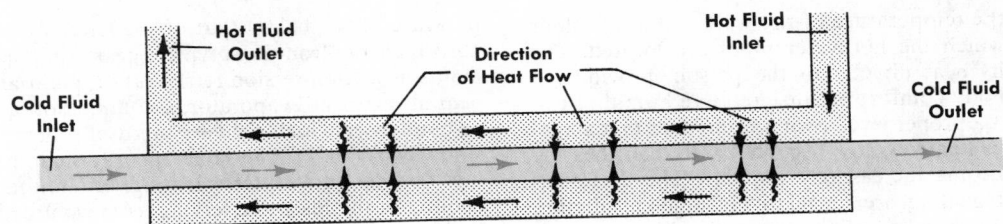

Heat exchanger: In single-pass shell-and-tube heat exchanger, temperature difference between hot and cold fluids directs heat flow to cold fluid, which continually carries heat away.

HEAT EXCHANGER: a device that effects the transfer of energy in the form of heat from a warmer to a cooler medium. In conventional heat exchangers, *e.g.* boilers, condensers, water heaters, automobile radiators, air heaters, and air coolers, the heat is transferred from one fluid to another through a solid wall; but a pot of water on a kitchen stove, or the core of a NUCLEAR REACTOR, also is a heat exchanger. The simplest type of heat exchanger is a container in which a hot and a cold fluid are mixed directly. In such a system both fluids will eventually reach the same temperature. More common and important, however, are exchangers in which one fluid is separated from the other by a partition through which the heat flows while both fluids are continuously passing through the system. These devices, called *shell-and-tube heat exchangers,* are available in many different forms and shapes. The simplest, consisting of a single tube within a cylindrical shell, is shown above. Depending on whether the fluids flow in the same or in opposite directions, the device is called a parallel- or a counter-flow exchanger. The number of times the fluid passes through the exchanger defines the system as a single- or multiple-pass unit. When the two fluids flow at right angles to each other, as in an automobile radiator, the heat exchanger is of the cross-flow type.

In general the rate of heat transfer (q) between the fluids can be calculated from the equation $q = UA\Delta T_{mean}$, where U is the over-all heat transfer coefficient or thermal conductance between the two fluids, A the heat transfer area, and ΔT_{mean} the mean temperature difference between the hot and the cold fluids. (See HEAT TRANSFER.)—*F. K.*

HEATH, SIR THOMAS LITTLE, 1861–1940, English civil servant and authority on Greek mathematics; b. Lincolnshire. Heath's work on Greek mathematics led to his election as a fellow of the Royal Society in 1912. His works on Diophantus (1885), Apollonius (1896), Archimedes (1897), and Aristarchus (1913) were authoritative English editions of the Greek masters. His 3-vol. English edition of Euclid's *Elements* (1908) was followed by a Greek edition of Book I of the *Elements* (1920). Heath's *History of Greek Mathematics* (1921) became the standard work on the subject. At his death, he was preparing an edition of the mathematical content of Aristotle's work (published 1948).—*H. C.*

HEATING SYSTEMS: the thermal and mechanical means whereby domestic, commercial, and industrial enclosures are heated. Every heating system must have a source of heat energy, *e.g.* a combustible fuel, electricity, or solar radiation. In a system utilizing coal, oil, or gas, there must be a FURNACE, or an insulated compartment in which the combustion reaction proceeds to completion; adequate air must be introduced for the initial combustion of the fuel and the secondary combustion of the hot gases. A furnace utilizing coal, for many years the most commonly used fuel in heating systems, must have a grate to support the bed of coal and a stoker to feed the coal to the grate. In those modern installations

where coal is still used because of its low cost, automatic chain-grate stokers are employed. For house heating, oil and gas are increasingly used, despite their higher cost, because of their cleanliness and simplicity of means of combustion. All furnaces must have a surface by which the heat of combustion is transferred to a working substance, *e.g.* the water in a BOILER, or the air passing directly over the transmitting surface. The heated working substance—usually steam, hot water, or air—circulates by pipes or ducts to the rooms or enclosures to be heated; there it gives up its heat by radiation, conduction, and convection (see HEAT TRANSFER).

In a one-pipe steam system, used mainly for small installations, the steam generated in the boiler at pressures of 5 lb/in.² or less circulates to a radiator, where it gives up its latent heat of CONDENSATION to the radiator; the radiator, designed to expose a large surface area, gives up some of its heat by radiation and the major portion by conduction to the air surrounding it. The condensed steam returns by gravity to the boiler by the same pipe through which it passed as steam. Larger steam installations use a two-pipe, or vapor, system, in which the condensed steam returns by way of a return pipe rather than by the steam pipe. A vacuum-steam system is a two-pipe system in which a vacuum pump maintains a reduced pressure in the pipes; this allows the steam to be formed at varying temperatures below 212°F (*i.e.* fewer calories are required to turn a given volume of water into steam). Thus, when the steam vapor condenses, it releases fewer calories than steam under atmospheric pressure: the amount of calories released can be controlled by varying the amount of vacuum produced by the vacuum pump; the pump in turn is controlled by an outdoor thermostat. The vacuum-steam system thus allows a flexibility not usually found in steam systems.

In hot-water systems, pipes convey hot water from the boiler by pump or by convection to radiators or convectors. (Convectors are finned metallic devices, installed close to the floor, which give up most of their heat by conduction to the air surrounding them, thus starting a convection current which carries the heat to the rest of the room.) The advantage of hot water over steam or warmed air is its extended retention of heat, due to its greater density; this avoids the sharp temperature fluctuations characteristic of the other systems. In warm-air systems, cool air passes over the heat-transmitting surface of the furnace.

Electric heating coils are in some systems used to warm the cool air, but the high cost of electricity prohibits its extensive use. The warm air either by convection or, more recently, by a centrifugal fan circulates by duct to a room register or diffuser, where it gives up its heat by convection; the cooler air in the room returns to the furnace by a return duct.

Steam, hot-water, and warm-air systems heat the air in a room; the comfort of an individual, however, depends not only on the air temperature but also on the relative humidity of the air and the temperature of the enclosing walls. Radiant heating uses the working substance, usually circulating hot water, to raise the temperature of the wall, ceiling, or floor panels, within which the hot-water pipes are located. The panel radiates its heat directly to the person, providing a high degree of body comfort because relative humidity can be maintained at a proper level, owing to the fact that actual air temperature is relatively low (*e.g.* 65°F). Radiant heating has therefore become increasingly popular. The disadvantages of radiant heating are its relatively high installation cost and the inaccessibility of the pipes should there be a leak; leaks generally cause rapid corrosion and extensive damage to the surrounding material. Radiating panels are efficiently activated by electricity, but again the high cost of electricity makes its general use prohibitive. Investigations of SOLAR ENERGY as a utilizable source of heat energy are now in progress, and the success so far achieved in limited experiments gives great promise.—*A. L.*

Fig. 1

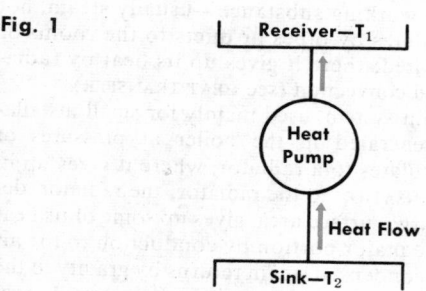

Fig. 2

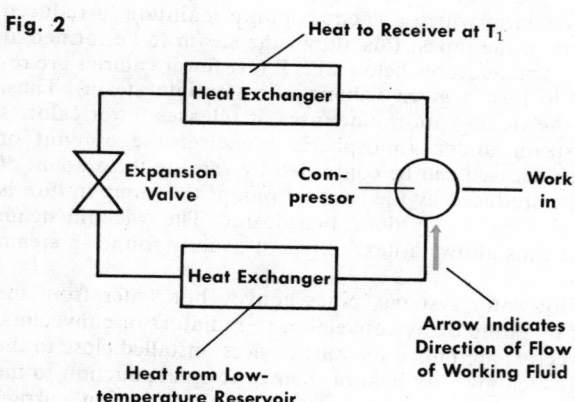

HEAT PUMP: a device that withdraws energy from a low-temperature reservoir, called a sink, and transfers energy as heat to a reservoir at a higher temperature, called a receiver. A heat pump is essentially a reversed heat engine. Its operation is shown schematically in Fig. 1. Heat flows from the sink at temperature T_2 to the working fluid of the engine, *e.g.* air or freon; the temperature of the working fluid is then raised to at least T_1 by compressing it, and the heated working fluid is brought into thermal contact with the high-temperature reservoir at T_1 where, in accordance with the second law of thermodynamics, some of its energy is transferred as heat to the receiver. After this energy transfer is completed, the fluid undergoes an expansion, in the course of which its tem-

perature drops below that of the sink, so that it can again absorb energy from it. A typical heat pump has the same elements as a compression refrigeration plant and consists of a heat absorber or evaporator, a compressor, a heat exchanger or condenser which delivers the useful heat, and an expansion valve (Fig. 2). The same apparatus can be used for summer cooling and winter warming, or simultaneously for the cooling of the reservoir serving as the source of heat and the heating of the reservoir serving as the heat receiver. There are many heat-pump installations in S California and other parts of the U. S. A. where all-year temperature control is desired.—*F. K.*

HEAT RADIATION: see HEAT TRANSFER.

HEAT SINK: a means by which heat is stored, removed, or absorbed; also a place toward which heat moves in a system. The term is often used in connection with re-entry heating of missiles. In recent designs ABLATION is used as a heat sink; this is in contrast to a solid heat sink, which requires placing material in the nose cone with enough capacity to absorb excessive heat.—*D. B.*

HEAT TRANSFER: the propagation of heat from a point at higher temperature to one at lower temperature. The methods of heat transfer include conductive heat flow through solids and liquids, convection currents in fluids, and radiant heat waves in "empty" space. In thermal CONVECTION, heat is transferred through a fluid by the movement of fluid matter, whereas in conduction, atoms and molecules simply "pass on" the kinetic energy delivered to them (see CONDUCTIVITY,

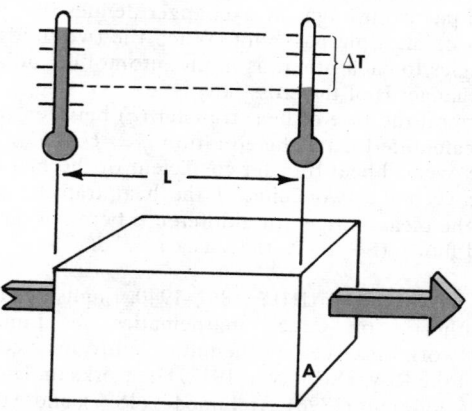

Rate of heat transfer depends on the temperature gradient, $\Delta T/L$, and the cross-sectional area of the heat path, A.

Transfer by convection involves motion of material being heated.

THERMAL). HEAT EXCHANGERS utilize the transfer of heat from one fluid to another, usually by convection and by metallic conduction through the walls separating the fluids. Radiant heat is transferred by electromagnetic waves (see RADIATION); the amount of heat transferred follows the STEFAN-BOLTZMANN LAW, and the variation of color with temperature in the radiating body is expressed by Wien's displacement law (see WIEN'S RADIATION LAWS).—*A. E.*

HEAT WAVE: a period of weather so hot (and usually so humid) that it interferes with normal human activities. Standards of "comfortable" temperature vary greatly from region to region, and hence a "heat wave" is hard to define in specific terms. On the east coast of the U. S. A., where at least one "heat wave" occurs nearly every summer, the cause is typically a strengthening of the circulation around the semi-permanent high-pressure area centered near Bermuda. The clockwise flow of air around the high brings hot, humid, tropical maritime air northward along the coast. —*D. H. L.*

HEAVISIDE, OLIVER, 1850–1925, English physicist and electrical engineer; b. Camden Town (near London). Largely self-trained, Heaviside contributed to a wide range of problems in electricity and electromagnetism. His investigation of the possibility of artificially increasing the inductance of telephone lines led to a vast improvement in long-distance telephone communication. The term *impedance,* which represents the resistive forces of inductance, capacitance, and resistance in an a-c circuit, was introduced by Heaviside in 1892 and has been accepted in the general terminology of physics. There was opposition to his introduction of operational methods to solve differential equations associated with electrical circuits, because his methods lacked a rigorous mathematical foundation. Today, operational methods, properly developed and utilizing Laplace transforms, are used to great advantage in all branches of applied science. With successful radio transmission by Marconi, Heaviside suggested that electromagnetic waves are reflected from a layer of ionized gas in the upper atmosphere. This is now called the Heaviside layer, or the Kennelly-Heaviside layer. His *Electrical Papers* (1892) and *Electromagnetic Theory* (1893–1912) are important in development of electrical theory. He was a fellow of the Royal Society.—*A. L.*

HEAVY WATER: a term used to describe any sample of water (H_2O or HOH) composed of isotopes of hydrogen (H) and oxygen (O) having atomic weights higher than the normal 1.008 for hydrogen and the normal 16 for oxygen. Deuterium oxide (DOD) is found in natural water in concentrations of approximately 1 part in 5,000. Deuterium is an isotope of hydrogen with twice the atomic weight of ordinary hydrogen (or protium). Another type of heavy water has one protium and one deuterium: HOD. A triple-weight hydrogen, tritium, also exists; and there are several heavy isotopes of oxygen that may produce heavy water.—*D. P. B.*

HEGEL, GEORG, 1770–1831, German philosopher; b. Stuttgart; professor at Jena and Berlin. His influential but difficult philosophy sought to integrate the cardinal assumptions of 18th-cent. rationalism with the conception of reality as an organically unified whole that was implicit in the romantic movement in theologic and social thought current in his day. According to Hegel, the basic categories or distinctions (*e.g.* change, chance, necessity, or freedom) used in interpreting experience to make it intelligible also represent fundamental aspects of reality and form a hierarchically ordered as well as

Georg Hegel
(German Information Center)

an organically interrelated system. Categories at higher levels in this hierarchy have a richer content than those at lower levels; they are more adequate to the nature of reality than the latter; and they are the outcome of a dialectical development, in which ostensibly incompatible categories at lower levels are absorbed into a higher unity. The laws of dialectic thinking, which moves progressively in triads from one fragmentary concept (the thesis) to its opposite (the antithesis) and then to their fusion (the synthesis), were thus identified by Hegel with the laws according to which the progressively more comprehensive aspects of reality are manifested. Moreover, since every stage in this development is but a partial aspect of the real, any account of an event that falls short of being a complete account of the event's relations to the whole of reality is for Hegel a mutilation of the truth. In consonance with these doctrines he therefore held that Newtonian science with its mechanical view of nature possessed at best only an inferior grade of truth; and he argued instead for a science which would be based on the assumption that nature is an organic whole whose parts and processes are all logically interrelated. Hegel's philosophy received little attention from natural scientists; but his view that the nature of man is revealed in man's history and in the historical unfolding of social institutions profoundly influenced the direction taken by historical and social studies in the 19th cent. In particular, Hegelian ideas were adopted by Karl Marx, though often in greatly modified form; and the Hegelian laws of dialectic continue to have a central place in the official philosophy of Soviet Russia. Hegel's chief works are: *Phänomenologie des Geistes* (*The Philosophy of Spirit,* 1807), *Wissenschaft der Logik* (*The Science of Logic,* 1812–16), *Enzyklopädie der philosophischen Wissenschaften* (*Encyclopedia of the Philosophical Sciences,* 1817), and *Grundlinien der Philosophie des Rechts* (*The Philosophy of Right,* 1820).—*E. N.*

HEIM, ALBERT, 1849–1937, Swiss geologist; b. Zürich. He became famous for his *Untersuchungen über den Mechanismus der Gebirgsbildung* (1878), dealing with mountain formation, and his *Geologie der Schweiz* (2 vol., 1916–22), on the geology of Switzerland, has been called "by far the finest national geology yet produced." He was a fellow of the Royal Society and an associate of the U. S. National Academy of Sciences. —*D. H. D. R.*

HEISENBERG, WERNER KARL, 1901–   , German physicist; b. Duisburg. He developed a system of quantum mechanics, based on matrix algebra and known as matrix mechanics. For this work and his prediction of two allotropic forms of hydrogen, he received the Nobel prize, 1932. His UNCERTAINTY PRINCIPLE states that certain pairs of quantities (known as canonically conjugate variables) cannot both be simultaneously determined with unlimited accuracy. An example of such a pair is the position and momentum of a particle. He is a fellow of the Royal Society and an associate of the U. S. National Academy of Sciences.—*D. H. D. R.*

HELICOPTER: an aircraft that obtains both lift and thrust from power-driven, rotating wings; it contrasts with conventional aircraft, which use fixed wings for lift and propellers or jet engines for thrust. While the entire fixed-wing aircraft must

Helicopter airliner: In the 20-odd years since its first appearance, the helicopter has become an important and familiar facet of air transportation. The twin-turbine Sikorsky S-61L above, capable of carrying 25 to 28 passengers, went into regular passenger service in 1961. (*Sikorsky*)

move through the air to develop lift forces on its wings, the helicopter's wings or rotor blades, moving independently, maintain lift whether the helicopter ascends or descends vertically, flies forward or backward or sideways, hovers in place, or rotates about a vertical axis. Although such toys as the ancient Chinese flying top and the 16th-cent. sketches of Leonardo da Vinci reveal efforts to build vertical air-screw flying machines, they contributed more to development of conventional aircraft. Basically different principles of flight and of design have left rotating-wing and conventional aircraft little in common. The helicopter's first workable ancestor, the autogiro, designed by Juan de la Cierva y Cordornia, was flown near Getafe, Spain, 1923. Cierva sought a device that would prevent disaster when an airplane's speed dropped below the minimum needed to sustain lift. Cierva's autogiro was pulled through the air by a conventional propeller, but had in addition to its fixed wings an arrangement of rotor blades mounted over the fuselage. When the autogiro taxied forward, these blades turned freely, developed lift, and helped get the autogiro airborne. If forward flight was stopped and the autogiro began to fall, the upward push of air kept the blades turning and their aerodynamic surfaces developed enough lift for a safe descent. Cierva overcame the first major problem of rotary-wing flight; *i.e.* blades develop more lift when moving into the wind than during the other half-rotation away. This tends to flip the machine on its side. Cierva attached his four rotor blades to their shaft with hinges that allowed each wing to rise slightly going into the wind and fall moving away from it, thus equalizing lift on both sides of the autogiro. The long step to a powered rotor wing was achieved by the Focke-Wulf FW-61 in Germany, 1936, and by the Sikorsky VS-300 in the U. S. A., 1937. Because the engine powering the blades developed torque—a tendency to make both engine and fuselage rotate in the opposite direction from the blades—two methods were devised to keep the fuselage stationary. The FW-61 used two rotors, on opposite sides of the fuselage, turning in opposite directions to cancel the effects of each other's torque. The Sikorsky had small rotors at the end of its long tail, and with the elongated tail section acting as a lever, the small rotor blades counteracted torque from the larger main blades mounted over the helicopter. More recently the use of jet engines at the tips of the blades has overcome the torque problem. Allowing a little torque to develop permits the helicopter to circle or turn at desired rates. Vertical motion is changed to forward or sideways motion by inclining the entire rotor blade assembly so that the thrust forces have a horizontal as well as a vertical component. Lift is controlled by changing the pitch of the rotor blade's leading edge. A pitch-control lever, a control stick for inclining the blade assembly, and pedals for the rudder or tail rotor comprise the major cockpit control devices.—*K. A.*

HELIUM: a gaseous element (He); at. no. 2; at. wt 4.003; density 0.117; one of the rare or *inert gases.* The element is the second-lightest gas known, hydrogen being the lightest. Most of the world's commercially used helium comes from U. S. natural-gas reservoirs in Texas. It is produced in nature by decay of radioactive elements and by cosmic-ray bombardment of light metallic elements, and exists in the Earth's atmosphere in 5 parts/million. In the SUN, helium is produced from hydrogen (see ATOMIC ENERGY). Helium was actually discovered in the Sun before it was known to exist

First practical-service helicopter: After much experimentation in the late 1930s Igor I. Sikorsky built the XR-4 (*below*), which in 1942 became the first helicopter to make an extended cross-country flight. Even at this early stage, the potentialities of the helicopter as a rescue craft were recognized. (*Sikorsky*)

Liquid helium, contained in transparent vessel (*center*), is used to obtain temperatures just a few degrees above absolute zero. Here a substance is being tested for superconductivity, a property that appears in many materials at very low temperatures. Superconducting materials are used in computer memory systems. (*IBM*)

on Earth (1868). This discovery took place during an eclipse of the Sun (observed in India) when the French astronomer J. Janssen turned a spectroscope on the solar chromosphere for the first time. The discovery of terrestrial helium is attributed to Sir William Ramsay (1894). Because of helium's extreme lightness and nonflammability, it is used in airships and balloons; it has 93% the lifting power of hydrogen. Liquid helium is used to produce extremely low temperatures (see CRYOGENICS). Major current uses of helium include arc-welding of reactive metals, refining and fabrication of zirconium and titanium, and an inert atmosphere in fabrication of oxidation-sensitive components, *e.g.* TRANSISTORS. An 80%–20% mixture of helium and oxygen is breathed instead of air by deep-sea divers to prevent "the bends." A similar mixture is sometimes prescribed when the respiratory tract is obstructed. —*T. M.*

HELMHOLTZ, HERMANN VON, 1821–94, German physician, physiologist, psychologist, physicist, mathematician, philosopher of science; b. Potsdam; ed. Friedrich-Wilhelm Inst. of Medicine and Surgery, Berlin. He was one of the most important and influential 19th-cent. scientists. His broad, definitive formulation of the principle of conservation of energy (1847) was the foundation of many subsequent developments in thermodynamics and the study of energy transformations. To physiology and psychology he contributed his monumental book of physiological optics, *Handbuch*

Hermann von Helmholtz
(*N. Y. Public Library*)

der physiologischen Optik (1856–67), "one of the great landmarks of 19th-cent. science," and *Die Lehre von den Tonempfindungen* (1863), a basic work in physiological acoustics. Among his other achievements in physiology were the first measurement of the velocity of nerve impulses, the invention of the ophthalmoscope, the Young-Helmholtz theory of color vision, and his own theory of auditory sensation and perception. He aided in development and popularization of non-Euclidean geometry, helped establish the Faraday-Maxwell conception of electricity, and was highly influential in uniting scientific and philosophical investigations. One of the great teachers of the century, he helped both to train a generation of scientists and to educate the public through many popular lectures and demonstrations. He was a fellow of the Royal Society and an associate of the U. S. National Academy of Sciences.—*R. K.*

HELMONT, JAN BAPTISTA VAN, 1577–1644, Dutch chemist, physiologist, and physician; b. Brussels. A founder of the Iatrochemical school of medicine, he believed that physiological processes are basically chemical reactions, and that disease is caused by chemical imbalance of the "ferments" of the body. Thus, gastric acidity might be corrected by administration of alkali. Helmont performed a famous experiment with a willow tree, which he raised in a carefully weighed quantity of earth, supplying it with nothing but water. At the end of 5 yr the tree and the earth were again weighed separately: the tree had gained 164 lb, but the earth had lost only 2 oz. Helmont's conclusion that plants need nothing but water for growth was accepted until disproved by Ingenhousz and Priestley over 100 yr later. He also originated the word "gas" and observed gases other than common air, *e.g.* "gas sylvestre" (carbon dioxide), produced by burning charcoal. His works were published by his son as *Ortus medicinae* (1648).—*R. J. F.*

HEMATITE: a major ore of iron, ferric oxide (Fe_2O_3). It is found in a wide variety of occurrences, but most of the major ore deposits are associated with moderately folded and metamorphosed sedimentary beds (iron formations) widely distributed throughout the world. Iron formations themselves are of low grade, and include the hard jaspery to quartzitic taconites. In some areas, near-surface portions of the iron formations have been reworked by ground waters which leached out silica and deleterious materials such as phosphorus and sulfur, leaving greatly enriched concentrations of hematite. These range from the earthy red masses typical of the Mesabi Range, Minnesota, to the dense blue-black ore which forms resistant, high ridges in the deserts of Mauritania. The strongly exothermic reduction of hematite to iron by aluminum is the basis for the Thermite process of welding, which requires no external source of heat or power. See IRON; MINERAL (table); STEEL.—*L. M.*

HEMOGLOBIN: see OXYGEN TRANSPORT.

HENLE, FRIEDRICH GUSTAV JAKOB, 1809–85, German anatomist and pathologist; b. Fürth. One of the first to appreciate the cell theory, he described and evaluated the different kinds of epithelium in the body, discovered the endothelium and smooth muscle of the blood vessels, described the relations of the various cerebral lobes and the structure of the larynx, and discovered the renal tubules named after him. His publications include *Handbuch der systematischen Anatomie* (3 vol., 1866–71), the first handbook of histology to be based entirely on cytology. He was a fellow of the Royal Society.—*D. H. D. R.*

Globular star cluster (M13) in constellation Hercules, barely visible to unaided eye, displays multitudes of stars in telescopic photographs. These plates represent exposures of 6, 15, 37, and 95 min with 60-in. reflector. (*Mt Wilson*)

HENRY, JOSEPH, 1797–1878, U. S. physicist; b. Albany, N. Y. An early experimenter with electromagnetism, whose interests parallel those of Michael Faraday, he developed an improved electromagnet, and was the first to insulate wire in the magnetic coil. Without knowledge of Faraday's work, he discovered self-induction, and produced and demonstrated an electromagnetic telegraph (1830–31). He also independently invented low-resistance and high-resistance galvanometers and the first electric motor, and discovered the oscillatory nature of electrical discharge (1842). In addition, Henry demonstrated that liquids and solids in general have the same amount of cohesion, showed by means of a thermogalvanometer that sunspots radiate less heat than the general solar surface, and produced a new method for determining the velocity of projectiles. In 1846 Henry became the first secretary and director of the Smithsonian Institution, Washington, D. C. The weather-reporting system which he organized led to the formation of the U. S. Weather Bureau. The *henry*, a unit of electrical measurement, is named for him. He was a member of the National Academy of Sciences.—*S. B.*

HENRY'S LAW: the principle that at constant temperature the weight of gas dissolved in a liquid phase is directly proportional to the pressure of the gas phase when it is in equilibrium with the solution. If the gas obeys BOYLE'S LAW (*i.e.* the volume filled by any amount of gas is inversely proportional to the pressure at constant temperature), the gaseous pressure above the solution will be directly proportional to the gas concentration in the solution. Hence, the more a gas is compressed, the greater its solubility in the liquid.—*G. W. M.*

HERACLITUS OF EPHESUS, early 5th cent. B. C., Greek philosopher and scientist; birthplace unknown. A monist, he suggested that heat ("fire") is the principle of all things. Heraclitus emphasized the perpetual change that goes on in the world while the world persists in a basically unchanged form: there is a strife of opposites that produces harmony. —*D. H. D. R.*

HERCULES CLUSTER (M13): the only great globular star cluster in the northern hemisphere visible to the unaided eye. Discovered by Halley, 1715, it consists of several hundred thousand stars at a distance of 25,000 lt-yr. This very old system, an example of Type II STAR population, has an age currently estimated at around 10 billion yr. (The constellation of Hercules also contains two other globular clusters, and a cluster of external galaxies).—*H. S. H.*

HEREDITY: the complex of inborn features in a plant or animal, received from its parents, that determine what it may become in a suitable environment. The first workable explanation for inheritance in any kind of life was offered in 1865 by the Austrian monk Gregor Mendel. Among garden peas he had been able to separate seven different pairs of pure-breeding lines. So long as he self-pollinated the plants in each line, the seeds produced would always grow into plants like the parents. One of these pairs of pure-breeding

lines was a tall line and a dwarf line. Whenever pure-line tall plants were crossed with pure-line dwarf plants, all seeds produced grew into tall plants. But if these tall hybrids were crossed with one another (or self-pollinated), their seeds would grow into either tall plants or dwarf plants in the proportion of three tall ones to one dwarf plant. The dwarf, if self-pollinated, would breed true; so would one third of the tall plants in this generation. The other plants, if self-pollinated, would again give rise to both tall and dwarf, in the proportion of three tall to one dwarf. Corresponding heredity was shown by each of the other six pairs of pure-breeding lines.

A set of symbols can be used to represent each plant and also the heredity it can pass on to another generation. The symbol *TT* indicates a pure-line tall plant, and *T* the heredity in its pollen or ovules. Similarly *tt* represents the pure-line dwarf plant, and *t* its hereditary contribution. When the inheritance *T* from the one parent is combined with the inheritance *t* from the other in a cross between the two pure lines, the hybrid offspring is represented by the combination *Tt*. Now Mendel noted that dwarfness was hidden ("recessive"), whereas the presence of the heredity from the tall parent (*T*) was obvious ("dominant"). When a hybrid plant of genetic constitution *Tt* produced pollen grains or ovules, it apparently parceled out its hereditary features in units, some with *T* and some with *t*. When the pollen grain or ovule with the *T* heredity from the one hybrid flower was combined with an ovule or pollen grain with the *T* heredity from another hybrid flower, the seed produced would have the constitution *TT* and grow into a tall plant, which would breed true if self-pollinated. If the heredity *t* from one hybrid flower combined with the heredity *t* from another hybrid flower, the seed produced would be *tt* and grow into a dwarf plant, which would breed true if self-pollinated. But if *T* combined with *t*, or *t* combined with *T*, the seed would have the constitution *Tt*— a hybrid like its parent—and grow into a tall plant, which would have two kinds of offspring if self-pollinated. So long as each hybrid parent (*Tt*) produced hereditary units *T* and *t* in equal proportions among both pollen grains and ovules, the offspring from any cross between two hybrids should be in the ratio of *one* pure-line tall to *two* tall hybrids to *one* pure-line dwarf—just as discovered by experiment.

Mendel summarized the principles that fit the experiments: (1) hereditary characteristics are passed from parent to offspring in units; (2) a dominant characteristic conceals the presence of a recessive characteristic; (3) dominant and recessive characteristics separate again in the offspring of crosses between hybrids; (4) hybrids produce two kinds of hereditary units in equal proportions, and fertilization is a random event; (5) the recessive characteristic is unaltered by association with the dominant characteristic in a hybrid; (6) when more than one pair of hereditary characteristics is followed in a single cross, the inheritance of each pair of characteristics is independent of the inheritance of every other pair of characteristics.

No reason for these principles could be given. None was suggested, in fact, until 1902, when the American cytologist

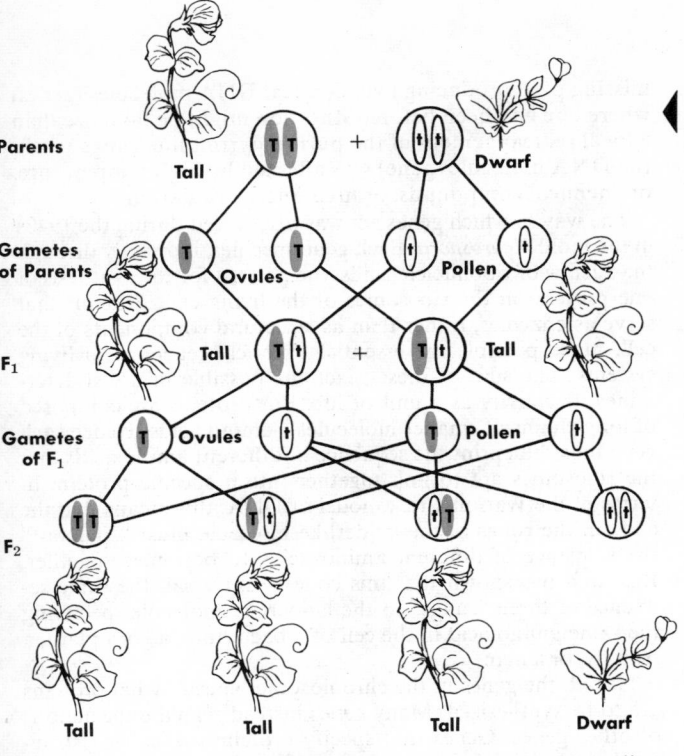

Parents
Tall   +   Dwarf

Gametes
of Parents   Ovules   Pollen

F₁   Tall   +   Tall

Gametes
of F₁   Ovules   Pollen

F₂

Tall   Tall   Tall   Dwarf

Mendelian cross: Starting from pure-line tall-stem and dwarf garden peas ("Parents"), Mendel produced a first filial (F₁) generation in which the dwarf form did not appear. He then crossed members of the F₁ generation; in the new population (F₂), the repressed dwarf form reappeared in one specimen out of four. Mendel accounted for its reappearance by postulating that each plant carries two hereditary factors for stem length and that when a given plant carries factors for both lengths, the factor for tallness (T) completely dominates the "recessive" factor for dwarfness (t). When gametes are formed, the two factors in each pair split up ("segregate"), each gamete receiving only one factor. These segregated factors then recombine in the next generation. The one combination out of four in which dwarf factor t is not masked by tall factor T will then express the dwarfness. Mendel dealt with single-factor traits exhibiting dominance; more complex possibilities have since been explored.

W. S. Sutton proposed the chromosome theory of heredity. He pointed out that the contribution of a sperm cell to an egg cell at the moment of FERTILIZATION consists only of the sperm nucleus. The obvious features in any nucleus are the threadlike bodies known as chromosomes (see CHROMOSOMES AND GENES). Chromosomes are accurately duplicated in the process of CELL DIVISION (mitosis), and each daughter cell receives exactly the same chromosomal complement as the parent cell; hence if chromosomes carry the heredity, all cells in an individual plant or animal have the same heredity. Body cells in most animals and green plants, moreover, have a double (diploid) set of chromosomes, whereas their reproductive cells—produced by reduction division (MEIOSIS)—have a single (haploid) set. This would explain the significance of Mendel's symbol TT or tt for a parent, and T or t for the heredity in a reproductive cell. The behavior of chromosomes would account for Mendel's principles if chromosomes alone carried hereditary characteristics.

This logical theory was consistent with a discovery made in Kansas the previous year by another cytologist, C. E. McClung: the body cells of female grasshoppers differ slightly from those of males. Every chromosome in the nucleus of a female body cell has a mate of the same size in the diploid set. But in the nucleus of male body cells, one large chromosome either lacks a mate or has a very small one. McClung named the large chromosome an X-chromosome and the small one a Y-chromosome. Female grasshoppers have two X-chromosomes in the nucleus of each body cell, whereas males have an X and a Y. In meiosis, half of the sperm cells would receive an X-chromosome and half of them a Y-chromosome—in addition to the rest of a haploid set. All eggs would receive an X-chromosome. If an egg with an X were fertilized by a sperm with a Y, the offspring would be a male. If the egg were fertilized by a sperm with an X-chromosome, the fertilized egg would have two X-chromosomes and develop into a female. McClung concluded that sex is determined at the instant of fertilization and follows the rules of chance. (See SEX DETERMINATION.)

Shortly after 1906, when Dr. T. H. Morgan began research on the heredity of the little fruit fly *Drosophila,* he found a characteristic inherited in a way that he could explain only by assuming that it was carried by the X-chromosome but not the Y. This was "sex-linkage," an idea that accounted also for the previously puzzling heredity of red-green color blindness and of hemophilia in mankind. Soon other peculiarities of inheritance were discovered in the fruit fly. When more than one characteristic was followed in a cross, the independence described by Mendel in his sixth principle often broke down. Instead, all hereditary characteristics in *Drosophila* were either sex-linked or fell into some one of three other "linkage groups." *Drosophila,* however, has only three pairs of chromosomes plus the pair of sex chromosomes in the nucleus of each body cell, and four different chromosomes (including a sex chromosome) in the nucleus of each egg or sperm. Each different chromosome must contain a "linkage group."

By 1915, Dr. Morgan had enough information about linkage in the fruit fly to propose the theory of the gene. According to his idea, each hereditary characteristic is controlled by a definite part of a specific chromosome. This part, the gene, occupies a particular site along the length of the chromosome; all genes in a chromosome (in a linkage group) lie in a single line. During the synapsis stage of meiosis, however, exchange and recombination of parts of chromosomes occasionally take place—a process he called "crossing over." This alters the outcome of the cross, but is an event from which more information could be gained. The farther genes are apart in a chromosome, the more often crossing over should occur between them; conversely, the closer together they are, the rarer would be the crossing over between them. By studying the frequency of cases of crossing over, Dr. Morgan mapped the position of the genes in each chromosome of the fruit fly. These discoveries and the theory of the gene proved so widely applicable to the plant and animal kingdoms, and to man as well, that Dr. Morgan was awarded a Nobel prize in 1933.

Occasionally a gene changes (mutates) from the dominant to the recessive condition, or from the recessive to the dominant. MUTATION may occur in a body cell, causing one tree branch to have variegated leaves or one eye to be a different color from the other. Or it may occur in a reproductive cell and influence the heredity of the offspring. The rate of mutation can be increased somewhat by higher temperature, by treatment with some chemical compounds, and by exposure to high-energy radiations such as x-rays. (See RADIATION GENETICS.)

Biochemists discovered that the site of the gene in the chromosome is occupied regularly by a nucleoprotein, of which the NUCLEIC ACID portion is deoxyribonucleic acid (abbreviated DNA). The chemical constitution of DNA was known prior to 1900, but not until 1953 did biochemists have

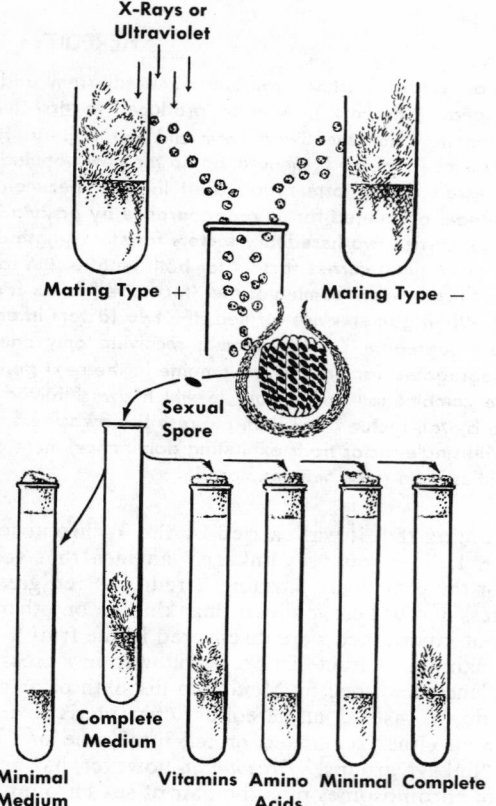

X-Rays or
Ultraviolet

Mating Type +   Mating Type −

Sexual
Spore

Complete
Medium

Minimal   Vitamins Amino Minimal Complete
Medium   Acids

How genes express heredity: In 1941 George W. Beadle and
Edward L. Tatum began using a very simple organism—the pink
bread mold *Neurospora crassa*—to single out the ways in which
genes control the organism's activities. In their normal state the
spores can survive on the well-defined ingredients of a certain
"minimal medium"; but by exposing some of them to radiation,
Beadle and Tatum produced mutant forms that could not survive
in this medium, having apparently lost the ability to synthesize one
or more essential products from it. The experimenters then tested
the mutant spores' ability to survive in a succession of minimal
cultures enriched by various additives, until they found one in
which they throve. The additive required by the mutant spore was
the one it could no longer synthesize, because a necessary enzyme
was lacking. It was soon realized that these enzymes are what the
genes control.

a definite idea as to the arrangement of its component parts:
the sugar deoxyribose, phosphate, a purine (either adenine
or guanine), and a pyrimidine (either cytosine or thymine).
Then the biochemists James Watson and F. H. C. Crick proposed a model for the DNA molecule, which provided for all
the known information about its genetic behavior. According
to their theory, DNA is a spiral, ladderlike molecule of indefinite length, with the sides composed of alternating sugar
and phosphate, and the rungs each of one purine and one
pyrimidine linking the sugar on one side to the sugar on the
other side. Further, they suggested that adenine could be
linked only to thymine, and guanine only to cytosine. With
this structure, the DNA molecule could provide in the sequence
of its four possible different rungs ($A—T, T—A, G—C,$ and
$C—G$) a code such as must be present to store the hereditary
information of a gene. The outstanding stability of the gene
would be matched by the known stability of the DNA molecule. The ability of genes in normal sequence in a chromosome
to duplicate themselves without change during mitosis could
be visualized as occurring by a lengthwise splitting of the
ladderlike DNA molecule; each side of the ladder would contain the full code; against it, following the rule of thymine with
adenine, cytosine with guanine, the cell could synthesize the

missing part, producing two identical DNA molecules (genes)
where one had been before. Mutation might be no more than
a local rearrangement of the purine-pyrimidine rungs where
the DNA molecule (gene) was affected by high temperature,
or chemical compounds, or high-energy radiations.

The way in which genes act was discovered during the 1940s
in the mold *Neurospora*. Each gene specifies, indirectly through
the agency of ribonucleic acids, the pattern for the synthesis of
one protein on the ribosomes of the living cell. Proteins that
serve as enzymes, rather than as structural components of the
cell, make possible the essential chemical reactions of living
systems. The sum of these reactions possible in a cell determines its activity as a unit of life. But proteins are composed
of long chains of smaller molecules—amino acids. Hence each
gene must blueprint the sequence of different amino acids that
the ribosomes are to link together into a specific protein. In
terms of the Watson-Crick model of DNA, this means that the
code in the rungs of the ladderlike molecule must "spell out"
the sequence of different amino acids to be joined together.
Research has shown that this code is universal, the same sequence of three "rungs" in the ladderlike molecule specifying
the same amino acid in the cell of a bacterium, a corn plant, a
fruit fly, or a man.

Not all the genes in the chromosomes specify what proteins
are to be synthesized. Many genes instead regulate the actions
of other genes. Genes that specify proteins are called "structural genes," and are seen to control inherited characters.
Genes that regulate the action of structural genes are called
"regulator genes." Additional genes control the synthesis of
ribonucleic acids.

The study of heredity has progressed in a little more than a
century from Mendel's symbolic representation of inheritance
in pea plants to an interpretation at the molecular level, related
to the chemical processes involved in growth and maturation.
The mechanism of heredity is now seen as a remarkable
unifying feature of all kinds of living things. See GENETICS.—
L. and M. M.

HERMAPHRODITE: an individual possessing both male and
female reproductive organs. Hermaphroditism occurs in
plants wherever staminate and pistillate flowers occur separately on the plant, as in squash, corn, and birch trees. Among
invertebrate animals, hermaphroditism is common. Hermaphroditic animals usually cross-fertilize one another (the
method used by earthworms), but a few fertilize themselves.
Self-fertilization is an important adaptation for animals that
otherwise might be unable to find a mate; this is true for
tapeworms, since only one of these parasites may happen to
enter a particular host. Some animals develop male and
female organs at different times—*e.g.* the oyster, which starts
as a male, then becomes female. In the higher vertebrates, a
hermaphroditic condition is never normal; it occurs rarely,
as a result of a hereditary disorder. Hormonally unbalanced
human beings with some physical characteristics of the
opposite sex, as well as homosexuals, are sometimes mistakenly termed hermaphrodites.—*A. P. E.*

HERMITE, CHARLES, 1822–1901, French mathematician; b.
Dieuze, Lorraine. At age 21 he communicated his original
work on Abelian functions to K. G. J. Jacobi, who encouraged
him warmly. Hermite made notable contributions to the
study of elliptic functions and applied them to algebraic
problems. He also worked on invariants. He was a fellow of
the Royal Society.—*H. C.*

HERO OF ALEXANDRIA, fl. probably 1st cent. A. D., Greek
physicist and mechanician; birthplace unknown. He wrote on

a number of subjects concerned with applied mathematics and physics, but he is best known as the inventor of many mechanical devices, particularly some using steam power, described in his *Pneumatics.* His *Mechanics* describes the wheel and axle, the wedge, the screw, the lever, and pulley systems, and discusses the theory of their operation. —*D. H. D. R.*

HEROPHILOS, early 3rd cent. B. C., Alexandrian-Greek anatomist; b. Chalcedon. He greatly improved the techniques of anatomical dissection and observation, provided anatomical descriptions of the human body superior to any previous ones, and contributed to anatomical terminology.—*D. H. D. R.*

HERSCHEL, FRIEDRICH WILHELM (SIR WILLIAM), 1738–1822, English astronomer; b. Hanover, Germany. An amateur astronomer turned professional, he constructed the largest reflecting telescopes of his time. He discovered the planet Uranus (1781) and two of its satellites (1787), and two satellites of Saturn (1789). He made the first systematic study of the relative brightness of stars, and discovered more than 2,000 nebulas and 800 double stars. By intensive star counts

Friedrich Wilhelm Herschel
(*Yerkes Observatory*)

he obtained the first estimate of the shape of the Milky Way system. He is known also for his determination of the rotation period of Saturn and for his discovery of the motion of the solar system in space. First president of the Royal Astronomical Society, he is considered the founder of modern astronomy. His sister **Caroline Lucretia Herschel** (1750–1848), as his lifelong assistant, helped with the construction of his telescopes, recorded most of his observations, performed necessary calculations, and compiled his catalogs. She independently discovered eight comets. His son, Sir **John Frederick William Herschel** (1792–1871), extended the catalogs of nebulas and clusters and set up an observatory at the Cape of Good Hope (1834) to survey the southern sky. Sir John also contributed to photography: he used sodium hyposulfite (hypo) as a solvent for silver salts, and invented a sensitized photographic paper. He was like his father a fellow of the Royal Society. —*S. D. G.*

HERTWIG, OSKAR, 1849–1922, German zoologist; b. Freiberg. He and his brother, **Richard von Hertwig** (1850–1937), proposed the "coelom theory" to explain the origin of the middle germinal layer in the development of higher animals. Hertwig made important contributions to understanding fertilization and cell division, and is generally credited with being the first to recognize that fertilization involves the union of the male and female nuclei. Late in life he devoted much time to criticisms of Darwin's theory of evolution by natural selection.—*D. H. D. R.*

HERTZ, GUSTAV, 1887–   , German-Russian physicist; b. Hamburg. For their discoveries of the laws governing the impact between an electron and an atom, Hertz and J. Franck received the Nobel prize, 1925. This research gave experimental support to N. Bohr's theory of the atom and provided a method for determining the value of PLANCK'S CONSTANT. —*D. H. D. R.*

HERTZ, HEINRICH RUDOLPH, 1857–94, German physicist; b. Hamburg. In 1888, while professor of physics in the Karls-

ruhe Technische Hochschule, Hertz demonstrated experimentally the existence of electromagnetic waves. At the suggestion of Helmholtz, whose student and assistant he had been in Berlin, he began the series of experiments that confirmed Maxwell's prediction of the existence of such waves. He used the passage of a spark to produce an oscillatory discharge in space; the appearance of a second spark across the gap of a nearby conductor demonstrated that energy in the form of electromagnetic waves does indeed exist and can pass from one circuit to another. He then succeeded in proving that electromagnetic waves obey the same laws as light waves, *e.g.* their susceptibility to reflection, to refraction, to interference, and to being focused by a lens. Hertz's demonstration, 9 yr after Maxwell's death, of Maxwell's theoretical conclusions concerning the electromagnetic nature of light remains an outstanding achievement of 19th-cent. physics, and one that has led directly to many of the major advances in the science of communication as well as in general physics. Hertz, in 1887, also observed the photoelectric effect, *i.e.* that a spark jumps more readily between two spheres when their surfaces are illuminated by the light from another spark. Late in his life, he turned away from electromagnetism and wrote his *Principles of Mechanics,* published after his death at the age of 37; it has lately been of great interest to philosophers of science. Hertz's *Collected Works* were published 1894–95. —*A. L.*

HERTZIAN WAVES: a name often used for electromagnetic waves in the high-frequency radio range, because these waves were first produced under laboratory conditions by Heinrich Hertz (*c.* 1885). His experiments verified the existence of ELECTROMAGNETIC WAVES, which had been first predicted by James Clerk Maxwell (1856).—*R. G. M.*

HESS, VICTOR FRANZ, 1883–   , Austrian-U. S. physicist; b. Schloss Waldstein. From studies of the ionization of the air, he concluded that a very penetrating radiation, akin to x-rays and γ-rays, was entering Earth's atmosphere. He confirmed this hypothesis experimentally, 1911–12. For his discovery of this radiation (named "cosmic rays" by R. A. Millikan), Hess shared the 1936 Nobel prize with C. D. Anderson. His works include *The Conductivity of the Atmosphere and Its Causes* (1928) and *Cosmic Rays and Their Biological Effects* (1940). —*D. H. D. R.*

HESS, WALTER RUDOLF, 1881–1964, Swiss-English physiologist; b. Frauenfeld, Switzerland. He did research on blood pressure, blood viscosity and its relation to circulation changes, the regulation of breathing, and the central control of the internal organs through the involuntary nervous system. For his discovery of the functional organization of the interbrain as a coordinator of the activities of the internal organs, he shared the 1949 Nobel prize with Antonio Egas Moniz (1874–1955). —*D. H. D. R.*

HETEROCYCLIC COMPOUNDS: the ring structures in organic chemistry which have more than one kind of element in the ring. Examples of heterocycles are

$$
\begin{array}{c}
CH_2\!-\!CH_2 \\
O \qquad\qquad O \\
CH_2\!-\!CH_2 \\
\text{Dioxane}
\end{array}
\qquad
\begin{array}{c}
CH\!=\!CH \\
HC \qquad\qquad N \\
CH\!-\!CH \\
\text{Pyridine}
\end{array}
$$

These should be compared with cyclohexane (see ALICYCLIC COMPOUNDS), which is *homocyclic,* since all the atoms in the ring are the same—namely, carbon. Dioxane has properties associated with aliphatic compounds, but the properties of pyridine are those of AROMATIC COMPOUNDS. See also ALIPHATIC COMPOUNDS.—*Ru. M.*

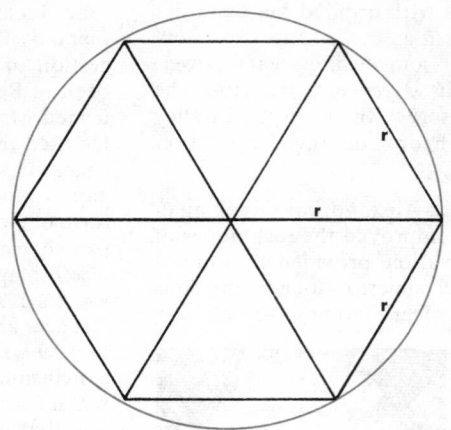

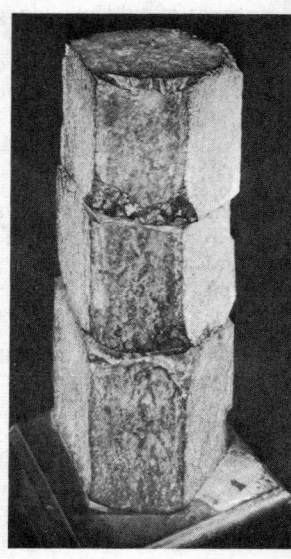

Hexagons in nature approximate those in geometrical construction. *Left:* in a honeycomb (*T. Davidson / National Audubon Soc.*). *Right:* in fragments of columnar basalt. (*Amer. Mus. of Nat. Hist.*)

HETERODYNE CIRCUIT: a circuit employed to change the frequency of an electrical signal. This frequency change is accomplished by multiplying (called "mixing") two electrical signals of slightly differing frequencies. The output of the "mixer" consists of frequencies (beat frequencies) which are the sum and difference of the two input frequencies. Customarily the beat frequency is selected by some tuning device in order to permit further amplification of the desired signal but at the reduced, beat frequency. In the common superheterodyne radio receiver the radio-frequency signal is combined with another signal from a local oscillator in the mixer tube, the output of which is fed to an intermediate frequency amplifier. The frequency change is accomplished because in practice it is easier to amplify at lower frequencies than at the high frequencies employed for radio transmission; in addition, frequency selectivity is more easily determined at the intermediate frequency.—*G. S.*

HEVELIUS, JOHANN, 1611–87, German astronomer; b. Danzig. Well known for his charting of the Moon's surface (*Selenographia,* 1647), Hevelius also studied the sunspots, observed the planets Jupiter and Saturn, and catalogued more than 1,500 stars. He was the second man to observe the transit of Mercury (Mercury's path across the solar disk), an observation important for the information it gives on the planet's movement in its orbit.

Johann Hevelius
(*U. S. Navy*)

Hevelius also suggested that comets have parabolic paths around the Sun. Among his pupils was E. Halley, later Astronomer Royal, who calculated the appearance of what is now known as Halley's comet. In 1664, Hevelius was elected to the Royal Society.—*A. L.*

HEVESY, GEORG DE, 1885–1966, Hungarian-Swedish chemist; b. Budapest. In 1923 he and D. Coster discovered the element hafnium. In 1934 Hevesy prepared a radioactive phosphorus isotope by neutron bombardment of carbon disulfide and used the phosphorus as a radioactive tracer. For his work on the use of isotopes as tracer elements in research on chemical

processes, he received the Nobel prize, 1943. He was a fellow of the Royal Society.—*D. H. D. R.*

HEXAGON: a polygon of six sides and six angles. A special interest attaches to the regular hexagon, which has six equal sides and six equal angles of 120° each. A regular hexagon can be inscribed in a circle by marking off six chords, each equal to the radius. Hence it is made up of six congruent equilateral triangles, each with its side equal to the radius, r. Since the area of one triangle is $r^2 \sqrt{3}/4$, the area of the hexagon is $6r^2 \sqrt{3}/4 = 3r^2 \sqrt{3}/2$. The perimeter is $6r$.

Regular hexagons are much used in design, *e.g.* hexagonal tiling. They also occur frequently in nature. Some crystalline structures exhibit hexagonal forms. Snow crystals often have this general shape. The cells in a honeycomb are prisms with cross sections in the shape of regular hexagons. A probable reason for this shape is that a set of wax containers of prismatic shape that completely fill the frame require the least amount of wax if the containers are regular hexagonal prisms.—*H. C.*

HEYMANS, CORNEILLE, 1892– , Belgian physiologist; b. Ghent. His studies of the pressure-sensitive and chemical-sensitive vascular receptors in the bodies of animals led him to the discovery of the role played by the carotid sinus and aortic mechanisms in the regulation of respiration. For this research, he received the Nobel prize, 1938.—*D. H. D. R.*

HEYROVSKY, JAROSLAV, 1890– , Czechoslovakian chemist; b. Prague. He did research in electrolysis and other aspects of electrochemistry, and in 1922 he made public an electrochemical method of analysis (polarography). For his work in this field he received the Nobel prize, 1959.—*D. H. D. R.*

HIBERNATION AND ESTIVATION: Hibernation is a state in some mammals marked by profound lethargy, depression of body temperature to near that of the surroundings, and a decrease in metabolism; the animal has the inherent capacity to regain normal body temperature without heat from outside sources. Ground squirrels, woodchucks, and bats are examples of mammals that hibernate. During hibernation, the common woodchuck may have a body temperature as low as 4 to 7°C (39 to 45°F) and a heart rate of only 4 to 5 beats/min. Bears are not true hibernators; during winter sleep in the cold (about −3.5°C) the body temperature of the black bear does not fall below 31°C. Poikilotherms, or cold-blooded animals (invertebrates, amphibians, reptiles), do not hibernate in the strict sense of the word. In cold weather they may go into a state of *torpor*, during which body temperature nearly equals that of the surroundings, and respiration, heart rate, and general metabolism are much reduced. The fresh-water painted turtles are known to remain torpid for periods of about three weeks. Only when the environmental temperature increases can these animals come out of torpor and become active; *i.e.* they depend on an external heat source for reactivation.

During periods of extreme dryness or heat some animals become inactive, or *estivate*. For example, the African lungfish, during severe drought, forms a mucus-lined cocoon in the mud and remains there until the rains come, months later. An estivating snail from Africa became active in the British Museum after four years of quiescence.

Hibernation in mammals, cold torpor in poikilotherms, and estivation are devices used by animals to survive unfavorable or even lethal conditions in the surroundings. The term hibernation is often used more loosely to include all the inactive states.—*C. G. W.*

HIGH: see ANTICYCLONE.

HIGH-PRESSURE PHENOMENA: We human beings, who spend our lives at the bottom of a sea of air, do not ordinarily think of pressure as a very important agent in the world around us, because the pressure of the sea of air is small and varies only slightly. But when we consider that the overwhelmingly largest part of the matter in the universe, the part that we cannot see below the surface of the stars, is exposed to pressures reaching into billions of "atmospheres," we need not be too surprised to find that pressure is a very important natural agent.

The highest pressures obtainable in the laboratory are very much lower than the maximum pressures of nature. The very highest laboratory pressures are in the neighborhood of 2,000,000 atm, and even 100,000 atm is considered high. There are formidable technical difficulties attending high-pressure experimenting. In the early days the most serious problem was to prevent leak of the fluid which carries the pressure. This problem was solved by a geometrical design such that the tendency of the fluid to leak is automatically reduced as the pressure increases. In the laboratory, pressure is almost always produced by driving a piston of some sort into a containing vessel. The force required to drive the piston may be very high, but there is no particular problem here, because forces of any desired magnitude can be attained by hydraulic presses. The principle of the hydraulic press has been known for a long time—a large piston drives a small piston, and the pressures on the two pistons are in inverse proportion to the areas. For example, if the large piston has an area 100 times that of the small piston, or a diameter 10 times greater, the pressure exerted by the small piston is 100 times the pressure on the large piston.

The ultimate limit to attainable pressures is set by the strength of the materials of which the apparatus is constructed. Compressive strength is necessary in the pistons and tensile strength in the containing vessels. No materials are known which would permit reaching more than 50,000 atm in simple apparatus. To reach higher pressures the apparatus has to be made more complicated in such a way that the less intensely stressed parts afford a degree of support to the most highly stressed parts which increases automatically when pressure rises. The complications of such a design soon become prohibitive.

The pressures now accessible in the laboratory are sufficient to produce alterations in the properties of substances which sometimes are dramatically large. For example, the temperature at which a liquid freezes or a solid melts is changed by pressure. According to a fundamental theorem of thermodynamics, this temperature rises if the substance contracts when it freezes, but falls if the substance expands on freezing. Nearly all liquids contract when they freeze, so that the melting temperature of most substances rises when pressure rises. The melting temperature of many substances may be raised hundreds of degrees by pressures now available. This effect is of great geological importance. It is present opinion that the core of the earth consists of iron maintained in the solid condition by the enormous pressure of 3,500,000 atm which prevails there, in spite of the fact that the temperature is some thousands of degrees above the normal melting point.

Water is one of the unusual substances which expand when they freeze, so that the freezing temperature of water drops when pressure is raised. The drop of freezing point continues down to about −22°C and about 2,000 atm. Here a most extraordinary thing happens. Ordinary ice becomes incapable of existing any longer, and collapses into a new molecular arrangement, with volume less than that of the liquid. The melting point of this new ice therefore rises with increasing pressure. But this new ice also presently becomes incapable of existence and gives place to another. This process is repeated several times; we now know of seven different kinds of ice, one of them a hot ice which melts at nearly 200°C under a pressure of 40,000 atm.

The phenomenon shown by ice in changing from one molecular arrangement to another is an example of a very common and important phenomenon under pressure known as polymorphic transition. A great many substances undergo

1,000-ton press is used to achieve pressures of 100,000 atm (1.6 million lb/in.²). Artificial diamonds were produced for the first time in this apparatus in 1955. (*General Electric*)

Roman highway engineering (above): The old Appian Way, sections of which are still in use, typifies the roads built by the Romans to hold together their widespread empire. Note stone blocks lining sides of road. (*Italian State Tourist Office*)

The automobile created the need for smoother, more durable highway surfaces. The 10-ft-wide concrete road above, in a relatively flat section of Maryland, represents mid-stage in evolution of the automobile highway. (*U. S. Dept. of Commerce, Bureau of Roads*)

Multi-lane superhighways, a mid-20th-cent. development, reflect huge increase in truck and auto traffic, and consequent need for easy access, dividing strips, better visibility, and wider road shoulders. Sections of Wilbur Cross Highway, Conn. (above), were built in 1930s. Schuylkill Expressway, Penn. (below), was completed in late 1950s. (*U. S. Dept. of Commerce, Bureau of Roads*)

abrupt changes of molecular or atomic arrangement when pressure is sufficiently increased; in fact the probability is that more substances show this effect than not. It is believed that deep in the crust of the earth most substances assume new polymorphic forms with which we are not familiar. One of the most striking polymorphic transitions is that of graphite into diamond. After attempts by scientists for more than a hundred years, the General Electric Co. recently succeeded in transforming graphite into diamond by the use of pressures approximating 100,000 atm.

Among many other effects of high pressure are changes of electrical resistance. Sometimes electrical resistance changes by thousands of fold; the change may be either an increase or a decrease, depending on the substance.

The highest man-made pressures subject to experimental control are produced by detonating explosives. With nuclear bombs the pressures are much higher and are of astronomical magnitude. Under such pressures the atoms themselves disintegrate and matter is compressed to densities measured in tons per cubic inch. Perhaps at some time in the future we may acquire experimental control of even such pressures. —*P. W. B.*

HIGHWAY ENGINEERING: the design and construction of main arteries intended to carry heavy, non-stop traffic. The Romans first built extensive road systems and included such roads in city planning. The Romans paved only important sections of their roads, for their method of paving was very costly. Roman roads resembled walls laid horizontally: the bottom and top layers were composed of fitted polygonal stone blocks, while the layers in between were of a loose, rubble-like fill. The Romans laid their roads straight, with little attention to topography. Their planned cities usually had two main streets parallel to each other, with cross-streets at right angles. A network of road systems—29 in all—radiated out from Rome to the farthest corners of the empire. The most famous of these is the old *Via Appia,* which extended first to Capua and then to Taranto and Brindisi at the heel of the peninsula.

After the fall of Rome, no advancements were made in road construction until the 18th cent., when France assumed the leadership in all branches of civil engineering. The father of French road building was Pierre-Marie-Jerome Trésaguet (1716–96), whose most valuable contribution was the design of highway foundations made of stones set on edge and held by strong stone curbs. This was in contrast to former French roads, made of flat stones piled one on another and thus easily displaced by the weight of stagecoach wheels. The surfaces of Trésaguet's roads, covered with three layers of crushed stone, were arched, so that the water would run off into gutters; thus drainage was provided—an essential requirement for durable roads. Trésaguet's methods were later utilized by Napoleon, who greatly extended France's highway network and built roads capable of bearing wheeled vehicles over every major Alpine pass.

Leadership in road building, as in other branches of civil engineering, passed to Great Britain in the early 19th cent. An early pioneer was John Metcalf (1717–1810), who was responsible for building some 180 mi of turnpikes. But the two greatest road-builders of the century were John Loudon McAdam (1756–1836), whose name is immortalized in the MACADAM road, and Thomas Telford (1757–1834). McAdam's surfacing consisted of compacted layers of broken stone. Telford's method resembled Tresaguet's: a roadbed of flat stones set on edge, and a surface of broken stone and gravel. Telford was responsible for opening up the vastness of Scotland and Wales; during a busy lifetime he built about 920 mi of roads.

In America, meanwhile, the building of the Cumberland or

National Pike, authorized in 1802, opened up Ohio to settlers. The first important surfaced road in the U. S. A. was the 62-mi Lancaster (Penn.) Turnpike, built in 1792–94; its surface was of broken stone. After the stagecoach era, the railroads pre-empted attention, and for about 50 yr little progress was made in road-building. Late in the 19th cent., the bicycle created a new demand for roads; but it remained for the automobile and the truck to create the need for our modern network of roads, and for more durable surfaces that would wear better than macadam or brick: asphalt, concrete, and reinforced concrete then came into use.

Highway engineering must be concerned with layout: the design of horizontal curves and the related superelevations (the tilting of the surface as the highway curves), so that the vehicle's stability is preserved at the maximum designated speed; and the design of vertical curves (the highway's profile), so that the driver's line of sight is preserved for a required distance and so that blind summits (stretches of road near the top of a hill when the driver cannot see ahead) are avoided. The highway surface must be designed to sustain the weight of the vehicle as well as the continuous friction of the wheels; it must resist deterioration owing to expansion and contraction caused by seasonal variation of temperatures; it must be brushed or broomed to avoid an overly smooth surface and attendant skidding. Highway surfaces are continuously studied to improve their durability; both asphalt and reinforced concrete—the competing virtues of each are endlessly debated—are almost exclusively used in most highway construction. The route proposed for a highway, with its effects on present and future land-use, and the highway's cost, affected by the rising value of land, are perhaps the major problems in modern highway planning.—*S. R. W.*

HILBERT, DAVID, 1862–1943, German mathematician; b. Königsberg. In 1895 he became professor of mathematics at Göttingen, where he remained the rest of his life. After the death of Poincaré in 1912, Hilbert was generally considered the foremost mathematician in the world. The quality of his researches was of the highest order and enormously influenced 20th-cent. mathematics. In 1898–99 he made a profound analysis of geometry and set up a system of postulates for Euclidean geometry that lacked the defects of the ancient system and that led the way for modern postulational method.

David Hilbert
(New York Public Library)

He also made important contributions to the theory of numbers and to integral equations, and out of the latter came the concept of "Hilbert space." He concerned himself with the logical foundations of mathematics and proposed a formalistic philosophy intended to free mathematics of all inconsistencies, but the work of Gödel and others after 1930 appears to demonstrate the failure of this program. He was a fellow of the Royal Society and an associate of the U. S. National Academy of Sciences.—*H. C.*

HILL, ARCHIBALD VIVIAN, 1886–   , English biophysicist; b. Bristol. He discovered that heat production by a muscle persists when (and only when) oxygen is available to the muscle, although the initial heat production does not require oxygen. For this discovery, he shared the 1922 Nobel prize with Otto Meyerhof. He became Foulerton Research Professor of the Royal Society (1926), of which he is a fellow. He is also an associate of the U. S. National Academy of Sciences.

His publications include *Living Machinery* (1926), *Muscular Activity* (1926), *The Role of Oxidation in Maintaining the Dynamic Equilibria of Life* (1929), and numerous articles. —*D. H. D. R.*

HILL, GEORGE WILLIAM, 1838–1914, U. S. astronomer; b. New York, N. Y. An astronomer on the staff of the American *Nautical Almanac Office,* he wrote many papers on celestial mechanics and is known principally for his contributions to the study of the Moon's motion. He was a fellow of the Royal Society and a member of the National Academy of Sciences. —*D. H. D. R.*

HINSHELWOOD, SIR CYRIL NORMAN, 1897–   , English chemist; b. London. His research has been on chemical reaction kinetics, particularly chain reactions in combustion processes and chemical reactions in living organisms. For their research on the mechanism of chemical reactions, he and N. N. Semenov shared the 1956 Nobel prize. Hinshelwood's publications include *Kinetics of Chemical Change* (1926) and *The Chemical Kinetics of the Bacterial Cell* (1946). He is a fellow of the Royal Society (president, 1955–60) and an associate of the U. S. National Academy of Sciences. —*D. H. D. R.*

HIPPARCHUS, 2nd cent. B. C., Greek astronomer, mathematician, and geographer; b. Nicaea. He built astronomical instruments, constructed the earliest known astronomical globe, used and probably invented the stereographic projection, and founded plane trigonometry. He discovered the precession of the equinoxes and catalogued hundreds of stars. Ptolemy, in his great work on astronomy, drew heavily on Hipparchus. —*D. H. D. R.*

HIPPOCRATES OF CHIOS, *c.* 460 B. C., Greek geometer. He stayed in Athens for some time, attending lectures on mathematics and teaching to increase his income. His chief contributions were in geometry. He determined the area between the arcs of two circles, showed that the ratio of the areas of two circles is equal to the ratio of the squares of their radii, and reduced the problem of duplicating a cube to that of finding two mean proportionals between two numbers, one of which is twice the other—that is, to that of finding x and y so that $s:x = x:y = y:2s$. He also compiled a book on elements of mathematics prior to Euclid.—*H. C.*

HISTAMINE: in biochemistry, an AMINE formed by the decarboxylation of the amino acid histidine. In the large intestine this reaction is carried out by microorganisms, but histamine is also found in lung, liver, muscle, gastric mucosa, and many other tissues. It is a powerful vasodepressant and, in excess, can cause vascular collapse. It is liberated during traumatic shock and local inflammation, as well as in allergic reactions and anaphylaxis. Histamine stimulates the secretion of both pepsin and acid by the stomach and is, therefore, useful in studies of gastric activity. See also VASOMOTOR SYSTEM.—*E. S.*

HISTOIRE NATURELLE, Générale et particulière, avec la description du cabinet du Roi, by George Louis Leclerc, Comte de Buffon, 44 vols., 1749–1804: Marked by a brilliance of literary style, this compendious work of Buffon and his collaborators attempted to bring order to the contemporary knowledge of the natural world. Of the 44 volumes, all but eight were published during Buffon's lifetime. A methodological essay outlining principles for studying natural history opens the first volume and justifies the whole work by its guarded claim of a fundamental unity of nature. There follow treatises on cosmology and geology, mineralogy, and the biology of man and other vertebrate animals, including a lengthy study of birds. The source of the claims that make Buffon an early advocate of evolution is found in two direct references by him to the theory. The first occurs in an article "De l'âne" (On the Ass) and the other in "De la dégénération des animaux" (On the Degeneration of Animals); in neither piece does Buffon emerge as an unqualified evolutionist.—*E. Me.*

The *Histoire naturelle* of Buffon is here represented by a plate from the posthumous vol. 35 of the second edition. The orangutan is described as "first among simians or last among men: excepting a soul he wants nothing of what we have, differing less from man than he does from the other animals named apes." (*N. Y. Public Library*)

HISTORIA ANIMALIUM (History of Animals), by Aristotle, 4th cent. B. C. Although Aristotle's influence over 2,000 yr was predominantly through his physical philosophy, since that influence faded he has been chiefly admired as a scientist for his biological investigations. Aristotle was the founder of scientific biology; after neglect and degeneration during the Middle Ages, in the 16th cent. zoology revived on the basis of the *Historia animalium*, just as embryology revived through study of his *De generatione animalium* (*On the Reproduction of Animals*). Aristotle the biologist was a keen observer, an eager seeker after specimens, an anatomist, and an experimenter. Some of his observations were verified only in the 19th cent., when his method was still praised as a model for the naturalist.—*A. R. H.*

HISTORIA NATURALIS (Natural History), by Pliny the Elder, A. D. 77. This large scientific encyclopedia, compiled from some 327 Greek and 146 Latin authors, was enormously popular throughout the Middle Ages. In the 16th cent. scholars became aware of Pliny's uncritical and credulous outlook, so that his authority declined, but his is still an important sourcebook for the classical world. Besides discussing plants, animals, and stones of all kinds Pliny wrote much on mining, metals, chemistry, and manufactures—indeed all the scientific and technological matters considered in antiquity.—*A. R. H.*

HOFMANN, AUGUST WILHELM VON, 1818–92, German chemist, b. Giessen; ed. at Univ. of Giessen, where he became assistant to Justus von Liebig. His research in organic chemistry, which led to discoveries of numerous coloring matters from coal-tar products, contributed to the development of synthetic aniline dyestuffs. The German Chemical Society was founded by him in 1867. He was a fellow of the Royal Society and an associate of the U. S. National Academy of Sciences. —*E. F.*

HOFSTADTER, ROBERT, 1915–   , U. S. physicist; b. New York, N. Y. In 1950 he began a systematic investigation of the structure of atomic nuclei, using a linear accelerator to produce a high-energy electron beam with which he bombarded the nuclei under study (see PARTICLE ACCELERATOR). The deflection of the electrons by the nuclei, measured by a magnetic spectrometer, indicated that the boundary of the nucleus is indeterminate rather than sharply defined. The results have indicated that both protons and neutrons, of which most nuclei are composed, consist of a central region surrounded by two interpenetrating clouds of MESONS. In protons, both meson clouds are positively charged, giving a net positive charge to the particle as a whole; in neutrons, one meson cloud is negative, and the net charge is neutral. For his investigations of this structure, Hofstadter shared the 1961 Nobel prize with R. L. Mössbauer. He is a member of the National Academy of Sciences.—*P. R. L.*

HOGBACK: in a landscape, a narrow ridge formed by the outcrop of a tilted layer of highly resistant rock, from both sides of which less resistant rock has been eroded away. The dip is generally more than 45°; it may be almost vertical. Some hogbacks consist of nearly vertical dikes of igneous rock which have been exposed by the erosion of softer rocks. The

Hogback formed by erosion of dipping resistant layer of Dakota sandstone is seen in this aerial view, looking northwest, near Denver, Colo. In the distance (*left*) are pre-Cambrian formations of Front Range. (*T. S. Lovering/U. S. Geological Survey*)

term *cuesta* may be used instead of "hogback" if the dip is gentle.—*N. E. A. H.*

HOGBEN, LANCELOT, 1895–   , English statistician and geneticist; b. Southsea. Recognized for his work on the pituitary gland and his mathematical theory of human inbreeding, Hogben achieved success also as a popularizer and apologist of science. Believing in the "essential unity of theory and practice," he has argued that science progresses only insofar as scientific knowledge is applied to the satisfaction of common human needs. He is a fellow of the Royal Society.—*A. D.*

HOLMES, ARTHUR, 1890–1965, English geologist; b. Hebburn-on-Tyne. Professor of geology at Edinburgh, 1943–56, he is best known for his research on the age of Earth and the absolute ages of the various geologic periods. He was one of the first to suggest radioactive processes as the key to age determination of rocks. His important field work in Africa and Asia, and his studies of rocks, are well known. A fellow of the Royal Society, he wrote *The Age of the Earth* (1913) and *Principles of Physical Geology* (1965).—*R. W. D.*

HOLMIUM: a lanthanide (rare-earth metal) element (Ho), at. no. 67; at. wt 164.94; one of the least abundant of the rare earths. J. L. Soret (1878) and Per Theodore Cleve (1879) independently discovered holmium. Although at present writing the element has not been isolated in pure form, very pure samples of holmium oxide have been obtained since 1953 by ion-exchange CHROMATOGRAPHY. Holmium occurs in gadolinite and similar minerals.—*I. B.*

HOLOGRAPHY: interference photography—that is, the recording of visual information in terms of phase and amplitude of light rather than intensity, as in the ordinary photographic image. Phased light, such as that from a laser, is split into two parts, one of which illuminates the scene to be photographed. This light is scattered from the objects of the scene, and recombines with the other half of the beam to form an interference pattern on a photographic plate. This interference pattern corresponds to the shifts of phase produced as the light travels paths of different lengths. The scene can be reproduced by directing through the plate, or hologram, light similar to that used originally. On one side of the hologram appears a virtual image in three dimensions; on the other, a real, two-dimensional image like that obtained with an ordinary camera lens. A relatively new technique, holography has rich possibilities for three-dimensional television, microscopy, and other applications.—*J. W.*

HOMOGENTISIC ACID: an intermediate in the metabolic degradation of the amino acids phenylalanine and tyrosine. In alkaptonuria, an inborn error of metabolism, the homogentisic acid cannot be degraded further because of the deficiency of a hepatic enzyme, and the acid is found in large amounts in the urine.—*F. F.*

HOMOLOGY AND ANALOGY: Organs of different animals having a similar structure and origin regardless of function are *homologous,* whereas organs having a similar function but not necessarily similar structure are *analogous*. There is a homology between the wing of a bird and the arm and hand of man, since these organs are similar in regard to the number, type, and position of bones, yet through modification are used for entirely different purposes. Between the wing of a bird and the wing of an insect there is said to be an analogy because, though both wings are used for flying, they have an entirely different structure and origin. When homology can be demonstrated, it is considered good evidence for evolutionary relationships between organisms—*i.e.* the organisms are assumed to be descendants from a common ancestor. —*J. M. P.*

HOOKE, ROBERT, 1635–1703, English physicist; b. Freshwater, Isle of Wight; ed. Oxford. He assisted Thomas Willis in chemical research and Robert Boyle in pneumatics, working with Boyle on the air pump. With the establishment of the Royal Society in 1662, Hooke was appointed first curator of experiments, and became a fellow in 1663. He later served as secretary of the Society, 1677–83. In 1665 he published his *Micrographia,* in which he explained combustion; described the iridescent colors of thin, transparent plates and films; detailed a compound microscope; illustrated numerous microscopical objects; and described the first refractor for liquids. Hooke, one of the first to employ a balance spring in the pocket watch, was the inventor of a very large number of instruments, including the wheel barometer, a sounding instrument, a sea-water sampler, a hygrometer, a wind gage, a rain gage, and a weathercock. He also showed that thermal expansion is a general property of liquids and solids, and proposed a temperature scale with the freezing point of water as zero. He published in 1674 an account of a systematic attempt to observe parallaxes of the stars, and in 1678 his *De potentia restitutiva, or Of Spring*. In addition he formulated the relation known as ELASTICITY.—*S. B.*

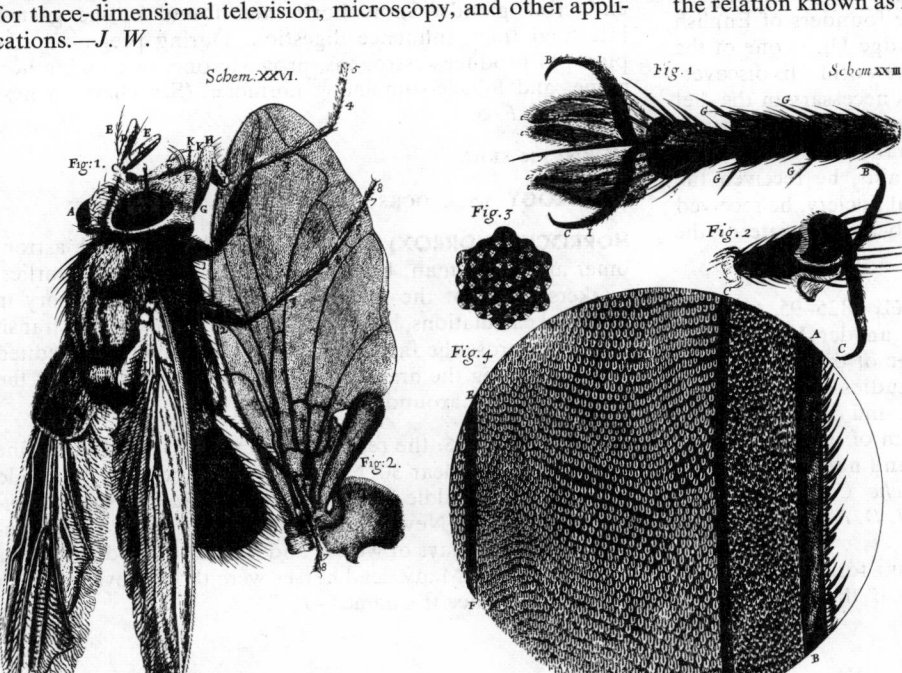

Studies of insects from Hooke's *Micrographia:* These drawings, showing clearly the details of external structure, were made using the compound microscope described by Hooke in his text. (*N. Y. Public Library*)

HOOKE'S LAW: a law, published by Robert Hooke in 1678, which states that within elastic limits the deformation of a system is proportional to the force producing the deformation. This is the principle of the spring scale. Suppose (see figure) a small weight *w* is added to weight *W*, causing the spring *S*, from which they hang, to stretch an additional

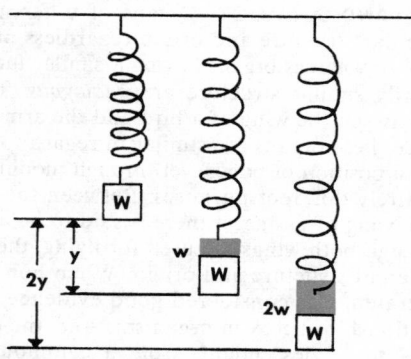

Experiment Demonstrating Hooke's Law

amount *y*. Then, if the spring obeys Hooke's law, an addition of *2w* to *W* will cause a stretch of *2y*, *3w* will cause a stretch of *3y*, etc. If all the weights are removed except *W*, the weight *W* returns to its original equilibrium position, confirming the ELASTICITY of the spring *S*.—*H. Sw.*

HOOKER, SIR JOSEPH DALTON, 1817–1911, English explorer and botanist; b. Halesworth. He took part in many scientific expeditions and wrote extensively on both botany and geography. His encouragement of Charles Darwin, a close friend, was responsible in large part for the publication of the *Origin of Species.* Later (from 1865), while director of Kew Gardens, Hooker lent influential support to Darwin's evolutionary theory. Hooker's publications include *Genera plantarum* (with G. Bentham, 1862), *Index Kewensis* (1895), and his *Life and Letters* (1918). A fellow of the Royal Society, he received its Royal, Copley, and Darwin medals. He was also an associate of the U. S. National Academy of Sciences. —*D. H. D. R.*

HOPKINS, SIR FREDERICK GOWLAND, 1861–1947, English biochemist; b. Eastbourne. One of the founders of English biochemistry, he developed at Cambridge Univ. one of the foremost biochemistry departments in the world. His discoveries about the nature of the amino acids necessary in the diet of mammals led him to the decision that the basic foodstuffs are not sufficient for the survival of mammals. For his discovery of the growth-stimulating vitamins, he received the Nobel prize, 1929. A fellow of the Royal Society, he received its Copley medal in 1926. He was also an associate of the U. S. National Academy of Sciences.

HOPPE-SEYLER, ERNST FELIX IMMANUEL, 1825–95, German physiologist and chemist; b. Freiburg an der Unstrut. He made major contributions to knowledge of the chemistry of the blood through his spectroscopic studies of hemoglobin and the isolation of hemoglobin crystals and other blood pigments. He also discovered the spectrum of oxyhemoglobin (1862) and of methemoglobin (1864), and named those pigments. His works include *Physiologische Chemie* (4 vols., 1877–81), an important textbook.—*D. H. D. R.*

HORIZON: a circle on the CELESTIAL SPHERE formed by a plane perpendicular to the zenith-nadir line. If the plane passes through the center of Earth so as to intersect the celestial sphere exactly 90° from the zenith, the circle so formed is the *celestial horizon.* If the plane passes through the observer's eye, the circle formed on the celestial sphere is the *sensible horizon;* if the plane is tangent to the observer's sea-level position, the *geoidal horizon* is formed on the celestial sphere. The apparent meeting of Earth's surface with the sky is the *visual,* or *apparent, horizon* and is formed by a series of rays from the observer's eye tangent to Earth's surface and extended to intersect the celestial sphere.—*T. N.*

HORMONES: a wide variety of substances which the body manufactures to regulate the growth and activity of tissues and organs. Together with the nervous system the hormones are the "information" by which the body, a complex of cells and tissues, is organized and controlled. Most hormones are produced in ENDOCRINE GLANDS by special cells and carried by the blood to the cells of the target organs, where they produce effects proportional to their concentration in the blood. The endocrine glands can control the metabolism of the other tissues with these chemical messages. Endocrinology, the study of hormones, is conducted in two general ways: (1) by removal of an endocrine gland (this allows a study of the effects produced by absence of the hormone); (2) by injection of the individual hormone (this allows a study of the effects it produces on the whole body).

Since all cellular activity is based on enzyme-catalyzed reactions, it is probable that hormones affect enzymes. By this means hormones may allow some reactions to proceed and others to slow down, and thus govern the cell's activity. A direct enzymatic effect has been found in a few cases (*e.g.* estrogen on transhydrogenase, and epinephrine on phosphorylase). Hormones may also act on the cell membrane, which regulates what enters and leaves the cell. Such an effect has been shown for insulin, which makes muscle cells much more permeable to glucose. In most cases, although the over-all effect of a hormone is known, the mechanism by which it acts is not. Hormones are found in all higher forms of life; in insects they control the metamorphosis from larva to adult. Chemically, the hormones may be simple organic compounds like epinephrine (a phenol derivative), proteins like insulin, or steroids like estrogen. Of the endocrine glands of vertebrates, the pituitary is one of the smallest but the most important, since its hormones control the activities of other endocrine glands. Some hormones, found in the gastrointestinal tract, influence digestion. During pregnancy the placenta produces estrogens, progesterone, luteinizing hormone, and follicle-stimulating hormone. (See chart on next page.)—*J. F. S.*

HORN: see SKIN.

HOROLOGY: see CLOCKS AND WATCHES.

HORROCKS (HORROX), JEREMIAH, 1617–41, English astronomer and clergyman; b. near Liverpool. Among the earliest workers to adopt the Copernican and Keplerian theory in practical calculations, he predicted and first observed a transit of Venus across the face of the Sun (1639). Newton credited him with being the first to describe the elliptical path of the Moon's motion around Earth.—*O. G.*

HORSE LATITUDES: the region of calms, light winds, and fine weather located near 30°N and 30°S lat., between the trade winds and the middle-latitude westerlies. Sailing ships carrying horses to the New World in the old days were often becalmed here for days or weeks, and ran out of food and water for the animals. Many dead horses were thrown overboard in this region; hence the name.—*P. L.*

HORMONES AND THEIR EFFECTS

Gland	Hormone	Site of Action	Effect
Anterior Pituitary	Growth hormone	General	Increase in growth; increase in muscle glycogen.
	Thyroid-stimulating hormone (TSH)	Thyroid	Increases thyroid hormone production.
	Adrenocorticotrophin (ACTH)	Adrenal cortex	Increases steroid hormone production.
	Luteinizing hormone (LH)	Ovary	Increases progesterone production.
		Testicle	Increases testosterone production.
	Follicle-stimulating hormone (FSH)	Ovary	Stimulates ovulation; increases estrogen production.
		Testicle	Increases spermatozoa production.
Intermediary Zone of Pituitary	Melanocyte-stimulating hormone	Skin	Increases skin pigment formation.
Posterior Pituitary	Oxytocin	Uterus	Causes uterine contractions.
		Mammary glands	Causes ejection of milk.
	Vasopressin	Arterioles	Increases blood pressure.
		Kidney	Increases water retention.
Thyroid	Thyroxine and triiodothyronine	General	Increases metabolic rate. Affects energy production from food.
Parathyroid	Parathormone	Bone and kidney	Regulates calcium metabolism.
Testis	Testosterone	Accessory sex organs	Stimulates function.
		General	Stimulates development of male characteristics.
Ovary	Estrogen and estradiol	Accessory sex organs	Stimulates maturation and normal cyclical function.
		Mammary glands	Stimulates development.
		General	Stimulates development of female characteristics.
Corpus Luteum	Progesterone	Uterus	Preparation and maintenance for pregnancy.
Adrenal Medulla	Epinephrine (Adrenalin)	Heart and smooth muscle	Increases pulse and blood pressure.
		Arterioles	Contraction.
		Liver and muscle	Glycogen breakdown.
	Norepinephrine (Noradrenalin)	Arterioles	Increases blood pressure and flow resistance.
Adrenal Cortex	Aldosterone	General	Increases sodium and water retention.
	Corticosterone	General	Increases metabolic rate; effect on sensitivity to foreign substances.
Pancreas	Insulin	General	Increases ability to use carbohydrate; reduces blood sugar level.
	Glucagon	Liver	Increases glycogen breakdown; raises blood sugar level.

HOUR ANGLE: the angular distance along the celestial equator from a point of origin to the hour circle of a celestial body, measured from the origin westward from 0° through 360°. Together with declination, hour angle defines a semi-local system of coordinates which facilitates conversion to and from the equatorial system of coordinates (see CELESTIAL COORDINATES). *Local hour angle* is obtained when the celestial meridian of the observer is used as origin. *Greenwich hour angle* is measured from the celestial meridian of Greenwich. *Sidereal hour angle* is measured from the hour circle of the vernal equinox. Local hour angle and Greenwich hour angle change about 360° per day because of Earth's rotation, but sidereal hour angle is unaffected. The difference between the Greenwich hour angle and the local hour angle of the same body measures the longitude of the local meridian. The sum of the sidereal hour angle and the right ascension of the same body always equals 360°.—*T. N.*

HOUR CIRCLE: a great circle of the CELESTIAL SPHERE passing through both celestial poles. The arc of the hour circle from the celestial equator to a celestial body is its declination; the arc from the body to a pole is its polar distance. As Earth rotates, the hour circle of each celestial body moves apparently westward with the body, coinciding with the celestial meridian twice per day; at that moment, the body is said to be in transit or at culmination.—*T. N.*

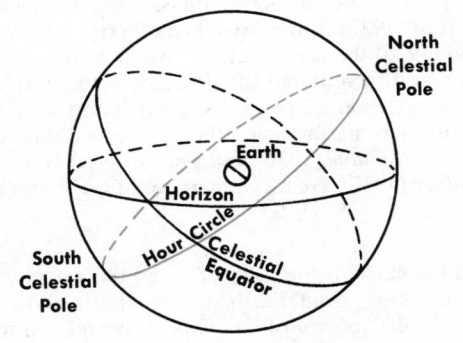

Hour Circle in Relation to Other Features of Celestial Sphere ▶

HOUSSAY, BERNARDO ALBERTO, 1887–   , Argentinian physiologist; b. Buenos Aires. His research has encompassed many fields of physiology, with emphasis on endocrinology. For his discovery of the part played by the hormone of the anterior lobe of the pituitary gland in the regulation of sugar metabolism, he shared the Nobel prize for 1947 with C. F. and G. T. Cori. He is a fellow of the Royal Society and an associate of the U. S. National Academy of Sciences. —*D. H. D. R.*

HOWARD, LUKE, 1772–1864, English meteorologist; b. London. He was one of the earliest scientists to keep regular records of the weather, which he published in his *Climate of London* (1818–20), but his name is now chiefly remembered for his system of classification of clouds by their shapes. He introduced the Latin names *cumulus, stratus,* and *nimbus*— still used by meteorologists all over the world. He was a fellow of the Royal Society.—*O. G. S.*

HOWE, ELIAS, 1819–67, U. S. inventor; b. Spencer, Mass. In 1843 he began work on his sewing machine, successfully demonstrated in 1845 and patented in 1846. His machine was awarded the gold medal at the 1867 Paris Exposition.—*S. B.*

HOWELL, WILLIAM HENRY, 1860–1945, U. S. physiologist; b. Baltimore, Md. A student of the physiology and pathology of the blood, he was a pioneer in the investigation of the phenomena of blood coagulation. He was a member of the National Academy of Sciences.—*D. H. D. R.*

HOYLE, FRED, 1915–   , English mathematician and astronomer; b. Bingley, Yorkshire. Author of *Some Recent Researches in Solar Physics* (1949), *The Nature of the Universe* (1951), and *Frontiers of Astronomy* (1955), Hoyle originated the mathematical form of the STEADY STATE THEORY, which holds that the universe of galaxies is expanding and new material is continually created in space to keep the mean density of the universe constant. He is a fellow of the Royal Society. —*G. H.*

Fred Hoyle
(Ramsey & Muspratt)

HUBBLE, EDWIN POWELL, 1889–1953, U. S. astronomer; b. Marshfield, Mo. From his work at Yerkes Observatory came his *Photographic Investigations of Faint Nebulae* (1920). Joining the Mt. Wilson Observatory in 1919, he made extensive photographic studies of the nebulas. He gave the first conclusive proof (1925) of the existence of extragalactic objects, published (1926) the classification system of GALAXIES still in use today, and formulated the distance-velocity relation for galaxies (see HUBBLE'S CONSTANT; RED SHIFT OF GALAXIES). In addition to numerous scientific papers, Hubble wrote *The Realm of the Nebulae* (1936) and *The Observational Approach to Cosmology* (1937). He was a member of the National Academy of Sciences.—*S. D. G.*

HUBBLE'S CONSTANT: the ratio between the velocity and distance of a galaxy from Earth. Observations show that the RED SHIFT in the spectra of GALAXIES is correlated with their apparent brightness. If the red shift is interpreted as a velocity, and if brightness is assumed to decrease with increasing distance, it is found that the velocity is a constant multiple of the distance. The observed value of this constant is 100 km/sec per million parsecs (see ASTRONOMICAL DISTANCE UNITS). Its reciprocal, which is a time interval (distance/speed), is equal to 13 billion yr and is a basic constant of COSMOLOGY.—*S. D. G.*

HUMAN BODY: The human body begins its development as a fertilized egg within the mother's body. Development proceeds by two general processes: differentiation (the production of specialized tissues from unspecialized tissue) and growth (massive cell division). The developing body, or embryo, spends its first nine months in the uterus of the mother (see EMBRYONIC DEVELOPMENT). During this period, membranes form about the embryo, and the umbilical cord connects it to the mother's body. The embryo is almost completely protected from environmental harm. It has its own separate blood circulation, with the heart beating at a rate uninfluenced by the mother, and its own nervous life. The blood of the embryo flows through blood vessels in the umbilical cord to a disc-like structure, the placenta, where it exchanges materials with the mother's blood by diffusion, absorbing food and oxygen and eliminating wastes. During BIRTH, the embryo (now called a fetus) is pressed out of the uterus by the mother's muscular contractions, the fetal membranes are thrown off (afterbirth), and the infant emerges into a new world with few of the protections it previously enjoyed. However, the newborn child quickly acquires the means to deal with its environment: breathing begins, with the result that oxygen formerly supplied by the mother's blood is now extracted from the air; senses start to respond to tactile, thermal, and auditory stimuli; a sucking reflex appears, which provides for intake of food; urination and defecation reflexes permit elimination of wastes.

At birth, the differentiation of the human body has been all but completed, further development being largely a matter of growth. Every major organ system is present, as well as almost every tissue, except some sexual accessory structures, such as mammary glands. Major organ systems and some of the organs they include are: *skeletal*—bones; *muscular*—muscles; *digestive*—teeth, mouth, salivary glands, esophagus, stomach, intestines, liver, pancreas; *circulatory*—heart, arteries, veins, capillaries; *respiratory*—nose, pharynx, larynx, trachea, bronchi, lungs; *endocrine*—endocrine glands; *excretory*—skin, alimentary canal, liver, kidneys, bladder; *integumentary*—skin, hair, nails, teeth; *nervous*—brain, spinal cord, nerves, eyes, ears; *reproductive*—testes, ovaries, uterus, oviducts. (See SKELETON; MUSCLE; DIGESTION; CIRCULATION IN LIVING THINGS; RESPIRATION; ENDOCRINE GLAND; EXCRETION; SKIN; HAIR; NERVOUS SYSTEM; REPRODUCTION.)

Following birth, growth occurs in regular and predictable patterns. Differences in structure are attributable to heredity, environment, or both. For example, a child of two blue-eyed parents will undoubtedly have blue eyes, as a result of HEREDITY; but bowed legs may be caused by environment—the result of bone changes brought about by a lack of vitamin D in the diet. During its lifetime, the human body undergoes several profound changes in structure and function. The largest change begins at PUBERTY and lasts through adolescence. Many secondary sexual changes occur at this time, marking the conversion of child to man or woman. Another major change occurs at about age 50, when a woman's body undergoes menopause, the termination of menstruation (see CHANGE OF LIFE). About age 60, AGING processes in both men and women become more rapid, and body parts deteriorate (skin

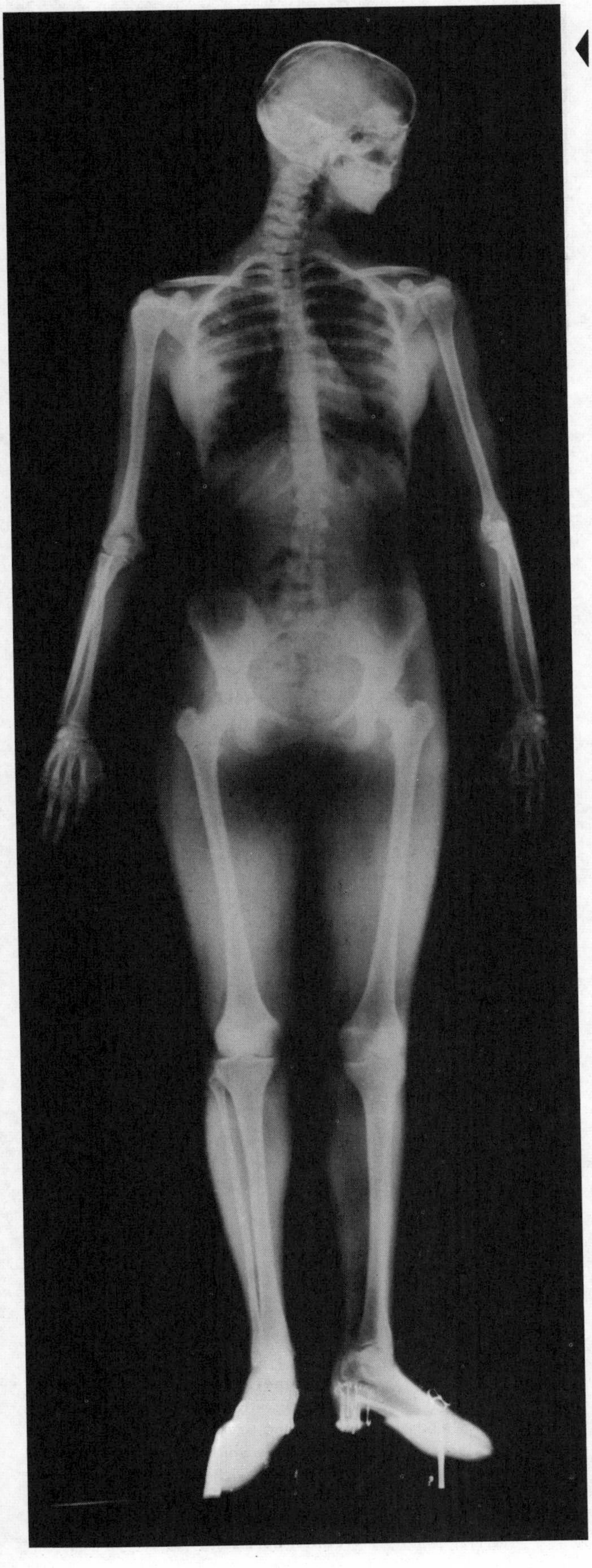

Human body at full maturity is seen in this radiograph of an adult woman. Opacity of bones to x-rays enables the skeletal system to be differentiated readily from the other organ systems of the body. (*Eastman Kodak Co.*)

loses its color, hair falls, muscles lose tone, teeth are lost). Finally, disease or failure of a "vital" organ ends the life of the body (see DEATH). See also ANATOMY; ANIMAL PHYSIOLOGY. —*A. R. D.*

HUMBOLDT, ALEXANDER, FREIHERR VON, 1769–1859, German naturalist and explorer; b. Berlin; ed. privately. With his life-long interest in nature and natural phenomena, Humboldt traveled widely and observed carefully. His most extensive trip (1799–1804) took him to little-known parts of South, Central, and North America. He helped to lay the foundations of physical geography, meteorology, and climatology. Equally important was his great influence in encouraging other scientists and in making science a cooperative international enterprise. He was a fellow of the Royal Society.—*R. K.*

HUME, DAVID, 1711–76, Scottish philosopher; b. Edinburgh. A man with literary ambitions, Hume never held an academic post, but his work rocked academic philosophy. The *Treatise of Human Nature,* completed at 26, is now regarded as the most penetrating criticism of 17th-cent. philosophy ever written. Hume's influence on modern EMPIRICISM is enormous. A succinct theory as to how our ideas are derived from experience, and how the mind associates ideas, provided

David Hume
(*N. Y. Public Library*)

Hume with a critical method for examining accepted beliefs about the self, bodies, uniformity of nature, and God, and illuminating explanations of our ideas of time, space, causality, and existence. All reasoning, Hume maintains, is of two kinds: (1) concerning *relations among ideas* (here demonstration and logical certainty are found, *e.g.* "2 + 2 = 4," and denials of demonstrative reasoning are inconceivable or contradictory); (2) concerning *matters of fact* (here "proof" is constructed from probable evidence, *e.g.* "Brutus stabbed Caesar," and denials of this reasoning are not inconceivable or *necessarily* false). For Hume, no reasoning about facts is capable of demonstration or logical necessity; thus natural science rests on probable or experimental reasoning. Failure to exhibit either mathematical or empirical reasoning, as in most metaphysics and theology books, leaves "nothing but sophistry and illusion." Hume views RATIONALISM as a philosophy based on confusion of these types of reasoning or denial of the difference between them. His own famous analysis of causality (*Treatise* I. xiv) exhibits this distinction: causal connections are observed constant conjunctions of events reasoned only inductively as in (2) above; but in the mind there may be a propensity *always* to associate the *idea* of one object (the "cause") with the *idea* of another (the "effect"). That propensity, or habit, is the source of necessity. But then necessity "exists in the mind, not in objects."—*H. S. T.*

HUMECTANTS: substances that can be added to commercial products to prevent their drying out. Humectants are hygroscopic (moisture-absorbing) substances, exerting their effect by absorbing moisture from the air in periods of high humidity. In foodstuffs, *e.g.* shredded coconut and candy, the most widely used humectants are glycerin, propylene glycol, and sorbitol. These and a few related compounds are also those most used in cosmetics, toothpaste, and tobacco. Sorbitol is used for treating paper and leather. Mixtures of several humectants sometimes give better results than those used singly.—*Ru. M.*

HUMIDITY: in meteorology, a measure of the quantity of invisible water vapor which the atmosphere contains. To illustrate how this quantity varies, we can pour a little water into a vessel and then seal it. The water evaporates into the air above it—rapidly at first, then ever more slowly, until evaporation stops. Molecules of water vapor continue to be exchanged between the water surface and the air, but at this stage molecules leave the water surface at exactly the same rate as other molecules arrive at the surface from the air; *i.e.* a state of equilibrium is reached with no tendency for evaporation or condensation, and the vapor is said to be saturated. (This is often loosely but conveniently expressed by the term "saturated air.") If the contents of the vessel are warmed, more water evaporates until the vapor again becomes saturated; the warmer the air, the more vapor is needed for saturation.

Temp.	Relative Humidity					
86°F	16%	24%	31%	45%	57%	100%
68°F	28%	42%	54%	79%	100%	
61°F	36%	53%	69%	100%		
50°F	52%	77%	100%			
43°F	67%	100%				
32°F	100%					
	4.85	7.27	9.41	13.65	17.31	30.4

Grams of Water Vapor per Cubic Meter

Relative humidity, expressed as a percentage, is the amount of water vapor actually contained in the atmosphere divided by the amount that could be contained at the prevailing pressure and temperature, and multiplied by 100. Thus, as indicated in the above chart, the relative humidity is 100% if the air at 86° holds 30.4 gm of water vapor per cubic meter, and only 16% if the amount of water vapor held is 4.85 gm.

Water-vapor content can be defined and measured in a number of ways. Moist air may be regarded as a mixture of water vapor and dry air; their relative proportion by weight is termed the *humidity mixing ratio* of the air. For example, 1 kg of saturated air having a total pressure of 1,000 mb (millibars) contains 3.82 gm of vapor at 0°C (humidity mixing ratio 0.00382) and 14.6 gm at 20°C. But water content can be expressed also as relative humidity: the ratio of the actual quantity of water vapor in the air to the quantity it could hold if saturated at the same temperature. Expressed as a formula:

Relative Humidity
$$= \frac{\text{Actual humidity mixing ratio of the air} \times 100}{\text{Humidity mixing ratio of saturated air at the same temperature}}$$

Relative humidity is always expressed as a percentage. Thus, air at 20°C which contains 12.4 gm of water vapor/kg has a relative humidity of 85% (because saturated air at 20°C contains 14.6 gm of water vapor/kg).

Recording humidity: Weather apparatus set-up in cotton-growing region includes wet- and dry-bulb thermometers (psychrometer), suspended vertically from cross-beam, and maximum and minimum thermometers on the upright at center. (*U. S. Weather Bureau*)

Molecules of water vapor in air exert pressure; their contribution to the total pressure of the atmosphere is known as the vapor pressure. In saturated air, the pressure exerted by the water vapor is called the *saturation vapor pressure*. Its value increases quite rapidly as the temperature of the air is raised. Since vapor pressure is directly proportional to quantity of vapor in the air, *i.e.* to the humidity mixing ratio, the relative humidity may also be defined as:

$$\frac{\text{Actual vapor pressure}}{\text{Saturation vapor pressure at the same temperature}} \times 100$$

The humidity mixing ratio x is related to the vapor pressure e and the total pressure p of the moist air by the formula $x = 0.622e \div (p - e)$, where e and p are expressed in the same units.

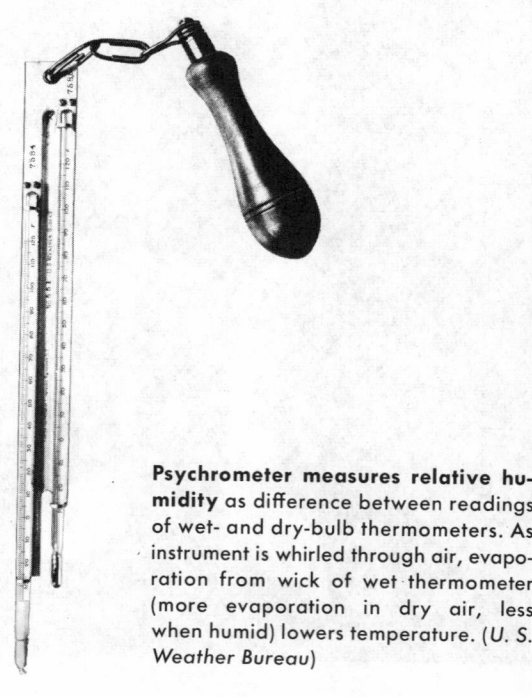

Psychrometer measures relative humidity as difference between readings of wet- and dry-bulb thermometers. As instrument is whirled through air, evaporation from wick of wet thermometer (more evaporation in dry air, less when humid) lowers temperature. (*U. S. Weather Bureau*)

Unsaturated air may become saturated by taking up more moisture or by cooling to the temperature at which it just begins to deposit moisture. This temperature, called the *dew point*, provides a further measure of humidity. We have seen that air containing 12.4 gm of vapor/kg at 20°C has a relative humidity of 85%; to become saturated it would have to be cooled to its dew-point temperature of 17.3°C. Saturated air is by definition at its dew-point temperature; otherwise the dew point is always lower than the air temperature. At temperatures below 0°C, it is sometimes convenient to take as a reference the equilibrium vapor pressure over a plane ice surface rather than that over a water surface. Air cooled until its vapor is just saturated relative to such an ice surface is said to be at its *frost point*.

To measure the humidity by evaporating water into the air, meteorologists use an instrument called the *wet- and dry-bulb hygrometer* or PSYCHROMETER.

If air near the ground is cooled below the dew point, condensation occurs on the surfaces of objects in the form of dew. In the free air, condensation occurs upon tiny particles floating in the air to form clouds or fog. If these particles are absent or rare, or if the air cools so rapidly that vapor condensation cannot keep pace, the vapor pressure may rise above the normal saturation value and the air is said to be *supersaturated*. Relative humidity thus rises above 100%; a relative humidity of 101% corresponds to a supersaturation of 1%. Air in a cloud does not remain in a supersaturated state indefinitely, but only while it is cooling quite rapidly; in any case, the supersaturation rarely exceeds 1%.—*B. J. M.*

HUNGER AND THIRST: vague sensations, still inadequately understood, that develop with a need for food and water. Hunger is much more than mere recognition that the stomach is undergoing contractions ("hunger pangs"), for it is still felt by persons whose stomach has been removed surgically. It may involve an unidentified hormone, since an intravenous injection of blood from a hungry dog into a satiated one will make the latter interested in food immediately. Hunger is more than a decrease in the concentration of blood sugar, for this can rise to its maximum level soon after the beginning of a meal without ending the animal's (or person's) interest in more food. Recently, a center that controls thirst has been discovered in the hypothalamus of the mammalian brain; by

stimulating it electrically, an experimenter can induce a horse that has drunk its fill at the watering trough to want more—upsetting the old proverb. Possibly this center in the hypothalamus detects an increase in the salt concentration of the blood passing it, the increase in saltiness being caused by the blood's having less water than normal. Apparently the center, by reflex action, reduces the flow of saliva and at the same time causes changes in the cells lining the throat; these cells thereupon cause the vague sensation of thirst. An addition of salt to the blood is as effective in inducing thirst as a decrease in the amount of water. Commonly people assume that thirst is due to a decrease in the amount of saliva and consequent drying of the mouth; holding water in the mouth, or chewing pickles that stimulate salivation, both fail to give more than momentary relief from thirst, because they have no effect on the thirst center in the brain.—*L. and M. M.*

HURRICANE: a cyclonic storm originating over a tropical ocean, with a wind speed of at least 74 mi/hr. These storms are known as "typhoons" in the W Pacific Ocean and as "cyclones" in the Indian Ocean. Such storms form primarily along the equatorward fringes of the subtropical ANTICYCLONES during summer and autumn, and often move far westward in TRADE WIND regions at 10 to 20 mi/hr before curving northward and accelerating into the westerly wind belt of the middle latitudes. This tendency is shown by Fig. 1, which also illustrates the great variability in direction and speed of individual hurricanes. Wind speeds of over 150 mi/hr and barometric pressures as low as 892 millibars (26.35 in. mercury) have been recorded near the center of hurricanes. Primary wind damage from hurricanes occurs in a relatively narrow strip, which may vary from less than 20 mi in width in very small storms to more than 200 mi in large ones. Destruction in coastal areas due to wind-generated waves and tides is often much greater than wind damage; also it tends to be concentrated along the storm track. Destruction due to flooding from the heavy rains which accompany the hurricane frequently occurs over a much wider area. Rain associated with the hurricane tends to occur in characteristic patterns which can be observed by RADAR (Fig. 2). The strongest winds and heaviest rain are usually found in a ringlike zone near the storm center. This area is found at varying distances up to 25 mi from the center of the hurricane circulation. Within

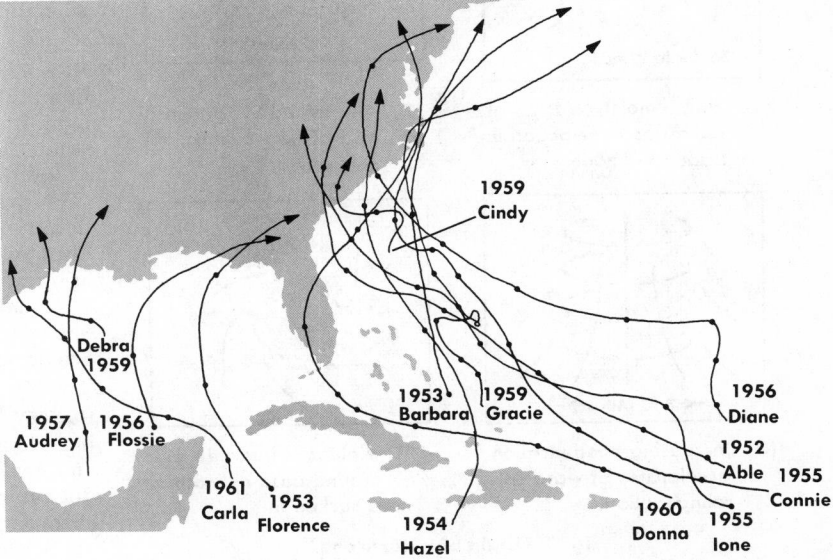

Fig. 1: Tracks of hurricanes whose centers entered the U. S. during the 1952–1961 period. Dots indicate positions of storm centers at 24-hr intervals. Individual hurricanes vary considerably in direction and speed. In each annual hurricane season, hurricanes are given girls' names in alphabetical order corresponding to the order in which the storms develop.

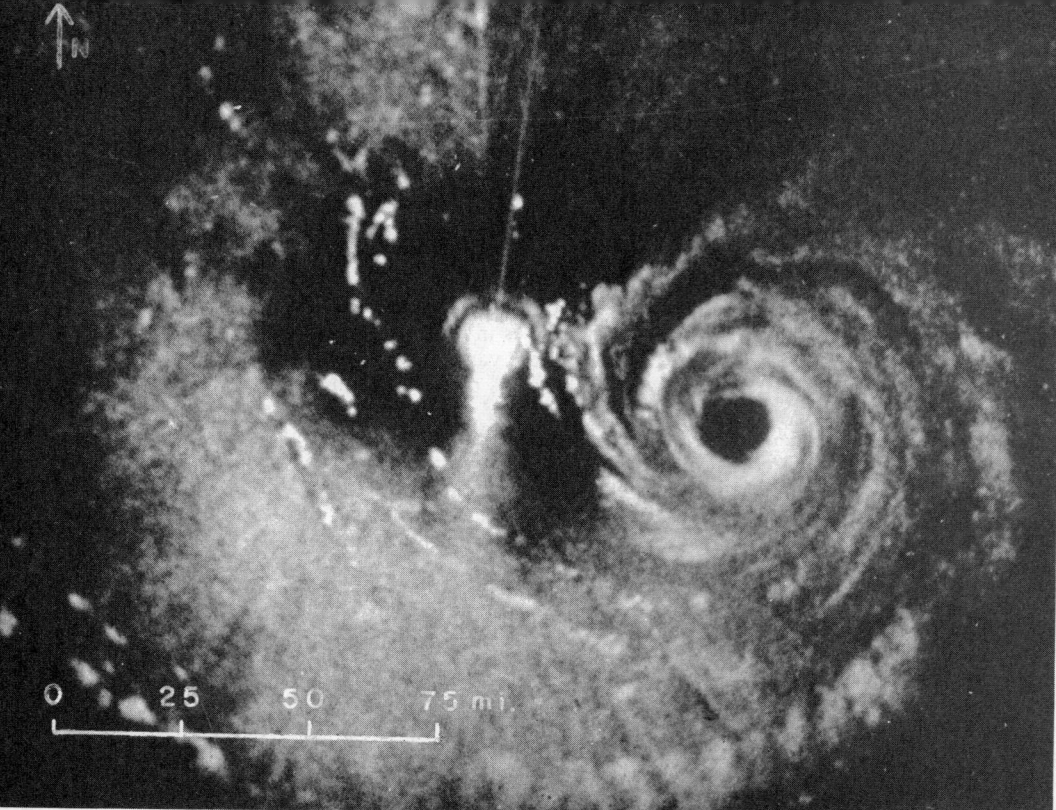

this ring is the well-known "eye" of the hurricane, a region in which cloudiness decreases, rain stops, and wind speed often decreases to less than 20 mi/hr. Outside the central ring there are squalls and thunderstorms, which tend to occur in spiral-like bands (Fig. 2). The significant weather and wind conditions in the hurricane are found almost entirely inside the area covered by the spiral bands.

Hurricanes form only over the tropical oceans during the months when the sea temperature is warmer than about 78°F. The energy source for these storms is the latent heat of condensation which is released as warm, moist air ascends in

the cloud systems surrounding the eye (Fig. 3). This energy source is available wherever precipitation is occurring but does not generally result in the generation of strong winds. The organization of the hurricane is such that the heat energy released in the areas of heavy rain can be converted to air motion. The clue to hurricane formation is, therefore, thought to lie in the upper-air circulations which may induce organized patterns in the distribution of the precipitating clouds.—*C. L. J.*

HUTTON, JAMES, 1726–97, Scottish geologist; b. Edinburgh. He postulated that past geologic changes were caused by processes presently observable, *e.g.* erosion, operating at the same rate throughout geologic time. Hutton published this "uniformitarian" theory (see GEOLOGY) in the paper "Theory of the Earth" (1788), and in two volumes under the same title (1795) expanded the theory, laying the foundation for the modern science of geology. He also developed the theory of igneous intrusion and emphasized the role of heat in the consolidation and uplift of strata.—*D. H. D. R.*

HUXLEY, JULIAN SORELL, 1887–   , English biologist; b. London. Like his grandfather, T. H. Huxley, he has studied organic evolution, but his interests have ranged over the whole field of biology. Among his many works are *Problems of Relative Growth* (1932) and *Evolution: the Modern Synthesis* (1942). He has been interested in interpreting science, particularly biology, for the layman and has published a number of popular books and articles. From 1946 to 1948 he served as director-general of the United Nations Educational, Scientific, and Cultural Organization. He is a fellow of the Royal Society and an associate of the U. S. National Academy of Sciences.—*D. H. D. R.*

HUXLEY, THOMAS HENRY, 1825–95, English zoologist; b. Ealing. He established Hydrozoa as a separate class of animals and, by his work on the vertebrate skull, introduced the inductive method of formulating a morphological type from characteristics common to a number of representative animals. He became the foremost champion of the free discussion of

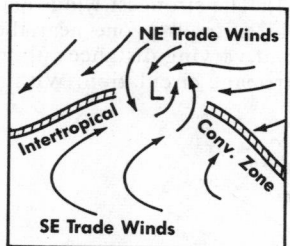

(1) Hot, moist eddy of air forms over ocean in trade-wind zone.

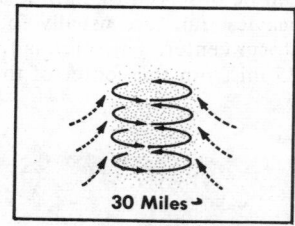

(2) Air, heated by condensation of its moisture, spirals upward.

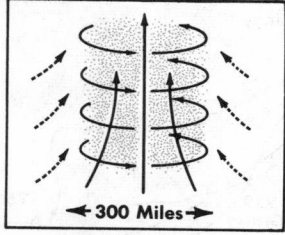

(3) Increasing condensation accelerates upward spiraling motion.

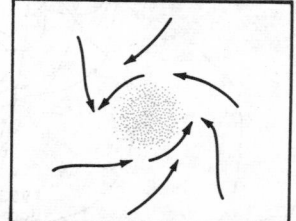

(4) Violent winds develop around base as more air is sucked in.

Fig. 3: Origin of a Hurricane

Darwin's theories, and many of his writings, notable for their distinguished literary style, dealt with the rising conflict between traditional religion and science. His practice of teaching zoology by emphasizing a few representative animal types has persisted. He was president of the Royal Society and received its Copley medal (1888). His *Scientific Memoirs* (4 vols., 1898–1902) contain his collected scientific papers.—*D. H. D. R.*

HUYGENS, CHRISTIAAN, 1629–1695, Dutch physicist, mathematician, astronomer; b. The Hague. One of the many great 17th-cent. scientists, he early wrote several papers in mathematics. After helping to improve the telescope, he made observations of the Orion nebula (1656), discovered a satellite of Saturn, and described Saturn's rings correctly. In 1656 he invented the pendulum clock (*Horologium,* 1658). Invited to become one of the first members of the French Academy, Huygens lived in Paris 1666–81. In 1673 he published his great *Horologium oscillatorium,* which contained sections on the relation between the length of a pendulum and its period of oscillation, the dynamics of a physical system, and centrifugal force. But his greatest contribution was in physical optics. Developing the wave theory of light (*Traité de la lumière,* 1690), he formulated the principle that bears his name: that every point on a wave front is the center of a new wave. Using this idea he explained reflection and refraction, and investigated double refraction and polarization of light. He was a fellow of the Royal Society.—*R. K.*

HYALURONIC ACID: a water-soluble polymer of N-acetyl glucosamine and glucuronic acid. It forms viscous solutions and acts in the body as a cement to bind cells together. It is the principal constituent of Wharton's Jelly, viscid umbilical cord fluid, and intra-ocular fluid. Certain toxic substances, *e.g.* bee venom, are able to diffuse rapidly in the body because they contain hyaluronidase, an enzyme which breaks down hyaluronic acid. Hyaluronic acid is produced by the fibroblast cells, which also form the connective tissue in the body. —*J. F. S.*

HYATT, JOHN WESLEY, 1837–1920, U. S. inventor; b. Starkey, N. Y.; self-educated. With little knowledge of chemistry, he discovered that a mixture of nitrocellulose, camphor, and alcohol becomes soft enough to mold when heated and becomes hard again on cooling. This discovery led to celluloid. His other inventions included many industrial machines. —*D. H. D. R.*

HYBRID: see BREEDING OF PLANTS AND ANIMALS.

HYDRATE: a substance containing molecules of water as part of its chemical make-up. Hydrates are of two kinds: (1) water may be an integral part of the molecule, as in copper sulfate pentahydrate, $CuSO_4 \cdot 5H_2O$; or (2) water may tend to fill holes in the crystal, as in washing soda, $Na_2CO_3 \cdot 10H_2O$,

and zeolites. In substances of the first class, the water molecules have a definite arrangement; thus in $CuSO_4 \cdot 5H_2O$ there are 4 water molecules combined in a definite geometrical manner with the copper ion, and 1 water molecule combined with the sulfate ion. In substances of the second class, the ratio is not as specific; water apparently fills the holes or tunnels in the crystal. Hydrates have definite vapor pressures, and heating can remove the water to make partially hydrated or anhydrous compounds. With hydrates of the first class, the loss of water upon heating takes place in regular steps (thus in $CuSO_4 \cdot 5H_2O$ first 1 molecule of water, then 2, and finally 2 more are lost); these steps are accompanied usually by changes in the crystal structure. Because the water molecule is polar, all polar species (such as ions) will tend to be hydrated in water solution. Thus, the positively charged sodium ion will be surrounded in water solution by 4 water molecules oriented so that the negative side of the water molecule is close to the sodium ion.—*L. Sc.*

HYDRAULIC MACHINE: a machine that is actuated by the pressure or motion of a liquid, or that moves a liquid. Some simple types have been known from antiquity. The Archimedes screw was probably used to raise water for irrigation by the Egyptians long before Archimedes' day. In the hydraulic press, or ram, a hydrostatically applied pressure is transmitted through the fluid. A force F applied on one arm produces in the fluid a pressure F/A_1 which is capable of supporting a load FA_2/A_1 on the other arm. If A_2 is much larger than A_1, very large forces can be generated. The hydraulic ram has many present-day applications to elevators and presses. In the water wheel, widely used in the 18th–19th cent., the weight of water in the buckets on one side of the wheel produces a torque, which is used to drive the shaft. Hydraulic machines today are used in applications where great force is needed and speed is not important.

Modern hydraulic machines include the impulse wheel, reaction turbine, and centrifugal pump. Much of the early development of the impulse (Pelton) wheel was due to L. A. Pelton (1829–1908). A jet of water under high pressure issues from a nozzle into a bucket and drives the wheel. The impulse wheel is capable of delivering much greater power than the water wheel, since, in the latter, the potential energy available is limited by the diameter of the wheel, whereas in the former the nozzle may operate at a very large head—*i.e.* depth below the reservoir water level. In a reaction turbine, water is admitted by a series of nozzles around the circumference of the wheel, so that all the buckets are in service at once. Consequently even greater power may be developed with a reaction turbine of given diameter than with a Pelton wheel. Some units at the Boulder Dam on the Colorado River develop 115,000 hp. Centrifugal pumps operate by means of the variation in pressure set up in a rotating fluid, commonly associated with the "centrifugal force." The vanes of the impeller cause the fluid in the pump to rotate rapidly and be

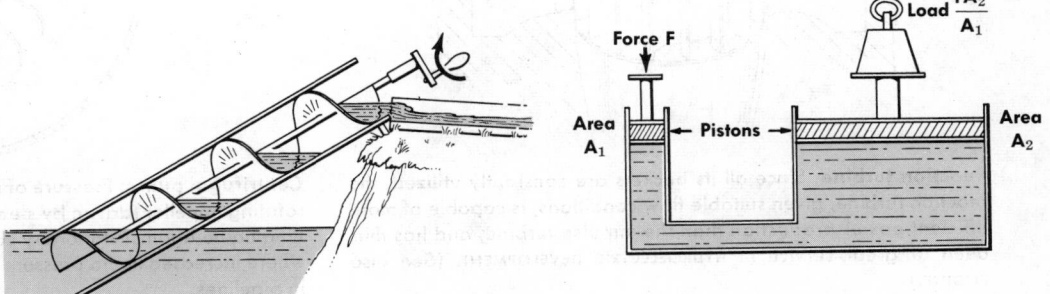

Archimedes screw (*left*) and hydraulic ram (*right*) are among the most ancient types of hydraulic machines. The Archimedes screw is used for lifting water; the hydraulic ram, for gaining mechanical advantage.

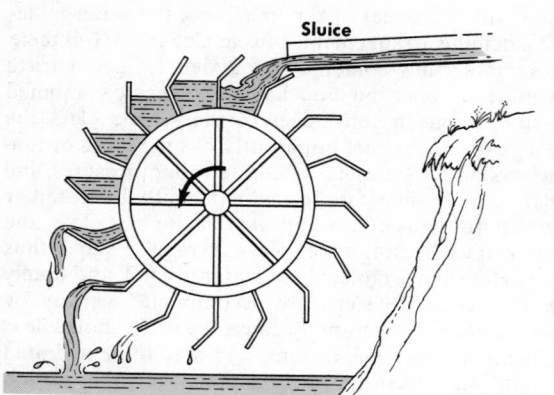

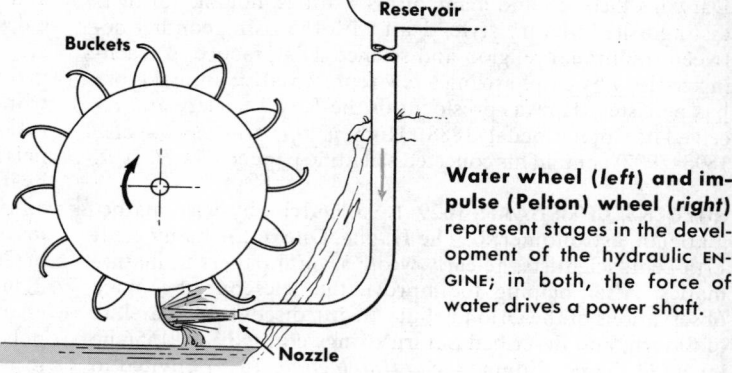

Water wheel (*left*) and impulse (Pelton) wheel (*right*) represent stages in the development of the hydraulic EN-GINE; in both, the force of water drives a power shaft.

thrown radially, so that if fluid is introduced near the impeller axis the centrifugal pump forces it in the radial direction and out through the nozzle. See TURBINE.—*O. M. P.*

HYDRAULIC MODELS: replicas on a laboratory scale of large hydraulic systems. Typical are (1) *river and estuary models,* for studying such problems as silting and erosion, movements of tides and flood waves, and efficiency of proposed harbor works; (2) *ship models,* to study drag and sea-keeping qualities of proposed hull forms; (3) *sluice and spillway models,* for studying flow patterns and flow rates in existing or proposed constructions; (4) *cavitation models,* for studying the occurrence and properties of cavitation near marine propellers or in similar situations. In hydraulic models, the REYNOLDS NUMBER (the ratio of inertia force to viscous force) should be the same as in the full-scale situation in order to preserve dynamical similarity. When free surfaces are involved, the Froude number (ratio of gravity force to inertia force) should also be held constant (and when CAVITATION is involved, the cavitation number also). The cavitation number is the ratio of the pressure of surrounding fluid (unaffected by the body moving through it) to DYNAMIC PRESSURE.

Complete dynamical similarity is rarely possible, since requirements for constant Froude number for the model and the full-scale flow are incompatible with constant Reynolds number. Sometimes, when the influence of viscosity is ignored and the Reynolds number requirement relaxed, valuable results may be obtained. In some estuary models, even geometrical similarity has to be sacrificed, the model depths being exaggerated to avoid excessive frictional losses; results of tests on these models must be interpreted with great caution. See TOWING TANKS AND WATER TUNNELS; MODELS AND MODELING.—*O. M. P.*

HYDRAULICS AND HYDRAULIC ENGINEERING: Hydraulics is an applied science dealing with the flow of liquids, particularly water, and hydraulic engineering involves the useful application of its principles. Next to applied mechanics, hydraulics is the oldest of the engineering sciences, and it is now regarded as one branch of the newer and much more general mechanics of fluids. Its fundamental principles are essentially three: continuity, momentum, and energy. The continuity principle states that the volume rate of flow (velocity times cross-sectional area) must be the same at successive sections of a liquid stream; the mean velocity of the flow is thus inversely proportional to the area of the cross section —*i.e.* higher velocities are to be expected at narrower sections, and vice versa. The momentum principle states that the net external force exerted upon the liquid within a given region must equal the rate at which the momentum (mass times velocity) of the liquid changes as it passes through that region —*i.e.* if the liquid changes speed or direction, either boundary stress or gravitational attraction must provide the necessary force. The energy principle states that the kinetic energy of the liquid (one-half the mass times the velocity squared) changes at a rate equal to that at which work (the product of force and distance moved) is done upon it; the most common form of the energy principle is the Bernoulli equation, which relates change in velocity to change in pressure and elevation, and upon which most instruments for flow measurement (Pitot tubes, Venturi meters, weirs) are based.

Flow phenomena in general are so complex that the only case in which the foregoing principles can be rigorously applied is the apparently trivial one of hydrostatics—liquids at rest—in which the pressure varies in direct proportion to depth. However, the laws of hydrostatics (some date from Archimedes) permit hydraulic engineers to design many struc-

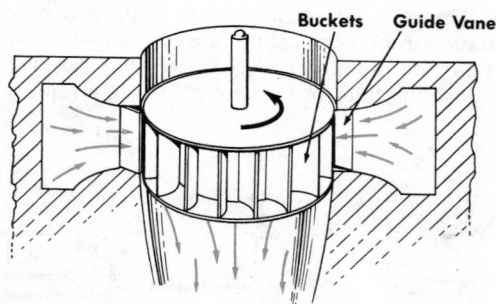

Reaction turbine: Since all its buckets are constantly utilized, the reaction turbine, given suitable flow conditions, is capable of more efficient power production than the impulse turbine, and has thus been of great service in HYDROELECTRIC DEVELOPMENT. (See also ENGINE.)

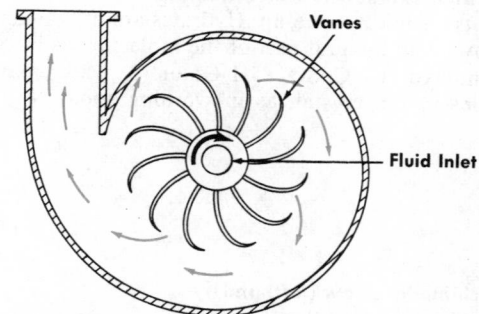

Centrifugal pump: Pressure of inlet liquid is increased by vanes of rotating impeller (driven by steam turbine or electric motor), which fling liquid against stationary casing and out nozzle. Pump is used where increased liquid pressure is desired, e.g. to overcome friction in pipelines.

tures in which liquid velocity does not approach zero—*i.e.* those in which surface resistance (so-called friction) is small and acceleration (velocity change) is not appreciable, *e.g.* certain channels, penstocks, and immersed or floating bodies. Problems involving pronounced acceleration must be handled through a combination of the continuity, momentum, and energy principles. Those involving considerable surface resistance—long pipelines and canals, pipes of small cross section, or conduits carrying flow at high velocity—require use of semi-empirical resistance laws comparable to the laws of boundary-layer and form drag of aeronautics. Peculiarly hydraulic, on the other hand, are gravitational phenomena involving the departure of the free surface from the horizontal: either with location, as in flow over weirs, around piers, and under gates; or with time, as in the propagation of waves.

Because of the complexity of such flow phenomena, the hydraulic engineer makes continued use of the scale model (of which he was the originator a century ago) as an aid to prototype design. Most of his models are operated according to the Froude law of similarity—velocity proportional to the square root of the length scale—as in the case of wave action in harbors or other gravitational phenomena. However, the variation of viscous effects (surface resistance) with the Reynolds law of similarity—velocity inversely proportional to the length scale—makes model reproduction of prototype occurrences involving both gravitational and viscous effects generally impossible. The frequent necessity of studying as well the effect of the movable bed of sediment in natural streams has led the hydraulic engineer to distort many of his models vertically and then vary the resistance artificially until known past conditions can be approximated; the model is then in effect an analog computer which will roughly indicate future occurrences. See MODELS AND MODELING.

The domain of the hydraulic engineer encompasses water supply, including problems of desilting, storage, seepage, and ground-water control; drainage and waste disposal; irrigation, by both gravity flow and spray; river development, involving flood prediction and control, channel stabilization, and canalization; harbor construction and maintenance; and the provision of hydro power, whether on rivers of small slope, below reservoirs of high head, or in tidal bays. All these are inherently civil engineering activities, their common feature being the use of natural waters in one phase or another of the hydrologic cycle. The word "hydraulic" has also long been associated with activities of the mechanical engineer in the design and operation of hydraulic machinery (pumps, turbines, fluid couplings, and torque converters), and more recently in the perfection of hydraulic controls based upon transmission of force by hydrostatic pressure through pipes containing oil. See also FLUID FLOW; HYDRAULIC MACHINES; HYDRAULIC MODELS; HYDRAULIC STRUCTURES; HYDRODYNAMICS.—*H. R.*

HYDRAULIC STRUCTURES: man-made facilities used to store, divert, or otherwise control natural waters for municipal and industrial WATER SUPPLY, IRRIGATION and drainage, FLOOD CONTROL, navigation, HYDROELECTRIC DEVELOPMENT, improvement of beaches and harbors (see HARBOR ENGINEERING), and recreation. Most present projects involving hydraulic structures attempt to combine several of these purposes; *i.e.* they are multi-purpose. DAMS, used for storing and diverting water, are classified as gravity, arch, buttress, earthfill, and rockfill, the selection of a particular type depending upon the geology of the dam site and the availability and cost of materials and labor, as well as the purpose of the project. Conduits, used for transmitting water, include CANALS, pen-

stocks, pipelines, TUNNELS, and natural channels. Design of a hydraulic structure requires knowledge of geology, hydrology, soil physics and mechanics, coastal and structural engineering, and how these branches of science and technology apply to local conditions.—*J. E. Fl.*

HYDROCARBON: in organic chemistry, a compound containing only hydrogen atoms and carbon atoms. Such compounds, based on structure, fall into easily recognized families which have characteristic chemical properties. In the ALIPHATIC series of chain compounds these are representative:

$$CH_3-CH_2-CH_3 \qquad CH_3-CH=CH_2$$

Propane, C_3H_8 Propylene, C_3H_6
An alkane   Propene
A paraffin, C_nH_{2n+2} An alkene
                    An olefin, C_nH_{2n}

$$CH_3-C\equiv CH$$

Methylacetylene, C_3H_4
Propyne
An alkyne
An acetylene, C_nH_{2n-2}

The simplest members of these families are described in the articles METHANE, ETHYLENE, ACETYLENE. From the general formulas it is possible to calculate the molecular formula of any member of the families. Thus, octane (an alkane or paraffin) is C_8H_{18}, from $C_8H_{2\times8+2}$. These families also include branched-chain and closed-chain members, such as:

$$CH_3-\underset{\underset{CH_3}{|}}{CH}-CH_3 \qquad \underset{\underset{CH_2}{}}{CH_2-CH_2} \qquad \underset{\underset{CH_2}{}}{CH=CH}$$

2-Methylpropane   Cyclopropane   Cyclopropylene

The smallest cyclic hydrocarbon with a triple bond in the ring is the 8-carbon compound, cyclo-octyne.

In the hydrocarbons called AROMATIC COMPOUNDS, the simplest member is BENZENE. When a side chain is attached to the benzene ring, as in

$$\underset{CH-CH}{\overset{CH=CH}{CH}}C-CH=CH_2 \qquad \text{Vinylbenzene}$$
                                     (Phenylethylene)

the compound has mixed properties: those of the aromatic ring and of the aliphatic side chain. In such compounds the ring is called the *nucleus*.

Chemically, the paraffin (alkane) hydrocarbons are relatively inactive, as a result of the saturation of the carbon valences. They burn, however, and form explosive mixtures with air; in this respect they are similar to olefins and acetylenes. The latter are much more reactive due to their unsaturation; if an olefin will readily add one molecule of chlorine (Cl_2) across the double bond, an acetylene will add two across the triple bond. These are so-called *addition reactions*. The H atom attached to the triple bond in an acetylene is acidic (see ORGANOMETALLIC COMPOUNDS). The benzene nucleus in the aromatic series does not add molecules the way olefins do, except under extreme treatment. The nucleus is more like a paraffin hydrocarbon in that it more readily undergoes *substitution reactions* in which H atoms are replaced, although the reaction conditions are different:

$$CH_4 \xrightarrow{Cl_2} CH_3Cl \qquad\qquad C_6H_6 \xrightarrow{Cl_2} C_6H_5Cl$$

Methane   Chloromethane   Benzene   Chlorobenzene
          Methyl chloride   Phenyl chloride

                                                —*Ru. M.*

HYDROCHLORIC (MURIATIC) ACID: a slightly yellow, highly corrosive and poisonous liquid formed by dissolving hydrogen chloride (HCl) gas in water. Commercial, fuming hydrochloric acid contains 37 to 39% hydrogen chloride. A constant-boiling mixture of hydrogen chloride and water forms when the hydrogen chloride content reaches 20%. Hydrochloric acid plays a role in the manufacture of a wide variety of substances, *e.g.* gelatin, dyes, pharmaceuticals, and pyrotechnics; it is also used in cleaning metal parts, tanning, and etching. Hydrogen chloride is prepared by burning hydrogen in an atmosphere of chlorine or by the action of sulfuric acid (H_2SO_4) on common salt (NaCl). It is produced also as a by-product: chlorine is diatomic (*i.e.* occurs in two-atom molecules); thus when one chlorine atom replaces a hydrogen atom on an organic compound, the other chlorine atom reacts with the hydrogen to produce hydrogen chloride.—*D. P. B.*

HYDRODYNAMICS (or **HYDROKINETICS**): the branch of fluid mechanics devoted to the study of liquids in motion. It includes the mechanics of fluid flow, fluid friction (or viscosity), the equation of continuity, Bernouilli's principle, and the propagation of surface waves in liquids. Technological applications cover the field of hydraulic power and hydraulic turbines (see HYDRAULICS AND HYDRAULIC ENGINEERING). The corresponding study of gases in motion constitutes the subject of AERODYNAMICS.

In the case of steady, uniform flow, the velocity of the stream, as well as its size and shape, is the same at every point in a uniform-width channel. But in a pipe of variable cross section, the same volume of liquid (assumed incompressible) must traverse every section in a given period of time Δt; hence the velocity of the stream must vary inversely with the cross-sectional area. This is known as the *equation of continuity* and is illustrated schematically in Fig. 1.

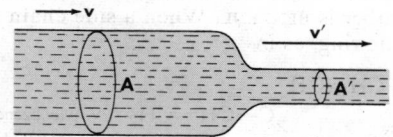

Fig. 1: Equation of continuity: $vA = v'A'$.

In considering the *velocity of efflux,* or the velocity of flow from an opening in a tank kept filled with water at a constant head (pressure in terms of height), Evangelista Torricelli, in 1641, equated the speed of efflux with that of a freely falling body. The modern point of view yields the same relationship ($V = \sqrt{2gh}$) by setting the potential energy of a mass of water at the top of the reservoir equal to its kinetic energy at the level of the orifice. In terms of symbols, the potential energy of a small mass m, raised to a height h above the orifice, is mgh; its kinetic energy at the discharge end is $\frac{1}{2}mV^2$. Equating mgh with $\frac{1}{2}mV^2$, we obtain $V^2 = 2gh$, or $V = \sqrt{2gh}$. The relationship assumes no friction at the opening, the presence of friction causing the actual velocity of efflux to be somewhat smaller than the predicted value.

Theoretically, water flowing in a pipe connected to a filled reservoir should reach the same height if directed upward. Pressures at successive points in the pipe, however, are found to drop as indicated by manometer tubes connected as shown in Fig. 2. There is an immediate drop of pressure due to the so-called *velocity head* (pressure required to produce horizon-

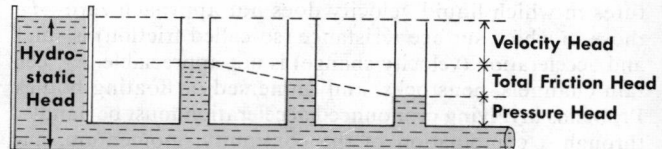

Fig. 2: Progressive loss of head due to friction and velocity of flow.

tal flow) and a series of progressive drops caused by friction, culminating in the total *friction head*. The remaining *pressure head* at the orifice is the difference between the original hydrostatic head (h) and the sum of velocity and friction heads. Making use of the principle of conservation of energy, Daniel Bernouilli (1700–82) found an explanation for the fact that an increase in the velocity of a fluid (in the constricted portion of a non-uniform pipe) was associated with a decrease in pressure (Fig. 3). Bernouilli assumed an ideal, in-

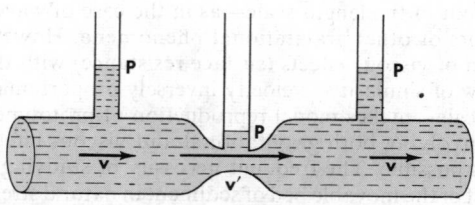

Fig. 3: Venturi tube, showing pressure drop at constriction that causes a velocity increase.

compressible, non-viscous fluid. According to Bernouilli's principle, the sum of the *pressure energy, PV,* present in a small volume of fluid V under a pressure P, and the *kinetic energy, $\frac{1}{2}mv^2$,* is constant in value. Thus a decrease in pressure is accompanied by an increase in velocity, and vice versa. Bernouilli's principle is utilized in the *Venturi meter* (Fig. 3), as well as in the aspirator and the down-draft carburetor. It explains why two nearby ships moving rapidly in the same direction are in danger of collision: the water pressure between them is reduced. A similar hazard exists when a fast-moving railway train passes close to a crowded passenger platform. A moving liquid possesses, by virtue of its motion, a definite *momentum* and exerts a force, on an interposed surface, equal to the rate of change of this momentum. The practical result of this in a hydroelectric TURBINE is the production of a torque that causes the rotation of the turbine and its associated electric generator. In the Pelton water wheel, or the so-called impulse turbine, the momentum of water dropping from an elevated reservoir through a penstock is transferred to each cup of the revolving wheel, with a complete reversal of direction of flow. This adds to the reaction of the wheel and doubles the delivered momentum. The Pelton wheel is particularly well-suited to high-head installations, heads as high as 3,000 ft having been utilized. For medium heads, the Francis turbine is now the accepted type of machine. In the latter, the energy received by the turbine is partly in the velocity form, but mostly in the pressure form. The conversion of this residual pressure into rotor velocity provides the main source of turbine torque. For very low heads (about 30 to 50 ft), the Nagler propeller-type turbine is extensively employed. More recently, an adjustable-blade propeller turbine (Kaplan) was introduced, permitting an adjustment of the blades to fit the changes brought about by widely varying heads.—*A. E.*

HYDROELECTRIC DEVELOPMENT: utilization of the energy of falling water to produce electricity; it embraces a wide range of applied science, including river operation and planning, hydraulic design of conduits and machinery, electrical generators, dams, and electrical transmission. Much present hydroelectric technology stems from ancient methods of converting running water to mechanical energy: water wheels (primitive turbines) were used 3,000 yr ago by the Babylonians and extensively during medieval times for milling. Development during the 19th cent. of hydro-turbines, electric generators, and practical transmission systems (about 1890) laid the base for the modern hydroelectric industry.

Early water wheels were undershot (utilizing the velocity of water against paddles) or overshot (utilizing the weight of water falling into buckets). Modern hydroelectric turbines are of the *impulse-type* (Pelton wheel), which converts the kinetic energy of a free jet; *reaction-type* (Francis wheel), which turns under the pressure of a radially converging flowing stream; and *propeller-type* (Kaplan wheel), which turns in a stream of essentially uniform section. Pelton wheels are used for high heads and low flows, Kaplan wheels for low heads and high flows, and Francis wheels for the intermediate range. Hydroelectric generation is at relatively low voltages (approx. 10 kv); this is stepped up for transmission, since the higher the initial voltage, the more efficient the transmission of electricity (power losses are reduced in proportion to the square of the transmission voltage).

The first practical transmission line, 1891, operated at 10 kv from Frankfurt-am-Main to Lauffin, Germany, a distance of 110 mi. Transmission is now commonly at 110, 220, or 330 kv. Maximum U. S. voltage (1964) is 500 kv nominal, and 700 kv is under consideration for 1970–80; maximum distance is 266 mi. Sweden and the U. S. S. R. transmit 600 mi at 500 kv and 400 kv, respectively. The U. S. S. R. is doing research on 800-kv and 1,000-kv direct-current lines.

Estimates of primary water power are based on minimum reliable flow; flow may be increased or regulated by reservoir storage. Interconnecting transmission networks increase the efficiency of power use. Modern hydroelectric developments are planned for *multiple use*—that is, common use of the facilities and resources for other purposes such as irrigation, flood control, navigation, and recreation. World hydroelectric-energy production was estimated in 1958 at 370 billion kw-hr annually—approximately 1.5% of the total energy requirement of the world and about 7% of world electricity production. It is estimated that this output may be increased economically about 10 times. Water-power resources are relatively well developed in the U. S. A., W Europe, and the U. S. S. R. Vast undeveloped water-power resources exist in Africa and Asia. Africa, with 41% of the world's potential, has developed only 0.02% of its hydroelectric resources.

The U. S. A. produces (1964) 175 billion kw-hr of hydroelectricity annually; an additional 325 billion kw-hr can probably be produced. Of total 1964 electricity requirements, hydroelectricity accounted for about 19%. By 1980, hydropower will supply an estimated 15% of electricity needs, even though U. S. hydroelectric capacity may be expected to increase from 40 million kw (1964) to 78 million, reflecting the fast-growing needs for electricity of the U. S. economy. See ELECTRIC POWER GENERATION AND POWER PLANTS; ELECTRIC POWER TRANSMISSION; ENGINE; GENERATOR; TURBINE.—*D. F. P.*

HYDROFLUORIC ACID: a solution of hydrogen fluoride (HF) in water. It is commonly available in strengths between 2 and 80%, and is a colorless, odorless, highly corrosive liquid that must be handled with great care. On contact with skin, it causes painful, serious burns. A distinguishing feature of hydrofluoric acid is its ability to react with silica (SiO_2), producing gaseous silicon fluoride (SiF_4). This reaction makes the acid useful for etching glass which is mainly silica, but requires the acid to be stored in wax bottles, lead jars, or steel drums rather than in glass containers. Hydrofluoric acid is produced by the reaction of sulfuric acid (H_2SO_4) on calcium fluoride (CaF_2), followed by absorption of the resulting gas (hydrogen fluoride) in water.—*D. P. B.*

HYDROFOIL: a term applied to a surface that, when moved through a liquid, develops lift just as an airfoil does when moving in air. For fully wetted operation, the familiar airfoil shapes are in fact used as hydrofoil sections; such sections form the blades of marine propellers, the wings of hydrofoil boats, and the impellers of hydraulic pumps and turbines. When operating at very high speeds, a foil may develop pressures low enough to cause the surrounding liquid to "cavitate" (boil) over a portion of its surface. If the cavity thus formed grows to a length greater than the foil chord, the hydrofoil is said to be "supercavitating." See AIRFOIL; AERODYNAMICS; CAVITATION; AIRSHIP.—*P. E.*

Hydrofoil craft: Lifted off water by two hydrofoils (submerged), one forward and one aft, this 5-ton experimental boat is capable of speeds in excess of 25 mi/hr. Attitude of hydrofoils is controlled by an automatic pilot. *(U. S. Navy)*

HYDROGEN: a gaseous element (H); at. no. 1; at. wt 1.0080; mp −259.14°C; bp −252.8°C. The lightest-known element, it is colorless, odorless, and tasteless. Hydrogen is incapable of supporting respiration but is not in itself poisonous. Sir Henry Cavendish discovered the element in 1766, but not until 1783 was it given the name hydrogen (water former) by Antoine Lavoisier. In 1932 Harold Urey prepared DEUTERIUM, an isotope of hydrogen that has an atomic weight of 2. In 1934 a second isotope, TRITIUM, at. wt 3, was discovered. Deuterium is found in hydrogen in only one part per 5,000, and tritium is even rarer, although some of the latter is produced in atomic-energy piles. Compounds of hydrogen occur widely in nature, examples being water, acids, alcohols, all plant and animal matter, and the hydrocarbons of petroleum, coal, and natural gas. Hydrogen is prepared commercially by the action of steam on heated carbon, decomposition of some hydrocarbons, and electrolysis of water.

Because of its lightness, hydrogen is used for inflating balloons, but its extreme flammability makes it less desirable than helium for this purpose. Large amounts are used in the fixation of atmospheric nitrogen and in HYDROGENATION of fats and oils.

Orthohydrogen, parahydrogen, and liquid hydrogen: Hydrogen is diatomic, and molecular hydrogen thus has two protons. If the protons spin in the same direction, the form is known as orthohydrogen; if in opposite directions, parahydrogen. The normal ratio of "ortho" to "para" is believed to be about 3:1. Methods have recently been developed to convert orthohydrogen into homogeneous parahydrogen catalytically; and this was the critical step in making available liquid hydrogen for large-scale laboratory and industrial use. Ordinary liquid hydrogen reverts more rapidly than expected to the gaseous state, because conversion from ortho to para proceeds naturally in the liquid phase; this conversion gives off heat, and the heat causes the liquid hydrogen to boil, *i.e.* return to its gaseous state. Homogeneous parahydrogen undergoes no similar conversion, and thus has less tendency to volatilize: while a 20% loss *per day* can be expected with ordinary liquid hydrogen, the loss in the case of liquid parahydrogen is less than 20% *per month* under the same storage conditions. Thus liquid parahydrogen can be shipped, handled, and stored with some efficiency. This has made possible the development of liquid hydrogen as a rocket fuel. With oxygen (or fluorine) as an oxidizer, liquid hydrogen provides a very high SPECIFIC IMPULSE, and its lightness contributes to a higher THRUST LOADING value for the rocket. Liquid hydrogen is also under study as the working fluid for nuclear rockets, and another recently developed use for it is as the sensitive fluid in a BUBBLE CHAMBER.—*D. P. B. and I. B.*

HYDROGENATION: broadly, the reaction of a chemical compound with elemental hydrogen. The term is usually restricted to the addition reaction of an unsaturated organic compound with hydrogen to form a more saturated analog. Few hydrogenation reactions can proceed without a catalyst. The noble metals platinum and palladium are very effective catalysts but have the disadvantage of being expensive and easily inactivated by impurities. Nickel is a widely used catalyst, and various preparations of cobalt, iron, chromium, and copper are also used. An early and still a major industrial use of hydrogenation is in the "hardening" of vegetable oils to form solid fats such as shortenings and margarine. More recently it has been widely used in the manufacture of gasoline and petrochemicals. The reaction of nitrogen with hydrogen to form ammonia (HABER PROCESS) and the reaction of carbon monoxide with hydrogen to form methanol are other industrially important hydrogenation reactions.—*A. M. S.*

HYDROGEN BOMB: an explosive weapon which derives its energy from fusion of atomic nuclei, rather than from nuclear fission (as in the ATOMIC BOMB) or from chemical reaction. It is frequently referred to as an H-bomb or thermonuclear weapon. The fusion reaction produces tremendous energy, but it will take place only under special conditions and at extremely high temperatures. For this reason, the H-bomb must use an A-bomb as its igniting "fuse," while the A-bomb itself can be set off simply by bringing together a "critical" amount of radioactive material—enough to start a chain reaction. Hydrogen bombs have been exploded in tests, but never in warfare.—*A. R. G.*

Hydrogen-bomb explosion in SW Pacific was photographed from 12,000 ft 50 mi away about 2 min after detonation. Subsequently, cloud reached elevation of 10 mi and diameter of 100 mi. (*U. S. Air Force*)

HYDROGEN BONDING: a low-energy attractive force between hydrogen and another element. The hydrogen atom has but a single electron; hence it can often closely approach valence electrons of another molecule and thus form a bond. The most important hydrogen bond is that associated with oxygen. Hydrogen bonding plays a major role in determining the properties of water, proteins, and other organic and inorganic compounds.—*E. G.*

HYDROGEN ION: see IONIZATION; PH VALUE.

HYDROGEN PEROXIDE: a heavy, colorless liquid (H_2O_2) soluble in water and ether. In anhydrous (dry) form, its specific gravity is 1.46, mp $-2.0°C$, and bp $158°C$. Normally, it is sold as a water solution in strengths ranging from 3 to 30%. It is an unstable compound, decomposing to water and giving off oxygen. The evolution of oxygen makes it a highly reactive (and thus sometimes dangerous) compound, but also makes it a good oxidizing agent and bleach. In living systems, hydrogen peroxide is formed during certain processes of biological oxidation; its accumulation is prevented by specific enzymes (catalase or peroxidase).—*D. P. B.*

HYDROGEN SULFIDE: a colorless, flammable gas (H_2S) with a characteristic "rotten egg" odor; mp $-83.8°C$, bp $-60.2°C$. Moderate concentrations of hydrogen sulfide can cause conjunctivitis ("pink eye") on exposure; in large concentrations the gas can prove fatal. Hydrogen sulfide reacts with air and the halogens (explosively with fluorine), is slightly soluble in water, and is stable below $400°C$. It is widely used as a reagent in chemical analysis.—*D. P. B.*

HYDROGEN TRANSPORT (ELECTRON TRANSPORT): a process of great importance in biological oxidation reactions. In living cells, the first steps in oxidation usually involve the removal of hydrogen from the substance to be oxidized by coenzyme-linked dehydrogenases (see PYRIDINE NUCLEOTIDES) and flavoproteins (see FLAVIN NUCLEOTIDES). The hydrogen then passes along a series of compounds, to each of which it is briefly linked, and ends up in combination with oxygen. The general process may be represented by these four general steps: (1) the metabolite to be oxidized yields hydrogen to DPN, leaving an oxidized metabolite plus $DPNH_2$ (reduced DPN); (2) $DPNH_2$ yields its hydrogen to an oxidized flavoprotein to form DPN and a reduced flavoprotein; (3) reduced flavoprotein yields hydrogen to an oxidized cytochrome, forming reduced cytochrome and reoxidized flavoprotein; (4) reduced cytochrome reacts with oxygen to yield oxidized cytochrome and water. Through these steps many compounds are oxidized, eventually by oxygen, and biological energy is produced by the process called OXIDATIVE PHOSPHORYLATION. These processes take place in the mitochondria of the cells.

Although some reduced flavoproteins, *e.g.* xanthine oxidase, can react directly with oxygen, most require the intervention of cytochromes (step 3). Cytochromes are proteins which contain an iron-porphyrin prosthetic group; they are easily oxidized and reduced. One of the best known is cytochrome *c*. Flavoproteins catalyzing the reduction of cytochrome *c* by $DPNH_2$ or $TPNH_2$ are called cytochrome reductases. The reaction of reduced cytochrome *c* with oxygen is catalyzed by an enzyme called cytochrome oxidase. Cytochromes are present in all organisms except anaerobic bacteria. See also table of ENZYMES; FLAVIN NUCLEOTIDES; PYRIDINE NUCLEOTIDES; OXIDATIVE PHOSPHORYLATION.—*K. H.*

HYDROLOGIC CYCLE: the series of processes by which quantities of water are evaporated from the ocean into the atmosphere and, eventually, returned to the ocean again. The cycle may be relatively short and direct, as when the evaporated water is promptly precipitated over the ocean again, or long and complex, as when it is precipitated on land and passes through numerous phases before its return to the ocean. There is probably truth in the saying that "a drop of water, evaporated from the sea, rains five times before it returns." Water that does not fall directly back into the sea may be transported landward as water vapor, fall as rain, and, while falling through a layer of relatively dry air, be re-evaporated before it reaches the earth. It may fall on vegetation and be evaporated from the surfaces of the plants on which it fell. It may fall on the earth and run off immediately, returning via the streams and rivers to the ocean, or it may penetrate the top layer of the earth and circulate through the earth as ground water, issuing finally from some spring, and contributing to a stream or river on

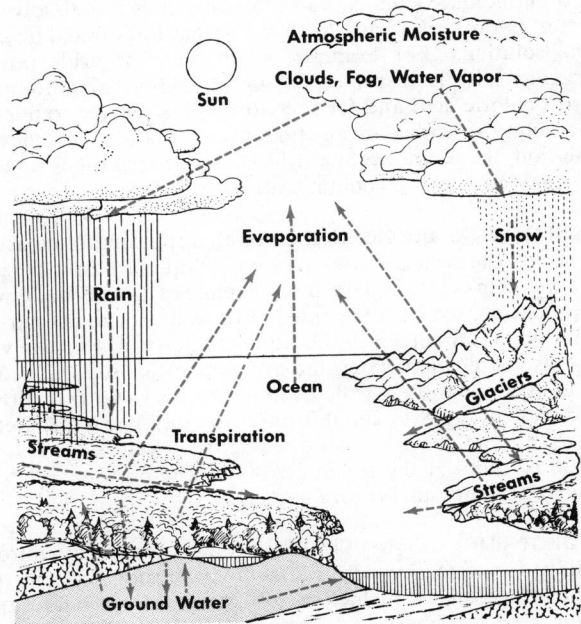

Travels of water: Moisture of oceans is evaporated into atmosphere, condensed to form clouds, and precipitated as rain or snow. Some moisture is used by plants and animals; some sinks into earth to become ground water; some runs off into lakes, rivers, and ocean; some evaporates from land. Most moisture eventually returns to ocean to begin cycle anew.

its way to the ocean. As ground water it may be absorbed by the roots of some plant and stored up for a while in plant tissue, or it may be evaporated from the pores of the leaves (*transpired*). The possible paths are numerous and varied, but, in nearly all cases, the paths followed lead eventually to the sea. Of all the water evaporated from the earth's surface, probably 80% falls as rain directly on that surface. The remainder is either intercepted by vegetation or re-evaporated while falling. Of the water that falls on the earth's surface, the relative amounts which run off, evaporate, or seep into the ground vary so much in different areas that no very exact figures can be given for the earth as a whole. In the U. S. A. 10 to 50% of the rainfall runs off at once, 10 to 30% evaporates, and 40 to 60% is absorbed by the soil. Of the entire rainfall, 15 to 30% is used in some way by plants, either to form plant tissues or to be transpired. In the end nearly all of it returns to the oceans, from which it came, thus completing the hydrologic cycle. See PRECIPITATION.—*A. P. E.*

HYDROLYSIS: chemical decomposition by water. It is essentially a chemical reaction of a molecule of a substance with one or more molecules of water, whereby the original molecule is split into two or more new molecules. Sometimes, as with plant and animal fats and oils, hydrolysis can be effected by superheated steam, the products here being glycerol and free fatty acids; hot dilute mineral acids yield the same products, but hydrolysis with hot aqueous alkali ("lye") yields glycerol and soaps. The hydrolysis of esters in general is often termed saponification, although (as in the hydrolysis of ethyl acetate) no soap may be formed. Special artificial catalysts are often used to promote hydrolysis; and in the living organism hydrolysis and the opposite process of esterification occur through the influence of a natural catalyst called lipase. Many other natural catalysts (enzymes) are hydrolytic; thus maltase (in yeast) hydrolyzes maltose to glucose, and urease (in soil bacteria) hydrolyzes urea to carbon dioxide and ammonia. When certain inorganic salts are dissolved in water, hydrolysis occurs, with the formation of acid or alkaline solutions. For example, when ferric chloride (an inorganic salt) is dissolved in water, a limited amount of hydrochloric acid and ferric hydroxide is formed, rendering the solution acidic. In an analogous situation, an aqueous solution of sodium acetate is basic because of the formation of small amounts of sodium hydroxide.—*J. R.*

HYDROMETER: a device that gives an approximate measurement of the SPECIFIC GRAVITY of a liquid. Basically, it is a long, thin, closed glass tube, expanded at the bottom to form a float, which is weighted with lead shot to keep it upright when immersed in the liquid under test. For use with liquids lighter than water, the hydrometer is proportioned so as to make possible a scale beginning with 1.000 at the lower end and ending with about 0.700 at the top. For hydrometers intended for use with liquids heavier than water, the reading 1.000 is found at the top and 2.000 at the bottom. Scale intervals are not equal in size.—*A. E.*

HYDROPHILIC SUBSTANCE: a substance that has a strong affinity for water by adsorption or absorption, even to the point of gradual liquefaction by extraction of water vapor from the atmosphere. A hydrophilic colloid is one that will swell in water and can not easily be coagulated. Many proteins have this property, accounting for much of the bound water in cells. A desiccant is a substance that will dry the restricted atmosphere about it by virtue of being strongly hydrophilic (see also HYDROPHOBIC SUBSTANCE).—*R. W. F.*

HYDROPHOBIC SUBSTANCE: a substance that has a distinct tendency to repel water in a manner usually characteristic of non-wetted, oily, waxy, or fatty materials. The surface will normally not take a water film, even a monomolecular film. Many biochemical compounds, *e.g.* neutral fats, lipids, and steroids, have this property; hence they make up, in combination with proteins, the membranes of cells (see also HYDROPHILIC SUBSTANCE).—*R. W. F.*

HYDROPHONE: a device for detecting sound in water. Most practical hydrophones can act also as sound sources, in which case they are called projectors or TRANSDUCERS. Normally, directivity is obtained by using a mosaic of electrical elements that may operate on either an electrostatic, an electrodynamic, or a PIEZOELECTRIC principle.—*H. M. T.*

HYDROSTATICS: the branch of physics devoted to the study of liquids at rest. It deals typically with the forces exerted by liquids on the surfaces with which they are in contact. Hydro-

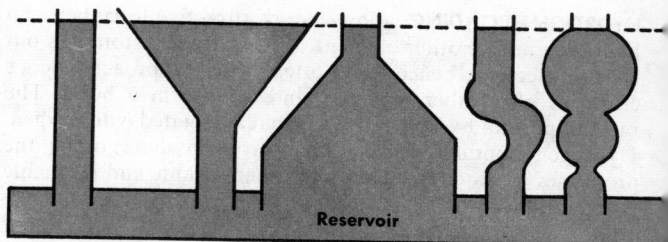

The hydrostatic paradox: Columns of water of equal height exert the same pressure per unit area, regardless of the shapes of the columns. In this demonstration, the interconnected columns of water all stand at the same height despite their different shapes. If pressures at bases of columns differed, columns would stand at different heights.

statics is important in the construction of dams, storage tanks, underwater tunnels, and similar structures.

Any liquid obviously exerts a downward force because of its weight. Not so obviously, it also exerts an equal force upward, sideward, and in all directions. Because of the structure of a liquid, its molecules slide freely over one another and are pushed out in all directions by the liquid's weight. When an object is partly or wholly immersed in a liquid, the upward force on the object's underside provides buoyancy (see ARCHIMEDES' PRINCIPLE).

The force produced by the weight of a column of liquid on a unit submerged area is the *hydrostatic pressure* (p) of the liquid at that depth. This pressure always acts perpendicularly to a submerged surface. The product of this pressure and the entire wetted area (A) is the *total hydrostatic force* (F). Thus, $F = pA$ or $p = F/A$. Pressure varies directly with the depth of submersion (h) and the weight-density of the liquid (ρ). This may be symbolized by the equation $p = h\rho$.

Pressure is independent of the shape of the containing vessel and may be measured directly with a U-tube manometer or indirectly with a Bourdon-element pressure gage (see PRESSURE MEASUREMENTS). Pressure applied to a confined liquid is transmitted undiminished to all parts of the container. This principle, discovered by Blaise PASCAL and known as Pascal's law, underlies the operation of the hydraulic BRAKE and the hydraulic press (see HYDRAULIC MACHINE).—*A. E.; R. M.*

HYDROXIDE: a compound that contains the hydroxyl (hydroxy) group OH^-. There are several different types:

(1) The basic metallic hydroxides of strongly electropositive metals, *e.g.* alkalies and alkaline earths. These ionize as follows, with M representing any strongly electropositive metal:

$$M(OH)_n \rightleftharpoons M^{n+} + n(OH^-)$$

(2) The amphoteric hydroxides of metals of intermediate electropositivity, *e.g.* zinc and aluminum, which may ionize as either an Arrhenius acid or base, depending on the environment:

$$Zn^{++} + 2\ OH^- \rightleftharpoons Zn(OH)_2 \rightleftharpoons ZnO_2^{-2} + 2\ H^+$$
$$\text{(base)} \qquad \text{(acid)}$$

(3) The hydroxides or hydroxy acids of weakly electropositive elements, *e.g.* boron and phosphorus, which ionize as follows, with M here representing any weakly electropositive element:

$$M(OH)_n \rightleftharpoons MO^{n-} + n\ H^+$$

(4) Hydroxides in which the hydroxide group is included

as part of a complex; *e.g.* in the complex $[Al(OH)_6]^{-3}$, the central Al^{+3} ion is surrounded by 6 OH^- ions.

(5) Oxyhydroxides, *e. g.* $FeO \cdot OH$. The characteristic feature of these hydroxides is that the H and O of the hydroxide (hydroxyl) group, since they act as a unit, differ from the H—O bonds in H_2SO_4, sulfuric acid. There is no hydroxyl group in sulfuric acid, because the OH^- does not bind together as a unit; this is shown by the fact that the characteristic OH^- spectrum is missing in spectral analysis of sulfuric acid.—*L. Sc.*

HYDROXYL RADICAL: the ion OH^-; see HYDROXIDE.

Hygrothermograph, here shown in front of removable case, combines two instruments mounted on same frame and recording on same rotating drum: a thermograph (*top*) and a hygrograph (*bottom*). Nonlinear response of human hair in hygrograph is mechanically compensated before transmission to pen. (*U. S. Dept. of Commerce, Weather Bureau*)

HYGROMETER: any instrument for measuring the humidity, or amount of water vapor in the air. Accurate measurements are usually made with a wet- and dry-bulb PSYCHROMETER, but direct-reading dial hygrometers, whose operation depends upon the contraction and elongation of a hair or vegetable fiber as the humidity changes, are widely used. A recording hygrometer is called a *hygrograph.*—*D. H. L.*

HYGROSCOPIC SUBSTANCES: substances capable of absorbing moisture from surrounding air. When added to certain items to prevent drying out they are called HUMECTANTS (*e.g.* glycerin added to candy or tobacco). Some hygroscopic substances, *e.g.* granular calcium chloride, can absorb enough moisture for complete solution; this process is called *deliquescence.*—*Ru. M.*

HYPATIA, d. A. D. 415, the first woman mathematician mentioned in the history of mathematics. The daughter of Theon of Alexandria, she was distinguished in medicine and philosophy as well as mathematics. She is said to have occupied the chair of Platonic philosophy at Alexandria and to have lectured on Plato, Aristotle, and other philosophers. She was murdered by a mob in a riot in Alexandria. Her works, which are lost, were commentaries on mathematics and astronomy.—*H. C.*

HYPERBOLA: one of the CONIC SECTIONS; the locus of a point which moves in a plane so that the ratio of its distance from a fixed point to that from a fixed line not through the point is a constant more than 1. The value of this ratio is the eccentricity. The fixed line is called a directrix and the fixed

point a focus. It can be shown that the locus is symmetric with respect to a line (the *y*-axis in the figure). Hence there are another directrix and another focus which also can be used to define the same curve. The curve has two branches opening in opposite directions.

The coordinate geometry provides an effective method of studying the hyperbola. Greatest simplicity is achieved by placing the origin at the center and letting the *x*-axis pass through the foci. If the coordinates of the vertices A' and A are $(-a, 0)$ and $(a, 0)$ we have $F'A - FA = 2a$. Since, for all points P on the hyperbola, $F'P - FP = a$ constant, this constant must be $2a$. If the coordinates of the foci are $(-c, 0)$ and $(c, 0)$ it is possible to show that the equation of the hyperbola is $x^2/a^2 - y^2/(c^2 - a^2) = 1$. If the positive quantity $c^2 - a^2$ is denoted by b^2, the equation becomes $x^2/a^2 - y^2/b^2 = 1$.

The quantity $2b$ is the length of the conjugate axis which is laid off on the perpendicular bisecter of $A'A$, between B' $(0, -b)$ and B $(0, b)$. The lines through the origin with slopes b/a and $-b/a$ respectively, are asymptotes of the hyperbola. (An asymptote of a curve is a line which the curve approaches more and more closely in both position and direction as it recedes infinitely far off—in fact, as closely as we wish.) A hyperbola with foci on the *y*-axis and center at the origin has

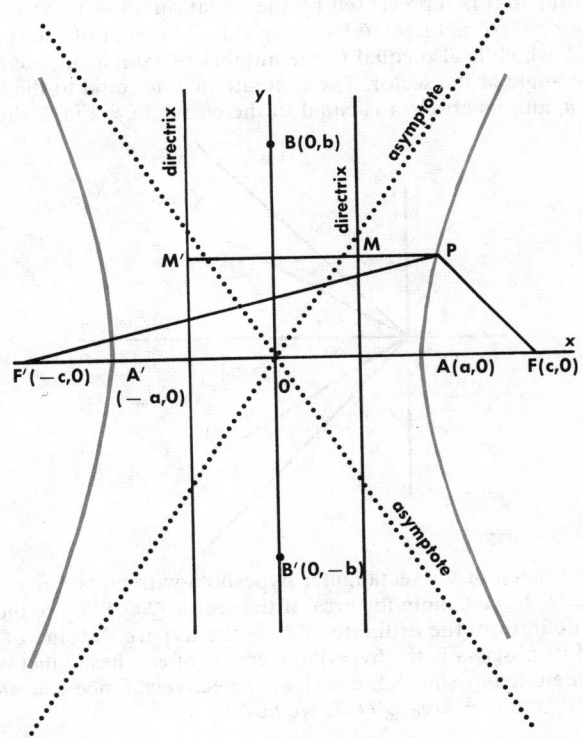

Hyperbola showing foci F and F' and directrixes. The difference in the distances between F and F' to any point P on either branch of the curve is constant. As the branches are extended toward infinity, they approach the asymptotes more closely.

an equation of the form $y^2/a^2 - x^2/b^2 = 1$. If the axes are placed in other positions the equation changes accordingly. A special hyperbola having its asymptotes perpendicular is called a rectangular hyperbola, and if the coordinate axes are made to coincide with the asymptotes, the equation has the form $xy = k$. This hyperbola is the graph of a relation of inverse variation: $y = k/x$.

The fact that the hyperbola is the locus of points having the difference of the distances from two fixed points equal to a constant leads to applications in the Loran system of modern navigation, astronomy, nuclear physics, and other branches of science.—*H. C.*

HYPERBOLIC FUNCTIONS: mathematical functions that are related to a rectangular hyperbola much as the trigonometric, or circular, functions are related to the circle. The analogy is brought out in the two figures. Fig. 1 shows a circle of unit

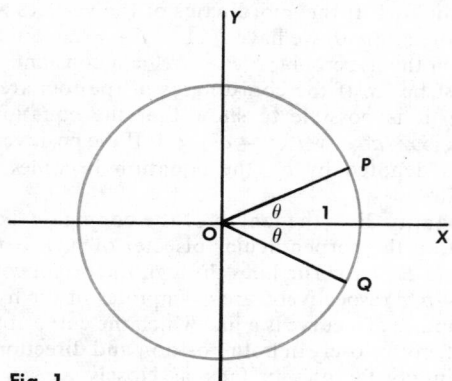

Fig. 1

radius that is represented by the equation $x^2 + y^2 = 1$; the sector QOP is bisected by the x-axis. The area of the sector is θ, which is also equal to the number of radians in one-half the angle of the sector. The ordinate of P is equal to the sine of θ, and its abscissa is equal to the cosine of θ. Fig. 2 shows

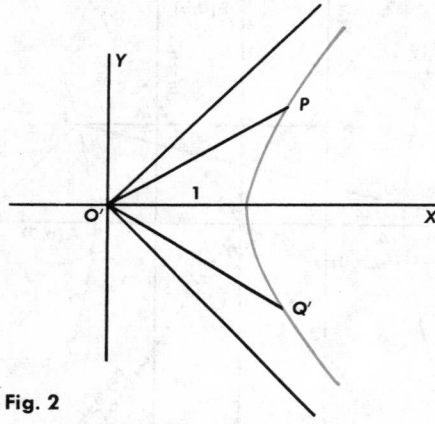

Fig. 2

one branch of the rectangular hyperbola with equation $x^2 - y^2 = 1$. If we denote the area of the sector $Q'O'P'$ by ϕ, then, by definition, the ordinate of P' is the hyperbolic sine of ϕ, and its abscissa is the hyperbolic cosine of ϕ. These functions are denoted by $\sinh \phi$ and $\cosh \phi$, respectively. Since $\phi =$ area QOP, and $\phi =$ area $Q'O'P'$, we have:

for the circle,   ordinate of $P =$ sin (area QOP)
          abscissa of $P =$ cos (area QOP)

for the hyperbola, ordinate of $P' =$ sinh (area $Q'O'P'$)
           abscissa of $P' =$ cosh (area $Q'O'P'$)

Whereas the trigonometric functions relate to the angle and the arc of the circular sector, as well as to the area, the angle and the arc of the hyperbolic sector play no part in the development of the hyperbolic functions. Moreover, there are no elementary ratio definitions of these functions, as of the circular functions.

The hyperbolic functions are closely related to the exponential functions, and may be defined as follows:

$$\sinh \phi = \tfrac{1}{2}(e^\phi - e^{-\phi}), \quad \cosh \phi = \tfrac{1}{2}(e^\phi + e^{-\phi}).$$

The fundamental identity relating $\sinh \phi$ and $\cosh \phi$ is $\cosh^2\phi - \sinh^2\phi = 1$, which follows from the equation of the hyperbola. Addition formulas are similar in form to those for the trigonometric functions. They are

$$\sinh(\alpha + \beta) = \sinh \alpha \cosh \beta + \cosh \alpha \sinh \beta$$
$$\cosh(\alpha + \beta) = \cosh \alpha \cosh \beta + \sinh \alpha \sinh \beta$$

Other hyperbolic functions are defined as follows:

$$\operatorname{cosech} \phi = 1/\sinh \phi, \quad \operatorname{sech} \phi = 1/\cosh \phi$$
$$\tanh \phi = \sinh \phi/\cosh \phi, \quad \coth \phi = \cosh \phi/\sinh \phi$$

The applications of the hyperbolic functions are among those of exponential functions. In many instances exponential functions occur in pairs, e^{kx} and e^{-kx}, in which case $\sinh kx$ and $\cosh kx$ are often more convenient. (See also TRIGONOMETRY; *e.*)—*H. C.*

HYPERFINE STRUCTURE: the effects upon ATOMIC SPECTRA of nuclear angular momentum (spin) and such related nuclear properties as magnetic moment. Although they are often too small to be observed in optical spectroscopy, hyperfine structure effects are easily detectable with microwave and radio-frequency spectrometers, yielding valuable information about both nuclear properties and the distribution of electronic charge in the atom.—*B. Be.*

HYPERON: one of several unstable transitory particles, with a mass intermediate between that of a neutron and that of a deuteron. (The meson is much lighter, intermediate in mass between an electron and a proton.) The hyperon was first "observed" in 1947 during cloud-chamber studies that made possible an estimate of its mass from the ionization density of its tracks and the curving of these tracks in magnetic fields. The Λ° particle is a neutral hyperon with a mass of 2,181 electronic masses, a mean life of 3.7×10^{-10} sec, and a decay pattern $\Lambda^0 \to$ p (proton) $+ \pi^-$ (negative π meson). There are also charged hyperons, such as Σ^+ and Σ^-. Hyperons may be excited, or high-energy, states of the more familiar fundamental subatomic particles. See CLOUD CHAMBER; EXCITED STATE. —*A. E.*

HYPERSONICS: see SONIC REGIMES.

HYPO: the name given by photographers to sodium thiosulfate, $Na_2S_2O_3$, used in water solution as a "fixing bath" in the processing of exposed photographic film. Its function is to dissolve out the portions of silver halide that have not been exposed. See FILM, PHOTOGRAPHIC; PHOTOGRAPHY.—*Ru. M.*

HYPOTHESIS: in formal reasoning, simply the condition under which a conclusion validly follows. In scientific discovery, a hypothesis is an informed guess, an idea to be tested. Some questions to be asked of a useful hypothesis are: Is it consistent with known principles, perhaps derivable from them, or if inconsistent, is it worth while to consider what changes would have to be made in the latter and could such changes be justified? Has the hypothesis unexpected consequences that are observable in nature or that lend themselves to confirmation in the laboratory? Would some other hypothesis account equally well for what has been observed and how shall we decide between them? See CRUCIAL EXPERIMENT.—*H. T.*

HYPSOMETER: an instrument for determining atmospheric pressure by measuring the temperature at which water boils. Because this method is very accurate at low pressures, the hypsometer is usually employed by mountaineers and balloonists for estimating altitudes. See ALTIMETER.—*D. H. L.*

HYSTERESIS: see MAGNETIC HYSTERESIS.

I

ICE (in chemistry): WATER in the solid state. It exists in at least five different allotropic forms. Only the common form, called "Ice I" or "light ice," is stable at pressures of less than about 2,000 atm; it is also the only form of ice that has a density less than that of liquid water. Only a handful of other solid substances, out of the thousands that have been examined, are less dense than their corresponding liquids. This remarkable

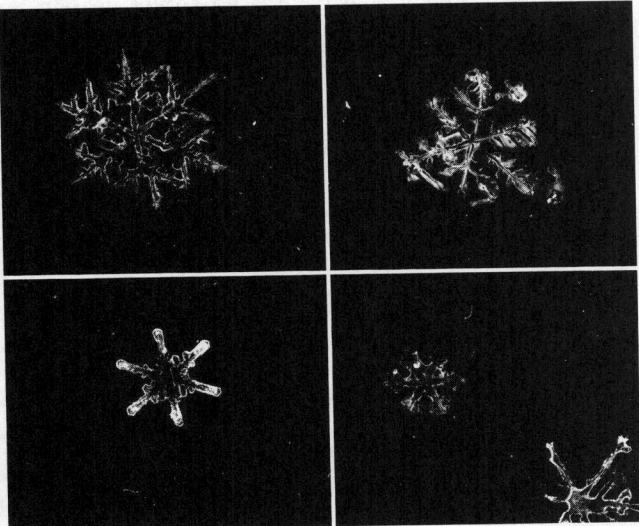

Snowflakes: These small ice crystals, formed directly from water vapor, typically take hexagonal form. (*Barbara Dymond*)

property causes ice to float on water and water to expand on freezing: these are natural phenomena of transcendent importance. The melting point of pure ice, 0°C or 32°F at 1 atm pressure, is a reference point for the centigrade and Fahrenheit temperature scales. Ice is a relatively poor conductor of heat and electricity, is quite transparent to visible light, and is essentially colorless except when viewed in great depth. See also FROST; GLACIERS AND GLACIATION; PRECIPITATION.— *A. M. S.*

ICE (in meteorology): Ice occurs in the atmosphere and on the earth's surface with temperatures at or below 32°F (0°C), at standard sea-level atmospheric pressure. In the air it takes the form of ice-crystal clouds or fog, snow, ice pellets, graupel, hail, etc. Examples of ice formed on the earth's surface are rime, frost, glaze ice, ice on the surface of bodies of water, and glacier ice (see GLACIERS AND GLACIATION).

Liquid water droplets in the atmosphere generally freeze only at temperatures well below 0°C unless freezing nuclei are present in substantial quantities (see SUPERCOOLING). Many supercooled droplets suspended in the atmosphere freeze spontaneously at −16°C (+3°F) without the presence of sublimation nuclei, but all water droplets freeze below

Icebergs, picturesque but ever a menace to navigation, are fed into the oceans continuously by the glaciers of polar regions. This one, called "Paul Bunyan's lower plate," was photographed by Coast Guard photographer on reconnaisance flight over heavily traveled Grand Banks waters. (*U. S. Coast Guard*)

−40°C (−40°F). Airplanes flying through clouds of supercooled water droplets collect ice on the forward edges of their wings and control surfaces as the droplets freeze on impact. If sufficient ice accumulates, the aerodynamic properties of the aircraft are altered and some loss of control results.

Cirrus, cirrostratus, and cirrocumulus, the wispy-appearing clouds high in the atmosphere, and cirrus falsus, the cap cloud of a cumulonimbus, are the common ice-crystal clouds. At temperatures of −30°C (−20°F) and below, fogs of tiny ice crystals sometimes form at ground level. Hailstones, which form in the colder regions of thunderstorms, may be either spherical or irregular in shape. They range in size from ¼ in. to over 5 in. in diameter, average size being from ½ to 1 in. The largest hailstone ever reported in the United States was 17 in. in circumference and weighed about 1½ lb.

Ice pellets and freezing rain start as liquid raindrops. If the rain falls through a shallow layer of very cold air, it will freeze on impact with a solid surface; hence ice storms, during which trees, telephone wires, roads, and the ground become covered with sheets of glaze ice. If liquid raindrops fall through a deep layer of very cold air, they freeze into very small pellets of clear ice before reaching the ground. See PRECIPITATION.

Ice forms at the Earth's surface when the ground temperature falls to 0°C. Water vapor in contact with a cold surface will change directly to frost; liquid water will freeze at 0°C. Sea water freezes at about −1.9°C (28.6°F).—*P. L.*

ICE AGES: see GLACIAL AGES.

ICEBERG: a large mass of glacier ice or shelf ice that has broken away from the parent body. It can be afloat or aground. Its density being close to that of water, an iceberg afloat is about 90% submerged. Most icebergs are less than 500 ft in diameter, but in the Antarctic huge ones more than 10,000 mi² in area have been seen. Icebergs are confined largely to polar seas but may reach latitudes of less than 30° before melting completely.—*R. F.*

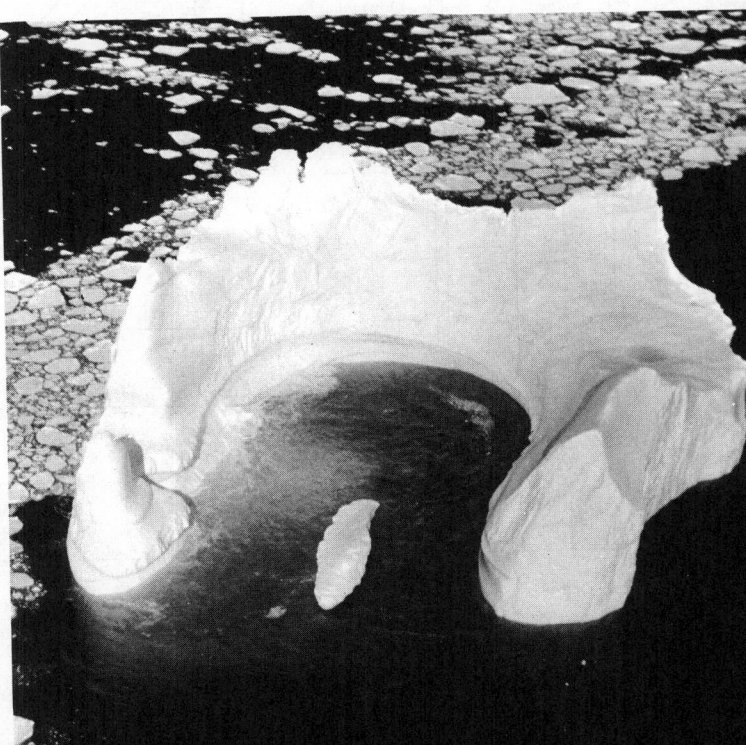

ICE SHEET: a broad glacier, of irregular shape, generally blanketing the terrain. Ice sheets tend to flow outward radially from a center or centers, the location of which depends in part on distribution of snowfall over the ice sheet. The largest ice bodies now in existence are the Antarctic Ice Sheet (5,000,000 mi²; maximum thickness more than 14,000 ft) and the Greenland Ice Sheet (666,000 mi²; maximum thickness more than 10,000 ft). The largest ice body that existed during former GLACIAL AGES was the Laurentide Ice Sheet, which extended from the Atlantic Ocean nearly to the Canadian Rockies, and from the Ohio River to the Arctic Ocean. In area it was a little larger than the present Antarctic Ice Sheet, but its thickness is not well known. Small ice sheets, including those ranging down to a few hundred feet in diameter, are called **ice caps.** —*R. F.*

ICING OF AIRCRAFT: the formation of ice on aircraft during flight. It may occur at any altitude in cold weather or at high altitudes, and build-up of ice may cause severe control problems. Icing tends to occur on the control surfaces, on the leading edges of both cockpit transparencies and the horizontal and vertical stabilizers, on air-intake ducts to the engines, and on aerials. On most modern airplanes, anti-icing equipment is standard; it may consist of a hot gas passed through a duct, vibration-producing devices, or a thermal "blanket" attached to the icing surface.—*W. Ho.*

IGNEOUS ROCK: rock formed by solidification of the molten matter that is called MAGMA when at depth and LAVA when on the surface. (The term "igneous" is from Latin *ignis,* "fire.") Igneous rocks formed from magma cooling beneath the surface, and exposed at the surface later either by faulting or by the eroding away of overlying rock, are INTRUSIVE ROCKS. Those formed by lava cooling on the surface are EXTRUSIVE. In all igneous rocks, composition of the magma determines the nature of the rock formed from it, except where the magma has assimilated appreciable amounts of the wall (surrounding) rock and thus has had its original composition changed. If half or more of the magma is silica, the resulting rock is called SIAL; if less than half, SIMA. Sial is generally lighter in color, less dense, and of coarser texture than sima. Intrusive rock is usually sial; most extrusive rock is sima. Exceptions are common, and there is no abrupt division between the two. Generally the terms sial and sima are used to designate the rock shells or layers underlying continental and oceanic regions, respectively.

The color and density of an igneous rock are ordinarily determined by its composition, but texture is due largely to the manner of solidification. If the process is slow, the various elements of the magma crystallize one after another (*fractionation*) according to the complexity of their molecular structure. First to crystallize are the minerals with the simplest structure (olivine among the ferromagnesian minerals, anorthite among the feldspars). As the crystals form, they either separate from the magma or react with the remaining magma to form different crystals. The speed of crystallization determines, among other factors, the size of the various crystals and the extent to which some of them resist further change.

MINERALOGICAL COMPOSITION OF IGNEOUS ROCKS

Intrusive (plutonic) rocks are indicated by *italic* type; extrusive rocks, by roman. Among the names of ultrabasic rocks (right side of chart), names of characterizing minerals other than the principal constituent appear in parentheses.

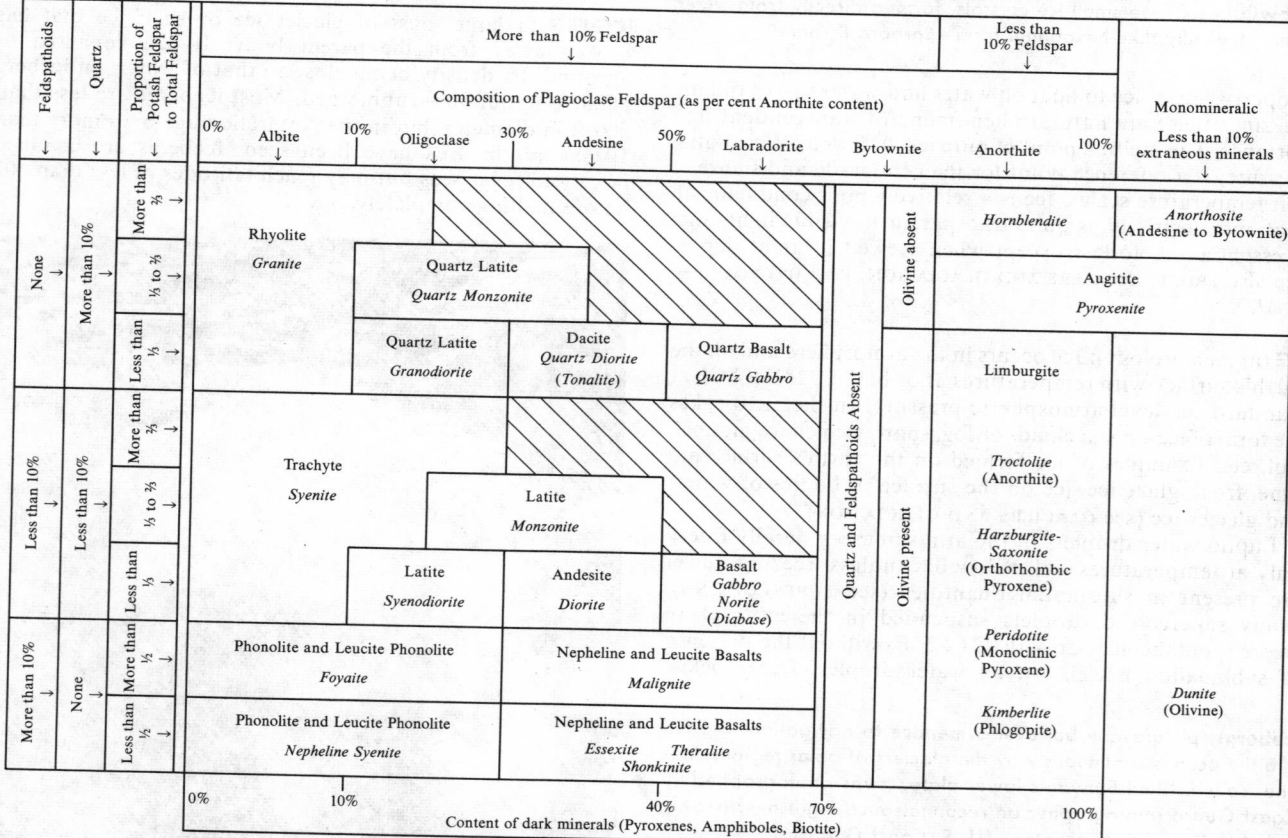

The last mineral to crystallize is usually quartz, composed entirely of silicon and oxygen; generally only highly sialic (acidic) magma is capable of producing quartz. Slow cooling, which is most likely at great depth, produces the largest crystals and thus the most coarse-grained rock; but another factor that favors formation of large crystals is low viscosity. Some granites, which are coarse-grained rocks containing quartz, are produced (usually at great depth) by slow cooling of sialic magma. Lava and pyroclastics, on the other hand, cool relatively quickly, either in the air or on the surface of the ground. As a result of fast cooling, small crystals form, and the rock produced when lava cools has fine grain—in some instances, no grain at all (*e.g.* obsidian, classified as a glass). If the lava is simatic, the rock will usually be basalt, a fine-grained rock rich in ferromagnesians and lacking quartz; if the lava is sialic, the product is generally andesite, a fine-grained rock poor in ferromagnesians, rich in feldspar, and also lacking quartz. Most lava is basalt, but in certain areas of the continents where orogeny (mountain-making) is in process, considerable andesite is found. The accompanying table lists the more important kinds of igneous rock. For forms of extrusive rock, see LAVA and PYROCLASTICS; for forms of intrusive rock, see PLUTON. See Color Plate 53.—*E. A.*

IGNITION: the firing of an inflammable substance or gaseous mixture. Ignition can be achieved by flame, electricity, friction (as with matches), percussion (cigarette lighter), or shock, where the shock wave of one explosive (*e.g.* fulminate of mercury) ignites another explosive (gunpowder). *Compression ignition,* as in the DIESEL ENGINE, is produced by compressing air so rapidly that heat is liberated and causes injected fuel oil to ignite. *Spontaneous ignition* is the unexpected firing, without artificial or intentional stimulation, of a substance or gas. It is often a problem in the cylinders of spark-ignition internal-combustion engines (see MOTOR VEHICLE). See also COMBUSTION; DETONATION; EXPLOSIVE.

Electric ignition systems, in which an electric spark fires the fuel, are commonly "jump-spark" high-tension systems. There are two types: battery-ignition and magneto-ignition systems, both used with internal-combustion engines. Both are continuous processes so long as the engine is running. In battery ignition a battery is used to supply current to produce the spark for the initial igniting of the chemical fuel (*e.g.* gasoline and air) in the cylinders, after which mechanical power taken from the engine is turned into electric current by the generator, and the current is used to charge the battery. In magneto ignition, hand- or foot-supplied mechanical power is turned into electric current for initial ignition, after which the normal operation of the engine (turning chemical energy of fuel into mechanical energy) supplies mechanical energy that can be turned into electric current for continuing ignition.

In the magneto system, voltage is generated by setting in rotation a set of permanent magnets. These are part of a magneto assembly, which houses, in addition to the permanent magnets, a primary and a secondary coil wound on a stationary iron core, a cam, breaker points, a capacitor (condenser), and a distributor. Initial manual or pedal rotation of the magnets generates current in the primary-coil circuit. The primary coil offers low resistance to current, which therefore rapidly reaches a maximum; at this stage, the cam causes the points to open, and the primary current is diverted to the capacitor. The charging of the capacitor causes the primary-coil current to subside quickly, with a consequent collapse of the magnetic field in the iron core. The quick collapse of the magnetic field induces a high-voltage current in the secondary coil (INDUCTION COIL), which leads to the distributor. The distributor, in turn, leads the induced current to the spark plugs

in the prearranged firing sequence necessary for smooth operation of multicylinder engines. A spark is produced inside the combustion chamber when the electric current produces an arc between the spark plug's central electrode and the spark plug's grounded electrode (the space called the spark gap). The role of the capacitor is particularly important in electrical ignition, since it prevents the high primary current caused by the collapse of the magnetic field from arcing between the breaker points and burning them out. The capacitor also aids the build-up of current in the secondary coil by promoting the rapid collapse of the primary current and consequently of the magnetic field of the iron core. The cam, mounted on a shaft that connects it and the distributor, actuates the breaker points. Thus the correct functioning of the cam is essential for the timing of the spark in the cylinders, since timing is controlled by the opening of the breaker points.

Battery ignition is essentially the same as by magneto except that the current in the primary coil is generated by a battery (generally 6 or 12 volts). Battery systems not only eliminate hand cranking in automobiles, but make current readily available for such accessories as driving, parking, and interior lights, radio, cigarette lighters, heaters, and battery-operated windshield wipers. Magneto systems are used in power lawnmowers and small outboard engines, where a battery would represent additional cost, weight, and maintenance. Though now practically obsolete, the "make and break" low-tension system of electrical ignition is still found in some marine and stationary engines. Instead of spark plugs, this system employs a pair of breaker points for each cylinder; one of the points is movable, and moves away or breaks contact with the other in order to generate a spark. See also ELECTROMAGNETIC INDUCTION.—*A. L.*

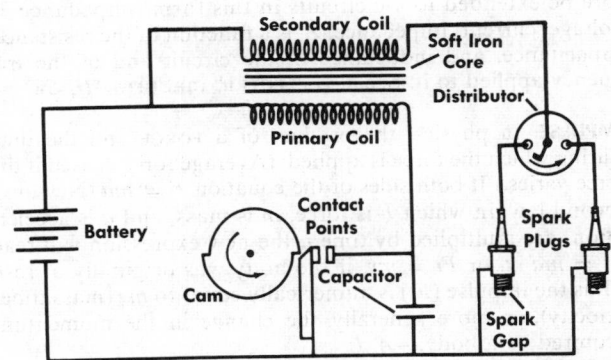

Battery Ignition: In this system, commonly used in automobiles, battery supplies current to primary coil. As engine rotates, the cam, which is timed to piston movement, opens and closes contact points. With points open, primary circuit is broken and battery current flows into capacitor, collapsing magnetic field of iron core. The high voltage thus induced in secondary coil is routed by distributor to spark plug in proper cylinder.

IGY: see INTERNATIONAL GEOPHYSICAL YEAR.

IMAGE: an optical replica or counterpart of a luminous or illuminated object formed by a mirror or LENS. A *real* image is one that can be formed on a screen and is produced by an actual focusing of rays of light at that point. A *virtual* image cannot be formed on a screen and is located in space only with the aid of the observer's eye. The image formed by a photographic camera is real; that produced by a magnifying glass or a plane mirror is virtual. See FOCUS; OPTICAL INSTRUMENTS.—*A. E.*

IMAGINARY NUMBER: see COMPLEX NUMBER.

IMMUNIZATION: the process of establishing immunity to the damaging effects of virulent bacteria, viruses, or toxins that may gain entry into the body. Active immunization of the human body is stimulated when a virulent agent or a fraction of its protein structure comes in contact with certain cells, primarily plasma cells, reticuloendothelial cells, and large lymphocytes. These cells have the ability to produce gamma globulins (*antibodies*) that are capable of reducing the virulence of the invading organism (*antigen*). Antibodies thus formed are generally specific, acting against the particular bacteria, virus, or toxin that stimulated their formation. The effectiveness of a specific antibody will vary from just a few weeks to the life of the individual. *Active immunity* can be artificially generated within the human body by the use of specific vaccines. Vaccines are made from virulent organisms that have been killed by formaldehyde and macerated (cholera, plague, typhoid, whooping cough, and Salk polio vaccines); or from live organisms whose virulence has been reduced (smallpox, yellow-fever, rabies, and live-virus polio vaccines); or from toxins whose potency has been reduced by chemical alteration, thereby becoming toxoids (diphtheria, scarlet fever, and tetanus vaccines). Any of these vaccines is capable of generating immunity when injected into the body. *Passive immunity* can be obtained by injection of serum containing antibodies from an animal or human with active immunity. Infants usually receive a measure of passive immunity from the passage of antibodies across the placenta and in the breast milk.—*C. G.*

IMPEDANCE: in a-c circuits, a quantity that plays the same role as the resistance in d-c circuits. OHM'S LAW may therefore be extended to a-c circuits in this form: impedance = voltage/current. Impedance, Z, is a function of the resistance, capacitance, and inductance in the circuit and of the frequency applied to it. See also ELECTRIC CIRCUIT.—*H. Sw.*

IMPULSE: in physics, the product of a FORCE and the time during which the force is applied. (Average force is used if the force varies.) If both sides of the equation $F = ma$ (Newton's second law, in which F is force, m is mass, and a is acceleration) are multiplied by time t, the new expression will read $Ft = ma \cdot t$, or $Ft = mv$, if the body was originally at rest. Thus the impulse (Ft) is numerically equal to mv (mass times velocity), or, more generally, the change in the momentum acquired by a body.—*A. E.*

IN ARTEM ANALYTICEM ISAGOGE (Introduction to the Art of Analysis), by François Viète, 1591: As the earliest work on symbolic algebra, Viète's book may also be regarded as the first introduction of modern mathematics. Algebraic methods were much older than the 16th cent., but the great bias in European (as in Greek) mathematics had been toward geometry. With Viète's book the modern emphasis on algebra and analytic methods begins, though Viète's notation was still very different from that now familiar.—*A. R. H.*

INBREEDING: see BREEDING OF PLANTS AND ANIMALS; HEREDITY.

INCOMMENSURABLE QUANTITIES: see COMMENSURABLE QUANTITIES.

INCUBATION: commonly, the process of development of an EGG into a complete animal outside the parent's body. In the strict sense incubation is peculiar to BIRDS, although brooding over eggs or young also occurs among some insects,

Mallard duck lays 8 to 10 eggs and incubates them for approximately 26 days. (*Hugh M. Halliday/National Audubon Society*)

amphibians, and reptiles. Among mammals, only the primitive spiny anteater (*Echidna*) and duckbill (*Ornithorhynchus*) incubate, the former carrying its eggs in a pouch resembling that of marsupials, the latter brooding its eggs in a nest in a burrow. Birds' eggs, when laid, must be kept at an elevated and relatively uniform temperature for a certain period of time. This temperature is usually effected and maintained by the high body temperature of the parents, which brood over the eggs in a NEST often lined with insulating material. Duration of incubation varies considerably among birds, being about 12 to 14 days for most songbirds. The most accurate studies on the temperature of incubation have been made on the domestic hen, which incubates for about 21 days. The body temperature of the brooding hen varies during incubation between 102.2° and 105.2°F, with eggs maintained at only 1½° to 3° lower. The mound birds, and also the reptilian alligator, deposit their eggs in a heap of decaying vegetation, where the heat generated is adequate for normal development. Sea turtles bury their eggs in sand above the high-tide level, where heat from the Sun's rays provides sufficient warmth.—*A. P. E.*

INDETERMINACY: see UNCERTAINTY PRINCIPLE.

INDETERMINATE EQUATION: an equation such as $2x + 6y = 10$, which is insufficient to determine the unknowns. We can put $y = (10 - 2x)/6$, or $x = (10 - 6y)/2$. Hence either unknown can be chosen at will. In general, an equation or system of equations which contains more unknowns than equations is indeterminate. A reasonable problem is posed by requiring those solutions which are integers, in which case the equations are called Diophantine, after Diophantus (*c.* A. D. 250), who first studied them.

One integral solution of the above equation is $x = 2, y = 1$. We can find all integral solutions as follows. We observe that if $x = x_1, y = y_1$ is a solution of the homogeneous equation $2x + 6y = 0$, then $x = 2 - x_1, y = 1 - y_1$ satisfies the equation $2x + 6y = 10$, since $2(2 - x_1) + 6(1 - y_1) = (2 \cdot 2 + 6 \cdot 1) - (2x_1 + 6y_1) = 10 - 0$. Now all integral solutions of $2x + 6y = 0$ can be found in the form $x = 3n, y = -n$. Hence $x = 2 - 3n, y = 1 + n$ are solutions of the given equation for all integers n. In this example, the solution $x = 2, y = 1$ was found by inspection. An integral solution of $ax + by = c$, where a, b, and c are integers, exists if, and only if, the greatest common divisor of a and b is contained in c.—*H. C.*

INDIAN SUMMER: a warm, sunny period which often comes in mid- or late autumn after a spell of seasonably cool weather. A typical Indian summer's weather map shows a weak, slow-moving high-pressure area. Light winds and clear skies bring warm, hazy days and cool nights.—*D. H. L.*

INDICATOR: a reagent used in chemical analysis to detect the presence of a sought-for substance. Moisture, for example, can be detected by the salt cobalt chloride (an indicator), which is blue when anhydrous, pink when moist. Presence of iron compounds in solution is detected by first treating the solution chemically to insure the presence of trivalent (ferric) iron; addition of potassium FERROCYANIDE, an indicator, then results in the formation of a Prussian blue, $FeK[Fe(CN)_6]$. Similarly, addition of a THIOCYANATE gives a red color with ferric iron. Acid-base indicators are those generally known simply as "indicators." They indicate whether a solution has excess hydrogen ions, H^+ (acidic), or excess hydroxyl ions, OH^- (alkaline). *Litmus* paper yields a qualitative estimate: if it turns red, the solution is acid; blue, the solution is alkaline. *Phenolphthalein* is colorless in acid, pink in alkali. Indicators when properly used can give a quantitative estimate of acidity or alkalinity, expressed usually in pH VALUE.—*Ru. M.*

INDIGO: a permanent blue dye originally obtained from leaves of the indigo plant, but now mostly made synthetically. Since it is insoluble in water, it is applied by reducing it to indigo white, soluble in alkaline solution. When cloth is dipped into the solution, then exposed to air, the indigo white is oxidized to indigo.—*Ru. M.*

INDIUM: a metallic element (In); at. no. 49; at. wt 114.82; density 7.3; mp 156.4°C; bp 2000 ± 10°C. It was discovered in a zinc blende, where it usually occurs, by Ferdinand Reich and H. Theodore Richter (1863) using spectroscopic analysis. This soft and silvery metal, being unreactive with air and water, is plated onto leaded bearings to increase their corrosion resistance, and it is used in solder for a like purpose. Indium also has been added to gold and silver dental alloys to increase their strength and improve their casting properties.—*I. B.*

INDUCTANCE: the phenomenon of electromotive force produced in a conductor perpendicular to a magnetic field by the relative movement of the conductor and the magnetic field. Michael Faraday and Joseph Henry both independently observed inductance (see ELECTROMAGNETIC INDUCTION); Faraday's law states that in a circuit, the induced electromotive force in volts, E, equals the rate of change of magnetic flux through the circuit (*i.e.* the area surrounded by the conductors of the circuit): $E = \Delta\phi/\Delta t$, where $\Delta\phi$ equals the change of magnetic flux, and Δt equals the time interval. This law indicates that it is immaterial whether the circuit moves relative to a magnetic field of constant or varying strength, or the magnetic field varies within the area enclosed by a circuit. The induced current has a direction opposite to that of the force producing it, *i.e.* either the direction of movement of the conductor or the direction of change of the magnetic field (see LENZ'S LAW). Inductance is responsible for making feasible the commercial production of electricity by the GENERATOR, which is, in effect, a coil of wire rotated through a magnetic field, transforming mechanical energy into electrical energy. When two coils are placed next to each other, and current flows in the primary coil, a magnetic field is produced and will pass (by virtue of the relative positions of the coils) through the secondary coil. If the current in the primary coil fluctuates, as it will if it is ALTERNATING CURRENT, the resulting fluctuating magnetic field will induce in the secondary coil a fluctuating voltage and fluctuating current. The ratio of the voltages in the two coils is proportional to the ratio of the number of turns, or windings, of the coils. This is called *mutual inductance* and is the principle of the TRANSFORMER, by which electric power at high voltages is "stepped down" to power at low voltages.

Where a single coil is in a circuit, current in the circuit will produce a magnetic field whose flux passes through the coil. Alternating current will cause the magnetic field to fluctuate; so will DIRECT CURRENT, if an initially closed circuit is opened, so that current subsides to zero, or if an open circuit is closed, so that current increases to its full value. The fluctuating magnetic field will induce in the coil an emf whose direction will oppose the change in the original emf. This is called *self-induction;* it was first observed by Henry in 1829. The induced emf is proportional to the rate of change of current: $E = L(\Delta I/\Delta t)$, where ΔI is the change in current and Δt is the time interval. The unit of self-inductance, or more simply the inductance, L, is called the henry. It is defined as the inductance of a coil in which the rate of change of current of 1 amp/sec induces an electromotive force of 1 volt (see ELECTRICITY).

INDUCTION: see ELECTROMAGNETIC INDUCTION.

INDUCTION, MATHEMATICAL: see MATHEMATICAL INDUCTION.

INDUCTION COIL (or spark coil): a type of step-up TRANSFORMER designed to produce a high intermittent voltage from a source of low direct-current potential. A primary coil carrying interrupted direct current produces, as a result of close linkage with a secondary coil composed of many turns of fine wire, a high induced electromotive force (emf). This emf is much higher just after the primary circuit is interrupted than

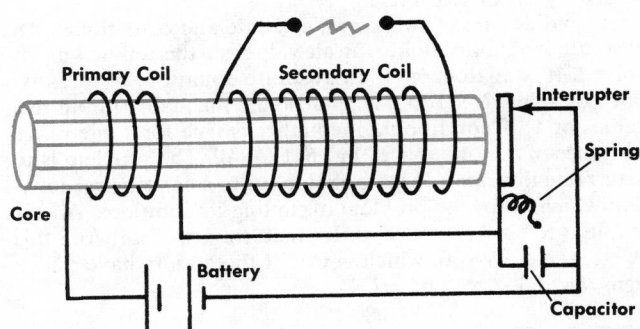

Ignition coil: Schematic view showing wiring. In actual coil, the secondary is wound over the primary to increase efficiency.

just after the circuit is closed. A capacitor placed across the terminals of the interrupter minimizes destructive sparking at these terminals and raises the peak output voltage. The secondary voltage is essentially unidirectional; hence it may be used for the study of electrical conduction through rarefied gases. The device is also used in the ignition system of gasoline engines.—*A. E.*

INDUCTION MOTOR: an alternating-current ELECTRIC MOTOR in which the rotating member (rotor) has a voltage induced into it by the rotating electric fields of the stationary stator; the necessary torque is the result of the forces between the fields of the induced voltage in the rotor and the rotating fields of the stator. The rotor therefore does not need to be connected by wires to an external power supply although, as with all electric motors, an outside electric-current source is required. (In an induction motor, outside current is fed only to the stationary member, or stator.) The induction motor is the most widely used alternating-current motor because of its ruggedness, ease of maintenance, and constant speed. Nikola Tesla (1856–1943) invented the induction motor in 1888.

The primary (usually the stator or fixed member) has conductors placed in a winding similar to that of an a-c GENERATOR. The secondary (usually the rotor or rotating member) may be wound with ordinary conductors or it may be of the squirrel-cage type. The conductors of the latter consist of copper bars welded to copper or aluminum end plates to reduce resistance and allow the circulation of current (hence the squirrel-cage appearance). The primary is supplied with two or more alternating currents which are out of phase with each other (see PHASE ANGLE). Tesla showed that these currents produce a rotating magnetic field even though the winding is physically stationary. The field induces a voltage in the secondary and, since the secondary is shorted, circulating currents result. The reaction between the circulating currents and the rotating field produces motor action.—*H. I. S.*

INEQUALITY: a statement that one quantity is less than ($<$) another or greater than ($>$) another. Examples are $2 < 3$, $1 > -1$, $x^2 + 1 > 0$. It is often desirable to extend an inequality slightly by use of the sign $\leqq$ or $\geqq$. Thus, $x^2 \geqq 0$ states that x^2 is greater than or equal to 0; that is, it cannot be negative. Continued inequalities are useful for expressing a range of values of some variable. Thus, $0 < x \leqq 1$ states that x must be greater than 0 but not greater than 1. The rules of operations with inequalities are similar to those of equations. Any number can be added to or subtracted from both members; any positive number can multiply or divide both members. If both members are multiplied or divided by the same negative number, the sense is reversed; *i.e.* $<$ is replaced by $>$, or vice versa.

Inequalities are of two kinds, absolute and conditional. An absolute inequality holds for all values of the unknowns involved. It is analogous to an absolute equation, or identity. For example, $x^2 + 1 > 0$ is an absolute inequality for all real values of x. A conditional inequality is true for some range of values of the unknowns, but not for all. The problem is to determine this range. This is analogous to a conditional equation which poses the problem of finding its solutions. An example is $x^2 - 7x + 12 < 0$. By factoring, we can write this $(x - 3)(x - 4) < 0$, which is true if the factors have unlike signs, *i.e.* if $3 < x < 4$.—*H. C.*

INERT GASES: the six gaseous elements of group O of the periodic table: HELIUM, NEON, ARGON, KRYPTON, XENON, and RADON; also called the rare or noble gases. They are present in air in small amounts, ranging from argon, the most plentiful (1.4% of air by weight), to radon (transient traces). All are colorless, odorless, and tasteless. Under normal conditions they undergo no chemical reactions; they are slightly soluble

in water. Their extreme chemical inactivity is the result of their outer electron shell's being completely filled (with eight electrons); this virtually prevents formation of compounds with other atoms (see CHEMISTRY). Five of the inert gases were discovered by W. Ramsay by distillation and spectral analysis of liquid air: helium (1894; helium's characteristic spectral lines had previously been discerned in observation of the Sun, 1868); neon (1898, Ramsay in conjunction with Morris W. Travers); argon (1894, Ramsay with Lord Rayleigh); krypton (1898, Ramsay with Travers); xenon (1898, Ramsay with Travers). Ernest Rutherford and R. B. Owens, 1900, were the first to discover an isotope of radon, the heaviest member of the group. Radon exists solely as the radioactive-decay product of radium, thorium, or actinium, and is itself extremely radioactive and short-lived. Radon's radioactivity has been utilized in certain medical treatments. The use of all the inert gases except radon in commercial electric lamps (*e.g.* neon lights) stems from the fact that a high-voltage electric current can ionize these gases even though they are chemically inert. When ionized, the gases emit light of characteristic color. Helium gives a light ranging from ivory-white to pink-violet; neon, red-orange; argon, purple-violet; krypton, pale violet; xenon, sky-blue or blue-green (see IONIZED GAS). The inert gases are also utilized as artificial atmospheres, because of their unreactivity (*e.g.* they will not react with the hot tungsten wire inside an incandescent lamp).—*R. W.*

INERTIA: the property that matter has of resisting changes in its motion. According to Galileo and Newton, a freely moving body does not come to rest, as previously thought, but moves in a straight line with constant speed; force is needed to change its motion. The more massive a body, the greater the force needed to produce a given change in its velocity, as follows from Newton's second law of motion (force equals mass times acceleration). Thus mass is a measure of inertia; it is the fundamental measure. But in the case of rotation, resistance to change of angular velocity is measured by a derived quantity, the MOMENT OF INERTIA, which takes into account the shape as well as the mass of the body.

Train passengers feel the effects of their own inertia when they fall forward as the train stops. Flywheels and centrifuges are inertial devices, as are gyroscopes and certain other control and navigational instruments. In an orbiting satellite, objects have no weight but they still have mass, for they do not lose their inertia.

Inertial reference systems are those in which Newton's laws of motion hold. Accelerated systems are not inertial, because free bodies do not move uniformly relative to them. This nonuniformity can be attributed to "fictitious" but potent inertial forces such as those that caused the train passengers to fall. Centrifugal and Coriolis forces are inertial forces.

The property of inertia sends the jockey flying over the head of the horse when the speed of the horse is abruptly reduced by contact with the obstacle. (*Wide World*)

THE INERT GASES

Name	Symbol	At. No.	At. Wt
Helium	He	2	4.003
Neon	Ne	10	20.183
Argon	Ar	18	39.944
Krypton	Kr	36	83.80
Xenon	Xe	54	131.30
Radon	Rn	86	222

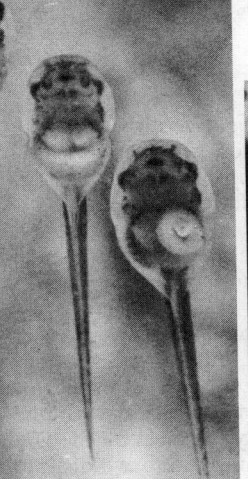

Early life of animals varies greatly from one group to another. Some young animals, such as tadpoles of the spring peeper (*above left*) and the caterpillar larva of the June beetle (*above right*), are different in form from what they will be as adults. Two contrasting conditions of infancy are illustrated at right: Black snakes hatching from eggs (*top*) are ready to fend for themselves, but piglets (*bottom*) are helpless at birth and require parental care. (*Above, George Porter/ National Audubon Society; right, U. P. I. and USDA Photo*)

Bishop Berkeley and, later, Ernst Mach objected to the idea that inertial forces could arise from acceleration relative to empty space, and argued that they must arise from interaction with the stars. Mach claimed that an object in an otherwise empty universe would have no mass. His ideas importantly influenced Einstein in the formulation of his general theory of RELATIVITY.—*Ba. H.*

INERTIAL GUIDANCE: a technique or process for directing aircraft or missiles to selected destinations or targets. Inertial-guidance systems provide information about the actual path of the missile or aircraft in relation to a predetermined path; any differences are transmitted to the vehicle's control system. An inertial-guidance system performs these functions without seeking information from outside the vehicle. Such equipment is merely a highly developed auto-pilot capable of storing and following preset flight instructions very accurately. See AUTOMATIC PILOT.

The mechanism consists of four essential parts: a platform stabilized by gyroscopes, a sensitive accelerometer complex, a computer, and a clock. The platform provides a continuous coordinate reference system during the flight. The accelerometers furnish computer inputs which can be integrated to obtain actual velocity and position. The computer determines course corrections by comparing actual and preset flight paths. The clock permits the computer to compensate for Earth's rotation during the time of flight.—*W. K.*

INFANCY: the early life of any animal. Infancy is a period of special danger, during which the animal must find a source of food differing greatly from that available to it prior to hatching or being born. In the sea, many worms, mollusks, and echinoderms hatch from eggs drifting freely in surface waters, with no parental care whatever. Usually, the more offspring a parent produces each year, the more each youngster must fend for itself. The oyster cannot look after its 100 million to 500 million eggs, whereas a lobster can carry her 12,000 to 15,000 eggs below her body until they hatch. On land, the toad leaves her 15,000 eggs in some pond to develop on their own, whereas the black widow spider and the house spider guard the three or four silken bags, each containing about 300 eggs, in a corner of the loose nest.

For many animals that must begin feeding themselves abruptly as soon as they hatch, the body of the young is quite unlike that of the adult. From an oyster's egg, a strange little swimming creature emerges. The butterfly's egg produces a caterpillar, and the toad's egg a tadpole. After a period of infancy, during which the animal relies upon foods that usually have no appeal to the adult, each youngster transforms through remarkable changes known as its METAMORPHOSIS. These are much greater than the changes that transform a chick into a hen or rooster, or a young termite or grasshopper into the adult insect.

The young of social insects, of various birds, and of many mammals are particularly helpless. Only through extensive parental care can they survive. The honeybee maggot lies quietly in its cell among the brood comb and passively accepts food regurgitated by passing worker bees. While scarcely larger than a honeybee, the newborn opossum creeps into its mother's pouch and remains protected there for many weeks, until it is almost ready to go off on its own. The rat, the cottontail rabbit, and the pigeon all start life in the nest as naked, blind youngsters. Kittens and pups are born with fur, but do not open their eyes until after their mothers have fed them for more than a week. By comparison, a human infant is better developed at birth. Yet a child remains dependent upon parental care for more years than any other kind of animal. The extended infancy of mankind is probably the chief bond holding families together: it allows transfer of information from parent to child, an important basis for civilization.—*L. and M. M.*

INFINITE PRODUCT: a number or a function with an infinite number of factors. For example, the product

$$x(1 - x^2)(1 - x^2/4)(1 - x^2/9)(1 - x^2/16)\cdots(1 - x^2/n^2)\cdots$$

represents a function of the variable x with an infinite number of roots: $x = 0, \pm 1, \pm 2, \pm 3, \pm 4, \ldots, \pm n, \ldots$. Such functions are natural generalizations of POLYNOMIALS, which have only a finite number of roots, and therefore a finite number of factors. It is known that the function $\sin \pi x$ has the same roots as the example given above, and one can show that

$$1/\pi \sin \pi x = x \prod_{n=1}^{\infty} (1 - x^2/n^2)$$

the symbol on the right side of the equal sign being an abbreviated notation for the infinite product given above.

From such an infinite product one can derive infinite products of numbers. Setting $x = \frac{1}{2}$, and knowing that sin $\pi/2 = 1$, we find

$$1/\pi = \frac{1}{2}(1 - \frac{1}{4})(1 - \frac{1}{16})(1 - \frac{1}{36})(1 - \frac{1}{64}) \cdots$$

$$= \frac{1}{2} \cdot \frac{3}{4} \cdot \frac{15}{16} \cdot \frac{35}{36} \cdot \frac{63}{64} \cdots$$

Infinite products have many properties in common with infinite sums. For example, the product

$$(1 + a_1)(1 + a_2)(1 + a_3)(1 + a_4) \cdots (1 + a_n) \cdots$$

where $a_1, a_2, \cdots$ is a given sequence of numbers, may or may not converge. But one can show that this product will converge if, and only if, the infinite series $a_1 + a_2 + a_3 + \cdots + a_n + \cdots$ also converges.—*H. Ho.*

INFINITY: a mathematical term used in several senses. In one usage it describes a mode of variation: we say a variable x tends to infinity (written $x \rightarrow \infty$), meaning that x increases beyond all bounds. The symbol ∞ does not denote a number, and none of the numerical operations can be applied to it. An example of tending to infinity is furnished by the natural numbers: $1, 2, 3, \ldots, n, \ldots$, to which there is no end; we say that n increases beyond all bounds, and that the natural numbers form an infinite sequence. Any set of numbers which does

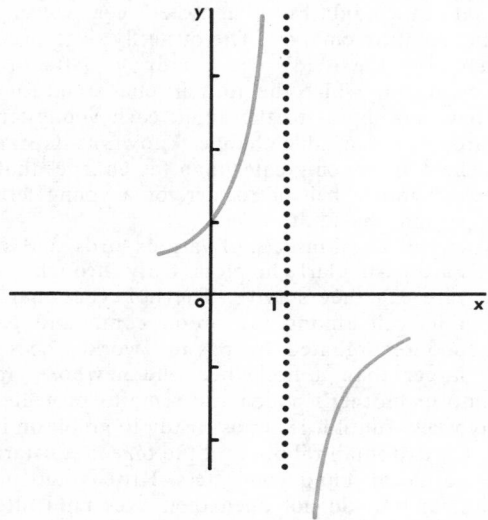

Graph of $y = 1/(1 - x)$

not increase numerically beyond all bounds is said to remain finite. Any sequence that can be matched with the natural numbers so that each term can be paired with a natural number, and vice versa, is said to be in one-to-one correspondence with the natural numbers, and is an infinite sequence; it may be denoted by $a_1, a_2, a_3, \ldots, a_n, \ldots$. Note that in this sequence, it is the subscripts, not necessarily the actual values, that go to infinity, denoting that the sequence has an infinite number of members, each of which is finite or zero; the sequence $\frac{1}{2}, \frac{1}{4}, \frac{1}{8}, \ldots, \frac{1}{2^n}, \ldots$, approaches zero as $n \rightarrow \infty$. A fundamental problem of sequences is to discover how they behave as $n \rightarrow \infty$. A sequence may tend to infinity, it may oscillate and remain finite, or it may approach a definite limit.

A function may increase beyond all bounds even though the variable in it does not. Thus, let $y = 1/(1 - x)$; as x approaches 1 through values less than 1, $y \rightarrow \infty$; as x approaches 1 through values greater than 1, $y \rightarrow -\infty$; that is,

y increases beyond all bounds in a negative direction. The graph of this function shows its behavior. In the accompanying figure, line $x = 1$ is a vertical asymptote. The concept of a LIMIT in calculus always involves infinity; this may be explicit, as in the limit of a function of x as x tends to infinity, or implicit, where the limit is defined as x tends (through an infinite number of values) to a finite number x_0.

Some parts of geometry make use of ideal elements, or elements at infinity. In Euclidean geometry, some pairs of lines called parallel lines, do not meet, but any pair of nonparallel lines in a plane meet in one point. However, in projective geometry it is postulated that lines (which are parallel in Euclidean geometry) meet at infinity (or meet on the line at infinity), so that it can be said generally that two distinct lines in a plane meet in one point, either finite or infinite. Similarly, it is sometimes said that a curve is tangent to its asymptote at infinity.

A third way in which infinity appears in mathematics is as a symbol, or number, associated with a collection of more elements than can be expressed by any natural number. Such collections are called infinite sets. There is a great variety of infinite sets, to different ones of which different transfinite, or infinite, numbers are attached. The method of comparison of two finite or infinite sets of discrete elements is by one-to-one correspondence. Any finite set can be put into one-to-one correspondence with a part of the natural numbers, but not with all of them. Hence the set of natural numbers is greater than any finite set, and its number is a transfinite number, symbolized by $\aleph_0$ (aleph null). The set of natural numbers can be put in one-to-one correspondence with a part of the points on a line, but not with all of them. Hence, the set of points on a line is greater than the set of integers and requires a different symbol. It is given the symbol C, since the line is considered to be a CONTINUUM. $\aleph_0$ and C are examples of transfinite, or infinite, numbers. There are many others, some of them symbolized by $\aleph_1$, $\aleph_2$, etc. These infinite numbers do not conform to the postulates of finite numbers. In particular, for them it is true that twice the number is equal to the number itself; *e.g.* $2\aleph_0 = \aleph_0$.—*H. C.*

INFLORESCENCE: the mode of arrangement or aggregation of flowers in clusters upon a plant. In magnolia, poppy, and many other species, there is a single flower at the tip of a stem. Other plants have branches or aggregates of flowers.

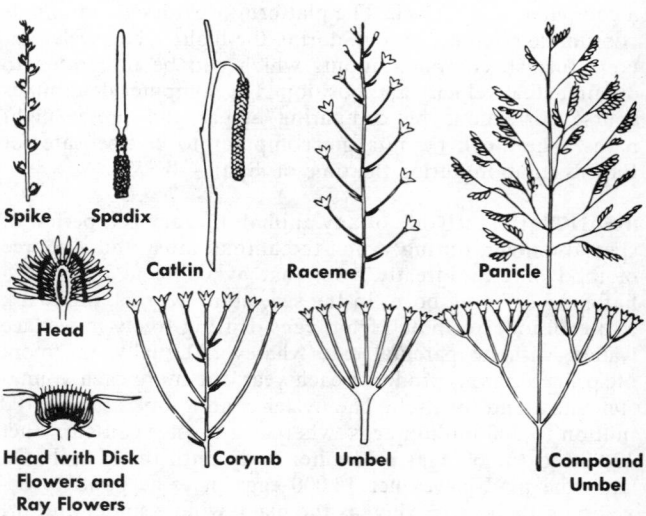

The many types of clusters, or inflorescences, in which flowers occur include these ten, the commonest. (*From Transeau*)

In extreme cases such as the daisy and the sunflower, the flower in the popular sense is in reality an inflorescence, called a *head,* which contains up to hundreds of small, separate, true flowers. Of the two basic kinds of inflorescence, the *racemose* is the commonest. Here, as in yucca, lily-of-the-valley, oak, dandelion, and daisy, the oldest flowers are at the base or circumference of the inflorescence, and there are progressively younger flowers toward the tip or center. In the less common *cymose* type of inflorescence, as in dogwood and sweet william, the oldest or first-formed flowers are central, and there are progressively younger flowers toward the circumference.—*W. Ko.*

INFORMATION THEORY: a branch of applied mathematics that utilizes both ANALYSIS and PROBABILITY THEORY. It originated in the early 1920s with the work of Leo Szilard and H. Nyquist; later contributions were made by Claude E. Shannon, A. N. Kolmogorov, Norbert Wiener, and others.

Neither information nor its communication is a simple matter. Just as the words force, power, work, and energy have very precise scientific meanings that differ markedly from their everyday meanings, so the word information should not be confused with knowledge. Information consists of raw data and facts; knowledge involves organization, classification, comparison, and thinking, and leads to ideas, concepts, and generalizations. Information may be regarded as the extent to which the number of possible answers to a problem can be reduced; the smaller the number of answers, the greater the amount of information. If the answers can be reduced to just one answer, there is complete information. In this respect, information may be treated as a physically measurable quantity. Note, however, that no attention whatever is given to the "value" of the information, a quality that is obviously subjective. When regarded objectively in this way, information is analogous to entropy in a physical system.

Information has the following characteristics: it may appear in a variety of forms; it can be measured precisely; in a physical system, it is always accompanied by "noise" or error. Information is something that is contained in a message; the message may consist either of discrete symbols or of a varying but continuous signal. If a message consists of binary digits, each digit conveys a unit (*i.e.* a "bit") of information. Thus the amount of information sent in a message is measured by the number of bits contained in the message. Note, however, that a signal conveys information only when it consists of a sequence of symbols or values that change in a manner unpredictable by the receiver of the signal.

There is an important difference between a message and the information it contains; the information content of a series of signals is materially reduced by the noise accompanying the message; in short, a message consists of information plus noise. The central problem is to extract the message effectively from the signal by reducing the error caused by the noise; this is often accomplished by the use of filters or receivers of some sort.

Communication, not at all the same as information, is achieved by the spoken word, the written word, gestures, pictures, signals, or musical sounds. Communication consists essentially of progressive elimination and narrowing of the totality of all possible messages down to the one message that is to be conveyed. The main problems of communication have to do with *technics,* or the accuracy of the transference of information from the sender to the receiver; *semantics,* or the interpretation of the meaning received compared with the intended meaning; and *influence,* or the success with which the message conveyed to the receiver causes the desired action on his part. A communication system consists essentially of

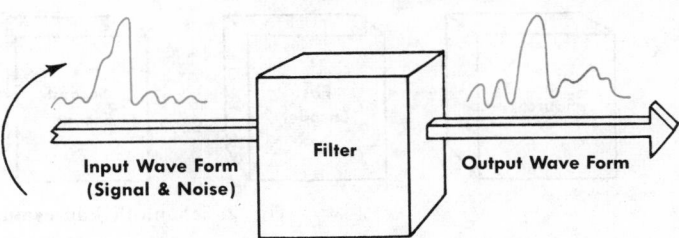

Fig. 1: Effect of an Idealized Filter on a Signal

(1) a message source; (2) a transmitter; (3) a communication channel; (4) a receiver; and (5) a user. The information source selects a message out of a set of possible messages; the transmitter converts the message into appropriate signals, which are then sent over the channel to the receiver, which processes the signals and forwards the information to the user.

Thus it is evident that in mathematics the word information is used in a very special sense. It has nothing to do with "meaning" as that term is ordinarily understood: two messages, for example, one full of meaning, the other sheer nonsense, could both be equivalent in information. In short, information refers to what one *could* say, rather than what one *does* say. It is a measure of one's freedom of choice when selecting a message. Information is analogous to the degree of randomness in a situation; if a situation has but little randomness or choice, there is little information. It so happens that anything one wishes to say can be expressed in terms of numbers. Hence information, when put into numerical form, can be processed accurately and quickly by means of mechanical or electronic computers, which might more properly be called "information machines." They can do much more than compute: they can process enormous amounts of data and automatically control many operations.—*W. L. S.*

"Information theory" refers to a collection of theories, both mathematical and practical, which deal with the transmission, processing, and utilization of information in the sense described above. Information theory is particularly applicable to electronic communications and control, and to data-processing systems; limited extensions to human behavior have proved interesting as well. We distinguish between information theory in the broad sense (as just defined) and in the narrower sense of encoding and decoding, which are also called "information theory." Furthermore, authorities differ as to exactly what is properly included in the broad-sense information theory. It seems reasonable to include at least the following four disciplines: (1) filtering and prediction theory; (2) decision and estimation theory; (3) encoding and decoding; (4) language studies.

Statistical Filtering and Prediction Theory: This is perhaps the simplest of the four to grasp in outline. Wiener and Kolmogorov developed the theory independently during World War II. It was applied then to the design of guidance and fire-control systems. The really new departure in this work—the notion which, once stated, became the starting point for the other aspects of information theory—was that in real-life communication and control situations, the element of randomness (see PROBABILITY) plays a fundamental role. This is because (1) the precise function to be performed by a system is not known in advance, but rather is usually known to be one of a set of possible functions, members of the set having various probabilities of actually occurring; and (2) unavoidable random disturbances are always present to some degree (see NOISE).

The system dealt with by Wiener and Kolmogorov can be represented as an electric FILTER (see Fig. 1).

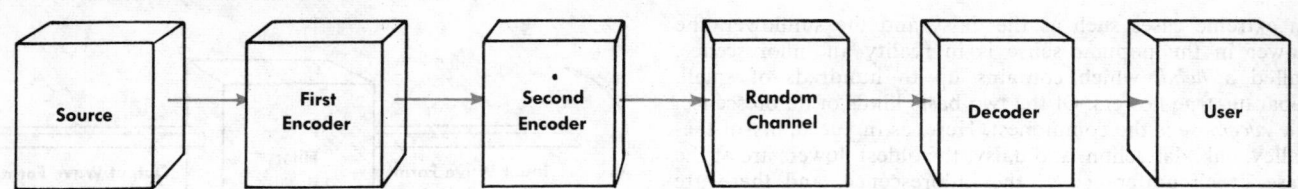

Fig. 2: Schematic Representation of Communication System

The useful signal and the unwanted noise are both assumed to be random, with only certain average statistical properties being known. The problem then consists of finding out what filter to specify so that on the average the output most closely resembles the signal in a particular way. By requiring the output to resemble most closely a time-advanced version of the input, one obtains the best "predictor." Such a predictor might be useful, for example, in causing a gun to "lead" an erratically moving target. Wiener and Kolmogorov solved these problems in a general way, and to make the solution practically applicable Wiener went on to extend it so that the filter was not just a mathematical fiction, but could be physically realized. In the last 15 yr a number of other extensions of the original theory have been made, and the method has become a standard tool for the designers of CONTROL SYSTEMS.

Decision and Estimation Theory: One is often interested not in dealing with an entire waveform (the output in Fig. 1), but rather in extracting one single fact out of the input mixture of signal and noise. For example, suppose we are given a waveform and told that it consists of a weak radar echo obscured by random noise, and the fact wanted is the target range (time delay of the echo). Or suppose we are told that the waveform at hand is really a noise-obscured communication signal standing for one of the 26 letters of the alphabet, and we are asked to say which letter was sent. These two are examples of what the statistician calls estimation and hypothesis-testing (decision) problems, respectively. Following the lead of V. Kotelnikov in the USSR and P. M. Woodward in England, radar and communication engineers have used estimation and decision theories to design systems which can, for example, give the range of a radar target in such a way that on the average the range error is a minimum; or systems which can determine, with the minimum attainable probability of being wrong, what letter was sent. Where the ideal systems are too elaborate actually to build, it has been possible to gauge how far short the performance of a more practical estimation or decision system actually falls.

Information Theory: In our example of deciding which letter of the alphabet was sent, we have encountered a part of the more general communication problem as it was viewed by Shannon in his famous *Mathematical Theory of Communication* (1948). The need for a more general basis on which to evaluate the performance of various forms of communication systems (relative to each other and to an ideal) had led him to reopen certain earlier speculations of two communications engineers, H. O. Hartley and H. Nyquist. In Fig. 2, the block labeled "random channel" embodies such operations as sending a signal which stands for a particular letter through a random medium to a receiving terminal where a decision is rendered as to which letter was sent. Thus in this illustration the input to the channel is a string of letters and the output another string of letters, but the second string may have occasional errors because of the random nature of the medium.

Shannon's work involved three basic insights. First, one can establish a measure of the average amount of information conveyed when a typical letter is properly received. This amount of information is proportional to the logarithm of

the number of possibilities, if the possibilities are equally likely. For example, receiving correctly one of 26 equally likely letters conveys log 26 ÷ log 2 = 4.7 times as much information as if there were only two letters to choose between. Using a two-fold choice as the elementary unit in which to measure "quantity of information," we would say that a correct 26-fold choice renders an amount of information equal to 4.7 *bits* (a contraction of "binary digits"). If the letters are unequally likely, the number of bits is given by a slightly more complicated statement which bears a very close parallel to the entropy concept of thermodynamics. This definition of information allows precise bookkeeping of the flow of information through the system. For example, it allows one to say what is lost due to incorrect decisions in the random channel.

The second and most remarkable part of Shannon's theory involves the two blocks labeled "second encoder" and "decoder." Until Shannon showed otherwise, it was assumed that if the random channel were beyond one's control, the faster one tried to send information through it, the larger would become the proportion of erroneous letters. Thus if one wanted to reduce the error probability, this could only be done by a reduction in information rate. Shannon showed that if one were willing systematically to intersperse into the stream of the original message letters occasional superfluous or redundant letters (encoding), and if one were willing to build a decoder at the receiving end to untangle the arriving stream of letters, a remarkable result would be obtained. Still keeping the rate of message letters the same, the error probability can be made arbitrarily small, so long as (1) one does not attempt to send faster than a rate called the channel capacity, an important intrinsic property of any communication channel, and (2) one is willing to increase the block length of the code. The block length is the number of preceding letters that the second encoder has to look at to decide what redundant letter to insert; the decoder likewise must examine the same number of received letters to decide what a given letter really is. This is called the "redundant-coding problem."

The third part of Shannon's theory says that if the originating information "source," in the figure, generates information at a certain rate, then using the "first encoder" it is possible to recode the data into a stream of binary digits whose rate is almost exactly the rate at which the source is generating information measured in bits. This is usually referred to as the noiseless-coding problem.

To summarize the functions of the two coders, a source can be encoded once (thus removing any redundancy or non-information-bearing elements) and then encoded again so as to add redundancy in just the right way to combat the deleterious effects of the channel. Examples of redundant coding can be found in nature. For example, several tens of thousands of binary digits per second are needed to represent adequately an unprocessed human speech signal. Yet the information rate of human speech as a simple information source is no more than several hundred bits per second. The huge discrepancy is simply the redundancy that makes speech so remarkably impervious to acoustic noise. When speech is processed by a *bandwidth compression device* (e.g. the Vocoder) to remove the redundancy, the resulting signal is extremely sensitive to noise. Thus, the communication engineer, realizing that the human redundant encoding may not be best for the random radio channel in use, may proceed to remove redundancy by a bandwidth compression scheme, and then reinsert redundancy by encoding for the electrical channel in use. The two coding operations are those shown in Fig. 2. Since Shannon's original study, which demonstrated these possibilities for certain simple forms of systems, a great deal of work has gone into extending them to different forms and into *coding theory,* the search for practical methods of implementing these two types of coding operations.

Language Studies: The attempt to set up valid mathematical models for natural languages received an enormous stimulus from the developments just described. The definition of quantity of information given earlier says nothing about meaning, dealing as it does only with cold probabilities. Since the source and the "user" usually involve a human being in some way, a suitable extension of the usual definition is desirable, and much interesting work is in progress on such questions.

For inanimate systems, *e.g.* control systems or computers talking to computers over telephone lines, the theories have proven enlightening and practically useful. The interaction of electronic-system ideas and psychophysical and neurophysiological studies has also been of mutual benefit (see CYBERNETICS).—*P. E. G.*

INFRARED RAYS: invisible RADIATION of longer wavelength than the red portion of the visible spectrum. Infrared rays were discovered in 1799 by Sir William Herschel, who placed a thermometer at various points in a prismatic spectrum and observed that the reading was highest at a certain distance beyond the red end. From this he inferred that radiant heat is essentially a kind of "invisible light."

All bodies give up some heat by radiation at any temperature above absolute zero. As the temperature is raised, however, the wavelength of the bulk of the radiation grows shorter. For example, as a nail is heated in flame it radiates heat to its surroundings long before it grows hot enough to glow. Eventually it will glow a dull red as the principal radiation appears in the visible range, and further heating will make the glow brighter in color and more intense. Infrared rays are very effective in warming their surroundings, be-

Infrared photograph: In this painted panel from a 17th-cent. harpsichord rebuilt into a piano at the end of the 18th cent., only the fleur-de-lys and coat of arms are visible to the eye today. In an infrared photograph, however, an earlier decorative pattern of stripes appears. (*Edwin M. Ripin*)

cause their energy is absorbed by material objects to a greater extent than is energy of such shorter wavelength radiation as visible light. Thus electric heaters, which are designed for heat rather than for light, are operated at low red heat so that their radiation will be primarily in the infrared range.

The fact that all objects emit infrared radiation leads to several practical applications. These include photography in total darkness and the detection of heat sources, as in the snooperscope, an infrared detector that "saw" the invisible flame of enemy alcohol stoves in the World War II Pacific campaign, or the guidance system of the Sidewinder missile, which homes in on the exhaust radiation of enemy aircraft. Because infrared rays are more penetrating than light, they are used for photographing works of art (to reveal painting beneath the visible surface) as well as in physical therapy. The frequencies of vibration of atoms in a molecule or crystal fall within the infrared range, and infrared spectra can thus be used to identify and analyze molecules.—*E. M. R.*

INFRARED WINDOW: the part of the infrared spectrum, between 7.5 and 11 microns, to which the atmosphere is almost completely transparent. Infrared radiation in this wavelength region can be detected at great distances, even under hazy conditions. Some military surveillance systems, *e.g.* the "snooperscope," take advantage of the "window." Measurements made in the infrared window by weather satellites are used to map surface temperatures, particularly over ocean areas, and to map the distribution of clouds on the night side of Earth.—*D. H. L.*

Infrared photography: Emulsion sensitized to infrared gives greater penetration through haze; foliage, which strongly reflects infrared radiation, appears very light. Combination of these effects gives better definition in distant row of poplars in infrared photograph (*right*) than in regular one (*left*).

INGENHOUSZ, JAN, 1730–99, Dutch biologist and physicist; b. Breda. He studied the role of plants in purifying air and discovered that the leaves of plants (particularly their undersides) produce "dephlogisticated air" (oxygen), but only in the presence of sunlight. He also discovered that at night or in shadow the roots, flowers, and fruit produce a gas (carbon dioxide) which, in quantity, is fatal to animal life. This research was published in his *Experiments on Vegetables, Discovering their Great Power of Purifying the Common Air in the Sunshine and of Injuring It in the Shade and at Night* (1779). He also did research on electricity and magnetism. He was a fellow of the Royal Society.—*R. J. F.*

INK: a coloring agent dispersed in a solvent; it is generally applied to a surface as a film of individual letters or figures. Inks were used by the Egyptians and Chinese as early as 2500 B. C. The first inks consisted of ground lampblack and glue mixtures added to water. Plant extracts were later used, *e.g.* indigo and natural resins. Inks consisting of ferrous salts and tannin extracts came into use about 200 B. C. This same mixture of ferrous salts and gallic or tannic acids, plus a small amount of organic acid, is the basis for present-day permanent inks.

Permanent-color inks form a water-insoluble compound on drying. Soluble dyes are added to permanent-color mixtures to enhance the color of a freshly written specimen. Washable inks are composed solely of soluble dyes, *e.g.* soluble blue and substituted triphenylmethane dyes. These dyes are not altered by light. Drawing inks contain a suspension of carbon in water. Printing inks contain varnish in addition to the mixture of pigments and solvent. The varnish functions to fix the color to the paper.—*G. W. M.*

INORGANIC CHEMISTRY: the chemical study of all the known ELEMENTS and their compounds, with the exception of the innumerable compounds of carbon, which fall into the division of ORGANIC CHEMISTRY. The scope of inorganic chemistry, and its approach to matter, can best be suggested by a consideration of *periodic classification.* which attempts to link all the elements together in a workable order, and to provide a method by which the chemical behavior of each of the elements, *e.g.* an element's formation of compounds, can be predicted.

The elements may be roughly classified as metals (*e.g.* gold, copper, zinc, and sodium) and nonmetals (*e.g.* sulfur, phosphorus, iodine, and oxygen). The first systematic classification was made on the basis of atomic weights. According to John Newlands' Law of Octaves (1863), when the elements are arranged in order of their atomic weights they fall to some extent into a series of octaves, or groups of eight. Dmitri Mendeleev (1869) stressed the resulting periodicity of properties, showing in his more elaborate Periodic System that the elements fall into groups, or families with similar chemical properties, valences, etc. As a consequence of the later electronic theory of valence (see CHEMISTRY), an improved but closely similar classification was effected on the basis of atomic numbers. The accompanying version of the periodic table indicates a stepwise change of chemical properties as the valence electrons increase from 1 to 8 in the lithium-to-neon octave (at. nos. 3 to 10), following which sodium (at. no. 11) starts a similar octave, and falls into group I with lithium. Every atom of the same *group,* or family of elements, has the same number of valence electrons, *e.g.* 1 electron in group I and 4 in group IV (C, Si, Ge, Sn, Pb). In general, this modern classification reflects the electronic structure of each kind of atom.

The molecule of a *compound* may contain one or more atoms of two or more elements. Of inorganic compounds containing only two elements, the oxides (in which one of the two elements is oxygen) are particularly important. An element may form several oxides; but as a general rule typical oxides of non-metals are acidic (see ACID) and those of metals are basic (see BASE). Acidic oxides combine with water to form acids, *e.g.* SO_3 (sulfur trioxide) $+ H_2O \rightarrow H_2SO_4$ (sulfuric acid). Basic oxides react with acids to form salts, *e.g.* CuO (cupric oxide) $+ H_2SO_4 \rightarrow CuSO_4$ (cupric sulfate) $+ H_2O$. Some basic oxides combine with water to form soluble bases known as alkalis, *e.g.* CaO (calcium oxide) $+ H_2O \rightarrow Ca(OH)_2$ (calcium hydroxide). Solutions of acids, bases, and salts conduct electricity and are known as *electrolytes.* This property is due to their electrovalent nature. Upon ionization, acids give rise to hydrogen cations (H^+, identical with the proton), and soluble bases (alkalis) to hydroxyl anions (OH^-); both classes, like salts, form equal numbers of cations and anions; for example: HNO_3 (nitric acid) $\rightarrow [H]^+ + [NO_3]^-$; NaOH

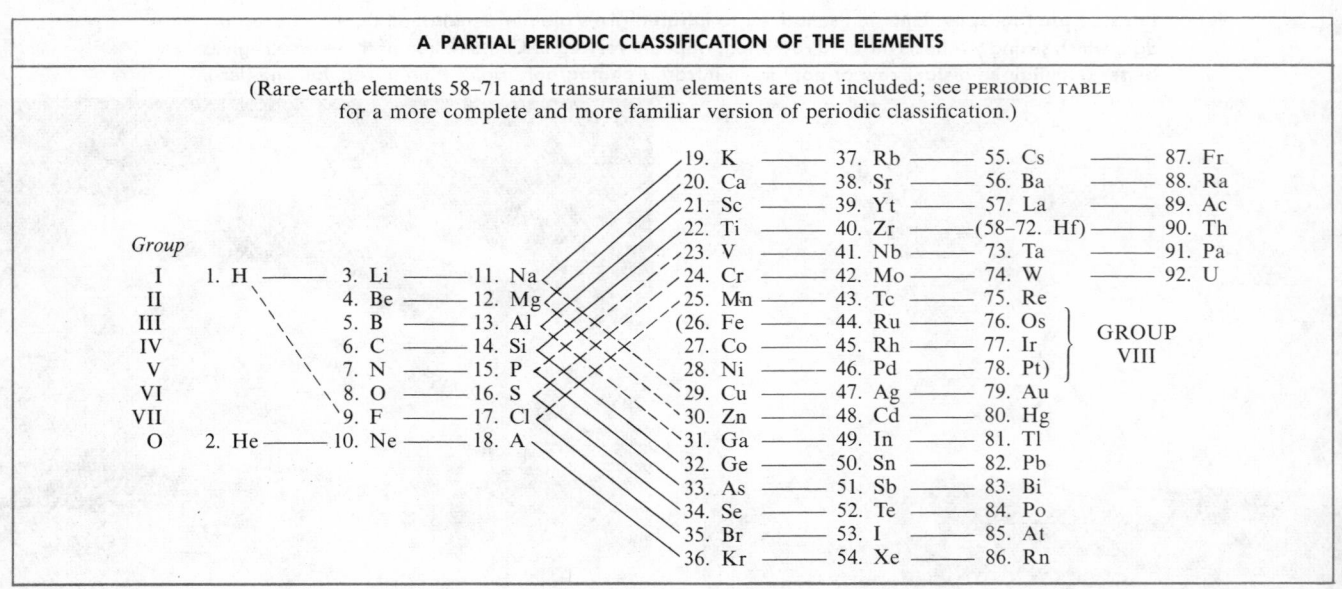

A PARTIAL PERIODIC CLASSIFICATION OF THE ELEMENTS

(Rare-earth elements 58–71 and transuranium elements are not included; see PERIODIC TABLE for a more complete and more familiar version of periodic classification.)

(sodium hydroxide) → [Na]$^+$ + [OH]$^-$; NaNO$_3$ (sodium nitrate) → [Na]$^+$ + [NO$_3$]$^-$.

In a periodic classification of the elements, hydrogen, at. no. 1, is exceptional: because of its electropositive character it is almost always shown heading the sequence of metals in group I; but as a univalent nonmetal, it can also be linked with the halogens of group VII. Group O contains the rare or inert gases of the atmosphere, which by virtue of their electronic structures are extremely stable and chemically inert. Group I contains the univalent alkali metals, of which sodium and potassium are particularly noteworthy. The outstanding member of group IV is the quadrivalent element carbon, the building block of organic compounds. The lower members of groups V (nitrogen, phosphorus, etc.) and VI (oxygen, sulfur, etc.) are nonmetals of great importance. Group VII contains the family of halogens (fluorine, chlorine, bromine, and iodine), leading to the characteristic halogen acids, *e.g.* hydrochloric acid (HC1), and their derived salts (sodium chloride, NaCl; potassium iodide, KI). In the accompanying table, the two lines leading from elements nos. 11–17 indicate the division of each of groups I–VII into two sub-groups A and B. (See separate articles on the representative chemical groups and compounds mentioned above.)—*J. R.*

INOSITOL: a cyclic alcohol often classified as a vitamin of the B-complex group. It is not known whether human beings require it in diet. The most important form is myo-inositol, widely distributed in animals and plants. Inositol is an important constituent of cephalin, a brain lipid, and is present in muscle and heart. See FATS IN BIOCHEMISTRY.—*R. Wu.*

INSECT: any member of the class Insecta, the largest subdivision of the great phylum Arthropoda. Insects comprise by far the largest class of animals, almost 900,000 different kinds being known. They are among the most numerous of land animals, with more than a million to the acre of grassland. Although most insects are terrestrial, many live in fresh water (particularly during early life), and a few venture out over the surface of the ocean. On land, insects occupy a place in the economy of nature comparable to that of the small crustaceans drifting in the upper levels of the sea. Insects transform plant foods into a form useful in the diet of larger animals.

The insect *body* is enclosed in a firm chitinous exoskeleton that shows segmentation, with joints permitting flexibility. The body is subdivided into a head, a thorax of three segments, and a segmented abdomen. Ordinarily the thorax bears three pairs of legs. As an adult, an insect may have one or two pairs of wings, attached to the second or the second and third segments of the thorax. To permit growth, the hard exoskeleton must be shed at intervals. Most insects molt at least half a dozen times, increasing in volume as much as 50% at each molt. Thus they grow by steps—not gradually, as so many other animals grow.

The simpler insects, *e.g.* silverfish and springtails, acquire no wings when they reach maturity. Their development produces almost no change, or METAMORPHOSIS, in body form. Other insects, as grasshoppers and dragonflies, reach maturity through a series of small changes at each molt; the wings, for example, can be seen developing as small projections on the back of the thorax—getting larger, step by step, until at the final molt they become useful in locomotion. This metamorphosis is regarded as incomplete, however, since it does not show the resting, or pupal, stage found in the most advanced insects, as butterflies, true flies, and bees. Insects with a pupal stage are said to have a complete metamorphosis. Their lives are divided into an efficient, younger, larval stage,

Insects as cross-pollinators: Insects of flower-pollinating groups appear in the fossil record in the later Mesozoic Era, gaining prominence in parallel with the flowering plants. The hawkmoth hovers over lilies and orchids at dusk, as above, extracting nectar through a long sucking tube formed from its elongated maxillae. (*Ross E. Hutchins*)

during which they feed rapidly and grow, then the pupal stage, during which no food is taken but the body is rebuilt into the very different form of the adult insect, and finally the mature stage, which is concerned almost exclusively with finding a mate and reproducing. Ordinarily this means laying eggs, which will hatch into a larva such as a fly maggot or a caterpillar.

Features of the *mouthparts and wings* are extremely helpful in the task of distinguishing between the many kinds of insects. A majority of insects have biting mouthparts (mandibles), as in grasshoppers and beetles, with a pair of strong jaws hinged to come together from the sides. Behind these jaws is another pair of mouthparts, the maxillae, which may serve to guide food into the mouth between the jaws. An equivalent of an upper lip (the labrum) and a lower lip (the labium) complete the mouthparts. In insects with sucking mouthparts, these same structures are modified to provide a tube through which liquid can be drawn. In a butterfly or moth, the coiled drinking tube that can be extended for reaching nectar deep in a flower is composed chiefly of modified maxillae, fitted together. In a mosquito or a plant louse (aphid), the sharp stylets, with which the insect drills through the surface to reach nourishing juice, are modified mandibles and maxillae. In a housefly, the expanding labium forms a sponge-like mouth pad used in stamping over the surface of food, the process whereby the fly picks up most of its nourishment.

Water insect: Giant water bug (order Hemiptera) seizes frog with its front legs, preparatory to killing it with its piercing and sucking beak. (*Robert C. Hermes*)

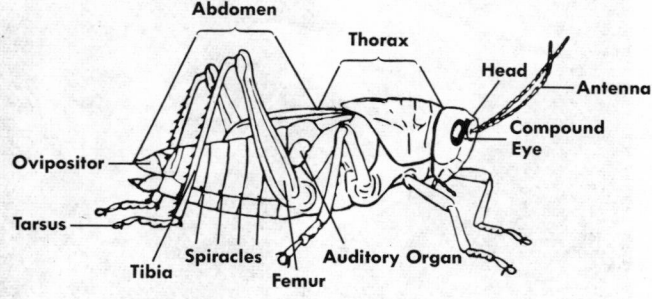

External Structure of a Grasshopper
(After Kenoyer)

The *digestive system* of insects extends, by way of an esophagus, a crop, and an intestine, to the anus, at the posterior end of the abdomen. Enlarged glands open into the digestive tube. So do excretory glands, called Malpighian tubules, which pick up dissolved wastes from the blood that fills the body cavity. The circulatory system is chiefly a series of spaces between the organs. Dorsally, however, a tubular heart takes in blood and propels it by muscular contractions toward the head. The blood distributes food materials and hormones, but has little importance in the transport of oxygen or carbon dioxide. Except in a few instances, as the fly larvae of deep lakes (known as "blood worms"), insect blood does not contain the red coloring matter hemoglobin, which in vertebrate blood transports oxygen from lungs to tissues. Insects breathe by means of a system of fine tubules called tracheae, which carry air directly to the internal organs and tissues. The tracheae open to the outside through special breathing pores (spiracles), which can be found, one pair to each segment, in the thorax and abdomen.

The *nervous system* of insects appears simple. In the head is a large ganglion serving as a brain, with nerves leading to the single pair of antennae, to the single pair of compound eyes, and to the one, two, or three simple eyes. A pair of nerves, extending around the esophagus, connects this brain-like ganglion to a smaller ganglion below. From the smaller ganglion, nerves run to the various mouthparts, and the ventral nerve cord extends posteriorly to additional ganglia in the thorax and abdomen. The senses of taste and smell are distributed over an insect's body very differently from the arrangement in a vertebrate animal. Taste, for example, is often most acute on the first pair of legs.

Insects are either male or female. The eggs are fertilized internally and usually laid in large numbers. A few kinds, *e.g.* blow flies, retain the eggs within the body until they hatch, and the mother deposits active young. Some insects, as plant lice, reproduce for much of the year by PARTHENOGENESIS— that is, the eggs develop without fertilization. During summer, wingless female aphids bear living young without mating; the offspring also develop into wingless females. At the approach of autumn, however, winged males and females appear and mate. Hard-shelled eggs are laid; these are the only stage of the insect able to survive the winter. In a few other kinds of insects, *e.g.* the white-fringed beetle, males are unknown; the females lay eggs that develop parthenogenetically.

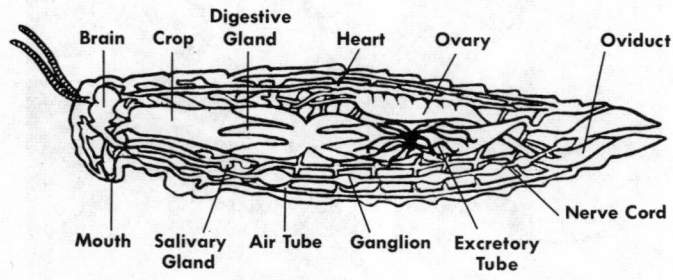

Internal Structure of a Grasshopper

Through a great variety of adaptations, insects are able to live in almost every conceivable situation except the sea. A few inhabit the Antarctic; some live on glaciers; others occur in hot deserts and even in thermal springs and pools of spilled petroleum in oil fields. In general, however, insects reach their greatest abundance and diversity in tropical and temperate areas. There, a great many of them serve man's interests by pollinating flowers, causing fruits to form. Insects such as the honeybee, silkworm, and lac insect produce materials of use to man. But others have become man's chief competitors for food and valuable materials. Many billions of dollars' worth of crops grow each year only because of the activity of beneficial insects. On the other hand, millions of dollars are lost each year through insect damage to crops. Insects transmit a number of serious diseases, *e.g.* malaria (carried by the mosquito *Anopheles*), yellow fever (by the mosquito *Aedes aegypti*), sleeping sickness (by the tsetse fly *Glossina*), and epidemic typhus fever (the famous "Red Death" of the Middle Ages, carried by the body louse, *Pediculus*).

The discovery of the insecticide DDT during World War II, and the later discovery of other chemical agents for insect control, have done much to revolutionize the treatment of infestations of insects in agriculture and medicine. However, insects have already begun to become immune to DDT and more recently developed insecticides, so that the future of chemical control is in doubt. Fortunately, insects parasitize one another, and the parasite is likely to change as rapidly as the "host" species, with the result that there is continuing biological control. By active encouragement of insect parasites of other insects, man can increase their effectiveness; thus biological control seems likely to be the most reliable means for insect control in the future.

About eight of the 20 different orders of insects are of major importance:

Orthoptera: cockroaches, praying mantids, walking-stick insects, crickets, grasshoppers. These have an incomplete metamorphosis, biting mouthparts, and membranous wings (if any), the rear pair of which is folded like a fan at rest. A few kinds of cockroaches live in the homes of man and enjoy his stores of food. Some species of grasshoppers are equally attracted to man's crop plants. Praying mantises are regarded as beneficial, because they feed voraciously upon other insects, which they capture and hold with their spiny forelegs. Other orthopterans feed on plants of no economic value.

Isoptera: the termites, an order of social insects that live in large colonies in the ground or in trees or houses. They are small and soft-bodied, with an incomplete metamorphosis, biting mouthparts, and membranous wings (if any), each pair almost identical in form and texture. Usually most members of each colony remain wingless workers; one "queen" lays the eggs for the colony, with a "king" and many workers in attendance. Winged members can become kings or queens at new colonies. Some tropical termites construct huge earthen mounds inhabited by millions of individuals. Most kinds that cause damage to houses in the U. S. A. are subterranean insects in the wild, with a liking for dry wood, which they can digest only through the help of protozoans living in their intestines.

Odonata: the damselflies and dragonflies that dart over the surface of ponds and streams. These insects are aquatic during development, although metamorphosis is incomplete. The mouthparts are of the biting type, and the four wings show a remarkably large number of fine cross veins. As immature individuals, these insects capture other insects under water. As adults, they feed on small insects, *e.g.* mosquitoes, and must be regarded as beneficial. The immature naiad (sometimes called a nymph) crawls out of the water, its exoskeleton splits along the back, and the adult insect emerges and expands its wings.

Homoptera: plant lice, leafhoppers, treehoppers (spittle insects), cicadas, scale insects. These have incomplete metamorphosis, piercing and sucking mouthparts, and membranous wings that are held tentlike over the back when at rest. Many of these insects suck the juices of plant crops, causing much destruction. A few, *e.g.* the beet leafhopper, carry diseases from one plant to another. The homopterans with the most unusual life history are the cicadas. One kind, called the 17-year cicada, spends 17 yr underground feeding on plant roots. After this slow development, it crawls out of the ground and to the bark of a tree, where it transforms to the winged cicada. The adults eat little; they are often noticed on hot summer days because of the whining call they produce in trying to attract mates.

Hemiptera: giant water bugs, water striders, water boatmen, and backswimmers. These insects have incomplete metamorphosis, piercing and sucking mouthparts, and membranous wings held flat over the back when not in use. The fore wings are thickened at the base, and their tips overlap in the folded position. To this order belong also the stink bugs, the bed bugs (which infest homes and suck human blood), the chinch bugs (which infest corn), and many others of economic importance.

Coleoptera: beetles and weevils, which have complete metamorphosis, biting mouthparts, and two pairs of wings. The fore wings are leathery and meet at rest in a straight line down the back. The rear wings are thin and membranous; they fold under the fore pair. Beetles include more species than any other group of animals. Beneficial types include the voracious tiger beetles, ground beetles, and ladybird beetles. Destructive types include the Mexican bean beetle, the Colorado potato beetle, the Japanese beetle, and the cotton boll weevil. The sacred scarab of Egypt is a beetle, which aids sanitation by burying dung as food for its larvae.

Lepidoptera: butterflies and moths, insects with complete metamorphosis, sucking mouthparts (a coiled "tongue"), and two pairs of wings clad in overlapping scales; the larvae are caterpillars, which may produce a naked chrysalis (if butterflies) or spin a cocoon in which to pupate (if moths). Adults range from tiny moths to insects with a 10-in. wing span. Often the scales are colorful and produce beautiful patterns.

Adult butterflies and moths sip a little nectar and dew, but eat nothing, relying upon food acquired by the preceding caterpillar stage. A few species migrate toward warm countries for the winter; the monarch butterfly travels all the way from Canada to the Gulf States or California, and back. Most other butterflies and moths overwinter as caterpillars or as pupae. Some members of Lepidoptera are important in pollinating flowers. Others, during the caterpillar stage, are destructive of stored products and growing crops. Destructive species include the common clothes moth, the European corn borer, the corn earworm, the bollworm of cotton, and the imported cabbage worm.

Diptera: the two-winged flies, which characteristically have a complete metamorphosis, piercing and sucking or lapping mouthparts, and one pair of wings plus a pair of balancers (halteres); usually the larva is a maggot, and the pupa is concealed within the last larval skin (the puparium or case). Beneficial flies include the predatory robber flies, the parasitic tachina flies, and the many kinds that pollinate flowers. Detrimental flies include kinds that bite and transmit diseases, *e.g.* mosquitoes, sandflies, deerflies, and horseflies. The cosmopolitan housefly has been suspected of carrying many diseases. The tsetse fly of equatorial Africa, which carries sleeping sickness and nagana disease of cattle, is a close relative of the housefly.

Hymenoptera: sawflies, ants, ichneumon flies, wasps, and bees. These insects have a complete metamorphosis, biting or biting and lapping mouthparts, and two pairs of wings. The rear pair are smaller than the fore pair and hook to the rear margin of the fore pair during flight. Sawflies have caterpillar-like larvae, but the immature stages of the other hymenopterans are either internal parasites in other insects or grubs that depend upon a supply of food furnished by parents or near relatives. Many members of this order are social insects, living in extensive colonies, often with a distinct division of labor among different castes.

The best-known insect in this order is the domesticated honeybee. In its beehive are three castes: the *queen,* which lays all the eggs and is the only perfect female in the colony; the *drones,* which are the only males and whose sole function is the fertilization of newly emerged queens; and the *workers,* which are imperfect females and do all the labor of the colony, from building honeycomb and feeding bee grubs to gathering nectar and pollen. A hive may contain as many as 40,000 workers.

Ichneumon flies are among the most beneficial of parasitic insects, aiding man in controlling insects that damage crop plants and stored products. Sawflies and ants often are destructive, and the stings of wasps are generally considered proof that they are undesirable as close neighbors.

Insect orders of lesser importance include: *Collembola*—springtails; *Dermaptera*—earwigs; *Plecoptera*—stoneflies; *Ephemeroptera*—mayflies; *Mallophaga*—biting lice and bird lice; *Anoplura*—sucking lice of man and other animals; *Corrodentia*—book lice; *Thysanoptera*—thrips; *Mecoptera*—scorpion flies; *Neuroptera*—lacewings, antlions, and dobson flies; *Trichoptera*—caddisflies; and *Siphonaptera*—fleas. See Color Plates 55–56.—*L. and M. M.*

Social insects: Bee colonies are marked by restriction of reproductive function to limited part of population and by division of labor among nonreproductive members. Stinging bee is a worker, or sterile female, who guards honey from intruders. Being barbed, sting is left in victim. (*Treat Davidson/Nat. Audubon Soc.*)

INSECTICIDE: any chemical applied to plants, animals, or man, or to their environments, to destroy harmful insects or related pests. Insecticides may act as stomach poisons that are eaten by the insect, or as contact poisons or poison gases that penetrate the insect's body. Their use is often required in the production of food, feed, fiber, and ornamental crops, the storage of plant and animal products, the preservation of forests, and the protection of mankind from malaria and other insect-borne diseases, as well as from the annoyance of insects in everyday living. Inorganic insecticides—those of mineral origin—include sulfur and arsenate of lead. Organic insecticides include synthetic or man-made materials whose base is carbon (*e.g.* DDT), insecticides derived from plants (*e.g.* nicotine and pyrethrum), and petroleum oils. Certain organic insecticides, known as chlorinated hydrocarbons, of which DDT is an example, retain their ability to kill insects for a long time; others, such as the organic phosphates (malathion and parathion), are effective for only a short period, until their residues disappear. The synthetic organic carbamates represent another group of organic chemicals now used for insect control.

Insecticides are poisonous but vary in their toxicity to different insects and to man and warm-blooded animals: some are extremely poisonous, and special clothing or devices must be worn by persons handling them; others can be used safely without strict precautions. In using insecticides great care is necessary to minimize adverse effects on pollinating insects such as honey bees and on fish, birds, and other wildlife. The Food and Drug Administration of the U. S. Dept. of Health, Education, and Welfare establishes legal tolerances for insecticides on particular crops and livestock, *i.e.* the amounts of residues (in parts per million) that may remain on the raw agricultural product without harm to man. Also, before interstate shipment, each insecticide must be registered by the U. S. Dept. of Agriculture; the insecticide is then labeled with a statement of the contents and directions for effective and safe use. Insecticides must be applied according to directions to food crops in order to avoid harmful residues, and to animals or plants on which animals feed in order to prevent contamination of meat or milk.

Insecticides are most frequently applied as dusts, granules, sprays, fogs, or gases, by means of hand or power equipment, including aircraft. Dusts and granules come ready-made and are used dry. Sprays are commonly prepared by mixing a wettable powder with water or an emulsifiable concentrate with water or oil. Fogs and gases are released by special applicators. Insecticides intended especially for greenhouse and household pests are dispensed as gas-propelled mists from aerosol bombs. As fumigants—chemicals that give off poisonous vapors—insecticides control insects infesting stored grain and other stored products. Carbon disulfide is a common fumigant.

Several insecticides, known as systemics, are absorbed by plants through their foliage or roots and kill insects that feed upon them. Such chemicals, when fed to cattle, injected into them, or administered dermally, cause the death of grubs feeding under the animals' skin.

Certain insecticides, when worked into the soil, destroy insects that feed on the underground parts of plants. Chemicals are also used to poison the breeding places of gnats, mosquitoes, flies, and other pests that annoy man and animals and may serve as vectors of diseases. Some insecticides lose their effectiveness when strains of insects develop various types of resistance. Chemicals that act as repellents protect man from the bites and stings of various pests; those called attractants are mixed with poisons to make up poisonous lures. —*A. M. V.*

INSECTIVORE: any member of an order (Insectivora) of small, primitive mammals that includes moles, shrews, and hedgehogs; in a broader sense, any insect-eating animal or plant (see CARNIVOROUS PLANT). Mammalian insectivores are found in all parts of the world except Australia and the southern two thirds of S America. They range in size from tiny shrews, some no heavier than a dime, to species the size of a small cat. Practically all have five toes on each foot, a long pointed snout extending considerably beyond the jaw, and a wedge-shaped skull. Teeth are sharp, with well-defined cusps, and the canines are small and shaped like the adjoining incisors.

Modern insectivores give some idea of the structure and habits of their less specialized forebears, the ancestors of the placental mammals of today, including man. The creature shown here is a star-nosed mole, of eastern U. S. A.; 22 fleshy projections, sensitive to pressure, project radially from the end of his snout. (*Lynwood M. Chace/Nat. Audubon Soc.*)

The fur of moles and shrews is soft and silky, whereas that of tenrecs and hedgehogs is coarse; prominent spines cover the body of the latter. All possess minute eyes, often hidden by the fur. In moles and shrews the eyes probably serve only to distinguish light from darkness. Insectivores are of particular interest to the biologist because animals of this order were among the earliest placental mammals and hence were forerunners of the primates, the order to which man belongs. Many insectivores have changed little during the past 60,000,000 yr.

Moles and shrews are among the most common insectivores. Moles are subterranean in habit, being well adapted for an underground existence. The large paddle feet and the tremendous development of the forelimbs are modifications for digging. The tiny mouselike shrews, most abundant in moist forests, are found throughout the temperate regions of the world. Some species of shrews have a life span of little more than a year. The Old World hedgehog is widely distributed from W Europe to China. Some insectivores are adapted for an aquatic existence (*e.g.* the desman, a water mole), whereas others are partly arboreal. All feed primarily on insects and other small invertebrates, *e.g.* earthworms, crayfish, spiders, and mollusks. The group is of minor economic importance: pelts of moles are of commercial value; the destruction of injurious insects by moles probably offsets the damage the animals do to lawns.—*A. P. E.*

INSOLATION: see SOLAR RADIATION.

INSTINCT: The scientific study of instinct has increased greatly in recent years, and the concept itself has regained an academic respectability it has not had since the time of Darwin. The bad repute of the word was basically the result of an almost complete cleavage that came to exist between psychologists and biologists. Some schools of psychologists used the word dogmatically without any firm evidence to back up its use, while others stoutly denied the existence of any inherited behavior patterns and claimed that all behavior is due to conditioning, *i.e.* learning. The new attitude has grown out of the work of the so-called ethological school of animal psychologists under the leadership of Konrad Lorenz in Germany, Niko Tinbergen and William Thorpe in England, and

Instinct enables robin to build typical three-layered robin's nest, even if bird has been reared in captivity and has never seen a nest. (*Hal H. Harrison/Nat. Audubon Soc.*)

G. P. Barrends in the Netherlands. It has been much strengthened by recent discoveries in neurophysiology, especially about localized centers in the brain for drinking, eating, and other types of behavior.

As defined by zoologists and ethologists, an instinct must fulfill the following four conditions: (1) It must be a relatively complex and stereotyped behavior pattern performed with little or no variation. (2) It must be characteristic of the species, but may be held in common by more than one species. (3) It must be unlearned in the sense that it can appear without previous experience. (Some instinctive actions may change slightly after repetition; it is difficult to know whether such change is the result of practice or of maturation within the central nervous system.) (4) An instinct must be an adaptation to the environment, in contrast to the trial-and-error type of behavior that frequently precedes or is a part of learning.

Why is it not enough to define instincts simply as inherited behavior patterns? Because intelligence is also due to an inherited characteristic of the nervous system. Trial-and-error responses are inherited response patterns. The line between a simple reflex and a full-blown instinct is more or less arbitrary. A knee-jerk has all the characteristics of an instinct except that it is not complex enough to justify the term.

Arthropods, especially insects and spiders, are animals in which instincts have been highly developed, although many insects and other arthropods are capable of learning. Cocoon-spinning by the caterpillar of the Cecropia moth is one of the most beautiful and best studied cases of an instinct. It fulfills all four of the criteria. First, it is a complex and stereotyped action. The caterpillar always begins with its head uppermost, spins a tentlike structure of silk lines, turns upside down, covers the floor of the "tent" with silk, returns to the upright position, and, with a series of figure-eight motions of the head, fills in the spaces between the vertical silk lines of the tent. It then forms the inner layers. The action regularly follows this order unless the caterpillar has been subjected to neurosurgery or otherwise interfered with. Second, this ritual is characteristic of the species. In fact, it is relatively easy to distinguish the cocoons of the various species of big saturnid moths, such as the Luna moth, the Promethea moth, and the Cecropia, so constant are the differences. Thirdly, cocoon-spinning is done without any possibility of learning. It is per-

formed only once in the animal's lifetime, with no guidance from the parent moth, which died shortly after laying the egg from which the caterpillar hatched. Lastly, the cocoon, by protecting the pupa from birds and other predators as well as from weather, demonstrates that the behavior is adaptive.

Spiders exhibit many beautiful examples of instinctive behavior patterns by their webs, which are as characteristic of each species as is any anatomical feature of the spider. The flight of sexual forms of ants also is instinctive. A winged ant walks out of the ground, climbs a blade of grass, spreads its wings, and flies. There is no period of learning remotely resembling that of a boy learning to roller-skate.

Vertebrates have developed learning and intelligence to the highest degree. Nevertheless, instinctive behavior patterns play an important role in the lives of many vertebrates and may be far more important than has been realized. One of the most striking examples of instinct among vertebrates is the behavior of the American cowbird and the European cuckoo. These birds lay their eggs in the nests of other birds, and the young are fed and brought up by foster parents. Yet when the young become sexually mature they mate, not with birds of the foster parent's species, but with other cowbirds or other cuckoos. The incubation period of cuckoos is a bit shorter than that of the host species. The nestling, before it has feathers and before its eyes open, lifts and pushes the eggs of the foster parent out of the nest and does so in a highly stereotyped way. Many female dogs, especially beagles, may undergo a false pregnancy shortly after the end of the estrus period, even though they have not been mated. Such females, which may never have seen a puppy since they were puppies themselves, will steal children's dolls and guard and mother them most earnestly. Later, when the endocrines responsible for this behavior subside, and the breasts decrease in size, those females would no more steal a doll than take a book down from a shelf to read.

It was once thought that instinct is a kind of precursor of intelligence. It now seems clear that instinct and intelligence are two quite different ways by which animals meet life's problems. Instincts are essentially prefabricated answers. No time is lost in learning; no parental care is necessary. Such "helps" are of little or no value in meeting new situations; they may even be detrimental. Intelligence permits flexibility and ability to solve new and unexpected problems, but it also carries a built-in disadvantage: learning implies making mistakes. See ANIMAL BEHAVIOR; ANIMAL INTELLIGENCE. —*G. B. M.*

Nest building is instinctive, but it took some trial and error before this house wren succeeded in getting stick through opening. (*Hal H. Harrison/Nat. Audubon Soc.*)

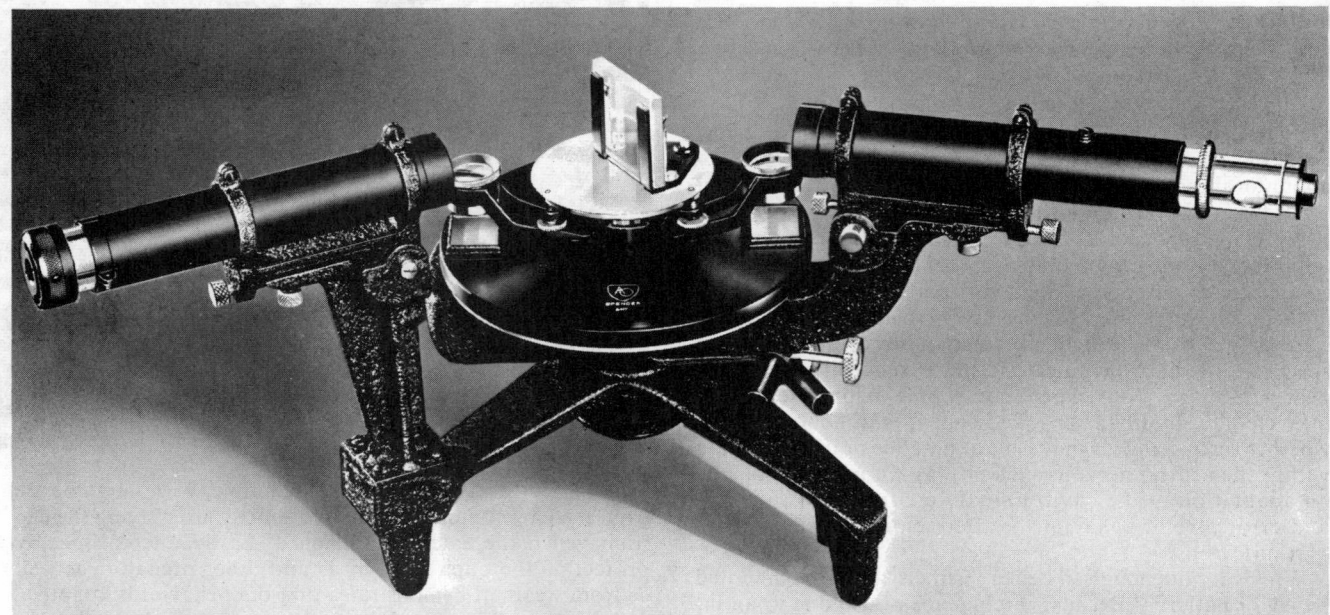

Spectroscope: By separating and dispersing light into its component wavelengths (forming a spectrum), the spectroscope allows physicists to identify materials; an early achievement was the chemical analysis of heavenly bodies. The above spectroscope uses a diffraction grating to produce a spectrum. Compared to prisms, gratings produce a *normal* spectrum; *i.e.* the distance between wavelengths in the spectrum is proportional to the difference between the magnitudes of the wavelengths. (*American Optical* Co.)

INSTRUMENTS, SCIENTIFIC: Our everyday knowledge of the physical world is derived from information gathered by our senses, and interpreted by our brains. Our sense organs, especially our eyes and ears, are impressive instruments which convert the physical stimuli such as light and sound into signals that can be understood by our brains. The human senses that have developed in the course of evolution have been those of greatest use in everyday life and in survival, and each sense has become particularly effective at a sensitivity level matched to the availability and value of the information to be derived. In bright light, for example, the eye is most sensitive to green light, in the middle of the visible spectrum, presumably because there is more of this color in sunlight than of any other color. And, while the peripheral regions of the eye are less sensitive to color, they are outstandingly sensitive to movement, because of the high survival value that this bestows both in hunting and in detection of attack.

Three Phases in Instrument Development: To make objective observations, we supplement our senses, and our memory, by specially contrived devices. The earliest of these devices were probably *rulers, clocks,* and *balances.* These were the simplest forms of measuring instruments, designed to convert lengths, times, or masses being investigated into numbers. They did not in the first place extend the range of observation; they added precision to observations that were within the compass of the naked eye, for example, and they removed the guesswork previously involved in deciding whether two objects in different places had the same length, or were of the same weight. The second phase of instrumental development was that typified by the *telescope* and the *microscope.* These are combinations of lenses which, used in conjunction with the eye, extend the range of existing human senses into new fields of experience, so that very distant and very small objects can now be examined, and knowledge thereby increased. Just as rulers can be used as aids to more accurate observation, so can scales placed in telescopes and microscopes convert them into more precise measuring instruments.

The invention of the *magnetic compass* by the Chinese started a third phase of development. Here was an instrument that depended for its stimulus upon a physical effect not appreciated, so far as we know, by any of the human senses. If any magnetic-sensitive organ had been evolved during human development, it had evidently had insufficient survival value to be retained through the period when human beings were savages, each restricted to a comparatively small region of Earth. But as the development of ships added to human mobility, a direction indicator that would work when cloud obscured the stars became of great value, and the magnetic compass filled the need. (Francis Bacon, in pointing out the enormous advantages to be gained from the development of science, remarked that without the compass Columbus might never have had the confidence to sail out into the Atlantic and thus discover America.) The compass is typical of a class of instrument which converts one kind of stimulus, to which we are normally insensitive, into another which we can detect. A simple illustration is the movement along a scale of a pointer denoting the intensity of an electrical current, which is readily appreciated by one of our existing senses. Many such instruments have been developed, particularly recently, as by-products of the efforts of scientists to improve their powers of observation, and some of these instruments have added considerably to the amenities and safety of everyday life. The *cathode-ray oscillograph* is an outstanding example, with its applications to radar and television.

We may note here that certain animals possess senses that human beings do not have, and that some of our recently devised instrumental aids have already been anticipated in nature. Thus there are insects which have a "polarization compass" for navigating by the light scattered from the blue sky; it is comparable to the device used by the U. S. Air Force for navigating over the North Pole when the Sun is below the horizon. Bats, and certain birds and marine animals, have acoustic radar; and rattlesnakes and the other pit vipers have infra-red detectors for locating prey.

Instruments belonging to the third phase of development include also those designed to supplement or replace human memory. The "reading" of measuring instruments was at first (and still often is) a process of visually observing the position of a pointer on a scale, and writing down the number on the nearest scale division. A modern trend is to incorporate devices that automatically read the setting of the instrument, and present the answer numerically as a series of digits; this is known as "digital presentation." Kelvin invented processes for recording the position of the instrument pointer photographically, or for attaching a pen to the pointer, so that the position of the pointer could be continuously recorded on a chart. Today this process has been extended to the punching of the numerical information directly on tape suitable for feeding data into *electronic computers*, which may be classed as instruments designed to extend the power of those faculties which deal with numerical calculation. Other techniques of recording information are plain and color *photography*, and *recording of sound* on mechanical discs, on magnetic tape, or on photographic film. Memory and computation instruments will not be considered further in this article, which is primarily concerned with devices for extending the range and precision of observation.

Some Basic Conditions in the Use of Instruments—*Standardization:* The principles underlying the construction, use, and performance of scientific instruments are best illustrated by simple examples. Consider the ordinary ruler, which consists essentially of a straight edge worked off in a number of divisions, each of an arbitrary length—say 1 mm. If this instrument is to be reliable, the length of the division must not change as the ruler ages; hence the material of which it is made must be carefully selected after a thorough study of its physical properties. Moreover, if, as is inevitable, the length of the ruler is liable to change with physical conditions such as temperature, the amount of change should be predictable, and allowed for in any precise measurement. And, if a measurement made on one ruler is to be duplicated exactly by another ruler used elsewhere (as is necessary, for example, in the communication of scientific results, or in reproduction of an engineering structure), the two rulers must be compared, so that the values expressed by one are the same as those expressed by the other. Usually, this comparison is not made directly, but each ruler is checked against a local standard, which in turn is compared with a national standard kept, for example, in Paris, London, Washington. Periodically, these national standards are inter-compared; this used to be done

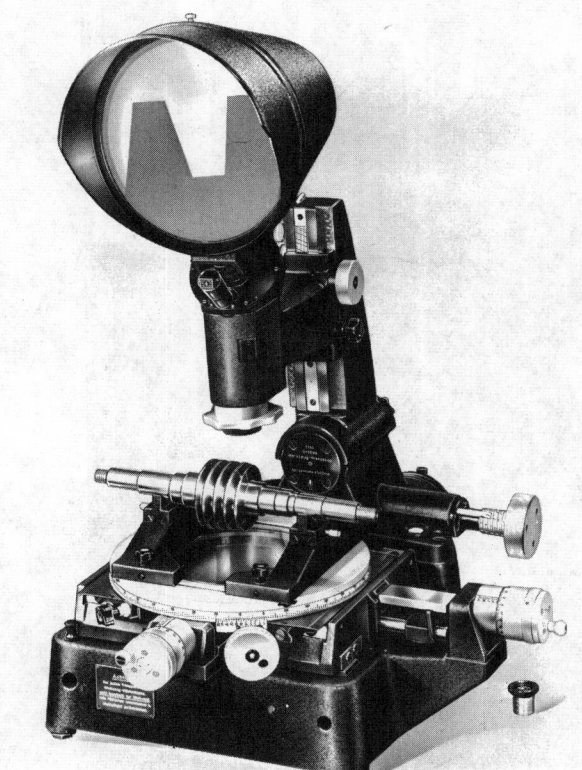

Optical comparator: Dimensions of an object are checked by using a machinist's microscope to project the image of the object on a screen, where it is compared to a standard pattern. (*Zeiss Ikon*)

Hygrograph and thermograph: Indicator at top is linked to strands of hair. As hair changes length with changing humidity, indicator records value of humidity on revolving drum. Lower indicator is linked with Bourdon gage (a gas- or liquid-filled, curved, flattened tube). As temperature changes, pressure within tube changes and alters shape of tube so as to move the indicator, which, in turn, records temperature on revolving drum. (*U. S. Weather Bureau*)

Rayleigh interferometer: This instrument reconstitutes two coherent beams, one of which has traversed an unknown gas. The character of the diffraction fringes produced gives the index of refraction and composition of the gas. (*Zeiss Ikon*)

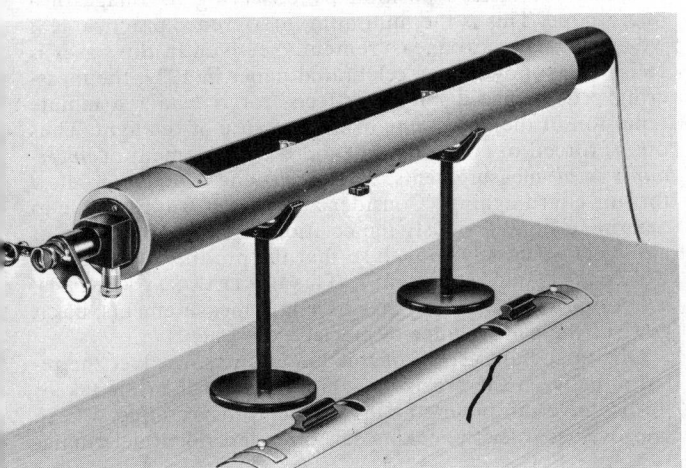

Mercury barometer: In each of these three barometers, height of mercury column indicates atmospheric pressure. (*U. S. Weather Bureau*)

Voltmeter: Deflection of current-carrying coil (with high-resistance shunt) in magnetic field indicates voltage. (*Weston*)

directly, but is now done by reference to the wavelength of light emitted by atoms of specified elements. The wavelengths are thought to be constant, under certain physical conditions which are easily duplicated in any part of the accessible universe, and are therefore taken as an international standard.

Precision Costs Time: Using even so elementary an instrument as a ruler accurately can be a time-consuming task. In measuring a length to the nearest centimeter, on a ruler divided into centimeters and millimeters, it takes very little time, to be sure, to lay the ruler roughly alongside the object, and read off the number of the nearest centimeter division at each end of the object, and subtract one reading from the other. If we require the length to the nearest millimeter, this takes more time, because we have to look more carefully, and the subtraction process takes longer because we have an extra digit to evaluate; and if we wish to find the result to the nearest 0.1 mm, we have to take still longer, estimating between the individual divisions.

Observation Influences the Object Observed: It is easy to see that there must be a physical contact between the ruler and the object to be measured. One literally lays the ruler on. Similarly, when *calipers* are used to measure the diameter of a rod, the caliper jaws must be pushed together until they are in actual contact with the rod. Now in each instance the physical contact is certain to have some effect, however slight, on the shape and size of the object we are measuring. The pressure and weight of the ruler, the compressive force of the jaws, both are to some extent deforming in their action. In short our very measurement alters the object being measured.

These two basic principles—namely, that precision costs time and that the act of measurement has consequences—are further exemplified by the familiar mercury-in-glass *thermometer*. There is a minimum limit to the size of the capillary in the graduated stem of the thermometer, and when this limit is reached, the only way of making the instrument more sensitive is to give it a bigger bulb, so that there is more liquid, giving more expansion for a given temperature rise. But the bigger bulb takes longer to heat or cool, and so the instrument takes longer to register the temperature; it also causes a bigger change in the heat content of the object being measured, and thus has an effect on its temperature.

Ultimate Limits: Philosophically, there is no way round these difficulties. Ingenious devices and stratagems can be used to avoid the need for physical contact; the object can be shielded from the various effects of the measuring instrument in different ways. Yet whatever precautions are taken, there is always *some* interaction between instrument and object. Consider the most delicate form of measurement. Say we use nothing more than light reflected from the object, and we establish the latter's position by observing its image in a microscope. This is the minimum interference practicable if we are to make any measurement. Yet even in this case, as Heisenberg showed in a celebrated paper in 1927, the measuring process has disturbing effects, for it entails a minute repulsion of the object due to the pressure of the light. Thus one is forced to conclude that there is an element of *uncertainty* in *all* measurements, an element one can neither allow for nor guard against. Consider also that it is impossible to determine simultaneously the position and the momentum of an object accurately enough so that the product of the errors will equal Planck's constant h. This UNCERTAINTY PRINCIPLE is not normally of importance in length measurements, but it governs the performance of precise experiments.

One important aspect of this uncertainty involves the relation between the precision achievable and the time taken; this is universal. In length measurement, for example, we can improve accuracy by making several independent determinations, and taking the average. If we do this *n* times, and the probable error of any one determination is *p*, then it can be shown that the probable error of the average of *n* determinations is $p/\sqrt{n}$. We have therefore improved our accuracy by $\sqrt{n}$, but the process has taken us *n* times as long as a single determination. Thus it takes a hundredfold increase in time to achieve a tenfold increase in accuracy, or ten thousand times as long to make an observation a hundred times as accurate. This relation between precision and time occurs in INFORMATION THEORY, from which it further appears that ENTROPY is transferred from the instrument to the system being observed, and that the minimum entropy transfer in an observation is *k*, BOLTZMANN'S CONSTANT.

"Noise": When we listen for a weak sound—*e.g.* of a mouse, or a watch ticking some distance away—we are limited by the general extraneous noise or the internal noise in our ears. Even if the extraneous noise can be reduced to zero, some residual noise arises at the eardrum itself. This diaphragm is in constant motion because it is under the random bombardment of the molecules of the air. Beyond a certain point the brain cannot distinguish between this residual noise and sounds from outside. Again, if we use a microscope to read the value of an electric current through an *ammeter* with the familiar type of needle-like pointer and scale, we find that the pointer is never quite steady, even when the meter is mounted as carefully as possible to avoid the effects of external vibration. Here again, the needle is being bombarded by the molecules of the surrounding air, and the random nature of the bombardment continually jerks the needle backward and forward about its true scale reading; the needle is executing BROWNIAN MOTION. Even if we remove all the air by evacuation, we cannot stop the movement, because the electrons in the meter circuit are also in continuously random motion, and they interact with the magnetic field in the meter to set up on the coil random torques which cause the needle to move just as much as it did when the air molecules were bombarding it.

Brownian movement is a universal phenomenon. All bodies are subjected to it, the mean Brownian kinetic energy of motion of a body at absolute temperature *T* being ½ *kT* per degree of freedom, where *k* is Boltzmann's constant. This applies to the body as a whole, and to its atoms individually; thus if we try to use a ruler we find each of its constituent atoms is in random vibration, and there are resultant fluctuations in the length of the ruler. We can therefore never be completely certain of the length of the ruler, unless we can cool it to the absolute zero of temperature (approximately −273°C), where the random vibrations would diminish to zero. We can never be completely certain of any measurement made with our ruler—which, if we could view it under sufficient magnification, would appear to be wobbling like a piece of jelly.

The problem of internal noise in scientific instruments is completely general to all instruments and is inescapable. It can be palliated only by operating the instrument at low temperatures, where the Brownian movement (or, more generally, "thermal fluctuation") is reduced, or by taking more time to average out the observations, as previously described.

Principles of Operation—*Conversion:* The object to be observed, or the quantity to be measured, must ultimately be caused by the instrument to give an indication that can be appreciated by one of the human senses or by an automatic device such as a computer. By far the commonest indication given is a visual one, since the eye is the most precise and comprehending of our sense organs. With the simplest measurements of length, no conversion is required, because the eye simultaneously regards the object to be measured and the ruler, and counts the number of divisions on the ruler to ob-

tain a length equal to that of the object. With more precise measurements of length, however, the unaided eye is insufficiently discerning; to measure a length to an accuracy of, say, a millionth of an inch, we must have some means of making this millionth appreciable to the eye. For example, parallel blocks of various calibrated lengths are built together until they approach the length of the object to be measured. The assembly of blocks and the object are placed in turn in an instrument (a "comparator") which is designed to measure the difference in length of the assembly and of the object. One form of this instrument has a table on which the object rests, and a precisely located, spring-loaded plunger vertically over the table. The object is removed, and the gage block assembly inserted, and the movement of the plunger, which may be a few ten-thousandths of an inch, is magnified to an extent that can be appreciated by the eye. There are, in fact, mechanical devices for effecting the necessary magnification, but more commonly nowadays some electronic device is used. A metal plate may, for example, be attached to the plunger, and a fixed parallel plate mounted near to it. Movement of the plunger thus causes the distance between the plates to change, which in turn varies the electrical capacitance between them. If this capacitance is connected to an oscillating electrical circuit, the change in capacity will change the frequency of oscillation; this change in frequency can be detected and amplified electronically, and indicated on a simple electrical meter, or recorded on a chart. This system constitutes a "transducer" for converting a small displacement of length into an electrical signal, and thence back, after electronic amplification, into a much larger displacement of the indicating needle. Among the earliest transducers were the *microphone*, for converting sound signals into electrical ones, and the *telephone* or loudspeaker, for reversing the process. There are now a great many transducers available; most of them cause the change in the quantity being observed to be converted into an electrical signal.

Amplification: The reason why transducers are generally designed to produce electrical signals is that these signals can be very conveniently magnified by electronic means. Great efforts have been put into the development of electronic devices in the past 40 yr, first using *thermionic tubes* and latterly *solid-state devices.* So powerful are these devices that it may be assumed here that the scientific instrument designer's task ceases when he has produced an electrical signal, from which point the electronic engineer can take over. It could, however, be contended that every electronic device is itself a scientific instrument, to which all the principles mentioned in this article also apply. Much of the spectacular development in electronics has in fact been due to a thorough application of these principles.

Although electronic engineers can now provide an almost unlimited amount of amplification, there is a limit to the amount that can be employed usefully. This limit is reached when unsteadiness of the object being observed, of its background, or of the first section of the transducer (*e.g.* the diaphragm of a microphone), is so much amplified that the output signal is not steady enough for its value to be read precisely within the available observation time. In optical instruments likewise there is a limit on the amount of magnification that can usefully be employed. In the ordinary microscope, diffraction of the light by the microscope objective (see LENS) results in a blurring of the detail in the image. The amount of blurring thereby apparently superimposed on the object corresponds roughly to about 0.1 micron (10^{-5} cm) with the best optical microscopes, and any detail finer than this in the object will be lost in the image. There is little point in producing an image that would appear much larger than two or three thousand times the object, because the blurring would then become prominent, and further magnification would not enable the viewer to see any more detail. Greater detail could be seen only by shortening the wavelength of the light used to examine the object, since there would then be less diffraction produced by the microscope objective lens. This has been done by giving up using light for this purpose, and using electrons instead, because of their much shorter wavelengths. The vastly reduced diffraction in the *electron microscope* makes it possible to employ usefully much greater magnification, and details only a few angstroms apart (1 angstrom $= 10^{-8}$ cm) can be seen.

There are also limits to the useful magnifying power of telescopes in astronomy. As with microscopes, diffraction by the objective lens or mirror sets a fundamental limit to the detail that can be distinguished; but long before this limit is reached, the performance of the telescope may have been spoiled by bad SEEING caused by rapid variations in refractive indices of the atmosphere. The largest telescopes even when operated from the most favorable sites on Earth's surface are little better than ones of moderate size for seeing detail on such objects as the Moon. When it becomes possible to operate large telescopes on artificial satellites outside Earth's atmosphere, a great gain in definition should result.

Isolation: An instrument must as far as possible be made immune to any influences other than a change in the quantity it is designed to observe or measure. A ruler intended to measure length should as far as possible be immune to effects of changes of other quantities such as humidity and temperature; hence wood is not a good material for rulers, since it shrinks in dry atmospheres, and although metal will not change its length with humidity, it will in general expand or contract if its temperature changes. A material of very small expansion coefficient ("Invar") is therefore sometimes used for scales, but this is subject to uncontrollable small changes in length as its crystalline structure ages. For precise measurements of length, therefore, it is desirable to isolate the ruler (or any more complicated measuring instrument) from changes in outside temperature by operating it in a room in which the temperature is thermostatically controlled.

Similarly, instruments that have moving parts, *e.g.* GALVANOMETERS, must be protected from external mechanical disturbances such as vibrations which would cause the instrument to give false indications. For this purpose, some instruments are placed on substantial piers sunk into the earth, while others are placed on anti-vibration mountings: these latter generally consist of a massive platform suspended or supported on springs, constituting a system which reduces and damps the shocks to the instrument as the suspension system of an automobile reduces the shock produced by bumps in the road. In general, the oscillation period of such a system has to be much longer than that of the external vibration against which the instrument is being protected.

Electrical and electronic apparatus has to be isolated from the effects of electrical disturbance, which may range from lightning flashes to the radiation from a-c power mains or even the field of radio-broadcast and television transmitters. Here the appropriate measures are to enclose the equipment in a metal screen and, in addition, to "ground" it at an appropriate point. There are many other forms of disturbance which may affect scientific instruments, particularly since the devices frequently have to operate in conditions in which unusual disturbances are being intentionally created. For satisfactory operation, it is therefore necessary in designing an instrument to anticipate kinds of disturbance and to include suitable protection in the design.

Compensation: It is often impossible to protect an instrument against all undesired external disturbances. For example, in many *infra-red detectors* the infra-red radiation is made to fall on a tiny blackened receiver, whose temperature very slightly rises as a result (see BOLOMETER). The small rise in temperature is then noted and taken as a measure of the strength of the infra-red radiation. But there are many external influences, other than infra-red radiation from the source under examination, that may cause the temperature of the detector to change. The general temperature of the surroundings, for example, may increase because of a change in weather. One remedy for this problem is to have two instruments, exactly similar to one another and mounted as closely as possible together, so that they react in exactly the same way to any exterior influence, except that one is allowed to "see" the source under examination, while the other is screened from it. Then the effect due to the source is the difference between the two recordings. In practice, the two instruments are usually constructed as one joint or "compensated" instrument, and their outputs are combined by subtraction, so that the difference alone is recorded. It is difficult to make two instruments exactly alike—in general there will be a difference of 1 to 10%—and so the compensation can hardly ever be perfect. Moreover, the random "noise" in the two instruments cannot be subtracted, and so a compensated instrument is about $\sqrt{2}$ times as "noisy" as an uncompensated one. Yet the principle of compensation can result in a ten to a hundredfold improvement in the performance of an instrument under disturbed conditions.

"Chopping": When the foregoing precautions of isolation and compensation are insufficient, a further step can sometimes be taken. Suppose we are looking for a single light against a background of many others. The single light can be made much more obvious if it is flashed on and off rhythmically. The process enables our eyes repeatedly to compare the view seen when the single light is on with that when it is off, and the difference becomes much more obvious than it would have been if the single light had merely been switched on and left on. By the process of flashing, the single light has been "labeled," and our eyes can be "set" to look for this label. And with different flashing rhythms it is possible to attach different labels to different lights, as has for long been done with lighthouses.

The same principle can be applied to scientific instruments. A steady light viewed by a photocell will give a steady photoelectric current, while a flashing light will give a rhythmically varying current. If the rate of flashing is high enough, say between 5 and 1,000 times per second, the photoelectric current will be modulated at this frequency, and it can be easily amplified electronically. Moreover, the amplifier can be "tuned" to be relatively insensitive to lights modulated at any other frequency, or to steady sources, so that the final indicator takes notice only of light flashing at the predetermined frequency. In this way, an instrument can be made peculiarly sensitive to a flashing light, which thus can easily be detected in full daylight, even when a steady light of the same brightness could not be detected. The instrument will recognize the flashing (or "modulated") light, even though the background illumination changes greatly.

With infra-red sources, the same labeling or chopping technique can be employed, using infra-red detectors in place of ordinary photocells. The consequent "labeling" of the current modulation in the detector enables this modulation to be distinguished from much of the electronic "noise" randomly generated in the detector itself, and the method is therefore a powerful one for enabling the greatest sensitivity to be attained with a given detector.

Chopping techniques have much wider application than radiation measurement alone, since they can in principle be used whenever it is possible to vary rhythmically, from zero up to its full value, the quantity being observed. For chopping to be effective, the observing system must have time to recognize the chopping rhythm, just as we must inevitably wait for a second or so to check that the light that we see flashing on an automobile ahead is coming from the direction indicator and not the brake warning light. Thus, the improvement in discrimination gained by chopping is only gained by expending time in observation.

Principles of Construction—*Design:* In general, no more effort should be spent on an instrument than is necessary to insure that it will do its designed job. This can usually be specified in terms of such properties as sensitivity, response time, stability within predetermined environments, and useful life. In detail, the specification will imply that some features of the instrument are critical, while the tolerances on other features are less stringent. One object of good design is to minimize the number of critical features, so that attention can be concentrated on them. Moreover, these features should as far as possible be designed so that they can be executed by easily controllable manufacturing operations.

This economy of design appears to have been considered first by Maxwell (*Kensington Museum Handbook,* 1876), who developed the principles of "kinematic design" for the mechanical parts of instruments. Briefly, these principles state that since a rigid body has six degrees of freedom, six suitably chosen constraints are sufficient to fix it, and therefore more than six will strain the body unnecessarily. Five constraints will permit the body to have one degree of freedom, *i.e.* it will be able to slide along a line or rotate about a single axis. Kinematic principles are a useful guide to the construction of mechanical instruments, but they need to be applied with care. Fixed constraints can often be replaced by leaf-spring linkages which allow the moving part to be translated or rotated over a limited range; since this construction avoids both wear and backlash, it is coming increasingly into use.

It is still worth quoting Maxwell's remarks on the aim of design:

"The fundamental principle is that the construction of the instrument should be adapted to the use that is to be made of it, and in particular, that the parts intended to be fixed should not be liable to become displaced; that those which ought to be movable should not stick fast; that parts which have to be observed should not be covered up or kept in the dark; and that pieces intended to have a definite form should not be disfigured by warping, straining, or wearing."

To these requirements we might add that scales and controls should be conveniently situated and shaped for the operator's convenience. The study of these last factors has recently developed as a branch of ergonomics.

Maxwell's principles were enunciated for mechanical instruments, but similar ones could be drawn up for optical, electronic, and all other instruments to form a complete body of rational design principles.

Any instrument should be "finished" enough to prevent its performance from deteriorating with age, and there is some esthetic satisfaction in giving it a pleasing appearance. Fraunhöfer is alleged to have said to someone who was critical of the finish of some of his instruments, "My instruments are made to be looked through, not looked at." In fact, however, Fraunhöfer's instruments (at least, those that have survived) were well finished. While there is no justification for extravagant finish, some degree of finish is almost always desirable and this, as with everything else, should be matched to the use that is to be made of the instrument.

Size: Very important in the design of an instrument is size. In an optical astronomical telescope, a large size is necessary in order for it to collect the largest possible amount of light

Ammeter: Deflection of current-carrying coil (with low-resistance shunt) in magnetic field indicates amperage. (*Weston*)

Theodolite: Telescope mounted on leveled platform measures horizontal and vertical angles. The theodolite is similar to a surveyor's transit, but is usually more accurate and its image is left inverted. (*Zeiss Ikon*)

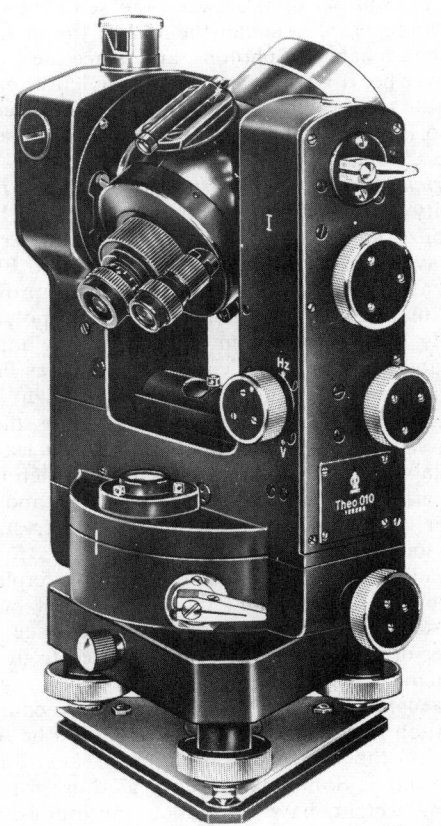

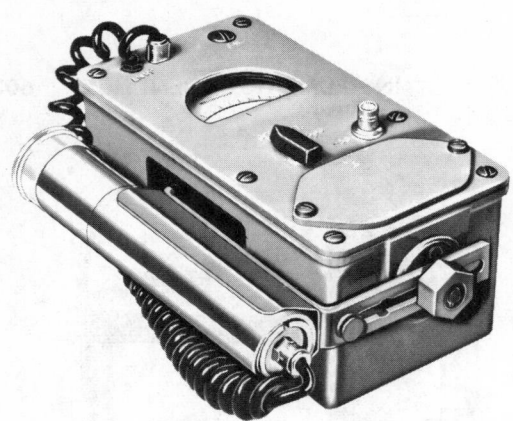

Geiger-Müller counter: Electrometer (surface dial) indicates radio-activity when ionizing particles from radioactive material enter ionization chamber (cylinder at left). (*Victoreen Instr. Co.*)

from a faint galaxy, and in a radio telescope large size is necessary for sufficient directional resolution. Size may be similarly necessary in a spectrometer to give high spectral resolution. In many other cases, smallness may be vital, since a small instrument may, for example, be far less prone to some external disturbance; again the size of an instrument may be limited by some other consideration such as the need to fit it into a confined space, as in an artificial satellite. Instruments that have delicate suspended systems or optical paths that are liable to be upset by convection currents in the air in the instrument casing are almost always best made small, because the convection currents increase roughly as the fifth power of the diameter of the casing, and convection troubles that are relatively serious in a large version of the instrument may be relatively negligible in a small one, made exactly to scale. Radiation-detecting instruments such as thermopiles and photocells are usually best made small, for a different reason. Here the limit of sensitivity is set by the random nature of the exchange of radiation (that is, in the form of photon packets) between the sensitive surface and its surroundings. The smaller the area of the surface, the less will be the exchange of photons, and hence the "quieter" will the receiver be. It is often possible to use lenses or mirrors to concentrate the desired radiation on to the smaller surface; if this is so, it is advantageous to make use of the improved "quietness" to achieve a greater sensitivity.

Materials: Improvements are gradually being made in the uniformity of the traditional materials—*e.g.* steel, brass, phosphor bronze, copper, glass—but many new materials are becoming available for instrument construction. Electrostatic instruments have, for example, been much improved, thanks to the insulating properties of plastics such as polythene. New lubricants like molybdenum disulfide have improved the performance of bearings. Clear plastics such as Perspex and Lucite have facilitated the development of "light guides" for coupling scintillator crystals to photomultipliers, thus facilitating the design of very sensitive detectors for nuclear radiation. The availability of single crystals of semi-conducting materials such as germanium has enabled the transistor and the photoconductor cell to be developed; and single crystals of salts such as sodium iodide form the scintillators for detecting nuclear radiations. There is much scope for interplay between the instrument designer and the developer of materials; in some instances, we are approaching the stage where the properties of new materials can be tailored to fit the design requirements.

The Sequence of Scientific Instruments: A comprehensive classification of scientific instruments would be futile to attempt with the enormous number of instruments currently available. Some instruments, as those for measuring length and weight, have developed continuously from the time of the earliest technology, while others, *e.g.* radio telescopes and electron microscopes, have originated within the last few decades, and devices such as masers are currently being added to our potential for observing the properties of the universe.

Astronomical instruments (not including telescopes) were accurate enough by the late 16th cent. for Kepler to have well-founded confidence in Tycho Brahe's observations—to the extent that 8 minutes of arc (an angle of less than 1 in 400) could be recognized as something well outside an instrumental error in observations of the position of Mars made many months apart. During the 17th cent. telescopes and microscopes were invented; they have, of course, since been developed into wide ranges of instruments—but it is worth remembering that Leeuwenhoek discovered bacteria less than 0.01 mm long with a single lens. Also during the 17th cent. thermometers began to appear, starting with Galileo's thermoscope. These were developed by Réaumur and Fahrenheit to the point where precise observations were possible. The use of a mercury-in-glass thermometer to measure the heat in a spectrum led Sir William Herschel to discover infra-red radiation, and this discovery in turn led to the development of more sensitive detectors. The development of electrical methods of measuring temperature (thermojunctions and resistance thermometers) resulted in instruments capable of great sensitivities, and operating over wide ranges of temperature. Pressure-measuring devices such as barometers, appearing in the 17th cent., enabled Pascal to invent the altimeter, and Boyle to discover his celebrated law. Investigation of the gas laws stimulated development of the kinetic theory in the 19th cent., and the understanding of gases thereby achieved led to the development of pumps for creating high vacua and of gages for measuring the minute pressures in these vacua.

Apart from the magnetic compass, which came to Europe from China in the Middle Ages, electrical instruments hardly began to appear before the 18th cent. Discoveries by Michel, Coulomb, Oersted, Ohm, Faraday, Gauss, Weber, Kelvin, and Maxwell resulted in a range of electrical instruments such as galvanometers and resistance devices (potentiometers, bridges, etc.), which have widespread applications today. The development of vacuum techniques led Röntgen to the discovery of x-rays in 1895, and from this discovery there rapidly developed the well-known x-ray diagnostic techniques for medical and engineering purposes. Later, x-ray diffraction was applied to the study of crystal and molecular structures, and x-ray spectroscopy has recently come to be a standard method of analyzing the chemical composition of materials. X-ray technology thus forms an impressive branch of scientific instrumentation.

The experiments of Hertz in 1887 to confirm Maxwell's electromagnetic theory led him to the generation of radio waves and, incidentally, to the discovery of photoelectric emission. J. J. Thomson, stimulated by Röntgen's work on x-rays, discovered the electron in 1896, and thus made possible the invention of electronic devices such as the thermionic valve, the photoelectric cell, the cathode-ray tube, and the mass-spectrograph. These and other devices form the basis of many techniques of instrumentation, from radar to radiofrequency spectroscopy. A further branch of instrumentation sprang from Becquerel's discovery of radioactivity, 1896, and from the subsequent techniques of Rutherford and his contemporaries. Devices such as the photographic plate, the Geiger-Müller counter, the scintillation counter, the Wilson chamber, and the bubble chamber have been developed for observing the behavior of nuclei and elementary particles. Some of these instruments have widespread application in geological prospecting, in radiation protection, and in isotopic work in medicine.

The development of various techniques of amplification after 1920 enabled several instruments to approach the sensitivity limit set by thermal fluctuations. The first instrument to do so was the galvanometer of Moll and Burger, in 1925; its unsteadiness was recognized in 1926 by Ising as due to the Brownian movement of the suspended coil. Since that time, radio receivers, infra-red detectors, electrometers, and other instruments have approached their limits at room temperature; there is current interest in operating instruments at liquid helium temperatures (about 4° absolute), where thermal fluctuations are much reduced.

We may indicate the magnitude of the present limits for a few instruments. A typical infra-red detector mounted at the focus of the 200-in. Hale telescope would be able to appreciate the heat of a candle at about 400 mi range if allowed an observation time of 1 sec; at this sensitivity the spontaneous "noise" in the detector would just become appreciable. A good radio telescope, with its sharp tuning and large receiving area, would be able to detect a source of radio energy of strength equivalent to a pea-lamp (say 3 watts) at about 5,000,000 mi, again given an observation time of 1 sec. The electron microscope can reveal detail of atomic arrangements and dislocations in crystals of about 1 angstrom unit (10^{-8} cm magnitude); and a proton microscope, with still smaller wavelength, is beginning to reveal structural detail in the proton and neutron of the order of 10^{-13} cm magnitude.

Up to about 1950, it was possible to argue that all the instruments so far invented had been dependent upon physical discoveries made before the advent of quantum mechanics. This is no longer true. Such devices as the "tunnel diode" and the maser, now currently in use, were conceived on the basis of a quantum-mechanical viewpoint, and they are likely to be the forerunners of a new generation of instruments. There is constant interplay between scientific discovery and instrumentation, almost in a hen-and-egg relationship. The discovery of a new physical phenomenon often leads to a new instrument, just as the discovery of the electron led to the cathode-ray tube. The instrument may thus be applied to make new observations, and hence to the discovery of new phenomena, which in turn leads to the development of further instruments. Sometimes, the desire to develop perfect instruments leads incidentally to important scientific discoveries, as when C. T. R. Wilson, trying to make a perfect electroscope, discovered the spontaneous ionization that led to the first identification of cosmic rays. Similarly, K. G. Jansky's efforts in 1931 to make his radio receivers as good as possible led him to investigate a noise which turned out to be coming from the Milky Way; this was the beginning of radio astronomy.

Instruments are thus vital to the development of scientific knowledge. The imagination of theoreticians can take us a long way in understanding the physical world; but even the greatest imagination is limited and, as de Broglie has pointed out, there are more things in heaven and earth than are dreamt of even in natural philosophy. Imagination must always be corrected and stimulated by observation; and observation can be made only when the appropriate instrument has been devised.—R. V. J.

SOME BASIC INSTRUMENTS OF PHYSICAL SCIENCE

General Area of Application	Instrument	Manner of Functioning
Mechanical Properties of Matter	Standard (for length)	Measures any length with which a conventional linear dimension can be compared. The *meterbar* is the international standard originally based on the international platinum bar at Paris. The basis is now a multiple of the wavelength of light emitted by the gas krypton[86]. *Gage blocks* are individual blocks, often of chrome steel, each with two parallel sides. The length between sides is marked on the block, often to an accuracy of 0.000008 in. They are widely used in machining parts to close tolerances.
	Comparator (for length)	Both measures and indicates the deviation of a dimension or set of dimensions from a reference (pre-set) dimension or pattern. Comparators take many different forms, *e.g.* optical, pneumatic, and radioactive. The basic comparator is a frame which holds the body to be checked and a movable measuring head which comes into contact with the body's surface. The measuring head is linked to a calibrated indicator. In many comparators, a microscope is mounted so that the limiting line or surface can be collimated with one of the crosshairs of the microscope. *Cathetometers* are comparators that are used to indicate and measure vertical distances.
	Caliper (for length)	Has pair of legs pivoted so that the ends can swing open and shut. When the ends are opened enough to span any distance (*e.g.* the diameter of a pipe or the distance across an irregular object), this distance is indicated by a calibrated standard on the instrument. For highly precise measuring the caliper can be directly linked with a micrometer and vernier.
	Planimeter (for area)	Has two legs pivoted together at the ends. The unpivoted end of one leg is kept pinned to one point. A tracing point is attached to the unpivoted end of the other leg. A calibrated wheel is also attached to the leg which has the tracing point. The motion of the tracing point as it is guided over the perimeter of the area causes the wheel to rotate, recording the size of the area traced.
	Graduated Cylinder (for volume)	Graduations, generally in milliliters or multiples thereof, indicate volume of liquid contained. *Burettes* suitably graduated are used for same purpose. Volume of a solid body can be ascertained by submerging it in a liquid and measuring the overflow in a graduated cylinder.
	Protractor (for angle)	Has a calibrated circular scale, with central or origin index. Generally used as a hand instrument for overlaying the angle to be measured.
	Goniometer (for angle)	Parallel rays of light are directed to two intersecting crystal faces. The direction of the reflected rays is indicated by a telescope mounted on a horizontal calibrated scale. The angle indicated on the scale is twice the angle between the intersecting faces. See MATHEMATICAL INSTRUMENTS.

SOME BASIC INSTRUMENTS OF PHYSICAL SCIENCE—Continued

General Area of Application	Instrument	Manner of Functioning
Mechanical Properties of Matter (*Cont.*)	Sextant (for angle)	Acts as a mariner's protractor, measuring local angle made by celestial body with horizon. It is used to determine latitude when local time is known. See SEXTANT; CELESTIAL COORDINATES; LATITUDE AND LONGITUDE.
	Surveyor's Level (for angle)	A telescope on whose axis is mounted a spirit (bubble) level. It is used to establish a horizontal line of sight. See SURVEYING.
	Theodolite or Surveyor's Transit (for angle)	A telescope, mounted in conjunction with horizontal and vertical calibrated circles, that measures and establishes vertical and horizontal angles. See SURVEYING.
	Balance (for mass)	Measurement is done by a balanced beam suspended on an accurately ground knife edge. The unknown mass is counter-balanced by a combination of calibrated weights. Other forms are the calibrated SPRING extension balance and the TORSION balance, which measures the rotation of an elastic beam when the mass is loaded at a known lever-arm distance. See CHEMICAL BALANCE.
	Mass Spectrograph (for atomic mass)	Atomic mass is determined by measuring ratio of charge to mass. This is indicated by the deflection of a charged particle in a magnetic field. See MASS SPECTROMETRY.
	Tachometer (for velocity)	Angular velocity of a shaft may be measured by a COUNTER which records the number of revolutions in a given interval of time.
	Ballistic Pendulum (for velocity)	Projectile is stopped by a PENDULUM whose mass is considerably larger than the projectile's mass. Observation of pendulum's displacement, and application of principle of the conservation of MOMENTUM, give projectile's horizontal velocity.
	Stroboscope (for velocity)	Produces periodic illumination of rotating mechanisms. Illuminating source is a flashing lamp that gives pulses of very short duration with frequency continuously variable. When frequency is in synchronism with motion of parts of the rotating mechanism, the latter gives the impression of being stationary, and such aspects as deformations and distortions may be observed (*e.g.* in a whirling flywheel). Moreover, by noting the flashing frequency at which the motion is arrested, the angular velocity may be calculated. See STROBOSCOPE.
	Pitot-Static Tube (for velocity)	Indicates the pressure head resulting from the kinetic energy of fluid in motion relative to the instrument. It is useful in determining the air speed of aircraft as well as fluid velocity in pipelines. See PITOT-STATIC TUBE.
	Dynamometer (for force)	Measures force. Any instrument measuring force is a DYNAMOMETER; *e.g.* a simple spring. A balance is a dynamometer, but one that can only measure the force of gravity on a body, *i.e.* its weight. In usual engineering nomenclature, a dynamometer is an instrument for measuring power output of a machine.
	Accelerometer (for acceleration)	Indicates ACCELERATION, *i.e.* the rate of change of velocity with respect to time. ACCELEROMETERS are of many types, each designed for a particular application. A typical instrument is a MASS on the end of a spring. When a body accelerates, the mass is displaced. Since compression or extension (displacement) of a spring is proportional to the force acting on it, and acceleration of a mass is proportional to the force acting on it, the displacement of the mass (and spring) is proportional to the acceleration.
Properties of Light	Colorimeter (for color)	Matches the color of a solution or body against a comparative standard. See COLORIMETER.
	Coronagraph (for solar observation)	When used with a telescope, a coronagraph occults (masks) the image of the solar disc, so that the telescope can project the solar corona as it would be seen during a total solar eclipse. See CORONAGRAPH; SUN.
	Interferometer (for phase contrast of light beams)	Reconstitutes coherent light beams that may or may not be out of phase (see PHASE ANGLE) to determine accurately optical wavelengths or small displacements. INTERFEROMETERS usually split a light beam into two or more coherent beams. By varying the length of path or by sending each ray through different mediums, interference fringes are produced when the rays are reconstituted. The number of fringes, with data on the wavelength of light, indicates the index of refraction and therefore the chemical composition of the medium traversed, or, when the length of path is varied, of the difference in length of path. The interferometer can be used to measure accurately small distances and wavelengths of monochromatic light. The *Rayleigh interferometer* measures refractive index by observing the shift in the interference fringe system after reconstitution of light that has traversed air (or vacuum) and light that has passed through the medium whose index of refraction is to be measured.

SOME BASIC INSTRUMENTS OF PHYSICAL SCIENCE—*Continued*

General Area of Application	Instrument	Manner of Functioning
Properties of Light (*Cont.*)	Interferometer (*Cont.*)	The *Fabry-Perot interferometer* consists of a pair of very flat, partially reflecting mirrors, separated by a spacer and mounted parallel to each other. Under monochromatic illumination, the interference pattern consists of a set of circular fringes, the diameter being a function of wavelength and order of interference. The *Michelson interferometer* divides a beam by a partially reflecting mirror set at 45° to the axis of the beam. A portion of the light passes through the mirror; the balance is reflected by the mirror. The two separate beams, after traveling different paths, are brought together (reconstituted). If the two paths are different in length, the reconstituted beam will show interference fringes.
	Microscope (for magnification)	By a system of lenses it produces a highly magnified image of a near, small object. See MICROSCOPE.
	Photometer (for light intensity)	In the past, the intensity of light from a given source was determined by comparing it visually (*i.e.* by means of the human eye) to the intensity of light from a standard source. More accurate determination can be made by means of a photoelectric cell connected to an ammeter or a voltmeter. Current or voltage, as indicated by a needle reading, is proportional to light intensity. See PHOTOMETER AND PHOTOMETRY.
	Polarimeter (for polarization)	Measures the rotation of the plane of polarization of light. It consists of a pair of polarizers one of which can be rotated with respect to the other. The material whose rotatory polarization is to be measured is placed between the crossed polarizers, extinction being set for 90°. The deviation from 90° for the new angle of extinction gives the measure of the rotation of the plane of polarization. See POLARISCOPE; POLARIZED LIGHT.
	Refractometer (for refractive index)	Measures the refractive index, or optical density, of a medium. Most REFRACTOMETERS depend upon the principle of total reflection (*i.e.* when light passes from a more to a less refractive medium, it will be totally reflected if it strikes the contact surface at an angle of incidence greater than the critical angle). The critical angle is characteristic of the material; determination of the critical angle indicates the index of refraction.

The *Pulfrich refractometer* measures the refractive index of a solid by placing the solid in optical contrast with a reference prism. This consists of placing one plane of the solid in physical contact with a plane of the reference prism and determining the critical angle by directing a slightly convergent beam of light along the interface of the two prisms. The *Abbe refractometer* is designed for determining the refractive index of a liquid by using a solid-liquid interface, with a calibrated protractor scale to observe the angle of total reflection. The *Rayleigh interferometer* measures the refractive index by presenting the shift in the interference fringe system after reconstitution of light that has traversed air (or vacuum) and light that has traversed a medium whose index of refraction is to be measured. See INTERFEROMETER. |
	Spectroscope (for radiation analysis)	Disperses the radiation from a light source or from any source of electromagnetic radiation, *e.g.* infrared or ultraviolet, into its component frequencies. Spectroscopes generally disperse the radiation by utilizing the differential refraction of various wavelengths as they pass through a dispersive prism or diffraction grating. A *spectrometer* is used for accurate wavelength determination when the rotating mechanism of the dispersive element is carefully calibrated. A *spectrograph* is a spectroscope capable of recording the spectrum data. Often the exit slit of the spectroscope is removed and replaced by a sensitized plate in order to photograph the spectrum. See SPECTROSCOPE AND SPECTROSCOPY; SPECTRUM.
	Telescope (for light-gathering and magnification)	By a system of lenses and often mirrors it produces an image of a distant object. The greater the diameter of the objective, the greater the power of the telescope to gather light and detect faint objects. See TELESCOPE.
	Turbidimeter (for turbidity)	Measures the scattering of light in a transparent or translucent medium. Turbidimeters are generally of the direct-reading type (usually photoelectric). The intensity of the light scattered at right angles to the direction of the incident beam may be used as an index of turbidity.
Properties of Heat	Calorimeter (for heat capacity)	Measures specific heat or heat capacity by determining the temperature rise of a body when the energy input is known. Water is generally used as a standard. See CALORIMETER; CALORIMETRY.
	Thermometer (for temperature)	Measures temperature, *i.e.* the coldness or hotness of a body. Although all instruments indicating a body's degree of temperature are thermometers, it is general practice to apply the term *thermometer* to all instruments that accurately record temperatures up to 1800°F, and the term *pyrometer* to all instruments that record temperatures above 1800°.

SOME BASIC INSTRUMENTS OF PHYSICAL SCIENCE—Continued

General Area of Application	Instrument	Manner of Functioning
Properties of Heat (*Cont.*)	Thermometer (*Cont.*)	The most commonly known thermometer is a glass capillary tube filled with mercury or alcohol, under vacuum. For higher temperature readings (above 1000°F) mercury is sealed under compressed nitrogen.
		The *gas thermometer* utilizes the thermal expansion of a gas. As in a gas barometer, a *Bourdon gage* is used. This is a pressure-measuring device which utilizes the pressure difference between the inside and the outside of a tube. A curved tube with a flattened section tends to straighten out as the pressure difference is increased; this motion is mechanically amplified and moves a pointer across a calibrated angular scale.
		For an extremely accurate and sensitive instrument in the low-middle range (up to 1800°F), the *thermistor* or BOLOMETER is used. This utilizes the change in resistance in an electrical circuit at different temperatures. Either a millivoltmeter or potentiometer as part of a bridge circuit is employed to indicate changes in resistance.
		For temperatures above 2500°F, THERMOCOUPLES are useful. These take advantage of the fact that in a circuit made up of two dissimilar metals, each junction being at a different temperature, an electric potential is set up. The circuits and the voltmeters or potentiometers are similar to those used for thermistors.
		Optical pyrometers and *radiation pyrometers* are used for temperatures above 1000°F. The optical pyrometer measures the temperature of a body by matching its brightness when viewed through an optical system against the brightness of a standard incandescent tungsten or platinum filament. The radiation pyrometer receives the radiation from a body whose temperature is to be determined and focuses it by means of an optical system on a thermistor or thermopile (a series of thermocouples).
Properties of Electricity	Ammeter (for current)	Measures current flow with minimum POTENTIAL drop by means of a galvanometric circuit of low RESISTANCE.
	Electrical Bridge (for resistance, impedance)	Measures resistance, impedance, or capacitance of a network element by balancing the network so that when a galvanometer on one branch of the network registers zero current (null detection), the voltage drop across the desired element, and therefore the resistance, impedance, or capacitance, can be calculated. See WHEATSTONE BRIDGE.
	Electroscope (for presence of electricity)	In the vane or gold-leaf type of electroscope, the divergence of the leaves indicates the presence of electricity. In an *electrometer,* the angular deflection of a light gold-leaf attached to a stiff rod is measured.
	Galvanometer (for current)	Angular displacement of a current-carrying coil suspended in a static magnetic field gives a direct measure of the magnitude of the current flowing through the coil. See GALVANOMETER.
	Ohmmeter (for electrical resistance)	Measures resistance by measuring current for a fixed voltage drop $R = V/I$, where R equals resistance in ohms, V equals voltage drop in volts, and I equals current in amperes. See OHMMETER.
	Potentiometer (for voltage)	Measures voltage by comparing the voltage of the unknown cell against that of a known cell. See POTENTIOMETER.
	Voltmeter (for voltage)	Measures potential difference by a galvanometric circuit of high resistance in order to reduce current drain.
	Wattmeter (for power)	Records the instantaneous product of voltage and current, and therefore the power. The mechanism may be a light high-resistance, voltage-indicating coil, moving in the magnetic field of a low-resistance current-indicating coil which is connected in series with it. The conventional *watt-hour meter* measures total energy consumed by integrating power over time. The commercial residential type uses a rotating vane (which absorbs a negligible percentage of the input energy) as a tachometer to perform this integration. See WATT; WATTMETER.
	Fluxmeter (for magnetic flux)	Measures the magnetic strength of a SOLENOID or an ELECTROMAGNET. The deflection of a moving-coil galvanometer suspended by a quartz fiber of negligible restoring TORQUE indicates the change in magnetic flux. See MAGNETISM.
	Magnetometer (for magnetic force)	Measures magnetic force. In present nomenclature, magnetometers are instruments used to measure the intensity of the horizontal component of Earth's magnetic field. These instruments depend on the simple magnetic pendulum relationship $T = 2\pi \sqrt{I/MH}$, where T equals the period of oscillation, M the moment of the magnet suspended in Earth's field, and H the intensity of Earth's field. Currently, very sensitive magnetometers are made by taking advantage of the radio-frequencies generated by the precession of the nuclear MAGNETIC MOMENTS of atoms, such as rubidium vapor atoms placed in a magnetic field.

1. **The thistle** (Cirsium arvense) thrives on any neglected land. Butterflies and bumblebees enjoy its nectar, and goldfinches feed their young on its half-ripe seeds. (Rutherford Platt)

Plate 45   FLOWERS

A flower is an invitation to an insect, bird, bat, or other animal to visit a plant and serve in pollination. Usually the visitor is rewarded with sugar water and a share of the nutritious pollen. This mutually beneficial alliance has helped to make flowering plants the most numerous of all kinds of plants.

2. After a good rain at any season of the year, **the ocotillo** (Fouquiera splendens)—a desert shrub of southwestern U.S.A. and Mexico—puts out green leaves and a banner of brilliant scarlet flowers. (Ernest Kleinberg/Rapho-Guillumette)

3. In peat and cranberry bogs grow insectivorous plants such as **the pitcher plant** (Sarracenia) and **sundew** (Drosera). (Maurice Broun/Shostal)

4. **The jack-in-the-pulpit** (Arisaema triphyllum) raises three-parted leaves and a remarkable flower cluster above the woodland floor in spring. The small flowers are on a central spike almost enclosed by a spathe with overhanging hood. (Rutherford Platt)

5. **A field of wild lupines** (Lupinus perennis) produces around Decoration Day a floral display of intense blue. (Emily Bash/Shostal)

Plate 46   FLAME TEST

Many elements and compounds give a characteristic glow when inserted into the pale blue, almost colorless flame such as that produced by a Bunsen burner; this is helpful in determining the presence of certain substances in qualitative chemical analysis. Here, a platinum wire loop, moistened in hydrochloric acid, has been dipped in an unknown powder. When placed in the flame, the resulting glow of color indicates that a certain element is present. Less distinct colors must be observed with colored glass filters or with a spectroscope in order to identify the substances present. *(Russ Kinne)*

COPPER   STRONTIUM   SODIUM

Plate 47   FLUORESCENCE

1   2

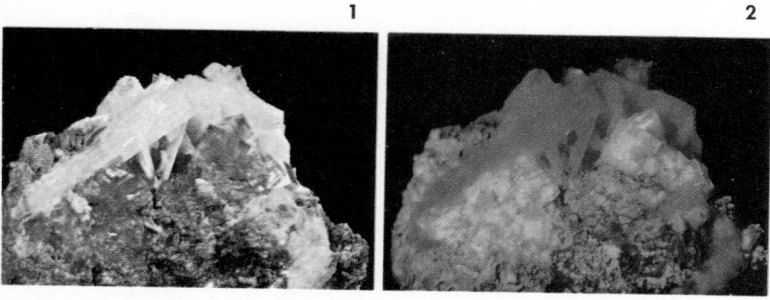

7   8

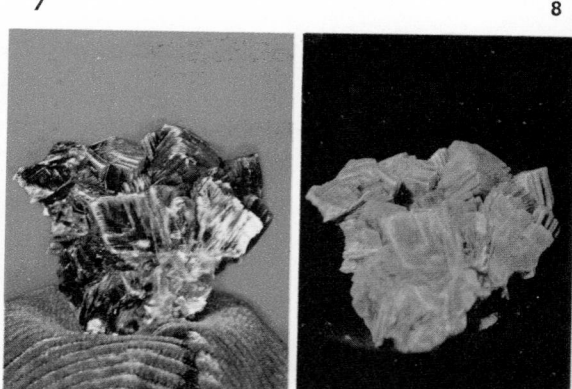

Brown fluorite from Ohio fluoresces a golden cream color (1). The blue color (2) is a reflection of some visible light from the blades of white celestite. In this photograph, as in others on this page, there is too much blue-green because of the limitations of photographic materials in dealing with ultraviolet light.

Autunite, a uranium mineral (7), is both radioactive and fluorescent (8).

3   4

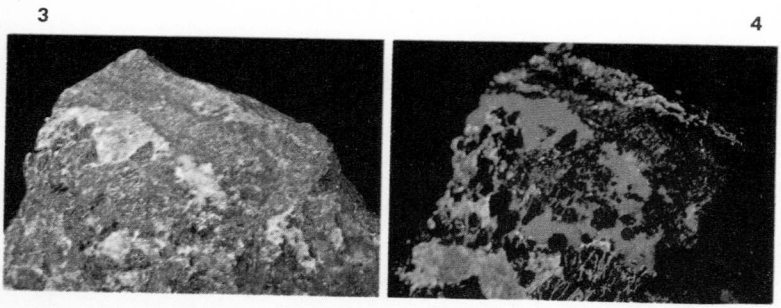

3. **Zinc-ore complex from Franklin, N. J.** contains a variety of minerals, some of which fluoresce in brilliant colors (4). Because of traces of manganese, willemite emits a brilliant yellow green to contrast with the brilliant red of calcite.

Fluorescent materials, natural and synthetic, can convert certain wavelengths of light into other wavelengths. Fluorescent mineral specimens shown here—each photographed first in natural light, then in ultraviolet light—change the invisible ultraviolet to visible color wavelengths. The same mineral species from different localities may fluoresce in different colors. *(All photographs of fluorescent minerals: Reo N. Pickens, Jr.)*

5   6

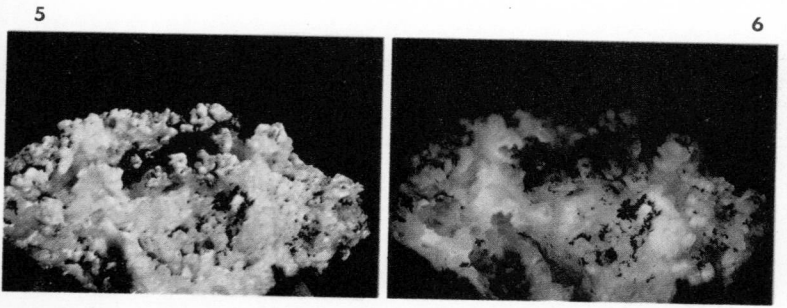

9   10

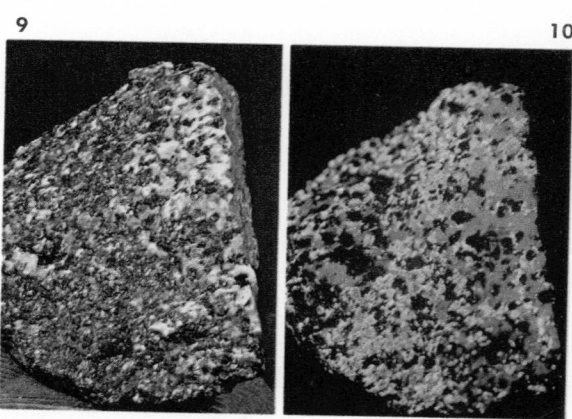

Aragonite: When ultraviolet light penetrates translucent form (5) of this common white mineral, aragonite has an eerie internal blue-green glow (6).

A New Jersey zinc-ore complex (9) reveals calcite (intense red to pink fluorescence) and willemite (green) (10).

Plate 48 FORESTS

Probably a twelfth of the world's land surface was forested before man began felling the trees. Now at least a third of these forests have been replaced by other types of plants or by deserts. Among the oldest and tallest of trees are the **coastal redwoods** of California **(1)**, which are evergreen conifers. Some of those alive today were seedlings in 1500 B.C. *(Brett Weston/Rapho-Guillumette)* Forests of **deciduous trees (2)** are common in temperate zone where summers are warm and wet, winters cold and snowy. *(P. E. Mahon/Shostal)* Richness of vegetation and variety of animal life characterize the **tropical rain forest,** such as this forest **(3)** in Uganda, at the edge of the warm, well-watered basin of the Congo River. Similar forests occur in the American tropics. *(Hans von Meiss, Teuffen/Photo Researchers)*

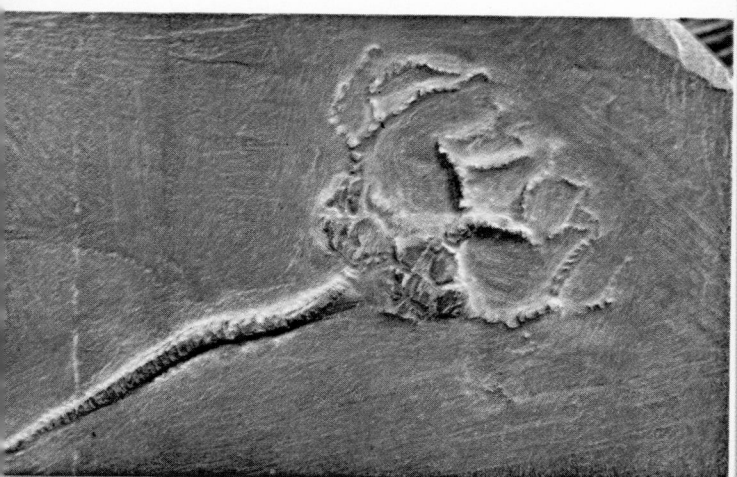

Plate 49 FOSSILS

A fossil is any evidence found in rocks of Earth's crust which tells something about former life on Earth. This evidence may be an actual animal, such as a mammoth preserved in the permafrost of the arctic regions; the hard parts of an animal, such as teeth, bones or shells; footprints; casts or molds; impressions of surface ornamentation; the carbon remains of leaves; or parts of any formerly living organism replaced by minerals, such as silica, pyrite, or calcite.

1. Crinoid from Dunderbach, Germany. Most members of this class of animals were attached to the sea bottom by a stalk, part of which is shown. *(F. H. Pough/ Amer. Mus. of Nat. Hist.)*

2. Petrified pine trees at Specimen Ridge, Wyoming. The original wood has been replaced by silica. *(Harold Wanless)*

3. Fossil fish preserved in the Green River shale of Wyoming. Only the carbon present in the original animal is here preserved. *(Jerome Wyckoff)*

4. Trilobite Phacops from the Devonian of Ohio. Such marine animals belong to the phylum Arthropoda and are found only in rocks of the Paleozoic Era, roughly 550 to 200 million yr ago. *(Paul Desautels)*

5. Eurypterid. This sea-dwelling relative of the scorpion belongs to the phylum Arthropoda. It lived 300 million yr ago and is now extinct. *(Paul Desautels)*

6. Fossil fern. Only the carbon present in the original leaf remains. *(Hermes)*

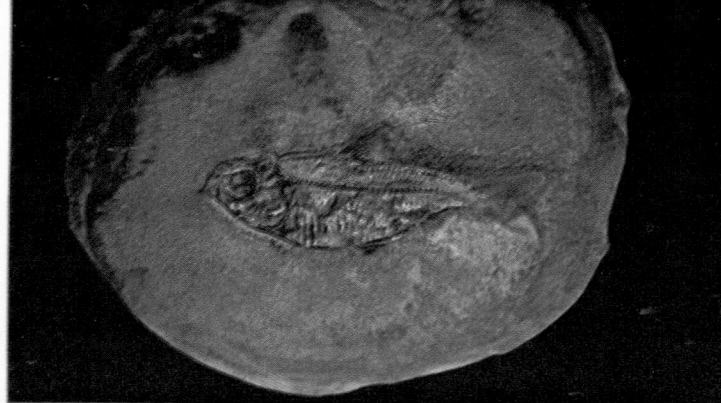

SOME BASIC INSTRUMENTS OF PHYSICAL SCIENCE—*Continued*

General Area of Application	Instrument	Manner of Functioning
Miscellaneous	Audiometer (for sound)	The hearing acuity of subjects to standardized speech and tone signals is determined a a function of pitch (frequency) and loudness (intensity). See SOUND.
	Flowmeter (for fluid flow)	Measures quantity of fluid flow per unit of time through channel or pipe. For steady-state pipe flow, either the pipe is gradually reduced in section and then expanded back (Venturi section) or a construction with a reduced opening is inserted. Pressure readings at critical points are obtained from manometers, and flow is calculated by means of BERNOULLI'S PRINCIPLE OF HYDRODYNAMICS.
	Geiger-Müller Counter (for ionization)	Detects ionizing material such as is produced by radioactive material, also cosmic rays and gamma radiation. The Geiger-Müller Counter is a metal cylinder enclosing a wire. An applied potential is maintained between the cylinders and the wire, and when an ionizing particle enters the chamber between the cylinder and the wire, ions are produced which move rapidly, causing by collision a rush of additional ions which when reaching the wire or the cylinder cause a momentary flow of current. This flow is indicated on an electrometer. See IONIZATION.
	Hygrometer (for relative humidity)	Measures relative humidity by the change in physical properties of a moisture-sensitive substance. The variation in length of a hair or of some plastic may be used to deflect a pointer. See HYGROMETER; METEOROLOGICAL INSTRUMENTS.
	Piezometer (for pressure)	Measures the compressibility of materials by using the PIEZOELECTRIC EFFECT as a transduction effect.
	Manometer (for pressure)	Measures pressure by indicating the difference in height of two connecting liquid columns. The surface of each column is exposed to one of the two mediums whose difference in pressure is to be measured. Most manometers are of the U-tube variety; the liquid used is determined by the density of the liquid and the range of pressure to be measured.
	Barometer (for pressure)	Measures atmospheric pressure. The usual meteorological barometer is a manometer which employs a column of mercury in an evacuated tube. Although a U-tube arrangement can be used (one end of the U-tube exposed to the atmosphere, the other end an enclosed vacuum), the more practical and common arrangement is to support the evacuated column in a pool of mercury that is exposed to the atmosphere. See BAROMETER.
	Bourdon gage (for pressure)	Indicates pressure differences by means of a sealed, curved, flattened, hollow tube. As the pressure of the medium surrounding the tube increases (or decreases), the difference in internal and external pressure causes the tube to flatten (or to coil). The tube's movement is mechanically amplified and indicated on a calibrated scale.
	Pirani gage (for pressure)	Measures the electrical resistance of a fine wire as a function of ambient pressure (low pressure, 0.1 to 0.001 mm). The *Ion gage* is also used at low pressures (less than 10^{-4} mm of mercury) and determines pressure by measuring the ion current in a vacuum tube.
	MacLeod gage (for pressure)	Measures pressure by utilizing BOYLE'S LAW. It compresses a known volume of gas into a smaller volume and measures the increase in pressure.
	Pitot-static tube (for pressure)	Measures dynamic pressure of a moving fluid by the difference in level of the two legs of a manometer, one column being acted upon by the moving fluid. See GAGE; PRESSURE MEASUREMENT; PITOT-STATIC TUBE.
	Psychrometer (for relative humidity)	Measures relative humidity by indicating the lowering in temperature of a wet-bulb (bulb wrapped in moist cloth) thermometer compared to a dry-bulb thermometer. The rate of evaporation, and therefore cooling of the wet-bulb, depends on the relative humidity. See PSYCHROMETER; METEOROLOGICAL INSTRUMENTS.
	Seismograph (for Earth vibration)	Records the wave motions of Earth as an elastic body by means of an inverted pendulum supported on a stable platform. See SEISMOGRAPH; WAVE AND WAVE MOTION.
	Tensiometer (for tension)	Measures SURFACE TENSION of a liquid. A balance linked to a platinum ring determines the force required to break a liquid film of known area and perimeter. See TENSION.
	Viscosimeter (for viscosity)	Measures the VISCOSITY of a liquid. A cylinder is suspended by a fiber or rod within another concentric rotating cylinder. The space between the two is filled with the liquid whose viscosity is to be determined. The deflection of the inner cylinder is proportional to the liquid's viscosity and the angular velocity of the outer cylinder, and inversely proportional to the thickness of the liquid layer. See VISCOUS FLOW.

INSULATION, ELECTRICAL: a material used to stop flow of electric current or prevent electrical losses. It is a non-conducting material—*i.e.* a dielectric. Air provides good electrical insulation; air gaps are used to prevent arcing (jumping of current from one conductor to another); another frequently used gas is sulfur hexafluoride. Solid dielectrics (INSULATORS) are mica, ceramics, glass, plastics, and paper. Liquid dielectrics include salt-free water, many hydrocarbon compounds, and synthetics such as the silicone oils. The porcelain parts on cross-country power lines are electrical insulators, as are the rubber coatings on electrical wiring and the paper wrappings on radio capacitors and resistors. Each of these materials offers a specific combination of properties, in addition to electrical insulating ability, that fits it for its job. Because electrical insulation involves several kinds of protection—*e.g.* prevention of arcing, tracking, and power loss—several different factors are used to evaluate insulating ability. Most frequently used is *dielectric strength*, a measure of the maximum voltage a material can stand without breakdown, in terms of v/mil or kv/cm. Also used are *dielectric constant*, defined as the ratio of the capacity of a condenser filled with the material under test to one "filled" with a vacuum; *dielectric loss*, the amount of energy dissipated (as heat, or in other ways) when a material is subjected to an alternating electric current; and *specific resistance* or *resistivity*, the resistance a material offers to passage of electric current, generally measured in ohm-centimeters.—*A. R. G.*

INSULATION, THERMAL: material used to prevent flow or transfer of heat. It may be used to keep heat in (*i.e.* to prevent heat loss) or keep heat out. It may be a non-conductor of heat or a reflector of heat. Thus, a reflective coating on a roof will help keep heat out of the house, while a mineral wool "blanket" in the ceiling can be used to prevent transfer of heat in either direction. Like electrical insulators, heat insulators may be solids, liquids, or gases. Air is one of the best thermal insulators and accounts largely for the insulating ability of wool-like and foamed materials; air trapped between the wool fibers and in the cells of foamed materials does the insulating. Because of the wide range of temperatures involved

Asbestos-wool fibers, blown pneumatically into the space within walls of this house, will provide an efficient barrier of insulation summer and winter. (*Johns-Manville Corp.*)

in heat insulation, many materials have been developed for the purpose, *e.g.* foamed plastics for low temperatures, as in the walls of refrigerators, and foamed or solid ceramics including bricks for high temperatures, as in furnaces. The primary measure of the thermal insulating ability of a material is its *thermal conductivity* or *k* factor (the amount of heat that will pass through a given volume of material at a given temperature differential in a given period of time). It is measured in calories/cm/sec/°C or Btu/hr/ft²/°F/ft. Also frequently used is the heat transfer coefficient, measured in terms of calories or Btu.—*A. R. G.*

INSULATOR, ELECTRICAL: a component of electrical apparatus fabricated of a material which inhibits or prevents the passage of electric current. Ceramic insulators employed to suspend radio aerials, and the glass insulators mounted on telephone poles to suspend telephone and electrical power lines, are common examples. Materials in general when considered electrically are classified as CONDUCTORS, SEMICONDUCTORS, and insulators. Metals are examples of conductors; glass, ceramics, rubber, and similar non-conductors are employed to form insulators. Semi-conductors, *e.g.* silicon and germanium, are between the two extremes in their conductivity. See INSULATION, ELECTRICAL.—*G. S.*

INSULIN: a hormone produced by the beta cells of the pancreas. It is a comparatively small protein (molecular wt 6,000). Its principal action appears to be to increase the rate at which blood sugar (glucose) enters muscle cells to be metabolized. This action of insulin at the cell surface is opposed in an unknown way by the action of a protein hormone produced by the posterior pituitary gland and a sterol hormone produced by the adrenal cortex (see ADRENOCORTICAL HORMONE). In proper balance, these three hormones regulate the rate at which blood glucose is made available to muscle cells. The continued absence of insulin from the blood due to pancreatic malfunction leads to a clinically recognized disorder known as diabetes mellitus, characterized by a high concentration of glucose in the blood (hyperglycemia), an inordinately large urine volume (diabetes), and the appearance of substantial quantities of glucose in the urine (mellituria). Overproduction of insulin by a diseased pancreas or the injection of too large an amount during treatment will cause a fall in the blood sugar concentration (hypoglycemia); this if untreated (by the administration of glucose) may result in convulsions due to failure of the brain to receive enough glucose. Diabetes mellitus can be produced in experimental animals by surgical removal of the pancreas or by injection of alloxan, a compound which selectively destroys the beta cells of the pancreas.

Owing to its small molecular size and its ready availability in highly purified, crystalline form, insulin has been much studied as an example of a protein. It was the first protein in which the complete sequence of amino acids was determined and the first protein to be synthesized in the laboratory. Beef insulin contains 51 amino-acid residues (groups) in two chains held together by sulfur-to-sulfur linkages; insulins from other species are chemically similar but not identical. Insulin was discovered by the Canadian scientists F. G. Banting (1891–1941) and C. H. Best (1899–   ), working under J. J. R. Macleod (1876–1935). For this discovery, Banting and Macleod were awarded the 1923 Nobel prize in physiology. See also GLYCOLYSIS.—*R. K. C.*

INTEGRAL EQUATION: an equation in which an unknown function occurs under an integral sign. Such equations arise in every branch of mathematical physics. One of the earliest examples was formulated and solved by the Norwegian mathematician Niels Henrik Abel in 1823. The problem he posed was the following: Suppose a particle slides down a smooth curve, starting from rest at some point P. The time of descent from P to an arbitrary point will, of course, depend on the shape of the curve. If this time of descent is a known function of position, can the curve be determined? One can show that if y measures the elevation above the horizontal, $s(y)$ the arc length along the curve, and $y = 0$ is the final elevation above the horizontal, then the time of descent $T(y)$ is given by

$$T(y) = \int_0^y \frac{ds(z)}{dz} [2g(y - z)]^{-1/2} \, dz$$

Here $T(y)$ is a prescribed function and $s(y)$ an unknown function. One can solve this integral equation for $ds(y)/dy$, and one finds

$$ds(y)/dy = (\sqrt{2g}/\pi) \, (d/dy) \int_0^y T(z) \, [y - z]^{-1/2} \, dz$$

The mathematician Eric Ivar Fredholm (1866–1927) studied a certain class of integral equations, which were named in his honor. The Fredholm integral equation of the first kind has the general form

$$g(x) = \int_a^b K(x, t) \, f(t) \, dt$$

and the equation of the second kind has the form

$$f(x) = g(x) + \int_a^b K(x, t) \, f(t) \, dt$$

In both cases $f(x)$ is the unknown function, $g(x)$ and $K(x, t)$ are known functions, and $K(x, t)$ is known as the kernel of the equation.

In some physical problems integral equations arise naturally; in others the problem can be reformulated as an integral equation. For example, in the study of vibrating strings one encounters the differential equation

$$\frac{d^2y}{dx^2} + \lambda\rho(x) y = 0$$

subject to the boundary conditions $y(0) = 0$, $y(L) = 0$. Here y represents the amplitude of the vibration, $\rho(x)$ the linear density of the string, L the length of the string, and $\sqrt{\lambda}$ the frequency of vibration. The boundary conditions indicate that the end points of the string are held fixed. This problem can be reformulated in terms of the integral equation

$$y(x) = \lambda \int_0^L K(x, t) \, y(t) \, dt$$

with a suitable kernel $K(x, t)$. This is a Fredholm integral equation of the second kind, but the function $g(x)$ outside the integral is missing. One advantage of this formulation, in contrast to the differential equation, is that the boundary conditions are automatically built into the equation and do not have to be stated separately.

This is a type of equation that arises in many applications. One obvious solution is $y = 0$, but this solution is evidently not of much interest. In general such an equation can have nonzero solutions only when λ takes on certain special values known as characteristic values. These represent the possible frequencies at which such a string can vibrate. In many physical problems it is essential that these characteristic values be known. In particular in many engineering problems they have to be known for design purposes. One can obtain numerical estimates of these values directly from the integral equation.—*H. Ho.*

INTEGRATION: see CALCULUS, DIFFERENTIAL AND INTEGRAL.

INTELLIGENCE: see ANIMAL INTELLIGENCE.

INTENSITY: the energy output of a source of heat, sound, light, or other radiation. Intensity is commonly measured in terms of the amount of energy that passes through a unit area perpendicular to the direction of energy flow per unit time. Accordingly, typical units of intensity are watts/cm², calories/sec/cm², and lumens/cm². The intensity of a point source of radiation falls off with the square of the distance from the source, according to the inverse-square law.

Intensities may also be measured relative to some fixed intensity level. Such comparisons are usually made using a logarithmic scale to give intensity levels in decibels: $db = 10 \log_{10} I/I_0$, where I is the intensity being measured and I_0 is the reference level. The advantage of this system is that it corresponds fairly closely to the response of human sense organs to changes in intensity level, which is logarithmic rather than linear.—*E. M. R.*

INTERFERENCE: the interaction of two wave motions, *e.g.* two beams of light or two sets of ripples or other water waves, when they cross one another at a glancing angle (see WAVE AND WAVE MOTION). The waves reinforce each other at certain points and counteract or annihilate each other at other points. The amplitudes (maximum displacements) of the interfering waves combine in an algebraic fashion and give values varying from the sum of the amplitudes to their difference, which will be zero for interfering waves of equal amplitude. This interaction gives rise to such unexpected effects as two light beams combining to give areas of darkness or two sound waves combining with the result that no sound at all is produced. Of course, the effects of interference are observed only over relatively small areas.

The vibration of a violin string is a simple example of so-called standing waves (see WAVE, STANDING), which result from the interference between the wave traveling up the string from the bow toward the nut, and the wave that is reflected back down the string. This interference effect occurs also in

Interference between two trains of waves in water: The two wave sources (*bottom*) acting in phase each generate circular waves. These waves interact to yield a pattern of radial lines of maximum and minimum activity. (*Berenice Abbott*)

organ pipes, which operate on the principle of standing waves formed in air. The point of no motion in a standing wave is called a node, and the area of maximum motion is called an antinode or loop.

For waves to interfere, they must be of the same wavelength (or very nearly so), and hence of equal frequency (or very nearly so). This means that there will be some definite phase relation between them, so that they will be accurately "in step" or "out of step" over a period of time or in a particular region of space. These conditions are easily fulfilled by water waves and some long electromagnetic waves such as radio waves. The conditions are more difficult to meet for light waves, however, because of the complicated mechanism of the production of light, by the acceleration of electrons in atoms, molecules, or solids. Thus devices employing the interference of LIGHT usually have a single, primary source, and the light from it is divided by an appropriate optical technique to give two secondary sources. Interference effects can then be produced between the light beams from the two secondary sources. Devices called INTERFEROMETERS work on this principle and are employed in measuring very short lengths or measuring longer lengths very accurately. If white light, which contains all colors or wavelengths, is used as a source, then colored effects may be produced as a result of interference between two beams. The interference may be destructive for some wavelengths but additive for others, so that colored effects are noted, *e.g.* in the reflections from thin soap bubbles or from oil films floating on water or wet pavement. The colors of insects' wings are due to multiple interference effects.

Interference techniques are used in the optical industry in measuring the flatness of surfaces. In another type of application, so-called interference filters employ the wavelength-sensitive properties of this phenomenon so that only a narrow range of color is transmitted. Interference effects can also be produced in polarized light, giving a combination of the phenomena of interference and polarization.—*S. S. B.*

INTERFEROMETER: any of several devices for measuring the wavelengths of light, radio, or sound waves, or for obtaining wave velocities, precise length measurements, directions, and other information in terms of wavelengths (see WAVE AND WAVE MOTION). This is accomplished by comparing the phases of two or more beams of coherent waves superposed one upon the other. To be coherent, individual beams must be essentially of the same frequency and must have a definitely fixed phase relationship with each other. To achieve this condition, all the beams must originate from the same source, but may be split and sent into different paths by suitable devices such as semi-transparent mirrors. When recombined at the detector, the intensity of the superposed waves will be increased where they are in phase and decreased where they are out of phase (see INTERFERENCE). A. A. Michelson and E. W. Morley used such a device, now called a *Michelson interferometer,* to show that there was no change in the velocity of light traveling either in the same direction or in the direction perpendicular to that of the earth with respect to the ether (the hypothetical substance through which light was supposed to travel). By showing that ether does not exist, they laid the foundation for the modern theory of relativity (see MICHELSON-MORLEY EXPERIMENT). Other forms of interferometers are used to achieve extremely precise measurements. The refractive index of a transparent substance (useful for understanding molecular structure) is determined by a *Rayleigh interferometer,* which passes a beam of light through the substance and compares the phase with a beam traveling the same distance through air. This procedure measures the decrease in

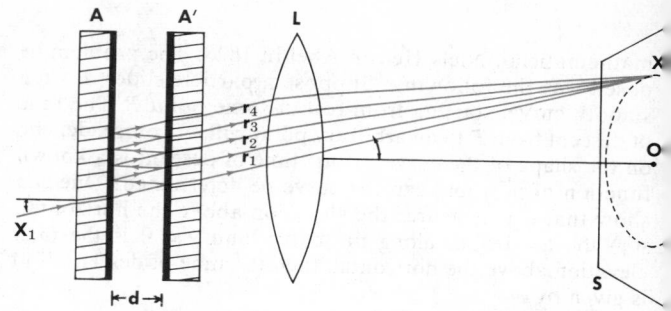

Fabry-Perot interferometer consists of two parallel pieces of plate glass, A, A', lightly silvered on their interior surfaces, at a distance d from each other. Beam of light from X_1 passing through A is partially transmitted through A' and partially reflected by silvered surface of A'. The result is a number of parallel beams (r_1, r_2, r_3, r_4 . . .), each of which has traveled an optical path longer than the preceding transmitted beam by an unvarying quantity. The parallel rays pass through lens system L, which focuses them at point X_2. When the difference in beam paths is a whole multiple of the beam's wave length, constructive interference results. If X_1 is a point source of monochromatic light, a diffraction pattern of concentric circles whose center is O will be seen on screen SS.

the velocity of light in the substance, which is shown as a change in phase at the interferometer detector. Interferometers also measure ordinary lengths, wavelengths and separations of spectral lines, the diameter of stars, and the separation between double stars. A thin-film form of interferometer, such as the *Fabry-Perot interferometer,* can select very accurately a desired color of light, the wavelength being twice the film thickness. The same principle is used in films coated on lenses to reduce reflections. In both acoustics and radio astronomy, interferometers give accurate indications of the direction of the source from which a signal has been detected. The most recent application of the interferometer has been in the optical maser, where it is used to generate an extremely intense and coherent beam of light.—*I. R.*

INTERMEDIATES: chemical compounds especially useful for preparation of other substances. Thus acetic acid has certain intrinsic uses, but it is mostly made in order to manufacture something else from it (see ACETATES). The term is used largely in the dyestuffs and pharmaceutical industries, where the final desired product is usually the result of a long series of consecutive chemical preparations. Some intermediates are not even isolated as such but are used immediately when formed in a reaction mixture (see Grignard reagents in ORGANOMETALLIC COMPOUNDS).—*Ru. M.*

INTERNAL COMBUSTION: one of two general methods used by engines (also called prime movers or power plants) to convert the chemical energy in a fuel to mechanical energy. The substances used for combustion (*e.g.* gasoline and air) are also used as the working substances; *i.e.* they expand against a piston or through a nozzle to perform useful work. In this respect the internal-combustion system differs from an external-combustion system, such as a gas or coal steam-power plant, in which heat must be transferred from the gas or coal (the combustion substance) and the water being converted to steam (the working substance). See ENGINE. In an internal-combustion system, the mechanical energy derived from the combustion of chemical fuel is transferred from the engine either by a rotating shaft (*e.g.* the propeller shaft of a piston-type aircraft engine) or by the kinetic energy of an effluent jet of combustion gases (as in the turbojet, a type of gas turbine). The particular advantages of internal-combustion engines are light weight and operating flexibility: the engines are capable of a wide range of speeds and, at constant speed, can deliver from zero to full power in a matter of seconds with a single control. These features have made possible 20th-cent. modes of land, sea, and air transportation.

Three types of action are common to all types of internal combustion: (1) compression of an air-fuel mixture or (as in the diesel) of air alone; (2) ignition and combustion of the mixture, or (as in the diesel) injection of fuel and ignition and combustion of the resulting mixture; (3) expansion, the first step in transferring energy out of the system to perform useful work. Internal combustion may be carried out by any of several series of devices, so long as the three basic processes of compression, combustion, and expansion are performed. Compression and expansion are best considered together (below). *Combustion* may take place in a closed combustion chamber or sealed volume by igniting a mixture of air and fuel with a spark; this method, spark ignition, is used in most automobile engines. In the diesel engine, fuel is injected into a closed combustion chamber containing air that has been heated by compression; the fuel ignites spontaneously because of the high temperature of the air. This is called compression ignition. The second general class of combustors is the steady-flow type in which air enters at one end, fuel is spray-injected into the air, and combustion proceeds continuously after the fuel is once ignited, much as in a bunsen burner. The hot gases then flow out of the combustor, carrying kinetic (mechanical) energy. Gas turbines utilize this method of combustion.

Compression in the internal-combustion system requires a mechanical-energy input to the working substance; *expansion* (following combustion) produces mechanical-energy output and a portion of this energy is utilized to achieve compression, leaving the residual or net mechanical energy of expansion to do useful work. There are four general classes of compressors and expanders:

(1) A piston may be used in a cylinder; this device is called a *reciprocator,* since reciprocating motion is required. Compression, combustion, and expansion are all carried out in a single reciprocator with appropriate valving to charge and scavenge the cylinder. Reciprocating motion is converted to rotary motion by means of a connecting rod-and-crank mechanism; this combination, called a reciprocating engine, represents the most common type of internal combustion, most familiarly seen in all types of automotive engines both Otto and diesel (see MOTOR VEHICLE). (2) Functionally similar to the reciprocator, but employing rotary rather than reciprocating motion, is the *rotary-displacement compressor* (or *expander*). A rotary engine may have a separate compressor and expander with a steady-flow combustor between, or a composite unit for all three processes. History has proved rotary-displacement engines very difficult to develop, principally because of the difficulty in sealing the system against gas leakage. There would be advantages to this kind of engine because rotary motion is developed without the necessity of a crank, with resulting high speed and high power-to-weight ratio; for these reasons a continuing effort is being made to develop this type of engine. (3) The *turbomachine,* used in the gas turbine, compresses (with the turbocompressor) and expands (with the turboexpander) dynamically by forcing a substance to flow over closely spaced foils. Turbocompressors and turbo-expanders are classified according to the general direction of the flow: axial flow if it is parallel to the axis of rotation, radial if it is perpendicular to the axis of rotation, and mixed flow if it is a combination. The compressor and the expander are separate; thus continuous flow through each component is maintained. (4) The fourth class of compressors and ex-

panders involves no moving parts but consists of a DIFFUSER, which converts the kinetic energy of a flow stream to pressure (ram compression). The air at increased pressure enters the combustion chamber, where it is mixed with the injected fuel. The air-fuel mixture burns, and the expanded gases are then ejected through the discharge nozzle. An engine that uses the diffuser/steady-flow combustor/nozzle combination is the ram-jet engine. A ram-jet aircraft must be moving at a high rate of speed, so that air has high kinetic energy with respect to the engine. Ram compression can then occur, followed by combustion, nozzle expansion, and jet thrust.

If an engine is designed to use two different methods of compression or expansion in series, it is called a *compound engine.* An example is the free-piston engine, now under development, in which combustion is by compression ignition, compression is achieved by two reciprocators in series, and expansion is first by reciprocator and then by turbomachine. Another example is a turbo-supercharged reciprocating engine, which carries out the first part of the compression in a turbomachine and the second part in a reciprocator; the same devices are used in the inverse order for expansion. In this sense a turbojet aircraft engine operating at high speed is a compound engine, since part of the compression occurs in the form of diffusion of ram air and part by turbocompressor. The expansion occurs first by the turboexpander and finally by the jet nozzle. In the broadest sense a non-air-breathing chemical rocket engine is an internal-combustion engine. The necessary substances for combustion are all carried internally to make the engine independent of Earth's atmosphere, but the compression, combustion, and expansion are analogous to those in air-breathing engines. See AIRCRAFT PROPULSION; DIESEL ENGINE; GAS TURBINE; PRIME MOVER; ROCKET; SPACE TRAVEL; STEAM ENGINE; TURBINE.—*H. E. J.*

Internal combustion in the space age: Hot, expanding gases pass through these exhaust nozzles of the Bell X-15 rocket engine, giving the aircraft thrust. The chemical rocket represents one of the newest forms of the internal-combustion principle. (*North American Aviation*)

INTERNAL ENERGY: the energy content of a system arising mainly from vibrational and rotational motions within its molecules. An increase in the structural complexity of a molecule increases internal energy. The internal energy in a system can in many instances be determined from spectroscopic data by the use of quantum theory.—*G. W. M.*

INTERNATIONAL DATE LINE: see TIME.

INTERNATIONAL GEOPHYSICAL YEAR (IGY): an international scientific effort, the largest of its kind ever undertaken, which explored Earth and its environment as interrelated physical systems in the 18-month period July 1, 1957, to Dec. 31, 1958. This "year" was chosen because during 1957–58 the 11-yr sunspot cycle approached maximum. Sunspots (see SUN) were discovered by Galileo over 300 yr ago, and in recent times have been related to solar flares and other giant solar disturbances; these, in turn, have major effects on Earth, *e.g.* auroral displays (northern and southern lights), ionospheric blackouts, magnetic storms, and cosmic-ray changes. Furthermore, as the source of life on Earth and Earth's nearest star, the Sun holds the key to many geophysical problems. Thus observation of the Sun on a worldwide basis during intense solar activity promised new and far-reaching discoveries, and similar cooperation in other scientific fields was indicated. Three major areas, encompassing thirteen geophysical disciplines, were the focus of IGY: (1) the solid Earth (seismology, gravity, and geodesy); (2) heat and water (meteorology, oceanography, and glaciology); (3) Sun-Earth relationships and the physics of the upper atmosphere (cosmic rays, ionospheric physics, aurora, airglow, geomagnetism, solar activity, and launchings of rockets and satellites). Although it will be years before all the data collected during IGY are analyzed and collated, and years before some projects begun during IGY reach fruition, many notable advances in science and engineering have already been registered, and sign posts have been set up pointing to many more such advances.

Earth: The programs in seismology, gravity, and latitude and longitude ranged from the ocean depths and Earth's interior to the surface crustal rocks and mountain tops. Seismic expeditions were undertaken in the mountains of S America and in unexplored regions of Antarctica. Among notable discoveries were ice-free valleys in Antarctica, one of which contains a fresh-water lake with abundant plant life; a 2,500-ft island under the antarctic ice; and new evidence, through seismic and gravitational measurements in the Andes, that mountains "float" in Earth's crust much as icebergs float in the ocean.

Special seismographs, sensitive to surface waves of about 400 sec (such waves are generated only by earthquakes of the very longest duration), were set up at observatories from Hawaii to Fiji and from Bermuda to Antarctica. Much use was made of the extensometer, or strain seismograph, to show accumulated earth-strain measurements. Data from this instrument are expected ultimately to provide a basis for earthquake prediction with consequent saving of life and property. Seismic observations show non-uniformities and regional geographic differences in the mantle, or subcrustal zone of Earth, comparable to variations (flat plains to mountain peaks) of Earth's crust. Seismology and gravity studies on sea and land provided new information about Earth tides that indicate the planet is not as solid or rigid as previously believed.

Scientists of 29 countries at 45 worldwide IGY stations determined more precisely Earth's latitudes and longitudes, making possible better and safer air and sea navigation and more accurate satellite and missile launchings.

Heat and Water: The oceans, covering 71% of Earth's surface, were explored systematically by more than 25 IGY nations. Studies were made of the relation of ocean temperatures to climate, the oceans as an important and abundant

Snow cave at Kainan Bay, Antarctica, is investigated by IGY glaciologist. Such caves, formed by wind and movement of ice, are source of information on the stratigraphy and textures of ice and snow. (*National Academy of Sciences/IGY*)

Mapping of Antarctica including determination of contours on land masses beneath the ice cap, was an important feature of IGY. Survey party here is using the tellurometer, an electronic distance-measuring device. (*Nat. Science Foundation*)

food source, ocean currents and tides, and the disposal of radioactive wastes in ocean waters. It was learned that there is an exchange of waters between northern and southern hemispheres coinciding with the seasons. An undersea mountain range was discovered in the Arctic Ocean. Other discoveries were a counter-current under the Gulf Stream; a river inside the ocean along the equator from the W Pacific to Panama that transports a thousand times as much water as the Mississippi; ocean tides such as the annual tide, the 14-month tide, and even an 18-month tide, which might aptly be called the IGY tide; and streams of deep water in some instances flowing in opposite directions to the known currents directly above them. A major practical benefit of IGY oceanography was the discovery that millions of square miles of ocean bottom in the SE Pacific contain loose nodules of manganese, nickel, and cobalt mixed with copper, valued conservatively at $500,000/mi^2.

IGY research in glaciology prompted the first comprehensive, coordinated program in the U. S. A. on the study of ice and snow. A World Data Center, still operating, was established giving all nations a chance to share in glaciological knowledge obtained during IGY and from subsequent research. Programs by as many as 30 nations were carried out in the arctic and sub-arctic regions, the temperate and equatorial zones, Asia, S America, and Africa; and 12 nations joined in exploring the antarctic ice. It was found that the ice of Antarctica alone, if melted, would raise the ocean level by some 200–300 ft; the south pole, almost 10,000 ft above sea level, has 9,000 ft of ice beneath it. Antarctica may have frozen fiords or vast frozen inland lakes and is not, therefore, the solid land mass it was believed to be. New knowledge was gained concerning the formation and melting of ice and snow in the western mountain ranges of the U. S. A. that could aid in hydroelectric development and should provide improved estimates of summer water supplies so essential for agriculture in these areas.

Fundamental mechanisms of weather are better understood as a consequence of IGY studies in meteorology carried on simultaneously in the southern and northern hemispheres. The IGY rawinsonde network also has advanced meteorological research. Rawinsonde is the technical name for measuring wind movements, temperature, pressure, and humidity by means of radio-equipped sounding balloons. These measurements provide advance notice of violent atmospheric disturbances such as storms, permitting precautions to save life and property. During IGY, several nations including the U. S. A. pioneered in stratospheric meteorology with high-reaching balloons that made possible the charting of atmospheric circulation at levels in excess of 100,000 ft— the zone in which the latest type of rocket planes can fly and in which the nuclear debris (*e.g.* strontium^{90}) released by nuclear-weapons tests travels. IGY research in meteorology revealed strontium^{90} deposits in antarctic snow: evidence that there is no barrier between the northern-hemisphere testing grounds and areas deep in the southern hemisphere. A Weather Central for the exchange and transmission of antarctic weather data was established on the frozen continent, staffed by meteorologists from Argentina, France, and the U. S. S. R. This central exchange made possible operational analysis and forecasting, which increased the safety of air flights necessary for the logistical support of interior antarctic stations.

Sun-Earth Relationships and Upper Atmosphere Physics: IGY provided to solar astronomers the most detailed history of the Sun ever compiled, thanks to the greatest cycle of sunspot activity ever observed. A day-to-day, hour-to-hour, and sometimes minute-to-minute cooperation in solar observa-

tions and reporting was made possible by the World Days and Special World Intervals communications arrangements involving all participating countries. Never before had the Sun been so intensively photographed.

IGY provided new knowledge of cosmic rays, electrically charged particles of exceedingly high energy (100 million to 100 billion electron volts) that bombard Earth from all directions. The search for both their source and the keys to their behavior is one of the major problems of modern physics; and while these objectives were not entirely reached by IGY research, important discoveries were made concerning cosmic-ray behavior and origin, among them the fact that the cosmic-ray equator deviates systematically from the geomagnetic equator, suggesting important magnetic fields of extraterrestrial origin that alter the paths of incoming primary cosmic-ray particles. Cosmic-ray experiments also revealed the existence of "soft" radiation in the high atmosphere. It appears that incoming auroral particles create x-rays, demonstrating correlation between the presence of x-ray radiation and solar, magnetic, and auroral activity. One consequence of IGY research in this field is knowledge that may lead to new methods of propulsion for use in space and new methods for generating thermonuclear energy.

Aurora is the only visible manifestation of incoming particles from the Sun. Airglow is the weak greenish light that results from the storage during the day of energy from the Sun; it is released at night but is not always as clearly visible as auroral displays. These phenomena affect communications, particularly radar reception. IGY research has made possible the prediction of auroras—a vital contribution to national defense, military strategy, and airline safety.

Disturbances in the ionosphere, the electrified regions of the upper atmosphere where free electrons act as a mirror for radio waves from the ground, affect radio communications by causing fade-out or static. Knowledge gained during IGY of ionospheric structure by use of rockets, balloons, and satellites will aid in the future elimination of interference from this natural sound barrier. Another outgrowth of IGY upper-atmosphere research was the beginning of intensive study of "whistlers," whistlelike sounds at very low radio frequencies which were taped by rocket and satellite equipment at the farthest reaches of the atmosphere. IGY research also proved the existence of the "electro-jet," an equatorial electric current previously contemplated only in theory.

Knowledge in all areas of upper-atmosphere physics as well as in the other two major divisions of IGY research was tremendously advanced by rockets and satellites. Sputnik I, launched by the U. S. S. R., Oct. 4, 1957, proved highly valuable as a tool for ionosphere research. During IGY six satellites were launched successfully, three by the U. S. S. R. and three by the U. S. A. They made possible scientific measurements and observations over a large portion of Earth during a long period at altitudes previously unattainable. From IGY satellite research came an accurate description of Earth's cloud cover, the discovery of the Van Allen radiation belts, and new information about the shape of Earth. Substantial engineering advances associated with spacecraft were also made, including development of solar energy supplies, heat- and radiation-resistant storage elements, highly sensitive tape recorders, new advances in plastics and ceramics, and improved chemical fuels for rockets.

Planning and Political Aspects: The proposal for IGY originated with a group of scientists in 1951, and was introduced by them at a meeting that year of the International Council of Scientific Unions (ICSU), their principal international organization. The proposal was referred to the various scientific groups belonging to ICSU and was favorably received

tion, in which 25 nations have participated, has uncovered important new sources of seafood and is expected to yield long-range benefits for both science and world economy. Twelve nations, including the United States and the Soviet Union, have joined in an Antarctic Research Program and have ratified a treaty that binds them to hold all territorial claims in abeyance for 30 yr, prohibits military activities and dumping of atomic wastes, and opens all antarctic stations to inspection by any participating power at any time. More than 60 countries are participating in the International Years of the Quiet Sun, studying solar activity at the minimum of the sunspot cycle. A World Weather Watch, whose concept grew out of proposals made by the United States in 1961, is under development by the World Meteorological Organization and its 126 member nations. This will establish an international system to bring the atmosphere of the globe under complete and continuous surveillance by means of weather satellites, giant computers, and high-speed communications. Scientists around the world are also taking part in the World Magnetic Survey, mapping Earth's magnetic field. Other major cooperative efforts include the International Upper Mantle Project to investigate development and structure of Earth's crust, the International Cooperative Investigations of the Tropical Atlantic, and the Cooperative Study of the Kuroshio Current south and southeast of Japan.

The United States is participating with 43 other countries in the International Biological Program (IBP), which will estimate the world's capacity to support life and determine how man

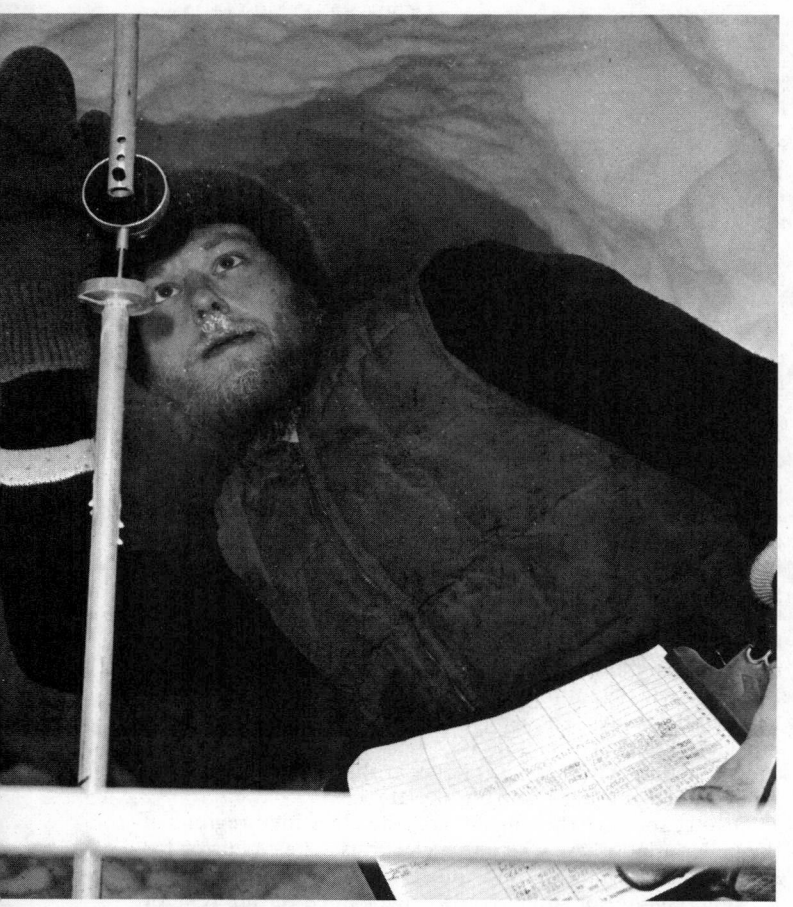

Closure rate of walls of snow mine beneath South Pole scientific station is measured by reading gages periodically. Glaciology was much enriched by IGY. (*Nat. Science Foundation*)

High-altitude rockets on Navy IGY research ship are readied for launching to gather solar radiation data during total solar eclipse of Oct. 12, 1958. Rockets carried instruments to heights of 140–150 mi. (*U. S. Navy*)

by them, and in 1953 ICSU established a special committee called the Comité Spécial de l'Année Géophysique Internationale (CSAGI) to develop and establish goals for the worldwide research program. So conceived, IGY developed as a non-governmental operation, yet with support of the governments of participating nations. Though each country had its own IGY program, and there was no over-all administering body, IGY was marked by international cooperation. (A precedent for such cooperation was set by the International Polar Years, 1882–3 and 1932–3, in which many nations worked together to study phenomena of the polar regions.) More than 60,000 scientists from 66 nations joined in IGY research and observation activities at 4,000 stations covering the planet from pole to pole. In the U. S. A. the National Academy of Sciences established a National Committee of IGY to plan the U. S. program. The National Science Foundation, as the Federal agency with major responsibility for support of general scientific research, was asked by the Academy to secure and administer the necessary Federal funds. Congress, in response to a petition from the NSF, appropriated $41,000,000 for IGY. In 1958 CSAGI extended IGY for another year under the name of International Geophysical Cooperation—1959.

International Cooperation Since IGY. Cooperation among nations since 1959 has extended to almost every field of science. In 1960 the International Indian Ocean Expedition was established to study that relatively unknown body of water whose 28 million mi^2 cover over 14% of Earth's surface. The expedi-

World-wide network of Baker-Nunn cameras, such as the one above, was set up during IGY for satellite tracking. Orbit of satellite can be calculated on basis of photos taken at three different locations simultaneously. (*Smithsonian Astrophysical Observatory/ National Academy of Sciences*)

can more efficiently manage his environment. The United Nations Educational, Scientific and Cultural Organization (UNESCO) has sponsored the International Hydrological Decade (1965–1975), which will establish a worldwide network of stations to measure and track water, and to study expansion of water supplies and flood and drought control. The U. S. A.'s National Aeronautics and Space Administration has agreements with 69 nations for programs in space exploration, including the launching of foreign satellites and the inclusion in U. S. satellites of experiments developed by scientists of other countries. Under U. S. sponsorship, the Communications Satellite Corporation established an international consortium, now numbering 46 nations, for the development and use of a communications network expected to achieve global coverage via telecommunications satellites by 1968.

Future goals for scientific cooperation among nations include programs for earthquake forecasting and damage assessment, science education, international scientific information cooperation, and a multi-disciplinary global effort to narrow the gap between technologically advanced and underdeveloped nations. In 1966, the UN General Assembly unanimously approved a treaty binding all signatory nations to explore the moon only for peaceful purposes and prohibiting the placing of weapons of mass destruction in orbit around Earth or on celestial bodies, including the Moon. It appears likely that international cooperation, which had a great beginning in IGY, will continue to grow.—*L. L.*

INTERPOLATION: the process of finding an intermediate value of a mathematical function from a set of known values; when used in connection with a table of values of the function, it may be described as a method of reading between the lines of the table. In more precise language, we are concerned with a function $y = f(x)$ whose values $y_0, y_1, \ldots, y_n$ are known for $x_0, x_1, \ldots, x_n$. Interpolation replaces $f(x)$ with a simpler function $g(x)$, which has the same values as $f(x)$ at $x_0, x_1, \ldots, x_n$ and from which it is easy to calculate other values. In elementary mathematics, interpolation is almost always linear. As an illustration, consider finding the logarithm of 3627, using a four-place logarithm table. The logarithm of this number is not in the table, but the logarithms of 3620 and 3630 are. Thus we find log 3630 = 3.5599, and log 3620 = 3.5587. Now we assume that the change in the logarithm is uniform for uniform change in the number. Thus, since a change of 10 in the number produces a change of .0012 in the logarithm, we assume that a change of 1 in the number will produce ¹⁄₁₀ of the change in the logarithm or .00012. Then a change of 7 in the number will produce a change of ⁷⁄₁₀ of the change in the logarithm or ⁷⁄₁₀ of .0012, which is .00084. We conclude that the logarithm is increased by .00084 from 3.5587 and becomes 3.5595 (to four decimal places). The assumption made is that the differences in the values of the dependent variable are constant for constant differences of the independent variable. This is the basic characteristic of a straight line. Thus we have replaced the given function ($y = \log x$) by a straight line passing through the given values and have computed the intermediate value as lying on the straight line. This is usually close enough to the true value to be useful in elementary mathematics.

If linear interpolation is insufficient, other functions that will approximate the true value more exactly can be used. Such methods of interpolation are discussed in books on numerical analysis or on the CALCULUS OF FINITE DIFFERENCES.—*H. E. W.*

INTERSTELLAR DISTANCES: An astronomical unit (a.u.) is the distance from Earth to the Sun, 93 million mi. From the Sun to the nearest star, Alpha Centauri, is 2,300,000 a.u., or 25 trillion mi. For interstellar distances a more convenient unit is the light-year (lt-yr), the distance that light, at a speed of 186,000 mi/sec, travels in 1 yr—about 6 trillion mi. The five stars nearest the Sun are listed in the table; only the first and the last are visible to the naked eye. These distances are typical of those between a star and its nearest neighbors throughout most of our galaxy (the Milky Way system), whose diameter is about 100,000 lt-yr. Stars (with diameters of the order of a million miles) are huge compared to Earth, but are extremely tiny compared to interstellar distances; they are scattered relatively as widely as raindrops 50 to 100 mi apart.

THE FIVE NEAREST STARS

Star	Visual Magnitude	Distance (lt-yr)
Alpha Centauri	0.0	4.3
Barnard's star	9.5	6.0
Wolf 359	13.7	7.7
Lalande 21185	7.5	8.1
Sirius	−1.4	8.7

For the nearer stars, distances can be found by triangulation, the same method used by surveyors to measure distances to inaccessible points by sighting them from the two ends of a measured base line. In astronomy the base line is the diameter of Earth's orbit. As Earth moves from one side of its orbit to the other, the nearer stars appear to move slightly with respect to more distant ones. The angular motion (called *parallax*) is not large—for only two stars does it exceed ½″— but it can be measured for a few hundred stars. (See PARALLAX, STELLAR.) At a distance of 3.26 lt-yr a star has a parallax of 1″; this distance is therefore called a *parsec* and is the unit used in most astronomical work. For very distant objects, the kiloparsec (a thousand parsecs) and megaparsec (a million parsecs) are used.

For the more distant stars several less direct methods of determining distance are used: (1) Their cumulative motions across the sky over a term of years give some measure of their distances; the nearer a star, the greater its apparent angular motion for a certain actual speed. (2) From the spectrum of a star, its approximate *intrinsic* brightness (absolute magnitude) can be derived. Comparing this with its *apparent* brightness (apparent magnitude) yields the distance: the most distant it is, the fainter it will appear (see PARALLAX, SPECTROSCOPIC). (3) For many distant stars, the distance can be estimated by measuring the absorption of their light by the tenuous dust and gas (INTERSTELLAR MATTER) between the stars. The absorption effect increases with distance. See also ASTRONOMICAL DISTANCE UNITS.—*P. Me.*

INTERSTELLAR MATTER: gas and dust particles thinly distributed in the space between the stars, particularly in spiral and irregular galaxies. The beautiful emission NEBULAS, *e.g.* the Orion Nebula and the Eta Carinae Nebula, are luminous clouds which show the presence of gas in the vast spaces between the stars. Small amounts of tiny cosmic dust particles form dark nebulas—extended clouds seen as dark markings against the bright parts of the Milky Way. According to the best available estimates, interstellar gas is composed of 65% hydrogen atoms (by mass) and close to 35% helium; all other elements combined account for less than 0.1% of the total mass. Carbon, nitrogen, and oxygen head the list of remaining elements, followed by calcium, sodium, potassium, titanium, and then presumably all other chemical elements, *e.g.*

Horsehead Nebula in Orion is a cloud of cold gas and dust surrounded by hot gases which are being caused to glow by radiation from nearby stars. Such clouds of interstellar matter have dimensions measured in light-years. (*Mt Wilson*)

Dust particles in region of this star cluster, the Pleiades, scatter and reflect light of the stars, producing brushlike nebulosity seen here on long-exposure photograph. (In shorter exposure, p. 937, nebulosity is barely visible.) Dust not in vicinity of stars is poorly lighted and hence invisible except against background of bright nebulosity (e.g. Horsehead Nebula, *above*). Invisible clouds of interstellar matter may, however, be detected by means of radio telescope. (*Mt Wilson*)

iron. The gas accounts for no more than 2% of the total mass of our Milky Way system, but for the region near the Sun the mass of the interstellar gas may be as much as a fifth of the total. *Cosmic dust* is probably composed of simple molecular combinations of hydrogen with carbon, nitrogen, and oxygen, and with small admixtures of metals. The particles have diameters of the order of 1/100,000 in., and are probably slightly elongated. The mass of cosmic dust does not exceed 1% of that of the interstellar gas.

Interstellar gas can be investigated in a variety of ways. Clouds of it shine as emission nebulas when there are high-temperature stars either embedded in the cloud or very near it. Ultraviolet radiation from the star is absorbed by gas atoms in the nebula; these atoms lose their outer electrons (become ionized) as a result; the positively charged atomic remains attract other free electrons and occasional recombinations take place; the visible light of the nebulas is a by-product of the recombination process.

If a non-luminous interstellar gas cloud happens to be in the line of sight between Earth and a distant star, then the cloud may produce certain definite additional absorption lines in the spectrum of the star. These absorption lines may ordinarily be distinguished by their sharpness from absorption lines originating in the star; they are also displaced with respect to the other lines of the star's spectrum because the radial velocity (of approach or recession) of the cloud differs from that of the star. In some cases multiple interstellar absorption lines are found, indicating the presence of several interstellar clouds along the line of sight; as many as seven of these clouds have been found in the spectrum of one single distant star. See STELLAR SPECTRA.

Neutral atomic hydrogen produces a line in the radio spectrum at a wavelength of 21 cm. The total amount of 21-cm radiation reaching Earth is very small, but modern radio-detection techniques permit us to study it in great detail. Not only can radio telescopes detect the direction from which the

21-cm radiation is strongest, but the technique permits the astrophysicist to estimate the number of neutral hydrogen atoms along any given line of sight and—from precisely measured shifts away from the rest-frequency—to place the clouds at their most probable distances from Earth on the basis of their observed velocities of approach or recession. The pattern of distribution of these gas clouds in the Milky Way system is thus revealed. The recombination spectrum produced by the process described above is relatively strong in the radio range and can be readily detected at wavelengths between 1 and 50 cm.

One advantage of radio astronomical studies of the interstellar gas is that through them we reach parts of our Milky Way system which, optically, would be forever hidden from view. The radio waves produced anywhere in our system, or beyond, pass through the dust clouds of interstellar space, without suffering marked decreases in intensity. It appears that our whole Milky Way system is embedded in a very thin gaseous halo at very high temperature. Magnetic fields in the halo serve to accelerate the free electrons present, and radio radiation is thus produced, especially at meter wavelengths. Gas atoms accelerated by the large-scale magnetic fields of our galaxy are probably the most important source of cosmic rays.

Cosmic dust is a minor component of interstellar matter, but is readily observed in the dark nebulas. The southern Coalsack, next to the Southern Cross, is the finest example, although visible only from far southern latitudes. Examples in the northern hemisphere are the Horsehead Nebula in Orion and the Great Rift, a dark belt stretching from Cygnus to Scorpius and Sagittarius. Cosmic-dust particles produce a marked reddening in the light of stars viewed through them. Occasionally the dark nebulas become visible as reflection nebulas when they are seen in light reflected from nearby or embedded stars, *e.g.* the Pleiades Nebula. Not infrequently the light from stars observed behind a dark nebula is slightly polarized, which suggests that the particles of the cloud are somewhat elongated and aligned by galactic magnetic fields of force.

The bright and dark nebulas are of special interest for the study of stellar evolution, since the smaller and more compact of them are probably closer to the pre-stellar stage than any other observed object. Very small and compact dark nebulas—*globules*—are often observed as tiny dark markings of roundish shape.—*B. J. B.*

INTESTINE: in a broad sense, the entire ALIMENTARY CANAL; more specifically, the mid- and hind-portions of the canal. In general, the intestine is a long, more or less convoluted tube, the walls of which are lined internally by a mucous membrane and contain layers of muscle and of connective tissue. The intestine transports food material and digestive residues by means of muscular contractions known as PERISTALSIS; the intestinal cavity acts as a site for digestion and absorption. Digestion may involve enzymes secreted by the mucous membrane or by distinct glands that empty their secretion into the intestine. Absorption involves transport of the products of digestion from the cavity through the intestinal wall and into the blood or lymph.

In vertebrates, the intestine proper begins with the *duodenum*, at the pyloric end of the stomach. The semi-fluid stomach contents (chyme) are ejected into the duodenum, where they are mixed with secretions of the pancreas, liver, and intestinal glands. The pancreatic juice contains alkali, which neutralizes the hydrochloric acid of the stomach, and enzymes or precursors of enzymes, which digest starch (amylase), protein (trypsinogen and chymotrypsinogen), and

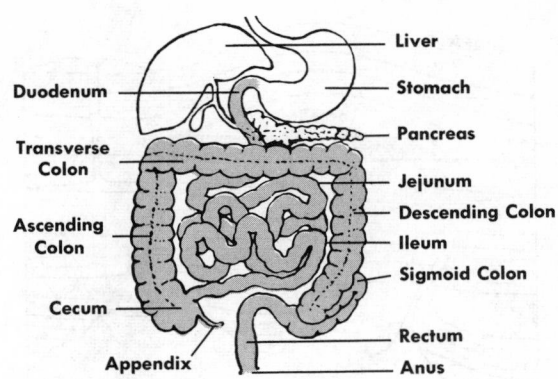

Human intestine begins with duodenum, ends with anus.

fat (lipase). The bile from the liver contains bile salts, which emulsify fats and render them accessible to the action of fat-splitting lipases. The intestinal juice contains amylase, lipase, polypeptidases, and other enzymes that complete the digestion of all foodstuffs, and enterokinase, which converts trypsinogen and chymotrypsinogen to their active forms, trypsin and chymotrypsin. Digestion continues and absorption begins in the next section (*jejunum*), and absorption is completed in the final portion (*ileum*) of the small intestine. The products of digestion of carbohydrate (sugars) and of protein (amino acids) are absorbed into the blood. The portion of fat that is

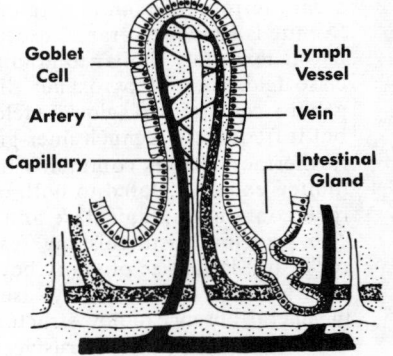

Internal wall of intestine is covered with closely packed projections called villi, which increase the total surface through which food substances can pass on their way to the blood. Diagram shows a single villus, which is about 1/40 in. long. Goblet cells secrete mucus. (*From Downes*)

hydrolyzed also enters the blood, but much fat is not hydrolyzed and passes directly into the lymphatic system.

Undigested residues, in the form of a thin fluid, pass from the ileum into the first part of the large intestine, the *colon*. Here ¾ or more of the water is absorbed, leaving a semisolid or solid residue, which is passed into the *rectum,* or terminal portion of the intestine. A good part of the mass of this residue is made up of bacteria, both living and dead. Distention of the walls of the rectum serves as a stimulus for defecation, a process which in many mammals is under voluntary control. The anus, or distal opening, of the alimentary canal is normally kept closed by two rings of muscle, or sphincters. See DIGESTION; EXCRETION.—*B. T. S.*

INTRUSIVE ROCK: IGNEOUS ROCK formed by the cooling of MAGMA which has intruded pre-existing rocks beneath the surface of Earth's crust. Any sizable mass of such rock is called a PLUTON. Intrusive rocks cool more slowly than extrusive rocks and are likely to develop relatively large individual crystal grains, easily discernible to the unaided eye; very coarse phases with grains as much as several feet in diameter are termed pegmatites. Like extrusive rocks, dark or basic intrusives owe their coloration to abundant ferromagnesian

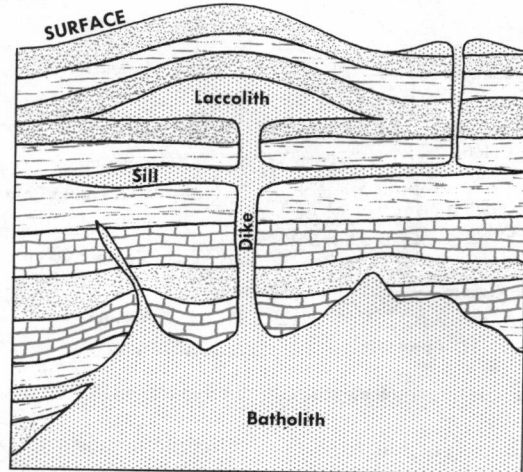

Intrusive rock structures: Dikes are wall-like igneous rock masses cutting across the structure of pre-existing rocks. Sills have the form of slabs, intruded parallel to the bedding or schistosity of the pre-existing rocks. A laccolith is a domelike structure formed where intruding magma pushed up overlying rock. Batholiths are large masses, originally at great depth, formed by fusion of older rocks.

minerals; conversely, light or acidic types owe their coloration to quartz, feldspars, and feldspathoids. GRANITE is the most abundant igneous rock; it contains quartz, feldspar, and a dark ferromagnesian mineral, usually hornblende or mica. Syenite is similar to granite except that it lacks quartz. GAB-BRO is texturally similar to granite but contains gray plagioclase feldspar and pyroxene; diabase is closely related to gabbro, containing plagioclase feldspar, augite, and magnetite, but it frequently is much finer-grained and porphyritic, and furthermore occurs commonly in sill- or dike-like bodies of limited extent. Related to both of the foregoing is diorite, a rock containing plagioclase and hornblende. (See BASALT.) The principal distinguishing features of intrusive igneous rocks are: large size of many bodies (see PLUTON), generally even granular texture, easily discernible mineral grains, and in general, absence of flow structure. The rounded or bouldery form of many exposed intrusives is due to their tendency to exfoliate into spheroidal forms. Granites and syenites are much in demand for structural and building stone; other intrusive rocks, particularly those rich in ferromagnesian minerals, are less used for ornamental purposes because of rusty stains produced by decomposition of these minerals. Crushed diabase is used in enormous quantities as ballast, as road metal, and as aggregate for concrete.—*J. Si.*

Dike in limestone near Franklin, N. J., was originally formed by magma intruding into limestone joints. The dike was exposed long afterward by quarrying. *(Jerome Wyckoff)*

INVERSION: in meteorology, a name given to a state of the atmosphere in which temperature increases with height. Inversions occur regularly very near the ground on clear calm nights and also in relatively shallow layers at greater heights, especially at the top of a fog layer and above stratus clouds. In anticyclones the surface inversion may extend to considerable heights; then it increases the hazards of ATMOSPHERIC POLLUTION by preventing the rise and dispersion of smoke and gases.—*O. G. S.*

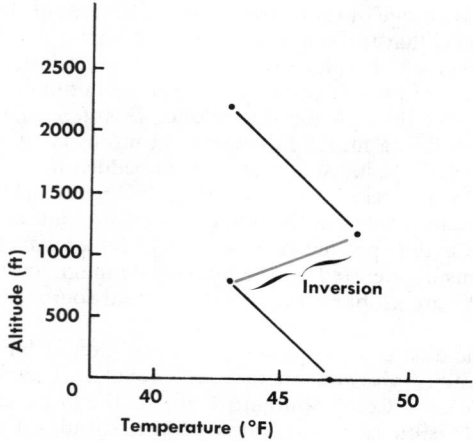

Graph of temperature vs. altitude shows temperature inversion between 750 and 1,250 ft above sea level.

INVERSIVE GEOMETRY: a branch of geometry that developed out of an investigation of a transformation called inversion. This was discovered independently by J. Plücker (1831) and W. Thomson (1845) in connection with some problems in mathematical physics, and then found to be important in conformal geometry.

Let O and P be two distinct points in the Euclidean plane, and let Q be a point on the line OP such that $OP \cdot OQ = k(\neq 0)$. For a fixed k, this construction defines Q as the image of P in a transformation $P \rightarrow Q$, known as inversion. Q is said to be the inverse of P; likewise, P is the inverse of Q; k is the modulus of the inversion and O is its center. To every point in the plane, other than O, corresponds a unique image point. To provide an image also for O, a point at infinity P_∞ is postulated, so that O and P_∞ become a pair of inverse points in the transformation. The Euclidean plane augmented by the ideal point P_∞ becomes the inversive plane. If the modulus $k = r^2 > 0$, all the points on a circle C with center at O and radius equal to r (see the figure) remain invariant; C is the circle of inversion and the inverse points P and Q are said to be reflections of one another with respect to C. Lines that pass through O are transformed by the inversion into themselves; lines that do not pass through O are transformed into circles that pass through O; circles that pass through O are transformed into lines that do not pass through

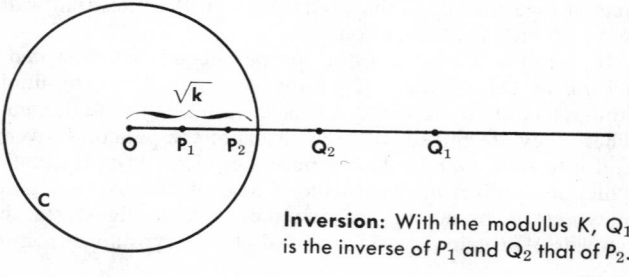

Inversion: With the modulus K, Q_1 is the inverse of P_1 and Q_2 that of P_2.

O; and circles that do not pass through O are transformed into circles. By letting the term m-circle designate both straight line and circle, we can describe an inversion as a one-to-one point transformation of the inversive plane that transforms m-circles into m-circles. Inversion is a conformal transformation; *i.e.* it transforms curves that intersect at an angle α into curves that intersect at the same angle α. There exist, however, other point transformations, such as translations and rotations, which transform m-circles into m-circles. The set of all continuous one-to-one point transformations of the inversive plane into itself which transform m-circles into m-circles form a GROUP, called the inversive group. Inversive plane geometry is concerned with the properties of plane figures which are preserved under the transformations of this group. Euclidean plane geometry is a subgeometry of inversive plane geometry; namely, the geometry of that subgroup of the inversive group that leaves P_∞ invariant. Inversive geometry also exists in spaces of n dimensions.—*J. M. F.*

INVERTEBRATE: any animal with no vertebral column ("backbone") for support. More than 95% of species in the animal kingdom are invertebrates, including the few members of the phylum Chordata that possess a notochord but not a vertebral column. Most CHORDATES have a vertebral column and are known as VERTEBRATES.

Twelve phyla constitute more than 99% of the 837,000 kinds of invertebrate animals: PROTOZOA (single-celled animals), Porifera (SPONGES), Coelenterata (jellyfishes and their relatives), Platyhelminthes (flatworms), Nematoda (roundworms), Rotifera (wheel animalcules), Bryozoa (moss animals), Mollusca (MOLLUSKS), Annelida (segmented worms), Arthropoda (crustaceans, insects, spiders, and others), Echinodermata (starfishes and their relatives), and some members of the Chordata. A minority of invertebrates, chiefly inconspicuous and marine, or living as internal parasites, constitute the phyla Ctenophora, Mesozoa, Nemertea, Gastrotricha, Kinorhyncha, Priapulida, Nematomorpha, Acanthocephala, Entoprocta, Chaetognatha, Hemichordata, Pogonophora, Phoronida, Brachiopoda, Sipunculoidea, and Echiuroidea. See ANIMAL; COELENTERATE; WORMS; NEMATODE; ROTIFERS; BRYOZOAN; ARTHROPOD; ECHINODERMS; CTENOPHORES.—*L. and M. M.*

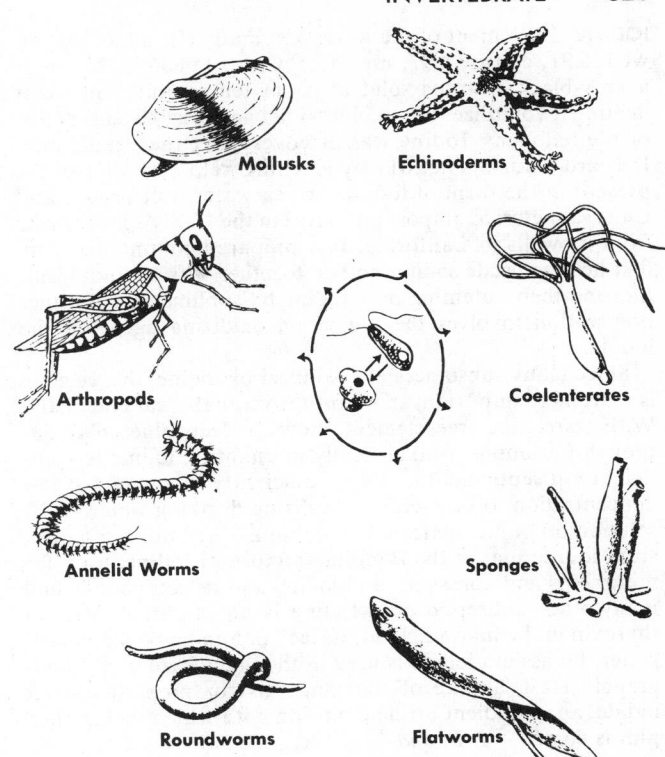

Labels: Mollusks, Echinoderms, Arthropods, Coelenterates, Annelid Worms, Sponges, Roundworms, Flatworms

Evolutionary sequence of the invertebrates is unknown because of poor fossil record. Single-celled ameba and flagellate (in circle) are closely related and could have been the ancestors of the surrounding groups of multicellular forms. (*From Bonner*)

Common invertebrates: *Below, left*—These marine animals look quite similar, but the sea slug (in the middle) is a mollusk, whereas the sea anemones (on either side) are coelenterates. *Below, top*—Common octopus is a mollusk and fairly close relative of the sea slug. (*Both, Douglas P. Wilson*) *Below, bottom*—Millipede, an arthropod, is related to insects and crustaceans. (*Robert Meyerriecks*)

IODINE: an element of the HALOGEN family (I); at. no. 53; at. wt 126.91; density 4.93; mp 113.5°C; bp 184.35°C. Iodine is a gray-black, lustrous solid at room temperature; on slight heating it volatilizes into a blue-violet gas. It is the least active of the halogens. Iodine was discovered by the Frenchman Bernard Courtois in 1811 by leaching kelp. The element is present in the form of iodides in sea water, salt brines, and Chile saltpeter; an important source in the U. S. A. is the brine from oil wells in California. It is prepared commercially by first heating crude sodium iodate together with sodium bisulfite, and then obtaining pure iodine by sublimation. Another preparation involves the use of an oxidizing agent on the iodide.

Since many substances are oxidized by iodine, this element is extremely important in quantitative analytical chemistry. With starch the free element shows a deep blue color. Although poisonous if taken orally in quantity, iodine has sufficient antiseptic action and is sufficiently innocuous at low concentration to be used for sterilizing drinking water. A 7% solution of iodine in alcohol mixed in a 5% solution of potassium iodide makes the familiar tincture of iodine, used for minor cuts and abrasions, and iodine and its compounds find many other antiseptic uses. Iodine is an important part of thyroxin in the thyroid gland; its lack in human beings causes goiter. Potassium iodide is used in the manufacture of photographic FILM, as one of the materials for preparing silver iodide, an ingredient of the emulsion with which the finished film is coated.—*I. B. and G. W. M.*

ION: an electrically charged element or bonded group of elements which migrates freely in solution. An atom that has a high electron affinity can acquire an electron and become negatively charged, *e.g.* bromine in forming a bromide ion. An atom with very little electron affinity, usually a METAL, readily loses an electron to become positively charged, *e.g.* calcium in becoming a calcium ion. The number of electrons that can normally be gained or lost by an atom determines its valence. Groups of atoms covalently bonded together and possessing a charge are called "radicals," *e.g.* $SO_4^=$, CO_3^-, NO_3^-.—*G. W. M.*

ION-EXCHANGE: a chemical reaction in which ions previously held on the electrically charged sites of a porous solid material are exchanged for ions in a solution surrounding the solid. Two major types of porous solids are used as ion-exchangers: (1) certain naturally occurring alkali aluminum silicates known as zeolites; (2) so-called ion-exchange resins, which are synthetic organic polymers specially made for this purpose. *Cation-exchangers* contain, as part of their chemical structure, groups that form negatively charged sites. In zeolites these are the silicate groups; in ion-exchange resins they are usually either carboxyl or sulfonic-acid groups. *Anion-exchangers* contain either amino or quaternary ammonium groups, which form the positively charged sites. Ion-exchange reactions are reversible, the distribution of ions between solution and solid depending on their relative concentrations. In softening water, for example, the hard water containing an undesirable but still relatively low concentration of calcium ion is passed through a column of resin containing a high concentration of sodium ion. The calcium ion replaces part of the sodium ion in the resin, and its place in the solution is taken by the sodium ion. Later, in a separate cycle, the accumulated calcium ion in the resin is displaced by sodium when the resin is treated with a concentrated sodium-ion solution; the column is thus regenerated. Ion-exchange processes are used in demineralizing water, and in the separation and purification of a wide variety of industrial chemicals. See CHRO-MATOGRAPHY; DEMINERALIZATION OF SALINE WATER; ELECTRODIALYSIS.—*A. M. S.*

IONIZATION: the process in which an electron is removed completely from an atom or molecule. The amount of energy required to do this, called the *ionization energy,* varies for different atoms and molecules, ranging from a few to about 25 electron volts. After an electron has been removed from the system, the resultant structure, no longer neutral, is called an ion. Since the chemical properties of an atom or molecule are due principally to its most loosely bound electron, the chemical properties of ions from which this electron has been removed, are much different from those of the electrically neutral species. Except in the case of atomic hydrogen, electrons can be removed from ions. These are then called doubly, triply, etc. ionized systems. The amount of energy required for multiple ionization is also different for different species. The principal methods of creating ions are by collisions with electrons or other ions, by interaction with light of sufficiently high frequency, by collision with other neutral atoms or molecules, and by transferring charge to other ionized systems (charge exchange). Another method of producing ions is to dissolve compounds such as sodium chloride in water. Ions are responsible for the electrical conductivity of solutions.

The process inverse to ionization, namely the association of an ion and an electron, is called recombination. It requires that the energy released be transferred to a third body or that light be emitted.

Neutral mixtures of ions and electrons are called plasmas. These are formed in gas discharges and are also likely to occur in any gas at high temperature, since the atoms and electrons present will have sufficient energy to ionize the gas. Thus we find plasmas in front of a missile re-entering the atmosphere, in the stars, and in all thermonuclear devices that attempt to convert nuclear into mechanical energy by fusion. The part of the atmosphere between 50 and 250 mi above the earth is a plasma called the IONOSPHERE. The ionization there is produced by the light emitted from the Sun. The existence of the ionosphere plays an important role in long-range radio communication.—*S. Bo.*

IONIZED GAS: a gas whose atoms have lost or gained an electron (*i.e.* become ionized) because of an electrical discharge or irradiation through the gas. Discharge of an electron from a cathode through a gaseous medium usually results in the dislodging of a second electron from a gaseous atom, so that the atom becomes an ION. Two electrons thus travel toward the anode. These can strike other gas atoms, causing them, also, to become ions; these positively charged ions will then serve to attract more electrons from the cathode. Thus ionization of the gas progresses so long as the electrical discharge continues. Each gas has a critical voltage at which ionization begins; the critical voltage of mercury is 15 v, and of radon, 10.7 v. Gases are ionized also by irradiation with alpha, beta, gamma, and x-rays. A beta ray releases an electron from a gas molecule through which it passes, but a very fast beta ray will not ionize a gaseous atom. X-rays or light waves cause ionization by ejecting electrons from an atom over which the light wave passes. Bombardment by rapid alpha radiation looses an electron from the atom through which it passes; slow-moving alpha particles may detach several electrons.—*G. W. M.*

IONOSPHERE: the region in the ATMOSPHERE, between about 50 and 250 mi, where the Sun's radiation ionizes most of the molecules of gas present. Here the molecules absorb so much energy that electrons are separated from their atoms and re-

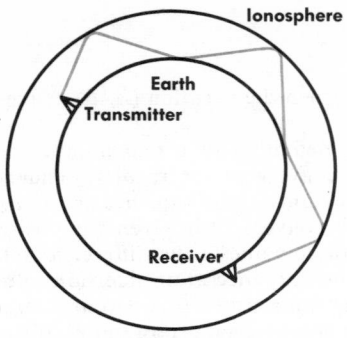

A radio wave is reflected back and forth between ground and ionosphere while on its way from transmitter to receiver.

main free for an appreciable time. These free electrons make the gas a better conductor of electricity than it was in the un-ionized state. For radio waves longer than a few meters (*i.e.* for frequencies lower than about 40 mc/sec), this increase in conductivity of the atmosphere has an effect similar to that which a decrease in the index of refraction has for light waves. A radio wave entering the ionosphere from below is bent back toward the ground, from which it is then reflected upward again. In this way (see the diagram) long-wave radio signals can travel for great distances around the curvature of Earth. The shorter, high-frequency waves, *e.g.* those used for FM, TV, and radar, though, normally pass through the ionosphere without being reflected. Such signals are usually received on the ground, then, only within line-of-sight range (50 to 75 mi) of the transmitter. On the other hand, because they do penetrate the ionosphere, high-frequency waves are useful in radio astronomy and satellite communications. Occasionally, the electron concentration of the ionosphere is temporarily enriched by dense streams of particles from the Sun; these make the ionosphere an effective reflector for even very short waves. During these disturbances, which are usually associated with sunspots, ordinary TV signals may be received 1,000 mi away. The change in ionospheric conductivity also affects the electric currents which flow around Earth through the upper atmosphere. Changes in these currents, in turn, cause variations in Earth's magnetic field. As the particles penetrate to the lower ionosphere, the ionization process produces the polar AURORA, or northern and southern lights. The ionized trails left by meteors as they burn up in the high atmosphere also cause ionospheric disturbances: these are local and short-lived, but so intense that they reflect even microwaves. Antenna systems have been designed to take advantage of meteor trails to provide microwave communication over paths of several hundred miles.—*D. H. L.*

ION PROPULSION: a method of providing rocket propulsion by means of the charged atomic particles called ions. These are accelerated to high speeds by electrical forces in the rocket engine, somewhat as electrons are accelerated in a television tube. Discharge of the beams of particles from the engine produces thrust. The working material is an easily ionizable substance, *e.g.* cesium, whose atoms are made to lose electrons by contact with a heated metallic grid. An ion engine's SPECIFIC IMPULSE (propulsive impulse per unit weight of propellant) is high, but its impulse-to-weight ratio is low because heavy equipment must be carried to achieve enough ion acceleration to produce a reasonable thrust. For this reason ion propulsion is useful in outer space, where weight is not a factor, after another engine with a greater thrust loading value has provided initial boost off Earth. Ion engines have potential advantages over other types of engines in spin control of satellites because they afford precise control of a minimum impulse thrust. Their efficiencies and lifetimes have reached levels which make them feasible for this purpose.—*D. B.*

IRIDESCENCE: the rainbowlike formation of surface colors as in mother-of-pearl, peacock's feathers, thin sections of certain minerals, and oil slicks on pavements. The phenomenon is ascribed to the INTERFERENCE of light waves reflected from upper and lower layers of the surfaces. Destructive interference eliminates certain colors from the total spectrum and consequently gives rise to a colored residue.—*A. E.*

IRIDIUM: a metallic element (Ir); at. no. 77; at. wt 192.2; density 22.42; mp 2454°C; bp above 4800°C. Iridium is extremely hard and, with the exception of osmium, is the heaviest known element (*i.e.* it has the second highest specific gravity). The metal is insoluble in all acids and in aqua regia. In 1803 Smithson Tennant discovered the metal in the residue of crude platinum dissolved in aqua regia. It occurs uncombined in platinum deposits and alloyed with osmium in the natural alloy osmiridium. Iridium is alloyed with platinum for use in surgical and scientific instruments. Osmium-iridium alloys are used for tipping pens and compass bearings.—*I. B.*

IRON: a metallic element (Fe); at. no. 26; at. wt 55.85; density 7.86; mp 1530°C; bp 3000°C. The most abundant of Earth's metals, iron was known to the Egyptians as far back as 3,000 B. C. Minerals used as iron ores are: hematite (Fe_2O_3); magnetite (Fe_3O_4); siderite ($FeCO_3$); and pyrite (FeS_2, "fool's gold"). Until their recent depletion, hematite deposits in Minnesota's Mesabi Range were the most important body of iron ore in North America. This ore could be fed directly to blast furnaces with little or no beneficiation. Now the taconites (quartz-magnetite) and other lower-grade ores are being used more extensively, being concentrated and often pelletized before smelting. The pure form of iron, which in fact is little used in industry, is obtained by electrolytic deposition of ferrous sulfate. Preparation of iron for commercial use involves the roasting and reducing of the ore to the metal in a blast FURNACE. In the furnace, coke reacts with oxygen to form carbon monoxide, which in turn reduces the iron oxides to pig iron. Acidic oxides are neutralized by limestone, and slag (mostly $CaSiO_3$) is formed. The pig iron can then be further processed to produce CAST IRON, WROUGHT IRON, or STEEL for industrial purposes. (See BESSEMER PROCESS; OPEN-HEARTH PROCESS.)

Ion-propulsion research: In this plasma-acceleration machine, a gas admitted at right is ionized by shock coil and accelerated down the tube. The ionized gas then strikes a ballistic pendulum, causing it to move. Here scientist adjusts the pendulum prior to a new test. (*Atomic Energy Commission*)

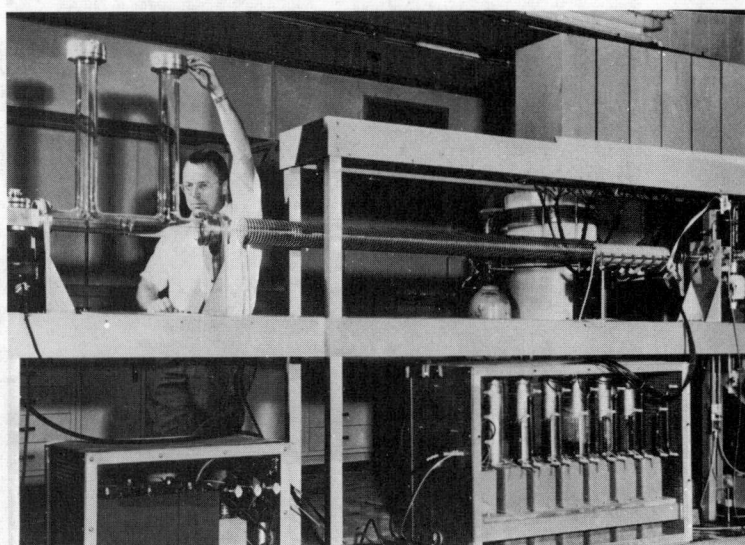

Iron has valences of $+2$ (ferrous), $+3$ (ferric), and very rarely $+6$. Ferrous ions are easily oxidized to ferric ions in neutral or alkaline medium. Blue or black inks contain the ferrous salt of tannic acid, which is colorless until exposed to air, when it turns black. Ferrous sulfate is a disinfectant. With ferrous or ferric ions, the cyanide complexes of iron form a brilliant blue pigment known as PRUSSIAN BLUE. Iron is an excellent reducing agent. When exposed to the atmosphere it forms RUST. Iron is present in hemoglobin, serving to carry oxygen in the blood.—*G. W. M.*

IRRATIONAL NUMBER: a real number that cannot be expressed as the quotient of two integers (whole numbers). Prior to the discovery of irrational numbers, mathematicians knew only the integers and the fractions (ratios of whole numbers). The Pythagoreans are said to have first noted that if each arm of a right triangle is 1 unit long, then the length of the hypotenuse is $\sqrt{2}$, and that $\sqrt{2}$ cannot equal a whole number (which is obvious) or a fraction. Hence the Greeks were forced to recognize that there are new types of numbers, which they called irrational (not expressible as a ratio). The irrational numbers, like the whole numbers and fractions, are called real numbers because they can be used to express real lengths such as the lengths of diagonals of right triangles. Examples of irrational numbers are $\sqrt{5}$; $3\sqrt{2}$; $5\sqrt{7}$; π; and e.

Irrational numbers are now classified as algebraic or transcendental. Algebraic irrationals are roots of polynomial equations with integral coefficients; thus $\sqrt[9]{2}$ is algebraic because it is a root of $2x^6 - 3x^3 - 2 = 0$. Transcendental irrationals are the remaining irrationals. The numbers π and e are transcendental, although they were not so proved until the latter part of the 19th cent.

Major systems for defining the irrational numbers were devised by Richard Dedekind and Georg Cantor. Both systems start with the rational numbers and then define the concept of real numbers, which include rationals and irrationals. Dedekind defined all real numbers as partitions, or cuts, in the rational number system. We select a rational number a and put in the class A all rational numbers smaller than a, and in the class B all rational numbers equal to or larger than a; then the partition (A, B) defines the rational number a. If we put into the class A all negative rational numbers, zero, and all positive rational numbers whose square is less than 2, and into B all positive rational numbers whose square is

greater than 2, then the partition (A, B) defines the irrational number $\sqrt{2}$.

The Cantor definition of a real number depends on the concept of a convergent, or regular, sequence of rational numbers. If the terms of the sequence are a_1, a_2, a_3, . . . , then the sequence is convergent if, given any positive small number ε, the absolute value of the difference between any two members of the sequence after a certain one is less than ε. Thus given any ε, it must be true that $|a_n - a_m| < \varepsilon$ for n and m greater than some definite subscript N. If ε is changed then N may change, but the inequality must hold for the new ε and for m and n greater than the new N. For example, $\frac{1}{2}$, $\frac{3}{4}$, $\frac{7}{8}$, $\frac{15}{16}$, . . . is a convergent sequence. Cantor then states that any convergent sequence is a real number. Now, given a convergent sequence of rational numbers a_1, a_2, a_3, . . . , if there exists a rational number A which the members of the sequence approach more and more closely, the convergent sequence is a rational real number. On the other hand, if there is no rational number A which the members of the sequence approach, the convergent sequence is an irrational number. For example, the convergent sequence given above is the rational number 1, but the sequence 1, 1.4, 1.414, 1.4141, . . . is the irrational number $\sqrt{2}$.—*H. E. W.*

IRRIGATION: the artificial application of water to the soil to supply moisture needed for plant growth; especially, the watering of agricultural crops. Irrigation in some form has been practiced since man began to cultivate the land; references to such a process occur in the Bible. Without irrigation, the extensive agriculture of the western U. S. A. would not be possible, and cultivation in other dry and arid regions of the world would be uncertain or nonexistent. Because of the capricious nature of rainfall over most of the world, irrigation may give better results than nature, since the water can be supplied when it is needed; also, crops need not be restricted to varieties that can be matured on rainfall alone. Modern irrigation has therefore been applied even in humid areas of the world and, together with fertilization and drainage under scientific management, is responsible for yields that would otherwise be impossible. The total irrigated area of the world today is about 310 million acres (125 million hectares), mostly developed in the last century. In the U. S. A., modern irrigation dates from the coming of the Mormon pioneers to Utah in 1847; approximately 30 million acres are now irrigated.

Crop irrigation: Montana farmer regulates irrigation of alfalfa seedlings and oats by means of wooden gate in border dike. *(USDA)*

Tube siphons lead water from earth ditch into Arizona cotton field before planting. Ditch is filled by water pumped from wells. (*USDA*)

Methods of applying water may be classified as: (1) *overhead irrigation,* including all types of sprinkler systems from the hand-held nozzle to large portable or permanent farm sprinklers; (2) *surface irrigation,* including methods of moistening the soil by running water over the surface in small channels called corrugations or furrows, or the flooding of the entire land surface, as with border irrigation, checks, basins, and paddy irrigation; and (3) *subirrigation,* in which water is applied in ditches spaced at various intervals and allowed to move laterally under the soil surface. The method used depends upon the crop, soil conditions, nature of the water supply, and personal preference of the farmers. To prevent a buildup of soluble salts in the soil or to overcome local dryness due to the uneven distribution of water inherent in the irrigation process, water usually must be applied in excess of the amount lost by plants to the atmosphere through transpiration. This excess water, without adequate drainage, may reduce production through water-logging and a high water table. For this reason, drainage may be required to maintain production at a high level. See RECLAMATION; RESERVOIRS AND AQUEDUCTS. —*A. A. B.*

IRRITABILITY: the capacity to respond to changes in the environment (stimuli); it is a fundamental characteristic of living things and of the cells composing them. Responses may involve changes in shape or rate of activity, or changes in special effector organs. The leaves of Venus's flytrap and leaflets of the sensitive plant *Mimosa pudica,* when touched, show irritability in the form of changes in turgor of special cells; these close the flytrap leaf (see CARNIVOROUS PLANT) and cause the leaflets of *Mimosa* to droop as though wilted. Irritability is more obvious in animals in which a NERVOUS SYSTEM is well developed. See ANIMAL BEHAVIOR.—*L. and M. M.*

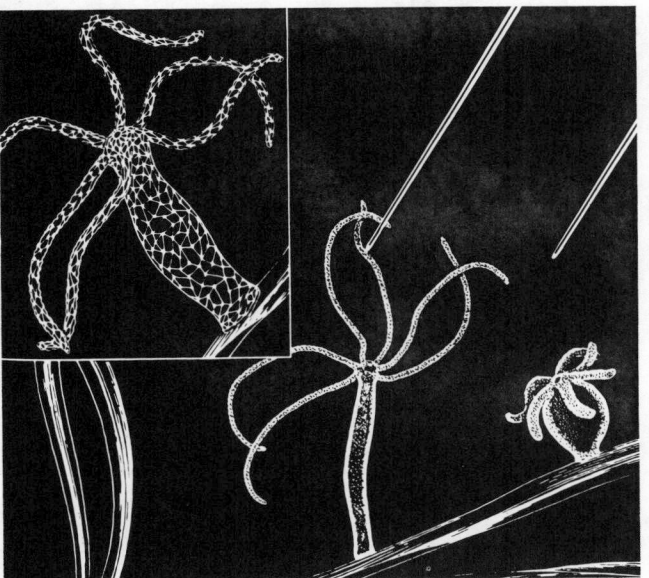

ISALLOBAR: a line on a chart or map that connects points of equal pressure change. In meteorology, isallobars are most commonly drawn for recorded 3-hourly pressure changes. These isolines depict the change of pressure with time, or the pressure tendency. Positive and negative changes are used by the meteorologist as aids in forecasting direction and speed of movement of highs and lows. See ATMOSPHERIC PRESSURE; ANTICYCLONE; WEATHER ANALYSIS.—*P. L.*

ISENTROPIC CHART: a chart showing the distribution of meteorological elements (usually pressure, wind speed and direction, temperature, and moisture) on a selected potential-temperature surface. (Potential temperature is the temperature a parcel of dry air would have if brought adiabatically to a pressure of 1,000 millibars.) Air parcels moving on such a surface undergo no change in ENTROPY. Air flowing in the free atmosphere follows such a surface as long as no heat energy enters or leaves via radiation, condensation, or evaporation. The isentropic chart, which permits easy visualization of many features of the flow pattern, was formerly used in forecasting such events as precipitation and the formation of highs and lows. It has been largely replaced in practice by the constant-pressure-surface chart.—*D. H. L.*

ISLAMIC SCIENCE: Islamic science may be said to have begun when the conquest of Alexandria (A. D. 640) brought Islam into contact with Hellenistic learning. Here and at other intellectual centers, Greek and Indian manuscripts (*e.g.* the works of Ptolemy and the Sanskrit *Siddhanta*) were preserved, translated, and studied. The Abbasid caliphs at Baghdad (A. D. 750ff.) are closely associated with the development of Islamic science; they founded an academy and an observatory, and encouraged translation of scientific works into Arabic. Other factors contributing to the rise of Islamic science were a community to some degree united by a common faith, Arabic as a universal medium of expression, and the mobility of individual scholars within the Islamic world. By the 11th cent. science was essentially an Islamic monopoly, and Muslims were adding their own contributions. Though a decline began in the 12th cent., Islamic science remained important at least until the 15th.

Scientific terms borrowed from Arabic and in use today (*e.g.* alcohol, algebra, alkali, almanac, azimuth, cipher, zenith, and many star names) suggest the wide scope of Islamic interest in pure and applied science. Islamic mathematicians consistently used digits and a zero symbol (whence our "Arabic" numerals) and dealt with problems in algebra, analytical geometry, and spherical trigonometry. Astronomical studies, fostered by the importance attached to astrology and by the astronomical definitions of the times of prayer, included systematic observations (often in specially equipped observatories), their codification as astronomical tables, and the improvement of instruments, in the making of which Islamic astronomers excelled. Alchemy led to chemical knowledge with practical applications in the manufacture of glass, steel, inks, lacquers, scents, and drugs. Pharmaceutical needs were an incentive to botanical study which went beyond popular tradition and the works of the ancients. Improvements were effected in agriculture, and the breeding of horses

Irritability: *Hydra,* a tiny freshwater coelenterate, has a nerve network extending through body (inset) and responds to touch of needle by drawing itself into ball. (*From Young*)

received particular attention. In medicine excellent clinical observations were recorded; anatomy was studied (in apes); hospitals (a Byzantine invention) were established; certificates instituted for specialist practitioners, and codes of professional conduct (*e.g.* secrecy) approved for physicians. Acoustics, optics, hydrostatics, geology, geography, chronology, veterinary science, mechanics, and philology were other fields of learning in which Muslim scholars made worthy contributions.

Islamic science drew on contributors of many nationalities. A few of the most famous are: the Nestorian Christian Hunayn b. Ishaq (809/10–877), who translated Sanskrit and Greek scientific works into Arabic; the encyclopedist al-Kindi (d. *c.* 873); the three 9th-cent. brothers (Banu Musa) who wrote on mathematics and mechanics; the medical writers ar-Razi (Rhazes, d. 923/4) and Ibn-Sina (Avicenna, 980–1037); Ibn Rushd (Averroës, 1162–98), a noted Aristotelian philosopher, physician, and medical encyclopedist; and the Jewish philosopher and physician Maimonides (1135–1204).

Knowledge of the achievements of Islamic science remains incomplete; many works were lost in the Mongol invasions of the 13th cent. and other disasters; other works may yet be discovered. However, Islamic science is not only important as one achievement of a brilliant civilization. Until the Renaissance, it was almost the only channel through which Greek and oriental science were transmitted to Christian Europe. In Muslim and re-Christianized Spain, and in the Norman kingdom of Sicily, Latin and vernacular translations were made of Arabic texts. These became the foundation of that corpus of medieval Latin learning and Aristotelian philosophy which reigned until challenged by the scientific revolution of the 17th cent.—*F. R. M.*

ISLAND: a body of land entirely surrounded by water. Islands are by definition smaller than continents, but vary in size from Greenland, with its area of 840,000 mi², to small rocky islets and sandbars a few feet across. Probably most islands result from flooding of a coastal tract of land by a relative rise in sea level. Former hilltops may thus protrude above the water as islands, and the drowned seaward ends of valleys form estuaries. The many islands off the Maine coast are excellent examples of this type. A second kind of island, generally much smaller and closer to the mainland, results from wave erosion. Small rocky islets, *e.g.* the "sea stacks" off the Pacific Coast of the U. S. A., consist of former parts of the mainland which were slightly more resistant to erosion than the surrounding material, which has been removed by wave attack. Such islands are relatively common along any coast where the sea is actively washing away the land; they commonly cluster off a wave-cut headland of resistant rock, where the sea has obviously undermined the coast.

Waves and currents under favorable conditions may build an offshore deposit of sand and gravel and thus fashion a third class of island. The many offshore bars of the Atlantic and Gulf coasts are such products of the constructional work of waves and currents, and, composed as they are of easily moved material, they may show some change in both shape and size after each major storm. Volcanoes, too, may be responsible for islands; thus the Hawaiian Is. are tops of volcanoes that have been built upward thousands of feet from the ocean floor. Such volcanic islands, as well as islands formed by an uplift of the sea floor, may be found many miles from continental borders. Together, these two types form the principal arcuate island groups of the Pacific, *e.g.* the Aleutians, the Japanese Archipelago, and many islands in the East Indies. Finally, coral reefs growing in the shallow coastal waters of the tropics produce raw material for the development of low islands. An atoll, which is such an island surrounding a shallow lagoon, is roughly circular; it is moderately common in the SW Pacific.

As a consequence of their isolated position, islands may have their own peculiar fauna and flora. Evolutionary change is ever-active, and land areas separated by an ocean barrier inevitably develop their own individual types of animals and plants. See Color Plate 54.—*J. Sh.*

ISLAND UNIVERSE: see COSMOLOGY; GALAXY.

ISOBAR: a line on a chart or map that connects points of equal pressure. Isobars used on charts depicting weather at the earth's surface connect points of equal barometric pressure. Isobars may be labeled in millibars, inches, or millimeters; millibar labeling is standard in meteorology. See ATMOSPHERIC PRESSURE; WEATHER ANALYSIS.—*P. L.*

ISOLATION: in biology, the separation of animal or plant POPULATIONS by barriers to interbreeding. Thus, the straits between the Galápagos Islands divide the land tortoises of each island into geographically isolated populations; time isolates insects active during dawn hours from those active at dusk; environmental barriers separate rose-feeding aphids from those on the mock-orange; and the sterility of mules isolates horses from donkeys. Populations divided by external factors change in heredity, form, and physiology until interbreeding becomes impossible. Intrinsically isolated populations are SPECIES, and diverge in EVOLUTION to fit different environments.—*J. B.*

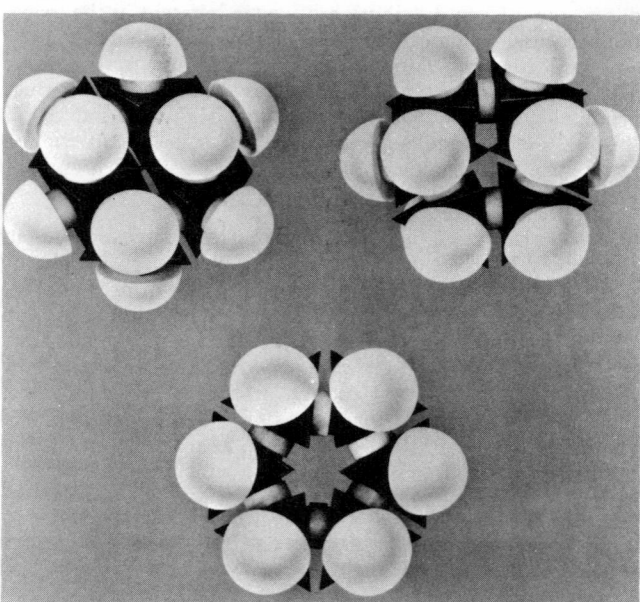

Isomerism: Three molecules of cyclohexane (C_6H_{12}) have the same molecular weight and same percentage composition of elements, but differ in structural arrangement of atoms. Black pyramids signify carbon atoms; white hemispheres are hydrogen atoms.

ISOMERS: chemical compounds which have the same composition and the same molecular weight, but different properties. In most instances isomerism is due to differing arrangements of the atoms within the molecule. There are, for example, two different compounds with the chemical formula C_3H_7Cl:

$$CH_3—CH_2—CH_2Cl \quad \text{and} \quad CH_3—CH—CH_3$$
$$\underset{\text{2-Chloropropane}}{\overset{|}{Cl}}$$

1-Chloropropane   2-Chloropropane

These have different liquid densities, different boiling points, and different chemical reactivities. Isomerism is prevalent among more complex compounds. Thus glucose is one of 16 isomeric sugars of the composition $C_6H_{12}O_6$, whose differences can be represented only by more elaborate systems of formula writing (see also STRUCTURAL FORMULA; STEREOCHEMISTRY; TAUTOMERISM).—*Ru. M.*

ISOMORPHISM: the phenomenon in which substances with analogous chemical formulas have similar or closely related crystal structures. Isomorphous substances thus tend to have similar crystal forms and also other crystallographic properties. In modern usage the term is essentially synonymous with isostructuralism and isotypism. Many isomorphous substances display some degree of solid solution if their structures are similar enough and if certain constituent atoms are sufficiently structurally equivalent. The term isomorphism is sometimes improperly used to denote solid solution or crystal solution.—*A. Ha. and D. H.*

ISOSTASY: the concept that, over broad regions of Earth, crustal movements keep topographic features in approximate hydrostatic equilibrium. The suggestion that mountains are buoyed up by some deficiency in mass beneath them was made in the 18th cent., and the idea of isostasy crystallized in the 19th cent., being first developed as a theory by C. E. Dutton in 1889. Gravity measurements have shown that under most mountains there is indeed a deficiency in mass, and seismic studies in the past few years have shown that mountains can have roots 60 km deep. It is now believed that the crust varies in thickness and is of lighter material than the mantle. MOUNTAINS and CONTINENTS have a thicker crust than ocean basins and are thus supported as if floating. This compensation is by no means perfect, and two explanations are current. Some hold that these anomalies and other irregularities in the shape of Earth (see GEODESY) are due to the mantle having permanent strength. The other view is that the mantle is subject to very slow plastic flow (see CONVECTION THEORY) and that this flow constantly disturbs the isostatic equilibrium. The rise of as much as 1 m per century still occurring in those lands around the Arctic Sea from which ice sheets melted about 11,000 yr ago shows that some flow does take place. It also appears that rising convection currents may support the MID-OCEANIC RIDGE and islands (*e.g.* Hawaii) at too high a level for stability, and that sinking currents tend to drag down the surface along deep ocean trenches such as those off Chile and the island arcs of E Asia.—*J. T. W.*

ISOTHERM: a line on a chart or map that connects points having the same temperature. In meteorology, isotherms appear on surface charts, upper-air (constant-pressure) charts, charts showing vertical cross sections of the atmosphere, and many others. See also WEATHER ANALYSIS.—*P. L.*

ISOTHERMAL PROCESS: any process in which matter undergoes a change at constant temperature, as in the melting of ice, the boiling of water, or the dissolving of ordinary salt in water. The expansion of a gas can also take place isothermally, with the addition of heat to maintain the same temperature.—*J. E. W.*

ISOTONE: one of two or more atomic nuclei containing the same number of neutrons but a different number of protons.—*S. K.*

ISOTOPE: any one of the varieties of an ELEMENT. Isotopes of the same element differ from one another in the number of neutrons contained in the nuclei of their atoms. For example, three isotopes of hydrogen exist in nature: the most common, ordinary hydrogen, has a single proton and *no neutrons* in the nucleus of its atom; the second, called deuterium, has one proton and *one neutron;* the third, called tritium, has one proton and *two neutrons.*

Isotopes of an element are essentially alike in chemical properties; thus the three hydrogen isotopes undergo about the same chemical reaction with oxygen or with other elements. The reason is that chemical reactions are simply interactions between the electrons of atoms, and the isotopes have the same number of electrons circulating about the nuclei of their atoms. (The number of electrons of an atom is exactly equal to the number of protons inside the nucleus.) Actually, the orbits of electrons in different isotopes are not quite identical, because of the different masses of the isotopes (the mass differences being the result of variation in neutron number). These slight differences in orbits result in minute variations in chemical properties, which can be detected by sophisticated experiments.

As a result of their varying masses, isotopes differ in physical properties, *e.g.* rate of atomic diffusion through a membrane and radius of curvature in a magnetic field (at constant energy). Both of these physical differences are exploited in the separation of isotopes; during World War II huge plants were constructed to separate a fissionable isotope of uranium from a nonfissionable isotope so that the former could be used in nuclear reactors and atomic bombs. Hundreds of isotopes are now known, many of which have been artificially produced by man and are radioactive. See RADIOISOTOPE.—*S. K.*

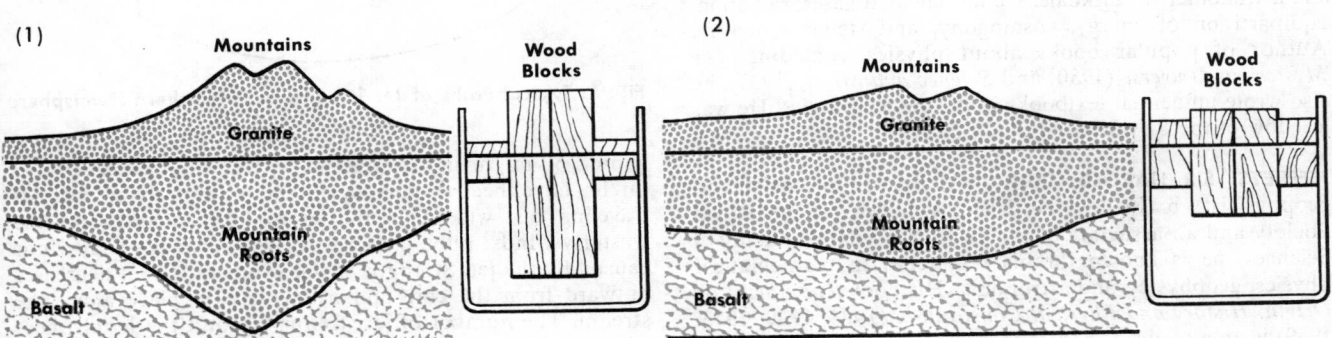

Isostatic balancing in Earth's crust: (1) Mountain mass of granitic rock "floats" in basalt, much as wooden blocks float in water. Depth reached by mountain roots at any given point corresponds to height of mass above that point. (2) As erosion partly levels the mountains, removing material from central region and depositing it on flanks, contour of mountain roots changes correspondingly. Balance is maintained by up and down movements of blocks of Earth's crust.

J

JĀBIR IBN-HAYYĀN (GEBER), 8th-cent. Arabic alchemist; birthplace unknown. He wrote on various aspects of chemical theory and such technological problems as refinement of metals, dyeing of cloth and leather, and distillation. Many of his books were translated into Latin in medieval times and helped to furnish the foundations of European chemistry. Latin versions of his writings bore the name of "Geber," although not all books published under that name were written by him. His *Works* appeared in English in 1678 and again in 1928.—*D. H. D. R.*

JACOBI, KARL GUSTAV JAKOB, 1804–51, German mathematician; b. Potsdam, Prussia. His memoir *Fundamenta nova theoriae functionum ellipticarum* (1829) gave him a wide reputation. He was the first to apply elliptic functions to the theory of numbers, and his memoirs helped (independently of Abel's) to establish the theory of Abelian functions. He made advances in dynamics, cast the theory of determinants in its present form, and contributed to the study of differential equations. He was a fellow of the Royal Society. —*H. C.*

JAMES, WILLIAM, 1842–1910, U. S. psychologist and philosopher; b. Cambridge, Mass. He was professor at Harvard 1880–1907. James is considered the founder of experimental psychology in America, as well as one of the innovators of PRAGMATISM. His influential *Principles of Psychology* (1890) is noted for its theory of emotions and treatment of "stream of consciousness." As pragmatist he interpreted Charles S.

William James
(Harvard Univ. News Office)

Peirce's theory of meaning as a theory of truth, and argued in *Pragmatism* (1907) and other philosophical works that concepts must be defined in terms of experience. Experience included, for James, religious experience, and he maintained that the *will* to believe justifies a right to believe in matters upon which science cannot pronounce.—*A. D.*

JEANS, SIR JAMES HOPWOOD, 1877–1946, English physicist and astronomer; b. Birkdale. He investigated gases, radiation, equipartition of energy, cosmogony, and stellar structure. Author of popular books about physics, including *The Mysterious Universe* (1930) and *Science and Music* (1937), he also wrote influential textbooks in theoretical physics. He was a fellow of the Royal Society.—*D. H. D. R.*

JEFFREYS, SIR HAROLD, 1891–   , English physicist and geophysicist; b. Britley, Durham. A fellow of the Royal Society and an associate of the U. S. National Academy of Sciences, he is known for his researches in mathematical physics, geophysics, and astronomy. His book *The Earth: Its Origin, History and Physical Constitution* (1924, 1929, 1953, 1959) is an advanced theoretical treatment of the mechanics and physical properties of the planet. In geophysics his major contribution has been to postulate Earth's possible origins and present structure by means of mathematical models. He was one of the first to point out the effect of heat from decay

of natural radioactive materials and its possible relation to Earth's internal heat and the forces of mountain building.— *R. W. D.*

JENNINGS, HERBERT SPENCER, 1868–1947, U. S. zoologist; b. Tonica, Ill. While on the faculty of Johns Hopkins Univ. (1906–38), he investigated reactions of unicellular organisms to physical and chemical stimulation, and strongly influenced the thinking of zoologists on behavior in simple organisms. His early results, described in 10 papers on "Studies on Reactions to Stimuli in Unicellular Organisms" (1897–1902), were followed by books such as *The Behavior of Lower Organisms* (1906) and *The Biological Basis of Human Nature* (1930). In later years he transferred his attention to inheritance in protozoans, and discovered the multiple mating types of *Paramecium*. He was a member of the National Academy of Sciences.—*L. and M. M.*

JET PROPULSION: see AIRCRAFT PROPULSION.

JET STREAM: a meandering, hemispheric band of high-speed, westerly winds, some 20,000 to 40,000 ft above the earth's surface. It can be visualized as a flattened, tubular ribbon of winds some 300 mi wide and 4 mi thick. The two jet streams of the northern hemisphere are the Polar and Subtropical jets. The Polar Jet occurs at the overlap of the leaves of the arctic and extratropical TROPOPAUSES, and the Subtropical Jet at the overlap of the extratropical and tropical tropopause leaves (Fig. 2). These jets result in part from strong temperature contrasts found at the overlaps. Maximum wind speeds in the jet-stream core average 100 mi/hr in the

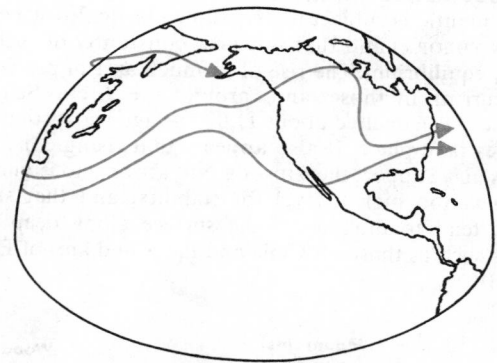

Fig. 1: Typical Paths of Jet Streams over Northern Hemisphere

winter, 50 mi/hr in the summer; extremes in excess of 250 mi/hr have been observed. Pilots of high-flying aircraft traveling east will fly in the jet to take advantage of the westerly winds; pilots flying west will avoid the headwinds caused by the jet. Strength of the winds in the jet decreases outward from the core and from place to place along the stream. The number of jet streams around the hemisphere will vary from week to week; their paths will vary from day to day and season to season. A typical jet stream varies in strength along its path; areas of maximum winds along the jet tend to travel eastward. Severe clear-air turbulence, which can cause structural damage to aircraft, sometimes occurs at

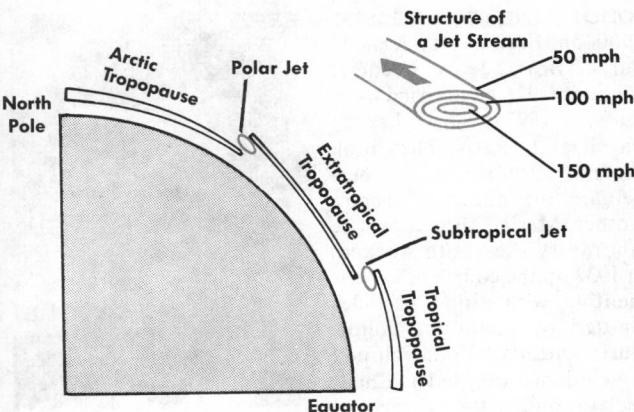

Fig. 2: The Tropopauses and the Jet Streams.

the edges of these maximum wind areas. In-flight penetration at these points is dangerous because the turbulence does not become evident until the aircraft is actually in the turbulence zone. The most pronounced maximum wind areas of the jet streams occur with high frequency across central Japan and over the northeastern U. S. A. Not generally recognized until World War II, the jet stream is now used daily by pilots and meteorologists for flight planning and forecasting.—*P. L.*

JEVONS, W. STANLEY, 1835–82, English logician and economist. He simplified but did not essentially modify Boole's system of mathematical logic; and his "logical piano" (a device for mechanically obtaining answers to problems in the logic of classes) was a precursor of modern computing machines. In his chief logical work, *The Principles of Science* (1874), he gave a valuable account of a variety of logical operations employed in the sciences, and in opposition to John Stuart Mill emphasized the important role of the hypothetico-deductive method in scientific procedure. He was a fellow of the Royal Society.—*E. N.*

JIG: a device for constraining and guiding a cutting tool into contact with a workpiece. The term is sometimes used loosely for a device (properly called a "fixture") that supports or positions the work for a machining operation or an assembling operation. Jigs are primarily used for drilling or reaming operation (*drill jigs*), in which the jig physically positions the workpiece so that the drill or reamer may be guided by a hardened drill bushing (see figure). Drill jigs are used where a large number of identical parts are required and holes must be located with fair accuracy. If only a few parts are required, the cost of making the drill jig is compared with the cost of al-

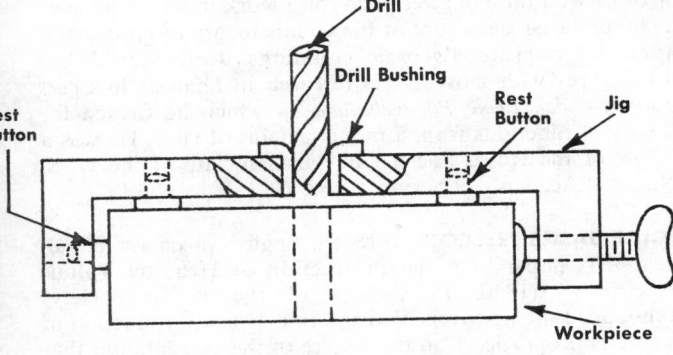

Plate jig is a simple plate to hold workpiece in place for drilling. Rest buttons are steel pins upon which the workpiece rests.

ternate means of producing the part. If a drill jig is not used, all holes on each piece must be located prior to drilling; if the holes must be accurately located, a *jig-borer* is used. A *plate jig* is a one-surface drill jig having a plate with accurately located holes that usually have drill bushings. An *open-face jig* is used to locate holes on a many-surfaced part. A *box jig* is used when a part must be completely enclosed so that holes may be located on its many surfaces. See DRILLING AND BORING.—*F. P.*

JOINING METHODS: Engineering structures (other than those like CONCRETE that are poured monolithically and continuously) require connectors where members join together. Design of connectors depends upon the type of material and the nature and magnitudes of the forces to be transferred at the joints. Metal structures are joined by riveting, bolting, pinning, or welding. Riveted connections are made by inserting heated rivets into holes in the members and driving or deforming the rivets until the holes are completely filled and rounded

Ring connector for wood structures (*above*) is placed in a circular groove that spreads the stress over a large area around the bolt that actually holds the joint together. (*Timber Engineering Co.*)

Riveting and bolting (*below*) are both used in fabricating and assembling structural-steel beams. (*R. Mottar/Chase Manhattan Bank*)

button heads are formed. When rivets cool, they shrink and clamp the pieces together. High-strength bolts exert a similar clamping action when tightened to high tension. Turned bolts, machine bolts, and pins are also commonly used as connectors. The most efficient joining method for metals is welding, in which the metals (usually heat-softened) are made to flow together, giving (on hardening of the metal) a continuous joint having strength almost equal to that of the parent material. Timber members are joined with nails, screws, glue, bolts, pins, and special timber connectors; the last are quite efficient in transferring loads, standard manufactured types being split rings, toothed rings, clamping plates, shear plates, and spike grids.—*W. W.*

JOINT: characteristically, a planar or smoothly curved fracture in a rock. Movement of the rock at right angles to the fracture may produce an open joint or fissure. If movement has occurred parallel to the fracture surfaces, the break is known as a FAULT. Joints range up to thousands of feet in length. They usually occur in large numbers; hundreds may appear within a single small ledge (outcrop). Most commonly they form groups, or joint sets, of more or less parallel fractures. Joints arranged in two or more sets or in some

Radial pattern of joints in basalt, suggesting a fold, reflects differences in rate of cooling of various parts of the intruded magma mass. Compare columnar jointing of basalt, p. 138.

Jointing in granite gneiss here generally follows foliation planes but at some points crosses them. Weathering has opened up joints near surfaces. (*Both photos: Jerome Wyckoff*)

characteristic pattern (concentric, radial, etc.) constitute a joint system. Polygonal crack patterns formed in desiccating mud or cooling basalt exemplify jointing due to shrinkage. Most joints result from Earth's crustal movements (see OROGENY), which deform and rupture the rocks. Jointing in rocks is a controlling factor in WEATHERING, EROSION, and TOPOGRAPHY.—*C. C.*

JOLIOT-CURIE, JEAN FRÉDÉRIC, 1900–58, French physicist; b. Paris. Born Jean Frédéric Joliot, in 1926 he married **Irène Curie,** 1897–1956, French physicist, b. Paris. They took the name Joliot-Curie to perpetuate the name of Irène's mother, Marie Curie, in whose laboratory they both worked. In 1932, in the course of experimenting with alpha particles emitted by polonium, Joliot-Curie and his wife developed the evidence that led J. Chadwick to confirm the existence of the neutron. In 1934, Joliot-Curie and his wife discovered

Jean Frédéric Joliot-Curie
(*N. Y. Public Library*)

artificial radioactivity; they bombarded aluminum with alpha particles and showed by chemical analysis that the remaining active by-product was an isotope of phosphorus, the first man-made isotope not found in nature. For this they received the Nobel prize in 1935. In 1946, Joliot-Curie was appointed French High Commissioner for Atomic Energy, and in 1948 he reported the discovery of a new sub-atomic particle, the mesatron lambda. In 1956, the year of his wife Irène's death, Joliot-Curie was appointed to the chair of nuclear physics at the Univ. of Paris. He died in Paris in 1958.—*A. L.*

JONES, SIR HAROLD SPENCER, 1890–1960, English astronomer and physicist; b. London. At the Cape of Good Hope, 1923, he began an analysis of the accumulated meridian observations. His work in photographic astrometry is mainly responsible for knowledge of stellar distances in the southern sky. He is most famous for his redetermination (1941) of the solar PARALLAX from observations of the 1931 close approach of the asteroid Eros; he was also instrumental in the introduction of ephemeris TIME in fundamental ephemerides. Jones became Astronomer Royal in 1933. He was president of the Royal Astronomical Society (1937–39) and of the International Astronomical Union (1945–48), and was elected a fellow of the Royal Society, 1930. In addition to numerous scientific works, he wrote *Worlds Without End* (1935), *General Astronomy* (1951), and *Life on Other Worlds* (1952).—*R. N. M.*

JORDAN, CAMILLE, 1838–1922, French mathematician; b. Lyons. Professor of mathematics at l'École Polytechnique from 1876 until his retirement, 1912, he was also *suppléant* of the Collège de France, and he edited the *Journal de Mathématique,* 1885–1922. His early research was in geometry. In 1870 he won the Poncelet prize for a work in which he gave a comprehensive account of the Galois theory of groups and applied groups to algebraic equations. Jordan published his lectures with most of his research in analysis in *Cours d'Analyse de l'École Polytechnique,* in which he treated the theory of functions from a modern point of view. He was a fellow of the Royal Society and an associate of the U. S. National Academy of Sciences.—*H. C.*

JOULE, JAMES PRESCOTT, 1818–89, English physicist; b. Salford. His paper "On the Production of Heat by Voltaic Electricity" (1840, *Proceedings* of the Royal Society) announced the discovery that the rate of heat production in a wire is proportional to the square of the current, and that the same relation applies in electrolytes. He later showed that the mechanical power required to generate an electric current is proportional to the square of the current, and that heat produced mechanically is evolved at a rate proportional to the mechanical power. Collectively, these discoveries established the equivalence of work and heat ("On the Mechanical Equivalent of Heat," *Philosophical Transactions,* 1850). Joule received both the Copley medal and a Royal medal from the Royal Society, of which he was a fellow. He was also an associate of the U. S. National Academy of Sciences. His *Scientific Papers* were published in 2 vols. (1885–87). The *joule,* a unit of energy, was named after him.—*D. H. D. R.*

JOURDAIN, PHILIP EDWARD BERTRAND, 1879–1919, English mathematician and historian of mathematics and physical theory; b. possibly Ashbourne, Derbyshire. His mathematical work was principally in the theory of SETS. He applied some of his conclusions in this area to the analysis of problems in mathematical physics. His lengthier studies include *The Nature of Mathematics* (1912) and *The Principle of Least Action* (1913).—*A. D.*

JUPITER: the largest and most massive of the planets of the solar system; fifth in order from the Sun (not counting the asteroids). At opposition, Jupiter has an apparent visual magnitude of −2.5, and (except for Venus at certain phases and Mars at closest approach) may be the brightest object in the night sky. Jupiter reflects about 41 per cent of the sunlight falling upon it. Because of its rapid rotation (in a period of less than 10 hr) Jupiter is noticeably flattened at its poles; the polar diameter of the planet is 82,800 mi, and the equatorial diameter 88,700 mi. But this is a small flattening for such a rapid rotation, and proves that Jupiter's mass is more strongly concentrated toward its center than is the mass of Earth. The mass of Jupiter is 318 times Earth's, but with its much greater volume, the average density of the planet is only 1⅓ times that of water.

Through a telescope, the disk of the planet exhibits a number of markings in the form of dark and light bands parallel to the planet's equator. Red and brown shades predominate, and while the general band pattern is always there, the details of the markings are constantly changing, indicating that the markings are in the planet's atmosphere and not on its surface. This is confirmed by observations which show that Jupiter's rotation period varies irregularly from one marking to another, differences in period amounting to as much as 5 min. A long-lived, still puzzling feature is Jupiter's Great Red Spot, some 30,000 mi long and 7,000 mi wide.

Jupiter's spectrum is the characteristic solar spectrum (since the light is reflected sunlight), but with some pronounced additional absorptions due to molecules in its atmosphere. These have been attributed to ammonia and methane. At the low temperature of the planet's surface (about −200°F) the methane is still gaseous, but the ammonia must be crystallized except for molecules of vapor in "clouds." It has been suggested that the atmosphere itself is mainly of hydrogen (which cannot be detected spectroscopically), forming a compressed layer several thousand miles thick. Below this, it is supposed, lies a thick layer of ice, with the rocky core of the planet being much smaller than the observed radius. Such conclusions are, at best, tentative.

Jupiter revolves about the Sun in a period of 11.86 yr, at a mean distance of 484 million mi, but its orbit is rather more elongated than Earth's, so that at perihelion the planet is 47 million mi nearer the Sun than when at aphelion. The orbit is inclined to the plane of Earth's orbit by a little over 1°.

The four largest and brightest of the satellites of Jupiter, visible in binoculars, were discovered by Galileo in 1610, and hence are called the *Galilean satellites.* Their orbits are nearly circular and lie close to the plane of Jupiter's equator, at distances between 260,000 and 1,170,000 mi, with periods ranging from 1.77 to 16.69 days. The first determination of the velocity of light was made by Olaus Römer (1675) as the result of observing that the discrepancy between the observed and the predicted time of the eclipse of a Galilean satellite by Jupiter's shadow was greatest when Jupiter was farthest from Earth. The fifth satellite, discovered by E. E. Barnard in 1892, is more difficult to observe because it is much fainter, and much closer to Jupiter. The remaining 7 of the 12 known satellites of Jupiter are still smaller, fainter, and more remote from the planet; their orbits are more elliptical and much more tilted to the plane of Jupiter's equator; four of them (VIII, IX, XI, and XII) revolve in the direction opposite that of Jupiter's rotation. The satellite farthest from Jupiter (IX) is nearly 60 times farther away than the innermost Galilean satellite (I). S. B. Nicholson discovered IX in 1914, X and XI in 1938, and XII in 1951.

In 1955 it was discovered that Jupiter emits radio waves in microwave regions. The waves originate in radiation belts like Earth's VAN ALLEN belts, which surround the planet. The intensity of some radio bursts is correlated with the position of Jupiter's innermost satellite, Io.—*M. W. O.*

JURASSIC PERIOD: see GEOLOGICAL TIME CHART; MESOZOIC ERA.

JUVENILE WATER: water believed to have been derived from Earth's interior and not having previously constituted part of the atmosphere or hydrosphere. It is thus distinguished from GROUND WATER. Much water liberated from volcanoes and fumaroles and from crystallizing masses of MAGMA may be of this origin.—*C. C.*

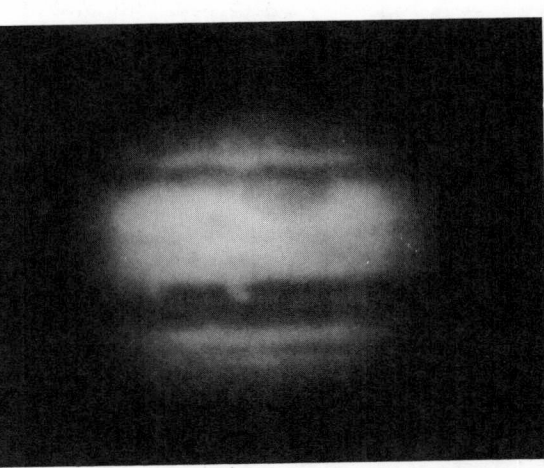
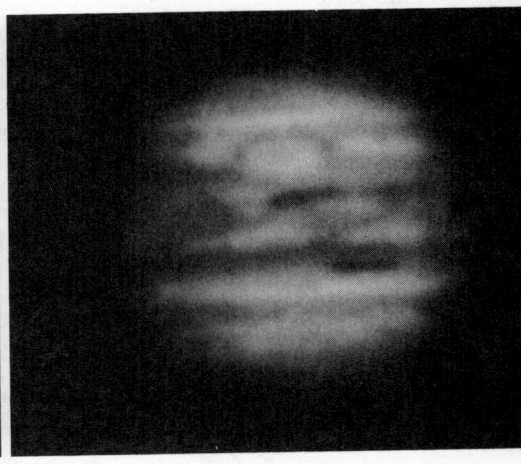

Changing face of Jupiter: Photo at left, taken July 15, 1937, shows Red Spot prominently as well as strong contrast in banding of clouds. In photo at right, taken Aug. 10, 1938, banding is markedly different; also in this photo Satellite I, one of the four larger moons of Jupiter, appears at the edge of the planet's disk, casting its shadow on the clouds toward the left. Both photos show Jupiter's equatorial bulge, due to its rapid rotation. (*Lowell Obs.*)

K

KAME: a steep-sided knoll or hummock of sand and gravel, deposited in contact with glacier ice. Many kames probably are deposited by meltwater running off the edge of glacier ice. Most kames occur in groups, and are commonly associated with KETTLES. Kames are familiar features of landscapes that were glaciated during the recent glacial periods. (See photos, pages 516 and 635.)—*R. F.*

KAMERLINGH ONNES, HEIKE, 1853–1926, Dutch physicist; b. Groningen. Founder of the Cryogenic Laboratory, he studied general thermodynamic properties of liquids and gases (*Algemeene Theorie der Vloeistoffen*, 1881). He obtained liquid helium in 1908 and was awarded the 1913 Nobel prize for research on optical, magnetic, and magneto-optical properties at low temperatures. In 1914 he began the systematic research on superconductivity of solids at extremely low temperatures. He was a fellow of the Royal Society.—*R. J. F.*

KANT, IMMANUEL, 1724–1804, German philosopher; b. Königsberg, East Prussia, where he lived all his life and was professor in the University. Kant's one notable direct contribution to science was an early essay setting forth the "Kant-Laplace hypothesis" concerning the origins of the planets. It is as a philosopher of science, however, that Kant's influence is unmatched in modern thought; it equals that of Aristotle and Descartes.

Immanuel Kant
(*N. Y. Public Library*)

Kant was concerned with the problem of how the mind acquires knowledge of nature; and he advanced a philosophy in which the Empiricist's view of the origin of knowledge is integrated with the Rationalist's emphasis upon the purely conceptual character of reasoning (see EMPIRICISM). Kant carefully developed his "revolutionary" discovery that the mind is active rather than passive in knowing; it brings to experience the principles necessary for interpreting and ordering sense data.

To paraphrase Kant's thought: concepts and percepts cooperate, concepts without percepts are empty (meaningless), percepts without concepts are blind. The technical core of his discovery Kant called "synthetic *a priori*" judgments in which both *conceptual* and *perceptual* components are logically related. Whereas Hume showed that a necessary connection of cause and effect is not derivable from sense experience, Kant argued that the causal principle is logically prior (*a priori*), yet applied *to* experience (synthetic). Without such judgments no knowledge is possible; hence their crucial importance in mathematics, physics, and morals. Kant's "critical philosophy" is an elaborate investigation of all theoretical and moral knowledge in order to exhibit and justify these judgments. *The Critique of Pure Reason* (1781, 1787) undertakes this investigation in mathematics and Newtonian physics, and examines the claims of metaphysical knowledge.—*H. S. T.*

KAPITZA, PETER LEONIDOVICH, 1894–   , Russian physicist; b. Kronstadt. Director of the Institute for Physical Problems of the Academy of Sciences, U. S. S. R. From 1921 to 1934 he worked in England with E. Rutherford. He has worked on electron inertia, radioactivity and nuclear physics, but is most famous for many papers on magnetism and low temperatures. He is a fellow of the Royal Society and an associate of the U. S. National Academy of Sciences.—*D. H. D. R.*

KAPTEYN, JACOBUS CORNELIUS, 1851–1922, Dutch astronomer; b. Groningen. He founded the Groningen astronomical laboratory (1886). A pioneer of modern statistical astronomy, he proposed (1905) the plan of SELECTED AREAS, in which 17 observatories agreed to pay special attention to "weak" stars in 206 selected regions. In 1908 he discovered *star streaming* from statistical data obtained by this worldwide survey, and proposed a theory of the structure of the

Jacobus Cornelius Kapteyn
(*Yerkes Observatory*)

Milky Way based on this discovery. He was a fellow of the Royal Society and an associate of the U. S. National Academy of Sciences.—*R. J. F.*

KÁRMÁN, THEODOR VON, 1881–1963, Hungarian-U. S. physicist and engineer; b. Budapest. Von Kármán's areas of research have included theory of elasticity, strength of materials, hydrodynamics, aerodynamics, thermodynamics, supersonic wind tunnels, and mathematical methods in engineering. He taught at the Univs. of Göttingen and Aachen in Germany, then left that country (1930) and became director of the Guggenheim Aeronautics Laboratory at the Calif. Inst. of Technology. His many writings include *Aerodynamics: Selected Topics in the Light of Their Historical Development* (1954). He was a fellow of the Royal Society.—*D. H. D. R.*

KARRER, PAUL, 1889–   , Swiss chemist; b. Moscow, U. S. S. R. With W. N. Haworth he shared the Nobel prize, 1937, for his work on carotenoids, flavins, and vitamins A and B. His research on plants and biochemistry includes investigations of carbohydrates, chitin, lichens, cellulose, lecithin, tannins, protein acids, and anthocyanin dyes. He isolated several carotenoids and 40 new alkaloids. After establishing the structure for vitamin A, he clarified vitamins B_2 and E, isolated vitamin K, and studied vitamin B_{12}. His later subjects of research include curare and strychnine. Among Karrer's writings are the textbook *Lehrbuch der organischen Chemie* (1930). He is a fellow of the Royal Society and an associate of the U. S. National Academy of Sciences. —*V. B.*

KARST TOPOGRAPHY: the surface configuration characteristic of certain regions of limestone bedrock, in which subsurface erosion by ground water has resulted in the formation of

Caverns, underground rivers, and sinkholes are characteristic in regions where surface bedrock is limestone. Karst features form as ground water dissolves calcium carbonate out of the rock. Remnants of eroded limestone landscape may take the form of flat-topped or peaked hills.

sinkholes and caverns. The name comes from the Karst region of Yugoslavia. W-central Kentucky, central Tennessee, S Indiana, and N Florida have notable karst topography.—*E. A.*

KEELER, JAMES EDWARD, 1857–1900, U. S. astronomer; b. La Salle, Ill. He pioneered in astronomical photography, applying its techniques to spectroscopy. By measuring the Doppler shifts of various parts of Saturn's rings, he proved that they are composed of small particles (1895). He made many notable photographs of spiral nebulas with the 36-in. Crossley reflector of Lick Observatory.—*O. G.*

James Edward Keeler
(Yerkes Observatory)

KEKULÉ VON STRADONITZ, FRIEDRICH AUGUST, 1829–96, German chemist; b. Darmstadt. An organic chemist, he worked mainly on the constitution of carbon compounds, particularly benzene. His theories on valency and the 6-carbon ring of benzene, in which single and double bonds alternate with each other, were the foundation of far-reaching advances and discoveries. A great teacher, Kekulé wrote the unfinished *Lehrbuch der organischen Chemie* (1861–66), a textbook. He was a fellow of the Royal Society and an associate of the U. S. National Academy of Sciences.—*E. F.*

KELVIN, BARON WILLIAM THOMSON, 1824–1907, British physicist; b. Belfast. Professor of natural philosophy at the Univ. of Glasgow at age 22, William Thomson, along with H. von Helmholtz, contributed to the establishment of the first law of thermodynamics, also known as the law of conservation of energy. Reviewing N. L. Sadi Carnot's work on an ideal heat engine, Thomson established the theoretical absolute temperature scale, called in his honor the Kelvin temperature scale. On the basis of his studies in heat phenomena, he estimated the age of Earth, provoking much controversy among biologists and geologists. In 1851 he presented a paper to the Royal Society of Edinburgh in which he formulated the second law of thermodynamics. Thomson's statement of the second law is as follows: *There is no natural process the only result of which is to cool a heat reservoir and do*

Baron William Thomson Kelvin
(N. Y. Public Library)

work as exemplified by raising a weight. From considerations of the second law, Thomson, along with others such as Clausius and Willard Gibbs, contributed to the theory of chemical equilibrium. Thomson was one of the great physicists of the 19th cent., and although his outstanding achievements were in thermodynamics, he made contributions in many branches of physics, including the theory of elasticity. He never accepted the electromagnetic theory of light and persistently tried to conceive of a mechanical model for the propagation of light through an elastic medium. From 1854, most of Thomson's energies were spent on perfecting the transatlantic submarine telegraphic cable. For this he was knighted in 1866, and in 1892 was made Baron Kelvin of Largs. A fellow of the Royal Society, he received its Copley medal in 1883, and in 1890 became its president.—*A. L.*

KELVIN SCALE: an absolute TEMPERATURE SCALE, based on the CELSIUS SCALE, in which absolute zero is designated as 0°K, the freezing point of water as 273°K, and the boiling point of water as 373°K. In addition to the convenience of a temperature scale in which there are no negative readings, use of the Kelvin scale facilitates applications of the laws of THERMODYNAMICS and the laws of GASES, since these laws are based on absolute temperatures. Temperatures of very hot bodies (*e.g.* stars) are frequently given in °K; above 20,000°C the two scales vary by less than 1% and are essentially interchangeable.—*E. M. R.*

KENNELLY-HEAVISIDE LAYER: see IONOSPHERE.

KEPLER, JOHANNES, 1571–1630, German astronomer; b. Weil, Württemberg; ed. Univ. of Tübingen. Assistant to Tycho Brahe at his observatory near Prague in 1600, he succeeded him the following year as imperial mathematician and court astronomer. At Ulm he completed and published Brahe's *Rudolphine Tables* (1627). Kepler is considered the founder of physical astronomy because of his demonstration that the

Johannes Kepler
(Yerkes Observatory)

planes of all planetary orbits pass through the center of the Sun and his recognition of the Sun as the moving power of the planetary system. He is best known for his laws of planetary motion (see KEPLER'S LAWS). Kepler also studied refraction and suggested the principle of the inverting telescope. Among his works are *Mysterium Cosmographicum* (1596), ASTRONOMIA NOVA (1609), and *Harmonice Mundi* (1619). —*S. B.*

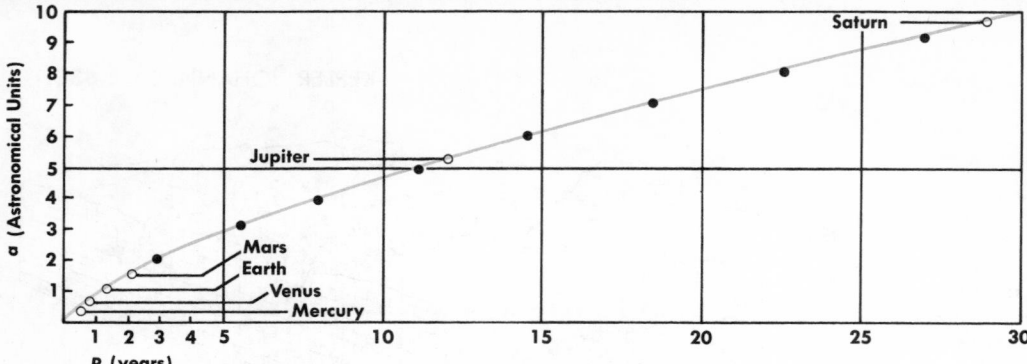

Kepler's third law relates a planet's distance from the Sun (*a*) to its period of revolution (*P*). These data all lie on a curve of $a^3 = P^2$ as shown. Small circles represent planets; solid dots represent whole-number values of *a*.

KEPLER'S LAWS: laws describing the motions of the planets about the Sun, discovered by Johannes Kepler at the start of the 17th cent.: (1) The orbit of a planet is an ellipse, with the Sun at one of the two foci. (2) The law of areas: the radius vector of the planet (*i.e.* the line drawn from the Sun to the planet) sweeps over equal areas in equal times (see figure). (3) The harmonic law: the ratio of the squares of the orbital periods (*P*) of any two planets is the same as the ratio of the cubes of the mean distances of the planets (*a*) from the Sun; thus $P_1^2/P_2^2 = a_1^3/a_2^3$.

If Earth is considered one of the two planets in the formula of the third law, and units of length and time are taken to be the astronomical unit and the year (so that for Earth $a = 1$, $P = 1$), then, in these units, for any planet $P^2 = a^3$. Thus, for

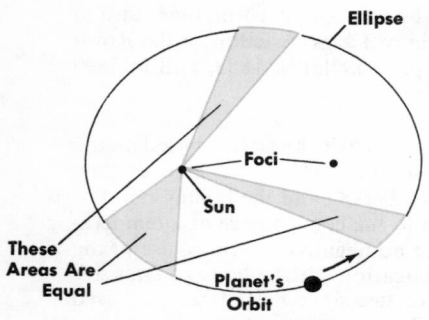

Kepler's first and second laws state that the planets move in elliptical orbits with the Sun at one focus of the ellipse, and that a line connecting a planet and the Sun sweeps over equal areas in equal times. (The closer a planet comes to the Sun, the more rapidly it moves.)

Mars, the mean distance from the Sun is 1.524 astronomical units; $(1.524)^3 = 3.540$, so that $P = \sqrt{3.540} = 1.881$ yr.

Newton showed that Kepler's laws could be understood if one supposed that the Sun exerts on a planet an attraction that varies inversely as the square of the distance of the planet from the Sun, and is proportional to the mass of the planet. Newton predicted that the third law would prove to be not quite accurate; that, instead, if the Sun's mass be *M* and the masses of two planets m_1 and m_2, then $(M + m_1)P_1^2/(M + m_2)P_2^2 = a_1^3/a_2^3$. Since the masses of the planets are very small compared to the mass of the Sun, the correction is very small, but it is confirmed by accurate observation. Newton was led, from this study of Kepler's laws, to formulate his law of universal gravitation, the basis of the study of the motions of planets and stars, and the mathematical methods devised by Newton for this problem are the foundation of modern physical science. Kepler's laws, with Newton's modifications, are valid everywhere as to comets, asteroids, natural and artificial satellites, double stars, and all other known celestial bodies. They apply to the motion of an artificial satellite of Earth, except for slight perturbations of the satellite orbits due to Earth's atmosphere and to the fact that Earth is not exactly spherical.—*M. W. O.*

KERATINS: proteins which are the main constituents of hair, wool, nails, and hoofs. Keratins are insoluble and resistant to animal digestive enzymes, and have a high content of the amino acid cystine.—*F. F.*

KEROSENE: the petroleum distillate fraction which boils (300°–550°F) next above gasoline. Once the principal product of PETROLEUM REFINING, it is now a minor one (5%). It is still used for home heating and cooking, as fuel for certain turbojet aircraft, and as a base for insecticide sprays.—*W. B. P.*

KERR EFFECT: the phenomenon of an electric field making a substance capable of DOUBLE REFRACTION. The effect, discovered by J. Kerr in 1875, arises from the fact that molecules have directional properties with respect to an electric field and tend to align themselves with it. This realignment from the random arrangement characteristic of materials to which no field is applied causes the change in the optical characteristics of the materials. The phenomenon is utilized in a very-high-speed shutter called a Kerr cell, which can open or close under an electric impulse in times as short as 10^{-8} sec, allowing the transmission of accurately timed, short bursts of light.—*E. M. R.*

KERST, DONALD WILLIAM, 1911–   , U. S. physicist; b. Galena, Ill. He did research in x-ray tube development and has worked with enriched chain reactors, electrostatic accelerators, and thermonuclear devices, but is best known for developing the betatron (see PARTICLE ACCELERATOR). He is a member of the National Academy of Sciences.—*D. H. D. R.*

KETONES: compounds in which the carbonyl radical (CO) is connected (1) to two aliphatic radicals, or (2) to two aromatic radicals, or (3) to one of each:

(1) Dimethyl ketone
    Acetone

(2) Diphenyl ketone
    Benzophenone

(3) Methyl phenyl ketone
    Acetophenone

Acetone, the simplest ketone, was heavily used in both World Wars as a solvent in the production of cordite, a propellent explosive. A chlorine derivative of acetophenone is an important tear gas, and acetophenone itself finds use as a soporific. Some important ketones occur in nature. Camphor is a complex ring structure in the alicyclic series with a keto group in one ring; and there are keto sugars, *e.g.* fructose. QUINONES are ketones.

Ketones are made by various methods. A general method is oxidation (dehydrogenation) of a secondary alcohol:

Isopropyl alcohol   Acetone (a ketone)

Because of their C=O bond, ketones are UNSATURATED COMPOUNDS, and can add hydrogen and other molecules. The addition of hydrogen is the reverse of the reaction above, in

634

which acetone is made by dehydrogenation of isopropyl alcohol. Some ketones can be made to undergo a self-addition:

$$CH_3-\underset{\underset{O}{\|}}{\underset{|}{C}}-CH_3 + CH_2-\underset{\underset{O}{\|}}{C}-CH_3 \longrightarrow CH_3-\underset{\underset{OH}{|}}{\overset{\overset{CH_3}{|}}{C}}-CH_2-\underset{\underset{O}{\|}}{C}-CH_3$$

Acetone (two molecules)　　　　　Diacetone alcohol

Diacetone alcohol is an important solvent in the paint and lacquer industry. See ALICYCLIC COMPOUNDS; ALIPHATIC COMPOUNDS; AROMATIC COMPOUNDS; CARBONYL RADICAL; ORGANIC CHEMISTRY.—*Ru. M.*

KETOSIS: accumulation in the blood of above-normal concentrations of acetoacetic acid and its breakdown products, acetone and B-hydroxybutyric acid. The high concentration results in urinary excretion of the acids, accompanied by sodium ions and large volumes of urine. This in turn produces *acidosis* (because of the loss of sodium ion) and dehydration, with accompanying clinical symptoms of depression, shortness of breath, and dryness of the mouth; also, the acetone can be detected as breath odor. The cause of the high acetoacetic acid levels is usually the faulty operation of the CITRIC-ACID CYCLE, because of lack of oxaloacetate; the result is that acetate is not oxidized but converted to acetoacetate. Underlying these circumstances is a lack of sugar oxidation but undiminished fat oxidation, brought about by diabetes, a high-fat diet, or starvation, in which the body burns up its store of fats. See FAT METABOLISM.—*J. F. S.*

KETTLE (in chemistry): a vessel used for carrying out chemical reactions on an industrial scale when only moderate ranges of temperature and pressure are required. Kettles range in size from as small as 20 gal to 3,000 gal or more; they are usually shaped like a vertical cylinder with a flat or slightly domed lid and a hemispherical or conical bottom. They are invariably fitted with gasketed manholes or hand-holes in the lid and with valved pipes for emptying and filling. Most kettles are fitted with stirring apparatus, the shafting for which enters the vessel through packing glands in the top or side. Most kettles have jackets or internal coils through which heating or cooling fluids can be circulated. Some kettles are heated directly by gas or oil fire or by electrical resistance mantles. Steel is the usual structural material for kettles; but the lining surfaces, which come in contact with the chemicals being processed, may be made of special resistant materials, *e.g.* vitreous enamel, nickel, stainless steel, copper, lead, rubber, and various plastics.—*A. M. S.*

Infrared photo of Cape Cod reveals numerous kettle lakes, formed in basins left by melting of residual blocks of ice at close of last glacial period. Kettles have been much modified along coasts by action of waves and currents. (*Lawrence Lowry*)

KETTLE (in geology): a basin in glacial drift, created by the melting-out of residual bodies of underlying glacier ice. Some kettles have bottoms that lie below the present water table and hence are occupied by lakes.—*R. F.*

KEYNES, JOHN MAYNARD, 1883–1946, British economist and philosopher; b. Cambridge. He edited the *Economic Journal* and participated in affairs of state. His very influential works include *Essays in Biography, Treatise on Probability* (1921), and *General Theory of Employment, Interest, and Money* (1936). He maintained that probability is an unanalyzable logical relation between propositions, and claimed that judgments of probability rest ultimately upon a direct intuition of such relations. Though many philosophers are skeptical of the latter thesis, it is widely agreed that his *Treatise on Probability* is a most important book, containing unusually penetrating discussion of the nature and validity of inductive arguments.—*S. M.*

KIDNEYS: the paired excretory organs of vertebrates. They are located one on either side of the vertebral column, just inside the body wall of the back. They regulate the composition and volume of body fluid by eliminating, in the urine they form, waste and excess materials. Each kidney is made up of a large number (about a million in man) of functional units called nephrons, with associated ducts and blood vessels.

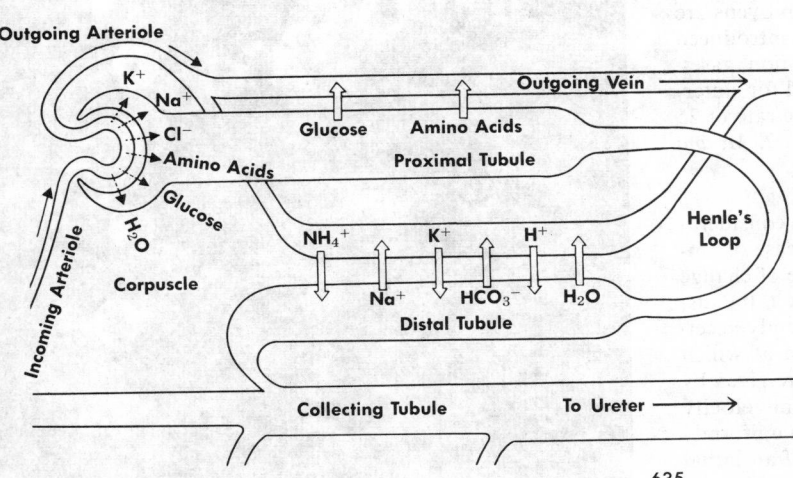

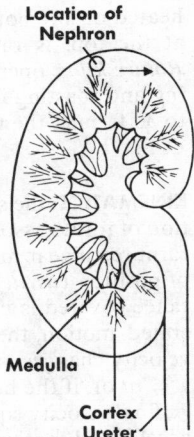

Kidney structure: Section of kidney (*right*) reveals outer layer (cortex), as well as inner portion (medulla) and its connection with expanded beginning of ureter; a single representative nephron is indicated for position. Schematic diagram at left outlines flow through glomerulus and tubule of a nephron.

A nephron has two parts: corpuscle and tubule. The corpuscle is a bundle of capillaries, called the glomerulus, tightly enclosed in a capsule. The tubule is a long, thin tube leading from the capsule to a collecting tubule.

Blood flows through the incoming arteriole to the glomerulus. Here blood pressure forces everything in the blood except cells and proteins to filter through the thin walls of the capillaries into the capsule. The remaining blood then flows through the outgoing arteriole to capillaries which surround the tubule. The filtrate is formed at a rate that depends on the blood pressure and on the highly variable rate of blood flow through the glomerulus. The filtrate passes from the capsule into the tubule, which has three portions in mammals. In the proximal part, the cells of the tubule wall take up glucose and amino acids from the filtrate, returning these to the blood. Certain toxic or other materials may also be secreted into the tubule from the blood. Urea, the major nitrogenous waste of mammals, remains in the tubular fluid, being neither secreted nor actively taken up. The fluid now passes through the thin-walled loop of Henle into the distal portion of the tubule. Here the cells of the tubule wall actively reabsorb sodium ion (Na^+) and possibly bicarbonate ion (HCO_3^-) and return these to the blood. They may also add potassium ion (K^+), hydrogen ion (H^+), and ammonium ion (NH_4^+) to the blood. The relative amounts of H^+, and NH_4^+, and HCO_3^- moved into or out of the blood are important in the regulation of blood acidity. In fresh-water animals, little water is reabsorbed from the fluid in the distal tubule, but nearly all the salt (NaCl) is removed; as a result, the urine is quite diluted. In mammals, water is taken up from the distal tubule, and the urine may become quite concentrated.

The uptake of salts and water is regulated by hormones. Aldosterone, a hormone secreted by the cortex of the adrenal gland, stimulates sodium uptake. The antidiuretic hormone, secreted by the posterior portion of the pituitary gland, stimulates water absorption. These two hormones, as well as others, regulate the amounts of salt and water lost in the urine. Secretion of these hormones is, in turn, regulated through nervous and hormonal pathways in relation to the volume and composition of the blood.—*B. T. S.*

KILN: originally, a brick oven for hardening, burning, or drying any substance, *e.g.* grain, meal, or clay products. Many modern kilns are made of heat-resistant alloys, without a brick lining. In ceramics, the backing or firing of clay and porcelain objects is carried out in *periodic* (brick) kilns, with moving ware exposed to stationary fire, or in *continuous* kilns (moving fire and stationary ware). *Vertical kilns* are used in making Portland cement, for calcining iron ores, and for burning lime and dolomite. These brick-lined iron ovens are heated on the bottom, and the powdered charge, introduced at the top, is rapidly heated by rising combustion gases. *Rotary kilns,* open or muffle (closed), are designed for sintering and roasting iron ores. The body rotates at the rate of 25 to 30 ft/min, the firing chamber being stationary.—*T. M. and C. S.*

KINEMATICS: the study of MOTION, unrelated to the consideration of forces associated with such motion. In the case of uniform rectilinear motion, velocity *v*, or the time rate of change of position (ds/dt), is constant. In a period of time *t*, the distance covered is given by the product vt. In uniformly accelerated motion, the acceleration *a* is the time rate at which velocity changes, or $a = dv/dt$. Final velocity is here given by $v = at$ or, if the body starts with an initial uniform velocity v_o, final velocity equals $v_o + at$. Distance covered in uniformly accelerated motion is expressed by $s = \frac{1}{2} at^2$ or, if an initial

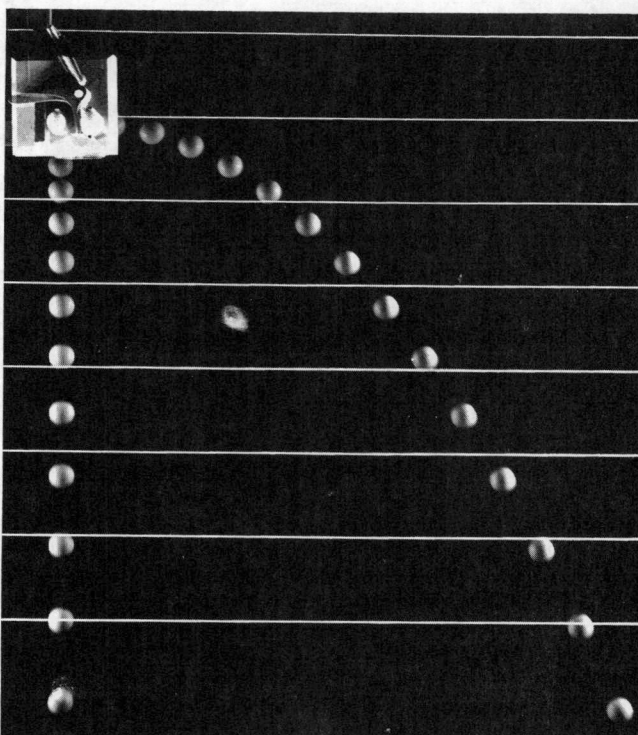

Motion shown in stroboscopic photographs: (*Above*) Two spheres, one projected horizontally and the other allowed to drop vertically, at the same instant, both fall at the same rate, as indicated by the horizontal lines. (*Below*) Dotted sphere moving from bottom collides with stationary sphere (suspended by wire from a point near camera lens). Both spheres move away from point of impact, sharing momentum of the moving sphere. (*Berenice Abbott*)

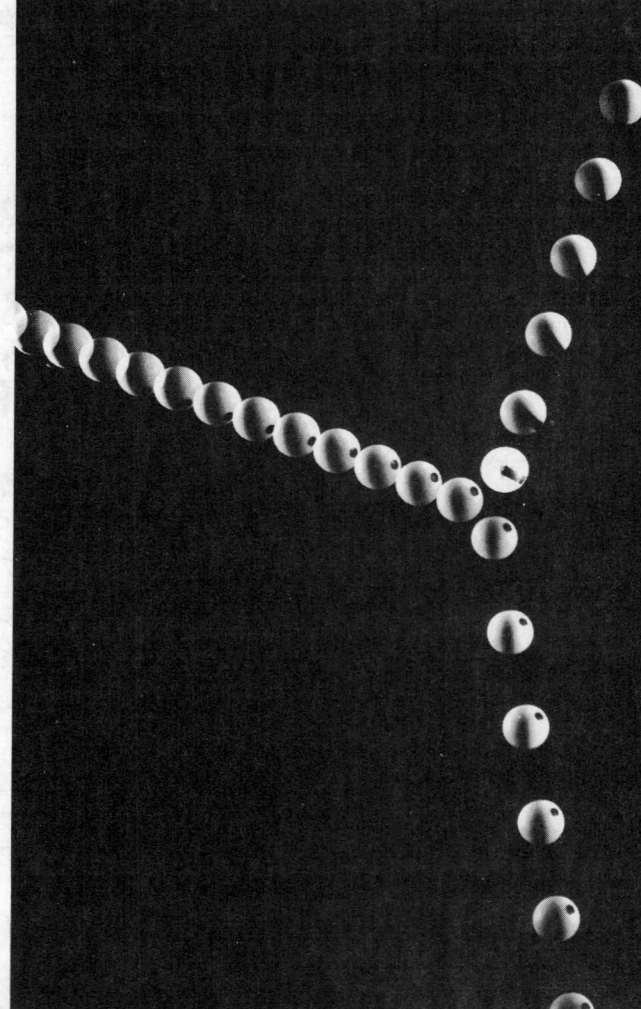

velocity v_o is assumed, by $s = v_o t + \frac{1}{2} at^2$. In the case of falling bodies, we substitute the acceleration of gravity (g) for the term a in the above equations. See DYNAMICS.—*A. E.*

KINETICS (in chemistry): the study of the rates of chemical reactions. The principal factors affecting reaction rates are the chemical nature of the reacting species (molecules or ions), temperature, pressure, concentration of the reacting species, and presence or absence of catalysts. In quantitative studies, concentration is usually taken as the dependent variable, since rate is measured by the decrease in concentration of the reactants or increase in concentration of the products. In unimolecular reactions and in certain other simple reactions the measured rate is found to be directly proportional to the concentration of one of the reactants. Such reactions are termed "first order." In second-order reactions the rate is proportional to the product of the concentrations of two reactants or to the square of the concentration of one reactant. Some third- and higher-order reactions are known but they are rare. In all cases the proportionality constant in the equation is called the specific *rate constant* and is characteristic of the reaction. This rate constant changes with temperature according to a law discovered by Svante Arrhenius (1889) partially based on work done by J. H. van't Hoff (1884). For two molecules to react they not only must come into contact (collide) but at the time of contact must possess energy higher by a critical amount than the average energy of surrounding molecules. This excess energy, acquired by fortuitous collisions, is called the energy of activation. It can be calculated from the rate constant/temperature relationship. The overall disappearance of reactants and appearance of products may be the result of several reactions taking place in series at different rates. If one reaction is much slower than the other, its rate determines the over-all rate, and its order the observed order. Thus although a knowledge of the order and rate constant of a reaction enables calculation of the concentration of major reactants and products at any time, it reveals little about the reaction mechanism. When the mechanism is known, reaction rates can in some instances be calculated from the concentrations and energy states of the intermediate complexes formed from the reactants. The method employed is known as the theory of absolute reaction rates.—*A. M. S.*

KINETICS (in physics): the branch of DYNAMICS dealing with the effects of forces and torques on the MOTION of material bodies. Kinetics covers the movement of idealized point particles as well as that of extended rigid bodies, whether free to move in any direction or confined to a fixed path. Kinetics includes rectilinear motion, circular motion (*e.g.* rotation), curvilinear motion (*e.g.* the parabolic path of a projectile), and harmonic motion (*i.e.* the motion of a body acted on by a force that varies in proportion to the body's regularly varying displacement from a definite point, a fundamental pattern of motion in physics). Among the general principles governing such movements are NEWTON'S LAWS OF MOTION and the concept of kinetic equilibrium first advanced by D'Alembert (see D'ALEMBERT'S PRINCIPLE); the latter interprets dynamic situations in terms of pure statics. Of particular value in problems involving impacts and collisions are the principles of conservation of energy and conservation of linear momentum. The conservation of angular momentum is the starting point in attacking problems dealing with ROTATION. Molecular motion, as described in the KINETIC THEORY OF MATTER, is also the province of kinetics. But for subatomic particles, as well as the extreme masses, distances, and speeds of astronomy, kinetics as developed from Newton's laws must be modified to conform to the more general concepts of RELATIVITY (see also QUANTUM MECHANICS).—*A. E.*

KINETIC THEORY OF MATTER: a theory that accounts for much of the physical behavior of matter on the assumption that it is composed of many small particles in rapid motion. An understanding of the theory is most easily grasped by first considering the following characteristics of gases: (1) Gases are very light compared with liquids and solids, and they may be highly compressed, whereas liquids and solids cannot. (2) Gases diffuse spontaneously in all directions and fill, swiftly and fairly uniformly, all space available to them. This diffusion occurs, although less rapidly, even if the space already contains other gases. (3) Gases exert a pressure on the walls of their containers that is virtually the same in every direction.

These observed facts can be explained by assuming that any specimen of gas consists of a great many independent, tiny particles, all in rapid, random motion, the total space between the particles far exceeding the aggregate volume of the particles themselves. The tiny particles of matter are called molecules. From experimental measurements their diameter is estimated to be about 0.00000001 cm and their number so large that under ordinary conditions a cubic inch of space holds about 450 billion billion of them. With particles so numerous it would be futile to consider individual motions, but the very magnitude of the molecular population in even a small sample of gas makes a statistical description highly reliable. For example, a huge swarm of molecules moving at random could hardly favor one direction more than another. Rather, it is to be expected that, just as in the case of a crowd of people strolling at random across a level field, about as many will always be headed in one direction as in any other.

We cannot suppose that the particles constituting a single specimen of gas all have identical speeds. Even if they did at one instant, this uniformity would be destroyed immediately by the inevitable jostling among them. Yet we can assume a certain average speed for the molecules, so long as conditions remain unchanged. Then, if many molecules are moving in every direction in equal numbers and with the same average speed, it is understandable that the pressure of the gas on its container must be uniform. It is further necessary to assume that the molecules are perfectly elastic, so that when they strike the walls, they rebound with no loss of speed. Otherwise they would slow down and ultimately stop after repeated collisions with the walls, thereby losing their ability to diffuse.

Demonstration of Charles' law: Doubling the absolute temperature of a gas at constant volume doubles its pressure. On the other hand, allowing the gas to expand until its pressure is restored to its original value causes the volume to be doubled (Boyle's law). The net resultant (as given by Charles' law) is a doubling of volume at constant pressure as a result of the doubling of absolute temperature.

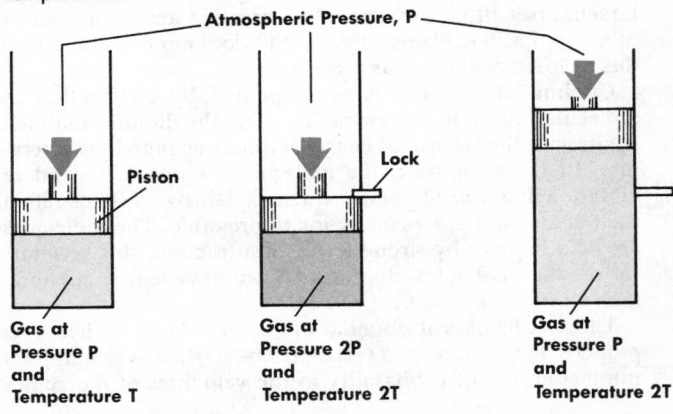

Atmospheric Pressure, P

Piston

Lock

Gas at Pressure P and Temperature T

Gas at Pressure 2P and Temperature 2T

Gas at Pressure P and Temperature 2T

The kinetic theory enables us to rationalize the gas laws very easily. Suppose a gas occupying one liter of volume is transferred to a vessel of one-half-liter capacity without any alteration of the average molecular speed. In the smaller container the particles will now bombard the walls twice as frequently as before, and the gas pressure, which is the manifestation of this bombardment, will be doubled. This is, of course, an example of BOYLE'S LAW.

Again, suppose that a gas confined at constant volume is heated until its molecules have doubled their average speed. These molecules should now hit the walls not only twice as frequently but also twice as hard as before, since the force of impact depends on their momentum, which, in turn, depends on their speed. Thus the force, and therefore the average pressure, exerted by the gas particles is quadrupled for a doubling of the average speed. In other words, the pressure is proportional to the *square* of the molecular speed. Since momentum equals mass times velocity, the pressure also depends on the total mass of the particles, which has not changed. Now, the kinetic energy of a moving body or a system of bodies is one-half the mass times the velocity squared (K. E. $= \frac{1}{2}mv^2$); hence the pressure exerted by a gas is evidently proportional to the average kinetic energy of the gas molecules. Finally, it is an observed fact that when a gas confined at constant volume is heated, the temperature rises in proportion to the amount of energy introduced. Thus, if pressure and absolute temperature are each proportional to the kinetic energy of the gas molecules, they must be proportional to each other also. This result yields $P/T =$ constant.

If the volume is not fixed but the outside pressure remains unchanged, the volume-temperature relation of CHARLES' LAW follows logically. Let us visualize an experiment in which a gas is confined in a cylinder equipped with a light, smoothly fitting piston, which initially is locked in place. The atmosphere presses down on it with a pressure P and the gas is heated until it develops a pressure $2P$. This causes its absolute temperature to double. When the lock is removed, the piston will be driven upward until the atmospheric pressure balances the gas pressure (*i.e.* until the gas pressure falls to P). The over-all result is that doubling the absolute temperature doubles the volume of the gas if the initial and final pressures are the same; this confirms Charles' law.

If the temperature of a gas is lowered sufficiently, the gas liquefies, undergoing a great reduction in volume and giving off a large quantity of heat without changing temperature in the process. The kinetic theory accounts for this behavior by postulating that the molecules come close together and attract one another. Since it would take work to separate them, they have far less energy as a liquid than they did as a gas at the same temperature. It is this energy, called the latent heat of vaporization, that is given off when the gas liquefies (see HEAT, LATENT). The attraction among molecules of a liquid also explains why a liquid does not expand until it fills a closed container, as a gas does.

Cooling of a liquid is accompanied by contraction as molecular motion decreases. Finally, the liquid solidifies, again with the release of energy without change in temperature. In the solid state, the molecular motion is limited to vibration about fixed points, which explains why solids retain their shape and are virtually incompressible. The molecules are held in place by strong forces of attraction; this accounts for the fact that solids do not flow and have tensile strength. (See CHANGE OF STATE.)

The mathematical foundation of the kinetic theory is properly the subject of STATISTICAL MECHANICS, which applies the techniques of probability in the velocities of molecules and examines the effects of their motion in a quantitative fashion. Daniel Bernoulli published in 1738 the first quantitative treatment of the kinetic theory of gases. His model was later revived by James Prescott Joule, and the greatest contributions to the theory were made in the latter part of the 19th cent. by Rudolf Clausius, James Clerk Maxwell, J. Willard Gibbs, and Ludwig Boltzmann.—*J. E. W.*

KINGDOM: see CLASSIFICATION OF LIVING THINGS.

KIRCHER, ATHANASIUS, 1601–80, German Jesuit, scholar, and mathematician; b. Geisa, near Fulda. In 1645 he invented the magic lantern, described in his *Ars magna lucis et umbrae* (1646). Credited with the design of an early counting machine and the perfection of the aeolian harp and the speaking tube, Kircher also pioneered in the study of Egyptian hieroglyphics. His observations and theories on volcanoes, rivers, fossils, and other geological subjects were published as *Mundus subterraneus* (1665).—*S. B.*

KIRCHHOFF, GUSTAV ROBERT, 1824–87, German physicist; b. Königsberg. He generalized the equations dealing with the flow of electricity in conductors and developed a theorem that gives the distribution of currents in a network. In his *Vorlesungen über Mathematik, Physik, und Mechanik* (1874–76) he gave a logical synthesis of mechanics which he considered an accurate description of natural phenomena. To-

Gustav Robert Kirchhoff
(Yerkes Observatory)

gether with R. H. Bunsen he made spectral analysis a highly useful means of investigating matter. Their *Über die Fraunhoferschen Linien* (1859), a study of the Fraunhofer lines in sunlight, laid the basis for SPECTROSCOPY, by which technique they discovered the elements cesium (1860) and rubidium (1861). Kirchhoff also used spectroscopy in the study of the chemical constitution of stars. The so-called KIRCHHOFF LAW of radiation states the relation between emission power and absorptivity of radiating bodies, absolute temperature, and the wavelengths emitted. He was a fellow of the Royal Society and an associate of the U. S. National Academy of Sciences.—*R. J. F.*

KIRCHHOFF'S LAWS: essentially, statements of conservation of charge and conservation of energy applied to electrical circuits, useful for finding the distribution of currents in circuit networks. The first law states that at any branch point in a circuit the sum of all the instantaneous currents into the junction is equal to the sum of those flowing out. Thus at point A in the figure, $I_4 = I_1 + I_2$ expresses the fact that as much charge flows into the junction A as flows out. The second law states that in any closed loop of a circuit the total energy per unit charge supplied by a battery or other source of emf is equal to the algebraic sum of potential differences across all portions of the loop. In the only closed path in the figure, there is one emf, E, and alone it would produce a current in the counterclockwise direction, but the actual currents may result in part from emf's in branches not here shown. Nevertheless, if OHM'S LAW applies, $E = I_2R_2 + I_3R_3 - I_1R_1$, where the term I_1R_1 is negative because the direction assumed for I_1, as indicated by the arrow, is opposite to that which would be produced by E alone. If the two laws are applied to the various loops and branch points of an entire network, the resulting equations may be

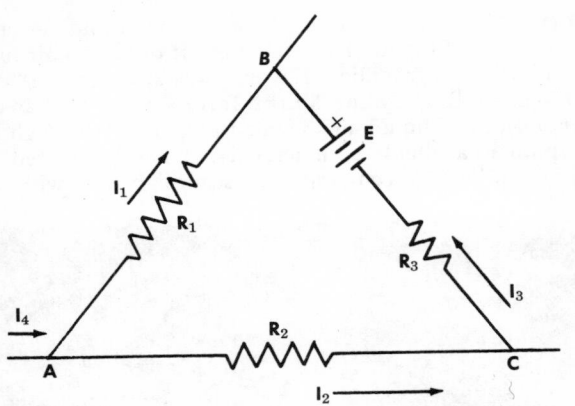

Kirchhoff's laws are illustrated by this figure of a portion of a circuit, in which each *I* represents current in amperes, and each *R* resistance in ohms.

solved to determine all the currents in terms of the emf's and the resistances.—*M. P.*

KIRKWOOD, DANIEL, 1814–95, U. S. astronomer; b. Harford County, Md. He did research in mathematical astronomy and demonstrated mathematically the necessity for the gaps in Saturn's rings and in the asteroid belt (Kirkwood's law). His objections to the nebular hypothesis aided in its downfall. His publications include *Meteoric Astronomy* (1867), *Comets and Meteors* (1873), and more than 100 articles.—*D. H. D. R.*

KJELDAHL, JOHAN G. C. T., 1849–1900, Danish chemist; b. Jaegerpris, Zealand. A chemist at the Carlsberg Brewery and first director (1876) of the Carlsberg laboratory, he was known for his research in biochemistry, plant physiology, and enzyme chemistry; and particularly for his method of determining nitrogen in plant and animal substances.—*R. E. O.*

KLAPROTH, MARTIN HEINRICH, 1743–1817, German chemist; b. Wernigerode. He helped to introduce Lavoisier's ideas into Germany and placed quantitative analysis on a sound basis by eliminating sources of error and extending methods of mineral analysis. His 6-vol. *Beiträge zur chemischen Kenntnis der Mineralkörper,* dealing with the chemistry of minerals, appeared 1795–1816. He discovered the elements uranium, zirconium, and cerium and verified the discoveries of titanium (by William Gregor) and tellurium (by F. J. Müller von Reichstein). He was a fellow of the Royal Society.—*A. I.*

KLEIN, FELIX, 1849–1925, German mathematician; b. Düsseldorf. He was professor of mathematics at Univ. of Erlangen (1872–75), Munich Technical Inst. (1875–80), Univs. of Leipzig (1880–86) and Göttingen (1886–1913). Klein was a lecturer of note and a prolific writer. In 1872 he proposed the Erlangen Programm for the study of geometries, which had great influence in Europe and the U. S. A. He founded the *Encyklopädie für Mathematik* in 1895 and was editor of *Mathematische Annalen* from 1872. Klein's researches were chiefly in geometry and theory of functions. He is also known for his lectures on the teaching of mathematics, published as *Elementary Mathematics from an Advanced Standpoint* (1908; English trans. 1932, 1939). He was a fellow of the Royal Society and an associate of the U. S. National Academy of Sciences—*H. C.*

KLEIN-NISHINA FORMULA: When a beam of light strikes free electrons, the light can be scattered as if it consisted of particles (photons). This is known as the COMPTON EFFECT. The Klein-Nishina formula gives the probability of the scattering of the photons through any given angle.—*G. M. S. and L. S.*

KLYSTRON: see ELECTRON TUBE.

KOCH, ROBERT, 1843–1910, German bacteriologist and microbiologist; b. Klausthal. His development of new methods concerned with the isolating, staining, mounting, and photographing of bacteria initiated a new era in bacteriology. He worked out the complete life cycle of the anthrax bacillus, transmitting it through many generations of mice (1876). This was the first demonstration of a specific disease as caused by a specific microorganism. In 1882 he announced discovery of the tubercle bacillus, thus establishing the infectious nature of tuberculosis. For his investigations and discoveries in regard to tuberculosis he received the 1905 Nobel prize. He was a fellow of the Royal Society and an associate of the U. S. National Academy of Sciences.—*D. H. D. R.*

Robert Koch
(N. Y. Public Library)

KÖLLIKER, RUDOLPH ALBERT, 1817–1905, Swiss anatomist and physiologist; b. Zürich. Known principally for his use of the microscope on a very extensive scale, he was also a pioneer in applying the cell theory to embryology. Kölliker's many achievements include: demonstrating that the nerve fibers are connected with processes of the ganglion cells; isolating the smooth-muscle fiber; showing that spermatozoa are not parasites and that they are cellular in origin; recognizing the segmentation of the ovum. His *Handbuch der Gewebelehre des Menschen* (1852) has been called the first modern work on histology. He was a fellow of the Royal Society and received its Copley medal (1897).—*D. H. D. R.*

KÖPPEN, WLADIMIR PETER, 1846–1940, German meteorologist; b. St. Petersburg, Russia. He developed the most widely used classification of world climates, and investigated and mapped the wind distribution of the world. Author of many papers on meteorology, he was also meteorologist at the German Naval Observatory, Hamburg (1875–1918).—*D. H. D. R.*

KORNBERG, ARTHUR, 1918–   , U. S. biochemist; b. Brooklyn, N. Y. In 1955 he discovered a bacterial enzyme that synthesizes deoxyribonucleic acid (DNA) from the nucleotide triphosphates in the presence of a small amount of "primer" DNA. For their discoveries of the mechanism of the biological synthesis of ribonucleic acids and deoxyribonucleic acids, he and S. Ochoa shared the 1959 Nobel prize. He is a member of the National Academy of Sciences.—*D. H. D. R.*

KOSSEL, ALBRECHT, 1853–1927, German biochemist; b. Rostock. Kossel applied the methods of organic chemistry to research in physiology. For his contributions to the knowledge of the chemistry of the cell, primarily his work on proteins and nucleic acids, he received the Nobel prize, 1910. He suggested that the amino acids might be considered as "building stones" in the metabolism of proteins. He was an associate of the U. S. National Academy of Sciences.—*D. H. D. R.*

KOVALEVSKY, ALEKSANDR ONUFRÏEVICH, 1840–1901, Russian embryologist; b. Dünaburg. He is known for his theory concerning the relationship between the vertebrates and the invertebrates and particularly for his study of the primitive marine chordate known as the lancelet. Kovalevsky studied the anatomy and embryology of numerous different animal forms. A student of E. H. Haeckel's, he firmly supported his teacher's theory of germinal layers. He was professor at St. Petersburg Univ. and the author of many specialized anatomical and embryological publications. He was a fellow of the Royal Society.—*D. H. D. R.*

KOVALEVSKY, SONYA (SOFYA), 1850–91, Russian mathematician; b. Moscow. At Heidelberg she studied under Helmholtz, Kirchhoff, Königsberger, and Du Bois-Reymond. Karl Weierstrass, in Berlin, took her as a private pupil when the university refused to admit a woman to his lectures, and a close relationship between the two continued throughout her life. In 1874 Göttingen Univ. granted her a degree, for which

Sonya Kovalevsky
(*N. Y. Public Library*)

she submitted three dissertations; one, on partial differential equations, was outstanding. She did valuable work in mechanics, her use of theta-functions showing how the theory of functions could be applied to physical problems. Professor at the Univ. of Stockholm from 1884, she was elected to the Paris Academy in 1888 and to St. Petersburg Academy just before her death. The outstanding woman mathematician of the 19th cent., she shares with Emmy Nöther the highest place among women mathematicians of the modern world.—*H. C.*

K-RADIATION: X-RAYS emitted by excited K-electrons.

KREBS, HANS ADOLPH, 1900–　, German-British biochemist; b. Hildesheim. After leaving Nazi Germany in 1935, he went to Britain, where he investigated the conversion of foods into energy and the interconversion of intermediates in the metabolism of fats, amino acids, and sugars via the CITRIC-ACID CYCLE (**Krebs cycle**). For his discovery and formulation of this cycle, he shared the 1953 Nobel prize with F. A. Lipmann. He is a fellow of the Royal Society.—*D. H. D. R.*

KROGH, AUGUST, 1874–1949, Danish physiologist; b. Grenaa. For his discovery of the regulation of the motor mechanism of capillaries he received the 1920 Nobel prize. Much of his research was concerned with gases, the influence of gaseous pressures on respiration, and the physiology of respiration and blood circulation. He was professor of physiology at the Univ. of Copenhagen, a fellow of the Royal Society, and an associate of the U. S. National Academy of Sciences.—*D. H. D. R.*

KRONECKER, LEOPOLD, 1823–91, German mathematician; b. Liegnitz, Prussia. An algebraist and a contributor to the theory of algebraic numbers, he insisted that the structure of mathematics must be founded upon positive whole numbers and finite processes. Irrational numbers were anathema to him, and he criticized analysis because of its dependence upon infinite processes and, in particular, upon real numbers defined by infinite sequences of rational numbers. He was a fellow of the Royal Society.—*H. C.*

KRYPTON: an inert gaseous element (Kr); at. no. 36; at. wt 83.80. One of the rarer INERT GASES, it occurs in air in less than one part per million. Krypton was discovered, 1898, by Sir William Ramsay and Morris Travers by spectral analysis of a residue of liquid air they had prepared. Although little krypton is available commercially, it has been used in a variety of incandescent and fluorescent lights. As with other

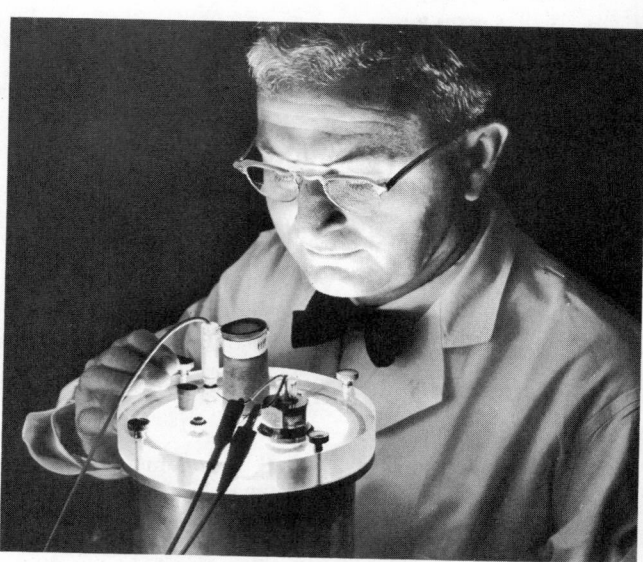

Krypton-86 lamp is being adjusted by government scientist at National Bureau of Standards. Krypton-86, a non-radioactive isotope, emits an orange-red light at a stable wavelength, which has been adopted as the International Standard of Length. (*National Bureau of Standards*)

inert gases, its virtue in incandescent bulbs is that it does not react with the hot tungsten filament (as oxygen or nitrogen would); in fluorescent bulbs krypton emits a pale-violet light when electric current passes through it.—*T. M.*

KUHN, RICHARD, 1900–　, German biochemist; b. Vienna. For his work on carotenoids and vitamins, he was awarded the 1938 Nobel prize in chemistry, but was forced by the Nazi government to decline. Author of more than 500 papers, he has studied conjugate double bonds, the polyenes and diphenylpolyenes, amino sugars, and cumelenes; determined the constitution of at least eight alkaloids and vitamin B_2; and isolated vitamin B_6. He has been an editor of *Annalen der Chemie* since 1948.—*V. B.*

KUMMER, ERNST EDUARD, 1810–93, German mathematician; b. Sorau. He attended the Univ. of Halle to study theology but changed to mathematics, taking his doctor's degree at 21. Kummer was a great teacher and a researcher of depth and originality, capable in applied fields but preferring pure mathematics. His greatest contribution came out of his work on Fermat's Last Theorem; it resulted in the creation of "ideal" numbers. He was a fellow of the Royal Society.—*H. C.*

KUSCH, POLYKARP, 1911–63, U. S. physicist; b. Blankenburg, Germany. His research was on atomic and molecular structure and molecular beams. For the precise determination of the magnetic moment of the electron, he shared the 1955 Nobel prize with W. E. Lamb, Jr. During World War II he engaged in research on microwave vacuum tubes and generators. He was a member of the National Academy of Sciences.—*D. H. D. R.*

L

LACAILLE (or **LA CAILLE**), **NICOLAS LOUIS DE**, 1713–62, French astronomer; b. Rumigny. During his successful expedition to the Cape of Good Hope (1750–54) to determine the solar and lunar parallax, he personally observed 10,000 stars. Coordinates of 2,000 of these and descriptions of 14 new southern constellations were published in his *Coelum australe stelliferum* (1763). Lacaille was known as the leading French observational astronomer of his day. His other publications include *Astronomiae fundamenta* (1757), giving accurate positions of 400 bright stars, and *Tabulae solares* (1758), which gave solar positions corrected for planetary perturbations. He was a member of the Academy of Sciences and a fellow of the Royal Society.—*O. G.*

LACCOLITH: see INTRUSIVE ROCK.

LA CONDAMINE, CHARLES MARIE DE, 1701–74, French mathematician and geographer; b. Paris. He was sent in 1735, with Pierre Bouguer and Louis Godin, to Quito (Peru, now Ecuador) to measure a degree of the meridian near the equator. The findings of this expedition, 1735–43, verified Newton's theory that Earth is flattened at the poles. Another result of the expedition was Bouguer's deduction, from gravitational anomalies encountered in the Andes, that the rocks constituting the mountains' "roots" are lighter than the surrounding rocks. Bouguer's theory was important to the concept of ISOSTASY. La Condamine, the first scientific traveler to descend the Amazon, wrote of his trip to the equator in his *Journal du voyage fait par ordre du roi a l'équateur* (1751). He also wrote *La figure de la terre déterminée par les observations de MM Bouguer et de la Condamine* (1749), which concerned the shape of Earth. Other works of La Condamine promoted inoculation in France (1754–73). He was a member of the Academy of Sciences and a fellow of the Royal Society.—*D. J. S.*

LACQUER: a clear or pigmented coating containing cellulose derivatives or other resinous materials (*e.g.* acrylics, epoxies, and urethanes) in solution; it dries and hardens by *evaporation* of the solvent rather than by oxidation or polymerization as in the case of paints and enamels. Alcohol-wet nitrocellulose or other cellulose esters are dissolved in suitable thinners (*i.e.* volatile liquids); resin solutions, plasticizers, and

Fast-drying lacquer is applied by spray gun in spot-painting of a repaired automobile fender. (*DeVilbiss* Co.)

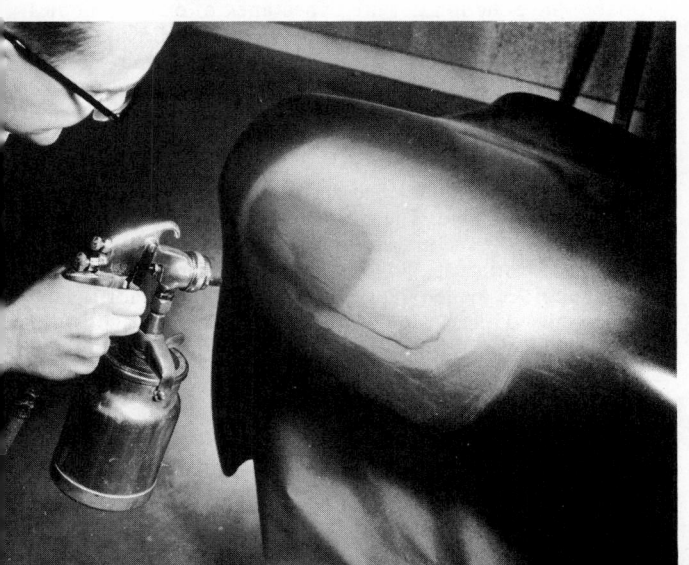

balanced thinners are then added. Non-cellulosic resins are similarly compounded to form lacquers. Since the 1920s lacquers have been used as automobile finishes: because lacquer is faster-drying and requires fewer coats than other finishes, automobile "painting" is now a matter of hours rather than the pre-1920 month or more. Hot spraying, steam spraying, airless atomization, and other methods have greatly added to the satisfactory and economical use of lacquers. Pigmented lacquers are often called enamels.—*L. F.*

LACROIX, FRANÇOIS ANTOINE ALFRED, 1863–1948, French mineralogist; b. Mâcon. He wrote nearly 700 scientific publications, and his *Minéralogie de la France et de ses colonies* (5 vols., 1893–1913) is one of the most comprehensive mineralogical works ever published. His mineralogical studies of Madagascar and of volcanoes are well known. A member of the Academy of Sciences, he was also a fellow of the Royal Society and an associate of the U. S. Academy of Sciences. —*D. H. D. R.*

LACTIC ACID: see GLYCOLYSIS.

LACTOSE: see SUGAR.

LA DISME ("DE THIENDE," THE TENTH), by Simon Stevin, 1585. Although Stevin did not invent decimal fractions, which had been used earlier by astronomers, in this small pamphlet he introduced them for the first time to the arithmetic of practical men. Through his teaching this elegant simplification passed into general use; moreover, Stevin was the first to realize the advantages of decimal systems of weights, measures, and currency. The modern notation for decimals (*e.g.* 3.142, which Stevin would have written 3⓪1①4②2③) was devised by John Napier.—*A. R. H.*

LAGRANGE, JOSEPH LOUIS, 1736–1813, French mathematician; b. Turin. He organized the research society that developed into the Turin Academy of Sciences, and was a fellow of the Royal Society. Early in his career he became interested in calculus variations and laid out for himself the study of mechanics from an analytic viewpoint with this calculus as the central and unifying theme. This work, com-

Joseph Louis Lagrange
(*New York Public Library*)

pleted more than 25 yr later, was embodied in the great *Mécanique analytique* (1788); it was a systematic development of mechanics in purely analytic terms requiring no diagrams whatever. The basic differential equations relate the three "generalized" coordinates of a point and the time, and Lagrange observed that mechanics can thus be regarded as a four-dimensional geometry. As president of the French commission on weights and measures, Lagrange influenced the adoption of the metric system (1799). In 1797 he became first professor of the newly founded École Polytechnique. A great teacher of mathematics, he followed the analytic methods which he had developed. Two of his books that in-

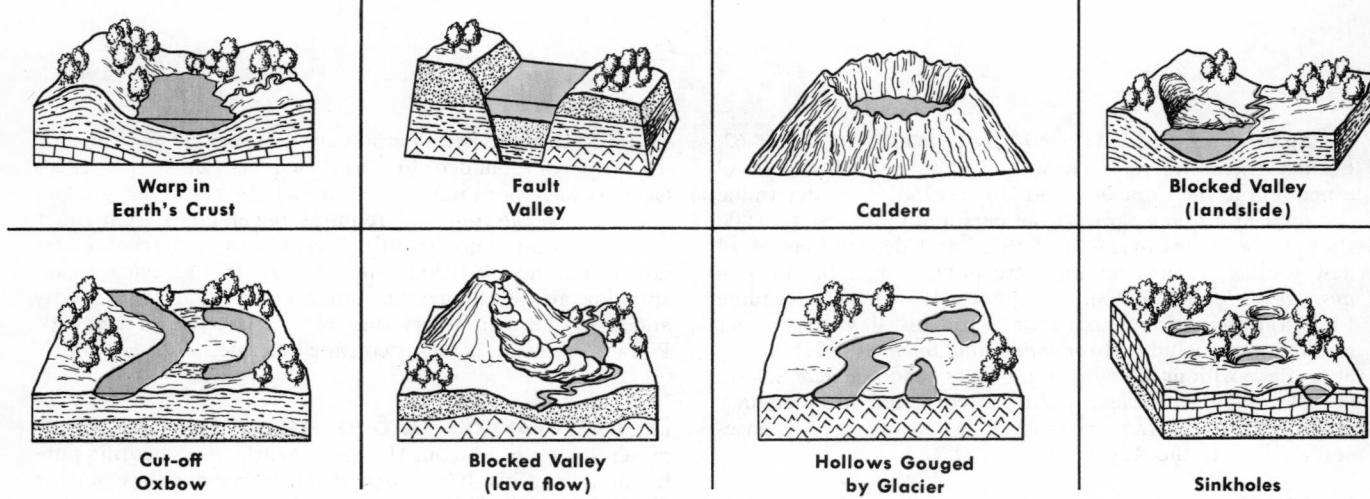

Warp in Earth's Crust	**Fault Valley**	**Caldera**	**Blocked Valley (landslide)**
Cut-off Oxbow	**Blocked Valley (lava flow)**	**Hollows Gouged by Glacier**	**Sinkholes**

Some Types of Basins in Which Lakes May Form

spired and influenced later mathematicians (notably A. L. Cauchy) were *Théorie des fonctions analytiques* (1797) and *Leçons sur le calcul des fonctions* (1801), on calculus of functions. His contributions to mathematics also included application of calculus to the theory of probability and important work on the solution of equations. He was a member of the Academy of Sciences.—*H. C.*

LAGUERRE, EDMOND-NICOLAS, 1834–86, French mathematician; b. Bar-le-Duc. One of the founders of modern geometry, he contributed greatly to linear systems and the theory of equations. He published some 500 memoirs in various journals.—*H. C.*

LAKE: a body of water occupying a hollow, or basin, of the Earth's surface and not forming part of the ocean system. Lakes are among the most short-lived of natural features; probably none endures as long as 100,000 yr, and most disappear more rapidly. They are essentially the result of a temporary interruption of the hydrologic cycle. Water of precipitation (rain or snow), in its course from higher to lower elevations and eventually to sea level, is held for a time in basins. Water so held is maintained as a lake as long as the ingress of water equals or exceeds the egress. Since natural conditions favor egress, the lake must eventually disappear.

Some water is supplied to a lake as the runoff of precipitation: rain or snow may fall directly upon the basin; or it may be carried into the basin by streams or as meltwater from a glacier. It may also be supplied as discharge from ground water; and wherever a WATER TABLE intersects the floor of a basin, a lake forms. A humid climate and the former presence of glaciers in an area of irregular surface account for most of the world's lakes, which are distributed very unevenly over the earth's surface. As lake water continues to participate in the hydrologic cycle, the lake "dies." Drainage and evaporation are two processes that doom a lake. As soon as the basin is filled to the lowest point of its rim, water flows out of the lake at that point; the outflowing water, like all streams, erodes its bed, increasing the break in the rim. The continuance of this process inevitably drains the lake. Simultaneously, evaporation occurs at the surface of the lake, and the larger the surface, the greater the amount of evaporation. Lakes with reliable water sources sometimes maintain a short-range equilibrium: as the elevation of the outlet is reduced, the water level falls, the surface area decreases, and therefore loss by evaporation declines. Conversely, if evaporation brings the surface below the lowest point of the basin's rim, outflow ends. A minor loss of lake water occurs through percolation downward if, as in some arid areas, a nonsaturated zone separates the lake bed from the water table. Lakes are also doomed because the basins they occupy are filled as rock particles are carried in by streams and deposited as sediment. Other solids dissolved in the water are precipitated out during evaporation. This combination of drainage, evaporation, seepage, deposition, and precipitation afflicts every lake in greater or lesser degree.

The quality of lake water ranges from "fresh," with the minimum of dissolved matter characteristic of runoff and precipitated water, to saline. Salinity increases in proportion as evaporation exceeds drainage. The extreme is reached when a lake in an arid region has no outlet: salt-bearing water enters and is rapidly evaporated, leaving a residue of solid precipitates (see EVAPORITES), of which salt (sodium chloride), sodium sulfate, various carbonates, and borax are the most common. The composition of the rock along the course of the feeding stream determines the type of prevailing evaporite.

Lakes are thus most conveniently classified as fresh-water or saline. Among the former, glacial lakes predominate, and are found in such regions as Canada and the northern U. S. A., Scandinavia, and S Chile, all areas that experienced geologically recent glacial activity and have relatively humid climates. Saline lakes are characteristic of poorly drained arid regions, *e.g.* central Asia, the Australian deserts, and the basin-and-range province of the western U. S. A. The Great Lakes are the most impressive lakes of glacial origin, and probably have the longest life expectancy of existing bodies of inland water. The largest saline lake is the Caspian Sea, which is visibly disappearing; an even more dramatic example of a short-lived lake is the Great Salt Lake, saline remnant of the once extensive fresh-water Lake Bonneville. The extreme in this category is the PLAYA lake, which exists as a lake only for a brief period after heavy rain.

Lakes may also be classified according to the type of basin in which they are held. The two principal types are structural depressions and erosional hollows. Crustal movements form rifts, lesser downthrusts, hollows between upthrusts, or warps, all irregularities which may receive water and form lake basins. Lake Titicaca in South America, Lake Baikal in Siberia, the Dead Sea in Palestine, and Lake Tahoe in the U. S. A. fill such basins. Much more common are the irregularities resulting from differential erosion. When approximately bowl- or saucer-shaped, such hollows may hold bodies of water. These are generally very short-lived unless gouged by glacial action to considerable depth. The blocking of a river valley impounds the water into a lake. Glaciation, mass wasting, and volcanism account for three principal kinds of natural dams: the moraine; the mudflow or landslide; and the lava flow. Other natural hollows that may hold lakes are: the CALDERAS of volcanoes; SINKHOLES of a karst formation; CIRQUES at the heads of mountain glaciers; and abandoned river channels (see OXBOW). A lagoon on an emerging seacoast may become a lake.

Lakes forming part of a stream system modify the erosional activity and localize the depositional activity of the stream. As flowing water enters a lake, its velocity falls and part of its load of sediment is deposited; the lake acts as a filter. The outflowing stream is thus deprived of much of the sediment itself, because of having passed through the lake. Especially in flood periods, a lake basin may collect the runoff for more gradual distribution to lower levels. This natural regulative function is adapted by man in the construction of artificial lakes, usually by building dams across river valleys. Man-made lakes, *e.g.* Lake Mead in the Colorado River system, are both large and deep, but they have the same life expectancy as natural lakes: Lake Mead will be filled by sediment within five centuries.

Lakes, both natural and artificial, have varied economic and social uses. Larger lakes are transportation arteries. As impounded runoff, lake waters are applied to irrigation, power supply, and industrial and household water supply. Lakes are also major recreational features, valued by fishermen, water sportsmen, and tourists. Several regions of the world, such as England's Lake District, the Alpine lake region, and Maine, Minnesota, and Wisconsin exploit the esthetic value of lakes. See Color Plates 59–60.—*E. A.*

LALANDE, JOSEPH JÉRÔME LE FRANÇAIS DE, 1732–1807, French astronomer; b. Bourg, Ain. His reputation was established by his observations at Berlin to determine the lunar parallax (1751). His works include the *Traité complet d'astronomie,* a multivolume textbook (1764 ff.), and *Histoire céleste Française,* a catalog of 50,000 star positions (1801). In 1769 he took over the almanac *Connoissance des Temps* and, by the excellence of his tables, virtually drove the competing French almanac out of business. He was a fellow of the Royal Society.—*O. G.*

LAMARCK, JEAN BAPTISTE PIERRE ANTOINE DE MONET, CHEVALIER DE, 1744–1829, French biologist; b. Bazantin, Picardy. He proposed the theory of organic evolution, conceiving of the process as proceeding continuously from simple forms at the bottom of the "Scala" (ladder) to the highest types of life. He assumed that new life was being formed spontaneously at the bottom, and that changes in individuals produced by the environment ("acquired characteristics") were inheritable. (See LAMARCKISM.) The term *Lamarckian* is often used to refer to the disproved idea about inheritability of acquired characteristics. Charles Darwin, however, fully acknowledged his debt to Lamarck for the concept of evolution itself. Lamarck's theory was fully expounded in his PHILOSOPHIE ZOOLOGIQUE (*Zoological Philosophy,* 1809).

Jean Baptiste Pierre Antoine de Monet, Chevalier de Lamarck

(Clay-Adams, Inc.)

His greatest technical work was a multivolume natural history of invertebrates: *Histoire naturelle des animaux sans vertèbres* (1815–22).—*L. and M. M.*

LAMARCKISM: the concept that modifications induced in an individual by the environment are transmitted to the individual's descendants and thus direct evolution. The theory was proposed in 1794 by Erasmus Darwin, grandfather of Charles, and in 1801 by Jean Baptiste de Lamarck. Lamarck suggested, for example, that a shore bird developed longer legs by stretching above the water; the longer legs were inherited and lengthened from generation to generation. He suggested that the "inner consciousness," prodded by need, induced the formation of new organs. August Weismann and others demonstrated that inheritance fails to transmit environmental changes, and they concluded that Darwin was right in his theory that the environment directs EVOLUTION through NATURAL SELECTION. Nevertheless, the inheritance of acquired characteristics was the official doctrine of the Soviet Union until 1964, when the ideas of biologist Trofim D. Lysenko were finally discredited in that country. Today, some biologists consider that certain types of acquired modifications in unicellular organisms are transmissible, as demonstrated by work on protozoans. Mechanical and chemical manipulation of paramecia, for example, produce individuals with several mouths, and this trait is inherited by the daughter cells, though the genetic material was not itself altered.—*J. B.*

LAMB, WILLIS EUGENE, JR., 1913– , U. S. physicist; b. Los Angeles, Calif. His research has been in atomic and nuclear structure, microwave spectroscopy, and fine structure of hydrogen and helium. The *Lamb shift* is a slight difference in energy levels in hydrogen atoms, which he described in a paper in 1947. For his discoveries regarding the hyperfine structure of the hydrogen spectrum, he shared the 1955 Nobel prize with Polykarp Kusch. Lamb is a member of the National Academy of Sciences.—*D. H. D. R.*

LAMBERT, JOHANN HEINRICH, 1728–77, French-German mathematician and scientist; b. Alsace. He was largely self-taught, with a fine imagination and high standard of rigor. Lambert made an investigation of parallels, entitled *Die Theorie der Parallellinien* and published after his death, that was similar to the one made by Saccheri some years earlier. He was the first to prove that π is irrational. He developed the theory of hyperbolic functions systematically and invented the present notation for the functions. He contributed to the theory of projections employed in making maps; many modern maps are called Lambert projections. He also contributed to methods of determining orbits of comets and, in physics, obtained valuable results in the measurement of the intensity of light and heat.—*H. C.*

LAMETTRIE, JULIEN OFFRAY DE, 1709–51, French physician and philosopher; b. St. Malo. In his controversial *Man the Machine* (1748), he argued, on the basis of medical observations, the materialistic theses that mental processes are mechanical functions of brain processes, that men and animals alike are machine-like, and that "in the Universe there is but one substance, diversely modified."—*A. D.*

LAMINAR FLOW: see FLUID FLOW.

LANDSLIDES, EARTH FLOWS, AND SLUMPING: gravitational downslope movements of rock or earth, consisting of materials that range in size from the finest particles to large rock masses. If the body of material slides as a mass on a definite shearing surface, it is a *landslide;* if it moves as in the pouring of sand from a tumbler, by interparticle adjustments distributed throughout the mass, it is an *earth flow.* Combinations of flow and slide are common. Landslides move at a readily perceptible rate, and if the movement is extremely rapid, the term *debris avalanche,* or *rock avalanche,* is used. (Similar rapid slides of ice and snow, common in mountain areas, are simply *avalanches.*) Undercutting or oversteepening of slopes is a frequent cause of slides, as along sea coasts, river banks, or artificial cuts. Overloading may start a slope failure. The presence of excess water is almost always a contributing condition, and is usually the proximate cause, for heavy rains or melting snows add weight as openings become saturated; water destroys cohesion; and water may exert hydraulic pressures that reduce friction. The presence of rock cracks sloping downhill, and of weak or slippery rock layers sloping downhill, constitutes structural conditions for failure.

Earth flow may or may not occur at readily perceptible rates. A common type, perceptible only by its results, is called *creep.* The gradual overturning of retaining walls is a common evidence. Creep is grain-by-grain downslope movement with many causes. Frost action lifts a grain which subsequently settles back, downslope. Burrows made by ants and worms fill in from the upslope side, as do plant root tubes; raindrop splash and run-off trickle are effective in inching particles downslope. The cumulative effects may be large indeed.

More rapid than creep are *mud flows* or *soil flows,* which result from loss of cohesion due to rains or meltwater. These generally take place in a dry climate where the limited rainfall takes place in cloudbursts, quickly saturating the surficial soils. If the movement is essentially a sinking on a subcylindrical surface of failure, the term *slump* is applied.

Slope failures annually cost millions in highway maintenance and repair. They are hazards to railroad lines, to homes and other buildings on slopes, and to various structures along river banks and sea coasts. Gravity is the principal agent, water the principal villain, in slope failures. Gravity cannot be suspended, but adequate drainage can be provided and is the best preventive, as well as the most frequently successful cure.—*J. T.*

Failure of coastal cliff at Point Firman, Calif., resulted from instability due to saturation. Undercutting of such cliffs by sea also is a weakening factor. (*Spence Air Photo*)

Slumgullion earth flow, 5 mi long, blocked valley to form Lake San Cristobal, Hinsdale Co., Colorado. It consisted of volcanic ash saturated by heavy rains. (*U. S. Geological Survey*)

LANDSTEINER, KARL, 1868–1943, Austrian–U. S. bacteriologist and pathologist; b. Vienna. For his discovery that normal human blood can be divided into several blood groups he received the 1930 Nobel prize. In 1940 he and A. S. Wiener discovered that the Rh (Rhesus) factor is common in human blood. Landsteiner became a member of the Rockefeller Inst. for Medical Research, New York (1922), and was a member of the National Academy of Sciences.—*D. H. D. R.*

LANGEVIN, PAUL, 1872–1946, French physicist; b. Paris. He investigated gaseous ions, Brownian movement, diamagnetism and paramagnetism, electric and magnetic double refraction, and relativity. He wrote more than 100 articles, and his *Oeuvres scientifiques* were published in 1950. A fellow of the Royal Society, he succeeded Pierre Curie as professor in the Sorbonne's School of Physics and Chemistry.—*D. H. D. R.*

LANGLEY, JOHN NEWPORT, 1852–1925, English physiologist; b. Newbury. The first 15 yr of his research were devoted to a systematic exploration of the secretory process; this was followed by an equal period of studies of the sympathetic nervous system. Langley was a fellow of the Royal Society.—*D. H. D. R.*

LANGLEY, SAMUEL PIERPONT, 1834–1906, U. S. astronomer and aeronautical researcher; b. Roxbury, Mass.; self-educated after high school. As director of the Allegheny Observatory, Pittsburgh (1867–87), he observed the solar eclipses of 1869, 1870, and 1878. He invented (1878) the BOLOMETER, which he used to determine the transparency of the atmosphere to solar radiation and to measure the increase in the intensity

Samuel Pierpont Langley
(Yerkes Observatory)

of solar radiation at high altitudes. He plotted 740 absorption lines in the solar spectrum, recording them photographically. A pioneer in aerodynamic research, Langley began the study of lift and drag effects while still at the observatory. In 1896 he built two steam-propelled flying machines ("aerodromes") which achieved pilotless flights of 3,000 and 4,200 ft, respectively. His endeavors to achieve manned flight were dropped for lack of funds after he failed in two attempts to fly an airplane (powered by a radial gasoline engine) from a launching platform atop a houseboat in the Potomac River, 1903. Langley wrote *Experiments in Aerodynamics* (1891), *The Internal Work of the Wind* (1893), and *On the Possible Variation of Solar Radiation* (1905). He served as secretary of the Smithsonian Institution, 1887–1906. He was a fellow of the Royal Society and a member of the National Academy of Sciences.—*S. B.*

LANGMUIR, IRVING, 1881–1957, U. S. chemist; b. Brooklyn, N. Y. Langmuir developed the coiled tungsten-filament electric lamp, essentially the electric light bulb in use today. His work in molecular hydrogen led to the invention of the atomic hydrogen welding torch. In 1913 his invention, with Gaede, of the mercury diffusion pump for the production of high vacuums materially contributed to progress in electronics. Beginning (1921) a study of plasma, Langmuir laid the foundation for present investigations of plasma in the utilization of nuclear fission. For his work in the structure of matter and surface chemistry, Langmuir received the Nobel prize in chemistry in 1932. Before his death in 1957, he experimented extensively in techniques of seeding clouds with silver

iodide to start rainfall. A fellow of the Royal Society, he was a member of the National Academy of Sciences.—*A. L.*

LANGUAGE: consists of *speech* and *writing* (in a broad sense that includes printing and other recording devices for reproducing the original sounds). Because linguistic behavior is of such central importance to all the social studies, it has been increasingly investigated by scientific method. But language is crucially important to science in another way, since all scientific thought must be expressed *in* language, or by means of sophisticated substitutes (mathematical and chemical formulas, graphs, diagrams, codes) that depend upon language for their interpretation. The very existence of science as a social activity demands a free and efficient flow of ideas and techniques between the members of the scientific community. Theoretical mastery of the character of language, as a distinctively human invention, and active interest in its conservation and improvement, are vital to the scientific enterprise.

A spoken language is an organized system of recognizably similar sounds, combined in conventional ways to produce utterances that mean something to suitably trained hearers. Each language uses a *finite* stock of single speech sounds (more accurately, a range of similar sounds that function interchangeably). From such *phonemes,* defined as the "minimum units of distinctive sound-features" (Leonard Bloomfield) are built up the smallest units having independent meanings (words or other *morphemes*). These, in turn, combine according to grammatical rules to produce full utterances. Thus, the English word *cat* is composed of three phonemes and has an arbitrary meaning attached to it. The total meaning of a simple sentence such as "The cat is hungry" is a function of the individual meanings of the four morphemes composing it.

The importance of language as an indispensable instrument of thought and communication depends upon the following features: (1) The movements needed to produce the phonemes (and such auxiliary sound features as intonation and stress) are relatively easy to perform and to teach; thus language can be readily transmitted as a social heritage. (2) Spoken words are heard by the speaker, who reacts upon himself in talking and so comes to know the effects produced in his partner; speech has *feedback*. (3) The *conventional* links between words and their meanings permit thought (possible only via language) in the absence of what is being thought about; upon this depends all human foresight and imagination. (4) The grammatical rules for sentence construction allow for infinitely many types of new utterances; a literate human being can roam freely in the realm of the possible, and man alone, among the animals, can deceive and lie. Only humans can produce sounds having these basic properties. The various signals by which crickets, sticklebacks, howler monkeys, and other animals cooperate, and even the fantastically elaborate "dances" that bees use to report food sources, fall short of speech in the full sense.

Scientific study of language enlists many different specialists. Linguists have been very successful in devising formal schemes for describing the phonemic structure, the vocabulary, and the grammar of living and dead languages. Detailed knowledge of the thousands of different languages spoken today has aroused keen interest in the possible influence of language upon thought ("psycholinguistics"). Use of high-precision instruments for recording and analyzing speech promises to illuminate the physical and physiological aspects of language. But much still remains mysterious about the origins of language and about its psychology and pathology. Important suggestions have recently come from advances in CYBERNETICS and from INFORMATION THEORY. Still more are likely to come from current work on theory of com-

Lost language reconstructed: Trilingual inscription on basalt fragment found by the French at Rosetta, in Nile delta, in 1799 and now in British Museum, offered key to then still-undeciphered Egyptian hieroglyphics. The Greek (*bottom band*) was transparent; the demotic cursive (*middle*) was deciphered by 1802; hieroglyphic text (*top*) yielded in parts to attack by English physicist Thomas Young (1819), then completely to analysis by French Egyptologist J.-F. Champollion in 1821. Text proved to be decree of thanksgiving by Memphis priesthood honoring reform monarch Ptolemy Epiphanes. (*Smithsonian Institution*)

puting machines and from researches into mechanical translation.

Work on the language of science itself has largely been undertaken by philosophers of science. A principal aim has been to clarify the language, and hence the concepts, of separate branches of science. In geometry, for instance, it has proved possible to list a minimal vocabulary of basic terms, to state the grammatical rules for their combination, to determine a sufficient set of initial statements ("axioms"), and to state exact rules for deriving theorems. Such an improved language for geometry prepares the ground for sophisticated studies of logical structure. Here, as elsewhere, improvement in language goes hand in hand with the clarification of basic concepts.—*M. B.*

LANKESTER, SIR EDWIN RAY, 1847–1929, English zoologist; b. London. He is best known for his work in classifying the principal divisions of the animal kingdom. Through an immense number of separate investigations, chiefly on comparative embryology and anatomy, he described the underlying relationships now regarded as fundamental to classification of Protozoa, the acoelomate phyla, mollusks, arthropods, annelids, and invertebrate chordates. He emphasized the importance of the coelom, germ layers, and evidences of recapitulation during development. Many embryological terms and major taxonomic categories proposed by Lankester have wide use today. His most important single work was *Notes on the Embryology and Classification of the Animal Kingdom* (1877). He was a fellow of the Royal Society and an associate of the U. S. National Academy of Sciences.—*L. and M. M.*

LANOLIN: a purified form of the translucent wool-fat obtained when raw sheep's wool is scoured. Lanolin contains waxes, alcohols, and free acids; and it forms relatively stable emulsions characterized by unusually large proportions of water. It is said to penetrate the skin easily, and is therefore used as a base for salves and ointments.—*Ru. M.*

LANTHANIDES: the chemical elements which occupy spaces 57 through 71 in the periodic table. They take their name from the first element in the group: lanthanum. They are the RARE EARTHS, but this term is frequently broadened to include other elements which fall in the same group (IIIB) of the periodic table, while the term "lanthanide" refers strictly to elements 57 through 71. In some cases, too, lanthanum itself is excluded from the lanthanide series, being considered only as the base point or prototype. The lanthanides are very similar in their chemical properties, particularly in their hydrated compounds, so that chemical separation has been extremely difficult. All form rather hard, high-melting oxides, borides, sulfides, and carbides, and have a number of potential ceramic and abrasive applications. Cerium oxide has, as a matter of fact, been used in glass-polishing for a good many years. In physical, magnetic, electrical, and nuclear properties, the lanthanides differ a great deal; *e.g.* gadolinium has one of the highest thermal neutron cross-section, while cerium's cross-section is quite low. Among the members of the group are ferromagnetic, antimagnetic, and paramagnetic materials, with at least one member of the group (holmium) showing all three properties, depending on the temperature at which it is held. Several of the elements (notably lanthanum, gadolinium, erbium) form semiconducting compounds, and are now under test for electronic applications. One element of the group, promethium (element 61), seems to have no stable form; it is not found in nature but has been produced in nuclear reactors.—*A. R. G.*

LANTHANUM: a rare-earth metal (La); at. no. 57; at. wt 138.92; sp gr 6.16; mp about 850°C. It gives its name to the LANTHANIDE series, the group of 14 elements whose atomic numbers (58–71) directly follow that of lanthanum in the periodic table. It was discovered, 1839, by the Swedish chemist Carl Gustav Mosander, a pupil of the great Berzelius, when investigating a sample of the mineral cerite, the same mineral in which Berzelius had discovered the element CERIUM some 35 yr before. Mosander's discovery consisted of separating the oxide of "a new metal" (lanthanum) from cerium oxide. Lanthanum is the third most abundant of the rare-earth metals, cerium and neodymium being more plentiful. Pure lanthanum metal is white, malleable, and ductile. It is found associated with other rare earths such as cerium in the minerals albanite and monazite, as well as in cerite; it can be isolated by fractional crystallization, and (in its purest form) by CHROMATOGRAPHY. Lanthanum oxide (La_2O_3) is the strongest BASE of the rare-earth group. Mixed with other rare earths, lanthanum finds use in alloying materials such as *misch metal,* which contains about 20% lanthanum: this "mixed metal" was originally a pyrophoric but is now more commonly a constituent of certain iron, steel, and aluminum alloys to which misch metal is added to drive out undesirable impurities (*e.g.* sulfur from steel) or to impart desired properties (*e.g.* hardness to stainless steel). Lanthanum oxide has been used like cerium in gas (Welsbach) mantles (see LIGHTING); to remove reactive gases from inside vacuum tubes; and in producing optical glass. See RARE EARTHS.—*E. H. H.*

LAPLACE, PIERRE SIMON, MARQUIS DE, 1749–1827, French mathematician; b. Beaumont-en-Auge, Normandy; ed. at military school there. A protégé of D'Alembert and a colleague of Lagrange at the École Normale, Laplace was one of the seminal thinkers of modern mathematics. Besides contributing important papers to the French Academy, he wrote three great works which rank as classics: MÉCANIQUE CÉLESTE (1799–1825), in which he demonstrated the stability of the solar system under the force of gravity; *Exposition du système du monde* (1796), a popular treatise on astronomy, in which he first enunciated his famous NEBULAR HYPOTHESIS; and *Théorie analytique des probabilités* (1812), in which he contributed much to the theory of probability. In treating certain physical problems, Laplace made much use of potential functions, which he showed were solutions of the equation

$$\frac{\partial^2 V}{\partial x^2} + \frac{\partial^2 V}{\partial y^2} + \frac{\partial^2 V}{\partial z^2} = 0$$

This has since been called Laplace's equation. His *Works* were published in 7 vols. (1843–47, 1878–1912). He was a member of the Academy of Sciences and a fellow of the Royal Society.—*H. C.*

LAPSE RATE: in meteorology, the rate at which air temperature decreases with height. Its magnitude indicates whether the atmosphere is stable or unstable. The critical value of 5.4°F per 1,000 ft, known as the *dry adiabatic lapse rate,* is that for which a volume of unsaturated air moving vertically is always at the same temperature and pressure as its surroundings. A superadiabatic lapse rate throughout a deep layer is often the first sign of a thunderstorm or even a tornado, but very large lapse rates, up to hundreds or thousands of times the dry adiabatic rate, are commonly found within a few inches of the ground on a warm day. The average lapse rate in the troposphere is about ⅔ the dry adiabatic rate, *i.e.* about 3½°F per 1,000 ft. A reversal of the lapse rate (temperature increasing with height) is called an INVERSION.—*O. G. S.*

LARMOR, SIR JOSEPH, 1857–1942, British physicist; b. Magheragall, N Ireland. A contributor to 19-cent. theories of ether (*Aether and Matter*, 1900), Larmor urged abandonment of mechanical concepts of ether. This insight enabled some of his work to survive theories of relativity later. In 1897 he determined rate of precession of electron in magnetic field (Larmor precession).—*A. L.*

LARMOR PRECESSION: the precession of the motion of a charged particle subjected to a magnetic field. An orbiting electron in a magnetic field experiences a torque that causes the axis of the orbit to rotate like the "wobble" of a toy top. Joseph Larmor (1897) proved that the angular velocity of this precession is given by the equation $\omega = eH/2m$, where e and m are the charge and mass of the particle and H is the magnetic field intensity. A spinning electron or proton experiences a similar precession in a magnetic field. Measurement of the frequencies of these precessions, and their combinations, yields information on atomic and molecular structure.—*I. R.*

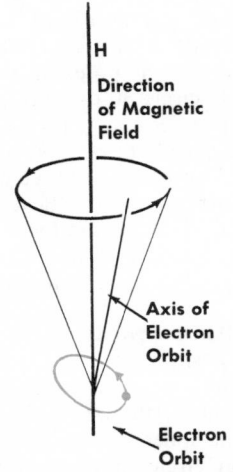

H
Direction of Magnetic Field

Axis of Electron Orbit

Electron Orbit

Larmor precession: Axis of electron orbit precesses around magnetic field.

LARVA: in the development of certain animals from egg to adult, an immature form that is unlike the adult. Common examples of larvae are the maggot of a fly, the caterpillar of a butterfly or moth, the pluteus of a sea urchin, and the tadpole of a frog. The change from larva to adult is called METAMORPHOSIS.—*R. G. M.*

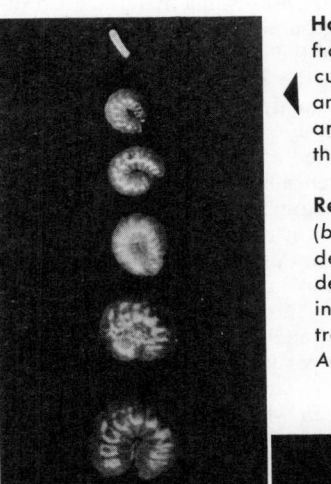

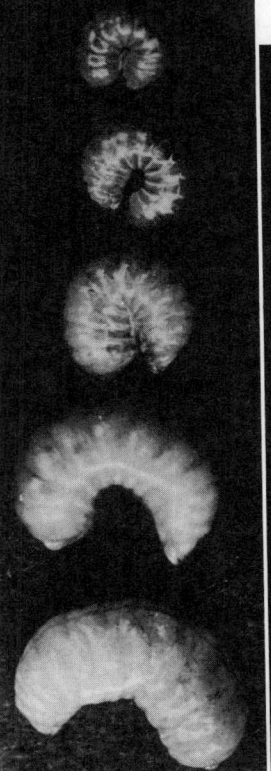

Honey bee larva (*left*) in stages from egg to 9-day larva. In bee culture, differentiation of queens and workers depends on amounts and types of food eaten during the larval period. (*USDA*)

Redheaded pine sawfly larvae (*below*) eat a pine needle. These destructive creatures completely defoliate pines, seriously damaging these commercially important trees. (*Gordon S. Smith/Nat. Audubon Society*)

LARYNX: the "voice box," located just above and continuous with the windpipe. It is visible on the outside as the Adam's apple. The larynx of mammals, reptiles, and terrestrial amphibians is constructed of cartilage and contains two vocal cords (organs of phonation) stretched across its interior. In quiet breathing the cords are relaxed and separated. In sound or voice production the cords are taut and close, and are set into vibration by exhaled air. Loudness of sound is determined by the pressure of the air blown across the cords, sound pitch by the length and tautness of them. Birds have a larynx, but it is not vocal; bird calls are produced by a structure called the syrinx.—*A. R. D.*

LASER: a device for amplifying the intensity of a light beam by stimulated emission. "Laser" is an acronym for Light Amplification by Stimulated Emission of Radiation. Lasers can produce light beams whose coherence, collimation, monochromaticity, and intensity are far greater than in light from conventional sources.

Laser operation depends upon the ability of atoms to exist at different ENERGY LEVELS. Most atoms in a material are ordinarily in the lowest energy, or ground, state. If an atom is struck by a photon, or unit of light, of the right energy, the atom will absorb the photon and thereby be excited to a higher energy state. After a short but random time, the excited atom will spontaneously decay to a lower state, emitting its surplus energy as a photon. If an excited atom is struck by a photon with energy equal to the difference between the atom's excited state and any lower state, the atom will decay immediately to the lower level, and the photon it emits will be added to the photon that caused the decay. In this way, stimulated emission increases the number of photons in a light beam, thereby intensifying the beam.

Consider a laser in which material in the ground state (E_0) is irradiated with light of the proper frequency to raise many of its atoms to the higher states E_1 and E_2. Atoms at E_2 decay quickly, many of them to E_1, in which (by the nature of the material) decay is much slower. Some of the photons produced by decay strike already-excited atoms, so that two photons are released; others strike E_0 atoms and are absorbed. However, if irradiation has been sufficient so that the excited atoms outnumber the E_0 atoms, photons strike more excited atoms than E_0 atoms, and there is a net gain of photons. Thus the light beam is amplified.

To increase photon multiplication, a mirror is placed at each end of the laser. One mirror is slightly transparent to allow the escape of some photons. But most of the light produced is reflected back and forth between the mirrors, stimulating a large number of photon multiplications before escaping to form the laser's beam. Meanwhile photons that are not moving exactly perpendicular to the mirror surfaces escape through the sides of the sample before producing many "progeny"; thus the beam acquires a high degree of collimation and coherence. Monochromaticity (consistency of wavelength) results from the nature of the laser material and the use of a particular frequency for the irradiation.

Since 1960 there has been an explosive development of new types of lasers and new applications. Laser action has been produced in crystals, glasses, liquids, and gases, and in semiconductor junctions. Beams have been produced at many wavelengths over the entire range of visible light and into infrared. Applications employing the high intensity and directionality of the beam include optical radar, cutting and welding of metals, and selective bombardment of small regions in biological specimens. (Laser beams are used to "weld" detached retinas back to supporting tissue in the eye.) The combination of high intensity, directionality, and monochromaticity makes the laser beam an excellent potential carrier for communication. Since the beam's carrier frequency is far higher than that used in radio and television, it could transmit many more messages simultaneously. The laser has made feasible the new branch of photography called HOLOGRAPHY, in which three-dimensional images are produced. A laser beam can be intensified enough to reveal very minute nonlinear responses of materials to light, opening up a whole new field of optics (analogous to the nonlinear phenomena introduced into electrical circuits by the vacuum tube).—S. K.

LASSELL, WILLIAM, 1799–1880, English astronomer; b. Bolton; self-educated. One of the pioneers with the reflecting telescope, he built a 9-in. Newtonian (1840), one of the earliest reflectors

with an equatorial mounting; a telescope with a 2-ft mirror (1846), with which he discovered the first satellite of Neptune, the seventh satellite of Saturn, and two satellites of Uranus; and a telescope with a 4-ft aperture (at Valletta, Malta, 1861), with which he catalogued 600 new nebulas. He also developed polishing machines for grinding mirrors and made observations of comets. He was a fellow of the Royal Society.—D. H. D. R.

LATIN SQUARE: an arrangement of numbers, or other symbols, in a square so that each symbol appears once, and only once, in each row and each column. The number of symbols is, of course, equal to the number of rows and columns. In Fig. 1, this number is 5. Latin squares are of importance in certain kinds of statistical analysis. For example, an agriculturist wishes to test five different fertilizers in a plot of land. If he divides the plot into five strips, differences in plant growth may be due not to the fertilizers but to differences in the fertility of the soils in the strips. Instead, he divides the land into 25 cells, and places the fertilizers in a pattern such as that in Fig. 1. He can then analyze the results so as to eliminate fertility differences. Another example is furnished by a gasoline manufacturer who wishes to test four mixtures in four cars with four drivers. Each driver performs four test runs, each with a different car and a different gasoline. The design of the experiment is shown in Fig. 2. Driver A drives car I with gas 1, car II with gas 4, and so on. The miles per gallon obtained are entered into the square, and the analysis will show which gasoline gives the best mileage, the differences between cars and drivers being eliminated.—B. P. S.

PLOTS WITH FERTILIZERS

a	b	c	d	e
d	e	a	b	c
b	c	d	e	a
e	a	b	c	d
c	d	e	a	b

Fig. 1

DRIVERS

		A	B	C	D
	I	gas 1	gas 2	gas 3	gas 4
C A R S	II	gas 4	gas 1	gas 2	gas 3
	III	gas 3	gas 4	gas 1	gas 2
	IV	gas 2	gas 3	gas 4	gas 1

Fig. 2

LATITUDE, VARIATION OF: the continuous change in latitude of every point on Earth's surface due to the wandering movements (NUTATION and PRECESSION) of the ends of the planet's axis—*i.e.* the poles. In these movements each pole traces a crude circle 30 to 60 ft in diameter. Variation of latitude is kept under constant observation at five installations located strategically throughout the world in northern latitudes along the 39th parallel. Three of these observatories are in foreign countries—Japan, Italy, USSR; they cooperate with two in the U. S. A., at Gaithersburg, Md., and Ukiah, Calif. Variation data are computed by the U. S. Coast and Geodetic Survey, which operates the American observatories.—A. J. W.

LATITUDE AND LONGITUDE: angular coordinates that specify the positions of points on Earth's surface. Earth is approximately spherical and rotates about an axis whose end points are the north and south poles. Any plane through the center of the sphere intersects it in a great circle. The *equator* is the great circle midway between the poles. The great circles through the poles are called *meridians*. The small circles in which planes parallel to the equatorial plane cut the sphere are called *parallel circles*. The latitude of point P in the figure

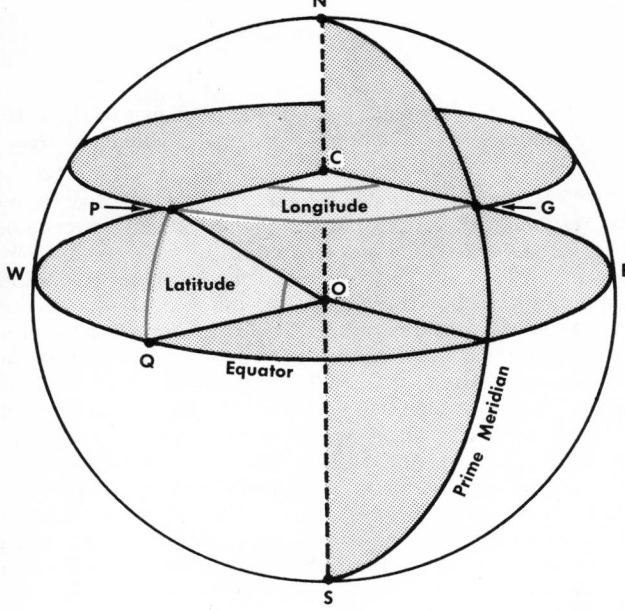

Latitude and Longitude

is the angle *QOP*, where *O* is the center of Earth and *Q* lies on the equator on the same meridian as *P*. The latitude of the north pole is 90°N, that of the south pole 90°S, and that of any other point some acute angle designated as north or south latitude according as *P* is north or south of the equator. All points on the equator have latitude 0°. All points on a parallel circle have the same latitude. It is customary to conceive degrees of latitude as degrees of arc on a meridian rather than of central angle. The distance corresponding to a degree of latitude is 1/360 of the circumference of Earth, or approximately 69 mi.

Longitude is measured from a zero, or prime, meridian, which is usually taken to be the meridian through Greenwich, England. In the figure, the prime meridian is *NGS,* and the longitude of *P* is the angle *GCP*, where *C* is the center of the parallel circle through *P,* and *G* is the point on that circle and on the prime meridian. The longitude can be any angle from 0° to 180°, designated as east or west longitude according as *P* is east or west of the prime meridian. All points on a meridian have the same longitude. The east-west distance corresponding to a degree of longitude is the length of an arc of 1° on a parallel circle, and therefore varies with the latitude. Since the radius of a parallel circle is *R* times the cosine of the latitude, where *R* is Earth's radius, a degree of longitude corresponds to the distance $(1/360) 2\pi R \cos$ (lat). At latitude 60°, this is one half as great as on the equator.—*H. C.*

LATREILLE, PIERRE ANDRÉ, 1762–1833, French entomologist; b. Brives. He is known for his reform of entomological classification and his organization of the insect collection at the Natural History Museum, Paris (where he became professor of invertebrate zoology in 1829, succeeding Lamarck). His writings include *Histoire naturelle générale et particulière des crustacés et insectes* (14 vols., 1802–05).—*D. H. D. R.*

LAUE, MAX THEODOR FELIX VON, 1879–1960, German physicist; b. Pfaffendorf. In 1912, while still a junior lecturer at Munich, he suggested that the atomic lattice of a crystal would act as a diffraction grating for x-rays. This was confirmed experimentally by two associates, W. Friedrich and P. Knipping. Laue's discovery allowed the wavelengths of x-rays to be determined and, perhaps more important, revealed the atomic structure of crystals; x-ray spectrography became crucial in development of theories of atomic structure. For predicting atomic-lattice diffraction as well as theoretically justifying

the diffraction patterns recorded, Laue received the 1914 Nobel prize in physics. He was a fellow of the Royal Society. —*A. L.*

LAVA: the material that forms from magma as it rises through Earth's crust and erupts at the surface through fissures or the vents of volcanoes. As magma nears the surface, the lowering of its temperature and pressure causes physical and chemical changes, and it becomes lava. The composition of the original magma, especially as to its silica content, determines the character of the lava formed.

Highly siliceous lava, which is characteristic of the continental land masses, is relatively viscous. hence it tends to clog the vent of a volcano, causing a buildup of pressure and a consequent explosive eruption. Such eruptions produce much lava in the form of PYROCLASTICS—fragments that accumulate around the vent to form cinder cones.

Lava that is viscous may emerge through vents or fissures without rapidly congealing and blocking the magma below. Most submarine volcanoes produce such lava, which wells out to form sheet upon sheet of basaltic rock, until lava mountains are sometimes built up. One of these, higher than Mt Everest, comprises the island of Hawaii, which rises almost 6 mi above the sea floor, although only the upper 45% of its height (and much less of its bulk) is dry land. Some continental volcanoes also produce basaltic lava, but most such lava appearing on continents originated in fissure flows. A single fissure may yield a sheet of lava covering hundreds of square miles; beds extending over hundreds of thousands of square miles, and piled to a thickness of thousands of feet, have emerged from multiple fissures. Examples of such lava beds are found in the Columbia Plateau, covering parts of five Western states; in the Deccan of India; and in the Paraná Basin of S America.

Lava of this less viscous (basaltic) type congeals in a variety of forms. It often flows for many miles before hardening all the way through. If the surface congeals while the flow continues, a crust is formed that may break up into jagged, irregular blocks called *aa.* Occasionally the fluid interior drains away completely, leaving a crustal "roof" or walls intact, and thus forming *tunnels, pipes, tubes,* or even *caverns.* When the entire mass congeals while still in motion, it may take the shape of thick ropes or taffylike twists, called *pahoehoe.* Lava containing dissolved gas may retain or release the bubbles; as the lava congeals, vesicles are left within the mass or on its surface, forming *scoria* or *pumice.* Lava discharged underwater often takes the shape of *pillows,* and the formations are so named. Cooling of a basaltic mass may result in a columnar structure, usually hexagonal in cross section. Such columns are seen in Devils Tower, Wyoming; Devils Postpile, California; and Giants Causeway, Ireland. In general, lava never congeals slowly enough to become a coarse-grained

Field of pahoehoe at Craters of the Moon, Idaho, suggests coils of rope. Also note the volcanic tubes, produced where liquid lava flowed out from within congealed masses. Pahoehoe is only one of several forms taken by basaltic lava. *(John A. Shimer)*

rock. It is usually fine-grained, constituting basalt if rich in ferromagnesian minerals, andesite if more siliceous, rhyolite if extremely siliceous. By far the most common lavas are basaltic. See Color Plate 57.—*E. A.*

LAVOISIER, ANTOINE LAURENT,

Antoine Laurent Lavoisier
(Clay-Adams, Inc.)

1743–94, French chemist; b. Paris. He served on a government commission which recommended the introduction of the metric system of measures and weights (1790). With K. W. Scheele and Joseph Priestley he recognized "fire-air" (oxygen) to be the promoter of combustion and digestion (1777). He stated that common air is a mixture of oxygen and nitrogen (1778), and water a compound of oxygen and hydrogen (1783). Together with C. L. Berthollet and A. F. Fourcroy, he extended Guyton de Morveau's tentative chemical nomenclature (1782) in TRAITÉ ÉLÉMENTAIRE DE CHIMIE (1789), which mentions 31 "elements," including heat and light. This new rational nomenclature and his quantitative investigation of chemical reactions with the balance established modern chemistry. His works include *Mémoire sur le meilleur système d'éclairage de Paris* (1766), *Sur la nature de l'eau* (1770), and *Experiences avec le diamant* (1772), which showed that a diamond burns to form carbon dioxide. *Traité de chimie* (1801) was published after he was guillotined during the Reign of Terror. He was a member of the Academy of Sciences and a fellow of the Royal Society.—*R. J. F.*

LAWRENCE, ERNEST ORLANDO, 1901–58, U. S. physicist; b.

Canton, N. D. He is best known for his invention of the cyclotron (see PARTICLE ACCELERATOR) and for developing it into a basic, highly efficient tool for nuclear research. The first cyclotron, completed 1930, was constructed mainly of glass and sealing wax; its vacuum chamber was only 4½ in. in diameter. A subsequent metal model of the same size produced proton beams with an energy of about 80,000 v. In 1932 an improved model enabled Lawrence to disintegrate atoms of lithium, the second artificial transmutation of elements ever performed (see COCKCROFT-WALTON EXPERIMENT). His method of separating uranium^{235} by converting the cyclotron into a large mass spectrograph was important in the development of the first atomic bombs. For the discovery and development of the cyclotron, and for his research on artificial radioactive elements, Lawrence received the 1939

Nobel prize. The element lawrencium is named for him. He was a member of the National Academy of Sciences.—*R. G.*

LAWRENCIUM: a man-made element (Lw); at. no. 103; at. wt 257 (estimated). The eleventh TRANSURANIUM ELEMENT to be discovered, lawrencium was created in the spring of 1961 by a team headed by Albert Ghiorso at the Lawrence Radiation Laboratory of the Univ. of Calif.; the team bombarded a sample of californium (at. no. 98) with boron nuclei in a heavy-ion linear accelerator. Lawrencium has a half life of about 8 sec, decaying to mendelevium (at. no. 101). Because of its extremely short half life and the fact that only a few atoms have so far been created, almost nothing is known about the properties of lawrencium. It is thought, however, that lawrencium completes the ACTINIDE group, and that any elements above 103, if created, will have the properties of a different group. This conjecture is based on the observation that each successive actinide has added an electron in the fifth (of 7) electron shell from the interior; with lawrencium, this fifth shell, with 32 electrons, is complete. (See CHEMISTRY; PERIODIC TABLE.)—*E. H. H.*

LEACHING: a separation process in chemical industry analogous to the action of a coffee percolator in the kitchen. A substance (*e.g.* ground coffee) from which some constituent (the coffee essence) is to be extracted is placed in a vessel through which a suitable solvent (hot water) can be passed, either once or several times. The desired constituent is said to be leached out (see ELUTRIATION).—*Ru. M.*

LEAD: a metallic element (Pb); at. no. 82; at. wt 207.21; density 11.35; mp 327.4°C; bp 1620°C. Lead, one of the seven metals of the ancients, is very soft and malleable as well as being extremely durable; it is a poor conductor of electricity. Its durability may be seen from the fact that lead pipes installed in ancient Rome are still usable.

Lead can be obtained by roasting the concentrate of its principal ore, galena (PbS), either alone or with limestone and carbon. The impure lead is refined to remove antimony, arsenic, zinc, and copper, which make it hard and brittle, and to recover the silver which is normally present. The metal and its oxide are used in storage-battery plates, in roofing (terne roofs), and in alloys such as solder, typemetal, and bearing metals. A self-sealing oxide film that forms over lead in air makes it relatively resistant to atmospheric corrosion or corrosion by oxygen-bearing waters. (Lead is also one of the few metals not corroded by dilute sulfuric acid.) For these reasons, the metal is widely used in pipe and cable sheathing and in the construction of chemical apparatus. Im-

Ancient Roman water pipes of lead are almost perfectly preserved and usable after 1,900 yr. Latin inscriptions on the pipe sections are clearly readable. (*Lead Industries Assn.*)

Lead-asbestos pads insulate foundations of motel in New York against vibration from garages and railroad tracks, over which rooms and recreational facilities were built. (Lead Industries Assn.)

portant compounds of lead include the three oxides PbO, PbO_2, and Pb_3O_4. The latter compound, known as red lead, is the familiar red pigment used in protective coatings on structural steel. Basic lead carbonate is a valuable and widely used paint pigment. Tetraethyl lead is the most widely used antiknock agent for GASOLINE. Lead and its compounds are toxic; since the human body does not easily rid itself of lead, the toxic action tends to be cumulative and constitutes a hazard to people who are exposed to lead compounds over long periods of time.

Lead plays an important role in several newer technologies. Lead-asbestos pads insulate the foundations of modern city buildings against vibrations arising from traffic and other sources; within the buildings, walls containing lead sheets block noise transmission. Lead sheets, masses, and containers are used for shielding against radiation sources, *e.g.* atomic reactors, particle accelerators, x-ray generators, and radioactive chemicals. Small engine-ignition systems are under development which use crystals of lead zirconate-titanate, a ceramic piezoelectric material that changes mechanical energy into electricity (see PIEZOELECTRIC EFFECT); other potential applications are under study for this material. Lead telluride, which picks up heat and converts it directly into electricity, is used in auxiliary electric-power generators. Lead has been used in paints, glazes, and enamels since about 1000 B. C. (Egypt); and it finds similar application in present-day leaded enamels and ceramics.—*A. M. S.*

Roof with outer sheathing of sheet steel coated with lead-tin alloy was used on Beth Torah Temple, north Miami Beach. (Lead Industries Assn.)

LEAF: the major food-manufacturing organ of higher plants, developing from a stem-borne bud. Food-making leaves are rich in chlorophyll, the green pigment involved in photosynthesis. The most common type of leaf consists of a leafstalk, or *petiole,* and (expanded from the tip of the petiole) a flattened *blade.* The petiole supports the blade and conducts materials into and away from it; the blade is the food-making part. From the apex of the petiole a system of *veins* branches out into every part of the leaf; these consist of *xylem* tissue, which conducts water and minerals into the leaf cells, and *phloem* tissue, which conducts manufactured foods out of the leaf cells into the petiole, whence they move downward into the stem.

External Forms: Leaves vary greatly in their external structure in different species of plants, and it is chiefly on the basis of these external differences that we are able to distinguish one species from another. A *simple* leaf is one that has a single blade, as in elm, maple, and apple. A *compound* leaf has more than one blade, as in clover, bean, and rose; the individual blades of a compound leaf are called *leaflets.* Leaves also vary in their margins. A leaf with a smooth, unbroken edge is called *entire* (lilac, dogwood); one with small, regular, pointed indentations is *toothed* (elm, peach); one with small, rounded indentations is *crenaté* (catnip, ground ivy); one with deep marginal indentations is *lobed* (maple, red oak). The forms of leaf blades also vary exceedingly, from *linear,* as in many grasses, to *orbicular,* or circular, as in nasturtiums; between these extremes are many intermediate forms, such as *lanceolate* (peach), *ovate* (apple), *cordate,* or heart-shaped (linden, redbud). In most conifers, leaves are not broad and flat but are needlelike (pine, fir) or scalelike (cedars) in form.

Internal Structures: The internal structure of leaves is very complex and variable. The more common type of internal leaf structure will be described here. The surface tissue, the *epidermis,* is a single layer of cells, which furnish protection, chiefly against water loss; in the epidermis are pores, the *stomata,* through which exchange of gases occurs; each stoma is enclosed by a pair of *guard cells,* the movements of which open and close the stoma. The factor that initiates guard cell movements is fluctuation in light intensity; in most plants, the guard cells open the stomata in light and close them in darkness. Epidermal cells often possess in their exposed walls a layer of a waxy material, *cutin,* which aids in the conservation of moisture. Beneath the upper epidermis is a layer

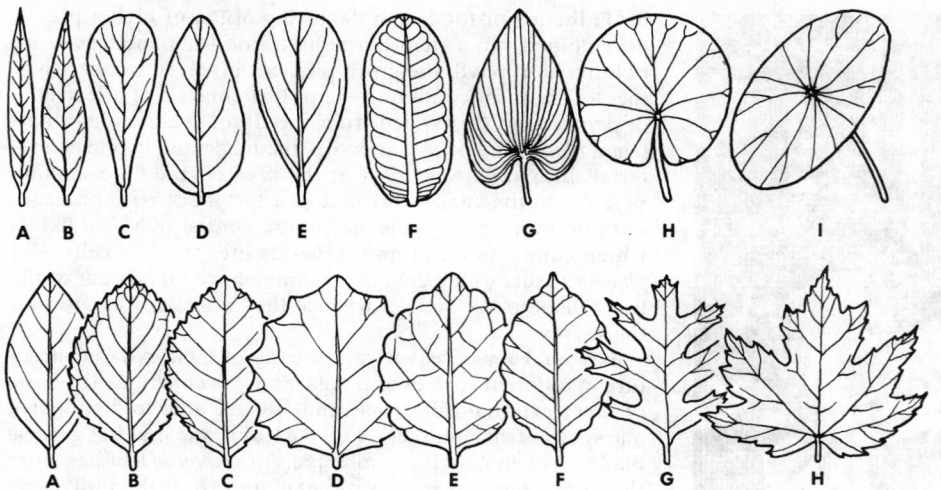

Forms of leaves show great variety. Top row—Forms of leaf blades include: A, linear; B, lanceolate; C, spatulate; D, ovate; E, obovate; F, oblong; G, cordate; H, orbiculate; I, peltate. Bottom row—Forms of leaf margins include: A, entire; B, serrate; C, doubly serrate; D, dentate; E, crenate; F, undulate; G, pinnately lobed; H, palmately lobed. (*From Transeau*)

(sometimes several layers) of *palisade* cells, which are cylindrical in form and elongated vertically in the leaf; palisade cells are rich in chlorophyll and thus engage in food manufacture. Beneath the palisade cells is the *spongy* tissue, composed of irregularly shaped chlorophyllous cells, which also manufacture food; the spongy tissue has numerous large air spaces, which give the tissue its spongy appearance. The palisade and spongy tissues are known collectively as *mesophyll.* The leaf veins pass through the mesophyll. The lower surface of the leaf is made up of the lower epidermis, in which most of the leaf's stomata usually occur.

Specialized Leaves: The types of leaves described above are the common foliage, or food-making, leaves. Other leaves have assumed some functions in addition to, or in place of, food manufacture and have undergone structural modifications accompanying their specialized functions. Some leaf modifications are so extensive that the organs in which they occur are scarcely recognizable as leaves. Among the more common types of specialized leaves are: (1) *bud scales,* protective leaves that form an overlapping covering over the growing tissues of buds in many plants; (2) *thorns,* protective leaves found in some plants, *e.g.* barberry; (3) *bulb scales,* food- and water-storage leaves of onion, narcissus, and other bulbs; (4) *tendrils,* leaves modified as climbing organs in

some plants, *e.g.* sweet peas; (5) *insectivorous* or *carnivorous* leaves, variously specialized for the trapping and digesting of insect bodies. See CARNIVOROUS PLANT; CLIMBING PLANTS.

Origin of Leaves: Leaves develop as a result of the growth of vegetative buds (also called leaf buds or branch buds). The elongation of a bud produces a section of stem, or branch; in this growth, small protuberances appear laterally at the growing apex of the bud and ultimately develop into leaves. As the leaves grow, a small bud forms in the axil (upper angle) of each leaf; such buds are called *axillary* buds. These may grow out into branches or develop into flowers.

Leaf Fall: The fall of leaves in autumn is the result of the development of a corky layer of cells, the ABSCISSION plane, across the base of the petiole. The formation of this abcission layer can be prevented by artificially increasing the hours of daylight.

Leaf Coloration: The color of food-making leaves is usually green, although in some plants (such as purple cabbage, Coleus, and copper beech) other pigments may be present which mask the green color of chlorophyll and give the leaves a reddish, bluish, or purplish hue. Pigments of this type are called *anthocyanins;* they develop in considerable concentrations in many types of leaves in late summer or fall and are responsible for the scarlet and purplish autumnal hues of

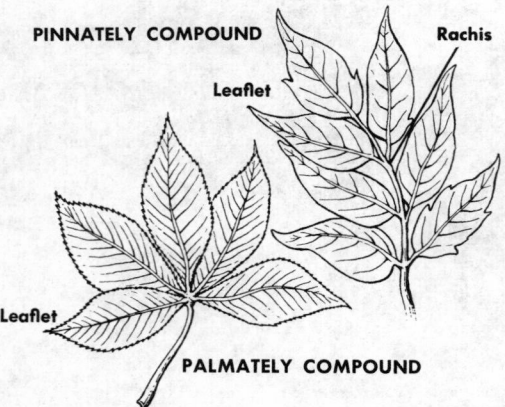

Compound leaves may be palmate, with leaflets originating from a single point, as in Buckeye (*above left*); or they may be pinnate, with leaflets borne on the rachis, as in Ailanthus (*right*).

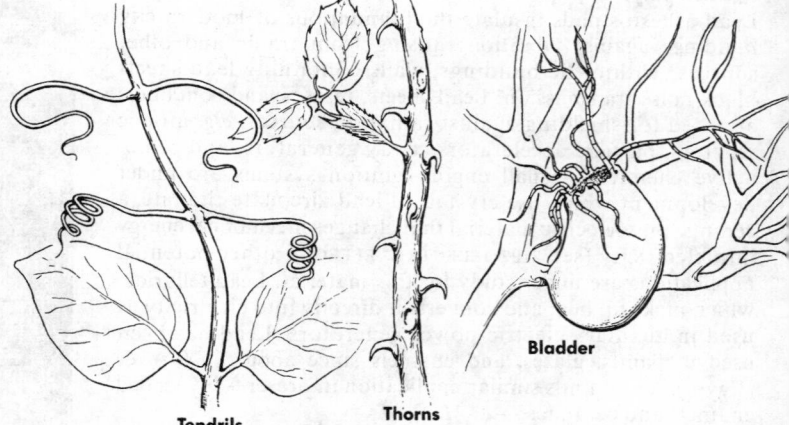

Specialized leaf forms include (*left to right*) tendrils for clinging and climbing, thorns for protection, and the bladder of *Utricularia,* the bladderwort, for trapping small aquatic insects.

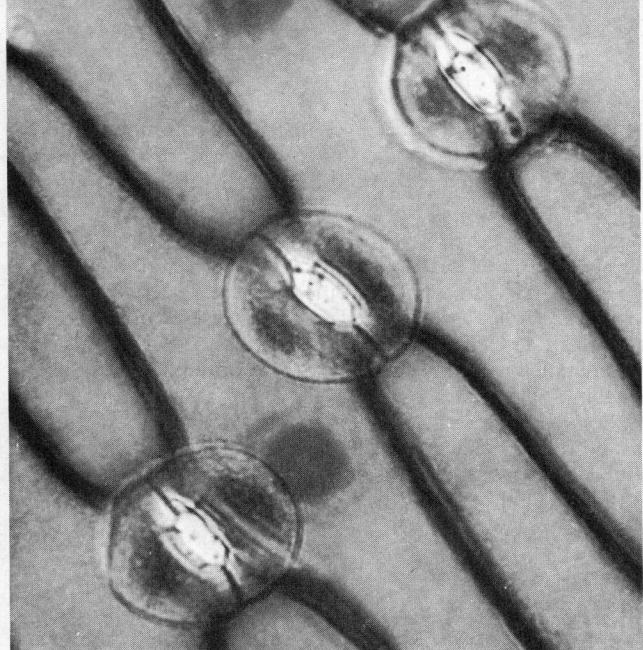

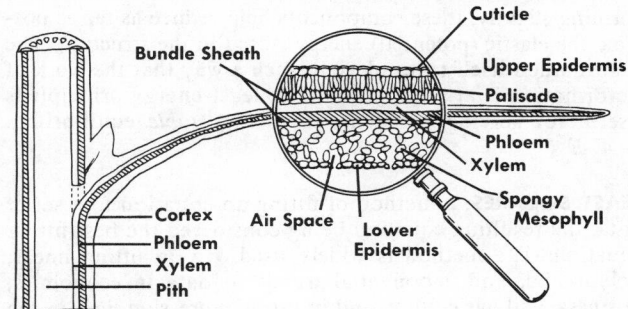

Tissues of leaf: Differentiation of cellular layers is shown in diagram of longitudinal section of leaf. Xylem, which lies toward upper surface, conducts water away from stem. (*From Transeau*)

Leaf structure: Above, magnified 260X, are three stomata from leaf of iris; surrounding them are paired crescent-shaped guard cells that control carbon dioxide and oxygen traffic. At right a leaf is seen in transverse section; the two dark conglomerations are parallel veins (plant is a monocot). A single layer of epidermal cells, interrupted by stomata, lines surfaces; large shrinkable cells of bottom layer help leaf curl when it needs to retain moisture. (*Carl Struwe/Monkmeyer; L. and M. Milne*)

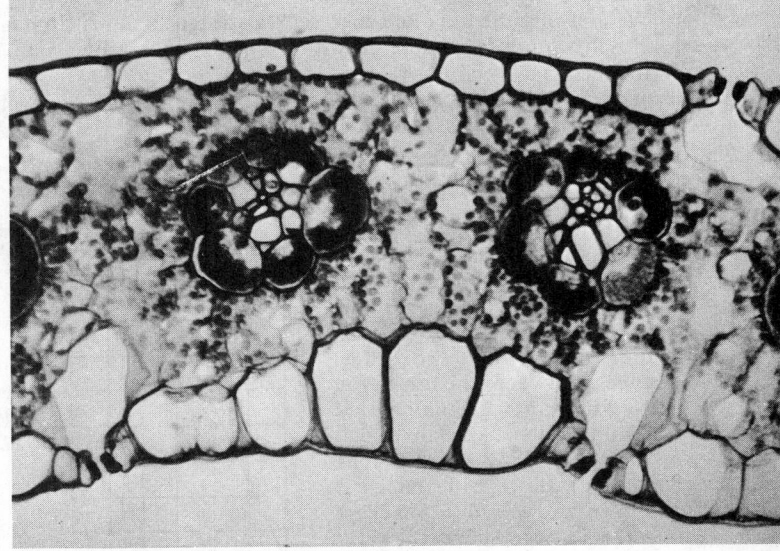

leaves, *e.g.* in sumac and sweet gum. In addition to chlorophyll, food-making leaves always possess the yellowish pigments xanthophyll and carotene; these are masked by the green of chlorophyll until autumn, when rapid chlorophyll disintegration reveals the orange and yellow colors of xanthophyll and carotene, as, for example, in elm and linden leaves. A common misconception is that frost is responsible for the development of autumnal coloration of leaves; actually such coloration begins before the first frosts, although frosts may intensify color changes. See COLORATION OF PLANTS.

Leaf Function: The major function of leaves is PHOTOSYNTHESIS, the manufacture of sugars from carbon dioxide and water with the energy of light and the mechanism of chlorophyll. A leaf is an effective machine for performing this function for these reasons: it is rich in chlorophyll; it is usually broad and flat, thus exposing a large surface to light and air; it is thin, so that light can penetrate to all cells of the leaf; it has numerous pores, which permit the entry of carbon dioxide into the mesophyll; its system of veins carries water into all parts of the blade; and its many intercellular spaces facilitate the diffusion of carbon dioxide to all mesophyll cells. In addition to photosynthesis, leaves also carry on digestion, respiration, and other processes. When the stomata are open to their greatest extent and are permitting the movement of carbon dioxide into the leaf, oxygen, formed as a by-product of photosynthesis, and water vapor diffuse outward into the air. This loss of water vapor, called *transpiration,* often constitutes a danger to a plant, since excessive water loss may result in wilting and death.—*A. P. E.*

LEAST-ACTION PRINCIPLE: a principle that elegantly summarizes the entire content of MECHANICS (for most systems) in a single statement. Before the principle can be stated it is necessary to define what is meant by the technical term "action." For the simple case of a single particle moving in a given trajectory connecting two specified points, the action is defined as the product of three quantities: the particle's mass, its average speed over the trajectory, and the distance traveled. Now the principle of least action asserts that of all conceivable trajectories which a particle, with a given energy, might follow between two specified points, that trajectory is followed for which the numerical value of the action is least. It can be shown that this principle is equivalent to NEWTON'S LAWS OF MOTION, which form the usual basis for the science of mechanics. Aside from its esthetic appeal, the principle of least action has practical value in that it gives physicists new insights into the essence of mechanics and its relationships to other fields. For example, by comparing this principle with a similar one in the field of optics (Fermat's principle), it is possible to show that Newton's classical system of mechanics approximates QUANTUM THEORY much as geometrical optics approximates wave optics.—*S. K.*

LEAST-ENERGY PRINCIPLE: the principle that the potential ENERGY of a physical or chemical system tends toward a minimum value. Thus a cone, precariously balanced on its apex, tends to topple over if disturbed, assuming a more stable position and thereby minimizing its store of potential energy. For the same reason, the rubberlike "membrane" constituting the surface of a liquid tends to shrink, because of forces of surface tension. The principle also applies to the elastic components of a loaded structure: by yielding or deforming slightly, these components help reduce as far as possible the elastic (potential) energy stored in the structure. The deformation itself takes place in such a way that the work of deformation is at a minimum. The least-energy principle is useful for solving problems involving *stable* equilibrium. —*A. E.*

LEAST SQUARES: a method of fitting an equation to a set of data, the resulting equation being considered the best-fitting equation. The method is widely used, *e.g.* in fitting linear, polynomial, and exponential trends to data in economics, business, and agriculture, and in fitting regression lines in the study of correlation. To illustrate the method, we shall consider a simple example where it is desired to fit a linear equation to the following set of data:

| x | 1 | 2 | 3 | 4 | 5 | 6 |
| y | 3 | 5 | 8 | 9 | 12 | 14 |

We first plot the data and then seek a straight line which fits closely. Suppose the line drawn in Fig. 1 is such a line. Call the original y-values y_0 (observed y-value) and let the corresponding y-values on the line be designated by y_c (calculated y-value). The difference between these two y-values is $y_0 - y_c$. Now, if the total of these differences is small, it would seem as if we had a well-fitting line. However, this may not be so for, if we take the line $y = 8.5$, the differences between the observed y-values and the calculated y-values ($y = 8.5$) are -5.5, -3.5, $-.5$, $.5$, 3.5, 5.5. The total of these differences is 0 but we would not accept $y = 8.5$ as a good fit to the given points. In order to improve the quality of the fit we square the differences $y_0 - y_c$ and find the line that satisfies the condition that the sum of the squares of these differences should be a minimum. The equation of a line is $y_c =$

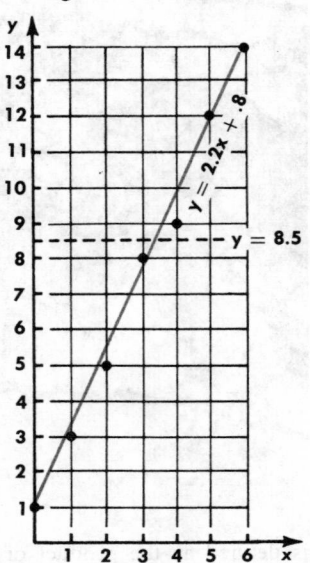

Fig. 1. Regression line. The line that best fits given data can be obtained by the method of least squares.

$mx + b$, and so we must satisfy the condition that $\Sigma(y_0 - y_c)^2 = \Sigma(y_0 - mx - b)^2$ shall be a minimum (here Σ means "the sum of"). This leads to two conditions that m and b must satisfy, namely

$$\Sigma y = m\Sigma x + bN; \qquad \Sigma xy = m\Sigma x^2 + b\Sigma x$$

where N is the number of corresponding values of x and y. These equations are sometimes called the normal equations.

We now construct a table from the given data with columns for x, y, x^2, and xy. The totals of these columns are 21, 51, 91, 217, respectively, and $N = 6$. Applying the normal equations to these totals we have

$$51 = 21m + 6b; \quad 217 = 91m + 21b$$

Solving for m and b, we find $m = 2.2$ and $b = .8$; so the straight line best fitting the data is $y = 2.2x + .8$. The equation found by this method is often called the regression line or the line of linear regression of y on x. It is also possible to develop a line of regression of x on y by minimizing the sum of the squares of the differences between computed and observed x-values. The method of least squares can be extended to apply to fitting exponential and other types of equations. —*H. E. W.*

LEBESGUE, HENRI LÉON, 1875–1941, French mathematician; b. Oise. In 1906 he went to Poitiers, where he became professor at the Collège de France. The recipient of many honors both in France and abroad, Lebesgue was one of the greatest mathematicians of his day. His fame resulted chiefly from his work in integration, a field that he largely remade. Influenced by Borel, Jordan, and others, he formulated a new definition of an integral, which is of the highest importance in modern analysis and is called a *Lebesgue integral.* He was a member of the Academy of Sciences and a fellow of the Royal Society. —*H. C.*

LEBLANC, NICHOLAS, 1742–1806, French physician and chemist; b. Ivoy le Pré. He was the inventor of the soda-manufacturing process that bears his name and that dominated the industry from its invention in 1792 through the 19th cent. It consists of heating sodium sulfate with calcium carbonate and charcoal, and extracting the sodium carbonate (soda) from the resulting calcined mass by means of water. Leblanc's discovery was important because it furnished a cheap, large-scale source of a basic raw material of contemporary industry, and thus stimulated the process of industrialization.—*V. B.*

LE CHATELIER, HENRY LOUIS, 1850–1936, French chemist; b. Paris. He is best known for the thermodynamic principle named after him (formulated with K. F. Braun), which may be stated thus: If one of the factors of a system in equilibrium (*e.g.* pressure, temperature, or concentration) is altered, one or more of the other factors will spontaneously adjust itself in such a way as to reduce the alteration. A pioneer in the accurate measurement of very high temperatures, he invented (1887) a platinum-rhodium thermocouple for use as a pyrometer. Le Chatelier made important contributions to the chemistry of cement and steel manufacturing. Among his many books are one on the measurement of high temperatures (with O. Boudouard, 1900) and *La silice et les silicates* (1914). Le Chatelier was a fellow of the Royal Society.—*E. F.*

LEÇONS SUR LES PHÉNOMÈNES DE LA VIE COMMUNS AUX ANIMAUX ET AUX VÉGÉTAUX by Claude Bernard, Paris (1878): This volume, published a few weeks after Bernard's death on Feb. 10, 1878, presented the initial lectures of a course in general physiology which he had begun at the Museum of Natural History. These lectures show Bernard's mature reflections on the development of physiology and the methodology of experimentation in biology. He reviewed the status of many of the then current problems basic to general physiology, the new field he was developing. He showed how his concern with the fundamental nature of living things led him to study the basic morphological units, the cells, in relation to organic functions. In these lectures on general aspects of life phenomena, Bernard provided the fullest statement of his conception of the *milieu intérieur* (internal environment), by which he explained the maintenance of an internal equilibrium which provided the multicellular organism with a degree of independence of the external environment. (See ANIMAL PHYSIOLOGY; PLANT PHYSIOLOGY.)—*E. Me.*

LE CORBUSIER (JEANNERET-GRIS, CHARLES ÉDOUARD), 1887–1965, Swiss architect; b. La Chaux-de-Fonds. He has considerably influenced modern architectural thinking, particularly on design in steel and concrete and on the planning of towns and groups of buildings. A sculptor and painter as well as the author of numerous books and articles, he wrote *Vers une architecture* (1923), *Propos d' urbanisme* (1946), and *Quand les cathédrales étaient blanches* (1947).—*D. H. D. R.*

LEDERBERG, JOSHUA, 1925– , U. S. geneticist; b. Montclair, N. J. For his discoveries concerning genetic recombination and the organization of the genetic material of bacteria, he shared the 1958 Nobel prize with G. W. Beadle and E. L. Tatum. He is a member of the National Academy of Sciences.—*D. H. D. R.*

Drs. Tsung Dao Lee (*left*) and Chen Ning Yang. (*Alan Richards*)

LEE, TSUNG DAO, 1926– , Chinese-U. S. physicist; b. Shanghai. He has done research in field theory, statistical mechanics, hydrodynamics, and astrophysics. In a paper published in the *Physical Review* (1957), Lee and C. N. Yang challenged the universal applicability of the principle of conservation of parity, showing that no existing experiments indicated whether parity was conserved in "weak" processes, such as beta decay. New experiments suggested by them and carried out by others, and later experiments at the National Bureau of Standards, showed that parity was not conserved. For their work on the so-called parity laws, which has led to important discoveries regarding elementary particles, Lee and Yang shared the 1957 Nobel prize.—*D. H. D. R.*

LEEUWENHOEK, ANTON VAN, 1632–1723, Dutch microscopist; b. Delft. He used his homemade microscopes (really single lenses) with magnifications up to 250, sometimes using dark-ground illumination, often measuring his objects by carefully comparing them with sand grains or red blood cells. The father of microbiology, he discovered protozoa, infusoria, spermatozoa (1677), and bacteria (1683); reported many histological and morphological details of plants and animals; and studied the blood capillaries (1668) and red blood corpuscles (1674). He wrote more than 280 letters (many illustrated), mainly to the Royal Society (1673 on). Two collections of his writings concerning his discoveries and observations were published: *Sendbrieven, Ontedingen en Ontdekkingen, Ondervindingen en Beschouwingen* (7 vols., 1685–1718) and *Opera omnia sive arcana naturae* (7 vols., 1715–22). He was a fellow of the Royal Society.—*R. J. F.*

Anton van Leeuwenhoek
(*Clay-Adams, Inc.*)

LEGENDRE, ADRIEN MARIE, 1752–1833, French mathematician; b. Toulouse. He is known in the history of elementary mathematics for his *Eléments de géometrie,* which was widely used as a substitute for Euclid's *Elements* in Europe and America. In later editions he attempted to prove the parallel postulate. Legendre is also noted for his extended work *Théorie des nombres* and for his study of elliptic integrals, the results of which appeared in *Traité des fonctions elliptiques.* He was the first to publish the method of least squares, which he developed independently of Gauss. He was a member of the French Academy of Sciences and a fellow of the Royal Society. —*H. C.*

LEGENDRE FUNCTIONS: see SPECIAL FUNCTIONS.

LEHMANN, JOHANN GOTTLOB, ?–1767, German-Russian geologist; birthplace unknown. In his *Versuch einer Geschichte von Flötzgebirgen* (1756), which concerned research on the natural history of the flötz rocks (flat strata that are horizontal and parallel to one another), Lehmann offered a classification system for German mountains, 17 yr after G. Arduino had used essentially the same system for N Italian rocks. Lehmann emphasized rightly that many rock strata originated as sediments in water. He also wrote extensively on the origin of metallic deposits.—*D. H. D. R.*

LEHRBUCH DER PHYSIOLOGIE DES MENSCHEN (Textbook of Human Physiology) by Carl Ludwig, 2 vols., 1852–56: One of the most influential 19th-cent. teachers of physiology, with over 200 pupils from different countries, Ludwig was an outspoken critic of the German speculative "nature-philosophy." In concert with the physiologists Brücke, Helmholtz, and Du Bois-Reymond, he joined in an attempt to "constitute physiology on a chemicophysical foundation, and give it equal scientific rank with physics." The *Lehrbuch* is important as an embodiment of this materialistic approach to the study of organic functions.—*E. Me.*

LEIBNIZ, GOTTFRIED WILHELM, 1646–1716, German philosopher; b. Leipzig. As jurist, diplomat, and historian, as well as mathematician and philosopher, Leibniz is often ranked with Newton as one of the two greatest thinkers of the 17th cent., but, unlike Newton, he completed few of his brilliantly conceived projects, and never set forth a thoroughly systematic presentation of his ideas. *Théodicée* (1710) was the one

Gottfried Wilhelm Leibniz
(*New York Public Library*)

book he published in his lifetime, but his *Discours de métaphysique* and *Monadologie* serve as outlines for some of his views. Of the 30,000 letters surviving from his correspondence with other learned men of the day, many are, like the unpublished manuscripts, of great value. In his philosophical views Leibniz was a thoroughgoing rationalist (see RATIONALISM). Among his mathematical achievements were the invention of a calculating machine, better than Pascal's, and the development of the infinitesimal calculus (1675–76), also discovered independently by Newton. Many fascinating interrelations exist between Leibniz's logical and mathematical theories and his philosophy of nature. *The Clarke-Leibniz Correspondence* contains Leibniz's criticism of Newton's doctrines of absolute space, time, and motion, and his own view of space and time as relational, in which view "things" are construed as continuous series of unfolding states and activities. Leibniz also sought to discover a universal logical language (*Characteristica universalis*) in which it would be possible automatically to analyze and determine the truth of any statement; disputation, he thought, could be replaced by the invitation "Let us calculate." He was a fellow of the Royal Society.—*H. S. T.*

LEIDY, JOSEPH, 1823–91, U. S. biologist and paleontologist; b. Philadelphia, Pa. He pioneered in vertebrate anatomy, invertebrate zoology, and vertebrate paleontology. His contributions in the field of Cenozoic stratigraphy, including *The Extinct Mammalian Fauna of Dakota and Nebraska* (1869), laid a foundation for later work. He was a member of the National Academy of Sciences.—*D. H. D. R.*

LEMAÎTRE, CANON GEORGES ÉDOUARD, 1894–1966; Belgian astrophysicist and cosmologist; b. Charleroi. His cosmogony (BIG-BANG THEORY) regards the universe as having originated from the disintegration of a primeval atom which contained all the energy of the universe. Lemaître's cosmological ideas, which are derived from an application of relativity theory to astronomy, were originally proposed in 1927 and fully developed in *L'Hypothèse de l'atome primitif, essai de cosmogonie* (1946). His research also included action of Earth's magnetic field on cosmic rays.—*D. H. D. R.*

LÉMERY, NICOLAS, 1645–1715, French chemist and physician; b. Rouen. A practicing pharmacist, he lectured on chemistry at the Univs. of Montpellier and Paris; his *Cours de chymie* (1675) was reprinted 13 times during his lifetime and was for years a standard work. His other works include *Pharmacopée universelle* (1697) and *Traité universel des drogues simples* (1698), which gives detailed instructions for preparation of chemicals for medicinal use. Lémery was one of the first to distinguish clearly between acids and alkalies, and he proposed a theory of the composition of salts based on the mechanistic philosophy of Descartes.—*R. J. F.*

LEMNISCATE OF BERNOULLI: see CURVES.

LENARD, PHILIPP EDUARD ANTON, 1862–1947, German physicist; b. Pozsony, Hungary. His researches were chiefly on light and electricity, and his publications include papers on the effect of ultraviolet light on solids and gases, the photoelectric effect, electrical conductivity of flames, and phosphorescence. He was the first to consider the atom as mostly empty space. For his researches on cathode rays, he received the Nobel prize, 1905. A fellow of the Royal Society, he was awarded its Rumford medal.—*D. H. D. R.*

LENOIR, JEAN JOSEPH ÉTIENNE, 1822–1900, French inventor; b. Mussy-la-Ville, Luxembourg; self-educated. Best known of his many inventions is a gas engine (1860), the first commercially feasible internal-combustion engine, which ran on illuminating gas. Although it used large quantities of fuel, it demonstrated the practicality of the internal-combustion engine, and was installed in a number of factories. Lenoir also invented other electrical and chemical devices, including a type of telegraph (1865).—*D. H. D. R.*

LENS: an object of transparent material, often glass, with a regularly curved, usually spherical surface. A lens produces an enlarged or diminished image of a visible object by bending and changing the direction of light rays from the object. This bending arises from the fact that light travels at different velocities in different mediums. If a ray of light passes from one medium to another at any angle except 90° to the surface of the second medium, the ray will bend (see REFRACTION). A double convex lens (Fig. 1a) bends the rays passing through it so that they converge and produce a *real image* (provided the object is beyond the focal length). A double concave lens (Fig. 1b) bends the rays so that they diverge; at the point where the diverging rays would intersect were they extended, a *virtual image* appears. Each lens surface has a radius of curvature (R) and a center of curvature; the line through the two centers of curvature is called the *principal axis*. Light rays parallel to the principal axis of a thin lens will converge at a point whose distance from the lens is called the *focal length* (Fig. 2a). A bundle of parallel rays not necessarily parallel to the principal axis will converge on the focal plane, which is the plane that is perpendicular to the principal axis and that passes through the focal point (Fig. 2b). The relationship between the focal length, f, the radii of curvature of the lens surfaces, R_1 and R_2, and the refractive index of the lens material, n, is $1/f = (n - 1)(1/R_1 - 1/R_2)$, known as the *lensmaker's equation*. The relationship between the focal length,

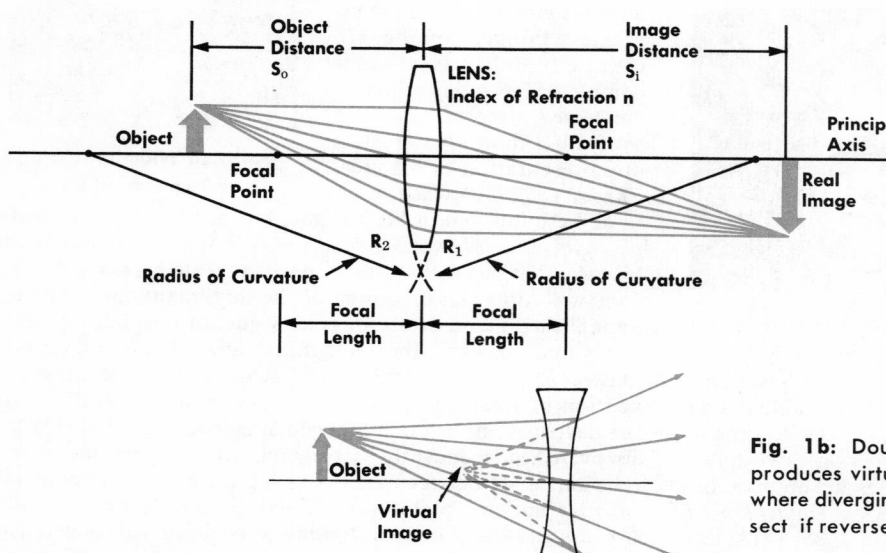

Fig. 1a: Double convex lens produces real image if object is at distance greater than focal length of lens.

Fig. 1b: Double concave lens produces virtual image at point where diverging rays would intersect if reversed in direction.

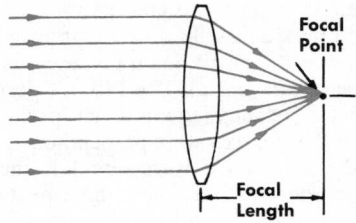

Fig. 2a: Rays parallel to principal axis intersect at focal point.

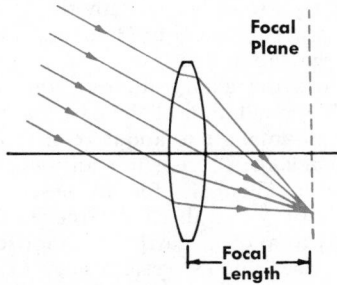

Fig. 2b: Rays not parallel to principal axis intersect on focal plane.

the object distance, s_0, and the image distance, s_i, is $1/f = 1/s_0 + 1/s_i$.

These equations are true only for thin lenses and for paraxial light rays (those rays close to the principal axis). In general, light rays not close to the principal axis do not converge at one point. The rays incident to the lens near its outer edge converge at a series of points short of the image formed by the paraxial rays. This limitation of the focusing power of a single lens is called *spherical aberration*. It is not caused by a defect in the manufacture of the lens, but is a limitation inherent in the refracting character of a spherical surface. Also, because the various wavelengths, or colors, that comprise light travel at different velocities in any medium except a vacuum, different wavelengths of light have different indices of refraction for the same medium. Therefore the same lens has a different focal length for each color; this can be verified by inspecting the lensmaker's equation. Consequently, a single lens forms not one image but a series of images, one for each color present in the light rays passing through the lens; this limitation is called *chromatic aberration*. There are, in fact, seven aberrations present in any lens: spherical aberration, longitudinal and lateral chromatic aberration, astigmatism, coma, curvature of field, and distortion. These cannot be wholly corrected, but the greater the number of lenses allowable in an optical system, the greater the degree of correction possible. All high-quality optical systems make use of a number of lenses, which together are designed to reduce those aberrations that will interfere with the particular task of the system. Besides double convex and double concave lenses, there are variations, *e.g.* concave-convex, plano-concave, and plano-convex, which are used in high-quality compound systems. Lenses are widely used in CAMERAS, TELESCOPES, MICROSCOPES, BINOCULARS, and, of course, the human EYE.—*A. L.*

LENZ, HEINRICH FRIEDRICH EMIL, 1804–64, Russian physicist; b. Dorpat. He did research on electricity and magnetism, formulating LENZ'S LAW and discovering that the change in electrical resistance due to a change in temperature is approximately proportional to the temperature change.—*D. H. D. R.*

LENZ'S LAW: a law of ELECTROMAGNETISM published in 1834 by H. F. E. Lenz. It states that when an electric current is induced by a varying magnetic flux, the direction of the induced current is such that its magnetic field opposes the variation in the inducing magnetic flux. It is against this opposition that work must be done in the generation of electrical energy, in accord with the law of conservation of energy.—*H. Sw.*

LEONARDO DA PISA (FIBONACCI), 1180?–?1250, Italian mathematician; b. Pisa. The son of a merchant, he gained an interest in arithmetic from his father's business. His travels to Sicily, Greece, Egypt, and Syria introduced him to Eastern and Arabic mathematics. He recognized the superiority of Hindu-Arabic methods of calculation and, after his return to Pisa, published his famous book *Liber abaci,* (1202). This book, which became a standard work in algebra and arithmetic for centuries, showed the advantages of Hindu-Arabic notation and did much to introduce that system into Europe. His *Practica geometria* (1220) collected a great deal of material on geometry and trigonometry, and his *Liber quadratorum* (1225) is a brilliant work on indeterminate equations.—*H. C.*

LEONARDO DA VINCI, 1452–1519, Italian painter, architect, engineer, and scientist, b. Vinci, Tuscany. Principally known as a painter, Leonardo was also a pioneer in the sciences of hydraulics and mechanics, and made extensive studies of human anatomy and the structure of the heart. In hydrostatics he recognized that liquids transmit pressure and that work done by the mover equals that done by the resistance; in hydrodynamics he developed the principle that with a given fall, the smaller the cross-section of the passage the greater will be the velocity of a flowing liquid. In dynamics

Leonardo da Vinci
(IBM)

his work was based on the theory of impetus, which, he stated, carried the moving body in a straight line. He devised a parabolic compass, mastered the principles of perspective, and attempted to devise or improve instruments of measurement including a clock, a hydrometer, a hodometer, and an anemometer, and attempted to improve the theory of lenses. He analyzed the flight of birds, and his drawings included models of a flying machine and suggestions for a helicopter and parachute. Because he did not publish his work, he had little effect upon the development of either science or technology.—*S. B.*

LESQUEREUX, LEO, 1806–89, Swiss-U. S. paleobotanist; b. Fleurier, Switzerland; self-educated. A distinguished paleobotanist, he was commissioned by the governments of Switzerland, Germany, Sweden, Denmark, and France to study the peat bogs in those countries. In 1848 he came to the U. S. A. and began a study of the flora of the Appalachian coal fields, reported in his *Description of the Coal Flora of the Carboniferous Formation in Pennsylvania and Throughout the U. S. A.* (1880–84). He studied other fossil floras also, and his *Flora of the Dakota Group* was published posthumously in 1891. He was a member of the National Academy of Sciences.—*D. H. D. R.*

LEUCIPPUS, fl. 5th cent. B. C., Greek philosopher; b. Miletus (?). Founder of the ATOMIC THEORY of matter, he wrote at least one book, *The Great World Order.* However, none of his writings has survived, and even in antiquity little seems to have been known about him. Democritus was a disciple of his, and it is impossible to distinguish between their respective works.—*D. H. D. R.*

LEVEE: an embankment built up along the side of a river's channel, higher than the normal water level and higher also than the surrounding land. Such embankments may form on a river's flood plain when floodwaters, overflowing the riverbanks, suddenly lose velocity and deposit large amounts of sediments. These natural barriers sometimes act as divides between streams. Like the artificial levees made with bags of sand or other materials, they may prevent flooding during future high-water periods, but continuing deposition in the channel between levees raises the river higher and higher above the surrounding terrain and thus may ultimately increase the flood hazard.—*J. W.*

LEVER: see SIMPLE MACHINES.

LEVERRIER, URBAIN JEAN JOSEPH, 1811–77, French astronomer and mathematician; b. St.-Lô. His investigation of the irregularity in the motion of Uranus led to the discovery of NEPTUNE, 1846, by J. Galle. (J. C. Adams had independently predicted its existence the previous year.) He presented to the Academy of Sciences the position of an expected planet and requested Johann Galle, in Berlin, to look for it. On Sept. 23,

Urbain Jean Joseph Leverrier
(Yerkes Observatory)

1846, Galle found an unidentified starlike object of the 8th magnitude very close to Leverrier's calculated position; this proved to be the predicted planet. Leverrier succeeded D. F. J. Arago as director of the Paris Observatory in 1854. He was a fellow of the Royal Society.—*R. N. M.*

LEYDEN JAR: see ELECTRICITY.

L'HÔPITAL (L'HOSPITAL), GUILLAUME FRANÇOIS ANTOINE DE, 1661–1704, French mathematician; b. Paris. He was attracted to the new calculus of Leibniz, although it was then in unreadable form, and studied for a time with Jean Bernoulli, solving several problems proposed by Bernoulli as a public challenge to the mathematicians of Europe. L'Hôpital's *Analyse des infiniments petits* (1696) was instrumental in making calculus better known. This textbook on the analysis of infinitely small quantities contained the method, known as L'Hôpital's rule, for finding the limit of a fraction whose numerator and denominator approach zero simultaneously. —*H. C.*

LIBBY, WILLARD FRANK, 1908–   , U. S. chemist; b. Grand Valley, Colo. He won the 1960 Nobel prize for his development of techniques for determining the age of organic remains by means of radiocarbon (see RADIOACTIVE DATING). He is a member of the National Academy of Sciences.—*D. H. D. R.*

LIBRATION: the oscillation of an angle that measures or is involved in measuring the position of a dynamical system, the oscillation being about a mean (or sometimes steadily in-

creasing value), as opposed to change in a single direction, *e.g.* a pendulum making oscillations as opposed to complete revolutions. One of the best-known instances is the libration of the Moon (see MOON, *illus.*). The Moon's period of revolution in its orbit is exactly equal to its period of rotation round its axis, and if this axis were perpendicular to the orbital plane and if the orbit itself were circular, then the Moon would always present precisely the same aspect to Earth. But neither of these conditions holds. The axis of the Moon is about 6½° out of the exact perpendicular, and this results in an apparent nodding of the north and south lunar poles alternately toward and away from Earth: the effect is known as the *libration in latitude* of the Moon. Then again, the lunar orbit is not circular but has an eccentricity of about ⅛, and the motion in longitude of the Moon does not occur at a constant rate (as, however, does the axial rotation); this results in an apparent sideways oscillation of the east and west limbs of the Moon through an angle of about 7¾°: this is known as the *libration in longitude.* There is in addition a diurnal libration, amounting to about 1° for an observer at Earth's equator, and resulting from the transference of the observer owing to the daily rotation of Earth; at moonrise the observer looks 1° beyond the Moon's western edge (as it would be seen from the center of Earth), and at moonset 1° beyond the eastern edge. The net effect of these librations is that about 59% of the lunar surface is directly visible from Earth in one sidereal month (27⅓ days), leaving only 41% hidden. A minute physical libration also results from a deviation from exact uniformity in the Moon's axial rotation.—*R. A. L.*

LICHEN: a type of plant consisting of algal cells and fungal cells in an intimate partnership known as SYMBIOSIS. The fungus provides filamentous strands which hold the organism together and trap moisture. The alga uses the water for producing by PHOTOSYNTHESIS the organic compounds needed for energy and growth by both algal cells and fungal cells. Usually the algal partner is a green alga, but may be a blue-green alga (see ALGAE). The fungal partner is generally a sac

"Old man's beard" is the common name for *Usnea barbata,* a widely distributed form of fruticose lichen here shown hanging from the branches of a fallen tree. (*Rutherford Platt*)

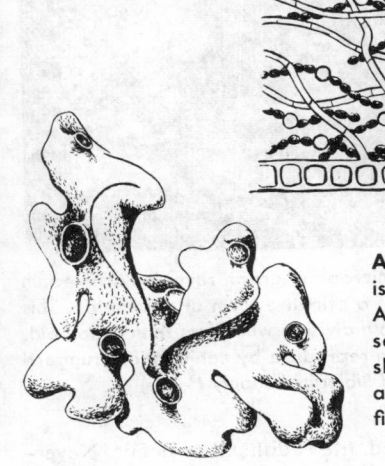

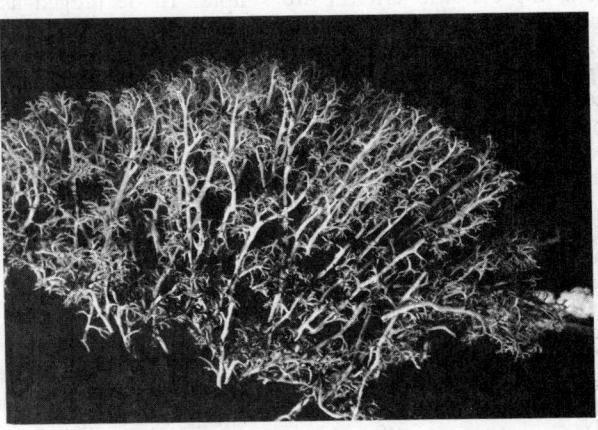

A lichen's general structure is shown in drawing at left. Above is a microscopic cross-section of the same plant showing chains of pigmented algal cells among the fungal filaments. (*After Bonner*)

Erect, branching lichen (*above*) grows on rocks, trees, and fallen trunks, and on the ground, while reindeer moss (*right*) covers ground in mosslike tufts. Both forms belong to *Cladonia*. Presence of these lichens often indicates suitable soil for development of forest areas in the practice of scientific tree farming. (*Photos courtesy The American Museum of Natural History, right, and Rutherford Platt*)

fungus, but may be a club fungus (see FUNGI). The particular combination determines which form of lichen will develop; these forms are so distinctive that they have been given pseudo-generic names such as *Pneumonaria* ("rock tripe"), *Usnea* ("old man's beard"), and *Cladonia* (including both "reindeer moss" and "woodsman's fire" or "Indian matches"). Some lichens have an encrusting habit; they are flat, small-lobed, and conform closely to the rock or bark on which they grow. Others spread out as lobed sheets (thalli), often elevated from the support by wrinkling. Still others, including those named, are erect or pendant, and branching; these cling to rock walls and trees, or grow on fallen logs and the ground itself. Lichens provide an important winter food for caribou and reindeer, lemmings, and a few kinds of insects. They grow under conditions of extreme adversity so long as water is available, occasionally being found high on mountain peaks and also on polar tundras. Commonly they reproduce by fragments blown by wind. Edible fragments of this kind are suspected of being the "manna" eaten by the Israelites. See Color Plate 63.—*L. and M. M.*

LIE, SOPHUS, 1842–99, Norwegian mathematician; b. near Bergen. A mathematician of wide range and great originality, he is known mainly for his work in differential equations, for which he developed the theory of continuous groups. He also made contributions in differential geometry. He published a major work (with F. Engel), *Theorie der Transformationsgruppen* (1888–93). He was fellow of the Royal Society and an associate of the U. S. National Academy of Sciences.—*H. C.*

LIEBERMANN, KARL THEODOR, 1842–1914, German chemist; b. Berlin. An organic chemist, he discovered β-naphthylamine, the stereoisomers of cinnamic acid, and the *Liebermann test* for phenolic compounds. Also, he unraveled the constitution of a number of cyclic compounds. With Karl Graebe (1841–1927) Liebermann produced alizarin from anthraquinone and laid the foundation of the industrial manufacture of alizarin, rendering the dye industry independent of vegetable sources. —*R. E. O.*

LIEBIG, BARON JUSTUS VON, 1803–73, German chemist; b. Darmstadt. His early work on fulminating silver brought him first into conflict and then into close friendship with Friedrich Wöhler. In 1831 he completed the development of a convenient apparatus for elementary organic-chemical analysis and founded the *Annalen der Pharmazie* (after 1834, *Annalen der Chemie und Pharmazie*). His studies of benzaldehyde showed (1832) that the greatest part of the molecule remained as a "radical," benzoyl, throughout reactions with hydrogen, chlorine, and oxygen. In 1837 he began the long work on *Handwörterbuch der Chemie* (with J. C. Poggendorf and Wöhler), a dictionary of chemistry. His applications of chemistry to agriculture and physiology were highly important, and resulted in his *Die Chemie in ihrer Anwendung auf Agrikultur und Physiologie* (1840). His *Chemische Briefe* (1844), "letters" on chemistry, stimulated general interest in this branch of science. He was a fellow of the Royal Society and an associate of the U. S. National Academy of Sciences. —*E. F.*

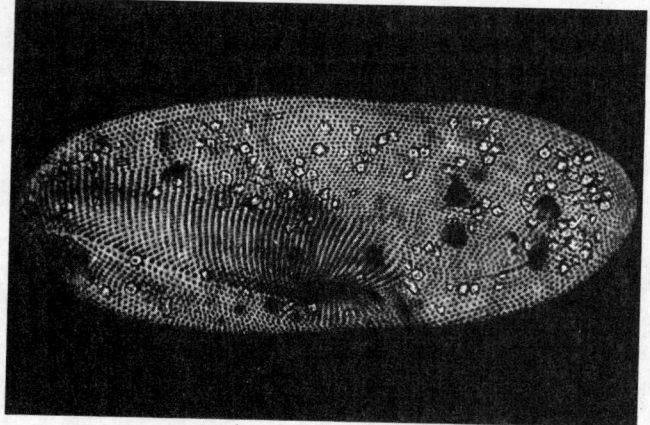

Life on one-celled level: Microphotograph reveals *Paramecium caudatum*, largest species of a primitive form of animal life. This begins to reproduce by simple division when less than a day old. Some species of *Paramecium* reproduce by conjugation, suggesting a sexual phase. (*General Biological Supply House*)

LIFE: Like the redness of red, life is difficult to define. Nevertheless, the classical criteria are simple. To be judged as living, any object must possess, or once have possessed, the ability to grow and reproduce and to maintain its own integrity. It must also exhibit continual chemical activity, *i.e.* metabolism, and some degree of responsiveness to environmental change. To growth and reproduction, most modern biologists add the ability to mutate. Taken separately, these criteria can be duplicated in the nonliving world. The flame of a candle carries on a continual exchange of matter and energy while maintaining its own integrity. A crystal and many colloidal globules can grow. A gun may be highly responsive to very slight stimuli. It is the coexistence of all these properties organized within a single entity that makes us call that entity alive.

Whatever may be discovered in the future about the ultimate nature of life, it seems certain that the facts as now established will not be shown to be in error, although they may be seen in a very different perspective. Contrary to what was widely believed a century ago, living things obey the laws of conservation of matter and energy. The chemical elements that compose protoplasm are the same elements that are found in the nonliving world. There is no evidence that the laws of matter cease to hold within the living world. On the contrary, the chemical study of living things is the most successful and important area of advance in biological research at the present time.

With the advance of BIOCHEMISTRY it has become clear that the "secret" of life lies in its organization. This organization is in important respects greater and more complex than anything found in the nonliving world. The phenomena of life occur on a series of levels of organization, each built from units of the next lower level in much the same way that water, on the molecular level, is composed of atoms of hydrogen and oxygen from the atomic level. Each level has its own characteristic properties and laws, so that when one passes from one level to another, either up or down in the scale, new properties emerge. Thus the properties of a molecule of water are not the average of the properties of its constituent hydrogen and oxygen, but something very different. This is the kind of thing biologists mean when they claim that the whole is more than the sum of its parts.

On the molecular level of biochemistry, the most characteristic molecules are proteins and nucleic acids. These are the largest and most complex of all known molecules; hence it is not surprising to discover that they possess properties unknown for smaller molecular species. Cells, which are constructed of proteins and other complex molecules, present the

next higher level and the first level of undoubted living things. Viruses are debatable borderline cases. The most complex form of life on the one-celled level is that of the ciliates—organisms like *Paramecium*.

The level of multicellular organisms presents creatures of incomparably greater mastery of themselves and their environment, organisms as varied as orchids, birds, and men. But even within this single level, it is the degree of organization, the complexity of pattern, that chiefly matters. The essential difference between the brain of a clever dog and the brain of a stupid dogfish is not any difference in the cells. Nerve cells in both are virtually indistinguishable. Still less is it a difference in the lipids, Nissl (RNA) bodies, water, and other molecules composing the nerve cells, and it is certainly not a difference in the atoms of which the molecules are made, for these are identical. The difference lies in the way the brain of the dog and the brain of the fish are organized, in the differing complexity of their architecture. To suppose that the ultimate nature of life can be best explored by further and further analysis into ever lower levels of organization is to fall into the error of the well-known small boy who cut open his drum to discover what made the noise. Chemical analysis of the leather drum head or of the metal sides will not yield him the answer, because the leather might just as well have been a pair of gloves and the metal sides a garden hoe. It is the organization, the pattern, that holds the secret.—*G. B. M.*

LIFE, EXTRATERRESTRIAL: life presumed to exist beyond the limits of Earth and its atmosphere. In our solar system there is no direct evidence for extraterrestrial life which even approaches the rather strict definitions for life established by biologists. All the solar planets beyond Mars are unlikely as possible abodes for life as we know it, because of their low temperature, low light intensity, and atmospheres containing noxious gases such as methane and ammonia. Mercury and our Moon are eliminated because of their lack of an atmosphere and the consequent extreme temperature conditions. As to cloud-covered Venus, observations from the Mariner space probe indicate an extremely high surface temperature. Yet some astronomers believe the observations have been misinterpreted—the temperatures may be rather moderate.

The environment of Mars is definitely known to be very harsh by our standards. Temperatures may reach 90°F near the equator in the middle of the day, but probably drop to many tens of degrees below freezing every night in all areas. The atmosphere is very thin and contains virtually no oxygen, although carbon dioxide is present in amounts about twice to 13 times that above the surface of our own planet. Water is probably present, accounting for the polar caps, but the quantities must be very limited, because water has been detected spectroscopically in the atmosphere only a few times. Occasionally unattenuated ultraviolet light strikes the planet, for there is no ozone layer to block it.

Harsh as these conditions may be, life as we know it could conceivably exist on Mars. Undoubtedly significant are the relatively dark-colored markings, roughly triangular in shape, mostly in the southern hemisphere, surrounded by lighter-colored reddish desert areas (see MARS). Three evidences that these markings represent some sort of living organisms (probably vegetation) might be mentioned: (1) The areas change color throughout the year, turning from a light bluish gray in the Martian winter to darker shades of blue, brown, red, black, or even—in certain areas—moss green in summer. The change begins next to the disappearing polar cap and moves toward the equator, opposite to the movement of spring on Earth. (2) Occasionally clouds of yellow dust from the deserts are deposited upon the markings, obscuring them. Yet in a few days the markings are again visible, and it has been suggested that only living organisms could so re-emerge from a covering of dust. Craters revealed by Mariner IV photographs often cut across the edges of these markings. A protected crater bottom, where temperatures and atmospheric density would be somewhat higher than elsewhere, and where moisture might collect, could harbor living things.

Volcanism, oxides of nitrogen, and very recently frost heaving have been invoked as alternative explanations for the markings, but none of these explanations is entirely satisfactory. Volcanism fails to account for the color changes, and the oxides-of-nitrogen theory depends upon the existence in the atmosphere of compounds that simply do not appear in the Martian spectra. The frost theory appears to be the best non-biological explanation for the Martian markings, although it fails to explain why the markings do not correspond better to the elevations (as these are somewhat uncertainly identified) on the Mariner photographs.

But what sorts of organisms, if any, could there be on the red planet? The lack of oxygen, the low temperatures, and the extreme scarcity of water immediately eliminate the possibility for nearly all the organisms familiar to us. It has often been suggested that vegetation on Mars might be lichen-like, for the lichens are very hardy, representing a symbiotic relationship between an alga and a fungus; but even the lichens fail under close scrutiny. They do not change color with changes of season; they are extremely slow-growing; they are flat organisms pressed against the surface of rocks and could hardly be expected to re-emerge from a covering of dust; they are quite sensitive to foreign gases in the atmosphere and do not grow well, if at all, in the absence of oxygen; and they do not grow at low temperatures, although they may survive. Thus no living organism known to man seems to account for the markings on Mars. We might expect a new sort of life, or at least a number of new and unique adaptations to meet the Martian environment.

In recent years we have become much more aware of the abilities of life as we know it to withstand extreme environments. Species of higher plants have been found that can withstand the equivalent of the ultraviolet light falling on the surface of Mars for a period equal to the Martian growing season. Several known microorganisms can grow at temperatures of $-20°C$ to $-30°C$. Various higher plants, notably winter rye, can withstand nightly freezing ($-20°C$) provided they are kept in an atmosphere free of oxygen. Some microorganisms can extract moisture from extremely dry atmospheres, and several species of plants and animals can live at very reduced pressures. The possibility that Mars supports life seems somewhat less remote than formerly.

Some Martian phenomena can be interpreted as evidence of intelligence: the network of "canals," the brilliant flares lasting seconds to minutes, and the two small satellites with their close, circular equatorial orbits. All this could be the work of intelligent beings, but other explanations—less imaginative ones—seem adequate.

In an attempt to discover direct evidence for extraterrestrial life, living organisms or their remains as well as other organic materials have been sought in meteorites. In recent years, the literature has been filled with reported successes in this research. But these reports, or inferences made from them, have been rejected by enough competent scientists so that we can hardly consider them conclusive.

There is no direct evidence for the existence of planets beyond the solar system suitable for life as we know it. Except for our Sun, no star is close enough to be viewed even by our most powerful telescope as any more than a point of light; planets, if any, around other stars simply cannot be seen. Thus we must reason by extrapolation from our own solar system, from present theories of planet formation, and from observations of multiple-star systems. Extrapolation is logically invalid but nevertheless compelling. Many astronomers, noting so much similarity in the observable universe, have estimated that there must be a billion billion planets like ours. Since the spectra of the distant stars are similar to that of the Sun, and since meteorites contain the same elements as Earth, the universe is presumed to be chemically uniform, or nearly so, throughout; and if chemically uniform it could be biologically uniform too.

Spurred by such thoughts, many scientists are currently trying to reconstruct the story of life's origins on Earth. If they knew how life originated here, they could speak more confidently of its likely origins elsewhere. Recent work on the origin of living tissues does seem to imply extraterrestrial life biochemically similar to our own. Carbon is plentiful in the universe. Under laboratory conditions believed to be like those that prevailed on the primitive Earth, the organic molecules that arise are, for the most part, the same molecules that are basic to Earth biochemistry.

On the other hand, life based on a silicon chemistry has been suggested, and one can imagine adaptations in our own metabolic processes which might allow survival under a wider range of environments. Such adaptations might include emphasis on oxidation and reduction of nitrogen or sulfur, and compounds in the protoplasm which might allow survival and even metabolism at much lower temperatures than those normally found on Earth.

Even in the absence of direct biological analogies, the argument for life on other worlds is powerful. If there are other planets with conditions like Earth's (this seems almost certain), and if similar conditions tend to produce similar effects, then the possibility that life exists on some other planets seems stronger than the possibility that it does not. Even if life's origin on Earth were supernatural, a similar argument would apply.

In this context the theory of panspermia (transfer of life from planet to planet by natural means) has been revived. The survival of certain spores under laboratory conditions like those of space gives some support to this theory. However, much work remains to be done in this area. And, whether proved or not, panspermia is not essential to the case for extraterrestrial life. As already indicated, if life has developed on one planet, it is more likely than not to develop on other planets where conditions are similar.

For centuries, man in his religious moods has claimed direct evidence (revelation) for the existence of extraterrestrial beings. Such evidence has logical validity but it cannot be scientific, since it is not subject to objective testing. Recent accounts of visitations by extraterrestrial beings in flying saucers seem to be in somewhat the same logical position: they may be valid, but they cannot be scientifically examined. Acceptance of both religious and flying-saucer evidence must therefore be a personal matter. Would man, in any case, be able to communicate with intelligent beings from other

Seasonal changes on Mars have stimulated speculation as to possible existence of life on the red planet. Photos taken on Martian dates corresponding to May 11, July 31, and Aug. 20 for Earth's northern hemisphere show shrinking of south (upper) polar cap of Mars and darkening of areas in southern hemisphere. (E. C. Slipher/ Lowell Obs.)

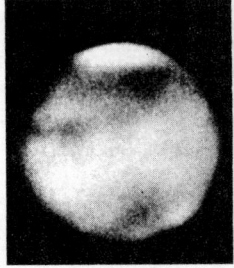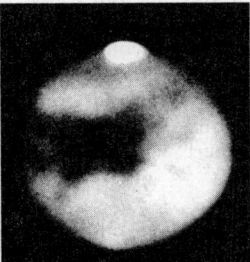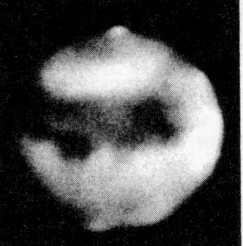

worlds? The very use of the word "intelligent" makes this seem quite likely. Various schemes for the systematic development of a common language for interplanetary communication have already been devised, and the radio telescope has already been employed, so far without success, in an effort to detect significant signals from the vicinity of relatively near stars. Future success in such efforts depends not only on whether intelligent life does exist elsewhere but on other factors too, such as its location in space and in time.— *F. S.*

LIFE, ORIGIN OF: It is generally believed among biologists that life on Earth originated by spontaneous generation under favorable conditions. Since there was no life on Earth when the planet formed, life must have arisen some time between the origin of Earth (4.5 billion yr ago) and the data of the earliest fossil evidence of life (2.7 billion yr ago). Until about 100 yr ago it was widely believed that living organisms could arise by SPONTANEOUS GENERATION as well as by sexual and asexual reproduction. Then Louis Pasteur made what is generally considered a conclusive demonstration (1862) that living organisms do not arise spontaneously on Earth at the present time. Pasteur's demonstration combined with Darwin's theory of evolution by natural selection implies that all life on Earth has evolved from the most primitive organism (see EVOLUTION).

Hypotheses: The proposal that the most primitive organism on Earth was created by a supernatural event is not scientific, since by its very nature it is not subject to experimental investigation. A second proposal is that life came to Earth from outer space (the panspermia hypothesis). But since living organisms apparently cannot survive for very long in space, because of cosmic rays and other radiation, this theory is held to be highly dubious, although it has not been disproved; also, it does not answer the question of where or how life did originate. A third hypothesis is that the first living organism arose directly from inorganic matter (carbon dioxide, water, and other inorganic nutrients) as a result of some very extraordinary event. However, even the simplest bacteria are extremely complex, and the chances of their arising directly from inorganic materials, with no steps in between, are too remote to consider seriously. A fourth proposal is that life orginated spontaneously from organic compounds in the oceans of the primitive Earth. The proposal assumes that primitive oceans contained large quantities of simple organic compounds that reacted to form structures of greater and greater complexity, until there arose a structure that we would call living. In other words, the first living organism developed by means of a series of nonbiological steps, none of which would be highly improbable on the basis of what is known today. This theory, first set forth clearly by A. I. Oparin (1938), is in general accepted by most scientists.

Formation of Organic Compounds: The first step in this process would have been the synthesis of simple organic compounds, including AMINO ACIDS, PURINES and PYRIMIDINES, SUGARS, and lipids (see FATS AND OILS). It is apparently not possible to synthesize organic compounds, except in extremely small quantities, using carbon dioxide, water, and a source of energy (such as ultraviolet light, electric discharges, and high-energy radiation). Therefore the initial step probably could not have taken place in an oxidizing atmosphere of carbon dioxide, nitrogen, oxygen, and water, as Earth has at present. However, Oparin and later Harold Urey (1952) suggested that organic compounds would be formed easily in a reducing atmosphere of methane, ammonia, water, and hydrogen. Reducing atmospheres are present on the planets Jupiter, Saturn, Uranus, and Neptune, and it seems likely that Earth had a reducing atmosphere when it was first formed. Oxidizing

conditions would have developed on Earth at a later stage because of the escape of hydrogen and the production of oxygen by the photochemical splitting of water.

Experimental evidence supports the suggestions of Oparin and Urey. S. L. Miller demonstrated (1953) that the action of electric discharges on a mixture of methane, ammonia, water, and hydrogen gives significant yields of amino acids, hydroxy acids, aliphatic acids, urea, and possibly sugars. The action of ultraviolet light gives similar results. J. Oro showed (1960) that it is possible to synthesize some of the purines and pyrimidines from an aqueous solution of ammonium cyanide, which was probably present in the primitive ocean.

Many steps in the synthesis of more complex organic compounds, especially polymers, would probably require a continuously available source of chemical energy. In present living organisms the energy is carried in the "high-energy" bond of adenosine triphosphate (see ENERGY IN BIOCHEMISTRY). It is not understood how this chemical energy was made available on the primitive Earth.

Following the formation of simple organic molecules, the next step would have been the synthesis of polymers of these molecules, the most important polymers being polypeptides, nucleotides, and polynucleotides (see NUCLEIC ACIDS; PROTEIN). The next degree of complexity would have been the synthesis of structures with biological-like activities, probably including polypeptides with catalytic activity (enzymes). Finally, polynucleotides capable of self-duplication would have developed. How these steps could have taken place in primitive oceans has not been demonstrated and is not understood.

First Living Organisms: The essential characteristic of a living organism is its ability to duplicate itself. In present living organisms, the replication process begins with the duplication of the genes located on the chromosomes in a cell (see CHROMOSOMES AND GENES). Additional enzymes and other cell constituents are synthesized, and the cell then divides into two fragments (see CELL DIVISION). Since genes are composed of polynucleotides called deoxyribonucleic acid (DNA), it seems likely that the first living organisms were simply molecules of deoxyribonucleic acid (or ribonucleic acid) that could duplicate themselves. Such an organism would have needed enzymes to carry out this duplication and probably a membrane to hold the structure together. This organism would also have been subject to MUTATION. Being able both to replicate and to mutate, it would have evolved into higher forms of life because of the selective pressures of the environment. This hypothetical organism is similar to a VIRUS except that it would have been able to duplicate itself outside a living cell.

Many other hypotheses on the nature of the first living organisms could be enumerated. These hypotheses are not likely to prove significant until much greater knowledge of the preliminary steps is available.—*S. L. M.*

LIFE, PREHISTORIC: broadly, organisms living prior to historical times; arbitrarily, life antedating the beginning of the last glacial retreat, about 10,000 yr ago. The traces of ancient life, FOSSILS, are the subject of a special science, PALEONTOLOGY. Paleontologists reconstruct the character, habits, and habitat of fossil animals and plants by attention to form, occurrence, association with other fossils, and similarities to modern organisms. The succession of fossils in rock layers provides a historical sequence (see CORRELATION; STRATIGRAPHY); this sequence corresponds with the divisions of the geologic column (GEOLOGICAL TIME CHART) and reflects the evolution of life through geologic time.

Calcareous structures formed by algae are the oldest known evidence of life. Some occur in Archeozoic rocks, nearly 3 billion yr old, in Africa; in Proterozoic rocks (2

Traces of life from the very remote past are fragmentary and often obscure, but may vividly suggest living scenes. Here, at the present site of Peace River Canyon, British Columbia, a dinosaur walked in mud, which was then buried, turned to stone, and finally exposed again. (*National Museum of Canada*)

billion to 600 million yr old) they are locally abundant (see PRECAMBRIAN TIME). Algal filaments and traces of fungi are fossilized in lower Proterozoic rocks, and chemical analysis shows the presence of amino acids (the structural units of protein) in these fossils. Proterozoic finds include questionable specimens of protozoans, jellyfish, worm tubes, sponges, brachiopods, and arthropods. Upper Proterozoic rocks in Australia have yielded traces of soft-bodied creatures, some familiar ones such as jellyfish, seapens, and annelid worms, and some of undeterminable affinities though obviously animals. The rarity of fossils older than the Cambrian Period indicates that inhabitants of these ancient communities lacked skeletons or shells; hard parts are more likely to be preserved. What is known of these, as well as early Cambrian fossils, indicates they were marine creatures, some of which fed on algae and others of which preyed upon the browsers.

Apparently several different animal groups evolved resistant skeletons at about the same time, and their appearance marks the beginning of the Cambrian, the first period of the PALEOZOIC ERA. Changes in the chemistry of the sea or atmosphere may have evoked or permitted skeletal evolution, but these changes are as yet undetermined. Over the following 100 million yr or so, most major animal groups enter the geologic record. Calcareous algal structures and rare impressions of seaweed record Paleozoic marine plants; the abundance and variety of herbivores testify to the abundance and variety of plant life. The bivalve brachiopods (or lamp shells), the small, colonial "moss-animals" (bryozoans), sponges, some clams, and the "sea lilies" (crinoids) and their extinct relatives (blastoids and cystoids) lived fixed on the ocean bottom and filtered microscopic organisms and debris from the water. Solitary horn corals and branching and massive colonial coelenterates preyed on animals that strayed within reach. Locally, the corals and calcareous algae built atolls or barrier reefs in shallow, clear seas. Primitive arthropods, the trilobites, swam or crept or burrowed along the bottom; they were probably mud feeders and scavengers. Other Paleozoic arthropods include various extinct types and ancestors of the barnacles, of the crabs and lobsters, and of the horseshoe crab. The predatory scorpion-like eurypterids inhabited streams, lakes, and estuaries as well as the sea. Annelid worms were probably numerous but are rare as fossils. Protozoans with calcareous or siliceous skeletons are abundant, but others are unknown. Snails, clams, primitive starfish and sea urchins, and some fish complete the roll of Paleozoic sea-bottom animals.

By the middle of the Paleozoic, 350 million yr before the present, fish had become abundant and varied. Early ones occur in stream, estuary, or lagoonal deposits; lacking jaws, they fed on bottom debris or filtered small organisms from the water. Later they spread to the open seas and, with the evolution of jaws, became predatory. Competing with them were relatives of the squids (cephalopods) which bore chambered shells, either straight, curved, or coiled. Fish and cephalopods swam the seas and hunted along the bottom. With them in surface waters were small arthropods, jellyfish, the now-extinct colonial graptolites, and presumably pastures of algae.

Through the Paleozoic and the later eras, the MESOZOIC and CENOZOIC, the marine communities changed with the extinction of some groups and the evolution of others. Brachio-

pods were rare in Mesozoic and Cenozoic seas; trilobites and blastoids disappeared by the end of the Paleozoic; graptolites and cystoids died out even earlier. During the Mesozoic the shelled cephalopods were extraordinarily abundant and varied, only to be replaced by the related squids and cuttle-fish and the competitive fish in the Cenozoic. New groups of corals, bryozoans, crinoids, sea urchins, clams, gastropods, and crustaceans occur in these later rocks. The fishes underwent a series of rapid evolutionary changes and became diversified for various modes of life.

The fresh waters had a less varied group of animals. Only fish, eurypterids, snails, clams, and bivalve crustaceans, the ostracods, occur in Paleozoic stream and lake deposits, and the eurypterids failed to survive the era. These various animals, however, are of particular importance, since they gave rise to most of the land animals. Land plants evolved early in the Paleozoic, and by the Silurian Period, 400 million yr ago, a variety of rather simple, typically fern-like types grew across swampy lowlands. The coal forests of the late Paleozoic (350 to 220 million yr ago) consisted of giant tree ferns, large horse-tails, the now extinct seed-ferns, and tall scale trees, cousins of present club mosses. Scorpions appeared in Silurian times, the insects in Devonian (over 350 million yr ago), and spiders in the later, coal-forest deposits. The amphibians joined the rush to land near the end of the Devonian. They evolved from large fish pre-adapted to land life by heavy lobed fins, by scales which prevented rapid drying, and by lungs.

The earliest amphibians retained a fish-like tail but had sturdy if short and wide-spraddled legs. During the Mississippian and Pennsylvanian periods, 350 to 270 million yr before the present, they diversified in form and mode of life. Some strong-legged types hunted the forests; others lived along the water's edge; some returned to an aquatic life. Some ate the giant insects; others ate fish or their brother amphibians, and still others, soft-bodied invertebrates. Some aquatic amphibians were limbless and snake-like, but others had flat, broad heads and bodies. Most of these amphibians inhabited the boggy lowland forests, and few penetrated onto the drier up-

Middle Cambrian life is shown (*above, left*) by several large-tailed trilobites swimming on the sea bottom; **Middle Devonian** (*center*), by seaweed, sponges, coral, crinoids, snails, and frilled cephalopods; **Pennsylvanian** (*right*), by a swamp forest of the Coal Age with tree ferns, rushes, and trunks of conifers and scale trees.

lands. After the Pennsylvanian Period, as the continents began to rise, the great swamps shrank and disappeared. Most of the swamp-loving amphibians became extinct, as did many of the coal-forest plants and insects.

With the development of eggs that could be laid on land, reptiles evolved from the amphibians. This may have occurred about 300 million yr ago, near the beginning of the Pennsylvanian Period. In the next 50 million yr or so, a variety of reptile herbivores, insectivores, and carnivores evolved, so that the reptiles dominated the land environments. The commonest reptiles were cotylosaurs, a primitive reptile group, and pelycosaurs, early members of the mammal-like reptile stock. Descendants of these forms flourished through the Permian and into the Triassic, until about 200 million yr ago. Then the dinosaurs and their relatives supplanted the earlier reptiles.

Some dinosaurs were huge, quadrupedal, long-necked herbivores; other plant eaters were rather smaller types, some bipedal, others armored, tank-like quadrupeds. Some late types bore long horns and a shield over the neck. The carnivores, which called forth this evolution of size, horns, and armor, were large bipeds. Other dinosaurs of smaller size and lighter build probably resembled the modern ostrich in form and habits. Crocodiles lived in the streams and lakes. Lizards and mammals darted through the trees and underbrush. Flying reptiles, the pterodactyls, and birds winged the air, while marine reptiles pursued fish and cephalopods. For over a 100 million yr, through the Jurassic and Cretaceous periods, these groups evolved and diversified. Forests took on a modern aspect as flowering plants appeared. Flies, wasps, beetles, and other modern insect types buzzed, crept, and burrowed. Then, suddenly, at the end of the Cretaceous many of the animals died out. Birds and mammals, crocodiles, lizards, snakes, and turtles, and frogs and salamanders among the amphibians, survived. Many explanations have been offered for this wave of extinction. The change in vegetation affected the plant eaters; the continents were a little higher; the lush swamps were reduced in extent. Some dinosaurs specialized for particular environments apparently could not tolerate these changes. As they disappeared, the balance of the terrestrial communities changed, and other groups followed them into extinction.

The fossil record of the birds is scant. A find in Jurassic rocks links birds to the reptiles. Two Cretaceous birds are well known; they still possessed teeth but otherwise show modern characteristics. Modern birds began to appear early in the CENOZOIC ERA, some 50 to 70 million yr ago. Large, flightless carnivorous birds distinguish this phase of avian history.

Mammals dominate Cenozoic history. The earliest occur at the end of the Triassic, but only with the extinction of many reptile groups did the mammals radiate into various modes of life. The early Cenozoic ones were rather short-legged, had simple teeth, and possessed relatively small brains. The forest and jungle environments predominated, and arboreal forms, including primitive primates, were abundant. As the continents rose in the most recent phase of mountain building, the climate became cooler and drier. Wide areas became grassland, and the forests and jungles shrank. About 35 million yr before the present, modern herbivores and carnivores began to replace the archaic ones. Rodents multiplied; monkeys and apes appeared. This change coincided with the spread of grasslands; it resulted in longer legs, lighter bodies, better-adapted teeth, and larger brains.

The climax of this phase of mammalian evolution occurred about 10 million yr ago (Pliocene), when mammals like those of the modern African veldt inhabited most of the continents. Climatic changes of the last million years (Glacial Ages) and the activities of man, fossil and modern, contributed to the destruction of many mammals, particularly the larger ones. The primitive ape-men had apparently evolved bipedal habits, social organization, tool-making, and hunting techniques by the beginning of the glacial epoch. Advanced humans with large brains and reduced jaws developed through the epoch, and our own species appears in the fossil record about 50,000 yr ago.—*J. B.*

LIFE CYCLE: the characteristic life history of an organism from its initiation as a fertilized egg until it produces reproductive cells that will fuse to start a new individual. Since the same history is repeated generation after generation, one can think of it as a cyclic phenomenon and can diagram the steps of the cycle as points around a circle. Such circular diagrams

Cretaceous sea scene (*below, left*) shows *Tylosaurus*, a large swimming lizard, and *Protostega*, a marine turtle with carapace and plastron like those of our modern giant turtle. **Late Cretaceous** scene (*center*) is featured by *Tyrannosaurus*, the great bipedal carnivore. **Miocene** period, the Golden Age of Mammals, is represented (*right*) by *Dinohyus*, the giant pig, and *Moropus*, the tall, clawed ungulate eating from tree.

Permian desert landscape (*above, left*) includes *Dimetrodon* and *Edaphosaurus*, typical fin-back reptiles of the period. **Triassic** period (*center*) shows *Cynognathus*, mammal-like reptile preceding true mammals. **Jurassic** shoreline scene (*right*) includes primitive *Archaeopteryx*, with birdlike plumage, teeth, clawed wings, and long tail, showing relationship to reptilian relatives on ground.

make comparisons of the life cycles of different kinds of organisms easy to visualize.

The life cycle of man begins with two types of fertilized eggs, one type resulting from the fusion with an egg of a male-determining sperm, the other type from the fusion with an egg of a female-determining sperm. The first type grows to be a male, the second a female. Considering sex only, females produce eggs of only one kind, whereas males produce two kinds of sperms, male-determining and female-determining. The fusion of an egg with one or the other type of sperm, producing a fertilized egg, completes the cycle.

Egg cells and sperm cells have one set of chromosomes in the nucleus of each cell. The number of chromosomes in a set is called the n number, which is 23 for humans. The fertilized eggs have two sets, the $2n$ number, which is 46 for humans. All cells of the body of the individual who developed from the fertilized egg have the $2n$ number of chromosomes in their nuclei. Prior to the production of functional eggs and sperms, the number is reduced to n in a distinctive type of nuclear division called MEIOSIS (actually two, coupled, nuclear divisions, meiosis I and II). The two sets of chromosomes are separated into the two nuclei formed after the first division, one set to each nucleus. That is, meiosis I is a "reductional" nuclear division. Meiosis II is an "equational" nuclear division, like all other nuclear divisions in organisms, and maintains the same number of chromosomes. In man, most animals, and some plants, cells formed by meiosis are, with a few internal developments, the reproductive cells, called gametes. One can outline the life cycle in this way: fertilized egg ($2n$); body cells of the individual ($2n$); meiosis; gametes (n); fertilization. The cycle then repeats itself.

In most plants there is an addition to the cycle. The cells resulting from meiosis are not gametes—*i.e.* they do not fuse in fertilization. They are called spores, and the plant body that produced them is called a *sporophyte*, or spore-bearing plant. The spores, having the reduced number of chromosomes (n), go on to produce a number of cell descendants by equational nuclear division, making another plant body. This plant body then produces gametes, and so is called a *gametophyte*, or gamete-bearing plant. The gametes (n) then fuse in fertilization, the fertilized egg having the $2n$ number of

chromosomes. The egg grows into a sporophyte ($2n$). In mosses, the familiar "leafy" plants are the gametophyte generation (n), which produces eggs (n) and sperms (n). The fertilized egg ($2n$), at the tip of a gametophyte plant, produces the sporophyte ($2n$), consisting mainly of a stalk with a capsule on its end. Meiosis occurs in some of the cells in the capsule, and spores (n) are produced. The spores grow into gametophytes. The gametophytes of ferns are small, green plants about ½ in., or less, in width. The familiar fern plant is the sporophyte generation, producing its spores on the edges or backs of its leaves. In flowering plants and conifers, the gametophytes are microscopic. The female gametophyte grows inside the structure (the ovule) that produced one kind of spore and did not shed it. The male gametophyte is the pollen grain. These gametophytes may have no more than three to eight or ten cells. Some algae and fungi have a conspicuous sporophyte ($2n$) generation and an inconspicuous gametophyte (n) generation, whereas others have the opposite. A few have the fertilized egg as the only $2n$ cell. In any case, in almost all plants, the cycle is: fertilized egg ($2n$), sporophyte ($2n$), meiosis, spores (n), gametophyte (n), gametes (n), fertilization. The cycle then goes on, with alternating sporophyte and gametophyte generations. See ALTERNATION OF GENERATIONS.—*H. Cr.*

LIFE SPAN: Plants that mature in a single growing season, then produce seeds and die, are "annuals." Those, such as carrot and hollyhock, that mature and die in their second year are "biennials." Others, including all trees and most shrubs, require several years to reach maturity and show no obvious limit to attainable age. They are perennials, with an indefinite future; the tips of their branches are as young as any seedling. This is true of a redwood tree, some of whose woody trunk may be 3,000 yr old, or of a bristlecone pine that has been growing for more than 4,000 yr.

The life span of animals is less definite. Those that die soon after reproducing (as Pacific salmon, eels, and most insects do) may still mature quickly or slowly, depending upon living conditions. Animals that reproduce repeatedly age gradually and lose their fertility before natural death overtakes them. Under competitive conditions in the wild, few animals live out their

Pleistocene reconstructions (*below, left*) show *Smilodon*, the sabertooth cat in foreground, and *Equus*, extinct species of the horse, in background; (*center*) *Megatherium*, the ground sloth, and *Doedicurus* and *Glyptodon*, large edentates related to armadillos; (*right*) Mammoth, North American Ice Age elephant, 12 ft tall, with typical long, curved tusks and long, dense hair. (*Dioramas from Chicago Nat. Hist. Mus.*)

MAXIMUM WELL-AUTHENTICATED LIFE SPANS OF REPRESENTATIVE ANIMALS

(From Alex Comfort, "The Life Span of Animals," *Scientific American*, Aug. 1961, Vol. 205, No. 2, pp. 108–119.)

	Years		Years
Sea horse	less than 2	Ostrich	30–40
Shrew	2	Domestic pigeon	35
Mouse	3¼	Newt	35
White rat	4+	Toad	36
Guppy & mosquito fish	5	Zebra	38+
Guinea pig	7+	Chimpanzee	39+
Queen bee	7+	Goose, crane, pelican	40–50
Silverfish (insect)	7	Horse	40+
Large beetles	5–10	Queen termite	40–60
Earthworm	5–10	Domestic goose	47+
Smaller bats	10–15	Hippopotamus	49
Rabbit	12	Crocodile, alligator	50–60
Smaller frogs	12–20	Freshwater mussels	50–100
Sheep	15+	Eel in captivity	55
Starling	19	Sea anemone *Actinia*	60–70
Queen ant	19	Halibut	60–70
Garden spider	20	Cockatoo	70–85
Seal	20–25	Indian elephant	77+
Deer	20–25	Sturgeon	80–100
Dog	24+	Golden eagle, other large	
Many snakes and lizards	25–30	raptorial birds	to 100
Arctic tern	27	Large tortoises	100–150
Domestic cat	27+	Man	115+
Lion	30–35		

total possible life span. Protected in a zoo or under domestication, they may live longer. Few meadow mice (voles), for example, escape for more than a few months from birds and beasts of prey, whereas in captivity they may survive for 18 months. A whale is old at 24 yr, whereas horses have lived to be 40, tame pigeons 35, dogs 24, cows 17, and cockatoos over 80. See AGING; DEATH.—*L. and M. M.*

LIFE ZONES: areas that can be marked on a map of a continent, indicating in a broad way the distribution of many kinds of plants and animals. In North America, as many as 29 different life zones, or biotic provinces, have been recognized. In most of them, more than one BIOME is represented, depending upon local differences in climatic conditions, soil types, and the like. Life zones, in a definite sequence, are recognizable, too, on the slopes of any major mountain; usually they correspond closely to life zones on more level land between the mountain and the nearer pole of Earth.

In North America, tundra and polar grasslands, together with coastal marine environments, are biomes contributing to the Arctic Life Zone, which extends northward from a line across the continent from Alaska to Labrador. The boundary is "tree line" or "timberline," north of which the soil thaws too shallowly each summer to let trees gain a roothold. Over the Arctic Life Zone range musk ox, caribou, polar bear, varying hare, and ptarmigan; this region is the summer nesting ground of vast numbers of migratory waterfowl. An alpine

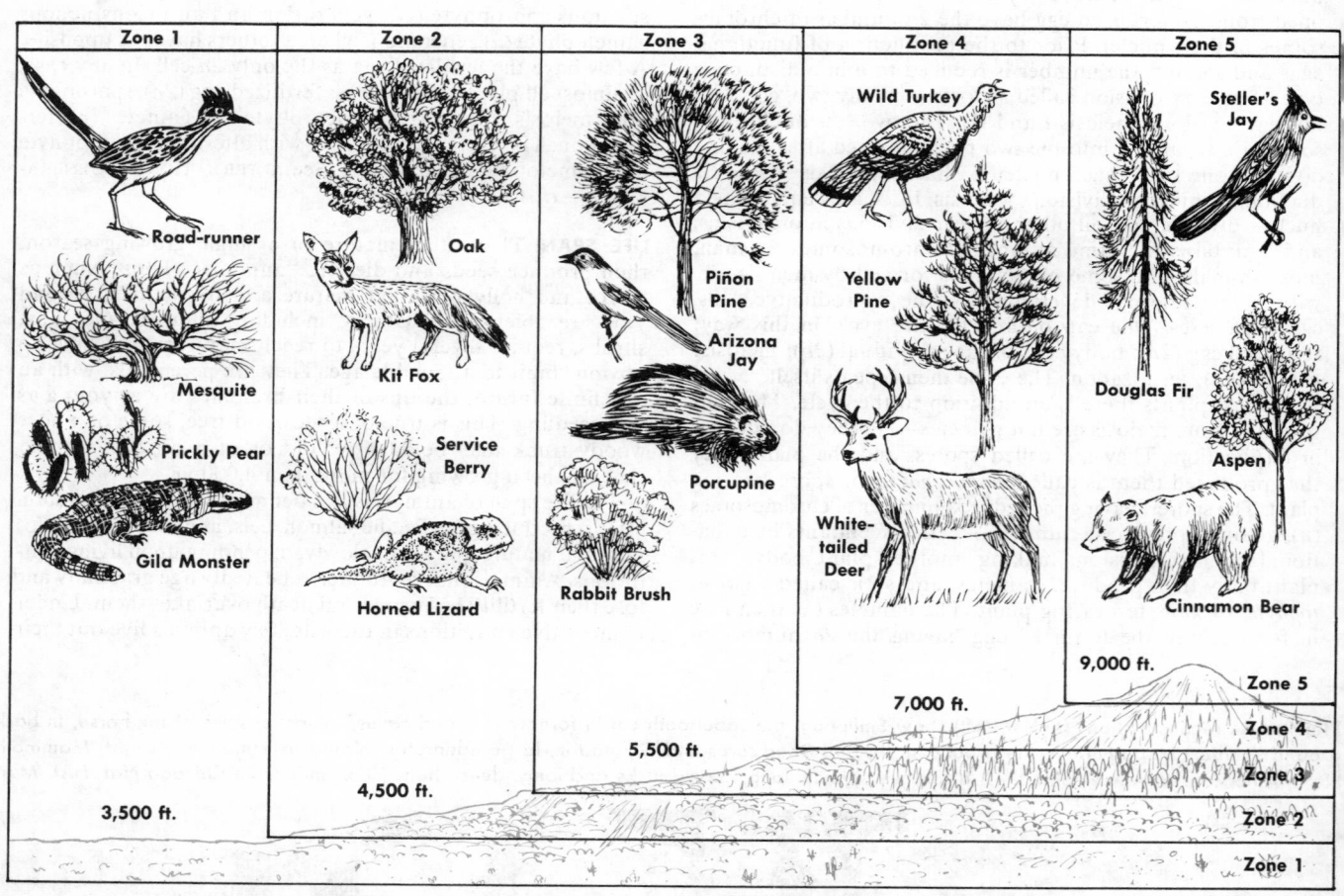

Life zones, in the level terrain of eastern North America, tend to be 500 to 1,000 mi across, but in the mountainous West a great many zones can be encountered in a much shorter space. Five separate life zones, for instance, can be found in a single 20- by 4-mi mountain area in the Chiricahua Range in southeastern Arizona—with a climate and biota varying from a Mexican Plateau environment to a top zone which in temperature, humidity, flora, and fauna matches Hudson Bay. (*After Natural History, May 1957*)

counterpart, similarly covered by lichens, "cushion plants," sedges, and short grasses, is the habitat of Rocky Mt goats and of mountain sheep.

South of tree line from the Arctic Zone, and downslope from the Alpine Zone, is a Boreal Life Zone, named for the north wind. In it, winter lasts for many months, but the soil thaws completely in summer. This zone is almost entirely occupied by a northern coniferous forest biome, rich in firs and spruces, and is the home of porcupine, moose, and elk. Shorter winters and warmer summers farther south, or lower on mountain slopes, permit the existence of different types of plants and animals—those of the Austral Zone, named for the south wind. The biomes of the Austral vary, according to the amount of moisture, from deciduous forests in which bear and deer are common to grasslands and deserts. The Austral extends to the true tropics, in which frost is never met. Somewhat comparable life zones can be distinguished in deep lakes and oceans, related to the amount of light available for photosynthesis. See AQUATIC ANIMALS; AQUATIC PLANTS; ECOLOGY; PELAGIC ANIMALS; PLANKTON; PLANT GEOGRAPHY; ZOOGEOGRAPHY.—*L. and M. M.*

LIGHT: the visible portion of the electromagnetic spectrum. Since man necessarily approaches nature through sensory experiences, it is not surprising that in the earliest theories concerning light the sensory (physiological) process of seeing was not clearly separated from the external phenomena of light. The Platonic school (4th cent. B. C.) explained VISION by assuming that the eye emits rays or *streams of vision* which, in the presence of sunlight, interact with something emitted by luminous bodies. In sharp contrast was another theory held by the atomists such as Democritus (5th cent. B. C.) and Lucretius (1st cent. B. C.). They believed that luminous bodies continually give off thin skins, or layers, of atoms, which maintain the shapes of the surfaces from which they are emitted, and that vision results when these extremely thin masks enter the eye. With various modifications these theories persisted into the Middle Ages. Euclid (330–260 B. C.), believing that the eye emits rays which travel in straight lines, applied his geometry to problems of perspective by drawing divergent straight lines from the eye toward the object. Thus began the idea of a ray of light, now recognized as a geometrical abstraction but still useful in optical design.

Whereas Euclid knew the law of REFLECTION from plane surfaces, Hero of Alexandria (about A. D. 100), in his *Catoptrics,* dealt with a wide variety of reflection problems involving curved as well as plane surfaces. He furnished a simple and beautiful proof that, for reflection from a plane surface, the light must travel along the shortest path between the eye and the object in order to make the angle of incidence equal to the angle of reflection. The geometrical proof is reproduced in Fig. 1. *EDO* is the path actually followed by a ray of light from the eye *E* (Platonic point of view) to the plane mirror *AB,* thence to *O,* the object seen by reflection. It is an observed fact that $\angle EDA = \angle ODB$. Now it can be shown that this is the shortest possible path by reflection from *E* to *O,* for if *EC* is drawn perpendicular to *AB,* and *OD* is prolonged until it meets *EC,* then *CD = DE,* so that the distance from *E* to *O* by reflection equals *CO.* Then any other path, say *EFO,* which equals *CFO,* is obviously longer than *CDO.* This demonstration was highly gratifying to the Greek mind, for it proved that reflection is in conformity with reason.

The most impressive work preserved from this period, however, is the *Optics* of Ptolemy of Alexandria (2nd cent.), which recorded experimental observations of the REFRACTION of light when passing from air to water, from air to glass, and from water to glass. Apparently Ptolemy also understood

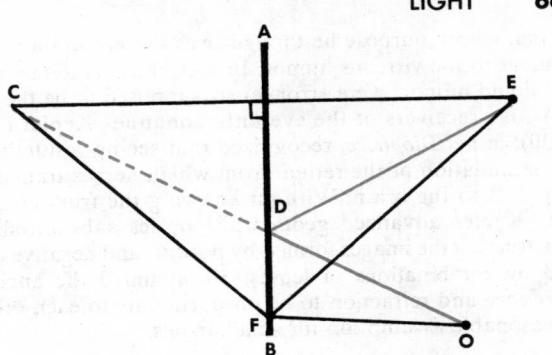

Fig. 1: Diagram gives geometrical proof that a ray of light takes shortest path from an object to a plane mirror to the eye when the angle of incidence equals the angle of reflection. *AB* denotes the plane mirror, *O* the object, *C* its virtual image, *E* the eye, *D* the point at which reflection actually takes place, and *F* another point, which requires a longer light path than *ODE.*

that refraction by Earth's atmosphere causes stars to be displaced from their true positions, especially when near the horizon. But his observations did not lead him to the correct refraction law, discovered by Willebrord Snell in 1621.

Medieval and Renaissance Contributions: The Romans contributed little to any branch of the natural sciences, but during the Arabic period, which followed, there was some progress in the study of optical phenomena. Both Alkindi (9th cent.) and Alhazen (10th cent.) wrote on OPTICS. Alhazen, in his *Treasury of Optics,* contributed substantially to knowledge of the structure of the eye and to an understanding of the functions of its various parts. He definitely rejected the Platonic notion of emission from the eye, he solved reflection problems with impressive mathematical skill, and he realized from careful measurements that the refraction law of Ptolemy was wrong, though he too was unable to formulate the correct law.

Although it was known even among the Greeks that objects appear to be magnified when seen through glass globes filled with water, the optical geometry involved did not begin to be clear until the time of Roger Bacon (the "admirable doctor" of the 13th cent.), Franciscan monk of Oxford and Paris. In his *Opus Majus*—Part V, he came very close to the invention of spectacles and even the TELESCOPE. It is not known who first made spectacles, but they were certainly in use in N Italy by the end of the 13th cent. Similarly, the inventor of the telescope is unknown; several persons may have used one before Hans Lippershey, the Dutch spectacle maker, in 1608 accidentally placed a negative and a positive lens in front of his eye, and before Galileo in 1609 constructed his series of famous telescopes. There is evidence from the notebooks of Leonardo da Vinci (1452–1519) that he had constructed a combination of a negative and a positive lens to observe the Moon. Unfortunately, Leonardo kept his notes secret during his lifetime, and they were edited much too late to have any influence on Galileo. As a consequence, astronomers such as Johannes Müller (Regiomontanus, 1436–76) and Tycho Brahe (1546–1601) had to design and use all their observational equipment without optical aids of any kind. To determine the positions of heavenly bodies it was necessary to sight through slits in metal plates with the naked eye.

In 1543 the great anatomist Andreas Vesalius (1514–64) had published his *Fabric of the Human Body* and clarified many obscure details, including those of the human eye. When Franciscus Maurolycus (1494–1575) wrote his *Light on the Subject of Light* in 1554, he discussed Vesalius' cross section from the optical point of view, and he corrected many old mistakes, but he failed to understand the function of the retina, whose purpose he thought was merely to furnish nutriment to the vitreous humor. In fact, the crystalline lens or the liquid humors were erroneously supposed to be the light-sensitive receivers of the eye until Johannes Kepler (1571–1630), in his *Dioptrice*, recognized that seeing resulted from the stimulation of the retina, from which nerves transmitted impulses to the brain. Without knowing the true refraction law, Kepler advanced geometrical optics substantially by constructing the images formed by positive and negative lenses and by combinations of lenses. He assumed the angles of incidence and refraction to be proportionate to each other—a reasonable assumption for small angles.

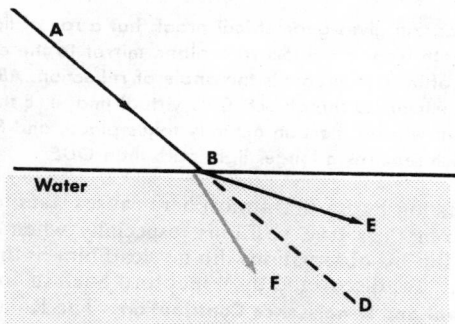

Fig. 2: When beam of light passes from air into water, it does not take straight path ABD but, rather, path ABF. Descartes argued that if light consisted of particles, it would follow path ABE; and, since this path is not followed, light does not consist of particles.

In 1637 René Descartes (1596–1650) published *Les Méteores*, in which there is an admirable explanation of the RAINBOW. Using a glass globe filled with water as a model for a raindrop, and using Snell's correct REFRACTION law, he succeeded in showing how both primary and secondary rainbows are formed, even calculating the true angles of elevation at which they are observed in the sky. He then tried to explain, in *La Dioptrique,* why Snell's law should be true (Fig. 2). A ball driven into water in the direction *AB,* he thought, would be diverted from its straight path *ABD* into the direction *BE,* because the ball moved with more difficulty in water than in air. Light, on the contrary, was known to bend in the direction *BF.* Light, therefore, was not like a particle but was assumed to be a motion or *an action* that passed more easily (and therefore more rapidly) through water and glass than through air. Descartes' explanation, though weak in logic as well as in fact, nevertheless set the stage for more important contributions, such as the CORPUSCULAR THEORY of Isaac Newton (1642–1727).

Corpuscular Theory: But before Newton's speculations can be properly judged, it is necessary to know the experiments and theories that influenced him. For example, Francisco Grimaldi (1618–63) had observed the shadow cast by an opaque body placed in the path of a cone of light formed by a hole admitting sunlight into a darkened room. He found the shadow to be larger than that predicted from drawing straight lines from the edges of the illuminated hole past those of the opaque object. Moreover, there were colored bands of light parallel to the edge of the shadow—a phenomenon called DIFFRACTION. Similarly, when a circular hole was illuminated from a small source, the cone of light transmitted by the hole was larger than it should have been by simple geometry. Grimaldi published no definite theory, but he hinted that light seemed to behave like waves in a liquid which could spread out into the shadow of objects in their path.

A much stronger argument for the wave nature of light came from Christian Huygens (1629–95). To him light seemed to be propagated through matter by elastic shock waves transmitted from particle to particle so that each point on a wave could be considered as a source of new waves. The resultant wave that progressed through the medium was the geometrical sum of all the spherical microwaves generated by the particles that had been disturbed. In this way he furnished a brilliant explanation of reflection and refraction (see WAVE MOTION), and even of double refraction, which Erasmus Bartholinus had described in Iceland spar in 1669. Furthermore, for the first time, refraction was explained on the assumption that light travels more slowly in water and glass than in air, a fact later verified by Jean Leon Foucault (1819–68) and fully described in 1862. Though the idea of waves was clear in Huygens' mind, he failed to see the important part played by the wavelength, and he did not understand the nature of COLOR. Huygens published *Traité de la Lumière* in 1690, and yet when Newton published the *Opticks* in 1704 he supported a particle, or corpuscular, theory. But there is some indication that, earlier, Newton had considered a combination particle-wave theory. The pages of the Philosophical Transactions of the Royal Society, which recorded the frequent disagreements between Robert Hooke (1635–1703) and Newton, contained in 1672 a reply by Newton to one of Hooke's criticisms in which Newton wrote: ". . . assuming the rays of light to be small bodies, . . . those, when they impinge on any refracting or reflecting superficies, must as necessarily excite vibrations in the aether, as stones do in water when thrown into it."

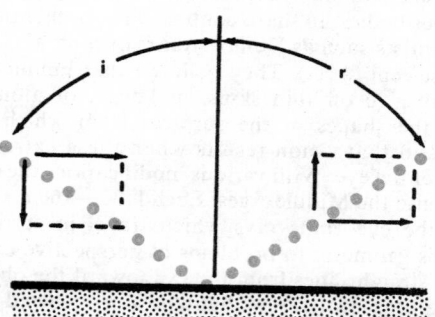

Fig. 3: Reflection of light was explained by Newton in terms of the impact of perfectly elastic particles on a hard surface. This model satisfies the laws of reflection.

It is by no means certain that Newton ever gave up this dualistic point of view completely, although throughout his later work he stressed the corpuscular aspect of light. Reflection was explained by assuming perfect elasticity for the material corpuscles, so that on impact with a hard, polished surface (Fig. 3) the component of the velocity parallel to the surface would remain unchanged while the perpendicular component reversed itself. Such an elastic mechanical rebound would be consistent with the known fact that the angle of incidence *i* is equal to the angle of reflection *r.* Refraction could be explained only by assuming that as the corpuscles approach the surface of a denser medium the velocity component perpendicular to the surface is increased owing to gravitational attraction between the corpuscles and the surface particles (Fig. 4). If the velocity component parallel to the surface remains constant, the direction of the corpuscles in the denser medium should turn toward the perpendicular, according to Snell's law. From this reasoning Newton also concluded that refraction should be greater for denser media.

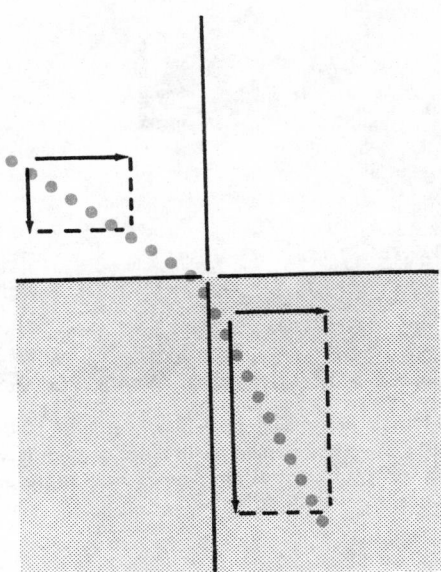

Fig. 4: Newton's explanation of refraction in terms of a stream of particles required an increase in the vertical velocity component together with a resulting increase in the speed of light as the beam passed into the denser medium.

Newton's conclusion that the velocity of light in water is greater than that in air was wrong, of course, but no one at that time had designed any experiment to test this point.

Wave Theory: The diffraction of light, observed by Grimaldi, and the interference effect, observed by Newton himself (Newton's rings), were never satisfactorily explained by Newton. Nevertheless, there was no attempt to challenge his corpuscular theory until 1802, when the brilliant British physician and scholar Thomas Young (1773–1829) published his famous demonstration of INTERFERENCE of light from two slits. When light from a narrow slit was allowed to fall on two narrow slits very close together a series of light and dark bands were formed on a screen, the brightest central band occurring where there should be deepest shadow, according to the corpuscular theory. But even before this crucial experiment, Young had noted some additional defects in the corpuscular theory that had not been stressed by others. Why should the corpuscles be emitted with the same velocity from a relatively cool surface as from the intensely hot surface of the Sun? If all corpuscles were the same, why should some be reflected and some transmitted when they struck the surface of a transparent material? The facts all seemed to point to a wave nature of light, and Young proceeded to use Huygens' theory with extraordinary skill, explaining the colors of thin films described by Hooke in his *Micrographia,* calculating the wavelengths for various colors of light observed in Newton's rings, and even observing the change in phase of the reflected wave from a glass surface. Young's superb exposition of the nature of light, instead of receiving the general recognition it deserved, was bitterly attacked. This strange reception, so rare in the natural sciences, was not entirely due to Newtonian hero-worship. A few years before, Young had been unnecessarily harsh in criticizing some publications, especially one by Henry Brougham, later Lord Chancellor. Brougham saw his chance for revenge, and the vindictive article that he published in the newly established *Edinburgh Review* delayed acceptance of the wave theory until 1817, when Augustin Fresnel (1788–1823) came to its rescue.

In 1809 Étienne Louis Malus (1775–1812) had discovered that light could be polarized by reflection. This posed an em-barrassing problem for the wave theory as well as for the corpuscular theory, because the waves postulated by Huygens and Young were considered to be *compressional,* or *longitudinal,* like sound waves in air. Fresnel realized that if light waves were not compressional but *transverse,* polarization phenomena could be fitted nicely into the wave theory. POLARIZED LIGHT could then be considered to consist of transverse vibrations restricted to one plane. With this added support the wave theory found general acceptance.

In 1865 James Clerk Maxwell (1831–79) added greatly to the prestige of the wave theory by proving mathematically that it is possible to have transverse waves in which the energy is shared equally between fluctuating electric and magnetic fields. When electric and magnetic constants were inserted into the MAXWELL EQUATIONS, the calculated velocity for the electromagnetic waves turned out to be the same as the velocity of light. Assuming light to be such a wave, one could calculate the index of refraction (an optical constant) of a transparent material from its dielectric constant (an electrical property). This extraordinary success was crowned in 1887 when Heinrich Hertz (1857–94) generated the predicted Maxwellian waves by means of an oscillating electrical discharge. From that time to the beginning of the present century the wave theory remained unchallenged.

A Dual Concept: The shadow that then fell on the wave theory stemmed from an attempt to explain the distribution of energy in the spectrum of the radiation from hot bodies (see BLACK-BODY RADIATION). Some progress in this direction had been achieved by W. Wien, J. W. S. Rayleigh, and J. Jeans; the Wien law fitted the short wavelength side and the Rayleigh-Jeans law the long wavelength side of the spectrum. But in 1900 there was no single derived law that described the entire spectrum of radiation from hot bodies at various temperatures. This problem attracted Max Planck (1858–1947), and he succeeded in solving it in 1901 by introducing the radical assumption that the light is emitted from the hot body not in continuous waves but in *quanta,* or packets of energy, such that the energy in each QUANTUM is equal to the product of a universal constant (PLANCK'S LAW) times the frequency of the light. It must not be supposed that this was a return to the old Newtonian corpuscles; the quanta were not considered to be *material* particles as Newton had supposed.

Though Planck's explanation was meant to fit only the *emission* of light, Einstein (1879–1955) made it clear in 1905 that the known photoelectric phenomena can be easily understood if it is assumed that light is also *absorbed* in quanta. There seemed to be a particle-to-particle interaction between quanta of incident light and the electrons in the photosensitive surface. (See PHOTOELECTRIC EFFECT.) The particle aspect of the quantum was even more sharply brought out by Arthur Compton (1892–1962) in experiments on the scattering of x-rays. The results of these observations (the COMPTON EFFECT) were interpreted by Compton in 1923 as proof of elastic COLLISIONS between x-ray photons and electrons in the scattering material, so that both momentum and energy are conserved. It was only necessary to assume that the momentum of a quantum is equal to its energy divided by the velocity of light.

What, then, is the real nature of light? There is no denying the *wave aspect* of light in any experiments involving interference, diffraction, or polarization. Neither can one ignore the *particle aspect* exhibited in the emission and absorption of light or in the Compton scattering. Light thus exhibits a dual nature, combining the features of both particles and waves—features that would appear contradictory in any mechanical model.—*H. Sw.*

LIGHT, VELOCITY OF: The speed c of light in empty space is approximately 299,800 km/sec, or 186,300 mi/sec. That light takes time to traverse space was demonstrated by Olaus Römer, 1675. Noting that eclipses by Jupiter of one of its moons seemed delayed when Earth was moving away from Jupiter and seemed hastened otherwise, he said the difference was due to the changing distances the light traveled from Jupiter to Earth, and concluded that light takes 22 min to traverse the diameter of Earth's orbit (an estimate 5 min too large). Römer's work found confirmation in 1728 when James Bradley calculated c from the ABERRATION OF LIGHT.

The first successful nonastronomical measurement of c was by H. L. Fizeau, 1849. Shining a light at a distant mirror, he interrupted both the beam and his view of the mirror by rotating a toothed wheel in front of the light. At certain rotation speeds, light escaping through a gap between teeth returned when a tooth had moved to a position blocking it. From the rotation speeds when this occurred he found how long light took to go to the mirror and back. In 1850 L. Foucault, using a rotating mirror, obtained better results over smaller distances. A. A. Michelson between 1880 and 1932 made accurate measurements on a heroic scale, but modern precision methods are compact.

Foucault showed that light goes more slowly in water than in air, a result long regarded as proving light is wavelike and not corpuscular. In 1887 the MICHELSON-MORLEY EXPERIMENT implied that the measured speed of light does not change when one moves: a paradoxical result that led to the theory of relativity. In that theory c is unique among speeds, being a physical quantity of fundamental importance: it is the maximum speed of transfer of energy, and enters such basic equations as $E = mc^2$. The speed of light is very slightly affected by gravitation.—*Ba. H.*

LIGHTING: The most ancient source of artificial light for man was the campfire. The torch, at first no more than a portable campfire, was the common source of light during prehistoric times up to the classical age and even into the Middle Ages. To make torch-sticks burn longer, they were often soaked in resin or tar. The lamp, a container with oil or fat and a wick, dates back to at least 3000 B.C. The container had many shapes and was made from hollowed-out stones, pottery, seashells, or metal. Animal fat was used at first; the Babylonians are believed to have used petroleum; the Romans in turn used olive oil or castor oil for their lamps. The candle, a wick immersed in wax or fat, is another development of Roman times. Tallow, *i.e.* fat from cows or sheep, was used for candles during the Middle Ages and up to the 19th cent.; beeswax, more expensive, was used only for ceremonial purposes. Candles made from spermaceti, a waxlike substance taken from the oil in the head of a sperm whale, were introduced at the end of the 18th cent. In colonial America, candles made from the wax of bayberry fruit were used.

Gas lighting was introduced at the end of the 18th cent. The gas was first obtained from destructive distillation of wood, and later, from coal. Gas lighting lent itself to central supply stations copied after the city water-supply systems; in turn, the gas-distribution system became the model for the electric systems. Gas put light on a mass-distribution basis. With it came not only new hours of leisure but also longer working hours, which transformed the habits of millions. The only competitor of gas was the mineral fuel kerosene, used in lamps; the discovery of oil in Pennsylvania (1859) considerably reduced its cost. One of the most notable devices developed for gas lighting was the so-called Welsbach mantle, consisting of a knitted-tube or stocking-like device impregnated with thorium and cerium compounds; this is attached

Ancient oil lamps: In the oil lamp, which is at least 10,000 yr. old, the wick raises the oil by capillary attraction so that it will receive oxygen necessary for combustion. Lamps here represent various ancient designs, from crude to refined.

Early American oil lamps: The Argand Lamp (large lamp, *center*), developed in 1783 and introducing the glass chimney, gave a better, steadier, less smoky light than the early crusie (*left center*), Betty lamps (*upper left and upper right*), and whale-oil lamps (*third from left*).

Gas light: Glass dome (*center*) contains material used for the original incandescent mantle, developed in 1893 by Welsbach. Other lamps here show upright mantles and inverted types, found to be superior. (*J. J. Barton/The Franklin Institute*)

inside the gas lamp at a point above the lamp's gas burner. A Welsbach mantle is actually a fluorescent screen, since it absorbs energy in one wavelength (from the burner) and emits energy in another wavelength. The quality of the light from Welsbach lamps (*i.e.* their light's similarity to daylight) surpasses most electrical illumination; but other factors— lower cost, durability, convenience—favor electric lights. Even though gas and oil lighting survived into the 20th cent., they steadily declined in importance after the introduction of electric lighting in the 1870s.

The arc light is a brilliant light produced by the discharge of an electric current between two conducting electrodes, usually carbon. The arc heats one electrode (the cathode) to incandescence. First used for outdoor lighting, the arc light could not be used in the home until its almost blinding light was "divided." Thomas A. Edison and Joseph Swan accomplished this when they produced the incandescent electric light in 1879: it consisted of a high-resistance filament of carburized thread in an evacuated glass bulb. When electricity was passed through the filament, this was heated to incandescence. But a most troublesome problem of the incandescent light was the short life of the filament and the loss of power through heat. In 1902, the tungsten filament was introduced, and the result was a brighter and longer-lasting bulb. Bulb life and efficiency were further improved with the invention, about 1918, of bulbs filled with inert gases. Another major step in illumination was made in the 1930s when fluorescent lighting was introduced. Three times as efficient as incandescent light, the fluorescent type is produced by a coated glass tube within which an electric current passes through mercury vapor to produce ultraviolet light. The ultraviolet radiation produces useful light by exciting the fluorescent coating on the inside of the tube. See ELECTRIC LAMP; FLUORESCENCE.—*H. I. S.*

LIGHTNING: a sudden high-voltage discharge of electricity in the form of a luminous, multi-branched spark, up to several miles long, in or between clouds or from a cloud to the ground. The current flowing in the flash (or "stroke") is of the order of tens of thousands of amperes. "Sheet" or "heat" lightning is simply the reflection of the flashes of a distant storm by clouds. For further discussion of lightning see ATMOSPHERIC ELECTRICITY; BALL LIGHTNING; THUNDERSTORMS.— *O. G. S.*

LIGHTNING ROD: a metallic, mast-like conductor of electricity, firmly planted in the ground, higher than and insulated from the structure it serves to protect from damage by lightning. The lightning rod provides a low-resistance path for the harmless conductance and consequent dissipation in the ground of electrical discharges caused by heavy accumulations of negative electrical charge in the lower part of a thundercloud; this accumulation of charge is generally understood to be drawn there by falling water droplets within the cloud. The negative charge induces an equally intense positive charge on the ground (see ELECTROSTATICS); and an electrical discharge, or lightning stroke, will tend to leap between negative cloud and positive ground, terminating at any point projecting from the earth's surface: thus the higher a structure, the greater the probability of its being the terminal point

Cloud-to-ground lightning at the height of a Kansas thunderstorm. When electric field between base of thundercloud and earth becomes sufficiently intense, discharges of electricity between cloud and earth occur, with spectacular results. (*U. S. Dept. of Commerce, Weather Bureau*)

for a lightning stroke. Also, any *sharp* point will be the location of a high induced potential gradient (*i.e.* an area where an electric field is built up), since the density of accumulated electrical charge is greater on surfaces of small radius. Therefore a lightning rod, by virtue of its height and sharp point, will be the terminal point for an electrical discharge from any thundercloud above it; its low resistance, because of its conductivity, allows it to be the path for the high currents caused by the lightning stroke. The protection provided by a lightning rod roughly extends to the volume of a cone whose altitude is the mast and whose diameter is equal to the height of the mast. Lightning rods are used to protect homes, especially those standing alone on flat plains, but are most extensively used to protect electric power-transmission installations.—*A. S.*

LIGHT-YEAR: see ASTRONOMICAL DISTANCE UNITS.

LIGNIN: the durable natural plastic composing about 25% of wood, in which it binds and stiffens the cellulose fibers. A group of closely related stable polymers of two or more aromatic monomers not yet precisely known, it varies in composition between tree species. Lignin is a major waste product and disposal problem of the pulpwood industry, although many uses have been or are being developed for it (see WOOD).—*T. M.*

LIGNITE: a variety of soft COAL, generally brown-black in color, in which the original wood structure is largely retained and prominently visible. It contains a considerable proportion of volatile matter, and is used mostly for fuel.—*Ru. M.*

LIMESTONE: in the broadest sense, a SEDIMENTARY ROCK composed chiefly of carbonate. In geology, the term *limestone* is used for those carbonate rocks in which calcite (calcium carbonate) is the dominant component, and the term dolomite or *dolostone* for those in which the mineral dolomite (calcium magnesium carbonate) predominates. There are gradations between limestone, shale, and sandstone. A rock containing roughly equal proportions of lime and clay is called *marl,* while limestone containing quartz sand is called sandy limestone.

Highly jointed Niagara limestone in Chippewa Co., Mich., presents an aspect typical of many limestone formations. Rock is light gray, almost white, running into blue-gray tones where it is darker in photograph. (*U. S. Geological Survey*)

Limestones are classified according to their physical characteristics and supposed mode of origin. Two major types of limestone are recognized: *autochthonous* limestones, believed to have formed essentially in place from lime which had been in solution; and *allochthonous* limestones, thought to have been brought in as discrete clastic grains to the site of deposition. Autochthonous limestones may be formed by inorganic precipitation or through organic agents. Calcium carbonate may be precipitated from sea water as needle-like crystals of aragonite or as spherical crystal aggregates called *oolites.* Aragonite is unstable and soon changes to calcite. Bacteria may be responsible for the precipitation of a fine lime mud called drewite. Blue-green algae found in shallow waters cause the formation of irregular laminated crusts which may harden to become *algal limestone.* The calcareous skeletal remains of planktonic microorganisms may settle to the bottom of the sea to form calcareous oozes; CHALK, an earthy variety of limestone, consists chiefly of the remains of such microorganisms. Corals and other framework-building organisms may construct reefs (see CORAL and CORAL REEFS). Fossil reefs are characterized by massive bedding and are usually riddled with cavities; because of their cavernous nature, they

are sometimes important oil reservoirs. Fossil shells may accumulate as moundlike deposits called *bioherms,* or as widespread sheets known as *biostromes.* Allochthonous limestones usually show rounding of the individual grains, broken fossils, sorting of the grains by size; they may even be cross-bedded. Shells formed at one place may be broken down to sand or even clay size, transported, and redeposited. The resulting sediment is called a *calcilutite* if the particles are of clay size, or *calcarenite* if they are of sand size. Deposits of larger fragments or of whole shells are called *coquinas.* Fine-grained limestones tend to recrystallize to a more coarsely granular texture, making the interpretation of the origin of many ancient limestones difficult. Limestone is of great economic importance as a raw material for the cement industry and is widely used as a construction stone, fluxing agent, soil conditioner, and source of lime.—*W. Ha.*

LIMIT: the number that the terms of an infinite sequence of numbers approach, ever more closely. For example, the limit of the sequence $\frac{1}{2}$, $\frac{2}{3}$, $\frac{3}{4}$, $\ldots$, $(n-1)/n$, $\ldots$, is 1; the difference between 1 and $(n-1)/n$ is $1 - (n-1)/n = 1 - 1 + 1/n = 1/n$, which we can make less than any assigned positive number by taking n large enough. In general, a sequence a_1, a_2, a_3, $\ldots$, a_n, $\ldots$ has the limit A if, for any positive quantity ε (epsilon), there exists a term a_m such that, if $n > m$, then $|A - a_n| < \varepsilon$. (The expression $|A - a_n|$ means the numerical amount of the difference.) A sequence that approaches a limit is said to be convergent; one that does not is divergent.

The concept of a limit is extended to a function, $f(x)$. Since x is an independent variable, values can be given to it as close as we wish to a fixed number x_0, provided that $f(x)$ is defined on an interval including x_0. The corresponding values of $f(x)$ may, or may not, tend to a limit. To say that $f(x)$ tends to the limit A as x tends to x_0 means that, for any positive quantity ε, there is a positive quantity δ (delta) such that if $0 < |x - x_0| < \delta$, then $|A - f(x)| < \varepsilon$. In this definition the condition $0 < |x - x_0|$ is stipulated because in many applications of the limit concept the value of $f(x_0)$ is irrelevant and perhaps non-existent. A function for which it is possible to remove this condition is said to be continuous at $x = x_0$. For such a function, $f(x)$ approaches a limit as x approaches x_0, and this limit is equal to $f(x_0)$.

Differential and integral calculus depends basically upon the concept of a limit. Derivatives and integrals are limits. Moreover, the sum of an infinite series is defined as a limit. —*H. C.*

LINDBLAD, BERTIL, 1895–1965, Swedish astronomer; b. Örebro. He is known for his research in stellar and galactic dynamics. In 1926 he proposed the theory that the Milky Way system of stars is composed of a number of rotating subsystems, each of which contains all the stars of a certain class. He became director of the Stockholm Observatory in 1927 and was an associate of the U. S. National Academy of Sciences.—*D. H. D. R.*

LINDERSTRØM-LANG, KAJ ULRIK, 1896–1959, Danish biochemist; b. Frederiksberg. A staff member (from 1919) and director (1938–59) of the Carlsberg Chemical Laboratory, he has led in the development of systematic ultramicrochemistry (working with less than one millionth of a gram) and its uses to analyze traces of enzymes. He also invented a number of research instruments, including an ultramicromanometer using the Cartesian diver principle. He was a fellow of the Royal Society and an associate of the U. S. National Academy of Sciences.—*D. H. D. R.*

LINEAR PROGRAMMING: the branch of mathematics that deals with the problem of finding the greatest or least value for a linear function whose variables are subject to certain restrictions in the form of equations or inequalities. A simple problem in linear programming is the following: A manufacturer has warehouses W_1, W_2, and W_3, which contain 100, 200, and 100 tons of his product. He receives orders of 125 tons from market M_1, and 225 tons from market M_2; the freight rates from warehouses W_1, W_2, and W_3 to market M_1 are 1, 2, and 3 dollars per ton, and from W_1, W_2, and W_3 to M_2 are 6, 5, and 4 dollars per ton. How many tons should the manufacturer ship from each warehouse? The solution of this problem requires finding the amounts x, y, z shipped to the first market from the three warehouses and the amounts u, v, w shipped to the second market, which give the minimum freight cost C. The required amounts satisfy five equations and inequalities in x, y, z, u, v, w. The methods of linear programming were developed in the 1940's and were of value in solving a number of problems that arose in the conduct of World War II. Types of problems that have been solved by linear programming are: (1) finding the shipping program for a product that will give the lowest shipping costs; (2) deciding more general questions involving where to ship, produce, and sell a product; (3) finding the most economical use of raw materials, *e.g.* in the blending of gasoline; (4) discovering the most efficient use of machines to produce a given product when machine capacity is limited; (5) deciding how to achieve a required production at the lowest possible cost; (6) finding the most effective scheduling of ships and routing of aircraft. —*H. E. W.*

LINE SQUALL: a line of thunderstorms with very gusty winds; an instability line. In British usage, the term *line squall* denotes either an instability line or a sharp cold front with heavy thunderstorm activity. The usual area of formation of an instability line is in the warm air well ahead of a fast-moving cold front. The line is produced when winds above a

cold front, moving ahead of the front, prevent the lifting of a warm air mass at the front itself; instead, the warm air is forced up with almost explosive violence at distances 50 to 300 mi ahead of the front. An instability line is usually oriented parallel to the front it precedes and moves at about the same speed. An approaching instability line has the threatening appearance of an approaching thunderstorm: high cumulonimbus clouds, black underneath, and anvil-topped billows above. As the line passes, sudden heavy gusts of wind and bursts of heavy rain interlaced with lightning are experienced. Extremely severe lines may even contain tornadoes. These lines are extremely dangerous to sailing ships and small boats because of the sudden shift from light southerly winds to strong winds from the west or northwest. A line will usually pass eastward over a point in less than an hour. Instability lines tend to be most active in the late afternoon and at night. The line squall is known alternatively as *squall line, instability line* (most acceptable), *pre-frontal squall line,* and *pseudo front.* See Color Plate 29.—*P. L.*

LINKAGE: an arrangement of rigid links or rods connected at movable joints so that one point will move in a required curve or, particularly, a straight line. Any object can be used to draw a circle: if the object is pivoted about any point, any other point will describe a circle (see Fig. 1). The usual way of drawing a straight line, however, is to copy the straight edge of a ruler, and the straightness of the line depends entirely upon that of the ruler. With a linkage, one can draw a straight line without first having another to use as a guide.

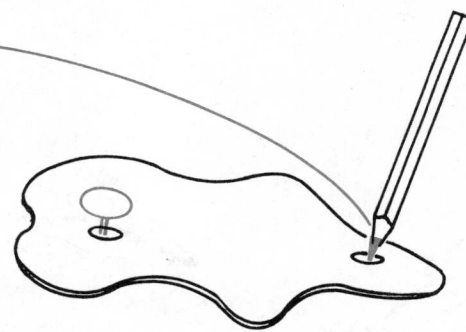

Fig. 1: A given point on an object pivoted about a fixed point describes a circle.

The first linkage was invented in 1782 by James Watt, who needed a mechanical arrangement that would convert the rotary movement of an engine's flywheel into the straight-line movement of a piston. He obtained only an approximation to a straight line, albeit sufficiently close for his purposes. The first exact straight-line linkage was discovered in 1864 by A. Peaucellier, a French officer. Fig. 2 is a diagram of this Peaucellier cell. For convenience, the edges of the individual links have been drawn straight. They can, of course, be of any shape; indeed, a device for drawing a straight line would be of limited value if straight lines were required for its construction! The cell contains seven links; four of them—*QR, RS, ST,* and *TQ*—of one length, two—*PR* and *PT*—of another, longer length, and one—*OQ*—of any length. The points *O* and *P* are joined to a fixed base, *e.g.* a drawing board, and so placed that $OP = OQ$. All the links can pivot freely about the indicated joints. As the linkage is pivoted, the point *Q* moves in a circle (center *O*) that passes through *P.* At the same time, *S* traces out a straight line. For each posi-

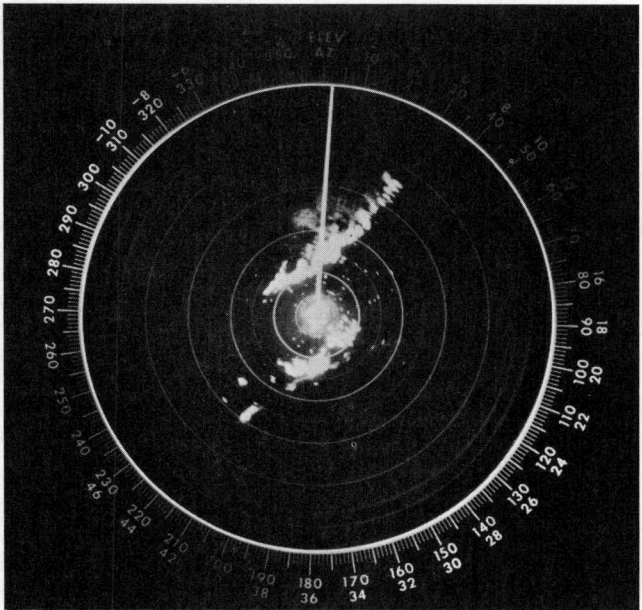

Lines of thunderstorms observed by radar at Washington National Airport, June 17, 1960. Range is approximately 250 nautical mi. (*U. S. Dept. of Commerce, Weather Bureau*)

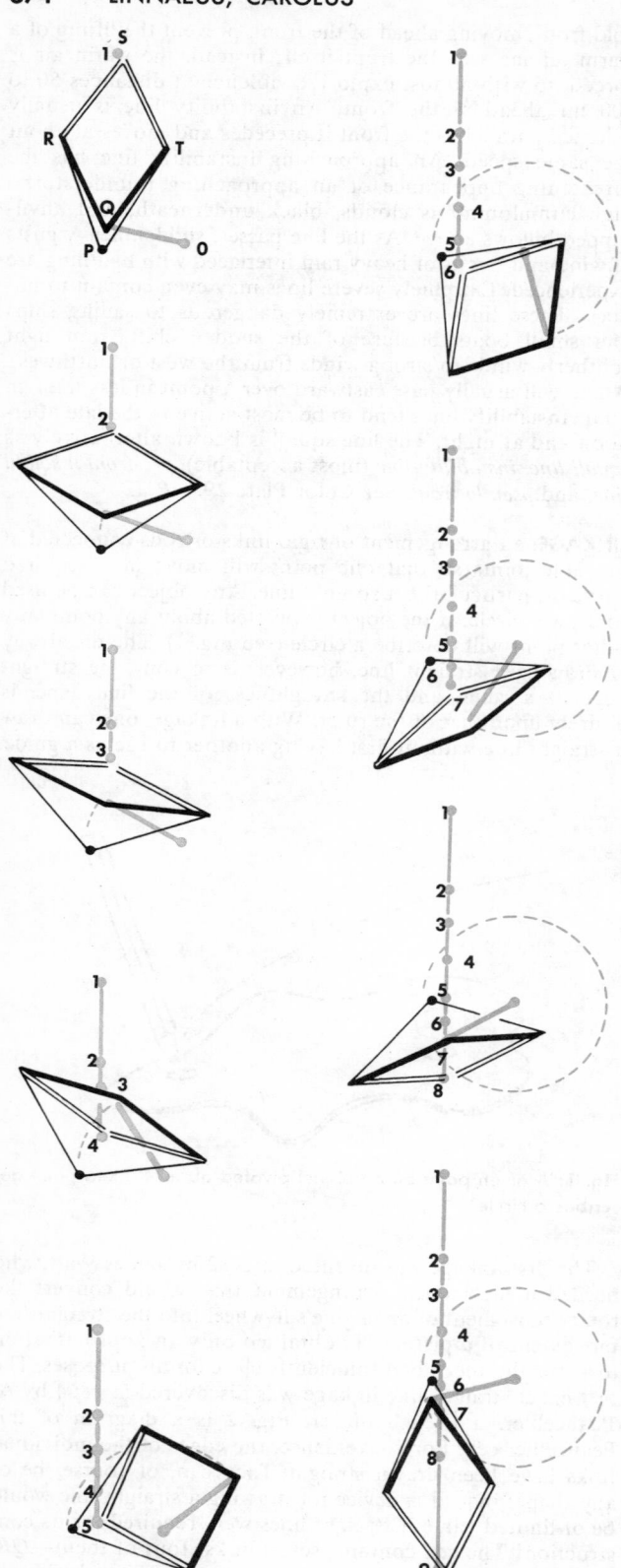

Fig. 2—Peaucellier cell: As point Q moves in a circle, point S moves in a straight line. Stages in the motions of Q and S are shown in order proceeding from top to bottom in the first column of drawings and then from top to bottom in the second column. Numbered dots on the path of S indicate positions of S shown in the preceding stages.

tion of the cell, *Q* marks a point on a circle while *S* marks a point on a corresponding line. This correspondence is called an inversion and is important in INVERSIVE GEOMETRY.

Linkages can be constructed to draw any simple curve; *e.g.* an adaptation of the Peaucellier cell describes a cissoid (see CURVES). The pantograph is a well-known linkage used by draftsmen for drawing enlarged or reduced copies of a diagram. Other types are used for finding approximate solutions to algebraic equations.—*B. P. S.*

LINNAEUS, CAROLUS (LINNÉ, CARL VON), 1707–78, Swedish physician and naturalist; b. Råshult. He was the first to apply consistently the principle of binomial nomenclature (a generic and a specific name) throughout the plant and animal kingdoms, thereby beginning modern taxonomy in both. Present botanical nomenclature goes back to the first edition of his *Species plantarum* (1753), and zoological nomen-

Carolus Linnaeus
(N. Y. Public Library)

clature begins with the 10th edition of his *Systema naturae* (1758). Linnaeus made extensive collections of plants and of insects, and assembled a great library on plants, animals, and minerals. His library and plant collection (herbarium) still exist in England. Many biologists today belong to Linnaean societies, such as those in London and New York City. The twinflower of North America and N Europe (*Linnaea borealis*) is named after Linnaeus. He was a fellow of the Royal Society.—*L. and M. M.*

LIOUVILLE, JOSEPH, 1809–82, French mathematician; b. Saint-Omer. He was elected to the Academy of Sciences at 30 and was later appointed professor at the Sorbonne and the Collège de France. He founded the *Journal des mathématiques pures et appliques* in 1836 and was its editor for 40 yr. In this capacity he did much to improve and maintain standards in the 19th cent. He was a prolific and highly original mathematician and is especially known for his work on differential equations and boundary-value problems—important in 20th-cent. mathematical physics. He was a fellow of the Royal Society.—*H. C.*

LIPMANN, FRITZ ALBERT, 1899–   , German-U. S. biochemist; b. Königsberg. A leading authority on enzymes, he discovered coenzyme A and its significance in the intermediate metabolism. For this work he shared the 1953 Nobel prize with H. A. Krebs. Lipmann also formulated the concept of the high-energy phosphate bond, *e.g.* in ATP, as the energy "coin" of the biological realm. He is a fellow of the Royal Society and a member of the National Academy of Sciences.— *D. H. D. R.*

LIPOIC ACID (6,8 dithio-n-octanoic acid): a vitamin which is a coenzyme for oxidative decarboxylation of alpha-keto acids. Oxidized lipoic acid is thought to be one of the early hydrogen acceptors in photosynthesis. Lipoic acid can exist in a cyclic disulfide (oxidized) form which is readily reduced to the di-sulfhydryl form. The enzymatic decarboxylation of an alpha-keto acid by the enzyme (probably with the aid of another vitamin, thiamine pyrophosphate) gives an aldehyde. The aldehyde is oxidized by the oxidized form of lipoic acid, to give an acyl thioester, a condensation product of reduced lipoic acid and the newly formed acyl group of the oxidized aldehyde. The acyl group is then transferred to coenzyme A, and the reduced lipoic acid is enzymatically re-oxidized by DPN, ready to partake once again in the reaction. It is thought that the vitamin reacts while conjugated to the decarboxylation enzyme.—*E. S. and P. S.*

LIPPMANN, GABRIEL, 1845–1921, French physicist; b. Hollerich, Luxembourg. He engaged in important research in electrocapillarity and invented a number of scientific instruments, including the capillary electrometer, for measuring very small electromotive forces; the *coelostat,* which provides a stationary image of a portion of the sky; and the *uranograph,* which gives a photographic chart of the sky with meridian lines marked on it at equal intervals of time. For his method of photographically reproducing colors, based on the phenomenon of interference, he received the 1908 Nobel prize. Lippmann was a fellow of the Royal Society.—*D. H. D. R.*

LIQUID: one of the three common states of matter, the other two being the gaseous and solid states. The molecules that make up matter are quite close to one another in a liquid, in contrast to their wide separation in a gas. They are almost as closely spaced as those in a solid, the difference being that they are not fixed in regular patterns but are free to wander about. See LIQUID FLOW.—*G. M. S. and L. S.*

LIQUID-DROP MODEL OF NUCLEUS: an attempt by Niels Bohr and John A. Wheeler to visualize, in terms of classical physics, a structure for the nucleus of an ATOM that would account for some of the properties of the nucleus. This model assumes, for an unexcited and hence a stable nucleus, a spherical, or liquid-drop, form, determined by a balance between Coulomb repulsive forces between like charges (protons) and inward-directed forces of surface tension. The capture by the nucleus of a slow neutron adds to its store of excitation energy and causes the nucleus to oscillate, with its original spherical shape now changing to that of an ellipsoid. Surface tension tends to restore the original shape, but Coulomb forces operate to resist the restoration. An additional increment of excitation energy may distort the nucleus into the shape of a dumbbell, which finally divides or splits apart into two spherical "drops," as the Coulomb forces prevail over the oppositely directed forces of surface tension. The result is nuclear fission (see FISSION, NUCLEAR), whose "mechanics" is thus made analogous to the process of binary fission in biology. The energy released in such fission is derived from the loss of mass, in accordance with the Einstein equation $E = mc^2$. Another explanation for the production of this fission energy may be found in the change of the nucleus from an unstable to a stable form.—*A. E.*

LIQUID FLOW: the flow of liquids through confining channels. A liquid may be considered as structurally equivalent to a "disordered-crystal" type of solid. It exhibits a short-range order, but lacks the over-all long-range pattern of a true crystalline solid. It is therefore *mobile,* or fluid, in character. Tar and pitch have a structure intermediate between those of

true liquids and solids, and their flow resembles more the "creep" of metals under stress. A liquid at rest exhibits a "free" horizontal surface whose elastic potential energy tends toward a minimum. The shape of a liquid is easily deformed, hence adapts itself readily to the shape of the containing vessel. Liquids are practically incompressible, except under extremely high pressures.

Liquids begin to flow almost immediately after shearing stress has been applied. Viscous liquids offer a frictional resistance to flow, with the result that layers adjacent to the walls of a pipe move more slowly than those near the center. Ideal, or nonviscous, liquids are presumed to move with the same velocity past every point in a given cross section of a channel. Nonviscous flow is characterized by the formation of *streamlines,* or lines of flow, along which the particles of the liquid may be assumed to be moving. Streamlines are separated perceptibly in the wider part of the channel and are crowded together in its constricted portions. We also speak of *laminar* flow, which is a flow in sheets, or laminae. Viscous flow introduces the element of *turbulence,* which is the result of obstructions, sharp bends in the channel, etc. This is a complex type of flow, rendered even more involved when it becomes rotational, or accompanied by the formation of *vortices.* The full theory of liquid flow is highly mathematical, but simple experiments (with hulls, floats, and model boats) are sufficient to establish its empirical nature. The study of liquid flow is an important part of the science of HYDRODYNAMICS. See also FLUID FLOW.—*A. E.*

LITHIFICATION (or **diagenesis**): in geology, the consolidation of loose materials into hard rock. Newly deposited SEDIMENTS consist of detrital particles and/or locally formed chemical precipitates, along with interstitial solutions. On burial and compaction of materials, temperatures and pressures rise and the various constituents react with each other to maintain over-all thermodynamic stability. Depending on the initial constituents, these reactions may involve dehydration, oxidation, reduction, solution, and precipitation, in various sequences. The boundary between diagenetic processes and low-grade METAMORPHISM is arbitrary and subject to controversy. In sandstones and conglomerates, lithification may be accomplished by precipitation of hematite, limonite, calcite, dolomite, chalcedony, opal, or other cementing materials in the interstitial voids (see CEMENTATION); by recrystallization or reconstitution of interstitial clays; or by solution and then reprecipitation of some of the silica as interlocking overgrowths on, and in crystallographic continuity with, the original sand grains. In limestones, diagenesis is generally accomplished by simple solution and reprecipitation of some of the calcium carbonate, but the conversion of aragonite to calcite may have some effect on the process. Bedded clays and mudstones are converted to shales by reconstitution or recrystallization of the original clay minerals, or by the alteration of clay minerals to micas or chlorites. These platy minerals grow with their longer dimensions in the plane normal to the superincumbent pressure and thus account for the fissility or cleavage of the shales.—*L. M.*

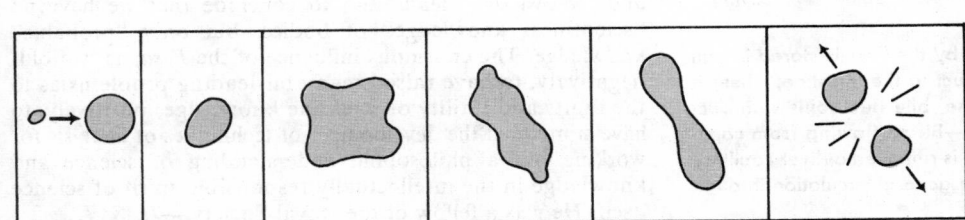

Liquid-drop model of nucleus: Arrival of neutron (*left*) causes increasingly severe oscillations of nucleus until it splits (*right*).

LITHIUM: silvery-white alkali metal (Li); at. no. 3; at. wt 6.940; sp gr 0.534; mp 186°C; bp 1336°C. Lithium is the lightest known metal and one of the most reactive of elements. It is never found free in nature, but always occurs in compounds—in the minerals lepidolite, spodumene, petalite, and amblygonite and in some naturally occurring brines. Spodumene, $LiAl(SiO_3)_2$, occurs in North Carolina, other lithium ores in New England. Lithium resembles the alkali metals sodium and potassium chemically but is much more reactive. It was discovered in 1817 by August Arfvedson, who on analyzing a sample of petalite found that sodium was "contaminated" by an unknown substance. Lithium is used in various alloys to increase tensile strength and resistance to corrosion. Lithium hydride in containers is used to provide a very light source of hydrogen for filling signal balloons.—*I. B.*

LITHOSPHERE: see EARTH.

LIVER: a large, reddish-brown gland in the body cavity of vertebrates. It has important functions in digestion, the storage and metabolism of foodstuffs, the regulation of blood composition, excretion, and the formation and destruction of red blood cells. The liver receives blood from the aorta through the hepatic artery and through the hepatic portal vein; the latter collects all blood coming from the capillary network of the intestine, and distributes it through a second capillary network in the liver. All blood coming from the intestine must pass through the liver before entering the general circulation; much of the absorbed food material, especially carbohydrate and amino acids, is removed from the blood for storage as glycogen in the liver cells or for other biochemical transformations. Amino acids may be used for synthesis of blood proteins or may be deaminated (deprived of the amino group). The ammonia formed in deamination is converted into urea, or uric acid, in the higher vertebrates (see EXCRETION), whereas the residues are either oxidized or converted to glycogen for storage. The formation of urea in amphibians and mammals, and of uric acid in snakes, lizards, and birds, and the conversion of amino acids to glycogen occur only in the liver. The regulation of the sugar content of the blood depends largely on the liver which, under the control of the hormone insulin from the pancreas, takes up sugar from the blood or adds sugar to the blood to maintain a constant level. The sugar added to the blood is derived from the breakdown of glycogen.

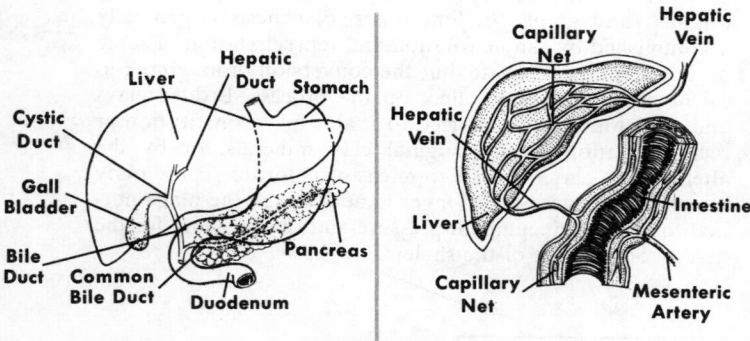

Functions of liver: *Left*—Bile secreted by the liver is stored in gall bladder, then delivered via the bile duct to the intestine, where it aids in digestion of fat. Near intestine, bile duct joins with duct carrying insulin from pancreas. *Right*—Blood flowing from capillary net of intestine carries food which is removed at liver capillary net and stored; blood then passes into general circulation through hepatic vein.

Liver cells secrete into special ducts a material known as bile. This includes a number of excretory products and special bile salts. The latter have an essential function in digestion and absorption of fat. The bile ducts converge to form a single duct, which drains into the intestine. Bile is temporarily stored in a diverticulum of this duct, the gall bladder. In lower vertebrates, and in embryonic mammals, the liver is the site of formation of red blood cells; in all vertebrates, it is responsible for synthesis of blood proteins, for breakdown of hemoglobin from worn-out red cells, and for storage of iron. Structures called livers in the invertebrates are in general not strictly comparable with the vertebrate liver, though they may perform some of the same functions.—*B. T. S.*

LOBACHEVSKI, NIKOLAI IVANOVICH, 1793–1856, Russian mathematician; b. Makariev. He entered the Univ. of Kazan at 13, obtained his master's degree at 18, and was appointed extraordinary professor at 22 and regular professor at 23. From 1827 to 1864, he was rector of the university. He won fame for the discovery of non-Euclidean geometry. Although K. F. Gauss and J. Bolyai arrived at similar conclusions about the same time, Lobachevski was the first to communicate his discoveries to the public (1826).—*H. C.*

L'OBEL, MATTHIAS DE, 1538–1616, Flemish botanist; b. Lille, France. He made one of the earliest attempts to classify plants according to structure, choosing leaf shape as the basis for grouping. His principal work was *Plantarum seu stirpium historia* (1576). His name is perpetuated in the plant genus *Lobelia.*—*D. H. D. R.*

LOCKE, JOHN, 1632–1704, English philosopher; b. Wrington, England. Locke's greatest work, *An Essay Concerning Human Understanding* (1690), professedly sets out to do for our knowledge of the understanding what Newton did for science: to introduce conceptual and linguistic clarity, removing "the rubbish" blocking knowledge. Locke's inquiry is "into the original, certainty, and extent of *human knowledge*

John Locke
(N. Y. Public Library)

together with the grounds and degrees of *belief, opinion,* and *assent.*" To explain *knowledge,* Locke elaborated a theory of the origins of ideas in sense experience and the operations of the understanding. The central issue—how we can know the world if all we know is ideas some of which *might* be effects of external objects—has come to be called "the problem of knowledge."

Newton's world of insensible particles obeying mechanical laws seems to exclude perception and mind altogether. Yet science is an accomplished fact. The "problem" then is: How is this fact to be explained? Locke begins by accepting Newton's world, but confusion over the meanings of "idea" and "knowledge" leads him to conclude that we have no "scientifical knowledge" of bodies, but only "probable" knowledge. The enormous influence of the *Essay* is twofold: negatively, to have raised many misleading problems as to the limits and futility of scientific knowledge; positively, to have stimulated the development of techniques of analysis for working out a philosophic understanding of science and knowledge in the intellectually responsible spirit of science itself. He was a fellow of the Royal Society.—*H. S. T.*

Diesel locomotive, built in 1956, develops 2,000 hp and is capable of maximum speed of 87 mi/hr. It is a four-axle type of engine, weighing 79 metric tons. (*Steidl/German Federal Railroad*)

LOCKYER, SIR JOSEPH NORMAN, 1836–1920, English astronomer; b. Rugby. Beginning as an amateur astronomer, Lockyer became famous for his studies of the spectrum of sunspots and of solar prominences. He discovered the element helium on the Sun, prior to its discovery on Earth, and coined the word "chromosphere." He was a fellow of the Royal Society.—*D. H. D. R.*

LOCOMOTIVE: a self-propelled vehicle designed to pull railroad cars. Steam, diesel-electric, and gas turbine-electric types manufacture their own power; electric locomotives take their power from an outside source.

Locomotives had their beginnings on the crude horse-powered tramways of English mining districts. In 1804 Richard Trevithick and Andrew Vivian successfully operated a high-pressure steam locomotive on such a tramway. A coal fire heated water in a horizontal boiler to produce steam, which pushed a piston back and forth in a horizontal cylinder. This motion was transmitted to the four smooth-flanged driving wheels, which ran on a smooth iron track. To increase the fire's draft, the inventors passed the engine's exhaust steam up the smokestack. Typical of the designs that followed was George Stephenson's "Rocket," which had a horizontal multi-tubular boiler and two reciprocating engines with connecting rods directly coupled to the drive wheels; this locomotive won the Rainhill Trials in England (1829) with a speed of 24 mi/hr.

The first locomotives on the continent of Europe and in the U. S. A. were English-made. The "Stourbridge Lion" was the first to operate in the U. S. A. (1829). During 1830 the "Tom Thumb," the first U. S.-built locomotive, began operation on the Baltimore and Ohio; it was followed by the "Best Friend of Charleston" on the South Carolina Canal and Rail Road. The "De Witt Clinton" was built for the Mohawk and Hudson in 1831.

In 1836 the highly successful "American"-type locomotive was introduced. Its wheels had a 4–4–0 pattern, *i.e.* four pilot wheels, four connected drive wheels, and no wheels under the firebox. Demands for increased power produced types with more drive wheels, bigger boilers, and higher steam pressures. (More power also required better braking, and steam and compressed-air brakes were the result.) Typical locomotives were the "Mogul" (2–6–0), "Consolidation" (2–8–0), "Atlantic" (4–4–2), and "Pacific" (4–6–2). Then came the even more powerful "Mountain" (4–8–2) and "Northern" (4–8–4) for passenger service; and the "Santa Fe" (2–10–2), "Berkshire" (2–8–4), and "Texas" (2–10–4) with their increased number of drive wheels for freight. And when in freight service greater speeds were called for to meet competition from other carriers, drive-wheel diameters were increased to 76 in. and then eventually to 84 in. Mountain railroads laid out in early days needed special locomotives for their steep grades and sharp curves; the articulated (jointed) locomotive, which could be big and powerful, yet "swing" around curves, was the answer. Robert Francis Fairlie's articulated design (1865) had two boiler barrels with

a central firebox and a smokestack at each end. Two engine frames supported the boiler, each with a pivot that allowed it to swing and follow the track. In 1890 Anatole Mallet of France built a semi-articulated compound locomotive with two engines under one conventional boiler, the front engine-frame swinging; this locomotive's two larger cylinders used exhaust steam from the smaller high-pressure pair. H. W. Garratt's locomotive (1908) had a big boiler on a steel frame slung between two engine frames turning on pivots. One engine carried the water tank; the other, the fuel. Special geared steam locomotives developed for heavy hauling on steep, rough, winding track included the "Shay," the "Heisler," and the "Climax." They were widely used in lumbering operations. Locomotives to operate on very steep mountain grades were built from 1887 on; their engines drove a toothed pinion gear that meshed into the teeth of a rack rail laid between ordinary rails.

Despite its long and picturesque history, the steam locomotive has certain economic disadvantages, chiefly low thermal efficiency (4–8%) and costly maintenance, *e.g.* periodic removal of scale from boiler tubes and frequent lubrication. Steam locomotives also require a large supply of water—a particular inconvenience in dry regions. Thus the more efficient and cleaner electric and diesel-electric types have gradually replaced steam locomotives. Various steam-turbine locomotives have been developed, but have not proved capable of competing successfully with electric and diesel-electric types. Electric locomotives were first used on the Baltimore and Ohio Railroad in 1895. Electric power (either alternating or direct current) is supplied by a central generating station either through an overhead wire or a third rail. Electric motors inside the locomotive transmit the power to the driving axles through reduction gears. A feature which is useful in mountainous regions is "regenerative braking": the motor, turned by the driving wheels, feeds current back into the line as it slows the train on long grades.

Steam locomotives dominated the railroads for over a century. Typical of the steam age of railroading was this 4-8-4, one of the largest and most powerful engines of its kind ever built. (*Forest Crossen*)

For long hauls at high speeds the operating efficiency of the steam locomotive surpasses that of the diesel locomotive, which operates most advantageously for short hauls at low speeds. Nevertheless, because of their over-all superiority, as well as recent improvements in flexibility of operation at high speeds, diesel-electric locomotives, introduced in switching service in 1925 and on main-line hauls in 1935, were by the early 1960s the most widely used type in the U. S. A. Their multi-cylinder diesel engines turn electric generators which furnish current for electric motors geared to the driving axles. The diesel-electric locomotive thus carries its own power plant with it and avoids the need for overhead wires or third rails. In the main, passenger and freight services use the same locomotives, and where differences in speed are required, changes can be made in the gear ratio of the traction motor. A recent development is the gas-turbine-electric locomotive, similar to the diesel-electric except that its generators are turned by GAS TURBINES; in these, combustion of fuel oil or powered coal in highly compressed air furnishes gases of great volume and velocity which power the turbine rotor.— *F. C.*

The Stourbridge Lion was first locomotive ever operated in America. It was put in service in 1829. (*N. Y. Public Library*)

LODESTONE: a variety of the mineral magnetite, Fe_3O_4, which shows strong natural magnetic polarity. The name, derived from early Germanic dialects, means "leading stone"; pieces of lodestone, floated on wooden chips, were the earliest mariners' compasses. Later it was found that iron needles could be magnetized by stroking them with lodestones. Chinese works as early as 2600 B. C. describe intricate, south-pointing mechanisms. The magnetic attraction of lodestone was known to the ancient Greeks, but its polarity apparently was not recognized until the 1500s, at about the same time that the magnetic polarity of Earth itself was first recognized. William Gilbert (1544–1603) made models of Earth (*terrellas*) by cutting small spheres from lodestone, locating the magnetic poles, and inscribing the meridians accordingly. Magical and curative powers have been ascribed to lodestone from the earliest times and were emphasized in the works of the Swiss alchemist Paracelsus (1493–1541) and the Rosicrucians in the 1600s; lodestones are still used today in voodoo rites.

Most magnetite does not show appreciable magnetic polarity. Measurements on a world-wide basis are now being made of the direction of the weak remanent magnetism of grains of magnetite disseminated through various kinds of rock; these measurements indicate the orientation of Earth's magnetic field at the time the rocks were formed. Geographical and stratigraphic results are being used to test hypotheses relating to CONTINENTAL DRIFT and to wandering of the poles (see TERRESTRIAL MAGNETISM). In petroleum exploration, the direction of remanent magnetism in drill cores is used for orienting the cores and for correlating formations intersected in different drill holes.

There is still no satisfactory explanation for the cause of the strong polarity of lodestones; any acceptable hypothesis must account for the fact that most magnetite is not appreciably polarized. The principal source of lodestone in North America is at Magnet Cove, Ark., where it occurs in coarsely crystalline rocks of an alkaline intrusive complex and in associated tactites. Residual masses of lodestone, weathered out of the original rocks, are scattered through the soil.— *L. M.*

LODGE, SIR OLIVER JOSEPH, 1851–1940, English physicist; b. Penkhull. He invented the coherer, a device used in wireless receivers (before the invention of the vacuum tube) to change electromagnetic waves into pulses of electric current. In 1889, he published *Modern Views of Electricity,* in which he gave a mechanical interpretation of J. C. Maxwell's equations. He was knighted in 1902 and made a fellow of the Royal Society. The death of his son in World War I turned him to a belief in communication between the living and the dead.—*H. I. S.*

LOEB, JACQUES, 1859–1924, U. S.-German physiologist; b. Mayen, Ger. Although interested in all phases of physiology, he is perhaps best known for his work in developmental physiology, particularly in the physiology of fertilization. Among his outstanding achievements was the induction of artificial parthenogenesis in the sea urchin. He also did important research in the chemistry and physiology of colloids. His many publications include the influential book *Comparative Physiology of the Brain and Comparative Psychology* (1899). He was a member of the National Academy of Sciences.— *D. H. D. R.*

LOESS: fine sediment deposited on land by the wind; it consists predominantly of silt, but may include both sand and clay. Characteristically nonstratified and unconsolidated, loess occurs as yellow, brown, or gray blankets a few feet to—rarely —hundreds of feet thick. It often shows vertical jointing and the ability to stand as firm cliffs in valleys and road cuts, probably because of the cementing effect of mineral deposits such

Exposure of loess deposit near Vicksburg, Miss., shows how this material can stand as a firm cliff. (*U. S. Geol. Survey*)

as calcite in vertical root channels. Familiar in the Mississippi Valley, loess is commonest in middle latitudes, covering, in North America and Eurasia, an aggregate of millions of square miles. Most North American loess originated as glacial outwash sediments during glacial ages; much of that in central and E Asia originated in deserts, and is not related to glacial activity.—*R. F.*

LOEWI, OTTO, 1873–1962, German-U. S. pharmacologist and physiologist; b. Frankfort-am-Main. He showed that cardiac nerves, when stimulated, free a chemical substance which in turn affects the responsive organ; the nerves do not stimulate the organ directly. His specific experimental work on the heart, combined with H. H. Dale's researches on acetylcholine, established the chemical transmission of nerve impulses and won for both men the 1936 Nobel prize. Loewi was a fellow of the Royal Society.—*D. H. D. R.*

LOGAN, SIR WILLIAM EDMOND, 1798–1875, Canadian geologist; b. Montreal. The first director (1842–70) of the Canadian Geological Survey, he did much of the pioneer work in Canadian geology. He traced the structure of the rocks forming the Laurentian and Adirondack Mts, then considered unstratified, and showed that they are actually disturbed and altered sediments of great thickness. He also proved that the clay underlying coal beds is the soil in which the coal vegetation grew; thus the theory of growth in place was established. Logan has been called "the father of Canadian science." He was a fellow of the Royal Society.—*D. H. D. R.*

LOGARITHM: a mathematical device by which many computations are made shorter and easier. Logarithms reduce multiplication to addition, division to subtraction, raising to powers to multiplication, and extraction of roots to division. They were invented by John Napier, who published the first table of logarithms in 1614.

The logarithm of a number N to the base b is the exponent of the power of b equal to N. Thus if $b^L = N$, then the logarithm of N to the base b is L, or $\log_b N = L$. The base of Napier's logarithms was a number very near 1. For computing in the decimal system of numbers the base 10 is more suitable. Henry Briggs, a contemporary of Napier, transformed Napier's logarithms to the base 10, and it is these Briggsian, or common, logarithms which are commonly used in computation.

Since $10^2 = 100$, in the common system $\log 100 = 2$; similarly $10^3 = 1000$, and $\log 1000 = 3$. Since $\log 1 = 0$ and $\log 10 = 1$, it is seen that if N lies between 1 and 10, $\log N$ lies between 0 and 1, and can be expressed exactly or approximately by a decimal fraction. A table of Briggsian logarithms provides such decimals for the numbers between 1 and 10. A five-place table has entries like the following:

N	0	1	2	3	4	5	6	7	8	9
317	50106	120	133	147	161	174	188	202	215	229

From this line of the table we can read the logarithms of all numbers from 3.17 to 3.18, correct to five decimal places. Thus, $\log 3.170 = .50106$, $\log 3.174 = .50161$, etc. By interpolation we can find $\log 3.1743 = .50165$. The table does not show the decimal points, since they can be supplied by the reader.

We observe that $317 = 3.17 \times 10^2$. Since $\log 3.17 = .50106$, $3.17 = 10^{.50106}$. Therefore $317 = 10^{.50106} \times 10^2 = 10^{2.50106}$. Hence $\log 317 = 2.50106$. In the same way we find that $\log 31.7 = 1.50106$, $\log 3170 = 3.50106$, and $\log .317 = .50106 - 1$. Thus the logarithm of each number consists of two parts— the decimal which is read from the table and is the same for all numbers having the same sequence of digits, and the whole number which is supplied by the reader in accordance with the position of the decimal point. The decimal part is called the *mantissa* and the integral part the *characteristic*. The table is actually a table of mantissas, and is frequently so designated. The following rule for finding the characteristic is convenient: if the decimal point is between the first two significant figures, the characteristic is 0; if not, count from this position the number of spaces to the point; this number is the characteristic, positive if the point is to the right of the zero position and negative if it is to the left. For example, the characteristics for the numbers 3.178, 317800, .03178, .00003178 are 0, 5, −2, and −5, respectively.

It was found above that $\log 3.1743 = .50165$. This statement can be inverted to read antilog $.50165 = 3.1743$. The antilogarithm of L is the number having L as its logarithm.

Rules for computing with logarithms follow from the rules for manipulating exponents. For example, if we wish to multiply 3.17×49.2, we find the logarithms of these numbers and add them.

$$
\begin{aligned}
\log 3.17 &= 0.50106 \\
\log 49.2 &= 1.69197 \\
\log \text{(product)} &= 2.19303 \\
\text{product} &= 156
\end{aligned}
$$

The result is the logarithm of the product. This is seen immediately if we translate the logarithmic statements into exponential form: $3.17 = 10^{0.50106}$, $49.2 = 10^{1.69197}$; therefore $3.17 \times 49.2 = 10^{0.50106} \times 10^{1.69197} = 10^{0.50106+1.69197} = 10^{2.19303}$. The computation is completed by finding the antilogarithm of 2.19303. This is 156; we keep only three figures since greater accuracy cannot be expected from the three-digit numbers with which we started.

In division we subtract the logarithms, in raising a number to a power we multiply its logarithm by the exponent, and in extracting a root we divide the logarithm by the index. For example:

(*1*) $8130 \div 24.79$

$$\begin{array}{rl} \log 8130 = & 3.91009 \\ -\log 24.79 = & \underline{1.39428} \\ \log(\text{quotient}) = & 2.51581 \\ \text{quotient} = & 32.80 \end{array}$$

(*2*) $(37.8)^4$

$$\begin{array}{rl} \log 37.8 = & 1.57749 \\ & \underline{4} \\ \log(37.8)^4 = & 6.30996 \\ (37.8)^4 = & 2,045,000 \end{array}$$

(*3*) $\sqrt[3]{29.3}$

$$\begin{array}{rl} \log 29.3 = & 1.46687 \\ \tfrac{1}{3}(\log 29.3) = & 0.48896 \\ \sqrt[3]{29.3} = & 3.083 \end{array}$$

(Although four digits have been kept in Ex. *2* and *3*, not more than three are reliable, since only three were given at the outset.)

A base that is frequently used in mathematics is the irrational number *e* (approximately 2.71828). The corresponding logarithms are called natural, or Naperian, logarithms and written $\log_e N$, or $\ln N$. Tables of natural logarithms are available but are not strictly necessary, since logarithms to a base *b* can be found from a table to a base *a* by the formula: $\log_b N = (\log_a N)/(\log_a b)$. Thus $\log_e N = (\log_{10} N)/(\log_{10} e) = (\log_{10} N)/.43429.$—*H. C.*

LOGIC: in its broadest sense, the study of the ways in which knowledge is advanced. For any claim to knowledge it is always possible to raise the question "How do you know?" and both the assessment of the reliability of such claims based on the asserted premises, and the systematic study of the principles involved in assessing such claims, are the concern of the logician. Logic is both a science and an art. To take the latter first, it includes the art of making distinctions, an activity that is subject to few rules, but in which skill can be developed through practice. A distinction is a difference that makes a difference, and logical activity is no more aptly described as "logic-chopping" than cutting down trees to build a house could be called merely wood-chopping. The interpretation of meanings, the seeking out of implied assumptions in arguments, seeing the point (or the ability to judge what is actually relevant and what only speciously persuasive in a discussion), estimating the probative force of a set of considerations, recognizing a fallacy, as in the ability to discern a chasm, when it exists, between the premises of an argument and the desired conclusion—these and similar skills are of the essence of what constitutes the rational mind. They rest ultimately on logical distinctions: between what is explicitly said and what is implied by the context; between the consistent and the contradictory or contrary; between the valid and the invalid, the necessary and the factual, the conclusive and the merely probable or possible.

Justice Oliver Wendell Holmes, who was himself an eminently rational man and practiced the art of making distinctions with skill, nevertheless did harm to the cause of reason when he wrote: "The life of the law has been experience and not logic." It was an oversimplified logic he was protesting against, and rightly, one which did not recognize that the application of rules to particular cases is more than an exercise in syllogizing, that it involves questions of social policy and principle. But the fact that the "felt needs of the times" help determine what judges do, and that judges are sometimes only dimly aware of the principles that have actually moti-

vated their decisions, is a good reason for trying to find out what these principles are. Once the principles are made explicit, they can be subjected to critical examination and evaluated by comparing them with their possible alternatives.

A language has logical principles built into it, and everyone who knows the language thereby has learned something of logic, whether he is conscious of this knowledge or not. But one who has not studied logic may not be able to distinguish between its correct application and its tendency to mislead the unwary, a fact which the unscrupulous use in order to deceive. Thus the dilemma is a valid argument form, and its use, *e.g.* in an argument involving social problems, carries great weight in suggesting to the logically unsophisticated that the propounder has a sound position. But it rests on the assumption that the alternatives enumerated in the argument exhaust the possibilities, so that one not trained in "passing between the horns," *i.e.* looking for other possibilities not covered by the argument, may be seriously misled. Furthermore, ordinary language is inconsistent; it is full of vague terms and those who speak it are often unaware of its assumptions. Try to take any word in ordinary use, *e.g.* "chair," and give it precise definition—the attempt will likely end in failure. Ordinary language may suffice for everyday use, but when exactness is demanded, as in meeting the needs of science, one must make use of a logic that is systematically developed and perhaps involves some of the techniques of mathematics. There is no precise dividing line between what is called logic and what is called mathematics, so that inquiries of the former merge imperceptibly into those of the latter. Thus ideas such as "some" (in the sense of "at least one") and "at most one" (which is "not at least two") have been traditionally assigned to logic, while "exactly one" was considered as mathematical. But as soon as it was realized that the latter could be defined in terms of the former, the dividing line disappeared, and logicians today are seriously concerned with the foundations of mathematics. The intimate connection of the two studies can be further seen from the fact that the fundamental relations among statements found in the statement calculus of logic can be developed completely by the methods of mathematics; the following two questions have precisely analogous answers:

A. What are the relations among all possible truth functions of any two statements *p* and *q*, where *p* and *q* can take only the values truth and falsity? Note that "*p* and *q*" (written "$p \cdot q$") is a truth function of *p* and *q* because the truth of this expression is known as soon as we know the truth of its two component parts, whereas "*p* is necessary" is not a truth function of *p*, because we may know that *p* is true without knowing whether "*p* is necessary" is true.

p	*q*	$p \vee q$	$p \cdot q$
T	T	T	T
T	F	T	F
F	T	T	F
F	F	F	F

Truth table involving two propositions *p* and *q*. If *p* is true (*T*) and *q* is true, then the proposition "*p* or *q*" ($p \vee q$) is true, and so is the proposition "*p* and *q*" ($p \cdot q$). If *p* is true but *q* is false (*F*), then "*p* or *q*" is true, but "*p* and *q*" is false.

B. What are the relations among all possible functions "$f(x, y)$," in which f, x, and y can take only the values 0 and 1?

It turns out that there are just 16 such relations. To see this write

$$f_n(0, 0) = a$$
$$f_n(0, 1) = b$$
$$f_n(1, 0) = c$$
$$f_n(1, 1) = d$$

Now if a, b, c, and d can each take only the values 0 and 1, then we can write 2^4 or 16 sets of these equations. If we think of 0 as representing falsehood and 1 as truth, then the function representing the joint assertion of the truth of two statements will be given by

$$a = b = c = 0, d = 1.$$

What this says is simply that the joint assertion of two statements is true if and only if each of them is true, but it says this in a way that exhibits the conjunction of two statements to be just one instance of a set of systematically related forms in which two statements can be combined.

The statement calculus on first acquaintance has an air of paradox about it, largely the result of the fact that among its theorems there occur such statements as "a false proposition implies any proposition" and "a true proposition is implied by any proposition." But the feeling of paradox quickly disappears as soon as it is recognized that in this calculus the word "imply" is being employed in an unfamiliar way. Besides, the calculus has other interpretations that are perfectly straightforward. In fact, it is basic to an understanding of elementary electrical theory and the design of electronic computers.

The logician classifies inferences as conclusive or as probable. Conclusive inferences are studied in deductive formal logic, which seeks to determine the form an argument must have to guarantee the truth of its conclusion whenever its premises are true. Methods for dealing with problems of this sort are contained in the calculus of statements, of predicates and relations. The statement calculus takes entire statements as units and studies the effect of negating them, of conjunction, of alternation (one or both of two statements are true), of implication (it is not the case that the first of two statements is true and the second false), of equivalence (two statements are both true or both false), and the like. It contains propositions of which the following is an illustration: if a statement p is true, then any alternation "p or q" which has p as one of its members is likewise true, no matter what the truth status of q. This, like other logical principles, lends itself to misuse, as when the government discharges several thousand people who talk too much to strangers, drink too much in public, have excessive debts, etc., collectively termed "security risks," and a spokesman then announces that "several thousand Communists or security risks" have been discharged, when there may not be any Communists among them at all.

Deductive logic is popularly thought of as a process by means of which conclusions are derived from given premises; and indeed from any set of premises an indefinitely large number of conclusions may be validly drawn, and a person with even a slight knowledge of logic can set them down as fast as he can write. However, most of these will not be worth writing down and there is, in general, no method for extracting the valuable ones; nor can there be except in special cases. In these respects, the traditional syllogism (according to which, for example, "All *A* is *C*" can be inferred from premises of the form "All *A* is *B*" and "All *B* is *C*") does not do justice either to the fact that it is usually not obvious what conclusions really follow from the premises in a deductive argument, or to the fact that only a fraction of validly drawn conclusions may be of serious interest. A better illustration for these points is the following: More than 2,000 yr elapsed before anyone realized that the axioms of Euclidean geometry imply the surprising theorem that if the angles of any triangle whatever are trisected, then the trisectors meet to form an equilateral triangle (Morley's theorem). Accordingly, although the conclusion of a deductive argument may be said to be "contained in" the premises, this is to be understood only in a figurative sense, for the conclusion cannot usually be obtained by mere inspection of the premises. Once a proof for a conclusion has been constructed, the validity of the proof can be checked by routine methods; and methods have also been developed in some cases, notably in the sentential calculus, for deciding whether a given statement is a theorem by applying mechanically certain rules. But in general there are no rules for constructing proofs or for deciding mechanically which statements are theorems. It is also worth noting that the validity of a deductive argument does not depend on whether its premises were discovered before the conclusion, but only on the nature of the logical relations between premises and conclusion.

Deductive logic owes its comprehensive range of application to the fact that it is formal, so that since arguments differing widely in their subject matter may exemplify the identical form, the same logical principles can serve in evaluating the validity of such arguments irrespective of their subject matter. This is illustrated by the following two arguments: (1) Given any 6 persons, then at least 3 must know each other or at least 3 be strangers to each other. (2) Given 6 points in space, it is impossible to color the lines connecting them red or blue without having at least one of the triangles formed all red or all blue. ("The line *A B* is colored red" corresponds formally to "*A* and *B* know each other," etc.)

The logic of probable inference has its deductive part, but we shall confine our discussion here to what are usually called its inductive aspects. The problem of induction may be defined as that of trying to arrive at reliable generalizations when our immediate evidence is confined to limited particulars. Every particular is a special case of an indefinitely large number of generalizations, some true and some false. Of those which are true, some are trivial and some are not. Of those that are true and valuable, some are always true, and some are true only for the most part. Of those true for the most part, some are true with an ascertainable relative frequency, and some are of such character that we can assign no numerical value to their relative frequency with which they are true.

Suppose an experiment has been performed a large number of times n and has always been found to have the result r; we are about to repeat it for the $(n + 1)$th time and wish to know with what confidence we should expect the result r. A little reflection shows that the sheer number of past experiments does not suffice to determine a reasonable answer to this question. For the experiment may be like that of observing the rising sun, or it may be one of the kind exemplified by taking a pitcher to a well once too often. A few years ago it was possible for a logician to write: "The proposition 'All Presidents of the United States have been Protestants' does not prove that the next president will also be one. But we should not regard these two propositions as altogether irrelevant to each other. The first is evidence of some sort for the other, although it falls short of being conclusive." Accordingly, the mere multiplication of instances, in the absence of other evidence, is a shaky reed on which to base reliable inferences.

Consider, on the other hand, the confidence with which a chemist will assert the percentage composition of a new compound, based on a few carefully performed experimental determinations. This confidence is warranted because he knows that compounds have stable compositions, so that working with any pure sample is sufficient. But he must, of

course, have adequate evidence to support his assumption that the substance with which he is experimenting is indeed pure as well as a compound. It is instructive to compare the chemist's conclusion about the composition of his compound with some familiar generalizations about the color characterizing the plumage of birds belonging to a given species, *e.g.* that all swans are white or all ravens are black. Since we possess much evidence to show that color is a frequently

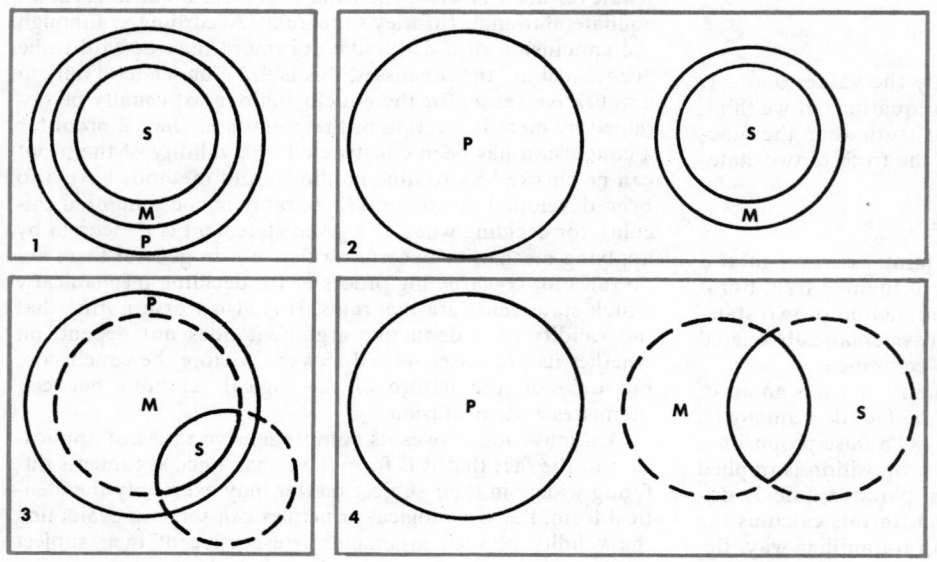

Syllogisms and Euler's circles: In Aristotelian logic, any syllogism can be reduced to one of four basic types. (These can in turn be reduced to types 1 and 3 by the use of immediate inference, and 3 can be reduced to 1 by the use of the propositional calculus; see SYLLOGISM.) Euler's circles demonstrate the meaning of the four syllogisms. (1) All M are P; all S are M; therefore all S are P. (2) No P are M; all S are M; therefore no S are P. (3) All M are P; some M are S; therefore some S are P. (4) No P are M; some M are S; therefore some S are not P. The dotted lines in 3 and 4 indicate that the conclusions deal with some S, but tell us nothing about the remaining S.

Syllogistic arguments represented as Venn diagrams: Any syllogistic argument can be represented by a Venn diagram (John Venn, late 19th-cent. English logician). Thus in diagram 1, since all M are P, there are no M which are not P; and hence the M-non-P region is shaded out. Similarly (diag. 2), since all S are M, the S-non-M region is shaded out with the combined result that the S-non-P region has been completely eliminated, showing that all S are P. In diagrams 3 and 4, the asterisk (*) indicates that there is something which is both S and M, since some M are S is given. Thus in diagram 3, since all M are P is also given, there are no M which are not P; hence the asterisk appears in the part of the S region which overlaps P; hence some S are P is the result.

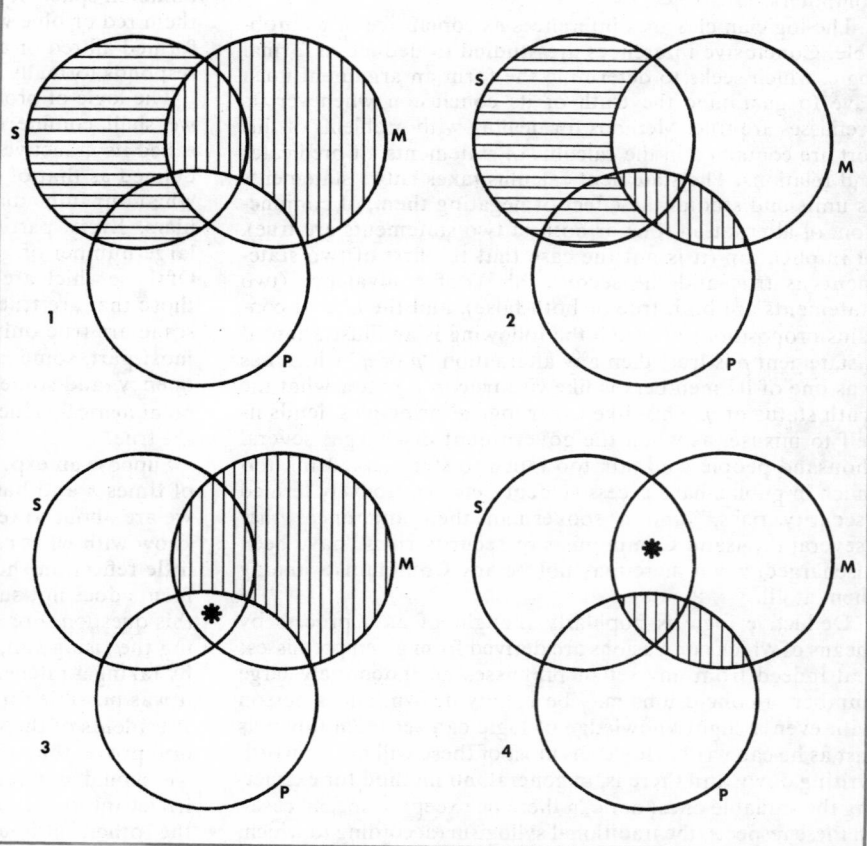

variable trait even in a single species of birds, such generalizations are usually unreliable, and it would have been unwise to place much confidence in the assumption that all swans are white, even before black swans were discovered and even though all the swans observed until that discovery was made were white. In contrast to such generalizations, there is strong warrant for the assumption that light of a certain frequency presents a definite color to a normal observer at rest with respect to the light source.

We need to distinguish carefully between a merely empirical generalization and a scientific law. "All rabbits are herbivorous" is an instance of the former because, although it is confirmed by our experience of rabbits, this does not eliminate the possibility that under special conditions, which could be set up in a laboratory, rabbits might be made to eat meat and could digest it (for an account of how this was done see Claude Bernard: *Introduction to the Experimental Study of Medicine*). Consider the statement "All men are mortal." What is its status? It is at least an empirical generalization: we know that men die, from accident, famine, disease, and "old age." But is old age a disease? We used to say that they died from "stoppage of the heart." But besides the fact that men have been revived after their hearts had completely stopped, we are no wiser if we do not know why the heart stops beating. Every part of the body is constantly being regenerated through interaction with the blood supply. Why does this process not continue indefinitely, but eventually come to an end instead? We do not know, and so we can say only that although we suspect "all men die" to be more than an empirical generalization, we still lack the theoretical basis for saying what this something more is. Our chief point is that empirical generalizations claimed to be universally true become more reliable when they can be shown to be deductively derivable parts of a theoretical system.

Generalizations involving "most" elements of a class have a different logic from those about "all." Neglect of the difference may lead one to commit the Fallacy of Accident (see FALLACY). Furthermore, suppose a person argues: "Since I know most *A*'s are *B*'s, I shall treat all *A*'s as if they were *B*'s, and then I shall be right most of the time." That this is not always a reliable rule may be seen if we suppose *A* is the class of human beings accused of a crime and identified by five impartial witnesses, and *B* the class of guilty persons. There are enough cases of mistaken identifications to shake confidence in the rule even here. The safest form to give an inference involving "most cases" is to put it thus:

Most *A*'s are *B*'s.
This is an *A*.
Therefore, if it is like most *A*'s, it is a *B*.

The conclusion here lacks the categorical form requisite for confident action based on the outcome of the reasoning, but it has the logically useful result of leading one to ask whether there is any obtainable evidence that this *A* is like most *A*'s, and also to consider the question "Suppose this turns out to be an untypical *A*, and I have treated it as if it were typical. What will be the cost of repairing the error as opposed to that of alternative courses of action open to me now?"

Where a numerical estimate of the proportion of *A*'s that are *B*'s is possible, the computational methods of the calculus of probability may be employed. Like all computations the process raises two kinds of questions: Has it been done correctly, and what interpretations may be justifiably placed on the result? Say to any logically unsophisticated person, "I have a coin in my hand and I am going to toss it; what is the probability of its coming down heads?"—you are likely to be told "one half," without his reflecting that the coin may be weighted in some way, or that each of its two faces may show a head, or that it may be tossed in a manner to favor its coming down tails.

Suppose a coin has been tossed 10 times and has come down heads each time. All we can say is that there are 2^{10} or 1024 possible outcomes of such an experiment with a true coin and only one of these gives 10 heads, whereas if it is biased or tossed unfairly, the result is more to be expected. But which of these is the case depends on an examination of the coin and the tosser.

Probable inferences are more reliable when they are made about the cardinal characteristics of a class than when they refer to its ordinal features. To understand this, consider the successive tosses of a coin, *i.e.* the class of its tosses considered ordinally. In particular, consider the next toss. By hypothesis, the outcome will be that the coin will come to rest either with the face showing heads or the face showing tails uppermost. But if we assign a probability to one of these alternatives (*e.g.* if we assert that the probability of the coin coming to rest on the *next* toss with heads uppermost is ½), it is an open question whether we are not simply speaking elliptically about the relative frequency with which the coin shows the head uppermost in a numerous class of tosses, *i.e.* about a property of such a class that does not depend on the *order* in which heads turn up. At any rate success with probable inferences depends on the assumptions that there are classes having subsets with specifiable characteristics, occurring with stable relative frequency in the class, that reliable estimates of these frequencies may be made from samples which may therefore be labeled "representative," and that these frequencies will continue to hold true in the future, or if they change, that allowance can be made for the changes. That these assumptions are held to be justified in many fields, *e.g.* in long sequences of throws with dice, may be evidenced by the fact that when the 19th-cent. Swiss astronomer Wolff obtained results at variance with what theory demanded in 43 years' recording of such throws, the only inference from this that has been thought worth considering is that his dice were biased. The activities of insurance companies are of course based on these assumptions. In the first place, anyone who looks at the small print under official tables of vital statistics will see that these are often based on sampling techniques involving all sorts of assumptions about under-registration and so forth. Secondly, it is assumed that if you take the approximately 4¼ million people who were born in the U. S. A. in 1960, divide them up into 17 groups of ¼ million each, add together the ages at which each of these people dies in each of the 17 groups, then the 17 totals so obtained will be approximately the same. Such assumptions seem to be justified in the absence of war, famine, and epidemic disease, and the figures may be applied to future generations when allowance is made for growth in longevity due to medical advances. We can only mention here, as something deserving of extended consideration, the problem of determining what constitutes a fair sample. This arises in part from the fact that "a random sample" cannot be successfully defined merely negatively, but positive precautions must be taken to insure that bias does not occur in the selection of the sample. Stability of relative frequencies in large assemblages has been found to hold in such widely disparate problems as the number of electrons that will leave a radiating substance in the course of a year, the number of light bulbs that will burn out in a given time from a set manufactured under similar conditions, and the number of sets of families of 5 all-male piglets that will occur in a set of families of 5 piglets each (here only a little over 100 such families were required to show the stability predicted by theory which assumed merely that any one piglet was as likely to be male as female).

It will be evident from this survey that logical principles are generalized principles of criticism. Logical principles do not provide substantive knowledge of the world, and cannot by themselves settle any issue of empirical fact. Their distinctive function is rather to serve as instruments in evaluating claims to knowledge, by clarifying the standards which such claims must meet when we judge them to be warranted. Nevertheless, as Morris R. Cohen has so well said:

"Logic is not a restriction upon the world that reason and observation disclose but an indispensable instrument for the exploration of possibilities, and in this sense an indispensable element of liberal civilization and free thought.

"We are all creatures of circumstance; we are are born into certain social groups and we acquire the beliefs as well as the customs of these groups. Those ideas to which we are accustomed seem to us self-evident when our first reaction against those who do not share our beliefs is to regard them as inferiors or perverts. The only way to overcome this initial dogmatism which is the basis of all fanaticism is by formulating our position in logical form so that we can see that we have taken certain things for granted, and that someone may from a purely logical point of view start with the denial of what we have asserted. Logic thus becomes an instrument for showing us the number of hypotheses other than those which we have taken for granted. The way to make progress in any field of learning is not by resolving to free ourselves of dogmatic assumptions—such resolutions are vain—but by making clear to ourselves what are the various assumptions that are possible, and thus envisaging our position as one of a great number. This widens our sympathetic understanding and breaks the backbone of fanaticism. It makes us humble because it indicates to us that ultimately we cannot prove the truth of our fundamental assumptions, for our fundamental assumptions determine the kind of world which we can perceive and the world of phenomena is wider than that of our knowledge.

"Tolerance, the avoidance of fanaticism, and above all a wider and clearer view of the nature of our beliefs and their necessary consequences, is thus a goal or end which the development of logic serves. In this sense logic is a necessary element of any liberal civilization."—*H. T.*

LOGICAL EMPIRICISM: a contemporary philosophical movement whose participants include many distinguished scientists as well as professional philosophers. As the name suggests, logical empiricism makes a fundamental distinction between the purely logical and the factual expressions composing a language. Logically true (or *analytic*) statements, established by logic and mathematics, constitute "formal science"; factual (or *synthetic*) statements, established in the various branches of empirical inquiry, constitute "empirical science." A further classification of expressions and uses into cognitive (or informational) and non-cognitive (*e.g.* emotive, action-producing) has been developed in some detail. A conspicuous feature of development of logical empiricism has been the rigorous analysis of language and the linguistic structure of science, using the techniques of modern mathematical logic. Thus it has been possible to show clearly just how certain subtle philosophic-scientific problems were in fact generated from equally subtle misuses or confusions of language; and a set of distinctions has been provided for expediting a number of clearly demarcated studies into aspects of the relation of formal to empirical science. As to the latter, studies of the relation of geometry to physics, investigations of theories of probability in empirical science, and the logic of verification

and theory construction have each occupied the attention of logical empiricists.

One suggestive programmatic thesis of earlier logical empiricism is that of "Physicalism" or "Reductionism"; namely, that every descriptive term in the statements of any science is translatable (reducible), by certain logical construction, into terms designating immediately experienced data. All scientific statements are hence, in principle, verifiable by direct observation. While attempts were made to carry out this reduction for physics and parts of psychology (notably by Rudolf Carnap) it soon proved impossible of more than fragmentary success. But the related thesis of the logical unity of the language of science and the systematic articulation and organization of the common conceptual structure of science remains an active goal of logical empiricism.

Logical empiricism is one of the rare instances in history of a cooperative philosophic enterprise, international in membership and interdisciplinary with respect to the sciences. Despite some significant differences of opinion over a number of technical issues, logical empiricists are united in their view of science as the one source of reliable knowledge and by a general program for the advancement and understanding of science. Some of the earlier stages in the evolution of this movement are known as "Vienna Circle," "Logical Positivism," "Unity of Science Movement." The mature statement of logical empiricism and its program is to be found in the *International Encyclopedia of Unified Science.*—*H. S. T.*

LOGICAL POSITIVISM: a philosophical doctrine formulated in the 1920s that was important in the development of the movement known as LOGICAL EMPIRICISM.

LONGEVITY: see LIFE SPAN.

LORENTZ, HENDRIK ANTOON, 1853–1928, Dutch physicist; b. Arnhem. His thesis, *Over de theorie der terugkaasting ·en der breking van het licht* (1875), gave the mathematical deduction of the behavior of light, as indicated in J. C. Maxwell's electromagnetic theory (1873). In 1880 he published his equation relating the refractive index and density of a medium. Further work on Maxwell's theory appeared in Lorentz's

Hendrik Antoon Lorentz
(New York Public Library)

La Théorie électromagnétique de Maxwell et son application aux corps mouvants (1892) and *Versuch einer Theorie der elektrischen und optischen Ersheinungen in bewegten Körpern* (1895). He explained the widening of spectral lines in a magnetic field, observed by Pieter Zeeman, by proposing an electron theory in *The Theory of Electrons* (1905). He and Zeeman shared the Nobel Prize for physics, 1902. Lorentz also forecast the existence of particles smaller than atoms, found by J. J. Thomson in 1897. In response to the MICHELSON-MORLEY EXPERIMENT, Lorentz, along with G. F. Fitzgerald, suggested that measured distance depended on the relative velocity of the observer (see LORENTZ-FITZGERALD CONTRACTION). The LORENTZ TRANSFORMATION formulating the extent of the contraction was part of Lorentz's Special Theory of RELATIVITY. In addition to writing essays on gravitation theory, thermodynamics, radiation, and kinetic theory, *e.g.* "The Einstein Theory of Relativity" (1920), Lorentz contributed important data for the drainage of the Zuider Zee by solving hydrodynamic and hydrostatic engineering problems. He was a fellow of the Royal Society and an associate of the U. S. National Academy of Sciences.—*R. J. F.*

LORENTZ-FITZGERALD CONTRACTION: the contraction in length of a moving body as measured by observers at rest, the contraction being in the direction of motion. The physicists H. A. Lorentz and G. F. Fitzgerald hypothesized this phenomenon in 1892 to explain the negative result of the MICHELSON-MORLEY EXPERIMENT, *i.e.* the failure to detect an absolute motion of Earth. Albert Einstein was the first to grasp the full significance of the contraction in formulating the special theory of RELATIVITY: he suggested that a body in motion is contracted by a factor $\sqrt{1 - v^2/c^2}$ where v is the speed of the body and c is the speed of light. Thus the contraction, too small to observe except in specially designed apparatus (such as Michelson and Morley's interferometer), depends only on the *relative* motion between the measured body and the measuring instrument.—*M. P.*

LORENTZ TRANSFORMATION: a mathematical relation between the space and time coordinates used by two observers in uniform motion relative to each other. H. A. Lorentz used it as a mathematical artifice in electromagnetic researches, but Einstein deduced it from the basic principles of his special theory of RELATIVITY and showed it reflects the physical behavior of space and time. It superseded the Newtonian "Galilean" transformation, in which time and lengths were unaffected by relative motion.—*Ba. H.*

LOUDSPEAKER: a device that converts an electrical signal into an audible sound. Loudspeakers may be classified on the basis of the physical principle employed in making the electrical-to-acoustical conversion, the common types being electrostatic and electrodynamic. All loudspeakers include a means for setting a relatively large amount of air into vibration; the two most common methods are by means of a cone vibrating along its axial direction, and by means of a horn with the conversion mechanism placed at its small end. All loudspeakers perform the conversion efficiently only over a given range of frequencies. Generally a large radiating surface is efficient at the lower frequencies, while small surfaces are efficient at higher frequencies. Thus loudspeaker systems tend to contain two or more units of varying sizes. The low-frequency performance of a loudspeaker can be improved by careful design of its enclosure: the corner of a room can act as a part of the enclosure. (See also SOUND REPRODUCTION.) —*H. M. T.*

LOW: see CYCLONE.

LOWELL, PERCIVAL, 1855–1916, U. S. astronomer and author; b. Boston. In 1894 he founded Lowell Observatory, Flagstaff, Ariz., dedicated to the study of the solar system, in particular the planet Mars. He is best known for his extensive observations of the Martian "network," which he believed to be a planet-wide system of canals constructed by intelligent life on a desiccated planet. From a mathematical analysis of discrepancies in the motion of Uranus, he predicted (1905–15) the existence and position of a trans-Neptunian planet, and as a direct result of this work, the ninth planet, named PLUTO, was found in 1930 at the Lowell Observatory by C. Tombaugh, only 6° from the predicted position. Lowell wrote *Mars* (1895), *The Solar System* (1903), *Mars and Its Canals* (1906), and many other astronomical works.—*G. R.*

LOWER, RICHARD, 1631–91, English physiologist; b. Tremeere, Cornwall. He performed the first blood transfusion (from one dog to another) at Oxford, 1665. His book *Tractatus de corde* (1669) contained important observations on both the anatomy and the physiology of the heart and vascular system. He assisted Thomas Willis in anatomical researches on the nervous system and practiced as a physician in London. He was a fellow of the Royal Society.—*D. H. D. R.*

L-RADIATION: X-RAYS emitted by excited L-electrons.

LUBRICATION: the introduction of oils, fats, greases, and other chemical compounds between moving machine parts to reduce friction and wear. Even the most carefully finished metallic surfaces are covered with minute projections and depressions, which tend to resist the movement of one surface over the other. Application of a lubricant to these surfaces reduces friction by interposing a single film of oil between the surfaces (*hydrodynamic or fluid lubrication*).

In a journal bearing, the rotation of the journal draws the oil between it and the bearing so that the two metal surfaces are separated by a very thin film of oil, the degree of friction depending on the viscosity of the oil, speed of rotation, and load on the journal. If the journal starts rotating after a period of rest, it may not drag in enough oil to float the surfaces apart; friction will be considerably greater, independent of the viscosity of the lubricant and related only to the load and to the property of the residual lubricant "oiliness," *i.e.* capacity to stick tightly to metal surfaces. This condition of "boundary lubrication," in which the moving parts are separated by a film of only molecular thickness, may cause serious harm to the overheated bearing surfaces; hence machines are designed so that lubrication occurs practically always under fluid conditions. If it is not possible to make bearings of softer metals to avoid damage to the more expensive journal should normal lubrication fail, certain "extreme-pressure" additives are dissolved in the lubricant to form a protective film at hot spots and prevent seizure and surface damage.

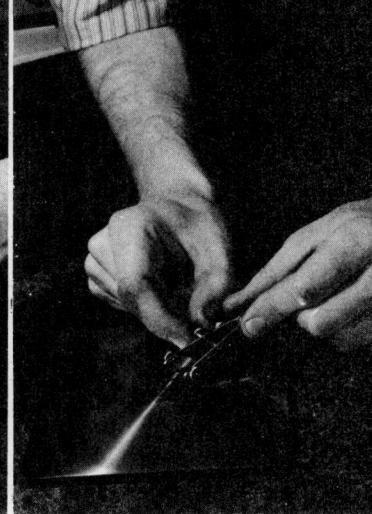

Spreading test for instrument oil: A calibrated pipette syringe is used (*left*) to draw a measured quantity of specially refined oil, a drop of which is then allowed to fall on a highly polished steel plate (*right*). Then the diameter of the drop as it spreads is measured with micrometer calipers at regular intervals over a period of several days. The results are carefully tabulated and interpreted to determine the spreading properties of this particular grade of oil. (*Standard Oil Co.*)

The two most significant characteristics of a hydrodynamic lubricant are its viscosity and its viscosity index, *i.e.* the relationship between the lubricant viscosity and temperature. The higher the index, the less the viscosity will change with temperature. In certain cases, one purpose of lubrication is to remove heat that is developed within machinery; this is done by gear-box oils and cutting oils. A film of lubricant on a surface will also serve as protection against moist air and corrosion (*e.g.* textile oils to prevent rusting of knitting needles; also, ball and roller bearings).

Before the advent of modern high-speed machinery, animal or vegetable fatty oils met the modest lubrication demands made on them. Now the petroleum industry is able to deliver good mineral lubricants which do not easily become acid and rancid. *Compounded oils* (mineral oils containing rape oil or fish oils) are still used when ready emulsification with water is wanted (*e.g.* steam cylinder oils under wet conditions, textile oils for scouring purposes). The older semisolid and solid fats have been displaced by greases where the parts to be lubricated are difficult to get at or inadequately sealed, or where a liquid lubricant might contaminate the product processed. The severe and widely differing conditions under which modern machinery operates can be met in general only by mineral oils or specially tailored synthetic chemicals. Plain bearings work properly with a fairly low viscosity lubricant and so do most ball bearings, but roller bearings and gears often require special extreme-pressure lubricants or greases because of high speeds and loads. For lubricating *steam cylinders*, compounded oils are used with wet steam, but such oils are unsuitable for superheated steam. For all cylinder lubrication, highly volatile oils should be avoided. Demands are even more stringent for *turbine oils*, which must be highly refined, with good demulsifying, anti-rusting, anti-oxidant properties. Oils used for the heavily loaded reduction gears of turbines contain special additives. For lubricating the cylinders of *compressors*, oils of high stability are used to avoid formation of gummy deposits. *Refrigerator oils* must be refined to avoid reaction with the coolant.

In the textile industry, lubrication is employed to prevent rusting and corrosion. In parts of the machinery there is the danger that the oil might soil the fabric processed; hence highly refined oils which will not thicken are indicated. Compounded oils, which can be removed by subsequent scouring, are used for moving parts that are in proximity to the yarn. Sometimes oils are used to lubricate certain textile fibers, *e.g.* wool or certain synthetic fibers, which would otherwise break. Special *cutting oils* are made for machining of metals, where in addition to cooling and lubrication they wash away metal chips.—*R. J. F.*

LUDWIG, KARL FRIEDRICH WILHELM, 1816–95, German physiologist; b. Hessen. His early research was on the functions of the "vegetative" organs in animals. He introduced the graphic method of recording with his kymograph (1847), an improvement on J. L. M. Poiseuille's hemodynamometer. He discovered the nervous excitation of the submaxillary glands (1851), and found that stimulation of the sympathetic system would make those glands secrete (1856). Ludwig taught at Leipzig and acquired extraordinary fame as a teacher. He was an associate of the U. S. National Academy of Sciences. —*D. H. D. R.*

LUMINESCENCE: the emission of light in the visible or near-visible regions of the spectrum as a result of the absorption of energy by matter. (This does not include emission from an entire body or its surface due to a high temperature; such emission is called *incandescence*.) Emission is called *photo-*

luminescence if the exciting energy is in the form of light (electromagnetic radiation), *cathodoluminescence* if it is a beam of electrons, *electroluminescence* if it is electrical, *thermoluminescence* if it is heat, *triboluminescence* if it is mechanical strain, *chemiluminescence* if it is a chemical reaction, *bioluminescence* if it is a biological process (as in the firefly). Some forms of emission are familiar in applications important in everyday life, *e.g.* photoluminescence in the fluorescent lamp, cathodoluminescence in the cathode-ray tube and television picture tube. If the emission occurs during excitation or immediately afterward, the process is commonly called *fluorescence*. Emission that occurs after this time is called *phosphorescence* or *afterglow*. Many common minerals display phosphorescence, which may last for weeks.

Luminescent mushrooms: Mushrooms of the species *Mycena luxcoeli* are shown photographed in natural light (*upper*) and in the dim light (*lower*) that they give off as part of the energy released during aerobic respiration. (*Haneda*)

Luminescence occurs in gases, liquids, and solids. Simplest to understand is luminescence of a gas at low pressure. The exciting energy, which may come from light, an electron beam, or passage of an electric current through the gas, raises atoms or molecules of the gas to higher ENERGY LEVELS; emission of radiation occurs as particles fall back to lower levels. Since atoms and molecules can have only certain discrete energies, these processes can occur only by "jumps." For each jump, the emitted radiation has a frequency given by the energy jump divided by Planck's constant (see PLANCK'S LAW). The luminescent emission thus consists of a spectrum of narrow lines.

In liquids and solids, essentially the same process occurs. Because of stronger interactions between neighboring atoms, however, the system of energy levels is more complex, and the emission spectrum may consist of very broad lines rather than narrow ones. Very few solid materials are luminescent in the pure state. The efficiency of luminescence is found to increase very strongly when certain impurities, called *activators,* are present.—*E. M. C.*

LUNAR DAY: the interval of time between two consecutive transits of the Moon across an observer's celestial meridian, analogous to the solar day interval between consecutive middays. Because the Moon revolves in its orbit about Earth in the same direction as the rotation of Earth on its axis (west to east), the Moon appears to move eastward among the stars, and the lunar day is (on average) 50 min longer than the mean solar day; it is variable in length because the Moon's orbit is elliptical and is inclined to Earth's equator. The term "lunar day" might also be used for the length of a "day" on the Moon itself, which would be, on the average, 29½ mean solar days.—*M. W. O.*

LUNAR ECLIPSE: see ECLIPSE.

LUNG: an organ of RESPIRATION. Respiration in air requires a thin, moist membrane through which oxygen and carbon dioxide can be exchanged with the blood. In most land animals, two such membranes line a pair of saclike structures, the lungs, within a body cavity. In small or inactive animals (*e.g.* snails, slugs, scorpions), the lungs are simple sacs or sheets of thin tissue well provided with blood vessels, but with no provision for active movement of air into and out of the lungs. In larger and more active animals, BREATHING movements draw or force air into and out of the lungs. This ventilation greatly increases the gaseous exchange, which is aided also by a large lung surface area and by a good blood supply. Lungs of vertebrates are believed to have evolved from a structure somewhat resembling the swim-bladder of certain fishes. In some fishes the swim-bladder opens to the exterior through a duct, and in the lungfishes the bladder is modified to form a true functional lung. In all higher vertebrates, the lungs communicate with the exterior through a single trachea leading from the mouth. The trachea divides into two bronchi at the entrance to the lungs, and each bronchus branches into bronchioles within a lung. All these tubes are stiffened with cartilage and lined with microscopic, hairlike CILIA.

Lungs of mammals, and of certain other vertebrates, are divided into lobules. Each bronchiole terminates in a series of small branches, the respiratory bronchioles, from which open a number of small air sacs, arranged somewhat like a bunch of grapes on a stem. The walls of the air sacs, in turn, are folded into many tiny pouches, the alveoli; this arrangement greatly increases the surface area of the lung. The lining of the lung lobule, unlike that of the bronchioles, consists of

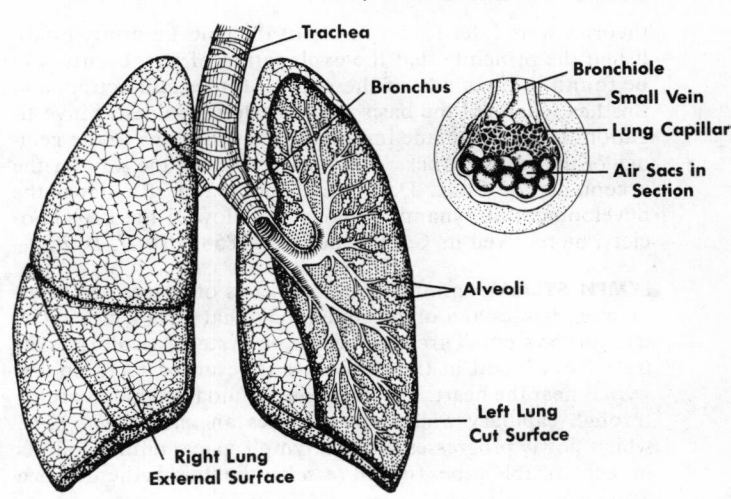

Human lungs with cutaway of surface of left lung showing bronchioles and alveoli. Small circle (*upper right*) is magnified section of air sacs and capillary lining of lobule where oxygen is added to blood and carbon dioxide removed.

a very thin cellular membrane, in which run the capillaries of the pulmonary circulation. Gas exchange occurs through the lining of the lobule directly with the blood of the capillary.

The total lung capacity of a man is about 6 qt. At the end of a normal passive expiration, the lungs contain about 2½ qt of air. An additional quart can be expelled by forced expiration, leaving 1½ qt which cannot be expelled from the lungs. Vital capacity, the maximum amount of air that can be taken into the lungs after a forced expiration, amounts to about 4½ qt in a typical man. Vital capacity depends on body size, and is relatively lower in women, and higher in trained athletes, than in a typical man.

Lungs of birds have a unique arrangement of large air sacs connected with the lungs. About three-fourths of the air taken in during breathing passes through the lungs and into the air sacs, thus flushing the lungs completely at each respiration and greatly increasing the efficiency of gas exchange.—*B. T. S.*

LUTETIUM: a lanthanide (rare-earth metal) element (Lu); at. no. 71; at. wt 174.99. The metal was discovered when G. Urbain (1906) and Carl Auer von Welsbach (1907) realized independently that "pure" ytterbium contained yet another elemental substance, lutetium. Of little practical use, lutetium can be separated from other lanthanides by fractional crystallization of lutetium bromate. See LANTHANIDES; RARE EARTHS. —*G. W. M.*

LYELL, SIR CHARLES, 1797–1875, English geologist; b. Kinnordy, Forfarshire, Scotland; ed. Exeter Coll., Oxford. His *Principles of Geology* (1830–33), which went through 12 editions in his lifetime and is probably the most influential book on geology ever written, revived the uniformitarian doctrines of James Hutton and vigorously attacked the catastrophic school of geology (see GEOLOGY). Although some of Lyell's

Sir Charles Lyell
(*New York Public Library*)

theories were later found to be insufficient, he firmly established the principle that the explanation of past events is to be found in the study of the natural forces still acting, and this has remained the basis of all modern geological investigation. Lyell also made important contributions to the geology of the Tertiary rocks. His works prepared the way for the acceptance of C. R. Darwin's theories and stimulated the development of dynamic geology. A fellow of the Royal Society, he received its Copley medal in 1858.—*D. H. D. R.*

LYMPH SYSTEM: an interconnected series of spaces and tubes between tissues and organs in animals that have a closed circulatory system. Through the lymph system, a colorless filtrate from blood in the capillaries is returned to the blood vessels near the heart. The filtration of fluid from blood occurs through capillary walls, and provides an *intercellular fluid,* which slowly progresses through lymph spaces until it collects in recognizable tubes (*lymph vessels*); the fluid is then known as *lymph.*

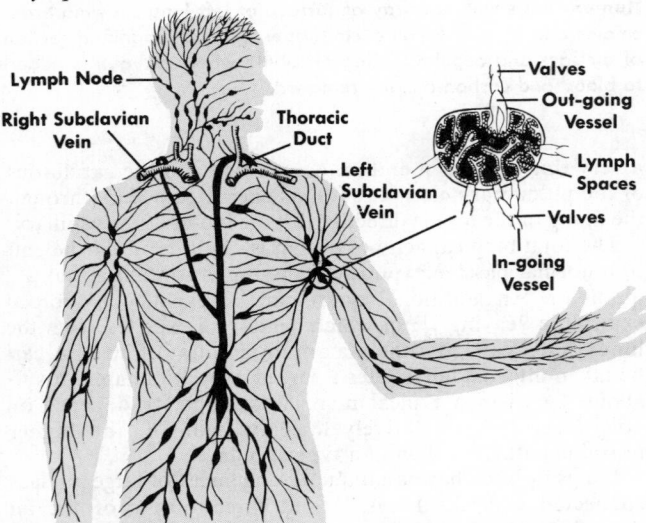

Lymph system returns tissue fluids from all parts of the body to the blood. Flow is from network of small tubes into larger vessels that converge in main thoracic ducts draining into subclavian veins. Lymph nodes (*cross-section, right*) are found at intervals in large channels. (*Biological Sciences Curriculum Study*)

The intercellular fluid serves as an intermediary between blood and cells bathed by the intercellular fluid. Materials move between the blood and the intercellular fluid through capillary walls, and between intercellular fluid and tissue cells through the cell membranes. Capillary walls permit free passage to all constituents of blood except proteins and formed elements such as cells. Blood in the capillaries is under pressure, and this tends to force fluid out through the relatively porous capillary walls. There is an opposing force, however, in the osmotic effect of blood proteins, which tends to pull water into the blood from the relatively protein-free intercellular fluid. Normally these two forces are approximately balanced, but variations in pressure in the capillaries, permeability of capillary walls, or protein content of blood will influence the rate of formation of intercellular fluid. Excessive formation of fluid in pathological conditions leads to a swelling of tissues known as edema (dropsy). The volume of lymph in normal individuals is not exactly known, but is probably somewhat less than that of blood; the volume of intercellular fluid is about three times that of blood. Lymph has about half as much protein as blood plasma, somewhat more organic material, and less salt.

The vessels in which lymph first appears form a network of small tubes much like capillaries, but with closed ends. These tubes converge to form progressively larger lymph vessels, which in turn converge to form two main trunks draining the lymph into the subclavian veins, where it mixes with the blood. The larger lymphatic vessels resemble veins in structure, and like the larger veins have valves which prevent flow away from the heart. The flow of lymph into the blood is small and irregular. In man, it amounts to about 1 cc per minute, compared with a blood flow through the heart of about 4 liters per minute, or 4,000 times as great. Flow from particular regions, *e.g.* intestine or limbs, is increased during activity of the regions, but it is not clear to what extent this is due to increased lymph formation and to what extent to the effects of muscular contractions in returning the lymph more rapidly. Flow of lymph in frogs is accelerated by special lymph hearts.

At intervals, larger lymph vessels are interrupted by lymph glands or nodes. In these, lymph flows through a meshwork of special lymphoid tissue which has three major functions: removal of bacteria from lymph, formation of lymphocytes, and formation of gamma globulin. Cells of lymphoid tissue have the ability to ingest and destroy bacteria, and in infections the lymph nodes become enlarged as this activity is increased. Lymphocytes, an important class of white blood cells, are formed in lymph nodes and enter the blood with lymph. Production of these cells at a rate of 2,000,000 per hour has been observed in a dog. The lymphocytes contain gamma globulin, which is the protein fraction of blood containing antibodies, part of the mechanism of resistance against infectious disease. These antibodies are formed, in part at least, in lymph nodes. Lymphoid tissue also occurs in the spleen and in mucous membranes of the alimentary canal.

Lymph vessels were first observed in early experiments on digestion: when animals were fed fatty foods, vessels filled with a milky fluid (now known as chyle) appeared in the intestinal region. About 60% of the fat absorbed from the intestine is absorbed directly into the lymph system, without previous digestion, in the form of tiny fat droplets, and reaches the blood through the lymph flow.—*B. T. S.*

LYNEN, FEODOR FELIX KONRAD, 1911–   , German biochemist; b. Munich. His research has included studies of fermentation, coenzyme A, the fatty acid cycle and enzymes of fatty acid metabolism, the coupling of phosphorylation to oxidation, the regulation of metabolic rates, and the citric-acid cycle. For work on mechanisms and regulation of cholesterol and fatty-acid metabolism he shared the 1964 Nobel prize in physiology and medicine with K. E. Bloch. He is an associate of the U. S. National Academy of Sciences.—*D. H. D. R.*

LYOPHILIZATION: freeze-drying, a preservation technique used in biological experimentation and for storage of such substances as antibiotics, serum, hormones, and plasma. The material to be preserved is frozen; the solvent (usually water) is removed by sublimation under high vacuum; the material is taken from the frozen to the dry state directly. Material thus preserved retains its characteristics for a long period.—*F. F.*

LYOT, BERNARD FERDINAND, 1897–1952, French astronomer; b. Paris. He invented the coronagraph, which makes possible the study of the solar corona and prominences at times other than during a solar eclipse, and developed monochromatic filters that permit passage of light from a small portion of the spectrum. Using the coronagraph with filters, he greatly extended the knowledge of the corona. He also studied polarization of light reflected from planets. He was an associate of the U. S. National Academy of Sciences.—*D. H. D. R.*

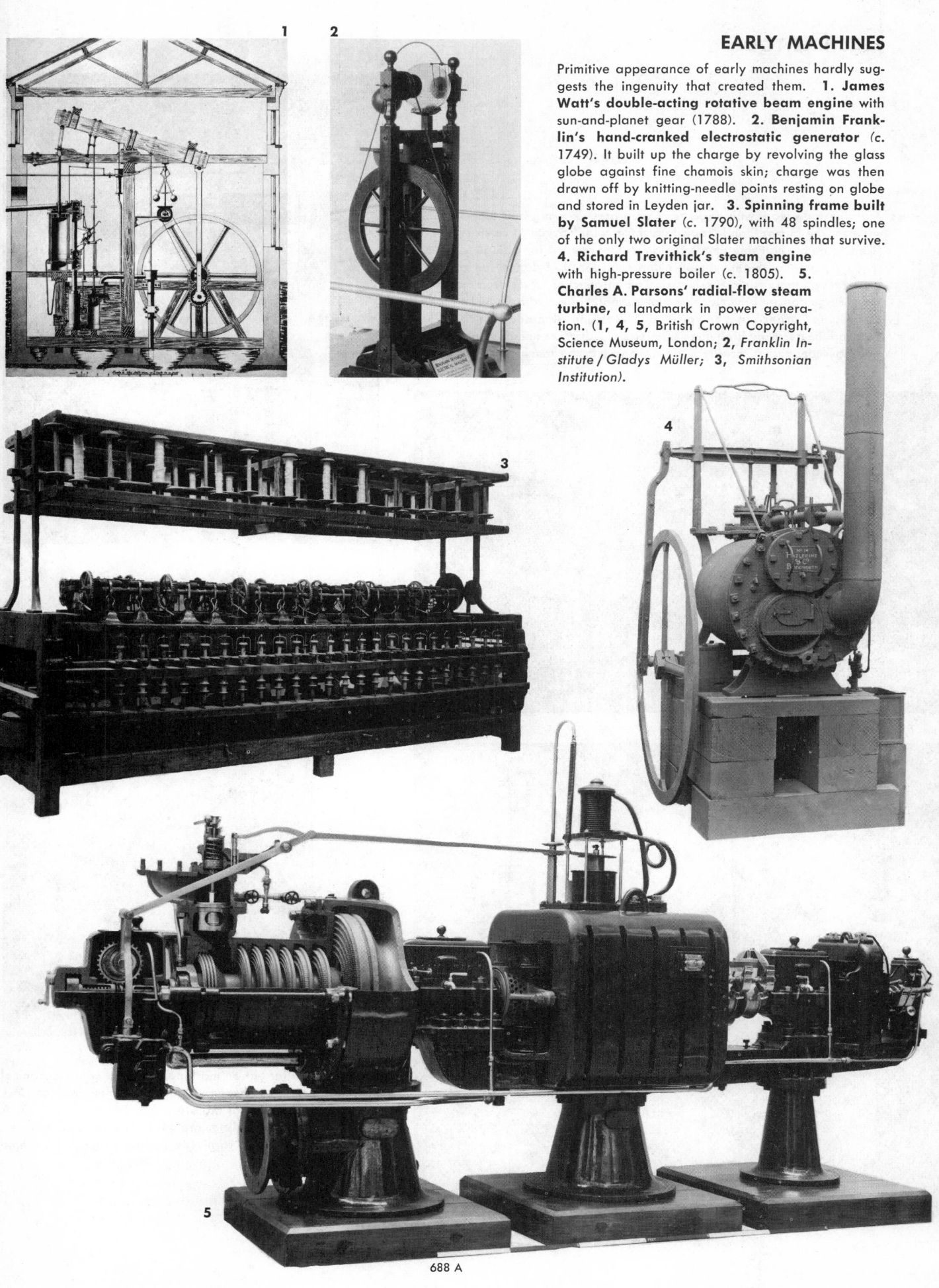

EARLY MACHINES

Primitive appearance of early machines hardly suggests the ingenuity that created them. **1. James Watt's double-acting rotative beam engine** with sun-and-planet gear (1788). **2. Benjamin Franklin's hand-cranked electrostatic generator** (c. 1749). It built up the charge by revolving the glass globe against fine chamois skin; charge was then drawn off by knitting-needle points resting on globe and stored in Leyden jar. **3. Spinning frame built by Samuel Slater** (c. 1790), with 48 spindles; one of the only two original Slater machines that survive. **4. Richard Trevithick's steam engine** with high-pressure boiler (c. 1805). **5. Charles A. Parsons' radial-flow steam turbine**, a landmark in power generation. (1, 4, 5, British Crown Copyright, Science Museum, London; 2, *Franklin Institute / Gladys Müller*; 3, *Smithsonian Institution*).

MACHINE TOOLS

Machine tools work with degrees of accuracy, strength, and speed impossible for the human hand. Tools used for a wide variety of operations are likely to be of relatively simple design. A tool needed for a single complex task may itself be highly complex and specialized in design but compensate through more rapid production. The introduction of electronic control, in which guidance of the machine tool is usually provided by punched tape, has resulted in increases in speed and precision of production, and has reduced the necessity for human supervision. Advances in industrial production have depended directly upon advances in the machine-tool industry.

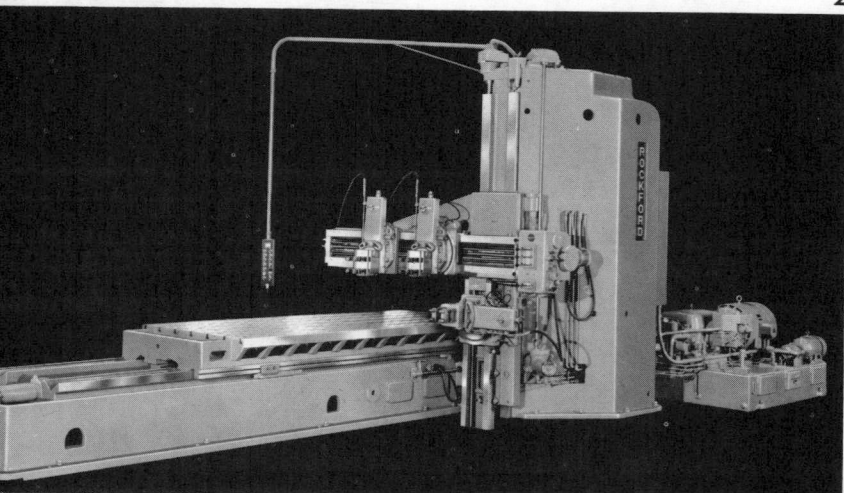

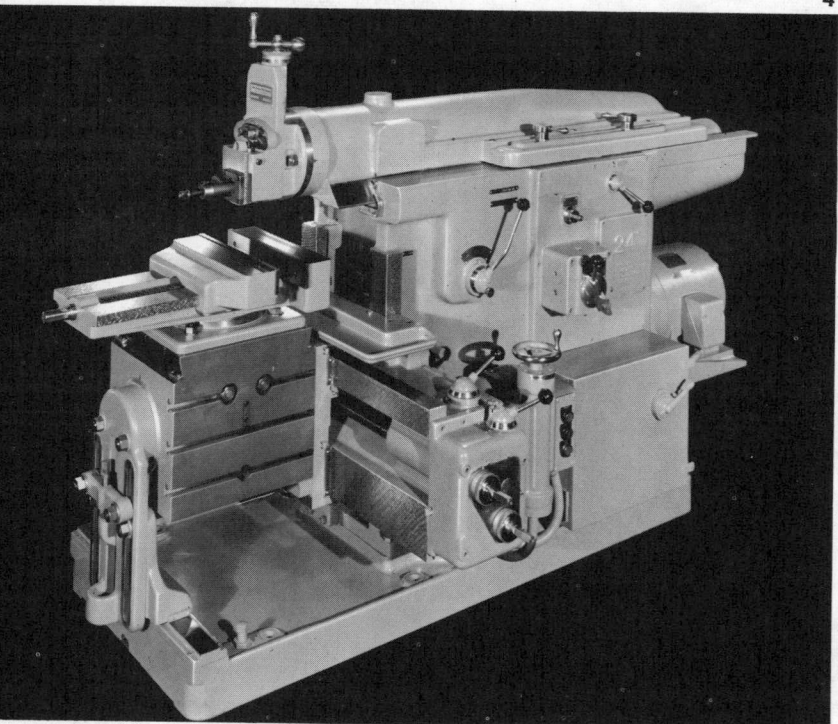

1. **Workpiece** (at left on machine) is drilled with mechanical guidance given by the jig *(National Automatic Tool Co.)*. 2. **An open-side planer** *(Rockford Machine Tool Co.)*. 3. **A cutter and tool-grinding machine** *(Brown and Sharpe)*. 4. **A hydraulic 24-in. ram-type shaper** *(Rockford Machine Tool Co.)*.

5   6

5. 1,000-ton press achieves pressures up to 100,000 atmospheres (1.6 million lb./in.) (*General Electric Research Lab.*).
6. Tape-controlled milling and drilling machine, used in production of high-voltage breakers, can select and automatically change any of a set of 961 differently coded tools (*Westinghouse*).

8

7

7. A 60-in. hydraulic slotter with workpiece in position (*Rockford Machine Tool Co.*).   **8. Turret drilling machine,** guided by tape inserted in control unit by operator (*Brown and Sharpe*).

MACHINE TOOLS—Continued

9. Drill guided by instructions from punched tape drills holes exactly in desired locations without use of any jig *(Pratt & Whitney)*. **10. Artist uses a simple machine tool**—a copper wheel and an abrasive—to impose delicate intaglios on glass *(Corning Glass Center)*. **11. Flame-hardening process** is applied to gear teeth *(Air Reduction Sales Co.)*. **12. Gear teeth** must be cut with high precision *(Brown and Sharpe)*. **13. 50,000-ton closed-die forging press** forms a titanium elliptical dome *(Wyman-Gordon Co.)*.

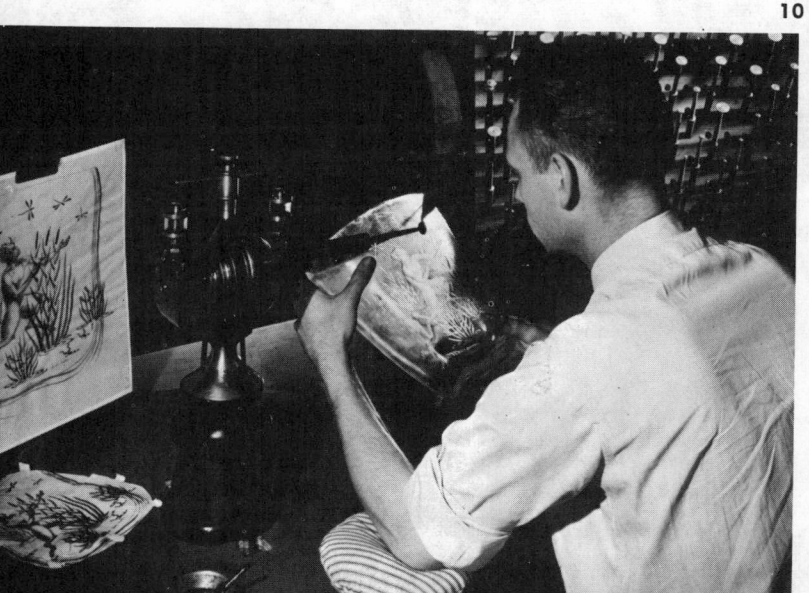

Mass wasting is the downward movement of earth due to the action of gravity. **1. "Creep"** of soil and rock near ground surface is evidenced by bending of shale strata *(Schultz, U.S. Geol. Survey)*. **2. Landslide** triggered by earthquake blocked Madison River, West Yellowstone, Mont., forming a lake *(Stacy, U.S. Geol. Survey)*. **3.** *Talus* at foot of cliffs in Snowy Range, Mont., consists of fallen rock fragments that were detached by weathering *(Union Pacific RR)*. **4. "Talus glacier,"** Silver Basin, Colo., is a mass of rock fragments that became waterlogged and frozen, and flowed downslope *(Cross, U.S. Geol. Survey)*. **5. Slides** on steep wooded mountainsides, as here in New York's Adirondacks, are expanses of bedrock exposed by slippage or slow flow of mantle (soil cover) *(Jerome Wyckoff)*.

The solid state: Long before germanium had been isolated, Mendeleev had with eerie accuracy predicted its atomic weight, its specific gravity, and the properties of its salts. What he could not have anticipated, 90 years ago, was its properties as a semi-conductor. With the advent of solid-state physics and of its most successful offspring, the transistor, germanium crystals with highly controlled traces of impurity have come to play a key role in communications and control. This photomicrograph of a thermally etched crystal of germanium (X1,100) reveals a winding spiral in the central etch pit indicating a screw dislocation. (*MIT Lincoln Laboratory.*)

M

MACADAM: a type of gravel road developed about 1815 by John L. McADAM, English contractor; it was the first substantial improvement in roadbuilding since Roman times. After removal of topsoil, 7 to 10 in. of crushed stone is placed on the dirt foundation. After compaction, usually by traffic, an additional 1-in. layer of finely crushed stone and stone dust, crowned to shed water, is added. This is compacted by traffic into a hard, durable surface. Although excellent for light traffic, the macadam road is dusty in dry weather. Today, macadam generally refers to a gravel surface bound by a bitumen such as asphalt.—*A. L.*

MACH, ERNST, 1838–1916, Austrian physicist and philosopher; b. Turas, Moravia. His writings influenced subsequent developments in physics and psychology as well as philosophy. In his most famous book, *The Science of Mechanics: A Critical and Historical Account of Its Development* (1st ed. 1883; 7th ed. 1912), he sought to show that the laws of mechanics are not a priori truths but are grounded in the common experience of mankind; and he also argued that concepts which he regarded as unverifiable by observation and hence as metaphysical (*e.g.* the Newtonian conceptions of absolute space and absolute time) have no legitimate place in physical science. Mach's critique of Newtonian mechanics was acknowledged by Einstein to have influenced his own researches on the theory of relativity. In his *Analysis of Sensations* (1885) Mach formulated systematically his philosophy of positivistic empiricism, maintaining that all our ideas are definable in terms of elementary data of sensation, which he held to be neither physical nor mental but neutral to this distinction. By thus denying that body and mind are two distinct substances Mach initiated the philosophy subsequently known as "neutral monism"; and his psychological analyses in this book also suggested some of the key notions of Gestalt psychology. In recognition of his pioneering studies on the motion of bodies in wind tunnels, the ratio of the speed of a body to the speed of sound in undisturbed air, important in the theory of flight, is called the MACH NUMBER.—*E. N.*

MACHINE ELEMENTS: the components that make up a machine or mechanical device, including both structural members used to position or support and members used to transfer motion and energy. Design or operation of any machine or device can be analyzed in terms of its elements. A machine's structural members are categorized according to the load they carry. Thus a *compressive member* is one that carries compression loads (*i.e.* compressive stresses). A *column* carries a compressive load; its length is much greater than its cross-section. A *beam* carries a load in such a way as to develop both compressive and tensile stresses; a *tension member* carries a load in such a way that only tension stresses are developed. Members used to transmit energy or motion are gears, cams, inclined planes, belts, levers, and wheels. Each of these elements may also carry any of the types of load described.—*F. P.*

MACHINE TOOL: an engine-powered device, other than a simple HAND TOOL, designed to perform an essential step or steps in transforming unshaped or unfinished material (usually metal) into a structural or mechanical part, a mechanical device, or some other product (*e.g.* a metal bowl). The principal types of machine tools are lathes, milling machines, shears and presses, planers and shapers, drilling and boring machines, and grinders. Although no precise distinction can be made between the more complex hand tools (*e.g.* a portable electric drill) and the simpler machine tools, certain characteristics of appearance, operation, and performance tend to distinguish one group from the other. A machine tool is generally stationary (though it may be attached to a movable carriage); it is usually larger and more complex than a hand tool; its operation is continuous and repetitive and requires the use of power other than human or animal muscle power. In terms of output of a specified item, a machine tool (though it allows for few of the creative embellishments of the craftsman) far surpasses a workman using hand tools, with a generally higher over-all conformity to specified standards. Machines specially designed to produce identical parts in quantities (mass production) are termed *production machine tools.* Examples are automatic lathes, turret lathes, screw machines, gear-cutting machines, threading machines, multiple-spindle drill presses, broaches, and punch presses. All machine tools can be divided into three categories: (1) those that shape material by deforming it; (2) those that shape material while it is in a molten state; and (3) those that remove some of the material in order to produce a desired shape (cutting or chip-removal type).

Machine Tools Utilizing Deformation: Application of a force to a material in order to cause plastic deformation usually affects the internal structure of the material (especially of metals), but both the surface appearance of the material and its general volume and weight remain unchanged, *i.e.* the material is neither added to nor reduced by the operation. *Shearing* by the use of pressure is deformation carried to the point of severing the material. The amount of deformation

Engine parts are bored to .0001 accuracy on a production basis with this numeric jig borer. Data on perforated tape automatically provide precision locating, boring, and checking. (*Pratt & Whitney*)

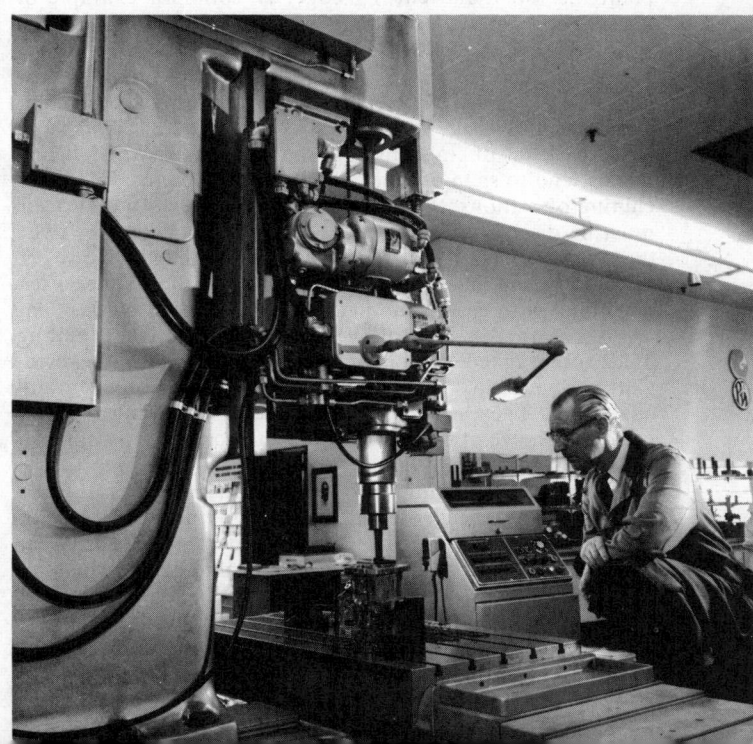

and the temperature at which the operation takes place determine the characteristics of metal products (see METALLURGY). Cold deformation, e.g. cold-rolling of steel sections, leaves the metal harder but less ductile; metal so treated is called work-hardened. Where work-hardened metal is not desired, deformation may be carried out at higher temperatures. The simplest machine-tool forming operation is one that bends the material. A more advanced shaping operation is one in which deformation takes place along a curved line or over a surface, e.g. the shaping necessary to produce a metal bowl or a shell casing. In this case, the material is originally a flat blank which is then shaped by a press into its final form. The actual shaping is done in a DIE, which is actuated by a *press* (see EXTRUSION). New techniques use the energy of an explosive to form the part. A whole range of articles, e.g. sheet steel, sheet plastic, automobile bodies, shell casings, and file cabinets, are made by deformation-producing machine tools.

Machine Tools Using Molten Material: In this type of operation the material is formed by forcing it in its liquid or molten state into a *mold*, i.e. a cavity in the shape of the required part or article. The operation is termed *casting*, and the object formed is also called a casting. In the casting of metals, the mold is often made of sand (the box holding the sand being called a *flask*). However, when a great number of castings is to be made, it is economical to construct a metal mold. Castings made from metal molds (die castings) are produced in machines that hold a quantity of the molten metal and automatically inject it under pressure into the mold. A modification of the molding operation is *sintering*, in which powdered metals are placed in a mold and subjected to pressure and usually to high temperatures. Sintered carbide cutting tools are in wide use in the machining of metals from brass and bronze to stainless steels. Objects formed by casting range from precision castings used for jewelry and dental purposes to rough castings used for cast-iron pipe. WELDING and brazing techniques also are considered to be included in this category.

Machine Tools for Cutting or Chip Removal: All chip-removal machine tools utilize the relative motion of the workpiece and the cutting tool to remove excess metal until the workpiece reaches the desired dimensions. In these operations the workpiece can be moved and the tool kept stationary, or vice versa. The cutting tool may have a single point, i.e. only one cutting edge. A common example of a multiple-point cutting tool is the rotary sawblade used in a power saw. Because of the great forces needed to cut metal, the chip (or ribbon) of material should be cut away continuously, since the greatest force is required at the commencement of a cut. Ductile metals machined at high speeds tend to shear off in continuous, ribbon-like strips; brittle metals tend to snap off in small, undistorted chips. In all machining operations, the heat generated in the cutting process must be dissipated, since excessive heat may warp or twist the workpiece and dull the tool's cutting edge. (However, metals that are machined with difficulty when cold are often machined with ease when heated; this is called *hot machining*.) To carry off heat as well as chip material, a cutting fluid, often called a lubricant or a coolant, must be used. Cutting fluids may be air jets, water, emulsions of water and oil, or oil. They usually incorporate rust inhibitors. Very often the choice of cutting fluid depends on the type of finish to be preserved. See LUBRICATION.

The choice of cutting tool depends on the material to be machined, the speed of machining, and the depth of cut. Carbon tool-steel is used for low-speed work on easily cut metals; high-speed steels (tungsten, chromium, and vanadium alloys) are used for machining harder steels; and stellite

tools (mainly cobalt, tungsten, and chromium alloys) resist abrasion and are used for extremely high-speed cutting. Sintered-carbide tools are used on materials ranging from brass to stainless steels, and have, of all types, perhaps the widest application as cutting tools. Where the above-mentioned materials are inadequate, diamonds are often used.

The most characteristic chip-removal machine tool is the *engine lathe,* which is used to produce either cylindrical surfaces or plane surfaces. For cylindrical surfaces the workpiece is rotated about its axis while a single-point cutting tool is advanced parallel to the rotating axis of the workpiece. If a plane surface is desired, the cutting tool is advanced perpendicularly to the workpiece's rotating axis. *Turret lathes* are engine lathes on which are mounted turrets having as many as six different tool positions. For example, turret lathes are equipped to cut, drill, ream, and tap in a sequence of successive operations. A very common use of the turret lathe is the production of screw material on bar stock.

In *drilling machines,* the workpiece is held stationary and a rotating drill is advanced into the workpiece to form a cylindrical hole. Single-spindle drills use only one drill; radial drills allow the drill to be moved horizontally over the surface of the workpiece before being advanced vertically. Multiple-spindle drills, or gang drills, are used to drill a number of holes simultaneously. Drilling machines are also used to ream, to tap (i.e. make threads on the interior walls of a hole), and to broach (i.e. to finish the surfaces of the interior walls of a hole). See DRILLING AND BORING.

Planers are machine tools designed to produce plane (flat) surfaces by the reciprocating straight-line movement of the workpiece against a stationary single-point cutting tool. With suitable adjustments, many planers will machine a slightly curved surface. *Shapers* are machine tools which are moved while the workpiece remains stationary. Shapers using multi-point tools are called *milling machines;* such shapers are often used to machine gears. *Grinding machines* use abrasives bonded together in the form of a wheel to remove stock, i.e. unwanted portions of the workpiece. The use of finer abrasives, e.g. flours affixed to leather or fabric wheels, is termed *polishing*.

The machining of wood and plastics, although essentially the same as the machining of metals, calls for variations in the choice of tool shapes, tool materials, and cutting speeds. For purposes of machining, most plastics are considered the equivalent of brass. The abrasiveness of glue-bonded lumber (e.g. wood laminates and plywood) calls for the increased use of stellite and sintered-carbide tools.—A. L.; F. P.

History: The machine tool could not come into being until practicable engines to drive it began to be developed in the late 18th cent. However, before this time many kinds of metalworking devices existed that were capable of quantity production with some degree of product uniformity, although such devices were powered solely by workmen or draft animals. Of the several types of machine tools, the lathe can be considered the historical prototype. A pole-driven lathe appears in one of Leonardo da Vinci's sketches in the 16th cent.; this and other machine designs proved readily adaptable to engine-drives. Also, the influence of ancient woodworking tools and techniques as well as the machinery associated with textile manufacture—both in many respects much mechanized at the close of the 18th cent.— cannot be ignored. (See also AGRICULTURAL TOOLS AND MACHINES; CLOCKS AND WATCHES; PRIMITIVE TECHNOLOGY.) Finally, in the 18th and first years of the 19th cent., much attention was devoted to the problem of producing metal mechanical and structural parts to accurate dimensions, a notable effort in this direction being the screw-cutting lathe of the Englishman

Henry Maudslay (1771–1831). Against this background of manufacturing technology, high-quality iron, steel, and other metals began to be produced in unprecedented quantities because of advances in extraction and refining techniques. (See METALLURGY; MINING.) It was thus inevitable that once prime movers (*e.g.* hydraulic and steam engines) became available, the machine tool would rapidly become a key force in bringing about the social, economic, and manufacturing changes collectively known as the Industrial Revolution. With machine tools, it became possible to produce great numbers of identical metal parts, from which more complex machines and devices could be assembled with a minimum of handwork. In turn, this standardization of manufacture meant that machine-made parts could be used interchangeably—that any part "A" designed for a certain role in machine "B" would always be available rather than having to be specially fashioned at great expense of time and money if an old part "A" wore out or broke, or if a new machine "B" was being built. Thus the machine tool, making possible the production of interchangeable parts in almost unlimited quantities, led to modern manufacturing methods—mass production and the assembly line. The first successful quantity production of interchangeable metal parts utilizing engine-powered machinery was an American development. In 1798, Eli Whitney proposed to make some 15,000 muskets for the U. S. government by mass-production and assembly-line techniques; included in Whitney's plans were water-powered machine tools for "forging, rolling, floating, boring, grinding, polishing, etc." Whitney's mill at Whitneyville, Conn., went into operation in 1800, and the practicability of his methods was soon demonstrated to the U. S. Secretary of War when Whitney assembled ten muskets from parts he had picked at random from each of many separate heaps of identical parts produced by his machine tools. Other early 18th-cent. American machine-tool pioneers were the pistol-makers Simeon North and Samuel Colt, and the clockmakers Eli Terry and Chauncey Jerome. By about 1835, modern methods of mass production by power machinery were established in general outline, although many refinements were yet to be made. A continuing trend has been the design of increasingly automatic machine tools, *e.g.* turret lathes, which can perform a number of distinct machining operations without being guided by a machinist (see AUTOMATION). Today, almost any given type of machine or construction or manufacturing equipment is built up from parts produced by machine tools, including the parts of the machine tools themselves; this has suggested the definition of machine tools as "machines that make other machines."—*E. H. H.*

MACH NUMBER, ANGLE, AND WAVE: Mach number (after Ernst Mach) expresses the ratio of the speed of a body relative to air or some other fluid to the speed of sound waves in the fluid; or the ratio of the speed of a fluid flow to the speed of sound in the fluid. Mach number 1.0 indicates speed equal to the speed of sound, and Mach 5.0, fives times the speed of

Shadowgraph of Dragonfly missile model clearly shows the Mach wave. The cosecant of the angle (Mach angle) between the wave and the direction of flow equals the Mach number 1.93, indicating a velocity of flow nearly twice the speed of sound. (*Ballistic Research Labs., Aberdeen Proving Ground, U. S. Army*)

sound. At transonic and supersonic speeds, the Mach number of the flow is more significant for aerodynamic analysis than is the absolute speed. *Mach angle* is the angle between a *Mach wave* and the direction of flow, the Mach wave being a very weak SHOCK WAVE in a supersonic flow caused by any small disturbance such as the nose of a very sharp body. This wave is the envelope of the small pressure waves continually being generated by the small disturbance and is inclined in the downstream direction. The cosecant of the Mach angle equals Mach number. Mach waves define the regime in which the fluid shows the existence of the disturbance, since signals cannot travel upstream in a supersonic flow.—*D. B.*

MACLAURIN, COLIN, 1698–1746, Scottish mathematician; b. Kilmodan. An extremely able mathematician, he was in his time ranked second only to Newton. He was professor at Aberdeen and, from 1725, at Edinburgh. His name is known to students of calculus through the so-called Maclaurin expansion, which is nothing more than a special case of the Taylor expansion and was actually given by James Stirling 25 yr before Maclaurin applied it. Maclaurin did valuable work in geometry, especially in the study of higher plane curves. He was an authority on the fluxional calculus of Newton, on which he wrote a treatise. He was a fellow of the Royal Society.—*H. C.*

MACLURE, WILLIAM, 1763–1840, Scottish-U. S. geologist; b. Ayr, Scotland. He made observations in almost every state and territory before producing the first geological map of the U. S. A., 1809. Often called the father of American geology, he was a patron of science and was president of the Philadelphia Academy of Natural Sciences (1817–40).—*D. H. D. R.*

MAGELLANIC CLOUDS: the Large and the Small Magellanic Cloud, two extragalactic star systems that appear as small, hazy patches in the southern sky, named after Magellan, who first described them. They can be seen only in equatorial and

Observers in southern hemisphere easily see Magellanic Clouds (Large, *left*; Small, *lower right*) with unaided eye. At upper right is star Achernar, overexposed. (*Harvard Obs.*)

southern regions, their positions in right ascension and declination being: R.A. = 5h20m, Dec. = − 68°, for the Large Cloud, and R. A. = 1h, Dec. = −72°, for the Small Cloud. Their angular diameters are impressive: 7° for the Large Cloud, 4° for the Small. The Large Cloud is in the constellation Dorado, the Small Cloud in Tucana. They are companions to our Milky Way system, generally classified as irregular GALAXIES, although some astronomers claim they show incipient spiral structure. Their distances from the Sun are of the order of 200,000 lt-yr (the diameter of the Milky Way system is 100,000 lt-yr). They contain stars the most brilliant of which outshine our Sun by a factor of 5 million, and many others with brightnesses equivalent to 100,000 Suns and greater. Both Clouds also contain INTERSTELLAR MATTER—gas (largely hydrogen) and dust, especially the Large Cloud. Variable stars and star clusters are found in abundance in both Clouds, and the presence of the highly luminous stars (probably cosmically quite young) and associated gaseous nebulas suggests that star birth and evolution are active processes there. The closest spiral galaxies of the northern sky in which these processes can be studied are at about 10 times the distance of the Magellanic Clouds. The presence of the latter alone justifies the erection of large optical and radio telescopes in the southern hemisphere.—*B. J. B.*

MAGIC: the prescientific art of supposedly bending nature's forces to an individual's or group's will, as to induce or ward off disease or death, or to insure a good crop, typically by means of incantations (spells) and actions (rites) performed or directed by a magician. Magic is akin to divination (see ASTROLOGY), which purports to foretell events. Like science, magic and divination aim at prediction and control. Magic is integral in primitive cultures and survives in all higher ones, if only marginally and in modified forms, *e.g.* in certain aspects of religion, fortune-telling, and the popular concern with "luck." The forces supposedly controlled by magic are conceived as "spiritual," or "soul-like"; originally these forces are seen as permeating nature, determining its course, later also are seen as "supernatural," intervening in nature's course. As a reverent appeal to supernatural forces, magic is absorbed in the higher religions. The first to divorce rational and empirical inquiry, notably in areas related to medicine, from magical and religious lore were the Greeks. The medieval Church condemned *black magic* (malevolent) as evil and satanic, not as false, but it tolerated *white magic* (non-malevolent). The latter, growing more flexible and experimental (see ALCHEMY), became—in conjunction with the practical technology of craftsmen, *e.g.* mechanics and builders—one of the two great sources of modern science, the other being the Greek-originated quest for rational understanding of nature. —*G. G.*

MAGIC SQUARE: a form of mathematical puzzle in which a set of numbers must be arranged in a square so that the sums of the numbers in each row, column, and diagonal are the same. Fig. 1 is a magic square containing five different numbers; each number occupies cells connected by the knight's move in chess. Another kind of magic square contains the numbers 1, 2, 3, and so on, with no number repeated. A 5 × 5 square of this type is shown in Fig. 2. There is a general method of forming such a square whenever the number of rows and columns is odd: Place 1 in the middle cell of the top row; place 2 in the bottom cell of the next column to the right; place 3 in the cell diagonally above and right of 2; continue placing the numbers in order along this diagonal; when the end of a row is reached, move to the first cell of the row above, and then continue on the same upward right diagonal;

when a filled cell is reached, drop to the cell directly below the last, and then continue the diagonal; when the top of a column is reached, move to the bottom of the next column.

27	14	8	33	2
33	2	27	14	8
14	8	33	2	27
2	27	14	8	33
8	33	2	27	14

Fig. 1

17	24	1	8	15
23	5	7	14	16
4	6	13	20	22
10	12	19	21	3
11	18	25	2	9

Fig. 2

The last cell to be filled will be the bottom row, middle column. If the number of rows and columns is n, the last number placed will be n^2, the number in the central cell will be $\frac{1}{2}(n^2 + 1)$, and the sum of each row, column, and diagonal will be $\frac{1}{2}n(n^2 + 1)$. For example, the 5 × 5 square contains 25 numbers, the central cell contains the number 13, and the sum of each row, column, and diagonal is 65. See also LATIN SQUARE.—*B. P. S.*

MAGMA: molten material formed by the fusion of solid rock in the middle or lower parts of Earth's crust, or the upper part of the mantle. Magma tends to move toward Earth's surface because its density is less than that of the solid rock from which it formed. It may cool and crystallize into intrusive IGNEOUS ROCKS within the crust, or be erupted through fractures to the surface as LAVA and consolidate as extrusive flows, tuff, and ash. The composition of magma or lava depends largely on the composition of the material that was fused. The lava erupted from oceanic volcanoes and from long, steep fissures, *e.g.* the Ramapo fault in New Jersey or the faults along the eastern side of the Cascades, consolidated into BASALT, a dark rock with a high content of silicon, potassium, and sodium. Such volcanoes or flows are known or assumed to have derived magma from the lower, or SIMA, portion of the crust, or the upper part of the mantle. In contrast, the most abundant intrusive igneous rock is granitic in composition (see GRANITE), having a high content of silicon, potassium, and sodium and a low content of magnesium, iron, and calcium. Igneous granites derived from magma formed in geosynclines where the SIAL portion of the crust has been deeply downfolded into the SIMA and fused. Probably magmas of intermediate compositions are also formed, but they are less common than the two extremes.

Magma is a mutual solution or melt of charged particles (ions). The most abundant ions are $SiO_4 \equiv$ and $AlO_4 \equiv$, as simple tetrahedra, chains, or more complex patterns of linked tetrahedra. Next in abundance are Mg^{++}, Ca^{++}, Fe^{++}, Na^+, and K^+. Small amounts of several other metal ions may also be present. In the solution are also small quantities of potentially gaseous substances that escape from the magma or lava as H_2O, NH_3, CO, CO_2, SO_2, H_2S, HF, HCl, and N_2. Many magmas contain suspended crystals that either have not yet dissolved or have precipitated from solution.

In consistency, magmas range from viscous liquids, like syrup, to nearly rigid plastics, like pitch. As magma cools, the viscosity increases. If the cooling is rapid, the increasing viscosity may prevent the crystallization of minerals, and the result is a natural glass such as obsidian. If the cooling is slower, the ions will combine to form mineral grains whose size varies directly with the length of time that the magmatic temperature remains near that of the crystallizing temperature of the minerals involved. Because crystallization is an exothermic (heat-producing) process, it is possible for crystallizing magmas in the crust to remain at nearly constant temperature for long periods of time. Minerals with simple compositions and compact crystal structures form first, *e.g.* olivine and anorthite. As crystallization proceeds, olivine is succeeded by pyroxene and then by amphibole, and the high-calcium feldspars by plagioclases containing more sodium. Early minerals may react with the liquid to form minerals later in the series. If water vapor is sufficiently abundant, micas may form at any stage of the crystallization and may remove much of the potassium from solution. The residual liquids of this sequential crystallization will contain increasingly large proportions of Na^+, $AlO_4\equiv$, $SiO_4\equiv$, and probably K^+, which will form albite, orthoclase, quartz, and probably muscovite. If it happens that the crystals and liquid are separated during the period of crystallization, igneous rocks of quite different mineralogies may be formed from a single magma. The separation may be accomplished by crystal settling or floating, or by squeezing of the liquid from a crystal mush.

Earthquake records indicate Earth's crust and mantle are essentially solid. This property precludes the idea of a zone or large reservoirs of magma within Earth. Since igneous rocks are being generated today at a tempo comparable to that of the last billion years of geologic time, it seems unlikely that they are derived from the last stages of crystallization of an originally molten mantle or simatic crust. Hence the alternative that magmas have been generated locally throughout geologic time because of changes of physical conditions. What is known of the increase of temperature with depth in Earth seems to indicate that at a depth of 10 to 20 mi the rock temperatures would be close to the critical temperature of fusion and that this situation may be true for the lower crust and the mantle. If this is true, a small increase in temperature or decrease of pressure will create magma. Increase of temperature may be produced by mechanical friction in faulting or folding, by radioactivity, or by plastic convection of the mantle. Decrease of pressure may result from faulting, folding, or erosion. Inasmuch as most igneous rocks are associated with the mobile belts where faulting and folding are prominent, we may conclude that most magma is generated by these diastrophic events.—*W. G. V.*

MAGNESIUM: an alkaline-earth metallic element (Mg); at. no. 12; at. wt 24.32; density 1.74; mp 651°C; bp 1107°C. Magnesium is the lightest commercially used metal; it is found naturally only in compounds, never as the free element. It is among the ten most abundant elements in Earth's crust (2.1%), and forms 0.13% of sea water. Although many minerals contain the metal, the most common sources are dolomite ($CaCO_3 \cdot MgCO_3$), magnesite ($MgCO_3$), natural brine, and sea water. Magnesium metal is made by the electrolysis of a fused salt mixture of magnesium, potassium, and sodium chlorides, or by the reduction of magnesium oxide with carbon or ferrosilicon. Magnesium compounds have long been known to man, but were confused with lime until 1755, when J. Black distinguished magnesia (magnesium oxide) from lime. Sir Humphry Davy (1808) isolated the element by boiling off the mercury from a mercury-magnesium amalgam; and in 1831 A. A. B. Bussy prepared the element in purer and more substantial amounts. Because of its lightness, magnesium is used in light-weight alloys, particularly with aluminum (density 2.70). Magnesium alloys are used extensively in the manufacture of aircraft, light-weight machinery, and portable tools and devices. Magnesium burns in air to form magnesia. Since the metal ignites readily in wire or powder form, it is used in signal flares, photographic flash

bulbs, and pyrotechnics; because it reacts with oxygen and nitrogen, it is used to rid vacuum tubes of these gases. A suspension of magnesia in water is known as "milk of magnesia" and is used as a neutralizer of stomach acids and as a laxative. "Epsom salts," *i.e.* magnesium sulfate, is used as a cathartic.—*G. W. M.*

MAGNET: a magnetized bar or other ferromagnetic object; also an electromagnet, especially an iron-core electromagnet, in which pieces of iron are surrounded and magnetized by coils of wire carrying currents. Air-core magnets are solenoids, or coils of wire which produce a field without the use of iron. Whereas the fields produced by iron-core magnets are limited by the saturation magnetization of iron, the fields of air-core solenoids can be increased to values limited only by the available current, by the heat generated, and by the strength of the coils in the face of the forces produced by the interaction of the currents with the fields they produce.—*F. B.*

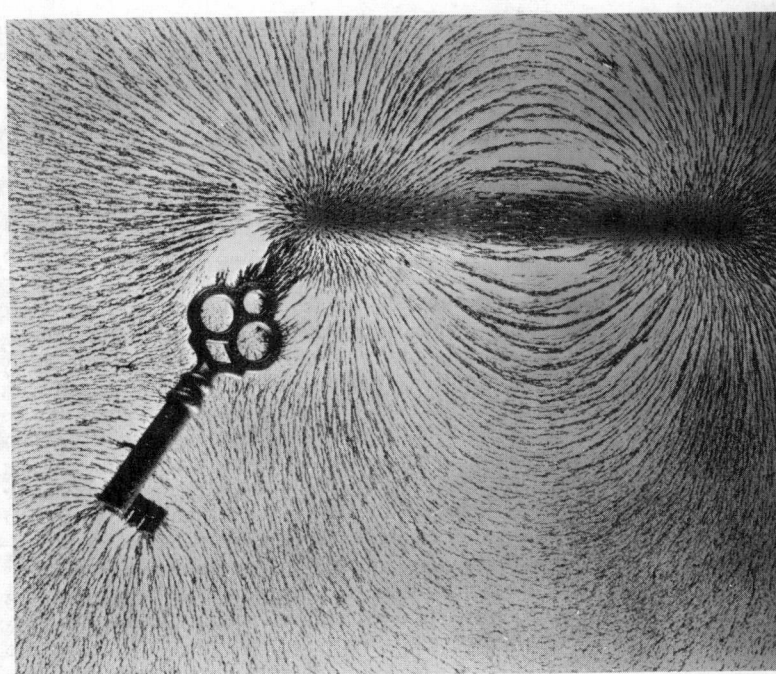

Magnetic field of magnet is mapped by iron filings. The bar magnet is causing the key to act as magnet also, as shown by the field lines emanating from it. (*Berenice Abbott*)

MAGNETIC CIRCUIT: a ring or ringlike structure of ferromagnetic material, usually containing an air gap, and surrounded by a coil carrying a current. The properties of a magnetic circuit are often discussed as approximately analogous to a simple electric circuit consisting of a battery and a resistor, the electromotive force (emf) of this battery being compared to the magnetomotive force (mmf) of the magnetizing coil; the electric current being compared to the total magnetic flux; and the electrical resistance being compared to a magnetic reluctance. The magnetic analogue of Ohm's law states that the total flux equals the magnetomotive force divided by the reluctance. The applicability of this law is limited by assumptions about leakage flux, just as Ohm's law is limited to circuits in which the conductor is surrounded by an insulating medium. For a ring of uniform cross-sectional area A, length L, and permeability μ containing an

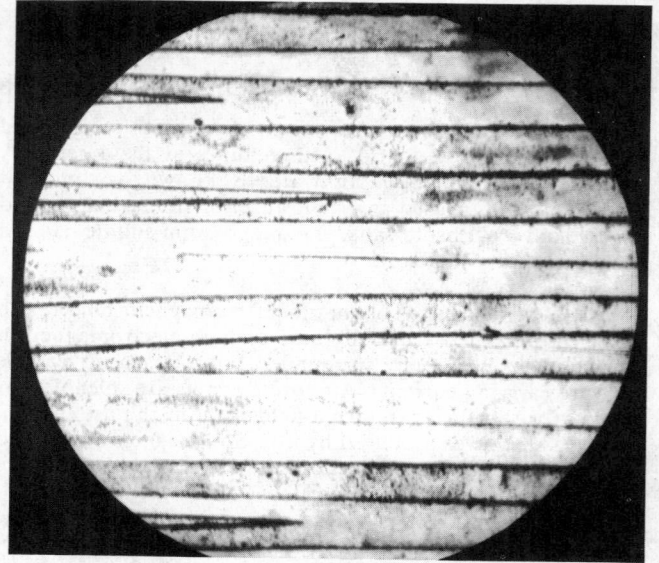

Magnetic domain boundaries appear in magnetized cobalt crystal. (*Bates*)

air gap of length L_g, the field in the gap may be computed as follows, if the length of the gap is sufficiently small compared to its diameter:

$$\phi = \frac{\text{mmf}}{R} = \frac{B}{A} \text{ gauss/cm}^2$$

$$\text{mmf} = Ni \text{ ampere turns}$$

$$R = R_{\text{iron}} + R_{\text{gap}} = \frac{10}{4\pi} \left(\frac{L}{\mu A} + \frac{L_g}{A} \right) \text{ cm}^{-1}$$

—*F. B.*

MAGNETIC COMPASS: a device for determining direction, consisting of a small bar magnet or a magnetized needle attached to a pointer and mounted so that it can rotate freely in a horizontal plane. The compass needle aligns itself with Earth's magnetic field, and a scale, marked in degrees, can be used to specify directions relative to this magnetic field. Magnetic compasses have been used in navigation for at least seven centuries. Early compasses frequently employed a piece of lodestone, or magnetite. The first systematic investigation of magnetism and the properties of magnets appeared in William Gilbert's *De magnete* (1600). Modern compass magnets are made from iron or an iron alloy capable of maintaining permanently a strong degree of magnetization. Earth's magnetic lines converge to two points on Earth's surface: the magnetic poles, located 700 mi from the geographic poles. The *north magnetic pole* is near Prince of Wales Island, Canada, at 74°N, 101°W; the *south magnetic pole* is near 68°S, 144°E, in King George V Land, Antarctica. Since these magnetic poles do not coincide with the geographic poles of Earth, the directions indicated by a magnetic compass are not true north-south lines. The angular difference is called the *magnetic declination,* or (in navigation) the *variation* of the compass. The exact locations of the magnetic poles vary somewhat from year to year in a rather irregular manner, so that the magnetic declination at any point on Earth varies also. In London the magnetic declination was 4°E in 1643 and 7½°W in 1960, and in New York, 11°W in 1960. In addition to variation, a compass is subject to *deviation,* which is the error introduced by the presence of local magnetic fields (*e.g.* those due to steel hulls of ships, or to varying constitution of Earth's crust): these cause the needle to point elsewhere than true magnetic north. Because of declination and deviation, magnetic compasses have been largely replaced by GYROSTATIC COMPASSES, which indicate true north directly. Magnetic compasses, however, still find frequent use for general direction finding.—*O. M. P.*

MAGNETIC DOMAIN: a region in a ferromagnetic material in which the magnetic moment of an atom is coupled to the magnetic moments of neighboring atoms by strong internal forces, so that there is an average magnetization in the domain determined by these internal magnetizing forces and the disorienting tendency resulting from thermal agitation. The magnetization of a macroscopic sample containing many domains is determined by the orientation of the magnetization of its constituent domains. Existence of these domains causes magnetization of a sample to increase in a series of small jumps—a phenomenon known as Barkhausen effect.—*F. B.*

MAGNETIC FLUX: the aggregate of the lines of induction passing through some given surface or linking some given closed loop. For a surface of area A at right angles to the direction of B, magnetic flux is the product AB. The concept is particularly useful in calculating induced electromotive force in a circuit from the rate of change of total flux linking the circuit. (See ELECTROMAGNETIC INDUCTION.)—*F. B.*

MAGNETIC HYSTERESIS: the lag of magnetization and therefore of the magnetic induction field (B) behind an applied magnetizing field (H). The phenomenon is observed in the course of a complete cycle of magnetization and demagnetization of a sample of ferromagnetic material, *e.g.* iron, steel, nickel, cobalt, or an alloy like alnico. Application of an initial magnetizing force causes a sharp but nonlinear rise in the state of magnetization (see figure), the permeability μ, or the ratio B/H, the attained values much exceeding those observed for paramagnetic substances (see MAGNETIC MATERIALS). If the process is reversed (after reaching saturation), the ferromagnetic sample will exhibit a lag or hysteresis, retaining or "remembering" its previous history of domain orientation. Accordingly, reducing H to zero will still leave a certain amount of residual magnetism, called *remanence* and denoted in the diagram by the symbol B_r. The value of H will actually have to be reduced to some negative value, H_c, known as the *coercive force,* if the last trace of magnetization is to be obliterated. The negative value is obtained by reversing the direction of H. If H is now increased to its negative maximum value, and then again reversed in direction, a complete cyclic curve, or *hysteresis loop,* will have been traced for the specimen. Its area represents an expenditure of energy.

Because of the lag of B behind H, the B-H curve never retraces itself. Soft magnetic materials, *e.g.* wrought iron, exhibit narrow hysteresis loops, showing that there is only a

Hysteresis loop shows stages of magnetization and demagnetization of a sample plotted on a graph of magnetization vs. magnetizing force. At points of loop, magnetic saturation is reached (additional magnetizing force results in no additional magnetization); but when magnetizing force is reduced to zero, some magnetism, B_r, remains.

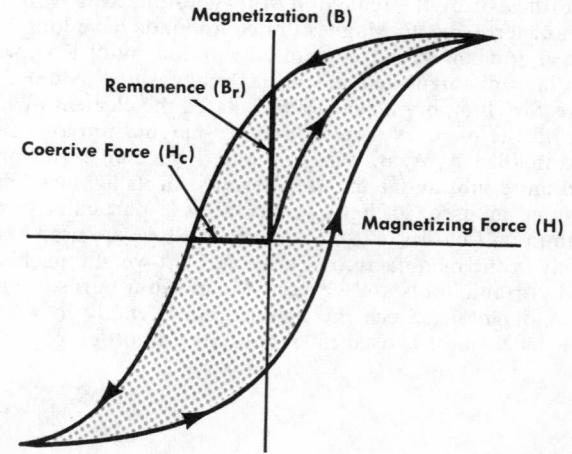

little energy per unit volume lost in the form of heat. Magnetically hard materials, *e.g.* steel or alnico, are deliberately designed to yield large hysteresis loops and provide large energy losses. Soft magnetic materials are used when the purpose is to improve the efficiency of electrical machinery subject to frequent reversals of magnetization. When hard magnetic materials are used, efficiency is sacrificed in favor of high residual magnetism and a high resistance to demagnetization. See MAGNETISM.—*A. E.*

MAGNETIC INDUCTION: the magnetic field vector *B*, measuring the magnetic flux density. In material having a permeability μ, the induction is μH, where *H* is the effective magnetizing field. It is *B* whose change is effective in producing an ELECTROMOTIVE FORCE in ELECTROMAGNETIC INDUCTION. —*F. B.*

MAGNETIC MATERIALS: those substances—mostly metals— useful in technology for their magnetic properties. All materials exhibit some response to a magnetic field; however, the response of such diamagnetic substances as copper (which tends to be repelled by the field) and such paramagnetic substances as aluminum (which is only weakly attracted by a magnetic field) is comparatively small. Accordingly, most of the materials used in technology are ferromagnetic and, like iron, exhibit strong responses to applied magnetic fields. (*See* DIAMAGNETISM, PARAMAGNETISM, and FERROMAGNETISM.)

The high degree of magnetizability of ferromagnetic materials, as measured by the permeability μ, is of importance in producing large inductances in small volumes, and also in the generation of fields, or the production of magnetic forces. For permanent magnets, materials having a large remanence and a large coercive force, and therefore a large hysteresis loop, are required. In a-c circuits in which eddy currents are to be avoided, high electrical resistivity is important. At low frequencies, *e.g.* 60 cy/sec, the addition of a few per cent of silicon is effective. At high frequencies, or where abrupt changes in magnetization taking place in a microsecond or less are wanted, iron compounds having a very high resistivity, particularly oxides, are used. Of particular interest in this connection are the "memory" elements in computers. Rings can be made which are always magnetized in one sense or another, and such a ring can be used to specify whether the answer to a question is yes or no, depending on the sense of its magnetization. Iron changes its shape very slightly with magnetization. This is known as *magnetostriction,* and is used in converting electrical oscillations into air oscillations in loudspeakers. The temperature of a magnetic specimen thermally insulated from its surroundings varies with the degree of magnetization: this is called the *magnetocaloric effect.* It is negligibly small except at very low temperatures, but below 1° absolute, or about −273°C, it is the only effective means of cooling.—*F. B.*

MAGNETIC MOMENT: a measure of the magnetic strength of a current loop or a rotating or revolving charge, most useful in describing atomic magnetism. Its definition is analogous to that for the mechanical moment, or angular momentum, of a particle, except that the charge is substituted for the mass. That is, the angular momentum of a mass *m* moving in a circular orbit of radius *r* with speed *v* is mvr, or, in terms of the angular velocity ω, $mr^2\omega$. If the particle has a charge *e*, its magnetic moment is $\frac{1}{2}evr = \frac{1}{2}er^2\omega$. The ratio of the magnetic moment to the angular momentum is called the gyromagnetic ratio, equal to $e/2m$ for an electron in orbit. The intrinsic angular momentum (spin) of an electron corresponds to a gyromagnetic ratio of e/m. Nuclei also possess magnetic properties that arise from the magnetic moments of their constituent particles and the motions of these particles. A linear bar magnet is a magnetic dipole, whose magnetic moment is the product of its pole strength and the distance between its poles.—*F. B.*

MAGNETIC PERMEABILITY: a number that characterizes the ability of a substance to concentrate within itself an applied magnetic field. Permeability is the ratio of the MAGNETIC FLUX in the substance to the strength of the field that produces the flux. Air has a permeability of essentially 1, brass a permeability of less than 1, and iron a permeability of 1,000 or more; the action of iron in concentrating a magnetic field is used to increase the strength of ELECTROMAGNETS.— *E. M. R.*

MAGNETIC RESONANCE: Resonance refers to the selective response of any mechanical system to an oscillatory stimulus in the vicinity of its own natural frequency. A magnetic resonance similarly refers to the selective response of a magnetic system to an oscillating magnetic field in the vicinity of the characteristic magnetic frequencies of the material. These magnetic frequencies may be associated with the precession of atomic nuclei or atomic electrons resulting from the angular momentum associated with their magnetization. They may also be associated with other frequencies, *e.g.* the frequency of circulation of a charge in a magnetic field. Magnetic resonance phenomena are particularly important, not only in reviewing the magnetic structure of the components of a material, but also in describing internal local fields.—*F. B.*

MAGNETIC SUSCEPTIBILITY: a number that characterizes the magnetization of a substance when subject to a magnetic field. The magnetic susceptibility multiplied by the applied magnetic field strength gives the intensity of magnetization of the substance. This coefficient is very nearly zero for most substances, but may be as large as several thousand for highly magnetic materials such as soft iron.—*M. P.*

MAGNETISM: the force of interaction between two magnets, a magnet and a magnetic material, or two parallel and closely spaced wires carrying electric currents. The tractive or lifting force of a magnet is its most obvious characteristic and lends particular interest to the introductory study of the subject. On a more advanced level, magnetism is seen to be the force resulting from electricity in motion, the unbalanced electron spin accounting for the magnetism of the individual iron atom.

A natural magnetic ore, called LODESTONE or *magnetite* (a

Demonstration model of "magnetic bottle": Magnets of Stellarator produce "corkscrew fields" to contain a hot ionized gas, preventing it from vaporizing walls of its container. This principle may enable control of fusion process. (*Princeton Univ.*)

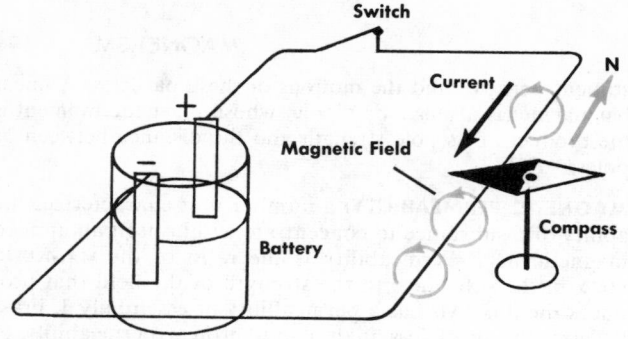

Oersted's experiment: When current flows through a wire, a magnetic field is created around the wire. This field acts to turn a compass needle so that it points at right angles to the wire.

mixture of iron oxides, FeO and Fe_2O_3), was known many centuries ago. Deposits of this ore were then located in Magnesia, a province of Asia Minor. Legend has it that a shepherd by the name of Magnes (hence the word "magnetism") was the first to note the attraction between his iron crook and bits of this ore. Magnetite was the first *permanent* magnet available to man; magnetite magnets were succeeded by permanently magnetized pieces of steel, at first magnetized by rubbing them over lodestone.

Crude compasses, made of carefully balanced, elongated pieces of lodestone, were used by the Chinese as early as 2700 B. C. The first magnetic "needle" showed a disposition to arrange itself in a definite direction, one end pointing approximately north, and the other, south. This, of course, made navigation possible. Steel compass needles, of the floating and suspended variety, became known in the 13th cent. and were fully described by Petrus Peregrinus. In 1600, William Gilbert of Colchester, England, published the book *De magnete,* in which he discussed the *dip* and *declination* of the compass needle (its departure, respectively, from the true horizontal and the north-south direction). Gilbert explained, with the aid of a spherical magnet called the *terrella,* the magnetic action of Earth itself (see TERRESTRIAL MAGNETISM).

The notion of magnetic *poles* was developed by Peregrinus. Lodestone attracts bits of iron most strongly at the regions called its poles, and on the basis of Gilbert's study it became

Magnetic field around a wire carrying an electric current is shown by these iron filings forming concentric circles. (*Berenice Abbott*)

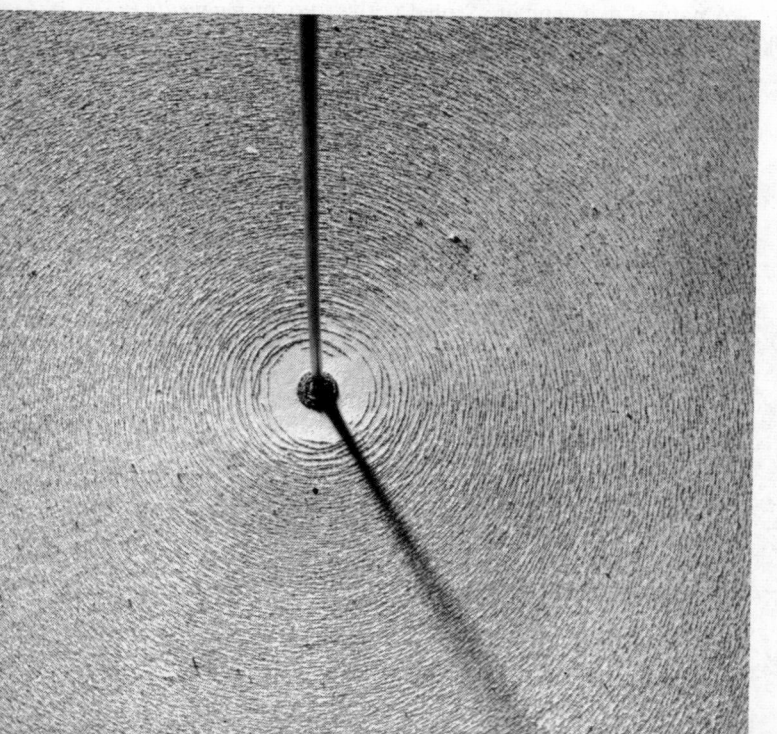

clear that a compass needle is deflected because of the interaction between its poles and the magnetic poles of earth. Unlike poles attract and like poles repel each other. Gilbert also made clear that poles cannot be isolated: new poles appear when a magnet is broken. Magnetic *lines of force* are continuous lines along the direction taken by a compass needle which is free to turn.

The quantitative law of force between two magnetic poles was discovered by J. Michell in 1750, and independently by C. A. Coulomb in 1785. Two well-localized poles attract or repel each other with a force that is directly proportional to the product of their pole strengths and inversely proportional to the square of the distance between them. The concept of *magnetic field,* which can be visualized by plotting lines of force, was developed quantitatively by Michael Faraday in his work on magnetism and electromagnetism.

The most significant experiment in the field of magnetism, revealing a relationship between magnetism and electricity, was performed in 1819 by Hans Christian Oersted. He observed that a current-carrying wire placed parallel to a compass needle causes this to be deflected in a direction perpendicular to that of the current passing through the wire (see figure). The circular magnetic field surrounding a current-bearing conductor was also investigated by André Marie Ampère, who demonstrated that electrically energized coils of wire act like magnets, and by Dominique Arago, who found that iron can be magnetized temporarily (and steel, permanently) by placing it inside a current-carrying coil. These discoveries soon led to the production of practical *electromagnets* by William Sturgeon and Joseph Henry, and made possible far greater magnetic strengths than those heretofore exhibited by relatively weak permanent magnets. The principle of the electric motor became clear when it was found that a conductor, carrying an electric current and placed at right angles to a magnetic field, experiences a force at right angles both to the current and to the field. The electric generator was first anticipated in 1831 by Faraday, who discovered that electricity can be produced by *changing* the magnetic flux established in a coil.

The experiments just cited gave rise to a suspicion that magnetism was somehow related to the very structure of matter. Wilhelm Weber, in 1852, suggested that each atom of a magnetic material is in itself a tiny little magnet or *dipole,* having its own north and south poles. Weber was able to explain over-all magnetization by assuming a definite alignment or orientation of the individual atomic magnets. He also accounted for the demagnetization of permanent magnets by heat or hammering, as well as the formation of separate magnets when an original magnet is broken in half. The dipole theory, however, failed to explain why atoms of iron and steel are magnetic in the first place.

With the discovery of the electron (1897), an *electrical* explanation of the origin of magnetism became possible. This was anticipated in 1825 by Ampère, who foresaw *circulating currents* inside atoms contributing to atomic magnetization. Much later, Paul Langevin and Pierre Weiss extended this reasoning and explained atomic magnetism in terms of the circulation of electrons around the nucleus of the atom, these electrons being the ones with an *uncompensated net spin.* Present-day theory indicates that such electrons are found in the third incomplete subshell of the M shell of the atoms of iron, cobalt, and nickel; other electrons exhibit spins that cancel one another. The unbalanced spin gives rise to a *magnetic moment,* which accounts for the magnetism of the individual atom. Over-all magnetism is now seen to be attained when the separate magnetic moments are oriented together and add their strength to that of the applied field.

Weiss' principal contribution to magnetic theory was his concept of *domains*—submicroscopic "colonies" of similarly oriented atomic magnets. Each domain is envisaged as made up of some 10^{18} (billion billion) individual little magnets, with their separate magnetic moments joined together. Domains are presumed to be separated by so-called Bloch walls, whose existence has actually been confirmed by the use of *powder-pattern* techniques. Partial over-all magnetization ensues when domain moments acquire a partial orientation with respect to one another. Complete magnetization occurs when the alignment with the applied field is complete. See MAGNET; MAGNETIC articles.—*A. E.*

MAGNETIZATION: the degree to which something is magnetized; more specifically, the magnetic dipole moment per unit volume of the magnetized material. It is analogous to the polarization of a DIELECTRIC.—*M. P.*

MAGNETOCHEMISTRY: the study of behavior of a chemical substance in the presence of a magnetic field. A paramagnetic substance, *i.e.* one having unpaired electrons, is drawn into a magnetic field. Diamagnetic substances, *i.e.* those having no unpaired electrons, are repelled by a magnetic field.—*G. W. M.*

MAGNETOHYDRODYNAMICS: the study of the motion of electrically conducting fluids that are acted on by two categories of forces: 1) the forces of ordinary hydrodynamics, *e.g.* pressure and viscosity forces; 2) the magnetic forces on the currents which exist in the medium. "Magnetohydrodynamics" is somewhat of a misnomer since "hydro" suggests water, a medium which rarely, if ever, is treated in the subject. The term is gradually being displaced by the more accurate terms magnetofluid-dynamics, magnetofluidmechanics, and magnetogasdynamics; however, the adjective "hydromagnetic" and noun "hydromagnetics" are, and will undoubtedly remain, in constant use.

Good examples of a hydromagnetic medium are mercury and sodium in liquid form, interstellar gas, and stellar matter. The first two are examples of incompressible liquids. The last two are examples of compressible gaseous media. All have in common the property of being excellent conductors of electricity. The last two examples are also typical PLASMAS —*i.e.* hot gases that owe their conductivity to ionization.

The science of magnetohydrodynamics is essentially the creation of astrophysicists, who have employed it in theoretical investigations of solar flares, the stability of stars, the mechanical equilibrium of sun spots, and other astrophysical phenomena. The resulting body of theory is used by geophysicists to explain the continued presence of Earth's magnetic field. It is believed that the rotation of the molten metallic core of Earth, in the presence of the existing geomagnetic field, causes the flow of currents which sustain the field. More recently, magnetohydrodynamics is playing a leading role in the development of controlled nuclear FUSION; here, magnetic "bottles" are used in place of material containers to confine hot plasmas. The newest applications of the subject include the explanation of various features of geomagnetic storms in terms of propagating hydromagnetic disturbances, and the work on missile re-entry phenomena and on propulsion by plasma jets.

The basis of all applications of hydromagnetism is the interplay of mechanical and magnetic forces. In some applications one wishes to intensify or maintain a magnetic field at the expense of the energy of motion; in others, to guide or contain a conducting fluid with the help of magnetic fields, at the expense of magnetic energy. An appreciation of the interaction of magnetic and mechanical forces is best gained by considering the idealized case of an infinitely conducting, nonviscous ideal gas. This idealization, it may be added, is believed to reflect accurately the physics of the Sun's atmosphere and the gas of interstellar space. Now it is a direct consequence of the assumption of infinite conductivity that the motion of material transverse to the embedded magnetic lines of force carries these lines of force along with it, much as the lines of tension in a stretched rubber band are displaced with the band when the latter is displaced. Further, motion that is everywhere parallel to the magnetic lines of force leaves the lines of force unaffected. Conversely, one can show that a transverse displacement of the magnetic lines of force is accompanied by an appropriate transverse motion of the material through which the lines of force thread. It is this mechanism which is exploited in applications. One may, in short, initiate motion by distorting the lines of force; one may guide motion by holding the lines of force fixed or nearly so; finally, one may intensify the embedded magnetic field by setting up suitable motions in the fluid. See also PINCH EFFECT.—*J. Ba.*

MAGNETOMETER: a device used to measure the intensity of a magnetic field. Any physical phenomenon dependent upon the strength of the field can be made the basis for a magnetometer's operation. For example, a bar magnet that is free to rotate in a magnetic field will oscillate about the direction of the field. The number of oscillations per second depends

Fluxgate magnetometer being launched from U. S. Coast Guard cutter will measure magnetic field of ocean area off Key West, Fla. (*U. S. Coast & Geodetic Survey*)

upon the strength of the field in a known way, so a measurement of the frequency constitutes a measurement of the field. Some other magnetometers depend upon the generation of electric current in a rotating coil (see ELECTROMAGNETIC INDUCTION) and upon the HALL EFFECT. One of the most sensitive types of magnetometers makes use of the fact that some atomic nuclei, when in a magnetic field, behave like tiny bar magnets.—*S. K.*

MAGNETOSTATICS: the study of magnetic fields at rest, as distinguished from changing fields. Magnetostatics deals with such concepts as poles, forces between poles, and the properties of lines of force. It also includes the interaction of steady currents. See MAGNETISM.—*A. E.*

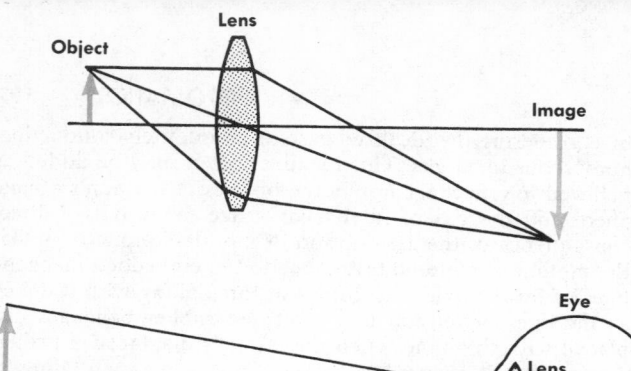

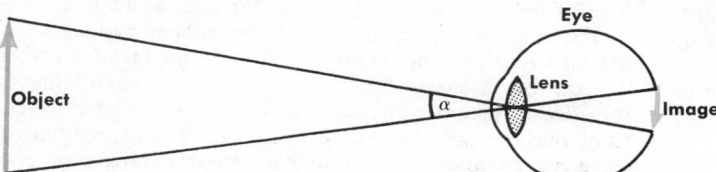

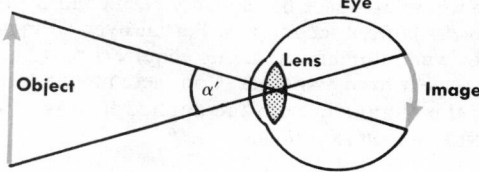

Linear magnification: A convex lens (*left*) makes an object look larger by increasing the linear dimensions of the image.

Angular magnification (*two drawings below*): The closer an object is to the eye, the larger is the angle it subtends at the eye. Convex lens increases the subtended angle α by causing light rays to converge more sharply on entering eye; thus, in effect, lens brings object closer, or "magnifies" it.

MAGNETOSTRICTION: a change in length of a ferromagnetic material upon application of a magnetic field. The applied field interacts with the magnetic moments of the atoms so as to produce distortion and therefore a change in dimensions. If the applied field varies periodically, so will the length. Magnetostriction is the major cause of noise heard in power transformers. It is applied usefully to generate and detect sound, particularly in underwater applications (see SONAR). It is also used in a new industrial device to drill holes of non-circular cross section, particularly in hard materials. See FERROMAGNETISM.—*I. R.*

MAGNIFICATION, OPTICAL: the measure of enlargement of the IMAGE of an object. *Linear magnification* is the ratio of any linear dimension of the image to the same linear dimension of the object. *Lateral magnification* is the linear magnification of a dimension at right angles to the optic axis of the lens or lens system. When, for example, an object is placed at a distance from a lens greater than the focal distance of the lens, light rays from the object passing through the lens form an image that can be projected on a screen. The image may be equal to, smaller, or larger than the object, depending on the object's distance from the lens. Direct measurement of image and object, independent of the position of the observer, will determine the lateral magnification of such an optical system. However, when the eye is an integral part of the optical system, as is the case of a person peering through a magnifying glass, a telescope, or a microscope, *angular magnification* is used to measure the image enlargement. The apparent size of an object seen by the eye depends on the size of the angle subtended by the object at the eye. When an object is moved closer to the eye, it appears larger because it subtends a greater angle, thereby producing a larger image on the retina of the eye. A magnifying LENS, TELESCOPE, or MICROSCOPE produces an enlarged image on the retina by bending the light coming from an object (see REFRACTION) and forming an image that subtends a greater angle at the eye than the object subtends. The angular magnification of an optical system is the ratio of the angle subtended by the image to the angle subtended by the object at the unaided eye. For a convex lens, the angular magnification *M* is also equal to the *distance of distinct vision* (the minimum distance an object can be from the eye and still be seen in sharp focus) divided by the focal length of the lens. Since the distance of distinct vision is about 25 cm (or about 10 in.), a lens with a focal length of 5 cm has a magnification of 5X (*M* = 25 cm/5 cm = 5). As magnification increases, the brilliance of the image decreases. This decrease in brilliance is offset in a microscope by illuminating the object with light of greater intensity. Since the illumination of bodies viewed through a telescope is ordinarily fixed, larger apertures must be used in the telescope to gather as much light from the object as possible.—*A. L.*

MAGNITUDE: in astronomy, a numerical designation of the brightness of a celestial object; by convention, the assigned number increases as the brightness decreases. In the 2nd cent. B. C., Hipparchus divided the naked-eye stars into six magnitude ranges, from the brightest stars (1) to the faintest (6). The precise definition of a magnitude scale depends upon the fact that the human eye sees equal ratios of brightness as equal steps of brightness, so that a 1st-mag. star is as many times brighter than a 2nd-mag. star as the 2nd-mag. star is than a 3rd-mag. star. Sir John Herschel found that one of Hipparchus' 1st-mag. stars was about 100 times as bright as one of 6th mag. The convention has been adopted that a range of 5 magnitudes shall be exactly equivalent to a ratio of 100 in brightness. Hence, if two stars have brightnesses I_1 and I_2, and have magnitudes m_1 and m_2, then $(m_2 - m_1) = 2.5 \log_{10} (I_1/I_2)$. The zero of the scale is adopted by convention, the definition only referring to relative brightness. Objects brighter than 1st mag. are given magnitudes 0, −1, −2, etc., and fractional magnitudes are also used.

The magnitude of one star relative to another can be estimated directly by eye, and a skilled visual observer can obtain a consistency of about 0.1 mag. The accuracy can be improved by visually comparing the star with a standard laboratory source of light that can be dimmed accurately. The *Revised Harvard Photometry* of the magnitudes of nearly 46,000 stars was obtained in this way, and was for many years the standard catalog of stellar apparent brightnesses.

A photograph can be used to compare the apparent brightnesses of stars because both the degree of blackening of the star image on the photographic negative and the diameter of

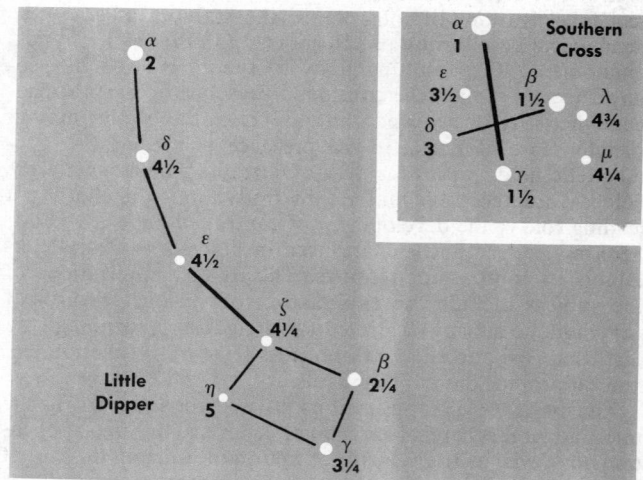

Magnitudes of stars can be estimated by comparing these stars with stars of known magnitude in Little Dipper (*above*) and in vicinity of Southern Cross (*inset*).

1

Plate 50   FUNGI

Unlike green plants, fungi lack chlorophyll and cannot make their own food by means of photosynthesis. So they must depend on other kinds of organisms—either living or dead—for their food. Most fungi live as parasites or saprophytes of animals or plants, but a few live in partnership with green plants, each partner deriving benefit.

1. Lichens encrust rock in desert. Lichen is a partnership between a fungus, which soaks up water, and an alga, which uses water to make food by photosynthesis. *(Herbert Lanks/Monkmeyer)*

2

2. Molds are microscopic fungi. They produce spores of characteristic forms, colors, and textures that can be grown on sterile plates of agar jelly containing suitable nutrients. *Streptomyces fradiae*, shown here, is the mold from which the antibiotic neomycin is extracted. *(Pfizer)*

3

3. Mushrooms are recognized by their fruiting bodies. These grow from threads of fungus living in rotting wood or richly organic soil. After bearing spores, fruiting bodies die, but successive crops are produced. *(D. Forbert/Shostal)*

4. Bracket fungus grows on both live and dead trees; it can damage a living tree. The visible structure, which serves as a fruiting body from which spores are dropped, grows from fungus threads spreading under the bark. *(Russ Kinne)*

4

Plate 51   GEMSTONES

Beauty, rarity, and durability are the characteristics shared by the few minerals prized as gemstones. Beauty is often enhanced by cutting a mineral in such a way that its brilliance or color is heightened. Here is a representative sampling of colored gemstones.

1. Tourmaline offers a wider range of color than any other gemstone. Crystals are cut into stones with large flat tops or "tables" to display the rich color. *(Paul Desautels)*

2. Rubies, emeralds, and sapphires have long been the most highly prized colored gemstones. Rubies (red), emeralds (green), and sapphires (blue) are displayed here in various cutting styles. *(Van Cleef and Arpels)*

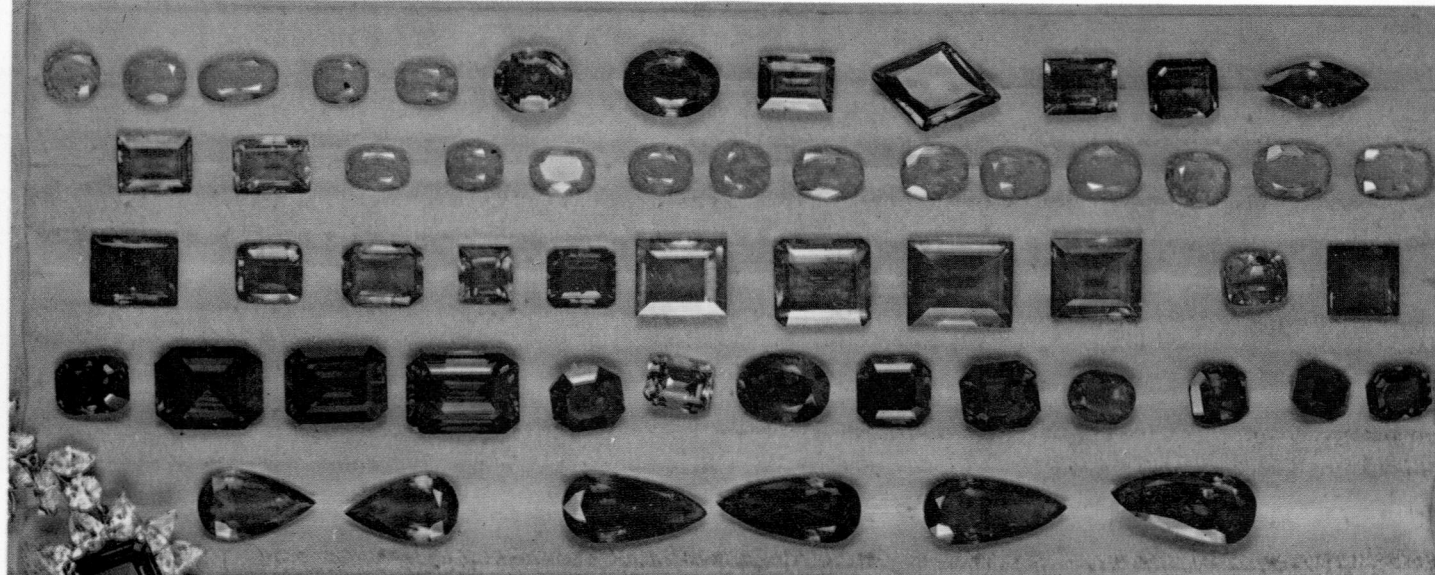

3. Star stones: "Star" pattern of reflected light adds to beauty of 330-carat sapphire "Star of Asia" *(left)*, a garnet *(middle)*, and a light-colored orthoclase *(right)*.

4. Opal, though colorless, produces flashing colors that shift and change when stone is moved.

5. Cutting of pale blue topaz: Standard "brilliant"-cut topaz *(top left)* is a final stage in transformation from rough-cut stone *(top right)*. *(3, 4, 5, Paul Desautels)*

1

Plate 52 GLACIERS

A glacier, formed by the compaction and recrystallization of snow, is a mass of ice which moves under the force of gravity. Now limited to high mountains and polar regions, glaciers have at times in the past covered more extensive areas of Earth.

1. Juneau Icefield, Alaska: Glaciologists are encamped near a crevasse in the ice *(foreground)*. Jagged, glacially eroded peaks rise in background. *(William O. Field/American Geographical Society)* **2. Cirque** in Giant Mountain, Adirondacks, N. Y.: This birthplace of a former glacier was hollowed out by ice plucking and frost action. *(Jerome Wyckoff)* **3. Ruth Glacier,** Mt. McKinley, Alaska: A valley-type glacier with small tributary glaciers *(background)* and a lateral moraine *(right foreground)*. *(Steve McCutcheon/Mac's Foto Service)*

2

3

Plate 53   IGNEOUS ROCK

An igneous rock is formed as molten material, called magma when under Earth's surface and lava when above, cools and solidifies. Igneous rocks are generally classified as acidic and basic, the former (such as the granites) containing a high percentage of the lighter-colored minerals quartz and potash feldspar, and the latter (such as basalt) being rich rather in the darker-colored, heavier ferromagnesian minerals.

1. Diabase Cliff near Haverstraw, N. Y.: Part of Palisades of Hudson River. This dark rock, similar in composition to basalt, was intruded as a sill between pre-existing layers of sediments. Yellow-brown color is a surface staining due to weathering of iron-bearing minerals in rock. *(Jerome Wyckoff)* **2. Massive granite** of Yosemite Valley, Calif.: Here a glacier gouged out and straightened a previous river-cut valley, leaving such features as the planed-off vertical wall of El Capitan *(left)*, Bridalveil Falls *(right)*, and Half Dome *(center, background)*. *(Glen Giffen)*

1

2

3. Basalt flow, Parrsboro, Nova Scotia, and Devils Tower, Wyo. (4), show columnar jointing. Such jointing, the result of shrinkage of the hot rock during cooling, is commonly associated with dark-colored igneous rock appearing as flows and small intrusive bodies. *(Harold Wanless [below] and Daniel Rothermel)*

4

3

the image depend upon the brightness of the star and the exposure time. Photographic magnitudes are reliable to about 0.03 mag., but a single plate can be used only over a range of about 4 mag. The most accurate measurements are made by allowing the star's light to fall on a photoelectric cell, and measuring the current given off. This method is capable of an accuracy of 0.001 mag., but variable absorption by Earth's atmosphere limits the practical accuracy to about 0.01 mag. A photoelectric photometer can be used over a range of 11 mag. or more, but can observe stars only one at a time.

The brightness of a star depends upon the color of the light observed. Thus, a red star might be brighter than a blue one when observed in red light, and fainter when in blue light. Magnitude systems are set up, using standard filters, photographic plates, and photoelectric cells. The color index of a star is the difference between the magnitudes observed in two specific colors. Relative magnitudes that would be obtained if all the radiations from the stars (ultraviolet, visible, and infrared) were recorded are called bolometric magnitudes. Because Earth's atmosphere completely absorbs some of these radiations, bolometric magnitudes can be estimated only approximately; better values may be obtained by observing stars from artificial satellites.

Magnitude as described above is *apparent magnitude*. This depends upon the distance of the object as well as upon its rate of output of light energy. To compare the rates of output by different stars, a scale of *absolute magnitude* is used. This is the apparent magnitude that the star would have if it were at a distance of 10 parsecs. (See ASTRONOMICAL DISTANCE UNITS.) The apparent magnitude of the Sun is -26.73 (in the yellow part of the spectrum), but its absolute magnitude is $+4.84$. The absolute magnitude of the most luminous stars is about -7, corresponding to a luminosity some 50,000 times the Sun's. The least luminous of the known stars has an absolute magnitude of $+18.7$, corresponding to a luminosity only 3 millionths times the Sun's.—*M. W. O.*

MALPIGHI, MARCELLO, 1628–94, Italian anatomist and physiologist; b. Crevalcuore. One of the founders of histology, he discovered the capillaries that connect the arteries and the veins and described them in his treatise on the lungs, *De pulmonibus* (1661). His microscopic studies of the chick embryo lent support to the doctrine of preformation or encasement, the view that a female contains all her descendants. His treatise on the anatomy of the silkworm is the first book devoted to an invertebrate. Malpighi's book on vegetable histology, *Anatome plantarum* (1675–79), was published by the Royal Society, of which he was a fellow. He held professorships at Univs. of Pisa and Messina and was physician to Pope Innocent XII.—*D. H. D. R.*

MALTHUS, THOMAS ROBERT, 1766–1834, English political economist; b. Guildford. His Malthusian principle influenced the development of the theory of evolution. He proposed that since two parents can and often do produce more than two children, only such factors as war, disease, and famine keep population in check. Both C. R. Darwin and A. R. Wallace said that reading Malthus' book, *An Essay on the Principle of Population* (1798), led them to the idea of natural selection by the survival of the fittest. Malthus was a fellow of the Royal Society.—*D. H. D. R.*

MALTOSE: see SUGAR.

MAMMAL: any of a group of warm-blooded vertebrates that differ from all other animals in possessing hair sometime

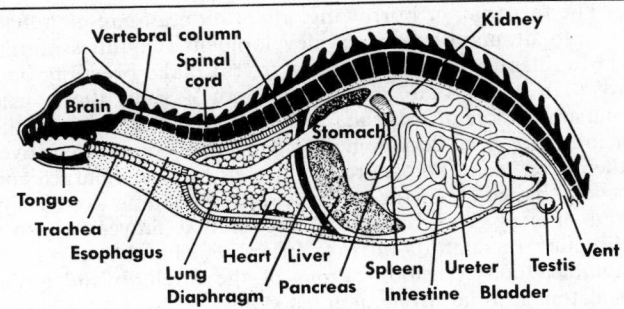

Mammal: Sagittal section through head and trunk of generalized mammal shows, in addition to usual vertebrate features, a separation of coelomic cavities by muscular diaphragm. (*After Guyer*)

during life and in having mammary glands for nourishing their young. Mammals have many structural peculiarities. The lower jaw is supported by a single bone, and there is a chain of three bones in each middle ear. The body cavity is divided by a muscular diaphragm into a chest cavity and an abdominal cavity. The highly developed circulatory system has a completely four-chambered heart, and a complicated system of controls in the arteries and veins to assist in regulation of body temperature. An extensive system of skin glands is another outstanding mammalian trait. Sweat glands, oil glands, and mammary glands are all modifications of this system. With the exception of one small group, the monotremes, all female mammals give birth to living young after specific periods of development within the uterus of the mother.

Evolution: Mammals were derived from reptilian stock during the late Mesozoic Era, approximately 100 million yr ago (see GEOLOGICAL TIME CHART). The mammals of the Mesozoic were small, primitive animals, none being larger than a chipmunk; they ate chiefly insects as food. With the decline and disappearance of the huge ruling reptiles, mammals slowly increased in numbers and in size. By the time of the Oligocene Epoch, a great variety of mammals had appeared, the hoofed forms being especially abundant. Mammals reached their peak with the development of the elephants and big carnivores of the Miocene; thereafter mammals decreased in both variety and average size.

Adaptation to Environment: Various groups of mammals are modified to fit a great variety of habitats. The typical mammal is a terrestrial animal with generalized legs and feet for running and walking on the ground. Examples include dogs, most mice, and chipmunks. Perhaps the first adaptation to be developed was that for arboreal existence, as seen in the tree shrew, the arboreal marsupials (*e.g.* the opossum), the squirrels, and the highly developed monkeys. These forms are usually equipped with long tails, which serve either as balancing organs or as grasping structures, and have light, strong bodies with strong limb girdles, and feet particularly adapted to grasping branches or rough bark.

From the extreme arboreal type developed the volant (or gliding) forms, represented today by the flying squirrels. Other primitive mammals developed flapping flight, as is seen today among the world-wide, highly diverse and successful bats. The phalanges (finger bones) of the bat's hand are greatly elongated and fastened together by a web of nearly hairless skin, all forming a wing. Hind legs and tail may be connected by a similar web, which serves as a stabilizer and rudder, and also as a scoop for capturing insect prey or maneuvering captured insects into position to chew and swallow. The typical bat has strong, small, grasping hind feet.

The fossorial, or burrowing, adaptation among mammals is seen at many stages of development. Countless forms (ground squirrels, prairie dogs, foxes) make breeding burrows in the ground and spend much time there. The marsupial mole of Australia and the true moles represent the acme of fossorial development. Their noses are ultrasensitive; their eyes, tails, and ears reduced; their forefeet enlarged and scoop-shaped; their fur soft and short, shedding sand easily and offering little friction as the animal moves in either direction through its burrow. Internal skeletal changes are notable, too, *e.g.* modifications of the forelimb and girdle skeleton, and the strong, pointed skull.

As among birds and reptiles, some mammals have returned to the water. Semiaquatic forms, *e.g.* mink, otter, beaver, and muskrat, have successfully combined the characteristics of several methods of life. The most strictly aquatic of all mammals are the whales, which have lost virtually all traces of hair and replaced its protection with a coat of blubber. Their front legs have been changed into highly efficient flippers; hind limbs are absent. Fleshy flaps serve in place of median fins, and by a rather remarkable modification great flukes have been developed on each side of the tail for locomotion. External ears are lacking, and external nostrils are so situated as to enable the animal to breathe while almost entirely submerged. Great changes in the skeletal and respiratory systems enable the whale to submerge to considerable depths. The body, with its short, stiff neck and almost completely streamlined trunk, conforms to the "ideal" aquatic pattern. Seals, walruses, and their allies exhibit these modifications to a lesser degree.

Mammals that live in open spaces develop long legs for running or jumping, and the feet are often modified in accordance with the ground over which they run. Generally speaking, odd-toed grazers, like the horse, dwell on hard ground; even-toed forms, as the camel, are more prevalent on soft, yielding surfaces. Many grazing mammals that feed in open areas, where they are exposed to their enemies, have specialized stomachs that enable them to secure large amounts of food in a relatively short time and to masticate it at leisure; the cud-chewing of the cow is typical.

Adaptation to Climate: Mammalian adaptations to climate are as varied as those to environment. Arctic mammals are equipped with warm, dense fur; many show color changes with the seasons. It is said that the color changes of the varying hare (snowshoe rabbit) are so perfectly correlated with the climate that the animal's fur begins to change from brown to white only with the first snowfall. The reduction in the length of the ears of the varying hare is thought to be a means of conserving body heat—another adaptation to the cold climate in which it lives. Heavy protective coats of fat and specializations of the feet enable the animal to burrow under ice and snow.

Many desert mammals appear capable of living their entire lives without a drink of water. The reason is their ability to produce metabolic water from foods with a high water content. Jumping and running are characteristic of most desert mammals. Most are nocturnal in habit and spend the day within burrows to escape the heat. Many forms undergo estivation when the heat is intense, and they may remain in their burrows for weeks at a time. The winter hibernation of many mammals, notably the bears, bats, woodchucks, and squirrels, is an adaptation of somewhat the same type. HIBERNATION involves a lowering of the metabolic rate and body temperature, and is perhaps the most remarkable of all mammalian adaptations, since mammals are warm-blooded and the regulation of these changes is internal.

Classification: Living mammals are subdivided into three very unequal subclasses and 16 orders:

A. *Subclass Prototheria and its single order Monotremata*—The egg-laying mammals found today only in Australia, New Guinea, and Tasmania: the duckbill platypus and the spiny anteaters. They are unusual in lacking nipples on their mammary glands and in having a cloaca through which urine, feces, and eggs all pass to the outside.

B. *Subclass Metatheria*—The pouched mammals, or MARSUPIALS, which are born in a very immature condition and creep into a special pouch (the marsupium) on the under surface of the mother, where each youngster swallows a long nipple and remains attached to it for many weeks. All mar-

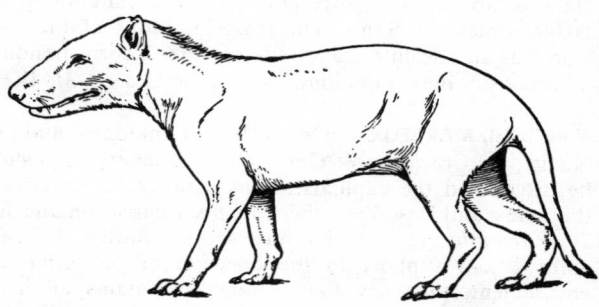

Archetypes of mammals: Even before the time of the dinosaurs some of the reptiles—the Synapsida—had already taken on a mammalian character, as evinced by Lycaenops (*below*), an advanced form with a characteristic mammalian pose. True mammals are represented by the Uintatherium (*lower left*) and Synoplotherium (*above*). Uintatherium, herbivorous and hoofed, belongs to an extinct mammalian order of the Eocene, the Dinocerata; it was of the size of a modern African rhinoceros. Synoplotherium belongs to an extinct suborder (the creodonts) of the still-thriving Carnivora. (*After Lull*)

The three subclasses of mammals: Most primitive are the Prototheria, here represented by Tasmanian species of spiny anteater (*left, above*). Young opossums, seen on mother's back (*left, below*), are N America's native marsupials, subclass Metatheria. Placental mammals (Eutheria) have adapted to a variety of modes of life—some, like this Corynorhinus bat (*above*), having even taken to the air. The great hornlike structures are ears; the smaller projections are homologous with the tragus of the human ear. (*Leonard Lee Rue III; Harry Frauca/Monkmeyer; Lorus J. and Margery Milne*)

supials are native to Australia and adjacent islands, except the opossums of America.

Order Polyprotodontia: Carnivorous marsupials with sharp conical teeth used in tearing food: opossums, burrowing "marsupial moles," insect-eating bandicoots, the Tasmanian "wolf," and Australian "cats."

Order Diprotodontia: Herbivorous marsupials with chisel-shaped incisor teeth and very small canine teeth: kangaroos, wallabies, the koala "bear," wombats, and phalangers.

C. *Subclass Eutheria*—Placental mammals, with neither a marsupium nor a cloaca, the mammary glands often having their nipples in lateral "milk lines." The young develop more completely in the uterus and are nourished by a PLACENTA. Of approximately 12,000 species of living mammals, more than 11,000 are placental forms.

Order Insectivora: The INSECTIVORES, which have many sharp teeth, used in feeding on insects, earthworms, millipedes, other small animals, and eggs. Insectivores include shrews, moles, and the European hedgehog.

Order Chiroptera: The only mammals able to fly with flapping wings, these being composed of the long bones of arm and fingers linked by a flexible leathery web; the sternum is keeled, as in flying birds. These are BATS.

Order Primates: Distinct from other mammals in having two (not three) incisors on each side of each jaw, and in possessing nails on some or all digits; the thumb or great toe or both are opposable and used in grasping objects. Primates include the lemurs, the tarsier of the Philippines, monkeys, apes, and mankind. See PRIMATE.

Order Edentata: Unique in lacking teeth or having an incomplete set without enamel. These are arboreal and terrestrial mammals: sloths, armadillos and anteaters of America, the aardvark (Cape anteater, of Africa), and pangolin (scaly anteater).

Order Lagomorpha: Their distinguishing feature is the presence of an additional pair of incisor teeth in the upper jaw, behind the front pair; the tail is very short, and hind legs are adapted to a hopping gait. Hares, rabbits, and pikas are included. See RABBITS AND HARES.

Order Rodentia: Gnawing animals with one pair of sharp, chisel-shaped incisors in each jaw, but no canine teeth; tail usually long and scaly. The most numerous and successful order of mammals, this includes rats, mice, squirrels, porcupines, and beavers. See RODENT.

Order Carnivora: Distinguished by enlarged, projecting canine teeth used in tearing prey: dogs, wolves, foxes, cats, bears, martens, minks, otters, seals, sea lions, and walrus. See CARNIVORE.

Order Cetacea: Aquatic mammals with nostrils represented by one or two blowholes atop the head, with hind legs represented only by a few skeletal remnants, and with the forelegs modified into fins used in clambering or in balancing the body as it is propelled by a tail expanded into horizontal flukes. The great blue whale (largest of known animals) and other baleen whales have whalebone (baleen) strainers in the mouth, used in collecting plankton food; the sperm whale and porpoises have conical teeth, used in seizing fish and other prey. See CETACEAN.

Order Artiodactyla: Even-toed hoofed mammals (ungulates), in which only two toes on each foot have well-developed toenails (hoofs); many have divided stomachs and chew the cud, as ruminants. Pigs, peccaries, and the hippopotamus have enlarged canines and incisors in both jaws, whereas cattle, sheep, deer, antelopes, giraffe, and camels have small canines or none, and have incisors only in the lower jaw. See UNGULATE.

Order Perissodactyla: Odd-toed hoofed mammals (ungulates), which bear their weight on the third (middle) toe, even if a few other toes reach the ground; incisors are well developed in both jaws of tapirs, zebras, and horses, but reduced in rhinoceroses.

Order Proboscidia: Unique in possessing an elongated, prehensile nose (proboscis); the tusks are modified incisor teeth, usually from the upper jaw. These are the elephants.

Order Hyracoidea: Small, rodentlike mammals with a short tail and teeth somewhat like those of ungulates: the coney (dassie) and tree *Hyrax* of Africa and the Middle East.

Order Sirenia: Aquatic mammals with nostrils on the upper surface of a broad snout, no hindlimbs, paddle-shaped forelimbs, and a flattened tail. Included are sea cows, manatees, and dugongs. The latter are supposed to have inspired legends about mermaids. See Color Plate 58.—*A. P. E.; L. and M. M.*

MAMMARY GLAND: a milk-secreting gland that originates in the skin of mammals and serves to nourish their young. Mammals are named after the unique presence of these glands, which distinguish mammals from all other groups of animals. The glands are present, but dormant, in males. In egg-laying mammals, such as the duckbilled platypus, the

Mammary glands: In human female, milk ducts from alveoli converge at nipple of mammary gland (*below*). In kangaroo, young animal feeds from nipples in mammary pouch (*right*). (After Eaton)

glands are scattered over the belly region, and the young lick milk from a large skin area of the mother's abdomen. In higher mammals, the glands are concentrated in two to twenty discrete areas (depending on species) on either side of the midline of the front, or underside, of the body; each gland opens onto the body surface by way of a nipple, or teat. In pregnant women prior to the birth of a child, estrogenic hormones and progesterone from the ovaries and the placenta stimulate the mammary glands to develop to the stage where they are ready for secretion. Mammary glands normally begin actual production of milk about three days after childbirth, after the release of an additional (lactogenic) hormone by the pituitary gland. During the first three days, the glands yield a very different secretion, called colostrum, which acts as a laxative for the child, inducing evacuation from its digestive tract of the mucus and cellular debris swallowed before and during birth.—*A. R. D.*

MANGANESE: a metallic element (Mn); at. no. 25; at. wt 54.94; density 7.2; mp 1260°C; bp 1900°C; valences 2, 3, 4,

6, and 7. When manganese has a low oxidation state, as in manganese dioxide (MnO_2), it acts as a base-forming element; but as its valence rises, its basic properties diminish until in its highest oxidation state (7) it is an acid-forming element. The oxide of manganese was recognized by Karl Wilhelm Scheele in 1774, and the pure metal was isolated in the same year by J. G. Gahn. The principal manganese ores are pyrolusite and psilomelane; principal ore deposits are in the U. S. S. R., W Africa, India, and Brazil. Important manganese compounds include manganese dioxide, a good oxidizing agent used in dry cells, and manganous soaps, used for catalyzing the drying of paints by oxidation of their oils; potassium permanganate ($(KMnO_4)_2$) is also a powerful oxidation agent much used in analytical chemistry, and as a disinfectant and antiseptic.—*I. B.*

Manganese appears in a wide range of alloys, most importantly with steel and iron. It prevents steel of high sulfur and phosphorus content from disintegrating during forging or hot-rolling. When manganese is added in large amounts (above 10%) to steel, together with about 1% silicon, and the resulting mixture is heated, cooled, reheated to about 1800°F, water-quenched, and finally cold-worked, a manganese steel is produced with extremely high tensile strength and abrasion-resistance; this is used for heavy-duty mining and milling machinery, *e.g.* rock crushers. Manganese added to either copper or nickel, or to a mixture of both, produces alloys having resistance to corrosion, high coefficients of expansion, high electrical resistivity, and vibration-damping qualities much superior to those of steel. Manganese increases aluminum's tensile strength, and is added to all magnesium-aluminum alloys to improve their resistance to corrosion and make them easier to weld. Manganese "bronze" is actually a BRASS containing up to 3.5% manganese and small percentages of other elements depending on the intended use; with its high strength, hardness, and resistance to corrosion and wear, it is used in pumps, gears, and many marine applications, *e.g.* boat propellers.—*E. H. H.*

MANOMETER: see PRESSURE MEASUREMENTS.

MANTLE: see EARTH.

MAP: a drawing or other representation on a reduced scale of all or part of Earth's surface on a plane surface. Maps intended for navigational purposes are called *charts,* while those representing cities may be termed *plans.* Progress in the making of maps (cartography) has always been closely related to the development of surveying methods; and since the 18th cent., advances in geodesy (the study of Earth's size and shape) have contributed much to the making of accurate representations of large areas, especially world maps and globes. A more recent development has been the use of aerial photography as an aid in compiling maps (see PHOTOGRAMMETRY; PHOTOGRAPHY). By means of outlines, contours, symbols, place names, and other conventions, maps commonly give information as to (1) the over-all shape of a physical feature, *e.g.* the shape of a peninsula, continent, or bay of water; (2) the location of various physical features in relation to each other; and (3) the distances between physical features. Distance is calculated from the map's *scale:* the proportion of any linear distance on the map to the same distance on Earth. Scale may be represented graphically by a length of line on which is marked the equivalent distance on Earth, *e.g.* 1 in. equals 50 mi; or it may be represented by a ratio, *e.g.* 1:3,168,000, meaning that 1 unit on the map equals 3,168,000 units on Earth.

Meridians and Parallels: As an aid in representing the shape and location of physical features, Earth's surface is

MAP 703

divided into a coordinate system. Lines constructed over the curving surface of Earth from pole to pole are termed *meridians;* from the meridian running through Greenwich, England, position is described in degrees of longitude. The lines circling Earth running parallel to the equator and perpendicular to the meridians are termed *parallels;* position north and south from the equator is described in degrees of latitude. See LATITUDE AND LONGITUDE.

Conformal versus Equal-area Maps: In general the scale of a map should remain as constant as possible over the whole surface of the map, *i.e.* an inch on a map, whether at the equator or near the poles, should represent equal lengths on Earth. To be useful to navigators, a map must be *conformal, i.e.* preserve angles and therefore represent shapes and directions accurately. Since meridians and parallels cross each other at right angles on the globe, meridians and parallels represented on conformal maps will cross at right angles. The Mercator projection, one of the most widely used of world maps, is a conformal map. However, to give an accurate idea of areas, *e.g.* the acreage available for agriculture or the square miles covered by glacial ice, an *equal-area map* must be used: a map on which equal areas on the map represent equal areas on Earth, whether the areas are at the equator or near the poles. Perhaps the best equal-area map is the Mollweide homolographic projection. There is no way of making a map both conformal and equal-area; a map that preserves shapes will tend to distort areas, and *vice versa.*

Problems of Mapping the Spheroid Earth: On any map representing actual land surfaces more than 4 mi in length, the scale tends to change from location to location. Thus maps of large areas and especially world maps incorporate extensive distortions of scale, shape, and area. These distortions stem from the fact that Earth's approximately spherical shape is not developable, *i.e.* cannot be made to lie in a flat plane. The surface of a cylinder or a cone when unrolled lies in a flat plane, but not the surface of a sphere unless it is pulled and distorted out of shape. Therefore, in making world maps, various methods have had to be devised to project (transfer) points on Earth, or on a globe representing Earth, to a plane surface. The three methods in widest use are (1) projection directly onto a flat plane, called *zenithal* or *azimuthal* projection; (2) projection onto the surface of a cylinder; (3) projection onto the surface of a cone.

Zenithal (or Azimuthal) Projection: To make a stereographic projection (one type of zenithal projection), a flat plane is placed touching a point on the globe. Any given point on the globe's surface is transferred to the flat plane by drawing a line from a point at the antipode of the point of contact between globe and plane through the given point on the globe's surface; this line's point of intersection with the plane is the projection of the given point. Stereographic projections are perfectly conformal and give a lively impression of Earth's roundness; but because popular taste is not accustomed to maps stressing Earth's curvature in the more inhabited portions of the globe, stereographic maps are usually restricted to representations of the polar regions. When points on the globe's surface are transferred by drawing rays from the globe's center to the point on the globe's surface, zenithal maps are termed *gnomonic* projections. On such maps great circles are represented by straight lines. (Great circles are circles having the diameter of the globe; they describe the shortest path between any two points on the globe's surface.) Therefore straight lines drawn by a navigator between two points on a gnomonic chart indicate the shortest course and describe the longitudes and latitudes at which the course intersects the meridians and parallels.

Cylindrical Projections: In a cylindrical projection, either a

Scale is the proportion of a distance as shown on a map or globe to the actual distance on Earth. Scale here is 1: 550,000,000.

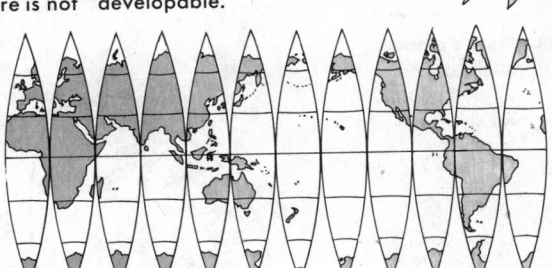

Surface of globe, peeled off into gores, will not lie flat and will therefore not produce a map. Unlike the cylinder, a sphere is not "developable."

cylinder is constructed around the exterior of the globe touching it at the equator, or the cylinder is made to intersect the globe through two parallels equidistant from the equator. A ray may be drawn from the center of the globe or from some other point (*e.g.* a point on the equator in Gall's stereographic cylindrical projection) to the point on the globe's surface; the ray is then extended until it intersects the surface of the cylinder. In all cylindrical projections, meridians and parallels intersect at right angles and are represented by straight lines; the parallels vary in their spacing depending on how the projection is made. Perhaps the best-known map suggested by cylindrical projection is Mercator's projection. This projection, invented by Gerhard Kremer (Gerhardus Mercator) of Flanders in the 16th cent., is not a true cylindrical projection, since the space between parallels is determined by mathematical formula rather than by geometric projection. An important consideration in regard to cylindrical projections is that, on the globe, the interval between two meridians on any parallel other than the equator is less than the interval between two meridians represented on a cylindrical projection. On all cylindrical projections, the meridians are constructed *as if* the intervals between them were equal all over the globe, with the result that intervals at high latitudes are represented as larger than the actual intervals between global meridians. In the case of the Mercator projection, the intervals between parallels are increased in proportion to the enlarged intervals between projected meridians on a cylindrical projection; this results in a map that is strictly conformal but contains serious distortions of area in high latitudes, *e.g.* Greenland appears eight times larger than S America. The Mercator projection has long been popular with navigators, since a constant compass direction, *i.e.* a line that crosses meridians and parallels at a constant angle, is a straight line.

Conic Projection: In a conic projection a cone is placed over a globe so that the cone touches the globe on one parallel. To project a point on the globe to the surface of the cone, a ray is drawn from the globe's center to the point on the globe and then extended until the ray intersects the cone's surface. The parallel touching the cone's surface is called the *standard parallel* and is at the same scale as the globe; however, the scale increases at all distances north and south from the standard parallel. Such simple conic projections have a fair degree

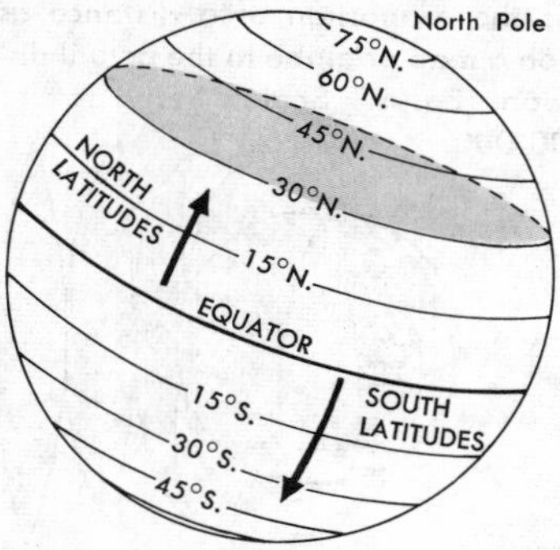

Latitudes are marked by parallels; only one of these, the Equator, is a great circle.

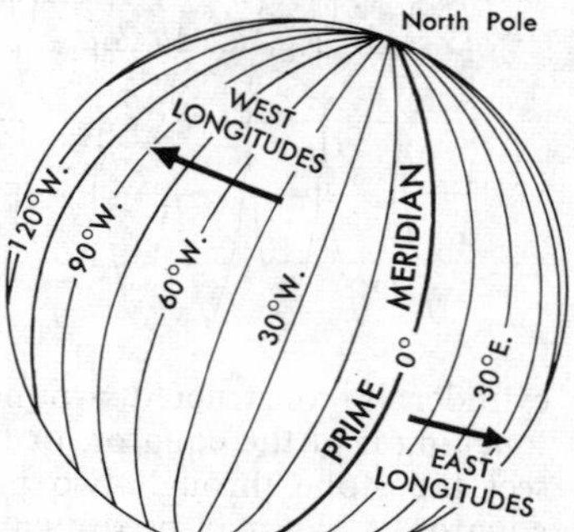

Longitudes are indicated by meridians—great circles that intersect at the poles.

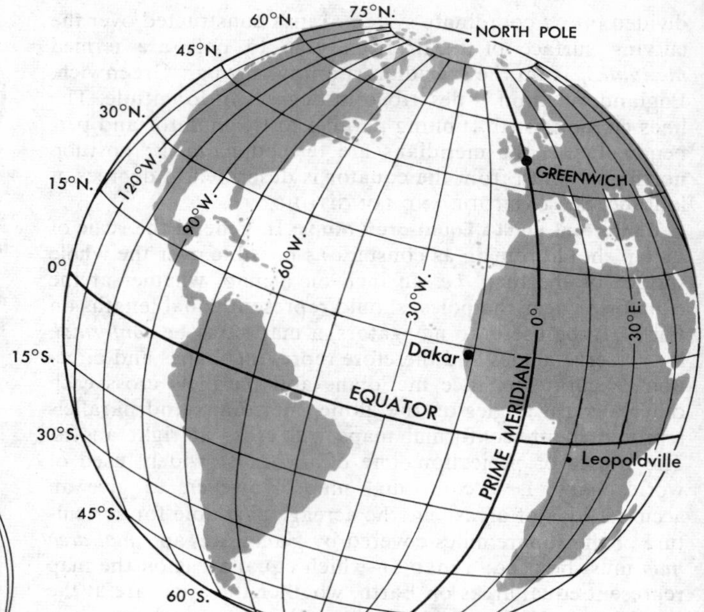

Equator and Prime Meridian are bases to which latitudes and longitudes of points on globe are referred. Latitudes are given in degrees N or S of Equator; thus Dakar is 15°N, Leopoldville is 4°S. Longitudes are reckoned from arbitrary Prime Meridian of Greenwich, but only to 180°: Dakar is 17°W, but Leopoldville is 15°E (not 345°W).

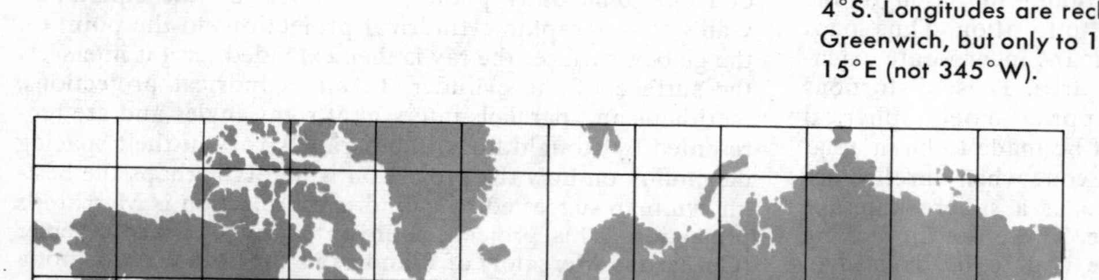

Mercator projection, conformal but not equal-area, is unique in showing lines of constant compass direction as straight. It is derived from the simple cylindrical projection shown at right by adjusting the vertical stretching to accomplish this result. (The projection lines are not actually straight lines radiating from the center of the globe.) The Mercator projection is grossly misleading at high latitudes.

Both maps are drawn to the same equatorial scale.

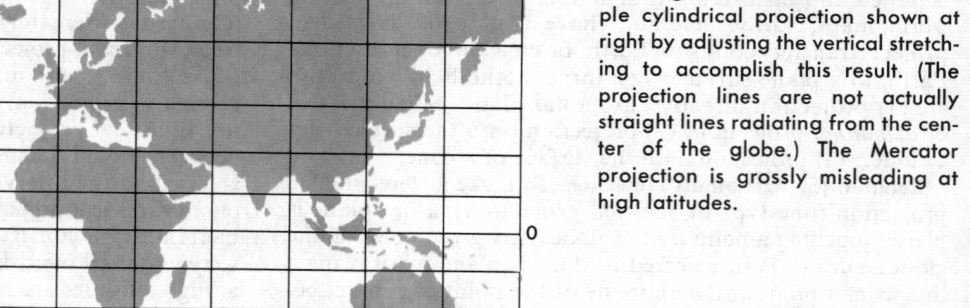

Mollweide projection, devised by Karl B. Mollweide in 1805, is not conformal but is "homolographic," or equal-area. Ellipse encloses entire surface of globe; inscribed within it is circle formed by 90°W and 90°E meridians, which embrace one hemisphere. Polar areas are distorted.

MAP 705

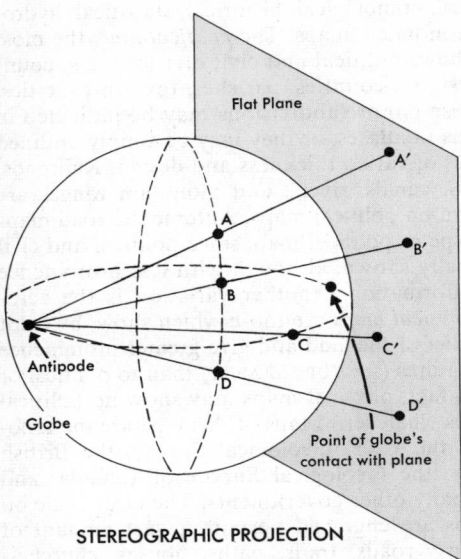

Flat Plane

A'

B'

A

C'

B

C

D'

Antipode

D

Globe

Point of globe's
contact with plane

STEREOGRAPHIC PROJECTION

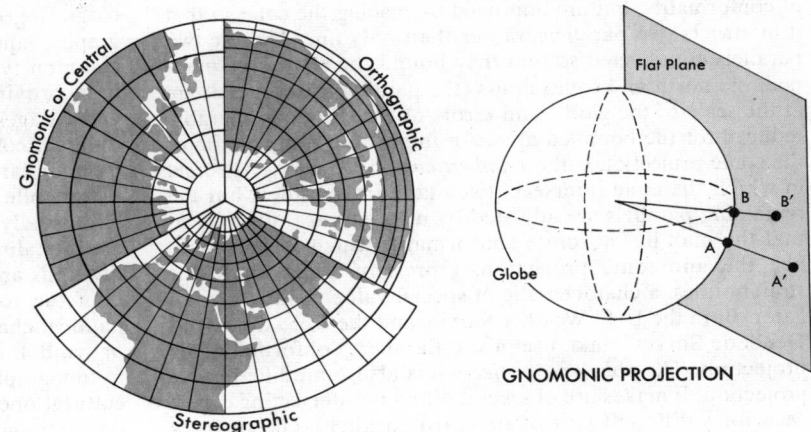

Gnomonic or Central

Orthographic

Stereographic

Flat Plane

B B'

A

A'

Globe

GNOMONIC PROJECTION

Projections to a developable surface (cylinder or cone) may be made, as below, by drawing lines from the center of the globe to the surface (after which the surface is cut along a single line and unrolled) or by drawing lines from infinity that pass through all points of the globe and are perpendicular to the surface, as in the equal-area cylindrical projection.

Projections to a plane include the *stereographic projection*, on which points on the globe are projected by means of straight lines from a point (the antipode) diametrically opposite to the point of contact of the globe and the plane; and the *gnomonic projection*, in which points on the globe are projected by means of straight lines radiating from the center of the globe. Each of these projections yields increasing distortion as the distance from the point of contact between the plane and the globe increases. However, for special purposes, this point can be located anywhere on the globe, minimizing the distortion over the area in question. A particular advantage of the gnomonic projection is that all great circles on the globe are projected as straight lines, making the map valuable for air and sea navigation. The third projection shown in the center panel, the *orthographic*, is made by drawing parallel lines perpendicular to the plane to all points on the globe. Essentially it is what the globe would look like seen from a great (theoretically, infinite) distance.

**CYLINDRICAL
EQUAL-AREA
PROJECTION**

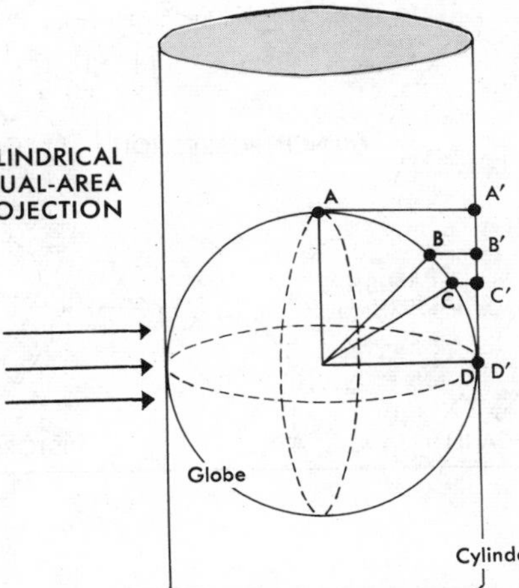

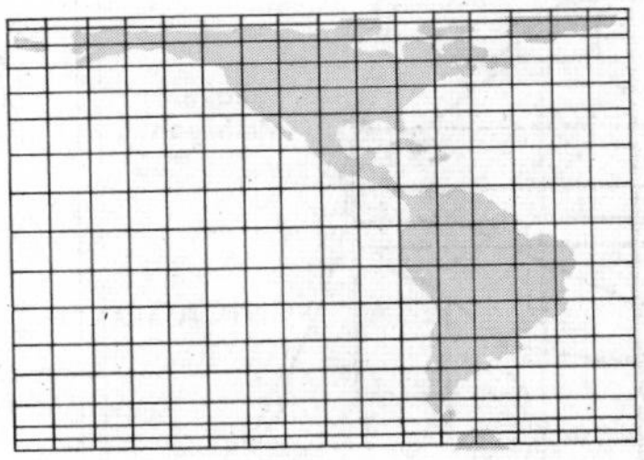

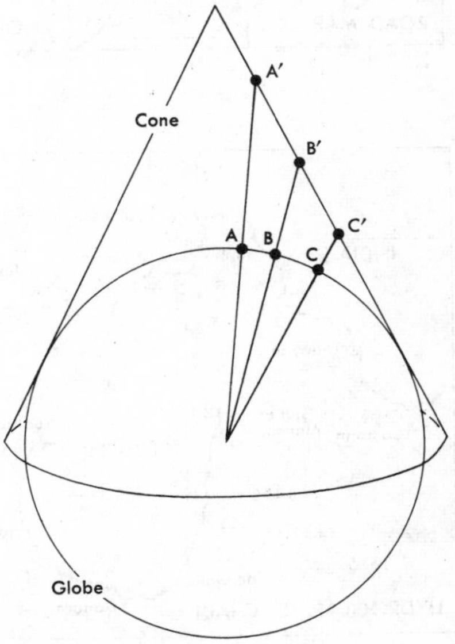

A'

B'

A

B

C'

C

D'

D

Globe

Cylinder

A

B

C

D

Globe

A'

B'

C'

D'

Cylinder

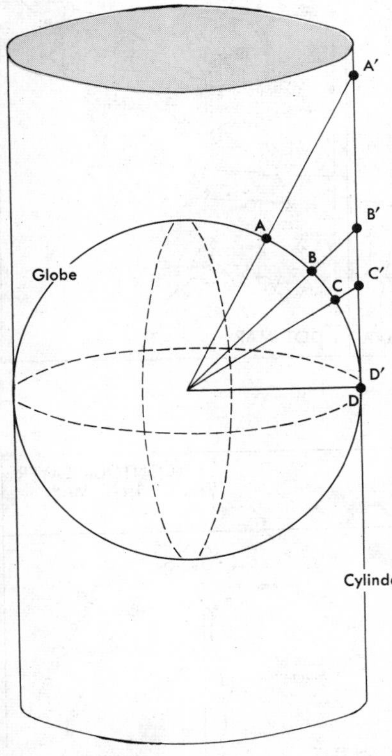

**SIMPLE
CYLINDRICAL
PROJECTION**

**SIMPLE CONIC
PROJECTION**

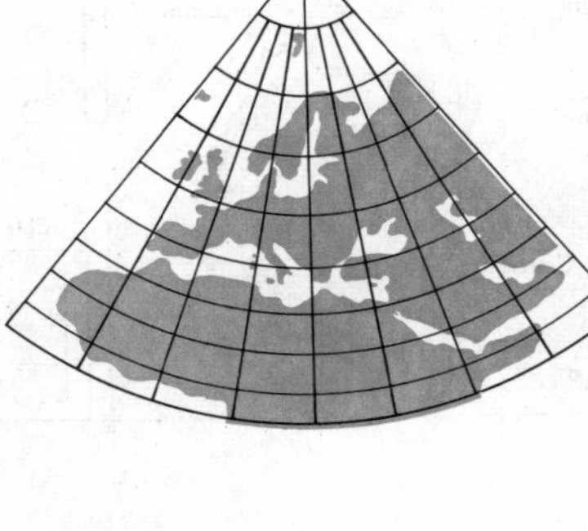

Cone

A'

B'

A B

C

C'

Globe

of conformality, but are improved by placing the cone so that it intersects two parallels, rather than only one. If these two parallels are selected so that they bound the area to be mapped, the north and south limits (the parallels intersected) are at the scale of the globe, and errors of scale are considerably reduced for the bounded area. An important modification of the conic projection is the *Lambert conformal conic projection,* in which the cone intersects two standard parallels but the remaining parallels are adjusted by mathematical formula so that the map has absolute conformality. Such a projection, like the gnomonic projection, represents great circles as straight lines, a characteristic of special value to the air navigator. Both the U. S. Weather Survey and the U. S. Coast and Geodetic Survey make use of the Lambert conformal conic projection. The *polyconic projection* is also a modified conic projection. It makes use of several different intersecting cones, each for a different pair of standard parallels. The surfaces charted between each pair of standard parallels are then matched to each other with only a small amount of stretching. Although polyconic projections are not absolutely conformal or absolutely accurate in representation of area, the degree of error is small, especially near the map's central meridian. Polyconic maps are used by the U. S. Geological Survey and the International Map of the World, but elsewhere have been increasingly replaced by the Lambert conformal conic projection.

Types of Maps: Maps vary widely in content. The information they convey classifies them as political, physical, meteor-ological, geological, ethnological, historical, statistical, hydrographic, and astronomical maps. The *political map,* the most common type, shows political and civil divisions, *e.g.* countries, provinces, states, counties, parishes, townships, cities, and villages. These minor subdivisions may be indicated in different colors, as in atlases, or they may be simply outlined by boundary lines of varied thickness and design. Railroads, automobile roads, canals, rivers, and mountain ranges are also usually shown on political maps. Automobile road maps are in reality a type of political map, since political and civil divisions are usually shown, although with less prominence than the road information. Another variation is the aeronautical chart. *Physical maps* are those which show, by color or symbol, the relief of the land and give greater prominence to topographic features (see TOPOGRAPHY) than to political or cultural ones. (In fact, physical maps may show no political or civil boundaries whatever.) Maps of this type are the topographic maps of the U. S. Geological Survey, the British Ordnance Survey, the Geological Survey of Canada, and departments of many other governments. The large scale on which these maps are engraved permits a vast amount of essential detail, *e.g.* roads, trails, paths, houses, churches, schools, brooks, creeks, marshes, and springs. *Meteorological maps* include climate, rainfall, temperature, and wind maps. The maps issued daily by the U. S. Weather Bureau show by color and arrows the precipitation, the temperature, and the pressure of the atmosphere in all parts of the U. S. A. for the previous 24 hr. *Geological maps* indicate the kind and quality

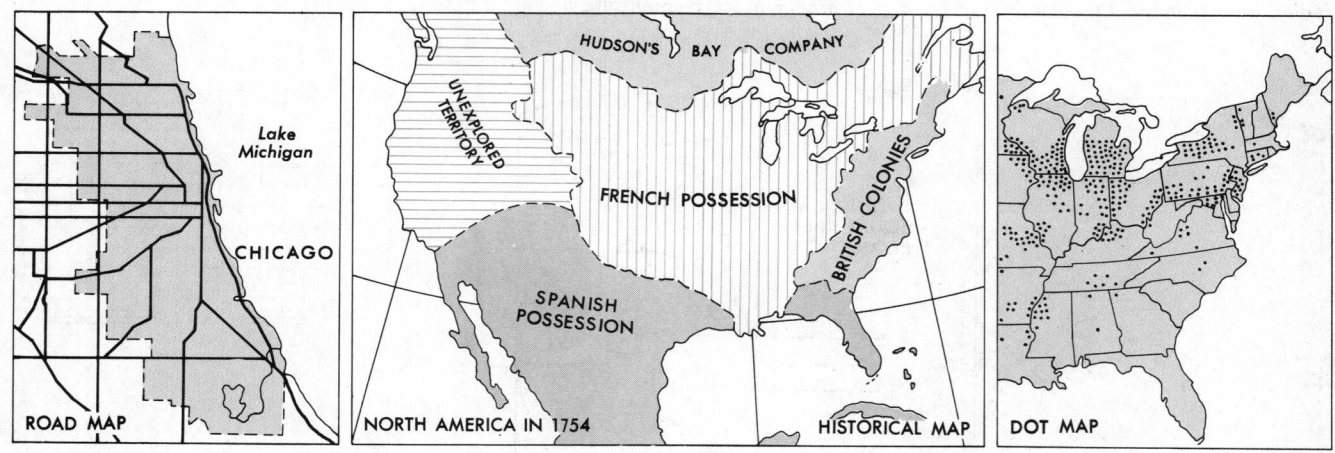

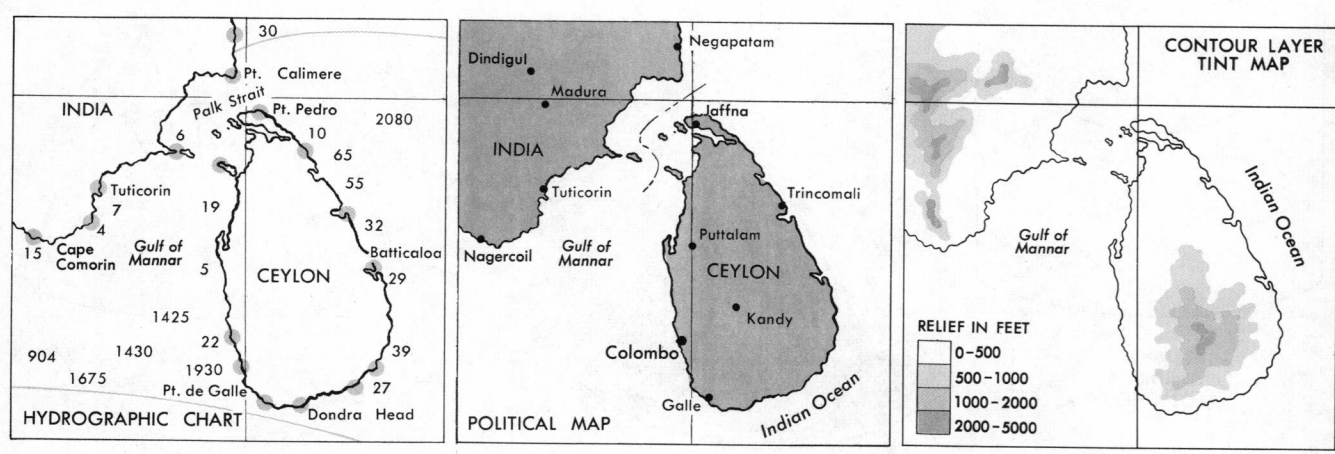

of the soil and rock prevailing upon and beneath the surface of the ground; different colors, tints, and symbols represent different strata and substrata. *Ethnological maps* show the races of mankind existing in different parts of the region mapped. The major races alone may be shown or the many divisions of each race. Maps illustrating the habitat of animals, birds, fish, or reptiles would come in this category. *Historical maps* are simply political maps of an earlier period; biblical maps fall into this classification. There are almost no limits to the variety of *statistical maps* which have been or may be compiled. The most common types are population, economic, vegetation, commercial, and maps illustrating prevailing languages and religions. Population maps illustrate the density of population by using different tints and colors to represent different degrees of density. Economic maps show the agricultural and mineral products at points where they are produced or mined. Vegetation maps show the typical fauna and flora that flourish in different parts of the region, *e.g.* coniferous forests, broad-leaved forests, meadows, and alpine flora. Forestry maps, such as are published by the U. S. Forestry Service, are typical of this class. Commercial maps give an idea of the relative importance and amount of trade movements. The waters of the world have been charted by the different governments; the resulting *hydrographic maps* are very much used by mariners, yachtsmen, and all who travel by water. These maps show the depths at frequent intervals, and indicate dangerous rocks and wrecks, as well as buoys, lighthouses, lightships, and lifesaving stations. An interesting series of maps published monthly by the U. S. Hydrographic Office shows the route of wind and rain storms during the previous month, together with the locations of derelicts and wreckage as reported by ship captains during that period. *Astronomical maps* are charts of the sky, locating all the principal celestial objects with reference to celestial coordinates. (See ASTRONOMICAL CATALOGS, MAPS, AND ATLASES.) Accurate *military maps* are essential in the planning and carrying out of military operations. All types of maps are used, from those depicting a whole country or region of the globe to large-scale, highly detailed topographic charts. Aerial photography is utilized wherever practicable.

History: Rudimentary forms of cartography existed in prehistoric times, especially among nomadic tribes; and crude maps are used by primitive peoples surviving into the modern age, *e.g.* by the Eskimos. There is historical evidence that cadastral maps were used by the Babylonians as early as 3,800 B. C.; but the oldest map still in existence dates from about 1,000 B. C.; this map is engraved on a clay tablet, unearthed in Iraq. Greek and Greco-Egyptian astronomers were the great cartographers of the Mediterranean civilizations. Beginning with Thales (7th-6th cent. B. C.) and culminating in the work of Ptolemy (2nd cent. A. D.), many modern concepts of mapmaking were introduced, *e.g.* the concept of Earth as a globe and the principles of latitude and longitude. Moreover, several types of projections were attempted or suggested, among them a stereographic projection (Hipparchus, 2nd cent. B. C.), a cylindrical projection (Marinus of Tyre, 2nd cent. A. D.), and two types of modified conical projections (Ptolemy). The famous Eratosthenes (3rd cent. B. C.) is also reputed to have made a world map. After Ptolemy, in the general decline of Western culture, these advances in cartography were either forgotten or neglected. Thus, at a time (*c.* A. D. 1,000) when the Polynesians were using crude but effective navigational charts and sextants to explore the Pacific, European maps were inaccurate and fanciful affairs constructed without meridians or parallels. These conditions, slightly improved by the invention of the compass, prevailed through the Middle Ages. In the 14th cent. the voyages of

discovery began to force a revival and reappraisal of world geography: parallels and meridians were reintroduced; mathematicians devised new methods of projection; and locations were determined less by paced distances and more by astronomical observations. With the maps of Mercator, the modern age of mapmaking began. The varieties and uses of maps have increased with the progress of civilization, cartography keeping pace with commerce and invention.—*A. P. E.; A. L.*

MARBLE: a metamorphic rock formed under pressure and heat, usually as a result of regional metamorphism, from limestone. It is coarse-grained, the product of the recrystallization of the grains of calcite (calcium carbonate) or dolomite (calcium magnesium carbonate) composing the parent rock. Impurities in the parent rock may become altered and enter into the composition of the marble, often accounting for the peculiar beauty characteristic of this rock. Thus serpentine, hematite, or carbon add green, reddish, or black coloration to a rock that otherwise would be white. Largely because of its handsome appearance, and despite its relative softness and incapacity to resist weathering, marble has been a favorite building material and sculptor's stone. Some rocks commercially known as "marbles" are actually limestones.—*E. A.*

MARCONI, GUGLIELMO, 1874–1937, Italian inventor; b. Bologna. He obtained a British patent (1896) on a simple system of transmitting and receiving wireless messages. The system's success depended on a greatly improved coherer (detector of electromagnetic waves) and the great advantage gained by grounding the antenna. He succeeded (1901) in transmitting a wireless message across the Atlantic. His companies in Europe and the U. S. A. did much toward making radio commercially successful. For the development of wireless telegraphy he and C. F. Braun shared the 1909 Nobel prize.—*H. I. S.*

MARGULES, MAX, 1856–1920, Austrian meteorologist; b. Brody. His research was concerned with atmospheric electricity, fluid mechanics, storm theory, and energy of storms, and the statistics and processing of meteorological data for various regions of Austria. He was the first to compute the slope of front between two air masses from wind and temperature readings (1906). From 1882 he was at the Central Meteorological Establishment, Vienna.—*D. H. D. R.*

MARINE NAVIGATION: the practices used to determine the position and direct the course of a vessel. There are, broadly, four methods—dead reckoning, piloting, celestial navigation, and electronic navigation. In practice, combinations of methods and instruments are often used.

Dead reckoning (a corruption of "deduced reckoning") is the oldest method. It consists in keeping track, on the chart or by mathematical techniques, of a vessel's course and distance traveled from the last well-known position. Compass heading, corrected for known compass error, is generally taken as the course, and distance is obtained from the product of speed through the water and the elapsed time. Speed is determined from mechanical devices, known as logs, by computation from propeller revolutions, or by observation of successive positions. Corrections to course and distance may be made for the effects of wind and current. In any case, dead-reckoning positions are not considered actual positions for a vessel, but rather only predictions of position under the circumstances that are presumed to exist.

Piloting consists of the navigational practices used in confined waters or close to the shore, where aids to navigation, known landmarks, and features of the ocean bottom are

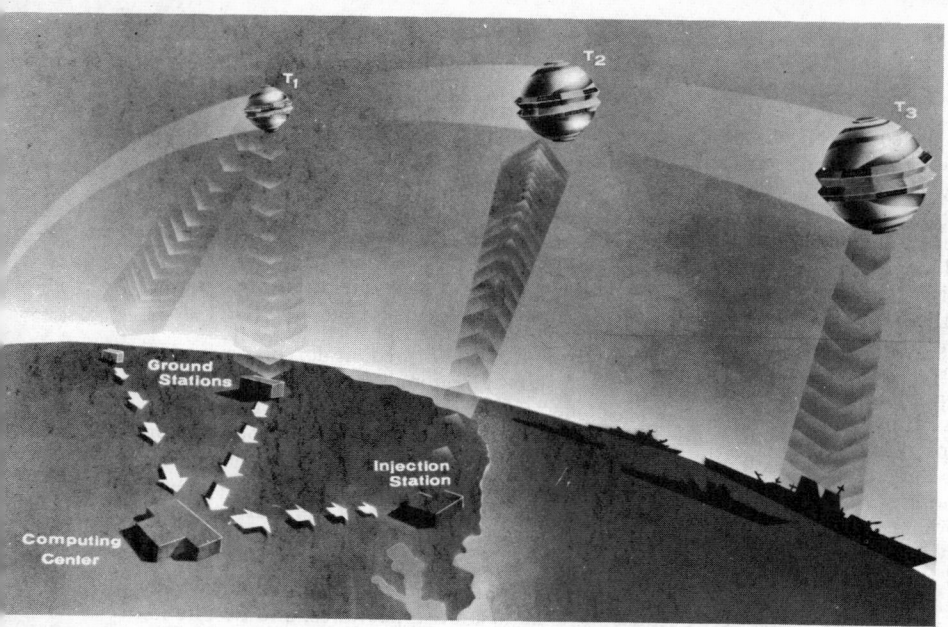

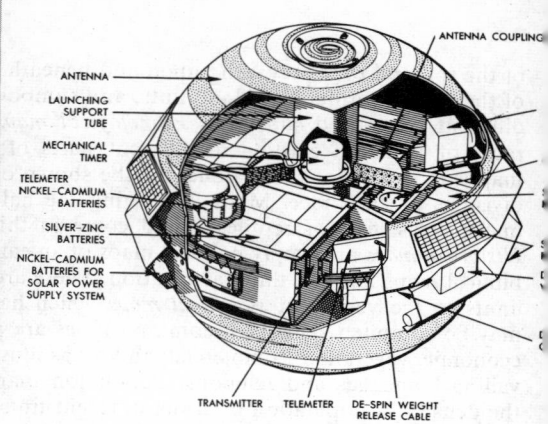

Cutaway of Transit 1 shows parts, including painted antenna. This satellite has a 36-in. diameter. (U. S. Navy)

World-wide navigational system provided by orbiting Transit satellites: Ground stations (two are shown above) track satellites, while at the computing center the satellites' future positions are predicted at least 12 hr in advance. From the injection station, predicted-orbit data are transmitted to the satellites and there stored in a memory unit. The satellites then transmit the data automatically every 2 min to craft using the Transit system, e.g. ships at sea, giving the craft the exact path of the satellites in space.

available. These waters are usually the most hazardous: they are often narrow and irregular in outline, frequent course changes may be required, depths are limited, currents are stronger and more variable, and traffic—posing the danger of collision—is heavy. Hence the greatest skill and alertness are required of the pilot, and navigational procedures must be used more often, more accurately, than in other waters.

In piloting, positional information is obtained in a variety of ways. Landmarks, beacons, and lights are used for taking bearings by compass or as ranges along which to proceed; buoys identify fairways, channels, and hidden dangers; distance to the shore is computed from angles of elevation taken on objects of known height; depths of the water and samples of the bottom are compared with data recorded on charts. Numerous publications identify navigational aids and shorelines by day and night Tables and charts of tides and tidal currents assist the navigator to estimate the variations in depth and in movement of the water which he might expect to encounter. Detailed charts drawn to various scales are used to track the progress of the vessel. CELESTIAL NAVIGATION, *i.e.* navigation by observations of celestial bodies, is used in open oceans where piloting aids are not available.

Electronic navigation has become extremely important in recent years. Echo depth finders and radio direction finders are among the oldest electronic aids to piloting. More recently, newer aids, *e.g.* RADAR and loran, have permitted piloting techniques to be extended to greater distances. As a result, electronic navigation is no longer considered merely a branch of piloting.

The principal radio devices now in general use are the radio direction finder, radar, and loran. Radio direction finders are simply shipboard radio receivers with special directional antennas that indicate the direction of transmitting antenna. Radar consists of a transmitter-receiver located on the vessel, with a rotating antenna and an electronic display console for indicating the distance and direction of any target which reflects radio waves back to the

transmitting antenna. In addition to its value in locating and plotting position from landmarks, radar is a valuable anticollision device.

Loran combines transmitting equipment on shore with special shipboard receivers that measure the time difference in the reception of suitable signals; for any measured time difference, the navigator can locate his vessel on a hyperbolic curve about the transmitting antennas. Loran can be used at a maximum range of 700 to 1,400 mi, depending on conditions, from the transmitting stations. A similar system, more accurate but more limited in range, is known as Decca.

Many other electronic piloting systems are in use or in development, using the principles of radio transmission and reception, or of the transmission of sound through water. Electronic equipment was also developed to aid in deadreckoning navigation, through electronic measurement and recording of course and speed, and in celestial navigation, by providing means to observe the Sun and Moon continuously with radio sextants and the stars with photometric sextants. The Transit system, based on the transmission of radio signals from a group of artificial Earth satellites, is expected to provide a continuous, reliable, all-weather navigation system available at all times at any point on Earth.

Special techniques and equipment are used by marine navigators in polar navigation, submarine navigation, and lifeboat—or survival—navigation. See AIR NAVIGATION.—T. N.

MARIOTTE, EDME C., 1620–84, French physicist; b. Dijon. He was abbé and prior of St. Martin-sous-Beaune, and one of the original members of the Académie des Sciences (founded 1666). He published several essays on physics (1676–79). In his *De la nature de l'air* (1676) he formulated the relation between volume and pressure of air, quite independently of Boyle, whose law dated from 1660. He suggested the use of the barometer in measuring the altitude of mountains. His *Traité du mouvement des eaux* (1686) contains fundamental observations on the flow of water from a reservoir. He also studied the increase in volume of freezing water and the specific gravity of ice. He concentrated rays of sunlight with the help of a biconvex ice-lens and studied the absorptive power of glass. His collected works were published in 1717 and again in 1740.—R. J. F.

MARIUS, SIMON (Simon Mayr), 1570–1624, German astronomer; b. Gunzenhausen. He claimed to have discovered the satellites of Jupiter shortly before Galileo's discovery. One of the earliest observers with the astronomical telescope, Marius observed sunspots in 1611 and the Andromeda nebula in 1612. His work on the satellites of Jupiter was published in 1614.—*D. H. D. R.*

MARS: The 4th principal planet in order from the Sun; it is one of the terrestrial PLANETS. To the eye it is orange, varying in stellar magnitude from near +2 (similar to Polaris) to −2.8 (brighter than Jupiter). It is the only planet whose solid surface can be examined in any detail. In physical nature it is more like Earth than any other planet, yet modern studies stress that Mars is cold, very arid, and comparatively airless. Its diameter is 4,200 mi, with little polar flattening—perhaps 0.5%. Its mass is 0.11 times Earth's, and its density 4.12 times that of water. Mars reflects 15% of the incident sunlight, which figure proves that we see a solid surface. Studies of changes of brightness show the surface to be smoother than the Moon's. The velocity of escape is 3 mi/sec (just under half Earth's), and we should theoretically expect the atmosphere of Mars to be thin.

The average distance from the Sun is 141.6 million mi, the period 687 days. The orbital eccentricity is 0.093; the inclination to the ecliptic, 1°51'. With its orbit not far outside Earth's, Mars varies greatly in its distance from Earth and is chiefly studied near opposition, when it is closest, although even this distance varies substantially because of the eccentric orbit. A "favorable" or near-perihelion opposition with a minimum distance of 35 million mi last occurred in 1956 and will next take place in 1971.

The Martian day is 24 hr 37 min 22.6 sec; the planet is tilted 24° to 25° to the plane of its orbit. The seasons are hence similar to our own but about twice as long. In low latitudes near perihelion the surface temperature is about 50° to 70°F in the brighter parts of the disc, and 70° to 85°F in the darker patches. Near aphelion the highest temperature is about 30°F. At night the temperature falls to −40°F or lower. The atmosphere of Mars is always very cold. The climate is thus so rigorous that, for survival, human beings would need the equipment used by high-altitude flyers.

The atmosphere is very rarefied, its surface pressure per-

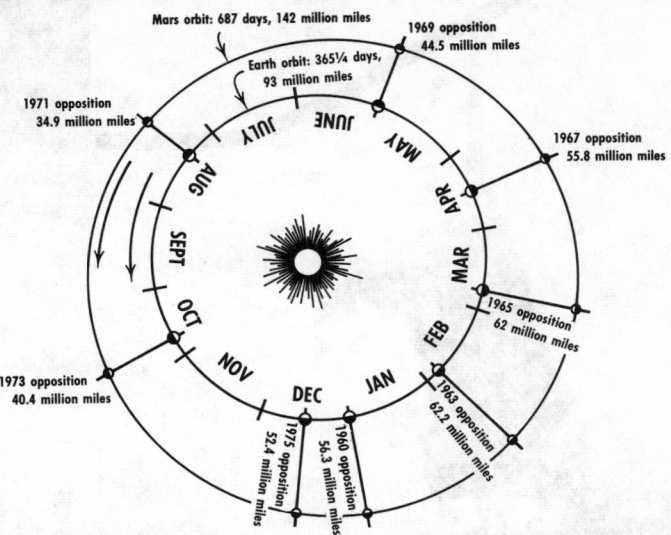

Oppositions of Mars, 1960–1975: Red planet is closest to Earth at times of opposition. Distance varies because orbits of planets are not concentric or exactly in same plane. Oppositions are best times for viewing. (*After Slipher*)

haps 1 or 2 cm of mercury (against 76 cm for Earth). The one gas positively identified by the spectroscope is carbon dioxide, in amounts similar to Earth's. There is at most 1% as much oxygen and 0.2% as much water vapor in the atmosphere of Mars as in Earth's. It is conjectured that most of the atmosphere is nitrogen. There are three kinds of clouds: blue, which are part of a "violet layer" of unknown nature; yellow, which are probably dust storms; and white, which may be like cirrus clouds.

White polar caps are often conspicuous features (see p. 661). Each shrinks in spring and grows in autumn. In 1948, G. P. Kuiper found spectroscopic evidence that they are ice crystals. Their thickness is very small, perhaps 1 or 2 in.; and in winter each is covered by an atmospheric veil. About three-fourths of the surface of Mars consists of bright areas, which change little in color or brightness and are called "deserts." They have been variously interpreted as an iron oxide and as an igneous rock. The dark areas on the surface, named *maria* when they were falsely thought to be oceans, have

Maps of Mars: Drawing at left was made by Giovanni Schiaparelli in Milan, Italy, and the one at right by Henri Josef Perrotin in Nice, France. Drawings were made one hour apart on June 4, 1888. Differences are due to drawing styles, to rotation of planet during the hour interval, and to the important differences even between skilled observers in perception and interpretation. (Compare with photos of Mars in article LIFE, EXTRATERRESTRIAL.)

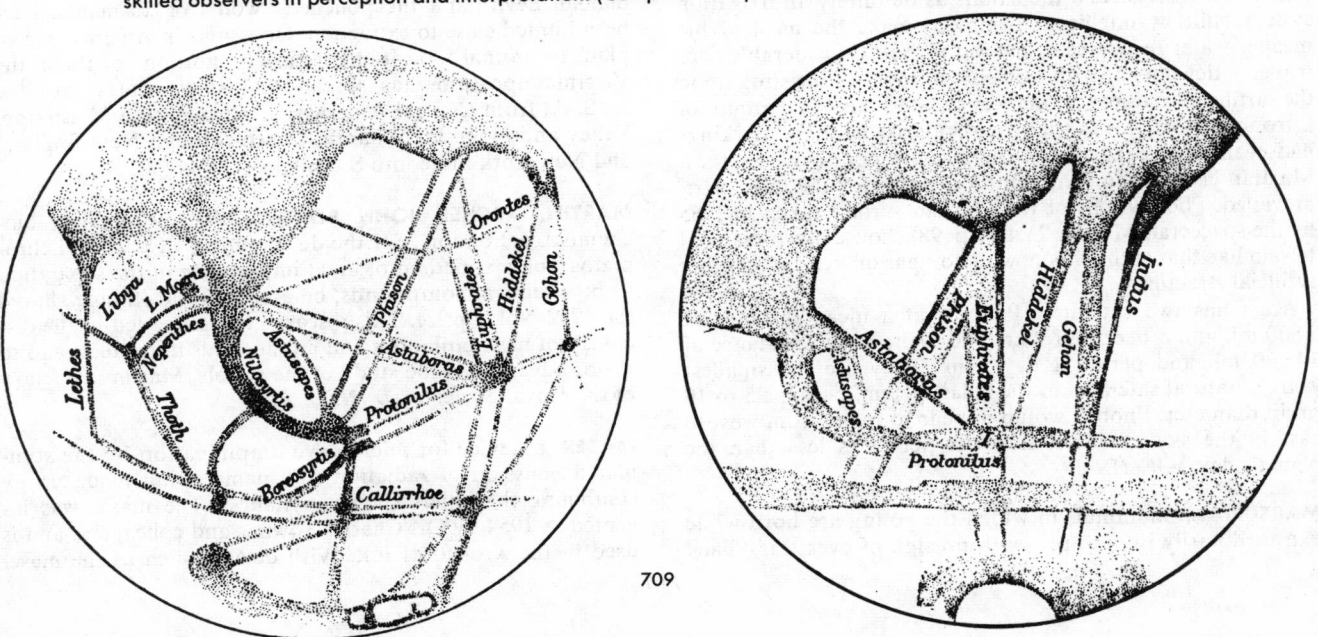

Pouched marsupials include American opossum (*left*) and Australian wallaby (*right*). Female opossum produces 6 to 16 young, which cling fast to teats in mother's pouch, where they feed until large enough to leave. For some time after, they cling with claws to fur on mother's back or with tails to her tail. Wallaby's single offspring remains in pouch until more fully developed, eating same plants the mother eats. (*Allan D. Cruickshank/Nat. Audubon Soc.; N. Y. Zoological Soc.*)

been mapped. Though their general outlines are comparatively permanent, they change in darkness, perhaps also in color, with the seasons, being most intense in early summer. Non-seasonal changes also occur, *e.g.* the darkening of an area twice as large as Texas in and before 1954. The maria are usually interpreted as concentrations of plants, perhaps somewhat like lichens; they do not reflect light in the way chlorophyll does. If they are plants, here is the only known example of life outside Earth (see LIFE, EXTRATERRESTRIAL).

Between the maria is a complex pattern of oases (dark spots) and canals (dark band-like features). Different observers see them very differently, nor have photography and other techniques yet resolved the question of their exact appearance. The canals, first studied by G. V. Schiaparelli in Italy in 1877, were thought by him to be perhaps artificial, because of their seeming geometric regularity. The American astronomer Percival Lowell, founder of the Flagstaff Observatory, later studied the canals intensively and became the leader of a school which regarded the canals as definitely an irrigation system built by intelligent beings to make the most of the meager water resources of the red planet. Considerable controversy developed, with Lowell's supporters insisting upon the artificial nature of the canals and another group of astronomers declaring that the regularity of these markings had been much exaggerated and was but poor evidence for a Martian civilization. The doubters have, for the most part, prevailed. Photographs of the Martian surface taken in 1965 by the spacecraft Mariner IV (see p. 98) show a much-cratered terrain like that of the Moon, with no signs of "canals" or other artificial structures.

Mars has two satellites: Phobos, at a mean distance of 5,800 mi, and a period of 8 hr; and Deimos, at a distance of 14,600 mi, and period 1 day 6 hr. They are the smallest known natural satellites in the solar system, perhaps 5 to 10 mi in diameter. Phobos would appear to move from west to east in the sky of Mars, since its period is less than the planet's day.—*W. H.*

MARSUPIALS: mammals in which the young are born while extraordinarily immature—with no sign of eyes, ears, back

legs, or tail—and develop within a pocket (marsupium) on the underside of the mother. Except for the opossums in America, all modern marsupials are native to Tasmania, Australia, New Guinea, and adjacent islands of the East Indies. There they occupy the many habitats in which placental MAMMALS are ordinarily found. (See PLACENTA.) Kangaroos, including the great gray kangaroo, which may stand 5 ft tall and weigh 200 lb, graze as cattle or rabbits do. Koala "bears" climb in tall trees, eating eucalyptus leaves almost exclusively. Wombats burrow like moles in search of roots and other plant foods. Honeysuckers rely upon a diet of nectar and insects from flowers. Bandicoots and phascogales are shrew-like denizens of the underbrush, where they search for insects. One of the phascogales is the smallest of marsupials; it is less than 2 in. long and weighs about 1 oz. Phalangers glide from tree to tree much like flying squirrels; they feed on insects and seeds. Marsupial "mice," "cats," and "wolves" are beasts of prey. Many of them, *e.g.* the "Tasmanian devil" and the pouched "wolf" of Tasmania, have been hunted close to extinction. Opossums in America accept plant or animal food in great variety, and one of them, the Virginia opossum, has spread in historic times into the U. S. A. from Central America, up through the Mississippi Valley and along the Atlantic Coast, through New England and New York State into S Canada.—*L. and M. M.*

MARTIN, ARCHER JOHN PORTER, 1910– , English biochemist; b. London. For the development of partition chromatography, a method of great importance in the separation of biochemical compounds, he and R. L. M. Synge shared the 1952 Nobel prize. This research technique led to the discovery of new antibiotics and amino acids in bacteria and to major advances in the study of the sterols. Martin is a fellow of the Royal Society.—*D. H. D. R.*

MASER: a device for *m*icrowave *a*mplification by the *st*imulated *e*mission of *r*adiation (the name being made up by combining the letters shown in italics). The maser was invented in 1954 by Dr. Charles Townes and colleagues, and is used in the ATOMIC CLOCK. With devices such as the maser (which may consist of a solid state crystal or a gaseous system, among others), it may become possible to transmit signals over great, even astronomical, distances. For the operation of the maser, it is necessary to have atoms or electrons raised in energy, or excited, by some suitable outside agency such as an electric field or a light beam. These atoms or electrons can then be induced to fall back to a low ENERGY LEVEL by subjecting them to radiation with a frequency equal to the energy difference between the excited state and the low energy state divided by Planck's constant. Since in so falling they emit radiation of the same frequency, this process results in the increase in energy, or amplification, of the original inducing radiation. When this principle is used to produce amplification of light, the device is also called a LASER.—*E. M. C.*

MASKELYNE, NEVIL, 1732–1811, English astronomer; b. London. He became astronomer royal of England in 1765 and began issuing the *Nautical Almanac* in 1766. From 1776 to 1811 he issued a four-vol. reference catalogue of about 90,000 observations of the solar system and 36 reference stars. For his research on the deviation of a plumb line near a mountain, he received the Copley Medal of the Royal Society, of which he was a member.—*D. H. D. R.*

MASONRY: construction in stone, brick, and/or concrete. Chief building stones are granite, limestone, sandstone, and marble. The simplest kind of stonework is rubble masonry, which is nothing more than broken fragments of rock, loosely piled to form a wall or chimney. This is now used mainly for shore protection and the facing of earth dams. Binding rubble by pouring mortar over and through it gives it greater stability. Pieces of natural stone set with roughly matching edges in mortar are termed polygonal masonry. For all carefully designed, durable building, stone taken from a quarry is cut and dressed in rectangular blocks and laid in mortar, usually with staggered joints. In the modern curtain wall, the thin sheathing blocks are often laid with continuous vertical joints.

BRICK is made from a variety of clays, plus small quantities of lime and slag. The soft clay, shaped in a mold under pressure or extruded from a die, was originally dried in the sun, but is now baked in a kiln. Bricks have been made in a variety of sizes and shapes over the centuries; the standard brick is now a rectangular prism of $2\frac{1}{4} \times 4 \times 8$ in. Bricks are laid in mortar with staggered or continuous joints. When laid with the long narrow face in a horizontal line, they are said to form a *stretcher* course; with the short end horizontal, a *header* course; and with the long narrow face vertical, a *soldier* course. Patterned brickwork, *e.g.* English or Flemish bond, is made by varying the positions of long and short faces.

CONCRETE was a Roman invention, but its use in modern building dates from 1824, when Joseph Aspdin (1779–1855) of Leeds, England, invented the artificial cement known as Portland cement. Concrete consists of lime (the cementing agent) mixed with oxides of aluminum and silicon, sand, gravel (the *aggregate*), and water. Concrete sets under water as well as in the air. It may be poured in individual blocks and laid like stone, but more commonly is poured in solid walls and slabs. Since concrete, like brick and stone, lacks tensile strength, it must be reinforced with steel to resist bending forces. When reinforced, however, it is applicable to an almost unlimited range of structural forms, and is now the dominant building material. The 20th-cent. invention of prestressing has greatly added to its strength.—*C. W. C.*

MASS: a concept so fundamental that the standard definition "quantity of matter" tells little we do not know already. To every object can be assigned a number, its *inertial mass,* which measures the amount of its INERTIA, *i.e.* strength of resistance to change of motion. To every object can also be assigned a number, its *gravitational mass,* which measures the strength of its gravitational effects. Experiment shows that these masses, measured in appropriate units, are equal. The scientific unit of mass is the gram, a standard kilogram (1,000 gm) being kept in Paris. In English-speaking countries the unit of mass is the pound. Though mass is different from WEIGHT, which is a gravitational force, the two are proportional; so mass is usually determined by weighing. The mass of Earth is determined essentially by comparing its gravitational attraction with that of a known mass. Before the formulation of the theory of relativity, it was believed that mass is neither created nor destroyed but *conserved.* Relativity brought significant changes in the concept. It showed that the faster a body moves relative to an observer, the greater is its mass relative to him—this *relative mass,* in general, approaching infinity as the relative speed approaches the speed of light, which is the maximum speed. The REST MASS of a body, its mass relative to an observer moving with it, is the minimum value of its various relative masses. Photons (light quanta) and neutrinos have zero rest mass; so, according to relativity, though they therefore move with the speed of light, their relative mass does not become infinite.

Relativity showed that mass is equivalent to energy ($E = mc^2$). So, because energy is released when the constituent particles of an atomic nucleus are brought together, the rest mass of a nucleus is less than the sum of the rest masses of its constituent particles, the difference being the *mass defect.* An atomic particle and its "anti-particle," *e.g.* an electron and a positron (positive electron), can "annihilate" each other, the whole of their rest mass being converted into radiation having zero rest mass but equivalent energy. In all processes, though, mass must be considered as conserved when account is taken of the mass equivalent of any released or entrapped energy. Atomic bombs convert only a small part of their rest mass into released energy; they effect a rearrangement of nuclear particles so that the total rest mass is slightly less than before.

The equality of inertial and gravitational mass, an inexplicable coincidence in Newton's theory, was the cornerstone of Einstein's theory of general relativity.—*Ba. H.*

MASS, CENTER OF: see CENTER OF GRAVITY AND MASS.

MASS, RELATIVISTIC: mass as affected by velocity. In Newtonian mechanics the mass of a particle remains constant under all conditions of velocity. According to the theory of RELATIVITY, however, the mass of a particle depends on its velocity: $M = M_0/\sqrt{1 - v^2/c^2}$, where M is the mass of a particle moving at velocity v, M_0 the mass of the particle at rest relative to the observer, and c the velocity of light. This relationship stems from the postulate introduced by H. A. Lorentz (see LORENTZ-FITZGERALD CONTRACTION) to account for the results of the MICHELSON-MORLEY EXPERIMENT. It can be seen that the above relationship states that at the speed of light a particle's mass becomes infinite. Thus matter can only approach, but never attain, the speed of light. The change of mass of a particle depending on its velocity has been confirmed by the measurement of the mass of high-speed subatomic particles. See PARTICLE ACCELERATORS.—*A. L.*

MASS ACTION, LAW OF: a fundamental postulate upon which the theory of CHEMICAL EQUILIBRIUM and reaction kinetics rests. In its most generally accepted form, the law of mass action states that the rate of a chemical reaction is proportional to the active masses of the reacting substances; such a hypothesis was proposed, 1879, by C. M. Guldberg and P. Waage after study of homogeneous reversible reactions taking place in either the liquid or the gas phase. With reversible homogeneous liquid or gas reactions, an "active mass" is equal to or directly proportional to the concentration of a reacting substance. In many chemical reactions the products can react with each other to give back the starting materials. Such reactions, termed "reversible," are usually written with a pair of oppositely pointing arrows replacing the equality sign. Examples of technically important, reversible homogeneous gas reactions are:

(I) $\qquad H_2 + CO_2 \rightleftharpoons H_2O + CO$

(II) $\qquad N_2 + 3H_2 \rightleftharpoons 2NH_3$

or, generically,

(III) $\qquad A + B \rightleftharpoons C + D$

Each system can be considered as two reactions taking place simultaneously, a forward or direct reaction (reading left to right) and a reverse reaction (right to left). When the over-all reaction has apparently stopped, i.e. has reached a steady state at any given temperature and pressure, the forward reaction and the reverse reaction are still proceeding, but at the same rate. The system is then said to be in a state of dynamic chemical equilibrium. Denoting the concentrations (C) of reactants A, B, C, and D in system III above by C_A, C_B, C_C, and C_D, the law of mass action states the forward-reaction rate as:

$$\text{Rate Forward} = k\, C_A C_B$$

where k is called the rate constant of the reaction. Similarly,

$$\text{Rate Reverse} = k'\, C_C C_D$$

where k' is the rate constant of the reverse reaction. Since at equilibrium Rate Forward = Rate Reverse, or

$$\frac{C_C C_D}{C_A C_B} = \frac{k}{k'} = K,$$

K is called the equilibrium constant of the reaction at the temperature and pressure specified. The above considerations translate directly to reaction I above. In the ammonia-synthesis reaction (II), again by law of mass action,

$$\text{Rate Forward} = k_f\, C_{N_2}\, C^3_{H_2} \text{ and}$$
$$\text{Rate Reverse} = k_r\, C^2_{NH_3}$$

The equilibrium constant for this reaction is

$$K = \frac{k_f}{k_r} = \frac{C^2_{NH_3}}{C_{N_2}\, C^3_{H_2}}$$

Equilibrium constants and their temperature coefficients can be used to calculate activation energies and the free-energy changes that accompany chemical reactions.—A. M. S.

MASS NUMBER: the number of neutrons plus protons that make up the nucleus of an ATOM. The mass number multiplied by the mass of the proton is very nearly equal to the mass of the atom. Different ISOTOPES of each element have different mass numbers. Isotopes are commonly designated by the name of the element or its symbol, plus the mass number of the isotope (e.g. uranium[238] or U[238]; carbon[14] or C[14]). —G. M. S. and L. S.

MASS SPECTROMETRY: a means of measuring the mass-to-charge ratio (e/m) of ionized atoms or molecules; used especially for mass analysis, since the charge is generally known. Applications include the determination of the abundance of an element's isotopes, precision measurements of isotopic masses, identification of extremely small traces of certain elements, analysis of complex chemicals, and separation of isotopes in useful quantities.

Modern mass spectrometers usually rely upon the magnetic deflection of moving charges. An ion traveling at right angles to the direction of a magnetic field experiences a force perpendicular to its motion and to the field, which causes it to travel in a circular path. The radius of the circle depends upon the ion's e/m ratio, as well as the field strength and the ion's velocity. In a typical mass spectrometer (see figure), part of a gas sample is first ionized by electron bombardment and then accelerated by a strong electric field into the magnetic-field region, where the ions acquire circular paths. The detector is an electrometer capable of measuring very small currents. Only ions with a particular e/m ratio reach the electrometer and are recorded. A complete mass spectrum of a sample may be taken by varying the accelerating voltage while keeping the magnetic field constant. Each e/m will fall at the electrometer position in its turn.

The resolution of a mass spectrometer—i.e. its ability to discriminate between slightly differing e/m—is determined by its focusing properties. Since the ion source has a velocity spread, both velocity and directional focusing (so-called "double focusing") are required for very high resolution. Most spectrometers accomplish one but not both types of focusing. With the best double-focusing spectrometers, e/m differences of better than 1 part in 100,000 can be seen.

Other types of spectrometers have recently come into general use. Time-of-flight devices discriminate e/m groups by the time it takes an ion to travel between two electrodes. Perhaps the most versatile of the new spectrometers is the electric quadrupole spectrometer originally devised by W. Paul and co-workers at Bonn University, Germany. Simultaneous d-c and a-c electric fields are applied to two opposite pairs of parallel electrodes, suitably shaped and symmetrically arranged. The resulting trajectories of the ions are such that any pre-selected e/m group can be refocused, while all other groups are deflected and collected at the electrodes. The resolution of the Paul-type mass-filter can be changed by varying the applied voltages. The best such device can produce resolutions quite comparable to those of conventional double-focusing magnetic mass spectrometers.

60° single-focusing mass spectrometer: This instrument makes use of the principle that ions of different mass are deflected through different angles in passing through a magnetic field. Here the magnetic field acts on charged ions of gas sample being analyzed, much in the manner of a prism acting on a beam of light. Heavy particles are deflected less than lighter ones, if velocities are the same, and are picked up by the movable detector at different locations.

MASS WASTING: in geology, the downslope transfer of rock fragments, varying from tiny particles to blocks of enormous size, under direct control of gravity; it is an important aspect of degradation. Small particles normally travel very slowly, *i.e.* creep, because most slopes are gentle; larger masses may do the same or, especially in rugged terrains, may plunge down. Mass wasting may involve movement only of relatively dry rock, or it may be the transfer of masses of waterlogged debris, which are dislodged much more readily when wet than when dry. The most spectacular expressions of mass wasting are rockslides, which move down slopes with much friction between the base of the moving mass and the rock below, and rockfalls, which occur where the slope is so steep that there is little friction. See LANDSLIDES, EARTH FLOWS, AND SLUMPING. —*N.E.A.H.*

MATCH: a splinter of wood or other combustible material tipped with some chemical composition that is flammable on friction. One of the earliest matches was the oxymuriate type used widely in Europe and America in the first half of the 19th cent. It consisted of a stick tipped with a mixture containing potassium chlorate and sugar, and was fired by touching the tip upon concentrated sulfuric acid, which was soaked up in asbestos and carried in a bottle. These *chemical matches* began to displace the tinderbox about 1820. The first practical match ignitible by simple friction was invented by John Walker, an Englishman, in 1827. It consisted of a splinter of wood dipped into a dried mixture of potassium chlorate ($KClO_3$), an oxidizing agent, and antimony trisulfide (Sb_2S_3), a substance having a low kindling temperature, made up with a solution of gum in water. It was ignited by drawing the match through folded glass paper. The first successful phosphorus matches, employing white phosphorus in place of the antimony trisulfide, appeared in France between 1830 and 1835. While white phosphorus has a lower kindling temperature than antimony trisulfide, it causes a disease known as "phossy jaw" among match-factory workers, and its use in matchmaking has been virtually eliminated.

The modern friction match is made of wood tipped with an igniting compound containing essentially two chemical substances that will react with each other, giving off heat, at a temperature attainable by rubbing the match head on a suitable surface. Thus an oxidizing agent, *e.g.* potassium chlorate or lead dioxide, is mixed with an easily ignitible substance, usually nonpoisonous phosphorus sesquisulfide, P_4S_3, which is concentrated at the tip of the match head. A filler containing fine abrasive material, *e.g.* ground glass, is added and the materials are bound together with glue. To insure the ignition of wooden match splints, a portion of the wood near the head is coated with paraffin. To prevent afterglow, matches are dipped into a solution of ammonium phosphate.

Safety matches were invented by J. E. Lundstrom in Sweden, 1855. The head of the match contains antimony trisulfide, glue, and an oxidizing agent, usually potassium chlorate. The prepared surface on the box contains red phosphorus (nonpoisonous), powdered glass, and glue. The tip of the match ignites readily only when rubbed on this surface. The heat caused by the friction converts a trace of the red phosphorus into white phosphorus, which ignites the head.—*A. P. E.*

MATERIALISM: a form of metaphysical monism, according to which such differences as may exist between various orders of phenomena (*e.g.* organic, inorganic, and mental) are not ultimate, and either the universe is material and all of a piece, or so-called "higher" phenomena are dependent upon and determined by wholly material processes. It contrasts with certain forms of Dualism (mental and psychical phenomena are irreducibly different and possibly causally independent), Idealism (only mental phenomena are real, matter being a construct), and Neutral Monism (mental and material phenomena are jointly reducible to, or are aspects of, some neutral substance). Materialism is vague without some restrictions on the term "matter" and some rules for showing the connection between matter and whatever is not so designated according to the restrictions. Comparable requirements hold for its metaphysical rivals. The earliest version of materialism is credited to Leucippus (fl. 440 B. C.) and Democritus (460–370 B. C.), for whom only material atoms moving in space are real, so that all qualitative differences between phenomena are to be explained by means of quantitative mechanical relations among groups of atoms. Thus, "Sweet, bitter, color exist by convention; atoms and Void alone exist in reality." Something like this view was put forward by Galileo, who distinguished between two sets of qualities: those which, like motion and extension, are inherent in bodies, and those which, like tastes and colors, are only ascribed to bodies by sensate beings, and do not truly characterize the physical world. Gassendi and Hobbes revived atomism, the latter stating that "all is body, all that occurs is motion"; and Galileo's distinction between what Boyle later termed "primary and secondary qualities" was a philosophical commonplace in the 17th cent., especially in Locke and Newton. But not everyone who subscribed either to it or to atomism was necessarily a materialist. In the 18th cent., La Mettrie and d'Holbach, among others, denied any autonomy to mental events, and sought to explain their occurrence as unilaterally determined by material changes in the body. Cabanis claimed that "thought is a secretion of the brain"—a slogan amplified by Vogt, who said that "the relationship between thought and brain is roughly of the same order as that between bile and the liver or urine and the bladder." Evolution modified materialism in the 19th cent., with Marx and Engels developing a variant form in their dialectical materialism, which held all cultural phenomena to reflect the economic situation which caused them. Materialism has recently been epitomized as the belief that "the inorganic pattern of matter is prior to living, minded, and purposive organisms which arise gradually and only as a result of complex evolutionary development." It will be seen that materialists frequently appeal to scientific finding in support of their views, and many scientists have found materialism an attractive philosophy. But whether as such science is materialistic is very difficult to say. Insofar as the various sciences may be reduced to physics, materialism may be a program for science. But even if this program is successfully fulfilled, the philosophical significance of the achievement would remain a matter for philosophical dispute.—*A. D.*

MATHEMATICAL FORMULA: a relationship whereby the value of one variable can be found from that of another, or those of several others. The formula $s = \frac{1}{2} gt^2$ gives the number of feet a body falls in t sec, under the influence of the force of gravity that produces the acceleration g. Many scientific conclusions are embodied in concise mathematical formulas. Newton's law of universal gravitation is an outstanding example: $F = km_1m_2/d^2$. In this formula m_1 and m_2 are measures of the masses of two bodies, d is the distance between them, k is a proportionality factor depending in part upon the units in which the quantities are measured, and F is the force by which the bodies attract each other. Many theorems of mathematics are expressed by formulas. The well-known formula for the roots of a quadratic equation is an example. The two roots of the equation $ax^2 + bx + c = 0$ are given by the formula $x = (-b \pm \sqrt{b^2 - 4ac})/2a$.—H. C.

MATHEMATICAL INDUCTION: a method of proof in mathematics which is actually deductive, although its form is somewhat analogous to induction. The nature of the proof can be indicated by a nonmathematical example: Suppose it can be proved that if the sun rises on any day, then it must rise the next; since it rose today, it follows by mathematical induction that it will always rise. A mathematical example is the proof of the theorem that the sum of the first k odd integers (whole numbers) is equal to k^2. There are two steps in the proof, which are independent of one another. First, we show that the theorem is true for the first sum, that is, for one odd integer: $1 = 1^2$. Second, we show that if n is a number of odd integers for which the theorem is true, so is $(n + 1)$. Let us suppose, then, that $1 + 3 + 5 + \cdots + (2n - 1) = n^2$. The next, or $(n + 1)$th, odd number is $2n + 1$. If the number is added to both sides of the equation, we have $1 + 3 + 5 + \cdots + (2n - 1) + (2n + 1) = n^2 + 2n + 1 = (n + 1)^2$. Hence, if the theorem is true for n it is also true for $(n + 1)$. But we have proved that the theorem is true for the first odd integer; therefore it must be true for the second, therefore for the third, and so on for all the odd integers. This example illustrates the kind of proposition to which mathematical induction can be applied. It must be a proposition which depends upon an integral variable. It is useful for proving formulas for sums of n terms, or products of n factors, or theorems involving other iterative processes. The BINOMIAL THEOREM for positive integral exponents furnishes an example.—H. C.

MATHEMATICAL INSTRUMENTS: Mathematical instruments fall into two main categories: instruments for constructing geometrical figures, and instruments for solving numerical problems.

Geometrical Instruments: The most familiar of all instruments is the straightedge for constructing straight lines. However, the chalk line used by artisans is more directly related to the fact that a straight line is the shortest distance between two points. The compass is used for drawing circles, and dividers, a closely related instrument, for marking off equal distances. Many devices have been invented for constructing special curves—conics and other algebraic and transcendental curves. A protractor, in the form of a graduated semicircle and its diameter, is an instrument for measuring or drawing angles of any size. A LINKAGE is a device consisting of rigid bars joined together with pins, about which the bars are free to rotate, *e.g.* a parallel ruler (Fig. 1).

Fig. 1: Parallel ruler. The outer edges remain parallel with each other as the space between them is varied.

Numerical Instruments: The most ancient and primitive of computing instruments is the ABACUS. The SLIDE RULE is a more modern device, which has been adapted to many different computations. The best known rule is merely a pair of logarithmic scales which can be set to represent the sum or difference of any two logarithms and therefore the product or quotient of any arithmetic numbers. Areas of figures bounded by curved boundaries can be found by a planimeter. Amsler's

planimeter, invented in 1854, consists of two bars, AB and BP, hinged at B (Fig. 2). Point A is fixed. A calibrated wheel is fitted perpendicular to BP at its center. As P is moved around the perimeter of the area to be measured, the wheel, in contact with the surface, rotates. During the complete circuit the wheel rotates, part of the time in one direction and part of the time in the other. The net rotation—that in the clockwise direction subtracted from that in the opposite direction—determines the area.

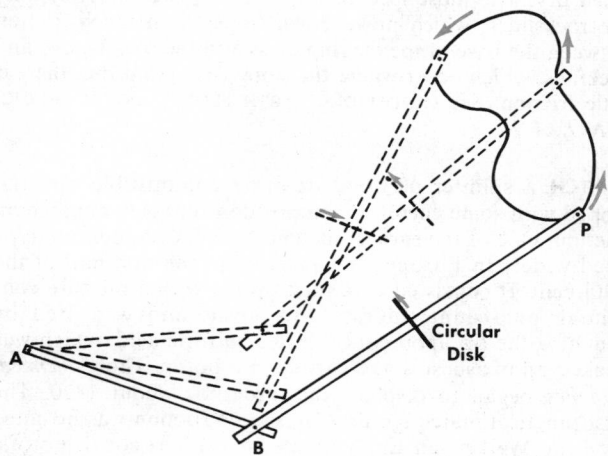

Fig. 2: Amsler's planimeter: As point P moves, disk rotates; its net rotation gives a measure of area enclosed by path of P.

Other instruments solve equations—finite algebraic equations, linear systems, differential equations, and partial differential equations. The integraph, invented by Charles Boys in 1881, determines the indefinite integral of a given function, in the form of a curve. The differential analyzer, first developed by Vannevar Bush in 1928, is capable of solving a broad class of differential equations. A harmonic analyzer calculates the coefficients in a Fourier series representing a given function.

Modern high-speed electronic computers have rendered some earlier instruments largely obsolete and, by their enormous capacity and speed, have led to utilization of methods of solving complicated problems which formerly involved a prohibitive amount of labor. Since they are adapted to repetitive operations, they have many uses in business as well as science.—H. C.

MATHEMATICAL NOTATION: the special signs, symbols, and abbreviations that constitute a language understood by mathematicians of all countries. An important phase in the development of mathematics has been the devising of notation; the course of development of a field has often been affected by the symbolism adopted. Thus, Newton's notation for his theory of fluxions was ill adapted to the dissemination of the new science. By contrast, that of Leibniz was so disarmingly convenient that it invited manipulations to the point of forgetting the concepts to which they referred. In modern mathematics, progress in solution of a problem is facilitated by a fortunate choice of notation and retarded by a poor one.

Numbers are generally represented in arithmetic by Arabic numerals, utilizing the principle of position with the decimal system; in algebra and higher numerical branches, letters are also used. Letters at the beginning of the alphabet usually denote *constants* (numbers that remain unchanged for the problem at hand), and those in the last part of the alphabet *variables,* although this is by no means a universal practice. Letters from the Greek alphabet are used freely, and occasionally Germanic and Hebrew symbols. Some of these symbols are associated with specific numbers. Thus, unless otherwise indicated, π denotes the ratio of the circumference to the diameter of a circle, e the base of natural logarithms, and $\aleph_0$ (aleph null) the transfinite number of the integers. Angles are often denoted by Greek letters.

Subscript notation is widely used; thus two values of x might be written x_1 and x_2. In some instances subscripts are written to the left, or more than one is employed. For example, $_nP_r$ denotes the number of permutations of n objects r at a time; and a_{34} might be the element in the 3rd row and 4th column of a matrix or determinant. A superscript is most commonly used as an exponent, *e.g.* x^2 means x times

x. It is also employed in symbols for 2nd and higher derivatives, *e.g.* d^2y/dx^2, and may replace a subscript; thus the element in the 3rd row and 4th column of a matrix is sometimes written $a_4{}^3$. When a symbol is understood to be employed with each of a set of numbers, a general subscript or superscript may appear with a statement as to the values it is to have. For example, n_i, $i = 1, 2, 3$, means the separate values n_1, n_2, n_3.

All numerical branches of mathematics have symbols for the various numerical operations and relations (*e.g.* = for equality, + for addition).

The accompanying table includes the common symbols, although it is not intended to be complete. Vector and tensor notations are omitted, as are the special uses of literal symbols in statistics and the specialized symbols of logic.—*H. C.*

COMMON MATHEMATICAL SYMBOLS

Arithmetic and Algebra

+	Plus; positive number or direction (Lat. $+8°$); also the operation of addition.
−	Minus; negative number or direction ($-6°$F); also the operation of subtraction.
× or ·	The operation of multiplication.
÷	The operation of division.
±	Plus or minus.
∓	Minus or plus.
=	Is equal to.
≡	Is identically equal to: $(a + b)^2 \equiv a^2 + 2ab + b^2$.
≠	Is not equal to.
>	Is greater than.
<	Is less than.
≧, ≥	Is greater than or equal to.
≦, ≤	Is less than or equal to.
→, ≐	Approaches: $x \to a$, x approaches a.
⋯	And so on: $1 + 3 + 5 + \cdots$
ab, $a \cdot b$, $a \times b$	a times b.
$a(b + c)$	a times the sum of b and c.
a/b, $\frac{a}{b}$, $a \div b$, $a:b$	Ratio of a to b; a divided by b.
$\frac{a}{b} = \frac{c}{d}$, $a:b::c:d$	Proportion: a is to b as c is to d.
∝	Varies as; is proportional to: *e.g.* weight $\propto$ mass.
∞	Infinity. If $x \to \infty$, x increases beyond all bounds.
$|x|$	Absolute value of x; numerical value of x without regard to sign; modulus of COMPLEX NUMBER.
a^n	The nth power of a: $a \cdot a \cdot a \cdots$ to n factors.
$\sqrt{\ }$, $\sqrt{}$	Radical sign; square root.
$a^{1/n}$, $\sqrt[n]{a}$	The nth root of a.
a^{-n}	The reciprocal of a^n, i.e. $1/a^n$.
exp x	Exponential x, or e^x, where e is the base of natural logarithms, 2.71828 approx.
(), [], {}, $\overline{}$	Parenthesis, brackets, brace, and vinculum, respectively; signs of aggregation that enclose quantities to be taken together.
L.C.M., lcm	Least common multiple.
G.C.D., gcd	Greatest common divisor.
log a	Logarithm of a.
$\log_{10} a$	Briggs' or common logarithm of a; logarithm of a to the base 10.
ln a, $\log_e a$	Logarithm of a to the base e; natural or Napierian logarithm of a.
antilog	Antilogarithm: antilog c is the number whose logarithm is c.
colog	Cologarithm: $\operatorname{colog} a = \log(1/a) = -\log a$.
e	Base of natural system of logarithms, $\lim_{n\to\infty}(1 + 1/n)^n = 2.71828\ldots$; charge on an electron; eccentricity of a conic section.
i	Imaginary unit; $\sqrt{-1}$; in physics, a symbol for electric current; a running, or general, subscript or superscript.
$\overset{\infty}{\underset{1}{\Sigma}}$, $\Sigma_1{}^\infty$	Summation; sum of infinitely many terms of a type indicated.
$\Sigma_{i=1}{}^{i=n}$, $\Sigma_1{}^n$, $\overset{n}{\underset{i=1}{\Sigma}}$	Sum of n terms: *e.g.* $\Sigma_1{}^n x_1{}^2 = x_1{}^2 + x_2{}^2 + \cdots + x_n{}^2$.
$n!$, $\lfloor n$	Factorial n, or the product of all integers from 1 to n, inclusive.
$P(n,r)$, $_nP_r$	Number of permutations of n objects taken r at a time.
$C(n,r)$, $_nC_r$, $\binom{n}{r}$	Number of combinations of n objects taken r at a time; coefficient of the product $x^{n-r}y^r$ in the expansion of $(x + y)^n$.
$f(x)$, $F(x)$, $\phi(x)$, etc.	Function of x.
$f(x,y)$	Function of x and y.

Elementary and Analytic Geometry

∠, ⦟	Angle, angles: $\angle ABC$, $\angle D$, ⦟ G and H.
⌐	Right angle.
△, ⧍	Triangle, triangles: $\triangle ABC$ ⧍ ABC and DEF.
rt. △	Right triangle.
▱	Parallelogram.
⊙, Ⓢ	Circle, circles.
⊥	Perpendicular; is perpendicular to.
∥	Parallel; is parallel to.
≅, ≡	Congruent; is congruent to.
∼	Similar; is similar to.
⌢	Arc: $\overset{\frown}{AB}$ means arc AB.
∴	Therefore.
∵	Since; because.
°	Degrees of arc or angle; of temperature.
′	Minutes of arc or angle; feet.
″	Seconds of arc or angle; inches.
π	Pi, the ratio of the circumference of a circle to its diameter $= 3.14159$. In angular measure π radians is equal to $180°$.
(x,y)	Rectangular, or Cartesian, coordinates of a point in a plane.

(Continued on next page)

$P(x,y)$	Point P whose plane coordinates are x and y.
(r,θ), (ρ,θ)	Polar coordinates of a point in a plane.
(x,y,z)	Cartesian coordinates of a point in space.

Trigonometric (circular) and Hyperbolic Functions

$\sin A$	Sine of A, where A is an angle; sine of the numerical variable A.
$\cos A$	Cosine of A.
$\tan A$	Tangent of A.
$\cot A$, ctn A	Cotangent of A.
$\sec A$	Secant of A.
$\csc A$	Cosecant of A.
vers A	Versed sine, or versine, of A ($=1-\cos A$).
hav A	Haversine of A ($=\frac{1}{2}$ vers A).
covers A	Coversed sine, or coversine, of A ($=1-\sin A$).
exsec A	Execant of A ($=\sec A - 1$).
$\sin^{-1}a$, arc sin a	Inverse sine of a; arc sine of a; the angle whose sine is a.
$\cos^{-1}a$, arc cos a	Inverse cosine of a; arc cosine of a; the angle whose cosine is a.
$\tan^{-1}a$, arc tan a	Inverse tangent of a; arc tangent of a; the angle whose tangent is a.
$\sinh x$	Hyperbolic sine of x.
$\cosh x$	Hyperbolic cosine of x.
$\tanh x$, $\coth x$, $\operatorname{sech} x$, $\operatorname{csch} x$	Hyperbolic tangent, cotangent, secant, and cosecant of x, respectively.
$\sinh^{-1}z$, ar sinh z	Inverse hyperbolic sine of z.
$\cosh^{-1}z$, ar cosh z	Inverse hyperbolic cosine of z.

Calculus

$\triangle x$, δx	An increment of x, as in the form $\lambda + \triangle x$, $\delta y/\delta x$, or $\Sigma f(x) \triangle x$; a difference between successive values of x in a table.

$\dfrac{dy}{dx}$, $\dfrac{df(x)}{dx}$, Dy, $Df(x)$, $D_x y$, y', $f'(x)$	Forms for expressing "the derivative of y with respect to x," if y is a function of x.
$\dfrac{d^2y}{dx^2}$, $\dfrac{d^2f(x)}{dx^2}$, D^2y, $D^2f(x)$, $D_x^2 y$, y'', $f''(x)$	Forms for expressing "the second derivative of y with respect to x," if $y = f(x)$.
$\dfrac{d^n y}{dx^n}$, etc.	The nth derivative of y with respect to x.
$\dfrac{\partial u}{\partial x}$, u_x, $f_x(x,y)$, $D_x u$.	The partial derivative of u with respect to x, if $u = f(x,y)$.
$\dfrac{\partial^2 u}{\partial x^2}$, u_{xx}, $f_{xx}(x,y)$, $D_{xx} u$.	The second partial derivative of y with respect to x, if $u = f(x,y)$.
$\dfrac{\partial^2 u}{\partial x \partial y}$, u_{xy}, $f_{xy}(x,y)$, $D_{xy} u$.	The second partial derivative of u with respect to y and x, if $u = f(x,y)$.
$\dot{x}$	Derivative of x with respect to time.
$\ddot{x}$	Second derivative of x with respect to time. If $s = $ distance, $\dot{s} = v = $ velocity, and $\ddot{s} = \dot{v} = $ acceleration.
$\int$	Integral sign; $\int f(x)\,dx$ is the indefinite integral or antiderivative of $f(x)$ with respect to x.
$\int_a^b$	Definite integral sign; $\int_a^b f(x)\,dx$ is the definite integral of $f(x)$ between the limits $x = a$ and $x = b$.
$\oint$	Curvilinear integral around a closed path; also written $\int_c$.
$\iint$	Double integral $= \iint f(x,y)\,dx\,dy$.
$F(x)\Big]_a^b$	$F(b) - F(a)$. Notation used within definite integrals: e.g. $\int_2^3 (2x+1)dx = (x^2+x)]_2^3 = (3^2+3) - (2^2+2)$.
Π_1^∞	Product of an infinite number of factors of the type indicated.
$\Pi_{i=n}^{i=n}$, Π_1^n, $\displaystyle\prod_{i=1}^n$	Product of n factors of the type given.
$\lim_{x\to a} f(x)$	Limit of $f(x)$ as x approaches a.

MATHEMATICAL PHYSICS: the study, by the techniques of mathematics, of measurements made in the physical sciences. Mathematical physics has two main functions: to summarize and present in an orderly fashion the vast amount of data obtained by observation and experiment, and to explore the relations between the facts to throw light on the way in which the universe is built. Modern mathematical physics, in this sense, began with Galileo (1564–1642) and especially Newton (1642–1727), who formulated a coherent account of matter by means of a strictly mechanistic theory. Newtonian mechanics is based upon three fundamental laws of motion, which embody the once revolutionary idea that the effect of a force on a moving body is to change, not to maintain, its motion. Newton gave this concept a precise mathematical form by stating that force produces in a body of fixed mass an acceleration in the same direction as the force and inversely proportional to the mass of the body. These laws, together with the law of universal gravitation, enabled the calculus to be used to solve a great number of problems in mechanics and, in particular, to explain the motion of the planets around the Sun. Later, it was found that electrically charged particles attract or repel in the same way and, all told, the mechanistic theory of Newton gave a firm structure to early physics. However, other phenomena, notably those of optics, were more difficult to fit into a purely corpuscular scheme. This led Christian Huygens (1629–95) to suggest that a beam of light consists of waves, not a shower of particles, and that it is energy, and not mass, that is propagated in this way. This break from the corpuscular theory ultimately led to the development, mainly by Michael Faraday (1791–1867), James Clerk Maxwell (1831–79), and H. R.

Hertz (1857–94), of the field theories of physics, in which it is supposed that gravitational, magnetic, and electrical effects result from lines of force which emanate from, and constitute a field of influence around, a body. This concept has been extremely fruitful in explaining effects such as electromagnetic induction and in making possible the design of electrical circuits and machines. It also united such apparently diverse branches of physics as optics and electromagnetism, with the velocity of light as a basic constant of the universe.

At the end of the 19th cent., mathematical physics (also called theoretical physics and natural philosophy) had become an established discipline, the principal branches of which were mechanics (statics and dynamics), hydrodynamics, conduction of heat, optics, and electromagnetism. The same period also saw the rise of the science of statistics and its application to physics in the kinetic theory of gases, which allowed physical properties such as pressure, density, and temperature to be expressed in terms of the Newtonian concepts of mass, momentum, and energy. The work of Maxwell and Ludwig Boltzmann (1844–1906) in this field brought the notion of probability into physics. The evolution of thermodynamics, especially by Willard Gibbs (1839–1903), which deals only with broad principles and not with the details of a process involving heat, was a significant move toward greater generality.

These later developments began the modern trend away from mechanical or easily visualizable concepts in mathematical physics toward more abstract ideas. The critical step was the formulation, by Max Planck (1858–1947), of the quantum theory, in which the flow of energy is regarded as pulsating and regulated by the universal "constant of action."

These ideas were applied by Einstein to explain the photo-electric effect and by Niels Bohr to construct a model of the atom. An even greater move toward abstraction came when it was recognized that both electricity and momentum are "atomic" in structure, and that the elementary entities can be regarded both as "waves" and as "particles." In wave mechanics, which is concerned with the subatomic world, strict causality has had to yield its place, in the formulation of the natural laws, to probability. A further reconsideration of the Newtonian philosophy has been necessitated by Einstein's theory of relativity, in which it is shown that space and time cannot be separated and also that mass and energy are basically of the same nature and are convertible one into the other in a calculable way, as in nuclear fission processes.

There are few branches of pure mathematics that are not involved in mathematical physics. Recently, the subject has gained enormous power with the development of the high-speed computer, which makes it possible to solve problems hitherto ruled out because of the immense labor of the calculations. At the same time the subject is becoming increasingly abstract, so that some of the fundamental concepts of physics now seem to exist only in the symbols of the mathematician. See APPLIED MATHEMATICS; PHYSICS; QUANTUM STATISTICS; STATISTICAL MECHANICS.—*O. G. S.*

MATHEMATICAL RECREATIONS: Mathematical puzzles have fascinated people throughout the ages, from Zeno's paradoxes of motion and ancient Chinese talismen magic squares to the sophisticated logic problems and topological curiosities of today. In addition to arithmetic and geometric recreations, MAGIC SQUARES, permutational games, and logic problems, some authorities would also include CRYPTOGRAPHY and cryptanalysis, numerology and number lore, mathematical prodigies and lightning calculators, logic machines, the fourth dimension, dynamic symmetry, the three classical CONSTRUCTION PROBLEMS of antiquity, the history and computation of π, calendar problems and calculations, and mathematical card tricks.

Curiously enough, seemingly innocent amusements have often led to mathematical discoveries of great significance, as, for example, the gambler's curiosity which helped Fermat to formulate his theory of probability, or the Königsberg bridge problem which led Euler to formulate the principles of networks and opened vistas of what was to become topology. Conversely, well-known mathematical tools or techniques have been applied to tantalizing puzzles or challenging problems which were then vanquished in a single stroke by generalizing the problem. As illustrations, one could cite the application of base 2 notation to the game of Nim; the use of electrical networks to "square the square"; or the use of lattices to create new magic squares.

Arithmetic Recreations: These include many simple and unexpected number curiosities such as:

$$1 \times 9 + 2 = 11 \qquad 6 \times 7 = 42$$
$$12 \times 9 + 3 = 111 \qquad 66 \times 67 = 4422$$
$$123 \times 9 + 4 = 1111 \qquad 666 \times 667 = 444222$$
$$1234 \times 9 + 5 = 11111 \qquad 6666 \times 6667 = 44442222$$
$$\text{etc.} \qquad\qquad \text{etc.}$$

Also included are a number of pleasantries such as the "four fours" problem of expressing various numbers by using exactly four 4's:

$$1 = \frac{4}{4} \cdot \frac{4}{4} \qquad 3 = \frac{4+4+4}{4}$$
$$2 = \frac{4}{4} + \frac{4}{4} \qquad 4 = 4 + (4 - 4)4$$

$$5 = \frac{4 \times 4 + 4}{4} \qquad 6 = 4 + \frac{4+4}{4}$$

Besides the familiar puzzles of "guessing a selected number" and "telling your age," numerical pastimes include both ancient and modern versions of problems of pursuit and overtaking, filling cisterns, clocks, inheritance, digits, age; problems depending upon arithmetic and geometric progressions, the manipulation of objects (measuring out liquids with a limited number of measures, or reapportioning liquids by decantation); and miscellaneous problems about money and interest. In the course of time, certain problems have become so renowned that they are now identified by names, as, for example, the "cattle problem of Archimedes"; the "counterfeit coin" problem; the Josephus problem; the "monkey and the coconuts"; "Spanish prisoner"; and the problem of the "crossed ladders." The following example illustrates not only the difficulty of classifying such diversions, but also how "old wine" can be dressed up "in new bottles": (1) A man, having run ⅜ the way across a railroad trestle, hears behind him the whistle of a train, which is coming toward him at 60 mi/hr. He quickly figures that he can run to either end of the trestle and just escape being hit by the train. How fast must he run to save himself? (See answer 1 at the end of this article.)

Some problems involve the theory of prime numbers, Mersenne numbers, Fermat numbers, and perfect numbers (see NUMBER THEORY). Arithmetical restorations are puzzles in which the missing numerals are to be "restored" or appropriate numerals substituted for the letters in a given algorithm:

$$
\begin{array}{cc}
(2) & \begin{array}{r} \text{SEND} \\ + \text{MORE} \\ \hline = \text{MONEY} \end{array}
\end{array}
\qquad
\begin{array}{cc}
(3) & \begin{array}{r} \text{ABC} \\ \text{BAC} \\ \hline \text{***C} \\ \text{**A} \\ \text{AABB} \\ \hline \text{A*CA*C} \end{array}
\end{array}
$$

(*Answers on page 720*)

The *Tower of Hanoi* consists of a board with three pegs (Fig. 1, next page), on one of which rest some discs of various sizes, the largest on the bottom, the next largest on that one, and so on. The object is to transfer the entire set of discs to one of the other two pegs by moving only one disc at a time, making sure that no disc is ever allowed to rest on one smaller than itself. The number of transfers necessary increases very rapidly as the initial number of discs is increased. In general, for n discs, the number of necessary transfers is $2^n - 1$. For $n = 64$, the number of transfers is 18, 446, 744, 073, 709, 551, 615.

In the game of Nim, two players play alternately with a number of counters placed in three heaps. Each player in turn is to take away as many counters as he wishes (but at least one) from any one heap he wishes. The last one to remove a counter wins the game. This game, which has many variations, admits of precise mathematical analysis based upon the binary scale of notation, and a definite game strategy can be formulated. Several Nim-playing robot machines have been built.

Geometrical Recreations: Geometric fallacies are ostensible proofs of untrue relations, such as: every triangle is isosceles; or, a right angle is equal to an obtuse angle; or, a part of a line is equal to the whole line. Many optical illusions, geometric puzzles, and paradoxes are well known (see Figs. 2).

The Chinese tangram, over 4,000 yr old, consists of seven pieces cut out of a square as shown in Fig. 3A; by rearranging the pieces, various interesting silhouettes can be made.

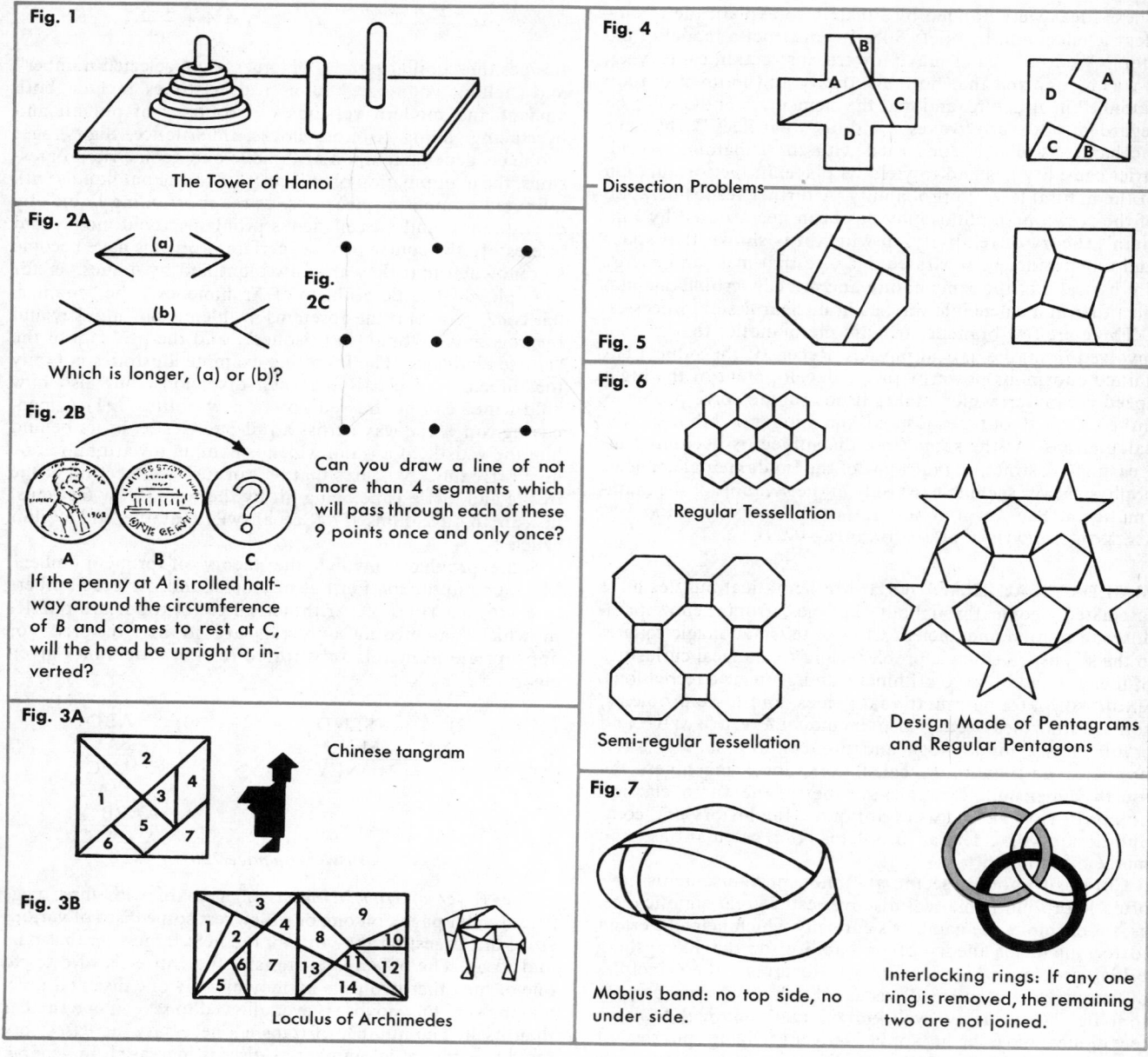

Fig. 1 The Tower of Hanoi

Fig. 2A (a) (b) Which is longer, (a) or (b)?

Fig. 2B If the penny at A is rolled half-way around the circumference of B and comes to rest at C, will the head be upright or inverted?

Fig. 2C Can you draw a line of not more than 4 segments which will pass through each of these 9 points once and only once?

Fig. 3A Chinese tangram

Fig. 3B Loculus of Archimedes

Fig. 4 Dissection Problems

Fig. 5

Fig. 6 Regular Tessellation — Semi-regular Tessellation — Design Made of Pentagrams and Regular Pentagons

Fig. 7 Mobius band: no top side, no under side. — Interlocking rings: If any one ring is removed, the remaining two are not joined.

Tangrams using other combinations of pieces are also known, one such notable set being the *loculus* of Archimedes (Fig. 3B).

More challenging are geometric dissection problems, one of which is to cut a Greek cross into four pieces with only two cuts of the scissors so that the four pieces can be arranged to form a square (Fig. 4). If the restriction as to the number of cuts is removed, there is an infinite number of ways of dissecting the Greek cross into four pieces to form a square. Every such dissection yields a reverse dissection: to cut a square into four pieces to form a Greek cross. Other possible dissections are known: to divide a regular pentagon into six pieces which can be put together to make a square; to divide an equilateral triangle into four pieces to make a square; to divide an isosceles right triangle into four pieces to make a Greek cross; to divide a regular octagon into five pieces to make a square (Fig. 5).

Equally fascinating are repeating designs, assemblages, mosaics, star polygons, tessellations, and space-packing elements (Fig. 6). A polygon assemblage is a set of regular polygons such that the set may be repeated so as to fill the plane without overlapping. A regular tessellation is a pattern of congruent regular polygons, all of one kind, filling the whole plane; only equilateral triangles, squares, and regular hexagons are admissible. In addition to the three regular tessellations, there are 8 semiregular tessellations.

An absorbing pastime is the construction of models of polyhedra: the five regular Platonic solids, the four regular Kepler-Poinsot star polyhedra, the 13 semiregular Archimedean solids (and their 13 duals), and, in addition, the regular compounds, solid tesselations, Prince Rupert's cubes, and regular polytopes, of which the tesseract, or hypercube (fourth dimension), is the simplest.

Many interesting pastimes have been drawn from the field of TOPOLOGY, such as the one-sided Möbius surfaces (Fig. 7), the wondrous torus, or doughnut, and the amazing Klein bottle, a closed surface with no inside and no outside. Topology also deals with the theory of knots, pretzels, and string figures; with unicursal paths and networks (Fig. 8); and with map-coloring problems. The theory of networks grew out of the Königsberg bridge problem, the attempt to traverse all seven bridges, crossing each bridge exactly once, as shown in Fig. 9.

Permutational Puzzles and Games: One celebrated type deals with ferrying across a river, *e.g.* the boatman who had to cross with the wolf, the goat, and the cabbage, taking only one at a time; or the three jealous husbands and their wives, who must cross in a boat that holds only two persons in such a way that a wife is never left with another woman's husband unless her own husband is present. So-called shunting problems with trains on railroad sidings are of the same sort.

Other permutational problems involve distributions, *e.g.* variations in arrangements of children in a circle, round robins in matches and tournaments, and the Kirkman Schoolgirls problem of grouping 15 girls in sets of three so that for seven consecutive days no girl will walk more than once with any of her school-fellows in any triplet. In chess and checkers permutational problems arise, among which the most notable are the so-called problem of the rooks, the problem of the queens, and the problem of the knight. Other games include the Japanese game of Go, played on a board of 18×18 squares with 180 white pieces and 181 black; Go-Moku, a modified version of Go; and Go-Bang, or Japanese checkers. Others include Jinx, Ruma, Lasca, Hopscotch (similar to Tic-tac-toe), Nine Men's Morris, Tricolor, Peg Solitaire, Dominoes, and the recently rediscovered African game of Wari, or Oware.

The renowned "Fifteen" puzzle consists of 15 equal cubes or slabs numbered from 1 to 15, and placed in a square, shallow box that holds just 16 such slabs, so arranged that they cannot be taken out of the box, but can be slid parallel to the sides of the box. The empty space may be in any of the 16 possible positions when the puzzle is presented for solving. The problem is to determine what permutations can be obtained, leaving the empty cell at the lower right-hand corner when the sequence of moves has been completed, as shown in Fig. 10.

Tic-tac-toe, a universal old-timer, may be described as "a two-person contest which is 'finite,' presenting no element of chance, and played with 'perfect information'; if played 'rationally' by both sides, the game must end in a draw." Modern versions of Tic-tac-toe are exciting: Toe-tac-tic, or the game in reverse; 3-dimensional Tic-tac-toe; 4-dimensional Tic-tac-toe on a hypercube; and the electrical Tic-tac-toe playing machine.

Logic Problems and Paradoxes: Recreational logic includes brainteasers involving deductive inferences rather than computation, such as puzzles involving truth-telling and lying. An example is the story of the two tribes: the members of one tribe always lie, those of the other tribe always tell the truth. An explorer, upon meeting two natives, asks the tall one if he is a truth-teller; "Ug" replies the tall one. "He say 'Yes,'" explained the short native, "but him big liar." If the word "ug" means either yes or no, to what tribe did each native belong? (Answer 4.)

Logical paradoxes, besides being amusing, are frequently related to profound mathematical concepts. Consider the celebrated town which boasted of only one barber. Said he: "I do not shave any men who shave themselves, but I do shave all those who don't shave themselves." Does the barber shave himself or not?

Or again, consider the executioner's plight. A prisoner sentenced to death is permitted to make one statement before he is executed. If that statement is false, he is to be hanged; if it is true, he is to be beheaded. The prisoner makes a statement, whereupon the executioner is dumbfounded and does nothing. What did the clever prisoner say? (Answer 5.)

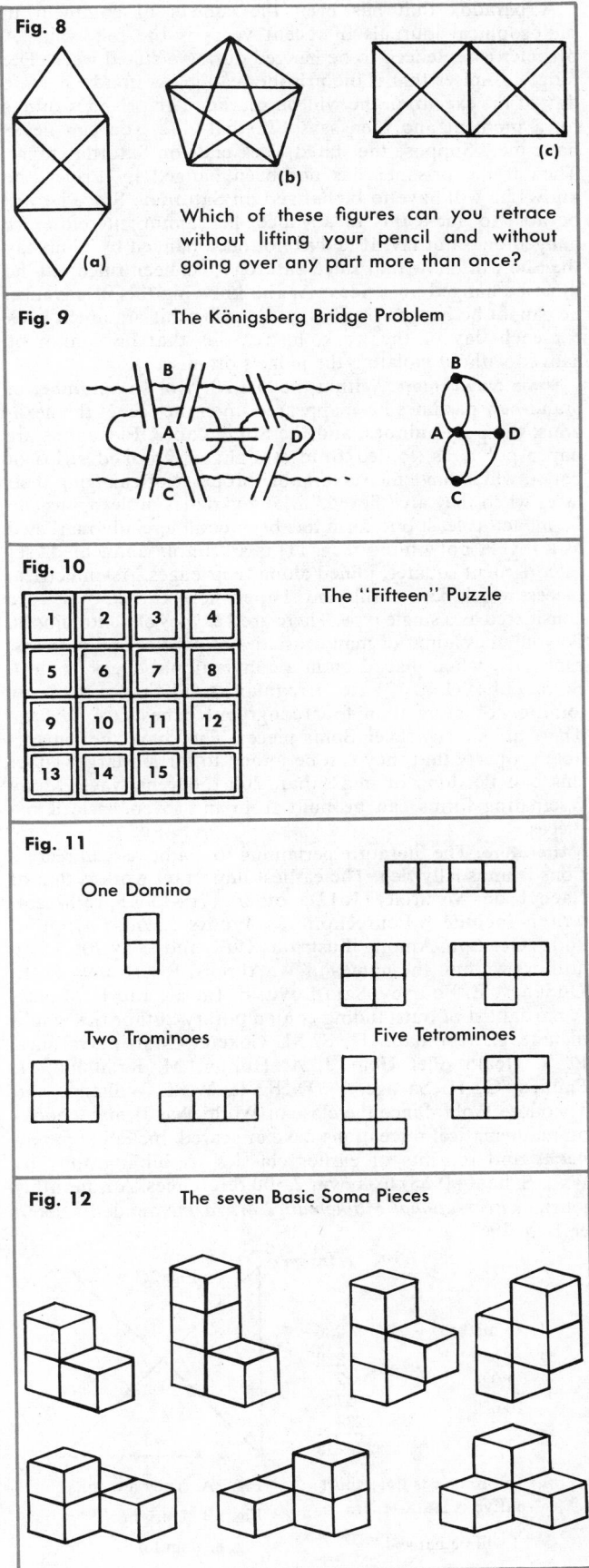

Fig. 8

Which of these figures can you retrace without lifting your pencil and without going over any part more than once?

Fig. 9   The Königsberg Bridge Problem

Fig. 10   The "Fifteen" Puzzle

Fig. 11   One Domino   Two Trominoes   Five Tetrominoes

Fig. 12   The seven Basic Soma Pieces

A paradox that has been the subject of comment in philosophical journals in recent years is the following: A prisoner is sentenced to be hanged during a stated week. The judge promises that if the prisoner can guess in advance the day of his execution, he will be spared. The prisoner thinks for a moment and then says, "In that case, you can never hang me." Suppose the stated week ends on Saturday night. Then if the prisoner has not been hanged by Friday, he knows he will have to be hanged on Saturday. Since he will be able to guess this in advance, he cannot, therefore, be hanged on Saturday. If he has not been hanged by Thursday then he will know that since Saturday has been ruled out, he must be hanged on Friday. Again, knowing this in advance, he cannot be hanged on Friday. Carrying this argument back for each day of the week, he reasons that he cannot be hanged without violating the judge's promise.

Some Newcomers: Within the last 20 yr or so a number of brand-new pastimes have appeared upon the scene: the flexagons, the polyominoes, and the Soma cubes. Flexagons are paper polygons, folded from straight or crooked strips of paper, which have the remarkable property of changing their faces when they are "flexed." Many varieties of flexagons can be made; at least one form has been commercially marketed as a toy. A polyomino (Fig. 11) is a "simply connected" set of congruent squares, joined along their edges. Asymmetrical pieces, which have a different shape when "turned over," are considered as a single type. There are 12 types of pentominoes. Polyominoes admit of many varieties of puzzles and patterns, especially when placed upon a conventional checkerboard. Soma cubes (Fig. 12) are "irregular" solid shapes made by joining not more than four congruent cubes face to face. There are exactly seven Soma pieces. They have the remarkable property that they can be joined to form a larger cube; this can be done in more than 200 different ways. Many fascinating forms can be built from the seven basic Soma pieces.

Literature: The literature pertaining to mathematical recreations is unusually rich. The earliest important work is that of Bachet de Méziriac (1612); other 17th- and 18th-cent. writers include J. Leurechon, C. Mydorge, Wm. Leybourn, and J. Ozanam. Among illustrious 19th- and early 20th-cent. authors we find the names of W. Ahrens, Rouse Ball, H. E. Dudeney, E. Fourrey, Sam Loyd, E. Lucas, and F. Maack. A partial list of outstanding contemporary authorities would include R. Abraham, H. S. M. Coxeter, Martin Gardner, R. V. Heath, Piet Hein, J. A. Hunter, M. Kraitchik, H. Phillips, G. H. Savage, V. Thébault, W. T. Williams, and Theodore Wolff. Since the close of World War II many books on mathematical recreations have appeared, including paperbacks and reprints of earlier classics. A bibliography by W. L. Schaaf (1958) lists over 2,500 references. A bimonthly journal, *Recreational Mathematics Magazine,* made its debut early in 1961.

Answers

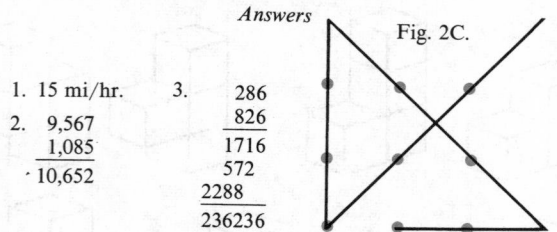

1. 15 mi/hr.

2. 9,567
    1,085
   _____
   10,652

3.   286
      826
     _____
     1716
      572
     2288
    _____
    236236

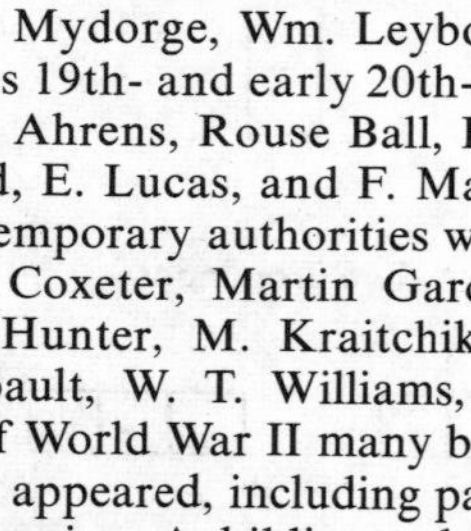

Fig. 2C.

4. Tall native is liar; short native is truth-teller.

5. "I will be hanged."

Fig. 2A. They are equal.

Fig. 2B. Upright.

Fig. 8. *a* and *b*

—W. L. S.

MATHEMATICAL TABLES: collections of numerical values of various mathematical functions. The use of tables can save time and avoid errors whenever the numerical value of a mathematical function is required in a problem. Commonly included are logarithms, trigonometric functions, logarithms of trigonometric functions, natural logarithms, exponential functions, squares and square roots, cubes and cube roots, reciprocals, factorials, circumferences and areas of circles, interest tables, mortality tables, areas and ordinates of the normal frequency curve, and conversion tables such as degrees to radians. Certain lists of functional relations are also called tables, *e.g.* tables of differentials and integrals.—*H. E. W.*

MATHEMATICS: the study that began as a science of space and quantity, concerned with concrete bodies and collections, but is now recognized to be a vast aggregation of deductions from assumptions about pure abstractions. The mathematics of Babylonia and Egypt included astrology, astronomy, mechanics, and surveying. At first there was no clear distinction between numbers and the collections of objects to which they referred, or between the properties of space and those of the objects that occupied space. Empirical methods were acceptable. At the hands of the Greeks, however, mathematics became abstract and deductive. Mathematical objects became idealized elements about which assumptions were adopted in accordance with what appeared to be true of the physical objects from which they were abstracted. Conclusions were acceptable only if they were obtained by deductive logic based on these assumptions. This abstract, deductive nature has characterized mathematics ever since. (See LOGIC.)

The principal source of the abstractions and assumptions of mathematics is the physical world. Many abstractions of mathematics are idealizations of concrete things: a geometrical line is given properties conceived to be those common to many physical lines—a stretched wire, an edge of a block, a ray of light. Because of this close relationship the conclusions of mathematics have concrete, practical interpretations. Much of mathematics is inspired by the need for answers to practical problems.

The deductive processes of mathematics start with assumptions about the abstract concepts. The concrete objects themselves always possess a complex of properties, many of which may be irrelevant to the question at hand; thus, to make clear and meaningful assumptions it is necessary to abstract from the concrete objects, or to create ideal objects, which then possess only the properties that are given to them by the assumptions, or axioms. This kind of reduction, or transformation, of a concrete situation to an abstract one governed by axioms brings concrete, physical situations within the purview of mathematics. This is the method of applied mathematics. The results of strict deduction, unlike those of scientific induction, are sure, and those parts of science that are purely mathematical require no revision or correction.

It is not only for its contributions to science that mathematics has value, much mathematics having been developed without thought of serving science. The abstract elements may be purely intellectual in origin, or so remote from physical sources that all connection with the world of matter is lost to view. Some modern mathematicians completely dissociate their thinking from concrete objects, thus emphasizing the fact that mathematics is not necessarily tied to the physical universe. Mathematics therefore appears as a huge intellectual structure of pure reason. It exemplifies reasoning in its purest form and furnishes a critique for our most basic intellectual processes. This is the point of view of pure mathematics.

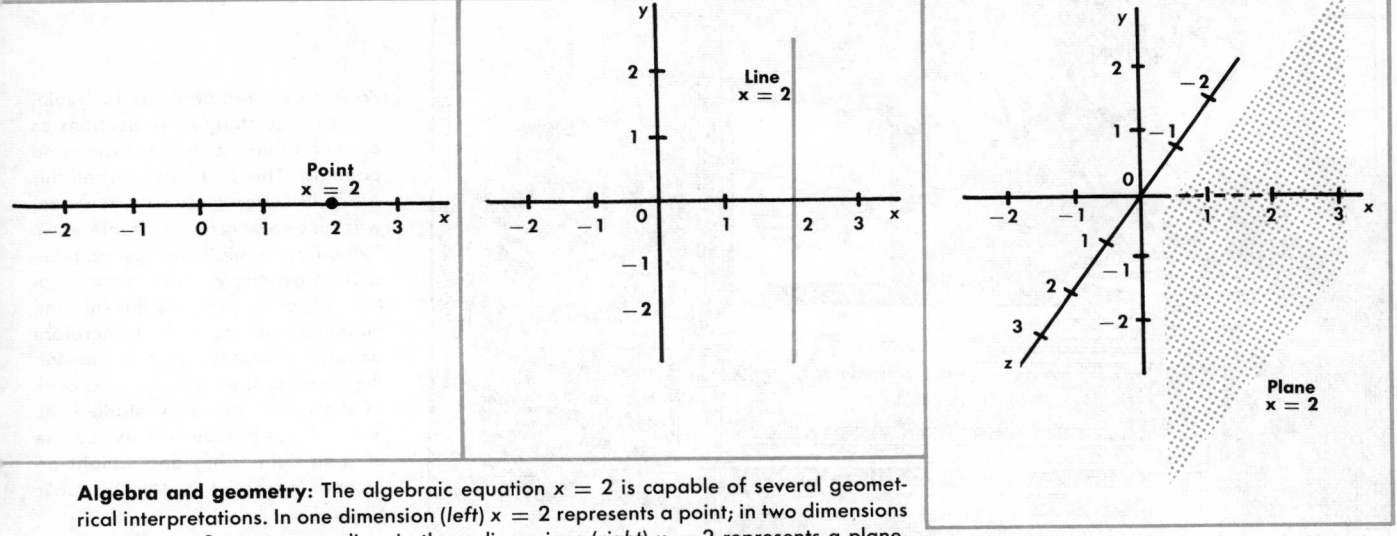

Algebra and geometry: The algebraic equation $x = 2$ is capable of several geometrical interpretations. In one dimension (*left*) $x = 2$ represents a point; in two dimensions (*center*) $x = 2$ represents a line; in three dimensions (*right*) $x = 2$ represents a plane.

The abstract, deductive nature of mathematics does not mean that, in the production of mathematics, mathematicians only think deductively about abstract elements. Mathematical thinking is an art in which intuition plays a prominent role. Experimentation with physical objects which approximate their abstract counterparts in mathematics often leads to mathematical insights. No mental process is prohibited in the furtherance of mathematics, but all results must pass the test of being deducible from the basic axioms. Thus any branch of mathematics has all its parts linked together by a chain of deductive reasoning, and is a completely stable body of knowledge, requiring revision only if faulty reasoning or poor concepts are used in its creation.

Branches of Mathematics: Although no body of deductive reasoning from fundamental axioms can be ruled out of mathematics, most of the subject is comprised in several large branches. The first of these, which comes to our attention early in life because of its great practicality, is arithmetic.

ARITHMETIC is concerned with numbers and numerical calculations. It is, of course, of use and importance to almost all people in modern life. In elementary arithmetic, operations of addition, subtraction, multiplication, and division are defined and systematized, first with whole numbers and then with fractions. Higher arithmetic treats these operations more abstractly and more generally, and extends the number system to include complex numbers.

NUMBER THEORY deals with numbers in a different way. Practical computation is no part of this subject. Rather, it is concerned with categories of whole numbers (integers), their extent and distribution, the existence of whole numbers satisfying given conditions, relations among classes of whole numbers, and so on. The prime numbers form an important class of whole numbers, a prime number being one having no exact factors except itself and unity. The first ten primes are 1, 2, 3, 5, 7, 11, 13, 17, 19, and 23. Are there an unlimited number of prime numbers, or is there a greatest prime, with all greater numbers equal to products of factors not larger than this greatest prime? Euclid proved that there is no greatest prime. Hence the number of primes is unlimited. A famous question in number theory is known as Fermat's Last Theorem. According to this theorem, there are no integers that can be substituted for x, y, and z and satisfy the equation $x^n + y^n = z^n$, if n is a whole number greater than 2. Although Pierre de Fermat claimed he had proved this statement, his proof was never found, and no one has since been able to prove it in general. Hence it has the nature of a conjecture rather than a theorem.

ALGEBRA goes beyond arithmetic by greatly extending the symbolism. In particular, algebra utilizes letters for unknown, or unspecified, numbers. This makes it possible to deal with known and unknown numbers on an equal footing. Through the relations we find among them, we can often determine the values of the unknowns. The characteristic method of solving a concrete problem by algebra is to assign a letter to the desired answer; set down a relation involving the unknown, in the form of an equation; and then solve the equation. The central problem of algebra is that of solving equations. A large body of algebra is the theory of equations (see EQUATIONS, THEORY OF). It includes systematic studies of equations of first, second, third, and fourth degrees in one unknown. Such equations can always be solved. Equations of the fifth and higher degrees cannot always be solved by algebraic processes (*i.e.* addition, subtraction, multiplication, division, and the extraction of roots), although the theory guarantees the existence of solutions. Some of the most profound mathematics of the 19th and 20th cent. has come out of studies in this area. The study of equations also includes systems of equations involving two or more unknowns. The most important systems are those in which the equations are of the first degree, called linear systems. Linear algebra is an important modern subject concerned with such systems and related matters, including determinants, matrices, vectors, and tensors. What is generally termed modern algebra is a highly abstract field. In some of its developments the familiar axioms of elementary algebra are altered. (See ALGEBRA, ABSTRACT.)

GEOMETRY is a vast field of mathematics with many subdivisions. The geometry usually studied in high school is essentially the same as that developed by the Greeks and systematized by Euclid. It has often been conceived as an accurate description of physical space, although today it is considered more abstractly and recognized to be only approximately true when interpreted physically. The basic elements of geometry are points, lines, and planes. These are undefined. More complicated elements, such as triangles, circles, and cubes, are defined in terms of the undefined elements. The axioms of Euclid have sometimes been called "self-evident truths," and were so considered in ancient times. We now recognize them to be assumptions about abstract elements, neither self-evident nor necessarily true. One of Euclid's axioms, which determined his theory of parallels and affected

Projective geometry had its beginnings in the study of projections as applied to problems in drawing and painting. The 16th cent., when this Albrecht Dürer woodcut was made, was an age of renewal of interest in Pythagorean mathematics and Euclidean geometry. Dürer's combination of a musical instrument and mathematical method is therefore doubly interesting. In the drawing the panel at the right is swung back to show how the artist studied the mandolin in perspective by the use of a straight string and weight attached to the wall. (*N. Y. Public Library*)

a large part of all Euclidean geometry, was so little self-evident that it was deemed a flaw in the system. Many mathematicians tried to prove this parallel axiom as a theorem. Finally, in the early 19th cent. the impossibility of proving it was established. The first non-Euclidean geometries were built on systems of axioms in which the Euclidean parallel axiom is replaced by a contradictory one. Later ones were created by changing additional postulates, and finally by abandoning the central notion that one part of space is like any other part. This last resulted in RIEMANNIAN GEOMETRY. The discovery of non-Euclidean geometries was instrumental in bringing out the abstract nature of geometry and the independence of mathematics from a literal description of the physical world.

In the 17th cent. a scheme was devised for uniting geometry and algebra. This is the COORDINATE GEOMETRY, or analytic geometry, first described by Descartes in 1637. By means of a coordinate system, each point is given numerical representation. As a result it is possible to represent many other geometric entities numerically, *e.g.* distance and direction. In plane analytic geometry, a line or curve is associated with an equation in two unknowns; in analytic geometry of three dimensions, a surface has a similar representation in three unknowns. So powerful are the methods of analytic geometry that they have supplanted the older methods in large areas of geometry. The association of geometrical and numerical elements in this geometry made it a most valuable instrument for scientists and mathematicians of the 17th and 18th cent. in their attack on the great problems of physical science. It was also a basic tool in the development of calculus.

PROJECTIVE GEOMETRY originated in the efforts of painters, architects, and engineers to produce realistic pictures of three-dimensional objects on a flat surface—the problem of perspective drawing. The principal stimulus came from the Renaissance painters. In this geometry, magnitude, congruence, and similarity, which play such an important role in Euclidean geometry, do not enter. Rather, the unchanging character of certain ratios, orders, and arrangements is the important feature.

DESCRIPTIVE GEOMETRY is as much a branch of mechanical drawing as of mathematics. It is concerned largely with representing three dimensions on a flat surface, not so as to

look like three dimensions, as in projective geometry, but so that each part is accurately represented. This subject was invented by army engineers and is important in the training of architects and engineers today.

TOPOLOGY, or *analysis situs,* originated in the middle of the 19th cent. and has since been one of the dominant fields of mathematics. It is concerned with properties of a geometrical object, such as a curve or surface, that remain invariant, or unchanged, as the object undergoes a topological transformation, *i.e.* when it is deformed without cutting or tearing, and without attaching any two points together. In this way a circle may be deformed into an ellipse. In this instance, the curve remains a closed curve, and this fact is a topological property. The initial curve is gradually deformed into the final shape, each point of one curve corresponding to precisely one point of the other. The curves are said to be topologically equivalent. Similarly, a spherical surface is topologically equivalent to a cube, but it is not topologically equivalent to a doughnut-shaped surface. Topology has contributed to many areas of modern mathematics, especially the theory of functions of a complex variable.

CALCULUS is one of the greatest discoveries in the history of mathematics, and has been the dominant force in mathematics for almost 300 yr. It resulted from efforts to analyze curved paths and surfaces in geometry, and continuously changing phenomena in the physical world. Efforts to do this with the tools of algebra and geometry, including analytic geometry, were unavailing, although correct results for many special problems were obtained. Newton and Leibniz, in the latter part of the 17th cent., discovered general methods, and these were extended in subsequent centuries. The tool of the calculus that transcends algebra is the limit of an infinite sequence. Once this concept is formulated, it leads to the notion of the limit of a function, and thence to the two main operations of calculus, differentiation and integration. By means of the concept of a limit we are able to arrive at a meaningful analysis of the slope and direction of a curve "at a point," or of motion "at an instant." Differentiation is the process of finding derivatives. A derivative is the limit of a ratio, formed in such a way as to provide the slope of the tangent of a curve on a coordinate system, or the instantaneous velocity of a moving object, or precise rates of change in other situations. The word "integration" is used in two senses. In one usage, it means the reversal of the process of differentiation. For example, we might find the equation of motion of a body if we knew a formula for its velocity. In the other, and more basic, usage, it means finding a definite integral of a function. Geometrically, this means finding the area bounded by the x-axis, a curve lying above it, and two vertical lines. This is the limit of a sequence of sums of approximating rectangles. The two operations of differentiation and integration opened the doors to the investigation of large areas in mathematics and science that had previously been approached somewhat tentatively and ineffectively. In mathematics, calculus was the foundation on which was erected the enormous structure of mathematical analysis, which has dominated applied mathematics for almost three centuries.

ANALYSIS includes several specialized branches that are outgrowths of calculus or extensions of it into other fields. The heart of it is FUNCTION THEORY, in which large classes of functions are studied by means of the limit operations, and their domains are vastly extended by letting the variables be any real or complex numbers. DIFFERENTIAL EQUATIONS are a far-reaching extension of integration by which one can find y as a function of x when x, y, and dy/dx all appear in an equation, in a variety of combinations. INTEGRAL EQUATIONS involve integrals in which unknown functions appear, and the solution of such equations calls for finding the unknown functions. CALCULUS OF VARIATIONS is a broad application of analysis to the solution of maximum and minimum problems of a high order. DIFFERENTIAL GEOMETRY is an extensive application of analysis to problems involving curves and surfaces. The investigation of infinite series appears in nearly all parts of analysis.

STATISTICS and PROBABILITY are two closely related branches of mathematics that have grown in response to vital needs in science and the study of social phenomena. In statistics, one tries to reach conclusions about a broad situation from observations of numerous special instances. Although mathematical methods are essential within statistical studies, the field itself is less mathematical than others mentioned above, in that it is concerned with concrete applications almost exclusively, and deduction from axioms is not the primary method. Probability is one of the principal mathematical tools used in statistics. The theory can be developed deductively from axioms, although it often happens that the statistical questions to be answered are permitted to obscure the mathematical nature of probability. In the late 19th cent. efforts aimed at clarifying the nature of the number system led to the investigation of infinite SETS—sets of numbers, points, or other mathematical objects. The theory of infinite sets is basic to much of modern mathematics. Both finite and infinite sets are important in developing the mathematical theory of probability.

Symbolic logic (see FORMAL LOGIC) is generally recognized as a branch of mathematics. It is highly technical, with an elaborate symbolism. Many of its results have useful implications regarding the foundations of mathematics.

Whether MATHEMATICAL PHYSICS belongs in physics or mathematics is determined by one's viewpoint. It is mathematics applied to physical problems. Many of the most significant and extensive developments in modern mathematics are in this area. QUANTUM THEORY and the theory of RELATIVITY are examples. Although one can hardly claim that the field of automation is a branch of mathematics, it would be impossible without mathematics. Mathematicians are prominent among designers of automatic equipment. The invention of high-speed COMPUTERS has led to the development of mathematical methods, comprised under numerical analysis, designed to make efficient use of them. Computing machines are highly mathematical in concept and design. Moreover, the volume of computation of which they are capable renders mathematical computation practical which would be impossible without them.—*H. C.*

MATHEMATICS, HISTORY OF: One cannot find a clearly designated beginning of mathematics, but a primitive science of number and magnitude is at least as old as mankind, and prehistoric drawings show early developments in a geometry of design and in a process of counting. From paleolithic times, there survives a tally stick with more than 50 notches incised on it, some of which are arranged in groups of five. Here one sees the start of a quinary system, probably associated at first with finger-reckoning. Neolithic ornamentation in pottery, baskets, and textiles shows familiarity with basic geometrical ideas of congruence and similarity; and early efforts at measuring objects led to the discovery of the properties of the straight line and the circle. In the Rhind papyrus (*c.* 1650 B. C.) the area of a circle is found by squaring eight-ninths of the diameter, an approximation equivalent to assuming a value of 3⅙ for π. The papyrus contains also a curious table in which fractions of the form $2/(n + 1)$ are expressed as sums of unit fractions, so that, *e.g.,* ²⁄₉₉ is equated to ¹⁄₆₆ + ¹⁄₁₉₈. In the older Moscow or Golenischev papyrus (*c.* 1850 B. C.) it is apparent that the Egyptians had a rule, perhaps discovered in pyramid-building, for finding the volume of a frustum of a pyramid with a square base.

Mathematics in the Mesopotamian valley was on a higher level than that of Egypt. Cuneiform tablets from some 4,000 yr ago indicate that the Babylonians were familiar with geometric theorems usually named for Thales and Pythagoras, who lived some 1,500 yr later. Quadratic equations were solved by a method equivalent to completing the square; and, through linear interpolation within tables of squares and cubes, special forms of cubic equations were handled. Important in the future of mathematics was the development in Mesopotamia of the principle of position, or place-value, which is the basis of modern numeration. The Babylonians adopted a number system with a base of 60; the present-day subdivision of time and angle units into minutes and seconds is a legacy of this ancient numeration. The Babylonians discovered that the very same symbols which they adopted for the integers from 1 through 59 could be used over again for the corresponding multiples of 60 simply by writing them to

Mathematician's study is the subject of this decorative woodcut from the book *Arithmetica practica methodus facilis,* by Gemma Frisius, printed in Antwerp in 1540. (*Bettmann Archive*)

the left of the units position, just as today one writes the 10s to the left of the units; the next position to the left indicated multiples of 60 times 60, each successive place to the left designating the next higher power of the base. Moreover, the Babylonians understood that positions to the right of the units represented successive powers of the reciprocal of the base, just as in the modern scheme for decimal fractions. By the 3rd cent. B. C. the Babylonians had perfected their system by the introduction of a special symbol, the equivalent of our zero, for an empty position.

Pre-Hellenic mathematics exhibited serious deficiencies, for surviving documents present us with specific cases only, without the general formulations which these imply. Moreover, the Egyptians and Babylonians did not organize their extensive empirical discoveries into a rational system. It is for this reason that ordinarily one refers to Thales of Miletus (*fl.* 600 B. C.) as the first mathematician, for he is reputed to have stated half a dozen geometrical theorems abstractly and to have provided some form of proof for them. From these beginnings Pythagoras of Samos (*c.* 580–*c.* 500 B. C.) is reported to have built up a more complete logical structure and to have established mathematics as a liberal discipline with four branches: arithmetic, or numbers at rest; music, or numbers in motion; geometry, or magnitudes at rest; and astronomy, or magnitudes in motion. The Pythagoreans believed that integers (whole numbers) were the key to all of life—as witness the principles of musical harmony and the laws of cosmic astronomy. It therefore was a blow to Pythagorean philosophy when, toward the end of the 5th cent. B. C., it was discovered that two straight-line segments may be such that their ratio is not expressible as a quotient of integers. That is, the diagonal of a square is incommensurable with its side, as is also the diagonal of a pentagon (a favorite Pythagorean symbol) with respect to a side of the pentagon. It is possible that this discovery prompted the Greeks to give to their geometry its definitive deductive form; but it had also the unfortunate effect of divorcing the fields of number and magnitude. Thus the nascent algebraic tendencies in Babylonian mathematics gave way in Greece to an emphasis upon geometry, in which interest came to be centered in three celebrated problems: the squaring of the circle, the duplication of the cube, and the trisection of the angle. The first of these inspired the method of exhaustion, a geometrical equivalent, perhaps introduced by Eudoxus (*fl.* 375 B. C.), of the integral calculus; the second seems to have led to the discovery of the conics by Menaechmus, student of Eudoxus and teacher of Alexander the Great; and the last was associated with the spiral of Archimedes (287–212 B. C.).

Toward the end of the 4th cent. B. C. the scene of mathematical activity had shifted to the new city of Alexandria, and it was here that Euclid (*fl. c.* 300) taught and wrote. His *Elements,* the most influential textbook ever written, constituted a summary of elementary mathematics, including the theory of numbers and a sort of geometrical algebra. On a higher level Archimedes fashioned the method of exhaustion into an effective device by which he found areas, volumes, and centers of gravity associated with conics and spirals. His younger rival, Apollonius of Perga (*fl. c.* 225), wrote a celebrated book on the *Conics,* covering properties associated with foci, tangents, asymptotes, conjugate diameters, poles and polars, and evolutes.

The golden age of Greek mathematics during the 3rd cent. B. C. was followed by a period of increased emphasis upon applications. Trigonometry arose as a handmaiden of astronomy in the work of Hipparchus (*fl. c.* 130 B. C.), and the subject was more fully developed in the *Almagest* (or *Syntaxis*) of Ptolemy (*fl.* A. D. 150). Numerical and mensurational problems received increased attention in the *Metrica* of Heron (*c.* A. D. 100); and the *Arithmetica* of Diophantus (*c.* 250) introduced the solution of indeterminate equations, since known as Diophantine analysis. Earlier Greek algebra had been rhetorical and geometrical; but that of Diophantus was syncopated and numerical, making possible the study of equations beyond the third degree.

Early in the 4th cent. A. D., there was a short-lived resurgence of pure geometry, represented especially by the *Mathematical Collection* of Pappus (*c.* 320); but in the long medieval interlude following Pappus, there was a hiatus in traditional mathematical developments in Europe. In India, meanwhile, mathematics was taking a different direction. There the "rope stretchers" had developed simple "rules of the cord," comparable to the geometry of the Nile surveyors, and these were incorporated in the *Sulvasutras,* roughly coeval with the Greek golden age; but there was no sustained mathematical tradition. The inspiration for the *Siddhantas* (or astronomical systems) of the 5th cent. may have come from contact with foreigners from Alexandria rather than from the local *Sulvasutras.* From the Hindu *Siddhantas,* nevertheless, two significant mathematical novelties seem to have stemmed, one in trigonometry and the other in arithmetic. The trigonometry of Hipparchus and Ptolemy had been a geometry of chords in a circle; but in the *Siddhantas* this was converted to a study of half-chords from which the modern sine function has evolved. In arithmetic the chief Hindu contribution was the development of the positional principle into a decimally ciphered number system from which the modern numerals are derived. However, the Hindus overlooked the decimalization of fractions, and it was not until the days of François Viète (1540–1603) and Simon Stevin (1548–1620) that the systematic use of decimal fractions was achieved.

From India the new trigonometry and the new numerals passed to the Arabic civilization in the 8th cent., together with elements of Babylonian algebra and of Greek astronomy and geometry. The eclectic Arabic scholars were not highly original, but their peculiar blending of ancient sources was influential in shaping the future of mathematics. In particular, Al-Khwarizmi (*fl. c.* 825) composed an elementary treatise, *Al-Jabr,* the name and spirit of which dominated early renaissance mathematics in Europe. Al-Khwarizmi wrote also a work on the Hindu numerals which was so influential in their transmission to Europe that, through corruption of the name of the author, the new computation became known as algorism or algorithm. As late as the 12th and 13th centuries the Arabic world was producing men of the caliber of Omar Khayyam (*c.* 1044–1123), who solved cubics geometrically, and of Nasir Eddin (1201–74), who attempted to prove the parallel postulate of Euclid; but by this time learning in Europe had surpassed that in Asia and Africa.

Latin scholars of the 12th cent. had translated important scientific treatises of antiquity and the early Middle Ages; during the 13th cent., through such new works as the *Liber abaci* of Leonardo of Pisa (*c.* 1180–1250), the Hindu numerals and Arabic algebra were established in Europe. In 1494, Luca Pacioli believed, like Omar Khayyam, that third-degree equations were algebraically unsolvable; but within the next 20 yr a Bolognese teacher, Scipio del Ferro, worked out an algebraic solution of a particular type of cubic. News of the discovery reached Niccolo Tartaglia and he independently discovered a method for solving other forms of cubic equations. Tartaglia shared the discovery with Girolamo Cardano, who published it in 1545 in the celebrated *Ars magna.* Cardano's secretary, Ludovico Ferrari, promptly produced an algebraic solution of the equation of fourth degree.

Later in the century Viète gave a solution of the cubic by means of trigonometric functions. Trigonometry had remained, prior to this time, largely an aid to astronomers; but Viète gave the subject new stature by emphasizing analytic aspects, including the formulas for sin $n\theta$ and cos $n\theta$. Viète evinced the modern spirit in mathematics, for he sought generalizations rather than special cases. Symptomatic also of the changed mathematical view in the 16th cent. was the fact that whereas the ancient Greeks had handled algebraic problems geometrically, the tendency of Viète was to systematize geometric constructions through the use of algebra.

The 16th-cent. renaissance in mathematics had brought new points of view in elementary branches, but it was the 17th cent. that provided new tools of advanced mathematics. One of the first of these was the invention, virtually simultaneously by John Napier (1550–1617) and Jobst Bürgi (c. 1552–1632), of logarithms. At first this remained but a calculating device, and theoretical aspects of logarithms were not exploited until the 18th cent. By contrast, the discoveries of analytic geometry and the calculus were from the beginning deeply enmeshed with mathematical theory. René Descartes (1596–1650), eager to find new ways of seeking truth, saw that geometrical constructions could be systematized through algebraic techniques. By superimposing a coordinate system upon a figure, the geometric properties could be expressed algebraically; and, conversely, an equation in two unknown quantities could be plotted as a plane curve on a coordinate system. This discovery was published by Descartes in *La Géométrie,* an appendix to his *Discours de la méthode* of 1637. Because the effectiveness of Cartesian geometry depended heavily upon algebra, much of *La Géométrie* is concerned with the elementary theory of equations, including transformations of equations and Descartes' rule of signs.

Euclid's *Elements:* Page here (much reduced) is from first printed edition (1482), a Latin translation probably from an Arabic text.

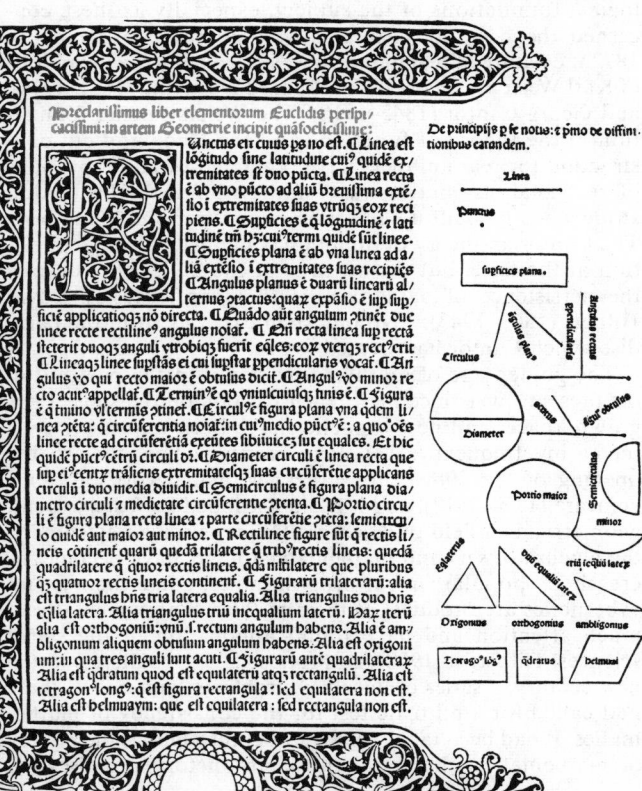

The principles of analytic geometry had been discovered independently by Pierre de Fermat (1601–65) before 1637; but posthumous publication deprived him of due recognition. Fermat, however, was a pioneer also in other directions. He initiated the modern theory of numbers, bequeathing the still unsolved problem of proving that $x^n + y^n = z^n$ has no solutions in integers x, y, z if n is an integer greater than two; he was also a founder, together with Blaise Pascal (1623–62), of the theory of probability. Most important of all, Fermat developed a method for finding tangents to curves and for maximizing or minimizing a function, his procedure being equivalent to that of the differential calculus. It was this work that led Isaac Newton (1642–1727) to devise, about 1665–66, a universal algorithm, which he called the method of fluxions, for handling problems involving areas and tangents. In Germany the same discovery was made a few years later by Gottfried W. Leibniz (1646–1718), and in 1684–86 he published his method, the differential and integral calculus, in his newly established journal, the *Acta Eruditorum.* Newton's first published hint of the calculus appeared in the *Principia* in 1687, and full accounts were not available until the next century, a delay which provoked a bitter priority controversy between supporters of Newton and those of Leibniz. Newton was admittedly the more powerful mathematician, but his successors in Britain overvalued the synthetic aspects of his work at the expense of the analysis and notations of Leibniz, and hence during the 18th cent., development on the Continent was more rapid than in England.

Foremost among the disciples of Leibniz to advance the cause of the new analysis were the members of the Bernoulli family, of whom Jean (1667–1748) was the most ardent and influential. He wrote books on the calculus and taught Leonhard Euler (1707–83), the most prolific analyst of all times. Euler is the classic representative of mathematics in his century. Cartesian geometry was extended to include three dimensions, and the calculus was broadened to include differential equations, differential geometry, and the calculus of variations. Analysis and the function concept intruded everywhere in science and mathematics. Trigonometry became the analytic study of periodic functions, and it was linked with the logarithmic and exponential functions through the Euler identities. Analytical mechanics and analytical optics replaced the synthetic point of view of Newton's *Principia* and *Opticks.* What one misses in Euler's work is a concern for the logical structure of mathematics. In some measure this deficiency was supplied by Joseph L. Lagrange (1736–1813), whose *Théorie des fonctions analytiques* (1797) paved the way for the modern theory of functions of a real variable through his effort to find a solid foundation for the calculus. In his *Mécanique analytique* (1788) Lagrange had similarly sought to place mechanics upon an axiomatic basis.

Euler had been born in Switzerland, but most of his life had been spent at the academies in St. Petersburg and Berlin. Lagrange had been born in Italy, but his mathematical career centered largely in Berlin and Paris; and it was at Paris that the next significant mathematical trends developed. The French Revolution ushered in not only a new political era, but a changed mathematical pattern as well. Lagrange was politically inactive during the Revolution, but two of his associates took leading roles in politics and mathematics. One of these was the Organizer of Victory, Lazare Carnot (1753–1823), who served on the Committee of Public Safety, led the victorious French armies, wrote on the foundations of the calculus, and initiated a revival of pure geometry. Carnot's *Géométrie de position* (1803) gave to synthetic geometry a degree of generality which made it more attractive and better able to compete with analysis. Gaspard Monge (1746–1818), also an associate of Lagrange and an energetic revolutionary figure who served as Minister of the Navy and who supervised the manufacture of gunpowder, aided the cause of pure geometry through the introduction of descriptive geometry, highly regarded by France at the time as a secret weapon of defense. Monge, who contributed heavily also to analytic geometry and differential geometry, was a remarkable teacher, and thus his influence was widely felt. Monge and Carnot were instrumental in the establishment of the Ecole Polytechnique, a school which had as teachers many of the foremost mathematicians, and as students those who were to fashion 19th-cent. thought. One of the lecturers was Pierre Simon de Laplace (1749–1827), the leading applied mathematician of the age who contributed to astronomy, mechanics, and probability.

The Ecole Polytechnique was an engineering school, but the students who graduated from it evinced a remarkable breadth of view in mathematics. Augustin-Louis Cauchy (1789–1857) characteristically contributed heavily in both quantity and quality, rivaling Euler in bulk and Lagrange in rigor. He provided the essentially modern definitions of derivative, integral, continuity, and convergence; and he was responsible for a tremendous broadening of the theory of functions through the use of complex variables. Cauchy was not alone in marking so clearly the tendencies of the new century, for at Prague the mathematician Bernard Bolzano was doing like things more unobtrusively, and Karl Friedrich Gauss was entering similar views and discoveries in his diaries. Gauss, possibly the greatest mathematical figure of all time, gave the first satisfactory proof of the fundamental theorem of algebra and made important discoveries in differential geometry, statistics, geodesy, potential theory, and other pure and applied fields. The theory of numbers has at all ages attracted some of the very best minds—Fermat, Euler, Lagrange, Cauchy—and in this field Gauss in 1801 published his greatest work, the *Disquisitiones arithmeticae,* a book containing beautiful and profound discoveries, including the algebra of congruences and the law of quadratic reciprocity.

Numerating rods were devised in 1617 by John Napier, inventor of logarithms, for the performance of multiplication and division. Known also as "Napier's bones," they are forerunners of slide rule of today. (*British Crown copyright, Science Museum, London*)

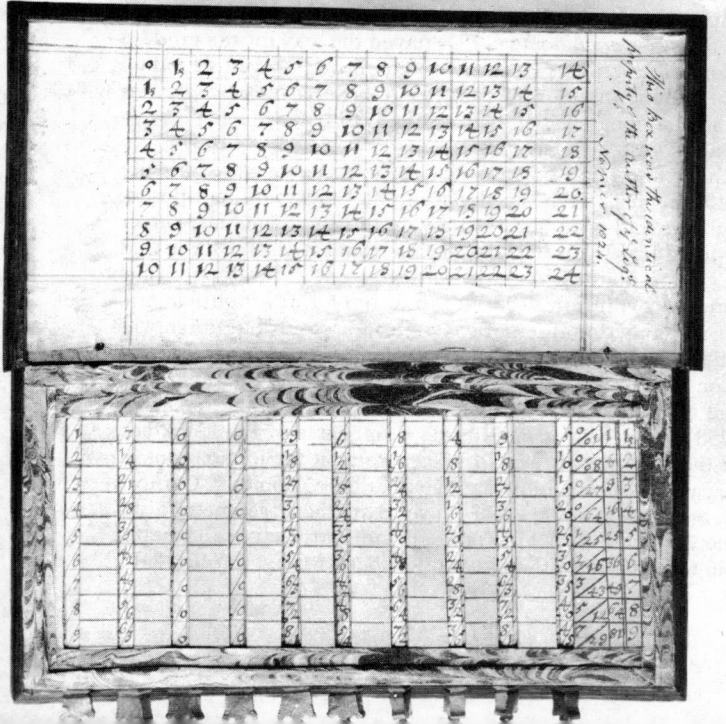

Many other ideas of Gauss remained unpublished, such as the graphical representation of complex numbers, devised and published independently by Caspar Wessel (1745–1818) and J. R. Argand (1768–1822); the double periodicity of elliptic functions, announced by N. H. Abel (1802–29); and the existence of non-Euclidean geometries, published by Nicolai Ivanovich Lobachevski (1793–1856) and Johann Bolyai (1802–60).

The discovery of non-Euclidean geometries placed the nature of mathematics in a new light. Heretofore regarded as the purest of the physical sciences, it now was realized that mathematics is a study not of the actual world, but of all possible worlds. That is, it is a logical structure based upon undefined terms and postulates, whether or not these have counterparts in nature. Mathematics, freed from limitations of sense perception, took wings in the 19th cent. Jean V. Poncelet (1788–1867), like Cauchy a graduate of the Ecole Polytechnique, developed projective geometry, an abstract branch of extraordinary generality in which points may be real or imaginary, finite or infinite. In Germany, the analytic geometer Julius Plücker (1801–68) transcended experience in a four-dimensional geometry having lines, rather than points, as fundamental elements; and Arthur Cayley (1821–95) in England carried abstraction further in an analytic geometry of indefinitely many dimensions. Algebra likewise became ever more general, throughout the 19th and 20th cent., with the growing awareness that the fundamental laws of arithmetic are not laws of nature but arbitrary assumptions. Algebras can be constructed in which some of the fundamental laws do not apply. In Cayley's algebra of matrices, for example, $A \cdot B$ is not generally equal to $B \cdot A$, and the same is true of the vector analysis of H. G. Grassmann (1809–77). Yet, oddly enough, by the mid-20th cent. these abstract branches of mathematics had become important tools of the scientist.

While the 19th cent. was soaring in flights of mathematical imagination, it also became increasingly concerned with the logical foundations of the subject, especially as these concerned the basic ideas of number and the continuum. In 1872 the nature of real numbers was clarified in the definitions of Karl Weierstrass (1815–97), Richard Dedekind (1831–1916), and Georg Cantor (1845–1918). The Weierstrassian foundation in the theory of functions and the Dedekind cut construction for real numbers have remained essential portions of real analysis; but it was Cantor who took the boldest stride when he built up an arithmetic of transfinite numbers. The Cantorian theory of infinite sets met with strong opposition at the time, but the attitude of the 20th cent., despite the persistence of paradoxes, is that expressed by David Hilbert (1862–1943): "No one shall expel us from the paradise which Cantor has created for us."

The golden age of mathematics is not in the past but in the present. Ever since the French Revolution the subject has grown apace, and new branches have been appearing with increasing frequency. Topology made its bow toward the opening of the 20th cent., largely with the work of Henri Poincaré (1854–1912), and it has outstripped its foster-parent, geometry, as a field of research. Other relative newcomers, the algebra of sets and mathematical logic, have become increasingly popular; linear programming, game theory, and cybernetics are products of the mid-20th cent. which attract much attention and have found application in the social sciences. Hilbert in 1900 had proposed, as a challenge to the new century, a series of unsolved problems; and one of these had called for a finitistic test for the consistency of mathematics. It had been tacitly understood, throughout the history of mathematics, that mutually contradictory premises (or

First adding machine with counter gears, a replica of which is shown, was constructed (1642) by Blaise Pascal, French philosopher and mathematician. In the original, now in Paris, Pascal made use of a ten-toothed gear counter wheel numbered from 0 through 9 around its circumference. When the counter wheel was at 9, and 1 was added, the position or the counter wheel advanced from 9 to 0, and at the same time a small extra side tooth nudged the adjacent counter wheel at the left, causing it to advance one step, thus providing the carry. This machine is the forerunner of the widely used printed-tape adding machine of today. (*British Crown Copyright, Science Museum, London*)

conclusions) are not to be tolerated; but how is one to test for consistency? A recourse had been to find a concrete representation of the abstract postulational system; but inability to find this does not prove inconsistency, and hence Hilbert's challenge had a certain urgency. The outcome, however, came as a shock to mathematicians. In 1931, Kurt Gödel proved that a test of the kind called for is not possible. Any formal mathematical system, such as that in the *Principia* of Bertrand Russell (1872–   ) and Alfred North Whitehead (1861–1947), can be shown to contain arithmetical propositions that are plainly true, but yet are not deducible within the formalism. Such a devastating conclusion has not, surprisingly, lessened the confidence of mathematicians in the soundness of their subject. It has, on the contrary, stimulated interest in mathematics and has directed attention toward another new aspect known as metamathematics. It is hazardous indeed to predict what the future lines of development in mathematics will be; but it appears to be safe to say that the subject will be characterized by two themes which have been apparent throughout past history—ever-increasing generality and ever-deepening abstraction.—C. B. B.

MATHEMATICS, LOGICAL STRUCTURE OF: Mathematics is not an empirical science; that is, its truths are not established by observation, but are derived by reasoning or, more specifically, deduced by logic. For example, geometry was codified by Euclid about 300 B. C. His point of departure was a number of notions, *e.g.* point, line, plane, which he defined; thus "a point is that which has no part." He then stated a number of axioms and postulates, from which theorems were established by proof, *i.e.* derived through a logical argument. In the course of history, several aspects of the method were clarified. The distinction between axioms and postulates became unessential. It became more and more apparent that the initial definitions themselves do not play any role in the proofs; points, lines, and planes are objects about which nothing is supposed to be known except what is explicitly stated in the axioms. Finally, it was discovered early in the 19th cent. that one could take as an axiom a proposition contradicting one of Euclid's assumptions (the "parallel postulate") and obtain a system of geometry just as consistent as Euclidean geometry. Hence axioms and postulates are not truths (rational or experimental), but assumptions, and from diverse assumptions one can obtain different conclusions. The mathematical truths are not the axioms or theorems, but rather the implications of certain statements by other statements. They have the form: If *p*, then *q*. In 1899, David Hilbert gave a version of Euclidean geometry that made explicit all assumptions, even those used by Euclid only tacitly removed initial definitions, and put in full light the strictly deductive aspect of the study. By that time, geometry had become an example for other branches of mathematics to emulate.

With the advent of non-Euclidean geometries, the problem of *consistency* became an explicit concern of mathematicians. The axioms of Euclidean geometry seemed, somehow, to be objectively "true," whatever that means exactly, and, as the methods of deduction were expected to lead from true propositions to true propositions, every theorem was considered to be true. Since, of two contradictory propositions, one is false, no theorem could be the negation of another theorem. When axioms are not any longer received as true, then false propositions may be theorems, and there is no guarantee that a deduction does not lead to a contradiction. It has to be established that it is not possible to prove a theorem *and* its negation, and the system requires a consistency proof. The first consistency proofs given were *relative* consistency proofs; that is, it was proved that a system is consistent if some other system is consistent, and this was done by giving an interpretation of the first system in the second. Thus, in 1868 Eugenio Beltrami proved that, if Euclidean geometry is consistent, so is Lobachevskian geometry. By the use of Cartesian coordinates, it was clear that Euclidean geometry is consistent if the real number system is consistent.

Relative consistency proofs have a limit: there is, finally, one or several theories whose consistency cannot be proved by this method. For such theories we need an *absolute* consistency proof. But the very notion of absolute consistency proof calls for a few remarks: a proof implies that certain means have been used to secure a demonstration and these means are, in a sense, premises of the result obtained. From this point of view, there is no absolute consistency proof. The consistency of most, if not all, branches of mathematics has been reduced to that of two: the theory of natural numbers and the theory of sets. For these two theories, the question of consistency is complex and difficult.

The problem of consistency and the whole nature of deductive systems had already made it clear by the time Hilbert axiomatized Euclidean geometry that it was necessary to go one step further. Hilbert used the ordinary language of mathematicians. He also took for granted the arguments and means of proof that were the common property of the mathematical world. If we want to further clarify the nature of a mathematical theory, we have to examine with a critical eye the language and the logic used.

Although Greek mathematics exerted a profound influence on Greek philosophy (Plato, even Aristotle) by presenting a body of stable non-empirical knowledge, Aristotelian logic was not a codification of the logic used by mathematicians. It was a logic of classes, perhaps suggested by biological classifications more than by the kind of arguments used by geometers. Stoic logic, dealing with propositions rather than with classes, was probably closer to mathematical practice, but for a long time, in fact till the end of the 19th cent., mathematics and the science of logic remained apart. Mathematicians used every argument that they thought should carry conviction, and it is astonishing to see how few disagreements there have been among professional mathematicians as to the cogency of mathematical arguments during 24 centuries. By the end of the 19th cent. the science of logic was already on the road to its modern renaissance, a rebirth that was at once the cause and the effect of a new transformation of mathematics. The first step was the creation of a symbolic language, in which signs are used according to explicit and definite rules and which does not suffer from the ambiguities of ordinary language. Then demonstrations are carried out by means of mathematical (or symbolic) logic. They are reduced to successive applications of a definite number of rules of deduction; these rules are stated in such a way that it can be checked mechanically whether a step does or does not follow from previous steps. We thus obtain the notion of a formal proof, and the axiomatized mathematical theory, rewritten in symbolic language, becomes a formalized axiomatic theory or a formal system. Formalization of mathematics is quite useless for the discovery of new theorems; but it has proved extremely useful in investigating the nature of mathematics. The properties of formal systems are studied by appropriate means (metamathematics). The problems that have aroused most interest in the study of formal systems have been consistency (absence of contradiction), completeness (every "true" proposition expressible in the system is provable in the system), categoricalness (the system is satisfied by just one model), decidability (there is a mechanical procedure for deciding whether a proposition is provable or not in the system). The solutions to these problems have often been surprising and, for the past 40 yr, the study of formal systems has been a lively field.—*J. v. H.*

MATHEMATICS, NEW: a term used popularly to describe recent reform in elementary- and high-school mathematics curricula. Another name for it is modern mathematics. Many different groups of school teachers and college professors have fashioned their own versions of this reform, but all versions are basically similar.

The reform is in part a new approach to traditional subject matter and in part a change in content. Reformers have criticized traditional methods on the grounds that arithmetic and algebra were taught mechanically and that students gained no insight into what they were doing. The new programs seek to provide insight by giving students the logical bases for arithmetic and algebra. This means presenting these subjects much as Euclidean geometry has been presented for hundreds of years; that is, the students are asked to learn definitions and axioms about numbers, and then to justify their steps by reference to the axioms and definitions and to theorems previously established. For example, if a student writes 5×4 instead of 4×5, he is expected to cite the commutative axiom of multiplication as the reason. If he replaces $(5 + 7) + 2$ by $5 + (7 + 2)$, he must justify the change by citing the associative axiom of addition. Part of the logical development of arithmetic and algebra is to show that the properties of negative numbers follow from the properties of positive numbers. In the older presentation a teacher might very well convince students that 3 times -2 is -6 because if -2 represents a debt, 3 such debts would mean a debt of -6. But in new mathematics a theorem is proved to the effect that the product of a positive and a negative number is negative.

Another principle of new mathematics is that all proof must meet the standards of correctness—or rigor, as the mathematicians term it—that are considered satisfactory by professional mathematicians. The effect of this on the curriculum may be most readily seen in the treatment of Euclidean geometry. Euclid used certain axioms which he failed to mention either because he thought they were too obvious to mention or because he overlooked his use of them. In the new version all axioms are explicitly stated, and the student is expected to prove any assertion, no matter how obvious it may be to the

intuition, by invoking the proper axioms or previously proved theorems. Thus one proves in the rigorous development of Euclidean geometry that there are an inside and an outside of a triangle and that every line segment has a unique midpoint.

The new math regards mathematics as a series of deductive structures. Here again, Euclidean geometry serves as a prototype. Each branch of mathematics is to be built on the basis of definitions, axioms, and proofs of theorems. Consistent with the emphasis on logical structure is a disregard of the applications of mathematics. The subject is presented as an end in itself. The reformers concede the importance of mathematics in modern life, but do not regard it as the function of mathematics courses to teach applications.

It is a doctrine of the new math that set theory can be used as the basis for unifying the presentation of mathematics. Hence, set theory is taught from the lowest grades of elementary school onward and is also used, for example, in formulating new definitions of standard concepts. Thus a triangle is defined as the union of three points not on the same straight line and the segments joining these points. The proponents contend that such definitions are essential to achieve precision and clarity.

The new mathematics involves some change in content. A few topics such as the logarithmic solution of triangles, which used to take considerable time in trigonometry and is not used nowadays, have been dropped. In place of these topics, most new math programs include some symbolic logic, set theory, a few of the notions traditionally taught in abstract algebra such as groups and fields, and bits of non-Euclidean geometry and topology.

The movement to reform the mathematics curricula was begun in 1952 by Max Beberman of the University of Illinois Committee on School Mathematics. Several groups started independent ventures soon thereafter. The launching of Sputnik I by the Russians in 1957 gave impetus to the reform movement. The mathematical community by no means agrees about the wisdom of the reforms, and many individuals and groups have raised serious criticisms.—*M. Kl.*

MATING AND COURTSHIP BEHAVIOR: Where sexual reproduction is found in the animal kingdom, mates often must recognize and accept each other before they can become

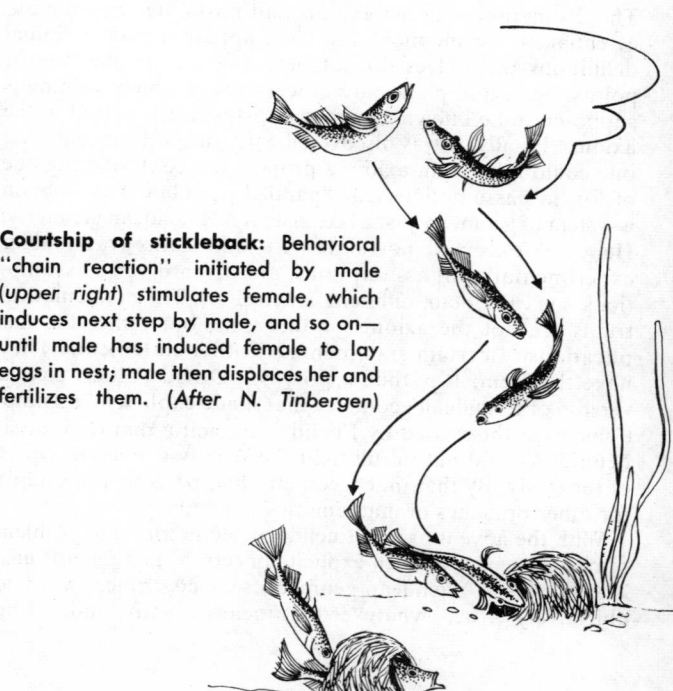

Courtship of stickleback: Behavioral "chain reaction" initiated by male (*upper right*) stimulates female, which induces next step by male, and so on—until male has induced female to lay eggs in nest; male then displaces her and fertilizes them. (*After N. Tinbergen*)

parents. Sometimes two individuals meet because hunger brings them together at a food supply. More frequently, males travel widely at mating season, seeking the opposite sex. Thus female silkworm moths release odorous substances into the breeze, and the male moths fly as much as 10 mi upwind to reach mates. Many birds and various insects appear to pair off after a silent female has come to the territory the male is defending and advertising with distinctive songs. Both scent and sounds serve cats and dogs in bringing mates together. In animals that rely extensively upon vision for ordinary activities, the bond between mates is often strengthened by various courtship antics, usually led by the male. In spiders, insects, and birds, courtship frequently includes stylized dances marked by gestures displaying distinctive colored areas. These displays are highly specific for each species and must be exactly right or the female is not stimulated to respond to the male. Where both parents participate in building a nest or in caring for young, courtship activities usually continue after mating until the need for the male's presence ends.—*L. and M. M.*

MATRIX: a rectangular array of numbers or other quantities. Invented by Arthur Cayley about 1858, in itself the matrix is purely formal. However, these rectangular arrays usually represent the essential information in some more significant mathematical expression or relation. A loose analogy is furnished by house numbers written on paper in the relative positions occupied by the houses.

Matrices can be used to represent transformations. The matrix of a transformation in which y is replaced by

$$\frac{ax + b}{cx + d} \text{ is } \left\| \begin{matrix} a & b \\ c & d \end{matrix} \right\| \text{ or } \begin{pmatrix} a & b \\ c & d \end{pmatrix}$$

which is simply the square array of constants as they appear in the fraction, enclosed by bars or parentheses. If x is now replaced by a similar fraction $(mz + n)/(pz + q)$, the result is to replace y by

$$\frac{(am + bp)z + (an + bq)}{(cm + dp)z + (cn + dq)}$$

The compounding of transformations can thus be symbolized by a "product" of matrices, in which

$$\left\| \begin{matrix} a & b \\ c & d \end{matrix} \right\| \cdot \left\| \begin{matrix} m & n \\ p & q \end{matrix} \right\| = \left\| \begin{matrix} am + bp & an + bq \\ cm + dp & cn + dq \end{matrix} \right\|$$

These matrices all have four elements arranged in two horizontal rows and two vertical columns. In the product, the element in the *first* row, *first* column $(am + bp)$, is the sum of the products of the *first* row of the first matrix by the elements of the *first* column of the second matrix; the element in the *first* row, *second* column $(an + bq)$, is a similar combination of the *first* row of the first matrix and the *second* column of the second matrix; and so on.

A matrix with m rows and n columns has the form:

$$\left\| \begin{matrix} a_{11} & a_{12} & a_{13} & \cdots & a_{1n} \\ a_{21} & a_{22} & a_{23} & \cdots & a_{2n} \\ \vdots & & & & \\ a_{m1} & a_{m2} & a_{m3} & \cdots & a_{mn} \end{matrix} \right\|$$

Each of the mn numbers a_{ij} is an element of the matrix, the first subscript denoting the row, the second the column containing the element. Thus a_{23} is in the second row, third column. The above matrix can be symbolized more compactly by $\|a_{ij}\|$, $i = 1, \ldots, m; j = 1, \ldots, n$. A matrix with a single row is a row matrix; one with a single column, a col-umn matrix. It must be understood that a matrix has no numerical value; it is simply an array.

Matrices having the same number of rows and the same number of columns are matrices of the same *type*. Two matrices of the same type are equal if each element of one is equal to the element in the same position in the other. That is, $\|a_{ij}\| = \|b_{ij}\|$ if $a_{ij} = b_{ij}$ for all i's and j's. The sum of two matrices of the same type is: $\|a_{ij}\| + \|b_{ij}\| = \|c_{ij}\|$, where $c_{ij} = a_{ij} + b_{ij}$. Each element in the sum is the sum of the corresponding elements in the summands. It follows that addition of matrices of the same type is commutative and associative.

There are two square matrices of special importance: the zero matrix, 0, has every element equal to 0; the unit matrix, I, is $\|\delta_{ij}\|$, where $\delta_{ij} = 1$ if $i = j$, and $= 0$ if $i \neq j$. The following are examples:

$$\text{zero matrix: } \left\| \begin{matrix} 0 & 0 \\ 0 & 0 \end{matrix} \right\|; \quad \text{unit matrix: } \left\| \begin{matrix} 1 & 0 \\ 0 & 1 \end{matrix} \right\|$$

The product of a matrix with m rows and n columns by a matrix with n rows and m columns, in that order, is defined as follows. Let $A = \|a_{ij}\|$, $i = 1, \ldots, m; j = 1, \ldots, n;$ and $B = \|b_{ij}\|$, $i = 1, \ldots, n; j = 1, \ldots, m;$ then $A \cdot B = \|c_{ij}\|$, $i = 1, \ldots, m; j = 1, \ldots, m;$ where $c_{ij} = a_{i1} b_{1j} + a_{i2} b_{2j} + \cdots + a_{in} b_{nj}$. For example,

$$\left\| \begin{matrix} a & b \\ c & d \\ e & f \end{matrix} \right\| \cdot \left\| \begin{matrix} x & y & z \\ u & v & w \end{matrix} \right\| = \left\| \begin{matrix} ax + bu & ay + bv & az + bw \\ cx + du & cy + dv & cz + dw \\ ex + fu & ey + fv & ez + fw \end{matrix} \right\|$$

Square matrices can be multiplied in either order, but multiplication is not, in general, commutative, *i.e.* $A \cdot B \neq B \cdot A$. Also, the product of two matrices can be 0 even though neither factor is 0, *e.g.*

$$\left\| \begin{matrix} 1 & 0 \\ 1 & 0 \end{matrix} \right\| \cdot \left\| \begin{matrix} 0 & 0 \\ 1 & 1 \end{matrix} \right\| = \left\| \begin{matrix} 0 & 0 \\ 0 & 0 \end{matrix} \right\|$$

The DETERMINANT of a square matrix is simply the determinant with precisely the same elements. By striking out some rows, or columns, or both, in a matrix, submatrices are formed. Now, if the determinant of some r-rowed square submatrix is not zero and all $(r + 1)$-rowed determinants in the matrix are equal to zero, the *rank* of the matrix is r. If the determinant of an n-rowed square matrix is not zero, the rank of the matrix is n. An n-rowed square matrix whose rank is less than n is *singular* and the value of its determinant is 0; if its rank is n it is *nonsingular*. Each square matrix possesses an *adjoint* matrix, and, if it is nonsingular, an *inverse* matrix. Let A denote a square matrix, and let a be the value of its determinant. Each element of the determinant of matrix A, a_{ij}, has a cofactor denoted by A_{ij}, which is the determinant formed by striking out the ith row and jth column and multiplying by $(-1)^{i+j}$. The adjoint of A is the matrix $\|A_{ij}\|$. If A is nonsingular, $a \neq 0$, and the inverse of A, denoted by A^{-1}, is the matrix $\|A_{ij}/a\|$. It is called the inverse of A because if it is multiplied by A in either order the result is the unit matrix, I.

There is an extensive algebra and calculus of matrices with many applications in science. Applications to linear transformations and linear systems are examples.

Linear Transformations: The general linear transformation of n variables is expressed by the n equations

$$\begin{aligned} y_1 &= a_{11} x_1 + a_{12} x_2 + \cdots + a_{1n} x_n \\ y_2 &= a_{21} x_1 + a_{22} x_2 + \cdots + a_{2n} x_n \\ &\vdots \\ y_n &= a_{n1} x_1 + a_{n2} x_2 + \cdots + a_{nn} x_n \end{aligned}$$

with matrix $A = \|a_{ij}\|$. If, now, the x's are expressed linearly in terms of n other variables, $z_1, z_2, \ldots, z_n$, with matrix $B = \|b_{ij}\|$, the y's are linear combinations of the z's with matrix $A \cdot B$. If A is nonsingular, and therefore has an inverse A^{-1}, the x's are linear combinations of the y's with matrix A^{-1}.

Linear Systems: A system of n linear equations in n unknowns:

$$a_{11} x_1 + a_{12} x_2 + \cdots + a_{1n} x_n = a_{1,n+1}$$
$$a_{21} x_1 + a_{22} x_2 + \cdots + a_{2n} x_n = a_{2,n+1}$$
$$\vdots$$
$$a_{n1} x_1 + a_{n2} x_2 + \cdots + a_{nn} x_n = a_{n,n+1}$$

may, or may not, have one or more solutions (set of x's satisfying all equations). A criterion is furnished by the ranks of two matrices. The matrix of the system is the square matrix $\|a_{ij}\|$, $i,j = 1, \ldots, n$. The *augmented matrix* is $\|a_{ij}\|$, $i = 1, \ldots, n$; $j = 1, \ldots, n + 1$. If both matrices have the same rank n, there is one solution. If both have the same rank which is less than n, there are many solutions. If the ranks are different, there is no solution. See EQUATIONS, THEORY OF.—*H. C.*

MATTER: anything possessing mass and occupying space. The fundamental "building blocks" of ordinary matter are the electron, proton, and neutron, although many other "elementary particles" (*e.g.* the positron and mu-meson) exist in nature and can also be considered as constituting matter. It is generally possible to classify a material object as belonging to one of four *states of matter:* SOLID, LIQUID, GAS, PLASMA. Each of these states is further describable in terms of its physical properties, among them density, electrical and thermal conductivity, magnetism, compressibility, shearing strength, and viscosity.

The most ordered state of matter occurs in crystalline solids, whose molecules are arranged in a symmetric three-dimensional array (see CRYSTALLOGRAPHY). Such solids may be good conductors of heat and electricity (*e.g.* metals), insulators (*e.g.* sulfur), or semiconductors (*e.g.* germanium). Most elements exist as crystalline solids at sufficiently low temperature. As temperature is raised, a point is reached at which the solid melts to become a liquid. Here the molecules do not possess symmetric or even fixed positions with respect to their neighbors, although they remain in physical contact; hence a liquid has about the same density and compressibility as the solid of the same element. A liquid tends to hold together because of the mutual attraction of its constituent molecules, but nevertheless it is unable to support shearing stress, which accounts for its tendency to flow and to maintain a horizontal surface under the action of gravity.

As the temperature is raised to the boiling point, a liquid vaporizes and becomes a gas, characterized by the relative ineffectuality of attractive molecular binding energy compared to the kinetic energy associated with thermal motion. Hence a gas will expand to fill its container. Gas molecules are generally not in physical contact except during the brief intervals when they are undergoing collisions, so that gases are readily compressible. As temperature is raised further, the agitated gas molecules become ionized, and the plasma state is attained. A plasma possesses bulk electrical neutrality, although the individual constituent particles are charged. Unlike gases, plasmas readily conduct electricity and can be strongly influenced by electromagnetic fields. One could in principle conceive of a further plasma state, in which the temperature is so high that the atomic nuclei themselves dissociate into elementary particles; perhaps such a state exists at the center of certain hot stars. See KINETIC THEORY OF MATTER.—*B. Be.*

MAUPERTUIS, PIERRE LOUIS MOREAU DE, 1698–1759, French astronomer and mathematician; b. St. Malo. After heading an expedition to Lapland to determine the size and shape of Earth, he published his results in *La figure de la terre* (1738). His LEAST-ACTION PRINCIPLE was published in his *Les lois du mouvement et du repos* (1746). The *Oeuvres* of Maupertuis appeared in several editions (1752–68). He was a fellow of the Royal Society.—*D. H. D. R.*

MAURY, MATTHEW FONTAINE, 1806–73, U. S. oceanographer; b. near Fredericksburg, Va. He entered naval service in 1825 and served as superintendent of the U. S. Naval Observatory and Hydrographical Office (1842–61). His research on winds and currents was of great assistance to mariners, and his *Physical Geography of the Sea* (1855) is recognized as the first textbook of modern oceanography.—*D. H. D. R.*

MAXIMA AND MINIMA: a kind of mathematical problem involving the determination of which member of a set of mathematical objects produces an extreme value of some related quantity. For instance, a shortest distance may be sought. In Fig. 1, what is the shortest route from P to the line l to Q? The answer, obtained by geometry, is the route PRQ, with PR and PQ making equal angles with l. For, if S is any point on l, $PRQ = P'RQ < P'SQ = PSQ$. Another example is that of finding which rectangle of given perimeter has the greatest area. It is, of course, a square. This can be proved by simple geometry and algebra, or by using the method of calculus. A problem of a higher order of difficulty is that of finding the plane figure with a given perimeter which has the greatest area. The answer is a circle, but the proof is difficult, and is treated in a higher form of calculus, known as calculus of variations.

Differential calculus provides a powerful method of solving maximum and minimum problems of a special variety. This method can be employed if the quantity to be maximized or minimized is related to a single variable by a function which is continuous and can be differentiated. Let us find the maximum point of the graph of $y = 4x - x^2$. By careful plotting the curve can be drawn as in Fig. 2. The maximum point appears to be $(2,4)$. At points of the curve to the left of the maximum point the curve is rising and the slope is positive, at points to the right the curve is falling and the slope is negative, and at the maximum point itself the slope is zero. Since the slope at any point is the value of the derivative there, we find a maximum point by setting the derivative equal to zero and solving the equation. Thus, in this example, $Dy = 4 - 2x$. The solution of the equation, $4 - 2x = 0$, is $x = 2$. Hence the abscissa of the maximum point is 2. Its ordinate is $4 \cdot 2 - 2^2 = 4$. We can now verify that for $x < 2$ the slope is positive, and for $x > 2$, the slope is negative, and thus be sure that this is a maximum point. By similar reasoning we see that at a minimum point the slope is zero, whereas

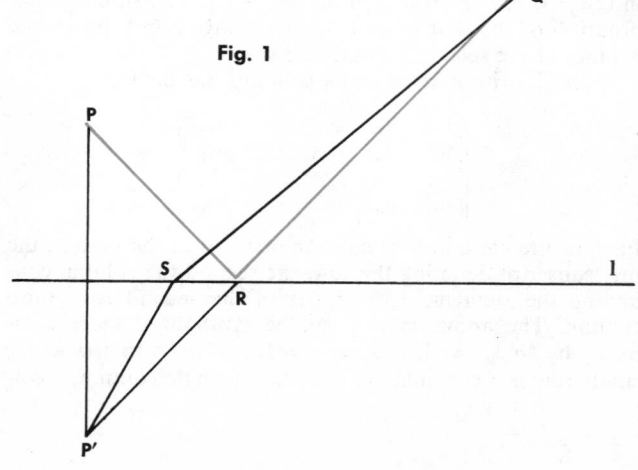

Fig. 1

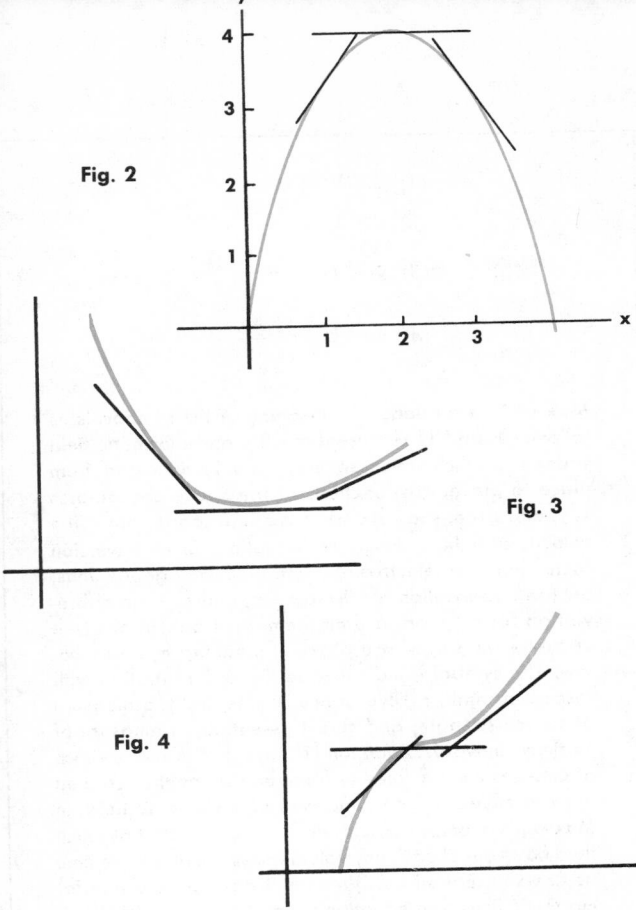

Fig. 2

Fig. 3

Fig. 4

top is to have a volume of 32 in.³, what should its dimensions be in order that the amount of metal used (the surface) shall be least? The quantity to be minimized is the area $A = x^2 + 4xy$, where x is the side of the base, y the height. Since the volume is $32 = x^2y$, we have $y = 32/x^2$. Substituting for y in the first equation, we have $A = x^2 + 128/x$. The next step is to differentiate, obtaining $DA = 2x - 128/x^2$. Next, we set the expression for the derivative equal to zero: $2x - 128/x^2 = 0$. The solution of this equation is $x = 4$. Hence $y = 32/4^2 = 2$. Therefore, the dimensions of the box for the least amount of metal are 4 in. by 4 in. by 2 in. That $x = 4$ produces a minimum can be verified by observing that $2x - 128/x^2$ is negative if $x < 4$ and positive if $x > 4$.

Problems in maximizing or minimizing a function involving more than one variable can be attacked by setting partial derivatives equal to zero and solving the resulting equations. Suppose that in the above problem a rectangular base had been specified. We can prove that its sides must be equal, and hence that it is really a square if the area is minimum. Let the dimensions of the base be x and z. Then $A = xz + 2xy + 2zy$, and $xyz = 32$. Therefore $y = 32/xz$, and $A = xz + 64/x + 64/z$. Finding the partial derivatives, we have $\partial A/\partial x = z - 64/x^2$, $\partial A/\partial z = \text{x} - 64/z^2$. Setting these derivatives equal to zero, we have $z - 64/x^2 = 0$ and $x - 64/z^2 = 0$. From the first equation $z = 64/x^2$. Substituting this quantity for z in the second equation, we have $x - x^4/64 = 0$, whence $x = 0$ or $x = 4$. If $x = 0$ there is no box. Therefore $x = 4$, $z = 4$, and $y = 2$.—*H. C.*

MAXWELL, JAMES CLERK, 1831–79, Scottish physicist; b. Edinburgh. Because of his insights into electricity and magnetism, Maxwell is regarded as one of the towering figures of 19th-cent. physics. His prediction of the existence of electromagnetic radiation led Heinrich Hertz to discover the existence of such radiation experimentally. Maxwell's assertion of the electromagnetic character of light laid the foundation for

James Clerk Maxwell
(*Bettmann Archive*)

much of the progress of present-day theoretical physics. Like Descartes and Faraday, Maxwell was opposed to the concept of "action at a distance," and to avoid it he constructed a mechanical model for the interrelation of magnetic and electrical phenomena and postulated, as had many of his predecessors, the existence of an "ether." However, in his monumental *Treatise on Electricity and Magnetism* (1873), he implicitly abandons the necessity of using the ether or any mechanical model and rests his theory on his set of symmetrical equations. These (*Maxwell's equations*) express the continuity of electrical and magnetic fields, and set forth the principle by which changes in the electric field produce changes in the magnetic field, and vice versa. Hardly a branch of physics has not been enriched by Maxwell's extraordinary scientific imagination. By the age of 19, he had completely developed the method of photoelastic stress analysis. For his work in color sensation he won the Rumford medal of the Royal Society, of which he was a fellow. His investigation of the motion of Saturn's rings led him to make important contributions to the kinetic theory of gases. In 1871, Maxwell accepted a professorship at Cambridge Univ.; there he supervised the construction of the Cavendish Laboratory, of which he was director until his death in 1879. —*A. L.*

for points to the left it is negative and for points to the right it is positive (Fig. 3). If, at some point, the slope is zero, and is positive both to the left and right, as in Fig. 4, or negative both to the left and right, the point is a horizontal inflection point. A zero slope is associated with a point that is a maximum, a minimum, or a horizontal inflection point. The first steps in finding such a point are to differentiate the function, set the result equal to zero, and solve this equation. In many practical problems this is sufficient, for we often know in advance that a maximum, for example, will be found. If we do not know which of the three types of point we have, we can test the result by observing how the derivative changes as x passes through the point.

The maxima and minima here discussed are relative. A relative maximum point of a curve is the highest point in the immediate vicinity. In Fig. 5, A and C are relative maxima, and B and D are relative minima.

To apply this method to a practical problem, it is necessary to express the quantity to be maximized or minimized as a function of one variable. If more variables appear, relations must be found whereby they can be eliminated. For example, if a metal box with square base, rectangular sides, and open

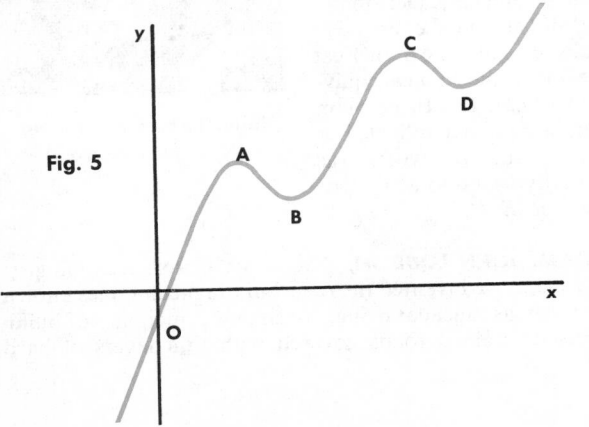

Fig. 5

MAXWELL-BOLTZMANN STATISTICS: the most probable distribution of speeds in a very large number of molecules of a gas; it follows from the assumption that molecular motion is completely random. The distribution law was first derived (1860) by James Clerk Maxwell, and more rigorously later (1877) by Ludwig Boltzmann, who took into account molecular collisions. The number of molecules within a small range of speeds depends on the mass of the molecules, but for a given gas the distribution depends only on the temperature. Written in terms of molecular kinetic energy, the distribution law is independent of the nature of the molecules. Under some conditions, quantum effects make necessary the introduction of either Fermi-Dirac or Einstein-Bose statistics, with resulting modification of the distribution law, but for particles of finite mass these modifications are negligible at high temperatures, so that both quantum distribution laws reduce to the Maxwell-Boltzmann distribution. See KINETIC THEORY OF MATTER; STATISTICAL MECHANICS.—*M. P.*

MAXWELL DISTRIBUTION LAW: see MAXWELL-BOLTZMANN STATISTICS.

MAXWELL'S EQUATIONS: four fundamental equations of the physics of electricity, magnetism, radio waves, and light. With them the physicist can calculate by known mathematical methods the facts observed in these areas. Also, with Maxwell's equations, he can make successful predictions concerning radio waves and lenses, as well as many other apparently diverse things. The equations were derived by the English theoretical physicist James Clerk Maxwell about 1865. He first reduced all the previous work on electricity and magnetism—work by Coulomb, Ampère, Faraday, and many others—to a common mathematical basis, a set of equations. Then he modified one of these equations by adding a certain term, called the displacement current. This term was added for theoretical and esthetic reasons; there was no direct experimental justification for it. From these modified equations, now known as Maxwell's equations, Maxwell derived the wave equation. This important equation was well known in physics, since many different types of waves had been previously studied. But it had never previously been encountered in the study of electricity and magnetism. The equation led him to make two extremely important predictions: First, he predicted that there are "electromagnetic waves." H. R. Hertz looked for these a few years later and found waves having just the properties that Maxwell had predicted. Today these waves, usually called radio waves, are of enormous practical importance. Maxwell's equations are still the basic tool for the study and use of radio waves. Second, Maxwell computed the velocity of these electromagnetic waves and found that it was close to the velocity of light. He concluded that light is an electromagnetic phenomenon—light waves are a special kind of electromagnetic wave. This prediction, too, was fully justified by further developments. Thus one area of physics, that of light, was successfully "reduced" to another, electricity and magnetism; a unified theory was found covering both areas.—*A. M. B.*

MAYER, JOHANN TOBIAS, 1723–62, German astronomer; b. Marbach. He improved N. L. de Lacaille's tables of the Sun. In his catalogue of approximately 1,000 zodiacal stars Mayer gave the proper motions, based on a comparison of the positions determined by Lacaille with those of Olaus Römer. Mayer contributed to lunar theory and prepared lunar tables for use in navigation.—*D. H. D. R.*

MAYER, JULIUS ROBERT VON, 1814–78, German physicist and physician; b. Heilbronn. His fame rests on his announce-

$$(1) \quad \text{div } \mathbf{E} = 0$$

$$(2) \quad \text{div } \mathbf{H} = 0$$

$$(3) \quad \text{curl } \mathbf{E} = -\frac{1}{c}\frac{\partial \mathbf{H}}{\partial t}$$

$$(4) \quad \text{curl } \mathbf{H} = \frac{1}{c}\frac{\partial \mathbf{E}}{\partial t}$$

Maxwell's equations: The meaning of the symbols is as follows: $\mathbf{E}$ and $\mathbf{H}$ represent electric and magnetic field strengths, which, because they vary in time and from place to place, are functions of the space coordinates x, y, and z (not shown) and of the time coordinate t. The velocity of light, c, enters the equations as a conversion factor between electrostatic and electromagnetic units; div (an abbreviation for divergence) and curl (an abbreviation for rotation) are mathematical operations (see VECTOR ANALYSIS) whose physical meaning appears below. The symbol ∂ indicates partial differentiation with respect to time, t. Divergence is essentially a measure of source strength, and curl is essentially a measure of vorticity. In words, equation (1) says that in the absence of charges electric lines of force can be neither created nor destroyed. If one conceives of an electric field, in Maxwell's idiom, as a fluid, div $\mathbf{E} = 0$ says that as much fluid flows out of each tiny volume of space in a given time as flows in. Equation (2) makes the same assertion for magnetic lines that equation (1) makes for electric lines, but is more general: there *are* no magnetic charges. Equation (3) is a statement of Faraday's law of electromagnetic induction. It says that the limiting value of electromotive force per unit area is proportional to the rate of change of $\mathbf{H}$ at a limit point P of the area; loosely stated, a changing magnetic field creates an electric field at right angles to the magnetic field change. Equation (4) says that a changing electric field produces a magnetic field. Note that the time rate of change of $\mathbf{E}$, $\partial \mathbf{E}/\partial t$, is Maxwell's displacement current.

ment of the general principle of the conservation of energy (1842). Perpetual motion was often discussed in his boyhood home, and as a practicing physician he was interested in the origin of animal heat and in the work output of the organism. He distinguished between potential and kinetic energy, and between heat, electromagnetic, and chemical energy. He established a definite numerical value for the mechanical equivalent of heat. His three main papers were either ridiculed or ignored, but his work was eventually assessed at its true value.—*R. E. O.*

Julius Robert von Mayer
(*N. Y. Public Library*)

McADAM, JOHN LOUDON, 1756–1836, British technologist; b. Ayr, Scot. He invented the road-building techniques known collectively as macadamizing, consisting principally of building raised, drained roads covered with thin layers of hard stone in pieces roughly the same size and less than 6 oz in weight. He wrote *A Practical Essay on the Scientific Repair and Preservation of Roads* (1819) and *The Present State of Road Making* (1820). In 1827 he became general surveyor of roads for Great Britain.—*D. H. D. R.*

McMILLAN, EDWIN MATTISON, 1907–   , U. S. chemist; b. Redondo Beach, Calif. He created the first of the transuranium elements: neptunium, the earliest of a series of new, artificial elements. During World War II he engaged in research on microwave radar. For discoveries in the chemistry of the transuranium elements, he and G. T. Seaborg shared the 1951 Nobel prize. He joined the Univ. of California faculty in 1932. He is a member of the National Academy of Sciences.—*D. H. D. R.*

MEAN FREE PATH: the average distance that a molecule in a gas may travel without colliding with another molecule. Mean free path varies inversely with the pressure of a gas, since when a gas is compressed the molecules are pushed closer together and are more likely to collide with one another. At sea level, the mean free path for a molecule in the atmosphere is 7×10^{-8} meter (0.000,003 in.); at an altitude of 100 km (328,00 ft), it is 0.1 m (about 4 in.); and at 200 km, it is 300 m (about 1,000 ft). The concept of mean free path is of importance in the KINETIC THEORY and gives a means of estimating the sizes of molecules in a gas; the mean free path can, in turn, be calculated from the viscosity of a gas.—*E. M. R.*

MEAN, MODE, AND MEDIAN: kinds of averages. There are five averages, three of which are described as means: arithmetic mean, geometric mean, and harmonic mean. The other two averages are the median and the mode. Each of the averages is defined for a set of numbers: $X_1, X_2, X_3, \ldots, X_N$.

Most people think of the average as the sum of the set of numbers divided by the number of numbers: $(X_1 + X_2 + X_3 + \cdots + X_N) \div N$. This average is more precisely called the arithmetic mean; it is the most familiar average, and the most used.

The median is a number such that half of the set of numbers are above it and half are below it. If N is odd, the median is the middle number in the set; if N is even, the median is taken halfway between the two middle numbers. The median, quite familiar, is often used to describe average income; *e.g.* if average (median) family income in a certain community is $6,000/yr, we know that half the families have income above $6,000 and half below $6,000.

The mode is the number which occurs most frequently in the set of numbers. A set has no mode if all the numbers are different; it has two modes if it has two pairs of like numbers. When we hear about "the average man," it is usually the mode that is meant.

The geometric mean is defined as the Nth root of the product $X_1 \cdot X_2 \cdot X_3 \cdot \ldots \cdot X_N$. When a set of numbers is in geometric progression, the geometric mean is used as the average. Often a population grows approximately in a geometric progression, and the geometric mean may be used as its average.

The harmonic mean is the reciprocal of the arithmetic mean of the reciprocals of the numbers. As an illustration of its use, consider an auto which travels 1 mi at 40 mi/hr and a second mile at 60 mi/hr. The average speed of the auto is the harmonic mean of 40 and 60; *i.e.* $1 \div [(\frac{1}{40} + \frac{1}{60}) \div 2]$ or 48 mi/hr.—*H. E. W.*

MEASUREMENT: The custom of measuring things probably started in prehistoric times with man's first attempts to keep track of his possessions: fish, cattle, beads, children. To this end he devised a number system (a set of symbols) and a series of empirical operations (counting). For millennia the number system and the empirical operations of measurement were so closely linked that even the greatest thinkers did not discern the crucial difference between them. It now is generally agreed that the number system is a formal, syntactical system, defined by a set of essentially arbitrary assumptions. On the other hand, empirical operations of measurement consist of manipulations performed upon objects, with or without the aid of elaborate devices and instruments. The over-all process of measurement can thus be regarded as the act of relating the number system to the objects according to one or another systematic rule or procedure. Measurement is therefore often defined as the assignment of numbers to objects or events according to rule; it is the process of mapping empirical properties or relations into a formal model derived from mathematics. Measurement is possible only because there is a kind of isomorphism between the properties of the number system and what we can do with the properties of objects or events. Provided some systematic rule is followed in relating numbers to the properties of objects, one or another form of measurement is achieved.

Since there are different kinds of rules by which numbers may be assigned, there are different kinds of scales of measurement. The simplest rule of all involves the use of numbers merely as names or labels—type numbers, as it were. Whenever two things are equal—*e.g.* if they are similar simply in appearance—they receive the same number, but not otherwise. This simple process leads to what is called a *nominal scale.* A slightly more complex rule involves the rank ordering of objects and assignment of numbers to express the resulting order: the classic example is the *ordinal scale* of hardness, on which one mineral stands higher than another if it scratches but is not scratched by the other (it would tell that diamond is harder than steel, but not *how much* harder). Whenever operations can be invented for determining equal distances along a scale, we can generate an *interval scale, e.g.* the Fahrenheit and Celsius scales. The zero points on these scales are arbitrary (0° Celsius happens to equal 32° Fahrenheit), but on both scales intervals or differences in temperature can be given an operational meaning. On the other hand, on these two scales no meaning can be given to statements about ratios of temperatures, *e.g.* whether it is twice as hot at the equator as at the south pole.

If, in addition to all other operations thus far described, we can also determine when ratios are equal, we can proceed to generate the most useful scale of all, the *ratio scale.* A scale of this form has been achieved with temperature in the development of the absolute Kelvin scale. As on all ratio scales, the zero point of the Kelvin scale is *not* arbitrary. Since the ratio scale contains all the information contained in the three other kinds of scales, plus more besides, the scientist usually tries to develop techniques for measuring quantities on a ratio scale. It is understandable, therefore, that most of the common scales in everyday use are ratio scales, *e.g.* length, weight, voltage, current, volume, time intervals.

The scientist sometimes distinguishes two kinds of ratio scales: *fundamental* and *derived.* A scale is said to be fundamental when it can be created by applying the operations of "addition" to the property being measured. Examples: the placing of lengths end to end in order to erect a scale of length, and placing weights together in the same scale pan of a balance in order to erect a scale of weight. In these instances, a ratio scale is created without recourse to any prior

Standards for measurement of mass and weight: The U. S. standard of mass (*left*) is a platinum-iridium cylinder 39 mm in diameter and 39 mm high. Known as Prototype Kilogram No. 20, it is an accurate copy of the international standards kept at the International Bureau of Weights and Measures at Sèvres, France, and was furnished to the U. S. A. by the Bureau in 1875. The standard has remained constant within about 1 part in 50 million. The U. S. National Bureau of Standards also maintains secondary standards (*right*) for the kilogram (two weights, upper left), the avoirdupois pound (four weights in diagonal center row), and the troy ounce (three weights in lower-right row). (*Nat. Bur. of Standards/U. S. Dept. of Commerce*)

measurements. A derived scale, on the other hand, makes use of two or more fundamental scales in a combination of some sort; thus density is measured by taking the ratio of the values on the two fundamental scales, mass and volume. Similarly, velocity is the ratio of distance to time. Force involves three fundamental quantities: mass, distance, and time. Physics deals with many derived scales, such as these, but the number of fundamental scales is limited to about half a dozen.

Other methods of achieving ratio scales have been developed in connection with efforts to scale subjective effects, *e.g.* apparent brightness of lights, or apparent loudness of sounds. A much used method, called fractionation, requires that the "observer" in the experiment adjust one sound until it seems half as loud as another. When sufficient trials have been made, with sounds of several different intensities, the data provide the basis for creating a ratio scale of loudness. Although fractionation is the best-known procedure, it is not as good for the purpose as some of the more recently developed methods. It is characteristic of all empirical measurement, in every field of science, that problems and difficulties attend each and every procedure. The art of mensuration is the art of reducing the size of the errors of measurement, and better procedures are continually being devised. However, it is never possible in empirical measurement to eliminate all sources of error.

It can be said that the history of science is the history of man's efforts to devise procedures for measuring and quantifying the world around him. Quantification is basic to the formulation of scientific laws in a form that allows the powerful tools of mathematics to be applied to the solution of problems, both theoretical and practical.—*S. S. S.*

MEASUREMENT SYSTEMS: systems of mechanical units employed in scientific and engineering work. Scientists prefer *metric absolute systems,* which are independent of gravity. The two in use are the centimeter-gram-second system and the meter-kilogram-second system. Engineers usually use *gravitational* (the English and the metric) systems, which refer to the strength of Earth's gravitational field. The fundamental basis for the choice of a system of units is Newton's second law, which defines force as the product of mass and acceleration ($F = ma$) and, by extension, gives the relationship between mass and weight.

In the centimeter-gram-second (cgs) absolute system, the unit of mass is taken as the gram. The unit of length is the centimeter, the unit of time the second. The unit of force, called the dyne, is defined as the force required to give a mass of 1 gm an acceleration of 1 cm/sec². The unit of work or energy is the dyne-centimeter, or erg. The unit of power (little used) is the erg/second.

The meter-kilogram-second (mks) absolute system uses the kilogram as a unit of mass; units of length and time are the meter and the second. The newton, defined as the force required to impart to the mass of 1 kg an acceleration of 1 m/sec², is the derived unit of force or weight. The unit of work is the newton-meter, or the joule, equal to 10,000,000 ergs. The unit of power is the joule/second, or the watt.

The English gravitational, or foot-pound-second (fps), system has the slug as the unit of mass. This is the mass to which a force of 1 lb will give an acceleration of 1 ft/sec². In terms of the standard pound, the value of the slug = 1 × g (acceleration of gravity); since the accepted value of g is 32.1740 ft/sec², the value of the slug is 32.1740 lb of mass. Thus, in the English gravitational system, the pound is regarded as a standard force unit, and from it a gravitational mass unit is obtained. The unit of work is the foot-pound, and the unit of power the foot-pound/second; 550 ft-lb/sec constitutes 1 horsepower, which is also equivalent to 746 watts.

A metric gravitational system is occasionally employed by engineers on the European continent. As in the English system, the standard is a unit of force (the kilogram) and the derived mass unit is the "metric slug." The kilogram value of the metric slug is 9.8 kg, the factor 9.8 representing the acceleration of gravity in meters/sec².—*A. E.*

TABLE OF UNITS

CGS System	MKS System	FPS System

LENGTH

CGS System	MKS System	FPS System
1 centimeter (cm) = 10^{-5} kilometer (km) 10^{-2} meter (m) 10^{-1} decimeter (dm) 10 millimeters (mm) 10^4 microns (μ) 10^7 millimicrons (mμ) 10^8 Angstrom units (Å)	1 meter (m) = 10^{-3} kilometer (km) 10 decimeters (dm) 10^2 centimeters (cm) 10^3 millimeters (mm) 10^6 microns (μ) 10^9 millimicrons (mμ) 10^{10} Angstrom units (Å)	1 foot (ft) = 1/5,280 mile (mi) 1/3 yard (yd) 12 inches (in.) 1 rod = 5½ yards = 16½ feet 1 furlong = 40 rods

Intersystem Conversions: 1 mile = 1.609 kilometers   1 yard = 0.9144 meter*   1 foot = 30.48 centimeters*   1 inch = 2.54 centimeters*

AREA

CGS System	MKS System	FPS System
1 square centimeter (cm^2) = 10^{-4} square meter (m^2) 10^2 square millimeters (mm^2)	1 square meter (m^2) = 10^4 square centimeters (cm^2) 10^{12} square millimeters (mm^2)	1 square foot (ft^2) = 144 square inches (in.^{2}) 1/9 square yard (yd^2) 1 square mile (mi^2) = 640 acres 1 acre = 160 square rods = 43,560 square feet 1 square rod = 272¼ square feet = 30¼ square yards

Intersystem Conversions: 1 square foot = 929.030 square centimeters   1 square inch = 6.452 square centimeters

VOLUME

CGS System	MKS System	FPS System
1 cubic centimeter (cm^3) = 10^{-6} cubic meter (m^3)	1 cubic meter (m^3) = 10^6 cubic centimeters (cm^3) 1 liter = 1,000 milliliters (ml)	1 cubic foot (ft^3) = 1,728 cubic inches (in.^{3}) = 1/27 cubic yard (yd^3) 1 gallon (gal) = 4 quarts (qt) = 8 pints (pt) = 96 fluid ounces 1 U. S. gallon = 231 cubic inches 1 imperial gallon = 277.42 cubic inches

Intersystem Conversions:
   1 cubic centimeter = 0.061 cubic inch   1 cubic inch = 16.387 cubic centimeters   1 liter = 0.264 gallons   1 gallon = 3.785 liters

MASS

CGS System	MKS System	FPS System
1 gram (gm) = 10^{-3} kilogram (kg) 10^3 milligrams (mg)	1 kilogram (kg) = 10^3 grams (gm) 10^6 milligrams (mg)	1 slug = the mass that weighs 32.1740 pounds

Intersystem Conversion: 1 slug = 14.594 kilograms

WEIGHT or FORCE

CGS System	MKS System	FPS System
1 dyne (dy) = 10^{-5} newton (new) 1 gram-weight = 981 dynes (dy)	1 newton (new) = 10^5 dynes (dy) 1 kilogram-weight = 9.81 newtons	1 pound (lb) = 1/2,000 short ton 1/2,240 long ton 16 ounces (oz) (avoirdupois) 12 ounces (Troy) 7,000 grains (gr)

Intersystem Conversions: 1 pound = 453.592 grams-weight = 0.454 kilograms-weight = 4.450 newtons

VELOCITY

CGS System	MKS System	FPS System
1 centimeter per second (cm/sec) = 10^{-2} meter/second (m/sec) 0.036 kilometer/hour (km/hr)	1 meter per second (m/sec) = 10^2 centimeters/second (cm/sec) 3.6 kilometers/hour (km/hr)	1 foot per second (ft/sec) = 0.682 mile/hour (mi/hr) 1 mile/hour = 1.467 feet/second (ft/sec) = 88 feet/minute (ft/min)

Intersystem Conversions: 1 meter/second = 3.281 feet/second = 2.237 miles/hour   1 mile/hour = 1.609 kilometers/hour

WORK and ENERGY

CGS System	MKS System	FPS System
1 erg = 10^{-7} joule (j) 1 dyne-centimeter (dy-cm) 2.389×10^{-11} kilogram-calorie 0.2778×10^{-13} kilowatt-hour	1 joule (j) = 10^7 ergs = 1 watt-second (watt-sec) 2.389×10^{-4} kilogram-calorie (kcal) 2.778×10^{-4} watt-hour (watt-hr)	1 foot-pound (ft-lb) = 5.050×10^{-7} horsepower-hour (hp-hr)

Intersystem Conversions: 1 foot-pound = 1.356 joules = 3.24×10^{-4} kilogram-calorie = 3.766×10^{-7} kilowatt-hour

---

* Exactly. Other equivalents in intersystem conversions are rounded off to the third decimal place.

MÉCANIQUE ANALITIQUE (Analytical Mechanics), by Joseph Louis Lagrange (1788), (*Oeuvres* XI, XII, 1868–69): This book is the high point in the active development of the statics and dynamics of point-masses as well as of rigid bodies, which took place during the 18th cent. in close relationship to the equally vigorous development of the calculus under the leadership of such men as A. C. Clairaut, L. Euler, and Lagrange himself. The treatment is analytic throughout; no geometric figures are allowed. Starting with the principle of virtual velocities and using the calculus of variation, the author derives the general equations of motion (D'ALEMBERT'S PRINCIPLE), in which generalized coordinates q^i and the so-called *Lagrangian equations*

$$\frac{d}{dt}\frac{\partial T}{\partial q'} - \frac{\partial T}{\partial q} + K(q) = 0$$

(T potential energy, $q' = dq/dt$, K generalized force) play a dominant role.—*D. J. S.*

MÉCANIQUE CÉLESTE (Celestial Mechanics), by P. S. Laplace, 5 vol. (1799–1825), *Oeuvres* I-V (1878–82): This work is a systematic presentation of theoretical discoveries in celestial mechanics by Newton, Clairaut, J. D'Alembert, L. Euler, J. L. Lagrange, and Laplace himself, based on Newton's law of universal gravitation. The first two volumes contain the theory of equilibrium and motions of celestial bodies in general; the third and fourth are devoted to each of the planets separately, the Moon, the other satellites, and the comets. The fifth volume deals mainly with the effect of perturbations, but also presents a theory of the tides. The *potential equation* (Laplace equation)

$$\frac{\partial^2 V}{\partial x^2} + \frac{\partial^2 V}{\partial y^2} + \frac{\partial^2 V}{\partial z^2} = 0$$

is developed in Vol. I. The first four volumes were translated into English by N. Bowditch (1829–39).—*D. J. S.*

MECHANICAL DRAWING: a hand-drawn, pictorial representation of a tool, part, or machine. An *outline* drawing depicts the general appearance and over-all size of an object. *Working* drawings, of two types, are the designer's instructions to fabricators or assemblers of the device. A *general* or *assembly* drawing shows the relative positions and functional interrelations of parts in an assembly; these are usually drawn in perspective. A *detail* drawing contains all the particulars of shape and dimensions—usually of a single part—that are needed for assembly. Such a drawing is usually two-dimensional and must therefore contain three separate views of the object to fully depict it, and this is accomplished by orthographic projection. The object is envisioned to be fixed in space, at eye level in front of the draftsman. His first view of it (*front view*) will be placed at the bottom of the drawing. It will show solid or curved lines that represent the edges of surfaces he can see, and show with broken lines those edges that are concealed inside or behind the object. Above the front view he draws a *plan view* representing both visible and concealed edges from a theoretical vantage point directly above the object. To the right or left of the front view he draws what he would see if he looked at the object from the right or left side (*side view*). Although the drawing is on a scale smaller or larger than the actual part, dimensions are printed with their actual values, superimposed on arrows parallel to or pointing radially toward the surface involved.—*K. A.*

MECHANICAL EFFICIENCY: the ratio of the work output of a machine to the work put in (work being used in the technical sense of force multiplied by the distance, in the direction of the force, through which the force is applied). An ideal machine would perform an amount of work equal to the work put into it. Because of friction, however, there is no ideal machine: work output is always less than work input, which means that mechanical efficiency is less than 1. See SIMPLE MACHINES.—*G. M. S.* and *L. S.*

MECHANICS: the oldest branch of physics, dealing with the state of rest or motion of particles and rigid bodies, and with forces acting on bodies. The subject has three main branches: statics, dynamics, and fluid mechanics. In statics, the forces acting on the body, or system of bodies, are so arranged that the body is in equilibrium—it does not move in any way. Typical problems involve the balancing of weights on a lever, the stresses and strains on a bridge, and, in hydrostatics, the forces acting on a body submerged in or floating on a liquid. Dynamics deals with systems in motion, and may be divided into *kinetics,* the study of the effect of forces in

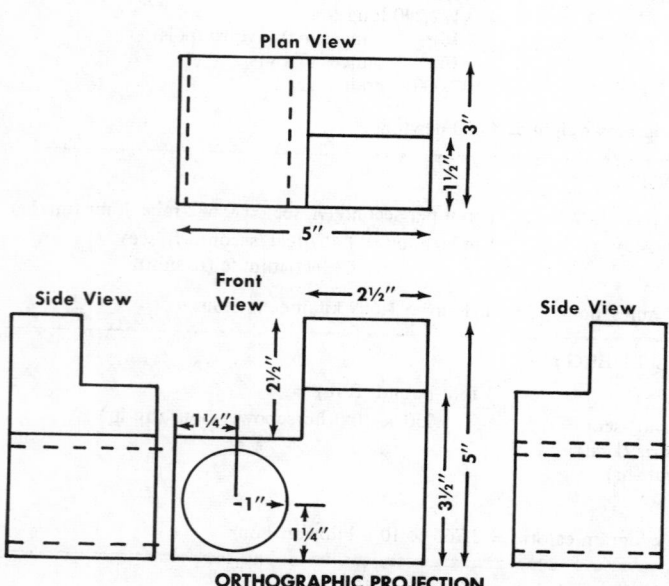

ORTHOGRAPHIC PROJECTION

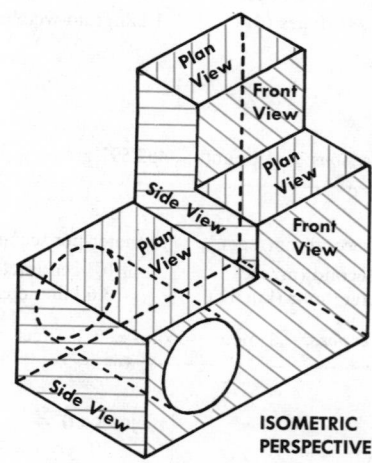

ISOMETRIC PERSPECTIVE

Mechanical drawing: Two-dimensional detail drawing (*left*) of object gives four views: from front, from each side, and from above (plan view); actual values of object's dimensions are noted. Perspective drawing (*above*) shows interrelationships of surfaces, with dotted lines representing concealed intersections of surfaces.

changing the motion of bodies, and *kinematics,* in which the motion of particles or rigid bodies is considered without reference to the forces producing the motion. (Since all of classical dynamics is based on NEWTON'S LAWS OF MOTION, which relate force and motion, the distinction between these divisions is somewhat arbitrary.) Problems in dynamics may involve the paths of projectiles (*e.g.* bullets and rockets) and the motions of planets, pendulums, and indeed all moving bodies. Fluid mechanics includes the theory of gases, hydrodynamics (the motion of liquids), and aerodynamics. The mathematical development of results and theories arising from classical mechanics is called *analytical mechanics.* See DYNAMICS; FLUID FLOW; STATICS.—*B. P. S.*

MECHANISM: refers firstly and more commonly to a structure such as a machine or a watch; once the detailed construction is studied, we are satisfied that the observed operations are explained by the connection between the parts, by their motions, and by the simple physical laws governing rigid bodies. The preeminent place of classical mechanics led to an extension of this explanatory procedure to cases where one had to postulate hidden or submicroscopic mechanisms, as in the theory of the ether, or the kinetic theory of gases. Indeed, it was widely held that the knowledge and disposition of all particles would permit, in principle, the prediction of any future state of affairs; here, human actions were included by those who considered the working of the mind fully explainable in terms of Newtonian mechanics. Secondly, one speaks now also of the mechanism of radioactive disintegration of nuclei or of gene replication, *i.e.* of phenomena whose explanations are not based on classical laws of physics. But these two usages are not as far apart as is often held, for the belief that the visible interaction of connected parts in a machine of itself explains the action of the apparatus is fundamentally unwarranted. As Hume pointed out, such connection is really first of all "connection in our thought." The modern view, thus, is to allow a predominantly mathematical (or other nonmaterial) and if necessary nonclassical and probabilistic description to serve as "mechanism," as for example Maxwell's equations (rather than a material ether) serve to explain the propagation of light waves, or as Pauli's rule in quantum mechanics helps to explain the chemical behavior of matter. In W. H. Watson's words, "What constitutes the mechanism of our theories is the system of logical connection of ideas appearing in the theory."

In biology, the word "mechanism" is, however, used in a somewhat more restricted sense; the proponents of the mechanistic philosophy hold that all life processes and the behavior of living organisms, in principle, "can be unequivocally explained in physiochemical terms," to quote Jacques Loeb.—*G. Ho.*

MEDIEVAL AND RENAISSANCE SCIENCE: During the Middle Ages (*c.* A. D. 500–1450) and Renaissance (1450–1600), the heritage of ancient Greek science was first assimilated by the Moslem culture of the Near East, North Africa, and Spain, then transmitted to W Europe at the time of the Crusades, and there developed in directions which led to the scientific revolution of the 17th cent. Throughout this period the basic framework of scientific theory was that of Aristotle, whose cosmology was given a theological interpretation which became an obstacle to scientific progress in early modern times. In this history three phases may be distinguished: (1) Moslem science, which flourished *c.* A. D. 850–1200; (2) Scholastic science, centered in the universities of N Europe in the 13th–14th cent.; (3) Renaissance science, developed chiefly in Italy *c.* 1450–1600.

Arabian astronomers, as pictured in woodcut from 1513 edition of essays of Macrobius, are making use of sundial (*left*), an alidade (*middle*), and a quadrant (*right*). (*Bettmann Archive*)

Moslem Science: After the schools of Athens were closed by order of the Byzantine Emperor Justinian, A. D. 529, the Greek scientific tradition was carried on in Egypt, Syria, and Persia, until in the 7th cent. this whole area was conquered by the Arabs under Mohammed. The Abbasid caliphate fostered the translation of Greek works into Arabic and encouraged the pursuit of scientific studies, so that Baghdad became the intellectual capital of the civilized world. W Europe, during this period, was in its dark age of relative illiteracy.

The Moslem contribution to the sciences was twofold: (1) the scientific tradition of the Greeks was preserved, and its content enriched by the work of many able men, especially in astronomy, medicine, botany, alchemy, and mineralogy; (2) the Moslem culture made a decisive contribution to all future scientific progress by introducing the Hindu numerals, decimal system, and algebraic methods of analysis. Outstanding in mathematics were Al-Khwarizmi (d. *c.* 850) and Omar Khayyam (d. 1123); in astronomy, Al-Fargani (800–870) and Al-Battani (858–929); in optics, Al-Haitam (965–1039); in medicine, Al-Razi or Rases (d. 923) and Ibn-Sina or Avicenna (980–1037). In philosophy, Al-Farabi (d. *c.* 950) and Avicenna were most influential in eastern Islam, while Ibn-Rushd (1136–98), known to the West as Averroes, was the leading philosopher of W Islam; Averroes' erudite commentaries on all the works of Aristotle exerted tremendous influence on Western scholastic philosophy for 400 yr. Whereas the mathematical disciplines were significantly advanced by the Moslem culture, the theoretical scheme of Greek astronomy, physics, and biology was taken over without basic revision and developed through enrichment of empirical content and technical detail.

Scholastic Science: In the 12th and early 13th cent. the philosophical and scientific literature of Greek and Moslem origin was translated into Latin and quickly mastered by the Christian scholars of W Europe. In the fields of medicine, astronomy, optics, alchemy, and mathematics, the Western scholastics carried on the Moslem tradition without basic alteration, though further contributions were made. Except for Leonardo of Pisa (*fl. c.* 1210) and Jordanus of Nemore (*c.* 1230), the West produced no important mathematicians until the 14th cent., when Thomas Bradwardine, John Maudith, and Richard Wallingford made original contributions to arithmetic and trigonometry, and Nicholas of Oresme introduced the method of graphic representation, the theory of fractional exponents, and ideas which foreshadowed the methods of analytical geometry and the calculus.

The major innovations of Western Scholasticism, in the field of science, were in mechanics. Jordanus of Nemore, influenced by some writings of late Alexandrian origin trans-

Renaissance astronomy: In his observational notes (some of which appear at left) of 1609, Galileo recorded existence of sunspots as well as their apparent motion across the solar disk. These observations, along with those of the terrestrial texture of the Moon's surface, helped scotch the notion of the imperturbability of the heavenly bodies. (*Yerkes*)

mitted through the Moslem tradition, did important work in statics, introducing the concepts of component of force and of statical moment, and utilizing the principle of virtual displacements in proof of the lever principle and of the relation of forces directed along variously inclined planes. A mathematical analysis of velocities and accelerations was developed by William Heytesbury (*c.* 1340), Richard Suiseth (*c.* 1340), and Nicholas of Oresme (*c.* 1370), who formulated and proved the important kinematic law of uniformly accelerated motion. At the same time John Buridan (1300–1358) developed a new explanation of projectile motions and of gravitational acceleration, in terms of the concept of *impetus* (or momentum), which undermined the basic assumptions of Aristotelian dynamics and prepared the way for the inertial mechanics of Galileo and Newton. In optics a fruitful union of mathematical and experimental methods was achieved by Robert Grosseteste (d. 1237), Roger Bacon (*c.* 1214–1292), and Dietrich of Freiburg (*c.* 1250–1310). Problems of continuity and infinity were studied with remarkable analytical skill by Buridan, Gregory of Rimini (d. 1358), and Albert of Saxony (d. 1390), and the hypothesis of the diurnal rotation of the earth on its own axis was espoused by Nicholas of Oresme. In general, the scholastic phase of Western science was fertile in new ideas, acute in the analysis of concepts and in criticism of a logical sort; but the approach was abstract and divorced from practical applications or experimental techniques, largely because the scholastics were clerics whose scientific and philosophical interests were incidental to teaching in the university faculties of Arts and of Theology.

Renaissance Science: Three important new influences led, in the late 15th and the 16th cent., to a fresh phase of scientific advance in W Europe. The first was a revival of Greek studies, with rediscovery of the advanced mathematical writings of Archimedes, Apollonius of Perga, Diophantos, and Pappus, which stimulated the ideal of a purely mathematical explanation of nature and promoted mastery of geometrical analysis. A second influence was provided by the translation of the works of Plato and of writings by Greek philosophers of the

Stoic, Epicurean, and atomistic schools, introducing other conceptions of the universe than that of Aristotle and thereby legitimizing a variety of new speculative cosmologies. A third influence was provided by the rise of a secular and commercial culture in N Italy, which stimulated the pursuit of scientific studies by laymen, in close association with military and commercial technology. The ideas in mechanics which had been developed by the northern scholastics influenced Leonardo da Vinci (1452–1519), Nicolò Tartaglia (1506–59), and Jerome Cardan (1501–76), whose interests in ballistics, hydraulics, and applied mechanics led to a fruitful interplay between theory and practical application. The geometrical approach to physical theory, inspired by Archimedes, was carried out with rigor and elegance by such men as Benedetti (1530–90) and Guido Ubaldo del Monte (1545–1607), leading to the great achievements of Galileo Galilei (1564–1642). Nicholas Copernicus (1473–1543) introduced the heliocentric theory of planetary movements, and through the work of Kepler and Galileo at the beginning of the 17th cent. the Copernican system won acceptance, in spite of stubborn resistance by ecclesiastical authority and by reactionary Aristotelians in the universities. In other fields of science the Renaissance contributions were less significant, though Vesalius (1514–64) did important work in anatomy, and Fabricius in 1574 contributed to the discovery of the circulation of the blood.

Each of the three phases of Medieval and Renaissance science which we have considered contributed to the flowering of modern science in the 17th cent. Moslem arithmetic and algebra, the scholastic contributions to special problems of the mathematical analysis of motion, the Renaissance dissolution of Aristotelian cosmology, and development of mechanics through the union of mathematical analysis with experimental methods of confirmation, all combined to make possible the birth of modern science in the 17th cent.— *E. A. M.*

MEIOSIS: a special kind of CELL DIVISION found in all plants and animals that have sexual reproduction. Meiosis, also called reduction division, serves to restore the chromosome number after it has been doubled through fusion of the nuclei of two sex cells (GAMETES). In plants, meiosis occurs during formation of spores (*sporogenesis*) by the sporophyte generation; ordinarily the sporophyte plant is diploid, with two

The Renaissance: Before revealing itself productively in science, the daring of the Renaissance mind manifested itself in art and navigation. In this copperplate engraving, the Florence-based Flemish illustrator Jan van der Straet ("Stradanus") suggests the world of the navigator of the great age of discovery. In addition to the conventional cosmographic devices, Stradanus shows, in the left foreground, a lodestone supported on a floating board. (*Bettmann Archive*)

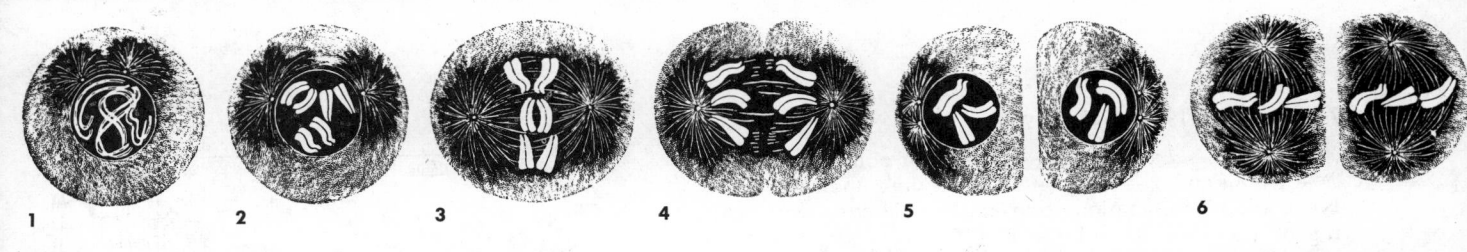

1 2 3 4 5 6

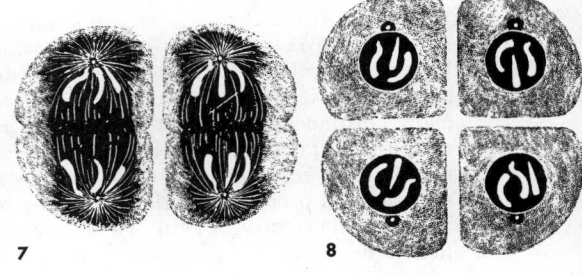

7 8

Meiosis: Since gametes from both parents join in the act of fertilization, the number of chromosomes would double every generation unless a compensatory halving occurred at some point in the maturation of the gametes. The process of cell division allowing for this is meiosis. In the numbered sequence above, which begins with paired chromosomes, a first cell division at 4-5 is followed by a second one at 7-8. Since no pairing off or longitudinal division of the chromosomes has occurred in the meantime, the end result of the original duplication and two subsequent halvings is one halving. As a result, each parent will contribute a single ("haploid") set of chromosomes through its gamete to give a complete ("diploid") set to the resulting zygote. (*After Young*)

complete sets of chromosomes in each nucleus, and the spores are haploid (monoploid), with one set of chromosomes apiece. In animals, meiosis occurs during formation of sperms or eggs (*gametogenesis*), providing each of these with a haploid nucleus.

The process of meiosis is regularly a double division, resulting in four cells. It begins in a way closely resembling the prophase of ordinary cell division (mitosis), with the chromosomes of the nucleus becoming shorter, thicker, more stainable, and each obviously consisting of two parallel chromatids. When the nuclear membrane breaks down and the chromosomes arrange themselves in the equatorial plane of the cell, they do not remain separate as in the equational division of mitosis at metaphase. Instead, homologous chromosomes come together and lie side by side, the no. 1 chromosome pairing off with another no. 1 chromosome, the no. 2 with another no. 2, and so on; this is known as *synapsis*. It is a step that groups two chromatids of one homologous chromosome with two more chromatids of the synaptic mate, forming a *tetrad* of chromatids. Until the meiotic divisions are complete, the chromatids do not replicate themselves.

The first separation of chromatids following synapsis suggests the action of anaphase in ordinary mitosis. From each tetrad, two chromatids (a *dyad*) move together toward each pole of the division spindle. Promptly the cell divides, but the groups of paired chromatids at the poles do not reorganize into chromosomes or nuclei. Instead, they spread out on the equatorial plane of a new division spindle, and once more separate toward the poles in a migratory movement resembling anaphase. This time, however, single chromatids (*monads*) go to the poles. As the cells divide again, these single chromatids at the polar positions replicate themselves and become chromosomes, then grow longer, less stainable, and more slender, as a nuclear membrane re-forms. Each of the four cells produced now has one complete set of chromosomes in its nucleus, rather than the double set from which the homologous pairs of chromosomes sorted themselves out at synapsis.

The diploid condition of the nucleus arises when one complete maternal set of chromosomes is augmented by one complete paternal set of chromosomes at the moment of FERTILIZATION. Ordinary cell divisions replicate each chromosome in the double set. Hence the homologous chromosomes that come together in synapsis include one of maternal origin and one of paternal; each consists of two chromatids. In the separation of chromatids during the two anaphase-like stages of meiosis, chance alone controls which chromatids will go to each daughter cell. Consequently, the four cells produced from each original cell undergoing meiotic division can show

every possible combination of maternal and paternal chromatids—which carry the inheritable characteristics—insuring a wide variation in the hereditary features passed on to the plant spores or the animal gametes.

In seed plants, meiotic divisions lead both to microspores, which become pollen grains, and to megaspores in the ovules. Each microspore mother-cell produces four microspores, all of which are equally important and capable of growing into male gametophytes, producing sperms toward fertilization of an egg cell. Each megaspore mother-cell, by contrast, produces four megaspores, only one of which develops into a female gametophyte; the other three die and disappear. In animals, a similar difference is seen in formation of sperm cells (four from each primary spermatocyte) and egg cells (one egg, plus three degenerate "polar bodies" from each primary oocyte).

In man, the primary spermatocytes line the seminiferous tubules of the testes, producing sperms by the billions almost continuously from puberty to old age. In woman, from 40,000 to 300,000 primary oocytes develop in the surface layer of the ovary long before the girl is born; thereafter, no new oocytes are formed. At puberty ("menarche") one of these oocytes already present undergoes meiosis, and the egg erupts into the body cavity, to pass toward the uterus by way of the Fallopian tube. Thereafter, at the middle of each menstrual cycle, one or a few more eggs reach the same stage. During the sexual lifetime of a woman, only about 500 of her oocytes undergo meiosis. Thus she produces only about 500 eggs, usually one at a time, ready for fertilization.

Meiosis is important not only in maintaining the number of chromosomes characteristic of each species of plant and animal, but also in providing opportunities for increasing variability among the offspring. Two features of the double division contribute to variability. One is simply the randomness with which maternal and paternal chromatids are parceled out into the plant spores or the animal gametes. The other is an event occurring during synapsis, while the four chromatids (two of maternal origin, two of paternal) are lying side by side. At this stage the chromatids show considerable twisting. While adjusting themselves prior to the separation of dyads for the first division, adjacent chromatids often break and recombine, transferring between one another various lengths of the total alignment of genetic determiners. This process, known as *crossing over*, might affect a maternal chromatid with the genetic characters represented by $A - B - C - D$ and a paternal chromatid with the homologous characters $a - b - c - d$. After crossing over, the chromatids separating toward the daughter cells might be $A - b - c - d$ and $a - B - C - D,$ or instead

$A - B - c - d$ and $a - b - C - D$, or equally well $A - B - C - d$ and $a - b - c - D$, depending upon where the break and recombination occurred. Double crossover, yielding $A - b - c - D$ and $a - B - C - d$, is also found. In fact, the farther apart two genes are in the locations along the length of the chromosome, the more probable it is that a crossing over will occur between them during synapsis. From statistical information on the actual frequency of crossing over between pairs of genes, it has been possible to *map* many chromosomes of fruit flies, maize, and tomatoes, and even some for mankind. Crossing over is an orderly type of reshuffling for genes, increasing variability among the reproductive cells produced. Variability contributes the basis for NATURAL SELECTION in EVOLUTION, and permits each mutation to be tested in a wide variety of combinations, some of which may be ADAPTATIONS with survival value. See also CHROMOSOMES AND GENES; HEREDITY.—*L. and M. M.*

MEITNER, LISE, 1878–   , Austrian physicist; b. Vienna. The codiscoverer (with physicist O. R. Frisch) of nuclear fission, she helped to interpret certain experimental results obtained by Otto Hahn and Fritz Strassmann as being due to the splitting of atoms (1939). Driven from her position in Germany by the Nazi regime in 1938, she became a member of the Nobel Institute Staff, Stockholm. She is a fellow of the Royal Society.—*D. H. D. R.*

MELANIN: the main pigment of the skin, hair, and the choroid coat of the eye, formed from the amino acid tyrosine by oxidation by the enzyme tyrosinase. Melanin is produced in specialized cells called *melanoblasts.* It serves to protect body tissues from ultraviolet radiation.—*F. F.*

MEMBRANE: a boundary layer that encloses a cell part, a cell, a tissue, or an organ. For example, a *nuclear membrane* encloses the nucleus of a cell, and a *cell membrane* is found around an entire cell. Heavier membranes are made up of whole sheets of cells (tissues). Epithelial tissue, which covers surfaces and lines hollow organs, acts as a membrane. Membranes pass materials (gases or liquids) back and forth from one side to the other by simple diffusion, by a special variation of diffusion known as osmosis, by secretion, and by absorption. The first two of these processes are said to be simple "physical processes," but the last two occur only in living tissue and require oxygen, hence are "metabolic processes." When a membrane secretes, it is acting as a gland. Among the many factors that determine how effectively a membrane performs a transport function are size of particles, porosity of membrane, living activity (metabolism) of the membrane, electrical charge across the membrane, relative mechanical pressures on each side of the membrane, interactions of substances on each side of the membrane, chemical and physical reactions of materials on a side of the membrane and the membrane itself. Diffusion through a membrane is always from the side of higher concentration of the material being diffused to the side of lower concentration. In living membranes, water diffuses more actively than any other liquid, and dissolved oxygen more actively than any other solute.—*A. R. D.*

"MÉMOIRE SUR LA FERMENTATION ALCOOLIQUE," Annales de Chimie et de Physique (Vol. 58, 1860) by Louis Pasteur: Pasteur's studies on fermentation had several important consequences. In the first phase, his examination of lactic fermentation (1857), he clearly showed that wherever the fermentation took place, there was a peculiar gray substance

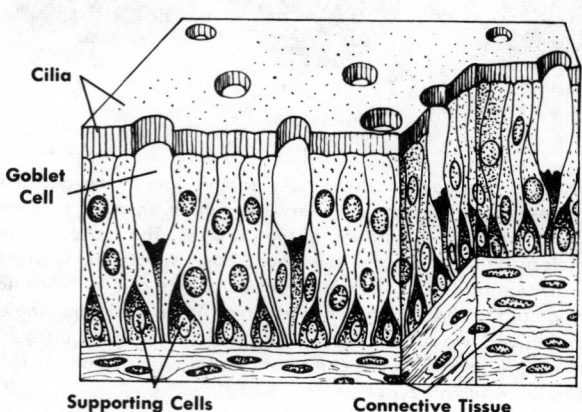

Cilia

Goblet Cell

Supporting Cells   Connective Tissue

The mucous membrane of mammals, here drawn in generalized form, is the tissue that lines the cavities and canals of the body that are in contact with the exterior environment. It has a single layer of epithelial cells; only some of these, the goblet cells, secrete mucus; others are fringed with threadlike cilia, here shown diagrammatically as a solid layer. (*After Young*)

present which under the microscope showed the characteristics of yeast, a microorganism. He further indicated that the yeast or ferment could come from the surrounding air. He clearly contradicted a contemporary view, held by Liebig and others, which suggested that fermentation was due solely to a molecular rearrangement in which a living organism was unnecessary. In the paper of 1860 on alcoholic fermentation, which he described as the alteration sugar undergoes under the influence of brewer's yeast, Pasteur clearly indicated that yeast *is* a living organism capable of reproduction. He further described the constant products of alcoholic fermentation and indicated the relative amount of each. Following up these experiments with a note to the Académie des Sciences he described, for the first time, microorganisms which can live and develop without a source of free oxygen and act as ferments; with this description, he laid the basis for understanding the fundamental nature of the process of fermentation.—*E. Me.*

MEMORY: commonly, the recall or recognition of something learned. It is thus the conscious aspect of learning, which itself may be defined as a change in behavior due to a more or less permanent change in the nervous system.

The location and nature of the change in the nervous system, called a "memory trace" or engram, have long been sought. In lower animals such as planarians and earthworms, surgical removal of the brain does not destroy "memory." In complex organisms, however, memory has been shown to depend on complicated, interweaving networks of nerve fibers called neuropiles located in particular regions of the brain. Such memory centers occur in the pedunculate bodies of the insect brain, in the optic lobes of the octopus brain, and in the cerebral cortex of most vertebrates. In the human cortex, as W. G. Penfield and others have shown, the temporal lobe and the hippocampus are importantly concerned with memory, but other regions also are involved.

Two general theories have been proposed for the physical basis of memory. According to the first, memory consists of patterned series of neural impulses continually reverberating through the several billion nerve cells within the brain. There is scant evidence favoring this view, and some evidence is contrary. According to the second theory, memory is created by a physical (probably biochemical) change within the brain. In the past much was made of the possibility of nerve fibers growing new terminal branchlets and thereby establishing new and permanent connections. But learning can take place from a single presentation of a stimulus in a time so short that branchlet growth as an explanation seems improbable. Some researchers have favored permanent changes in the permeability of synapses as an explanation of memory. Most recent evidence indicates that changes in ribonucleic acid (RNA) and proteins are the key events.

As long ago as 1947 memory was attributed to changes in neural proteins. More recently increases have been noted in RNA within nerve cells subjected to certain stimuli; concomitant depletion has occurred in adjacent glial cells. Since RNA controls synthesis of specific proteins, proteins may be involved. Some researchers have apparently been able to transfer learning by extracting RNA from an "educated" worm and feeding it to an ignorant one, but others have not been able to confirm this result.

In rats, the drug 8-azaguanine, which inhibits RNA synthesis, also inhibits memory if administered before the end of a 45-minute "fixation" period. Memory fixation time in rats was reduced when the animals were fed a malononitrile which enhances RNA and hence, presumably, protein synthesis. Experiments on goldfish and rats have shown that puromycin, an antibiotic that inhibits protein (but not RNA) synthesis, also inhibits memory.

J. Z. Young of London has proposed a model for the actual mechanism of memory. When an animal sees a white square that it recognizes through past experience, it will either advance or retreat. Somewhere in the nervous system there must be a fork, one pathway leading to the muscles of advance, the other to the muscles of retreat. At this point the neuroglial cells act, either blocking the unused pathway more or less permanently or perhaps unblocking the used one.

Memory has been investigated with respect to motivation, the effect of repetition, age, intensity of stimulus, and the like. All such studies will be clarified by anything learned about the biochemical basis of memory.—*G. B. M.*

MENAECHMUS, fl. 4th cent. B. C., Greek mathematician. He was the discoverer of the conic sections, laying the foundations for the achievements of Apollonius in this field, and also introduced the term *elements* into geometry. Menaechmus is the supposed originator of the answer to kings who asked to have mathematics made simple for them: "There is no royal road in geometry." He reputedly gave this answer to Alexander the Great, and Euclid gave it to Ptolemy.—*D. H. D. R.*

MENDEL, GREGOR JOHANN, 1822–84, Austrian Augustinian monk and experimental horticulturalist; b. Heinzendorf. His meticulous experimental studies on inheritance in the garden pea led him to an algebraic representation based on statistical numbers of offspring from each cross. He developed the concepts of pure-breeding lines and dominant and recessive characters, and demonstrated independent segregation of inheritable characteristics. These discoveries laid the foundation for genetics, but his writings attracted little interest until after their rediscovery by H. de Vries and others, *c.* 1900 (see GENETICS; HEREDITY). In 1865 he published a paper concerning plant hybridization experiments: "Versuche über Pflanzenhybriden." This was followed in 1869 by a paper on *Hieracium* hybrids obtained by artificial fertilization: "Über einige aus künstlicher Befruchtung gewonnene Hieracium-Bastarde."—*L. and M. M.*

MENDELEEV, DMITRI IVANOVICH, 1834–1907, Russian chemist; b. Tobolsk, Siberia. Mendeleev developed the periodic classification of the elements in 1869, independently of J. L. Meyer, and used it to predict successfully the properties of several undiscovered elements (see PERIODIC LAW). His studies of physical properties of gases and liquids led him, independently of Thomas Andrews, to the concept of CRITICAL TEMPERATURE. He also investigated the characteristics of Russian petroleum. His PRINCIPLES OF CHEMISTRY (1868–70) exerted great influence on chemical theory. He was a fellow of the Royal Society and an associate of the U. S. National Academy of Sciences.—*A. I.*

MENDELEVIUM: an artificial element (Mv) of the actinide group; at. no. 101; at. wt 256 (most stable isotope). Mendelevium, the ninth transuranium element to be discovered, was produced in 1955 by a group of scientists headed by Albert Ghiorso at the Univ. of California at Berkeley. The element was made by the artificial transmutation of E^{253} under bombardment by helium ions. Mendelevium decays by alphaparticle emission, and has a very short half-life. See ARTIFICIAL ELEMENTS; TRANSMUTATION OF ELEMENTS; TRANSURANIUM ELEMENTS.—*G. W. M.*

MENSTRUATION: the discharge of cast-off cells and accompanying blood from minor hemorrhage, during one portion of the cyclic changes in the reproductive organs of female higher primates, including women. The discharge, known as the menstrual flow or menses, occurs from the vaginal opening and commonly is repeated with fair regularity every four weeks from the time of menarche (about age 13 in mankind) to menopause (about age 50). In higher primates, the lining (*endometrium*) of the uterus is shed and regenerated periodically under the control of HORMONES from the OVARY and the PITUITARY GLAND. Although subject to considerable variation from person to person, and temporary upset as a result of major alterations in living habits, the timing of events in the menstrual cycle is typically as follows:

1st to 4th day—Menstruation. *5th day*—A new ovarian follicle, containing one egg, begins to develop under stimulation

The menstrual cycle: In three layers the adjacent diagram records the sequence of events in the ovary (*middle*) and the lining of the uterus (*bottom*) under the control of four interacting hormones (*top*). A 28-day cycle with ovulation on the 14th day is assumed. The successive developments and their hormonal triggering are discussed in the text. (*After Young*)

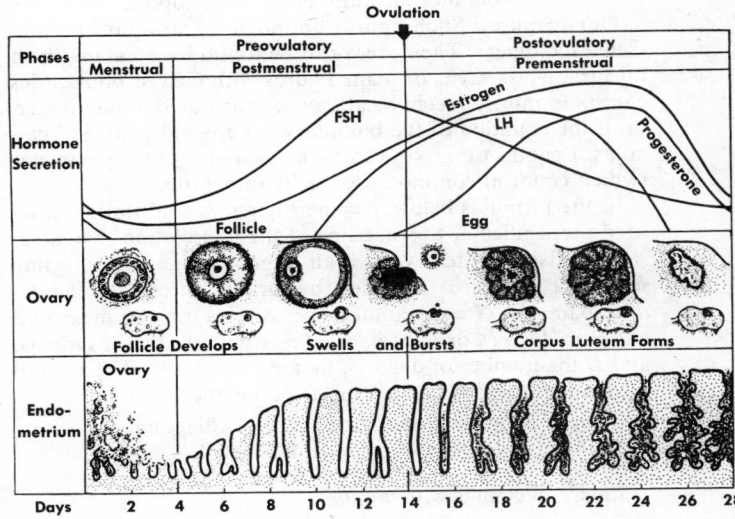

of a hormone (FSH) from the pituitary gland. *5th to 14th day* —Follicle develops rapidly and produces the hormone estrogen, which induces the endometrium to thicken into a layer many cells deep. *14th day* (day of OVULATION)—Egg erupts from follicle, enters oviduct, and is slowly propelled toward the uterus; the complete trip to the uterus requires about 4 days. *15th to 20th day*—Empty follicle fills with yellow cells (*corpus luteum*). These cells, under stimulation by the luteinizing hormone (LH), secrete the hormone progesterone; this further prepares the endometrium to receive a fertilized egg, and inhibits the pituitary gland from releasing more FSH, thus stopping the development of any further follicles in the ovary until the fate of the egg is settled. An unfertilized egg is not accepted by the uterine wall; but apparently the egg continues for its lifetime to send out an unidentified hormone that maintains the corpus luteum. If the egg reaches the uterus and remains unfertilized, it may survive for a day or two, then die. *21st to 24th day*—If the egg dies (pregnancy does not occur), the corpus luteum becomes nonfunctional, and the endometrium begins to shrink; the concentration of progesterone in the blood begins to decrease, but takes a few days to fall far enough to let the pituitary gland again begin releasing FSH. *25th to 28th day*—Maximum shrinkage of the endometrium, preparatory to shedding.

If the egg is fertilized, it is accepted promptly by the uterine wall and continues to produce the hormone that stimulates growth and the secretion of progesterone by the corpus luteum; for the duration of pregnancy, menstruation is suspended. After the baby is born and the placenta ("afterbirth") discharged, however, there is no longer a source of hormones to inhibit the pituitary gland, which once more releases FSH, starting anew the menstrual cycle.—*A. R. D.*

MENSURATION: the application of geometry, trigonometry, and other fields of mathematics to the calculation of geometric magnitudes from known quantities. These magnitudes are lengths of lines and arcs, perimeters and areas of closed figures, areas and volumes of solids, and angles. The measure of a magnitude is the ratio of the magnitude to a unit magnitude of the same kind. Thus the length of a line is the number of times it contains a line segment that has been adopted as a unit. In the formulas of this article, the unit of area is a square whose side is the unit of length chosen; and the unit of volume is a cube whose edge is the unit of length. The basic length unit may be a centimeter, an inch, a foot, a mile, but in any formula only one basic unit at a time may be used. The symbol π denotes the number 3.14159, approx.

Plane Figures: Such figures bounded by straight lines are called rectilinear. Their areas can be found by breaking them into triangles. Areas of plane figures with curved boundaries can be found by mechanical devices such as the planimeter, or, if the equation of the boundary is known, by integral calculus. Lengths of curves can be measured by the opisometer (which is not in common use) or by integration.

In the formulas below, p = perimeter, h = altitude (measured perpendicular to some line of the figure), and A = area. A may also denote a vertex, an angle, or one end of a line segment. In figures bounded by circular arcs, r = radius, d = diameter, C = circumference. Angles may be measured either in degrees or in radians: if θ is the number of radians, and D the number of degrees, then $\theta = \pi D/180$. The symbol $\perp$ denotes "perpendicular" or "is perpendicular to."

Rectangle: adjacent sides a and b are $\perp$; diagonals, d.

$$p = 2(a + b); \qquad d = \sqrt{a^2 + b^2}; \qquad A = ab$$

Square: rectangle with $a = b$.

$$p = 4a; \qquad d = a\sqrt{2}; \qquad A = a^2$$

Triangle ABC: sides a, b, c; h_a is altitude upon a, extended if necessary; similarly for h_b and h_c. (Fig. 1.)

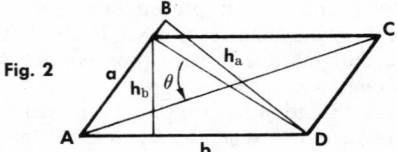

Fig. 1

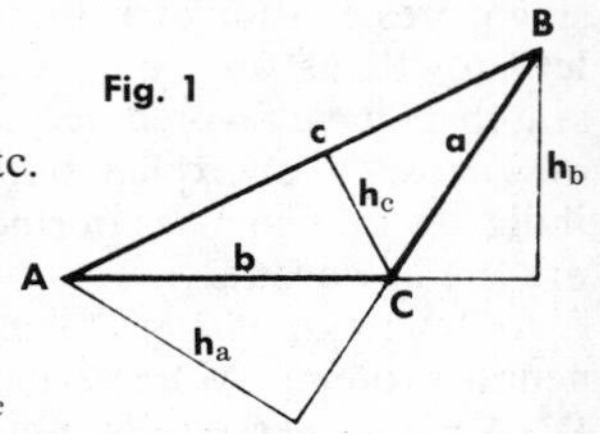

$$p = a + b + c$$
$$a^2 = b^2 + c^2 - 2bc \cos A, \text{ etc.}$$
$$a/\sin A = b/\sin B = c/\sin C$$
$$h_a = b \sin C = c \sin B, \text{ etc.}$$
$$A = \tfrac{1}{2} a h_a = \tfrac{1}{2} b h_b = \tfrac{1}{2} c h_c$$
$$= \tfrac{1}{2} ab \sin C = \tfrac{1}{2} bc \sin A = \tfrac{1}{2} ca \sin B$$
$$= \sqrt{s(s - a)(s - b)(s - c)}, \text{ where } s = \tfrac{1}{2} p$$

Right Triangle, $C = 90°$: All triangle formulas apply, with $\sin C = 1$, $\cos C = 0$.

$$c = \sqrt{a^2 + b^2}; \qquad A = \tfrac{1}{2} ab$$

Parallelogram ABCD: a and b, adjacent sides; h_a, altitude upon a; h_b, altitude upon b; θ, angle of intersection of diagonals (Fig. 2).

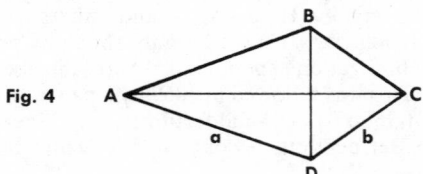

Fig. 2

$$\angle A = \angle C; \ \angle B = \angle D; \ \angle A + \angle B = 180°$$
$$\sin A = \sin B; \qquad \cos A = -\cos B$$
$$p = 2(a + b)$$
$$h_a = b \sin A; \ h_b = a \sin A$$
$$\text{Area} = a h_a = b h_b = ab \sin A$$
$$= \tfrac{1}{2} (AC \times BD) \times \sin \theta$$

Rhombus: equilateral parallelogram; side a, diagonals c and d.

$$p = 4a; \qquad \text{Area} = a h_a = \tfrac{1}{2} cd; \qquad c \perp d$$

Trapezoid: a and b, parallel sides; c and d, nonparallel sides; h, $\perp$ distance between a and b; E and F, midpoints of nonparallel sides. (Fig. 3.)

$$p = a + b + c + d$$
$$\text{Area} = \tfrac{1}{2} h (a + b) = h \times EF$$

Fig. 3

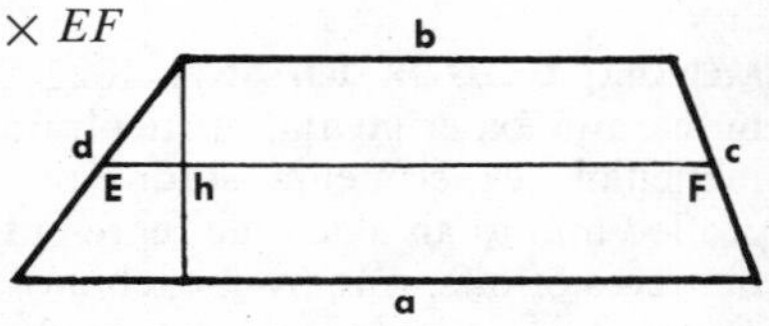

Kite ABCD: $AB = AD = a$, $BC = CD = b$. (Fig. 4.)

$$p = 2(a + b); \text{ area} = \tfrac{1}{2}(AC \times BD); \ AC \perp BD$$

Fig. 4

Trapezium: no two sides parallel or equal; a and b, diagonals; θ, angle between diagonals.

$$\text{Area} = \tfrac{1}{2} ab \sin \theta$$

Regular Polygons: n equal sides and n equal angles; a, side; R, radius of the polygon, *i.e.* that of the circumscribed circle; r, apothem, *i.e.* radius of the inscribed circle. (Fig. 5.)

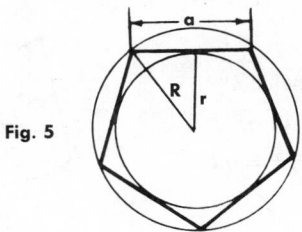

Fig. 5

Each angle $= \dfrac{n-2}{n} \times 180°$.

$$a = 2R \sin(180°/n) = 2r \tan(180°/n)$$

$$p = na = 2nR \sin(180°/n) = 2nr \tan(180°/n)$$

$$R = \tfrac{1}{2} a \csc(180°/n) = r \sec(180°/n)$$

$$r = \tfrac{1}{2} a \cot(180°/n) = R \cos(180°/n)$$

Area $= \tfrac{1}{2} rp = \tfrac{1}{2} nar$

$$= \tfrac{1}{4} na^2 \cot(180°/n) = \tfrac{1}{2} nR^2 \sin(360°/n)$$

$$= nr^2 \tan(180°/n)$$

Circle: $C = 2\pi r = \pi d$

$$A = \tfrac{1}{2} rC = \pi r^2 = \tfrac{1}{4} \pi d^2 = 0.7854 d^2, \text{ approx.}$$

Circular Sector OPMQ: arc $PMQ = s$; $\angle POQ = \theta$ radians $= D$ degrees. (Fig. 6.)

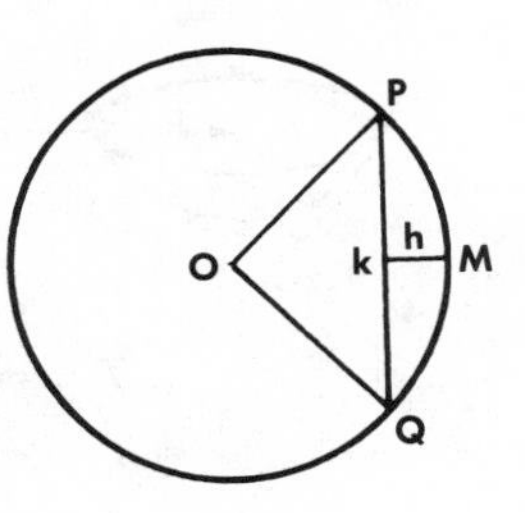

$$s = C\theta/2\pi = r\theta$$

$$= CD/360 = \pi r D/180$$

$$A = \tfrac{1}{2} rs = \tfrac{1}{2} r^2 \theta = r^2 \pi D/360$$

Fig. 6

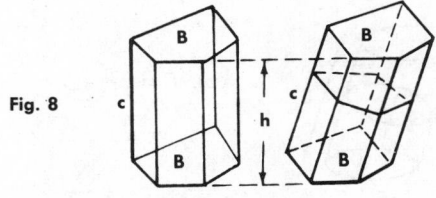

Chord PQ: $PQ = k = 2r \sin \tfrac{1}{2} \theta$.

Segment $PQMP$: $h \perp PQ$ at its midpoint.

$$A = \tfrac{1}{2} rs - \tfrac{1}{2} r^2 \sin \theta = \tfrac{1}{2} r^2 (\theta - \sin \theta)$$

$$= \pi r^2 D/360 - \tfrac{1}{2} r^2 \sin D$$

Annulus: circular ring with outer radius r_1, inner radius r_2.

$$A = \pi(r_1^2 - r_2^2) = \pi(r_1 - r_2)(r_1 + r_2)$$

Ellipse: semimajor axis a, semiminor axis b. (Fig. 7.)

Fig. 7

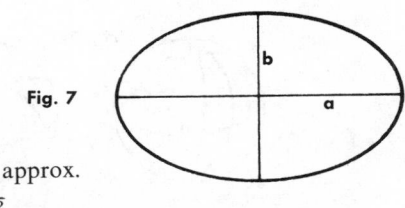

$$p = \pi \sqrt{2(a^2 + b^2)}, \text{ approx.}$$

$$= 4.443 \sqrt{a^2 + b^2}$$

$$A = \pi ab$$

Solids: A plane surface intersects a solid in a plane figure called a section (or cross section); a right section is one that is perpendicular to a lateral edge of a prism or pyramid, or to the elements of a cylinder. An element of a cylinder or cone is a line of the cylindrical or conical surface in one of the positions taken by the generatrix, the line whose motion is thought of as generating the surface. A truncated prism or pyramid is the portion of the solid included between the base and a section that is not parallel to it; a frustum of a pyramid or cone is the portion of the solid included between the base and a section parallel to it. For a regular pyramid or its frustum the slant height is the altitude of the triangle or trapezoid that is a lateral side of the solid; for a cone or its frustum it is the length of an element or of that portion of it between two bases of the frustum.

A solid bounded by plane surfaces is a polyhedron. A regular polyhedron has its bounding faces congruent regular polygons. There are only six regular polyhedrons. Their areas and volumes are given in the table; a, length of one edge; k, number of sides of each polygonal face; n, number of faces.

n	Name	k	Total area	Volume
4	Tetrahedron	3	$1.73205\,a^2$	$0.11785\,a^3$
6	Hexahedron (cube)	4	$6.00000\,a^2$	$1.00000\,a^3$
8	Octahedron	3	$3.46410\,a^2$	$0.47140\,a^3$
12	Dodecahedron	5	$20.64578\,a^2$	$7.66312\,a^3$
20	Icosahedron	3	$8.66025\,a^2$	$2.18170\,a^3$

In the formulas below, $V =$ volume, $A =$ area of some designated surface, $L =$ lateral area, $T =$ total area, $B =$ area of base, $h =$ altitude (which is always measured perpendicular to some base), $s =$ slant height, $r =$ radius, and $l =$ length of an element of a right cylinder or cone.

Prism: c, lateral edge; p, the perimeter of a right section. (Fig. 8.)

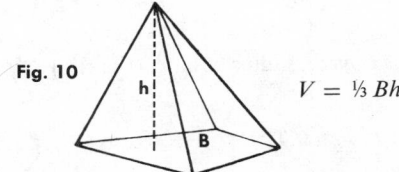

Fig. 8

$$L = pc; \qquad T = 2B + L; \qquad V = Bh$$

Rectangular parallelepiped: edges a, b, c. (Fig. 9.)

$B = ab$; $\quad L = 2c(a + b)$; **Fig. 9**

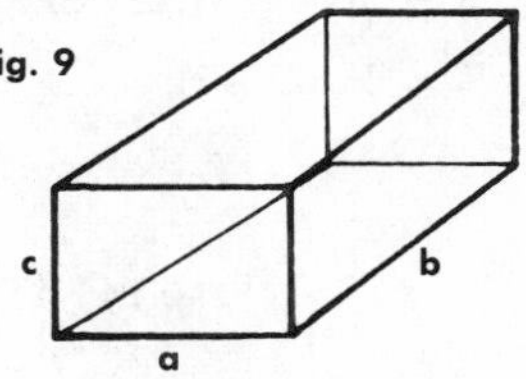

$$T = 2(ab + ac + bc)$$

$$V = Bh = abc$$

Cube: rectangular parallelepiped with $a = b = c$.

$$T = 6a^2; \quad V = a^3$$

Pyramid: h, $\perp$ distance from vertex to plane of base. (Fig. 10.)

Fig. 10

$$V = \tfrac{1}{3} Bh$$

Frustum of Pyramid: h, ⊥ distance between bases, *B and B'.* (Fig. 11.)

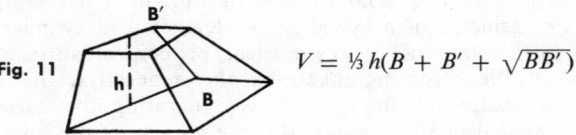

Fig. 11

$$V = \tfrac{1}{3} h(B + B' + \sqrt{BB'})$$

Regular Pyramid: a, side of base; slant height *s = HK; n,* number of sides of base; *p,* perimeter of base.

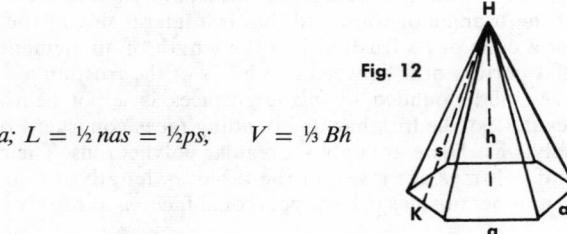

Fig. 12

$$p = na; \quad L = \tfrac{1}{2} nas = \tfrac{1}{2} ps; \quad V = \tfrac{1}{3} Bh$$

Frustum of Regular Pyramid: p, p', perimeters of lower and upper bases, *B and B'.* (Fig. 13.)

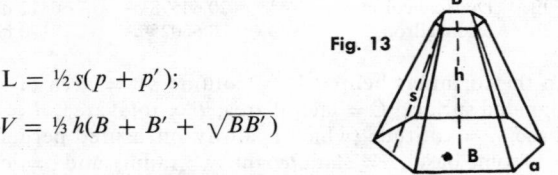

Fig. 13

$$L = \tfrac{1}{2} s(p + p');$$
$$V = \tfrac{1}{3} h(B + B' + \sqrt{BB'})$$

Cylinder: l, length of element; *p,* perimeter of right section. (Fig. 14.)

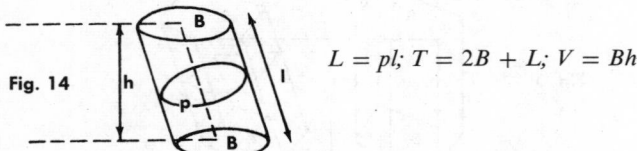

Fig. 14

$$L = pl; \quad T = 2B + L; \quad V = Bh$$

Right Circular Cylinder: r, radius of base; *h = l.* (Fig. 15.)

$$B = \pi r^2; \quad L = 2\pi rh = pl$$
$$T = 2\pi r(h + r); \quad V = Bh = \pi r^2 h$$

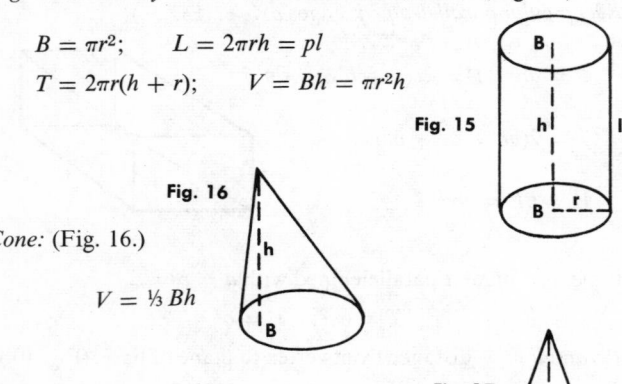

Fig. 15

Fig. 16

Cone: (Fig. 16.)

$$V = \tfrac{1}{3} Bh$$

Fig. 17

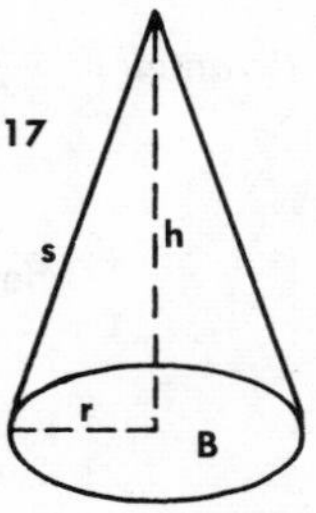

Right Circular Cone: r, radius of base. (Fig. 17.)

$$B = \pi r^2; \quad L = \pi rs; \quad T = \pi r(r + s)$$
$$V = \tfrac{1}{3} Bh = \tfrac{1}{3} \pi r^2 h$$

Frustum of Right Circular Cone: r and r', radii of lower and upper bases; *h,* ⊥ distance between bases. (Fig. 18.)

$$B = \pi r^2; \quad B' = \pi r'^2; \quad L = \pi s(r + r')$$
$$V = \tfrac{1}{3} \pi h(r^2 + r'^2 + rr')$$

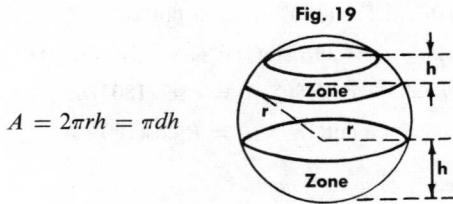

Fig. 18

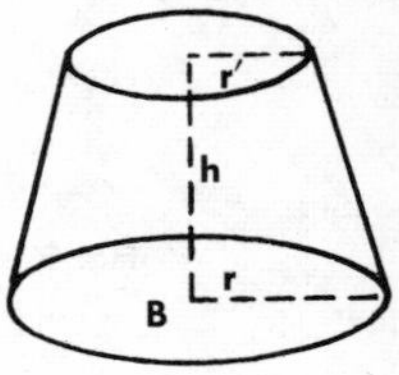

Sphere: radius *r,* diameter *d.*

$$A = 4\pi r^2 = \pi d^2;$$
$$V = 4\pi r^3/3 = \pi d^3/6$$

Zone: spherical surface between parallel plane sections of a sphere, distance *h* apart. (Fig. 19.)

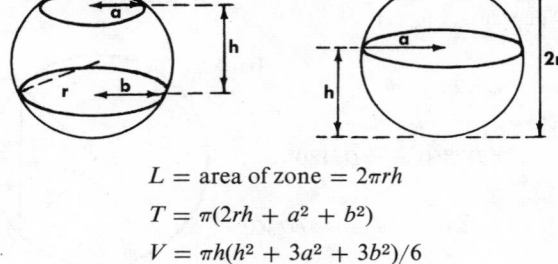

Fig. 19

$$A = 2\pi rh = \pi dh$$

Spherical Segment: solid between parallel plane sections of a sphere, distance *h* apart; *a* and *b,* radii of the bases. If one plane is tangent to the sphere, then segment has one base, and *b = 0.* (Fig. 20.)

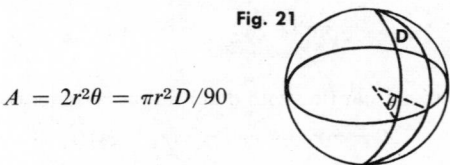

Fig. 20

$$L = \text{area of zone} = 2\pi rh$$
$$T = \pi(2rh + a^2 + b^2)$$
$$V = \pi h(h^2 + 3a^2 + 3b^2)/6$$

Lune: surface between halves of two great circles of a sphere, intersecting at an angle *θ.* (Fig. 21.)

Fig. 21

$$A = 2r^2\theta = \pi r^2 D/90$$

Spherical Triangle: angles *L, M, N* in degrees. (Fig. 22.)

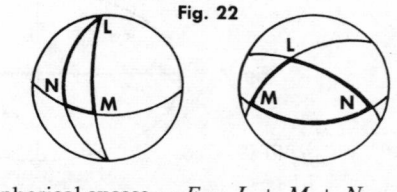

Fig. 22

$$\text{Spherical excess} = E = L + M + N - 180$$
$$A = \pi r^2 E/180$$

Spherical Sector: solid generated by rotating a sector of a circle about a diameter; *h*, altitude of zone that is base of the sector. (Fig. 23.)

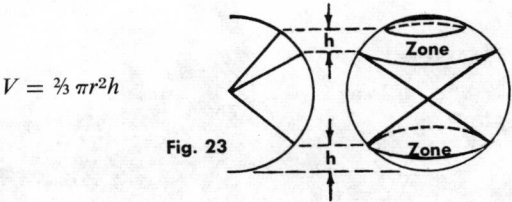

$$V = \tfrac{2}{3}\,\pi r^2 h$$

Fig. 23

Spherical Shell: r_1 and r_2, outer and inner radii.

$$V = \tfrac{4}{3}\,\pi(r_1{}^3 - r_2{}^3)$$

Ellipsoid: semiaxes *a*, *b*, *c*. (Fig. 24.)

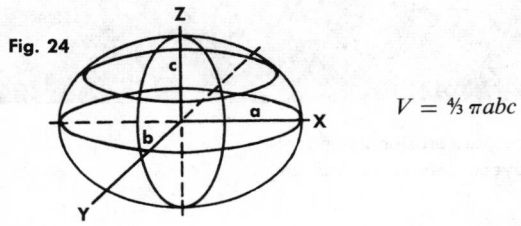

Fig. 24

$$V = \tfrac{4}{3}\,\pi a b c$$

Ellipsoid of Revolution: generated by rotating the ellipse with equation $x^2/a^2 + y^2/b^2 = 1$ and eccentricity $e = \sqrt{1 - (b^2/a^2)}$, $b < a$, about one of its axes.

Oblate Spheroid: rotation about minor axis

$$A = \pi[2a^2 + (b^2/e)\,ln\,(i + e)/(i - e)]$$

$$V = \tfrac{4}{3}\,\pi\,a^2 b$$

Prolate Spheroid: rotation about major axis

$$A = 2\pi[b^2 + (ab/e)\sin^{-1} e]$$

$$V = \tfrac{4}{3}\pi a b^2$$

—H. C.

MERCAPTANS (hydrosulfides): organic compounds of carbon, hydrogen, and sulfur containing the radical SH. They cause the characteristic bad odor of unrefined gasoline. Traces are sometimes added to manufactured or natural gas to betray leakages in pipelines.—*R. J. F.*

MERCAPTURIC ACIDS: in biochemistry, DETOXICATION products by which the body rids itself of certain ingested substances containing poisonous halogen-substituted hydrocarbons, *e.g.* parabromophenol. The process is accomplished by linking the substances to the sulfur atom of N-acetyl cysteine as thio ethers. N-acetyl cysteine is frequently linked to glucuronic acid through its carboxyl group. Thus, bromobenzene given experimentally to dogs leads to excretion of a mercapturic acid glucuronide in the urine.—*J. F. S.*

MERCATOR, GERHARDUS (GERHARD KREMER), 1512–94, Flemish mathematician, geographer, and cartographer; b. Rupelmonde (now in Belgium). In 1537 he published a map of the Holy Land, and a year later his first map of the world. He made a terrestrial globe in 1541 and a celestial globe in 1551. His first map by the celebrated Mercator projection was made in 1568. This projection, which depicts terrestrial lines of constant direction as straight lines, has been used by navigators more widely than any other. His great atlas, be-gun in 1585, was completed and published by his son in 1594. See MAP.—*H. C.*

MERCURY: in astronomy, the nearest to the Sun of all known PLANETS; one of the four so-called terrestrial planets. It is visible as an "evening star" in the western sky after sunset or as a "morning star" in the eastern sky before sunrise; its greatest angular distance from the Sun is only 28°. Usually between −2 and +1 in stellar magnitude, according to its orbital position, Mercury is occasionally conspicuous to the unaided eye but is usually invisible in the Sun's rays. Telescopic studies are often made in full sunshine, however, if the planet is higher in the sky. Mercury's average distance from the Sun is 36 million mi. The orbit is inclined 7° to the plane of the ecliptic and has an eccentricity of 0.21 (both values are exceeded among the principal planets only by Pluto). The period of revolution around the Sun is 87.97 days. Because the planet's orbit is inside Earth's, and because it shines only by reflected sunlight, Mercury exhibits the same PHASES as the Moon; the average interval between two consecutive "full" phases is 115.88 days.

Mercury, with a diameter of about 3,000 mi, is the smallest principal planet. Its mass, difficult to determine in the absence of any known satellite, is probably about 5% of Earth's; its density is about 5 times that of water. The temperature of the sunlit portion at perihelion is near 770°F, but the night side is at about 70°F.

Mercury's surface is probably like the Moon's, its reflectivity being only 7% and its surface being very rough (hence the brightness varies greatly with the phase). Mercury can have little or no atmosphere, for the ESCAPE VELOCITY is only 2.3 mi/sec. However, E. M. Antoniadi and some others have recorded apparent veilings (gaseous?) of surface markings. Surface details are difficult to observe because of Mercury's angular nearness to the Sun; visual observers often disagree about what they see, and few photographs show any markings. The chief markings definitely identified are permanent dark patches, probably similar to the Moon's dark *maria*. Mercury's rotation period was once thought to equal its period of revolution, but recent radar observations and theoretical studies of effects of solar gravitation on the planet both yield a rotation period of about 59 days. The axis of rotation is nearly perpendicular to the plane of the orbit.

A TRANSIT of Mercury across the Sun can occur only near May 7 and Nov. 9, the dates when Mercury crosses the plane of Earth's orbit. The most recent transit was on Nov. 7, 1960; the next two will be on May 9, 1970, and Nov. 10, 1973. A small telescope (with proper protection for the eyes) will show Mercury as a tiny round black spot slowly moving across the Sun's disk. Observations during transits make possible measurement of the diameter of Mercury. Also, the careful timing of its contacts with the Sun's edge, when done at different geographical locations, makes possible the determination of exact distances between these locations.—*W. H.*

MERCURY: in chemistry, a metal (Hg); at. no. 80; at. wt 200.61; density 13.546; mp −38.87°C; bp 356.58°C; valences 1 and 2. It is the only common metal that is liquid at room temperature. One of the seven metals of the ancients, mercury was known to the Chinese and Hindus in pre-Christian times, and has been found in Egyptian tombs believed to date back to 1500 B. C. The metal occurs in nature almost entirely in the form of its sulfide ore, cinnabar (HgS). Commercial preparation involves heating this ore in air; the sulfur (S) combines with oxygen to form sulfur dioxide (SO₂), leaving free mercury. Because mercury is liquid at ordinary temperatures, does not wet glass, and has a regular coefficient of ex-

Mesas and buttes near Monument Valley, Ariz., are erosional remnants of a plateau of nearly horizontal rock layers. (*Santa Fe Railway*)

pansion, it has long been used in thermometers, barometers, and other such measuring instruments. However, it now finds its most important application in complex electrical apparatus and control instruments, where use is made of its compactness, fluidity, and excellent electrical conductivity. The properties of mercury are also utilized in batteries and mercury-vapor lamps. Most mercury compounds are highly poisonous, generally acting through destruction of kidney cells. The extremely poisonous mercuric chloride ($HgCl_2$), a white, crystalline powder, is used as an insecticide, fungicide, rat poison, and wood preservative. Mercury compounds have been used to coat the back of mirrors because of their opaqueness; mercury sulfide, "vermilion red," is one of the oldest paint pigments. Mercury fulminate, $Hg(CNO)_2$, is used in percussion caps as a detonator for smokeless powder and TNT. Organic mercury compounds are used in antiseptic solutions, *e.g.* mercurochrome, merthiolate, and mercressin, and in certain cathartics and diuretics.—*I. B.*

MERIDIAN, CELESTIAL: a projection of the terrestrial meridian into the CELESTIAL SPHERE, so that every point on the celestial meridian lies directly above the terrestrial meridian. The celestial meridian of a position on Earth is the great circle of the celestial sphere that passes through both celestial poles and the zenith of the position, remaining stationary above the position. At any instant, the meridian coincides with whatever hour circle is then passing through the zenith. The two intersections of the celestial meridian with the horizon define the north and south points of the horizon.—*T. N.*

MERSENNE, MARIN, 1588–1648, French mathematician; b. La Soultière. A Minimite friar, he was a noted amateur of science and mathematics. The series of weekly scientific discussions that he conducted led to the establishment of the French Academy of Sciences. He wrote in many fields and is known for the so-called Mersenne primes, or prime numbers, of the form $(2^n - 1)$.—*H. C.*

MESA (Span. "table"): term used in the southwestern U. S. A. for an isolated or partly isolated plateau remnant in the form of a flat-topped mountain with two or more steep sides. Some mesas owe their elevation to a resistant caprock that protects underlying weaker rock; others exist because of their remoteness from major streams. A mesa's broad top, level because of the horizontality of the rock strata, may be thousands of square miles in area. Continued erosion of a mesa may in time convert it into buttes.—*E. A.*

MESIC ATOM: an atom that differs from a conventional one by having one or more of its electrons replaced by an equal number of negatively charged MESONS. Since the mass of a meson is much greater than that of the electron it replaces, the meson's stable position is very close to the nucleus; in heavier atoms, the meson actually penetrates the nucleus. This property makes mesic atoms useful for investigating the charge distribution of nuclei.—*S. Bo.*

MESONS: one of the major groups of elementary particles, possessing integral (0, 1, 2...) units of spin and obeying Einstein-Bose quantum statistics. They are called mesons because the first families discovered had masses intermediate between that of the electron and that of the proton. Their existence was originally postulated in 1935 by H. Yukawa in an attempt to explain the character of the nuclear force that binds protons and neutrons into nuclei. This force is more than 100 times as strong as that between electric charges, but is of extremely short range, extending for distances of only 10^{-13} cm or less. Yukawa suggested it was due to continual exchange of relatively light particles, which he called mesons, between the neutron and the proton. To explain the very short range of the force he showed that the exchanged particles must be a few hundred times as heavy as the electron.

At the time Yukawa put forward his theory, electrons, protons, and neutrons were the only known particles, but in 1937 C. D. Anderson and others at California Institute of Technology discovered particles about 200 times as heavy as electrons while investigating the passage of cosmic rays through cloud chambers. Subsequent work, however, showed that these particles hardly interacted at all with nuclei, and therefore certainly could not be responsible for nuclear forces. Particles of the Yukawa type were not found until 1947, when C. F. Powell and co-workers, at Bristol University, discovered pi-mesons, or pions, 270 times as heavy as electrons. These do interact strongly with nuclei, and also exhibit other properties predicted by Yukawa. Mu-mesons are now known to be exactly like electrons except for their larger masses. They are called muons rather than mesons and are grouped with electrons and neutrinos into a class of elementary particles called leptons.

Other families of mesons have been discovered since the pions were found. Particles of the lightest such family, called K-mesons, or kaons, are nearly four times as heavy as pions. Particles of other families are heavier still, some being even heavier than the proton, but all these are very unstable, and generally decay very rapidly into pions or kaons (see PARTICLE, ELEMENTARY). Presumably these heavier particles also contribute to nuclear forces, but because they are so heavy their effects are limited to distances even smaller than those at which pions are effective. The basic ideas of Yukawa's theory are still believed to be correct, but so far there is no completely comprehensive theory explaining exactly how the effects of all the particles combine to produce the nuclear forces.—*D. C. C.*

MESOSPHERE: the layer of the ATMOSPHERE from about 15 to 50 mi up, separated from the stratosphere below by the mesopause and merging with the ionosphere above. In the mesosphere, air temperature increases with height up to a maximum between 45°F and 65°F (7°C and 18°C) between 25 and 30 mi up, above which height the temperature again decreases. This warm layer is caused by the absorption of solar radiation by ozone.—*D. H. L.*

MESOZOIC ERA: a major unit of geologic time, between the end of the PALEOZOIC ERA about 230 million yr ago, and the beginning of the CENOZOIC ERA, about 70 million yr ago (see GEOLOGICAL TIME CHART). The Mesozoic is divided into three periods: Triassic (following the Paleozoic Era), Jurassic, and Cretaceous. The name, from Greek *mesos* (middle) plus *zoa* (life), indicates the mixed fauna and flora of the period: the dominance of reptiles on land but the initial appearance of mammals and birds; the development of the flowering plants but the continued abundance of conifers, cycads, and ginkgos; the variety of shelled cephalopods (ammonites) in the seas in contrast to the occurrence of modern groups of bony fishes, clams, and corals (see LIFE, PREHISTORIC). The physical history was also, in a sense, transitional, for the continents had assumed some elements of their present form, but at times shallow seas spread across their interiors and deep troughs (geosynclines) received sedimentary deposits where mountains now rise. Climates were apparently milder and more uniform than at present, but deserts and dead seas left their traces as sand dunes and salt beds in some areas.

After the intense mountain building of the later part of the Paleozoic Era, E North America was relatively stable through most of the Mesozoic. Early in the era, faulting formed a series of narrow basins along the Appalachians from Nova Scotia to North Carolina. In these there accumulated dark lake shales, thin coals from peat swamps, and great thicknesses of red sandstone and mudstone. Lava from deep in the crust worked upward, forced its way between rock layers to form sills such as the Palisades of New York and New Jersey, and flowed out across the surface. After this the Atlantic border tilted slowly beneath the ocean, and by the close of the era, sediment, eroded from the rising Appalachian Mts, was spread across a shallow sea floor, the present coastal plain. The Gulf coastal plain had a similar history;

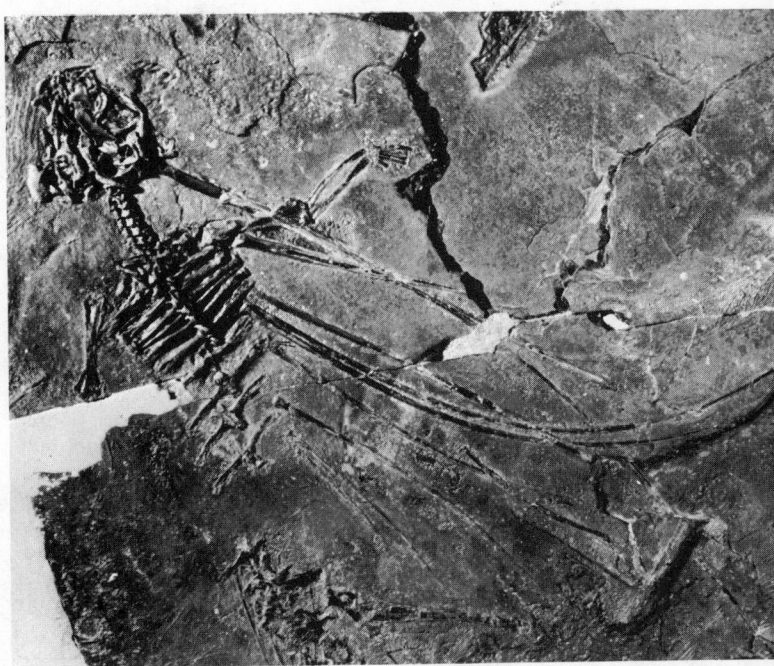

Fossil reptile was found in black shale of Triassic Period in N New Jersey. The animal, lizardlike in form, and about 7 in. long, glided from tree to tree on membranous wings supported by elongated ribs. It lived about 175 million years ago, antedating the earliest birds and flying reptiles (pterosaurs). (*Amer. Mus. of Nat. Hist.*)

Fossil of Archaeopteryx appears in upper Jurassic (middle Mesozoic) rocks of Germany. Although these are richly fossiliferous rocks, only three such specimens have ever been found. The earliest-known bird, Archaeopteryx was a primitive, reptilelike form about the size of a crow, with teeth and clawed wings. (*Amer. Mus. of Nat. Hist.*)

invaded by the sea in the mid-Mesozoic, it accumulated a series of beach, lagoonal, and shallow marine sediments. In the continental interior, the northeastern portion stood constantly above sea level as a low platform; the southern and western portions sank slowly, so that a broad seaway reached from the Gulf to the Arctic in the later Mesozoic. The western border of the continent comprised two parallel geosynclinal systems. The outer (westernmost) accumulated great thicknesses of coarse, poorly sorted sandstone, dark shale, and siliceous sediment as well as lava flows and layers of volcanic ash. Near the middle of the Mesozoic, these rocks were deformed, invaded by granitic magma from below, and elevated into mountain ranges (the Sierra Nevada and the Coast Ranges) in the Nevadan disturbance. Some sediment, eroded from the rising mountains, continued to accumulate in narrow basins between the ranges; the remainder poured eastward to form great deltas in the inner geosynclinal belt. This inner trough, which had received principally continental deposits during the early Mesozoic, began to sink more rapidly, so that marine sands and muds accumulated over most of the geosyncline. But the mountain-building pulses, extending progressively eastward, deformed these sediments near the end of the Mesozoic and at the beginning of the Cenozoic to form the Rocky Mts.

In South America the Andes also began to rise from a geosyncline, in the later Mesozoic. Australia and South Africa remained stable through the era; only continental sediments and narrow belts of marine deposits along the coast record the history of these two regions. On the other hand the East Indies and the Japanese Is. were active belts, deep troughs sinking between rising island ridges. A great geosyncline, the Tethys, extended 'across Eurasia from India through the Middle East and into S Europe and N Africa along the Mediterranean axis. Divided into linear troughs by narrow ridges or island arcs, the Tethys included a variety of sediments, shales, and sands from the deeps, and reef rock and other limestones from the shallows. Portions of the geosyncline also received important additions of lava and volcanic ash. This belt, too, underwent some deformation, though the major mountain building did not occur until the development of the Alps and of the Himalayan ranges in the Cenozoic. To the north, Asia was a lowland area of lakes, swamps, and flood plains. Similar conditions prevailed across N Europe at the beginning of the era. The New Red Sandstone of the British Is. and similar sandstones and mudstones in Germany record river and flood-plain conditions. Shallow seas invaded the region toward the middle of the era, interfingering marine sediments with terrestrial ones. Salt beds in the marine deposits and abundant dune sands indicate desert conditions. Thick limestone beds, abounding in corals, mollusks, and other shells, mark the maximum marine advance in the late Mesozoic. The chalk cliffs of Dover remain as one evidence of this sea.

Study of residual magnetism in Mesozoic rocks, as well as of fossil distribution, indicates the continents changed in position with respect to one another during the era. Australia, South America, and Africa may have been much closer at its beginning. North America and Europe also appear to have drifted apart, and the Atlantic Ocean may be a relatively new feature (see CONTINENTAL DRIFT). The poles may have also shifted (or the continents moved relative to the poles), for iron particles in early Mesozoic rocks of N America point toward a magnetic pole in central Siberia (see TERRESTRIAL MAGNETISM). By the close of the era, however, the poles and continents had largely assumed their present positions and shapes, and the framework of the recent (Cenozoic) era was set.—*J. B.*

MESSIER, CHARLES, 1730–1817, French astronomer; b. Badonviller, Lorraine. Among his contemporaries, Messier was recognized as an assiduous observer of comets. Today his fame rests on the catalog of about 100 of the brightest nebulae and clusters, which he compiled in Paris during his comet searches and published by installments in the *Memoires* of the French Academy for 1771 and the *Connoissance des Temps*

Charles Messier
(Yerkes Obs.)

for 1783 and 1784. Celestial objects in the Messier catalog are designated by the letter M, such as M31, the Andromeda galaxy. He was a member of the Academy of Sciences and a fellow of the Royal Society.—*O. G.*

METABOLISM: the total of chemical events that occur in a living system. Metabolism includes *catabolism,* or those processes that degrade foodstuffs (*e.g.* digestion and breakdown of carbohydrates, fats, and proteins), and *anabolism,* or processes that build simple molecules into complex proteins, nucleic acids, and other large molecules. Metabolism is one of the attributes of life; when an organism dies, metabolism ceases. During life, metabolism can be considered to accomplish the needs of an organism through digestion of foodstuffs and their conversion into complex cellular constituents. Processes of metabolism also are responsible for generation of energy for digestion, synthesis of new compounds, nerve transmission, and muscular movement; for cell division; and for growth. A substance which takes part in a metabolic process, whether catabolic or anabolic, is called a *metabolite* (see also ANTIMETABOLITE).—*V. H. C.*

Basal metabolic rate is the rate at which an individual expends energy to maintain the life processes while awake, at rest, and fasting. Energy expended is measured by the body's heat production, usually determined by the amount of oxygen consumed and carbon dioxide eliminated in a definite time interval. In medical diagnosis, the test for basal metabolic rate is most often used to measure thyroid-gland disturbances.—*J. F.*

METABOLISM, INBORN ERROR OF: a metabolic aberration that is congenital, hereditary, permanent, and uncorrectable, but not lethal. Some inborn errors are: albinism, the failure to manufacture the normal skin pigment melanin; alkaptonuria, a condition involving a disturbance in the metabolism of the amino acid tyrosine; sickle-cell anemia, a disease related to the presence of an abnormal type of hemoglobin; hemophilia, caused by the absence of a blood-clotting factor; and a type of hemolytic anemia in which the red cells are abnormally susceptible to destruction by certain drugs because they lack the enzyme glucose-6-phosphate dehydrogenase.

In each case the cause is the congenital lack of a particular enzyme; this defect prevents an essential step in the metabolism of a compound from taking place, and a certain normal metabolic change fails to be brought about. Thus, an intermediate compound increases in concentration in some cells, and is usually found in high concentration in the urine. See also BIOCHEMICAL GENETICS.—*F. F.*

METAL: a substance belonging to one of the two somewhat ill-defined classes into which the chemical elements are often divided, the other being NONMETALS. The division goes back a long way, and still has its uses. There is no rigid boundary between the two classes, certain so-called metalloids, *e.g.* arsenic and antimony, occupying a borderline position in the periodic table. Physically, metals are usually opaque, lustrous, and capable of taking a high polish; they are good conductors of heat and electricity, and very often malleable, ductile, and of great tensile strength. Their melting points have a high average value but are spread over a wide range, from mercury (the only liquid metal), $-38.9°C$ ($-38.0°F$), to tungsten, $3370°C$ ($6098°F$). Their specific gravities, likewise usually high in comparison with those of nonmetals, also range widely, from lithium (0.534) to osmium (22.5). Various metals when fused together yield useful ALLOYS.

COMPARISON OF METALS AND NONMETALS

Physical Properties	Metals	Nonmetals
Common form.......	Malleable solid with metallic luster	Brittle solid or diatomic gas
Electrical conductivity.......	High	Low
Heat conductivity.......	High	Low
Chemical Properties		
Simple ions........	Positive	Negative
Oxides...........	Basic	Acidic
Compounds.......	Metal-metal compounds have metallic bonds	Nonmetal-nonmetal compounds are covalent

Metal plus nonmetal yields ionic compound

Chemically, most metals combine readily with many nonmetals, forming *e.g.* oxides, chlorides, and sulfides. Often one metal forms several oxides, one or more of which is basic, reacting with acids to form salts: thus silver oxide, Ag_2O, gives rise to the sole series of silver salts; while ferrous oxide, FeO, and ferric oxide, Fe_2O_3, give rise respectively to the ferrous and ferric series of iron salts, *e.g.* the sulfates, $FeSO_4$ and $Fe_2(SO_4)_3$. Metal hydroxides, as well as oxides, dissolve in acids to yield the corresponding salt plus water, and metal carbonates yield carbon dioxide as well. With some acids, metals react to give the salt plus hydrogen; but with others, *e.g.* nitric acid, the "nascent" hydrogen enters into secondary (reducing) reactions with the acid. Also certain metal hydroxides, such as zinc and aluminum, are amphoteric, *i.e.* they dissolve in alkalis as well as in acids, to form two kinds of salts, such as sodium zincate, Na_2ZnO_2, and zinc chloride, $ZnCl_2$, respectively. Metallic chlorides are usually stable and unaffected by water; but hydrides of metals are rare and unstable. An outstanding characteristic of metals is their electropositive nature. Because of their chemical properties, metals usually occur naturally in combination, and have to be extracted from their ores by metallurgical processes.

Of several ways of classifying metals, the most satisfactory is to refer them to the PERIODIC TABLE in its modern form based upon atomic numbers (see also INORGANIC CHEMISTRY). Here they fall into groups, or families, of related metals—*e.g.* group IA: the alkali metals, lithium, sodium, potassium, rubidium, cesium; and group IB: copper, silver, gold. The LANTHANIDE metals (at. nos. 58–71) are placed in a special sequence in group III, being confusingly like one another. The ACTINIDES for the same reason also are placed in a special sequence.—*J. R.*

Metallurgy in Germany, 16th cent.: Efforts to extract useful metals from their ores had created, by the beginning of the Renaissance, a complex technology whose roots lay deep in ancient history; but metallurgy as a science was yet to evolve. Illustration is from Agricola's *De re metallica* (1556).

METALLURGY: the science and technology of metals, including extraction of metals from ores, processing of metals into useful form, and the study of their properties and behavior. Metallurgy as a scientific discipline includes areas of physics, chemistry, and applied mechanics; and a recent uptrend of scientific investigation has resulted in a tremendous acceleration of metallurgical development, with intensified exploration and development of new metal and alloy systems. The branch of metallurgy called *metallography* deals with the microscopic structure and constitution of metals and alloys; another phase of metallurgical science deals with the internal changes that metals undergo during thermal and mechanical treatment. The engineering phases are concerned with winning of metals from their ores (extractive metallurgy), consolidation and solidification of the metal into massive form, alloying, processing and fabrication, heat treatment, engineering properties and behavior, and practical utilization.

Although the art of metallurgy is ancient, only in the past century has a true science of metallurgy developed. Indeed, since 1900 more metal has been extracted from Earth's crust than had been extracted up to that time from the beginning of man's history. Before 6000 B. C. man knew of no useful metal; he made his tools, weapons, and utensils from wood, stone, and bones. In about 4000 B. C. a method for smelting copper was discovered in W Asia; and as early as 3000 B. C. techniques of welding, joining, riveting, surface treatment, and anti-rust coating were being developed. The use of metals spread slowly from Asia to other parts of the world, and by A. D. 1000 metals were widely exploited not only in Asia but in N Africa and most of Europe. The progress of civilization has been closely linked to increasing knowledge and application of metals; thus certain progressive stages of civilization have been labeled the Bronze Age and the Iron Age by archeologists. Only seven metals were known during the period of antiquity: gold, copper, silver, lead, tin, iron, and mercury (listed here in probable order of discovery and application). For many thousands of years copper was the most important of these, and the original smelters of copper were believed to be magicians with a "God-given art." Iron was first smelted about 1500 B. C., but was not widely used until after 500 B. C. No new metals emerged until about A. D. 500; steel was not deliberately produced until about A. D. 1740. But the flourishing of alchemy in the Middle Ages distinctly aided the development of metallurgy. In searching both for a "philosopher's stone" to change base metals into noble ones and for an "elixir," or universal medicine, to cure all ills and prolong human life, the alchemists made contributions that laid the foundations for modern metallurgy. They discovered and recorded much about the chemical properties of metals. The production of pure metals demanded the development of laboratory techniques and scientific apparatus; the concept of quantitative accuracy and the means of achieving it in practice, *e.g.* ASSAYING, were introduced. Alchemy and the notion of transmutation died about the end of the 16th cent.; transmutation became a reality in modern times only with the discovery of atomic fission. Also during the Middle Ages much metallurgical interest centered on processes for winning iron from its ores. Coal began to replace charcoal for iron-smelting after about 1650, but the great advances in iron and steel metallurgy occurred during the 18th cent., particularly with the use of coke in steelmaking. By 1800 other elements had begun to achieve technological importance, *e.g.* arsenic, antimony, bismuth, zinc, and platinum. However, the development of the blast furnace by Bessemer in 1859 and of Siemen's open-hearth furnace in 1864, together forming the basis of our present steel industry, marked the real beginning of the modern era of metallurgy.

Extractive Metallurgy: Metals occur only rarely in the free or uncombined state and thus must be separated from their ores. Such processes as mineral dressing (ore concentration), leaching, roasting, smelting, electrolysis, and amalgamation may be involved, depending upon the nature of the metal and its ore. Most ores contain waste materials, or *gangue* (*e.g.* sand, clay, gravel); *mineral dressing* eliminates as much gangue as possible, usually by chemical methods or density differences. A widely used method is the FLOTATION process, in which finely crushed ore is agitated in water containing chemical frothing agents. The metal-containing particles float in the froth and are skimmed off, while the unwanted minerals sink to the bottom of the tank. *Leaching* (*e.g.* cyanide leaching of gold) consists of treating finely powdered ore with chemicals, dissolving the metal of interest, and subsequently reprecipitating this metal from solution (see LEACHING). Concentrated ores usually contain the metal combined with oxygen, *e.g.* iron oxide; the oxide is converted to the pure metal by reduction (smelting) or by electrolysis. On the other hand, some ores contain metals in the form of sulfides (*e.g.* zinc or lead); these sulfides must be heated in air, or *roasted*, to convert the sulfides into oxides prior to smelting. The fundamental purpose of *smelting* is to convert (reduce) the metal oxide in the ore to free metal. Some form of carbon,

usually coke, is employed as the reducing agent; the carbon unites with the oxygen and passes off as a gas. The temperature of the process is sufficient to cause the metal to melt as it is formed. Other addition agents may be used to combine with the gangue and form a liquid layer of waste products, known as *slag*, which floats on top of the molten metal. In the Bessemer blast furnace for the smelting of iron, coke and limestone are used for the reducing and slag-producing reactions. The smelted free metal still contains substantial amounts of impurities and must be further refined or purified. (See BESSEMER PROCESS; SMELTING.) *Electrolytic processes* are also employed in the primary production of metals from their ores. Aluminum is obtained by the electrolysis of molten salts, and magnesium is produced by the electrolysis of concentrated brines from sea water. Likewise, copper is refined to a high degree of purity by electrolytic methods. (See CELL, ELECTROLYTIC; ELECTROLYSIS.) Gold and silver frequently are recovered from their ores by a process of amalgamation in which mercury is used to form a compound with the gold or silver. Subsequent heating drives off the mercury in vapor form, leaving a residue or sponge of pure gold or silver.

Production and Process Metallurgy: The processing of refined metals into useful finished shapes can require any number of processing operations, including consolidation and solidification, alloying, shaping and forming, heat treatment, and joining. Electric furnaces, arc furnaces, and vacuum furnaces are utilized to melt large masses of metal prior to pouring the metal into molds to form ingots. The open-hearth furnace is mainly used for steel. (See ELECTRIC FURNACE; FURNACE; OPEN-HEARTH PROCESS.) Alloying, *i.e.* the addition of other metals and elements to the base metal to impart special properties, is performed during the melting operation. Metals such as titanium, molybdenum, and zirconium (of great interest today because of their military and nuclear-reactor uses) require special vacuum or inert-atmosphere furnaces for their preparation because they react readily with gaseous elements, *e.g.* oxygen and nitrogen, and are thereby embrittled. Finished and semi-finished shapes may be made directly by *casting* the molten metal or alloy into properly prepared molds; or metal or alloy powders may be pressed into the desired shape by a combination of high pressure and temperature.

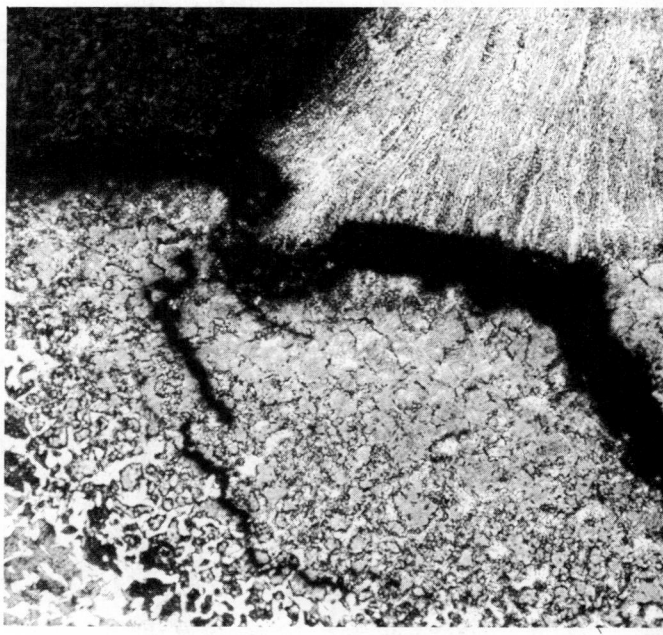

Mechanical metallurgy: Microscopic inspection revealed origin of fracture in steel bar from a lock in the St. Lawrence Seaway. Steel at the most highly stressed point was embrittled by effect of heavy weld (entire *upper-right* section of photograph) and finally cracked because of dimensional changes during cold weather. Brittle steel adjacent to the toe of this weld (*middle right*) is easily distinguished from the normal structure of the metal (*lower left*). (*National Bur. of Standards*)

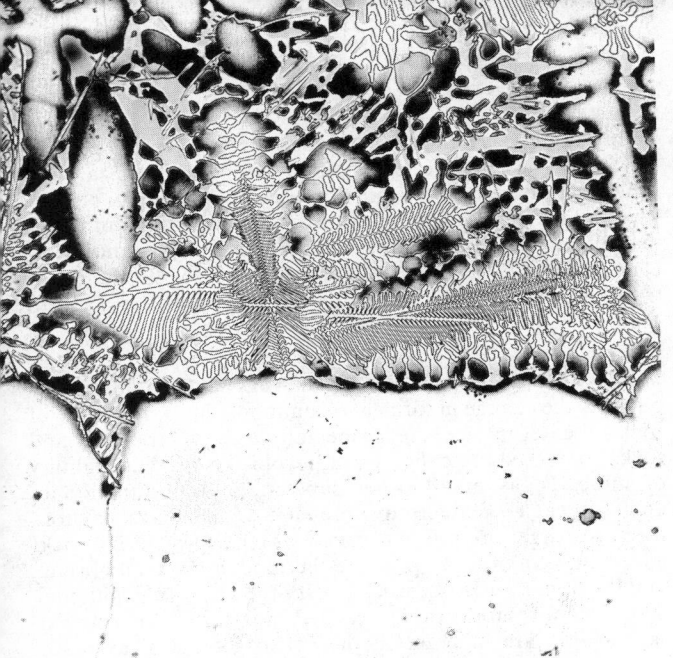

Modern metallurgical microscopes reveal internal structure of metals and alloys. Pictured here is a section of Iconel X, a wrought alloy of nickel, chromium, and several other elements, used for supercharger and gas-turbine parts because of its high strength at elevated temperatures. Unusual pattern is caused by diffusion of silicon into alloy; no more than 0.5% silicon is allowable in Iconel X. (*Westinghouse*)

Ingots are processed into bars, rods, sheet, wire, and other semi-finished shapes by a series of mechanical working or shaping processes. *Forging, extrusion, swaging, rolling,* and *drawing* are some of the primary processing operations. Most of these operations are performed after the metal has been heated to high temperatures so that it is malleable and can be readily worked, although the final "sizing" operation may take place at only moderate or room temperature. Fabrication of metals into finished shapes is accomplished by *forming, stamping, cupping, deep drawing,* and related cold-working operations. Alloys can be made that are considerably harder and stronger than pure metals, and further modifications of almost any given physical or chemical property can be obtained by heat treatment. Typical heat-treatment processes are normalizing, age-hardening, quenching, tempering, annealing, and stress-relieving. These treatments can produce alloys of the desired strength, toughness, magnetic properties, wear-resistance, corrosion-resistance, and other specific characteristics.

Metallurgy as a Science: The physical, chemical, and mechanical properties of any metal (or alloy) are a function of its internal structure; in turn the structure has been determined by the metal's chemical composition and the mechanical-working and heat-treating processes to which the metal (or alloy) has been subjected. The study of the microstructure of metals and of the relationships between composition, structure, and properties underlies the modern science of metals. The differences among metals and the effects of processing and heat treatment on metal microstructure can be observed with metallurgical microscopes. Because metals are opaque, their surfaces must be examined by reflected light, and highly polished and etched metal samples must be used. Metallographic techniques for the examination of the metal microstructures date from the work of H. C. Sorby in 1865. Today the metallurgist has at his disposal a wide range of equipment to study the atomic and crystalline structure of metals and alloys. Through the use of new techniques and instruments such as x-ray diffraction, electron diffraction, electron and nuclear magnetic resonance, electron-transmission microscopy, and field and thermionic-emission microscopy, a rapid increase in knowledge of the structure and properties of metals and alloys has occurred, with a consequent advance in metals technology. Current areas of major interest are (1) *physical metallurgy,* which includes the study of alloying behavior, metal and alloy structure, internal transformations which occur with mechanical working and heat treatment, and observations of physical properties; (2) *mechanical metallurgy,* which considers the strength and ductility properties of metals and alloys and their deformation and fracture behavior; and (3) *chemical metallurgy,* covering the physical chemistry and thermodynamics of metal-producing reactions, chemical behavior of metals and alloys, corrosion, and surface reactivity. See ALLOY; METAL; MINING.—*J. J. H.*

METALS IN BIOLOGY: A variety of metals, or rather ions derived from them, form integral and essential constituents of the cells of all living organisms. In this they may: (1) function as actual participants in chemical reactions; (2) form part of the functionally active region of macromolecules of biological importance, *e.g.* the enzymes, certain hormones, and nucleic acids; (3) maintain biologically active macromolecules in appropriate configurations or conformations; and (4) fulfill the same role with respect to subcellular organelles and constituents, cells, and tissues by maintaining their physical integrity and physiological role. Our understanding of the metal requirements of animals and plants rests on reasonably firm grounds; much more uncertainty attends the role of certain metals as growth factors for microorganisms: The latter is, however, more an experimental than a real difference, since it is frequently difficult, if not impossible, to obtain growth media completely free of the last traces of certain metal impurities. In general, the following list of required elements might be expected to extend over all of living nature, the quantities required differing vastly between species and according to different stages of development and varying environments within the same species: Group I—potassium, magnesium; Group II—sodium, calcium; Group III—iron, cobalt, copper, manganese, zinc, molybdenum; Group IV—aluminum, vanadium; Group V—boron, selenium. Metals in Group I are required in bulk quantity by higher animals, but only in trace amounts, if at all, by plants and microorganisms; those in Group II are required in reasonably high concentration for almost all species; those in Group III appear essential in trace amounts for most species; those in Group IV are required for certain scattered species or genera, *e.g.* aluminum for certain higher plants and vanadium for plants and tunicates; while the elements in Group V also seem required for certain species only. These last are really nonmetallic but possess certain metallic features which make their inclusion appropriate. It is an axiom of contemporary biochemistry that micronutrients in general must play their role as parts of catalysts rather than as actual participants in reactions, and catalytic, *i.e.* enzyme, systems which specifically either contain or require all the trace elements listed above have indeed been found. Among the most important are: iron, which is found linked to certain proteins either as a complex with such organic molecules as porphyrins and riboflavin or linked to the protein directly, forms an integral part of many important oxidative enzymes as well as of hemoglobin; copper, which forms the "active center" of enzymes that catalyze the oxidation of a variety of organic compounds, and also forms part of hemocyanin (the oxygen-carrying pigment of certain invertebrates); molybdenum, which seems important in reduction of nitrate and oxidation of aldehydes and purines; zinc, which forms part of pyridine nucleotide-requiring dehydrogenases which interact with a large variety of organic molecules; and cobalt, an essential part of vitamin B_{12}. Magnesium seems to be required in almost all reactions involving inorganic or organic phosphates; it is also vital in bone formation and forms part of the chlorophyll molecule. Potassium is the principal cation in most cells and, together with magnesium, is required for maintenance of the structure of a variety of macromolecules and organelles such as cell membranes. Calcium fulfills an essential role in bone formation and blood coagulation.

Heme (ferrous protoporphyrin IX) unites with the protein globin (to form hemoglobin) as well as with many other proteins.

Metal Complexes: Most of the metallic ions of importance to living organisms exist within the cell, not free in solution but in association with other organic or inorganic entities which may be neutral molecules or anions, forming metal complexes or chelates which will then be either neutral or positively or negatively charged. Among the most important complex-formers (donors, ligands) are phosphoric acids, organic phosphate esters (including polymeric forms such as the nucleic acids), keto acids (*e.g.* oxalacetic, pyruvic, acetoacetic), hydroxy acids (*e.g.* lactic, malic, citric), and especially amino acids, either free or as constituents of proteins, as well as porphyrins and their derivatives (in chlorophyll and vitamin B_{12}). The most common porphyrin is protoporphyrin IX; its iron $^{+2}$ derivative is known as *heme* and forms part of the oxygen-carrying protein, hemoglobin. —H. M.

METAMATHEMATICS: a method for the investigation of the foundations of mathematics through the study of mathematics as a formalized language (see SYNTAX, LOGICAL). This language is called the *object language,* while the language which we use to study the object language is called the *metalanguage.* (Similarly, when an English-speaking person studies the French language, the object language is French and the metalanguage is English.) Since one of the main purposes of metamathematics is to prove the consistency of a sufficiently strong formalized language of mathematics, it seems reasonable that the metalanguage should use only those notions and methods of proof which are simpler and less susceptible to doubt than those of the object language itself. Such notions and methods are called *finitistic,* but, except for a weak fragment of arithmetic, there is no general agreement about the precise scope of finitistic ideas. It was proved by Gödel (see GÖDEL'S PROOF) that, in order to prove the consistency of a sufficiently strong formalized mathematical system, the metalanguage used cannot be included within or be identical with the object language. In fact, when Gentzen proved in 1936 the consistency of a system of formalized number theory, he used a fragment of the theory of ordinal numbers, which could not be imbedded

within the given system of number theory. Whether Gentzen's methods and different methods proposed by Gödel and others are to be called finitistic seems to be a matter of individual preference. Many other important results in metamathematics have been obtained by Alfred Tarski and members of his school. These relate especially to the notion of truth in formalized languages, to decision procedures, and to the theory of models.—*El. M.*

METAMORPHISM AND METAMORPHIC ROCKS: Metamorphism is the change in form, and commonly in composition, of rock by external agencies, especially heat or pressure, and rocks so altered are called metamorphic rocks. The stability of minerals, as of all other substances, is a function of environment. As temperature, pressure, and chemical environments change, the mineral suites which characterize rocks also change in order to preserve thermodynamic equilibrium, and the trends are in accordance with the phase rule (although actual equilibrium is rarely reached in nature). Environmental changes are inherent in the cyclic geological events of Earth's crust, encompassing uplift, weathering, erosion, deposition, consolidation, burial, downwarping (with associated rise in temperature), orogeny (= tectonics = diastrophism = mountain building, with associated forces of compression and differential movement), igneous activity, then uplift again. Cycles varied in frequency from region to region throughout geological time, and individual cycles were not always complete (thus downwarping and orogeny need not have been accompanied by igneous activity, and igneous activity has occurred without appreciable orogenic activity). Changes in rocks that are associated with weathering, erosion, deposition, and consolidation are considered to be sedimentary processes (see SEDIMENTARY ROCK). All other changes induced in rocks in the geological cycle are thought to be metamorphic (short of total remelting, in which case the resulting rocks cannot be distinguished from primary IGNEOUS ROCKS). Changes induced by deep burial, downwarping, and orogenic processes are termed *regional metamorphism.* Changes induced by heat and components derived from invading magmas are termed *contact metamorphism.* Wherever orogeny was accompanied by igneous activity, the metamorphic effects have been merged and often no distinction is possible. Metamorphic effects range from simple recrystallization and coarsening of original constituents to reactions between constituents, with development of entirely new suites of minerals. Metamorphism may be progressive or retrogressive, depending on increase or decrease of temperature and pressure. As metamorphism progresses, hydrous and open-mesh crystal structures give way to anhydrous and progressively denser packings.

Some minerals have stronger crystallizing forces than others, and when the required thermodynamic conditions are reached, the constituents of the stronger minerals will diffuse through the rock and accumulate on more or less evenly distributed nuclei to form conspicuous crystals (metacrysts-porphyroblasts) which may become considerably larger than the crystals of the intervening (matrix) minerals. Garnet, staurolite, kyanite, and andalusite commonly form conspicuous metacrysts in phyllites and schists.

When recrystallization occurs under compression, platy or elongate minerals grow with their longer axes normal to the direction of the applied stress, thus accounting for the planar structures of slate, phyllite, schist, and some gneisses. Most platy minerals have perfect cleavage in the same plane, thereby accounting for the fissility (cleavage) of those rocks.

Layering of constituents (foliation, or "gneissosity") in metamorphic rocks may be inherited in part from primary layered structures such as sedimentary bedding or igneous

PROGRESSIVE METAMORPHISM OF COMMON ROCKS

Rocks Before Metamorphism   Rocks After Metamorphism

SEDIMENTARY PROCESSES				METAMORPHIC PROCESSES			
Original Deposition	Consolidation (diagenesis); Shallow Burial	Compaction; Moderate Burial	Moderate Compression (orogenic); Moderate Burial	Increasing Orogenic Intensity and/or Depth of Burial (Downwarping)			Deep Burial; Equalized Pressure
Gravel	Conglomerate			Quartzitic Conglomerate	Stretched-pebble Conglomerate		Quartzitic Conglomerate
Sand	Sandstone			Quartzite			Quartzite
Silt	Siltstone			Quartzite			Quartzite
Clay and Mud	Mudstone	Shale	Slate	Phyllite	Schist	Paragneiss	Granulite
Calcareous Marl	Chalk	Limestone		Marble		Flowage Marble	Marble
Shell Beds	Coquina						
Coral	Coral Rock	Dolomitic Limestone		Dolomitic Marble		Brucitic-flowage Marble	Brucitic Marble
Sandy and Muddy Marls	Sandy and Muddy Limestone	Sandy and Shaly Limestone; Dolomitic Limestone	Sandy and Slaty Limestone; Dolomitic Limestone	Schistose Marbles	Schistose Lime and Magnesium Silicate Rocks; Some Skarns	Gneissic Lime and Magnesium Silicate Rocks; Skarns	Massive Lime and Magnesium Silicate Rocks; Skarns
Peat	Lignite	Bituminous Coal	Anthracite Coal	Graphitic Anthracite		Graphite	Graphite

Acidic Volcanic Rocks				Phyllite	Schist	Acidic Orthogneiss	Granulite
Basic Volcanic Rocks				Greenstone Chlorite Schist	Hornblende Schist	Basic Orthogneiss Amphibolite	Eclogite

flowage, but in part may be caused by segregation of constituents during recrystallization under stress, in which case the metamorphic structures may transect the relict primary structures; thus the foliation developed by an amphibolite may cut across the still recognizable primary flow structures of the basalt it replaces (palimpsest structure). When foliated metamorphic rocks are invaded by intrusives, magmatic material may be infused along the foliation planes (*lit-par-lit* injection), forming composite gneisses (or injection gneisses).

In regional metamorphism the mineral suites that are developed at any given grade are directly related to the original composition of the rock except where there has been extensive addition of material; thus a sandstone composed almost entirely of pure quartz, SiO_2, will become a nearly pure quartzite, but if the original sandstone contains some calcite, $CaCO_3$, this will react with the quartz at about 500° to 600°C to form wollastonite, $CaSiO_3$. The stability ranges of individual minerals or reactive suites of minerals may thus serve as geological thermometers and indicate the maximum grade of metamorphism. These standards are useful only if metastable relics have been preserved in the rocks now accessible, or if the existing minerals are pseudomorphic and preserve recognizable crystal outlines or textures of the higher grade minerals; *e.g.* uralitic amphibole pseudomorphic after pyroxene crystals, and chlorite pseudomorphs after garnet crystals. Relative degrees of metamorphism to which a terrane has been subjected are shown on geological maps by *isograd contours,* which outline zones of equal intensity as indicated by the mineral suites.

The presence of a contact metamorphic aureole and the configuration of its isograds can serve to delineate an intrusive body even though it may not appear at the surface. The composition of the mineral suites developed in a contact aureole depends not only on the original host rock but also on materials transferred in gaseous (pneumatolytic) or hydrothermal form from the crystallizing intrusive. Fluid residues (mother liquors) which remain after most of the magma has crystallized are rich in hyperfusibles ("mineralizers") such as water, fluorine, sulfur, boron, and carbon dioxide, and may thus have profound effects on the wall rocks. Limestone and dolomite are particularly susceptible to silication and other forms of alteration. There is much evidence that certain ore deposits have been formed by precipitation of metals, generally as sulfides, in the country rocks adjacent to intrusive bodies. Tactite is the general term for the calcium-magnesium silicate masses formed by contact metamorphism of carbonate rocks. Skarns are tactites that contain iron-bearing silicates and are commonly associated with magnetite deposits of contact-metamorphic origin. Hornfels is a catch-all term for various dense, fine-grained, usually dark rocks resulting from moderate contact metamorphism of shales. For metamorphism that may result in granites, see GRANITE.

The regional metamorphism of most intrusive and plutonic igneous rocks is generally limited to the retrograde direction, since such rocks are inherently stable at relatively high temperatures and pressures. Under conditions of stress and differential movement these rocks develop a gneissic foliation, and elongate crystals may grow in a preferred orientation.

Where two kinds of rock of appreciably different composition are in contact, they may under certain conditions enter into joint reactions, forming gradational zones from one rock to the other. See Color Plate 61.—*L. M.*

METAMORPHOSIS: in biology, the radical changes of body form that some animals undergo during their development after hatching from the egg. The most familiar examples are found among insects and amphibians. Many young insects have a form entirely different from that of their parents, and transform into the adult form only when about to become sexually mature. Thus the young dragonfly (called a nymph or naiad) is a rapacious creature that lives in pond water and has no resemblance to its winged parents. A young mosquito (known as a wiggler) also lives in fresh water; it would not be recognized for what it is if we did not know too well that

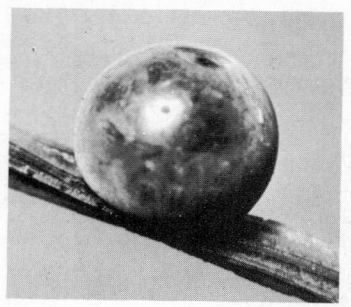

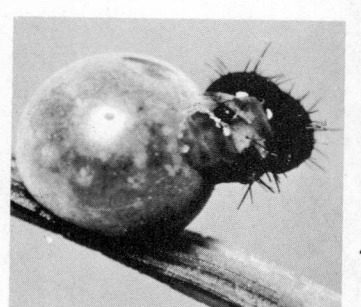

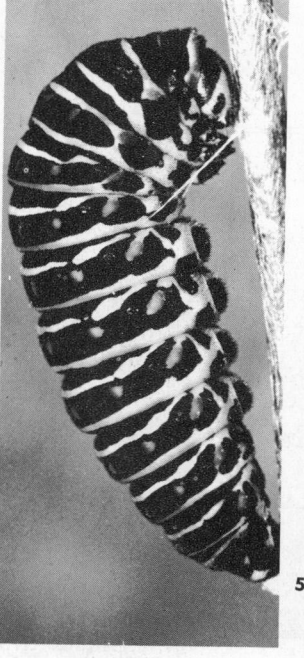

it turns eventually into an adult mosquito. A young housefly is a soft maggot without external legs or wings; a young wasp or a juvenile honeybee is a grub that is reared in a cell of the comb and fed by adult members of the colony. A young moth or butterfly is a caterpillar, well adapted to voracious feeding and to crawling and climbing.

Development of the frog after hatching: (A) Recently hatched tadpole. (B) Young tadpoles clinging to submerged plant. (C) External-gill stage. (D) Internal-gill stage, with breathing pore. (E) Tadpole with hind legs developed. (F) Tail nearly absorbed. (G) Adult. (*From Walcott*)

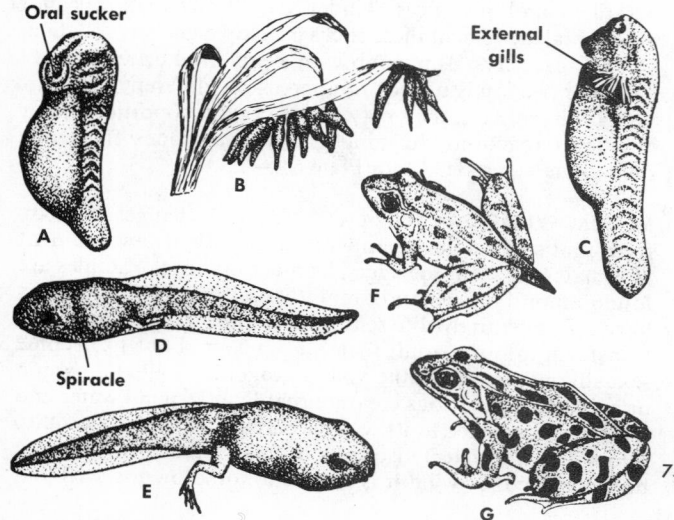

Oral sucker

External gills

A

B

C

Spiracle

D

E

F

G

Nymphs and naiads of grasshoppers, dragonflies, and some other insects transform directly to adult form and are said to have a *direct metamorphosis*. The larvae of moths and butterflies, however, are like those of beetles, flies, bees, and wasps, in that they enter first a preliminary reconstructive stage (known as a pupa) from which the adult emerges; this is an *indirect* or *complete metamorphosis*. A pair of small glands close to the brain of the juvenile insect secretes a hormone that inhibits metamorphosis until the individual has attained an adequate state of nutrition and of size; then another hormone, from the brain itself, allows the suppressed adult characteristics to develop through the metamorphosis.

Among insects and amphibians, dispersal of the species is accomplished chiefly during the adult, reproductive stage; juvenile individuals are most conspicuously adapted toward feeding, growth, and protection from enemies. Thus only the adult stage of insects is winged. Elsewhere in the animal kingdom, by contrast, wherever metamorphosis is found, the juvenile individuals comprise the stage at which dispersal of the species is usually accomplished. In many cases, the young, prior to metamorphosis, are carried easily for long distances by water currents, whereas the adults move about over a more limited area of the bottom.

Other examples of animals in which the young differ radically in form from their parents are found among marine worms, mollusks, crustaceans, coelenterates, and echinoderms. Young polychaete worms in the *trochophore* stage are minute, top-shaped creatures that drift in the sea and swim freely by means of circles of cilia. Many marine snails go through an immature stage known as a *veliger,* during which they are carried by currents and move by means of cilia, before settling down on the bottom where they mature. The eggs of some fresh-water clams hatch into a minute bivalved *glochidium,* which can seize hold of the skin or gills of a fish, burrow into the body as a temporary parasite, and be carried for several weeks before emerging and dropping to the bottom, where it changes into the adult form. Various crustaceans go through a series of larval stages. Barnacles hatch as minute *nauplii,* which seem to be all head; they have a simple eye and swim by energetically waving their only paired appendages—two pairs of short antennae and a pair of long slender mandibles. In a few hours or days, each transforms into a *cyprid* stage,

754

7   8   9

Stages in the life cycle of the swallowtail butterfly are shown on these pages. (1) Egg. (2) Larva breaking open shell. (3) Larva completely emerged from egg. (4) Caterpillar larva begins to spin cocoon (after 15-min interval). (5, 6, 7) Caterpillar completes cacoon (in 3 days). (8) Pupa, or chrysalis. (9) Adult emerging from pupal case. (10) Adult with wings, fully emerged from cocoon. (*Hermann Eisenbeiss, Munich*)

10

in which the thorax, with additional swimming appendages, and a short abdomen are partly concealed by a bivalved carapace. The cyprid settles to the bottom, cements itself to some solid object by means of glands on its second antennae, and transforms into the adult body form—never to move about again. Some other crustacean larvae become adapted to a parasitic life on or even within the bodies of other animals. Many coelenterates go through a ciliated *planula* stage before becoming attached to the bottom. Most echinoderms go through a free-swimming, pelagic, ciliated *dipleurula* stage, which is bilaterally symmetrical; later they transform into an adult body form showing a radial pattern.

Probably all of these examples of metamorphosis are controlled by hormones. In amphibians, two endocrine glands are involved. The anterior lobe of the pituitary in a fully grown tadpole begins secreting more thyrotropic hormone, which stimulates the thyroid gland to add more thyroxin to the blood stream. Tissues all over the tadpole of a frog or toad respond to the extra thyroxin: the tail atrophies, and its vertebrae fuse into an inconspicuous urostyle; the lungs develop, and gills (as well as the gill openings) disappear; the front legs burst from inconspicuous pockets, and the back legs develop into efficient jumping organs; the skin acquires a pattern of pigment cells; the eyes enlarge and their light-sensitive pigment undergoes changes that make it more efficient for perceiving light received from air; the tongue enlarges, and the digestive tract shortens, preparing the animal for a diet of insects and worms to replace the vegetable diet. Amphibians with defective anterior pituitary or thyroid glands fail to metamorphose. Tadpoles that have not yet reached full size can often be induced to metamorphose early if they are fed thyroid gland tissue or injected with either thyrotropic hormone or thyroxin.—*R. E. S.*

METASTABLE STATE: in a physical system, an EXCITED STATE that persists for a longer time (100 times or more) than a nor-

mal one. A system in this state cannot decay into a less energetic one via a more rapid mode without violating some conservation law. In chemistry the term "metastable" is applied to any phase or system that can persist without change for appreciable periods of time even though it is not at thermodynamic equilibrium. Thus, supercooled liquids are said to be in a metastable state. See ENERGY LEVEL.—*S. Bo.*

METAZOA: many-celled animals, as distinguished from single-celled ones (PROTOZOA). Although SPONGES are multicellular, they are often excluded from the Metazoa category because of the rather loose organization of their structure. The animal kingdom is sometimes divided into the subkingdoms Protozoa, Parazoa (sponges), and Metazoa. See ANIMAL.—*L. and M. M.*

METCHNIKOFF, ELIE, 1845–1916, Russian bacteriologist; b. Kharkov. His early research was on the anatomy of the invertebrates. He discovered that bacteria are destroyed by phagocytes (1892)—a defense mechanism that is of great importance in acute diseases. In recognition of his work in immunity he was awarded the 1908 Nobel prize, sharing it with P. Ehrlich. In 1887 he left his position as professor of zoology at the Univ. of Odessa and became Pasteur's associate in Paris, succeeding Pasteur as director of the Pasteur Institute (1895). Metchnikoff was particularly interested in studies on longevity, believing that a human lifetime of 150 yr was not an unreasonable expectation. He was a fellow of the Royal Society.—D. H. D. R.

METEOR: in astronomy, a streak of light seen in the sky when a relatively small, solid body from interplanetary space penetrates Earth's atmosphere and disintegrates or vaporizes from friction; popularly, a "shooting star." "Meteor" may also mean the object that produces the streak of light. Fragments that reach the ground are METEORITES. A depression or hole made in Earth's surface by the impact of a large meteorite is called a METEOR CRATER.

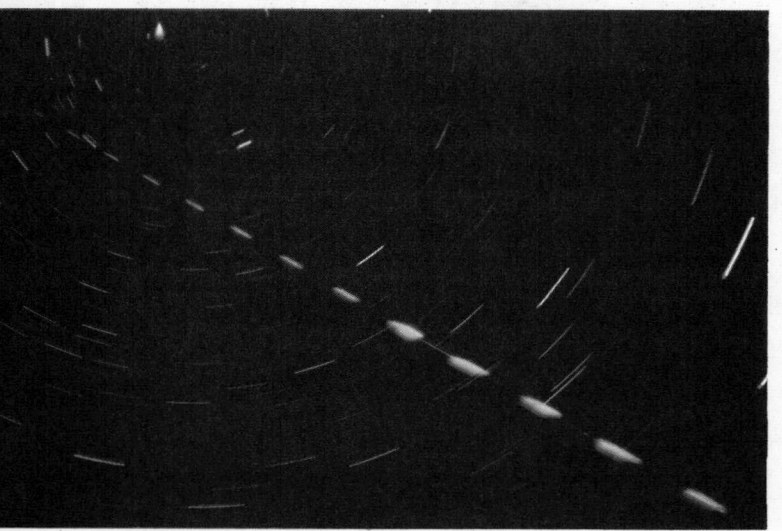

Track of Perseid meteor photographed at intervals of 1/10 sec. Rotation of Earth caused stars to trace circular paths around pole during 25-min. exposure. (*Millman/Nat. Research Council, Ottawa*)

Millions of meteors are encountered by Earth in its orbit daily, but even on a moonless night away from city lights and haze, only 5 to 10 meteors per hr are visible. The largest numbers are visible after midnight, because then the observer's side of Earth is facing in the direction of Earth's motion in its orbit. Only a small fraction of the meteors encountered, however, can be seen from one place. Roughly 200 million meteors capable of making a flash bright enough to be seen at night enter the atmosphere each 24 hr.

The average meteor is not spectacular; it is a swift-moving point of light which appears as a streak because of its high velocity across the observer's line of sight. Bright meteors may actually leave a faintly glowing train of incandescent material which may last for a few seconds or, in rare cases, for minutes. Such a train generally becomes distorted into a snakelike form by the winds of the upper atmosphere.

The very brilliant meteors, called *fireballs,* are truly spectacular. The head may assume a tear-drop form and exhibit various colors. Bursts of light appear along the path; small pieces and sparks are scattered behind the head. These exceptional meteors may penetrate well down into the atmosphere and reach a level where sound is carried; then rumbles and shock-wave detonations are heard by the observer some minutes after the object has been seen.

At certain times of year, meteors appear in greater numbers than usual from some particular area of the heavens; the phenomenon is called a meteor shower. Although the average shower is not striking, some in the past have been of frightening intensity. Accounts of "stars falling like rain" may be found in ancient records. All meteors belonging to a particular "shower" are traveling along nearly parallel paths in space as they meet Earth; hence the perspective effect of radiation from a point among the stars. The name of the shower is derived from the star constellation in which this point, the "radiant," is located.

PROMINENT METEOR SHOWERS

Shower	Date of Maximum	Hourly Number of Meteors Seen at Maximum	Shower Duration (days)	Meteor Velocity (mi/sec)
Quadrantid	Jan. 3	40	1	25
Lyrid	Apr. 21	15	2	30
Perseid	Aug. 11	60	5	37
Orionid	Oct. 20	30	8	41
Leonid	Nov. 16	20	4	44
Geminid	Dec. 13	60	6	22

A meteor leaves charged particles along its path, a column of electrons and ions that is dense enough to reflect radio waves. Hence meteors can be detected by radar and studied during daylight and in cloudy periods. The light of meteors originates in a glowing gas, a mixture of atoms from the meteoric particle and from the air; in this respect the light is somewhat similar to that produced in fluorescent lighting systems. Each atom shines with its characteristic group of monochromatic hues. In the spectra of meteors are commonly found the yellow light of sodium, the green light of magnesium, and the violet light of calcium. Evidence of iron appears throughout the whole range from red to ultraviolet, while oxygen and nitrogen are particularly strong in the infrared.

As the original meteoric particle enters Earth's atmosphere at high velocity, it presumably collides directly with air molecules. The force of these collisions converts the solid into a cloud of gas and dust; the original energy of motion is transformed, producing light, heat, and charged particles. There is evidence that the average particle breaks up fairly easily; hence it is probably a body of fairly low over-all density, possibly quite porous, perhaps a "dustball."

Numerous meteors invisible to the unaided eye are seen in telescopes or recorded by radio methods. Still lower in the scale of size is meteoric dust that never reaches the luminous stage. It can be detected by instruments mounted in artificial satellites or rockets and is collected from deep-sea sediments and isolated areas of Earth's surface. At least several thousand tons of this material enters Earth's atmosphere daily. The total weight represented by visible meteors is probably very much smaller than this, but current knowledge of the masses of individual meteors is approximate only. A particle producing a meteor comparable to a bright star possibly has a weight somewhere between 1 oz and 1/100 oz.

Until recently, most studies of meteors were visual. Recent advances in photographic and radio techniques have made possible the instrumental recording of meteors and more accurate knowledge of them. Accurate heights and velocities of meteors can be determined through two-station photography (giving parallax), by using cameras equipped with occulting shutters, or by multiple-station radio observations. On the average, the faster meteors appear and disappear higher in the atmosphere than do the slower objects. A typical meteor moving 40 mi/sec becomes visible at a height near 70 mi and disappears 10 to 20 mi below this; one moving only 10 mi/sec appears about 50 mi up and disappears at a height of 40 mi or lower.

Knowing the speed and direction of motion of a meteor, we can calculate its space orbit. Shower meteors have orbits in the form of elongated ellipses about the Sun. The great majority, and possibly all, of these shower orbits correspond closely to the orbits of known COMETS—a fact which points to a cometary origin for shower meteors. Among meteors whose velocities have been accurately measured, none have been found moving fast enough to indicate that they could escape from the Sun's gravitational field; hence most meteors seen must be members of the solar system.—*P. M.*

METEOR CRATER: any of the many craterlike depressions in Earth's crust believed to have been caused by the impact of meteorites. Most meteorites penetrate only a few inches, or at the most a few feet, into the ground when they fall; but a large mass will not be slowed down much by air resistance and may hit the ground with a velocity of as much as 10 to 20 mi/sec. The energy thus dissipated almost instantaneously will act explosively, creating a crater like that from a high-explosive shell but much larger, and scattering meteoritic fragments over the vicinity. The mineral COESITE and the odd rock formations called SHATTER CONES may be the results of meteoritic impacts. Small craters ranging from 10 to 100 ft in diameter were produced by a meteorite fall in Siberia in 1947. In prehistoric times much larger craters were produced in the same way: Meteor (Barringer) Crater in Arizona, perhaps 20,000 yr old, is 4,200 ft across and 600 ft deep, and a number of circular features in Canada, with diameters ranging from 1 to 10 mi, give evidence of meteoritic impacts hundreds of millions of years ago. The surface of the Moon shows evidence of a similar bombardment, though not all the circular features seen on the lunar surface were thus produced.—*P. M.*

Meteor (Barringer) Crater near Winslow, Ariz. (*below*), was the first identified as due to a meteor. (*Ariz. State Trav. Comm.*)

METEORITE: a fragment of metallic or stony material reaching Earth from an extraterrestrial body that has penetrated the atmosphere, become heated by friction, and broken up or vaporized. Meteorites are produced by METEORS. Dust from a meteor may remain in the atmosphere indefinitely, possibly serving as condensation nuclei that cause PRECIPITATION. A very small percentage of meteors result in fragments large enough to reach the ground. These fragments are either nickel-iron of a very hard type, or heavier-than-average stones, which generally contain significant quantities of metallic nickel-iron inclusions. Freshly fallen specimens are covered with a dark, relatively smooth crust a few hundredths of an inch thick.

The meteoritic body passes through the air at high speed due chiefly to its original velocity in space relative to the Earth, and increased by the gravitational pull of Earth. Its surface is rapidly vaporized until its velocity has been so much slowed that the temperature of the stone or iron is no longer above

Fluffy micrometeorite (*above*), highly magnified here, is about 1/25,000 in. long. (*C. L. Hemenway/Dudley Obs.*)

Fourteen-ton iron meteorite found in Willamette Valley, Oreg.: The holes are thought to be the result of weathering during the years following impact. (*Amer. Mus./Hayden Planetarium*)

METEOROLOGICAL INSTRUMENTS: Like most scientific apparatus, meteorological instruments must be precise, yet because they are generally used outdoors in all kinds of weather they must also be rugged—able to withstand heat, cold, moisture, and strong winds. Many weather instruments must be capable of installation in remote locations and of maintenance and use by little-trained personnel.

Instruments Used Near Earth's Surface: The most familiar instrument for measuring air temperature is the type of thermometer consisting of a glass tube filled with a liquid, *e.g.* mercury or alcohol. With increasing temperature the liquid expands, rising into the stem and indicating temperature on a scale engraved on the glass. In general, mercury thermometers are more accurate than alcohol types for most meteorological purposes, but since mercury freezes at $-38°F$, alcohol (which freezes at $-202°F$) is ordinarily used for measuring very low temperatures. The bimetallic thermometer, another type, is based on the different thermal expansion characteristics of two metals. Special thermometers have been developed for measuring the highest and lowest temperatures during a given period; these are called maximum and minimum thermometers. A continuous record of temperature changes can be obtained with a thermograph, which usually consists of a bimetallic thermometer connected to a pen which records temperature on a moving strip of paper.

The most accurate commonly used instrument for measuring humidity is the PSYCHROMETER, in which a small muslin sleeve is placed over the bulb of a glass thermometer. When the muslin is soaked with pure water, the resulting evaporation cools the bulb by an amount proportional to the humidity of the air. Another common, though less accurate, humidity-measuring device is the hair HYGROMETER, which makes use of the fact that human hair varies in length with changes in humidity. An automatic recording form of this instrument is the hygrograph; frequently the hygrograph and thermograph are combined into a single instrument called a hygrothermograph. These instruments are placed in a louvered box (Stevenson screen) about 4 ft above the ground so that they are shielded from direct sunshine.

Wind direction is indicated by a wind vane, perhaps the oldest weather instrument. In its most common form it consists of a plate mounted on a shaft which is free to turn with the wind; the direction toward which the vane points is visually observed or electrically recorded. Wind speed is

the melting point. The last layer of melted material solidifies on the surface, and the meteorite plunges earthward over the final portion of its path as a dark object trailing a dusty vapor cloud. On the average, probably not more than about 10 meteorites of specimen size reach the ground daily over the entire globe. Meteorite finds are extremely rare except in the immediate vicinity of sites where very large meteorites have shattered on impact (see METEOR CRATER). The average composition of meteoritic material is somewhat similar to that of the surface rocks of Earth. Meteorites have a higher percentage of iron, nickel, magnesium, and sulfur than the surface rocks, but are deficient in oxygen, silicon, and aluminum. See TEKTITE.

Ages of meteorites have been determined in a number of ways, using quantitative measures of the isotopes of various elements: these ages in general lie between 10 million and 5,000 million yr. The internal structure of these samples from space shows clearly that they were once parts of a much larger body or bodies. Such orbits as have been determined conform more nearly to asteroid orbits than to those of comets; hence meteorites in contrast with most meteors are probably fragments of disintegrated small planets. They may represent what the substance of Earth is like at depths of hundreds or thousands of miles.—*P. M.*

Some instruments for measuring and recording wind, temperature, and rain: (1) cup anemometer with counting dials, (2) Dines portable anemometer, (3) air meter, (4) maximum and minimum thermometers (mounted horizontally when in use), (5) rain gage, recording type. (*Smithsonian Inst. and U. S. Weather Bureau*)

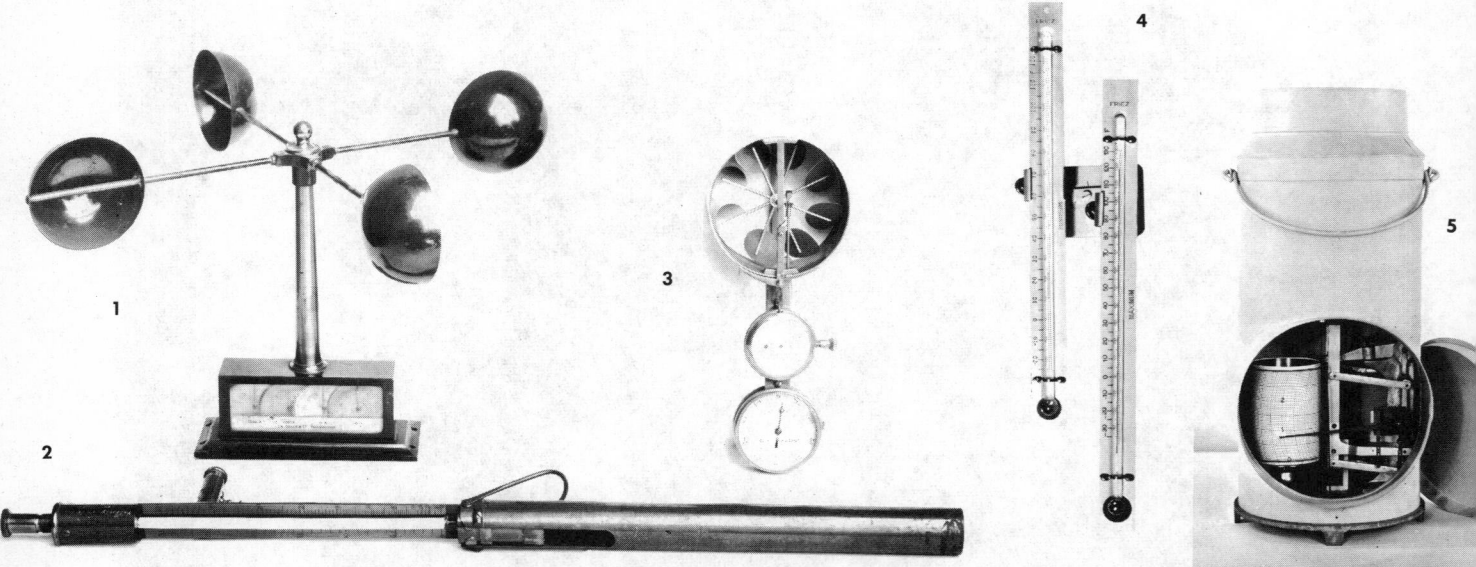

measured by an ANEMOMETER. One form consists of a set of revolving hemispherical cups fastened to a vertical shaft, whose speed of rotation indicates wind speed. Another type is a hollow tube which is kept facing into the wind; the wind pressure on a diaphragm in the tube indicates wind speed.

The total weight of the atmosphere above a given point (*i.e.* the atmospheric pressure) is measured by the BAROMETER. In its simplest form this is a vertical glass tube sealed at the upper end; the tube is evacuated of air and the lower, open end is immersed in a small cup of mercury. The weight of the atmosphere on the surface of the mercury in the cup balances the mercury column in the tube, and the height of this column thus measures atmospheric pressure. The more convenient aneroid barometer has a sealed flexible metal container from which most of the air has been evacuated; variations in air pressure cause the sides of the container to bulge in or out, and this motion is conveyed to a pointer on the face of the instrument. A recording form of the barometer is called a *barograph*. The HYPSOMETER, used primarily for measuring low pressures, is based on the principle that the boiling point of a liquid varies directly with atmospheric pressure.

Precipitation, or the total amount of liquid represented by the rain, snow, and ice which fall to the ground from the atmosphere, is measured by a rain gage. The most common form consists of a vertical cylinder open at the top; the various forms of atmospheric moisture fall into the cylinder, and the depth of water which collects in the bottom indicates the total precipitation. A recording form of the rain gage is called a *pluviograph*.

Observations of duration of sunshine are made by a SUNSHINE RECORDER, a glass bulb coated with lampblack and enclosed in a vacuum. The total amount of radiant energy received from the Sun is measured by a PYRHELIOMETER.

Upper-air Instruments: Direction and speed of wind at high altitudes are routinely observed by releasing a gas-filled balloon into the upper air. From the rate of ascent of the balloon and observation of its position in space with a theodolite (an instrument for measuring horizontal and vertical angles), wind characteristics at various altitudes can be calculated. When clouds will obscure the balloon, a small radio transmitter can be attached to it, and radio direction-finding equipment can then track it. The transmitter is called a *rawinsonde* (radio-wind-sounding device). In some cases a metal target is attached to the balloon; then position is obtained by radar (see RADAR WIND OBSERVATIONS). The *radiosonde* (radio-sounding device) consists of balloon-borne equipment for measuring temperature, pressure, and humidity, together with a small lightweight radio transmitter. As the equipment is carried aloft, measurements made by the meteorological instruments are automatically broadcast to a ground receiving station. In many cases, the radiosonde transmitter also serves as a rawinsonde signal source so that measurements of winds aloft can be made at the same time.

Special-purpose Instruments: Instruments have been developed also to meet the need for highly specialized measurements. At most modern airports, the height of the cloud layer (ceiling) is determined by a ceilometer, and the transmission of visible light through the atmosphere (visibility), by a transmissometer. Both of these measurements are extremely important for landings and take-offs. Weather radar is used to detect hurricanes, tornadoes, and other severe storms by recording the radar "echoes" from the heavy precipitation associated with such disturbances. The recently developed transosonde (trans-ocean-sounding device) is a large balloon designed to float at a constant level high in the atmosphere, carrying meteorological instruments and radio equipment which transmits data back to ground stations along its path. At very high levels in the atmosphere, measurements are made by sounding rockets capable of carrying instruments to heights of several hundred miles and by METEOROLOGICAL SATELLITES.—*J. C. T.*

METEOROLOGICAL OPTICS: the study of the optical characteristics of the atmosphere and the effects produced by suspended matter such as water vapor, ice crystals, and dust particles. See ATMOSPHERIC DIFFRACTION; ATMOSPHERIC REFRACTION.—*W. P. C.*

METEOROLOGICAL SATELLITES: artificial satellites of Earth placed in orbit to make observations of the atmosphere. Television pictures of cloud patterns, and measurements of infrared radiation from Earth's surface, of the Sun's radiation in various wave lengths, and of the physical properties of the gases at the fringe of the atmosphere, are all important in furthering knowledge of the weather. From television pictures such as those taken by the *Tiros* series of satellites, meteorologists are able to analyze the weather in terms of cloud patterns over wide areas. Only about 20% of the globe's surface is adequately covered by weather observing stations. Dangerous storms often form unobserved outside the weather-station network, later to move—unforecast—into shipping lanes or over populated regions. Satellite observations thus help fill in the blanks in the weather map, increasing the accuracy of weather forecasts and storm warnings in many parts of the world.

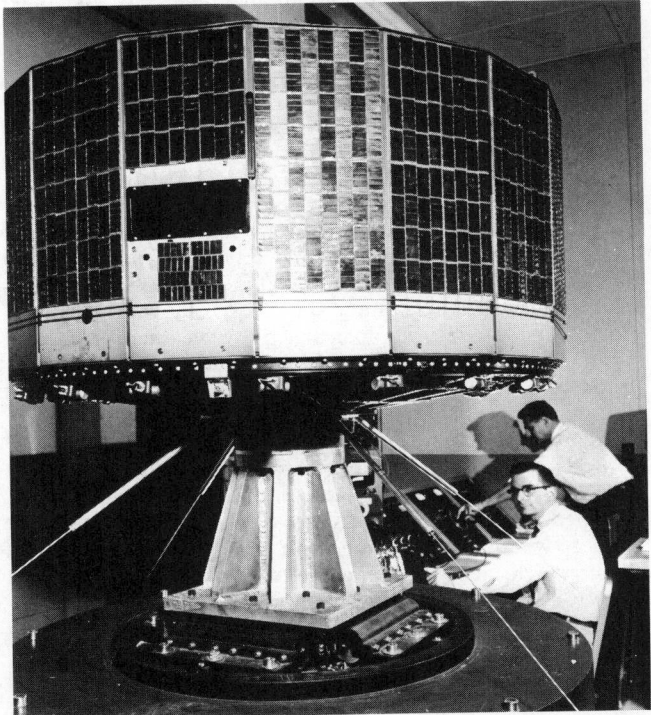

Tiros I satellite carries two television cameras. Orbiting the Earth at varying altitudes, satellites thus equipped have transmitted thousands of pictures of the planet's cloud cover. (NASA)

Less obvious in application, but equally significant, are observations of the HEAT BALANCE OF EARTH. Since the ultimate source of power to drive the atmospheric circulation is the heat of the Sun, detailed understanding of the distribution of solar energy in space and time will permit more complete knowledge of the forces which determine weather. The

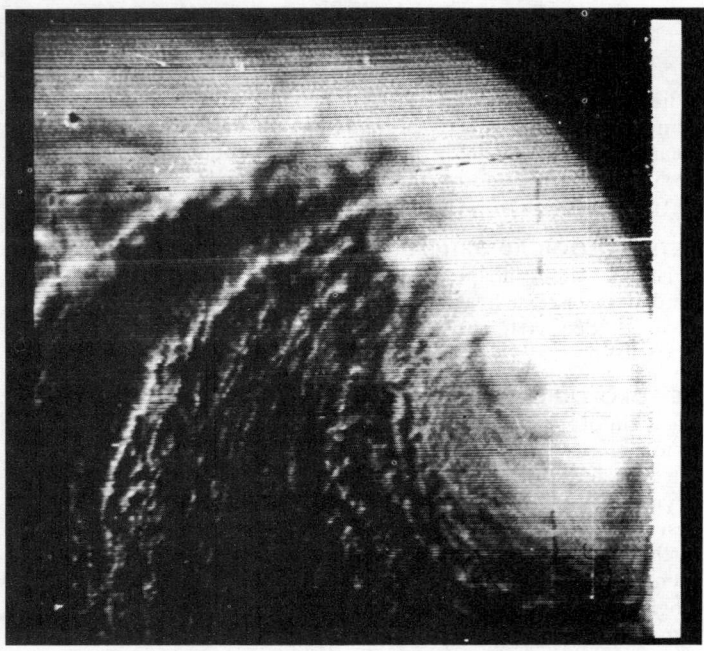

Typhoon over Pacific Ocean televised from Tiros I. (NASA)

obscuring effects of the atmosphere are eliminated if these measurements are made in free space aboard a satellite.

Evidence gathered so far by satellites and sounding rockets suggests that weather phenomena of the lower atmosphere are linked with less-well-understood phenomena of the outer atmosphere. It is suspected, for example, that meteoritic dust (micrometeorites) becomes condensation nuclei in the atmosphere and thus increases precipitation.—*D. H. L.*

METEOROLOGY: the science of the atmosphere. It involves the study of the composition, physical properties, and motion of the envelope of air which surrounds Earth. The more dramatic manifestations of the energy of the atmosphere, *e.g.* thunderstorms, gales, floods, and droughts, were the subject of superstitious dread in the early days of civilization, and meteorology long lagged behind its sister science, astronomy, as a true branch of natural philosophy. Modern meteorology and its main technological activity, weather forecasting, came into being only when the invention of the electric telegraph in the 19th cent. made possible the construction of synoptic weather charts, which display the state of the atmosphere at fixed hours over very large areas.

Meteorology is treated in this work under various titles. The state of the atmosphere at a given time in a given locality is called weather (see WEATHER SYSTEM). CLIMATE is the average weather of a region. The energy of the motions of the air which cause weather comes entirely from the Sun, and there is a balance between incoming and outgoing radiation for Earth as a whole. (See ATMOSPHERE; ATMOSPHERIC RADIATION; HEAT BALANCE OF EARTH.) The techniques of weather forecasting are dealt with mainly under WEATHER ANALYSIS and WEATHER FORECASTING, and form part of *dynamical meteorology. Physical meteorology* is concerned chiefly with the processes which produce the characteristic phenomena of weather, *e.g.* as explained in CLOUD and PRECIPITATION. The study of the atmosphere calls for the development of special measuring techniques, which are discussed under METEOROLOGICAL INSTRUMENTS and in other articles. Much of the beauty of the terrestrial scene arises from effects which are described and explained in METEOROLOGICAL OPTICS, and the electrical properties of the atmosphere are considered under ATMOSPHERIC ELECTRICITY and THUNDERSTORM. Meteorology is organized on a national and an international basis, the lat-

ter aspect being the concern of the World Meteorological Organization, located in Geneva, Switzerland. See also: ATMOSPHERIC TIDES; MICROCLIMATOLOGY; WINDS, LOCAL; WEATHER OBSERVATIONS; ATMOSPHERIC POLLUTION.—*O. G. S.*

METHANE: a gas which is the simplest member (CH_4) of the PARAFFIN hydrocarbons. So-called natural gas from gas and oil wells varies from nearly pure methane to a gas with rather low methane content. Methane is formed by bacterial action in swamps (marsh gas) and is one of the dangerous gases present in coal mines (fire damp).—*Ru. M.*

METHYL: the radical CH_3, present in compounds in which one H atom of methane (CH_4) is replaced by substitution; *e.g.* Cl—CH_3, methyl chloride, or chloromethane.—*Ru. M.*

METHYL ALCOHOL (METHANOL): CH_3OH, a chemical compound in which the hydroxyl (alcohol) radical, OH, replaces one of the H atoms in a molecule of methane, CH_4. In systematic nomenclature it is *methanol.* It is also called wood alcohol, since it used to be obtained by distillation of wood. It is now made almost entirely by synthetic methods. Methyl alcohol is used as a solvent, antifreeze, and chemical intermediate. Being poisonous, it has been used to denature ethyl alcohol.—*Ru. M.*

METON, fl. 5th cent. B. C., Greek astronomer; b. Leucas. A resident of Athens, he is best known as the discoverer of the CYCLE which bears his name. This cycle is a period of 235 lunations, at the end of which time the phase of the Moon falls on the same day of the year as it did at the beginning of the cycle. The cycle commenced July 16, 433 B. C. Received with great acclaim and adopted throughout Greece, it was said to have been engraved in golden letters, whence it received the appellation *Golden Number.* The cycle was in use for about a century before an error was detected by CALLIPPUS, who substituted a new cycle to reduce the error. —*R. N. M.*

METRIC SYSTEM: an international system of weights and measures based on the kilogram and the meter or on the gram and the centimeter. (The two versions are described in MEASUREMENT SYSTEMS.) Except for units of time, the metric system is decimal in character and thus differs radically from the English system with its variety of nondecimal multiples and submultiples. The metric system, which grew out of the deliberations of the French National Assembly during the revolutionary period (1791–1795), became compulsory in France in 1837 and gradually spread over all of non-English-speaking Europe. Though legally recognized in the U. S. A. and Great Britain, the system has not been officially adopted in these countries.

The meter was originally defined as one ten-millionth of Earth's meridian quadrant passing through Paris. Because of uncertainties in the measurement of Earth's circumference, the meter was later defined as the distance between two parallel lines scratched on a platinum-iridium bar maintained at the temperature of melting ice. The original meter bar is preserved at the International Bureau of Weights and Measures at Sèvres, France, with accurate copies or prototypes deposited in the National Bureau of Standards at Gaithersburg, Md. In 1960 the meter was defined as equivalent to 1,650,763.73 wave lengths of orange-red light emitted by krypton 86, yielding an accuracy of 1 part in 100,000,000. The new procedure makes it possible to reproduce the meter even if the old meter bar is completely destroyed.

Ten meters (*abbr.* m) constitute a dekameter (dkm), 100 meters a hectometer (hm), 1,000 meters a kilometer (km). Common submultiples include the decimeter (dm), which is

¹⁄₁₀ meter; centimeter (cm), ¹⁄₁₀₀ meter; and millimeter (mm), ¹⁄₁,₀₀₀ meter. Smaller units employed in measuring wavelengths of light include the micron (μ), 10^{-6} meter; millimicron (mμ), or nanometer, 10^{-9} meter; and Angstrom unit (Å), 10^{-10} meter or 10^{-8} centimeter.

The meter is a fundamental unit of length. Units of area and volume are derived from it (or its multiples and submultiples). Thus a liter, or 1,000 cubic centimeters, represents a volume occupied by a cubic decimeter.

The unit of mass in the metric system was originally the mass of one cubic centimeter of water, or one gram (gm). The present unit of mass is the kilogram, or 1,000 gm, represented by the mass of a cylindrical block of platinum-iridium, maintained at Sèvres, with accurate prototypes deposited at the National Bureau of Standards and other standardizing laboratories. As in the case of the meter, the prefixes deci-, centi-, and milli-, when applied to fractional values of the gram, denote respectively 10^{-1}, 10^{-2}, and 10^{-3} gm. Among multiples of the kilogram (kg), the most widely used is the metric ton, or 1,000 kg.

PREFIXES USED IN THE METRIC SYSTEM

Prefix	Multiple	Prefix	Submultiple
deka-	10	deci-	10^{-1}
hecto-	10^2	centi-	10^{-2}
kilo-	10^3	milli-	10^{-3}
myria-	10^4	micro-	10^{-6}
mega-	10^6	nano-	
giga-	10^9	(or millimicro-)	10^{-9}
tera-	10^{12}	pico-	10^{-12}

The decimal notation applies to such terms as kilocycles and megacycles (thousands and millions of cycles per second), kilowatts and megawatts, kilotons and megatons. Although time units are not decimal in character, the milli-, micro-, and even the nanosecond (10^{-9} sec) are in scientific use today. It is interesting to note that currency in both the non-English-speaking part of Europe and the U. S. A. is decimal in nature. The English pounds, shillings, and pence contrast sharply with other types of money.

From time to time, proposals have been put forward for adopting the metric system in the U. S. A. Cogent reasons are invariably advanced either for or against adoption. The U. S. electrical industry does use metric units, *e.g.* the kilowatt-hour.—*A. E.*

MEYER, JULIUS LOTHAR, 1830–95, German chemist; b. Varel, Oldenburg. Meyer developed a periodic classification of the elements (1870), independently of D. I. Mendeleev, as a consequence of his studies on the change of properties with increasing atomic weight. The relationship between the atomic weights and the properties of the elements is discussed in his book of theories of chemistry, *Die modernen Theorien der Chemie* (1864). See also ELEMENT.—*A. I.*

MEYER, VICTOR, 1848–97, German chemist; b. Berlin. He found isomeric nitro compounds and discovered thiophen, to which he devoted a book (1888). His work included gas reactions, the determination of vapor densities at high temperatures, the influence of substituent groups on the esterification of aromatic acids, and iodonium compounds. Together with Paul Jacobson, he started in 1893 a many-volumed textbook, *Lehrbuch der organischen Chemie.*—*E. F.*

MEYERHOF, OTTO, 1884–1951, German-U. S. physiologist and biochemist; b. Hanover. He shared the 1922 Nobel prize with A. V. Hill for his discovery of the relationship between the consumption of oxygen and the metabolism of lactic acid in muscle. In this research Meyerhof showed that, under the influence of oxygen, lactic acid formed in muscle is largely restored to the muscle as carbohydrate. His preparation from muscle of a potassium-chloride extract capable of carrying out glycolysis significantly advanced research techniques and elucidated the relation between metabolism and muscle contraction. Meyerhof was author or coauthor of nearly 300 scientific papers. He left Nazi Germany (1938) and went first to France and then to the U. S. A. He was a fellow of the Royal Society and a member of the National Academy of Sciences.—*D. H. D. R.*

MICA: any of a group of common and widespread aluminosilicate minerals characterized by perfect basal cleavage. The resulting thin, flexible, tough, and heat-resistant cleavage plates are the basis for most of the uses of the micas. The micas include several partially to completely isomorphous series:

True Micas:

$KAl_2(AlSi_3O_{10})(OH,F)_2$	Muscovite (potash or white mica)
$NaAl_2(AlSi_3O_{10})(OH,F)_2$	Paragonite (soda mica)
$K(Al > Cr)_2(AlSi_3O_{10})(OH,F)_2$	Fuchsite (chrome mica)
$\underline{K}V_2(AlSi_3O_{10})(OH,F)_2$	Roscoelite (vanadium mica)
$KMg_3(AlSi_3O_{10})(OH,F)_2$	Phlogopite (magnesium or amber mica)
$K(Mg,Fe)_3(AlSi_3O_{10})(OH,F)_2$	Biotite (iron or dark mica)
$K(Fe > Mg)_3(AlSi_3O_{10})(OH,F)_2$	Lepidomelane (same)
$KFe_3(AlSi_3O_{10})(OH,F)_2$	Annite (same)
$K(Mg,Mn)_3(Fe'''Si_3O_{10})(OH,F)_2$	Manganophyllite
$K_2Li_3Al_3(AlSi_3O_{10})_2(O,OH,F)_4$	Lepidolite (lithium mica)
$K,Fe,Li,Al(AlSi_3O_{10})(O,OH,F)_4$	Zinnwaldite (same)

Brittle Micas:

$CaAl_2(Al_2Si_2O_{10})(OH)_2$	Margarite
$(Fe'',Mn)(Al,Fe''')_2(Al_2Si_2O_{10})(OH)_2$	Ottrelite
$(Fe,Mg)_2Al_2(Al_2Si_2O_{10})(OH)_4$	Chloritoid

The micas and brittle micas are all monoclinic, but with almost 90° inclination of the *a*-axis. The mica structure is based on infinite sheets of SiO_4 tetrahedra linked into a pseudohexagonal network through the sharing of three of the four oxygen ions. AlO_4 tetrahedra may substitute for up to one half of the SiO_4 tetrahedra. Paired sheets are bound together into strong layers by cross-linkages through shared Mg, Al, and (OH) ions. Each layer has a negative charge, which is balanced out by relatively scattered K or Na ions which act as weak links between layers, thus accounting for the great strength within layers and the lack of strength (= excellent cleavage) between layers. The chlorites, talc, and pyrophyllite are structurally related to and resemble the micas.

Micas occur in most igneous rocks as primary constituents (even as phenocrysts in extrusives) or as deuteric alteration products. Micas or brittle micas are also major constituents of a great variety of metamorphic rocks. Most phyllites and schists owe their fissility to the presence of micas. *Muscovite* is an almost universal constituent of gneisses, and its fine-grained variety, *sericite,* is common in the wall-rock alteration "haloes" surrounding ore deposits of hydrothermal origin. All commercial *lepidolite* and sheet muscovite are obtained from pegmatite dikes, and sheet *phlogopite* is obtained from pegmatite-like high-temperature veins of calcite. Muscovite resists weathering and appears as fine scales in sandstones and shales. *Roscoelite* forms intergranular aggregations in sandstones in the vanadium deposits of the Colorado Plateau type and is one of the parent minerals of carnotite and tyuyamunite in the oxidized deposits.

Sheet muscovite and phlogopite are used as electrical insulators in such articles as radio tubes, capacitors, commutators, transformers, irons, and toasters. Laminated mica sheets have been prepared by a process similar to papermaking. Mica crystals large enough to provide useful sheets have been synthesized in the electric furnace. Pulverized scrap and fine-grained flakes obtained as by-products in feldspar and clay operations are used as surface coatings on roofing and siding materials, in oil-well drilling muds, in paints, and as fillers in plastics. Lepidolite is a major source of lithium compounds, and roscoelite is an ore of vanadium. See MINERAL (table).—*L. M.*

MICELLES: Aggregates, frequently electrically charged, of certain types of surface-active molecules. Micelles appear spontaneously in solutions of these molecules above a characteristic concentration called the *critical micelle concentration.* See SURFACE-ACTIVE AGENTS.—*H. W. F.*

MICHELANGELO (Michelangelo Buonarroti), 1475–1564, Italian painter, sculptor, and poet; b. Caprese. The foremost artist of the Florentine Renaissance, Michelangelo also executed notable civil and military engineering works. In 1505–06 he surveyed the quarrying of marble at Carrara and its transport to Rome for a sepulchral tomb for Pope Julius II. In 1529 he strengthened the defenses of San Miniato and designed bridges for the Rialto (Venice) and a new Tiber bridge (Rome). As the architect of St. Peter's (Rome), 1547, he designed the cupola, later built by Giacomo della Porta (1588–90). From 1555 to 1559 he directed the reconstruction of the defenses of Rome.—*R. J. F.*

MICHELL, JOHN, 1724–93, English geologist, physicist, and astronomer; b. Nottinghamshire. He invented the torsion balance, used so effectively for the measurement of small forces by H. Cavendish and C. Coulomb. In its 20th-cent. form (torsion pendulum) the torsion balance is used as a gravity meter in prospecting for oil. Michell also invented the "double touch" method of making artificial magnets, stated the inverse-square law for magnetism, and proposed the concept of star clusters. His "Conjectures Concerning the Cause and Observations upon the Phenomena of Earthquakes" (1761) was a conspicuous addition to knowledge of earthquakes and included an attempt to determine the velocity of the Lisbon earthquake of 1755. Michell was one of the pioneers in emphasizing the idea of succession in the formations composing Earth's crust. He was a fellow of the Royal Society.—*D. H. D. R.*

MICHELSON, ALBERT ABRAHAM, 1852–1931, U. S. physicist; b. Strelno, Germany. He invented the Michelson interferometer for measuring distances by means of the lengths of light waves and produced methods for precise measurement of the speed of light. For the Paris International Bureau of Weights and Measures, Michelson measured the meter in terms of the wavelength of incandescent cadmium. In 1920 he employed light interference to make determinations of the size of stars. His work with E. W. Morley (see MICHELSON-MORLEY EXPERIMENT) contributed to the origin of the theory of RELATIVITY. For his optical precision instruments and for the spectroscopic and metrological investigations made with them, Michelson received the Nobel prize, 1907. In addition to numerous scientific papers, he was the author of *Velocity of Light* (1902), *Light Waves and Their Uses* (1903), and *Studies in Optics* (1927). He was a fellow of the Royal Society and a member of the National Academy of Sciences.—*S. B.*

MICHELSON-MORLEY EXPERIMENT: an attempt to determine experimentally the velocity of Earth relative to the "ether." The ether was a hypothetical substance assumed to pervade all space and was thought necessary as a medium for the propagation of light waves and other electromagnetic radiation. To account for the velocity of light and for the apparent lack of friction between the ether and celestial bodies, the ether was assumed to have an extremely low density and at the same time a greater rigidity than steel. These disturbingly contradictory qualities led 19th-cent. scientists to try to verify the ether's physical existence. The ABERRATION OF LIGHT from stars indicates that Earth does not carry along with it the medium presumed to transmit light. If the ether were stationary, the relative motion of Earth could be determined by measuring the speed of light, since the measured velocity of a wave in classical physics depends on the velocity of the observer relative to the medium which carries the wave.

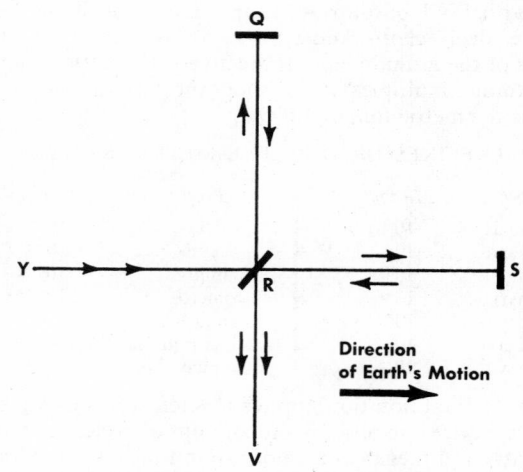

Michelson interferometer compared speed of light traveling in two different directions to determine existence of "ether." Michelson mounted apparatus on a concrete block floating in a pool of mercury so it could be rotated through 90 degrees.

In 1881 the American physicists A. A. Michelson and E. W. Morley, by use of an INTERFEROMETER, devised an experiment to compare the velocity of light in the direction of Earth's motion and perpendicular to it (see diagram). A beam of light travels from its source at *Y* to a half-silvered mirror, *R*, where it is divided, one half going to *S*, the other half being reflected perpendicularly to *Q*. The light is reflected from *Q* and *S* back to *R*, and then directed to the observer at *V*, who sees INTERFERENCE bands, or fringes, of light and dark. The paths *RQ* and *RS* are equal, but if Earth (and the interferometer) are moving in the direction *RS*, and if the speed of light is constant with respect to a *stationary* ether, then light takes longer to traverse the path *R* to *S* and back to *R* than to go from *R* to *Q* and back. (It takes longer to swim a mile upstream and back again than to swim two miles at right angles to the direction of the current, the swimmer's speed with respect to the water being constant.) Rotation of the whole apparatus through 90°, so that *RQ* is along the line of motion, should then produce a shift in the interference fringes, owing to the interchange of the two paths. No such shift could be detected, although the apparatus was designed to show changes that would result from the known velocity of the earth in its orbit. This observation, repeated many times, seemed incompatible with other experiments, notably the aberration of light. To account for it G. F. Fitzgerald and H. A. Lorentz independently postulated what became known as the LORENTZ-FITZGERALD CONTRACTION. According to this, lengths along the direction of motion are shortened by just enough so that light would travel the two

1

Plate 54   ISLANDS

Islands exist but a short time, geologically speaking, because they are under sharp attack by wave and current action. They owe their formation to special geological conditions, such as volcanic activity, changes in sea level, and coastal erosion.

1. Volcanic islands, St. John, West Indies, are of igneous origin. *(Bradley Smith/Rapho-Guillumette)* **2. Fire Island** off south shore of Long Island, N.Y., is a sand bar culminating (foreground) in a sand spit. It was built by wave and current action, and is continually being modified in shape, especially at times of storm. *(Budnik/Magnum Photos, Inc.)* **3. Sea stacks** in vicinity of Lizard Head, England, are remnants of slightly more resistant material that survived as the sea cut away less resistant rock of the coast. *(Philip Gendreau)*

2

3

4. Coral atoll, South Pacific, between islands of Aitutaki and Tahiti, is an island created by marine animals. *(Leon Daller/ Monkmeyer Press Photo Service)*

4

Plate 55   INSECTS

More than two-thirds of all known kinds of animals are insects. They are found in great abundance on land and in fresh water, but rarely on or in the sea. A few tolerate the high temperature of hot springs; others live on glaciers high on mountain tops. Most insects eat plant leaves or other insects.

1. Chrysalis of a monarch butterfly (*Danaus plexippus*): In this capsule a milkweed caterpillar is converted into an adult—the black-and-orange monarch butterfly. When its wings dry, butterfly may migrate from Canada to Mexico and back, thereby avoiding cold weather. *(Shostal)*

1

2. Ox beetle is a scarab beetle of tropics. On its back are three hard, curved horns, which male may use in dueling with another male to win a mate. *(Russ Kinne)*

3. Male cecropia moth (*Samia cecropia*) relies upon sense of smell located in its feathery antennae to lead it to a fragrant female cecropia moth. Female's antennae are more threadlike, and wing span (to 6½ in.) is likely to exceed male's by an inch or more. *(Louis Quitt/Monkmeyer)*

2

3

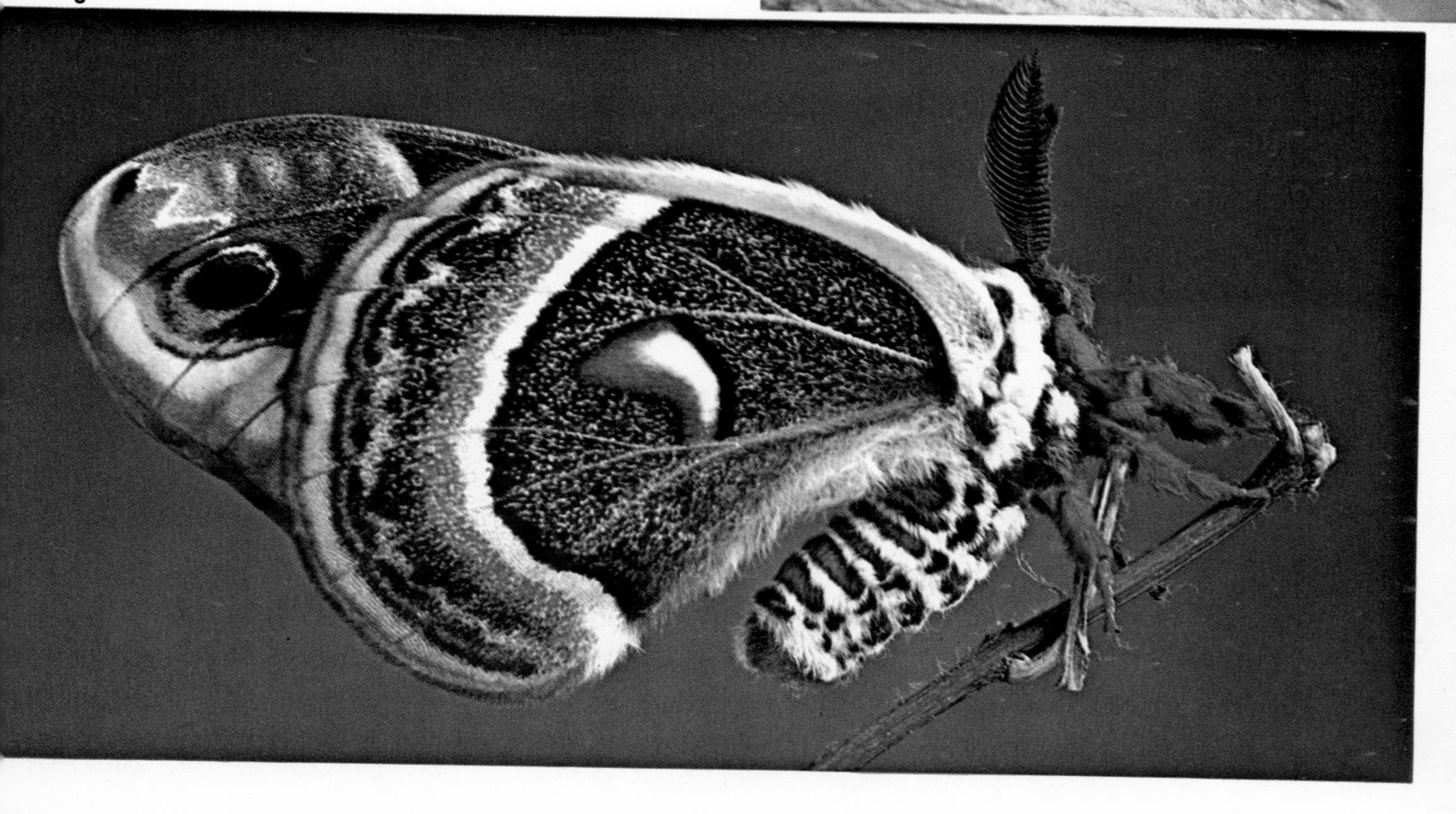

Plate 56 INSECTS

4. Lubber grasshopper *(Romalea microptera)* of Florida is short-winged and rarely tries to fly. Its appetite for garden foliage is in proportion to its big body. It is shown with smaller grasshopper that has longer wings and flies well. *(Amer. Mus. of Nat. Hist.)*

5. Tarantula hawk *(Pepsis)* is a large blue-black wasp that stocks a burrow with paralyzed tarantulas as food for its young. Carefully the wasp stings each tarantula it catches, injecting only enough venom to immobilize the prey—never enough to kill it. *(Herbert Lanks/Monkmeyer)*

6. Robber fly *(Asilus)* skillfully captures other insects, including honeybees. It pounces upon insect from above, holds insect firmly with its hairy legs, and sucks body juices through a hole bitten in insect's back. *(Herbert Lanks/Shostal)*

5

6

Plate 57   LAVA

Lava is a hot, liquid, rock-forming material which appears at Earth's surface from an underground source. If it is under high pressure with much dissolved gaseous material, it will emerge as a violent eruption; otherwise it will flow out more gently. Cooled lava is found in many forms, depending upon its chemical composition and the conditions under which it reaches the surface. Blown-out matter commonly forms lava dust, "cinders," and "bombs." Lava flows may form large masses of *aa* and *pahoehoe*.

1. Paricutín, Mexico: Flying fragments in a lava fountain, the start of a violent eruption. *(F. H. Pough/Amer. Mus. of Nat. Hist.)*

2. Paricutín, Mexico: Red-hot core of an advancing lava flow appears wherever the surface crust drops off. *(F. H. Pough/Amer. Mus. of Nat. Hist.)*

3. Aa lava flow and cinder cone, south of Reykjavik, Iceland: This type of flow is characterized by a rough, jagged, clinkery surface. *(Harold Wanless)*

4. Pahoehoe lava flow, Craters of the Moon National Monument, Idaho: This type of flow is characterized by rounded surfaces showing billowy or ropy shapes. *(Josef Muench)*

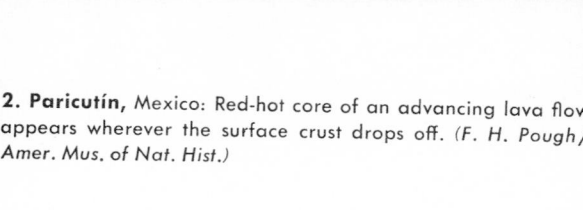

paths, *R-Q-R* and *R-S-R,* in equal times, regardless of the orientation of the apparatus. In 1905 Albert Einstein introduced the special theory of RELATIVITY, in which the velocity of light in empty space is constant and independent of the velocity of the observer. With this theory there is no necessity for the ether as a medium for the propagation of light.—*A. L.*

MICROBAROGRAPH: a barograph, or recording BAROMETER, designed to be sensitive only to small short-period variations in atmospheric pressure. Microbarographs are used chiefly in the study of the fine-scale details of weather systems, or mesometeorology.—*D. H. L.*

MICROBIOLOGICAL ASSAY: a quick and simple biochemical research technique employed principally for analyses of vitamins, amino acids, or other nutrients. Microbiological methods are based on the fact that certain microorganisms require much the same nutrients for growth as do higher animals. The synthetic growth medium is made as complete as possible, except that the substance under study is omitted. On such a medium, growth is practically zero; as small, graded amounts of the nutrient are added to individual test tube cultures, progressively greater growth is obtained. Any unknown sample may be analyzed by comparing the growth of a culture to that of the "standard curve" cultures obtained with known amounts of the nutrient. Analyses so obtained are generally reproducible to ±10% for vitamins and ±5% for amino acids.—*V. H. C.*

MICROBIOLOGY: the study of living forms (microorganisms, microbes) that can be seen as individuals only with the microscope; more specifically, the study of small plant forms (algae, molds, yeasts, bacteria), single-celled animals (protozoa), and viruses. All can be seen with the light microscope (magnification 25 to 2,000 diameters) except the viruses, which are made visible with the electron microscope (magnification up to 100,000 diameters). Microbiology emerged as a discipline during the mid-20th cent., after the methods used so successfully to study the bacteria were adopted for investigation of other minute forms. See BACTERIOLOGY.—*H. B. F.*

MICROCHEMISTRY: the science of using and analyzing extremely small amounts (in the range of 1 mg) of substances in chemical reactions. Systematic microchemical methods were first developed by Friedrich Emich at the beginning of the 20th cent. Microorganic chemistry was advanced significantly by the work of Fritz Pregl (1909) when it became necessary for him to determine quantitatively the carbon and hydrogen contents of an extremely small quantity of a new organic compound which he had isolated from gallstones. Previously, large amounts of starting materials had to be used in order to isolate a sufficient amount of product for analysis. Prior to the work of Emich and Pregl, microchemical methods were associated with the use of a microscope. Crystals of a substance were identified by comparison with a known compound, and physical changes were observed with a microscope.

Because of the small quantities involved in microchemistry, certain analytic methods must be altered from the conventional macro (100 mg or more) determinations. Gravimetric determinations are not reliable, because precision balances have not been developed which will accurately measure micro-quantities. Volumetric methods of analysis are the most precise and accurate in microchemistry; colorimetric methods are not as accurate but are adequate for most micro work. Microburettes, micro-electrodes, and spectrofluorimeters are some of the special apparatus used. The major advantages of microchemical techniques are the conservation of time, labor, and materials. See CHEMICAL ANALYSIS.—*G. W. M.*

MICROCLIMATOLOGY: study of the properties of the lowest levels of the atmosphere, the region in which life is most abundant. Normally, "climate" refers to the condition of the atmosphere at about 4 ft above the ground, the breathing level of a man. The air within a few inches of the ground, the normal habitat of small creatures and young plants, has very different properties from air found at slightly higher levels,

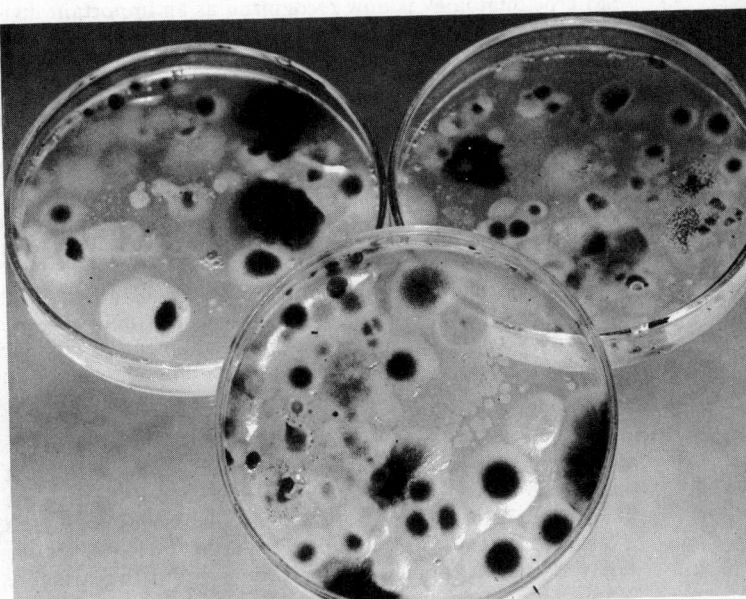

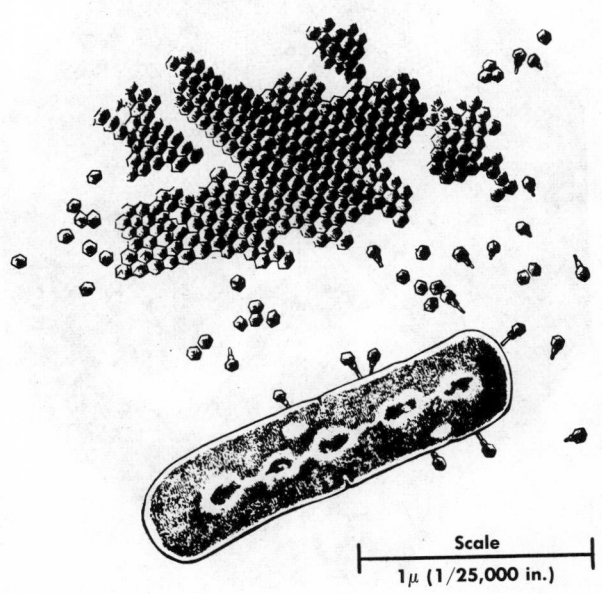

Microorganisms proliferate in dishes of nutrient agar (*above*). Drawing (*left*) shows thin-section preparation of rod-shaped bacterium (bacillus) and some virus particles as seen through electron microscope. Unlike bacteria, many of which play an essential role in life cycles of higher organisms, all viruses are parasitic. Here, the bacillus is being attacked by tailed viruses. As Jonathan Swift noted: "So naturalists observe, a flea/Hath smaller fleas that on him prey;/And these have smaller still to bite 'em,/And so proceed *ad infinitum.*" (*Photo: Chas. Pfizer & Co.; drawing after Cox*)

Scale

1μ (1/25,000 in.)

especially with regard to temperature. The surface of the earth is subject to a much greater range of temperature than the air at 4 ft, even in temperate climates. In hot climates the difference is very marked; thus in the desert near Tucson, Ariz., a surface temperature in excess of 71°C (160°F) has been recorded in the afternoon, sinking to about 15°C (60°F) at night. The magnitude and range of surface temperature, however, depend greatly on the nature of the soil and its vegetation cover, as well as its locality. A knowledge of microclimates is essential in field studies in biology and is of importance in agriculture.

Another feature which distinguishes the meteorology of the lowest layers from that of the higher levels is that in the first few feet of the atmosphere temperature changes vary rapidly with height, the rate of fall in conditions of bright sunshine being hundreds or thousands of times that measured in the free atmosphere. On a clear night, the surface and the air near it cool rapidly, and the normal fall of temperature with height is reversed. These changes affect the turbulence or eddying of the wind, and hence its power to disperse suspended matter, *e.g.* smoke or dust, in the atmosphere. The study of such effects is essential for the control of ATMOSPHERIC POLLUTION.

Microclimates depend markedly upon the nature of the surface and its topography. The direction of air currents in the lowest layers often bears little relation to that of the main flow in the atmosphere, but instead is determined largely by the shape of the surrounding country. For this reason, hollows or valley floors may become "frost holes" on clear nights, because of the tendency of chilled (and therefore dense) air to drain into them from higher land. The micrometeorologist pays great attention to the motions of shallow air currents in order to advise on matters such as the correct siting of orchards.

Microclimatology is now recognized as an important division of the science of the atmosphere, with wide applications to matters such as atmospheric pollution, evaporation, crop growth, and urban planning. It involves the difficult mathematical study of the effects of wind eddies (see TURBULENCE) and requires special instrumentation, *e.g.* extremely sensitive anemometers and rapid-response thermometers, for many important effects depend on the behavior of shallow, slow-moving air streams within a foot or so of the ground, which are not shown on the ordinary weather map. The term "microclimate" is sometimes also applied to the climate within the tallest stand of vegetation in an area and to local climates, *e.g.* on the lee shores of large lakes; in a more restrictive sense, it may refer to such phenomena as climatic conditions along the north (or south) wall of a house or on different sides of a railroad embankment. See also CLIMATE. —*O. G. S.*

MICROGRAPHIA, by Robert Hooke, 1665: This was the first book to describe a wide range of objects as seen through the microscope, with a very beautiful set of plates. Besides insects (examined, but not well depicted, by others before) Hooke described plants (applying the word "cell" to the structure he saw in cork), stones, seeds, and man-made objects, illuminating his accounts with his gift for ingenious scientific speculation. *Micrographia* is notable also for Hooke's views on such diverse topics as light, combustion, and the formation of the Moon. Although Hooke did not pursue microscopy further, his book was the first of the series of great 17th-cent. treatises that began to disclose the micro-architecture of nature.—*A. R. H.*

Eyes and head of gray drone-fly: A plate from Hooke's *Micrographia*, London, 1665. (N. Y. Public Library) ▶

MICROPHONE: a device for converting an audible sound into an electrical signal. Generally the sound waves impinge on a diaphragm and cause it to vibrate. Microphones may be classified by the mechanism used to convert the diaphragm vibrations into an electrical signal. Thus in an *electrostatic microphone* a large constant voltage is maintained between the diaphragm and a nearby fixed plate; the resulting variations in electrical capacity give rise to fluctuating charges on the diaphragm. In the *electrodynamic* type, the diaphragm moves a coil of wire placed in a magnetic field, the motion thus producing an ELECTROMOTIVE FORCE in the coil. In a *crystal microphone,* the diaphragm is a PIEZOELECTRIC crystal the bending of which generates a fluctuating voltage. In a *velocity microphone,* the diaphragm is a thin flexible ribbon, placed in a magnetic field, which tends to move with the same velocity as the air particles impinging on it. The motion of the ribbon generates an electromagnetic force in the ribbon. Microphones that are equally sensitive to sounds coming from all directions are called omnidirectional; those most sensitive in two opposite directions (*e.g.* the velocity microphone), bidirectional; and those most sensitive in only one direction, unidirectional.—*H. M. T.*

MICROSCOPE: an optical instrument that produces an enlarged image of a minute object. The distinctness with which the unaided eye is able to see an object depends upon the clarity of the image produced in the eye and the size of that image. A person with normal vision sees an object most clearly at a distance of about 10 in. from the eye. At a closer distance, the object looks larger, but it also appears indistinct or fuzzy, because the eye cannot bring it into focus. The microscope, in effect, enables an object to be brought much closer to the eye and yet still be in focus. Microscopes are simple or compound. The common magnifying glass is, in fact, a *simple microscope,* consisting of a single positive LENS or a combination of lenses acting as a single positive lens. A *compound microscope* consists usually of two lens systems, each system acting as a single positive lens.

History: No one knows when man first discovered the basic principle of the microscope. However, it is believed that magnifying lenses were used as eyeglasses in ancient times both in China and in civilized areas around the Mediterranean.

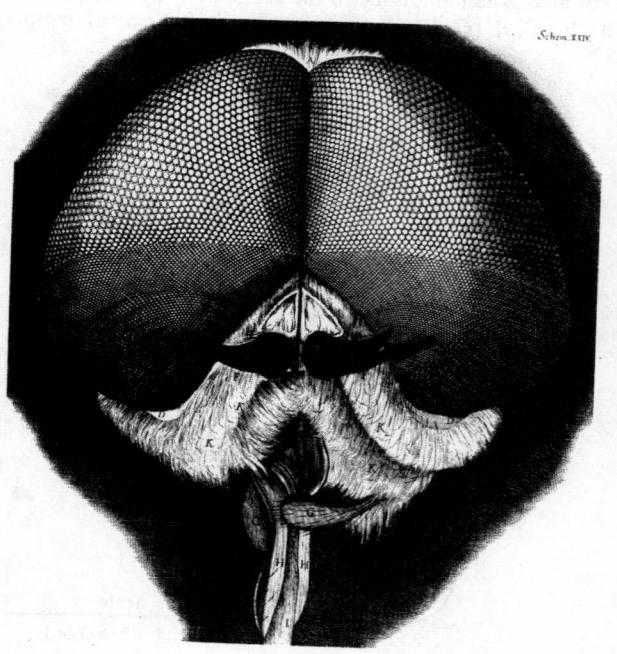

Schem. XXIV

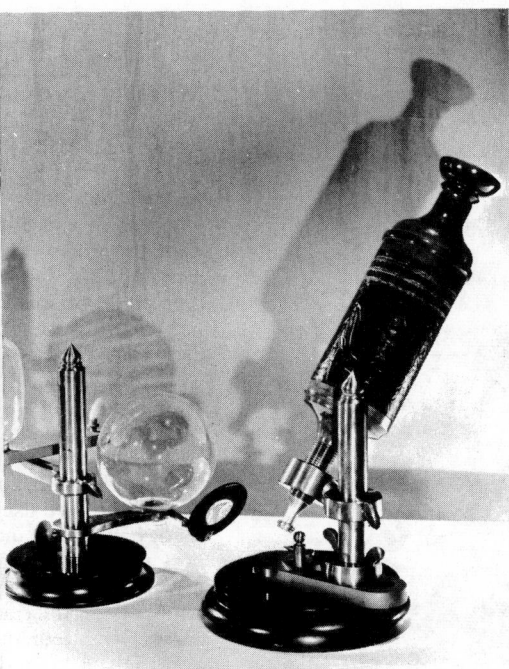
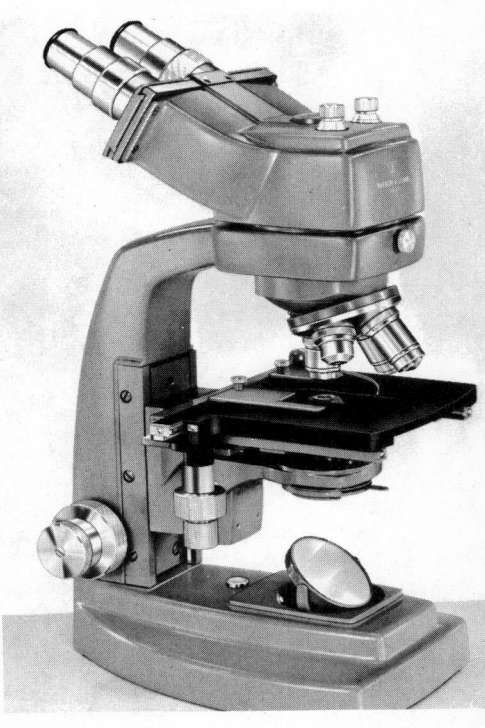

Evolution of the microscope: A replica of Leeuwenhoek's microscope of 1673; a replica of the microscope, and its spherical condenser, used by Hooke in making the observations described in his *Micrographia* (1665); and a mid-20th-century binocular microscope. (*Bausch & Lomb*)

About 1590 Zacharias Janssen, a Dutch spectacle maker, built a successful compound microscope measuring 1 ft in length and containing two lenses. Other men made improvements in microscope construction, but all these early workers were baffled by *aberration,* the deviation of light rays from certain points through which they should pass to achieve a distinct focus. *Spherical aberration* results in distortion of the image, and *chromatic aberration* produces colored fringes around an otherwise white image. The difficulty caused by aberration turned workers toward the development of the simple microscope, or magnifying glass. Anton van Leeuwenhoek (1632–1723) built many efficient microscopes of this type. About 1845 Charles Chevalier (1804–59) made the first successful achromatic lens, eliminating all the color fringes around an image, and in 1847 Charles A. Spencer (1813–81) produced the first American-made microscope with an efficient achromatic lens combination. Progress since then has been mainly concerned with mass production of microscopes. Notable advances include the ultraviolet microscope, the phase microscope, the FIELD-EMISSION (and field-ion) microscopes, and the ELECTRON MICROSCOPE.

Operation of Microscope: The compound microscope is essentially a tube with a lens system called the *objective* at the bottom, and a lens system called the eyepiece at the top. As shown in the diagram, the mirror directs a beam of light through the object on the stage, and the objective projects an enlarged image of the object up near the top of the microscope tube. This image is viewed through the eyepiece, which acts much like a simple magnifying lens, the principal difference being that the eyepiece magnifies an aerial image instead of the actual object. The final much-enlarged image formed by the eyepiece is the large arrow labeled "virtual image." It is called a virtual image because the light rays do not actually come from this image, but merely appear to come from it; they are simply extensions of the actual rays, which pass from the eyepiece to the eye.

Magnification: The final magnification is the product of the objective and eyepiece magnifications. If the objective magnification is 10 and the eyepiece magnification is 10, the final magnification is 100. There is no upward limit to magnification of a microscope, but there is a limit to useful magnification. This limit is set by *resolving power,* the ability of the microscope to render visible the fine detail of the object. If the object has been magnified to the point that its image is becoming indistinct because of limited resolving power, further magnification only makes the image larger and fuzzier, without showing any more detail. Modern compound microscopes have magnifications up to 2,000 ×.

Resolving Power: A microscope's resolving power depends generally on the design of the objective. An objective capable of utilizing a large angular cone of light coming from the specimen will have better resolving power than an objective limited to a smaller cone of light. The mathematical expression generally used to express the limit of resolving power of an objective is $S = 1.22\ \lambda/2N \sin U$, where S is the least difference between two lines of detail that can be resolved (*i.e.* seen as two distinct lines rather than being blurred into one); λ is the wavelength of light used; N is the lowest refractive index between object and objective; and U is the greatest semiangle of a light cone that the objective can utilize. The quantity $N \sin U$ in the equation is called the *numerical aperture,* or N.A., of an objective. The N.A., which is usually engraved on an objective, is the most important factor in determining resolving power.

Objective and Eyepiece: In modern microscopes, the objective is a complicated system of lenses acting as a single convex lens. The demand for great magnification and high resolving power requires lenses of short focal length and large numerical aperture, in which aberrations are corrected. The eyepiece usually consists of two simple lenses, which also act as a single lens. The lens nearer the objective is called the field lens; the one nearer the eye is the eye lens.

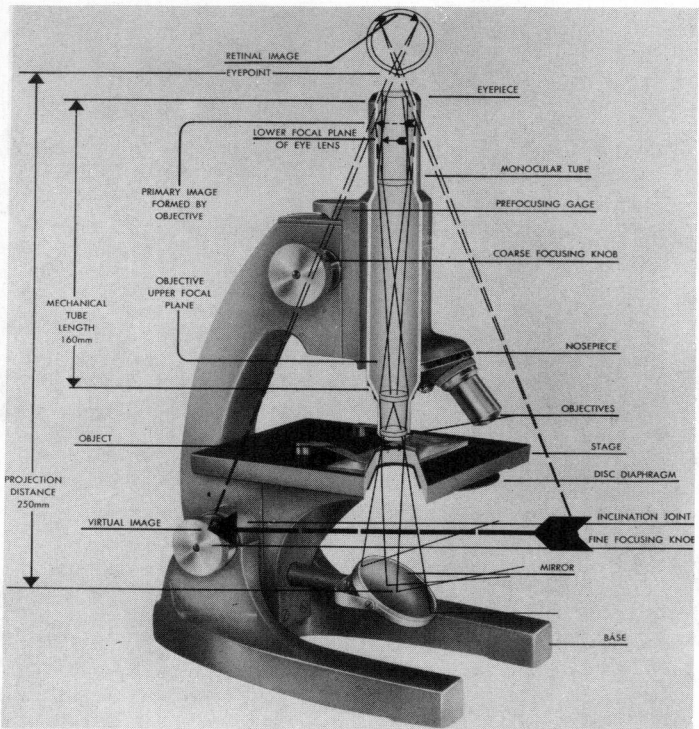

Compound microscope: Image formation and component parts of a modern monocular microscope. (*Bausch & Lomb*)

Illumination: Usually, the light is reflected from a mirror mounted below the object being viewed. With a small light source, a plane mirror gives an illuminating beam of rays that are, for all practical purposes, parallel; a concave mirror provides a convergent cone of illumination. A condenser can be used to provide an illuminating cone of larger angle than the concave mirror can give. The condenser is a series of lenses interposed between the plane mirror and the object. It is designed to concentrate the rays reflected from the plane mirror so that they converge on the object as a wide-angled cone. By accurate focusing of the condenser, intense illumination of the object is possible. Examination of opaque objects requires illumination from above, and the objective becomes, in effect, the condenser. Light is admitted through an opening in the tube of the microscope and is reflected, by means of a mirror or prism, through the objective so that it is focused on the object to be viewed.

Dark Field Illumination: Very small particles that cannot be viewed directly can be examined with the aid of dark field illumination. An opaque disk is placed at the center of the condenser. The object is illuminated by oblique rays from the ring outside the disk. The light is diffracted, producing a scintillation against a dark background as it falls on the minute particle being viewed. Dark field illumination is used commonly in examinations of material for the presence of spirochetes of syphilis, which are too slender to be seen by using ordinary microscopic methods.

Ultraviolet Light and Phase Microscopy: A 20th cent. contribution to microscope development has been the application of invisible ultraviolet light to microscopy. Since ultraviolet light has a very short wavelength, it increases the resolving power of the lenses, with the result that a higher effective magnification can be realized. Since the image formed cannot be seen directly with the eye, the ultraviolet microscope must be used in conjunction with photography or a fluorescent screen.

Phase microscopes make it possible to examine living organisms and tissues, emulsions, plastics, and other materials too transparent to be seen with the ordinary microscope. To produce a phase microscope, a diffraction plate is added to the objective and an annular diaphragm is placed below the condenser. By this means very slight differences in refraction in the material being studied are made into images that can be seen and photographed.

Binocular and Stereoscopic Microscopes: Binocular instruments have two eyepieces and are designed for use with both eyes simultaneously. Light rays passing up from the objective are bent by prisms so that part of them pass into one eyepiece and part into the other. The binocular microscope gives the advantage of depth perception and greater eye comfort in use. It has gained steadily in popularity and may eventually replace the monocular instrument entirely. The stereoscopic microscope has two eyepieces and two objectives. It is used to examine gross objects by reflected light (rather than transmitted light) with magnification usually less than 100 diameters. Extensive use is made of stereoscopic microscopes in biology and medicine, mineralogy, precision tool manufacture, food processing, and textile production. The stereoscopic microscope gives depth perception, and the most modern instruments produce an erect rather than an inverted image.

Uses: In medicine, bacteriology, metallurgy, chemistry, crime detection, and many other fields, the microscope is today an invaluable aid. Indeed the rapid progress and development of many medical, chemical, and industrial techniques would have been impossible without the use of the microscope. —*A. P. E.*

MICROSOMES: submicroscopic particles found in cells. They can be isolated from a homogenate (crushed cells) by very high-speed centrifugation. The resulting pellet is known as the *microsome fraction.* Depending on the nature of the cell, this pellet may consist of intracellular membranes or very small particles called ribosomes, or mixtures of the two. The membranes contain enzymes involved in fat synthesis and, in liver cells, in detoxification reactions. The ribosomes are involved in protein synthesis.—*P. S.*

MICROWAVES: ELECTROMAGNETIC WAVES located in that portion of the radio spectrum having wavelengths between 1 mm and 30 cm, corresponding to frequencies between 300,000 Mc and 1,000 Mc. Longer wavelengths (lower frequencies) are known as VHF and UHF (very-high and ultra-high frequencies), whereas wavelengths shorter than 1 mm are in the infrared region. Microwaves are characterized by wavelengths comparable to the dimensions for which it is practicable to build apparatus. Consequently, advantage can be taken of the wave nature of the radiation to build waveguides, cavity resonators, and antennas of high efficiency. To produce sharply directional beams of radiation at high gain, an antenna must have a diameter of many wavelengths. This can readily be done with microwaves but not at lower frequencies, for which the waves are longer. To provide a signal with a large amount of information (which is needed for television relay circuits or for radar pulses), a wide band of modulation frequencies is needed. This, too, is easier to obtain at the high frequencies of the microwave region than at lower frequencies, because the modulation is a smaller percentage of the carrier frequency. For these reasons, the microwave band is used to provide efficient radar equipment that can give precise information about the direction of and distance to a specified target. This information is used to detect and locate ships, aircraft, and ground features, being particularly valuable for navigation, control of air traffic near

Midnight Sun photographed at 10-min intervals: Point Barrow, Alaska, June 27–28, 1960. Middle image represents 12 o'clock midnight position. (*Fred E. Wiedeman/Alaska Photo*)

airports, and military purposes. Microwaves are also used for point-to-point communication, as in the relaying of telephone and television signals and in private communication systems. The advantages of microwaves in this application are that the high directionality of the antennas makes it possible to use low-power, low-cost transmitters, and that the wide modulation band widths make it feasible to transmit many messages simultaneously. Another application of microwaves, microwave spectroscopy, lies in the investigation of the nature of molecules.—*I. R.*

MIDNIGHT SUN: the Sun seen at midnight at any place north of the arctic circle, or south of the antarctic circle. Because the apparent path of the Sun on the CELESTIAL SPHERE is inclined to the celestial equator, the angular distance of the Sun from the celestial pole (its co-declination) changes throughout the year. From the north celestial pole the co-declination of the Sun is greatest, 113½°, at the winter solstice; it is 90° at the equinoxes; and it is smallest, 66½°, at the summer solstice. If a star or other celestial object has a co-declination less than that of the latitude of the observer, it will move between the pole and the observer's horizon, never setting. (Such a star is called circumpolar for that observer.) Hence, in a place at a particular latitude, the Sun will remain continuously above the horizon as long as its co-declination is *less* than this latitude. For a place on the arctic circle (of latitude 66½°), the midnight Sun occurs just one night, at the summer solstice. (On the antarctic circle, it occurs at the winter solstice.) At the north pole, the Sun is above the horizon for 6 mos. and below it for 6 mos. There are 2 mos. without sunset in latitude 70° and 4 mos. in latitude 78°N.

Owing to bending of light by Earth's atmosphere, the Sun may actually be wholly below the horizon when it appears wholly above it. Allowing for this effect, and for the apparent size of the Sun in the sky, the theoretical figures given above are modified; some part of the Sun is above the horizon in north latitudes 70°, 78°, and 90° for 73, 128, and 192 days, respectively. The lengths of time for observers in corresponding southerly latitudes are comparable, but not exactly the same. Because Earth's orbital speed is greater near perihelion, on Jan. 4, than it is at aphelion, the Sun spends a shorter time south of the equator than it does north of the equator, so that in the same latitude, the period of midnight Sun is of shorter duration in the southern hemisphere than in the northern.—*M. W. O.*

MID-OCEANIC RIDGE: a 40,000-mi-long range of mountains which occupies the middle third of the Atlantic, Indian, and South Pacific oceans. It is one of Earth's three first-order features, the others being the continents with their margins and the ocean floor. The Ridge varies from a few hundred to 2,000 mi in width, and rises 1,000 to 2,000 fathoms above the adjoining ocean basin floor. In form, it is a broad, fractured swell. The Mid-Atlantic Ridge, the best-known of this world-encircling Mid-Oceanic Ridge, can be divided into distinctive physiographic provinces, which can be identified on most trans-Atlantic profiles. The Rift Valley, Rift Mts., and High Fractured Plateau, which constitute the crest provinces, form a strip 50 to 200 mi wide. The Rift Valley is bounded by the inward-facing scarps of the Rift Mts. The floor of the Rift Valley lies 500 to 1,500 fathoms below the adjacent peaks of the Rift Mts, which drop abruptly to the High Fractured Plateau, lying in depths of 1,600 to 1,800

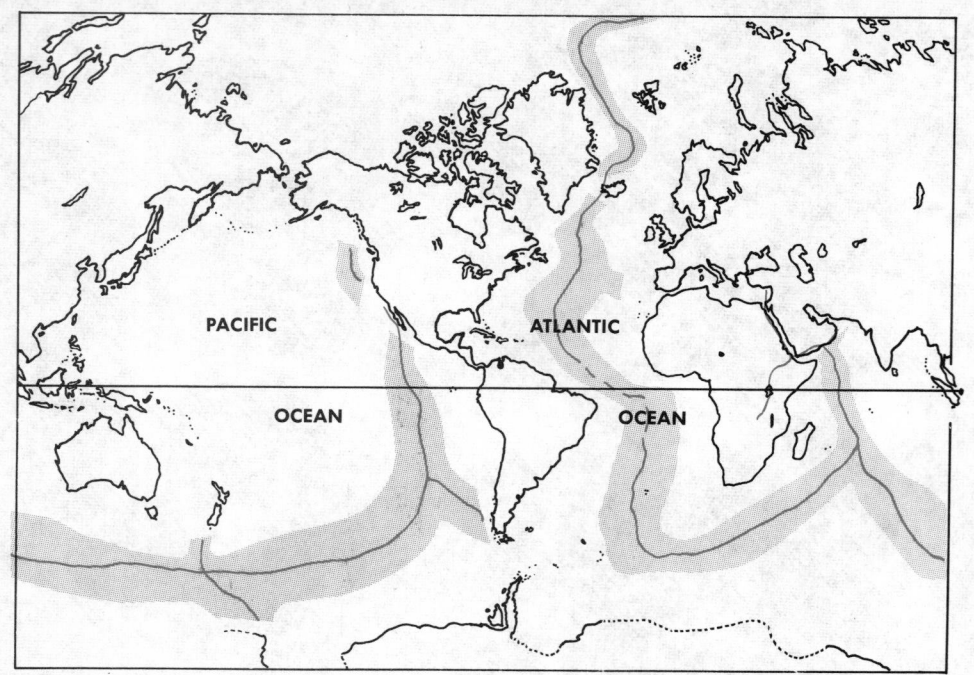

Mid-Oceanic Ridge and Rift Valley: Extensive oceanographic research, especially since World War II, has determined the broad topographical outlines of the world's sea bottoms. Solid blue line on map represents Rift Valley, and shaded areas the Mid-Oceanic Ridge.

fathoms on either side of the Rift Mts. An earthquake belt closely follows the Rift Valley throughout the North Atlantic. Extensions of this epicenter belt can be traced throughout the entire 40,000-mi length of the Mid-Oceanic Ridge. Since it has been shown in the North Atlantic and in several parts of the Indian Ocean and South Atlantic that the epicenter belt follows the median Rift Valley, probably the line of epicenters can be used to trace the Rift Valley in portions of the ocean not yet explored with the echo-sounder.

Measurements of the flow of heat through the ocean floor indicate that approximately seven times as much is flowing through the sea floor near the Rift Valley as through the normal ocean floor. Frequently a large positive magnetic anomaly is found associated with the Rift Valley, indicating the frequent presence of rocks having anomalously high magnetic susceptibility. Studies of crustal structure by use of the seismic-refraction technique reveal that the crest provinces of the Mid-Oceanic Ridge have a distinctly different crustal structure from that observed either under the continents or under the ocean basins. Rocks dredged from the Mid-Oceanic Ridge consist of basalt, gabbro, and serpentine.

The crest provinces of the Mid-Oceanic Ridge can be traced directly into the Rift Valley, Rift Mts, and high plateaus of Africa. Since these features of African geology are the result of tensional forces in Earth's crust, it is inferred that the Mid-Oceanic Ridge is of similar origin. The flank provinces can be divided into several steps, or ramps, each bounded by scarps; these provinces, compared to the crest ones, have a crustal structure more similar to that of the ocean basin floor. The values of heat and flow are nearly normal, and earthquake activity is absent.

The origin and structure of the Mid-Oceanic Ridge have been the subject of much speculation. Some suggest that the Mid-Oceanic Ridge represents a pile of debris left on the sea floor when the continents drifted apart, and others think the Ridge is composed of sediments which filled the cracks between drifting continents. But the high heat flow, earthquake activity, and seismic exploration reveal a modern, active feature with crustal characteristics not compatible with either of these hypotheses. Most presently active investigators believe that the Mid-Oceanic Ridge is the result of tension, and that material rising from the mantle beneath the crest is adding new rock to the floor of the Rift Valley. However, there are two schools of thought concerning the reason for this upflow of mantle material. The explanation favored by most workers is the CONVECTION THEORY, which attributes the fundamental features of the ocean floor to the effect of convection currents which rise beneath the crest of the Ridge and then flow laterally toward the continents. It is supposed that the drag of these currents on the underside of the continents causes the continents to be compressed and the ocean bottoms to be stretched. The second explanation attributes the stretching of the ocean floors to a general expansion of the interior of the planet. Since the Mid-Oceanic Ridge is the longest mountain range on the surface of Earth and covers an area almost equal to the area covered by the continents, its origin is of fundamental importance in considerations of the deformation of Earth's crust.—*B. H.*

MIGRATION: in zoology, the periodic movement of animals to a new area and their return to the original locality. Ordinarily the localities are inhabited at different seasons of the year, and the time of migration to and from these localities is regulated by periodic or rhythmic changes in the environment. The movement during migration is not an aimless drifting, but a more or less continuous, inherent action under the control of the animal, and it does not cease until the new locality is reached. The distance traveled and the direction taken, especially with reference to altitude and latitude, vary considerably among different species. Migratory behavior is found among several diverse groups of animals, and judging from their history there is little doubt that it arose independently at several times in the course of evolution. It is most prevalent among those animals in which locomotion is exceptionally well developed, and where the animals are susceptible to marked changes in their environment. That birds should be outstanding migrants is readily understandable, for they travel great distances with comparative ease and are completely dependent on their environment for food, shelter, and breeding places. (See BIRD MIGRATION.)

When animals travel great distances but do not return to the locality from which they started, the movement is properly termed *emigration.* When the return migration is made by different individuals, the term *remigration* is used. Since migration has arisen independently many times, it is not surprising that there is a wide divergence in the extent, the causes, and the methods employed among the various groups.

Invertebrates: Of invertebrate animals the most outstanding migrants are found among insects. There are many examples of emigration and remigration, but the only known example of true migration, where the same individuals return to the locality from which they started, is the migration of the monarch butterfly. This unique ability of the monarch is probably the result of its unusually strong flying ability and the fact that it is longer-lived than other related species.

During the late summer and early fall the newly formed adult monarchs in northern U. S. A. and Canada aggregate in flocks and, soon after cold weather begins, fly southward. The vast hordes, which fly and rest as a group, are unbelievably abundant. Their wintering grounds are primarily the southern U. S. A. from Florida to California, extending northward up the California coast as far as Monterey, and up the Atlantic coast as far as North Carolina. While on their wintering grounds from November to March, the butterflies are inactive, hibernating in enormous masses in the treetops. As spring approaches they become active and begin their migration, often individually, reaching their breeding grounds as the milkweed (*Asclepius*), their host plant, becomes suitable for their eggs. The young larvae that hatch from the eggs develop on the milkweeds, pupate, and later emerge as adult butterflies. This migration of the monarchs is somewhat similar to that of birds, with the exception that the adult monarchs make only one round trip in their lifetime, for they die soon after the eggs are laid. In another butterfly, *Pyrameis cardui,* the adults fly north and lay their eggs, and the young travel south in the fall. The stimulus for these migrations in butterflies is unknown.

Grasshopper migrations (remigration) and their devastating effects are well known. The chief migratory locust of North America is *Melanoplus mexicanus.* At various times this species has migrated from the Rocky Mt area, its permanent breeding area, into the states immediately west of the Mississippi. After ravaging the area visited, adults lay eggs in the soil and, with the approach of winter, die. The following spring and summer, when the eggs hatch and the grasshoppers develop, there is a return flight to the Rocky Mt area. Migration occurs usually between temperatures of 22°C to 34°C, with swarms arriving on warm days and alighting late in the afternoon. The direction taken seems to be dependent mostly on wind direction, the locusts being driven by the wind.

Among invertebrates other than insects, only instances of rather local movements are known in response to seasonal changes in environment. In Douglas Lake, Mich., for example, seven species of pulmonate snails migrate into deep water when cold weather comes and return to shallow water in the spring. Crabs, prawns, lobsters, and squids, which live along the shores of the ocean, also go into deep water in winter and return to the shore in spring.

Fishes: With the evolution of vertebrate animals and their unique internal skeleton of bone or cartilage, the methods of locomotion were much improved. It is not unusual, therefore, to find migratory behavior well developed in fishes, mammals, and birds, the three groups of vertebrates with the most efficient locomotion, and present to only a limited extent in the two remaining groups, amphibians and reptiles.

Migratory marine and fresh-water fishes are classified under two main groups: *anadromous* species, which migrate toward shore from deep water, often ascending rivers to spawn, and *catadromous* species, which normally live along shores or in shallow waters and move into deep water at favorable seasons to spawn. In each of these groups a marked change from the usual habitat of the species may occur, such as from salt to fresh water, or the reverse.

An example of an anadromous species is the herring. The breeding period in the spring and the subsequent feeding occur in shallow marine waters. The herrings then move into deeper water and remain there throughout the winter. Other fish that resemble the herring in migratory habits are the mackerel, tunny, pilchard, hake, garfish, bluefish, and sharks.

The salmon and shad are also anadromous species, but they are fresh-water fish and breed in rivers and lakes. In many species of salmon the adults are found in the ocean, where they feed and live actively for 2 to 7 yr without breeding. When they are ready to spawn they migrate from the ocean to the rivers and finally to their breeding places, which are often large lakes. After the salmon enter fresh water they can no longer feed, for the digestive organs undergo a partial degeneration. All the time they are in fresh water, and it may be a whole·year, they live on the food materials stored in their tissues. In the longer rivers of the Pacific coast, where the distance traveled upstream may be as much as 1,000 mi, the salmon are so exhausted after spawning that there is little doubt that all of them die. After the young are hatched, they remain in fresh water from 6 to 18 months and then descend the rivers to the sea, often remaining close to the mouths of the rivers in which they hatched.

The most remarkable example of a catadromous species is the eel. Its breeding grounds lie between the Bermudas and the West Indies. After the young develop they migrate from these grounds in the spring, entering the estuaries and rivers of W Europe and E America, where they remain for 5 to 20 yr or more. When they reach sexual maturity they return to their breeding grounds, a journey of 3,000 mi, and upon arrival, spawn and die.

The causes for these extensive and costly migrations and remigrations among fishes are not known. That they continue to occur indicates that the spawning area is well suited to the reproductive needs of the species and hence provides for the continuance of the species. Migratory fishes may be influenced by temperature and salt content of the water, but neither of these factors apparently provides the stimulus for the initiation of migration. There is a suggestion that salmon in the sea require more oxygen as they reach sexual maturity and therefore seek river water, which has a higher oxygen content. The evidence suggests that the particular route taken by the salmon as it ascends the streams is determined by chemical (and perhaps temperature) stimuli, which differ from one branch to another of a large stream.

Migration: Hatched near Sargasso Sea, eel larvae drift toward fresh waters—a year's journey of 1,000 mi for American eels, 3 yr and 3,000 mi for European species. Several years later, when mature, adults return to Sargasso Sea area to lay eggs, and migration cycle is repeated.

Mammals: Among mammals, migration and emigration are known, and in many instances the primary cause is a seasonal variation in food supply. The arrival and departure of whales from particular seas has long been known to those engaged in whaling. California gray whales frequent the coast of California from early winter to late spring, where they bring forth their young in the bays and lagoons of the lower coast. With the approach of summer they move northward, remaining close to shore. They spend the summer in the Arctic Ocean and Okhotsk Sea, feeding on the rich *plankton* (collective animal and plant life floating on the surface of the water) or on those species of fishes that feed on these same minute organisms. As cool weather approaches, the whales return to their winter haunts. Migrations are also known in the humpback, whalebone, blue, and sperm whales.

The general occurrence of migration among whales, as well as among other marine mammals, is apparently necessitated by the seasonal variations in food supply of oceanic areas. The whalebone whale, for example, could not survive in those oceans where uniform tropical temperatures prevail throughout the year, because of a deficient supply of its primary food source, the plankton organisms. The richest sources of plankton are to be found at certain seasons of the year in the waters of the far north or the highest southern latitudes. In these waters, which represent a transition from warm to polar regions, variations in temperature are marked, and as a result organic materials at the bottom are brought toward the surface. Acting somewhat like fertilizer, these materials provide the plankton organisms with the substances they need for growth and reproduction. The ultimate result is a very rich plankton fauna that provides food for the whalebone whale and for many other marine animals upon which other species of whales feed. A remarkable feature of the whalebone whale is its ability to store food in the form of blubber while it is in northern seas. Hence, when in the southern waters, where its food is scarce, it is still provided with a reserve store of food.

The most remarkable migration among marine mammals is that of the fur seal. In this case the stimulus is not one of food but rather of reproduction, the animals migrating in the spring to their breeding grounds in the Pribilof Is, off the west coast of Alaska. The old bulls pass the winter just south of the Aleutians, or in the Gulf of Alaska, but the females, pups, and young males winter as far south as S California. During their 3,000-mi journey north in the spring, the females maintain a true course and pass unerringly through the narrow waters of the Aleutian Is. Soon after they arrive they are delivered of their pups, and shortly afterward the female is again impregnated. She then feeds in the sea, returning at two-day intervals to nurse her pups. The old bulls watch over the breeding grounds continuously, not leaving even to feed. By August the new pups are born, and the exhausted bulls, having abstained from food for 3 months, return to the sea. The pups are nursed until November, when they are full grown, and then the cows, pups, and young males begin their long migration to the winter area.

Among land mammals, extensive migrations are made by several species. Caribou present an impressive spectacle as they move in great numbers from summer to winter quarters. It is believed that the search for suitable food is the stimulus for their migration; since climatic conditions affect the availability of food, the migration routes and extent of migration, with regard to numbers of animals and distance covered, may vary from year to year. Other hoofed mammals that undergo migrations in response to varying food supply are elk, mule deer, and mountain sheep.

Because of their ability to fly, one naturally expects bats to migrate. The most extended migrations occur among the lasiurine bats, or tree dwellers. The cave-dwelling bats are subjected to a more or less uniform temperature throughout the year, for caves, even in the northern states, seldom vary much in temperature. Hence these bats can winter much farther north than tree-dwelling species, which have been found in Bermuda and in the S Atlantic states during the late fall and winter, far removed from their breeding grounds in the north.

Some mammals perform seasonal migrations that are local in extent but are nevertheless regular. Norway rats, for example, may leave their human habitations in the spring for the meadows and fields, where they breed and subsist on grains, vegetables, and other crops. With the first frosts of autumn, they return to the farms and villages, where there is more food and better shelter.

Emigration of Mammals: The migrations of mammals discussed above represent true migrations, since two-way movements are involved. Equally famous and well known among mammals are one-way movements, or emigrations, where thousands of individuals leave an area, usually to take up residence in a new locality.

Emigration may be caused by lack of food, in which case the population seeks a new territory with sufficient food; by detrimental changes in climatic conditions; or by an over-

PHOTOGRAPHIC MAGNITUDES

population of the home area. Of these factors, overpopulation has been noted most frequently as the initial stimulus among wild animals. It was once thought that the marked increase in the number of individuals resulted from an abnormal abundance of food. It is known now, however, that overpopulation is due to an increase in fecundity, and the available data suggest that some substances in the vegetation exert a stimulating effect on the reproductive organs and hence on sexual activity. Why these substances should occur abundantly in the vegetation only in particular years and at irregular intervals is not understood.

The classic example of emigration is that of the lemming, *Lemmus lemmus.* The mouselike rodents live in colonies in the birch and willow habitat of the high Norwegian mountains. They feed on grasses and roots, and normally produce one or two litters each summer, with four or five individuals per litter. Periodically there is a tremendous increase in their reproductive power, three or four litters being produced each summer, with as many as 11 young in each litter—an increase of approximately 300 to 400%! With the tremendous increase in numbers, the food supply is inadequate and emigration occurs. The hordes move first to the edge of the plateau they inhabit, and some lemmings move as far as the nearby forest. The continued increase in numbers in the following year forces the lemmings to go farther, and the valleys and slopes soon become covered with them. In the great lemming years the rivers and fiords are littered with their drowned bodies, for they always emigrate westward, across all barriers, and eventually reach the ocean, where they enter the water and perish. The annual loss to agriculture and forestry caused by mice and lemmings is so great over the entire world that there is an almost never-ending war to prevent the periodic plagues of these rodents.

Other emigratory mammals include the gray squirrel, snowshoe hare, beaver, bushy-tailed wood rat, and Norway rat. See ANIMAL NAVIGATION.—*A. P. E.*

MILKY WAY: the faintly shimmering band of stars that stretches more or less in a great circle around the sky. Known to the ancient Romans as the *Via Lactea,* it figured

Milky Way: This hand drawing, based on individual plotting of about 7,000 stars, has grid lines superimposed which define galactic coordinates. This type of projection allows a spread of 360° all around the galactic plane, although the edge-on view conceals the spiral design of our galaxy. Both the Small and the Large Magellanic Cloud, outside the Milky Way, appear in background in lower right quadrant. (*Lund Obs.*)

LUND OBSERVATORY

MARTIN KESKÜLA
TATJANA KESKÜLA

prominently in the mythologies of primitive peoples. It can be seen on any clear night, away from city lights, and is best viewed against inky-black tropical night skies. Telescopic observations show that the band of the Milky Way is composed mainly of multitudes of faint stars. It outlines the central plane of our Milky Way system, often also called our Galaxy, the star system of which our Sun is a part. The phenomenon of the band of the Milky Way is produced by stars at greatly varying distances, some of them within a few hundred light-years of the Sun, others possibly as distant as 20,000 lt-yr or more.

Our Milky Way system contains approximately 100 billion stars, some of them intrinsically much brighter than our Sun, others intrinsically very much fainter, and with our Sun near the middle of the scale of intrinsic brightnesses. The Milky Way system is a flattened spiral galaxy with a circular diameter of approximately 100,000 lt-yr, and a maximum thickness, in the central region, of the order of 4,000 lt-yr. The whole Milky Way system is probably embedded in a vast, almost spherical halo of very thinly distributed interstellar gas and relatively inconspicuous stars of great cosmic age.

Our Sun is a star close to the central plane of the Galaxy, but at a distance of 25,000 to 30,000 lt-yr from the center of the system. The high flattening observed for our Galaxy suggests that the whole system must be in rapid rotation, and this has indeed been confirmed by direct observation. The solar system and most of the stars in its vicinity move around the galactic center at approximately 170 mi/sec, requiring close to 250 million yr to complete one single circuit around the galactic center. The eccentric location of the Sun is proved in a variety of ways. In Sagittarius and Scorpius the Milky Way is both brighter and broader than in other parts; in the opposite direction in the sky, near Auriga and Gemini, are the thinnest and least spectacular regions. First conclusive proof of the eccentric position was provided by Harlow Shapley when he showed, about 1918, that the distant globular star clusters exhibit a striking concentration toward the Sagittarius-Scorpius section of the Milky Way.

The most interesting feature of our Milky Way system is that it apparently exhibits spiral structure in and near the central plane. In this respect our Galaxy resembles the spiral GALAXIES beyond it, which are found in great numbers with the aid of large modern telescopes. The Andromeda Galaxy, about 2 million lt-yr from the Sun, is perhaps the best-known example of a spiral galaxy and the one closest to our own. Some varieties of stars and INTERSTELLAR MATTER (gas and dust) delineate most clearly the spiral structure in the Andromeda Galaxy and other systems, and for many years astronomers have been gathering evidence to help them to trace the spiral structure of the Milky Way system. One reason why this is a very complex problem is that the Sun and Earth are near the central plane of the system and the pattern of distribution of the "spiral tracers" is not readily revealed. However, the existence of at least four sections of spiral arms is now fairly well established. The first evidence for spiral structure in the near regions of our Galaxy comes from studies of the distribution of relatively nearby gaseous nebulas and young stars, or groupings of such stars, mostly of the variety with white-hot surfaces (surface temperatures approximately 55,000°F), all of which are known to trace the spiral structure most effectively in galaxies beyond our own. Absorption lines produced in the spectra of very distant stars by intervening interstellar gas assist further in outlining the spiral structure by traditional optical methods. Intervening cosmic dust considerably limits optical telescopes in the direction of the central plane but does not diminish the intensity of radiations recorded by radio telescopes. Radio astronomical techniques are therefore being employed to detect interstellar gas—notably hydrogen—at great distances from the Sun.

In the late 1940s, Walter Baade suggested that there are two basic star populations in the Milky Way system. Population I, which is found mostly in the outlying regions, is composed of interstellar gas and cosmic dust, and blue-white supergiants, singly or in groups, that are associated with the spiral structure. According to present views on star birth and evolution, the stars of Population I are young on the cosmic scale of time measurement—10 million to 100 million yr old, which is about 1/100 of the age of Sun and Earth. Population II contains the vast numbers of the less spectacular older stars, none of them intrinsically very brilliant, which inhabit the spaces between the spiral arms and the central core of our Galaxy as well as the thinly populated outer halo. Population II stars include the oldest known stars, with estimated ages equal to at least 10 billion yr, twice the age of Sun and Earth. Baade's two populations are now regarded as a simplified description of a complex situation. Population II includes a great variety of objects of varying ages. The oldest of these objects were probably built up from the cloud of presumably almost pure hydrogen from which our Milky Way system has gradually evolved. In the interiors of the more massive stars that were originally formed, nuclear transformations must have taken place on a vast scale and chemical elements other than hydrogen must have been formed. As some of these stars exploded in the first few billion years since the birth of the Milky Way system, they returned their gases to the interstellar gas, including some chemical elements heavier than hydrogen. The next generation of stars condensed from the interstellar gas composed of hydrogen enriched with heavier elements. And so the process continued until we reach the present generation of young stars, condensed from interstellar gas with a fair amount of the heavier chemical elements. We thus view our Milky Way system and its component stars as being in continuing slow evolution.—*B. J. B.*

MILL, JOHN STUART, 1806–73, English philosopher; b. London. His father gave him the equivalent of a college education during his early childhood. One of the most influential 19th-cent. British philosophers, Mill became a main figure in the traditions of empiricism, which maintains that all knowledge is derived from sense perception, and utilitarianism, which holds that the production of pleasure and alleviation of pain are the basic standards of ethical judgment. Among his most important works were: *A System of Logic* (1843), *An Examination of Sir William Hamilton's Philosophy* (1865), and the essay *On Liberty* (1859). Mill explained mathematical principles as generalizations from mental images, and defined matter as "the permanent possibility of sensation." In logic, he criticized deductive inference as useless for scientific discovery, and he formulated some of the main rules of induction—"Mill's Canons."—*R. A.*

MILLER INDICES: a system of numbers indicating the angles that the planes of a crystal make with its axes. It is computed by taking the reciprocal of the distance from the origin (measured in lattice units) at which the plane intersects each axis, clearing fractions, if necessary. Thus, if one plane intersects the three crystal axes at 1, ⅓, and 2 lattice units, and if a second plane intersects the first axis at ¼ unit but is parallel to the other two axes, the Miller indices would be 261 and 400, respectively. (To get 261, we take the reciprocals of 1, ⅓, and 2, which gives us 1, 3, ½; multiplying by 2 to clear fractions, we get 2, 6, 1.) For hexagonal crystals, a set of 4 numbers is used, the third of which is equal to the sum of the first two, but is opposite in sign. The fact that the Miller indices are small whole numbers is an indication of the regular arrangement of atoms in a crystal.—*I. R.*

MILLIKAN, ROBERT ANDREWS, 1868–1953, U. S. physicist; b. Morrison, Ill. For his determination of the charge of the electron and for his experimental verification of Einstein's photoelectric equation, he received the Nobel prize, 1923. His research on cosmic rays (which he named) showed that these rays are absorbed by Earth's atmosphere, implying extraterrestrial origin. He was a member of the National Academy of Sciences.—*D. H. D. R.*

MILNE, EDWARD ARTHUR, 1896–1950, English mathematician and physicist; b. Hull. He did research on astrophysics, particularly on the study of the surfaces of stars, and developed kinematical relativity, which provided an alternative to Einstein's general relativity theory. He became a fellow of the Royal Society (1926) and a professor at Oxford Univ. (1928).—*D. H. D. R.*

E. A. Milne
(Yerkes Observatory)

MIMICRY: see ANIMAL CAMOUFLAGE.

MINERAL: any of a large variety of naturally occurring substances possessing characteristic chemical and physical properties. Most minerals are crystalline (see CRYSTALLOGRAPHY) and of inorganic origin; among the commonest are silicates, oxides, and sulfides. Uncombined elements are called "native," *e.g.* native silver, native sulfur. Most mineral species are compounds with fixed or closely limited compositions, depending on the degree of ionic substitution (isomorphism) permitted by the crystal structure. Only elements having appropriate charges and ionic radii within a limited range can substitute for each other. All ionic charges (valences) must be in balance: a condition sometimes fulfilled by multiple substitutions. Many common minerals are members of isomorphous groups, and their physical characteristics, *e.g.* axial and interfacial angles, hardness, specific gravity, indices of refraction, optical axes, and color, vary directly with their composition. Some substances are polymorphous (form different crystal structures in response to different environments), *e.g.* calcite (trigonal) and aragonite (orthorhombic), the high- and low-temperature forms of calcium carbonate. There are some non-crystalline (amorphous) minerals—mostly hydrous, colloidal materials, such as opal.

Minerals have been formed in many ways and are still being formed. The history of minerals is actually the history of Earth, for Earth is composed of rocks, and rocks are composed of minerals. Some minerals have crystallized directly from molten rock (MAGMA) at depth (see INTRUSIVE ROCK) or from magma that poured out over the surface as lava (EXTRUSIVE ROCK). Rocks of Earth's crust have undergone innumerable partial or complete cycles of weathering, erosion, deposition, burial, consolidation, metamorphism (possibly even remelting), and uplift. Each process, with its own environment, controls the formation, existence, and destruction of minerals.

Rocks consist of minerals: Fordham gneiss, shown here, is a metamorphic rock consisting principally of the minerals biotite mica, quartz, and hornblende. (*Amer. Mus. of Nat. Hist.*)

On WEATHERING, soluble fractions are removed and accumulate in the ocean or in inland basins. Resistant minerals and insoluble residues are broken down mechanically, removed by erosion, and redeposited as bedded SEDIMENTS. The soluble constituents may be reprecipitated by organisms (*e.g.* as skeletal parts, teeth, shells, and fecal pellets), by inorganic reactions, and by evaporation of waters in landlocked basins. On consolidation of sediments (diagenesis), some of the constituents are redistributed by means of entrapped interstitial (connate) water. Interstices may be filled by cementing, or by overgrowths on the original grains, and joint fissures and other openings may be lined by crystals precipitated from such solutions.

An increase in temperature resulting from deep burial and tectonic activity (regional METAMORPHISM) or the proximity of igneous intrusives (contact metamorphism) intensifies the reactions between rock constituents, and new minerals develop that are stable in the changed environments. These reactions are aided by the connate water, by water released from clays and other hydrous minerals, and, in contact metamorphism, by "juvenile" waters released by the crystallizing magma. Since the most soluble constituents remain till last in the "mother liquors" of crystallizing magmas, those fluids become enriched in strong fluxing agents ("mineralizers") such as carbon dioxide, fluorine, chlorine, sulfur, and boron. Portions of magmas thus enriched tend to form coarsely crystalline bodies (pegmatites) in which many of the rarer elements are concentrated.

The high-temperature hydrothermal solutions of the metamorphic zone tend to migrate toward zones of lesser pressure, usually toward the surface. Such solutions dissolve and transfer enormous quantities of the more soluble elements and redeposit them in different environments. The common metals, which constitute only a few parts per million in most rocks, are thus extracted and later re-precipitated in the form of rich veins and wallrock-replacement deposits.

Thermodynamic stability in any given environment is the controlling factor for the presence, composition, and physical characteristics of all minerals. Physical chemistry, and particularly crystal chemistry, can account for the presence of 25-ft-long crystals of spodumene in a pegmatite dike, pseudomorphs of limonite after pyrite in the weathered and leached outcrop (gossan) of a mineral deposit, amethyst crystals lining a pocket in a basalt flow, concretions of siderite in a shale, ruby and sapphire pebbles in a river gravel, and borax beds in a playa lake basin. (See table of minerals on following pages; also Color Plates 64–65.)

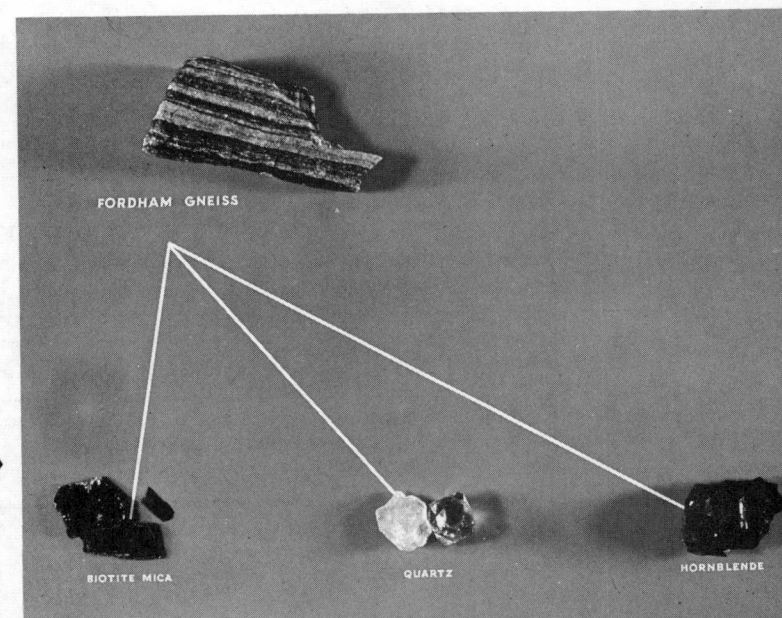

FORDHAM GNEISS

BIOTITE MICA   QUARTZ   HORNBLENDE

SOME IMPORTANT MINERALS

(*Note:* Minerals to which complete articles are devoted elsewhere in this encyclopedia are identified in the first column below by the use of *ITALIC CAPITAL* letters.)

MINERAL (Composition) GROUP	CRYSTAL SYSTEM, SYMMETRY CLASS, HABIT	CLEAVAGE PLANES AND ANGLES	COLOR, TRANSPARENCY, TRANSLUCENCY, LUSTER, OTHER OPTICAL PROPERTIES	HARDNESS (MOHS SCALE); SPECIFIC GRAVITY	PHYSICAL AND CHEMICAL CHARACTERISTICS; OCCURRENCE; USES
ALBITE $NaAlSi_3O_8$ *Plagioclase* FELDSPARS	Triclinic, $\bar{1}$. Stocky to tabular. Platy. Albite, pericline, and Carlsbad twins. Dissem. grains.	Pinacoidal (001) and (010) at 86°. Twinning striations on (001).	Colorless to white; various tints. Transp. to transl.; vitreous.	6 2.6	Member of solid-solution series with anorthite ($Ca\ Al_2\ Si_2O_8$). In alka igneous and metamorphic rocks; in pegmatites. Platy variety forms end-s replacement bodies in pegmatites.
ALMANDITE $Fe_3Al_2(SiO_4)_3$ GARNETS	Isometric, $\frac{4}{m}\ \bar{3}\ \frac{2}{m}$. Dodec-ahedral and trapezohedral.	None.	Various shades of red. Transp. to transl.; vitreous.	7½ 4.3	Member of solid-solution series with spessartite (Mn-rich) pyrope (Mg-r Common metamorphic mineral in gneisses and schists. In placers. Use abrasive in sand-blasting, dental tools, garnet papers. Gemstone.
AMBER $C_{40}H_{64}O_4$ (approx.)	Amorphous. Drop-shaped to irreg. masses.	None.	Light yellow to reddish brown. Transp. to sub-transl. Vitreous to resinous.	2—2½ 1.0	Fossilized resin from coniferous trees. May contain insects and other fossil sedimentary rocks. Flammable. Electrified by friction. Gem and orname stone.
ANALCITE $NaAlSi_2O_6 \cdot H_2O$ ZEOLITES	Isometric, $\frac{4}{m}\ \bar{3}\ \frac{2}{m}$. Trap-ezohedral. Granular; dissem. grains.	None.	Colorless to white; various tints. Transp. to subtransl.; vitreous.	5 2.3	As primary mineral in silica-deficient to basic alkaline igneous rocks. In v veins, and sheared zones. Common in playa sediments as alteration pro of volcanic ash and clay minerals.
ANDALUSITE Al_2SiO_5	Orthorhombic, $\frac{2}{m}\ \frac{2}{m}\ \frac{2}{m}$. Rough prisms. Granular.	Prismatic (110) at about 90°.	Gray; also pink, red, violet, brown. Transp. to transl. Vitreous to greasy.	7½ 3.2	Polymorph of kyanite and sillimanite. As metacrysts in phyllites and sch replacement bodies in altered volcanics. Sintered to produce mullite refracti and porcelains. Gems include transparent stones and chiastolite, which carbonaceous inclusions in cross-shaped patterns.
ANDRADITE $Ca_3(Fe,Ti)_2(SiO_4)_3$ GARNETS	Isometric, $\frac{4}{m}\ \bar{3}\ \frac{2}{m}$. Dodec-ahedral; trapezohedral. Granular.		Dark red to brown; yellow (topazolite); green (demantoid); black (melanite). Transp. to sub-transl. Vitreous to resinous.	7—7½ 3.7	Member of solid-solution series with uvarovite (Cr-rich) and grossularite rich). As metacrysts and masses in tactites and skarns. Dark, Ti-rich vari in alkaline igneous complexes. Topazolite and demantoid are gems.
ANHYDRITE $CaSO_4$	Orthorhombic, $\frac{2}{m}\ \frac{2}{m}\ \frac{2}{m}$. Crystals rare. Granular; plumose; radial; fibrous.	Pinacoidal (001), (100), and (010), forming cubic fragments.	Colorless to bluish or violet. Transp. to transl.; vitreous; pearly.	3½ 3.0	Common evaporite mineral; as extensive beds or as disseminations in salt b Major constituent of salt-dome cap rocks.
ANTHOPHYLLITE $(Mg,Fe)_7Si_8O_{22}(OH)_2$ AMPHIBOLES	Orthorhombic, $\frac{2}{m}\ \frac{2}{m}\ \frac{2}{m}$. Prismatic. Bladed; acicular; fibrous; columnar; radial.	Prismatic (110) at 56° and 124°.	White; gray; brown; green. Transl.; vitreous; silky.	5½—6 2.8—3.2	In metamorphosed basic and ultrabasic rocks and some iron format Fibrous variety is a commercial asbestos.
APATITE $Ca_5(PO_4)_3(F,Cl,OH, CO_3) \cdot nH_2O$	Hexagonal, $\frac{6}{m}$. Prismatic; tabular. Granular; collo-form; concretionary.	Not distinctive.	Wide range of colors and shades. Transp. to sub-transl.; vitreous to earthy.	6 2.9—3.2	Minor constituent of most igneous and metamorphic rocks. Crystals in matites and high-temp. veins. Teeth and bones are apatite. Sedimentary bec amorphous carbonate-apatite (as fossilized bones, teeth, fecal pellets, cor tions) are mined for phosphate chemicals and fertilizers.
ARAGONITE $CaCO_3$ CALCITE	Orthorhombic, $\frac{2}{m}\ \frac{2}{m}\ \frac{2}{m}$. Prismatic; acicular; tabular. Cyclic twins. Colloform; concretionary.	Not distinctive.	Colorless to white; some tints. Transp. to transl. Vitreous to resinous; pearly.	3½—4 2.9	Much rarer than polymorph, calcite. Deposited from solution in near-su environments, including caves, hot springs, shallow marine shelves. Cora some shells, including mother-of-pearl and pearls, are aragonite.
ARSENOPYRITE $FeAsS$	Monoclinic, pseudo-ortho-rhombic, $\frac{2}{m}$. Prismatic to stocky, striated. Granular.	Not distinctive.	Silver white; tarnishes. Opaque; metallic; streak dark.	5½—6 5.9—6.2	Fusible. Widespread in hydrothermal mineral deposits of high to mode temperature in many environments. Ore of arsenic, which is recovered f smelter gases.
AUGITE $(Ca,Na)(Mg,Fe'', Fe''',Al)(Si,Al)_2O_6$ PYROXENES	Monoclinic, $\frac{2}{m}$. Prismatic to stocky. Dissem. grains.	Prismatic (110) at 87° and 93°. Var. diallage has pin-acoidal parting (100).	Green to black. Transl. to subtransl.; vitreous.	6 3.2—3.6	Member of solid-solution series with diopside (Mg-rich) and aegerite (Na-Fe'''-rich). Major constituent of many intermediate to basic igneous rocks phenocrysts in porphyries. In gneisses, skarns, and some pegmatites and h temp. veins.
AZURITE $Cu_3(CO_3)_2(OH)_2$	Monoclinic, $\frac{2}{m}$. Tabular; prismatic; stocky. Collo-form; concretionary.	Domal (011) ca. 60° and 120°.	Various shades of blue. Transp. to subtransl. Vitreous to earthy.	3½—4 3.8	In gossans and oxidized zones as weathering product of primary copper Concretions replace sandstones in "red-bed" type deposits. Minor ore of per. Crystals and stalactitic forms cut as gems.
BARITE $BaSO_4$	Orthorhombic, $\frac{2}{m}\ \frac{2}{m}\ \frac{2}{m}$. Tabular; prismatic. Gran-ular to earthy. Colloform.	Dormal (011) 78° and 102°; basal (001) at 90°.	Colorless to white; various tints, esp. blue. Transp. to subtransl. Vitreous to earthy.	3—3½ 4.5	In mod.- to low-temp. hydrothermal veins and as replacement bodies in li stone. In residual deposits. Used in drilling-muds, glass, fillers; is major or barium and its compounds.
"BAUXITE" $Al_2O_3 \cdot H_2O$	Amorphous. Pisolitic; oolitic; colloform; earthy.	None.	White to red or brown; opaque; waxy to earthy.	1—3 2.5	Clayey odor. Complex mixture of microcrystalline and colloidal hydrated ox of Al, Fe, Mn, etc. As lateritic caps produced by tropical-humid weatherin alumina-rich rocks and residual clays. Major ore of aluminum. Sintered to duce abrasives and refractories.
BERYL $Be_3Al_2(Si_6O_{18})$	Hexagonal, $\frac{6}{m}\ \frac{2}{m}\ \frac{2}{m}$. Pris-matic to stocky. Columnar; radial.	None.	Wide range of colors, tints, shades. Transp. to transl.; vitreous to greasy.	7½—8 2.8	In pegmatites, high-temp. veins, and greisens. Also as end-stage concretio masses in granites. Ore of beryllium. Gem varieties include emerald, a marine, morganite (pink), golden and smoky beryl. Some asteriated.
BIOTITE $K(Mg,Fe)_3AlSi_3O_{10}(OH,F)_2$ MICAS	Monoclinic, $\frac{2}{m}$. Prismatic to tabular. Foliated masses; scales.	Basal (001), forming elastic plates.	Dark green or dark brown to black. Subtransl.; splendent to dull.	2—3 2.7—3.5	Member of complex solid-solution series with phlogopite (Mg-rich) and a varieties. Widespread constituent of igneous and metamorphic rocks. L crystals in pegmatites and high-temp. veins.

SOME IMPORTANT MINERALS—Continued

MINERAL (Composition) GROUP	CRYSTAL SYSTEM, SYMMETRY CLASS, HABIT	CLEAVAGE PLANES AND ANGLES	COLOR, TRANSPARENCY, TRANSLUCENCY, LUSTER, OTHER OPTICAL PROPERTIES	HARDNESS (MOHS SCALE); SPECIFIC GRAVITY	PHYSICAL AND CHEMICAL CHARACTERISTICS; OCCURRENCE; USES
RAX ₂B₄O₇·10H₂O	Monoclinic, $\frac{2}{m}$. Stocky to tabular. Granular to earthy.	Prismatic (110) at 87° and 93°; pinacoidal (100) at 123°.	Colorless to white; various tints. Transp. to subtransl. Vitreous to earthy.	2 1.7	Soluble. Sweetish taste. As beds or concretionary masses in playa lake evaporite deposits. Source of boron and borates.
RNITE ₅FeS₄	Isometric, $\frac{4}{m}\overline{3}\frac{2}{m}$. Cubic; dodecahedral; octahedral. Granular.	Not distinctive.	Copper red to light brown. Tarnishes to iridescent film. Opaque; metallic; streak grayish black.	3 5.1	Minor accessory in igneous rocks. In high- to mod.-temp. hydrothermal vein and replacement deposits. Called "peacock ore." Ore of copper.
LCITE CO₃	Trigonal, $\overline{3}\frac{2}{m}$. Rhombohedral; scalenohedral; prismatic; stocky; tabular; etc. Colloform; concretionary; earthy; fibrous.	Rhombohedral (10$\overline{1}$1) at 75° and 105°.	Colorless to white; various tints and shades. Transp. to transl. Vitreous; pearly; earthy. Fluorescent, phosphorescent, and triboluminescent varieties. Marked birefringence (double refraction).	3 2.7	Polymorph of aragonite. Principal constituent of marl, chalk, limestone, marble. In veins and hot-spring deposits. As hydrothermal alteration product of calcic igneous rocks. Used in cement, fertilizers, chemical processing. Transparent crystals (Iceland spar) used in optical instruments. Ornamental varieties include Mexican onyx (colloform) and satin spar (fibrous).
RNOTITE (UO₂)₂(VO₄)₂·3H₂O	Orthorhombic or monoclinic. Platy. Microcrystalline; compact to powdery.	Basal (001).	Yellow; yellow green; yellow orange. Transl.; pearly; earthy.	2—3 4.6	Weathering product of primary uranium and vanadium ores. As veinlets and disseminations in sandstones, conglomerates, limestones; as replacements of fossil logs. With similar Ca-analogue, tyuyamunite, a major ore of uranium and vanadium.
SSITERITE O₂	Tetragonal, $\frac{4}{m}\frac{2}{m}\frac{2}{m}$. Prismatic; dipyramidal. Colloform and concretionary ("wood tin").	Prismatic (100) at 90°.	Various shades of reddish to yellowish brown; black. Zoned. Transp. to subtransl. Adamantine to greasy; metallic.	6—7 7.0	In pegmatites, greisens, high- to mod.-temp. veins. In placers. Major ore of tin. Minor gemstone.
LESTITE SO₄	Orthorhombic, $\frac{2}{m}\frac{2}{m}\frac{2}{m}$. Tabular; lath-shaped; prismatic. Columnar; fibrous; concretionary; granular.	Prismatic (210) at 76° and 104°; basal (001) at 90°.	Colorless to light blue. Transp. to transl. Vitreous; silky.	3—3½ 4.0	As deposits from hydrothermal and ground-water solutions, in vugs and veins, and as replacement bodies in limestones. As beds in evaporite deposits. Ore of strontium and its compounds.
ALCEDONY O₂ QUARTZ	Orthorhombic, $\frac{2}{m}\frac{2}{m}\frac{2}{m}$. Always micro-crystalline. Colloform; concretionary; pseudomorphic.	None.	Wide range of colors and shades. Transp. to subtransl.; vitreous to waxy.	7 2.6	Deposited from solution at mod. to low temp. on free surfaces or as replacements of sandstone, limestone, wood, coral, etc. Common in gravels. Chert, flint, and novaculite used as refractories, abrasives, and in construction. Agate used in instrument bearings and grinding mortars. Gem varieties include agate, onyx, chrysoprase, bloodstone, carnelian, jasper, petrified wood.
ALCOCITE ₂S	Orthorhombic, $\frac{2}{m}\frac{2}{m}\frac{2}{m}$ (high-temp. phase hexagonal). Tabular; stocky; prismatic. Cyclic twins. Granular; spoty.	Not distinctive.	Lead gray; tarnishes to black. Opaque; metallic.	2½ 5.5—5.8	As primary mineral in hydrothermal vein and replacement deposits. More common as weathering product. Bonanzas ("secondary enrichments") form by reprecipitation from leachwaters at water table. Ore of copper.
ALCOPYRITE FeS₂	Tetragonal, $\overline{4}\frac{2}{m}$. Tetrahedral; colloform; granular.	Not distinctive.	Brass yellow; dark to iridescent tarnish. Opaque; metallic; streak greenish black.	4 4.2	Fusible. Widespread as disseminations in igneous and metamorphic rocks. In sulfide-rich segregations in basic intrusives. In hydrothermal vein and replacement deposits over wide temp. range and in great variety of environments. A major ore of copper.
LORITE SERIES (Mg,Fe,Al,Cr,Mn)₆(Si,Al)₄O₁₀(OH)₈	Monoclinic, $\frac{2}{m}$. Tabular (pseudo-hexagonal). Platy; radial sheafs; scales.	Basal (001), forming flexible plates.	Generally dark green. White to yellow (low in Fe); red (Cr-rich); orange to brown (Mn-rich); nearly black (Fe-rich). Transl. to subtransl. Vitreous; splendent to pearly.	2½ 2.6—3.3	A major constituent of green schists and greenstones derived by regional metamorphism of basic igneous rocks. As deuteric and hydrothermal alteration products in various igneous and metamorphic rocks. In iron formations.
ROMITE Cr₂O₄	Isometric, $\frac{4}{m}\overline{3}\frac{2}{m}$. Octahedral. Compact; granular. Dissem. grains.	Not distinctive.	Black; opaque. Metallic to pitchy; streak brown.	5½ 4.5—5.1	Member of spinel group. Dissem. through ultrabasic rocks and their metamorphic equivalents. Veinlike and poddy concentrations may represent hydrothermal reworking. In placers. Major ore of chromium and its compounds. Used in refractories.
RYSOCOLLA SiO₃·nH₂O	Orthorhombic (?). Microcrystalline; colloform; earthy.	None.	Blue to green, with brown to black staining. Transl. to subtransl. Vitreous to waxy.	2—4 2.0—2.5	Colloidal weathering product of primary copper minerals. Important constituent of near-surface portions of "porphyry copper" deposits. Ore of copper. Minor gemstone.
NNABAR gS	Trigonal, 32. Rhombohedral; tabular; prismatic. Granular to earthy.	Prismatic (10$\overline{1}$1) at 60° and 120°.	Bright to dark red. Transp. to transl. Adamantine to earthy.	2—2½ 8.0	As crystals and granular masses in low-temp. veins, and earthy impregnations in surrounding rocks. Some deposits associated with hot springs. Major ore of mercury.
OLUMBITE— ANTALITE SERIES (Fe, Mn)(Cb,Ta)₂O₆	Orthorhombic, $\frac{2}{m}\frac{2}{m}\frac{2}{m}$. Tabular; prismatic; stocky. Columnar; dissem. grains.	Pinacoidal (010) and (100) at 90°.	Brownish black to black.	6—6½ 5.2—8.0	Complete solid-solution series. Density increases with tantalum content. In pegmatites, high-temp. veins, and greisens; in placers. Major ores of columbium and tantalum.
OPPER	Isometric, $\frac{4}{m}\overline{3}\frac{2}{m}$. Cubic; dodecahedral; hexahedral; octahedral. Distorted. Filiform; arborescent; pseudomorphic; irreg. grains.	None. Sectile, ductile, malleable.	Bright copper-red. Tarnishes. Opaque; metallic.	2½—3 8.9	Fusible. End-stage hydrothermal product in basic extrusive rocks, esp. amygdaloidal lavas, and in surrounding sediments, esp. sandstones and conglomerates. Also as a precipitate from surface waters that have leached primary copper minerals. Ore of copper.

SOME IMPORTANT MINERALS—Continued

MINERAL (Composition) GROUP	CRYSTAL SYSTEM, SYMMETRY CLASS, HABIT	CLEAVAGE PLANES AND ANGLES	COLOR, TRANSPARENCY, TRANSLUCENCY, LUSTER, OTHER OPTICAL PROPERTIES	HARDNESS (MOHS SCALE); SPECIFIC GRAVITY	PHYSICAL AND CHEMICAL CHARACTERISTICS; OCCURRENCE; USES
CORUNDUM Al_2O_3	Trigonal, $\overline{3}\frac{2}{m}$. Prismatic, tapered. Pyramidal; stocky; tabular. Dense aggregates; dissem. grains.	Partings basal (0001) and rhombohedral ($10\overline{1}1$) at 86° and 94°, forming nearly cubical fragments.	Wide range of colors, tints, and shades. Commonly zoned. Transp. to subtransl. Adamantine to vitreous. Pearly to bronzy on basal plane; dichroic.	9 4.0	As phenocryst in igneous rocks, but mostly a metamorphic mineral resul from recrystallization of highly aluminous rocks or by desilication reac with ultrabasic rocks or limestones. Used in abrasives, refractories, bear ("jewels"). Emery is impure compact variety assoc. with spinel and magn Gems include ordinary and star rubies and sapphires. Common and varieties now produced synthetically.
DIAMOND C	Isometric, $\frac{4}{m}\overline{3}\frac{2}{m}$. Octahedral; dodecahedral; cubic. Curved and highly modified. Spinel twins (macles). Radial, granular to microcrystalline (bort and carbonado).	Octahedral (111) at about 70°.	Colorless to black, and wide range of colors, tints, and shades. Transp. to transl. Adamantine to greasy. Coke-like (carbonado). High index of refraction and dispersion causes "fire." Some fluorescent.	10 3.5	In peridotite dikes and pipes, and eluvial and alluvial deposits. Used in drills and rock-saws, wire dies, grinding-wheel and machine-tool shapers. thesized at high temp. and pressure. Gems of many colors, some artifici modified by irradiation.
DIASPORE $AlO(OH)$ BAUXITE	Orthorhombic, $\frac{2}{m}\frac{2}{m}\frac{2}{m}$. Tabular; bladed; acicular. Foliated; stalactic.	Prismatic (110) at 86° and 94°, pinacoidal (010) at 133°.	Colorless to white; various tints. Transp. to transl. Adamantine to vitreous; pearly.	6½—7 3.3—3.5	Hydrothermal alteration product of alumina-rich minerals. With related min —boehmite, $AlO(OH)$, and gibbsite, $Al(OH)_3$—a widespread weathering p uct, and constituent of bauxite and clays. Source of aluminum and alumin
DIOPSIDE $CaMgSi_2O_6$ PYROXENES	Monoclinic, $\frac{2}{m}$. Prismatic to stocky. Columnar, radial, granular. Dissem. grains.	Prismatic (110) at 87° and 93°. Basal parting (001).	White through various shades of green, rarely blue. Transp. to transl.; vitreous; pearly on parting.	5—6 3.3	Member solid-solution series with augite (Mg-, Fe-, Al-rich) and aegerite and Fe'''-rich). In basic and ultrabasic igneous rocks and their metamo equivalents. In magnesian marbles, tactites, and associated pegmatites high-temp. veins. Minor gemstone.
ENARGITE Cu_3AsS_4	Orthorhombic, 2 mm. Tabular; prismatic, striated. Granular.	Prismatic (110) at 82° and 98°; pinacoidal (100) and (010) at 90°, 49°, and 51°.	Gray; tarnishes. Opaque; metallic. Streak grayish black.	3 4.5	Readily fusible. In hydrothermal vein and replacement deposits of modera low temp. Ore of copper.
ENSTATITE— HYPERSTHENE SERIES 100 to 10% $Mg_2Si_2O_6$ 0 to 90% $Fe_2Si_2O_6$ PYROXENES	Orthorhombic, $\frac{2}{m}\frac{2}{m}\frac{2}{m}$. Prismatic; tabular. Usually as cleavable masses; lamellar; fibrous.	Prismatic (210) at 88° and 92°. Parting pinacoidal (010).	White to pale green, grading to brown as Fe increases. Transl. to subtransl. Vitreous; pearly.	6 3.2—3.9	Solid-solution series. Most common pyroxenes in ultrabasic rocks and metamorphic equivalents. In other igneous rocks, esp. the charnockites. Ir tites and skarns; in meteorites. Bronzite has submetallic schiller caused b solution lamellae, and is minor gemstone.
EPIDOTE $Ca_2(Al,Fe)_3Si_3O_{12}(OH)$	Monoclinic, $\frac{2}{m}$. Prismatic to acicular; striated. Granular to microcrystalline; fibrous.	Basal (001).	Various shades of green. Piedmontite (Mn-bearing) is red. Transp. to transl.; vitreous.	6—7 3.3—3.6	Very common metamorphic mineral derived from Ca-bearing minerals in variety of environments. As end-stage alteration product within igneous r In pegmatites and high-temp. veins; in gneisses, schists, hornfels, tac skarns; in placers. The closely related minerals zoisite and clinozoisite, us gray to light green, occur in similar associations. A minor gemstone. Un (epidotized granite) is an ornamental rock.
FLUORITE CaF_2	Isometric, $\frac{4}{m}\overline{3}\frac{2}{m}$. Cubic; octahedral; dodecahedral; complex modifications and parallel growths. Layered and columnar. Granular to microcrystalline. Dissem. grains.	Octahedral (111) at about 70° and 110°.	Wide range of colors, tints, and shades. Transp. to subtransl.; vitreous. Color changed by irradiation. Fluorescent, phosphorescent, and triboluminescent varieties.	4 3.2	Very widespread. In pegmatites and greisens, in hydrothermal vein an placement deposits over wide temp. range. Used in ceramics and as m lurgical flux. Source of fluorine and its compounds. Clear crystals used in c correcting lenses and gemstones.
GALENA PbS	Isometric, $\frac{4}{m}\overline{3}\frac{2}{m}$. Cubic to octahedral. Complex modifications, parallel growths, elongations. Pseudomorphic; plumose. Granular to microcrystalline.	Cubic (001).	Lead gray; tarnishes. Opaque; metallic; streak gray.	2½—3½ 7.6	Fusible. Widespread in great variety of occurrences. In hydrothermal-vein replacement deposits throughout full temp. range, including "Mississippi V type" replacement and vug-filling in limestones; also "red bed" type rep ments in sandstones. Major ore of lead. Argentiferous galena, containing of argentite, is major ore of silver.
GLAUCONITE $K(Fe,Mg,Al)_2Si_4O_{10}(OH)_2$	Monoclinic. Not in crystals. Concretionary granules. Pseudomorphic after microfossils and fecal pellets.	Basal (001).	Green to black; weathers brown. Transl. to subtransl.; earthy.	2 2.5—2.8	Marine sedimentary mineral, as disseminations in limestones and sandst Rich concentrations called "green sands." Celadonite, in velvety crusts, is stage hydrothermal alteration product in basic igneous rocks. Used as exchange medium in water-softening.
GLAUCOPHANE— RIEBECKITE SERIES $Na_2Mg_3Al_2Si_8O_{22}(OH)_2$ to $Na_2Fe''3Fe'''_2 Si_8O_{22}(OH)_2$ AMPHIBOLES	Monoclinic, $\frac{2}{m}$. Prismatic to acicular. Fibrous; asbestiform.	Prismatic (110) at 56° and 124°.	Various shades of blue, ranging to black with increase in Fe. Transl. to subtransl. Vitreous; silky.	6 3.0—3.4	Solid-solution series. Metamorphic mineral in schists and gneisses. Riebe occurs in Na-rich granites, pegmatites, rhyolites.
GOETHITE— LIMONITE $HFeO_2$	Orthorhombic, $\frac{2}{m}\frac{2}{m}\frac{2}{m}$. Tabular; prismatic, striated. Acicular, columnar to radial. Colloform; concretionary (clay, ironstone); pisolitic; oölitic; earthy. Amorphous (limonite).	Pinacoidal (010) and (100) at 90°.	Yellow-brown to black. Transl. to subtransl. Adamantine; submetallic; silky; earthy.	5—5½ 3.3—4.3	Widespread weathering product of Fe-minerals in many environment laterites and gossans. As precipitate in springs and bogs ("bog iron ore"). "limonite" used for mixtures of rusty-looking hydrous iron oxides; a field Ore of iron.

SOME IMPORTANT MINERALS—Continued

MINERAL (Composition) GROUP	CRYSTAL SYSTEM, SYMMETRY CLASS, HABIT	CLEAVAGE PLANES AND ANGLES	COLOR, TRANSPARENCY, TRANSLUCENCY, LUSTER, OTHER OPTICAL PROPERTIES	HARDNESS (MOHS SCALE); SPECIFIC GRAVITY	PHYSICAL AND CHEMICAL CHARACTERISTICS; OCCURRENCE; USES
LD	Isometric, $\frac{4}{m}\bar{3}\frac{2}{m}$. Octahedral; dodecahedral; cubic. Arborescent; dendritic; filiform; scaly; irreg. grains.	None. Highly malleable and ductile.	Gold yellow. Color and streak vary with purity. Opaque; subtransl.; green in very thin sheets; metallic.	2½—3 19.3 (pure)	Widespread in many rock types. In hydrothermal veins and replacement deposits through great temp. range. Placers range from beach and river sands and gravels to metamorphosed quartzites and conglomerates. Major ore of gold, generally containing some silver.
APHITE	Hexagonal, $\frac{6}{m}\frac{2}{m}\frac{2}{m}$ (?). Tabular. Columnar, radial, foliated. Dissem. flakes. Microcrystalline.	Basal (0001), forming flexible plates.	Steel gray to black. Opaque. Metallic; earthy. Streak dark gray, shiny.	1—2 2.0—2.2	Greasy feel. Widespread metamorphic mineral in schists, gneisses, marbles, tactites, skarns. In pegmatites and high-temp. veins cutting marbles. As product of contact metamorphism of coal ("amorphous graphite"). In meteorites. Used in lubricants, packings, paints, motor and generator "brushes," electrodes, crucibles, "lead" pencils; as moderator in nuclear reactors. Synthesized from coal in electric furnaces.
PSUM O₄·2H₂O	Monoclinic, $\frac{2}{m}$. Tabular; prismatic to acicular, striated. Fishtail twins. Helicitic; foliated; fibrous; granular; concretionary. Pseudomorphic.	Pinacoidal (010) (100) and (001), forming rhombic flexible plates, 66° and 114°.	Colorless to white, various tints. Zoned. Transp. to transl. Vitreous; pearly; silky. Fluorescent and phosphorescent vars.	2 2.3	Widespread in evaporite deposits, either as direct precipitate or as replacement of anhydrite. As sublimate in fumaroles, and as weathering product of sulfides. Calcined to produce plaster. Used in cement, fillers, fertilizers. Transp. var., selenite, used in optical instruments. Microcrystalline var. (alabaster) and fibrous var. (satinspar) used for ornamental objects.
ITE l	Isometric, $\frac{4}{m}\bar{3}\frac{2}{m}$. Cubic; octahedral. Cavernous, hopper-shaped. Columnar; stalactitic; granular.	Cubic (001).	Colorless to white; tints, esp. blue (free Na ions). Transp. to transl. Vitreous. Some fluorescent.	2 2.2	Soluble; salty. As sublimate in fumaroles. Widespread in both marine and interior-draining evaporite deposits. Beneficiation of rock salt is based on its strong diathermy. Used in cooking, food preservation, snow-melting. Major source of soda-ash and chlorines.
MATITE ₃	Trigonal, $\bar{3}\frac{2}{m}$. Rhombohedral; tabular. Rosettes ("iron rose"). Lamellar to micaceous (specularite). Columnar; fibrous; radial; colloform; granular; concretionary; oolitic; fossiliferous; ochery (rouge); pseudomorphs after magnetite (martite).	Partings rhombohedral (10$\bar{1}$1) at 86° and 94°, and basal (0001) at 122°.	Steel gray; opaque. Metallic. Streak and earthy varieties red.	5—6 5.3	As sublimate in fumaroles. Widespread in sedimentary and some igneous and metamorphic rocks; in veins and tactites; in gossans. Ore bodies include laterites and bedded sedimentary deposits and their metamorphic equivalents (iron formations and taconites). Enriched cappings formed by action of surface waters. A major ore of iron. Used in pigments and polishing agents (rouge, crocus cloth).
NBLENDE a₂(Mg,Fe,Al)₅(Si, Al)₈O₂₂·(O,OH,F)₂ IIBOLES	Monoclinic, $\frac{2}{m}$. Stocky to prismatic. Bladed; columnar; acicular; fibrous; granular.	Prismatic (110) at 56° and 124°.	Dark green to black, rarely brown. Transl. to subtransl. Vitreous; silky.	6 3.0—3.4	Complex solid solution series with many varieties. Widespread in igneous and metamorphic rocks. Major constituent of amphibolites, hornblende schists, and some skarns. Var. uralite is pseudomorphic after pyroxene.
ENITE O₃	Trigonal, $\bar{3}$. Tabular; prismatic. Granular. Dissem. grains.	Partings rhombohedral (10$\bar{1}$1) at 86° and 94° and basal (0001) at 122°.	Steel gray to black; opaque. Metallic to submetallic; streak brownish to black.	5—6 4.7	Slightly magnetic. May contain lamellae or blebs of hematite, magnetite, or rutile, and it forms blebs in magnetite. Widespread minor constituent in most kinds of rocks. Ore deposits include masses in anorthosites and gabbros; concentrations in river gravels, beach and dune sands. Reduced in electric furnaces to pig iron and Ti-rich slag. Titania pigments made from ilmenite and slag.
LINITE ₄O₁₀(OH)₈ MINERALS	Triclinic, $\bar{1}$. Tabular, pseudohexagonal. Usually microcrystalline; earthy.	Basal (001).	White; stained. Transl. to subtransl.; pearly to earthy.	2—2½ 2.6	Widespread product of hydrothermal alteration and weathering. With closely related, similar, clay minerals—nacrite, dickite, halloysite—in or adjacent to hydrothermal veins; in weathered cappings; in muds, clays, and shales. Used in ceramics, cement, refractories, fillers.
NITE O₅	Triclinic, $\bar{1}$. Tabular to elongate. Generally bladed, columnar to radial, or disseminated.	Pinacoidal (100) and (010), parting (001), forming rectangular fragments.	Commonly blue to green; also colorless to white or gray. Pleochroic. Transp. to transl.; pearly.	4—5/elongation 6—7 ⊥ 3.5—3.7	Polymorph of andalusite and sillimanite. Widespread metamorphic mineral in schists and gneisses, and in pegmatites and veins cutting these. Sintered to form mullite (Al₆Si₂O₁₃) for ceramics and refractories. Minor gemstone.
DOLITE ₃Al₃(AlSi₃O₁₀)₂ (O,OH,F)₄	Monoclinic, $\frac{2}{m}$. Tabular. Usually granular, platy, or microcrystalline. Dissem. flakes. Pseudomorphic.	Basal (001), forming flexible plates.	Colorless to pink, lilac, or red; yellow; gray. Transl.; vitreous; pearly.	2½—4 2.8—3.0	Has wide range of solid solution. In granitic pegmatites, generally in late-stage replacement zones. Used in ceramics and glass, and as source of lithium and its compounds.
NETITE ₂'''O₄	Isometric, $\frac{4}{m}\bar{3}\frac{2}{m}$. Octahedral; dodecahedral. Spinel twins. Pseudomorphic. Radial. Granular. Dissem. grains. Flat, reticular or dendritic. Exsolution lamellae of ilmenite common.	Parting octahedral (111) at about 70° and 110°.	Steel gray to black; opaque. Metallic to submetallic. Streak black.	5½—6½ 5.2	Strongly magnetic. Var. lodestone has natural polarity. Widespread as an accessory mineral in nearly all kinds of rocks. Ore deposits include masses or layers of titaniferous magnetite in basic intrusives, metamorphosed iron formations (taconite), replacement bodies in tactites, skarns, and gneisses, and placers. A major ore of iron.
ACHITE O₃(OH)₂	Monoclinic, $\frac{2}{m}$. Prismatic to acicular. Fibrous; radial; colloform; concretionary. Pseudomorphic.	Domal ($\bar{2}$01) and pinacoidal (010) at 90°.	Various shades of green. Transp. to subtransl. Adamantine; vitreous; velvety; silky.	3½—4 4.0	Common weathering product of primary Cu-minerals. In gossans. In upper zones of "porphyry-copper" deposits. As concretionary masses in "red-bed" sandstone deposits. Patina on ancient bronzes. Ore of copper. Concentric color variations emphasized in gem and ornamental uses.
CASITE	Orthorhombic, $\frac{2}{m}\frac{2}{m}\frac{2}{m}$. Tabular; pyramidal; prismatic to capillary. Spear and cockscomb twins. Pseudomorphic. Colloform; concretionary.	Domal (101) at 64° and 116°.	Silver white; tarnishes yellow to bronze. Opaque; metallic. Streak grayish to brownish black.	6—6½ 4.9	As low-temp. hydrothermal or ground-water precipitate. Polymorph, pyrite, more stable in higher-temp. and alkaline environments. As crystals in vugs, as concretions and fossil replacements in sediments. Marcasite disintegrates into ferrous sulfate and sulfuric acid on removal from normal environment.

SOME IMPORTANT MINERALS—*Continued*

MINERAL (Composition) GROUP	CRYSTAL SYSTEM, SYMMETRY CLASS, HABIT	CLEAVAGE PLANES AND ANGLES	COLOR, TRANSPARENCY, TRANSLUCENCY, LUSTER, OTHER OPTICAL PROPERTIES	HARDNESS (MOHS SCALE); SPECIFIC GRAVITY	PHYSICAL AND CHEMICAL CHARACTERISTICS; OCCURRENCE; USES
MICROCLINE $KAlSi_3O_8$ FELDSPARS	Triclinic, $\bar{1}$. Stocky to prismatic. Carlsbad, baveno, and mannebach twins. Micro-gridiron twinning. Exsolution intergrowths with plagioclase (perthite and microperthite).	Pinacoidal (001) and (010) at almost 90°	White; buff; various shades of pink to red; green (amazonite). Transl.; vitreous.	6 2.6	Lower-temp. polymorph of orthoclase and sanidine. Widespread in igneous metamorphic rocks. In pegmatites and high-temp. veins; in arkosic sandst and conglomerates. Used in glass, ceramics, scouring powders. Amazonite dark red perthite cut as gems.
MOLYBDENITE MoS_2	Hexagonal, $\frac{6}{m}\frac{2}{m}\frac{2}{m}$. Tabular; stocky; tapered. Foliated masses; dissem. flakes.	Basal (0001), forming flexible plates.	Lead gray with bluish tinge. Opaque; metallic. Streak greenish to bluish gray.	1—1½ 4.6	In granites, pegmatites, high-temp. veins, greisens, tactites, skarns, and gne Major ore of molybdenum.
MONAZITE $(Ce,La,Y,Th)PO_4$	Monoclinic, $\frac{2}{m}$. Tabular; prismatic. Granular to microcrystalline.	Pinacoidal (100) and (010) at 90°. Parting basal (001).	Yellow to reddish brown. Transp. to subtransl. Adamantine; vitreous; waxy.	5—5½ 4.6—5.4	Weakly magnetic. As accessory mineral in alkaline intrusives, carbona pegmatites, and high-temp. veins. In recent and fossil placers. Occurrenc schists and gneisses may be metamorphosed placers. Ore of thorium and earths. Commonly assoc. with similar mineral xenotime, YPO_4.
MONTMORILLONITE $Al_2Si_4O_{10}(OH)_2 \cdot nH_2O$ CLAY MINERALS	Monoclinic, m. Tabular; microcrystalline; earthy.	Basal (001).	White to gray; various colors. Transl. to subtransl. Waxy to earthy.	2 2.0—2.7	Slippery when wet. Forms extensive solid-solution series. Easy cation exch and adsorption. Major constituent of bentonite ("swelling clay") forme weathering of volcanic ash beds. Used in drilling-muds, foundry molds, ble ing clay ("fuller's earth"); carrier for catalysts and insecticides, etc.
MUSCOVITE $KAl''_2Al'''Si_3O_{10}(F,OH)_2$ MICAS	Monoclinic. Tabular; stocky; prismatic; tapered. Pseudomorphic. Foliated masses or dissem. flakes. Fine scales (sericite).	Basal (001) forming elastic plates. Pinacoidal (010) and prismatic (110) partings, forming "wedge," "ribbon," "A," and "ruled" mica.	Colorless to smoky; various tints. Transp. to transl. Splendent; vitreous; pearly.	2½//Cl. 4 ⊥ Cl. 2.8—3.1	Forms solid-solution series with paragonite (Na-rich). In alkaline igneous pegmatites, high-temp. veins, and greisens. Widespread metamorphic mi in phyllites, schists, gneisses. Detrital mineral in arkoses. Sheets used as in tors in vacuum tubes, commutators, appliances; flakes as fillers, coating ag paint extenders. Va-rich roscoelite forms impregnations in sandstones and ore of vanadium.
NATROLITE $Na_2Al_2Si_3O_{10} \cdot 2H_2O$ ZEOLITES	Orthorhombic, mm2. Prismatic to acicular. Radial; granular.	Prismatic (110) at 89° and 91°.	Colorless to white. Transp. to transl.; vitreous.	5—5½ 2.2	Easy cation exchange. Common deuteric and hydrothermal mineral. In vu extrusives; in veins, shears, and joints in plutonic and metamorphic rocks. duced synthetically as a water softener. Related zeolites include Ca-be scolecite, mesolite, and thompsonite.
NEPHELINE $(Na,K)AlSiO_4$ FELDSPATHOIDS	Hexagonal, 6. Tabular; stocky; prismatic. Irreg. masses; dissem. grains.	Parting prismatic $(10\bar{1}0)$ at 60° and 120°.	Colorless to white; some tints. Transp. to transl.; vitreous to greasy.	5—6 2.6	In alkaline intermediate to basic igneous and metamorphic rocks. As ph crysts in porphyries, crystals in vuggy xenoliths. In limey gneisses and sk and associated pegmatites and high-temp. veins. A major constituent o nepheline syenites used in ceramics and glass, and for glazed roofing gran
OLIVINE SERIES $(Mg,Fe)_2SiO_4$	Orthorhombic, $\frac{2}{m}\frac{2}{m}\frac{2}{m}$. Tabular to stocky. Granular; dissem. grains.	Not distinctive.	Yellowish to brownish green. Transp. to transl.; vitreous.	6½—7 3.2—4.4	Complete solid-solution series from forsterite (Mg-rich) to fayalite (Fe-Common in basic to ultrabasic igneous rocks. As phenocrysts in porph Chief constituent of dunite and peridotite. In contact-metamorphosed stones. Dunite used in refractory bricks and furnace linings. Gemstones, kn also as peridot and chrysolite.
OPAL $SiO_2 \cdot nH_2O$ QUARTZ	Amorphous. Colloform; concretionary; earthy. Pseudomorphic.	None.	Wide range of colors, tints, and shades. Transp. to transl. Vitreous to resinous. Opalescence and color play caused by laminae of varied H_2O content, with different refractive indices. Some fluorescent.	5½—6½ 2.0—2.2	Deposited from low-temp. hydrothermal solutions or ground waters. As spring and geyser deposits (siliceous sinter). As cement in sandstones, ings, encrustations, replacements of crystals, wood, shells, and other foss skeletal material of diatoms, sponges, radiolaria, etc. Diatomite used as f filters, source of silica. Gemstones in wide range of colors and color-play.
ORTHOCLASE $KAlSi_3O_8$ FELDSPARS	Monoclinic, $\frac{2}{m}$. Tabular; stocky; prismatic. Carlsbad, baveno, mannebach twins. Granular to microcrystalline.	Pinacoidal (001) and (010) at 90°.	Colorless to white; pink; yellow. Transp. to transl. Vitreous; pearly. Opalescent (moonstone).	6 2.6	Intermediate polymorph between high-temp. sanidine and low-temp. m cline, commonly metastable. Sometimes includes variety of adularia fou low-temp. veins. Orthoclase widespread in alkaline igneous rocks; frequ intergrown with sodic plagioclase as perthite. Term "orthoclase" frequ used for K-feldspars collectively.
PENTLANDITE $(Fe,Ni)_9S_8$	Isometric, $\frac{4}{m}\bar{3}\frac{2}{m}$. Not as crystals. Granular; dissem. grains; exsolution lamellae.	Parting octahedral (111) *ca.* 70° and 120°.	Light bronze-yellow; opaque; metallic. Streak bronze.	3½—4 4.6—5.0	Non-magnetic. In basic igneous rocks and metamorphic equivalents. Usua microscopic intergrowths in pyrrhotite; the major ore of nickel.
PSILOMELANE $BaMn^{II}Mn^{IV}_8O_{16}(OH)_4$	Orthorhombic. Not as crystals. Colloform; earthy.	None.	Steel gray to black; opaque; submetallic. Streak brownish to black.	5—6 4.7	Intimately mixed with other minerals and colloids. Weathering product o mary Mn minerals. In gossans and as limestone replacements. As residual centrations. As precipitate in bogs and swamps. Wad is a collective ter complex mixtures of psilomelane, pyrolusite, and other hydrated metallic o Used in making steel, dry batteries, in production of chlorine and bro manganese alloys and compounds.
PYRITE (IRON PYRITES, FOOL'S GOLD) FeS_2	Isometric, $\frac{2}{m}\bar{3}$. Cubic; pyritohedral; octahedral. Complex modifications, elongations, and distortions. Colloform; concretionary; pseudomorphic.	Not distinctive.	Brass yellow; tarnishes. Opaque; metallic. Streak greenish to brownish black.	6—6½ 5.0	Thermoelectric. Occurs in almost all types of rocks; stable in almost a vironments except for weathering and oxidation. Major deposits occur regations in basic igneous rocks, and hydrothermal veins and replacem through wide temp. range. As crystals, concretions, and fossil replaceme sediments; as metacrysts in metamorphic rocks. Burned to produce sulfur sulfuric acid, the residue used as iron ore. Some varieties contain enough c or nickel to be ores of those metals.
PYROLUSITE MnO_2	Tetragonal, $\frac{4}{m}\frac{2}{m}\frac{2}{m}$. Stocky to prismatic. Columnar; fibrous; radial; colloform. Granular to microcrystalline; dendritic; earthy.	Prismatic (110) at 90°.	Steel gray to black; opaque. Metallic to submetallic. Streak bluish to black.	6—6½ 5.0	Weathering product of primary Mn minerals. In gossans. As precipitate in lakes, ocean (including deep-sea nodules). Used in steel making, producti chlorine and bromine; in dry batteries, manganese alloys and compounds

SOME IMPORTANT MINERALS—Continued

MINERAL (Composition) GROUP	CRYSTAL SYSTEM, SYMMETRY CLASS, HABIT	CLEAVAGE PLANES AND ANGLES	COLOR, TRANSPARENCY, TRANSLUCENCY, LUSTER, OTHER OPTICAL PROPERTIES	HARDNESS (MOHS SCALE); SPECIFIC GRAVITY	PHYSICAL AND CHEMICAL CHARACTERISTICS; OCCURRENCE; USES
OPHYLLITE $i_4O_{10}(OH)_2$	Monoclinic, $\frac{2}{m}$. Not as crystals. Platy to bladed or fibrous. Microcrystalline.	Basal (001), forming flexible plates.	White to pale yellow; stained. Transl. to subtransl. Pearly; dull.	1—2 2.8	In metamorphosed Al-rich rocks, particularly volcanics. Used in ceramics, welding-rod coatings, fillers. Microcrystalline material used for carving.
RHOTITE —x	Hexagonal, $\frac{6}{m}\frac{2}{m}\frac{2}{m}$. Tabular; pyramidal. Rosettes and other parallel growths. Granular or dissem. grains.	Parting basal (0001).	Silver gray, brown tinge. Tarnishes rapidly. Opaque; metallic.	3½—4½ 4.6	Variably magnetic. In wide range of igneous and metamorphic rocks. In pegmatites, high-temp. veins, tactites, skarns. Host mineral of intergrown pentlandite in Cu-Ni deposits in basic rocks, and thus, as by-product, is source of sulfuric acid and iron. Var. troilite occurs in meteorites.
RTZ	Trigonal, 32. Prismatic; stocky; tabular. Columnar; radial. Granular; dissem. grains. (See also CHALCEDONY, above.)	None.	Generally colorless to white, but almost infinite variety of colors, tints, shades. Transp. to transl.; vitreous.	7 2.7	Piezoelectric and pyroelectric. Polymorphs include cristobalite, tridymite, coesite, and chalcedony. Widespread in almost all kinds of rocks and full range of hydrothermal vein and replacement deposits. As phenocrysts in porphyries, grains in acid to intermediate igneous and metamorphic rocks, large masses and graphic intergrowths with feldspar in pegmatites, crystals in veins, vugs, and geodes. Chief constituent of most sands, sandstones, and quartzites. Crystals used in radio-frequency control, and fused for crucibles, ultraviolet lamps. Used in glass, ceramics, metallurgical fluxes, abrasives, refractories. Gemstones include rock crystal, amethyst, citrine, rose, smoky, rutilated quartz. Crystals can be produced synthetically.
DOCHROSITE O_3	Trigonal, $\bar{3}\frac{2}{m}$. Rhombohedral; scalenohedral. Colloform. Granular to microcrystalline.	Rhombohedral (10$\bar{1}$1) at 73° and 107°.	Pink to rose. Transp. to transl. Vitreous; pearly.	3½—4 3.7	Limited solid solution with calcite, siderite, magnesite. In mod.- to low-temp. hydrothermal veins. An ore of manganese. Semiprecious gem and ornamental stone ("Inca rose").
DONITE iO_3	Triclinic, $\bar{1}$. Tabular; colloform. Granular to microcrystalline.	Prismatic (110) and (1$\bar{1}$0) at 88° and 92°.	Pink to rose; veined by black alteration products. Transp. to transl. Vitreous.	5½—6½ 3.4—3.7	Contains varied amounts of Fe, Zn. In high- to mod.-temp. hydrothermal vein and replacement deposits. In metamorphosed sedimentary manganese deposits. Semiprecious and ornamental stone.
ILE	Tetragonal, $\frac{4}{m}\frac{2}{m}\frac{2}{m}$. Prismatic to acicular, striated. Geniculated and cyclic twins. Reticular masses. Pseudomorphic. Granular to microcrystalline. Exsolution "needles."	Prismatic (110) at 90°.	Red, through brown to black. Transp. to subtransl. Adamantine to submetallic. High dispersion. Leucoxene: white to brown. Opaque; waxy.	6—6½ 4.2—5.6	Polymorphous with anatase (octahedrite) and brookite. Contains varied amounts of Cb, Ta, and Fe. Widespread in microscopic amounts in almost all kinds of rocks. Deposits include hydrothermally altered zones in noritic anorthosites, ultrabasics, and volcanics; high-temp. vein and replacement deposits associated with alkaline intrusive complexes; residual and alluvial concentrations, particularly in beaches and dunes. Ore of titanium. Microcrystalline rutile and anatase produced synthetically for pigments. "Titania Gems" cut from synthetic rutile crystals. Oriented needles of rutile cause asterism of star rubies and sapphires, rose quartz, star-mica.
EELITE O_4	Tetragonal, $\frac{4}{m}$. Pseudo-octahedral, modified. Pseudomorphic; granular.	Pyramidal (101) at 73° and 107°, 67° and 113°.	Colorless to white; various tints. Transp. to transl. Adamantine to vitreous or greasy. Strongly fluorescent.	4½—5 6.1	Limited solid solution with powellite, $CaMoO_4$. In high- to mod.-temp. veins; in greisens, tactites, skarns. In residual and placer deposits. Fluorescence guides prospecting and beneficiation. Ore of tungsten.
PENTINE $i_4O_{10}(OH)_8$	Monoclinic. Not as crystals. Columnar, acicular (picrolite) to fibrous (chrysotile). Lamellar to micro-foliated (antigorite). Colloform (deweylite, genthite, garnierite). Pseudomorphic.	None?	Various shades of yellow to green; red; brown; black. Transl. to subtransl. Resinous; waxy; silky.	2½—5½ 2.5—2.8	Widespread metamorphic mineral, as alteration product of olivines and orthopyroxenes in igneous rocks, and of these and the chondrite group in magnesian limestones. Chrysotile is the principal commercial asbestos. Genthite and garnierite are nickeliferous and are mined from lateritic cappings on peridotites in New Caledonia. "Precious serpentine" and "verde antique" are ornamental materials.
ERITE O_3	Trigonal, $\bar{3}\frac{2}{m}$. Rhombohedral; scalenohedral. Colloform; concretionary. Granular to microcrystalline.	Rhombohedral (10$\bar{1}$1) at 73° and 107°.	Yellowish to reddish brown. Transl.; vitreous; pearly.	3½—4½ 4.0	Solid-solution series with magnesite and rhodochrosite. Widespread in many kinds of occurrences. In pegmatites, hydrothermal vein and replacement deposits over wide temp. range, and as bedded sediments (iron formation). An ore of iron. Sintered to form ocherous pigments.
IMANITE O_5	Orthorhombic, $\frac{2}{m}\frac{2}{m}\frac{2}{m}$. Prismatic to acicular, striated or rounded. Columnar; radial; fibrous; felted.	Prismatic (110) at 88° and 92°.	White, green, to brown. Transl.; vitreous to silky.	6—7 3.2	Polymorph of kyanite and andalusite. Common metamorphic mineral in schists and gneisses. Fibers parallel direction of movement in sheared zones. Indian ax heads were made of microcrystalline, jade-like variety.
VER	Isometric, $\frac{4}{m}\bar{3}\frac{2}{m}$. Cubic; octahedral; dodecahedral. Distorted and elongated. Wiry, arborescent, dendritic, and in sheets. Pseudomorphic.	None. Ductile and malleable.	Silver white; tarnishes. Opaque; metallic.	2½—3 10.5	Fusible. Complete solid solution with gold. In mod.-temp. hydrothermal veins. In gossans and oxidized zones as weathering product of primary ores. Ore of silver.
THSONITE O_3	Trigonal, $\bar{3}\frac{2}{m}$. Rhombohedral; scalenohedral. Colloform. Granular to microcrystalline.	Rhombohedral (10$\bar{1}$1) at 72° and 108°.	Colorless to white; various tints. Transl.; vitreous; pearly.	4—4½ 4.0—4.5	Weathering product of primary zinc ores. In gossans and oxidized zones, and as replacement bodies in adjacent limestones. Ore of zinc.
ALITE $AlSiO_4)_3Cl$ SPATHOID	Isometric, $\bar{4}$3m. Dodecahedral. Pseudomorphic. Irreg. masses and dissem. grains.	Dodecahedral (110) at 60° and 120°.	Various shades of blue; also colorless; white; green; red. Transp. to transl.; vitreous. Some fluorescent.	6 2.1—2.4	Solid-solution series with lazurite. As phenocrysts in silica-deficient alkaline porphyries, but more commonly as hydrothermal replacements in igneous and metamorphic rocks of similar composition. Gem and ornamental stone.

SOME IMPORTANT MINERALS—Continued

MINERAL (Composition) GROUP	CRYSTAL SYSTEM, SYMMETRY CLASS, HABIT	CLEAVAGE PLANES AND ANGLES	COLOR, TRANSPARENCY, TRANSLUCENCY, LUSTER, OTHER OPTICAL PROPERTIES	HARDNESS (MOHS SCALE); SPECIFIC GRAVITY	PHYSICAL AND CHEMICAL CHARACTERISTICS; OCCURRENCE; USES
SPHALERITE ZnS	Isometric, $\bar{4}$ 3m. Tetrahedral; octahedral; modified. Simple and polysynthetic spinel twinning. Colloform. Granular to microcrystalline.	Dodecahedral (110) at 60° and 120°.	Yellow to brown; red (ruby blende), black (Fe-rich marmatite, "black jack"). Transp. to subtransl. Adamantine to resinous. Some fluorescent or triboluminescent.	3½—4 3.9—4.1	Pyroelectric. Widespread in great variety of occurrences. Ore deposits in hydrothermal vein and replacement bodies through full temp. range, incl. "Mississippi Valley-type" low-temp. replacements and vug-fillings in limest Major ore of zinc, cadmium, indium, gallium, germanium.
SPHENE $CaTiSiO_5$	Monoclinic, $\frac{2}{m}$. Wedge- or envelope-shaped. Granular; dissem. grains.	Prismatic (110) at 66° and 114°.	Reddish to brown; yellow to green. Transp. to subtransl. Adamantine to resinous.	5—5½ 3.4—3.6	Widely dissem. in igneous and metamorphic rocks. In pegmatites, high-t veins, tactites, and skarns. In placers. Minor gemstone.
SPINEL SERIES $MgAl_2O_4$	Isometric, $\frac{4}{m}\bar{3}\frac{2}{m}$. Octahedral, modified. Granular; dissem. grains.	None.	From colorless to black, in wide range of colors and shades. Transp. to subtransl.; vitreous.	7½—8 3.6—4.0	Extensive solid solution with hercynite, gahnite, and galaxite (Fe, Zn, an respectively). Widely dissem. in igneous and metamorphic rocks. In pegma high-temp. veins, and contact-metamorphic zones in magnesian limestones highly aluminous schists. In placers. Gemstones in wide range of colors. C also produced synthetically.
SPODUMENE $LiAlSi_2O_6$ PYROXENES	Monoclinic, $\frac{2}{m}$. Prismatic; tabular; striated. Bladed.	Prismatic (110) at 88° and 92°. Parting pinacoidal (100) at 46° and 134°.	Colorless to white or gray; green (hiddenite); pink to violet (kunzite). Transp. to transl.; vitreous; silky.	6½—7 3.2	In granitic pegmatites. Major ore of lithium and its compounds. Gems in hiddenite, kunzite, and colorless spodumene.
STAUROLITE $FeAl_4Si_2O_{10}(OH)_2$	Monoclinic, $\frac{2}{m}$ (pseudo-orthorhombic, $\frac{2}{m}\frac{2}{m}\frac{2}{m}$). Prismatic. Diagonal and cruciform twins. Granular; dissem. grains.	Pinacoidal (010).	Red to brown. Transp. to subtransl.; vitreous.	7—7½ 3.7	Common metamorphic mineral in schists and gneisses. In placers. Minor stone. Cruciform twins ("fairy crosses") as charms.
STIBNITE Sb_2S_3	Orthorhombic, $\frac{2}{m}\frac{2}{m}\frac{2}{m}$. Prismatic to acicular, striated, bent, twisted. Radial. Irreg. masses; granular to microcrystalline.	Pinacoidal (010). Flexible. Somewhat sectile.	Steel gray; tarnishes. Opaque; metallic.	2 4.6	Readily fusible. In low-temp. hydrothermal vein and replacement deposits, hot-spring deposits. Major ore of antimony.
STILBITE $(Ca,Na,K)_2Al_2Si_7O_{18}$ $\cdot 7H_2O$ ZEOLITES	Monoclinic, $\frac{2}{m}$. Tabular. Sheaflike; radial; globular.	Pinacoidal (010).	White, yellow, reddish, to brown. Transl.; vitreous; pearly.	3—4 2.1	Common deuteric and hydrothermal mineral. In vugs in extrusives, miar cavities in intrusives; in low-temp. hydrothermal veins. Radial aggregates joint surfaces of igneous and metamorphic rocks. Related zeolites of simila currence include phillipsite, harmotone, laumontite, and heulandite.
SULFUR S	Orthorhombic, $\frac{2}{m}\frac{2}{m}\frac{2}{m}$. Pyramidal; tabular; sphenoidal. Colloform; granular.	Not distinctive.	Yellow, various shades. Transp. to transl. Resinous to greasy.	1½—2½ 2.1	Electrified on friction. Fusible and inflammable. Sublimate in fumaroles, precipitates in hot-spring deposits. Residual product in weathered sulfid posits. Most common in evaporite deposits, particularly in cap-rocks of domes; possibly derived by bacterial reduction of gypsum or anhydrite. M source of elemental sulfur. Prepared synthetically from "sour" natural gas by burning pyrite.
SYLVITE KCl	Isometric, $\frac{4}{m}\bar{3}\frac{2}{m}$. Cubic; octahedral. Granular; dissem. grains.	Cubic (001). Somewhat glides rather than scratches).	Colorless to white; various tints, esp. pink. Transp. to transl. Vitreous to greasy.	2 2.0	Soluble. Bitter compared to halite. Sublimate in fumaroles. Widesprea evaporite deposits. Major source of potash for chemicals and fertilizers.
TALC $Mg_3Si_4O_{10}(OH)_2$	Monoclinic, $\frac{2}{m}$. Tabular; foliated; microcrystalline.	Basal (001), forming flexible plates. Sectile.	White, pale green, to gray. Transl.; greasy; pearly.	1 2.7	Slippery. Common metamorphic mineral derived from magnesian silicates posits include contact-metamorphosed magnesian limestones and alt peridotites. Used in ceramics, refractories, cosmetics, fillers. Talc-rich rock, s stone, or steatite, slabbed for switchboards, laundry tubs, chemically resi table tops and sinks.
TETRAHEDRITE—TENNANTITE SERIES $(Cu,Fe)_{12}(Sb,As)_4S_{13}$	Isometric, $\bar{4}$ 3m. Tetrahedral, modified. Cyclic twins. Granular to microcrystalline.	None.	Gray to black. Opaque; metallic. Streak brown to black.	3—4½ 4.6—5.1	Tetrahedrite, Sb-rich; tennantite, As-rich. Contains varied amounts of Ag Cu, Pb, Zn, and Fe. In hydrothermal vein and replacement deposits. Or copper and silver.
TOPAZ $Al_2SiO_4(OH,F)_2$	Orthorhombic, $\frac{2}{m}\frac{2}{m}\frac{2}{m}$ (?). Prismatic, striated. Granular to microcrystalline.	Basal (001).	Colorless to white; various tints. Transp. to transl. Vitreous.	8 3.5	In vesicles in rhyolite, and in pegmatites. As high-temp. hydrothermal mi in greisens, tactites, and veins. In placers. Used in ceramics. Gemstones in range of colors, some of which may be modified by heating.
TOURMALINE $Na(Mg,Fe)_3Al_6(BO_3)_3$ $Si_6O_{18}(OH)_4$	Trigonal, 3m. Prismatic to acicular, striated. Stocky to tabular. Rounded triangular cross-sections. Columnar; radial.	None.	Colorless, through wide range of colors, to black. Zoned. Transp. to subtransl.; vitreous. Strong absorption and dichroism.	7½ 3.0—3.2	Extensive solid solution, including Ca- and Li-rich varieties. Pyroelectric piezoelectric. In pegmatites, high-temp. veins, greisens, tactites, schists, gne In placers. Used in high-pressure gages. Gems of many colors, incl. bicol "watermelon tourmaline."
TREMOLITE—ACTINOLITE SERIES $Ca_2(Mg,Fe)_5Si_8O_{22}(OH)_2$ AMPHIBOLES	Monoclinic, $\frac{2}{m}$. Stocky; tabular; prismatic. Bladed; acicular; columnar; fibrous; radial; granular; microcrystalline.	Prismatic (110) at 60° and 120°.	Colorless to dark green, as Fe increases; pink (hexagonite). Transp. to transl. Vitreous; silky.	5—6 2.9—3.4	Tremolite, Mg-rich, to actinolite, Fe-rich. Common metamorphic miner talc and chlorite schists, in magnesian marbles, in tactites and skarns. M crystalline var. (nephrite) is a variety of jade. Asbestiform vars. commercially.

SOME IMPORTANT MINERALS—Continued

MINERAL (Composition) GROUP	CRYSTAL SYSTEM, SYMMETRY CLASS, HABIT	CLEAVAGE PLANES AND ANGLES	COLOR, TRANSPARENCY, TRANSLUCENCY, LUSTER, OTHER OPTICAL PROPERTIES	HARDNESS (MOHS SCALE); SPECIFIC GRAVITY	PHYSICAL AND CHEMICAL CHARACTERISTICS; OCCURRENCE; USES
NA $(CO_3)_2 \cdot 2H_2O$	Monoclinic, $\frac{2}{m}$. Tabular to elongate. Columnar; fibrous.	Pinacoidal (100).	Colorless to white or gray. Transp. to transl. Vitreous.	2½—3 2.1	Soluble. "Alkaline" taste. As efflorescent crusts in arid areas ("alkali"). Common evaporite mineral in playa-lake deposits. Is natural form of the "soda ash" manufactured by Solvay and other processes, and is used for glass, caustics, etc.
QUOISE $,Fe)_6(PO_4)_4(OH)_8 \cdot 4H_2O$	Triclinic, $\bar{1}$. Crystals rare. Colloform; microcrystalline. Pseudomorphic.	Basal (001).	Light blue to light green. Subtransl. Waxy.	5—6 2.7	Weathering product of Al-rich rocks in arid environments. As crusts and vein-fillings. Pseudomorphs of feldspar, fossil bones, teeth, etc. Most so-called "bone turquoise" is not Cu-bearing and is misnamed. Semiprecious stone.
YAMUNITE $O_2)_2(VO_4)_2 \cdot nH_2O$ OTITE	Orthorhombic, $\frac{2}{m}$ (?). Tabular to bladed. Radial; microcrystalline; earthy.	Basal (001).	Various shades of yellow. Transl. Adamantine; pearly; earthy.	2 3.6—4.3	Weathering product of primary uranium and vanadium minerals. Common in Colorado Plateau-type deposits as linings along fractures, impregnations in sandstone, and as replacements of fossil logs. With similar K-analogue, carnotite, a major ore of uranium and vanadium.
NINITE— HBLENDE	Isometric, $\frac{4}{m}\bar{3}\frac{2}{m}$. Cubic to octahedral. Arborescent clusters; sooty; pseudomorphic. Colloform (pitchblende).	None.	Steel gray to black; opaque. Submetallic to greasy; earthy.	5—6½ 8.0—10.5	Solid solution with thorianite ThO_2; intermediate mineral, uranothorianite. In pegmatites, high- to mod.-temp. veins and tactites. In placers. As dissemina-tions in Colorado Plateau-type sandstone deposits through reduction by or actual replacement of organic "trash." A major ore of uranium.
MICULITE $e,Mg)_3Si_4O_{10}(OH)_2 \cdot nH_2O$	Monoclinic; usually pseudomorphic.	Basal (001), forming flexible plates.	Yellow, green to brown. Transl. to subtransl.; pearly.	1½ 2.4	Easy cation exchange. Expands greatly by exfoliation through steam loss on heating. Hydrothermal alteration or weathering product of biotite and phlogopite. Major deposits in alkaline intrusive complexes and in reaction zones between pegmatites and ultrabasic rocks. Expanded vermiculite used in insula-tion for heat, sound, and impact; in lightweight aggregates for construction, fillers.
FRAMITE SERIES $Fe)WO_4$	Monoclinic, $\frac{2}{m}$. Stocky; prismatic; tabular; striated. Bladed; lamellar; granular.	Pinacoidal (010).	Yellow brown to black. Transl. to opaque. Resinous to metallic.	4—4½ 7.1—7.5	In pegmatites, high- to mod.-temp. veins, greisens, tactites. In residual and alluvial deposits. Ore of tungsten.
CON O_4	Tetragonal, $\frac{4}{m}\frac{2}{m}\frac{2}{m}$. Prismatic to pyramidal. Zoned. Some metamict.	Not distinctive.	Colorless to brown; various other colors. Transp. to transl. Adamantine to vitreous. Fluorescent.	7½ 3.9—4.7	Contains hafnium in varied amounts. Widespread as accessory in almost all kinds of rocks. Large crystals in pegmatites and high-temp. veins. Gems and ordinary vars. mined from alluvial deposits. Used in refractories and foundry sands. Major ore of zirconium and hafnium. Gems in wide color range. Colors may be modified by heating.

MINERAL DEPOSITS: see ORES AND ORE DEPOSITS.

MINERALIZATION: in geology, the process by which organic materials are replaced or supplemented by inorganic materials, as in fossilization; also, the process by which any substance, *e.g.* a metal or other element, is converted into a mineral. See FOSSIL; MINERAL; PETRIFACTION.

MINERALOGY: the study of the chemical and physical charac-teristics of minerals and their origin and associations. Related, overlapping fields include CRYSTALLOGRAPHY and crystal CHEMISTRY, PETROLOGY AND PETROGRAPHY, gemmology (see GEMSTONES), pedology (SOILS), and the study of METEORITES.

Mineralogy is a very old science, having begun with the use of inorganic substances known in ancient times, most of them of natural occurrence. The earliest mineralogists were inter-ested primarily in the occurrence, processing, and applications of ores and other useful minerals and gemstones. Early writ-ings, ranging from Theophrastus in Greece (*c.* 315 B. C.), Pliny in Rome (*c.* A. D. 75), Albertus Magnus in Germany (*c.* 1260), to Georgius Agricola, also in Germany (*c.* 1550), dealt primarily with the practical aspects of mineralogy, but unusual properties, *e.g.* the magnetic polarity of lodestone and the electrification of amber, were noted and discussed. Early knowledge of minerals was much involved with their use in ALCHEMY and with notions of their supposed magical origins and properties, but by the 17th cent. basic studies were being made of composition, crystal forms, physical properties, and modes of origin of minerals. Much of today's physical and chemical science grew directly from these early studies, made by men now renowned as pioneers in their re-spective fields.

There is no sharp division between mineralogical and non-mineralogical physics and chemistry; almost all developments in these sciences have been derived from or can be applied to some phase of mineralogy. Mineralogical investigations draw on a wide variety of precise techniques and refined instru-ments. Mineralogy encompasses the following fields as applied to minerals:

1. Crystal morphology, structure, and growth; the study of external crystal forms, with measurements made by contact and reflecting goniometers; the determination of crystal lat-tice type and structure by x-ray diffraction; examination of crystal surfaces with optical and electron microscopes.

2. Correlation of lattice constants with chemical composi-tion, and with precisely measured physical properties such as density, hardness, magnetism, thermo- and piezo-electric properties.

3. Determination of optical constants such as anisotropism, indices of refraction, pleochroism, absorption, and reflectivity, mostly by means of polarizing and reflecting microscopes, but also with spectrophotometers, refractometers, and other in-struments. (Other studies relating to light include ultraviolet and infrared fluorescence, phosphorescence, thermolumines-cence, and triboluminescence.)

4. Precise determinations of chemical composition; and correlation, through crystal chemistry, with polymorphism and isomorphous substitution.

5. Synthesis of minerals in carefully controlled systems, to establish phase equilibria between components at various pressures and temperatures. (This might be considered ex-perimental petrology and is interlocked with studies of the origin of rocks and of ore deposits.)

6. Investigations of solid-solution and exsolution phenom-ena; the composition and pressure-temperature relations of fluid inclusions in crystals.

Crystal structure of tourmaline is modeled as revealed by x-ray diffraction. Each sphere represents an atom. (M. I. T.)

7. Precise determinations (to parts per billion) of contained isotopes, for correlation of isotopic ratios with modes of origin and for determination of absolute age.

8. Differential thermal analysis.

Mineralogical techniques are applied directly, or with minor modifications, to many allied fields, *e.g.* gemstone identification, control of the beneficiation of ores and industrial minerals, and production of ceramics and glass, refractories, abrasives, and cements.

Determinative mineralogy is the testing and identification of minerals by techniques that do not require highly specialized training or elaborate facilities, and thus can be used by the field man or the interested amateur. Such techniques include:

1. Recognition of crystal system and class, as indicated by the symmetry, and of characteristic twinning patterns. (See CRYSTALLOGRAPHY.)

2. Recognition of typical CLEAVAGES and partings by relative location and by interfacial angles.

3. Recognition of typical FRACTURE-surfaces, as defined by the terms *conchoidal, hackly, irregular, splintery,* etc.

4. Recognition of characteristic crystalline aggregates, such as bladed, columnar, acicular (needle-like), radial, concretionary, colloform (deposited originally as a colloid, and usually showing smooth knobby to stalactitic surfaces with interior concentric and radial patterns), pseudomorphic (replacement of other minerals, wood, shells, etc.).

5. Determination of relative hardness by scratch tests, using as standards the minerals of Mohs' scale:

1. Talc	4. Fluorite	7. Quartz	9. Corundum
2. Gypsum	5. Apatite	8. Topaz	10. Diamond
3. Calcite	6. Orthoclase		

6. Determination of ease of fusibility, and checking for inflammability and exfoliation on heating.

7. Recognition of characteristic colors, and of other optical properties such as luster, transparency, opalescence (milky "glow"), chatoyance (cats-eye), *Schiller* (metallic "glow"), and color play.

8. Making streak tests on unglazed porcelain tiles (on paper for very soft minerals), or pulverizing some of the material to determine true color. (Of particular value for the very dark to opaque minerals.)

9. Testing for magnetism and magnetic polarity, piezo- and thermo-electricity, thermoluminescence, fluorescence, phosphorescence, triboluminescence, and radioactivity.

10. Checking for characteristic chemical constituents by means of tests with the blowpipe and charcoal or plaster-tablets; flame-coloration tests with and without color filters; heating in open and closed glass tubes; selective staining; color spot and microchemical tests; coloration tests in beads of sodium carbonate or salt of phosphorus held in a loop of platinum wire; acid tests to determine solubility and effervescence.

11. Determination of specific gravity by weighing in and out of water, either by suspension or with a pycnometer, or by use of calibrated heavy liquids such as tetrabromoethane or bromoform.

12. Tests for tenacity. Most minerals are brittle, but some show malleability, ductility, or sectility (can be cut by knife without fragmenting).

13. Recognition of characteristic odor when moist.

Field guides and handbooks list most common minerals in accordance with these various characteristics, and identity can often be established after a few simple tests.

Most important rock-forming and economic minerals are listed in the accompanying table, with notations in these categories:

1. Name of species. (Well-known alternate names shown in parentheses.)

2. Composition, shown by structural formula, using standard chemical symbols for the elements. (Common isomorphous substitutions are indicated by a series of elements separated by commas, in parentheses, *e.g.* the tetrahedrite to tenantite series: $(Cu,Fe)_{12}(Sb,As)_4S_3$.)

3. The group, if a species, is a member of a prominent mineral group, *e.g.* feldspars, micas, garnets. (Such groups are covered in separate entries throughout the volume.)

4. Crystal system and symmetry class (using the Herman-Maugin symbols).

5. Crystal habit.

6. Twinning patterns, where definitive.

7. Characteristic crystalline aggregates.

8. Cleavage planes, defined by crystal form names (MILLER INDICES in parentheses). (Angles between planes are shown.)

9. Sectility, malleability, and ductility (if distinctive).

10. Characteristic color or range of colors.

11. Transparency. (Minerals which appear opaque in bulk but afford a light streak are described as subtranslucent, as distinct from the truly opaque, generally metallic, minerals.)

12. Luster.

13. Scratch hardness, based on Mohs' scale.

14. Specific-gravity range.

15. Isomorphous or polymorphous relations, noting composition of end members of an isomorphous series.

16. Unusual properties, *e.g.* solubility and taste, magnetism, piezo- and pyro-electricity.

17. Common types of occurrence.

18. Minerals related in composition and occurrence.

19. Commercial applications.   —L. M.

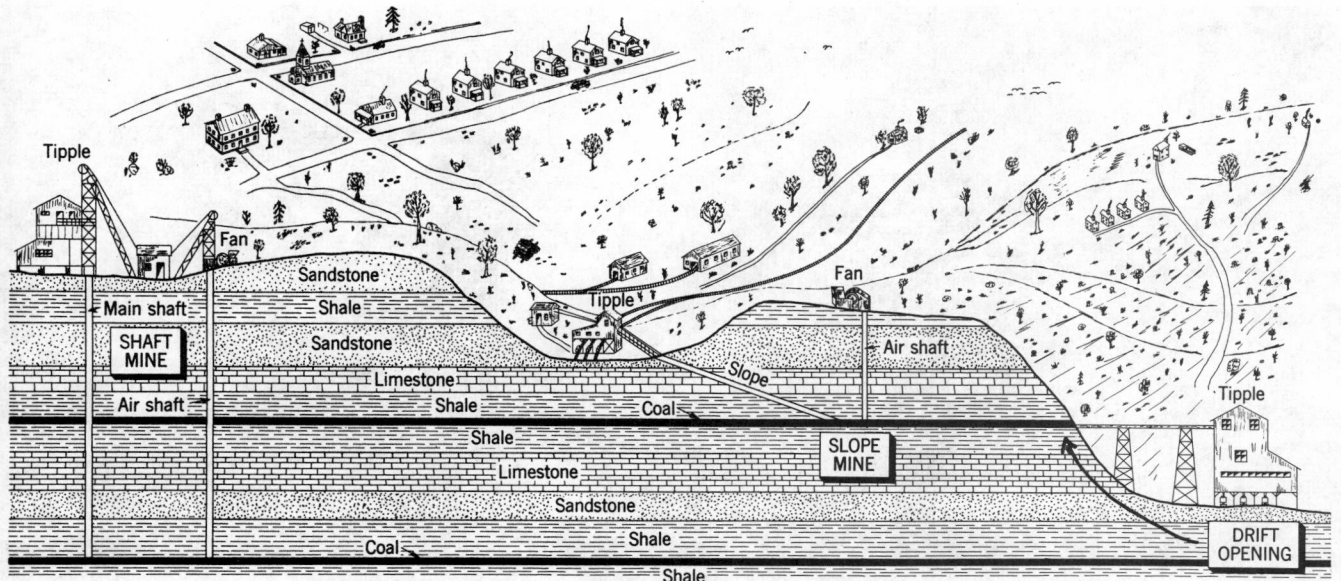

Coal deposits can be approached vertically (*left*), at an angle (*center*), and horizontally (*right*). (*U. S. Bureau of Mines*)

MINING: the operations involved in extracting minerals or usable rock from Earth's crust. *Quarrying* generally designates removal of noncarboniferous, nonmetallic stone that is to be used, either in blocks or broken, for various building, ornamental, and other purposes, while *mining* covers both coal mining and the extraction of ore containing valued minerals, metals, or other substances, which are procured from the ore by subsequent processing. Quarrying tools and techniques have always been closely associated with tools and techniques used in mining.

Early Mining: Mining was one of man's earliest activities, and its origins are lost in antiquity. Archeology customarily divides the history of human culture into ages associated with the extraction and use of metals and minerals: the Stone, Bronze, and Iron Ages. Early underground workings for the production of flint (for implements) have been found in Europe (*e.g.* at Grimes Graves on the Norfolk-Suffolk boundary in England); these remains reveal knowledge of general principles of shaft-sinking and underground excavations. Even at this early stage (late Paleolithic), it was clear to the miners that much labor could be saved by following the flint veins (stringers) underground instead of making an ever-larger pit. A remarkable chapter in early stone quarrying was the removal by the Egyptians of huge granite blocks—obelisks—chipped out of solid rock. Obelisks date as far back as the 4th Egyptian dynasty (3998–3721 B. C.) and continued to be quarried down to Roman times. "Cleopatra's needle," a famous Egyptian obelisk now standing in New York City's Central Park, is about 70 ft high and weighs over 400,000 lb. The tools used by the Egyptians were first copper, then bronze, and finally iron. The earliest underground excavation that can be dated was part of the Egyptian copper-mining operations, which began *c.* 2600 B. C. on the Sinai Peninsula. Copper, however, was commonly used by the Sumerians as early as 3000 B. C. Other Bronze-age copper mines were worked in Cyprus and throughout Europe, one of the most important being in the Tyrol, Austria.

The Tyrol mines show interesting developments in underground mining, *e.g.* ventilation shafts and timber-supported underground galleries over 300 ft long, access by tree-ladders down the center shaft, and lighting by torches made of bundles of twigs. There is evidence that gold and tin were

Placer mining is performed today with such mechanized aids as this gold dredge with its endless bucket-line and revolving screens. This dredge is operating in Alaska. (*Russ Kinne*)

Open-pit mining for copper: The Chuquicamata Mine in N Chile now measures
2 mi by half a mile. It yields 140,000 tons of ore and waste per day. (*Anaconda*)

being mined in England (in all likelihood from surface deposits) from about 1800 B. C.; horn picks, wooden picks and
shovels, and bronze axes have been found with tin-bearing
strata around Cornon in Cornwall. Mining techniques gradually advanced; salt mines of 1000 B. C. (around Hallstatt,
Austria) had shafts almost 1300 ft long, to a depth some 300
ft below the surface, with large timbered chambers. The Mt
Laurion silver mines of the Greeks mark a notable step forward in mining methods: the Greek miners sank shafts
approximately 5 ft square to depths of almost 400 ft in order
to reach scattered silver-ore bodies. Although opened by the
Mycenaeans in the 2nd millennium B. C., the Mt Laurion
mines were first actively worked by the Athenians, 600–350
B. C.; these mines have continued to produce iron, lead, and
zinc to this day.

The Romans practiced mining on an unprecedented scale,
and, beginning about 200 B. C., carried mining operations to
every part of Europe, the British Isles, and Asia Minor. The
Roman invasion of Britain is said to have been motivated, at
least in part, by a desire to exploit the island's mineral wealth.
Among the most important Roman mines were those in the
Rio Tinto area of Spain; from these the Romans extracted

enormous quantities of gold and silver. Later, when easily
mined deposits of these precious metals became scarce, the
Rio Tinto mines produced large quantities of copper, tin,
lead, iron, and cinnabar (the chief ore of mercury). Other
than the sheer scope of Roman exploration and exploitation,
perhaps the Romans' greatest contribution to mining was their
drainage methods, exemplified by water wheels or Archimedean screws in series to raise water as much as 80 ft out of
the Rio Tinto mines.

After the decline of the Roman Empire, mining activity
diminished, although there was some activity in the 9th and
10th cent. In the 15th cent. a revival of mining occurred in
Germany and Bohemia, stemming from an increased demand
for copper and especially for the silver found with copper.
However, the importing of silver from Central and South
America depressed the price of silver and made European
operations unprofitable; and the military advances of Turkey
into central Europe completely extinguished mining in the
area. Until the industrial revolution, the miner's principal interest was in precious metals, although some mining of other
metals (for making armaments and agricultural implements)
did occur.

Modern Mining Begins: Modern mining activity can be said to have started with the mining of COAL. The introduction of coal as fuel, as well as the emergence of techniques that successfully used coal in the smelting of copper and iron ores (see METALLURGY; SMELTING), caused rapid expansion of coal mining, especially in England. Many of the easily mined coal outcrops were soon exhausted, and it became necessary to follow the beds underground. The problem of drainage arose: depth of mines was limited because of flooding by subterranean water. Where coal deposits were mined in mountains, TUNNELS that sloped to lower ground (called adits or drifts) could be built which allowed the drainage of accumulated water. Where the terrain was flat, vertical shafts were sunk and horse-powered pumps, very similar to those used by the Romans, were installed. Such pumping systems were not economical, and the exploitation of deeper coal beds awaited the development of an efficient pump; this situation led in large part to the development of the reciprocating STEAM ENGINE. The steam engine, with its application in almost every part of the industrial economy, enlarged the demand for iron and then STEEL; with the steam engine's success also came an enlarged demand for copper, lead, tin, antimony, and a myriad of alloying metals (see ALLOY).

Placer Mining: Present-day mining methods fall into three categories: (1) placer mining, (2) open-cut (open-pit) mining, and (3) underground mining. Placer mining is the recovery of the desired metal or ore from alluvial sands and gravels, *i.e.* sands and gravels resulting from the erosion, through time, of surrounding rocks. Although gold remains the most important product of placer mining, many other minerals and metals are found in alluvial deposits, *e.g.* tin, platinum, copper, bismuth, silver, zircons, diamonds, and sapphires. Essentially, alluvial mining consists of excavation of the deposits, transportation to a separator, and the separation of the valuable minerals from the waste. The time-honored separating device, the sluice, is an inclined trough to whose bottom are attached upward-pointing cleats, so spaced that coarse gravel either slides or rolls over the cleats and only fine sand can enter the spaces between the cleats. A mixture of the excavated ore and water is dumped into the head of the sluice. As the mixture moves down, material of higher specific gravity settles to the bottom and is trapped between the cleats. Since the valuable minerals are usually of a higher specific gravity than the waste rock, they appear in the trapped concentrate. If the ALLUVIUM is a fine sand with, say, minute specks of gold, the cleats may be replaced by a material such as burlap or blanketing. The golden fleece of mythology may well have been a lamb or goat skin placed in the bottom of a stream carrying suspended ore from a gold placer; natural grease on the wool made the settled gold particles adhere to the hairs even after vigorous washing—hence the golden appearance. Although sluices were widely used in the past, the greatest volume of placer mining is now accomplished by dredges, which are steel hulls on which are mounted an endless bucket-line that revolves and digs the alluvial material below the pond (natural or artificial) on which the dredge floats. The buckets discharge their loads on revolving screens through which the material of finer dimensions is washed. Recovery units, either mechanical or chemical, further process the material, leaving behind the placer concentrate. The coarser material that passes over rather than through the screen is called *tailings* and is discharged from the back of the dredge. Dredges are best utilized in working large flat deposits. Although dredges are limited in the depths they can reach, modern dredges have extended their range and recover material well over 100 ft below water. Where rich paystreaks of alluvial deposits are encountered underground, drift mining (see below) may be used.

Open-cut (Open-pit) Mining: Where massive ore deposits are close to the surface, *e.g.* the Mesabi iron-ore deposits in N Minnesota or the copper-ore deposits in Utah and Nevada, open-cut mining is used. A distinction is made between *open-cut mining* and *strip mining*. Open-cut mining refers to the exploitation of concentrated deposits whose general direction is vertical. Strip mining refers to the exploitation of horizontally extended deposits near the surface, *e.g.* coal beds. In strip mining, the power shovels or bulldozers strip the overburden (the waste rock overlying the ore deposit) in cuts 40 to 50 ft wide, exposing the ore bed. Power shovels or drag lines then work the exposed beds. When the beds slope, the overburden must be stripped in benches following the contours of the terrain. This stage of strip mining is virtually indistinguishable from open-cut mining, in which the overburden is stripped and the ore mined in continuous shelves or benches that circle the resulting pit and generally follow the contours of the descending ore body. Benches are formed

Underground mining: Using a Lessman loader as a platform, a miner is drilling holes in one of the wide pillars that support the ceiling in this lead mine in SE Missouri. In the last stages, before abandonment, as much ore as possible is "slabbed" from the pillars. (St. Josephs Lead Co.)

Open-stope mining: This giant rig drills multiple holes for blasting out a "room" in copper mine. Pillars of ore will be left for support. In room-and-pillar mining, either the ore body or the enclosing rock constitutes the pillars. (*Canadian Nat. Film Bd.*)

by drilling and blasting (see EXPLOSIVE); the broken ore is then picked up by power shovels and loaded into trucks or railroad cars. The shelves or benches already excavated act as the road on which the powered excavation equipment rests and over which the ore is transported either by truck or by railway operating on the temporary track laid on the shelf. If the deposit occurs in the side of a mountain, the benches are cut to create an ascending road with a series of switchbacks following the natural contours; with mountainside deposits, removal of overburden and mining of ore may proceed simultaneously.

Underground Mining: Deposits that are too deep to be exploited by open-cut mining methods can be reached by various underground methods. For deposits located above the initial level of operation (*e.g.* a deposit within a mountain), adits or drifts are driven horizontally to explore the extent of the deposit; these tunnels later afford entry for men and supplies as well as serving for ventilation, and, eventually, for haulage-ways for the broken ore. Deposits directly beneath the surface of initial operation are reached by a vertical shaft from which adits are driven at various levels. The adits, like all passageways, must be adequately supported by timber, steel, or concrete to protect the mine from cave-ins. From the

adits, additional tunnels (crosscuts) at right angles to the adits are driven until every part of the deposit is brought within reach. When the general axis of the whole deposit dips at an angle, the primary shaft may follow the dip; or, if it is economically advantageous, the primary shaft may be driven horizontally from the vertical shaft to reach ore-bearing material. Extensive exploration and evaluation of the ore body are required to choose the most economic and efficient system of underground tunneling.

Stoping and caving are the two general methods of underground excavation. *Stoping* involves drilling and blasting of the ore in order to break it up into pieces that can be readily loaded and hauled by mechanical equipment. There are as many varieties of stoping as there are underground conditions, but two broad types may be distinguished: *overhand stoping*, which is the excavation of ore that forms the roof (hanging wall) above the miner, and *underhand stoping*, which is the excavation of ore that forms the floor (footwall) beneath the miner. *Open stoping* originally meant the excavation of ore bodies without using interior supports, but now designates either stopes with ore pillars left for the purpose of giving support or stopes that utilize simple timber supports. Open stoping is used for ore bodies of uniform character with strong walls. *Breast stoping* is the removal of the entire vertical face of ore bodies that are approximately horizontal and not over 100 ft thick. *Filled stopes* refer to operations where chambers, having been fully excavated and depleted of ore, are filled with tailings and water to provide wall support. *Shrinkage stopes* are excavations where overhand methods have provided broken ore which, before being loaded and hauled away, is used as a working floor for miners.

Caving is the practice of undercutting a slice or block of ore and allowing the ore's weight and the weight of the overburden, or capping, to cave it in and break it up. In many instances, the ore is drilled and blasted to initiate caving; timbering is used as a temporary support until the undercutting is complete, then the timber supports are blasted away. The amount of material caved at any one time depends on the character of the area. In general, caving is used for large bodies of relatively low-content ores which are soft enough to cave readily; on the other hand, if the ore is hard, it must be brittle enough to shatter into small pieces that can be worked by available equipment. The overburden should always be heavy enough to cause complete and immediate caving, since if the overburden stays temporarily in place, only to collapse after an interval, miners are endangered. Caving naturally may cause the ground above the mine to slump, and thus cannot be used where earth slumpage would threaten surface buildings.

Coal Mining: Coal mining differs from other types of mining in that COAL is generally found in horizontal beds, whereas metallic ore deposits, because of a different geological origin, are generally vertical in direction. Furthermore, many dangerous gases (*e.g.* the highly explosive methane, and poisonous CARBON MONOXIDE) are associated with coal deposits. Such hazards have stimulated invention of countless safety devices since the early 19th cent., *e.g.* various kinds of safety lamps, but coal mining remains a highly dangerous occupation, as attested by major catastrophes in the 20th cent. Since coal is relatively soft, and since bituminous coal commonly occurs in horizontal beds of uniform structure, there was an early development of machines designed to cut coal directly from the face of the bed. The first practical machine, a steam-driven revolving cutter having a serrated edge like that of a circular saw, was developed in 1863 and is similar in principle to those used today. However, electrical power has led to improvements in the efficiency and flexibility of such tools and, at present, continuous rippers are in operation which have auxiliary conveyor belts that carry the broken coal directly to transportation facilities.

Quarrying: A distinction is made between the quarrying of stone that will be used in broken or crushed form and stone that will be used in larger blocks (dimension stone). *Crushed-and broken-stone quarrying* produces road stone, concrete aggregate, fill, rip-rap, and railroad ballast. Limestone, the most quarried type of stone, has many additional applications, *e.g.* as calcined lime, metallurgical flux, agriculture lime, and an ingredient of cement. Other types of broken and crushed stone are sandstone and shale, and igneous rocks such as trap (basalt), granite, and granitoid rocks; some of these, differently quarried, can be used as dimension stone. Crushed or broken stone is quarried in various ways, depending on the position of the rock body (side hill or level land), the character of the rock (stratification or lack of it, thickness, hardness), and the rock's intended use. The actual breaking of stone from a solid ledge is done by drilling and blasting. Where the body of rock is thin (less than 15 ft) the quarry may consist of a single bench. With a high bluff composed of many low, irregular bluffs and narrow benches, the hand-held pneumatic sinker ("jackhammer") may be used to drill small-diameter (1½- to 2-in.) holes the full depth of the bluff. When benches are 15 to 30 ft apart in elevation, wagon drills perform the same operation on a larger scale. When nearly vertical bluffs 30 to 200 ft high occur, the churn or well drill is employed to drill holes 6 to 10 in. in diameter. Often all three types of drilling may be needed in the same quarry. The quantity of explosive inserted in each drill hole is carefully

Continuous coal mining: Machinery gouges bituminous coal from face of bed (seam), breaking it into small pieces that can be carried away by conveyor belt. Such mechanization is possible because coal is soft enough to be cut and broken by metal drills and choppers, and because bituminous coal commonly occurs in unbroken horizontal beds. This Joy Twin Borer cuts a hole 12 by 13 ft, producing an 8-ton/minute flow of coal. (Joy Mfg. Co.)

calculated to break the burden into the desired degree of fragmentation without scattering the broken stone, and at the same time leave the newly exposed face of the bluff in good condition for the next cycle of drilling and blasting.

Dimension-stone quarrying must produce large, sound, uniform blocks of attractive appearance. The commercial granites (granite and the granitoids) are the most-used dimension stones, finding use as building stone, cemetery memorials, and ornamental paneling and trim; the commercial granites are followed by marble (building, memorial, ornamental uses), sandstone (building), limestone (building), verd antique (ornamental), slate, and soapstone (both of the latter used for laboratory, laundry, and toilet facilities). Since structural soundness is essential for all dimension stones, high-speed explosives which cause incipient fractures cannot be used; even slow-speed explosives must be used sparingly. Thus dimension-stone quarriers must utilize various natural fractures in the rock body—faults, joints, seams, beds.

In opening a new quarry it is usually necessary to remove a key block. If no natural vertical fracture (joint, fault, or seam) is present, the key block must be cut on four sides by channeling down to a bed. If no bed is present, the block must be broken off at the bottom with explosives. If neither of these methods succeeds, the key block must be drilled, blasted, and removed, partly or wholly as waste rock. With the removal of the key block, an open face is exposed, facilitating subsequent quarrying. Primary breaks for freeing key blocks and large masses are made by channeling or wire-sawing. Channeling is the removal by machine of a narrow (1- to 3-in.) strip of rock the depth of the desired block and around as much of the block or mass as is neither open nor bounded by a natural fracture. A number of different channeling machines are in use, the choice of a particular type depending on the character of the rock. Most channeling machines are mounted on a track paralleling the line of the cut; they move back and forth, deepening the channel 6 in. to 2 ft at each pass with a steam- or pneumatic-powered cutting tool consisting of 3 to 5 bits with diagonal chisel edges. The wire saw is used for somewhat smaller cuts; it makes smooth, narrow (¼-in.) channels by employing an endless stranded or deformed wire belt to which an abrasive (generally sand) is fed on a stream of water. The wire saw operates continuously, revolving in one direction at a speed of 20 to 60 ft/sec.— *A. P. E.; A. L.; M. D. H.*

MINKOWSKI, HERMANN, 1864–1909, Russian-German mathematician; b. Alexota, near Kaunas. He is known for his research on the mathematical basis of relativity theory, particularly his provision of a four-dimensional mathematical framework for Einstein's special theory of relativity. This was published in Minkowski's book on space and time: *Raum und Zeit* (1907). He also worked in number theory and determinant theory.—*D. H. D. R.*

MIOCENE EPOCH: see CENOZOIC ERA; GEOLOGICAL TIME CHART.

MIRA (*o* Ceti): a long-period VARIABLE STAR discovered by Fabricius, 1596. It was the first variable star to be recognized as such. Mira's light varies from a magnitude of 2 or 3 at maximum to 9 or 10 at minimum, in a period of about 331 days. It is a red super-giant, having a diameter about 300 times the Sun's, and a density about three-millionths of the Sun's. Often referred to as "The Wonderful," it is typical of a large group of red long-period variables. Because of its great range in magnitude, from a bright star that can be seen easily without optical aid to a star so faint that a small telescope is needed to see it, Mira is often mistaken for a NOVA. Actually it is a double star; the red component has a blue companion which also varies and is about 10th mag. when at maximum. —*R. N. M.*

MIRAGE: an optical illusion caused by refraction of light through air layers of different temperatures. The most familiar mirage is the apparent sheet of water seen over a paved road on a sunny day. Here, the sun-warmed pavement heats the lowest few inches of air so that the density, and therefore the index of refraction, of the layer close to the ground is less than that of the air above. A nearly horizontal ray of light striking the upper surface of this warm layer will be bent upward as though a mirroring water surface were there. Mirages sometimes occur also when warm air moves over a cold surface, *e.g.* in the springtime, when warm tropical air often spreads northward over the cold waters of the North Atlantic. The boundary between the warm and the cold air is then a few dozen feet above the water. The reflection of light rays at this surface makes objects from beyond the horizon seem suspended in the sky. Ships and shorelines 100 mi away are sometimes visible. With wind, the reflecting boundary surface may become wavy, producing fantastic changes of shape in the distant objects.—*D. H. L.*

MIRBEL, CHARLES FRANÇOIS BRISSEAU DE, 1776–1854, French botanist; b. Paris. He was the founder of microscopical plant anatomy in France. Mirbel provided a theory of cell formation (1801), based on that of K. F. Wolff, insisting that all forms of vegetable tissue are cellular. He wrote a treatise on plant anatomy and physiology, *Traité d'anatomie et de physiologie* (1802), and was a fellow of the Royal Society.—*D. H. D. R.*

MIRIFICI LOGARITHMORUM CANONIS DESCRIPTIO (An Account of the Wonderful Table of Logarithms), by John Napier, 1614: In this little, difficult book Napier explained and exemplified the principles of calculation by logarithms (exponents) for the first time. With the object of easing the astronomer's labor of computing with large numbers, he invented the greatest aid to calculation between the introduction of place-value and the electronic computer, and opened up questions of capital importance for pure mathematics. The root of his invention was a comparison between arithmetic and geometric progressions, which he successfully analyzed. But Napier's logarithms were not identical with the modern Napierian logarithms, and "common logarithms" (to base 10) were first introduced (after the pattern of Napier's) by Henry Briggs in 1617.—*A. R. H.*

MIRROR: a smooth, highly reflecting surface that forms a clear-cut image of an object. In ancient Greece and Rome, highly polished bronze surfaces were used as mirrors. Mirrors of glass backed with an amalgam of tin and mercury were first manufactured commercially by the Venetians in the 16th cent. The present practice of making mirrors by coating a glass surface with silver was begun in 1840. Common types of mirrors are the plane mirror of everyday use, the spherical mirror, and the paraboloid mirror.

Plane Mirror: The image formed by a plane mirror is erect, reversed (right side appears as left side), and the same size as the object. The image is exactly the same distance behind the mirror as the object is in front of the mirror. It is known as a virtual image, because it is not formed directly by light rays from the object, but rather by the extension of these rays behind the mirror. In Fig. 1, three light rays from point *O* are reflected from the surface of a plane mirror. The angle of incidence *i* equals the angle of reflection *r*. From the geometry of the rays it can be shown that the distance of the object *O* to the mirror is equal to the distance of the virtual

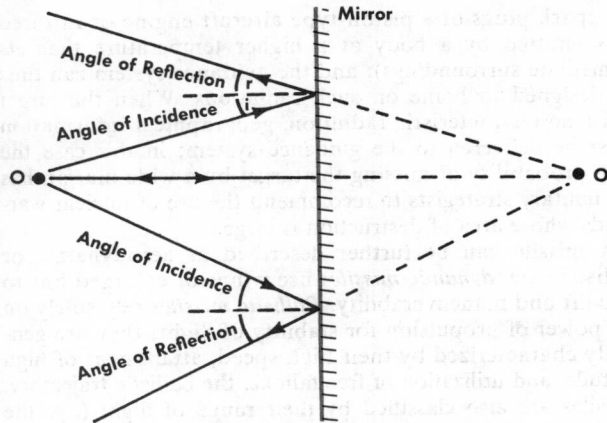

Fig. 1: Formation of a virtual image by a plane mirror.

image O' to the mirror. All the rays from point O seem to diverge from O'.

Spherical Mirror: This is a mirror whose surface is a section of a sphere. When the outer side of the spherical surface is the reflecting surface, the mirror is convex; when the inner side is the reflecting surface, the mirror is concave. The image formed by a spherical mirror differs from that formed by a plane mirror in several respects. Whereas the image formed by a plane mirror is always a virtual image, the image formed by a spherical mirror can be either real or virtual. Convex mirrors always produce virtual images. Concave mirrors produce a virtual image when the object is closer to the mirror than one half its radius of curvature; when the object is farther away, a real image is produced. The image formed by a spherical mirror can be either larger or smaller than the object, depending on the distance of the object from the mirror and the mirror's radius of curvature. Thus a spherical mirror, like a lens, can produce a magnified image of an object. The relation of the size of the image to the size of the object, called *lateral magnification,* equals s'/s, where s' is the distance between image and mirror and s is the distance between object and mirror (see Fig. 2). If a ray of light parallel to the

Fig. 2: Formation of a real image by a concave spherical mirror.

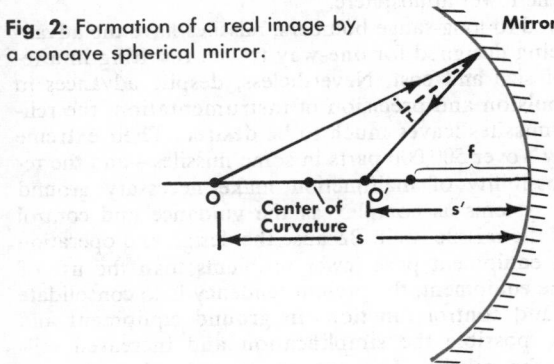

optical axis strikes a concave spherical mirror, the reflected ray will strike the optical axis at a distance equal to half the radius of curvature of the mirror; this distance is the focal length f of the mirror. All parallel rays close to the optical axis —*i.e.* paraxial rays—will coincide at the focus; objects such as stars that are so far from the mirror that rays from any one point on them are parallel will produce images in the focal plane, *i.e.* the plane passing through the focal point and perpendicular to the optical axis. The general relationship between the distance of the object from the mirror (*s*) and the distance of the image from the mirror (*s'*) is: $1/s - 1/s' = 1/f$.

This relationship, as in the case of reflected parallel rays coinciding at the focus, holds only for rays close to the optical axis. Parallel rays that strike a concave spherical mirror at its periphery will intersect the optical axis at various points between the focus and the mirror. This *spherical aberration* causes blurring of the image.

Paraboloid Mirror: Since the 6th cent., it has been known that a concave paraboloid surface does not produce spherical aberration for rays incident along the direction of its axis. As a result, concave paraboloid mirrors are preferred in telescopes. The parallel rays from a celestial body are reflected so as to concide at (or very near) the focal point, making a sharp *real image.* Conversely, a point of light at the mirror's focal point is reflected as a beam of parallel rays, a property that makes these mirrors useful as reflectors in searchlights and automobile headlights. As used in telescopes, paraboloid mirrors have a great advantage over LENSES in that they are free from chromatic aberration. The first reflecting telescope, built by Sir Isaac Newton, had a mirror made of an alloy of tin and copper known as speculum metal. In the early 18th cent., James Short, of Edinburgh, constructed telescope mirrors with true paraboloid surfaces. Modern reflecting telescopes, such as the 200-in. instrument at Palomar Mountain, have pyrex glass surfaces with aluminum silvered on their concave (reflecting) surface. See REFLECTION OF LIGHT.—*A. L.*

MISCEGENATION: the interbreeding of different races, especially human races. This process is as old as recorded history and will undoubtedly proceed at an accelerated rate as world travel becomes more frequent and populations more mobile. In various times and places halfbreeds have been despised by both parent races as unreliable, but the scientific evidence indicates that whatever difficulties the offspring of human racial crosses may have, they are sociological rather than biological in origin. Human racial crosses apparently confer neither advantages nor disadvantages on offspring. Available evidence supports the view that there are not enough differences—or at least not the right kind of differences—between various races of mankind to produce hybrid vigor after crossing, such as is well known in corn and various animals.—*G. B. M.*

MISES, RICHARD VON, 1883–1953, Austrian-born mathematician and philosopher; b. Lemberg, Austria. His most important scientific writing was in the field of aerodynamics (*Theory of Flight,* 1935). The application of mathematics led him to study the relationship of physical theory to experience, and then the foundations of probability theory (*Wahrscheinlichkeit und Ihre Anwendungen,* 1931; *Wahrscheinlichkeit, Statistik und Wahrheit,* 1936). *Positivism* (1951) expresses his philosophical position. Von Mises founded and edited (1920–33) *Zeitschrift für Angewandte Mathematik und Mechanik.*— *F. Sc.*

MISSILE: in modern military-scientific usage, a self-propelled, unmanned device that carries a warhead or a payload of scientific instruments through the atmosphere, space, or ocean, and which directs itself or is directed to a target. An *unguided missile,* after being launched, receives no further instructions from its internal system or from a ground-based guidance system; typical of such missiles were the V-1 rockets and the air-launched rockets used in World War II. *Guided missiles* are directed on a designated target path by complex guidance systems utilizing GYROSCOPES for INERTIAL GUIDANCE, missile-borne and ground-based digital computers, and radar. Certain targets can be discerned by characteristic electromagnetic emissions (*e.g.* electromagnetic waves emitted by

the spark plugs of a piston-type aircraft engine or infrared rays emitted by a body at a higher temperature than its immediate surroundings); and the guidance system can thus be designed to home on such radiations. When the target emits no characteristic radiation, geographical information must be delivered to the guidance system; in this case the high probability of missing the target by a wide margin has led military strategists to recommend the use of nuclear warheads whose area of destruction is large.

A missile can be further described as aerodynamic or ballistic. *Aerodynamic missiles* use wings or enlarged fins to give lift and maneuverability. *Ballistic missiles* rely solely on the power of propulsion for stability of flight; they are generally characterized by their high speed, attainment of high altitude, and utilization of free fall, *i.e.* the ballistic trajectory. Missiles are also classified by their range of flight (*e.g.* the ICBM, or "intercontinental ballistic missile") and by their launching and target media, *e.g.* surface-to-surface, surface-to-air, air-to-air, and air-to-surface.

A missile's principal components are payload, guidance and control system, and propulsion system. The payload can consist of scientific instruments used to accumulate and transmit data, *e.g.* meteorological rockets used to ascertain the force and direction of the winds in the upper atmosphere; currently, however, the payload of a missile is usually a warhead. The larger ballistic missiles have always been designed for the delivery of nuclear warheads; and with the reduction in cost of small-scale NUCLEAR WEAPONS, nuclear warheads are increasingly used in missiles originally designed to carry conventional explosives. Guidance systems determine the divergence of the missile's path from the pre-set path. The control system uses servomechanisms to translate the guidance system's signals into the mechanical movements necessary to return the missile to its proper path. Propulsion is accomplished by either air-breathing engines or ROCKET engines, and sometimes by a combination of the two. Rocket engines, which carry along their own oxygen or other oxidizer, are used in outer space or at altitudes where air is extremely thin. They are used in ballistic missiles because of the great speed, altitude, and range of such missiles. Also, because of their simplicity of operation, rocket engines are widely used in missiles that fly solely in the lower atmosphere.

Compared to long-range bombers, missiles have the advantage of being designed for one-way travel, resulting in a reduction of size and cost. Nevertheless, despite advances in both propulsion and precision of instrumentation, the reliability of missiles leaves much to be desired. Their extreme complexity—over 500,000 parts in some missiles—and the resulting possibility of malfunction make necessary ground check-out systems as complex as the guidance and control systems of the missile itself. Because the design and operation of ground equipment pose fewer problems than the use of flight-borne equipment, the present tendency is to consolidate guidance and control functions in ground equipment and thus make possible the simplification and increased reliability of the missile. The current operational surface-to-surface ICBM missile, Minuteman, weighs 65,000 lb; it carries a nuclear warhead of about one megaton yield and has a range of 6,000 to 7,000 nautical miles.—*A. L.*

Launching of Atlas D missile: ICBM missiles of this type have three liquid-propellant engines, with booster-stage engine developing a take-off thrust of approx. 330,000 lb. Flights have averaged 5,000 mi down the Atlantic Missile Range from Cape Kennedy. This booster, though operational, has been outdated by the Titan III-C and Saturn V boosters. (*U. S. Air Force*)

MISSISSIPPIAN PERIOD: see GEOLOGICAL TIME CHART; PALEO-ZOIC ERA; LIFE, PREHISTORIC.

MIST: see FOG.

MITOCHONDRIA: small bodies, about the size of bacteria, which are found in practically all animal and plant cells, and are of very similar structure in all these cells. Often called the "powerhouse of the cell," they are responsible for most of its energy production. These bodies, which can be isolated from a homogenate (crushed cells), contain many enzymes responsible for the oxidation of diverse compounds. In addition, they are the sole site within the cell of the enzymes of the electron transport chain and of OXIDATIVE PHOSPHORYLA-TION; thus they produce most of the adenosine triphosphate made by the cell, which is used for synthetic purposes both within and outside the mitochondria.—*P. S.*

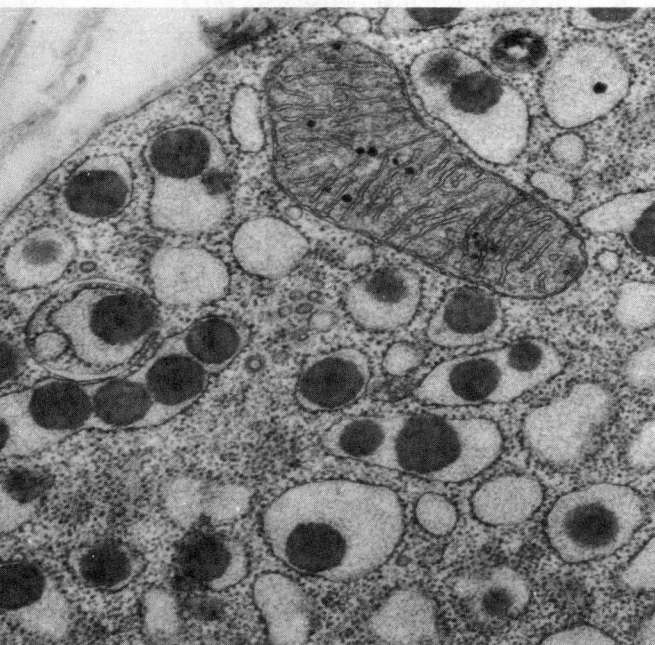

Mitochondrion: In this electron micrograph (X 35,000) of a secretory cell from the pancreas of a guinea pig, the mitochondrion is the large gray, striated, socklike structure at top. Inner membranes of mitochondrion are site of oxidation reactions in which energy of foodstuffs is converted to energy of ATP. (*George E. Palade/ Rockefeller Inst.*)

MITOSIS: see CELL DIVISION.

MITSCHERLICH, EILHARDT, 1794–1863, German chemist; b. Neuende, Oldenburg. His discovery that certain phosphates have the same crystal form as the corresponding arsenates (1818) brought him an invitation to collaborate with Berzelius in Stockholm. Returning to Berlin, he studied the case of calcium carbonate, which crystallizes in two different forms. He called the first phenomenon *isomorphism,* the other *di-* or *poly-morphism.* As professor in Berlin from 1822 on, he discovered the manganic acids, the conversion of heated calcium benzoate into benzene, and new aspects of the reaction by which ether is formed from alcohol. The polarimeter became in his hands a practical tool of analysis in the sugar industry. His textbook *Lehrbuch der Chemie* (1829–30) had many later editions in several languages. He was a fellow of the Royal Society.—*E. F.*

MIXING: a unit process in chemical technology whose purpose is to produce a homogeneous blend of the ingredients in a substance. The term "mixing" usually implies a physical or mechanical (rather than a chemical) action, although chemical actions may occur as a result of mixing. Emulsification and foam generation, although technically mixing operations, are usually not considered as such; likewise the dissolving of solids in liquids. The mixing of gases, and of two or more mutually miscible liquids, results in a single-phase mixture which can be perfectly homogeneous, *i.e.* homogeneous down to the molecular level. Mixtures of this type will form themselves by simple diffusion if the ingredients are left together long enough in a single vessel. To speed the process the inhomogeneous mass may be stirred by propellers, paddles, or turbines, or it may be pumped in confluent streams. Achieving complete homogeneity in a reasonably short time may require considerable expenditure of energy if large masses of viscous liquids are being handled. The mixing of very viscous or plastic materials, *e.g.* rubbers and plastics, is done in heavy vessels carrying two counter-rotating agitator shafts that fit closely against the vessel walls; the Banbury mixer commonly used in rubber manufacture is of this general design. Mixing of viscous materials is also done on roller mills. These consist essentially of two or more rollers, running at different speeds, with a controlled narrow clearance between them. The mass of material to be mixed is nipped and sheared between the rollers, then scraped off when it has been mixed to a satisfactory state. The mixing of solid particles in liquids to form relatively thin slurries is frequently done in tumble mills, a good example being the familiar truck-mounted concrete mixer. Thicker and more intimate mixtures, *e.g.* paints, are usually made on roller mills. Dry solid powders are mixed in tumble mills, often with grinding, or in sifting and screening devices.—*A. M. S.*

MIXTURE: in chemistry, a system of two or more ingredients which do not bear any fixed proportion to one another, and whose molecules retain their separate existences regardless of how intimately they are mingled. A mixture is distinguished from a COMPOUND, in which the chemical ingredients are invariably present in a definite proportion. Mixtures are of two classes: mechanical and physical. In mechanical mixtures each component exists as a separate phase, and can therefore be separated from the other components by purely mechanical means. A mixture of sand and salt, for example, can be separated by picking out the individual granules. Physical mixtures, of which solutions are the best example, consist of a single phase, and to bring about separation at least one of the components must undergo a physical change. Thus to separate an aqueous salt solution into its components, one can evaporate water (physically changing it to vapor, which may be condensed separately) and leave the solid salt. Alternatively, the mixture can be completely frozen, physically changing the water to ice, and thus allowing the mechanical separation of ice crystals from salt crystals.—*A. M. S.*

MÖBIUS, AUGUST FERDINAND, 1790–1868, German astronomer and mathematician; b. Schulpforta; ed. Leipzig, Göttingen, and Halle. He taught astronomy at Leipzig from 1815 and directed the observatory erected under his supervision 1818–21. He wrote on astronomy and celestial mechanics. His purely mathematical works, which were chiefly geometrical, foreshadowed discoveries of modern times and led to the introduction of methods of modern projective geometry. A "Möbius band" is a one-sided surface of topological interest that can be made by attaching the ends of a strip of paper after one twist.—*H. C.*

MODAL LOGIC: in logic, the study of the properties of such notions as *necessity, possibility,* and *impossibility* (referred to as *modes,* or *modalities*). Systems of modal logic concern (among other things) relations between modalities and *truth.* A proposition may be not only true, but also necessarily true. "There was an earthquake in Chile in 1960" is a true statement, but it is not necessarily true: affairs might have turned out differently. On the other hand, "Either there was an earthquake in Chile in 1960, or else there was not" is necessarily true; it *must* have been the case that one of these alternatives happened.

Classical examples of necessary truths are the *law of identity* ("*A* is *A*" or "*A = A*"), and the *law of the excluded middle,* also called the *tertium non datur* ("Every proposition is either true or false," *i.e.* there is no third possibility). The statement above about the Chilean earthquake is an instance of the law of the excluded middle. One also considers propositions which are *not possibly* true ("This object is both round and square"). Impossible propositions may not sound very interesting, but it should be noted that one of the most important ways we have in mathematics of showing that a proposition is true is to assume that it is false, and then show that a contradiction (an impossible proposition) follows. (This method of proof is familiar under the name *reductio ad absurdum.*)

Certain relations among these concepts are obvious: if a proposition is necessary, it is true (but not necessarily conversely), and if a proposition is impossible, it is false (again not necessarily conversely). Other, less obvious truths may also be proved, from plausible sets of axioms. Contemporary interest in these topics stems largely from the pioneering work of C. I. Lewis (Lewis and Langford, *Symbolic Logic,* 1932). More recently, modal logic has been found to have some surprising connections with the algebra of *topology* and with the logic of mathematical *intuitionism.* In 1951, G. H. von Wright (*An Essay in Modal Logic*) stimulated investigation of similar logics (called *deontic* logics) dealing with the concepts of permission, obligation, and prohibition.—*A. R. A.*

MODE: see MEAN, MODE, AND MEDIAN; STATISTICS.

MODELS AND MODELING: in experimental science, the technique of reproducing the behavior of a physical system on convenient laboratory scale; *e.g.* the motion of a ship in a heavy sea, the swimming action of spermatozoa, or the flow of air past an aircraft wing. If the model is to behave in a manner corresponding to the actual situation, it must have (1) geometrical similarity (*i.e.* as to shape, though not size) and (2) dynamical similarity (*i.e.* with forces acting on the model in the same ratios as in the full-scale situation).

In the motion of a viscous fluid, the ratio of the product fluid mass-acceleration (the inertia force) to the viscous force is the *Reynolds number* (from the British engineer Osborne Reynolds, 1842–1912). If ρ represents the fluid density, μ its viscosity, U a representative velocity, and L a representative length of the flow, the Reynolds number R is given by

$$\frac{\rho U^2/L}{\mu U/L^2} = \frac{\rho U L}{\mu}$$

To model, say, the swimming action of a spermatozoön, the Reynolds number must be the same for the large model as for the actual small-scale motion. In the model, L is to be in-

Model of Niagara River and Falls shows effects of diversions of water. Engineer is removing gates from regulating dam. One foot in model represents 360 ft horizontally and 60 ft vertically. American Falls are at left, Canadian Falls at right. (*U. S. Army Engineers*)

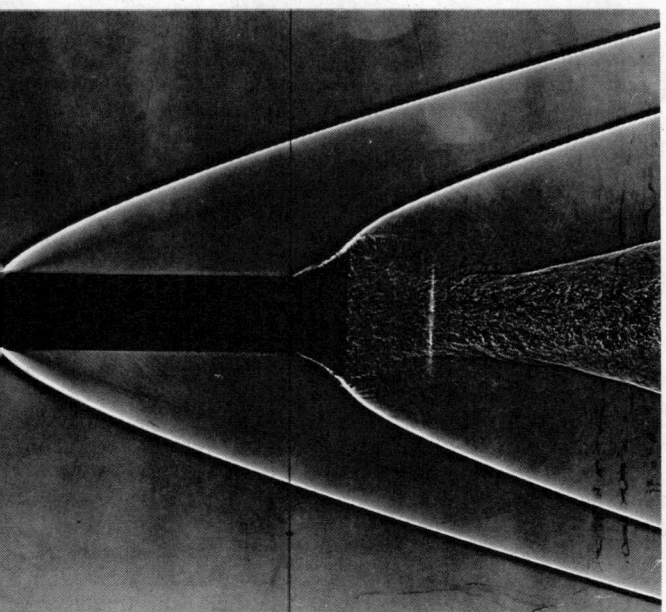

Flight stability is investigated through use of aerodynamic models. Behavior of this small, blunt-nosed cylinder, fired from a gun, simulates, in accordance with scaling laws, the behavior of large vehicles of similar shape, moving at supersonic speeds. (NASA)

creased many times, and it is convenient to keep the density ρ and velocity U of the same order in the two cases. To preserve equality of the Reynolds number, the viscosity μ of the liquid surrounding the model must be increased in proportion to L.

If the free surface of a liquid is involved, as in ocean-wave problems, the force of gravity must also be considered. The *Froude number* (after William Froude, 1810–1879) is the ratio of gravity force to inertia force, or

$$F = \frac{gL}{U^2}$$

where g is the gravitational acceleration. Other similarity parameters of importance are (1) the MACH NUMBER, $M = U/a$, the ratio of flow speed to speed of sound a, where compressibility effects are important; (2) the *Prandtl number,* the ratio of kinematic viscosity (μ/ρ) to heat conductivity, where heat conduction in fluids is involved; (3) in high-speed underwater flows, the CAVITATION number (ratio of pressure in the surrounding liquid to "dynamic pressure," $\frac{1}{2}\rho U^2$). A large number of parameters are used in special problems involving such factors as hydrodynamics, chemical reactions, and diffusion; these must be held constant for accurate model representation. Models are also used frequently to investigate the static and dynamic response of a structure to applied fixed and moving loads, particularly in advanced design. In accurate tests on structural models, corresponding principles of geometrical and dynamical similarity must be obeyed. *Display models* are sometimes used to illustrate the workings of a complex machine, or the atomic arrangements in a molecule. *Working models* of machines can be constructed to test the feasibility of a proposed design, but unless dynamical similarity is preserved, the performance of the model may differ considerably from that of the full-scale machine. A *mathematical model* is the term used for an abstraction of a physical situation into mathematical terms. By analysis of his mathematical model, a theoretician seeks to predict the behavior of the physical situation. See also HYDRAULIC MODELS; WIND TUNNEL; TOWING TANKS AND WATER TUNNELS.—O. M. P.

MODELS IN LOGIC AND PHYSICS: In the sciences the term "model" has several senses, no one of which is precisely defined; in logic, however, the term has a precise and standard use which can be explained best by a simple example. Consider the sentence: (1) All logicians are liberals. A *model* or interpretation for this sentence in the domain of the integers (called the *domain of discourse*) is the class of prime numbers greater than 2 and the class of odd numbers greater than 2. Since a true assertion is obtained when the term "logicians" is replaced by a name of the first class, and the term "liberals" by a name of the second class, the model is said to be a *realization of* the sentence, or the sentence is said to be *satisfied by* the model. Another model for (1) in the domain of integers is the class of prime numbers, and the class of odd numbers. However, (1) is not satisfied by this model, since it is not true that all the prime numbers are odd, the number 2 being an integer which is prime but not odd.

For sentences of grammatical structure more complex than (1) a model must be correspondingly more complex. Further, groups of sentences can have a model. A model is a *realization of* a group of sentences, or the sentences of the group are *simultaneously satisfied by* the model, just in case, under the interpretation given, all the sentences of the group make true assertions of the model.

Models play an important role in connection with the postulates of a theory, mathematical or empirical. To establish the consistency of a set of postulates it is sufficient to find a model for them by which they are simultaneously satisfied. To establish that a specified sentence is not a logical consequence of a set of postulates, it is sufficient to find a model which satisfies the postulates simultaneously but which does not satisfy the specified sentence, for if a model simultaneously satisfies some sentences it also satisfies any logical consequence of them. Thus, a sentence of the form "No S is P" is not a logical consequence of postulates having the form "All M is P" and "No S is M"; for the model consisting of the classes Circles, Plane Curves, and Hyperbolas satisfies the postulates but not the given sentence.

One sense in which scientists use the term "model" is closely related to the logician's sense. When a physicist speaks of some physical phenomena as a model of a scientific theory, he is claiming that these phenomena constitute a model which is a realization of the set of postulates of his theory. For example, when it is asserted that the solar system is a model of celestial mechanics, the solar system and certain relationships among its parts are being considered as a model of which the postulates of celestial mechanics are true assertions. On the other hand, the word "model" is sometimes used to denote a geometrical or mechanical concept which serves as a starting point for theory, as in the Bohr model of the atom. In this sense of the word economists call the equation $D \times P = constant$ a model for the relation between the market demands for an article and its price.—D. K.

MODULATION: the alternation or regulation of some property of an electric signal, *e.g.* regulation of the amplitude, frequency, or phase of an electromagnetic wave. For transmission of electromagnetic waves to be efficient and relatively free from noise, high frequencies must be used. The information to be transmitted, however, such as speech or music in ordinary radio broadcasting, is usually low-frequency. Therefore, the high-frequency carrier wave is modulated so that the alternations, properly detected, reproduce the low-frequency audio signal. The high-frequency carrier wave, or unmodulated signal, is commonly represented by a sine wave, as in Fig. 1. It is characterized by three quantities: amplitude, frequency, and phase. The amplitude is the magnitude of the wave; in

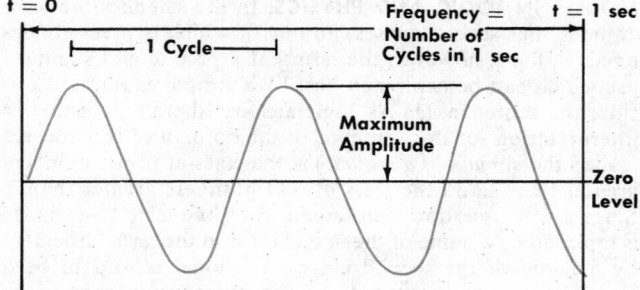

Fig. 1: Typical sinusoidal wave.

Fig. 1, the amplitude is the instantaneous distance of the wave above or below the zero level indicated by the solid straight line. When above zero, the amplitude is positive, and when below, negative. The waves of Fig. 1 show how the wave amplitude varies as a function of time. The frequency of the wave is the number of times per second the wave experiences one complete alternation from zero to its maximum positive value, back through zero to its maximum negative value, and back again to zero. Such an alternation is termed a cycle, and frequency is the number of cycles per second. Phase relates to the positioning of the entire wave relative to a given reference time, usually taken as the initial or zero instant ($t = 0$). Shifting the wave back and forth along its time-axis (the solid straight horizontal line of Fig. 1) corresponds to changing its phase. A familiar example of an unmodulated electric wave is the common alternating house current; the frequency of this is generally 60 cycles/sec and the amplitude is normally 110 v. Because of the difference between audio frequencies and transmission frequencies, modulation is part of almost all electrical communications systems. It is accomplished by (1) *amplitude modulation,* (2) *frequency modulation,* and (3) *pulse modulation.*

Fig. 2: (A) Unmodulated high-frequency carrier wave. (B) Low-frequency modulating signal. (C) Carrier wave amplitude-modulated by low-frequency signal. (The relative frequencies of the waves are not shown to scale.)

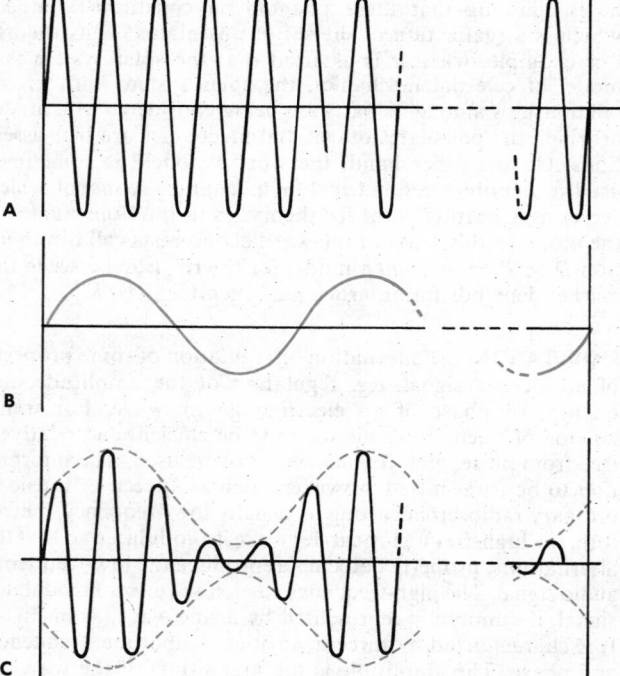

Amplitude modulation (AM) has been, until recently, the method most extensively used, and is still used in the majority of household radios. In AM, the amplitude of the carrier wave varies directly as the amplitude of the desired audio signal. If we have a carrier wave of 1,500,000 cycles/sec, as shown in Fig. 2A, and an audio, or modulating, signal of 400 cycles/sec, as in Fig. 2B, then by means of a MODULATOR the envelope of the modulated wave (*i.e.* the instantaneous amplitude of the carrier wave) will be a wave of 400 cycles/sec.

Frequency modulation (FM) is accomplished by changing the instantaneous frequency of the carrier wave in response to some desired modulating wave; the frequency at any instant is proportional to the amplitude of the modulating wave (Fig. 3). To recover the audio signal in a FM receiver, the signal can be passed through a FILTER whose output amplitude varies with input frequency. Both AM and FM accomplish the primary task of communication. FM, however, has the advantage of higher fidelity, reduced noise, and reduced interference between broadcasting stations. A variation of FM is *phase modulation,* in which the phase angle varies as the amplitude of the modulating signal, whereas in FM the *rate of change* of the phase angle (the frequency) varies as the amplitude of the modulating signal.

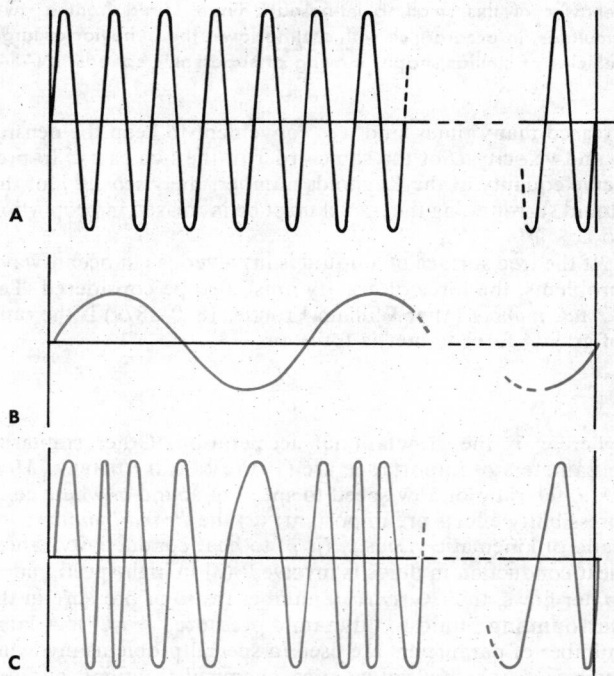

Fig. 3: (A) Unmodulated carrier. (B) Modulating signal. (C) Carrier frequency-modulated by signal.

Pulse modulation reproduces some characteristic, usually the amplitude, of the modulating wave by series of pulses. Because pulses are discrete, *i.e.* separated by a level of zero current, there must be a number of pulses for each cycle of the modulating wave if that wave is to be fairly reproduced. The instantaneous amplitude of the wave can be reproduced by (1) the instantaneous amplitude of the pulse (P. A. M.: pulse-amplitude modulation), (2) a pulse of constant amplitude whose time duration is proportional to the instantaneous amplitude of the modulating wave (P. W. M.: pulse-width modulation), (3) a pulse of constant amplitude and constant time duration, where the time interval between pulses is proportional to the instantaneous amplitude of the modulating wave (P. T. M.: pulse-time modulation), and (4) a combination of pulse duration and variable time intervals that indicates a predetermined invariant level of amplitude (quantized level) for each range of instantaneous amplitudes of the modulating wave (P. C. M.: pulse-code modulation). The advantage of pulse modulation is that additional modulating waves may be transmitted by additional sets of pulses placed between the pulses of the initial set of pulses. Thus a number of modulating waves, or sets of information, may be sent (a process called multiplexing) simultaneously. Pulse modulation has become increasingly important in the transmission of data for use in computers and transmission of data from space vehicles (see TELEMETERING).—*G. S.*

MOHL, HUGO VON, 1805–72, German botanist and microscopist; b. Stuttgart. He established the cellular structure of many parts of plants, *e.g.* bark; he described the development of partition walls in cells during cell reproduction, and argued that cells in algae and even higher plants reproduce by division. Mohl introduced the term "protoplasm" for the living material in the cell (1846), and his *Micrographie* (1846) was an important text on microscopic technique. Mohl was a fellow of the Royal Society.—*D. H. D. R.*

MOHOROVIČIĆ DISCONTINUITY: the boundary between the crust of EARTH and the mantle. At a depth of a few kilometers below the surface an abrupt rise in velocity of primary SEISMIC WAVES, from about 7 to about 8.2 km/sec, marks this boundary. The rise was first noticed by the geophysicist A. Mohorovičić while studying the records of a Balkan earthquake in 1909. Under the deep oceans the discontinuity is always close to 4.7 km below the sea floor, and this uniformity suggests that the "Moho," as the discontinuity is called, is a phase change, perhaps from gabbro to eclogite, a denser rock of the same composition. Under the CONTINENTS the depth of the Moho varies from 20 to 60 km, but averages 34 km; whether it is a phase or a composition change is uncertain. The **Mohole project** is an attempt to drill a hole in the ocean floor to this discontinuity.—*J. T. W.*

MOHR, KARL FRIEDRICH, 1806–79, German pharmacologist and chemist; b. Koblenz. He made many inventions useful in chemical analytical work, including the cork borer and a balance for determining specific gravities. Mohr also developed techniques of volumetric analysis, described in his *Lehrbuch der chemisch-analytischen Titriermethode* (1855), a textbook on titration methods.—*D. H. D. R.*

MOHS, FRIEDRICH, 1773–1839, German mineralogist; b. Gernrode. He supported the classification of minerals on a basis of physical appearance rather than by using chemical analogies, as proposed by J. J. Berzelius. His name survives in Mohs' scale, a classification of the hardness of minerals (see MINERALOGY). His many books and articles on mineralogy and related subjects include a treatise on mineralogy, *Grundriss der Mineralogie* (1822–24).—*D. H. D. R.*

MOISSAN, HENRI (in full, **Ferdinand Frédéric Henri**), 1852–1907, French chemist; b. Paris. His principal contribution was the isolation of fluorine as a greenish-yellow gas by electrolysis of a solution of potassium hydrogen fluoride and anhydrous hydrofluoric acid (1886). He developed the arc furnace, whose high temperature of 4100°C enabled such uncommon metals as uranium, chromium, tungsten, vanadium, manganese, titanium, and molybdenum to be reduced from their ores. In 1893 he created a sensation by preparing small artificial diamonds from carbon which had been dissolved in molten iron. For his research on the isolation of fluorine and for placing at the service of science the electric furnace which

bears his name, he received the 1906 Nobel prize in chemistry. He was a fellow of the Royal Society and an associate of the U. S. National Academy of Sciences.—*E. F.*

MOLAR SOLUTION: a solution of 1 liter capacity that contains 1 MOLE (gram-molecular weight) of solute. The term is a weight/volume (w/v) method of expressing concentration, and is useful in many laboratory experiments where the number of solute molecules must be known. Varying concentrations (of solute in solvent) can be described by their relation to the standard of *molarity* (*i.e.* to the degree of solute concentration in a standard molar solution); this is done by expressing the number of moles of solute per number of liters of solution. Inasmuch as there are 1,000 millimoles per mole and 1,000 ml per liter, a concentration may also be expressed as number of millimoles of solute per number of milliliters of solution. Because the molecular formula may be ambiguous (*e.g.* sulfur at room temperature is actually S_8, not S) many chemists prefer to use "formality" instead of "molarity." Formality expresses concentration as number of gram-formula weights *as written* per number of liters of solution. Thus in the example cited, the gram-formula weight of sulfur is 1×32.06 gm and the gram-molecular weight is 8×32.06 gm. See SOLUTION.—*L. Sc.*

MOLD: see FUNGI.

MOLE: the abbreviation for *gram-molecular weight,* or the sum of the atomic weights expressed in grams of all the atoms in a molecule, based upon the gram-molecular weight of naturally occurring diatomic oxygen (O_2) accepted as 32 gm. Thus the mole of carbon dioxide (CO_2) is 44 gm, because the atomic weight of carbon (C) is 12 and of oxygen (O) 16. Some writers prefer to use the term "gram-formula weight" rather than "gram-molecular weight," because the formula as written may not conform to the true molecular composition (see MOLAR SOLUTION).—*L. Sc.*

MOLECULAR BEAM: a directed beam of neutral molecules traveling through a vacuum. For purposes described here, the beam must have low density, so that very few molecules collide with each other. Such a beam may be readily formed by allowing gas at low pressure to leak out of a small hole into a high-vacuum region. Passage of gas molecules through a narrow slit produces a *directed* beam.

Molecular-beam experiments have played a major role in modern physics. Perhaps most dramatic was the Stern-Gerlach experiment. A beam of silver atoms was passed through a non-uniform magnetic field, and whereas classical physics would have predicted a broadening of the original beam by the field, instead the beam split into two equal components, one on each side of the original beam (see figure). This was a direct confirmation of the quantum-mechanics prediction that atoms can align themselves only in certain

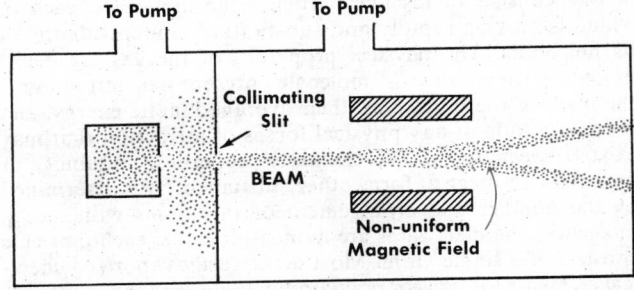

Stern-Gerlach experiment employs a molecular beam to demonstrate quantum-mechanical behavior of silver atoms.

well-defined directions in a magnetic field. (See QUANTUM NUMBER.) Use of molecular beams was greatly expanded by I. Rabi and his collaborators, who combined the Stern-Gerlach experiment with radio-frequency spectroscopy to develop a method of remarkable sensitivity and accuracy for study of molecular, atomic, and nuclear properties. From this came application of beams to atomic clocks and masers; other modern applications include study of atomic collisions, chemical reactions, and surface-particle interactions.—*B. Be.*

MOLECULAR SPECTRA: band spectra originating in molecules, as distinguished from line spectra associated with individual atoms (see ATOMIC SPECTRA). Molecular spectra are obtained by passing an electric discharge through a polyatomic gas at low pressure and by dispersing the resulting complex radiation with the aid of a prism spectroscope. Spectra of diatomic gases, such as H_2, O_2, N_2, or CO, are less complicated than spectra of gases with molecules composed of three or more atoms. The recurring bands are aggregates of fine lines, each corresponding to a specific wavelength, their separation and intensity decreasing toward the short-wavelength end of the spectrum. Band spectra may also be obtained for substances such as sodium chloride, which can be dissociated at the relatively low temperatures of a Bunsen-burner flame. See SPECTROSCOPE AND SPECTROSCOPY; SPECTRUM.—*A. E.*

MOLECULAR WEIGHT: the relative mass, or weight, of a molecule compared to the oxygen atom, which has been assigned a reference value of 16. Molecular weight is, therefore, the sum of the ATOMIC WEIGHTS of the atoms that make up the molecule. Water (H_2O), for instance, contains two atoms of hydrogen (at. wt 1.008) and one atom of oxygen (at. wt 16). Thus the molecular weight of water is $(2 \times 1.008) + (1 \times 16)$, or 18.016; or, for most practical purposes, 18. If the formula for a compound represents the actual number of atoms present in a molecule, as is usually the case, the molecular weight is also the formula weight. However, some compounds, *e.g.* starch or cellulose, are macromolecules designated by empirical formulas ($C_6H_{10}O_5$ for starch and cellulose) that represent only the proportionate numbers of each atom in the molecule. In such cases, the formula weight is not properly the molecular weight. Molecular weights of volatile compounds can be determined by measuring their vapor density. Molecular weights of non-volatile compounds are determined by dissolving them in a suitable solvent and noting either the boiling-point elevation or the freezing-point lowering (see RAOULT'S LAW).—*A. M. S.*

MOLECULE: the smallest particle of an element or compound that retains all the chemical properties of a larger mass of the same material. The modern concept of chemical molecules was developed largely through work on gases by J. L. Gay-Lussac and A. Avogadro in the early 19th cent. A mass of GAS consists of discrete particles, the molecules, each of which is moving rapidly and substantially independently of its neighbors. The physical properties of the gas are determined by the number of molecules present per unit volume, the mass of the molecules, their average kinetic energy, and the magnitude of any physical forces of attraction that may exist between them. The chemical properties, *i.e.* ability or proclivity to react to form other substances, are determined by the number and arrangement of the atoms within each molecule. The inert gases are monoatomic; *i.e.* each molecule consists of a single atom. Most other easily vaporized chemical elements form di- or poly-atomic molecules in the gaseous state. The vapors of those chemical compounds that are stable in the gaseous state consist of molecules, each of which

Molecular model: In this model of the antibiotic terramycin, black springs mark double bonds of carbon atoms, indicating that the molecule is an unsaturated hydrocarbon. The OH group that differentiates terramycin (oxytetracyline) from aureomycin (chlorotetracycline) and other tetracyclines is indicated by a wire ring. (*Chas. Pfizer & Co., Inc.*)

possesses the same number and proportion of chemical elements as a bulk amount of the same material. The forces that unite the atoms in a molecule, called chemical bonds, are generally much stronger than the forces of attraction (intermolecular forces) between molecules, the latter forces being those that cause gases to condense to the liquid and solid state at sufficiently low temperatures. The term "molecule" is usually reserved for an electrically neutral assemblage of atoms having more than a transitory existence. Assemblages of atoms bearing a definite electric charge are called IONS. In many solids and liquids, particularly in aqueous solutions of inorganic salts, the chemically bonded units are ions rather than molecules. In most organic liquids and solids, however, the units are neutral molecules.—*A. M. S.*

MOLESCHOTT, JACOBUS ALBERTUS WILLEBRORUS, 1822–93, Dutch-born Italian physiologist; b. 's Hertogenbosch. A practicing physician throughout his career, he was noted as a popularizer of scientific material and as an exponent of mechanical materialism. Moleschott's books include *Physiology of Food* (1850) and *The Cycle of Life* (1852), in which he attacked the views of J. von Liebig.—*W. P. C.*

MOLLUSK: any invertebrate animal of the phylum Mollusca, a primary division of the animal kingdom, which includes such familiar forms as oysters, clams, snails, slugs, limpets, squids, and the octopus. The group consists of about 96,000 living species, as well as a large number of extinct species. A typical mollusk has a shell of calcium carbonate, secreted by a special glandular layer of the body wall, a muscular "foot," and usually a "head" or headlike structure. Size ranges from minute snails only a millimeter (1/25 in.) long to the giant squid, reputed to reach a length of 55 ft. Many slugs and snails are terrestrial, especially in the tropics and subtropics, but the great majority of mollusks live in the seas or in fresh water. Some marine species are noted for their brilliant coloration and fascinating patterns, whereas fresh-water mollusks are generally rather drab.

Bivalve mollusks (class Pelecypoda) have a shell composed of left and right valves hinged along the top edge. The valves are further held together by short transverse muscles. Typically, these animals move about in a vertical position in the surface layers of the bottom of the ocean, lakes, ponds, and rivers. Locomotion is produced by movements of the muscular foot, which is protruded when the two valves gape. A bivalve feeds by straining minute organisms and particles from a stream of water passing over the internal gills. Some giant marine clams of the tropics attain a length of 4 ft and a weight of several hundred pounds. Fresh-water clams are seldom more than 5 in. long, the largest specimens being found in our larger rivers. Familiar bivalves of our coasts include the oyster, scallop, razor clam, hardshell clam, and mussel. The teredo is a small wormlike bivalve specialized for boring into wood. It is an extremely important pest of seacoasts, where it bores into piling and eventually causes its collapse.

Pearls are formed when a foreign body (often a small parasite or bit of debris) becomes lodged in the soft tissues of a bivalve. The irritation stimulates certain tissues to deposit mother-of-pearl around the foreign body, the result eventually being a pearl. Although a great many bivalves are known to form pearls, only a few produce pearls of marketable color and symmetry. "Culture pearls" are formed in precisely the same way as "natural" pearls, except that the foreign body is deliberately inserted.

Snails, limpets, and slugs are members of a second great group (class Gastropoda). A typical gastropod mollusk has a coiled shell, but in the limpets the shell is caplike and shows little or no evidence of coiling, and in the slugs the shell has disappeared except for a small disklike vestige embedded in the dorsal body wall. Gastropods have a prominent muscular foot with a flat bottom surface. Ciliary action and waves of muscle contraction along the bottom surface of the foot produce smooth, gliding locomotion. Most of the visceral organs are located in the coils of the shell. The great majority of gastropods are vegetarians; the mouth is supplied with jaws

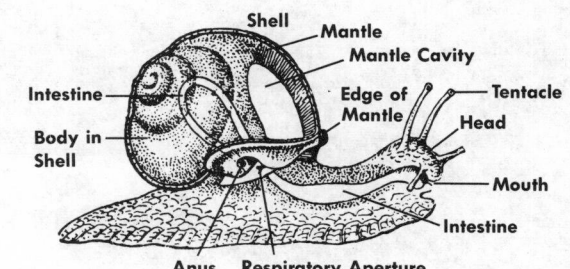

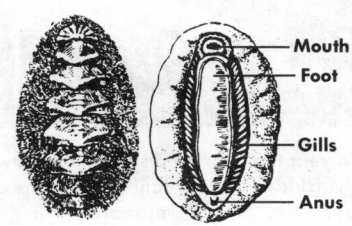

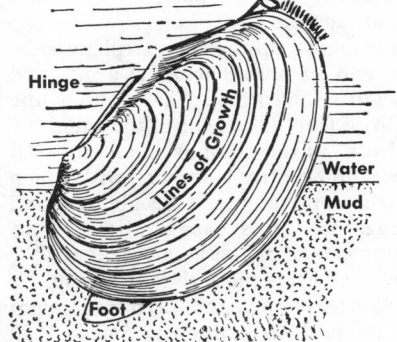

Features of mollusks: Large muscular foot behind mouth is seen in snail (*above*) and in chiton (*left*), associated with atypical multiple gills and mantle plates; side and edge-on views of clams (*below*) show lines of growth (*left*) and valves ajar for feeding. (*Top: from Guyer, after Selenka; left: from Guyer, after Schmeil; below: after Storer*)

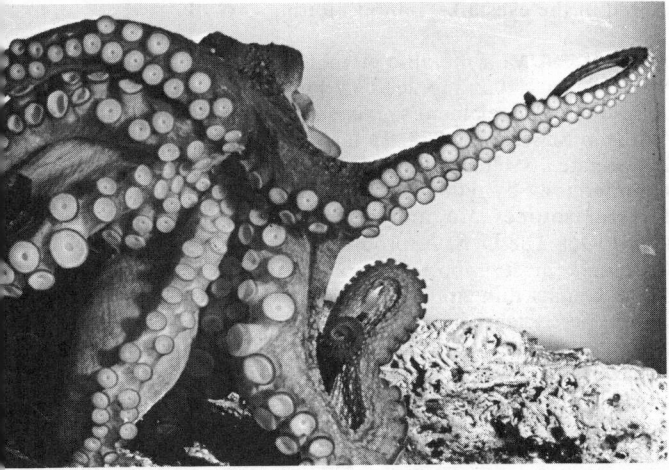

Classes of mollusks: Most advanced of the mollusks are the cephalopods, here represented by an octopus brandishing its sucker-studded tentacles (*above*). Of greatest economic value are the pelecypods, like the queen scallop (*below*) propelling itself away from a sea star by clapping its shells. Tree snail (*right*) belongs to only class of mollusks that has terrestrial forms, the gastropods; mirror reveals underside of foot. (*Douglas P. Wilson, two at left; L. and M. Milne*)

and a rasping apparatus that grinds up vegetation. Among familiar and economically important gastropods worth mentioning is the oyster drill, a small marine snail that drills a hole through an oyster shell, inserts its proboscis, and feeds on the oyster's soft tissues. Slugs occasionally become garden pests. Especially in Europe, a land snail, Helix, is grown commercially and is considered a table delicacy. Flesh of the abalone is an important food along our West Coast. The cowries are a large group of marine gastropods, the shells of which were formerly very important as currency among tropical islanders.

A third class of mollusks (Amphineura) consists of the chitons. These are elongated, flattened animals with a series of eight dorsal plates of limy material. Chitons are found clinging to rocks along the seashore.

Molting: Several times a year the hognosed snake, a burrowing N American colubrine, sheds its outer cornified epidermis. The old covering, which includes a scale conformal to the eye, is peeled off inside out backward from the snout. Epidermal cells have meanwhile already elaborated a new layer of horny scales to take its place. (*John H. Gerard*)

The tusk shells or tooth shells (class Scaphopoda) are small, deep-sea mollusks having the soft parts enclosed in a hollow, slightly curved and tapering shell.

The most active mollusks make up the class Cephalopoda, including squids (10 arms and tentacles), octopi (8 arms), and the chambered nautilus (80 to 90 arms). The bases of the long arms and tentacles arise from the head; in the squid the body is large and cylindrical, in the octopus small and oval or spherical. The arms bear many strong suckers, with which the prey is held and brought to the mouth. Tales about octopi "attacking" human beings are gross exaggerations, since these animals are quite innocuous and will almost invariably beat a hasty retreat. Few have arms more than 4 ft long.

Members of the sixth class (Monoplacophora) were thought to have been extinct for the past 280 million yr, but in 1952 living specimens were dredged up from the deep sea. They are small, limpet-like animals showing obvious relationships to the annelid worms.—*R. P.*

MOLTING: the shedding by certain animals of dead derivatives of the skin (hair, feathers, scales, exoskeleton, or cuticle) in one or many pieces within a relatively short period of time. Mammals and birds of temperate and polar regions commonly molt twice annually, replacing worn and abraded coverings and at the same time changing from a covering adapted to heat losses characteristic of winter or of summer to one better suited to the other season. In many instances, *e.g.* varying hare and ptarmigan, the molt introduces a major change in color, providing the animal with a covering that tends to match its customary background. Many birds molt from a distinctive juvenile plumage to a very different one typical of the adult, *e.g.* from pure white feathers on a little blue heron to blue ones at maturity. Adult birds may molt to a different color pattern too; *e.g.* the male goldfinch has bright plumage only in the breeding season, is drab at other times.

Animals with a continuous firm exoskeleton, *e.g.* insects, crabs, and nematode worms, are encased in a nonliving shell that cannot increase in size. These animals secrete a new, flexible exoskeleton beneath the old, then molt the hard covering. The creature increases in size rapidly by taking in air or water, and holds this until the new exoskeleton hardens in the expanded form.

In all animals that have been studied, molting is under the control of hormones. Removal of the thyroid gland inhibits molting in birds. Other ENDOCRINE GLANDS are probably involved, too, for molting in domestic chickens corresponds to a period of reduced egg-laying. In insects, the hormone ecdysone stimulates both molting and metamorphosis. In crustaceans such as crabs and lobsters, hormones produced in the cerebral ganglion and an associated "x" organ, and stored in the eyestalks, inhibit molting.—*G. W.*

MOLYBDENUM: a metallic element (Mo); at. no. 42; at. wt 95.95; density 10.2; mp 2620°C; bp 4800°C; valences 2, 3, 4, 5, and 6. The element's existence was detected by Karl Wilhelm Scheele in 1778; P. J. Hjelm (1782) was the first to investigate its chemical properties. The metal is prepared commercially by reducing molybdenum oxide with carbon; mineral sources are molybdenite (MoS_2) and wulfenite ($PbMoO_4$). The U. S. A. produces 90% of the world's molybdenum, a most important molybdenum-ore deposit being at the Climax mine in Colorado. Molybdenum added to cast iron in percentages less than 1% imparts toughness, strength, and wear-resistance. Like carbon, molybdenum adds hardness to steels; like tungsten, it gives resistance to deformation caused by CREEP or by high temperatures. Molybdenum is added to stainless steel to make it corrosion-resistant. Softer and more ductile than tungsten, yet having high strength and a low vapor pressure, it is extremely useful for radio grids, screens, and filaments; it also finds use as highly refractory resistance wire, and in electrical contacts. Molybdenum sulfide is used as a lubricant additive.—*E. H. H.*

MOMENT OF INERTIA: a parameter useful in describing the rotational motion of rigid bodies. The moment of inertia of a body, referred to an axis of rotation, is the sum of the masses of all of its component parts—each multiplied by the second power of its distance from the axis of rotation. Thus,

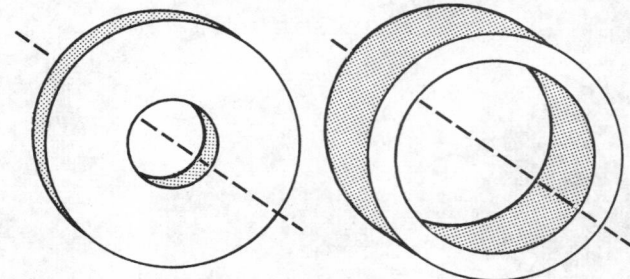

In two wheels of equal mass, moment of inertia is greater in the one in which mass is farther from axis of rotation.

the moment of inertia depends upon the distribution of the matter as well as upon its mass. For example, if the two wheels shown in the figure have the same total mass, the moment of inertia of the second is larger because its mass is farther from the axis of rotation. Moment of inertia plays the same role in rotational motion as does mass in linear motion. If a TORQUE is applied to a rigid body, the resulting angular acceleration equals the applied torque divided by the moment of inertia. Analogously, in linear motion the acceleration of an object equals the applied force divided by its mass.—*S. K.*

MOMENTUM: a fundamental quantity characterizing the motion of any object, defined as the velocity of the object multiplied by its mass. (It is sometimes called linear momentum to distinguish it from ANGULAR MOMENTUM.) NEWTON'S LAWS OF MOTION state that while a force acts on a system, the momentum of the system changes. The increment in momentum at the end of each instant points in the same direction as the force, and its magnitude equals the product of the magnitude of the force and the length of the interval of time. It follows that if no force acts on a system, its momentum remains constant. The law of conservation of momentum for isolated systems is an extremely useful tool in physics. For example, one can calculate the motion of a rocket in free space by noting that the system (rocket plus discharged gas) is an isolated system with no external forces acting on it; therefore the increase in forward momentum of the rocket must be equal in magnitude and opposite in direction to the momentum of the expelled gas.

When it is not discharging gas, the rocket continues in a straight line with constant momentum—hence, constant velocity. Although the law of conservation of momentum for an isolated system follows from Newton's laws of motion, the former has more general validity than the latter. The law of conservation of momentum for isolated systems appears to be universally valid, whereas Newton's laws must be replaced by QUANTUM MECHANICS in describing atomic and nuclear phenomena, and by RELATIVITY in describing systems moving at speeds approaching that of light.—*S. K.*

MONADNOCK: an isolated hill or mountain rising conspicuously above a peneplain. It is a residual feature produced by erosion of the surrounding, less resistant terrain. Mt Monadnock in SW New Hampshire gave the type its name; another monadnock is Stone Mt in NW Georgia.—*E. A.*

MONDINO DE' LUZZI (Mondino of Bologna), *c.* 1275–1326, Italian anatomist and physician; b. Bologna. He was the first since antiquity to dissect human cadavers as well as domestic animals in demonstration lectures on anatomy. His textbook *Anatomia mundini* (1316), the standard anatomical text for over 200 yr, went through some 40 editions.—*D. H. D. R.*

MONGE, GASPARD, 1746–1818, French mathematician; b. Beaune. He invented descriptive geometry, a method of representing three-dimensional figures on a plane, which is the foundation of all mechanical drawing and is valuable in engineering. He was a close friend of Napoleon and accompanied him to Italy and Egypt. Monge was professor of mathematics at l'École Normale and l'École Polytechnique, which he helped to found. He made important contributions to differential equations and the geometry of surfaces.—*H. C.*

MONOCHROMATOR: an optical instrument that produces a beam of monochromatic light, *i.e.* light from a very narrow range of the spectrum. This device is usually found as part of a spectrophotometer, an apparatus used to make precise measurements of color.—*D. H. L.*

MONOCOT (or **monocotyledon**): any FLOWERING PLANT of the subclass Monocotyledoneae. The approximately 50,000 species include such ornamental plants as lily, iris, daffodil, palm, and orchid, as well as many grasses of tremendous value as crop plants, *e.g.* corn, sugar cane, wheat, oats, barley, and rye. Monocots are distinguished from DICOTS, which make up the other subclass of flowering plants, by having one cotyledon, or seed leaf, in each seed. Also, the flower parts of monocots are usually in threes, the leaves usually have parallel veins, and the vascular bundles lack a cambium. Centers for secondary growth often remain in the nodes along the stem

Monocot: By their number, the six outthrust stamens of the stemless Clintonia lily show it to be a monocot. (*Rutherford Platt*)

where leaves arise; these growth centers can add to the length of the leaves, extending them farther and farther (as is familiar in grasses after the tips of the leaves have been cut off by grazing animals or a lawnmower). Growth centers at the nodes can also elongate a stem, but not increase it in diameter or add new conducting tissue to correspond to extra leaves and roots. Monocots seem particularly well adapted to rapid growth when conditions are favorable, but seldom produce a woody trunk from which leaves develop year after year.—*W. Ko.*

MONOMOLECULAR LAYER: a layer or film of material one molecule in thickness. A drop of 1% solution of oleic acid in alcohol, deposited on an oil slick (the latter obtained by placing a drop of used crankcase oil on the surface of distilled water), forms a circle or, strictly speaking, a shallow cylinder one molecule deep. If the volume of the oleic acid used is divided by the area of the circle, the result is the height or the maximum dimension of the oleic-acid molecule.—*A. E.*

MONSOON: a seasonal wind that blows from ocean to continent during summer and reverses during winter months. It is basically a large-scale land-sea breeze circulation. The strongest monsoon occurs over S and E Asia, where the southwest summer monsoon brings hot, humid air and heavy rains. Here the winter monsoon brings the dry season and relief from the heat.—*P. L.*

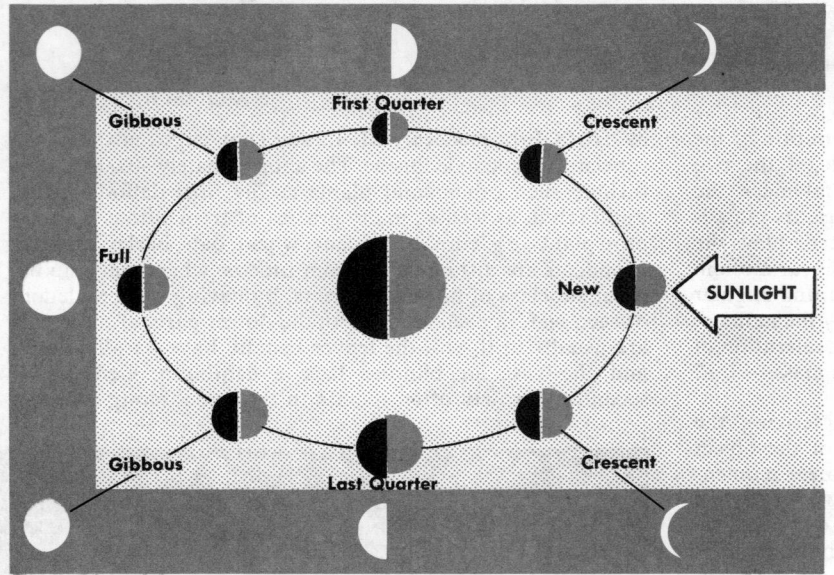

First Quarter

Gibbous

Crescent

Full

New

SUNLIGHT

Gibbous

Crescent

Last Quarter

Phases of Moon depend upon position of Moon with respect to Earth and Sun. Full lighted side of Moon can be seen ("full moon") from Earth only when Earth is between Moon and Sun. Moon is invisible ("new moon") when Moon is between Earth and Sun. When Moon is in other positions with respect to Earth and Sun, varying amounts of its lighted hemisphere are visible.

MONTGOLFIER, JOSEPH MICHEL, 1740–1810, and his brother **Jacques Étienne,** 1745–99, French inventors; b. Vidalon-les-Annonay. In 1783 they produced the first practical balloon: a spherical linen bag covered with paper and inflated with heated air from burning wool and damp straw in an iron grate in the balloon's basket. On its test flight, June 5, 1783, the balloon ascended 6,000 ft and remained aloft 10 min. Honored and rewarded by the Académie Royale des Sciences and by King Louis XVI, the brothers repeated the Annonay experiment at Versailles, Sept. 19. The balloon ascended 1,500 ft and remained aloft 8 min. A Montgolfier captive fire balloon was used for the first human ascent, Oct. 15, 1783, and the first free flight was made with another of their balloons a month later. Joseph invented a hydraulic ram, and the brothers made improvements in paper-manufacturing processes.—*S. B.*

MOON: Earth's natural satellite, the astronomical body nearest Earth except for artificial satellites and atmospheric objects such as meteors. The Moon has little or no atmosphere, no surface water, no sounds or weather, tremendous extremes of heat and cold but apparently few changes otherwise.

Orbit: The lunar orbit relative to Earth is elliptical, the average Earth-Moon distance being 238,860 mi, and the greatest and least distances 252,710 and 221,460 mi. Both Earth and Moon revolve relatively around their common center of mass; but Earth is so much more massive that this center is within the planet. However, the Moon's absolute orbit about the Sun is everywhere concave to the Sun. The Moon's orbit is inclined approximately 5° to the plane of Earth's orbit, so that our satellite in the "new" phase usually is not exactly between Earth and Sun, nor does the Moon at "full" phase usually enter Earth's shadow (see ECLIPSES). The period of the Moon's revolution around Earth long ago established the month as a natural unit of time. Astronomers recognize different kinds of months, among them the synodic month of 29 days, 12 hr, 44 min, the period of the lunar phases; and the sidereal month of 27 days, 7 hr, 43 min, the period of the lunar revolution around Earth (see CALENDAR). Both months vary in length. The Moon's motion is affected by the gravitational attraction of Sun, Earth, and

With changes of Moon's phases, lengths and directions of shadows change, revealing altitudes and shapes of mountains, valleys, and craters. Ridges as little as 10 ft high can be detected when parallel to the terminator (line dividing light and dark). At full Moon, the ray systems are clearest. At first and last quarters, with features thrown into great relief, shadows hide many details. Knowledge of the Moon comes from combining many kinds of observations. (*Lick*)

the nearer planets (see PERTURBATIONS); the complete mathematical theory of the lunar motions is highly complex.

Phases: The lunar phases result from the simple fact that the Moon shines only by reflected sunlight, and we see varying amounts of the lighted surface. At new moon the illuminated hemisphere is turned completely away from Earth, and we see nothing. At first or last quarter, half of the sunlit hemisphere is turned toward us. At full moon the Sun-facing hemisphere is also the Earth-facing hemisphere, so that the whole disk appears lighted. Lunar phases have no influence on weather or crops. Near new moon, the non-sunlit regions are illuminated with EARTHSHINE—light reflected to the Moon by Earth, which is then full in the lunar sky.

Physical Data: With its diameter of 2,160 mi, the Moon is much the largest satellite in the solar system compared to its primary. Although its mass is only $\frac{1}{81}$ of Earth's, it is some-

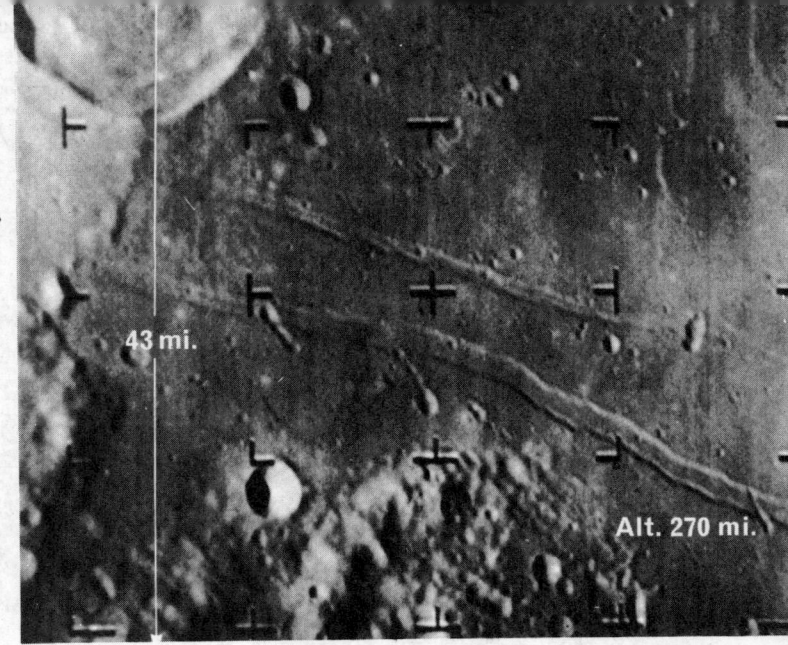

Lunar closeup taken by Ranger VII spacecraft at an altitude of 270 mi. before it struck Moon, July 31, 1964. Note craters and "splash" effects from meteorite impacts. Deep crater at lower left is Hypatia E, 3 mi. wide. Above highlands are the Hypatia rilles—two long valleys which apparently are fault zones—and several lightly defined scarps (upper right). (NASA)

43 mi.

Alt. 270 mi.

times considered to be a sister planet of Earth. Its average density is 3.3 times that of water. The lunar equator is inclined 6°41′ to the plane of the lunar orbit. The period of rotation is one sidereal month, equal to the period of revolution around Earth; hence the Moon always keeps one hemisphere toward Earth. Minor variations occur, however, because of LIBRATIONS, so that the terrestrial observer sees a total of 59% of the Moon during each lunar month. There are two principal librations: in latitude, because of the tilt of the lunar axis, and in longitude, because the Moon rotates on its axis at a uniform rate but revolves around Earth more rapidly near perigee.

Only 7% of the sunlight striking the lunar surface is reflected. The variation in brightness with phase shows the lunar surface to be extremely rough. Though bright moonlight is often compared in intensity to daylight, 450,000 full moons would be required to give as much light as the Sun. Temperatures vary from about 210°F in the middle of the sunlit hemisphere to perhaps −240°F during the two-week-long night.

The lunar surface gravity is 16% of Earth's, and the velocity of escape is 1.5 mi/sec compared to Earth's 7 mi/sec. Hence the Moon can have retained very little of whatever atmosphere it had in the past. The blackness of lunar shadows, the suddenness with which stars appear and disappear at the edge of the Moon, and the extreme distinctness with which the lunar surface is seen when Earth's atmosphere permits are further evidence against a lunar atmosphere. The greatest possible surface density of a lunar atmosphere is about $\frac{1}{10,000}$ of the surface density of Earth's air blanket; the true value may be many times smaller.

Lunar Surface Features: The Moon is the only astronomical body whose surface can be examined in detail. The surface has been mapped both visually and photographically, and the following principal features have been recognized: (1) *Maria,* so-called seas but not actually bodies of water. They are comparatively dark and smooth plains, the larger ones a few hundred miles across. (2) *Craters, or ring-mountains,* approximately circular. The largest, Bailly, is about 180 mi in diameter; the smallest are tiny pits at the limit of visibility and only some hundreds of yards in diameter. The craters

are shallow compared to their diameters; it is rare for the rim to be as much as 15,000 ft above the floor. There are frequently central mountains and other visible details on the floors. (3) *Mountains and mountain ranges.* These are uncommon compared to the omnipresent craters. The highest lunar mountain known (near the crater Casatus) rises at least 30,000 ft above its surroundings. (4) *Clefts or rills,* cracks in the surface sometimes several hundred miles long and chiefly occurring at the edges of *maria.* (5) *Bright rays,* systems of bright streaks radiating outward from many craters and occasionally more than 1,000 mi long. Near full moon the crater Tycho and its rays dominate the lunar scene. The rays ignore all topographical barriers and are hence usually thought to be among the most recent of lunar features.

The Moon's surface is almost changeless and is usually presumed to have shown its present aspect for thousands and perhaps millions of years. However, N. T. Kozyrev witnessed a volcanic degassing in the crater Alphonsus, Nov. 3, 1958, and a number of competent observers have reported other possible, but unconfirmed, minor changes. The two principal theories of how the Moon's surface was molded to its present appearance stress the impact of meteorites or asteroids, and possibilities of volcanic activity. Both theories have been discussed at great length, and perhaps both causes have been operative. Investigations have involved comparisons with terrestrial geology, studies of the distribution of craters,

Moonscape as photographed by U. S. Lunar Orbiter I at altitude of 730 mi above Moon, Aug. 23, 1966. Earth, 232,000 mi away, appears as a crescent about four times as wide as a crescent Moon seen from Earth. (NASA/Boeing)

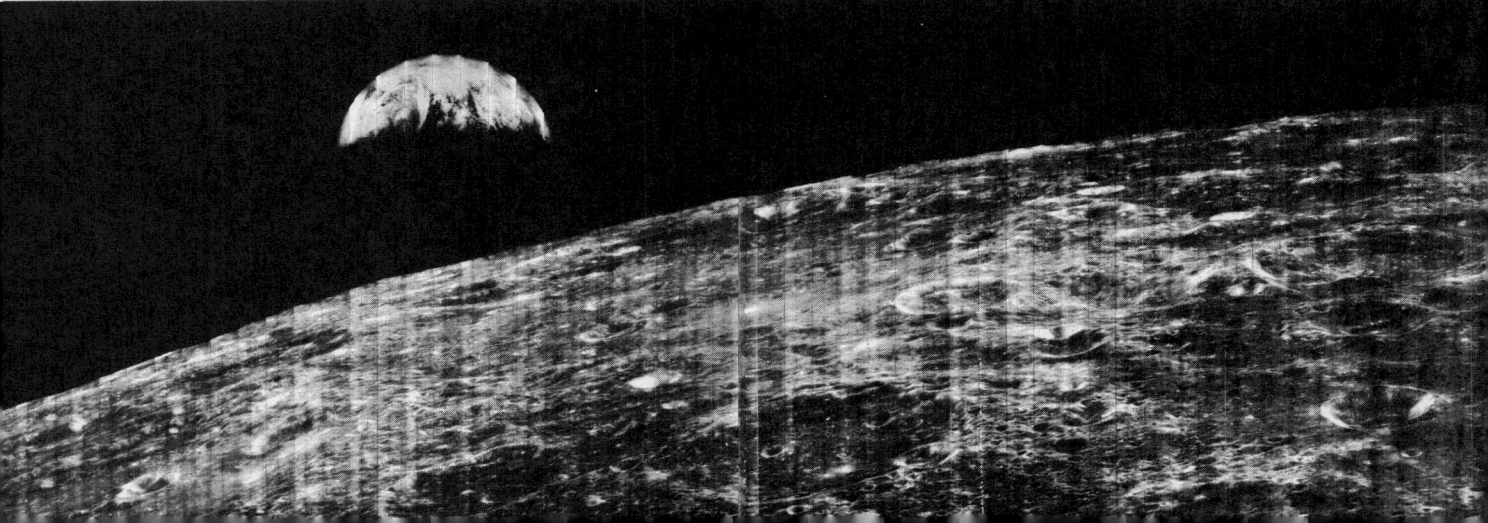

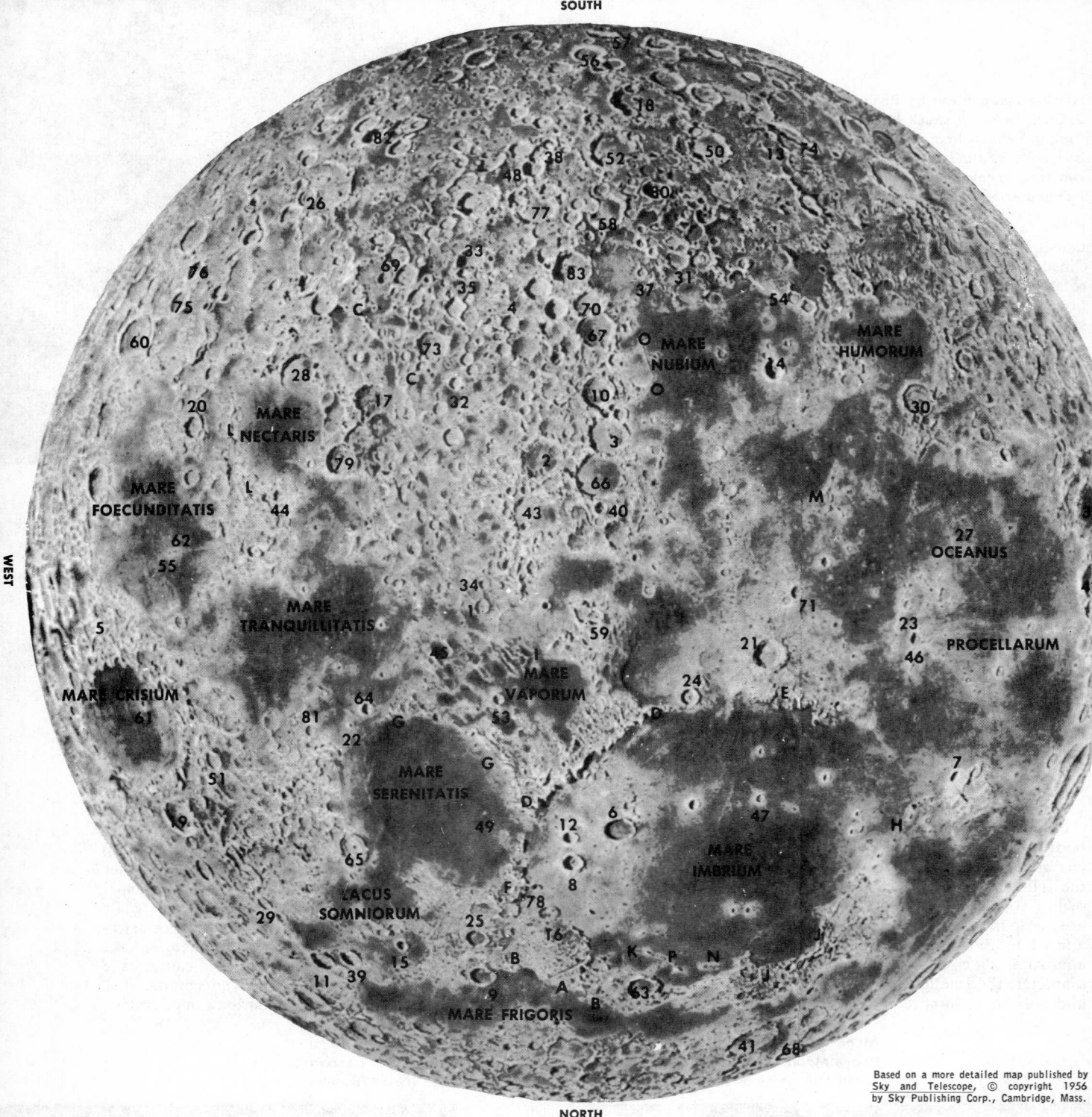

SOUTH

MARE NUBIUM

MARE HUMORUM

MARE NECTARIS

OCEANUS

MARE FOECUNDITATIS

MARE TRANQUILLITATIS

PROCELLARUM

MARE VAPORUM

MARE CRISIUM

MARE SERENITATIS

MARE IMBRIUM

LACUS SOMNIORUM

MARE FRIGORIS

WEST

NORTH

Based on a more detailed map published by Sky and Telescope, © copyright 1956 by Sky Publishing Corp., Cambridge, Mass.

THE MOON

Mountains, Valleys, and Faults

A Alpine Valley **B** Alps **C** Altai **D** Apennine Mts **E** Carpathian **F** Caucasus **G** Haemus **H** Harbinger **I** Hyginus Cleft **J** Jura Mts **K** Pico **L** Pyrenees **M** Riphaeus **N** Straight Range **O** Straight Wall **P** Teneriffe

Craters

1 Agrippa **2** Albategnius **3** Alphonsus **4** Apianus **5** Apollonius **6** Archimedes **7** Aristarchus **8** Aristillus **9** Aristoteles **10** Arzachel
11 Atlas **12** Autolycus **13** Bayer **14** Bullialdus **15** Bürg **16** Cassini **17** Catharina **18** Clavius **19** Cleomedes **20** Colombo **21** Copernicus
22 Dawes **23** Encke **24** Eratosthenes **25** Eudoxus **26** Fabricius **27** Flamsteed **28** Fracastorius **29** Franklin **30** Gassendi **31** Gauricus
32 Geber **33** Gemma Frisius **34** Godin **35** Goodacre **36** Grimaldi **37** Hell **38** Heraclitus **39** Hercules **40** Herschel **41** Herschel, J.
42 Hevelius **43** Hipparchus **44** Isidorus **45** Julius Caesar **46** Kepler **47** Lambert **48** Licetus **49** Linné **50** Longomontanus **51** Macrobius
52 Maginus **53** Manilius **54** Mercator **55** Messier **56** Moretus **57** Newton **58** Orontius **59** Pallas **60** Petavius **61** Picard **62** Pickering, W. H.
63 Plato **64** Plinius **65** Posidonius **66** Ptolemaeus **67** Purbach **68** Pythagoras **69** Rabbi Levi **70** Regiomontanus **71** Reinhold **72** Riccioli
73 Sacrobosco **74** Schiller **75** Snellius **76** Stevinus **77** Stöfler **78** Theaetetus **79** Theophilus **80** Tycho **81** Vitruvius **82** Vlacq **83** Walter

experiments with small-scale impacts on different kinds of surfaces, and computations of energy releases in meteoritic impacts.

The surface of the Moon is now being closely examined by means of space probes. The new age of direct exploration of the universe is beginning with the close, near-changeless Moon. We have already learned that the averted hemisphere lacks large *maria* and that the Moon has no strong magnetic field. Photographs sent to Earth by the Ranger VII spacecraft in 1964 before it struck the Moon gave astronomers a close look at long-controversial features—lunar maria, mountains, craters, domes, rilles, and scarps. The thousands of pictures taken by the Surveyor and Lunar Orbiter ships in 1966 showed a terrain on which craters only inches wide and rock fragments of pebble size could be discerned. These photographs, as well as landings by spacecraft, indicated that the Moon is not covered with a deep layer of dust as some astronomers thought, but has a surface compact enough to support light spacecraft and astronauts at least. The first really clear views of the rear side of the Moon were obtained in 1966 by Lunar Orbiter I, whose pictures revealed a surface more cratered, and with less maria, than the surface that faces Earth.—*W. H.*

MORAINE: an accumulation of GLACIAL DRIFT, deposited chiefly by direct glacial action, and having constructional topography independent of the floor on which it lies. An *end moraine* is a ridge-like accumulation built up at the margin of a glacier. *Ground moraine* consists of widespread drift with a smooth surface of knolls and basins.—*R. F.*

MORGAN, THOMAS HUNT, 1866–1945, U. S. biologist; b. Lexington, Ky. He became well known first as an embryologist while serving as professor of experimental zoology (from 1904) at Columbia Univ. Around 1911, however, he became interested in heredity and began his famous study of the fruit fly *Drosophila melanogaster.* He discovered sex-linked inheritance in this animal, and progressed with statistical studies of large populations obtained by careful cross breeding until he was able to explain linkage, crossing-over, and the sequence of inheritable units along the chromosomes in *The Theory of the Gene* (1926). For his work relating embryology to genetics and his concept of the gene, he was awarded the 1933 Nobel prize. Among his other works were *Development of the Frog's Egg* (1887), *Heredity and Sex* (1913), and *Evolution and Genetics* (1925). He was a fellow of the Royal Society and a member of the National Academy of Sciences. —*L. and M. M.*

MORLEY, EDWARD WILLIAMS, 1838–1923, U. S. chemist; b. Newark, N. J. He collaborated with A. A. Michelson in measuring the velocity of light (see MICHELSON-MORLEY EXPERIMENT). They subsequently collaborated in the ether drift experiments, their negative results being a factor in the development of Einstein's theory of relativity. Morley also made very precise measurements of the combining weights of hydrogen and oxygen. He was a member of the National Academy of Sciences.—*A. I.*

MORNING AND EVENING STAR: in astronomy, a term applied to any planet when it crosses the local meridian after midnight ("morning star") or before midnight ("evening star"). In popular lore, it is applied principally to Mercury and Venus when either of these planets is prominent in the east shortly before sunrise or in the west shortly after sunset. In ancient mythology, Venus was called Phosphorus when seen as a morning star, Vesper or Hesperus when seen as an evening star.—*R. N. M.*

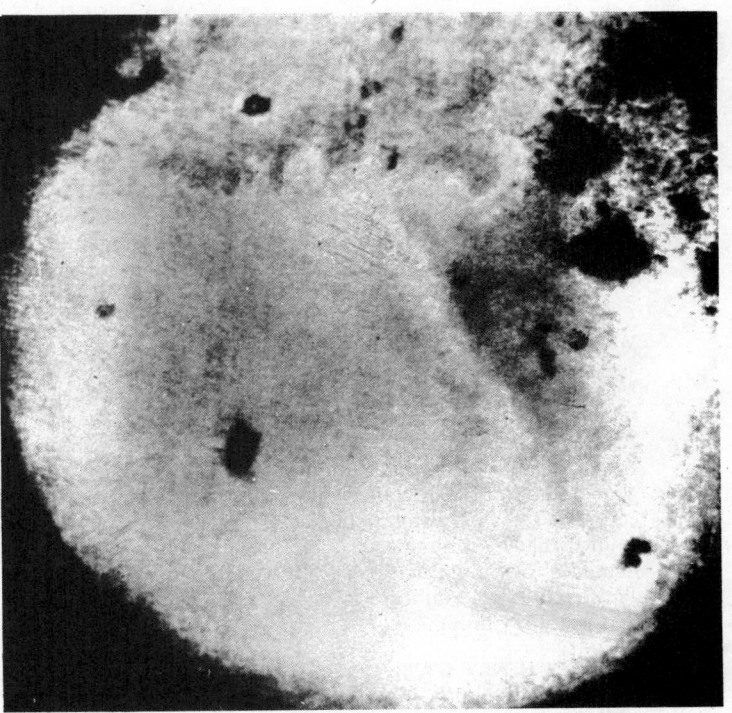

First photograph of Moon's rear side, taken by Russia's Lunik III, revealed a lack of maria. More detailed, clearer photos taken later by U. S. and Russian lunar craft showed a densely cratered surface. (*Wide World*)

Northern area of Moon as photographed with 100-in. telescope: Major features can be identified by reference to map on facing page. Apennine Mts and other lighter-appearing, rough areas may antedate formation of the dark "seas." Impact which presumably formed Mare Imbrium seems to have splashed lava over Apennines. White rays (pulverized rock?) spreading across Imbrium from Copernicus indicate crater was formed after the sea. Smooth floor of Plato indicates surface of Moon was relatively soft when Plato was formed. Alpine Valley, SW of Plato, is 80 mi long and 11,500 ft deep; it may have been cut through mountains by a meteor. (Mt Wilson)

MORSE, SAMUEL FINLEY BREESE, 1791–1872, U. S. artist and inventor; b. Charlestown, Mass. A successful portrait painter, he first became interested in the magnetic telegraph in 1832, when he constructed a primitive telegraphic apparatus and conducted experiments. By 1837 Morse's apparatus was working successfully over a distance of 10 mi. Congress appropriated $30,000 for the construction of an experimental line between Washington and Baltimore in 1843. On May 24, 1844, Morse sent the historic message over this line, "What hath God wrought!" Morse invented the system of dots and dashes which developed into the Morse Code.—*S. B.*

MOSANDER, CARL GUSTAV, 1797–1858, Swedish chemist and mineralogist; b. Kalmar. A student and close associate of J. J. Berzelius, he is remembered for outstanding work on the rare earths. Ytterbia and ceria were regarded as homogeneous materials until Mosander discovered lanthanum in ceria (1839) and terbium in gadolinite (1843). In 1841 he found what he thought was a new element in lanthana, and named it didymium, but in 1885 it was found by C. Auer von Welsbach to be a mixture of two new elements, neodymium and praseodymium.—*R. E. O.*

MOSELEY, HENRY GWYN-JEFFREYS, 1887–1915, English physicist; b. Weymouth. At Ernest Rutherford's laboratory in Manchester he designed apparatus for producing x-rays by bombarding samples of various elements with electrons. He found a correspondence between the wavelengths of the x-rays emitted by the elements and the atomic numbers previously assigned to them by chemists and thus identified the charge on the nucleus with the atomic number. His work indicated more precisely the number of then undiscovered naturally occurring elements.—*D. H. D. R.*

MÖSSBAUER, RUDOLF L., 1929– , German physicist; b. Munich. He devised a method for producing gamma rays the wavelength of which does not vary more than one part in 10^{15} (see MÖSSBAUER EFFECT). Mössbauer announced his discovery in 1958, and shared the 1961 Nobel prize in physics with R. Hofstadter.—*P. R. L.*

MÖSSBAUER EFFECT: the increase in precision of gamma radiation energy obtained when the radiating nucleus of an atom is in a solid crystal instead of gaseous form. The gamma rays emitted by radioactive nuclei are quite sharply defined in energy and can be used for measuring nuclear energy levels and half-lives. However, much of this precision is ordinarily lost because the nucleus recoils when the gamma ray is emitted, just as a gun recoils when a bullet is fired. Nuclear recoil affects the energy of the emitted gamma ray, and a similar recoil occurs when a nucleus absorbs this ray. Rudolf Mössbauer found that the isotope iridium[191], when used in crystalline form, emits some gamma rays that suffer no observable change in energy, because the nuclear recoil is distributed over the large number of nuclei in the entire crystal. Later it was found that many isotopes exhibit this effect. The most useful one discovered so far is iron[57]. A significant use of the Mössbauer effect has been to verify the theory of gravitation, which predicted that the energy of radiation emitted by a nucleus at ground level would differ from that emitted or absorbed by an identical nucleus at some height above the ground. The gravitational shift in energy is very small, and could not be measured with the degree of precision available before the discovery of the Mössbauer effect. Other applications have been the study of the internal magnetic field in iron, the vibrations of crystal lattices, and the measurement of chemical shifts, line widths (spread in wavelengths), and energy levels in isotopes.—*I. R.*

MOSSES AND LIVERWORTS: nonvascular, green land plants comprising the phylum Bryophyta, mosses being in class Musci and liverworts in class Hepaticae. They differ from ALGAE in the character of their sex organs (stalked *antheridia,* within which a large number of swimming sperm cells develop, and flask-shaped *archegonia,* each containing a single egg cell); they differ from VASCULAR PLANTS in having the sporophyte stage in the life history dependent for raw materials and food upon the gametophyte, as well as in lacking specialized conducting tissues (phloem and xylem).

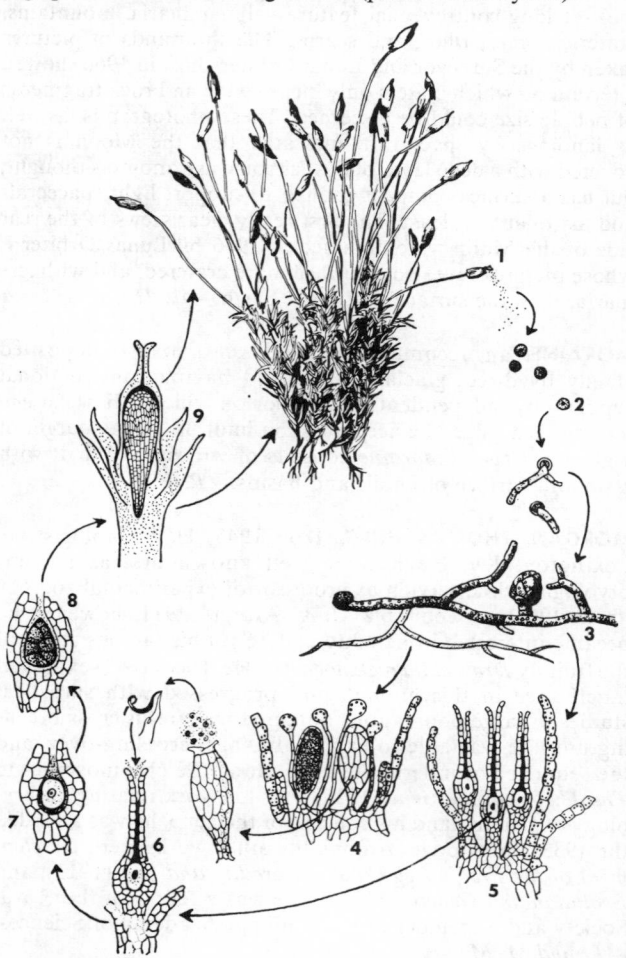

Life cycle of moss: Sporophytes (1) are attached to gametophyte plant on which they are dependent. Spores (2) germinate into filamentous protonema (3) carrying buds of one sex or the other. Motile sperms are produced in antheridia (4), egg cells in archegonia (5). Film of water allows sperm to swim to elongated flasklike archegonium (6), fertilizing egg inside it. Fertilized egg (7) grows into young sporophyte (8), all the while attached to maternal gametophyte (9). (After Whaley)

Under suitable conditions, a moss spore germinates into the familiar plant, which is the gametophyte (gamete-producing) generation in the regular ALTERNATION OF GENERATIONS. First, the young plant is merely a thread-shaped green filament (*protonema*). But as it carries on photosynthesis and grows, it enlarges into a stemlike structure of filaments that interweave as though braided together. Still, the plant is too feeble to grow upright and must rest on the ground or a stone or another plant. From the stemlike portion, fine, colorless, multicellular *rhizoids* grow outward, anchoring the plant in place but not serving as absorptive roots. At the same time, upright branches appear, each producing flat leaflike expansions; usually these have a stiffer midrib, giving some support. At the tip of each branch, the leaflike expansions commonly form a small cup-shaped structure. At the bottom of this cup, in the appropriate season, little clusters of antheridia or archegonia develop. The splash of raindrops striking the terminal cups squarely is enough to carry the sperm from ripe antheridia to the tips of archegonia, in which ripe eggs are waiting. Sterile cells in the neck of the flask-shaped archegonium have already disintegrated, leaving a fluid pathway down which the sperm can swim to reach and fuse with the egg. The fertilized egg, which begins the sporophyte generation, develops into an embryo that gets its nourishment from the gametophyte, while extending vertically as a stalk tipped with a spore case (sporangium). Often the neck portion of the archegonium tears away and is carried aloft as a cap over the spore case. Spores are formed within the spore case by MEIOSIS and released into the wind, which distributes them widely.

Many liverworts are flat and strap-shaped; others are said to be "leafy," although they produce no true leaves. Liverwort rhizoids are unicellular anchoring filaments, and their leaflike expansions lack a stiffening midrib. The sporophyte generation of liverworts is less conspicuous than that of mosses, but equally dependent upon the gametophyte. Some of the broad "thallose" liverworts bear their antheridia and archegonia (and then their pendent sporophytes) on remarkable umbrella-shaped structures, which grow upward an inch or two, where they are more exposed to rain and wind.

Peat moss (*Sphagnum*) is almost the only member of this phylum of plants useful to man. This pastel-colored moss (which may be reddish, purple, orange, or almost yellow) grows commonly in BOGS, often extending out over open water as a floating mat of vegetation which quakes if walked on. It floats because of air trapped in special cells of the leaflike expansions of the gametophyte plant, these cells being between those that carry on photosynthesis. Peat moss, as it begins to decay, releases chemical compounds that reduce

bacterial action. Often dead, waterlogged peat plants accumulate in old bogs, where blocks of the compacted remains may be cut and dried for use as fuel. If living peat moss is squeezed under water and then released, the air in the special cells is driven out and water takes its place. The plant then acts as a sponge, and can be used by gardeners as an inexpensive wrapping around the roots of transplanted trees to keep them moist. Because of its bactericidal action and water-absorbing qualities, peat moss has also been used during emergency surgery as a sponge with which to mop up blood or catch exudates from wounds as they healed. See Color Plate 63.—*L. and M. M.*

MOTH: see INSECT.

MOTHER-OF-PEARL CLOUD: a rare variety of cloud which is strongly iridescent, suggesting mother-of-pearl. Observed mostly in Norway and Alaska, these clouds form in the mid-stratosphere (12 to 15 mi up) in the lee of mountain ranges. At that altitude, they remain illuminated well into twilight, when their brilliant colors are best seen. Optical effects suggest that they are made up of tiny, transparent, spherical ice particles. (See NOCTILUCENT CLOUD.)—*D. H. L.*

MOTION: the continuous change of position of a body, relative to a fixed reference position. Motion is characterized by displacement, velocity, and acceleration. Displacement describes the instantaneous position of a body, velocity the rate of change of displacement with time, and ACCELERATION the rate of change of velocity with time. Speed is defined as total distance traveled per unit time. (See VELOCITY AND SPEED.) The simplest type of motion is uniform motion, characterized by constant velocity (zero acceleration), describing a body traveling in a straight line with constant speed. The simplest type of nonuniform motion is that of constant acceleration, *e.g.* a falling body. Here the velocity increases in proportion to the time, and displacement in proportion to the square of the time. A projectile's motion near Earth's surface, neglect-

Liverworts and mosses: Lacking tissues that would allow it to rise to compete for sunlight, this dense mat of Ricciocarpus liverwort lies flat on damp shady rock (*left*). Strands of spiral tangle (*middle*) are "teeth," which come in sixteens, of capsules of tufted moss of genus Barbula; sensitive to humidity, they control discharge of spores. Sporophyte capsules (*right*) are from cord moss, a variety common on recently burned-over soil. (*John H. Gerard/Nat. Audubon Soc.; Strüwe/Monkmeyer; Stephen Collins/Nat. Audubon Soc.*)

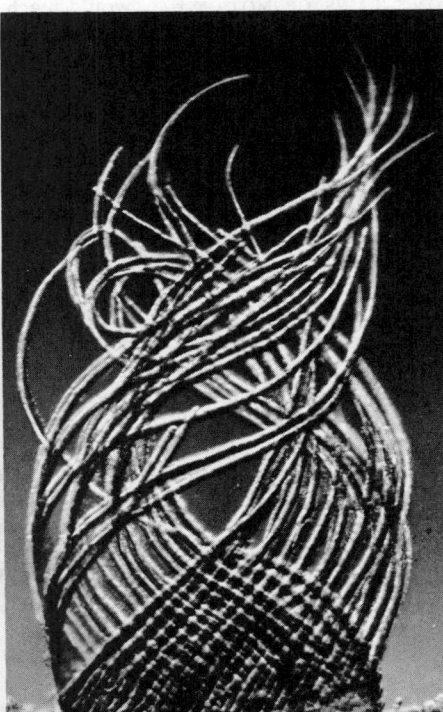

Rapid motion of golfer's swing is caught in stroboscopic photo at 100 flashes/sec. Greatest velocity of club head (just before impact) is indicated by greater distance between exposures, since velocity is measured by distance covered per unit of time. (*Harold E. Edgerton/FLO*)

ing air resistance, is also one of constant acceleration, where the motion consists of a superposition of uniform motion in the horizontal plane and constant acceleration in the vertical plane. Uniform circular motion is an important special type of accelerated motion in which an object's speed is constant but its direction is continually changing so that its acceleration always points toward the center of ROTATION. Satellite motion, and planetary motion in general, is usually of this type, to a fair degree of approximation. Simple HARMONIC MOTION describes an oscillation through a fixed point such that the acceleration always points opposite to the displacement and is proportional to it. Examples are a vibrating spring, an oscillating pendulum, and an oscillating diatomic molecule. (See MECHANICS; NEWTON'S LAWS OF MOTION.) —*B. Be.*

MOTION PICTURE: see CAMERA; PHOTOGRAPHY.

MOTOR: see ELECTRIC MOTOR.

MOTOR VEHICLE: a self-propelled conveyance used for passenger transportation (automobiles, buses, motorcycles) or for hauling freight (trucks). The major components of a motor vehicle are (1) the engine, which transforms heat energy into mechanical energy; (2) the transmission, which transmits the engine's power to the wheels at the required speed and torque; and (3) the chassis, or structure supporting passengers and freight, engine, transmission, and various additional components. The first self-driven carriage, built by Nicolas Cugnot in France in 1769, was propelled by steam, with a speed of about 3 mi/hr. In England, the development of similar vehicles was impeded both by the high cost of toll roads and by legislation inspired by concern for the safety of pedestrians, animals, and horse-drawn vehicles. After 1896, with the repeal in England of legislation penalizing self-propelled vehicles, there was an interest in electrically propelled types. These gained little favor, however, because of their low power and

the inconvenience of frequently recharging their accumulators (storage batteries). At present, some electrically powered vehicles are in use for local freight delivery, their advantages being noiselessness and freedom from exhaust. In 1885, the first automobile propelled by INTERNAL COMBUSTION was built by Karl Benz. This type of ENGINE, which produces power by controlled explosions of fuel within a cylinder, predominates in present-day automobiles.

Engines: The most common type of internal-combustion engine in motor vehicles is the spark-ignition type using gasoline as fuel. A mixture of air and gasoline is introduced into a cylinder and compressed by a piston. At the point of maximum compression the mixture is ignited by a spark and explodes; the resulting hot gases exert a force against the piston, pushing it down the cylinder. Before entering the cylinder, the gasoline is drawn into a *carburetor*, where it is mixed with the proper amount of air. In a complete cycle, the piston draws in the fuel mixture, compresses it, delivers power to the crankshaft, and scavenges (expels the burnt gases from) the cylinder. The piston accomplishes these operations in two or four one-way trips through the cylinder, depending on whether it is a 2-stroke or 4-stroke engine. Because of their generally higher efficiency, 4-stroke engines are used in most larger motor vehicles. The greater the number of cylinders, the smoother the engine's operation. Smoothness of power and delivery is improved when each piston delivers its power stroke at a different time, so that during the period of a cycle, the crankshaft is receiving a constant quantity of power. In order for the fuel mixture in each cylinder to be ignited at the proper time an IGNITION system is provided that uses a *distributor* to route the current to the proper spark plug within the proper cylinder at the exact time. To start the engine, a battery supplies voltage to a small motor which turns the crankshaft and at the same time delivers voltage to the cylinder's spark plugs. Once the engine is running, the battery is no longer needed, since part of the power from the engine is used to turn a *generator*, which then supplies the voltage to the spark plugs and at the same time recharges the storage battery. This electrical system also powers the various appliances that are part of the modern motor vehicle, *e.g.* the radio, windshield wipers, and headlights. A large percentage of the energy produced by combustion remains in the form of heat. If this heat were not dissipated, the engine parts would reach destructive temperatures; thus every engine must have a *cooling system*. Although some motor-vehicle engines are cooled by the passage of air, the majority have their cylinders surrounded by a water jacket through which water is circulated by means of a water pump; the water is then passed through a radiator, where it is cooled by a fan. In cold weather, the cooling-system water must be protected from freezing by ANTIFREEZE. In some heavy motor vehicles, DIESEL ENGINES are used. These internal-combustion engines differ from the spark-ignition type in that they utilize neither carburetor nor ignition system; they are started by an auxiliary electrical motor powered by a storage battery. The piston compresses the air until it is above the fuel's ignition temperature. At this point, the fuel is injected in a fine spray into the cylinder and ignited. Diesel engines generally have higher thermal efficiencies than standard internal-combustion engines, and can support a greater range of fuels. GAS TURBINES, because of their simplicity, have long been considered for motor vehicles; and, at present writing, gas-turbine automotive engines appear to be nearing commercial production.

Transmission: Internal-combustion engines operate best within a relatively narrow range of speeds (*i.e.* a crankshaft speed of 3,000 to 4,000 rpm). *Power* delivered by the crankshaft at such high speeds must be transmitted to the wheels

Model T Ford of 1914: Mass-production and assembly-line techniques made the Model T the first low-priced automobile. In final step at Highland Park, Mich., assembly plant, chassis and engine were tested and driven to point outside building where the body slid down a chute onto top of chassis and was fastened into place. Complete car was then ready to be driven away. (*Ford*)

Assembly line, 1962: Completed stub frame is attached to engine and transmission, suspended from overhead traveling crane.

At another station, front-end components and rear-axle assembly are positioned on lifts for attachment to body. (*General Motors*)

Among the most scenic of fault-block mountains are the Grand Tetons of Wyoming, carved out by erosion of the eastern side of a great westward-dipping fault block. Grand Teton, highest peak in the range (*center*), 13,766 ft, after millions of years of erosion still rises about 7,000 ft above the broad sunken block, Jackson Hole, to the east (*foreground*). (*Union Pacific*)

at various lower speeds and increased torques. The transmission, by means of reducing gears, takes engine power at high speeds and low torques and delivers it to the output shaft at lower speeds and higher torques. The majority of motor vehicles now use automatic transmissions utilizing the rotational force of fluids or planetary gear systems, rather than manual gear shifting with its continual need for clutch disengagement.

Chassis: Engine, transmission, and passengers or freight must be supported by a structural frame, called a chassis. In most cases this is made of channel steel sections on which the front wheels are mounted by coil-spring suspensions; the integral chassis-body uses the body, suitably stiffened, as the chassis. BRAKES are generally of the internal-expanding type; present speeds demand that all four wheels have brakes. Power brakes use the vacuum from the engine intake manifold to operate the brakes and thus reduce the amount of force that must be expended by the operator. Virtually every component of the motor vehicle, and especially the engine and transmission, is exposed to the friction accompanying high speeds; this makes adequate LUBRICATION essential. Transmissions are lubricated by heavy oils; springs and steering bearings by grease. Early engines used mechanical methods, *e.g.* splashing of crankcase oil, to lubricate bearings and cylinder walls. Present-day engines use forced-feed pressure distribution of oil through lubrication channels to ensure that every moving surface in contact with another surface is adequately lubricated.—*A. L.*

MOUNTAINS AND MOUNTAIN BUILDING: Mountains are relatively high, large masses of rock that rise notably above their surroundings. Although many are arranged in linear patterns, called *ranges,* some are isolated. The several types include volcanic mountains, folded and faulted mountains, fault-block mountains, and mountains of circum-erosion.

Volcanic Mountains: Many of the world's mountains are piles of volcanic material built up around an opening in the ground through which volcanic rock has flowed or has been blasted to the surface (see VOLCANO). A spectacular example is Paulof Volcano, Alaska. Volcanic mountains made chiefly by consolidation of liquid rock around the opening have generally low slopes (*shield volcanoes*). In contrast, volcanic mountains built chiefly by the fall of explosion products around the opening are generally steep cones (*cinder cones*). The lava that consolidated to a dense, resistant rock in the throat of a volcano when it became inactive may remain as a mountain (see VOLCANIC NECK) long after the outer shells have been eroded away, *e.g.* Ship Rock, New Mexico. The Hawaiian volcano Mauna Loa, a shield volcano which is perhaps the greatest mountain mass of volcanic rock on Earth, was built up from a sea floor more than 14,000 ft below sea level to an elevation of more than 13,000 ft above the sea, and thus has a relief of nearly 28,000 ft. In North America, Mts Hood, Shasta, and Rainier are well-known *strato-volcanoes*—i.e. composite cones, formed of alternating layers of ash and lava.

Folded and Faulted Mountains: The greatest ranges on Earth consist of folded and faulted mountains. These consist

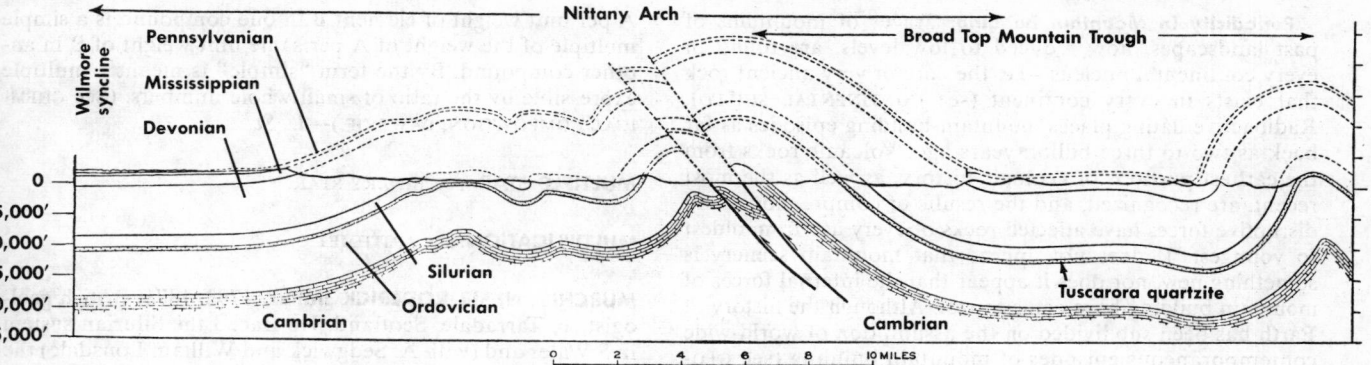

Fig. 1: Generalized cross-section, northwest to southeast, across a portion of the Appalachian Mts in Pennsylvania. These are folded mountains. Note faults near midsection. (*After U. S. Geological Survey*)

of bent and broken rock layers, at many places buttressed by rocks of igneous origin that consolidated far below the present ground surface. Such mountains arise from former elongated, down-warped troughs (GEOSYNCLINES) in which many thousands of feet of sediments together with volcanic flows and pyroclastic materials accumulated. Either the sinking of the geosyncline under the load of sediments and volcanics approximately kept pace with the filling, or the filling kept pace with the sinking, for shallow-water sediments predominate. To this geosynclinal class belong all the great ranges of Earth—the Alps, the Himalayas, the Andes and the Rocky Mts, and the Appalachians. The thickness of the packet of sedimentary layers in all these regions before the mashing into mountain structures occurred amounted to many thousands of feet.

The folding and breaking of rocks in these ranges indicate that they have been squeezed as well as uplifted; in fact, horizontal dislocations amounting to scores of miles are clearly demonstrated in many ranges. A simplified and generalized cross-section of a portion of Pennsylvania (Fig. 1) illustrates this type of deformation.

Although such mountains have been subject to compressional forces, vertical movements account for most of the present elevations. Two types of dislocation are therefore indicated by geosynclinal mountains: *orogenic* movements, which involve a shortening or mashing together of the rock mass or packet of layers; and later *epeirogenic* uplifts, involving essentially vertical displacement with little deformation. Unanimity of opinion has not been reached as to causes or mechanisms of orogenic deformation. Various suggestions include (1) shrinking of Earth with consequent skin wrinkling; (2) deep convection currents (see CONVECTION THEORY) that involve drag of rocks into folds or breaks; and (3) volume changes due to changes of state or phase, as in the solidification or liquefaction of large masses of rock, or as in transformation of minerals from bulkier to denser phases or vice versa, with or without changes of composition. Epeirogenic

uplifts, likewise, are not yet fully understood. Many data show the continents are underlain by rocks lighter than those beneath the oceans; and it is rocks lighter than the average continental material that make folded mountains. These data suggest approximate equilibrium (ISOSTASY) between blocks of differing densities. The higher a block floats, the deeper its base is submerged; thus mountain masses are not extra loads on Earth, because their height is compensated by their lightness. But a disturbance of this balance, as by erosion and deposition, change of phase or volume, or shortening or extension, results in vertical movements. It is most remarkable that geosynclines persistently subsiding for scores of millions of years persistently if intermittently rise for more millions of years after the lateral squeezing that produces the complex folds and breaks characteristic of folded and faulted mountains. Sculpturing by wind, water, and ice has shaped the uplifted structures into their present forms.

Fault-block Mountains: Mountains bounded by normal faults are called fault-block mountains. Large crustal blocks are broken by forces which produce shearing surfaces that bound the range on one or both sides, and the blocks are tilted during the deformation. The structural pattern of fault-block mountains is shown in cross-section in Fig. 2. The origin of the forces that cause the faults is not yet known, although the structures produced have been intensively studied in ranges of Utah, Nevada, Arizona, and California, as well as in the Rhine Valley, Africa, and elsewhere. The Sierra Nevada Range of the U. S. A. is an outstanding example of fault-block mountains.

Mountains of Circum-erosion: Remnant isolated masses standing high above adjacent lowlands are called mountains of circum-erosion. These remains of a higher general level of land in previous times were left high because of superior resistance to erosion or because of their position with respect to previous drainage lines. They are classed as monadnocks. Two classic mountains of this type are Mt Monadnock, New Hampshire, and Stone Mountain, Georgia.

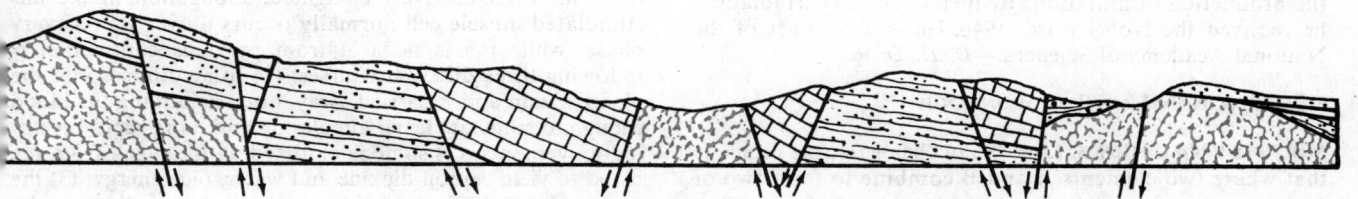

Fig. 2: Cross-section of block faulting near Globe, Ariz. (*After U. S. Geological Survey*)

Periodicity in Mountain Building: Traces of mountains of past landscapes, now reduced to low levels, are found in every continental nucleus—*i.e.* the core of very ancient rock that exists in every continent (see CONTINENTAL SHIELD). Radioactive dating places mountain-building episodes as far back as two to three billion years ago. Volcanic rocks from the earliest portions of geologic history, as well as the most recent, are recognized, and the results of compressional and disruptive forces have affected rocks of every age from oldest to youngest. It does not appear that mountain scenery is something new, nor does it appear that the internal forces of mountain building have come to rest. Although the history of Earth has been subdivided on the assumption of world-wide contemporaneous episodes of mountain building (see GEOLOGICAL TIME CHART), accumulating evidence seems to indicate that periods of orogeny were not clear-cut. Deformation and volcanism have certainly taken place within, as well as between, the established periods of geologic time. It also appears, nevertheless, that during most of the history of the continents, widespread shallow seas and lowlands with generally mild climates over broad latitudes have prevailed. The present time of unusual cold, of wide desert distribution, and of alpine scenery is exceptional. We appear to be living, geologically speaking, in a revolutionary epoch of mountain building.—*J. T.*

MOUTH: the anterior (front) opening of the ALIMENTARY CANAL; also, the cavity (buccal cavity) into which the canal opens. The mouth and its associated structures vary greatly in different animals, partly in relation to feeding habits. Notable modifications are the many accessory mouth parts of insects and crustaceans used for chewing, biting, and sucking; the tearing tongue-like radulae of mollusks; and the jaws of vertebrates, which may take the form of a horny beak, as in birds, or may bear various forms of TEETH. The buccal cavity of many vertebrates has a muscular TONGUE, which may aid in SWALLOWING and may have the important function of TASTE. Salivary glands, which discharge a secretion into the buccal cavity, are widely found in animals; the secretion may serve for lubrication or may contain digestive enzymes, irritants, or poisons. See SALIVARY GLAND; DIGESTION; POISONOUS ANIMALS.—*B. T. S.*

MOVEMENT: see ANIMAL LOCOMOTION; MOTION.

MUCOUS MEMBRANE AND MUCUS: The mucous membrane is the epithelium lining the alimentary canal and the respiratory tract. It contains many single-celled glands whose secretion is partly a glycoprotein called *mucin*. Mucin combines with water and forms mucus, a lubricant and protective coating for the entire surface of both the alimentary canal and the respiratory tract.—*A. R. D.*

MULLER, HERMANN JOSEPH, 1890–   , U. S. geneticist; b. New York, N. Y. He developed and applied quantitative methods for the study of mutations. His discovery that most mutations are lethal implies that an increase in the mutation rate can be exceedingly dangerous to life. For his discovery of the production of mutations by means of x-ray irradiation, he received the Nobel prize, 1946. He is a member of the National Academy of Sciences.—*D. H. D. R.*

MÜLLER, JOHANN: see REGIOMONTANUS.

MULTIPLE PROPORTIONS, LAW OF: in chemistry, the principle that where two elements A and B combine to form two or more compounds (*e.g.* hydrogen and oxygen to form water, H_2O, and hydrogen peroxide, H_2O_2), the weight of element A per unit weight of element B in one compound is a simple multiple of the weight of A per same unit weight of B in another compound. By the term "simple" is meant a multiple expressible by the ratio of small whole numbers. (See CHEMICAL COMPOSITION, LAWS OF.)—*L. Sc.*

MULTIPLE STAR: see BINARY STAR.

MULTIPLICATION: see ARITHMETIC.

MURCHISON, SIR RODERICK IMPEY, 1792–1871, British geologist; b. Tarradale, Scotland. He traced the Silurian system in S Wales and (with A. Sedgwick and William Lonsdale) the Devonian system in Devon and Cornwall. With Sedgwick he investigated the structure of the Alps, and with Édouard P. de Verneuil (1805–73) and Alexander von Keyserling (1815–91), established the classification of the Paleozoic rocks in Russia. Director-general of the Geological Survey of Great Britain, he was one of the founders of the British Association for the Advancement of Science. As a fellow of the Royal Society he received its Copley Medal in 1849. His works include *Russia and the Ural Mountains* (with Verneuil and Keyserling, 1845) and *Siluria* (1854 *et seq.*). He was a member of the U. S. National Academy of Sciences.—*D. H. D. R.*

MURRAY, SIR JOHN, 1841–1914, Canadian-British marine naturalist and oceanographer; b. Cobourg, Ontario, Canada. A naturalist on the *Challenger* deep-sea exploration expedition (1872–76) and leader of several later expeditions, he became the leading authority on deep-sea deposits. He divided all marine sediments into two categories: muds derived from land and oozes derived from surface organisms. *Report on the Scientific Results of the Voyage of H. M. S. Challenger* (1880–95), of which he was editor, is an outstanding work in the history of oceanography. He was a fellow of the Royal Society and an associate of the U. S. National Academy of Sciences.—*D. H. D. R.*

MUSCLE: body tissue consisting of specialized animal cells, usually in the form of fibers, that contract when suitably stimulated. The term muscle, when used without qualification, generally refers to muscle fibers arranged in groups attached to bones of the skeleton. These skeletal muscles are important to many animals in capturing food, breathing, and locomotion. Additional muscle cells form cylindrical sheaths that are components of the soft body wall, of tubular organs such as digestive tract, heart, and arteries, and of ducts of the urogenital system.

Contraction (shortening) of muscle cells occurs as a direct result of structural changes in protein molecules, *e.g.* actomyosin, within the cells, when the molecules are acted upon by adenosine triphosphate (ATP), which provides the energy for contraction. ATP, in turn, derives its energy from chemical actions within the muscle cell whereby the polysaccharide glycogen is converted into the by-product lactic acid. After a muscle cell has contracted, it cannot repeat the process until it has been passively elongated. Elongation in the unstimulated muscle cell normally occurs during its recovery phase, while the lactic acid from previous contraction is following three different courses: (1) some diffuses into the blood stream and is carried away, often acidifying the blood enough to stimulate faster circulation and more rapid breathing movements; (2) some is oxidized with oxygen from the blood to yield carbon dioxide and water, plus energy; (3) the remainder of the lactic acid is converted into glycogen by means of energy from (2). Additional glycogen is synthesized in the muscle cell from sugar provided by the blood stream, and thus the glycogen reserves of the cell are built up and become available for future rounds of contraction.

From the appearance of muscle cells under the compound microscope, the terms "striped" (striated) and "smooth" (unstriated) have been derived. During embryonic development, many individual muscle cells combine in forming striped muscles, which have many nuclei and show branching; such muscles contract rapidly, but require comparatively long periods of relaxation before they can contract again. Muscles associated with the vertebrate skeleton (skeletal muscles) are striated, and the terms skeletal muscle and striated muscle are often used synonymously; however, muscles constituting the vertebrate heart wall (cardiac muscles) are finely striated. Smooth muscles are unbranched and have one nucleus per cell. They contract more slowly and are relatively insensitive to fatigue, requiring little relaxation before contracting again. They are important in moving food through the digestive tract, in controlling the pattern of blood flow in the arterial system, and in tasks such as propelling an egg or a baby to the outside world. All these are known as "visceral muscles."

Almost all skeletal muscles are under voluntary control, through motor neurons connected to motor areas in the cerebral cortex. They show so-called "stretch reflexes," contracting slightly after being stretched; the contraction is initiated by impulses sent to the central nervous system from special receptor cells (proprioceptors), which keep the brain apprised of the position and tension of these muscles. Skeletal muscles are conspicuously enclosed in thin sheets of connective tissue (fascia), which extend beyond the muscle and provide its attachments, in the form of tendons or tendonous tissue. The end of a skeletal muscle that moves least when the muscle contracts is called the *origin* of the muscle; the end that moves most is the *insertion;* between these is the large population of muscle cells (muscle fibers) constituting

the muscle itself, called the *belly* of the muscle. According to a muscle's action, it is classified as a flexor or extensor (having folding and unfolding parts, as in muscles moving the forearm in relation to the upper arm), abductor or adductor (moving an appendage away from or toward the midline of the body), elevator or depressor (raising or lowering a skeletal part, such as the lower jaw). Usually groups of muscles cooperate in each action. Normally every skeletal muscle is under slight tension (tonus) because a few cells in it are contracting every second. Only when more contract at one time can movement occur. Even then, movement is likely to be well controlled, because antagonistic muscles are holding back. A great deal of energy can be spent by muscles in merely preventing movement—as in standing or maintaining any unbalanced posture. Muscle fatigue develops if lactic acid from contraction accumulates in the muscle cells and blocks them from receiving stimuli carried by associated nerves (see FATIGUE).

Antagonistic muscles, working against one another, permit fine control movements and help maintain delicate equilibrium. Here, two sets of muscles help keep a man upright: those in front pull downward, tending to keep him from falling backward; those in back pull downward, tending to keep him from falling forward. (After Guyer)

Almost all visceral muscles are beyond voluntary control. They are stimulated to contract by nerves of the sympathetic and parasympathetic systems, and also by chemical agents such as the hormone adrenalin. Ordinarily all of these contractions are automatic, attended to by parts of the nervous system beyond consciousness, and rely upon the proper working of a complex set of receptor cells and of sensory nerves, as well as upon various hormones. Together these provide the nervous system with feedback information similar to that used in modern electronic control systems for industrial machinery.

A vertebrate heart (cardiac muscle) is so interconnected with branching fibers that its muscular walls consist essentially of one big multinucleated cell. Upon this cell depends the heart's law of action: it contracts completely or not at all (the "all-or-none law"). Although the heart is of striated muscle, it is involuntary and linked to the automatic portion of the nervous system, as well as being responsive to hormones. In man, at rest, the heart beats about 72 times/min, which allows about 0.8 sec per beat. The auricles contract in about 0.1 sec, propelling the blood they contain into the relaxed and distensible ventricles. Then the ventricles contract for about 0.3 sec, expelling the blood from the heart. For the rest of the 0.8 sec, the whole heart is relaxing, recovering, ready for the next beat. In some vertebrates, *e.g.* the turtle, even pieces of ventricle wall have enough nerve connections, glycogen reserves, and local control to be able to continue beating for hours if cut free and kept under suitable conditions. See HEART.—*L. and M. M.*

MUSCLE CONTRACTION: shortening of a muscle as a result of conversion of chemical energy to mechanical energy; or an

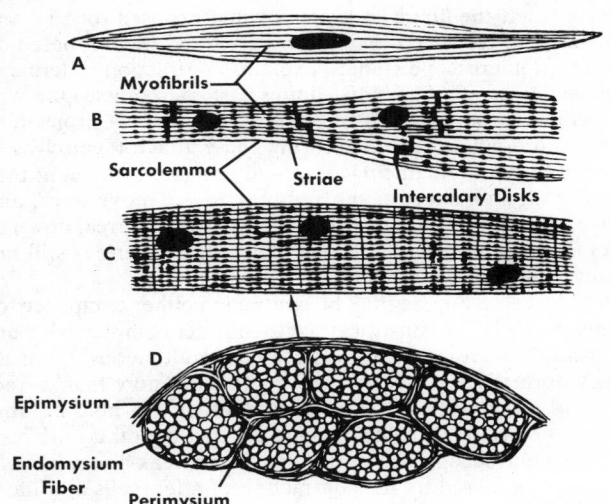

Three varieties of muscle tissue: (A) smooth muscle cell, (B) cardiac muscle fiber, (C) skeletal muscle fiber, (D) muscle cross section showing bundles of fibers. (B) and (C) are examples of striated muscles. Note that the dark bands do not extend continuously from one sarcolemma (outer wall) to another, but are features of the filaments (myofibrils). The intercalary disks mark boundaries between separate cells. Skeletal muscle fibers lack this feature, and can therefore be considered single, multi-nucleated cells (syncytia). The endomysium, perimysium and epimysium are sheaths of connective tissue surrounding individual fibers, bundles of fibers, and muscles respectively. (After Eaton)

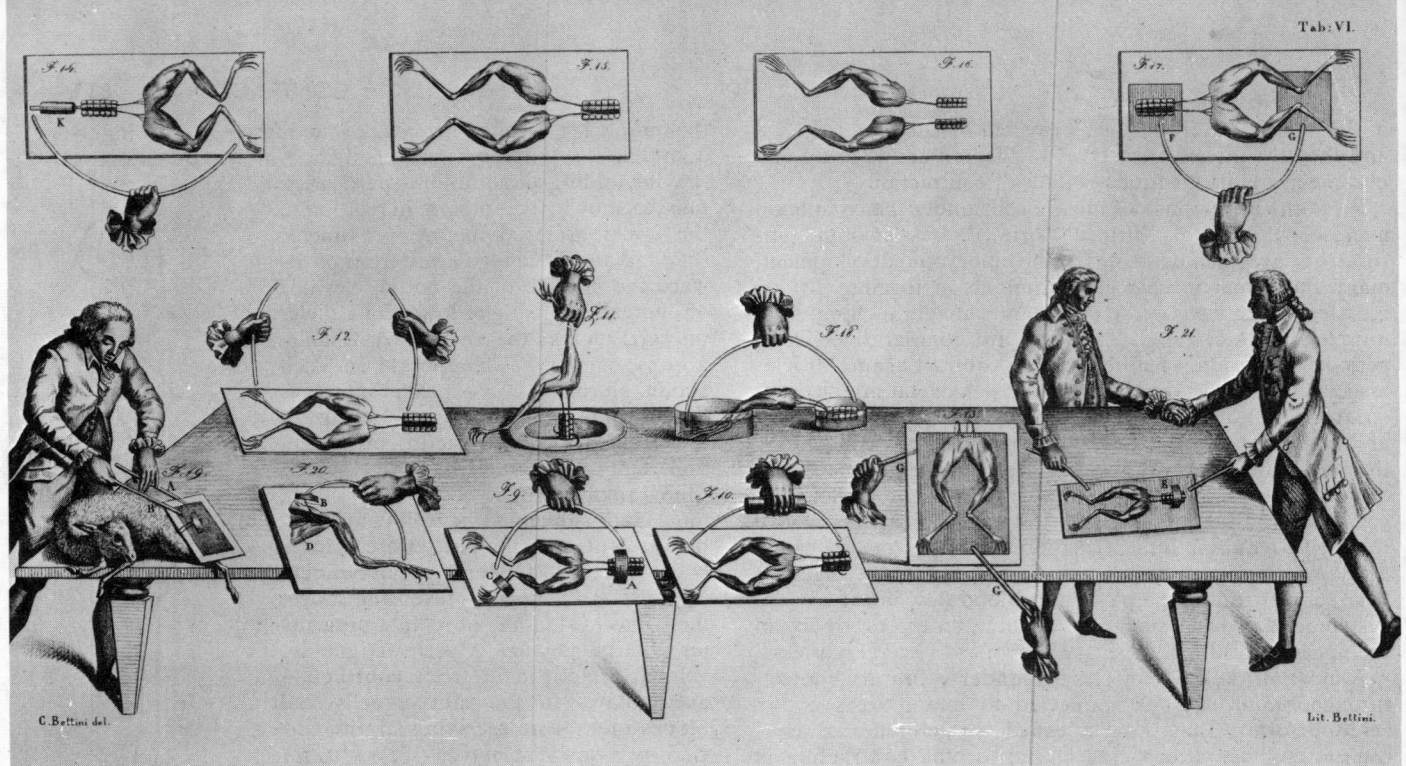

Muscles contract when subjected to an electric discharge or when touched by two different metals. Electrically caused contraction was accidentally observed and then investigated by Luigi Galvani, and it inspired Volta to invent the electric battery. Demonstrations of some of Galvani's experiments appear in the above plate, reproduced from *Opere edite ed inedite del Professore Luigi Galvani* (1841). (*Library of Congress*)

increase in tension in a muscle that is prevented from shortening. Contraction is stimulated naturally by chemicals released from nerves or ductless glands, and artificially by electric stimulation. It is of great scientific interest because of the mystery of how mechanical energy is produced with high efficiency (20 to 40%) and in a way completely different from that in any man-made engine. The energy for contraction comes ultimately from oxidation of carbohydrates to carbon dioxide and water, but the immediate source of energy is the conversion of adenosine triphosphate (ATP) into adenosine diphosphate (ADP) plus phosphoric acid. Then energy from carbohydrate oxidation is used to convert the ADP back into ATP so that contraction can continue (see OXIDATIVE PHOSPHORYLATION). When contraction occurs with inadequate oxygen, as during a runner's sprint, carbohydrate is broken down only as far as lactic acid and an *oxygen debt* accumulates. It

may take many minutes of deep breathing to correct the oxygen deficiency resulting from a 10-sec sprint.

One theory explains contraction in terms of protein fibers kinking or folding, as in the shrinking of wool. Albert Szent-Györgyi produced artificial fibers of actomyosin by mixing the two principal muscle proteins, actin and myosin, and observed that the fibers contracted when exposed to ATP and potassium. However, the currently favored theory, based on electron microscope studies, explains contraction in terms of ultramicroscopic filaments sliding past each other. One type of filament, largely myosin, is studded with tiny projections that can oscillate back and forth. These attach themselves to a second type of filament, composed principally of actin; they pull it along a short distance, break loose, move back, and give the actin filament another pull. How the breakdown of ATP provides energy to cause this pulling along is still not fully understood.

Although a muscle may be contracted either completely or only partially, its constituent cells contract completely or not at all. They are never all contracted simultaneously, nor do they normally exert a contractive effort for more than a fraction of a second; even in sustained effort, *e.g.* holding up a heavy object, while some cells are contracting others are resting, to contract again in turn. A partial or weak muscular contraction is caused by the contraction of a few cells at a time; a strong contraction involves the simultaneous contraction of many cells.—*F. F.*

MUSHROOM: see FUNGI.

MUSSCHENBROEK, PIETER VAN, 1692–1761, Dutch physicist; b. Leyden. He published extensively in the fields of electricity and magnetism and constructed an electric capacitor (perhaps based on E. G. von Kleist's earlier work). His descriptions of experiments with the capacitor were published by J. A. Nollet (1700–70) in *Observations sur quelques nouveaux phénomènes*

Muscle contraction decreases angle between the two bones. If joint represented is the elbow, contraction will bring the hand toward the shoulder. (*After Eaton*)

d'électricité (1746). Because Musschenbroek was at Leyden, the name "Leyden jar" became attached to the capacitor, the first device for storing electricity. He was a fellow of the Royal Society.—*D. H. D. R.*

MUTATION: a change in a characteristic of an animal or a plant which can be passed on to its offspring; more precisely, a change in a hereditary unit known as a gene, or some rearrangement of the chromosomes in which the genes are located. (See CHROMOSOMES AND GENES.) Both a mutated gene and an organism showing the results of such a gene are known as mutants. Mutations occur naturally in all known organisms but at a very slow rate. This rate can be accelerated artificially by exposing the organism to high-energy radiation such as x-rays or ultra-violet rays, or by subjection to certain chemicals such as the nitrogen mustards. Mutations are random in being unpredictable and in being unrelated to the needs of the organism. Mutations for winglessness occur among flies on oceanic islands where lack of wings is an advantage and also among flies reared in laboratory cages where it is a disadvantage. The nature of any mutation reflects the properties of the nucleic acids of which chromosomes are constructed. Hence when enough is learned about the chemistry of nucleic acids, controlled and directed mutations may become possible.

Because most organisms are well adapted and delicately adjusted to their environment and mutations are at random, it follows that almost all mutations are disadvantageous. A random change in any well-planned machine is not very likely to be an improvement; hence most mutants lose out in the struggle for existence. They may not live to a reproductive age, or they may have a shortened life span. In any case, the mutant gene tends to be lost in succeeding generations. But if a gene confers an advantage on its possessor, whether bacterium, oak tree, or man, the possessor will be better equipped in the competition for survival, and the gene may be passed on to succeeding generations, gradually spreading throughout the population. Mutations are thus the raw material of NATURAL SELECTION and one of the major factors in organic EVOLUTION.

Like any other gene, a mutated one may be dominant or recessive. If a recessive gene is to express itself in any individual organism, it must have been received from both of the parents of that individual. A dominant gene is one which produces its effect when received from only one parent. A gene for ALBINISM is recessive to a gene for normal pigmentation. If a man receives a gene for albinism from one parent and a gene for normal pigmentation from the other parent, he will have normal pigmentation. Likewise, mutated genes may be sex-linked, which means they may be located on the X chromosome. Normal human males, like normal vinegar fly males, receive an X sex-chromosome from their mother and a Y sex-chromosome from their father. Females receive an X from both parents. Since the Y chromosome is virtually empty of genes, any gene, even though recessive, which is carried on the X-chromosome of a male will manifest itself. Red-green color blindness is such a recessive trait. To make a color-blind woman it must be present in both X chromosomes, but a color-blind man will result whenever that gene is in his single X chromosome.

Facts regarding mutation rates for specific genes are slowly accumulating. In Denmark 8 mutations for a certain kind of dwarfism occurred in 94,075 births. The mutation causing very short legs in sheep (the so-called Ancon sheep) is known to have occurred at least twice, once in 1791 on a farm in Massachusetts and a second time in 1925 in Norway. The mutation that produces yellow body in Drosophila, the vinegar fly, occurs about 3 times in every 10,000 flies.—*G. B. M.*

MUTUALISM: see SYMBIOSIS.

MYOGLOBIN: a protein which serves as the storehouse of oxygen in the muscle. It releases oxygen during the contractile phase of the muscle, when the demand is greatest. Myoglobin contains only one heme group, while the analogous protein hemoglobin contains four. See OXYGEN TRANSPORT.—*F. F.*

MYSTERIUM COSMOGRAPHICUM: see PRODROMUS DISSERTATIONUM COSMOGRAPHICARUM CONTINENS MYSTERIUM COSMOGRAPHICUM.

Mutation of gene that controls gland affecting deposition of fat contributed to obesity of mouse shown here with its normal littermate. Diets of the two mice were the same. Genetic defect producing obese mutant is a recessive hereditary factor in mice, with gene symbol "ob." (*Roscoe B. Jackson Memorial Lab.*)

N

NADIR: the point on the CELESTIAL SPHERE directly beneath an observer, 180° from the zenith (the point directly above the observer). A straight line connecting nadir and zenith passes through the observer's position perpendicular to the plane of the celestial horizon. The direction of the nadir is that assumed by a plumb line on Earth's surface.—*T. N.*

NAIL: see SKIN.

NAMIAS, JEROME, 1910–   , U. S. meteorologist; b. Bridgeport, Conn. His research has been in general circulation of the atmosphere and aerology, and he is known particularly for his work in extended-period forecasting. He is the author of *An Introduction to the Study of Air Mass Analysis* (1935), later enlarged to include isentropic analysis (1940). Namias has been chief of the Extended Forecast Section of the U. S. Weather Bureau since 1941. See WEATHER ANALYSIS; WEATHER FORECASTING.—*D. H. D. R.*

NAPHTHA: a liquid obtained by distillation from petroleum, coal tar, shale, or wood. The composition depends on the source: wood naphtha is largely wood alcohol, but the other naphthas are mixtures of hydrocarbons. Coal tar and petroleum naphthas are useful solvents and paint thinners.—*Ru. M.*

NAPHTHALENE: a white, crystalline hydrocarbon which separates from a certain distillation fraction of coal tar. It was first obtained from a naphtha fraction. It has a characteristically pungent odor and is used in "moth balls"; also it is useful in the manufacture of dyes, to make lampblack, and as an intermediate for the synthesis of many commercially important compounds. Naphthalene belongs among the AROMATIC COMPOUNDS. Its formula shows that it consists of two benzene rings in a type of structure called condensed, or fused, rings.—*Ru. M.*

NAPIER, JOHN, 1550–1617, Scottish mathematician; b. near Edinburgh. He published polemics on religious matters and wrote a sort of science fiction, in which he foresaw the invention of war engines and submarines. His mathematical work, a side line with which he amused himself, led to his invention of logarithms as a device for shortening the labor of computation. His first table of logarithms, published 1614, contained the logarithms of the sines of angles. (Logarithms were improved by Henry Briggs, and the Briggsian, or common, logarithms are generally used today.) Napier is also known for his mnemonic rule of circular parts, used in writing formulas for the solution of spherical right triangles, and for the analogies for the solution of spherical oblique triangles. He was a fellow of the Royal Society.—*H. C.*

NATURAL GAS: a mixture of gases of variable composition which occurs trapped under pressure in porous rock formations beneath denser rock layers. It is often found with petroleum. The gas may contain methane and other paraffins, hydrogen sulfide, helium, carbon dioxide, nitrogen, and several other substances. When rich in hydrocarbons (some natural gas is nearly pure methane) it is a valuable fuel and chemical intermediate, and is piped from the well to all parts of the country. It can be used to make carbon black, acetylene, and alcohols. Gas from some wells contains less than 25% methane.—*Ru. M.*

NATURAL HISTORY (Pliny): see HISTORIA NATURALIS.

NATURAL SELECTION: a process that controls the frequency of different types of hereditary material (genes) in a population through differences in survival and reproduction of individuals bearing this material. The process, described by Darwin and Wallace simultaneously in 1858, directs most if not all EVOLUTION and forms a key principle in evolutionary theory. Since 1850 nearly 60 species of British moths, for example, have changed character through natural selection. Light-colored moths contrast with soot-grimed trees and buildings; dark ones do not. Birds eat more of the light-colored moths, and few of the latter live to transmit genes for "light color" to the next generation (see HEREDITY). Dark-colored moths were only a few per cent of the original populations; today, they form over 90%.

Natural selection is noted in studies of peppered moth and its darker mutant *carbonaria*. When both forms are resting together on bark, the blacks are much more often picked out and eaten by birds on lichen-covered trees (*right*) in the country, but pale moths much more often on smoke-grimed trees (*left*) in industrial areas. In the country, natural selection apparently favors the pales; in industrial surroundings, the blacks. Natural selection of this kind may operate swiftly to alter animal populations. (*H. B. D. Kettlewell, Univ. of Oxford*)

Darwin described natural selection as survival of the fittest. Some, taking this to mean dominance of the strongest individual, emphasized individual competition as the driving force in evolution; but the process appears more complicated. The number of viable eggs produced is just as important as survival under predation. Individuals may be favored because of their role in the population: thus a few light moths survive because crosses between light and dark are physiologically superior to pure dark. Populations also compete, so that selection favors superior populations rather than individuals. —J. B.

NAVIER-STOKES EQUATIONS: relations expressing Newton's second law of motion in a form most suitable for fluid dynamics; they are based on the work of Sir George Stokes (1819–1903) and C. L. M. Navier (1785–1836). The three equations state that the acceleration of a fluid element is the result of pressures acting normal to its surface, viscous shearing stresses acting along its surface, and body forces such as gravitation acting throughout the volume of the element. The acceleration is conveniently divided into the part concerned with time-rate of change at a single point in the flow, and another part concerned with the change due to convection of the fluid from point to point.—D. B.

NAVIGATION: see AIR NAVIGATION; ANIMAL NAVIGATION; CELESTIAL NAVIGATION; MARINE NAVIGATION.

N-DIMENSIONAL GEOMETRY: Although some concepts of n-dimensional geometry can be traced back to the 18th cent., particularly in the work of Joseph Louis Lagrange, its systematic development began when some of the geometries of the plane and space were formally generalized to "spaces" of more than three dimensions by Hermann Grassmann (1809–77), Arthur Cayley (1821–95), and Julius Pluecker (1801–68). The geometries capable of generalization to n-space might be any one of the familiar geometries of 3-space, such as Euclidean, non-Euclidean, affine, projective, or conformal, to name a few. Moreover, since these geometries could be investigated either synthetically or analytically, their generalizations were conducted along both synthetic and analytic lines.

At first, the extension of geometric concepts to "spaces" of more than three dimensions was attacked by some philosophers and also by some mathematicians on the ground that our space, the space of perceptual experience, is 3-dimensional and that it is the sole purpose of geometry to produce a faithful description of it. Therefore, to speak of points, lines, and such things as r-dimensional manifolds in a space of n dimensions was only a meaningless and useless exercise, a mere playing with words. Such a view, however, was soon swept aside as a stultifying prejudice, especially when geometries came to be regarded as purely abstract postulational sciences. From this point of view each abstract geometry, including n-dimensional geometries, was capable of any number of concrete interpretations or representations by means of models which could be found not only in our 3-space, but in physics, chemistry, and other sciences. For example, in the kinetic theory of gases, the momentary state of a given mass of gas containing N molecules depends upon the position and velocity of each molecule. The position is given by its three Cartesian coordinates and the velocity by three orthogonal components, so that the state of the gas has $6N$ degrees of freedom or $6N$ dimensions.

To see how natural it is to generalize from a geometry of two and three to one of n dimensions, consider the case of analytic Euclidean geometry. In Euclidean 3-space, a point

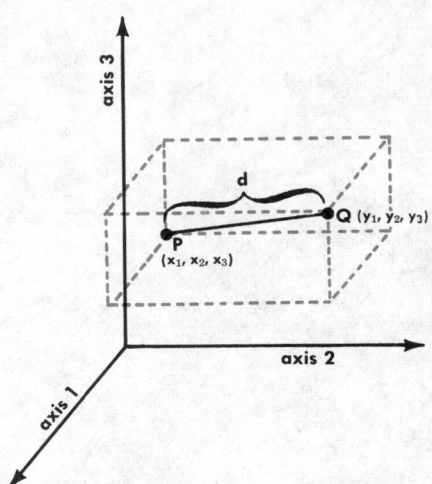

Distance formula for 3-space can be generalized for spaces of higher dimension.

can be represented by an ordered set of three real numbers. Using Cartesian coordinates, let the points P and Q have the coordinates (x_1, x_2, x_3) and (y_1, y_2, y_3), respectively; then the distance between P and Q is given by the formula

$$d = [(x_1 - y_1)^2 + (x_2 - y_2)^2 + (x_3 - y_3)^2]^{1/2}$$

which resembles and generalizes the formula for the Euclidean distance between two points in a plane. We now define Euclidean n-space as a manifold of arithmetic "points": namely, ordered n-tuples of real numbers $(x_1, x_2, \ldots, x_n)$; and we define the distance between two points $P(x_1, x_2, \ldots, x_n)$ and $Q(y_1, y_2, \ldots, y_n)$ by means of the formula

$$d = [\sum_{1}^{n} (x_i - y_i)^2]^{1/2}$$

—J. M. F.

NEBULA: a hazy patch of light seen in the night sky. The name means "cloud" in Latin, but it is now known that although some so-called nebulas are indeed clouds of gas, others are systems of stars, in which the stars cannot be individually distinguished by the naked eye. Sir William Herschel was the first to observe (1786) that some nebulas are composed of stars. He described several types of these "clouds" and suggested that some are vast stellar systems. Modern astronomers distinguish three main types of star systems: galactic clusters, consisting of stars within our galaxy; globular clusters, associated with, but outside the plane of, our galaxy; and external galaxies. (See STAR CLUSTER; GALAXY.) Diffuse nebulas are also of several types: dark nebulas, which obscure the stars beyond them (see INTERSTELLAR MATTER), and planetary, reflection, and emission nebulas.

Planetary Nebulas: In small telescopes planetary nebulas appear as disks that usually somewhat resemble the planets Uranus and Neptune. They are, however, formed by an extra-bright zone within a huge sphere of gas surrounding a hot, blue star. Atoms in the gas absorb energy from ultra-violet radiation from the central star; at some later time the atoms re-emit this energy as visible light. The most luminous gases in a planetary nebula are hydrogen and oxygen. The Ring Nebula in Lyra is typical.

Reflection Nebulas: A cloud of cosmic dust which shines by reflecting light from a relatively cool star, or group of stars; nearby or embedded in it is a reflection nebula. The Pleiades cluster possesses an associated cloud of cosmic dust, in which delicately striated nebulous structures can be seen on long-

Filamentary Nebula in Cygnus is one end of long wreath of gas traveling through space at rate of 0.″05/yr. Outward movement of ends indicates nebula may result from explosion of a star 150,000 yr ago. The Filamentary Nebula is of the emission type. Photos of nebulas such as this require a large telescope and long exposure. (*Mt Wilson*)

exposure photographs taken with telescopes or cameras of relatively small focal length. The same kind of nebulosity occurs in some parts of the Ophiuchus complex and in Taurus, Perseus, and certain sections of the Orion complex. The spectra of reflection nebulas are of the usual stellar variety: continuous spectra crossed by dark absorption lines. They resemble the spectra of the embedded stars, with the difference that blue and red rays are not reflected equally, so that a different color distribution in the nebula and in the star results. Moreover, the light from stars seen through the reflection nebulas is reddened to a considerable extent. From these various color effects one deduces that the cosmic dust particles responsible for the nebulas have diameters of the order of $\frac{1}{100,000}$ in. From the degree of reflectivity shown by these nebulas one finds furthermore that the particles are probably mostly simple molecular combinations of carbon, nitrogen, and oxygen with hydrogen; one might say they are tiny ice particles. Certain polarization effects are observed which suggest the presence of elongated particles aligned in part by magnetic fields associated with the nebulas.

Emission Nebulas: When a very hot star, rich in ultraviolet radiation, is either embedded in or very near to a fairly dense cloud of interstellar gas, this cloud becomes an emission nebula. The Great Nebula in Orion is probably the most beautiful, but it has two close rivals in the southern sky: the Great Nebula near Eta Carinae and the Tarantula Nebula in Doradus. The Orion and Carina nebulas belong to the Milky Way system, but the Tarantula is part of the Large Magellanic Cloud, a companion galaxy to our own. These emission nebulas are all exceedingly large, tenuous clouds of gas, composed of hydrogen atoms (approximately 65% of the total), helium atoms (most of the remaining 35%), oxygen and calcium (less than 0.1%), and sodium, potassium, and titanium (less than 0.01%). The Orion Nebula is 1,500 to 1,600 lt-yr from the Sun, and its main body measures approximately 25 lt-yr across. The minimum mass of the gas of which the nebula is composed is approximately 300 solar masses. Recent radio astronomical studies—and photography with special cameras of short focal ratio equipped with color filters to isolate the hydrogen radiations from the nebula—have shown that the Orion Nebula proper is only an

island of great brilliance in a much vaster gaseous complex, which has a mass of the order of 100,000 solar masses and a diameter of at least 300 lt-yr. The Carina Nebula is at a considerably greater distance, probably at about 5,000 lt-yr from the Sun. Its principal luminous body measures at least 200 lt-yr across and its minimum gaseous mass is several thousand solar masses. The Doradus Nebula is at the distance of the Large Magellanic Cloud, probably 200,000 lt-yr, and is approximately 1,000 lt-yr across; its mass has been estimated as high as one million solar masses.

Emission nebulas shine by absorbing and re-emitting radiation from embedded blue-white, very hot stars. The Trapezium Cluster, of which the main visible part is a close group of four of these blue-white stars, is in the brightest part of the Orion Nebula. Similarly, blue-white and very hot supergiant stars are found in and near the Carina and Doradus nebulas. All these embedded stars have surface temperatures of the order of 30,000° K, and they emit plentiful ultraviolet radiation. The hydrogen atoms of the nebula absorb this ultraviolet radiation, so that each affected hydrogen atom loses its electron and separates into a positively charged hydrogen nucleus (a proton) and a negatively charged free electron. In due course the proton, with its positive charge, meets another free electron and captures it. While the original ejection most likely proceeds directly from the lowest energy level of the neutral hydrogen atom, capture of an electron by a proton is just as likely to occur in one of the higher energy levels of the neutral hydrogen atom. The electron will remain at the higher energy level for only a very small fraction of a second, and it will then cascade down to the lowest atomic energy level, often emitting on the way the familiar pattern of the Balmer spectral lines of the neutral hydrogen atom. The visible radiation is the direct product of this cascading process. Other spectrum lines, notably the green nebular lines, are produced in a somewhat different fashion. These come from doubly ionized oxygen atoms, and atomic collisions, however rare, play a prominent role in their production. From a study of the hydrogen and other lines, we can learn much about the physical conditions in the emission nebulas. In the denser portion, the average number of atoms per cubic inch is of the order of 1,000, whereas in the outlying parts the corresponding figure may drop to 10. The atoms and electrons move with speeds corresponding to temperatures of the order of 10,000° K.

Spectrophotography is only one of several approaches to the study of emission nebulas. Radio techniques contribute much useful information. In the course of the recombination process (in which a proton captures a free electron), radio radiation is emitted and can now be readily detected. Studies of the intensity distribution in the 21-cm line of neutral atomic hydrogen tell us especially about the outlying regions of the nebulas, where the ultraviolet light from the stars penetrates at best in a very diluted form. It has often been thought that much might be learned from telescopes on orbiting satellites. However, it is most likely that the scattered ultraviolet radiation from interstellar hydrogen will produce a general celestial fog at wavelengths of the order of 1000Å (1/10,000 cm) and less, thus rendering it impossible to pinpoint the nebulas in the far ultraviolet.

Emission nebulas are not to be imagined as huge, amorphous clouds of interstellar gas. Very likely there is much structure in them, and the gas may occur to a considerable extent in cumulus-like aggregates with diameters that may be as small as ⅟₁₀₀ lt-yr for the average unit. Star formation is probably an important process at work in the major emission nebulas, practically all of which contain an unusual abundance of stars that are apparently very young on the cosmic scale.—*B. J. B.*

NEBULAR HYPOTHESIS: a descriptive explanation of the origin of the solar system devised by the French mathematician Pierre Laplace, 1796, and sometimes referred to as the *Laplacian hypothesis.* It became widely accepted, and only a century later were serious dynamical flaws pointed out. Even so, certain modern theories of the origin of the planets have features in common with it. (See DUST CLOUD THEORY.) The hypothesis was that the solar system in its primitive state consisted of a slowly rotating, highly spheroidal distribution of nebulous matter at first in gaseous form because of high temperature. As the nebula cooled it tended to shrink, and in so doing shed off a ring of material from its equatorial outer edge. This ring was then supposed to pull itself together lengthwise to form a primitive planet in circular motion round the main mass. A similar development of this primitive planet would produce satellites circling it. Further shrinkage of the nebula would result in shedding of further rings at successively closer distances from the center, thereby giving the whole series of planets. Then finally the large part of the nebula settled down to a single compact central body to give the primitive Sun.—*R. A. L.*

NECKAM, ALEXANDER, 1157–1217, English author; b. St. Albans. Two of his books, *De utensilibus* and *De naturis rerum*, contain the earliest known European mentions of the magnetic compass, to which Chinese writers had referred in the previous century. It is likely that sea captains had been using compasses for a considerable time before that.—*D. H. D. R.*

NEMATODE: any of the non-segmented, smooth, elongated, cylindrical worms found in vast numbers in soil and on the bottom of the seas, ponds, lakes, and rivers. Many are internal parasites in plants or in animals. About 13,000 described species make up the phylum Nematoda, one of the main animal divisions. Length of the adult ranges from about 50 microns (⅟₅₀₀ in.) to 3 ft, although the great majority are between ⅟₁₆ and ½ in. long. They have many different feeding habits. Some are carnivorous, some herbivorous, some feed on debris; parasitic species feed on the body fluids or tissues

of the host. One large species of *Ascaris* (6 to 16 in. long) is an important parasite in the small intestine of the hog and of man. The hookworm of tropical and subtropical lands, about ½ in. long, is bent into a small hook at the anterior (front) end; it feeds on the lining of the small intestine of man and produces serious sickness. Trichinosis is a human disease produced by enormous numbers of microscopic larvae of *Trichinella* embedded in the muscle tissues. See PARASITISM. —*R. P.*

NEODYMIUM: a lanthanide (rare-earth metal) element (Nd); at. no. 60; at. wt 144.27; density 6.95; mp 840°C. Discovery of the element is credited to Carl Auer von Welsbach (1885), who separated what was then believed to be a pure compound of the element "didymium" into two parts—neodymia (a compound containing neodymium) and praeseodymia (a compound containing praeseodymium). Traditionally prepared by fractional crystallization, very pure neodymium has been produced since World War II by ION-EXCHANGE methods; commercial preparation may involve ELECTROLYSIS of neodymium-halogen compounds, or reduction of neodymium salts. The metal has been used for coloring glassware and as a glare-removing agent in special glasses, and is included with other RARE EARTHS in the alloy misch metal.—*I. B.*

NEOGENE PERIOD: second division of CENOZOIC ERA, including Miocene, Pliocene, Pleistocene, and Recent epochs.

NEON: a gaseous element (Ne); at. no. 10; at. wt 20.183; density 6.95; one of the INERT GASES. Neon is colorless, odorless, and tasteless, and has no chemical compounds. It occurs in Earth's atmosphere in the proportion of 18.18 parts per million by volume, and traces are found in minerals and meteorites. Neon is prepared commercially by subjecting liquefied air to fractional distillation, neon being one of the earliest components to "boil off"; the element was discovered in this manner by Sir William Ramsay and M. W. Travers in 1898. When an electric current is passed through neon confined in a glass tube, the ionized neon produces the reddish-orange glow so familiar in advertising signs. Many other uses stem from neon's inertness and its property of ionizing and thereby conducting electricity readily and, in so doing, emitting a characteristic glow; *e.g.* it is used in warning devices to guard against an overload of electric current. See IONIZED GAS. —*I. B.*

NEOPRENE: see RUBBER.

NEOTENY: in animals, the assumption of sexual maturity while in a larval or juvenile condition. It is a rare phenomenon, although found in very diverse groups, and may have played an important role in the evolutionary origin of radically new groups of animals.

The Mexican axolotl, a salamander of the genus *Ambystoma,* is the classic case. These salamanders permanently retain their larval traits, such as external gills, tail fin, thin larval-type skin, fishlike lateral-line sense organs. That these are truly larval structures is proved not only by the fact that they are found in larval but not adult stages of other salamanders, but also by the fact that the axolotl itself will lose them and assume a normal "adult" form if fed thyroid gland or injected with thyroxin.

Neoteny may have been the way some animal groups have escaped the "evolutionary trap" of specialization. Basic new departures in animal evolution have always come from simple, generalized forms rather than from highly specialized ones that seem to be evolutionary dead-ends. Insects, for example, like other segmented animals, must have evolved from segmented worms—but how? The evidence now available indicates that millipedes, which are segmented wormlike animals and specialized for terrestrial life, formed the link between segmented worms and insects via neoteny. Millipedes already possess the essential internal organs for life on land: a tracheal respiratory system and an excretory system of Malpighian tubules almost precisely like that of the insects. The striking fact is that the larval stage of a millipede has only three pairs of legs, just as in insects, and these legs are in the segments immediately back of the head, again as in insects. It would take only a very slight change, perhaps only a single MUTATION, to inhibit further growth in such a creature and render it sexually mature. Such an organism would be little different from some of the most primitive insects living today. (See METAMORPHOSIS.)

It has even been theorized that the origin of man was the result of at least partial neoteny: that man is essentially a fetal ape that has become sexually mature. In any case, man does exhibit important traits that characterize vertebrate embryos, notably the relatively great size of the brain and its orientation at right angles to the spinal cord. Moreover, the age at which the bone sutures fuse and the second teeth appear in man is much retarded, as compared with the corresponding age in great apes. Thus neoteny may be responsible for some of the big evolutionary changes that lead in new directions—for what has been called macro- or quantum EVOLUTION.—*G. B. M.*

NEPTUNE: the 8th principal PLANET in order from the Sun; it is one of the giant planets. Invisible to the eye, Neptune is seen in binoculars as an 8th-mag. "star." In telescopes it exhibits a greenish disc about 2.4″ in diameter. Its mean diameter is about 28,000 mi, with the polar diameter about 2.5% less than the equatorial one. Its mass is 17.2 times Earth's. The surface temperature is so low that measurements are difficult; Neptune is probably colder than −300°F.

Uranus, subsequent to its discovery in 1781, deviated from its predicted orbit. A possible explanation was the effect of an unknown, more distant planet. John Couch Adams in England and Urbain Leverrier in France independently predicted the position of the disturbing planet. Galle at Berlin used Leverrier's work to make Neptune's visual discovery, in Sep. 1846, a major triumph of Newtonian dynamics.

Neptune revolves around the Sun with a period of 165 yr, at an average distance from the Sun of 2,794 million mi. The eccentricity of the orbit is 0.009, and the inclination to the ecliptic is 1°46′. Neptune has an extensive atmosphere, in which methane exists above the reflecting surface. The planet resembles the other giants in its average density of 2.29 times water, in its much increased density toward the center, and in its very high reflecting power—about 73%.

All surface detail is extremely difficult to observe, but perhaps there are cloud-belts like those so prominent on Jupiter. The period of rotation is about 15.8 hr. The equator is inclined about 29° to the plane of the orbit.

Neptune has two known satellites: Triton, with a mean distance of 220,000 mi and a period of 5 day 21 hr; and Nereid, with a mean distance of 3.4 million mi, period 360 days. Triton, comparable in size to our Moon, has been conjectured to have an atmosphere. Nereid is small, perhaps 200 mi in diameter; the eccentricity of its orbit (0.75) is the greatest for all known natural satellites in the solar system. Triton's revolution is retrograde, Nereid's direct.—*W. H.*

NEPTUNIUM: an artificial element (Np) of the actinide group; at. no. 93; at. wt 237 (most stable isotope). Neptunium became the first artificial transuranium element to be discovered when, in 1940, E. M. McMillan and P. H. Abelson bombarded uranium with neutrons at the Univ. of California, producing the neptunium isotope Np²³⁹. The isotope Np²³⁷ is currently produced in minute quantities as a by-product from nuclear reactors that produce plutonium. Uranium ores, through transmutation with available neutrons, produce very small amounts of the element naturally.—*I. B.*

NERNST, WALTHER, 1864–1941, German physico-chemist; b. Briesen. His heat theorem, dealing with the entropy of matter as it approaches absolute zero, became the third law of thermodynamics. For his thermochemical work he received the 1920 Nobel prize. His principal inventions were a microbalance and the Nernst electric lamp, equipped with a metal oxide which when heated becomes a conductor of electricity. He was a fellow of the Royal Society.—*R. J. F.*

NERNST HEAT THEOREM: the third law of THERMODYNAMICS, which states that all crystalline substances have zero thermal capacity (zero ENTROPY) at a temperature of absolute zero. —*E. M. R.*

NERVOUS IMPULSE: an electrical disturbance, accompanied by chemical changes, that travels along a nerve fiber; it is the "message" unit that enables living things to react to stimuli. The nervous impulse is set off by a stimulus, but its characteristics are not affected at all by the type or intensity of the stimulus; each impulse is basically the same. However, most stimuli set off a series of impulses, which differ in number and frequency, thus making possible a variety of responses. Impulses travel at speeds ranging from 5 cm/sec (about 1/10 mi/hr) to 100 m/sec (about 225 mi/hr), depending on the type of fiber they are moving through and the kind of organism in which the fiber occurs.

A nervous impulse is initiated when a stimulus causes abrupt changes in the membrane properties of the nerve fiber of a nerve cell. A resting nerve fiber (Fig. 1) is a cylindrical structure containing potassium ions (K⁺) on the inside and bathed in a solution containing sodium ions (Na⁺) on the outside. A biochemical "pump" in the membrane forces out any Na⁺ that may leak in and sets up an electrical potential difference, which holds the K⁺ inside. When the fiber is

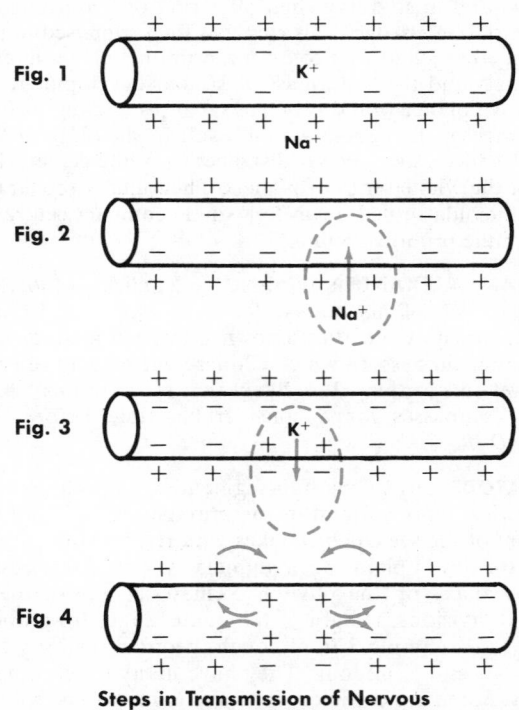

Steps in Transmission of Nervous Impulse Through Nerve Fiber

stimulated, its properties change, so that Na⁺ can rush in (Fig. 2). This results in a momentary reversal of potential in the stimulated region, and K⁺ is thus drawn out, so that the potential is restored to its former level (Fig. 3). Meanwhile there is a flow of current between adjacent unexcited regions of the membrane surface and the stimulated region (Fig. 4). This flow of current stimulates the adjacent region, and the action potential is thus propagated along the surface of the fiber in both directions away from the initial point of stimulation. See NERVOUS SYSTEM; NEURON.—*B. T. S.*

NERVOUS SYSTEM: a complex structure of nervous tissue found in all except one-celled animals. By their senses, animals detect conditions of their internal and external environment. The primary function of the nervous system is to transmit this information to other parts of the organism, to integrate information from various sensory sources, and, when appropriate, to initiate muscular movements or glandular secretions. The basic unit of the system is a special type of cell called a neuron. By virtue of its irritability, a neuron is able to conduct a NERVOUS IMPULSE. For example, stimulation of a sensory cell (receptor) may cause a nervous impulse to be transmitted by a neuron to a muscle cell (effector), inducing contraction.

Evolution: In very elementary life forms, simple functional units such as that described above are sufficient. A noxious stimulus may act by means of a receptor and neuron to cause a muscle-cell contraction, removing the organism from a potential source of danger. As we proceed up the evolutionary scale, however, sensory and motor systems of organisms become more complex, and their original relationships are modified. Additional neurons are interposed between receptors and effectors. Cell bodies of some of these interpolated neurons cluster together in various parts of the animal, forming groups of cells called ganglia. Neurons themselves bundle together forming nerves, each nerve containing hundreds or thousands of neurons. Information from receptors in adjacent areas of the body is transmitted to ganglia, which in turn may relay nervous impulses to groups of muscle cells. Ganglia come to serve as primitive decision-making mechanisms: more than one sensory input may be required before a nervous impulse is relayed to an effector.

Further modification of ganglia permits coordination of the contractions of large numbers of muscle cells, exemplified by movements of the common earthworm. This animal embodies the prototype of a true nervous system. Nerves, containing neurons from receptors in the skin and gut, enter ganglia distributed along the entire length of the animal. From the ganglia, nerves lead both to muscles and to other ganglia. As first one muscle group, then another, receives nervous impulses, a wave of motion sweeps the length of the body. Of interest in the earthworm is a ganglion somewhat larger than the others, called the cerebral ganglion, or "brain," located in the foremost segment of the animal. Although of limited functional value in the earthworm, it is the first step in the evolution of a true brain.

In more advanced animal species the brain comes to play a greater and greater role in the coordination of sensory information and motor (muscular) behavior. The spinal cord develops, enclosed in the bony structure of the backbone, and functions as a vast communications channel, along which nervous impulses are relayed to and from the brain. Nerves from receptors lead to special centers in the brain, each center concerned with a special type of sensory input, *e.g.* vision or hearing. The sizes of these centers are largely related to the importance of the particular sensory systems which they serve. In fish, which depend a great deal on their sense of

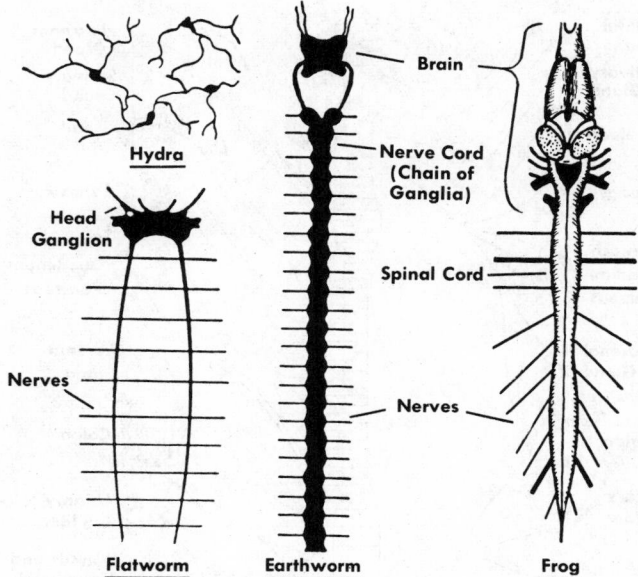

Increasing organization of nerve pathways makes possible increasingly complex modes of behavior. In nerve network of *Hydra*, impulse can travel only between neighboring neurons. Behavior is limited to local contraction. But flatworm, unlike radial *Hydra*, has head and tail. Nerve network feeds into central nerve cords which connect at ganglion, permitting a choice of reactions and some coordination of movements. Earthworm and frog represent further refinements: nerves are more specialized as to function, the number of ganglia increases, and there is greater centralization. *(From Carlson)*

smell for locating food, the olfactory pathways and centers of the brain occupy a correspondingly large part of total brain volume. Other parts of the brain develop which integrate and direct complex muscular activity and regulate operation of the animal's internal organs and glands.

Human Nervous System: The human nervous system caps millions of years of evolutionary development. Anatomically it consists of two parts: the central nervous system, composed of the brain and spinal cord, and the peripheral nervous system, comprising those parts external to brain and spinal cord. Sensory input travels via the peripheral nervous system to the brain, either directly or by way of the spinal cord. From the brain, nervous impulses in turn are relayed to muscles, glands, and organs of the body by means of the peripheral nervous system. Functionally, it is convenient to consider a third grouping, the autonomic nervous system, a classification based primarily on activities in which it is engaged rather than on its location in the body. The autonomic system is composed of parts of both central and peripheral portions of the nervous system.

Elements of the central nervous system are discussed elsewhere (see BRAIN; SPINAL CORD). The peripheral nervous system consists of 12 pairs of cranial nerves, which enter the brain directly, and 31 pairs of spinal nerves, which enter the spinal cord before their neurons proceed to the brain. In general, one member of each pair of nerves is associated with one side of the body. As it enters the spinal cord, each spinal nerve splits into two parts. One part contains sensory neurons leading toward the brain; the other contains neurons leading toward muscles, glands, or internal organs. Cranial nerves differ from spinal nerves in that some carry sensory neurons only, some carry only motor neurons, and some contain both types of neurons.

The autonomic nervous system is concerned with internal functionings of the body. It consists of numerous ganglia

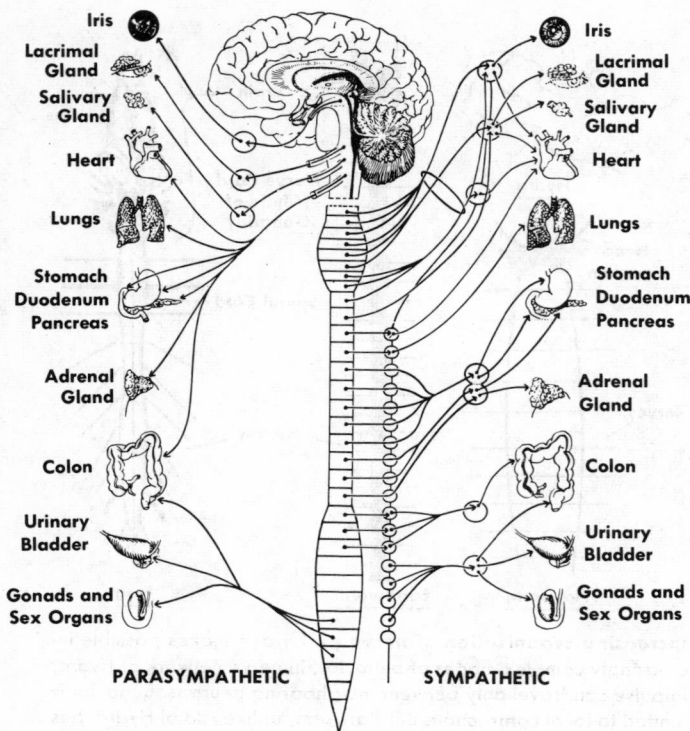

Organs innervated by autonomic nervous system: Circles represent ganglia, from which nerves lead to organs. (*From Whaley*)

found paralleling the spinal cord and in other parts of the body (*e.g.* the solar plexus in the abdomen, certain centers within the central nervous system) and of nerves which lead to intestines, bladder, heart, and other internal organs and glands. The autonomic system itself is divided into two parts: the sympathetic and the parasympathetic systems. The sympathetic system generally serves to prepare the body for, or sustain it during, increased activity. It accelerates heartbeat, promotes secretion of adrenalin, diverts blood from intestines and stomach to brain and muscles, etc. The parasympathetic system produces quite opposite effects by slowing heartbeat, relaxing intestinal muscles, and so on. Thus the two systems act as checks on one another, expending or conserving resources of the body as conditions demand.—*D. M. F.*

NEST: a place or structure used by animals for shelter, hibernation, raising of young, or laying and hatching of eggs. Nests vary from a hollow scooped out of the ground to elaborate structures. Nests of reptiles generally consist of no more than a hole in which eggs are buried. More skillful nest builders include harvest mice, squirrels, and rabbits among mammals; certain frogs among amphibians; the sticklebacks among fishes; and ants, bees, and wasps among insects.

Nest building is particularly common among BIRDS. Each kind of bird builds a nest typical for its species, and the process is instinctive, not learned; this has been proved experimentally with weaver finches. Birds nest in holes in the ground, in caves, on the ground, in low vegetation, in tree trunks, high in trees, on roofs, in chimneys, on cliffs; some build floating nests on water. Normally the nest is used just to hold the eggs during INCUBATION and the young until they can run about or fly; only by a few kinds of hole-nesters is it used as a year-round sleeping place. Certain species, notably many kinds of wrens, build special sleeping nests, but most birds sleep in the open. The whippoorwill and others make no nest but simply lay their eggs on the ground. Of birds that raise more than one family in a year, most build a new nest for each family; but some regularly, and others rarely, re-use a nest in the same season. Small, exposed nests usually fall

apart over winter. Occasionally a nest that survives is used again; the huge nests of ospreys and eagles are commonly used for many years. There are species that use an abandoned nest of a different species. The starling and certain other birds —regularly or occasionally, depending on species—drive other species from their nests and then use the nests.—*H. Br.*

NEURAMINIC ACID: a 9-carbon sugar and a constituent of the mucins of saliva. It is formed by aldol condensation of pyruvic acid and glucosamine. The nitrogen acetylated form, called sialic acid, is found in glycoproteins and mucins.—*J. F. S.*

NEURON: a special cell constituting the basic unit of the NERVOUS SYSTEM. Extending from the surface of the *cell body*, containing the nucleus, are two or more processes. The *axon*, from several micra to several feet in length, is larger than the remaining short *dendrites*. Nervous impulses, initiated at a dendrite or cell body, are propagated along the axon.— *D. M. F.*

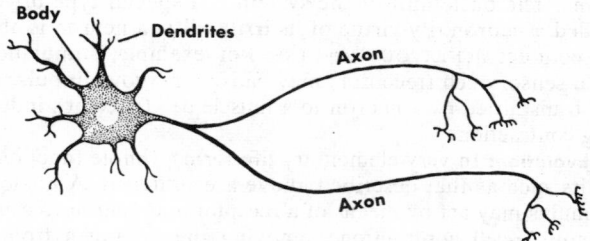

Neuron acts simply, like a single switch-element in a computer. Coordinated actions of multitudes of neurons result in activities ranging from lifting finger to painting picture. (*After Young*)

NEUTRALIZATION: the reaction of an ACID and a BASE to form a salt and water; after neutralization the characteristic properties of both acid and base are destroyed. The reaction of a strong or fully ionized acid with a strong base can be represented as follows, with M^+ denoting any positive (metal) ion other than hydrogen (H^+), and A^- representing any negative (nonmetal) ion other than the hydroxide (OH^-):

$$\underset{\text{Base}}{\underline{M^+ + OH^-}} + \underset{\text{Acid}}{\underline{H^+ + A^-}} = \underset{\text{Salt}}{\underline{M^+ + A^-}} + \underset{\text{Water}}{\underline{H_2O}}$$

A typical "strong" neutralization reaction is that of potassium hydroxide (KOH) with hydrobromic acid (HBr) to form potassium bromide (KBr) and water. Interestingly, all neutralizations involving any strong acid and any strong base evolve identical amounts of heat, indicating that the union between H^+ and OH^- ions to form water is the entirely dominant reaction. However, reactions between weak or slightly ionized bases and strong acids (or between weak acids and strong bases) evolve varying amounts of heat, indicating that not only are H^+ ions uniting with OH^- ions but also an additional reaction is proceeding between water and the salt ions, with the salt being dissociated into ions to a greater or less extent depending on the acid and base used. A typical weak base-strong acid neutralization occurs between silver hydroxide and hydrochloric acid, which react to form slightly dissociated silver chloride and water. Acid and base concentrations or their equivalent weights can be determined by neutralization.—*G. W. M.*

NEUTRINO (from Italian, "small neutral one"): a particle emitted from a radioactive nucleus when an electron is emitted from or captured by the nucleus. Its existence was suggested in 1931 by Wolfgang Pauli to account for otherwise unexplainable energy and momentum losses in beta decay (see

RADIOACTIVITY). Its role in beta decay was elaborated by Enrico Fermi in 1934. The neutrino is believed to have no measurable mass when at rest, no electric charge, and negligible magnetic properties, and to interact with matter only in the reverse of the process by which it is produced. For more than 20 yr, all attempts to detect any such interaction failed to give conclusive evidence, but in 1955 F. Reines and C. L. Cowan, and others, succeeded in demonstrating the predicted occurrence of the reverse process (neutrino capture).—*G. T. S.*

More recently L. Lederman, M. Schwartz, and R. J. Steinberger, using high-energy neutrinos (ν) from the decay of fast pions into muons (μ), have detected interactions of the kind $\nu + p \to \mu + n$, but have not observed the process $\nu + p \to e + n$. If the neutrinos associated with electrons are identical with those associated with muons, then the two reactions should occur equally often, so the absence of the second interaction indicates there are two distinct kinds of neutrinos.—*D. C. C.*

NEUTRON: a neutral uncharged particle of atomic weight approximately unity (precisely 1.00898 on the scale where $O^{16} = 16.0000$). Closely packed neutrons and protons (*i.e.* nucleons) compose the nuclei of all atoms. The neutron is slightly heavier than the proton; in the free state it decays, yielding a proton, with a half life of about 12 min. It has some magnetic properties.

The neutron was discovered in 1932 by the English physicist James Chadwick as a product of the bombardment of beryllium nuclei with alpha particles (helium ions) from the natural radioactive element polonium; Chadwick's definitive experiments followed some initial, incompletely interpreted observations of the German physicists W. Bothe and H. Becker and the French scientists Frédéric and Irène Joliot-Curie. Neutrons have been produced subsequently in many artificially induced nuclear reactions; these are now more important sources.

After a number of collisions with nuclei, a *fast* neutron has its speed reduced to such an extent that it has approximately the same average kinetic energy as the atoms of the medium in which it is undergoing such nuclear collisions; such neutrons are known as *thermal* or *slow* neutrons. Thermal neutrons are readily captured by nuclei because of their slow speed and absence of electrical charge. Both fast and slow neutrons are very important as projectiles in fundamental nuclear investigations. (See PARTICLE ACCELERATORS.)

Neutrons have an especially important application in the nuclear fission of heavy elements such as uranium and plutonium. The energy released may be utilized in a controlled manner in chain reactors (piles) for nuclear (atomic) power production or in nuclear weapons (atomic bombs). Reactors are also important sources of neutrons and of fissionable material (*e.g.* plutonium). See ATOM; FISSION, NUCLEAR; NUCLEAR REACTOR.—*G. T. S.*

NEUTRON DIFFRACTION: the bending of the path of a neutron when it goes through an opening comparable in size to its wavelength or passes near an obstacle (see QUANTUM MECHANICS; DIFFRACTION). Neutron diffraction can be observed when a beam of neutrons is shot at a crystal that consists of a regular array of atoms (or obstacles) with spacing comparable to the wavelength of the neutrons. Because the neutron has a magnetic moment (and therefore an additional interaction with atoms having a magnetic moment), neutron diffraction has been particularly useful for determining the location of such atoms within a crystal.—*E. M. C.*

NEWCOMB, SIMON, 1835–1909, U. S. astronomer; b. Wallace, Nova Scotia, Canada. Professor of mathematics and astronomy (1884–93) at Johns Hopkins Univ., and director (1877–97) of the U. S. Nautical Almanac Office, he promoted (1896) the adoption of standard astronomical constants and of basic stars in the calculation of ephemerides. His studies of motions of Earth and other planets resulted in publication (1895–99) of extensive tables for the calculation of ephemerides of these bodies. Author of numerous scientific papers and books, he is best known for his *Popular Astronomy* (1878). He was a fellow of the Royal Society and a member of the National Academy of Sciences.—*R. N. M.*

NEW EXPERIMENTS PHYSICO-MECHANICAL TOUCHING THE SPRING OF THE AIR AND ITS EFFECTS, by Robert Boyle, 1660: After Gilbert's *De magnete*, Boyle's is the first great treatise devoted to experimental physics. Modern pneumatics began with Torricelli's invention of the mercury barometer; following the earlier efforts of Otto von Guericke, Boyle had the first laboratory air pump made, performing with it many experiments, exploring both the elastic properties of the air and the physical characteristics of near-vacua. While their most famous result is BOYLE'S LAW of gases (if the temperature of a gas remains constant, the product of the pressure exerted by the gas and its volume is constant, or $pv = k$), Boyle's experiments were no less important in justifying mechanistic forms of explanation in science.—*A. R. H.*

NEW SYSTEM OF CHEMICAL PHILOSOPHY, by John Dalton, Part I, 1808; Part II, 1810; vol. II, 1827: The 17-cent. atomistic idea of matter had remained largely speculative, being almost unrelated to definite experiments and mathematical theory. Lavoisier's chemical revolution (*c.* 1780–90) avoided such speculation, turning instead to the pragmatic idea of element, and to the determination of chemical composition by measurement of the weights of the elements involved. It was Dalton's genius to combine these two strands of thought, and so introduce the modern form of atomic theory into chemistry. Dalton, beginning with a consideration of the mixture of gases in the atmosphere, reasoned thus: assuming that (1) each element is composed of identical atoms, with a characteristic weight; and (2) atoms of different elements combine in simple ways (1 and 1, 1 and 2, etc.), then from the experimentally known, definite proportions of the elements *by weight*, required to form a compound, the relative weights of the atoms can be found. Multiple compounds (*e.g.* the oxides of nitrogen) were explained as multiple combinations of atoms. Thus the atomic structure of all substances could be gradually worked out. Despite the reluctance of many chemists to believe in the reality of atoms, Dalton's ideas greatly promoted chemical theory, and represent the first step toward a quantitative knowledge of the structure of matter.—*A. R. H.*

NEWTON, SIR ISAAC, 1642–1727, English mathematician; b. Woolsthorpe. He is generally considered the greatest mathematician the world has yet produced. Born prematurely, after his father's death, he was a frail and sickly child, but his interest and ability in experimentation while still quite young were unusual. At Trinity College, Cambridge, he studied mathematics under the brilliant and original Isaac Barrow. Barrow's lectures on methods of drawing tangents and finding areas inspired Newton to his own attack on these

Sir Isaac Newton
(N. Y. Public Library)

problems, which led in turn to the invention of differential and integral calculus. After taking his degree in 1664, Newton returned to his native village, where he pursued his researches independently until 1667.

Early in this period he discovered the BINOMIAL THEOREM, which provides this formula for raising a binomial to a power:

$$(a + b)^n = a^n + \frac{n}{1} a^{n-1}b + \frac{n(n-1)}{1 \cdot 2} a^{n-2}b^2 + \cdots$$

The expression terminates if n is a positive integer, and the formula can easily be proved by mathematical induction. If n is not a positive integer, the expansion yields an infinite series. The theorem then has meaning only if the series converges, which happens for some values of a and b but not for all. The determination of the values of a and b for which the theorem is valid did not come until the 19th cent., but Newton was sure of the theorem's correctness for values he required.

During these early years, Newton also developed his theory of fluxions (differential calculus), which he communicated to Barrow in 1669, although the theory was not published until 1704. By its methods he found the rate of change of one quantity relative to another, and made exact determinations of tangents to curves. He also developed the principles of the integral calculus, which he used for determining the areas of curves, and discovered the reciprocal relation between these problems, whereby integrals are calculated by inverting the process of differentiation. Other great achievements during this period were his observation of the decomposition of light into colors upon refraction by a prism, his construction of a corpuscular theory of light, and a tentative formulation of the law of gravitation.

Newton returned to Cambridge as a fellow of Trinity College (1667) and succeeded Barrow as Lucasian professor of mathematics (1669). In 1668 he constructed a reflecting telescope with which he observed the moons of Jupiter. In 1684, encouraged by Halley, he started to prepare his astronomical and dynamical discoveries for publication. During the following 2 yr he worked continuously, with little thought for his health and comfort, and completed his *Principia Mathematica,* one of the greatest works of all time. From physical laws, he deduced the "system of the world." His law of gravitation was the great principle which unified and explained the facts of the universe. The Newtonian system has been one of the most powerful influences in scientific and philosophical thinking ever since publication of this work in 1687. Newton was slow to publish his researches, probably because of his distaste for the controversies that frequently ensued, *e.g.* the controversy (*c.* 1705) with Leibniz over priority in the discovery of calculus. During the last 35 yr of his life he did not engage seriously in scientific work, but held a variety of government posts. A fellow of the Royal Society from 1671, he served as its president from 1703 until his death. See also articles on CALCULUS; BINOMIAL THEOREM; GRAVITATION; TELESCOPE.—*H. C.*

NEWTON'S LAWS OF MOTION: three natural laws on which mechanics, as a branch of physics and engineering, is based. Although Galileo laid the qualitative foundations for these laws, Sir Isaac Newton in 1686 was the first to state them clearly in mathematical terms. Newton's *first law* of motion is: "Every body persists in its state of rest or of uniform motion in a straight line unless it is compelled to change that state by forces impressed upon it." Force here is simply a push or a pull. It acts on a mass that resists a change in motion. This resistance is called *inertia.* The first law is often simplified to read: A body at rest tends to remain at rest; a body in motion tends to continue in motion.

Newton's *second law* involves acceleration and was expressed by him as follows: "The change in motion is proportional to the motive power impressed and is made in the direction of the straight line in which the force is impressed." Newton's term "motion" meant mass × velocity, and is today called *momentum.* What Newton said was that a force acting on a body is equal to the rate of change of momentum. Thus, force equals rate of change of (mass × velocity). But since the mass is constant and cannot change, force equals mass × (rate of change of velocity). The rate of change of velocity is called acceleration, and so we have the familiar law $F = ma$.

Newton stated his *third law* as follows: "To every action there is always an opposed and equal reaction, or the initial action of two bodies upon each other are always equal and directed to contrary parts." This is often simplified to read: Every action has an equal and opposite reaction.

Many modern physicists consider Newton's three laws as three different cases of one law of motion. All involve the equation $F = ma$. In the first law, if there is no force (F), there is no acceleration (a), and the system remains at rest or in the same kind of motion. In the second law, acceleration is constant if force is constant. If mass is increased, and the same force is applied, the acceleration is smaller. If force increases, acceleration increases. In the third law, we can think of the acceleration and reaction as common momentum. Rockets are a good example of the law of action and reaction. The rocket moves forward in reaction to the rearward action of the exhaust gases. Actually the product of the velocity and mass of the exhaust is one momentum, which is equal to the other momentum (the mass of the rocket multiplied by the rocket velocity). Thus, $m_1v_1 = m_2 v_2$.

Newton's laws, which underlie all of classical physics, have proved adequate for explaining all forces and motions on a terrestrial scale. The refinements introduced by the theory of RELATIVITY have extended the applicability of Newton's laws to all phenomena thus far encountered on both macroscopic and microscopic scales.—*A. J.*

NICHOLSON, SETH BARNES, 1891–1963, U. S. astronomer; b. Springfield, Ill. Of the 12 satellites of Jupiter now known, four were discovered by Nicholson: one in 1914, two in 1938, one in 1951. With E. Pettit he made a long series of pioneering observations of the total radiant energy from the Moon, planets, and stars, using a vacuum thermocouple. Measurement of the Moon's rate of cooling during an eclipse led him to infer the existence on its surface of a dust layer. From a study of the effect of Pluto's gravitational attraction for Neptune (with N. U. Mayall, 1931) he made a first determination of Pluto's mass. An authority on the surface activity of the Sun, he was on the staff of the Mt Wilson Observatory, 1915–57, and was a member of the National Academy of Sciences. —*G. R.*

NICKEL: a metallic element (Ni) belonging to the iron-cobalt family (group VIII) of the periodic table; at. no. 28; at. wt 58.71; density 8.90 (20°C); mp 1445°C; bp 2900°C; valences 2 and 3. Like iron and cobalt, nickel is magnetic and forms colored salts and complex ions; also the melting and boiling points of the three elements, as well as their densities, are very close. Nickel is distinguished, however, by its excellent corrosion resistance and by its ability to form a remarkable number of useful ferrous and nonferrous alloys. Pure or nearly pure nickel is silvery white and will retain a high polish. The element was first isolated in 1751 by Axel Cronstedt from the mineral niccolite. Ranking 9th among metals in world consumption, nickel is found associated with several other metals (*e.g.* iron, cobalt, copper, gold, silver, magnesium, manganese, and the platinum metals) in various sulfide, silicate, and arsenide ores. The largest known deposit, in the Sudbury region of Ontario, Can., consists of mineral sulfide ores such as pentlandite and pyrrhotite. Important deposits of silicate (oxide) nickel ores are found in New Caledonia, the chief mineral there being garnierite. The metallurgical operations required to extract nickel from its ores are varied and complex, involving many steps such as roasting, smelting, crushing, and bessemerizing. Pure (and nearly pure) nickel is obtained by electrolysis or by the Mond process. In the latter, carbon monoxide acts on impure nickel, causing the formation of nickel carbonyl gas (Ni (CO)$_4$); on heating to 200°C this gas decomposes into carbon monoxide, which is recirculated, and pure nickel, which is recovered. Nickel plating protects iron and other metals from corrosion, but is now largely used as an underplate preparatory to chromium plating. Dry, finely divided nickel is used as a catalyst in the HYDROGENATION of liquid fats (oils) to form solid fats such as oleomargarine and vegetable shortening; about 1 lb of nickel catalyst is required to produce 3,000 lb of oils.

Nickel Alloys: Among the important nonferrous nickel alloys are the white, corrosion-resistant *nickel brasses* (copper, zinc, and nickel, and sometimes small amounts of silicon and other elements), used in hardware and imitation silver; the *nickel bronzes* (copper, tin, nickel, and sometimes zinc, lead, and other elements), utilized for gears, castings, bearings, hardware, and plumbing fixtures; *nickel-chromium* alloys (often containing large percentages of iron and small percentages of other elements), valued for heat- and corrosion-resistant materials and for electrical resistance wires; *nickel-cobalt* alloys, used to electroplate ferrous and nonferrous metals to protect them against corrosion; *nickel copper*, employed in the production of other nickel alloys; and *nickel silver* (copper, nickel, zinc, and sometimes small amounts of other elements including silver), used for dinnerware, resistance wire, plumbing fixtures, and dairy equipment. *Monel metal*, originally produced during the smelting of Sudbury nickel ores but now made principally by alloying techniques, is predominantly nickel (approx. 70%) with copper (approx. 25%) and small amounts of manganese, iron, and silicon. It can be hot-worked or cold-worked with good results, is acid- and corrosion- resistant, and is used for marine, chemical,

and mining equipment, restaurant and kitchen appliances, and valves. The U. S. "nickel" 5-cent piece (normally 25% nickel, 75% copper) is a nickel alloy, as are many other coins. Ferrous nickel alloys include *nickel steel* (usually 1.5 to 5% nickel, less than 1% carbon, sometimes trace percentages of silicon, manganese, and other elements, and the balance iron); this alloy, to which nickel imparts strength, toughness, hardness, and increased elasticity, is used for heavy-duty parts in automobiles, locomotives, and other machines, as well as for armor plating and ordnance. *Nickel-chromium steel* (stainless steel) is characterized by its exceptional resistance to corrosion as well as its hardness and toughness. Various *nickel irons* are also produced, with a wide range of useful properties including excellent acid resistance, heat resistance, and wear resistance.—*E. H. H.*

NICOL PRISM: an optical device for producing POLARIZED LIGHT. The action of the Nicol prism is based upon the phenomenon of birefringence, or double refraction. A parallel beam of unpolarized light directed through a birefringent crystal of, for example, calcite will be split into two beams of light linearly polarized in mutually perpendicular directions. In the Nicol prism (see below), a crystal of calcite is cut diagonally, then cemented back together with Canada balsam, which has a lower index of refraction than the cal-

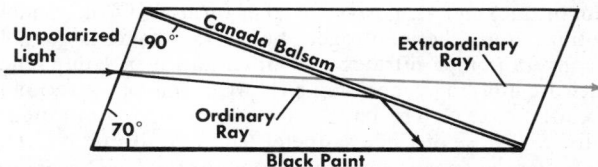

Nicol prism is made from two pieces of calcite cemented together with Canada balsam. The ordinary ray is reflected at the interface between the calcite and the balsam, and is absorbed by the blackened lower surface of prism.

cite. A beam of unpolarized light entering at the left will be split into an upper and a lower beam, both polarized. The lower beam is reflected to the side of the prism, where it is absorbed by a layer of black paint. The upper beam, striking the calcite-balsam interface at a more direct angle, is transmitted out through the end of the prism. Several other forms of polarizing prisms have also been devised to suit particular requirements, but these prisms have now been largely replaced by Polaroid.—*D. H. L.*

NIÉPCE, JOSEPH NICÉPHORE, 1765–1833, French inventor; b. Châlon-sur-Saône. The first person to make photographs, he invented heliography (*c.* 1813), in which pewter plates covered with light-sensitive varnishes of various sorts were exposed to sunlight through a transparent engraving. With a camera (1816) he produced negative pictures on paper sensitized with silver chloride, and he partially fixed them with nitric acid. After shifting from silver chloride to bitumen dissolved in white petroleum, he obtained permanent pictures (1826), one of which still exists. (Practical photography was produced by L. J. M. DAGUERRE, onetime partner of Niépce.) Niépce and his brother Claude also invented an internal-combustion engine using petroleum as fuel, the "Pyreolophore" (1807), and used it to propel boats and barges.—*D. H. D. R.*

NIGGLI, PAUL, 1888–1953, Swiss geologist; b. Zofingen. He did research in crystallography, mineralogy, and petrography. His method of recalculating chemical analyses in "Niggli values," his system of molecular norms, and his graphical methods for comparing the chemical characters of rocks all influenced petrography.—*D. H. D. R.*

NIGHT: see DAY AND NIGHT.

NIOBIUM (columbium): a rare metallic element (Nb, Cb); at. no. 41; at. wt 92.91; density 8.4; mp 2400°C; bp 3700°C; valence 3 or 5. Until 1949, when the International Union of Pure and Applied Chemistry standardized the name niobium, the metal was officially called columbium in some countries and niobium in others. The English chemist Charles Hatchett (1801) announced the discovery of a new element "columbium" in the mineral he named columbite; Hatchett cautioned that his "columbium" might turn out to be a mixture or a compound rather than a true element, but could not prove it with the analytical methods at his disposal. In 1844, the German mineralogist and pharmacist Heinrich Rose showed that columbite contains both niobium and TANTALUM. When added to austenitic stainless steel, niobium increases corrosion resistance; it is added to certain chromium steels to reduce creep, improve impact resistance, and inhibit oxidation. It is also used as a plate and grid metal in vacuum tubes (for absorbing gases). Niobium carbide (NbC) is used for making cutting tools.—*I. B.*

NITRATE: a chemical compound containing the nitrate $(NO_3)^-$ radical. Nitrates are essential to plant and animal life and have broad industrial significance as FERTILIZERS (*e.g.* ammonium nitrate) and EXPLOSIVES. Higher forms of life are unable to utilize atmospheric nitrogen; but certain bacteria are able to convert it into nitrates and other nitrogen compounds which are utilized by more complex organisms (see NITROGEN; NITROGEN CYCLE). The large, naturally occurring nitrate deposits, *e.g.* those of Chile saltpeter (sodium nitrate, $NaNO_3$) and soda niter or saltpeter (potassium nitrate, KNO_3), are believed to have been produced by bacteria working on atmospheric nitrogen.

All known nitrates are soluble, the most soluble being silver nitrate ($AgNO_3$); even lead, which tends to form insoluble compounds with inorganic acids, is soluble in nitrate form. Monovalent metals form anhydrous nitrates; divalent metal nitrates add water of crystallization. On heating, nitrates give up oxygen and tend to be flammable, often explosive. The inorganic compound ammonium nitrate, for instance, is a powerful explosive when mixed with oil or other fuel. Nitroglycerine, more aptly called glyceryl trinitrate, $CH_2NO_3CHNO_3CH_2NO_3$, is a prime example of an explosive organic nitrate.—*D. P. B.*

NITRATE METABOLISM: the various biochemical processes involved in the synthesis, use, and degradation of nitrogen compounds by living organisms (see AMINO ACIDS; PROTEIN). Most plants and microorganisms utilize nitrates from the soil as a dietary source of nitrogen. Nitrate is reduced enzymatically through the stages of nitrite and hydroxylamine to ammonia, with reduced coenzymes as hydrogen carriers. The ammonia is then used to build amino acids and other nitrogen-containing molecules. See also METABOLISM; NITROGEN FIXATION.—*J. F. S.*

NITRIC ACID: a colorless to yellow corrosive liquid (HNO_3); sp gr 1.503; bp 86°C; mp −41.65°C. It is sold in various grades: white fuming nitric acid (WFNA) contains more than 97.5% nitric acid; red fuming nitric acid (RFNA) contains more than 86%. It can be prepared by the catalytic oxidation of ammonia (to form nitrogen oxides) followed by absorption in water; or by treating a NITRATE with sulfuric acid (H_2SO_4). It attacks most metals with the exception of platinum, rhodium, iridium, and gold, converting them into nitrates or oxides. On contact with skin, nitric acid causes severe burns;

inhalation of its fumes can cause nitrous gas poisoning. It is, in addition, a potent oxidizing agent and will ignite spontaneously with many oxidizable materials.—*D. P. B.*

NITRILE: in organic chemistry, an alternative name for a CYANIDE. Thus methyl cyanide (CH_3—CN) is named as a derivative of hydrocyanic acid, HCN, but can also be called *acetonitrile,* because it hydrolyzes to acetic acid:

$$CH_3-CN \ + \ 2H_2O \longrightarrow CH_3-\underset{\underset{OH}{|}}{C}=O \ + \ NH_3$$

Similarly, all nitriles are named on the basis of the acids to which they hydrolyze. An isocyanide, *e.g.* methyl isocyanide, CH_3—NC, is an *isonitrile.* Hydrolysis breaks the NC linkage and gives the amine CH_3—NH_2. Nitriles are used industrially both as solvents and as raw materials for commercial polymers: acetonitrile and benzonitrile (C_6H_5CN) are solvents; acrylonitrile (CH_2=CHCN) is a raw material for certain synthetic rubbers and textiles.—*Ru. M.*

NITROCELLULOSE: see NITRATE.

NITRO COMPOUND: an organic compound containing the nitro radical $(NO_2)^-$ attached to a carbon atom through a linkage with the nitrogen atom. Nitro compounds can be expressed by the general formula RNO_2, where R is either aliphatic, as in the nitroparaffins, or aromatic, as in nitrobenzene or trinitrotoluene (TNT). Nitrobenzene, a liquid, is widely used as a solvent for organic compounds. It was formerly used as a flavoring agent ("artificial oil of bitter almonds") but, like many aromatic nitro compounds, was found to be toxic; its use has therefore been avoided in applications that could lead to harmful physiological reactions. Several aromatic nitro compounds, like TNT, find use as explosives; and various derivatives of the aromatic nitros are used in the making of pharmaceuticals, photographic chemicals, and rubber. (For description and uses of the aliphatic nitro compounds, see NITROPARAFFIN.) Both the aliphatic and the aromatic nitro compounds differ from *nitrites,* in which the linkage with the carbon atom is through the oxygen atom; nitrites are thus represented by the general formula RONO. Compounds of the general formula $RONO_2$ are sometimes called nitro compounds, but more properly should be called nitrates; *i.e.* nitroglycerin and nitrocellulose should be called glyceryl tri*nitrate* and cellulose *nitrate* respectively. The outstanding chemical characteristic of nitro compounds is their susceptibility to reduction. Many reduction intermediates are possible, with use of a strong oxidizing agent causing complete reduction to the primary amine (RN_2). Physically, most nitro compounds are heavier than water; most aromatic nitros are at most only sparingly soluble in water.—*D. P. B.*

NITROGEN: the gaseous element (N) which makes up 78% of air by volume; at. no. 7; at. wt 14.008; density 1.2506 g/1; mp −209.86°C; bp −195.8°C. The Scottish scientist Daniel Rutherford discovered nitrogen in 1772. K. Scheele showed that this gas is present in the atmosphere, and A. Lavoisier first identified it as an element. Although it is the major constituent of the atmosphere, where it occurs as the diatomic molecule N_2, nitrogen is only the 17th most abundant element in Earth's crust, where it is found in mineral compounds such as saltpeter (KNO_3) and soda niter, or Chile saltpeter ($NaNO_3$). Compounds of nitrogen are essential constituents of all living organisms, the proteins and nucleic acids in particular being basic building blocks of all life forms. Nitrogen forms a series of oxides and oxyacids, the most important of which is nitric acid, HNO_3. It also unites with hydrogen to form ammonia, NH_3, and with many of the metallic elements to form nitrides. The organic compounds of nitrogen, however, are more numerous and variegated than the inorganic ones. They include the amines or substituted ammonias; the nitro series, to which many explosives belong; the amides, e.g. nylon; and the azo dyestuffs, as well as a wide variety of other chemical species.

Although nitrogen compounds are generally quite reactive, gaseous elemental nitrogen is relatively inert, and cannot be directly utilized for nourishment by higher plants. It is fixed (converted into compounds useful to plants) in nature in two ways: (1) certain bacteria that inhabit nodules on the roots of leguminous vegetables convert atmospheric nitrogen to nitrates; (2) lightning discharges can also cause nitrogen to unite with oxygen, the resulting oxides being washed to earth by the rain in the form of nitrates and nitrites. Nitrogen can be fixed artificially by several methods, of which the most important is the *Haber process*. In this reaction nitrogen is combined with hydrogen at high temperatures and pressures to form ammonia. Very large tonnages of ammonia are produced annually, much of it being used directly or indirectly for FERTILIZER (see AMMONIA for other uses of this nitrogen compound; also see AMIDES; AMINES; DYES AND DYEING; NITRATE; NITRO COMPOUND; NITROPARAFFIN).—*A. M. S.*

NITROGEN BALANCE: the nitrogen equilibrium observed in healthy mature animals and humans. For example, during a 24-hr period the nitrogen excreted in urine, feces, and perspiration, plus that retained in new dermal outgrowths, e.g. skin and hair, is just equal to the nitrogen consumed in food and drink. See PROTEIN METABOLISM.—*E. M.*

NITROGEN COMPOUNDS (organic): compounds in which carbon is linked to nitrogen in a C—N bond. The compounds fall into easily recognized classes. AMINES are regarded as ammonia, NH_3, in which H atoms are replaced by alkyl or aryl radicals. A typical compound is methylamine, $H_3C—NH_2$. Amines are primary, secondary, or tertiary, depending on the number of H atoms in ammonia replaced by radicals; e.g. dimethylamine, $(CH_3)_2NH$, is a secondary amine. AMIDES are similarly considered to be ammonia in which H atoms are replaced by acyl radicals. An example is acetamide, $CH_3C—NH_2$. Cyanides (and isocyanides) contain the cyanide
$$\parallel$$
$$O$$
radical (CN) linked with alkyl or aryl radicals. Typical compounds are methyl cyanide, $H_3C—CN$, and methyl isocyanide, $H_3C—NC$. Such organic cyanides are often called NITRILES. NITRO COMPOUNDS are those in which a nitro group, NO_2, is directly linked to carbon, e.g. the aliphatic compound nitromethane, $H_3C—NO_2$ (which is a NITROPARAFFIN), and the aromatic compound nitrobenzene, $H_5C_6—NO_2$. Ring compounds with N atoms included in the ring are highly important. A few examples are:

Pyrrole   Pyridine   Purine

Nitrogen compounds play a very important role in living nature. Amino acids—e.g. the simplest member, aminoacetic acid (glycine), CH_2NH_2COOH—are the building blocks of proteins; the alkaloids, e.g. cocaine and morphine, are based on ring structures typified by pyrrole and pyridine; caffeine is a derivative of purine.

Nitrogen can form "onium" salts (see VALENCE), in which all its 5 valence electrons are employed. In most compounds in nature, however, the valence of nitrogen is 3, leaving an unemployed pair of electrons which can be used for dative-bond and hydrogen-bond formation, a phenomenon of great importance in life processes involving proteins and chlorophyll.—*Ru. M.*

NITROGEN CYCLE: the series of chemical changes that nitrogen from the atmosphere undergoes in its use by animals and plants. Proteins, the most distinctive of organic compounds in living things and the type serving as enzymes catalyzing all of the chemical reactions of life, differ from carbohydrates and fats in containing nitrogen. To synthesize proteins, an animal must have particular nitrogen-containing compounds

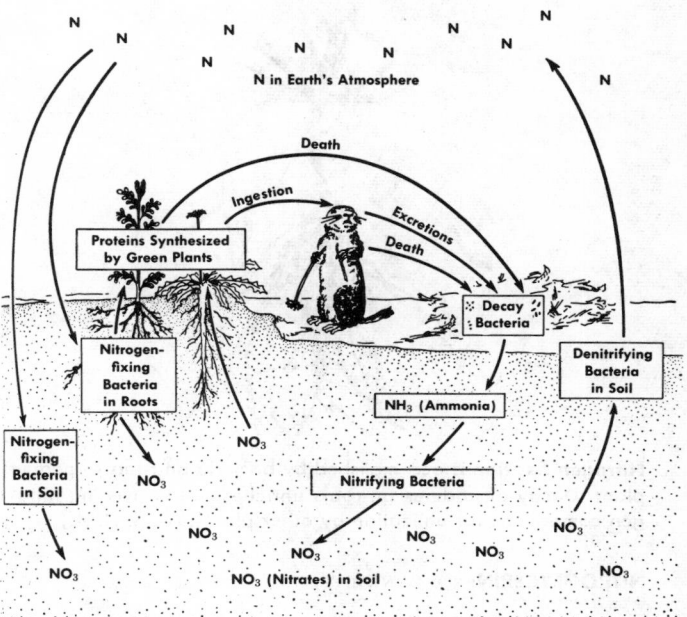

Green plants absorb nitrogen in the form of nitrates, build it into proteins, and thus pass it on to animals. Excretions of plants and animals, as well as their remains after death, are broken down into ammonia by decay bacteria, and the nitrifying bacteria of the soil oxidize the ammonia to form nitrates again. Nitrogen-fixing bacteria also take nitrogen from the air and make it into nitrates. (*After Young and Stebbins*)

(amino acids) derived directly or indirectly from plant food. To synthesize amino acids and proteins, a green plant must have nitrogen-containing compounds; it cannot use nitrogen directly from the air. Only bacteria of certain kinds are able to take nitrogen from the atmosphere and incorporate it as part of organic compounds. Some nitrogen-fixing microbes live in the soil; others are symbiotic in nodules on the roots of green vascular plants, particularly legumes (see SYMBIOSIS). Nitrogen thus follows a cycle, from atmospheric gas into nitrogen-fixing bacteria, into green vascular plants, into animals, and by decay or in excreted nitrogenous wastes (e.g. urea) back to the soil. There, denitrifying bacteria may break down nitrogenous compounds and release gaseous nitrogen. Or fire may release nitrogen from dried remains of plants and animals. Often the supply of nitrogenous compounds is a critical factor, limiting the number of plants and animals a region can support. See CARBON CYCLE; NITROGEN FIXATION; NUTRITION; PROTEIN.—*L. and M. M.*

NITROGEN FIXATION: the combination of atmospheric nitrogen gas with other substances into nitrogen-containing compounds such as ammonia and nitrite and nitrate. In nature, this is known to occur in the nitrogen-fixing soil bacteria (*azotobacter*) which convert nitrogen to ammonia. Other bacteria work symbiotically with legumes (*e.g.* alfalfa, clover, lupins, beans, peanuts) to fix nitrogen. Still other soil bacteria convert ammonia to nitrates. Nitric acid is also formed in the atmosphere during lightning discharges, and this is an important source of nitrogen. In nature, plants depend on these sources for the nitrogen they need to survive and grow. Nitrogen is fixed industrially by catalytic reduction to ammonia and by oxidation of air in an electric arc to form nitric acid. See AUTOTROPHIC ORGANISMS; NITRATE METABOLISM; NITROGEN CYCLE.—*J. F. S.*

Nitrogen fixation is accomplished by bacteria on roots of peanut plant. Decay of nodules on roots enriches soil by freeing nitrogen compounds for utilization by other plants. (*U. S. D. A.*)

NITROGLYCERIN: see DYNAMITE.

NITROPARAFFIN: an aliphatic (straight-chain) NITRO COMPOUND; *i.e.* an organic compound in which the nitro group, NO_2, is linked to carbon by a C—N bond in a PARAFFIN. Nitroparaffins are generally made by an indirect method, *e.g.*

$$CH_3CH_2Cl + AgNO_2 \longrightarrow CH_3CH_2NO_2 + AgCl$$

Chloroethane   Silver nitrite   Nitroethane   Silver chloride
(A Nitroparaffin)

Some nitroparaffins are now made commercially by direct nitration with nitric acid at temperatures above 300°C; this method gives mixtures of various lower-molecular-weight nitroparaffins. Like the aromatic nitro compounds, the nitroparaffins are good solvents, and some of them (*e.g.* a sensitized form of nitromethane, CH_3NO_2) are employed as explosives. Nitroparaffins also find use as fuels and as starting materials in a variety of chemical syntheses; on reduction, they yield a variety of useful aliphatic AMINES.—*Ru. M.*

NITROUS OXIDE: a colorless, nonflammable, sweet-tasting gas (N_2O) that liquefies at −89°C. As an anesthetic ("laughing gas") it has the virtue of taking effect quickly and permitting an equally quick recovery. It is not suitable for prolonged surgery or for surgery where profound relaxation is required, and must be administered with oxygen or air to prevent anoxia. It is prepared by gently heating ammonium nitrate. The gas is then purified, condensed, and stored in cylinders. —*D. P. B.*

NOBEL, ALFRED BERNHARD, 1833–96, Swedish inventor and philanthropist; b. Stockholm. He is best known for having established the NOBEL PRIZES. Having obtained a background in chemistry, Nobel began the manufacture and study of nitroglycerin (1864). In 1867 he patented dynamite, his most notable technological achievement; it was followed by blasting gelatin (1876) and ballistite (1889), each of which is a combination of nitroglycerin and guncotton. He also participated actively in the development of the Baku oil fields.— *D. H. D. R.*

Alfred Bernhard Nobel
(*New York Public Library*)

NOBELIUM: an artificial element (No) of the actinide group; at. no. 102; at. wt 254 (most stable isotope); the tenth transuranium element to be discovered. The element was reported discovered in 1957 by members of the Nobel Institute at Stockholm, Sweden, in collaboration with workers from Argonne (U. S. A.) National Laboratory and from the British Atomic Energy Establishment; the group in Sweden reported producing an isotope of element 102 (251 or 253) by bombardment of curium[244] with carbon ($C^{13(+4)}$) ions, and named the element nobelium after the Nobel Institute. In 1958 a group including A. Ghiorso and G. T. Seaborg at the Univ. of Calif. Radiation Laboratory produced the isotope 102[254] by bombarding curium[246] with carbon[12] ions in a heavy-ion linear accelerator. Also in 1958 a third group, in the U. S. S. R., headed by G. N. Flerov, produced an isotope of 102 by bombarding plutonium[241] and plutonium[242] with oxygen ions. Nobelium[253] has been reported to have a half-life of about 10 min.—*I. B.*

NOBEL PRIZES: a group of international awards conferred each year in the fields of physics, chemistry, physiology or medicine, literature, and peace in accordance with the will of ALFRED NOBEL, chemist and industrialist. The will stipulated that the interest on his fortune should be "annually distributed in the form of prizes for those who, during the preceding year, shall have conferred the greatest benefit on mankind." The last condition seems to indicate that Nobel was guided by a similar condition which governs the award of the Rumford Medal by the Royal Society of London. The stipulation that the award be in recognition of an achievement during the previous year has been interpreted liberally in the Statutes of the Nobel Institute, so that "the awards shall be made for the most recent achievements . . . and for older works only if their significance has not become apparent until recently." The stipend varies according to the income of the foundation; in 1961 it was roughly $48,000. The awards for physiology or medicine are made by the Caroline Medico-Chirurgical Institute in Stockholm; those for physics and for chemistry are made by the Nobel Committees of the Swedish Royal Academy of Sciences from invited nominations extended to certain scientists and previous Nobel prize winners; those for literature are made by the Swedish Academy of Literature, Stockholm, and the academies of France and of Spain; those for peace are made by a committee of five chosen by the Norwegian Parliament. A listing of awards made in physics, chemistry, and physiology or medicine follows.—*A. K.*

1. Silky anteater *(Cyclopes didactylus)* is a squirrel-sized, tree-dwelling mammal of Central and S America, related to sloths and armadillos. Adult and young animal (clinging to underside of branch) are shown. *(Russ Kinne)*

1

2

Plate 58   MAMMALS

Mammals live in almost every corner of the world. Most mammals are terrestrial, but a few (such as whales and sea cows) live in the sea. The distinctive features of mammals include hair, warm-bloodedness, mammary glands, and a diaphragm separating the body cavity into a chest and an abdomen. A small sampling of mammals, both common and uncommon, appears on this page.

2. Spotted fawn of the white-tailed deer is well camouflaged in the dappled shade at the forest edge. *(Russ Kinne)*
3. Mouse opossum *(Marmora mitis)* of Central America is barely larger than some of the big grasshoppers upon which it feeds. *(Carl W. Rettenmeyer)* **4. Cheetah** is tiger-sized cat of African plains, where it outruns the swiftest antelopes and knocks them down with a well-aimed blow of the forepaw. *(Hans von Meiss-Teuflin/Photo Researchers)*

3

5

4

5. Pair of cougars is cornered in an outbuilding. These big, long-tailed cats of America are also called mountain lions, panthers, and pumas. *(Shostal)*

Plate 59　LAKES

Lakes depend for their existence upon rather special geological conditions, and they tend to disappear—relatively rapidly, by geological standards—as these conditions change. Lakes of diverse origins are illustrated on these pages.

3. Lake San Cristobal, Colorado, was formed by Gunnison River when its canyon was blocked by rain-soaked volcanic dust flowing down from San Juan Mts. *(State of Colorado)*

1. Jackson Lake, Wyoming, lies in basin formed by faulting that raised up Grand Teton Range. *(George Wolfson)* **2. Land of Lakes** in Christian River area, Alaska, is dotted with lake-filled basins gouged out by ice sheets of the Pleistocene Epoch. *(Russ Kinne)*

Plate 60 LAKES

4. Deep Lake, in Sun Lakes State Park, E Washington, occupies part of a former river valley. Terraces and potholes made by river are still visible. *(Ray Atkeson)*

5. Lower Ausable Lake, in New York's Adirondacks, lies in valley hollowed out by glacial ice of Pleistocene. *(Jerome Wyckoff)*

6. Crater Lake near Sellfoss, Iceland, is one of many lakes that occupy calderas—collapsed craters of volcanoes. A lake of similar origin in the U.S.A. is Crater Lake, Oregon. *(Harold Wanless)*

7. Salt lakes, such as this one in Colombia, South America, are salty because they lack an outlet which could carry salts out as fast as they are emptied into the lake by drainage from the surrounding region. Evaporation from lake takes out water but not the salts. *(Annan Photo Features)*

Plate 61   METAMORPHIC ROCKS

Metamorphic rocks are formed from previously existing sedimentary or igneous rocks by heat, pressure, or chemically active solutions, or a combination of these factors.

Serpentinized marble, Montville, N.J., formed by the alteration and recrystallization of a limestone. *(Jerome Wyckoff)*

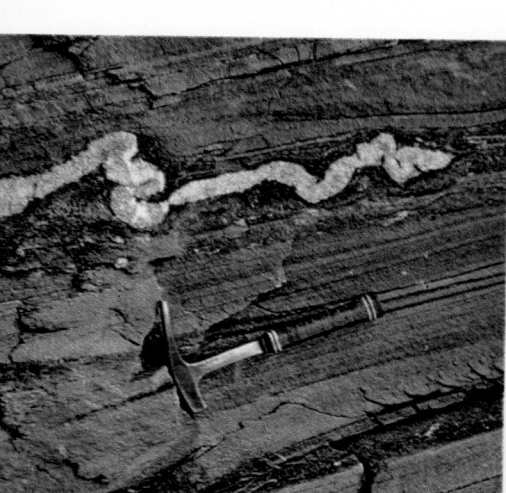

Schist, Murray Bridge, South Australia, displaying segments formed by cross-fracturing, and a ribbonlike quartz intrusion. *(Harold Wanless)*

Gneiss near Mt. Holy Cross, Colo.: A type of rock characterized by relatively coarse foliation, or banding. *(Joan E. Gordon)*

Quartzite, Baraboo, Wis.: A hard rock formed by metamorphism of a sandstone. Note cross-bedding of sand layers. *(Harold Wanless)*

Slate in southern N.Y., formed by recrystallization of a shale under directed pressure: Slaty cleavage commonly develops at an angle to original bedding of the shale. *(Jerome Wyckoff)*

AWARDS OF NOBEL PRIZES
Physics

Year	Name	Nationality	Achievement
1901	Wilhelm Konrad Röntgen (1845–1923)	German	Discovery of x-rays
1902	Hendrik Antoon Lorentz (1853–1928)	Dutch	Investigation of magnetic effects upon radiation phenomena
	Pieter Zeeman (1865–1943)	Dutch	
1903	Henri Becquerel (1852–1908)	French	Discovery of spontaneous radioactivity
	Pierre Curie (1859–1906)	French	
	Marie Curie (1867–1934)	French	
1904	John William Strutt (Lord Rayleigh) (1842–1919)	British	Discovery of argon
1905	Philipp Lenard (1862–1947)	German	Cathode-ray research
1906	Joseph J. Thomson (1856–1940)	British	Investigation of conduction of electricity through gases
1907	Albert Abraham Michelson (1852–1931)	U. S.	Investigations in spectroscopy and metrology
1908	Gabriel Lippmann (1845–1921)	French	Reproduction of colors by photography
1909	Guglielmo Marconi (1874–1937)	Italian	Development of wireless telegraphy
	Karl Ferdinand Braun (1850–1918)	German	
1910	Johannes Diderik van der Waals (1837–1923)	Dutch	Work on the equations of state for gases and liquids
1911	Wilhelm Wien (1864–1928)	German	Formulation of laws of heat radiation
1912	Nils Gustaf Dalén (1869–1937)	Swedish	Invention of automatic regulators used in lighting lighthouses and light buoys
1913	Heike Kamerlingh-Onnes (1853–1926)	Dutch	Investigation of properties of matter at low temperatures, and the production of liquid helium
1914	Max von Laue (1879–1960)	German	Discovery of diffraction of x-rays passing through crystals
1915	William Henry Bragg (1862–1942)	British	Analysis of crystal structure by means of x-rays
	William Lawrence Bragg (1890–)	British	
1916	(No Award)		
1917	Charles Glover Barkla (1877–1944)	British	Discovery of the characteristic x-ray radiation of the elements
1918	Max Planck (1858–1947)	German	Discovery of the elemental quantum
1919	Johannes Stark (1874–1957)	German	Discovery of the Doppler effect in canal rays and the separation of spectral lines in an electric field
1920	Charles Édouard Guillaume (1861–1938)	French	Discovery of the anomalies in nickel-steel alloys
1921	Albert Einstein (1879–1955)	German	Formulation of theory of relativity and discovery of the law of the photoelectric effect
1922	Niels Bohr (1885–1962)	Danish	Investigation of structure of the atom and its radiation
1923	Robert Andrews Millikan (1868–1953)	U. S.	Studies of elementary electric charge and the photoelectric effect
1924	Karl Manne Siegbahn (1886–)	Swedish	Investigations in x-ray spectroscopy
1925	James Franck (1882–1964)	German	Formulation of laws governing collision of electrons and atoms
	Gustav Hertz (1887–)	German	
1926	Jean Baptiste Perrin (1870–1942)	French	Research on discontinuous structure of matter and discovery of the equilibrium of sedimentation
1927	Arthur Holly Compton (1892–1962)	U. S.	Discovery of effect bearing his name (x-ray dispersion)
	Charles Thomson Rees Wilson (1869–1959)	British	Method of perceiving paths of electrically charged particles
1928	Owen Willans Richardson (1879–1959) (awarded in 1929)	British	Work on phenomena of thermionics and the discovery of the law which now bears his name
1929	Louis Victor de Broglie (1892–)	French	Discovery of the wave character of electrons
1930	Chandrasekhara Venkata Raman (1888–)	Indian	Work on diffusion of light and discovery of the effect which now bears his name
1931	(No Award)		
1932	Werner Heisenberg (1901–) (awarded in 1933)	German	Discovery of quantum mechanics in the matrix formulation
1933	Erwin Schrödinger (1887–1961)	Austrian	Discovery of new forms of the atomic theory
	Paul Adrien Maurice Dirac (1902–)	British	
1934	(No Award)		
1935	James Chadwick (1891–)	British	Discovery of neutron
1936	Victor Franz Hess (1883–1964)	Austrian	Discovery of cosmic rays
	Carl David Anderson (1905–)	U. S.	Discovery of positron
1937	Clinton Joseph Davisson (1881–1958)	U. S.	Discovery of electron diffraction by crystals
	George Paget Thomson (1892–)	British	
1938	Enrico Fermi (1901–54)	Italian	Discovery of new artificial radioactive elements and of nuclear reactions effected by slow neutrons
1939	Ernest Orlando Lawrence (1901–58)	U. S.	Invention and development of the cyclotron
1940–42	(No Award)		
1943	Otto Stern (1888–)	U. S.	Detection of magnetic moment of protons
1944	Isidor Isaac Rabi (1898–)	U. S.	Work on magnetic moments of atomic particles
1945	Wolfgang Pauli (1900–58)	Austrian	Work on atomic fission
1946	Percy Williams Bridgman (1882–1961)	U. S.	Studies and inventions in high-pressure physics
1947	Edward Appleton (1892–1965)	British	Discovery of layer in the ionosphere which reflects radio short waves, called the Appleton layer
1948	Patrick Maynard Stuart Blackett (1897–)	British	Improvement upon Wilson cloud chamber and discoveries in cosmic radiation
1949	Hideki Yukawa (1907–)	Japanese	Theoretical work on meson
1950	Cecil Frank Powell (1903–)	British	Photographic technique for studying atomic nuclei; research concerning mesons
1951	John Douglas Cockcroft (1897–)	British	Transmutation of elements by artificially accelerated atomic particles
	Ernest T. S. Walton (1903–)	Irish	
1952	Felix Bloch (1905–)	U. S.	Measurement of magnetic fields in atomic nuclei
	Edward Mills Purcell (1912–)	U. S.	

Year	Name	Nationality	Achievement
1953	Fritz Zernike (1888–1966)	Dutch	Introduction of phase-contrast microscopy
1954	Max Born (1882–)	British	Work in quantum mechanics
	Walther Bothe (1891–1957)	German	Use of coincidence method for analysis of cosmic radiation
1955	Polykarp Kusch (1911–1963)	U. S.	Work on the anomalous magnetic moment of the electron
	Willis Eugene Lamb, Jr. (1913–)	U. S.	
1956	William Shockley (1910–)	U. S.	Development of electronic transistor
	Walter Houser Brattain (1902–)	U. S.	
	John Bardeen (1908–)	U. S.	
1957	Tsung Dao Lee (1926–)	Chinese	Disproving of principle of "conservation of parity"
	Chen Ning Yang (1922–)	Chinese	
1958	Pavel A. Cherenkov (1904–)	Russian.	Work resulting in development of cosmic-ray counter
	Ilya M. Frank (1908–)	Russian	
	Igor E. Tamm (1895–)	Russian	
1959	Emilio Gino Segrè (1905–)	U. S.	Demonstration of the existence of the anti-proton
	Owen Chamberlain (1920–)	U. S.	
1960	Donald A. Glaser (1926–)	U. S.	Invention of the bubble chamber for studying subatomic particles
1961	Robert Hofstadter (1915–)	U. S.	Investigations of the size and structure of atomic nuclei by means of a high-energy electron beam
	Rudolf L. Mössbauer (1929–)	German	Discovery of the "Mössbauer effect" (production of recoil-free gamma rays), useful in confirming theory of relativity; the most accurate measurement of time yet achieved
1962	Lev Davidovich Landau (1908–)	Russian	Investigations of the low-temperature behavior of helium
1963	Eugene P. Wigner (1902–)	U. S.	Contributions to nuclear and particle theory
	Maria Goeppert Mayer (1906–)	U. S.	Studies of shell structure of nucleus
	J. Hans Daniel Jensen (1907–)	German	
1964	Nikolai G. Basov (1922–)	Russian	Work in quantum electronics related to maser-laser principle
	Aleksandr M. Prokhorov (1916–)	Russian	
	Charles Hard Townes (1915–)	U. S.	
1965	Richard Phillips Feynman (1918–)	U. S.	Research in quantum electrodynamics
	Julian Seymour Schwinger (1918–)	U. S.	
	Shinichero Tomonaga (1906–)	Japanese	
1966	Alfred Kastler (1902–)	French	Studies of energy levels in the atom

Physiology and Medicine

Year	Name	Nationality	Achievement
1901	Emil von Behring (1854–1917)	German	Development of serum therapy against tuberculosis
1902	Ronald Ross (1857–1932)	British	Discovery of life cycle of the causative agent of malaria in the mosquito
1903	Niels Ryberg Finsen (1860–1904)	Danish	Treatment of lupus vulgaris by concentrated light rays
1904	Ivan Petrovich Pavlov (1849–1936)	Russian	Studies of the physiology of digestion
1905	Robert Koch (1843–1910)	German	Work on tuberculosis; development of scientific bacteriology
1906	Camillo Golgi (1843–1926)	Italian	Work on the structure of the nervous system
	Santiago Ramón y Cajal (1852–1934)	Spanish	
1907	Charles Louis Alphonse Laveran (1845–1922)	French	Studies of protozoa, *e.g.* trypanosomes, as causative agents of disease
1908	Paul Ehrlich (1854–1915)	German	Work on immunity
	Elie Metchnikoff (1845–1916)	Russian	
1909	Emil Theodor Kocher (1841–1917)	Swiss	Work on the physiology, pathology, and surgery of the thyroid gland
1910	Albrecht Kossel (1853–1927)	German	Studies in cellular chemistry, especially of proteins and nuclear substances
1911	Allvar Gullstrand (1862–1930)	Swedish	Work on the dioptrics of the eye
1912	Alexis Carrel (1873–1944)	French	Development of methods for vascular ligature and the grafting of blood vessels and organs
1913	Charles Richet (1850–1935)	French	Development of anaphylactic test
1914	Robert Bárány (1876–1936)	Austrian	Studies on the physiology and pathology of vestibular system
1915–18	(No Award)		
1919	Jules Bordet (1870–1961)	Belgian	Discoveries in the field of immunity
1920	Schack August Steenberg Krogh (1874–1949)	Danish	Discovery of the mechanism regulating capillaries
1921	(No Award)		
1922	Archibald Vivian Hill (1886–)	British	Discoveries relating to heat production in muscles
	Otto Fritz Meyerhof (1884–1951) (awarded in 1923)	German	Establishment of the correlation between consumption of oxygen and production of lactic acid in muscle
1923	Frederick Grant Banting (1891–1941)	Canadian	Discovery of insulin
	John James Rickard Macleod (1876–1935)	Canadian	
1924	Willem Einthoven (1860–1927)	Dutch	Invention and development of the electrocardiograph
1925	(No Award)		
1926	Johannes Andreas Grib Fibiger (1867–1928)	Danish	Discovery of the spiroptera carcinoma (a type of cancer)
1927	Julius Wagner-Jauregg (1857–1940)	Austrian	Use of malaria inoculation in treatment of paresis
1928	Charles Nicolle (1866–1936)	French	Work on typhus exanthematicus
1929	Christiaan Eijkman (1858–1930)	Dutch	Discovery of antineuritic vitamins
	Frederick Gowland Hopkins (1861–1947)	British	Discovery of growth-promoting vitamins
1930	Karl Landsteiner (1868–1943)	Austrian	Discovery of human blood groups
1931	Otto Heinrich Warburg (1883–)	German	Discovery of the character and mode of action of the respiratory enzyme
1932	Charles Scott Sherrington (1857–1952)	British	Discoveries of the function of the neuron
	Edgar Douglas Adrian (1889–)	British	

Year	Name	Nationality	Achievement
1933	Thomas Hunt Morgan (1866–1945)	U.S.	Discoveries on hereditary function of the chromosomes
1934	George Richards Minot (1855–1950)	U.S.	Development of liver therapy of anemia
	William Parry Murphy (1892–)	U.S.	
	George Hoyt Whipple (1878–)	U.S.	
1935	Hans Spemann (1869–1941)	German	Discovery of the "organizer effect" in embryonic development
1936	Henry Hallett Dale (1875–)	British	Research on chemical transmission of nerve impulses
	Otto Loewi (1873–1961)	Austrian	
1937	Albert von Szent-Györgyi von Nagyrapolt (1893–)	Hungarian	Work on biological oxidation, especially vitamin C and catalysis of fumaric acid
1938	Corneille Heymans (1892–)	Belgian	Discovery of the importance of sinus and aorta mechanisms in the regulation of respiration
1939	Gerhard Domagk (1895–1964) (declined award*)	German	Discovery of the antibacterial effect of prontociliate
1940–42	(No Award)		
1943	Henrik Dam (1895–)	Danish	Discovery of vitamin K
	Edward Adelbert Doisy (1893–)	U.S.	Analysis of vitamin K
1944	Joseph Erlanger (1874–1965)	U.S.	Development of a method for detecting changes in electric potential of nerve fibers
	Herbert Spencer Gasser (1888–1963)	U.S.	
1945	Alexander Fleming (1881–1955)	British	Discovery of penicillin
	Ernst Boris Chain (1906–)	British	
	Howard Florey (1898–)	British	
1946	Hermann Joseph Muller (1890–)	U.S.	Study of the effects of x-rays on genes
1947	Carl Ferdinand Cori (1896–)	U.S.	Isolation of enzyme that initiates conversion of animal starch into sugar
	Gerty Theresa Cori (1896–1957)	U.S.	
	Bernardo A. Houssay (1887–)	Argentinian	Study of the pituitary hormone
1948	Paul Mueller (1899–1965)	Swiss	Discovery of insect-killing properties of DDT
1949	Walter Rudolf Hess (1881–)	Swiss	Studies of the function of the midbrain
	Antonio Caetano de Abreu Freire Egas Moniz (1874–1955)	Portuguese	Development of prefrontal leucotomy
1950	Philip Showalter Hench (1896–1965)	U.S.	Discoveries about hormones of the adrenal cortex, e.g. cortisone
	Edward Calvin Kendall (1886–)	U.S.	
	Tadeusz Reichstein (1897–)	Swiss	
1951	Max Theiler (1899–)	South Afr.	Development of anti-yellow-fever vaccine
1952	Selman Abraham Waksman (1888–)	U.S.	Co-discovery of streptomycin
1953	Fritz Albert Lipmann (1899–)	U.S.	Discovery of coenzyme A
	Hans Adolph Krebs (1900–)	British	Discovery of the Krebs (citric-acid) cycle
1954	John F. Enders (1897–)	U.S.	Work with the cultivation of the polio virus in human tissues
	Thomas H. Weller (1915–)	U.S.	
	Frederick C. Robbins (1916–)	U.S.	
1955	Axel Hugo Theorell (1903–)	Swedish	Work on oxidation enzymes
1956	Dickinson W. Richards, Jr. (1895–)	U.S.	Development of new techniques in treatment of heart disease
	André F. Cournand (1895–)	U.S.	
	Werner Forssmann (1904–)	German	
1957	Daniel Bovet (1907–)	Italian	Development of drugs to relieve allergies and relax muscles during surgery
1958	Joshua Lederberg (1925–)	U.S.	Investigations of genetic mechanisms
	George Wells Beadle (1903–)	U.S.	Discovery of how genes transmit hereditary characteristics
	Edward Lawrie Tatum (1909–)	U.S.	
1959	Severo Ochoa (1905–)	U.S.	Discoveries on the mechanism of synthesis of ribonucleic and deoxyribonucleic acids, believed to carry genetic information
	Arthur Kornberg (1918–)	U.S.	
1960	Frank Macfarlane Burnet (1899–)	Australian	Development of a theory of immunity of the human body against invading organisms or grafted foreign tissue
	Peter Brian Medawar (1915–)	British	
1961	Georg von Bekesy (1899–)	U.S.	Discoveries concerning the mechanism of hearing
1962	Francis Harry Compton Crick (1916–)	British	Elucidation of three-dimensional molecular structure of DNA.
	James Dewey Watson (1928–)	U.S.	
	Maurice Hugh Frederick Wilkins (1916–)	British	
1963	John Carew Eccles (1903–)	Australian	Studies on operation of nerve cells
	Alan Lloyd Hodgkin (1914–)	British	
	Andrew Fielding Huxley (1917–)	British	
1964	Konrad Emil Bloch (1912–)	U.S.	Discoveries concerning mechanism and regulation of cholesterol and fatty-acid metabolism
	Feodor Felix Konrad Lynen (1911–)	German	
1965	François Jacob (1920–)	French	Discoveries relating to action of genes in body cells
	André Lwoff (1902–)	French	
	Jacques Monod (1910–)	French	
1966	Charles B. Huggins (1901–)	U.S.	Treatment of cancer of the prostate
	Francis Peyton Rous (1879–)	U.S.	Discovery of tumor-inducing viruses

Chemistry

Year	Name	Nationality	Achievement
1901	Jacobus Henricus van't Hoff (1852–1911)	Dutch	Formulation of laws of chemical dynamics and osmotic pressure
1902	Emil Fischer (1852–1919)	German	Research on synthesis of sugar and purine groups
1903	Svante August Arrhenius (1859–1927)	Swedish	Formulation of his electrolytic theory of dissociation
1904	William Ramsay (1852–1916)	British	Discovery of different inert gases in atmosphere and their places in periodic system
1905	Adolph von Baeyer (1835–1917)	German	Development of organic dyes and aromatic hydrocarbon compounds
1906	Henri Moissan (1852–1907)	French	Isolation of the element fluorine; introduction of electric (Moissan) furnace

Year	Name	Nationality	Achievement
1907	Eduard Buchner (1860–1917)	German	Discovery of non-cellular fermentation and investigations in biological chemistry
1908	Ernest Rutherford (1871–1937)	British	Disintegration of elements and the chemistry of radioactive substances
1909	Wilhelm Ostwald (1853–1932)	German	Work on catalysis and investigations of chemical equilibrium and reaction rates
1910	Otto Wallach (1847–1931)	German	Work on alicyclic compounds
1911	Marie Curie (1867–1934)	French	Discovery of elements radium and polonium
1912	Victor Grignard (1871–1935)	French	Discovery of reagent subsequently named after him
	Paul Sabatier (1854–1941)	French	Method for hydrogenating organic chemicals in presence of finely divided metals
1913	Alfred Werner (1866–1919)	Swiss	Researches on chemical valence
1914	Theodore William Richards (1868–1928)	U. S.	Determination of exact atomic weights of many chemical substances
1915	Richard Willstätter (1872–1942)	German	Research into the coloring matter of plants, especially chlorophyll
1916–7	(No Award)		
1918	Fritz Haber (1868–1934)	German	Invention of a synthetic method of producing ammonia
1919	(No Award)		
1920	Walther Nernst (1864–1941)	German	Work in thermochemistry
1921	Frederick Soddy (1877–1956)	British	Investigation of origin and character of isotopes
1922	Francis William Aston (1877–1945)	British	Discovery of isotopes in non-radioactive elements and law of complete numbers
1923	Fritz Pregl (1869–1930)	Austrian	Method of microanalysis of organic substances
1924	(No Award)		
1925	Richard Zsigmondy (1865–1929) (awarded in 1926)	German	Work on the heterogeneous nature of colloid solutions
1926	Theodor Svedberg (1884–)	Swedish	Research on disperse systems
1927	Heinrich Wieland (1877–1957) (awarded in 1928)	German	Investigation of bile acids and related substances
1928	Adolf Windaus (1876–1959)	German	Research on constitution of the sterols and their connection with vitamin group
1929	Arthur Harden (1865–1940)	British	Investigations of sugar fermentation and the enzymes involved
	Hans Karl August Simon von Euler-Chelpin (1873–1964)	Swedish	
1930	Hans Fisher (1881–1945)	German	Investigation of coloring matter of blood and leaves, and the synthesis of hemin
1931	Carl Bosch (1874–1940)	German	Origination of chemical high-pressure methods
	Friedrich Bergius (1884–1949)	German	
1932	Irving Langmuir (1881–1957)	U. S.	Research in the realm of surface chemistry
1933	(No Award)		
1934	Harold Clayton Urey (1893–)	U. S.	Discovery of heavy hydrogen (deuterium)
1935	Frédéric Joliot (-Curie) (1900–58)	French	Synthesis of new radio-active substances
	Irène Joliot-Curie (1897–1956)	French	
1936	Peter J. W. Debye (1884–1966)	Dutch	Research on dipole moments and diffraction of x-rays and electrons in gases
1937	Walter Norman Haworth (1883–1950)	British	Research on carbohydrates and vitamin C
	Paul Karrer (1889–)	Swiss	Work on carotenoids, flavins, and vitamins A and B
1938	*Richard Kuhn (1900–)	German	Study of carotenoids and vitamin research
1939	*Adolph Butenandt (1903–)	German	Research on sexual hormones
	Leopold Ruzicka (1887–)	Swiss	
1940–2	(No Award)		
1943	Georg de Hevesy (1885–1966)	Hungarian	Research on the use of isotopes as indicators; discovery of hafnium
1944	Otto Hahn (1879–)	German	Work on atomic fission
1945	Artturi Ilmari Virtanen (1895–)	Finnish	Development of improved methods for conserving fodder
1946	James Batcheller Sumner (1887–1955)	U. S.	Crystallization of enzymes
	John Howard Northrop (1891–)	U. S.	Preparation of enzymes and virus proteins in pure form
	Wendell Meredith Stanley (1904–)	U. S.	
1947	Robert Robinson (1886–)	British	Research on alkaloids and other plant products
1948	Arne Tiselius (1902–)	Swedish	Colloid analysis and isolation of mouse paralysis virus
1949	William Francis Giauque (1895–)	U. S.	Investigation of properties of matter under conditions approaching absolute zero
1950	Otto Diels (1876–1954)	German	Discovery of diene synthesis, enabling further study of structure of organic matter
	Kurt Alder (1902–58)	German	
1951	Glenn Theodore Seaborg (1912–)	U. S.	Discovery of the element plutonium
	Edwin Mattison McMillan (1907–)	U. S.	
1952	Archer John Porter Martin (1910–)	British	Development of partition chromatography
	Richard L. M. Synge (1914–)	British	
1953	Hermann Staudinger (1881–1965)	German	Research in giant molecules
1954	Linus Pauling (1901–)	U. S.	Study of forces holding protein molecules together
1955	Vincent du Vigneaud (1901–)	U. S.	Work on pituitary hormones
1956	Cyril Hinshelwood (1897–)	British	Research on chemical reaction kinetics
	Nikolai N. Semenov (1896–)	Russian	
1957	Alexander Todd (1907–)	British	Research with chemical compounds that are factors in heredity
1958	Frederick Sanger (1918–)	British	Determination of molecular structure of insulin
1959	Jaroslav Heyrovsky (1890–)	Czech	Development of polarography (an electrochemical method of analysis)
1960	Willard Frank Libby (1908–)	U. S.	Development of a method of measuring the radioactivity in carbon-containing material, useful in determining ages of materials
1961	Melvin Calvin (1911–)	U. S.	Use of carbon[14] to trace chemical reactions of photosynthesis
1962	John Cowdery Kendrew (1917–)	British	Work on protein structure of myoglobin and hemoglobin
	Max Ferdinand Perutz (1914–)	British	
1963	Karl Ziegler (1898–)	German	Contributions to macromolecular chemistry
	Giulio Natta (1903–)	Italian	
1964	Mrs. Dorothy Crowfoot Hodgkin (1910–)	British	Determination of structure of biochemical compounds, notably penicillin and vitamin B_{12}
1965	Robert Burns Woodward (1917–)	U. S.	Syntheses of chlorophyll, sterols, and other organic compounds
1966	Robert Sanderson Mulliken (1896–)	U. S.	Theoretical studies of chemical bond

* Award delayed by Hitler's decree of Jan. 31, 1937, forbidding acceptance of Nobel prizes. Award made later.

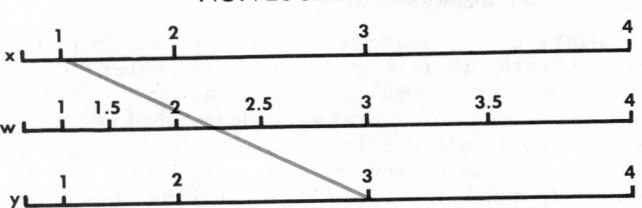

Nomogram for $2w^2 = x^2 = y^2$, showing determination of w for $x = 1$, $y = 3$.

NOCTILUCENT CLOUDS: clouds which sometimes form in the upper stratosphere (40 to 60 mi up) in high latitudes during summer. Silvery blue, and not iridescent like MOTHER-OF-PEARL CLOUDS, noctilucent clouds are so called because they are high enough to remain in the sunlight during the long summer twilights of the sub-Arctic. Light from noctilucent clouds is polarized, while that from lower clouds is not. Noctilucent clouds are probably composed of tiny dust particles covered with a thin film of ice.—*D. H. L.*

NOISE: popularly, any unwanted sound; by extension, unwanted electrical disturbances in telephones, amplifiers, radio receivers, etc., and thermal agitation in electron flow through vacuum tubes and wires (see NOISE, THERMAL-AGITATION). If a wanted signal—whether voice, music, or electrical impulse—is diminished, or the noise increased, until signal and noise are at about the same level, it becomes difficult to separate them intelligibly; a further drop in relative signal level renders the signal imperceptible. Most noises are sounds to which little or no pitch can be assigned, aside from a general "highness" or "lowness." If such a noise is resolved into a frequency spectrum, it will usually be found that the energy is spread more or less uniformly through a band or bands of frequencies, rather than occurring in the sharply defined fundamental and harmonic overtones typical of a musical instrument. If the energy is distributed uniformly through the band under study, it is random or "white" noise; the background hiss of an amplifier-loudspeaker system is of this kind. The study, measurement, and control of noise associated with industrial processes and machinery, *e.g.* looms, printing presses, and power sources generally, has become an important profession. In machinery, excessive noise often indicates excessive wear. For people in factories and elsewhere, noise tends to be irritating and distracting, causing loss of working efficiency and increase in nervous tension. Loud, continued noise may cause loss of hearing. Control of noise in the modern industrial environment, particularly in cities and along air-traffic lanes, is an increasingly serious problem.—*M. C. H.*

NOISE, THERMAL-AGITATION: unwanted electrical signals produced by the random motion of electrons in any component having resistance. The motion is produced by heat energy. Because of the randomness of the thermal motion, these noise signals occur at all frequencies. This accounts for a fundamental limitation of the sensitivity of radio, radar, television, and similar receivers, since the noise will overpower and prevent the detection of very weak signals. In radio, this interference is heard as an unwanted sound (hence the name "noise"), whereas in radar and television, it appears on the picture tube screen as "snow." The magnitude of the noise voltage V_n produced by thermal agitation at the terminals of the resistor is given by

$$V_n = \sqrt{4kTR\,\Delta f}$$

where k is Boltzmann's constant, T the absolute temperature, R the resistance in ohms, and Δf the bandwidth of the receiver in cycles/sec. A related effect is "shot noise," which is caused by electrons emitted from the hot cathode of a vacuum tube at random intervals and with random values of initial velocity. Random thermal noise also occurs in transistors and other semiconductor devices. Masers and parametric amplifiers greatly reduce thermal noise and therefore effect improvement in the sensitivity of receivers in which they are used.—*I. R.*

NOMOGRAM: a graphical representation of mathematical relations from which required values can be read directly, by use of a straightedge. Nomograms are especially useful for obtaining approximate solutions of many equations of the same kind. The most common type is an alignment chart, which consists of suitably scaled lines, usually, though not invariably, straight. For example, by plotting on two parallel scales the values of x^2 and y^2, we can read from the scale midway between them the value of w satisfying the equation $2w^2 = x^2 + y^2$. By construction of appropriate scales, nomograms can be used to give the value of w corresponding to values of x and y in any equation $f(w) = g(x) + h(y)$.—*H. C.*

NON-EUCLIDEAN GEOMETRY: any geometry based on postulates different from Euclid's. The term usually is applied to a geometry that differs from Euclid's in regard to the fifth, or parallel, postulate. This postulate reads (trans. by T. L. Heath): "If a straight line falling on two straight lines makes the interior angles on the same side together less than two right angles, the two straight lines, if produced indefinitely, meet on that side on which the angles are together less than two right angles." This postulate seemed somewhat less "self-evident" than others, and there is evidence that Euclid sought to prove it as a theorem. Failing in this, he adopted it as a postulate. Now, by definition, two lines in a plane are parallel if they fail to meet, no matter how far produced. From the assumption in the postulate it follows that, through a point not on a given straight line, just one parallel to the line exists. For more than 2,000 yr, mathematicians tried to prove this postulate and so make it a theorem, since the necessity of including it among the postulates to them a blemish on the subject of mathematics. None succeeded, and mathematicians of the 19th cent.—N. I. Lobachevsky, János Bolyai, K. F. Gauss—inferred that the postulate is truly independent of the other postulates. Hence it was logically possible to adopt a contradictory postulate.

There are two ways in which the fifth postulate can be contradicted, leading to two different conclusions about parallels. We may assume that, even if the interior angles are together less than two right angles, the lines may fail to meet. With this assumption, it follows that through any point not on a given line, many parallels to the line exist. This is the assumption used by Lobachevsky, and the geometry that results is called Lobachevskian, or hyperbolic, geometry. We may, equally well, assume that if the interior angles are equal to two right angles, the two lines still must meet if produced sufficiently far. With this assumption there are no parallels. The non-Euclidean geometry of Riemann is based on this, together with a denial of Euclid's second postulate: that a line may be extended indefinitely in either direction. Riemann assumed that a line may have a finite length without being terminated; a circle is a model of such a line. This geometry is called elliptic geometry.

The majority of the theorems of Euclidean geometry depend in part upon the fifth postulate. Hence both the Lobachevskian and the elliptic geometries differ extensively from Euclidean. A comparison of theorems brings out the sharp differences in these three geometries. In Euclidean geometry, the sum of the angles of a triangle is equal to two right angles; in Lobachevskian geometry the sum is less than two right angles; in elliptic geometry the sum is greater than two right angles. (In both non-Euclidean geometries there is a direct relationship between the area and the sum of the angles.) In Euclidean geometry an angle inscribed in a semi-circle is a right angle; in Lobachevskian geometry it is acute; in elliptic geometry it is obtuse. In elliptic geometry two lines completely bound an area, and all perpendiculars to a given line come together at a point.

A person brought up on the familiar Euclidean geometry is likely to believe it to be a true description of physical space and to think of non-Euclidean geometries as being fantasies that cannot have real interpretations. This is, in part, the result of conditioning and biased interpretations of physical evidence. For example, a line of sight, or ray of light, is the most commonly accepted criterion of straightness. Yet light rays may not obey the Euclidean postulates for straight lines. They may be bent by refraction without our knowing it. Which of the geometries best approximates the structure of space depends upon what physical elements are identified with the basic elements of geometry. If a straight line is taken to be a path of shortest distance, then on Earth's surface it is a geodesic, part of a great circle, and the geometry is elliptic. On Earth's surface all great circles perpendicular to a given great circle meet; for example, all meridians are perpendicular to the equator and meet at both north and south poles. Also the sum of the angles of a triangle formed by three great circles is greater than two right angles. Geodesics on another surface may have quite different properties. There is a surface known as a *pseudosphere*. Its geodesics obey Lobachevskian geometry. It is not inconceivable that physical space has characteristics that make whatever paths we might adopt as straight lines (*e.g.* light rays) conform to either of these non-Euclidean geometries. It is even possible that one geometry applies in a part of space and a different one in another part.

A major contribution of the discovery of non-Euclidean geometries was in opening the eyes of mathematicians, scientists, and philosophers to the true nature of geometry and of all mathematics. It became clear that the postulates of a mathematical system can be chosen without reference to physical applicability, and that, consequently, mathematics is free to develop in its own way subject only to its own standards of consistency. See EUCLIDEAN GEOMETRY; RIEMANNIAN GEOMETRY.—*H. C.*

NONFERROUS METALS: metals other than iron, steel, and the various alloy steels. At present and throughout the modern industrial era the tonnage of iron and steel produced has so far exceeded the tonnage of all other metals combined that it has become customary to use the single term "nonferrous" to refer to all these other metals and their alloys. Usage is thus grounded in commercial rather than in technological or scientific considerations. There are, however, certain metallurgical properties that are shared by several of the more common nonferrous metals and that differentiate them from iron and steel. Most nonferrous metals, for example, do not exhibit more than one allotropic form and therefore cannot be hardened by simple heating and quenching. Similarly, the effect of carbon is much less pronounced in most nonferrous metals and alloys than it is in iron. The first metals to be used by man were nonferrous. They included those that occur naturally in the elemental state (particularly copper, silver, and gold) and those easily produced by low-temperature reduction of their oxide ores (*i.e.* lead and tin). Today the more important nonferrous metals, listed in order of tonnage produced, are aluminum, copper, lead, zinc, sodium, nickel, tin, magnesium, antimony, and titanium. Some others, *e.g.* molyb-

denum, manganese, and chromium, are produced in large tonnages but are used almost entirely in alloy steels.

Methods for winning the nonferrous metals from their ores differ widely. Lead, tin, nickel, titanium, and antimony are produced almost entirely by pyrometallurgical methods, using carbon, carbon monozide, hydrogen, or a basic metal as a reducing agent at high temperatures. Titanium ore is converted to titanium chloride before reduction, but most of the other ores are converted to the metal oxides. Copper and zinc are produced both by pyrometallurgy and by electrolytic reduction of their salts in aqueous solution. Zinc, because of its relatively low boiling point, is one of the few metals refined on a large scale by distillation. Magnesium is produced largely by electrolysis of fused magnesium chloride, although some is produced by carbon reduction of the oxide. Aluminum is produced by electrolyzing a solution of purified aluminum oxide, made from the impure oxide ore bauxite, in a molten mixture of sodium, aluminum, and calcium fluorides.

Since prehistoric times, when bronze (an alloy of copper and tin) was the major material for tools, the nonferrous metals have been used most effectively as alloys. The various brasses and bronzes consist mainly of copper with zinc and tin as the major alloying elements. Small percentages of other metals such as lead, beryllium, antimony, and manganese may be added to confer special properties. Nickel-copper alloys such as Monel metal (approx. 70% nickel and 30% copper) are used in chemical manufacturing equipment because of their strength and resistance to corrosion. Lead-tin alloys are used as solders and bearing metals. Almost all structural aluminum, *e.g.* that used in aircraft construction, is alloyed to give it the required strength and toughness. The precious metals gold, silver, and platinum, when used for ornamental purposes or coinage, are alloyed to improve their strength and resistance to wear.

In recent years the development of atomic energy and rocketry has given a great impetus to nonferrous metallurgy. Many metals that were hitherto laboratory curiosities are now being produced for use because of special nucleonic, thermal, or electrical properties they possess. (See ALLOY; BRASS; BRONZE; and articles on chemical elements.)—*A. M. S.*

NONMETALS stand apart from METALS in many ways, both physically and chemically, although these two classes of elements merge into one another. Physically, nonmetals do not exhibit luster or polish; they are poor conductors of heat and electricity; if solid, they are often brittle, they are not ductile, and they possess poor tensile strength. At ordinary temperatures some are solid, some liquid, and some gaseous: their melting points range from $-272°C$ ($-457.6°F$), under 26 atm pressure, for helium, to above $3550°C$ ($6422°F$) for carbon. Their values for specific gravity are low, compared with those for metals. Chemically, their oxides usually react with water to form acids, and their chlorides are often decomposed by water. Most of them combine with metals, forming *e.g.* oxides, sulfides, chlorides; hydrides also are common and usually stable. Carbon is unique in forming myriads of hydrides (hydrocarbons), the simplest of which is methane, CH_4. Of the three hydrides of nitrogen, ammonia, NH_3, is particularly important; it acts as a basic anhydride, dissolving in water to form ammonium hydroxide, NH_4OH, which reacts with acids to give the notable ammonium salts. Of the two hydrides of oxygen, water, H_2O, is uniquely important.

In the periodic table of the ELEMENTS, nonmetals occur in groups IV to VII, although not all elements in these groups are nonmetals. The INERT GASES of the atmosphere, chemically indifferent to both metals and nonmetals, are placed in

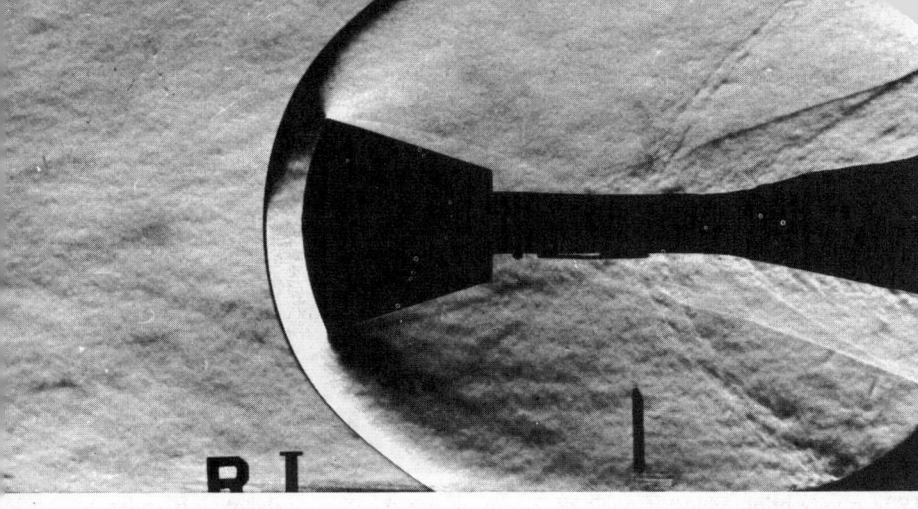

Prototype nose cone for Titan ICBM missile: Blunt cone serves to decrease missile's velocity and thereby also the re-entry heating; heat-sink type nose cone also uses ablation materials to dissipate heat. Test shows shock-wave pattern at Mach 5. (*USAF*)

group O. The classification of hydrogen is equivocal: physically it appears to be a nonmetal; on the other hand, it gives rise to the hydrogen ion which resembles metallic ions in carrying a positive charge, thereby differentiating hydrogen decisively from nonmetals. The elements of group V, in particular, illustrate the gradual passage, with increase of atomic number and atomic weight, from typical nonmetals (nitrogen, phosphorus) through metalloids (arsenic, antimony) to metal (bismuth). Group VII forms the very distinctive HALOGEN family of nonmetals, the hydrides of which act as monobasic acids, *e.g.* hydrogen chloride, HCl (hydrochloric acid). Some nonmetals possess quite extraordinary importance. Thus, air contains about 78% nitrogen and 21% oxygen (by volume); water (ice, water vapor) is composed of 88.9% oxygen and 11.1% hydrogen (by weight); and carbon is the foundation element of ORGANIC CHEMISTRY, mainly in combination with hydrogen, oxygen, and nitrogen. See CHEMISTRY; INORGANIC CHEMISTRY.—*J. R.*

NORMAN, ROBERT, late 16th cent. A. D., English instrument maker; birthplace unknown. He discovered the dip of the compass needle and published his discovery in *The Newe Attractive* (1581). The fact that Georg Hartmann had discovered the dip earlier was not known until the 19th cent.— *D. H. D. R.*

NORTHERN LIGHTS: see AURORA.

NORTHROP, JOHN HOWARD, 1891–　, U. S. biochemist; b. Yonkers, N. Y. For years he has pioneered in work on the purification and mode of action of enzymes. After the enzyme urease was crystallized by J. B. Sumner in 1926, Northrop investigated pepsin and crystallized it (1930). This work and later studies convinced him that all enzymes are proteins. For their preparation of enzymes and virus proteins in a pure form, Northrop and W. M. Stanley shared the 1946 Nobel prize with Sumner. Northrop is a member of the National Academy of Sciences.—*D. H. D. R.*

NORTH STAR: see POLARIS.

NOSE: the facial organ that houses external openings to the respiratory passages and contains the sense organ for smell (olfaction). Air passages leading back from the nose direct incoming air across a sensitive area (*cribiform plate*) in which there are many olfactory nerve terminations that are sensitive to odors. The air passages continue to the back of the palate and thence to the pharynx (throat), through the glottis into the trachea (windpipe), and to the lungs.

The sense of smell is commonly confused with the sense of taste. This can be clearly demonstrated by attempting (with eyes closed and nose held shut) to distinguish between the taste of a fresh slice of potato and one of apple. Distinction can seldom be made. However, if the nose is open, the difference is apparent. Thus apples and potatoes are (in large measure) examples of foods that are distinguished by odor rather than flavor. The nature of this stimulatory energy to which the sense organ for smell is sensitive is not yet exactly known. Since the time of Aristotle it has been commonly held that odorous substances give off small particles that stimulate the sense of smell. Modern science has been investigating the infrared sensitivity of the organ for smell.

The nerves (cranial nerve no. 1) from the cribiform plate lead into the very front part of the brain (rhinencephalon). In general, the relative size of this part of the brain increases progressively from higher to lower vertebrates; there is a keener sense of smell in lower animals. Fish, accordingly, have an extraordinary sense of smell.—*A. R. D.*

NOSE CONE: the most forward structural element of a missile or other space vehicle. When, upon a vehicle's RE-ENTRY into Earth's atmosphere, friction and compression convert the vehicle's high velocity into heat, the nose cone sustains the greatest heat absorption. The elevated temperatures associated with re-entry can destroy the cone; or, if the surface of the cone is hot and its interior relatively cool, severe distortions and ultimate structural failure of the vehicle can result. Hence, nose cones of high-velocity space vehicles must (1) be made of materials that retain their strength and shape at high temperatures, and (2) be so shaped that they absorb a minimum amount of the heat generated by pressure and friction drag. Non-brittle ceramics and ceramic-coated metals give resistance to elevated temperatures; as for shape, the blunter the cone, *i.e.* the wider the cone angle, the greater the amount of heat dissipated to the surrounding air and kept from the body of the vehicle. Another advantage of a blunt nose cone is that it aids in decreasing the velocity of a vehicle as it passes through the thinner, less dense (higher) regions of the atmosphere; this in turn minimizes the pronounced increase in friction and heat that inevitably occurs as the vehicle descends through higher-density atmospheric gases. At present, ABLATION materials for nose cones are being used in some vehicles; these are materials whose heat of vaporization (see HEAT, LATENT) is large and which, in vaporizing at re-entry temperatures, dissipate a portion of the heat that would otherwise penetrate into the interior of the nose cone (see HEAT SINK).—*A. L.*

NÖTHER, EMMY, 1882–1935, German mathematician; b. Erlangen. She taught at the Univ. of Göttingen until 1933, when the Hitler regime forced her to leave. Emigrating to the United States, she became a professor of mathematics at Bryn Mawr College and lectured at the Institute for Advanced Study at Princeton. One of the greatest of algebraists, she made striking advances in abstract algebra. She has been recognized as one of the two greatest woman mathematicians of modern times, the other being Sonia Kovalevski.—*H. C.*

Appearance of a nova: Late in 1934 a very bright object (magnitude 2) was observed in the constellation Hercules (*left*); comparison with earlier photographic plates showed it had previously been recorded as a faint star (*right*). Of slower development than most novas, Nova Herculis 1934 maintained near-maximum brightness for 3 mo. (*Yerkes*)

NOVA: a STAR that undergoes a very rapid increase in brightness, followed by a much slower decline to approximately the original luminosity. The typical nova, prior to its outburst, is a faint object observable only through a large telescope; at maximum it may be brighter than most naked-eye stars. It is not surprising that before the invention of the telescope such a phenomenon was regarded as the appearance of a new star (Latin, *stella nova*).

Ordinary Novas: The great majority of novas observed in our own galactic system and in the Andromeda nebula belong to the group usually referred to as ordinary or common novas. An ordinary nova at maximum has an intrinsic brightness approximately 50,000 times the Sun's. It rises to maximum brightness in about 2 days, and then fades, losing at least half its maximum luminosity within a year after the outburst; after several years, it has returned approximately to its original brightness. An estimated 50 to 100 ordinary novas occur each year in our own galaxy, but most of these do not reach naked-eye visibility, because of great distance and obscuration by clouds of interstellar dust. Several recurrent novas are known, and the property of being a nova seems to be restricted to a limited class of unstable stars.

What little information exists about pre-outburst spectra indicates that the pre-nova stars are probably small, dense, and of rather high surface temperature. Several novas have been observed shortly before maximum brightness. At this stage they are of late B or early A spectral type (see STAR SPECTRA); at maximum the spectrum closely resembles that of a supergiant star of type A or F. The absorption lines of the spectrum of a nova near maximum are displaced to the violet, meaning that an expanding shell of material has been ejected by the nova. Then widened emission bands of hydrogen and ionized calcium from the expanding shell are observed. Finally, as the nova decays, emission lines characteristic of planetary nebulas appear, showing that the ejected material is now very diffuse. During a single outburst, several shells may be ejected and may become visible about the star as a diffuse expanding disc.

Supernovas: These have been divided into two groups on the basis of observational differences. Type I contains those that attain at maximum a luminosity of the order of 400 million times the Sun's. Their spectra are peculiar and have not thus far been explained. Supernovas of Type II are less brilliant, the luminosity at maximum being about 10 million times the Sun's. Their spectra appear to resemble those of ordinary novas; in fact these stars might be described as ordinary novas on a greatly enlarged scale. Since modern equipment has been available, no supernovas have appeared in our own galactic system, although several are famous in astronomical history. Our knowledge of supernovas has been obtained by observing those discovered in various extragalactic nebulas, where their frequency of appearance is of the order of one per galaxy per 400 yr; they are thus exceedingly rare phenomena.

Causes: The causes of these outbursts are still unknown. In the case of ordinary novas, the star for some reason blows off its outer layers, but the amounts of energy and matter involved are not sufficient to produce any far-reaching change in the star. There is some evidence suggesting that ordinary novas are members of binary star systems. With supernovas, however, the energy liberated is so enormous that the star literally blows itself to pieces. (The Crab Nebula is the expanding debris of the supernova which occurred in our galaxy and was seen by the Chinese in A. D. 1054.) Probably at the centers of supernovas nuclear reactions are taking place which produce from simple elements more complex elements of high atomic weight.—*M. W. O.*

NOXIOUS GASES: gases harmful to man. As in discussions of chemical warfare, the term "gases" is often expanded to include all airborne noxious substances that cause harm by inhalation or by absorption through the skin, *i.e.* not only true gases like chlorine, but also aerosols like silica dust. Industrialization has introduced many noxious gases into the atmosphere; the most widespread, because of its presence in automobile-engine exhaust gases, is carbon monoxide. This gas is present in the illuminating gas made from coal and oil as well as in the products of incomplete combustion of coal. Carbon monoxide causes most of the deaths due to noxious gases. Some noxious gases are quite localized, *e.g.* sulfur dioxide around smelters, and phosgene or chlorine around certain chemical processing plants. Air pollution by industry is made more dangerous by vagaries of the atmosphere. Sometimes a stagnant blanket of air in which pollutants (gases and aerosols) have built up to toxic concentrations settles over an area and causes many deaths (see ATMOSPHERIC POLLUTION). Federal and state regulations prescribe maximum safe limits for exposure to noxious gases, and various commissions periodically review the data and issue revised lists.—*Ru. M.*

NOZZLE: a pipe or enclosed channel of decreasing cross section that directs a flow of fluid into an open space. The fluid passing through a nozzle undergoes a decrease in its static pressure and an increase in its velocity (see BERNOULLI'S PRINCIPLE OF HYDRODYNAMICS). The calculation of the change in velocity—and therefore of the quantity of flow through a nozzle—is based in most cases on the assumption that the fluid is incompressible. Liquids are in fact compressible but to such a small extent that for all practical matters they are considered incompressible. Gases traveling at velocities much below the speed of sound are also considered incompressible. (See FLUID FLOW.) The quantity of flow of an incompressible fluid through a nozzle is given by the formula

$$Q = KA_2 \sqrt{\frac{1}{1 - \left(\frac{A_2}{A_1}\right)^2}} \; \sqrt{2gh}$$

where Q is the quantity of flow in ft³/sec, A_1 and A_2 the cross-sectional areas in ft² of the nozzle at its base and tip respectively, g the acceleration of gravity in ft/sec², and h the head of static pressure at a point behind the nozzle's base. The discharge coefficient K varies with different nozzles and depends on such characteristics as the roughness of the nozzle walls and the nozzle's angle of convergence.

Applications: The most obvious and most common use of nozzles is to direct a high-velocity liquid jet, *e.g.* the nozzles of garden hoses and fire hoses. Similar nozzles are used to displace ore-laden gravel in placer mining. Nozzles are used extensively in TURBINES: in the impulse-type Pelton turbine a nozzle directs a high-velocity water jet against the buckets of the rotor; in steam turbines nozzle-shaped vanes are used to direct jets of steam against the vanes of the rotor. (See ENGINE.) In rockets and jet-propulsion engines, nozzles are used to convert high-pressure, high-temperature gases into high-velocity jets; in this case the exhaust gases have a velocity that exceeds the speed of sound and must be considered *compressible*; thus thermodynamic considerations must be incorporated into flow and velocity calculations.—*A. L.*

NUCLEAR FORCES: the nonelectromagnetic forces between nucleons (protons or neutrons) in the nucleus of an atom. The basic characteristics of nuclear forces are their strength and short range. Beyond a distance of 10^{-13} cm, which is about the size of a light nucleus, their strength is essentially zero; at shorter distances they are strongly attractive, holding the nucleons together, though at the very shortest ranges there is evidence that they are mutually repulsive. The origin of nuclear forces is believed to be the interchange of particles called MESONS between two nucleons. This is analogous to the force between charged particles, which originates from the interchange of PHOTONS. At present the theory of nuclear forces lacks a firm foundation.—*G. M. S. and L. S.*

NUCLEAR PHYSICS: a science the central problem of which concerns the forces holding together the neutrons and pro-

tons (nucleons) of the atomic nucleus. These forces are strong and are exerted only over very short distances; hence they are very difficult to investigate. Whereas the well-known gravitational and electric forces between material bodies or between electric charges are exerted over great distances, diminishing with the square of the distance between the bodies, the nuclear force exerted by nucleons on one another is appreciable only when they are separated by distances less than about 1 or 2×10^{-13} cm (*i.e.* about one or two times the diameter of the nucleons themselves). If the particles are separated farther, they do not interact. As the separating distance diminishes to this size, however, the nuclear force comes into play rapidly and powerfully, increasing from negligible strength to full magnitude in a little over 10^{-13} cm.

Compared with the electrical energy binding the atomic electrons to the nuclear protons, or binding the atoms of molecules to one another, the binding of the nucleons is enormously strong. Expressed in the unit of energy common to atomic and nuclear physics, the electron volt (ev), the energy required to separate the atoms of a molecule, or to take an electron out of its parent atom, ranges from a few ev to, at most, tens of thousands of ev. The energy required to separate a proton or neutron from the atomic nucleus is much greater—of the order of several million electron volts (Mev).

Because electromagnetic and gravitational forces act over long distances, studies of them can be performed on a macroscopic scale, as in the science of celestial mechanics or in investigations of the effect of electrically charged bodies on one another. Atomic and nuclear effects, on the other hand, entail studies on a submicroscopic scale. The short range and great strength of the nuclear force, in particular, make necessary the use of probes of nuclear dimensions—nuclear particles themselves, or extremely short wavelength x-rays—possessed of the Mev energies required to perturb the nucleus appreciably. In addition, the extremely small size of the probing particles and of the nuclei they explore means that the probability with which such nuclear reactions can occur is quite small. The field of nuclear physics is thus characterized on the one hand by highly specialized particle-accelerating devices capable of producing streams of high-energy exploring particles and, on the other hand, by sensitive methods enabling the detection of even a single nuclear event.

The investigation of nuclear phenomena is in large part carried out by observing the properties (*e.g.* number and

An important tool of nuclear physics is the spark chamber, in which the tracks of nuclear particles can be observed. In this photo, paths of particles show up clearly (as broken white lines) in the huge crescent-shaped spark chamber at left. Two smaller, rectangular chambers are visible at center. The spark chamber contains a mixture of gases and a series of closely spaced charged plates. A particle passing through the chamber ionizes gas along its path, permitting a spark to jump between a pair of charged plates. As the particle moves through the chamber, it triggers successive pairs of plates, producing a series of sparks. (*Lawrence Radiation Lab., Univ. of Calif.*)

kind, energy and angular distributions) of particles emitted by radioactive nuclei or by nuclei exposed to radiations of various kinds. The detection of such particles results from the fact that fast charged particles can produce observable effects such as ionization or fluorescence when they pass through matter. An effect can take the form of visible tracks, as in photographic emulsions or in saturated vapors or liquids (see CLOUD CHAMBER; BUBBLE CHAMBER). Detectors also make use of the light emitted by certain substances when traversed by charged particles (see SCINTILLATION); or the electric charge released by ionization in gases and some crystals (e.g. ionization chambers, Geiger counters, crystal counters; see COUNTER). Such techniques were used by the earliest workers in the field. The first detection of radioactive emanations was by means of photographic emulsions; and the visual observation of scintillations produced by alpha particles and protons in thin layers of zinc sulfide was used in radioactivity researches as early as 1903. Recent detection techniques have achieved a considerable degree of sophistication, as, for example, in the spark chamber, an extended arrangement of electrified surfaces immersed in a suitable gas, between which the traversing particle triggers a chain of spark discharges, which mark its path.

History: Much of the early development of nuclear physics occurred side by side with the advancement of the knowledge of atomic structure. An outstanding stimulus to both nuclear and atomic physics was the demonstration by Lord Rutherford in 1911 that the bulk of the atomic mass resides within a region much smaller than the dimensions of the atom. The study of effects peculiar to the nucleus had its beginning with Henri Becquerel's discovery in 1896 of radioactivity in uranium (see RADIOACTIVITY). Between 1896 and 1911 there followed the isolation of other radioactive elements (including radium) and the detection of a number of important nuclear phenomena. It was established that radioactivity is not affected by the physical state of the element from which it emanates and that the radioactivity of a given sample of material decreases with time at a rate peculiar to the substance of which it is composed (see HALF-LIFE). In 1903 Rutherford and Frederick Soddy discovered that radioactive disintegration results in a transmutation, or change in atomic species of the radioactive atom, and by 1910 the existence of ISOTOPES—atoms of similar chemical properties but different atomic weights—was demonstrated. It was found that three distinctive types of radiation are emitted by radioactive atoms (ALPHA, BETA, AND GAMMA RAYS), and the correct relation was formulated between the associated transmutation and the type of radiation emitted. By 1905 Egon von Schweidler had set forth the random character of radioactive disintegrations, describing the process as statistical—i.e. the radioactive decay of an atom must be described as the probability of its decay in a given time interval.

During the same period, the character of α- and β-rays was elucidated and their masses and charges were measured. The α-particles were found to be identical with the doubly charged helium ion, and the β-particles very light, negatively charged, with a wide range of velocities. In addition to the evidence that the long-sought transmutation of elements had at last been discovered, it also became clear that the processes which had come to light involved energy releases several million times greater than those of ordinary chemical processes. It is interesting to note that Rutherford and his colleagues pointed out the possibility that the heat of Earth is the result of radioactivity and that radioactive processes may be the source of solar energy.

With the proposal by Rutherford of the nuclear model of the atom in 1911, the phenomenon of radioactivity was for the first time associated distinctly with the massive but tiny nucleus, rather than with the atom as a whole. The following two decades saw a remarkable series of efforts that resulted in, among other things, the artificial disintegration of nuclei bombarded by α-particles from radioactive sources; a quantitative measurement of the nuclear radius and the formulation of an empirical law for its variation with atomic number; and the proposal (by Wolfgang Pauli) of the existence of the neutrino—a massless, chargeless particle, assumed to be created and emitted during each β decay process to explain the spread of velocities of the β-particles, a spread that would otherwise be in violation of the principles of energy and momentum conservation. Also, during this period, George Gamow and others took a theoretical step of great significance when they correctly explained α-radioactivity (see TUNNEL EFFECT); the explanation employed the quantum-mechanical theory used so successfully earlier to interpret phenomena observed in connection with purely atomic effects.

Three remarkable advances in 1932 marked a significant turning point of nuclear physics: the discovery of the neutron by James Chadwick; the experimental observation of the positive electron, or positron, by Carl Anderson, verifying an earlier implicit theoretical prediction of its existence by Paul Dirac; and the production of a nuclear reaction by the bombardment of the nuclei of matter with energetic helium ions accelerated artificially to high kinetic energy (John Cockcroft and Ernest Walton). The constituents of nuclei were now known to be the neutron and proton; there was positive evidence for the existence of a world of subnuclear particles; and the use of high-voltage machines to produce particles which could induce nuclear reactions by bombardment opened an avenue for the study of nuclear structure much more fruitful than that which had been possible when the only available artillery had been radioactive materials. The period from 1932 to the present has seen a breadth of activity and an extension of the field and the tools for working in it that have been truly phenomenal. The ramifications have been so numerous that the field has in fact been described by some as a collection of separate topics rather than a logically ordered and connected subject.

Current Investigations: Particle-accelerator development, following the work of Cockcroft and Walton, continued with the invention, in rapid sequence over the next 15 yr, of the electrostatic accelerator, cyclotron, betatron, synchrotron, and synchrocyclotron (see PARTICLE ACCELERATOR). Developments after World War II included the microwave linear accelerator and the application of strong focusing magnetic devices to the synchrotron and cyclotron, with the consequent increase, by many orders of magnitude, of attainable particle beam intensities and energies. Modern synchrotrons produce beams of up to 30 billion electron volts (30 Gev) in energy, and designs are in progress for similar accelerators that will produce beams with energies of several hundred Gev. The availability of such machines has given great impetus to the study of nucleon-nucleon scattering and the study of nuclear reactions induced by artificially accelerated protons, deuterons, and alpha particles, as well as by high-energy x-rays. Techniques of several kinds have been perfected for precise measurement of magnetic and other properties of the nucleus that follow from nucleons showing, like atomic electrons, all the characteristics of rotating bodies. (Although it is only an analogy, electrons are often visualized as spinning particles moving about the nucleus in well-defined orbits.) Systematic relationships of significance were discovered among the various properties of nuclei. For example, nuclei with even numbers of both neutrons and protons are more stable and abundant than those in which the nucleons appear in an "odd-even" combination. Nuclei with "odd-odd" numbers of protons and neutrons are, in turn, the least stable and least abundant of the nuclei. In particular, nuclei with the specific numbers 2, 8, 20, 50, 82, and 126 of either protons or neutrons show very strong binding and exceptional stability. The shape of the nucleus, inferred from measurements of the shape of its electric charge, is found to be closest to spherical for such so-called "magic" nuclei.

These and many other observations have been the basis of intensive and widespread efforts to achieve a systematic and coherent representation of the nucleus; but the picture is as yet far from complete. The construction of machine sources of energetic particles in the hundred and thousand Mev range has made it possible to generate from nuclei a host of subnuclear "elementary" particles (see MESON; HYPERON; PARTICLE, ELEMENTARY), whose existence demonstrates that nucleons are not simple particles and further complicates an already complex scene. The existence of a subnuclear particle very much like the subsequently discovered π-meson was suggested on theoretical grounds (by Hidekei Yukawa, 1937) as the agent responsible for binding nucleons to one another. Although no satisfactory meson theory has as yet been devised, theorists continue to hope that the proper understanding and description of the interactions of elementary particles may also shed light on the character of the force holding together the nucleus. The main properties of nuclei have nevertheless been fairly successfully explained by assuming only certain general features of the nuclear force, such as its short range and its essential similarity in the case both of neutrons and protons. A number of theories have been developed which account satisfactorily, if restrictedly, for many of the observed experimental phenomena.

Much effort has been concentrated, for obvious reasons, on explaining the simplest nuclear system, the deuteron, which consists of one proton and one neutron. It has been found that the behavior of this system at low energies is consistent with the assumption that the laws of quantum mechanics hold and that the nuclear force depends not only on the distance between the nucleons, but also to some extent on the relative directions of the "spins" and orbital rotations of the elementary particles. The force does not appear to depend, at least at particle energies below the order of 10 Mev, upon whether the interacting particles are protons or neutrons.

Nuclear Models: With more complicated nuclei, especially at higher energies, severe investigational difficulties arise because of the mathematical complexity of the many-body problem, which becomes formidable even when there are as few as three interacting bodies. This complexity, coupled with the uncertainty as to whether the laws of quantum mechanics are completely valid in the case of the nucleus, has forced upon investigators the procedure of assuming the simplest possible interactions and testing by experiment the phenomena predicted. With the LIQUID-DROP MODEL of the nucleus, for example, it has been possible to account for the nuclear masses and binding energies of the nuclei, expressing these by the numbers of nucleons, the nuclear electric charge, and the nuclear radius. Another, more detailed, and apparently quite fundamental model of the nucleus has been one in which, by contrast to the liquid-drop model, the nucleons are considered to move essentially independently of one another under the influence of a common central "potential" (see NUCLEAR-SHELL MODEL). Although this oversimplification of their average effect upon each other ignores the basic problem, the approach has been strikingly successful. Especially as applied by M. Mayer and H. Jensen, the theory has per-

mitted the development of a concept of nuclear structure quantitatively consistent with a very large body of experimental knowledge.

Although the present status of nuclear theory continues to rest on a somewhat disconnected phenomenological basis, many of the important features of the nucleus are understood in the very real sense that significant predictions can be made as to its behavior. The discovery of the powerful FISSION and FUSION phenomena, and our considerable understanding of the role of nuclear reactions in the creation and the evolution of matter on a cosmological scale, are only two examples of the effectiveness of even the present imperfect theoretical foundations. The situation is fluid and changing rapidly. Many heretofore dissimilar theoretical points of view are being reconciled, and some of the nuclear models are being extended to overlap one another and to encompass wider fields of observation. The mass of data to be reconciled is still very great. There is obvious need for much further experimentation to understand the evident but confusing dependence of nuclear forces on the velocities and spins of the nucleons and upon the subnuclear particles and their interactions.—*P. T. D. and F. J. E.*

NUCLEAR POWER PLANT: see ENGINE; NUCLEAR PROPULSION; NUCLEAR REACTOR.

NUCLEAR PROPULSION: use of a nuclear power plant as the source of energy for propulsion of a vehicle. In all such plants so far built or designed, some of the potential energy in uranium nuclei is converted into heat energy by a fission reactor (see NUCLEAR REACTOR), and the heat energy is then converted into mechanical energy. In submarines and ships the heat energy is transferred by a circulating coolant to a boiler where steam is generated, and the steam drives a turbine, which is coupled to the screws. In nuclear-powered

Propulsion reactor system for N. S. *Savannah:* First U. S. nuclear merchant ship utilizes a pressurized-water reactor. Heat of fission from uranium fuel elements is transferred from reactor and used to heat water, producing steam power. Twenty-four control rods are used to govern rate of chain reaction. (*Babcock & Wilcox*)

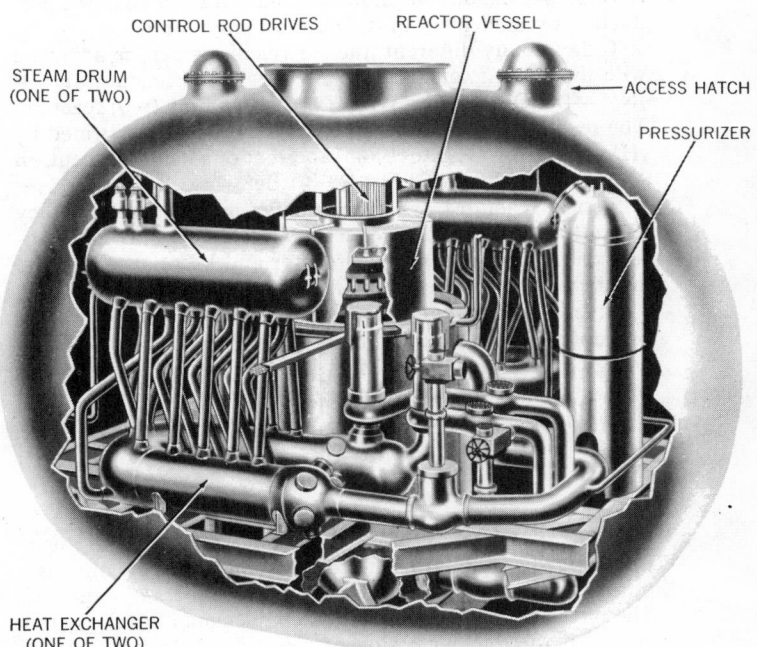

CONTROL ROD DRIVES   REACTOR VESSEL

STEAM DRUM
(ONE OF TWO)

ACCESS HATCH

PRESSURIZER

HEAT EXCHANGER
(ONE OF TWO)

ROCKETS the reactor heats hydrogen gas to high temperature, causing it to stream at high speed through a nozzle in the rear; the rocket is thus propelled forward. Since a nuclear reactor consumes only about a millionth as much fuel, by weight, as a coal-, oil-, or gas-burning power plant in producing the same quantity of heat, a nuclear-propelled vehicle need not carry large quantities of fuel or refuel frequently. Since the nuclear power plant needs no oxygen, it is well suited for submarines and space vehicles; indeed many submarines that are operating today have such plants, and the National Aeronautics and Space Agency has as one of its main projects the development of a nuclear-powered rocket. Freedom from frequent refueling makes nuclear propulsion attractive also for surface ships and long-range aircraft; thus the U. S. S. R. has built a nuclear-powered icebreaker, and the U. S. A. has a merchant ship, an aircraft carrier, and other naval vessels powered by nuclear reactors. A nuclear power plant for aircraft has been successfully ground-tested, but no aircraft using nuclear power has yet been constructed. A major problem is the massive, heavy shielding necessary to protect the aircraft's crew from radiation; a similar problem makes nuclear-powered automobiles impracticable.

Another possible future power source is the FUSION reactor, which derives its energy from the fusion of light nuclei to form helium, as occurs in the Sun: such reactors would find wide application because they use a more plentiful fuel and could probably convert nuclear energy directly into electrical energy.—*S. K.*

NUCLEAR REACTION: a reaction in which an atomic nucleus ($_zX^A$) changes its mass number A (its number of nucleons) or its atomic number Z (number of protons), or both. Natural and artificial radioactivity, as well as direct nuclear bombardment, provide conditions under which nuclear transformations take place. Ernest Rutherford was the first (1919) to produce a nuclear reaction of the α-p type (alpha particles used as projectiles and protons escaping as product-particles). The reaction may be symbolized as $_2He^4 + _7N^{14} \longrightarrow _1H^1 + _8O^{17}$, which means that an alpha particle (helium nucleus, $_2He^4$) interacts with a nitrogen nucleus ($_7N^{14}$) to form a proton (hydrogen nucleus, $_1H^1$) and an oxygen nucleus ($_8O^{17}$). This was the first man-made transmutation, since it resulted in the production of an element of different atomic number.

Today, many different nuclear reactions can be achieved with the aid of PARTICLE ACCELERATORS. The reaction $_1H^1 + _7N^{14} \longrightarrow _8O^{15} + \gamma$ is a typical proton-gamma (p-γ) reaction. The reaction of a proton-neutron (p-n) type is illustrated by $_1H^1 + _{11}Na^{23} \longrightarrow _{12}Mg^{23} + _0n^1$ and that of a deuteron-neutron (d-n) type is illustrated by $_1H^2 + _4Be^9 \longrightarrow _5B^{10} + _0n^1$.

Fission reactions are of particular interest because they liberate vast amounts of energy. Thus an atom of U^{238} absorbs a neutron in a nuclear reactor and becomes U^{239}. The latter emits a negative beta particle and is converted to Np^{239}. Another beta emission results in the formation of Pu^{239}, which, on capturing a neutron, undergoes fission with a release of energy. Fusion reactions, in which light nuclei combine, are responsible for the energy production in stars. For example, if a high-energy proton collides with another proton of lower energy, the reaction $_1H^1 + _1H^1 \longrightarrow _1H^2 + _1e^0$ may occur. —*A. E.*

NUCLEAR REACTOR: a furnace that converts part of the potential energy latent in atomic nuclei into heat energy; and, as a bonus, simultaneously produces large numbers of neutrons. The physical phenomenon which enables man to release this energy is the nuclear fission process. To understand how a

nuclear reactor works it is necessary to know the following properties of the fission process:

(1) The nucleus of the atom of one form of naturally occurring uranium, called U^{235}, sometimes splits in half (fissions) when struck by a neutron. Two other nuclei, which can be produced artificially, also have this property. One is the form of uranium called U^{233}, which is produced from thorium by absorption of a neutron. The other is plutonium^{239}, produced from uranium by neutron absorption.

(2) The slower the speed of the incoming neutron, the more probable it is that the target nucleus will fission. This is a special case of the general rule that slow neutrons interact more readily with nuclei than do fast ones, simply because the former spend more time within the nucleus, and therefore have time to share their energy with a larger number of the neutrons and protons there.

(3) After fission has occurred, the two resulting medium-weight nuclei fly apart with extremely high speeds. These fragments quickly collide with neighboring atoms, imparting additional kinetic energy to them and thus heating the environment. Non-nuclear heating plants derive their heat energy from the motion of molecules recoiling from chemical reactions, *i.e.* from exchange and rearrangement of electron orbits. But the forces which bind neutrons and protons together in nuclei are so much stronger than those binding electrons in molecules that the corresponding energy changes in fission processes are a million times larger. A nuclear reactor produces about a million times more heat than a conventional furnace from roughly the same weight of fuel.

(4) One additional property of fission, discovered by Leo Szilard and Enrico Fermi in 1939, is vital to operation of a

Pressurized steel sphere, 160 ft in diameter, will house nuclear reactor of 150,000-kw Garigliano Nuclear Power Station, Italy's first. The sphere is so constructed as to contain any accidental release of radioactive materials. (*General Electric*)

"**Nuclear furnace**": Reactor pressure vessel is installed at Humboldt Bay Nuclear Power Station, Eureka, Cal. The heart of the plant's nuclear system, this 134-ton steel unit will contain uranium fuel elements and boiling-water coolant. (*General Electric*)

The accompanying figure is an idealized sketch of a nuclear reactor showing the essential components. The *fuel rods,* made of the fissionable material, are usually alloyed with other metals to minimize corrosion and maximize heat conductivity and strength. In so-called homogeneous reactors, the fuel is uniformly distributed in the form of a salt dissolved in a fluid, as a slurry, or as a molten metal. The *control rods* are made of a material which absorbs neutrons readily; the two materials most commonly used are cadmium and boron. Their function is to prevent the chain reaction from getting out of hand. By varying the degree of insertion of the control rods, the free neutron population can be controlled. The *moderator* is a material of low atomic weight which does not absorb neutrons. Its function is to slow down the high-speed neutrons emitted by the fission fragments and thus increase the probability of fission. Light nuclei are used as moderators because the neutron transfers a larger fraction of its kinetic energy in a collision with a light nucleus than with a heavy one. Water, carbon, beryllium, and heavy water are commonly used as moderators. The *coolant* is a gas or liquid pumped through the reactor for the purpose of transferring the generated heat to a boiler or turbine. Common coolants are water, liquid sodium, certain organic liquids, carbon dioxide gas, and helium.

Some neutrons inevitably leak out of the reactor, and others are captured by structural materials and control rods. In a correctly designed reactor, a setting of the control rods can be found such that the rate at which neutrons are lost by absorption and leakage equals the rate at which they are being produced by fission products; the reactor is then said to be "critical." If a control rod is now inserted further into the reactor, the added absorber causes the rate of loss of neutrons to exceed the rate of production, and the neutrons gradually disappear; this state of affairs is called the "subcritical" state. Finally, if a control rod in a critical reactor is further removed, the reactor becomes "supercritical." If unchecked, the neutron population increases until something catastrophic (*e.g.* melting of a fuel element) forces the reactor into subcriticality. The central problem of reactor design is to keep the neutron population under control at all times. It must be possible to make the reactor critical and hold it there at all stages of its lifetime.

A component common to all reactors is the reflector. This is a shell completely surrounding the reactor proper; its purpose is to reflect back to the fuel neutrons which might otherwise leak out. Reflector materials must readily scatter, but not absorb, neutrons. Since the requirements are not much different, moderator materials are frequently used as reflectors.

The first nuclear reactor was completed Dec. 1942 in a converted squash court at the Univ. of Chicago by a group of scientists under the direction of Enrico Fermi. Few persons knew that the Atomic Age was born that day, because all work on nuclear fission was done in secrecy. The world was at war, and it was fairly obvious that an atomic bomb was a distinct possibility. Since then, essentially all reactor work has been declassified, and hundreds of reactors have

nuclear reactor. To produce a useful amount of power it is necessary to have very large numbers of nuclei fissioning simultaneously. But each fission must be initiated by a neutron, and there are a negligible number of free neutrons available in nature. Neutrons are bound inside nuclei; are extracted with difficulty; and decay after about 15 minutes of freedom. Neutrons become available by the fact that the fission fragments when formed are highly excited internally, with the result that neutrons and protons inside the fragments jostle one another energetically. By the time the fragments have settled down to their final states, they have boiled off several neutrons—usually two or three. Thus each fission provides neutrons to initiate other fissions, and a chain reaction can be started simply by inserting one neutron among a large number of U^{235} nuclei. This one neutron is always available, because the energetic particles of the ubiquitous cosmic radiation are continually knocking neutrons out of nuclei.

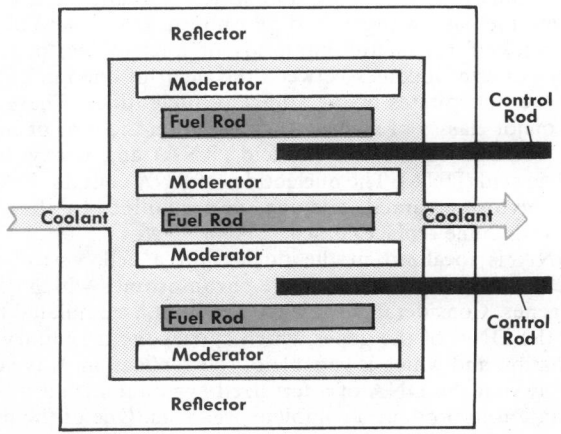

Schematic diagram of nuclear reactor: Control rods are set between fuel rods to regulate rate of nuclear reaction. Withdrawal of the rods permits free passage of neutrons from one fuel rod to another, increasing reaction rate. Moderator acts to slow these neutrons, increasing the likelihood of their reacting with fissionable nuclei.

been built in many countries. They fall into three categories: for research, for production, and for power. The first two types are designed to maximize the neutron leakage in certain areas. The neutrons from a research reactor are used for scientific experiments, and those from a production reactor are used to produce new kinds of nuclei by neutron absorption. All plutonium used for atomic bombs is made in this way. Power reactors for civilian purposes have become economically competitive with conventional power plants in some areas. Nuclear power for propulsion of submarines has been highly successful. Small nuclear generators are used to power unmanned weather stations in the arctic and other remote places, and to provide auxiliary power aboard satellites and other spacecraft (see ENGINE; NUCLEAR PROPULSION).—*S. K.*

NUCLEAR-SHELL MODEL: a conception of the atomic nucleus that has had remarkable success in predicting certain properties of the nucleus. Like the electron "shells" of the atom (see ELECTRON STRUCTURE OF ATOMS), the nucleus displays all the properties of a structured quantum-mechanical system of particles. It is excitable in general to states, or combinations of states, of specifiable energy and spin; and its constituent particles, the nucleons, are known to be subject to the same quantum-mechanical rules as electrons (see EXCLUSION PRINCIPLE and QUANTUM STATISTICS). In the case of atomic electrons, it is possible to infer the structure of even quite large atomic aggregates fairly accurately by considering separately the interaction of each electron with the nucleus. This is quite permissible, since the force of attraction exerted by the nucleus is so much larger than the force of mutual repulsion that the electrons exert upon each other. The situation in the nucleus itself is not so simple. There is no single influence that affects the neutrons and protons strongly enough to predominate over their mutual interactions with each other. The assumption that the problem may be treated "as though" each nucleon experienced on the average a simply definable central field of force has nevertheless met with striking success. A valid treatment of the nucleus appears to be that of considering the nucleons to be independent of one another and influenced only by a common "nuclear potential" characteristic of the nucleus as a whole. (Physically the common potential is an oversimplified average representation of the effects of the nucleons on each other.) In this way, just as with the atomic system, one finds a series of independent "single particle" states of specified character (*e.g.* energy and spin) that may be occupied by each of the nucleons in accordance with the rules of quantum mechanics. The behavior of the nucleus as a whole is then described in terms of the collective property of all of the nucleon states. For example, the energy of the nucleus is the simple sum of the energies of all the states, and the spin of the nucleus is one of the allowable vector summations of all the single-particle-state spins. Applied quantitatively and subjected to some further refinements (such as allowing the energy of each particle state to be influenced by the relative directions of the orbital and intrinsic toplike spins of the nucleons), the theory has led to an explanation of the observed binding energies and masses and spins of the nuclei. A particular success of the model has been its prediction of a structure among the nucleons consistent with the special properties of nuclei with 2, 8, 20, 50, 82, or 126 of either neutrons or protons. Such nuclei (known for some time as "magic" nuclei) have binding energies greater than those of their neighbors and show other properties (*e.g.* more regular shape) that confirm the shell structure predicted by the theory. The model does not agree very well with measured magnetic and electric moments of nuclei, but these are known to be exceedingly sensitive to

small differences in the nucleon motions. The superposition of effects due to additional kinds of nuclear motion (vibrations and rotations of the whole nucleus, and coherent "collective" rotations of several of the nucleons at a time) has reduced many of these discrepancies, substantiating the essential validity of the model.—*P. T. D. and F. J. E.*

NUCLEAR WEAPONS: devices designed to destroy military targets by the rapid and massive release of atomic energy. The energy is released by the FISSION of isotopes of uranium or plutonium atoms in an ATOMIC BOMB, or by the FUSION of deuterium atoms in a HYDROGEN BOMB. The energy yield from either nuclear reaction is vastly greater than that from a dynamite or TNT explosion. Complete fission of 1 lb of uranium or plutonium would release approximately as much energy as an explosion of 9,000 tons of TNT. Fusion of all the nuclei in 1 lb of deuterium would yield the energy of 26,000 tons of TNT. Whereas TNT explosions destroy by shock only, nuclear weapons cause damage also by intense heat, immediate lethal radiation, and lingering poisonous contamination. The first nuclear weapon was an experimental uranium device exploded in the U. S. A. at Alamogordo, N. Mex., July 16, 1945. A uranium bomb was then exploded over the Japanese city of Hiroshima (Aug. 6, 1945), followed by a plutonium bomb over Nagasaki (Aug. 9, 1945). The terrifying destruction caused by these two bombs is generally credited with forcing Japan's surrender and bringing an end to World War II. Since then, nuclear weapons have been exploded in a series of tests by governments of the U. S. A., the U. S. S. R., Great Britain, France, and Communist China. In the U. S. A. these tests have led to the development of nuclear weapons that are small enough for use by infantrymen or artillery and are reduced in destructive power and contaminating after-effects.

In 1963 the U. S. A., the U. S. S. R., and Great Britain signed a treaty banning nuclear testing in the atmosphere, in space, and under water. Underground tests are not covered by the treaty, nor are France and Communist China bound by it. —*G. Wh.*

NUCLEI: in meteorology, particles in the atmosphere which have the necessary chemical and physical properties to trigger a change of phase of water molecules, either from vapor to liquid or from liquid to solid. *Condensation nuclei* form liquid droplets from water vapor. *Freezing nuclei* make ice crystals from droplets of supercooled water. (See CONDENSATION.) —*D. H. L.*

NUCLEIC ACIDS: high-molecular-weight substances often conjugated with proteins, present in all organisms from viruses to man. They consist of a large number of repeating units called nucleotides, each of which contains a purine or pyrimidine base, a sugar, and phosphoric acid. These building blocks form chains hundreds of nucleotides long, by means of ester linkages between the sugar of one nucleotide and the phosphates of the adjacent nucleotides. There are two major classes of nucleic acids based on the type of sugar they contain: ribose nucleic acid (RNA) and deoxyribose nucleic acid (DNA). The nucleotides of RNA contain the four bases cytosine, uracil, adenine, and guanine. In those of DNA, thymine replaces uracil.

DNA is localized in the nucleus of a cell, where it is specifically a constituent of the chromosomes which carry the genes. Considerable evidence has been accumulated that it is the DNA of the genes which carries the hereditary information and which is capable of self-replication. It is noteworthy that the DNA of a fertilized egg contains all the information to produce a complete organism. One of the most

exciting research problems in biochemistry today is the deciphering of the "code"—presumed to reside in the arrangement of the bases along the DNA chain—by which genetic information is transmitted.

Hydrogen bonding between the bases of two DNA chains causes these chains to intertwine to form a double helix. In these complementary chains, guanine bonds with cytosine and thymine with adenine. It is thought that during replication the chains unwind and each serves as a model for the production for a new chain complementary to itself.

RNA is found throughout the cytoplasm and also in the nucleus. There are a high-molecular-weight variety primarily found in small particles called ribosomes, and also a shorter chain type, referred to as "transfer" or "soluble" RNA. Both kinds appear to play important roles in PROTEIN SYNTHESIS. In a number of viruses which do not contain any DNA, RNA is evidently capable of serving as the carrier of genetic information.

Enzymes (deoxyribonucleic acid polymerases and ribonucleic acid polymerases) have been discovered that will syn-

Fragment of nucleic acid: Seen in an electron micrograph, DNA is a threadlike structure some 17 angstroms wide and over 1,000 times as long. The portion appearing in this model shows the structure of something like 1/500 of the entire length of the molecule. Seen along the outer edges are the two helical strands of nucleotides—deoxyribose sugar groups (pentagonal structures) linked by phosphates. The horizontal groupings spanning the space between the helices are each composed of a pair of nitrogenous bases (seen separately at top of page). In the actual molecules these basal planes are separated by an interval of 3.4 angstroms. (*Central Scientific Co.*)

Bases joining nucleic acid chains: The two intertwining helices that are the most conspicuous feature of the DNA molecule are joined by a long succession of crosslinks. These links consist exclusively of four nitrogenous bases—adenine, thymine, guanine, and citosine, which combine in complementary pairs. One pair (*above*) consists of adenine (*left*) linked in two places to thymine (*right*) by hydrogen bonds; the other pair (*bottom*) consists of guanine (*left*) linked (also in two places, also by hydrogen bonds) to cytosine (*right*). The DNA of a given species contains equal amounts of adenine and thymine and equal amounts of guanine and cytosine. (*Griffin & George Sales Ltd.*)

thesize DNA and RNA respectively from deoxyribonucleotide and ribonucleotide triphosphates. In the reaction, pyrophosphate is split from the nucleotide triphosphates in each case, and the remaining phosphate of one nucleotide is bound covalently to the deoxyribose or ribose group of the next nucleotide. The phosphate group links the third carbon atom of one sugar with the fifth carbon atom of the adjacent sugar. Synthesis of DNA requires the presence of existing DNA to serve as a primer or "template." Recently there has been discovered yet another RNA fraction. It requires DNA as primer for its synthesis and has a base sequence complementary to that of the primer DNA used. It is believed to be the "messenger" sent out by the genes to direct the synthesis of specific proteins in the ribosomes.—*E. S.*

NUCLEON: neutron or proton. These are the building blocks of atomic nuclei. Nucleons are attracted to each other by a strong, short-range force to form atomic nuclei.—*S. K.*

NUCLEONICS: the whole complex of scientific and technological activities related to practical utilization of nuclear energy. Principal areas are: (1) Mining and purification of the nuclear fuels—uranium and thorium. A novel technology involved here is the separation of isotopes of uranium having different nuclear properties but nearly identical chemical properties. (2) Design and construction of NUCLEAR WEAPONS for military use and for peaceful applications such as large earth-moving projects. (3) Design and construction of NUCLEAR REACTORS. This is the largest subarea, involving close collaboration of large numbers of reactor physicists, heat-transfer engineers, and metallurgists. (4) Utilizing of reactor-produced radioactivity elements in a variety of industrial, medical, and scientific applications. (See RADIOISOTOPE.) (5) Recovery of uranium from spent fuel elements of reactors, and utilization of the radioactive fission products in the residue. A serious challenge in large-scale utilization of reactors for industrial power is not only to find practical use for the vast energy available in the form of radioactive FISSION PRODUCTS, but also to find safe means of storing or disposing of these dangerous substances.—*S. K.*

NUCLEOSIDES: in biochemistry, an important class of compounds that are constituents of nucleic acids. Nucleosides are formed by combination of a sugar and a purine or pyrimidine base. In most naturally occurring nucleosides the sugar is either ribose or 2-deoxyribose. Ribose nucleosides are found

COMMONLY OCCURRING NUCLEOSIDES

Nucleoside	Purine Base	Pyrimidine Base	Sugar
Adenosine	Adenine		Ribose
Guanosine	Guanine		Ribose
Inosine	Hypoxanthine		Ribose
Cytidine		Cytosine	Ribose
Uridine		Uracil	Ribose
Deoxyadenosine	Adenine		Deoxyribose
Deoxyguanosine	Guanine		Deoxyribose
Deoxycytidine		Cytosine	Deoxyribose
Thymidine		Thymine	Deoxyribose

in ribose nucleic acid (RNA), and nucleosides based on 2-deoxyribose (deoxyribonucleosides) are found in deoxyribose nucleic acids (DNA). Nucleosides are converted to nucleotides by addition of an inorganic phosphate group. See also NUCLEIC ACIDS; NUCLEOTIDES; PURINES; PYRIMIDINES.—*K. H.*

NUCLEOTIDES: in biochemistry, a class of compounds formed from NUCLEOSIDES by addition of phosphoric acid. Thus, the combination of residues of adenine (a purine), ribose (a sugar), and phosphate yields the nucleotide adenine monophosphate (AMP). Further additions of phosphate yield adenine diphosphate (ADP) and adenine triphosphate (ATP). The adenine nucleotides are of great importance in metabolism (see OXIDATIVE PHOSPHORYLATION; ENERGY; MUSCLE CONTRACTION). Other nucleosides, *e.g.* cytidine, guanosine, and uridine, can also form mono-, di-, and triphosphates. The mononucleotides of adenylic, guanylic, uridylic, and cytidylic acids are hooked together to form ribose nucleic acids (RNA). The mononucleotides of deoxyadenylic, deoxycytidylic, deoxyguanylic, and thymidylic acids are found in deoxyribose nucleic acids (DNA). For nucleotides of a slightly different type, see COENZYME A; FLAVIN NUCLEOTIDES; PYRIDINE NUCLEOTIDES.—*K. H.*

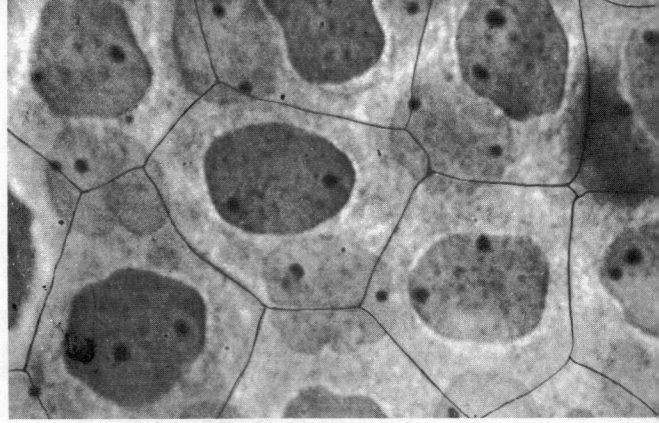

Cells with nuclei in tail fin of salamander larva are revealed in microphoto. Network of boundaries between cells has been emphasized by retouching. (*L. and M. Milne*)

NUCLEUS (of cell): an important body found in the cells of all animals and plants (with the exception of the mature red blood cell of mammals). It is the sole site of DNA (deoxyribonucleic acid—the prime constituent of the nuclear chromosomes) in the cell. DNA determines the nature of the enzymes and other proteins in the cells; thus it controls the synthesis of substances in the cytoplasm and, therefore, cell heredity. The nucleus carries the code of the inheritance in the DNA in its chromosomes, and this is passed on from one cell generation to the next by nuclear division, or mitosis (see also NUCLEIC ACIDS).—*P. S.*

NUCLIDE: any species of atom that is characterized by the charge and mass number of its nucleus. The nuclide classification uniquely identifies a particular species of atom, whereas isotopes (nuclides of equal charge), isobars (nuclides of equal mass), and isotones (nuclides containing the same number of neutrons) refer to families of atoms. Physicists have thus far identified about 1,200 nuclides, most of which do not occur naturally—they have been created by bombardment of naturally occurring nuclei with projectiles from nuclear particle accelerators and reactors. All the man-made nuclides and some of those that occur naturally are unstable and decay into stable nuclei by the process of radiation. See ATOM NUCLEUS; RADIOACTIVITY.—*W. P. C.*

NUMBER: one of the basic elements of mathematics. In simple situations, numbers often answer questions of how many and how much. The simplest types of numbers are the whole numbers, integers, or **natural numbers,** denoted by the symbols 1, 2, 3, 4, and so on. The origin of whole numbers dates back to primitive times; undoubtedly man learned the basic ideas of whole numbers in comparing such things as flocks of sheep. Early symbols were vertical marks, and later the letters of the alphabet were used. The Roman system of notation probably developed from these. However, it was not a convenient system and was slowly replaced in the later middle ages in Europe by the Hindu-Arabic system, which depended on the idea of POSITIONAL NOTATION and made possible the simplification of methods of computation. Ancient man was also familiar with the concept of a fraction to express parts of a whole, and to represent parts of units of measurement; *e.g.* a span was half of a cubit.

Although the ideas of whole numbers and of fractions were adequate for the needs of man in early antiquity, the development of geometry in Egypt and Greece led to new types of numbers. The length of the diagonal of a square that was one unit on each side could not be expressed exactly by means of either whole numbers or fractions. The circumference and the diameter of a circle were also seen to be incommensurable, and **irrational numbers,** *e.g.* $\sqrt{2}$, π, came into existence in

Greece. The number zero migrated to the West with the Hindu-Arabic system, and negative numbers were developed soon after. It seems surprising today to realize that only 500 yr ago mathematicians called negative numbers false numbers and that men had trouble comprehending the idea of signed numbers and of zero. It was easy to visualize 5 horses, 2 horses, or 1 horse, but it seemed completely ridiculous to think of 0 horses or -3 horses. The idea of signed numbers to represent opposite directions gradually took hold, so that today no one is disturbed by their use in measuring temperature, debits, and deficits. Similarly, the number zero is now familiar, both in connection with positional notation, as a blank space holder, e.g. in 103, and in describing a concept of nothingness, as "there have been 0 kings of the United States."

When only integers and fractions were known, it was possible to perform most of the elementary operations of arithmetic. If any two integers or fractions were added, multiplied, or divided, the result was an integer or fraction. Subtraction also was always possible as long as the number to be subtracted was the smaller number. The inclusion of the ideas of signed numbers and zero now extended subtraction, so that any whole number or fraction could be subtracted from any other. However, the introduction of zero into the number system introduced a new difficulty. Operations involving zero gave no trouble, except division by zero. Indeed, it became necessary to recognize that it is impossible to divide by zero. This is seen from the fact that if the quotient of $a \div b$ is a number c, then $c \times b = a$. If $b = 0$, then there is no number c that will make $c \times 0 = a$, unless a is also zero, in which case any number at all will do. Thus in neither case is there a unique number which will satisfy the operation.

Any positive or negative integer or fraction, or zero, is called a *rational* number. We have observed that the four basic operations of arithmetic, addition, subtraction, multiplication, and division (except by 0) can always be performed on any pair of rational numbers. The set of rational numbers is therefore said to be closed under these operations.

The Greeks recognized that there are *irrational* numbers, e.g. $\sqrt{2}$, that cannot be expressed exactly as a fraction, although they can be approximated as closely as one desires by means of a fraction. This leads to the realization that, if rational and irrational numbers are written in decimal notation, some decimals terminate (e.g. 370, 2.5), some repeat (e.g. .333...), and others continue without terminating or repeating, (e.g. 1.41421...). It is possible to show that all terminating and repeating decimals can be expressed in the form of a fraction and hence are rational numbers, and that the nonterminating and nonrepeating decimals are the irrational numbers.

The collection of all rational and irrational numbers is called the set of **real numbers.** This set is closed under the operations of addition, subtraction, multiplication, and division (except by 0). However, irrational numbers introduce the idea of root extraction, and so the question now arises as to whether we can extract the root of any number in the set of real numbers. A difficulty is soon observed when we seek to extract a square root of a negative number. For example, the square root of -4 cannot be a number among the real numbers, for this would require a number b which had the property that $b \times b = -4$. That there is no such number is evident, since the product of two positive or of two negative numbers is always positive. To mend this gap in the real numbers, imaginary numbers were introduced.

An **imaginary number** is a number b that has the property that $b \times b = -b^2$. In order to avoid complications in operations with numbers, an imaginary unit, denoted by i, is introduced with the property that $i \times i = -1$; hence

$i = \sqrt{-1}$. Thus, we express the square roots of negative numbers with this unit, e.g. $\sqrt{-4}$ is written $\sqrt{4} \times \sqrt{-1} = 2i$, and $\sqrt{-4} \times \sqrt{-4}$ becomes $2i \times 2i = 4i^2 = -4$; hence we say that the square root of -4 is $2i$. All even roots of negative numbers are imaginary numbers, but odd roots of negative numbers are real numbers; for example, $\sqrt[3]{-8} = -2$, since $(-2)(-2)(-2) = -8$. When real and imaginary numbers are added, e.g. 3 and $2i$, we can only express the sum as $3 + 2i$, since the two parts involve different units. Such a number is called a **complex number**. It can always be expressed in the form $a + bi$, where a and b are real numbers. If neither a nor b is zero, the number is complex; if $a = 0$, the number is imaginary, and if $b = 0$, the number is real. The set (collection) of complex numbers is closed under the operations of addition, subtraction, multiplication, division (except by 0), involution (raising to a power), and evolution (extracting a root). For this reason, it is the basic number system of arithmetic and of algebra, and it continues to serve throughout mathematics. If no set of numbers is specified in a problem in elementary mathematics, it is assumed that the set of complex numbers is meant. There are many times, however, when the set is restricted to the set of real numbers, e.g. in most problems considered in analytic geometry and in elementary calculus. See also TRANSCENDENTAL NUMBER; TRANSFINITE NUMBERS.—*H. E. W.*

NUMBER MYSTICISM: the superstitious attribution of mystical properties to numbers. Before the advent of the POSITIONAL NOTATION now used to write numbers, the rules for arithmetical operations were so difficult that a man skilled in reckoning was regarded as having almost supernatural powers. This may be one reason why mystical interpretations of numbers have been so popular and widespread. In ancient times they were incorporated into religious systems: The Babylonians used a number system based on 60, and associated each number up to 60 with a god. Certain numbers recur in the Old Testament. Both the deluge and Moses' sojourn on Mt Sinai lasted 40 days and 40 nights; the children of Israel wandered in the desert for 40 yr. Another ominous number was seven. "For seven days, seven priests with seven trumpets invested Jericho, and on the seventh day they encompassed the city seven times." Among the sevens in the New Testament are the seven deadly sins, and the seven spirits of God. In Chinese mythology, odd numbers signified white, day, sun, and fire; even numbers signified black, night, water, and earth. To the Pythagoreans (c. 550 B. C.), odd numbers were indissoluble and masculine; even numbers were ephemeral and feminine. The Pythagoreans attributed divine significance to most numbers up to 50. The number one, the source of all numbers, represented reason; two, man and, also, opinion; three, woman; five, marriage. Four, the product of equals (2 × 2), was considered a divine number signifying justice and cosmic creation, whereas the "mother of all" was ten $(1 + 2 + 3 + 4)$. Even relatively modern mathematicians have succumbed to the lore of mysticism. In the 17th cent. Leibniz recommended the adoption of the binary system, instead of the decimal system, since it requires only two digits: 1, which he believed to represent God, and 0, the void out of which the universe was created.

Gematria: The Hebrews, Greeks, and Romans all used letters to symbolize numbers. The first letter of the Hebrew alphabet, א (aleph), was used for 1, as was the first Greek letter, α (alpha); the second letters, ב (beth) and β (beta), were used for 2. To represent 11, both systems used their letters for 10 and for 1. Every letter of the alphabets had a numerical value, and as a result the values of the individual letters in any word could be added to produce a sum that, in a magical way, represented that word. The names of the heroes Patroclus, Hector, and Achilles add up to 87, 1225, and 1276 respectively, and "therefore" Achilles was the greatest man. The book of Revelations gives 666 as the "number of the beast." (A gematric explanation of this is that 666 is the total of the Hebrew letters required to write "Nero Caesar.") The modern superstition of numerology depends mainly on gematric interpretations of names.

Gematria in part was concerned with perfect numbers—that is, any number which is the sum of its divisors, excluding the number itself. The smallest perfect number is 6, its divisors being 1, 2, and 3. The next is 28, with divisors 1, 2, 4, 7, and 14.

St. Augustine wrote: "God created all things in six days because this number is perfect." If the gematic sum of a word was perfect, the concept represented by the word was considered perfect. When asked what a friend was, Pythagoras replied: "One who is the other I; such are 220 and 284." The divisors of 220 add up to 284; the divisors of 284 total 220. Such pairs are still called *amicable*. There is a story of a medieval prince who discovered that his name totaled 284, and therefore sought a bride whose name totaled 220. The mystical properties of perfect and amicable numbers have no place in modern life, but their mathematical properties are studied as part of NUMBER THEORY.

Mysticism in Geometry: Mystics have looked for magic in shapes as well as in numbers. The Greeks studied the regular or platonic solids (solids whose faces are all congruent regular polygons). It was probably the Pythagoreans who proved that there are only five. They held that Earth was produced from the cube; fire from the regular tetrahedron; air from the regular octahedron; water from the regular icosahedron; and the celestial sphere itself from the regular dodecahedron. Plato (*c.* 400 B. C.) was attracted to this teaching and helped to perpetuate it. As late as the 17th cent., Johannes Kepler, who discovered the laws of planetary motion, tried to show how the platonic solids could be placed inside the orbits of the major planets.—*B. P. S.*

NUMBER SYSTEMS: The essentials of a number system are symbols for small totals which are convenient in written and spoken language, and a scheme for combining these symbols to represent larger aggregates without unduly burdening the system with a vast array of unrelated marks and sounds. The second requirement was less important in primitive systems than in systems adapted to modern use, since large numbers played a less prominent role in them. Modern methods of computing are largely determined by the scheme adopted for writing large numbers.

Primitive Systems: The symbols for small numbers—the numerals, or digits—took many forms in different cultures. They were often mere repetitions of a basic mark. Thus, in the Egyptian system the first nine numerals were

| | || ||| |||| ||| ||| |||| |||| ||||
|| ||| ||| |||| |||||

The Babylonian numerals were similar, but employed the chisel mark, Y, for each unit. It is one of the virtues of the Hindu-Arabic system, which is the system used by Western civilizations today, that separate, compact, nonrepetitive symbols denote these numerals. Although present-day symbols look quite different from those of the Hindus of some 2,000 yr ago, they are not intrinsically superior. They underwent considerable modification in form prior to the invention of printing, probably because of variations among copyists. They have changed little in appearance since the 15th cent.

Along with the numerals for small numbers, some system of counting in groups is necessary to deal with large totals and represent them compactly. Primitive number systems

recognized this necessity. The early Egyptian hieroglyphic system had special characters for the powers of 10. For example, ∩ (a heel) denoted 10, ⟨scroll⟩ (a scroll) denoted 10², ⟨lotus⟩ (a lotus) denoted 10³, and other symbols were utilized for higher powers. Three thousand would be denoted by the thrice-repeated symbol for 10³; that is, ⟨⟨⟨. The number we call two thousand three hundred twenty-five would be represented by ⟨⟨ ⟨⟨⟨ ∩∩ ||| ||. The system is additive, this collection of symbols signifying ⟨⟨ + ⟨⟨⟨ + ∩∩ + |||||. Some systems employed both additive and subtractive principles; the Roman system is an example. In this, powers of 10 were represented by single letters—X for 10, C for 100, M for 1,000. There were also letters for groupings based on five—V for 5, L for 50, D for 500. The additive principle appears in XII, which is 10 + 2. The subtractive principle produces IV for 5 − 1, IX for 10 − 1, and XL for 50 − 10. The number 1964 would be written MCMLXIV.

The Egyptian system was a decimal system like our own, although it was cumbersome because of the repetitive manner of expressing what we express with one digit. The Babylonian system was mixed, utilizing basic groups of ten in numbers less than sixty, and groups of sixty for larger numbers. A system based on sixty is called sexagesimal. The Mayan civilization of Yucatán had a highly developed number system based on twenty. The Babylonian system was entirely positional but was ambiguous, since it did not have a zero.

Hindu-Arabic System: The great advantage of the Hindu-Arabic system over others lies in its use of a zero to eliminate ambiguities in position. This is illustrated in the number 302. Beginning at the right end of the number, the numerals denote units, tens of units, hundreds of units, and higher powers of 10 if there are more than three digits. Thus:

$$302 = 3 \cdot 10^2 + 0 \cdot 10^1 + 2 \cdot 10^0 = 3 \cdot 100 + 0 \cdot 10 + 2.$$

Zero serves a double purpose in the system. It denotes a void, or a nullity, providing the answer to such subtractions as 1 − 1 and 5 − 5, and it makes positional notation unambiguous. If there were no zero numeral in the second place (302) to indicate the absence of tens, it would be necessary to make

Primitive numbers: On this clay tablet, the Babylonians (c. 1690 B. C.) recorded a formula for making pottery glaze, using number symbols to indicate volume, weight, and length. (*Bettmann Archive*)

List of eleven properties, Babylonia, c. 2000 B. C., demonstrates how use of number symbols and mathematical thinking grew out of practical needs. (*Bettmann Archive*)

an estimate of the position of the digit 3 in order to decide whether it denotes tens, hundreds, or even thousands. Thus the invention of 0 was a crucial step in the construction of our number system, and was a major discovery. Because of the simple rules of calculation that the principle of position makes possible, school children today can learn to carry out operations with large numbers that were difficult for accomplished mathematicians prior to the adoption of this system. The positional principle was introduced in India as early as A. D. 800, but several hundred years elapsed before the Hindu-Arabic system containing this principle became well known in Europe. More centuries were required for the new methods of computation to win out over the older methods, which utilized some form of abacus.

The almost universal use of the Hindu-Arabic system based on ten—a decimal system—is likely to make one believe that the base of any system must necessarily be ten. However, ten has no intrinsic superiority over other possible bases. Its general adoption, in many early systems as well as our own, is probably due to the anatomical fact that humans normally have ten fingers and use them naturally in counting. Other bases are not only possible, but for some practical purposes are superior. Although any whole number other than 1 can be used as the base, two of them have special interest—twelve, the base of a duodecimal system, and two, the base of a binary system.

Duodecimal and Binary Systems: In a duodecimal system, numerals for zero and the first eleven whole numbers are necessary. Twelve is represented by 10, thirteen (one twelve plus one) by 11, twenty-four by 20, and one hundred and forty-four (twelve squared) by 100. The virtues of the decimal system are shared by the system based on twelve. The latter also has some advantages (*e.g.* divisibility by three and four), which have led to its being seriously advanced to replace the decimal system. Only two numerals appear in the binary system, 0 and 1. The number two is denoted by 10, three by 11, and four by 100. This system would be clumsy in written calculations, but it is well adapted for use by high-speed electronic computers, since the presence or absence of, say, a magnetized dot can represent 1 or 0.

The principle of position extends to the representation of fractions, which are called decimal fractions in the base ten. The method is equally good in all bases. Thus, in the duodecimal system, $28.413 = 2 \times 12 + 8 + 4/12 + 1/12^2 + 3/12^3$. In the binary system, $11.101 = 1 \times 2 + 1 + 1/2 + 0/2^2 + 1/2^3$.—*H. C.*

NUMBER THEORY: the branch of mathematics that deals with the properties of integers (positive and negative whole numbers and zero). Some problems are restricted to the natural numbers 1, 2, 3, ... A basic property of the integers is that they form a ring; *i.e.* the sum, difference, or product of any two of them is itself an integer. The next important property is that of division: when a and b are integers, one can always find a quotient q and a least positive remainder r such that $a = q \cdot b + r$ (for $0 \leqq r < b$). Example: $75 = 3 \cdot 23 + 6$. This holds regardless of the signs of a and b. Sometimes one uses the least absolute remainder (the remainder that is numerically least but may be positive or negative), *e.g.* $89 = 7 \cdot 13 - 2$.

An integer c is a divisor of a if $a = b \cdot c$, where b is also an integer, *e.g.* $15 = 3 \cdot 5$ or $(-3)(-5)$. In most problems only positive divisors are considered, and the number itself and 1 are trivial. A *common divisor* of a and b divides both numbers. Among these there is a greatest common divisor (gcd) denoted by (a, b). For example, since 6 is the greatest divisor of both 24 and 42, we write $(24, 42) = 6$. When $(a, b) = 1$, we say that a and b are relatively prime, *e.g.* $(15, 22) = 1$. A *multiple* of a and b is a number divisible by a and b; there is always a least common multiple (lcm) denoted by $[a, b]$; for example, $[6,9] = 18$. For any two numbers, the product of their lcm and gcd is equal to the product of the numbers: $(a, b) \cdot [a, b] = a \cdot b$.

Prime Factorization: A number is *composite* if it has divisors other than itself and 1; if not, it is *prime*. Every composite number has prime factors or divisors, namely the smallest primes greater than 1 that divide it. By successively factoring out prime factors, any integer can be written as a product of primes, *e.g.*

$$120 = 2 \cdot 2 \cdot 2 \cdot 3 \cdot 5 = 2^3 \cdot 3 \cdot 5$$

There is a unique prime factorization for each integer. If $p_1, p_2, \ldots, p_r$ are the prime factors of n, with exponents $\alpha_1, \alpha_2, \ldots, \alpha_n$ then

$$n = p_1^{\alpha_1} p_2^{\alpha_2} \cdots p_n^{\alpha_n}$$

For small numbers, the factorization can be found by trial and error. Note that if the number is n, none of the factors can exceed $\sqrt{n}$, so that one need only divide by primes between 1 and $\sqrt{n}$. There are many methods, some well suited to machine calculation, for determining whether a number is a prime. For numbers up to 10 million, there are tables of all primes, and factor tables giving the smallest divisor of each number.

The series of primes 2, 3, 5, 7, 11, 13, 17, 19, 23, 29, 31, 37, 41, 43, . . . is quite irregular, but the number of primes $\Pi(n)$ up to a number n increases approximately as the function $n/\ln n$. This fact is known as the prime number theorem. To find all primes below a certain limit n one can use the Sieve of Eratosthenes (230 B. C.). Write all the numbers 1, 2, 3, . . . , n, and strike out all numbers divisible by 2, except 2 itself. The next remaining number is the prime 3. Strike out every number divisible by 3 except 3 itself. The next remaining number is now 5, and the process is continued by striking out every fifth number, and so on, successively obtaining each prime.

Some types of primes are of particular interest. Among them are Fermat's primes of the form $F_a = 2^{2^a} + 1$. Only the following five are known to be prime: $F_o = 3$, $F_1 = 5$, $F_2 = 17$, $F_3 = 257$, $F_4 = 65537$. Gauss, in 1801, established the curious fact that a regular polygon with n sides can be constructed with straightedge and compass alone if n has the form $n = 2^k \cdot p_1 \cdots p_r$, where the p's are different Fermat primes.

Mersenne's primes have the form $M_p = 2^p - 1$, where p is a prime; e.g. $M_2 = 2^2 - 1 = 3$; $M_3 = 7$; $M_5 = 31$. Only 17 Mersenne primes have been found; the largest, M_{2281}, has 687 digits and is the largest prime known. Others, not yet published, have been computed.

Number Theoretical Functions: The prime factorization can be used to determine various number functions. The number of divisors of a number n is $\mu(n)$, where

$$\mu(n) = (\alpha_1 + 1) \cdots (\alpha_r + 1)$$

For example, $120 = 2^3 \cdot 3 \cdot 5$, so that $\alpha_1 = 3$, $\alpha_2 = 1$, $\alpha_3 = 1$; therefore $\mu(120) = 4 \cdot 2 \cdot 2 = 16$, and 120 has 16 divisors. Euler's function

$$\phi(n) = n(1 - 1/p_1) \cdots (1 - 1/p_r)$$

gives the number of positive integers less than and relatively prime to n; e.g.

$$\phi(120) = 120(1 - 1/2)(1 - 1/3)(1 - 1/5) = 32.$$

The sum $\sigma(n)$ of all divisors of n is

$$\sigma(n) = (1 + p_1 + \cdots + p_1^{\alpha_1}) \cdots (1 + p_r + \cdots + p_r^{\alpha_r})$$

e.g.

$$\sigma(120) = (1 + 2 + 2^2 + 2^3)(1 + 3)(1 + 5) = 360$$

Various Greek speculations on gematria—number symbolism —are connected with $\sigma(n)$. Greek numerals were denoted by letters of the alphabet, and therefore a word could be associated with a number. A concept was considered perfect when the number associated with its name was perfect, i.e. was the sum of its divisors (excluding as a divisor the number itself). For example, the divisors of 6 are 1, 2, and 3, and $6 = 1 + 2 + 3$, so that 6 is a perfect number. Similarly, the divisors of 28 are 1, 2, 4, 7, and 14; since 28 is the sum of its divisors, it too is perfect. In general, a number n is perfect if $\sigma(n) = 2n$. All known perfect numbers are even and have the form $n = 2^{\alpha-1}(2^\alpha - 1)$, where $(2^\alpha - 1)$ is a Mersenne prime; e.g. $496 = 2^4(2^5 - 1)$. Two numbers were called amicable by the Greeks when the sum of the divisors of one was equal to the other, and conversely. For example, 220 and 284 are amicable because the sum of the divisors of 220 is 284 and the sum of the divisors of 284 is 220. The general condition is $\sigma(n) = m + n = \sigma(n)$. A large number of pairs of amicable numbers are known, but there are few general rules.

Partitions: A representation of a number n as a sum of positive terms

$$n = a_1 + a_2 + \cdots + a_r$$

is called a partition. In simple partitions the a's may be any integers, e.g. $4 = 3 + 1 = 2 + 2 = 1 + 1 + 2 = 1 + 1 + 1 + 1$, and there are expressions for the number of such partitions. Often, however, the terms are restricted to some special kinds of numbers, and one wishes to know when such a representation is possible and in how many ways it can be done. An illustration is Goldbach's conjecture that every even number not less than 6 is the sum of two primes, e.g. $6 = 3 + 3$; $12 = 5 + 7$; $20 = 3 + 17$.

Lagrange showed that every integer is the sum of at most four squares: $47 = 5^2 + 3^2 + 3^2 + 2^2$. A related fact is due to Fermat: A prime that leaves the remainder 1 when divided by 4 can be written in only one way as the sum of two squares; e.g. $41 = 5^2 + 4^2$. The products of such primes have the same property, and this holds also when the prime is multiplied by 2 or a square number; these are the only numbers that can be represented as the sum of two squares. Similar partition problems exist for higher powers. Any integer is the sum of at most 9 third powers. In general there exists a number k_n such that every integer is the sum of k_n nth powers; determining k_n is called Waring's problem.

Diophantine Equations: These are equations to be solved in integers; they are named for the Greek mathematician Diophantos of Alexandria (c. A. D. 275). Since there is usually one equation containing several unknowns, they are often called indeterminate equations. The simplest are linear, a type often found in puzzle questions: In a party, the men pay $11, the women $7 each; the total bill is $200; how many men and how many women were there in the party? The condition is $11M + 7W = 200$. Dividing by the smallest coefficient $W = (200 - 11M)/7 = 28 - M + (4 - 4M)/7$. Since W must be an integer, $(4 - 4M)/7$ must be an integer, say T, so that $(4 - 4M)/7 = T = 4(1 - M)/7$, or $(1 - M)/7 = t$, where $t = T/4$. Thus, $M = 1 - 7t$, and $W = 27 + 11t$. Only for $t = 0$, $t = -1$, and $t = -2$ does this give positive values: $M = 1$, 8, or 15, and $W = 27$, 16, or 5; there are thus three solutions. Any linear Diophantine equation can be solved by reductions of this kind.

Another important equation of this type is the Pythagorean $x^2 + y^2 = z^2$, in which the integers x, y, and z can be the sides of a right triangle. One can assume that no two of the numbers have a common factor, since if they have they can be divided out. All the solutions can be obtained from the equations $x = 2uv$, $y = u^2 - v^2$, $z = u^2 + v^2$, where u and v may be any integers provided that one is odd, the other even. If $u = 4$ and $v = 1$, then $x = 8$, $y = 15$, $z = 17$. About 1680, Fermat stated that there are no non-zero integers x, y, and z that satisfy $x^n + y^n = z^n$, for n greater than 2. This conjecture has never been proved in general.

Congruences: A most useful calculus in number theory is the theory of congruences, introduced by Gauss in 1801. If the difference between two numbers a and b is divisible by m, then a is said to be congruent to b for the modulus m, written $a \equiv b \pmod{m}$. For example, $5 \equiv 23 \pmod 9$, and $25 \equiv -1 \pmod{13}$. Congruences behave much like equations. When they have the same modulus they can be added, subtracted, and multiplied. There are other analogies to equations; for instance, the congruence $x^2 + 1 \equiv 0 \pmod{13}$ has the two roots $x = \pm 5$, since $25^2 + 1 \equiv 0 \pmod{13}$. An important congruence result is Wilson's theorem, which states that for any prime p, then $1 \cdot 2 \ldots (p - 1) \equiv -1 \pmod p$. Thus, $1 \cdot 2 \cdot 3 \cdot 4 \cdot 5 \cdot 6 \equiv -1 \pmod 7$. For any number a and prime p, Fermat's theorem states $a^p \equiv a \pmod p$. Closely related is Euler's congruence $a^{\phi(n)} \equiv 1 \pmod n$, where a is relatively prime to n, and $\phi(n)$ is Euler's function.

There are numerous applications of congruences: (1) If for a number p one can find an integer a such that Fermat's theorem does not hold, then p cannot be a prime. This is a most effective way of establishing that a number is composite. (2) A positive rational fraction $r = m/n$ has a finite decimal expansion if and only if 2 and 5 are the only prime factors of n; in this case one can multiply r by a power of 10 to make it an integer; e.g. $3/8 = .375$. When no prime factor of n is equal to 2 or 5, the decimal expansion is purely periodic, or repeating; e.g. $12/37 = .324\ 324\ldots$. The length t of the period is the smallest number such that $10^t \equiv 1 \pmod n$. The period of $12/37$ is 3 because $10^3 \equiv 1 \pmod{37}$. Finally where n has factors 2 or 5 and others, the expansion is periodic but the period will not begin immediately; e.g. $7/15 = .4666\ldots$.—O. O.

NUMBERS, LAW OF LARGE: a basic law of probability and statistics which relates the probability of an event and the relative frequency of the occurrence of the event. Intuitively, it seems reasonable to assume that, if any experiment, *e.g.* rolling a true die, is repeated many times the relative frequency of any outcome will very nearly equal the probability of the outcome, and that, if the number of trials is increased, the relative frequency approaches the probability. Thus, if a die is rolled 600 times and an ace appears 102 times, the relative frequency is 102/600; if the die is rolled 6,000 times and an ace appears 1,007 times, the relative frequency is 1,007/6,000; if this is continued the relative frequencies approach the probability 1/6.

A more precise formulation of the law is that as the number of trials increases, it becomes more and more certain that the average number of successful outcomes differs from the probability by less than any pre-assigned number, however small. Jacob Bernoulli (1654–1705) formulated the law, and Siméon Poisson (1781–1840) coined its name. A common fallacy in the minds of some gamblers, due to a misunderstanding of this law, is the "law of averages." This is the basis of the belief that, if a coin has fallen heads many times in succession, it is much more likely to fall tails on the next throw.

A more general form of the law of large numbers which is of especial importance in statistics deals with the relationship of the mean $\overline{x}$ of a random sample of size n selected, with replacement, from a population with mean μ and standard deviation σ. In this form the theorem states that as n increases without bound the probability $\Pr(\mu - c \leqq \overline{x} \leqq \mu + c)$ approaches 1 where c is any positive number. From this theorem we can conclude that by choosing the sample size sufficiently large, we can be as sure as we want to be that the sample mean is as near to the population mean as we would like.—*H. E. W.*

NUTATION: the small periodic oscillations that are superposed on the precessional motion of the Earth's axis (see PRECESSION OF EQUINOXES). The phenomenon was discovered by the English astronomer J. Bradley from a study of star observations in 1727–47. Because the Earth is not spherical, the attractions of Moon and Sun produce a couple on Earth, the lunar contribution being the larger owing to its proximity. The nodes of the lunar orbit retrograde on the ecliptic in a period of 18.6 yr, and as a result the principal nutational oscillation has this period. The resulting motion would cause the celestial poles to describe a small ellipse of angular semi-major axis 9".21, the *constant of nutation*. However, this small oscillatory motion is superposed on the far larger precessional motion, and consequently the poles describe a wavy path (about a steady circle) among the stars. The next largest oscillation of the axis arises from the action of the Sun; its amplitude is 0".55, its period exactly ½ yr. There are numerous other far smaller terms (components) due to other variations in the strength of action of Moon and Sun.—*R. A. L.*

Nutation of Earth's axis is an elliptical motion superimposed on circular motion due to precession of equinoxes. During one cycle of precession (26,000 yr), over 1,400 cycles of nutation take place, and amplitude of nutation cycle is about ¹⁄₁₀,₀₀₀ that of precession cycle. (Drawing not to scale.)

NUTRITION: the science which deals with the composition of foods, how they are used by plants and animals, and their effect on health. Animal foods contain water, carbohydrates, fats, proteins, minerals, and vitamins. Most animals (including human beings) require for good health foods containing adequate amounts of calories (from carbohydrates, fats, and proteins); water; the fatty acid linoleic acid; the nitrogen-containing essential amino acids (from proteins) threonine, tryptophan, histidine, arginine, leucine, lysine, isoleucine, methionine, valine, and phenylalanine plus additional (non-specific) nitrogen from amino acids in proteins; the mineral elements (in combined form) calcium, phosphorus, potassium, sodium, chlorine, magnesium, iron, manganese, copper, iodine, cobalt, zinc, and fluorine; and vitamins A, C, D, E, K, B_{12}, thiamine, riboflavin, nicotinic acid (niacin), pyridoxine, pantothenic acid, biotin, choline, inositol, and folic acid. The nutrients in foods are digested, then absorbed from the intestinal tract and distributed to various parts of the body by the blood stream. Carbon compounds (food carbohydrates, fats, and proteins) are either used to build new body cells, stored as fat or carbohydrate, or burned to supply energy. The caloric (energy) needs of animals have been determined under different conditions of environment and exercise. Thus, a 150-lb man uses energy at the rate of 1,100 kilocalories/hr when walking upstairs, but expends only 65 kilocalories/hr when asleep. Some mineral elements are used to build or repair structural tissues such as bone; others function as a part of an enzyme system, being necessary for the activation of particular enzymes. Most vitamins function as a part of an enzyme system. Improper balance or inadequate intake of a required nutrient will cause a specific deficiency disease; *e.g.* iron deficiency causes anemia; vitamin C deficiency, scurvy.

Plants require water, carbon dioxide, and 12 minerals. They obtain the carbon dioxide required as food from the air. The remaining plant foods are absorbed by the roots as a water solution of minerals containing the needed chemical elements: nitrogen, sulfur, phosphorus, potassium, calcium, and magnesium in relatively large amounts; and iron, boron, manganese, copper, zinc, and molybdenum in trace amounts. The carbon dioxide is reduced to carbohydrates (sugars) in the leaf by the action of light (photosynthesis). The sugars then react in the plant cells with water, oxygen, fixed nitrogen, and sulfur to produce other carbohydrates, fats, proteins, and related carbon compounds needed by the cells. Each of the plant foods has a specific function. For example, carbon dioxide furnishes carbon compounds, magnesium is an essential part of chlorophyll, and the trace minerals are essential parts of enzyme systems. Lack of any one of these plant foods produces deficiency symptoms in plants. Thus, green leaves turn yellowish and stems slightly purplish on a low-nitrogen diet. In contrast, leaves turn dark green with a low-phosphorus diet. Deficiency of any of the 14 required food nutrients for plants reduces dry-matter yields of forage, flower, fruit, and seed.—*E. M.*

NYLON: see TEXTILE.

O

OBERTH, HERMANN, 1894–   ; German-U. S. physicist and rocket engineer; b. Hermannstadt, Rumania. Regarded as one of the pioneers of modern rocketry, he accurately described future space craft and space travel by rocket in his book, *Die Rakete zu den Planetenräumen,* which was published as early as 1923. During World War II, he worked briefly on the V-2 rocket project at Peenemunde, Germany; in 1955 he moved to the U. S. A. and began rocket research for the U. S. Government.—*C. S. V.*

OBSERVATORY, ASTRONOMICAL: a building or station from which astronomical observations are made. Before the 17th-cent. invention of the telescope, observations were made by eye with the help of sighting devices, *e.g.* the cross-staff. As early as 2608 B. C., an observatory was established in China for the purpose of correcting the calendar. Other studies in ancient times were concerned with time and the prediction of eclipses. The Greek astronomer Hipparchus (190–125 B. C.) began the systematic cataloging of star positions; in Alexandria, Ptolemy (*c.* A. D. 150) prepared the earliest catalog of stellar and planetary positions to come down to us; and Ulugh Begh (1394–1449) erected an observatory at Samarkand, Persia, and published star catalogs. The last famous observatory in the pre-telescopic era was founded by Tycho Brahe (1546–1601) at Uraniborg on the Danish island of Hveen. The accurate observations made there were used by Tycho's assistant Kepler to formulate his laws of planetary motion. These in turn led Newton to the law of universal gravitation.

Galileo, in 1610, became the first to turn a telescope to the sky. From then on, the instrument was standard equipment in every observatory (see TELESCOPE). Newton's laws stimulated extensive recording of accurate positions and motions of Sun, Moon, and planets. National observatories in Europe, *e.g.* the Royal Greenwich Observatory established in England in 1675, were founded particularly for solving the problem of determining longitude at sea. However, they soon extended their scope to the study of the solar system, stars, and nebulas.

The activities of observatories were tremendously enlarged about 1860 by the development of "dry" photographic plates which could be used conveniently and effectively at the focus of a telescope. Photography rapidly assumed a major role in the work of most large observatories (see ASTRONOMICAL PHOTOGRAPHY). Another revolutionary development arose from the clear enunciation by G. R. Kirchhoff and R. W. E. Bunsen in 1859 of the principles of chemical analysis by means of light rays. Sir William Huggins (1824–1910), a British amateur astronomer, pioneered the use of the spectroscope for physical and chemical studies of the stars. He wrote: "The observatory became the meeting place where terrestrial chemistry was brought into direct touch with celestial chemistry. Iron from our mines was line-matched with stellar iron from opposite parts of the celestial sphere." Spectroscopic studies of sunlight and starlight constitute a major part of the work at many observatories (see SPECTROSCOPE AND SPECTROSCOPY). Photographs of spectra yield chemical analyses of stellar atmospheres together with information on temperature, density, and, in some stars, the presence of a magnetic field. Also, the motion of a source toward or away from the observer can be found, according

LARGEST RADIO TELESCOPES

Observatory	Location	Aperture (feet)	Date
Arecibo Ionospheric Obs....	Arecibo, Puerto Rico	1,000	1963
Associated Universities.....	Green Bank, W. Va.	300	1962
Manchester Univ.........	Jodrell Bank, England	250	1957
Radiophysics Laboratory...	Sydney, Australia	210	1961
Jet Propulsion Laboratory..	Goldstone, Calif.	210	1966
Associated Universities.....	Green Bank, W. Va.	140	1965

LARGEST REFLECTING TELESCOPES

Observatory	Location	Aperture (inches)	Date
Palomar..................	Palomar Mt, Calif.	200	1948
Lick.....................	Mt Hamilton, Calif.	120	1959
Crimean..................	Nauchny, Crimea	102	1960
Mt Wilson...............	Mt Wilson, Calif.	100	1918
Royal Greenwich Obs......	Herstmonceux Castle, England	98	1966
Kitt Peak Obs............	Kitt Peak, N. Mex.	84	1964
McDonald................	Fort Davis, Texas	82	1939
Haute Provence...........	St Michel, France	77	1958
David Dunlap............	Ontario, Canada	74	1935
Radcliffe.................	Pretoria, S Africa	74	1948
Mt Stromlo..............	Canberra, Australia	74	1955
Helwan..................	Helwan, Egypt	74	1960
Okayama.................	Kamogata, Japan	74	1960
Dominion Astrophysical.....	Victoria, B. C.	72	1918

Note: In 1966, ten reflecting telescopes with diameters greater than 100 in. were under construction or in planning stages.

LARGEST REFRACTING TELESCOPES

Observatory	Location	Aperture (inches)	Date
Yerkes...................	Williams Bay, Wis.	40	1897
Lick.....................	Mt Hamilton, Calif.	36	1888
Paris....................	Meudon, France	33	1893
Allegheny	Pittsburgh, Penn.	32	1899
Potsdam	Potsdam, Germany	30	1914
Greenwich...............	Herstmonceux, England	28	1894

to the Doppler principle, from the exact position of spectrum lines whose wavelengths have been measured in the laboratory.

Until about 1900, observatory telescopes were predominantly of the refracting type. The 20th cent. has been the era of giant reflectors, which have important advantages for photography. Refractors, however, continue to play a useful role. Catadioptric telescopes, *e.g.* the Schmidt, employ a spherical mirror and a correcting lens, and are used extensively for photography. Other important instruments are zenith tubes, transits, spectrographs, photoelectric photometers, and comparator microscopes for accurate measurement of spectra.

Several years of study are needed to determine the best location for an observatory. It must be a place with wide horizons, free from the vibrations caused by traffic, from the smoke and dust of industry, and from the glare of city lights. (As the city of London spread nearer to Greenwich, it became necessary to move the Royal Observatory south to Herstmonceux Castle; the move, in the 1950's, took several years.) The site must have a mild, dry climate with clear skies and without a great daily range in temperature. The top of a mountain may seem to be a suitable location, but around some mountains air currents continually impair the SEEING. Before building a new observatory, meteorological data are studied and the proposed site is tested for seeing by experienced astronomers. Artificial satellites and Moon bases may some day prove to be ideal observatories. As well as having perfect seeing they will have access to radiations that cannot penetrate the atmosphere, *e.g.* far ultraviolet, from which we will learn more about the abundance of such elements as hydrogen, helium, carbon, oxygen, and neon.

A new kind of institution, the *radio observatory,* has come into existence through the discovery that astronomical bodies can be observed by means of radio waves, 1 cm to 15 m, which they emit. Among identified radio sources are the Sun, planets, various stars and galaxies. Radio telescopes are particularly efficient in studying distant clouds of hydrogen, the most abundant element in the universe, and have already made possible the best maps of the general structure of our Milky Way system. Moreover, it seems probable that they will eventually disclose galaxies more distant than any now known. In the future, it is safe to predict, many observatories will specialize in radio astronomy. See RADIO ASTRONOMY; RADIO INTERFEROMETER; RADIO TELESCOPE.—*P. Me.*

OBSIDIAN: an extrusive IGNEOUS ROCK, formed by sudden cooling of lava, usually on the surface of a flow. It is dark, glassy in texture, entirely lacking grain, and in composition is similar to granite, for only acidic lava will produce obsidian. (A similar, very rare glassy rock produced by basaltic lava is called basalt glass.) The surface at a fracture is more perfectly conchoidal (shell-like) than that of any other rock. Primitive peoples used obsidian, as found in nature, for tools and weapons, *e.g.* awls and arrowheads.—*E. A.*

OCCLUSION: in chemistry, the physical retention of one material (which may be gas, liquid, or solid) within macroscopic holes or voids in a second material, a solid. During crystallization from a solution some of the mother liquor is frequently occluded by the growing crystals; the occluded material has relatively little effect on the properties of the material in which it is enclosed. In some solid-gas systems, where the voids containing the occluded substance are of molecular dimensions, occlusion is essentially similar to adsorption or solution. Thus, activated charcoal is referred to as "occluding" various gases. Hydrogen is easily dissolved or adsorbed by palladium or platinum; this effect may also be referred to as occlusion.—*A. M. S.*

OCCLUSION: in meteorology, a frontal structure formed as a cold front overtakes a warm front and either lifts it off the ground (*cold occlusion*) or rides aloft over it (*warm occlusion*). The former takes place when the cold air under the cold front is colder than the cold air beneath the warm front. Widespread precipitation occurs along and in advance of the line of the occluded front. See FRONT.—*P. L.*

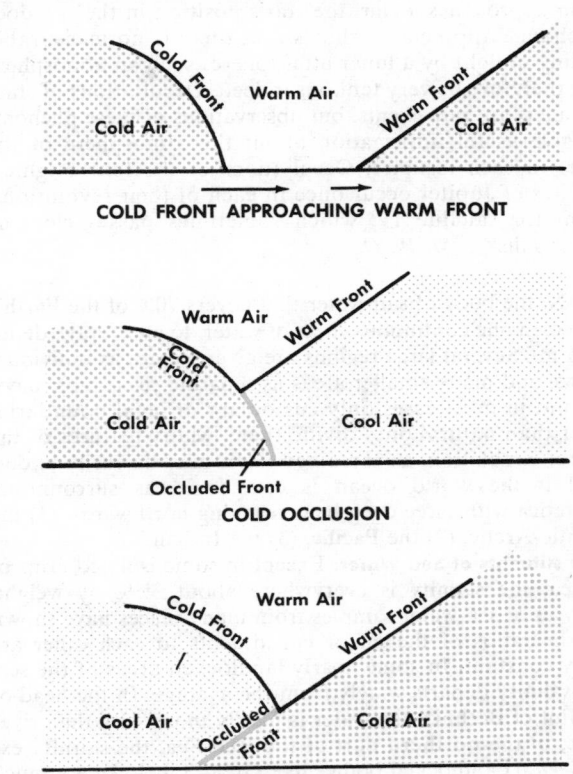

COLD FRONT APPROACHING WARM FRONT

COLD OCCLUSION

WARM OCCLUSION

OCCULTATION: the apparent disappearance of a star or planet behind the Moon, or of a star or satellite behind a planet. Planets are occulted infrequently, but many stars are occulted by the Moon each year. Observations of lunar occultations are used to determine accurately the position of the Moon in its orbit; from observations of the same occultation at different places on Earth's surface, the distance of the Moon can

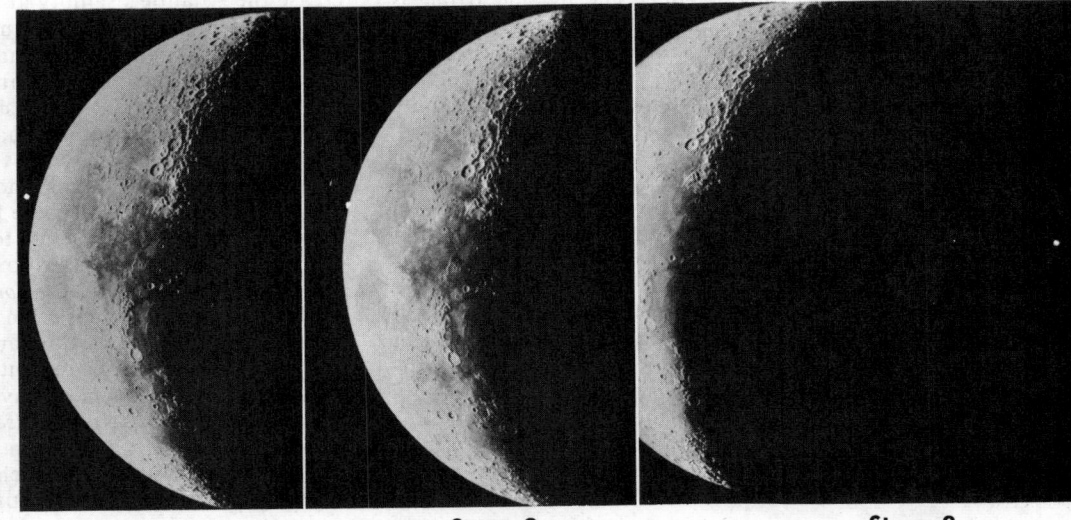

Occultation of star Aldebaran by Moon: Three stages (*left to right*) represent interval of 1 min, 40 sec, with Moon moving right to left. In third stage, star (*extreme right*) has just emerged from behind lunar disk. Star image seems unchanged just before occultation—suggesting lack of lunar atmosphere to cause refraction and diffusion of starlight passing through it. Moon's large apparent diameter (approx. ½°) makes occultations of stars common. (*Yerkes*)

Stage 1   Stage 2   Stage 3

be determined. In most cases, a star disappears or reappears very suddenly at a lunar occultation. Occasionally, the star does appear to dim slightly before disappearing, and this may happen because it is a double star. Attempts have been made to determine the apparent sizes of the stars by measuring the way their brightness drops at an occultation, but the results have not proved reliable. The fact that, as the limb of the Moon approaches a star, the star's position in the sky does not change appreciably shows that there is no measurable bending of light by a lunar atmosphere; such an atmosphere must therefore be very tenuous indeed. Occultations of stars by planets are rare events, but observations of these phenomena give useful information about the atmosphere of the planet in each instance. Occultations of the four brightest satellites of Jupiter occur once in each of their revolutions, except for satellite IV, which sometimes passes clear of Jupiter's disk.—*M. W. O.*

OCEAN: the body of salt water that covers 70% of the Earth's surface, in one continuous sheet of water, to an average depth of 2½ mi. Several large regions are given names as individual oceans, and many smaller areas as separate seas, gulfs, bays, etc.; but in most cases only customary or legal boundaries rather than natural ones divide them. Many features of the general circulation, as explained later, may be easily understood if the world ocean is considered as surrounding Antarctica with three deep bays reaching northward—(1) the Atlantic-Arctic, (2) the Pacific, (3) the Indian.

Constituents of Sea Water: Except in some isolated arms of the sea, the salinity is everywhere about 3½% by weight. Analyses of sea-water samples from many places have shown that the ratios of the major constituents to each other are nearly constant. In some nearly landlocked areas of the sea, total salinity departs widely from the average. In the head of the Gulf of Bothnia, the water is hardly more salty than river water; in the northern part of the Red Sea, the salinity exceeds 4%. (Landlocked bodies like Great Salt Lake are much saltier than the ocean, and the proportions of the constituents are different.) Constancy of proportions of the major constituents is important because it enables one to determine the total salt concentration, density, electrical conductivity, freezing point, and other properties of a sample of sea water by measuring any one of these properties or the concentration of any major constituent. Commonly the chlorinity (a quantity closely related to total halides) or the conductivity is measured.

The density of sea water at standard temperature can be determined from the salinity. Consider a number of columns of sea water of equal area standing side by side. If one is diluted by adding water, or expanded by heating, its density is less and its specific volume greater. It now stands higher than the others, forming a hill down which the water will flow to re-establish a level surface. From observations of salinity and temperature at many points, densities can be plotted, and surfaces of equal density can be described along which water movements will occur.

About half of the chemical elements have been found in sea water. Besides those listed (next column), elements of much interest are ones that are important to organisms, especially nitrogen (other than dissolved elementary nitrogen), phosphorus, silicon, and iron. All these occur in only very small concentrations, which vary with location and season. When they occur in appreciable amounts in the surface layers, conditions are favorable for growth of microscopic plants (phytoplankton), which are fodder for the small floating animals (zooplankton) of the sea, which in turn are the food of fish. Those parts of the sea where these elements are never plentiful in the surface layers are barren.

Many marine animals take advantage of the fact that calcium carbonate is readily precipitated: they form strong shells or skeletons of it. Vast deposits of shells exist on the ocean floor, and huge reefs are built of the calcareous skeletons of the tiny coral polyp (see CORAL REEFS AND ATOLLS).

Temperatures: While the ocean reaches depths of more than 6 mi in places, temperature is controlled by processes occurring in the uppermost few hundred feet. Below this depth the temperature seldom exceeds 10° to 12° C, so that both horizontal and vertical temperature gradients are extremely small and there is little conduction or radiation of heat. In the uppermost layers heat is gained principally by absorption of solar radiation, and lost principally through convection and evaporation. Transparency of water is so low that even in the clearest seas 98% of the Sun's radiation is absorbed by the upper 50 ft. Heat can be transferred to greater depths only by the bodily vertical transport of the warmer surface water, principally by wind stirring. Commonly the upper layers are well stirred and have uniform temperature down to the limit of wind and wave action, below which the temperature drops rapidly with increasing depth. In high latitudes and in winter, heat is lost at the surface by evaporation, conduction, and radiation. The cooled surface water is replaced by convection, and the process continues until the whole water column is of uniform low temperature.

MAJOR FOREIGN CONSTITUENTS IN SEA WATER

(gm/kg)

(Modified from Sverdrup, Johnson, and Fleming)

Chlorine	19.0	Potassium	0.38
Sodium	10.6	Bicarbonate	0.14
Sulfate	2.65	Bromine	0.065
Magnesium	1.27	Boric Acid	0.026
Calcium	0.40	Strontium	0.013

Circulation: The over-all circulation of the world ocean is greatly affected by these factors. Cold surface waters from the Arctic and Antarctic sink and flow along the bottoms of adjacent oceans. At the same time, warm equatorial surface water flows toward the higher latitudes—notably in the Gulf Stream and the Kuroshio. In another example, surface water from the Atlantic flows into the Mediterranean, where evaporation increases its salinity until it becomes denser and sinks. Over the sill in the Strait of Gibraltar, at a depth of about 1,000 ft, this now denser, saline layer flows out again to increase the Atlantic's salinity at intermediate depths. Many other widespread current systems arise from small changes (0.1 to 0.2 gm/kg) in salinity and temperature. To these current systems is due, in large part, the fact that ocean water has a relatively constant composition. The world ocean has a continuous slow circulation that involves every part. See OCEAN CURRENTS.

The Sea Bottom: The gross morphological features of the sea bottom are beginning to be known, though not yet well understood. The sea floor close to the shores of continents is characteristically shallow (see CONTINENTAL SHELF SLOPE, AND RISE) and is bordered by the *continental slope,* which has a grade of 5% or more and is often cut by deep valleys (SUBMARINE CANYONS). These bottom areas together with all others less than 10,000 ft deep constitute about 25% of the sea bottom. Most of the remainder may be considered as a number of basins divided by *ridges* or *rises.* The bottoms of the great basins, with depths of more than 15,000 ft, constitute another 25% of the sea bottom, of which only a small fraction is at depths greater than 20,000 ft (DEEPS AND TRENCHES). Large

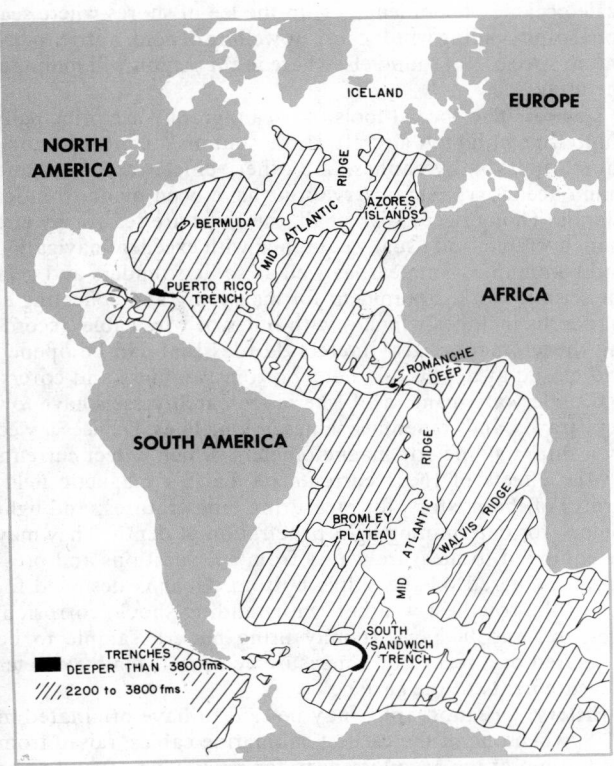

Principal Relief Features of Atlantic Ocean
(*From Shepard*)

include the Gulf Stream, the Kuroshio off Japan, and the Benguela Current (see map on next page). Between about 10° and 40° N lat. in each ocean is an anticyclonic circulation pattern, with currents flowing poleward on the west side of each ocean, equatorward on the east side, eastward at the higher latitude, and westward near the equator. The maximum velocity only in spurts exceeds 3 or 4 knots, the depth is a few hundred feet, the width may be more than 100 mi, but the swiftest water is usually found in a narrow band near one side of the current. Major currents are usually driven by winds, *e.g.* the trade winds. Under the attraction of Sun and Moon, oscillatory tidal currents occur throughout the sea. Changing distribution of air pressure on the surface due to the passage of storms sets up transitory currents. A major driving force is the differences in water density associated with changes in temperature and salinity caused by insolation, rainfall, evaporation, etc. (see OCEAN). Ocean currents also are affected by friction and deflected by rotation of the earth (CORIOLIS FORCE). In very recent years currents have been found flowing at moderate depth, in directions different from those of the overlying water. Existence of currents at great depths has been demonstrated by photographs showing ripples in bottom sediments. Vertical currents of small velocity and no great vertical extent exist and are important to the circulation of the sea. (For the work of shore currents, see COASTLINES and OCEAN WAVES.)—*M. S.*

OCEANOGRAPHY: the scientific study of phenomena connected with the sea, especially the whole sea, and with the high sea more than its edges. (See OCEAN.)

Scope: Oceanography has physical, chemical, geological, and biological aspects. Such features as currents and tides can be studied closely without attention to biological, chemical, and geological phenomena, but these latter categories are nevertheless intimately involved. Thus marine sediments may contain organic remains as clues for the paleontologist studying prehistoric life; meteoritic material of interest to the mineralogist and the astronomer; glacial drift for study by the glaciologist and climatologist; volcanic debris for examination by the volcanologist. Again, the fishery problem—primary in biological oceanography—involves such diverse factors as

areas of some basin bottoms are classed as *abyssal plains,* with very low relief and gentle slopes, probably smoothed by the deposition of sediments by turbidity currents. Areas of low hills and large mountain ranges are also common. Isolated peaks rising more than 1 km above the surroundings are called *seamounts* or, if flat-topped, *guyots*. Some features reach above the surface, forming oceanic islands and island chains, The greatest geographical feature of the sea bottom is the nearly continuous system of highlands (collectively called the MID-OCEANIC RIDGE) extending through the Atlantic, Indian, Antarctic, and Pacific oceans for a distance of about 20,000 mi, sometimes 2 mi high and more than 500 mi wide. The Mid-Atlantic Ridge extends from Iceland to the latitude of Cape Horn, where it turns around Africa and joins the Mid-Indian Ridge. At St. Paul Island, another branch extends south of Australia and New Zealand, turning north in lat. 120° W to approach the continent of N America, as the E Pacific Rise. Throughout its course, the crest of this feature marks a line of earthquake epicenters. In the Mid-Atlantic and Mid-Indian ridges a median trench is a noticeable feature. The highest portions of the E Pacific Rise are marked by very high heat flows through the bottom. The pattern of magnetic anomalies along the Rise is parallel to the course of the crest. The E Pacific Rise is crossed by fracture zones more than 1,000 mi long, showing large vertical and horizontal displacements. The texture of the sea bottom depends on the availability of terrigenous material carried by turbidity currents and of sediments, and on the rate of sweeping by currents. See also COASTLINE; OCEAN WAVES.—*M. S.*

OCEAN CURRENTS: All water in the ocean is undergoing translatory motion all the time, and in some areas this motion is so regular, so swift, and transports so much water that it has long been recognized as a current. Well-known currents

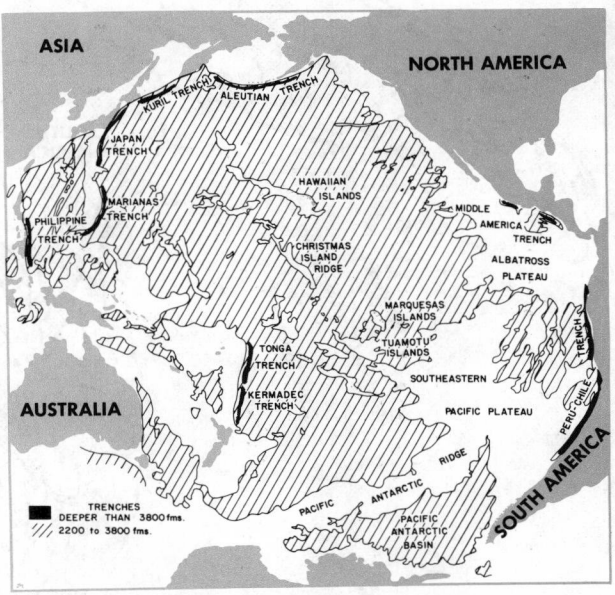

Principal Relief Features of Pacific Ocean
(*From Shepard*)

weather, currents, water temperature, supply of PLANKTON (and nutrient elements generally), and predators. *Physical oceanography* is the study of OCEAN CURRENTS, turbulence and mixing, OCEAN WAVES (wind waves, swell, TSUNAMIS, and TIDES), heat transport in the sea (which involves penetration of radiation), heat exchange with the atmosphere, marine weather, sea ice, and acoustics. The *chemical oceanographer* studies plant nutrients, especially nitrogen, phosphorus, and iron, which govern growth of phytoplankton (floating microscopic plants) and, through them, the growth of all other organisms; atmospheric gases and radionuclides as an index to the rate of surface-to-bottom mixing; trace organic substances, *e.g.* vitamins and antibiotics, which are important to organisms; precipitation and solution; and exchanges between sediments and interstitial water. *Geological oceanography,* or *submarine geology,* includes studies of bottom configuration and material, stratification of SEDIMENTS and their transport, shoreline and shallow-water phenomena (building and erosion of BEACHES and bars), SUBMARINE CANYONS, gross morphology, and tectonics of the sea bottom (see COASTLINE; CONTINENTAL SHELF, SLOPE, AND RISE; DEEPS AND TRENCHES). Submarine geology merges with that part of marine geophysics which is concerned with magnetic and gravity anomalies at the sea surface and on the bottom, heat transport through the bottom, and deep-sea seismic exploration. *Biological oceanography,* or *marine biology,* in its most characteristic form comprises the study of exploited fish populations, but includes problems of identifying and mapping distribution of organisms, following migrations, population dynamics, life histories of pelagic (high-seas) animals, and production of organic matter. Oceanography is not generally considered to include the biology of tide-pool animals, although the life histories, developments, and ecology of such organisms are often closely controlled by large-

scale oceanic phenomena; *e.g.* in the lee of shores where seasonal or prevailing winds cause upwelling of cold, nutrient-rich water, species not found elsewhere in the region will maintain themselves.

Devices: The special tools of oceanography are principally shipborne, although aircraft, shore stations, anchored buoys, submarines, bathyscaphes, and other vehicles are used; and many oceanographic observations have been made from ice islands. Though generally small, the ships are seaworthy and maneuverable, and usually equipped with excellent navigation and communication gear, as well as sonic sounders and gear for seismic work. Equipment for measuring and collecting at all depths includes winches with miles of wire cable, recording thermometers, gravimeters, bottles that can be opened and closed at depth, tow nets, bottom samplers and corers, and underwater cameras. Fisheries-research vessels have tow nets, trawls, and sometimes seines or long lines. Devices towed by a ship may include magnetometers, which detect currents by the effects of these currents on Earth's magnetic field; strings of thermistors, for measuring temperatures; and light meters, for determining light penetration at depth. They may be equipped to measure waves from accelerations and pressures registered on the ship's bottom. Gear is designed for use in the roughest weather, withstanding shock, corrosion, pressure, and leakage. It may bring back a sample to be measured or a record of a measurement, or it may telemeter measurements to the surface.

History: Oceanography may be said to have originated in 1858, when one of the earliest submarine cables, raised from the bottom of the Mediterranean for repairs, was found to be encrusted with various organisms and thus prompted biologists to realize that the deep sea was inhabited, possibly by unknown types of animals. One such biologist in England

Principal currents of the world's oceans: Currents shown are at surface, not at depth. Black arrows indicate cool currents, blue arrows warm currents.

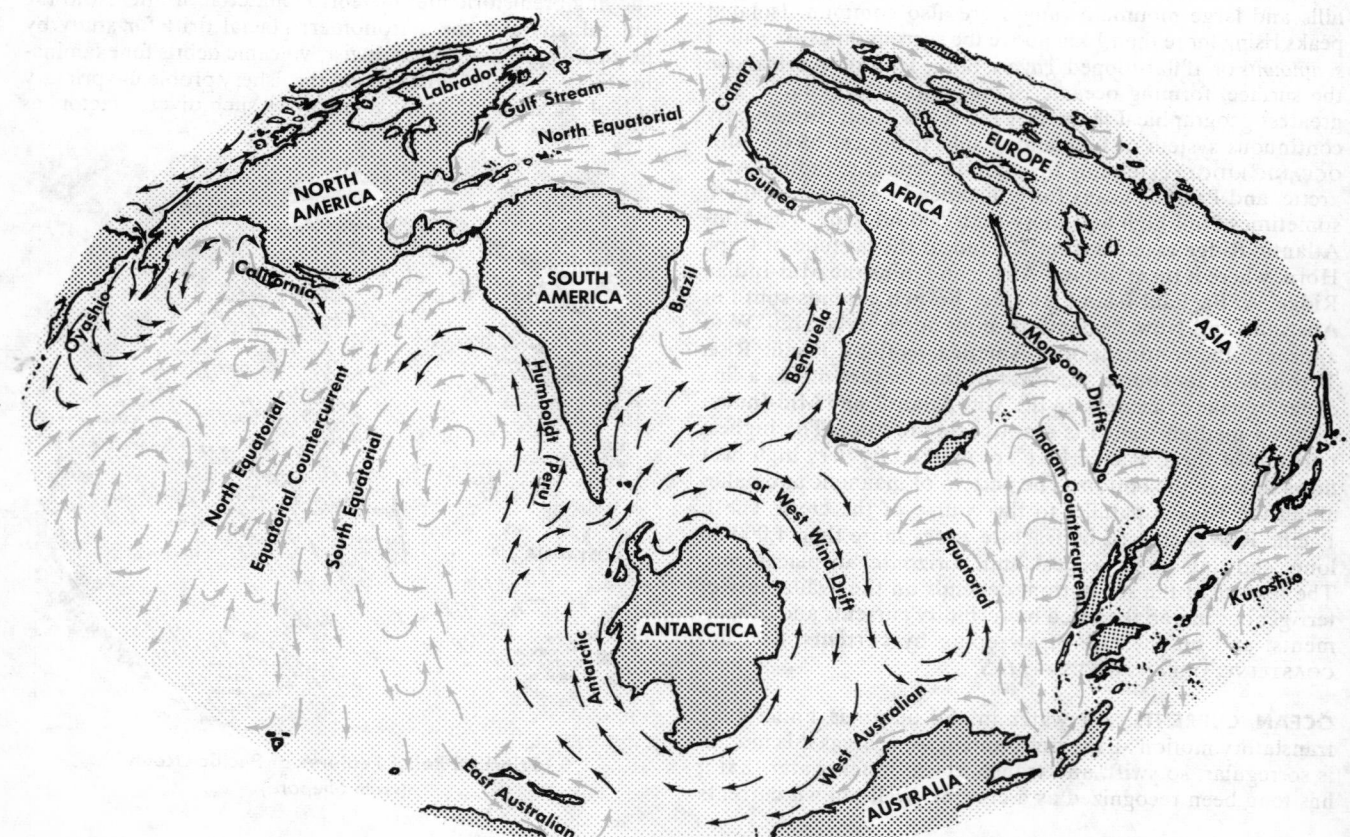

Basic techniques in oceanography include use of corers. Corer, dropped through hundreds or thousands of feet of water, can bring up sample of bottom mud for analysis. *(Lamont Geological Obs.)*

as shown, for instance, by B. Heezen and M. Tharp in their recent physiographic diagram of the Atlantic. More surprising has been the discovery of the "deep scattering layer" of fish and plankton which lies at a depth of 1,000 or more ft in the daytime and spreads upward toward the surface at night.

Oceanographic Institutions: A list of all the organizations doing oceanographic work would be very long. The table lists only a few leading laboratories with their dates of founding, affiliations, and locations. Today in the U. S. A. there are at

LEADING CENTERS FOR OCEANOGRAPHY

Stazione Zoologica, 1872, Naples
Kristinebergs Zoological Station, 1877, Gullmarfjord, Sweden
Marine Biological Association, 1880, Plymouth, England
Laboratoire Arago, 1881 Banyuls-sur-Mer, France
Marine Laboratory, 1882, Aberdeen, Scotland
Biologische Anstalt, 1890, Helgoland, Germany
Biologisk Laboratorium, 1894, University, Oslo, Norway
Plankton Laboratoriet, 1902, Copenhagen, Denmark
Institute Oceanographique, 1906, Monaco and Paris
Scripps Institution of Oceanography, 1909, Univ. of California, La Jolla
Imperial Marine Observatory, 1919, Kobe, Japan
Woods Hole Oceanographic Institution, 1928, Massachusetts
Institute for Oceanography and Fishery, 1930, Split, Jugoslavia
Atlantic Biological Station, 1930, St. Andrews, New Brunswick
All-Union Scientific Research Institution of Marine Fisheries and Oceanography, 1933, Moscow
National Institute of Oceanography, 1949, Wormley, England
Lamont Geological Observatory, Palisades, N. Y., 1949

was Sir C. Wyville Thompson who, after several summers of dredging around the British Isles, in 1872 set forth in HMS *Challenger* for the scientific exploration of the seven seas. In its 3½-yr cruise the *Challenger* visited all the oceans and circled the globe, collecting animals from the ocean bottoms, dredging up rocks and sediments, sampling fish and plankton, observing sea birds, and taking numerous soundings to depths of over 3 mi. This single expedition revolutionized both scientific and popular conceptions about the sea.

Landmarks in oceanography include the exploit (1893–96) of F. Nansen in letting his ship, the *Fram,* freeze in polar ice and drift across the central Arctic Ocean. In 1909–31 the non-magnetic ship *Carnegie* cruised all oceans, making the greatest contributions in the Pacific. In 1925–27 the German ship *Meteor* charted the currents and water masses of the S Atlantic, and in 1931–39 the British *Discovery* surveyed the entire Antarctic. Other milestones were the first descent of A. Piccard in his bathyscaphe to 10,000 ft, in 1953, and the cruise of the American submarine *Nautilus* under the ice from the Bering Strait to the North Pole to the Norwegian Sea (1958). These exploits indicated the extent to which oceanographic knowledge was becoming dependable.

Among the major discoveries during the last century was J. Schmidt's gradual unraveling (beginning 1904) of the great migrations of the European river eels, which, he found, cross the Atlantic to breed near Bermuda, whence the fry find their way back to European streams. Another triumph has been the application of theoretical hydrodynamics to ocean circulation, notably by V. Bjerknes and A. Defant; it has resulted in the last few years in the discovery of major sub-surface water currents. One major result of the *Discovery* cruises was the demonstration, due especially to G. E. R. Deacon, of the formation of the bottom water of the Pacific and S Atlantic by subsidence of cold surface water in the Antarctic. The introduction of underwater sound gear on ships in 1924 has led to many and diverse discoveries, of which the most straightforward is that of the morphology of the sea bottom

least ten major institutions or university departments of oceanography, and more than twenty oceanographic ships, plus facilities of several governmental departments. Russia, Japan, England, and Canada have large groups of oceanographers, and nearly every country with a coastline is active in this branch of science. Because of the vast size of the oceans, and because they touch the shores of many nations, international cooperation is common. The International Council for the Exploration of the Sea, formed in 1901 to encourage study of the North Sea, set a precedent for several other organizations.—*M. S.*

OCEAN WAVES: Most ocean waves are caused by wind, except for swells observed on calm days, and these are known to result from winds blowing at a distance. The height from crest to trough, length from crest to crest, and period (time interval between passages of two crests) depend on strength of the wind, length of time it has been blowing, and the fetch (distance over which it has been blowing across the water). In general, the stronger the wind, and the longer and farther it blows, the higher and longer are the waves, and the longer their period. When ocean waves leave the area where the wind is blowing, they become longer and lower the farther they go, eventually attaining lengths of several hundred feet and heights so small as to be detected only by instruments; thus, swell originating near Madagascar has been detected off California.

In deep water, the motion of each particle of water in a wave is forward, downward, backward, upward, and forward again, approximately in a circle without net forward movement; it is the form of the wave rather than the water that moves forward. As the wave nears shore and becomes affected by the bottom, the "orbit" of each particle becomes flattened into an ellipse, the wave increases in height, and the wavelength diminishes, but the period of the wave remains the same. On a beach the wave tends to break—*i.e.* the water of the wave plunges forward at about the point where the depth

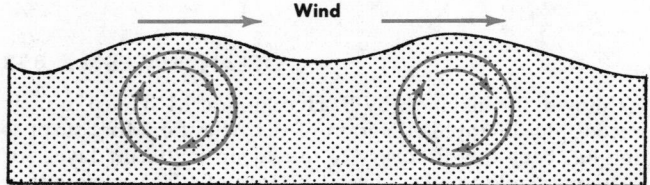

In an ocean wave in deep water, each particle of water tends to describe a vertical circle. Wave moves but water does not.

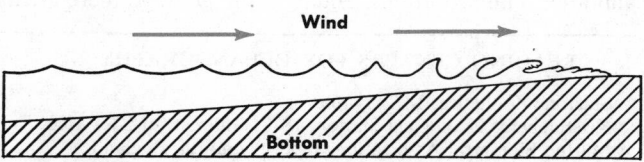

As wave approaches shelving shore, it is affected increasingly by the bottom. Wave gets higher and wavelength shorter, until wave plunges forward.

of the water on the beach becomes equal to the height that the wave had in deeper water.

Waves moving against a shore produce wash, backwash, and shore currents. Wash is the water of breakers flooding up a beach; backwash is this water returning down the beach. Some of the water moving against a shore forms longshore currents, which run approximately parallel to the shoreline. Water returning seaward may concentrate into rip currents, which are streams of agitated water sometimes extending hundreds of yards out to sea. The currents popularly called undertow consist essentially of backwash and rip currents—neither of which involves distinct bottom currents that would drag a swimmer under.

So-called tidal waves are caused by earthquakes on the ocean floor (see TSUNAMIS), and very-long-period waves (microseisms) are a result of changes in barometric pressure. TIDES are a world-wide system of long-period waves caused by the gravitational attraction of Sun and Moon.

Direct observation of ocean waves is difficult because trains of waves of different sizes moving in different directions are all present at once. Small waves are usually underrated and large ones overrated by observers. Reliable reports of waves over 60 ft high are rare. But several methods exist for determining wave heights by simultaneously recording surface levels at many points or continuously at one point. One method employs stereoscopic photography; another is to record continuously the accelerations of a ship and the water level on its side. Still another is to record surface level at a station fixed to the bottom. The gage can be a graduated staff projecting through the surface which is photographed continuously or records electrically, or it can be a sensitive device on the bottom to record the pressure (hence the height) of the water column above it.

If a strong vertical temperature gradient is present, internal waves can be readily observed by recording the up-and-down motion of a given isotherm. A carefully trimmed submarine may experience vertical displacement by internal waves when lying in a density gradient.—*M. S.*

OCHOA, SEVERO, 1905–   , Spanish-U. S. biochemist; b. Luarca, Spain. For years a leader in the investigation of oxidative mechanisms of the cell, in 1955 he discovered a bacterial enzyme that synthesizes ribonucleic acid (RNA) from nucleotide diphosphates. For their discoveries of the mechanism of biological synthesis of ribonucleic and deoxyribonucleic acids, Ochoa and A. Kornberg shared the Nobel prize for 1959. He is a member of the National Academy of Sciences.—*D. H. D. R.*

OCKHAM, WILLIAM, (*ante* 1290–1349), famous English logician, philosopher, and theologian. A member of the Franciscan order, he taught at Oxford 1316–24, but became involved in the dispute between the Franciscan friars and Pope John XXII, and was excommunicated in 1328. Besides writing numerous political treatises advocating independence of civil government from ecclesiastical domination, he made important contributions to logic and philosophy of science, establishing the Nominalist school of late medieval philosophy, and developing an empiricist theory of scientific method. By holding that the basic doctrines of theology are not demonstrable by human reason, but rest wholly on faith, Ockham helped promote the modern orientation of philosophy toward the physical and mathematical sciences. His principal writings include *Summa logicae; Quaestiones super quattuor libros sententiarum; Quodlibeta;* and *Summulae in libros physicorum.* —*E. A. M.*

OCTANE RATING: a number which denotes the ability of a gasoline to perform in engines without knocking or "pinging." GASOLINE consists of hydrocarbons, and their tendency to cause knocking depends on their structure. Straight-chain paraffins produce excessive knocking; branched-chain paraffins are good; olefins and aromatic hydrocarbons are best. The octane rating system arbitrarily assigns to the straight chain, n-heptane, a zero ability, and to the branched-chain, iso-octane, a 100% ability, with respect to anti-knock. A 30-octane gasoline, for example, is one that would have the same anti-knock ability as a mixture of 70% n-heptane and 30% iso-octane.

$$CH_3-CH_2-CH_2-CH_2-CH_2-CH_2-CH_3$$
n-heptane

$$CH_3-\underset{\underset{CH_3}{|}}{\overset{\overset{CH_3}{|}}{C}}-CH-CH_2-CH_3$$
iso-octane

—*Ru. M.*

OERSTED, HANS CHRISTIAN, 1777–1851, Danish physicist; b. Rudkjöbing. He discovered that an electric current can deflect a compass needle (1819). Details of his discovery were published in his *Experimenta circa effectum conflictus electrici in acum magneticam* (1820). French, Italian, German, English, and Danish translations quickly followed. The consequences of the discovery, developed primarily by Ampère, formed the foundations for the science of electromagnetism. Oersted was a fellow of the Royal Society.—*D. H. D. R.*

Hans Christian Oersted
(*Bettmann Archive*)

OHM: see ELECTRICAL AND MAGNETIC UNITS.

OHM, GEORG SIMON, 1787–1854, German physicist; b. Erlangen. He is known for the mathematical relationship (OHM'S LAW) between potential difference, electric current, and electric resistance. In his *Die galvanische Kette mathematisch bearbeitet* (1827) he offered his mathematical treatment of d-c electric circuits. He was a fellow of the Royal Society.—*D. H. D. R.*

OHMMETER: a device for measuring electrical resistance. It consists basically of a battery, a current-measuring device (ammeter), and a known resistance, all in series with the unknown resistance. The larger the unknown resistance, the smaller will be the current measured by the ammeter. The numerical value of the resistance can be computed by means of OHM'S LAW.— *S. K.*

OHM'S LAW: an empirical rule which says that the ELECTRIC CURRENT passing through a material is directly proportional to the applied POTENTIAL difference. Ohm's law has been found valid in metallic conductors over a wide range of conditions, and to a lesser extent in semiconductors and conducting liquids. It is not valid for describing the flow of electricity through gases or vacuum tubes. Ohm's law is extremely useful in the design and analysis of electrical circuits. The algebraic expression of Ohm's law is $R = V/I$, where R is the resistance in ohms, the potential difference V is in volts, and the current I is in amperes.— *S. K.*

OIL: see ESSENTIAL OIL; FATS AND OILS; PETROLEUM.

OLBERS, HEINRICH WILHELM MATTHÄUS, 1758–1840, German physician and astronomer; b. Arbergen, near Bremen. In 1797 he published a new, simplified method for computing the paths of comets. Becoming known as an astronomer by his calculation of the orbit of the comet of 1779, he discovered many comets himself, including that of 1815, which bears his name. He also discovered the asteroids Pallas (1802) and Vesta (1807). In 1826, he formulated the problem that is known in cosmology as OLBERS' PARADOX. He was a fellow of the Royal Society.— *D. H. D. R.*

OLBERS' PARADOX: the problem, first formulated in 1826 by Heinrich Olbers, as to why the night sky is dark. Suppose Earth to be surrounded by a series of vast spherical shells, each of the same thickness. The volume of each shell will be approximately proportional to the square of its distance from Earth. If the stars are uniformly distributed in space, then the number within each shell, and the total starlight emitted by each shell, will also be proportional to the square of the distance. But the light received by Earth from a star is *inversely* proportional to the square of the distance; therefore the total light reaching Earth from any one shell should be independent of the distance. Since one can conceive of innumerable shells stretching throughout space, with the same amount of light reaching Earth from each one, why is the night sky dark? The question seemed to be answered when it was realized that the visible stars belong to our Milky Way galaxy, itself an island in space. However, it is now known that there are billions of galaxies, and the paradox has been revived, with "galaxies" replacing "stars." One explanation is that since the galaxies are moving away from us, the light they emit undergoes a Doppler shift toward the longer wavelengths (see DOPPLER EFFECT). Therefore, most of the light emitted by distant galaxies reaches us as invisible infrared, whereas the light we receive in the visible range was originally emitted in the ultraviolet, where the intensity of emission is comparatively small. — *B. P. S.*

OLEFINS (ALKENES): those hydrocarbons in which a pair of carbon atoms are joined by a double bond. The simplest member of the series is ethylene, CH_2=CH_2; the next is propylene, CH_3—CH=CH_2. The ending *ene* characterizes these compounds. Those with two double bonds are called DIENES. When the C=C double bond occurs in more complex compounds containing other reactive groups, its typical olefenic properties are retained; *e.g.* an organic acid containing the C=C double bond exhibits both olefenic and acidic properties. Olefins are UNSATURATED COMPOUNDS. Their principal property is ability to add across the double bond to form a saturated compound; thus, CH_2=CH_2 + Cl_2 → $ClCH_2$—CH_2Cl (ethylene chloride). Olefins are often made by reversing this reaction; thus alcohol, CH_3—CH_2OH, by catalytic dehydration yields water, HOH, and ethylene, CH_2=CH_2. Olefins enter into the manufacture of a variety of important industrial products: high-octane gasolines, synthetic rubber, plastics, and detergents.—*Ru. M.*

OLIGOCENE EPOCH: see CENOZOIC ERA; GEOLOGICAL TIME CHART.

ONE-TO-ONE CORRESPONDENCE: the relation between two classes when for each member of the first there is exactly one member of the second, and conversely. Thus, if each person in a room is sitting on a chair and there are no vacant chairs, then the chairs and the persons in the room are in one-to-one correspondence. When this relationship holds, the two classes are said to have the same number of members, even if the classes are of infinite cardinality. For example, since the relation $y = 2x$ pairs the integers with the even numbers, the two sets have the same cardinal number $\aleph_0$.—*H. T.*

ON FLOATING BODIES, by Archimedes (*c.* 240 B. C.): One of the greatest pure mathematicians, Archimedes was also the founder of mathematical physics in his work on statics and hydrostatics. In the latter, making only one physical postulate about the nature of a fluid, Archimedes deduced mathematically the laws of buoyancy and stability. He used the concept of specific gravity for the first time, and enunciated the famous ARCHIMEDES' PRINCIPLE that the weight of a body in a fluid is diminished by the weight of the volume of fluid displaced. By applying this principle he solved the famous problem of estimating the ratio of gold to silver in Hiero's crown. Comparatively little known in the Middle Ages, Archimedes' mathematical physics was highly esteemed again in the 16th cent., when it was adopted as a model by Galileo and others.—*A. R. H.*

ON THE ELECTRODYNAMICS OF MOVING BODIES, by Albert Einstein (1905): In this epoch-making paper, Einstein founded the special relativity theory, later expanded by him into the general one. Experiments showed that, as expected, a body's electromagnetic and optical behavior, unlike its mechanical behavior, was affected by its motion in a "fundamental" frame of reference wherein light, an electromagnetic phenomenon, propagated uniformly in all directions; but, strangely, the observer always found himself at rest in the latter. In his paper Einstein boldly accepts the evidence, sweeping aside hypotheses accumulated to explain it away, and postulates that all natural laws, electromagnetic as well as mechanical, and the velocity of light, irrespective of any motion of the light source, are the same for all observers non-accelerated relative to the fixed stars. Therefrom he derives the relativity to the observer of the distance and time lapse between two events, and, by a penetrating analysis of the concepts of space and time measurements, shows this to be perfectly compatible with the assumption that differently moving observers use identical measuring procedures; thus he removes all appearance of contradiction from his postulates. See RELATIVITY.—*G. G.*

ON THE HYPOTHESES THAT LIE AT THE FOUNDATIONS OF GEOMETRY, by Bernhard Riemann (1854): In this lecture Riemann originated the *analytical approach* to NON-EUCLIDEAN

GEOMETRY, or the abstract investigation of all possible metrical geometries, which has proved invaluable to modern physics. The central concept is that of *space curvature,* an extension of Gauss's concept of curvature of surfaces. When the Riemannian "curvature" is zero, the geometry is Euclidean; when it differs from zero, the geometry is non-Euclidean. Riemannian "curvature," however, is not to be understood in the ordinary sense as a measure of the "bending" of space in some higher dimension. See SPACE.—*G. G.*

ON THE ORIGIN OF SPECIES by Means of Natural Selection, or the Preservation of Favoured Races in the Struggle for Life, by Charles Robert Darwin (1859): Written as a biological treatise, this book had a major impact on 19th-cent. thought in general. Ideas of organic evolution can be found in the writings of scientists prior to Darwin, but it was the *Origin of Species* which first brought together the enormous amount of evidence from fields as diverse as artificial breeding and the geographical distribution of plants and animals. Equally important was the suggestion of a mechanism, previously lacking, to account for evolution: NATURAL SELECTION. Darwin seized upon this as the means whereby the almost imperceptible variations that occur in nature could be accumulated. Selective pressure would tend to preserve those variant forms best able to adapt to their environment and permit them to produce progeny. Unfavorable variations would be destroyed, and ultimately a new species would emerge. Modern evolutionary theory requires two sets of laws: one, the laws of survival, was supplied by Darwin; the other, the laws of heredity and variation, was not developed until 50 yr after the publication of the *Origin of Species.*—*E. Me.*

OORT, JAN HENDRICK, 1900–1966, Dutch astronomer; b. Franeker, Netherlands. He worked on development of the theory of galactic rotation, determination of density of matter in the solar neighborhood, and radio studies of the structure of the Milky Way. He was at Leiden Univ., the Netherlands, from 1924, and director of its observatory from 1945. President of the International Astronomical Union, 1958–61, he became a fellow of the Royal Society in 1959. He was elected a foreign associate of the U. S. National Academy of Sciences in 1953.—*S. D. G.*

OPEN-HEARTH PROCESS: a method of producing steel from pig iron. Pig iron, iron ore, scrap steel, and limestone (in varying proportions, depending on the product desired) are placed on a shallow hearth, made of a high-temperature refractory material such as magnesite ($MgCO_3$). A gaseous fuel and air, in combustion, are passed over the surface of these ingredients until temperatures are reached at which impurities in the pig iron, *e.g.* manganese, phosphorus, silicon, and carbon, are oxidized by the oxygen of the iron ore (Fe_2O_3) or, if there is a large proportion of scrap steel, by the oxygen in the furnace. Open-hearth processes rely on the regenerative furnace developed by Sir William Siemens in 1868. The burned fuel-gas, while being evacuated, gives its heat to a brick grill; then repeated reversals of the direction of gas flow allow these grills to preheat the incoming fuel and air so that increasingly high temperatures are reached. Basic open-hearth processes (referring to the basic, rather than acidic, nature of the slag and magnesite) account for most contemporary steel production in the U. S. A. The main advantages over the Bessemer process are: (1) ability to remove phosphorus, which cannot be removed by the usual acid Bessemer process and which can be removed by the Thomas or basic Bessemer process only by using slag; (2) better con-

Open-hearth furnace, tapped by remote control, emits spray of steel sparks. Explosive charge removes clay stopper, permitting flow of molten steel at 3000°F. (*U. S. Steel*)

trol of temperature and of the degree of purification; (3) ability to use a wide variety of raw materials, including scrap; (4) more steel per amount of pig iron, since some of the iron from the iron-ore oxidizer is utilized. In recent years basic oxygen furnaces, which combine all these advantages with high production rates, have been replacing open-hearth furnaces in new installations. See BESSEMER PROCESS; FURNACE; STEEL.—*A. L.*

OPERATIONALISM: the school of scientific philosophy that emphasizes the importance of operational definition. Such a definition states the overt procedures that constitute the necessary and sufficient conditions for the employment of a term. There are two major versions of operationalism: the stronger maintains that all scientific terms must be operationally defined; the weaker demands only that the basic empirical terms of science be operationally defined and that theoretical terms be coordinated in some suitable manner with operationally defined ones. An operational definition of a term T can take the form "$T =$ If A then B," where A represents a description of an operation a scientist can perform with some instrument, and B can be replaced with a statement of the outcome of that operation.

Critics of operationalism hold it doubtful that scientists do—or ought to—provide such definitions for empirical or observational terms: they deny that operational definitions can be given for metrical terms representing such continuous quantities as length, mass, and temperature; and they also maintain that since operational definitions are frequently altered in light of changes in theories, operationally defined terms cannot be considered the basic concepts of science. P. W. Bridgman, a leading proponent of operationalism, insisted that an operational definition can be given by reference either to operations with instruments or to operations with paper and pencil. It is therefore possible to view his version of operationalism as a demand that scientists clearly stipulate the conditions under which they use their terms rather than as a directive which prescribes in what manner the stipulations must be made. Though the emphasis upon operational definition by physicists such as Bridgman and philosophers such as Philipp Frank has undoubtedly played an important role in the clarification of terms in science, many philosophers and scientists now tend to minimize its importance.—*S. M.*

OPERATOR: in mathematics, a symbol that denotes an operation of some sort, when applied to a suitable object. For example, the operator $2 \cdot$ denotes the operation of doubling a quantity, and when applied to a number x produces the number $2x$. One can use operators to write equations, and there is a general theory for solving equations in operational notation. If P denotes an operator and x a suitable object, one possible equation is $Px = a$.

This equation in effect poses the question: if P is a given operator and a is a given object how is x to be chosen so that P operating on x produces a? This question can be answered if one can find another operator, say Q, which when applied to Px produces x; symbolically we would then have $QPx = x$. If Q is applied to both sides of the first equation, we have $QPx = Qa$ but since $QPx = x$ we have $x = Qa$.

The operator Q is called the inverse of P, since with it the equation can be inverted. For example, the inverse of the operator $2 \cdot$ is $\frac{1}{2} \cdot$, since $\frac{1}{2} \cdot 2 \cdot x = x$ if one is given the algebraic equation $2 \cdot x = a$ one finds that the solution is $x = \frac{1}{2} \cdot a$.

An illustration of a differential equation is

$$dy/dt + y = f(t)$$

with the initial condition $y(0) = 0$. Symbolically, the equation can be written in the form $(d/dt + 1)y = f(t)$. The inverse operator of $(d/dt + 1)$ is $e^{-t} \int_0^t e^t \, dt$ since

$$e^{-t} \int^t e^t (\frac{d}{dt} + 1)y \, dt = y$$

By applying the inverse operator to the differential equation one finds

$$y = e^{-t} \int_0^t e^t f(t) \, dt$$

Sometimes it is possible to simplify the operations required. For example, in the case of the algebraic equation $2x = a$, one can apply logarithms to change the operation from a multiplication to an addition. Then one obtains

$$\log 2 + \log x = \log a$$

The operator inverse to $(\log 2 +)$ is $(- \log 2 +)$ so that

$$-\log 2 + \log 2 + \log x = -\log 2 + \log a$$

$$\log x = -\log 2 + \log a = \log \tfrac{1}{2}a$$

whence
$$x = \tfrac{1}{2}a$$

An analogous operation can be carried out in a wide class of differential equations by means of the Laplace transform. This transformation is defined by

$$\int_0^\infty e^{-st} y(t) \, dt = Y(s)$$

where the function $y(t)$ is transformed into $Y(s)$. One can show that

$$\int_0^\infty e^{-st} \frac{dy}{dt} \, dt = sY(s) - y(0)$$

so that the transformation of dy/dt is algebraically related to the transformation of y. If one applies this transformation to the differential equation

$$\frac{dy}{dt} + y = f(t); \qquad y(0) = 0$$

one finds

$$\int_0^\infty e^{-st} (\frac{dy}{dt} + y) \, dt = \int_0^\infty e^{-st} f(t) \, dt$$

and this becomes

$$S \, Y(s) + Y(s) = F(s)$$

where
$$\int_0^\infty e^{-st} f(t) \, dt = F(s)$$

Thus one sees that the differential equation has been converted into an algebraic equation, whose solution is

$$Y(s) = F(s)/(s + 1)$$

To recover $y(t)$ from this equation one has to find a function, whose Laplace transform is given by

$$F(s)/(s + 1)$$

This done, one again obtains the solution found before.

Operators are important because one can operate with them in a symbolic fashion. Furthermore they can be classified into numerous groups, and the properties of each group can be studied in generality so that many kinds of problems can be studied by a unified method. A class of operators about which a rather complete theory exists is the *linear operators*. These are operators with the property that when applied to a linear combination $ax_1 + bx_2$ they satisfy the relationship

$$P(ax_1 + bx_2) = aPx_1 + bPx_2$$

All operators discussed here are linear operators.—*H. Ho.*

OPPENHEIMER, J. ROBERT, 1904–67, U. S. physicist; b. New York, N. Y. A noted teacher, he made important contributions to quantum theory, nuclear physics, and relativity. As director of Los Alamos Scientific Laboratory, 1943–45, he was the key figure in development of the atomic bomb. The Atomic Energy Commission in 1954 denied him access to secret material on grounds of security but in 1963 gave him its highest honor, the Enrico Fermi Award, for advancing peaceful uses of atomic energy. Director and professor of physics at the Institute for Advanced Study, Princeton, 1947–66, he wrote *The Open Mind* (1955), *Science and the Common Understanding* (1954), and *Some Reflections on Science and Culture* (1960). He was a fellow of the Royal Society and a member of the U. S. National Academy of Sciences.—*R. M.*

OPPOSITION: a term used in astronomy to express the fact that the celestial longitudes or right ascensions of two celestial bodies differ by exactly 180°. Accordingly, at *opposition in longitude,* the two bodies and Earth are in a plane perpendicular to Earth's orbit with the bodies on opposite sides of Earth; at *opposition in right ascension,* the bodies and Earth are similarly disposed in a plane perpendicular to the celestial equator. In the most current usage of these terms, one of the bodies is the Sun, the other being a planet or the Moon. Mercury and Venus can never be at opposition, because their orbits lie entirely inside Earth's orbit. The best time for observing a superior planet is when it is at or near opposition, for it is then nearest to Earth and visible in the night sky. Since a planet's orbit is elliptical, the most favorable oppositions for observation are those which occur when the planet is at or near perihelion, for then its distance from Earth is as small as possible. The Moon is full when it is at opposition in longitude.—*S. D. G.*

OPTICAL ACTIVITY: the property of certain substances (in solution, in liquid form, or as crystals) of rotating the plane of a beam of polarized light when such a beam is passed through them. The property is inherent in substances with molecules that have an asymmetric structure (see ASYMMETRIC CARBON ATOM). The rotation may be to the left or right (dextro- or levorotary), and optically active compounds can exist in either form. These are optical isomers or enantiomorphs (mirror images of each other's molecular structure). A mixture of both (racemic mixture) has no optical activity, since isomers cancel each other in this respect. L. Pasteur was the first to separate such mixtures into their components and to understand the phenomenon.—*J. F. S.*

OPTICAL INSTRUMENTS: devices that use the principles of OPTICS to extend or to supplement the vision of the eye. Optical instruments may be divided into two main classes: those that form an image of an external object and those that modify the light passing through them and produce an information-bearing pattern of some other sort. To the first class belong the magnifying glass, MICROSCOPE, TELESCOPE, CAMERA, and others. The second class includes the SPECTROSCOPE, REFRACTOMETER, POLARISCOPE, PHOTOMETER, and many more.

The magnifying glass is usually a simple thin LENS, with a focal length of a few inches or less, which is held between the eye and the object. The normal eye, neither near-sighted nor far-sighted, can focus comfortably on objects as close as about 10 in. away. By placing a convex lens before the eye, the accommodative power of the eye can be effectively increased, and the object can be brought much closer. For the action of the lens, see Fig. 1. The image the eye sees is located on the same side of the lens as the object, and thus cannot be projected on a screen. Such an image is called a *virtual image*. A more complex form of the magnifier is used when the eye is to examine not a real object but, instead, an optical image formed by another lens. In the microscope, for example, this image is formed by a small lens of short focal length, which is placed close to the object to be examined. This so-called *objective* lens forms an enlarged *real image* (which can be seen on a screen or ground glass) in the focal plane of the eyepiece, or *ocular* lens. The ocular lens brings to the eye a still more enlarged virtual image. This action is shown in Fig. 2, where simple lenses are used in the diagram

to represent the complex arrays found in a high-quality instrument.

Optically speaking, the refracting telescope is very closely related to the microscope. The objective lens of the telescope forms a real image of an object that is at an essentially infinite distance. This image is magnified by the ocular and viewed by the eye as an enlarged virtual image. As Fig. 3 shows, the final image is inverted. In astronomical work, this is no problem; for other purposes, as when the telescope is to form one side of a pair of binoculars, prisms are placed in the path of the light in such a way that the image reaches the eye upright.

A slightly different form of refracting telescope is shown in Fig. 4. Though now used mostly in opera glasses and children's toys, this design was the one employed by Galileo in his astronomical researches as early as 1609. As the diagram shows, the ocular is a concave lens, which forms a virtual image, enlarged and erect, of the real image, which is located on the eye side of the ocular. The Galilean telescope has the advantages of simplicity and compactness, but is seriously handicapped by its narrow field of view.

Because glass refracts light of different wavelengths by slightly different amounts (see DISPERSION; SPECTRUM), the image of a white star, for example, will not be focused sharply by a single simple lens. To minimize this so-called chromatic aberration, it is necessary to make the lenses in quality instruments out of two or more individual lenses, ground separately and cemented together (see LENS). Even the best-designed of these lenses, however, does not eliminate aberration for all wavelengths. In telescope design the problem of chromatic aberration is especially critical. Large telescopes are used mainly for spectrographic work, in which color accuracy is vital. To achieve full correction in a lens of more than a few inches aperture becomes difficult and very expensive. It was Newton who suggested, about 1670, that

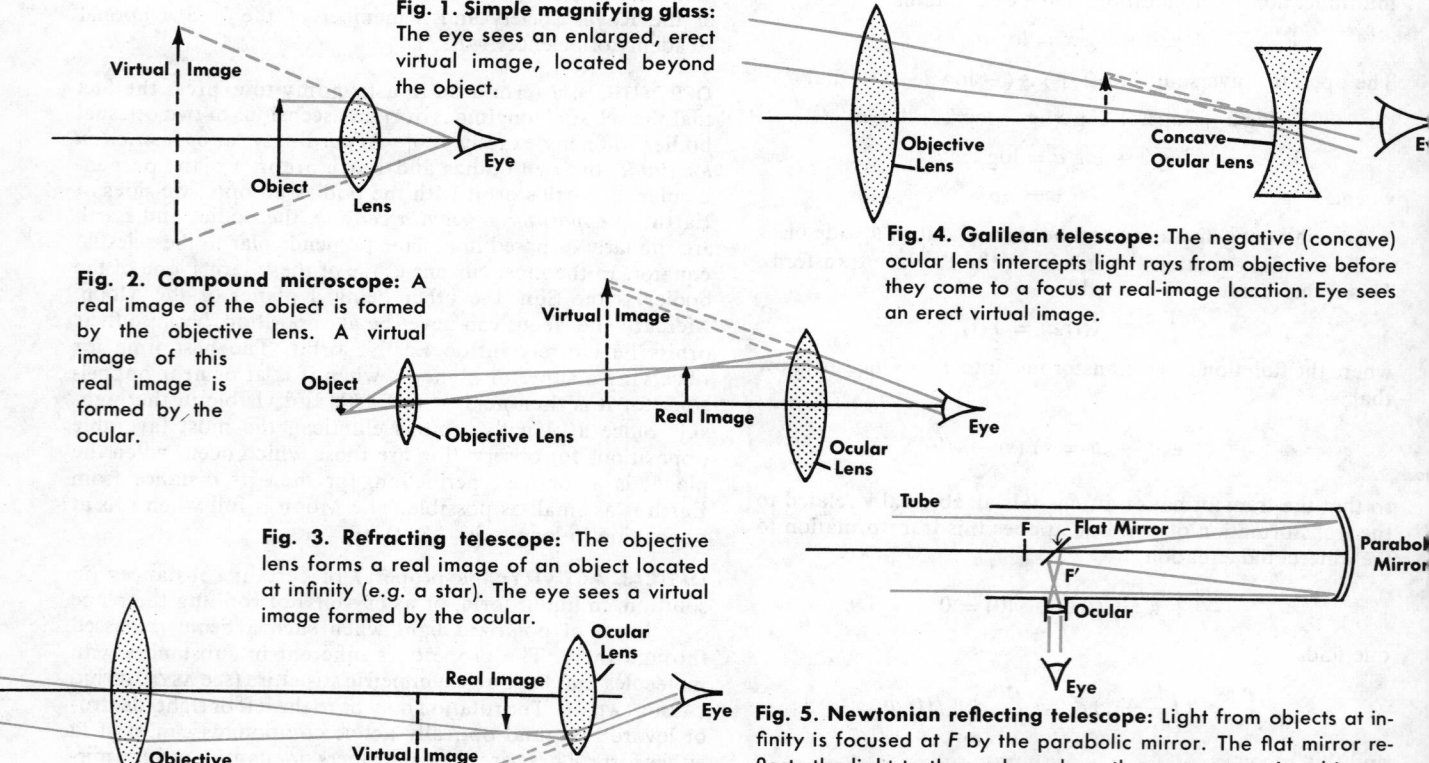

Fig. 1. Simple magnifying glass: The eye sees an enlarged, erect virtual image, located beyond the object.

Fig. 2. Compound microscope: A real image of the object is formed by the objective lens. A virtual image of this real image is formed by the ocular.

Fig. 3. Refracting telescope: The objective lens forms a real image of an object located at infinity (e.g. a star). The eye sees a virtual image formed by the ocular.

Fig. 4. Galilean telescope: The negative (concave) ocular lens intercepts light rays from objective before they come to a focus at real-image location. Eye sees an erect virtual image.

Fig. 5. Newtonian reflecting telescope: Light from objects at infinity is focused at *F* by the parabolic mirror. The flat mirror reflects the light to the ocular, where the eye sees a virtual image of the real image (located at *F'*).

the problem of chromatic aberrations could be eliminated by using a curved metallic reflecting surface, rather than a lens, to form the image in a telescope. Mechanical difficulties in figuring the surface to an exact paraboloid delayed the construction of a practical astronomical reflecting telescope until the early 18th cent., but the most common type in use even today differs little from Newton's original design (see Fig. 5), except that a glass mirror has been substituted for the metallic one.

Other optical instruments, *e.g.* the camera (Fig. 6) and the projector (Fig. 7), form a real image on a flat surface, which is viewed more or less directly by the naked eye. These instruments consist essentially of only an objective lens, usually highly corrected and fitted with adjustable stops, shutters, and focusing mechanisms. To produce objectives with minimum aberrations and distortions, the designer usually makes the lens of four to six separate elements. Internal reflections among the surfaces of the elements, the so-called ghost images, are suppressed by the use of antireflection coatings. A feeling of depth is achieved in photography by taking two pictures of the same subject from slightly different angles and by viewing the pictures through a STEREOSCOPE.—*D. H. L.*

OPTICKS, by Isaac Newton (1704): From the famous paper (1672) in which Newton described his new theory of light and color there followed a long controversy; thereafter Newton remained silent on optics until 1704, when he at last published his ideas and experiments fully. Newton discovered that white light is not homogeneous but a mixture of all the colored constituents which, separated, appear in the spectrum. Each set of rays forming a colored patch in the spectrum was for him an individual entity, characterized by its unique refrangibility in the prism. Pursuing this mathematical analysis of color, Newton was able to explain many hitherto baffling

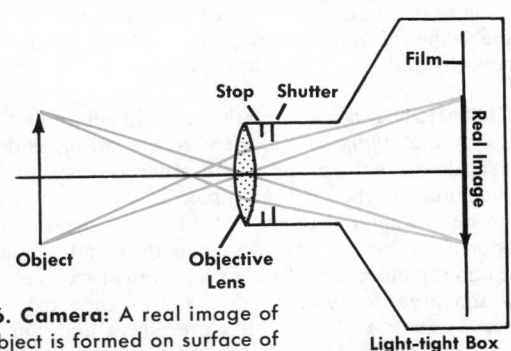

Fig. 6. Camera: A real image of the object is formed on surface of the film by objective lens. The stop controls amount of light admitted; the shutter controls exposure time.

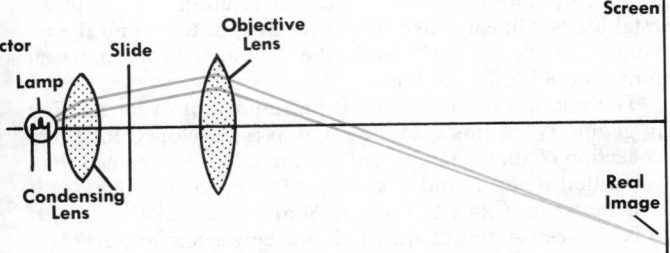

Fig. 7. Projector: The reflector and the condensing lens concentrate light from the lamp in the plane of the objective lens and thus bring the maximum illumination to screen. Objective lens forms a real image of slide on surface of screen.

optical phenomena, *e.g.* chromatic aberration. Making more complex assumptions, he also produced a mathematical theory of "Newton's rings" (interference colors), on which his experiments were as numerous and accurate as those with the prism. Hardly less interesting (though less enduring) than his work in physical optics are the *Queries* added to successive editions of *Opticks;* by these, in explaining his more speculative views on the ultimate nature of things, Newton powerfully influenced the imagination of later physicists and poets.—*A. R. H.*

OPTICS: originally the study of LIGHT and its interactions with matter; now generally expanded to mean the branch of physics that deals with electromagnetic radiation of wavelengths shorter than radio waves, but longer than x-rays. In *geometrical optics,* light is considered as a mathematical abstraction, obeying a body of geometric laws, but not necessarily having any proper physical reality. The REFLECTION and REFRACTION of light rays by mirrors, prisms, and lenses of various shapes can be described in terms of pure geometry, and the performance of an optical system made up of such elements can be predicted by purely mathematical methods. In *physical optics,* the wave and particle nature of light is emphasized, and the interactions between radiation and matter are studied. DIFFRACTION, INTERFERENCE, POLARIZED LIGHT, SCATTERING, DISPERSION, as well as phenomena such as the FARADAY EFFECT, the ZEEMAN EFFECT, and the KERR EFFECT, are all fundamental topics in physical optics. Taken together, geometrical optics and physical optics occupy a central position in science because of their value as tools for other disciplines. Modern biology, for example, could not have developed without the MICROSCOPE, nor astronomy without the TELESCOPE. Much of our knowledge of the atomic structure of matter has been learned through study of the SPECTRUM and by related optical methods. In another field, the phenomenon of PHOTOELASTICITY, in which some plastics exhibit DOUBLE REFRACTION when under mechanical stress, enables engineers to determine by optical means the distribution of stress in complex structures. Other optical methods and instruments are used in nearly every branch of science and technology.

Also of great interest are branches of optics that study the behavior of light in certain media. *Atmospheric optics,* for example, deals with effects produced by light passing through the air, or through raindrops, fog, dust, and the like. Typical phenomena are the MIRAGE, RAINBOW, CORONA, and GLORY. *Physiological optics* is the scientific study of VISION. The eye is a remarkably complex optical instrument and although the geometrical optics of vision are well understood (and extensively applied in optometry), the links between vision and perception—the formation of the mental, as distinguished from the optical, image—remain obscure. COLOR VISION, for example, has been adequately explained as a purely optical phenomenon for nearly 300 yr, ever since Newton's demonstration that the eye interprets the wavelength of light in terms of subjective color. Nevertheless, the exact nature of the process by which the eye-brain combination performs this task is still the subject of active research. Study of the perception of shapes, patterns, movements, and spatial relationships is likewise a rapidly progressing field of research in physiological optics. The term "optics" is occasionally applied in physics to fields other than those involving light. The flight of beams of electrons through vacuum tubes, for example, can be analyzed in terms of geometrical optics. Electrical analogies to lenses, prisms, and other optical elements exist and are used in the construction of ELECTRON MICROSCOPES and other quasi-optical devices.—*D. H. L.*

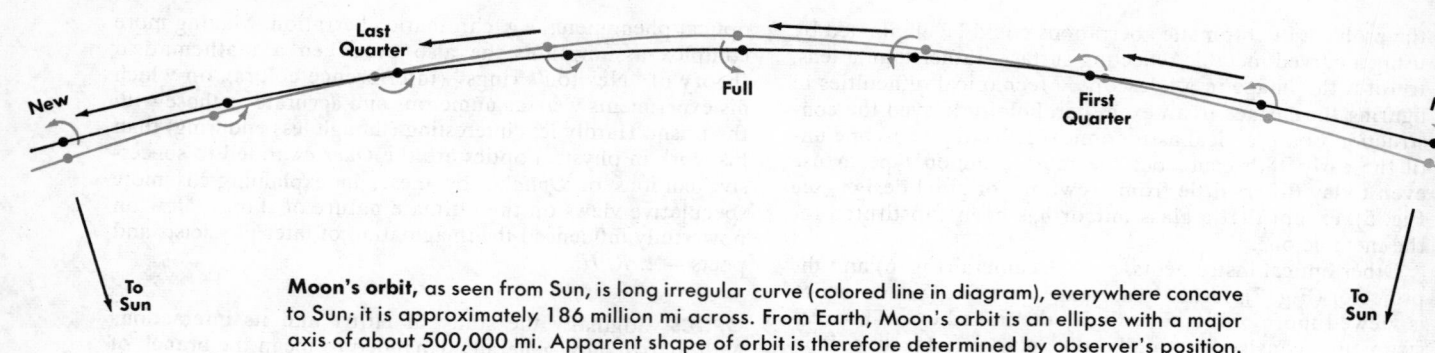

Moon's orbit, as seen from Sun, is long irregular curve (colored line in diagram), everywhere concave to Sun; it is approximately 186 million mi across. From Earth, Moon's orbit is an ellipse with a major axis of about 500,000 mi. Apparent shape of orbit is therefore determined by observer's position.

ORBIT: the path of a celestial body through space, under the gravitational attraction of one or more other bodies. (An artificial satellite is said to be "in orbit" when it moves in a circular or elliptical path around Earth.) The orbit of a body of negligible mass under the attraction of a single massive body is, according to NEWTON'S LAWS OF MOTION, a CONIC SECTION, with the massive body at one of the foci of the curve. A circle, an ellipse, a parabola, and an hyperbola are all conic sections; the circle and ellipse are closed curves, in which the motion of the small body would be periodic, but the parabola and hyperbola are open curves, so that the motion of the small body is not periodic. A straight line through the massive body is also a special case of a conic section. The planets move about the Sun in elliptical orbits, obeying KEPLER'S LAWS (the third law being modified to allow for the fact that the masses of the planets are not completely negligible compared with that of the Sun).

A body's motion may be considered with respect to Earth or another planet, the Sun, or nearby stars. Thus, Earth's orbit relative to the Sun is an ellipse. However, the Sun itself is moving through space toward a point in the constellation Lyra, carrying Earth with it. Hence Earth's *absolute orbit* in space is roughly a helix. Similarly, the Moon's orbit relative to Earth is an ellipse with Earth at a focus; its orbit relative to the Sun is a closed curve that is everywhere concave to the Sun (see MOON); and its orbit relative to nearby stars is approximately helical.

If the mass of the smaller body is not negligible, then the two bodies move about their common center of mass in orbits of similar shape, the more massive body moving in the smaller orbit. This often occurs in double stars. In the case of the Moon moving around Earth, the Moon is massive enough to cause a slight, periodic departure of Earth from a strictly elliptical orbit about the Sun. The presence of faint third components in visual double stars has been detected by the distortions they produce in the otherwise elliptical relative orbits of the double stars. To analyze precisely the motion of a planet about the Sun, allowance must be made for the attractions of the other planets (see PERTURBATIONS). The following quantities, or parameters, are required to specify the orbit of any object in the SOLAR SYSTEM: its inclination to the ecliptic; the longitude of its ascending node; the angle from ascending node to perihelion; its semimajor axis; its eccentricity; and the time of perihelion passage of the object.

Refined observation has shown that the motions of the planets, even allowing for their mutual attractions, are not fully represented by Newton's laws of motion. The theory of relativity accounts for most of the discrepancies. The inadequacy of Newton's laws is significant only in the case of Mercury; the planet moves in a rosette-like orbit that can be considered to be a Keplerian ellipse that is slowly rotating. (The correctness of the relativity prediction has also recently

been confirmed for the orbits of Earth and Venus, where the effect is much smaller.)

In the two-body problem, regardless of the mass of either body, the position, velocity, and direction of motion of one body relative to the other completely define both shape and size of the relative orbit. If one of the bodies is disturbed by a third, at any time it is possible to define an "osculating orbit," which is the orbit that the body would pursue if the third, disturbing body were suddenly removed. With a very large number of bodies, sufficiently far apart for close approaches of two or more bodies to be rare (as in our Galaxy of stars), a single body can be considered to be moving in an orbit under the combined attraction of all the other bodies considered together. The Sun and the other stars move in orbits about the center of the Galaxy, and osculating orbits are circular or elliptical. However, the actual orbits are not elliptical; as a star with an elliptical osculating orbit changes its distance from the center of the Galaxy, the effective attraction of all the other stars does not vary in the same way as the attraction of a single central mass. The size, shape, and orientation of the osculating orbit of a single star thus change with time as the star moves through the Galaxy, the real orbits being complicated. See THREE-BODY PROBLEM.—*M. W. O.*

ORDER RELATIONS: in mathematics, certain relations such as *less than, greater than, before, after, to the left of,* and *to the right of.* To describe the properties of order we may consider a set of elements and the relation "precedes." A set of elements is said to be arranged in linear order if it satisfies the following properties: (1) given any two elements x and y, one must precede and the other must follow; (2) given any two elements x and y, if x precedes y, then y does not precede x; (3) given any three elements x, y, and z, if x precedes y and y precedes z then x precedes z. The relation "less than" establishes a linear order among the whole numbers; for, given any whole numbers, we can always distinguish which is the smaller one; if one is smaller than another it is not larger than the second, and if $x < y$ and $y < z$, then $x < z$. The relation "earlier than" establishes a linear order among instants of time, and the relation "to the left of" establishes a linear order between points on a horizontal line.

The relation of "between" is an important order relation in geometry. In this case the relation is developed for every collection of three members of the set, and it is assumed that, given that A, B, C, and X are members of the set, then (1) If B is between A and C, then A, B, and C are distinct; (2) If B is between A and C, then C is not between A and B; (3) If B is between A and C, it is between C and A; (4) If A, B, and C are distinct, then either A is between B and C, or B is between A and C, or C is between A and B; (5) If A, B, C, and X are distinct, and B is between A and C, then B is either between A and X or between X and C.—*H. E. W.*

ORES AND ORE DEPOSITS: Ores are rocks that contain varied amounts of valuable minerals. Ores valuable at one time may be worthless at another and vice versa, depending on technological developments in mining, ore processing, fabrication, and use; availability of similar materials or substitutes; and accessibility and transportation costs. The minimum *grade* of an ore varies inversely with the value of the contained material; thus a minable ore of gold need contain only a fraction of an ounce of gold per ton, but the porphyry coppers must contain about 20 lb of copper per ton. Some ores can be used directly as mined, *e.g.* hematite, chromite, bauxite, rock salt, gypsum; but others may require intricate processing to separate valuable constituents from intimately interlocked worthless constituents (gangue minerals). (See METALLURGY; MINING.)

Ore deposits are by definition natural concentrations of valuable minerals. The formation and localization of such concentrations are directly related to the stabilities of the minerals and to the geological processes and environments in which they have been involved.

Syngenetic deposits are those which have been formed contemporaneously with their enclosing rocks. *Epigenetic deposits* are those which have been introduced after their host rocks were consolidated. Syngenetic deposits include eluvial (residual) and alluvial (placer) deposits, laterites, bedded sediments, evaporites, magmatic segregations (in original position), and pegmatitic "blows" in igneous bodies. Epigenetic deposits include hydrothermal veins and replacement deposits, contact metamorphic deposits, magmatic segregations that have migrated beyond the limits of their own source bodies, and pegmatite dikes and sills. Many deposits, especially those which have been metamorphosed, are difficult to classify and their origins are subject to controversy. Isotopic ratio studies appear to be of some value in solving these problems.

Among the simplest types are the *eluvial* (or *residual*) *deposits,* in which minerals that are resistant to weathering and were originally sparsely disseminated through a rock have accumulated more or less in place as the associated, more common rock-forming minerals were removed through chemical weathering and erosion. Thus gold, diamonds, corundum (including rubies and sapphires), chromite, and barite occur as eluvial deposits. Eluvial minerals, too, are eventually removed by erosion and accumulate in drainage basins as *alluvial* (*placer*) *deposits.* Concentration is effected by differences in resistance to abrasion, and particularly by differences in density, the heavier minerals tending to lag behind in the upper reaches of the stream valleys and to work down toward bedrock, forming "pay-streaks" just above it. On beaches strong, storm-induced waves act as concentrating agents. The powerful upsurge can carry all kinds of sand grains to the top of the beach, but the backwash, starting from zero intensity, is too weak to remove some of the heavier grains, and thus the upper beach may become enriched in heavy minerals (*black sands*). A similar winnowing action is effected by strong winds which carry away light mineral grains, so that the dunes nearest a beach may become enriched in heavy minerals. Gold, platinum, rutile, ilmenite, zircon, and monazite are mined from active and fossil *beach* and *dune deposits.* Under conditions of tropical, humid weathering, aluminum, iron, nickel, manganese, and cobalt form insoluble hydrated oxides. In well-drained flat areas the more soluble constituents including silica, the

Tungsten-bearing quartz veins in schist: In this stripping, near Michipicoten Harbour, Ontario, crystals of scheelite, $CaWO_4$, are disseminated through the veins. Distribution of scheelite, which is strongly fluorescent, was determined by mapping at night with ultraviolet lamp. (Louis Moyd)

alkalies, and alkaline earths are selectively removed, with resulting development of cap-like enrichments (laterites) of the hydrated oxides.

Materials which are removed in solution during weathering may be reprecipitated in concentrated form. When bodies of sea water become landlocked in arid regions and evaporate to dryness, *saline deposits* (*evaporites*) are formed. Repeated inundations may give rise to great thicknesses of bedded evaporites, *e.g.* rock salt, anhydrite, and gypsum. Similar deposits are formed by evaporation of saline waters in interior drainage basins ("playa lakes"). Partial re-solution of evaporite beds may effect the leaching and localized re-precipitation of some of the more soluble constituents, *e.g.* potash salts, borates, nitrates. *Organic agencies,* as bacteria, foraminifera, sponges, and mollusks, are able to extract dissolved substances selectively and precipitate them as respiratory or alimentary wastes or as skeletal parts. The bedded iron formations are believed to be bacterial precipitates; the sulfur deposits associated with salt domes are believed to result from bacterial reduction of gypsum and anhydrite; deposits of diatomaceous earth are accumulations of the opaline skeletons of diatoms.

Ground water circulating through fractures and pore spaces or rocks can cause concentrations by dissolving material from one rock type or zone and precipitating it elsewhere.

Beach deposit: "Leasers" mine a rutile- and zircon-rich bed of heavy minerals underlying the barrier beach of North Stradbroke Island, near Brisbane, Australia. The heavy minerals were selectively concentrated by the action of strong, storm-induced waves. Nearby, more disseminated deposits are mined and beneficiated by mechanical methods. (Louis Moyd)

The uranium-vanadium deposits of the Colorado Plateau
type may have been formed by leaching of uranium and
vanadium from beds of volcanic ash by ground waters which
later traveled through fossil stream beds ("channels") filled
with relatively coarse sandstones and conglomerates. Localized concentrations of organic "trash" such as fossil carbonized logs, branches, and leaves in the channels caused precipitation of the uranium and vanadium. Many economic
geologists believe the lead and zinc of the "Mississippi
Valley"-type limestone-replacement deposits were leached
from adjacent sediments and re-precipitated in structurally
and chemically favorable zones by the action of circulating
ground waters.

A common factor in deposits of this type is the absence of
potential igneous sources for the metal-bearing solutions.
Various authorities have noted that the quantities of limestone known to have been dissolved away by ground waters,
based on measurements of stylolitic partings, would have
afforded more than enough lead and zinc to account for the
ore bodies.

Surficial mineral deposits that have been formed in the
course of weathering, erosion, transportation, and sedimentation may become buried and thus "fossilized." Along with
the enclosing rocks these deposits may then be subjected to
the increasing temperatures and pressures associated with
deep burial, downwarping, and tectonic activity.

As rocks become metamorphosed so, too, do the mineral deposits, the individual minerals reacting with each other
to maintain thermodynamic equilibrium as conditions change.
The sequence peat→lignite→bituminous coal→anthracite
coal→graphitic anthracite→graphite illustrates the progressive effects of deep burial and regional METAMORPHISM. Many
authorities believe the extensive gold deposits of the Witwatersrand in S Africa and the uranium deposits of the Blind
River area in Canada were originally alluvial concentrations
in gravels that were later metamorphosed to quartzitic conglomerates. Reactions and recrystallizations imposed in metamorphism may, in themselves, account for direct development or reconcentration of valuable minerals, *e.g.* garnets,
corundum, and kyanite, from shales, or magnetite from iron-
bearing clays of sedimentary iron formations.

Igneous activity is responsible for certain ore deposits. As
the more basic (*i.e.* silica-deficient) igneous bodies cool and
crystallize, metallic oxides and sulfides, in fluid form, become
immiscible in the silica melt and segregate into gravity-
controlled layers or irregular masses. Extensive layers of
titaniferous magnetite and of chromite, in part enriched in
nickel and platinum, have been thus formed. Most of the
large copper-nickel-iron sulfide deposits are directly associated
with basic igneous rocks and apparently had a similar origin,
but their initial form has been obscured by later movement
and hydrothermal reworking. As the more silicic and alkaline magmas cool and crystallize, their residual fluids become
enriched in "mineralizers" such as CO_2, B, Fl, Cl, H_2O, and
S. In some cases mineralizer-enriched zones crystallize within the igneous body itself, forming coarse-grained patches
called *pegmatites*. In other cases the fluid pegmatitic magma
is forced out into the country rocks, forming lenticular dikes
and sills. Lithium, tantalum, beryllium, and cesium minerals,
sheet mica, potash feldspar, gem tourmaline, and many other
gem and commercial minerals have been obtained almost
exclusively from pegmatites.

If, during the crystallization of intermediate to silicic magmas, there is opportunity for the mineralizer-rich fluids to
escape from the magma chamber more or less continuously,
mineralization takes a different form. The outer, already
crystallized shell of the igneous body and the surrounding
country rocks are permeated by tenuous fluids which take
advantage of all types of openings in their movement toward
zones of lower pressure. Such openings may include original
intergranular pores in the rocks, joint systems, sheared zones,
and major fault systems and their subsidiary "tear zones."
The precipitation of valuable minerals from these hydrothermal fluids is based on many factors, ranging from simple
pressure-temperature relations within the solutions themselves to very complex reactions with wall-rocks of varied
compositions. The changes in equilibrium that take place
during regional metamorphism can liberate some of the less
stable elements that might be dispersed in the rocks. These
elements would become concentrated in the interstitial fluids,
and such fluids would then be almost indistinguishable from
the primary hydrothermal emanations from crystallizing
magmas.

Ore processing, 18th cent.: Queensboro Furnace, in Hudson highlands, southern New York, is a survivor of many that date from
Revolutionary period. Magnetic iron ore, occurring in dikes that
form networks in the gneisses of this region, was blasted out with
black powder. Furnaces were charged with mixture of ore, limestone, and charcoal to produce the iron. (Jerome Wyckoff)

Opinions vary greatly concerning the source of the heavy metals in hydrothermal deposits—how much, if any, was introduced from extraneous magmatic sources and how much was extracted and remobilized from the wall rocks themselves. The "source-bed" concept is strengthened by the common association of certain types of deposits with specific kinds of wall rocks, *e.g.* quartz-carbonate-chalcocite-bornite veins in greenstones that were derived from basaltic lavas through moderate regional metamorphism.

Mineralogical zoning, based on the stability ranges of various minerals and mineral suites, is a rough geological thermometer, reflecting the temperatures and pressures of hydrothermal ore-deposit formation. High-temperature effects are most strongly developed in the wall zones of intrusives and in the immediately adjacent country rock. High-temperature quartz veins fill fissures, and the adjacent wall rocks may be greisenized. Mineral suites of the greisens and high-temperature veins are characterized by feldspars, micas, topaz, cassiterite, scheelite, wolframite, beryl, molybdenite, bismuth, and bismuthinite.

Contact metamorphism and *high-temperature (hypothermal) mineralization* overlap in both cause and effect, particularly where carbonate country rocks are involved and tactites and skarns are developed. Wall-rock replacement (metasomatism) has occurred to a greater or lesser extent in most ore bodies, regardless of temperature of formation. All gradations occur, from sharp veins with well-defined walls and sharp, unaltered inclusions of country rock ("horses") to complete infiltration and replacement of the host rock, with little or no relict original material.

At increasing distances from the igneous source, the mineral suites of the hydrothermal vein and replacement bodies reflect progressively lower pressure-temperature conditions. Vein and replacement bodies formed at moderate temperatures (mesothermal deposits) are characterized by sulfides, sulfarsenides, and tellurides. The low-temperature hydrothermal deposits (epithermal deposits) are characterized by low-melting sulfides of arsenic, antimony, and mercury, and, where vein-forming solutions actually reach the surface as hot springs, those minerals occur as precipitates in the hot-spring deposits (tufas). Fumarolic and solfataric deposits are sublimates from the exhalations of cooling lavas.

Rock structures are major factors in controlling the localization of mineral deposits and the development of rich zones (*ore-shoots*) within the deposits. In replacement deposits, the structure of the host rock directly influences the structure of the resulting ore body; thus if, because of initial porosity and/or composition, one particular bed of limestone is a favorable host rock for hydrothermal replacements, ore bodies might be developed wherever ore-bearing fluids had access to the bed. Exploration of a mining district of this type is thus aimed primarily at locating all occurrences of the favorable bed, regardless of how complex its present structure might be. Ore-shoots in jointed, faulted, or sheared rock are commonly localized near the intersections of fissures and along the axes of minor folds and crenulations. In the "porphyry copper" deposits, copper and molybdenum minerals are sparsely disseminated through igneous bodies and adjacent structurally favorable country rocks in the form of film-like impregnations in reticulating networks of joint fractures.

The weathering of sulfide-bearing deposits of the heavy metals, ranging from rich concentrations to relatively sparse disseminations, may give rise to important *secondary enrichment* deposits. In the near-surface zone of weathering and oxidation, sulfide minerals are broken down and leached by the surface waters. Insoluble oxide, carbonate, and sulfate minerals remain in the iron- and manganese-stained, rusty cappings (gossans), some of which are characterized by colorful oxidized copper, nickel, cobalt, and uranium minerals. Native gold and silver, and the hydrated manganese-oxide minerals, are mined from gossans. The heavy metals leached from the oxidized zone may be precipitated as secondary enrichments in the reducing zone, just at the water table. Many important deposits have been formed at the water table areas by the precipitation of a relatively thin but rich layer of secondary minerals formed of metals that had originally been very sparsely disseminated through a great thickness of overlying rock.

Age sequences of mineralization are of major importance in the exploration of mineral deposits. Rocks emplaced later than a given sequence of mineralization not only will be lacking in mineral deposits formed during that period, but also may mask or cover existing mineralization in earlier rocks. Geological mapping, in conjunction with geophysical and geochemical surveys of various kinds, has been effective in locating and delineating hidden ore deposits.—*L. M.*

ORESME, NICOLE, 1322–1382, French mathematician; b. Normandy. A college professor and a bishop, he translated some of Aristotle and wrote papers of his own. In one paper he used for the first time the equivalent of fractional exponents. In another he anticipated a part of analytic geometry when he represented certain relations graphically, plotting values of a dependent variable (*latitudo*) corresponding to values of the independent variable (*longitudo*). This tract had something of a vogue in the 15th cent. and may have influenced later mathematicians, including Descartes.—*H. C.*

ORGAN: several different TISSUES arranged in a characteristic structural pattern and forming a major part of a plant or animal. Each organ generally has one chief function, but may perform additional minor functions. Some organs are concerned primarily with reproduction. In animals the reproductive organs are the ovaries and testes. In the lower plants they are sporangia; in the higher plants they include flowers, fruits, and seeds. Other organs maintain the life of the individual. In many animals these organs are combined into organ "systems." Thus the digestive system consists of such organs as esophagus, stomach, small and large intestine, liver, and pancreas; the chief organs of the circulatory system are the heart and spleen; the excretory system usually includes kidneys and a urinary bladder; the respiratory system in terrestrial vertebrates consists of lungs and trachea; the nervous system of all vertebrates includes a brain and spinal cord. In a higher plant, or tracheophyte, the maintenance organs are the root, which anchors the plant and absorbs water and soil minerals; the leaf, which is the chief site of photosynthesis; and the stem, which provides support and conducts water and minerals.—*C. J. H.*

ORGANIC CHEMISTRY: the chemistry of the compounds of carbon. These are known in hundreds of thousands, greatly outnumbering the compounds of all other elements put together. Many fulfill essential functions in living plant and animal organisms (*i.e.* in "organized" matter, hence the name), whereas others are purely artificial substances. A very large number of the naturally occurring organic substances have been synthesized by purely artificial processes. Organic compounds consist mainly of carbon in combination with one or more of the elements hydrogen, oxygen, and nitrogen; but often other elements, notably sulfur and phosphorus, enter into organic combination. August Kekulé's *Theory of Molecular Structure* (1858) explained the unequaled capacity of carbon for forming multitudes of compounds by postulating the quadrivalency of carbon and the capacity of carbon atoms to undergo mutual linking, not only by single bonds but also by double and even triple bonds, as in the following simple structural formulas:

Ethane   Ethylene   Acetylene

Very long chains of carbon atoms may be formed; sometimes they are unbranched, but they may also throw out branches, forming complex ramified structures containing hundreds or even thousands of carbon atoms in combination with atoms of other kinds.

Hydrocarbons contain carbon and hydrogen only. The simplest, methane (CH_4), is the first member of the *paraffin* series of *saturated hydrocarbons,* having the successive formulas CH_4, C_2H_6, C_3H_8, C_4H_{10}, etc. These form an arithmetical progression, with the common difference CH_2 and the general formula C_nH_{2n+2}. Other such *homologous series* start with ethylene, C_2H_4, and acetylene, C_2H_2, having the respective general formulas C_nH_{2n} and C_nH_{2n-2}; these hydrocarbons are called *unsaturated,* since their molecules, unlike those of the paraffins, do not contain the maximum possible number of hydrogen atoms. Molecules of certain unsaturated hydrocarbons and other organic types readily coalesce to form giant molecules (macromolecules or polymers), the building blocks of plastics, rubbers, fibers, etc.

From butane, C_4H_{10}, onward in the paraffin series, any one molecular formula corresponds to more than one substance. Owing to branching of the carbon chain, there are two butanes, as shown below, and three pentanes (C_5H_{12}):

$$CH_3—CH_2—CH_2—CH_3 \qquad CH_3—\overset{\displaystyle CH_3}{\underset{}{CH}}—CH_3$$

Normal butane   Isobutane

Substances having the same molecular formula are called *isomers.* The formula $C_{15}H_{32}$ has 4,347 possible isomers. Isomerism, and also homology, in all types of compounds, are among the most characteristic features of organic chemistry.

The above hydrocarbons and their numerous derivatives are classed as *open-chain* (or *aliphatic*) compounds. The most important of a great variety of *closed-chain* (or *ring* or *aromatic*) compounds is benzene, C_6H_6; another coal-tar compound, naphthalene, $C_{10}H_8$, is an example of a *polycyclic* hydrocarbon. All such hydrocarbons and their derivatives are called *homocyclic,* because the rings contain only carbon atoms. Homocyclic rings may contain from 3 to about 50 carbon atoms. There is also an enormous variety of *heterocyclic* compounds, containing ring-atoms of nitrogen, oxygen, and sulfur, as well as atoms of carbon. An example is quinoline, C_9H_7N:

Benzene   Naphthalene   Quinoline
C_6H_6 $C_{10}H_8$ C_9H_7N

A large variety of atoms or groups may be introduced into open-chain or closed-chain molecules of all kinds. *Alcohols*

possess a hydroxyl (OH) group attached to a saturated carbon atom, as in ordinary ethyl alcohol, C_2H_5OH, or $CH_3—CH_2—OH$. Organic *acids* contain the typical group

; aldehydes have . More complex oxygen types occur as *fats* and *carbohydrates.*

Nitrogenous types include the organic bases, *e.g.* amines and *alkaloids,* also *amides, amino acids, nitrocompounds,* synthetic dyes from coal-tar constituents, etc. The extremely complex *proteins* are built up from about two dozen kinds of amino acids, of which glycine, $H_2N—CH_2—COOH$, is the simplest. See CHEMISTRY; STEREOCHEMISTRY; BIOCHEMISTRY; and separate articles on the representative organic groups and compounds mentioned above.—*J. R.*

ORGANOMETALLIC COMPOUNDS: in organic chemistry, synthetic compounds that contain a metallic element linked directly to a carbon atom. This metal-carbon link can be introduced into a wide variety of compounds. The simplest of these are the carbides, in which only the metal and the carbon are present:

$$CaC_2 \qquad Al_4C_3 \qquad Ag_2C_2 \text{ or } Ag—C≡C—Ag$$
Calcium carbide   Aluminum carbide   Silver carbide

The silver compound is shown as a derivative of acetylene, from which it can be made. The silver-carbon link is largely covalent (see VALENCE), and the compound is explosive when dry. The compounds of the more electropositive metals, *e.g.* aluminum and calcium, are more saltlike. Calcium carbide in water yields acetylene, but aluminum carbide in water gives methane; the different behaviors are probably due to differences in crystal structure. Nickel carbonyl, $Ni(CO)_4$, and iron carbonyl, $Fe(CO)_5$, represent a family of metal carbonyls which are liquids or solids, but all of which are soluble in organic solvents and volatile. At high temperatures the vapors decompose to the metal and carbon monoxide; this phenomenon provides a method of purification and separation, as in the Mond process (see NICKEL).

The organometallic compound best known to the public is tetraethyl lead, $Pb(C_2H_5)_4$, the major constituent of the *ethyl* fluid used to raise the octane rating of gasoline. Many compounds of this type are known, including triethylaluminum, $(C_2H_5)_3Al$, important as a catalyst in the manufacture of polymers from olefins; and a series of boron compounds such as diethylborane, $(C_2H_5)_2BH$, used as rocket fuels. Silicon compounds are numerous, an important one being dimethyldichlorosilane, $(CH_3)_2Cl_2Si$, which can be hydrolyzed and condensed to a rubber polymer of the silicone type. Most important of the organometallic compounds to the research chemist are the Grignard reagents, in which magnesium is linked to carbon. Preparation of the reagent is generally written shorthand:

$$R—X \quad + \quad Mg \quad → \quad R—Mg—X \text{ (a Grignard reagent)}$$

where R can be practically any organic radical, *e.g.* methyl, acetyl, or phenyl, and X is a HALOGEN radical, preferably bromide or iodide. The reagent is prepared in solution (usually ether) and is not isolated. By mixing the proper Grignard reagent with a properly selected reactant, almost all types of structures in organic chemistry can be made. For this development, Victor Grignard received the Nobel prize, 1912. Some organomercuric (carbon-mercury) compounds, *e.g.* mercurochrome and merthiolate, are important in medicine.—*Ru. M.*

ORIGIN OF SPECIES: see ON THE ORIGIN OF SPECIES.

Great nebula in Orion is here seen in a long-exposure photo taken with 100-in. reflector at Mt Wilson. The glowing, wreathlike cloud of gas spans a distance of 26 lt-yr. *(Mt Wilson)*

ORION NEBULA (M42): a gaseous emission nebula located in the "sword" of Orion, visible in low-power field glasses as a hazy patch in a row of faint stars. Its radiation is excited by ultraviolet rays emitted by a group of very hot stars, the Trapezium cluster, embedded in the nebula. The distance from the Sun is approximately 1,600 lt-yr. This nebula marks the densest part of a very large region of interstellar gas in which many young stars (ages less than 1% of Earth's) are found and in which star formation is apparently still taking place on a large scale. The Orion nebula emits radiation in the radio as well as the optical range of wavelengths.—*B. J. B.*

ORLON: see TEXTILE.

OROGENY: MOUNTAIN BUILDING by folding, faulting, and thrusting. It is a form of DIASTROPHISM. Orogenic forces affect at any one time only relatively narrow belts of Earth's crust, *e.g.* in the creation of the Appalachian structure at the end of the Paleozoic Era and the Rocky Mts at the end of the Mesozoic. The term orogeny should be compared with epeirogeny, which refers to diastrophic movements of continental extent which produce plateau uplifts and the broad depressions in the continental masses which may at times be covered by the sea.—*J. Sh.*

OROGRAPHIC PRECIPITATION: precipitation (*e.g.* rain or snow) that falls on the windward side of orographic barriers, as hills or mountain ranges. Air forced uphill by wind flow cools adiabatically, clouds form, and, with sufficient additional lift, precipitation results. Nearly all the moisture may thus be removed from the air on the windward side of the orographic barrier, and the lee side may get very little precipitation. Such a dry region is called a *rain shadow*. The coastal ranges of the western U. S. A., for example, are green on the west, or windward side, but on the east merge into the desert and near-desert areas of the Great Basin.—*P. L.*

ORRERY: a mechanical device for demonstrating motions in the solar system. It was invented probably by George Graham (1675–1751), under the patronage of Charles Boyle, 4th Earl of Orrery. Such a mechanical model was formerly called a planetarium, a term now applied to a complex optical projector; other names for the orrery are *tellurium* and *lunarium*. —*W. P. C.*

Mechanical orrery: This drawing, from James Ferguson's *Astronomy* (1773), shows an orrery made by him. When handle at lower left was turned, the motions of Sun, Mercury, Venus, Earth, and Moon were demonstrated. *(Gossner Collection)*

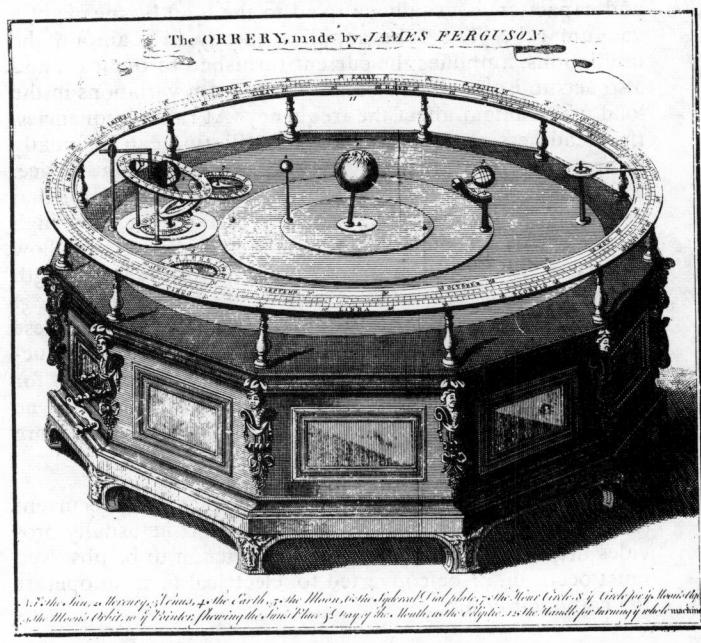

The ORRERY, made by JAMES FERGUSON.

ORTHOHYDROGEN AND PARAHYDROGEN: the two forms of ordinary HYDROGEN, which normally is a mixture of about 75% orthohydrogen and 25% parahydrogen. In the orthohydrogen molecule the two atomic nuclei (actually protons) spin in the same direction; in the parahydrogen molecule the spins are opposite. The two forms differ slightly in physical properties.—*B. Be.*

OSBORN, HENRY FAIRFIELD, 1857–1935, U. S. paleontologist; b. Fairfield, Conn. His 60 yr of research included work in the history of science, comparative anatomy, comparative embryology, evolutionary theory, and paleontology, particularly Mesozoic and Cenozoic vertebrate paleontology. Among his publications are his great monographs on the titanotheres and the Proboscidea. Professor at Columbia Univ. from 1890, he was president of the American Museum of Natural History from 1891. He was a fellow of the Royal Society and a member of the National Academy of Sciences.—*D. H. D. R.*

OSCILLATION: a type of motion in which a body or an electric current repeatedly goes through the same pattern of backward-and-forward motion in equal, successive periods of time, *e.g.* the swinging of a PENDULUM, the VIBRATION of a mass suspended from a spring, or the flow of current between an inductance and a capacitance (see OSCILLATOR, ELECTRIC). Oscillation requires the action of a driving force to move the body or current in one direction, and the action of a restoring force (proportional to the displacement from the rest position) to move it back again. Thus the push that starts the pendulum swinging upward is the driving force, and gravity is the restoring force that pulls it down. However, the momentum of the motion carries the pendulum up again on the other side. The motion would be repeated indefinitely, except for DAMPING.—*I. R.*

OSCILLATOR, ELECTRIC: a device in which the amplitude of current and voltage varies regularly with time. At low frequencies, the oscillator consists of an INDUCTANCE (coil) and a CAPACITOR connected together. The movement of electric charge from the coil to the capacitor and back again produces the OSCILLATION. This usually varies sinusoidally with time at a frequency f. This frequency in cycles/sec is given by $f = 1/(2\pi\sqrt{LC})$, where L is the inductance in henries and C is the capacitance in farads. The resonant circuit (coil and capacitor) is usually coupled to the load by means of a vacuum tube. The tube supplies energy to maintain the oscillations, amplifies the current furnished to the load, and also acts to isolate the resonant circuit from variations in the load which might affect the frequency. At radio frequencies, the steadiness of the frequency of oscillation can be greatly improved by using a quartz crystal as the resonant device. The crystal is a very stable electromechanical oscillator that generates an electric voltage at its surface. At very high (microwave) frequencies, the resonant circuit used is a hollow metal cavity with dimensions of the order of the wavelength needed. Special types of ELECTRON TUBES are employed, *e.g.* klystrons, magnetrons, and backward-wave oscillators. These tubes usually have the resonant cavity built into their structure. Oscillators are used to provide the proper frequency for the operation of radio transmitters and of superheterodyne receivers; they are also used in test equipment to measure frequencies.—*I. R.*

OSCILLOSCOPE: a device for the visual displaying of recurrent (oscillating) phenomena. A CATHODE-RAY TUBE usually provides the viewing "screen." The phenomenon to be observed must occur in, or be converted to, electrical form to operate the cathode-ray tube.

The most common use of an oscilloscope is to display wave forms. To accomplish this, a time axis or "sweep" must be provided: a voltage that changes at a constant rate from one value to a second value, then returns very quickly to the first value to repeat the cycle. This voltage, applied to the horizontal-deflecting circuits of the tube, causes the tip of the electron beam to draw a straight horizontal line across the screen, usually from the viewer's left to his right. The voltage whose wave form is to be observed is then applied to the vertical-deflecting circuits. When the frequency of the observed pattern is an even multiple of the sweep frequency, a stationary pattern results.

The oscilloscope is used also to display phase and frequency relationships between two voltages. One voltage is applied to each deflecting system. Stationary patterns result when the two frequencies are related by a simple fraction. When both voltages are sine waves, the patterns are called Lissajous figures. When two sine waves are at the same frequency, a straight slanting line shows them to be in phase. The line opens up into an ellipse when the voltages are not in phase. A circle indicates voltages of equal amplitudes 90° apart in phase.—*R. M. P.*

OSMIUM: a metallic element (Os) of the platinum family; at. no. 76; at. wt 190.2; sp gr 22.48 (20°C); mp 2700°C; bp greater than 5300°C. Osmium is the heaviest (densest) of all Earth's forms of matter. The English chemist Smithson Tennant discovered the metal in 1803 in the insoluble black residue (a mixture of osmium and iridium) left after crude platinum was dissolved by aqua regia. (Aqua regia will not dissolve osmium or iridium.) Tennant separated the osmium from the iridium by successive treatments of the residue with acid and alkali, and announced his discovery of the two new elements in 1804. The name osmium (Gr. *osmē,* "smell") was chosen because of the malodorousness of osmium tetroxide (OsO_4). The vapor of this compound is intensely penetrating, extremely poisonous, and produces temporary blindness and other adverse physiological effects. Very small amounts of osmium are found associated with platinum deposits, often in a natural alloy (*osmiridium*) with iridium. The man-made alloy of these two elements, also called osmiridium, is used in fountain-pen points and phonograph needles; osmium is alloyed with platinum to increase the hardness of the latter, although iridium is more commonly used for this purpose because of the danger that osmium might volatilize into the poisonous tetroxide. Osmium is sometimes used to stain microscope slides, because it forms the black hydrous oxide OsO_2 on contact with certain cells and tissues. It has been used as an oxidizing agent in the synthesis of steroids and formerly was used for incandescent-lamp filaments. See IRIDIUM; PLATINUM.—*E. H. H.*

OSMOSIS: diffusion of a liquid through a semipermeable membrane; the process plays an important role in plant and animal life. When a substance is dissolved in water, the dissolved substance (solute) tends to distribute itself uniformly through the solution. If a partition (membrane) that allows passage of the solvent but not the solute particles is placed between this solution and a more dilute solution of the same solute, the pure solvent will pass through the membrane. Such a membrane is called *semipermeable*. Parchment paper, animal membranes, or cellophane may be used, though they are not desirable for accurate measurement because they lack sufficient strength to withstand the pressures developed; moreover, they allow the solute to leak through. A most successful membrane for careful experimental work consists of a gelatinous deposit of copper ferrocyanide held in the walls of a porous cup. Wilhelm Pfeffer first made measurements with this kind of membrane in 1877. Osmotic flow occurs from the more dilute solution toward the more concentrated solution and continues, theoretically, until the concentrations are the same on both sides of the membrane. The least external pressure required to prevent the flow of solvent through a membrane is the OSMOTIC PRESSURE. Osmotic pressures as high as 273 atmospheres have been obtained by the use of the porous-cup arrangement. The air in a closed space may serve as a semipermeable membrane between the pure solvent and a solution. If one beaker half filled with pure water and another half filled with a solution are placed under a bell jar and left for some time, the water in the form of vapor passes through the air into the solution. This is the result of differences in vapor pressures, proportional to the osmotic pressures.

A variety of mechanisms seem to operate in different cases of osmotic flow. Water will pass through a crystalline hydrate, e.g. calcium sulfate ($CaSO_4 \cdot 2H_2O$), probably because the hydrate loses water to the more concentrated solution, and the loss is replaced by water molecules from the pure solvent. Again the osmotic flow occurs more rapidly through a membrane in which the solvent is more soluble. Adsorption of solvent is a factor in some cases.

Two solutions separated by a semipermeable membrane are said to be *isotonic* when there is no net flow in either direction, as is seen when cells are immersed in a normal saline solution. The cells neither shrink (plasmolize) nor swell. It is important that solutions added to the blood or placed in contact with delicate body cells be isotonic with the cells. A solution having a higher osmotic pressure than a cell is said to be *hypertonic* with respect to the cell. Osmotic flow occurs from the cell to a hypertonic solution, and the cell wilts or shrinks. Thus plants wilt when their roots are surrounded with salt solution or too much fertilizer. A solution having a lower osmotic pressure than a cell is said to be *hypotonic* with respect to the cell, and the osmotic flow is from the solution into the cell, causing it to swell and possibly to rupture the cell membranes (plasmoptysis). Osmosis partially accounts for the absorption of soil water by the root hairs and for the elevation of liquids to the leaves of plants. It also is responsible for the absorption of water by the cells of the animal body. The passing of nutrients through cell walls, however, involves DIALYSIS and perhaps other processes. Certain drugs seem to be able to change the permeability of cell walls.—*A. P. E.*

OSMOTIC PRESSURE: the excess pressure that must be applied to a solution separated from a pure solvent by a semipermeable MEMBRANE to balance the inflow of solvent. In blood plasma, the protein albumin exerts this pressure and thus regulates the osmotic pressure of blood in relation to the surrounding body fluids (see also OSMOSIS).—*F. F.*

OSSIFICATION: formation of BONE tissue in place of cartilaginous or membranous precursors. The process spreads from one or more *ossification centers*. The long tubular bones of arms and legs develop from separate centers in the shaft (diaphysis) and in the widened articulating ends (epiphyses). When the cartilaginous epiphyseal plate, between the diaphysis and epiphysis of such a bone, becomes ossified, the bone ceases to grow. Its ossification is now said to be complete. The bones of the human face and the short bones of the hands and feet never become entirely ossified and may resume their growth under special conditions. Ossification of the human skeleton ceases, on the average, at the age of 18 in females and at 22 in males.—*A. P. E.*

OSTWALD, WILHELM, 1853–1932, German physical chemist; b. Riga, Latvia. He did research on the dynamics of chemical change. For his work on catalysis and on the conditions of chemical equilibrium and velocities of chemical reactions, he received the Nobel prize, 1909. From 1887 to 1906 he made the Univ. of Leipzig a center of research in physical chemistry. Author of many technical papers and books, he was cofounder of one scientific journal, *Zeitschrift für physikalische Chemie* (1887), and the founder of the *Annalen der Naturphilosophie* (1901). In 1887 he created the *Klassiker der exacten Wissenschaften,* a series of reprints and translations of classic scientific writings. He was an associate of the U. S. National Academy of Sciences.—*D. H. D. R.*

OUTWASH PLAIN: the surface of a broad body of sand and gravel deposited by streams of meltwater flowing away from a GLACIER.—*R. F.*

OVARY: an egg-producing organ in a female animal or a flowering plant. Commonly (*e.g.* in segmented worms and vertebrates) eggs are released from the ovary by the process of OVULATION into the body cavity, from which they are conducted toward the outside world through tubular OVIDUCTS. Less commonly the ovaries are borne on the outer surface of the animal (*e.g.* in the hydroid *Hydra* and the jellyfish *Craspedacusta,* both of fresh water), and the eggs are discharged into the surrounding medium, either before or after FERTILIZATION. The ovaries of vertebrate animals, which are paired structures supported in the body cavity by a special double fold of peritoneum (the *mesovarium*), produce both eggs and the hormone estrogen; the latter is an important part of the chemical control system regulating the reproductive cycle. In mammals, the eggs burst from a special *Graafian follicle* containing endocrine tissue, which promptly grows to

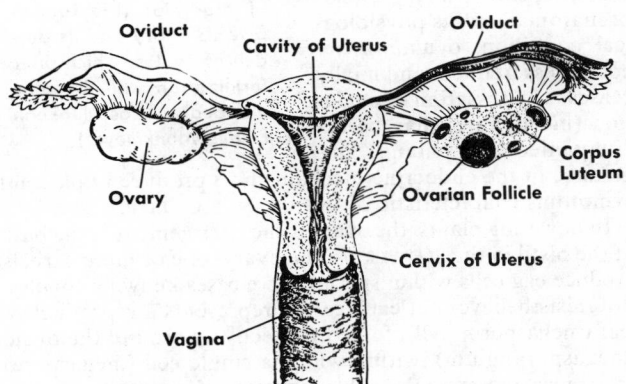

Ovaries of mature human female are potato-shaped, almond-sized glands. (In above diagram, they are pulled outward from the normal sites.) Sectioned ovary (*right*) is seen to contain several maturing follicles, the labeled one larger than the others. Monthly bursting of most mature follicle ("ovulation") releases egg into oviduct. (*After Young*)

become a yellow body (the *corpus luteum*) that produces another hormone (progesterone). Both estrogen and progesterone stimulate the proliferation of cells lining the uterus, readying that organ for implantation of a developing embryo if the egg is fertilized; both hormones also inhibit the anterior lobe of the PITUITARY GLAND from releasing its follicle-stimulating hormone (FSH), without which further follicles will not develop in the ovary. If the egg is fertilized, the corpus luteum continues to grow slowly, secreting its hormone, preventing ovulation during pregnancy, and assisting in the implantation of the embryo and the development of the placental connection between the embryo and the mother; later, the placenta itself appears to secrete one or more hormones with the same effect, and the corpus luteum degenerates. If the egg is not fertilized within a few days following ovulation, the corpus luteum degenerates, ending its inhibition of the anterior pituitary, which thereupon begins again releasing FSH and inducing a new round of ovulation. At the same time, the cells lining the uterus react to the reduced concentration of estrogen and progesterone in the blood by degenerating; in women, as well as in other primates, this degeneration is followed by minor hemorrhage from small blood vessels in the uterine wall and bleeding from the vaginal opening (MENSTRUATION). The hormone FSH and the luteinizing hormone (LH) from the anterior pituitary interact with estrogen and progesterone from the ovary of mammals, inducing cyclic changes in both structure and behavior that provide the timing mechanism for an estrus cycle or a menstrual cycle. However, after months or years, depending on the species of mammal and its physiological condition, ovulation becomes less frequent and finally ceases. The cessation of ovulation (menopause) may be accompanied by enough imbalance in the endocrine mechanism to produce unpleasant symptoms characteristic of this CHANGE OF LIFE.

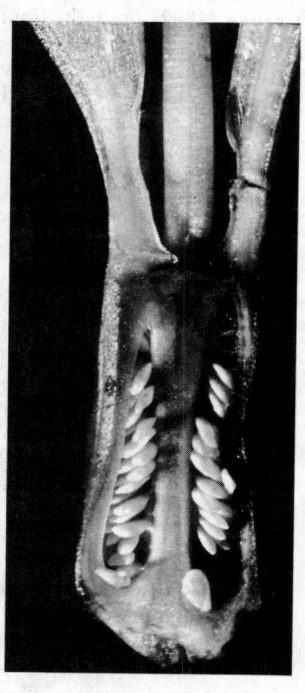

Cutaway view of ovary of gladiolus (Iris family) reveals ovary and its burden of ovules, which after fertilization will become monocot seeds. (*Joseph Foldes/Monkmeyer*)

In flowering plants, the ovary is the enlargement at the base of the pistil in the FLOWER. In the ovary, one or more carpels produce egg cells within special spore cases known as ovules. Botanists believe that each carpel represents a reproductive leaf (megasporophyll), folded protectively around the ovule (megasporangium), within which a single cell (megaspore) undergoes the special double division of MEIOSIS and produces four spores (megaspores). Only one of these spores develops, but it becomes a female gametophyte with a single egg nucleus ready for FERTILIZATION by a sperm nucleus from a pollen grain. (See ALTERNATION OF GENERATIONS.)

The ovary of both animals and plants is the site of meiotic division—in the former during gametogenesis, in the latter during sporogenesis. See GAMETE; MEIOSIS; REPRODUCTION.—L. and M. M.

OVIDUCT: a tube through which eggs pass from the OVARY of a female animal toward the outside world. Commonly the oviduct either is lined by a ciliated epithelium that propels the egg or has muscular walls that move the egg by waves of contraction. Often the lining cells are glandular and contribute a gelatinous covering to the egg (e.g. in frogs); or the glands may provide an egg shell of chitinous or limy material,

giving mechanical strength to the covering and hence protecting the egg from later damage. In animals in which internal FERTILIZATION occurs (e.g. birds and mammals), the oviduct is usually the site where sperm meets egg. In many instances, fertilized eggs or developing embryos are retained in an enlarged portion of the oviduct, called the uterus. In mankind and most other mammals, the nonenlarged portion of the oviduct on each side of the body is named the Fallopian tube; a funnel-shaped enlargement (ostium) of its open end may partly surround the ovary, increasing the efficiency with which the tube captures eggs at OVULATION. At its outer end, the oviduct (or uterus) may open to the outside of the body or into a cloaca; or the two oviducts may be joined together in varying degrees and may provide a receiving chamber (vagina) for the sperm from the penis of the male during copulation. See REPRODUCTION.—L. and M. M.

OVOMUCOID: in biochemistry, one of the conjugated egg-white PROTEINS. It contains 25% polysaccharide, which consists of equal portions of mannose and N-acetyl glucoseamine. This polysaccharide protects the protein portion from coagulation by the action of heat or acids. Ovomucoid from hen eggs is an inhibitor of the proteolytic enzyme trypsin. The ovomucoid from some other species inhibits chymotrypsin. The function of ovomucoid in the egg is unknown.—J. F. S.

OVULATION: the release of an egg (mature ovum) from the OVARY of an animal. In mammals, ovulation is controlled in part by pituitary hormones (FSH and LH) acting on the ovarian follicle in which the egg matures. In most animals, the process takes place at a definite time in the reproductive cycle and may be the only period during which a female will sexually accept a male. In a few species, e.g. the domestic rabbit, ovulation follows no cycle, but is induced by nervous and endocrine changes initiated by copulation. Ovulation in a female rabbit can be induced by injecting the rabbit with urine containing excreted sex hormones from a woman who is pregnant. This is the basis for the widely used Friedman test for pregnancy. In women, ovulation normally occurs about the 14th day after MENSTRUATION begins.—A. R. D.

OWEN, SIR RICHARD, 1804–92, English anatomist; b. Lancaster. The foremost anatomist of his day, he wrote many books and scientific articles. For his anatomical researches he was awarded the Copley medal of the Royal Society, of which he was a fellow. He was also an associate of the U. S. National Academy of Sciences.—D. H. D. R.

OXALIC ACID: a white, poisonous, crystalline solid, $(COOH)_2$, found in nature in many plants and molds. A good chelating agent for metals, it is used as a mordant in dyeing, as an anticoagulant in blood chemistry, and in rust removal in automobile radiators. It was the first synthetic organic compound made; its synthesis by F. Wöhler (1824) refuted the belief that organic compounds could be produced only by living systems. See also CHELATES.—J. F. S.

OXBOW: a lake formed by the cutting off of a river meander; so named because its U-shaped outline resembles that of a yoke. Erosion of the banks of a meander tends to be greatest at the outside of each curve, because the flow is likely to be faster there than on the inside. Hence the open end of a loop may become narrower and narrower. Eventually, especially at flood time, the flow may be strong enough to cut completely through the remaining barrier, establishing a new channel. Deposits of sediments along the channel sides may cut off the old loop completely, forming the oxbow. Many

Oxbow lakes flank the meanders of a stream in the "old age" period of development. Each oxbow is the loop of an old meander which the river skipped, probably during flood time, and did not return to again. (*U. S. Geological Survey*)

oxbows, lacking flow, soon fill with vegetation and dry up. Oxbows are characteristic of rivers in the "old age" stage of development.—*J. W.*

OXIDATION AND REDUCTION: chemical reactions in which electrons are permanently transferred from one of the reactants (the reducing agent) to the other reactant (the oxidizing agent). The loss of electrons is termed an *oxidation* and the gain of electrons a *reduction;* thus the reducing agent is oxidized and the oxidizing agent is correspondingly reduced. The term "oxidation" was originally applied to the addition reaction of a substance with elemental oxygen, *e.g.* the rusting of iron or the burning of hydrogen. Later it was recognized that the oxygen for reactions of this type could be furnished by certain oxygen-rich chemicals such as nitric, perchloric, or chromic acids, and that in furnishing oxygen the valence of the central atom in these oxidizing agents was lowered. The term "reduction" comes from metallurgy where it has long been used to denote the conversion of an (oxide) ore to a metal, with charcoal as the reducing agent. The electron-transfer concept of oxidation-reduction developed with the electronic theory of molecular structure. In cases where reactants and products are ionized or ionizable or where there is a formal change of valence, it is relatively easy to follow the electron transfer. Thus, any reaction where a metal is transformed to the corresponding positive metal ion is an oxidation of the metal. An increase in positive valence, such as the conversion of MnO_2 to $KMnO_4$, is also an oxidation. Among elements the base metals are strong reducing agents and the halogens strong oxidizing agents. In ionizable systems it is frequently possible to arrange the reaction in the form of an electromotive cell, oxidation taking place at one electrode, or half cell, and reduction at the other. The voltage developed by the cell is a measure of the free-energy change of the over-all reaction. It is valuable for many purposes to consider the voltage or potential of the single-electrode reactions rather than of the total cell. This can be done by referring to a suitable standard electrode, and the $H_2 — H^+$ half cell has been universally adopted as such, with its potential taken as zero. The voltage of any half cell coupled with the $H_2 — H^+$ half cell is called its *oxidation potential.* Oxidation potentials of metal-metal ion half cells are positive if the metal is above hydrogen in the electromotive series, negative if the metal is below hydrogen.

In nonionized compounds, *e.g.* organic compounds, the transfer of electrons is not always easy to follow. Organic groups containing one carbon center, however, can exist in four states of oxidation ranging from CH_4 or its equivalent to $C(OH)_4$ (orthocarbonic acid or fully hydrated carbon dioxide) or its equivalent. Atoms or radicals that can be replaced by OH in a simple hydrolysis reaction are equivalent to OH in determining the state of oxidation.—*A. M. S.*

OXIDATIVE DECARBOXYLATION: in biochemistry, the name given to a process whereby certain α-keto acids are oxidized and at the same time lose carbon dioxide; for example,

$$CH_3 \cdot CO \cdot COOH$$
(pyruvic acid)
$$+$$
$$HS \cdot Co\,A$$
(coenzyme A)
$$+ \, DPN \rightarrow CH_3 \cdot CO \sim S \cdot Co\,A$$
(acetyl coenzyme A)
$$+ \, DPNH_2 + CO_2$$

This reaction appears to be irreversible; hence, in the animal body, fatty acids cannot be converted into carbohydrate. In the CITRIC-ACID CYCLE a similar process takes place with α-ketoglutaric acid. See FAT METABOLISM; GLYOXYLIC ACID; PYRIDINE NUCLEOTIDES.—*K. H.*

OXIDATIVE PHOSPHORYLATION: a vital process by which the living cell utilizes the chemical energy released during combustion of food (see ENERGY IN BIOCHEMISTRY). This chemical energy is stored in the phosphate-bond linkages of adenosine-triphosphate (ATP) and is utilized in the energy-consuming activities of the cell (*e.g.* synthesis of cell materials; muscle contraction). In this respect living matter shares with some man-made machines the requirement of converting energy from one form into another before work can be accomplished. ATP provides energy for muscle contraction, for example, by reacting with appropriate receptor sites in the muscle fiber, and in the process loses its terminal phosphate group and becomes adenosinediphosphate (ADP). To re-form the ATP, it is necessary to supply a phosphate group plus the energy required to couple the phosphate to ADP. Oxidative phosphorylation is responsible for over 90% of all of the ATP synthesized by mammalian cells. The cellular machinery for this energy-transforming process is located in the MITOCHONDRIA. In the first stage of biological oxidation food is broken down by enzyme action into simpler components such as amino acids, fatty acids, and sugar molecules, a process which in higher animals occurs in the digestive tract. Only a relatively small amount of the total stored chemical energy, less than 1%, is released during this initial phase. When the foodstuff is a carbohydrate, the end product is a sugar molecule, *e.g.* glucose, which is absorbed into the blood stream from the intestine and is carried to the cells where the second stage of the energy transformation process begins. The glucose molecule undergoes partial degradation by GLYCOLYSIS into pyruvic acid as a result of the sequential action of a dozen specific enzymes. During this process only 2 of the 38 molecules of ATP which are ultimately formed during the complete oxidation of a molecule of glucose are obtained.

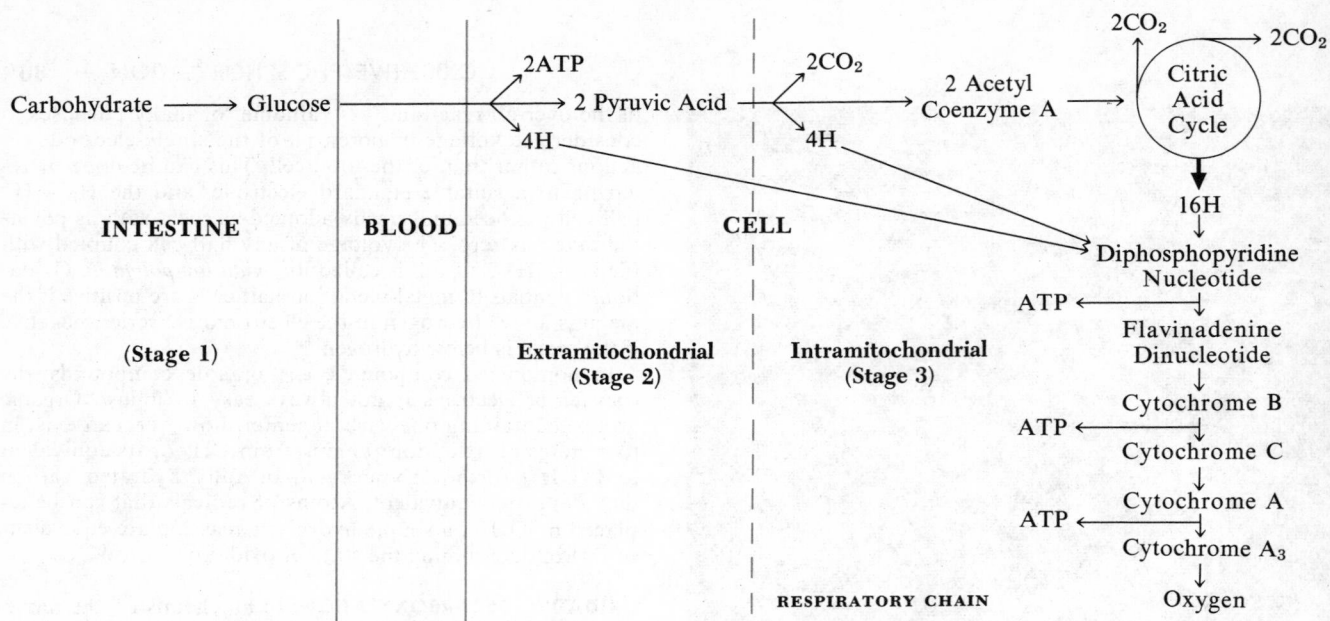

Oxidative phosphorylation converts the chemical energy released during combustion of food into ATP molecules; these, in turn, supply energy for such activities as muscle contraction and synthesis of cell materials. For example, in mammals (as shown above), 36 of the 38 molecules of ATP derived from complete oxidation of one molecule of glucose are formed within the mitochondria of the cells (Stage 3, far right). The glucose molecules can come into the cell from the blood (as shown above) or can be synthesized within the cell.

The biologically significant feature of the third stage is the synthesis, in the mitochondria, of the other 36 molecules of ATP via oxidative phosphorylation. Each of the two molecules of pyruvic acid enters the mitochondria and is converted by a set of specific enzymes acting sequentially (CITRIC-ACID CYCLE) to carbon dioxide and hydrogen atoms. The latter are picked up by carrier molecules and transported stepwise via another major multi-enzyme sequence (respiratory chain) and are finally combined with oxygen to form water.

Over 60% of the energy released during the transfer of a pair of hydrogen atoms to oxygen is conserved by coupling 3 molecules of phosphate to 3 molecules of ADP to form 3 molecules of ATP. Since the oxidation of one molecule of glucose produces 12 pairs of hydrogen atoms (see diagram) the total yield is three times 12, or 36 molecules of ATP. The intimate mechanism by which the passage of hydrogen atoms through the respiratory chain is coupled to the synthesis of ATP is not fully understood. Recent work, however, has established the probable locations in the respiratory chain which are coupled to energy transfer, i.e. to synthesis of ATP (see diagram).

The enzyme systems concerned in oxidative phosphorylation would seem to represent a strategic location for the operation of regulatory mechanisms within the cell (e.g. hormonal control), since most vital cellular functions, including growth, must ultimately depend on a supply of ATP.—M. E. P.

OXIDE: a compound of oxygen with a chemical element. Most elements except the inert gases form one or more oxides; these oxides vary greatly in stability, from those of the alkali and alkaline-earth metals, which are extraordinarily stable, to the oxides of chlorine and fluorine, which decompose explosively on heating. Oxides vary also in physical properties from hard-to-condense gases such as carbon monoxide (bp −190°C) to refractory solids such as zirconium oxide (mp 2900°C). In general, the oxides of the strongly metallic elements react with water to form bases, and the oxides of the non-metallic elements (e.g. sulfur, nitrogen, and phosphorus) react with water to form acids. An element having several valence states usually can form oxides corresponding to each

of its valences. These oxides sometimes differ widely in their acid-forming or base-forming properties. The oxide of trivalent chromium, for example, is weakly basic but the oxide of hexavalent chromium is strongly acidic. A major percentage of the solid portion of Earth's crust is made up of oxides, usually in neutral combinations of an acidic and a basic oxide. Combinations with silicon dioxide (SiO_2), aluminum oxide (Al_2O_3), and ferric oxide (Fe_2O_3) are particularly common. A very large proportion of the economically valuable ores and minerals are oxides. Carbon dioxide is the atmospheric raw material which plants use to photosynthesize carbohydrates, and is thus one of the indispensable foundations of life. WATER, the oxide of hydrogen, is the reference substance of chemical neutrality, and is possibly the most ubiquitous and most important single chemical compound in man's environment.—A. M. S.

OXYGEN: the most abundant element (O) in Earth's crust; at. no. 8; at. wt 16.00; bp − 183°C; mp − 218.4°C. In the uncombined state, as the diatomic molecule O_2, oxygen constitutes approximately 20% of the atmosphere. Combined with hydrogen in water, and with silicon, aluminum, iron, and other elements in rocks, it is estimated to constitute about 50% of Earth's crust. Oxygen was first isolated by Joseph Priestley (1774) and independently by Karl Scheele at about the same time. Priestley noted that it supported combustion much more vigorously than air; but Lavoisier (1783) was the first to demonstrate the true nature of combustion as an oxidation reaction, and to give oxygen its modern name. Elemental oxygen can be conveniently prepared by the electrolysis of water, or by the thermal decomposition of certain metallic oxides, e.g. mercuric oxide, this latter method having been used by Priestley and Lavoisier. Oxygen is currently prepared on a commercial scale by liquefying and fractionally distilling air. The triatomic form of elemental oxygen, OZONE (O_3), a highly reactive gas which can be prepared by subjecting ordinary oxygen to an electrical discharge, occurs in the upper atmosphere. Ozone is remarkably opaque to ultraviolet rays and thus filters destructive excesses of ultraviolet radiation from sunlight. Oxygen plays an inestimable role in the life process as well as in a vast number of other naturally occurring or artificially induced chemical processes. The oxidation of carbon and hydrogen compounds within the cells furnishes the energy that sustains all higher animal life. Oxidation processes are also important in plant life, although green plants can utilize the energy of sunlight for certain of their biochemical activities.

Oxygen forms compounds with all elements except the inert gases, and its ATOMIC WEIGHT was long the standard from which other atomic weights are calculated. OXIDES of the metals are basic, and oxides of the nonmetals acidic, the degree of basicity or acidity depending on the position of the combining element in the ELECTROMOTIVE SERIES. Rapid oxidation by means of gaseous oxygen with liberation of heat and light is called combustion. The combustion of carbon and hydrogen compounds in the form of plant tissue (wood), coal, petroleum, or fuel gases continues to furnish the major portion of mankind's heat and energy requirements. Air is used for ordinary combustion; where more intense and rapid combustion is needed or is advantageous, *e.g.* in rocket engines, cutting and welding torches, and high-capacity smelters, purified oxygen is used.—*A. M. S.*

OXYGEN TRANSPORT: in biochemistry, a process by which molecular oxygen (O_2) is transferred from the cellular environment to cytochrome oxidase molecules in mitochondria, the tiny cellular furnaces in which occurs the first step of biological oxidation: the activation of O_2 by cytochrome oxidase. In mammals, mechanisms connected with O_2 transport make possible the transport of 50 times more O_2 than can be carried by an equal volume of sea water. In single-celled organisms, the transport of O_2 is by physical diffusion from the liquid environment, where it is higher in concentration, into the cell and thence into the mitochondrion, where it is lower in concentration. In multilayered organisms, diffusion of O_2 from the environment is inadequate. During evolution, a number of means were developed to transport O_2 into the center of a cell mass. These included the formation of a circulatory system; the use of molecules, *e.g.* hemoglobin, that could form weak bonds with O_2; and the packaging of hemoglobin molecules into special cells, the red blood cells, or erythrocytes. This permitted the concentration of hemoglobin to be increased in the blood stream without increasing the viscosity or osmotic pressure. In mammals, even the nucleus is eliminated in the red blood cell to increase its efficiency per unit volume for O_2 transport. The cell is densely packed with hemoglobin molecules, which make up 95% of its protein content. The cell is doughnut-shaped, permitting more rapid diffusion of gases into and out of the cell. In some invertebrates a less efficient green, copper-containing protein serves for O_2 transport.

The hemoglobin molecule has a number of other features built into its structure which make the loading and unloading of O_2 more efficient and aid in the transport of carbon dioxide (CO_2). Each hemoglobin molecule (molecular wt 68,000) is made up of 4 subunits. A subunit consists of a colorless protein portion (globin) and a flat red iron protoporphyrin molecule (heme). The iron forms a weak bond with the O_2 molecule and is thus directly responsible for the O_2-transporting property. This bond forms about 1,000 times as fast as it breaks. The oxygenated molecule, called oxyhemoglobin, is red in color; non-oxygenated hemoglobin is purple. The structure of globin is such that it does not crystallize out of solution. About 35% of the wet weight of the red blood cell is globin. The interaction of the four subunits of oxyhemoglobin is such that the first O_2 molecule is removed with difficulty; once it is removed, the other three come off much more easily. This interaction makes possible the release of O_2

in considerable amounts when the blood gets to the tissues. Another property of the globin causes oxyhemoglobin to be somewhat more acid than hemoglobin. This "Bohr effect" permits about 60% of the CO_2 coming from the tissues to be transported in the red cells without alteration of the pH of the blood; it also aids in the elimination of CO_2 from the red cells when hemoglobin becomes oxygenated in the lungs. Smaller amounts of CO_2 are transported in weak association with amino groups of the globin.

Not only does the mass movement of O_2 occur by diffusion from regions of higher to lower concentration, but O_2 also moves from proteins where it is weakly bonded toward proteins where it is more strongly bonded. The relative strengths of the bonds to O_2 are adult hemoglobin $<$ fetal hemoglobin $<$ muscle hemoglobin (myoglobin) $<$ cytochrome oxidase. In the fetus there is a special hemoglobin in the red cells, which because of its higher affinity for O_2 can capture O_2 from adult hemoglobin. Thus, for the same concentration of O_2, the adult hemoglobin of mother's blood will lose its O_2 to fetal hemoglobin. This feature aids in the transport of O_2 through the placenta to the fetus. Many active muscles, *e.g.* the heart and the "dark meat" of fowls, are red because they contain within their cells a special protein, myoglobin, which is considered to act as a momentary storage place for O_2.

In man the pathway for O_2 starts in the lung, where breathing movements bring air molecules into contact with the lung surfaces. The O_2 molecules dissolve in the aqueous film coating the lung cell, diffuse through a 4-μ-thick cell layer into the blood capillary and thence into the red cell. In the cell the O_2 attaches to the iron of the heme of hemoglobin to form oxyhemoglobin. Because oxyhemoglobin is slightly more acid than hemoglobin, bicarbonate in the red cell is converted to carbonic acid which, as CO_2, is eliminated in the lung. The oxyhemoglobin is transported from the lungs through the circulatory system to all body cells, *e.g.* a heart muscle cell. Here because of the lowered oxygen content, the O_2 diffuses from the red cells, through the capillary wall, into the muscle cell, where it combines loosely with myoglobin. Thence the O_2 diffuses into the mitochondrion to attach to a specific enzyme, cytochrome oxidase, which activates the O_2 molecule to accept electrons and form water. Simultaneously with the release of O_2 the red cells take up CO_2 from the tissue cells. They are then carried back to the lungs to become oxygenated again.—*S. G.*

OZONE: the triatomic form of oxygen, O_3, a blue gas with the characteristic odor of "clean air" often perceived after a thunderstorm or around electric trains. Formed by an electrical discharge through oxygen or by irradiation of oxygen with ultraviolet light, it is highly irritating and toxic even at low concentrations. It is made commercially by passing oxygen over aluminum plates which are charged to a potential of 10,000 volts. Ozone is more reactive than oxygen, being second only to FLUORINE in oxidizing power. It converts mercury and silver into oxides, frees iodine from potassium iodide, and is a good bleaching agent, capable of discharging the color of many organic substances. It is also a powerful germicide, used to sterilize drinking water.—*G. W. M.*

OZONOSPHERE: the layer in the atmosphere, between roughly 20 and 30 mi up, in which the air contains a higher proportion of OZONE, formed from atmospheric oxygen through action of the Sun's ultraviolet radiation, than is found at lower levels. This concentration of ozone, although small, absorbs the harmful extreme ultraviolet radiation from the Sun (of wavelength below 0.3 microns), and in doing so raises the temperature of the attenuated air to a maximum of about 50°F (10°C).—*D. H. L.*

P

PAINT: a mixture of materials designed to form a protective or decorative film over the surface to which it is applied. Paints consist of pigments suspended in a vehicle. The bulk of the vehicle is the binder, which promotes "drying" and hardening of the paint; but a solvent or thinner, drier, antioxidizer, or plasticizer may also be included in the vehicle. PIGMENTS are the coloring or concealing (hiding) components and protect the vehicle from the deteriorating effects of sunlight. Most paints, with the exception of the very dark colors (blacks, browns, reds), have a white pigment base, important white pigments being titanium dioxide, zinc oxide, and white lead. Extender pigments are added to paints containing pigments that are too light or too heavy; they also decrease cost. Common extenders are gypsum, clay, barium sulfate, whiting, talc, and silica.

Paints are differentiated by the type of binder they contain as well as by their color. Both natural and synthetic RESINS of many types are used; and binders of synthetic rubber (latex paints) have also come into use for both interior and exterior decorating. Casein and glue are also used as binders; the binders in oil paints are drying oils. The drying and hardening of these binders is not a process of evaporation, but rather an oxidation or polymerization (or both) of unsaturated organic compounds on exposure to air; this produces a tough, resistant, more or less permanent film (see POLYMERS). By far the most important drying oil has been linseed oil,

which is pressed from flaxseed; next in importance is dehydrated castor oil, and third are fish oils. Other widely used oils are soya, tung, citicica, perilla, and poppyseed. Catalysts added to quicken the hardening are the driers. Thus, heating linseed oil with oxides of lead, magnesium, or cobalt produces "boiled linseed oil," which dries in a few hours.

Use of solvents (or thinners) enables paint to be brushed or sprayed freely and increases penetration of the paint. The principal solvents are turpentine, benzine, and other petroleum solvents; benzene and related aromatic compounds; and ethyl, methyl, and amyl alcohols.

VARNISH is made of oil cooked with resin, then thinned with solvent; it has no pigment, but is used as the vehicle in enamel paint, which is a varnish with a pigment. Spirit varnish consists of resins in a solvent. LACQUER also is a solution of resins in a solvent; *shellac* is a solution of the natural resin, lac, in alcohol. Recently, fractionation and synthesis of oils have made available new paint vehicles that are inexpensive and adaptable to a wide variety of uses.

Types of Paint: *Flat paint,* which dries without gloss, is often preferred on interiors; a common type has an oil or varnish base. The flat tones are caused by a high pigment content, or by "flatting" agents that disperse light. *Antifouling paint,* used on ships' bottoms to prevent the growth of weeds and barnacles, is a quick-drying iron-oxide paint containing a small amount of poisonous material, *e.g.* mercuric or cuprous oxide. *Casein paints* have binders of lime and casein; they are used mostly for flat finishes on plaster or stucco. For masonry or concrete they may have a filler of Portland cement, with other ingredients to reduce the brittleness of the finish. Casein paints come as dry powder, or as pastes; since they are thinned with water to form a suspension, they are also known as water paints. *Emulsion paints* consist of an emulsion of oil in water and may contain casein as an emulsifying agent. *Primers* and *sealers* are undercoats to prepare surfaces for painting. Anticorrosive primers may contain rust-resisting chemicals, *e.g.* zinc chromate. Insecticidal paints contain a contact insecticide, *e.g.* DDT, which gives protection against insects. The quick-drying, synthetic-resin varnishes and the resin-emulsion, water-thinned paints were developed in the 1930s; and latex paints for home and industrial use were introduced in the late 1940s.

Paint Manufacture: The two chief operations in paint manufacture are grinding the pigment and dispersing the ground pigment in the vehicle; these operations may be carried out simultaneously or separately. For pigments that are extremely difficult to grind or for the manufacture of paints that contain a combination of colors, a separate grinding and dispersal operation is required before final mixing; this is usually done in ball or pebble mills, but for simpler mixtures, the pigment and the vehicle are mixed together and sent through a sequence of hardened steel rollers (*roller mills*), each turning at a different rate. Either five-roll or three-roll mills may be used, the former providing a finer grind. In *ball mills* and *pebble mills,* only part of the vehicle is used in the grinding process, the remainder being added after the pigment has been dispersed. These mills are porcelain-lined, cylindrical in shape, and revolve at approx. 1,400 rev/hr; they vary in capacity from 35 gal. to over 1,000 gal. Quantities of small steel balls falling inside the ball mills as the mills revolve serve to pulverize colored materials. White pebbles are used to grind white enamels and primers which would be discolored by

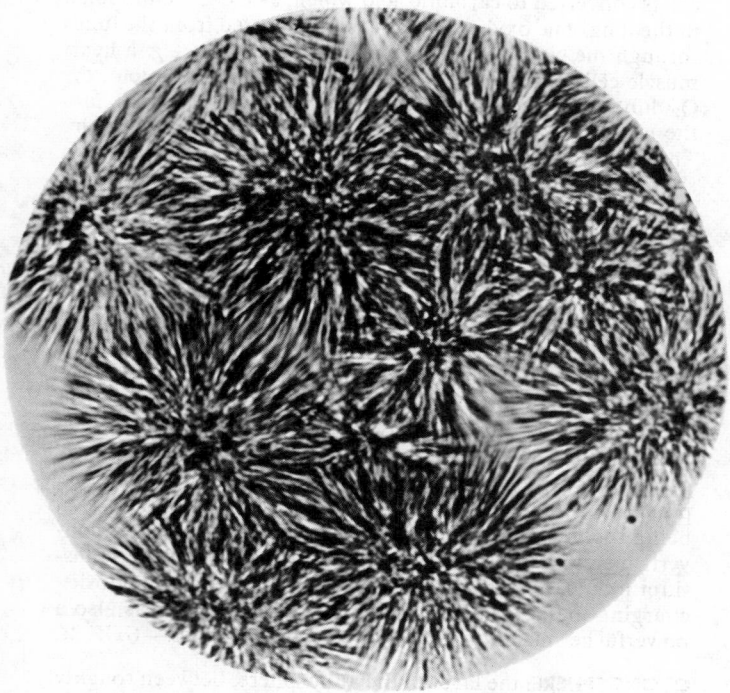

Photomicrograph of white-lead house paint: Meshing of burr-shaped lead-soap crystals increases tensile strength of the paint and reduces cracking. Combination of lead with the fatty acids of the oil binder (forming lead soap) gives paint flexibility, elasticity, and resistance to water. White lead (basic lead carbonate) pigment, unmixed with other pigments, produces a durable exterior paint. (*Lead Indust. Assn.*)

steel balls. *Stone mills* having silicon-carbide grinding stones are also used in certain operations. Materials may be ground for 15,000 to 70,000 revolutions in ball and pebble mills, depending on the fineness desired. Ordinary paints are usually given a relatively short grind, while refrigerator enamels and other kinds of industrial paints may be ground as long as 48 hr. Upon completion of the grind, the base of ground pigment is transferred to mixing tanks, where the balance of the vehicle is added and the entire mixture is mixed with high-speed agitators. The material is then shaded or matched to the desired color standard, and tests of its quality are made by the control laboratory. The equipment and tests are designed to duplicate end-use as nearly as possible. Tests vary for different products, but generally involve determination of gloss, hiding power, viscosity, weight per gallon, drying time, and appearance of the dry paint film on a test panel. All tests on the dry product have to be made at a specific film thickness, and electrical gages are used to check the film reading. Electrical instruments are also used to measure gloss. Test panels are dried in large ovens. See COATING.—*A. P. E.; L. F.*

PAIR PRODUCTION: the first known example of the creation of matter from energy, being the production of an electron and its antiparticle, the positron, from a gamma ray, which is electromagnetic energy. The inverse process, the production of a gamma ray from the annihilation of an electron-positron pair, also occurs. This corresponds to the destruction of matter. See ANTIPARTICLES; ANNIHILATION OF MATTER; CONSERVATION OF MASS-ENERGY.—*G. M. S. and L. S.*

PALATE: loosely, the roof of the mouth in vertebrate animals. In fishes and amphibians, where the nasal pits do not communicate with the mouth, or open into it only at the front, the roof of the mouth is a *true* palate, protecting the brain from below; it develops partly from the palato-pterygo-quadrate cartilages of the trough-like cartilaginous cranium under the brain, and partly from dermal bones (particularly the premaxillary and maxillary bones). In reptiles, birds, and mammals, an additional, *false* palate arises during embryonic development through extensions from these same dermal bones toward the midline. The false palate develops beneath the original palate and separates the nasal cavity from the mouth cavity except at the back (posterior end), where the nasal passages continue to communicate with the pharynx. In birds and mammals, the posterior part of the false palate is soft and contains muscles that can elevate it. When raised, it closes off the pharynx from the nasal cavity during swallowing, and this prevents food from entering the nasal cavity. In children, the palate epithelium includes some taste buds, but these usually degenerate by maturity; even so, tasty food is often described as "palatable."

Under certain conditions, the false palate in a mammalian fetus may be abnormally formed, leaving a slot connecting each nostril through the upper lip into the mouth ("hare lip") or connecting the nasal cavity on each side with the mouth ("cleft palate") all the way from the front of the mouth to the pharynx. Both conditions, which may occur together, can be corrected with scarcely a scar if remedial surgery is performed soon after birth.—*L. and M. M.*

PALEOCENE EPOCH: see CENOZOIC ERA; GEOLOGICAL TIME CHART.

PALEOGENE PERIOD: the first division of the CENOZOIC ERA, including the Paleocene, Eocene, and Oligocene epochs.

PALEOMAGNETISM: see TERRESTRIAL MAGNETISM.

Tracks of Brontosaurus are removed from bed of Paluxy River, Texas. Surface was clay when 25-ton reptile lumbered across it; in 120 million yr it has become rock. Such finds are choice. Removal is difficult and time-consuming. (*Roland T. Bird*)

PALEONTOLOGY: the science (Greek *logos*) of ancient life (*palaios* and *onta*). It derives from study of FOSSILS (traces of ancient organisms), of rocks in which they occur, and of the similarities of fossils to modern plants and animals. Although Xenophanes (576–480 B. C.) and other classical philosophers recognized that fossils represent living things, systematic study of such remains did not begin until the late Middle Ages. Da Vinci demonstrated their true origin, but most of his contemporaries and successors considered fossils as remains of victims of the Biblical deluge or as chance results of inorganic processes within the rocks. Georges-Louis Buffon (1707–88) in France greatly stimulated interest in natural history and, with his contemporaries Johann Gottlob Lehmann and Johann Christian Füchsel, who observed that the Earth's rocks represent a *succession* of strata, prepared the way for the founders of paleontology. Notable among these pioneers were Jean Guettard, William Smith, Alexandre Brongniart, Chevalier de Lamarck, and—most of all—Georges Cuvier, who by 1810 had developed the essential principles and methods for interpretation of animal fossils. Groundwork for the study of fossil plants was provided by K. H. von Sternberg (1761–1838) and Adolphe Brongniart (1801–76) a few years later.

In reconstructing the story of PREHISTORIC LIFE, paleontologists assume that life processes and factors have remained essentially the same (see GEOLOGY), although organisms themselves have changed. To illustrate: In certain red sandstones of the Silurian Period, some 400 million yr old, large

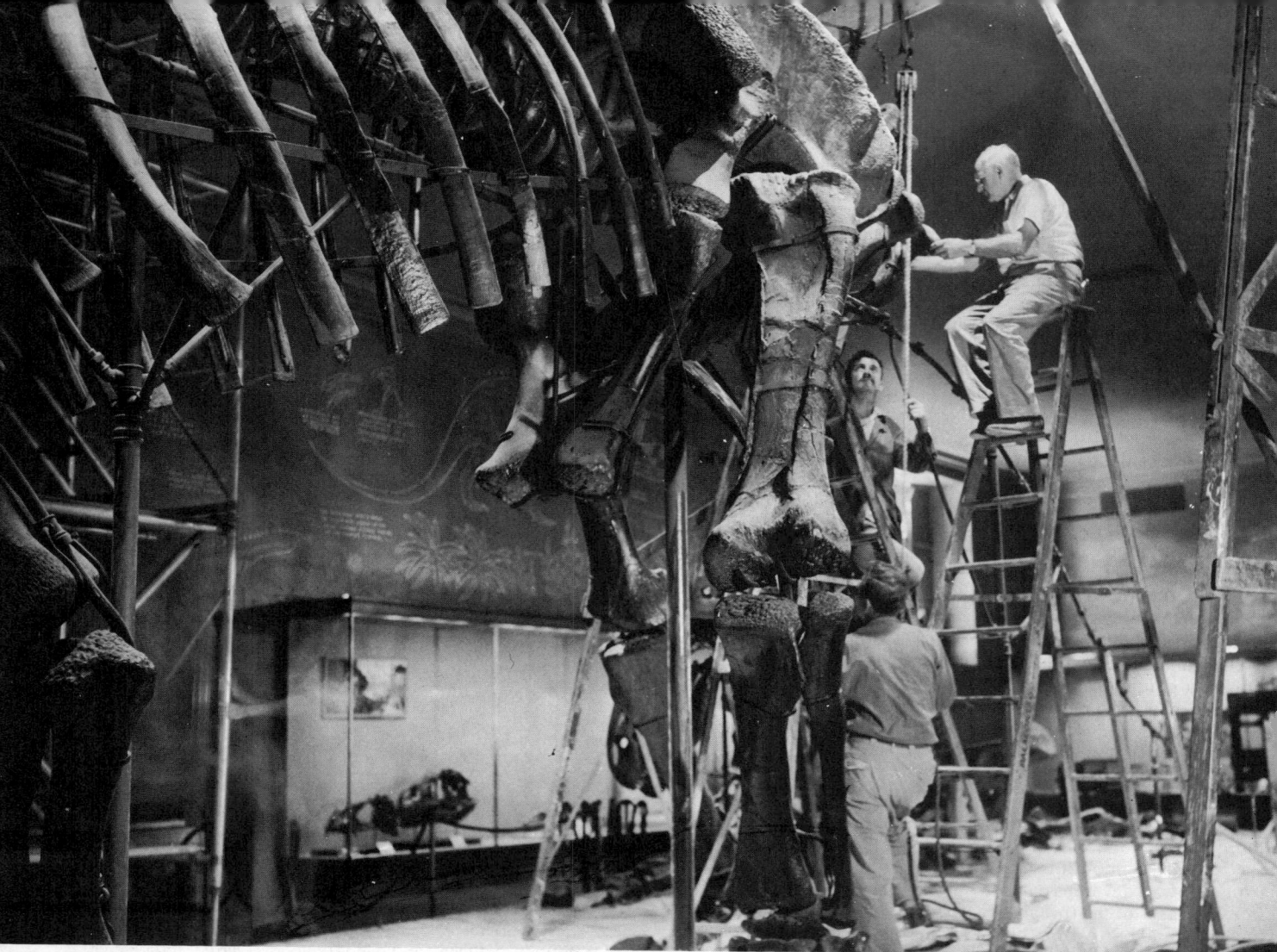

Brontosaurus tail vertebra is fastened to rest of skeleton by museum workers. Reconstructions of entire animals are not possible, as some believe, on the basis of inferences made from a few bones. Detailed reconstructions depend upon knowledge gained from accumulated, specific fossil finds. (*Roland T. Bird*)

plates of fossilized bone occur. Being of bone, the plates apparently are remnants of vertebrate animals. The impressions of gill pouches demonstrate that the animals were fish—a few individuals preserved from an ancient population. A slit-like mouth without jaws implies that they filtered small organisms from the water or the bottom. Short, stiff bodies covered by large, heavy scales and lacking paired fins indicate that they were poor swimmers; the nature of the red sandstone shows that these fish lived in rivers or tidal estuaries and became buried in sand bars of an ancient channel. Being unbroken, the bone plates probably were not transported far; they became buried near where the animals lived. The absence of jaws and paired fins links these fossil fish with modern lampreys. In some places, giant, aquatic, scorpion-like eurypterids occur with these fossil fish; probably they fed on them. The community resembled that in a modern stream, though the animals are quite different. Interpretation thus depends on similarities to modern organisms, on interpretation of structure in mechanical terms, on apparent kinship to modern types, on preservation, and on the associated rocks and fossils. The occasional preservation of organic compounds indicates something of the biochemistry of such ancient life. Rock layers above and below the fish-beds, moreover, bear different fossils; the fish, then, occur only in a thin sequence of rocks. Some fossils occur through a thick rock succession;

others, in a thin bed. In general, any succession of fossil-bearing rocks shows a fossil succession, which corresponds to the biological process of EVOLUTION. (See also STRATIGRAPHY.)

Paleontologists study fossils to describe them, to learn their environment, to determine their geographic distribution, to demonstrate their succession, and to interpret their evolution. In reconstructing the life of the past, the paleontologist is essentially a biologist, but he draws constantly upon the principles and data of physical geology (see STRATIGRAPHY; GEOCHRONOLOGY; MINERALOGY). Likewise, his contributions are not only to the understanding of life forms and their evolution through more than two billion years of Earth history, but also to the reconstruction of the past history of the planet's crust (GEOMORPHOLOGY) and the modern exploration of the crust for mineral wealth (GEOCHEMICAL PROSPECTING). —*J. B.*

PALEOZOIC ERA: the grand division of geologic time between PRECAMBRIAN TIME and the MESOZOIC ERA; it includes the Cambrian, Ordovician, Silurian, Devonian, Mississippian, Pennsylvanian, and Permian periods (see GEOLOGICAL TIME CHART). It yields the first records of a large variety and abundance of organisms, which give to the era its name (from Gr. *palaeos*, ancient, and *zoa*, life). The era began nearly 600 million yr ago with the spread of shallow seas across the continents, and concluded with the elevation of the continents and the restriction of the seas to the ocean basins, about 230 million yr ago. Traces of only aquatic organisms occur in early Paleozoic rocks; animal life included primitive kinds of arthropods, annelid worms, brachiopods, bryozoans, echinoderms, snails, clams, cephalopods, corals, sponges, and protozoans. Land plants and animals (scorpions, insects, amphibians, and reptiles) evolved before the end of the era (see LIFE, PREHISTORIC). The era closed with the extinction of the trilobites (a primitive group of arthropods), of the early coral types, and of many kinds of brachiopods, bryozoans, and echinoderms.

In the Paleozoic, the North American continent comprised a stable central area and four unstable, marginal belts, the Appalachian on the east, the Ouachita on the south, the Cordilleran on the west, and the Franklin to the north. The stable interior sank slowly and intermittently during the early Paleozoic; at times 60% of the continent was inundated. Broad rises (the arches) stood above sea level as low islands between shallow basins. The basins received fine mud and lime deposits almost continuously, and, on occasion, the seas lapped across the arches, depositing beach sand and then lime mud. Only the north-central part of the area, the Canadian Shield, failed to receive a veneer of sediments; it must have risen as low mountains above the sea (see PRECAMBRIAN TIME).

The marginal belts, in contrast, consisted of narrow, relatively deep, rapidly subsiding troughs (geosynclines) and relatively high, rapidly rising ridges. The Appalachian belt, along the trend of the present mountain system, had a complex history of subsidence, deposition, and deformation. An outer trough, in New England and the Piedmont, received thick deposits of unsorted sand, mud, and volcanic lavas and ash until about 450 million yr ago. The trough was then driven westward; the rocks folded, faulted, and altered; and the Atlantic border was raised to become mountains. Gravel, sand, and mud from these mountains were borne westward into the still-subsiding inner geosyncline. A second period of mountain building followed, about 350 million yr ago. Rivers built deltas across the inner trough into the stable interior. Thick peat deposits accumulated in delta swamps; these became the coals of the eastern and central U. S. A. A third period of mountain building, about 250 million yr ago, folded and elevated the rocks of the inner geosyncline to complete the Appalachian mountain system.

The history of the Ouachita is less well known but re-

From a Permian graveyard: Rock slab from Wichita Co., Tex., displays 16 skulls, 15 skeletons, and other parts of the amphibian *Trimerorhachis insignis*. These fossils date from the Permian Period, which closed the Paleozoic Era. (*Amer. Mus. of Nat. Hist.*)

sembles that of the Appalachians. Deposition ceased, and mountain building began in the outer geosyncline about 300 million yr before the present. The inner geosyncline was folded about 50 million yr later to form the present Ouachita, Arbuckle, and Wichita Mts. The Cordilleran mobile belt, extending from Mexico to Alaska, persisted through the Paleozoic and into the succeeding Mesozoic Era. Volcanic rocks and coarse sand accumulated in the western troughs; deposits of limestone, fine mud, and well-washed sand formed nearer the continental interior. Toward the era's close, mountains rose in Colorado, Utah, and New Mexico, and shed coarse sediments into basins on all sides. The history of the Franklin belt in the Arctic is still obscure, but it is known that rocks on the north, resembling the outer geosyncline rocks of the Appalachians, were deformed at least twice in the mid-Paleozoic; inner geosynclinal rocks to the south were folded a little later.

The other continents, like North America, consisted of stable, slowly subsiding nuclei and of unstable belts surrounding or interposed between nuclei. The Caledonian geosyncline formed the Atlantic border of Europe and, after subsidence in the early Paleozoic, was deformed about 400 million yr before the present. In the mid-Paleozoic, deltas were built across N Europe, lapping around the stable Baltic element,

Devonian life: This museum exhibit was reconstructed from fossil remains in a single layer of red sandstone. The small fishes (center rear) are primitive sharks; those at bottom center are jawless vertebrates with head and part of body encased in bony "armor." Large fish left of center is a crossopterygian; recently found coelacanths represent a branch of the same order, from which it is assumed amphibians and other higher vertebrates evolved. (*Amer. Mus. of Nat. Hist.*)

Highly resistant conglomerate strata, dipping westward, form cliffs of Shawangunk Mts in southern New York. These rocks formed from debris that was eroded from highlands existing here in Silurian Period of Paleozoic Era. (*Jerome Wyckoff*)

and another trough formed along the southern border of the stable area, across central Europe. The rocks of this geosyncline were folded too, about 300 million yr ago. Southern Europe and northern Africa were submerged as the western end of a developing geosyncline. By the late Paleozoic this latter system of troughs and ridges appeared as a distinct entity, the Tethys, extending from the Atlantic through the Middle East to N India. Another geosyncline, the Uralian, separated the Baltic and N Asian stable areas; the Ural Mts formed here in the later Paleozoic. The Pacific border of Asia was occupied by a geosyncline; another trough-and-ridge system formed along the E Indies trend, and a third across E Australia. The former two persisted into the Mesozoic; the latter was deformed and destroyed in the mid- and late Paleozoic. Still another geosyncline, the Andean, formed the margin of South America until near the end of the Mesozoic. Central and S Africa, W Australia, the Indian Peninsula, and NE South America were stable areas.

Some evidence, such as the orientation of iron particles in Paleozoic rocks (see TERRESTRIAL MAGNETISM), suggests a shift of continents relative to the poles and to each other. The fact that certain distinctive plants and animals were limited to the southern continents during the Paleozoic implies that these continents were then much closer together. Glacial deposits in Australia, S Africa, and India near the present equator also suggest that changes have since occurred in continent-pole positions. If these interpretations are correct, the general geography of Earth must have changed since Paleozoic times. Paleozoic geography differed also in regard to the occurrence of geosynclines where mountains now rise and in regard to the spread of shallow seas into the continental interiors. Except for evidence of late Paleozoic glaciers in the southern continents, Earth's climate was apparently milder than at present. Paleozoic rocks also indicate the existence of extensive deserts and dead seas; the thick salt beds of Michigan and New York, for example, remain as evidence of aridity. In all, the strange shapes and positions of the continents, the warm climates, and the archaic life forms represent the Paleozoic to modern eyes as an exotic, only half-familiar world.—*J. B.*

PALLADIUM: a metallic element (Pd) of the platinum family; at. no. 46; at. wt 106.7; mp 1549°C; sp gr 12.16; it is a precious, lustrous, silvery-white metal used often in jewelry; alloyed with gold it makes a "white gold." Palladium is ductile, does not tarnish in air, and is resistant to corrosion and acids. Discovered, 1803, by the English chemist William Hyde Wollaston in crude platinum ore, where it principally occurs, palladium is less plentiful but also less expensive than platinum. Besides its use in jewelry, palladium is used in electrical contacts (*e.g.* breaker points in circuits) because of its extreme durability and resistance to spark erosion; also in the plating of electric appliances. It is a catalyst in the production of certain drugs and chemicals, particularly in HYDROGENATION processes, where the exceptional ability of the metal to absorb hydrogen is utilized. Other forms of use include decorative surfaces (*e.g.* of books and picture frames), dental alloys, non-magnetic watch parts, and surgical, astronomical, and other delicate instruments. Palladium is only about half as heavy as platinum: thus it may be chosen over platinum for fine instruments that must be light. See PLATINUM.—*E. H. H.*

PALLAS, PETER SIMON, 1741–1811, German-Russian explorer, zoologist, and geologist; b. Berlin. He was director of a 6-yr scientific expedition in Russia (1768–74), and his report, *Travels through Various Provinces of the Russian Empire* (1772–76), contains a wealth of information on Russian zoology, geology, and fossil remains. He also wrote on the origin of mountains, using for Russia the threefold classification scheme used by G. Arduino for Italian rocks and by J. G. Lehmann for German rocks. His *Observations sur la formation des montagnes* was published in 1777. He was a fellow of the Royal Society.—*D. H. D. R.*

PALMÉN, ERIK HERBERT, 1898–   , Finnish meteorologist and oceanographer; b. Vaasa. He collaborated with J. Bjerknes to produce the first comprehensive analyses of the three-dimensional structure of developing cyclones. Palmén subsequently discussed the structure of cyclones, upper-air waves, and jet streams. He has also contributed to the knowledge of ocean-atmosphere interactions, energy and momentum balances, tropical and extratropical cyclones, and the general circulation of the atmosphere.—*S. P.*

PALYNOLOGY: the study of plant spores and pollen, especially those preserved as fossils. Spores and pollen are unusually durable fossils, and are commonly found where all other traces of life have been destroyed. They occur in abundance in both continental and marine deposits, and are a great aid to geologists in determining the age of the deposits. Palynological study of peat deposits formed since the retreat of the ice-age glaciers about 10,000 yr ago permits determination of climatic changes in Earth's immediate past.—*W. Ha.*

PANCREAS: a complex gland associated with the alimentary canal of vertebrates; it usually lies in the mesentery (intestinal membranes) in the curve of the duodenum (first part of the small INTESTINE). It contains two kinds of tissue: exocrine and endocrine. The exocrine tissue forms a digestive secretion (pancreatic juice) that passes into the duodenum along the pancreatic duct. The endocrine tissue, known as the Islets of Langerhans, forms two hormones, insulin and glucagon, concerned in the regulation of carbohydrate metabolism. The *pancreatic juice* is an alkaline fluid containing an assortment of digestive enzymes, including trypsinogen, chymotrypsinogen, polypeptidase, amylase, and lipase. When the acid contents of the stomach are ejected into the duodenum, the acid causes the hormones *secretin* and *pancreozymin* to form in

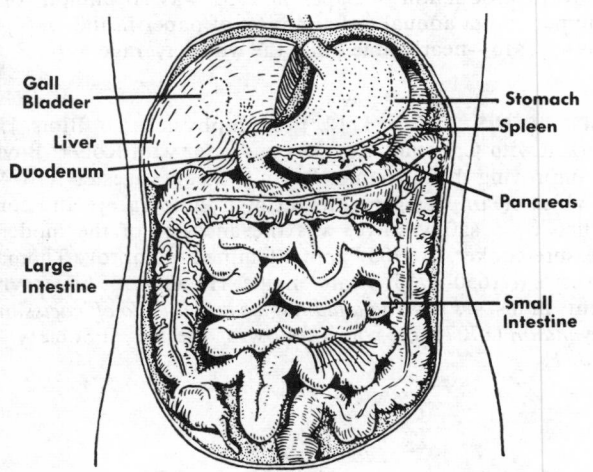

Gall Bladder

Liver

Duodenum

Large Intestine

Stomach

Spleen

Pancreas

Small Intestine

Pancreas, in man (front view), lies against the rear abdominal wall, its broad right end cradled by the curve of the duodenum, into which it secretes its digestive enzymes. (*After Manter*)

the walls of the duodenum. These substances enter the blood and are carried to the pancreas, where secretin causes formation of the alkaline fluid, and pancreozymin causes enzyme secretion. Enzyme secretion may also occur in response to nervous stimulation. The *Islets of Langerhans* are small clumps of tissue scattered among the exocrine tissue, but without connections to the pancreatic duct. The islets contain two types of cells, designated *A* and *B*. The *B* cells secrete the hormone *insulin,* a protein whose structure is now completely known.

Insulin is essential for utilization of glucose by vertebrate cells. In its absence, as in the disease *diabetes mellitus,* glucose cannot be used and accumulates in the blood, reaching a concentration such that the kidney tubule cannot entirely reabsorb it; hence it appears in the urine. Injection of insulin increases glucose utilization and lowers the glucose concentration in the blood. The normal rate of insulin secretion by the islets appears to be determined by the glucose concentration in the blood, with insulin secretion increasing when the glucose level falls. The *A* cells form another hormone, the protein *glucagon.* This was recently discovered as a contaminant of insulin preparations. It has the effect, when injected into mammals, of increasing the blood glucose—the opposite of insulin. The role of glucagon in control of metabolism, and its mechanism of action, are not fully understood.—*B. T. S.*

"Digested" and bleached pulp drops from bleaching tank to conveyor belt on its way to pulp storage tank, whence it will move on to the beater (to be fibrillated), the refiner, and eventually the Fourdrinier machine. (*Gulf States Paper Corp.*)

PAPER: sheets of matted fibers held together by mechanical intertwining and by hydrogen bonds (see HYDROGEN BONDING). As a medium for transmitting information, paper has played an important role in the development of civilization. Today much paper pulp is used for making products such as bags, containers, and filters. The principal raw material for papermaking is WOOD; better papers are made with cotton linters or rags; for cheaper grades, printed matter is reused. Raw materials also include various grasses and agricultural byproducts; and experiments with fibrillating synthetic fibers are in progress.

Paper was first made in China, 2,000 yr ago, by (1) disintegrating linen rags in hot water, (2) forming a web of entangled fibers by pouring this slurry on a screen, and (3) forming a sheet by pressing and drying the web. Modern paper-making is highly mechanized, but consists of the same basic steps. In chemical preparation of pulp, debarked and cleaned chips are cooked in large "digesters" at a high temperature and pressure to dissolve lignin and other non-cellulosic components of the wood. The acid-sulfite process uses bisulfite salt solution containing sulfurous acid; it produces light-colored pulp, suitable for making fine papers. The widely used sulfate (kraft) process uses a solution of sodium sulfide; it produces strong, dark pulp for making coarse

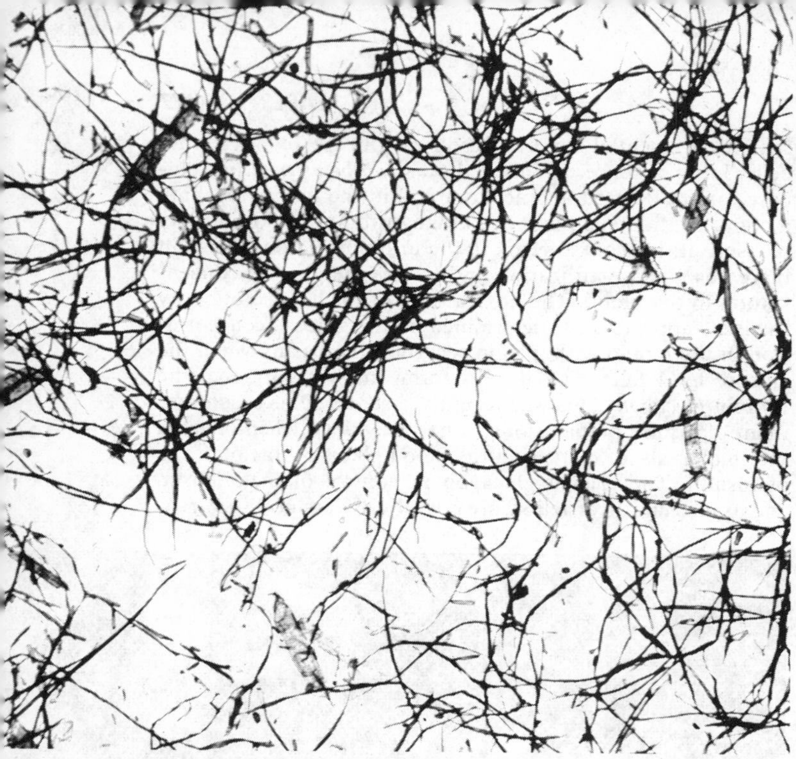

Chemical vs. mechanical pulping: Microphotographs (both 23×) show pulp after it has been cooked in digester in the sulfate (kraft) process (*left*) and after pulping by mechanical processes (*right*). In kraft process, most of the lignin is dissolved away, leaving smaller fiber bundles. About 50% yield of pulp by weight is obtained from hardwood logs (*e.g.* birch) in this process, and the resulting paper is generally used to make cardboard, wrapping paper, and other strong, dense papers. Mechanical pulping yields about 80% pulp by weight from debarked logs (*e.g.* spruce), since relatively little lignin is dissolved away. Pulp produced by mechanical methods is predominantly used in manufacture of newsprint. (*Paper Trade Journal*)

papers and cardboard. In mechanical pulping, debarked logs are pressed against revolving grindstones and water is sprayed on the grinding surfaces to cool them and to carry the separated fibers away. Further processing is done in paper mills, where the washed wood fibers are dispersed in water and the slurry is forced through narrow clearances between ribbed rotating rolls and stationary plates. The fibers are broken, crushed, and forced to fibrillate. The degree of beating determines the degree of fibrillation: lightly beaten fibers give weak papers; highly beaten fibers give strong, dense papers. The fibrillated fibers are bleached; and fillers and chemical agents are added to the slurry to improve the opacity, wet strength, and other properties of the products. The web is formed by pouring the slurry either on an endless wire belt, which acts as a screen through which water drains off, or on a rotating screen cylinder partially submerged in the slurry. After preliminary pressing, the web is transferred onto a woolen felt, which carries it through additional pressing and drying operations. Papers are often calendered, embossed, corrugated, coated, waxed, or laminated; these finishing treatments impart to them special properties for special uses.

World production of paper in 1959 was 80 million tons. The per-capita annual consumption of paper in the U. S. A. was 437.8 lb—nearly nine times the world average.—*W. P. C.*

PAPIN, DENIS, 1647–*c.* 1712, French physicist; b. Blois. He worked with Christian Huygens and later with Robert Boyle on improving the air pump. Papin's "steam digester" (1674), in which steam was generated at high temperature and controlled by a safety valve, was the ancestor of the modern pressure-cooker. In 1705 Papin attempted to improve Thomas Savery's (*c.*1650–1715) steam engine. He wrote of his experiments in his *Ars nova ad aquam ignis adminiculo efficacissime elevandum* (1707). He was a fellow of the Royal Society.—*R. J. F.*

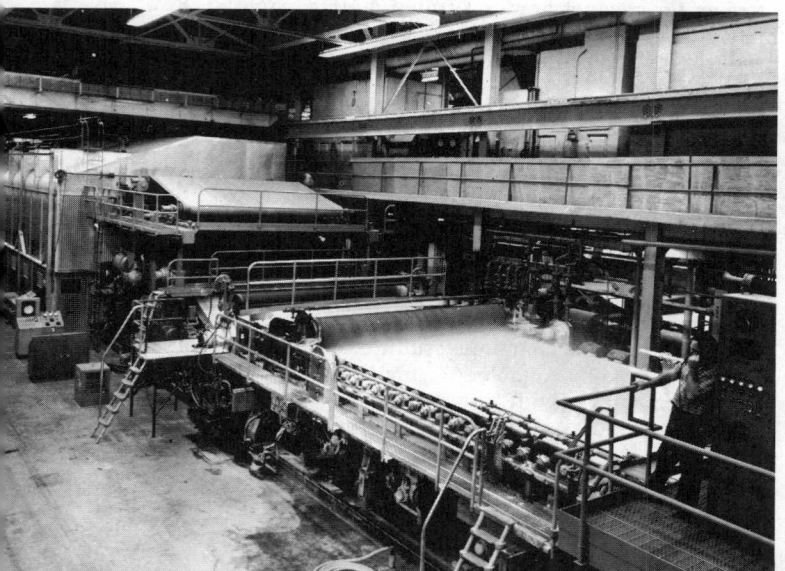

Fourdrinier machine performs key step of transforming pulp slurry into a sheet of matted fibers. Slurry is made to drop evenly on moving wire screen (*right foreground of picture*), where matting immediately begins as slurry starts to lose water content through screen. After passing through rollers (*center*), sheet of wet pulp is firm enough to leave supporting screen and pass on to presses and dryers (in enclosed structure, left background), which remove remaining excess water. Finally, the rough paper is passed through another series of rollers (calenders), which give the paper strength, density, and smoothness. (*Beloit Iron Works*)

PAPPUS OF ALEXANDRIA, late 3rd cent. A. D., Greek mathematician; birthplace and education unknown. He wrote many books on mathematics, geography, musical theory, and astronomy, but his only surviving work is the *Mathematical Collection,* in which he both summarized previous research in geometry and added original work of his own, particularly on conic sections. His name is still attached to several theorems he discovered, among which is the famous geometrical problem of Pappus: Given several (say four) straight lines in the plane, find the locus of all points such that the product of the perpendiculars from any one of these points to two of the given lines equals the product of the perpendiculars to the remaining two lines.—*D. H. D. R.*

PARABOLA: roughly, the shape assumed by the cables of a suspension bridge; one of the CONIC SECTIONS, it is the locus of a point which moves in a plane so that its distance from a fixed line is equal to its distance from a fixed point not on the line. The fixed line is called the directrix, the fixed point the focus. In the figure $MP = FP$. The line perpendicular to the directrix and through the focus is the axis. The point O where the parabola intersects the axis is the vertex.

If the distance of the focus from the vertex is denoted by p, its distance from the directrix is $2p$. The chord through the focus perpendicular to the axis intersects the parabola in two points, Q and Q', each being $2p$ units from the directrix. This chord is called the latus rectum, and its length is the focal width. The focal width is $4p$, or four times the distance of the focus from the vertex. This relation, which applies to all parabolas, suggests that all parabolas have the same shape, and this is true.

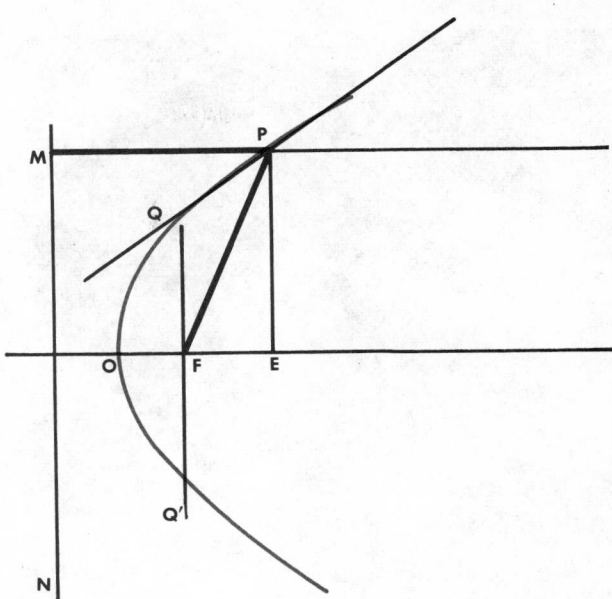

Parabola: The colored line describes a parabola with directrix MN and focus F. Point O is the vertex, and the line passing through F perpendicular to MN is the axis.

A geometric relation which characterizes the parabola is the following: if a perpendicular is dropped from any point of the parabola to the axis, its length is a mean proportional between the distance of its foot from the vertex and the focal width. That is, $OE/PE = PE/QQ'$. This relation is expressed by the equation of the parabola in rectangular coordinates. If the origin is at 0 and the focus on the x axis, the equation is $y^2 = 4px$.

If a line parallel to the axis is drawn to any point P of the parabola, this line and the line FP make equal angles with the tangent at P. Hence, if the curve were replaced by a parabolic mirror, all rays from a source of light at F would be reflected in a parallel beam. This principle is used in the construction of reflectors for searchlights. Similarly, if rays parallel to the axis enter the reflector they are all reflected to the focus. This is the principle of the reflecting telescope. Parabolic reflectors for sound and electromagnetic waves operate in the same way. Trajectories of projectiles are approximately parabolic. They vary from a parabola because of air resistance. Projectiles in the atmosphere are affected more by air resistance the higher the velocity.—*H. C.*

PARACELSUS, PHILIPPUS AUREOLUS, 1493–1541, German physician; b. Einsiedeln, Switzerland. An itinerant physician, he changed his name from Theophrastus Bombastus von Hohenheim to the classical form, a common practice in his time. He is considered to be the discoverer of the treatment of syphilis by mercury; he sought specific causes and treatments of specific diseases, and emphasized the chemical nature of life processes. He wrote many books, and his collected works have been published as *Sämtliche Werke* (8 vols., 1945–49).—*D. H. D. R.*

PARACHOR: a name given to the molecular parameter $V\gamma^{1/4}$, where V is molecular volume and γ (gamma) is surface tension. A physical constant dependent on structure, it is helpful in choosing one of several configurations of a molecule. —*Ru. M.*

Parabolic curve described by bouncing golf ball is shown in stroboscopic photograph. Differences in spacing between the images indicate ball is moving fastest at bottom of curve. (*Harold Edgerton*)

◀ **Steerable parachute:** Slot in the parachute canopy (visible as break in right front side of canopy) enables the parachutist to steer toward a safe landing spot. This so-called Derry-slot parachute is used by Air Force rescue teams. (*U. S. Air Force*)

PARACHUTE: a foldable, lightweight device for slowing the descent of a body falling through the air. It is usually made of natural or synthetic fiber, *e.g.* silk, cotton, rayon, or nylon; the material must be porous enough to allow safe and controllable descent. The conception is centuries old but did not come into use until late in the 18th cent., after the Montgolfier brothers had invented the balloon. In World War I the device was adopted as a means of saving the life of the pilot of a disabled airplane. Today it has six main applications: (1) life-saving, (2) dropping of paratroops, (3) dropping supplies and heavy equipment, (4) dropping certain types of bombs and flares, (5) as brakes for high-speed aircraft and gliders, and (6) as an anti-spin device in experimental flying.—*W. Ho.*

PARADOXES, LOGICAL: certain puzzling arguments, invented in the 20th century and much discussed by logicians and philosophers, which seem to lead by correct reasoning to self-contradictory conclusions. Analysis of fallacies concealed in these extraordinary arguments has led to important innovations in logic and the foundations of mathematics (see TYPES, THEORY OF). The oldest example, already included in Aristotle's treatise on fallacies, and thoroughly analyzed by medieval logicians, is the so-called Paradox of the Liar (or Epimenides). One version runs as follows: A man might say, "What I am now saying is false" and nothing more; then either what he says is true or else it is false. On the first alternative, what he says is incorrect, since he says he is *not* speaking truly; hence if he speaks truly, he speaks falsely. On the second alternative,

Parachute recovery system: Space capsules can be recovered with little damage risk by utilizing built-in parachute that opens to slow capsule's descent. In wind-tunnel test below, parachute has opened and capsule has decelerated to Mach 1.34 (shadowgraph taken at 1,500 frames/sec). (*U. S. Army*)

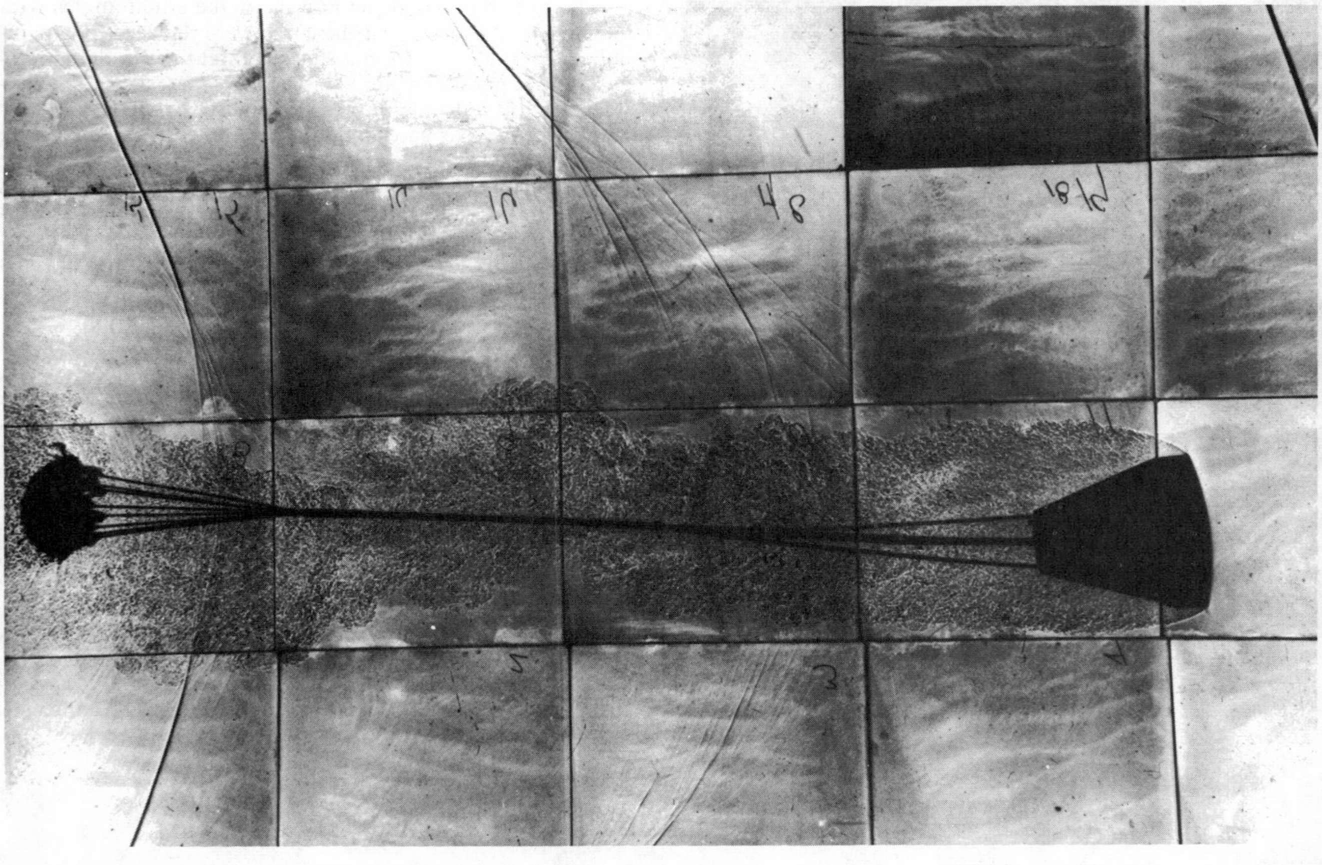

what he says is correct, for he says he is speaking falsely; hence if he speaks falsely, he speaks truly. From these two results it follows that if the speaker tells the truth, he says what is untrue; and if he does not speak the truth, he says what is true. So it seems impossible for him either to speak the truth or not to speak the truth. The following is a modern variant: On one side of a card appear the words "The statement on the other side of the card is true," and on the other side the words "The statement on the other side of the card is false." It is easily seen that neither statement can be true and neither can be false.

The general pattern of such paradoxes can be illustrated by a modern example. Suppose all the books in a certain library are classified on the following plan: If a book contains its own title as part of its text (as the words "war and peace" might occur in the text of *War and Peace*) it is called a self-mentioning book, or an *S*-book for short. All other books are called non-self-mentioning books, or *N*-books for short. Suppose now that a printed catalog of all the *N*-books in the library is added to the same library. Is it an *N*-book or an *S*-book? If the former, it should include its own title in its text (which is intended to be a list of all the *N*-books in the library). But then it will be a self-mentioning book, an *S*-book. If the catalog is an *N*-book, it must be an *S*-book. But if it is an *S*-book, it must include its own title in its text. Since the text is simply a list of all the *N*-books, the catalog will then be listed as an *N*-book. If the catalog is an *S*-book, it is an *N*-book. Once again, a contradiction has been reached.

The above examples depend upon uncritical uses of notions of *truth, statement,* and *classification;* similar puzzles turn upon the notions of *name* and *definition.* Such paradoxes are often assigned to the theory of meaning (or SEMANTICS) and regarded as raising no purely logical problems. However, in 1903 Bertrand Russell constructed a famous paradox expressed wholly by means of logical notions. His argument can be presented as follows: The class of men (*i.e.* all men taken together) is plainly not a man; in logicians' language, the class is not a member of itself. Call it a *regular* class or, for short, an *R*-class. Now consider the class of all *R*-classes (*i.e.* all *R*-classes taken together). Call this class *K*. Just as the defining property for membership in the class of man is *being a man,* so the defining property for membership in *K* is *being a regular class.* Now, is *K* a regular class or not? Suppose it is an *R*-class. *K* is the class of all *R*-classes. Hence *K,* assumed to be an *R*-class, would have to be a member of *K, i.e.* of itself. But classes that are self members are not regular, by definition. So, if *K* is an *R*-class, it is not an *R*-class. But if *K* is not an *R*-class, it is self member. Hence, *K* is a member of *K* and therefore regular (since *K* consists of nothing but regular classes). Once again, an impasse has been reached.

Russell's paradox of "the class of classes not containing themselves as members" has cast serious doubt upon some accepted principles of logical and mathematical reasoning. One way out is to impose restrictions upon definitions of classes (and so to rule out *K* as illegitimate); but this kind of solution looks arbitrary. Experts still disagree on the proper methods for disposing of the logical paradoxes.—*M. B.*

PARADOXES, MATHEMATICAL: see FALLACIES AND PARADOXES.

PARAFFINS (ALKANES): members of a series of open-chain hydrocarbons of the general formula C_nH_{2n+2}, of which methane (CH_4) is the first member and ethane (CH_3—CH_3) is the second. Paraffins are fairly stable against chemical attack, and form the bulk of most crude petroleums. Methane (50–90%) and ethane (5–20%) are the principal hydrocarbons in NATURAL GAS. Other low, volatile members like propane

(C_3H_8) and butane (C_4H_{10}) are sold as liquids (under pressure) and used for cooking and domestic heating; propane and butane are also present in natural gas. Liquid members of the series, like octane (C_8H_{18}), are valuable components in engine fuels. The higher members of the series are solid and more generally known as "paraffin wax."—*R. J. F.*

PARAHYDROGEN: see ORTHOHYDROGEN AND PARAHYDROGEN.

PARALLAX, SOLAR: half the angular diameter of Earth as it would appear from a position at the center of the Sun; a measure of the distance of Earth from the Sun. The currently adopted value of the solar parallax, 8".790, corresponds to an average Earth-Sun distance (the astronomical unit) of 93 million mi. The method of measuring distances within the solar system depends upon the fact that a celestial object, *e.g.* an asteroid, that is relatively near Earth appears to be in different positions (against the background of very distant stars) when seen from different places on Earth's surface. The difference between two apparent positions corresponds to an angle which is the parallax, *p*, of the object. Knowledge of this angle and of the linear distance between the two points on Earth's surface gives, by simple geometry, the distance between Earth and the observed object (see Fig. 1). If the Sun likewise could be observed against the background of stars,

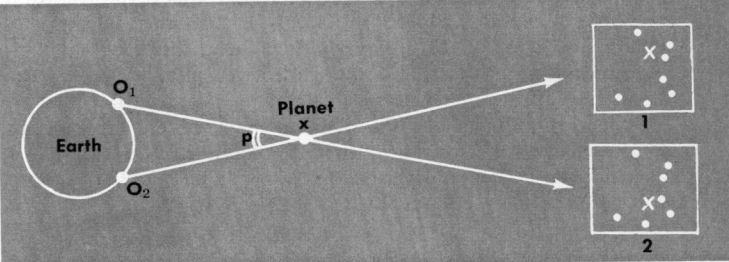

Fig. 1: Distance between Earth and other objects in solar system can be determined by triangulation. Angle *p*, parallax of object, is determined by reference to background of stars.

its parallax could be similarly determined. However, the Sun because of its brightness cannot be thus observed, and its parallax must therefore be determined indirectly, from data on the parallaxes and orbits of observable objects. For accurate definition of the Earth-Sun distance in terms of a parallax angle, the flattening of Earth has to be taken into account, as well as the variation in the distance of Earth from Sun. The mean horizontal equatorial parallax of the Sun is the angle of parallax *p* of the Sun as measured from Earth's equator, with the Sun on the horizon, the Earth-Sun distance being at its average value (see Fig. 2). This is the quantity usually called the solar parallax. The most famous determination of the Earth-Sun distance by the parallax method is the one which employed the asteroid Eros at its close approach to Earth in 1931.

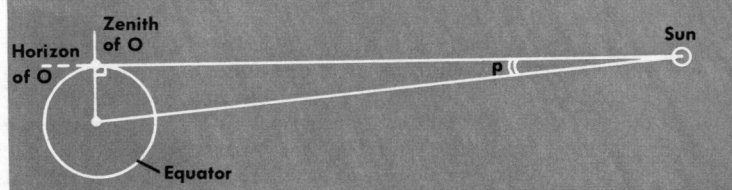

Fig. 2: Solar parallax is half the diameter of Earth as it would appear from position at center of Sun. Complicating factors, *e.g.* irregularity of Earth's shape and the changing Earth-Sun distance, make accurate determination of solar parallax difficult.

Observations of the planets' motions, when interpreted in terms of Newton's and Kepler's laws, yield a scale model of the solar system in which all distances are expressed in units of the Earth-Sun distance. Determination of the distance (in miles) of any one planet at any one time thus serves to set the scale, and so to give the Earth-Sun distance in familiar units. The distances of the planets Mars and Venus have been measured by the method of parallax, but the fact that the images of the planets are discs, of about the same size as the parallax angle to be measured, limits accuracy. Hence other methods of determining the distance have been used. The velocity of Earth in its orbit may be obtained from observations of the DOPPLER EFFECT in the spectra of suitable bright stars which lie more or less in the plane of Earth's orbit. Since the time it takes Earth to move once round the Sun is known, the circumference of its orbit can be immediately calculated. It has also proved possible to measure the distance of Venus by radar (see RADAR ASTRONOMY).—*M. W. O.*

PARALLAX, SPECTROSCOPIC: the parallax of a star as determined from detailed observation of its spectrum and measurement of its apparent magnitude. For stars whose distances are known from trigonometric measurements (see PARALLAX, STELLAR), the intrinsic luminosity (rate of output of light) can be calculated from the apparent brightness. The widths and intensities of certain lines in the stellar spectrum are found to be closely correlated with the star's intrinsic luminosity. By observing these characteristics for a more distant star, and assuming that the correlation holds at any distance, the intrinsic luminosity can be estimated. If the difference between the intrinsic luminosity and the apparent brightness is an effect only of distance, then the distance of the star can be calculated. Frequently, allowance has to be made for absorption of light by interstellar matter.—*M. W. O.*

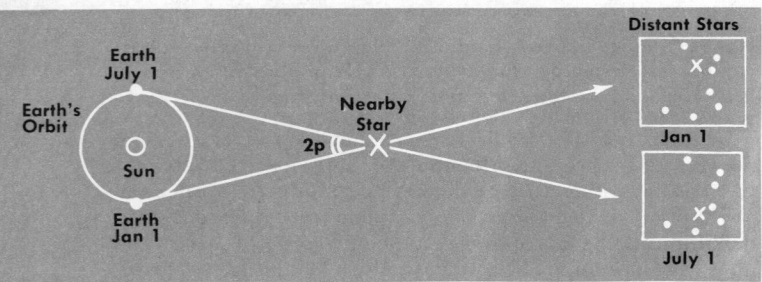

Fig. 1: Apparent position of a star changes as Earth moves in its orbit. The nearer the star, the greater is the change.

PARALLAX, STELLAR: the angular radius of Earth's orbit, as seen from a star. It is used to express the distance of a star from the Sun. The fundamental method of measuring this distance is by annual (or trigonometric) parallax. Because of the motion of Earth in its orbit, a nearby star appears to move against the background of more distant stars, just as, seen from a train, the telegraph poles beside the line appear to move (in the opposite direction to the motion of the train) against the background of distant landscape. A nearby star observed on a given date appears in a slightly different place when observed six months later. By measuring this shift, the angle "*p*" (see Fig. 1) can be measured, and the distance of the star from the Sun found by simple geometry. The greater the distance of the star, the smaller its parallax. A unit of distance, the parsec, is defined to be the distance of a star whose parallax is 1″; a star with a parallax of 0″.1 is at a distance of 10 parsecs.

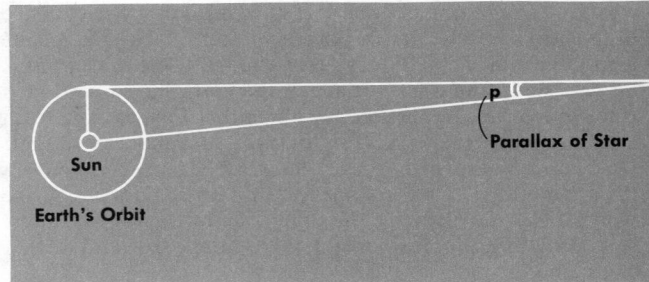

Fig. 2: Parallax of a star (*p*) is half the angle 2*p* shown in Fig. 1. Star with parallax of 1″ would be 3.26 lt-yr away.

The first successful measurement of a stellar parallax was made by F. W. Bessel, 1838. He obtained a parallax of about 0″.3 for the star 61 Cygni. Knowledge of stellar distances grew slowly in the 19th cent., but the introduction, by F. Schlesinger in 1903, of photography with long-focus telescopes brought rapid improvement. A modern parallax catalog lists over 6,000 stars with measured parallaxes. However, many of these parallaxes are very small (about 0″.01) and they cannot be considered accurate. There are only a few hundred stars, those with parallaxes exceeding 0″.05, whose distances can be considered reliably known. The nearest star has a parallax of less than 1″. Distances of more remote stars are found by other, non-geometrical methods which are calibrated by comparison with stars of known trigonometric parallax. Distances so determined are still, however, expressed in parsecs, or as parallax angles. See PARALLAX, SPECTROSCOPIC.—*M. W. O.*

PARALLEL POSTULATE: Euclid's fifth postulate, on which the theory of parallels depends. In the translation of Euclid's *Elements* by T. L. Heath, this postulate reads as follows: "If a straight line falling on two straight lines makes the interior angles on the same side together less than two right angles, the two straight lines, if produced indefinitely, meet on that side on which the angles are together less than two right angles." Two lines in a plane are by definition parallel if they do not meet, however far produced. From the postulate it can be proved that, through a point not on a given line, just one parallel to the given line exists. There is reason to believe that Euclid did not at first conceive of the above statement as a postulate, but tried to prove it as a theorem, for he did not use it until he needed it for further progress. For more than 2,000 yr it was considered an imperfection in geometry. Many mathematicians tried to prove it, and so remove it from the postulates. One of the most celebrated attempts was that of G. Saccheri, who published *Euclides ab omni naevo vindicatus* ("Euclid Freed from Every Blemish") in 1733. Although this work did not accomplish its purpose, it opened a line of reasoning that might have led to the discovery of non-Euclidean geometry had Saccheri pursued it further. J. H. Lambert (1728-77) and A. M. Legendre (1752–1833) also made notable efforts. K. F. Gauss (1777–1855) gave the postulate some attention, at first attempting to prove it. Two younger mathematicians, N. I. Lobachevsky (1793–1856) and J. Bolyai (1802–60), are credited with the discovery that this postulate is not capable of proof and can be replaced by a contradictory one, *e.g.* given a line and a point not on that line, at least *two* lines can be drawn through the given point that do not meet the given line. There is evidence that Gauss made the same discovery, perhaps at a prior date. The three share the credit for the discovery of NON-EUCLIDEAN GEOMETRY—*i.e.* a geometry based on a parallel postulate different from Euclid's.—*H. C.*

PARAMAGNETISM: the magnetic properties of materials that are feebly attracted by the poles of an electromagnet. Such materials owe their magnetization to the partial alignment of permanently magnetized constituents, atoms or electrons, in a magnetic field. The degree of such alignment is sometimes markedly dependent on the temperature and becomes nearly complete in fields of the order of 10,000 to 100,000 gauss at temperatures approaching absolute zero. In other substances the paramagnetism may only be feebly dependent on the temperature, because the equilibrium orientation of the constituent atomic moments in a magnetic field is not determined primarily by thermal interaction, *e.g.* in degenerate systems, such as conduction electrons of a metallic conductor, or in strongly coupled antiferromagnetic systems.—*F. B.*

PARAMETER: a literal symbol in mathematics, used with either of the two following meanings: (*1*) an auxiliary variable in terms of which other variables are expressed; (*2*) a constant in a relation between variables, which is not irrevocably fixed, but, by its assumption of different values, makes the relation into a system, or family, of relations. The *first usage* is illustrated by mathematical formulations of many physical results. If a ball is thrown with a velocity of 40 ft/sec in a direction inclined at 45° to the horizontal, its height and horizontal distance away at any time t sec later are given by the equations: $y = 40t \sin 45° - 16t^2$, $x = 40t \cos 45°$. Here t is the parameter in terms of which the coordinates y and x are expressed. In analytic geometry the equations of curves are often expressed parametrically. The circle with radius 1 and center at the origin, for example, has the parametric equations $x = \cos \theta$, $y = \sin \theta$, where θ is the parameter representing the angle between the radius vector of a point and the x axis. The *second usage* is illustrated by the equation of the family of straight lines through the origin, in coordinate geometry. This equation is $y = mx$, in which x and y denote the coordinates, and m is the parameter whose value determines one particular line of the family. In this usage the parameter is conceived as an arbitrary constant, which can be given any value at will. It may be looked upon as an adjusting device which permits an equation to vary within certain limitations, and represent any one of a variety of curves.—*H. C.*

PARASITISM: a type of SYMBIOSIS in which two different kinds of organisms habitually associate with one another, to the detriment of one and the benefit of the other. It differs from predation in that the organism receiving the benefit (the *parasite*) is smaller than the victim (the *host*) and in that the host is seldom killed quickly by the parasite. Among parasitic animals that remain outside their hosts (*external parasites*) are leeches and some female mosquitoes; they take blood meals if they have an opportunity, but do not need blood to live. Some animals (*e.g.* mosquitoes, fleas, sea lampreys) are parasitic only as adults. Others (*e.g.* lice, ticks) require a host or succession of hosts to reach maturity. Among parasitic animals that invade the blood stream, digestive tract, or respiratory or excretory organs of the host (*internal parasites*), there are, commonly, extraordinary adaptations which aid the parasite in gaining entrance; usually the parasite is swallowed. Tapeworms and trichina worms (the latter cause trichinosis) reach the digestive tract in the form of larvae encysted in uncooked fish and undercooked meat (especially beef and pork); in the digestive tract the parasites mature and reproduce; to infect another victim, the developing young of these parasites usually enter a second host, in which they become dormant (encysted) until their host is eaten by another animal. Malaria parasites (unicellular protozoans) and filaria worms (round-

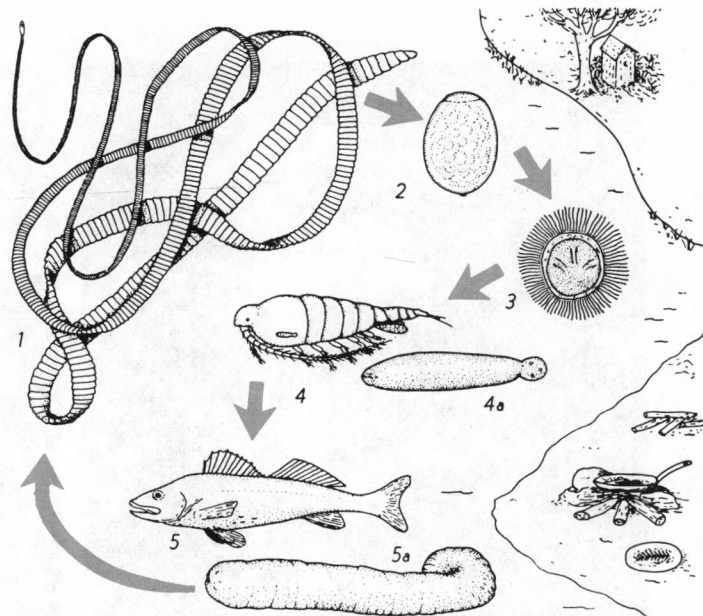

Tapeworm parasite (1) of man lays eggs (2) which pass out in the feces. If the feces come in contact with water, the eggs develop into a free-swimming ciliated larva (3). When ingested by a shrimplike host (4), the larva develops further (4a). These shrimplike animals are the natural food of fish (5), and in the muscles of the fish the final larval form (5a) develops. It is this form which is infectious to man. It grows into the adult tapeworm if the fish is eaten raw or undercooked. (*From Manter*)

worms of small size) are transmitted from one host to another by certain mosquitoes, which withdraw from one victim blood containing the infective stages of the organism and then inject the parasites along with saliva into a new victim. The malaria organisms reproduce within red blood cells, which they destroy, causing anemia as well as fever and chills; the filaria worms multiply within the lymphatic spaces, and may clog those of the legs until the calf, ankle, and foot swell with the characteristic appearance of *elephantiasis*. Reproductive individuals of both the malaria organism and the filaria worm appear in the small blood vessels of the skin, ready for a

The young of a parasitic wasp emerge from eggs attached to a tomato hornworm. The female wasp paralyzes the hornworm by stinging before laying eggs upon it. (*Ross E. Hutchins*)

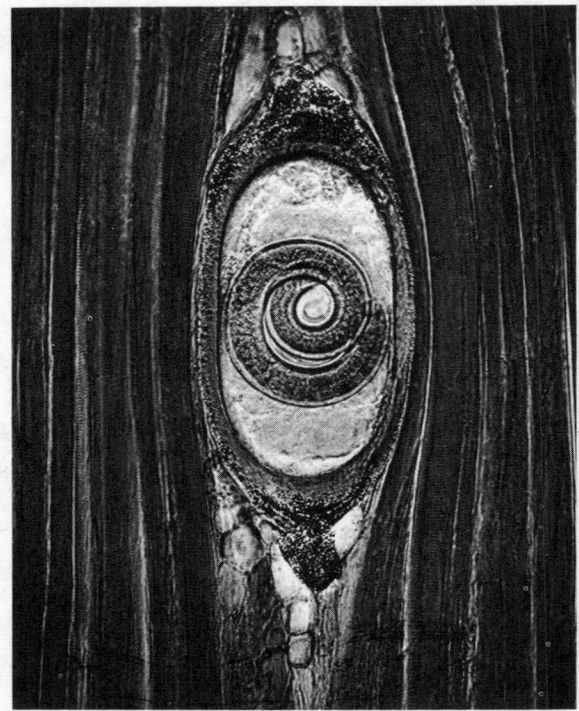

Parasitic modes of life: Larva of trichina worm, in man the source of trichinosis, is shown encysted (*above*) in skeletal muscle. Slender twining dodder (*right*), a parasite that absorbs its food from other plants, is here attacked in its turn by sap-sucking aphids. (*Carl Strüwe/Monkmeyer; Ross E. Hutchins*)

mosquito to take them on their way to another victim. Blood flukes and hookworms penetrate the skin of the host and travel through the blood vessels. Usually the flukes take up residence in the circulatory system associated with the intestine. From here the fluke's larvae can next penetrate into the cavity of the digestive tract and be carried out with feces; the larvae may then enter a secondary host—a pond-dwelling snail. Hookworms entering the blood stream emerge into the lungs and, propelled by cilia, are carried in mucus to the throat, and are there swallowed—finally, in this roundabout way, reaching the cavity of the intestine where they mature.

Parasitic plants usually are not of the green type. Most are bacteria or true fungi (*e.g.* wheat rust, potato blight, and the causative agents of the skin infections called ringworm and barber's itch). A few (*e.g.* dodder and mistletoe) are flowering plants that parasitize grasses, shrubs, and trees.—*L. and M. M.*

PARATHYROID GLANDS: in vertebrate animals, small masses of endocrine tissue, close to or embedded in the THYROID GLAND, that secrete the hormone *parathormone*. This secretion, rich in a specific protein and essential for life, is released at different rates according to the concentration of calcium ions in the blood. When blood calcium decreases, more parathormone is released. This causes a decrease in the reabsorption of phosphate from the kidney filtrate passing down the KIDNEY tubules. As a result, the concentration of phosphate in the blood is reduced, and this in turn leads to withdrawal of calcium from bone, raising the blood calcium concentration. Correspondingly, any increase in blood calcium, such as follows absorption of calcium ions from food, induces the parathyroid glands to decrease their release of parathormone; with less parathormone in the blood, the kidney tubules re-

absorb more phosphate from the kidney filtrate, raising the phosphate concentration in the blood and bringing about calcium deposition in bone tissue. Removal of the parathyroid glands, which used to occur through ignorance during surgical work on the thyroid gland, is followed quickly by a decrease in the concentration of parathormone in the blood, an increase in phosphate excretion through the urine, a blocking of calcium release into the blood, a lowering of the blood

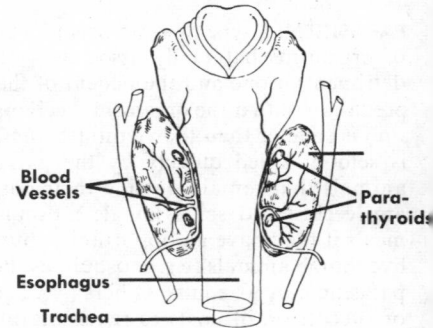

Parathyroids: In human subject (here seen from behind), they are embedded in dorsal surface of thyroids. (*From Young*)

Blood Vessels

Parathyroids

Esophagus

Trachea

calcium concentration, and a consequent hypersensitivity in muscles deprived of normal calcium supplies. The latter becomes evident through trembling and twitching movements in the skeletal muscles. Unless calcium ions are added to the blood, or an injection of parathormone is given at frequent intervals, animals lacking parathyroid glands soon die. Some of the actions of parathyroid hormone closely parallel those of vitamin D.—*L. and M. M.*

PARHELION: an image of the Sun, colored or white, seen in the sky. Parhelia, often called *sun dogs* or *mock suns,* are produced by refraction of sunlight in the needlelike hexagonal ice crystals often found in high clouds. When the Sun is near the horizon, the parhelia are about 22° from the Sun; when the Sun is higher, they are farther away, because the sunlight passes through the ice at a more acute angle to the axis of the crystal. Parhelia sometimes have a reddish tinge on the inner edge. The *anthelion*, a special form of the parhelion, appears as a luminous white spot in the sky opposite the Sun and at the same elevation above the horizon. It is produced by reflection of sunlight from ice crystals.—*D. H. L.*

PARITY: a type of symmetry exemplified by an object and its mirror image, or by the right and left hands. The parity of a quantum-mechanical system (as discussed under SYMMETRY PRINCIPLES) is "even" or "odd" according to whether the algebraic sign of its wave function is multiplied by + 1 or − 1 when the directions of all the coordinate axes are reversed. Since parity inversion is equivalent to mirror reflection, any system in which the principle of parity conservation is violated will not obey the same physical laws as its image. Consider, for example, a spinning ball, and let the sense of spin define an axis, as would a right-handed screw. On reflection, the spin motion is reversed and the corresponding screw becomes left-handed. However, this does not allow a distinction to be made between the systems, because one could equally well use a left-handed screw definition to begin with. The only circumstance under which a violation of mirror symmetry can be detected is one in which there is a clear indication on physical grounds of whether the system is right- or left-handed.

Mirror image of an ordinary (right-hand) screw is a left-hand screw. A distinction of this kind at the subatomic level exists only for weak interactions. (Massey)

This consideration led T. D. Lee and C. N. Yang to propose an experiment involving the beta-decay of a nucleus such as that of cobalt[60]. Such nuclei have magnetic moments as a result of their spins and electric charges, and can be aligned at very low temperatures, where thermal agitation is negligible, by subjecting them to a magnetic field. This serves to define an up-down axis, but cannot be used to specify which direction is up and which is down, because a right-handed convention is used to specify the way the field points. On decay, however, each nucleus emits a negatively charged electron and a neutrino, and if the electrons tend to go one way along the field rather than the other, the process is asymmetric and a choice for the system can be made between left-handedness and right-handedness.

The experiment was carried out late in 1956 by C. S. Wu and her collaborators. The electrons were found to go more often against the conventional field direction than with it, indicating a "preference" for left-handedness. Such an up-down asymmetry can occur only if states of opposite parities are present, and since the initial and final nuclear states have well-defined parities, the occurrence of the two opposite states in the decay is a clear indication that parity is not conserved in the transition. Soon after this work was carried out, other experiments showed that a similar situation prevails in all kinds of transformations involving weak interactions. Parity violation is now an accepted feature of the theory of this process. So far, however, no indications of a similar breakdown have been found for strong nuclear or electromagnetic interactions.—*D. C. C.*

PARKER, GEORGE HOWARD, 1864–1955, U. S. physiologist; b. Philadelphia, Pa. He investigated the persistence in the higher vertebrates of primitive neuromuscular mechanisms and supported the theory that muscle differentiates in the embryo before the nervous system does. He was the author of *The Elementary Nervous System* (1919) and *What Evolution Is* (1925), and was a member of the National Academy of Sciences.—*D. H. D. R.*

PARMENIDES OF ELEA, fl. *c.* 500 B. C., Greek natural philosopher. His ideas were expressed in his poem *Nature,* of which only about 120 lines of fragments have survived. He subjected the theory of monism ("All is one") to a searching scrutiny and concluded that the validity of monism implies the unreliability of our senses, according to which the world appears to be of infinite variety. Thus he aided in the development of the idea that scientists must go beyond brute experience to seek understanding, and he laid the foundation for Plato's mathematical interpretation of nature.—*D. H. D. R.*

PARSEC: see ASTRONOMICAL DISTANCE UNITS.

PARSONS, WILLIAM, 3RD EARL OF ROSSE, 1800–67, English astronomer; b. York. He improved the construction of reflecting telescopes, making possible the use of large mirrors. His giant metal mirror, 6 ft in diameter and of 54 ft focal length, was completed in 1842 and set up in 1845 at Birr Castle, Parsonstown, Ireland. Using this great reflector, he made his first contribution by resolving certain nebulas into stars and groups of stars, and detected their spiral form. He also discovered many binary and triple stars. He was a member of the Royal Society and its president (1849–54).—*R. N. M.*

PARTHENOGENESIS: literally, "virgin birth"; the development of eggs without FERTILIZATION. In some kinds of animals, parthenogenesis is a normal, common means of REPRODUCTION. During the summer or wet season, female young are produced parthenogenetically by most rotifers, by many crustaceans (*e.g.* the water flea *Daphnia*), and by aphids (plant lice) and scale insects; just prior to winter or dry season, these females, now mature, usually produce by parthenogenesis a new generation of young, including both males and sexually active females. This generation reproduces sexually; the fertilized eggs have heavy shells and physiological characteristics that make them resistant to freezing temperatures and desiccation. Parthenogenesis is also the normal method for production of males (drones) among ants, bees, and wasps; females develop from fertilized eggs.

In some kinds of animals, it is possible to induce parthenogenesis artificially by subjecting an unfertilized egg to thermal shock or mechanical or chemical treatment. In this way, "fatherless" frogs (all females) and turkeys (all males) and a few rabbits (all females) have been produced under careful laboratory supervision. Most embryos that begin development by artificial parthenogenesis fail to reach maturity.

Except in birds, some fishes, and some insects, the offspring produced by parthenogenesis are exclusively female if the egg is diploid (has two sex chromosomes) and exclusively male if the egg is haploid (has one sex chromosome). (See SEX DETERMINATION.)

In flowering plants, comparable development of eggs without fertilization is called *parthenocarpy*. It occurs spontaneously in some species, and can be induced by appropriate treatment in a few others.—*L. and M. M.*

PARTICLE, ELEMENTARY: any of the subatomic particles, over 50 of which have thus far been discovered, each characterized by its mass, electric charge, spin, magnetic moment, and lifetime. These particles appear in the study of atomic and nuclear physics and are of fundamental importance, since they are the basic constituents of all matter. They do not always behave as macroscopic particles do, but sometimes exhibit properties more usually associated with waves. This wave-particle duality presents certain conceptual difficulties, but it arises mathematically in the most natural way from the postulates of QUANTUM THEORY, which were first formulated in 1925 by E. Schrödinger and W. Heisenberg. A relativistic treatment of the subject was given in 1927 by P. A. M. Dirac, who succeeded in devising a theory that predicted the properties of the only elementary particles known at that time, the PROTON and the ELECTRON. It follows, surprisingly, from this theory that each particle has associated with it an ANTIPARTICLE, with the same mass, spin, lifetime, and other properties, but with opposite electric charge—a prediction that was verified in 1932 with the discovery of the positive electron, or POSITRON. Another important consequence is that certain physical quantities, *e.g.* angular momentum, can adopt only those values that are multiples of a basic unit, and for this reason the spin associated with any particle is restricted to a value of 0, ½, 1, ... units. Some particles (specifically those that interact strongly, as noted below) also possess a quantum mechanical property known as parity, which together with spin

is important for classification purposes. There is not yet any general theory that explains the occurrence of elementary particles, but there is an empirical scheme that classifies them into four broad groups shown in the accompanying table.

Photons: The first group includes only one member, the photon, which is the quantum of electromagnetic radiation. The photon is included as a particle because, just as particles sometimes behave as waves, waves sometimes show particle characteristics. Even though the photon has no mass, it can transmit energy and momentum, and it also carries one unit of spin. Its interaction with other particles is relatively well understood, and the strength of its interaction is characterized by a "coupling constant" the magnitude of which is 0.007. There is no way of distinguishing the photon from an antiphoton, so the photon is said to be its own antiparticle.

Leptons: The next group contains particles called leptons, of which there are three kinds: neutrinos, electrons, and muons. The *electron,* which was the first particle to be discovered, has a mass of 9×10^{-28} gm, and carries one unit of negative electric charge. Like the other leptons, it has spin ½, but it is a stable particle, in contrast to the *muon,* which has a mean life of only 2×10^{-6} sec before decaying into an electron plus two neutrinos. The muon mass is 207 times that of the electron, but its properties are otherwise the same. *Neutrinos,* which have no mass and are stable, appear only in decays where another lepton is involved, and scarcely interact with particles in the other groups. It has recently been found that the neutrinos produced in association with muons are distinct from those which occur with electrons; so there are apparently two kinds of neutrinos.

All leptons have antiparticles with properties predicted by theory, and when particle and antiparticle meet they generally annihilate each other—a process which has been experimentally observed with electrons, where the energy released appears in the form of photons. The converse reaction can also occur, and a photon passing close to an atomic nucleus sometimes is converted into a positron-electron pair. The strength of leptonic interactions can be gaged by a coupling constant of the order of 10^{-14}, and since this is so small compared, say, to the photon coupling constant, leptons are said to be weakly interacting. Processes involving leptons occur in times of 10^{-10} sec or longer, depending on how much energy is available. It has been observed that the appearance or disappearance of a lepton is always canceled by the appearance or disappearance of an antilepton; this has led to the belief that the total number of leptons in nature is a constant.

Mesons: The third group of particles, called mesons, contains two essentially similar families, pi-mesons (or pions) and K-mesons (or kaons). The *pions*—positive, negative, and neutral—are about 270 times heavier than an electron and are regarded as primarily responsible for the forces that hold nuclei together. Charged pions are antiparticles of one another and decay into the correspondingly charged muons, plus neutrinos, in 2.6×10^{-8} sec. The neutral pion is its own antiparticle and has a very short life before it decays into two photons. This is an electromagnetic interaction, and the time involved, 10^{-16} sec or less, is characteristic of the process. Pions, and also *kaons,* are produced abundantly in collisions between high-energy nucleons (as neutrons and

Particle interactions are shown in photograph and corresponding scale drawing. Antiprotons produced in a tungsten target in the Brookhaven National Laboratory's 30-Bev Alternating-Gradient Synchrotron were led into a liquid-hydrogen bubble chamber by bending and focusing magnets. Here, they reacted with hydrogen nuclei to yield a xi (2) and an anti-xi (3) particle. These in turn decayed into a number of other particles. (*Brookhaven National Lab.*)

SOME ELEMENTARY PARTICLES AND THEIR PROPERTIES

Group	Spin and Parity	Particle Name	Relative Mass	Lifetime (seconds)	Charge	Symbol	Strangeness	Principal Decay Modes
PHOTONS	1	Photon	0	Stable	0	γ	0	
LEPTONS	½	Neutrino	0	Stable	0	ν	0	
					0	$\bar{\nu}$	0	
		Electron	1	Stable	−	e^-	0	
					+	e^+	0	
		Muon	207	2.2×10^{-6}	−	μ^-	0	$e^- + \nu + \bar{\nu}$
					+	μ^+	0	$e^+ + \nu + \bar{\nu}$
MESONS	0−	Pion	264	0.9×10^{-16}	0	π^0	0	$\gamma + \gamma$
			273	2.6×10^{-8}	+	π^+	0	$\mu^+ + \nu$
					−	π^-	0	$\mu^- + \bar{\nu}$
		Kaon	972	$K_1^0: 0.9 \times 10^{-10}$	0	K^0	+1	$K_1^0: \pi^+ + \pi^-$
				$K_2^0: 5.8 \times 10^{-8}$	0	$\bar{K}^0$	−1	$K_2^0: \pi^0 + \pi^0 + \pi^0, \mu^\pm + \pi^\mp + \nu$ or $\bar{\nu}$
			966	1.2×10^{-8}	+	K^+	+1	$\mu^+ + \nu, \pi^+ + \pi^0, \pi^+ + \pi^0 + \pi^0$
					−	K^-	−1	$\mu^- + \bar{\nu}, \pi^- + \pi^0, \pi^- + \pi^0 + \pi^0$
		Eta	1070	$\sim 10^{-16}$	0	η^0	0	$\pi^+ + \pi^- + \pi^0, \pi^+ + \pi^- + \gamma, 3\pi^0, \gamma + \gamma$
BARYONS	½ + for baryons	Nucleon	1838	1000	0	n	0	$p^+ + e^- + \bar{\nu}$
					0	$\bar{n}$	0	$\bar{p}^- + e^+ + \nu$
	½ − for anti-baryons		1836	Stable	+	p	0	
					−	$\bar{p}$	0	
		Lambda	2182	2.5×10^{-10}	0	Λ	−1	$p + \pi^-, n + \pi^0$
					0	$\bar{\Lambda}$	+1	$\bar{p}^- + \pi^+, \bar{n} + \pi^0$
		Sigma	2329	$< 10^{-14}$	0	Σ^0	−1	$\Lambda + \gamma$
					0	$\bar{\Sigma}^0$	+1	$\bar{\Lambda} + \gamma$
			2328	0.8×10^{-10}	+	Σ^+	−1	$p + \pi^0, n + \pi^+$
					−	$\bar{\Sigma}^-$	+1	$\bar{p} + \pi^0, \bar{n} + \pi^-$
			2341	1.6×10^{-10}	−	Σ^-	−1	$n + \pi^-$
					+	$\bar{\Sigma}^+$	+1	$\bar{n} + \pi^+$
		Xi	2579	3.0×10^{-10}	0	Ξ^0	−2	$\Lambda + \pi^0$
					0	$\bar{\Xi}^0$	+2	$\bar{\Lambda} + \pi^0$
			2583	1.8×10^{-10}	−	Ξ^-	−2	$\Lambda + \pi^-$
					+	$\bar{\Xi}^+$	+2	$\bar{\Lambda} + \pi^+$
	½ +	Omega	~ 3270	$\sim 1.5 \times 10^{-10}$	−	Ω^-	−3	$\Xi^0 + \pi^0, \Lambda^0 + K^-$
	½ −				+	Ω^+	+3	Not yet observed

Where a pair of particles is listed, the antiparticle is below the particle.
$\sim$ Means approximately. $<$ Means less than. $\pi^\pm$ Means π^+ or π^-, etc.

protons are collectively called) with which they are said to be strongly coupled, the coupling constant being close to 1. Because this number is so large, strong interactions occur in very short times—of the order of 10^{-23} sec.

The positive kaon (K^+) and its neutral counterpart, the K°, have the K^- and K° as their respective antiparticles, and each is about 970 times as heavy as an electron. Charged kaons decay in 10^{-8} sec, mainly into leptons, but about one-quarter of the time into pions; evidently this process of kaon decay is a weak one, even though the process of kaon production is strong. The two kinds of neutral kaons exhibit an unusual feature when they decay, and are found to form two groups, one living for 10^{-10} sec and the other for 6×10^{-8} sec. The former always decay into pions, but the latter go mostly to leptons. The eta meson is like a neutral pion except that it is four times as heavy. It decays electromagnetically into pions and photons, and its lifetime is expected to be about 10^{-16} sec.

All mesons in the table have zero spin and negative parity.

Baryons: The last group on the list is the baryons, subdivided into nucleons and hyperons. Just as the number of leptons is constant, so is the number of baryons. The *nucleons* have masses about 1,840 times that of electrons, and spins of ½. They are called nucleons because all atomic nuclei are made from them. The neutron is slightly heavier than the proton and can decay to the latter with emission of an electron and antineutrino; this process, called beta-decay, constitutes an important kind of nuclear RADIOACTIVITY. The lifetime of the neutron is long, even for a weak interaction, because the energy release is small. Like electrons, protons are stable, and all known elementary particles end up, after successive decays, as either electrons or protons (plus neutrinos or photons). Antinucleons exist, and when antinucleons and nucleons collide they often annihilate each other, generally producing pions or kaons.

The lightest of the *hyperons* is the lambda particle, at 2,182 electron masses, and this is a neutral, spin-½ particle, which decays almost exclusively into a nucleon plus a pion, although leptonic decay sometimes occurs. Next comes a triplet of particles, the sigmas, which are about 2,330 times as heavy as electrons. Charged sigmas, like the lambda particle, decay mainly into nucleons and pions with lifetimes of approximately 10^{-10} sec, but the neutral sigma goes in a much shorter time into a lambda and a photon.

All three sigmas and the lambda have antiparticles, but these have not yet been seen in sufficient quantities to enable their properties to be completely determined. Xi-particles occur in both negative and neutral form. They are about 2,550 times as heavy as an electron and have lifetimes of 1.8×10^{-10} sec. and 3×10^{-10} sec., respectively. The heaviest baryon in the table is the *omega-minus,* with a mass 3,300 times that of an electron and with a lifetime of approximately 1.5×10^{-10} sec. About a dozen cases of the production of this particle have been seen since its discovery in 1964 by N. P. Samios at Brookhaven National Laboratory, but the corresponding antiparticle has not yet been observed. Unlike the other baryons, which all have spin ½, the omega is expected to have spin ³⁄₂, though this has not yet been confirmed experimentally. Its parity should be positive, like that of the other baryons. The antibaryons all have negative parity, opposite to that of the corresponding baryons, but they do have the same spins.

Hyperons and kaons are collectively described as "strange" particles, since, although they could decay strongly, they do not; they have unexpectedly long lifetimes. Furthermore, it is observed that these particles occur only in certain groupings, and the nature of these groupings has led to the assignment of a so-called strangeness number to each of them. Nucleons, pions, leptons, and photons are assigned zero strangeness, and it is found that the total strangeness number is conserved in strong production reactions, but not in the weak decay processes.

Resonant Particles: In addition to the particles shown in the table, all of which are either stable or live a relatively long time on the sub-nuclear scale (*i.e.* they decay only by weak or electromagnetic interactions), there have recently been found many other particles, characterized by extremely short lifetimes—about 10^{-23} sec. These particles decay, via strong interactions, into various combinations of those shown in the table, and possess well-defined spins, parities, etc., which in many cases have been determined. They cannot be observed directly, but when they are produced in a nuclear interaction their decay products show up among the outgoing particles as groups possessing certain total energies, equal to the masses of the decaying systems. These particles are usually described as *resonances,* because of the way in which they appear, as if they were combinations of longer-lived particles strongly attracted to each other at particular energies. Many examples of both meson and baryon resonances have been found since 1961. The lighter ones have low spins, ½ or ³⁄₂ for baryon states and 0, 1, or 2 for mesons, but the heavier systems tend to have higher spins. There may be a large spectrum of such states yet to be discovered, since new, heavier resonances continue to appear as experiments to look for them are performed at higher and higher energies.

Classification schemes: Many attempts have been made to classify the elementary particles. The most successful of these is the so-called Unitary Symmetry scheme. This uses ideas from the mathematical theory of *groups* to classify the strongly interacting particles, including resonances, into multiplets of various kinds. There are singlets and octets of mesons and singlets, octets, and decuplets (10-fold groups) of baryons. All particles within a given group have the same spin and parity, and roughly similar masses. The multiplets appear to recur at higher masses, with the same parities, but with spins successively higher by two units for each recurrence.

The possibility that such recurrences might exist is based on a theory put forward by T. Regge of Turin University. The Regge theory also makes predictions about the manner in which elementary particles should interact at high energies, and so far there is quite good agreement between these predictions and experimental results.

As the number of elementary particles has increased, several attempts have been made to formulate models in which the particles are built up as composite states of only a few fundamental objects. In one such theory, due to M. Gell-Mann of the California Institute of Technology and G. Zweig of C. E. R. N., all particles are built from a set of three such objects, called quarks, carrying respectively $-\frac{1}{3}$, $-\frac{1}{3}$, and $+\frac{2}{3}$ of the electronic charge. This model arises naturally from the Unitary Symmetry scheme and can be used to predict the properties of the established multiplets, as well as the existence of others not yet found. Several experimental searches to detect these fractionally charged objects have been made, but no trace of them has yet been seen, and in spite of the successes and apparent simplicity of the model, it seems doubtful whether the quarks have a physical existence.—*D. C. C.*

PARTICLE ACCELERATORS: electromagnetic machines that produce beams of high-energy particles, *e.g.* protons, deuterons, or electrons. The particle beams are used for research in NUCLEAR PHYSICS and, at very high energies, for studies of the elementary PARTICLES of matter. The accepted energy unit is the Mev (million electron volt); 1 Mev is the energy acquired by a singly charged particle in traversing a potential difference of 1 million volts. The range of energies useful in nuclear physics is 1 to 100 Gev; in particle physics, 200 Mev to 30 Gev (billion electron volt).

Accelerators are often called "atom smashers." Particles of several-Mev energy can disintegrate the nuclei of target atoms; in these interactions the nuclei emit radiations or particles and are transformed into different nuclei. Many types of disintegration processes occur, depending on the accelerated particle and the target material. Frequently the product nuclei from the disintegration processes are unstable radioactive isotopes and decay into more stable forms. An example is the "radiative capture" of a proton in carbon to form radioactive nitrogen. The reaction is written in customary symbols: $_6C^{12} + _1H^1 \longrightarrow _7N^{13} + \gamma$. One product is $_7N^{13}$, which decays with a half-life of 10.1 min into $_6C^{13}$ and a positron (positive electron). Another product is a gamma ray, γ, which is a high-energy electromagnetic radiation similar to light or x-rays.

Neutrons are emitted from certain disintegrations, *e.g.* when beryllium is bombarded with deuterons (heavy hydrogen ions): $_4Be^9 + _1H^2 \longrightarrow _5B^{10} + _0n^1$. Although neutrons have zero charge, they can cause still other types of disintegration. When neutrons are slowed to thermal velocities by atomic collisions, their effectiveness in causing certain kinds of disintegration is greatly increased. For example, slow neutrons can produce fission of uranium ($_{92}U^{235}$), which releases other neutrons. Accelerators were used in many early studies (1940–45) that led to the development of the NUCLEAR REACTOR and the ATOMIC BOMB.

Particles with energies above 200 Mev can disrupt the protons and neutrons in atoms and produce several types of mesons, which are unstable forms of elementary particles intermediate in mass between electrons and protons. These mesons are "created" out of the energy of the incident particles, in the presence of a nuclear particle. The most common type is the π-meson, with a mass of 276 electron masses and a half-life of 2.6×10^{-8} sec. The π-meson decays into a μ-meson and a neutrino. The μ-meson decays into an elec-

PARTICLE ACCELERATORS

Type	Particle	Energy Range (Mev)
Voltage multiplier	e, p, d	0.5—1.5
Electrostatic generator	e, p, d	0.5—6
Cyclotron	p, d	2—25
Betatron	e	10—300
Linear accelerator	p	20—70
Linear accelerator	e	20—20,000
Synchrocyclotron	p, d	100—700
Synchrotron	e	50—1,000
Synchrotron	p	1,000—10,000
A. G. synchrotron	e	1,000—6,000
A. G. synchrotron	p	1,000—30,000

tron and two neutrinos, in 2.2×10^{-6} sec. Still heavier mesons, with different properties and decay schemes, are produced at higher bombarding energies.

Beams from accelerators with energies of 5 Bev or higher can produce unstable particles heavier than the stable protons and neutrons in nature. These particles, called hyperons, have extremely short half-lives (10^{-10} to 10^{-12} sec) and decay into protons or neutrons and other lighter particles. High-energy bombardment also produces negative protons (antiprotons) and antineutrons, which have masses equal to those of normal protons or neutrons. A particle and its antiparticle share an unusual property: when they meet, they annihilate each other. In the annihilation process, the total mass-energy of both initial particles is released in the form of energy and other, lighter particles.

The numerous types of modern accelerators cover different energy ranges and accelerate different particles. The first accelerators, developed in the early 1930s, were the voltage multiplier, the cyclotron, and the electrostatic generator, which produced proton and deuteron beams of a few Mev

Proton synchrotron: "Cosmotron" accelerates protons in circular path to speeds near velocity of light; when protons attain energy of 3 Gev, they are directed at target. (*Brookhaven National Lab.*) ("Bevatron," a 6-Bev proton synchrotron, is at Univ. of California Radiation Laboratory.)

Proton linear accelerator: Proton beam moves from low-energy end (*foreground*) to high-energy end (*background*) of 110-ft linear-accelerator ("linac") tank. Large auxiliary units (*left*) house the circuits that pulse the quadrupole magnets, which focus the proton beam in the linac. (*Brookhaven National Lab.*)

energy for nuclear-physics studies. The development of the high-energy machines used for particle physics began in 1946 with the discovery of the principle of phase-stable acceleration, which led to the synchrotron, the synchrocyclotron, and the proton synchrotron. Modern multi-Gev accelerators utilize the principle of alternating gradient focusing, which was announced in 1952.

The *voltage multiplier* and the *electrostatic generator* develop a steady voltage across an evacuated DISCHARGE TUBE. Charged particles are produced by a source inside the high-voltage terminal, are accelerated through a series of short gaps across which the potential is distributed, and are directed against targets at the grounded end for experimental studies. The practical energy limit is set by breakdown of insulation.

The *betatron* is a MAGNETIC INDUCTION accelerator, operating on the principle of the TRANSFORMER. A laminated magnet is pulsed cyclically to produce a rising magnetic field across a ring-shaped aperture. Electrons circulate within a doughnut-shaped vacuum chamber between magnet poles. The central magnetic flux linking the orbit increases simultaneously, providing a circumferential electric field for acceleration. The accelerating voltage per turn is equivalent to the potential induced in a wire loop if located at the orbit. For the proper balance of linkage flux and magnetic field at the orbit, the electrons will maintain a constant orbit radius in the increasing magnetic field. Acceleration continues while the central flux rises, with maximum energy limited by magnetic saturation of the iron core and the dimensions of the orbit.

All other accelerator types utilize the principle of multiple resonance acceleration, in which particles cross many times through a relatively low potential drop, acquiring a final energy many times larger than the applied voltage. The basic technique is that of resonance with an alternating potential between one or more pairs of electrodes, provided by a radio-frequency power supply. The particles are made to cross the accelerating gaps at a fixed phase of the radio-frequency cycle on each crossing, each time acquiring an additional increment of energy.

The *cyclotron* is a MAGNETIC RESONANCE accelerator. Ions traverse circular paths of ever-increasing radius in a steady magnetic field, in resonance with an alternating electric field between two hollow semicircular electrodes. The rotation frequency of an ion orbiting in a uniform magnetic field is constant, independent of the linear velocity or the energy. The frequency applied to the accelerating electrodes is set equal to this rotation frequency. The electrodes are enclosed in a vacuum chamber between the magnetic pole faces and are electrically insulated. Positive ions released from a source at the center are pulled into one electrode, where they traverse a semicircular path, returning to the gap between electrodes a half-cycle later. Here they receive a further acceleration and traverse a path of larger radius within the second electrode. Acceleration continues until the particles have crossed the gap hundreds of times and have acquired a total energy sufficient to bring them to the periphery of the magnetic field, where they are deflected outward against a target. A simple analogy is the garden swing, which can be urged to higher and higher amplitude by successive small pushes timed to the natural frequency of the swing. Ultimately the relativistic increase in mass of the ions with increased energy reduces the orbital frequency, so the ions fall out of resonance. This results in a practical maximum energy for the fixed-frequency cyclotron of about 25 Mev.

In linear accelerators (called linacs) particles traverse a sequence of cylindrical electrodes in line, acquiring an increment of energy on each traversal. Particles remain in resonance with the applied radio-frequency field if the physical spacing of electrodes is designed to match the particle velocity. *Proton linear accelerators* have an array of cylindrical "drift tubes" of increasing length, since particle velocity increases with energy. The time interval between gap crossings is a half-period of the applied radio frequency, so fields are reversed and the ions are accelerated at each gap. The present limitation on energy for proton linacs is the cost and availability of suitable radio-frequency power sources.

Electron linear accelerators use uniformly spaced diaphragms along a cylindrical waveguide, since electrons approach the constant limiting velocity of light at quite low energies. The diaphragm-loaded waveguide has a wave velocity for the impressed radio frequency just equal to the velocity of light, and a traveling wave moves along the guide at this velocity. Electrons can be visualized as riding along the face of this advancing wave like a surfboard on a water wave. Power supplies and techniques developed for radar applications have suitable frequencies, so electron linacs can be built for higher energies than those for protons. The emergent beams of electrons are ideally collimated for research experiments.

In the *synchrocyclotron* the relativistic energy limit of the standard cyclotron is overcome by modulating the applied radio frequency to match the decreasing orbital frequency at high energies. Much larger magnets can be used and higher energies obtained. The principle of stable synchronous acceleration controls the phase of crossing the gaps, and ions remain in resonance for many thousands of turns. An "equi-

Plate 62 MOLLUSKS

Mollusks are a large group of animals whose variety is suggested by these four representatives. **1. Octopus** has eight sucker-studded tentacles surrounding its mouth. *(Leonard Lee Rue III/Monkmeyer)* **2. Razor clam** *(Ensis directus)* uses tonguelike foot to pull itself down into sand. *(L. and M. Milne)*

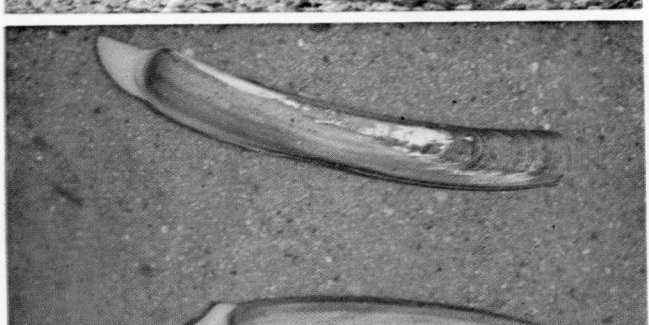

4

3. White-lipped garden snail *(Succinea ovalis)* creeps on soft, flat foot. *(Leonard Lee Rue III/Monkmeyer)* **4. Chitons** cling tenaciously to rocks when tide goes out. *(Reeves-Franklin Photo)*

Plate 63 MOSSES AND LICHENS

Mosses and lichens are the pioneer plants that colonize rocks, barren slopes, and frigid plains. They capture and hold together particles of dust and crumbled rock; these gradually accumulate as soil in which other land plants can grow. **1. Masses of reindeer lichen** in far north provide food for reindeer and lemming. *(Russ Kinne)* **2. Old man's beard** *(Usnea),* another northern lichen, trims spruces with pale green streamers. *(Norval R. Barger Jr.)* **3. Green moss and fungi** (yellow) often grow in same moist places. *(Franklin Photo Agency)*

1

2

3

Plate 64 MINERALS

The science of mineralogy recognizes approximately 1,800 mineral species. New species are reported each year, but several of these "discoveries" are later discredited. Perhaps 200 species can be considered common. Many of these abundant species are valuable ore minerals, e.g. hematite (3), the major ore of iron; galena (21), the major ore of lead; and stibnite (25), the major ore of antimony. Frequently two or more species are closely associated, such as chalcopyrite on dolomite (2) and calcite on amethyst (4). Often the association is even closer, and one species may be completely enclosed within another as an inclusion, e.g. marcasite in

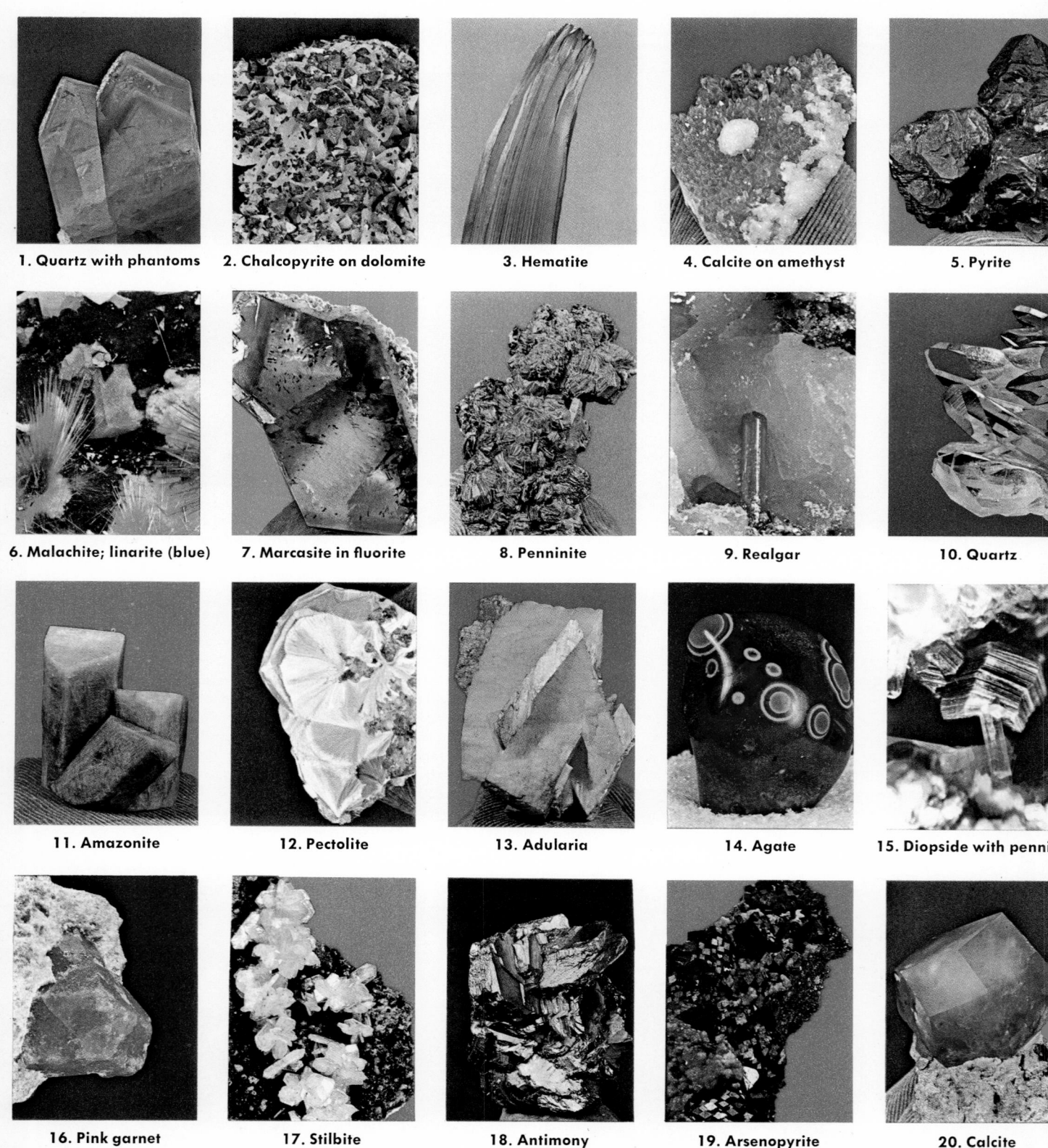

1. Quartz with phantoms   2. Chalcopyrite on dolomite   3. Hematite   4. Calcite on amethyst   5. Pyrite

6. Malachite; linarite (blue)   7. Marcasite in fluorite   8. Penninite   9. Realgar   10. Quartz

11. Amazonite   12. Pectolite   13. Adularia   14. Agate   15. Diopside with penni

16. Pink garnet   17. Stilbite   18. Antimony   19. Arsenopyrite   20. Calcite

Plate 65   MINERALS

fluorite (**7**) and asbestos in quartz (**22**). Minerals can be grouped according to chemical composition; thus galena (**21**), stibnite (**25**), pyrite (**26**), and marcasite (**40**) belong in the same chemical group, since all are compounds of a metal and sulfur; *e.g.* galena is composed of lead and sulfur. Species can be grouped by crystal structure; thus galena (**21**), pyrite (**26**), copper (**34**), and garnet (**36**) are isometric, while calcite (**20**) and quartz (**29**) are rhombohedral (see Color Plate 32). Many of the minerals pictured here occur also in other colors; some, *e.g.* sulfur, are polymorphic. *(All photos, Reo N. Pickens, Jr.)*

21. Galena   22. Asbestos in quartz   23. Agate   24. Corundum   25. Stibnite

26. Pyrite   27. Diopside   28. Mercury   29. Quartz   30. Agate

31. Halite   32. Prehnite   33. Goethite   34. Copper   35. Uranophane

. Grossularite garnet   37. Microcline with albite   38. Molybdenite   39. Sulfur   40. Marcasite

1

Plate 66   MOUNTAINS

Mountains are elevated parts of the land with limited summit areas. Their elevation may be the result of the uplifting of a block of the crust along a fault, of folding of the rocks, of broad uplift of relatively large areas, or of the piling up of volcanic debris to form volcanoes. Any such elevated parts of the land are subject to weathering and erosion, with consequent carving out of various isolated peaks.

1. Stone Mountain, Ga., is a dome of granite, elevation 1,686 ft—a residual mountain left after the less resistant material around it was removed by erosion. *(State of Georgia Dept. of Commerce)* **2. Mt Mayon,** Luzon, Philippines, is an active volcano noted for its perfect conical shape. *(Ace Williams/Shostal)* **3. Mont Blanc,** French Alps, has a granite core flanked by crystalline schists, and was carved from the folded and faulted mass of the Alps by river and glacial erosion. *(Marthe Eidelberg)*

2

4

3

4. Adirondack Mountains, N.Y., were carved from a vast dome of granitic rocks by water and glacial action. *(Jerome Wyckoff)*

5. Grand Tetons, Wyo., are jagged, glacially eroded peaks sculptured from a block of Earth's crust which was faulted up along the east side and tilted down to the west. *(Jerome Wyckoff)*

librium" phase gives the correct volts-per-turn to match the designed rate of frequency modulation. Off-phase ions that acquire an incorrect energy increment travel in circles of different radii in the uniform field, and so take different times to return to the gap. This shift in phase for off-phase ions results in phase oscillations about the correct value. A synchronous bunch of particles is accelerated outward at each frequency sweep, with individual ions traversing circular paths of increasing radius. Energy is limited by the size and cost of the large solid-core magnets required and by the associated power equipment.

Synchrotrons also utilize phase-stable acceleration to maintain resonance for thousands of turns. The *electron synchrotron* uses a laminated ring-shaped magnet to provide a guide field, as in the betatron, and the magnetic field is pulsed cyclically. One or more accelerating gaps around the orbit are powered at a constant radio frequency, in resonance with the electron orbital frequency at the equilibrium orbit. Off-phase particles oscillate in phase of crossing the gaps, about an equilibrium phase which maintains the correct rate of increase in energy to match the rising magnetic field. A synchronous bunch of electrons is accelerated in each magnetic cycle, limited in energy by orbit radius and by the strength of the magnetic field.

Proton synchrotrons also use a ring magnet that is pulsed cyclically. However, the increasing velocity of protons requires an applied frequency that increases over a wide range of frequency during the acceleration cycle. Ions are pre-accelerated to several Mev energy to minimize this frequency sweep, using a linac or an electrostatic generator, and are inflected into the orbit when the magnetic field matches the injection energy. Phase oscillations result in a synchronous bunch of ions being accelerated in each sweep of the magnetic field and the frequency. Time-average intensity is limited by the cycling rate. The energy limitation is that due to the size and cost of the large-diameter ring magnets and the required power supplies.

The principle of alternating gradient (AG) or "strong" focusing is utilized in the design of synchrotron magnets of large magnetic gradient (wedge-shaped gaps) in sectors that face alternately inward and outward around the orbit. Such gradient fields are magnetic lenses for charged particles, alternately focusing and defocusing. The net result is strong transverse focusing, which decreases oscillation amplitudes and compacts the beam strongly about the equilibrium orbit. Much smaller magnets can be used, if proper care is taken in alignment and magnetic uniformity, which allows the use of orbits with a larger radius and which results in higher particle energies.

Proton synchrotrons using alternating gradient focusing have achieved the highest proton energies to date. The AG proton synchrotrons at the European nuclear research laboratory (C. E. R. N.) near Geneva and at Brookhaven Laboratory on Long Island both accelerate protons to about 30 Gev and share the world's record for energy produced in accelerators. —*M. S. L.*

PARTITION FUNCTION: a mathematical term expressing the probable statistical distribution, in a system of non-interacting atoms or molecules, of the number of particles occupying different energy states. Since ENERGY LEVELS or states may be those associated with translation (straight-line motion), rotation, or vibration, the partition functions corresponding to these separate and independent modes of energy are multiplied together to yield the total or net partition function of the distribution.—*A. E.*

Heavy-ion linear accelerator: Interior of "HILAC" accelerator in which heavy atomic nuclei (*e.g.* carbon, argon, neon) are accelerated to 10 Mev per nucleon through the doughnut-shaped "drift tubes" within the 110-ft-long, 10-ft-diameter atom "gun" barrel. This machine was used in creation of elements 102 and 103. (*Lawrence Radiation Lab., Univ. of California*)

Elements of 30-Bev Alternating-Gradient Proton Synchrotron: Cockroft-Walton generator (*above*) is used to give initial acceleration of 750,000 electron volts to protons, upon which protons are injected into 50-Mev linear accelerator before entering orbit of the A. G. synchrotron. Part of the ½-mi-circumference ring of the A. G. synchrotron (*below*) shows one of the 48 titanium evaporation pumps (*right foreground*) and its control console (*left of pump*). These pumps serve to maintain high vacuum in tube through which proton beam is accelerated, thus preventing undue loss of protons caused by collisions with residual atmospheric molecules. (*Brookhaven National Lab.*)

PASCAL, BLAISE, 1623–62, French mathematician, scientist, and theologian; b. Clermont. A prodigy, at eleven Pascal wrote on cessation of sound in vibrating bodies, and at sixteen discovered "Pascal's theorem" concerning the inscription of a hexagon in a conic. He discovered the principle of the calculating machine in 1642. His experiments in HYDROSTATICS led to *Pascal's Law;* and his celebrated experiments with air established that air has weight, and

Blaise Pascal
(N. Y. Public Library)

refuted "Nature abhors a vacuum" as a physical explanation. Pascal invented the barometer, syringe, and hydraulic press, and co-founded with Fermat the mathematical theory of probabilities. His major contributions to scientific literature were *A Treatise on the Equilibrium of Liquids* (1663) and *A Treatise on the Weight of the Mass of the Air* (1663), both posthumous. —*A. D.*

PASTEUR, LOUIS, 1822–95, French chemist and biochemist; b. Dôle, Jura. He did research on isomeric organic acids, the molecular structure of sugar, and conversion of sugar into isomeric alcohols and acids by fermentation. This work led him into extensive studies of fermentation. He proposed the theory that all fermentation is produced by microorganisms, so that if the microorganisms in a substance are killed (by heating) and others are prevented from entering, fermentation will not occur; this is the principle upon which PASTEURIZATION is based. Pasteur became involved in a controversy with F. A. Pouchet (1800–72), who maintained that the microorganisms were produced by spontaneous generation, but Pasteur convinced most observers of the falsity of Pouchet's views. Pasteur's studies contributed materially to the development of the germ theory of disease. He was a fellow of the Royal Society.—*D. H. D. R.*

PASTEUR EFFECT: in biochemistry, a phenomenon which describes a biological regulation of sugar metabolism. Louis Pasteur found that, for a given extent of growth, yeast cells utilize much less sugar in the presence of air than in its absence. In other words, breakdown of sugar and accumulation of fermentation products are inhibited during aerobic metabolism. This utilization of the more efficient oxidative process rather than fermentation for the generation of energy makes possible the conservation of sugar. The Pasteur effect has gained more general significance since it has been found to operate in many other organisms and tissues, including organs and cells in animals and men. See GLYCOLYSIS—*R. Wu.*

PASTEURIZATION: the application of heat to liquid food products in order to kill harmful microorganisms and to make longer storage possible by reducing the concentration of factors that tend to cause decomposition and loss of flavor. Originated by Louis Pasteur, the process has been adapted to a number of products, including wine, beer, crab meat, and milk. The nature of heat treatment and the temperature applied vary with the substance being pasteurized. Most familiar is the pasteurization of milk to kill the tuberculosis organism. For milk in bulk (which must be constantly well stirred) the temperature is held 30 min at about 140°F; but the time can be reduced to 15 sec at 160°F under the proper conditions of continuous flow.—*Ru. M.*

PAULI, WOLFGANG, 1900–58, Austrian-Swiss physicist; b. Vienna. For the discovery of the EXCLUSION PRINCIPLE, also called the Pauli principle, he received the Nobel prize, 1945. The mathematical description of electron spin is named in his honor. He made many other notable contributions to quantum theory and the theory of fields. He was a fellow of the Royal Society.—*D. H. D. R.*

PAULING, LINUS CARL, 1901– , U. S. chemist; b. Portland, Oreg. His areas of research have included the determination of structure of crystals and molecules, the application of quantum mechanics to chemistry, rotation of molecules in crystals, the size of ions, the structure of proteins, immunochemistry, and sickle-cell anemia. For his research on the nature of the chemical bond and its application to the elucidation of the structure of complex substances, Pauling received the Nobel prize, 1954. Among his many publications is *The Nature of the Chemical Bond* (1939). He has been on the California Institute of Technology faculty since 1922. He is a fellow of the Royal Society and a member of the National Academy of Sciences. His efforts toward a ban on nuclear testing won him the Nobel Peace Prize in 1963.—*D. H. D. R.*

PAVLOV, IVAN PETROVICH, 1849–1936, Russian physiologist; b. Ryazan. His study in the 1890s of secretory functions of the alimentary tract became the foundation of present-day knowledge in this field. By operating on animals to expose them to observation during normal functioning of the organs, he discovered how the stomach secretes gastric juices. While investigating the reflex or automatic nature of secretion (after 1902), Pavlov conducted his famous experiment in which a dog associated food with the ringing of a bell and salivated automatically when the bell was rung. He found that the "conditioned reflex" and the "conditioned response" could be erased by repeatedly denying food. This work became the basis of study of the actions of the cerebral cortex, and the central focus of one school of experimental psychology. In recognition of his work on the physiology of digestion, he received the 1904 Nobel prize in physiology and medicine. He wrote *The Work of the Digestive Glands* (1902). His *Conditioned Reflexes* appeared in English (1927) as did his selected works (1955). He was a fellow of the Royal Society and an associate of U. S. National Academy of Sciences.—*R. G.*

PEANO, GIUSEPPE, 1858–1932, Italian mathematician; b. Cuneo. He was the founder of *Rivisti di Mathematica.* Mainly interested in FOUNDATIONS OF MATHEMATICS, he contributed to the grounding of geometry, approached numbers from the postulational point of view, developed mathematical logic (devising logical symbols which have been widely adopted), and contributed to SET THEORY. The Peano "space-filling" curve passes through every point in an area, or in a region of any number of dimensions. He also studied singular points and existence theorems of differential equations.—*H. C.*

PEARL: in its broadest sense, the protective envelope of carbonate material secreted by a mollusk around an irritant, such as a foreign body. Pearls may be of any shape. The gemologist defines pearls as concretions produced by the relatively few mollusks whose shells are lined with the iridescent material known as mother-of-pearl or nacre. This substance consists largely of calcium carbonate, either hexagonal calcite or orthorhombic aragonite, deposited by specialized cells of the outer membrane or mantle in very thin layers, each composed of minute parallel prisms. Prismatic layers are cemented to each other by an albuminoid known as conchiolin. On the average, the composition of pearls is: 86%

calcium carbonate, 12% conchiolin, and 2% water; sp gr 2.61–2.78; hardness 3.5–4. Interference of light through prismatic layers and diffraction from edges of layers results in the well-known iridescence. The finest pearls are produced by various species of the salt-water *Pinctada* and fresh-water *Unionidae*. Handsome though non-iridescent pink pearls are produced by the giant conch, *Strombus gigas;* other shellfish are unimportant as producers. Cultured pearls are produced in enormous numbers by surgical introduction of fresh-water mother-of-pearl beads along with small squares of nacre-secreting mantle membrane into the native *Pinctada martensi* of Japanese waters. Since about 1958, important quantities of very large and fine cultured pearls have been produced in the *Pinctada maxima* of the NW coast of Australia by use of Japanese techniques. The most important fisheries for natural pearls are: *salt-water*—Persian Gulf, Gulf of Manaar near Ceylon, NW coast of Australia, Mergui Archipelago near Burma, Sulu Sea, Tahiti, New Guinea, Borneo, Gulf of Mexico, Caribbean Sea; *fresh-water*—Mississippi River drainage, British Isles, W central Europe.—*J. Si.*

PEARSON, KARL, 1857–1936, British statistician and philosopher; b. London. He contributed to theoretical statistics, especially biometrics, and was founder and editor of *Biometrika*. In *The Grammar of Science* (1892) he defends the view that the data of experience are sensations, laws describe sequences of sensations, and theories are tools for predicting experience. Theories may employ useful "constructs of imagination," *e.g.* atoms and electrons, but these are not "realities of experience." He was a fellow of the Royal Society.—*A. D.*

PEGMATITE: an igneous or metamorphic rock characterized by unusually large component crystals. Pegmatites are minor rock bodies formed as late magmatic injections (see MAGMA), by partial fusion of rock, or as concentrations of material that diffused through solid rocks. (See METAMORPHISM.) Most pegmatite bodies are tabular or lenticular, and range from a few inches to hundreds of feet in length; some are miles long. Pegmatites may exhibit a concentric zoning of mineralogy and texture. Most are granitic in composition, but complex bodies contain a number and variety of rare minerals in addition to feldspar, quartz, and mica. Quartz and feldspar crystals attaining dimensions of many cubic feet are common in some pegmatites; there are also great crystals of mica and other silicates. About one tenth of all pegmatites, concentrated in relatively few localities, contain rare minerals found virtually nowhere else, including gems and ores. Among the gems are beryl, topaz, and tourmaline. The ores include cassiterite, a source of tin; tantalite and columbite, from which the rare metal tantalum is derived; apatite, a source of fluorine; lepidolite, from which lithium is obtained; thorite and zircon, the ores of thorium and zirconium, respectively; and pitchblende or uraninite, prime sources of uranium, radium, and other rare elements.—*E. A.*

PEIRCE, BENJAMIN, 1809–80, U. S. mathematician and astronomer; b. Salem, Mass. While in his teens he assisted N. Bowditch in revising and correcting his translation, with commentary, of the first four volumes of Laplace's *Traité de mécanique céleste* (1829–30). Peirce, the foremost U. S. mathematician of his time, published a series of textbooks, founded and edited a mathematical journal, helped to found Harvard Observatory and to organize the Smithsonian Institution, and was active in getting a coast and geodetic survey started. His most original mathematical work was *Linear Associative Algebras* (1870). He was a fellow of the Royal Society and

an associate of the U. S. National Academy of Sciences. His son **Charles Sanders Peirce,** 1839–1914, philosopher and scientist, b. Cambridge, Mass., achieved during his lifetime more recognition in astronomy and geodesy than for his highly original and, as it proved, important philosophical work. His fragmentary writings were assembled posthumously in *Collected Papers of Charles Peirce* (8 vols., 1931–58). Peirce's PRAGMATISM (he was founder of this movement) self-consciously reflects the experimental attitude ideally prevailing in laboratories, and is expressed as a theory of meaning: "Consider what effects, that might conceivably have practical bearings, we conceive the object of our conception to have. Then our conception of these effects is the whole of our conception of the object." We extend our conception by acting on objects, and a fixed belief is a habit of action, held as true insofar as it successfully anticipates experience. But "we cannot attain absolute certainty regarding any matter of fact" (*Fallibilism*), so beliefs are probable at best. The probability of a hypothesis is the limit approached by the ratio of the number of cases where both antecedent (an action) and consequent (an experience) are true, to the number of cases where the antecedent is true. Hence to speak of the truth of a hypothesis is to refer to "the ideal limit towards which endless investigation must tend"; so that a true belief is "the opinion fated to be ultimately agreed to by all who investigate." It follows that only such beliefs as can be communicated can be true. Logic, to the modern development of which Peirce made a pioneering contribution, was regarded by him as alternatively the theory of communication or the theory of signs. His view of science was that of a common activity, in which a set of beliefs is continually tested and revised, the entire system approaching truth as a limit. He was a member of the National Academy of Sciences.—*A. D.*

PELAGIC ANIMALS: animals of the open sea, far from any shore. They depend directly or indirectly upon food manufactured through PHOTOSYNTHESIS by microscopic drifting plants. Some of these animals, *e.g.* young herring and a great variety of small crustaceans, are able to filter the microscopic plants from the water and gain enough to eat. Others, *e.g.* jellyfishes, the whale shark, and whalebone whales, capture the young herring and the small crustaceans. The strange ocean sunfish *Mola* achieves a weight of several tons by eating jellyfishes. A great blue whale calf, weaned after 12 months at a length of about 56 ft and a weight of perhaps 40 tons, grows to maturity on this diet in two or three years. It doubles its weight and length, rapidly becoming the largest animal that ever lived. Many small crustaceans and the fishes that feed on them migrate vertically for hundreds of feet, down before dawn and up about sunset, feeding in surface waters by night and waiting in the twilight of the depths during the day. Whales and many fishes migrate horizontally on a yearly schedule that takes them thousands of miles. See PLANKTON; MIGRATION; AQUATIC ANIMALS.—*L. and M. M.*

PENCK, FRIEDRICH KARL ALBRECHT, 1858–1945, German geologist and geographer; b. Leipzig. His wide range of research in geology and geography included studies of mountains, the glacial ages, and formation of glaciers. He also did important work in hydrography and geomorphology. In 1891 he proposed a world map on the scale of 1 to 1,000,000. His many publications include three volumes on the ice age in the Alps, *Die Alpen im Eiszeitalter* (with E. Brückner, 1901–09); a study of Greek landscapes, *Griechische Landschaften* (1933); and a treatise on the movements of coastlines, *Theorie der Bewegungen der Strandlinie* (1934). He was an associate of the U. S. National Academy of Sciences.—*D. H. D. R.*

PENDULUM: a body suspended from a point so as to be able to swing to and fro. In the simplest case it consists of a small (point-like) mass hanging from a long (weightless) string fastened at its upper end; this system, called a simple (ideal) pendulum, is governed by the law:

$$T = 2\pi\sqrt{l/g}$$

where T is the period of swing, l the length of the string, and g the acceleration. Physical or real pendulums, being rigid bodies suspended so as to swing, follow the same law, but the length l is interpreted as the length of an equivalent ideal

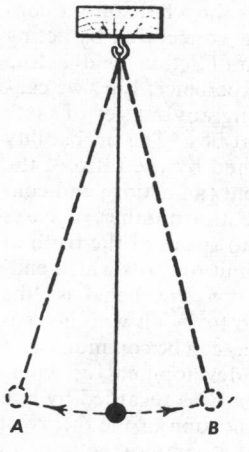

◀ **Simple pendulum** shown here is a small, dense mass (e.g. metal ball) suspended by light-weight thread. Movement of mass from A to B and back to A constitutes a complete swing.

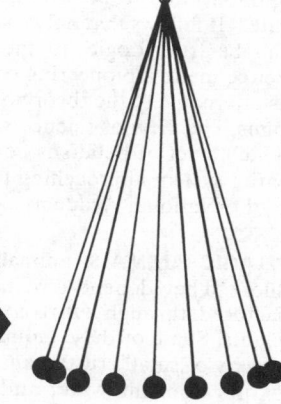

Swing of pendulum: Motion of pendulum, as it would appear in multiflash photograph, shows that fastest speed occurs at center of swing, and slowest speed at ends of swing. ▶

pendulum rather than the actual length of the body itself. For a uniform rod swinging from one end, the equivalent length is 2/3 the length of the rod, meaning that the period of swing of the rod is the same as the period of a simple pendulum of 2/3 its length. Galileo was the first to observe that the amplitude of swing of a pendulum does not affect the period of swing—that successive swings occur in equal lengths of time, regardless of whether a swing is large or small. As a result of this property, pendulums have long been used in clocks. They are also used to determine the acceleration of gravity g, which varies from place to place. See FOUCAULT PENDULUM.—*C. E. B.*

PENEPLAIN: in geology, an extensive land surface of very low relief evolved by erosion. (The word is from Latin *pene*, "almost," and "plain.") Streams, the main agents of erosion, lose gradient as the land surface is lowered. Downcutting therefore virtually ceases, but valleys continue to be widened by weathering, slopewash, and mass wasting until little relief remains. The Virginia Piedmont is a peneplain near sea level; Colorado's Flattop Plateau represents the cut-up remnants of an uplifted peneplain. Today few peneplains can be recognized, apparently because of recent widespread crustal deformations and the beginnings of new erosion cycles. Some authorities doubt the concept of peneplains, arguing that their development would require excessively long periods of crustal stability.

Most geologists, however, are convinced that such periods have indeed occurred in the past.—*J. W.*

PENICILLIN: see ANTIBIOTICS.

PENNSYLVANIAN PERIOD: see GEOLOGICAL TIME CHART; PALEOZOIC ERA.

PENTOSE PHOSPHATE PATHWAY: in biochemistry, a series of chemical reactions through which sugars are utilized for the formation of ribose phosphate (a component of ribonucleic acid, nucleotides, and coenzymes) and for the production of energy in the form of reduced triphosphopyridine nucleotide (TPNH). This pathway forms much of the TPNH in the cell; the compound provides hydrogen in the synthesis of many compounds, particularly fats.

Pathways of Carbohydrate Metabolism: To meet its complex requirements, the cell has developed several distinct mechanisms for utilization of carbohydrates. One is GLYCOLYSIS, which provides a quick source of energy independent of the immediate availability of oxygen. In glycolysis the end product is lactic acid, which is oxidized by way of pyruvic acid and the CITRIC ACID CYCLE to carbon dioxide and water, the ultimate products of carbohydrate metabolism. Another is the pentose phosphate pathway, so called because sugars having five carbon atoms, the pentoses, are prominent intermediates in its function (see accompanying figure). Other intermediates in the pathway, namely glucose 6-phosphate, fructose 6-phosphate, and glyceraldehyde 3-phosphate, also figure in glycolysis; the first two represent branch points at which this pathway of carbohydrate metabolism diverges from glycolysis. For this reason the pentose phosphate pathway is often called the hexose monophosphate shunt.

Non-oxidative Pentose Phosphate Pathway: The accompanying scheme shows two routes from hexose monophosphate to ribose phosphate, one at the left and bottom starting with fructose phosphate through the four-carbon sugar (tetrose) erythrose phosphate and the seven-carbon sugar (heptulose) sedoheptulose phosphate; and another at the top and right starting with glucose 6-phosphate and proceeding through 6-phosphogluconate and ribulose 5-phosphate. In the first of these pathways fructose 6-phosphate is seen to undergo two types of cleavage of the carbon chain. In one instance (Reaction I) a unit composed of two carbon atoms (center) is transferred to glyceraldehyde 3-phosphate (triose phosphate), forming xylulose 5-phosphate and leaving erythrose 4-phosphate as the product. In the second type of cleavage of fructose 6-phosphate (Reaction 2) a unit composed of three carbon atoms (bottom) is transferred to erythrose 4-phosphate, forming sedoheptulose 7-phosphate and leaving glyceraldehyde 3-phosphate. These reactions are catalyzed by the enzymes transketolase and transaldolase, respectively, both of which are found in nearly all types of cells.

Sedoheptulose phosphate does not generally accumulate in cells; in the presence of transketolase it yields a second two-carbon fragment which is transferred (Reaction 3) to glyceraldehyde 3-phosphate to form a second molecule of xylulose 5-phosphate and ribose 5-phosphate. Thus two molecules of fructose phosphate and one molecule of triose phosphate are converted to 3 molecules of pentose phosphate. The three pentoses are in equilibrium by virtue of the reactions shown in the upper right-hand portion of the scheme. The conversion of xylulose 5-phosphate to ribulose 5-phosphate (Reaction 4) is catalyzed by the enzyme xylulose 5-phosphate 3-epimerase; the formation of ribose 5-phosphate from ribulose 5-phosphate (Reaction 5) is catalyzed by the enzyme phosphoribose isomerase.

All these reactions are readily reversible. In animal tissues they insure production of ribose phosphate from hexose phosphate and therefore from blood sugar. Identical reactions occur in photosynthesizing plants where hexose phosphate, the ultimate product of photosynthetic assimilation of carbon dioxide, must be converted to ribulose diphosphate, the primary acceptor of carbon dioxide.

Oxidative Pentose Phosphate Pathway: The second route to ribose phosphate, through 6-phosphogluconate, requires two oxidation steps in which reduced tryphosphopyridine nucleotide (TPNH) is produced. The first oxidation step (Reaction 6) is catalyzed by glucose 6-phosphate dehydrogenase or *zwischenferment;* the second (Reaction 7), by phosphogluconic dehydrogenase. This pathway, therefore, begins with glucose 6-phosphate rather than fructose 6-phosphate. These two intermediates, however, are kept in constant equilibrium through the action of the enzyme phosphoglucose isomerase (Reaction 8). The importance of these reactions in the cell lies in the fact that they produce TPNH, and, incidentally, ribose 5-phosphate. Reduced pyridine nucleotide (TPNH) can be regarded as a form of energy and is used for synthesis of essential cellular components. It is required for reduction steps in the synthesis of fatty acid, the synthesis of steroids, the detoxification of drugs, and the formation of amino acids from ammonia. These reactions require energy which they derive by being coupled, as they are in the cell, to the reoxidation of TPNH.

Function of Pentose Phosphate Pathway in Cell: The pentose phosphate pathway thus provides useful energy in the form of reduced pyridine nucleotide, whereas glycolysis yields energy in the form of adenosine triphosphate as well as reduced pyridine nucleotide (DPNH). The pathway also provides intermediates for biosynthesis. Erythrose 4-phosphate is used to form the aromatic amino acids. Ribose phosphate is incorporated into nucleotides and also into histidine and

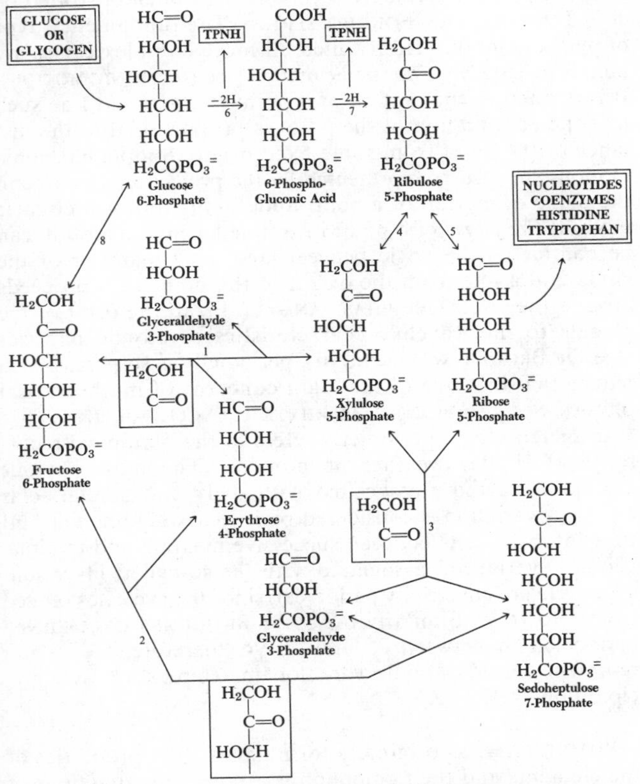

tryptophan. It is also utilized for the formation of the deoxyribose nucleotides found in deoxyribonucleic acid (DNA). As indicated earlier, the non-oxidative portion of the cycle is widely distributed and is the basic mechanism for pentose formation. The oxidative portion is confined to tissues which have large demands for TPNH. Where this demand exceeds the need for pentose, *e.g.* in the lactating mammary gland, the excess pentose phosphate is converted back to hexose phosphate by the transketolase-transaldolase reactions, and the pathway operates as a cycle.—*B. Ho.*

PEPTIDE: the structure formed by the linking together of two amino-acid molecules through the carboxyl group of one and the amino group of the other, with the removal of a molecule of water, *e.g.*

$$H_2NHCH_2CO\boxed{OH + H}NHCH_2COOH \longrightarrow$$

Glycine Glycine

$$H_2NCH_2CONHCH_2COOH + H_2O$$

Glycylglycine

Peptides range from dipeptides like that shown here to polypeptides containing numerous amino acids linked end to end by peptide bonds. Peptides are intermediate between amino acids and proteins. Many have been synthesized in the laboratory; others occur in nature. The latter group includes many with important biological activity, *e.g.* the antibiotics gramicidin, bacitracin, and tyrocidin, the pituitary hormones oxytocin and vasopressin, the growth promoter strepogenin, and the intracellular regulator glutathione (see PROTEIN SYNTHESIS). —*E. H.*

PEREGRINUS, PETER, 13th cent. A. D., French military engineer; b. Maricourt. He is also known as Peter the Stranger. His *Epistola de magnete* (1269), the earliest surviving work devoted solely to magnetism, introduced the concept of pole into magnetic theory, defined the concept of north and south poles, and stated the theory that like poles repel and unlike poles attract. The book was an important source of information for William Gilbert.—*D. H. D. R.*

PERENNIAL: a plant that lives and continues to grow for more than 2 yr. Perennials such as asparagus and many grasses produce herbaceous aerial shoots that die to the ground each year and are replaced during the following year by new aerial shoots growing from the perennial underground part. In contrast, trees and shrubs have woody aerial shoots or stem systems that continue to live and grow from year to year. See ANNUAL; BIENNIAL.—*W. Ko.*

PERFUME: a volatile substance of pleasant odor, used in toilet preparations or for scenting soap, rubber, and other commodities. A highly valued perfume may contain up to several hundred ingredients, and the blending of these ingredients calls for consummate skill. Fragrant perfume oils may be derived from plants (see ESSENTIAL OIL) or they can be chemically synthesized from various alcohols and coal-tar hydrocarbons. The "sweet smell" of perfume may arise from any of many types of organic compounds, or a mixture of these compounds. A particular perfume ingredient is not necessarily fragrant in itself. The organic compound indole, for example, which is found naturally in jasmine and orange blossoms and is now made synthetically, has a very disagreeable odor when concentrated, but imparts a fragrant floral odor when highly diluted. In addition to compounds which impart fragrance, most perfumes contain *fixatives,* whose role

Intermediates of the Pentose Phosphate Pathway

is to delay evaporation of the fragrant substances while not spoiling the distinctive fragrance of the perfume. Some fixatives are pleasant-smelling in themselves and thus can be blended to form a part of the perfume's fragrance; others are neutral in odor; still others are malodorous and must be masked or used in extreme dilution. Animal secretions are among the most interesting and valued fixatives: civet (from the civet cat) is malodorous and must be used in small amounts; musk (from male musk deer) is pleasantly aromatic; and ambergris (from the sperm whale) has no odor of its own.

Types of organic chemicals, in addition to those mentioned above, which are widely found in natural and synthetic perfume substances are ethers, esters, aldehydes, and ketones. In plants, essential oils containing such chemicals are present not only in the petals of flowers (carnation, rose, orange blossom) but also in leaves (violet, peppermint, rosemary, lavender), seeds and fruits (orange, lemon, nutmeg), roots (sassafras, ginger), stems (geranium, citronella grass), bark (cassia, cinnamon), wood (cedar, sandal), and in gummy exudations of the bark (balsam, myrrh). Essential oils are obtained from the plant by distillation, by extraction with a suitable solvent, or by expression (manual or machine pressing).

Synthetics and Semisynthetics: Commercially manufactured perfume substances are constantly increasing in variety and number. These products, though in many cases chemically similar to substances produced in nature, are far cheaper than the natural substances. Natural jasmine, for example, is quoted in the perfume markets at about $100/oz; benzyl acetate, produced at a cost of about $1/lb, is an excellent substitute that is freely used in the blending of jasmine perfumes. Also, a synthetic musk is available in place of natural musk, one of the most expensive of all natural perfume ingredients. Among the fragrant synthetic substances used in perfumes, each with its characteristic flowery odor, are: phenyl amyl alcohol (lemon-verbena), phenyl acetaldehyde (hyacinth), phenyl ethyl benzoate (roselike), phenyl methyl carbinol (gardenia), phenyl naphthyl ketone (orange blossom), anisaldehyde (hawthorn), methyl salicylate (wintergreen), and trinitro isobutyl toluene (musk). The *semisynthetics* are chemical improvements of plant extracts. Some of the most remarkable of the semisynthetics are the ionones, complex ketones prepared from a lemon-grass oil base, which are indispensable in making all of the violet bouquets.—*G. W. M.; A. P. E.*

PERICARDIUM AND PERICARDIAL CAVITY: The pericardium is the membrane forming the wall of the pericardial cavity, which encloses the heart of vertebrates. The pericardium is arranged in two layers, the space between these layers being filled with fluid. This pericardial fluid cushions the heart and serves to prevent friction between the beating heart and surrounding body parts.—*R. G. M.*

PERIDOTITE: an ultrabasic intrusive IGNEOUS ROCK, composed of olivine (peridot) and pyroxene, with minor chromite, magnetite, and various deuteric minerals. It is gradational into dunite with increase in olivine, and into pyroxenite with increase in pyroxene. Peridotites have two principal modes of origin: (1) as accumulations of olivine and pyroxene crystals settled out during the early stages of the crystallization of large bodies of essentially gabbroic composition; (2) as direct crystallization products of a magma, believed to originate in a peridotitic shell completely surrounding Earth underneath the basaltic layer. Many peridotite belts are closely associated with large-scale tectonic events (island-arc development). —*L. M.*

PERIGEE: see APOGEE AND PERIGEE.

PERIHELION: see APHELION AND PERIHELION.

PERIMETER: the length of the entire boundary of a plane geometrical figure, or the boundary itself. The perimeter of a circle is called the circumference. For polygons the perimeter is the sum of the lengths of the sides. The calculation of a curved perimeter is more difficult and requires the application of a limit process. The calculation of the circumference of a circle was performed by a limit process, which defined the irrational number π. The circumference is the product of π and the length of the diameter. Isoperimetric figures have the same perimeter. The isoperimetric problem of calculus of variations is that of finding, among all isoperimetric figures, that which has the greatest area. The solution, if there are no subsidiary conditions attached, is a circle.—*H. C.*

PERIOD: see PERIODICITY.

PERIODICITY: the repetition of an event at regular time intervals. Many phenomena in nature are periodic, *e.g.* the motion of many celestial bodies, the phases of the moon, the tides, alternating current, and all types of waves, including sound and electromagnetic waves. Whether various economic phenomena such as periods of prosperity and depression are truly periodic is a subject of controversy. For all periodic motion, the *period* is the time required for one complete VIBRATION or OSCILLATION; the reciprocal of the period is the *frequency* ($f = 1/T$). The physical extension of the vibration, *e.g.* displacement of a moving pendulum, spring, or reciprocating machine part, is the *amplitude*. Although some phenomena exhibit simple periodicity, many others, *e.g.* sound waves and the electromagnetic waves associated with sound, may be complex; and with certain limitations, these can be broken down into simple periodic components, as demonstrated by J. P. J. Fourier (see FOURIER SERIES). The fundamental type of periodic motion from which all more complex cycles are built is called *simple harmonic motion* (see HARMONIC MOTION). It is defined as the motion of a point in a straight line such that the acceleration of the point is proportional to the distance of the point from some fixed origin. Simple harmonic motion may also be represented by the projection on a line in the plane of motion of a point undergoing uniform circular motion; the *phase* of a point in simple harmonic motion can be considered the angle between any fixed diameter of the circle and a line from the origin to the point as it proceeds around the circle (see PHASE ANGLE). From the orbit of the planets to the wavelike characteristics of atomic particles (see DE BROGLIE WAVELENGTH), periodicity is so pervasive in nature that it is one of the main concerns of mathematical physics. See also BIOLOGICAL RHYTHM; CYCLE.—*A. L.*

In meteorology, periodicity refers to the periodical recurrence of similar weather phenomena. The most obvious examples are those associated with daily and annual solar cycles. A variation is considered periodical only if a constant time interval exists between successive maxima and minima. Climatic variations associated with the so-called 11-yr sunspot cycle are not strictly periodical, since the cycle has ranged from 8 to 16 yr. Similarly the 35-yr BRÜCKNER CYCLE has a period length between 25 and 50 yr; therefore it does not represent a true periodic variation in temperature and precipitation.—*W. C. J.*

PERIODIC LAW: as originally formulated, "the properties of the elements and their compounds are periodic functions of the atomic weights of the elements." Credit for the periodic law (1865) is generally given to D. Mendeleev, who developed it on the basis of empirical observations; and the law is now accepted as the most important generalization in chemistry. Present-day understanding of the periodicity of the elements' properties is more complete because of H. G. J. Moseley's concept of atomic number (*c.* 1910) and because of modern views concerning the nature of the atom and how atoms react; thus in the more precise and modern statement of the periodic law, the words "atomic weights" have been replaced by "atomic numbers."

To emphasize the periodic reappearance of properties the elements are customarily arranged in the form of a periodic table (see below). There are many forms of this table (for another version see INORGANIC CHEMISTRY) but in each of them the elements are so arranged that elements with like properties appear in vertical columns. Such columns are known as *subgroups;* one, two, or three subgroups may be gathered together to make a *group.* There are eight groups, though some authors

prefer to consider group VIII as three separate groups. A horizontal sequence of elements is known as a *period;* and a portion of a period or group may be called a "family." Similar properties reappear where the elements have similar electronic structures. For example, each of the ALKALI METALS of group I A (lithium, Li; sodium, Na; potassium, K; rubidium, Rb; and cesium, Cs) has one electron in the outermost "shell" or energy level and, except for lithium, whose atomic number is only 3, eight electrons in the next innermost shell. These elements tend to lose this lone electron in chemical reaction. Because cesium has the largest atom among the naturally occurring alkali metals, its lone electron is farther removed from the nucleus and is shielded from the attractive force of the nucleus by a large number of other electrons; thus cesium will lose its electron more readily than any other alkali metal and is the most active of the group. The other alkali-metal elements will have predictable intermediate activities. In a like manner, properties of the elements of other

PERIODIC TABLE OF THE ELEMENTS

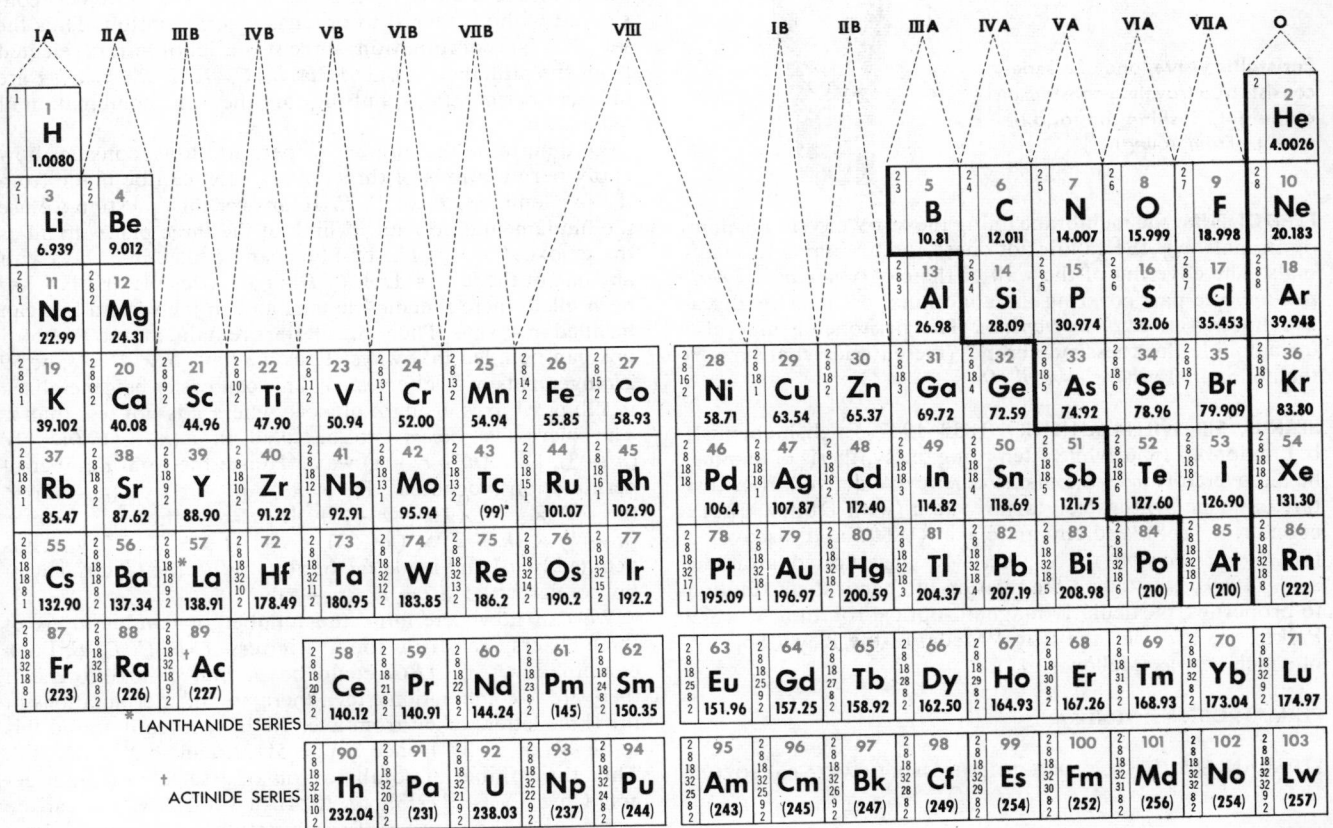

Atomic weights are based on carbon^{12} = 12. In several cases, the weights are rounded to four or five significant figures. Electron configurations taken from *Theoretical Inorganic Chemistry* by M. Clyde Day and Joel Selbin, Reinhold Publishing Corporation.

*Numbers in parentheses indicate mass number of most stable known isotope.

Periodic table: Latin numerals and dotted lines above table signify the various *groups* of elements. Vertical column of numbers to left of each element's symbol indicates number of electrons in each "electron shell" of the element's atom. Number above symbol is element's atomic number; number below is atomic weight. Note that in this recent version of the table, atomic weights have been calculated on the basis of carbon^{12} = 12. Thus the traditional value for oxygen's atomic weight, O = 16, has been adjusted to O = 15.999. Similarly, slight adjustments are made in the atomic weights of certain other elements. See ATOMIC WEIGHT. (*From Wood*)

groups can be predicted. For example, since the HALOGENS of group VII A (fluorine, F; chlorine, Cl; bromine, Br; and iodine, I) *add* an electron during chemical reaction, fluorine, the smallest, will be the most active because the electron which is to be added is more strongly attracted by the fluorine nucleus than by the nuclei of the other halogens. The nuclei of the other halogen atoms are shielded by additional shells of electrons so that the attraction of an additional electron is made less likely with increasing atomic size. In such manner, the periodic law and the table derived from it provide useful means for organizing the chemistry of the elements and aid in understanding such concepts as reactivity, oxidation numbers and valences, and the predictability of properties. See CHEMISTRY; ELEMENT; OXIDATION AND REDUCTION.—*L. Sc.*

PERISTALSIS: a characteristic wave of contraction of a tubular organ. Under appropriate stimulus, the visceral muscle in the walls of a tube (*e.g.* the INTESTINE or an oviduct) contracts, constricting the tube in that region. A wave of such contraction moves along the tube, pushing the contents of the tube before it. See DIGESTION.—*B. T. S.*

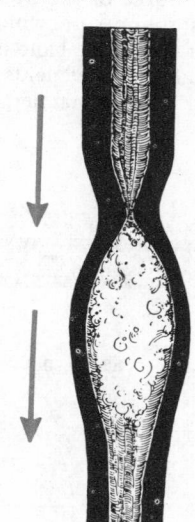

Peristaltic wave, one of a series, consists of a traveling constriction of the gut, pushing the food before it. (*From Young*)

PERITONEUM: the membrane lining the BODY CAVITY (coelom) of animals, *e.g.* the cavities of chest and abdomen in mammals. The covering of the wall of the cavity is *parietal peritoneum;* the part covering the abdominal organs (*e.g.* digestive tract) is *visceral peritoneum.* The peritoneum may also form double-thickness membranes (mesenteries) that support the abdominal organs.—*A. R. D.*

PERKIN, SIR WILLIAM HENRY, 1838–1907, English chemist; b. London. In 1856, while attempting the synthesis of quinine, he discovered *mauve,* the first synthetic dye derived from coal tar. Later he synthesized tartaric acid (with Duppa, 1861), coumarin (1868), and cinnamic acid (1869), and discovered the *Perkin reaction* for synthesis of unsaturated aromatic acids (1869). He studied the relation of chemical constitution to properties, particularly magneto-optical rotation. In 1879 Perkin was awarded the Royal Medal of the Royal Society, of which he was a fellow.—*A. I.*

PERMAFROST: see TUNDRA.

PERMIAN PERIOD: see GEOLOGICAL TIME CHART; PALEOZOIC ERA.

PERMUTATIONS AND COMBINATIONS: a study of methods of selection and arrangement. For example, how many different automobile license plates can be made if each plate has a letter followed by five digits? Such questions are of interest in themselves and are of especial importance in the study of probability. The basic principle involved can be illustrated by many simple examples. Thus, if a boy in a cafeteria has a choice of 5 sandwiches and 4 desserts, how many different

lunches consisting of 1 sandwich and 1 dessert can he have? Since, with any sandwich, he can select any one of 4 desserts, he has 4 possible lunches with each sandwich. Since there are 5 sandwiches, this gives him 20 different lunches. In general terms, if an operation can be performed in m ways and after it is performed in any one of these ways a second operation can be performed in n ways, the two together can be performed in $m \times n$ ways. This principle can easily be extended to any number of operations, so that if operations can be performed one after the other in $n_1, n_2, n_3, \ldots, n_k$ ways, the k operations can be performed together in $n_1 \times n_2 \times n_3 \times \ldots \times n_k$ ways. Thus if the boy in the cafeteria also has a choice of 2 different soups and 3 different beverages he can select soup, sandwich, dessert, and beverage in $2 \times 5 \times 4 \times 3 = 120$ ways.

In some problems the arrangement of the objects is of importance; in others the selection of the objects is independent of the order. As an example, consider the awarding of 1st, 2nd, and 3rd prizes in a competition in which there are five contestants, *A, B, C, D, E.* Here the order in which the contestants are selected is of importance, since the order *ABC* would be different from *BAC.* However, if three prizes of equal value were to be awarded, only the contestants selected and not the order of selection would be of importance. An arrangement of a set of objects in a definite order is called a permutation of the objects. Thus *ABC* and *BAC* are permutations of the letters *A, B, C.* A selection of objects considered without regard to order is a combination. Thus the set *ABC* is a combination, since it is a set of letters selected from the alphabet; *ABC, ACB, BAC, BCA, CAB, CBA* are different permutations, but they are the same combination of letters.

To determine the number of permutations, consider how many permutations of three letters each can be made from the five letters *A, B, C, D, E.* To answer this question we use the fundamental principle. Think of the three places to fill as three boxes □□□. The first box can be filled in 5 ways with any one of the letters *A, B, C, D,* or *E.* After the first box has been filled, there remain 4 letters, and so the second box can be filled in 4 ways. Then three letters remain, and so the third box can be filled in 3 ways. Thus we have $5 \times 4 \times 3$, or 60 arrangements of 3 letters each. This can easily be generalized to filling r boxes, using n objects, where n is not less than r. The successive boxes can be filled in $n, (n-1), (n-2), (n-3), \ldots, (n-r+1)$ ways. Hence the total number of permutations, denoted $_nP_r$, is $n \times (n-1) \times (n-2) \times (n-3) \times \ldots \times (n-r+1)$. If $n = r$, then $_nP_n = n \times (n-1) \times (n-2) \times (n-3) \times \ldots \times 3 \times 2 \times 1$, which is denoted by $n!$ and read "factorial n." With the factorial symbol we can write $_nP_r = n!/(n-r)!$

We can now determine the number of combinations of three letters each from the five letters *A, B, C, D, E.* Each combination, *e.g. ABC,* could be permuted in 3! ways. If there are X combinations, then there are $3!X$ permutations of the three letters taken from five. We have already found this to be $_5P_3$ or $5!/2!$. Hence $3!X = 5!/2!$, and so $X = 5!/2!3!$. Thus the number of combinations of 3 selected from 5 denoted by $_5C_3$ is $5!/2!3!$, or 10. In a similar way it can be proved that the number of combinations of r selected from n is $_nC_r = n!/r!(n-r)!$

To determine the probability of an event, it is often necessary to determine the number of possible outcomes, which is often found by the formulas for permutations and combinations. The probability that an event will succeed r times out of n tries, if the probability for success on one try is p, is given by the term $_nC_r p^r q^{n-r}$ in the expansion of the binomial $(p + q)^n$, where $q = 1 - p$.—*H. E. W.*

PEROXIDE: any compound containing the peroxide radical, O_2^{-2}. In this radical the two oxygen atoms are bonded together by a single pair of electrons in a single covalent bond. The radical as a whole has two extra electrons. Characteristic compounds are sodium peroxide, Na_2O_2; hydrogen peroxide, H_2O_2; and barium peroxide, BaO_2. Peroxides are distinguished from dioxides such as lead dioxide, PbO_2, in which each oxygen atom has its normal oxidation number of minus 2 and the oxygens are not bonded to each other—both oxygens are bonded individually to the lead atom. The direct oxygen-oxygen bond present in peroxides tends to be unstable and peroxides decompose readily, especially upon the application of heat or a catalyst. The best-known example is hydrogen peroxide. This substance decomposes with almost any solid material acting as a catalyst to yield water and oxygen. This reaction is responsible for the bleaching and cleansing action of the compound.—*L. Sc.*

PERPETUAL-MOTION MACHINES: any of a large number of proposed devices that would violate either of the first two laws of THERMODYNAMICS—*if* they performed as specified. The fact that none of them does work constitutes part of the experimental evidence for these two laws. A "perpetual-motion machine of the first kind" is one that purports to perform useful work without extracting energy from any source —an engine requiring no fuel. However, the first law of thermodynamics, which in its most general form is known as the law of conservation of energy, tells us that there is no phenomenon in nature in which energy is created from nothing. Energy can be transferred from one system to another, but the total energy content remains constant. The second law imposes a further restriction on cyclic machines that derive their energy by means of heat transfer, *i.e.* by absorbing energy from a hot substance and releasing it at a lower temperature during each cycle of the operation, as does the steam engine (see CARNOT CYCLE). The second law tells us that it is not possible for such a machine to convert all of the energy so absorbed into useful work. Before the engine can be returned to its original condition at the beginning of each cycle, it is necessary that some of the energy absorbed from the hot reservoir be transferred to a cold reservoir. Thus, only part of the energy absorbed is available for the per-

Perpetual motion: Leonardo da Vinci imagined perpetual-motion machines which his reason rejected. These wheels were supposed to keep on rotating, once started, because weights on the side going down moved farther from center.

formance of useful work, and the remainder must be discarded. A heat engine that purports to work without discarding a portion of the absorbed heat energy is called a "perpetual-motion machine of the second kind."—*S. K.*

PERRIN, JEAN BAPTISTE, 1870–1942, French physical chemist; b. Lille. In 1895 he devised an apparatus which showed experimentally that cathode rays transport a negative electric charge; thus he contributed to the development of the concept of the electron. By brilliant experimentation, Perrin verified a theoretical prediction that the Brownian motion should be describable by the gas laws (1908). For this research and its extension to the subject of equilibrium of sedimentation, Perrin received the Nobel prize, 1926. He was a fellow of the Royal Society.—*D. H. D. R.*

PERSISTENCE: in meteorology, the tendency for a condition to continue for a short period; *e.g.* tomorrow's temperature is more likely than not to be similar to that of today. Persistence is a useful forecasting tool, particularly for 1- to 2-hr forecasts of conditions at airports and for forecasting winds at great heights, where 12-hr changes in wind direction and speed tend to be very small. It is one of the factors used in assessing the value of weather forecasts.—*P. L.*

PERSPECTIVE: a method of organizing objects in a picture. *Conceptual perspective* depends on certain conventions which may have a historical basis or symbolic meaning. The resulting picture may have little relation to reality. *Optical perspective* is a method of organization that attempts to convey the same impression to the eyes of the viewer of the picture as

Focused perspective is illustrated by view down railroad tracks. Although tracks are parallel, they appear to converge at the "vanishing point." (*Northern Pacific Railroad*)

would the actual scene. Rules of drawing to accomplish this end were discovered by Renaissance painters, notably Alberti, Piero della Francesca, Leonardo da Vinci, and Albrecht Dürer, each of whom wrote a treatise on the subject. These men recognized that the art of painting depended upon the science of perspective, which is wholly mathematical. Much of projective geometry stemmed from the study of perspective.

The basic principle of *focused perspective* is illustrated by a representation of a railroad track, along which the viewer is looking. The rails, which are known to be parallel, appear to come together; hence, in the picture, they are so drawn. The point where they converge is the vanishing point. In the physical scene this point would not be reached by the rails,

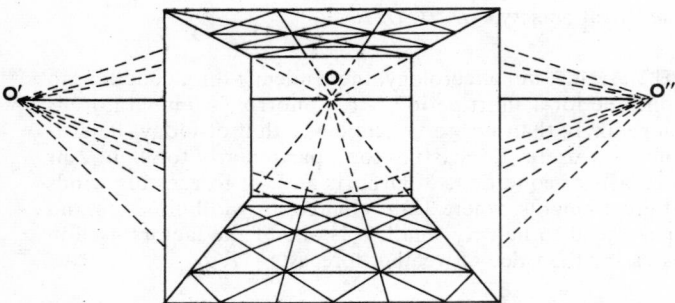

In formal system of perspective, all parallel lines, except those parallel to horizon (line O'OO'') and those vertical to horizon, appear to vanish at points along horizon.

but would be infinitely far away. The illusion of distance is created by the foreshortening of distances perpendicular to the plane of the picture, as indicated by the closer spacing of the ties in the background. Similarly, the lines of a room which are perpendicular to a viewer appear to converge at a vanishing point *O,* as in the figure, but other parallel lines, *e.g.* the diagonals of the floor tiles, meet on the horizontal line through *O,* which is the horizon line, or vanishing line. —*H. C.*

PERSPIRATION: see SWEAT GLAND.

PERTURBATIONS: in astronomy, deviations from the mean path of one celestial body about another, caused by the attraction of other bodies or by a resisting medium. If subject solely to the attraction of the Sun, a planet would move in an elliptical orbit with the Sun at one focus; but actually the combined attraction of the other members of the solar system distorts this orbit. Such perturbations are not confined to the Sun and planets: they occur anywhere in space whenever more than two bodies are involved (*e.g.* satellite systems, multiple stars). The mathematical expressions describing a perturbed orbit contain secular terms (which remain proportional to time and powers of time for extremely long periods) and periodic terms (comparable to oscillations). Secular terms arise from the manner in which the orbits of the perturbing bodies are oriented in space. They cause changes in the eccentricity, inclination, and position of the nodes and line of apsides of the perturbed orbit. Periodic terms arise from changes in the mutual distances of the perturbing bodies. They do not affect the orbital elements, but continually shift the body from the position it would have in its mean orbit (*i.e.* above or below, ahead or behind, or sideways from that position). The effect of these periodic terms may become cumulative if the revolution period of the perturbing planet is a common multiple of that of the perturbed body, because

the two objects then return periodically to the same relative position. The net result is that the revolution period of the perturbed body eventually undergoes a permanent change and is no longer commensurable with that of the perturbing planet. This phenomenon is responsible for the absence of asteroids at distances from the Sun where their period would be commensurable with that of Jupiter; the resulting voids in the asteroid belt are known as *Kirkwood's Gaps.*

Other classic examples of the effect of perturbations within the solar system are the gradual change in the orbits of periodic comets from their original parabolic shape to an elliptical one, and the variations in their periods; *e.g.* the period of Halley's comet has varied by as much as 2½ yr from its average value.

Satellite systems undergo additional perturbations caused by the flattening of the parent planet, owing to the uneven distribution of mass within the perturbing body. The motions of artificial satellites, which obey the same laws, are further complicated by the effect of Earth's atmosphere, which acts as a resisting medium. Unless the satellite's distance exceeds the limits of Earth's atmosphere, this *atmospheric drag* gradually retards the motion of the satellite and causes it to spiral back to Earth.—*S. D. G.*

PETRIFACTION: the process of changing or being changed into material having stony characteristics. It is an aspect of the mineralizing process called replacement; it is commonly associated with wood that has been replaced molecule for molecule by silica (generally opal or chalcedony). The petrified forests of our Western states are splendid examples. Forests were buried by ash fall from volcanic eruptions, and burial prevented total decay of the wood. Later, ground water circulated through the ash, picked up silica from it, and carried it to and into the logs. There slowly the silica was deposited, replacing the wood bit by bit. Today these logs are a storehouse of semiprecious gem material—all the cryptocrystalline varieties of quartz such as agate, carnelian, chrysoprase, jasper. Sometimes wood is replaced by opal. The replacement is so minute that as a rule the cell structure of the wood is preserved, and even the growth rings, bark, and similar features can easily be recognized. Of the many such sites, probably best known is Petrified Forest National Monument in the Painted Desert in Arizona.—*R. E. M.*

PETROCHEMICALS: products made by chemical conversion of natural gas or oil refinery products or by-products. The term literally, but inaccurately, means "rock chemicals." Generally petrochemicals are organic compounds, *i.e.* compounds of carbon and hydrogen which may also contain oxygen, nitrogen, or sulfur. Many basic petrochemicals were originally made commercially from other raw materials, as methyl alcohol by dry distillation of wood, ethyl alcohol by fermentation of various vegetable materials, butyl alcohol by fermentation of corn, benzene, phenol, and toluene from coal tar, acetylene from coke plus lime and water, and ammonia from coke plus air and water. Isopropyl alcohol, the earliest commercial "petrochemical," was first made on a large scale in 1920 from propylene in refinery by-product gas; it is one of the few never previously made commercially from other raw materials. By 1930 petrochemical ethyl alcohol, butyl alcohol, acetone, and ethylene glycol and diglycol had pushed petrochemical production to about 140 million lb/yr, still only 1% of total organic and inorganic chemical production. In 1960 petrochemicals accounted for about 30% of the total dollar volume of U. S. chemical production.

The basic petrochemical "building blocks"—ammonia, acetylene, ethylene, propylene, the butylenes, and "synthesis

1, 3-Butadiene, one of the most important petrochemicals, is stored in spherical tanks before shipment. Most of the 1½ billion lb of butadiene produced yearly in the U. S. A. is used in the manufacture of nylon, synthetic rubber, and latex paints. Rising above the storage tanks, in background, is a catalytic cracker. (*Standard Oil Co., N. J.*)

gas" (carbon monoxide and hydrogen)—are produced from either crude oil, natural gas, or oil-refinery by-product gases. Benzene, toluene, the xylenes, cyclohexane, naphthalene, the pentanes and pentenes, and many other hydrocarbons from oil are also important basic petrochemicals. Acetylene and ammonia (from coke) and benzene and naphthalene (from coal tar) are still produced in large amounts. Many important chemical products today, while predominantly petrochemical, are not entirely so, *e.g.* the important chemicals phenol, aniline, acrylonitrile, hydrogen cyanide, acetone, and their many derivatives; the plastics polystyrene and polyvinylchloride; molding resins of the phenol-formaldehyde and urea-formaldehyde type; surface-coating resins of the acrylic and alkyd types; synthetic fibers of the acrylic and polyamide types; synthetic rubbers of the styrene-butadiene and acrylonitrile-butadiene types; synthetic detergents based on dodecylbenzene or petrochemical alcohols; fertilizers based on ammonia and its derivatives. But 100% petrochemical in origin are many important chemicals ranging from ethylene oxide and its many derivatives, *e.g.* ethylene glycol (used for permanent anti-freeze and synthetic fibers), to terephthalic acid (film and synthetic fibers) and high-boiling alcohols

(plasticizers and detergents). Examples of ultimate products derived entirely from petrochemicals are the plastics polyethylene and polypropylene, also useful as fibers; synthetic rubbers of the polyisoprene, polybutadiene, and polyisobutylene types; synthetic fibers of the polyester type; and many insecticides.—*W. B. P.*

PETROLEUM: a complex liquid mixture of hydrocarbons (compounds of carbon and hydrogen) ranging from those containing one carbon atom (methane or natural gas) to complex molecules containing perhaps 100 carbon atoms. Sulfur, nitrogen, and even certain metals may be present in small amounts. Hundreds of compounds of varying composition, molecular weight, and structure (see PARAFFINS; NAPHTHENE; AROMATIC COMPOUNDS) have been identified. Their properties are extremely varied: some boil below room temperature; some cannot be distilled without decomposition; all are combustible. Countless special products come from petroleum: lubricants, waxes, solvents, asphalts for roofs and roads, medicinal oils, and numberless chemical derivatives. But the tremendous growth of the petroleum industry has been based on demand for fuels: gasoline, diesel fuel, house heating oils,

World's first oil boom: In Aug. 1859 at Titusville, Pa., Edwin L. Drake completed the first successful oil well drilled specifically for petroleum. Spurred by the demand for "lamp oil" (kerosene), other drillers soon flocked to the oil fields of W Pennsylvania. (*Texas Co.*)

and heavy fuel oils for industrial furnaces and steam and power generation. In 1920 petroleum (including natural gas) supplied 17.7% of the U. S. energy requirement for power and heat, coal 78.4%, and water power 3.9%. By 1960 our total energy requirement had quadrupled, but petroleum supplied 73%, coal 23.1%, and water power 3.9%. This "revolution" was partly due to the convenience and efficiency of petroleum products, partly to low costs.

Origin and Occurrence: Petroleum formed from sedimentary organic deposits (see SEDIMENTARY ROCK) in prehistoric lakes or oceans by reactions still obscure; heat and pressure of subsequent overlying deposits were factors. Of oil in the U. S., about 43% occurs in geologic formations of the Cenozoic Period (1 to 75 million yr ago), 43% Mesozoic (75 to 200 million yr), and 14% Paleozoic (200 to 500 million yr ago). Petroleum is found in porous rock formations, typically sandstone or limestone, in zones where geologic upheavals have, by upthrusting or slippage, produced traps of porous formations between impervious ones. Natural gas is found in similar traps and is often associated with oil. In the U. S. A., oil is produced in significant amounts in 23 states, starting in Pennsylvania in 1859, Ohio and W Virginia in 1860, and California in 1861. Leading states in cumulative total production up to 1961 were Texas, 36.4% (starting 1889); California, 18.4%; Oklahoma, 12.6% (starting 1891); Louisiana, 8.4% (starting 1902); and Kansas, 5.1% (starting 1889).

History of Use: Petroleum, in the form of surface deposits of asphalt, was known and used before 3000 B. C. It was also found as liquid seepages or skimmings from springs and salt wells. By A. D. 100 it was being refined (distilled) in the Near East to make naphtha as the base for "Greek Fire." Oil springs were observed in North America in 1627, and by 1755 the Pennsylvania and Ohio oil fields were being indicated on maps. Between 1800 and 1850 "rock oil" from seepages and

Offshore oil-drilling: Steadily increasing demand for petroleum, with depletion of underground deposits, has led to exploitation of underwater oil fields. Production from offshore rigs such as this one off Louisiana coast had increased to about 200 million bbl by 1961. (*Standard Oil Co., N. J.*)

springs was exploited in the U. S. A., and to some extent in England, as a liniment and internal medicine—a centuries-old practice among American Indians and others. Meanwhile whale oil, distilled spirits of turpentine, and finally "coal oil" (distilled from tar produced by coking coal in closed retorts) displaced the candle for purposes of illumination; then the discovery that "rock oil" could substitute for "coal oil" started commercial production and use of petroleum. The Drake well completed at Titusville, Pa., Aug. 1859, was the first successful one drilled specifically for petroleum; more wells and small refineries followed, and commercial success of "lamp oil" (kerosene) led to rapid expansion of both drilling and refining. Lighter (lower-boiling) oils were mixed with air to produce an illuminating gas that could be distributed in pipes. With the sudden spread of automobiling around 1910, gasoline became a major product.

Exploration for Oil: Drake's 1859 well, a producer at 69 ft, was located by looking for surface seepages, as were many that succeeded it. As data on oil occurrences accumulated, they were correlated with geological formations, and this information, with test "core" drillings, formed the basis for new drilling. Since the 1930s, more sophisticated methods of prospecting have been in use. Magnetometers or gravitometers detect local differences in Earth's magnetic or gravimetric field and help to locate underground formations in which oil might occur. Analyses of soil for traces of hydrocarbons may reveal underlying oil deposits. But seismic surveying is now the most important method. An explosive charge is detonated at the surface, and each of several interconnected receiving stations records the exact time when shock waves reflected or refracted from underground strata are detected. Since these waves travel at different speeds through strata of differing density and type, the nature and configuration of the underground strata can be mapped and the likelihood of petroleum deposits estimated. See SEISMOLOGY.

Drilling for Oil: From 1859 to 1960 a total of about 1,864,000 oil and gas wells were drilled in the U. S. A.; of these 27% were unproductive dry holes and 599,977 or 32% were still in production in 1960. Despite more sophisticated exploration methods, oil has become progressively more difficult to find, as witness the fact that dry holes in 1958 were 37.6% of the total drilled. For "exploratory wells" or "wild-cats" the percentage of dry holes was about 87%.

In 1859 "cable drilling," in which a drill bit on the end of a cable is raised and then dropped in the hole, was the only available method. In 1900 the deepest U. S. oil well drilled by this method was 2,800 ft. Shortly after, "rotary drilling" came into use. The bit is fixed on the end of a rotating drill pipe inside a casing, the casing being set lower and lower as the drilling progresses. A heavy artificial "mud" is circulated down through the drill pipe, out through the bit, and back up the casing to remove the rock fragments. In 1960 about 74% of all U. S. oil and gas wells were rotary-drilled, their average depth was 4,000 ft, and the deepest were 25,340 ft (dry) and 20,745 ft (producing). Average cost per well is over $50,000; the deepest may cost over a million dollars.

After completion a well may flow freely, producing up to thousands of barrels daily, as a result of high "reservoir pressure" generated by natural gas trapped with the oil or the pressure of water layers above the oil. Ultimately, pumping may be necessary to get the last of the recoverable oil. Other expedients to increase oil recovery include: fracturing of the oil-bearing formation by explosives or by applying pressure at the well head; partial dissolving of the formation by acid; pumping of water, natural gas, or other gases down one well to increase the flow from adjacent wells in the same formation; even pumping air down and producing combustion in the formation around one well to heat the oil and promote flow from adjacent wells. These expedients have increased the possible final recovery of total oil in a formation from 25% formerly to 50 or 75% today. In 1960, 88% of the 599,977 producing wells in the U. S. A. were operating by some form of artificial lift. In 1860 typical Pennsylvania wells produced 10 bbl per day; in 1960 the U. S. average was only 12.0 bbl per day. However, about 65% of the 1960 producing wells were "stripper wells" yielding only a few barrels per day, and most wells capable of large production were held back by state oil-conservation regulations.

Underwater drilling offshore is practiced in California and in the Gulf of Mexico, mainly off Louisiana and Texas. Offshore production in 1960 was only a few percent of the U. S. total.

Transportation: As demand grew, more efficient ways of shipping petroleum and its products were needed than the original one of ordinary barrels. A tank car holding 90 bbl was introduced in 1865 (modern tank cars hold 200 bbl). Pipelines (the first trunk line was completed in Pennsylvania in 1878) in 1960 amounted to over 152,000 mi of crude oil and products lines. Seagoing tankers, carrying loads of 4,000 to 10,000 bbl were first used 1880–85. By 1960, tankers carrying over 1,000,000 bbl were in use.—*W. B. P.*

PETROLEUM REFINING: distillation of crude oil to make desired lighter oils. Refining of oil from ground seepages has been practiced at least since A. D. 100. Soon after the drilling of Drake's well in Pennsylvania in 1859 (the first drilled specifically for petroleum), thousands more were drilled, and refineries sprang up. In 1873 there were 103 in the U. S. A., with an average capacity of 445 bbl per day; in 1961 there were 296, with an *average* daily capacity of 36,000 bbl. Total U. S. capacity is about 10,600,000 bbl—almost half of the free-world total of 23,500,000.

Former Methods: Early refining was simple. Crude oil was distilled in horizontal or vertical cylindrical stills of a few hundred barrels' capacity, to eliminate light products and recover kerosene, or "lamp oil." Shortly it was discovered that by running stills slowly, heavier oils could be *cracked* (large molecules split into smaller ones) and yields of kerosene could be increased. Light naphthas (gasoline) were mainly waste products until the automobile age began, around 1910. Lubricating oils were an early but relatively crude product, as was paraffin wax. Treating or purification of products was limited to washing with small amounts of sulfuric acid followed by caustic, and sometimes filtering through clay, to improve color and odor. By 1900 the main development was the *continuous battery still,* in which a series of horizontal stills were interconnected, undistilled oil flowing by gravity to progressively hotter stills, thus producing progressively heavier distillates. "Sweetening" of kerosene and gasoline (deodorization by sulfur removal) by treating with solutions of sodium plumbite also came into use around this time. By 1910 the electric light and the automobile had begun to reverse the sovereignty of kerosene over gasoline. In 1913 the *Burton cracking process,* which doubled gasoline yield, came into use; "gas oil" (a heavy distillate oil) was heated under a pressure of about 115 lb/in.^{2} to prevent the oil from distilling before it cracked, *i.e.* decomposed thermally into lower-boiling products.

The 1920s saw a revolution in refining. Continuous battery stills were replaced by multi-thousand-barrel-per-day *"pipe stills."* These heat the crude oil rapidly in pipe coils in the furnaces and flues of oil- or gas-fired heaters, and discharge the oil at atmospheric pressure into vertical fractionating towers 100 ft or more high. Unvaporized residual oil is

Refining methods in transition: Huge stacks of pipe stills (*middle, right*) are silhouetted in the blaze of lights from the newer catalytic cracking units (*left and background*). (*Standard Oil Co., N. J.*)

drawn from the bottom; vapors condense and are fractionated on the "bubble trays" in the upper section of the tower. Heavy-gas oil, light-gas oil, and heavy naphtha or kerosene may be withdrawn progressively up the tower. Light naphtha or gasoline leaves the top as a vapor and is condensed by external coolers. The unvaporized residual oil may be further distilled under vacuum in another tower, for production of lubricating oil stocks, etc. Heaters and "bubble towers" are used by hundreds in a modern refinery as part of almost every process unit.

Likewise in the '20s a multitude of new cracking processes were developed. In general, all heated gas oil under pressure to its cracking temperature, far beyond its boiling point at atmospheric pressure, and discharged it into a large insulated but unheated soaking drum, where it continued to crack, pressures of 500 to 1,500 lb/in.^{2} being commonly used. Then, passing to a flash drum, heavy tars formed in the process were removed; next, a bubble tower separated product gasoline from uncracked gas oil, and the latter was recycled to the heater. By 1930, percentage yield of gasoline from crude oil was as high as today. Lubricating oils, however, were still being made by elementary acid-caustic-clay treating methods, and the key to quality was still the selection of crude oils that inherently gave good lube stocks.

Modern Methods: In the 1930s modern oil refining began. Efficiency was largely a matter of increasing the size of important units. Crude stills reached capacities of 50,000 bbl per day; today there are many that exceed 150,000 bbl daily. Thermal cracking units, of the type developed in the '20s, reached around 50,000 bbl per day charging capacity. Large continuous-treating plants, using old principles, also contributed to the output.

Coking, to recover useful oils from unwanted or unusable heavy residual oils, was also modernized during the '30s. Formerly it involved simply heating the bottom of a horizontal cylindrical still until the heavy oil contents were distilled down to coke, and digging the coke out by hand; now the heavy oil is rapidly heated in a pipe heater far above its coking temperature, is discharged into a large insulated drum, and is left to coke by its own contained heat. Coke is removed from the bottom of the drum by hydraulic jets.

Constantly increasing power output, compression ratio, speed (r.p.m.), and operating temperature of automobile and aircraft engines multiplied product-quality problems. For gasoline this meant constant increase of anti-knock quality

"Bubble towers" and a "cat cracker": Most of the technology of 20th-cent. petroleum refining has been designed to solve but one basic problem: how to derive a greater percentage of the more valuable, lower-boiling hydrocarbons (e.g. gasoline) from crude oil. In fractionating columns or "bubble towers," crude oil is separated into high-boiling and low-boiling fractions; but since only about 20% of the yield of a fractionating column is suitable for gasoline, devices such as the fluid catalytic cracking unit (*right*) have been designed. Such "cat crackers" attain over 50% yield of gasoline from crude oil. (*Standard Oil Co., N. J.*)

(octane rating) and stability. For lubricating oils it meant increased stability, decreased production of engine deposits, improved lubrication under high bearing pressures, less thinning and thickening at high and low temperatures (higher "viscosity index"), and less corrosion of bearing metals. Quality demands soon led to catalytic polymerization of propylenes and butylenes in refinery gas from cracking units, such polymer gasoline being of quite high octane rating. For aviation gasoline, such polymers were hydrogenated to produce *iso-octane* of still higher anti-knock value. Polymer hydrogenation was soon made obsolete by the *alkylation process,* which used sulfuric or hydrofluoric acid as catalyst for the reaction of isobutane and butylenes in refinery gas to produce the equivalent of iso-octane in one step.

A major contributor to gasoline quality in the '30s was *thermal reforming,* in which heavier fractions of the gasoline itself are cracked in units similar to those for cracking heavy oils to gasoline, but operated under more severe conditions. The real breakthrough came in April 1937, when *catalytic cracking* was first demonstrated as a commercial possibility. The stability problem, particularly severe with cracked gasolines, also was solved in the '30s by development of antioxidants, usually aminophenolic compounds, which almost completely prevent gum formation.

Refiners could hardly have kept up with the demand for higher gasoline octane ratings without use of tetraethyl lead ("TEL") as an anti-knock additive. First used commercially in 1923, it became indispensable to the refiner for obtaining the last increment of required octane rating and is now used in 98% of all U. S. automotive gasoline. An average proportion of about 0.10% by weight adds 5 to 10 extra "octane numbers" to the anti-knock rating of the base gasoline.

The '30s also saw development and wide use of practically all the modern processes for improvement of lubricating oils. First was *solvent extraction,* in which lubrication stocks are treated with immiscible selective solvents (notably phenol, furfural, or dichlordiethylether) which dissolve and remove the aromatic-type hydrocarbons, leaving the predominantly

paraffinic types, which do not get too thick or too thin with temperature changes in use. This made the industry independent of Pennsylvania crude, the former source—a limited one—of high-viscosity-index oils.

Solvent dewaxing displaced the old and laborious methods of chilling and filter-pressing, the most common solvents being propane or methylethyl ketone, sometimes combined with others. *Propane deasphalting* made it possible to eliminate asphaltenes, which tend to produce carbon deposits in engines. Additives to improve lubrication under extreme pressure conditions, to reduce bearing corrosion, to improve stability, to lower "pour points," and to improve viscosity index were all developed and used in this period. Today such additives may exceed 15% by volume in a high-grade motor oil.

New Processes: By World War II, new catalytic cracking processes had been developed, notably the *"fluid"* process. In the fixed-bed process first developed, carbon deposited on the catalyst was burned off *in situ* and elaborate means for removing its heat of combustion were needed. In the *fluid* process, first used in 1941, the catalyst is finely divided and is continuously cycled in suspension between the cracking zone and a regeneration zone where carbon is burned off and the catalyst reheated under controlled conditions. After the fluid process, *moving-bed processes* were developed in which the granular spent catalyst drops out of the bottom of the reactor into a regenerator and, after carbon is burned off, is returned to the reactor top by pneumatic lift. All these processes use natural or synthetic clay-type catalysts at somewhat lower temperatures and much lower pressures than those used in thermal cracking, and all produce more olefinic gases and higher-octane gasoline than the thermal processes. The largest catalytic cracking units built have had about 55,000 bbl per day capacity, but units as small as 1,200 bbl per day are operable.

Another very important development of this period was *catalytic reforming,* first called *hydroforming.* It first used a molybdenum-oxide-type catalyst, although modern forms of the process use platinum-type catalysts. In all forms, gasoline-range naphthas are passed over the catalyst at moderate temperatures and pressures in the presence of hydrogen, which prevents formation of carbon and its deposition on the catalyst. The process forms aromatic hydrocarbons (notably benzene-toluene-xylene) and produces hydrogen, part of which is recycled. The liquid product is high-octane gasoline and also is a source for pure aromatic hydrocarbons for petrochemical uses. Typical units have around 10,000 bbl per day capacity but have ranged from 200 to 30,000.

World War II placed tremendous demands on the petroleum industry for aviation gasoline—mostly 100-octane grade, produced in very small volume before the war. This, plus demands for the synthetic-rubber program, required between 1940 and 1945 about a 30% increase in crude oil refined annually. It necessitated tremendous expansion of catalytic cracking capacity and also of alkylation and hydroforming capacity. This expansion continued, along with general expansion of U. S. refining capacity from 5,300,000 bbl per day in 1945 to 9,800,000 in 1960. One major new process is *hydrotreating*. Surplus hydrogen produced by catalytic reformers (hydroformers) is used to treat various stocks, in the presence of catalysts at moderate temperatures and pressures, to desulfurize and otherwise improve them. It is used mainly on charge stocks for catalytic reformers to improve catalyst life in the reforming operation, but it is also used to reduce sulfur content and otherwise improve quality of jet fuels, kerosene, furnace oils, and diesel fuels.—*W. B. P.*

PETROLOGY AND PETROGRAPHY: Petrology is the branch of geology that deals with the natural history of ROCKS—rock origin, occurrence, composition, alteration, and decay. Petrography, more limited in scope, is concerned largely with the systematic description and classification of all rocks as based on field and laboratory observations. Very simply, rocks are aggregates or mixtures of minerals; such mixtures are not completely random or accidental but range between more or less well-defined, and commonly highly restricted, limits. Although usually polymineralic (*e.g.* granite, basalt), rocks may be essentially monomineralic (quartzite, marble, glacial ice); and some consist of no true minerals (coal, obsidian). Rocks may be consolidated (granite) or unconsolidated (sand, gravel).

The most useful tool in petrography is the polarizing or petrographic microscope. It permits examination of rock material in thin sections (1/1000 in. thick) or in powdered or disaggregated form. It enables one to observe detailed rock textures and structures and rapidly determine the chemical composition of the individual minerals by measuring their optical properties. Supplementary procedures include standard chemical analysis, microchemical tests, and various types of x-ray techniques. Studies of rock synthesis and phase equilibria under controlled conditions of temperature and pressure have contributed tremendously to such petrological problems as order of crystallization in rocks, changes in composition of residual fluids, and nature of transformation in the solid state. Much of petrology is closely allied to GEOCHEMISTRY. Field studies give evidence of the size, shape, composition, internal structure, and mutual relations of rock units; and when combined with the knowledge gained from laboratory investigations, such studies enable one to learn much about the time, environment, and manner of rock formation.—*C. C.*

PETRUNKEVITCH, ALEXANDER, 1875-1964, Russian-U. S. zoologist; b. Piski, Russia. For many years the leading scientist interested in the taxonomy, anatomy, sense of sight, and

mating of spiders, and the evolution of fossil arachnids, he was associated with Yale Univ. from 1917. He was a member of the National Academy of Sciences.—*D. H. D. R.*

PETTERSSEN, SVERRE, 1898– , Norwegian-U. S. meteorologist; b. Hadsel. His research has been in synoptic and dynamic meteorology, especially in the technique of weather forecasting. He was in the Norwegian Meteorological Service (1925-39), was advisor to the Meteorological Office of the British Air Ministry (1942-45), taught at Mass. Inst. of Technology, and has been professor of meteorology at the Univ. of Chicago since 1952. Petterssen's publications include *Weather Analysis and Forecasting* (1940).—*D. H. D. R.*

PETTY, SIR WILLIAM, 1623-87, English statistician, physician, and political economist; b. Ramsey. His survey of Irish lands appropriated by Cromwell was the first scientific survey on a large scale. After the Restoration he returned to England and was knighted by Charles II, who made him surveyor-general of Ireland. He was a pioneer in the science of statistics, his Irish survey being based on sociological data. Petty is best remembered as a political economist. His *Treatise on Taxes and Contributions* advanced the doctrine that price is determined by the labor needed for production. He was a fellow of the Royal Society.—*H. C.*

PEWTER: a tin alloy used since ancient times to make metal ware, especially domestic utensils and vessels used in church services; it was often a substitute for silver. Pewter was originally tin alloyed with lead, but now is usually tin with small amounts of antimony and copper.—*Ru. M.*

pH: see pH VALUE.

PHARYNX: in vertebrates, a common passage for food and respiratory water or gases, located between the mouth and the esophagus; in some invertebrates, the anterior part of the alimentary canal. In fishes, the pharynx has a series of lateral openings, the gill slits; water is taken in through the mouth and forced out through the gill slits over the gills in respiration. Food passes from the mouth through the pharynx into the esophagus. In air-breathing vertebrates, the gill slits close early in embryonic life, but the pharynx remains a common passage for respiratory air and for food.—*B. T. S.*

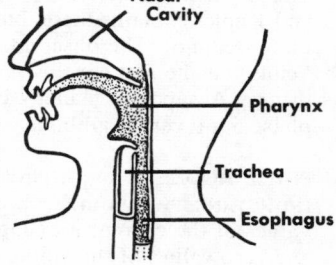

Human pharynx is portion of alimentary tract leading from mouth to esophagus. It is crossed by respiratory tract leading from nasal passages to trachea. (After Manter)

PHASE: in astronomy, the fraction of the apparent disc of the Moon or a planet that appears, at any time, to be illuminated by the Sun. When the Moon is opposite the Sun in the sky, the illuminated hemisphere faces Earth, so that the Moon appears "full." Because of its orbital motion about Earth, the Moon appears to move eastward against the stars at a rate greater than that of the Sun. As the angular distance of the Moon from the Sun increases, the illuminated hemisphere no longer faces Earth, and a crescent of the disc is dark. The Moon is then "gibbous." When the angular distance of Moon from Sun is 90°, the Moon appears half-illuminated; it is then at Third, or Last, Quarter. As the angular distance still further decreases, only a crescent of the disc is illuminated. Finally, as the Moon passes between Earth and the Sun, the illuminated hemisphere faces away from Earth, the apparent disc is dark, and the Moon is New. If the Moon's orbit were exactly in the plane of Earth's orbit, the Moon would pass exactly between the Sun and Earth once every synodic period (the period of the cycle of the phases), and a total eclipse of the Sun would occur. Actually, because of the tilt of the Moon's orbit, total eclipses occur only on those relatively rare occasions when the Moon is New and also in the plane of the Earth's orbit. Even at New Moon, except for occasions of total solar eclipses, a very thin crescent of the Moon should be seen, but in practice, it cannot be picked up by eye until the Moon is about 18 hr past New. After New Moon, the Moon becomes a crescent again, the points of the crescent always pointing away from the Sun. When the angular distance of the Moon from the Sun is again 90°, on the other

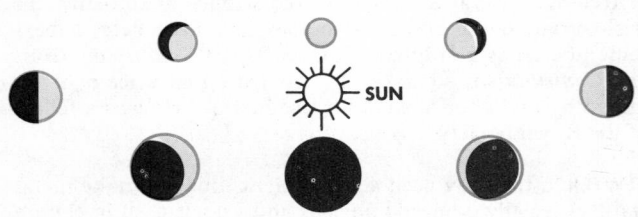

Inferior planet shows phases to us as it follows orbit around Sun. It looks brightest in crescent phase (*foreground*), because apparent area of visible part of lighted surface is then greatest. Superior planets (*e.g.* Mars) can exhibit only full and gibbous phases.

side of the Sun, the Moon is at First Quarter. Finally, the Moon passes through gibbous phases to Full Moon again. The synodic period lasts, on the average, about 29½ days.

Under favorable atmospheric conditions, the part of the Moon not illuminated by the Sun may be faintly visible. It is illuminated by sunlight reflected from Earth to the Moon and back again (see EARTHSHINE).

The inferior planets, Mercury and Venus, also show phases. The sun-centered description of the solar system of Copernicus and Kepler explains these, but the Earth-centered Ptolemaic theory cannot. The observation by Galileo of the phases of Venus was the first conclusive evidence against the Ptolemaic theory. A superior planet can never be seen in a crescent phase but it can be gibbous.—*M. W. O.*

PHASE ANGLE: In an a-c circuit, when either CAPACITANCE or INDUCTANCE (or both) is present, the maximum and zero values of the current may lag behind or lead the maximum and zero values of the voltage. If ac is represented by a sine

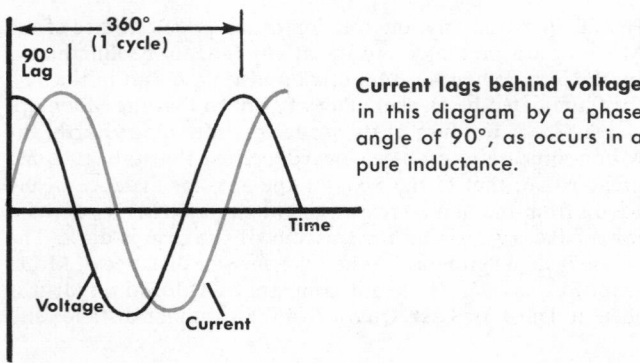

Current lags behind voltage in this diagram by a phase angle of 90°, as occurs in a pure inductance.

wave, and a cycle (the variation in voltage or current from zero to its positive maximum, to zero, to its negative maximum, and back to zero—one complete cycle) is divided into 360°, the number of degrees by which the current lags or leads the voltage is called the *phase angle*. The phase angle varies from 0° for pure resistance to 90° for pure inductance or capacitance.—*A. L.*

PHASE MODULATION: see MODULATION.

PHASE RULE: an equation for determining the number of variables that can be given arbitrary values in a system in equilibrium without upsetting the equilibrium. The equation is $v = 2 + n - f$, where v is the number of variables, n the number of components, and f the phases of the system. For example, if water is in equilibrium with its saturated vapor, there is one component, water ($n = 1$), and two phases, liquid and vapor ($f = 2$); therefore $v = 1$. This means that at an arbitrarily chosen pressure (one variable), the system will remain in equilibrium, but that the other possible variable, temperature, is uniquely determined for that pressure. Or the temperature may be chosen arbitrarily, but then the pressure is uniquely determined for the particular temperature chosen. Another example is a chemically defined homogeneous fluid, which has one component ($n = 1$), and one phase ($f = 1$), since only liquid is present; thus $v = 2$. This means that *both* pressure and temperature can be arbitrarily chosen without disturbing the system's equilibrium. For a system in equilibrium consisting of ice, water, and water vapor, there are three phases—solid, liquid, and vapor ($f = 3$)—and one component ($n = 1$), so $v = 0$. This means that the three phases of water can exist together in equilibrium at a fixed temperature and a fixed pressure only; neither can be varied arbitrarily (see TRIPLE POINT). The phase rule, which was derived by J. Willard Gibbs, can be expanded to apply to systems where chemical reactions are taking place. Although simple in appearance, and applied here to examples where the necessary conditions for equilibrium can be determined by inspection, the phase rule is of tremendous value in the study of complex systems and of great practical value especially in the study of alloy systems.—*A. L.*

PHASES OF MATTER: distinct physical states of matter that differ in large-scale properties. Matter is commonly regarded as having three phases: gaseous, liquid, solid. Highly ionized gas called PLASMA may be considered another phase, as can various solid states characterized by definite atomic or molecular arrangements. Most changes of phase occur at fixed temperatures and are accompanied by heat transfer and change in volume, as in the freezing and boiling of water, and the change from one solid phase to another. The transition from one phase to another also involves changes in specific heat, electrical conductivity, and other gross properties. In metallurgy the various heat treatments (*e.g.* tempering, quenching) and forming methods (forging, cold-rolling) favor the phases that give a metal its mechanical properties (hardness, ductility, malleability, and elasticity).—*E. M. R.*

PHASE SPACE: an abstract mathematical "space" in which one dimension is allowed for each possible variable. Thus the phase space for a molecule of a monatomic gas is six-dimensional, since three dimensions are required to determine its position and three more to determine its velocity with respect to the position axes.—*E. M. R.*

PHASE VELOCITY: the speed of travel of a selected reference point (or phase) on a wave, such as its peak or trough. For an ELECTROMAGNETIC WAVE traveling in free space, the phase velocity is equal to the velocity of light, *c*. In an enclosed WAVE GUIDE, the phase velocity is greater than *c*.—*I. R.*

PHENOLOGY: the science concerned with *periodic* biological phenomena, *e.g.* stages in plant growth or in the migrations or development of insects or other animals, especially in relation to climate. The chronology of such biological events as the first bloom of certain species of plants or their fruiting as they vary from year to year serves to integrate important bioclimatic factors, and provides important sources of information on regional climatic variations. The oldest climatic records prepared by man are phenological; they predate by many centuries the oldest records made through use of meteorological instruments.—*W. C. J.*

PHENOLS: chemical compounds in which the hydroxyl group, OH, is attached to carbon in the nucleus of an aromatic compound. (In alcohols, the OH is linked to carbon in the chain structure of an aliphatic compound.)

Phenol
Hydroxybenzene

ortho-Cresol
ortho-Methylphenol

Ethyl alcohol
Hydroxyethane

The simplest of the phenols, hydroxybenzene (C_6H_5OH), is called "phenol" or "carbolic acid" (although it is not a true acid). It is poisonous and corrosive to the skin, but also toxic to micro-organisms; it was the first antiseptic, used by Lister in 1867. Hydroxyl derivatives of toluene are phenolic, and are called *cresols*. Phenol and the cresols are found in coal tar and wood tar. Phenol is made synthetically in large quantity for use as a chemical intermediate, principally for plastics.—*Ru. M.*

PHENOMENALISM (in physics): Phenomenalism offers both a theory about the *world* and a theory concerning the *meaning* of scientific terms. As regards the world, it asserts that only sensations, *e.g.* a particular sensation of smell or of touch, exist, and that all the other alleged "objects" of science must be understood as complicated assemblages of sensations. As regards the meaning of scientific terms, phenomenalism either asserts that these terms have no meaning at all, but function as parts of a calculating machine (the scientific theory) which enables us to predict the occurrence of sensations (*phenomenalistic instrumentalism*); or it asserts that whatever meaning a scientific term possesses is conferred upon it by the fact that it can be connected with, and explained with the help of, terms designating sensations; an explanation of this kind is called a *reduction* of the scientific term to sense data, and this version of phenomenalism is therefore also called *reductionism*. There exists not a single physical theory that has been constructed with the explicit purpose of providing an instrument for the prediction of sensations, or constructed in such a manner that its relation to sensations is explicit in the formalism. Instrumentalistic theories *do* exist, *e.g.* the quantum theory; but these theories are conceived as instruments for prediction of macroscopic *physical processes,* and not of sensation. Nor is there a single physical theory that contains even a passing reference to sensations. It is therefore necessary for the phenomenalist to *reinterpret* physics and to show that it only apparently talks about, and assumes the existence of, objects and processes that are not sensations or assemblages of sensations. It can be safely said that none of the numerous attempts at a phenomenalistic

reinterpretation of physics has been successful; phenomenalism does not give a correct account of physics.—*P. K. F.*

PHILOLAUS, 5th cent. B. C., Greek mathematician and astronomer; b. S Italy. The first of the Pythagoreans to publish, he wrote on mathematics, astronomy, and physiology, and suggested sagely that Earth moves around a "central fire" (the earliest known reference to the revolution of Earth). Only fragments of his writings remain.—*D. H. D. R.*

PHILOPONUS, JOHN, fl. 6th cent. A. D., Alexandrian physicist and philosopher. He introduced the concept of an "incorporeal motive force" into the study of dynamics, a concept that developed into *impetus* in the 14th cent. and into *momentum* in the 17th. Philoponus is the first person known to have suggested dropping objects of different weights in the study of free fall, and he attacked many of the Aristotelian ideas on mechanics.—*D. H. D. R.*

PHILOSOPHER'S STONE: see ALCHEMY.

PHILOSOPHIAE NATURALIS PRINCIPIA MATHEMATICA (The Mathematical Principles of Natural Philosophy), by Isaac Newton (1687): In this supreme work Newton enunciated the law of gravity (the force of attraction between two bodies is proportional to the product of their masses and inversely proportional to the square of the distance between them, or,

$$f = \frac{m_1 \cdot m_2}{d^2})$$

and demonstrated its ability to account for the observed phenomena of the planets, the Moon and other satellites, and the tides. Thus he solved the major problems of 17th-cent. physical science, at once confirming the stability of the Sun asserted by Copernicus, revealing the dynamical relationships underlying Kepler's empirical laws of planetary motion, and justifying the mathematical and mechanistic idea of nature adumbrated by Galileo, Descartes, and their successors. Newton did more than this, however, for he set the pattern of mathematical physics for the next 200 yr. In Book I he had constructed the abstract theory of motion for a particle impelled toward a center; in Book III he applied this theory to explain the celestial motions. In so doing Newton not only laid the foundations of dynamics as the fundamental part of physics, but showed how physical theory was rendered exact by the mathematical treatment of forces.

Title page of first edition of Newton's work. (*N. Y. Public Library*)

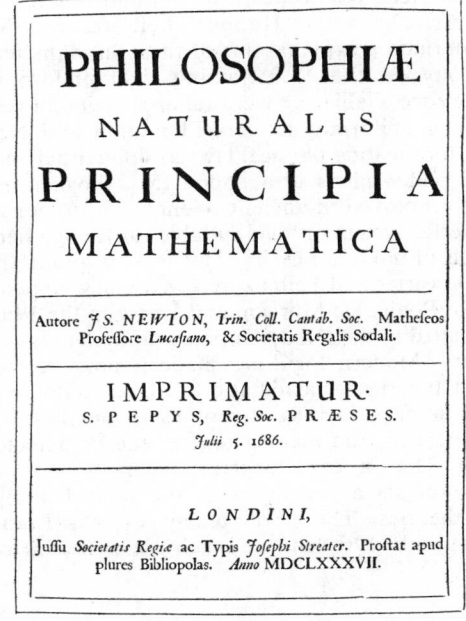

Never able himself to explore in this way any force of nature other than gravity, Newton clearly foresaw that theoretical physics would progress through the mathematical analysis of other forces. In the discussion of fluid dynamics in Book II, he gave further examples of the usefulness of this "mathematical way" in resolving complex phenomena.—*A. R. H.*

PHILOSOPHIE ZOOLOGIQUE (Zoological Philosophy), by Jean Baptiste Pierre Antoine de Monet de Lamarck (1809): Lamarck is the most important forerunner of the Darwinian theory of evolution. The *Philosophie zoologique* contains the second of three statements of evolution as expounded by Lamarck, the third appearing in his *Histoire naturelle des animaux sans vertebres* (1815). The argument for the mutability of species is based on the interaction of two factors. Most fundamental was the innate tendency toward greater complexity of structure. The second factor, with which Lamarck's name has become intimately associated, was the inheritance of acquired characteristics. According to Lamarck, if environmental influences upon the mechanism of heredity were excluded, the organisms would develop from the simplest to the most complex along a straight line. It was not until the publication of Darwin's ON THE ORIGIN OF SPECIES (1859), however, that organic evolution became an accepted part of biological thought.—*E. Me.*

PHILOSOPHY OF SCIENCE: the clarification of the concepts, principles, and methods of scientific inquiry, and the organization of knowledge into a unified view of nature. The problems of philosophy of science are of three types: (1) *intra-field problems* of analyzing the meanings of concepts and evaluating the consistency of inferences within a single discipline; (2) *inter-field problems* of coordinating knowledge in different sciences—*e.g.* determining the relation between mind, as studied by psychology, and body, as studied by physiology; and (3) *supra-field* or *general problems* of clarifying the methodological principles common to all fields of inquiry, and evaluating the impact of science on other forms of culture, *e.g.* art, technology, religion, and ethics.

Intra-field problems develop out of important changes in the theories and methods of a specific field of scientific inquiry. In the 17th cent., when physics was transformed from a body of qualitative generalizations and vague hypotheses into a system of mathematical laws, it became necessary to redefine "space," "matter," "motion," and "force," and to clarify the differences between the old and the new uses of these terms. Descartes, Hobbes, Leibniz, and Spinoza offered alternative explanations of these fundamental concepts of physics, thus constructing rival philosophies of physical science. Galileo's successful application of geometry in describing uniformly accelerated motion and Newton's success in formulating physical laws as differential equations persuaded philosophers to abandon the syllogistic rules of deduction employed in ancient science, and to construct a more powerful system of logic suitable for the mathematical calculations of modern physics. This task, begun in the 17th cent. by Descartes and Leibniz, received a new impetus with the work of Boole, De Morgan, and Peirce in the 19th cent., and culminated in the full development of SYMBOLIC LOGIC in this century. Modern logic has made it possible to recast established theories in axiomatic form, so that the logical relations among principles, hypotheses, and laws can be rigorously traced, and inconsistencies can be detected and eliminated. Thus a very substantial part of the work of philosophy of science consists in the logical analysis of scientific theories. The development of NON-EUCLIDEAN GEOMETRIES in the 19th cent., and their use in physics together

with new systems of algebra such as the tensor calculus, provoked new definitions of space, time, and motion. Similarly, the development of RELATIVITY theory and QUANTUM theory required new analyses of the concepts of matter, energy, position, and causality, and the formulation of new principles of inference, such as *n*-valued logic for probability computations.

Psychology and the social sciences became specialized scientific disciplines only toward the end of the 19th cent. Previously, studies of mind and society had been rather speculative branches of philosophy. The emergence of psychology as an experimental science stimulated philosophical analysis of central concepts such as sensation, perception, motivation, instinct, and habit, and of the logical relations of these concepts to the data of experimental and clinical research. Similarly, the adoption of controlled procedures of data-gathering and statistical generalization in studies of social behavior established sociology, economics, and anthropology as special sciences, whose new concepts and methods required philosophical clarification.

Inter-field problems arise out of uncertainty as to the relations between different branches of inquiry which depend on one another in varying degrees. Some fields of science have a more general scope than others, in that their concepts, laws, and theories form part of the equipment of other, more specialized fields. For example, logic and mathematics are applied to all the empirical sciences, both natural and social. Physical theory is applied to the special content of natural sciences, *e.g.* chemistry, biology, meteorology, and geology. In areas where sciences overlap to the degree that it is impossible to say which one predominates, the equal importance of each is indicated in such joint names as "biochemistry," "physical chemistry," or "biophysics." Because of this interdependence, issues arise concerning the exact degree of dependence of one science on another. Decisions on these matters cannot be made by specialists in a single field, and thus become subjects of philosophical discussion. In general, problems of interdependence are of two kinds: (1) preserving the consistency of theories in one field with theories in another field, *e.g.* determining whether purposive explanations in biology are consistent with physical principles such as the conservation of energy, and (2) clarifying the degree of dependence of a subordinate field on a more general field, *e.g.* the dependence of biology on physics, or of sociology on psychology. Traditionally, this issue of degree of dependence has been discussed in terms of the "reducibility" of some sciences to others. The philosophical view known as MECHANISM maintains that all the natural sciences (and, according to the more extreme mechanists, the social sciences as well) are reducible to physics. However, there are various degrees of mechanistic interpretation of science, depending on how the philosopher understands the notion of reducibility. In the narrowest sense, to say that one science is reducible to another is to claim that the concepts of the first are definable in terms of the concepts of the second, *e.g.* that the biological concepts of life, reproduction, and metabolism are definable in terms of the physical concepts of mass, force, velocity, electrical potential, and molecular structure. In a somewhat more moderate sense of "reducibility," one may mean to claim that the laws of the subordinate field are deducible from those of the more general field together with auxiliary hypotheses, *e.g.* that chemical laws governing molecular combinations may be deduced from physical laws of electrostatic attraction together with hypotheses as to the atomic structure of the component substances. But reducibility, even in this sense, is regarded by most contemporary philosophers as an unrealistic project. The most moderate form of mechanism regards other natural sciences as dependent on physics only in the sense that the laws of physics are necessary conditions for the validity of the laws of the other natural sciences, so that, for example, biological processes such as cellular division or genetic transmission must be described in a manner consistent with physical principles and laws.

Supra-field problems attract the widest interest because of their direct bearing on our common-sense view of nature. These problems arise from the attempt to organize scientific information into a unified system of knowledge. This is a vast enterprise which requires the interpretation of technical theories in terms of everyday language and common beliefs, the adjudication of apparent conflicts between technical findings and generally accepted principles of knowledge—*e.g.* the apparent conflict between the quantum mechanical description of a subatomic particle as having no exact position and velocity and the traditional conception of matter—and finally, the evaluation of scientific knowledge in relation to possible alternative modes of knowledge, such as theology, artistic insight, and metaphysics. This latter task raises many controversial issues, such as whether science provides adequate explanations of events or only descriptions of regular sequences which must then be explained by some higher mode of knowledge; whether scientific theories are accurate pictures of a reality hidden from direct observation (*e.g.* do electrons really exist?) or are merely symbolic devices to facilitate mathematical computations; whether science provides ethical as well as factual information or whether ethical judgment requires qualities of character and personal insight to which scientific training has no relevance; and whether science is of unqualified value to society or whether its value is dependent on how it is put to use.—*R. A.*

PHLOEM (or **bast**): the tissue of VASCULAR PLANTS that is specialized for the conduction of dissolved food. It consists primarily of sieve tube cells with perforated end walls, usually accompanied by companion cells.—*C. J. H.*

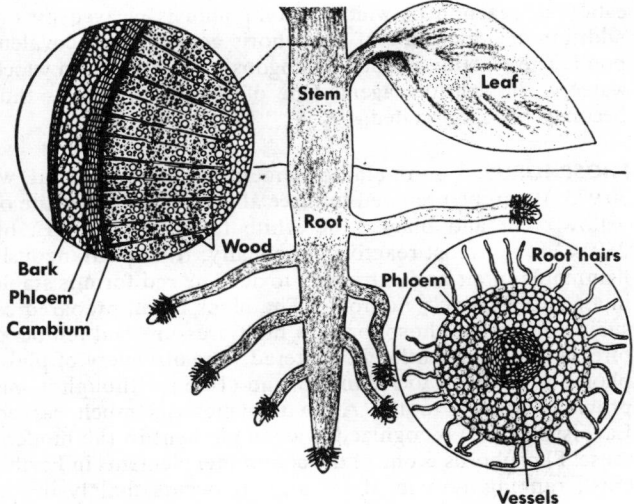

Phloem: Sections of generalized plant show phloem, or food-conducting tissue, to be in inner bark of stem and in central vascular cylinder of root (where it surrounds xylem vessels). (*From Young*)

PHONON: a unit, or quantum, of energy of a vibration of a crystal lattice (see CRYSTALLOGRAPHY). The random heat motion that all atoms undergo in a crystal can be thought of as the result of a large number of waves resembling sound waves traveling through the crystal. Each such wave has a definite frequency, or number of vibrations per second, v. As in the case of a light beam (see PHOTON), the energy of these waves is bunched in amounts $h v$, here called phonons, where h is Planck's constant. The phonons act like particles in interacting with each other and with electrons. See also QUANTUM THEORY; QUANTUM MECHANICS.—*E. M. C.*

PHOSPHATASES: see ENZYME.

PHOSPHATE: a salt or ester of phosphoric acid. Orthophosphoric acid forms three series of salts by replacement of one, two, or three of its protons by metals. Sodium dihydrogen phosphate (NaH_2PO_4) and disodium monohydrogen phosphate (Na_2HPO_4) are used in baking powder. Trisodium phosphate (Na_3PO_4) is extensively used in heavy detergents. By far the largest tonnage of phosphate is used in FERTILIZER,

Storage piles of phosphate rock, composed principally of $Ca_3(PO_4)_2$, await conversion into calcium superphospate, a fertilizer, at plant near Brewster, Fla. (*American Cyanamid Co.*)

in the form of "calcium superphosphate." This is a mixture of soluble calcium-acid phosphates formed by reacting the naturally occurring insoluble calcium phosphates, which plants cannot use as food, with sulfuric acid. By elimination of water from phosphoric acid or its salts, a series of dimers, trimers, and higher polymers can be formed. These substances, represented by sodium pyrophosphate, sodium tripolyphosphate, and sodium hexametaphosphate respectively, are extensively used in household laundry detergents and water softeners. The organic esters of orthophosphoric acid, exemplified by tricresyl phosphate, are important plasticizers.
—*A. M. S.*

PHOSPHOLIPIDS (or **phosphatides**): a group of lipids that contain phosphoric acid. Belonging to the class of complex lipids, they can be subdivided into (1) glycerophosphatides in which glycerol is the only alcohol present, *e.g.* phosphatidic acid, phosphatidylcholine (lecithin), phosphatidyl ethanolamine, phosphatidylserine, phosphatidyl inositol, phosphatidyl glycerol, diphosphatidyl glycerol (cardiolipin), acetal phosphatide or plasmalogen, and lysophosphatide; and (2) sphingophosphatides, or phosphorus-containing lipids in which sphingosine is the alcohol, *e.g.* sphingomyelin.

Glycerol is esterified at two of its hydroxyl groups by long-chain fatty acids, *e.g.* stearic or palmitic acid. The other hydroxyl group is esterified by inorganic phosphate, which is in turn linked to a nitrogen base. In lecithin, this base is choline; in phosphatidyl ethanolamine, it is ethanolamine.

$$H_2C-O-\overset{\overset{O}{\|}}{C}-R_1 \quad (R_1 = \text{mainly saturated hydrocarbon})$$
$$HC-O-\overset{\overset{O}{\|}}{C}-R_2 \quad (R_2 = \text{mainly unsaturated hydrocarbon})$$
$$H_2C-O-\text{phosphate choline}$$

LECITHIN

Phospholipids are widely distributed in nature. They occur in viruses, microorganisms, and lower plants as well as in cereals, grains, and oil-producing plants; they form integral parts of cells and fluids of all animals. Commercially the most important source of phospholipid is soybeans, which contain 1.5 to 3.2% of phospholipid and thus compare favorably with the phospholipid content of eggs, formerly the primary source of phospholipids. In mammals, phospholipids are synthesized by all tissues but not by blood plasma. The liver and small intestine are the most active sites of phospholipid synthesis, as indicated by studies in which radioactive isotopes were used. The synthesis of phospholipids is profoundly influenced by a number of hormonal and dietary factors.

Phospholipids may serve as structural components of the cell membrane, determining membrane permeability; phosphatidic acid has been implicated in the transport of ions and fatty acids across membranes; unsaturated phospholipids may aid in oxygen transport. Various phospholipids may act as catalysts or intermediates in oxidative processes in the mitochondria and may stabilize blood lipoproteins so as to prevent deposition of their cholesterol in large arteries, as may happen in atherosclerosis. Some of the cephalins are responsible for the acceleration of blood coagulation by "thromboplastin" contained in blood platelets and released from damaged tissues.

The most widely studied phospholipid is lecithin, isolated from egg yolk (Gr. *lekithos*) as early as 1846; it is quite soluble in alcohol. Cephalin, isolated from brain (Gr. *kephale* = head) in 1884, is characterized by its relative insolubility in alcohol. Sphingomyelin (Gr. *sphingein* = to bind tightly; *myelos* = marrow) is found primarily in nervous tissue; it is relatively insoluble in ethyl ether, which forms the basis for its isolation. In contrast to sphingomyelin, both lecithin and cephalin are hydrolyzed readily by acid or alkali; this difference forms the basis of an analytical method for the determination of glycerophosphatides in the presence of sphingomyelin. Lysophosphatides are formed from glycerophosphatides by the loss of one fatty acid. This loss is catalyzed by the action of an enzyme (lecithinase A) found in cobra venom. Lysolecithin when added to blood will rupture (hemolyze) red blood cells. Phosphatidic acid, a phospholipid in which the nitrogen base is absent, has been obtained by enzymatic degradation of glycerophosphatides in cabbage leaves and carrots, and a more complex form, "cardiolipin," has been isolated from beef heart. Plasmalogens differ from other phospholipids in that one of the fatty acids is replaced by an unsaturated alcohol. The alcohol, when split off by $HgCl_2$, is converted to an aldehyde. Various phosphatides have been prepared synthetically.—*D. B. Z.*

PHOSPHOR: a term applied in industrial technology to a luminescent material, particularly one artificially produced for use in television tubes, radar screens, or fluorescent lamps. The two main classes of phosphors are the inorganic sulfides and the group of oxygenated phosphors. Zinc sulfide, cadmium sulfide, and their mixtures are the most important members of the former class. They are activated by cathode rays or by ultraviolet light. In these mixtures increasing cadmium content shifts the wavelength of the emitted light toward the red. Silver and copper are frequently included to intensify the luminescence. The oxygenated phosphors include zinc and beryllium silicates, cadmium borate, and magnesium tungstate and phosphate. A complex of calcium halides and phosphates is widely used as the phosphor in mercury-vapor fluorescent lamps because it is an efficient emitter in the visible range when activated by the characteristic ultraviolet radiation of mercury.—*A. M. S.*

PHOSPHORESCENCE (or **afterglow**): a type of LUMINESCENCE in which there is a delayed emission of light from a substance. Whereas in FLUORESCENCE light is emitted essentially only during the excitation, in phosphorescence the emission persists after removal of the exciting source (*e.g.* light or other radiation). The delay is caused by molecules' being excited to metastable states, *i.e.* states that do not decay readily (see ENERGY LEVEL). Phosphorescence may last from fractions of a second to several days or even longer, depending on temperature and other factors. In both fluorescence and phosphorescence, the wavelength of emitted light is longer than the wavelength of the exciting radiation; thus if the exciting radiation is visible light, the emitted light is redder. A striking example of phosphorescence occurs in zinc sulfide: when a trace of copper (an activator) is added, the zinc sulfide will glow brightly after exposure to light. Mobile electrons originating from excited zinc atoms are captured by copper ions and released slowly, causing the delayed emission of light. See PHOSPHOR.—*A. E.*

PHOSPHOROLYSIS: in biochemistry, a reversible, enzyme-catalyzed reaction in which a compound is cleaved by the addition of a molecule of phosphoric acid across a covalent bond. The reaction is quite analogous to hydrolysis, in which water is the splitting agent. One of the split products thus becomes phosphorylated.—*E. S.*

PHOSPHORUS: a nonmetallic element (P); at. no. 15; at. wt 30.975. It can be prepared in three allotropic forms: white or yellow, red, and black. The white form (mp 44.1°C, bp 280°C) is the most reactive chemically; it is spontaneously flammable in air and extremely toxic. The red form is stable in air and relatively nontoxic. The black form, prepared by subjecting white phosphorus to high pressure and temperature, is least frequently encountered. The discovery of phosphorus is ascribed to Hennig Brand (1669), although it was probably known to the Arabian alchemists much earlier. Lavoisier (1777) recognized it as an element in the modern sense. Phosphorus is one of the commoner elements in Earth's crust, ranking 12th in abundance. It occurs mainly in the form of apatite or phosphate rock, a calcium orthophosphate that usually contains varying amounts of coordinated chlorine, fluorine, or hydroxyl. Large deposits are found in southeastern U. S. A. The major proportion of phosphate rock mined is converted by reaction with sulfuric acid to the fertilizer "superphosphate" (see PHOSPHATE). Elemental phosphorus, the starting material for most commercial phosphorus chemicals, is produced by heating phosphate rock, coke, and silica (which acts as a fluxing and slag-forming agent) together in the electric furnace. Phosphorus pentoxide, which can be hydrated to phosphoric acid, is made by burning phosphorus in air. Phosphorus forms a series of sulfides, of which the sesquisulfide, P_4S_3, is best known for its use in MATCHES. The pentasulfide, as well as the phosphorus chlorides and oxychlorides, is used largely as an intermediate for preparing organic phosphorus compounds. Although phosphorus is in the same group of the PERIODIC TABLE as nitrogen, and generally resembles nitrogen in chemical behavior, it forms a much less extensive series of stable organic compounds. Some of these, however, are of great economic importance. The alkyl and aryl phosphates are used as plasticizers. Various esters of alkyl phosphonic acids, thioalkyl phosphonic acids, and thiophosphoric acids are valuable as insecticides and as additives for lubricating oils.—*A. M. S.*

PHOTOCELL: see PHOTOELECTRIC CELL.

PHOTOCHEMISTRY: the study of chemical reactions resulting from exposure of a system to light, *i.e.* to electromagnetic radiation of the visible and near-visible frequencies, usually in the wavelength range 2,000 to 10,000 Ångstroms. The absorption of energy in this range causes a photochemical system to react by raising one or more of the reacting components to a so-called excited state, or state of high energy and high reactivity. The great majority of chemical reactions that proceed with an absorption of energy acquire that energy in the form of heat, and are referred to in the language of photochemistry as "dark" or "thermal" reactions. The reaction of hydrogen with chlorine was one of the earliest photochemical reactions to be studied, and its behavior led to a realization (T. von Grotthuss, 1817, and J. W. Draper, 1841) that only those frequencies which are absorbed by the system can be effective in producing the chemical reaction. Not all absorbed frequencies, however, induce photochemical activity. Many are re-emitted as fluorescent radiation, and some are transformed to heat. Another important law of photochemical behavior (Albert Einstein, 1905, and J. Stark, 1908) states that each molecule participating in a photochemical reaction absorbs one quantum of the radiation causing the reaction, *i.e.* each molecule absorbs $h\nu$ ergs of energy, where ν is the effective frequency and h is Planck's constant. One mole therefore absorbs $Nh\nu$ ergs, where N is Avogadro's number. The unit of energy, 6×10^{23} quanta, is called an *einstein*. Its value in ergs or calories varies with the frequency of the radiation. Sometimes the excited molecules undergo secondary dark reactions and the photochemical reaction accounts for less than one mole transformed per einstein absorbed. The fraction of expected product actually obtained is referred to as the quantum yield.

The basic techniques of photochemistry involve both absorption spectroscopy and analytical chemistry. The absorption characteristics of the system under study, and the frequencies associated with the chemical change, are first measured; the number of moles of chemical transformed per unit of absorbed radiation can then be determined. Photochemical effects are utilized industrially to initiate chlorination and oxidation reactions. They are of primary importance in all photographic and photo-reproduction processes. One of the most extensively studied photochemical processes, and certainly the most important, is PHOTOSYNTHESIS, *i.e.* the synthesis of carbohydrates from atmospheric carbon dioxide and water by living plants; this process is catalyzed by chlorophyll, the green pigment common to most forms of plant life.—*A. M. S.*

PHOTOCONDUCTIVE EFFECT: the increase in electrical conductivity of a material due to illumination by visible or infrared light. The increase is due to the creation by the light of additional current-carrying electrons and/or holes (see CONDUCTOR AND SEMICONDUCTOR) or to the mitigating effect of the light on barriers to current flow. The effect is technologically important for detection of light, particularly infrared light, in such devices as television cameras, light meters, and infrared detectors that enable missiles to "home" on aircraft.—*E. M. C.*

PHOTOELASTICITY: production of INTERFERENCE patterns in POLARIZED LIGHT by such stressed transparent dielectrics as glass, bakelite, or celluloid. These materials normally transmit light in the same way in all directions, but become birefringent (see DOUBLE REFRACTION) under application of stress. The material in question is placed between two "crossed" Nicol prisms or Polaroid disks. If the specimen is unstressed, no light is transmitted, but as stress is applied, causing deformation of the specimen, colored fringes become visible, determined by the position of lines of stress. Stress patterns are usually transitory in character, disappearing when stress is removed, although it is possible to keep a strained plastic model under load at a high temperature, allow it to cool while loaded, and "freeze" the pattern permanently even after complete removal of the stress.

Photoelastic analysis is useful in structural engineering. Plastic models of bridges, trusses, and other members subject to stress are placed between crossed Polaroids and loaded at strategic points. The resulting fringe patterns serve to predict the behavior of actual structures under normal and even abnormal operating conditions.—*A. E.*

PHOTOELECTRIC CELL: a light-actuated vacuum or gas-filled tube designed to convert light into electrical energy. Its uses include sorting, counting, measuring illumination levels, and actuating machinery. Its operation depends on the PHOTOELECTRIC EFFECT. A typical photoelectric cell has an electron-emitting cathode, usually a layer of silver coated with an alkali metal such as cesium. This light-sensitive coating may be deposited over the inside of the entire tube, with a "window" left open for the admission of light. A semicylindrical cathode may be employed for the same purpose. In each case, an axial tungsten wire serves as an electron-collecting anode. An external voltage source of the order of 100 volts d-c provides the necessary potential to operate the tube. Light falling on the cathode releases electrons, whose movement constitutes the current output of the cell. The number

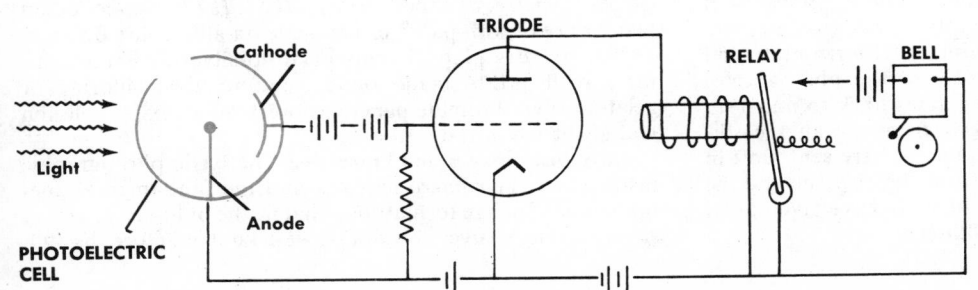

Photoelectric cell is used here to actuate a burglar alarm. When the light striking the cell is interrupted, the bell rings. For details of operation, see article.

of electrons ejected from the surface of the cathode is directly proportional to the intensity of the light. The velocity of these "photo" electrons increases with a rise in the frequency of the light.

The figure shows in schematic form a photoelectric cell, its current output amplified with the aid of a triode and delivered to a relay acting as the load. The connection illustrates the use of the cell in a burglar alarm. When the beam of light incident on the cell is interrupted, electron release is checked, and the relay armature returns to its operating (bell-ringing) position. Special cathode coatings enable the cell to respond to predetermined ranges of spectral colors. The addition of gas at low pressure increases the current output of the cell.—A. E.

PHOTOELECTRIC EFFECT: the ejection of ELECTRONS from a material as the result of irradiation with LIGHT. This effect was discovered by Heinrich Hertz in 1887 as a by-product of his classical research on electric waves and oscillations. Two important characteristics of the effect have been well established experimentally: (1) the number of electrons emitted is directly proportional to the intensity of the light falling on the material; (2) the electrons are emitted with a range of energies, the maximum energy being independent of the intensity of the light, but depending on its frequency (i.e. color). This second feature surprised early experimenters because a more intense beam, having more energy, would be expected to give the electrons more energy. In 1905, Albert Einstein proposed an explanation of this feature; for this work he subsequently received the Nobel prize. He assumed that the energy of the light beam is bunched in packets called PHOTONS, each with energy $h\nu$, h being Planck's constant and ν the frequency, or number of vibrations per second. Emission of a photoelectron occurs when an electron in the material absorbs a photon. The maximum energy with which an electron can leave the material is equal to the photon's energy $h\nu$ minus the energy required to bring the electron out of the material, or the work function. Increasing the intensity of the light only increases the number of available photons; it does not increase their energy. It is for this reason that the number of emitted electrons increases with increasing intensity, while the energy of the electrons remains the same. The actual energy of an emitted electron can be less than the maximum if it loses energy in interaction with other electrons before emerging from the surface. If $h\nu$ is less than the work function, the light will not be able to free electrons from the material. Thus there is a minimum, or threshold, value of frequency required for photoelectric emission to occur, which is equal to the work function of the material divided by h. It has been found that the low work-function metals sodium, potassium, rubidium, and cesium emit more photoelectrons than do other metals under the same conditions. The photoelectric effect is used in PHOTO-ELECTRIC CELLS, which are technologically important for measuring light intensities and actuating machinery in response to changes in illumination.—E. M. C.

PHOTOGRAMMETRY: the science of compiling MAPS from aerial photographs. Principles of optics and geometry are used to determine both the planimetric (horizontal) and topographic (three-dimensional) scale of the photographs. Map making based on photographs dates back to mid-19th cent. when photographs were taken from elevated earth-supported platforms; soon after, cameras were sent aloft in kites and balloons. The development of the airplane and the demand for maps during both World Wars have given great impetus to aerial mapping in the 20th cent.

Aerial photographs, the source material of photogrammetry: Series of photographs of Mt Marcy region, N. Y., has been laid out to form a quadrangle (area bounded by white latitude and longitude lines). By photogrammetric methods, these photographs were used to compile the actual topographic map (Mt Marcy Quadrangle) published in 1953 by the Geological Survey, U. S. Dept. of Interior. Mt Marcy, the highest point in N. Y. State (5,344 ft), appears to left of center. (U. S. Geological Survey)

Aerial photographs are either *vertical* or *oblique, i.e.* the optical axis of the camera is either vertical or at some specific angle to the vertical. Today, many aerial cameras designed for general reconnaissance work are *multilensed,* having one lens for vertical photos and the remaining lenses for oblique shots. If certain distances and elevations have been determined previously by ground SURVEYING, both planimetric and topographic scales are readily determined; if the altitude of the camera and the distances between overlapping photographs in a sequence are known, the apparent displacement (parallax) of any one feature on the ground (caused by the fact that the photographs are taken from different positions) allows the computation of that feature's elevation above datum level. To establish the continuity and precision of aerial maps, all photographs must overlap 60% and every point mapped must be included in at least two photographs. Even so, the over-all scale of an aerial photograph is only an average scale, since the altitude above datum level of any feature affects its representational size on the photograph. (Only a photograph of a flat plane surface can have an unvarying scale.) Furthermore, since photographs can never be taken at the exact vertical, there is always some error because of *tilt.* Despite such limitations, aerial photographs and mosaics (maps made from a number of assembled photographs) have several advantages: (1) they reveal dominant features of a large surface; (2) they are made with speed and economy; (3) they allow inaccessible areas to be mapped; (4) they present a wealth of detail. At present, with increased control of scale and improved representation of topography, aerial photography is widely used for geological, industrial, and engineering surveys. See PHOTOGRAPHY; STEREOSCOPE AND STEREOVISION.—A. L.

PHOTOGRAPHY: the production of an image by the action of visible light or other radiation on a sensitized material, commonly supplied as a film, plate, or paper. The practice of photography can be considered to date from 1839 (introduction of the daguerreotype); its subsequent development in the 19th cent. was marked by several series of discoveries, investigations, and improvements, all centering around materials and apparatus for exposing, developing, and printing images. Before 1900 photographers had achieved professional status; commercial production of sensitized materials and cameras had begun, and photography was being used for purposes other than portraiture. The history of photography before 1900 is summarized by C. E. K. Mees in three phases: *1839-1851,* daguerreotype (metal plate) and calotype processes (paper negatives, paper print); *1851-1879,* wet-collodion plate process, with paper prints made on albumenized paper; *1879-1900,* dry plates having gelatino-silver-bromide coatings, with prints made on a gelatino-silver-chloride or gelatino-silver-bromide paper; before 1890 a flexible roll film had also been introduced.

Early Instruments and Processes: The basic photographic instrument, the *camera obscura,* and the fundamental phenomenon of image formation—that is, the light-sensitivity of silver salts (*e.g.* silver chloride)—were known before the 19th

U.S. DEPARTMENT OF THE INTERIOR
GEOLOGICAL SURVEY
TOPOGRAPHIC DIVISION

PROJECT GS-ZB   STATE NEW YORK
FLYING COMPLETED 5-9-52   FOCAL LENGTH 6"
SCALE OF ORIGINAL PHOTOGRAPHY 1: 40,000
SCALE OF PHOTO INDEX 1:125,000
CONTRACTOR   ALSTER & ASSOCIATES

SANTANONI | LAKE PLACID | AUSABLE
| MT. MARCY |
| SCHROON LAKE |

N

cent. The *camera obscura* is a dark chamber, or box, into which light is admitted through a very small opening so that an image of an exterior scene is formed on the wall opposite the aperture. During the 16th cent., Barbero, a Venetian, fitted a *camera obscura* with a simple lens. A common form employed either a sloping mirror or a 90° prism to make the image appear right side up. The early experimenters used this simple instrument for exposing various coatings on metal or glass plates, and obtained an image that faded after a short time. Thomas Wedgwood and Sir Humphry Davy repeated early experiments and set forth their efforts in a paper (1802), but they offered no method for making a lasting image. In the 1820s the Frenchman J. N. Niepce succeeded in producing a permanent photographic engraving by the process he called *heliography,* which utilized a light-sensitive coating of asphaltum on a metal plate. The drawback of this process was the poor quality of the image, *e.g.* poor contrasts and a general lack of definition. However, these imperfections were largely eliminated in the *daguerreotype* process developed by Niepce's colleague, L. J. M. Daguerre, who made a successful permanent image (1839) using a silver plate which was fumed with iodine vapor and then exposed for several minutes in a *camera obscura* and developed with mercury vapor. Daguerre's process became very popular, and daguerreotype centers were established in many European and U. S. cities. Even in Japan and China there were a number of daguerreotypists, beginning with a Japanese chemist who bought a Daguerre apparatus from Dutch traders and made portraits of noble personages.

Meanwhile in 1835 W. H. F. Talbot in England treated paper with silver-nitrate and potassium-iodide solutions, exposed the paper in a *camera obscura,* developed the resulting image with an acid silver-nitrate solution, and fixed the image with salt water. This produced a negative image from which a positive print could be made on paper that was sensitized, like the exposure paper, with silver nitrate and potassium iodide. This *calotype* process had two advantages over Daguerre's system: it permitted more than one copy, and it corrected the left-to-right reversal of the image. Talbot's process never achieved the popularity of Daguerre's; but it is from Talbot's negative-to-positive principle that the modern photographic process is derived.

Evolution of Sensitized Materials: Improvements in glass photographic plates progressed from the use of albumen as a silver-iodide carrier (Niepce de Saint-Victor, 1847) to collodion, a carrier made by dissolving nitrated cotton in an ether-alcohol solution (F. S. Archer, 1851). Then, in the late 1850s, came a gelatin-coated collodion plate, which made possible the first commercial dry plate. The replacement of collodion by a gelatin carrier (R. L. Maddox, 1871) led to the introduction of the first general-use dry plates—a convenience that did much to encourage the spread of amateur photography. Salted paper for prints was replaced by albumenized paper (1850), to be followed by gelatino-silver-chloride or -bromide paper which could be coated by machine. A number of other processes developed during this period gave prints of good quality, *e.g.* a bichromated gelatin material that could be imbedded with pigments to produce color prints; a gum-bichromate process still used in some pictorial applications; and *platinotype,* using ferric oxalate and potassium chloro-platinite to produce monochromes and portraits of high quality.

Following Talbot and his calotype process the quality of photographic plates improved with discoveries of more efficient agents for developing and fixing the image, beginning with hypo (sodium thiosulfate) as a fixing agent (Sir John Herschel and the Rev. J. B. Reade, 1839), acid pyrogallol as a developer (1851), and alkaline pyrogallol (1862). Other developing agents introduced in the ensuing 30 yr included ferrous oxalate (1877); hydroquinone (1880); sodium-sulfite developers (1882); metol, glycin, and diaminophenol developers (1891); and *p*-aminophenol and *p*-phenylenediamine (1888), the latter still used in developing color photographs. Likewise, the use of potassium cyanide (A. Gaudin, 1853) as a fixing agent for silver-iodide collodion negatives; a single-bath reducer, *i.e.* ferricyanide; and thiosulfate (1883) and bisulfate as fixer-stabilizers (1889) contributed to the evolution of modern photographic processes.

Increases and changes in the sensitivity of silver-halide emulsions resulted from discoveries of various dyes that conferred sensitivity to particular spectral regions. Corraline (H. W. Vogel, 1873) was the basis for orthochromatic materials, which gave increased sensitivity to the green portion of the spectrum. A red-sensitive dye, pinacyanol (B. Homolka, 1904), made panchromatic emulsions possible. A continuing succession of color-sensitizing dyes have appeared and have constantly improved the quality of emulsions, including those used for infrared, ultraviolet, x-ray, and high-speed films and plates.

Early Cameras: The daguerreotype camera had either a simple LENS or a prism. The first camera lens based on mathemati-

The calotype process, birth of modern photography: Despite the popularity of the daguerreotype, it was W. H. Fox Talbot's calotype process that formed the basis for all subsequent advances in photography. Three of the cameras used by Talbot in the late 1830s and the 1840s appear above. The earliest paper photograph in existence (*right*) was taken by Talbot in Aug. 1835 in Lacock Abbey, Wiltshire, England, and developed by methods that evolved into the calotype process. (*Science Museum, London*)

cal calculations was an f/3.4 objective, designed by Josef Petzval, a Hungarian mathematician, and made by Johann Voigtländer (1840), the first of many lines of German-made precision lenses. Other early advances in camera design included a focal-plane shutter produced in England, 1861, and a central blade-type shutter that formed an iris diaphragm, made in Germany in 1887. Improvements in sensitized materials and in cameras were closely related. With the introduction of gelatin dry plates, smaller, hand-held cameras could be manufactured, one of the first of these being introduced by the E. and H. T. Anthony Co. of New York in 1884. The Anthony camera featured a small finder, a shutter with adjustable speeds, a means for near and distant focusing of the lens, and a receptacle that received plateholders. The introduction of roll film (*i.e.* an emulsion-coated paper roll) in 1864 brought further changes in camera technology. A small box camera, loaded with a sensitized paper roll providing about 100 exposures, appeared in 1888; this "Kodak" camera was returned by the photographer to the factory, where the exposed roll was processed to give paper negatives from which prints were made. Patents for transparent support were filed in 1887 (H. W. Goodwin) and 1889 (George Eastman and H. N. Reichenbach), and a roll film with a clear, nitrocellulose base gave results superior to those of the paper roll.

Color Photography: Color photography had its beginnings in a demonstration by James Clerk Maxwell (1861); he made three black-and-white negatives, each exposed through a liquid filter of a different primary color—red, green, and blue. Black-and-white positives made from the negatives were projected through red, green, and blue filters, corresponding to the negative exposures, using three lanterns simultaneously so that three colored-light images were superimposed on the screen. Early processes of this type were called *additive* color systems. Examples were Lumière Autochrome (1907) and Dufaycolor, which used a screen containing a microscopic mosaic arrangement of three primary colors. The prevailing concepts of color processes were changed by the discovery of *color development* (R. Fischer, 1912), *i.e.* the use of color formers, or couplers, to react with the oxidation product of development to form a dye image. Two multi-layer films, Kodachrome (1935) and Agfacolor (1936), in which each of three emulsion layers was sensitive to a specific primary color, were the commercial realization of the discovery of this *subtractive process.* In Kodachrome the couplers were in the developer; in Agfacolor the couplers were incorporated in the emulsion layers. These materials were processed by the reversal method by the manufacturer, to give a transparent color positive rather than a negative. Most commercial color films since 1935 have been subtractive color processes.

A color-negative material, Kodacolor (1942), intended chiefly for amateur use, permitted color prints on paper sensitized in the same manner as the film. Two multilayer color products, intended for customer processing, were first restricted to military use, then released for general sale after World War II; these were Ansco Color, which gave a negative, and Aero Kodachrome film, released as Kodak Ektachrome film, giving a positive. Ektacolor film followed, intended as the professional counterpart of Kodacolor and the Eastman color films for professional motion-picture use.

Motion Pictures: Edison's Kinetoscope, using a flexible film strip supplied by Eastman (1889), was among the first of the practical systems of cinematography. In France, the Lumière brothers, capitalizing on Edison's failure to obtain foreign patents on his process, further developed motion-picture apparatus and materials and presented the first commercial projection in Paris, 1895. The first motion-picture "story" was produced in France a year later, preceding by seven

Early movie camera: R. W. Paul's "Kinematograph Camera" (1896) was one of the first successful motion-picture cameras. Mounted on a specially designed revolving stand, it was used to film Queen Victoria's jubilee, 1897. (*Science Museum, London*)

years *The Great Train Robbery*, the film that signaled the beginning of the U. S. movie industry. Sound movies ("talkies") did not appear until the 1920s. An early color motion-picture process, Kinemacolor (1907), was a two-color additive system. A motion-picture process based on dye imbibition was first introduced as a two-color system by Technicolor Corporation and converted to a three-color system in 1932. Three color-separation negatives, *i.e.* a bipack and a single film, were exposed simultaneously by means of an optical beamsplitter. Positive matrices were dyed and combined to give a single strip of film. Both Technicolor process and Eastman color films are adaptable to wide-screen motion-picture processes, but use different means to achieve the wide-screen theater positive. Amateur motion pictures came into general use about 1923 when a 16mm film system was introduced that allowed the exposed film to be developed to a projection positive (*i.e.* reversal development); this was followed by an 8mm system in 1932. Color film for 16mm was introduced in 1935, for 8mm in 1936. A sound track printed on the unperforated edge extended the use of these narrow-gauge films, *e.g.* for teaching, documentary, industrial, and travel films. See SOUND REPRODUCTION.

Basic Mechanisms Underlying Photography: Several long series of investigations have elucidated some of the basic mechanisms involved in photography. With increased knowledge of solid-state physics, it has become clear that the phenomenon of latent-image formation arises from a change in the properties of silver-halide crystals as the crystals absorb photons of radiant energy. A photon-excited electron moves through the crystal to find an impurity, or structural flaw, *e.g.* a speck of silver sulfide; the speck then becomes negatively charged and attracts positive silver ions to form an atom of metallic silver. This pattern is repeated with every photon absorbed. Much study has also been devoted to the phenomenon of the selective reaction of certain chemical agents (developers), which donate electrons to the silver-halide crystals having an excess of silver atoms at the "speck." (This activity continues until all the silver halide in the crystal is reduced to metallic silver.) It has been found that the greatest number of crystals involved in this reduction are in the area of greatest exposure; thus the discriminatory nature of the action causes the image to conform to the production of metallic silver. Recently, research on various photoconductive and photosensitive materials has opened great possibilities for data recording and improved communications; these materials include zinc oxide, selenium, tellurium, and certain polymers.

Typical Films and Cameras of Today: 20th-cent. research concerning sensitization, the mechanism of latent-image formation, and the kinetics of development has led to the introduction of photographic materials that permit high-quality photographs to be taken with a minimum of effort and training; photography has thus achieved wide popularity as a hobby. A key discovery was that of S. E. Sheppard who, in 1925, found that the presence of minute amounts of organic sulfur compounds in emulsions increased film sensitivity. This discovery and the development of dye sensitizers led to high-speed emulsions. Other improvements in film characteristics (*e.g.* panchromatic sensitivity, finer grain) now give both amateur and professional better results in still and motion pictures and increase the possibilities for applying photography in industry, science, and technology. American general-use films such as Ansco Super Hypan, Kodak Tri-X and Plus-X Pan, and Polaroid 3000 embody many of these improvements; foreign manufacturers offer comparable products. Film-support materials have also changed; for example, inflamma-

First aerial photograph in the U. S. A. (1860), taken by J. W. Black from a captive balloon at 1,200 ft, depicts Boston Harbor. Equipment was supplied by the E. and H. T. Anthony Co., pioneer film and camera maker. (*American Museum of Photography*)

ble cellulose nitrate was gradually replaced with "safety," a slow-burning cellulose acetate, and DuPont polyester has structural and dimensional properties desirable for several film applications. See FILM, PHOTOGRAPHIC.

Cameras for general use include box, folding, reflex, miniature, subminiature, press, view or studio, and motion-picture types. Those for specialized use include stereo, television, rapid-sequence, panoramic, high-speed, underwater, tracking, and shutterless types. The Polaroid-Land camera with its film is a photographic system in itself. Trends in design of general-purpose cameras include built-in synchronized accommodations for flash, particularly in amateur types; range finders coupled with focusing-control mechanisms; film-advance mechanisms coupled with shutter operation; interchangeable lenses for different focal lengths; telephoto, wide-angle, and "zoom" lenses; large-aperture lenses; parallax correction; built-in exposure meters; shutters as fast as 1/2000 sec.; and automatic interlocking of aperture and shutter control according to available light. Associated apparatus, *e.g.* exposure meters, projectors, and enlargers, have kept pace with improvements in cameras and films. See CAMERA.

Standardization of Photographic Materials: Quantitative evaluation of photographic materials began with a method devised by F. Hurter and V. C. Driffield (1890) by which numerical values could be determined to express the relationship between exposure time and image density of a negative. From this research, the science of measuring sensitivity and other tone-reproduction characteristics, *e.g.* contrast, fog, and speed, was developed; this eventually led to standards being established for manufacture and use of films. There are at present three recognized standardizing bodies (in the U. S. A., the U. K., and Germany) that examine performance characteristics of photographic materials; among their functions is the determination—independent of the manufacturers' suggestions—of *exposure indexes.* The values in the system of any one of the standardizing bodies, known respectively as the A. S. A. (U. S.), B. S. I. (U. K.), and D. I. N. (German) values, can be converted into any of the other systems.

Applications of Photography: From its beginning, photography has been closely associated with many branches of science and technology. Its association with PRINTING has been particularly close: several early systems of photography (*e.g.* those of Niepce and Daguerre) resulted from efforts to reproduce matter by existing mechanical processes; and several printing processes, *e.g.* photolithography, photogravure, and rotogravure, developed side by side with photography in the 19th cent. The pre-1900 era witnessed the beginnings of commercial and applied photography, prints for advertising purposes, photographic postcards, and documentary prints of the Crimean War by Roger Fenton and of the American Civil War by Mathew Brady who, with his assistants, made over 7,000 pictures by the wet-collodion process. During the siege of Paris (1870) a microphotograph system was developed for the pigeon post; Eadweard Muybridge made photographic studies of human and animal body movements (1877–95); an object in rapid motion was photographed by using an electric spark (Talbot, 1851); early methods for three-color processes and animation were introduced; photographs were made from a free balloon (1857); and flash photography had its beginnings with the use of magnesium wire (1859) and magnesium powders (1865) to give artificial illumination. By 1900, photography was playing a role in surveying, astronomy, and medicine (x-rays); and before 1925 phototelegraphy using telephone lines, radiographic tomography of a living subject, a stereo-comparator for terrestrial photogrammetry, and photoreduction of documents for library use had become practical realities.

High-speed photography: Shadowgraph of a 20-mm artillery shell traveling at Mach 1.29 typifies 20th-cent. advances in photographic techniques. Picture at right represents one frame of film set to record at 1,445 frames/sec; characteristic wave configuration and turbulence are plainly visible. (*U. S. Army*)

Today, the application of photographic principles—both in scientific research and in the creation of new products by industry—is one of the most dynamic areas of technology. Use of photomicrographs allows study of objects and events at the atomic level; in medicine, an emulsion-coated balloon, introduced into the stomach by a gastroscope, makes it possible to confirm the presence and determine the general area of a malignant stomach tumor. In fluid dynamics, an ultra-high-speed camera, capable of making 480 to 1,600,000 pictures/sec, is used to study gas bubbles appearing in turbulent fluids; and a Kerr-cell camera, said to be the fastest high-resolution photographic instrumentation (at the end of 1960), can make an exposure every one five-billionths of a second of shock waves traveling at 18,000 mi/hr. (See *High-Speed Photography,* below.) New advances in aerial photography include a camera for high-altitude reconnaissance capable of detecting 2-ft-high objects from an altitude of 200,000 ft and at speeds above Mach 2. In astronomy, color photographs have been made, using the Palomar Mountain telescopes, of such objects as the Veil Nebula in Cygnus and the great nebulas in Orion and Andromeda—the last the most distant object visible to the naked eye. (See ASTRONOMICAL PHOTOGRAPHY.) In oceanography, color photographic studies have been made of the ocean floor about 4 mi below sea level in the Romanche Trench (which breaks the Mid-Atlantic Ridge near the equator) by means of pressure-resistant cameras and electronic flash units lowered by nylon cables. In the modern business office, silver-halide photocopying processes (*e.g.* Verifax), as well as several non-silver-halide processes of photography, have come into prominence for documentary copying—*e.g.* diazotype (Ozalid), electrophotography (Electrofax, xerography), photothermography (Kalfax), thermography (Thermofax), and processes using light-sensitive polymers and thermoplastic recording systems. —*M. B. K.*

High-Speed Photography: This field now provides some of the most important and versatile tools used in scientific research and in industry. "High-speed" is generally used to designate (1) single-exposure cameras that take photographs with exposures shorter than $\frac{1}{10,000}$ sec; and (2) motion-picture cameras that operate at speeds in excess of 300 pictures (frames)/sec. High-speed photographic studies are made in such diversified areas as ballistics, aerodynamics, hydrodynamics, machine design, engine design, combustion studies, explosives, biology, and medicine. High-speed techniques and appropriately sensitized films have been employed using every portion of the electromagnetic spectrum that can be recorded photographically (*e.g.* infrared, visible, ultraviolet, and x-radiations).

The growth and usefulness of high-speed photography are directly related to the development of high-intensity light sources. The recording of rapid movement necessitates short exposure times, since blurring in the photograph is proportional to the distance traveled by the moving object across the field while it is being photographed. With a wide-aperture lens in bright summer sunlight, the shortest exposure that can be given a near subject is approx. $\frac{1}{10,000}$ sec. Yet to obtain a sharp image of a bullet in flight requires an exposure of no more than a microsecond ($\frac{1}{1,000,000}$ sec). Since conventional shutters do not begin to approach this speed, high-speed events are very often recorded without the use of a shutter by a system utilizing a short flash of light of great intensity under subdued lighting conditions. Originally, an electric spark discharged from a capacitor was used as a high-intensity light source. However, in recent years, gas-discharge lamps controlled by electronic circuitry have been developed that produce a flash almost as "fast" as the electric spark and many times more intense. Gas-discharge lamps can be designed to produce flashes from $\frac{1}{5,000}$ sec to one microsecond in duration. Hence, they can be used in conjunction with light-pulse or stroboscopic techniques, which make a rapidly repeating event appear to be taking place in slow motion. See STROBOSCOPE. These lamps vary in size from giant airborne assemblies (for night aerial photography) to small, portable, camera-mounted units.

In many lines of research, a record of the rapid variations in pressure and wave fronts—rather than the brightness variations associated with pictorial photography—is needed; and a method known as *Schlieren photography* is used with high-intensity light sources. The technique relies upon the change in refractive index of a gas when subjected to pressure or rarefaction. In its simplest form, it consists of a photographic plate, a point source of light, and the appropriate optics. When the object producing the pressure change, *e.g.* a bullet, passes between the light source and the camera, a shadow is cast on the photographic plate. When wave fronts pass, the refractive index will be altered and a series of shadows representing the wave front will also be cast on the plate; the result is called a *shadowgraph.* High-speed photography of this type has been used extensively to study flames, ventilation problems, cooling problems with lamps, carbonation and evaporation, fan efficiency, wind-tunnel problems, and jet-engine design.

Some high-speed motion-picture cameras have rates as high as millions of frames/sec; this is in contrast to conventional motion-picture equipment operating at 16 or 24 frames/sec. Specialized cameras of extreme complexity, *e.g.* framing cameras, streak cameras, and smear cameras, have been designed to achieve these high rates. To prevent blurring, involved mechanical and optical systems have been created to move both the film and the image as the exposure is made. —*R. W. G.*

PHOTOLYSIS: see PHOTOSYNTHESIS.

PHOTOMETER AND PHOTOMETRY: Photometry is the science of the quantitative measurement of what may loosely be called the brightness of LIGHT, and a photometer is the instrument by which this is done. A source of light has both an intrinsic physical brightness and a subjective physiological brightness that depends upon the state of the observer. Only the physical brightness, which can be measured unambiguously by a photometer, will be discussed here.

The original fundamental unit of photometry was the *candle,* defined as the intensity of the light of a special standardized wax candle. This unit has been replaced by the *new international candle,* defined as one-sixtieth of the luminous intensity provided by one square centimeter of a black body (see BLACK-BODY RADIATION) at the temperature of platinum at its normal melting point. The luminous flux emitted by such a standard source depends on the area of the opening through which it is emitted and on the cone of radiation, *i.e.* the solid angle measured in steradians. (A steradian is the solid angle that subtends L^2 units of area at a distance L from the vertex.) The unit of luminous flux is the *lumen;* it is defined as the luminous flux issuing from one-sixtieth of a square centimeter of opening of a standard source, and included within a solid angle of one steradian. Thus one candle equals one lumen/steradian. Brightness is the luminous flux emitted by a unit area. The unit of brightness is the *lambert;* it is defined as a perfectly diffusing surface giving out one lumen/cm² of projected area. The English unit of illumination is the *foot-candle,* defined as the illumination at a surface one foot distance from, and normal to, a source of luminous intensity of one lumen; this unit is rapidly becoming obsolete. *Illuminance* is the luminous flux falling on a unit area; the metric unit of illuminance is the *lux* and is defined as one lumen/m². The illuminance (E) produced by a source of luminous intensity (I) at a distance (L) is given by $E = I \cos \theta / L^2$, where θ is the angle between the light and the normal to the illuminated surface.

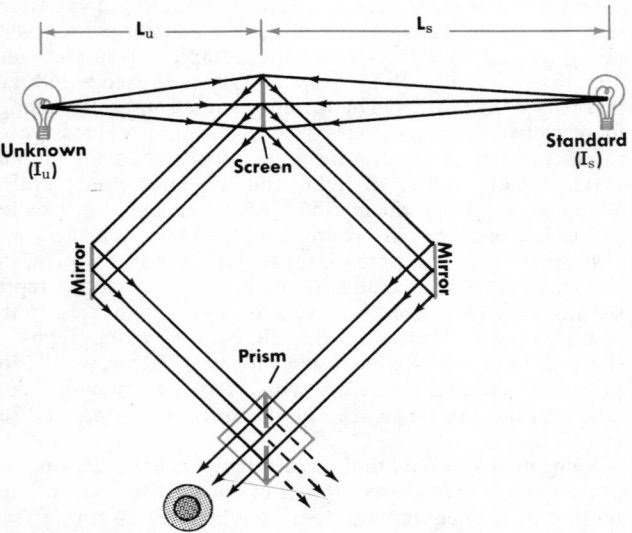

Lummer-Brodhun photometer: Observer sees circular illuminated field in which light from standard lamp appears at center, surrounded by the light from the source of unknown intensity. Screen is moved along line between light sources until field appears uniform. Difference between distances L_u and L_s indicates intensity I_u.

The principle of the photometer is to compare the illuminance on a test screen from a source of unknown intensity with that from a standard source. The figure shows the essentials of the photometer: a white screen is mounted on a rail running between the unknown light source and a standard lamp. An arrangement of mirrors and prisms allows the observer to see both sides of the screen at once. The screen is moved back and forth until both sides appear equally bright. The distances L_s and L_u are measured and the intensity of the unknown source is found from the formula $I_s/L_s^2 = I_u/L_u^2$. To compensate for unavoidable differences in transmission in the two light-paths, the sources are interchanged and a new balance-setting is made. The relative distances of the two sources must be the only variable factor in the measurement. If the unknown source is of a color different from the standard, the photometer is modified so that the observer sees the sources in rapid alternation. The color difference then disappears, but a flicker in brightness remains until the source distances are balanced. For photographic and engineering uses, photoelectric photometers, calibrated against standard sources, are universally used.—*D. H. L.*

In astronomy, photometers are used to measure the light intensity of celestial bodies. One of the simplest devices is a neutral-tinted optical wedge, which is pushed into a beam of light until the light is extinguished or is equal to the light of an artificial "star" formed by a small lamp shining through a pinhole. Another type is the polarizing photometer, whereby apparent brightness of a star is determined comparatively by passing its light and the light of a star of known apparent brightness (which may be artificial) through polarizing prisms. Use of photographs of star fields for determining relative brightness was begun in 1857 by George P. Bond at Harvard College Observatory; the size and blackness of a star image on the negative were functions of the magnitude of the star. Extensively used today is the photoelectric photometer, which measures radiation electrically and is accurate to about 0.01 mag.—*R. N. M.*

PHOTOMULTIPLIER: a device for amplifying light signals. It is a vacuum tube with a photosensitive negative electrode (cathode) and a series of positive electrodes each of which is maintained at higher potential than the preceding one. Incident light releases electrons from the negative electrode, and these are accelerated to the first positive electrode, where an average number of about five secondary electrons results from the impact of each electron from the cathode. These electrons are accelerated to the second positive electrode, where again each one releases five electrons. The process is repeated at each positive electrode. With 10 positive electrodes, a single electron released from the cathode causes the emission of about 10,000,000 electrons at the last electrode. This amplification of the original signal makes possible the detection of very weak sources of light. See ELECTRON EMISSION; SECONDARY EMISSION.—*G. M. S. and L. S.*

PHOTON: a unit, or QUANTUM, of energy of a light wave or other electromagnetic wave. Although LIGHT displays wave properties—notably DIFFRACTION and INTERFERENCE—Planck (see PLANCK'S LAW), Einstein (see PHOTOELECTRIC EFFECT), and others found that in some situations it behaves like a stream of small particles, or photons. The energy of a photon is the product of a universal constant h (called Planck's constant) and the frequency (number of vibrations per second) of the light wave. Since Planck's constant is quite small (6.62×10^{-27} erg sec), the energy of a photon of visible light is quite small—of the order of that of an electron which has fallen through a potential of 2 volts.—*E. M. C.*

PHOTONUCLEAR REACTION: a photon-induced nuclear reaction in which high-energy photons (x-rays or gamma rays) of the order of a few million electron volts or higher produce disintegration of the target nucleus. In some cases a photon apparently interacts with a single nucleon, producing a photoneutron or a photoproton. Both are produced when a photon interacts with the deuteron (the nucleus of the deuterium atom), which consists of one proton and one neutron. In other cases the photon excites the nucleus as a whole; this later loses one or more particles, or even divides roughly in two—a process called *photofission.—M. P.*

PHOTOPERIODISM: the response by many living things to the photoperiod—the proportion of day in each 24 hr. The photoperiod varies with the season in lands remote from the tropics. When night is short, lettuce comes into flower; it is a "long-day" plant. *Salvia* produces luxuriant foliage if the

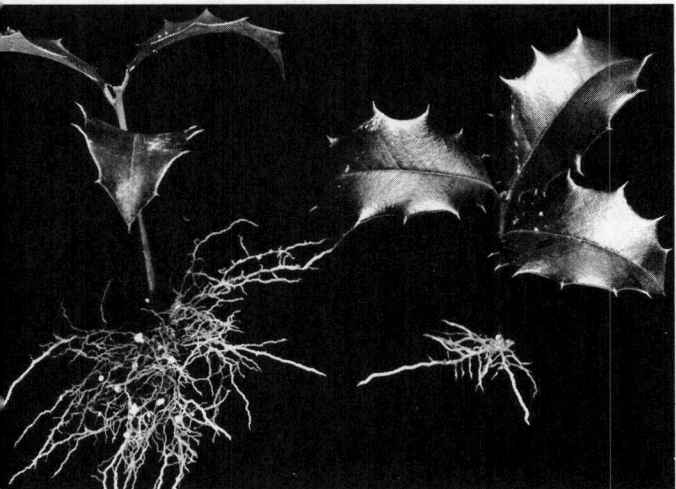

Roots of two American holly plants show effect of light on growth. Both were rooted and grown during winter, but plant at left received extra light during the long nights. (*U. S. D. A.*)

night is short, but puts out scarlet flowers as the nights lengthen in autumn. Domestic hens are short-night breeders, but a light in the henhouse abbreviates their autumn and winter nights, inducing them to lay eggs at the rate they would in summer. Many birds migrate according to the photoperiod. See BIRD MIGRATION.—*L. and M. M.*

PHOTOSYNTHESIS: the cluster of interrelated chemical reactions by which plants capture energy from light and incorporate it as chemical bonds holding together organic compounds. Without this process, life as it has evolved on Earth could not exist, for photosynthesis alone utilizes such simple chemical substrates as carbon dioxide (CO_2) and water in producing food materials necessary for all life. Today only certain purple bacteria containing bacteriochlorophyll and green plants with the pigment CHLOROPHYLL carry on photosynthesis; they rely upon CO_2. In the Precambrian era of geological time, it seems likely that photosynthesis evolved in primitive plants as an efficient means for capturing energy, a means made possible by the gradual accumulation in the atmosphere of CO_2 from fermentation carried on in the absence of oxygen by still earlier forms of life. Photosynthesis, however, added free oxygen to the atmosphere, making possible efficient respiration in both plants and animals and permitting sustained activity at high rates—the way of life we now associate with most animals.

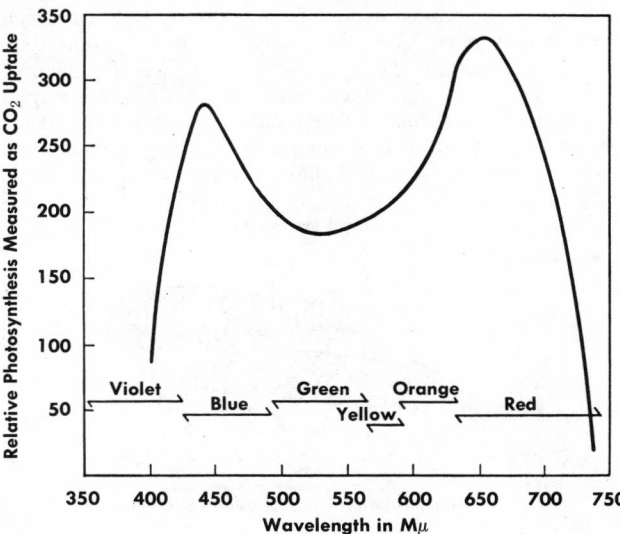

Action spectrum of photosynthesis: Graph shows relative rate of photosynthesis at different wavelengths. Maximum occurs in blue and red portions of spectrum. (*After Hoover*)

Chlorophyll acts as a photoreceptor, trapping solar energy and catalyzing at least two chemical steps which take place so rapidly that they reach an end-point in a mere $\frac{1}{100,000}$th sec and cease until their products are removed by reactions for which light is not necessary. These two or more chemical steps requiring light energy are grouped as the "light reactions" of photosynthesis. Those that follow in either illuminated or dark surroundings are called the "dark reactions."

One of the light reactions for which chlorophyll is necessary splits the water molecule by *photolysis,* adding one of the hydrogen atoms from H_2O to a still-unidentified hydrogen-acceptor compound, and producing an OH group that is transferred through unknown dark reaction chains (one of them requiring the presence of manganous ions) until at last the oxygen is released as a by-product. The hydrogen acceptor is utilized in at least one of the dark reactions for synthesis of other organic compounds.

A second light reaction, linked intimately to the photolysis of water, is known as *photophosphorylation.* This reaction is effective in capturing units of solar energy and, by at least three steps, linking inorganic phosphate groups to adenosine diphosphate to yield the important nucleotide adenosine triphosphate (ATP). The high-energy bonds of ATP are available for use in a host of different reactions.

The dark reactions, which proceed equally well in the light or dark, but are dependent on the products of the light reactions, require about $\frac{1}{100}$th sec to reach completion. Thus, if a plant is subjected to alternating periods of $\frac{1}{100,000}$th sec of light and $\frac{1}{100}$th sec of darkness, it carries on photosynthesis at top speed—although it is in the dark 99.9% of the time. It may even operate more effectively than in continuous light, since light seems to inactivate or destroy some of the products of the dark reactions, within the $\frac{1}{100}$ sec of their formation, before they can be used.

The dark reactions, in addition to those mentioned, include one conspicuous series whereby carbon dioxide as a substrate from the environment is linked to a 5-carbon phosphorylated sugar (ribulose diphosphate) that acts as a carbon-dioxide acceptor. This reaction produces a 6-carbon compound, which promptly splits into two 3-carbon molecules (phosphoglyceric acid), which in turn are reduced to 3-carbon sugars (trioses) that serve as intermediate compounds in respiration.

All these reactions occur in the *chloroplasts* of green plants. Chloroplasts are microscopic (usually spheroidal), specialized parts of the cytoplasm, in which the chlorophyll is spread in thin layers, these in turn being grouped into subdivisions (*grana*) of the chloroplast. Subsequent reactions are carried on in other parts of the cytoplasm, but usually within the same cell that contains the chloroplasts.

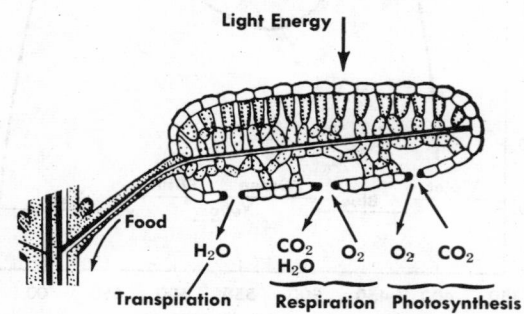

Photosynthesis is the important leaf function in which energy is stored, later to be released ("respiration") as carbohydrates are oxidized to carbon dioxide and water. Leaves also allow transpiration of soil water accumulated beyond plant's physiological needs. (*From Densmore*)

Most chlorophyll-containing cells of green vascular plants are in the leaves, although some may be present and carry on photosynthesis in the stems as well.

Some of the products of photosynthesis are used in satisfying the plant's own respiratory needs; others proceed through a series of steps involving 5-carbon sugars (pentoses) and replenish the supply of carbon-dioxide acceptor; still others participate in a ladderlike series of phosphorylations and produce more complex carbohydrates (*e.g.* pentoses; hexoses, such as glucose, fructose; disaccharides, such as sucrose, maltose; polysaccharides, such as starch, inulin, lignin, and cellulose).

Over-all Process: Just as it is possible to list the amount of raw materials going into a factory and the number of products coming out, all without specifying the manufacturing operations going on inside, so it is also possible to describe the over-all process of photosynthesis by a chemical equation linking substrates and products:

$$\text{Light} + n\text{CO}_2 + n\text{H}_2\text{O} \xrightarrow[\text{chlorophyll}]{\text{in the presence of}} (\text{CH}_2\text{O})_n + n\text{O}_2$$

For each molecule of carbon dioxide (CO_2) and each molecule of water (H_2O) removed from the environment, one molecule of oxygen (O_2) is returned, and a portion of a molecule of carbohydrate (represented by CH_2O) is produced. These over-all changes are exactly opposite those of aerobic RESPIRATION, in which the chemical energy stored in foods is released through oxidation, with the ultimate use of oxygen and release of carbon dioxide.

Photosynthetic Rate: Many environmental factors influence the rate of photosynthesis. Plants require adequate soil moisture and nutrients for healthy growth. Temperatures between 10° and 50°C (50–122°F) are generally most favorable for plant metabolism, and in this temperature range photosynthesis also proceeds most rapidly. The most important factor controlling rate of photosynthesis is light intensity. At low light intensities the rate of photosynthesis may be lower than the rate of respiration; at a slightly higher intensity the rates of these two processes are equal (*compensation point*); and at all higher light intensities photosynthesis proceeds more rapidly than respiration, and the products of photosynthesis

accumulate. Maximum rates are achieved only at light intensities approaching full sunlight. Rates of photosynthesis at saturating light intensities can be increased by raising CO_2 concentration beyond the 0.03% normally present in Earth's atmosphere. During the Carboniferous period of geological time, the CO_2 content of Earth's atmosphere was considerably higher than it is at present. The excess productivity of plants of that age has been preserved as coal deposits, which are being utilized in our time as a source of energy in the form of fuel for home and industry.—*L. and M. M.*

PHOTOTROPISM: see TROPISM AND TAXIS.

PHOTOTUBE: another name for PHOTOELECTRIC CELL.

pH VALUE: a number on a scale, 0 to 14, indicating the hydrogen-ion concentration of an aqueous solution at 25°C; it is a useful index of acidity or basicity. Mathematically, pH value is the negative of the logarithm of hydrogen-ion concentration in an aqueous solution. Thus, if the concentration of hydrogen ions in a given solution is 10^{-8} moles per liter the pH value is 8, since $-\log 10^{-8} = 8$. Distilled water has a pH of approximately 7; the lower the pH below 7, the more acid the solution; the higher the number (to 14), the more basic. The concept derives from a statement of the law of CHEMICAL EQUILIBRIUM:

$$\frac{[\text{H}] \times [\text{OH}]}{[\text{HOH}]} = \text{K}$$

The brackets indicate the concentrations of hydrogen ions, hydroxyl ions, and molecular water; and K is a constant for a given temperature. Since for practical purposes, water (HOH) does not dissociate, the concentration of molecular water can be considered to be 100%, and the denominator in the equation can be disregarded. The product of the concentrations of the hydroxyl and the hydrogen ions in water at 25°C has been found to be approximately 10^{-14}. In water the equivalent concentrations of the two ions must be the same, *i.e.* both are 10^{-7}. The presence of additional hydrogen ions (from an acid) causes the hydrogen-ion concentration to increase, and, since the product must remain constant, the hydroxyl ions must decrease. Conversely, addition of a basic substance causes the hydrogen-ion concentration to decrease. Since pH is an exponential value, a change from 5 to 4, for example, represents a 10-fold increase in acidity.—*D. P. B.*

All enzymatic processes in animals, plants, and microorganisms have an optimal pH, which may vary from organism to organism. Thus in gardening and agriculture, the pH value of soils is an important consideration in achieving optimal growth of plants and crops. In man, the hydrogen-ion concentration of the blood must be kept within the narrow limits of 7.35–7.45 for healthy functioning of the body. This optimal pH of human blood is maintained by natural *buffers* (mixtures of a weak acid and its salt), which compensate for small changes in the blood's hydrogen-ion concentration by effecting changes in the amount of undissociated acid. Careful control of pH value is also important in many industrial processes, *e.g.* in textile manufacture, leather manufacture, cleaning processes, and food processing. —*E. H.*

PHYLLITE: a metamorphic rock intermediate between slate and schist, and like them derived primarily from clay-rich sediments. Its foliation surfaces are finely crinkled, lustrous, and closely spaced. It is composed of very fine-grained micas with segregated quartz, and may include large crystals (porphyroblasts) of albite or garnet.—*H. J.*

PHYLUM: see CLASSIFICATION OF LIVING THINGS.

PHYSICA (Physics), by Aristotle (4th cent. B. C.): No work has ever dominated men's ideas of nature more firmly or for longer than this; it was not until the 17th cent. that Aristotle's ideas were finally set aside. The *Physics* is as much a philosophical as a scientific treatise; it is as much concerned with the general problem of change as with the specific problem of change of place, the motion of bodies. Scientifically it is chiefly important for Aristotle's "law of motion" (the speed of a body is equal to the force acting on it divided by the resistance of the medium through which it moves: $V = F/W$), his discussion of acceleration, his theory of the continuum, and his treatment of lightness and heaviness and of the four elements (earth, water, air, fire). With *De caelo* (On the Heaven) the *Physics* presented almost the complete Aristotelian picture of the cosmos, divided between the perfect, changeless celestial regions and the imperfect, corrupt, changing sublunary world. Although Aristotle's mechanics was challenged and partially supplanted in the 14th cent., his cosmos survived to the time of Copernicus and Galileo.— *A. R. H.*

PHYSICAL CHANGE: alteration of a substance from one state of aggregation (solid, liquid, or gaseous) to another, without the formation of any new substance. Such changes are brought about through the influence of temperature and/or pressure. For example, ice may be liquefied by heat or compression, and water when boiled is converted into steam (gaseous water). All gases can be liquefied, even under atmospheric pressure, if cooled sufficiently; but for each gas there is a *critical temperature* above which it cannot be liquefied however great the applied pressure. The accurate determination of melting point, or of boiling point at a definite pressure, is often used as a criterion of purity of a substance. The heat absorbed or liberated when a solid melts or a liquid freezes, or when a liquid boils or a gas condenses (all without change of temperature), is known as *latent heat*. Most liquids contract on solidification, important exceptions being water and antimony, which expand.—*J. R.*

PHYSICAL CHEMISTRY: the study of the physical properties and structure of all matter, including fundamental particles, as well as of the energies involved in all types of reactions and of the mechanisms and rates of these reactions. Wherever possible, the approach is quantitative and general. Traditionally, physical chemistry has been distinguished from both inorganic and organic chemistry, which describe specific chemical reactions and properties, and also from analytical chemistry, which is concerned with the analysis of substances. However, since physical chemistry is concerned with basic principles underlying all chemical phenomena, the inorganic, organic, and analytical chemist must utilize physical chemistry in his work. See CHEMICAL ANALYSIS; CHEMISTRY; INORGANIC CHEMISTRY; ORGANIC CHEMISTRY.

THERMODYNAMICS, the great classical area of physical chemistry, is based upon generalizations dealing with heat, energy, and ENTROPY. It is concerned with the interrelation of properties such as pressure, volume, and temperature of gases; the relation of vapor pressure to the temperature and composition of liquids and solids; phase relations in general; and heat effects associated with chemical reactions. Thermodynamics also deals with CHEMICAL EQUILIBRIUM and the factors that determine how far chemical reactions will proceed.

Another major area of physical chemistry is *chemical kinetics,* concerned with the rates at which chemical reactions proceed. The basic principle here is the law of MASS ACTION, which relates the rate of reaction to the concentration of the reacting chemicals; thus the rusting of iron proceeds more rapidly in pure oxygen than in air, which is a mixture of oxygen and nitrogen. Although the rates of complex reactions do not seem superficially to follow the law of mass action, it is found that the over-all reaction is the result of a sequence of several simple reactions, each of which does follow the law of mass action. This sequence of reactions is called the *mechanism.* A central problem of physical chemistry is the unraveling of the mechanisms of chemical reactions. See KINETICS.

Electrochemical phenomena arise from the fact that certain compounds exist in the form of ions. Thus sodium chloride, NaCl, exists as sodium and chloride ions, Na^+ and Cl^-; calcium phosphate, $Ca_3(PO_4)_2$, as calcium and phosphate ions, Ca^{++} and $PO_4^{\equiv}$. Electrochemical phenomena may be classified as either conductimetric or potentiometric. *Conductimetric* phenomena are those which accompany the passage of electricity through ionic liquids (see CELL, ELECTROLYTIC). Unlike metallic conduction, which is the result of a flow of electrons, conduction through liquids is the result of a flow of ions. Faraday's laws (see ELECTROCHEMISTRY) are the basic tools with which the physical chemist works in this area. The ordinary dry cell illustrates a *potentiometric* phenomenon (see CELL, VOLTAIC). Here, in addition to the conduction of electricity, the physical chemist is concerned with relating the electrical voltage developed by the cell to the energy relations among the chemicals within the cell. See also ELECTROLYSIS; ELECTROLYTIC DISSOCIATION THEORY.

Atomic and Molecular Structure: A further concern of the physical chemist is to elucidate the relationship between atomic structure and a substance's properties. An atom is conventionally portrayed as a small nucleus of neutrons and protons surrounding which is a number of discrete, moving electrons. The dynamic arrangement of these electrons, which is known to vary from element to element, is considered to account for many of the distinctive physical and chemical properties of the individual elements. Also, the nuclei of certain atoms are unstable, and those of others can be made to undergo changes with the aid of modern "atom-smashing" devices (see PARTICLE ACCELERATORS). The study of such nuclear transformations and reactions is also in the domain of physical chemistry.

The actual structure of a molecule can now be studied by x-rays, electron beams, and infrared, ultraviolet, microwave, and radio-frequency radiation. By proper interpretation of the resulting data, the actual spatial configuration of the atoms in a molecule can be determined. This information can, in turn, be correlated with the gross properties of substances.

Since most substances can exist in the colloidal state, physical chemistry also deals with colloidal systems, as do all other fields of chemistry. See COLLOID CHEMISTRY.—*M. K.*

PHYSICS: the systematic study of natural phenomena to discover the basic laws governing them. Traditionally physics is divided into major topics, namely mechanics, heat, optics, electricity and magnetism, atomic physics, and nuclear physics. Because of the remarkable unity of nature, however, only a small number of basic laws are required to describe the behavior of all physical phenomena that are presently understood; so the separation into topics is to some extent artificial and only exists for convenience. Newton's second law, relating force to acceleration, and his third law, relating action and reaction, form the basis of MECHANICS. Clerk Maxwell's equations, which combine in elegant mathematical form the laws discovered by A. M. Ampère, C. A. de Coulomb, and Michael Faraday, form the basis of ELECTRICITY and MAGNETISM and OPTICS. An understanding of statistics is necessary to describe the behavior of bulk matter and, with the laws of mechanics and electricity and magnetism, forms the basis of HEAT and THERMODYNAMICS. All the above topics constitute the realm of "classical physics," which reached a high state of development by the end of the 19th cent.

Modern physics began its growth with the work of Max Planck and the special and general theories of RELATIVITY of Einstein, reaching its climax in the theory of QUANTUM MECHANICS developed by E. Schroedinger, W. Heisenberg, P. A. M. Dirac, Max Born, Wolfgang Pauli, and others in the 1920s. QUANTUM THEORY introduced radically new ideas into physics, among them the concepts of quantization of atomic energy states, and a recognition by L. V. de Broglie of the wavelike properties of atomic and nuclear particles. The discovery of "spin," or the possession of angular momentum by electrons, and of the exclusion principle by Pauli completed the theory necessary for a thorough understanding of ATOMIC PHYSICS. For example, it became possible to construct the periodic table of the elements, to predict their properties, and to understand the nature of atomic spectra. Since the 1930s there has been a rapid development of NUCLEAR PHYSICS, including discovery of the neutron, positron, and other fundamental particles; creation of artificial radioactivity; discovery of nuclear fission and fusion; and development of particle accelerators such as the cyclotron and betatron, which today are capable of bombarding nuclei with particles possessing billions of electron volts of energy. Even so, the nature of nuclear forces remains a mystery; the existence of the large number of fundamental particles and antiparticles now known also remains to be explained.

Active research flourishes in many other fields, such as: SOLID STATE PHYSICS and CRYOGENICS (study of properties of matter at very low temperatures, including superconductivity); microwave and radio frequency spectroscopy (see SPECTROSCOPE AND SPECTROSCOPY), a field that employs magnetic and electric resonance techniques to study properties of matter in bulk, as well as to measure with high precision fundamental atomic and nuclear properties; PLASMA physics, which is growing rapidly because of the current search for controlled thermonuclear fusion and because of the exploration of space; GEOPHYSICS and ASTROPHYSICS, and the related fields of fluid mechanics (see HYDRODYNAMICS; HYDROSTATICS) and MAGNETOHYDRODYNAMICS.—*B. Be.*

PHYSIOLOGY: see ANIMAL PHYSIOLOGY; PLANT PHYSIOLOGY.

PI (π): the number 3.14159 26535 89793 23846 . . . , defined geometrically as the ratio of the circumference of a circle to its diameter. It is also the area of the circle with radius equal to 1. Johann Heinrich Lambert (1728–77) proved it to be an irrational number. In practical applications rational approximations are used, such as $3\frac{1}{7}$, or 3.142. The method of exhaustion, used by Archimedes to calculate the area of a circle, utilizes a sequence of regular polygons inscribed in the unit circle and approximating the area more and more closely as the number of sides increases indefinitely. The precise value of π is the limit of the sequence of areas. The sequence of perimeters of these regular polygons approximates the circumference, and its limit is 2π. The side $S(4)$ of the inscribed square is clearly equal to $\sqrt{2}$, whence the perimeter is $4\sqrt{2}$. From the figure we see that the side $S(8)$ of the inscribed octagon, found by the Pythagorean theorem, is $\sqrt{2 - \sqrt{2}}$; there are 8, or 2^3, sides, so that the perimeter $P(8)$ is $2^3\sqrt{2 - \sqrt{2}}$. Similarly, for the 16-sided polygon,

$S(16) = \sqrt{2 - \sqrt{2 + \sqrt{2}}}$, and $P(16) = 2^4\sqrt{2 - \sqrt{2 + \sqrt{2}}}$

In general, for the 2^n-sided polygon:

$$P(2^n) = 2^n \sqrt{2 - \sqrt{2 + \sqrt{2 + \sqrt{2 + \cdots + \sqrt{2}}}}}$$

in which there are $n - 1$ radical signs. It can be shown that this sequence tends to a limit as n increases beyond all bounds, and hence defines the number 2π. Approximate values can be obtained from integral values of n. For example, if $n = 4$, we obtain 6.224 as an approximation to 2π.

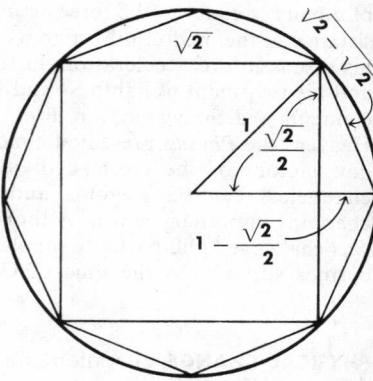

Perimeter of polygon inscribed in circle of radius 1 is approximately 2π. The more sides in the polygon, the better is the approximation.

Approximate values of π can be found without extracting roots, from the infinite series

$$\frac{\pi}{4} = 1 - \frac{1}{3} + \frac{1}{5} - \frac{1}{7} + \cdots$$

due to Leonhard Euler (1707–83), and from the infinite product

$$\frac{\pi}{2} = \frac{2}{1} \cdot \frac{2}{3} \cdot \frac{4}{3} \cdot \frac{4}{5} \cdot \frac{6}{5} \cdot \frac{6}{7} \cdot \frac{8}{7} \cdots$$

discovered by John Wallis in 1655.

The number π appears in mensuration formulas for all plane and solid figures involving circles, *e.g.* cylinders, cones, and spheres. It is important, also, in the development of the circular functions, *e.g.* sine and cosine, which form the mathematical basis for the study of oscillatory motion. Because the circumference of the unit circle is equal to 2π, this quantity is the period of the functions $\sin x$ and $\cos x$.—*H. C.*

PIAZZI, GIUSEPPE, 1746–1826, Italian astronomer; b. Ponte, Valtellina. Professor of astronomy and mathematics at Palermo (1780–1817), he established there (1790) an observatory. He began the preparation of a new catalog of 6,748 stars which was published in 1803. In 1814, he published a new catalog which extended the list to 7,646 stars. Piazzi is best known for his discovery of the first planetoid (asteroid), which he named Ceres (Jan. 1, 1801). He was a fellow of the Royal Society.—*R. N. M.*

Giuseppe Piazzi
(U. S. Navy)

PICARD, JEAN, 1620–82, French astronomer; b. La Flèche. He was the first to apply the telescope systematically in conjunction with graduated circles for the precise measurement of angles, and he provided the first accurate measurement of a degree of a meridian (1669–70). In 1671 Picard determined the latitude and longitude of Tycho Brahe's observatory at Uraniborg. In 1679 he founded *La Connaissance des Temps,* which he edited until his death.—*S. B.*

PICCARD, AUGUSTE, 1884–1962, Swiss physicist; b. Basel. He worked on radioactivity and carried out the Michelson experiment at high altitudes. (See MICHELSON-MORLEY EXPERIMENT.) On May 27, 1931, he made his first balloon ascent in an airtight gondola, reaching 51,793 ft; the following year he reached 55,500 ft. After World War II he built a bathyscaphe, in which he and his son, Jacques, descended into the ocean to a depth of 10,168 ft (1953).—*E. F.*

PICKERING, EDWARD CHARLES, 1846–1919, U. S. astronomer and physicist; b. Boston, Mass. He established the first physics laboratory in the U. S. A. for instruction of students, made special studies of light and spectra of stars, and developed a meridian photometer with which he made over a million and a half measures of the light of stars. He established (1891), with his brother William, a station of the Harvard Observatory at Arequipa, Peru; this made observations in both northern and southern hemispheres possible and produced over 200,000 photographs of the sky. Pickering initiated a continuous "patrol" of the sky in both hemispheres. He was a fellow of the Royal Society and a member of the National Academy of Sciences.—*R. N. M.*

PICKERING, WILLIAM HENRY, 1858–1938, U. S. astronomer; b. Boston, Mass. He established (1891), with his brother Edward, an observatory in Arequipa, Peru; the Flagstaff, Arizona, observatory in 1894; and a station in Jamaica, B. W. I. (1900). His research included studies of the surface features of the Moon and Mars, and observations of solar eclipses. In 1905 he received the Lalande Prize of the French Academy for his discovery (1898) of Phoebe, the 9th satellite of Saturn. Among his many scientific papers are "Investigations in Astronomical Photography" and "Visual Observations of the Moon and Planets." His books include *The Moon* (1903) and *Mars* (1921).—*R. N. M.*

PIEZOELECTRIC EFFECT: the appearance of electrical charges on the surface of certain insulating crystals when they are subjected to mechanical stress. The effect is found in DIELECTRIC crystals with low symmetry (specifically, not possessing a center of symmetry; see CRYSTALLOGRAPHY) such as quartz, Rochelle salt, and tourmaline. Crystals that show this effect also show the inverse effect whereby the crystal becomes strained, *i.e.* changes in dimensions, when an electric field is applied. If an alternating electric field were applied, the crystal would alternately expand and contract in response to it, thus acting as a source of high-frequency (ultrasonic) sound waves (see ULTRASONICS).

The effect was discovered by Pierre and Jacques Curie in 1880. It became of practical importance during World War I when Langevin suggested using it to detect submarines (see SONAR). The high-frequency sound waves, generated as described by a piezoelectric crystal, are reflected by a submarine (or other large object). They are then detected by another piezoelectric crystal which, set in vibration by the reflected sound waves, has alternating signs of charge on its faces and thus generates an alternating voltage that can be used to actuate other equipment. These effects are now used commercially for LOUDSPEAKERS, MICROPHONES, phonograph pickups, frequency control, and many other applications.—*E. M. C.*

PIGMENT: an insoluble substance used to give color or tint to PAINT and other surface coatings. It is generally distinguished from a dye, which is soluble and penetrates the tissues and fibers of an organic material. Pigments may be white or colored, organic or inorganic, natural or synthetic; production and use of synthetic pigments have vastly increased in recent years. In addition to their coloring properties, pigments impart valuable physical properties to plastics, rubber, glass, tile, leathers, linoleum, and textiles. Pigments for paint should be insoluble in their vehicle and chemically inert toward it. They should have good covering or spreading power, high opacity or hiding power, and clean, intense colors. The class of pigments called extenders has relatively poor hiding power; they are used to increase yield, consistency, and body without affecting gloss and hardness.

White Pigments: Titanium dioxide is the leading white pigment; though relatively expensive it has the greatest hiding power of any white. Zinc oxide is one of the most optically pure whites; when blended with lead sulfate it is called leaded zinc oxide, which is predominantly used in exterior house paints. Lithopone, a pure white made of precipitated barium sulfate and zinc sulfide, is valued for paint blending because of its brilliant white, fineness, hiding power, and cheapness; blends with titanium oxide are called titanated lithopones. White lead (basic lead carbonate) was known at least as early as 400 B. C. and long led the white pigments in quantity produced. It is the only white pigment that will produce a durable exterior paint unmixed with other pigments. Although it tends to darken on contact with atmospheric sulfides, its surface chalks evenly away, effecting a "self-cleaning" action.

Colored Pigments: The red pigments include iron oxide or Indian red, used widely in barn paint; red lead, used in protective paints for structural steel; vermilion, a brilliant artist's red; and the organic reds used to tone white pigments, *e.g.* the toluidine toners that produce fire-engine red enamel. Inorganic yellows include the chromates of lead and zinc (*e.g.* chrome yellow), valued for their great brilliance, opacity, and fastness to light; organic yellows include the alkali-resistant hansa yellows used to tint casein paints, and the benzidine yellows, used for toy finishes. Ultramarine (sodium aluminum silicate and sulfide) is an important blue pigment, as is prussian blue. Phthalocyanine blue is resistant to acids, alkalies, and light deterioration. Chrome greens are the most important industrial greens; phthalocyanine green is an exceptionally strong pigment that produces a clean, brilliant, and light-fast tint. The black pigments are almost universally forms of carbon, *e.g.* carbon black, which is made by the incomplete combustion of natural gas. The carbon blacks are widely used in printer's ink and rubber. The common brown pigments include the siennas, umbers, and ochres, made by the controlled heating of clays containing iron. Most pigments of this class are exceptionally long-lasting. See also COLORATION OF ANIMALS and COLORATION OF PLANTS.—*A. P. E.*

PINCH EFFECT: a constriction in the cross-sectional area of an electrical current arising from the attractive magnetic force between current elements. It is experimentally observed that there is a force of attraction between two parallel wires carrying currents in the same direction. Hence, if one thinks of a single current-carrying wire as a collection of thin current filaments, one should expect the filaments to "pinch" together under the action of their mutual attractions. The force between moving charges arising from their magnetic interaction is ordinarily smaller than the electrostatic force which exists whether or not they are moving (see COULOMB'S LAW). Hence, the former force is masked by the latter unless, in the space occupied by moving charges, the positive and negative charges are in numbers very nearly the same.

The pinch effect is readily produced in plasmas. A plasma is a gas consisting of a mixture of neutral molecules, electrons stripped from molecules, and the resulting ions. An electrical current passing through the plasma consists of a stream of electrons moving in one direction and positive ions moving in the other. Because the numbers of electrical charges of opposite sign are equal, the magnetic forces predominate and their direction for both types of charge is inward. The plasma is compressed until the outward pressure arising from thermal motion just balances the inward pressure of the magnetic field.

The pinch effect forms the basis for one approach being pursued in Project Sherwood, which aims to extract useful power from NUCLEAR FUSION reactions at a controlled rate, thereby to provide an almost unlimited source of energy. The most formidable problem is to find a "container" for a plasma whose temperature is 100,000,000°C. A material container is out of the question; all approaches depend upon use of confining magnetic fields. Unfortunately, the pinch effect has not yet been successful in containing the plasma for a long enough time to produce a net gain in useful energy, because the configurations are highly unstable and usually last for only a few microseconds.—*S. K.*

PINEAL GLAND: in vertebrate animals, a small, knob-shaped upward projection from the midline of the second subdivision of the forebrain. In some fishes, amphibians, and reptiles, the pineal body appears to be sensitive to light. In the rhynchocephalian reptile *Sphenodon,* its structure suggests that of a degenerate eye facing directly upward. In the mammalian brain, the pineal gland is concealed below the greatly enlarged cerebral hemispheres. Yet the ancients discovered this small lump and referred to it as the "seat of the soul." Recently it has been discovered to serve both as an ENDOCRINE GLAND, secreting the hormone melitonin (which affects development of the sex glands and their activity), and as a "biological clock." Kept synchronized with daylight by nerves from the sympathetic part of the autonomic nervous system linked to the eyes, it can continue for almost a week of darkness to regulate body activities on a rhythmic cycle approximately 24 hours long.—*L. and M. M.*

PIPELINE: a segmented tube or enclosed conduit used to transport liquids, gases, or slurries (mixtures of pulverized solids and water) continuously, usually over considerable distances. Pipelines differ from other modes of transport in that the conveyor itself does not move; this results, after the initial investment, in reductions of transportation costs. LEAD pipes to convey water were used by the ancient Romans, and well-preserved sections of such pipe are still in existence. Except for the occasional transportation of water, the use of pipes was neglected until the discovery of oil in the U. S. A. in 1859. One factor that restricted the use of pipeline was the sizable loss of material due to leakage; this problem persisted through the 19th cent. despite the introduction of threaded joints for cast-iron pipe. However, in 1913–14 the welding of steel-pipe sections was successfully initiated, and the use of pipeline transportation on a large scale became practical. *Pressure pipelines* are those in which the material is moved by pressure supplied by a pump; *nonpressure pipelines* are those in which a slight gradient is utilized to move the material by gravity. Petroleum pipelines have from 4-in. to 36-in. diameters; an 8-in. pipeline with 800-lb pressure delivers approximately 21,000 barrels of oil/day, with the oil flowing at about 4 mi/hr. At present more than 450,000 mi of pipelines traverse the U. S. A., carrying mainly oil products and gas; there are also important pipeline systems extending throughout S America. Because of their convenience and economy, pipelines are used to carry not only petroleum products and natural gas, but a whole range of other liquids and gases, *e.g.* oxygen, nitrogen, ethylene, alcohol, brine, latex, helium, and molasses. Solids such as pulverized coal mixed with water are also being increasingly transported by pipelines. With some products, *e.g.* sugar cane and wood pulp, the intimate association of the product with water during transportation is an important part of the refining process; in this way (and by the use of transporting liquids other than water) pipeline transportation can become an integral part of a total chemical process. It has been suggested that pipeline transportation will expand to many industries, especially chemical industries, which at present use other means of transportation.—*A. L.*

PITCH (in chemistry): a name applied to any of several dark-colored, viscous, tarry substances which are frequently thick enough to be brittle at room temperature. Similar but less viscous substances, liquid at room temperature, are usually called *tars.* Pitches are used as binders for mineral aggregate in construction and road building, as well as for roofing, shingles, sheathing paper, caulking, and sealing. They are classified and named according to their source. The common-

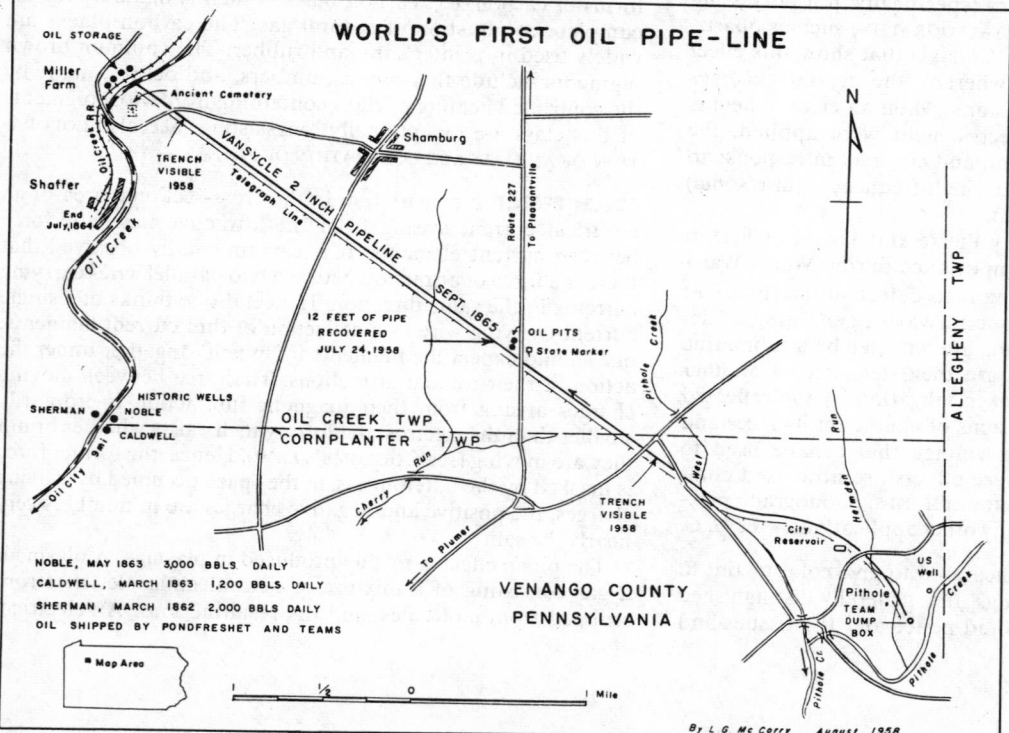

Pipeline transportation: Discovery of oil in U. S. A. in 1859 prompted construction of a 6-mi pipeline (upper left to lower right on map). With improvements in techniques to reduce leakage, especially welding of steel-pipe sections during World War I, pipeline construction rapidly increased. During World War II over 2,500 mi of large-diameter (20- to 24-in.) pipelines were built to deliver petroleum to East Coast depots. Under consideration at present are pipelines designed to cross the Mediterranean, linking North African oilfields with Europe. Besides petroleum, many other products, especially in the chemical industry, are transported by pipelines. (Pennsylvania Geological Survey)

est artificial pitches are residues from the distillation of petroleum, coal tar, wood resins, or fatty acids. Naturally occurring asphalts and bitumens are known as mineral pitches or native pitches.—*A. M. S.*

PITOT-STATIC TUBE: an instrument that measures the velocity of a fluid in motion. It combines a *pitot tube,* named after its originator, the Frenchman Henri Pitot (1695–1771), with a device for indicating the static pressure of the fluid. The pitot tube measures stagnation pressure of a fluid in flow, *i.e.* the pressure resulting from the fluid's velocity and the static (hydrostatic) pressure. The simplest type of pitot tube is a glass tube with a right-angle bend; both ends of the tube are open and the shorter leg is placed with the cross section of the opening perpendicular to the direction of flow. The stagnation pressure p_s is indicated by the height h of the liquid column in the larger (vertical) leg. If a simple manometer or a piezometer is used to give the static pressure p, then the fluid velocity of an incompressible fluid (*i.e.* all liquids and those gases with a relative velocity much below the speed of sound) can be found with a pitot tube by the following application of BERNOULLI'S PRINCIPLE OF HYDRODYNAMICS: $p_s/m = p/m + V^2/2g$, where p_s = stagnation pressure, p = static pressure, m = fluid density, g = acceleration of gravity, and V = fluid velocity. Thus if $p_s - p$ is measured, the fluid velocity (V) can be calculated from the formula $V = 2g(p_s - p)/m$. Calculated velocities are usually corrected by a numerical factor based on the particular tube used. Pitot-static tubes are also used to measure air velocities; however, at velocities equal to or greater than the speed of sound, fluids are considered compressible, and thermodynamic considerations must be introduced. See FLUID FLOW; PRESSURE MEASUREMENTS.— *A. L.*

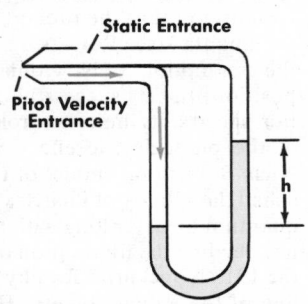

Pitot-static tube of type shown is used to determine air speed of airplanes. Air stream entering pitot velocity entrance causes difference (*h*) in levels of fluid in tube; this indicates air speed.

PITUITARY GLAND: a complex ENDOCRINE GLAND of vertebrates, named from the Latin *pituita,* meaning phlegm, from the mistaken notion that the gland secretes the mucus discharged from the nose. The pituitary gland is located back of the base of the nose, below the second of the subdivisions of the brain. During embryonic development, the anterior lobe of the pituitary gland arises from tissue growing up from the roof of the mouth, and the posterior lobe arises from a knob of brain tissue growing downward. There is some question as to whether the posterior lobe actually secretes hormones or merely receives and distributes to the blood stream hormones elaborated in the adjacent hypothalamus region of the brain. These hormones include (1) vasopressin (or pitressin), which stimulates contraction of smooth muscles in walls of arteries and helps maintain blood pressure; (2) ADH (antidiuretic hormone), which stimulates the kidney tubules to reabsorb water from the filtrate, keeping urine volume low; (3) oxytocin (or pitocin), which stimulates contraction of smooth muscles in the oviduct wall and is important in propelling eggs of oviparous animals to the outside or in propelling the mature fetus of viviparous animals during birth; (4) an antidiabetogenic fraction, which inhibits release of glucose into the blood.

The anterior lobe produces at least 10 hormones, several of which stimulate other endocrine organs; for this reason the pituitary gland is sometimes called the "master gland" of the body. It is distinctly possible that the brain determines what the "master gland" will secrete. Hormones from the anterior pituitary include (1) a thyrotropic hormone, which stimulates the THYROID GLAND to secrete thyroxine when the concentration of this hormone in the blood falls below a critical level; (2) parathyrotropic hormone, which stimulates the PARATHYROID GLANDS when the concentration of parathormone in the blood falls; (3) adrenocorticotropic hormone (ACTH), which stimulates the ADRENAL cortex to release cortisone and other components of the hormone complex known as "cortin"; (4) luteinizing hormone (LH), which stimulates the corpus luteum in the OVARY to produce progesterone; (5) follicle-stimulating hormone (FSH), which induces eggs to mature and rupture from ovarian follicles; (6) luteal hormone, which stimulates growth of the corpus luteum in a ruptured follicle; (7) prolactin, which stimulates enlargement of the mammary glands and, finally, induces lactation; (8) somatotropic hormone, which stimulates growth, particularly of the long tubular bones in arms and legs; (9) gonadotropic hormone, which stimulates maturation of the gonads; (10) diabetogenic hormone, which counteracts the effect of antidiabetogenic hormone from the posterior pituitary, so that the concentration of glucose in the blood is maintained within narrow limits.

In fishes and amphibians, the pituitary gland includes also an intermediate lobe, from which the hormone intermedin circulates through the blood, affecting pigment cells in the skin and inducing them to spread out their pigment granules. Removal of the pituitary from these animals leads quickly to the lowering of intermedin concentration in the blood, the concentration of pigment in the pigment cells, and the consequent blanching of the skin.—*L. and M. M.*

PLACENTA: a nutritive connection between a developing embryo and the parent plant or animal. In the OVARY of a seed plant, the ovules develop into seeds while attached by individual short stalks to the placenta or placentas. In a pea pod or bean pod, a single placenta extends along one side of the pod as a thickened region full of vascular tissue, which conducts food materials to the ripening seeds. In a tomato, the seeds are attached to placental tissues along the inner partitions. In all plants, the placenta is part of the parent.

In animals, a placenta is chiefly or entirely composed of tissues produced by the developing embryo, with never more than slight contributions from the lining of the maternal OVIDUCT. The extraembryonic membranes serve to hold the

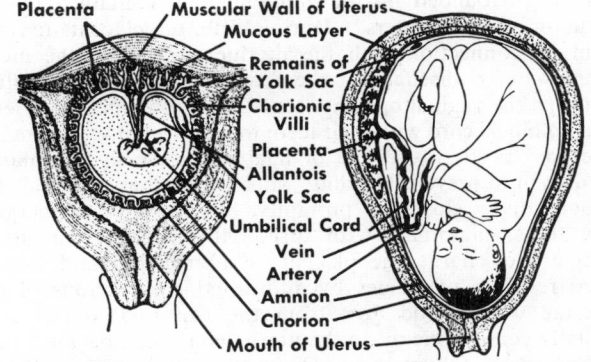

Human placenta, where chorionic villi project into sinuses filled with maternal blood, is site of exchange of materials between maternal and embryonic blood. At 38 days (*left*), villi are still present throughout chorion (though enlarged in region of future placenta); at term (*right*), they are confined to placenta. (*From Kenoyer*)

developing embryo securely in the uterine portion of the oviduct, and to make easier the exchange of carbon dioxide and nitrogenous wastes from the embryo for oxygen and nourishment from the mother. A placental connection is most conspicuously developed by mammalian embryos, except those of monotremes and marsupials, which thereby differ from "placental mammals" (subclass Eutheria). In placental mammals, the extraembryonic membranes that form the placenta are homologous to the membranes that line the shell of the egg of reptiles and birds (serving there in the respiratory exchange of gases between the embryo and the environment). In all placental membranes, the blood of the embryo circulates through vessels of the chorio-allantoic mesoderm and is always separated from the maternal tissues by an overlying epithelium of embryonic ectoderm.

In the pig, horse, and certain other mammals, the entire outer surface (chorion) of the placenta is raised into minute fingerlike villi that fit into equally minute crypts of the uterine wall; this is a *diffuse* placenta. In the cow and other cud-chewing animals, the villi are restricted to small button-shaped areas of the chorion, which fit corresponding pockets in the uterine wall (the maternal mucosa); this is a *cotyledonary* placenta. In cats and other members of the order Carnivora, the villi arise only in a band around the placenta; this is a *zonary* placenta. In bats, rodents, and certain primates (including man), the villi grow in one or two large rounded areas of the chorion as a *discoidal* placenta. The different types of placenta correspond to degrees of invasion by the placenta into maternal tissue. In mammals with a diffuse placenta, the lining epithelium of the uterus remains intact; in mammals with a cotyledonary placenta, the villi digest their way through the lining epithelium of the uterus into the underlying connective tissue, thereby coming closer to blood vessels in the uterine wall; in mammals with a zonary placenta, the villi digest away also the connective tissues surrounding the maternal blood vessels, and come into actual contact with blood-vessel walls; in mammals with a discoidal placenta, the final step is taken in that the placental villi digest their way right into the blood vessels themselves, and then dangle in pools of maternal blood in the most intimate possible relationship that still keeps the embryo's blood stream independent of that of the mother. This independence enables the embryo to remain unaffected by most diseases of the mother and to reject many (but not all) toxic substances circulating in her blood stream.

Within its extraembryonic membranes, the fetus is connected to its placental tissues by way of the umbilical cord, and is surrounded by the amniotic fluid contained by the amnion ("bag of waters"). During birth, the placenta may retain its connection with the uterine wall while the membranes burst, discharging the fetus and the amniotic fluid through the vaginal opening. Most mammalian mothers sever the umbilical cord with their teeth to free the baby; in humans, the cord needs to be tied or ligatured close to the infant's abdomen to prevent bleeding, whereas in other mammals the blood supply closes off promptly. Shortly after discharging the fetus, mammals with discoidal placentas (including women) discharge the placenta ("afterbirth") and associated residues of tissues by additional contractions of the uterine wall. Blood flow from the ruptured uterine wall usually ceases quickly as the uterus contracts, because each blood vessel follows a spiral course and is squeezed to a diameter at which clots will stanch the flow; no one knows why clots form at this time but not earlier when the villi of the embryo are dangling in the maternal blood. Other mammals absorb the placenta without discharging it.

Placental connections between developing young and parent are known in an assortment of animals other than mammals: in some ovoviviparous snakes and lizards; in some fishes, most notably the placental dogfish shark described first by Aristotle; in some scorpions and velvet worms (onychophorans). In fishes that develop placental connections, the extraembryonic membranes involved are exclusively those of the yolk sac. See BIRTH; EMBRYONIC DEVELOPMENT; GESTATION; MAMMAL.—*L. and M. M.*

PLANCK, MAX KARL ERNST LUDWIG, 1858–1947, German physicist; b. Kiel. As a student of G. Kirchhoff in Berlin, Planck became interested in black-body radiation. Experiments near the end of the 19th cent. showed that the continuous spectrum of radiant energy from a black body exhibited for each temperature an energy peak at one particular wavelength; in general, the wavelength associated with the maximum value of energy radiated by a black body is inversely proportional to the absolute temperature of the black body. Attempts made to describe the spectra of black-body radiation from the various models of classical physics, notably Lord Rayleigh's formula, failed to accord with these observed spectra. In 1900 Planck, in his famous "Zur Theorie des Gesetzes der Energieverteilung im Normal-Spektrum," made the assumption that the radiant energy came in discrete packets, or "quanta" (see PLANCK'S LAW). This radical departure from the assumptions of Newtonian physics encountered strong opposition; but its successful explanation of black-body radiation spectra, its important role in Albert Einstein's explanation of the photoelectric effect, and its further development by Niels Bohr in his model of the hydrogen atom finally established the validity of Planck's concept of the quantum. Planck's quantum theory, along with the General Theory of Relativity, has become the foundation of 20th-cent. physics. Planck won the 1918 Nobel prize for physics, and in 1926 he became a fellow of the Royal Society. He was an associate of the U. S. National Academy of Sciences. Planck's *Vorlesungen über Thermodynamik* (1897) and *Einführung in die theoretische Physik* (1916–30) have been translated into many languages. —*A. L.*

PLANCK'S LAW: a law of physics describing the distribution in frequency (or wavelength) of radiant energy emitted by a material that is a perfect emitter and absorber, the so-called black body. The great significance of the law lies in the fact that to derive a law to fit the experimental observations the German physicist Max Planck was forced to assume that energy transfers associated with radiation are made up of definite *quanta*, or increments, of energy proportional to the frequency of the corresponding radiation. This assumption, called *Planck's hypothesis,* is the fundamental law of QUANTUM THEORY and can be said to have initiated 20th-cent. physics. If v is taken as the frequency of the radiation, the energy of a quantum is hv, where h, known as *Planck's constant,* is a number that was first determined by fitting the theoretically derived distribution formula with the experimental data. Its value is approximately 6.61×10^{-27} erg seconds.

The distribution of energy depends on the temperature, but goes to zero at very short and very long wavelengths for all temperatures, as indicated in the figure. The maximum of the distribution occurs at a wavelength λmax such that λmax T is a constant, where T is the absolute temperature (WIEN'S RADIATION LAWS). Both the energy density at any wavelength and the total energy radiated, given by the area under the curve, are proportional to the 4th power (T^4) of the temperature (STEFAN-BOLTZMANN LAW).—*M. P.*

PLANE GEOMETRY: see EUCLIDEAN GEOMETRY.

PLANET: a solid body that revolves around the Sun in a closed, elliptical orbit and is seen by reflected sunlight. The ancients recognized seven planets or "wandering stars": Sun, Moon, Mercury, Venus, Mars, Jupiter, and Saturn. We now know that the Sun is a star, and we consider the Moon as a satellite of Earth, which is itself a true planet. We have discovered three more principal planets—Uranus, Neptune, and Pluto—making nine in all, besides almost 2,000 minor planets, or ASTEROIDS. The modern astrophysical concept of a planet is that it shines only by reflected sunlight and that it is much colder than the Sun. Planets differ basically from comets in being very much denser and in lacking gaseous comas or tails, and from meteorites in being large enough to be observed outside Earth's atmosphere. See also SOLAR SYSTEM.

The *inferior* planets are those with orbits inside Earth's, and *superior* planets are those with orbits outside Earth's. For an inferior planet four configurations are recognized: *inferior conjunction,* when it is directly, or almost directly, between Earth and Sun; *superior conjunction,* when the Sun is between Earth and the planet; and *greatest elongations east* and *west,* referring to the planet's greatest angular separation from the Sun in the sky. An inferior planet exhibits phases like the Moon's (see PHASE), being full at superior conjunction, showing half its disc at greatest elongation, and being new at inferior conjunction. A superior planet shows these four configurations: *conjunction,* when the Sun is between Earth and planet; *opposition,* when Earth is between Sun and planet and hence nearest to the planet; and *east* and *west quadratures,* in each of which the directions of planet and Sun are at right angles as seen from Earth. A superior planet is full at opposition or conjunction; its phase-defect is greatest at quadrature, when the planet is gibbous. Planets are observed to move sometimes eastward among the stars (direct motion) and sometimes westward (retrograde motion), the rate being variable for each planet. These apparent motions, which were long misinterpreted, are

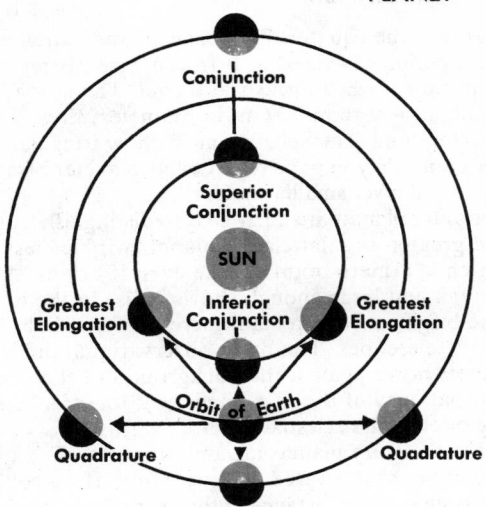

Planetary configurations: Conjunctions and elongations of an inferior planet (innermost circle) and conjunction, opposition, and quadratures of a superior planet (outermost circle) are shown for the conditions described in the text.

a combined effect of the planet's revolution around the Sun and Earth's revolution around the Sun.

The so-called *terrestrial,* or earth-like, planets are MERCURY, VENUS, EARTH, and MARS. They are small, 3,000 to 8,000 mi in diameter, and have relatively thin atmospheres, show average densities of 4.1 to 5.5 times water, rotate in a period of 24 hr or more, and exhibit little polar flattening. The *giant* (Jovian) planets are JUPITER, SATURN, URANUS, and NEPTUNE: all are huge, 28,000 to 86,000 mi in diameter; they have thick atmospheres, possess average densities of 0.7 to 1.6 (they are largely gaseous, with dense centers), rotate in 10 to 16 hr, and bulge

THE MAJOR PLANETS

(Adapted by permission from G. H. Herbig and C. E. Worley, "Some Basic Astronomical Data," *Astronomical Society of the Pacific Leaflet No. 325, 1960.*)

Name	Year of Discovery	Maximum Apparent Visual Mag.	Mass (Earth = 1)	Surface Gravity (Earth = 1)	Velocity of Escape (mi/sec)	Mean Density (water = 1)	Period of Rotation		Oblateness[1]	Chief Molecules in Atmosphere
Mercury		− 1.9	0.056	0.37	2.6	5.2	59^d		0.0	—
Venus		− 4.4	0.82	0.89	6.4	5.1	249^d		0.0	N_2,O_2,CO_2,H_2O,A
Earth		—	1.00	1.00	7.0	5.52	23^h	56^m	0.0034	CO_2,H_2O,O_2
Mars		− 2.8	0.11	0.39	3.2	4.1	24^h	37^m	0.0052	CO_2,H_2O,A
Jupiter		− 2.5	318.35	2.54	37.1	1.34	9^h	50^m	0.062	CH_4,NH_3
Saturn		− 0.4	95.2	1.06	22.0	0.68	10^h	14^m	0.096	CH_4,NH_3
Uranus	1781	+ 5.6	14.6	1.09	13.9	1.75	10^h.8		0.06	CH_4,H_2
Neptune	1846	+ 7.9	17.6	1.41	15.5	2.2	15^h.8		0.02	CH_4
Pluto	1930	+ 14.9	?	?	?	?	6^d	9^h	?	—

Name	Mean Distance from Sun		Sidereal Period		Eccentricity of Orbit	Inclination of Orbit to Ecliptic	Diameter	
	(miles)	(astr. units)[2]	(tropical years)	(days)			(equatorial miles)	(apparent seconds)[3]
Mercury	35,950,000	0.3871	0.24085	87.969	0.20563	7° 00'.2	3,100	4".5 − 12".9
Venus	67,180,000	0.7233	0.61521	224.70	0.00679	3° 23'.7	7,600	9".6 − 66".0
Earth	92,880,000	1.0000	1.00000	365.24	0.01673	0°	7,927	
Mars	141,520,000	1.5237	1.88089	686.98	0.09337	1° 51'.0	4,200	3".5 − 25".7
Jupiter	483,320,000	5.2037	11.8652		0.04849	1° 18'.4	88,700	30".4 − 50".1
Saturn	889,880,000	9.5809	29.6527		0.05162	2° 29'.2	75,100	15".0 − 20".9
Uranus	1,775,600,000	19.1168	83.585		0.04431	0° 46'.3	29,000	3".1 − 3".7
Neptune	2,797,200,000	30.1157	165.27		0.00734	1° 46'.4	28,000	2".0 − 2".2
Pluto	3,651,000,000	39.3133	246.50		0.24811	17° 10'.1	3,600?	0".2 − 0".3?

[1] Oblateness is defined as equatorial diameter minus polar diameter, divided by equatorial diameter.
[2] 92,880,000 mi.
[3] Depends on distance from Earth at time of observation.

appreciably at the equator. PLUTO, small and extremely cold, its surface perhaps covered with frozen gases, is regarded by some astronomers as a terrestrial planet. The ASTEROIDS are very small, all less than 500 mi in diameter; they lack sufficient mass to hold atmospheres, most show irregular shapes, and as a group they may be regarded as planetary fragments, merging into the yet smaller meteorites.

The brighter planets are fairly easy to distinguish from stars. Being of greater angular size, a planet twinkles less than a star, which is a mere point source even if bright. A planet near enough and large enough shows a disc in the telescope, while the brightest stars remain mere points of light even in the largest telescopes. The basic observational difference is that planets move against the background of the stars. The apparent pathway of the planets is the ZODIAC, a belt about 16° wide circling the celestial sphere.

Whether there are planets around other stars is a question that cannot yet be answered with certainty. If we could view the solar system at the distance of the nearest star, our greatest telescopes would not reveal even Jupiter, the largest planet. A stellar planet might, however, be detected by its gravitational effect on its primary. Several invisible companions of nearby stars have been discovered through such effects, and their masses are planetary in magnitude rather than stellar. Current theories of the origin of planets (see DUST-CLOUD THEORY) would make such systems extremely common among the many billions of stars in the Galaxy. Life can develop only on a planet of suitable size and atmosphere at a proper distance from its central star (see LIFE, EXTRATERRESTRIAL). —*W. H.*

PLANETARIUM: an instrument for depicting artificially the positions and motions of celestial bodies. By extension, the word has come to include the building in which such an instrument is housed and operated. Devices that demonstrate the motions of a few of the bodies of the solar system with some measure of accuracy are called "orreries," from the 4th Earl of Orrery (1676–1731), under whose patronage one of the earliest such machines was built. The modern complicated projection planetarium was invented and designed in 1919 by Dr. Walter Bauersfeld of the Zeiss Optical Co., Germany. Modern planetaria are provided with complicated projectors capable of throwing upon a domed ceiling a representation of the sky with the visible stars, planets, Moon, and Sun. These projectors are equipped to simulate the three major motions of Earth: daily rotation; annual revolution; and precession, the slow oscillation of Earth that slowly changes the direction in which Earth's poles point. Both the apparent and the real motions of Moon and planets can be shown. Most planetaria supplement the picture of the sky with auxiliary effects such as clouds, rainbows, auroras, lightning, and horizon effects that increase the illusion of the real sky. The audiences are seated completely around the machine; the operator, who is also the lecturer, is stationed at a control board so that he can move the instrument in keeping with his text. In addition to providing a spectacle of great interest to the layman, a planetarium furnishes an unsurpassed means of instruction to navigators and students of astronomy.

There are ten planetaria in the U. S. A. with projectors sufficiently intricate to duplicate almost every celestial situation visible to the unaided eye: Charles Hayden Planetarium, Boston, Mass.; Morehead Planetarium, Chapel Hill, N. C.; Adler Planetarium, Chicago, Ill.; Air Force Academy Planetarium, Colorado Springs, Colo.; Robert T. Longway Planetarium, Flint, Mich.; Griffith Planetarium, Los Angeles, Calif.; American Museum-Hayden Planetarium, New York, N. Y.; Fels Planetarium, Philadelphia, Pa.; Buhl Planetarium, Pittsburgh, Pa.; Morrison Planetarium, San Francisco, Calif. In addition, there are many smaller planetaria operated by schools, museums, and libraries. In many large cities of Europe, South America, and Asia, there are planetaria comparable to the large installations in the U. S. A.—*J. P.*

Planetarium projector can be rotated at varying speeds so that periodic movements of projected heavenly bodies are compressed into intervals of minutes, graphically demonstrating the pattern of their paths. By varying the setting of the planetarium projector, the heavens as seen from any point on Earth can be portrayed. Most heavenly bodies are depicted at intensities far brighter than they would be seen in the heavens; this is done in order to accommodate the visual sensitivity of the audience. Additional effects, e.g. the silhouette of the local horizon, clouds, and the aurora, are projected to give the demonstration a heightened air of reality. (*Zeiss Ikon*)

PLANETARY MOTION: see KEPLER'S LAWS.

PLANETESIMAL HYPOTHESIS: a theory of the origin of the solar system in which planets are assumed to have been formed by accretion of small solid bodies, or planetesimals, originally condensed from matter ejected from the Sun. Developed in the early 1900s by T. C. Chamberlin and F. R. Moulton, it is based on the assumption that a star passing close to the Sun caused, on the Sun's surface, an enormous tidal surge directed toward the star and a somewhat lesser one in the opposite direction. This phenomenon was accompanied by a number of smaller surges both before and after the time of nearest approach of the two bodies. Additional eruptions of solar material took place as the inner regions of the Sun were relieved of overlying pressure. Part of the material thus ejected escaped into space, some returning to the Sun and the remainder being swung into a swirling nebula about the Sun. As the material cooled, its less volatile constituents condensed into knots orbiting the Sun. The largest of these, stemming from the greatest tidal surge, swept up surrounding material and formed the giant planets: Jupiter, Saturn, Uranus, and Neptune. The knots produced by the opposite surge, being less massive and thus less able to retain gases, captured some of the remaining heavier elements and formed Earth and Venus. The knots resulting from small surges solidified into minute bodies (planetesimals). As their orbits intersected, a number of collisions occurred, the result being a gradual accretion of material into bodies of modest size, such as satellites, asteroids, Mars, and Mercury. Ingenious though it appeared at first, this theory is unacceptable because gases escaping from the Sun would dissipate before they could condense, and because collisions would destroy the smaller planetesimals rather than cause gradual accretion. A modification of these basic assumptions was attempted by Sir James Jeans (see TIDAL THEORY).—*S. D. G.*

PLANKTON: plant and animal life, mostly minute, suspended in waters of ponds, lakes, rivers, and oceans. Because of their small size, their lack of locomotion, or their ability to move only feebly and erratically, these organisms are at the mercy of currents, tides, and waves. The plants (*phytoplankton*) of both fresh and salt waters are all microscopic in size; they include bacteria, related molds, and algae in the form of single cells or minute colonies. The animals (*zooplankton*) of fresh waters consist chiefly of protozoa (single-celled animals) and rotifers (wheel animalcules), measuring 0.0004 to 0.02 in. in length, and a wide variety of small crustaceans 0.02 to 0.01 in. long. Protozoa and crustacea are also the dominant zooplankters in the ocean, but marine plankton includes, in addition, jellyfish, some worms, a few small mollusks, and the microscopic immature stages of many animals which as adults live on the ocean bottom. In common practice, however, the worms, mollusks, and jellyfish are not considered as plankton, because of their large size. Rapid streams have no true plankton, but other fresh waters and most parts of the ocean contain an abundance of these organisms, masses of which can be strained out by pulling a fine silk net through apparently clear water.

In general, plankton populations of fresh waters are much more dense than those of the ocean. Under exceptionally favorable conditions a highly productive lake may contain 500 crustaceans, 2,000 rotifers, 500,000 protozoans, 40,000,000 green plant cells, and 500,000,000 bacteria per qt of water, the combined volume of all these organisms being less perhaps than 0.02 in.^{3} During part of the summer some lakes have green scums, or "blooms," of algae, which upon death and decay produce an offensive odor. On several occasions the

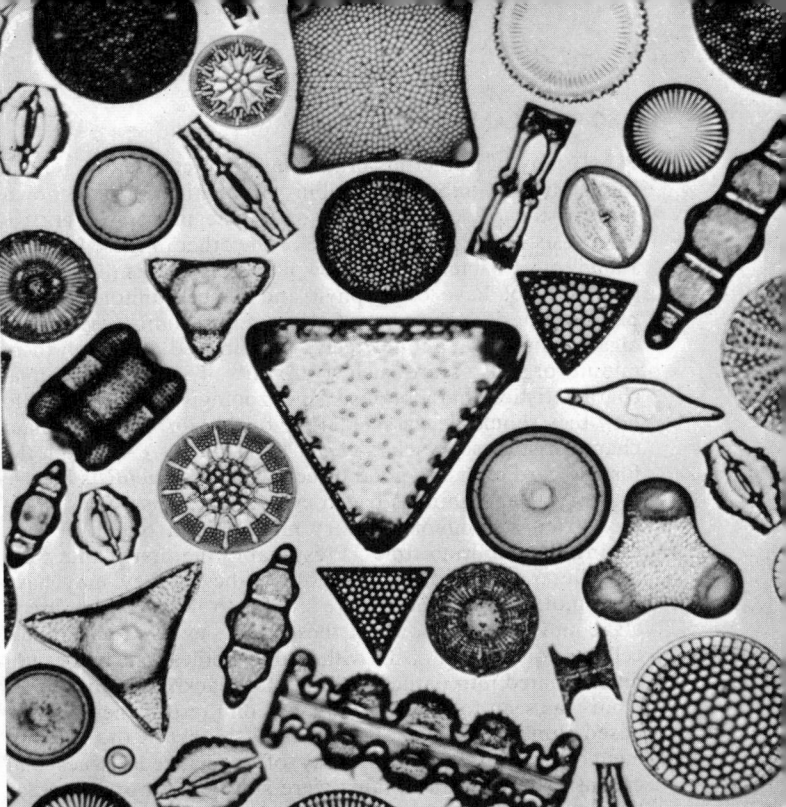

Plankton population of seas and oceans includes many microscopic unicellular plants called diatoms. The skeletal structure of these plants is unique in that it is composed of silicon dioxide. A few of the many forms of diatom skeletons are shown above. (*Carl Strüwe/Monkmeyer*)

disintegration products of blooms in small ponds have been sufficiently toxic to kill cattle that have drunk the water.

The largest marine plankton populations occur at high latitudes and in offshore waters rather than in the open ocean. Sometimes the water may appear to be almost "soupy" with organisms; the RED TIDES of some coastal areas, for example, are the result of enormous numbers of a kind of protozoan. Whereas most lake plankton is restricted to the uppermost 20 to 30 ft of water, there are in the ocean a few planktonic organisms below a depth of 400 ft. From a seasonal standpoint, maximum populations occur between April and October in temperate waters in northern and southern latitudes; winter populations are usually less than 20% as great.

Some planktonic crustaceans exhibit, during each 24-hr period, vertical "drifts" or migration cycles in response to changing light intensities. In the late afternoon they begin to swim erratically upward toward the surface, and between midnight and early morning are concentrated in the upper waters. At dawn the crustaceans begin migrating downward, and by noon, when light intensity is greatest, the population is largely diffused in lower waters. A few lake zooplankters may migrate a vertical distance of 30 ft, and some marine zooplankters as much as 150 ft during a 24-hr period.

A plankton population provides a good example of an interdependent food chain. The algae carry on PHOTOSYNTHESIS, using water, dissolved carbon-dioxide gas, and mineral salts for the manufacture of food necessary for maintenance and growth. These organisms serve as the chief food of the zooplankton. The zooplankton, in turn, is important in the diet of small fishes, and the small fishes may be eaten by large fishes. Waste products of digestion and dead organisms of all kinds are reconverted by bacteria into simple chemical compounds that are again available for use as food by the microscopic green plants. Thus, the bacteria connect the two ends of the food chain. See Color Plate 73.—*A. P. E.*

PLANT: any of numerous organisms characterized in general by a stationary habit and an ability to manufacture their own food in the presence of sunlight by the process of PHOTO-SYNTHESIS. Some plants lack one or the other of these features. Fungi, most bacteria, and a few flowering plants (*e.g.* Indian pipe) do not have chlorophyll and hence cannot carry on photosynthesis. A number of microscopic plants (*e.g.* certain algae) can swim about freely, and indeed some of these minute organisms are such a mixture of plant and animal characteristics that botanists and zoologists disagree as to how they should be classified. (For further discussion of plant characteristics, see ANIMAL-PLANT DIFFERENCES.) Although the fossil record offers no good direct evidence, scientists believe that plants and animals began evolving along separate pathways from a common ancestry more than a billion yr ago, during Precambrian times. Presumably the first plants were unicellular and carried on photosynthesis; they may have been motile and perhaps were similar to modern blue-green algae and bacteria. Some of these plants evolved into multicellular aquatic organisms with thallus bodies—*i.e.* bodies not differentiated into tissues and therefore lacking in division of labor—as seen today in the algae. Conquest of the land imposed numerous obstacles, but these were met by the development in the multicellular body of specialized tissues and organs. The first land plants were simple, without vascular tissues; later, the more complex tracheophytes appeared.

Today, as a result of evolution, there are about 350,000 living species of plants that make up the vegetation of land and water. These are grouped into phyla, each phylum representing a basic body plan and method of reproduction. Arranged in a series from simple to complex, the major phyla illustrate evolutionary trends that afford an over-all view of the plant kingdom.

A number of diverse phyla make up the group of thallus plants. The phylum Cyanophyta, or blue-green algae, numbering 1,400 species, consists of aquatic primitive plants with unicellular, filamentous, or colonial bodies whose cells possess CHLOROPHYLL but no chloroplasts, chromatin but no true nucleus (see CELL). Thus these plants exhibit a primitive form of both cellular organization and vegetative body. The phylum Chlorophyta, or green algae, numbering 5,000 species, includes the pondscums and some seaweeds; these aquatic thallus plants have an advanced cellular organization with chloroplasts and nuclei, yet retain the unicellular, filamentous, or thalloid bodies. Chlorophytes are considered the ancestral type from which all green plants have evolved. The phylum Phaeophyta, or brown algae, with 900 species, includes thallus plants highly specialized for living in the ocean; they possess an accessory brown pigment (fucoxanthin) masking the chlorophyll, and have rugged bodies capable of surviving the stress of tides and waves. Typical phaeophytes are the kelps and rockweeds. The phylum Rhodophyta, or red algae, numbers about 2,500 species; they, too, are marine thallus plants, but possess a red pigment (phycoerythrin) instead of a brown one. Familiar examples are dulse and Irish moss. Two phyla of thallus plants lack chlorophyll and thus live as parasites or saprophytes. The 1,400 species of BACTERIA make up the phylum Schizomycophyta; members of this group are mostly unicellular and lack a typical nucleus, a primitive condition they share with the blue-green algae. The phylum Eumycophyta—the yeasts, molds, and mushrooms—constitutes a large assemblage of over 50,000 species. The vegetative body is chiefly filamentous, but the reproductive structures are often massive, as in the fruiting cap of a mushroom. (See ALGAE; FUNGI.)

Leaving the thallus line of plant evolution, we come to the photosynthetic plants that have established themselves on

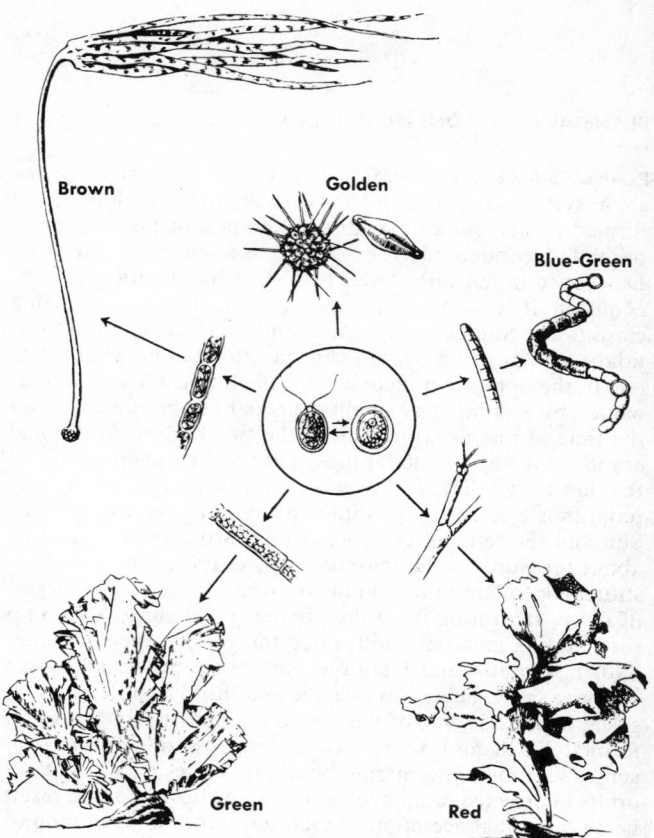

Plant evolution: All plants evolved from single-celled organisms. Diagram above shows how two different stages of a unicellular alga (central circle) may have developed into the various forms of algae that exist today. (*From Bonner*)

land. To do so, these plants had to possess specialized tissues or organs to prevent desiccation, anchor the plant to the substratum, absorb water and nutrients, support a photosynthetic expanse, and provide an internal vascular system of PHLOEM and XYLEM. The phylum Bryophyta, including 23,000 species of mosses and liverworts, is today the simplest group of green land plants; with only a few of the above adaptations to land life, these plants are restricted to moist, protected habitats. The phylum Tracheophyta, possessing the necessary land adaptations, is an imposing assemblage of 260,000 species, by far the largest phylum in the plant kingdom; the number and widespread occurrence of these plants as herbs, shrubs, and trees testify to their success as terrestrial organisms. Contributing much to this success is their possession of special conducting channels that form a vascular system extending from roots, through stems, to leaves (see VASCULAR PLANT). Tracheophytes can attain great size because they develop woody tissue. The phylum includes several classes, formerly grouped in the two phyla Pteridophyta and Spermatophyta; the former includes the ferns, horsetails, and clubmosses—flowerless plants that formed the dominant land vegetation in previous geologic periods but that have been succeeded by the seed plants (Spermatophyta). Two large classes of seed plants are the GYMNOSPERMS, which have seeds but lack flowers and fruits; and the angiosperms, or FLOWERING PLANTS, which have the flower-fruit-seed organ system for reproduction. Tracheophytes have become a tremendous asset to man, since they are a source of all our agricultural products, fibers, and textile materials; wood for building and for manufacture of wood products; and drugs and medicinal products. In addition, they conserve water supplies, prevent erosion, renew atmospheric oxygen, and provide homes for game animals. See BOTANY.—*C. J. H.*

PLANT ASSOCIATIONS: see COMMUNITY, ANIMAL AND PLANT; POPULATION; SUCCESSION.

PLANT BREEDING: see BREEDING OF PLANTS AND ANIMALS.

PLANT GEOGRAPHY (or phytogeography): the study of the distribution of plant species, genera, and families, as a result of their natural dispersal and their dispersal by man. Plant geographers attempt to explain distribution patterns in terms of present ecological limitations and of changes in distribution during geological history. They need a knowledge of fossil plants, of evolutionary mechanisms and taxonomic relations, of plant ecology, climatology, soil science, and the science of geomorphology. *Plant areas* are never quite continuous, but rather consist of separate localities. When species grow in areas separated by extensive regions in which the species do not exist (*e.g.* oceans, plains), the areas are called *disjunct*. Species that occupy very small areas (such as mountains or islands) are called *endemic*. Species with world-wide distribution are called *cosmopolitan*. All degrees of intermediate areas exist. According to J. C. Willis' *age and area hypothesis,* a plant species begins as a small, endemic population, then expands to become widespread and eventually disjunct. Each disjunct segregate then may evolve into a separate species, resuming the cycle (see EVOLUTION).

Historic Factors: The distribution of a species is the result of its migrations and evolutionary history. FOSSILS often attest to past distribution (*e.g.* redwoods in Greenland, Europe, elsewhere). To explain how species have moved from one continent to another, three main hypotheses have been advocated. According to the CONTINENTAL DRIFT hypothesis, at one time all land on earth was in one single continent, portions of which then separated and drifted apart. Present plant distributions would still reflect the existence of this single original land mass. Continental drift is often called upon to account for similarities in land flora and fauna in S Africa, S America, and Australia. The second hypothesis states that *land bridges* at one time connected parts of the continents, permitting the passage of plant populations. Several land bridges are known to have existed between England and Europe, and between Siberia and Alaska, and they appear to explain floristic similarities in these areas. A third hypothesis is based on *transoceanic movement of seeds,* which is known to occur between Pacific islands and in the W Indies. Although most seeds perish in salt water, some are carried far by birds, winds, or other agencies, and the possibility is strong that in the course of millions of years of geologic time a few seeds could island-hop successfully and become established in new habitats (see POPULATION). Other events that have been important in the spread of plants are glaciations, changes in sea level (emergence or submergence of land masses), and climatic changes. These events have caused migrations of vegetation and account for many peculiarities in plant distribution, especially in N America and Europe.

Ecological Factors: The distribution of vegetation depends largely upon climate and soil conditions. The difficulty facing plant geographers is that no one factor alone will account for the total distribution of a species. In areas of high rainfall, the soil requirements of plants may differ from those in dry areas. Also, a species may have evolved so recently that it is not yet at the limit of its potential area. In such cases, most ecological explanations fail.

Plant geography contributes to an understanding of the origin, history, and civilization of an area. For example, the history of early Indian cultures in Latin America is written in the distribution of maize varieties; and the distribution of cotton species gives us clues to the migrations and affinities of the American Indians and Pacific and Asiatic peoples.—*K. L.*

PLANT MOVEMENTS: slow, coordinated changes in position or direction occurring in roots, stems, leaves, and flowers, seemingly in response to specific hormones. Most movements are caused by differences in rate of growth in adjacent parts, causing bending in young regions of the plant. Less common are the reversible movements created by local wilting.

Different rates of growth, in response to the stimulus of gravity, light, or contact, cause the bending of roots toward the earth, of stems away from the earth, of roots away from light, of stems toward light, and of climbing vines toward the supports to which they cling. The hormones that mediate these growth changes are called AUXINS. They are produced in leaves and buds, and travel in the phloem downward under the force of gravity, decreasing in concentration with distance from the secreting regions. Auxins serve to stimulate stem elongation, to inhibit root elongation, and to inhibit development of lateral (axillary) buds; they are inactivated by light.

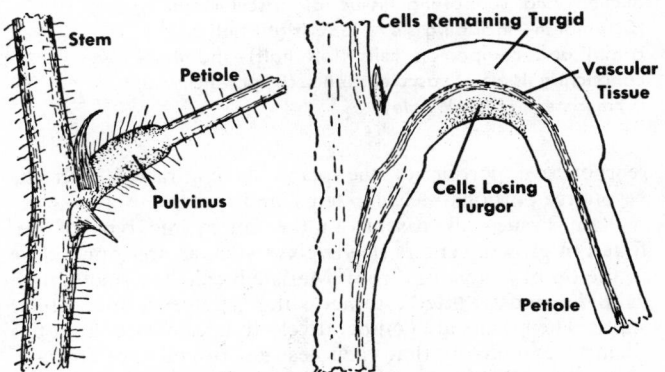

Movement of leaf stalk: Petiole of sensitive plant (*Mimosa pudica*) is held up by turgid pulvinus tissue (*left*). When leaf is touched, cells of lower side of pulvinus lose water, and petiole collapses (*right*). (*From Weatherwax*)

Reversible movements caused by TURGOR changes are usually more rapid than growth changes. Reversible movements occur within specialized parts (pulvini) along the midrib of the leaf in the Venus's flytrap (*Dionaea*); at the point of attachment of the leaflets in clover, wood sorrel (*Oxalis*), and other plants; and at the base of the petiole in the sensitive plant (*Mimosa pudica*). They are responsible for the sudden closure of the flytrap leaf, for the so-called sleep movements of clover, wood sorrel, and other plants, and for the spectacular response of the sensitive plant to touch. Still other types of movements, as the rotation of sunflower heads to face the Sun and the repeated opening and closing of flowers with no directive stimulus, require further study to identify the underlying mechanisms. See CARNIVOROUS PLANT; TROPISM AND TAXIS.—*L. and M. M.*

PLANT ORGANS AND TISSUES: subdivisions of the body of a VASCULAR PLANT. Closely associated cells form tissues, and one or more tissues form the structural and functional unit known as an organ. The ROOT, STEM, and LEAF are distinct plant organs. The cones of GYMNOSPERMS (*e.g.* conifers) and the flowers of FLOWERING PLANTS are generally regarded as being composed of modified leaves, and hence are compound structures—each group of organs. Although some parts of a FLOWER or of a cone may be sterile and contribute nothing directly to reproduction, the entire structure is considered a

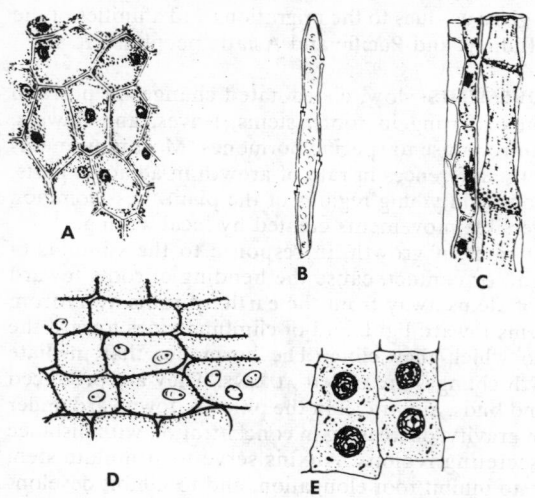

Plant tissues: (A) leaf epidermis; (B) xylem, the conducting and supporting tissue of vascular plants; (C) phloem—including sieve tube (right half of diagram) and companion cells (left half)—the other conducting tissue of vascular plants; (D) parenchyma; (E) meristem. (From Whaley)

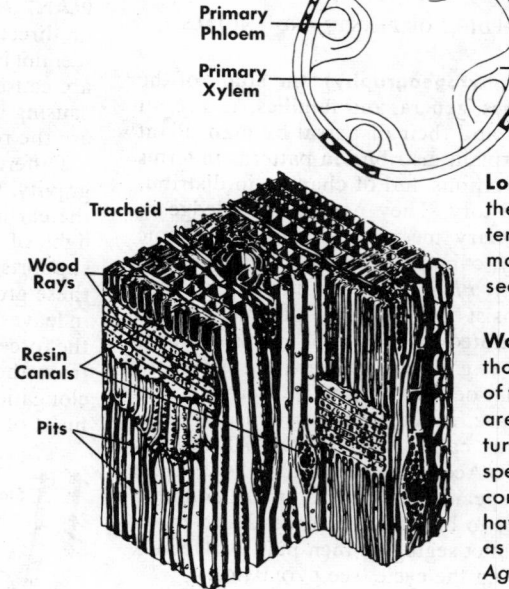

Location of tissue layers of the central cylinder of a buttercup root is shown schematically in enlarged cross section. (From Whaley)

Wood of gymnosperm: Although all wood is composed of the same type of cells, there are many variations in structure. For example, gymnosperms frequently lack vessels common in angiosperms, but have distinctive resin canals as shown. (U. S. Dept. of Agriculture)

reproductive portion of the plant, as contrasted with the vegetative portions—leaves, stems, and roots.

Plant tissues all arise from the embryonic type of cell found in growth centers (*meristems*), such as are found close to the tip of a stem or a root. Meristem cells are small, often cuboidal, and are fitted together with scarcely any intercellular space. Their walls are comparatively thin, and cytoplasm fills them so completely that vacuoles (*e.g.* of cell sap) are rare. Meristem cells are capable of rapid and repeated CELL DIVISION. From the terminal meristems of root and stem come *primary* tissues, such as parenchyma, epidermis, collenchyma, endodermis, and the vascular tissues xylem (primary xylem) and phloem (primary phloem). *Secondary* tissues arise from lateral meristems (cambiums), which provide for the growth in diameter of roots and stems in DICOTS and gymnosperms. These tissues include secondary xylem, secondary phloem, periderm, phelloderm, sclerenchyma, and additional parenchyma.

Primary Tissues: Least specialized of the tissues arising from meristems is *parenchyma* (known also as "fundamental tissue" or "ground tissue"). Parenchyma cells are large, thin-walled, and rounded. Because of their roundness, they tend to fit together quite loosely, with intercellular spaces occurring between them. Generally the volume of vacuoles in each cell equals or exceeds the volume of cytoplasm. Parenchyma is the principal storage tissue in the cortex of stem and root, in the pith of stems, in the pulp of fruits; in young stems and leaves, its cells generally contain chloroplastids (making it a *chlorenchyma*) and carry on PHOTOSYNTHESIS. Parenchyma cells retain the ability to undergo a limited amount of cell division, which is important in the closing of wounds. In specific regions of root and stem, parenchyma cells may dedifferentiate to become meristematic; this is the origin of the pericycle tissue in the root (from which branch roots arise) and of the cambium in roots and stems. *Epidermis* tissue forms the outside covering of young roots and stems, leaves, and fruits. Usually it is one cell thick, with the cells fitted together tightly; it lacks chloroplastids except in specialized pairs of cells ("guard cells") around the stomata of leaves and young stems. Epidermal cells on plant organs normally exposed to

air are generally waterproofed by a secreted cuticle. Commonly a great many epidermal cells of roots extend themselves among the soil particles; as "root hairs" they greatly increase the absorptive surface of the root. On stems, leaves, flower parts, and fruits, epidermal cells may project in pointed or branching structures that are hairlike or spiny; in some leaves (*e.g.* those of many bog plants), the hairs on the under surface appear to help in reducing water loss or in keeping insects away from the softer parts of the leaf. *Collenchyma* is a stiffening tissue often found paralleling the veins of a leaf or below the epidermis of a young stem. It consists of elongated living cells the walls of which are thickened internally in lengthwise strips, particularly in the corners where the parallel cells fit together. *Endodermis* is a sheath of cells one cell thick that forms the innermost boundary of the cortex in the root. In the region of absorption in the root (the level at which epidermal cells extend as root hairs), the radial walls of endodermis cells become thickened with deposits of fatty materials. This blocks the passive movement of water through the cellulose walls from the vascular cylinder (where the water may be under high pressure) back toward the soil. *Xylem* and *phloem* (the vascular tissues) are composed both of cells specialized for TRANSLOCATION of chemical substances within the plant and of supporting cells; they are *compound* tissues, whereas parenchyma, epidermis, collenchyma, and endodermis are *simple* tissues, because each is composed essentially of one type of cell. Xylem consists of water-conducting tracheids and vessels (tracheae), supporting fibers, and parenchyma cells. Of these, only the parenchyma cells are alive at functional maturity. Tracheids develop from single elongated cells, the cytoplasm of which deposits additional wall material in the form of rings, spirals, or patches; these structures give extra strength to the cell. After forming them, the cytoplasm dies and disappears; water passes into and out of the cell through the remaining thin-walled regions. Vessels are formed from cells that line up end to end, then lose their end walls and protoplasm. Before cytoplasm dies in a vessel cell, it adds strengthening bands or sheaths to the cell wall. Fibers also arise from elongated cells, the cytoplasm of which, before dying and disappearing, adds a great thickness of stiffening material rather uniformly to the wall. Sometimes fibers are in distinct bundles, called *sclerenchyma* or sclerenchymatous tissue, within the xylem. The parenchyma cells of xylem are arranged chiefly in thin radial vanes, one or two cells thick. In transverse sections of a stem, they are evident as radiating lines of cells, called xylem rays or xylem parenchyma. The cell types of phloem are sieve tubes, companion cells, fibers, and parenchyma. Sieve tubes and companion cells arise together from elongated cells down the length of which a cell wall develops. The wall separates a companion cell, of small diameter, from a parallel sieve tube, of larger diameter. The companion cell retains the nucleus from the pre-existing cell, and appears to control the translocation of organic compounds through the sieve tube. The end walls of a sieve tube are perforated by a large number of pores, through which the cytoplasm of one sieve tube communicates with the cytoplasm of the next sieve tube in the line; the perforated end walls are the "sieve plates" for which the conducting cell is named. Fibers in phloem tend to be in larger groups than the fibers in xylem, but the phloem parenchyma usually is in the same radiating lines as the xylem parenchyma. Only the fibers of phloem are dead cells at maturity. Companion cells and the parenchyma cells of vascular tissue continue to live, sometimes for the life of the plant.

Secondary Tissues: In the roots and stems of dicots and gymnosperms, the primary vascular tissues may be supplemented by new secondary vascular tissue, through the activity of the *cambium* (a lateral meristem). The cambium develops from parenchyma lying between the xylem and phloem, and completely surrounds the xylem in most woody plants. The thin sheath of cambium produces new cells around both its inner and outer surfaces. From the inner surface come new conducting cells of xylem, new xylem fibers, and new xylem parenchyma in line with the previous parenchyma ray tissue. As the sheath of secondary xylem becomes thicker with continued growth and the parenchyma rays reach the cambium at greater intervals, new rays of parenchyma begin to appear. From the outer surface of the vascular cambium come new companion cells and sieve tubes, new fibers, and new parenchyma as a continuation of the parenchyma rays. All this secondary growth pushes the primary phloem radially outward from the central axis of the root or stem. As a result, the integrity of the plant organ is threatened: the epidermis ruptures lengthwise at many points, and the primary cortex parenchyma is torn apart, just as garments split when forced to go around a growing body. The plant safeguards its integrity by developing additional lateral meristems (*cork cambiums*).

These overlapping meristems provide new secondary tissue of the *periderm* as a waterproof outer bark that replaces the ruptured epidermis and primary cortex. In roots, the cork cambiums (phellogens) arise in the pericycle. In stems, which have no pericycle, the cork cambiums arise as discontinuous, overlapping patches in the greater thickness of the primary cortex parenchyma. Periderm is a compound tissue, since it includes waterproof *cork* cells (produced from the outer surface of each cork cambium) and thin-walled *phelloderm* cells that resemble parenchyma (produced from the inner surface of the cork cambium). Phelloderm cells serve in storage and, sometimes, in food manufacture. Cork cambiums also extend themselves in tangential directions, thus maintaining the continuity of the root or stem and remaining in a position to furnish new phelloderm cells between the points of primary phloem or in any spaces that tend to develop through the expanding action of the vascular cambium. Cork cambiums often produce bundles of sclerenchyma; frequently they replace previous stiffening bundles of collenchyma, which are lost along with epidermis and primary cortex tissue. Sclerenchyma cells are fibers; they are dead cells easily distinguished from the cells of collenchyma. In some plants, the cork cambiums produce additional special tissues, such as resin ducts and latex-secreting cells.

The development of secondary tissues in roots usually occurs at the same time as the impregnation of fatty materials in the tangential walls of the endodermis, bringing to a halt all movement of water and solutes between the cortex and the vascular cylinder. Any cortex beyond the cork cambium developing in the pericycle is sloughed off along the epidermis, while cork cells take over the role of blocking loss of water from the maturing root. The endodermis, as the innermost sheath of cortex cells, is thus lost soon after its tangential walls become waterproof.—*L. and M. M.*

PLANT PHYSIOLOGY: the biological science dealing with the functions and activities of plants. Plant physiologists seek the answers to the how and the why of plant nutrition, metabolism, growth, development, and reproduction; they study plants in action. Historically, plant physiology had its inception with the work of the English chemist Stephen Hales (1677–1761), who was one of the first scientists to see the need for a union of chemistry and biology in interpreting plant functions. His *Vegetable Staticks* (1727) described the first scientific experiments with transpiration, root pressure, sap movement, and plant growth. He also was first to appreciate the importance of leaves as food-manufacturing organs and the role of light in photosynthesis. Other chemists (Joseph Priestley, Nicolas de Saussure, Justus von Liebig) followed Hales' lead; Liebig made important contributions in discovering the role of minerals in plant nutrition and the use of fertilizers. By the end of the 19th cent., plant physiology was firmly established as an important field of biology.

The subject matter of plant physiology falls into three main categories: nutrition, metabolism, and growth. *Plant nutrition* is of fundamental importance, since green plants produce the food upon which animals and man ultimately depend. The key process in nutrition is PHOTOSYNTHESIS, whereby plants make food available to all animals for formation of protoplasm and the potential energy for all living activities. As a result, much physiological research is devoted to all aspects of the photosynthetic process. In addition, the study of plant nutrition involves finding out what minerals are needed by plants, how they are absorbed, and how used. This is the basis of the scientific use of fertilizers. Another important aspect is that of the water relations of plants; knowledge gained in this area has led to better irrigation techniques, which have opened up many arid regions where previously it had been difficult to raise crops. Research in plant nutrition also investigates the effect of soil factors on plant development and TRANSLOCATION of materials within the plant. *Plant metabolism* includes many interrelated activities of plants; among them are the special aspects of the biochemical changes that take place in the metabolism of carbohydrates, lipids, and nitrogen compounds. The metabolic processes are controlled by ENZYMES, whose nature and function must be determined to understand their role in plant health. *Plant growth* includes a number of factors, within the plant as well as in its environment, which affect GROWTH rates and productivity. The life history of a plant, from seed germination through production of foliage, flowers, fruits, and finally the seeds that repeat the cycle, is an orderly sequence of events that are kept in harmony with each other and the environment by means of HORMONES. Recent physiological research has greatly increased our knowledge of the ways in which these chemical messengers affect plant growth and development, and the production of flowers and fruits. Familiar examples are the growth-stimulating solutions used in plant propagation, weed killers, and the substances used in controlling leaf fall, flower production, and fruit drop.

The importance of plant physiology lies in its relationship to agronomy, horticulture, and forestry. Since food production is affected vitally by knowledge of how plants grow, plant physiology is of paramount importance, especially in these times of increasing world population. See BOTANY; PLANT; PLANT MOVEMENTS; TRANSPIRATION.—*C. J. H.*

PLANT PROPAGATION: in horticulture, any means for increasing the number of individuals of some particular kind of plant. Thus peas or carrots can be propagated by seeds, whereas certain other kinds of plants, *e.g.* tulips, are propagated by bulbs. Sometimes the usage is restricted to mean propagation by any agency other than seeds. Seeds are produced by the fusion of sex cells. Any other means of getting more plants would be by asexual methods. Popularly, propagation has come to mean asexual or vegetative reproduction of the plant by bulbs, tubers, corms, bulblets, tuberous roots, rooting of stem or leaf cuttings, grafting, or dividing a plant into two or more parts.—*H. Cr.*

PLANT REPRODUCTION: see REPRODUCTION.

PLASMA: state of matter in which a considerable proportion of atoms are split into free electrons and positive ions. For this degree of ionization to exist, matter must be in a gaseous form and usually at a high temperature. The ionized gases in fluorescent tubes, in neon tubes, and across the gap of a carbon arc, as well as the stream of electrons and ions in vacuum tubes, all are plasmas. Gases approach the plasma state at a temperature of 3,500°F and are fully within that state at temperatures of 15,000°F and above. At these temperatures the random movement of the atoms is so violent that collisions between atoms jar their electrons loose, leaving the electrons and the positive ions to collide with other atoms and jar loose still more electrons. The stars, as well as most interstellar matter, are plasma; in fact, the investigation of stellar behavior initiated the study of plasma. Since plasma is an ionized fluid, it is a conductor of electricity. Because of this characteristic, most applications of plasma depend on the interaction of the plasma with magnetic fields which are either externally applied or are the result of the movement of the plasma itself. The study of the interaction of magnetic fields and plasma and the application to many diverse areas—*e.g.* space travel, high-temperature technology, and power production from nuclear fusion—is the science of MAGNETOHYDRODYNAMICS.—*A. L.*

PLASMA PROPULSION: a form of rocket propulsion achieved by heating the propellant to the point where appreciable ionization is produced, and simultaneously or subsequently accelerating the ionized gas through an exhaust NOZZLE to provide the reactive thrust. A distinctive feature of plasma propulsion is the use of electromagnetic forces to accelerate the plasma to obtain added thrust. The forces result from the interaction of induced currents in the plasma with a magnetic field. (See MAGNETOHYDRODYNAMICS; PLASMA.) Plasma propulsion differs from ION PROPULSION in that the positively and negatively charged particles constituting a plasma are well mixed, so that the plasma is neutral in the large. This confers an advantage over the negatively charged ionic propellant because it insures electrical neutrality of the vehicle during flight without further experimental complications. Several varieties of plasma-acceleration devices have been studied, but none has

yet been developed for installation in a flight vehicle. Most of the devices are of the gun or shock-tube variety, in which a plasma is produced by discharge of electrical energy at one end of a long tube, and then quickly accelerated down the tube by magnetic forces; velocities of over one million ft/sec have been attained. Thus far, these experiments have been largely of the single-pulse type, but additional research is under way on repeated pulsing as well as on continuous-acceleration techniques. Plasma-propulsion devices, like ion engines, are characterized by a high SPECIFIC IMPULSE, typically 10,000 sec or higher; plasma propulsion would thus be most useful for long space journeys. Chief developmental problems are heat losses to the plasma engine walls, inadequate knowledge of physical properties of plasmas, and the relatively low efficiency of plasma accelerators.—*D. B.*

PLASTIC DEFORMATION: see PLASTICITY.

PLASTICITY: the property of retaining a deformation produced by stress in a material after the stress has been removed. Plasticity may be contrasted with ELASTICITY, which is the property of recovering shape and dimensions after a moderate deforming force is withdrawn. Thus lead solder exhibits plasticity, and hardened steel wire, elasticity. Deformation can be partly elastic and partly plastic. At elevated temperatures most metals deform plastically because the distorted crystal structure does not re-form until after cooling takes place; the new crystals then formed are unstressed. It is this effect that is utilized in the hot-working of metals.—*A. E.*

PLASTICIZER: a substance added to a plastic or resin to render it more pliable and workable. Probably the oldest plasticizer is camphor, which when added to *pyroxylin,* a brittle substance, converts it into *celluloid,* which is thermoplastic (see PLASTICS) and can be molded into useful products. Plasticizers preferably have a very low evaporation rate, so that the finished product will last a long time without becoming brittle.—*Ru. M.*

PLASTICS: organic substances made synthetically by polymerization, and capable of being formed into an almost endless variety of products, *e.g.* threads, sheets, tubes, and molded objects. The term *resin* is generally applied by the industry to the initially made polymeric substances, and the term plastics to the products made from the resin by incorporating other materials such as fillers, coloring matters, antioxidants, and plasticizers. The ancestor of modern synthetic plastics is *celluloid,* first made in the U. S. A. in 1869 by John Wesley Hyatt by plasticizing a nitrocellulose with camphor. Developed as a substitute for ivory in billiard balls, and subsequently used for many other products, celluloid has certain disadvantages—its flammability and the fact that it is not readily molded. Thus it was not until the discovery of BAKELITE in 1907 that the real foundation of the synthetic plastics industry was laid. Plastics that consist of long-chain molecules, however tangled they may be, can be softened by heat and molded into a desired shape; these are called *thermoplastic.* Plastics in which the polymer chains are cross-linked have much greater rigidity and cannot be softened; they are called *thermosetting* because they are permanently set so far as heat is concerned, once they have been cured into the shape of the mold. The terms thermoplastic and thermosetting are also applied to the resins from which plastics are made. See POLYMERS; RESIN.

The principal agent incorporated in a plastic is the resin; it may be natural, like shellac, cellulose, or rosin, but is most generally synthetic. The resin is also known as the binder.

Substances added to the plastic to enhance certain properties, *e.g.* hardness, resistance to shock, or resistance to abrasion, are called fillers; examples are asbestos, glass fibers, and wood flour. PLASTICIZERS are included in the formulation to render the mixture more workable. Metallic soaps, waxes, and oils may be added either to the formulation or to the mold, to prevent the mold from sticking; these are the lubricants. ANTIOXIDANTS may be added to promote chemical stability and thus prolong life. Catalysts are added to assist the final cure (final formation of the product), and stabilizers to protect against sunlight, heat, and other destructive factors.

The procedure used to shape a plastic into its final form depends on the plastic's properties. Some plastics can be injection-molded because when the formulation in its liquid or soft state enters the mold and solidifies, the plastic expands enough to fill all the voids. Other plastics, however, must be compression-molded; after they are filled into the mold they are subjected to pressure, as well as heat if necessary. Certain plastics are simply cast into their final shape, as when a biological specimen in a beaker is encapsulated by pouring a plastic formulation into the beaker and allowing it to cure.

Key Role of Polymerization: A plastic containing a given monomeric substance can often be "tailored" for different end-uses by varying the method of polymerization. A good example is the vinyl-type plastic Lucite (or Plexiglas), the polymer of methyl methacrylate. The monomer can be prepared as an emulsion with water, using the proper emulsifier, then polymerized by adding catalysts which operate through a free-radical mechanism. This produces a molding powder (the resin) which can be combined with various additives for use in making plastics by one of the several molding operations. If, however, the emulsified monomer is not polymerized to the molding powder, it can be incorporated as an aqueous latex (see RUBBER) in water-based paints. Furthermore, if the polymerization of methyl methacrylate is carried out in bulk, then a casting operation produces the final product, *e.g.* all the ingredients of the formulation are mixed in a container of the proper shape and curing allowed to take place. (This cast product by definition is thus both a resin and a plastic.) The casting process can be used for making dental fittings, for mounting biological specimens, and for many other purposes. Some vinyl monomers are not so universal in their adaptability. Vinyl cyanide is more easily polymerized by the emulsion process than in bulk, and is used to make TEXTILE fibers such as Acrilan and Orlon.

The first modern plastic, Bakelite, illustrates many of the problems and techniques associated with the manufacture of plastics, as well as illustrating the variations that are possible using essentially the same polymeric substance. (The trade name Bakelite was for many years synonymous with the

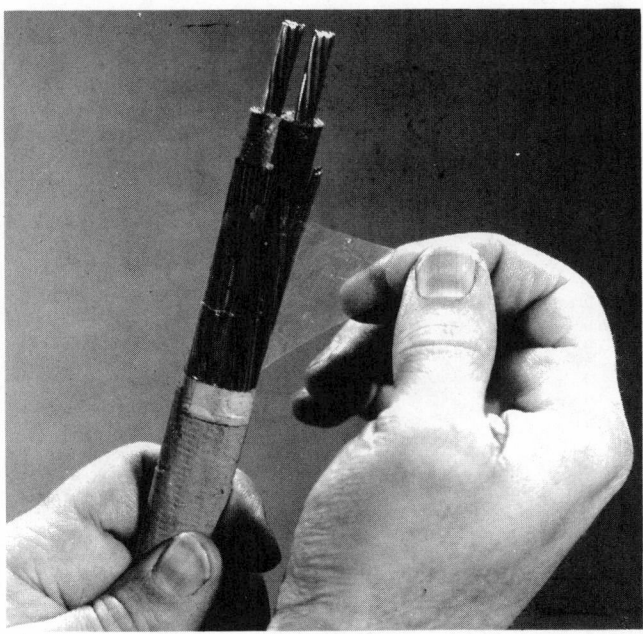

Polyglycol terephthalate film, made by condensation polymerization of ethylene glycol with terephthalic acid, serves as an impregnable dam and binder for typical electric cable serving buildings. Above, 1-mil thick "Mylar" film (upper part cable) is contrasted with 8-mil rubber-filled cotton fabric (lower portion), which it replaced. (*Du Pont*)

term plastic.) The original Bakelite was a thermosetting resin made from phenol and formaldehyde. With a basic catalyst the initial reaction products are methylolphenols:

$$\underset{\text{Phenol}}{\text{OH}} + \underset{\text{Formaldehyde}}{\text{CH}_2\text{O}} \longrightarrow \underset{\text{Methylolphenol}}{\text{OH, CH}_2\text{OH}}$$

Fig. 1

Only the *o*-methylolphenol is shown in the equation, but the *p*- compound also is formed. When heated briefly, the methylolphenols condense with elimination of water to yield chain polymers of relatively short chain length. The upper water layer is removed. This initial polymer (Fig. 2) is the A-stage resin, both fusible (thermoplastic) and soluble.

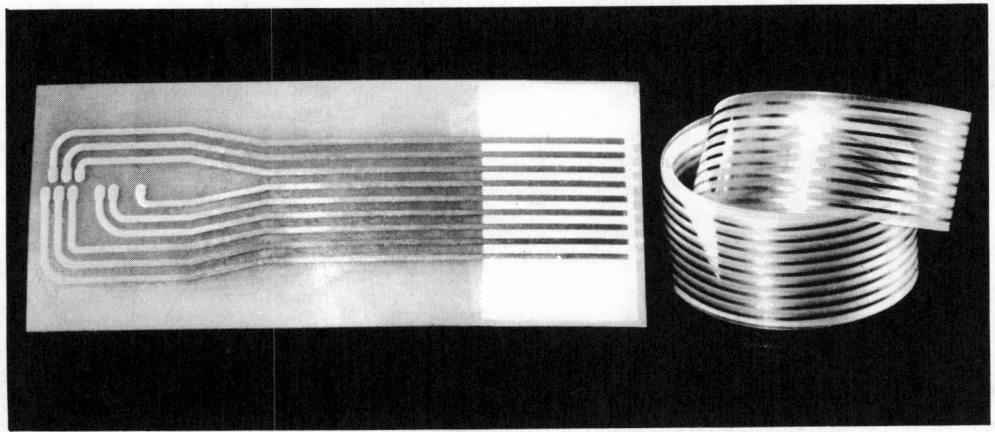

A fluorine plastic, tetrafluoroethylene ("Teflon"), built up by polymerization of fluorocarbons, has high resistance to heat and acid and good electrical-insulation properties; it is thus used as an insulating base for printed circuitry (*left*) and for flat, flexible wire (*right*). In the household, the tetrafluoroethylene polymer finds use as a lining for frying pans. (*Willard Stewart*)

Polyvinyl fluoride, a recently developed plastic, provides a pigmented, corrosion-resistant film surface on the underside of metallic roof decking. This "Tedlar" film eliminates costly, often hazardous painting of production-area ceilings. (*Du Pont*)

There is also a B-stage (produced by further heating) at which the resin is still fusible but less soluble in organic solvents. The fusible resin can be cast into desired objects by running into molds and heating; cross-linking occurs because of an excess of formaldehyde in the formulation, which supplies the CH_2 groups for the cross-links. The final resin (C-stage) is thermosetting. A molding powder can be made by grinding the B-stage resin, which can then be mixed with filler, plasticizer, lubricant, and other additives, and used to make plastics by compression molding. Most of the molding powder is actually made by running the initial polymerization with an acid catalyst, and conducting the final thermosetting operation with a basic agent that also supplies the formaldehyde needed for cross-links.

A di-acid and a di-alcohol can, by condensation polymerization, be condensed to a long-chain polyester with elimination of water as by-product owing to interaction of the OH groups. If some of the acid used in the reaction is maleic acid, $HOOC—CH=CH—COOH$, the resulting chain polymer is an unsaturated polyester because of the presence of the $—CH=CH—$ group. Through this group it is possible to cross-link the chains, by adding small molecules (*e.g.* STYRENE,

Fig. 2: Segments of two linear chains in the fusible A-resin, which can cross-link as shown to give an infusible resin.

$C_6H_5CH=CH_2$) containing more of the same $—CH=CH—$ groups. To make a polyester plastic (or resin), an unsaturated polyester, which is thermoplastic, is dissolved in the styrene monomer; when this mixture is heated it cures to a thermosetting solid. The final cure of the polyester resin takes place without by-products, since it is addition polymerization. The molding process to make large objects requires only simple contact pressure. The polyester resins are used mostly with reinforcing materials, especially fiber glass, and molded into such objects as statues, cradles, auto bodies, and boats. (For discussion of addition vs. condensation polymerization see POLYMERS.)—*Ru. M.*

PLATEAU: an extensive upland region which may have only slight relief (*e.g.* parts of the Plateau of Tibet) but usually has been deeply incised by rivers (*e.g.* Colorado Plateau). Where cutting is advanced, a plateau may have the aspect of a mountain range, with all crests at about the same elevation. Some plateaus result from the accumulation of lava flows (Columbia Plateau). Most originate by the uplift of a thick sequence of nearly horizontal sedimentary rocks (Colorado Plateau; Appalachian Plateau).—*E. A.*

PLATEAU, JOSEPH ANTOINE FERDINAND, 1801–83, Belgian physicist; b. Brussels. Though blind, he pioneered in study of optics, behavior of molecules in motion, and stroboscopic analysis of vibratory motion. He wrote *Statique expérimentale et théorique des liquides* (1873).—*W. P. C.*

PLATINUM: a lustrous, silver-gray, metallic element (Pt); at. no. 78; at. wt 195.09; mp 1773.5; sp gr 21.37 (20°C); it is the most-used and most plentiful of the *platinum metals,* a group of six elements occupying a block in group VII of the periodic table; iron, cobalt, and nickel form the *upper triad* of group VII, followed by the platinum metals RUTHENIUM, RHODIUM, PALLADIUM (*middle triad*) and OSMIUM, IRIDIUM, and platinum (*lower triad*). Platinum was the first of these metals to be discovered. The difficulty caused by native platina alloy in gold refining was reported from Colombia and Mexico in the mid-16th cent. In 1735, Don Antonio de Ulloa accompanied a joint French and Spanish scientific expedition to Peru and subsequently noted the existence of native platinum, but de Ulloa's papers were not published until 1748. Concurrently (1741), the English metallurgist Charles Wood sent a specimen of Colombia platina to William Brownrigg in England, who 9 yr later (1750) reported the existence of a new "semi-metal" to the Royal Society. In 1803 William Wollaston obtained pure platinum. Rich deposits exist in the U. S. S. R. (Ural Mts), S Africa (Transvaal), S America (Colombia), and Canada (Sudbury). Platinum has a face-centered cube structure and is a malleable and highly ductile metal. It can be drawn into a wire 0.00005 in. in diameter; 1 oz of metal can be drawn out for several hundred miles. Platinum does not tarnish when exposed to air or sulfur in urban environments. Its excellent resistance to corrosion, low electrical resistivity, and high ductility make platinum useful in highly precise thermocouples, resistance thermometers, and electrical instruments. Various alloying elements, *e.g.* ruthenium and iridium, are used to impart greater hardness or corrosion resistance for certain applications. The metal and its alloys are used as anodes in electroplating processes; in the electrical industry for contacts, brushes, precision potentiometer wire, and heavy low-loss cable in power stations; as grids in radar tubes; in heavy-duty spark-plug electrodes; to make spinnerets for forming synthetic fibers; and in crucibles (often with 3.5% rhodium) for the production of high-purity optical glass. Platinum is an outstanding oxidation catalyst and is used in the manufacture of acetic, nitric, and sulfuric acids, in production of vitamins and other chemicals, and in petroleum-reforming processes, particularly the production of high-octane gasoline. Because platinum's coefficient of linear expansion is near that of glass, the metal is widely used for vacuum-tube leads where a permanently airtight seal is essential. Because of its low thermal expansion, as well as its hardness, durability, and corrosion resistance, an alloy of 90% platinum and 10% iridium is used to make the National Prototype Meters and Kilograms maintained by individual nations (see MEASUREMENT SYSTEMS, photograph). Platinum and its alloys are also used in dental and surgical prosthetic devices and for jewelry and ornamentation.—*R. B. T.*

THE PLATINUM METALS

Name	At. No.	At. Wt.	Valence	mp °C	Sp Gr
Ruthenium	44	101.1	2,3,4,6,8	2450	12.2 (20°C)
Rhodium	45	102.91	3	1966	12.5 (20°C)
Palladium	46	106.4	2,4,6	1549	12.16 (20°C)
Osmium	76	190.2	2,3,4,8	2700	22.48 (20°C)
Iridium	77	192.2	3,4	2454	22.42 (17°C)
Platinum	78	195.09	2,4	1774	21.37 (20°C)

PLATO, 428/427–348/347 B. C., Gr. philosopher; b. Athens. A disciple of Socrates, Plato has had enormous effect on science. From Parmenides he took the view that our senses are unreliable, and maintained that intelligible reality consists in the eternal forms (or "ideas") which objects embody only imperfectly, and which can be grasped only by reason but not by sense observation. This doctrine is often called "Platonic idealism," but the "ideas" are not to be understood as things existing in some mind. From the Pythagoreans Plato learned the importance of mathematics, and he eventually proposed a cosmology in which the five regular geometric solids played a fundamental role and stimulated active interest in mathematics among his own students. Thus Platonism in science has emphasized the importance of abstract thought and of mathematics, while belittling the need for sensory observation. N. Copernicus, J. Kepler, Galileo Galilei, and I. Newton were in the Platonistic tradition, which is typical of mathematical physicists. Before the 12th cent. only the *Timaeus* was available in Western Christendom, and its influence was generally anti-scientific.—*D. H. D. R.*

PLAYA: a shallow basin in an arid region. Such basins in deserts receive runoff of streams after occasional, sometimes heavy, precipitation. This accumulated runoff, charged with dissolved salts, may cover a large area, forming a "playa lake." The combination of high temperature, low humidity, and extensive surface in relation to the volume of water results in swift evaporation, leaving a bed of precipitated salts (see EVAPORITES) on the site of the lake.—*E. A.*

PLAYFAIR, JOHN, 1748–1819, Scottish mathematician and geologist; b. Benvie, near Dundee. His masterly *Illustrations of the Huttonian Theory of the Earth* (1802) was largely responsible for the great influence exerted on geology by the ideas (especially uniformitarianism) of JAMES HUTTON, who was himself an inadequate writer. Playfair, professor of mathematics (1785–1805) and natural philosophy (1805–19) at the Univ. of Edinburgh, also wrote a number of works on mathematical and physical subjects. He was a fellow of the Royal Society.—*D. H. D. R.*

PLEIADES (M45): the earliest- and best-known of all STAR CLUSTERS, in the constellation Taurus. Though six stars of this galactic cluster are easily visible to the naked eye, early

The Pleiades, close to the plane of the Milky Way, are an open cluster several hundred light-years from the Sun. The nebulosity in which they are shrouded is very faint in this photo, which was taken in red light. (*Mt Wilson*)

legends associate the Pleiades with the number seven, which suggests that one star has become fainter. The cluster, containing up to 500 stars, has a diameter of about 30 lt-yr. The brightest stars are blue, and there is much nebulosity. The age of the Pleiades is estimated at 50 million yr. Observations with radio telescopes hint that stars may still be in process of formation within the cluster.—*H. S. H.*

PLEISTOCENE EPOCH: see CENOZOIC ERA; GEOLOGICAL TIME CHART.

PLEURA AND PLEURAL CAVITY: The pleura (*pl.* pleurae) is a part of the PERITONEUM found in the chest or pleural cavity of mammals. It adheres to a LUNG and the adjacent inner chest wall. The pleural cavity is the *potential* space between the two adherent sheets of this tissue. In life, a "suction," or subatmospheric pressure, exists in the pleural cavity, which helps prevent lung collapse. In dogs and many other mammals, one pleural cavity encloses both lungs; in man, however, the cavity is divided completely in two, making possible the inflation of one cavity to inactivate a lung diseased with tuberculosis, a procedure followed in the therapeutic practice of pneumothorax.—*A. R. D.*

PLINIUS SECUNDUS, GAIUS (Pliny the Elder), 23–79, Roman civil servant and author; b. Como. A voracious reader, he compiled his *Historia naturalis* in 37 books, which he dedicated to the future emperor Titus, his comrade-in-arms in Syria. He wrote many other works, also, and his scientific encyclopedia survived through the Dark Ages to become a great influence throughout the Middle Ages and long after. The first English translation, by Philemon Holland, dates from 1601. Pliny perished at Pompeii when, as a commander of the fleet at nearby Misenum, he went ashore to witness the effects of the great eruption of Vesuvius.—*R. J. F.*

PLIOCENE EPOCH: see CENOZOIC ERA; GEOLOGICAL TIME CHART.

PLÜCKER, JULIUS, 1801–68, German mathematician; b. Elberfeld. He introduced an abridged notation into analytic geometry, applying it to straight lines, circles, conics, and cubic curves. His greatest work was on algebraic curves: "Plücker's equations" relate the singularities of algebraic curves. He discussed cubic curves exhaustively, enumerating 219 different kinds. His researches in physics included important investigations of magnetic bodies and of spectroscopy. He was a fellow of the Royal Society.—*H. C.*

PLUMBING: the fixtures, pipes, and controlling and cleaning devices necessary for the use of water in a building, ship, or railroad car. Clay and wood pipes for water supply date from pre-classical antiquity. Metal pipes (bronze and lead) and methods of discharging sewage by means of water are chiefly Roman inventions. Modern pressure-plumbing dates from the mid-19th cent., when rapid growth of densely populated cities made sanitary water facilities a necessity. Today the functions of a plumbing system include the supplying of pure water under pressure, safe disposal of waste and sewage, and prevention of contamination of the pure water supply through cross-connections, ground seepage, gases, bacteria, and vermin. A building's plumbing system begins where the supply line leaves the municipal water main; it runs through various fixtures and ends where the disposal line joins the street sewer. In rural areas, wells and septic tanks may take the place of mains and sewers. Major parts of a system are: supply main; primary cold-water line and the line passing through the water heater, with branches serving the fixtures; drains, which eventually join the disposal main; and the venting system, consisting of traps and stacks for maintaining atmospheric pressure in the various lines to prevent back-movement of waste and to block the passage of gases and organisms. The venting system is so designed that air can be exhausted when line pressure exceeds that of the atmosphere, and air introduced when line pressure falls below atmospheric pressure. Commonly used materials are enameled steel for fixtures; copper and galvanized wrought iron or steel for piping; and vitreous clay for ground drains. In multistory apartment buildings, fixtures and piping are arranged, when possible, to permit vertical alignment of facilities. A single vertical supply line can thus serve all fixtures, and a single disposal line can remove all waste. Contemporary practice for office buildings is to concentrate all plumbing, heating, and electrical facilities in a single centrally located core or shaft.—*C. W. C.*

PLUMB LINE: a cord with a weight that is attached to its lower end and allowed to hang free. The weight, called a *plumb bob,* is usually in the shape of an inverted cone. The point of the cone then hangs vertically below the point at which the upper end of the cord is held. Plumb lines are commonly used to determine true vertical lines by carpenters, plumbers, and bricklayers. Surveyors hang a plumb line from the bottom of a transit or, in uneven terrain, from the end of a measuring tape carefully kept horizontal. That part of the instrument or tape from which the plumb line hangs is then precisely in a vertical line over the point indicated by the plumb bob.—*A. L.*

PLUTO: the most remote planet known (at times, however, coming nearer to the Sun than Neptune). It was discovered by Clyde Tombaugh, 1930, at the Lowell Observatory, and crowned a search for a trans-Neptunian planet begun there a quarter of a century earlier. The tiny planet was actually found near one of two positions predicted by Percival Lowell, 1915, according to calculations based on outstanding residuals in the orbit of Uranus, and by W. H. Pickering, 1919, from perturbations in the orbit of Neptune. The symbol adopted for the planet, ♇, is a combination of Lowell's initials as well as being the first two letters of Pluto.

Pluto moves round the Sun in an orbit of mean distance 39.5 astronomical units, or 3,700 million mi. The sidereal orbital period is about 248 yr, the synodic period 366.7 mean solar days. The eccentricity of the orbit, 0.25, is the largest for the planets, and the orbital inclination, 17°.3, is more than twice that of any other planet. Because of the high eccentricity, Pluto at perihelion is closer to the Sun than

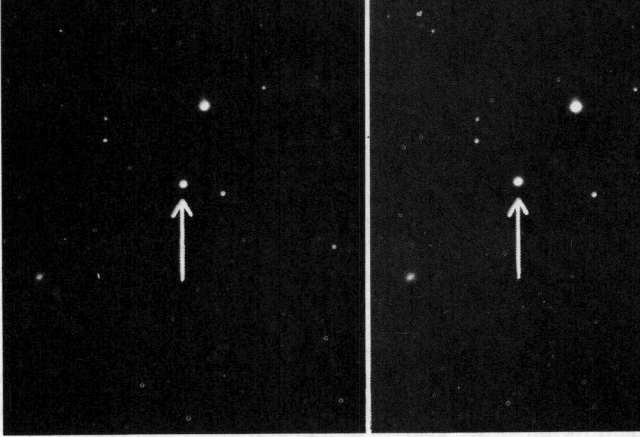

Pluto: Slowly moving against a background of "fixed" stars, the outermost planet of the solar system is here seen in two photographs taken 24 hr apart through the 200-in. reflector. When found by Clyde Tombaugh in Lowell Observatory search photographs in 1930, it was approaching the ascending node of its orbit. It is due to reach perihelion in 1989, when its distance of 2,760 million mi from the Sun will put it within the orbit of Neptune. (*Mt Wilson*)

Neptune is. The two orbits do not at present even nearly intersect, but as they precess under planetary action they could come to do so and may have done so in the past. This suggests that Pluto may once have been a second large satellite of Neptune, comparable with Triton, that escaped and in so doing reversed the motion of Triton, which is now retrograde. The rotation period of Pluto is difficult to observe and its value is highly uncertain. Estimates range from less than a day to nearly a week, though the longer values seem more likely.

At its brightest, Pluto is a 15th-magnitude object, and so can be observed only with fairly large telescopes; only the very largest show it as a disc. In 1950, its diameter was measured as about 3,600 mi, but this is uncertain. It has no satellites and produces only minute perturbations on the other planets; its mass is therefore extremely difficult to determine. According to Brouwer and Clemence, its mass is nearly equal to that of Earth, implying an exceptionally high density. In appearance the planet is described as yellowish; its power of reflecting light is considered to be exceptionally low, possibly indicating a very rough surface with transparent or negligible atmosphere. In view of Pluto's distance from the Sun, the surface temperature must be lower than − 290°F.—*R. A. L.*

PLUTON: a body of INTRUSIVE ROCK formed at depth by solidification of magma; or, broadly, a similar body formed by replacement of original igneous rock by a pseudo-igneous rock through the process of metamorphism. All plutons are deep-seated in origin, and the various types are distinguished solely by size and shape, not composition. Cooling of an entire magma chamber of the size that presumably feeds a group of volcanoes, or replacement of any similarly large mass of rock by rock of another composition, would result in a body of vast dimensions, called a BATHOLITH or *bathylith* (Gr. *bathys,* "deep"). Some plutons evidently were formed by magma passing through older rock, forcing it up, or otherwise displacing it. Magma that invades a joint (a transverse crack in rock strata) and cools there forms a wall-like *dike;* if it forces its way between strata along a bedding plane, taking a sheetlike form, it becomes a *sill.* Dikes and sills radiate from batholiths and other large plutons. When a smaller reservoir of magma accumulates at the end of a channel, it may cool as a *laccolith* (Gr. *lakkos,* "tank"), after forcing older rock upward into a dome. Magma in the channel between a reservoir and a volcanic crater may eventually cool to form a body of which the upper section is the *plug* of the volcano. (The plug, when the crater has eroded away, remains as a *neck*.) All plutons, having been formed at depth, can appear at the surface only by being uncovered through erosion or faulting.

Plutons range from such batholiths as that forming the Coast Mts of British Columbia, thousands of square miles in area (depth unknown), to little fingerlike dikes traversing beds of sedimentary rock. The distinction between a batholith and a *stock*, as revealed by the outcrop, is arbitrary. All plutons with more than 40 mi² of surface are generally considered batholiths, but some of lesser surface and unknown depth, apparently the upper domes of batholiths, are given the name stock. Large plutons are almost always coarse-grained—granite or granodiorite; dikes and sills are most often fine-grained and basaltic. A sill when exposed is distinguished from a lava flow by the fact that *all* rock surfaces in contact with the sill may show scorching, whereas a lava flow, being a surface event, would have scorched only the rock over which it poured; rock formed over it later would not have been scorched. In fact, the relationship of plutons to adjacent formations gives significant information to geologists as to the interaction of magma and pre-existing rock, as to melting in the crust, and as to formation of granitic masses by transformation of solid rocks without the intervention of magma (see *granitization* under GRANITE).—*E. A.*

PLUTONIUM: a transuranium element (Pu) first prepared artificially but existing naturally in trace quantities in uranium ores; at. no. 94; at. wt 242 (most stable isotope). It has an unusual history and remarkable nuclear and chemical properties. It was discovered in late 1940 and early 1941 by G. T. Seaborg, E. M. McMillan, J. W. Kennedy, and A. C. Wahl, who prepared the isotope with mass number 238 by bombarding uranium with deuterons accelerated in the 60-in. cyclotron at the Univ. of Calif. at Berkeley. The important isotope, Pu^{239}, was discovered in 1941 by J. W. Kennedy, G. T. Seaborg, E. Segrè, and A. C. Wahl; this same team found that Pu^{239} was fissionable with slow neutrons, thus revealing its potentialities as a nuclear-energy source. This property led to the wartime Plutonium Project for production of the element on a large scale in nuclear reactors and investigation of its potentiality as an explosive, culminating with the successful experimental nuclear weapon tested at Alamogordo, N. M., July 16, 1945. Plutonium has an important future in the development of nuclear power, since the energy freed instantaneously in the nuclear weapon can also be released in a slow, controlled fashion, and the element can be produced in quantity in nuclear reactors. The trace quantities that have been detected in nature arise from neutron capture in uranium ores. The manufacture of plutonium was the first instance of nuclear transmutation accomplished on a large scale, and plutonium is now produced in very large amounts. It was also the first synthetic element to be produced in visible quantities. The chemical properties of plutonium have been examined intensively and found to be exceedingly intricate. A great many plutonium compounds have been prepared and studied. The element has four oxidation states, (III), (IV), (V), and (VI), in aqueous solution, and all four of these states can exist simultaneously in equilibrium with each other in finite concentrations, thus creating a very complicated system. Plutonium metal has been prepared and found to have six phase changes between room temperature and its melting point. Plutonium isotopes ranging in mass number from 232 to 246 are known, and all are radioactive. The half-life of the best known and most important isotope, Pu^{239}, is 24,360 yr. This isotope is one of the most potent poisons known to man, because of its alpha radioactivity and its chemical properties, which cause it to be more or less permanently deposited in the bone after assimilation. Special equipment and precautions are necessary in the investigation of its properties.—*G. T. S.*

PLYWOOD: a glued assembly of thin sheets of wood. The sheets singly are called veneers; when glued together they are called plies. Veneer is produced by peeling sections off bark-free logs. Long, continuous sheets are made by rotating the log against a slowly advancing knife. The thickness is selected according to the kind of wood and its intended use, the most popular thicknesses being between ⅛₈ and ⅛ in., although veneer as thin as ⅓₀₀ in. is produced for special purposes. The adhesives used are natural proteins or synthetic resins, sometimes applied as dry films. Much plywood is produced in 3 to 9 plies with the fiber direction of each ply alternating; the plies are combined by brief heating under light pressure. Special high-strength, high-density plywoods are made under high pressure. Thick plywood may have a core of lumber or of rigid foamed resins.—*E. F.*

PNEUMATIC TOOL: a machine driven by compressed air. Air under pressure is supplied in most cases by an air COMPRESSOR (but sometimes by a compressed-air tank) and is delivered to the pneumatic tool by a rubber hose. Pneumatic tools utilize either the rotary motion of an air motor or the reciprocating motion of a piston. In lighter pneumatic tools, *e.g.* drills, screwdrivers, and torque wrenches, compressed air pushes on the vanes of an air motor's rotor, rotating a shaft to which the tool is fastened. In the heavier tools, *e.g.* rock drills and hammers, compressed air is used to drive a reciprocating piston. In the majority of reciprocating-piston pneumatic tools, the piston strikes the shank of the tool; but there are also *piston drills* in which the drill tool is fastened directly to the piston. Pneumatic tools are used in almost every industrial and agricultural activity: in addition to their capacity to deliver a rapid, repetitive, percussive force, they are free from the hazards attending electric tools, *e.g.* electric shocks and explosions caused by sparking. Pneumatic tools are used for many kinds of hammering operations, such as chipping and sealing, sand hammering, and riveting. Pneumatic rock drills are widely used in mining, tunneling, and general construction.—*A. L.*

P-N JUNCTION: see TRANSISTOR.

POINCARÉ, JULES HENRI, 1854–1912, French mathematician; b. Nancy. The scope of his work included mathematical physics in all its branches, theoretical physics, and theoretical astronomy; in addition he wrote classics on the philosophy of science. In mathematics he made valuable contributions to the theory of Abelian functions and created a new type of function which he called Fuchsian. He wrote on all phases

Jules Henri Poincaré
(*Yerkes Observatory*)

of analysis, analysis situs, groups, and number theory. He modernized the attack on problems of celestial mechanics. His popular works on philosophy of science have been translated into several languages. An English translation, including *Science and Hypothesis, The Value of Science,* and *Science and Method* in one volume, was issued in 1913. An extremely prolific writer, he published more than 1,500 memoirs and more than 30 books. Almost 500 papers, some extensive, were concerned with new mathematics. He was elected to the Academy of Sciences in 1887, becoming its president in 1906. He was also a fellow of the Royal Society and an associate of the U. S. National Academy of Sciences.—*H. C.*

POISEUILLE, JEAN LOUIS MARIE, 1799–1869, French physiologist; b. Paris. He contributed to knowledge of the circulation, pressure, and viscosity of blood, and was the first to use the mercury manometer to measure blood pressure. After constructing a hemodynamometer (1828) and inventing a viscosimeter, he used these to study the flow of blood, and he expressed quantitatively the factors that affect blood velocity (POISEUILLE'S LAW). Poiseuille published papers on motion of liquids in tubes and other scientific subjects.—*D. H. D. R.*

POISEUILLE'S LAW: an expression of the loss of head (pressure) for a viscous (non-turbulent) fluid flowing through a pipe. The loss of head (h_f) is directly proportional to the length of pipe (L) and to the velocity (V) of the fluid; it is inversely proportional to the specific gravity of the fluid (s) and to the square of the diameter of the pipe (D): $h_f = 0.032\mu \frac{LV}{sD^2}$. The constant of proportionality, the viscosity mu (μ), is called a *poise*, after J. L. M. Poiseuille (who developed the law in 1842).—*A. L.*

POISONOUS ANIMALS: animals that subdue their prey, or defend themselves against attack, by means of chemical compounds which can be fatal when injected in moderate amounts; less commonly, animals that may cause death if eaten. "Poisonous" is a relative term: an injection of venom from a centipede may kill a mouse, a young child, or an infirm adult, but may cause only local swelling and discomfort in a vigorous adult; a cobra bite that would kill a child might produce no obvious symptoms in a mongoose; the nettling cells on the tentacles of almost any jellyfish can cause irritation of human lips or other tender areas on contact, but rarely cause discomfort to the finger tips.

Dangerously poisonous animals are found among protozoans, coelenterates, mollusks, arthropods, echinoderms, and chordates. Certain dinoflagellate protozoans are responsible for sporadic RED TIDES, which cause the death of millions of marine fish, sea turtles, and other animals; often toxic materials blown inland from sea spray in regions of red tide

cause severe irritation of the eyes and respiratory tracts of persons living along the coast. Essentially all coelenterates make use of their unique nettling cells (cnidoblasts, with enclosed projectile nematocysts) in capturing and subduing prey; the toxic material produced by these cells is particularly virulent in the Portuguese man-of-war (*Physalia*) and in the jellyfish known as the lion's mane (*Cyanea*), which was made famous in a story by Conan Doyle. Among mollusks, the handsomely marked snails known as cone shells include several in the S Pacific that are capable of stabbing the hand of a human collector with a venom-bearing radula, occasionally with fatal effects. Recently the octopus has been found to use a strong salivary venom to kill shellfish, often injecting the venom through a small hole cut in the shell by the rasplike radula of the octopus.

Scorpions, which immobilize their prey and also defend themselves with venom from a poison claw at the tip of the abdomen, include several species with especially deadly venom. Among spiders, the black widow is rightly famous for the virulence of the venom it can inject; all spiders are equipped with similar poison glands opening at the tip of tonglike fangs (chelicerae) close to the mouth, but very few species give as painful a bite as a horsefly. A number of biting flies, including mosquitoes, inject saliva into the wound as they penetrate the skin to reach a blood meal; some persons react to the saliva as though it were a poison comparable to the venom in the sting of a bee or wasp, whereas others are scarcely affected by it. The weapons of bees and wasps are modified ovipositors, adapted as organs of defense. Human deaths occasionally result from a single stinging by a bee or wasp; such hypersensitivity to the venom may be the result of an acute allergy. Certain caterpillars (*e.g.* the io) and moths have bristly hairs that, when jabbed into human skin, produce a stinging effect.

Some of the larger sea cucumbers (holothurian echinoderms) in tropical waters contain so much poisonous material (saponins) in their body walls that native fishermen sometimes wring them, as they might a towel, over large tidal pools to poison the edible fish and bring them within easy reach. Some tropical fishes, especially stonefishes and scorpionfishes (*e.g.* the lionfish), rank as the most poisonous fishes in the world; their venom glands, which are associated with the bases of grooved spines, discharge poison into wounds made by the spines when the fish is accidentally stepped on or when it attacks a victim; a number of healthy human adults have died, some in less than 2 hr, after stepping on such fish. Apparently none of the amphibians have comparable toxins, although almost all have protective agents in skin glands, and a few such agents have been used in tropical America for making a deadly type of arrow poison; the poison that a large toad (*e.g. Bufo marinus*) can discharge while being mouthed by a curious dog can be fatal to the dog.

Certainly the most dangerously poisonous animals are certain snakes whose modified salivary glands produce venoms that are injected into prey or attackers. In India alone, 16,000 people die annually from the bites of cobras and other venomous snakes; most of these reptiles inject a poison ("neurotoxin") that destroys the nervous system of the victim. The Americas have the various rattlesnakes, copperheads, water moccasins, bushmasters, and fer-de-lance snakes, which are all pit-vipers; these snakes have a blood-destroying (hemolytic) venom, which is injected by two erectile fangs at the front of the upper jaw. When these fangs are driven into a victim, venom passes from glands at the sides of the upper jaw, down through channels within the fangs, and emerges near the sharp tips as though through twin hypodermic needles. Since the venom ordinarily is discharged

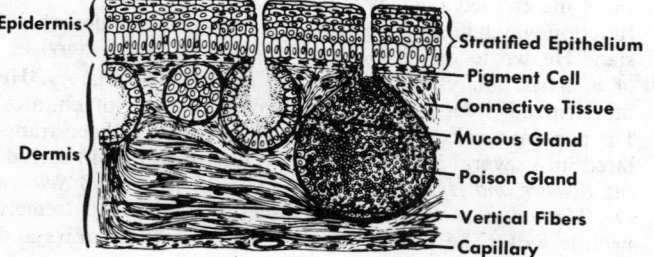

Poison glands: In rattlesnake, venom flows from gland in head (shown partly dissected) through tube into hollow fang, which injects venom into victim. (*From Smallwood*) Poison glands in the skin of toads and some frogs deter would-be predators. Section of frog's skin (*below*) shows gland's location. (*From Kenoyer*)

Poison Gland

Nostril

Pit

Poison Fangs

Tongue

Muscle

Epidermis

Dermis

Stratified Epithelium

Pigment Cell

Connective Tissue

Mucous Gland

Poison Gland

Vertical Fibers

Capillary

Poisonous animals: Tarantula spider (*far left*) has a much less powerful poison than does black widow; bite is painful but not dangerous to man. Gila monster (*left*) is one of the two poisonous lizards of the world; its venom is fatal to small animals, e.g. rabbits, mice. (*Robert C. Hermes; Lorus J. and Margery J. Milne*)

into the lymphatic spaces between the skin and the underlying muscles or bone of a human victim, much of it can be removed by cutting deeply and applying suction; chilling the area of the bite with ice is now a preferred method for retarding the slow movement of residual poison through lymph channels to the general circulatory system. These measures delay the effects of the poison, giving the victim more time to get an injection of antivenin, which is a neutralizing agent that must be given only little by little, as needed, under constant medical care. Antivenins for neurotoxins from bites of cobras and other poisonous snakes are less often effective, for a cobra bite can be fatal within less than an hour, whereas a pit-viper's double stab is rarely dangerous if care is given within a few hours. Deaths from pit-viper bites are few.

Only two species of lizard are venomous: the pink-and-black mottled Gila monster of Arizona (which reaches a length of about 2 ft, including the thick tail) and its close relative, the Mexican beaded lizard (which is usually dull black, with a slender tail). Both have been known to defend themselves by biting; they clamp their jaws as though waiting for the poisonous saliva to work into the wounds and take effect. Among mammals, the male duckbill platypus is equipped with a poison claw on each rear foot; its venom is fatal to rabbits. Several species of shrew appear to have a highly toxic saliva, with which they immobilize their prey.—*L. and M. M.*

POISONOUS PLANTS: plants that cause harm or even death to man or animals by ingestion or contact. Among the lower plants, blue-green algae have been reported as causing death to cattle that drink water from ponds infested with these algae during the hot summer months. In the cell sap, the algae concentrate nitrates, which are changed to highly toxic nitrites after ingestion by cattle. Some fungi are notorious for their toxic properties. The most poisonous of those eaten by people belong to the genus *Amanita,* which includes

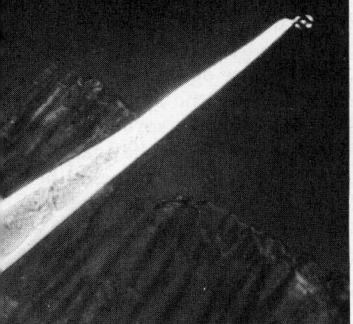

Stinging nettle (*above left*) has a hollow hair (highly magnified at *lower left*), which contains acetylcholine and histamine. When small knob at end of hair is broken by contact, these irritating substances are released. (*Hugh Spencer; Carl Strüwe/Monkmeyer*)

several different mushrooms. The so-called destroying angel (*Amanita verna*) is especially deadly and is responsible for a few deaths in the U. S. A. each year. Of the flowering plants, the water hemlocks (*Cicuta*) are among the most poisonous. Cattle die after eating their leaves; people are reported to have died after eating the fleshy roots, mistaking them for parsnips. An extract of a related plant, poison hemlock (*Conium maculatum*), is reputed to have been used to poison

Deadly toadstool: The "death cap" (*Amanita phalloides*) often is mistaken for an edible mushroom. It usually is fatal to people who eat it. Identifying characteristics are its white color, the bulb or cup at its base, and the veil around the upper part of the stem just under the cap. (*Hugh Spencer*)

Socrates. The foliage or sap of a few plants causes a severe irritation of human skin on contact. The most notorious of these plants in America are poison ivy and poison sumac (*Rhus* species). Stinging nettles (*Urtica* species) cause short-lived burning sensations when glandular hairs in their leaves and stems are broken by rough contact with human skin. —*F. L.*

POISSON, SIMEON DENIS, 1781–1840, French mathematician; b. Pithiviers. Although he was fundamentally a mathematician, much of Poisson's work was in the application of mathematics to theoretical physics. He contributed to the fields of heat transfer, electricity and magnetism, and theory of elasticity. Appointed to the faculty of the Ecole Polytechnique, he succeeded J. Fourier in 1806. He extended the application of the Fourier series (a trigonometric series representing a mathematical function with a finite number of discontinuities, widely used in harmonic analysis) to the field of mathematical analysis. As a result of developments in the wave theory of light in the first part of the 19th cent., Poisson, along with A. Cauchy, became interested in the general problem of wave motion through an isotropic medium and demonstrated that a disturbance within part of a body results in waves both transverse and longitudinal in character. *Poisson's ratio,* the ratio of lateral strain to longitudinal strain, is widely used by engineers. He was a fellow of the Royal Society.—*A. L.*

POLAR COMPOUNDS: chemical compounds in whose molecules the centers of positive and negative electrical charge are separated. Such molecules possess an electrical dipole moment and tend to rotate when placed in an electrical field.—*Ru. M.*

POLARIS: the polestar (α Ursae Minoris), or "north star," brightest star in the constellation Ursa Minor, being at the tip of the handle of the Little Dipper. It is about 30° north of the bowl of the Big Dipper, in line with the Pointers, which are two stars, some 5° apart, of the bowl. At present Polaris is less than 1° from the north celestial pole and thus is called the polestar; but owing to PRECESSION OF EQUINOXES other stars have been and will be successively the polestar. Polaris has a mean visual magnitude of 2.1; its magnitude varies because the star is a cepheid variable, with a period of 4.0 days. It is a yellow star, at a distance from the Sun of about 400 lt-yr. Intrinsically it is very luminous, the output of light being some 1,700 times the Sun's. It is also a spectroscopic binary star, with a period of 30 yr. Polaris can be seen throughout the year in the northern hemisphere.—*M. W. O.*

POLARISCOPE: an optical instrument used to study the effects produced by various materials on POLARIZED LIGHT of known orientation. A polariscope employs two NICOL PRISMS (polarizer and analyzer) or a pair of polarizing films such as Polaroids.—*A. E.*

POLARITY: the conventional designation of certain singular points in electric or magnetic fields and of the direction of motion of electrons in electric circuits. The terminal of an active electrical element, *e.g.* a battery or a generator, is said to have *negative* polarity if electrons leave it and move to other parts of the circuit. The terminal that accepts electrons is the *positive* terminal. In speaking of a FIELD, polarity specifies the vector direction of the electric or magnetic flux. In an electric field, the flux is said to flow from positive to negative pole, just the reverse of the motion of electrons. In a magnetic field the flux is said to flow from north pole to south. The north pole is that which would repel the northward-pointing end of a compass needle; the south pole is that which would attract it. See ELECTRICITY; MAGNET; MAGNETISM.—*D. H. L.*

POLARIZATION OF STARLIGHT: In 1949, A. W. Hiltner and J. S. Hall found that starlight is sometimes polarized (see POLARIZED LIGHT). The rough correlation they found between the amount of polarization and interstellar reddening indicates that interstellar particles are responsible for the polarization. To polarize starlight, these minute particles must be elongated and aligned in a more or less parallel arrangement over extensive regions. The elongation need not be great; a ratio of 5 to 4 between the longer and shorter dimensions would be adequate. The alignment of particles in clouds hundreds of light-years across is not fully explained, but is probably produced by weak magnetic fields. See also INTERSTELLAR MATTER.—*R. N. M.*

POLARIZED LIGHT: light whose vibration pattern exhibits preference in orientation. The vibration is associated with the so-called electric vector, which represents the direction and intensity of the rapidly varying electromagnetic field. In unpolarized light this vector is oriented in a random, unpredictable fashion, but in polarized light it shows a directional preference, often lying in a given orientation in the plane transverse to the propagation direction of the wave; this is linearly polarized or plane-polarized light. If the tip of the

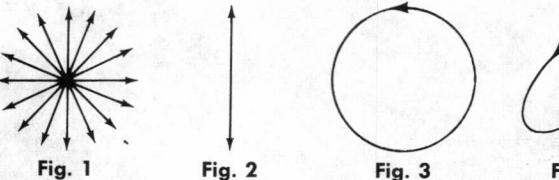

Polarized light: Diagrams show idealized end-on views of vibrations of a light beam that is (1) unpolarized, (2) plane polarized, (3) circularly polarized, (4) elliptically polarized.

electric vector moves in a circular path or in an elliptical fashion in the transverse plane, the light is said to be circularly or elliptically polarized, respectively. The figures show an idealized end-on view of a light beam to illustrate the various types of polarization. Fig. 1 indicates vibrations in many directions, and these are entirely uncorrelated in time; this is a representation of unpolarized light, which exhibits no directional preference. Fig. 2 illustrates linearly or plane-polarized light, with the vibration direction vertical. Fig. 3 indicates circularly polarized light; and Fig. 4, elliptically polarized light.

Although the unaided human eye is unable to detect the presence of polarization, the eyes of many insects and crustaceans are apparently sensitive to it, for they orient themselves in relation to the direction of polarized light. Partially plane-polarized light occurs in nature to a surprisingly large extent. For example, the light from a rainbow is polarized; light from the blue sky, especially from a direction at right angles to the direction from the observer to the Sun, is partially plane-polarized; light reflected from smooth surfaces such as those of the sea or lakes, window glass, or even pavement, is also partially plane-polarized. These polarizing effects can be detected by holding one lens of a pair of polarizing sunglasses just in front of one eye and looking with that eye at the blue sky, a rainbow, or other appropriate object. As the frame of the glasses is rotated, the apparent intensity of the light will be seen to vary, going through a maximum twice in one complete rotation, and through a minimum twice, at 90° to the positions of maximum intensity. (See also POLARIZATION OF STARLIGHT.)

The polarizing sunglass lens is an example of a sheet polarizer. Polarizers can also be made from crystals of quartz or calcite of special construction. Such polarizing units are used in devices called POLARISCOPES to measure the rotation of the plane of polarization produced by some chemical compounds, *e.g.* turpentine and sugar solutions. A specialized type of polariscope called a saccharimeter is used all over the world in testing the concentration and purity of raw sugar, and serves as the commercial basis for establishing the quality of natural sugar.—*S. S. B.*

POLAR WANDERING: the gradual shift in location of Earth's magnetic poles as a result of secular variation in TERRESTRIAL MAGNETISM.

POLE: see CELESTIAL SPHERE; COORDINATE SYSTEM; EARTH; MAGNET; MAGNETIC COMPASS.

POLESTAR: see POLARIS; PRECESSION OF EQUINOXES.

POLLEN: a mass of dust-sized reproductive bodies in seed plants. These bodies serve as vehicles by which male reproductive cells, or sperms, reach and fertilize egg cells. Pollen is produced in the anthers of flowers and in the staminate, or male, cones of gymnosperms (*e.g.* pine and spruce trees). Within pollen sacs that develop in pairs below the scales of a staminate cone or that develop in pairs to form the anther of a stamen in a flower, pollen grains are formed by the special cell division known as MEIOSIS. Each pollen grain is a microspore, and the pollen sac is known as a microsporangium. Within the pollen grains, CELL DIVISIONS take place, producing a minute male gametophyte with a *generative cell.* The pollen sacs then split open, releasing the pollen. *Pollination* is the transfer of the pollen from the anther or cone where it is produced to a receptive region in the vicinity of an egg cell—either the stigmatic surface on the pistil of a flower or the sticky material on a female cone scale. Pollen may fall into the receptive region or may be blown by the wind or carried by insects, birds, bats, snails, or other animals. When it reaches its destination, a pollen grain receives chemical stimulation, which induces it to form a pollen tube. The tube grows until it reaches and penetrates an ovule containing an egg cell. The generative cell in the pollen grain divides and becomes two sperm cells, which travel through the pollen tube to the vicinity of the egg. The fertilization of the egg by one of these sperms marks the beginning of the sporophyte generation, which is an embryo plant that will become dormant in the SEED. (See ALTERNATION OF GENERATIONS.) Fertilization may follow pollination in a matter of hours (as in the petunia) or may take as long as a year (as in the pine tree).

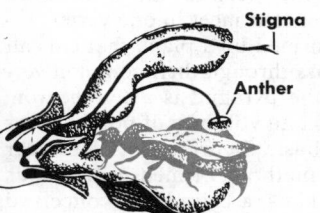

Pollination by insects: Male organs of sage ripen earlier than female organs; bee collects pollen from anther of young sage (*left*), dusts it on stigma of older flower. (*From Whaley*)

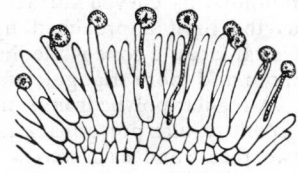

Germination of pollen: Pollen grains have landed on stigma (*right*). They germinate and develop pollen tubes; male gametes then descend to ovule. (*From Whaley*)

Pollen grains usually are yellow, but sometimes are blue, green, or red. Their outer walls have distinctive markings by means of which a pollen specialist (palynologist) can identify the kind of plant that produced them. These walls are so re-

Pollen sacs: Transverse section through staminate (male) cone of larch (a deciduous conifer of the pine family) shows radial pattern of microsporangia. Individual granules are microspores that will become pollen grains. (*Carl Strüwe/Monkmeyer*)

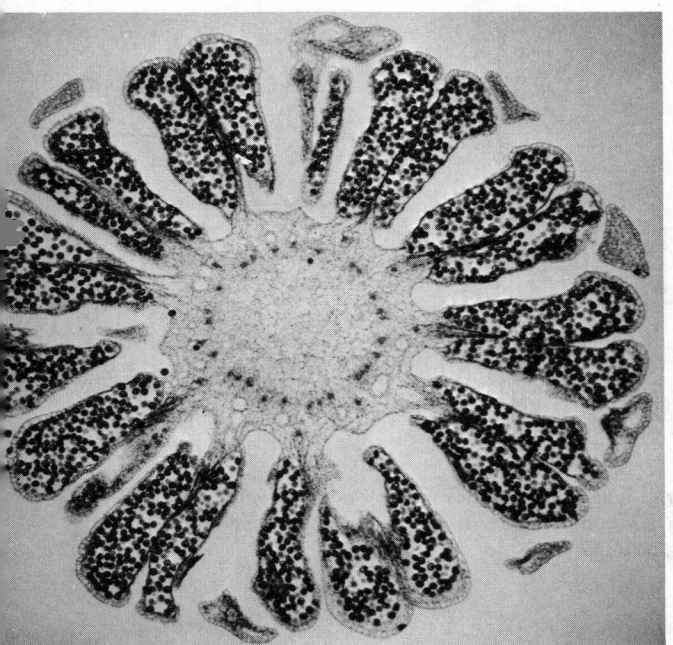

sistant to decay that pollen has often been preserved for thousands of years in peat or coal. By studying such deposits, palynologists not only can learn what kinds of plants lived in the past, but also can estimate the abundance of each kind of plant represented (see PALYNOLOGY). Pollen identification is useful, too, in determining which kinds of plants cause human allergies ("hay fever").—*H. Cr.*

POLLINATION: see POLLEN.

POLLUTION: see ATMOSPHERIC POLLUTION; WATER POLLUTION.

POLONIUM: a radioactive metallic element (Po); at. no. 84; at. wt 210; valence 4, occasionally 2; rarely 6. It was the first radioactive substance discovered by Marie and Pierre Curie (1898), who detected it by radiochemical analysis of pitchblende. Several isotopes of polonium are known, with half lives ranging from the extremely short up to approx. 200 yr (Po^{209}). Polonium^{210} is the final radioactive product of radium disintegration; its half life is about 138 days. One gm of Po^{210} is contained in about 25,000 tons of pitchblende or in 7.5 kg of radium over 30 yr old. Chemically the element resembles tellurium and bismuth, and must be separated from the latter by repeated fractionations. It is an alpha-particle emitter and therefore presents a dangerous radiation hazard, but when contained in gold foil polonium is used industrially as an anti-static agent in paper rolling, synthetic-fiber spinning, and sheet-plastics processing. Polonium^{210} has also been called radium F (RaF), since it is a decay product of radium E, a bismuth isotope.—*R. B. T.*

POLYETHYLENE: a polymer of ethylene, $CH_2=CH_2$, widely used in the form of film (*e.g.* for wrapping commercial articles), tubing, electrical insulation, and molded objects. The polymer was originally made at high pressure (1,000 atm) and high temperature (above 212°F). Processes developed later operate at atmospheric pressure and lower temperature to yield a stronger, more heat-resistant product.—*Ru. M.*

POLYGON: a plane figure bounded by three or more straight line segments, or sides, meeting in an equal number of points, or vertices. Polygons with a small number of sides are generally known by special names, those with three to ten sides being, respectively, triangle, quadrilateral, pentagon, hexagon, heptagon, octagon, nonagon, and decagon; a polygon with 12 sides is a dodecagon, one with *n* sides is an *n*-gon. The triangle is the fundamental figure, and the facts about other polygons are discovered by breaking them into triangles. Quadrilaterals, including squares, rectangles, parallelograms, and trapezoids, are basic figures in geometry and occur in many physical objects. In particular, the concept of area is closely tied to the square.

A polygon of more than three sides can be convex, having every interior angle less than 180° (Fig. 1, next page), or may possess one or more re-entrant angles. The quadrilateral in Fig. 2 contains a re-entrant angle at *B*. The interior angle at *B* is greater than 180°. An important theorem of Euclidean geometry establishes that the sum of the interior angles of a convex polygon of *n* sides is $(n - 2) \times 180°$.

Two polygons are similar if they have the same number of sides and the same shape. The angles and sides of one can be made to correspond to the angles and sides of the other, with corresponding angles equal and corresponding sides proportional. A polygon is regular if all its sides are equal and all its angles are equal. A circle can always be circumscribed about a regular polygon, the circumference passing through every vertex; another circle can be inscribed whose

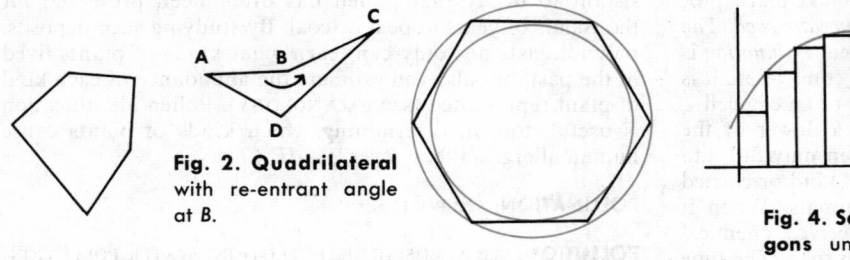

Fig. 1. Convex polygon.

Fig. 2. Quadrilateral with re-entrant angle at *B*.

Fig. 3. Polygon inscribed in a circle and circumscribed about a smaller circle.

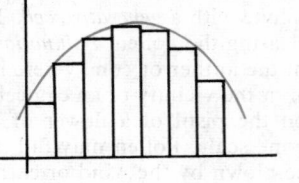

Fig. 4. Sequence of polygons under a curve is used in integral calculus to find area under curve.

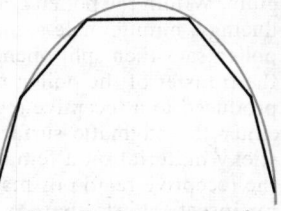

Fig. 5. Sequence of polygonal lengths is used to find length of a curve.

circumference is tangent to every side of the polygon (see Fig. 3). The radius of the circumscribed circle is the radius of the regular polygon. The radius of the inscribed circle is the apothem of the polygon. Since the sum of the interior angles of any *n*-sided convex polygon is $(n - 2) \times 180°$, each interior angle of a regular *n*-sided polygon contains $(n - 2) \times 180°/n$, or $180° - 360°/n$.

Formulas for the area and length of the circumference of a circle can be obtained by approximations from regular polygons. The sequence of areas of inscribed polygons of more and more sides converges to the same limit as that of circumscribed polygons of more and more sides. This limit is taken to define the area of the circle, since the circular area includes that of every inscribed polygon and is included in that of every circumscribed polygon. The length of the circumference is found in a similar way. Polygons of special kinds are constructed to deal with similar problems in connection with other curves. Thus, the general area problem that gives rise to integral calculus is solved by a sequence of polygons, each constructed under a curve as shown in Fig. 4. The problem of the length of a curve is solved by a sequence of polygonal lengths, each drawn as indicated in Fig. 5.—*H. C.*

POLYHEDRON: a solid figure bounded by intersecting planes. The bounding planes form the faces, the intersection of two faces is an edge, and a point of intersection of three or more faces is a vertex. Each face is a polygon and each edge a line segment. The smallest number of faces a polyhedron can possess is four, the number of faces of a tetrahedron.

A polyhedron that has important physical uses, *e.g.* refracting light rays in optical instruments, is the prism. A prism is bounded by three or more faces that are parallelograms intersecting in parallel edges, together with two faces that are congruent polygons formed by parallel planes cutting across all the parallel edges. The simplest example is a rectangular parallelepiped, or box, which has six rectangular faces. If the six faces are squares, the figure is a cube. Another kind of polyhedron is the pyramid; this is bounded by three or more triangular faces that meet in one vertex, together with a polygonal base formed by a plane that cuts all the other faces and does not pass through their common vertex. If the base is a triangle, the pyramid is a tetrahedron. The calculation of the surfaces and volumes of polyhedrons is accomplished by means of basic theorems on rectilinear figures. They, in turn, lead to methods of measuring solids bounded by curved surfaces. Thus, a cylinder is conceived as the limit approached by prisms with more and more lateral faces; a cone is the limit approached by pyramids with more and more triangular faces.

A regular polyhedron is one in which all the faces are congruent regular polygons. Each edge is the intersection of just two faces, and each vertex is the intersection of just three faces. Unlike regular polygons, which can have any number of sides greater than two, regular polyhedrons can only have four, six, eight, twelve, or twenty faces. There are thus only five regular polyhedrons: the regular tetrahedron, having four faces which are equilateral triangles; the cube, having six faces which are squares; the regular octahedron, having eight faces which are equilateral triangles; the regular dodecahedron, having twelve faces which are regular pentagons; and the regular icosahedron, having twenty faces which are equilateral triangles. That these, and no others, are possible

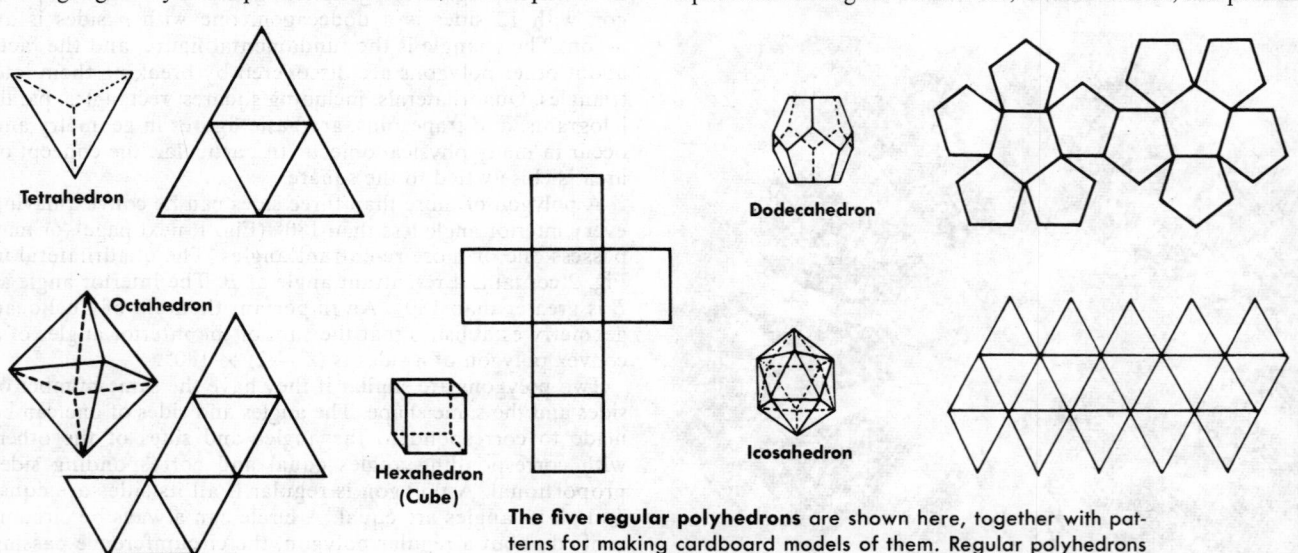

Tetrahedron

Octahedron

Hexahedron (Cube)

Dodecahedron

Icosahedron

The five regular polyhedrons are shown here, together with patterns for making cardboard models of them. Regular polyhedrons can have only 4, 6, 8, 12, or 20 faces.

follows from the Euler formula which connects the number of vertices V, the number of faces F, and the number of edges E, by the equation $V + F = E + 2$. This formula holds for any polyhedron.

The study of regular polyhedrons occupied a high place in Greek geometry. They were often called Platonic solids, although they were probably known before Plato's time. Euclid treated them to some extent in Book XIII of the *Elements*. In the 16th cent., Kepler considered these as perfect figures which the Creator would use in designing the universe, and he worked out an elaborate explanation of the motions of the planets based on them.—*H. C.*

POLYMERS: molecules of giant size formed through the linkage of many units of relatively simple molecules (monomers) in such a way that a certain recurring pattern is present. Polymers of this kind are common in nature, *e.g.* CELLULOSE, STARCH, RUBBER. The process of building a large molecule by constant addition of the same units is called *polymerization,* in which there are two distinct mechanisms: in *addition polymerization* the units join very simply to create the large molecule; in *condensation polymerization* the units interact through functional groups, *e.g.* OH, to make the molecule larger.

Addition Polymers: An appropriate catalyst under the proper conditions causes ETHYLENE to add to itself, with the formation of POLYETHYLENE. The recurring unit here

$$n\ CH_2{=}CH_2 \rightarrow [-CH_2-CH_2-]_n$$

Ethylene monomer   Ethylene polymer, or polyethylene

is the 2-carbon ethylene monomer. After the n units have combined, in a linear progression, the formation of the giant molecule is terminated at each end of the chain by groups which are fragments of the catalyst or of an ethylene molecule:

End group—CH_2—CH_2—CH_2— $\cdots$
$\cdots$ —CH_2—CH_2—CH_2—End group

End-group variations have little effect on a molecule in which a thousand or more ethylene units are present.

Ethylene is an olefin and an unsaturated compound, but the polymer made from it is saturated and has the chemical inertness of a paraffin. A few other olefinic monomers which can be polymerized are shown below; an important trademark substance made from each polymer is shown in parentheses. It should be remembered that the C=C double bond (as in polyethylene) disappears in polymerization:

Vinylmethane
Propylene
(Polypropylene)

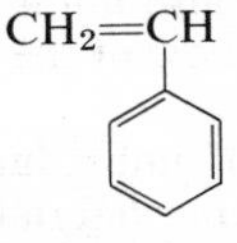

Vinylbenzene
Styrene
(Styron)

Vinyl cyanide or
Acrylonitrile
(Orlon & Acrilan)

Isobutylene
(Vistanex)

Vinyl chloride
(Koroseal)

Some olefinic compounds that undergo self-addition possess a conjugate system of single and double bonds. Two examples are isoprene and butadiene (see DIENE). When these

molecules add to each other, the valence bonds rearrange so that a double bond appears in the center of the molecule and the addition polymerization takes place at the ends. In the resulting polymer each recurring unit has one double bond:

$$n\ CH_2{=}CH-CH{=}CH_2 \longrightarrow [-CH_2-CH{=}CH-CH_2-]_n$$

Butadiene   Polybutadiene

Isoprene

Polyisoprene,
or rubber

The presence of double bonds in these polymers makes it possible to modify them further by vulcanization.

Many important polymers are built up from two different monomers; these are called *copolymers.* An example is the SBR rubber, famous in World War II (when it was called GR-S rubber), which is a copolymer of butadiene and styrene. Butyl rubber is a copolymer of isoprene and isobutylene. (See RUBBER.) Saran is a copolymer of a compound called vinylidene chloride and small amounts of vinyl chloride. The character of a copolymer will depend on the order and arrangement of the monomers contained in it. If the monomers are A and B, the descriptive words used to label the arrangements are:

Alternating   A—B—A—B—A—B—A—B—$\cdots$

Random   A—A—B—A—B—B—B—A—$\cdots$

Block   A—A—B—B—B—B—A—A—$\cdots$

Graft

When a monomer has side chains, like those in propylene and in styrene, the nature of the polymer depends on how the side chains line up with respect to the principal chain. The carbon chain zigzags, so the vinyl compounds mentioned earlier in this article when polymerized can be pictured as follows:

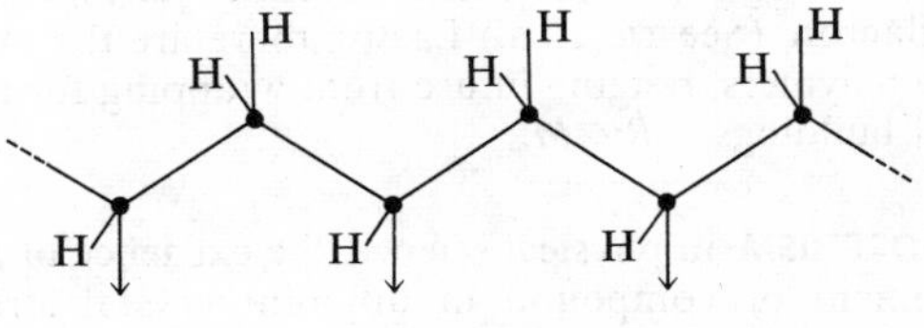

Isotactic

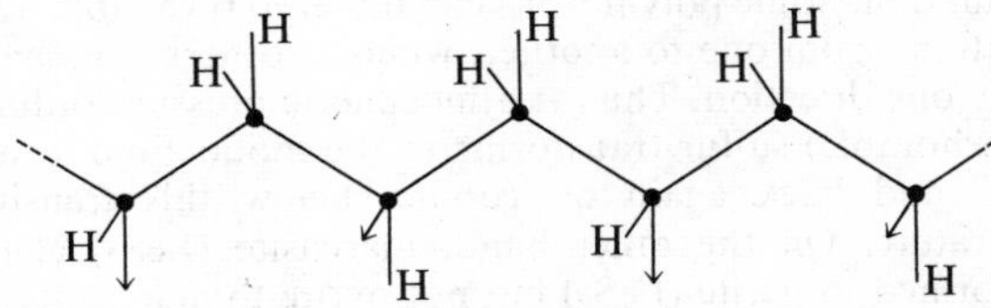

Syndiotactic

In the isotactic polymer all side chains (arrows) are on the same side. When the side-chains alternate on each side, the polymer is called syndiotactic. If there is no regularity, the polymer is atactic. The isotactic polymer is tougher and more rigid. This phenomenon is especially important in the chemistry of rubber and its analogs.

Condensation Polymers: These are formed from the monomers by chemical interactions which result in elimination of a by-product, usually water. Dacron is such a polymer, made from ethylene glycol and terephthalic acid. The recurring unit shown in the brackets is essentially an ester (ethylene terephthalate),

$$HO—CH_2CH_2—OH$$

Ethylene
glycol

$$HO—\overset{O}{\overset{\|}{C}}—\langle\text{benzene ring}\rangle—\overset{O}{\overset{\|}{C}}—OH$$

Terephthalic
acid

$$H\left[—OCH_2CH_2O—\overset{O}{\overset{\|}{C}}—\langle\text{benzene ring}\rangle—\overset{O}{\overset{\|}{C}}—\right]_n OCH_2CH_2—OH$$

Dacron

so that dacron is a polyester. In general, polymers made from a polyhydric alcohol (*i.e.* an alcohol containing two or more hydroxyl groups) and a dicarboxylic acid (or its anhydride) are called alkyd resins. In the general formula of an alkyd resin made from glycerol (glycerin),

$$H\left[—OCH_2—\underset{OH}{CH}—CH_2—O—\overset{O}{\overset{\|}{C}}—R—\overset{O}{\overset{\|}{C}}—\right]_n OCH_2—\underset{OH}{CH}—CH_2—OH$$

An alkyd resin from glycerol (R is a divalent radical)

each recurring unit in the polymer chain still has an active OH group, and two such chains can react with more of the dibasic acid to form a cross-linked structure. This gives the polymer more rigidity and special properties.

Phenol and formaldehyde condense to form resins of which BAKELITE is an important example. The formaldehyde molecule supplies —CH_2— bridges between the benzene rings of the phenol molecules. The polymer is one that forms in three dimensions and is particularly insoluble and infusible. (See RESIN.)

Uses: Synthetic polymers are often classified by application. Some are stretchable, like the rubbers, and are called *elastomers*. Some can be dissolved in suitable vehicles and extruded through spinnerets in the form of *fibers, e.g.* nylon, orlon, dacron. (See TEXTILE.) Lastly, there are the PLASTICS, or bulk polymers, ranging in use from wrapping for bread to walls of buildings.—*Ru. M.*

POLYMORPHISM: in physical science, the existence of a chemical element or compound in different crystal structures. The particular structure taken depends upon the conditions of formation. Some polymorphs can undergo reversible transformations from one to another, whereas others can change in only one direction. Thus at atmospheric pressure ordinary (orthorhombic) sulfur transforms to the monoclinic form at 95.6°C and back again on cooling below this transition temperature. On the other hand, marcasite (FeS_2) can be transformed to pyrite (FeS_2) but not pyrite to marcasite.

The phenomenon of polymorphism covers differences in structure from very marked to very minor. Thus, in the polymorphs of SiO_2, quartz, tridymite, cristobalite, and coesite all have different linkages of silicate tetrahedra. On the other hand, temperature modifications of the first three exist as polymorphs in which there is only slight displacement of the tetrahedra. Many mineral species differ from one another in that they are polymorphs; thus, for example, the silica minerals just mentioned. The converse phenomenon to polymorphism is isomorphism or isostructuralism, in which substances have the same structures but different compositions.

The common minerals calcite ($CaCO_3$), siderite ($FeCO_3$), and rhodochrosite ($MnCO_3$) are examples.—*A. Ha. and D. H.*

POLYMORPHISM (in biology): the occurrence of individuals of more than one form within a species, usually unrelated to differences in age. In colonial organisms, *e.g.* some coelenterates, polymorphism is related to division of labor within the colony: individuals are specialized for feeding, reproduction, or defense. Similarly, social insects (especially bees, termites, and ants) exhibit polymorphism in their several castes specialized for separate duties: workers, soldiers, queen, drones, etc. A special type of polymorphism in which different members of a single species sometimes differ markedly in color patterns is exhibited by butterflies, birds, and some mammals.—*C. F. L.*

POLYNOMIAL: an algebraic expression constructed from fixed numbers and unknowns by means of the rational, integral operations—addition, subtraction, and multiplication. It is also called a rational integral expression. In a polynomial a symbol for an unknown cannot appear as a divisor nor under a radical sign; hence, it cannot have a negative or fractional exponent. An example is $x^4 + 4x^3 + 6x^2 + 3$. A general form for a polynomial in one unknown is

$$a_0x^n + a_1x^{n-1} + a_2x^{n-2} + \cdots + a_{n-1}x + a_n$$

in which n is a positive integer and $a_0, a_1, \ldots, a_n$ are any numbers. With this definition polynomials include one-term expressions and even mere numbers like 1. Polynomials are the simplest expressions in algebra and dominate much of the subject. The theory of EQUATIONS is concerned with rational integral equations, which are equations that can be expressed by polynomials set equal to zero. Because of their simplicity, polynomials are often used to approximate more complicated expressions.—*H. C.*

PONCELET, JEAN VICTOR, 1788–1867, French mathematician; b. Metz. He is best known for his work on projective geometry, to which his outstanding contribution was the development of the two great principles of continuity and duality. By the principle of continuity, properties of a figure which persist as the figure varies in a specified way hold also when the method of variation places the figure in a limiting position. The principle of duality in plane projective geometry states that any proposition about lines and points has a "dual" proposition obtained by replacing the word "line" by "point," "intersection of lines" by "connection of points," and conversely. If a statement about the projective properties of a figure is proved, its dual also holds. Poncelet was a member of the *Académie* and a fellow of the Royal Society.—*H. C.*

POPULATION: a group of individuals of the same species living together in the same habitat. A population derived from a single set of parents is called a "Mendelian" population (see MENDEL). Population size is determined by birth and death rates, immigration and emigration. Introduced into a habitat with limited resources, a population grows at a rate that follows an S-shaped curve whose upper limit is determined by the environment. Once a limit is reached, a population seldom remains constant. It fluctuates from year to year or in cycles of several years. Oscillations may be inherent in the population or may be a response to environmental cycles or to prey-predator relationships (*e.g.* fox and rabbit cycles). (See ECOLOGY.)

Dispersal: Plant and animal populations tend naturally to expand the territory they occupy. This tendency is associated with reproduction. Travel is often accomplished by special structures called disseminules. Seeds and fruits with bristles (burs) are adapted to cling to animals and thus to be transported by them; fleshy fruits are eaten by animals and their hard seeds transported; winged and plumed seeds and fruits, tumbleweeds, and spores are dispersed by wind. (See SEED.) Many sea animals (worms, crabs, corals) are dispersed as larvae with special floating organs. Wind dispersal is most far-reaching; the atmosphere abounds with spores, small insects, and other minute organisms.

Invasions: Most species invade new habitats slowly. Usually there is a balance between numbers of new individuals and mortality. Thus some animals have only held their own, and others have become extinct. Only a few, escaping their ecological limitations, have expanded in numbers and territory in spectacular manner. Most notable among them is man, along with species that take advantage of man's ecological upheavals (*e.g.* weeds, insect pests, starlings, sparrows). Successful invasions also have occurred when man has introduced a species to a new habitat where the natural enemies of the species do not exist. This was the case with the South American fire ant, the Japanese honeysuckle, and the chestnut blight fungus. See BALANCE OF NATURE.—*K. L.*

PORPHYRINS: in biochemistry, red-colored molecules containing four pyrrole rings attached to each other by CH bridges. They are physiologically important when they occur as certain

Fe protoporphyrin-9 (heme)
$C_{34}H_{32}O_4N_4Fe$

Chlorophyll *a*
$C_{55}H_{72}O_5N_4Mg$

iron or magnesium complexes. Iron porphyrin or heme compounds are the prosthetic or active groups of a number of heme proteins which serve in general for oxygen transport and oxidative respiration, *e.g.* hemoglobin, catalase, peroxidase, and the cytochromes. The green pigments of plant cells active in photosynthesis, *i.e.* chlorophylls, are magnesium dihydroporphyrins. Vitamin B_{12} is a reduced porphyrin-like derivative containing the metal cobalt.—*S. G.*

PORPHYRY: any igneous rock containing a combination of large and small crystals. The former, called phenocrysts, appear scattered throughout a finer-grained groundmass. Such rock may result when magma cools slowly at depth, where the larger crystals develop, then cools faster at the surface, so that the remaining minerals form as smaller crystals or glass around the phenocrysts. Porphyritic rocks also originate in other ways. Many types of igneous rock have porphyritic texture, and are so characterized, *e.g.* porphyritic granite and porphyritic andesite. If the phenocrysts occupy more than one fourth of the mass, the terminology is reversed, *e.g.* granite porphyry and andesite porphyry. The name (Gr. *porphyros,* "purple") refers to a common color of the groundmass.—*E. A.*

PORTA, GIAMBATTISTA DELLA, 1538–1615, Italian physician, physicist, and alchemist; b. Naples. He built a museum and botanical garden at Naples. In the 20 books of *"Magia naturalis sive de miraculis rerum naturalium"* (two editions, 1558 and 1589) he published secret lore of the Middle Ages and some physics and chemistry. He also produced popular works on optics (*De refractione optices parte,* 1593), on pharmacy (*De distillatione,* 1608), physiognomy, and many other subjects.—*R. J. F.*

POSITIONAL NOTATION: a method of denoting the value of a number symbol by its position as well as by its shape, *e.g.* the number 234 means two hundred thirty-four, each symbol (2, 3, 4) being interpreted in terms of its position in the number.

A system of positional notation was used by the Babylonians in 2000 B. C., but did not have a zero. Our decimal system was developed by the Hindus, perhaps as long ago as the 2nd cent. A. D., and was transmitted to Europe in the 12th cent. by the Arabs. A very minor use of positional notation occurred in the late Roman notation, *e.g.* in the numbers VI and IV. Here it was understood that IV meant four, since a smaller symbol preceded a larger symbol. However, the Roman XXXII meant thirty-two, each X having the same meaning and each I the same meaning. Positional notation reduces the work involved in arithmetic computation so much that it can be taught to children. We can recognize this achievement if we observe the simplicity of multiplying, say, 263 by 185 in the Hindu-Arabic system, and compare this with multiplying CCLXIII by CLXXXV, for which the Romans had to use an abacus.

In positional notation every number is expressed in terms of powers of a base number. In the decimal system, the base

Porphyrins in animals and plants: Structural correspondence of key pigments of animals and plants is apparent in these diagrams of their porphyrin constituents. Heme, iron-bearing hemoglobin pigment that combines reversibly with oxygen, is seen holding single iron atom in center of its flat porphyrin ring. Chlorophyll *a,* a catalyst that enables green plants to use solar energy in reducing carbon dioxide, holds magnesium in center of its porphyrin ring (see structural model under CHLOROPHYLL).

is ten. Thus 234 means 2 hundreds + 3 tens + 4 units, or $2 \times 10^2 + 3 \times 10 + 4$, and 52,064 means $5 \times 10^4 + 2 \times 10^3 + 0 \times 10^2 + 6 \times 10 + 4$. Each place is named by the power of ten the place signifies. In each number given, the last place is the units place, for the 4 means 4 units, the place where we multiply by ten to the first power is called the tens place, the place where we multiply by 10^2 is called the hundreds place, and so forth. Carrying in addition, borrowing in subtraction, and the placement of the symbols in multiplication and division depend on the idea of positional notation. To add 385 and 267, we place the two numbers one under the other so that the units are under units, the tens place under the tens place, and so on. Then we add the units 5 and 7, obtaining 12, or 1 ten + 2. We write down the 2 in the units place and carry the 1 to the tens column, since it represents 1 ten. Then, adding the 8 tens, the 6 tens, and the carried 1 ten, we get 15 tens, or 1 hundred and 5 tens. We write down the 5 in the tens place and carry the 1 to the hundreds column, since it represents 1 hundred. Finally, adding the 3 hundreds, the 2 hundreds, and the carried 1 hundred, we obtain 6 hundreds; so we write 6 in the hundreds column. Thus we have obtained 652. See NUMBER SYSTEMS.—*H. E. W.*

POSITIVISM: a term denoting either (1) the "Positive Philosophy" of Auguste Comte (1798–1857); (2) a general form of philosophic-scientific empiricism, rooted in the thought of Francis Bacon, Locke, Hume, Comte, and Mill—a tradition especially critical of speculative and metaphysical philosophy, placing a high value on scientific knowledge and holding that all knowledge is based upon and confirmable by directly observable data; or (3) a more recent philosophic movement called logical positivism (see LOGICAL EMPIRICISM).—*H. S. T.*

POSITRON: the ANTIPARTICLE of the electron; distinguishable from the electron by its opposite (positive) electrical charge and by the fact that the two annihilate each other on contact. Positron-electron pairs can be created by the conversion of energy to mass, but positrons do not live long: collision with an electron and, hence, annihilation is inevitable.—*S. K.*

POSITRONIUM: a short-lived atom consisting of an electron and a positron circling about a common center. In less than a millionth of a second after its formation the atom destroys itself. The electron and positron collide and annihilate each other, producing electromagnetic radiation. See ANNIHILATION OF MATTER; ANTIPARTICLES.—*S. K.*

POTASH: in commercial and industrial usage, a group of naturally occurring or easily derived potassium compounds. By itself the term "potash" means potassium carbonate, although the "potash content" of a compound frequently is used to mean the equivalent K_2O content. The word potash is also used in combined form; *e.g.* "muriate of potash" (potassium chloride), "sulfate of potash," "caustic potash" (potassium hydroxide). Potash chemicals are used mostly in fertilizer. They are also used in the manufacture of glass, soap, and a variety of fine chemicals.—*A. M. S.*

POTASSIUM: an alkali-metal element (K), the 7th most abundant element in Earth's crust; at. no. 19; at. wt 39.100; mp 63°C; bp 770°C. Elemental potassium is very easily oxidized and extremely reactive, resembling sodium in its chemical behavior. It was first prepared in 1807 by Sir Humphry Davy by means of his recently invented electrolytic procedure. Potassium occurs in a wide variety of silicate rocks and minerals. Although on Earth as a whole it is only slightly less abundant than sodium (2.4% as against 2.63%), the oceans contain only about 1/30 as much potassium as sodium. The rocks and soil are correspondingly richer in potassium. Naturally occurring forms of potassium that are economical to recover are the water-soluble chloride and sulfate, frequently formed in mixtures with magnesium salts. They occur both as dry, saline mineral deposits and in brines, the most notable deposits being at Strassfurt in Germany and at Searles Lake and Carlsbad in the U. S. A. Chemically, potassium is one of the strongest base-forming metals, standing near the positive end of the ELECTROMOTIVE SERIES. Its oxide and hydroxide are strong bases and its salts are, with few exceptions, highly soluble in water. Potassium salts are necessary in the life processes of both plant and animal cells. They are selectively collected from the soil by plants; and the ashes of plants, particularly certain seaweeds, are rich sources of POTASH.

The major proportion of all potassium chemicals produced is used for FERTILIZER, mainly in the form of sulfate. Potassium carbonate is used in large quantities in glass manufacture and potassium hydroxide in soap manufacture and as an intermediate for other potassium chemicals. Potassium nitrate (saltpeter) formerly found extensive use as the oxidizing ingredient in black gunpowder.—*A. M. S.*

POTENTIAL: the work done against the force exerted by a FIELD when a unit physical quantity (mass, electric charge, or magnetic pole) is brought from infinity (or some "floor") to the point for which the potential is specified. Having the dimensions of work per unit mass or work per unit charge, potential is a scalar quantity, as contrasted with field intensity, which has the additional property of direction and is therefore a vector. More precisely, potential is a line integral function that is independent of the path followed by the unit quantity as it traverses the field to the point in question.

Gravitational potential is the work done against gravitational attraction, or the work that must be performed by an external agent if a unit mass is to be moved away from a much larger "reference" mass (*e.g.* Earth). The lifting of a unit mass above the surface of Earth, against the direction of the gravitational field, calls for an input of work, which then determines the gravitational potential acquired by the unit mass. Conversely, if the mass falls back to Earth, the work expended earlier is now released. A typical unit of gravitational potential is the joule/kilogram or the foot-pound/slug.

Electric potential is the work done on or by a unit positive test charge $(+q)$ as it moves from infinity to some point in the electric field (*absolute potential*) or as it moves from some point A to another point B in the field (*potential difference*). If the work is positive (performed by an external agent), B is regarded as being at a higher or more positive potential than A. If the work is negative (performed by the charge itself), B is at a lower or less positive potential than A. Electric potential is measured in volts, the volt being defined as the equivalent of one joule of work performed on or by a positive charge of one coulomb carried through the electric field. A potential of 100 accordingly represents a unit potential energy equivalent to 100 joules/coulomb.

As in the case of other potentials, *magnetic potential* represents the positive or negative work associated with the movement of a unit north pole in a magnetic field. This potential is sometimes referred to as *magnetostatic.*

A field can be pictured as completely filled with lines of force. Another important physical construct is that of an equipotential surface, a surface perpendicular to the field lines and, as its name suggests, characterized by the same potential at every point. (Equipotentials around a point mass, point magnetic pole, or point charge are concentric spheres.) If a unit mass, charge, or pole is transported along an equipotential no work whatever will be expended or released, since no difference of potential is involved in the journey.

The change of potential per unit of distance is known as the *potential gradient*. In electric fields, this quantity may be expressed in volts/meter. This is numerically equal to the electric field intensity, or the force exerted on a unit charge, expressed in newtons/coulomb. Thus, if two oppositely charged plates have a potential difference of 300 v and are placed 2 cm apart, the potential gradient between the plates, as well as the electric intensity of the field between them, is 300/0.02 = 15,000 v/m (or 15,000 newtons/coulomb).—*A. E.*

POTENTIAL BARRIER: an opposing electric field that slows or stops a charged particle moving in a certain direction. For example, a potential barrier at the surface of a metal prevents electrons from leaving the metal at ordinary temperatures. If heat is applied, electrons may acquire enough energy to overcome the potential barrier and escape; this is the process of THERMIONIC EMISSION. If energy is given to electrons by the absorption of light, we have photoelectric emission (see PHOTOELECTRIC EFFECT). A similar potential barrier at the surface of a nucleus keeps protons and neutrons from escaping (except in radioactive atoms). Sometimes the wave nature of particles allows them to escape through potential barriers (see TUNNEL EFFECT).—*I. R.*

POTENTIAL DIFFERENCE: see POTENTIAL.

POTENTIAL THEORY: the mathematical theory of potential energy, principally that arising from forces, such as gravitational and electrostatic, that are inversely proportional to the square of the distance. The POTENTIAL resulting from such forces is inversely proportional to the distance ($\varphi \propto 1/r$), and the force can be found by differentiation. Being a scalar, potential is more convenient than force because forces combine vectorially while potentials are simply added.

In simple cases the potential can be calculated directly by adding the contributions of all particles, the addition usually being performed by integration. But Laplace, in 1782, found a more powerful approach. He showed that, for the above forces, the potential φ satisfies the partial differential equation

$$\nabla^2\varphi \equiv \frac{\partial^2\varphi}{\partial x^2} + \frac{\partial^2\varphi}{\partial y^2} + \frac{\partial^2\varphi}{\partial z^2} = 0 \qquad (1)$$

(called Laplace's equation) wherever there is no matter. At places where potential-producing matter of density ρ is present, φ satisfies Poisson's equation

$$\frac{\partial^2\varphi}{\partial x^2} + \frac{\partial^2\varphi}{\partial y^2} + \frac{\partial^2\varphi}{\partial z^2} = -4\pi\rho \qquad (2)$$

Solutions of (1) are called *harmonic functions*. For each reasonable physical situation there is only one solution of (1), to within an unimportant added constant. A powerful theory has been constructed that allows the calculation of potentials in quite general situations by adding basic harmonic functions. Harmonic functions have many applications outside of potential theory; *e.g.* they yield important *quantum numbers* in atomic physics.

In two dimensions, (1) becomes

$$\frac{\partial^2\varphi}{\partial x^2} + \frac{\partial^2\varphi}{\partial y^2} = 0 \qquad (3)$$

which does not pertain to forces proportional to $1/r^2$ but to forces proportional to $1/r$. An extraordinary property of (3) is that it has a general solution derivable in terms of functions of the quantity $x + iy$, where $i = \sqrt{-1}$. The beautiful mathematical subject of functions of a complex variable (see FUNCTION THEORY) grew out of the problem of solving (3).—*Ba. H.*

POTENTIOMETER: a device used to measure the electromotive force (emf) of a source by finding the difference of potential across its terminals without drawing any current from it. (It is necessary not to draw current because every source of emf has some internal resistance, and therefore the terminal voltage is smaller than open-circuit emf if any current is drawn.) In the circuit shown, a battery B causes a current I to flow in a wire resistance AD, the magnitude of the current being adjusted by the rheostat R. A standard cell of known emf E_s is

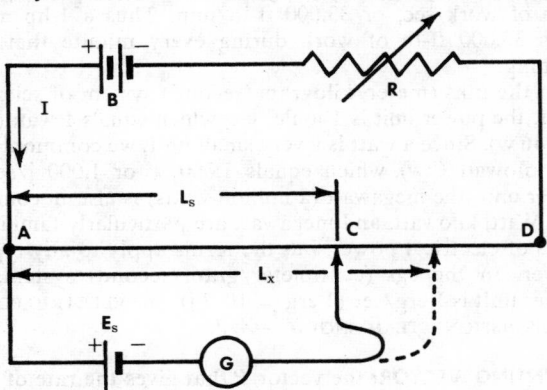

Potentiometer provides precise determination of cell emf.

then connected with its polarity as shown, and the sliding contact point C is moved through a length of wire L_s until the galvanometer G shows no deflection. The potential drop from A to C then equals E_s, or $E_s = IkL_s$, where k is a constant depending on the material and the diameter of the wire. Now E_s is replaced by the unknown source E_x, and a new balance obtained at some point L_x. Then $E_x = IkL_x$ and $E_x = L_x/L_s E_s$.—*H. Sw.*

POTHOLE: a depression in a streambed that has developed where an eddy has given rotary motion to coarse sediments transported by the water. Swirling debris can cut into the most resistant rock. After a pothole starts to form, the velocity of the eddy increases, especially during floods, so that the deepening and widening are accelerated. Potholes range in diameter up to about 20 ft, and in depth to about 50 ft. The formation of these depressions seems to be an important factor in the erosion of deep, young canyons.—*N. E. A. H.*

POWELL, CECIL FRANK, 1903–   , English physicist; b. Tonbridge. The use of photographic plates for the study of subatomic particles became in his hands an effective tool for research in nuclear physics. At the Univ. of Bristol he and his colleagues studied primary cosmic rays and the production of mesons by these rays. They obtained data by sending photographic plates to high altitudes by means of balloons. For his photographic study and his discoveries about mesons, Powell received the Nobel prize for 1950.—*D. H. D. R.*

POWELL, JOHN WESLEY, 1834–1902, U. S. geologist and ethnologist; b. Mount Morris, N. Y. Leader of the first group to explore the Colorado River by boat (1869), he later became director of the second division of the U. S. Geological and Geographical Survey of the Territories (1875–79) and then of the U. S. Geological Survey (1880–94), which he built into the largest scientific organization in the world at the time. Powell was the first to make plain that valleys can be formed by river erosion as the land undergoes gradual uplift, and he was the first to make use of the concept of BASE LEVEL in regard to erosion. He was director of the Bureau of Ethnology in the Smithsonian Institution (1879–1902) and a member of the National Academy of Sciences.—*D. H. D. R.*

POWER: in physics, the rate at which work is done, work being the product of a force and of the distance through which it acts. Whether one lifts a 10-lb weight above one's head in 1 sec or in 10 sec, one does the same amount of work, but at different rates. If work W is done in time interval t, the average power P can be expressed as $P = W/t$. In engineering, work is measured in foot-pounds, and the unit of power is 1 ft-lb/sec. Since this is a very small unit, a larger one, the horsepower (hp), is commonly used. One horsepower (hp) is 550 ft-lb of work/sec, or 33,000 ft-lb/min. Thus a 1-hp motor does 33,000 ft-lb of work during every minute that it is running.

In the mks (meter/kilogram/second) system of scientific units, the power unit is 1 joule/sec, which equals 1 watt (1 hp = 746 w). Since a watt is a very small unit, we commonly use the kilowatt (kw), which equals 1,000 w, or 1,000 j/sec. A larger unit, the megawatt (a million watts) is also in common use. Watt, kilowatt, and megawatt are particularly familiar as units of electrical power, but the terms apply to any type of power. In the cgs (centimeter/gram/second) system, the power unit is 1 erg/sec (1 erg = 10^{-7} j). See ELECTRIC POWER TRANSMISSION; STEAM ENGINE.—*A. J.*

POYNTING VECTOR: the vector P that gives the rate of flow of power per unit area in an electromagnetic wave. It is defined in magnitude and direction by the vector equation $\mathbf{P} = \mathbf{E} \times \mathbf{H}$, where $\mathbf{E}$ is the electric-field intensity and $\mathbf{H}$ is the magnetic-field intensity. The Poynting vector is at right angles to the plane containing the $\mathbf{E}$ and $\mathbf{H}$ vectors, which are perpendicular to each other.—*I. R.*

PRAGMATISM: a philosophical doctrine that emphasizes the practical applications or consequences of ideas. The doctrine was first enunciated (1877–78) by Charles S. Peirce, who applied the term "pragmatism" to his theory of meaning. It was subsequently amplified by William James and John Dewey to include also theories of truth, ethics and religion, thinking and inquiry, and a general philosophy of life. In the early part of the 20th cent. pragmatism virtually became identified with Dewey's philosophy. However, many distinguished British and American philosophers who defended pragmatism, *e.g.* C. I. Lewis (1883–   ), dissented from some of Dewey's views and attempted to restrict the application of "pragmatism" to a general theory of meaning.

In many formulations of pragmatism there is an emphasis upon action or conduct. Peirce specified his theory of meaning thus: a concept, *i.e.* the rational purpose of a word or other expression, lies exclusively in its conceivable bearing upon the conduct of life. James insisted that pragmatism is an attitude which turns a pragmatist toward fact, toward action, toward power. In defending his version of pragmatism, C. I. Lewis insisted that knowledge, action, and evolution are essentially connected and "that the primary and pervasive significance of knowledge lies in its guidance of action; knowing is for the sake of doing. And action is obviously rooted in evaluation." This emphasis upon action has given rise to the widespread claim that a pragmatist insists that the active life is to be valued more highly than the contemplative one. But though this claim may be true for some pragmatists, most of them have appealed to action in order to account for certain features of our knowledge, and not as a basis for a way of life.

Pragmatism is a continuation of the empiricist tradition that knowledge, with the possible exception of our knowledge of logical truth, is based upon experience. It challenges that thesis, however, in a number of important respects. It agrees with the Kantian doctrine that knowledge must be understood not as the outcome of a passive apprehension and combination of sensory units but rather as the product of interpreting the data of sensation in terms of the conceptual system which we bring to experience. Pragmatists add, however, that this conceptual system is influenced by our interests and values.

When pragmatists analyze scientific discourse and theories, they tend to emphasize the role various scientific terms and principles play in actual scientific practice. In some cases this has led to the view that theoretical nonobservational terms like "meson field" are not employed primarily—or even at all—to designate some nonobservable entity, but are essential ingredients of theories which serve to connect various observational statements. Hence the theories are considered not as true or false, or as descriptions of some non-accessible values, but as instruments enabling us to interpret experience and predict its course. A related thesis about the status of logical truths has been developed by some pragmatic philosophers. Here again logical principles are analyzed not as higher-order descriptions or truths about the invariant features of nature, but as conceptual tools or directions for the ordering of scientific discourse about nature and man.—*S. M.*

PRANDTL, LUDWIG, 1875–1953, German physicist; b. Freising. He studied hydrodynamics and aerodynamics, including their application to ship and aircraft design. His textbook on fluids, *Hydro- und Aeromechanik,* went through many editions and was translated into English, French, and Russian. He was a fellow of the Royal Society.—*D. H. D. R.*

PRASEODYMIUM: a lanthanide (rare-earth metal) element (Pr); at. no. 59; at. wt 140.92; valence 3,4,5. Carl Auer von Welsbach fractionated the salts of samarium-free dydimia into green and red portions in 1885. The green salt he called praseodymia (Gr. *prason,* "leek"); the red, nedoymia. (See NEODYMIUM.) Praseodymium metal was isolated in 1904 by electrolysis of the fused chloride at 1000°C; and until the late 1940s, when ION-EXCHANGE techniques were developed, electrolysis, prolonged fractional crystallization, and other exacting and expensive processes were required to separate praseodymium from other rare earths. Praseodymium oxide is used in the production of yellow pigment for zirconium-oxide-based ceramics and ceramic glazes. With other lanthanides it is present in the alloy misch metal, and such mixtures are also useful in controlling the optical properties (*e.g.* reflectivity and refractive index) of special optical glasses. (See LANTHANIDES; RARE EARTHS.)—*R. B. T.*

PRECAMBRIAN TIME: the interval of geologic time from the origin of Earth, perhaps 4.7 billion yr ago, to the first appearance of abundant and varied fossil organisms, nearly 600 million yr ago. These fossils, particularly the primitive arthropods called trilobites, define the Cambrian Period, the oldest subdivision of the PALEOZOIC ERA, and thus all older rocks are Precambrian. Although representing over 80% of geologic time, Precambrian history is relatively obscure and poorly known because the paucity of fossils makes relative dating difficult, because younger deposits cover Precambrian rocks over much of Earth, and because mountain building has deformed and profoundly altered most of these ancient rocks.

Precambrian Time is occasionally divided into two eras, the Archean (or Archeozoic) and the subsequent Proterozoic, but these divisions are indistinct. The term Cryptozoic Era also is used to designate Precambrian Time.

Precambrian rocks occur in the cores of some mountain ranges, in the bottom of a few very deep canyons, and, most extensively, in the continental interiors as broad, low plateaus

Fossil algae are prominent among the few traces of Precambrian life that can be identified. These are silicified specimens from the Bass Limestone, Bright Angel Canyon, Grand Canyon, Ariz. (*Amer. Mus. of Nat. Hist.*)

called shields. Thus the Canadian Shield occupies the north-central part of N America; the Baltic Shield forms the nucleus of Europe; Asia possesses two shields, the Angaran in Siberia and the Indian; the Guianan and Amazonian form the eastern part of S America; still other shields underlie central and S Africa, W Australia, and a large part of Antarctica. The Canadian Shield may be taken as typical in character and history, although each has its own unique features and historical sequence. The oldest dated Canadian rocks, formed over 2.5 billion yr before the present, occur north of Lake Superior, near the center of the continent. Although much changed by intense heat and pressure, they were originally coarse, poorly sorted sands, dark muds, and thick basaltic lava flows, deposited in narrow, rapidly subsiding troughs called geosynclines. Subsequently these sediments, transformed into rock, were folded and faulted; hot fluids and molten rock in-

Outcrop of Precambrian gneiss in southern New York shows pattern of "flow," suggesting intensity of metamorphic processes by which, over a period of a billion years or more, this rock was converted from original sedimentary rock. (*Jerome Wyckoff*)

vaded and metamorphosed them into schist and gneiss; the molten intrusives cooled to form granite; and a mountain system arose from the former troughs. Other geosynclines, flanking the new ranges, trapped the sand and mud eroded from the ridges. These sediments are typically finer and better sorted than those of earlier troughs, and include a higher proportion of limestone. They, in turn, were deformed, intruded, and elevated into mountains perhaps 1.5 billion yr ago. In the final stage of crustal evolution, between 600 million and a billion years ago, faulting produced small basins between the ranges and these accumulated coarse debris and lava flows. A similar sequence occurred in other portions of the Canadian Shield, although the sequence of subsidence began later than in the Lake Superior region.

Since the oldest rocks occupy the center of the Shield, and mountain building seemingly extended progressively outward, some geologists suggest the continent has grown from a small nucleus. Study of other shields supports this theory in part but also suggests that some of the original nuclei, particularly in the southern continents, split and partly foundered. Since iron particles in Precambrian rocks point in directions other than those of the present poles, the continental nuclei may have shifted position as well as changed shape. Little is known of the atmosphere or seas of the planet's early days; the amount of oxygen in the atmosphere, the amount of water, and the saltiness of the ocean probably all increased during the Precambrian. The primeval physical environment was almost certainly much different from the present: a world of small, barren continents, shallow seas, intense ultraviolet radiation, and a poisonous atmosphere. Though hostile to modern organisms, these conditions may have favored the origin of life. The rocks containing the oldest fossils, about 3 billion yr old (see LIFE, PREHISTORIC), suggest—as do younger rocks —a change toward modern conditions of atmosphere and sea.—*J. B.*

PRECESSION: the wobbling motion of the axis of a rotating body when a force is applied perpendicular to that axis. The simplest example is seen in a spinning toy top, whose axis moves in a cone-shaped figure because of the force of gravity. The effect is stronger as the top slows down. The angular velocity and direction of the precession W_p is given by the vector equation $W_p = W_s \times L$, where W_s is the angular velocity of spin and L is the torque (or turning force) applied to the rotating body. An important application of the precession phenomenon occurs in the gyroscopic stabilizer and in the AUTOMATIC PILOT. In these devices, undesired motion of the ship or airplane causes a GYROSCOPE to precess. The motion of precession is linked to mechanisms that bring the vessel back to the desired position. This is also the basis of INERTIAL GUIDANCE devices. The gravitational forces of Sun and Moon produce a torque on Earth, causing a precession of Earth's axis (see PRECESSION OF EQUINOXES). Precession is found also in the motions of electrons and symmetrical molecules, where torques are due to magnetic and electric forces rather than to gravitation. The motion of a spinning electron in a magnetic field is called LARMOR PRECESSION.—*I. R.*

PRECESSION OF THE EQUINOXES: a slow westward motion, along the ecliptic (the plane of Earth's orbit), of the line of intersection of the ecliptic and the plane of Earth's equator. The position of a star in the sky can be defined by its angular distance from the ecliptic (latitude) and its distance along the ecliptic measured eastward from the vernal equinox (longitude). Precession of the equinoxes thus results in an apparent steady increase in the longitude of a star by about 50″ per yr, with no change in latitude. The discovery of precession of the

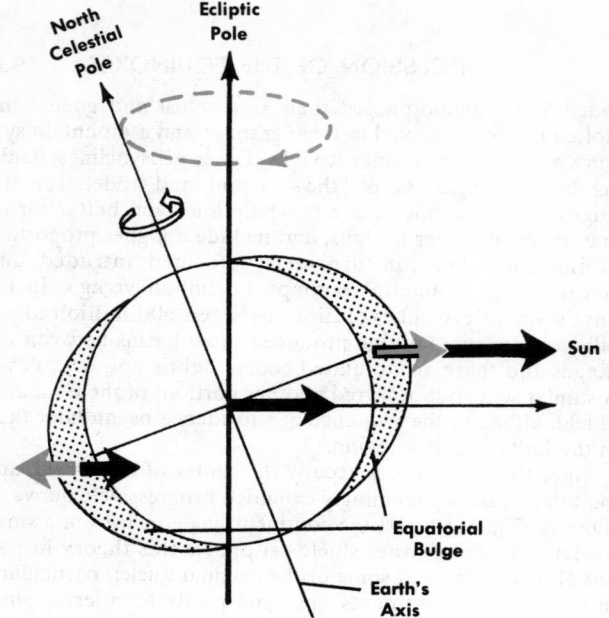

North Celestial Pole
Ecliptic Pole
Sun
Equatorial Bulge
Earth's Axis

equinoxes is attributed to Hipparchus, c. 125 B. C., who compared observations of the days in the year when particular stars could first be seen rising before the Sun with similar observations made about 300 B. C. Owing to precession, this date for any particular star advances by about one day every 70 yr.

Earth is not completely spherical but bulges at the equator. The gravitational attraction of the Sun and Moon on the side of the equatorial bulge facing these bodies is greater than their attraction on the opposite side of the bulge. Therefore the Sun's attraction tends to bring Earth's equatorial plane into coincidence with the plane of the ecliptic, and the Moon's attraction tends to bring it into coincidence with the plane of the Moon's orbit, which itself never strays far from the ecliptic. Because Earth rotates, however, the combined effect is not a decrease in the angle between the planes of the ecliptic and of Earth's equator, but a conical motion of Earth's axis. This conical motion, completing one westward revolution in about 26,000 yr, is called the *luni-solar precession.* The Moon's contribution is much the greater because its smaller mass is more than compensated by its shorter distance.

In a separate effect, the attraction of the planets progressively alters the orientation in space of the plane of the ecliptic. This *planetary precession* results in a small eastward shift of the line of equinoxes and thus somewhat counteracts the luni-solar precession. In addition, planetary precession continually alters the tilt of Earth's axis to the ecliptic by minute amounts. The phenomenon of precession is also associated with a periodic variation of the tilt of Earth's axis called NUTATION.

Owing to precession, the north celestial pole moves among the stars in a circle of radius 23½° about the north ecliptic pole (with a similar motion for the south celestial pole). Planetary precession distorts this circle somewhat, so that in fact it never closes exactly on itself. Polaris, the present polestar, is only temporarily so near the pole. About 3,600 B. C., the star Alpha Draconis was near the pole; in 12,000 yr the polestar will be Vega. The pole will return to the vicinity of Polaris in another 26,000 yr.—*S. D. G.*

PRECIPITATION: in chemistry, the rapid deposition of a substance from a liquid in which it is not more than slightly soluble. The deposit, known as a *precipitate,* is usually a solid, but it may be a liquid. In inorganic chemistry, precipitation is often brought about in an ionic reaction known as double decomposition. For example, when aqueous solutions of barium nitrate and sodium sulfate are mixed, there is

an immediate precipitate of insoluble barium sulfate, and sodium nitrate is left in solution. Similarly, any soluble substance giving rise to chlorine ions will yield a precipitate of silver chloride when added to a solution of a soluble silver salt. Such reactions are applied as tests in qualitative analysis, and also as the basis of quantitative analytical methods (see CHEMICAL ANALYSIS). Precipitates are often indicated in chemical equations by downward-pointing arrows. Sometimes precipitates have distinctive colors, as with certain metallic sulfides and compounds of iron and copper. Sometimes they appear only on heating, as in the coagulation of proteins and the reduction of Fehling's solution. A typical example of liquid precipitation is that of chloroform, as heavy droplets, when chloral hydrate solution is warmed with alkali. The rapid deposition of crystals caused by seeding a supersaturated solution is sometimes also regarded as precipitation. Precipitation is widely applied in chemical processes, both in the laboratory and industrially.—*J. R.*

PRECIPITATION: in meteorology, those water particles, liquid or solid, that form in the atmosphere and fall to the ground. Rain, hail, and snow all are types of precipitation. Fog, clouds, dew, and frost are not classified as precipitation, since they do not fall. A non-raining CLOUD is composed of tiny water droplets about 0.002 cm in diameter and in concentrations of a few hundreds per cubic centimeter.

Growing clouds are sustained by vertical air currents, which may vary in strength from several centimeters per second in the widespread layer clouds to several meters per second in large cumulus clouds. Considerable growth of the cloud droplets, which have falling speeds of only about 1 cm/sec, is therefore necessary if they are to fall through the cloud, survive evaporation in the unsaturated air beneath, and reach the ground as drizzle or rain. *Drizzle* drops have diameters of the order of 0.2 mm, while the largest raindrops are 5 mm across and fall at about 9 m/sec. Production of a relatively few large drops from a larger population of much smaller ones may be achieved by *coalescence.*

Cloud droplets are not, in general, of uniform size; they arise on condensation nuclei of various sizes and grow under slightly different conditions of temperature and supersaturation in different parts of the cloud, and some may remain inside the cloud longer than others before being carried to the drier air outside. A droplet larger than average will fall faster than the smaller ones and so will collide and coalesce with some of those lying in its fall path. Once a drop starts to grow by this process, it will continue at an ever-increasing rate, because after each collision it becomes bigger, falls faster, and so sweeps out a larger volume of cloud more quickly. If its journey in the cloud is sufficiently long and if the population of smaller droplets is sufficiently dense, it may eventually grow large enough to fall out of the cloud as a raindrop.

Growth may occur also by the Bergeron-Findeisen ice-crystal process. A fundamental feature of natural clouds is their frequent occurrence in the SUPERCOOLED state: the cloud droplets exist as liquid at temperatures well below 0°C, sometimes down to −40°C. At temperatures above −40°C the water droplet can freeze only if it contains small solid motes possessing certain favorable properties. These particles, called *ice nuclei*, consist largely of special kinds of clay particles. At temperatures just below 0°C the probability of a cloud droplet containing a suitable ice nucleus is very small, but at lower temperatures this probability increases as more and more airborne particles become capable of initiating the freezing of supercooled water. In general, then, that part of the cloud which lies between the 0°C and −20°C levels consists of supercooled droplets coexisting with a much smaller number of ice crystals. The equilibrium VAPOR PRESSURE over water is greater than that over ice at temperatures below 0°C, so that air saturated with respect to water will be appreciably supersaturated relative to ice, and the ice crystals will grow by condensation much more rapidly than the water droplets. The ice crystals grow mainly as thin hexagonal plates, six-sided columns, and richly branched star-shaped crystals, several of which may join together to form a *snowflake*. On falling through the level at which the temperature becomes 0°C, the snowflakes melt and eventually reach the ground as *raindrops*.

Observations made from aircraft and with radar have shown that the ice-crystal process is largely responsible for the widespread, persistent precipitation which falls from the extensive stratus-cloud systems which are associated with fronts and depressions. While DRIZZLE (drops about 0.2 mm in diameter) often falls from non-freezing stratus clouds in which the drops can grow only by coalescence, most of these clouds do not produce RAIN (drops greater than about 0.5 mm in diameter) unless their tops are colder than −12°C; so ice crystals may be responsible. Precipitation from cumulus clouds, which may reach the ground in the form of raindrops, pellets of *soft hail*, or larger hard hailstones, is generally of greater intensity and shorter duration than that from stratus clouds, and is composed of larger particles. The great vertical depth of the cumulus clouds, the strong vertical air currents, and the high concentrations of liquid water in them all ensure the rapid growth of precipitation particles by coalescence.

In tropical and subtropical regions, showers fall from clouds which are entirely beneath the 0°C level and therefore cannot contain ice crystals. Raindrops must therefore grow by coalescence; it is thought that the larger droplets necessary to initiate the process are provided by sea spray. In the middle latitudes, the 0°C level is much lower than in the tropics. Although showers may be released by coalescence in warm weather, conditions are relatively more favorable for the ice-crystal process. The crystals grow initially by condensation of vapor in much the same way as in stratus clouds, but when their diameters exceed about 0.1 mm, growth by collision with supercooled water droplets usually predominates. The droplets freeze on impact to form pellets of *soft hail*, which may reach the ground in wintertime but in warmer weather melt on their way down.

True *hailstones*, which fall in warm weather, have a core of soft, opaque ice, probably a pellet of soft hail, or a clear, transparent center, probably a frozen raindrop. The core is often surrounded with several alternate layers of clear and opaque ice. In a dense cloud the hailstones may collect supercooled water at a rate faster than it can be frozen and so acquire a liquid coat which, on subsequent freezing, produces a layer of clear ice. The alternate layers are probably formed as the stone makes a number of trips between regions of higher and lower temperature and/or between regions of higher and lower water content. The largest hailstones may reach golf-ball or even tennis-ball size; to do this, they must remain suspended for at least 20 min in a region of strong upcurrents and high water content which is not being denuded of moisture by much more numerous smaller stones. It seems that while the majority of hailstones fall out of the upcurrent after their first journey through it, a very few re-enter it again lower down and pass through it a second or third time, and so continue their growth into really large stones.—*B. J. M.*

PRECIPITATOR: a device for removing finely divided solid or liquid fumes from air or another gas. The term is usually restricted to a device other than a filter (see FILTRATION, CHEMICAL) or a simple settling chamber. One important type of precipitator is the *cyclone separator,* in which the mass of gas is given a spiral motion and the dust particles are thrown by centrifugal force against the walls of the collecting vessel. The most effective and widely used type is the electrostatic or Cottrell precipitator, named after Frederick G. Cottrell (1877–1948), the man who did most to develop it early in this century. In this device the dust-laden gas passes through a narrow chamber across which a high-voltage unidirectional electrostatic field is maintained. The gas ions formed by the field attach themselves to the dust particles, which then migrate under the influence of the field to the chamber walls. There they agglomerate and are removed mechanically. Cottrell precipitators are used for smoke abatement and to remove pollutants or unwanted constituents from industrial gases. They are also used to recover valuable substances from fumes and smokes in various industrial processes; such materials as sulfuric acid, carbon black, phosphorus, zinc oxide, and the coal tar entrained in coke-oven gas are recovered in this way.—*A. M. S.*

PREGL, FRITZ, 1869–1930, Austrian chemist; b. Laibach. He developed methods for complete, rapid analyses with only a few milligrams of an organic substance. His book on quantitative organic microanalysis, *Die quantitative organische Mikroanalyse,* first appeared in 1917 and had many expanded editions. For his invention of the method of microanalysis of organic substances he received the 1923 Nobel prize in chemistry.—*E. F.*

Fritz Pregl
(*Wide World*)

PREHISTORIC LIFE: see LIFE, PREHISTORIC.

PRESSURE: the ratio of the force exerted by a fluid to the area over which this force is applied ($P = F/A$). The hydrostatic pressure produced by a liquid is, by definition, the weight of a column of such liquid resting on a unit area; similarly, the pressure exerted by the atmosphere is the weight of a unit column of air extending from sea level to the outermost reaches of the atmosphere. Hydrostatic pressure may be computed with the aid of the equation $P = hd$, where h is the height of the column and d the weight density of the liquid. Pressures of gases are determined with manometers and pressure gauges. Gas pressures may be stated in absolute or gauge values and are measured in lb/ft^2, $lb/in.^2$, newtons/$meter^2$, or dynes/cm^2; pressure may also be stated as the height of a column of mercury that produces the same pressure. The gauge pressure of a gas represents the difference between its total or absolute pressure and the normal (sea-level) pressure of the atmosphere.

Critical pressure is the pressure required to produce the liquefaction of a vapor at its critical temperature. Above this temperature no amount of pressure will liquefy a vapor.—*A. E.*

PRESSURE MEASUREMENTS: determinations of force per unit area exerted on a solid surface, usually by a liquid or gas. Pressure can be expressed in terms of any convenient units of force and area, common units being lb/in.², g/or kg/cm², or dynes/cm². Attempts to introduce the *bar* (10⁶ dynes/cm²) as an international unit of pressure have not met widespread acceptance. Pressure is also expressed in two other ways: (1) in *atmospheres,* one standard atmosphere (atmospheric pressure under specified standard conditions) being equal to 14.696 lb/in.²; (2) in *millimeters of mercury, i.e.* the pressure exerted by the weight of a column of mercury a given number of millimeters high. One standard atmosphere is equal to 760 mm of mercury. Analogous expressions of pressure in *inches of mercury* (29.92 in. of mercury equals 1 atm), *centimeters of water,* and *feet of water* are used.

Measurement of Atmospheric Pressure: Devices for measuring atmospheric pressure are called *barometers.* Atmospheric pressure was first studied systematically by Evangelista Torricelli (1643) and Blaise Pascal (1647). These researchers showed that if a long glass tube closed at one end was filled with mercury, then inverted to a vertical position in a pool of mercury, the height or level in the closed end fell to about 30 in. above the mercury in the pool. The level varied slightly with weather conditions, and decreased as the altitude above sea level increased. This was the first barometer, and the present-day standard mercury barometer differs from it solely in minor refinements. Barometers of this type can be made with liquids other than mercury, but since these are all less dense than mercury the height of the standing column is correspondingly greater. Thus in a barometer filled with water the height would be about 34 ft. The aneroid barometer, used in aircraft and in other applications where a tall, vertical tube of mercury would be clumsy, consists of a hermetically sealed bellows. Since the pressure inside is constant, the length of the bellows will vary with changes in the outside atmospheric pressure. This displacement, amplified by multiplying levers, is transmitted to a pointer sliding across the scale (calibrated against a mercury barometer).

Other Pressure-measurement Devices: Devices for measuring the pressure of gases or liquids in industrial, laboratory, household, and military applications are called *manometers* or *pressure gages.* The term *manometer* is usually reserved for a simple U tube of mercury or other suitable liquid, one end of which is open to the region of unknown pressure. The other end is open to either the atmosphere or a vacuum. The difference in liquid level between the two legs of the U tube measures the pressure. *Pressure gages* operate on different principles to suit the requirements of each case. As a rule they measure the *gage pressure, i.e.* the excess pressure in a closed vessel over the atmospheric pressure. The *absolute pressure* equals the gage pressure plus the atmospheric pressure. In a partial vacuum, *i.e.* where the absolute pressure is less than 1 atm, the gage pressure is considered negative. The absolute pressure is always positive except in a perfect vacuum, where it is zero. There are gages that measure absolute pressure both above and below 1 atm (vacuum), and all other gages are calibrated against them. The *compound gage* measures vacuum as well as ordinary pressures.

The *absolute-pressure gage* works with two bellows—one evacuated, the other open to gas or vapor. The open bellows either expands or collapses as the pressure rises above or drops below atmospheric. The movement actuates a spring linked to a pointer or a recording pen. The atmospheric pressure collapses both bellows to the same extent; hence no correction for its variations is needed. The absolute-pressure gage is used to measure pressure in the range of zero to 5 in. of mercury. In the *diaphragm gage,* utilizing a flexible leather disk or a series of corrugated metal disks, one side is exposed

to atmospheric pressure, the other to a pressure to be measured. When each side is open to a different source of pressure, the absolute differential pressure can be measured; pressures between zero and 5 lb/in.² are measured with this device. The *Bourdon tube* (or Bourdon-spring pressure gage) is a narrow, oval, curved tube of phosphorus-bronze, stainless steel, or other material with one end closed and the other open to pressure. Pressure at the open end tends to unbend the tube when the pressure applied is more than 1 atm and to curl it when the pressure is less. This results in a slight movement of the sealed end of the tube, and the movement is transmitted through a piston bearing to the pointer. This instrument is highly accurate (1 part in 200), and is by far the most common pressure gage in industrial installations. It can be used up to 10,000 lb/in.² A spiral arrangement of Bourdon tubes, having improved sensitivity, is used in industry as a pressure-control device.

The *absolute-pressure gage* for high pressures is a cylinder filled with oil and open to pressure. The compressed oil tends to raise the lid, which has a piston running through it, counterbalanced by weights. This type of gage can measure the highest artificially obtainable pressures. For low temperatures a glycerine-water mixture is used instead of oil.

The most widely used device for measuring low pressures in gases is the *McLeod vacuum gage* (1874), available in many different designs embodying the same principle. A bulb of known capacity (usually 250 or 500 ml) is connected with the chamber whose pressure is to be measured, and is allowed to come to the unknown pressures. It is then disconnected and the residual gas within it is forced by mercury into a small calibrated tube, where its volume at atmospheric pressure is measured. From the ratio of the volume at atmospheric pressure to the bulb volume, by Boyle's law, the unknown pressure is calculated. The McLeod gage is highly accurate and is used to calibrate other vacuum gages. It is directly useful for pressures as low as 10^{-6} mm mercury.

The very-low-pressure ranges are usually measured by secondary electrical effects that are sensitive to changes in absolute pressure. At low gas pressures, for example, there is a definite relationship between the pressure and the heat loss from an electrically heated coil. This principle is used in the *resistance-type vacuum gage,* where the pressure (as a *differential* value) is obtained by measuring the coil resistance with a Wheatstone bridge (calibrated against a known very high vacuum). In the *ionization (high-vacuum) gage* the electrons in a triode flowing to the positively charged grid are deflected by the negative plate to the interior of the tube connected to the vacuum to be measured. Under the electron bombardment, ions form in the residual gas; their number, which depends on the gas pressure, can then be counted. These gages are capable of measuring pressures as low as 10^{-8} mm mercury.

Remote indicators measure gas or vapor pressure at a distance by converting the pressure to a direct-current voltage. In another design, the pressure acts on a variable magnetic field, affecting an alternating current. The scale is calibrated in terms of pressure.—*A. M. S.*

PRIESTLEY, JOSEPH, 1733–1804, English clergyman and chemist; b. Fieldhead, Yorkshire. In his *The History And Present State of Electricity* (1767) he explained the "Priestley rings" formed by electrical discharges upon metallic surfaces. He improved techniques for studying gases by collecting them over mercury instead of water, and he prepared and studied various gases and isolated oxygen. In his work entitled *Experiments and Observations on Different Kinds of Air* (1774) Priestley demonstrated that plants immersed in water yield oxygen, and that this gas is necessary for the survival of

Plate 67 NESTS

Birds and some insects are born with instincts that enable them, when mature, to construct nests in which to raise their young. All the individuals of a species build the same kind of nest, having inherited the same set of "instructions." Although primarily a nursery, the nest may also double as a shelter or a home for the adults.

1. Barn owl: Barn owls take shelter and make nests in buildings when suitable hollow trees are scarce. Often an owl can be seen before sundown, peering from doorway of nest. *(Harry J. Lance, Jr./ Shostal)* **2. Great white heron** builds nest platform of sticks high in branches of tree, out of reach of most predators. *(National Audubon Soc.)*

3. Social wasps chew up plant fibers and work them into a gray, paperlike material from which they build community nurseries. *(Carl W. Rettenmeyer)*

4. Female ruby-throated hummingbird clings to side of small, cup-shaped nest built on a tree branch from cobwebs and plant fibers, then camouflaged with living lichens. *(Allan D. Cruickshank/ National Audubon Soc.)* **5. Cowbirds** lay eggs in other birds' nests. Here a big nesting cowbird is fed by its foster parent, a solitary vireo, after having shouldered the vireo's offspring out of nest. *(Allan D. Cruickshank/National Audubon Soc.)*

Plate 68   PRINTING

FOUR-COLOR PROCESS PRINTING

SCREEN TONES IN INCREMENTS OF 10%

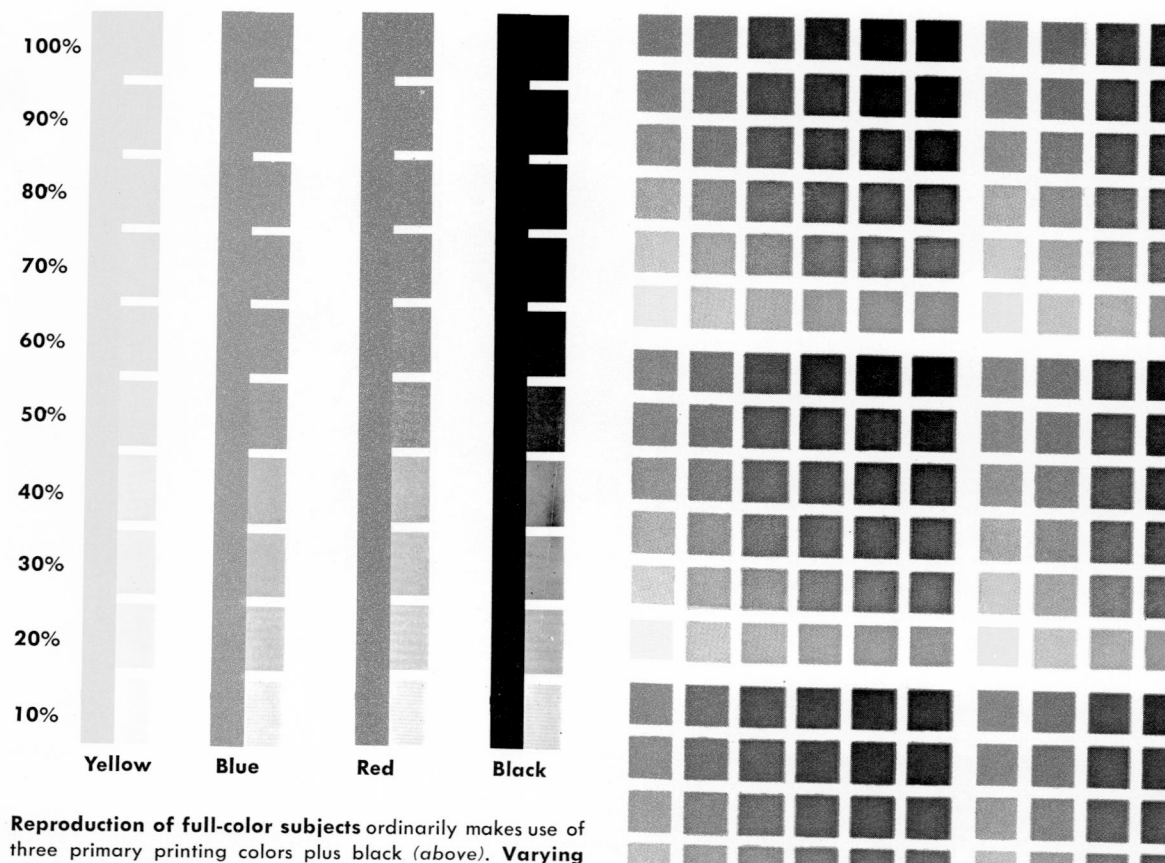

100%
90%
80%
70%
60%
50%
40%
30%
20%
10%

Yellow   Blue   Red   Black

Reproduction of full-color subjects ordinarily makes use of three primary printing colors plus black *(above).* **Varying percentages of tone** attained by screening and combining colors give wide range of chroma *(right).* **High-speed offset lithographic press** *(below)* is printing yellow, blue, red, and black. Press completes one side of sheet in a few seconds. *(Western Printing and Lithographing Co.)*

Plate 69 PRINTING

Yellow
90° angle

Black
45° angle

Blue
105° angle

Film
in its
original
size

Red
75° angle

Preparation for full-color printing, whether it will be by a relief, an intaglio, or a planographic process, follows the same general pattern; the camera plays a dominant role. Most full-color work makes use of the primary printing colors of yellow, red, and blue, with black for added accent. Each color requires its own printing plate. In order to separate all the yellow from the full-color subject, the camera man uses a purple filter which holds back the red and blue elements, allowing yellow to be recorded on the film negative in terms of black or gradations of tone down to the absence of black. Similarly, the extraction of red requires a green filter; of blue, an orange filter. A crossline screen (enlarged, right) in the camera breaks up the continuous tone of the subject into fine dots, a necessary requisite for printing. As each screened film is made, the crossline screen in the camera is turned to the appropriate angle to form the dot pattern. These steps result in four individual films; each represents a separate color and has its image broken up into dots through the use of the crossline screen. Each film is then further processed by transferring the image photochemically to a printing plate from which the image can be reproduced in quantity on a press.

THE THREE BASIC PROCESSES OF PRINTING

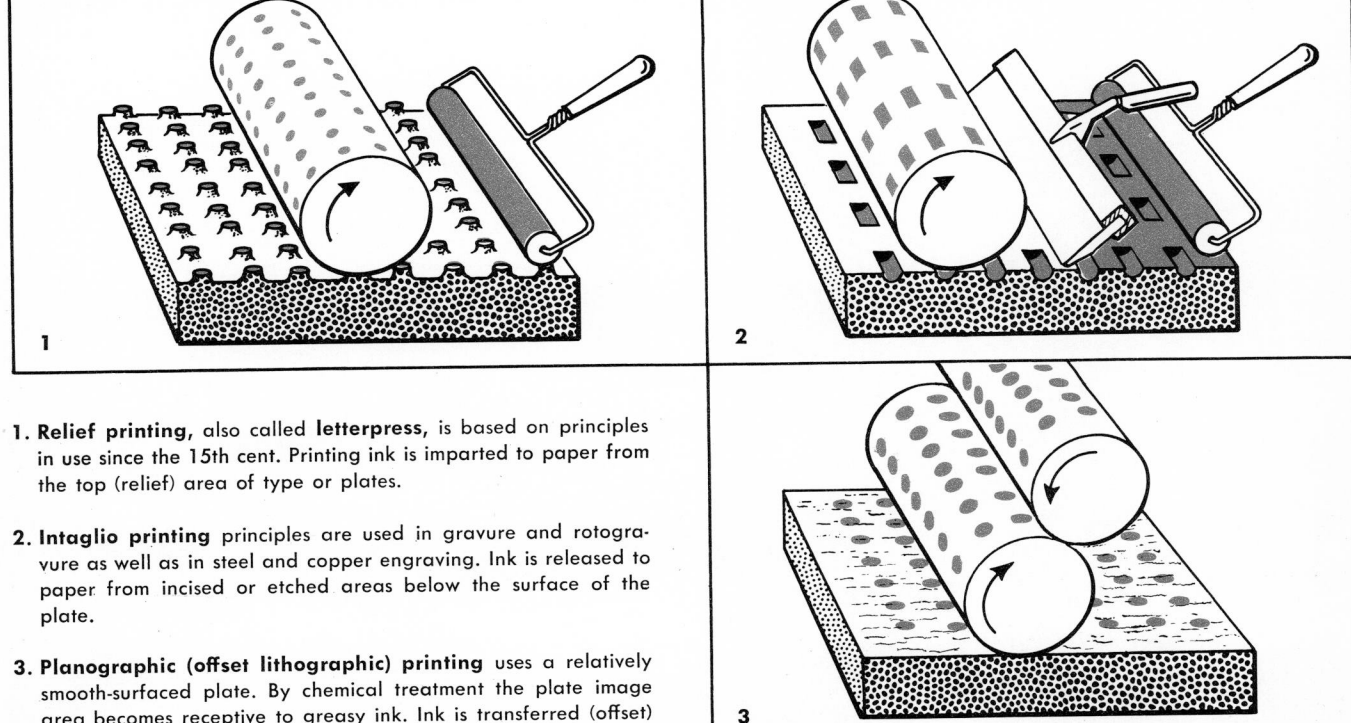

1. **Relief printing,** also called **letterpress,** is based on principles in use since the 15th cent. Printing ink is imparted to paper from the top (relief) area of type or plates.

2. **Intaglio printing** principles are used in gravure and rotogravure as well as in steel and copper engraving. Ink is released to paper from incised or etched areas below the surface of the plate.

3. **Planographic (offset lithographic) printing** uses a relatively smooth-surfaced plate. By chemical treatment the plate image area becomes receptive to greasy ink. Ink is transferred (offset) to a rubber blanket and thence to the paper.

Plate 70 PALEONTOLOGY

Paleontology deals with the past life of Earth as revealed by study of the fossils found in the rocks. Much of the preliminary work of paleontologists consists of finding fossil remains and removing them from the enclosing rock in as complete a condition as possible.

1. Trachodon mirabilis: An herbivorous dinosaur from the Cretaceous. This specimen, at the South Dakota School of Mines and Technology at Rapid City, is mounted next to a cycad, virtually the same plant that existed at the time of the dinosaurs, over 60 million yr ago. *(Shostal)*

2. Fossil specimens in field are covered with a coating of plaster before moving. *(Amer. Mus. of Nat. Hist.)*

3. Freeing fossils from enclosing rock: a time-consuming and often delicate process. *(Paul Desautels)*

4. Thrinaxodon: a mammal-like reptile from the Mesozoic rocks of South Africa. *(Paul Desautels)*

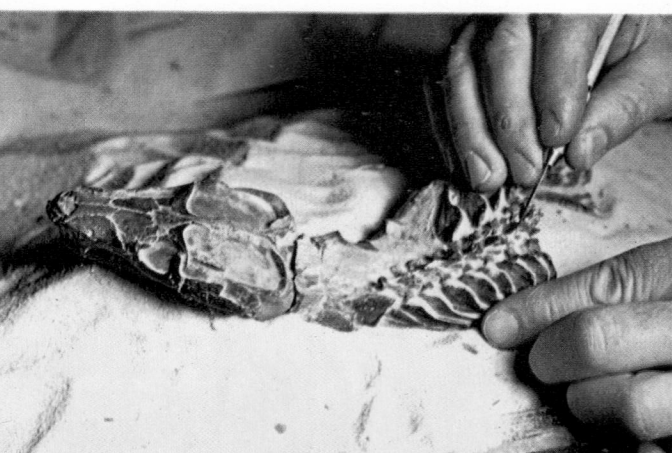

3   4

Primates: In these photographs appear a number of the animals that, together with man, belong to the mammalian order of the primates. Two suborders are recognized: prosimians and anthropoids. Surviving prosimians are represented by two large-eyed male tarsiers from the islands between Asia and Australia (*top left*) and a slow-moving slender loris of the forests of S India and Ceylon (*top center*). The remaining photographs illustrate the other suborder, the anthropoids, which include ceboids, cerco-pithecoids, and hominoids. Ceboids—the prehensile-tailed New World monkeys—are represented by the weeper sapajou (*top right*), one of the several varieties of capuchins, bands of which roam the forests of Cent. and S America. Cercopithecoids, which have a separate history (having developed in Africa, Asia, and Europe), are represented by the Japanese red-faced macaque (*bottom left*); hominoids, by the orangutan (*left*) and chimpanzee (*right*) of the last photograph. (*N. Y. Zoological Society*)

animal life. In 1794 he emigrated with his family to the U. S. He was a fellow of the Royal Society.—*S. B.*

PRIMATE: any MAMMAL of the order Primates, which is a group of relatively unspecialized animals including the lemurs, the tarsier, the lorises, the tree shrews, and the great apes in the Old World; the various kinds of monkeys in tropical regions of both hemispheres; and man. Primate, signifying "first," was the rank assigned to man and his nearest relatives when scientific classification of animals was begun. Now that the fossil record is known more fully, it is held widely that primates arose from a primitive INSECTIVORE, somewhat similar to the tree shrews of today, in which an accumulation of adaptations to arboreal life led to elongation of the long bones in arms and legs; modifications in comparatively short hands and feet until the thumb and great toe became opposable and useful in grasping branches; the transformation of at least one claw on each hand and foot into a flat nail; and the retention in part of the primitive shoulder girdle and the collar bone (clavicle), which provides additional support to an animal traveling hand over hand ("brachiating") among tree branches. On this basis, the primates are closely related to living insectivores and bats, possibly to the edentates (*e.g.* sloths, anteaters). Primates usually retain the primitive number of five digits on hand and foot.

Probably in relation to arboreal habits, primates came to rely less on the sense of smell and more on vision. This led to a shortening of the nose and flattening of the face, a reduction in the number of teeth but not in their diversification, a shortening of the jaws, and a more forward position of the eyes together with a greater overlap in the binocular visual field. Primates usually have two rather than three pairs of incisors in each jaw and, commonly, fewer cheek teeth (premolars and molars), so that the total number of teeth is 32 in man, apes, and monkeys. The linking of good binocular vision to the ability to handle and manipulate objects appears to be correlated with increased development of the cerebral cortex of the brain, until in man the brain became larger and more complex in proportion to body size than the brain of any other animal. The increasing development of the brain has conferred on primates the possibilities of memory, learning, reasoning, and intelligence.

Most primitive of primates are the lemurs and the aye-aye of Madagascar, bush-babies and pottos of Africa, and lorises of S Asia. These animals have nails on all fingers and on all toes except the second one. They are arboreal, rather slow-moving and generally nocturnal, sleeping curled up in a tree hole all day with the bushy tail (when present) curled over the head, but emerging at dusk. While holding on to branches with the hind legs they capture insects or collect fruits with the hands. A second suborder, the tarsiers, includes several members of one genus (*Tarsius*), all of which are rat-sized arboreal animals with elongated ankles important in hopping or jumping in pursuit of insects. Two toes on each hind foot bear claws; the rest of the toes and the fingers end in nails. All digits are provided with adhesive pads, which aid in holding to branches. The eyes are enormous, circular, and placed close together just above the short nose and small mouth.

The remaining primates are monkeys, baboons, and apes, with nails on all fingers and toes, and with more social habits than the lemurs and their allies. In South and Central America they include the extremely active marmosets and tamarins, squirrel monkeys, uakaris, sakis, and the monkeys that have a prehensile tail which can be used as a fifth hand—the capuchin ("organ-grinder's monkey"), spider monkeys, wooly monkeys, wooly spider monkeys, and howler monkeys. All the New World monkeys have a flat septum in the nose, lack cheek pouches, and are unable to oppose the thumb, although they do have opposable big toes. In Africa and S Asia, including many of the E Indian islands, the division *Anthropoidea* includes the Old World monkeys (which have opposable thumbs, nonprehensile tails, and often cheek pouches and bald callus areas on the buttocks) and the apes. Old World monkeys include primarily arboreal species (*e.g.* vervet, guereza, and guenon monkeys in Africa), some that spend about equal time in trees and on the ground (*e.g.* the langurs, and the sacred hanuman monkeys of India), and others (*e.g.* baboons, mandrills, and the macaque, or rhesus, monkey so widely used in medical research) that are essentially ground animals of arid countries. Great apes, unlike other primates (excepting man), lack a tail and never have cheek pouches. They include the long-armed, long-legged slender gibbon found from the Himalayas to Borneo; the orangutan of swampy forests in Sumatra and Borneo; the gorillas of central African forests; and the chimpanzee of forests in the Congo and W Africa. Man probably arose along the edge of forested land in Africa, south of the equator. His family (Hominidae) is grouped with that of the apes (Pongidae) into a superfamily (Hominoidea) that is considered to be distinct from the Old World monkeys and the New World monkeys. The tarsioids and the lemuroids are regarded as being only remotely related to man.—*L. and M. M.*

PRIME MOVER: a driving mechanism that converts energy from natural sources (wind, water, steam, and combustible fuels) into mechanical energy directly usable by other machines. The term is synonymous with ENGINE and power plant; TURBINES are an important class of prime movers. A water wheel is turned by the energy of dammed water or by a waterfall, and the potential energy of the water is converted into the mechanical energy of rotation used to operate the machinery of a flour mill; therefore the water wheel is a prime mover. A steam engine, which utilizes expanding steam to produce reciprocating motion (ultimately transferred to wheels of a locomotive or the propeller of a ship), is a prime mover. In the case of electric generators, whose rotors are turned by the mechanical energy previously produced by some type of turbine, diesel engine, or other power plant, it is the diesel engine or turbine, not the electrical generator, that is the prime mover. Electric motors are not prime movers.—*C. S.*

PRIME NUMBER: an integer greater than 1 that has no integral factors other than itself and 1. The first ten primes are 2, 3, 5, 7, 11, 13, 17, 19, 23, and 29. The prime numbers are the building blocks from which all other integers are derived in the sense that every other integer is a product of primes. In consequence, prime numbers have been much studied. One of the first questions was whether there are infinitely many of them or only a finite number. This was answered by Euclid, whose demonstration of the infinitude of primes is a model of mathematical reasoning by the indirect method of proof. Eratosthenes (3rd cent. B. C.) gave a process, known as the "sieve of Eratosthenes," for finding all primes up to a given number n.

Much attention has been given to the distribution of primes. Formulas have been sought that will yield only primes, even if not all of them. Pierre de Fermat suggested that the expression $2^{2^n} + 1$ might be prime for all values of n. This proved to be wrong, for although the result is prime for $n = 0, 1, 2, 3$, and 4, the number $2^{2^5} + 1$ has been factored. The expression $n^2 - n + 41$ is prime for all integral values of n from 1 to 40, but not for 41.

There are many conjectures about prime numbers that are strongly supported by empirical evidence but that have not been proved. The conjecture of Christian Goldbach (1690–1764) suggests that every even number except 2 is a sum of two primes. It has not been proved. Primes frequently occur in pairs differing by 2; *e.g.* 3 and 5, 11 and 13, 17 and 19. Are there infinitely many such pairs? The answer to this question is not known. The question of the average number of primes among the first n integers, for any n, has been answered by the prime number theorem. According to this theorem, if A_n denotes the number of primes among the first n integers, the average, A_n/n, is approximated more and more closely by $1/\log_e n$ as n increases.—*H. C.*

PRIMITIVE TECHNOLOGY: The basis of mechanized civilization lies in the tools and crafts gradually developed in prehistoric times. Improvements grew from experience in exploiting materials and developing processes to cope with domestic needs. As craft skills increased and tools and devices were refined, there followed local specialization and small-scale industrial production. But with slave labor abundant and draft animals available, up through Classical times there was little urge to mechanize. The earliest tools—pear-shaped fist-axes of the Paleolithic period—were not suitable for fashioning other tools. The need was met in the later Paleolithic by utilizing stone flakes for cutting and scraping, with cutting edges prepared by pressing off chips. Still later, smaller graving tools made refined workmanship possible. By Neolithic times granular stone was rubbed (ground) to shape. Stone was bored with a stick or hollow reed, armed with sharp sand, twirled between the palms. Bow-drill and pump-drill reduced the labor, and in the following Bronze Age hooked metal tools and weighted cranks permitted the hollowing of narrow-mouthed stone vessels.

Woodworking was often laborious. Wood was split with wedges, and, with fire as the active agent, trimmed or hollowed by scraping away the charcoal. Pieces were reduced to length by snapping after drilling a line of holes or cutting a kerf. Joining was by lashing or sewing through pairs of holes. Work was more easily accomplished when copper and bronze became available (4,000 to 3,000 B. C.); equipment then included adzes, axes, chisels, and saws cutting on the pull stroke. The arts of doweling, mortising, and dovetailing were evolved a few centuries later (see CARPENTRY).

A great step toward mechanization followed from the utilization of metals for tools (see HAND TOOLS) and construction. Copper, the earliest used, had no substantial advantages over stone, but could be cast and more easily shaped. Bronze came into general use about 2,000 B. C. after the proportions in the alloy were controlled; iron followed in common use about 700 B. C. Smelting of ores with charcoal was done in open fires, making use of the updrafts on windy hillsides. The iron mass thus produced was soft and brittle; reheating with charcoal and hammering removed impurities and transformed it to steel. Equally fundamental was the invention of the WHEEL, on which rested future machine techniques and application of power. It first appeared as a cart wheel in the Near East in the Bronze Age, revolutionizing modes of transportation. The water wheel was soon derived from it as a source of power, and adaptations such as gears, revolving shaft, windlass, and pulley followed not long before the Christian era. Among the earliest machines, which may have originated independently of the wheel, were the cranked grindstone (2,000 B. C.) and the wood-lathe (7th cent. B. C.). Slow hand-shaping of pottery was accelerated by the invention of the potter's wheel in the Bronze Age, transforming a household activity to one of quantity production by specialists. Fabric weaving is of great antiquity: even the simplest of devices first employed to stretch warps, equipped with a heddle and shed rod to separate them, could produce complex weaving. Looms of several forms date from the late Neolithic—suspended warps stretched by weights, warps pulled taut by the weaver's body, or stretched between two bars tied to stakes. The later horizontal framed loom (about 1,500 B. C.) permitted mechanical additions for actuating multiple heddles. Another fabric, felt, formed by compacting fibers, was an ancient Central Asiatic invention. (See TEXTILE.)

House construction involved only simple procedures: beams were laid on supports or were lashed. Brick and stone MASONRY of late prehistoric periods was used in forms limited in roof span by the length of available logs. When in 4,000 B. C. the corbeled arch, and some centuries later the round arch, were invented in Mesopotamia, more ambitious structures supporting overhead loads became possible; see ARCHITECTURAL CRAFTS AND TOOLS; ARCHITECTURAL ENGINEERING. —L. Sp.

PRINCIPIA MATHEMATICA (The Principles of Mathematics), by Alfred N. Whitehead and Bertrand Russell (1910–15): While preceded by important pioneering work in the generalization and mathematization of traditional logic, this monumental treatise (not to be confused with Russell's earlier *Principles of Mathematics*) is the classic of modern symbolic logic, having inaugurated a new, rigorous approach to the subject which rendered all previous ones obsolete. The work has also been seminal in its endeavor to establish the still controversial thesis that all mathematics is derivable from logic (logicism). —G. G.

PRINCIPIA PHILOSOPHIAE (Principles of Philosophy), by René Descartes (1644): Believing that certain ideas (*e.g.* the definition of matter as extension, and the impossibility of a vacuum) cannot in principle be false, Descartes built upon them in his *Principles* a complete, logically connected system of science. His theory of matter was *a priori;* everything else, *e.g.* his cosmology, optics, chemistry, theory of gravity, followed from it by application of the laws of motion. In considerable detail and with great ingenuity Descartes showed how (as he thought) all phenomena could be accounted for in terms of the movements of different kinds of particles. Thus he formulated the mechanistic explanation of the universe toward which 17th-cent. science was groping. The influence of this explanation was enormous, even on skeptics, and though every point in it was overthrown by the progress of experimental and mathematical science, Descartes had decisively turned scientific thought in a new direction.—A. R. H.

PRINCIPLES OF CHEMISTRY, by Dmitri Ivanovich Mendeleev (1868): When working on this textbook the great Russian chemist discovered the PERIODIC LAW. The book's organization, based on the periodic table, established a pattern still evident in general chemistry textbooks today. Description of the various elements was accompanied by extensive footnotes, frequently speculative, which stimulated new research. Numerous diagrams illustrated experimental and industrial operations. The book shows the influence of theoretical ideas recently revived by S. Cannizzaro, but Mendeleev took little notice of the rapidly expanding field of organic chemistry. The book was published in 2 vols. in Russian, 1868–70, and was repeatedly revised; the seventh Russian edition was published by the time of his death in 1907. The later editions were translated into German, French, and English.—A. L.

PRINCIPLES OF GEOLOGY, Being an Attempt to Explain the Former Changes of the Earth's Surface, by Reference to Causes now in Operation, by Charles Lyell (3 vols., 1830–33): The extended title of this treatise provides the key to its importance in the history of geology: all the processes of the past must be judged by those now in progress. In taking over these principles of the "uniformitarian" theory advanced by James Hutton (see GEOLOGY), Lyell was able to add much confirmatory evidence from the new studies of fossils and their indication of the relative age of geologic deposits. The uniformitarian theory gave a death-blow to the "catastrophic" schools and provided a sound basis for evolutionary theories. Nature, it taught, is parsimonious of violence and generous of time. Charles Darwin acknowledged a debt to Lyell's *Principles,* which he had begun reading on his round-the-world voyage on the *Beagle.*—*E. Me.*

PRINGSHEIM, NATHANAEL, 1823–94, German biologist; b. Wziesko, Silesia. He observed the filaments of the fresh-water alga *Vaucheria* develop globular unicellular outgrowths (oögonia), in each of which a single egg developed. From J-shaped unicellular outgrowths (spermatogonia) the filament simultaneously produced flagellated sperm cells; these entered the eggs, and the fertilized eggs subsequently germinated into new *Vaucheria* plants. This discovery (1855) made clear the sexual nature of algae reproduction. Pringsheim also published works on plant physiology.—*D. H. D. R.*

PRINTING: the process or system of mechanically producing multiple, identical copies of a graphic image, *e.g.* type, illustration, or design. Today's printing technology ranges from the humble operation of cancelling a postage stamp to the technically and artistically challenging operations required to produce millions of copies of a full-color photograph or painting. There are three broadly defined methods in general use: relief, planographic, and intaglio. However, many other printing methods are currently in small-scale use, and several methods are in the experimental stages.

Relief Printing: This method, also called letterpress or typographic printing, was the first system used by Europeans. Developed by Johann Gutenberg in the mid-15th cent., it continues today as the dominant process. It is known to have existed in Europe for decades before Gutenberg, specifically in block prints or xylographs consisting of illustrations and/or text carved into planks of wood. In the East it boasts a more venerable history. Impressions in clay from carved seals were widely used in China in the 2nd cent. B. C.; block prints of illustrations and some text matter have been dated in the 8th cent. A. D. Individual movable characters made of clay were in use in China as early as the 11th cent.; movable bronze type was being used in Korea early in the 15th cent. These movable characters soon fell into disuse, however, because of the excessive time consumed in searching for and setting characters, and the enormous storage problem created by the thousands of characters in this ideographic system.

Although Gutenberg cannot be credited with inventing the entire process of letterpress printing, his independent development of a printing system utilizing movable metal type (*c.* 1440) marks the beginning of quantity printing in Western civilization. Gutenberg's striking contribution was the invention of an adjustable type mold for duplicate casting of individual pieces of metal type that insured exact dimensional uniformity of the type bodies. His mold was variable in order to accommodate the varying widths of individual letters in the alphabet. Gutenberg's printing system incorporated many special adaptations and extensions of processes and materials known to other, existing trades, although there is no evidence to indicate that Gutenberg's invention was based in any way on a knowledge of the work of his predecessors in the Far East. For example, his press required an ink that would adhere evenly on the metal surface but, under pressure, would be released onto the paper or other material. For this purpose Gutenberg used (and perhaps formulated himself) an ink derived from boiled linseed oil.

The basic printing technology developed by Gutenberg—casting type in an adjustable mold, hand setting of type, and hand-powered presses—remained practically unchanged until the beginning of the 19th cent. During this 350-yr period, however, printing grew rapidly as a skilled craft. Successively, Germany, Italy, France, and then the Low Countries claimed pre-eminence in printing; typefounding was established as a separate business; and printing expanded from books to periodical literature, stationery, and ephemera. During this period, too, there was a proliferation of typeface designs.

Planographic Printing: This, the most recently developed of the three major processes, is based on the inventions of Alois Senefelder. In 1796 he devised a means of reproducing handwriting from a smooth stone (Gr. *litho*) surface; thus the planographic process is generically described as *lithography*. The term planographic is used because both the printing and the nonprinting areas are on the same plane. The antipathy of grease and water is the underlying principle of the process. Senefelder used a greasy crayon to produce an image on a polished slab of limestone whose porosity made it receptive to water. When water and ink were successively applied to the stone, moisture was held in the porous, non-image areas and ink adhered to the greasy image areas. A sheet of paper pressed against the stone received a sharp, clean copy of the inked image. Throughout most of the 19th cent. Senefelder's invention, to which he contributed not only the principles but a successful press and many refinements, was used for transferring hand-drawn art and lettering.

Intaglio Printing: This process differs from letterpress and planographic printing in that ink is released from recessed wells below the surface of the plate. In the planographic process the printing area is on the same level or plane as the non-printing area; in letterpress the inked printing area is in relief. Two broad categories of intaglio printing are in commercial use today: (1) *copperplate and steel engraving,* favored for social and business stationery, in which a wide range of tonal effects is achieved through the use of varying widths of line and cross-hatching, acid-etched or worked with a burin or engraving tool; and (2) *gravure printing,* most often seen in the rotogravure supplements of Sunday newspapers. In conventional gravure printing the entire image is broken into a pattern of square wells of uniform size but varying depths. Shallow wells hold and discharge a slight amount of

Gutenberg's printing shop, Mainz, c. 1450: Artist's rendering shows Gutenberg's financial backer Johann Fust (*left*) inspecting the first proof from the press (*right, background*). Also present are Gutenberg (*right*) and Gutenberg's assistant Peter Schoeffer (*middle*). (*N. Y. Public Library*)

ink, while the deep wells hold and discharge a greater amount. Thus tonal qualities of a photograph can be reproduced.

Mechanization of Presses: In the first few decades of the 19th cent., developments in printing technology transformed letterpress printing from a hand craft into a mechanized industry. First, the principle of *stereotyping* was successfully introduced. As early as 1725, William Ged of Edinburgh had devised a means of making plaster of Paris molds of the composed pages of books. Metal printing plates (stereotypes) were then cast from these molds, a whole page at a time. This released tons of typemetal for distribution and reuse, and eliminated the need for storage or resetting of type for new editions. Ged, however, was thwarted by compositors, pressmen, and typefounders who opposed stereotyping as a threat to their livelihood. Nearly a century later Firmin Didot in France and the Earl of Stanhope in England successfully revived stereotyping.

The second development was the invention of machines to replace the centuries-old, hand-powered, wooden adaptations of cheese or cider presses which had been used since Gutenberg's time. In 1800 the first *iron press* was developed by Lord Stanhope. Then, between 1811 and 1816, Friedrich Koenig developed the flat-bed cylinder that revolutionized the industry. In both the hand press and the platen press a sheet of paper must be pressed against the entire printing form, a procedure requiring tremendous pressure to produce a print; however, with the cylinder press, the impression is tangential to the circumference of the cylinder, permitting both an improved print and greater production speeds. On the night of Nov. 29, 1814, *The London Times* was printed on a Koenig machine into which two men simultaneously fed sheets of paper. Hourly production on this *double-feeder cylinder machine* exceeded the production of an entire day shift on the older hand presses. Two years later Koenig produced still another marvel, a *perfecting cylinder press*—a machine capable of printing both sides of a sheet of paper in a single operation. Then came the invention by the Englishman David Napier, 1828, of the two-revolution cylinder press with "grippers" for carrying sheets around the cylinder. Similar presses were soon being made by R. Hoe & Co. These cylinder presses along with the power-driven Adams bed and platen presses made deep inroads in the U. S. A. on the hand press as the basic publication tool, although the hand press, as in the case of Hoe's "Washington Press," continued in use until about 1900. Thus, 30 short years changed the printing operation from a slow hand craft to a high-speed mechanical operation.

Following Koenig's cylinder presses, R. Hoe & Co. of New York produced (1846) a *rotary newspaper press* called the "Hoe type revolving machine," in which type forms were secured to the cylinder by means of V-shaped column rules, rather than the cylinder's being used to press the paper against a flat type form. In 1865 the newspaper press was further improved so that it would print on a continuous web of paper instead of separate sheets. With the advent of the rotary, stereotyping at last fully proved its value. Curved stereotypes were fitted to the cylinders, and the resulting increase in web speeds made possible greater hourly production at lower unit costs. It must be borne in mind, however, that all these improvements were wholly dependent on an adequate and continuing supply of PAPER. From the 2nd cent. A. D. until 1798 little change occurred in paper-making methods. At that time Nicholas Louis Robert introduced a machine to replace the vat and hand mold; it produced a continuous web of paper, limited in output only by the supply of raw material, rags. The machine was improved and promoted by the brothers Fourdrinier, after whom it was named; it still bears that name and is in use today in various adaptations and improvements. The supply of raw material was reasonably assured when Gottlieb Keller in 1845 found how to use mechanical ground wood pulp to make paper. Finally, Benjamin Tilghman's production in 1866 of fine paper through the chemical reduction of wood pulp to a pure cellulose fiber answered the ever-increasing demand of the presses.

Impact of Photographic Techniques: A third succession of inventions in the early 19th cent. further altered printing technology. Since the time of Gutenberg, illustrations to print with type had been produced from either woodcuts or wood engravings. Illustrations with a broader and subtler range of tones were produced on separate sheets of paper by either copperplate engraving, some form of etching, or lithography; then the illustrated pages were pasted or bound into the book. Developments in photography and photo-engraving made this practice obsolete except for special purposes. In 1826 Joseph Nicéphore Niepce produced an intaglio printing plate by coating a pewter plate with bitumen of Judea (light-sensitive), laying an engraved proof on it, and exposing it to the sun. It was then acid-etched to make an intaglio plate. Niepce's experiments continued in collaboration with J. M. Daguerre; their joint efforts led in 1839 to a practical process of PHOTOGRAPHY utilizing the photo-sensitivity of a thin layer of silver halide on a sheet of copper to produce a faithful representation (*i.e.* a daguerreotype) of an image.

Daguerre's success spurred a series of inventions relating to

Automatic typesetting, introduced commercially in the 1880s, eliminated hand setting of type and speeded production. The "Linotype," above, utilizes circulating matrices. As operator strikes keys, matrices are assembled, forming justified lines on metal slugs; matrices are then returned to storage magazine, ready for reuse. (Mergenthaler Linotype Co.)

printing plates and illustrations. In 1841, Joseph Adams produced the first *electrotype,* which is a duplicate of an original woodcut, photo-engraving, or type form. The form or plate was pressed into a soft material, usually beeswax, to produce an impression; across this image a conductor of electricity (*e.g.* powdered graphite) was applied in order to provide a base on which a thin shell of copper could be deposited electrolytically. The fragile copper duplicate of the original plate was then strengthened by filling the back of it with typemetal alloy. By mounting the electrotype on a block of wood, a usable duplicate of the original printing plate or type form was produced. (See ELECTROTYPING.) Then, in 1848, Charles Gillot discovered a light-sensitive but acid-resistant coating which could be applied to a sheet of zinc. By exposing the coated plate to strong light through a photographic negative, the coating was caused to harden in the image area but remained soluble in the non-image area. The soluble coating was then washed off, so that the zinc plate, when immersed in acid, could be etched away in the non-image area, leaving the image in relief. This light-sensitive acid-resistant coating marked the beginning of modern photoengraving procedures.

One other photographic discovery in the last half of the 19th cent. was of great importance. In 1852, W. H. F. Talbot devised a cloth or "halftone" screen, through which a reflected image of a photograph could be exposed on film as a series of dots whose size varied with the tonal intensities of the different areas of the photograph. The halftone screen, eventually perfected by Louis and Max Levy of Philadelphia in 1893, was applied to letterpress and then lithography.

Offset and Rotogravure: During the second decade of the 20th cent. both offset and rotogravure printing gained commercial acceptance. Neither of these two processes was new, but only with developments in photography and printing press design did either process become practicable for high-quality, high-speed commercial work. In the *offset press,* an extension of lithography, an image is transferred from a metal plate to a rubber-covered cylinder and then to a sheet of paper. This system replaced the old, cumbersome cylinder presses that used a 2,000-lb stone and a reciprocating bed to transfer the image directly to paper. Since, in the offset process, the plate was a thin sheet of metal fastened around a cylinder, the press was basically a sheet-fed rotary. Because the plate printed on a rubber offset blanket, plate life was increased and paper surface irregularities became less troublesome. The use of offset printing has grown steadily until, at present, it accounts for most commercial or job printing (as distinguished from publication and specialty work).

Another 20th-cent. process of printing that benefited from photography is rotogravure, an extension of intaglio printing. Invented by Karl Klic in 1894 (following his development of photogravure, 1875), rotogravure was first used in America about 1912 to produce Sunday newspaper supplements. Newer forms of gravure permit the manufacture of plate cylinders in which both the depth and the size of the wells vary, enhancing the photographic quality of the print.

Automatic Typesetting and Phototypesetting: The final stage in the mechanization of letterpress printing was the invention of successful automatic typesetting machines which could produce justified lines (*i.e.* could automatically adjust the word spacing to fill out a line to required measure). The first of these, the *Linotype,* was invented by a German immigrant in the U. S. A., Ottmar Mergenthaler in 1886. During the middle decades of the 19th cent. scores of typesetting machines had been tried and abandoned. Most of them were devised to set individual pieces of cast type, although some, like the Linotype, attempted to produce a mold from which a line of type could be cast as a unit. With the success of the Linotype, typesetting equipment received increasing attention. The *Monotype* (patented 1887), whose action is controlled by a punched tape, differs from the Linotype in that it sets individual pieces of cast type justified by lines. In recent years the computer has been linked to typesetting machines with great increases in speed and efficiency.

While experiments in producing type directly on photographic films began in the 19th cent., *photographic typesetting* can be dated, as a commercial process, from 1948. The first successful phototypesetter was basically an adaptation of the hot-metal, line-casting machine, except that the matrices carry photographic images of individual characters, and the metal-casting mechanism is replaced by a camera. Other photographic typesetting machines combine punched tapes (for actuation) with electronic control devices for enlargement and reduction of images, justification of lines, and selection of the desired typeface and size.

The cathode-ray tube now shows promise of being a very rapid means of tracing the desired type image on film.

Electronic Systems: Letterpress engravings are now widely made by electronic engraving machines which read the light value of a tiny segment of a photograph and convert it into a controlled cutting action on metal or plastic plate stock. Color separations are also made electronically, producing either a set of four-color, separation negatives or even a set of four letterpress printing plates. Related to electronic printing is the utilization of data-processing methods for printing production. Punched tapes and cards have been used not only to control machines, but to make high-speed copies of lists, directories, blueprints, and engineering drawings. In the last instance, the printing process is electrostatic, *i.e.* the image area is established as an electrostatic field, then fixed by the application of a magnetically sensitive pigment. See Color Plates 68–69.—*C. L. H.*

PRISM (in mathematics): see POLYHEDRON.

PRISM: in optics, a transparent solid with two congruent and parallel bases and plane parallel faces that are parallelograms. Prisms change the direction of light passing through them—a property that is useful for many purposes. When a narrow beam of light passes through a triangular glass prism, the light spreads out in a rainbowlike band of colors known as a SPECTRUM. The light is dispersed into its constituent colors because each color, or wavelength, of light is bent (refracted) to a different degree (see DISPERSION). The triangular prism is the key element in the prism SPECTROSCOPE, an instrument used for studying spectra. Triangular prisms of crown and flint glass can be combined to form an Amici prism that will disperse a beam of light into its component colors without altering the beam's average direction, as a single prism does.

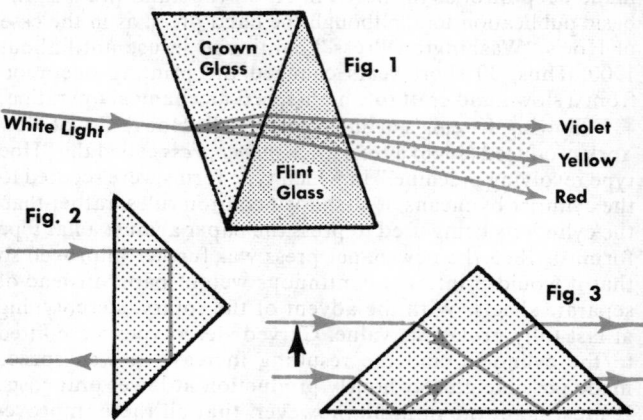

Three types of prism: Cemented elements of crown and flint glass (Fig. 1) are used in Amici prism to disperse light without changing direction of central (yellow) rays. Right-angle prism can be used as Porro prism (Fig. 2) to reverse direction of light, or as Dove prism (Fig. 3) to invert image.

The Amici prism, a simplified form of which is shown in Fig. 1, is used in direct-vision spectroscopes. Prisms are useful not only for the dispersion of light, but also for its reflection. Figs. 2 and 3 represent two right-angle prisms such as are used in prism binoculars. Both prisms produce internal reflection: prism 2 reverses the direction of the light, and prism 3 inverts the image. Prisms such as 3 are used in prism binoculars to reinvert the inverted image, which does away with the need for a third lens system, as in the field telescope, and results in a more compact instrument. A NICOL PRISM, which consists of two pieces of Iceland spar cemented with Canada balsam, produces plane-polarized light from an unpolarized beam. See POLARIZED LIGHT.—*A. E.*

PROBABILITY: the likelihood that an event will occur, or will occur in a certain form. The mathematics of probability is an attempt to provide definite rules for deducing probability estimates from certain probability assumptions (see PROBABILITY THEORY). It is not a purely mathematical problem to certify the material correctness of any probability estimate, *e.g.* of the assumption that the probability of obtaining heads with a newly minted coin is very nearly ½.

The empirical corroboration of such probability estimates presents the logician with a particularly complex problem in analysis. However, we may make a beginning as follows: Let E be an experiment capable of indefinite repetition and having two possible outcomes, which we call success and failure; and let p be the probability of a successful outcome in any one experiment. If E is performed n times and f is the success ratio in the set of n independent trials, then it can be shown that the probability that f will differ from p by an amount no greater than d cannot be less than $1 - \frac{1}{4}nd^2$. In other words, if n is suitably large it must be highly probable that the success ratio will resemble the probability of an individual success. Hence, in large samples of independent trials characterized by constant probability of success, it is highly improbable that a large error will be committed, if we measure theoretic probabilities by empirical success ratios. Such seems to be the sense of what is sometimes called the law of averages.

It will be seen that the empirical procedure of measuring probabilities by observed success ratios presupposes a judgment concerning the independence, or approximate independence, of experimental outcomes. Such judgments are said to be corroborated when they provide a basis for correctly anticipating empirical success ratios in large samples; they are said to be disconfirmed when the contrary is the case.

Nothing has yet here been said concerning the meaning of "probability." The following remarks are intended to be a partial clarification of that sense of "probability" which is pertinent to the foregoing discussion. Properties or attributes are lawfully associated in such wise that the presence of certain properties may, more or less reliably, be taken as a sign of others. Hence, probability may be construed as the degree of the lawful associatedness of properties, or, as the coefficient of reliability with which one property signifies another. It must be stated that important uses of "probability" exist in the literature which are, in varying degrees, dissimilar to the meaning used here. Some writers have construed probability as a logical relation, so that statements of probability are certifiable *a priori*. Other authors have construed probability as a measure of psychological confidence. J. Venn, C. S. Peirce, and H. Reichenbach have interpreted probability as the limit of the sample ratios generated by an infinite sequence of trials. To this definition R. von Mises added the further requirement that the sequence of trials be insensitive to place selection.—*A. Sm.*

PROBABILITY THEORY: the study of the mathematics of the laws of chance. The outcome of an individual chance event, such as the toss of a penny, is unpredictable. However, if this event is repeated many times, the outcome can be predicted with reasonable accuracy. For example, if a ton of pennies are tossed, we feel fairly certain that about half a ton will fall heads up and half a ton heads down. The applications of probability range over the physical and behavioral sciences and philosophy. Some specific applications are found in the kinetic theory of gases, Brownian motion, scintillations caused by radioactivity, quantum theory, theory of errors, Mendel's theory of heredity, mortality, life insurance, statistical inference, and design of automatic telephone exchanges.

The study of probability had its origin in problems that arose in games of chance. Around 1525, Geronimo Cardano showed that a player must have four throws with a single die to have at least an even chance of getting a 6. Galileo (1564–1642) prepared a complete table of probabilities for throws with three dice. Blaise Pascal (1623–1662) became interested in problems related to probability when an acquaintance of his proposed problems on games of chance. The first of these was the dice problem: If one throws two dice, how many throws must be allowed in order to have better than an even chance of getting at least two 6's at least once? Pascal showed the answer to be 25. It had been thought that the answer was 24 on the ground that for one die it was 4, and 4 is to 6 as 24 is to 36 (the square of 6). The second problem was the division problem: How shall the prize money be divided in a game that is interrupted before it is completed? This problem

had been considered for at least three centuries, and its solution by Pascal was one of the significant advances in the theory of probability.

The elementary ideas of probability can be developed in an intuitive way from the consideration of simple experiments like the toss of a coin or the roll of a die. Thus we sometimes say that the chance for a head on a toss of a coin is fifty-fifty and that the chance for a 5 on a toss of one die is one in six. Out of such ideas we develop the idea that the probability of an event may be defined as the number of favorable cases f divided by the total number of cases n. In simple problems, it is possible to determine the total number of cases, the total number of favorable cases, and so calculate the probability, even before the experiment has been tried. Thus this definition is often called the *a priori* definition since it is used prior to the trying of the experiment. However, there are many assumptions implicit in the use of this definition. With a coin, for example, we must assume that the two sides are distinguishable, that it is not bent, that its weight is so distributed that neither heads nor tails are favored, that the toss is sufficiently complicated so that the result is unpredictable, and that we will not accept standing-on-edge as an outcome. These assumptions are concerned with the nature of the object and with the nature of the toss. As for the object, we need to assume that the various possible outcomes are equally likely, and for the toss we need to assume that it is really a chance event. To make this definition more precise we state: If there are n equally likely outcomes of an experiment which are the result of chance and if f are of one kind (which we may call favorable) and the balance $n - f$ are of a second kind (unfavorable), the probability for a favorable outcome is f/n.

Although the *a priori* definition is convenient in simple situations, we cannot really know that the various outcomes for the toss of a coin or die are equally likely. Furthermore, there are many probability questions that cannot be resolved into equally likely cases. For example, if a thumbtack is tossed, the outcomes, point up and point down, are not equally likely. Similarly, when we consider the question of whether a particular person will survive for a given period of time, we know there are only two outcomes—he may live or he may die—but they are certainly not equally likely. Thus another definition of probability is needed.

Consider the tossing of a thumbtack. If in 10 tosses it lands point up three times the relative frequency of point up is 3 in 10 or $\frac{3}{10}$. If it lands point up 23 times in 100 tosses the relative frequency is $\frac{23}{100}$ or .23. Now if we continue this we may find the following results:

Number of tosses	10	100	1,000	10,000	100,000
Number of point up	3	23	198	2,012	20,032
Relative frequency	.3	.23	.198	.2012	.20032

The number that is approximated by these successive values of the relative frequency is called the *probability*. In the example presented, the probability might be taken as .2, and each relative frequency is an approximation to the probability. Since this method of defining probability depends on experiment, it is sometimes called empirical probability; since it depends on statistical data it is sometimes called statistical probability; and since it is defined after trials of the experiment it is also called *a posteriori* probability.

The difficulties inherent in the intuitive approach to probability have led mathematicians to develop a more formal, systematic, and logical approach, based on the properties of sets. We can illustrate some of the ideas used in this development if we consider the toss of two dice, one red and the other white. The various outcomes may be listed in a table as follows. (The outcome for the white die is shown first, so that 12 means the white die showed 1, the red die 2.)

11	12	13	14	15	16
21	22	23	24	25	26
31	32	33	34	35	36
41	42	43	44	45	46
51	52	53	54	55	56
61	62	63	64	65	66

These pairs of members are the elements of a set of outcomes of the experiment of tossing two dice. They are also referred to as points, and the entire set of points is called a sample space. To each element in this set a number between 0 and 1 is assigned and called its probability, subject to the restriction that the sum of all the numbers assigned shall be 1. If we view the outcome of the toss of two dice as equivalent to selecting an element at random from the table, then it is reasonable to assign a probability of $\frac{1}{36}$ to each element in the table. This approach replaces the actual toss of two dice with a model, a set of outcomes and probabilities that are not subject to the various defects possible in tosses of dice. The actual behavior of a pair of dice may then be compared to the ideal probabilities determined from this model.

Having assigned probabilities to the elements (outcomes) of the set of outcomes, we can now develop principles for determining the probability of any subset of the sample space. Such a subset is called an event. To illustrate the principles involved, we may consider several examples based on the table for two dice.

Consider the probability that a total of 7 or of 11 is obtained on the throw of two dice. The event 7 can occur in 6 ways and the event 11 can occur in 2 ways. Hence the probabilities for the separate events $P(7) = \frac{6}{36}$ and $P(11) = \frac{2}{36}$. Also we see that 7 or 11 is obtained in 8 ways, so the probability for 7 or 11 is $P(7 \text{ or } 11) = \frac{8}{36}$. This is the sum of the probabilities for 7 or 11, so we note that $P(7 \text{ or } 11) = P(7) + P(11)$. The event 7 and the event 11 are said to be mutually exclusive, since they have no common elements. This property can be proved in general, and so we state the property: if two events A and B are mutually exclusive, then $P(A \text{ or } B) = P(A) + P(B)$.

Consider the probability that the white die falls 1 or 2 or the red die 1, 2, or 3. Here, if we examine the chart, the event we seek occurs if the outcome is any one of the elements in the first two rows or first three columns of the table. There are 24 elements in this event, and hence the probability $P(W \leqq 2 \text{ or } R \leqq 3) = \frac{24}{36}$. Now, when we examine the separate events, $P(W \leqq 2) = \frac{12}{36}$ and $P(R \leqq 3) = \frac{18}{36}$. If we add these probabilities we get $\frac{30}{36}$, which does not agree with our previous result. This is due to the fact that 6 elements, 11, 12, 13, 21, 22, 23, were counted twice, once in $P(W \leqq 2)$ and again in $P(R \leqq 3)$. Hence we must subtract the probability that both $W \leqq 2$ and $R \leqq 3$ or $P(W \leqq 2 \text{ and } R \leqq 3) = \frac{6}{36}$. Thus we have

$$P(W \leqq 2 \text{ or } R \leqq 3) = 12/36 + 18/36 - 6/36$$

In general, it can be proved that the probability for the happening of either of two events A or B is

$$P(A \text{ or } B) = P(A) + P(B) - P(A \text{ and } B)$$

It should be noted that if the events are mutually exclusive, $P(A \text{ and } B) = 0$, and so this property includes the previous one.

Consider the probability that the white die falls 1 or 2 and the red die 1, 2, or 3. If we examine the chart, the event we seek occurs if the outcome is any one of the elements appearing in the upper left-hand corner, namely 11, 12, 13, 21, 22,

23. There are 6 outcomes; so the probability $P(W \leqq 2$ and $R \leqq 3) = \frac{6}{36} = \frac{1}{6}$. Now the probability that white is 1 or 2 is $P(W \leqq 2) = \frac{12}{36} = \frac{1}{3}$, and the probability that red is 1, 2, or 3 is $P(R \leqq 3) = \frac{18}{36} = \frac{1}{2}$. We see that the probability of the event $W \leqq 2$ and $R \leqq 3$ is the product of the separate probabilities. When this is the case, the events are said to be independent, and in general we can write $P(A \text{ and } B) = P(A) \times P(B)$.

Consider the probability that the sum of the dots on the two dice is less than or equal to 3 and that the white die is 1. In the chart for two dice there are only two outcomes that satisfy this condition—namely, 11 and 12. Hence the probability is $\frac{2}{36} = \frac{1}{18}$. Now we wish to compare this with the separate probabilities. The probability that the sum is less than 3 is $\frac{3}{36}$, since there are 3 outcomes 11, 12, and 21 of this type. Now, if this event has occurred, then one of the outcomes 11, 12, and 21 has occurred and the probability that white is 1 is $\frac{2}{3}$, since 2 of the three cases have $W = 1$. We see thus that to get the correct probability we must multiply $\frac{3}{36}$ by $\frac{2}{3}$. If the two events are denoted A and B and we write $P(B|A)$ for the probability that B occurs, A having occurred, we have $P(A \text{ and } B) = P(A) \times P(B|A)$. It may be noted that the probability for independent events follows from this if $P(B|A) = P(B)$, i.e. if the probability of B occurring is the same whether A occurs or not.

On the basis of the properties of probabilities that have been illustrated, the subject is extended to a study of repeated probabilities where the binomial distribution represents the various probabilities if a single trial has two outcomes. This is of especial value in applications to STATISTICS. The probability of events where the outcomes form a continuous set instead of a discrete set is of basic importance in statistics, especially when the distribution is a normal frequency distribution.—*H. E. W.*

PRODROMUS DISSERTATIONUM COSMOGRAPHICARUM CONTINENS MYSTERIUM COSMOGRAPHICUM (The Cosmographical Mystery), by Johannes Kepler (1597): This book, Kepler's first, is the supreme instance of a scientific idea, utterly

Kepler's model of planetary orbits, from *Prodromus*, attempted to show a harmonious mathematical correspondence between the diameters of the planetary orbits and the diameters of the five regular POLYHEDRONS arranged within one another in a certain order. (*N. Y. Public Library*)

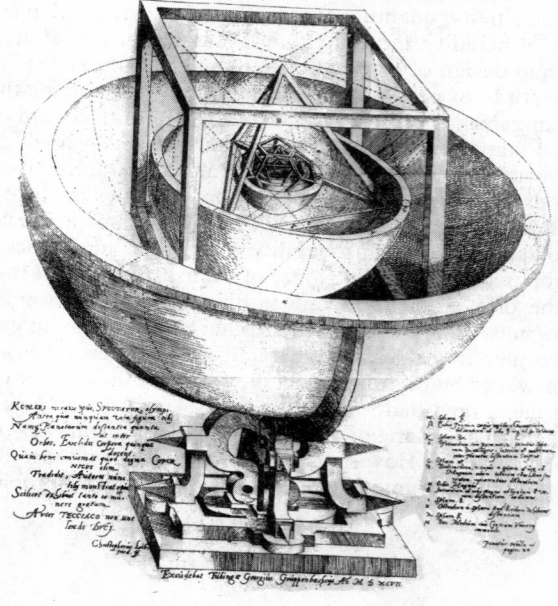

TABVLA III. ORBIVM PLANETARVM DIMENSIONES, ET DISTANTIAS PER QVINQVE REGVLARIA CORPORA GEOMETRICA EXHIBENS.
ILLVSTRISS: PRINCIPI, AC DNO. DNO. FRIDERICO, DVCI WIRTENBERGICO, ET TECCIO, COMITI MONTIS BELGARVM, ETC. CONSECRATA.

fantastic in itself, nevertheless leading to the discovery of a vital truth. Believing that God had constructed the world according to precise mathematical proportions, Kepler sought the harmony that he thought underlay the number and sizes of the planetary orbits. He revealed it in this book in the (rough) correspondence between the diameters of the six orbits then known and those of the five regular solids arranged successively one within the other in a certain order. Later he discovered the falsity of this hypothesis; his search for a better harmony was rewarded in the discovery of his Third Law, $T^2/r^3 = k$ (the square of the time during which a planet traverses its orbit is proportional to the cube, or third power, of the orbit's average radius), announced in *Harmonices mundi* (1619), a relation that served later to verify the hypothesis of universal gravitation.—*A. R. H.*

PRODUCER GAS: a gaseous mixture used industrially as a fuel; it is obtained by passing air, or air plus steam, through a bed of incandescent fuel, usually coke. The furnace used is called a *producer.* The exit gases consist largely of carbon monoxide, CO, and hydrogen, H_2, diluted with nitrogen, N_2, from the air employed. Producer gas can be modified to serve for illumination (see WATER GAS).—*Ru. M.*

PROGESTERONE: a steroid hormone produced and secreted by the corpus luteum of the ovary. It stimulates the secretory phase of growth of the uterus in preparation for the implantation of the fertilized ovum. Progesterone is secreted also by the placenta and is present in all steroid-producing endocrine glands.—*F. U.*

PROGRAMMING: see DYNAMIC PROGRAMMING; LINEAR PROGRAMMING.

PROGRESSION, MATHEMATICAL: see SERIES.

PROJECTION: see MAP; PROJECTIVE GEOMETRY.

PROJECTIVE GEOMETRY: the study of those properties of plane figures that remain invariant (unchanged) under central projection. An example of central projection can be obtained in this way: Suppose one looks through a window at a rectangle lying on the ground, and draws on the window a figure, each point of which appears to cover a point on the rectangle. The resulting perspective drawing will not be a rectangle, but it will be a quadrilateral. A similar drawing of a circle will be an ellipse, which, like a circle, is a conic section; and a drawing of a triangle will be a triangle, albeit of a different shape from the original. These drawings are all projections of the original figures; a line from the eye to any point of the original figure will pass through a corresponding point on the projection, and vice versa. Although the shapes and the sizes of the figures change under projection, some properties (*e.g.* triangularity) remain invariant. It is with these projective properties that projective geometry is concerned.

A definition of central projection is as follows: Let P be a point (Fig. 1) outside two intersecting planes π and π', and let a line connect P with any point A of the plane π; then the point A' in which the line intersects π' is the central projection of A on π', with respect to the pole P. Conversely, A is the projection of A' on π. The points A of any line on π are projected into the corresponding points A' of a line on π'. Thus, a point is projected into a point, a line into a line, a line pencil (a set of lines passing through a point) into a line pencil, and a point range (a set of points on a line) into a point range. Properties of figures depending exclusively on the intersection of lines and curves, or on the connection of points by lines, are projective properties, as is tangency.

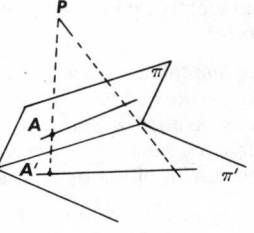

Fig. 1

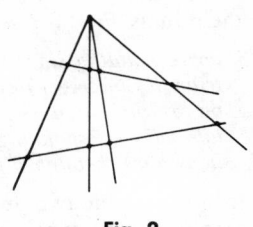

Fig. 2

Parallelism, the distance between two points, and the angle between two lines are not projective, and neither is the ratio $AB:BC$ of any three points A, B, and C on a line.

However, if we take four points A, B, C, D on a line, then the ratio $AC/BC:AD/BD$ is a projective invariant. It is called the *cross ratio* (or anharmonic ratio) of the four points, and written (AB,CD). When $(AB,CD) = -1$, the four points are said to be *harmonic.* (Here AB is measured in such a way that $AB = -BA$.) Some other arrangement of the four points in two pairs, *e.g.* (CB,AD), yields another cross ratio; of the 24 ways of arranging the four points only six different cross ratios result. If four lines of a line pencil are intersected by another line in four points (Fig. 2) then the cross ratio of these points is called the cross ratio of the pencil; the corresponding points of intersection of the pencil and any other line have the same cross ratio. If this ratio is harmonic, the pencil is called harmonic.

A line may be defined as the connection between two points, and a point as the intersection of two lines. This *duality* between points and lines is highly significant: in projective geometry, with respect to every statement a geometric figure lying in a plane, involving points and lines, has a dual statement obtained by replacing "point" by "line," "connection of points" by "intersection of lines," and conversely. If a statement about projective properties is true, its dual is true. Take, for example, the *complete quadrangle* in which four points A,B,C,D are connected by six lines, (AB), which is the line connecting A and B, (AC), (AD), (BC), (BD), and (CD). These lines can be grouped into three pairs of "opposite" sides which intersect in three diagonal points P, Q, and R (Fig. 3a), and PQR is called the diagonal triangle. The dual of this figure is the *complete quadrilateral* in which four lines a, b, c, d intersect in six points, (ab), which is the point of intersection of a and b, (ac), (ad), (bc), (bd), and (cd).

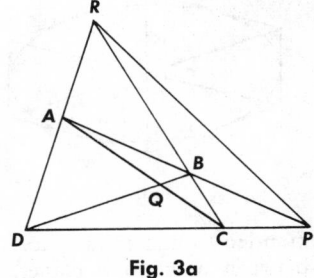

Fig. 3a

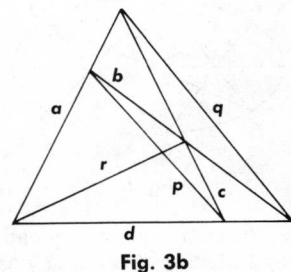

Fig. 3b

These points can be grouped into three pairs of "opposite" vertices which are connected by three diagonals p, q, and r (Fig. 3b) and pqr is called the diagonal triangle. We then have the dual theorems:

At a vertex of a complete quadrilateral, the two sides are harmonic with respect to the lines connecting this vertex with the vertices of the diagonal triangle.	*On a side of a complete quadrangle, the two vertices are harmonic with respect to the points in which this side is intersected by the sides of the diagonal triangle.*

Here are two more theorems of projective geometry, and their duals. First is *Desargues' theorem:*

If corresponding sides of two triangles intersect in points on a line, then the lines joining corresponding vertices pass through a point.	*If the lines joining corresponding vertices of two triangles pass through a point, then the corresponding sides intersect in points on a line.*

In this case the two dual theorems are also the converse of each other. These theorems are illustrated by the configuration of Desargues, consisting of 10 points and 10 lines, each line passing through 3 points, each lying on three lines (in Fig. 4, the triangles are PQR, $P'Q'R'$). This configuration is *self-dual*.

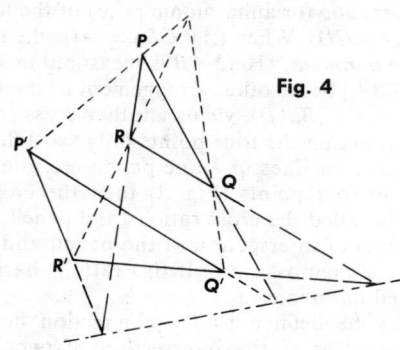

Fig. 4

Next are the *dual theorems of Pascal and Brianchon:* To understand these, note that the dual of a curve conceived as a locus of points is a curve conceived as an envelope of lines. Thus the dual of a conic section is a conic section. We further note that in projective geometry a hexagon is formed by six points and six lines such that any two points are connected by a line and any two lines intersect in a point.

The opposite sides of a hexagon inscribed in a conic intersect in three points on a line. (Pascal's theorem, Fig. 5; the opposite sides are 12, 45; 23, 56; 34, 61.)	*The opposite vertices of a hexagon circumscribed about a conic may be connected by three lines that meet in a point.* (Brianchon's theorem, Fig. 6.)

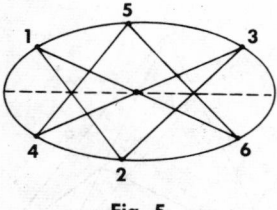

Fig. 5

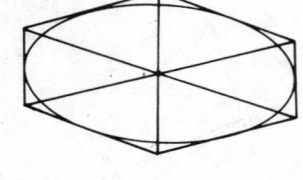

Fig. 6

Projective geometry can be extended to figures in space. In this case there is a duality between points and planes, while lines, which are the connections between two points as well as the intersections of two planes, are self-dual.

We can develop projective geometry by means of purely projective concepts. The primary concepts are those of *perspectivity* and *projectivity*. Two point ranges are perspective if the lines connecting corresponding points pass through the same point (the pole of perspectivity, Fig. 7); two pencils are perspective if the points of intersection of corresponding lines lie on the same line (the axis of perspectivity, Fig. 8). If each of two perspective pencils is intersected by a line (Fig. 9), then we obtain on these lines two point ranges which

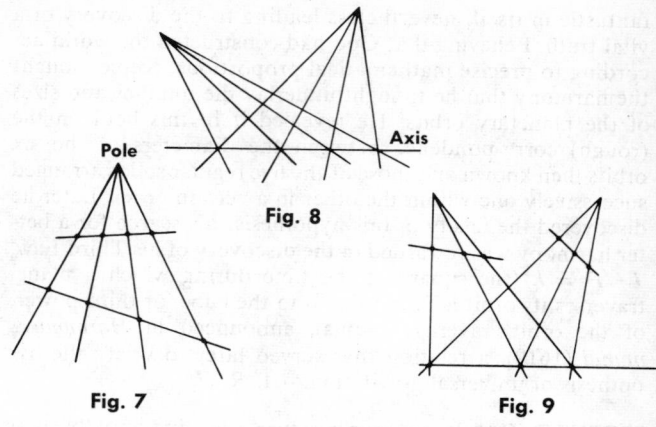

Fig. 7

Fig. 8

Fig. 9

are not, in general, perspective, but the fundamental property still holds that to each point of the one point range corresponds one and only one point of the other point range. Such ranges are called *projective*. One can in a similar way define projective pencils of lines. In projective ranges (pencils) any two sets of four corresponding points (lines) have the same cross ratio. Conic sections can now be defined as the locus of the points of intersection of corresponding lines of two projective pencils, or as the envelope of the lines connecting corresponding points of two projective ranges.

In contrast to this purely geometrical (or synthetic) approach, one can also study the subject algebraically, with so-called *homogeneous coordinates*. Here a point in the plane is given by the ratio of three numbers $x_1 : x_2 : x_3$, and similarly a line by $u_1 : u_2 : u_3$. Duality results from the fact that the point lies on the line if and only if $u_1 x_1 + u_2 x_2 + u_3 x_3 = 0$. —*D. J. S.*

PROMETHIUM: a radioactive element (Pm) of the LANTHANIDE series; at. no. 61; at. wt 147 (best-known isotope); half life 2.6 yr, decaying by emission of beta particles. Other isotopes' half lives range from a few minutes to about 30 yr. Although discovery of promethium in rare-earth concentrates was claimed in 1926, subsequent research has offered inconclusive evidence of its occurrence in natural deposits. The element was first synthesized in 1941 by irradiating neodymium and praseodymium with neutrons, deuterons, and alpha particles; but not until 1947 was it positively identified—by J. A. Marinsky, *et al.,* by means of ion-exchange chromatography. Promethium can be isolated in quantity from uranium fission-product mixtures by multistage ion-exchange extraction techniques developed during World War II; another source is the waste products from radiochemical processing. The best-known compounds are the hydroxide, chloride, and nitrate. Several possible experimental uses have been described for promethium, *e.g.* as a beta-particle source for thickness gages, in the preparation of fluorescent compounds, and in the construction of miniature atomic batteries.—*R. B. T.*

PROPANE: $CH_3CH_2CH_3$, a hydrocarbon and one of the paraffin series, found in natural gas and in petroleum. It is bottled under pressure for use as a household fuel.—*Ru. M.*

PROPELLANT: a chemical or mixture of chemicals that can be ignited to provide thrust to a jet-propulsion device by virtue of combustion. While air-breathing propulsion systems carry a fuel that reacts with oxygen (as oxidizer) in the atmosphere, rockets designed to leave Earth's atmosphere must carry with them both a fuel and an oxidizer, or a mixture containing both. Rocket propellants may be liquid or solid. Liquid propellants are stored in tanks and forced into the combustion chamber either by pumps or by pressurizing the storage tanks. Liquid-propellant systems usually consist of an oxidizer (*e.g.* liquid oxygen) and a liquid fuel (*e.g.* liquid hydrogen), but monopropellants containing fuel and oxidizer in one liquid are also available (*e.g.* hydrogen peroxide). In solid-propellant rockets all the propellant must be contained within the combustion chamber. This type of system is consequently more difficult to control in flight than a liquid-propellant system and can not readily be shut off after combustion starts. But since no feed systems are required for solid-propellant units, they are relatively simple in construction and can be stored more easily than liquid units. Solid propellants have found wide application in rockets designed for brief operations such as assistant take-off units or boosters for large rockets; they are, however, also suitable as propellants in missiles having specific missions, *e.g.* the Minuteman. Lately, the term has been applied to more exotic types of propulsion, *e.g.* cesium as a possible propellant for air engines. See FUEL; INTERNAL COMBUSTION.—*F. K.*

PROPELLER: a radially arranged set of blades shaped so that their movement through a fluid, either liquid or gas, will generate forces to move the craft to which the blades are attached. The *water propeller* or *marine screw* is actually a segmented mechanical screw. Its blades, usually short and wide for maximum surface area, move through the water like inclined planes, pushing water astern; this reaction moves the craft forward. *Air propellers,* on the other hand, derive only a small part of their efficiency from the mechanical displacement of air. Their function depends primarily upon the same aerodynamic forces that produce lift on an airplane wing.

Air propellers are shaped very much like long, thin wings (see AIRFOIL). There are three types: *fixed pitch,* having blades set at a fixed angle to the propeller's plane of rotation; *adjustable pitch,* where the angle may be changed on the ground by remounting the individual blades on the central hub; and *variable* (or *controllable*) *pitch,* where mechanical or hydraulic linkages allow the pilot to alter the pitch angle in flight. Each blade has a flat side, similar to the underside of a wing, called the *face,* and a cambered or rounded side, similar to the upper surface of a wing, called the *back.* To make them strong, the blades usually are round at the hub end, becoming flatter and thinner, with cross-sections becoming more like a true wing, toward the blade tip. The cambered or rounded side of the propeller faces toward the direction of flight. As the blade bites through the air, the flow of air over the cambered surface is faster than over the flat surface. A pressure difference like that between the top and the bottom of a wing is produced, and the higher pressure behind the propeller forces it forward just as higher pressure under the wing forces it upward. However, if the propeller blades were shaped exactly like wings, then the lift produced would be smaller toward the hub and greater toward the tip. (The linear speed of a rotating object increases with the distance from its center of rotation.) To maintain uniform lift over the entire length of the propeller blade, the blade is twisted and gradually reduced in cross-section toward the tip. As a result, while air moves more rapidly across the blade farther from the hub, it does not move over so rounded nor so wide a surface area. Therefore, less lift is produced in proportion to the increased airflow, and this gradual reduction from hub to tip keeps lift uniform.

Some propellers for light aircraft are still made of laminated wood, as were all early types; but aluminum and other metal alloys are most commonly used in two-, three-, and four-blade configuration propellers. In the helicopter, whose rotors must act both as wing and propeller, twisting is not feasible to achieve uniform lift along the length of the blade. The blade is therefore made flexible, arching like a bow toward the tips to achieve a loss of efficiency at that point and thus control lift. See AERODYNAMICS.—*K. A.*

PROPER MOTION: in astronomy, a progressive angular displacement of the position of a star relative to the general pattern of stars; it is a result of a motion of the star in space relative to the Sun (see SPACE VELOCITY OF A STAR). For a given tangential velocity (velocity across the line of sight), proper motion is larger for nearby stars than for remote ones, so that to discover the tangential velocity in mi/sec, measurements have to be made of both the proper motion and the distance of the star. The majority of stars are so distant that their proper motions are too small to be measured. A proper motion is measured by comparing two photographs of the same area of sky taken on different dates, *e.g.* 30 yr apart, and comparing the positions of the star images. Proper motions as small as 0".001 per yr can be measured, and the proper motions of some 50,000 stars are known, but the distances are known only for about 10% of these. The largest known proper motion is that of Barnard's star (a 10th-mag. star only 6 lt-yr away), which changes its position by 10".3 per yr.

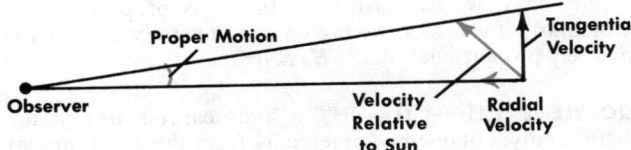

Proper motion of a star is a measure of one component—tangential velocity—of a star's true motion. The proper motion of a nearby star seems greater than that for a distant star.

Stars tend to move in groups with more or less parallel paths in space; because of perspective, the paths appear to converge to a point. Owing to proper motions, the shapes of the constellation star-patterns are slowly changing, although a group of stars moving together in space will, for a long time, keep the same relative positions in the sky.

The motion of the Sun affects the proper motions of all stars in the same area of sky, at the same distance, in the same way. Hence the *solar motion* can be determined from the systematic tendencies of stellar proper motions; stars, on the whole, appear to move away from the point on the celestial sphere toward which the Sun is moving (apex), and to converge to the point away from which the Sun is moving (antapex). The study of stellar proper motions has also shown that the Sun and stars are moving in orbits around the center of the Galaxy, in periods measured in hundreds of millions of years, stars nearer the center moving faster, and stars farther away moving slower. See STARS, REAL MOTIONS OF.—*M. W. O.*

PROPORTION: an expression of equality between two ratios, thus: $a/b = c/d$. The concept of proportion was familiar to the Greeks and is the subject of Book V in Euclid's *Elements.* If two ratios a/b and c/d are equal they are said to be in proportion, and we may write $a/b = c/d$. An older notation for a ratio was to use two dots instead of the fraction line; thus a/b can be written $a:b$; instead of the equal sign four dots were used to indicate the proportion, as $a:b::c:d$. The four terms a, b, c, d are called the first, second, third, and fourth proportionals. The first two terms, a and b, are called the antecedents; the last two, *c* and *d,* the consequents; the first and fourth, *a* and *d,* the extremes; and the second and third, the means. If $a/b = b/c$, the term *b* is called the mean proportional between the other two. Many theorems of proportion are stated in this language; *e.g.* the product of the means is equal to the product of the extremes.

Many geometric theorems involve proportion. For example, if two triangles are similar, their sides are proportional; and the perimeters of two regular polygons of the same number of sides are to each other as their radii. Many construction problems make use of proportion. One of the best known is the method of dividing a line segment into *n* equal parts. To do this any line is drawn from the end point of the given line segment, and on this line an arbitrary length is marked off *n* times. The end of the *n* segments is joined to the other end of the given segment, and lines parallel to this are drawn at each point of division. Thus the given line segment is divided into *n* equal parts, because $a' = b' = c'$ and so on, and $a/a' = b/b' = c/c'$ and so on.

The language of proportion is also useful in describing variation. For example, if $y = kx$, then *y* is said to vary directly as *x*. If now we take two pairs of corresponding values of *x* and *y,* namely (x_1, y_1) and (x_2, y_2) and substitute these in the equation $y = kx$, we obtain $y_1 = kx_1$ and $y_2 = kx_2$. Now if we divide the first equation by the second, we get $y_1/y_2 = x_1/x_2$, a proportion. Thus when *y* varies directly as *x,* we can also state that *y* is proportional to *x.* Similarly if $y = k/x$, we say *y* varies inversely as *x,* or *y* is inversely proportional to *x.*—*H. E. W.*

PROPYLENE: $CH_3—CH=CH_2$, a hydrocarbon, one of the olefin family, obtained commercially from the gases present in the high-temperature cracking of petroleum hydrocarbons into smaller compounds. It can be made into polymers. Polypropylene plastics compete with those made from polyethylene.—*Ru. M.*

PROSTATE GLAND: an exocrine accessory GLAND surrounding the junction of the vasa deferentia and the urethra in male mammals. It produces a thin fluid that forms a part of the secretion carrying sperms. See REPRODUCTION.—*A. R. D.*

PROTACTINIUM: a radioactive element (Pa), the second member of the ACTINIDE series; at. no. 91; at. wt 231 (longest-lived isotope); valence 4 or 5. The immediate parent of ACTINIUM (which is formed when Pa^{231} loses an alpha particle), protactinium[231] was discovered in 1918 by Otto Hahn and L. Meitner, and independently by Frederick Soddy and J. A. Cranston. However, almost 50 yr before, in 1871, D. Mendeleev on the basis of his periodic law had predicted the existence of an element falling between thorium and uranium in the periodic table; Mendeleev suggested the name *ekatantalum,* since he correctly surmised that the element would belong to a group VA of the periodic table. and resemble tantalum. Pa^{231} has a half life of 34,300 yr; it is a shiny, malleable, metallic mass that easily tarnishes. Several natural and artificial radioactive isotopes are known; one of them, Pa^{234}, was actually recognized before Pa^{231} (in 1913), but was mistakenly thought to be another form of uranium.—*R. B. T.*

PROTECTIVE COLORATION: see ANIMAL CAMOUFLAGE.

PROTEIN: a large group of complex, nitrogen-containing organic substances of high molecular weight, widely diversified in function, and essential to the structure and functioning of all living things. Examples are: hemoglobin (molecular weight 68,000), the oxygen-transporting pigment responsible for the color of red blood cells; ribonuclease (mol. wt 14,000), an enzyme secreted by the pancreas for digesting ribonucleic acids in the intestine; insulin (mol. wt 6,000), a hormone vital in control of carbohydrate metabolism in higher animals; and myosin (mol. wt 440,000), a protein involved in contraction of muscle fibers. Proteins may be classified according to biological functions as *structural* and *functional.* Structural proteins, *e.g.* COLLAGEN from connective tissue or KERATIN from hair, comprise a relatively restricted group, but preponderate in the total protein content of an organism. Some 40% of the protein in an adult man may be collagen. Functional proteins such as the ENZYMES, HORMONES, and ANTIBODIES are usually present, individually, in far smaller quantities.

When *simple* proteins are subjected to hydrolysis (usually accelerated by the presence of acid and use of elevated temperatures), they are broken down completely into AMINO ACIDS. *Conjugated* proteins (*i.e.* simple proteins combined with nonprotein groups) on complete hydrolysis give rise to other substances in addition to amino acids. The enzyme pepsin is a *phospho*-protein because it yields, on hydrolysis, phosphoric acid as well as amino acids. Egg albumin is a *glyco*-protein because the additional material formed on hydrolysis is carbohydrate. The quantitative analysis of the products liberated on complete hydrolysis is of considerable value in the characterization of a protein.

Reversal of the process of hydrolysis is usually called PROTEIN SYNTHESIS; it involves removal of water from amino acids and requires expenditure of energy. When a molecule of water is eliminated from the amino group of one amino acid and the acid group of a second amino acid, a peptide bond is formed, and the product is a dipeptide:

$$NH_2—\overset{R^1}{\underset{|}{C}}H—CO\boxed{OH + H}NH—\overset{R^2}{\underset{|}{C}}H—COOH \longrightarrow$$

Amino acid   Amino acid

Peptide bond

$$NH_2—\overset{R^1}{\underset{|}{C}}H—CO—NH—\overset{R^2}{\underset{|}{C}}H—COOH + H_2O$$

Dipeptide

When water is similarly removed from a dipeptide and a third amino-acid molecule, a tripeptide results; stepwise continuation of the process leads to a polypeptide, a linear array of amino-acid units connected by peptide bonds. When the number of amino-acid residues, as the units are called, exceeds approximately 20, such an array is called a polypeptide chain.

Proteins may contain one or more polypeptide chains; if more than one, strong interactions or CHEMICAL BONDS between chains prevent them from separating. In building up a chain, the relative number of the 20 different amino-acid residues as well as the linear order, or sequence, in which the individual residues are arranged along the chain may be varied. Since typical polypeptide chains may contain up to 200 amino-acid residues, the possibilities for compositional and sequence variation are enormous.

If the peptide bond were the only structural feature of importance in protein architecture, the wide range of specialized functions exhibited by proteins could not be attained. It is the side chains of the amino acids that chiefly determine the individuality of proteins. They may interact by simple cohesion due to dispersive forces; by formation of electrostatic bonds between oppositely charged side chains; by means of

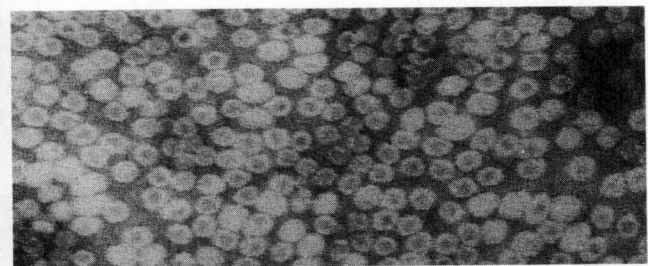

Molecules of ferritin, a conjugated protein, are shown in electron micrograph (280,000X). The simple protein apoferritin forms a protein shell (lighter material) around micelles of ferric hydroxide (darker material in center of molecules). Ferritin is found in high concentration in the liver and spleen of mammals and is their chief source of available iron. Components of molecules were made visible by negative staining with phosphotungstate. (*Walther Stoeckenius/Rockefeller University*)

hydrogen bonds between polar groups. Side chains also facilitate formation of secondary hydrogen bonds between peptide bonds of the polypeptide chain. Such hydrogen bonds may form between peptide bonds of adjacent chains or between peptide bonds of the same chain. The cumulative effect of these several interactions is to fold an essentially random coil molecule (the peptide chain) into a highly compact, organized structure. In structural terms two main classes are recognized: fibrous and globular proteins. In the fibrous, which predominantly include the structural proteins of biology, polypeptide chains are arranged in parallel rows stabilized largely by existence of hydrogen bonds between chains. In the globular proteins, which include predominantly the soluble, functional proteins of the cell, polypeptide chains are folded on themselves to give cluster-like molecules.

The presence of positively and negatively charged side chains is important when proteins dissolve in water. Charges are contributed by weakly acidic and basic groups (see AMINO ACIDS) and vary with the pH of the solution. The net charge on a protein molecule is therefore a variable quantity dependent on the solution environment. The charge distribution determines the ability of the protein molecule to interact with another identical molecule (aggregation), with the molecule of another protein, or with other charged molecules and ions in general. The charge carried by protein molecules is of considerable biological significance in affecting the distribution of diffusible ions at membranes impermeable to proteins.

Synthesis of proteins from amino acids in living things is characteristic of growth and maintenance. It is a highly specific and apparently invariant process. The insulin of a year-old cow will be the same as the insulin of that cow at age five, and the same as the insulin of another cow. However, bovine insulin is uniquely different from porcine insulin, even though substantial portions of the molecules are identical. The remarkable constancy of the synthesis of proteins is the result of genetic determination.—*C. H. W. H.*

PROTEIN METABOLISM: the transformations undergone by proteins from ingestion as food to breakdown and excretion as end products, *e.g.* ammonia and urea. Proteins exist in all living things in a state of flux called the dynamic state. This means that in a non-growing state, protein molecules constantly break down and are as constantly being resynthesized. The processes whereby proteins are broken down intracellularly are poorly understood; enzymes capable of catalyzing the hydrolysis of proteins to peptides and amino acids have been isolated from many tissues, *e.g.* kidney, lung, tumors, and from lower forms, *e.g.* molds and bacteria, and it is possible that these enzymes play a role in protein breakdown. Protein synthesis, on the other hand, takes place in all cells. A source of adenosine triphosphate (ATP), such as the reac-

tion complex called OXIDATIVE PHOSPHORYLATION, provides the necessary energy for synthesis. The mechanism controlling the rate of synthesis of a particular protein is still unknown. The rate at which a constant population of molecules of a protein is broken down and re-formed (the turnover rate) varies greatly from one protein to another. For some proteins the turnover rate is extremely rapid; thus, half the serum albumin molecules in a rat are replaced in a few hours. The turnover rate of others is extremely slow or essentially zero; collagen, for example, appears to have no turnover at all. When net protein synthesis takes place in an organism, as in growth, amino acids must be provided either from the environment or by synthesis from other precursors. When an organism cannot synthesize a needed amino acid, or synthesizes it too slowly to match the demand, it must obtain this "indispensable" amino acid from its diet. Higher plants can utilize inorganic nitrate and some microorganisms can utilize atmospheric nitrogen.—*C. H. W. H.*

PROTEIN SYNTHESIS: in biochemistry, the complex group of successive enzyme-catalyzed reactions by which amino acids are condensed together to form specific proteins. Proteins are the most numerous and most important class of compounds in the body; all enzymes are proteins. For the cell, the problem of protein synthesis is twofold; it takes energy to form the peptide bond which connects two amino acids with each other, and the amino acids must be linked in certain sequences, for the nature of these sequences determines the properties of

Three-dimensional scale model of a molecule of myoglobin from the muscle of the sperm whale: Myoglobin serves to store oxygen in muscle tissue and is particularly prevalent in the muscles of diving animals, such as seals and penguins, which remain submerged for protracted periods. Oxygen is bound to an iron-containing heme prosthetic group. The iron atom is indicated by the large sphere at approximately the center of the picture. Adjacent to it is a smaller sphere, which locates the site at which oxygen is bound. The small sphere is approximately the size of a water molecule and provides an impression of the relative size of the protein. The heme prosthetic group is seen edge on. A white cord threaded through the structure serves to depict the general folding of the polypeptide chain, which contains 153 amino acid residues. The terminus of the chain with a free NH₂ group is at lower left; the other end of the chain is at rear center. To facilitate interpretation, individual atoms in the polypeptide backbone and the sidechains are not shown—only the bond lengths between them. If the atoms were included it would be difficult to trace the structure, but the model would then reveal that in the interior of the molecule all the atoms are in close contact.

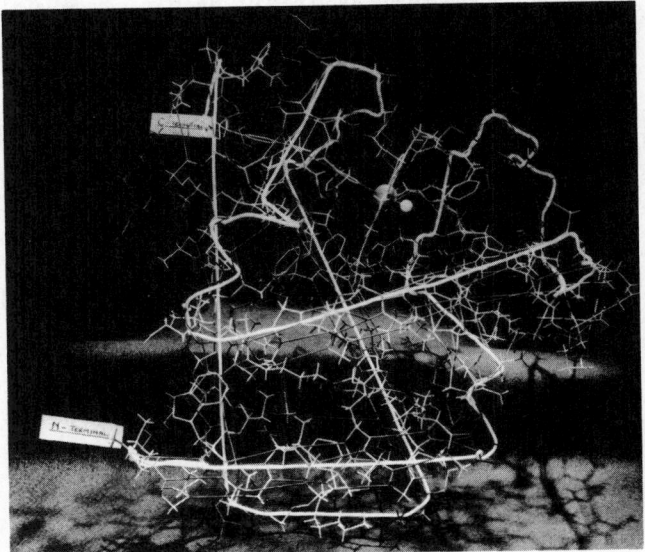

the enzymes which are synthesized. As far as present knowledge goes, the probable steps in the synthesis of protein are as follows: First there is an enzymatic "activation" of the individual amino acids, in which ATP, providing the energy, reacts with the amino acid to form an aminoacyladenylate compound. The latter compound then reacts with a small-molecular-weight ribonucleic-acid (RNA) molecule (this RNA, called soluble or transfer RNA, being specific for each amino-acyladenylate) to form an RNA-amino-acid compound. The various RNA-amino-acid compounds are then lined up in a specific order, and the amino acids are stripped off the RNA and condensed together to form the finished protein chain. This final step takes place mostly in ribosomes, which are very small particles containing about 50% RNA and 50% protein, residing mostly in the cytoplasm. The specificity of protein synthesis is thought to be brought about by the "messenger" RNA. This is a large RNA molecule which is a translation of a code in the DNA in the nucleus. This code is such that an arrangement of three ribonucleotides in the "messenger" RNA molecule signifies a particular amino acid in the protein to be synthesized. Thus, a linear array of these "triplets" in the RNA signifies a linear sequence of specific amino acids in the protein. It is thought that the "messenger" RNA is released from its place of synthesis in the nucleus, somehow gets into the cytoplasm, and becomes bound to the ribosomes. There, in conjunction with the other factors mentioned above, it acts to promote the synthesis of proteins. The ribosomes are thought to provide various enzyme factors necessary for synthesis to occur, in addition to a rigid framework necessary for the faithful transcription of the genetic message into a specific protein.—*P. S.*

PROTEOLYTIC ENZYMES: a class of enzymes which split PROTEINS to smaller PEPTIDES and eventually to their building blocks, the AMINO ACIDS. When this process occurs in the living animal (protein digestion), these enzymes liberate the constituent amino acids from dietary proteins so that they can be absorbed from the intestinal tract into the blood stream, transported to tissues, and reassembled into proteins characteristic for each particular organ. Animal proteolytic enzymes are found both inside cells and in body fluids. Perhaps the most familiar extracellular enzyme is pepsin, liberated from the stomach wall into the interior of the stomach, where it begins the process of protein digestion. As partially digested protein reaches the intestine, it is broken down further by trypsin and chymotrypsin (two enzymes produced in the pancreas and secreted into the intestinal tract), and subsequently by other proteolytic enzymes. The above-named enzymes (and certain others) can be isolated from their tissues of origin as inactive pro-enzymes or zymogens (pepsinogen, etc.) which are converted into functionally active enzymes by chemical or enzymatic action only after they have been secreted from their place of formation.

Intracellular animal proteolytic enzymes are collectively referred to as cathepsins. Each known cathepsin is the counterpart in activity to an extracellular enzyme but may differ from its partner in physical and chemical properties. Examples of plant proteolytic enzymes are: ficin (fig tree), papain (papaya), and bromelin (pineapple).

Proteolytic enzymes hydrolyze peptide bonds between amino acids in a protein chain. Distinction is made between endopeptidases (which act on peptide bonds deep inside the protein chain, and include the examples cited above) and exopeptidases (which act on peptide bonds adjacent to the ends of protein chains). Examples of this latter class are aminopeptidases, carboxypeptidases, and dipeptidases.—*B. J. J. and J. J. O'N.*

PROTEROZOIC ERA: see GEOLOGICAL TIME CHART; PRECAMBRIAN TIME.

PROTON: the hydrogen atom stripped of its electron—that is, the nucleus of the hydrogen atom. Its discovery is not associated with the name of any single individual or date but has a more complicated history beginning with the discovery of the element hydrogen by the English scientist Henry Cavendish in 1766. Toward the end of the 19th century a number of scientists, including Eugen Goldstein and Wilhelm Wien in Germany, J. B. Perrin in France, and J. J. Thomson in England, studied positively charged hydrogen rays in discharge tubes and hence established the principal properties of electrical charge and mass.

The role of the proton in atomic structure was anticipated as early as 1816 by the English scientist William Prout, who considered that all atomic weights might be multiples of that of hydrogen. Following the discovery of the neutron by James Chadwick in 1932 it became clear that the nuclei of all atoms are composed of neutrons and protons (*i.e.,* nucleons). The weight of the proton (atomic weight 1.00726 on the scale where that of C^{12} equals 12.00000), is 1,836 times that of the electron and slightly less than the weight of the neutron.

The first successful artificially-induced nuclear transmutation was produced with protons; the English physicists J. D. Cockcroft and E. T. S. Walton accomplished this in 1932 as the result of acceleration in a high-voltage tube. Artificially accelerated protons have been used ever since as bombarding projectiles for the production and investigation of nuclear reactions and interactions and thus have played a decisive role in the development of nuclear theory. Various electronuclear machines in laboratories throughout the world accelerate protons to energies of millions or even billions of electron volts. See PARTICLE ACCELERATOR.—*G. T. S.*

PROTOPLASM: the living material of plant and animal CELLS, capable of carrying on assimilation, respiration, biosynthesis, reproduction, and excretion of wastes. These chemical activities occur on the surfaces of intracellular membranes and organelles. In most cells, the protoplasm shows subdivision into a general CYTOPLASM and one or more distinct nuclei, in which nucleic acids important in heredity are carried as the genes in chromosomes.—*L. and M. M.*

PROTOZOA: single-celled animals. About 30,000 living species have been described. Almost all are microscopic, but a few kinds are large enough to be distinguished with the naked eye as small dots. Protozoans are usually grouped as the phylum Protozoa, a main division of the animal kingdom. Most are solitary, but others form aggregations or colonies that may have a diameter of a centimeter (about 2/5 in.) or more. A very wide range in cell shape is found in this phylum; although we usually think of a single CELL as having few specializations or adaptations, protozoans characteristically have parts of the cell specialized for feeding, locomotion, contraction, impulse transmission, detection of light, and other functions. Most familiar species have a grayish or whitish appearance, but others may be brown, red, green, or yellow. In general, protozoans are found in wet places—in oceans, fresh water, puddles, damp soil, mountain snowbanks, hot springs. Many occur as internal or external parasites of other animals; some are harmless commensals that live on the surface of other animals or in the digestive tract (see PARASITISM; COMMENSALISM). A wide variety of protozoans may usually be found in small ponds or puddles where there is much decaying vegetation. Often protozoans become so abundant that they impart a bad odor and taste to municipal water supplies.

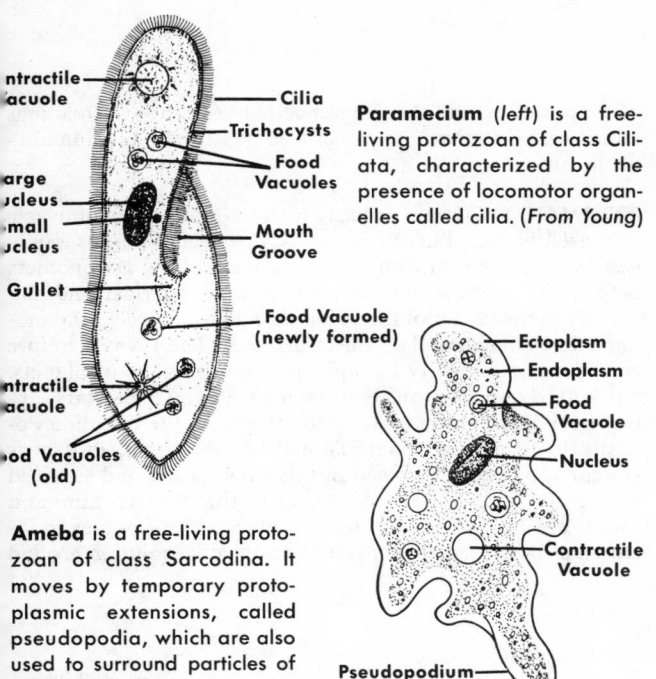

Paramecium (*left*) is a free-living protozoan of class Ciliata, characterized by the presence of locomotor organelles called cilia. (*From Young*)

Cilia
Trichocysts
Food Vacuoles
Mouth Groove
Food Vacuole (newly formed)
Ectoplasm
Endoplasm
Food Vacuole
Nucleus
Contractile Vacuole
Pseudopodium

ntractile acuole
arge ucleus
mall ucleus
Gullet
ntractile acuole
od Vacuoles (old)

Ameba is a free-living protozoan of class Sarcodina. It moves by temporary protoplasmic extensions, called pseudopodia, which are also used to surround particles of food. (*From Whaley*)

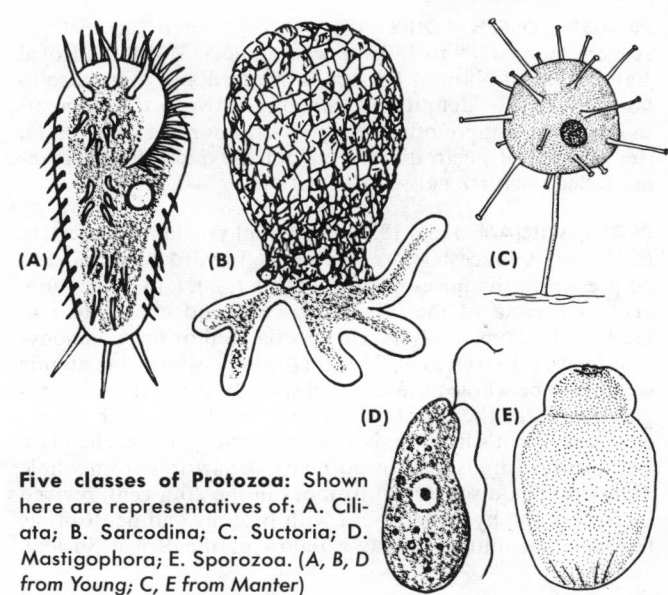

(A)   (B)   (C)   (D)   (E)

Five classes of Protozoa: Shown here are representatives of: A. Ciliata; B. Sarcodina; C. Suctoria; D. Mastigophora; E. Sporozoa. (*A, B, D from Young; C, E from Manter*)

Four basic types of feeding habits are known. Some species feed on small particles of all kinds, including bacteria, algae, other protozoans, and bits of living and dead organic matter. A second group of protozoans (closely related to true algae) are green, carry on PHOTOSYNTHESIS, and thus manufacture their own organic materials. (Some botanists consider them to be plants; see ALGAE.) Other protozoans absorb dissolved organic matter from their surroundings and synthesize their protoplasmic constituents. A fourth group of protozoans obtain nutriment by a combination of any two or all three of the above methods.

Usually protozoans multiply by simple CELL DIVISION, but many species also have more or less complicated life cycles that involve the formation of special cells resembling eggs and sperm. Most species are widely distributed; a pond in the U. S. A. usually harbors the same species as similar ponds in New Zealand, Argentina, India, or anywhere else. Such wide distribution is chiefly a result of their ability to form around themselves thick-walled, resistant cysts, which may be easily blown or otherwise carried about from place to place.

One class of protozoans (Sarcodina) includes ameba and its relatives. These creatures move about by means of tem-

porary lobelike extensions (pseudopods) from the main body. One very important form is a parasite in the large intestine of man, where it causes amebic dysentery. A small, harmless type of ameba lives in the mouth of most persons at the gum line, feeding on bacteria and small bits of food. A second class of protozoans (Mastigophora) includes the flagellates. These forms have one or more long, whiplike, protoplasmic extensions from the cell, which are used in locomotion. Sleeping sickness and Oriental sore are important human diseases caused by parasitic species. A third class (the Ciliata) includes those species that are more or less covered with an abundance of small, living, hairlike cilia. Such cilia, beating rhythmically, propel the animal rapidly through the surrounding liquid. A fourth class (the Sporozoa) is composed chiefly of very minute parasites which have no special means of locomotion and are transported passively. Malaria is produced by sporozoans, as are many common diseases of domestic and wild animals. The fifth and smallest class (the Suctoria) includes stalked forms found attached to the external surfaces of animals, plants, and inanimate objects in marine and fresh-water habitats. They suck liquid food from prey caught at the tips of minute, hollow tentacles.—*R. P.*

Solitary and colonial protozoans demonstrate a great variety of body forms. *Left to right:* (1) Five young colonies of *Volvox* being formed from a parent colony. Each tiny particle is a single individual. (2) Glass model of the very intricate siliceous skeleton of a radiolarian. (3) A group of *Paramecia*. (4) Glass model of *Stentor*, a ciliated protozoan. In life its pellicle (body covering) is dark blue. (*Carl Strüwe/Monkmeyer; Monkmeyer; Bausch and Lomb; Amer. Mus. of Nat. Hist.*)

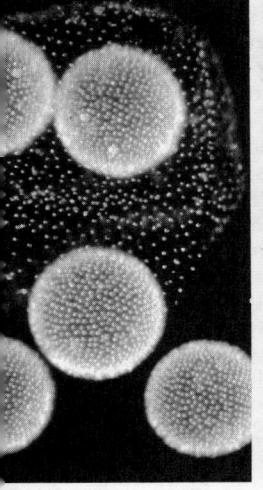
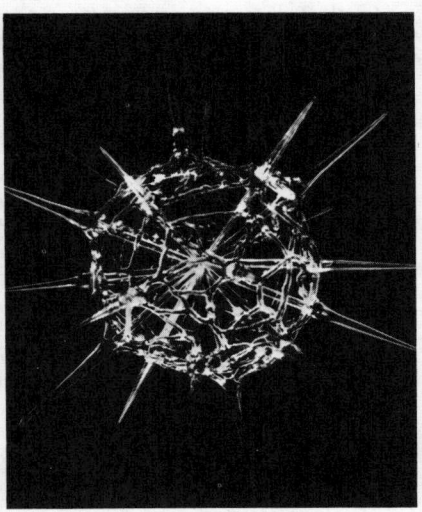
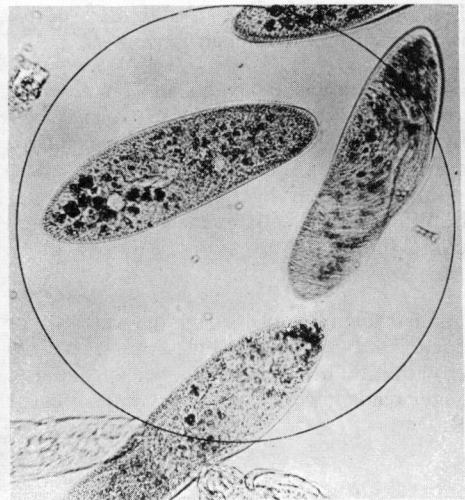
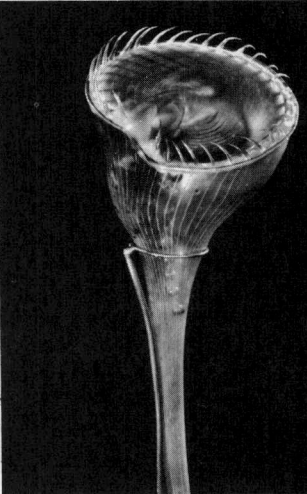

PROUST, JOSEPH LOUIS, 1754–1826, French chemist; b. Angers. From 1789 to 1808 he was connected with the Royal Laboratory of Natural History in Madrid and there formulated the law of definite proportions between the elements in chemical compounds. He also did important research on the varieties of sugar, discovering glucose and isolating mannitol. See DEFINITE PROPORTIONS, LAW OF.—*E. F.*

PROUT, WILLIAM, 1785–1850, English physician and chemist; b. Horton, Gloucestershire. He showed hydrochloric acid to be present in the juices of the stomach (1803), identified uric acid in excreta of the boa constrictor, and contributed to methods of urine analysis. He was the author of two anonymous papers in *Annals of Science* (1815–16) suggesting atomic weights to be whole numbers and speculating that the hydrogen atom was the "protyle" or building block of the other elements. Prout's hypothesis was attractive to many chemists, but accurate analysis showed many departures from whole numbers. The discovery of isotopes in the 20th cent. revived interest in the hypothesis, but with protons and neutrons as fundamental units. He was a fellow of the Royal Society. —*A. I.*

PROXIMA CENTAURI: one of the two nearest known stars, being at a distance of only 4.3 lt-yr. It is an 11th-mag. star in the southern constellation Centaurus, about 2° away, in the sky, from the bright star **Alpha Centauri.** The two stars are at virtually the same distance, have nearly the same proper motion (about 3."7/yr), and are probably moving together in space. Since "Proxima" is visually faint in spite of its nearness, it must be intrinsically very faint; it is a red dwarf star, with a rate of output of light only $\frac{1}{12,500}$ times the Sun's. It can be seen only in latitudes south of 30°N.—*M. W. O.*

PRUSSIAN BLUE: a brilliant blue pigment prepared by the addition of ferric ion to soluble ferrocyanides. Turnbull's blue is prepared by the addition of ferrous ion to soluble ferricyanides. It is now believed that Prussian and Turnbull's blue are identical, and that the different oxidation states (valences) of the iron alternate in a regular manner in the crystal lattice. Both have the formula $KFeFe(CN)_6 \cdot H_2O$, and the name *Berlin blue* has been suggested as an unambiguous name for both.—*L. Sc.*

PSEUDOMORPHISM: the process by which a mineral alters in internal structure without change in crystal form. Thus pyrite (iron disulfide, FeS_2), which crystallizes as isometric cubes, may be completely oxidized to goethite, an orthorhombic iron oxide, $HFeO_2$, with no change in the external cubic form; here goethite is said to be "pseudomorphous after pyrite." Pseudomorphs may result not only from such gradual chemical change but also from complete replacement of one mineral by another, in which case the crystal form of the original mineral is assumed by the replacing one.—*H. J.*

PSEUDOPOD: one of the protoplasmic extensions, few to many in number, characteristic of certain PROTOZOANS. It may be a blunt lobe, narrow and linear, or finely branched; usually it is a temporary means of locomotion or food-getting. Pseudopods are often found in certain digestive and blood tissues of higher animals. White blood cells in man ingest foreign particles by engulfing them with pseudopods (see BLOOD). —*R. P.*

PSYCHROMETER: an instrument for measuring the water-vapor content of air by means of two thermometers, one with a dry bulb and the other with a bulb covered with wet muslin. The wet-bulb thermometer reads lower than the dry bulb because of evaporation, and the difference between the two readings indicates, by reference to tables (see HUMIDITY), the humidity of the air.—*O. G. S.*

PTOLEMAIC SYSTEM: a geocentric description of the universe proposed by Claudius Ptolemaeus, or Ptolemy, in his *Almagest* (A. D. *c.* 150). Ptolemy followed most of the astronomers before him in believing that Earth was spherical and stationary at the center of the universe, and that all celestial motions were circular and at constant speeds. There was therefore considerable difficulty in explaining the motions of planets, particularly as each, in its movement against the stars, appears for some time to retrograde (travel in the direction opposite to its normal one). Though cumbersome, Ptolemy's system appeared to succeed in this explanation and survived for nearly 1,500 yr. The distances to the planets, Sun, and Moon not being known, Ptolemy placed these bodies in increasing order of their apparent periods of revolution around

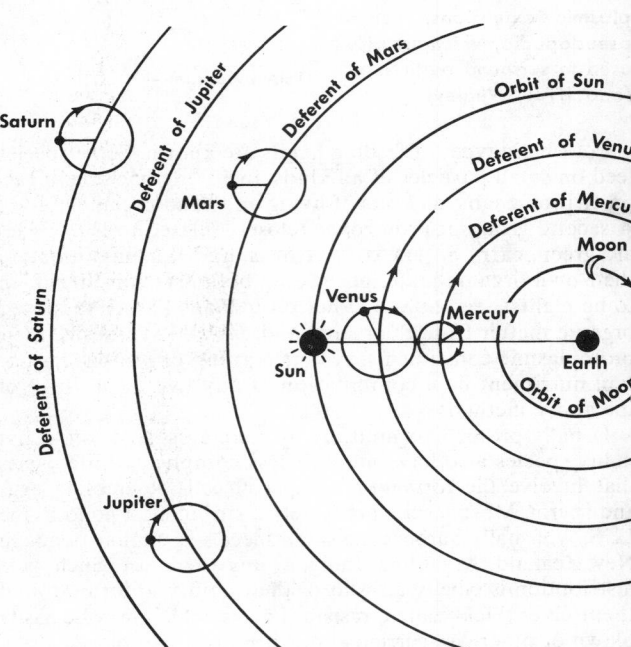

Ptolemaic system: Planets were assumed to revolve with uniform speed in a small circle, an *epicycle,* whose center revolved in a large circle, a *deferent,* whose center was near Earth. Attempts to justify observations made necessary additional circular paths for certain of the celestial bodies.

Earth. The sequence was: Moon, Mercury, Venus, Sun, Mars, Jupiter, and Saturn; and outside these was a sphere containing the fixed stars. Each day the sphere of stars rotated once about Earth, but the motions of the planets were necessarily more complicated. Each planet was thought to revolve with constant speed around a small circle, called the *epicycle.* The center of the epicycle, in turn, revolved around a larger circle, the *deferent,* which is also called the *eccentric* because its center was not at the center of Earth. However, uniform movement around an epicycle moving uniformly around a deferent did not produce a motion that conformed with observation, and so a third circle, the *equant,* was introduced. Its center was neither that of Earth nor that of the deferent. A point on the line joining its center to the center of the epicycle was assumed to move with constant speed around the equant. The result, mathematically, was a variation in the speed of the epicycle about the deferent. With suitable choices of epicycles, deferents, and equants, the motions of the planets could be represented with fair accuracy. The system was improved from time to time by the Arab astronomers, and was brought to Europe in medieval times. It survived competition with the original COPERNICAN SYSTEM, in which circular orbits were still used; it is, in fact, mathematically equivalent to that system. But after the elliptical orbits of Kepler were proved valid by Newtonian theory, the Ptolemaic system was gradually abandoned. Now discarded, it remains still a monument to human ingenuity.—*B. P. S.*

PTOLEMY (Claudius Ptolemaeus), fl. 127–151, Alexandrian astronomer; b. Egypt. He synthesized Greek astronomical work into a geocentric theory of planetary motions in terms of uniform circular motion, a requirement rigidly adopted by Greek philosophers. In the PTOLEMAIC SYSTEM, each planet revolved in a circular epicycle whose center in turn moved in a deferent circle. Ptolemy described the system in his *Mathematiké Syntaxis,* usually called the *Almagest,* the masterpiece of ancient astronomy; it also contained the rudiments of trigonometry, largely from the work of Hipparchus. Ptolemy's *Geographia* was of major importance, as was his *Tetrabiblon,* a textbook of astrology.—*O. G.*

PUBERTY: the beginning of the transition period (adolescence) between childhood and sexual maturity in mankind. Puberty typically occurs between the ages of 13 and 16 in boys, and 11 and 14 in girls. Beginning at puberty, androgenic hormones are secreted by the testes of adolescent boys, and estrogenic hormones are secreted by the ovaries of adolescent girls. These hormones induce continuing changes throughout adolescence, which lasts about 6 yr. Pubertal changes in boys include: a rapid growth in the size of penis and testes; some enlargement of the breasts (often painful); appearance of pubic and axillary hair, and later a beard on the upper lip and face; change in voice; and presence of living sperm in the testes. Pubertal (menarchal) changes in girls include: an increase in the width of the hips (pelvis); changes and rapid enlargement of the breasts; changes in vaginal secretion from alkaline to acid; appearance of pubic hair and axillary hair; and beginning of regular menstrual periods.—*A. R. D.*

PULSE (in physiology): a regular pulsation that can be felt by the tips of the fingers when they are pressed gently against the skin in a region, *e.g.* wrist, neck, or temple, where an artery runs close to the surface. Arterial pulse has been a primary source of diagnostic information for physicians since antiquity. It is a wave of arterial expansion which spreads from the heart outward along the arteries at each beat of the heart. When the heart contracts, blood is suddenly forced into the aorta. The initial effect is a stretching of the aorta's wall, since the force required to do this is less than that required to overcome the inertia of the long column of blood already filling the arterial system. The stretched wall now recoils elastically, and the adjoining portion of the arterial wall is stretched as part of the blood is forced into that portion. This process continues throughout the length of the arterial system, so that a wave of expansion travels along the arterial walls at each heart beat. The rate of movement of the wave, at 12 to 18 ft/sec, is much more rapid than the rate of flow of blood, which is only 1 to 2 ft/sec. In the same way, a jerky movement by a locomotive may be transmitted along a moving railroad train at a velocity quite different from that of the movement of the train. Velocity of the pulse wave depends on elasticity of arteries, blood pressure, and other factors. The form of the pulse wave, which can be recorded mechanically with a sphygmograph, depends on functional states of both heart and arteries. The skillful physician can recognize changes in heart rate, in pulse wave form, and in blood pressure from palpation of the pulse. Mechanical recording of pulse waves adds accuracy and precision to these observations. Besides arterial pulse there is a venous pulse, seen in the large veins near the heart; it is caused by auricular contraction.—*B. T. S.*

PULSE: a short, sharp burst of energy, usually in the form of a sudden change in voltage or current of short duration. The ideal pulse is rectangular in outline, with an instantaneous rise of the energy to its full amplitude, which then remains constant for the duration of the pulse. Pulses are used as RADAR signals, because it is relatively simple to measure the time between the sharp edge of the emitted pulse and that of the "echo" from the target, the time indicating the distance to the target. Pulses varying in amplitude, width, or position are used in communication systems to overcome noise and to provide high rates of transmission of information. See TELECOMMUNICATION.—*I. R.*

PUMICE: a cellular or spongy extrusive igneous rock, formed by sudden cooling of acidic lava in a volcanic eruption. Pumice differs from a similar glassy rock, obsidian, in having innumerable pores or holes left by emanation of gases previously dissolved in the magma. It may be blown out during the eruption as a solid, or produced by sudden cooling of the upper surface of a lava flow. Because it solidifies suddenly, it is glassy in texture, entirely lacking grain. The volume of the pores throughout the mass of the rock is sufficient to make pumice buoyant on water. Pumice (light gray) differs from the similar rock *scoria* (generally black), which is usually formed by sudden cooling of the upper surface of basaltic lava, and which contains fewer but larger pores. Pumice is much used as an abrasive.—*E. A.*

PUMP: a machine designed to increase the energy of a liquid. This increased energy may be used for such purposes as (1) raising the liquid or overcoming the friction in pipelines which arises when the liquid is conducted to another location, as in water-supply installations; (2) producing a high velocity, as for fire-fighting equipment; (3) supplying liquid to a high-pressure chamber, *e.g.* supplying water to a boiler. Pumps may be divided into four general classifications: reciprocating, centrifugal, rotary, and jet.

Reciprocating steam pump: Steam piston at right activates water piston at left. Water piston draws in water at low pressure, pushes it out at higher pressure. (*Science Museum, London*)

Reciprocating Pump: This type consists of a piston reciprocating in a stationary cylinder with suitable valves. Generally used for relatively high pressures and small volume flows per unit time, a reciprocating pump operates at relatively low speeds. The piston may be driven directly by the expansion of steam, or through a crank driven by a fairly slow-speed, or geared, electric motor. Some reciprocating pumps are single-acting in that the pump delivers liquid only when the piston moves in one direction; others are double-acting in that the pump delivers liquid during each stroke of the piston. In either case after the liquid is discharged from one end of the cylinder, the return stroke of the piston "draws in" a fresh charge of liquid. These pumps generally have a quite high efficiency. For higher pressures several units may be used in series.

Centrifugal Pump: A rotating impeller inside a stationary casing is characteristic of the centrifugal pump. The impeller imparts a velocity to the liquid, flinging it outward into the casing by the centrifugal force. The kinetic energy imparted to the liquid in the impeller is converted to potential energy or pressure in the casing by the decrease in velocity. This may be achieved in a single spiral-shaped passage, known as a volute; or by passing the liquid through a number of expanding passages acting in parallel, a device known as a vaned diffuser.

Centrifugal pumps are usually driven at rather high speeds by electric motors or steam turbines, and are often used for relatively large flows per unit time and lower pressures. If it is not possible to attain the desired pressure rise in a single impeller, a multistage pump, consisting of a number of impellers operating in series, may be used. It is not necessary to have the liquid discharge radially from the impeller. In mixed-flow centrifugal pumps the liquid is discharged at an angle less than 90° from the shaft axis. For installations requiring large flows with low pressure, as in large irrigation installations, an axial-flow or propeller pump may be used. Here the direction of the flow is essentially parallel to the axis of the shaft, and the action is similar to that found in a common desk fan. The action then is hydrodynamic rather than centrifugal.

Rotary Pump: Similar in action to reciprocating pumps are rotary pumps, in which the liquid is trapped in a chamber and then discharged under high pressure. The many forms of such pumps are distinguished from reciprocating devices by the absence of valves. A common form of rotary pump consists of a pair of meshing gears which rotate in a close-fitting casing. One gear is driven and the other idles. The liquid, trapped in the spaces between the gear teeth and the casing, is discharged in small "slugs" to the high-pressure side. It cannot flow back to the suction, because of the meshing of the gear teeth and the close clearances between the gears and the casing. Many forms of rotary pumps have been used with variously shaped lobed impellers or meshing screws, but the basic principle follows that described for the gear pump. Rotary pumps deliver relatively small quantities of liquid per unit time against relatively high pressures and are used for pumping high-viscosity liquids such as oil, hot tars, and resins. Again, these pumps may be multistaged to attain higher pressures, but this is seldom necessary.

Jet Pump: In the jet pump, which is usually without moving parts, there is a small stream of high-velocity liquid or vapor impinging on a larger mass of low-pressure liquid to convert the kinetic energy into potential energy or pressure of the entire mass. This principle is used in an injector to introduce water into a steam boiler. Jet pumps generally are used for small flows per unit time and high discharge pressures.

One of the major problems in the design of any type of pump is that of CAVITATION of the liquid on the low-pressure or suction side, so that the liquid is apt to flash into vapor if its absolute pressure becomes too low. Frequently this situation can be remedied by the use of the jet principle at the inlet of a pump for any of the types described. See also COMPRESSOR; FLUID MACHINERY; HEAT PUMP.—*A. C.*

PUPA: in the development of certain insects from egg to adult, an immature form between larval and adult stages. The pupal stage is usually quiescent, the moth pupa, for example, resting in a cocoon. When not entirely quiescent, a pupa is called a *nymph.* A butterfly pupa is often called a *chrysalis.* The development of an insect from stage to stage is known as META-MORPHOSIS.—*R. G. M.*

PUPIN, MICHAEL IDVORSKY, 1858–1935, Serbian-U. S. inventor and physicist; b. Idvor, Hungary (now in Yugoslavia). His research was principally on electricity, and he is best known for his invention of the loaded line, which is of great importance in telephone transmission. He was a member of the National Academy of Sciences.—*D. H. D. R.*

PURBACH, GEORG VON (PEURBACH, or PEUERBACH), 1423–61, Austrian mathematician and astronomer; b. near Linz. Together with his pupil Regiomontanus, Purbach contributed much to the advancement of astronomy as a science. Distinguished also as a mathematician, he compiled a table of sines, calculated new tables of the planets, measured the obliquity of the ecliptic, and constructed a globe showing the motion of the stars from the time of Ptolemy to the year 1450. His most celebrated work is *Theoricae Novae Planetarum* (1460).—*R. N. M.*

PURCELL, EDWARD MILLS, 1912–   , U. S. physicist; b. Taylorville, Ill. For their discovery of new methods for nuclear magnetic precision measurements and subsequent discoveries in this field, he and Felix Bloch shared the 1952 Nobel prize. —*D. H. D. R.*

PURINES: a large group of fused-ring organic compounds of great biological significance. Like the pyrimidines, the purines adenine and guanine are major components of NUCLEIC ACIDS. The purine nucleotides (which correspond to those of the pyrimidine series) are adenylic acid and guanylic acid.

Purine Ring   Adenine

Guanine

Adenylic acid is biologically synthesized from glycine, glutamine, carbon dioxide, aspartic acid, serine, and ribose-5-phosphate in the presence of adenosine triphosphate (as energy source) in about ten enzymatic steps. In addition to their genetic role as building blocks in DNA and RNA (see PYRIMIDINES), adenine derivatives are important components of many key cofactors in enzymatic reactions; thus adenosine triphosphate (ATP) is the principal agent in the transfer of biological energy. The phosphopyridine nucleotides (DPN and TPN) are coenzymes that act as hydrogen carriers in a host of enzymatic reactions involving oxidation and reduction. Coenzyme A, vitamin B_{12}, and flavin nucleotides are other important coenzymes which contain the adenine ring.—*R. Wu.*

PURKINJE, JOHANNES EVANGELISTA, 1787–1869, Czech anatomist and physiologist; b. Lobkowitz, Bohemia. His work included research on the physiology of the senses, *e.g.* studies of visual sensations produced mechanically and by electric currents. His microscopical discoveries include the germ cell in the hen's egg, the cilia in the oviduct and respiratory duct in vertebrates, the axis cylinders of the nerves, the large ramified cells in the cerebellum (Purkinje's cells), and the spiral apertures of the sweat glands. He was the first to use a microtome for the preparation of microscopic sections, and the first to prepare slides with balsam.—*D. H. D. R.*

PUTREFACTION (decay): the biochemical processes responsible for food spoilage and tissue breakdown. The two causes are: (1) breakdown of protein, carbohydrate, and fat by bacterial and mold enzymes; (2) release of breakdown enzymes in dead tissue. The latter enzymes are contained in cellular structures, called lysosomes, which dissolve on death of the cells and cause tissue autolysis. Putrefaction can be prevented by destroying the enzymes, as in canning, or by slowing their action, as in refrigeration. The odor associated with putrefaction is due to the breakdown of amino acids to amines by decarboxylases, *e.g.* lysine to cadaverine, ornithine to putrescine, tryptophan to indole. See AUTOLYSIS; SAPROPHYTE.—*J. F. S.*

PUZZLES: see MATHEMATICAL RECREATIONS.

PVT RELATIONSHIPS: see GAS.

PYRAMID: a solid figure bounded by a polygonal base and lateral triangular faces that have the sides of this polygon as their bases and meet in a common point, the vertex of the pyramid. Pyramids are classified according to the number of sides of the base. Thus, a triangular pyramid has a triangular base, a square pyramid has a square base, and so on. If the line from the vertex to the center (centroid) of the base is perpendicular to the base, the pyramid is a right pyramid. The celebrated pyramids of Egypt are right square pyramids. A triangular pyramid is bounded by four triangular faces and is also called a tetrahedron. If the four faces are congruent, equilateral triangles, the solid is a regular tetrahedron. The altitude of a pyramid is the perpendicular distance from its vertex to the plane of its base. Its volume is one third that of a prism with the same base and altitude, and hence is one third the product of the altitude by the area of the base. This formula is correct regardless of the shape of the base. Just as a circle is approximated more and more closely by regular inscribed polygons of more and more sides, so a circular cone is approximated more and more closely by a sequence of inscribed pyramids based on these regular polygons.

The pyramids of Egypt are, of course the most famous of pyramidal structures. One of these, the Great Pyramid, was one of the Seven Wonders of the Ancient World, and remains one of the remarkable man-made creations. Pyramidal forms are occasionally used in modern architecture.—*H. C.*

PYRETHRIN (I and II): complex chemical molecules which are the main constituents of the extract of *pyrethrum* flowers (which resemble chrysanthemums). The pyrethrins are prized for their quick lethal action on flies, general insecticidal properties, and relative nontoxicity to man and animals.—*D. P. B.*

PYRHELIOMETER: an instrument for measuring the strength of heat radiation from the Sun. In a common type of pyrheliometer, thin black and white metal plates are exposed to sunlight inside an evacuated glass bulb. The temperature difference between the plates, measured by a thermocouple, indicates the intensity of the sunshine.—*D. H. L.*

PYRIDINE NUCLEOTIDES (coenzymes I and II): in biochemistry, two phosphorus-containing compounds that serve as cofactors to a number of enzymes involved in oxidation-reduction reactions. Coenzyme I, also called diphosphopyridine nucleotide or DPN (sometimes also cozymase), consists of residues of adenine, ribose, two phosphates, ribose, and the vitamin nicotinamide, in that order. Coenzyme II (also called triphosphopyridine nucleotide or TPN) has a similar structure but contains a third phosphate group linked to the first ribose. Both DPN and TPN readily take up two atoms of hydrogen from a substrate in the presence of an enzyme which is specific for the substrate that is being oxidized. The reduced coenzymes can lose their hydrogens either to flavoproteins or to other substrates; thus a small amount of coenzyme can oxidize or reduce a great many substrate molecules. It is chiefly the nicotinamide end of the molecule that is involved in the gain and loss of hydrogen. DPN and TPN act as coenzyme to separate "families" of dehydrogenases; a very few enzymes seem to work equally well with either, but the majority will only work at an appreciable rate with one or the other. An example is glucose-6-phosphate-dehydrogenase, an important enzyme involved in the PENTOSE PHOSPHATE PATHWAY, which is specific to TPN. DPN and TPN are of great biological importance because of the number of reactions in which they are involved. See also *dehydrogenases* (ENZYME, table); HYDROGEN TRANSPORT; FLAVIN NUCLEOTIDES; NUCLEOTIDES.—*K. H.*

PYRIMIDINES: a group of cyclic organic compounds of great biological significance. Together with purines, pyrimidines are the building blocks of RIBONUCLEIC and DEOXYRIBONUCLEIC acids, in which they are linked to pentose and phosphate groups as NUCLEOTIDE units. Nucleic acids, universally present in all forms of life, serve to carry genetic information and are important to protein synthesis. The major pyrimidines are cytosine and uracil in the ribonucleic acids and thymine and uracil in the deoxyribonucleic acids. Pyrimidine nucleotides are synthesized in living organisms from simple organic compounds; *e.g.* uridylic acid (the nucleotide of uracil) is biologically synthesized from carbon dioxide, ammonia, aspartic acid, and ribose-5-phosphate in the presence of adenosine triphosphate (an energy source) and several enzymes. Uridylic acid derivatives can then be converted to cytidylic acid and thymidylic acid by other enzymatic reactions. Many other biologically important compounds are derivatives of pyrimidine ring. Purine, pteridine, and isoalloxazine are condensed ring systems containing the six-membered heterocyclic nucleus of pyrimidine.—*R. Wu.*

PYRITE (iron pyrites or fool's gold): a mineral which is the isometric polymorph of iron disulfide, FeS_2. One of the commonest minerals, occurring in minor amounts in almost all rocks, pyrite is particularly abundant in various kinds of ore deposits. On exposure to WEATHERING, pyrite is readily oxidized, the iron remaining as the hydrated oxide, *limonite,* and the sulfur forming sulfuric acid, which accelerates the breakdown of associated minerals. The limonite-rich cappings (gossans), which overlie and are guides to the discovery of many mineral deposits, have been formed by weathering of pyrite and other sulfide minerals. Pyrite is more stable at higher temperatures and in alkaline environments, whereas *marcasite,* the orthorhombic polymorph, is more stable at lower temperatures and in acid environments. *Pyrrhotite* is a similar hexagonal mineral, with a composition approximating FeS. All these minerals are readily distinguished from gold because they are hard and brittle, whereas gold is soft and malleable. Pyrite, pyrrhotite, and to a lesser extent marcasite are major sources of sulfuric acid and liquefied sulfur dioxide, which are obtained by burning the commercial concentrates (called *iron pyrites),* the resulting clinker being used as an ore of iron. See MINERAL (table).—*L. M.*

PYROCLASTICS: fragmented material ejected from a volcanic vent during an eruption. It consists mostly of lava solidified by sudden cooling, but pieces of rock broken off the vent walls may be intermingled with it. Pyroclastics are glassy because of the sudden cooling, but may contain occasional crystals. As solidified magma they may be called lava, although this term is usually restricted to molten matter issuing from vents or fissures, and to the rock subsequently formed when it cools. Pyroclastics, on the other hand, appear originally as solids. The finest particles are usually called *volcanic dust* or *ash,* although not actually the residue of combustion. Particles up to about an inch across are called *lapilli;* if frothy, they are *cinders.* Larger fragments that become somewhat rounded as they hurtle through the air are *bombs,* and angular pieces are known as *blocks*—though the latter term is sometimes restricted to fragments broken from the sides of the vent by the eruption. Frothy lava material is generally called *pumice.* Pyroclastics are deposited most heavily near the vent, and may accumulate in heaps 1,000 ft thick. Some volcanic cones, *e.g.* that of Mt Etna, are mainly composed of pyroclastics, but finer matter may be blown far. Kodiak Island, 100 mi from the volcano of Katmai, has received up to 12 ft of ash; fine dust blown out by Krakatoa in 1883 circulated around the globe in the atmosphere for two years. Although all pyroclastics are true igneous rock, they may also be classed as sediments, if the material drops into basins where sedimentation is taking place and, if later consolidated, may form sedimentary rock. Consolidated strata of volcanic ash are called *tuff.*—*E. A.*

PYROLYSIS: a chemical decomposition brought about by heat; particularly, the thermal decomposition of a relatively complex organic molecule into smaller fragments. Pyrolytic reactions, widely used in the chemical processing industries, can be grouped into two major categories: non-catalytic and catalytic. Non-catalytic pyrolysis, as the name implies, is brought about by heating the starting material to its decomposition temperature in the absence of air and of any special catalyst or promoter. Examples practiced on an industrial scale are the production of ethylene from ethane, and acetylene from butane. Such operations as the coking of coal, the preparation of charcoal from wood, and the manufacture of carbon black from natural gas involve complicated non-catalytic pyrolytic reactions. Pyrolysis in the presence of special catalysts, generally known as "catalytic cracking," is used on a very large scale to produce GASOLINE from heavy petroleum oils.—*A. M. S.*

PYROMETER: an instrument for measuring temperatures too high for an ordinary THERMOMETER. The nature of the instrument varies with the temperature to be measured. An *optical pyrometer,* for example, measures temperature of incandescent bodies by determining intensity of light emitted in a certain wavelength (see HEAT DETECTOR).—*Ru. M.*

PYROTECHNICS: inflammable compositions used in civil and religious festivals and in military tactics. The term is used interchangeably with *fireworks.* Inflammable compositions consisting variously of wood, sulfur, pitch, petroleum, and charcoal were used in war by ancient peoples more than 2,500 yr ago to burn enemy cities; bellows provided the necessary oxidizer (air). Modern pyrotechnics are self-contained; *i.e.* they contain not only the combustible material but also the oxidizer and the igniter. Some historians state that fireworks were invented by Callinicus (Kallinikos) about A. D. 670 with his so-called Greek fire, which contained combustibles together with a secret ingredient, reputedly saltpeter (potassium nitrate, KNO_3), as oxidizer. However, since saltpeter was not recorded in the literature before the 13th cent. the secret ingredient of Callinicus may have been quicklime, which evolves much heat when wet with water and can be used to ignite oily combustibles. Greek fire, a liquid, was also known as wet fire; it was used with great effect against ships at sea. Availability of saltpeter in the 13th cent. led to the development of black powder (GUNPOWDER) and to the first real fireworks. Black powder is basically a mixture of saltpeter, sulfur, and charcoal, sometimes with various other additives.

With the emergence of chemistry as a modern science (ca. 1800) other oxidizers, *e.g.* potassium chlorate, $KClO_3$, became available; certain salts were found to add color to the flame; and new metals such as magnesium and aluminum were found to give brilliant flash effects when used as combustibles. Black powder is primarily used as a propellent EXPLOSIVE, but when confined in a pasteboard cylinder (the simple firecracker) it is a noise maker; if potassium chlorate is used as an oxidant there is more noise; if powdered aluminum is added there is a white flash. The fuse may be a cotton string impregnated with black powder and binder. Quickmatch, used instead of a fuse in some devices, has the black powder in a suface strip, with a dextrin binder. Both fuse and quickmatch conduct a small flame to the pyrotechnic mixture.

Flares and colored flames generally use potassium chlorate as an oxidizer. These pyrotechnic mixtures contain salts that give color to the flame; some mixtures also contain chlorinated organic compounds that insure conversion of the salts to chlorides volatile at the combustion temperature of the mix. Sodium salts are used for yellow flames, barium for green, and strontium for red. Combustible binders such as shellac and paraffin may also be employed. "Stars," sent aloft by rockets or Roman candles, are composed either of substances that burn when flying through the air (*e.g.* sodium metal) or pyrotechnic mixtures that ignite abruptly while in the air. Military forces often use pyrotechnics (*e.g.* flares) for illumination; these are discharged either from aircraft or from the ground, and are generally made with powdered aluminum and magnesium as combustibles. Another military use of pyrotechnics is signaling with colored smoke grenades; these pyrotechnic compositions include dyes, which are volatilized by the burning mixture and condensed to a colored smoke.—*Ru. M.*

PYROXENES: a common and widespread group of silicate minerals which are major constituents of many kinds of igneous and metamorphic rocks, and of meteorites. The pyroxenes include several interlocking, partially to completely isomorphous series:

Orthopyroxenes (orthorhombic)		
$Mg_2Si_2O_6$	Enstatite
$(Mg > Fe)_2Si_2O_6$	Bronzite
$MgFeSi_2O_6$	Hypersthene
$Fe_2Si_2O_6$	Ferrosilite (Not naturally occurring)

Clinopyroxenes (Monoclinic)	$Mg_2Si_2O_6$	Clinoenstatite (metastable, mostly in meteorites)
	$MgFeSi_2O_6$	Clinohypers-thene (same)
	$Fe_2Si_2O_6$	Clinoferrosilite (metastable)
	$CaMgSi_2O_6$	Diopside
	$(Ca,Mg,Fe)_2Si_2O_6$	Pigeonite
	$CaFeSi_2O_6$	Hedenbergite
	$(Ca,Na)(Mg,Fe'',Fe''',Al)$ $(Si,Al)_2O_6$	Augite
Alkali Pyroxenes (Monoclinic)	$LiAlSi_2O_6$	Spodumene
	$NaAlSi_2O_6$	Jadeite
	$NaFe'''Si_2O_6$	Aegirine
Pyroxenoids (Triclinic)	$Mn_2Si_2O_6$	Rhodonite
	$CaMnSi_2O_6$	Bustamite
	$(Ca,Mn)(Mn,Zn)Si_2O_6$	Fowlerite
	$Ca_2Si_2O_6$	Wollastonite
	$Ca_4Na_2H_2(Si_2O_6)_3$	Pectolite

The pyroxene structure is based on an infinite chain of SiO_4 tetrahedra, each linked to its neighbor through a shared oxygen ion, and elongate in the direction of the c axis of the crystal. In the pyroxenoids, however, the chains parallel the b axis. The structural formula, $xy(Si_2O_6)$, permits the incorporation of various combinations of monovalent and divalent cations having a total of four positive charges. This is modified in the augites by substitution of AlO_4 tetrahedra for some of the SiO_4 tetrahedra. The symmetry of the pyroxenes is directly related to the ionic radii of their cations. The crystals are orthorhombic when the x and y sites are occupied by small ions, monoclinic when occupied by large and small ions respectively, and triclinic when both are occupied by large ions.

The pyroxenes are closely related to the AMPHIBOLES in structure, composition, appearance, and occurrence. The most prominent distinction is in the prismatic cleavage planes, which meet at about 90° in the pyroxenes, and at about 60° and 120° in the amphiboles. At lower temperatures, the amphibole structure is generally more stable than that of the equivalent pyroxene, and partial to complete replacement of pyroxene by amphibole (uralitization) is common. Rocks composed almost exclusively of pyroxene are called *pyroxenites,* of which there are two major types: (1) ultrabasic IGNEOUS ROCKS composed of orthopyroxenes, which appear to result from the accumulation of crystals settled out of a slowly cooling basic to ultrabasic MAGMA; (2) METAMORPHIC ROCKS generally composed of diopside, derived from the alteration of magnesian limestones; in some cases, the required silica was already present as an original constituent of the sediments, while in others the silica was introduced by fluids emanating from intrusive igneous rocks. There are no uses for pyroxenes, except as constituents of rocks used in construction and decoration. See MINERAL (table).—*L. M.*

PYTHAGORAS, fl. 6th cent. B. C., Greek mathematician and philosopher; b. Samos. He traveled extensively in Egypt, Babylonia, and Italy. In Crotona, Italy, he founded a secret brotherhood through which his influence became widespread. Little is known regarding Pythagoras himself; later philosophers tend to refer to the Pythagoreans rather than the founder. Besides their beliefs in transmigration of souls and reincarnations, the Pythagoreans constructed a philosophy based on numbers as the essence of the universe: although numbers are pure symbols, all matter is numerical and all relationships can be expressed numerically. To the Pythagoreans numbers were the whole numbers and the ratios constructed from whole numbers; but they discovered that these numbers are not sufficient for expressing all magnitudes, as demonstrated by the famous PYTHAGOREAN THEOREM. This failure of the whole numbers to supply all numerical needs was something of a scandal and raised issues that were not settled until the 19th cent.; some mathematicians are not satisfied even yet. Perhaps the greatest contribution of the Pythagoreans resulted from their insistence that in developing geometry the postulates be set down at the outset and that the entire development proceed by strict deduction from the postulates. Since that time mathematics has had this purely deductive character.—*H. C.*

PYTHAGOREAN THEOREM: probably the most famous theorem of geometry, if not of all mathematics; it states that the sum of the areas of the squares on the two perpendicular sides of a right triangle is equal to the area of the square on the hypotenuse. In Fig. 1, area M + area N = area R. Although the first strictly deductive proof of the theorem probably was given by the Pythagoreans, the theorem was well known long before Pythagoras' time (c. 550 B. C.). Special cases were known to the Egyptians as early as 2000 B. C.; the theorem is found in Chinese works written around 1100 B. C.; and it appears in the Vedic writings of India as early as 800 B. C.

One of the many proofs of the theorem is obtained by dissection. Cut out of the square *ABDE*, in Fig. 2, the right triangles *BFD* and *GED*, as shown. Now move triangle *BFD* into position *AHE*, and triangle *GED* into position *CAB*. The

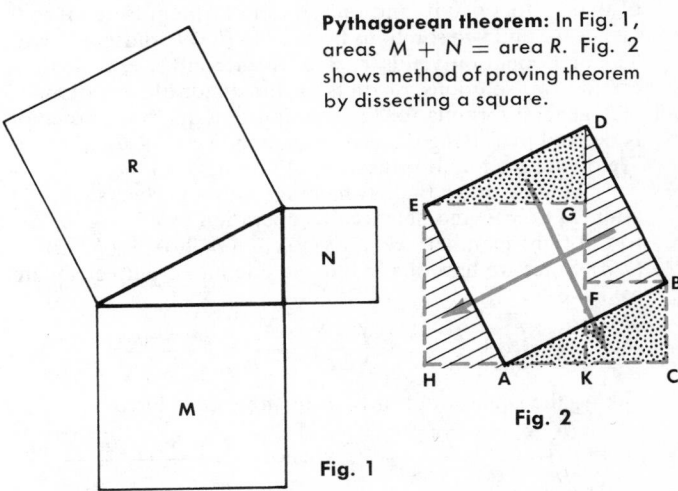

Pythagorean theorem: In Fig. 1, areas M + N = area R. Fig. 2 shows method of proving theorem by dissecting a square.

Fig. 1

Fig. 2

parts of the square *ABDE* now make up the two squares *BCKF* and *HKGE*. Side *HK* of the latter square is easily proved equal to *AC*. Thus the square on *AC* plus that on *BC* is equal to the square on *AB*.

The theorem demonstrated to the Pythagoreans that integers and fractions do not suffice for describing all lengths. If, for example, each of the perpendicular sides has its length equal to one unit, the Pythagorean theorem shows that the length of the hypotenuse is $\sqrt{2}$. But no integer or fraction exists whose square is 2; hence other numbers are necessary. This was the first recognition of a need for irrational numbers. The Pythagorean theorem provides the *distance formula* so fundamental in COORDINATE GEOMETRY. This formula not only gives us the lengths of straight lines on a graph, but is central in the application of calculus to the calculation of the lengths of curves.—*H. C.*

Q

Q OF A CIRCUIT: a measure of the quality of a resonant electrical circuit, defined as 2π times the ratio of the energy stored in the circuit to that dissipated per cycle. This definition also applies to the Q of components such as inductors, capacitors, and microwave cavities. In a resonant circuit consisting of an inductor and a capacitor, Q is equal to the ratio of the reactance of either element to the resistance in the circuit. If a high-Q circuit is set into oscillation, it will continue to oscillate for a long time after the source of energy is removed (it has low damping); in addition a high-Q circuit will resonate over a narrower range of frequencies than one with low Q.—*I. R.*

QUADRATIC EQUATION: an algebraic equation of the second degree. The general form of a quadratic equation in one unknown is $ax^2 + bx + c = 0$, where a, b, and c are known numbers. An example is $2x^2 - 5x - 7 = 0$, which is identified with the general form by making $a = 2$, $b = -5$, and $c = -7$. The study of quadratic equations is an important topic of elementary algebra. Two methods of solution are available: the method of factoring and the use of a general formula. Factoring is easier if the quadratic expression is readily factored. In the above example we find that $2x^2 - 5x - 7 = (2x - 7)(x + 1)$. The equation can therefore be written $(2x - 7)(x + 1) = 0$. We now reason that the product of two factors is 0 if, and only if, one of them is equal to 0. Hence we find two solutions from $2x - 7 = 0$ and $x + 1 = 0$. The first equation yields $x = \frac{7}{2}$, the second $x = -1$; these are the two solutions, or roots, of the quadratic equation.

A general formula for the solution of a quadratic equation is derived by solving the general equation $ax^2 + bx + c = 0$. We divide by a, and transpose, obtaining $x^2 + (b/a)x = -c/a$. We now make the left member into a perfect square by adding $(b/2a)^2$, and balance this operation by adding $(b/2a)^2$ to the right member: $x^2 + (b/x)x + (b/2a)^2 = (b/2a)^2 - (c/a)$. Since we have made the left side into a perfect square, we have

$$\left(x + \frac{b}{2a}\right)^2 = \left(\frac{b}{2a}\right)^2 - \frac{c}{a} = \frac{b^2 - 4ac}{4a^2}.$$

Taking the square root of both members, we have

$$\left(x + \frac{b}{2a}\right) = \pm\sqrt{\frac{b^2 - 4ac}{4a^2}}, \text{ whence } x = \frac{-b \pm \sqrt{b^2 - 4ac}}{2a}.$$

Because of the "plus or minus" sign before the radical, there are two roots unless $b^2 - 4ac = 0$. Solving the earlier example by the formula, we have

$$x = \frac{5 \pm \sqrt{(-5)^2 - 4 \cdot 2 \cdot (-7)}}{2 \cdot 2} = \frac{5 \pm \sqrt{81}}{4} = \frac{5 \pm 9}{4}.$$

Hence $x = -4/4 = -1$, or $x = 14/4 = 7/2$.

The quantity $b^2 - 4ac$ is called the discriminant of the quadratic. If the discriminant is equal to 0, the two roots are equal; if it is positive, the roots are real and distinct; if it is negative, the roots are conjugate COMPLEX NUMBERS. The formula brings out the relations between the roots and the coefficients in the equation. By adding the two values given by the formula, we get $-b/a$; and by multiplying them we get c/a. If the two roots are r_1 and r_2, then: $r_1 + r_2 = -b/a$, $r_1 r_2 = c/a$.

The quadratic equation can be studied geometrically by means of the quadratic function, $y = ax^2 + bx + c$. The graph of this function is a parabola with a vertical axis, which has its vertex at $x = -b/2a$, $y = -(b^2 - 4ac)/4a$. The parabola is tangent to the x axis at $x = -b/2a$ if $b^2 - 4ac = 0$; it crosses the x axis at two points corresponding to the real roots of the equation if $b^2 - 4ac > 0$; and it fails to meet the x-axis if $b^2 - 4ac < 0$. Approximate values of the real roots of a quadratic equation can thus be obtained by plotting a graph of the function and observing where it coincides with the x-axis.—*H. C.*

QUADRATURE: the position of a planet or the Moon when it has a celestial longitude that differs from the Sun's by 90°. This means that the angle between the direction to the body and the direction to the Sun, as seen from Earth, is approximately 90°; therefore a planet nearer to the Sun than Earth can never be in quadrature. When the Moon is in quadrature, it shows half of its disc illuminated by the Sun, and first or last quarter occurs.—*M. W. O.*

QUADRIC SURFACES: surfaces that are represented in three-dimensional rectangular coordinates by equations of the second degree. (See COORDINATE GEOMETRY.) The three principal varieties, ellipsoids, paraboloids, and hyperboloids, are analogous to the three second-degree curves: ellipses, parabolas, and hyperbolas. The sphere is a special ellipsoid; quadric cylinders are limiting cases of ellipsoids; and quadric cones are limiting cases of hyperboloids.

An ellipsoid (Fig. 1) has three axes of symmetry. If it is so placed that these axes coincide with the three coordinate axes, it has an equation of the form $x^2/a^2 + y^2/b^2 + z^2/c^2 = 1$. Sections of the surface by the three coordinate planes are the three ellipses,

$$x^2/a^2 + y^2/b^2 = 1, \, x^2/a^2 + z^2/c^2 = 1, \, y^2/b^2 + z^2/c^2 = 1$$

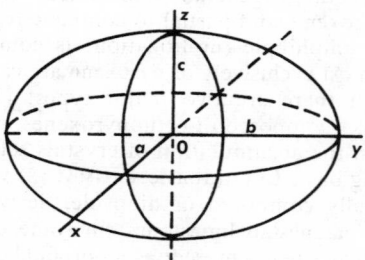

Fig. 1: Ellipsoid

The axes of these ellipses are the principal axes of the ellipsoid. If $a \neq b = c$, the surface is an ellipsoid of revolution which can be generated by rotating about the x-axis the ellipse whose equation is $x^2/a^2 + y^2/b^2 = 1$. If $a > b$, the figure is called a prolate spheroid; if $a < b$, it is an oblate spheroid. All plane sections perpendicular to the x-axis are circles, and all others are elliptical. If $a = b = c$, all axes are equal and the surface is spherical. An elliptic cylinder may be regarded as a limiting surface approached by ellipsoids as one axis increases beyond all bounds.

There are two varieties of paraboloids. Each has a single

axis of symmetry. Plane sections containing the axis are, in general, parabolas. The parabola degenerates to a straight line in some instances. Sections perpendicular to this axis are either elliptical or hyperbolic. The equation $x^2/a^2 + y^2/b^2 = cz$ is that of an elliptic paraboloid (Fig. 2). The section made by the plane $z = k$ has the equation $x^2/a^2ck + y^2/b^2ck = 1$, in the plane $z = k$. If $ck > 0$, this is the equation of an ellipse. If $ck < 0$, there is no real intersection. If $a^2 = b^2$, the

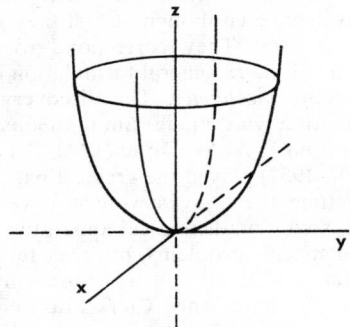

Fig. 2: Elliptic Paraboloid

paraboloid is circular, or a paraboloid of revolution, which can be generated by rotating the parabola $x^2 = a^2cz$ about the z-axis. The equation $x^2/a^2 - y^2/b^2 = cz$ is that of a hyperbolic paraboloid (Fig. 3). The section made by the plane $z = k$ has the equation $x^2/a^2ck - y^2/b^2ck = 1$. The sections of the surface by planes perpendicular to the z-axis

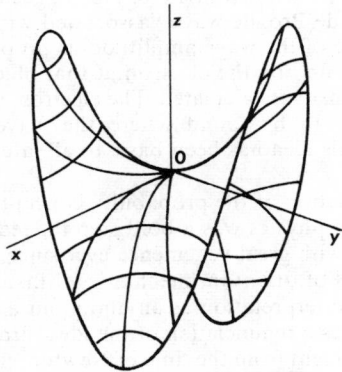

Fig. 3: Hyperbolic Paraboloid

are therefore two sets of hyperbolas. If $c > 0$, those above the xy-plane have transverse axes parallel to the x-axis, and those below have transverse axes parallel to the y-axis. The equation $xy = cz$ also represents a hyperbolic paraboloid. The sections by planes perpendicular to the z-axis are the rectangular hyperbolas, $xy = k$.

A hyperboloid, like an ellipsoid, has three axes of symmetry. If it is placed so that these axes coincide with the co-

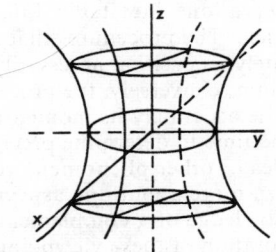

Fig. 4: Hyperboloid of One Sheet

ordinate axes, the equation has a form such as $x^2/a^2 + y^2/b^2 - z^2/c^2 = \pm 1$. A different arrangement of signs corresponds to a different orientation on the axes. If the sign of the term in the right member is plus, the plane sections perpendicular to the z-axis are ellipses, whereas those perpendicular to the x and y-axes are hyperbolas. This is called an unparted hyperboloid, or hyperboloid of one sheet (Fig. 4).

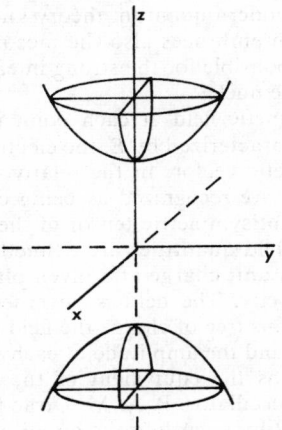

Fig. 5: Hyperboloid of Two Sheets

If the sign of the right member is minus, the plane sections perpendicular to the z-axis, which lie more than c units from the origin, are ellipses; planes less that c units from the origin do not intersect the surface. Planes perpendicular to the x-axis or the y-axis intersect the surface in hyperbolas. This hyperboloid is called a biparted hyperboloid, or hyperboloid of two sheets (Fig. 5). The equation $x^2/a^2 + y^2/b^2 - z^2/c^2 = 0$ represents a quadric cone, which is approached by a hyperboloid as the lengths of the principal axes tend to 0. —H. C.

QUALITATIVE ANALYSIS: see CHEMICAL ANALYSIS.

"QUANTISIERUNG ALS EIGENWERTPROBLEM" (Paper on Wave Mechanics), by Erwin Schrödinger, *Annalen der Physik,* Vol. 79 (1926): Here Schrödinger successfully explained the structure of atoms by assuming that electrons have wave properties and that their motion is governed by a wave equation, which he was able to derive. The solution of this equation showed that only certain electronic energies are possible. If one assumes, as did Bohr, that the atom changes its energy by emitting or absorbing photons, the frequency of light emitted by atoms can be successfully predicted. Schrödinger in this and subsequent papers showed that the wave properties of electrons, discovered experimentally by Davisson and Germer (see DAVISSON-GERMER EXPERIMENT), are necessary for determining all atomic properties.—*S. Bo.*

QUANTITATIVE ANALYSIS: see CHEMICAL ANALYSIS.

QUANTITY: see NUMBER.

QUANTUM: a unit or "bundle" of discontinuously propagated vibratory energy, whose content (*E*) is the product of Planck's constant (*h*) and the frequency of vibration (*f*). Accordingly a quantum, or a photon, of blue light carries more energy than one of red light, since the frequency of blue light is greater than that of red. In a restricted sense, the quantum is reminiscent of the Newtonian *corpuscle,* except that the latter represented a "packet" of matter rather than energy.—*A. E.*

QUANTUM ELECTRODYNAMICS: the branch of physics concerned with formulation of laws of electricity and magnetism suitable for description of such phenomena at the level of interaction of individual atomic particles. It stands in relation to classical theory of electricity and magnetism (as developed by James Clerk Maxwell and H. A. Lorentz) as QUANTUM MECHANICS stands to classical Newtonian mechanics. Quantum electrodynamics is a special case of a more general development of modern quantum theory known as *quantum field theory,* which embraces also the meson fields that are thought to be responsible for the strong interactions between nucleons in atomic nuclei.

The electromagnetic field at each point in space and at each instant is characterized by **E**, the electric vector, and **H** (or **B**), the magnetic vector; in the relativistic formulation, these two vectors are recognized as being components of a single entity, an antisymmetric tensor of the second rank in space-time. The field quantities are defined in terms of the force that acts on unit charge at a given place and moving with a given velocity. The field is governed by Maxwell's equations. In regions free of charge the field can be analyzed into plane waves, and the amplitude of each such component can be regarded as the equivalent of the amplitude of a simple harmonic oscillator. P. A. M. Dirac initiated the development in 1927 by regarding the amplitude of each such oscillator as given by procedures taken over from those applicable to a quantum-mechanical harmonic oscillator.

Similarly each kind of particle is also represented by a field, and the interactions between particles and with the electromagnetic field are described by coupling terms in the equations for the several fields.

Quantum electrodynamic effects are generally so small that they are barely observable, but these effects have been accurately measured and thus have served to verify the theoretical structure on which the subject is based. Most important of these observed effects are the Lamb shift (discovered by Willis E. Lamb), which is a small relative displacement of some of the quantized energy levels in the hydrogen atom, and the fact that the magnetic moment of the electron is slightly larger than given by elementary theory. See also ELECTRODYNAMICS.—*E. U. C.*

QUANTUM MECHANICS: By 1924, QUANTUM THEORY had developed to the point where it was generally recognized that the motion of electrons and other constituents of atoms must follow laws radically different from those of the mechanics of Isaac Newton, originally worked out to explain the motion of large-scale bodies, including the planets of the solar system. A decisive step was taken in that year in the doctoral thesis of Louis de Broglie, who postulated that the duality between the wave and the particle nature of light is also applicable to the behavior of material particles such as electrons and protons. He assumed that the relation of energy E and momentum P of such a particle to the frequency and wavelength of the associated waves was the same as for light, namely, $E = h\nu$ and $P = h/\lambda$, where h is Planck's constant and ν and λ are the frequency (cycles/sec) and wavelength (cm/cycle) of the wave. In this way he could interpret the existence of the discrete quantum states of electron motion in an atom as being akin to the discrete number of possible frequencies of vibration of a stretched violin string of definite length and tension. Later (1926) this viewpoint was elaborated by Erwin Schrödinger into a definite mathematical structure called wave mechanics, which was soon found to agree with Bohr's orbital theory at all points where that agreed with experiment, and to give correct results where Bohr's orbit calculations failed.

Concurrently Werner Heisenberg was giving an apparently totally different kind of reformulation to the laws of mechanics of atomic particles. The quasi-periodic motions in classical orbits had long been analyzed into pure harmonic (or Fourier) components in Bohr's basic work. Heisenberg modified this kind of analysis by representing the motion in terms of *matrices,* a doubly infinite array of periodic components governed by unfamiliar rules of algebra. Later Schrödinger's and Heisenberg's formulations were recognized as mathematically equivalent, even though at first they seemed totally different in character. They correspond to two different approaches to a still more general formulation of the subject, known as *quantum mechanics.* The discovery of the more general formulation was made simultaneously by several physicists, of whom P. A. M. Dirac (1902–   ) and John von Neumann (1903–1957) played the greatest part.

For a brief time these ideas were not well understood. Physicists possessed a mathematical apparatus that gave correct answers to specific problems, but they felt that they did not really understand it. (It is worth observing that similar doubts assailed physicists when Clerk Maxwell first put forward his equations.) Perhaps the greatest lack was that of a better understanding of what is meant by the vague phrase that a de Broglie wave is "somehow associated with" the motion of a particle. But the reality of these waves as governors of the motion of electrons could no longer be doubted after the discovery in 1927 of ELECTRON DIFFRACTION, which showed that the laws of scattering of a beam of electrons by a crystal are much like those governing the scattering of x-rays by crystals. A decisive step of interpretation was taken by Max Born in 1926. He suggested that the intensity of the de Broglie wave "associated with" an electron (*i.e.* the square of the wave amplitude) is proportional to the probability of finding the electron at that place in space for which the intensity is calculated. The electron, in other words, is most likely to be found where the wave has greatest amplitude. This idea has been basic to all later development of the subject.

The introduction of the probability concept into the basic laws of atomic physics was a bold step indeed and has been argued about with great vehemence ever since. While accepting the results of quantum mechanics, Einstein never fully accepted this interpretation as anything but a makeshift, because it involves a renunciation of the idea, firmly entrenched in physical thought from the time of Newton, that all motions in nature will be found to be fully causally determined when we know enough about the details of the situation involved. Born, on the other hand, said that all we can hope to know about atomic processes is a set of possible alternative outcomes of various experiments, and the relative likelihood of their occurrence in repeated trials.

Born's idea was further developed in 1927 by Heisenberg in his UNCERTAINTY PRINCIPLE and by Bohr in his COMPLEMENTARITY PRINCIPLE. By analyzing in detail the actual processes by which position and momentum of a particle are measured, Heisenberg was able to show that the act of making such observations inevitably interferes with the motion of the particle. The procedures that must be used to locate quite accurately its position necessarily and drastically disturb its momentum; conversely, the procedures that must be used to determine accurately its momentum frustrate the attempt at the same time to determine precisely its position. Bohr gave examples of other phenomena respecting which the attempt to learn more about one aspect interferes with or destroys our knowledge of a complementary aspect. Out of the further elaboration of these viewpoints over the years there was evolved what is generally known as the *Copenhagen interpretation* of quantum mechanics, so named because the focal point of its development was Bohr's seminar in Copenhagen.

The main cleavage between Einstein and the Copenhagen school did not arise from differences over what was actually known about physical phenomena in the small. Though profound, the cleavage related to the future course of physics. Einstein was of the opinion that the uncertainties and complementary aspects of physics are attributes of our *present* limited knowledge; both would vanish, he was convinced, as men learned more; the Copenhagen school, on the other hand, feels deeply that these limitations are fundamental and inherent in the ultimate nature of things and our relation to them. It must be said now that, after a third of a century, despite great efforts, nothing has been learned to contradict the Copenhagen viewpoint, but of course this does not prove no such advance ever will be made.

In this third of a century, there has been an enormous range of detailed applications of quantum mechanics to atomic, molecular, and nuclear structure problems, with an intimate association between theory and experiment. Nowadays it is impossible to present atomic theory except in the language of quantum mechanics, for most of the theory was developed in terms of that language. Although the successes have been many and detailed and exact, in many cases the theory poses mathematical problems too difficult for anything but approximate calculation. In these cases, therefore, it is really not known whether the present formulation of quantum mechanics gives exact agreement with experiment.— *E. U. C.*

QUANTUM NUMBER: any of the numbers that designate the possible values of the observable properties of the elementary particles of matter. All experimental evidence indicates that the intrinsic properties of elementary particles, as well as the combined properties of two or more interacting particles, are quantized, *i.e.* the parameters characterizing the observable properties of these systems can assume only a discrete set of values. Each of the allowed values consists of a fundamental quantity of nature multiplied by an integer, a half-integer, or a simple function of these. The integer (or half-integer) associated with a permitted value of an observable property is called a quantum number. For example, possible values of the component of angular momentum about a chosen axis are given by $mh \sqrt{2\pi}$, where m can be any integer, and h is a universal constant of nature, called Planck's constant. This has the value $6.6 (10)^{-27}$ erg sec. The integer m is thus quantum number associated with this observable quantity. Similarly the allowed values of the energy and the magnitude of the total angular momentum are characterized by other quantum numbers. Four quantum numbers are required for the complete quantum description of a single electron in an atom, and by the EXCLUSION PRINCIPLE no two electrons in the same atom may have all of the same four quantum numbers. The mathematical formalism that has been developed to describe the observed behavior of the fundamental particles, and that enables one to calculate the quantum numbers of a system, is called QUANTUM MECHANICS.— *S. K.*

QUANTUM STATISTICS: the modifications of STATISTICAL MECHANICS resulting from the fact that motions of basic particles must be described by means of QUANTUM MECHANICS rather than by classical mechanics. Statistical mechanics undertakes to describe average properties of aggregates of large numbers of particles in terms of the relative numbers of these to be found in various states of energy and momentum, and the change of this distribution with time caused by mu-

tual collisions of the particles and by external influences such as electric, magnetic, and gravitational fields. Ludwig Boltzmann in the 19th cent. was particularly successful in giving in such terms an interpretation of the molecular processes responsible for the second law of thermodynamics, particularly relating many properties of gases to what is now known as the classical Boltzmann distribution.

When quantum mechanics is applied to the motion of individual particles in such a system, important deviations from the Boltzmann statistics are obtained; these deviations have extended and perfected the range of applicability of the theory. There are two new forms of quantum statistics, known respectively as Bose-Einstein statistics and Fermi-Dirac statistics; both agree with Boltzmann statistics in limiting cases of low particle density. Certain classes of elementary particles "obey" Bose-Einstein statistics and are called bosons for this reason, whereas others "obey" Fermi-Dirac statistics and are called fermions. All particles having an integral value (in units of $h/2\pi$) of spin (including zero) are bosons, and those having half-integral values, notably electrons, protons, and neutrons, are fermions.

The quantum-mechanical wave function describing the state of a system of like particles is symmetrical in the case of bosons and antisymmetrical in the case of fermions. Here symmetry of the wave function means that the function does not change its value if the coordinates of two particles are interchanged, whereas antisymmetry means that the function reverses its sign for this same operation on the wave function. The Planck radiation formula is intimately associated with the fact that photons are bosons. The Pauli EXCLUSION PRINCIPLE, which explains the behavior of electrons in atoms and the periodic table of the elements, and also the distinction between metals and electrical insulators in solids, is intimately associated with the fact that electrons are fermions.— *E. U. C.*

QUANTUM THEORY: the underlying theory that governs all nuclear, atomic, molecular, and solid-state physics. The theory was initiated in 1900 by Max Planck. The starting point was the theory of the relative intensity of radiation of different frequencies that is emitted by hot bodies. The radiation that fills a hollow cavity at temperature T (measured from absolute zero) is independent, as to total amount and the mode of energy distribution among frequencies, of the material of which the cavity walls are made. The total amount of such energy in unit volume is proportional to T^4 (Stefan-Boltzmann law), and the relative energy distribution over different frequencies v cycle/sec is a function of v/T (Wien displacement law), so at higher temperatures the radiation shifts to higher frequencies.

Before Planck's work it was supposed that this radiant energy exists in the form of continuous ELECTROMAGNETIC WAVES (akin to those used in radio telegraphy), which were supposed to be continuously emitted and absorbed by atoms. Planck found that, in order to get agreement with experiments on the form of the relation between intensity and frequency, he had to assume instead that atoms emit or absorb radiation discontinuously, in *quanta* of energy; that is, finite discrete amounts of energy are emitted and absorbed in individual acts of emission or absorption. In other respects the radiation behaves like a wave motion of frequency v cycle/sec. The connection is that the energy content of one quantum is $E = hv$; that is, the energy of its quantum is directly proportional to the frequency of the associated wave. The factor of proportionality, h, is now known as *Planck's constant*.

This assumption made such a radical break with the then prevalent views that it was all but ignored for a few years until Albert Einstein showed in 1905 how this assumption led to a clear understanding of a hitherto puzzling fact about the PHOTOELECTRIC EFFECT. In this, electrons are liberated from a metal when it is illuminated. Increasing the intensity of the light increases the rate at which electrons are ejected (number released in unit time), but does not affect the maximum energy of motion with which they are thrown out. Increasing the frequency of the light, on the other hand, increases the maximum energy of liberation of the individual electrons. Einstein postulated that one quantum's energy goes to one electron, hence this is the same for a definite frequency, while greater intensity merely means that more electrons are affected. Thus the *maximum* energy of ejected electrons is controlled by the frequency, some electrons losing energy on the way out of the metal from greater depth and hence appearing with less than the maximum.

Einstein (in 1907) also used the quantum idea to interpret the experimental fact that the heat capacity of all solids (amount of heat needed to produce unit rise in temperature) becomes very small near the absolute zero of temperature. This can be explained by the fact that the vibratory motion of atoms in a crystal lattice may be analyzed into elastic waves of definite frequencies. For a given mode of vibration the possible energies of motion are restricted to values that are integral multiples of $h\nu$, where now ν is the frequency of vibration of the elastic wave in the crystal. When the temperature is sufficiently decreased, the high-frequency waves are unable to acquire even one quantum of energy, and therefore no energy is absorbed in exciting these vibrations. As the temperature is further decreased, even the vibratory modes of lower frequency cannot obtain quanta of energy. The total result is that only small amounts of energy can be absorbed, and the heat capacity diminishes rapidly as temperature is diminished. This theory has since been greatly elaborated by Peter Debye, Max Born, and others, so that it now gives a satisfactory account of the details about the heat capacity of all crystals that have been studied.

The next major step (1913) was taken by Niels Bohr, who extended the quantum idea to give an interpretation of the sharp-line spectra of light emitted and absorbed by atoms in the gaseous state. He built on Ernest Rutherford's nuclear atom model, which supposes atoms to consist of a central nucleus (about 10^{-12} cm in diameter) containing most of the mass and all of the positive charge, surrounded by a cloud of enough negatively charged electrons (occupying a space about 10^{-8} cm in diameter) to make the whole structure neutral. Bohr supposed the atom to exist in discrete energy states having values characteristic of the particular kind of atom in question. Light is emitted when the atom makes a radiative transition from a state of energy E' to one of lower energy E'', in such a way that one quantum, $h\nu = E' - E''$, is emitted in such a quantum jump. Similarly, absorption of light occurs when the light causes the atom to make a transition from a lower to a higher ENERGY LEVEL. This idea proved enormously fruitful in disentangling the complicated line spectra emitted by the atoms and in interpreting the spectra emitted and absorbed by molecules. Such analysis of spectra was a central task of physics from 1915 to 1935. Though the analysis still goes on, most of the major spectra have now been rather thoroughly interpreted. (See ATOMIC SPECTRA; MOLECULAR SPECTRA.) With the advent of the study of nuclear structure, it was found that Bohr's principles apply: the nuclei exist in discrete energy levels, and gamma rays are emitted and absorbed by nuclei in accordance with the same quantum rule.

At first Bohr supposed the actual motions of particles in atomic structures to follow the laws of Newtonian MECHANICS, but this view soon proved inadequate. In the period 1924–27,

a modification of mechanics, known as QUANTUM MECHANICS, was developed to deal with these motions.

An important extension to the original quantum idea came about in 1923 with the experimental discovery of the COMPTON EFFECT by A. H. Compton. From ideas originating in the theory of RELATIVITY, together with knowledge that light exerts pressure on a material object on which it falls, it was reasoned that the light quanta carry momentum as well as energy, the amount of the momentum carried by one quantum being h/λ, where λ is the wavelength of the associated light wave. This led Compton to reason that when x-rays are scattered by atoms, whose electrons are loosely bound, they should give up some of their energy to the electrons and be scattered as quanta of lower energy and hence of lower frequency. The change is one that is simply calculated from the principles of conservation of energy and momentum. Compton gave an experimental demonstration of the reality of this Compton shift in wavelength of the scattered x-rays, and from that time on the light quanta have been known to be carriers of discrete amounts of momentum as well as of energy.

Thus all forms of electromagnetic radiation appear to have dual aspects, behaving in some respects as a stream of quanta bearing particulate amounts of energy and momentum, and in other respects as a continuous spreading electromagnetic wave. In recent years it has become customary to name all the constituent particles of atomic physics with words ending in -on, and accordingly it is now more common to speak of *photons* instead of light quanta, but the terms are synonymous. See also QUANTUM ELECTRODYNAMICS; QUANTUM STATISTICS; ELECTROMAGNETIC WAVE; LIGHT.— *E. U. C.*

QUANTUM THEORY OF THE ELECTRON by P. A. M. Dirac, *Proceedings of the Royal Society*, A Vol. 117 (1928): Here Dirac combined the concept of the wave properties of the electron with Einstein's Special Theory of Relativity. The resultant wave equation, which he derived, successfully explained the fine structure of the hydrogen atom spectrum. It predicted too the spin of the electron (see ELECTRON SPIN) and the existence of the positron. This work laid the foundations for the FIELD THEORY of elementary particles. The wave equation derived by Dirac can be used to describe neutrons, protons, and all other particles whose spin is ½.—*S. Bo.*

QUARTZ: a crystalline form of SILICA, SiO_2. The most common single mineral except for water, it varies widely in form, color, and occurrence. It is a major constituent of many IGNEOUS and METAMORPHIC ROCKS and is common as hydrothermal vein fillings and replacement bodies. Quartz resists all forms of chemical weathering except lateritization, and thus persists as a fragmental (clastic) sediment to form large volumes of sand, sandstone, and quartzite. It also occurs in lesser amounts in shales, siltstones, and limestones. Good crystals of quartz, including the GEM varieties rock crystal, amethyst, smoky quartz, and citrine, have generally been formed under hydrothermal conditions and occur in endstage phases in pegmatites, in vugs and veins.

Relatively pure silica may take on any of ten different forms, depending on temperature, pressure, and chemical environment. Most of these forms are metastable at ordinary temperatures and pressures, and some have been obtained only through rapid quenching of synthetic melts.

The structure of the silicas and silicates is based on the SiO_4 tetrahedron, with four oxygen ions forming the corners and a silicon ion at the core. Bonding is both ionic and covalent. In all the POLYMORPHS of silica, and in many of the silicates, the tetrahedra are linked into three-dimensional networks through the sharing of all the oxygen ions. The packing densities of the networks and the orientation of the tetrahedra within them are junctions of the lattice energies, the more expanded forms resulting from crystallization at higher temperatures and/or lower pressures.

Coesite forms at extremely high pressures and is known in nature only in quartz-bearing rocks that have been struck by large meteorites. It was first discovered in the walls of Meteor Crater, in Arizona, then in the walls of several other impact craters, and its presence is an important criterion in establishing the impact origin of such craters. *Tridymite* and *cristobalite* apparently require the presence of small quantities of foreign ions to keep their structure from collapsing at lower temperatures. Tridymite and cristobalite occur only in volcanic rocks, and were formed at high temperatures in mineralizer-rich environments. The original quartz of igneous rocks crystallizing above 573°C was β quartz, which inverted to α quartz on cooling. The pre-existence of β quartz is indicated only where there are well-formed crystals showing the higher symmetry, usually hexagonal dipyramids with little or no development of prisms. Phenocrysts that were originally β quartz occur in porphyries. *Chalcedony* is always microcrystalline, usually as radial to tangled fibrous aggregates. Most chalcedony has apparently been derived from pre-existing colloidal forms of silica, *e.g.* silica gel or opal. Chemical sediments and their metamorphosed equivalents show a progressive sequence from opal, through chalcedony, to microgranular quartz. Some *cherts* and *flints* are composed of combinations, indicating intermediate stages. X-ray studies of *opal* and fused silica indicate that these may be composed of randomly oriented submicroscopic aggregations having a cristobalite structure. The skeletons of diatoms, sponges, and various plants are opaline silica. The color-play of gem opals is an interference effect based on the variations in index of refraction between layers with different degrees of hydration. *Lechatelierite* has been found in nature only in the vicinity of meteor craters and as the cementing agent in *fulgurites*—the branching, rootlike aggregations formed when lightning strikes sandy ground.

In common quartz, the SiO_4 tetrahedra are arranged in right- or left-handed spirals. This structure is reflected in the external form, optical properties, and strong piezoelectric and pyrolectric properties of the crystals. Natural and synthetically grown quartz crystals are sliced in especially oriented, thin wafers for use in radio signal frequency control. Fused quartz, because of its chemical resistance, high fusion point, and low coefficient of thermal expansion, is used in combustion tubes and crucibles. Sawed blocks of quartzite are used as refractory furnace linings for the same reasons. The hardness (7) and sharpness of broken grains account for the use of quartz as an abrasive in whetstones, coated papers, scouring powders, and sandblasting. Quartz-rich sands, sandstones, and quartzites are sources of silica for glass, ceramic wares, metallurgical fluxes, adhesives (silica gel), silicones, and other chemicals. Some flints and quartzites are used as grinding-mill liners and grinding agents ("pebbles") because of their hardness and toughness. Sand is used in large quantities in construction, in foundry molds, in oil-formation "fracturing," for filtering, and as a filler. See MINERAL (table).—*L. M.*

QUARTZITE: a massive METAMORPHIC ROCK formed from quartz sandstone. In the metamorphic process, the quartz grains of the parent rock become cemented together with silica. This may be caused by the heat and pressure of regional metamorphism or by hot, silica-bearing, aqueous solutions. Whereas sandstone will break between the grains, quartzite breaks through the grains, which appear (under the

Quartz: When free from flaws, transparent quartz crystals such as these are used in many optical devices, especially those that transmit ultraviolet light. (*Amer. Mus. of Nat. Hist.*)

microscope) to have retained their identity but which behave indistinguishably from the cementing silica. Like the parent sandstone, quartzite may contain admixtures of other minerals, which give color to a rock that, in its pure form, is white. Quartzite is extremely durable, but its hardness makes it difficult to shape and detracts from its use in building. The term "quartzite" is also applied to a sedimentary rock composed largely of quartz that has been cemented by quartz or silica.—*E. A.*

QUASI-STELLAR RADIO SOURCE (or **quasar**): a celestial object of faint, starlike appearance, characterized by intense radio emission and an extremely large RED SHIFT. About 100 quasars are known. If the red shift is given the classical interpretation as indicating speed of recession, some quasars are receding at 80%

Cliff of quartzite near Bennington, Vermont, shows characteristic blocky jointing and smooth fracture surfaces. (*Jerome Wyckoff*)

of the speed of light. This has led to the assumption that they are a type of galaxy near the limits of the known universe, perhaps 10 billion lt-yr away. This would mean (see BIG BANG THEORY) that quasars date back to the beginning of the universe. This interpretation does not explain the fact that if they are at such great distances the amount of energy received from them is 10 to 100 times more than from average galaxies, and their light output fluctuates faster than would be possible by known physical standards. Alternate theories suggest that they are nearby objects ejected at enormous speeds by an explosion at the center of our galaxy only a few million years ago. —*J. L. G.*

QUATERNARY PERIOD: the younger of the two geological periods, or systems, of the CENOZOIC ERA; it includes the Pleistocene and Recent epochs.

QUATERNION: an expression in four symbols u, i, j, k, with real coefficients s, a, b, c, of the following form:

$$q = su + ai + bj + ck$$

where q is a quaternion. If $q' = s' u + a' i + b' j + c'k$ is a second quaternion, the quaternions q and q' are said to be equal if $s = s', a = a', b = b'$ and $c = c'$.

The addition and multiplication of q and q' are carried out "as if u, i, j, k were independent variables" whose table of multiplication is shown.

First factor	Second factor			
	u	i	j	k
u	u	i	j	k
i	i	$-u$	k	$-j$
j	j	$-k$	$-u$	i
k	k	j	$-i$	$-u$

Note that $jk \neq kj$. Thus quaternion multiplication is not commutative, and the order of the factors must always be kept in mind when multiplying.

By definition:

$$q + q' = (s + s')u + (a + a')i + (b + b')j + (c + c')k$$

$$qq' = (ss' - aa' - bb' - cc')u + (bc' - cb')i$$
$$+ (ca' - ac')j + (ab - ba')k$$

The product qq' can be found by treating u, i, j, k as independent variables, multiplying q and q' as in high-school algebra but paying attention to order, and finally simplifying all products such as jk by referring to the above table, which tells us that $jk = i$, etc.

Quaternions of the form $su + 0 \cdot i + 0 \cdot j + 0 \cdot k$ are identifiable with the real numbers, the symbol u being identified with the unit 1. Thus we can rewrite $q = su + ai + bj + ck$ as $q = s + ai + bj + ck$. The symbol i can be identified with the ordinary complex number $i = \sqrt{-1}$; more precisely, the quaternion $s + ai + 0 \cdot j + 0 \cdot k$ behaves like a complex number. The quaternion $0 + 0 \cdot j + 0 \cdot j + 0 \cdot k$ can be identified with the zero of the real numbers and plays the role of a zero for the quaternions. Every quaternion q has a negative, $-q = -s - ai - bj - ck$.

Quaternion multiplication, as we have seen, is non-commutative. It is, however, associative, as a simple calculation shows. The quaternion $q = 1 + 0 \cdot i + 0 \cdot j + 0 \cdot k$ is the unit for multiplying quaternions. Addition of quaternions is commutative and associative. Finally, multiplication, on the right or on the left, is distributive with respect to addition. Although multiplication is not in general commutative, each non-zero quaternion has a unique *inverse* q' such that $qq' = q'q = 1$. If $q = s + ai + bj + ck$, then

$$q' = \frac{(s - ai - bj - ck)}{(s^2 + a^2 + b^2 + c^2)}$$

If we define the *conjugate* $\bar{q}$ of q to be $\bar{q} = s - ai - bj - ck$, then we see that $q\bar{q} = s^2 + a^2 + b^2 + c^2$ and that $q' = \bar{q}/q\bar{q}$. Thus quaternions obey all the axioms of a FIELD, save that of commutativity of multiplication. They are said to form a non-commutative or skew field.

The lack of commutativity of quaternion multiplication means we must distinguish between the two quotients of a quaternion q_1 by a quaternion $q_2 \neq 0$, the quotient q' on the left and the quotient q'' on the right: $q' q_2 = q_1$ and $q_2 q'' = q_1$ do *not* imply $q' = q''$. Also note that $(q + q')(q - q') \neq q^2 - (q')^2$ necessarily, for in general $q q' \neq q' q$.

Just as we can have polynomials with coefficients in a field, we can have polynomials over the quaternions. Consider the equation $x^2 = -1$, where we allow quaternion solutions, if any. It turns out that this equation has an infinity of solutions: if $a^2 + b^2 + c^2 = 1$ then $(ai + bj + ck)^2 = -1$.

Quaternions were invented in 1843 by the British mathematician Sir William Rowan Hamilton.—*J. S.*

QUINOLINE: a liquid with a pungent odor, first obtained by distillation of coal tar but also found among the distillation products of alkaloids (basic nitrogenous compounds) of the *quinine* family, after treatment of the alkaloids with alkali. Quinine is a specific in the treatment of malaria. Quinoline (and isoquinoline) are HETEROCYCLIC and AROMATIC. They are condensations of the benzene and pyridine rings:

Quinoline   Isoquinoline

In World War II about 14,000 compounds were screened in the search for anti-malarials to substitute for quinine. The quinoline structure is present in many of those found most satisfactory, *e.g. chloroquine.*—*Ru. M.*

QUINONES: highly colored (yellow-red) unsaturated ring compounds with two ketone groups. They have olefin and ketone properties, rather than aromatic. They are obtained from corresponding hydroquinones by oxidation, and are reconverted to hydroquinones by addition of hydrogen (reduction).

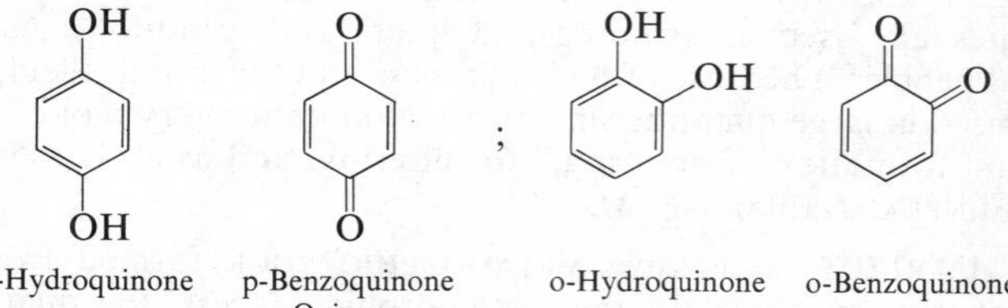

p-Hydroquinone   p-Benzoquinone   o-Hydroquinone   o-Benzoquinone
                  Quinone

The quinone (quinoid) structure is highly important in dye chemistry. Of biochemical importance is coenzyme Q, a quinone involved in HYDROGEN TRANSPORT.—*Ru. M.*

R

RABBITS AND HARES: small herbivorous MAMMALS of the order Lagomorpha. Like RODENTS, rabbits and hares lack canine teeth and use their chisel-shaped incisors for gnawing. They differ from rodents in having a short tail, long back legs (which account for their characteristic hopping gait), and a second, inconspicuous pair of incisor teeth located behind the front, exposed pair in the upper jaw. Also, rabbits and hares lack the ability of rodents to rotate the forelegs so that objects may be held between the paws. The terms "rabbit" and "hare" are commonly confused; strictly, a rabbit, such as the cottontail rabbits (*Sylvilagus*) of N America, prepares a fur-lined nest and bears blind, naked, and helpless young; a hare, by contrast, gives birth to well-furred young that not only can see but may be able to run after the mother immediately. On this basis, the Belgian "hare" (*Oryctilagus*), from which the domesticated rabbit was bred, is a true rabbit, but the jack "rabbit" (or antelope hare) and the snow-shoe "rabbit" (or varying hare) are true hares. The order Lagomorpha also includes the cony, or pika, which looks much like a small (about 6 in. long) rabbit, except for its shorter ears and hindlegs, and its lack of a tail. Conies live in mountainous regions of Asia, Europe, and western U. S. A. —*L. and M. M.*

RABI, ISIDOR ISAAC, 1898– , U. S. physicist; b. Rymanow, Austria. For his application of the resonance method to the measurement of the magnetic properties of atomic nuclei, he received the Nobel prize, 1944. His techniques, which were evolved from the molecular-beam method used by Otto Stern for the determination of magnetic moments of atoms, considerably improved the accuracy of measurement. Rabi is a member of the National Academy of Sciences.— *D. H. D. R.*

RADAR: a RADIO device for "seeing" objects. The name is from the original function: *RA*dio *D*etection *A*nd *R*anging. Radar uses a powerful radio transmitter to illuminate objects with radio waves, much as a searchlight illuminates objects with light waves. It uses a sensitive radio receiver to detect reflected radio waves, much as the eye detects reflected light waves. A single antenna usually serves both transmitter and receiver. The receiver would be "blinded" by the transmitter, just as the eye is blinded by looking into a powerful searchlight, if special precautions were not taken; hence the original and still most widely used type of radar functions by sending out radio waves in short pulses and receiving reflected waves, or "echoes," between pulses, so that the transmitter is off while the receiver is operating. In pulse radar, as this is called, it is necessary to connect the antenna only to the transmitter while sending and only to the receiver while receiving. Since the antenna must be switched from one to the other in a small fraction of a microsecond, no mechanical device would suffice. The switching is accomplished by an ingenious combination of resonant transformers, impedance inverters, and spark gaps, called a "duplexer." This is one of the greatest circuit inventions of modern radio.

The antenna forms a beam of radio waves, called a *radar beam,* just as a searchlight forms a light beam. Direction to objects is determined by an indicator of antenna direction when the objects are observed. Distance is determined by measuring the time required for the pulse, traveling at the speed of light, to go from the transmitter to the object and back to the receiver.

The use of short pulses renders indication of distance quite simple with the help of a CATHODE-RAY TUBE. This tube has an electronic pencil that writes on the tube screen. The pencil is made to draw a straight horizontal line, called a range line, across the center of the screen. The line is started at the left each time a radar pulse is sent out. Received echoes cause the electronic pencil to put vertical marks, or "pips," on the range line. The farther away the reflecting object, the greater will be the time delay between sent and received pulses, and the farther to the right will the corresponding pip appear on the screen. Properly spaced calibration marks on the range line can then indicate the distance to each reflecting object. This type of indicator is called an "A-scope." It displays in proper range all objects that lie within illumination by the radar beam.

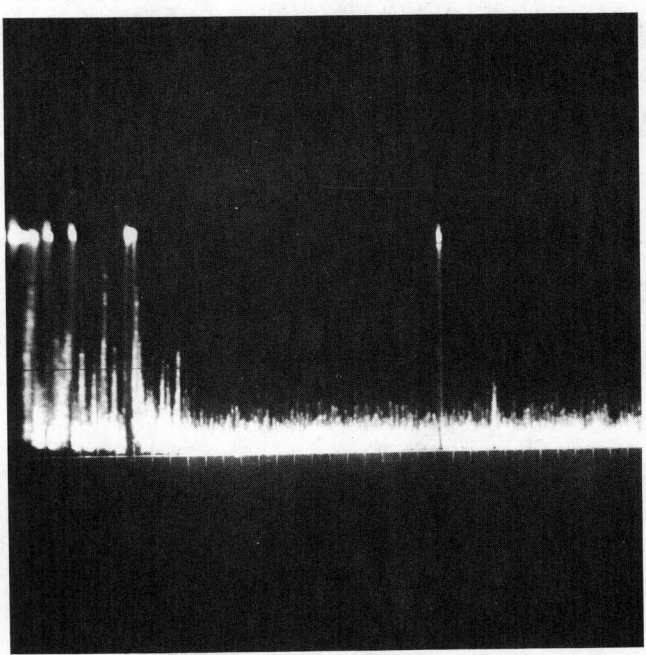

Radar A-scope photograph shows signals received on screen. From the range line, which extends from left to right, rise vertical marks, or "pips." The distance they rise indicates the signal strength, and the distance from left side measures the distance from the radar antenna of the object reflecting the signal. In this photo, signals at left are from ground objects (e.g. buildings and trees) in the vicinity of the antenna. Near right is a strong signal from an airplane at a distance of 61 mi. (*U. S. Navy*)

A more useful type of indicator for many purposes is the plan position indicator (PPI). In this indicator the range line starts in the center of the screen and extends in a direction corresponding to the compass direction of the radar beam. The range line is made dim, and echoes appear as bright spots instead of pips. The antenna is then made to rotate continuously, and as the range line rotates with it, all objects illuminated by the beam appear as bright spots on the screen in true plan position.

Surveillance of large volumes of space is best accomplished with radio waves in the meter-wavelength region as used in the first radars. Resolution of crowded targets and precision tracking of selected targets are best accomplished with MICRO-WAVES. Development of microwave radar was made possible by the klystron receiving tube and the cavity magnetron transmitting tube.

Since radar uses radio waves instead of light waves, it can "see" through fog, smoke, and darkness, but it cannot see the fog or the smoke. It can detect rainfall, however, and because it can see for great distances it can detect the outlines of hurricanes and weather fronts many miles in extent. Originally developed shortly before World War II as a military instrument for detecting aircraft and ships, it now also serves as an aid for navigating ships and aircraft, mapping storms and other meteorological disturbances, and studying the Moon and nearby planets.—*R. M. P.*

RADAR ASTRONOMY: the study of celestial objects by the use of RADAR echoes. A high-power transmitter sends a beam of radio pulses into space; these pulses are reflected by an object and are detected by sensitive receivers and antennas on Earth. The power of the echo indicates the size of an object and its surface roughness; the time delay between transmission and reception of the echo indicates the distance. Echoes can be obtained from Moon and planets, and also from clouds of ionized gas. Thus a meteor causes a radar echo as the small, solid fragment is heated to incandescence in Earth's atmosphere and produces a column of ionization; the echo from this column tells the direction, velocity, and hence the orbit of the meteor. Radar studies have disclosed meteor streams incident on the daylight side of Earth which were previously unknown to optical astronomers. Meteor echoes also yield data on winds and on air density in the ionospheric regions. The aurora borealis, or northern lights, also reflects radar pulses.

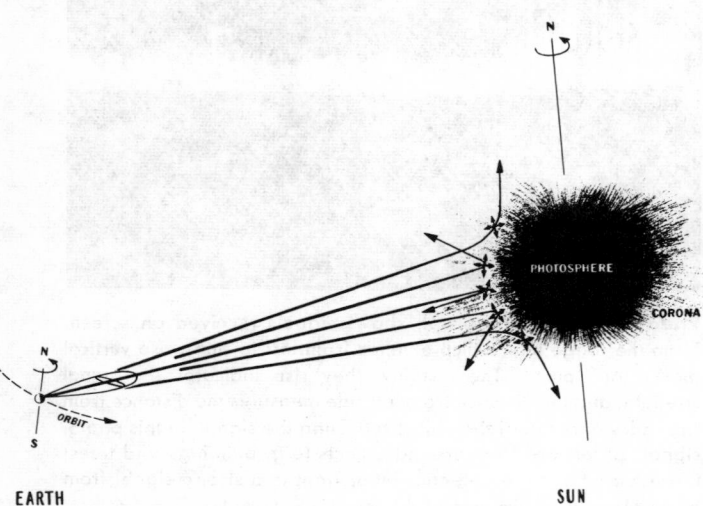

Ionized corona of Sun reflects radar signals from Earth, 93 million miles away. Reflection is irregular, some signals being dispersed in directions other than toward Earth. (M. I. T. Lincoln Lab.)

The distance to the Moon was first determined by this method by radar scientists of the U. S. Army Signal Corps in 1946. The Moon echo comes primarily from a small area at the center of the disc because the Moon behaves as a smooth reflector at radar wavelengths. The Moon echo shows a

Radar installation: M. I. T.'s Millstone Hill radar has made detailed measurements of Moon's surface and has measured distance from Earth to Venus. It has also determined electron density throughout ionosphere. (M. I. T. Lincoln Lab.)

variable amplitude, some of the variation being due to the effects of glinting as mountains and craters assume a favorable aspect, and some variation being caused by the ionosphere of Earth. Radio signals, including voice transmissions, can now be sent around the world by using the Moon as a reflector.

Application of the echo method to Venus and Mercury has yielded the first reliable values for their rotation periods. It has indicated the existence of mountain ranges on Venus. Broadly, it has helped to fix the scale of the solar system.

The Sun's corona is extremely ionized and reflects radar signals with high efficiency. Although echoes have been obtained from the Sun, the task was difficult because of the immense distance (16 min for the round trip) and because the Sun emits radio noise which interferes with reception of the echo. Present techniques do not enable us to obtain echoes from the stars and other objects beyond the solar system.—*G. S. H.*

RADAR WIND OBSERVATION: observation of motions of the atmosphere by means of radar electronic tracking devices. A form of metal target or small radar transmitter is attached to a helium- or hydrogen-filled balloon and released into the

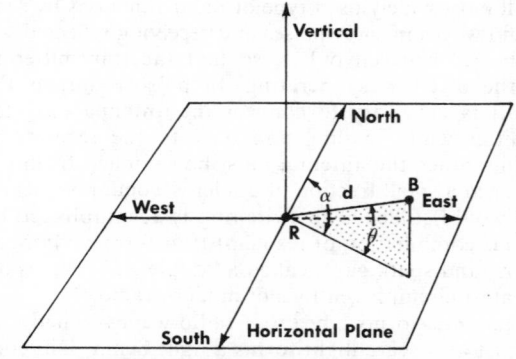

Geometry of radar wind observations: Balloon *B* is observed from radar installation *R*, which measures azimuth angle α, elevation θ, and distance *d* to balloon.

atmosphere. Its flight is followed by a precision, narrow-beam radar which measures, at successive intervals of time, the azimuth and elevation angles of the balloon and its distance from the release point. Trigonometric computation gives the position of the balloon in space. Wind direction and speed at any level are then given by the vector distance traveled by the balloon in a unit interval of time.—*J. C. T.*

RADIAL VELOCITY: in astronomy, the velocity of a celestial body along the line of sight—positive if the star is receding from the observer, negative if the star is approaching. The radial velocity of a star can be measured directly, in mi/sec, from an examination of its spectrum. A normal stellar spectrum shows a continuous rainbow band of color, crossed with dark lines. These are due to particular elements in the star's atmosphere, and can be identified. In many cases the spectrum lines are all shifted systematically (either to the red or to the violet) compared with the same lines observed in the laboratory. Such systematic shifts may be attributed to the DOPPLER EFFECT, whereby the light emitted by an object approaching the observer appears bluer than normal, while a receding object seems redder.

The normal wavelength of a stellar line (λ), the observed wavelength (λ'), and the star's line-of-sight velocity (v) are related: $(\lambda' - \lambda)/\lambda = v/c$, where c is the velocity of light, about 186,300 mi/sec. The observed line-of-sight velocity includes the effect of Earth's orbital motion; to obtain the true radial velocity, measured with respect to the Sun, the motion of Earth toward the star at the time of observation is added to the observed line-of-sight velocity. For accurate work, the velocity is also corrected for the motion of the observer due to the rotation of Earth.

The radial velocities of some 5,000 stars are now known. The most accurate are known to a fraction of a mile per second, but many are only accurate to 1 or 2 mi/sec. Radial velocity is a component of SPACE VELOCITY.—*M. W. O.*

RADIAN: a unit of angular measure; the angle at the center of a circle which intercepts an arc equal in length to the radius. The circumference of a circle of radius r is $2\pi r$. Hence there are 2π radii on the complete circumference, and 2π

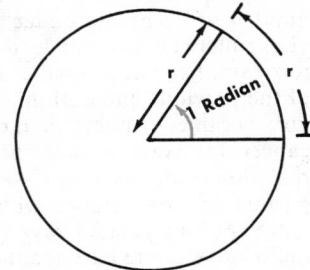

When intercepted arc is equal in length to radius r of the circle, angle at center is 1 radian. A 360° angle has 2π radians.

radians in a complete rotation, or 360°; therefore π radians equals 180°, and 1 radian is approximately 57½°. When the central angle of a circle is measured in radians, the corresponding arc may be measured by its subtended angle, for if the radius is 1, the number of units in the arc is the same as the number of radians in the angle; for any other radius r, the arc is equal to r times the number of radians in the central angle. Because of this intricate connection between the number of radians in an angle and the length of its intercepting arc, the radian is a natural angular unit. Degree measure is more artificial, since a degree is an arbitrary division of a complete rotation. Radian measure is generally employed in calculus because it simplifies many formulas involving trigonometric functions.—*H. C.*

RADIATION: the means by which energy is transferred through space. The three known types of radiation are mechanical, electromagnetic, and nuclear.

Mechanical Radiation: Waves on a water surface and sound passing through matter are examples of mechanical radiation. In each case, the radiation consists of a wave disturbance traveling through a medium. The disturbance originates when the part of the medium adjacent to a moving object is displaced from its equilibrium condition; because every small part of the medium is elastically connected with its neighboring part, the disturbance is transmitted throughout the medium. The object causing the initial disturbance expends energy in doing so, and this energy is propagated through the medium by the waves. For example, some of the energy expended by the diesel engine of a ship is carried away by the waves generated by the ship as it plows through the water. Anyone who has been in a rowboat tossed about by such waves knows the energy they carry.

Electromagnetic Radiation: This consists of traveling waves of electric and magnetic fields, which—unlike mechanical radiation—can travel through a vacuum. Electromagnetic radiation is generated when an electrical charge is accelerated, which may happen in many ways. The radiation travels through space at 186,000 mi/sec, the maximum speed at which energy can be transferred. The most familiar type of electromagnetic radiation is visible light given off by incandescent substances; it is generated by electrons falling from outer to inner orbits in atoms. The frequency of oscillation of the electric and magnetic fields in a light wave is proportional to the energy lost by the electron in making a transition. The wavelength of the light is equal to the velocity of the wave divided by the frequency. The longer wavelength radiation just beyond visible light is called infrared. It is often produced by the vibrational and rotational motions of molecules. Longer still in wavelength are microwaves and radio waves, which are generated by oscillating streams of electrons.

At wavelengths lower (or frequencies higher) than those of visible light are ultraviolet light and x-rays. These arise from very energetic transitions in which an electron falls into an orbit very close to the atomic nucleus, or when fast electrons are stopped on hitting a target. When the protons inside an excited atomic nucleus redistribute themselves into a more stable configuration, energy lost by the nucleus usually is radiated in the form of extremely energetic (and therefore high frequency) electromagnetic radiation, called gamma rays. One of the startling discoveries of the past century—now incorporated in QUANTUM THEORY—is that electromagnetic radiation exhibits wavelike properties under some experimental conditions and behaves like a stream of particles under other conditions. The particle-like behavior of light is most pronounced at the high frequencies of gamma radiation.

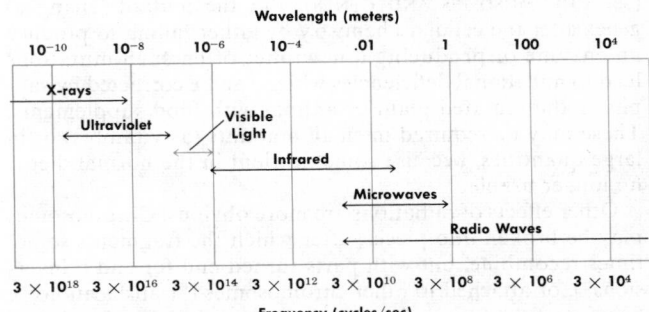

Electromagnetic radiations arranged according to wavelength (or frequency) form spectrum. The entire spectrum, except for the far ends, is shown in this diagram.

Effects of radiation: (1) Chromosomes in cell from anther of trillium are shown normally grouped (*left*) and with abnormal fragmentation and bridging (*right*) incurred upon exposure to x-rays at an earlier stage. (2) Radiation causes mutations in chromosomes. In this trillium cell, exposure to x-rays bent one chromosome into O-shape. (3) Genetic machinery of trillium cell exposed to x-rays went awry. Cell with chromosomes attempted to divide into three cells instead of normal two. (*Brookhaven National Lab.*)

Because atoms in all matter are in continual vibration (the so-called thermal motion), they are continually radiating electromagnetic waves. This "thermal" radiation has a broad range of frequencies corresponding to the continuum of frequencies of the oscillating atoms or molecules. The higher the temperature of a material, the more violent the atomic vibrations, and therefore the higher the average frequency of the thermal radiation. At room temperature the thermal radiation occurs in the infrared and is therefore not visible, but at about 500°C bodies become "red hot" (emitting red light), and at about 2000° they become "white hot" (emitting most of the colors of the visible spectrum). When an object is exposed to thermal radiation, its atoms are forced to oscillate by the varying electric field, and this increased thermal motion heats the object. This is the way we are warmed by sunlight and campfires.

Nuclear Radiation: Both mechanical and electromagnetic radiation transfer energy from one object to another without transferring any matter. When nuclear RADIOACTIVITY was first discovered, the nature of the emanations was unknown, and they were called nuclear radiation. We now know that, in addition to gamma rays, nuclear radiations can include protons, neutrons, alpha particles, and other nuclear fragments of the emitter. See BLACK-BODY RADIATION; ELECTROMAGNETIC WAVE; WAVE AND WAVE MOTION.—*S. K.*

RADIATION GENETICS: a branch of GENETICS that began in 1927 when Dr. H. J. Muller, then of the Univ. of Texas, discovered that by treating fruit flies with x-rays at the time when their reproductive cells were being formed, he could increase the rate of MUTATION. The discovery, which won a Nobel prize for Muller in 1946, speeded up progress in research on inheritance. One effect of radiation is to cause *gene* mutations, which make no visible change in any chromosome (see CHROMOSOMES AND GENES). But the mutant (changed) genes alter the cellular chemistry by either failing to produce an enzyme or producing a new one; often such mutations lead to nutritional deficiencies which can be corrected by supplying the mutated plant or animal with food supplements. These may be required in small amounts (as vitamins) or in large quantities, because some nutrient in the normal diet is no longer usable.

Other effects of radiations are more obvious. Chromosomes may be broken into pieces, after which the fragments sometimes recombine, but with parts turned end for end ("inversions"), or attached to other chromosomes ("translocations"), or left to float free in the cytoplasm at cell division and then lost to the genetic machinery ("deficiencies"). In animals, many of these drastic changes in chromosomes are fatal to any offspring or cause incurable deformities, while others are successful. Radiation geneticists are much concerned over the harmful effects on human heredity caused by exposure to high-energy radiations from radioactive materials now being used and distributed in increasing amounts. See HEREDITY; RADIATION HAZARDS.—*L. and M. M.*

RADIATION HAZARDS: the harmful effects to which living organisms are susceptible if exposed to x-rays, gamma rays, or other penetrating radiation. There is considerable controversy as to both the "permissible" exposure and the extent of harm inflicted on biological systems. This controversy stems largely from the fact that each of a number of persons can be exposed to the same amount of radiation, yet the effect on one individual may differ surprisingly from the effect on another. Furthermore, there are significant differences from one individual to another in the amount of radioactive material that is retained in the body system. The discovery of x-rays in 1895 and of radioactivity in 1896 made penetrating radiation a new feature of man's environment: within months scientists learned that x-rays and radioactive rays could injure living cells and produce profound biological effects. Excessive exposure produced serious radiation burns as well as delayed effects. Death was the ultimate consequence of overexposure. During the first decades of the 20th cent. a number of scientists and technicians working with x-ray devices suffered injury and death as a result of repeated exposure to x-rays. Each additional dose of x-rays added to the effects of the previous one until finally, often many years later, injury became manifest in the individual. Various forms of cancer, for example, were produced by x-rays. Penetrating radiation eludes the human sense organs—a man may receive a lethal dose of radiation without feeling it.

X-rays and gamma rays (emitted by radium and other radioactive atoms) are identical. Their effect upon tissue is measured in terms of the *roentgen* (r) unit. A dose of 500 r is generally taken as lethal in man, *i.e.* it produces death in 50% of those so irradiated. Death occurs within one month. Higher doses produce death more quickly. Doses of 200 r produce radiation sickness from which recovery usually occurs. Everyone is exposed to constant bombardment from natural sources of radioactivity in Earth's crust and atmosphere, and from cosmic rays. Furthermore, every person contains a small amount of radioactivity taken into the body from food and water. As a result the average person living at sea level is exposed to 0.1 r per yr or 7 r throughout a normal lifetime. To this normal background of radiation is added radiation from man-made sources. In the U. S. A. the use of x-rays in modern medicine adds several roentgens to the individual's lifetime dose. Radioactive fall-out from nuclear tests (through July 1962) will add up to 0.5 r to the dose of Americans.

There are two distinct types of biological effects. First is the *genetic* effect or injury to the germ plasm. Low levels of radiation produce genetic MUTATIONS or alterations in heredity which may then appear in future generations. Such radiation-induced genetic defects are of the same kind as occur naturally in a few per cent of human births. Therefore, any increase in human defects due to radiation will be hidden among those that occur naturally. But there is no doubt that a genetic effect takes place at low levels of radiation. The second type of radiation injury is known as *somatic,* meaning that the effect is produced in an individual's body cells as opposed to his sex cells. There is no question about somatic effect at high levels of radiation, but as one reduces the dose to a few roentgens or less, the experimental data are ambiguous. Some experts believe that there is a certain dose or threshold below which no somatic effect takes place. Others hold that any dose, however small, produces some biological effect. This uncertainty as to the effect of low levels of radiation complicates and confuses the fall-out issue. However, it has become clear that the increased use of x-rays, the growing waste products from atomic power plants, and widespread applications of radioactivity in industry all require adequate public control. The U. S. A. has recognized this problem by creating a Federal Radiation Council to establish policy and to formulate proper standards for radiation controls. The U. S. Public Health Service is charged with responsibility for surveying radiation hazards. For the average population, the Federal Radiation Council has recommended that the yearly whole-body exposure not exceed 0.17 r and that the 30-yr value be less than 5 r exclusive of the dose due to natural background. Somewhat larger amounts of radiation are set as limits for occupational exposure. These limits apply to external radiation, *e.g.* x-rays striking the body from an external source. The situation with respect to internal hazards is more complex; some radioactive materials have a long residence time in the body, *e.g.* radium, which "locks" itself in the bone, while others are eliminated quickly. Some have very short radioactive persistence (*i.e.* short HALF-LIFE) and thus differ in toxicity from radioactive species with longer half-lives. Radium, for example, loses half its activity in 1,600 yr. In addition, the character of the radiation emitted by various atoms may differ widely in its effective range in tissue and in its destructive power. Human experience with internal radioactive hazards is based upon studies of radium damage to the bodies of radium-dial painters. Follow-up studies, some stretching over 40 yr, have been made on several hundred individuals. These data provide the basis for setting 0.1 microgram of radium, *i.e.* about 3 billionths of an ounce of radium, as the body burden. Obviously, when such tiny amounts of material are involved, extreme precautions must be taken to safeguard against radioactive hazards.

Since harmful radiation eludes human senses, reliance must be placed upon special instruments to detect and measure radiation, *e.g.* Geiger counters, ionization chambers, and crystal counters. A new professional worker—the health physicist—uses these instruments and interprets radiation hazards in order to protect personnel from overexposure to damaging radiation.

Radiation hazards are present in space also. Earth is embraced by the Van Allen radiation belt. Anyone traversing this region will be exposed to significant radiation. In addition, our Sun is known to be somewhat capricious, and periodically emits bursts of penetrating radiation which could be dangerous to the unshielded space traveler.—*R. La.*

RADIATION UNITS: standards for measuring the intensity of radiation emitted by radioactive nuclei, and for measuring the effects of radiation on materials. The curie measures the rate at which radioactive material emits radiation. If 3.7 $(10)^{10}$ of its nuclei disintegrate in 1 sec, a sample has an activity of 1 curie. (Each nuclear disintegration involves the emission of electromagnetic radiation and/or electrons or fragments of the nucleus.) Knowing the nature of the emitted particles and the activity of a sample, one can calculate the radiation effects on the surroundings. The *roentgen* is a measure of the "dosage"—*i.e.* energy deposited—in a region through which nuclear radiation has passed. When the electrically charged, subatomic particles produced by radioactive nuclei pass through a medium, they knock many electrons out of atoms along their paths. The number of atoms with missing electrons (ions) can be measured by several techniques, and is proportional to the total energy deposited. If 2.08 $(10)^9$ ions are produced in 1 cm^3 of air, the dosage is 1 roentgen. A typical dental x-ray delivers 5 roentgens to one's jaw. Since ionization within biological cells can kill the cells, strict standards have been set for dosages.—*S. K.*

Other radiation dosage units have been based on the energy absorption (93 ergs/gram of tissue) corresponding to the irradiation of body tissue by one roentgen of x-radiation. For example, the roentgen equivalent physical (rep) unit, now obsolete, corresponds to energy absorption of 93 ergs/ gram by tissue through which ionizing radiation passes. The *rad* has replaced the rep unit (1 rad $=100/93$ rep) and corresponds to energy absorption of 100 ergs/gram of body tissue. *Relative biological effectiveness* (rbe) is a weighting factor, equal to unity for x-rays, that expresses how much more or less effectively a given radiation produces biological effects than do x-rays of the same rad. In assigning an rbe number many biological effects must be considered, and values are not yet well established in man. The *roentgen equivalent mammal* (rem) unit, defined originally in terms of the rep, is the amount of any given radiation producing the same biological effect as one rep of x-rays. The current definition is 1 rem $=$ $[1/(rbe)]$ rad; but this is for practical purposes unchanged from the former definition because of the small difference ($< 10\%$) between the rep and rad units.—*P. T. D. and F. J. E.*

RADICAL: a combination of atoms that react chemically as single atoms. Thus, one can convert methyl chloride, CH_3Cl, to methyl alcohol, CH_3OH, to dimethyl sulfate, $(CH_3)_2SO_4$, without altering the methyl radical, CH_3; in this example, the hydroxyl, or alcohol, OH, and sulfate, SO_4, are also radicals. Other common radicals are carbonate (CO_3), bicarbonate (HCO_3), sulfite (SO_3), nitrate (NO_3), nitrite (NO_2), phosphate (PO_4), ammonium (NH_4), cyanide (CN), ethyl (C_2H_5), and glyceryl (C_3H_5). A few radicals, such as carbonyl (CO) and triphenylmethyl ($(C_6H_5)_3C$), exist in the free state. It is sometimes convenient to refer to an atom like chlorine, Cl, as a radical, especially when it is a *free radical* (see CHEMICAL BOND). Some radicals are quite complex, but familiarity with the radicals in chemistry assists greatly in CHEMICAL NOMENCLATURE; for that purpose lists of radicals and their names are published by the American Chemical Society. Two-part names are generally based on the radicals present; *e.g.* methyl acetate, CH_3COOCH_3, is a combination of the acetate radical, CH_3COO, and methyl radical, CH_3. Radicals usually retain their structural identity when certain of their atoms are replaced by other atoms; thus, in methyl chloroacetate, $ClCH_2COOCH_3$, replacement of an H atom in the acetate radical by a Cl atom does not alter the general nature of the acetate radical. The link between radicals is the covalence bond, just as it is between atoms; *e.g.* the formula of a molecule of methyl chloride, $Cl:CH_3$, resembles that of a molecule of chlorine, $Cl:Cl.$—*Ru. M.*

RADIO: an electrical system that uses electromagnetic energy for sending information through space. The portion of the electromagnetic spectrum used by radio is divided by convention into several frequency bands, as shown in the accompanying table.

CONVENTIONAL RADIO FREQUENCY BANDS

Title and Code	Frequency	Wavelength
Very Low Frequency (VLF)	below 30 Kc/sec	above 10,000 m
Low Frequency (LF)	30-300 Kc/sec	1000-10,000 m
Medium Frequency (MF)	300-3000 Kc/sec	100-1000 m
High Frequency (HF)	3-30 Mc/sec	10-100 m
Very High Frequency (VHF)	30-300 Mc/sec	1-10 m
Ultra High Frequency (UHF)	300-3000 Mc/sec	10-100 cm
Super High Frequency (SHF)	3-30 Kmc/sec	1-10 cm
Extremely High Frequency (EHF)	above 30 Kmc/sec	below 1 cm

The frequencies are generated by electrical OSCILLATORS, which usually employ vacuum tubes, TRANSISTORS, diodes, or equivalent devices. (See ELECTRON TUBE.) The energy is radiated into space (transmitted) and collected from space (received) by radio ANTENNAS.

Modulation: Conventionally an electrical oscillator generates a single frequency, called the *carrier*. Being a single frequency, its wave form is necessarily sinusoidal. Information is put on the carrier by changing one or more of its three characteristics—amplitude, frequency, and phase—by the process called MODULATION. Modulation causes the carrier to depart from its pure sinusoidal wave form and produce other frequencies, called sidebands, close to the carrier frequency and symmetrically disposed above and below it. The frequency spectrum occupied by the sidebands is called the modulation band width.

The most primitive form of modulation is turning the carrier on and off with a telegraph key, *e.g.* to make the dots and dashes of the international Morse code. However, the most commonly used forms of modulation are amplitude (AM) and frequency modulation (FM) (see RADIO BROADCASTING). A particularly useful form for radio relay is pulse-code modulation. Radio relay is used for long-range, point-to-point communication circuits, in which line-of-sight frequencies are used, and a series of stations are so located that each one can "see" the next one. Each station receives the signal from the next station on one side, and retransmits the signal to the next one on the other side. With amplitude or frequency modulation, each transmission adds a little noise to the signal, so limiting the number of stations that can be used. In pulse-code modulation, all pulses are sent at the same amplitude, and pulse position or timing is modulated, so each station sends new, noise-free pulses, even though the received pulses are degraded by static and other noise.

Transmitting and Receiving: In radio transmitting, the carrier is usually generated and modulated at the relatively low power level of a few watts. The modulated carrier is then amplified with vacuum tubes to high power levels, sometimes many kilo-

watts, and radiated from the transmitting antenna in the form of radio waves. In receiving, the radio waves are picked up by the receiving antenna, along with static and other unwanted electrical signals, and fed at low levels, often only a small fraction of a microwatt, to the receiver input.

The radio receiver performs four functions. It (1) separates out the desired modulated carrier from all the unwanted signals; (2) amplifies the weak received signal up to usable power levels; (3) extracts the modulation signal from the carrier; and (4) presents in desired form the information in the modulation signal. In addition, the receiver "inadvertently" adds its own noise to the signal, since all electrical circuits generate electrical signals from the thermal motion of molecules. This is called "thermal noise," and is related to the temperature of the circuit. The *sensitivity* of a radio receiver is its capacity to receive low-energy signals, and is limited only by its own thermal noise at the input. It is expressed in terms of noise power per cycle of band width, or, alternately, in terms of noise temperature. A receiver's *selectivity* is its ability to separate the desired signal from unwanted signals. This is accomplished with tuned or resonant circuits, which pass only certain selected frequencies, and reject all others. Resonant circuits are characterized by frequency and band width, *i.e.* they must be tuned to the signal frequency and have just sufficient band width to pass the modulation. Additional band width would pass additional noise without helping the signal. Only those unwanted signals whose frequency lies within the pass band of the receiver will remain to interfere with the desired signal. In special cases even part of this noise can be rejected, by such means as time resolution (radar), amplitude limiting (frequency modulation), or time discrimination (cross-correlation processes). Extraction of the modulation signal from the carrier is called *detection*. For amplitude modulation the detector is merely a RECTIFIER that converts the modulated carrier to direct current. The modulation then appears as variation in a direct current, which is the electrical form of the original modulation signal at the transmitter. For frequency modulation the detector is a discriminator whose direct current is proportional to the frequency of the input. This also reproduces the modulation signal at the transmitter. Presentation of the information may be by head phone, loudspeaker, graphic recorder, cathode-ray indicator, meter, or control device.

Radio transmitters must be kept on their assigned carrier frequencies. If their frequencies were not accurately controlled, receivers would not stay "in tune," and transmitters on adjacent frequency channels might drift too close together and interfere with each other. Accurate frequency control is obtained by use of a piezoelectric crystal. Such a crystal will

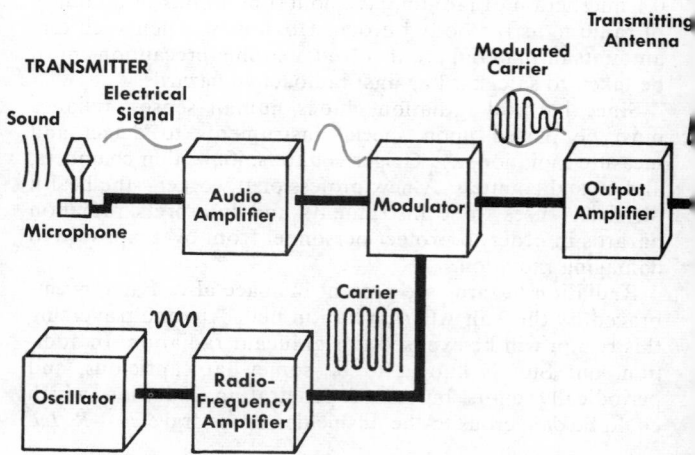

deform slightly when placed in an electric field, *e.g.* the field produced between two condenser plates, and when deformed will produce voltages across its edges. When voltages so produced are amplified and made to generate the electric field to deform the crystal, the crystal will oscillate mechanically at the resonant frequency determined by its size and shape, and continuously generate an alternating electrical voltage at the same frequency. Quartz and tourmaline crystals are most used for this purpose. High mechanical stability, enhanced by close control of temperature, results in very stable frequency generation. (See PIEZOELECTRIC EFFECT.)

Propagation of Radio Waves: The propagation of radio waves is influenced by many factors in Earth's environment. In the high upper atmosphere, the air is ionized, or separated into positive ions and negative electrons, by x-rays and ultraviolet light from the Sun. This ionized air, known as the Kennelly-Heaviside layer, or IONOSPHERE, acts like a half-silvered mirror to frequencies below about 30 Mc/sec, reflecting much of the radio energy back to the ground and allowing only part of it to pass through into space. Energy thus reflected back to the ground is reflected at Earth's surface and bounced back up to the ionosphere again. These repeated reflections enable the radio waves to travel all the way around the Earth, sometimes going around several times before becoming too faint to record. This type of propagation skips over large distances (skip zones) between reflections at Earth's surface.

Although UHF and VHF radio waves appear generally to travel in straight lines, they are faintly scattered back to the ground for great distances beyond the horizon. This scattering (termed tropospheric forward-scatter propagation) is thought to be caused by turbulence in the upper atmosphere, or troposphere, which would tend to produce random inhomogeneity in propagation velocity.

The velocity of radio waves in air is influenced by atmospheric moisture. There is frequently a detectable change in moisture at some height above the ground, usually between 3,000 and 6,000 ft, with dry air above the given altitude and moist air below. This condition causes radio waves to bend downward at that altitude and follow Earth's curvature, staying trapped in the boundary layer. The boundary then acts as a duct for conducting radio waves, and is called an elevated duct. Sometimes a similar boundary layer exists much closer to Earth's surface, and radio waves even above UHF become trapped between this layer and Earth's surface, enabling the waves to travel great distances. Meteors leave ionized trails in the atmosphere which persist for a fraction of a second. There are enough meteors to make it possible to design radio systems using *meteor trails* to reflect the waves

over the horizon. Another recent discovery is that charged particles from ionized air and from the Sun interact with Earth's magnetic field and appear to form guide paths for VLF waves along the magnetic lines of force. These paths seem to guide the radio waves in great loops, reaching out perhaps several Earth radii and returning again to the Earth, where the waves bounce back along the same magnetic path to the point of origin. This is called the *whistler* mode of propagation, since the signals by which it was discovered sound like descending-pitch whistles. Radio signals are also directed against the Moon, which reflects the signals back to any point on Earth where the Moon at that time is visible. Similarly, radio communication has been achieved by reflecting radio signals off artificial satellites (*e.g.* Echo) and more recently by utilizing satellites with built-in repeater systems (Telstar).

CHRONOLOGY OF RADIO

1832   Michael Faraday postulated the electromagnetic field.

1865   Mahlon Loomis made and named first radio "aerial," transmitted a radio frequency transient 18 mi.

1873   James Clerk Maxwell theoretically predicted the existence and behavior of radio waves.

1879   D. E. Hughes generated radio waves over a distance of 100 yd.

1886   Heinrich Hertz experimentally demonstrated that radio waves behave like light waves.

1894   Oliver Lodge demonstrated first radio-communication system.

1901   G. Marconi achieved transatlantic communication with a long wavelength.

1902   A. E. Kennelly and O. Heaviside postulated the ionosphere.

1904   J. A. Fleming invented the thermionic diode.

1905   Lee DeForest invented the vacuum-tube triode.

1912   E. H. Armstrong and DeForest independently invented the regenerative circuit.

1919   A. H. Taylor and L. C. Young inaugurated a regularly scheduled broadcast, weekly, to study high-frequency propagation.

1920   Frank Conrad inaugurated first daily-scheduled radio broadcast for public entertainment, which provided a public market for broadcast receivers and became station KDKA.

1921   P. F. Godley accomplished first transatlantic reception of short waves (270 m).

1923   L. Deloy, J. L. Reinartz, and H. Schnell achieved first two-way transatlantic communication on short waves (100 m).

1924   Reinartz and Taylor established existence of skip zone, assuming an ionosphere mechanism.

1924   Sir Edward Appleton and M. A. F. Barnett confirmed ionosphere and measured its height indirectly with continuous-wave, point-to-point transmission.

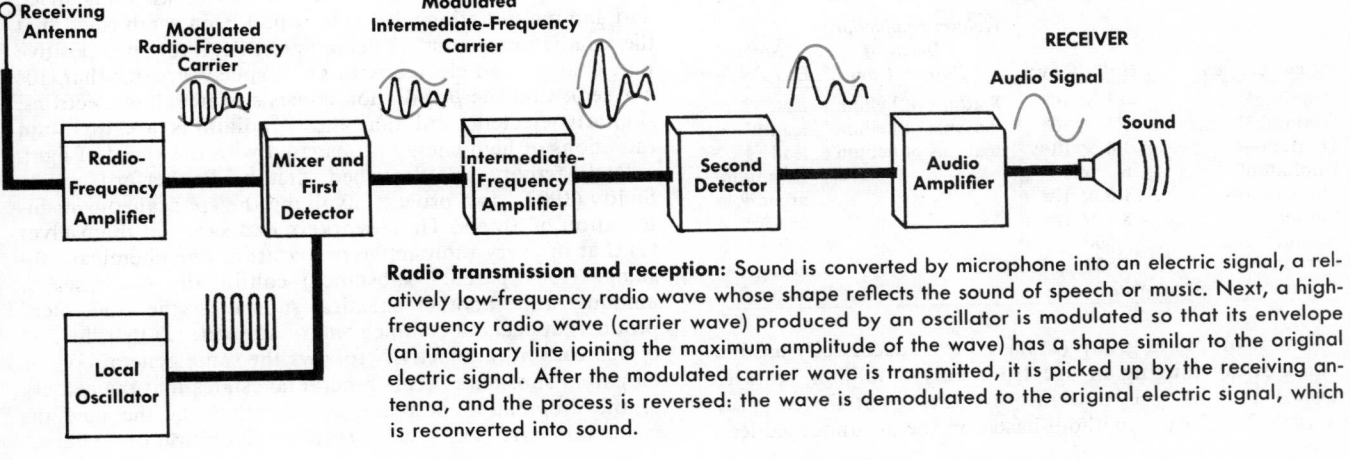

Radio transmission and reception: Sound is converted by microphone into an electric signal, a relatively low-frequency radio wave whose shape reflects the sound of speech or music. Next, a high-frequency radio wave (carrier wave) produced by an oscillator is modulated so that its envelope (an imaginary line joining the maximum amplitude of the wave) has a shape similar to the original electric signal. After the modulated carrier wave is transmitted, it is picked up by the receiving antenna, and the process is reversed: the wave is demodulated to the original electric signal, which is reconverted into sound.

1924   Taylor, Young, and L. A. Gebhard constructed first radio transmitter with frequency controlled by piezoelectric quartz crystals.

1925   G. Breit, M. A. Tuve, and Taylor measured ionosphere height directly with pulsed radio signals, using quartz-crystal-controlled transmitter.

1922–1940   Development of RADAR.

1946   M. Katzin and C. L. Pekeris discovered tropospheric forward-scatter propagation and explained it by atmospheric turbulence.

1950–51   Development of high-power klystron enabled exploitation of tropospheric forward-scatter propagation for communication.

1953   J. H. Trexler discovered lunar reflection band width to be adequate for voice communication.

1959   D. L. Ringwalt observed and verified elevated duct propagation and explained the responsible mechanism.

—*R. M. P.*

RADIOACTIVE DATING: the use of radioactive isotopes that occur naturally on Earth to determine the period of time that has elapsed since certain events in Earth's history. All RADIOISOTOPES have a characteristic rate of decay, and it is believed this rate has not changed since the formation of Earth. When atoms of a radioactive element decay, atoms of a new element are formed; thus, if the rate of decay of a given radioisotope in a sample is known and the resulting amount of new element can be determined, the age of the sample can be computed. The amount of new element corresponds to the amount of movement of the hands of a clock.

Radioisotopes that occur naturally on Earth (see RADIOACTIVITY) include (1) those of long half-life that have been present since the formation of Earth; (2) those that are being continually produced by the decay of other radioisotopes; (3) those produced by reactions between cosmic rays and stable isotopes. Most useful in group (1) are uranium^{235} and uranium^{238}, thorium^{232}, potassium^{40}, and rubidium^{87}; in group (2) ionium (thorium^{230}) and radium; in group (3) carbon^{14} and tritium (hydrogen^3). Isotopes in group (1) must have half-lives of the order of thousands of millions of years, or they would have decayed away completely since the formation of Earth. Isotopes in groups (2) and (3) may have shorter half-lives, for they are continually being produced, and this process balances the loss by decay. Some of the main characteristics of the isotopes mentioned above are shown in the table.

CHARACTERISTICS OF ISOTOPES USEFUL
IN RADIOACTIVE DATING

Parent Element	Half-life (yr)	Helium Production by Decay of 1 Parent Atom	Stable End Product
Uranium^{238}	4.5×10^9	8 atoms of helium	lead^{206}
Uranium^{235}	7.1×10^8	7 atoms of helium	lead^{207}
Thorium^{232}	1.4×10^{10}	6 atoms of helium	lead^{208}
Rubidium^{87}	6×10^{10}		strontium^{87}
Potassium^{40}	1.8×10^9		argon^{40}
Ionium	8×10^4		lead^{206}
Radium	1,600		lead^{206}
Carbon^{14}	5,600		nitrogen^{14}
Tritium	12.5		helium^3

Radioisotopes in group (1) have been successfully used in dating rocks ranging in age from only a million years to several billions (see GEOCHRONOLOGY; GEOLOGICAL TIME CHART). The "lead" method, based on the accumulated lead isotopes in uranium and thorium minerals, gives good results in carefully selected minerals that contained very little lead at the time of formation. The "helium" method is based on helium produced in uranium and thorium minerals; its limitation is the escape of helium from the rock over millions of years. Potassium and rubidium methods are still being further developed; the former especially may eventually prove the most accurate, where it is applicable. In many cases, several methods can be applied to the same sample and thus furnish independent checks.

Ionium and radium, in group (2), are proving useful for determining the chronology of sediments on the floor of the ocean. Carbon^{14} and tritium, in group (3), which are produced in the atmosphere by cosmic rays, also are useful. Carbon^{14} enters into the life cycle of all living matter, but this process ceases on death. Accordingly, the proportion of carbon^{14} to ordinary carbon^{12} (which is a known constant for living matter) remaining in the sample is a measure of the time that has elapsed since death occurred. The method may be applied to a wide variety of materials including parchment, wood, cloth, glue, and animal or human remains; it has made possible valuable archeological and geological dating of events within the last 40,000 yr. Carbon^{14} is distributed also throughout the carbon of the oceans and so may be used for studies of ocean circulation. Since tritium mixes with water in the atmosphere, on the land, and in the surface ocean, it may be used for dating water samples up to 50 yr and for identifying rainwater as such.—*G. J. F.*

RADIOACTIVITY: the property, exhibited by certain types of matter, of emitting energy spontaneously. This energy, which is emitted from the individual atoms of the radioactive material, can appear as the kinetic energy of particles or as the energy of quantum radiations. For historical reasons the distinction is frequently made between "natural" radioactivity and "artificial" radioactivity. Some radioactive substances occur "naturally" in Earth's crust; in more recent years, many more such substances have been produced "artificially" in the laboratory. Essentially, there is no difference between these two manifestations of radioactivity.

Natural radioactivity was discovered first by H. Becquerel (1896). Becquerel was led to his discovery while investigating the phosphorescence of certain compounds of uranium. He found that uranium metal and all its compounds, whether phosphorescent or not, emit a "dark" radiation spontaneously, in an amount proportional to the number of uranium atoms in the preparation. E. Rutherford (1899) identified two distinct components in this radiation, and P. Villard (1900) identified a third. In order of increasing penetrating power, these component radiations are referred to as alpha, beta, and gamma radiations. By 1910 it had been established that the α-radiation consists of helium atoms carrying two positive unit charges and ejected with great speed (greater than 10^9 cm/sec); that the β-radiation consists of negative electrons, similarly ejected; and that the γ-radiations are quantum radiations of high energy propagated with the speed of light.

Radioactivity was described, first by Rutherford and F. Soddy (1903), as a process involving the spontaneous disintegration of atoms. These workers had satisfied themselves (1) that in every radioactive preparation one chemical substance (the "parent" substance) continually decreases in amount, while another chemical substance (the "daughter" product) appears in complementary amount; (2) that the rate of decrease of radioactivity follows the same general law for all parent substances. This general law states that the activity of the preparation decreases exponentially as the time increases linearly. The law leads to the definition of a characteristic time, the HALF-LIFE, which has a different value for each parent substance.

Natural radioactivity is confined, with a few exceptions, to those chemical elements having ATOMIC NUMBERS between 81 and 92 inclusive. Obviously, for any radioactive substance to remain as a constituent of the Earth's crust at the present stage of cosmic evolution, either it must be itself a substance of very great half-life or it must be a radioactive daughter product that is continually being produced by a very long-lived parent. It is now known that only three of the naturally occurring radioactive substances of atomic number greater than 80 are very long lived in this sense: thorium^{232} (half-life 1.4×10^{10} yr), uranium^{238} (half-life 4.5×10^9 yr), and uranium^{235} (half-life 7.1×10^8 yr). All others (some 40, in all) are daughter products of successive "generations," deriving from one of these three.

When the nuclear atom model was adopted, following its formulation by Rutherford (1911), it rapidly became evident that the phenomenon of radioactivity is to be ascribed to the atomic nucleus. We now say that a radioactive nucleus may emit an α-particle (helium nucleus) or, in another case, a β-particle (negative electron), and that in some circumstances it may also emit a quantum (or quanta) or γ-radiation. Because the α-particle carries a positive charge of two units, the daughter product resulting from α-emission has an atomic number of two less than the atomic number of the parent. Similarly, after β-emission, the daughter product has an atomic number of one more than that of the parent. This is essentially the "displacement law," put forward independently by various workers (1913). An example of each type of emission is represented schematically as follows:

$$\text{Radium} \begin{pmatrix} 226 \\ 88 \end{pmatrix} \rightarrow \text{Emanation} \begin{pmatrix} 222 \\ 86 \end{pmatrix} + \alpha \begin{pmatrix} 4 \\ 2 \end{pmatrix}$$

$$\text{Radium E} \begin{pmatrix} 210 \\ 83 \end{pmatrix} \rightarrow \text{Polonium} \begin{pmatrix} 210 \\ 84 \end{pmatrix} + \beta \begin{pmatrix} 0 \\ -1 \end{pmatrix}$$

In the brackets, the upper figure is the mass number, and the lower figure the atomic number, of the RADIOISOTOPE. Note that the mass number of the β-particle (electron) is given as zero. This is not an approximation representing the small mass of the electron; MASS NUMBER is essentially an integer. The emission of a β-particle does not (according to accepted views) alter the number of particles in the nucleus: the β-particle is itself "created" in a process in which a neutron in the nucleus changes spontaneously into a proton:

$$\text{Neutron} \begin{pmatrix} 1 \\ 0 \end{pmatrix} \rightarrow \text{Proton} \begin{pmatrix} 1 \\ 1 \end{pmatrix} + \beta \begin{pmatrix} 0 \\ -1 \end{pmatrix}$$

See, however, NEUTRINO.

The first example of artificial radioactivity was discovered by I. Curie and F. Joliot (1934). Since that time every process that has been used to produce nuclear transmutation (see TRANSMUTATION OF ELEMENTS; NUCLEAR PHYSICS) has provided the means of producing many hundreds of different NUCLIDES which do not occur naturally in Earth's crust. These nuclides are almost invariably found to be radioactive. Many α-emitting nuclides so produced have atomic numbers in the ranges 60 to 65 and 83 to 101 (elements of atomic number greater than 92 are referred to as transuranic elements), but the majority of artificially produced nuclides of any atomic number less than 83 are electron emitters. Of these by far the largest single group, classified in respect to mode of production, is the FISSION PRODUCTS.

It is more appropriate to refer to artificially radioactive nuclides as "electron emitters" rather than "β emitters," because although some of these nuclides emit negative electrons, others emit positive electrons (see POSITRON). Indeed,

there is a third class of electron-active nuclide in which transformation takes place when the nucleus captures a negative electron from the extranuclear system of the atom. These two types of radionuclide, positron-emitters and capture-active species, were first discovered among the products of artificial transmutation of stable nuclei; they are scarcely ever found among the naturally occurring radioelements. In spite of this apparent distinction, however, it must be emphasized that there is no fundamental difference between the three types of electron activity that an unstable nucleus may exhibit.—*N. F.*

RADIO ASTRONOMY: the study of radio radiation emitted by celestial objects. The possibility of receiving radio waves from the Sun was first suggested by Thomas Alva Edison in 1890. No success was obtained until 1932, when Karl Jansky detected radiation, not from the Sun but from the center of our galaxy. The first RADIO TELESCOPE was built soon after by Grote Reber, in Illinois. Since World War II progress has been very rapid, at first in the Netherlands, England, and Australia, and now in the U. S. A. and the U. S. S. R.

Radio waves that reach the surface of Earth are several millimeters to tens of meters in length. Some radio sources have been identified with optical objects; these include Sun, Moon, four planets, and a small number of stars, nebulas, and galaxies. Many sources have no corresponding optical radiation, and radio studies thus serve to complement and extend optical observation.

In the Sun, regions near the visible photosphere emit short-wave radiation; regions of the corona within a solar radius from the photosphere emit long waves. The Sun has two kinds of activity. When there are few sunspots and no flares, it is "quiet"; the radio emission is comparatively steady and its intensity is related to the temperature (a million degrees for the corona). Slow changes occur as the presence of sunspots modifies the state of the solar atmosphere. However, violent activity occurs in association with sunspots and solar flares. A characteristic of sunspot radiation is a rapid change in intensity, resulting in bursts lasting a few seconds. Outbursts lasting several minutes are associated with flares. Bursts

Map of neutral-hydrogen clouds as detected by a radio telescope: Numbers on clouds indicate velocities of approach in km/sec. Cross-hatching indicates peak-brightness temperatures in excess of 2°K. Grid shows galactic longitude and latitude. (North galactic pole is located in the constellation Coma Berenices.) (*Ohio State-Ohio Wesleyan Observatory*)

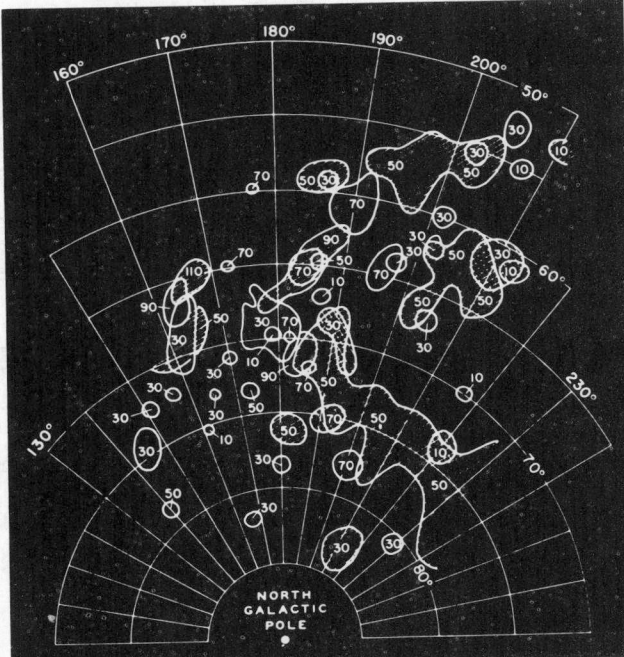

and outbursts often start at short wavelengths and drift to long, indicating that the particles causing the disturbance are moving outward through the solar atmosphere. The burst velocities are of the order of the velocity of light; the outburst velocities, about 1,000 km/sec.

Radiation from Moon, Venus, Mars, and Saturn is indicative of the surface temperature. (No other measurement of the temperature of Venus has been possible, since the planet is surrounded by clouds.) In addition to thermal radiation, Jupiter emits two other kinds. One is a steady radiation at decimeter wavelengths, which is partly linearly polarized and appears to come from a belt at two or three radii from the visible surface. The belt is probably similar to Earth's outer Van Allen belt, and the radiation is caused by electrons trapped in the planet's magnetic field. The other type of radiation occurs at long meter wavelengths and consists of groups of short bursts. These appear to originate from distinct areas on the surface of the planet and may occur some days after solar disturbances.

A radio telescope of low resolving power detects a broad band of radio emission across the sky which roughly corresponds to the visible Milky Way. With telescopes of higher resolving power this band partly breaks up into a number of discrete sources. In regions where absence of interstellar obscuring clouds permits optical investigation, these sources are found to correspond to either emission nebulas (ionized hydrogen surrounding very hot stars) or what are probably remnants of stellar explosions or supernovas. The most famous is the Crab Nebula, the remnants of an explosion recorded by the Chinese in A. D. 1054. Both the light and the radio waves from it are partly polarized. The most intense galactic source is at the nucleus of the galaxy, where extreme physical conditions exist.

Radio emission from a number of nearby galaxies, including the Andromeda Nebula and the Magellanic Clouds, has been detected. This emission is at a level comparable to that of our own galaxy; however, some rare galaxies emit up to 10^8 times as much. The first radio source discovered was finally tracked down to a system some 6×10^8 lt-yr distant. Another radio source led to the discovery of a cluster of galaxies at a distance of 6×10^9 lt-yr—by far the most distant object known. Many radio galaxies are at such distances, and it is possible that their study will reveal evolutionary effects in the universe. Such effects are claimed by some observers, but the evidence is challenged by others.

The most important line so far detected in the radio spectrum is the 21-cm line of atomic hydrogen. It is highly useful because interstellar hydrogen cannot normally be detected by optical means. The received wavelength depends on the relative velocity of source and observer; thus because of the non-rigid rotation of the galaxy the received line is widened and often split into several components representing concentrations of hydrogen at different distances. From such observations a fairly complete picture of the spiral structure of our galaxy has been developed. Near the center of the galaxy the gas is found to be in highly turbulent motion, and further out there is a steady outward motion of about one solar mass per year. Similar 21-cm studies of the Magellanic Clouds have revealed their motions and the total gas mass. The line has also been detected in several other nearby galaxies. The helium atom and the hydroxyl radical (OH), too, have been observed.—*J. G. Bo.*

RADIO BROADCASTING: a one-way communications medium employing spatial radiant energy to transmit mass program material (as distinct from special-purpose messages) from a central point to receivers scattered over a broad area. Broadcast studios are equipped with MICROPHONES to pick up speech and music or other sounds, controls for adjusting signal levels, and TRANSMITTERS and ANTENNAS for radiating the signals to distant RECEIVERS. Frequently the transmitter is situated several miles from the studios and connected to them by radio link or wire lines. A substantial proportion of radio broadcasting today involves regional or national networks, in which a single program source is linked over wire or microwave telephone circuits to a number of outlet stations, each broadcasting throughout a local area.

Two principal techniques are used in radio broadcasting. The more common is amplitude modulation, or AM, in which speech and music are conveyed by variations in the amplitude, or strength, of the transmitted signal. The second method, more recently developed, is frequency modulation, or FM, in which the frequency of the transmitted signal varies in accordance with the pattern of speech and music, while the amplitude remains constant. (See MODULATION.) Each technique requires its own type of receiving circuit, but many commercial home radio receivers today are equipped for both AM and FM program reception.

The great number of broadcasting stations in operation (about 3,600 AM and 1,000 FM stations in the U. S. A. as of 1961) makes it necessary to allocate definite wavelengths for the use of each station to prevent jamming. In the U. S. A., this allocation is set by the Federal Communications Commission; international allocations are set by the International Telecommunications Union and other bodies. Standard AM broadcasting in the U. S. A. employs the frequency range between 550 and 1,600 kilocycles; domestic FM broadcasts use the far higher frequency band from 88 to 108 megacycles (one megacycle = 1,000 kilocycles). International AM broadcasting uses the short-wave frequency spectrum of seven bands between 6 and 28 megacycles. In tropical regions, national radio services make extensive use of frequencies between 3 and 6 megacycles, where least disturbance is encountered from noisy atmospheric effects associated with warm climates. In domestic U. S. broadcasting, FCC regulations also set limits on the transmitting power of individual stations in order to avoid interference between stations operating at the same or nearly identical frequencies in adjoining regions. Another device for reducing interference is the directional antenna, which radiates low-powered signals in some directions and high-powered signals in others.

The standard domestic broadcasting frequencies are not suitable for long-range transmission. FM is particularly limited in range because its waves are not reflected by the Heaviside layer of the atmosphere but radiate straight out into space. (Disturbances in the Heaviside layer occasionally result in transmission of local AM broadcasts to places normally far beyond their range.) Nationally broadcast programs are transmitted over telephone circuits to local stations. If the program is to be rebroadcast later for different regional audiences, it is recorded on tape. Short-wave transmission is based on the phenomenon of reflection of certain frequencies of radiant energy by the ionized layer of the atmosphere. But since the height and degree of ionization of this layer are highly variable, short-wave broadcasting is subject to static and fade-out.—*E. A. L.*

RADIO COMPASS: a device used on ships and airplanes for indicating the compass direction of a transmitting station of known location. It consists of either a fixed- or a rotatable-loop antenna, a radio receiver, and an indicator. The *fixed-loop antenna* is used for following a course ("homing") directly toward the radio transmitter. The loop is fixed so that the center line faces fore and aft. When the craft heads directly toward the station, the radio waves from the station will in-

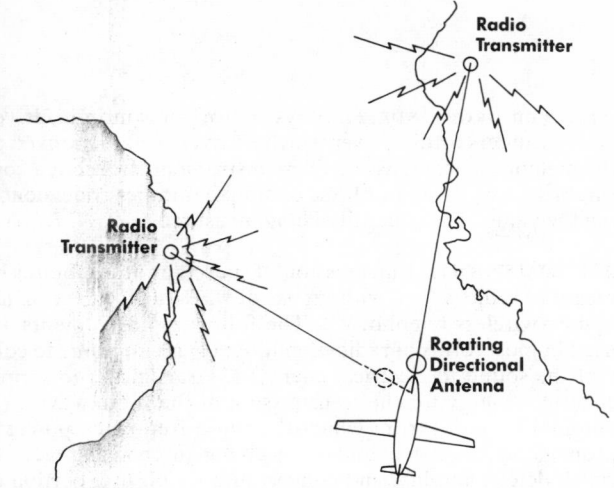

Radio compass: Antenna on airplane rotates so as to point in direction of radio transmitter from which signals are being received. If directions of two different transmitters are noted, and corresponding direction lines are plotted on map, the lines will intersect. Point of intersection is location of airplane.

tersect the right and left sides of the loop at the same instant. The voltages induced in each side will be equal in magnitude but opposite in polarity, the total voltage across the loop will be zero, and the indicator in the cabin will show that the heading is correct. If the craft veers to the left or right of course, the voltages in the sides of the loop will not be equal and the indicator will show "left" or "right" of course.

With a rotatable antenna the radio compass can be used to indicate the exact location of the craft. To accomplish this, the location of two transmitters must be known. First one station is tuned and the loop is rotated until it points at that station. The exact position is determined by checking for zero voltage across the loop by means of the indicator; in some compasses this "sensing" is done automatically. The direction of the transmitter from the craft is noted and a line is drawn on a map. The same procedure is followed for the second station. The intersection of the two direction lines will then indicate the exact location of the craft.—*H. I. S.*

RADIO INTERFEROMETER: a RADIO TELESCOPE in which two or more antennas are connected to a single receiver. The

Radio interferometer is essentially a radio telescope with bank of antennas, as below. Interferometer combines radio waves received by each antenna to produce interference fringes much as an optical interferometer does. (*French Embassy Press & Infor. Div.*)

antennas are frequently arrays of dipoles, but paraboloid reflectors are also used. The effect of two separate antennas is to split the original radio beam into a series of fine "fringes." The fringe resolving power is the ratio of the wavelength to twice the separation of the antennas. This secondary resolving power can be utilized only if the primary beams are narrow enough to isolate an object effectively. However, in such cases it is very valuable for the determination of precise positions and angular diameters of radio sources.—*B. P. S.*

RADIOISOTOPE (or **radioactive isotope**): any ISOTOPE whose atoms have unstable nuclei—*i.e.* nuclei that emit radiation until they become stable. Eventually every radioisotope is transformed by radioactive decay into a stable isotope. Two isotopes—whether radioactive or stable—of the same element have the same chemical properties, but their nuclei have different masses.

Physicists have identified more than 800 radioisotopes. A few occur naturally, but most are produced artificially by bombarding stable isotopes with beams of neutrons from nuclear reactions or with beams of protons or other light nuclei from particle accelerators. When a stable nucleus absorbs one of the incident projectiles, it becomes a different, usually radioactive nucleus.

Radioisotopes are widely used in industry and research. Some applications utilize the radiation as a source of energy (as in nuclear batteries), as a thickness-measuring instrument, as a food sterilizer, as a "super x-ray" to detect flaws in metal castings, and as a treatment (partially successful) for cancer. Since radioisotopes are chemically identical with stable isotopes of the same element, they are very useful as "tracers" in biochemical research. For example, the pathway of phosphorus through an organism can be traced by mixing a radioisotope of phosphorus with ordinary phosphorus and feeding the mixture to the organism. The "tagged" atoms can be followed through the organism by means of a radiation detector. As another example, the role played by zinc in the development of tomato plants can be studied by placing radiozinc in the soil in which the plants are growing. The radiozinc is carried through the plant (along with ordinary zinc) into the fruit, and is deposited in the seeds. When a slice of the tomato fruit is placed on a photographic film protected from light, the radiations from the radiozinc expose the film, showing the areas where the most abundant deposits of both radiozinc and zinc have occurred. See ATOMIC ENERGY; RADIOACTIVITY.—*S. K.*

RADIOMETER: a device for measuring intensity or pressure of an ELECTROMAGNETIC WAVE. Early forms measured pressure from a bright light caused to fall on a TORSIONAL BALANCE consisting of two polished silver discs suspended by a quartz fiber in an evacuated enclosure. The angle of twist of the disc measured electromagnetic pressure. This device was subject to error in measurement when air was permitted in the enclosure. The error arose after the silver discs became heated, when rebounding (thermally excited) air molecules hit the discs. A variation of this radiometer is one in which the discs freely rotate at a speed proportional to intensity of the incident light. A modern radiometer of great scientific and practical importance is the "Dicke" type, which measures intensity (or effective temperature) of electromagnetic radiation in the microwave or millimeter-wave region by comparing temperature (or power) or incoming radiation with the power of a local, "dummy" antenna, heated to a known temperature. This form of radiometer is used extensively in RADIO ASTRONOMY for mapping our galaxy and areas of the universe beyond.—*A. S.*

RADIOSONDE: a balloon-borne device used in meteorology to measure temperature, humidity, and pressure in the free atmosphere and to transmit the measurements to a ground station. These measurements, called *upper air soundings,* are indispensable in modern scientific weather analysis and forecasting. Radiosondes used by the various national weather services differ considerably in detail, but all radiosonde observations are made on the same general principles: a small measuring unit combined with a miniature radio transmitter is attached to a gas-filled balloon; the balloon carries the radiosonde aloft, reaching a peak height of about 100,000 ft (30,000 m). The balloon usually then bursts, and the instrument descends to the surface on a parachute. During the flight, radio signals, coded to represent temperature, pressure, and humidity values, are transmitted to a ground receiver, where the data are put into a standard format and finally disseminated via teletype and radio to weather analysis centers all over the world. At many stations, the radiosonde is tracked during its flight by a directional antenna, and upper-air winds are calculated from the observed motions of the transmitter. These are usually called *rawinsonde* observations.

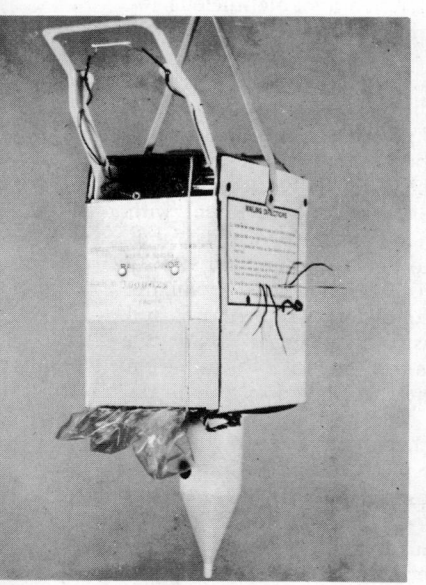

Radiosonde (*above, left*), carried aloft by gas-filled balloon to altitudes as high as 100,000 ft, collects and transmits upper-air meteorological data. Data are received and recorded automatically by ground-station recorder (*right*). (*U. S. Weather Bureau*)

The present standard American radiosonde is essentially an AM or FM ultra-high-frequency transmitter with the audio frequency determined by the electrical resistances of a temperature and a humidity sensor. These sensors, as well as two fixed-reference resistors, are switched into the circuit by a barometer-switch driven by an aneroid capsule. Thus, at predetermined pressures, readings are made of temperature and humidity. From the hydrostatic law, the variation of these quantities with height is easily calculated. Other varieties of radiosonde operate by changing the radio frequency, rather than the audio frequency of the transmitter: in the standard British instrument a bimetallic thermometer, an aneroid barometer, and a hair hygrometer move tuning slugs in the transmitter tank circuit while the circuit is switched cyclically from one sensor to another by means of a windmill-driven contact arm. A third class of radiosonde, *e.g.* the Russian *Molchanov* and German *Graw* models, and the

American DROPSONDE, employs motor- or windmill-driven code cylinders or discs over which contact arms are moved by the meteorological sensors. These instruments transmit a continuous-wave signal in Morse or simple number code, denoting the value of the quantity being measured.—*D. H. L.*

RADIOTELEPHONY: transmission of speech or other sounds by means of radio waves, without use of wires (hence the original name "wireless telephony"). The following instruments are used in most forms of radiotelephony: (1) microphone to convert the sound to electrical energy; (2) transmitter to supply electrical energy for the transmission of the radio waves; (3) antenna or aerial from which the radio-frequency power is propagated into space; and (4) receiving antenna and receiver which detect, amplify, and convert into sound that portion of the transmitted power which arrives at the point of reception (see RADIO; RADIO BROADCASTING).—*E. E.*

RADIO TELESCOPE: an astronomical instrument that receives and processes radio radiation from space. The radiation is collected by an antenna, which sends an electrical signal through tuning and amplifying systems. The final read-out is usually in the form of a curve on a paper recorder, or occasionally on magnetic tape or photographic film.

The radio waves that penetrate the atmosphere are 1 cm to 30 m long. For pickup of shorter wavelengths the most common antennas are parabolic reflecting dishes that focus the radiation as the parabolic mirror of a reflecting telescope focuses light. Dishes are made of sheet metal or wire mesh, accurate to about ⅒ wavelength. Resolving power—or optimum angular separation—depends upon the wavelength used and the aperture (diameter) of the dish: a 1°-beam requires an aperture of 40 ft at 10-cm wavelength, and 4,000 ft at 10 m. Thus, even the largest radio telescopes have less resolving power than optical ones; the 250-ft antenna at Jodrell Bank, England, can resolve sources 15' apart at 30-cm wavelength (the shortest wavelength at which it is fully efficient). For work with longer wavelengths, greater resolving power is obtained by connecting two or more separate antennas to the same receiver; such an arrangement constitutes a RADIO INTERFEROMETER.

While some radio telescopes are fixed, many can be steered. Equatorial mounts are preferred (Fig. 1); but the largest are

World's largest telescope: 300-ft. dish of Arecibo Ionospheric Observatory, completed in 1963, was built in a natural hollow in the hills of Puerto Rico. Dish is stationary, but observations can be made as far as 20 degrees from zenith. Instrument is used for radio astronomy and radar observation of nearer planets and other objects. (*Cornell Univ. Photo*)

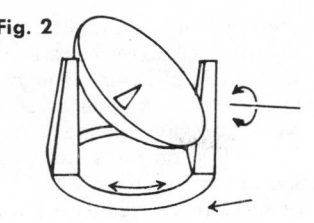

Radio-telescope mountings: In equatorial mounting (Fig. 1), antenna rotates on polar axis (parallel to Earth's axis) on declination axis (perpendicular to Earth's axis). In altazimuth mounting (Fig. 2), movement is provided for in altitude and in azimuth.

usually supported by more easily built altazimuth mountings (Fig. 2). In general, the receivers are similar in principle to commercial superheterodyne receivers, but require high gain stability and greater sensitivity. To achieve gain stability, a comparison system is often used: the input of the receiver is switched between antenna and reference load, and a modulated signal is detected at the output. Considerable improvements in sensitivity have been achieved with the use of parametric amplifiers or masers as input stages.—*B. P. S.*

RADIUM: a radioactive metallic element (Ra) of the alkaline-earth series; at. no. 88; mp 960°C; bp 1140°C. There are four naturally occurring isotopes of radium, those having atomic weights of 223, 224, 226, and 228. The isotope of at. wt 226 is by far the most abundant. It is formed by the radioactive disintegration of uranium^{238}, has a half-life of 1,620 yr, and decays by alpha emission to form radon^{222}. The iso-

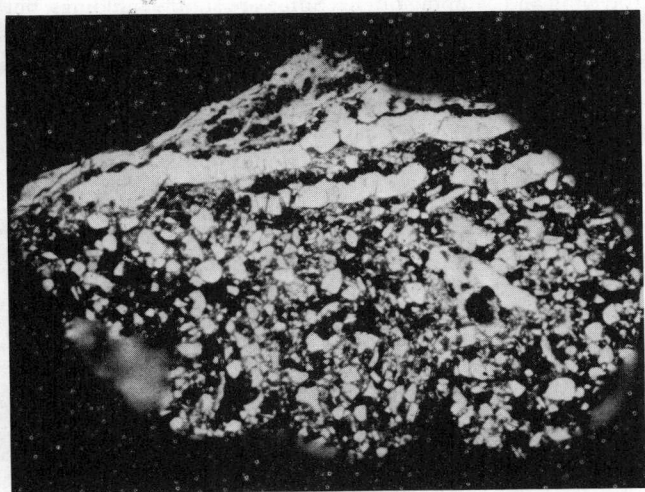

Radioactivity of pitchblende (a radium-uranium ore) causes ore to take its own picture (*as above*) when placed next to a photographic plate that is shielded against light. (*N. Y. Public Library*)

tope of at. wt 223 is formed from uranium^{235} and has a half-life of 11 days. The other two isotopes are products of thorium decay. Aside from its radioactivity, radium exhibits the same general chemical behavior as strontium, calcium, and barium, the other alkaline-earth elements. Radium occurs in the uranium minerals pitchblende and carnotite, which contain about 3×10^{-7} gm of radium per gm of uranium. The chief deposits are in the Congo, the Great Bear Lake area of Canada, and the Colorado-Utah area in the U. S. A.

Radium was discovered in 1898 by Pierre and Marie Curie. They found that radium chloride could be separated from pitchblende by using barium chloride as a carrier; the radium

chloride could then be separated from the barium chloride by fractional precipitation in an aqueous alcohol solution. Pure elemental radium can be prepared by electrolysis of a radium-chloride solution with a mercury cathode, so that a radium amalgam is formed. The amalgam is then heated to drive off the mercury. Radium salts are used as a major source of radiation for the treatment of cancer: these high-energy particles strike the malignant area and eventually destroy it. But since they can also destroy healthy tissue, exposure of healthy tissue to radioactive sources must be limited. Radium is used to make objects such as watch dials luminous; it is an excellent activator for most *phosphors*. Radium is steadily being replaced by more economical sources of radioactive emission, *e.g.* cobalt^{60}.—*A. M. S.* and *G. W. M.*

RADON: an inert gaseous element (Rn); at. no. 86; at. wt 222; half-life 3.825 days. Radon and two isotopes—*actinon* (at. wt 219, half-life 3.9 sec) and *thoron* (at. wt 220, half-life 3.8 days)—are formed when radium is exposed to air. The group of three isotopes is sometimes called emanation (Em). Sir Ernest Rutherford (1899), seeing that thorium compounds impart radioactivity to air (thoron), unsuccessfully sought a similar reaction from radium. F. E. Dorn, using radium bromide, discovered radon in 1900, and André Debierne isolated actinon from actinium in 1903. Rn^{222} is a beta- and gamma-ray source: it is used in medicine as a gamma source in ointments, or implanted in the body in capsules called "seeds" or "needles," which destroy necrosed tissue, radiation-injured tissue, and cancerous growths. Seeds are short sealed gold or glass capillary tubes inserted in the tissue; needles are larger. Cobalt^{60} and cesium^{137} are gradually replacing radon in these uses. Since radon is inert, it diffuses readily in tissue and therefore is used in biological research and as an alpha-ray tracer element in gas-flow studies. (See INERT GASES.)—*R. B. T.*

RAILWAY ENGINEERING: the design, construction, and maintenance of the special roadways over which locomotives pull passenger or freight cars. These roadways are traditionally constructed with pairs of parallel steel rails (tracks) which support the smooth, flanged, iron or steel wheels of the locomotive and cars. Railways originated in the mining districts of England. As early as the 16th cent. men found that horses could pull heavier loads in wagons over wooden rails than over earthen roads. When wooden rails were found to wear out rapidly, they were topped with strips of iron. Cast-iron plateways were also tried: the first steam locomotive of Richard Trevithick and Andrew Vivian pulled a string of loaded cars at walking pace over such rails in 1804.

The Rainhill Trials in England (1829) demonstrated the practicality of the steam locomotive and provided an impetus to railroad construction in continental Europe and the U. S. A. England led in the development of railroad service: the Stockton and Darlington Railway, opened in 1825, was the first public line to carry passengers; the Liverpool and Manchester began service in 1830 as the first railroad to use steam locomotives exclusively. Railroading in the U. S. A. began in 1824 when John Stevens operated a steam locomotive over a track in Hoboken, N. J. In 1829 the "Stourbridge Lion," imported from England, operated briefly on the Delaware and Hudson. In 1830 the Baltimore and Ohio opened scheduled daily traffic over nearly 14 mi of line, using horses. On this line Peter Cooper tried his "Tom Thumb" to prove the superiority of steam power. The first transcontinental railroad, heavily subsidized by the U. S. government, became a reality

Modern railway yard: Opened in 1956, the Englewood Radar Yard at Houston, Tex., can channel out up to 3,000 cars per day over the "hump" (elevation in foreground, behind control building). Radar-activated car-braking equipment and an electronic computer are utilized. (*Assn. of American Railroads*)

in 1869. In 1954 the U. S. A. had 234,497 mi of operating trackage; the world total was approximately 768,000 mi.

The first railways were very crude; rails were laid on blocks of stone, with space between the blocks for a horse to walk. The track was rough, difficult to maintain, and expensive to build. Ends of the iron straps fastened to the wooden rails frequently pulled loose, spearing up through the floors of the flimsy coaches and threatening to impale the terrified passengers. On a voyage to England in 1830 to purchase locomotives and rails, Robert Stevens whittled out a T-shaped rail design, to be cast of iron. Its superiority over the early strap was at once recognized. Soon steel replaced the iron, and wooden cross ties replaced the earlier granite blocks supporting the rails. The wooden ties were cheaper, more elastic, and less subject to frost heaving. In this early period,

Remote control of rolling stock: Operator at Markham Yard, Chicago, controls the coasting speed of freight cars by buttons that actuate automatic retarders on rails. Retarders allow car just enough momentum to reach its destination. (*Illinois Central RR*)

there was no uniformity of gauge, *i.e.* the distance between the inner edges of the rails; some gauges were as wide as 7 ft. George Stephenson strongly urged a 4-ft 8½-in. width, which later became known as *standard gauge;* today 60% of the world railway mileage is in standard gauge.

The first railways had guards stationed along the track to signal the engineers when to stop. They were soon replaced by mechanical signals, *e.g.* the semaphore mounted on a pole. Train orders dispatched by telegraph gave safer operation. This system was followed by the *block system,* in which the track is divided into segments or blocks and no train may follow or move against a train ahead until the block is cleared. Centralized train control, radio, radar, and loudspeaker systems in the yards have contributed greatly to safety and increased speed of operations.

Modern Railway Systems: The ideal railway is one with level track. Toward this end railways have spent millions of dollars constructing bridges, trestles, tunnels, cuts, and fills. The cost has been justified by fuel savings and less wear on equipment. In the 20th cent., track building and maintenance have become fine crafts. Wooden ties treated with preservatives are laid on a well-drained bed of selected material, with clean crushed rock, slag, or cinders about them. This ballast must be kept clean and the rails firmly fastened to the cross ties at the proper distance and elevation on curves. Modern railways have terminal yards with tracks where cars can be assembled into trains for departure, incoming trains pulled in, and cars switched out to be unloaded or loaded. There must be tracks into servicing facilities, *i.e.* roundhouses, car shops, and fueling and cleaning shops. A modern railway also has passenger and freight stations with proper facilities to serve the traveling and shipping public. Some are simple buildings, but those of population centers are large, elaborate structures. *Rolling stock* (*e.g.* locomotives and passenger and freight cars) has increased in size, speed, and versatility. Some of the first passenger coaches were stagecoach bodies mounted on rail trucks, and early freight cars were small and simple. Early-day trains had no dining cars and no places to sleep other than the hard seats. The first cars had inadequate, hand-operated brakes; present-day vacuum and automatic air brakes have added immensely to safety. Modern passenger coaches built of metal have largely eliminated the terrible menace of fire and the threat of break-up of wooden coaches in wrecks. A large variety of specialized freight cars for shipping various commodities have been developed; *e.g.* the refrigerator car for perishable foods, the tank car for fluids ranging from milk to gasoline, the flatcar for machinery and lumber, and the hopper car for coal and cement. Present-day locomotives are more powerful, require less servicing, and pull longer trains at higher speeds. Steam locomotives are being replaced by more efficient diesel-electric, gas turbine-electric, and electric locomotives. Railways are nearly all government-owned and operated, the U. S. A. being the only major country with a privately owned rail system. The U. S. S. R. is said to have the world's largest railway system. See LOCOMOTIVE.—*F. C.*

RAIN: precipitation in the form of liquid water drops. Raindrops vary in size from about 0.02 in. (0.5 mm) to as much as 0.2–0.33 in. (5–8 mm) in heavy thunderstorms. Droplets smaller than 0.02 in. are classified as drizzle. The largest drops are quite distorted: some have their undersides flattened; others, about to break into smaller drops, take the shape of dumbbells. Very small raindrops and ice crystals falling from clouds tend to evaporate before reaching ground. These trails of evaporating drops, appearing as wispy scarves or darkish streaks hanging under the clouds, are called "virga."

Rain is called light, moderate, or heavy, depending on how much falls within a specified period of time. Where there is no means of measuring the fall, various methods of estimating it are used. Light rain falls at a rate of 0.1 in. or less/hr; moderate rain, at 0.11–0.3 in./hr (but not over 0.03 in. in 6 min); and heavy rain, 0.3 in. or more/hr, or 0.03 in. or more in 6 min. Rain that falls intermittently or steadily over wide areas is usually associated with frontal systems, particularly warm fronts, and frontal waves. Showers usually produce heavy rain for brief periods. Although a thunderstorm or rain shower seldom lasts for more than 20 min at any particular place, it may dump over an inch of rain in that time. Rain in

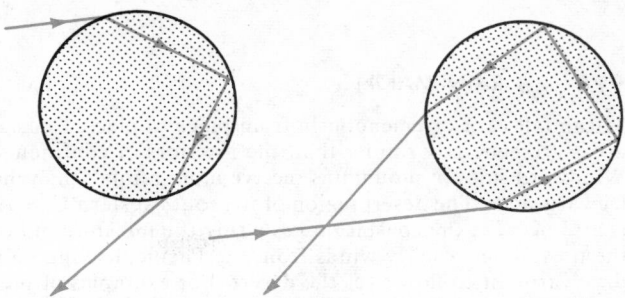

Passage of light through spherical water droplets produces primary rainbow (*left*) and secondary rainbow (*right*). Deduction of these light paths and the explanation of the formation of the rainbows were accomplished first by René Descartes, who in his *Meteores* (1637) used the diagram shown below. (*Burndy Library*)

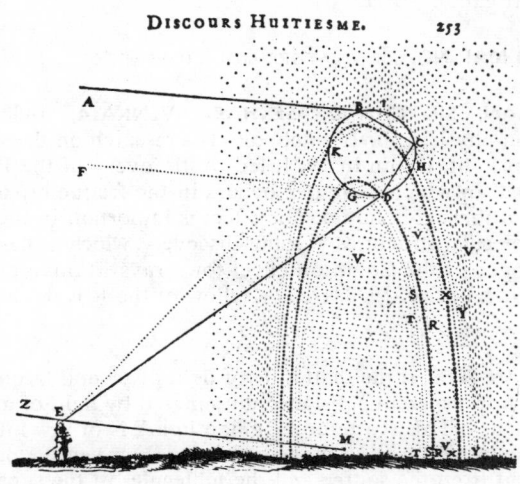

DISCOURS HUITIESME. 253

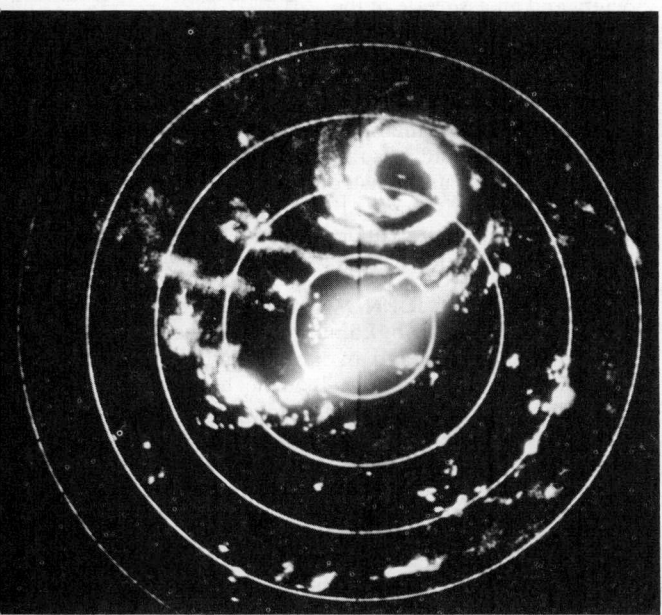

Radar photograph of rainfall distribution: Light areas indicate rainfall; the spiral (*top*) is a hurricane whose center is 45 mi from radar station (very center of concentric circles). Circles are range lines at 20-mi intervals. (*U. S. Navy*)

the mid-latitudes, usually associated with frontal systems, occurs throughout the year whenever temperatures are above freezing. Deserts, of course, are the exception to this rule. In the tropics rain tends to be showery and is usually seasonal, with one or two rainy seasons interspersed with a like number of dry seasons during each year. (See also PRECIPITATION; RAINFALL.)—*P. L.*

RAINBOW: the arcs of colored light seen by an observer when sunlight from behind him is reflected by drops of rain or spray in the air in front of him. The light of the rainbow reaches his eyes after being reflected from the inside surface of the drops. The brighter, inner arc, the *primary* rainbow, produced by a single internal reflection of the sunlight, has a violet or blue inner border and a red outer border (see illus.). Outside the primary bow a *secondary* one is often seen: its colors are reversed, with the red inside and the violet outside, because reflection has occurred twice inside the drops. More complex patterns of internal reflections are possible, but the rainbows thus formed are usually too faint to be seen. In any rainbow, the dispersion of white sunlight into the spectrum of colors takes place at the surface of the drop, where each of the component colors of the white light is bent, or refracted, at a slightly different angle; reflection then occurs inside the

drop. The rainbow appears always to be of the same size, no matter how far away the water drops are from the observer: this is so because the light reaches the eyes only from those drops which lie at the proper angle to the line from the Sun to the observer. Thus any drop which lies at an angle of 40° from the shadow of the observer (*i.e.* at 140° from the Sun) reflects yellow light to the observer; any drop at 42° reflects red light. Individual rainbows do differ, however, in the brightness and width of the individual bands of color. These variations are due to differences in sizes of drops and consequent differences in diffraction of the light.— *D. H. L.*

RAINFALL: the water equivalent of any type of precipitation that reaches the ground. Rainfall is measured in inches or millimeters, one inch of rainfall being the depth of water that falls on a given area. Measuring is done with devices of various types. The usual rain gage is an upright, open-topped cylinder with a funnel inside its mouth; this conducts the rain caught at the top to a smaller measuring cylinder. The standard opening is 8 in. in diameter; the measuring cylinder has a cross-sectional area one tenth that of the larger cylinder, so 1 in. of water in the smaller tube represents 0.1 in. rainfall. Another type of gage has a small bucket which tips over and empties itself when it has caught 0.01 in. of rain, recording the amount electrically. A third type, the weighing gage, catches, weighs, and records precipitation on a clock-work-driven chart. The water equivalent of snow averages 1 in. of water to 10 in. of snow depth, varying from a ratio of nearly 30 to 1 for dry, fluffy snow to 2 to 1 for old, hard-packed snow. To find the water equivalent of snow, the average depth of the fall is determined, and a sample is cut out and melted.

Rainfall varies tremendously from place to place. Coastal areas are generally rainier than the interiors of continents. Windward sides of mountains receive more rainfall than the leeward sides. The desert region of the southwestern U. S. A. is arid because the coastal ranges wring the moisture out of the prevailing westerly winds from the Pacific, leaving only dry, warm air to flow over the desert. For examples of precipitation totals, see CLIMATIC EXTREMES. Rainy days vary from less than one day per yr in some desert areas to over 200 in coastal regions, *e.g.* the Olympic Mts area of the state of Washington. The annual rainfall of an area is a principal factor in determining its arability. Generally 20 in. is considered the minimum needed for conventional farming without irrigation.—*P. L.*

RAIN MAKING: see WEATHER MODIFICATION.

RAMAN, SIR CHANDRASEKHARA VENKATA, 1888–   , Indian physicist; b. Trichinopoly. His research on the scattering of light, begun in 1921, led to discovery of the RAMAN EFFECT, in which a change occurs in the frequency of light passed through a liquid. The effect is important in the study of molecular structures. For this discovery, which is the optical analogue of the Compton effect for x-rays, Raman received the Nobel prize, 1930. He is a fellow of the Royal Society.—*D. H. D. R.*

RAMAN EFFECT: the scattering of light of several frequencies from a transparent substance illuminated by light of a single frequency. This scattered "Raman light" is of low intensity and results from an exchange of energy between the photons of light from the source and the molecules of the substance. Those photons that absorb energy from the molecules emerge with a higher frequency, whereas those that yield energy to the molecules emerge with a lower frequency. Study of these energy exchanges gives important information about the structure of the molecules and is used in chemical analysis. The Raman effect was discovered by C. V. Raman in 1928.—*I. R.*

RAMANUJAN, SRINIVASA, 1887–1920, Indian mathematician; b. Erode. He received some education at the government college at Kumbakonam, and for a short time had a scholarship at the Univ. of Madras, leaving in 1909 to become clerk in the Madras Port Trust. He pursued an independent study of mathematics, in the course of which he corresponded with G. H. Hardy of Cambridge. This led to a further scholarship from Madras. He went in 1914 to England, where Hardy assisted him in filling in the background needed for original work. He was made a fellow of the Royal Society in 1918, and, in the same year, was elected a fellow of Trinity College, Cambridge. He made valuable contributions to the theory of numbers, the theory of partitions, and the theory of continued fractions.—*H. C.*

RAMÓN Y CAJAL, SANTIAGO, 1852–1934, Spanish anatomist; b. Petilla. A founder of modern histology, he shared the 1906 Nobel prize (with Camillo Golgi) for his work on the structure of the nervous system. Author of more than 200 scientific papers and numerous books, he was also a fellow of the Royal Society and an associate of the U. S. National Academy of Sciences.—*D. H. D. R.*

RAMSAY, SIR WILLIAM, 1852–1916, Scottish chemist; b. Glasgow. He is best known for his research at University College, London (1887–1912), which led to the discovery of the inert gases argon, helium, neon, krypton, and xenon. (See INERT GASES.) For the discovery of the rare gases and the determination of their place in the periodic system, Ramsay received the 1904 Nobel prize in chemistry. With F. Soddy he discovered the element radon. Among his numerous publications is *The Gases of the Atmosphere* (1896). He was a fellow of the Royal Society and an associate of the U. S. National Academy of Sciences.—*D. H. D. R.*

Sir William Ramsay
(Yerkes Observatory)

RAMSDEN, JESSE, 1735–1800, English instrument maker; b. Salterhebble. He was the inventor of the achromatic eyepiece named after him, and was famous during his lifetime for his divided circles for use in astronomical observatories. A 5-ft vertical circle of his make (1789) was used by G. Piazzi at Palermo to compile his catalog of stars. Ramsden was a fellow of the Royal Society.—*R. J. F.*

RANKINE, WILLIAM JOHN MACQUORN, 1820–72, Scottish engineer and physicist; b. Edinburgh. He received a practical training in surveying and in harbor and railroad building under Sir J. B. Macneill. In 1855 he became professor of civil engineering at Glasgow Univ. One of the founders of the science of thermodynamics, he coined the term "energy" and wrote the first essay on this subject: *A Manual of the Steam Engine and Other Prime Movers* (1859). He was a fellow of the Royal Society.—*R. J. F.*

RANKINE SCALE: an absolute TEMPERATURE SCALE, based on the FAHRENHEIT SCALE, in which absolute zero is designated as 0°R, the freezing point of water as 492°R, and the boiling point of water as 672°R. The scale is used to a limited extent by engineers in those countries using the Fahrenheit scale.—*E. M. R.*

RAOULT, FRANÇOIS MARIE, 1830–1901, French chemist; b. Fournès. He did research on electrochemistry, vapor tension, and freezing points. *Raoult's law* is concerned with the lowering of the freezing points of liquids by substances dissolved in the liquid, a subject on which Raoult published many scientific papers. He was a professor at the Univ. of Grenoble from 1867.—*D. H. D. R.*

RAOULT'S LAW: "For solutions of a non-volatile solute in a volatile solvent, the vapor pressure above the solution is equal to the vapor pressure of the pure solvent multiplied by the mole fraction of the solvent." This quantitative relationship set forth by F. M. Raoult (1887) can also be expressed in a mathematically equivalent form; *i.e.* the vapor-pressure lowering is equal to the mole fraction of solute, or

$$(p_o - p)/p_o = n_2/(n_1 + n_2)$$

where p_o is the vapor pressure of pure solvent, p is the vapor pressure of the solution, n_2 and n_1 are, respectively, the number of moles of solute and solvent present in the system. This law permits calculation of the molecular weights of non-volatile substances by measuring the vapor-pressure lowering of solutions of the substances.—*A. M. S.*

RARE EARTHS: traditionally, the chemical elements grouped with lanthanum in the periodic table—numbers 57 through 71. In recent years the term has been extended to include two outlying elements—scandium (element 21) and yttrium (element 39)—which fall in the same group (III B) of the periodic table. There is also a tendency to extend the term to cover the ACTINIDES, which, too, fall in this group and are called "heavy rare earths"; but since one group of LANTHANIDES likewise is known as the "heavy rare earths," this practice is being discouraged. Actually the term "rare earth" is itself a misnomer, since the elements of this group are not rare compared to gold or platinum, and they are true metals, not "earths." The rare earths show a wide range of mechanical, electrical, and magnetic properties. In general, scandium, yttrium, and elements 64 through 71 are fairly strong metals, with relatively high melting points and moderate hardness; while elements 57 through 63 tend to be weaker and softer, with lower melting points. The most important rare-earth ores are monazite sands, bastnasite, and euxenite, with the thorium-bearing monazite sands being the major commercial source today. Although individual rare earths have become available only recently in any quantity, impure mixtures such as the high-cerium composition known as "misch metal" have been in commercial use for many years. The cerium mixture is the major ingredient of cigarette-lighter flints. A praseodymium-neodymium mixture known as "didymium" is used to make light-absorbing glass, *e.g.* for welding masks.

Rare-earth elements of high purity are now produced in quantity by ion-exchange resin columns. Until the development of such methods (as discussed in CHROMATOGRAPHY and ION-EXCHANGE), separation of rare earths was complex and time-consuming. (*Johnson, Matthey & Co. Ltd.*)

In order of increasing atomic number, the rare earths are scandium (at. no. 21, symbol Sc); yttrium (39, Y); lanthanum (57, La); cerium (58, Ce); praseodymium (59, Pr); neodymium (60, Nd); promethium (61, Pm); samarium (62, Sm); europium (63, Eu); gadolinium (64, Gd); terbium (65, Tb); dysprosium (66, Dy); holmium (67, Ho); erbium (68, Er); thulium (69, Tm); ytterbium (70, Yb); and lutetium (71, Lu). See individual articles on these elements.—*A. R. G.*

RATHKE, MARTIN HEINRICH, 1793–1860, German biologist; b. Danzig. A founder of modern embryology, he discovered in bird and mammalian embryos structures suggesting gill slits, and he studied their disappearance as the embryos developed. His view was that higher animals pass through the lower animal forms during their embryonic life. His name is perpetuated in *Rathke's pocket,* the embryonic outpocketing from the mouth which becomes the anterior lobe of the PITUITARY GLAND. He was also a pioneer in research on marine life.—*D. H. D. R.*

RATIO: see PROPORTION.

RATIONALISM: the philosophical belief, usually contrasted with EMPIRICISM, that human reason, unaided by sense experience, can arrive at objective truths. Traditionally, mathematics was the paradigm of such knowledge. But Descartes defended rationalistic physics and Spinoza rationalistic ethics, and Leibniz contended that every truth might be known by rationalistic means. Kant developed a modified rationalism, arguing that experience is organized according to forms of perception not given in experience, and that there exists synthetic A PRIORI knowledge. Few philosophers since the 17th cent. have been pure rationalists, but the possibility and extent of *a priori* knowledge remains a matter for refined philosophical analysis.—*A. D.*

RAY (or WRAY), JOHN, 1627–1705, English naturalist; b. Black Notley, Essex. Often called the father of natural history in England, he was noted for his systematic classification and precision of terminology. His *Historia plantarum* (1686–1704) had a great influence on Linnaeus and others. In zoology, Ray supplied the first classification of animals that was both general and grounded in nature and that made use of comparative anatomy. He made a lasting classification of insects, quadrupeds, and birds, and conducted important experiments on the movements of plants and the ascent of sap in trees. Ray also was among the first naturalists of modern times to realize that fossils are the traces of life of the remote past. He was a fellow of the Royal Society.—*D. H. D. R.*

RAYLEIGH, BARON JOHN WILLIAM STRUTT, 1842–1919, English physicist; b. Langford Grove, Essex. Rayleigh's work ranged from subjects of popular interest such as the color of the sky and the nature of foam to studies of electromagnetic waves. His main work, stimulated by reading Helmholtz, was first in resonance and then in acoustics. *The Theory of Sound* (1877), perhaps the best existing treatment of mathematical acoustics, includes the vibrations of strings, bars, membranes, and plates, as well as non-sonic vibrations. His method of calculating frequencies directly from energy considerations is widely used not only in the study of vibrations but in many other branches of physics and engineering, especially the theory of elasticity. His theory of elastic surface waves, found in his *Scientific Papers* (1899), has contributed much to the understanding of earthquakes (see SEISMIC WAVE). After the death of James Clerk Maxwell, Rayleigh headed the Cavendish Laboratory and occupied the chair of experimental physics at Cambridge Univ. For his discovery, along with Sir William Ramsay, of the inert gas argon, Rayleigh received the 1904 Nobel prize. His derivation according to classical theories of the formula for the energy of black-body radiation, although erroneous, stimulated the development of the quantum theory of radiation. He was a fellow of the Royal Society and an associate of the U. S. National Academy of Sciences.—*A. L.*

Baron John William Strutt, Lord Rayleigh
(Yerkes Observatory)

RAYON: a regenerated cellulosic fiber, first produced commercially in 1884 from nitrocellulose. Today rayon is usually manufactured by the viscose process, in which wood pulp or cotton linters are treated with caustic and carbon disulfide to produce a viscous solution of cellulose xanthate; the viscose is extruded through spinnerets into an acid bath to regenerate the cellulose in the form of threadlike filaments.

Rayon by viscose process: Liquid viscose (mainly cellulose xanthate in dilute sodium hydroxide) is extruded through fine holes of spinneret into a chemical bath. After traveling a few inches, viscose forms rayon fiber. *(Du Pont)*

Recent modifications of the process involve changes in the chemical composition of both the viscose and the coagulating bath, and in fiber-spinning and fiber-drawing techniques. Fibers produced by the new processes are stronger than the older rayons, do not swell as much, and resist stretching in the wet state (improving washability) while retaining the advantages of the older rayons, *e.g.* comfort, dyeability, and low price. See CELLULOSE; TEXTILE.—*W. P. C.*

REACTANCE: the opposition to the flow of alternating current offered by INDUCTANCE and CAPACITANCE in an electric circuit. Inductive reactance increases with the frequency of the applied emf, whereas capacitive reactance decreases as the frequency increases. Thus a pure inductance acts as a short circuit for direct current and an open circuit for very-high-frequency ac, and a pure capacitance acts as an open circuit for dc and a short circuit for very-high-frequency ac. Inductive reactance X_L is given by the formula $X_L = 2\pi FL$, where X_L is in ohms when the frequency F is in cycles/sec and the inductance L is in henrys; capacitive reactance X_C is given by the formula $X_C = \frac{1}{2\pi FC}$, where X_C is in ohms when F is in cycles/sec and the capacitance C is in farads. The current leads the applied voltage in a capacitor and lags behind it in an inductor; therefore, when inductive and capacitive reactance are both present in a circuit they tend to offset each other, and the net reactance X is the difference between X_L and X_C. See ELECTRIC CIRCUIT; ELECTRIC POWER.—*E. M. R.*

REACTOR: see NUCLEAR REACTOR.

RÉAUMUR, RENÉ ANTOINE FERCHAULT DE, 1683–1757, French biologist and physicist; b. La Rochelle. He invented the 80-degree thermometer scale known by his name; improved methods of iron refining, described in his *L'Art de convertir le fer forgé en acier* (1722) and other works; and studied the expansion of fluids. His most famous work is *Mémoires pour servir à l'histoire des insectes* (6 vols., 1734–42), a monumental natural history of insects. He was a fellow of the Royal Society.—*D. H. D. R.*

REAUMUR SCALE: a TEMPERATURE SCALE used in Germany and Scandinavia, in which the freezing point of water is designated as 0° and the boiling point as 80°.—*E. M. R.*

RECALESCENCE: a term meaning development of warmth. In STEEL manufacture it refers to the liberation of heat at a certain characteristic temperature when the metal is made hot and allowed to cool. A major temperature arrest in the cooling curve of a plain carbon steel takes place at 690°C, with heat liberation. Below the recalescence temperature carbon steel consists of pure iron and cementite, Fe_3C. This particular recalescence temperature is also the EUTECTIC temperature of iron and carbon.—*Ru. M.*

RECAPITULATION (or **biogenetic law**): the theory that a developing embryo of an animal passes through stages that repeat in sequence the adult stages in the evolutionary history of the animal. Thus, according to recapitulation, the gill slits that occur in the embryos of reptiles, birds, and mammals repeat the gill slits of adult fishlike ancestors. First advanced by Fritz Müller (1864), the theory was presented vigorously by Ernst Haeckel, who trenchantly summarized it as "ontogeny repeats phylogeny." Today the theory has been

Recapitulation: At each successive stage of its early embryonic development (upper row), a higher organism—in this case amphioxus, a chordate—bears a general resemblance to mature organisms (lower row) farther down in the evolutionary scale. *(From Kenoyer)*

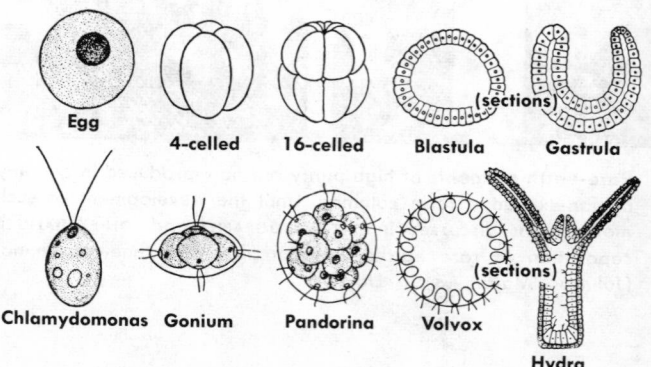

Egg 4-celled 16-celled Blastula (sections) Gastrula

Chlamydomonas Gonium Pandorina Volvox (sections) Hydra

modified to the view that such structures as gill slits in the embryos of higher vertebrates correspond to gill slits in fish embryos rather than in ancestral adults; that the similarity between embryos exists because the earlier stages of embryonic development have not been as affected by evolutionary changes as the later stages.—*R. G. M.*

RECEIVER: a device designed to intercept electrical signals, generally of radio frequency, and operate on them in some fashion to extract their intelligence. The common radio receiver takes an extremely weak radio signal and amplifies, demodulates, and amplifies again the audio modulation in order to obtain a sufficiently strong signal to drive a speaker or other transducer. Customarily the first amplification is accomplished in two stages, with the aid of the HETERODYNE principle. The demodulator extracts the signal modulation from the carrier frequency. In the common household radio this signal modulation is the audio signal which, after amplification, is emitted by the radio speaker. See ELECTRON TUBE; RADIO BROADCASTING; MODULATION.—*G. S.*

RECLAMATION: improvement of infertile or waste land for agriculture or other uses by IRRIGATION; by diking from the sea; by drainage of ponds, swamps, marshes, or land waterlogged by irrigation; or by reduction of salinity or alkalinity. Irrigation has been practiced since the dawn of civilization. Extensive irrigation works existed anciently in the valleys of the Nile, Tigris-Euphrates, and Indus rivers. Irrigation was also practiced by the ancients generally throughout China, the Middle East, India, Ceylon, and the southwestern U. S. A. Sophisticated systems of engineering, water law, and administration frequently developed in connection with the rise of civilizations dependent on irrigation. Present estimates indicate that 300,000,000 acres of land depend primarily on irrigation. Largest acreages are in China (77,000,000), India-Pakistan (80,000,000), and U. S. A. (30,000,000).

Since the 11th cent., the Dutch have been using dikes to reclaim low-lying delta lands submerged by the sea. More recently, nearly 600,000 acres have been reclaimed by diking the tidal estuaries of the Sacramento-San Joaquin Delta in California. Drainage of tidal marshes has been extensive, *e.g.* along the southeastern U. S. Atlantic Coast prior to the Civil War. Much land in the U. S. Midwest was reclaimed by drainage of fresh-water marshes in the Mississippi and Ohio R. valleys during the 18th and 19th cent. Large areas were

Dike on Zuyderzee in Holland is protected from erosion by stone-facing. Depending on position of dike, a lighter or heavier material is used. (*Netherlands Info. Service*)

reclaimed similarly in England. Drainage is also extensively used to relieve waterlogging of low-lying lands arising from irrigation. In the U. S. A. 103,000,000 acres of agricultural land are under drainage systems and additional millions of acres need drainage. However, unrestricted draining is not always a cure-all: water tables are sometimes drastically lowered by drainage of swamps and marshes, and the habitats of waterfowl and other wildlife destroyed.

Salinity results from the accumulation of soluble salts in the root zone, and causes decreased yields because of increased osmotic pressure. If excessive sodium ions become absorbed by the clay particles, the soil becomes *alkali* (sodium-saturated) and damage to the tilth results. Saline and alkali lands may be reclaimed by drainage and the application of neutralizing chemicals and leaching. Loss of the use of irrigated land due to salinity and alkali is a major economic factor in drier areas of the world, notably Iraq and Pakistan. —*D. F. P.*

Reclaimed land: New land on Zuyderzee, mainly fertile marine clays and peat, is visible beyond town. It emerged after two giant pumping stations had been in operation for six and a half months. (*Netherlands Info. Service*)

RECORDE, ROBERT, *c.* 1510–58, British mathematician; b. Tenby, Wales. Considered to be the founder of the English school of mathematics, he wrote in English rather than Latin, and showed great originality of thought. He published four books on mathematics as well as one on medicine. *The Grounde of Artes* (1540) was one of the most popular books on arithmetic of the 16th cent. *The Castle of Knowledge* (1551), on astronomy, advocated the Copernican system. *The Pathewaie to Knowledge* (1551) contained Euclid's *Elements* in shortened form, and *Whetstone of Witte* (1557) was a book on algebra, in which the equality sign appears for the first time.—*H. C.*

RECOVERY FACTOR: the fraction of kinetic energy converted into heat when a fluid in motion is brought to rest by friction. This factor varies according to existing conditions. For air it is generally about 0.8 to 0.9.—*Wm. R.*

RECTIFIER: a device that passes electrical current in one direction only. In conjunction with appropriate CAPACITORS and other components, rectifiers primarily are employed to convert alternating current to direct current. Of the many varieties of practical rectifiers, the most common are the two types employed in radio and phonograph power supplies: *i.e.* vacuum tubes and the solid-state rectifiers utilizing a semiconductor such as selenium or germanium. In a vacuum tube, electrons can be emitted only from the cathode. The vacuum-tube rectifier needs only a cathode and a collector or so-called "plate" electrode to catch the emitted electrons. When the current is reversed, as it is every half-cycle with a-c, the cathode is positive and no electrons are emitted. Thus the current is forced to flow in one direction only, and the rectifier transmits current flowing only in that direction. The operation of a semiconductor rectifier is more complicated, depending upon the properties of a so-called p-n junction (see TRANSISTOR). Under proper conditions, semiconductor solids can be grown in a liquid melt with discontinuities or junctions which transmit electrons in one direction only. In applications requiring high currents, mercury-vapor rectifiers are frequently employed; these are essentially vacuum tubes into which a small amount of mercury vapor has been injected. The resulting ionized vapor will conduct a heavy uni-directional discharge. (See ELECTRON TUBE.)—*G. S.*

RECYCLING: a procedure used to boost the yield of a chemical process; it involves adding some of the substances initially acted upon to an as yet unaffected batch of reactants. In this way heat developed in the reaction is utilized and the unaffected material is given another chance to enter the reaction. Recycling can be made automatic and repeated as often as desired.—*Ru. M.*

REDI, FRANCESCO, 1627?–98?, Italian biologist; b. Arezzo; ed. Univ. of Pisa. He showed experimentally that insect larvae that appear in rotting meat are not produced spontaneously but are the result of eggs laid in the meat. This work was an important step in the fight against the crude theory of "spontaneous generation." His researches were in physics, anatomy, and natural history.—*D. H. D. R.*

RED SHIFT OF GALAXIES: displacement toward the red of the spectral lines of distant galaxies. Perhaps the most important observation in COSMOLOGY, this shift is generally interpreted as DOPPLER EFFECT due to a velocity of recession of the

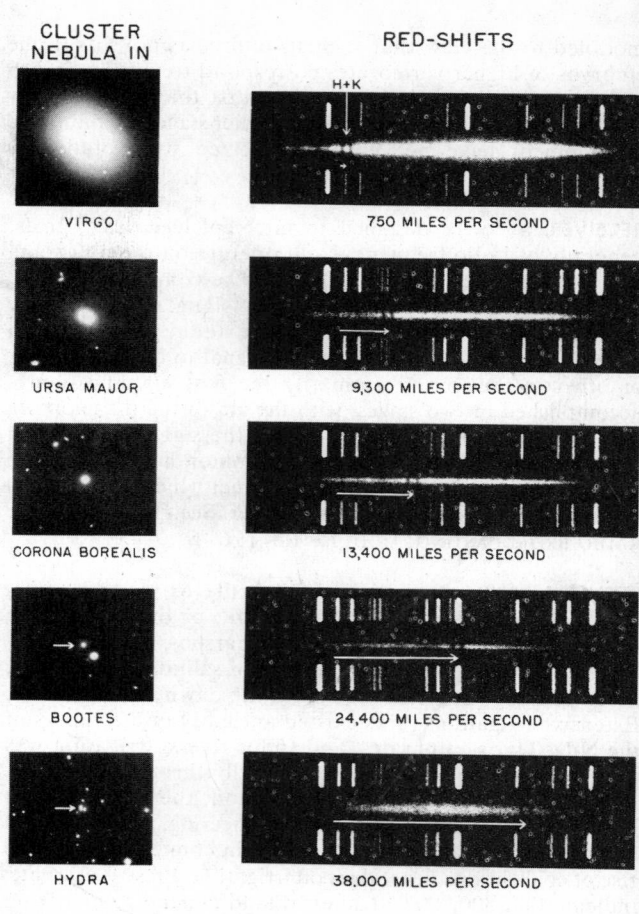

CLUSTER NEBULA IN	RED-SHIFTS
VIRGO	750 MILES PER SECOND
URSA MAJOR	9,300 MILES PER SECOND
CORONA BOREALIS	13,400 MILES PER SECOND
BOOTES	24,400 MILES PER SECOND
HYDRA	38,000 MILES PER SECOND

Red shift: Remote galaxies give spectral lines displaced toward red end of spectrum. Above, laboratory spectra are compared with spectra of galaxies. Two black discontinuities above head of each horizontal arrow show position of absorption lines used for comparison. Red shift results partly from velocity away from Earth in accord with Doppler effect, and partly from gravitational field of galaxies in accord with relativity theory. (*Mt Wilson*)

galaxies, and thus as indicating expansion of the universe. The velocity inferred is proportional to the estimated distance of the source (see HUBBLE'S CONSTANT). This velocity-distance relation, and its independence of direction, form the most powerful and convincing evidence for the uniformity of the universe.—*H. B.*

RED TIDE: a discoloration of ocean waters caused by the sudden multiplication of one-celled organisms called dinoflagellates. The presence of tremendously large numbers of these organisms can turn water red (or sometimes yellow or olive-green). Some species of dinoflagellates contain a poison; others use up so much of the available oxygen in the water that aquatic animals suffocate. In parts of the ocean where there are "blooms" of dinoflagellates, millions of fish may die and be cast ashore by waves. Although the cause of blooms is not known, it is thought that a biological "chain reaction" occurs in which ingested dinoflagellates kill some fish, which in turn decay and supply nutrients to support increased numbers of dinoflagellates, which produce more poison, and so on. The seasonal presence of large "blooms" of poisonous dinoflagellates in many coastal waters presents a serious problem because of the key role played by these organisms in the food chain of the oceans. They are consumed

Red tide: Seasonal population explosions of *Gymnodinium, Gonyaulax,* and other dinoflagellate protozoans cause the death of huge numbers of fish. The protozoans, which secrete a highly toxic alkaloid, contain large reddish vacuoles; hence the name of the phenomenon. (*U. S. Dept. of Interior, Fish and Wildlife Service*)

by shellfish, crustaceans, and other marine organisms. Many shellfish can survive after a meal of poisonous dinoflagellates, because the shellfish segregate the poison in one of their organs. The shellfish remain poisonous, however, and can be toxic if consumed by humans. The toxin is a powerful nerve poison for which no antidote is known. Primitive peoples were aware of the danger of eating fish and shellfish at certain times of the year. Indians living along the west coast of N America posted guards on the shore to warn tribes from inland areas; South Sea islanders had elaborate taboos concerning the eating of fish.—*H. H.*

REDUCING AGENT: see OXIDATION AND REDUCTION.

REDUCTIO AD ABSURDUM: in logic, a familiar species of argument, in which a conclusion is established by proving that the assumption of its falsehood entails a contradiction (and thus an "absurdity"). A simple example is that of the barber who shaved all those people in his town and only those who did not shave themselves. Suppose there were such a barber. If he shaved himself, he would, by assumption, not shave himself. It follows that he *does not* shave himself, for if a statement implies its own negation it must be false (this logical principle has itself sometimes been called *reductio ad absurdum*). But if the barber does not shave himself, then, by assumption, he does; therefore, he *does* shave himself. Our assumption having led to a contradiction, we may conclude that there is no barber of the sort described. —*F. Sc.*

REDUCTION: see OXIDATION AND REDUCTION.

REDUCTIVE EXPLANATION: in philosophy, the process of reducing one theory to·another. When such reduction has been achieved, the phenomena described by the reduced theory

may be considered explained by the theory to which it has been reduced. In some cases the reduction of theory B to theory A consists in showing that the laws of B are special cases of the laws and principles of A; then theory A need not be augmented by supplementary postulates in order to derive the laws of B from it. A standard example of such reduction is the derivation of Kepler's laws from Newton's. Often the derived laws of theory B are not identical with those assumed prior to reduction, so that a reduction will then require a partial alteration of theory.

When theory A deals with phenomena not described and discussed in theory B, the latter can be reduced to A only when A is supplemented by additional postulates. Such postulates stipulate necessary and sufficient conditions for the occurrence of the phenomena discussed in B. If theory B concerns a complex entity whose parts or subsystems are described by A, a reduction is a refutation of some versions of the doctrine of EMERGENCE. The best-known example of such a reduction is the reduction of thermodynamics to statistical mechanics. Here the behavior of gases is explained by reference to the behavior of the sub-entities or molecules of which the gas is ostensibly composed. However, the logical structure of that reduction is still under scrutiny.—*S. M.*

RE-ENTRY: the return of an object, usually a missile or space vehicle launched from Earth, into the atmosphere. The term has been associated with the physical effects arising from the dissipation of the vehicle's kinetic energy as the vehicle is slowed by the increasingly dense atmosphere; these effects include heating of the vehicle's surface as a result of compression and friction drag of the surrounding air sheath. The drag also heats the air and gives it some motion which is subsequently dissipated in the turbulent wake. Air temperatures as high as 14,000°F are encountered in missile re-entry, and

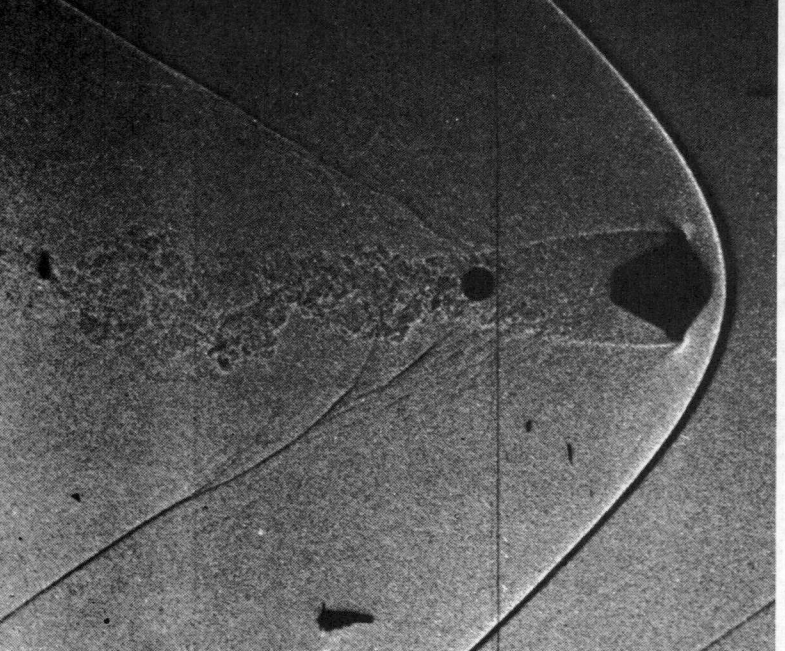

Dissipation of heat produced by passage of object through atmosphere at high velocity is a serious problem of space-vehicle re-entry. Shock waves produced by blunt-nosed cone above help in decelerating body and reducing heat effects. (*Ballistic Research Lab., Aberdeen*)

the heat entering one square foot of surface near the nose each second may be more than enough to convert 1 lb of ice to steam. Conditions surrounding ultra-high-speed vehicles returning from deep-space missions may be even more severe. By use of blunt shapes for ballistic re-entry, it is possible to reduce the severity of the heating effects at the nose. A further advantage of a blunt shape is that it increases pressure drag relative to friction drag; this reduces heat transfer from the atmosphere to the vehicle's surface. Another technique in use for reducing heat transfer to the surface is ABLATION. Re-entry heating has been an important factor in the design of capsules to return astronauts from Earth orbits. Other vehicles whose trajectories include a re-entry phase are glide rockets and skip rockets. See MISSILE; NOSE CONE.—*D. B.*

REFLECTION: the turning back of a material object or wave from the boundary between two media. The phenomenon is usually considered in connection with the behavior of waves. At least partial reflection occurs when any wave motion, such as sound, light, or ripples on a liquid surface, passes from one medium into another, or encounters the interface between two media. For example, when a beam of light strikes the interface between two media, part or all of the beam will rebound from the interface, as a tennis ball rebounds from a concrete wall. If the beam is traveling in air and strikes a

polished metal surface, a very large fraction—perhaps 9/10—will be reflected. If the beam strikes a smooth, transparent surface such as a pane of glass, only a small fraction—perhaps 1/25—will be reflected. The directions of the incident (incoming) and reflected beams are usually measured from the normal to the reflecting surface, *i.e.* from the perpendicular to the surface erected at the point where the light beam strikes the surface. The laws of reflection for rays (narrow beams of light) state that the reflected ray lies in the plane determined by the incident ray and the normal; and the angle between reflected ray and normal (angle of reflection) equals the angle between incoming ray and normal (angle of incidence), as in Fig. 1.

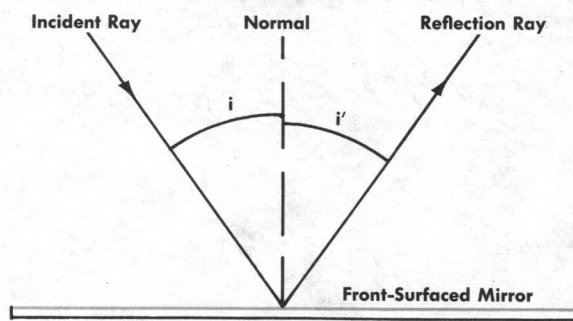

Fig. 1—Specular reflection from a front-surfaced mirror: Angle of incidence *i* equals angle of reflection *i'*.

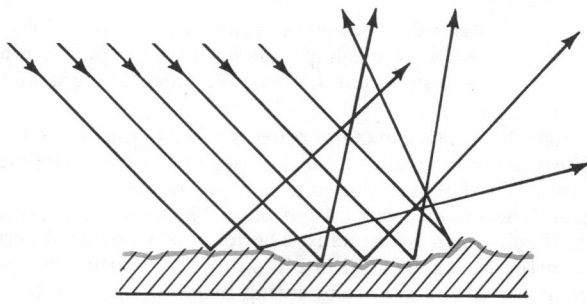

Fig. 2—Diffuse reflection from a rough surface: Reflected light is scattered in many directions.

The fraction of the incident light intensity that is reflected from a surface is a function of the relative refractive index of the two materials forming the interface, the state of polarization of the incident light, the angle of incidence of the light on the surface, and the smoothness of the surface (see REFRACTION; POLARIZED LIGHT). If the surface is flat and well polished, the reflection will be regular, or specular; *i.e.* the angular convergence (or divergence) of the reflected beam will be the

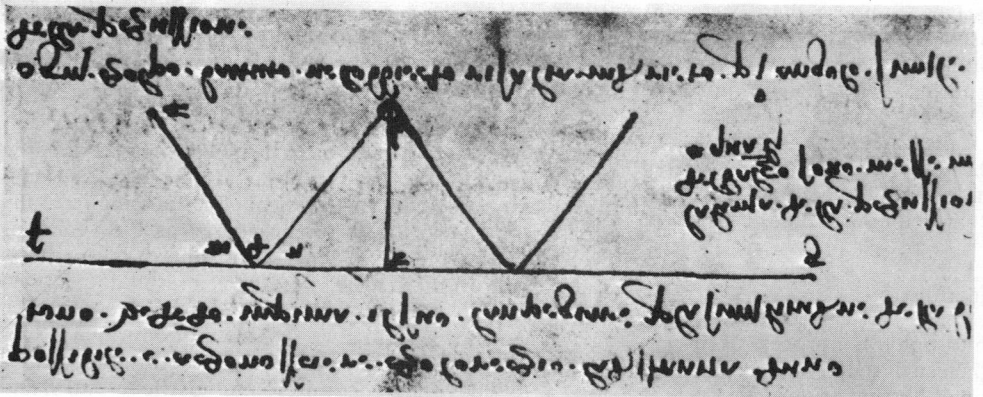

Diagram of reflection from Leonardo Da Vinci's notebooks. Leonardo was familiar with the properties of reflection, particularly that of left-right reversal. His text, written from right to left, can be read conveniently only by holding it up to a mirror.

same as that of the incident beam. If the surface is rough, as in Fig. 2, the reflected light will be scattered; this is described by the term diffuse reflectance. Most surfaces cause both specular reflectance and diffuse reflectance, the relative amounts depending on the smoothness of the surface.

For specular reflectance from nonmetallic, largely transparent objects, the fraction of light reflected is least for normal incidence and increases with increasing angle of incidence. For normal incidence from air onto a body of refractive index n, the specular reflectance ρ is given by Fresnel's formula: $\rho = [(n-1)/(n+1)]^2$. For a parallel-sided slab with negligible absorption, the light is reflected back and forth many times within the sample. The net specular reflectance ρ for the multiple-reflected case, again for normal incidence, is given by the expression: $\rho = 1 - [2n/(n^2+1)]$.

Curved surfaces of high reflectivity are used to alter the convergence or divergence of light rays and may be employed as components of optical instruments. The surfaces are ordinarily spherical in form, although paraboloidal surfaces are used for special applications. See MIRROR.—S. S. B.

REFLEX: an involuntary response to a stimulus, usually evident through movement or secretion. Touching a hot stove with the hand, for example, results in the involuntary jerking away of the arm; tickling of the throat elicits a gagging reflex; shining a bright light in the eyes causes the pupils to constrict; putting food in the mouth elicits the secretion of saliva. The simplest reflexes are mediated by a simple three-neuron arc. The first (sensory) NEURON conducts a NERVOUS IMPULSE from the stimulated receptor to a second (association) neuron (generally in the spinal cord), which then conducts the impulse to a third (motor) neuron running to the appropriate muscles or secretory organs. See NERVOUS SYSTEM. —D. M. F.

REFRACTION: the change in the direction of propagation of a wave, such as sound or light, as it passes from one medium into another. The path of the wave bends because the wave travels with different speeds in the two media. For example, the speed of light in water is ¾ that in air, and its speed in glass is about ⅔ that in air. The change in speed is specified by a number called refractive index or index of refraction, usually given the symbol n, which is the ratio of the speeds of light in the two media. When one of the media is a vacuum, in which light travels with the constant speed of about 186,300 mi/sec, *absolute* refractive indexes are obtained —1.33 for water and about 1.5 for glass. But since light travels only very slightly more slowly in air than in a vacuum, the absolute refractive index of air being 1.0003, it is satisfactory in most practical instances to quote refractive indexes relative to air rather than vacuum.

When a beam of light, traveling through air, strikes the surface of an object, some light is reflected from the surface (see REFLECTION). If the object is opaque, the rest of the light is absorbed at or near the surface. If the object is transparent, the light beam is transmitted through it, although there is always a certain amount of light lost by internal absorption, and some light may also be lost from the beam by scattering within the object.

If a narrow beam of light strikes the surface of a transparent substance at an oblique angle, the beam will be abruptly bent as it enters the substance. Snell's law, first stated in 1621, relates i, the angle of incidence between the incoming ray and the normal to the surface (the perpendicular to the surface erected at the point where the beam strikes); r, the angle of refraction between this normal and the ray traveling inside the medium; and n, the refractive index of the medium, as: $n = \sin i/\sin r$ (Fig. 1). Thus, since light

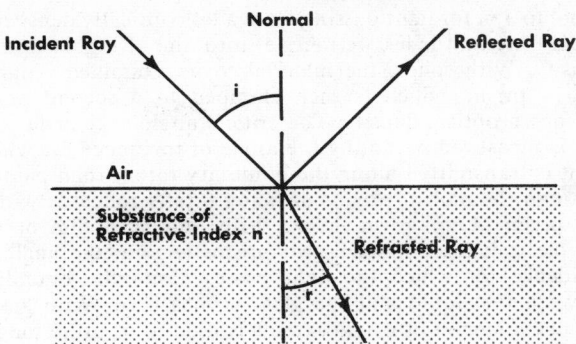

Fig. 1: Light ray entering a more refractive medium from a less refractive medium is bent toward the normal. Ray entering less refractive from more refractive medium is bent away from normal.

travels more slowly in the medium than in air, n is greater than 1 and r is less than i. That is, upon entering the substance the ray is bent *toward* the normal.

Since light rays passing from a more refractive medium into a less refractive medium are bent *away* from the normal, objects immersed in water appear to be at shallower depths than they really are (Fig. 2). For example, if the water in a swimming pool is 8 ft deep, to an observer who looks down perpendicularly on the water surface, the bottom of the pool seems to be only 6 ft below the surface. In general, and for viewing perpendicularly to the surface, the apparent depth

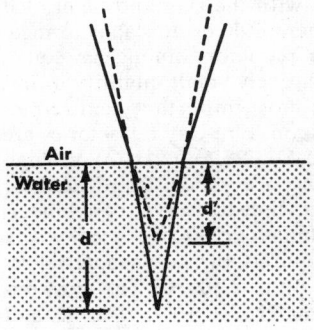

Fig. 2: An object submerged in water to a depth d appears to be at a shallower depth d'. Because of refraction, light rays after emerging from water follow paths represented by solid lines instead of paths represented by dashed lines.

equals the real depth divided by the refractive index of the medium: $d' = d/n$.

The bending of light rays by glass objects is put to use in optical instruments through components called PRISMS and LENSES. The former produce net deflections or deviations of the light beam, and the latter are used to bring light to a focus or otherwise to form optical images of real objects. Unless light of only a single color is used, chromatic effects are produced, since the speed of light in any substance varies somewhat with the color (wavelength) of the light. Blue light travels more slowly than red light; hence the refractive index of a substance is greater for blue light than for red light. Light of all colors travels with the same speed in a vacuum. —S. S. B.

REFRACTOMETER: a device used to measure the optical index of REFRACTION. Different refractometers are used for work with solids, liquids, and gases. Those used with solids and liquids do not directly measure the index of refraction n, but rather measure a related property of the substance under examination: the CRITICAL ANGLE at which total internal reflection takes place. The sine of this angle is numerically equal to $1/n$ for light passing from a less optically dense medium (one that is less refractive) into one of higher optical density. With solids, the material to be examined is made into a prism, which is then clamped to a second prism of known optical density. The critical angle at their boundary is measured by noting the angle of incidence for which light is transmitted along the boundary rather than passing through the pair of prisms or being totally reflected within the prism of unknown index. With liquids, a film of the sample is placed between two prisms. Again, the angle of incidence for which the light passes along the boundary between the liquid and the glass is measured. With gases, the phenomenon of INTERFERENCE is used to measure the index of refraction. If part of the light from a single source is passed through the gas and part through air, a recombination of the two beams will yield interference fringes (see DIFFRACTION), because of the difference in the speeds of light in the two media. The ratio of the speeds is the index of refraction with respect to air, which may be corrected for the difference between this index and the "absolute" index with respect to a vacuum.—*E. M. R.*

REFRACTORY: a structural material that retains its strength at high temperatures. Refractories are used for lining furnaces, crucibles, and high-temperature vessels, and also for constructing boiler settings and incinerators. Chemically they are classified as acid, basic, or neutral, according to the typical chemical reactions they undergo at high temperatures. The chemical character of a refractory is of particular importance in metallurgy: the refractory lining of a smelting furnace must be acidic if the slag is acidic, and basic if the slag is basic; otherwise it will react with the slag and be eroded rapidly. In a refining furnace where little or no slag is formed, *e.g.* a steelmaking furnace, the refractory lining can sometimes assist in removing the relatively small quantity of impurity by reacting with it. The most important acid refractories are fire clay, silica, and zircon. Fire-clay refractories are made by baking kaolinite ($Al_2O_3 \cdot 2SiO_2 \cdot 2H_2O$) to high temperatures. Silica refractories are made from sand or quartzite rock, with just enough lime to serve as a binder. Zircon ($ZrO_2 \cdot SiO_2$) and zirconia (ZrO_2) are used where extreme resistance to heat is required, the latter material remaining strong at temperatures up to 2,500°C. The most important basic refractory raw materials are magnesite and dolomite; these are calcined before use so that the final refractory substance consists of magnesium oxide or a mixture of magnesium and calcium oxides. These are widely used in open-hearth steel furnaces and in Portland-cement kilns. The common neutral refractories are chromite ore, a mixture of $FeO \cdot Cr_2O_3$ with $MgO \cdot Al_2O_3$ and $FeO \cdot Al_2O_3$; mullite or "high alumina," a name applied to clays containing more than 50% Al_2O_3; and carbon.

Refractories are most commonly fabricated in brick form, but special shapes are also made, as well as mortars and cements. The choice of a refractory for a given high-temperature operation involves not only its chemical behavior but its mechanical strength, volume stability, and resistance to thermal shock; other important factors are heat capacity, thermal conductivity, and electrical resistance.—*A. M. S.*

REFRIGERATION: The process of obtaining and maintaining a temperature below that of the surrounding atmosphere. Attainment of reduced temperatures implies removal of heat from any material or enclosed area. Heat removal is most commonly achieved by inducing a change of phase in the refrigerant, *e.g.* vaporization of liquid ammonia or the melting of ice.

Natural refrigeration makes use of ice, well water, evapora-

tion of water, and cool air from cellars or caves. The spring-house on the farm, the use of porous clay jugs in arid climates to cool water, the "icebox" used widely up to 20 yr ago are familiar examples. When ice melts at a constant temperature, heat is required. The space or material to be cooled supplies this heat and is thus refrigerated. The limit on such a system is the freezing point of water. Since heat flows to a cooler body, well water can refrigerate warmer objects to a temperature close to that of the water. The evaporation of water requires heat just as does the melting of ice. The rate of evaporation depends upon the relative humidity of the air. With a high relative humidity, the rate of evaporation is very slow, with a corresponding small amount of refrigeration.

Mechanical (or artificial) *refrigeration* usually operates on the principle of a liquid-to-gas, gas-back-to-liquid cycle. Two such systems are the compression refrigeration cycle and the absorption refrigeration cycle. The compression refrigeration cycle utilizes a compressor, a condenser, an expansion valve, and an evaporator to achieve refrigeration. In this process, the refrigerant vapor leaving the evaporator is compressed to a high pressure, with subsequent elevation of the boiling point. The vapor, now at high temperature and pressure, enters the condenser and is condensed, releasing heat. The liquid refrigerant is partially vaporized by passing it through the expansion valve, where it undergoes a pressure drop. This vaporization extracts heat from the remaining liquid, and the temperature of the liquid is reduced. The mixture is then passed through an evaporator, where heat is absorbed and the liquid is again vaporized. The absorption of heat in the evaporator provides the refrigeration.

Absorption refrigeration retains the condenser, expansion valve, and evaporator of the compression system, but replaces the compressor with an absorber, a pump, a generator, or still (in which vapor is driven out of solution) and a pressure-reducing valve. The vapor from the evaporator flows into the absorber, where an absorbent fluid traps the refrigerant vapor. Brine heat is generated in this absorption process and is removed by cooling water. The cooled absorbent containing the refrigerant enters a pump which increases its pressure. Most of the refrigerant vapor is driven off as the mixture passes through the generator. The refrigerant then flows to the condenser, at which point the operation is similar to the compression refrigeration cycle. The absorbent is cooled by expansion through a pressure-reducing valve and returned to the absorber.

Steam-jet refrigeration is a method of refrigeration utilizing ejection of the evaporator vapor by means of a jet using high-pressure steam. Since water is usually the refrigerant, temperatures below the freezing point of water cannot be obtained.

Although refrigeration is primarily an application of thermodynamics, other phases of engineering are involved in the design, manufacture, and operation of refrigeration systems. Some knowledge of the chemistry of refrigerants, as well as of their thermodynamic properties, is necessary if one is to analyze the cycles involved. A study of evaporators and condensers, and their heat transmission and fluid-flow characteristics, is also essential. Calculation of cooling loads requires a knowledge of the physiological conditions necessary for body comfort, while fluid mechanics plays an important role in the sizing of the equipment.—*K. T.*

REGENERATION: the replacement by an animal or a plant of parts that have been lost or destroyed. The regenerative capacities of living things vary greatly, but in general are more spectacular in plants and lower animals than in higher animals. Many plants show an almost unlimited capacity for repairing mutilations. Thus, if a tree is cut down, the stump may regenerate new twigs. At the opposite extreme are mammals, such as man, in which the regenerative capacity is limited to the healing of wounds, the production of scar tissue in damaged organs, the production of red and white blood cells to replace those constantly lost, the regeneration of liver cells, and other minor aspects of maintenance.

Lower animals show all degrees of regenerative ability. When certain unicellular organisms, *e.g. Stentor,* are cut up, a fragment ⅟₅₀th the size of the original will develop into a new whole individual. If the fresh-water coelenterate, *Hydra,* and the flatworm, *Planaria,* are cut into several portions, each portion develops into a new individual. Common starfishes are able to regenerate new limbs; in fact, a detached arm alone may produce a whole starfish. Before this was known, commercial oyster fishermen had vainly attempted to reduce the population of oyster-eating starfishes by chopping up and tossing back into the ocean all the starfishes they caught. Many crabs and crustaceans can regenerate lost legs. The capacity of both starfishes and crustaceans to regenerate lost arms and legs is adaptively associated with their ability to shed appendages that are injured or held by predators. When roughly molested by a lobster or other animal, the sea cucumber can explosively eject nearly all its internal organs. These contain a viscous material that can effectively entangle the foe. The sea cucumber then regenerates an entirely new set of visceral organs within a few weeks. Among vertebrates the capacity to restore major organs is restricted to the lower groups. For example, many fish can regenerate fins; salamanders and newts are able to restore tails and in some instances can replace lost limbs; and some lizards can regenerate a tail that has broken off.—*A. P. E.*

REGIOMONTANUS, 1436–76, German mathematician and astronomer; b. Johann Müller, at Königsberg; ed. Leipzig and Vienna. A student of G. Purbach, Regiomontanus became the outstanding mathematician of his day and contributed to the advancement of trigonometry, geometry, arithmetic, and astronomy. He edited Latin versions of the works of Ptolemy, Apollonius, and others. His *Tabulae directionum profectionumque* (1475) contained the first table of tangents published in Europe. He also wrote *De doctrina triangulorum* (1463), *De quadratura circuli* (1463), and many other works of mathematics and astronomy.—*R. N. M.*

REGNAULT, HENRI VICTOR, 1810–78, French physicist and chemist; b. Aix-la-Chapelle. In 1835 he started studying halogenated hydrocarbons, alkaloids, and organic acids. His 4-volume *Chemistry* (1847) became world-famous. His basic work on the specific heats of solids, liquids, and gases (1840) was followed by most careful measurements of vapor tensions and heat of evaporation of water (1841) and by collection of data on propagation of sound in gases and the conductivity of gases for heat (1856–70). He improved the air thermometer and the hygrometer, and measured the expansion of mercury accurately. A member of the Académie des Sciences, he was also a fellow of the Royal Society and an associate of the U. S. National Academy of Sciences.—*R. J. F.*

RELATION: one of the most common general ideas employed in mathematics. In algebra and arithmetic we have such relations as less than, equal to, and function of; in geometry we have such relations as parallel, collinear, congruent. The foundations of mathematics make use of certain simple notions: points and lines, and statements of relations between them, *e.g.:* "Through any two points in the plane, there is one and only one straight line." Relations thus appear in the first principles, and all mathematics itself might be described as a study of relations between certain elements such as numbers or points.

A relation is a way of bringing together the elements of two sets. There are several different types: The relation of mother to son is a one-many relation, since one mother may have many sons, but the relation of son to mother is many-one, since many sons may have the same mother. The relation of doubling in numbers is a one-one relation, since for any number n there is only one double, namely $2n$, and for $2n$ there is only one number n that is its half. Relations are classed as *symmetric, reflexive,* and *transitive.* A relation between two terms x and y is symmetric if xRy implies yRx; that is, if "x has a relation to y" implies "y has the same relation to x." The relations "parallel" between straight lines and "brother of" between two brothers are symmetric. If xRy implies that yRx is false, the relation is said to be asymmetric, *e.g.* "father of." Relations that are neither symmetric nor asymmetric are nonsymmetric; thus "John loves Mary" does not imply that Mary either does or does not love John. A relation is reflexive if xRx is always true, and aliorelative if xRx is always false; thus "equal to" and "congruent" are reflexive, but "less than" and "perpendicular to" are aliorelative. A relation is transitive if "xRy and yRz" always implies xRz (*e.g.* "less than, since $a < b$ and $b < c$ implies $a < c$). If a relation is symmetric, reflexive, and transitive, it is called equable; *e.g.* the relations of equality and congruence. (See also ORDER RELATION.)—*H. E. W.*

RELATIVE HUMIDITY: see HUMIDITY.

RELATIVITY: a theory of the nature of space, time, energy, and gravitation, originally developed by Albert Einstein. The first series of his papers (1905), known collectively as the *special theory of relativity,* discussed principally the behavior of matter, energy, and light in the restricted case in which all observers are moving in a straight line and at constant speed with respect to each other. Such relative motions, in which no acceleration or deceleration is present, are called inertial motions (from the principle of inertia, according to which a body not subjected to external forces proceeds at a uniform unaccelerated speed). Similarly, the observers are called in-

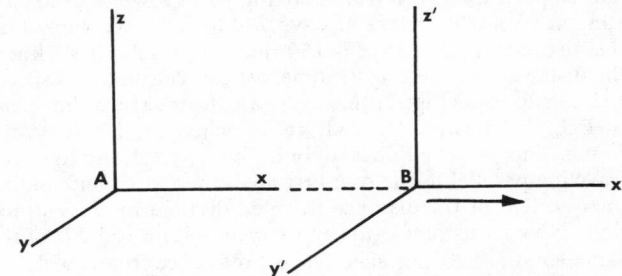

Fig. 1—Inertial observers: Observer A performs physical measurements in frame of reference x, y, z. Observer B performs them in frame x', y', z'. B and frame x', y', z' are moving at uniform rectilinear speed with respect to A and frame x, y, z.

ertial observers (Fig. 1). Each inertial observer must, of necessity, perform all his physical measurements and experiments in his own environment, *i.e.* in a frame of reference attached to himself. In the *general theory of relativity* (1916), Einstein expanded his original theories to make them applicable to inertial and non-inertial (*i.e.* rotating or accelerated) observers alike. Since gravitation is the principal cause of accelerated space motions, the general theory is in fact the relativistic theory of gravitation. As such, it finds its applications mostly in the domain of astronomy.

Special, or Restricted, Theory: Historically, the need to revise existing concepts concerning the behavior of light became imperative after the failure of the MICHELSON-MORLEY EXPERIMENT. The original purpose of this experiment had been to obtain Earth's orbital velocity by comparing the observed speed of light in the direction of Earth's motion with the speed of light at right angles to that direction. From everyday experience, one would assume that light traveling alongside the Earth would appear to move more slowly than if it traveled sideways because, in the first instance, Earth's speed would be subtracted from the light's speed. Yet Michelson and Morley observed no trace of the effect. This odd behavior of light led Einstein to formulate his *special principle of relativity,* which states that the laws of nature appear the same to all inertial observers. This means, in particular, that if light has a velocity c with respect to an observer A, it has the same velocity c relative to all observers who are in uniform motion with respect to A. Only in the case of light was Einstein's principle at variance with earlier concepts; it did not contradict the basic assumptions of Newtonian dynamics, which hold that *mechanical* laws apply to all inertial observers. The assumption of an invariable speed of light, however, had far-reaching consequences affecting the concepts of space and time.

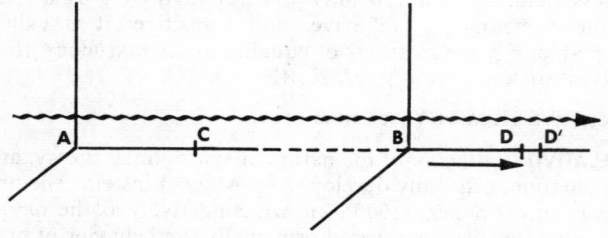

Fig. 2—Length contraction: Light ray takes same time to travel from A to C as from B to D′. Since speed of light is constant for A and B, BD (which would be same length as AC if both were at rest) must contract in direction of its motion.

One of these consequences is called *length contraction.* Lengths (or distances) may be measured in terms of speed and elapsed time: if a train starting from town A and traveling at 75 mi/hr arrives at town B 2 hr later, we know that the distance from A to B is 150 mi; conversely, if we know the distance and the elapsed time, we can calculate the speed. Let us suppose (Fig. 2) that we want to measure the speed of light by means of a rod AC attached to A's reference frame. This may be done by timing the arrival of a light ray traveling parallel to the rod, first at A, then at C, and finding the quotient of the distance traveled divided by the elapsed time. Now let us repeat the experiment with a rod BD of the same length as AC, attached to B's reference frame, which is moving in the same direction as the light at uniform rectilinear speed with respect to A. We time the arrival of the light ray at B, but while the ray travels the length of the rod, the latter has moved and the extremity D is now at D'. Yet we know from the Michelson-Morley experiment that the light ray travels the distance BD' in the same time as for AC. Since the speed of light is invariable, we must assume that BD has contracted in the direction of its motion in order to restore the same value to the quotient. According to Einstein's equations, a rod of length l at rest with respect to A contracts to a length $l\sqrt{1-(v^2/c^2)}$ with respect to B, if B has a velocity v relative to A.

Another important consequence of assuming an invariable speed of light is the effect called *time dilatation.* Let us suppose that observer B sets off a green flare at time t'_1 and

a red flare at time t'_2. For him the two events occur in the same place in his own frame of reference, and they are separated by a time interval $(t'_2 - t'_1)$ as measured by his clock. The flares are seen by A in the same order, but because B is moving with respect to A, the latter sees the red flare at a point in space other than the green; furthermore, B's distance from A has increased in the interval, so the red flash takes longer to reach A than the green, and the time interval $(t_2 - t_1)$ that A measures by *his* clock appears longer. The same result would be obtained if the time intervals $(t'_2 - t'_1)$ and $(t_2 - t_1)$ were equal on some absolute scale, with A's clock ticking faster than B's; this is equivalent to saying that if A attempts in his own reference frame to measure time intervals occurring in B's reference frame, his clock (which is at rest) appears to run faster than B's clock (which is in relative motion). Einstein's equations demonstrate that the moving clock is slower than the clock at rest in the ratio $\sqrt{1-(v^2/c^2)}$ in which, as before, v is the speed of B relative to A, and c is the speed of light.

An extension of this reasoning makes it clear that absolute simultaneity no longer has any meaning for a group of inertial observers. Two observers C and D, separately in uniform motion with respect to A and B, may set off flares which happen to reach A simultaneously, yet B may well see D's flare some time before or after C's. Hence time cannot be conceived as being measured by an absolute succession of events independent of the observer. Rather, time must be related to the reference frame of each observer; in other words, it must be treated as a fourth coordinate (or dimension) which, together with length, width, and height, completely describes the observer within a *space-time continuum* in the same way that length, width, and height describe him in three-dimensional Euclidean space.

The effect of time dilatation has been verified in the behavior of the elementary particles called MESONS. The mathematical expressions used by Einstein to relate the space and time measurements at A to those at B are known as the LORENTZ TRANSFORMATION.

These changes in the concepts of space and time made it necessary to change the laws of dynamics as well, particularly where the mass of a body in motion is concerned. As a rule, we think of a body's mass in terms of its weight; but we may think of it also in terms of the energy we must apply to stop it if it is moving toward us: the heavier it is, the more we must exert ourselves. However, the energy we must expend increases also with the speed of the body: the faster it travels, the harder it is to stop. This is equivalent to saying that the mass of the body is increased by the amount of kinetic energy it acquires from its speed. Einstein showed that a body of mass m at rest relative to A has a mass $m/\sqrt{1-(v^2/c^2)}$ relative to B. This formula has been verified by measurements in discharge tubes and particle accelerators. The increase of mass Δm arises from the kinetic energy K of the body according to the formula $K = c^2\Delta m$. This equation expresses the equivalence of mass and kinetic energy. Einstein showed that, in its most general form, it may be written as $E = mc^2$, in which m is the mass of a body at rest (*i.e.* its inertial mass) and E is its equivalent in any form of energy This general equivalence of mass and energy was regarded by Einstein as the most important consequence of his theory. It underlies much of nuclear and elementary-particle physics, where it has been amply verified. It also underlies many energy-producing processes, *e.g.* those occurring in Sun and stars, in atomic and hydrogen bombs, and in reactors.

General Relativity: Let us imagine (Fig. 3 *left*) an observer A on a rotating platform—*i.e.* a non-inertial observer—who sees an object B sliding without friction on the floor below.

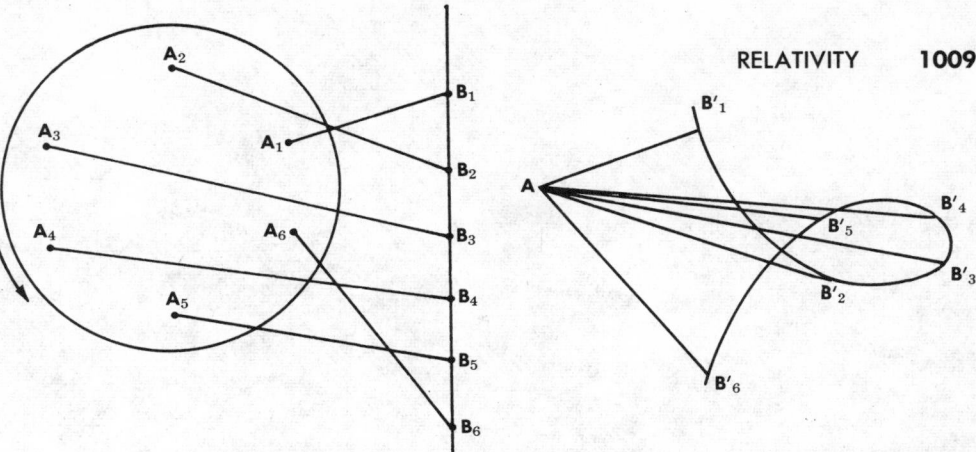

Fig. 3—Non-inertial observer: *Left*—A is carried successively to positions A_1, A_2, A_3, etc., by rotation of platform. B is sliding without friction, hence is moving in uniform rectilinear motion and is seen successively by A at positions B_1, B_2, B_3, etc. *Right*—To A, who considers himself at rest, B appears to follow path B_1', B_2', B_3', etc.

A is unaware of his motion and considers himself at rest. To him the motion of *B* appears to occur in a curved path (Fig. 3 *right*), in flagrant contradiction of Newton's principle of inertia. In order to reconcile *B*'s motion with Newtonian dynamics, *A* must assume the existence of an inertial force—*i.e.* a force that counteracts *B*'s inertia. Inertial forces—*e.g.* Coriolis force (as in this case) and centrifugal force—do not seem to have a physical origin in matter; this would suggest that the laws of nature are different for non-inertial and inertial observers, hence that the relativity principle could not be extended to non-inertial observers. However, Einstein was able to prove, by use of very imaginative comparisons, that a non-inertial observer isolated in his own frame of reference is incapable of distinguishing the effect of inertial forces from that of gravitation. Let us imagine, for example, that a man is sealed in one of the cabins of a Ferris wheel set out far enough in outer space that it is not subject to any gravitational effect. The man cannot see outside and therefore considers himself at rest. The turning Ferris wheel keeps him hurled outward, his feet pressing firmly on one of the cabin's walls. If the walls are all identical, he considers that particular wall as the floor and believes himself to be standing in a room under the action of gravitation. Yet an observer outside the Ferris wheel explains the man's position in terms of centrifugal force.

These considerations, together with the fact that gravitation always exactly counteracts inertia regardless of a body's mass (since bodies of all masses are equally accelerated in free fall), led Einstein, in 1907, to assume that *inertial forces are gravitational in origin.* This is known as the *principle of equivalence.* Having thus assumed that inertial forces have a physical nature after all, he was then able to formulate the principle of general relativity, which states that the laws of nature apply equally to inertial and non-inertial observers.

An alternative interpretation of inertial forces was proposed by Ernst Mach, who held that inertia is caused entirely by the gravitational effects of distant stars. Known as Mach's Principle, this theory has not been disproved, but it requires us to assume the existence in the universe of vast amounts of matter, far in excess of those revealed by observation.

Fig. 4—Advance of Mercury's perihelion (point in orbit closest to Sun) occurs at a faster rate than predicted by Newton's theory. White arrow, above, shows predicted advance; colored arrow shows the advance actually observed. Einstein's theories of relativity explain this discrepancy. (Natural History/*Helmut Wimmer*)

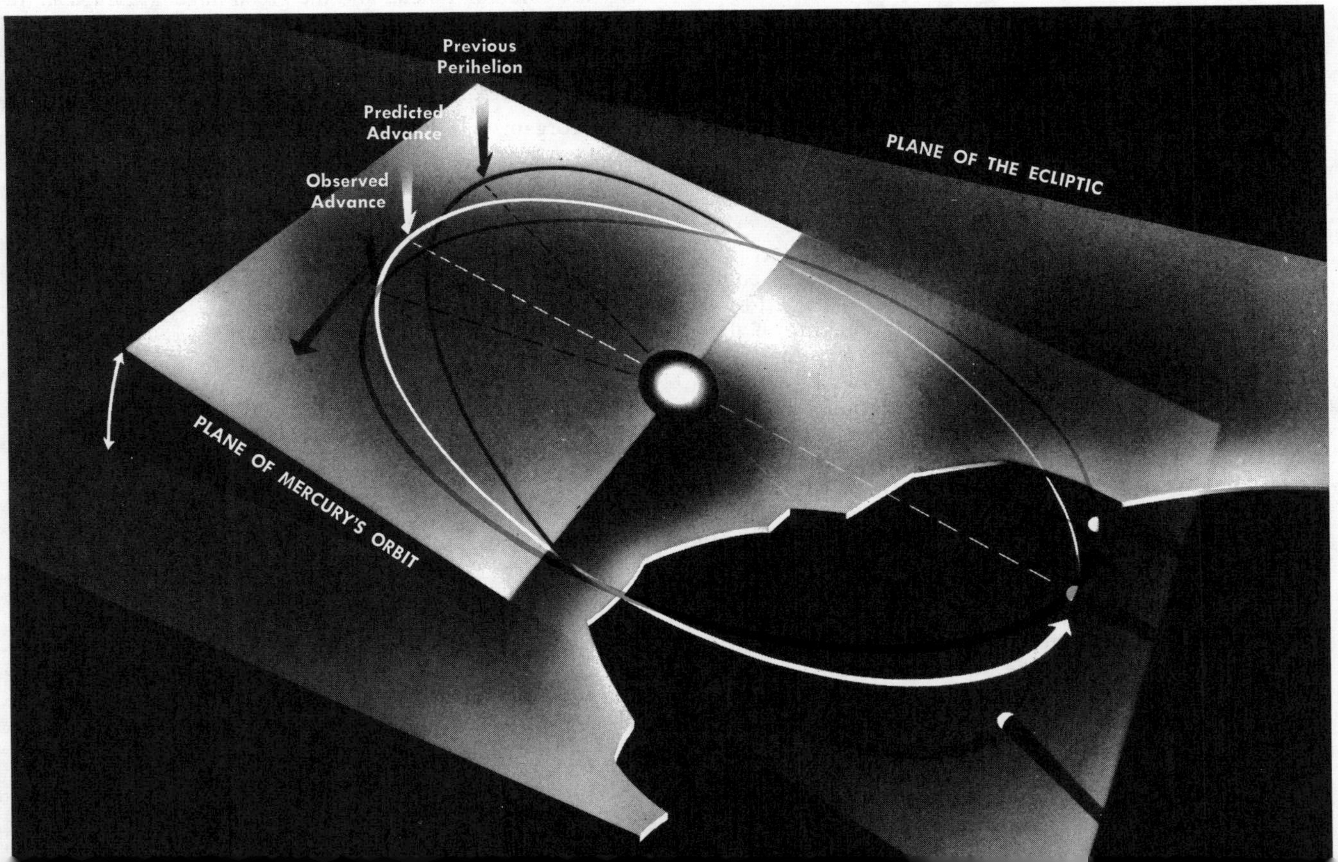

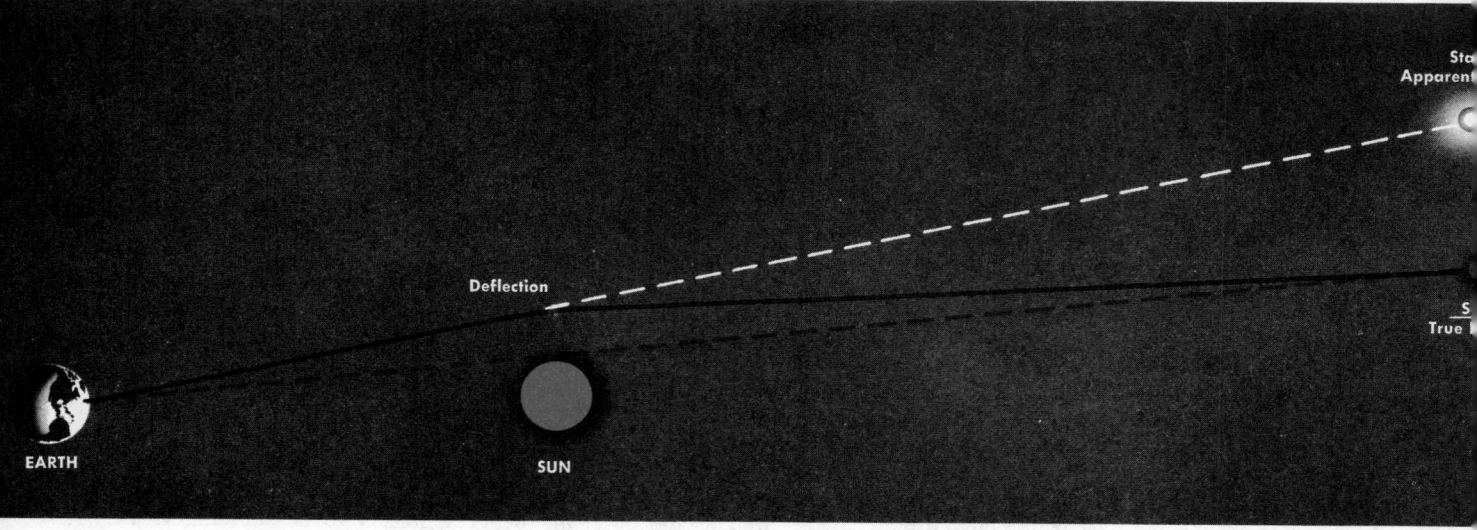

Star
Apparent

Deflection

S
True

EARTH

SUN

Fig. 5—Deflection of light by massive bodies, diagramed above (exaggerated for clarity), was a further Einstein prediction. Apparent position of a star (*white*), viewed close to Sun's edge, is compared here with its true position (*colored*). (Natural History/*Helmut Wimmer*)

Rather than retaining Newton's concept of gravitation as a force acting instantaneously at great distances—an idea that had puzzled physicists since its inception—Einstein introduced the notion of a *gravitational field*. Just as a magnet creates a pattern of lines of magnetic force (a magnetic field), a massive body such as a star or planet creates a gravitational field around itself. The orbits of celestial bodies are determined by the conditions within that field, in the same manner that iron filings follow the lines of force in the magnet's field.

After Einstein worked out the complex mathematical formulation of his theory (*c.* 1916), he was able to predict a number of astronomical phenomena susceptible of verification, which are not accounted for by Newtonian dynamics. They are:

a) *Advance of Mercury's perihelion* (Fig. 4): When the orbit of a planet around the Sun is computed by Newton's formulas, it is found to be an ellipse slightly distorted by the action of other planets. The perihelion of the orbit—*i.e.* the point nearest the Sun—is also found to move slightly eastward; in other words, the orbit rotates slowly in space. But in the case of Mercury, the observed advance of the perihelion had been known for some time to exceed the value predicted by Newtonian theory. The revised value predicted by Einstein (43 sec of arc per century) agreed satisfactorily with observation. In recent years the Einstein result has also been verified for Earth and Venus.

b) *Gravitational red shift:* See article of same title.

c) *Deflection of starlight* (Fig. 5): Einstein considered light as consisting of particles of matter. Thus a light ray coming from a star and grazing the Sun would be deflected by the Sun's gravitational field. The predicted "bending of light" leads to an apparent displacement of the star that is just twice the amount predicted by Newton's law of gravitation, assuming each light quantum has a gravitational mass given by $E = mc^2$. This effect has been sought at total solar eclipses, when the stars surrounding the Sun become visible. It was first verified, at least qualitatively, at the eclipse of May 29, 1919.

Einstein's equations have also been used in cosmology, the study of the structure of the universe as a whole. Here the main observational fact is that galaxies are receding from one another. This appears to imply that at some time in the past they were all concentrated in one point. This BIG-BANG HYPOTHESIS is opposed by the nonrelativistic STEADY-STATE THEORY, which asserts that on a large scale the universe always has the same appearance, the continuous creation of new

matter compensating for the expansion. Data obtained from recent observations have tended to favor the big-bang hypothesis.—*S. D. G.*

RENAISSANCE SCIENCE: SEE MEDIEVAL AND RENAISSANCE SCIENCE.

REPRODUCTION: the process by which all organisms, both plant and animal, duplicate themselves. It is one of the major criteria for distinguishing living from nonliving things. The duplication may provide two individuals from one, through *asexual reproduction*. Or it may produce one individual (or more) from two parents, through *sexual reproduction*. In the latter, the most significant event is the fusion of two sex cells (gametes), one from each parent, to form one cell from which the new individual grows.

Asexual Reproduction: Single-celled animals and plants, *e.g.* the common ameba and the green flagellate *Euglena*, reproduce in the simplest way. First the nucleus of the cell divides into two by mitosis, and the daughter nuclei move apart in the cytoplasm. Then the cytoplasm separates into two equal parts, each containing one daughter nucleus; each part reorganizes itself into a complete, new individual organ-

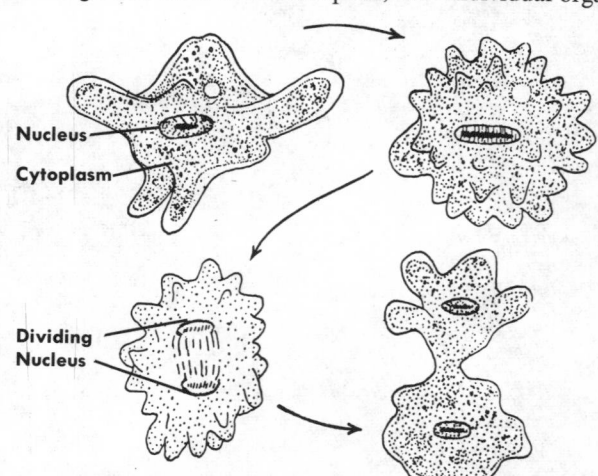

Nucleus

Cytoplasm

Dividing
Nucleus

Binary fission in ameba: During this process of asexual reproduction the nucleus first undergoes mitotic division. Then the cytoplasm constricts, dividing equally between the two daughter nuclei, and two individuals are formed. (*From Kenoyer*)

ism. Where one cell produces two of the same size, and these separate as new individuals, the process is called *binary fission*. A modification of this occurs in yeast cells, where one daughter nucleus moves out into a small projecting mass of cytoplasm (a *bud*) extending from one side of the parent cell; gradually the bud grows to full size, and may repeat the process before separating completely from the parent cell. This type of reproduction is called *budding*. (See YEAST.)

In multicellular plants and animals, ordinary cell duplication is similar to binary fission, but the cells do not separate (see CELL DIVISION). Instead, they remain together as component parts of a growing individual. Commonly the rate of cell division and growth decreases as mature size is reached; the slowing corresponds to maturation of the component cells and of the organization of the whole organism; generally it is related to a definite LIFE SPAN. In some plants (*e.g.* certain lilies) and animals (*e.g.* the fresh-water coelenterate *Hydra* and various sea anemones) a small portion of the parent body grows out as a multicellular bud, which separates from the parent and grows into a new individual. Many ALGAE and most FUNGI reproduce asexually by means of SPORES—single cells produced in vast numbers in special spore-bearing bodies, *e.g.* sporangia; often a whole mass of spore-producing structures are raised into the air, as is evident when mushrooms rise from inconspicuous fungus plants growing below the surface of the soil. Liverworts commonly produce on their upper surfaces small cup-shaped structures in which thin plates of green cells are freed from the parent plant. Rain drops splashing into the cups distribute the multicellular plates (gemmae), each of which can develop into a new liverwort plant (see MOSSES AND LIVERWORTS).

Some of the flatworms and a few kinds of marine segmented worms reproduce asexually by *fragmentation*. The body of the animal grows very long and then divides transversely into a number of separate individuals, each of which reorganizes itself to acquire an intact front and back end. Filamentous algae, *e.g.* the pond scum *Spirogyra*, often reproduce in this way, as if by accident, when individual filaments have grown very long by repeated cell divisions. Somewhat similar to fragmentation is a process called *stolonization* that occurs in many higher plants, *e.g.* hawkweeds and wild raspberry bushes; branches extended sideward by these plants take root at the tips and become independent plants.

Sexual Reproduction: In the simplest type of sexual reproduction, *e.g.* in the slipper animalcule *Paramecium* and the unicellular fresh-water alga *Chlamydomonas*, two individual cells join together, combine hereditary material, and then separate as individuals with a changed genetic content. Even here, however, the fusion of hereditary materials from two parental cells is followed by a reduction division (MEIOSIS), which reduces the number of chromosomes in the daughter cells to the same number that was in the parent cells before sexual fusion. In many unicellular plants and animals that reproduce sexually in this way, the sex of the parent cells cannot be distinguished except by behavior; mating strains are then referred to as "plus" and "minus," with the realization that a cell of a plus strain will fuse with one of a minus strain, but that two of plus strain or two of minus strain will fail to unite.

In the pond scum *Spirogyra* and related green algae, two filaments lying parallel in the water may engage in sexual reproduction; individual cells extend tubular extensions (conjugation tubes) that touch, join, and serve as a bridge across which the contents of one cell move to combine with the contents of the other. In *conjugation* (a "yoking together") of this kind, the cell whose contents move across the bridge is regarded as the active partner and hence male, the other as

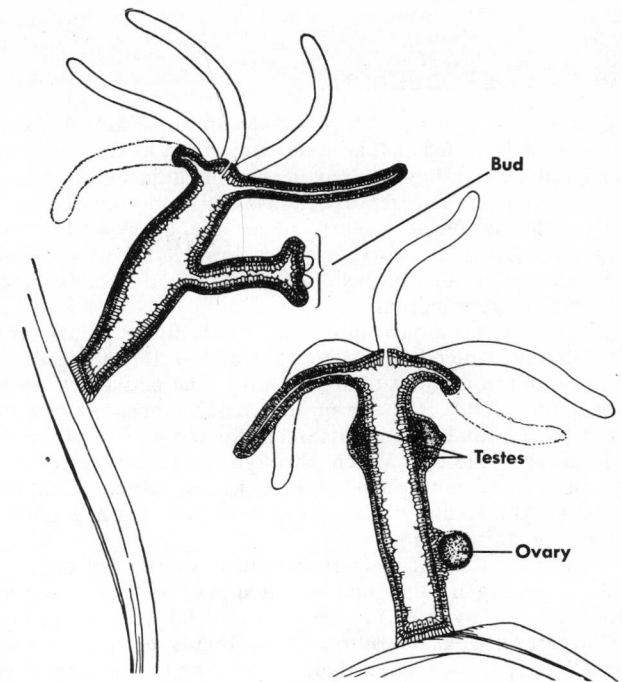

Reproduction in *Hydra* occurs both asexually (by budding) and sexually (through production of ova and sperm). Individual at left has produced a bud which will eventually constrict at its base and detach, becoming an independent *Hydra*. *Hydra* at the right has developed testes and an ovary. The testes release mature sperm into the water, and a sperm cell then penetrates the ovary and fertilizes a mature ovum. The embryo becomes encysted and the cyst separates from the parent, drops into the water, and develops into an adult *Hydra*. (*From Kenoyer*)

Conjugation in *Paramecium*: In this very primitive method of sexual reproduction, two individuals join together temporarily and exchange nuclear materials (sequence in left column). Following the exchange, the exconjugants separate and each one undergoes two asexual fissions (sequence in right column). (*From Kenoyer*)

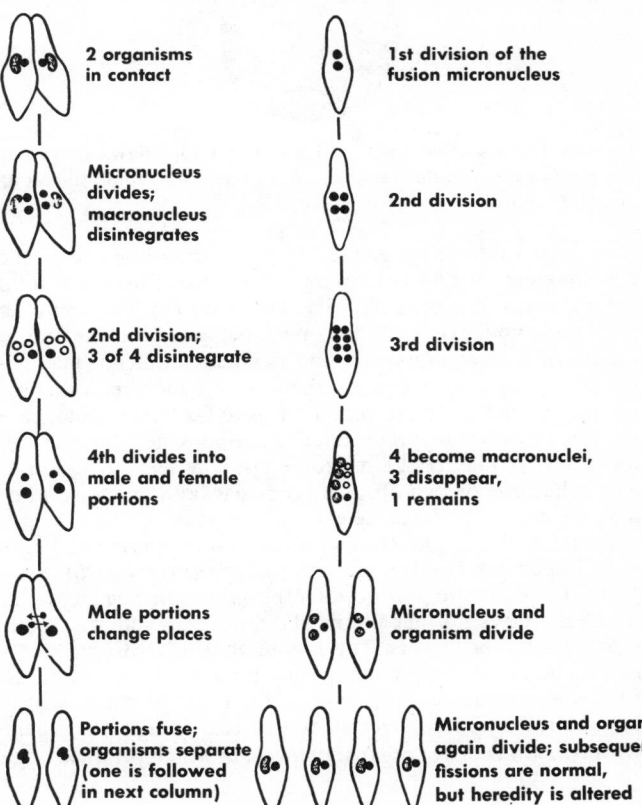

2 organisms in contact

1st division of the fusion micronucleus

Micronucleus divides; macronucleus disintegrates

2nd division

2nd division; 3 of 4 disintegrate

3rd division

4th divides into male and female portions

4 become macronuclei, 3 disappear, 1 remains

Male portions change places

Micronucleus and organism divide

Portions fuse; organisms separate (one is followed in next column)

Micronucleus and organism again divide; subsequent fissions are normal, but heredity is altered

the passive partner and hence female. In one filament, some conjugating cells may act as males and others as females; still other cells, which have no partners in the adjacent filament, may continue in the vegetative (nonsexual) condition. Usually the product of fusion in these algae is a heavy-walled cell (zygospore) that can survive desiccation and freezing temperatures before its nucleus undergoes reduction division as a prelude to germination.

Multicellular animals and most multicellular plants produce definite unicellular GAMETES, which differ in degree of activity and in amount of stored food. The active cell, with little stored food, is a sperm; the passive one, often with much food available as nourishment for the growth of a new individual, is the egg. When, through the process of FERTILIZATION, a sperm cell fuses with an egg cell, the combination is known as a fertilized egg, or zygote. From it, a new multicellular organism can grow.

Most multicellular animals produce sperms or eggs in definite sex organs, the gonads, which may be TESTES (sperm producers) or OVARIES (egg producers). Usually, accessory ducts carry the gametes from the gonads to the outside. Initially a sperm-carrying duct is very fine in diameter (vas efferens), but several combine into a large duct (vas deferens), the lower end of which may be enlarged as a sperm storage chamber, the seminal vesicle. The male of animals that are fertilized internally may have a copulatory organ (penis) through which the sperm duct opens. In the female, eggs released by OVULATION ordinarily pass toward the outside through paired OVIDUCTS. The terminal ends of these may be joined as a vagina, into which the penis of the male is inserted during copulation; this provides for direct transfer of sperm cells to the female.

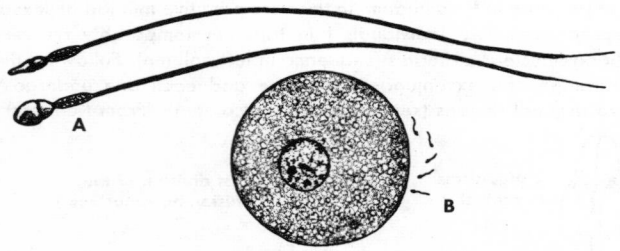

Human reproductive cells: (A) Side and top views of sperm. (B) Mature ovum (relative sizes of sperms and ovum indicated). (*From Young*)

In most animals, the gonads appear during late embryonic development, but do not enlarge or become functional until the approach of sexual maturity (see PUBERTY). The ability to reproduce may exist only for one short season at the end of life (as in insects, lampreys, and Pacific salmon) or may extend over many years. Often, animals with a short reproductive period produce far more young but give far less parental care than those with a long reproductive period. One adult salmon, for example, may lay 28 million eggs, whereas a penguin or a deer has one or two offspring per year, and an elephant or a whale may only have one every other year.

In multicellular plants, the production of sperms and eggs is an important event in a regular ALTERNATION OF GENERATIONS. Gametes are produced by the *gametophyte* generation, which is always a rather simple plant, never having true roots, stems, leaves, or flowers. The zygote develops into the *sporophyte* generation, which alone may possess these structures. In liverworts, mosses, and some of the more primitive vascular plants, the gametophyte generation is an independent plant with two kinds of sex organs: *antheridia,* which produce large

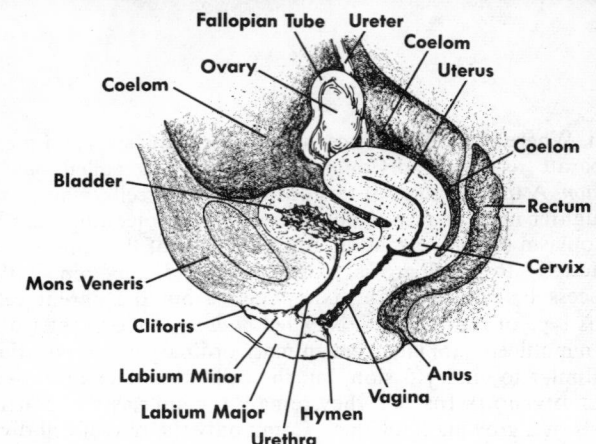

Reproductive system: *Above,* median sagittal section through reproductive system of human female. *Below,* reproductive system of the human male. (*From Young*)

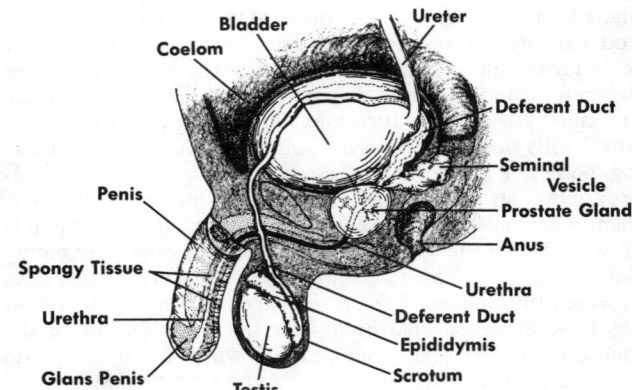

numbers of sperm cells, and *archegonia,* each of which produces one egg cell. The sporophyte of these plants develops through an embryonic stage, during which the embryo gets its nourishment from the gametophyte. In higher vascular plants, the gametophyte generation is greatly reduced in size, and male gametophytes are separate from female gametophytes. The male gametophyte consists of only a few cells within the pollen grain (which is a spore from the sporophyte generation), and the sperm nucleus is transported within the cytoplasm of the pollen tube. The female gametophyte similarly consists of a small number of cells within the ovule. After pollination and fertilization, an egg cell develops into a new sporophyte within the SEED. (See also FLOWERING PLANT; GYMNOSPERM.)

Some plants and animals that are able to reproduce sexually suspend this normal process for long periods of time during which they produce young that develop from unfertilized eggs.

Sexual reproduction in plant kingdom: Male flower of willow tree (*left*) produces pollen which is wind- or insect-borne to female flower (*right*). After pollen grains reach stigma of female flower, pollen tubes develop and enter ovule. Sperms that have developed in pollen tube travel to ovule and fertilize both egg and endosperm nucleus of future food-storage tissue. Fertilized egg will eventually become mature seed. (*Harold V. Green*)

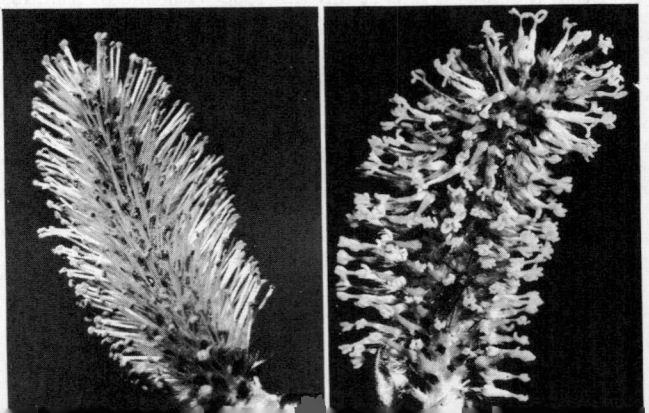

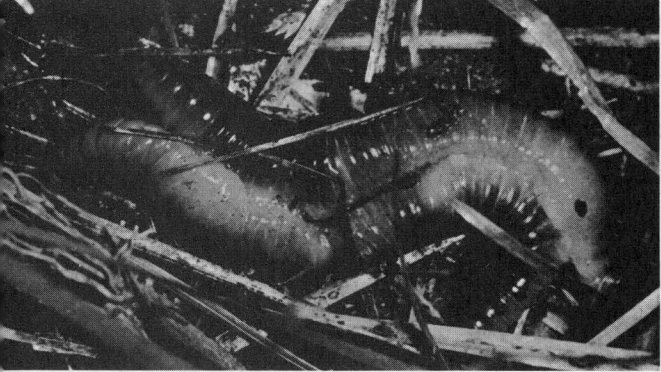

Copulating earthworms fertilize one another. Each earthworm has both male and female organs, and each injects and receives sperm during copulation. (*General Biological Supply House*)

In animals, this is called PARTHENOGENESIS; in plants, it is parthenocarpy. A few kinds of animals, notably certain salamanders, become sexually mature and reproduce without undergoing the metamorphosis that is usual in these organisms. This extension of a youthful stage into an egg- and sperm-bearing stage is called NEOTENY.

Significance of sexual reproduction: One might expect asexual reproduction to be more successful than sexual reproduction because it is simpler. But the sexual method finds wider use throughout the range of organisms, from bacteria and unicellular protozoans to the largest plants and animals. In asexual reproduction, new individuals are identical with their parents unless a change has been introduced by a rare, spontaneous MUTATION, by chromosome abnormalities arising during faulty cell division, or by genetic damage. Only organisms with prodigious rates of reproduction, made possible by small size and simple structure, can provide in these limited ways enough variation among their countless offspring to enable them to evolve adaptations in a changing environment. Among plants and animals with sexual reproduction, by contrast, variation is guaranteed in two additional ways. Before fertilization takes place, the special double cell divisions of MEIOSIS apportion to the sex cells every possible combination of maternal and paternal inheritance. Since a person has received a set of 23 chromosomes from the father and a corresponding set of 23 from the mother, the two sets can produce 2^{23} different combinations in the set of 23 chromosomes provided in each egg cell or sperm cell. This is more than eight million different sex cells available from each parent for fertilization. Thus any two human parents can theoretically produce over 64 million million combinations of inheritance in the fertilized eggs. This number of combinations is increased even more by the possibility of paired chromosomes crossing over—*i.e.* interchanging their parts—during one stage of meiosis. Since evolution depends on the operation of natural selection among the variable members of a population, sexual reproduction contributes more importantly to evolutionary change than does asexual reproduction. This is the advantage that makes the complex sexual method of reproduction preferable to the simpler asexual method.—*L. and M. M.*

REPTILES: cold-blooded VERTEBRATE animals that breathe air with lungs and have horny body scales. Living types are snakes, lizards, turtles, crocodilians, and a large lizardlike "living fossil" (*Sphenodon punctatum*) found in New Zealand. Many distinctly different types are extinct—*e.g.* dinosaurs, pterodactyls, and ichthyosaurs—and these make reptiles the most varied class of vertebrate animals in way of life and body form. Scientific interest in living reptiles stems chiefly from the fact that reptiles have changed relatively little in millions of years: in many basic structural and functional ways, they are like our ancestors of some 200,000,000 yr ago.

In a more immediate way reptiles are useful to man as food (almost all kinds are eaten by some humans), for leather, for important medicines, for varied horny ornamental products, as experimental animals, and as controls upon noxious animals, *e.g.* certain insects and rodents. For example, each mouse- and rat-eating bull snake on a farm is said to be worth five dollars a year to the farmer, and the commercial value of turtles used as food and as pets in the U. S. A. alone runs annually into hundreds of thousands of dollars.

Cold-bloodedness in reptiles, as in many other animals, means only that they have no "inner" means of controlling BODY TEMPERATURE. The warm-blooded animals—birds and mammals—balance controlled heat-gains produced by metabolism (chemical breakdown of food materials) against controlled heat-losses effected by various devices, and in this way maintain a fairly constant temperature at all times. The only exceptions are the animals, mostly mammals, that hibernate (become dormant) in winter, when they have a somewhat lower temperature. Reptiles cannot exercise this temperature control; their temperature is always a composite of that of their surroundings—air and substrate—except that their temperature also is increased by insolation (sunning) or decreased by evaporation. During warm weather reptiles maintain a chemically efficient body warmth by moving between warmer and cooler spots. In winter they must seek depths underground or under water below the frost line, for they cannot endure temperatures at or below freezing for more than a few moments.

Turtles are the most distinctive living reptile. Each of the some 250 known species has a carapace above and plastron below that make up a complete boxlike or panlike shell into or under which the turtle's head, tail, and four legs can be more or less completely drawn. Sea turtles are the largest of all, reputedly reaching ¾ ton, and are almost completely aquatic, coming ashore only to lay and bury hundreds of eggs in sandy beaches. They often sleep on the bottom of a shallow part of the ocean. Because they respire to a considerable extent through the walls of the cloaca while submerged, sea turtles need to surface only occasionally for air. Often they return to the same resting spot day after day for years. They appear to migrate in the breeding season to offshore shallows, where mating takes place. Their food consists of marine algae, which in some areas make the turtles poisonous for humans to eat. Most permanent, sizable streams and lakes in temperate and tropical regions have one or more species of fresh-water turtles, all of which are primarily scavengers on dead or dying plant and animal matter. Contrary to common belief, turtles do very little damage to fish and wildlife. All species lay eggs in sandy soil near water and sun themselves in warm weather either on land or in shallow water. In cool regions turtles usually hibernate, buried in mud or sand under water. They can spend weeks in winter without breathing air; the small amount of oxygen they require comes from the water, entering the body through the skin or through a pair of thin-walled sacs opening into a chamber (cloaca) at the rear end of the gut.

A few species of land turtles exist, some occurring in semi-arid regions, others in humid zones. These feed upon succulent vegetation, small animals (*e.g.* insects), and carrion. Many turtles bite viciously, but none—not even the snapper—has a jaw strong enough to bite a pencil in two, much less to bite a broomstick in half or a chunk from a board.

Crocodilians, of which there are 25 species, live in all tropical parts of the world. They can reach a maximum length of about 30 ft, and some are a real menace to human life. Three groups of crocodilians are recognized: alligators, caimans, and crocodiles. Alligators and caimans are relatively

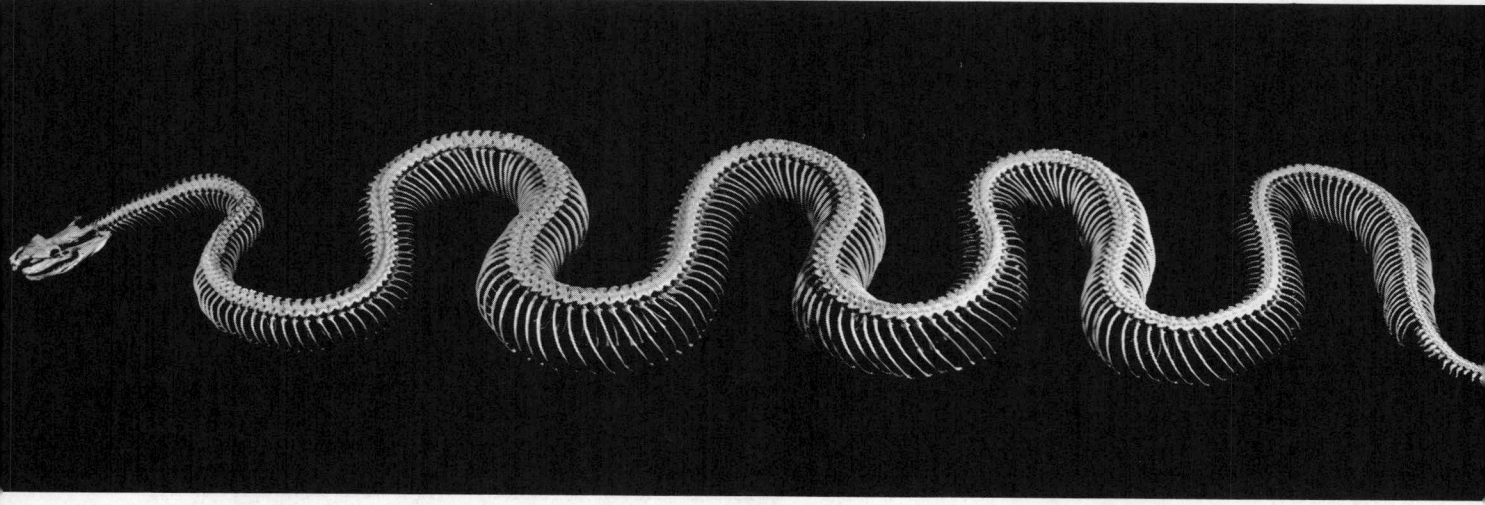

Skeleton of python: The numerous vertebrae and ribs are connected to each other by an intricate system of tendons and segmental body muscles—an arrangement that makes possible the snake's sinuous body movements. The lower jaw is articulated in four places, allowing great distension of mouth during swallowing. (*Amer. Mus. of Nat. Hist.*)

small (20 ft at maximum) and broad-snouted; they live only in the western hemisphere, except for one species of alligator in China. Crocodiles are both large and small, and are slender-snouted; they are found in both hemispheres, but are more abundant in the eastern. The gavial of India, which reaches 30 ft in length, has a very long, slender snout resembling the handle of a frying pan. All crocodilians lay eggs in large, crude nests of mud and vegetation near water.

Lizards, of which there are 3,000 kinds, are the commonest reptiles. Most lizards have four legs, but some have only two (either front or rear), and others have none. Legless species are usually mistaken for snakes, but can be distinguished by the fact that the two sides of the lower jaw are joined together, whereas in snakes each half of the lower jaw is independent. Lizards do not live as far north as snakes and turtles, possibly because their requirements for hibernating sites are more critical. Some live only in trees, and others only in the ground, where they burrow like worms. The largest are the strong-limbed land monitors of S Asia, which reach 10 to 12 ft in length. The smallest are scarcely more than an inch in length. Many kinds (mostly geckos) are active only at night; these have vertical pupils, which serve to protect the light-sensitive eyes when exposed to intense daylight. These lizards are provided with suction pads on tips of fingers and toes, enabling them to crawl on smooth and vertical surfaces. The flying lizards of the E Indies have a fanlike fold on each side of the body that can be spread flat, permitting them to glide long distances when they jump from tall trees.

Some lizards (*e.g.* tree iguanas) eat vegetation, but most are insect-eaters. Larger kinds eat almost any small animal they can catch. Two closely related species of southwestern U. S. A. and W Mexico—the Gila monster and the beaded lizard—are the only poisonous lizards in the world. Their venom glands lie in the lower jaw, the venom-conducting teeth (fangs) in both jaws. These lizards feed upon the ground-deposited eggs of reptiles and birds and upon small lizards, birds, and mammals. Some species of lizards give birth to their young, but most lay eggs. Snakes and lizards are unique among vertebrates in having two equally efficient copulatory organs (hemipenes).

Snakes rival lizards in number of species, but are much less often seen and are less numerous as individuals. All are legless, but primitive kinds, *e.g.* boas and pythons, have spurlike vestiges of hind legs beside the vent. Many species are poisonous; the venom is always produced by the salivary glands of the upper jaw, never by the tail, and the venom is introduced by means of hollow or grooved fangs, never by

the tongue. No snake can blow a poisonous vapor, although some African "spitting" cobras can squirt venom through their fangs into the eyes of an enemy at a distance of 10 ft or less. Rear-fanged snakes (*opisthoglyphs*) are mildly venomous, except for a few deadly African species. Most front-fanged snakes are deadly venomous, and they fall into two groups: those with fixed fangs (*proteroglyphs*) and those with movable fangs (*solenoglyphs*) that fold back, when the mouth is closed, like the blade of a jackknife. All vipers, including rattlesnakes and moccasins, are solenoglyphs and have a venom that usually affects the blood and causes painful swelling. The proteroglyphs include cobras, kraits, mambas, and many other kinds in Asia, Africa, and Australia, but only the coral snakes in the New World; the venom of all these snakes usually affects primarily the nervous system.

Snakes are among the most marvelously adapted creatures in the world. Being limbless, they cannot tear their food into bits, but must swallow it whole. Their jaws can spread amazingly wide, the two sides of the lower jaw can be advanced independently, and their skin and stomach can stretch to engulf large chunks of food. Apparently derived from burrowing ancestors, snakes have permanently fused transparent eyelids covering their eyes and have lost their ability to hear air-borne sounds. They are highly sensitive to vibrations, however, and slither away at the approach of footsteps. They detect odors primarily with a pair of pitlike vomeronasal organs at the front of the mouth; the tongue is important in smell, for it picks up air-borne particles as it is flicked in the air and then carries those particles into the vomeronasal organs. One of the most amazing special organs of the snake is the temperature-detecting facial pit between the eye and the nostril on each side of the head of "pit" vipers, *e.g.* rattlesnakes, copperhead, fer-de-lance, and bushmaster. Almost equally unique is the rattle on the tail tip of rattlesnakes of the Americas; this structure consists of dry portions of shed skins; probably the rattle evolved in response to selective pressure favoring a warning device against the enormous herds of hoofed mammals that long inhabited the western hemisphere.

Most snakes lay eggs, but some kinds give birth to their young, which number as many as 101. All eat animal matter, never vegetation. Sea snakes, which are deadly venomous, may never come ashore; they use their flattened tails for propulsion while hunting for fish in shallow water, particularly among coral reefs of the Indian and Pacific oceans. Some other snakes live underground exclusively; a few snakes regularly live in trees. Many snakes (*e.g.* pit vipers) are nocturnal, but most are diurnal.—*H. M. S.*

RESERVOIRS AND AQUEDUCTS: facilities for storing and transporting water; they form an integral part of public water supplies and are among the oldest of engineering structures. A reservoir is a basin where water is collected and stored to serve man's needs. It may be a natural lake which has been developed by man; or an artificial lake created either by construction of a DAM across a natural drainage way, or by construction of a basin, or by conveyance of water to natural basins. Most modern reservoirs are multiple-purpose projects whose uses include irrigation, municipal and industrial use, power production, flood control, navigation, recreation, and fish and wildlife protection, while older reservoirs were simply water-storage basins for irrigation or municipal and industrial use. The benefits derived from storing water to be used through periods of drought were recognized early in human history, and dams were built accordingly. Through history, dams have increased in size and complexity. The oldest known dam was built in Egypt 5,000 yr ago to store water for irrigation and drinking. Hoover Dam with its reservoir (Lake Mead) of 32,359,000 acre-ft total capacity, and Grand Coulee Dam with its reservoir (Roosevelt Lake) of 9,645,000 acre-ft capacity, are prime examples of modern reservoirs.

An aqueduct is a channel or conduit built to convey water from a source of supply to a point of use or distribution in an urban center. The term "aqueduct" is usually reserved for the primary channel conveying water to a city; branches, subchannels, and irrigation canals are not generally classified as aqueducts. In most cases, aqueducts are closed conduits built in place. They may be nonpressure channels, in which the water is flowing with a free surface, or pressure conduits and tunnels, in which the water is under pressure. Like

Hydrologists use gamma-ray density probe to measure sediment accumulation in reservoirs. Such data are used in control of sedimentation that robs reservoirs of storage space. (U. S. D. A.)

reservoirs, aqueducts have been known since ancient times, and it is not known where or when the first was built. Aqueducts built nearly 2,000 yr ago are still in use. The city of Athens in Greece is still using an aqueduct constructed in A. D. 134. Jerusalem was served by an aqueduct in ancient times, and ancient Rome had many. Aqueducts serving modern cities are almost fantastic in size and capacity; among them the Colorado River aqueduct, serving metropolitan S California, is the longest—over 250 mi in length, with a capacity of 1,034,000,000 gal/day (see TUNNEL).—*A. A. B.*

Reservoir (San Carlos Lake) behind Coolidge Dam in southeastern Arizona stretches back 20 mi to Gila River. Fed by mountain snows, the fast-moving waters flowing into the reservoir carry much suspended soil. Life of dam and its reservoir is being materially shortened by rapid accumulation of silt in the reservoir. (U. S. D. A.)

RESINS: polymeric organic substances, solid and semisolid, natural or synthetic. A pure *polymer* in bulk is called a resin; *plastics* are made from resins by the addition of other substances and further chemical and mechanical treatment. Typical natural resins are ROSIN, amber (a fossil resin found in lignite beds), and lac (the exudate of a tree-living insect cultivated in India). Amber is used in such items as cigarette holders and pipestems; lac is employed in varnishes and in shellac, the alcohol solution of lac. *Synthetic resins* greatly outnumber those found in nature, and are much more adaptable to the manufacture of commercial products. (The basic chemistry involved in the synthesis of resins is described in the article POLYMERS.)

Vinyl Resins: This is a large family, all of which are formed by addition polymerization of vinyl compounds. Vinyl chloride, $CH_2{=}CH$, for example, combines with itself to form

$$\overset{|}{Cl}$$

long chains where the typical linkage is

$$\cdots{-}CH_2{-}\underset{|}{CH}{-}CH_2{-}\underset{|}{CH}{-}\cdots$$
$$\quad\quad\quad Cl\quad\quad\quad Cl$$

This polyvinyl chloride resin is used to make sheet plastic and phonograph records; and, copolymerized with vinyl acetate, to make vinylite floor coverings and latex emulsions for paints. Other examples are polymethyl methacrylate (Lucite and Plexiglas) and polytetrafluoroethylene (Teflon), the monomers of which are respectively

$$\underset{CH_3}{\overset{|}{CH}}{=}CH \quad\quad \text{and} \quad CF_2{=}CF_2$$
$$\quad\quad\quad COOCH_3$$

Epoxy Resins: These are condensation polymers of epichlorohydrin and a bisphenol. In the resulting chain polymer,

$$H{-}CH{-}CH{-}CH_2\boxed{Cl + H}O{-}\bigcirc{-}\underset{CH_3}{\overset{CH_3}{C}}{-}\bigcirc{-}\boxed{OH}$$
$$\quad\quad O$$

Epichlorohydrin   Bisphenol-A

Vinylidene fluoride resin, one of the newer vinyl resins, is used in wire insulation and jacketing, machine parts, and coatings. This "Kynar" resin is mechanically strong and resistant to corrosive chemicals and high temperatures; it can be both extruded and molded. Resin is available either in pellets (shown above) or as a molding powder. (*Pennsalt Chemical Corp.*)

which is not in itself useful, each oxide ring opens to form one OH group. In the curing process other compounds are added which cross-link these chains through the OH groups. The epoxies adhere well to glass and metal surfaces. They have startling efficiency as adhesives, both in industry and in the home, largely because in the cross-linking (curing) process no volatile products are evolved and there is no shrinkage.

Silicone Resins: Organic silicon compounds like $(CH_3)_2SiCl_2$ and CH_3SiCl_3 can be hydrolyzed and then condensed by elimination of water molecules to give chain polymers called SILICONES:

$$\underset{HO\quad\boxed{OH}}{\overset{R\quad\quad R}{Si}} \quad + \quad \underset{HO\quad\boxed{OH}}{\overset{R\quad\quad R}{Si}}$$

When there are two OH groups per molecule a long chain is formed, and the products are water-repellent oils and greases. If some of the molecules have three OH groups (from $RSiCl_3$) cross-linking is possible, to yield the silicone resins used in films and coatings.

Phenol-formaldehyde Resins: These resins, developed after 1907 by L. Baekeland and called BAKELITE, ushered in the modern technology of resins and plastics. Closely related are the resins in which phenol is replaced by either urea, furfural, or melamine. (See PLASTICS.)—*Ru. M.*

RESISTANCE: in mechanics, the opposition to motion produced by frictional effects; in electricity, the factor by which the square of the current must be multiplied to obtain the power dissipated by a conductor, *e.g.* as heat. For a metallic conductor the resistance is the ratio of the difference of potential across the conductor's terminals to the (direct) current in the conductor.—*M. P.*

RESISTOR: a part of an ELECTRIC CIRCUIT that offers RESISTANCE to the flow of electricity.

RESONANCE: the state of an oscillating system when it is driven by an oscillating external force whose frequency approximates the system's own natural frequency. Some examples of oscillating systems are a vibrating spring, a tuning fork, and a closed electrical circuit containing a CAPACITANCE and an INDUCTANCE. In the first two examples, a mass vibrates about an equilibrium position. In the last example, electric current oscillates in the circuit, periodically charging and discharging the capacitance through the inductance. Now consider such a system being driven by an external force whose frequency is equal, or almost equal, to the natural frequency, *e.g.* a pendulum that is lightly struck at the beginning of each period. It receives an increment of energy at every stroke, causing it to oscillate with ever-increasing amplitude. Neglecting friction, its amplitude of OSCILLATION would increase indefinitely. In practice, however, amplitude increases only until the energy acquired from the driving force per cycle exactly balances the friction losses incurred during each cycle.

A useful "figure of merit" of a resonant system is the ratio of total energy of oscillation to the energy lost per cycle, called the Q of the system. In the figure, a series of "resonance curves" are shown, in which steady-state amplitude is plotted against the driving-force frequency, for systems of low, medium, and high Q. Note that the higher the Q, the sharper is the resonance about the natural frequency. Circuits of high Q will continue to "ring" for some time after the driving force is removed, as does a tuning fork after it is struck.

Resonance plays a very important role in ELECTRIC CIRCUITS. Friction here takes the form of electrical resistance. The external driving force is produced by an oscillator (in

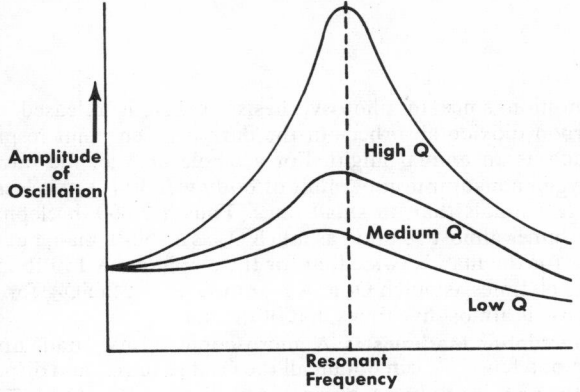

Resonance occurs when vibrating system is driven by a force whose frequency is close to system's natural frequency. The higher Q is (*i.e.* the ratio of total energy of oscillation to energy lost per cycle), the sharper is the system's resonance.

electrical circuits) or an a-c generator (in power circuits). The Q's of electric circuits vary from less than 100 at low frequencies (*e.g.* 60 cycles/sec) to many thousands at very high frequencies (*e.g.* microwaves). One application of electrical resonance is as a "wave trap," in which the resonant frequency is selected from a large number of frequencies present in a circuit for selective amplification.

All musical instruments are resonant systems. A violin string, excited by a drawn bow, experiences a large number of driving frequencies, but only certain ones resonate and are sustained. These are the basic frequency (the actual note played) and the various harmonics (multiples of the basic frequency); the latter resonate with generally much smaller amplitude. The nonresonant frequencies rapidly decay to an inaudible level.

Resonance phenomena in atomic and nuclear physics behave in analogous fashion to those described above. For example, electromagnetic radiation of certain frequencies can excite atoms to higher energy states, while nonresonant radiation will leave them unaffected (see ENERGY LEVEL). Thus, resonance radiation may be absorbed by a gas, which remains transparent to the remainder of the spectrum. The highest Q is that of the MÖSSBAUER EFFECT, which represents the highly selective absorption of gamma rays by certain atomic nuclei.—*B. Be.*

RESPIRATION: a series of chemical reactions by means of which the living cytoplasm in a CELL obtains energy from food, for example from the 6-carbon sugar glucose. Although respiration occurs continuously throughout the life of every cell, the term is still widely used in its former inexact sense to describe the intake of oxygen and release of carbon dioxide from a whole plant or whole animal. Often respiration in animals is equated with the movements of the body that serve to bring in oxygen and carry away carbon dioxide; properly these movements are examples of ventilation or BREATHING, rather than respiration.

Cellular Respiration: For each molecule of glucose utilized, the cytoplasm first obtains through the steps of GLYCOLYSIS two molecules of the 3-carbon compound pyruvic acid plus two molecules of the high-energy nucleotide ATP (adenosine triphosphate). Subsequent steps differ according to whether the cell is carrying on *anaerobic* respiration in the absence of oxygen, or *aerobic* respiration with oxygen available. Some kinds of plants (*e. g.* many bacteria, brewer's yeast) and of animals (*e.g.* the larvae of the midge *Chironomus* in the bottom mud of deep lakes, and some parasites in the intestinal tract) carry on anaerobically. Even in animals that must have oxygen, some cells (*e.g.* muscle cells) can engage for a time in anaerobic respiration while releasing energy quickly. In

yeast, the pyruvic acid molecules from glycolysis of each sugar molecule are converted into two ethyl alcohol molecules, releasing two molecules of carbon dioxide and obtaining a further molecule of ATP. In *Chironomus* larvae and in muscle cells, the pyruvic acid is converted into lactic acid; this material the larvae excrete, whereas a muscle cell loses some of its lactic acid to the blood, oxidizes some with oxygen from the blood, and may use the remainder in synthesis of glycogen (see MUSCLE CONTRACTION).

In aerobic respiration, the pyruvic acid is taken up by the MITOCHONDRIA of the cytoplasm and enters the CITRIC ACID CYCLE (or Krebs cycle) to yield 34 molecules of ATP which can provide energy for synthetic reactions within the cell. Waste products are chiefly carbon dioxide and water, giving the whole series of reactions the over-all form

$$C_6H_{12}O_6 + 6\,O_2 \rightarrow 6\,CO_2 + 6\,H_2O$$
$$+ \text{ energy in 36 ATP molecules}$$

The oxygen required for aerobic respiration does not enter directly into the citric acid cycle. Instead, it serves to remove hydrogen from an interacting cycle known as an "electron-transport system," which consists of a series of four iron-containing enzymes (cytochromes) related to hemoglobin. The cytochrome system reactivates the important coenzyme diphosphopyridine nucleotide (DPN), allowing the DPN to act like a man in a bucket brigade—alternately accepting a hydrogen atom freed in the stepwise dehydrogenation of glucose, and passing it on to a cytochrome. The fourth in the series of cytochromes links the hydrogens with oxygen to form the water that appears in the equation above.

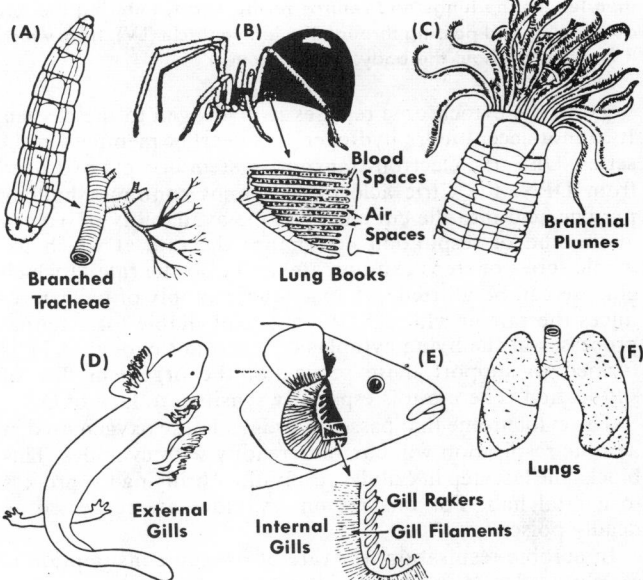

Respiratory apparatus of different animals: (A) Insects respire by means of branched tracheae, located throughout body; these carry oxygen directly to tissues. (B) In arachnids, respiration is accomplished by gas exchange on surface of the leaflike lung books. (C) Certain marine segmented worms respire by means of branchial plumes which function as external gills. (D) Adult aquatic salamanders and all amphibian larvae respire through external gills. (E) In fish, gas exchange in respiration is accomplished by passage of water over the gill filaments. The gill rakers prevent food particles from leaving through the gill slits. (F) In some amphibians and in all reptiles, birds, and mammals, gas exchange during respiration occurs on moist inner surfaces of lungs. (*From Whaley*)

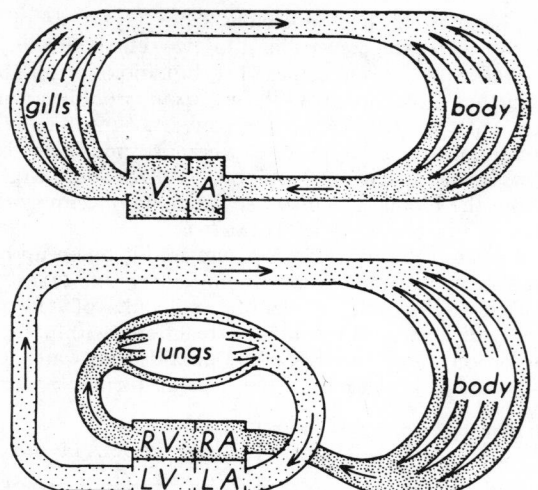

Respiratory and circulatory system relationships: *Upper*—In a fish, which has a two-chambered heart, deoxygenated blood (dense stippling) enters the heart at the auricle (A), flows through the ventricle (V), and from there flows to the gills, where it is oxygenated and carbon dioxide is removed. The oxygenated blood (light stippling) then circulates through the body, giving up its oxygen and receiving carbon dioxide, and then returns to the atrium. *Lower*—In birds and mammals, which have a four-chambered heart, deoxygenated blood from the body enters the right auricle (RA), passes through the right ventricle (RV), and from there flows to the lungs, where gas exchange occurs. The oxygenated blood then leaves the lungs and returns to the heart, entering the left auricle (LA) and passing through the left ventricle (LV), from which it flows throughout the body. (*From Manter*)

Until the cytochrome releases its hydrogen to the oxygen, it cannot accept more hydrogen from earlier members in the series. Until the electron-transport system accepts hydrogen from DPN, the citric acid cycle cannot continue shuffling pyruvic acid into the circuit. Thus the availability of oxygen at the end of respiration determines the rate at which the whole series of steps can operate, and also the rate at which glucose can be utilized. An inadequate supply of oxygen reduces the rate at which ATP is made available for essential processes in the living cytoplasm; when not enough ATP is formed to support these processes, the organism dies of suffocation. The brain is especially sensitive to lack of O_2.

The cytochrome that passes hydrogen to the oxygen used in aerobic respiration will combine readily with cyanides. This blocks the last step in cellular respiration, bringing the process to a fatal halt. For this reason, cyanides are respected as deadly poisons.

In aerobic respiration, the rate of oxygen consumption is widely used as a measure of the whole metabolic rate (see METABOLISM). For a green plant, the process of PHOTOSYNTHESIS must be brought to a halt to gain any measure of oxygen con-

sumption since in photosynthesis oxygen is released and carbon dioxide absorbed. In the dark a green plant respires much as an animal might. For a whole animal, the rate of oxygen consumption per unit of body weight (Q_{O_2}) is less in large animals than in small ones. Thus a 2,000-lb elephant consumes almost 30 times as much O_2 as a 150-lb man, but the Q_{O_2} for the man is twice that for the elephant. A 150-lb man uses 60 times as much O_2 as a 1-oz mouse, but the Q_{O_2} for the mouse is almost five times that of the man.

Ventilation Mechanisms: A microscopic animal, made up of one or a few cells, can obtain all the O_2 it requires, and dispose of the CO_2 it produces, by simple DIFFUSION. The O_2 diffuses from the water surrounding the organism, where the O_2 concentration is relatively high, into the cell, where the O_2 concentration is lowered continually in cellular respiration. In the same way, CO_2 produced in the cell becomes more highly concentrated there than on the outside, and so diffuses out of the cell. This diffusion is a simple consequence of the random motion of the O_2 and CO_2 molecules (see KINETIC THEORY).

As animals become larger, O_2 consumption increases in proportion to body volume, which is in turn proportional to the cube of the body diameter. The amount of surface through which diffusion can occur, however, increases only with the square of the diameter, and there comes a point at which the surface area is inadequate to supply the O_2 needs of the animal. This point is reached much sooner in aquatic animals and plants than in those that live in air, since the rate of diffusion of O_2 and CO_2 in water is much less than in air, and O_2 is not very soluble in water. The surface area may be increased by a change in shape; a flattened or threadlike form, as seen in the leaves and roots of most plants, offers a greater surface for a given volume than does a spherical shape. The leaves of plants are also generally porous; this provides a still larger surface for exchange.

Gaseous diffusion occurs most readily through thin, moist membranes. Such membranes are readily damaged and, when exposed to air, tend to dry out. In consequence, most higher animals have evolved special respiratory structures that provide a relatively large area of thin membranes in a protected position. These structures are called GILLS in aquatic animals, and LUNGS in terrestrial animals. Gills are usually feathery in structure, whereas lungs take the form of pouches or sacs, often branching from a central tube.

The efficiency of diffusion through the membranes of the exchange region is increased by ventilation, in which a current of air or water is passed through or drawn into and forced out of the respiratory chamber. In this way, the water or air in the chamber is continuously renewed, and the concentration of O_2 in the chamber kept as high as possible. The mouth and gill movements of a fish serve to draw water into the mouth and expel it across the gills. The alternate expansion and constriction of the chest cavity of a man draw air into the lungs and expel it again.

In man, the inspiration phase of BREATHING is accomplished by contraction of the diaphragm muscle, and elevation of the ribs by contraction of the rib muscles; these movements enlarge the chest cavity, and air rushes in through the mouth

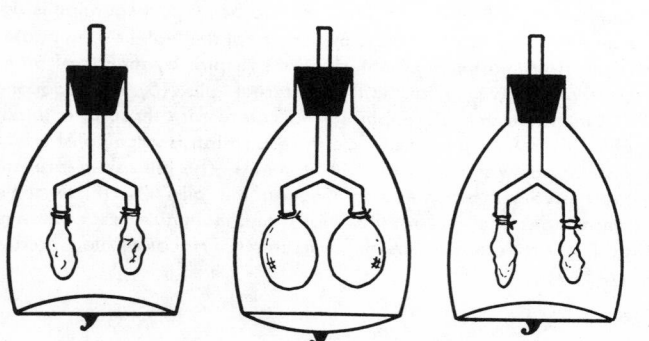

Mechanism of breathing: Bell jar represents chest cavity of a mammal; Y-tube represents trachea and bronchi; balloons represent lungs; rubber membrane at bottom of jar represents diaphragm. When diaphragm is relaxed (*left*), lungs are deflated. Contracting diaphragm (*center*) enlarges space in chest cavity, decreasing pressure on lungs and allowing air to pass into them through the trachea and bronchi. Relaxation of diaphragm (*right*) decreases volume of chest cavity, increasing pressure on lungs and forcing air out of them. (*From Whaley*)

and nose, through the trachea or windpipe, and into the bronchi and bronchioles, finally reaching the alveoli or air sacs of the lungs. The inspiratory muscles then relax, and the ribs and diaphragm return passively to their resting positions; this expiratory movement forces the air out again. In normal quiet respiration, only about 10% of the air in the lungs is exchanged. This can be increased to about 80% by the most vigorous respiration, in which the chest is expanded to its full capacity, and expiration involves active depression of the ribs and active elevation of the diaphragm, by contraction of rib and abdominal muscles respectively.

The ventilation rate is the amount of air or water moving into or out of the exchange region (gill or lung chamber) per minute; this rate is determined by the rate and the depth of the breathing movements, which are under nervous control of a center located in the hindbrain. The activity of this center is determined, in man and other air-breathing animals, by the amount of CO_2 in the blood; in aquatic animals, it is determined by the level of O_2 in the blood.

Insects have a unique ventilating mechanism, the tracheal system, which consists of branched tubes that "pipe" air directly to the cells. The system opens to the exterior through a set of paired openings, called spiracles, one pair in each body segment; the openings have valves that can be opened and closed. In smaller insects, gas exchange in this system is entirely by diffusion; in larger insects the outer portion of the system is ventilated. The grasshopper, for example, draws air through spiracles in the thorax into the main trunks of the tracheal system by expanding the thorax. The valves are then closed, and the air in the system is compressed by constriction of the body. Finally valves in the abdomen are opened, and the air is forced out through abdominal spiracles.

Transport Mechanisms: In larger animals other than insects, O_2 and CO_2 are transported between the exchange region and the cells by the circulatory system. This transport is aided by respiratory proteins such as hemoglobin or, in mollusks and arthropods, hemocyanin. These substances combine with O_2 and increase greatly the amount of O_2 that can be transported by a given volume of blood. The compound of protein and O_2 is a loose one, and the amount of O_2 held in combination depends on the concentration of free O_2. Hence, when the protein reaches the tissues where free O_2 concentrations are low, the O_2 is liberated from the protein. CO_2 is carried in the blood in solution in the form of carbonic acid and bicarbonate; these compounds break down in the lungs or gills, where the free CO_2 concentration is low, and are formed in the tissues where the CO_2 concentration is high.—*L. and M. M.*

REST MASS: the mass of an object as measured by an observer at rest relative to the object. Before the successes of the theory of RELATIVITY it was thought that the inertial mass of matter (its resistance to acceleration by a force) was an intrinsic property with a value independent of the mode of measurement. However, one of the important consequences of relativity theory is that a measurement of mass yields a number that is larger as the relative speed between object and observer becomes greater. The effect is too small to be measurable at speeds encountered in everyday life, but it has been experimentally confirmed with atomic particles moving at speeds approaching that of light.—*S. K.*

RETROGRADE MOTION: (1) An apparent movement of an object in the solar system, westward against the background of stars. If Earth had no orbital motion, a superior planet (one farther from the Sun) would overtake it once in each synodic period and appear always to move eastward with direct motion. But Earth is moving in the same direction, and with

greater speed than the superior planets. Some time before opposition, Earth overtakes the superior planet, which appears to stop and then move westward with retrograde motion. Direct motion is resumed some time after opposition. The inferior planets, Venus and Mercury, also retrograde for an interval surrounding the time of inferior conjunction when the planet is nearest Earth.

(2) An actual movement of a comet in a westward (clockwise) direction around the Sun, or a similar motion of a satellite around a planet. The eastward (counterclockwise) motion around the Sun, or around a planet, is termed direct motion; it is shared by most members of the solar system, with the exception of a few satellites and about half the known comets.—*S. D. G.*

REVERE, PAUL, 1735–1818, U. S. silversmith, engraver, and patriot; b. Boston. In addition to his production of gold- and silverware, Revere established a foundry in which he cast bells and cannon. He achieved success with his process for rolling sheet copper, and pioneered in the production of copper plates and spikes for ships. In 1808–09 he made copper plates for the boilers of a steam ferryboat for Robert Fulton. —*S. B.*

REVERSIBLE REACTION: see MASS ACTION, LAW OF.

REYNOLDS, OSBORNE, 1842–1912, Irish-British engineer and physicist; b. Belfast, Ireland. His research on lubrication led to important practical inventions, and his studies of the flow of water in pipes resulted in his discovery of the *Reynolds velocity*, a critical speed at which the character of flow changes, and the REYNOLDS NUMBER. He developed a method of direct determination of the mechanical theory of heat. His *Papers on Mechanical and Physical Subjects* were published 1900–03. He was a fellow of the Royal Society.— *D. H. D. R.*

Osborne Reynolds
(Brown Brothers)

REYNOLDS ANALOGY: in fluid-flow physics, the assumption, in turbulent heat-transfer analysis, that a turbulent eddy picks up heat and momentum in one layer of flow and releases these in another layer. This highly useful assumption (after Osborne Reynolds) allows the deduction that transfer of heat from a fluid to a surface is proportional to the surface friction.—*Wm. R.*

REYNOLDS NUMBER: a parameter used to describe and scale similar FLUID FLOWS, developed by Osborne Reynolds. When applied to the flow of a liquid or gas in a pipe, it equals the product of density, velocity, and pipe diameter, divided by the coefficient of the fluid viscosity. In modern aerodynamics, similarly, it is derived from the ratio of momentum forces to viscous forces about a body (aircraft) in a fluid flow. If the number is above 2,000, the flow is turbulent; a low number indicates viscous flow. Thus in aerodynamics, high Reynolds numbers (several thousand or more) indicate that laminar (nonturbulent) flow is limited largely to boundary regions. At even higher numbers laminar flow tends to disappear even at the boundary regions, and the boundary-layer flows become turbulent. See AERODYNAMICS; MODELS AND MODELING.—*D. B.*

RHENIUM: a metallic element (Re) of the manganese·family; at. no. 75; at. wt 186.22; mp about 3200°C. Rhenium (like the third member of the manganese family, TECHNETIUM) was "missing" until well into the 20th cent.; and a blank space was reserved for it in most periodic tables until its·actual discovery in 1925, when the German scientist Walter Noddack and his future wife Ida Tacke detected it by chemical treatment and x-ray analysis of samples of platinum ore and the mineral columbite. Rhenium, though hard, is malleable and ductile, and can be cold-worked or annealed into foil or wire. It is widely distributed in many minerals, but in extremely small concentrations, the main source being molybdenum ores (*e.g.* the mineral molybdenite), which may contain as much as 90 parts per million of rhenium. Though it has recently been produced in atomic piles, rhenium is commercially a by-product of either the smelting of molybdenum ore or the refining of copper by electrolysis. It has been used as a catalyst in dehydrogenating (liberating hydrogen from) certain substances; in high-temperature thermocouples; in fountain-pen points; and in various electric and electronic components.—*E. H. H.*

RHEOLOGY: the study of the flow of materials, primarily materials whose characteristics lie between those of crystalline solids and true liquids, and also such heterogeneous materials as blood. Many crystalline materials—*e.g.* ice in glaciers—flow when subjected to large sustained forces. In addition, metals tend to flow at elevated temperatures that are well below their melting points, in the phenomenon known as "creep." Such amorphous substances as tar act more like

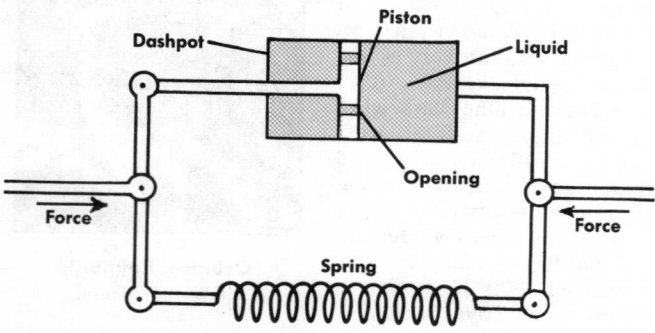

Rheological model: A force from either side is modified by the combination of initial absorption by the spring and the damping action of piston moving through liquid in dashpot.

liquids of very high VISCOSITY. Rheology concerns itself with the mechanisms by which flow takes place; it makes use of models, frequently consisting of springs and dashpots (see figure), to explain the manner in which forces act on a material and cause it to flow. The subject is of great importance in such diverse fields as metallurgy, geophysics, plastics and foodstuff manufacturing, and medicine.—*E. M. R.*

RHEOSTAT: a resistor that can be varied so as to control the electric current that flows through it. A rheostat may consist of individual resistance units connected in series by means of a switch, or it may be continuously variable by a movable contact that slides over turns of resistance wire wound on an insulating support. Another type consists of carbon blocks that can be pressed together to reduce the total resistance.—*W. P. C.*

Rh FACTOR: see BLOOD GROUP.

RHODIUM: a white metallic element (Rh) with a bluish-gray luster; one of the six PLATINUM metals; at. no. 45; at. wt 102.91; valence 3 or 4; mp 1966°C. One of the rarer metals (about 1×10^{-7}% of Earth's crust), rhodium is found in small quantities with platinum and in some nickel-copper ores. W. H. Wollaston first isolated the metal in 1803, naming it for the brilliant red of its salts. Rhodium is hard, ductile, malleable, highly acid resistant, and free from oxidation; because its surface does not form electrically resistant oxide films, it is used for electrical contacts in switches and relays. The metal's highly reflective and tarnish-free surface makes it useful in plated jewelry and as a brilliant reflector for searchlights and movie projectors, but it also has important uses in alloy with platinum. A standard thermocouple component is 90% platinum and 10% rhodium; this alloy is also used for spinnerettes in the drawing of synthetic fibers and for bushings in drawing glass fibers. A fine gauze of the alloy is an extremely efficient catalyst for converting ammonia to nitric acid.—*R. B. T.*

RHYOLITE: an extrusive igneous rock and a type of lava, having the mineral composition of GRANITE but a texture that is very fine-grained or glassy. It is the extrusive equivalent of granite, from which it differs in having no visible crystals, except for occasional phenocrysts of quartz; if these are numerous, the rock is porphyritic rhyolite. The cooling of viscous, acidic lava of a type that issues usually from explosive continental volcanoes produces rhyolite.—*E. A.*

RIBOFLAVIN: see FLAVIN NUCLEOTIDES; VITAMIN.

RIBONUCLEIC ACID POLYMERASES: enzymes which will synthesize high-molecular-weight ribonucleic acid (RNA). The reaction uses the triphosphates of adenylic, guanylic, cytidylic, and uridylic acids. Pyrophosphate is split off during the reaction; the remaining phosphate of the nucleotide is then bound covalently to the ribose of the adjacent nucleotide, connecting the third carbon of one sugar to the fifth carbon of the other sugar. If a given DNA is added to the enzymatic reaction, the RNA that is synthesized has a nucleotide composition similar to that of the added DNA, indicating that this enzymatic reaction is probably the one in which a DNA molecule "directs" the enzymatic synthesis of an RNA molecule whose bases are complementary to that of the bases in the DNA (see NUCLEIC ACIDS; PROTEIN SYNTHESIS). —*P. S.*

RIBOSOMES: very small particles found in the cytoplasm of all cells—animal, plant, and bacteria—and in the nuclei of some cells. Ribosomes are about the size of the smallest viruses, and can be seen only with the electron microscope. They are made up of roughly equal portions of ribonucleic acid and protein, and are involved in the syntheses of many of the cell's proteins. The ribosomes are believed to be the nonspecific factor upon which proteins are synthesized, the specificity of protein synthesis being conditioned not by the ribosomes, but by the "messenger" RNA which is bound to it (see PROTEIN SYNTHESIS; RIBONUCLEIC ACID POLYMERASES). —*P. S.*

RICCIOLI, GIOVANNI BATTISTA, 1598–1671, Italian astronomer and Jesuit; b. Ferrara. His major work was the voluminous anti-Copernican *Almagestum novum* (1651, supplement 1665), wherein was collected most of what was known in astronomy at the middle of the 17th cent., together with observations, opinions, explanations, and methods of computation.—*R. N. M.*

RICHARDS, ALFRED NEWTON, 1876–1966, U. S. pharmacologist; b. Stamford, N. Y. His fields of research included the chemistry of connective tissues, salivary digestion, adrenalin secretion, kidney function, shock, the action of dilators, and toxicity of various substances. He was a member of the Pennsylvania Medical School faculty 1910–46, a fellow of the Royal Society and a member of the National Academy of Sciences.—*D. H. D. R.*

RICHARDS, THEODORE WILLIAM, 1868–1928, U. S. chemist; b. Germantown, Pa. He made many contributions to exact chemical analysis and established improved atomic-weight values for 23 elements. His work on the atomic weight of lead led to the recognition of lead isotopes in minerals of radioactive origin. He was awarded the 1914 Nobel prize in chemistry. A fellow of the Royal Society, he was also a member of the National Academy of Sciences.—*A. I.*

RICHARDSON, LEWIS FRY, 1881–1953, English mathematical physicist and meteorologist; b. Newcastle upon Tyne. He developed the application of the mathematical method of finite differences to physical problems, particularly that of predicting the future physical state of the atmosphere from present observations, and worked on eddy diffusion in the atmosphere. Later he became interested in psychology and in the causation of wars, and he authored or coauthored 44 books and articles in this area in addition to many publications on meteorology, computational techniques, and instruments. He was a fellow of the Royal Society.—*D. H. D. R.*

RICHARDSON, SIR OWEN WILLANS, 1879–1959, English physicist; b. Dewsbury. He investigated (from 1900) the effect of heat on the interaction between electricity and matter, and showed that hot metals emit electrons; he discovered an equation (*Richardson's law*) to describe the phenomenon. This thermionic emission of electrons, which occurs in radio tubes, is of fundamental importance in electronics. Richardson's studies in related fields included the gyromagnetic effect. For his work in thermionics, he received the 1928 Nobel prize. His writings include *The Electron Theory of Matter* (1914) and *The Emission of Electricity from Hot Bodies* (1916). He was a fellow of the Royal Society.—*D. H. D. R.*

RICHET, CHARLES ROBERT, 1850–1935, French physiologist; b. Paris. He made investigations in pharmacology, physiological chemistry, pathology, and pathological psychology. After developing the idea of immune serum, he performed the first serotherapeutic injection on a human being (1890). For his studies on anaphylaxis (sensitivity to poisons, as opposed to immunity), he received the Nobel prize, 1913.—*D. H. D. R.*

RIDDLE, OSCAR, 1877–   , U. S. zoologist and physiologist; b. Cincinnati, Ind. His fields of research have included bionomic physiology, the physiology of reproduction, internal secretions, the nature of sex, and constitutional factors. From 1914 to 1945 he was an investigator of the Station for Experimental Evolution of the Carnegie Institution, and in 1954 wrote *The Unleashing of Evolutionary Thought.* He is a member of the National Academy of Sciences.—*D. H. D. R.*

RIEHL, HERBERT, 1915–   , U. S. meteorologist; b. Munich, Germany. A disciple and associate of C.-G. A. Rossby, Riehl is a prolific contributor to modern meteorology and is known for his works on energy, water vapor and momentum balances, typhoons and hurricanes, and a variety of other atmospheric structures and circulations. Together with Rossby and E. Palmén he led in the early investigation of the jet stream. He has also contributed substantially to the development of research on the meteorology of the intertropical belt. His many writings include the textbook *Tropical Meteorology.*—*S. P.*

RIEMANN, GEORG FRIEDRICH BERNHARD, 1826–66, German mathematician; b. Breselenz, Hanover. He was educated at Göttingen and Berlin under K. F. Gauss, K. G. J. Jacobi, P. G. L. Dirichlet, and J. Steiner. He developed the system of NON-EUCLIDEAN GEOMETRY based on a postulate which permits no parallel lines. His theory of space provided a geometric foundation for modern physical theories, in particular the theories of Einstein (see RIEMANNIAN GEOMETRY). The Riemann definite integral is a more general concept than that of A. Cauchy, and is the basic form of the integral presented in calculus courses today. Also building upon Cauchy's ideas, Riemann developed the theory of analytic functions of a complex variable from the partial differential equations known as the Cauchy-Riemann equations. Riemann surfaces, which he conceived for the purpose of giving geometric representation of multiple-valued functions of a complex variable, have been of prime importance in the development of modern function theory. His *Gesammelte mathematische Werke* were published in 1876 (reprinted, 1953). He was a fellow of the Royal Society.—*H. C.*

RIEMANNIAN GEOMETRY: a type of geometry in which the space involved is not necessarily uniform; *e.g.* it could be like the surface of a mountainous region. Riemannian geometry led to new insights into the nature of geometry, and played a crucial role in Einstein's theory of RELATIVITY. Riemannian geometry should not be confused with Riemann's non-Euclidean geometry (see NON-EUCLIDEAN GEOMETRY), which is only a special case of Riemannian geometry.

In Euclidean geometry, the distance ds between neighboring points (x, y), $(x + dx, y + dy)$ in a plane is given by the Pythagorean relation

$$ds^2 = dx^2 + dy^2 \qquad (1)$$

when the coordinates are like those on ordinary graph paper. But if curved coordinates are used

$$ds^2 = A\,dx^2 + B\,dxdy + C\,dy^2 \qquad (2)$$

where A, B, and C depend on x and y, in general having different values at different places.

On a non-flat surface there are no coordinates for which (1) holds everywhere; but (2) still holds, with suitable A, B, and C. Gauss proved that one can determine the local curvature of a surface in terms of A, B, and C—that is, by making measurements entirely on the surface without going outside it. For example, the curvature of a sphere can be determined by measuring the area of a spherical triangle and the sum of its angles. Riemann treated the geometry on surfaces intrinsically in terms of their A, B, and C, without reference to anything outside them. He then considered, analogously, non-uniform spaces of any number of dimensions without having to visualize them. He found a mathematical expression (now called the curvature tensor) involving only the analogs of A, B, and C, which vanishes if and only if the space is flat. Uniform spaces are special cases of Riemannian spaces. *Non-Riemannian geometry* deals with spaces having even more general properties than those contemplated by Riemann. Einstein's general theory of relativity represents the world in terms of the Riemannian geometry of a curved, four-dimensional space-time, its non-uniform curvature corresponding to non-uniform gravitation.—*Ba. H.*

On sandy surfaces subject to action of wind, waves, or currents, ripple marks are characteristic. They are often found at depth on the ocean bottom as well as in shallows. These dunes are in dust-bowl area of Texas. (U. S. D. A.)

RIFT VALLEY: see FAULT; GRABEN; MID-OCEANIC RIDGE.

RIGHT ASCENSION: the angular distance along the celestial equator from the vernal equinox to the hour circle of a celestial body. It is measured eastward in hours, minutes, and seconds from 0 hr through 24 hr. Right ascension and declination are coordinates in the equatorial system (see CELESTIAL COORDINATES). Sidereal hour angle is a similar coordinate, but measured from the vernal equinox westward in degrees. The right ascension of each star increases slowly, principally because of precession; the right ascensions of objects in the solar system change more rapidly because of their revolution.—*T. N.*

RIGIDITY, MODULUS OF: see SHEAR.

RING NEBULA (M57): a planetary NEBULA in the constellation Lyra, formed by a thick extra-bright zone within a huge ball of gas around a faint but very hot star. It appears by projection as a bright ring with a relatively dim central area. The longest outside dimension of the ring is about 90″. The most luminous gas in the ring is oxygen, which is made to glow by ultraviolet light from the central star. Many similar, but smaller, gaseous forms are called planetary nebulas because in small telescopes their disks look something like distant planets.—*P. Me.*

RIPPLE MARK: a small ridge, as in sand or similar loose material, produced by blowing of the material by wind or by the action of waves or currents in water. A ripple mark produced by wind is a dunelet, and forms as SAND dunes do. Ripple marks frequently are found in sedimentary rocks that have been split along the bedding planes; in such cases they have been preserved much as FOSSILS are.—*J. W.*

RITTENHOUSE, DAVID, 1732–96, U. S. astronomer; b. near Germantown, Pa. Primarily an instrument maker, he used surveying instruments of his own manufacture to establish the location of several state lines. By use of one of the several orreries he had constructed, he succeeded in measuring the 1769 transit of Venus (the passage of Venus across the disk of the Sun). In 1775 he was appointed "public astronomer observer" by the Pennsylvania Assembly. Among his contributions were use of measured gratings and the use of spiderwebs for crosshairs in the eyepieces of telescopes and transits. He was a fellow of the Royal Society and president of the American Philosophical Society from 1791 until his death.—*A. L.*

RIVERS AND RIVER VALLEYS: Rivers and their valleys are, respectively, the most important agents of EROSION and the most obvious erosional results. Rivers dissect landscapes and can move sediments thousands of miles; they are effective over most land areas of the world. Even in deserts, running water from the rare rains may, in places, be more effective than the wind as an eroding agent. Rivers are usually responsible for cutting the VALLEYS in which they flow and thus indirectly for the ridges and hills between them, these being in most cases residual features left after the valleys have been carved. Many smaller valleys, especially in arid and semi-arid areas, have water flowing in them only intermittently after a time of rain. Perennial streams, in which water is present throughout the year, are replenished, between rains, from underground (see GROUND WATER), the beds of such streams being below the WATER TABLE, whereas in the case of intermittent streams the channel most of the time is higher than the water table.

Any river valley is the result of the combination of two processes. It is deepened by the down-cutting of the stream,

Ring Nebula in Lyra is northern hemisphere's best-known example of a planetary nebula, formed apparently by explosion of a star. It is visible in small telescopes. (Mt Wilson)

whose load of sand and gravel acts as a tool to abrade the bed; and it is widened by WEATHERING and MASS WASTING. Streams carry their load in one of three ways: a small amount of material is carried in solution; the finer clastic particles such as mud and sand are carried in suspension; and the larger particles, the gravel and boulders, are pushed and rolled along the bottom of the stream channel. The size of particle which running water can move increases dramatically with a moderate rise in velocity, as is shown by the tremendous capacity of flood waters to move large boulders. The work done by a major river is demonstrated by the Mississippi, which carries approximately 600 million tons of material into the Gulf of Mexico each year.

Deposition of stream-carried material occurs as the velocity of the moving water decreases. This may happen between flood stages on the stream bed itself and result in the production of sand and gravel bars, the material in such deposits being shifted at each time of flood. Eventually deposition in a more permanent form will occur when the stream reaches a body of standing water, either a lake or the ocean, resulting in the production of such a feature as a DELTA. Some inter-mittent streams on leaving the steep gradient of a mountain slope will dump their load in the form of an ALLUVIAL FAN, the land counterpart of a delta.

The life cycle of a river and its valley is associated with a rather definite sequence of changes. A stream in *youth* is characterized by rapid down-cutting and a V-shaped cross profile, with the stream occupying the bottom of the V and the steep walls above constantly crumbling as the result of WEATHERING. At this stage the stream for much of its length will be flowing on bedrock, into which it may drill moderately deep holes (POTHOLES), the gravel which it is carrying acting as abrasive tools. WATERFALLS AND RAPIDS will be common, and will appear wherever the stream bed changes from a relatively resistant rock to a less resistant rock downstream. "Youth" persists as long as a stream has these characteristics; age in years is not a necessary criterion. The Colorado River as it flows through the Grand Canyon is still a "youthful" river although it has been flowing for some millions of years.

Streams increase the length of their valleys by the process of "headward erosion." In this process, when water first becomes channeled down the very end of a valley, it flows in a

Tanana River in Alaska has low gradient here and wanders slowly over a relatively flat landscape. Former channel is seen in foreground (to left of Alaskan Highway). Shifting of channels is characteristic of streams in "old-age" phase. (*Josef Muench*)

Rejuvenated river: Uplift of the land converted San Juan River, in S Utah, from a slow meander on a peneplain into a faster-moving stream which is rapidly cutting its channel deeper. Down-cutting is now occurring faster than erosion of channel's sides. (*Spence Air Photos*)

mere gully and will erode downward, with the result that after a heavy rain the gully is slightly longer, starting as it does somewhat farther up the slope than before. With continued down-cutting, the gradient of a youthful stream diminishes, until eventually the velocity of the water is just sufficient to transport the load of sand, mud, and gravel brought to it by its tributaries. At this stage the stream is "graded" and has reached *maturity*, with consequent changes in the shape and scenic features of the valley. The ungraded, rock-floored valley of youth, with its falls and rapids and potholes, gives way to a flat-floored valley veneered with deposits over which the slower-moving mature stream will *meander*. In time, as the stream continues to meander over its flood plain, it cuts the floor wider and wider until this floor may be many times wider than the meander belt. Some geographers distinguish an old stream from a mature stream as one flowing down a valley with a flood plain more than eight times the width of the meander belt.

Any time a river flowing on a flood plain overtops its banks, the flow of water will be abruptly slowed down, and some of the coarser material in suspension will be deposited near the main channel to form a natural levee, or low ridge adjacent to the river. Also at times of flood a meandering stream may abandon one of its loops when it cuts across the narrow neck between two of its bends, and thus leave a crescent-shaped OXBOW lake behind. A meandering stream may be *rejuvenated*, perhaps by a rise of the land relative to sea level, and start to cut downward again, through its flood-plain deposits and into the underlying bedrock. However, throughout this time it will maintain its meandering course,

and thus the anomalous situation of a youthful stream following an entrenched meandering path will arise, *e.g.* the San Juan River in S Utah.

The life history of any river depends upon the whole changing pattern of conditions among which it exists. Climate and elevation affect the stream's volume and gradient, and hence its cutting power. The varying resistance of the bedrocks through which a channel is being cut helps to determine the river's course, the steepness of its banks, and the presence or absence of waterfalls and rapids. Since river courses tend to follow the lines represented by less resistant rocks, the drainage pattern of a whole region reflects the

THE WORLD'S GREATEST RIVERS		
River	*Drainage Basin* (mi²)	*Length* (mi)
Amazon	7,050,000	5,500
Congo	3,700,000	4,640
Mississippi-Missouri	3,250,000	6,970
Rio de la Plata	3,100,000	3,880
Ob	2,915,000	3,640
Nile	2,800,000	5,920
Niger	2,800,000	4,160
Yenesei	2,570,000	4,750
Lena	2,320,000	4,600
Amur-Kerulen	2,080,000	4,480
Yangtze	1,775,000	5,300
Mackenzie	1,660,000	4,600
Volga	1,460,000	3,895
Zambesi	1,430,000	2,660
St. Lawrence	1,200,000	3,500

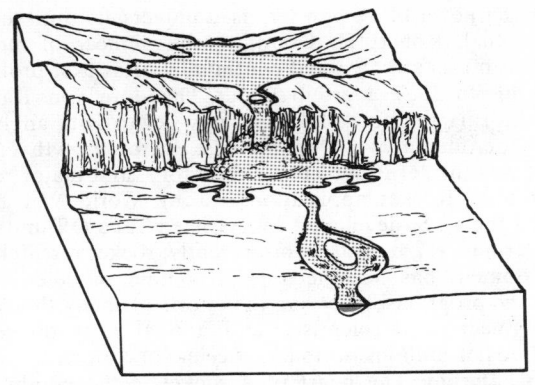

Youthful stage of river is marked by steep gradient, rapid flow, few tributaries, narrow and irregular valley, and waterfalls.

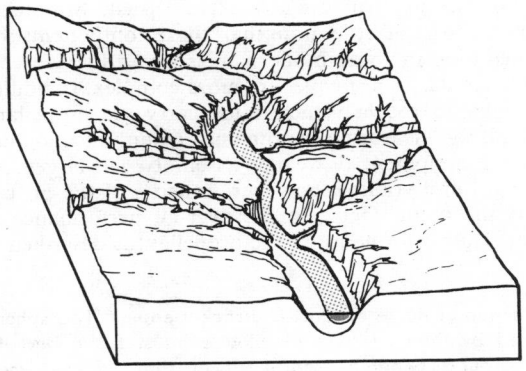

In early maturity, erosion has reduced gradient. Flow is slower, valley wider, tributaries more numerous, valley sediments deeper.

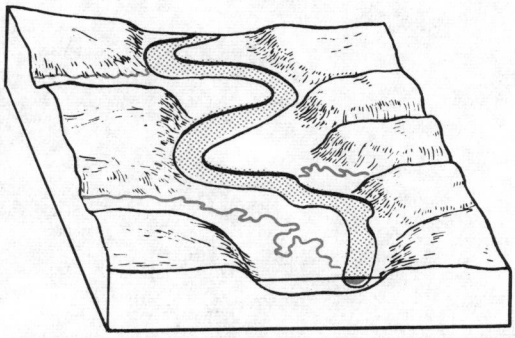

Later maturity finds river with gradient further reduced, and slower flow, wider valley, and meandering course.

By old age, landscape is nearly leveled, gradient slight, flow very slow, stream meandering more widely, oxbows developing.

bedrock structures that are under attack, and the drainage pattern changes as general degradation of the region exposes different rock structures to the erosion process. The course of any river, moreover, can be changed more or less abruptly by such agencies as blockage by landslides or glacial ice, faulting or warping of the bedrock, subsurface tunneling by ground water, and volcanic activity. And the life of a river may abruptly change when, as the result of its headward cutting, junction with another stream occurs.—*J. Sh.*

RNA: see RIBONUCLEIC ACID POLYMERASES.

ROBINSON, SIR ROBERT, 1886–   , English biochemist; b. Bufford. His research has been on analysis and synthesis of certain organic compounds. For research on certain vegetable products of great biological importance, particularly alkaloids, he received the Nobel prize, 1947. He is a fellow of the Royal Society and an associate of the U. S. National Academy of Sciences.—*D. H. D. R.*

ROCK: the hard structural material of Earth's crust. Consisting of minerals, it varies greatly in texture, color, density, and composition. Rock near the surface can be analyzed directly; but the nature of deeper rock must be inferred mainly from studies of seismic waves that have passed through the crust at depth. Most rock consists principally of silicate minerals, in which silicon and oxygen are combined with one or more metals. In the lower zone of the crust, the predominant metals are iron and magnesium, and rock in this zone is essentially a ferromagnesian silicate. Nearer to the surface, aluminum replaces the heavier metals, and the rock here is predominantly aluminum silicate. Within the upper 10 mi, silicates constitute about 75% of rock content; aluminum, about 8%; iron, 5%; and another 10% consists of calcium, sodium, potassium, and magnesium. The other natural elements (except the "noble" gases) constitute less than 2%. These various elements are combined in a large number of minerals, which are the actual components of all rock. Although rock may, therefore, be classified according to its mineral composition, geologists prefer to classify it according to the manner in which it was formed. Rock that formed from MAGMA is called IGNEOUS ROCK; it constitutes 95% of the uppermost 10 mi of the crust, although it does not appear everywhere at the surface. Heat, pressure, or contact with molten lava may alter such rock to one or more of the forms called METAMORPHIC ROCK. But all rock at Earth's surface is subject to disintegration. Contact with air, water, ice, and organic materials results in chemical decomposition; temperature changes and the force of gravity cause fragmentation; streams and surf, glaciers in motion, and wind further break up and then transport rock fragments, usually from higher to lower elevations, where the debris is deposited as sediments in basins. There pressure and cementation may consolidate the strata to form SEDIMENTARY ROCK—*e.g.* SANDSTONE or SHALE. Another type of sedimentary rock, LIMESTONE, may form from the precipitation of carbonates from sea water or by accumulation of limy organic remains on sea bottoms. Like igneous rocks, any sedimentary rock may become altered to form metamorphic rock. Eventually crustal movements may raise rock formations high above sea level, to begin a cycle of erosion, transport, and deposition that will create new sedimentary rocks. Most rocks at the planet's surface are, in fact, sedimentary, and the material constituting these rocks has undergone the cycle many times. Igneous and metamorphic rocks are covered by sedimentary rocks of varying depths in most areas, and appear on the surface only as a result of volcanic action, erosion, and removal of the sedimentary cover, or faulting.—*E. A.*

ROCKET: a vehicle or projectile powered by an engine that develops thrust by its reaction to the jet of hot gases it produces. The term sometimes refers to the rocket engine itself or to any one of the combustion chambers or tubes of a multi-chambered rocket engine. The principle of operation of a rocket engine stems directly from Newton's third law of motion: to every action there is an equal and opposite reaction. Rocket propulsion differs from jet propulsion in that the rocket engine carries within itself all the substances necessary for engine operation and can operate in outer space. By contrast, jet propulsion must use atmospheric oxygen to achieve fuel combustion. The terms "rocket" and "missile" are not synonymous, a missile being simply any object thrown, dropped, fired, launched, or otherwise projected with the purpose of striking a military target, irrespective of whether it is powered by a rocket engine. Only when the missile is powered by a rocket engine can it be called a rocket. Conversely, rocket power is used for purposes not connected with missile flight, *e.g.* auxiliary thrust units on aircraft.

History: Rocketry appears to have started with the Chinese many centuries ago, and from the 13th cent. onward there is increasing mention in military literature of the use of rockets in war. They were used by the British in the War of 1812. Around 1900, a Russian mathematics teacher, Konstantin Eduardovich Tsiolkovsky, presaged the age of modern rocketry by discussing the significance of exhaust velocities, and suggesting the greater efficiency of liquid fuels (hydrogen or oxygen) over black powder, used universally until then as rocket fuel. Robert H. Goddard, the pioneer of modern American rocketry, worked continually on rocket problems 1919–40. In 1937 a group under Theodore von Karman at California Institute of Technology began both analytical and experimental work on rockets. An outgrowth of this effort was the Jet Propulsion Laboratory, first major rocket laboratory. Rocket applications during World War II included the U. S.-developed Jet Assisted Take Off units and the German V-2 rockets. More recently, rocket research and development has become a priority item in defense and scientific programs, involving the efforts of many thousands of engineers and scientists, and annual expenditures of hundreds of millions of dollars. See SPACE TRAVEL.

Basic Design: The heart of a rocket is the combustion chamber, where fuel and oxidizer, together constituting the propellant, react to produce high temperature and pressure. A nozzle attached to the chamber allows the combustion products to escape, providing reactive thrust. Simple rocket engines consist of little more than these components, but the engines used in some modern missiles and space vehicles, though similar in principle, are more complex. In addition to the engine, a rocket vehicle must carry the propellant and payload, *e.g.* measuring instruments, communication devices, guidance equipment, or weapon assembly. The largest portion of weight and volume, however, consists of the propellant; this is the major factor in the over-all performance of the rocket. The performance of the propellant is described by the

Rocket engine tested: Hidden by steel platform and by intense reflection of flame exhaust is a rocket engine. Two spherical tanks supply fuel to engine's combustion chamber. Below, obscured by flame, is water-cooled exhaust flame bucket. This receives and deflects high-temperature exhaust gases, protecting ground beneath from heat erosion. (*Rocketdyne*)

Rocket engine: Cylindrical portion on left is combustion chamber into which fuel is injected and ignited. High-pressure hot gases exhaust at high velocity through converging-diverging De Laval-type nozzle at right. (*Buffalo Chamber of Commerce*)

SPECIFIC IMPULSE, which is the number of pounds of thrust produced per pound of propellant consumed per second. A typical value for specific impulse obtainable with chemical rockets is 250 sec. The attainable velocity for a given vehicle is directly proportional to its specific impulse and also increases with the propellent fraction. To obtain outer-space flight velocities with this magnitude of specific impulse requires more than a single rocket unit. Multistage rocket units are now fairly common; in such devices the velocities of the individual units become additive. Rocket engines are distinguished by the type of mechanism used to produce the exhaust thrust. By far the most common are chemical rockets, which use either liquid or solid propellant, or a hybrid. Liquid fuel, *e.g.* hydrazine, is mixed with a liquid oxidizer, *e.g.* liquid oxygen, by an injection process in the combustion chamber. In the solid-chemical type, the fuel and oxidizer are mixed together in a fluid condition, after which they harden into a solid mass, called a grain.

Other propulsion mechanisms, still largely in the research stages, are receiving increasing attention. One of these is a chemical rocket using a free-radical propellant. Free radicals are unstable molecular fragments which tend to recombine into a stable form with release of large quantities of energy. Electric propulsion engines under study fall into three classes: electrothermal, or arc-jet; electrostatic, or ion; and electromagnetic, or plasma. In electrothermal engines, an electric arc heats a propellant and ejects it through a nozzle, as in a conventional rocket. Electrostatic engines accelerate to high velocity and eject charged particles, such as ionized cesium, by purely elec-

trostatic fields (see ION PROPULSION). The electromagnetic rocket produces a plasma by an electric discharge, then accelerates the plasma by magnetic forces (see PLASMA PROPULSION). The Nerva nuclear rocket, developed in the U. S. A.'s Project Rover, consists of a fission reactor, perforated with many longitudinal passages through which hydrogen gas is heated as it passes through to an exhaust nozzle. It has attained a specific impulse of about 750 sec. Also of interest is the proposed use of a thermonuclear reactor in which hydrogen fusion produces the heat energy.

Solar Propulsion: Two types of solar propulsion have been suggested. One is the photon rocket, in which the pressure of the Sun's radiation (consisting of photons) supplies thrust against a large, lightweight surface attached to the space ship. This surface might be a large, metallized balloon of high reflection properties, sometimes referred to as a solar sail. A second suggestion is to use the Sun's radiation to heat hydrogen gas, which would then be expelled through a nozzle to produce thrust. But as of now, chemical rockets have the advantage of requiring less weight of components, and can more easily develop the thrust-weight ratio necessary to lift a missile or space vehicle system off Earth. The advantage of the newer mechanisms mentioned above is in the higher values of specific impulse attainable. Thus, for example, to send a vehicle into an orbit around Mars, one might use two types of propulsion: a high-thrust, low-specific-impulse chemical rocket to achieve an orbit around Earth, followed by a low-thrust, high-specific-impulse electromagnetic rocket to transfer from this orbit to the Mars orbit (see THRUST LOADING).

Achievements in Rocketry: The Titan III-C booster, using solid rockets, has achieved an average thrust of more than 1,000,000 lb. The Saturn V rocket will have a payload capability of almost 95,000 lb for a lunar-landing mission; its first-stage thrust is 7,500,000 lb. Saturn V's second stage will develop a thrust of 1,000,000 lb; its third, 200,000 lb. The Soviet Union is said to be developing a rocket that will boost 100 tons into orbit.— *D. B.*

RODENT: any member of the largest order of MAMMALS, the Rodentia, which includes the squirrels, gophers, rats, mice, porcupines, and beavers. These are all gnawing mammals, with specially developed incisor TEETH, one pair of which is located at the front of both upper and lower jaws. Growing in a curve from perennial roots, the rodent incisors not only replace themselves as they wear away at the tips, but also are self-sharpening, as a result of their having enamel on only the front surface; the exposed dentine at the back of the tooth wears away faster than the enamel-protected portion, so that the tooth remains chisel-shaped and efficient as a cutting tool. Rodents have no canine teeth; instead, their jaws show a gap between the incisors and the cheek teeth; through this gap a thickened portion of the cheek wall may project above the tongue, effectively isolating the gnawing teeth (and any debris produced from gnawing) and closing off the part of the mouth behind them. The jaws are narrow, and the hinging of the lower jaw allows movement forward and back as well as from side to side, in addition to the customary movement of opening and closing the mouth. The feet of rodents are usually five-toed, with sharp claws, and are placed flat on the ground (plantigrade posture); the forearms rotate at the elbow, allowing the animals to use their forefeet as paws in manipulating food. The tail ordinarily is long, but may be modified in relation to its use as a rudder (bushy in squirrels that leap from tree to tree, flattened in the beavers) or may be even prehensile (in tropical porcupines).

Beaver, *Castor canadensis,* is a large rodent of the family Castoridae. Native to North America and Europe, the beaver is adapted for a partially aquatic existence by its dense, waterproof pelage and by its scaly, paddlelike tail, which is used for locomotion in water. (*Leonard Lee Rue III*)

Flying squirrel, *Glaucomys volans,* is a forest-dwelling North American rodent of the family Sciuridae. A broad integumental membrane extending between the limbs on each side of its body acts as a parachute, enabling the animal to glide from branch to branch. (*Leonard Lee Rue III/Nat. Audubon Soc.*)

White-footed mice, *Peromyscus leucopus,* are small, insect- and seed-eating rodents of the family Muridae, and are widely distributed in eastern and central North America. They frequent open woodlands and scrubby hillsides, and nest beneath fallen logs, in burrows, or in trees. The very similar deermouse, *P. maniculatus,* has a more northerly and westerly range. (*Tom McHugh/Nat. Audubon Soc.*)

Thirteen-lined ground squirrel, *Citellus tridecemlineatus,* is a burrowing rodent of the family Sciuridae. Common in plains regions of central and W North America, it feeds on insects, birds, and mice, and occasionally damages cultivated crops. It strongly resembles the chipmunk but can be distinguished from the latter by its greater size and by its body markings—alternate rows of dots and stripes. (*Leonard Lee Rue III*)

Although world-wide in distribution, no rodents are fully aquatic; even muskrats, nutrias, and beavers build shelters above the water surface. The largest rodents are the capybaras of South and Central America, which reach a length of 4 ft; the smallest are mice only 2 in. long. Although most kinds are less than 1 ft in length, rodents have great importance in food webs, because they eat plant products (chiefly roots, seeds, stems, and leaves, supplemented by insects) and are eaten, in turn, by carnivorous reptiles, birds, and mammals. Many are burrowers; a few are arboreal; "flying squirrels" are gliders and, like most rodents, are nocturnal. Among the most common pests of man are the house mouse (*Mus musculus*), the black rat (*Rattus rattus*), and the Norway rat (*Rattus norvegicus*); an albino strain of the latter is the white rat commonly used in biological research.

Mammals of the order Lagomorpha (including rabbits,

hares, and pikas) differ from rodents in several respects. Lagomorphs have an additional, less conspicuous pair of incisor teeth directly behind the first pair in the upper jaw. Jaw movements of lagomorphs are limited to side-to-side and opening-and-closing motions, whereas the jaws of rodents also move forward and back. All lagomorphs are short-tailed, and the back legs of most of them are greatly elongated—which accounts for their hopping gait.—*L. and M. M.*

ROEBLING, JOHN AUGUSTUS, 1806–69, German-U. S. engineer; b. Mühlhausen, Ger. In 1841 he manufactured the first wire rope made in the U. S., using machinery he designed and made, and introduced wire rope for canal towlines and similar uses. He built a highway suspension bridge over the Monongahela River (1846), the first railroad suspension bridge at Niagara Falls (1855), and many other suspension bridges and aqueducts. He also designed the Brooklyn Bridge. His many publications include *Long and Short Span Railway Bridges* (1869).—*D. H. D. R.*

ROENTGEN UNIT: see RADIATION UNITS.

RÖMER, OLAUS or **OLE,** 1644–1710, Danish astronomer; b. Aarhuus, Jutland. He assisted J. Picard in establishing the position of Tycho Brahe's observatory at Uraniborg (1671), and went to Paris with Picard to work at Paris Observatory (1672). During his 9 yr at the observatory, Römer observed the variations of time in a series of eclipses of the innermost satellites of Jupiter, verifying the theory of the finite velocity of light (1675). He returned to Copenhagen (1681) to become the royal mathematician and professor of astronomy at the University. Römer invented the transit circle and also claimed to have independently invented a micrometer in 1672.—*S. B.*

RÖNTGEN (or ROENTGEN), WILHELM KONRAD, 1845–1923, German physicist; b. Lennep. While investigating the effect of cathode rays on a fluorescent screen, Röntgen, at that time (1895) professor of physics at Würzburg, observed evidence of an invisible type of radiation, which he called x-rays. Röntgen investigated the physical nature of this radiation and established that (1) all solid materials are in varying degrees transparent to x-rays,

Wilhelm Konrad Röntgen
(Wide World)

(2) photographic plates are sensitive to x-rays, and (3) x-rays ionize the air surrounding their path. He tried to establish the wave character of x-rays but in this failed, owing to their extremely short wavelength. So thorough were Röntgen's investigations that with the exception of their polarization, no additional characteristics of x-rays were observed until M. von Laue established their wave character in 1912. Röntgen did research in many other fields of physics, *e.g.* piezoelectricity and the absorption of infrared radiation by air. For his discovery and investigation of x-rays he received the 1901 Nobel prize.—*A. L.*

ROOT: the organ of VASCULAR PLANTS that usually grows underground, absorbs water and dissolved minerals, and anchors the plant. The root conducts the absorbed materials to the stem, with which it is continuous. In some plants, *e.g.* the sweet potato, the root functions as a storage organ. Covering the tip of the root as it grows through the soil is a protective structure known as the *root cap.* Just behind the root cap is the region where new cells are added in the process of root growth. The outermost layer of cells in a root is the epidermis, which serves the dual functions of protection and, at times, absorption. Some epidermal cells grow out to form fine tubular papillae called *root hairs;* these are important in providing more surface area for absorption. Other structural components, proceeding inward from the epidermis, are the cortex, a storage tissue; the endodermis, a tissue that regulates interchange of materials between the central conducting cells and the rest of the root; the pericycle, an embryonic tissue that gives rise to branch roots; and, in the center, the conducting tissue.

The part of the root that first grows out of a seed is the *primary root.* If the primary root persists as the dominant part of the root system, the plant develops a long, deep, penetrating tap root, as in sweet clover and plantain. In contrast, such plants as the grasses develop a shallow fibrous type of root system, consisting of numerous roots arising from the base of the stem. Tap roots reach water and minerals at lower levels in the soil than do fibrous roots, but the latter are more efficient as soil binders.

Roots that originate on the aerial organs of a plant are called *adventitious roots.* Usually they arise at nodes of the STEM, particularly on plants that grow in humid air. Adven-

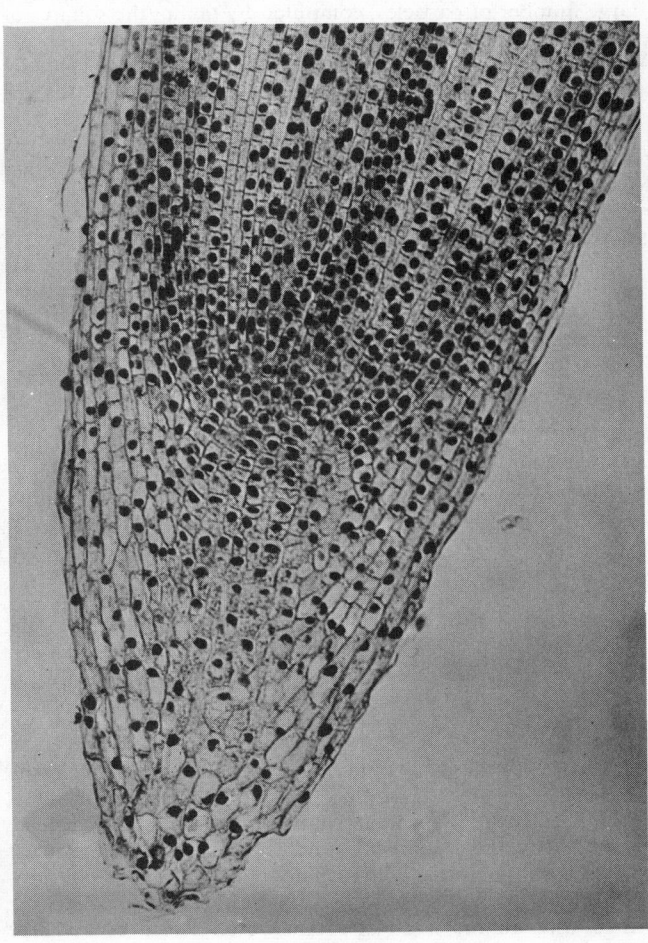

Longitudinal section through lower part of onion rootlet: Rather large oval cells at tip of rootlet form the root cap, a structure which protects the meristematic region from mechanical injury. The meristematic, or growth, region where cell division occurs, is immediately above (and partially within) the root cap. (*L. and M. Milne*)

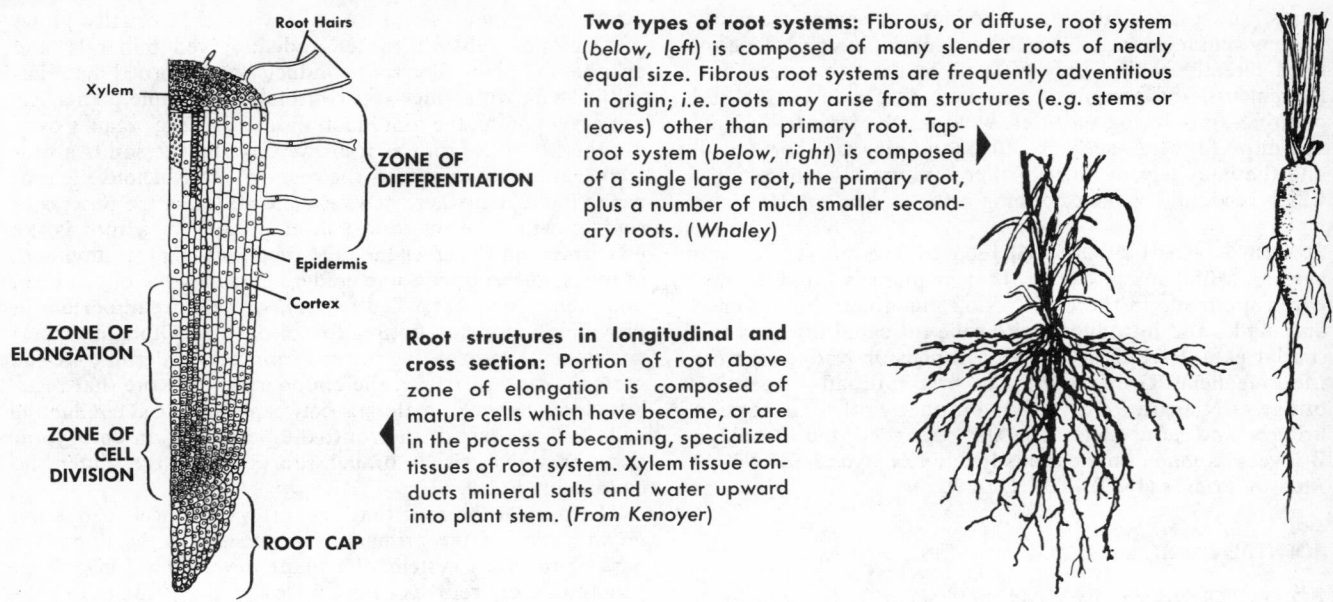

Root Hairs

Xylem

ZONE OF
DIFFERENTIATION

Epidermis

Cortex

ZONE OF
ELONGATION

ZONE OF
CELL
DIVISION

ROOT CAP

Two types of root systems: Fibrous, or diffuse, root system (*below, left*) is composed of many slender roots of nearly equal size. Fibrous root systems are frequently adventitious in origin; *i.e.* roots may arise from structures (e.g. stems or leaves) other than primary root. Tap-root system (*below, right*) is composed of a single large root, the primary root, plus a number of much smaller second-ary roots. (*Whaley*)

Root structures in longitudinal and cross section: Portion of root above zone of elongation is composed of mature cells which have become, or are in the process of becoming, specialized tissues of root system. Xylem tissue con-ducts mineral salts and water upward into plant stem. (*From Kenoyer*)

titious roots include the prop roots of corn, the aerial roots of orchids, the clinging roots of English ivy, and the roots that develop on stem cuttings. Roots have no nodes, whereas even underground stems (*e.g.* potato tuber) show nodes at which leaves and buds occur.—*F. L.*

ROOT MEAN SQUARE VELOCITY: the average velocity of a large number of particles, computed by taking the squares of the velocity of each particle, averaging them, and then taking the square root. This quantity is important in the kinetic theory of gases, because it gives the average speed of the gas particles without regard to their direction of motion. The mean square velocity multiplied by half the mass of the gas molecule gives its average kinetic energy. See KINETIC THEORY OF MATTER.—*I. R.*

ROSCOE, SIR HENRY ENFIELD, 1833–1915, English chemist; b. London. He prepared vanadium in a pure state, studied its oxides and chlorides, determined its atomic weight, and showed that it belongs in the phosphorus-arsenic family of elements. With R. W. Bunsen he investigated the chemical action of light. He was a fellow of the Royal Society.—*D. H. D. R.*

ROSENBUSCH, KARL HARRY FERDINAND, 1836–1914, German geologist and petrologist; b. Einbeck. An early student of metamorphic zoning (1876), he became known for meticulous mineralogical and textural analyses of eruptive rocks by use of the polarizing microscope. His genetic classification of eruptive rocks by mode of occurrence, texture, and mineral-ogy rather than chemistry is still predominant. The *Rosen-busch rule* gives the order of crystallization of the minerals in igneous rock. He wrote *Mikroskopische Physiographie der massigen Gesteine* (1877), making petrography a historical and not a descriptive science. He was an associate of the U. S. National Academy of Sciences.—*C. J. S.*

ROSIN: a natural RESIN obtained from pine trees. This resin is distilled to give turpentine, leaving a crystalline residue, *gum rosin.* Rosin is employed in paper SIZING, soaps, varnish, paint driers, and soluble oils, and as a soldering flux. Since it prevents slipping, it is used, usually in dried, powdered form, by athletes for better ball-handling, on the canvas of boxing rings, and on the hairs of violin bows. Rosin is a source

of abietic acid ($C_{19}H_{29}COOH$), a compound used to make laundry soap. The term *naval stores* is sometimes used to describe rosin and turpentine.—*Ru. M.*

ROSSBY, CARL-GUSTAV ARVID, 1898–1957, Swedish-U. S. meteorologist; b. Stockholm. He was one of the founders of the modern school of atmospheric dynamics. Beginning in 1938, Rossby and his collaborators investigated long waves in the westerlies, and developed isentropic analysis as a method of forecasting (see WEATHER ANALYSIS). The *Rossby diagram* provides a thermodynamic method of identifying air masses. His influence on the meteorologists of his genera-tion can hardly be overestimated. He was a member of the National Academy of Sciences.—*D. H. D. R.*

ROTATION: the spinning of a body about a fixed axis, as dis-tinguished from its motion in a straight line (translation). A rotating body moves with a uniform angular velocity if the radius drawn from the axis to some point on the body sweeps through equal angles in equal periods of time. Angular velocity may be expressed in degrees per second, revolutions per minute or second, or radians per second (1 revolution = 2π radians). In mathematical terms, angular velocity, ω, equals $d\theta/dt$, or the time rate of change of angular displace-ment θ.

The linear or peripheral speed (v) of a point on a rotating flywheel is related to its angular velocity (ω) and the radius (r) of the flywheel by the equation $v = \omega r$. Even with uniform peripheral speed, there is an acceleration toward the center, known as centripetal acceleration and expressed by $a = v^2/r$.

Angular motion may take place with accelerated angular velocity, provided that an unbalanced torque (the rotational equivalent of force) is applied to the shaft. Angular accelera-tion, α, equals $d\omega/dt$ (time rate of change of angular velocity) and is usually expressed in radians/sec². Displacement in ra-dians, θ, achieved in the course of accelerated rotation, is given by ½αt^2 if the rotating body accelerates uniformly from rest, and by the expression $\omega t \pm$ ½αt^2 if the positive or nega-tive acceleration is superimposed on an initial uniform rotary motion. It should also be noted that the linear acceleration of a point on a rotating body equals the product of its angu-lar acceleration and the radius extending from the shaft to the point in question.—*A. E.*

ROTATION OF EARTH: see DAY AND NIGHT; EARTH; TERRESTRIAL MAGNETISM.

ROTIFER: an invertebrate animal of the phylum Rotifera, a primary division of the animal kingdom consisting of about 1,500 species of microscopic aquatic animals. They are found chiefly in fresh waters, sometimes in enormous numbers. Some species are attached to underwater objects and others creep about, but the majority swim actively by means of CILIA on the anterior (front) end. They feed chiefly on bacteria, algae, protozoa, and bits of debris.—*R. P.*

ROUX, WILHELM, 1850–1924, German embryologist; b. Jena. He was one of the early investigators of the mechanics of structural changes in the embryo and the founder of the school of evolutionary physiology. His work was a consequence of the biogenetic principle of his teacher, E. H. Haeckel ("ontogeny recapitulates phylogeny"), and he attempted to explain phylogeny through the study of ontogenic development and by experimentation directed at finding the manner in which organs and tissues develop to assume their ultimate form and function. He was the founder of the journal *Archiv für Entwicklungsmechanik der Organismen* (1895). He was an associate of the U. S. National Academy of Sciences.—*D. H. D. R.*

ROWLAND, HENRY AUGUSTUS, 1848–1901, U. S. physicist; b. Honesdale, Pa. His first major paper, "On Magnetic Permeability, and the Maximum of Magnetism of Iron, Steel, and Nickel," was published in the *Philosophical Magazine,* 1873. Rowland's studies ranged widely, from construction of a dividing engine for ruling diffraction gratings to the calculation of the mechanical equivalent of heat. He was a consultant on the first Niagara Falls electric power plant.

Henry Augustus Rowland
(Yerkes Observatory)

He was a fellow of the Royal Society and a member of the National Academy of Sciences.—*H. I. S.*

RUBBER: *Natural rubber* is an elastic substance found as a milky dispersion in many unrelated species of plants, ranging from trees to fungi; *synthetic rubbers* are high polymeric elastic substances manufactured from a wide range of chemical compounds. The English name "rubber" comes from the now trivial use of the substance for erasers. In other languages the name for natural rubber is derived from the Brazilian native word, *e.g.* "caoutchouc" (French) or "Kautschuk" (German). Both synthetic and natural rubber have in common the ability to undergo nearly reversible, highly elastic deformations. When properly prepared, rubber will recover its original length after extensions as high as ten-fold. In 1960 world-wide use of rubber was divided nearly equally between the natural product (about 2.0 million long tons) and synthetic rubber (about 1.8 million tons). In the U. S. A. 69% of new rubber used in 1960 was synthetic; U. S. production amounted to 1.45 million tons and consumption to 1.08 million tons.

Natural Rubber: Natural rubber is closely related chemically to many other naturally occurring compounds, from animals as well as plants, including terpenes and steroids. These are known collectively as isoprenoids, because of a common structural feature, being formally derivable from a series of isoprene (2-methyl-1,3-butadiene or C_5H_8) units. No physiological function for rubber is known; it has been shown not to be metabolized even under conditions of extreme starvation. The basic building block for natural rubber as well as other polyisoprenoids is acetic acid, in the form of its coenzyme-A derivative. This is converted to rubber through the sequence of compounds:

Acetate—acetoacetate—hydroxymethyl glutarate—mevalonate (*i.e.* dihydroxymethyl valerate)—mevalonic acid pyrophosphate—isopentenylpyrophosphate—rubber.

Natural rubber occurs in a separate system of *latex* vessels just under the outer bark and outside the sap-bearing vessels. Careful cutting of the bark permits the latex to drip without injury to the tree. Latex is collected, bulked, then either coagulated or preserved. Most rubber is shipped as "smoked sheets" prepared by coagulation with the aid of acetic or formic acid, sheeting out on mills, and drying at low temperature in a stream of smoky air. Latex is preserved by addition of ammonia, and concentrated by centrifuging or by "creaming" for shipment as a liquid.

Rubber was first obtained principally from wild trees in Brazil, particularly the species *Hevea brasiliensis.* Through the efforts of Sir Henry Wickham in the 1870s, seedlings were established at Kew Gardens in London and plantations then started in SE Asia. Substantially all rubber is now produced from selected clones derived from these seedlings or their descendants. *H. brasiliensis* will grow anywhere within 5° of the equator, but diseases indigenous to S America have so far prevented successful establishment of plantations on that continent. About 75% of all natural rubber now comes from the Malay Peninsula and Indonesia. Roughly half is produced on large plantations, the rest in native "smallholdings."

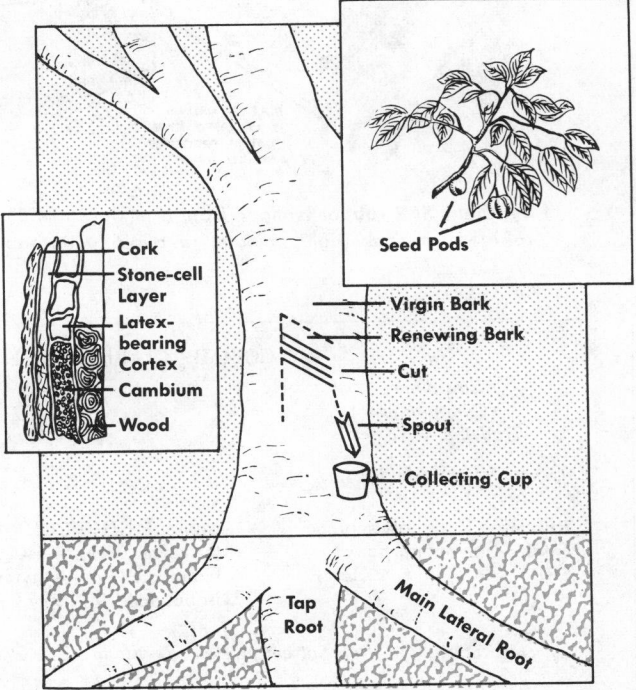

Natural rubber is obtained from *Hevea brasiliensis* by shaving off a thin strip of bark about ¹⁄₁₅ in. deep. Through a spout inserted into the lower end of the cut, latex flows into a cup; flow continues about 3 hr. Trees are self-healing and continue to produce 4 to 15 lb of latex per yr for about 25 yr. Seed pods (*top insert*) explode when ripe, hurling seeds as much as 100 ft. (*U. S. Rubber Co.*)

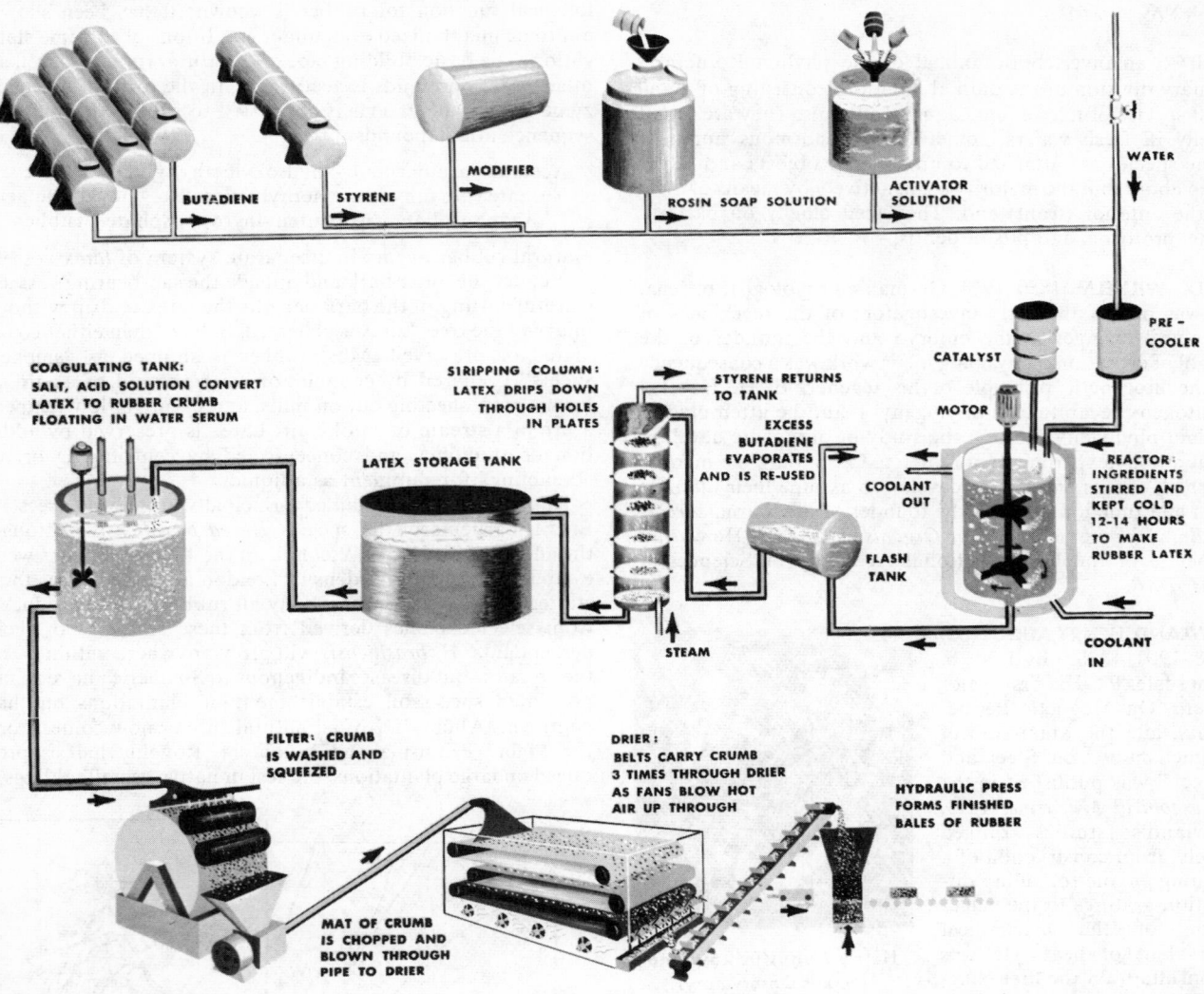

Synthetic SBR rubber is made from a mixture of 75% butadiene and 25% styrene. Polymerization must occur in refrigerated tank (*right, middle*) to avoid undesirable properties in the finished rubber. (*U. S. Rubber Co.*)

COMMERCIALLY AVAILABLE SYNTHETIC RUBBERS

Elastomer (Common or Trademark Name)	Made From	Polymerization Method
A. General-purpose Rubbers:		
Rubber, NR, cispolyisoprene	isoprene, $CH_2=CCH=CH_2$ (with CH_3)	Natural; Stereospecific
Cis-1, 4-polybutadiene	butadiene, $CH_2=CHCH=CH_2$	Stereospecific
SBR	butadiene (75%) + styrene, $C_6H_5CH=CH_2$	Emulsion
Butyl	isobutylene (97–99%) + isoprene (1–3%)	Solution, metal-halide catalyst
B. Special Rubbers for High Solvent or Heat Resistance, Low Permeability, etc.:		
Neoprene	chloroprene, $CH_2=CCH=CH_2$ (with Cl)	Emulsion
Polyurethanes*	polyester or polyether + diisocyanate	Addition reaction
Nitrile rubber	butadiene (60–80%) + acrylonitrile $CH_2=CHCN$	Emulsion
Silicone rubber*	dichloroalkyl silanes, R_2SiCl_2	Hydrolysis + polycondensation
Thiokol*	ethylene halides	Polycondensation with polysulfides

* The main chain or backbone of these rubbers includes some other atom as well as carbon in a recurring unit.

Making a tire: "Green tire" resembling a small barrel (*right*) is placed in mold. When mold closes, steam inflates a heavy reinforced bag (underneath green tire); bag forces green tire against mold, giving tire its final shape and tread (*left*). (*Firestone Tire and Rubber Co.*)

Synthetic Rubber: Preparation of rubber-like materials in the laboratory is nearly as old as commercial growing of rubber, but the manufacture of synthetic rubbers was of little consequence until the early 1930s. The spur of wartime necessity led to a revolution in the U. S. rubber industry following the loss to the Japanese of Asiatic plantations in 1942. In a short time the preparation in large volume of SBR general-purpose synthetic rubber (formerly called Government Rubber-Styrene, or GR-S) was successfully accomplished. SBR is prepared by emulsion polymerization, a process originally developed in Germany in the late 1920s. A mixture of butadiene and styrene (75%/25%) is mixed with water, an emulsifying agent such as soap, an initiator, and usually an auxiliary compound to control molecular weight of the polymer. Initiators are sources of free radicals which convert the monomers to a high-molecular-weight polymer. Because polymerization at higher temperatures adversely affects rubber properties, much SBR is made at low temperatures, using refrigeration to remove the heat of reaction. The reaction is stopped before it is complete, by adding a "short-stop" to prevent undesirable gel formation. The unreacted monomers are recovered and the latex processed. The latex may be used *as is* in the same way as natural-rubber latex, but most often is converted to dry forms. In making synthetic rubbers, control over the rubber's properties is afforded by varying the polymerization reaction; also it is possible to make a range of rubber materials by various additions to the latex before preparation of the solid rubber. Thus, carbon black can be mixed into the latex; and very-high-molecular-weight rubber may be made softer by the addition of large amounts of oil. An essential addend is a small amount of stabilizer or ANTIOXIDANT to protect the rubber from the effects of atmospheric oxygen.

A new method for preparation of general-purpose synthetic rubbers was discovered independently in several laboratories in the mid-1950s, and reached commercial production with startling rapidity. A synthetic polyisoprene identical with natural rubber became commercially available in the U. S. A. in 1959. These rubbers are produced by an ionic polymerization in hydrocarbon solvents, using organic metal derivatives as catalysts. Such catalysts give very good control of the chemical structure of the rubber produced, a feature not available in SBR and other rubbers produced by free-radical reactions. Continued research has led to the availability of a large number of additional synthetic rubbers, listed in the accompanying table. Each of these has some special properties which particularly fit it for certain uses, *e.g.* superior resistance to solvents or to severe in-service conditions. Other rubbers available include chlorosulfonated polyethylene, highly fluorinated polymers, and acrylate polymers. These are all used where very severe conditions are encountered. A new, potentially large-volume rubber is based on ethylene and propylene as monomers. (See POLYMERS.)—*E. M. B.*

RUBIDIUM: a soft, silvery, very reactive alkali-metal element (Rb); at. no. 37; at. wt 85.48; valence 1. Robert Bunsen and Gustav Robert Kirchhoff discovered rubidium (1861) in the course of their pioneer studies of emission spectra. The element ignites spontaneously in oxygen, reacts vigorously with the halogens, and when molten (39°C) burns in air; since rubidium also reacts violently with water and burns the liberated hydrogen, it is stored in petroleum, benzene, or some other oxygen-free liquid or in a dry, inert gas. The present supply of rubidium is limited, and uses for the element are few. When alloyed with antimony, bismuth, or gold, it can be used in photoelectric tubes as a light source. As a "getter" in vacuum-tube manufacture, rubidium or one of its salts is inserted in the tube in a capsule; when the capsule is heated by a high-frequency source, the rubidium chemically reduces the gas remaining in the tube and the resulting compound is deposited as a thin film on the inside of the glass. Because it is one of the most easily ionized elements, rubidium is being investigated for use in ion-propulsion engines, as well as for magnetohydrodynamic (MHD) and thermionic energy-conversion systems. See ALKALI METALS.—*R. B. T.*

RUBNER, MAX, 1854–1932, German physiologist; b. Munich. He proposed in his *isodynamic law* that carbohydrates, fats, and proteins are exchangeable in the body on the basis of their caloric equivalents. He determined the energy yield in metabolism of each of the three groups of foodstuffs—important knowledge in planning national food supplies. His *law of surface area* for mammals states that the rate of heat production in the mammal is proportional to the surface area of the body. His researches in animal calorimetry culminated in the experimental demonstration of the principle of conservation of energy for animal metabolism. He was an associate of the U. S. National Academy of Sciences.—*D. H. D. R.*

RUMFORD, BENJAMIN THOMP-SON, COUNT, 1753–1814, British physicist; b. North Woburn, Mass. Rumford's experiments using the heat produced during the boring of cannon undermined the prevailing *caloric* theory of heat and led him to declare (in "An Inquiry Concerning the Source of Heat which Is Excited by Friction," 1798) that heat could be nothing other than motion. He anticipated the equivalence of heat and work and, in a crude way, attempted

Count Rumford
(*Amer. Acad. of Arts and Sciences*)

to measure it. He investigated not only the characteristics of heat but also ballistic phenomena, and attempted to improve domestic heating and illumination. His restless temperament led him successively into the service of the British Crown and the Duke of Bavaria, and a great part of his energies was spent in diverse schemes of social betterment. A fellow of the Royal Society, Rumford established the Rumford medal with a gift of £1,000. In 1799 he formed the Royal Institution, which became a major research center under the direction of H. Davy and M. Faraday. To Harvard Univ. he bequeathed a fund to found a professorship in the physical and mathematical sciences.—*A. L.*

RUMSEY, JAMES, 1743–92, U. S. mechanical engineer; b. Bohemia Manor, Md. One of the first to experiment with the construction of steamboats, Rumsey demonstrated (1787) a boat driven by streams of water forced through the stern by steam pumps. He invented an improved pipe boiler and obtained patents in England and the U. S. A. on the steamboat and boiler (1791), but died before the completion of a second demonstration steamboat.—*S. B.*

RUNCORN, STANLEY KEITH, 1922–   , English geophysicist; b. Southport. He has been a prime investigator of the remanent magnetism in rocks and its implications as to possible wanderings of Earth's magnetic and rotational poles. (See TERRESTRIAL MAGNETISM and CONTINENTAL DRIFT.)—*R. W. D.*

RUSSELL, BERTRAND ARTHUR WILLIAM, 3rd EARL, 1872–   , English mathematician and philosopher; ed. Trinity College, Cambridge, where he later became a lecturer and fellow. With Alfred North Whitehead he wrote *Principia Mathematica* (3 vols., 1910–13), a major work in symbolic logic. He has written extensively in the field of mathematical philosophy and in other areas of philosophy. Although a profound scholar, Russell has never been an ivory-tower academician. He has been deeply interested in education, morals, social welfare, and the problem of peace, and he has written extensively on all of these matters. The penetration of his thinking and a lucid and vivid style of writing have made him one of the most influential writers of his age. He is a fellow of the Royal Society.—*H. C.*

RUST: the reddish-brown coating which appears on iron exposed to the atmosphere; it is mainly ferric oxide (Fe_2O_3), with some hydroxide and carbonate. It is apparently formed by the combined action of carbon dioxide, moisture, and oxygen. Rusting takes place more rapidly if the exposed iron is in contact with a less active metal, if its surface is rough, if it is under strain (as when bent) or if it comes into contact with chloride salts. The impurities generally present in commercial iron can also accelerate rusting. Protective treatments include tarring, painting, or enameling; coating with other metals, such as tin or zinc (galvanizing); and coating with magnetic oxide of iron. (See CORROSION.)—*W. P. C.*

RUTHENIUM: a white, lustrous, metallic element (Ru): one of the PLATINUM metals; at. no. 44; at. wt 101.1; valence 2, 3, 4, 6, or 8. Ruthenium was discovered (1844) and first isolated by Karl Karlovich Klaus. It reacts with oxygen when hot, and thus must be melted in an inert atmosphere. Ruthenium is extremely corrosion-resistant, but its close-packed hexagonal structure makes it almost too hard to be worked; the metal is therefore chiefly used in alloy, practically always with other platinum metals. Ruthenium-platinum and ruthenium-palladium alloys are used for hard-service electrical contacts in magnetos, heavy-duty switches, and relays. The high strength and electrical resistivity of these alloys make them useful also for filament and fuse wire. Alloys of ruthenium and osmium, iridium, or rhodium are very hard and suitable for bearing pivots and pen points. The metal is used as a catalyst in the synthesis of long-chain hydrocarbons, in jewelry as a platinum substitute. Ruthenium forms a wide variety of complex salts, many of them highly colored. Ruthenium ferrocyanide, a purple analogue of Prussian blue, has been used as a pigment. —*R. B. T.*

RUTHERFORD, ERNEST, 1st BARON, 1871–1937, British chemist; b. Nelson, N. Z. While professor of physics at McGill Univ., Montreal, Rutherford established the existence of α and β particles. In 1903, along with F. Soddy, he published a general theory of radioactivity, asserting (1) that radio-

active elements such as radium, thorium, and uranium are in the process of producing new kinds of radioactive matter, and (2) that the emanations from radioactive material are accompanied by fundamental changes within their atoms. For this discovery he received the 1908 Nobel prize in chemistry. In 1911, as a result of observing the deflection angles of α particles, he published his conclusions concerning

Ernest Rutherford
(*Wide World*)

the structure of the atom. His model of a positively charged compact central nucleus surrounded by negatively charged electrons in motion has remained valid until the present. From this he drew the conclusion that the chemical nature of an element derives from the number of positively charged particles in the nucleus; to this particle he gave the name *proton*. In 1919, after developing methods of anti-submarine warfare during World War I, Rutherford discovered that the collision of α particles with nitrogen atoms resulted in the disintegration of the nitrogen and the production of hydrogen nuclei and ions of an oxygen isotope. Along with J. Chadwick, he continued his "atom smashing" and succeeded in 1921 in producing transformations in boron, fluorine, aluminum, and phosphorus. Many of the outstanding physicists of the early 20th cent.—H. Geiger, H. G. J. Moseley, and Niels Bohr—worked in his laboratory at the Univ. of Manchester, England. In 1919 he became director of the Cavendish Laboratory in Cambridge. He was a fellow of the Royal Society and an associate of the U. S. National Academy of Sciences.—*A. L.*

RUYSCH, FREDRIK, 1638–1731, Dutch anatomist; b. The Hague. He was a pioneer of the injection method, and was the first to describe the bronchial blood vessels (1665). The *Opera omnia anatomico-medico chirurgica* (Amsterdam, 1737–43) contain his anatomical work. He was a fellow of the Royal Society.—*D. J. S.*

RUŽIČKA, LEOPOLD, 1887–   , Yugoslav-Swiss chemist; b. Vukovar, Yugoslavia. He discovered that the five carbon units having the particular configuration of isoprene, important in understanding the molecular structure of carotinoids (Vitamin A and related compounds), occur in a wide variety of natural products, including many essential oils. He also investigated the chemistry of materials used in making perfume. For his work on polymethylenes and higher terpenes, he shared the 1939 Nobel prize with Adolph Butenandt. He is a fellow of the Royal Society and an associate of the U. S. National Academy of Sciences.—*D. H. D. R.*

RYDBERG CONSTANT: a number proportional to the frequency of oscillation of the electromagnetic radiation emitted when a proton captures an electron and the latter falls into the innermost orbit possible, thereby forming a stable hydrogen atom. All the possible frequencies (colors) in the light radiated by excited hydrogen atoms can be computed from a simple formula involving the Rydberg constant. The formula was originally arrived at empirically by J. R. Rydberg, and one of the early triumphs of QUANTUM MECHANICS was to justify it theoretically. The formula states that the frequency of the light emitted in a transition from the Bohr orbit n_2 to n_1, counting from the innermost orbit, is $f = cR(1/n_1^2 - 1/n_2^2)$, where R is the Rydberg constant, and c is the speed of light. —*S. K.*

1

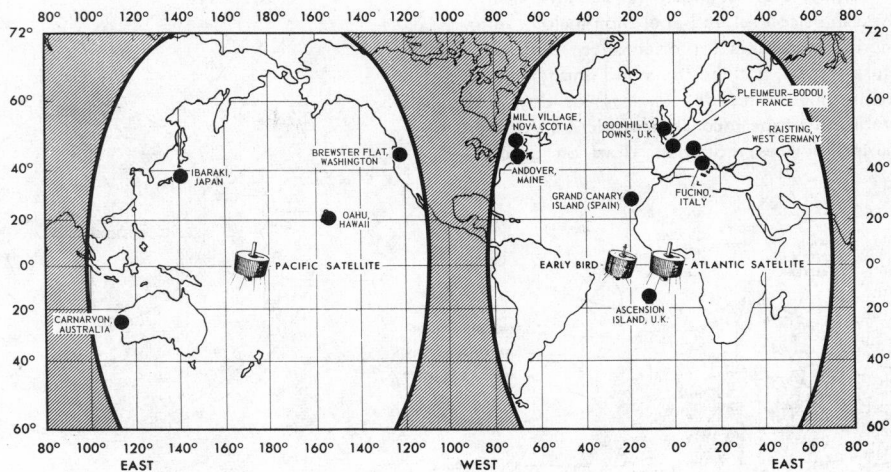

HORN ANTENNA

AUTO TRACK

VOICE, DATA, TV

VOICE, DATA, TV

PRECISION TRACKING

TRACKING, TELEMETRY SIGNALS AND COMMANDS

CONTROL BUILDING

MICROWAVE TO PORTLAND, MAINE

COMMAND AND TELEMETRY ANTENNA

PRECISION TRACKING ANTENNA

Communications satellites help to solve a basic problem of radio broadcasting: the fact that radio waves travel in straight lines—not in paths following the curve of the globe. In the past, long-distance broadcasting has depended upon reflection of waves from the upper atmosphere; but many such waves, especially the short ones, are not reflected and are lost into outer space. A communications satellite eliminates the need for reflection; it can receive signals directly from one station and relay them directly to another station thousands of miles away. The first commercial communications satellite was Early Bird, launched in 1965 into an equatorial orbit with an altitude of 22,300 mi. and a speed of 6,900 mph. (corresponding to the speed of Earth's rotation). Three such satellites, kept properly spaced—*i.e.* synchronized—can cover the globe.

1. Comsat (Communications Satellite Corporation) stations in operation early in 1967. **2. How signals are relayed** from one earth station to another one over the horizon. (COMSAT)

3. Comsat station in northern Oahu, Hawaii, with control building, horn antenna (middle right), and 85-ft "dish" antenna. **4. A communications satellite,** showing telemetry antennas for receiving commands, communications antenna for relaying signals, solar cells for power generation, and sensors and rocket units for orientation. (COMSAT)

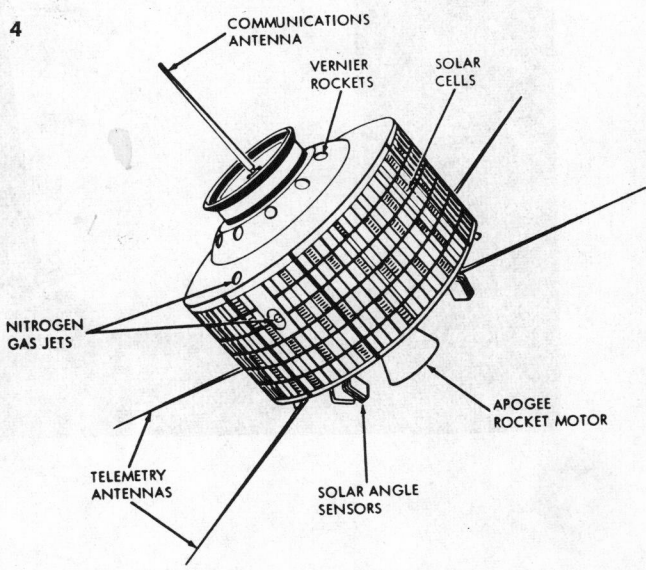

COMMUNICATIONS ANTENNA

VERNIER ROCKETS

SOLAR CELLS

NITROGEN GAS JETS

APOGEE ROCKET MOTOR

TELEMETRY ANTENNAS

SOLAR ANGLE SENSORS

SPACE TECHNOLOGY: Atmospheric Research

The meteorological satellite is an omnibus for scientific instruments. Devices involved in its control and operation include solar cells for power generation, sensors for orientation, automatic shutters for temperature control, and the command and telemetry antennas. Research instruments include cameras for day and night (infrared) photography, tape recorders for picture storage, and radiation-measuring devices that yield data on ground,

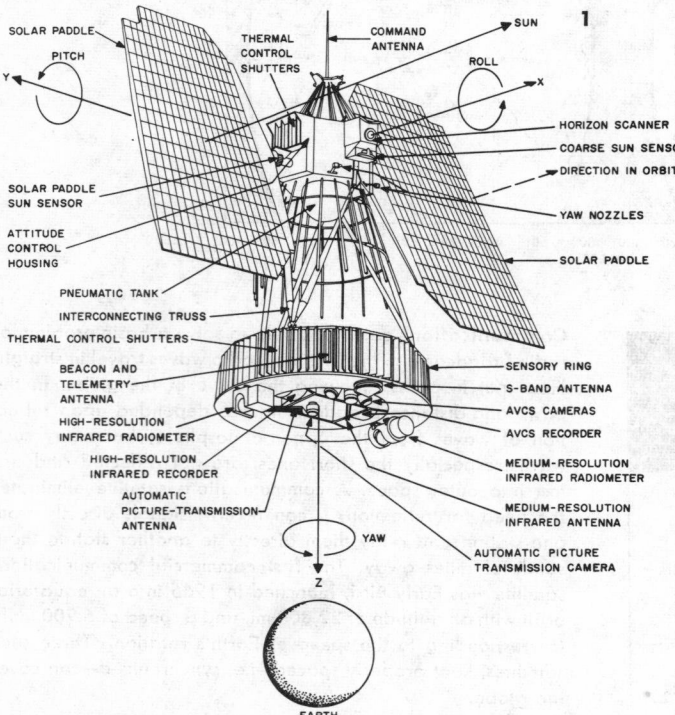

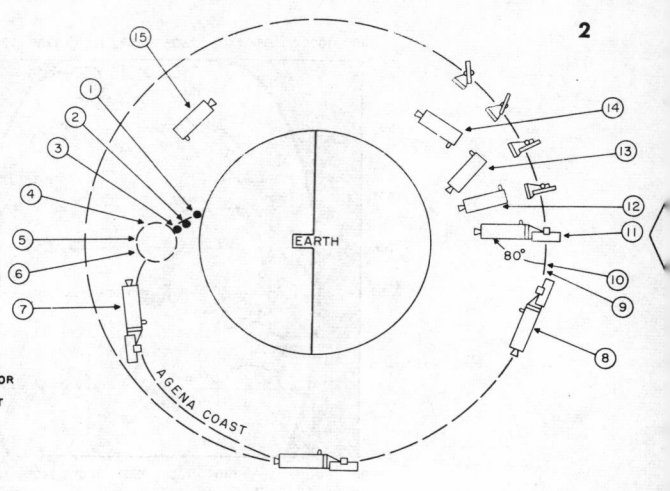

1. Launch. 2. Thor main engine cutoff. 3. Thor vernier-engine cutoff. 4. Thor-Agena separation. 5. Agena first burn. 6. Nose-shroud separation. 7. Agena first cutoff. 8. Agena second ignition. 9. Agena second cutoff. 10. Initiate 60° per min. pitchup. 11. Terminate pitchup. 12. Separate spacecraft. 13. Initiate yaw-roll maneuver. 14. Terminate yaw-roll maneuver; first retro. 15. Second retro.

ocean, and air temperatures and on moisture conditions. The satellite's transmitters, operating around the clock, send to earth stations a continuous weather report, from which meteorologists can make analyses with a scope and a continuity that would not be possible even from the most extensive, most elaborate ground observations. **1. Diagram of Nimbus C** meteorological satellite. **2. Launch of Nimbus** into orbit by means of Thor-Agena B rocket *(both NASA)*. **3. Close-up of 912-1b Nimbus** *(G.E. Valley Forge Space Tech. Center).*

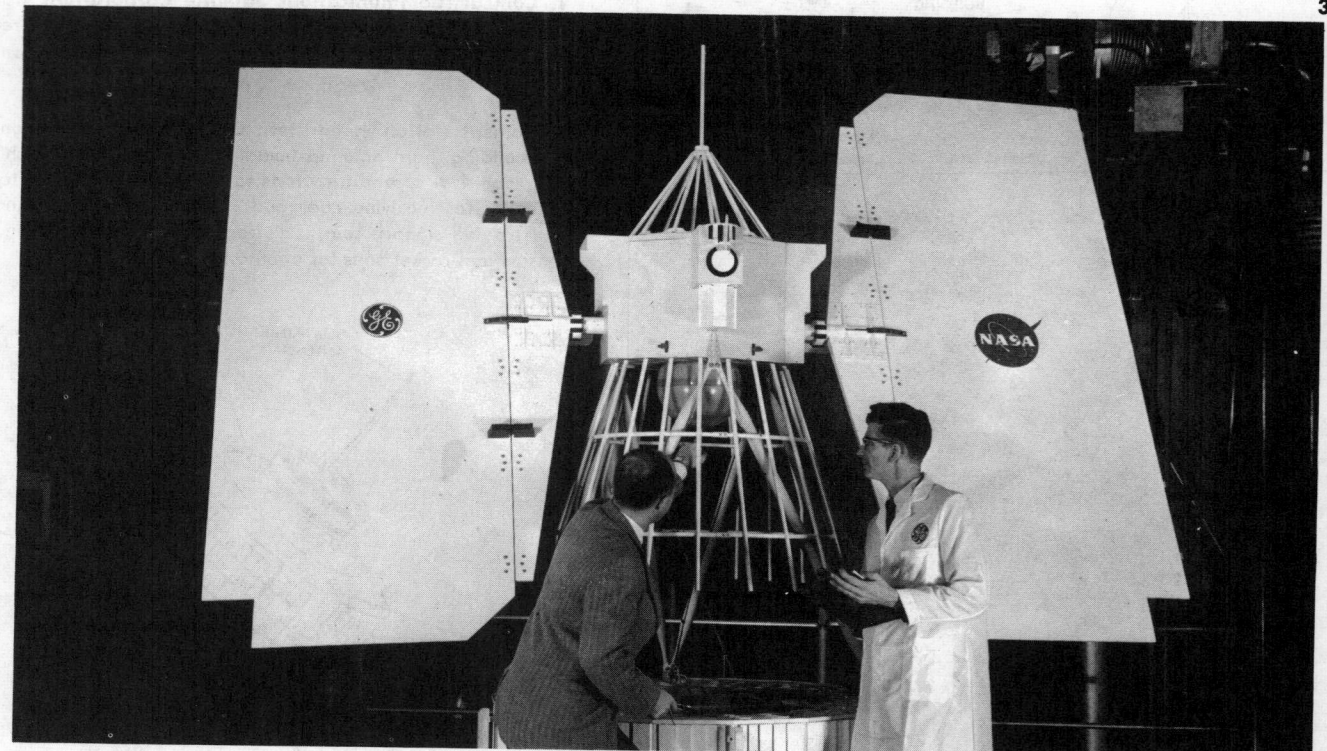

1

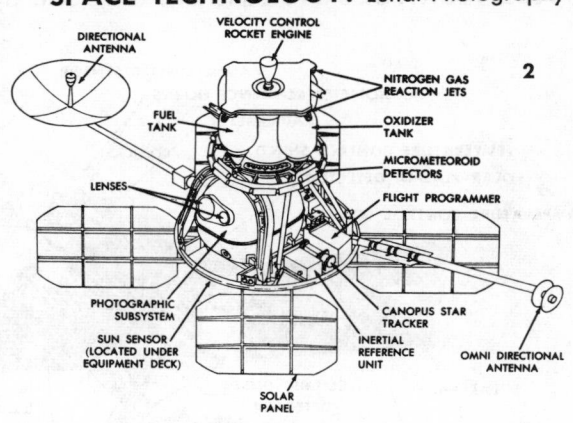

SOLAR PANEL

OMNIDIRECTIONAL ANTENNA

SURVEY TV CAMERA

HIGH-GAIN ANTENNA

STAR CANOPUS SENSOR

OMNIDIRECTIONAL ANTENNA

THERMALLY CONTROLLED COMPARTMENT

RADAR ALTITUDE-DOPPLER VELOCITY ANTENNA

VERNIER ENGINE

VERNIER PROPELLANT PRESSURIZING GAS (HELIUM) TANK

AUXILIARY BATTERY

ATTITUDE CONTROL GAS (NITROGEN) TANK

RETRO ROCKET MOTOR

ALTITUDE MARKING RADAR ANTENNA

LANDING GEAR

2

DIRECTIONAL ANTENNA

VELOCITY CONTROL ROCKET ENGINE

NITROGEN GAS REACTION JETS

FUEL TANK

OXIDIZER TANK

MICROMETEOROID DETECTORS

LENSES

FLIGHT PROGRAMMER

PHOTOGRAPHIC SUBSYSTEM

CANOPUS STAR TRACKER

SUN SENSOR (LOCATED UNDER EQUIPMENT DECK)

INERTIAL REFERENCE UNIT

OMNI DIRECTIONAL ANTENNA

SOLAR PANEL

Close-up lunar photography was accomplished first by a spacecraft orbiting the Moon (the Soviet Union's Lunik III, in 1959) and later by U.S. and Soviet craft before impacting on Moon or after making "soft" landings there.

3

APOLUNE 1150 ST. MI. ALTITUDE

INJECTION INTO PHOTOGRAPHIC ORBIT

PHOTOGRAPHIC AREA OF INTEREST

PERILUNE 120 & 28 ST. MI. ALTITUDE

INJECTION INTO INITIAL ORBIT

SECOND MIDCOURSE CORRECTION

FIRST MIDCOURSE CORRECTION

SUN-CANOPUS ORIENTATION

SOLAR PANEL AND ANTENNA DEPLOYMENT

AGENA SEPARATION

DSS (GOLDSTONE)

DSS (WOOMERA)

LAUNCH

JETTISON ATLAS BOOSTER

SEPARATE ATLAS AND NOSE SHROUD

EARTH ROTATION

1ST AGENA IGNITION (INJECT INTO PARKING ORBIT)

COAST IN PARKING ORBIT

2ND AGENA IGNITION (INJECT INTO TRANSLUNAR TRAJECTORY)

DSS (MADRID)

1. Surveyor B, one of two U.S. craft that sent thousands of photos of lunar surface to Earth in 1966. **2. Lunar Orbiter 3,** the third of the U.S. craft that orbited the Moon in 1966-67, photographing its surface from altitudes as low as 30 mi. to identify sites for future manned landings. **3. Maneuvers** involved in orbiting of Lunar Orbiter 3 in 1967. **4. Artist's visualization** of Lunar Orbiter over Moon. **5. Centaur** rocket used as second stage for Surveyor spacecraft. *(NASA)*

4

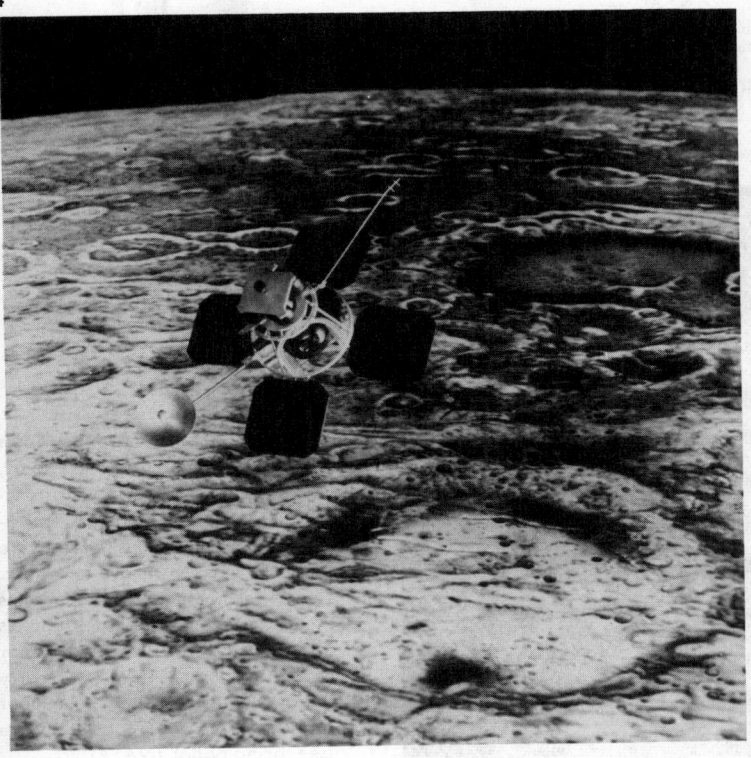

5

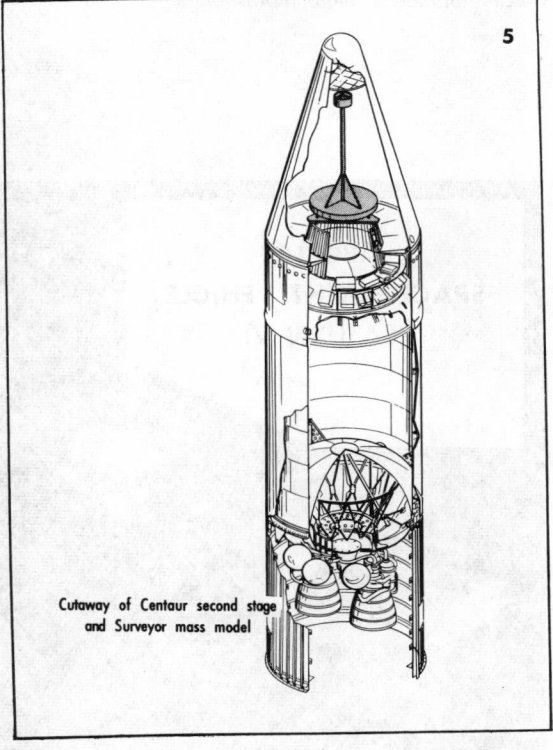

Cutaway of Centaur second stage and Surveyor mass model

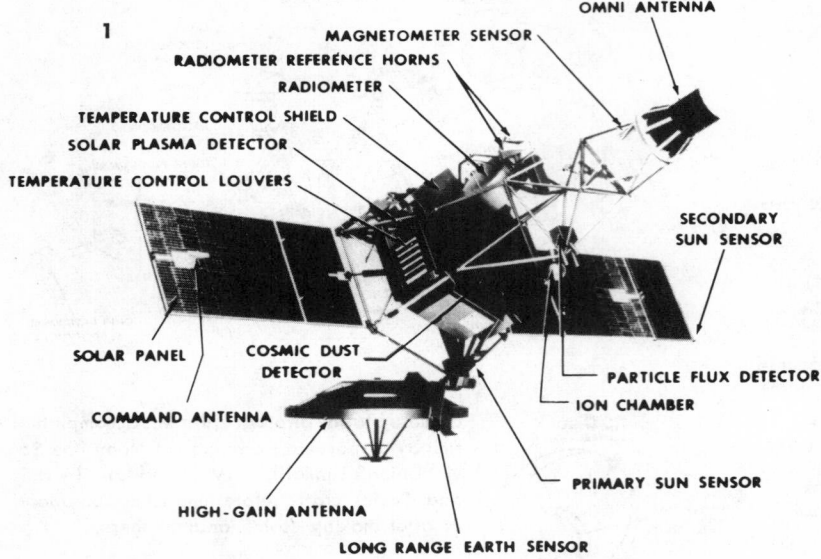

1

OMNI ANTENNA
MAGNETOMETER SENSOR
RADIOMETER REFERENCE HORNS
RADIOMETER
TEMPERATURE CONTROL SHIELD
SOLAR PLASMA DETECTOR
TEMPERATURE CONTROL LOUVERS
SECONDARY SUN SENSOR
SOLAR PANEL
COSMIC DUST DETECTOR
COMMAND ANTENNA
PARTICLE FLUX DETECTOR
ION CHAMBER
PRIMARY SUN SENSOR
HIGH-GAIN ANTENNA
LONG RANGE EARTH SENSOR

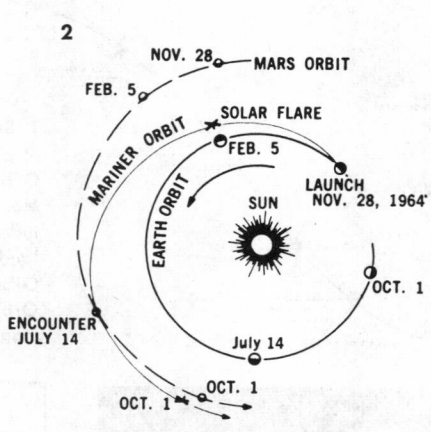

2

NOV. 28 — MARS ORBIT
FEB. 5
SOLAR FLARE
MARINER ORBIT
FEB. 5
LAUNCH NOV. 28, 1964
EARTH ORBIT
SUN
OCT. 1
ENCOUNTER JULY 14
July 14
OCT. 1
OCT. 1

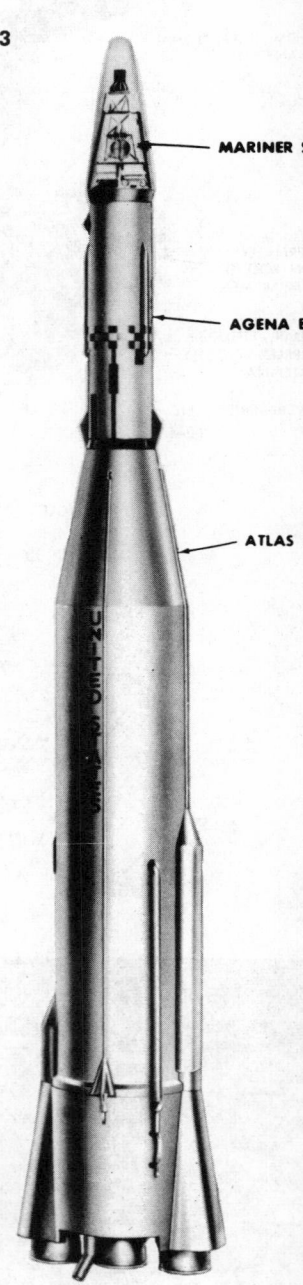

3

MARINER SP
AGENA B
ATLAS B

Close-up photography of other planets of the solar system began with the flight of the U.S. Mariner 4 spacecraft. Launched by means of an Atlas-Agena rocket, Nov. 28, 1964, the spacecraft on July 15, 1965, passed within 6,118 mi. of Mars, taking a series of 21 photographs of the red planet as it raced by. These pictures, radioed by Mariner back to Earth, revealed the Martian surface as a cratered terrain much like that of the Moon. **1. Elements of Mariner spacecraft. 2. Flight plan. 3. Launch rocket** for Mariner flight. *(NASA)*

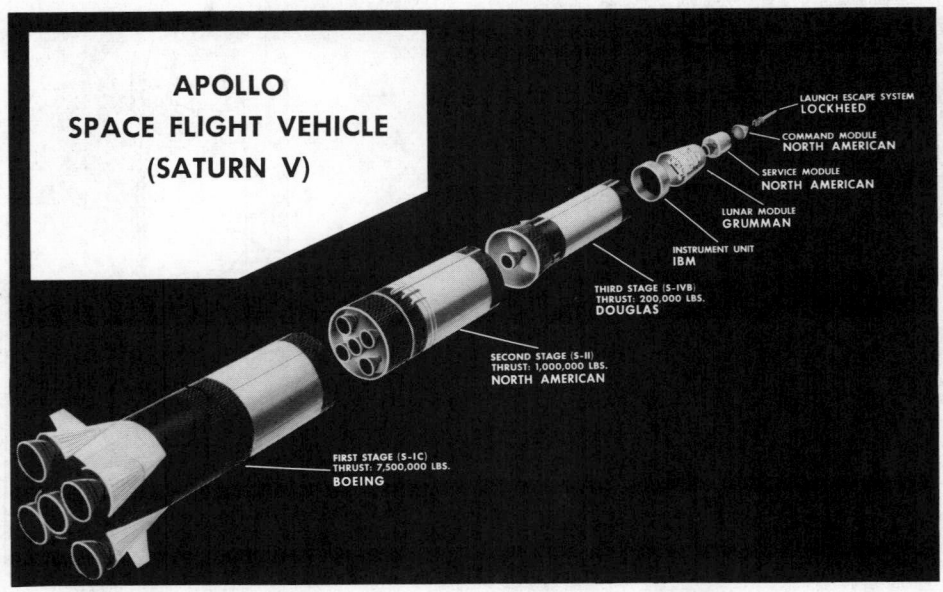

APOLLO
SPACE FLIGHT VEHICLE
(SATURN V)

LAUNCH ESCAPE SYSTEM
LOCKHEED
COMMAND MODULE
NORTH AMERICAN
SERVICE MODULE
NORTH AMERICAN
LUNAR MODULE
GRUMMAN
INSTRUMENT UNIT
IBM
THIRD STAGE (S-IVB)
THRUST: 200,000 LBS.
DOUGLAS
SECOND STAGE (S-II)
THRUST: 1,000,000 LBS.
NORTH AMERICAN
FIRST STAGE (S-IC)
THRUST: 7,500,000 LBS.
BOEING

Manned space travel to the Moon is the objective of the Apollo Project, the spacecraft for which consists essentially of three modules. The 5 ton command module is the structure in which the crew will live and work. The 24-ton service module contains the rocket engines and fuel supplies for the round trip. The 15-ton lunar excursion module (LEM) will carry the astronauts from the circumlunar orbit down to the Moon's surface (see facing page). *(NASA)*

Having put their Apollo spacecraft into orbit around the Moon, crewmen will enter the LEM, detach it, and descend to the lunar surface (right) to take pictures, gather samples of material, and perform scientific experiments. Re-entering the LEM, they will rendezvous with the main spacecraft, jettison the LEM, and begin the return journey to Earth. Before re-entry into Earth's atmosphere, the service module will be jettisoned, and the command module alone, with the astronauts, will complete the trip. (NASA)

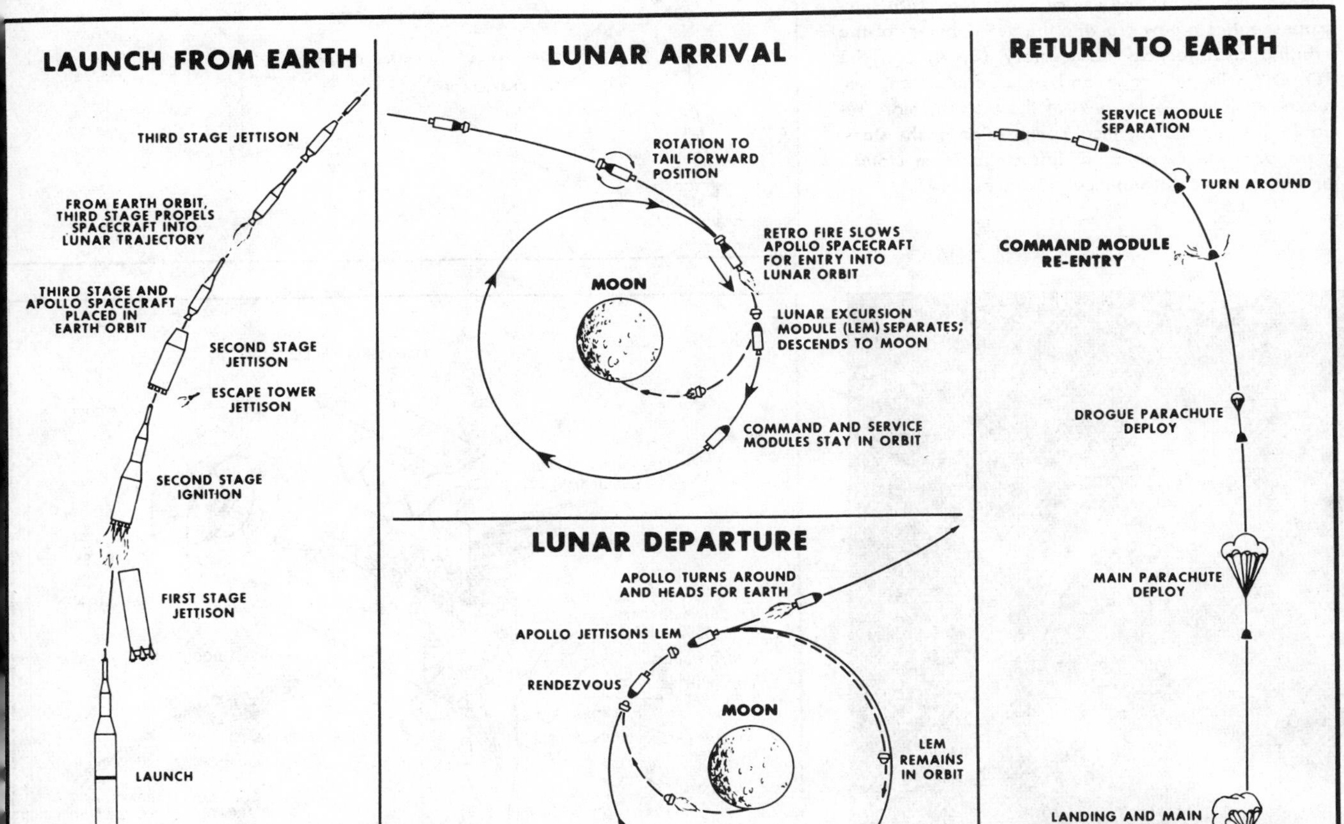

LAUNCH FROM EARTH

THIRD STAGE JETTISON

FROM EARTH ORBIT, THIRD STAGE PROPELS SPACECRAFT INTO LUNAR TRAJECTORY

THIRD STAGE AND APOLLO SPACECRAFT PLACED IN EARTH ORBIT

SECOND STAGE JETTISON

ESCAPE TOWER JETTISON

SECOND STAGE IGNITION

FIRST STAGE JETTISON

LAUNCH

LUNAR ARRIVAL

ROTATION TO TAIL FORWARD POSITION

RETRO FIRE SLOWS APOLLO SPACECRAFT FOR ENTRY INTO LUNAR ORBIT

LUNAR EXCURSION MODULE (LEM) SEPARATES; DESCENDS TO MOON

MOON

COMMAND AND SERVICE MODULES STAY IN ORBIT

LUNAR DEPARTURE

APOLLO TURNS AROUND AND HEADS FOR EARTH

APOLLO JETTISONS LEM

RENDEZVOUS

MOON

LEM REMAINS IN ORBIT

COMMAND AND SERVICE MODULES IN ORBIT

RETURN TO EARTH

SERVICE MODULE SEPARATION

TURN AROUND

COMMAND MODULE RE-ENTRY

DROGUE PARACHUTE DEPLOY

MAIN PARACHUTE DEPLOY

LANDING AND MAIN PARACHUTE RELEASE

SPACE TECHNOLOGY: Geophysical and Astronomical Research

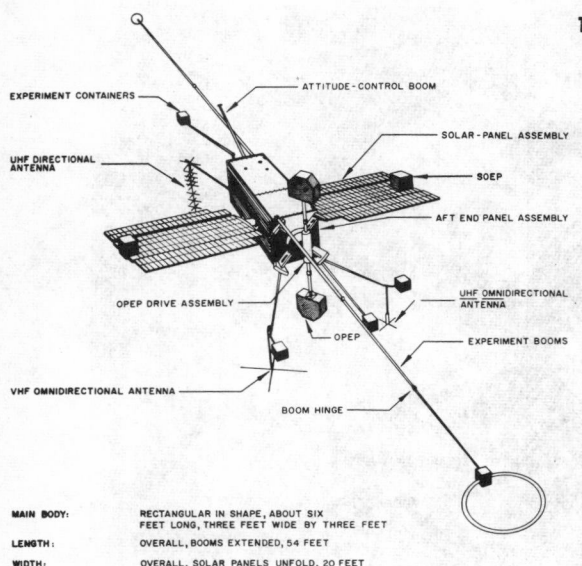

1

EXPERIMENT CONTAINERS
ATTITUDE-CONTROL BOOM
UHF DIRECTIONAL ANTENNA
SOLAR-PANEL ASSEMBLY
SOEP
AFT END PANEL ASSEMBLY
OPEP DRIVE ASSEMBLY
UHF OMNIDIRECTIONAL ANTENNA
OPEP
EXPERIMENT BOOMS
VHF OMNIDIRECTIONAL ANTENNA
BOOM HINGE

MAIN BODY: RECTANGULAR IN SHAPE, ABOUT SIX FEET LONG, THREE FEET WIDE BY THREE FEET
LENGTH: OVERALL, BOOMS EXTENDED, 54 FEET
WIDTH: OVERALL, SOLAR PANELS UNFOLD, 20 FEET

2

ORBITING GEOPHYSICAL OBSERVATORY
AREAS OF INVESTIGATION AND ORBITS, OGO I AND OGO B

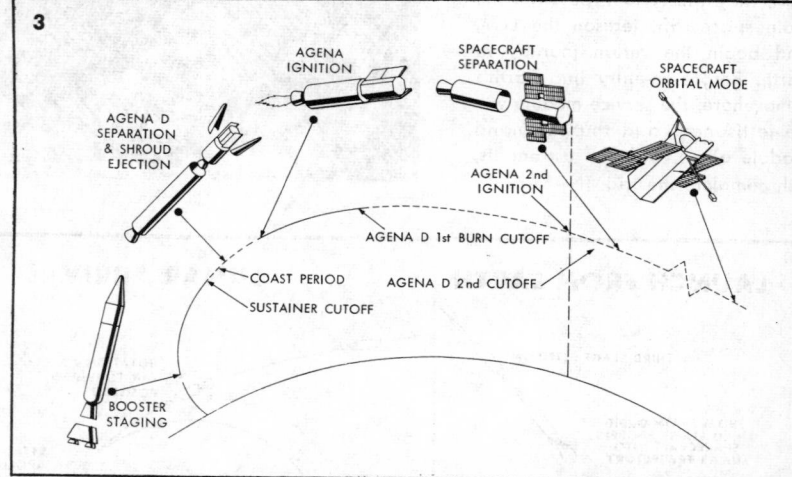

- IONIZATION
- SUDDEN IONOSPHERIC DISTURBANCES
- VERY LOW FREQUENCY NOISE
- AIRGLOW
- GALACTIC COSMIC RADIATION
- SOLAR WIND
- SOLAR FLARES
- SUN
- ELECTROMAGNETIC RADIATION
- INTERPLANETARY MAGNETIC FIELDS
- SHOCK WAVE
- MAGNETOSPHERIC COMPRESSION
- HYDROMAGNETIC WAVES
- PARTICLE ACCELERATION
- GEOMAGNETIC TRAPPING
- PARTICLE BUNCHING
- RADIATION BELT DUMPING
- POLAR CAP ABSORPTION
- AURORA

255°
160°
76,000 MILES OGO B ORBIT
93,000 MILES OGO I ORBIT

NOTE: NOT TO SCALE

Geophysical research has been greatly enriched by satellite technology. An orbiting geophysical observatory, or "OGO" (1), can carry instruments for the many types of investigations indicated in the diagram (2).

Observational astronomy, long restricted by Earth's atmosphere despite the use of great terrestrial telescopes, enters a new era with the development of the orbiting astronomical observatory (3, 4, 5). The "OAO," with telescope and other equipment, will make possible clearer views of the planets, more reliable data on the chemical composition of the stars, more accurate mapping of interstellar dust clouds, and other basic astronomical advances. *(NASA)*

3

AGENA IGNITION
SPACECRAFT SEPARATION
SPACECRAFT ORBITAL MODE
AGENA D SEPARATION & SHROUD EJECTION
AGENA 2nd IGNITION
AGENA D 1st BURN CUTOFF
COAST PERIOD
SUSTAINER CUTOFF
AGENA D 2nd CUTOFF
BOOSTER STAGING

4

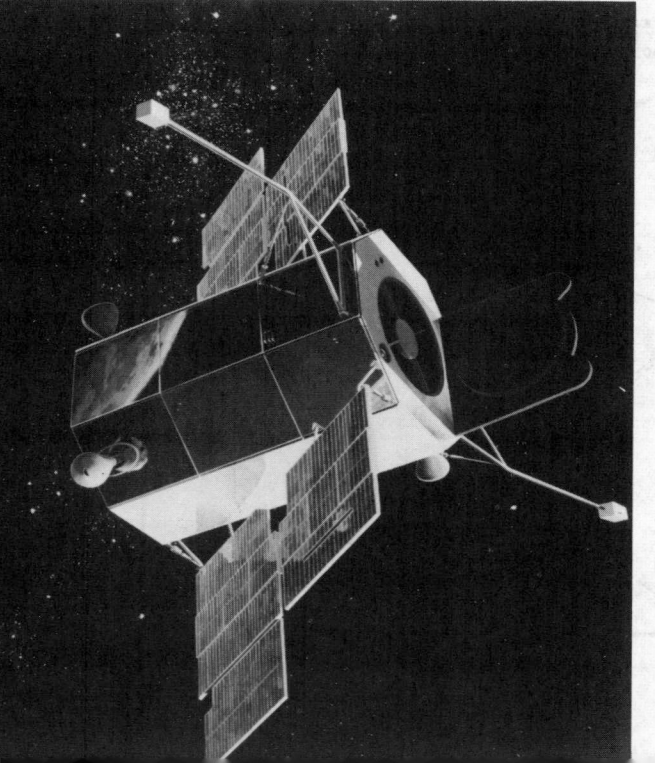

5

FIXED SKIN PANELS
AFT COVER
EQUIPMENT SHELVES (EACH BAY)
AFT SKIN
AFT BULKHEAD
PRIMARY TRUSSES
STAR TRACKER ACCESS HOLE
FORWARD SKIN
BORESIGHTED STAR TRACKER
HINGED DOORS (4)
ATTITUDE TV CAMERA
STAR TRACKERS (6)
SUN SHADE
CENTRAL SHELL
FORWARD BULKHEAD
SOLAR CELL ARRAYS (4) (2 ARRAYS-3 PADDLES EACH)
BALANCE WEIGHT BOOM (2)

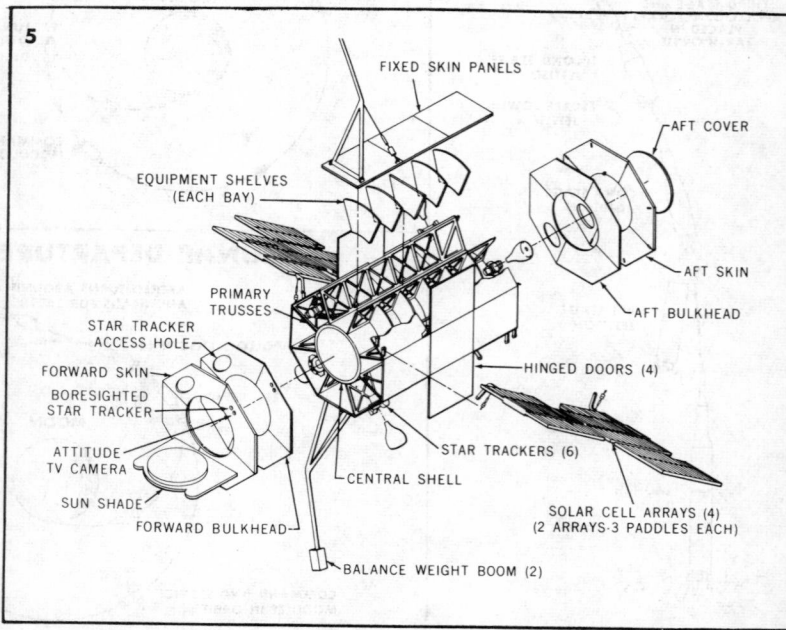

S

SABATIER, PAUL, 1854–1941, French chemist; b. Carcassonne. In 1897 he and J. B. Senderens (1856–1936) discovered that HYDROGENATION, the combining of hydrogen with certain organic compounds, could be facilitated by the presence of finely divided metals. Sabatier shared the 1912 Nobel prize with V. Grignard. He was a fellow of the Royal Society and an associate of the U. S. National Academy of Sciences.—*D. H. D. R.*

SACCHERI, GIOVANNI GIROLAMO, 1667–1733, Italian mathematician and Jesuit; b. San Remo. He is famous for his attempt to prove the 5th postulate of Euclid and thereby strengthen the foundations of geometry. In his book *Euclides ab omnia naevo vindicatus* (1733), he undertook a line of reasoning which might have led to the discovery of non-Euclidean geometry if he had pursued it further. This was one of the most important studies of the 5th postulate between the time of Euclid and the discovery of non-Euclidean geometry in the early 19th cent.—*H. C.*

SACHS, JULIUS VON, 1832–97, German botanist; b. Breslau. One of the early converts to Darwinism, he has been called the founder of experimental plant physiology; he investigated particularly the influence of light, heat, and gravitation on plants. He wrote textbooks on botany, and his *Geschichte der Botanik* (1875) was translated into French and English. He was a fellow of the Royal Society and an associate of the U. S. National Academy of Sciences.—*D. H. D. R.*

SACROBOSCO, JOHANNES DE (John of Halifax, or **John Holywood),** *c.* 1200–56, English mathematician and astronomer; b. Halifax, Yorkshire. He is best known for his book on astronomy *De sphaera* (English trans. by L. Thorndike, 1949). His *Algorismus* helped popularize the art of calculating with nine figures and a zero. An outstanding scholar of the Middle Ages, he was one of the first to make use of the astronomical writings of the Arabians.—*R. N. M.*

SAHA, MEGHNAD, 1893–1956, Indian physicist; b. in Bengal. From his work on thermal ionization he derived the equation named after him, which connects rates of ionization with a partition function for ionization states, temperature, and electron pressure. Saha founded and directed the Institute of Nuclear Physics at Calcutta. He was a fellow of the Royal Society.—*E. F.*

ST. ELMO'S FIRE: the bluish electrical glow sometimes seen at the tips of masts and spars of sailing ships before and during an electrical storm. Clouds of the storm carry a heavy charge of static electricity which attracts unlike charges on the ground. The static electricity on the ground, attracted by the cloud charge, discharges through pointed objects. When this point-discharge is visible, it is called St. Elmo's Fire. The phenomenon is not exhibited by steel ships, because these are grounded; but it can sometimes be seen on the wing tips and propellers of an airplane flying in or near a thunderstorm. The phenomenon is named after the patron saint of Mediterranean sailors. (See ATMOSPHERIC ELECTRICITY.)—*P. L.*

SAINTE-CLAIRE, DEVILLE: see DEVILLE, HENRI ÉTIENNE SAINTE-CLAIRE.

SAINT-VENANT, ADHÉMAR JEAN CLAUDE BARRÉ DE, 1797–1886, French engineer; b. Portoiseau. He was the first to provide a satisfactory theory of the bending of beams, developed in his celebrated paper "Mémoire sur la torsion des prismes" (1856). He was elected a member of the Academy of Sciences (1868).—*D. H. D. R.*

SALIVARY GLAND: one of the glands that empty their secretion, called saliva, into the mouth or buccal cavity. The primary function of saliva in most animals is to lubricate the food as it begins its passage through the alimentary canal, but other functions are known. Some snails utilize an acid saliva in dissolving the shells of prey or in boring into rocks for protection. Many kinds of animals (*e.g.* octopi, poisonous snakes, shrews) secrete poisonous materials in the saliva, which is injected into the prey to kill or paralyze it. Blood-

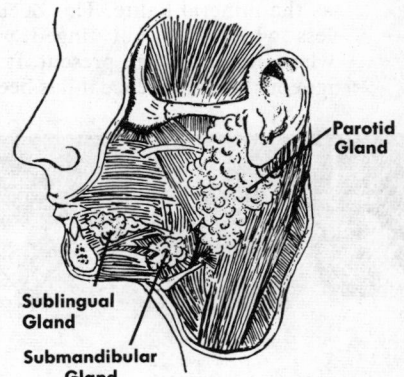

Salivary glands of human being: Secretion of saliva by these three paired glands is under control of the autonomic, or involuntary, nervous system. (*From Best*)

Parotid Gland
Sublingual Gland
Submandibular Gland

sucking animals (*e.g.* mosquitoes, leeches, lampreys) secrete anticoagulants in their saliva. Many animals secrete digestive enzymes in the saliva. Man, the pig, and a few other vertebrates secrete a salivary amylase, which catalyzes the hydrolysis of starch in the stomach, until its action is stopped by hydrochloric acid from stomach glands.—*B. T. S.*

SALT: a type of chemical compound in which a positively ionizing radical (or cation) other than hydrogen is combined with a negatively ionizing radical (or anion) other than hydroxyl. A salt is the product of the reaction between an ACID and a BASE. In the solid state most salts possess an ionic crystal lattice. Salts vary widely in solubility, ranging from the virtually insoluble mineral silicates and sulfides to hygroscopic materials such as calcium chloride. The solubility of a salt is a characteristic of its ion pair, *i.e.* of the total salt, rather than of either the anion or the cation alone; thus a given cation can form soluble or insoluble salts, depending on the anion with which it is combined, and vice versa. When dissolved in water or other suitable polar liquids, the majority of soluble salts dissociate into their constituent ions and exhibit the characteristic properties of these ions. Cupric salts, for example, have the blue color of the cupric cation, and salts of chromic acid the strong yellow color of chromate anion. The generic reaction for salt formation is called NEUTRALIZATION, and can be represented by the equation

$$H^+A^- + B^+OH^- \rightleftharpoons B^+A^- + HOH$$

$$\text{acid} \qquad \text{base} \qquad \text{salt} \qquad \text{water}$$

which shows a monobasic acid (one that can produce only a single hydrogen ion when it dissociates in solution) reacting with a monoacidic base (one that can produce only a single hydroxyl ion). The product is a neutral salt, one that contains no ionizable hydrogen or hydroxyl. When a di- or poly-basic acid reacts with a base, salts can be formed that retain one or more of the acidic hydrogens. For example, the tribasic phosphoric acid can react with sodium hydroxide to form the acid salts NaH_2PO_4 and Na_2HPO_4, as well as the neutral salt Na_3PO_4. Similarly, polyacidic bases, *e.g.* aluminum hydroxide, $Al(OH)_3$, can form basic salts such as $Al(OH)_2Cl$.

The neutralization reaction, as the equation indicates, is reversible; *i.e.* under suitable conditions certain salts can react with water to form an acid and a base. This HYDROLYSIS reaction occurs to a significant extent only when the precursors of the salt, and therefore its hydrolysis products, include a weak acid and/or a weak base. An example of a readily hydrolyzed salt is ammonium acetate, whose precursors are the weakly basic ammonium hydroxide and the weakly acidic acetic acid. See also SALT, COMMON.—*A. M. S.*

SALT, COMMON: sodium chloride (NaCl), naturally occurring as the mineral halite. This occurs in cubic crystals, is colorless when pure but tinged with yellow, brown, or blue when impurities are present. It occurs in small quantities in igneous rocks, whence it has been carried to the oceans, there

Brine wells—major source of common salt: Underground rock salt (containing up to 95% NaCl) is mined by forcing water down into it through pipes, pumping the water (now a saturated salt solution) back to the surface by compressed air, and evaporating it. Note well derrick in right background. (*Dow Chemical Co.*)

to concentrate as the water has evaporated (see EVAPORITE). It provides the needed sodium and chlorine for all animal life. Beds of salt in rock form accumulated in arid regions by evaporation of brines, either in interior drainage basins (PLAYAS) or in shallow arms of the sea that were periodically isolated from the main body of water. Major evaporite deposits may contain salt beds of varied purity hundreds of feet in thickness. Salt domes, which rise from deeply buried beds,

may be up to a mile in diameter and more than 4 or 5 mi deep. Much salt is produced in arid countries through solar evaporation of sea water that is entrapped by damming off flooded areas during high tides just before the dry season. Salt is recovered from bedded deposits or domes by ordinary mining or by solution mining—*i.e.* pumping fresh water down "wells" and recovering the resulting brine. Contaminated particles are removed from crushed rock salt by taking advantage of the "transparency" of clean salt to thermal radiation. Impure particles absorb the rays, become warm, and adhere to the surface of a thermoplastic-coated moving belt. Clean salt particles, which remain cool, do not adhere and are thrown free at the end of the belt-line.

Rock salt, which is the source of chlorine and caustic soda, forms the basis for much of the heavy-chemical industry. Most of the salt produced is used for production of sodium hydroxide, sodium carbonate, and other chemicals. There are direct uses in cookery, food preservation, and snow-melting. See also MINERAL (table).—*L. M. and D. P. B.*

SAMARIUM: a lanthanide (rare-earth metal) element (Sm); at. no. 62; at. wt 150.35; sp gr 7.8; mp 1350°C; valence 2 or 3. The element was discovered with the spectroscope by Lecoq de Boisbaudran (1879) on analysis of the Scandinavian mineral samarskite. In further analysis, Boisbaudran first prepared dydimia, which had formerly been accepted as the oxide of a new element "dydimium" (C. G. Mosander, 1840); but from this Boisbaudran extracted "samaria." (Samarium-free dydimia was later shown to be a mixture of yet two more elements, praseodymium and neodymium.) As with other lanthanides, separation of samarium's compounds from those of its neighbors in the periodic table, as well as preparation of the pure element, calls for long and intricate laboratory techniques. Eugène Demarçay, 1901, was the first to obtain relatively pure compounds; pure and nearly pure samarium and samarium compounds have been obtained by fractional-crystallization and ion-exchange methods. Samarium metal has also been prepared by electrolysis of its fused salts, though little use is made of the element or its compounds. (See LANTHANIDES; RARE EARTHS.)—*E. H. H.*

SAND: unconsolidated, detrital material within the size range of $\frac{1}{16}$ to 2 mm. Although the term "sand" is applied to loose materials of many kinds—including, for example, beach sands derived from basalt and coral—the principal mineral constituents of sand in the usual sense are quartz and feldspar; minor constituents include a wide variety of minerals. Of economic importance are beach sands rich in such minerals as monazite, zircon, or magnetite. Sand composed almost exclusively of silica (SiO_2) is used for the manufacture of glass. Upon consolidation (lithification), sand becomes the sedimentary rock SANDSTONE.—*C. C.*

SAND BAR: a deposit of sand found either in the bed of a stream or near the shore in the shallow water of a lake or ocean. Sand bars in a stream bed are deposited at times of slack water, and shifted at times of flood. In coastal waters they are built up by wave and current action. A bar built out from the mainland as a small peninsula is a sand spit, and when it joins an island to the mainland it is a tombolo. Offshore (barrier) bars are characteristic features along a land area bordered by a coastal plain where the water is relatively shallow, *e.g.* the S Atlantic and Gulf coasts of the U. S. A. In both river and ocean environments the size and shape of bars are variable as sand is either added or removed in response to changes in the quantity or velocity of the moving water. —*J. Sh.*

SANDER, BRUNO, 1884–   ; Austrian geologist and petrologist; b. Innsbruck. His important work *Gefügekunde der Gesteine* (1930) showed the prevalence of preferred orientation (systematic arrangement) of minerals in rocks.—*D. H. D. R.*

SANDSTONE: a SEDIMENTARY ROCK composed of detrital sand grains held together by a mineral cement which partially or completely fills the interstitial voids. In most sandstones the detrital grains are predominantly QUARTZ and minerals of the FELDSPAR group (albite, microcline, orthoclase). Other sandstones may contain large amounts of detrital rock fragments explosively ejected from a volcano. An average sandstone contains about 65% detrital quartz and feldspar and 35% mineral cement, which may be clay, mica, silt, calcite, or hematite. Size of the detrital grains varies from about 0.05 mm in diameter in a fine-grained sandstone to about 2.0 mm in a coarse-grained variety. Individual detrital grains may range from the extremely angular to the extremely rounded, depending upon conditions to which they were subjected after being detached from the parent rock—*e.g.* the velocity and distance of their transportation by streams or winds.

CLASSIFICATION OF SANDSTONES
(by Mineral Composition)

Per Cent of Detrital Grains:	Orthoquartzite	Graywacke	Arkose	Tuffaceous Sandstone
Quartz	95	47	47	40
Feldspar		16	43	20
Rock fragments		7		
Volcanic debris				30
Per Cent of Mineral Cement:				
Calcite				
Mica and clay	5	25	10	10
Hematite				
	100%	100%	100%	100%

The abundance of the different types of sandstone in Earth's crust is estimated to be as follows: *orthoquartzite,* 30%; *arkose,* 25%; *graywackes* and *tuffaceous sandstones,* 45%. Orthoquartzites consist almost entirely of quartz and are generally cemented by interlocking overgrowths on and in crystallographic continuity with the original grains. Arkoses contain appreciable amounts of detrital feldspar and mica. Graywackes are usually dark and "dirty," containing quantities of fine-grained rock fragments, dark minerals, and clays. Most sandstones originate from transportation and deposition by streams or the ocean of detrital material eroded from granitic rocks, gneiss, and other siliceous rocks. The particular type of sandstone formed can often be related to the geological and chemical environment of deposition. Some types of graywacke are formed by marine deposition in deep water, and an oxygen-poor or reducing environment. Arkoses are deposited by shallow, turbulent, fresh-water streams in an oxygen-rich or oxidizing environment. Orthoquartzites are formed along shore zones as the end product of long periods of weathering and abrasion, which eliminate or sort out all detrital minerals less durable than quartz. Many orthoquartzites have preserved such features as current ripple-marks and cross-bedding. See Color Plates 76–77.—*H. J.*

SANGER, FREDERICK, 1918–   , English biochemist; b. Rendcombe. In 1944 he began research on the breaking down of the protein insulin into identifiable peptides, and he determined the sequence of amino acids in these peptides and then in the whole molecule. He received the 1958 Nobel prize in chemistry for developing a method for studying the amino-acid sequence of proteins and, especially, the insulin molecule. He is a fellow of the Royal Society.—*D. H. D. R.*

SANITARY ENGINEERING: as commonly described, the engineering branch of public health. It is concerned with the promotion of human health and well-being through the control of man's environment, especially control of water quality. From the earliest civilizations, man has been aware of the importance of a plentiful supply of potable water, and of the fact that water could contribute to well-being. The Egyptians, Greeks, and Romans all made attempts to treat their water supplies, and some of their methods of sediment removal and chemical treatment (*e.g.* with copper salts) are not unlike modern ways. The Roman aqueducts are an impressive monument to Rome's concern with water supply. Engineering efforts to prevent pollution of water by human excrement, garbage, and other contaminants date at least as far back as the palace of Minos at Knossos in Crete, where, about 1500 B. C., a drainage system to dispose of waste water was built. Ancient Greek cities show evidence of drainage systems, complete with latrines flushed by water; and Rome beginning in the 6th cent. B. C. developed an extensive network of drains. After the fall of Rome little progress was made in sanitary engineering; in fact, the period from the dawn of the Christian era to the "great sanitary awakening" in Britain in the 19th cent. can be characterized as a period of regression in most phases of public sanitation. In the medieval city, it was common to throw household refuse and human excrement out the window into the street (where it lay for lack of a collection system), and often the closest approach to a sewage system was a brook that had been turned into an open sewer. However, the growth of cities that accompanied the Industrial Revolution made urgent demands on engineers to provide for adequate and safe supplies of water and for the removal of the spent water, as well as for the removal of waste matters from household and industry by sewage systems. Through the collaboration of physicians, chemists, and biologists with civil engineers, toward the end of the 19th cent., particularly in the U. S. A., the discipline of sanitary engineering evolved. Of primary concern was the prevention of water-borne epidemics. At one time cholera and typhoid fever exacted a heavy toll of disease and death; now outbreaks of cholera are

London sewer, 1854: Contemporary sketch shows workmen repairing the Fleet sewer. Once an open, polluted river, the Fleet was covered over at the start of the "great sanitary awakening" in 19th-cent. England. (*Bettmann Archive*)

REPAIR OF THE FLEET SEWER.

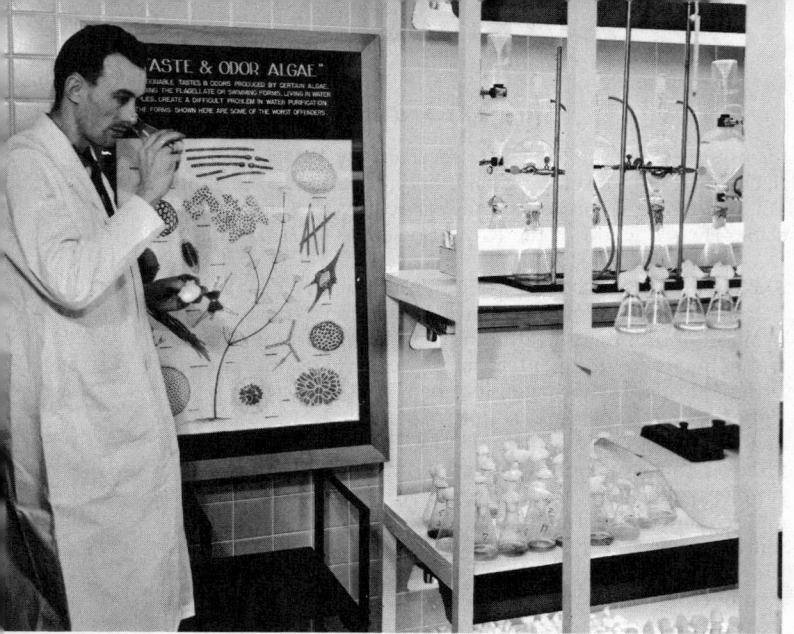

Control of algae in drinking water is one aspect of modern sanitary engineering. In this laboratory at Robert A. Taft Sanitary Engineering Center, Cincinnati, O., single species of algae are isolated and cultivated to determine their effect on taste and odor of water. More effective methods of combating specific strains of offensive algae in reservoirs and surface waters can thus be developed. (*U. S. Public Health Service*)

largely confined to SE Asia, and typhoid fever no longer menaces the population of the advanced countries. Outbreaks of enteric infections, including dysentery and hepatitis, still occur from time to time when water supplies are not well designed or well managed.

Modern WATER SUPPLY installations collect water from ground or surface sources; if for some reason this water is not acceptable, it must also be conducted to treatment plants. Chlorination is the most effective single hygienic measure so far devised; in relatively small concentrations it destroys large numbers of possibly pathogenic bacteria, protozoa, and viruses. Other purification operations comprise chemical coagulation and sedimentation; these are often followed by filtration through sand or other granular materials. Suspended substances and natural color, as well as iron and manganese that have been precipitated by oxidation (*e.g.* through aeration), are removed by filtration. Odors and tastes are adsorbed onto activated carbon. Substances that make water "hard," and some radioactive isotopes, are removed by ION EXCHANGE. Ion exchange and electro-osmosis through selectively permeable membranes will desalt water, but for the demineralization of sea water, evaporation is still the most economical process. (See DEMINERALIZATION OF SALINE WATER.) "Hard" waters may be softened by lime and soda ash, and lime may be added to reduce the corrosiveness of the water to metal piping and other equipment. The fluoride content of water may be boosted to the physiological concentrations at which the child population is protected against dental caries. Blooms of algae in lakes and reservoirs are destroyed or inhibited by copper salts. The clean or purified water is carried to the community most often in pipelines of steel, concrete, or cast iron, less often through tunnels. A distribution reservoir is generally placed near the community served, and a network of pipes within the municipality delivers the water to each consumer.

The growing urbanization and industrialization of the world have intensified the competition for water and the danger of impairing water resources. Competitive uses that interfere with the availability and management of drinking water are,

in particular, industrial water use, irrigation, and the removal of waste materials via natural drainage channels. New in their impact on water-quality management are the organic synthetics that find their way into water, *e.g.* detergents, fertilizers, pesticides, or herbicides. If natural bodies of water are to be kept acceptably clean, municipal sewage and industrial wastes must be reduced in concentration either by removal or transformation. For transformation, biological processes are employed in which hosts of microorganisms, chiefly bacteria, break down the complex organic substances that render all sewage and many industrial wastes offensive. If removal of contaminating substances is indicated, waste waters are conveyed through systems of underground pipes (sewers) of tile or concrete to a treatment plant, whence they pass into a natural drainage channel. Seacoast cities normally discharge their waste waters into the sea, sometimes through long, deeply submerged outfalls, usually after some treatment. Protection of bathing beaches and useful aquatic life in both salt and fresh water is essential. The sanitary control of swimming pools is a natural extension of the responsibility of sanitary engineering for water control.

Although the collection and disposal of garbage, rubbish, and ashes is a sanitary engineering activity, the organization of a motorized collection and transportation system often requires special competence outside the profession. This is true also of incineration procedures, as well as the composting of mixed refuse and its disposal as sanitary land fill. ATMOSPHERIC POLLUTION, industrial hygiene, food sanitation, and control of insect vectors of disease may also be concerns of the sanitary engineer. Most recently, the profession has been forced to consider the problems involved in disposal of radioactive wastes. See also WATER POLLUTION; WATER TREATMENT. —*G. M. F.*

SAP: any of the watery solutions found in cells of plants. A living plant cell contains *cell sap* in one or more vacuoles, each bounded by a membrane that regulates the inward and outward movement of materials essential to the cell's normal activities. In VASCULAR PLANTS, specialized tissues known as xylem and phloem conduct the sap from one part of the plant to another. *Raw sap,* a dilute solution containing some mineral salts but few organic compounds, is carried by the xylem tubes from the roots to the leaves, where some of the water is used in PHOTOSYNTHESIS and much is lost by TRANSPIRATION. *Elaborated sap,* which contains sugars, amino acids, and hormones, is carried in the phloem to all parts of the plant. See TRANSLOCATION IN PLANTS.—*L. and M. M.*

SAPROPHYTE: a plant that obtains its energy and nutrient materials by digesting and absorbing chemical compounds from dead plants. Saprophytes are important agents of decay. Most of them are true fungus plants (*e.g.* mushrooms) or harmless bacteria. The parts we see are chiefly reproductive structures, from which microscopic SPORES are released into the air as dust particles. When these spores fall where moisture and organic compounds of dead plants are available, they germinate, grow, and increase the rate of decay.—*L. and M. M.*

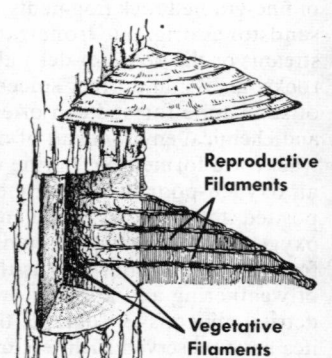

Reproductive Filaments

Vegetative Filaments

Bracket fungus is common saprophyte. Part of lower fungus and tree trunk is cut away to show vegetative filaments; these secrete enzymes that digest wood. (*From Young*)

SARCOSINE: a sweetish, crystalline chemical compound, found in animal tissue, mostly muscle. Chemically, it is *N*-methyl-glycine. It is formed by enzymatic methylation of glycine, one of the non-essential amino acids, or by decomposition of creatine during the constriction of muscle tissue. Its physiological significance is unknown at present.—*R. W. F.*

SAROS: a period of 223 lunations after which solar and lunar ECLIPSES recur with similar characteristics. In the modern calendar, this period corresponds to 18 yr, 11 and one-third days (10 and one-third days if there are 5 leap years in the interval); *e.g.* the solar eclipse of July 10, 1972, marks the return of the eclipse of June 30, 1954; both are total and have almost the same duration. Although of Babylonian origin, the name Saros was used for the first time in connection with eclipses by Sir Edmund Halley, 1691.—*S. D. G.*

SARS, MICHAEL, 1805–1869, Norwegian zoologist and geologist; b. Bergen. One of the pioneers of marine biology in Scandinavia, Sars discovered metamorphosis in the marine mollusks. He published observations of the deep-sea crinoids and established their similarity to fossil forms.—*D. H. D. R.*

SARTON, GEORGE, 1884–1956, Belgian-U. S. historian of science, b. Ghent, Belgium. The founder of the history of science in the U. S. A., he established *Isis* (1913), now the journal of the History of Science Society, and introduced the history of science as an academic discipline at Harvard Univ. It has spread to nearly 100 other U. S. colleges and universities. He wrote over 300 books and papers, and published a monumental *Introduction to the History of Science* (3 vols., 1948) of over 3,000 pages, covering the period up to A. D. 1400. Sarton emphasized the history of science as a coherent discipline distinct from the histories of the individual sciences. His work was primarily, although not exclusively, that of a compiler. His *A Guide to the History of Science* (1952) contains a general bibliography.—*D. H. D. R.*

SATELLITE, ARTIFICIAL: a man-made object placed in orbit around Earth or any other member of the solar system. The theoretical principle of the launching of a satellite was expressed by Sir Isaac Newton (1687) in his explanation of the Moon's orbital motion. He pointed out that, if a projectile is thrown in a direction parallel to Earth's surface, the distance it covers before falling back to the ground increases with the force of the throw; as the throw is made progressively stronger, it becomes eventually sufficient to keep the projectile permanently aloft. In this last instance the projectile would be in orbit around Earth: it would be an artificial satellite. An even stronger throw would cause it to escape forever from Earth's gravitational attraction. Such an escape occurs when an object leaves our planet's surface with a speed of at least 6.93 mi/sec or about 25,000 mi/hr (hence called *velocity of escape*).

Launching: The principle of launching satellites by means of rockets was first formulated by Konstantin Tsiolkovsky (1903), but the required technological means were not available until the mid-1950s. To be placed in orbit, a satellite must first be lifted against Earth's gravity to the required altitude; then it must be imparted the precise velocity necessary to achieve orbital motion (about 18,000 mi/hr for a satellite orbiting within a few hundred miles from Earth). This double operation cannot be performed by a single initial impulse, *e.g.* by shooting from a powerful cannon, because at such high speeds the friction from the dense lower atmosphere would cause the satellite to overheat and be consumed or severely damaged before reaching orbit altitude. Therefore, the launching apparatus must consist of rockets, which are capable of imparting gradually increasing speeds and thus provide a less

Communications satellite: In Aug. 1960, satellite Echo was put into orbit 1,000 mi from Earth. A 100-ft aluminum-coated plastic balloon when fully inflated (*above*), the satellite was carried folded within a 26-in. magnesium sphere (*left*) which was launched by a three-stage rocket. (*NASA*) Once in orbit, the magnesium sphere separated from the burnt-out third-stage rocket and split apart, allowing the balloon to inflate. Remarkable in performance, Echo clearly transmitted radiotelephone and photograph signals by reflecting them to reception stations otherwise beyond reach. A photograph of its path (*below*) taken one year after it was launched shows tracking antenna in foreground. Success of this and subsequent communications satellites led to launching of Telstar, which allowed television transmission between Europe and North America. (*Bell Telephone Lab.*)

Artificial planet: A vehicle of the Pioneer Tiros I type (*above*) was launched Mar. 11, 1960, and attained a solar orbit with a period of 331.64 days; expected lifetime is greater than 100,000 yr. Four "paddlewheels" contain a total of 4,800 solar cells to recharge batteries powering radio transmitters. Instrumentation includes a high-energy radiation counter, an ionization chamber, a search-coil magnetometer, and a micrometeorite-impact counter. Total data-transmission time was 138.9 hr, the last signals having been received when the vehicle was over 22,000,000 mi from Earth. (*U. S. Air Force Photo*)

hazardous flight through the lower atmosphere. Launching rockets consist of several individual units, or *stages,* ignited automatically in succession. Each stage is jettisoned after burn-out, thereby reducing the load which must be propelled further and hence the amount of fuel necessary to continue the task. As a rule, the first two stages are used to attain proper altitude. The remaining ones give the satellite itself (or *payload*) the correct orientation and the final thrust that will impart the proper orbital velocity.

Orbits: Satellite orbits obey the laws of Newtonian dynamics. In particular, the plane of the orbit necessarily contains the center of Earth, with the result that the inclination of the orbit to the equator is at least equal to the latitude of the launching site. The orbit is essentially an ellipse, more or less elongated depending on launching conditions. Its orientation in space is practically constant but, owing to Earth's rotation, there is a continuous westward shift of the satellite's apparent orbit as viewed from terrestrial sites. If the final thrust of the launching rocket takes place in a direction parallel to the planet's surface, the point where the satellite is ejected becomes the orbit's perigee—the point nearest Earth. If this final thrust occurs at any other angle, the perigee is closer to Earth than the launching point, a circumstance that is preferably avoided because the satellite's path would then penetrate denser regions of the atmosphere. In extreme cases the satellite would actually strike Earth.

The lifetime of the satellite, *i.e.* the time span between launching and total destruction, depends principally on its distance at perigee. If the latter is less than 110 mi, the lifetime never exceeds two weeks. Collisions with air molecules gradually reduce the size of the orbit, speed up the satellite, and cause it to spiral back into the regions of denser atmosphere, where overheating eventually destroys it. Orbital decay produced in this manner is less important at greater heights and falls off rapidly as perigee distance increases.

Thus it is not unusual for a satellite to have an estimated lifetime of several hundred years if its perigee distance is in excess of about 400 mi.

Observations: Optical observations of satellites are limited by their small size and by the fact that during most of the night they are eclipsed by Earth's shadow. They can be seen only during the brief periods after sunset and before sunrise while they are still bathed in sunlight, whereas night has already begun at the observer's site. At such times they may be observed telescopically and photographed with wide-angle cameras operated at fast shutter speeds. For continuous TRACKING, there are several radio methods based on the observation of a radio beacon emitted by the satellite. If the latter is silent from malfunction or exhaustion of its power supply, tracking may still be performed by the radar-echo method.

Observations obtained by the instruments carried aloft may be telemetered back to Earth by modulations of the radio beacon. When recovery of the contents of a satellite capsule is essential to the completion of the experiment, the capsule is ejected by a mechanism triggered from the ground and is deflected into a trajectory that will intersect Earth's surface (see RE-ENTRY). Special techniques have been developed to effect recovery in mid-air, on land, or at sea.

Space Probes: The principle of artificial satellites is applied also to the design of *space probes,* or vehicles for the exploration of the Moon and nearby planets. Probes must be imparted a speed at least equal to the velocity of escape (25,000 mi/hr) to break away from Earth's gravitational attraction. For landing on the Moon, the probe's trajectory must intersect the lunar orbit near the position of the Moon's center at time of impact. Although the vehicle slows up considerably at great distances from perigee, its speed is still sufficient to wreck the payload on impact. Soft landings require the use of retro-rockets to provide the necessary braking action. Thus Surveyor I's speed when it struck the lunar surface was only about 10 ft/sec. If the trajectory passes clear of the Moon's surface, the vehicle may circumnavigate the Moon (*e.g.* Lunik III) if it passes close enough and at the proper speed to allow the Moon's gravitational pull to take over. If these conditions are not fulfilled, the vehicle pursues its path beyond the Moon and eventually becomes a satellite of the Sun, *i.e.* an artificial planet (*e.g.* Lunik I, Pioneers IV and V).

Planetary probes are in fact artificial planets launched into elongated orbits designed to bring the vehicle alternately close to Earth and to another planet. Thus Venus probes must be placed in orbits such that their perihelion distance— their nearest distance from the Sun—is about 75 million mi (nearly equal to Venus' mean distance from the Sun) and their aphelion distance—their farthest distance from the Sun —is about 92 million mi (nearly equal to Earth's mean distance from the Sun). Initially, such a probe must be launched into a *transfer orbit* which is tangent both to Earth's orbit and to the final orbit that must be achieved. It is considered that many of the problems concerned with initial thrust, amount of fuel to be carried, and size of the probe could be simplified by launching from a space platform in orbit around Earth.

Information Gained: Experiments performed by means of artificial satellites have yielded a wide range of information— for example, precise data as to the shape and size of Earth, important weather data (see METEOROLOGICAL SATELLITE), and information on the density of micrometeorites, conditions on the lunar surface, and physical properties of Venus and Mars. About 70% of the far side of the Moon was photographed by Lunar III and Zond III; the Lunar Orbiters carried this work further in 1966. Among the most important results of the

SIGNIFICANT SATELLITE LAUNCHINGS

Name	Launching Date	Lifetime	Remarks
Sputnik I	Oct. 4, 1957	92 days	
Sputnik II	Nov. 3, 1957	162 days	Dog "Laika" on board.
Explorer I	Jan. 31, 1958	7–10 yr*	
Vanguard I	Mar. 17, 1958	200–1,000 yr*	
Explorer IV	Jul. 26, 1958	454 days	
Score	Dec. 18, 1958	34 days	
Lunik I	Jan. 2, 1959	Indefinite	"Mechta"; in orbit around Sun.
Pioneer IV	Mar. 3, 1959	Indefinite	Interplanetary probe; in orbit around Sun.
Explorer VI	Aug. 7, 1959	over 2 yr*	
Lunik II	Sept. 12, 1959	35 hr	
Lunik III	Oct. 4, 1959	199 days	
Tiros I	Apr. 1, 1960	50–100 yr*	
Echo I	Aug. 12, 1960	2–10 yr*	
Discoverer XIV	Aug. 18, 1960	29 days	Re-entry capsule recovered in mid-air.
Vostok I	Apr. 12, 1961	1 hr 48 min (1 orbit)	Manned satellite (Maj. Yuri A. Gagarin flight).
Friendship 7	Feb. 20, 1962	4 hr 56 min (3 orbits)	Manned satellite (Lieut. Col. John H. Glenn, Jr., flight).
Telstar	Jul. 10, 1962	Life expectancy 2 yr	First communications satellite; in orbit around Earth.
Mariner II	Aug. 26, 1962	Indefinite	Venus Probe
Ranger VII	Jul. 28, 1964	Impacted on Moon	4,300 pictures sent prior to impact
Mariner IV	Nov. 28, 1964	Indefinite	Mars probe Pictures of surface
Ranger VIII	Feb. 17, 1965	Impacted on moon	Photos before impact.
Voskhod 2	Mar. 18, 1965	26ʰ	First space walk (Lt. Col. A. Leonov)
Ranger IX	Mar. 21, 1965	Impacted on Moon	5,814 pictures before impact
Zond III	Jul. 18, 1965	Indefinite	25 pictures of far side of Moon
Lunar IX	Jan. 31, 1966	Landed on lunar surface	Sent back pictures from surface
Gemini VIII	Mar. 16, 1966	10ʰ.7 6½ orbits	Rendezvous and first docking (N. Armstrong and D. Scott)
Surveyor I	May 30, 1966	Soft landing on Moon	Over 10,000 pictures of lunar surface. Survived lunar night
Lunar Orbiter I	Aug. 10, 1966	Indefinite	Closeup lunar photos; in orbit around Moon

* Estimated.

satellite experiments were the discovery and study of VAN ALLEN RADIATION and the subsequent realization that the belts form part of an extensive *magnetosphere*. Satellites also have made possible measures of Earth's magnetic field and of interplanetary magnetic fields. Simultaneous observations of satellites from different geographic locations have enabled the determination of distances between these locations with a higher degree of accuracy than ever before. Commercial applications have included the launching of television satellites such as Telstar and Early Bird. Manned satellites have provided data on WEIGHTLESSNESS and other problems that man encounters in space travel.—*S. D. G.*

SATELLITE, NATURAL: a celestial body traveling in an orbit around one of the planets of the solar system. The MOON is Earth's natural satellite; by analogy, satellites of other planets are often called "moons" in popular scientific literature. All satellites other than the Moon are too small to be seen with the naked eye and have been discovered telescopically, by visual or photographic means. The Moon itself is unique among satellites in that it has the largest size in comparison with the planet around which it revolves; its diameter (2,160 mi) is roughly one quarter of Earth's diameter (7,927 mi).

The two satellites of MARS, Phobos (Fear) and Deimos (Panic), are believed to be no more than 10 mi across. Because of their small size, they are observable only in large telescopes. They are mere pinpoints of light and nothing is known of their physical characteristics. It has even been suggested that they might be artificial satellites launched by a hypothetical Martian civilization, but there is no observational evidence to substantiate this view. A unique feature of Phobos is that its period of revolution (7h 39m) is shorter than the Martian day (24h 37m); hence, as seen from Mars, it rises in the west and sets in the east.

JUPITER has the greatest number of satellites (12). The four largest (Io, Europa, Ganymede, and Callisto) are just at the

Changing configurations of satellites: Of Jupiter's 12 satellites, the four largest (*below*) are visible with field glasses (when not occulted by the planet); they were reported by Galileo in 1610. The periods of Io (I), Europa (II), Ganymede (III), and Callisto (IV) are approximately 1¾, 3½, 7, and 17 days, respectively; their orbits lie nearly in the same plane, so that the satellites seem to be moving back and forth along an almost straight line. The change in configuration shown below represents a time lapse of 2 hr 43 min. Motions of these satellites were used by Olaus Römer, 1675, in his determination of the velocity of light. (*Yerkes Obs.*)

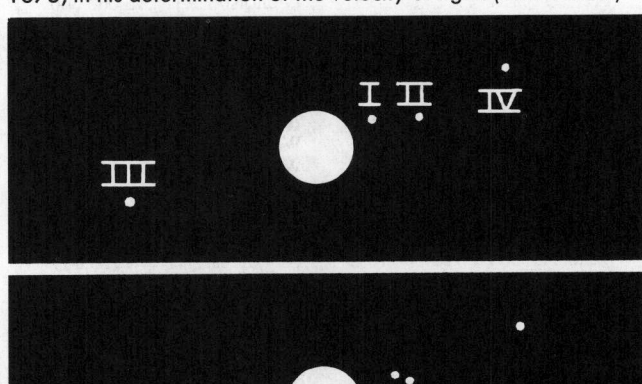

Satellite and shadow: Ganymede, one of Jupiter's largest satellites (it is larger than Mercury), is here seen casting its shadow—and thus producing a solar eclipse—on the planet. (*Mt Wilson*)

satellites are less than 100 mi across; hence they are difficult to observe in view of Jupiter's great distance from Earth. They were not given names but are designated by Roman numerals in chronological order of discovery. Satellites VIII, IX, XI, and XII, the most distant from Jupiter, have a retrograde motion, *i.e.* travel along their orbits in a direction opposite to that of the planets; it is possible that originally they were asteroids captured by Jupiter's attraction.

Of the ten satellites of SATURN (Janus, Mimas, Enceladus, Tethys, Dione, Rhea, Titan, Hyperion, Iapetus, Phoebe), Titan is the largest, 2,990 mi in diameter, the only satellite in the solar system on which an atmosphere has been detected; its composition, of methane and ammonia, is similar to that of Saturn's own atmosphere. The other nine satellites are so small that current values of their sizes and masses are highly uncertain.

Similar uncertainties affect our present knowledge of the satellites of URANUS and NEPTUNE. The orbits of Uranus' five satellites (Miranda, Ariel, Umbriel, Titania, and Oberon) lie almost exactly in the plane of the planet's equator. Thus, depending on the orientation of the planet as seen from Earth, these orbits appear periodically either as straight lines or as very broad ellipses. The larger of Neptune's satellites (Triton) is comparable to the Moon in size and has a retrograde motion. The other (Nereid) is very faint and small, with an estimated diameter of 200 mi.

Satellite observations yield data useful for accurate determination of the mass of the planet around which the satellites

limit of naked-eye visibility. They could be seen without a telescope, were it not for the proximity of Jupiter; all except Europa are more massive than the Moon. Io and Europa reflect light in a manner similar to that of snow and are probably covered by a layer of hoarfrost. The remaining eight

SATELLITES OF THE SOLAR SYSTEM

Satellite	Year of Discovery	Discoverer	Mean Distance from Planet (mi)	Sidereal Period of Satellite	Approximate Magnitude at Opposition	Diameter (mi)	Mass (Moon = 1)	Density (Water = 1)
(EARTH)								
Moon	—	—	238,857	27ᵈ 07ʰ 43ᵐ	− 12.7	2160	1.00	
(MARS)								
Phobos	1877	A. Hall	5,825	0ᵈ 07ʰ 39ᵐ	+ 12	5?		
Deimos	1877	A. Hall	14,580	1ᵈ 06ʰ 18ᵐ	+ 13	3?		
(JUPITER)								
V	1892	Barnard	112,000	0ᵈ 11ʰ 57ᵐ	+ 13.0	70?		
I Io	1610	Galileo	261,900	1ᵈ 18ʰ 28ᵐ	+ 5.5	2020	1.2	4.9
II Europa	1610	Galileo	416,600	3ᵈ 13ʰ 14ᵐ	+ 5.7	1790	0.7	4.1
III Ganymede	1610	Galileo	664,600	7ᵈ 03ʰ 43ᵐ	+ 5.1	3120	2.1	2.3
IV Callisto	1610	Galileo	1,169,000	16ᵈ 16ʰ 32ᵐ	+ 6.3	2770	1.2	1.9
VI	1904	Perrine	7,130,000	250ᵈ.6	+ 13.7	50?		
X	1938	Nicholson	7,200,000	254ᵈ	+ 19.4	5?		
VII	1905	Perrine	7,290,000	259ᵈ.7	+ 18.1	8?		
XII	1951	Nicholson	13,000,000	625ᵈ	+ 19.6	4?		
XI	1938	Nicholson	14,300,000	714ᵈ	+ 18.9	6?		
VIII	1908	Melotte	14,600,000	735ᵈ	+ 18.0	9?		
IX	1914	Nicholson	14,700,000	758ᵈ	+ 19.1	6?		
(SATURN)								
Janus	1966	A. Dollfuss	51,900	17ʰ58.5ᵐ	14	300?	?	?
Mimas	1789	W. Herschel	115,200	0ᵈ 22ʰ 37ᵐ	+ 12.1	400?	0.0005	
Enceladus	1789	W. Herschel	147,700	1ᵈ 08ʰ 53ᵐ	+ 11.6	500?	0.0010	
Tethys	1684	D. Cassini	182,900	1ᵈ 21ʰ 18ᵐ	+ 10.5	630	0.0088	1.2
Dione	1684	D. Cassini	234,300	2ᵈ 17ʰ 41ᵐ	+ 10.7	550?	0.014	2.8?
Rhea	1672	D. Cassini	327,100	4ᵈ 12ʰ 25ᵐ	+ 9.7	810	0.03	1.9?
Titan	1655	Huyghens	758,400	15ᵈ 22ʰ 41ᵐ	+ 8.2	2990	1.87	2.3
Hyperion	1848	W. Bond	918,700	21ᵈ 06ʰ 38ᵐ	+ 13.0	250?	0.002	
Iapetus	1671	D. Cassini	2,210,000	79ᵈ 07ʰ 55ᵐ	+10-12	?	0.02	
Phoebe	1898	W. Pickering	8,040,000	550ᵈ 09ʰ	+ 15.5	100?		
(URANUS)								
Miranda	1948	Kuiper	80,700	1ᵈ 09ʰ 56ᵐ	+ 17	200?		
Ariel	1851	Lassell	119,100	2ᵈ 12ʰ 29ᵐ	+ 14.8	450?		
Umbriel	1851	Lassell	165,900	4ᵈ 03ʰ 28ᵐ	+ 15.4	350?		
Titania	1787	W. Herschel	272,100	8ᵈ 16ʰ 56ᵐ	+ 13.9	700?		
Oberon	1787	W. Herschel	363,900	13ᵈ 11ʰ 07ᵐ	+ 14.3	600?		
(NEPTUNE)								
Triton	1846	Lassell	219,500	5ᵈ 21ʰ 03ᵐ	+ 13.8	2000?	1.8	
Nereid	1949	Kuiper	3,450,000	359ᵈ.88	+ 19	200?		

Adapted with permission from G. H. Herbig and C. E. Worley, "Some Basic Astronomical Data" (rev. 1960), in Leaflet No. 325, Astronomical Society of the Pacific, San Francisco, Calif.

Horn-shaped antenna of radio tracking system has receiving circuits in cab at small end of horn. Rotating about base, it can track fast-moving satellite anywhere in sky. (*Bell Telephone Lab.*)

revolve; this mass is obtained by study of PERTURBATIONS caused by the planet on the satellites' orbits. For that reason, the masses of Mercury, Venus, and Pluto, which have no satellites, are not known with the same degree of accuracy as the masses of the other planets. By the same method, the masses of satellites belonging to a single planet may be obtained from the perturbations they cause on each other's orbits.—*S. D. G.*

SATELLITE TRACKING: continuous, organized observation, by means of appropriate instruments, of artificial SATELLITES while in orbit. Tracking is done by a number of stations set up for this purpose in various locations around the world. The number and locations of stations for any particular project are determined according to the vehicle's motion, the rotation of Earth, and the need for an unrestricted line of sight. Raw data obtained by tracking systems are normally processed in special computing centers, two of the largest being the Smithsonian Observatory in Cambridge, Mass., and the Vanguard Computing Center in Washington, D. C. The three principal types of tracking systems are the radar or radio type, those using optics in the visible range, and infrared systems.

In *radio tracking,* so-called passive systems use an outside (ground-based) transmitter to reflect waves from the vehicle, which are then picked up by a receiver. In an active system, considered superior in range and accuracy, the satellite or other vehicle contains its own signal-sending equipment. Thus, a satellite sending signals may be tracked by the variation in angle of tracking antennas, which adjust to the direction of maximum signal strength. As a more accurate alternative to direct-angle measurements, a special interferometer

technique called Minitrack was developed for use with the U. S. Vanguard satellite. It combines signals received from the satellite at two antennas a known distance apart; such signals will either add or cancel, depending on the relative phase. In this application, there is an alternate adding and canceling in accordance with the motion of the vehicle, an advantage for accurate tracking. A similar technique, called Microlock, has been successfully used to track the U. S. Explorer satellite.

An *optical tracking system* uses as its basic component a telescope mounted on gimbals, which permit rotation about two axes. One version of optical tracker is the *cinetheodolite,* which produces a photographic record of the position of the target image, along with telescopic orientation readings and the time. By use of two such instruments on a measured baseline, the position of the moving vehicle is obtained by triangulation. Another variety of optical tracker is the ballistic camera, which photographs the vehicle against the back-

Optical tracking system: A telescope is the "eye" of an optical tracking system. Precise when not subject to weather interference, optical systems can preserve photographic record of satellite's path. (*Amer. Optical Co.*)

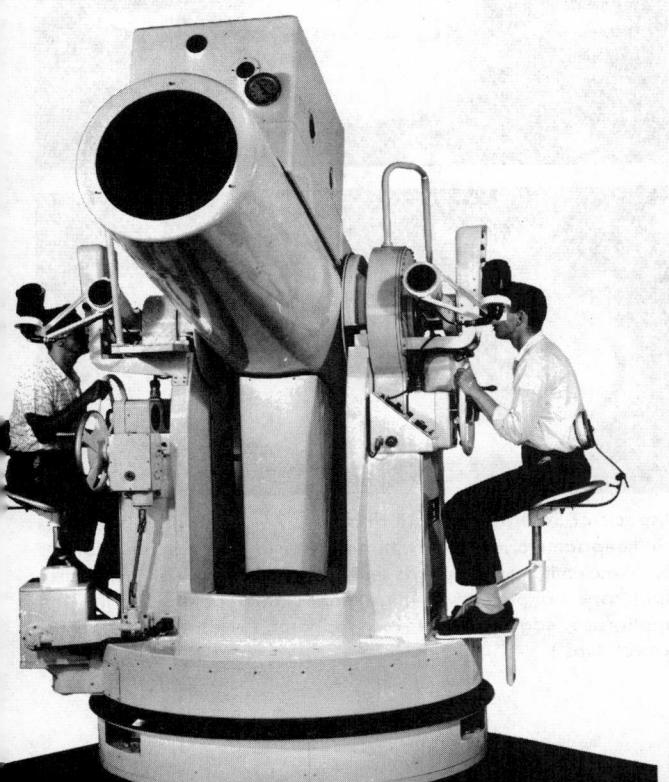

Quad-helix steerable array antenna is part of Mercury spacecraft radio tracking system. It finds and tracks spacecraft, receives 90 channels of telemetered information, and maintains two-way communications. (*Bendix Corp.*)

ground of stars, thus making possible highly precise position determinations. Optical tracking is very accurate but suffers from such interference as clouds and haze.

Infrared tracking can penetrate fog and haze, and also provides a better contrast against interfering background radiation. However, since infrared radiation is absorbed by the lower atmosphere, infrared equipment is most useful when carried in high-altitude vehicles.—*D. B.*

SATURATION: see SUPERSATURATED SOLUTION.

SATURN: the 6th principal planet in order from the Sun; it is one of the giant planets. The surrounding rings make Saturn a uniquely beautiful telescopic object. To the eye it is yellowish, of the 1st mag. or brighter, according to its distance and the changing aspect of the rings. Saturn is the most oblate planet: its average diameter is 71,500 mi but its polar diameter is almost 11% less than the equatorial. Its mass is 95 times Earth's, and is strongly concentrated toward the center. Its average density, 0.71 times that of water, makes Saturn the least dense planet. About 46% of the incident sunlight is reflected, and the surface temperature is near −240°F. Saturn revolves about the Sun in a period of 29.5 yr, at an average distance of 890 million mi. The eccentricity of the orbit is 0.056, and its inclination to the ecliptic, 2°29′. The equator is inclined 26°45′ to the plane of the orbit, giving seasons like Earth's (though solar heat is much reduced at Saturn's great distance), and causing changes in the aspect of the rings lying in the equatorial plane: the rings are on edge at 15-yr intervals (as in 1966) and well opened at intermediate times (as in 1958).

Saturn's visible surface is composed of clouds, with markings arranged in cloud-bands parallel to the equator. These belts (dark) and zones (bright) resemble those of Jupiter but are less prominent and less variable in color and intensity. Spots near the equator usually have rotation periods close to 10 hr 14 min; some objects near latitude 60°N in 1960 had typically longer periods, near 10 hr 40 min. Methane and ammonia have been detected above the reflecting surface, but probably most of the atmosphere is hydrogen.

There are three rings. Ring A, the outer one, is 10,000 mi wide; then comes a gap 3,000 mi wide called *Cassini's Division.* Ring B is 17,000 mi wide. Ring C, the inner ring, is 11,000 mi wide, with its inner edge 7,000 mi above the planet's surface. Ring B is brightest; Ring A is dimmer; and Ring C is so dusky it is called the *Crape Ring.* The rings may be only inches thick. A number of minor gaps exist, *e.g. Encke's Division* near the middle of Ring A. In 1895 Keeler demonstrated that the rings revolve more rapidly in their outer portions and hence must consist of a swarm of very numerous separate small particles. G. P. Kuiper has found evidence that these are ice particles.

Saturn has ten satellites, at distances between 51,900 and 8 million mi, with periods ranging from about 18 hr to 550 days. Their diameters range from a few hundred miles up to about 3,000 mi for Titan, the largest. Titan is the only satellite in the solar system known to have an atmosphere, methane bands having been discovered by Kuiper. Phoebe, the farthest, alone revolves backward as compared to the direction typical of planetary revolutions. Such retrograde motion may mean that the satellite is a captured asteroid; or the motion may result from a past close approach to another planet.—*W. H.*

SAUSSURE, HORACE BÉNÉDICT DE, 1740–99, Swiss geologist; b. Geneva. He devoted his life to the study of the W Alps, and his great work, *Voyages dans les Alpes* (1779–96), stimulated interest in the scientific observation of these ranges.

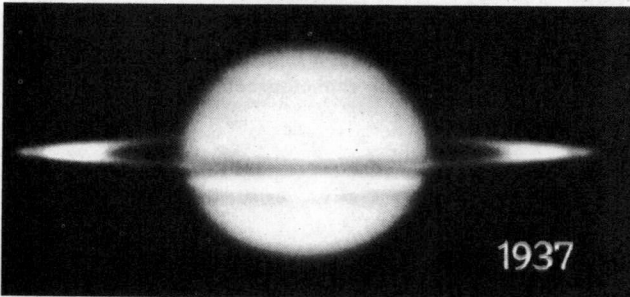

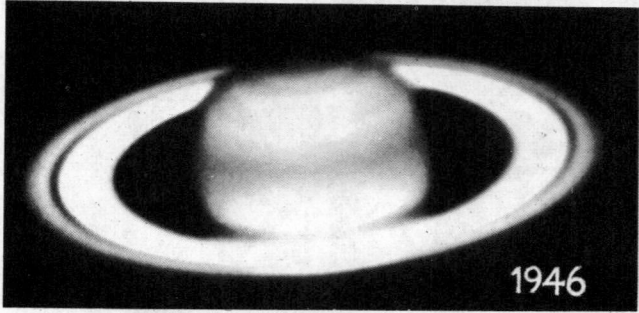

Aspects of Saturn: Rings, which make 27° angle with planet's orbit, keep same orientation with reference to planet and to planet's 29½-yr circuit around Sun. As seen from Earth (which is much nearer Sun), aspect of planet with rings keeps changing. Rings go through upper-face, edge-on, lower-face, edge-on cycle of presentations. (*Lowell Obs.*)

Plate 71 POISONOUS ANIMALS

Many comparatively weak animals are armed with venom, used for defense or for subduing struggling prey, or for both. Few of them use their poison offensively against any animal as large as a man.

1. Portuguese man-of-war *(Physalia)* is a colonial coelenterate from which purplish blue tentacles hang downward into the ocean as far as 100 ft. Each tentacle is studded with stinging cells, whose poison is highly irritating to human skin and fatal to small sea creatures upon which the man-of-war feeds. *(David Linton)* **2. Coral snake** *(Micrurus)* of southern U.S.A., Central America, and S America, is extremely venomous. Its poison, like that of the cobra, attacks nervous system. *(Russ Kinne)*

3. Sea urchin Diadema, found in waters of W Indies and near tip of Florida, has hollow needlelike spines filled with a mild poison. *(Robert C. Hermes)* **4. Cottonmouth moccasin** *(Agkistrodon piscivorus)* is a fish-catching pit-viper of swamplands from Missouri and Virginia south to Florida and Texas. It injects venom through erectile fangs. *(L. and M. Milne)*

Plate 72 POISONOUS PLANTS

No one is sure whether the toxic materials in plants are simply waste substances or whether they are elaborated as defensive adaptations against attacks by animals. A toxic substance in a plant probably will spare the plant from repeated attack by an animal susceptible to the poison. But every poisonous plant is eaten with impunity by a few animals.

1. Fly amanita mushroom *(Amanita muscaria)* has sticky, orange upper surface with thick, pale scales. Deadly poisonous to man. It is harmless to red squirrels and chipmunks. *(C. J. Ott/Shostal)*
2. Poison ivy *(Rhus toxicodendron),* with shiny leaflets in groups of three, grows both as vine and as low shrub. At some time in life, almost everyone is susceptible to its poison. *(Russ Kinne)*

1

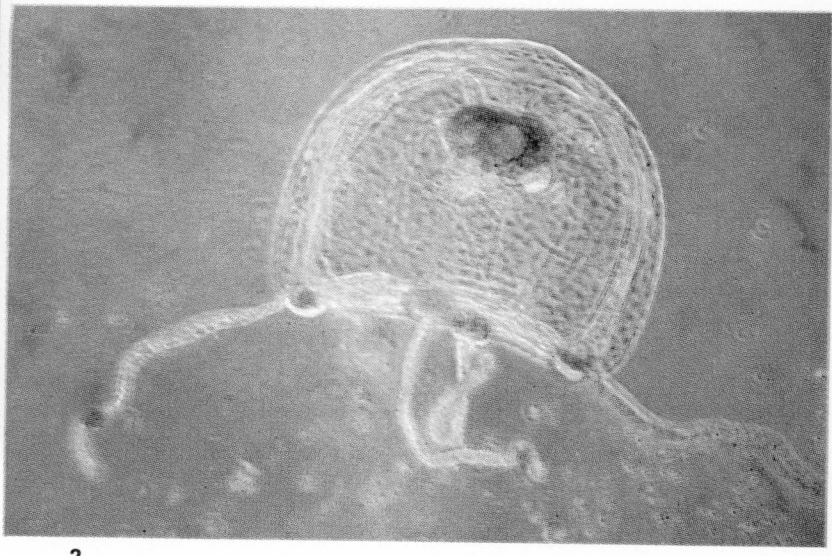

1

2

3

Plate 73 PLANKTON

Surface waters of oceans, lakes, and ponds teem with untold millions of microscopic plants and the minute animals that feed on them. These tiny organisms, which drift with current and tide, are included in the general term plankton. Among animal plankton are adult or larval representatives of every major animal group. A few appear here. **(1)** Larva of horseshoe crab, carried along by ocean currents, may become temporary member of plankton assemblage. **(2)** Transparent bell of young jellyfish pulsates slowly, moving animal to a position where its stinging tentacles can capture minute animals for food. **(3)** Tiny bivalved crustaceans called ostracods move by kicking their jointed legs, which extend through a crack between the valves. **(4)** Long threadlike antennae, stalked compound eyes, and strong pincers on front pair of legs help identify this planktonic animal as young crab. **(5)** Myriads of copepods like this one swim among the plankton, feeding on microscopic plants that form the "grass" of the sea. *(Roman Vishniac)*

5

4

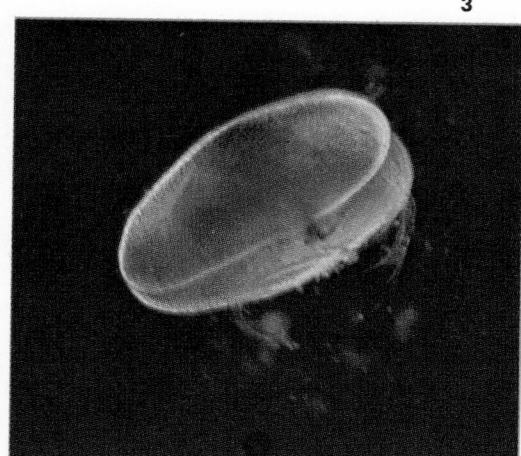

1

2

1. **Eight-inch *Anolis* lizard** of southeastern U.S.A., like its many relatives in West Indies, can change its color slowly from green to gray or brown, often matching its background. *(Axelrod/Shostal)*

2. **Alligator** of Gulf States, once feared by the pioneers, is now protected in Florida to insure against its possible extinction. Its muzzle is blunt, unlike the pointed snout of the crocodile. *(Russ Kinne)*

3. **Giant land tortoise** *(Testudo)* was once so numerous on remote islands off Pacific coast of Ecuador that these islands were given the Spanish name for tortoise—Galápagos. Now these ancient animals have been largely exterminated by man. *(Russ Kinne)* 4. **Emerald tree boa** is one of the famous constrictor snakes of tropical America that coil their muscular bodies around victims and prevent them from breathing. *(Walter Dawn)*

Plate 74   REPTILES

Today's reptiles are but a token left from the wealth of the Mesozoic era, the "Age of Reptiles," which ended about 75 million years ago. Reptiles conquered the land as no animals with backbones had been able to do before them. But they never achieved control of body temperature, as did the birds and mammals, which developed later. The principal living types of reptiles today are lizards, crocodilians (including alligators), turtles and snakes.

3

4

Plate 75 RIVERS

The character of valleys cut by rivers varies with such conditions as elevation of the land, type and structure of the rocks, climate, and length of time the river has been at work. Four types of river valleys appear here.

1. Ausable River, N.Y.: During the past 30,000 yr this "young" stream has cut a deep chasm into Cambrian sandstone which itself is over 400 million yr old. *(Jerome Wyckoff)* **2. Christian River,** Alaska, shows characteristics of "old age." Note the many meander loops, the wide flood plain, and the many abandoned former river channels, some of which form "oxbow" lakes. *(Russ Kinne)* **3. White River,** southwestern Missouri, is in "mature" stage. Here it has flooded over its banks and, as its color shows, is carrying a large load of finely ground rock debris. *(Jack Zehrt/F.P.G.)* **4. "Goose-neck" of San Juan River,** Utah: River has been rejuvenated; formerly a meandering river flowing on a floodplain, its gradient was steepened by a rise of the land. Rapid downcutting then resulted in a deep entrenchment of the stream. *(Harold Wanless)*

1

2

3

4

He was an outstanding observational geologist and one of the first great mountain climbers. He modified the hygrometer and thermometer and invented a number of other meteorological instruments, with which he made numerous observations. He was a fellow of the Royal Society.— *D. H. D. R.*

SCALER: any of a class of electrical circuits capable of responding with high speed to electronic impulses, and employed for the purpose of counting and registering the number of such impulses occurring during given intervals of time. The scaler is applied to a wide variety of physical problems ranging from the counting of rates of radioactive decay to determining the frequency of electromagnetic signals. Common scaler circuits are the "decade ring" and the "scale-of-two" (or binary) circuit. See COUNTER.—*P. T. D. and F. J. E.*

SCALES: small, hard, flat, integumentary (skin) structures, composed of either epidermal KERATIN or dermal bone. Scales form a partial or complete protective armor, particularly in fishes and reptiles, but also in fossil amphibians and to a limited degree in birds and mammals.—*H. M. S.*

SCANDIUM: a metallic element (Sc); at. no. 21; at. wt 44.96; mp 1200°C; valence 3. It is often considered a RARE EARTH, since it falls in the same vertical column (group III B) as lanthanum in the periodic table; but scandium is not a member of the LANTHANIDE series. Scandium is present in small quantities in many minerals, principally those found in Scandinavia (after which the element is named). The existence of scandium (*ekaboron*) was predicted by D. Mendeleev in 1869 on the basis of his periodic law and table, and discovered by the Swedish chemist Lars Frederick Nilson (1879) by fractionation and spectral analysis of the mineral euxenite. Spectral analysis has indicated that scandium is relatively abundant in the Sun and stars. Scandium has been described as an alloying element for nickel and nickel steels; the isotope Sc^{46} is radioactive and is used as a tracer. The pure metal was isolated in 1937.—*E. H. H.*

SCARP: an escarpment, or cliff, produced in various ways, such as direct faulting (fault scarp), differential erosion along a fault line (fault-line scarp), or differential erosion of layers of resistant and weak material, the stronger rock being left to form such a feature as the steep slope of a cuesta or the cliff surrounding a mesa.—*J. Sh.*

SCATTERING: change in direction of motion experienced by a moving object when influenced by a force. The orbit of a comet in the gravitational field of the Sun, the rebound of one billiard ball from another, and the controlled deflection of electron beams by magnetic fields in the cathode-ray tube of a television receiver exemplify scattering. In all these cases the forces responsible for the scattering are well understood, so the trajectories of the scattered particles can be predicted quantitatively. But the forces between elementary particles inside atomic nuclei are not well understood, and scattering is the principal technique used by nuclear physicists for studying the properties of these forces. The projectiles commonly used for such experiments are electrons, protons, and light nuclei to which high speeds have been imparted by particle accelerators. These particles are directed against a target made up of the nuclei being studied, and the few projectiles that come within 10^{-13} cm of a nucleus are scattered by the nuclear force. By examining the angular and energy distributions of the scattered particles one can infer some of the properties of the force fields encountered.—*S. K.*

SCENT GLAND: a special area on the surface of an animal, from which odorous substances are released under conditions of stress or sexual readiness, or while the animal is marking the boundaries of a territory. The anal scent glands of the skunk, which can be used to discharge a jet of liquid secretion made malodorous by methyl mercaptan, are famous as a means of animal defense in America, where skunks are found from coast to coast. A valuable component of expensive perfumes, civet, is a secretion from similar glands of civet "cats" in Africa (especially Ethiopia) and Asia, where the animals are kept captive and "milked" of the strongly aromatic material; civet "cats" are related to mongooses and, like them, smear the odorous secretion on food and the walls of burrows to which they will return. Scent glands on the backs of wild pigs (peccaries) give off a strong odor, which appears to warn away predators and also competitors for food on the forest floor. Many kinds of deer mark out territories during mating season by rubbing against trees and rocks, leaving there a secretion with a strong scent from glands near the eyes. Both domesticated dogs and their wild kin leave comparable signs in their territories with odorous materials from preputial glands, which give distinctive character to urine wherever it is discharged. Pronghorn antelopes leave a trail of odorous material from glands on their feet and, when alarmed, can discharge a warning scent from a glandular area on the rump. In man, the gland of Tyson in the glans penis of males, and the vulval glands of females, are scent glands.

Among cold-blooded animals, too, scent glands are important. Many reptiles possess them in the lower jaw and around the cloacal opening, probably relying upon odor to bring mates together. Moths and butterflies make extensive use of scent glands during courtship; the odor released by a freshly emerged female moth may bring mates to her from as far as 7 mi downwind. Some of these lures have now been synthesized in the laboratory and put to use in insect control. —*L. and M. M.*

SCEPTICAL CHYMIST, THE, by Robert Boyle (1661): This best-known of Boyle's scientific writings is often misunderstood. Boyle did *not* first define the chemical concept of element (nor did he claim this). He did *not* succeed in destroying belief in the Aristotelian elements or the chemical "principles" (salt, sulfur, mercury), though it was a main object of his essay to bring them under doubt. To this end he argued (1) from experiments, that such elements were not consistently produced by analysis; (2) from theory, that all matter is made of particles, and that such particles rather than fictitious (and for Boyle, transmutable) elements constitute the ultimate material reality. *The Sceptical Chymist* is truly significant as the first attempt to base the study of chemical composition firmly on experiments, in terms of a theory of particulate structure. —*A. R. H.*

SCHEELE, KARL WILHELM, 1742–86, Swedish apothecary and chemist; b. Stralsund. A remarkable experimenter, he worked with extremely primitive apparatus but discovered probably more new substances than any previous investigator, including the elements chlorine and oxygen, glycerine, and molybdic and tungstic acids. He also studied radiant heat and the blackening produced in certain silver compounds by light. Scheele published many papers on chemical analyses.— *D. H. D. R.*

SCHEINER, CHRISTOPH, 1575–1650, German astronomer; b. Walda bei Mindelheim. He is chiefly remembered for his controversy with Galileo concerning sunspots, but he also was an astronomer of note in his own right. He was probably the first to use the telescope of two convex lenses suggested

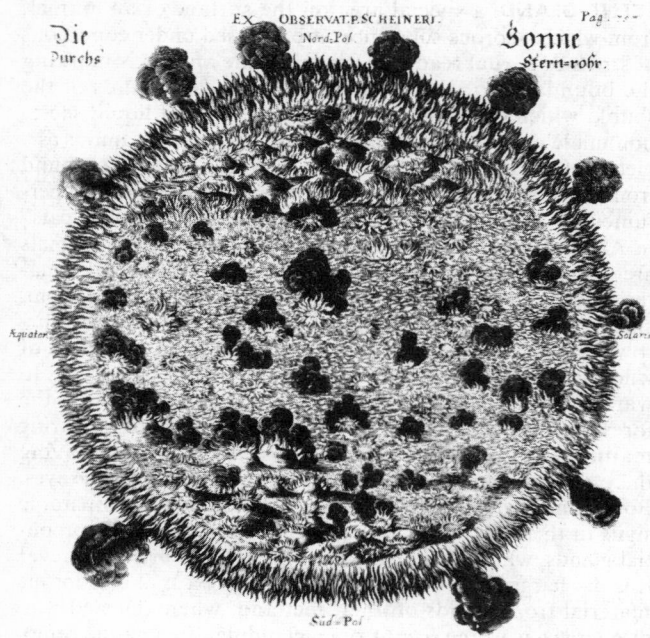

Father Scheiner's representation of sunspots, first appearing in his *Rosa ursina* (1630), is here reproduced from a somewhat later book. Scheiner buttressed his anti-Copernican views by interpreting the wandering sunspots as satellites around the "planet" Sun. (*Gossner Collection*)

by Kepler, and he discovered the faculae, bright areas on the Sun that occur along with sunspots. Scheiner was one of several persons who independently discovered the sunspots. His solar observations were published in his monumental *Rosa ursina* (1630).—*D. H. D. R.*

SCHIAPARELLI, GIOVANNI VIRGINIO, 1835–1910, Italian astronomer; b. Savigliano. He devoted himself to the telescopic study of the planet Mars, publishing a series of seven papers describing its surface. He determined its axis of rotation and the position of its southern polar cap, and mapped the planet in more detail than had ever been recorded before. In 1877 he discovered the so-called Martian "canals" and stimulated great interest in the possibility of intelligent life on the red planet (see LOWELL, PERCIVAL; MARS). Schiaparelli attributed meteor showers to disintegrated comets—a view now widely accepted. He was director of the Brera Observatory, Milan, 1862–1900, and was a fellow of the Royal Society and an associate of the National Academy of Sciences.—*D. H. D. R.*

SCHIST: a metamorphic rock formed under intense pressure and heat, the product of regional METAMORPHISM. One of the most common of metamorphic rocks, schist represents advanced metamorphism; it may be derived from either sedimentary or igneous rock or from another metamorphic rock, *e.g.* slate or phyllite. Its texture is moderately coarse and its mineral crystals are visible as thin, roughly parallel layers along which the rock tends to split. The dominant mineral often lends its name to the type of schist; common types are *mica schist,* derived from phyllite; *hornblende schist,* often formed from basalt; and *chlorite schist,* with chlorite replacing mica. See Color Plate 61.—*E. A.*

SCHLEIDEN, MATTHIAS JAKOB, 1804–81, German botanist; b. Hamburg. A founder of the cell theory, he suggested in a paper entitled "Beiträge zur Phytogenesis" (1838) that every plant cell "leads a double life"—one life as an individual and another as an integral part of the plant. His textbook on botany, *Grundzüge der wissenschaftlichen Botanik* (1842), helped to turn the attention of botanists from an excessive concentration on classification of plants and toward studies in plant anatomy and physiology.—*D. H. D. R.*

SCHLIEREN PHOTOGRAPHY: see PHOTOGRAPHY.

SCHMIDT, BERNHARD VOLDEMAR, 1879–1935, German astronomer; b. Nargen Island, Estonia. A manufacturer of astronomical lenses and mirrors and an associate of the Bergedorf Observatory, Hamburg, he invented (1931) a combination of spherical mirror with a correcting lens mounted at its center of curvature. This became known as the Schmidt telescope or SCHMIDT CAMERA. The largest Schmidt camera is in operation at Palomar Observatory, Calif.—*D. H. D. R.*

SCHMIDT CAMERA: a precision optical system of unusual simplicity, originally designed as a photographic telescope by Bernhard Schmidt (1879–1935) of Hamburg Observatory. It consists of a window-like "correcting plate" of optical glass at the upper end of the telescope, coincident with the center of curvature of a spherical mirror at the lower end. One surface of the correcting plate has a prescribed shape deviating slightly from flatness. The combination of plate and mirror produces a wide field of excellent imagery on a spherically curved photographic plate in the center of the tube (see TELESCOPE). The largest Schmidt telescope, at Palomar Observatory, has a 48-in.-diameter plate and a 72-in. mirror. Modified versions of the Schmidt camera are used in most instances where wide-angle optics are required, *e.g.* in satellite tracking, spectroscopy, aerial surveying, television, and wide-angle projection.—*S. D. G.*

SCHOENHEIMER, RUDOLF, 1898–1941, German-U. S. biochemist; b. Berlin. Using deuterium, Schoenheimer and his colleagues traced the metabolism of fat (1936), and later used "heavy nitrogen" (N^{15}) to study protein metabolism (1939). Schoenheimer originated the concept of the "metabolic pool," a hypothetical reservoir of free metabolic residues from which proteins and other complex molecules are constantly being formed, and to which many residues are returned after their breakdown, others being excreted. These ideas are expressed in his *The Dynamic State of Body Constituents.* He was a fellow of the Royal Society.—*P. R. L.*

SCHOLASTICISM: historically, a term referring (1) to the educational system in western Europe during the Middle Ages, under control of the Catholic Church, primarily for the education of the clergy, and (2) to the systematic body of theological and philosophical doctrine taught in European universities, 13th–15th cents. Distinctive of scholastic tradition and method are: (1) acceptance of Church dogmas as a norm and guide in philosophical doctrine; (2) use of the tradition of Aristotle, Plato, and St. Augustine in formulating the problems and content of metaphysics, philosophy of nature, and moral philosophy; (3) a method of study involving the interpretation and reconciliation of authoritative texts, by arguments on both sides of a given question, followed by a resolution. In extended usage, the word "scholasticism" often refers to educational method which emphasizes tradition and use of authoritative texts, including, currently, the philosophical movement espoused by Catholic educational institutions throughout the world, which bases its teaching on the scholastic tradition of the 13th cent. and especially on the teachings of St. Thomas Aquinas.—*E. A. M.*

SCHRÖDINGER, ERWIN, 1897–1961, Austrian-German physicist; b. Vienna. Beginning from the foundation provided by L. V. de Broglie's idea of matter waves (1924), he and P. A. M. Dirac developed wave mechanics. Schrödinger showed (1926) that wave mechanics and the matrix mechanics of W. Heisenberg are equivalent. He and Dirac shared the 1933 Nobel prize "for the discovery of new and fruitful forms of the atomic theory." He was a fellow of the Royal Society.—*D. H. D. R.*

SCHRÖDINGER EQUATION: an equation that plays the same role in QUANTUM MECHANICS that Newton's equation (force = mass × acceleration) plays in classical mechanics. It was formulated in 1926 by Erwin Schrödinger, following De Broglie's hypothesis that all particles have wave properties. In areas where the classical theory is successful, as in the motions of the planets, the Schrödinger equation leads to results that differ by infinitesimal amounts from the classical theory. In atomic systems, however, the classical theory is useless, whereas the Schrödinger equation leads to results that are in excellent agreement with experiment.

The quantity that one wishes to find in using the Schrödinger equation is the wave function for a particle or system of particles. It does not have immediate physical significance. The square of the wave function determines the probability of finding the system in any prescribed position. The Schrödinger theory is not, in general, fully causal, as is any classical theory. However, the probability that a given event will occur can be calculated. Interestingly, the Schrödinger equation predicts that certain quantities are discrete rather than continuous. For example, the possible values that the energy of an atomic system can assume are, in certain domains, discrete—*i.e.* can take on only certain allowed values. —*G. M. S. and L. S.*

SCHULTZE, MAX JOHANN SIGISMUND, 1825–74, German anatomist; b. Freiburg. He established our modern conception of the vital components of the cell, introducing the word protoplasm as the universal term for the cell's "fundamental substance," and studied the structure and function of protozoa, and of the nerve endings of the eye, ear, and nose. His most famous publication was his *Über Muskelkörperchen und das, was man eine Zelle zu nennen habe* (1861).—*D. H. D. R.*

SCHWANN, THEODOR, 1810–82, German anatomist; b. Neuss. One of the founders of the cell theory, he completely accepted the botanical cell theory of M. J. Schleiden and extended it to animals. He also discovered cells with nuclei in the notochord of tadpoles, followed the development of cells in tissue from the embryonic stage to maturity, and established the cellular nature of animal tissue. Details of his microscopical researches were published in his *Mikroskopische Untersuchungen über die Übereinstimmung in der Struktur und dem Wachstum der Tiere und Pflanzen* (1839). He was a fellow of the Royal Society and was awarded its Copley medal (1845).—*D. H. D. R.*

SCIENCE: an organized body of knowledge and opinion which is systematically supported by formal proofs or by observational evidence. The sciences may be divided into two categories: mathematics and logic (*e.g.* algebra, analysis, mathematical logic, metamathematics, and the formal logic of natural languages), which are concerned with the analysis, elaboration, and proof of the principles that regulate the permissible operations within systems of symbols; and the empirical or observational sciences, which are concerned with the description and explanation of phenomena discovered by sensory observation. A body of knowledge is regarded as an empirical "science" insofar as it meets two conditions: (1) it must be the outcome of a particular method of inquiry; (2) it must conform to certain principles of organization.

The method of scientific inquiry may be broadly described as follows: Every scientific hypothesis is regarded as subject in principle to being disproved by observational evidence. If any hypothesis has consequences that can be shown to be false, then it must be rejected, *i.e.* either abandoned outright or reformulated so that the false consequences no longer follow. Every hypothesis must be supported by actual observational evidence. A hypothesis is regarded as highly confirmed only if it has some true deductive consequences that alternative hypotheses lack. The evidence for a hypothesis must be *public*. This means that the relevant observational and experimental situations which exhibit the phenomena to be explained must be repeatable, at least in principle. Moreover, the evidence derived from any such experiment must be observable by a large number of persons. Thus, an introspection cannot constitute scientific evidence, but an introspective report can.

Scientific knowledge must be so organized that the scientist needs relatively few concepts and hypotheses for describing a variety of types of phenomena. This is accomplished with the help of specially constructed concepts that are both comprehensive in application and suitable for stating general laws that apply to a variety of cases. (See also APPLIED SCIENCE.)—*M. Be.*

SCIENCE FICTION: a type of speculative fiction dealing with scientific or pseudo-scientific themes. Like fantasy, science fiction is based on premises that differ from current notions of reality, but it eschews such supernatural phenomena as devils, ghosts, werewolves, and vampires. Its cardinal conditions are: (1) established facts may not be repudiated; (2) accepted theory, *e.g.* the Einstein demonstration that mass becomes infinite at the speed of light, may not be by-passed without an explanation that at least sounds rational. The prevailing form of science fiction today is what may be termed the "super-physics" or "galactic" school, whose groundwork was laid in the boisterous "Skylark" and "Lensmen" tales of E. E. Smith. In marked contrast to this "space-opera" approach, the austere John Taine (in real life the late Dr. Eric Temple Bell, the well-known mathematician) insisted that the science-fiction writer must have more than a nodding acquaintance with real science. This school is based on logical extrapolation of known scientific principles. It is a characteristic of the better science fiction that it tends to come true; in 1869 Jules Verne described the submarine so exactly that a patent could not be obtained for the invention when it actually appeared, and in *The World Set Free* (1914), H. G. Wells vividly portrayed the radioactive fury of atomic bombs. Many other examples might be cited.

Johannes Kepler (1571–1630) and Cyrano de Bergerac (1619–1655) told of imaginary voyages to the Moon; since their methods of reaching it were obviously fantastic, science fiction is commonly held to begin with Jules Verne (1828–1905). Its second and more important founder was H. G. Wells (1866–1946). Wells originated most of the favored science-fiction themes: invaders from another planet (*The War of the Worlds*), the spaceship (*The First Men in the Moon*), time travel (*The Time Machine*), suspended animation (*When the Sleeper Wakes*), gigantic insects (*The Food of the Gods*), invisibility (*The Invisible Man*), the mad scientist (*The Island of Dr. Moreau*), and parallel universes (*Men Like Gods*). Like many other science-fiction writers, Wells used his stories to carry a social message.

Two other hardy perennials flourish in the science-fiction

garden: supermen of prodigious powers, and man-created intelligences. Often the superman is a being of outstanding physique, or he may have telepathic and hypnotic powers. Modern electronic calculators have almost taken the gigantic artificial brain out of science fiction. The other man-created intelligences are the robot and the android, both usually man-like in appearance but otherwise quite different. The robot is of clanking metal; the android is of flesh and blood, though chemically created. The word "robot" came from Karel Capek's 1920 play, *R. U. R.* (Rossum's Universal Robots). Generally, robots are faithful, though frequently exasperating, servants of man. Androids, like their prototype, Frankenstein's monster, tend to be vicious. With all its pictures of space travel, telepathic mutants, life on other worlds, and totalitarian future societies, science fiction is a frankly escapist form of literature. As such, it is but one of many expressions of man's age-old desire to liberate himself from the yoke of reality through the use of his imagination.—*C. B. C.*

SCIENCE IN EDUCATION: Scientific research for improvement of education has been devoted mainly to physical, administrative, social, and psychological conditions that affect learning, and only recently extended to instructional materials and techniques. (This is less true of work with children who cannot attend regular classrooms because of emotional or physical handicaps.) Study of personal and cultural factors affecting school achievement has produced an impressive body of substantive findings. Despite attack, the I Q (intelligence quotient equals tested mental age divided by chronological age) stands as a convenient though very rough instrument for predicting long-range chances for academic success. The IQ is not a measure of innate capacity, for it is greatly affected by cultural and emotional factors, as is academic success; both are functions of verbal skill—a learned, not an inherent, ability. When IQ is contrasted with academic achievement, results show great wastage of talent among scholastically and culturally deprived groups such as segregated Negroes, recent immigrants, and children from economically depressed families.

Studies of academically talented children show that the rule is correlation, not compensation, in abilities. Even physical size, emotional stability, and creativity tend to correlate with verbal skill, though individual variations from this tendency are wide. Rates of academic achievement vary as widely as do rates of physical growth, and, likewise, those who go faster earlier are more likely, but not certain, to go further in the long run.

Individual learning is affected profoundly by the fact that teaching in schools occurs in group situations rather than by individual instruction. The nature of this factor is, however, not well understood. Social isolation from classmates tends to inhibit academic achievement, but exceptions are frequent. If teaching technique remains unchanged, achievement in academic subjects is not significantly affected by variations in size of class, but other outcomes, such as enjoyment of study and ambition for further pursuit of the subject, may be affected negatively with increased class size. For usual-size classes and methods of teaching, other things being equal, the less the variation among the members of a class in achievement in a particular subject, the greater the learning in that subject. But other things are never equal; application of this principle on a large scale would require extensive reorganization of school policies. Research is needed to determine the effect of variations in teaching procedures for groups that differ in size, in range of ability, and in degree of social cohesion. Effective use of electronic teaching devices is inhibited by lack of evidence on these factors.

With the financial support of several philanthropic foundations and cooperation among educators, learned societies, and testing services, new sets of textbooks and visual aids in science and mathematics are being produced and used with careful attention to testing their effectiveness in differing school situations. Even more important for scientific study of education is the recent research on "teaching machines"—*i.e.* programmed instruction. Programming in education is as yet more art than science, but its elements are now fairly clear: (1) analyzing material to be taught into the simplest meaningful units; (2) constructing a sequence of these units to exemplify the logic or structure of the material; (3) arranging this sequence into teaching frames such that (4) every frame presents a stimulus to and requires a response from the student and (5) every frame contains cues or overlap from previous frames to make possible a correct response, (6) the whole being so presented that correct responses may be reinforced, *i.e.* rewarded, immediately. Mechanical devices, some of great ingenuity, have been devised for doing (6), but the rest requires human imagination of the highest order. Programmed instruction makes it possible to use results from psychology of learning for the first time in classrooms. Preliminary studies indicate that many well-established beliefs may have to be revised; for example, the IQ predicts speed in moving through programmed material, not absolute ability. If on-going wide-scale research bears out preliminary findings, the overdue technological revolution of education is at hand.—*J. E. M.*

SCIENTIFIC METHOD: the rules of concept formation and inference and the techniques of controlled observation employed in the search for knowledge. Rules of concept formation and inference, which constitute the logic of science, are fairly constant from one area of inquiry to another, while methods of observation and experimentation vary considerably. All procedures, whether logical or observational, are scientific to the degree that they are objective, *i.e.* they yield the same results for all observers under standard conditions, and to the degree that they have proved themselves reliable in the past.

The logical or formal part of scientific method can be divided into two components: (1) rules of vocabulary and sentence construction, and (2) rules for inferring conclusions from data. Scientific language differs from conversational language in its greater precision and in excluding statements that cannot be clearly verified. The precision of scientific language is due to three features: (1) new expressions are introduced by defining them in terms of expressions already in use; (2) wherever possible, concepts are defined in terms of measuring procedures; and (3) the personal and emotional associations that individuals attach to certain words are ruled out as irrelevant, so that the meanings of scientific expressions are the same for everyone.

The rules of scientific inference are similarly more precise and more restrictive than those of informal, common-sense argument. While not all these rules can be explicitly stated, a great deal of philosophical and scientific effort is invested in the task of formulating such rules as clearly as possible; whereas common-sense reasoning is flexible and tolerant of individual variations. In the early stages of development of a science, its concepts are mainly qualitative and classificatory, and serve the purpose of grouping many diverse phenomena into distinct classes which are then connected by generalizations. The rules of inference employed at this stage are mainly those of elementary induction and the logic of classes (see FORMAL LOGIC). When techniques of measurement are developed, it becomes possible to relate measurable properties by means of mathematical equations (laws). The highest

Inductive methods were championed by Sir Francis Bacon, 1620, in the second part of his *The Great Instauration*, the *Novum organum*, as a replacement for Aristotelian logic, which he felt incapable of generating new arts. Title page of *The Great Instauration* (above) shows a three-master issuing from the (Aristotelian) Mediterranean, passing Pillars of Hercules, and setting out into Atlantic on voyage to the New (Baconian) World. The twin pillars that have checked progress are represented by Bacon in the preface as man's exalted estimate of his present condition and low estimate of his chances of improving it. Latin motto ("Many will pass through and knowledge will be increased") is from *Daniel* xii: 4. (*Burndy Library*)

each in a given field varies with its level of theoretical development and the degree of complexity of its subject matter. See also SCIENCE; SCIENTIFIC RESEARCH.—*R. A.*

SCIENTIFIC RESEARCH: research done in any field of science, its nature depending upon what one designates as science. Generally speaking, science is the exercise of so-called SCIENTIFIC METHOD. The "what" of science is less important than the "how" of the method, but this depends on "who" has applied it. In general, there is probably just one complete method but varying degrees of realization owing to the nature of the material at hand. Most advanced sciences are those that have been the simplest to study, partly because of the isolation of individual phenomena and partly because of the controllability of particular factors. Although measurement itself is not necessary for the use of the scientific method, in most cases quantitative measurement has contributed greatly to progress.

Scientific research such generally starts with a specific question, motivated by a desire for new knowledge, or by a need for solving a practical problem. The method usually is analytical, hence necessarily piecemeal, so that science as a whole has to be put together from parts that may not fit nicely together; there may be overlapping or even gaps between different sciences. In doing research, the subjective aspects cannot be completely eliminated; the vaunted objectivity of science is based primarily upon intersubjective agreement, but is presumably due to some more objective reality that lies beyond our sense experiences.

In asking particular questions of nature, one gets answers —observed facts—which are necessarily selective in character. The scientist is always looking *for* something; he is not looking *at* everything—not just staring. The observed facts depend upon the operations both of selecting and of obtaining. From the observed facts, one infers inductively general rules on the assumption of the uniformity of nature; this procedure represents the lowest level of scientific research. For example, one may ask, "What is the temperature each day at noon?" Observing it to be 50°F on Monday, Wednesday, and Friday, one may generalize inductively and infer that it was 50°F on Tuesday (interpolation), or that it will be 50°F on Saturday (extrapolation), or that it is always 50°F (a general rule). Our experience warns us of the potential inaccuracy of any such inductive inference in this instance. Satisfactory criteria for validation have to be devised phenomenologically. Some young sciences such as meteorology may not have progressed beyond this kind of activity, and are confined largely to the empirical level. At a higher level, one attempts to find relations between various events or phenomena. One may begin with simple identification, *e.g.* objects with the same colors, shapes, and sizes, and then develop a scheme of classification, say, for stones, leaves, or clouds. Next one searches for relations (often called scientific laws or principles) among such facts, *i.e.* related factors. For instance, one might have also asked above, "What is the atmospheric pressure each day at noon?" Our inductive answer might have been 30 in. of mercury. Now is there a relationship between these two physical quantities, the temperature and the pressure of the atmosphere? Are they, perhaps, always proportional? One could tentatively set up such a hypothesis and then continually check its validity as new data become available, often by specially designed tests. If a hypothesis fails, one may devise a new one—or use the old one only in its restricted domain of reliability. The scientist himself may formulate new concepts to describe such relationships; for example, specific gravity signifies the constancy of the relationship of the weight of a particular substance to that of an equal volume

stage of scientific development is reached when systematic theories are constructed by means of which many specific laws can be deduced from a few general principles and hypotheses. Newtonian mechanics is a classic example of this highest stage. In general, the natural sciences are well advanced on the theoretical level, while psychology and the social sciences are largely concerned with classification and correlation of measurable properties that characterize the first and second levels of development.

One of the main issues in discussions of scientific method is whether scientific reasoning is primarily inductive or deductive. Deductive inference is more conclusive than inductive inference, since the conclusion of a valid deductive inference follows logically from its premises, while the conclusion of an inductive inference is, at best, only strongly suggested. All mathematical reasoning is deductive, while the extrapolation of generalizations from observed data is inductive. Empiricist philosophers, beginning with Francis Bacon, have maintained that inductive procedures are more productive of new discoveries in science than the deduction of laws from general principles. Rationalist philosophers and scientists hold the contrary view. All scientific disciplines employ both deductive and inductive methods, but the exact proportion of

of water. In looking for patterns, one may be guided by a practical desire for convenient simplicity or by a theoretical ideal of esthetic unity, but one is subject always to logical consistency, on the assumption of the comprehensibility of nature itself. Scientific research consists often in merely obtaining data sufficiently accurate to reveal such relationships (*e.g.* the painstakingly gathered data of the astronomer Tycho Brahe, which revealed to Kepler the elliptical orbits of the planets).

Simple relationships are recognized frequently only because more complicated phenomena are ignored. Nature itself is inexpressibly complicated; it does not consist of neatly packaged sciences—physics, chemistry, biology. The unity of nature transcends the unity of science; it inspires the scientist's attempts to make his own view or theory ever more inclusive of different phenomena, as Newton viewed the revolution of the Moon about Earth as physically like the falling of an apple to the ground. When a scientific theory changes, the original facts may not be different, but only the manner of looking at them—often because of the presence of new facts, as when a mountain climber gets a wider view higher up. Scientific research involving relationships is more synthetic than empirical research and is based, necessarily, upon imaginative insight. Any theory, however, must always check with observable phenomena to some acceptable degree; sometimes scientific research consists solely of such verification. A scientific theory is usually, however, not merely descriptive of phenomena, but also predictive of facts not previously known. From a general theory specific statements can be deduced and compared with experience. Thus the atomic theory enables us to predict the properties of elements not yet found. If any theory breaks down, one may have to restrict its scope or devise a wholly new one. New questions, too, may lead to newly observed facts; one then finds new related factors and develops a new factitious theory; and, once more, one asks new questions from the new viewpoint —in an ever-spiraling process. Changing scientific theories are always in the direction of cumulative advance—not of defeat.

As a science develops in complexity, however, there is less opportunity for an individual to participate in comprehensive research. Modern research is increasingly dependent upon large, precise, and hence costly equipment—telescopes and microscopes, satellites and ships—all requiring the investment of many people and much money. Teams of scientists, often from different disciplines, unite to attack major problems. Theorists strive generally for experimentally confirmable answers; experimentalists, for theoretically significant facts. This dichotomy of research is merely one of practical convenience; actually, scientific research is dependent upon the intimate relationship of both groups.

The much-used terms *basic research* and *applied research* are more difficult to define than to illustrate. Suppose an insulating material is required that will withstand a certain electrical voltage. General information about the desired physical and chemical properties is fundamental for supplying the answer to this engineering problem. The research required to obtain this information could be regarded as basic research in engineering, *i.e.* engineering science; the *use* of it would constitute applied research, *i.e.* engineering. But why do particular materials have the different properties they do? Why, for example, is copper electrically conducting, whereas rubber is not? This question belongs properly to physical science. Copper is made up of particular kinds of atoms that readily share their free electrons; to understand this behavior, one must learn about atomic structure and atomic forces. Basic research in chemical physics is requisite to finding the

chemical answer; its application may be termed applied research. One may ask further, "Why does one atom differ from another?" *Basic* research will yield information on the structure of an atomic nucleus and the forces between elementary particles; the information here can be *applied* to nuclear engineering, *e.g.* atomic reactors.

Knowledge is thus seen to be made up of layers, like an onion. A question at any one level is dependent immediately upon information in the layer directly beneath it; the answer there, in turn, can be applied at the layer just above. The designation "basic" or "applied" is largely a matter of viewpoint. Everyday problems—the top layer—are necessarily *applied;* fundamental questions—the very bottom layer—are necessarily *basic.* We descend from technological needs to more scientific questions, and vice versa; at each step we require basic and applied research. Social progress has proved critically sensitive to the depth of our probing. See also SCIENCE; SCIENTIFIC METHOD.—*R. J. S.*

SCIENTIFIC RESEARCH CENTERS: are inextricably bound up with the physical experimentation by which man's concepts about the natural world are tested and extended. From the beginning of the scientific revolution in the 16th and 17th cent., various approaches to the furtherment of experiment have been employed, reflecting the changing complexion of science itself. The 20th cent. is no exception. Between 1896 and the end of World War II, profound changes swept through science and it was inevitable that the institutions supporting scientific research should be transformed. Hitherto unknown experimental devices were discovered, opening up novel avenues of research. Fundamental changes in the modes of experimentation required drastic rearrangements in the organization of scientific efforts. Machines such as particle accelerators and nuclear reactors marked a break with the traditional instruments used solely to observe and measure; they are devices used in an aggressive fashion to extract information, to perturb normal systems, and to simulate conditions not readily available to earthbound investigators. The fusion of fundamental science and inventive technology, each reinforcing the other, each gaining in power, versatility, and scope, has enormously stimulated science and made the creation of large research centers inevitable.

Conditions of Experimental Work Before 20th Cent.: Francis Bacon was among the first to foresee the consequences of the experimental testing of our concepts of nature and the practical use of these new ideas. In *The New Atlantis* he envisaged in "Salomon's House" groups of specialists working in concert on the solution of both theoretical and technical problems by direct experimentation. Bacon stated that "the unassisted hand and the understanding left to itself possess little power" —a phrase which could serve as a motto for every experimental laboratory. In the 17th cent., SCIENTIFIC SOCIETIES AND ACADEMIES spontaneously arose both to engage in experimentation and to exchange and disseminate the new knowledge. M. Ornstein described the *Accademia del Cimento* (1657–67) in Florence as a place where "nine scientists supplied with the means of scientific research, gave ten years of united effort to the elaboration of instruments, the acquisition of experimental skill and the determination of fundamental truths." Likewise, the Royal Society of London, from its beginning in 1660, has had as one of its most important functions the performance of experiments before its members. "The business of the Royal Society is to improve the knowledge of natural things, and all useful Arts, Manufactures, Mechanick practices, Engynes and inventions by Experiments," said Hooke. In every case, these institutions supported the efforts to shed the "unbridled rationalism" and deductive science of the Middle Ages. They took direct and full advantage of the developments which so stimulated the Renaissance—printing, commerce, the explorations following closely on navigational discoveries, the public postal service. It is also not without significance that by and large the vernacular tongue was used in scientific communications (medicine being a conspicuous exception in this respect in retaining Latin). The new academies stood in stark contrast to the universities as constituted in the 17th cent., for the latter stood, without question, in the way of the new knowledge and the new methods of inquiry: they were isolated, by language and temper of mind, from the very sources of science. While many of the most noted natural philosophers were associated with the universities, it was not until the second half of the 19th cent. that laboratories were provided in their own institutions. In the 18th and early 19th cent., the various courts of Europe provided the home for experimental science. Institutions and academies received royal patronage and were marked by the varying characteristics of the countries in which they were formed.

The circumstances under which the earlier experimentalists worked are significant. Michael Faraday began as an assistant in the Laboratory of the Royal Institution of Great Britain in 1813, and became Director in 1825. Laplace taught at the Ecole Militaire Académie but presented the results of his private researches to the scientific world through the Academy of Sciences of France, established in 1795 in Paris. Lagrange in 1766 took up at the Berlin Academy a post just vacated by Euler, who had gone on to the Russian Academy of Sciences, established in 1725 by Catherine I in St. Petersburg. In the U. S. A., Joseph Henry, who started his career at the Albany Academy, first took a professorship in natural philosophy at the New Jersey College (Princeton), finally held an appointment at the Smithsonian Institution in Washington, where he made a considerable number of experimental discoveries. These few examples make it clear that the seedbed of experimental science was prepared principally by the enlightened courts of Europe and by the spontaneously formed academies.

The 19th cent. brought still other changes in social forms, in industrialization, and in the attitude of the universities.

The influence and interest of the various societies also changed. While experimentation associated with fundamental concepts of nature was being supported more and more by the universities, the societies turned toward the practical consequences of science. The societies have continued to the present day to hold meetings, publish journals, and otherwise disseminate information. But to a large extent, the original version of experimental science as a spontaneous cooperative effort on the part of enlightened amateurs was all but lost, and was to reappear in academic dress.

The shift to the universities was begun in 1866 with the creation of the Clarendon Laboratory at Oxford, established specifically to provide a place for experimental demonstrations to students as well as for experimental research. The equally famous Cavendish Laboratory at Cambridge was built in 1874 under the careful eye of James Clerk Maxwell, the first occupant of the newly formed chair of experimental physics at that university. All the universities, such as land-grant colleges in the U. S. A. and "Redbrick" universities in Britain, which came into being in the late 19th cent., quite naturally included laboratories as part of their educational plant. Thus, from the beginning of the 20th cent. to the present, fundamental scientific experimentation has been intimately associated with the universities.

The Formation of Centers in the 20th Cent.: Modern scientific research centers reflect in varying degree the historical elements just discussed. Some centers are the direct outgrowth of a specific piece of academic research which became so large and costly as to require separate funding and organization to prevent a gross distortion of the universities' other functions (*e.g.* the Ernest O. Lawrence Radiation Laboratory and the Jet Propulsion Laboratory). Some centers are new forms of the older academies and have been established to fill a gap such as then existed between medicine and the biological sciences (*e.g.* the Rockefeller Institute) or to engage in an entirely new field of endeavor for which the universities, by location or academic schedule, were unsuited (the Woods Hole Oceanographic Institution; the Carnegie Institution of Washington). Some centers represent an extension and expan-

Woods Hole Oceanographic Institution is housed in two brick buildings at left. This center was endowed in 1930 by the Rockefeller Institute. In foreground is the two-master *Atlantis*, one of the Institution's three research ships. (*Woods Hole Oceanographic Inst.*)

National Bureau of Standards scientists determine gyromagnetic ratio of proton. Bureau was established in 1901, and is the foremost federal agency for research in physical sciences. Principal laboratory is in Washington, D. C. (*U. S. D. C.*)

National Institutes of Health pathologist analyzes body fluids. These agencies of Dept. of Health, Education and Welfare engage in medical research, dividing activities between cancer, heart, and dental research, and also mental health, neurological diseases, and blindness. (*Nat. Inst. of Health*)

sion of World War II projects in which new fields of research and technology were developed and deemed worthy of continued support in the national interest (Argonne National Laboratory). Still other centers were created *de novo* after World War II in response to the spontaneously expressed need of university scientists to have certain advanced experimental tools made available which, by their nature, size, and cost, were beyond the resources of any single university (Brookhaven National Laboratory). Indeed, one center of this type (see CERN below) represents the combined effort of a group of European nations to pool their resources and provide the scientific community they represent with a central facility adequate to present-day standards. Certain of the facilities within governmental agencies can be considered to be scientific research centers. The establishment and recent extensive growth of the National Institutes of Health (see below) are a good example of the government's direct response to public pressure to pursue certain fields of science directly, rather than to depend upon and support existing private organizations. It followed that government laboratories, *e.g.* the National Bureau of Standards (see below), would engage in fundamental research in order to provide adequate services in an increasingly technologically based economy. Finally, the role of industrial laboratories should be mentioned. Only a few such laboratories, by the nature of the organization or the specific field of interest (Bell Telephone Laboratories), both pursue fundamental research *and* make their results available to the public or scientific community. However, although much excellent and pioneering work is accomplished in such laboratories, they cannot, by virtue of their private interests, be considered as research centers.

Many of the overseas centers reflect an earlier counterpart in the U. S. A., but also bear witness to different national characters and, in Europe, to the long tradition of direct government support and encouragement of fundamental science. In addition to joining in international efforts such as at CERN, the major European powers have developed their own centers, while some of the smaller countries have formed bilateral establishments (see below: *Jener; Rutherford High Energy Laboratory; Saclay Nuclear Research Center*).

The U. S. S. R. through the all-powerful Academy of Sciences established a center at Dubna and made the facilities available to a group of socialist countries on a membership basis similar to CERN (see *Joint Institute of Nuclear Research*).

Centers in U. S. A.

Rockefeller University, New York City, founded 1901 as the Rockefeller Institute for Medical Research, a philanthropic corporation under the laws of the State of New York and endowed by John D. Rockefeller. Its original purpose was to "conduct, assist and encourage investigations in the sciences and arts of hygiene, medicine and surgery, and allied subjects, in the nature and causes of disease and the methods of its prevention and treatment, and to make knowledge relating to these various subjects available for the protection of the health of the public and the improved treatment of disease and injury." In 1958 the charter was amended to broaden the scope of the Institute's research in certain physical sciences and to grant graduate academic degrees. General control of the Institute and management of endowment, $160 million in 1960, are vested in a Board of Trustees. The institution in 1960 had a faculty of 200, with 100 students and 500 on the supporting staff. In 1965 the name was changed to Rockefeller University. Facilities include laboratories on the main campus in Manhattan, plus research rooms in the Marine Biological Laboratory at Woods Hole, Mass., and the N. Y. Botanical Gardens.

Carnegie Institution of Washington, incorporated 1904 in Washington, D. C., privately endowed, with the following departments: Mount Wilson and Palomar Observatories, Pasadena, Calif.; Geophysical Laboratory, Washington, D. C.; Dept. of Terrestrial Magnetism, Washington, D. C.; Dept. of Plant Biology, Stanford, Calif.; Dept. of Embryology, Baltimore, Md.; Dept. of Genetics, Cold Spring Harbor, N. Y. In 1960, the endowment was $61 million, operating funds $800,000, capital investment $6 million.

Lawrence Radiation Laboratory, Berkeley, Calif., operated under contract between the Univ. of California and U. S. Atomic Energy Commission. E. O. Lawrence originated the cyclotron here in 1930 while he was a member of the staff of the Dept. of Physics, Univ. of California. In 1936, the Radiation Laboratory was established within the Physics Dept. to support the development of accelerators and associated equipment. During World War II, the laboratory resources were employed by the Manhattan District. The present contract has been effective since the establishment of the Atomic Energy Commission under the Atomic Energy Act of 1954, the name being changed after Lawrence's death in 1958. Major facilities include the 60-in. cyclotron (48-Mev alpha particles); the 184-in. (735-Mev proton) synchrocyclotron; the Bevatron, 6.2-Bev proton synchrotron; the 335-Mev synchrotron; and the Hilac (heavy-ion linear accelerator). In 1959, employees totaled 2,200, the annual budget was $16 million, and capital equipment amounted to $31 million.

Jet Propulsion Laboratory, Pasadena, Calif., operated under contract between Calif. Inst. of Technology and the National Aeronautics and Space Administration. The laboratory evolved from work of Dr. Von Karman in the mid-1930s on jet and rocket propulsion as part of the Guggenheim Aeronautical Laboratory of Cal. Tech. The present contractual arrangement dates from 1958. In 1960, its staff numbered 2,500; the operating budget was $69 million and capital investment amounted to $30 million.

Argonne National Laboratory, Lemont, Ill., originated from work done during World War II at the Univ. of Chicago in the development of self-sustaining nuclear reactors under the Manhattan District project. The present Laboratory is operated under a contract between the Univ. of Chicago and the U. S. Atomic Energy Commission. The Laboratory has specialized in reactor science and development and recently has extended its program to include high-energy physics and thermonuclear research. Recently, to insure more widespread cooperation between the Laboratory and the regional universities, the Associated Midwest Universities (A. M. U.) was incorporated to work with the Laboratory's administration, without altering the basic contract with the U. S. Atomic Energy Commission. In 1959, the staff was approximately 3,500, operating costs $35 million, capital investment $100 million.

The National Institutes of Health, Bethesda, Md., the largest biomedical research institution in the U. S. A., is operated directly by the Federal Government under the Dept. of Health, Education and Welfare as the research arm of the Public Health Service. The Institutes are primarily concerned with "fundamental laboratory and clinical research in causes, prevention, and methods of diagnosis and treatment of cancer, cardiovascular and geriatric diseases, allergy and infectious diseases, arthritis and metabolic diseases, dental diseases and conditions, mental illnesses and neurological and sensory diseases." This broad program is carried on by the National Cancer Institute, National Heart Institute, National Institute of Allergy and Infectious Disease, National Institute of Arthritis and Metabolic Diseases, National Institute of Dental Research, National Institute of Mental Health, and National Institute of Neurological Diseases and Blindness. The clinical investigations of these seven Institutes are served by the Clinical Center, a 516-bed research hospital. Each Institute as well as the Division of Research Grants and Division of General Medical Sciences of the Public Health Service administers an extensive program of support via grants-in-aid and training fellowships to many public and private institutions in the U. S. A. and abroad. In 1960, 13,500 research grants, 3,600 training grants, and 4,200 fellowships were awarded. In 1961 the total expenditure of the seven Institutes was about $365,000,000, of which, for example, $86,000,000 was spent on research and training by the National Cancer Institute. Each of the Institutes represents a major scientific center; the entire constellation is a most significant example of direct government support of research.

Brookhaven National Laboratory, Upton, N. Y., operated under a contract between Associated Universities, Inc., and the U. S. Atomic Energy Commission. Associated Universities has held a charter since 1946 under the education laws of the State of New York. Its structure is of special interest, since many recently founded centers have adopted a similar form (the University Corporation for Atmospheric Research and the Associated Universities for Research in Astronomy, as well as CERN on an international scale). The Corporation was formed for the specific purpose of operating a laboratory whose principal objectives were to: "seek new knowledge in the nuclear and other related sciences; encourage appropriate use of its facilities by qualified scientists of university and other laboratories, and industrial research groups; assist the Atomic Energy Commission in the solution of specific problems; aid in the training of scientists and engineers in nuclear science and technology." The corporate affairs are in the hands of a board of trustees consisting of two members nominated by each of nine universities, which initially provided *pro forma* support to the new enterprise. These universities are Columbia, Cornell, Harvard, Johns Hopkins, Mass. Inst. of Tech., Princeton, Univ. of Pennsylvania, Univ. of Rochester, and Yale. At the present time, five additional trustees are appointed at large. A.U.I. also operates the National Radio Astronomy Facility located in Green Bank, W. Va., under a contract with the National Science Foundation.

Brookhaven National Laboratory, L. I., N. Y., engages in research in nuclear and related sciences. Office and laboratory building (*middle left*) and target building (*to its right*) adjoin the new PARTICLE ACCELERATOR (*center front*). The latter, ½ mi in circumference, is in tunnel under 12 ft of earth. (*Brookhaven Nat. Lab.*)

The principal facilities of Brookhaven National Laboratory are a large graphite-moderated research reactor, a reactor for medical research, a number of particle accelerators including the 3-Bev Cosmotron and the 33-Bev Alternating Gradient Synchrotron. In 1959, the staff was approximately 1,800, the total budget $18 million, and the total investment in plant $75 million.

National Bureau of Standards, Washington, D. C., and Gaithersburg, Md. The Bureau has developed into a major research center as a consequence of its mandate "to provide national leadership in the development and use of accurate and uniform techniques of physical measurement." Founded in 1903 by Act of Congress, the Bureau is part of the U. S. Dept. of Commerce. Its activities are organized under institutes for Basic Standards, Materials Research, and Applied Technology. The broad scope of the Bureau's research and services to science, industry, and commerce is indicated by the names of its Divisions: Analytical and Inorganic Chemistry, Applied Mathematics, Atomic Physics, Building Research, Cryogenic Engineering, Data Processing Systems, Electricity, Heat, Instrumentation, Ionosphere Research and Propagation, Mechanics, Metallurgy, Metrology, Mineral Products, Organic and Fibrous Materials, Physical Chemistry, Radiation Physics, Radio Standards, Radio Systems, and Weights and Measures. Measurement standards are provided for such quantities as length, mass, time, volume, temperature, light, color, electrical energy, radioactivity, x-ray intensity, viscosity, and sound and radio frequency. The radio and cryogenic engineering laboratories of the Bureau are located at Boulder, Colorado, and many other field stations are maintained. The Bureau's budget for 1967 was about $32,000,000.

Foreign Centers

CERN (The European Organization for Nuclear Research), at Meyrin, 6 mi from Geneva, Switzerland, initiated by the Convention of European States, consisting in 1960 of the following countries: Austria, Belgium, Denmark, Federal Republic of Germany, France, Greece, Italy, Netherlands, Norway, Sweden, Switzerland, United Kingdom, Yugoslavia; for the purpose of supporting an organization to provide for "collaboration among European States in nuclear research of a pure scientific and fundamental character." The organization is similar in form to Associated Universities, Inc., in that two delegates from each member state form the council of the organization. The principal facilities of the laboratory are a 600-Mev proton synchro-cyclotron, a 28-Bev proton synchrotron, and the associated experimental equipment, such as heavy liquid bubble chambers. In 1960 the total budget was approximately $15 million and the total staff 1,100.

JENER (Joint Establishment for Nuclear Energy Research) is located at Kjeller near Lillestrøm, Norway. It is a joint research and training center sponsored by the Reactor Centrum Nederland of the Netherlands and the Institutt for Atomenergi (IFA) of Norway. The IFA was founded May 30, 1947, to build a nuclear reactor in Norway. The Netherlands, to utilize a quantity of uranium stored from World War II and get under way in nuclear research, agreed to participate in IFA activities beginning in 1951 via *JENER.* An additional facility is the Halden Boiling Heavy Water Reactor, built and financed by IFA, but developed and designed by *JENER.* The pooling of special talents and specific resources of two small nations is noteworthy.

Norwegian-Dutch Joint Establishment for Nuclear Energy Research (JENER): Scientist in his research is using neutrons from JENER's reactor. JENER produces radioactive isotopes for medical and research purposes throughout Scandinavia and other parts of Europe. (*Norwegian Info. Service*)

Rutherford High Energy Laboratory, the first laboratory of the National Institute for Research in Nuclear Science, is adjacent to Harwell, some 60 mi west of London. Harwell is the headquarters and contains the main research facilities of the Research Group of the United Kingdom Atomic Energy Authority. The Authority's primary interest has been in nuclear reactors for plutonium and power production, reactor-materials studies, and isotope production. Six of the U.K.A.E.A.'s 23 reactors in existence in 1960 were at the Harwell facility. Additional equipment includes various medium-energy accelerators. The National Institute was set up in 1957 with the aim of strengthening "the resources of university research departments, not to replace them by a central facility." The first major piece of equipment at the Rutherford Laboratory was a 7-Bev proton synchrotron. The working relationship between Harwell and the Rutherford Laboratory (which are actually separate) is close and broad, the older and much larger Harwell group supplying the bulk of technical assistance and design. The arrangement reflects the need and desire to separate the U.K.A.E.A.'s responsibility to defense and power needs from the Institute's function of widening the nuclear-research resources of universities in Britain, even though the entire complex can be considered as a center.

Saclay Nuclear Research Center was installed by the French Atomic Energy Commission in 1946 near the original Commission laboratories at Fontenay-aux-Roses outside Paris. Equipment includes a 25-Mev cyclotron, a 28-Mev linear electron accelerator, a 3.5-Bev proton synchrotron ("Saturne") which went into service in Aug. 1958, and five nuclear reactors. In 1959 the total staff at SNRC numbered in excess of 3,300. In 1956 the Institute of Nuclear Sciences and Techniques was created at Saclay under the supervision of the National Education Ministry, "to assure, in close cooperation with the universities, highly specialized instruction in the field of nuclear sciences and techniques, designed to complete the training of engineers and technicians." The combination of a

Joint Institute for Nuclear Research: Detlov Bronk, president of Rockefeller Institute, and Wallace Brode (*right*), science consultant to State Department, are being conducted on tour of one of the two synchrotrons at the Soviet Union's Joint Institute at Dubna, 60 mi from Moscow. (*Sovfoto*)

basic research center and a training institute has become a common European device to provide the specialists the new sciences require.

Joint Institute for Nuclear Research: The U. S. S. R. Academy of Sciences operates the Institute for Nuclear Problems at Dubna, a town on the Volga River about 60 mi from Moscow. Among the major facilities is a 205-in. synchrocyclotron, delivering 280-Mev deuterons, which was put into operation in Dec. 1949 and was modified to deliver 680-Mev protons about 1953. A 10-Bev proton synchrotron was brought to full energy in 1957. This machine is similar, except in size, to the proton synchrotron at Lawrence Radiation Laboratory. In addition a pulsed-neutron reactor, heavy-ion cyclotron, and high-speed computers are available.

In the spring of 1956, the Soviet Government sponsored the establishment of the Joint Institute for Nuclear Research at Dubna under an agreement signed in Moscow. That autumn the new institute's charter was approved by the representatives of the governments of Albania, Bulgaria, China, Czechoslovakia, the German Democratic Republic, Hungary, the Korean People's Democratic Republic, Mongolia, Poland, Rumania, the U. S. S. R., and the Democratic Republic of Vietnam. The charter declares that "the institute will devote all its work to the uses of nuclear energy for peaceful purposes only for the good of all mankind."—*R. C. A.*

SCIENTIFIC SOCIETIES AND ACADEMIES: The human impulse to communicate and discuss matters of mutual interest with like-minded men is the basis for the origin of scientific societies and academies. Their roots go back to remote antiquity. Learned societies evolved as schools, museums, lyceums, academies, universities, societies, and congresses. These early associations embraced the whole field of learning.

In classical antiquity, the schools and academies of ancient Greece were essentially associations of scholars, under the leadership of men like Thales (640–546 B. C.), Pythagoras (582–497 B. C.), Plato (427–347 B. C.), and others too numerous to mention, who studied problems in natural science, philosophy, medicine, mathematics, ethics, politics, etc. It is from the "academy" of Plato that the modern term is derived. The famous museum and library of Alexandria provided support for such scholars as Euclid (3d cent. B. C.), Herophilus (c. 335–280 B. C.), and Erasistratus (c. 310–250

B. C.). It is known that there were associations of scholars during the Muslim hegemony over the Mediterranean world, notably at Cordova in Spain.

If we seek the modern roots of scientific societies we must turn first to Italy in the 16th and 17th cents. Here, during the Renaissance, small groups of men interested in experimental science came together to perform experiments and discuss their results. One of the earliest of the societies was the Accademia dei Lincei (the keen or lynx-eyed searchers), founded in Rome in 1603, with Galileo among its members. Although obliged to suspend its meetings because of ecclesiastical opposition, it was revived in 1609 and began publication of its proceedings as the *Gesta Lynceorum,* the first recorded publication of scientific research conducted by a corporate body of scientists. Although this society was dissolved in 1657, another one, equally famous, the Accademia del Cimento (Academy of Experiment), was established in Florence in 1657 under the patronage of Ferdinand II, Grand Duke of Tuscany. Among its members were Viviani and Torricelli, physicists and pupils of Galileo; Borelli, the anatomist; Steno, the Danish anatomist and mineralogist; the embryologist Redi; and Jean-Dominique Cassini, the astronomer. Its record of 10 yr of brilliant scientific activity has been preserved in published form; but this society was also forced out of existence by the Church. Scientific leadership now passed from Italy to England and France, and there associations of scientists were established which have persisted to the present and which provided the pattern for the many societies which exist today.

In England a group of scientific amateurs meeting informally from about 1645 in Oxford (later London) were granted a royal charter by Charles II in 1662 under the name of the Royal Society. Among the original members were John Wilkins, Sir Christopher Wren, Robert Boyle, Henry Oldenburg, and Thomas Willis. One of the principal functions of the new society was the publication of its journal, *Philosophical Transactions.* The organization flourished, and through its journal the scientific community was provided with a ready means of communication. Those who made discoveries in science were encouraged to announce them publicly, and their scientific peers were enabled to experimentally verify, extend, or refute these results. Thus science acquired a mechanism for self-criticism and growth.

In 1666 the French Academy of Sciences was established under the patronage of Louis XIV, and it also grew out of informal meetings of a group of philosophers and mathematicians, including Descartes, Pascal, Gassendi, and Fermat. The example of the Royal Society in London and the new Academy in Paris stimulated the formation of similar societies in other parts of Europe. The Berlin Academy was founded in 1700. Leibniz, its principal organizer, was also instrumental in stimulating Peter the Great of Russia to create the St. Petersburg Academy in 1724.

All over Europe, scientific societies were now springing up; although those of a national character were under royal patronage, many local groups, too, were founded. With the advance of science in the 18th and 19th cents., societies representing the various specialties began to develop. Chemists, astronomers, mathematicians, biologists, geologists, physi-

cians, physiologists, and others organized themselves to provide recognition for the scientific studies of their members, to meet periodically to exchange ideas, to support publications such as journals, to finance explorations or experiments, and to create and support museums and libraries. Many scientific academies were in fact able to build up important scientific libraries at little expense, by exchanging publications with other societies.

As European culture and civilization were transplanted to the New World, learned societies were established there. In the English colonies there were many members of the Royal Society, among them Cotton Mather, the three John Winthrops, Zabdiel Boylston, Benjamin Franklin, David Rittenhouse, John Morgan, and John Mitchell. In 1727 Benjamin Franklin organized a secret literary and scientific society known as the "Junto" which became the predecessor to the American Philosophical Society, established in Philadelphia in 1743 (its headquarters are still there). Election to membership in this society is one of the highest honors which can come to an American or foreign scientist.

The growth of scientific societies in the U. S. A., as elsewhere in the world, has been phenomenal. In 1863, under the spur of the Civil War and to provide a mechanism for scientific advice to the Federal government, the National Academy of Sciences was established in Washington; it has grown greatly in power and influence since its inception. The 19th and 20th cents. saw the founding of such national organizations as the American Academy of Arts and Sciences, the American Physiological Society, the American Statistical Association, the American Society of Civil Engineers, the American Chemical Society, the American Geographical Society, and others. The largest of the national organizations is the American Association for the Advancement of Science (founded 1848), established like its English counterpart, the British Association for the Advancement of Science (1831), to provide a more popular base for the rapidly growing scientific community. As various states were added to the Union, state academies were established; many, like the New York Academy of Science, attained world recognition through their publications.

Within recent years, the burgeoning growth of societies has led to the formation of super-societies to coordinate their activities. Thus in the U. S. A. we find the American Institute of Physics and the American Institute of Biological Societies to coordinate the activities of their constituent groups and promote more effective study of common problems. This same phenomenon has taken place at the international level with the growth of such bodies as the International Council of Scientific Unions, The Hague (1931), International Union of Pure and Applied Chemistry, Paris (1919), International Astronomical Union, Leiden (1919), European Federation of Chemical Engineering, Frankfurt-am-Main (1953). One of the activities of these bodies is to promote international congresses and other meetings to facilitate exchange of ideas among scientists of various nationalities.

Space does not permit discussion of the growth of scientific associations in Latin America, Asia, Africa, and Australia. Nevertheless, their history is comparable to that already outlined. Wherever scientific activity develops, there we will find a society. They have proved themselves potent forces for the increase and diffusion of scientific and technical knowledge among men.

Most of the national academies elect their members on the basis of proven scientific accomplishment, and therefore election is regarded as a form of accolade. Others, such as the American Association for the Advancement of Science and

Scientific society receives patron: Engraving by Sebastien Le Clerc shows meeting of French Academy of Sciences within a few years of foundation, in quarters of library of its patron, Louis XIV. Jean-Baptiste Colbert, leader in mid-17th-cent. French regime, stands hatless in center of picture, with Louis XIV on his right. On King's right are a military leader, the Prince de Condé, and the King's brother, the Duc d'Orléans; behind them, speaking over shoulder, is astronomer Jean-Dominique Cassini. Observatory, in course of construction, has by artist's license been made visible through window. Observatory architect, Claude Perrault, stands behind and between Colbert and King. Huygens, who was on leave in Holland, is not shown. Armillary sphere, burning mirror, fortification map, air pump, stills, and mammalian skeletons bespeak current (1671) interests of members. (*Burndy Library*)

PROMINENT NATIONAL ACADEMIES OF SCIENCE
(with Locations and Dates of Founding)

Austrian Academy of Science (Vienna), 1847

Australian Academy of Science (Canberra), 1954

Royal Academy of Sciences, Letters, and Fine Arts of Belgium (Brussels), 1772

Bulgarian Academy of Sciences (Sofia), 1869

Royal Society of Canada (Ottawa), 1882

Chilean Academy of Natural Sciences (Santiago), 1926

The Academy of Sciences of China (Peking), 1949; (Academia Sinica, 1928, and National Academy of Peking, 1929)

Colombian Academy of the Exact Sciences, Physics, Chemistry, and Natural Sciences (Bogotá), 1871

Academy of Medical, Physical, and Natural Sciences (Havana, Cuba), 1861

Czechoslovak Academy of Sciences (Prague), 1952

The Royal Danish Academy of Sciences and Letters (Copenhagen), 1742

Egyptian Society of Engineers (Cairo), 1920

Finnish Academy of Science (Helsinki), 1908

Finnish Scientific Society (Helsinki), 1838

Académie des Sciences (Paris), 1666

Association Française pour l'Avancement des Sciences (Paris), 1864

German Academy of Sciences (Berlin), 1700

The Royal Society (London), 1660

Royal Society of Edinburgh (Edinburgh, Scotland), 1783

British Association for the Advancement of Science (London), 1831

Hungarian Academy of Sciences (Budapest), 1825

National Academy of Sciences (Allahabad, India), 1930

Royal Irish Academy (Dublin), 1786

Accademia Nazionale dei Lincei (Rome), 1603

Japanese Academy (Tokyo), 1879

National Academy of Science (Mexico City), 1884

Royal Netherlands Academy of Sciences (Amsterdam), 1808

The Norwegian Academy of Science and Letters (Oslo), 1857

Pakistan Association for the Advancement of Science (Lahore), 1947

Polish Academy of Sciences (Warsaw), 1952

Lisbon Royal Academy of Science (Lisbon), 1779

Royal Academy of Exact, Physical and Natural Sciences (Madrid), 1847

Royal Academy of Science (Stockholm, Sweden), 1739

Academy of Sciences of the U. S. S. R. (Moscow), 1725

National Academy of Sciences (Washington, D. C.), 1863

American Philosophical Society (Philadelphia), 1743

American Association for the Advancement of Science (Washington, D. C.), 1848

the British Association, are open to all who are interested. Nevertheless, these groups award the title *Fellow* (as distinct from ordinary membership) in recognition of scientific achievement. The specialized societies and academies usually restrict their membership to those professionally engaged in scientific activity, *e.g.* physics, chemistry, biology, medicine, or engineering.—*M. C. L.*

SCINTILLATION: the emission of light by a material as a charged atomic particle passes through it. The electrical forces between the passing particle and the electrons in the atoms of the material knock some of the electrons into more energetic orbits (see ENERGY LEVEL). But these so-called excited states are short-lived; in less than a millionth of a second the excited electrons fall back into their equilibrium orbits, simultaneously emitting the surplus energy in the form of electromagnetic radiation. Most of the radiation from transitions of this kind is in the frequency range corresponding to visible light. Scintillators are among the most frequently used particle detectors in nuclear-physics laboratories; they come in all sizes and shapes and are made of various materials, including certain organic liquids, plastics, and both organic and inorganic crystals. The light pulses emitted by the line of excited atoms along the track of the projectile are so faint that scintillators could not be exploited as particle detectors until an instrument with extreme sensitivity for light was invented. Such an instrument is the PHOTOMULTIPLIER tube. This consists of a face plate, which is covered with a material that emits electrons when struck by light, and an ELECTRON MULTIPLIER. The latter is a series of metal plates with electric fields in between. The emitted electrons are accelerated from one plate to the next, and dislodge electrons from each successively struck plate. After about eight stages of multiplication, the stream of moving electrons constitutes an electrical current large enough to be measured. Thus a short electrical pulse from the multiplier indicates that a charged particle has passed through the scintillator.

Recently physicists have developed instruments, called *image intensifiers,* that amplify the light pulses from scintillators in an image-preserving way, so that photographs can be taken of the actual track of the charged particle in the scintillator.—*S. K.*

SEABORG, GLENN THEODORE, 1912– , U. S. chemist; b. Ishpeming, Mich. He and his associates, following a path blazed by E. M. McMillan, created plutonium. Seaborg worked on the atomic bomb project 1942–46 and then returned to the creation of additional transuranic elements. His work on phase stability made possible the construction of improved particle accelerators. For their discoveries in

Glenn Theodore Seaborg
(*Wide World*)

the chemistry of the transuranic elements, he and McMillan shared the 1951 Nobel prize. Seaborg joined the Univ. of California faculty in 1937 and was appointed chairman of the U. S. Atomic Energy Commission in 1961. He is a member of the National Academy of Sciences.—*D. H. D. R.*

SEA LEVEL: Maps and charts show heights and depths above and below "sea level" which is, usually, an arbitrary level measured from an existing benchmark. However, the U. S. Coast and Geodetic Survey and other agencies have adopted a definition of "mean sea level" which is the mean of hourly readings of the height of the sea for 19 yr. Readings have been made from the records of a tide gage of efficient design operating continually at a fixed spot during the whole period. Actually, however carefully defined, sea level is an inconstant quantity. At a given point the average sea level for one week differs from that for the next week because of changes in the average barometric pressure. Over a large part of Earth, sea level is higher in the fall (by an amount seldom more than a few inches or a foot) than in the spring. This is chiefly because in summer the water in the upper few hundred feet is warmed and expands; in winter it cools and contracts.

At many shore stations, sea level shows a progressive change over many years. Examples occur in Scandinavia, where the land is rebounding from the glacial load of a few millennia ago and is now rising in the north and sinking in the south. Furthermore, there is a general world-wide rise in sea level as water that was locked up on the land in the form of glacial ice has melted in these warmer times. Locally, sea level may change with respect to the land in response to differential uplift or subsidence of the crust.—*M. S.*

SEASONS: the four divisions of the year, each beginning at the time the Sun crosses an EQUINOX OR SOLSTICE. Because Earth's axis is constantly tilted to the plane of its orbit, the north pole is inclined toward the Sun 23½° on June 21 (the summer solstice for the northern hemisphere); on Dec. 22 (winter solstice for northern hemisphere) the south pole is inclined 23½° toward the Sun. During its summer, each pole has perpetual sunlight, and throughout its hemisphere the day is longer than the night (see DAY AND NIGHT). During the northern hemisphere's winter, the south pole is in perpetual sunlight and the north pole in perpetual darkness; when spring prevails in one hemisphere, autumn is at hand in the other. Changing temperature as seasons change is due to the changing obliquity with which the Sun's rays strike Earth; the greater the obliquity, the less heat they deliver to any given area. Greatest heat is received at the time of the summer solstice, but this time of year is not necessarily the warmest; the maximum average daily temperature is reached about Aug. 1 in mid-northern latitudes, the lag being due largely to accumulation of heat in the atmosphere and oceans. Similarly, the minimum average temperature of mid-northern winter occurs about Feb. 1.

In December, Earth is somewhat nearer the Sun than it is in June, and moves more rapidly in its orbit; hence the southern summer is about 7 days shorter than the northern. Similarly the southern winter is longer than the northern.

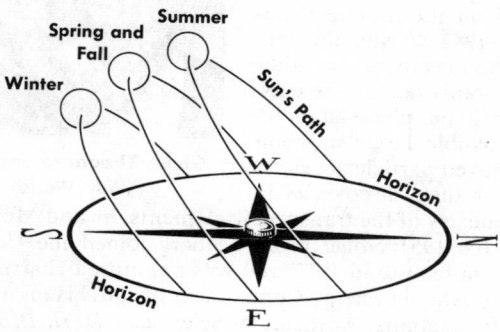

Length of day related to seasons: In northern hemisphere, Sun describes shortest arc in winter, when points of sunrise and sunset are toward south, and longest arc in summer, when points are toward north.

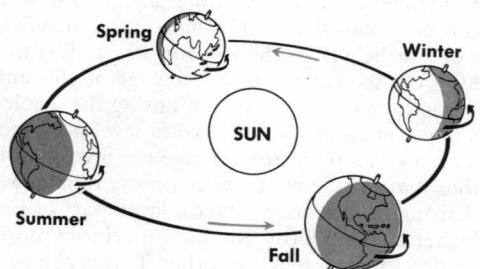

Insolation related to seasons: When a hemisphere is tilted toward Sun (*i.e.* when it has summer), it receives more sunlight than when tilted away from Sun (*i.e.* during its winter). Seasons as named in above diagram are for northern hemisphere; seasons for southern hemisphere are opposite.

Since Earth is nearer the Sun during the southern summer than during the northern summer, more heat is received by the southern hemisphere during its summer, but this effect is counteracted by the existence in the southern hemisphere of larger expanses of ocean. Because of PRECESSION OF THE EQUINOXES, these conditions will be reversed in about 13,000 yr; then perihelion will be reached in June, and the northern summer will be the shorter one.—*R. N. M.*

SEA WATER: see OCEAN.

SECCHI, PIETRO ANGELO, 1818–1878, Italian astronomer; b. Reggio nell' Emilia. His research on spectrum analysis led to the invention of the spectroscope method of using an objective prism. His greatest contributions were in the classification of stars by their spectra (a field in which he pioneered) and in solar physics. His best-known works are *Le Soleil* (1870), *L'Unita della Forze Fisiche* (1869), and *Le Stelle* (1877).—*R. N. M.*

Pietro Angelo Secchi
(Yerkes Observatory)

SECONDARY EMISSION: the emission of electrons from a solid as a result of bombardment by high-energy electrons. For some materials, as many as 12 secondary electrons will be produced for each primary electron striking the solid. Secondary emission is utilized as an ELECTRON MULTIPLIER, particularly in PHOTOMULTIPLIER tubes and in television camera tubes.—*I. R.*

SECONDARY SEXUAL CHARACTERISTICS: body features that differ between male and female, excluding reproductive organs, ducts, and associated glands. Examples are the lower pitch of a man's voice and development of the mammary glands in a woman.—*A. R. D.*

SEDGWICK, ADAM, 1785–1873, English geologist; b. Dent, Yorkshire. He traced the Cambrian system in N Wales (1831–54) and (with Sir R. I. Murchison and W. Lonsdale) the Devonian system in Devon and Cornwall (1839). Sedgwick also made important investigations of the Permian system in N England and the geology of the Lake District. He was Woodwardian professor of geology at Cambridge Univ. (1818–73), where he founded a rich geological museum. A fellow of the Royal Society, he was awarded its Copley medal (1863).—*D. H. D. R.*

SEDIMENT: see SEDIMENTS.

SEDIMENTARY ROCK: rock formed, usually in layers or beds, by consolidation of rock or mineral particles (clastic sediments) or accumulation and compaction of precipitates or solid organic remnants (nonclastic sediments); see SEDIMENTS. Most sediments are deposited under water in layers, consolidation of which over hundreds of thousands of years results in stratified rock. Some wind-deposited sediments also form stratified rock. Other sedimentary rock that is not stratified includes dripstone (precipitates) such as the stalactites and stalagmites of caverns; tillites, formed from unstratified glacial drift; and reefs, which are mounds or beds of organic remains. But most sedimentary rock is stratified, and this characteristic especially distinguishes it from other types of rock.

Layered appearance, due to changes in conditions during deposition of original sediments, characterizes most sedimentary rocks. Red sandstones here formed from erosion debris deposited to depths of thousands of feet; strata have been exposed by subsequent erosion. Site is South Desert, Utah; Henry Mts are in background. *(Josef Muench)*

The usual classification of sedimentary rock is based on its composition and texture. The wind or water transporting clastic material tends to sort it according to size or weight, and to form beds containing a greater part of coarser particles, *e.g.* sand or gravel, or of finer particles, *e.g.* mud or silt. Sand is usually composed of fragments of the mineral quartz, and so is SANDSTONE, the rock formed from cemented beds of sand. *Siltstone* is composed essentially of very fine sand. Mud, and its compacted equivalent, SHALE or *mudstone,* is composed of flaky clay minerals such as kaolinite. CONGLOMERATE, the coarsest of all clastic sedimentary rocks, results from cementation of a deposit of pebbles or cobbles rounded by stream or wave action. BRECCIA is similar to conglomerate, except that the rock fragments are angular.

The major non-clastic types of rock are LIMESTONE and dolomite. Some are formed inorganically by direct precipitation of calcium carbonate, and some have an organic origin, being composed of the accumulated skeletons and shells of organisms. Chalk is composed largely of the very small shells of foraminifera, and coquina of fragments of mollusk shells. Much limestone is composed of consolidated calcium carbonate sand or mud formed by the break-up of shell fragments. Sediments are, however, rarely composed of a single type of rock particles, and the rock derived from sediments is seldom "pure" sandstone, shale, or limestone, but a composite in which one or another mineral prevails. Thus a sandstone with considerable clayey minerals is called argillaceous (clayey) sandstone; one with an admixture of lime is called calcareous (limy).

Beds usually are deposited atop one another, with a fairly clear surface of demarcation—a "bedding plane." A change in the character of the sediments, delineated by the bedding plane, is caused by a change in the conditions of sedimenta-tion. For example, heavy rainfall may bring a flood which carries sediment of a size and weight greater than normal to a given distance beyond the mouth of a river; this might account for a layer of conglomerate between beds of sandstone at this site, and, somewhat farther offshore, a layer of sandstone between beds of shale. A climatic change, or a change in the level of the ocean floor, may make it possible for certain marine organisms to flourish here and leave a record of their existence in the form of limey deposits, which a later change may cause to be covered with silt; thus limestone may appear under shale. Usually a thick bed indicates a stable environment over a long period of time, while thin beds indicate frequent change. In a few places, usually the bottoms of glacial lakes, seasonal deposits of silt or mud have accumulated year after year, resulting in layers each measured in fractions of an inch. Such layers, or laminations, are called "varves."

Layers of sediment are deposited in essentially horizontal strata, but crustal movements tilt, fold, and break the beds, so that few are found in their original horizontal position. However, even folded and faulted beds do not offer insurmountable obstacles to the geologist, who is usually able to reconstruct the order in which the strata lay before they were deformed. The most difficult task has been to relate series of beds, or formations, in one locality to series in other localities, and so to extend the record of sedimentation over a significantly large area (see STRATIGRAPHY). This process (correlation) is made possible chiefly by another characteristic of sedimentary rock: the presence of fossils. A bed containing certain key or index fossils (remains of organisms that had only a brief period of existence) is assumed to be of about the same age as formations elsewhere that contain identical fossils. Thus a master geological time-table was gradually

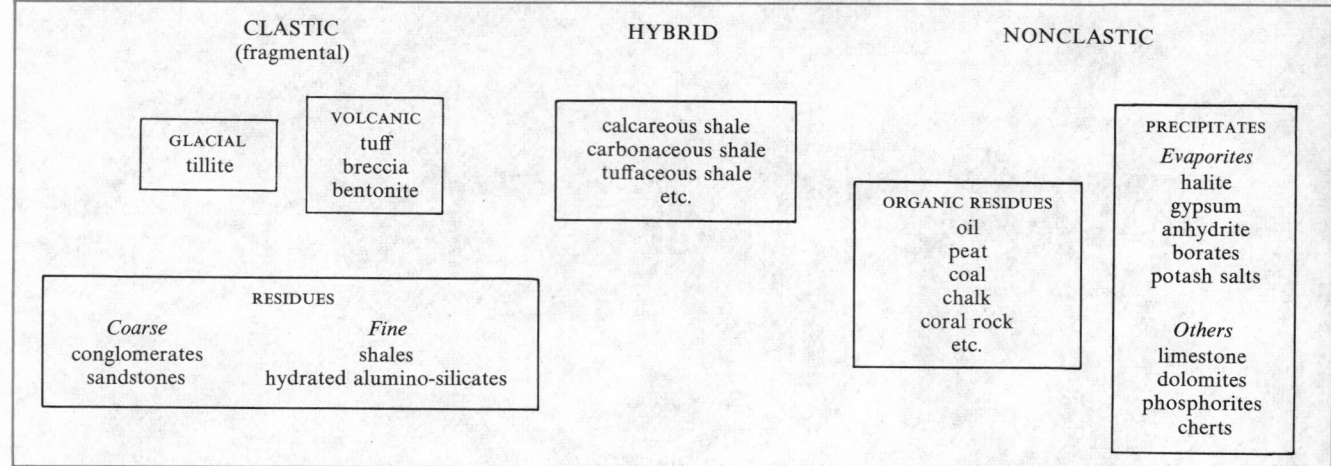

	CLASTIC (fragmental)	HYBRID	NONCLASTIC

GLACIAL
tillite

VOLCANIC
tuff
breccia
bentonite

calcareous shale
carbonaceous shale
tuffaceous shale
etc.

RESIDUES

Coarse
conglomerates
sandstones

Fine
shales
hydrated alumino-silicates

ORGANIC RESIDUES
oil
peat
coal
chalk
coral rock
etc.

PRECIPITATES

Evaporites
halite
gypsum
anhydrite
borates
potash salts

Others
limestone
dolomites
phosphorites
cherts

prepared to which formations in various parts of the world could be keyed.

Although most sediments are deposited under the sea, crustal movements may eventually raise them above water; indeed, about three-fourths of the rock at the earth's surface is of sedimentary origin. This means that most of the present land area of the earth has been submerged at one time. The greater part of this sedimentary rock—almost half—is shale; about one-third is sandstone; less than one-fourth is limestone; and only about 1% of all sedimentary rock is conglomerate or one of the minor types, which include the evaporites, coal, and certain iron ores, *e.g.* limonite. See Color Plate 77.—*E. A.*

SEDIMENTATION (in chemistry): the process whereby solid particles or cells suspended in a medium of different density (usually a liquid) tend to move in the direction of a gravitational field, or settle out. Sedimentation is an extremely useful tool of biological and biochemical research. If the particles or cells are large enough, as red cells are, they will sediment readily on standing. If they are smaller (*e.g.* proteins and other giant molecules), gravity can be helped along by high-speed centrifugation in the ultracentrifuge. This instrument can reach a speed of 60,000 rev/min, and a force equivalent

Running water is the chief agency by which erosion occurs on land, and it is also the chief means by which sediments are transported to lower and lower levels. (*Union Pacific*)

to 290,000 times gravity. Some ultracentrifuges have a viewing system which allows observation of the sedimenting molecules in motion. Since the rate of sedimentation depends on the size and shape of the molecules as well as the density of the medium, it can be used to calculate the molecular weight of the sedimenting particles and molecules. Ultracentrifuge experimentation also provides information about the homogeneity of the suspended material. Differential centrifugation of minced tissue allows separation and sedimentation of cell nuclei, MITOCHONDRIA, and MICROSOMES. For sedimentation in geology, see SEDIMENTS.—*F. F.*

SEDIMENTS (in geology): particles of mineral or organic debris carried or deposited by water, wind, or glacial ice. Clastic sediments (Greek *klastos,* broken) are solid fragments derived from the disintegration of igneous, metamorphic, or sedimentary rock through weathering and erosion. Most sediments are clastic, and may be graded according to approximate size, as shown in the Wentworth scale (see table), adopted by many geologists. *Nonclastic sediments* may be produced by precipitation from a solution (water carrying dissolved salts); or they may be composed of the massed skeletons, shells, or other remains of organisms.

Clastic Sediments: These particles are transported from sites where they were formed in processes of erosion and are deposited at new sites. They may be carried by glacial action or by wind, but running water is the principal carrier. Washed by rain or falling by gravity into a stream, the sediments are carried in suspension or as bedload to a lower site. The size of the fragments and the velocity of the stream determine when deposition occurs. Fine particles, *e.g.* clay or silt, are most easily borne by running water and are the last to settle. Only a river under flood conditions can move large boulders. Between these extremes are the sand grains, pebbles, and cobbles, carried from the highlands to ever lower ground, and constantly decreasing in size because of abrasion. All are eventually deposited as sediment: terrestrial sediment on the bed of a lake or river, or marine sediment on the ocean floor. Most clastic sediment reaching the sea does not reach the depths, but is deposited on the surface of the continental shelf adjoining the coastline, or in shallows, *e.g.* the Baltic Sea or Hudson Bay. Wave and current action, eroding the coasts, also yields clastic marine sediments.

Streams tend to sort their load as they travel seaward. Other things being equal, gravel settles first, then sand, and last of all silt and mud, as a stream loses velocity; this happens at times after floods, or as the stream enters a lake or sea. A seasonal or climatic increase in rainfall may cause a layer of sand to sweep over a bed of mud. Shore currents and coastal topography are other factors which influence the abundance and distribution of marine sediments. Thus the layers of sediment do not form a simple pattern of mud over sand over gravel, as might be expected, but have infinite variety. Geologists may infer the history of a stream's flow, and even the climate of its drainage basin far inland, from the order of the beds in its delta.

Clastic sediments are also transported by wind and by glacial action. Only particles of the size of sand grains or smaller are carried any distance by wind, but extremely fine particles—dust—may be swept around the world and are deposited universally. Wind (aeolian) deposits are also sometimes graded by size: heavier accumulations form sand dunes; and the masses of dust which collect in certain areas form LOESS deposits. The sediments resulting from glacial action (drift) include: rock particles pushed ahead or along the sides of moving ice, as moraines; the debris carried within or atop the ice mass and deposited as the ice melts; and particles carried and then deposited by the melt-waters of the glacier. Only the last kind of deposits, glacial outwash, is likely to be graded; the unsorted glacial sediments are called till. Another source of clastic sediment is volcanic action; its products are distinguished from weathered particles under the name of PYROCLASTICS. While these are not usually graded, since the matter ejected from a single volcano may range in size from huge "bombs" to fine "ash," protracted volcanism in one locality may result in the repeated scattering of ash over a body of water, where it settles to form a bed of sediment (bentonite). Conversely, the existence of bentonite indicates previous volcanism in the vicinity.

CLASSIFICATION OF SEDIMENTS
(Wentworth Scale)

Name	Diameter of Particle
Clay	Less than $\frac{1}{256}$ mm.
Silt	$\frac{1}{256}$ to $\frac{1}{16}$
Sand	$\frac{1}{16}$ to 2
Granule	2 to 4
Pebble	4 to 64
Cobble	64 to 256
Boulder	over 256

Nonclastic Sediments: Precipitated (crystalline) sediments result when a solution becomes supersaturated and the salts are crystallized out. This happens during the evaporation of a body of water (*e.g.* a playa lake), usually because of climatic factors. The salts thus deposited (EVAPORITES) include halite (sodium chloride, or common salt), calcite (calcium carbonate), gypsum (hydrous calcium sulphate), and several others, either separately or in combination. Chemical change and evaporation account for the formation of stalactites and stalagmites (calcite formations) in caverns and for the deposits of tufa (also calcite) and sinter (silica) in the vicinity of hot springs and geysers.

The most important nonclastic sediments are those formed by the accumulation of vast numbers of shells and skeletons of marine organisms, from the microscopic foraminifera whose remains comprise chalk to the shellfish whose fragments form coquina. Both are essentially calcite, as are the skeletons of the coral that form great reefs in tropical seas. The prevalence of any of these sediments, or of marine limestone formations derived from them, is considered evidence of the previous existence on that site of relatively warm and still bodies of water, in which such organisms could flourish. The ocean depths are covered with ooze, composed of organic sediment,

along with fine red clay, probably of aeolian or volcanic origin. Another type of organic sediment, entirely terrestrial, is formed by the decay of vegetation, accumulated rather than deposited, in great swamps that were later covered by clastic sediments. Such accumulations become peat, then lignite, before they are transformed by compaction into the rock called coal.

Rock Formation: Sedimentation varies according to the material deposited and the depositing agent. Where grading occurs, beds or strata are formed. The sediments, at first unconsolidated, adhere to one another under pressure of their own weight, closing the pore spaces or interstices. This process (compaction) is particularly effective with fine-grained deposits, *e.g.* clay and most organic sediments. In the case of sand or gravel deposits, consolidation (CEMENTATION) is generally the result of precipitation of calcite, silica, or iron oxides from circulating solutions. These are the two main processes of LITHIFICATION by which sediments are transformed into SEDIMENTARY ROCK. See Color Plate 76.—*E. A.*

SEED: a specialized reproductive structure of a seed plant. In the group of seed plants known as GYMNOSPERMS, including the conifers, seeds are borne on the surfaces of the scales of seed cones; in the angiosperms, or FLOWERING PLANTS, seeds are enclosed by the fruit. A seed develops from a ripened ovule in the ovary of a flower, after the egg cell within the ovule has been fertilized. A typical seed consists of seed coat, endosperm tissue, and embryo. The *seed coat,* or surface structure, varies in thickness from the thin, papery covering

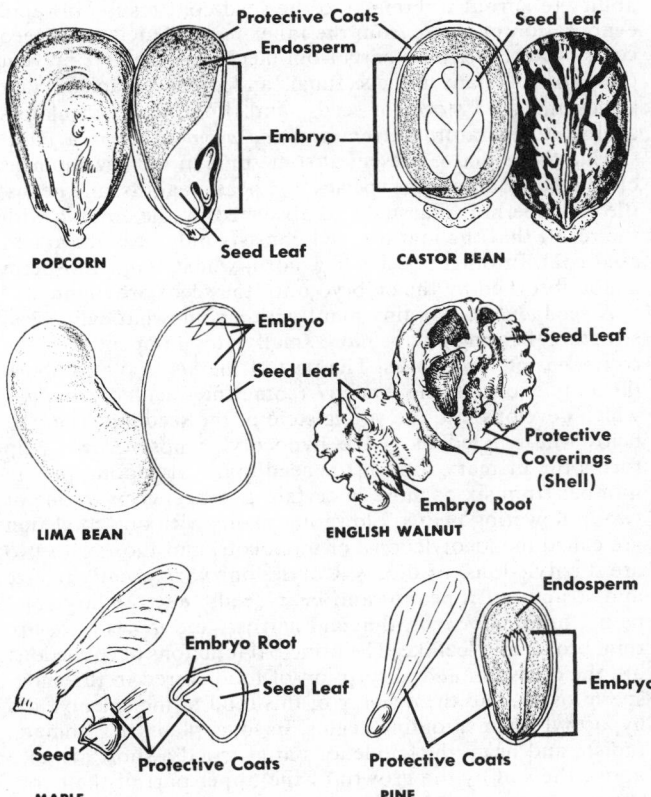

Kinds of seeds: A seed consists essentially of an embryo; endosperm, or food-storage tissue; and a protective outer covering, or testa. The endosperm, which may be digested and absorbed by the embryo either before or during germination, furnishes nourishment for growth of the seed leaf, or cotyledon. (*From Young*)

Seed-dispersal mechanisms: *Left*—Colorful fruits of magnolia are eaten by birds and carried to new locations, where the seeds, unharmed, are dropped in the birds' excreta. *Center*—Seeds of *Ailanthus,* the tree of heaven, are encased in flattened "wings," which facilitate dispersal by wind. *Right*—Spine-covered fruits of cocklebur attach to fur of passing animals and to human clothing, and are thus dispersed. (*Watson/From Monkmeyer; Rutherford Platt; Hugh Spencer*)

of a pea to the thick, hard covering of certain water-lily seeds. The major function of most seed coats is apparently the retention of moisture within the seed. Many seeds lose their ability to sprout if damage to the seed coat results in rapid evaporation of water from the inner parts. Thick, hard seed coats protect the inner parts from mechanical injury; prevent the entry of many insects, fungi, and other organisms that attack the food stores of seeds; and often act as insulators against temperature extremes. *Endosperm tissue* is a food-storing tissue that is present at some time in the development of all seeds. But in some species, *e.g.* peas, peanuts, and beans, the endosperm is digested and absorbed by the embryo with the result that the mature seed consists only of embryo and seed coat. In other species (*e.g.* corn, wheat) the endosperm is not absorbed by the embryo until the seeds are planted.

A seed *embryo* is a tiny plant with a somewhat cylindrical structure, bearing one or more small, lateral appendages, the *cotyledons* or seed leaves. The part of the embryo axis above the cotyledons is the *epicotyl* (sometimes called *plumule*), which develops into the young stem of the seedling. The part below the cotyledons is the hypocotyl, whose growing tip forms the primary root of the seedling. Cotyledons vary in number from six or more in certain gymnosperms to one or two in flowering plants. Flowering plants with one cotyledon are called monocotyledons, or monocots, and those with two are dicotyledons, or dicots. Cotyledons vary greatly in size and structure. In peanut and bean seeds they are large and fleshy; in tomato seeds, thin and narrow; and in castor beans, thin, broad, and leaflike. The principal functions of cotyledons are the digestion and absorption of food stored in the endosperm tissue, and the delivery of this food to the epicotyl and hypocotyl when sprouting begins. In some plants, *e.g.* tomato, radish, and bean, the cotyledons are carried a short distance above the soil by the growth of the upper part of the hypocotyl; these cotyledons serve as the first leaves of the young plant, manufacturing its food by PHOTOSYNTHESIS.

Seed dispersal in milkweed: Filamentous plumes attached to each seed form parachute by which seeds are wind-borne to new locations. (*Hugh Spencer*)

Dormancy: Seeds of many plants pass through a period of rest before they can sprout. This phenomenon, called dormancy, often is advantageous in that it keeps seeds in an inactive, resistant condition during cold weather or drought. Dormancy may result from several causes: the embryo may be immature when the seed is shed by the parent plant and thus may require a period for development into a mature embryo before sprouting; the seed coat may be so strong and hard that it prevents the emergence of the embryo until the coat is gradually eroded by soil acids or by alternate freezing and thawing; the embryo may require the completion of certain chemical changes before it can sprout; or the seed coat may be temporarily impervious to water or oxygen or both. When the causative condition disappears, the seed will sprout if environmental conditions are favorable.

Longevity: As they age, all seeds lose their viability, or ability to sprout. Some orchid seeds retain their viability for only a few weeks, whereas seeds of Indian lotus have remained viable for more than 300 yr. Seeds lose their viability because of several factors: exhaustion of food reserves through respiration over a period of years; desiccation of the embryo;

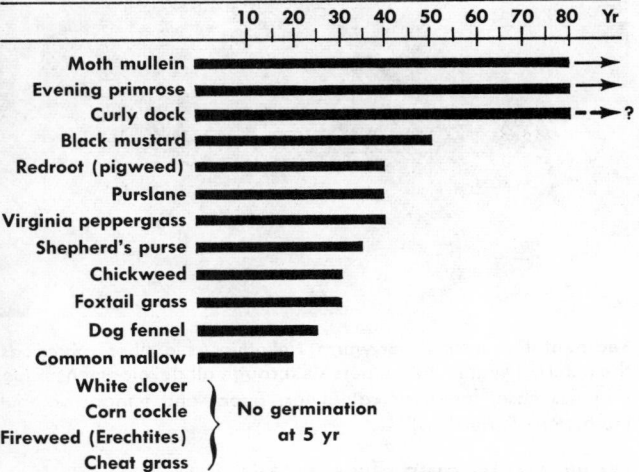

	10 20 30 40 50 60 70 80 Yr
Moth mullein	████████████████████████ →
Evening primrose	███████████████████████ →
Curly dock	█████████████████████████ - → ?
Black mustard	███████████████
Redroot (pigweed)	████████████
Purslane	████████████
Virginia peppergrass	████████████
Shepherd's purse	███████████
Chickweed	██████████
Foxtail grass	██████████
Dog fennel	█████████
Common mallow	████████
White clover	⎫
Corn cockle	⎬ No germination
Fireweed (Erechtites)	⎪ at 5 yr
Cheat grass	⎭

Longevity of seeds is subject of continuing experiment begun in 1879 by the late W. J. Beal of Michigan Agricultural College (now Michigan State Univ.). Beal mixed seeds of various plant species in sand, buried them in soil in inverted open bottles. Every 5 (later 10) yr a bottle has been dug up and its seeds have been tested for ability to germinate. After 80 yr, 80% of moth mullein, 10% of evening primrose, and 2% of curly dock seeds showed germination. Longevities of other seeds are given in chart. (*From Cronquist*)

coagulation of protoplasmic proteins; and failure of normal cell division. The longevity of seeds is increased by cool, dry conditions and decreased by warm, moist weather.

Germination: Seed sprouting, or germination, occurs when environmental conditions—particularly temperature, moisture, and oxygen—are favorable. For most seeds, the best temperatures for germination lie between 75° and 85°, although some seeds, *e.g.* barley grains, sprout at temperatures approaching 32°F. Seeds of most plants require a fairly large amount of moisture for germination. However, too much moisture, by preventing adequate aeration, may cause seeds to rot. The seeds of many water plants, such as water lilies and certain rushes, germinate best in very wet soil or under water. But the seeds of some desert plants germinate when the soil is slightly moist and may not germinate if the soil is very wet. Oxygen is necessary in considerable quantities for the germination of most seeds, except those of certain water plants that require little oxygen. Most seeds need not be covered by soil to germinate, but will sprout even in distilled water, since they contain enough food to nourish their

Germination of lima-bean seed, a dicotyledonous seed without endosperm, begins with downward growth of hypocotyl, lower part of which becomes taproot. Upper part lengthens, arches, and pulls two cotyledons and epicotyl out of ground. Cotyledons become first food-making leaves of plant. (*After Kenoyer*)

Epicotyl

Cotyledons

Hypocotyl

embryos through the early stages of germination. The continued growth of seedlings to maturity, however, is possible only if the plants can absorb mineral nutrients from the soil.

When conditions are right for germination, seeds absorb water and swell in size. As water content increases, so does physiological activity. Digestion of stored foods begins, and respiration (the release of energy through the oxidation of foods) increases, rendering energy available for growth. Cell division takes place, especially at the tips of the epicotyl and hypocotyl. The swelling of the seed ruptures the seed coat, and the embryo starts to emerge. The first part to grow out in most seeds is the hypocotyl tip, which forms the primary root. The early establishment of a root system helps the seedling by anchoring it firmly in the soil and ensuring the development of an absorption system that delivers much-needed water to the growing seedling. The epicotyl grows upward to form the stem of the seedling.

Dispersal: Many seeds have structural devices that promote their distribution. Seeds of milkweed have a tuft of hairs that causes the seeds to float considerable distances on air currents. Seeds of catalpas have flat, broad wings that give buoyancy and aid their dispersal by breezes. Some seeds, *e.g.* those of raspberry, are enclosed by pulpy, sweet ovary tissue that is eaten by animals, through whose digestive canals the seeds pass unharmed, to be cast out with the feces. In some plants the fruits have surface hooks, barbs, and bristles that fasten the fruits to the fur of passing animals and thus "hitch a ride" to new locations. The fruits of touch-me-not and oxalis explode when touched, throwing seeds several feet.

Economic Importance: Seeds are of vital importance to man for many reasons. They are the chief vehicle for the propagation of plants. They furnish food for man and for many animals important to man. They supply oils used in paints, soaps, oleomargarine, and other products; furnish medicinal substances (*e.g.* castor oil); are the source of beverages (*e.g.* coffee, cocoa); and are used for flavoring (*e.g.* nutmeg, mustard, anise). See Color Plate 78.—*A. P. E.*

SEED PLANT: any plant that characteristically reproduces by means of SEEDS. More than 250,000 species of seed plants have been given names; they comprise approximately two-thirds of the species in the plant kingdom. Until about 1915, when a different CLASSIFICATION of plants became widely adopted, botanists regarded the seed habit as so important that seed plants were given the rank of a phylum (Spermatophyta) in the plant kingdom. Now they are grouped with the ferns as leafy plants (subphylum Pteropsida) among vascular plants (phylum Tracheophyta), but are separated from ferns (class Filicinae) and divided into two very unequal groups: the GYMNOSPERMS (class Gymnospermae, with about 630 species) and the FLOWERING PLANTS (class Angiospermae, with about 250,000 species). Seeds of gymnosperms are exposed, whereas seeds of flowering plants are hidden within a FRUIT.

In all seed plants, the gametophyte generation in the regular ALTERNATION OF GENERATIONS is reduced to microscopic dimensions, and the male gametophytes develop independently of female gametophytes. Male gametophytes develop within POLLEN grains, which are small and easily transported to the general vicinity of the female gametophytes. Each female gametophyte develops within an *ovule* wall (megaspore wall), which later becomes the *seed coat*. In all instances the ovules remain attached to the parent plant until the fertilized egg cell in the female gametophyte has had a chance to develop through embryonic stages to become a seed. In some cycads and in the maidenhair tree (*Ginkgo*), the seed coat is fleshy and resembles a fruit; usually, however, the

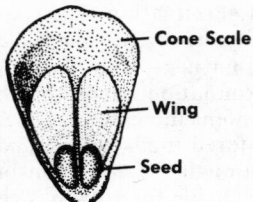

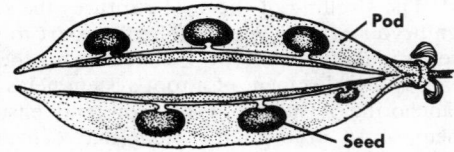

The two classes of seed plants are distinguished, in part, by their modes of seed bearing. *Left*—Seeds of pine, a gymnosperm, are naked. *Below*—Seeds of bean, an angiosperm, are protected by a pod, or ripened carpel. (*From Kenoyer*)

Segmentation in corn-ear worm, *Heliothis:* As in other arthropods, the external segmentation persists through all development stages—in this case, larva, or caterpillar; pupa; and imago, or adult moth. (*Ross E. Hutchins*)

seed coat is hard and drought-resistant, enabling the plant to bridge a dry season before the dormant embryo within the seed begins germinating. Neither cycads with fleshy seeds nor *Ginkgo* shows a resting stage in seed development; instead, their embryos proceed at once to become seedlings. Flowering plants today comprise so many species largely because ancestral seed plants had the evolutionary advantage of possessing seeds that could go through a resting (dormant) stage during regular seasons unfavorable to germination and growth of seedlings.—*L. and M. M.*

SEEING: in astronomy, the quality of a telescopic image as determined by atmospheric conditions rather than instrumental effects. Although seeing is affected by dust and moisture in the air, it depends mostly upon the manner in which the light from celestial objects is refracted by the atmosphere. The light travels at somewhat different speeds through air layers of differing densities; hence it follows a more or less zigzag course through the atmosphere before reaching the telescope, and the resulting telescopic image tends to "dance," "boil," and even vary in color. The nearer the celestial object is to the horizon, the greater the refractive effects are likely to be; also, these effects tend to be stronger in winter than in summer. Standard scales of seeing, usually from 1 (very poor) to 10 (perfect), correspond to the appearance of a diffraction pattern of an out-of-focus image as seen with a standard magnification in a telescope of definite size. Since atmospheric conditions thus put an absolute limit on telescope performance, observatories must be located where the conditions are known to be good. In the future, telescope-carrying satellites will be a means of avoiding atmospheric interference altogether.—*J. W.*

SEGMENTATION: the subdivision of an animal's body into a series of basically similar units, often separated by crosswise partitions, as in the body of earthworms (see WORMS) or of ARTHROPODS. The word is used also for the process by which a fertilized egg undergoes its first few cell divisions or cleavages.—*L. and M. M.*

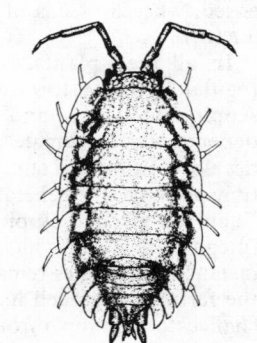

Sow bug, *Oniscus,* demonstrates conspicuous external segmentation characteristic of all arthropods. (*From Guyer*)

SEGRÈ, EMILIO GINO, 1905– , Italian-U. S. physicist; b. Tivoli, Italy. For the production and identification of the antiproton, he and Owen Chamberlain shared the 1959 Nobel prize. Segrè is a member of the National Academy of Sciences. —*D. H. D. R.*

SEISMIC WAVES: a generic term for elastic waves in Earth: compressional (dilatational, irrotational primary, or P) waves, with the highest velocity and a particle motion in the direction of propagation; shear (transverse, rotational, equivoluminal, or S) waves, with lower velocity and a particle motion perpendicular to the direction of propagation; and surface waves, having the lowest velocity, distinguished by an exponential decrease of amplitude with depth. Compressional and shear waves are "body" waves, in that they propagate in the interior of Earth; surface waves are confined to and propagate along an interface, either the surface or one or more internal discontinuities; shear waves are further resolved into two components, in the plane of, and perpendicular to, Earth's surface (SH and SV waves). Generally, the velocities

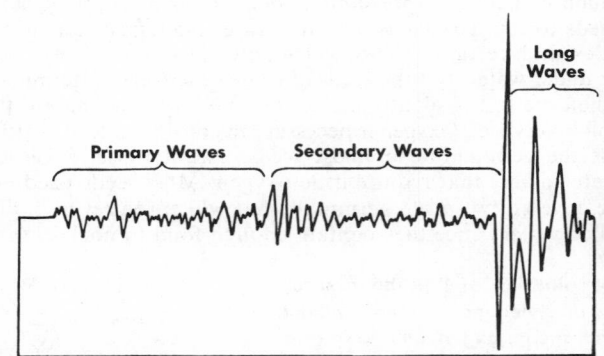

Earthquake waves: Primary waves arrive from epicenter first, then secondary waves, and finally long waves. Amplitude of the long waves, and hence their destructiveness, is great. (*After Garrels*)

of both body waves increase with depth in Earth. The dependence of body-wave velocities on density is approximately linear. P-wave velocities range from about 2 km/sec for some sedimentary rocks to 8 km/sec for high-density minerals; corresponding velocities for S-waves are approximately 1.2 to 4.7 km/sec.

Body waves in Earth are non-dispersive—their velocity of propagation is independent of wavelength; surface waves, because of the layered structure of Earth, are dispersive, the longer wavelengths penetrating deeper to higher-velocity rock and therefore traveling at a higher velocity. Heterogeneity of the crust produces refraction, scattering, and diffraction of seismic body waves. The refraction process obeys Snell's law (see REFRACTION); the scattering and diffraction processes are analogous to those encountered in optics. Surface waves are of two types. In Rayleigh surface waves, particle motion traces a vertical ellipse in the plane of propagation; while in Love waves, particle motion is entirely transverse.

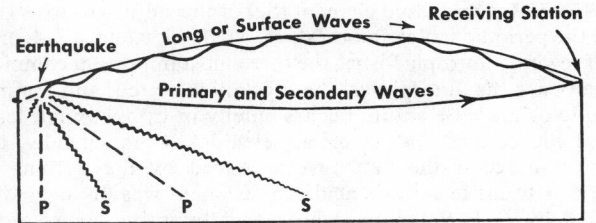

Seismic waves: Primary and secondary waves radiate in all directions from earthquake center. Those reaching surface become long, or surface, waves. The latter waves cause the physical devastation associated with earthquakes. (*After Garrels*)

Seismic waves are produced by natural and artificial sources. Among the former are EARTHQUAKES, large atmospheric-pressure disturbances, and storms at sea; the latter include explosions on or beneath the surface, automotive and rail traffic, and reciprocating machinery. Seismic waves are recorded by SEISMOGRAPHS, and are used in SEISMOLOGY to study internal structure and physical properties of Earth, mechanisms of earthquake occurrence, and location of earthquakes and explosions.—*Sa. K.*

SEISMOGRAPH: an instrument for detecting and recording SEISMIC WAVES. Seismograph systems generally consist of three components: an electro-mechanical transducer (often called seismometer) for converting mechanical motion of the ground into an electrical signal, suitable for transmission over some distance; another transducer (with amplifier if necessary) for converting the transmitted signal to a mechanical motion suitable for recording; and a recorder. Seismometers in general use differ in the component of ground motion to which the instrument is designed to respond, the type of suspension, and the type of electrical transducer used.

The motion of the ground produced by any disturbance may be resolved into three components: vertical, east-west, and north-south. Measurement of these three components permits a complete description of the motion of the ground. Most existing seismometers respond to one of these components and, accordingly, may be described as vertical or horizontal seismometers. Most seismometers consist of a mass suspended from a frame which is fixed to the ground. The combined mechanical system consisting of the mass and suspension has a resonant frequency comparable with the frequency of the waves to be detected. In an oscillating spring-supported mass or a pendulum the mass moves with respect to the support; in a seismometer, the mass remains stationary (because of its inertia) and the frame, fixed to the ground, moves with respect to the mass. In a vertical seismometer, the suspension usually consists of a coiled spring or leaf-springs so situated as to prevent relative lateral motion between mass and frame. A horizontal seismometer usually consists of a mass fixed to a rigid lateral boom supported by a fine wire from the frame. The mass and boom are free to move laterally, but not vertically. A wide variety of seismometers have been built for different purposes, including detection of large ground motions in active earthquake zones and in blast-effect

studies; the detection of very long-period ground motions; and seismic exploration requiring small, light-weight instruments. Based on an entirely different principle is the linear-strain seismometer, which consists of a long horizontal tube of fused quartz, which has a very small coefficient of thermal expansion. The tube is fixed to the ground at one end and free to move at the other end. A suitable transducer measures the motion of the free end of the tube, relative to the ground. This motion is proportional to the earth strain produced by SEISMIC WAVES.

Various types of transducers to convert the motion of the ground into an electrical signal have been used. Those in common use include a moving-coil electromagnetic system, in which a coil of many wire-turns is attached to the inertial mass, while a strong magnet is attached to the case. Relative motion between coil and magnet induces a voltage in the coil which is a measure of the ground motion. A variable-reluctance transducer consists of a permanent magnet which supplies magnetic flux across two or four air gaps to an armature around which is wound a wire coil. One of these two elements is attached to the frame, which is fixed to the ground; while the other element is attached to the mass. Relative motion between the two changes the lengths of the air gaps, the reluctance of the magnetic circuit, and the magnetic flux through the armatures, and thus produces an electromotive force in the coils surrounding the armatures. Another type of transducer consists of an electrical condenser with one plate attached to the frame and the other plate attached to the mass. Relative motion produces variations in capacitance and voltage which are suitably amplified and transmitted.

The electrical signal from the seismometer transducer is transmitted to a receiving transducer, which usually consists

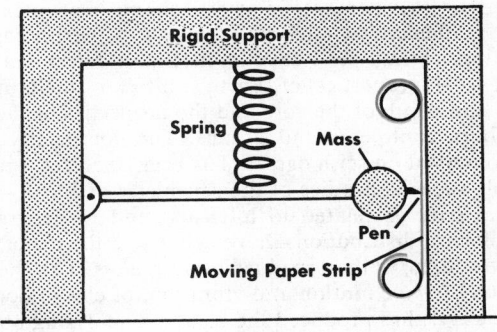

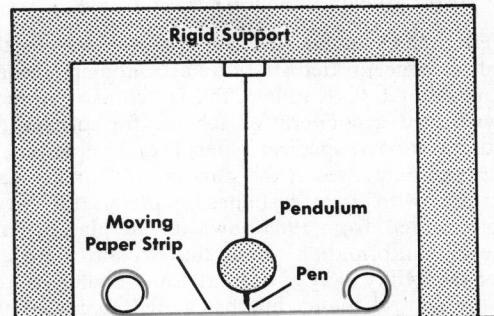

Seismographs: Schematic diagrams of vertical-movement (*top*) and horizontal-movement (*below*) types. In both, the earthquake causes displacement of rigid support with respect to a suspended mass, and this displacement is recorded by a pen on a moving paper strip or by similar means.

of a galvanometer, deflecting a light beam, or an amplifier controlling the motion of a recording pen. The output, which is a direct indication of the displacement, velocity, or acceleration of the motion of the ground, is obtained on photographic paper or film, or written on paper by a pen.

The important parameters which determine the response of a complete seismograph system are its magnification, or ratio of recorded motion to ground motion, and the range of frequencies over which the complete system responds, relative to frequencies present in the ground motion.—*Sa. K.*

SEISMOLOGY: the science which deals with the occurrence, location, and properties of EARTHQUAKES; the generation, propagation, and effects of SEISMIC WAVES produced by natural and artificial sources; and the theory, design, construction, and operation of SEISMOGRAPHS, used to record seismic waves. Geologic observations indicate that Earth has been subjected to earthquakes for at least several hundred million years. References to earthquakes and their causes appear in the mythologies of the ancient Greeks, in the Old Testament, and in the writings of ancient Egypt. The Greek philosophers, especially Aristotle and Lucretius, had well-defined theories for the origin of earthquakes; Aristotle devised a system for classifying earthquakes according to the ground motion produced. The Chinese in A. D. 132 devised an instrument for indicating the direction of first motion. By the middle of the 18th cent., useful observations were becoming available; early in the 19th, lists of earthquakes were published on a regular basis. In 1840 the first world catalog of earthquakes appeared, and by 1900 a world-wide network of stations was in operation. During the 19th cent. the groundwork was laid for the mathematical analysis of elastic wave propagation. The properties of various types of SEISMIC WAVES were predicted from theory, and many waves were identified on seismograms. The 20th cent. has seen great advances and refinements in SEISMOGRAPH instrumentation, and in mathematical analysis of elastic wave propagation. Seismological data have been applied to a determination of the physical properties of Earth's interior, including the fluidity and depth of the core and the properties of the crust, under both continents and oceans. The complexity of the waves observed on seismograms has been analyzed with considerable success. Studies of the seismicity of Earth—earthquake activity as related to intensity, and to geographical and geological distribution—have delineated the major global TECTONIC features that produce earthquakes. The theory of elasticity, of wave motion and vibration, of elastic body and surface waves, has produced the basis for analyzing observed seismic waves and for predicting and interpreting certain seismic waves difficult to identify.—*Sa. K.*

SELECTED AREAS: areas, evenly distributed over the sky, selected for concentrated study by astronomers according to the proposal of J. C. Kapteyn, the Dutch astronomer, 1904. Kapteyn urged a cooperative scheme for measurement of magnitudes, colors, spectral types, radial velocities, proper motions, and parallaxes of the stars in these areas. Kapteyn's scheme met with great response; many useful, large-scale catalogs resulted, from 1906 onward. The plan has afforded much useful information about the structure and arrangement of the Milky Way system at some distances above or below the central plane, but has failed to reveal the true arrangement in the central plane itself. At present, the basic data serve usefully as standards for calibration purposes in many varieties of studies of galactic structure.—*B. J. B.*

SELECTION RULES: in nuclear physics, rules relating the energy states of a nucleus before and after certain processes occur.

For example, if a nucleus is in an excited state, it can drop to a lower energy level, with the emission of electromagnetic radiation. The selection rule for this process is: if there are a number of states of lower energy, the state selected will be, in general, the one that differs least in angular momentum (spin) from the initial excited state. There are rather similar selection rules for a number of other processes. See ENERGY LEVEL. —*G. M. S. and L. S.*

SELENIUM: a metalloid element (Se) of the sulfur group (VI A) of the periodic table; at. no. 34; at. wt 78.96; valence 2, 4, or 6. Of several allotropic forms, the three most important commercially are the amorphous, the crystalline or red, and the metallic or gray. Selenium occurs chiefly in iron, copper, lead, and nickel ores and as metal selenides. Commercially, the chief source is the flue dust produced by the burning of pyrites to make sulfuric acid. The element was discovered in 1818 by J. J. Berzelius, who was attempting to isolate a quantity of TELLURIUM from impure sulfur. In 1873 Willoughby Smith observed that the electrical conductivity of gray selenium metal increases with the intensity of illumination; this discovery led eventually to the use of selenium in photoelectric cells. Other present-day devices utilizing the photoelectric properties of selenium are solar cells, xerographic copying machines, and vidicon television tubes. As a semiconductor selenium is widely used to rectify alternating current in electronic equipment. The largest use of selenium and its compounds, however, is in the glass and ceramics industry. Selenium is added to glass to remove green tints caused by iron; cadmium-selenide reds are used to make ruby glass, red ceramics, and enamels. Selenium metal, being highly toxic, is used in insecticides and ship-hull paints (to prevent incrustations of marine organisms). Selenium dioxide is an oxidizing agent in drug and hydrocarbon processing, and an antioxidant additive for lubricating oils.—*R. B. T.*

SEMANTICS: various types of investigation into meaning. Introduced by Michel Bréal in his book *Semantics: Studies in the Science of Meaning* (1900), the word is still used by linguists to stand for systematic studies of *changes* in the meanings of words. A popular use of the word was spread by the still influential movement known as "General Semantics," founded by Count Alfred Korzybski (1879–1950). So used, it refers to an educational program for curing the alleged "un-sanity" provoked by confusion between "the word" and "the thing," by undue reliance upon the "two-valued logic" of Aristotle, by uncritical use of abstractions, and by other bad practices depending upon faulty conceptions of the relation between language and reality. In still looser, but widespread, uses of the word, "semantics" means hardly more than "something to do with meaning" (often in a hostile or debunking sense). The word also stands for a rigorous discipline invented by modern logicians for studying the relations between formal systems of symbols (arranged as "axiom sets," governed by explicit rules of construction) and the things or situations to which they refer. Semantics is then contrasted with "syntactics" (or "logical syntax") and with "pragmatics." Syntactics deals with relations between symbols, without reference to their meanings (as in formal logic); pragmatics includes all inquiries into meaning demanding explicit reference to the thought or behavior of symbol users. Semantics occupies an intermediate position. Its starting point is statements such as " 'H$_2$O' stands for water," which link something verbal with something non-verbal, without explicit mention of symbol users.

A notable achievement of formal semantics has been Alfred Tarski's famous semantical definition of the notion of truth. Rudolf Carnap and others have made important contributions to the analysis of such notions as those of *logical model* and *intension*. Semantics promises to be an indispensable tool for clarifying the scope and meaning of scientific theory.—*M. B.*

SEMENOV, NIKOLAI NICOLAEVICH, 1896–   , Soviet physical chemist; b. Saratov. His research has been in chemical-reaction kinetics and the production of chain reactions in combustion. For their researches into the mechanism of chemical reactions, he and C. N. Hinshelwood shared the 1956 Nobel prize. Semenov played a leading role in the organization of the Soviet chemical industry in the post-revolutionary period. He is a fellow of the Royal Society.—*D. H. D. R.*

SENESCENCE AND SENILITY: see AGING.

SENSES: mechanisms by which animals receive stimuli. The ability to detect changes in temperature or to hear sounds made by an enemy may spell the difference between survival and extinction. Highly specialized cells known as sensory cells, or receptors, have evolved to handle this task. Their principal function is to transform various kinds of stimuli (energy) into NERVOUS IMPULSES which may be transmitted by the nervous system to other parts of the organism. (See ANIMAL BEHAVIOR.)

Since energy comes in numerous forms (*e.g.* light, sound, temperature) there are many different types of receptor mechanisms. Each type has evolved in such a manner that it is especially sensitive to a particular form of energy. In VISION the stimulus is light. Falling upon the retina, light initiates a series of biochemical reactions, involving the decomposition of pigments in retinal receptors, which finally instigate a nervous impulse. The EAR transforms vibrations of air molecules into vibrations of fluid within the ear; these vibrations in turn lead to stimulation of receptors which trigger the nervous impulse. Senses of TASTE AND SMELL are stimulated by chemicals reaching the surface of the tongue or of the olfactory organ of the nose. Receptors for warmth and those for cold (they are not the same) are stimulated by temperature. Receptors for TOUCH respond to changes in pressure.

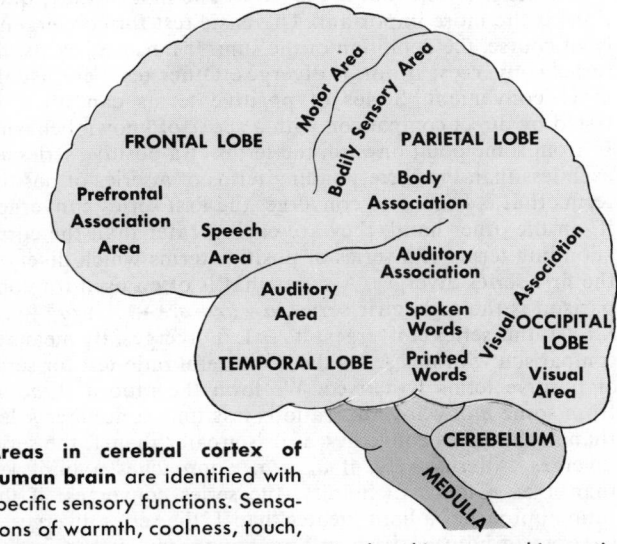

Areas in cerebral cortex of human brain are identified with specific sensory functions. Sensations of warmth, coolness, touch, and muscular movements are perceived and interpreted in particular regions of the somesthetic, or bodily sensory area, of the parietal lobe. In auditory area of temporal lobe, sound is perceived; it is interpreted and associated with other sensations in auditory association area. Areas for perception and association of visual impulses are located in occipital lobe of cortex. (*From Young*)

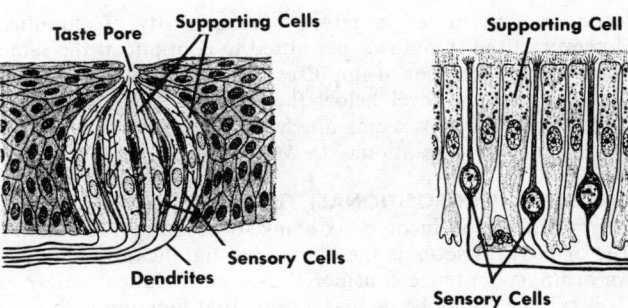

Receptors of chemical sensations: *Left*—A taste bud: Substances in solution (in saliva) enter taste pore and chemically stimulate sensory cells, which send impulses out along dendrites. Impulses travel along specific nervous pathways to taste center, at lower end of bodily sensory area of cortex. *Right*—Olfactory receptors (sensory cells) in nasal cavity: Olfactory sensations stimulate sensory cells, which then send impulses along nervous pathways that lead to olfactory bulbs (located beneath frontal lobes of cerebrum) and from there to center of smell, located on inner aspect of temporal lobe. (*From Young*)

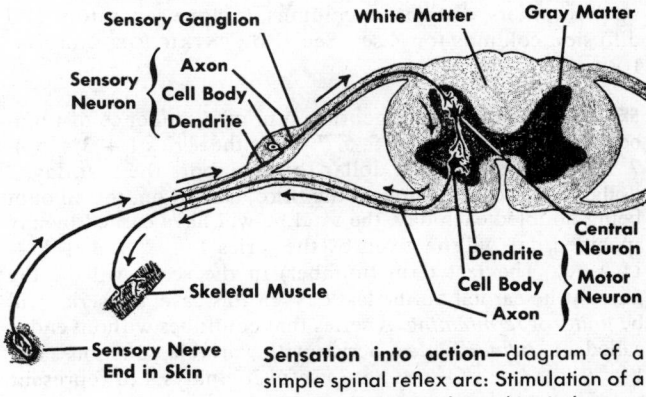

Sensation into action—diagram of a simple spinal reflex arc: Stimulation of a sensory nerve end in skin induces a nerve impulse in a sensory neuron. Impulse travels, via a sensory ganglion in the dorsal root of the spinal cord, to gray matter of spinal cord. Here impulse crosses a synapse to a motor neuron. Impulse then exits via ventral root of spinal cord and travels to a skeletal muscle, which is caused to contract. (*From Young*)

Pain receptors, which are independent of other types, respond to a variety of stimuli. Many other types of receptors are distributed throughout the body, in the vestibular apparatus (responsible for BALANCE AND EQUILIBRIUM), in the muscles and joints, in the intestines and bladder, and so on.

Stimulation of receptors gives rise to the subjective experience called sensation. Sensations differ from one another both in quality (*e.g.* smell vs. sight) and in quantity (*e.g.* severe pain vs. mild pain). In the brain there are relatively well-defined areas of tissue associated with the various senses. Since one nervous impulse is much like another, differences in *quality* of sensation must be attributed largely to where in the brain the impulses from receptors go. Differences in *quantity*, or strength, of a sensation are related to intensity of stimulation. The more intense the stimulation, the more nervous impulses will be propagated per second, and the more receptors will be activated. Both mechanisms serve to increase the frequency with which impulses arrive at the appropriate center in the brain.

Directly related to mechanisms governing strength of sensation is the phenomenon of adaptation. When a stimulus is applied to a receptor, the number of nervous impulses per second is determined largely by the intensity of stimulus. However, if the stimulus is permitted to continue at the same intensity, the number of impulses per second will gradually decrease to some level below the original frequency. Thus water in the bathtub seems much hotter at first than after a few minutes of adaptation.—*D. M. F.*

SENTENTIAL (PROPOSITIONAL) FUNCTION: in logic, a statement form, *e.g.* an income-tax blank. It becomes a statement, true or false, as soon as the blanks are significantly filled in. An ordinary sentence considered as a grammatical unit, *e.g.* "It is raining," may be seen as a sentential function with suppressed variables ("It is raining at place x and time y") whose values are implicitly supplied in the context in which it is uttered. Sentential functions are classed as monadic, *e.g.* "x is an even number"; dyadic, *e.g.* "x is greater than y"; triadic, *e.g.* "x gives y to z"; and so on.—*H. T.*

SEPARATION: an operation required in most industrial processes to isolate one material from another. Typical operations are the *mechanical* separation of solid from liquid by FILTRATION, and extraction of a component by LEACHING, which is often *chemical* in nature. Types of apparatus include: centrifugal decanters, distillation columns, cyclone separators, and diffusion columns for gases. See also CENTRIFUGE; CHROMATOGRAPHY.—*Ru. M.*

SERIES: the expressed algebraic sum of a sequence of numbers; *e.g.* the sequence 1, 3, 5, 7 yields the series $1 + 3 + 5 + 7$. If a man is paid one dollar for his labors the first day, 2 dollars the second, 4 dollars the third, and so on, the amount being doubled each day, the total he will have earned by any specified day will be given by the series $1 + 2 + 4 + 8 + 16 + \ldots$. The last term (number) in the series will be the amount he earned on the last day. In this case, the series will be *finite,* or *terminating.* A series that continues without end is called an *infinite series.* Series with variable functions, *e.g.* $1 - x + x^2 - x^3 + \ldots$, are useful in analysis to represent functions.

The most important finite series are those whose terms form arithmetic and geometric progressions. An arithmetic progression is a sequence of numbers each of which differs from its predecessor by the same amount. The simplest example is the set of natural numbers: $1, 2, 3, \ldots, n$, where n is any integer greater than 1. The corresponding arithmetic series is $1 + 2 + 3 + \ldots + n$. In general, if we denote the first term by a and the common difference by d, the arithmetic series is $a + (a + d) + (a + 2d) + \ldots + [a + (n - 1)d]$. If the nth term is called l, the series can be written $a + (a + d) + (a + 2d) + \ldots + l$, or, in reverse order, $l + (l - d) + (l - 2d) + \ldots + a$. Adding these two forms, term by term, we obtain twice the sum, $2S$, equal to $(a + l) + (a + l) + (a + l) + \ldots + (a + l) = n(a + l)$. Therefore $S = \frac{1}{2} n(a + l)$. This formula shows that the sum is n times the average of the first and last terms.

A geometric progression is a sequence of numbers in which the ratio of each number to its predecessor is the same. An example is 1, 2, 4, 8, 16, the corresponding finite geometric series being $1 + 2 + 4 + 8 + 16$. If we denote the first term by a and the common ratio by r, the geometric series is $a + ar + ar^2 + \ldots + ar^{n-1}$, if n is the number of terms. In order to find the sum $S = a + ar + ar^2 + \ldots + ar^{n-1}$, we can multiply by r and subtract $Sr = ar + ar^2 + ar^3 + \ldots + ar^n$, obtaining $S - Sr = a - ar^n$. Therefore $S = a(1 - r^n)/(1 - r)$. A third finite series of some interest is a harmonic series, in which the reciprocals of the terms are in arithmetic progression. The simplest example is $1 + \frac{1}{2} + \frac{1}{3} + \frac{1}{4} + \ldots + 1/n$.

There is no formula for the sum of a finite harmonic series.

Infinite series have far greater interest and utility than finite series. The simplest example of an infinite series is the expressed sum of the natural numbers, $1 + 2 + 3 + 4 + \ldots + n + \ldots$, which is an infinite arithmetic series. Other examples are the harmonic series, $1 + \frac{1}{2} + \frac{1}{3} + \ldots + 1/n + \ldots$, and the geometric series $1 + \frac{1}{2} + (\frac{1}{2})^2 + (\frac{1}{2})^3 + \ldots + (\frac{1}{2})^{n-1} \ldots$. The dots at the ends of these expressions indicate the nonterminating character of the series. The sum of an infinite series is not defined by the algebraic definition of a sum, which applies only to a limited number of terms. Intuitively it may appear that an infinite number of terms cannot have a finite sum. This was the reason for the discomfort caused by Zeno's race-course paradox. Zeno pointed out that before a runner finished the course he must finish half of it, then half of the half remaining, then half of the quarter still remaining, and so on. The total distance run must therefore be $\frac{1}{2} + \frac{1}{4} + \frac{1}{8} + \ldots$. Since there are infinitely many terms in this series its total must be infinitely great, and the time required for the runner would also be infinitely great. But this argument is easily refuted. We observe that the series is geometric with first term $= \frac{1}{2}$ and common ratio $= \frac{1}{2}$. The sum of n terms is therefore $\frac{1}{2} \cdot [1 - (\frac{1}{2})^n]/(1 - \frac{1}{2}) = 1 - (\frac{1}{2})^n$, which cannot be more than 1 no matter how large n is. Since $1 - (\frac{1}{2})^n$ approaches the LIMIT 1 as n increases beyond all bounds, it seems natural to conclude that the sum of the infinite series is 1. A similar conclusion cannot be reached for the arithmetic series $1 + 2 + 3 + \ldots + n + \ldots$, for the sum of n terms clearly increases beyond all bounds as n does. For such a series we conclude that no sum exists. These situations are dealt with by defining the sum of an infinite series as follows: For the infinite series, $a_1 + a_2 + a_3 + \ldots + a_n + \ldots$, consider the infinite sequence of partial sums: $S_1 = a_1$, $S_2 = a_1 + a_2, \ldots, S_n = a_1 + a_2 + \ldots + a_n, \ldots$. If this sequence tends to a limit as n tends to infinity, this limit is called the sum S of the infinite series: $S = \lim_{n \to \infty} S_n$. Such a series converges to S. If the sequence of partial sums does not tend to a limit as n tends to infinity, the infinite series has no sum and is said to diverge.

There are two questions concerning an infinite series: does it converge? If so, what is the sum? The first of these questions is the more important. The basic test for convergence is, of course, the definition of the sum. If $\lim_{n \to \infty} S_n$ exists, the series converges; if not, it diverges. Other tests are usually more convenient. Series of positive terms can often be tested by direct comparison with a series of known behavior. If, from some point onward, the terms of a positive series are each less than the corresponding terms of a series of positive terms that is known to converge, the first series converges; if, on the other hand, they are each greater than the corresponding terms of a series of positive terms which diverges, the first series diverges. A series that is often used for comparison is the geometric series, $a + ar + ar^2 + \ldots + ar^n + \ldots$. If $r < 1$, this series converges; if $r \geq 1$, it diverges. By means of comparison with this series the very useful ratio test for series of positive terms is derived. We form the ratio a_{n+1}/a_n. If, from some n onward, this ratio is less than a number k less than 1, the series converges; if it is greater than 1, the series diverges. Alternatively, if a_{n+1}/a_n approaches a limit less than 1 as n tends to infinity, the series converges; if this ratio approaches a limit greater than 1, the series diverges.

Series of both positive and negative terms may converge because the terms of one sign offset those of the other. If a series of such terms converges independently of the signs, *i.e.* even when all signs are made positive, it is said to converge absolutely. If its convergence is dependent upon the signs, it converges conditionally. One of the most interesting kinds of series containing positive and negative terms is an alternating series, in which the signs alternate. An alternating series converges if its terms continually decrease in size and approach 0. The series $1 - \frac{1}{2} + \frac{1}{3} - \frac{1}{4} + \ldots$ converges, but it does not converge absolutely since $1 + \frac{1}{2} + \frac{1}{3} + \frac{1}{4} + \ldots$ is a harmonic series, and every harmonic series diverges.

If the terms of a series are all functions of some variable x, the main question is not whether it converges but for what values of x it converges. If all the functions are defined for a common interval of values of x, and if the series converges whenever any value of x in this interval is inserted, then the series itself represents a function of x in the interval. The most important kind of series of functions is a power series, which has the form $a_0 + a_1 x + a_2 x^2 + \ldots + a_n x^n + \ldots$. An example is $1 + x + x^2 + x^3 + \ldots + x^n + \ldots$, which can be obtained from the fraction $1/(1 - x)$ by long division. Since this series is geometric, we see that it converges if $|x| < 1$. ($|x|$ means the absolute, or numerical, value of x.) In this interval it converges to the same values as those given by $1/(1 - x)$. In order to find the interval of convergence of a power series, we first apply the ratio test by writing $\lim_{n \to \infty} |a_n x^n / a_{n-1} x^{n-1}|$ $= \lim_{n \to \infty} |a_n/a_{n-1}| \cdot |x|$. If the limit of $|a_n/a_{n-1}|$ is L, the series converges for $|x| < 1/L$, since, for such values, $\lim_{n \to \infty}$ $|a_n x^n/a_{n-1} x^{n-1}| < 1$. The question of convergence for $x = 1/L$ or $-1/L$ must be settled by other tests.

A function may be defined by a power series, or a power series may be found for a function already known in another form. A method of obtaining a power series for a given function is provided by Taylor's series, if the function has derivatives of all orders. The general form of Taylor's series for a function $f(x)$ is $f(x) = f(a) + f'(a)(x - a) + f''(a)(x - a)^2/2! + f'''(a)(x - a)^3/3! + \ldots + f^{(n)}(a)(x - a)^n/n! + \ldots$. This gives a function as a series of powers of $x - a$, and the coefficients are formed from the function and its derivatives at $x = a$. The special form for $a = 0$ is often called Maclaurin's series, and is $f(x) = f(0) + f'(0) x + f''(0)x^2/2! + \ldots + f^{(n)}(0)x^n/n! + \ldots$. This form gives the following series for e^x, $\sin x$, and $\cos x$:

$$e^x = 1 + x + x^2/2! + x^3/3! + \ldots + x^n/n! + \ldots$$

$$\sin x = x - x^3/3! + x^5/5! - \ldots + (-1)^{n-1} x^{2n-1}/(2n-1)! + \ldots$$

$$\cos x = 1 - x^2/2! + x^4/4! - \ldots + (-1)^{n-1} x^{2n}/(2n)! + \ldots$$

Functions expressed by power series are continuous, and can be differentiated and integrated term by term within the interval of convergence.—*H. C.*

SEROTONIN: 5-hydroxy tryptamine, a derivative of the amino acid tryptophan. It occurs chiefly in the blood and stomach linings of mammals. When platelets disintegrate, as in blood clotting, serotonin is released, causing constriction of small blood vessels. It also occurs in nervous tissue, particularly the hypothalamus. Its exact function is unknown.—*F. F.*

SERPENTINE: a common and widespread metamorphic mineral, $Mg_6Si_4O_{10}(\dot{O}H)_8$. Antigorite, formed of finely intergrown plates, closely related in crystal structure to the MICAS and CLAY MINERALS, is the most common type of serpentine. However, the fibrous variety, chrysotile, is the most important commercial ASBESTOS. Electron-microscope studies indicate that the individual fibers of chrysotile are hollow cylinders. Serpentine occurs principally as a deuteric or contact-metamorphic alteration product of olivines and pyroxenes in IGNEOUS ROCKS, and as a replacement of these and other minerals formed by the contact METAMORPHISM of magnesian limestones. Chrysotile veins occur in serpentinized rocks of both types. Ultrabasic rocks which contain trace amounts of nickel may, under tropical-humid weathering, give rise to laterites enriched in nickel, in the form of genthite or garnierite, which are varieties of serpentine. The nickel ores of Cuba and New Caledonia are of this type. The mottled green "verde antique marble" of soda fountains is serpentinized peridotite that has been brecciated and sheared by tectonic forces.—*L. M.*

SERVETUS, MICHAEL (Miguel Serveto), 1511–53, Spanish anatomist, physician, and polemic theologian; b. Tudela. With his *Christianismi restitutio* (1553) he became the first European to publish a description of the pulmonary transit of the blood (also known as lesser circulation), from the right to the left side of the heart through the lungs. This phenomenon was discovered earlier by Ibn al-Nafis (*c.* 1210–88), but it is not known whether Servetus had knowledge of this. He was burned at the stake for heresy, 1553.—*D. H. D. R.*

SERVOMECHANISM (or servo): one of two kinds of CONTROL SYSTEMS, the other kind generally being termed a regulator. A servomechanism adjusts its output automatically to match its input, whereas a regulator (*e.g.* a household thermostat) maintains a fixed output independent of input variations. A servomechanism consists essentially of a sensing element (*i.e.* an error-determining device), an amplifier, and a servomotor (See illus.). The sensing element determines the extent to which the controlled quantity differs from the desired value ("the error"). The signal from the sensing element is amplified and then used to actuate the servomotor in such a direction as to reduce the error as nearly as possible to zero. A servomechanism may regulate any physical quantity, *e.g.* temperature, angular position, speed, or acceleration, to a desired value. The sensing element may be a gyroscope, thermometer, photo-electric cell, or other device which responds to change in physical quantity. The amplifier is usually electronic, but magnetic, hydraulic, and pneumatic amplifiers have been used. The servomotor is generally an electric motor or a hydraulic piston, though other types are also used. The ratings of these motors may range from a fraction of a watt to hundreds of kilowatts.

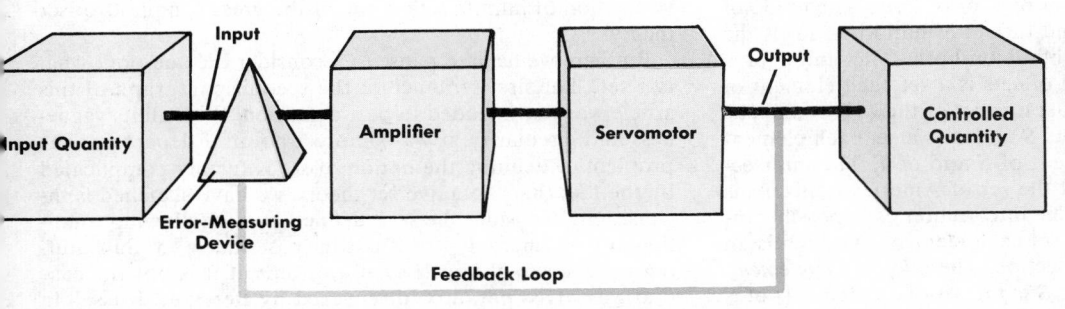

Input Quantity — Input — Error-Measuring Device — Amplifier — Servomotor — Output — Controlled Quantity — Feedback Loop

Servomechanism feedback loop transmits output data back to error-measuring device, which in turn regulates input until difference between output and desired output is zero.

An automatic turret-lathe or milling machine which forms a metal block according to a predetermined shape employs a servomechanism to match the cutting head (the output) to the proper position of the guiding template (the input). A similar application is one in which the servomechanism matches the instantaneous position of a rotating output shaft to that of an input shaft which is otherwise unconnected and physically may be considerably removed from the output. Another typical application is the positioning of a 100-ton telescope by a small hand crank. The astronomer swings the crank through a certain angle, and a large motor moves the telescope through approximately the same angle. To point the telescope in precisely the proper direction, the sensing element of the servo "compares" the positions of telescope and crank, and then, through the amplifier, actuates the motor to reduce this difference. The signal from the position of the crank is the input; the signal from the sensing element is the output. The error is the difference between input and output. Because the output is "fed back" and compared with the input, servomechanisms are called closed-loop control systems. In airplane AUTOMATIC PILOTS, the desired course is the input, the sensing element is a gyroscope, and the servomotor actuates the rudder to maintain the desired course. Altitude and speed are maintained by other servos which control the elevators and engine throttle; altimeters and air-speed indicators are the sensing elements.

These examples demonstrate the two typical characteristics of all servomechanisms: (1) weak signals may be employed to control extremely powerful outputs; (2) the output and input may be physically far apart. Servomechanisms are used extensively to improve the accuracy, reliability, and safety of engineering and manufacturing processes. See FEEDBACK.— *G. S. and A. P. E.*

SET THEORY: a new branch of science, developed in the last 80 yr and lying in the abstract regions between mathematics and logic. It has been very fertile in new ideas, and its study cannot now be dissociated from the study of logic and foundations of mathematics. Set-theoretical terminology has greatly unified the ways of speaking of mathematicians, and mathematics could be considered as the science of sets.

A set is a collection of objects considered together for some purpose. Each object is an element of the set. If the object a is an element of the set S, we write: $a \varepsilon S$, (a belongs to S). Sets are finite or infinite: a set of dishes is finite, the set of even natural numbers is infinite. A set T is a subset of the set S if every element of T is an element of S, and we write: $T \subset S$ (T is included in S). By this definition, a set is a subset of itself. If we want to exclude this case, we say that T is a *proper* subset of S if T is a subset of S and at least one element of S is not an element of T. Two sets S and T are equal, $S = T$, if S is a subset of T and T a subset of S; *i.e.* if every element of S is an element of T and every element of T an element of S.

The *union* $S \cup T$ of two sets S and T is a set each element of which is an element of S or of T or of both. The union of the set of persons over 65 and the set of blind persons is the set of persons over 65 or blind or both. The union of a (possibly infinite) collection of sets is a set each element of which is an element of at least one set of the collection. The *intersection* $S \cap T$ of two sets S and T is a set each element of which is at once an element of S and of T. The intersection of the set of males and the set of American citizens is the set of American males. The intersection of a (possibly infinite) collection of sets is a set each element of which is an element of all sets of the collection. The *relative complement*, $S - T$, of a subset T in a set S is the set of all elements of S that are not elements of T. The relative complements of the set of even natural numbers in the set of natural numbers is the set of odd natural numbers.

Generally, the objects considered in an investigation are all elements of some definite set, called the *universal* set, U. The *complement* S' of a set is the relative complement of S in U. The *null* set (or *empty* set) Φ is the complement of U. To familiarize himself with sets the reader should check the following statements: $S \cup S = S$; $S \cap S = S$; $T \subset S$ if and only if $T \cup S = S$; $T \subset S$ if and only if $T \cap S = T$; $(S')' = S$; $S \cup S' = U$; $S \cap S' = \Phi$; $S \cup U = U$; $S \cap U = S$; $S \cup \Phi = S$; $S \cap \Phi = \Phi$; $T \subset S$ if and only if $S' \subset T'$; $(S \cup T)' = S' \cap T'$; $(S \cap T)' = S' \cup T'$. The last two statements are known (erroneously) as De Morgan laws.

The *Cartesian product,* $S \times T$, of a set S with a set T is the set of all ordered pairs (x, y), with $x \varepsilon S$ and $y \varepsilon T$. The Cartesian product of the set of real numbers with itself is the set of points in the (coordinate) plane. The Cartesian product is not commutative, *i.e.* in general, $S \times T \neq T \times S$.

Many intuitive notions can be defined in terms of sets. For example, a relation between elements of a set S and elements of a set T is a subset of $S \times T$. If N is the set of natural numbers, the relation "is less than" between natural numbers can be considered as the subset of $N \times N$ whose elements are certain ordered pairs of natural numbers, namely those in which the first element is less than the second. A *function* defined over a set S and taking values in a set T is a relation, *i.e.* a subset of $S \times T$, satisfying an additional condition: (x, y) and (x, z), with $y \neq z$, are not both in the subset. An *operation* defined over a set S is a subset of $(S \times S) \times S$, that is, a set of ordered triples (x, y, z), with $x \varepsilon S$, $y \varepsilon S$, $z \varepsilon S$, satisfying the following condition: (x, y, u) and (x, y, v), with $u \neq v$, are not both in the subset. Addition of integers is the set of ordered triples such as $(3, 5, 8)$, where the last number is the sum of the first two. Thus set theory provides a convenient universal language for mathematics. Numbers—natural, rational, real, complex—can be defined in terms of sets.

Set theory has led to a better understanding of infinity. The basic tool is the one-to-one correspondence between the elements of two sets. If there exists such a correspondence, we say that the two sets are equivalent. It may happen that an infinite set is equivalent to one of its proper subsets (a paradoxical fact already known to Galileo); for example, the set of natural numbers is equivalent to one of its subsets, the set of even natural numbers. On the other hand, it has been shown that not all infinite sets are equivalent. For example, the set of real numbers is not equivalent to the set of natural numbers. We thus obtain classes of equivalent sets, called cardinal numbers. The finite cardinal numbers are the natural numbers. The infinite cardinal numbers, *i.e.* the classes of infinite equivalent sets, are the transfinite cardinal numbers. The smallest is $\aleph_0$ (aleph null), the class of sets equivalent to the set of natural numbers. There are infinitely many transfinite numbers, and thus the intuitive notion of infinity is decomposed into an infinite scale of transfinite numbers. The investigation of infinite sets is one of the great conquests of set theory.

But here we have to pause to reconsider the question: what is a set? The first sentence of the second paragraph of this article was not intended to be a definition. With all its vagueness and circularity, it was simply a point of departure. The problem of defining the notion of set is further complicated by the fact that the naive set theory we have sketched is inconsistent. Consider the set r defined by the following condition: $x \varepsilon r$ if and only if it is not the case that $x \varepsilon x$. Substituting r for x, we obtain: $r \varepsilon r$ if and only if it is not the case that $r \varepsilon r$. This paradox, discovered by Bertrand Russell in

1901, is very disturbing because it involves merely the notions of set and element of a set and it shows that these basic notions, in all their simplicity, are a source of inconsistency. The originator of set theory, Georg Cantor (1845–1918), had used in his proofs the kind of arguments generally used by working mathematicians. Russell's paradox, as well as other paradoxes, forced a greater scrutiny of the methods employed and led to axiomatic set theory (Zermelo, 1908; Skolem, 1922). Sets are not what we intuitively consider them to be—*i.e.* collections —but they are undefined objects satisfying certain axioms, and their properties are derived from these axioms. The conditions imposed are to be narrow enough to exclude paradoxes and broad enough to permit a free development of mathematics. There is not to this day a universally accepted set theory. Another approach is to reduce set theory to logic: the set of blue objects is replaced by the propositional function "*x* is blue." The language of sets, although convenient, is nothing but a paraphrase of logic. But if we follow this approach, set theory has to face all the unsolved difficulties of logic. (See FOUNDATIONS OF MATHEMATICS.)—*J. v. H.*

SEX: see REPRODUCTION; SECONDARY SEX CHARACTERISTICS.

SEX DETERMINATION: In most kinds of animals the sex is determined at the moment of fertilization, according to the combination of sex chromosomes brought together in the egg cell and the sperm cell. Except in birds, some fishes, and some insects, the sperm cells are of two types: those containing an *X*-chromosome and those with a *Y*-chromosome. The corresponding eggs all contain an *X*-chromosome. When an *X*-bearing sperm cell fertilizes an *X*-bearing egg cell, the hereditary basis (*XX*) for a female is established. A *Y*-bearing sperm cell and an *X*-bearing egg cell provide the basis (*XY*) for a male. In birds and the few fishes and insects that have a different system of sex determination the male has two similar sex chromosomes (*WW*) and sperms of only one type (*W*), whereas the female has an unlike pair of sex chromosomes (*WZ*) and produces two types of eggs. In honeybees, unfertilized eggs with a single *X*-chromosome develop by PARTHENOGENESIS into males (drones), which produce only sperm cells with an *X*-chromosome. Fertilized eggs (*XX*) develop into females, which may be queens or sterile workers, according to the diet received during development. During normal development in most other animals, the sex chromosomes call forth hormones that influence growth processes. These result in production of OVARIES or TESTES, and of sexual characteristics in other parts of the body. In a few kinds of animals, *e.g.* tapeworms, earthworms, oysters, and hagfishes, as in most plants, each individual has all the genes for both sexes. Locally within the body, factors of the internal environment determine that the genes for one sex will express themselves in one region (producing a testis or a stamen), and those for the opposite sex in a different region (producing an ovary or a pistil). In the minority of plants that have staminate flowers on one individual and pistillate flowers on another (*e.g.* the waterweed *Elodea* and the hops), the staminate plants have an X- and a Y-chromosome in each cell, whereas the pistillate ones have the genetic constitution XX; such plants can be regarded as genetically male and female. See HEREDITY.—*L. and M. M.*

SEXTANT: a navigational instrument for measuring the altitude (angular distance above the horizon) of celestial objects. It may also be used for measuring horizontal angles between two points. The frame of the instrument is an arc of a circle rigidly connected to two radial arms that are joined at the center of the circle. A half-silvered, half-transparent glass (horizon glass) is fixed to one radius, a telescope to the other.

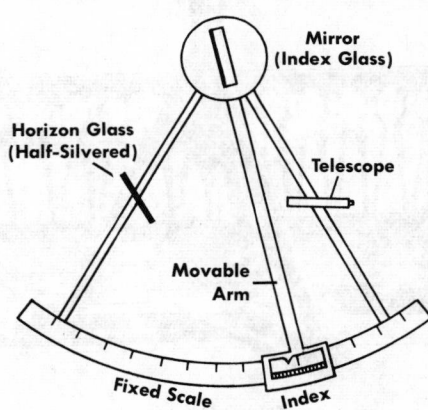

Mariner's sextant: Looking through telescope, observer turns movable arm until image of Sun, reflected from index glass and silvered half of horizon glass, appears to be at horizon. Index gives angle between Sun and horizon on fixed scale, marked in degrees.

A mirror (index glass) at the center can be rotated by a movable arm, the lower end of which bears a pointer (index mark) and vernier. Light from a distant source is reflected by the mirror to the horizon glass, and part of it is again reflected

Sex determination in fruit fly (*Drosophila*): Primordial male germ cells contain a pair of unlike sex-determining chromosomes, the X- and the Y-chromosomes. Cell division during maturation of germ cells proceeds so that, of the four resulting mature sperms, two contain an X-chromosome and two a Y-chromosome. The mature female sex cells, the eggs, contain only X-chromosomes. Since Y-chromosomes are male-determining, the union of an egg with a sperm bearing a Y-chromosome (an XY combination) will result in a male offspring. If an X-chromosome sperm unites with an egg (an XX combination) a female offspring will result. (*After Lee*)

FEMALE

X-Chromosome

X-Chromosome

MALE

Y-Chromosome

X-Chromosome

Autosomes

PRIMORDIAL GERM CELLS

Useless Polar Body

MEIOTIC DIVISIONS

Egg

Useless Polar Body

Y-Bearing Sperms

X-Bearing Sperms

Egg Fertilized by Y-Bearing Sperm Produces Male

Egg Fertilized by X-Bearing Sperm Produces Female

into the telescope. When the mirror and the glass are parallel, light from the same source enters through the transparent part of the glass and coincides with the reflected ray. If the mirror is rotated through an angle, the reflected ray rotates through twice that angle; the fixed arc is therefore graduated so as to show twice the angle through which the arm (with the mirror) has rotated. Since the angles normally measured are not more than 90°, many instruments are made with arcs of only 45°; these are sometimes called *octants*. In the most common usage they are all called sextants, and the distinction between quadrants (90°), sextants (60°), and octants (45°) is seldom made—except in textbooks.

To determine the altitude of a star, the observer holds the sextant vertically with the telescope horizontal so that he can see the horizon through the transparent part of the horizon glass. He then moves the arm, rotating the mirror, until the image of the star coincides with the horizon. The star's altitude can then be read directly from the scale, using the vernier for precision.

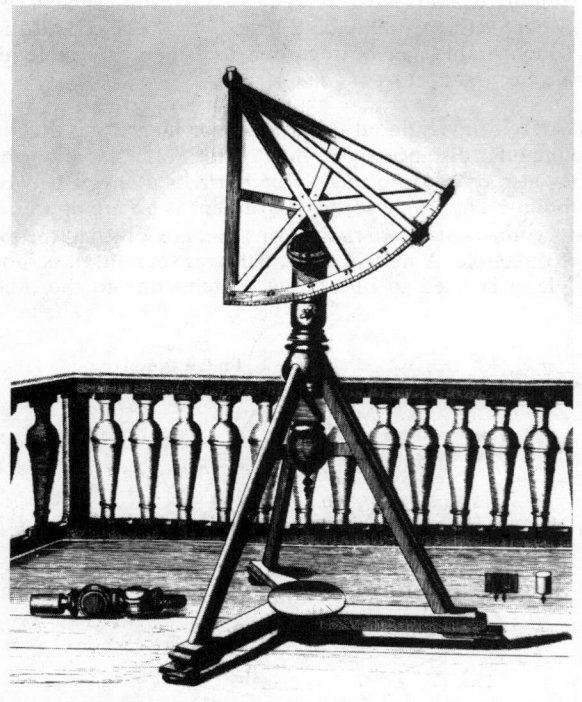

Hevelius' brass sextant: This sextant of 17th-cent. astronomer Johann Hevelius was used to find angle between celestial bodies. One star was sighted through fixed sight (extreme right) and other through movable sight. (*U. S. Navy*)

The *bubble sextant* is used in aircraft, from which the horizon can rarely be seen. It contains an artificial horizon formed of an optical system that incorporates a circular bubble, comparable to the one in a spirit level. When the image of the star is centered on that of the bubble, the star's altitude can be read from a scale. For steadiness, the instrument is mounted on gimbals. The *radio sextant* tracks the Sun by radio, and can thus be used in submerged submarines and in ships on overcast days. The data are fed directly into a computer which reads out the ship's latitude.—*B. P. S.*

SHADOW: the region behind an illuminated opaque body, from which light is completely or partly excluded. (The shadow is sometimes erroneously defined as being only the dark area formed on a screen.) Shadow formation is based on the straight-line propagation of light. However, it must be

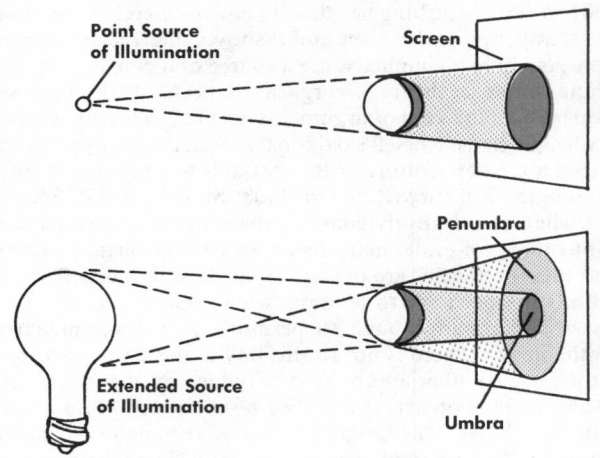

Shadows: Difference between shadow produced by point source of illumination and shadow produced by extended source.

noted that, as in the case of all wave motion, some bending around corners (DIFFRACTION) takes place; hence light, intercepted by a sharp razor blade or a fine wire, may appear in regions that would be "forbidden" by purely geometrical or straight-line considerations.

A point source of light, *e.g.* the crater of an arc lamp, produces sharply defined shadows, with clear boundaries between light and shade. If a large (extended) luminous source is employed, the shadows formed are no longer sharp. The portion of the shadow from which light is completely shut off is known as the *umbra;* the portion that remains partially illuminated is called the *penumbra* (see ECLIPSE). As the large source of light responsible for these vague shadows is moved farther away from the opaque body, its apparent dimensions approach those of a geometrical point, and the resulting shadow grows sharper and better defined. Acoustical "shadows" may be observed when sound waves strike an appropriate obstacle, and an analogous phenomenon exists with radio and television waves.—*A. E.*

SHALE: layered SEDIMENTARY ROCK composed chiefly of clay-sized particles, usually a mixture of QUARTZ and CLAY MINERALS. Shale often contains some calcium carbonate as

Black shale: This rock, in southern New York State, formed from sediments laid down 300 million yr ago on a broad delta. The strata were later raised and tilted. (*Jerome Wyckoff*)

well, and when this makes up half of the rock, the term *marl* is applied. Shale is well bedded, with layers so thin that they are called laminae. The platy clay minerals are oriented with their long dimensions parallel to the bedding planes, so that the rock often tends to split easily along these planes—a property called fissility. The extremely fine size of the particles indicates that all shales were deposited under very quiet conditions.

Shales are classified according to color, and the color often offers a clue as to the mode of origin. Black shales owe their color to a high content of organic matter. They are usually very fissile, and often contain pyrite or pyritized fossils. They represent deposition in an environment devoid of oxygen but with an abundance of hydrogen sulfide (euxinic conditions). Gray shales are the most common sort, and may represent a wide variety of depositional environments. Red shales owe their rusty color to oxidized iron (ferric oxide), and indicate that an abundance of oxygen was available at the time of deposition. Red shales are forming at present in warm areas with marked seasonal rainfall. Green shales, relatively rare, when they do occur are commonly associated with red shales, lying above or below them. The green color is due to less highly oxidized iron (ferrous oxide) and indicates a lack of oxygen at the time of deposition. Often green shales are associated with bits of organic matter, and oxidation of the organic matter is believed to have caused reduction of red ferric oxide to green ferrous oxide.—*W. Ha.*

SHAPLEY, HARLOW, 1885– ,

Harlow Shapley
(Yerkes Observatory)

U. S. astronomer; b. Nashville, Mo. His pioneering work on eclipsing binaries (with H. N. Russell) established a fundamental technique for finding the masses, radii, and other physical properties of stars. After proving that cepheid variables cannot be binaries (1914), he proposed stellar pulsation as the cause of their variations. Working at Mt Wilson Observatory, Shapley calibrated the period-luminosity relation for the cepheids and with this tool determined (1917) that the distance from the Sun to the center of our Milky Way galaxy is about 50,000 lt-yr; this contradicted the then-prevailing opinion that the Sun is near the hub of the galaxy. (About 1930 he determined, more accurately, that the distance is 25,000 to 30,000 lt-yr.)

As director of Harvard Observatory, 1921–52, Shapley studied variable stars, clusters, and galaxies. The Shapley-Ames *Survey of External Galaxies Brighter than the 13th Magnitude* is representative of numerous contributions he made at Harvard. His books include *Star Clusters* (1930), *Galaxies* (1943, 1961), *The Inner Metagalaxy* (1957), and *Of Stars and Men* (1958). He is a member of the National Academy of Sciences.—*O. G.*

SHATTER CONE: a type of conical fracturing in rock indicative of shattering by intense shock waves such as could have been created only by the impact of a giant meteorite, asteroid, or comet head. Volcanic and other natural explosions are incapable of producing shatter cones, but cones have been artificially produced by exploding shaped charges of high brissance, and have been found in the target craters of hypervelocity bullets shot from light gas guns at velocities of 18,000 ft/sec. Shatter cones are not to be confused with cone-in-

Shatter cone in limestone from Kentland, Ind., astrobleme shows characteristic distinctive horsetail-like bundles of striations. On left side of cone, striations have been obscured by weathering. Width of cone is about 4 in. (*Robert S. Dietz*)

cone structures (concretions) or slickensides, and are distinct from other common modes of conical failure. In essence, shatter-coning is a mode of failure under such intense and overpowering shock forces that the rock does not yield along its innate lines of weakness. The most distinctive aspect is the radiating, horsetail-like sheaves on the master cone.

Shatter cones are known from nine circular areas of highly crushed, brecciated, and deranged rock which provide evidence of an ancient explosion. The shatter cones rather conclusively show these sites to be astroblemes (ancient meteorite-impact wounds), although meteoritic material has yet to be found there. Astroblemes are the "root structures" of Quaternary meteorite craters in their present state after deep erosion. Presently known shatter-coned astroblemes are: Steinheim Basin, Germany; Wells Creek and Flynn Creek basins, Tennessee; Serpent Mound, Ohio; Kentland structure, Indiana; Crooked Creek structure, Missouri; Decaturville structure, Missouri; Sierra Madera structure, Texas; Vredefort Ring, South Africa. Shatter cones are also found at two Quaternary meteorite craters: Meteor (Barringer) Crater, Arizona, and Ashanti Crater (occupied by Lake Bosumtwi), Ghana. The high-stress mineral COESITE, requiring shock pressures in excess of 20 kilobars for its formation, is already known to co-exist with shatter cones at three of the above-named basins as well as at the two meteorite craters.—*R. S. D.*

SHEAR: the tendency of adjacent particles, in a body under stress, to slide past each other. The force causing this tendency is called the *shear force;* it acts parallel to the plane of sliding; its intensity per unit of area is the *shear stress.* The deformation due to shear is measured in terms of the *shear strain,* defined as the change of angle (in radians) between two orthogonal axes.

In an elastic material, shear stress and shear strain are proportional; their ratio is called the *shear modulus* or *modulus of rigidity. Shear strength* is defined as the largest shear stress which can be resisted by a material. An ideal fluid is characterized by complete lack of shear strength, while plastic behavior of ductile materials is intimately related to their shear strength. In structural mechanics, shear arises in stressed members such as beams, shafts in torsion, and rivets. See STRENGTH OF MATERIALS.—*K. G.*

SHELLFISH: see MOLLUSK.

SHELL STRUCTURE: see ELECTRON STRUCTURE OF ATOMS; NUCLEAR SHELL MODEL.

SHERRINGTON, SIR CHARLES SCOTT, 1857–1952, English physiologist and pathologist; b. London. He was one of the foremost physiologists of the last 100 yr, his studies ranging from development of the eye to cholera epidemics in Italy and Spain. However, Sherrington's greatest achievement lies in his pioneer work in the understanding of the over-all development and action of the nervous system; among his many publications, the most important is *The Integrative Action of the Nervous System* (1906). For his discoveries concerning the function of the neuron, he shared with E. D. Adrian the 1932 Nobel prize in physiology and medicine. He was a fellow of the Royal Society and an associate of the U. S. National Academy of Sciences.—*A. L.*

SHIELD: see CONTINENTAL SHIELD.

SHIELDING, ELECTRIC AND MAGNETIC: a means of reducing the strength of an electric or magnetic field in a given region by diverting the field's lines of force to some path outside the region. Electric shielding is based on Michael Faraday's historic "ice-pail" experiment, by which he demonstrated that a free charge cannot exist inside a conducting vessel, but resides only on its outer surface. Since electric lines of force begin and end on electric charges, such lines cannot penetrate metallic enclosures that carry no charge whatever in their interior (Fig. 1). Accordingly, a closed metal box or even a wire screen serves as a complete electric shield. Perfect magnetic shielding is possible when superconducting materials are used at temperatures near absolute zero (see SUPERCONDUCTIVITY), but the maintenance of such temperature is imprac-

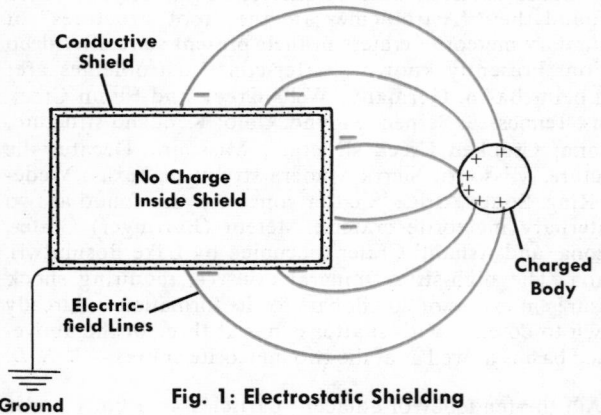

Fig. 1: Electrostatic Shielding

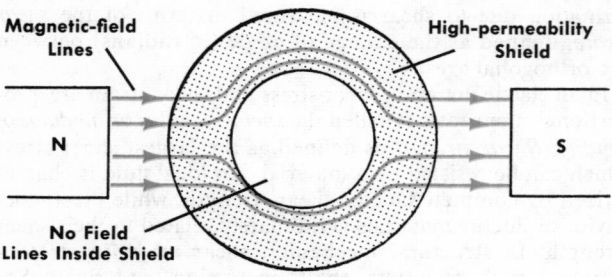

Fig. 2: Magnetic Shielding

ticable. All that can be done at ordinary temperatures is to shunt aside magnetic lines of force by interposing highly permeable materials in their path (see MAGNETIC PERMEABILITY). Thus, a watch movement or a delicate electrical instrument may be shielded against stray magnetic fields by placing it in a soft-iron case, which will then "draw" to itself the objectionable lines of force, leaving its interior relatively free of disturbance (Fig. 2).—*A. E.*

SHIELDING, NUCLEAR: the use of special materials surrounding NUCLEAR REACTORS, accelerators, and radioactive sources to prevent the passage of injurious radiations. The material employed depends on the type and intensity of radiation being emitted. Lead, steel, and special concrete are used most frequently for shields against gamma rays. Aluminum and plastics make good shields against beta rays. Boron, water, paraffin, and concrete are suitable for slowing down and absorbing neutrons.—*E. E.*

SHIKIMIC ACID: an intermediate in the biochemical pathway, starting with glucose, that leads to the synthesis of compounds containing benzene rings, *e.g.* the amino acids phenylalanine and tryptophan. The enzymes that catalyze the synthetic steps of this pathway are found in bacteria and plants, but not in animals; hence animals cannot synthesize phenylalanine and tyrosine and need these amino acids in their diet. See also AMINO ACIDS.—*J. F. S.*

SHIP: The design of ships has always been determined by (1) the materials available for hull construction, (2) the ship's particular function, and (3) the character of the surrounding waters.

Oar-propelled and Sailing Ships: Early man built ships from skins stretched and sewn over a rigid frame, from bundles of reeds, and from hollowed-out logs (dugouts). Ships that developed from the dugout, *e.g.* the war galleys of the Greeks and Romans, were long and slim—characteristics that gave them their desired speed and maneuverability. A Greek *trireme* (a galley using three banks of oars) was able to cover 168 mi/day, a performance equal to the efforts of the best racing crews of today. Relying mainly on oars, the war galley used its large, square sail only as an auxiliary means of propulsion. The true sailing ship of the ancient world was the Phoenician trading vessel, developed from the shallow, spoon-shaped, river craft of the Egyptians, who most probably made their first boats from bundles of reeds. The primary need of the Phoenicians was to transport cargo; speed was secondary, and thus they chose to rely on sail. The Phoenicians built their ships deep in order to carry a large volume of cargo, and broad because a deep ship must be broad if it is to be stable. A shortcoming of the Phoenician trading vessel (and of the sail-rigged war galley) was that it could only run before the wind, *i.e.* be directly pushed by the wind. Not until the decline of the Roman Empire, when the Mediterranean was invaded by people who had lived on the shores of the Indian Ocean, was a sailing rig used that allowed a ship to sail into the wind (tacking or close-hauling). This was the *lateen rig,* a triangular sail hanging from a diagonal yard (wooden beam) attached to the mast. The great sea distances and the inconstant winds of the Indian Ocean were too dangerous to rely on oars and winds only from the right direction. Except for the fact that it was helpless in a calm (as is any sailing ship), the lateen rig gave mariners a new freedom to maneuver in any direction regardless of the wind's direction. There is some evidence that, much earlier, Northern Europeans were able to sail into the wind using a square sail controlled by ropes from its lower corners. Despite this progress in the

Dugout: American Indians, like other primitives, burned and scraped out the interior of a log in order to make a dugout.

Dhow: Secured to the mast is a slanting yard, from which hangs a sail. This arrangement, the lateen rig, was introduced to the Mediterranean area by invaders from the south around the 5th cent. It permitted sailing into the wind.

use of sail, the 14th- and 15th-cent. warship was still a long, narrow, oar-propelled galley that relied on its speed and maneuverability to conduct landing operations against opposing ships. But by this time the merchant ship, tubby and solidly built, used both the square sail and the lateen rig. Over its bow and stern were "castles," at first built to defend the ship from pirates, but subsequently used as shelter for the crew; today, these structures are the well-known forecastle and poop. As men's knowledge of the stars increased, as their instruments of navigation became more reliable, and as they themselves became more adventurous, they made longer voyages both for trade and discovery. Ships had to be larger in order to carry more food and water, and stronger in order to resist the force of mid-ocean gales. More sail became necessary. First one and then two masts were added to the original mast; eventually, by the 15th cent. there evolved the three-master with a foremast (nearest the bow) and a mainmast, both square-rigged, and a mizzenmast (nearest the stern), lateen-rigged. Instead of a large steering paddle, a rudder was firmly secured under the stern. This is the ship that with slight variations carried Vasco da Gama around the globe, Columbus to America, and the Mayflower pilgrims to Massa-

chusetts. The six-sail rig (two sails on the foremast, two on the mainmast, one on the mizzenmast, and a jib) remained the conventional equipment of merchantmen well into the 18th cent. With the advent of cannon and the consequent demise of the war galley, the warship also took on sail; and, as warships became heavier, with tiers of cannon on the

Galley: A plan view of an oar-propelled galley. This type of ship was used for war from Greek times until the 16th cent. The advent of cannon finally made oars obsolete; and the last great battle fought by galleys was at Lepanto in 1571.

Sailing vessel of 16th cent. (*left*) has three masts. Each of the two forward masts carries two square sails, while the mizzenmast, at rear, still carries the lateen rig. Improvement generally took the form of more sail and slimmer hulls. By 1850 the sailing vessel was reaching its peak. The *Edward Everett* (*right*) carried much more sail on its three masts, plus two fore-and-afts from its bowsprit. On its mizzenmast the lateen rig survived vestigially in the form of the fore-and-aft sail (sail running parallel to ship). (*N. Y. Public Library*)

The *Elise* (*left*) in 1816 made the first voyage by steam from London to Paris. Here it appears as it finished that memorable trip, saluting the Tuileries palace and the curious crowds on the banks of the Seine. By 1845 the *Washington* (*right*), first steamboat to be subsidized by Congress, was regularly carrying mail across the North Atlantic. As can be seen, reliance on steam was not complete; the *Washington* still carried a precautionary complement of sail. (*N. Y. Public Library*)

broadside, more and more sail was needed to give the warship the desired power and speed. Finally, marking the climax of the age of sailing ships, the *clipper ship,* with its demand for even more speed, added more sail and slimmed its hull, achieving length-to-breadth ratios of almost 7:1, in contrast to the 3:1 ratios of the ordinary sailing ship.

Steamships: Steam as a means of propulsion had been tried as early as the 16th cent., but not until 1807, when Robert Fulton made two successful voyages on the Hudson, did it become a serious threat to sail. Steam propulsion was at first used mainly for coastal and inland waters in both Europe and America, but in 1836 the first transatlantic steamship line was formed. Successful steamship operation was impeded by the great weight and size of the engines as well as the enormous consumption of coal involved. A ship making the voyage from Europe to America had to carry so much coal that there was scarcely room left for passengers or cargo. These disadvantages were eliminated by steady improvement in engine design. The most important innovations, in addition to Watt's invention of the double-acting piston, were the surface condenser, which allowed fresh water to be used and reused for steam production; the Yarrow water-tube boiler, which provided high-pressure steam; and the compound en-

gine, in which high-pressure steam first pushes a small piston and, at the end of the stroke, the steam at its lower exhaust pressure pushes a second, larger piston. This type of engine using three expansion stages (a triple-expansion engine) became the most popular and efficient of reciprocal steam engines. For steam warships, the paddlewheel was vulnerable to enemy fire, and the screw PROPELLER was introduced (U. S. Navy Capt. John Ericsson, 1836). A far more efficient means of propulsion than the paddlewheel, the screw propeller soon was installed on all steamships except those operating in shallow waters. After 1850 steam increasingly displaced sail, in contrast to the early 1800s, when steamships carried only passengers of wealth and expensive cargo. By the 1870s steamships were carrying cargo over great distances at a profit. But efficient and commercially successful as steamships were, improvements were still to come. In 1890, Charles A. Parsons developed the *steam turbine.* Superior in speed to the reciprocating steam engine (early turbine-propelled ships achieved 36 knots compared to 24 knots, the record at the time), the steam turbine is at the same time lighter in weight and relatively free of vibration. Because it does not need internal lubrication, the steam turbine can use super-heated steam and thus increase its efficiency as a heat engine. By

World War I, all major naval and passenger vessels were powered by steam turbines. The steam turbine also has disadvantages. In general, turbines used for forward motion can not be reversed; thus for reverse motion a separate *astern* turbine must be used. Also, turbines operate efficiently at high rotational speeds. But for efficient propulsion, screw propellers must turn at relatively low speeds. A typical steamship may have its turbines turning at 3,000 rev/min while its propeller shaft turns at 400 rev/min. The necessary reduction is accomplished either by mechanical gearing or by connecting the turbine to an electric generator which supplies power to a slow-speed electric motor, which is, in turn, directly connected to the propeller shaft. Such *turbo-electric systems* have the advantage of simple reverse switching for astern motion. In the 1890's Rudolph Diesel perfected the *diesel engine.* Ships powered with diesel engines are termed motor ships. Propeller shafts can be turned directly by large slow-speed diesel engines, but most diesel installations operate best at high speeds and therefore must use either mechanical reduction gearing or an electric system in order to reduce the rate of propeller shaft rotation. Diesel engines can be reversed; but diesel-electric systems are preferred in some ships, since they allow more maneuverability and a greater freedom in choice of engine location. Although the diesel engine is the most efficient heat engine available for marine propulsion and might completely dominate ship propulsion, there are practical limits to its size, and the larger passenger liners and naval ships still use steam turbines. See DIESEL ENGINE; ENGINE; STEAM ENGINE; TURBINE.

Iron and Steel Hulls: The use of iron for ships was received cautiously in the 19th cent., although successful iron barges had been built as early as 1787. The advantages of iron hulls are strength, reduced weight (by 35%), reduced cost (by 10%), and great resistance to deterioration. The use of iron also allows the construction of larger ships. Wooden ships, even when longitudinally reinforced, are limited to approximately 300 ft in length. This is because of *hogging,* the tendency of the bow and stern to sag when a ship is lifted by a wave under its midsection, and *sagging,* the tendency of the midsection to sag when the bow and stern are lifted by waves. In 1851, I. K. Brunel built the iron-hulled *Great Eastern,* with a length of 680 ft. The *Great Eastern* was the first ship to have both an exterior hull and an interior hull to protect the ship from inrushing water in the event the exterior hull was damaged. At present all ships of any size have double bottoms, and double bottoms are mandatory for passenger ships over 300 ft in length. Modern armament, especially explosive shells, forced naval vessels to use armor and eventually to use iron hulls; it was these ships that emphatically demonstrated iron's superiority over wood. The lighter weight of iron hulls and consequently their increased capacity offered added cargo space that merchant shippers could not ignore. In the 1870s, steel and steel alloys of reliable quality became available. Steel's superiority in strength was immediately evident and by 1890 the use of iron was completely discontinued. With steel, the steam turbine, and the diesel engine, the modern age of marine transportation had arrived.

The modern steel hull is designed to resist the stresses resulting from the pressure of the water in which it is immersed, the force of rough seas, and the weight of machinery, cargo, and passengers. Although structural analysis is applied, the complex and variable character of the forces creates a stress pattern that cannot be precisely known, and data compiled from cumulative experience are of prime importance. Substantial stiffening derives from both longitudinal and transverse *bulkheads,* which also serve to restrict the spread of fire or sea water in case of accident. The ship's hull is also shaped

Ship construction: Hull of cargo ship, the *American Challenger* (*above*), still lacks its bow. Welders can be seen working on portions below decks and on bulkheads. Hull of another cargo ship, *Pioneer Moon* (*below*), is complete. Construction of its superstructure, including bridge and forecastle, is in progress. (*Newport News Shipbuilding Photo*)

Modern ocean-going vessels: Carrying both passengers and freight, the *Mariposa* (*left*) is an excellent example of a modern oil-fired steam-turbine ship. At its stern can be seen a steam-propelled stern paddler, a ship usually reserved for use on rivers of limited depth. The freighter *Hawaiian Refiner* (*right*) is designed to carry sealed containers, seen loaded on her decks. Use of containers for general cargo considerably reduces cargo-handling costs. (*Matson Lines*)

to minimize resistance to propulsion, which largely results from skin friction or frictional drag of the immersed surface. For ships designed to travel at high speeds, wave-making resistance is also considerable. Here, as in the structural design of ships' hulls, theoretical considerations are important guides, but the reduction of friction and wave-making resistance is largely accomplished by repeated observation of hull models drawn through towing tanks. (See TOWING TANKS AND WATER TUNNELS.)

Recent Developments: New developments are changing both the propulsion systems and hull shapes of new ships. GAS TURBINES have already been installed in smaller vessels and may soon be used in conjunction with steam turbines for larger ships. NUCLEAR PROPULSION systems are already used for submarines and recently such a nuclear power plant was installed in a prototypical nuclear merchant vessel under construction (see below). Perhaps the most radical innovation in hull design is the HYDROFOIL ship. This uses a hydrofoil totally immersed in water to lift the ship's hull completely off the water's surface, thus eliminating both frictional and wave-making resistance. Hydrofoil ships are already in use and some presently under contract are planned to reach speeds of 100 knots. With further progress in ship design, it is expected that the form of the ship will undergo changes in the future as radical as those of the past.—*A. L.*

Tugboats, like the one here, maneuver larger ships into their berths, haul barges, and help distressed vessels. In most cases, the modern tugboat depends on the diesel engine for its power. (*Fairbanks, Morse & Co.*)

Nuclear-powered merchant vessel: The *Savannah*, seen here on sea trials, is powered by a pressurized-water nuclear reactor. Heat released by reactor produces superheated steam which, as in conventionally powered ships, is then fed to steam turbines. Nuclear-powered ships can cruise great distances without refueling. (*Babcock and Wilcox*)

SHIVERING: an involuntary quivering of skeletal muscles. Such quivering increases heat production. Heat is always liberated during muscular contractions, as an inevitable by-product in the conversion of chemical energy into mechanical energy of movement. When the body of a bird or mammal is chilled, skeletal muscles increase tonic contraction, under control of the autonomic nervous system. When muscle tension becomes high, it also becomes spasmodic, and shivering is the result. Movement, however, is secondary to heat production, which is important in preventing a further decrease in BODY TEMPERATURE. Shivering is thus a part of the complex mechanism of temperature regulation.—*A. P. E.*

SHOCKLEY, WILLIAM, 1910–   , U. S. physicist; b. London, Eng. His research has been in the fields of ferromagnetics, semiconductors, plastic properties of metals, theory of solids, and transistors. In 1939, while on the staff of Bell Telephone Laboratories, he began the study of semiconductors as amplifiers. This work led eventually to the development of the transistor. Between 1942 and 1945 he did antisubmarine research. For their investigations on semiconductors and the discovery of the transistor effect, Shockley, J. Bardeen, and W. H. Brattain shared the 1956 Nobel prize. He is a member of the National Academy of Sciences.—*D. H. D. R.*

SHOCK TUBE: a device for research on shock waves (strong pressure waves) and related high-temperature effects in fast-moving air and other gases. The tube consists of a closed pipe or channel containing a diaphragm which separates two chambers having different initial pressures. Diaphragm rupture causes a shock wave to travel into the lower pressure chamber. The wave heats and accelerates the gas through which it passes under conditions which permit controlled measurements. The shock tube became an important research tool following World War II and has provided important information on the heating of ballistic vehicles upon RE-ENTRY into the atmosphere.—*D. B.*

SHOCK WAVE: an abrupt increase in pressure, density, and temperature, accompanied by a decrease in velocity, in a supersonic field of flow. In contrast to sound waves of normal loudness, which are relatively small disturbances, a shock wave constitutes a disturbance of large dimensions with sharp boundaries. At sea level the wave may be only a millionth of an inch thick, whereas in the thinner air encountered at high altitudes the transition is less abrupt, thickening to about ¼ in. at 250,000 ft. An intense sound will develop into a shock wave after traveling a short distance. Thus, a strong explosion inevitably produces a shock wave, which is in some cases the most damaging aspect of the blast.

Shock waves exist only in connection with supersonic motion, because only in this case can disturbances "pile up" to form such waves. Consider, for example, an airplane which accelerates from rest to supersonic speed in a series of short pulses. Each acceleration pulse will generate a sound pulse, much as a tuning fork does. After reaching supersonic speed, the plane will be traveling faster than the sound waves and will catch up with them, bunching the waves to form a shock wave in front of the plane. Shock waves may also be set up near the trailing as well as the leading edge of an airfoil, or in between. The intermediate location is characteristic of transonic flight, where the initially subsonic flow expands to supersonic, downstream of the leading edge, and then decelerates to subsonic flow again before reaching the trailing edge. Shock waves often occur in supersonic jet flows and can be seen in the luminous exhausts of rocket nozzles. In such streams they serve the purpose of adjusting the pressure of the jet flow to that of the surrounding atmosphere.

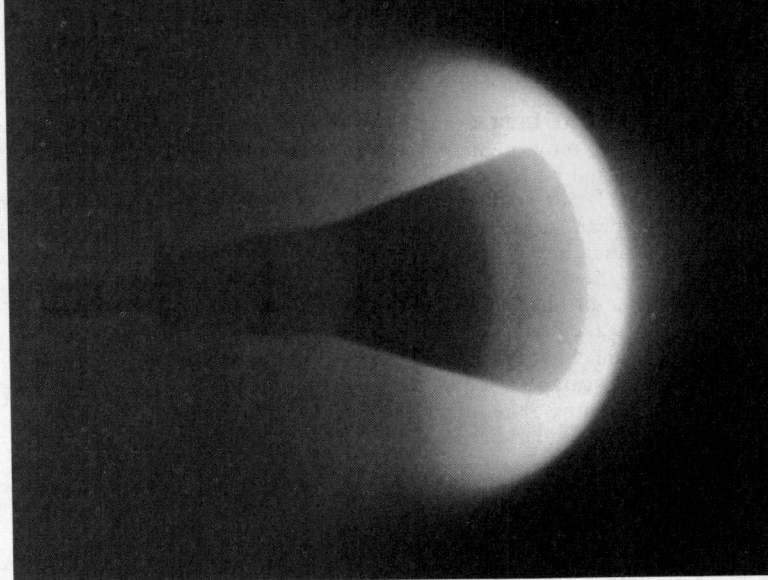

Shock wave produced as air flows past model of Mercury space capsule is made visible by air that has been excited to luminescence by a strong electrical discharge before it reaches model. Intensity of glow corresponds to density of air. (NASA)

Shock waves are more complex than most other types of waves. The reflection of shocks from surfaces does not obey the law of equality between angles of incidence and reflection; at a critical angle, regular reflection is replaced by Mach reflection in which a triple shock configuration is formed. A shock wave impinging on an interface between two gases will divide into a transmitted wave and a reflected wave. Depending on the conditions at the interface, the reflected wave may be a shock wave or may be changed in phase to become a wave of decreased pressure. See SONIC REGIMES.—*D. B.*

SHORT CIRCUIT: the inclusion in an operating ELECTRIC CIRCUIT of an element of extremely low resistance that bypasses the rest of the circuit and reduces the over-all circuit resistance to very nearly zero. This gives rise to an excessive current and a severe drop in circuit voltage. Short circuits frequently result from the leads to a circuit coming into electrical contact with each other. Unless checked, a short circuit will cause the melting of wires, destruction of measuring instruments, and possible damage to generators. Fuses or circuit breakers serve to open and thus protect a temporarily shorted or overloaded circuit.—*A. E.*

SHRUB: any woody PERENNIAL plant that lacks a main trunk and is smaller than a tree. Shrubs usually branch at their bases and grow to a height of less than 20 ft. Common shrubs include barberries, lilacs, azaleas, rhododendrons, and viburnums.—*A. P. E.*

SIAL: a term applied to rock composed largely of silica (silicon and oxygen) with aluminum; the term was coined from silica + alumina, and replaces the earlier term "acidic rock." Sial appears only on the continents and is believed to rest everywhere on an underlying zone of SIMA. Sial is lighter in color and less dense than sima, never exceeding three times the density of water. Most intrusive igneous rock near the surface is sial (see PLUTON), particularly the larger forms, *e.g.* BATHOLITHS. Lava of an especially viscous type, appearing only in continental regions where orogeny (mountain-making) is in process, forms the sialic rock andesite. The most common type of sial is granite, a coarse-grained rock; its fine-grained equivalent is rhyolite. Obsidian and pumice are extrusive, uncrystallized types (glass).—*E. A.*

SIDEREAL CLOCK: any clock rated to keep sidereal TIME. The 24-hr movement of the clock coincides with the apparent diurnal period of the vernal equinox, the *sidereal day*, equal to 23^h 56^m 04.091^s of mean solar time; thus the sidereal clock appears to gain about 4 min per day over the civil clock, coinciding with it when the Sun crosses the celestial equator on the date of the autumnal equinox, about Sept. 23. On the date of the vernal equinox, about Mar. 21, the sidereal clock and the civil clock differ by 12 hr. The sidereal clock can be rated readily from observations of the stars, and star observations can be scheduled and timed more easily from it, because the time on the sidereal clock indicates the right ascension of the local meridian at every moment. (See TIME.)—*T. N.*

SIEGBAHN, KARL MANNE GEORG, 1886–   , Swedish physicist; b. Örebro. He is known for his research on electricity, magnetism, and x-rays. He developed special research techniques for x-ray spectroscopy, determined with extraordinary accuracy the wavelengths of x-rays, and provided a theory of x-ray radiation that was congruent with the Bohr theory of the atom. His *Spectroscopy of Röntgen Rays* (1924) became the standard work on this subject. For his discoveries and investigations in x-ray spectroscopy, he received the 1924 Nobel prize. He is a fellow of the Royal Society.—*D. H. D. R.*

SIEMENS, ERNST WERNER VON, 1816–92, German engineer; b. Lenthe. He is best known for his work in electrical engineering. With his brother, **Karl von Siemens** (1829–1906), he established the firm of Siemens and Halske (1847). Siemens discovered gutta-percha's insulating properties for underground and underwater cables (1847), built the first telegraph line in Germany (Berlin–Frankfort am Main, 1849), developed apparatus for duplex and diplex telegraphy, and contributed to the technology of dynamos. His collected technical writings were published as *Wissenschaftliche und technische Arbeiten* (2 vols., 1889–91).—*D. H. D. R.*

SIGHT: see EYE; VISION.

SIKORSKY, IGOR IVANOVICH, 1889–   , Russian-U. S. inventor; b. Kiev. An aircraft designer and aeronautical engineer, he built the first operable four-engine airplane (1912). He is best known as the designer and developer of a helicopter, the first successful model of which he flew in 1939.—*D. H. D. R.*

SILICA: the compound silicon dioxide, SiO_2. It occurs very widely in nature both in free form and in combined form as silicates. Free silica exists in several crystalline and amorphous forms. By far the commonest crystalline modification is QUARTZ, which frequently occurs in massive formations of high purity, and is the major constituent of sand, sandstone, and quartzite rocks. Quartz belongs to the hexagonal crystal system. Tridymite (triclinic system) and cristobalite (tetragonal system) are the other crystalline forms of silica. Amorphous silica occurs as flint, chalcedony, jasper, and opal. An especially interesting form of amorphous silica is DIATOMACEOUS EARTH, a friable powder occurring in claylike deposits. It consists of the siliceous skeletons of diatoms, a type of microorganism. Another interesting form is the extremely hard mineral COESITE. The abrasive tripoli, named after the region of its origin, is a form of diatomaceous earth. Silica is very hard, with a high melting point (about 1600° C), and relatively unreactive chemically. It is used as a refractory material in furnace construction. It is also the principal ingredient of glass. The alkali metal silicates, made from silica and the alkali metal hydroxides, are water-soluble and are used in detergents.—*A. M. S.*

SILICA GEL: an artificial amorphous form of SILICA. It is a good adsorbent and widely used for dehumidifying and dehydrating. It has catalytic activity and is also a useful carrier for catalysts.—*D. P. B.*

SILICON: a nonmetallic element (Si); at. no. 14; at. wt 28.09; mp 1420°C; bp 2355°C; sp gr 2.42; valence 4. It falls below carbon in group IV B of the periodic table, and after oxygen is the most abundant element in Earth's crust, occurring combined with oxygen in silica (silicon dioxide, SiO_2) and in silicates. Elemental silicon was first prepared and described by Berzelius in 1823. The element is relatively unreactive at ordinary temperatures but unites readily with chlorine, fluorine, or oxygen when heated; it reacts with carbon at electric-furnace temperatures to form silicon carbide, which is widely used as an abrasive. Silicon also forms compounds and alloys with many metals, several of which are used in cermets. The most important compounds of silicon are the dioxide, silica, which is the anhydride of silicic acid, and the various silicates, which are salts of silicic acid. The silicates have a strong tendency to coordinate and form complex salts with other acidic anions. Most silicates, except those that contain only alkali-metal cations, are quite insoluble in water; sodium and potassium form a series of water-soluble silicates containing varying ratios of the alkali-metal oxide to silicon dioxide. Those high in alkali are used as detergents and corrosion inhibitors; those high in silica, known as water-glasses, are used in adhesives and sealants. The insoluble calcium and sodium-calcium silicates are most familiar in the form of glass. Most ceramics and hydraulic cements contain aluminum silicates as their major ingredients. Silicon forms a series of hydrides analogous to the hydrocarbons, but members having more than 4 or 5 silicon atoms in the chain are unstable. Hydrogen atoms in these hydrides can be substituted by alkyl or aryl groups to form the organo-silicon compounds, of which the best known are the SILICONES. Elemental silicon is used in metallurgy as an oxygen remover and an alloying element. In highly purified form it is used in transistors, photoelectric devices, and electronic components.—*A. M. S.*

SILICONE: the generic term for a group of polymeric compounds which are characterized by a repeating silicon-oxygen (—Si—O—) chain. This has at least one organic group attached through a carbon atom to each silicon atom. In most silicones the organic groups are either methyl or phenyl, although other organic groups with reactive substituents are used. Some silicones, notably those intended for hardenable coatings, contain hydrogen atoms attached to some of the silicon atoms in the chain. This enables cross-linking of the chains by oxidation or hydrolysis, with the formation of insoluble, infusible, three-dimensional polymers. Silicone oils, the simplest silicones, are made by hydrolysis of the organic silicon dichlorides, $RR'SiCl_2$, where R and R' represent alkyl, aryl, or hydrogen. The molecular weight of these linear polymers can be controlled by the conditions of hydrolysis. They can be further modified to rubbers, greases, lubricants, and a variety of other functional forms. As a class, the silicones are characterized by chemical inertness and by unusual stability to heat, so that they are useful for high-temperature applications. The liquid silicones are much more compressible and have lower viscosity coefficients than most liquids; the solid silicones have unusually low surface energy.

Silicone waterproofing: In water tank, a firebrick coated with silicone floats. Untreated brick sank.

Silicone finish, less than ¹⁄₁₀,₀₀₀ in. thick, prevents tarnishing of silver. Untreated portions of silver tray and cup are badly tarnished after 3-yr exposure; silicone-treated portions remain bright and shiny. (*Union Carbide*)

These properties make the silicones useful in hydraulic systems and in waterproofing compositions. See POLYMERS. —*A. M. S.*

SILL: a sheetlike mass of igneous rock formed from MAGMA that has intruded between horizontal or gently dipping beds. Exposed sills commonly form low narrow ridges or long cliffs such as the Palisades of the Hudson River in New Jersey. See INTRUSIVE ROCK, *illus.*—*J. Si.*

SILLIMAN, BENJAMIN, 1779–1864, U. S. chemist and geologist; b. Trumbull, Conn. He conducted the first course of experimental lectures in chemistry at Yale (1804) and began a full course of lectures in mineralogy and geology (1813). His influence was responsible for the establishment of the Yale Scientific School. He founded (1818) and edited the *American Journal of Science and Arts* (often called "Silliman's Journal"), and wrote *Elements of Chemistry* (1830–31) and many books about his travels. He was a member of the National Academy of Sciences. His son **Benjamin Silliman,** 1816–85, U. S. geologist, was b. New Haven, Conn. In his *Report on the Rock Oil, or Petroleum, from Venango County, Pa.* (1855), he showed that petroleum is a mixture of hydrocarbons different from vegetable and animal oils, that the hydrocarbons could be separated by fractional distillation, and that some fractions provided superior illuminants. He extracted paraffin from petroleum and made candles from it, recommended certain fractions for lubrication, and found that a gas useful in illumination could be prepared from petroleum. He was a member of the Yale faculty (from 1854) and a member of the National Academy of Sciences.—*D. H. D. R.*

SILT: in geology, an unconsolidated clastic sediment (see SEDIMENTS AND SEDIMENTATION) in which most of the particles are, by the usual definition, between ¹⁄₁₆ and ¹⁄₂₅₆ mm in diameter. In size, silt particles are between sand and clay. On consolidation, deposits of silt become *siltstone.*—*J. W.*

SILURIAN PERIOD: see GEOLOGICAL TIME CHART; PALEOZOIC ERA.

SILVER: a precious metallic element (Ag); at. no. 47; at. wt 107.88; density 10.50; mp 961°C; bp 1950°C; valence 1. Silver was known in ancient times and was used, as today, for coinage and for ornamental objects. It is one of the whitest metals, reflecting all ranges of the visible spectrum equally well; this property makes it a particularly valuable material for mirrors. Like gold it is quite soft, and is usually alloyed with small amounts of copper to increase its durability. Sterling silver, widely used for tableware, and U. S. silver coins both contain alloying elements for greater hardness. Silver occurs mainly as the sulfide, argentite, but also as free silver and as the chloride. It is frequently associated in small amounts with the ores of zinc, copper, and lead, and can be recovered as a valuable by-product in the winning of these metals; it is usually extracted and purified by electrolysis. Silver is one of the more noble metals, being relatively difficult to oxidize. It dissolves readily in nitric acid to form the easily soluble nitrate, the most widely used intermediate for preparing other silver chemicals. But the largest use of silver compounds is in photography. Silver halides, especially the bromide, are the essential ingredients of photographic emulsions. They are converted by light to a form which can easily be reduced to metallic silver by the mild organic reducing agents known as photographic developers. Silver compounds are also used as germicides and mildewcides. Metallic silver, suitably alloyed, is used in bearing metals and hard solders.—*A. M. S.*

SIMA: a term applied to rock rich in ferromagnesian minerals. These minerals, having a high proportion of iron and magnesium, give simatic (formerly called "basic") rock its dark color and high density (over three times that of water). The innermost zone of Earth's crust is believed to be composed

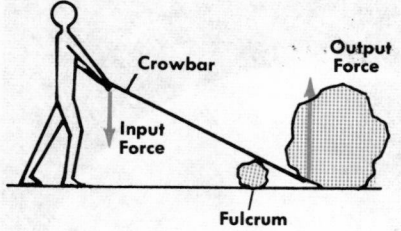
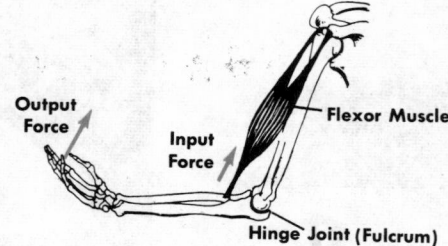
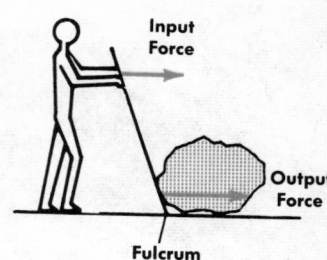

Fig. 1—Levers

(A) Fulcrum between input force and output force.

(B) Input force between output force and fulcrum.

(C) Output force between input force and fulcrum.

entirely of sima, grading off in the direction of the surface to SIAL. Some intrusive igneous rock near the surface is sima, particularly the smaller forms, *e.g.* sills and dikes. Most lava and pyroclastics, the results of volcanic activity, may be classed as sima, and it follows that most pockets of magma which give rise to such activity are rich in ferromagnesians. Sima is believed to be peridotitic in composition but includes also BASALT, a fine-grained igneous rock; the coarse-grained equivalent of basalt is GABBRO. The term sima was coined from "silicon" and "magnesium"; an alternate for the adjective "simatic" is "mafic" (magnesium, ferrous), or the older term "basic."—*E. A.*

SIMPLE MACHINE: in mechanics, a device for changing either the magnitude or the direction of a FORCE, or both. Four of the simplest machines are the lever, pulley, wheel and axle, and inclined plane. Practically every other machine is either a modification of one of these or a combination of two or more. A *lever* is simply a rigid body free to rotate about an axis. Fig. 1A shows a lever being used to lift a boulder. Here, the direction of the output force is opposite to that of the input, and its magnitude depends upon the location of the axis of rotation (technically called the fulcrum). The closer the fulcrum is to the boulder, the larger the output force for a given input. Fig. 1B shows a lever invented by nature in which the force is between the fulcrum and the output force —the human arm. When the flexor muscle contracts, the resulting upward force rotates the arm about the hinge joint. The output force exerted by the hand is smaller in magnitude and roughly in the same direction as the input force of the muscle. A third type of lever is the crowbar (Fig. 1C) in which the output force appears between the fulcrum and the input.

Both the *pulley* and the *wheel and axle* can be considered as special cases of the lever. The fixed pulley (Fig. 2A) simply

reverses the direction of the applied force, whereas the wheel and axle (2B) changes its magnitude as well as its direction. A number of pulleys may be connected together to increase the output force, as shown in Fig. 3. Fig. 4 illustrates the principle of the *inclined plane* as applied to the lifting of a load against gravity. In this case, the inclined surface (assumed frictionless) exerts a force on the object perpendicular to the surface. The output force (the vector sum of the input and the reaction forces) just balances the pull of gravity. Because of the help provided by the reaction of the incline, the input force required to lift the object is always less than the weight of the object, as every moving man knows. Other machines that utilize the principle of the inclined plane are the *screw* and the *wedge*.

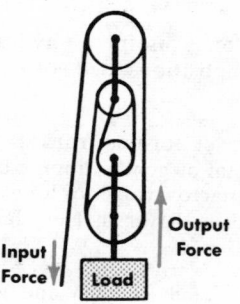

Fig. 3—System of pulleys increases output force. Ratio of output to input force equals number of strands of rope supporting movable load (excluding strand on which input force acts, which merely changes the direction of the applied force). Ratio, or mechanical advantage, here is 4.

Two parameters used to describe the performance of machines are the *mechanical advantage,* or ratio of the output force to the input force; and *efficiency,* or ratio of work done (force times distance through which it acts) by the output force to the work done by the input force. The first law of thermodynamics states that the efficiency of a machine is always less than 1; the difference represents the energy expended in overcoming frictional forces, and appears in the form of heat. —*S. K.*

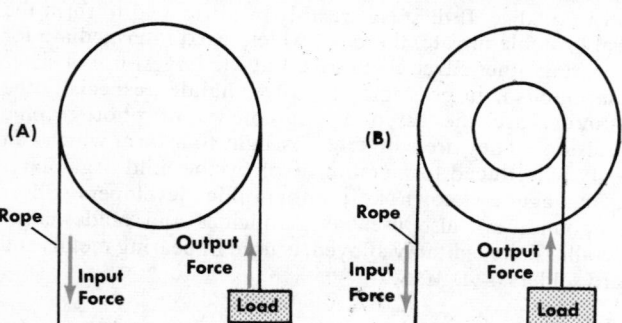

Fig. 2—Pulley (A) and wheel and axle (B): In both of these simple machines, direction of force is reversed. In fixed pulley the magnitude of the forces remains unchanged, but in wheel and axle the output force may exceed input force.

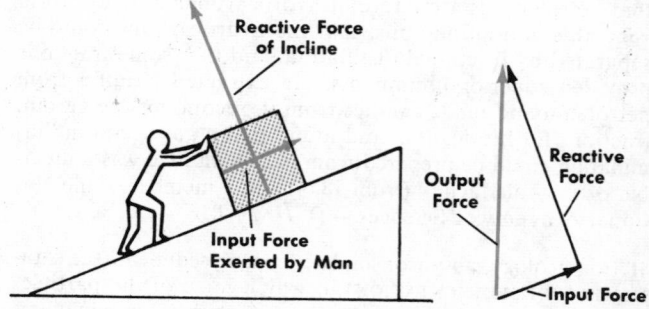

Fig. 4—Inclined plane: Magnitude of output force is sum of reactive and input forces, as vector diagram (*right*) shows.

SIMPSON, GEORGE GAYLORD, 1902–   , U. S. paleontologist; b. Chicago. A foremost student of fossil mammals, he has made particularly significant studies of Mesozoic and early Cenozoic forms, and of the origins of the higher categories of the class. He has also been a leader in the use of statistical methods in paleontology. His contributions to evolutionary synthesis (*Tempo and Mode in Evolution,* 1944; *The Major Features of Evolution,* 1953) are milestones in the application of paleontologic evidence to modern evolutionary theory.—*A. L. McA.*

SIMPSON'S RULE: a rule for obtaining a numerical approximation to the area bounded by a curve, the *x*-axis, and two ordinates; equivalently, a process for obtaining the approximate value of the definite integral $\int_a^b f(x)dx$. The rule is used if the curve does not fit any known mathematical expression, or if it fits an expression that is difficult, or impossible, to integrate. The segment along the *x*-axis from *a* to *b* (see figure) is divided into an even number (*n*) of equal parts, each of length $h = (b - a)/n$. The ordinates at $x = a$, $x = a + h$, $x = a + 2h, \ldots, x = b$, are $y = y_0, y = y_1, y = y_2, \ldots, y = y_n$. The lengths of the ordinates can be measured from the graph

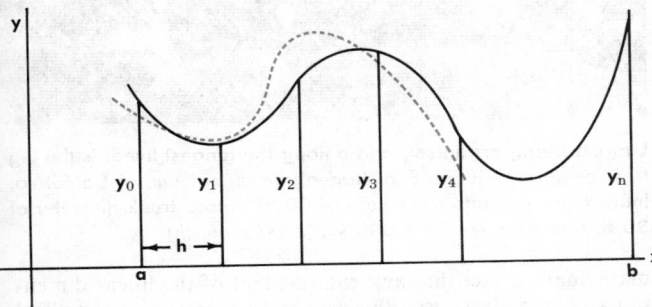

Simpson's rule obtains approximate value of area beneath curve. The greater the number of vertical segments into which the area is divided (*i.e.* the greater the number of ordinates, y_n), the closer the approximation will be. Broken blue line shows parabolic arcs approximating portions of the curve.

or calculated from the equation of the curve. Each segment of the curve going through three adjacent ordinates is replaced by a segment of a parabola. The more ordinates there are, the closer will the approximation be. If $n = 2$, there are three ordinates, and the area *A* is given by:

$$A = (\tfrac{1}{3})\, h(y_0 + 4y_1 + y_2)$$

For any even value of *n*:

$$A = (\tfrac{1}{3})\, h [\, y_0 + 4(y_1 + y_3 + \ldots + y_{n-1})$$
$$+ 2(y_2 + y_4 + \ldots + y_{n-2}) + y_n]$$

This formula is exact if the equation of the curve is of third degree or less.—*B. P. S.*

SINKHOLE: a pit in the ground caused by the dissolving or collapse of underlying rock layers, generally limestone. Some sinkholes result from enlargement of joints or crevices, the overlying soil slumping into the hollow thus created. Others are formed by collapse of cave roofs. Some of the latter are quite large, with diameters up to several miles and depths of more than 100 ft. Natural bridges often result from preservation of portions of the roofs of such collapsed caverns.—*A. P. E.*

SIPHON: a curved tube with two arms, one shorter than the other, that is used to transfer a liquid from one vessel to an-

other vessel at a lower level. The siphon can be filled by pouring liquid into it before it is placed in the operating position, or by applying suction at the lower end after it is in position. The flow into the lower vessel, once started, continues until the liquid in the two vessels is at the same level or until the higher vessel is emptied. The flow can be reversed in direction if the lower vessel is raised to a point where its liquid level is above that of the first vessel. The siphon functions because the force of gravity on the longer column of water is greater than that on the shorter column; the result is a net force that causes the liquid to move toward the lower vessel even though the liquid must move upward in the short section of the tube. The liquid columns do not separate and flow downward into the two vessels because this would create a partial vacuum in the tube. The atmospheric pressure exerted on the liquid at both ends of the tube is equal and acts to prevent the creation of this partial vacuum.—*A. E.*

SIRIUS AND SIRIUS B: a double-star system in the constellation Canis Major. Sirius A is the brightest star in the sky, with an apparent visual magnitude of -1.42. It is a white star of the main sequence, with a surface temperature of about 18,000° F. Its apparent brightness is due primarily to its nearness, its distance from the Sun being only 8.7 lt-yr. Sirius B, invisible to the naked eye, was first suspected to exist by F. W. Bessel, 1844, when he found that Sirius was moving (against the background of more distant stars) not in a straight line but with a wavy motion. He concluded that Sirius has an invisible companion, and that the two are moving in orbits about their common center of gravity, as well as moving together in space. To affect Sirius in this way, the companion must have a mass comparable with that of Sirius A; nevertheless its apparent magnitude is only 8.7, and it was not observed through the telescope until 1862. Sirius B was thus the first of the white dwarf stars (which are of enormous density) to be discovered. Its period about Sirius A is 50 yr; in 1960, the two were 9″ apart. The proper motion is large—about 1.3″/yr. In terms of the Sun, the masses of Sirius A and B are 2.28 and 0.98, respectively; the diameters, 1.8 and 0.03. Sirius is on the meridian at midnight about Jan. 2.—*M. W. O.*

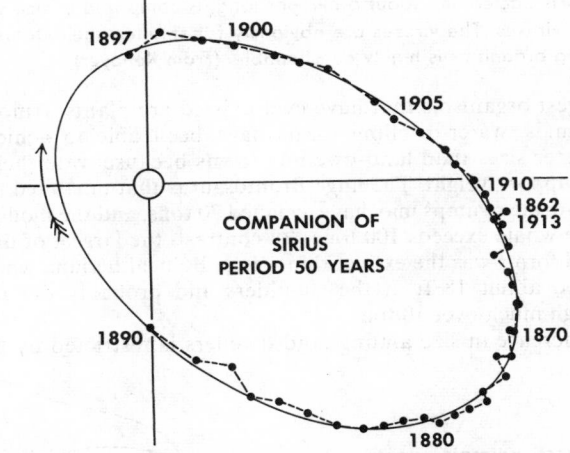

Apparent orbit of companion of Sirius, with respect to Sirius, is indicated by black dots; Sirius is indicated by open circle. Sirius has an elliptical orbit similar to that of its companion. The two stars in following their orbits move around a common center of gravity, which itself is moving through space. (*Yerkes Obs.*)

SITTER, WILLEM DE, 1872–1934, Dutch astronomer; b. Sneek. Director of the Leiden Observatory (1919), he studied the application of photometry in astronomy and conducted research on the satellites of Jupiter. He applied the theory of relativity to astronomy and attempted to calculate the radius of the universe from the observed mean density of matter (1917); and through this work he became one of the pioneers of the theory of the expanding universe. Among his writings are *Kosmos* (1932) and *The Astronomical Aspect of the Theory of Relativity* (1933).—*R. J. F.*

SIZE OF LIVING THINGS: Living things occur in a vast range of sizes. The biggest living objects are giant redwoods, which in a lifetime of several thousand years may reach 300 ft in height and 100 ft in girth. The smallest indisputably living organisms are true BACTERIA, 25,000 of which laid side by side would measure scarcely ½ in. Still smaller are VIRUSES, on the borderline between the living and nonliving.

The nature of an organism and the environmental circumstances under which it lives set limits on its size. Nonmotile organisms can grow very large because they evade the mechanical problem of moving a heavy weight; thus the

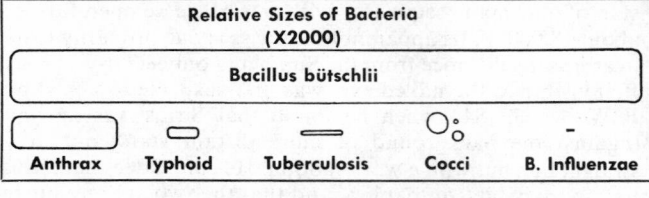

Relative Sizes of Bacteria (X2000)

Bacillus bütschlii

Anthrax   **Typhoid**   **Tuberculosis**   **Cocci**   **B. Influenzae**

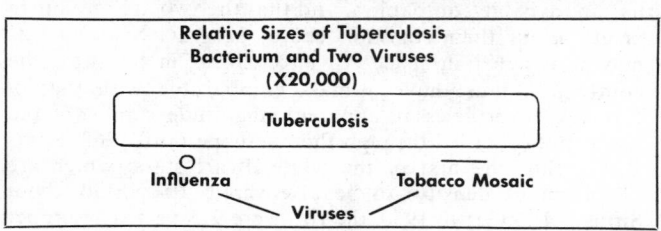

Relative Sizes of Tuberculosis Bacterium and Two Viruses (X20,000)

Tuberculosis

Influenza   **Tobacco Mosaic**

Viruses

Relative sizes of the smallest living organisms: Bacteria are the smallest of the organisms that are definitely considered as "living." The largest bacterium shown above, *Bacillus bütschlii*, which occurs in the cockroach intestine, is about 75 microns long. The tuberculosis bacterium, about 6 microns long, is compared in size with two viruses. The viruses are obviously far smaller; their status as living organisms is highly questionable. (*From Kenoyer*)

largest organisms that have ever existed are plants. Among animals, water-dwelling forms have been able to achieve greater sizes than land-dwelling forms because water helps to support weight. The huge Brontosaurus that inhabited the Mesozoic swamps may have weighed 70 tons, and the modern blue whale exceeds 100 tons. By contrast, the largest of dry-land forms was the extinct rhinoceros, Baluchitherium, which stood about 18 ft at the shoulders and probably did not weigh much over 10 tons.

Increase in size among land-dwellers is restricted by the

Largest living organism, and among the longest-lived, is the big tree, or giant sequoia, *Sequoiadendron giganteum,* of California. Individuals may attain a height of 300 ft and a trunk diameter of 30 ft, and may live for 4,000 yr. (*Josef Muench*)

mathematical fact that any enlargement of the linear dimensions of a body causes the weight to increase as the third power of the enlargement. For example, a uniform doubling of dimensions brings about an 8-fold (2^3) increase in weight. A big animal must therefore devote a larger proportion of its strength and energy to supporting and moving its own bulk than does a small one. Large animals have numerous advantages in self-defense, in food-getting, and in heat conservation, but the problems of movement and support have nevertheless limited the extent to which evolution has been able to increase the size of terrestrial animals.

Invertebrates, with the exception of some jellyfishes and a few sessile marine forms, are generally smaller than vertebrates. The difference is due to the fact that vertebrates possess an internal skeleton made of bone, a material that provides protection and support while it continues to grow. Invertebrates possess external skeletons, made of a material that does not grow. The lobster, for example, can increase its body size only by sloughing off its "shell," quickly expanding its body, and then developing a new "shell." During this molting period the animal is unable to defend itself or even to move.

Largest animals, past and present: The sulfur-bottom (blue) whale is the largest animal that has ever lived. This great creature dwarfs the elephant (the largest living land animal) which, in turn, dwarfs man. The swamp-dweller, brontosaurus, now extinct, was one of the largest land-living animals on record. (*From Kenoyer*)

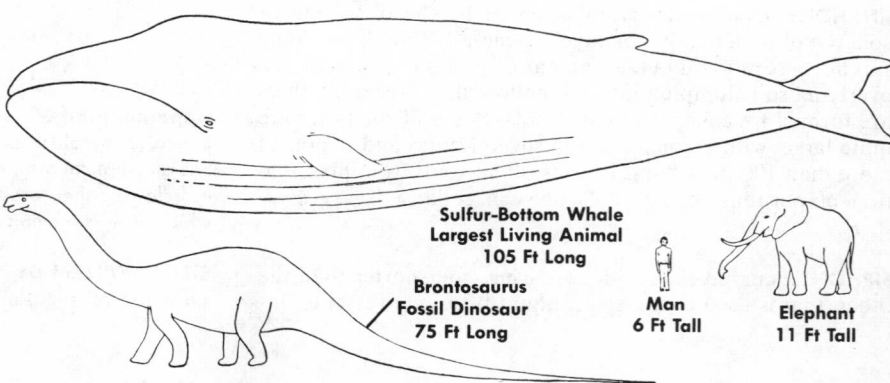

Sulfur-Bottom Whale Largest Living Animal 105 Ft Long

Brontosaurus Fossil Dinosaur 75 Ft Long

Man 6 Ft Tall

Elephant 11 Ft Tall

From a strictly human point of view, the attainment of large size is important because intelligence of the human level could probably not have been evolved in animals much smaller than ourselves. Intelligent behavior appears to depend on the possession of a brain of large *absolute* size, in which many billions of interconnections between cells are possible. A brain of the human level of attainment can therefore occur only in a body large and strong enough to support it.—*F. M.*

SIZING: a process of applying continuous, generally removable coatings to materials. In the TEXTILE industry, sizes are applied to the warp-yarns to bind the individual fibers together, stiffen the yarns, and protect them from chaffing in the loom harness; sizes are also applied to fabrics to stiffen and improve texture and increase weight. Starches, gums, gelatin, and polyvinyl alcohol have found use as textile sizes. Starch is still the most popular one, but because of stream pollution caused by starch-containing mill effluents, much effort has recently been made to develop sizes not having such a high biological oxygen demand. (Also certain synthetic sizes, although they have little or no biological oxygen demand, pose a pollution problem because they do not decompose and thus remain in water almost indefinitely.) In the PAPER industry, sizes are extensively used to give strength, weight, and desirable surface properties to the finished sheet. Paper sizes, in contrast to most textile sizes, are permanent rather than removable, forming an integral part of the paper.

In the cold-working of metals, the term "sizing" describes a method of producing accurate dimensions on a press, eliminating the need for further machining or grinding. See MACHINE TOOL.—*W. P. C.*

SKELETON: the hard parts that give mechanical support to the soft tissues of an animal; also, the stiffening structures found in or surrounding single-celled organisms. Since living cells surround the skeletons of sponges, echinoderms, and vertebrates, these animals are said to have *endoskeletons.* By contrast, the secreted materials that support and partially enclose other animals are all external to the living tissues and hence are *exoskeletons;* they are found in coelenterates (*e.g.* corals), bryozoans (moss animals), lamp shells (brachiopods), mollusks, most arthropods, and tunicates (sea squirts). The single cell of a diatom is enclosed in a two-piece shell or skeleton of intricately sculptured siliceous material. Among protozoans, the radiolarians develop supporting needles of silica, and the foraminiferans secrete external shells of lime. The scales of fishes and reptiles, as well as the bony shell under the scales of a turtle, are so close to the surface that they are sometimes regarded as exoskeletons, even though the animal has an endoskeleton, too.

Animals with external skeletons often suspend activity when disturbed, and withdraw into the haven of their protective armor. This behavior also occurs in echinoderms such as sea urchins, which have a firm internal skeleton close beneath the surface of the body. In many arthropods, the waxy covering of the exoskeleton is important in limiting the rate at which the body loses water. Insects and other terrestrial arthropods can be active under conditions that would be fatal to less protected animals, because their lightweight jointed exoskeletons are impervious to passage of water. These animals are able to exploit the advantages of small size (*e.g.* short life cycle, ease of concealment, profligate reproduction) without incurring the usual penalty of rapid water loss resulting from a high ratio of surface to volume. Land tortoises gain from their exoskeletons in a similar way, but on a larger scale.

The primitive skeletal support of chordates is the noto-

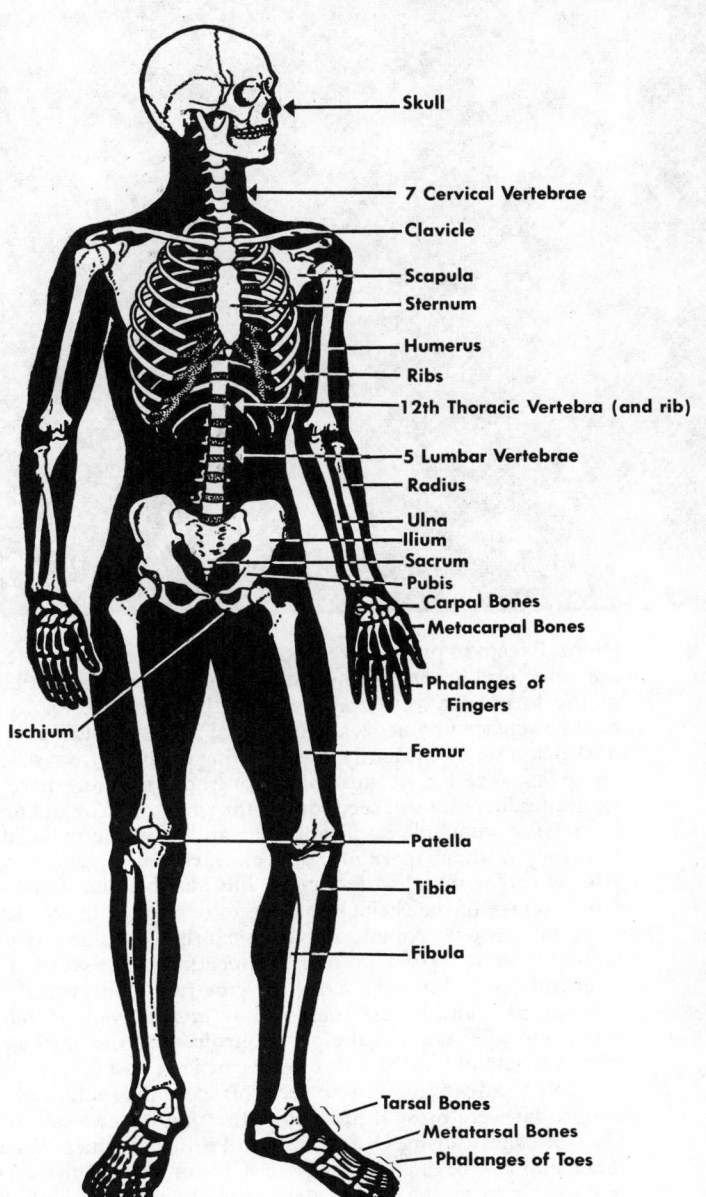

Human skeletal system (*above*) and an enlarged view of the skull (*below*): Including bones of ear, which are not shown, adult skeleton consists of more than 200 named bones. (*From Guyer*)

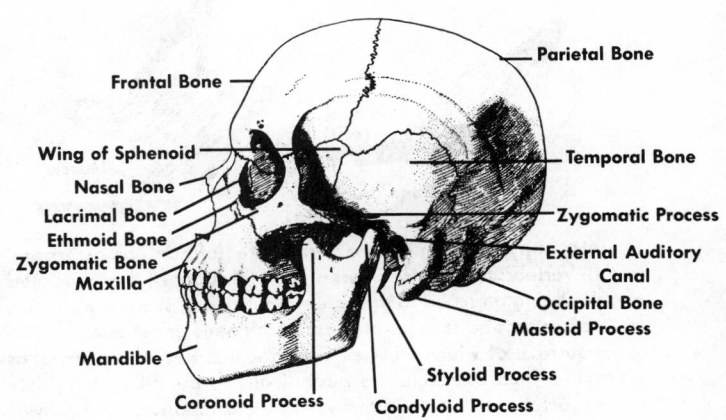

chord. Except in protochordates (*e.g.* lancelets and tunicates), the notochord becomes supplemented or replaced by cartilage in the form of a vertebral column; this cartilage, in turn, may be replaced by BONE as the animal matures. Such an endoskeleton serves primarily in preventing the body from shortening as a result of muscular contractions and thereby facilitates locomotion; secondarily the skeleton provides firm points for attachment of muscles, and this increases the efficiency of their operation. The exoskeleton of arthropods also serves for muscle attachment, but has the compensating disadvantage of the skeleton having to be molted at intervals to permit growth. An endoskeleton can be continuously enlarged. In vertebrates with paired appendages, the skeleton is often subdivided into an *axial skeleton* (the skull, vertebral column, ribs, and breastbone) and an *appendicular skeleton* (the pectoral girdle and the pelvic girdle, plus the cartilages or bones actually in the fin or flipper or leg or wing).

Another advantage can be recognized in the endoskeletal plates that were present just below the skin of jawless ostracoderm fishes during Ordovician and Silurian times. When these animals began invading fresh water, as the first vertebrates to do so, the fresh water tended to enter the body by osmosis faster than had the salt water. Bony plates (ostracoderm means "shell-skinned") apparently provided a seal against excessive inflow and permitted these animals with their

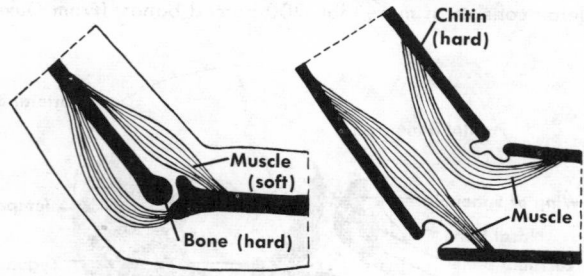

Skeletal support of limbs of a vertebrate (*left*) and an arthropod (*right*): Vertebrate limb has internal skeletal support, the associated muscles being attached to the external surface of skeletal elements. Limb of arthropod is supported by a chitinous exoskeleton, to interior surface of which muscles are attached. Because arthropods must shed their exoskeletons periodically to permit growth, they are, at such times, without effective skeletal support. (*From Kenoyer*)

rather inefficient kidneys to survive in the new habitat. Later, fishes and amphibians developed more efficient kidneys and also an epidermal seal in a stratified skin; at the same time they lost the bony plates, which must have hampered movement. The epidermal seal, with or without overlapping scales in the skin, appears to have been effective, too, in resisting water loss to the atmosphere when amphibians and early reptiles began invading the land.

Animals have produced a wide range of skeletal materials: siliceous material in many sponges; proteinaceous horny secretions (spongin) in other sponges, such as the bath sponge; lime in limy sponges, in the endoskeletons of echinoderms and vertebrates, in the exoskeletons of corals, brachiopods, and mollusks; proteinaceous materials impregnated with the polysaccharide chitin in the exoskeletons of arthropods and, with lime added, in many crustaceans and millipedes; and a type of cellulose as the tunic of tunicates.—*L. and M. M.*

SKIN: the outermost cellular layer of an animal's body, known also as the integument; also, loosely, the outermost layer of cells covering a fruit. Among invertebrate animals, the skin is usually one cell thick. Among vertebrates it is stratified, composed of an *epidermis* of ectodermal origin and a *dermis* of mesodermal origin. The skin is composed of epithelial tissues, with or without associated connective tissues. Generally it is the largest organ of the animal body.

In free-living flatworms (turbellarians) the skin is soft and ciliated on the ventral surface; in most other worms it secretes a flexible cuticle. In brachiopods (lamp shells) and mollusks, the skin over the mantle may secrete a hard shell, while the ciliated integument that lines the mantle cavity creates a current of water which brings in food and oxygen, and carries away wastes. Among arthropods, the skin secretes the jointed plates of the external skeleton, which is molted at intervals to permit growth. In echinoderms, the thin integument covers the endoskeletal plates, *e.g.* the shell of a sea urchin.

Among vertebrate animals, the glands of the skin are all parts of the epidermis, although they may project deep down into the dermis and be closely associated there with blood vessels and nerves. These glands are specialized for secretion of mucus, oily and waxy materials, odorous substances, poisonous substances, milk, and watery sweat (see SWEAT GLAND). The epidermis may also produce external structures such as the horny teeth of lampreys (cyclostomes), the horny scales of turtles and pangolins, FEATHERS, HAIR, the horn of rhinoceroses, antlers, claws, nails, hoofs, and the whalebone (baleen) of whalebone whales. It may cooperate with the dermis in producing TEETH, and horns that have a bony core. Epidermal cells may receive pigment from *melanocytes* (chromatophores) located between the epidermis and dermis.

The dermis, which is well supplied with blood vessels and nerves, is held to the rest of the body by connective tissues. Dermis cells, when dead, absorb tannins and metallic salts readily, forming an insoluble material called leather. In leather processing, various methods are used to remove the epidermis and any epidermal structures from the skin, as well as all blood vessels and loose connective tissue from its inner surface; the dried, stretched skin is then a "hide." A somewhat different method of preparation is necessary to keep the fur on a mammal skin in making it into a "pelt."

The dermis layer of vertebrates contributes special products, too. In vertebrates that have a bony skull, the dermis supplies many bony plates that sink into the skin of the head and become associated with the brain case. In turtles and armadillos, the dermis produces bony plates over the body. In turtles, these bony plates do not correspond in pattern to the horny plates secreted by the epidermis, but are usually fused to the vertebrae and ribs. In fishes, lizards, and snakes, the dermis commonly provides bony SCALES, which lie under the epidermis but overlap in a way that gives the animal a flexible armor. As the animal grows, its dermal plates grow, too. Those of fishes may show distinct markings from which it is possible to estimate the individual's age.

Terrestrial amphibians, lizards, and snakes all shed the outer layer of the epidermis, as a unit (a "slough") or in patches. Birds and mammals similarly molt their feathers or fur at definite seasons (see MOLTING). The outermost layers of human epidermis are constantly being worn away and replaced by new growth in the innermost *germinative* (Malpighian) layer; older, outer layers are composed of dying and dead cells, rendered waterproof by degenerative changes that make them "cornified" (horny), *i.e.* transform their contents into insoluble proteins. Repeated friction against skin areas often leads to additional local growth, which thickens the epidermis into a *callus*. On the hands and feet of primates, the grasping surfaces show an adaptation toward holding objects without slipping: the epidermis has raised rows of "friction ridges." The patterns of these ridges are unique in each individual and provide the basis for identification, as in fingerprints and sole prints.—*L. and M. M.*

SKIN EFFECT: the tendency, at high frequencies, for electric currents to flow only in a thin skin along the outer surface of a conductor. In contrast, direct current is considered to flow uniformly throughout the whole cross-section of a conductor. The skin effect is caused by self-INDUCTANCE. For copper, the thickness of the skin is given by $6.61/\sqrt{f}$ cm, where f is the frequency. At a frequency of 100 Mc, for example, the skin is only 6.61×10^{-4} cm thick.—*I. R.*

SKIN FRICTION: friction due to the tendency of a fluid to stick to solid surfaces. A body moved through a fluid pulls some fluid with it on its skin. The force required to overcome this fluid friction is called *skin drag*, or *skin friction*, and constitutes a major contribution to the drag of a high-speed aircraft.—*Wm. R.*

SLATE: a metamorphic rock formed from SHALE by dynamic metamorphism in mountainous areas. It is fine-grained and splits into thin sheets. This "slaty cleavage," developed at right angles to the direction of the pressure applied during metamorphism, is due to the structural arrangement, in layers, of invisible flakes of the component minerals, chiefly mica and chlorite. It is likely to be at an angle to the bedding plane of the shale. The color of slate is caused by the mineral content other than mica (muscovite), which is colorless. A predominance of chlorite produces green slate; scattered flakes of iron sulfide produce the familiar dark gray slate. Various colors of slate have been used for paving and blackboards. See Color Plate 61.—*E. A.*

SLEEP: a bodily state that superficially resembles unconsciousness and coma, but differs from these states in that the animal or person may be readily aroused from it. Significant bodily changes during sleep include lowered blood pressure and body temperature, reduced rate of heartbeat, and slower metabolic rate. These and other factors argue against the conception of sleep as a state during which bodily tissues destroyed during wakefulness are built up or repaired. In man, at least, sleep provides a chance to dream, and there is some evidence that dreaming is essential to mental health. While many animal species alternate between sleep and wakefulness several times during the day, others exhibit more regular patterns. The sleeping habits of adult human beings are deeply ingrained and very resistant to change. People who undergo extensive sleep deprivation are considerably more alert during the daylight hours of deprivation than at night, their usual sleeping time.

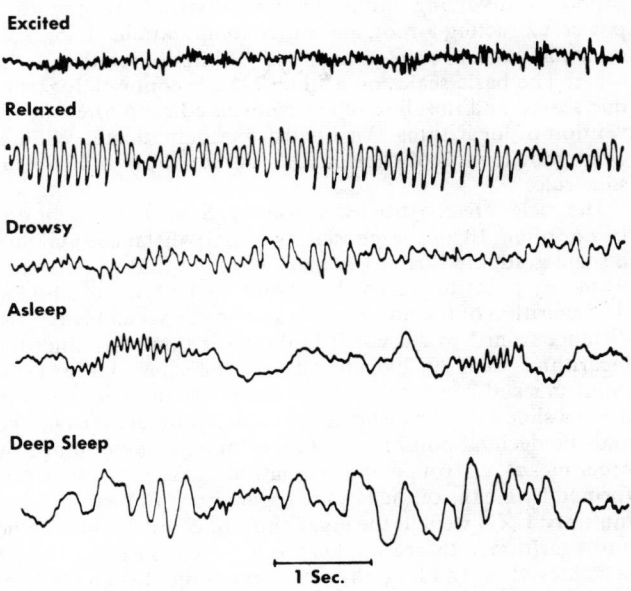

Recordings of brain waves from a normal subject made during various stages of wakefulness and sleep: Amplitude and frequency of waves are indicative of brain activity. Even during deep sleep, periods of relaxation are interspersed with periods of strong brain activity. *(From Villee, after Jasper)*

Brain waves are good indicators of the depth of sleep and other sleep phenomena. If tiny electrodes are attached to the scalp, they can detect small electrical changes that appear as waves when displayed on an oscillograph. During wakefulness, rapid, complex wave forms are superimposed on relatively slower *alpha* waves, which have a frequency of 8 to 12/sec. During deep sleep, this pattern is replaced by slower, simpler *delta* waves, with a frequency of 4 to 5/sec. Brainwave records reveal an alternation between deep and light slumber during the night. Dreams occur frequently, though many or most may not be recalled on awakening. Changes in position of the body and periods of active eyeball movements are numerous; usually these occur between dreams.

A particular area of the hypothalamus of the brain appears to be critical in sleep; when this region is destroyed, animals sleep for days, remain drowsy for months. Nervous impulses from sensory receptors reach this region by means of the reticular formation, another portion of the brain. Activation of this system tends to prohibit sleep. Conversely, diminished nervous impulses in the reticular formation (as in quiet darkness) tend to promote sleep.—*D. M. F.*

SLEET: popularly, almost any sort of precipitation in which liquid water and ice or snow fall together. In meteorology, the term is used in the U. S. A. as a synonym for ice pellets, or clear, spherical, frozen raindrops. In parts of the U. S. A. sleet means the layer of clear ice deposited by freezing rain; this is properly called GLAZE.—*D. H. L.*

SLICKENSIDE: in geology, a polished and scratched surface found along a fault plane, resulting from the friction between two shifted blocks which have mutually abraded each other. When the fault surface is not a single plane, the wall rocks may be crushed and a fault breccia produced; and if the crushed material has been ground to powder, this powder is termed *fault gouge.*—*J. Sh.*

SLIDE RULE: a mechanical device for rapid calculation of problems involving multiplication, division, raising to a power, extracting a root, and other computations. It consists essentially of two rules, one of which slides in relation to the other. The basic scales on a slide rule are common logarithmic scales, and the slide rule was invented soon after the invention of logarithms. An English mathematician, William Oughtred (1574–1660), invented both rectilinear and circular slide rules.

The scales are constructed as follows. Some convenient distance, often 10 in., is chosen as a unit distance. On this, a scale graduated from 1 is marked off so that the distance from any point to the left-hand end of the scale is equal to the logarithm of the number marked on the scale. Hence, the distance from 1 to 2 is equal to the logarithm of 2. Since the logarithms of 2, 20, 200, etc. all have the same mantissa, the point marked 2 can be used for any such number. Thus, in using a slide rule, the decimal points in a problem are ignored and the decimal point in the answer must be determined by other means, *e.g.* rough approximations. Computation is performed by means of the laws of logarithms. For example, to multiply 2×3 we add the logarithms of 2 and 3 and find the antilogarithm of this result. On the slide rule the same answer is achieved by adding the corresponding distances. Specifically the number 1 on the sliding rule is moved opposite the 2 on the fixed rule; the number on the fixed rule opposite the 3 on the sliding rule is the answer, 6. Division is performed by subtracting distances. Slide rules may also contain scales giving squares, cubes, reciprocals, trigonometric functions, natural logarithms, and other, more specialized, relations. Different models and sizes of slide rules are available. The more expensive ones have more scales, are more carefully made, and can be adjusted by the user. Operation is fully described in the instruction booklets provided by manufacturers.—*H. E. W.*

SMELL: see SENSES; TASTE AND SMELL.

SMELTING: extraction or refining of a metal from its ore by treatment in a FURNACE. Fundamentally, smelting is the re-

Smelting and refining copper: Ores are reduced to matte copper in blast furnaces. Placed in horizontal converters (*above*), impure matte is exposed to air blasts and reduced to a copper more than 99% pure. (*Copper & Brass Research Assoc.*)

duction of ores with the aid of heat, rather than by purely mechanical means (*e.g.* panning for gold), purely chemical means (*e.g.* dissolving gold or silver from their ores by cyanide), or electrolysis (*e.g.* the production of aluminum from bauxite). The most widely used smelting process is the reduction of iron ore to pig iron. This is accomplished in a blast furnace loaded with iron ore (essentially Fe_2O_3, plus impurities such as water and the oxides of several elements), coke, and limestone. Heated air is blown upward through the mixture. This burns the coke to carbon monoxide, which reacts with the iron oxide, reducing it to metallic iron. The limestone, dissolving or combining with the impurities (the gangue) of the residue, lowers the melting temperature of the gangue, and allows a liquid slag to form which is tapped from the surface of the molten iron. Copper-oxide ores are smelted the same way; copper sulfides, as well as lead, tin, and many other metal ores, are reduced in furnaces with the addition of ingredients suitable for the particular reaction desired, and sometimes, as in the case of tin, with no additional ingredients at all. Despite chemical and electrical processes, smelting remains the most important means of extracting and refining metals. See METALLURGY.—*A. L.*

SMITH, ALEXANDER, 1865–1922, U. S. chemist; b. Edinburgh, Scotland. His series of texts with appropriate laboratory manuals profoundly influenced the teaching of chemistry in the U. S. A. He devised the isoteniscope, to determine vapor pressure at elevated temperatures, and with it he corrected all inconsistencies observed in physical data for sulfur and dissociation of Hg_2Cl_2, NH_4 and PH_4 compounds, and P_2O_5. He solved the puzzling relationship between liquid, solid, and gaseous forms of sulfur. He was a member of the National Academy of Sciences.—*V. B.*

SMITH, EDGAR FAHS, 1854–1928, U. S. chemist; b. York, Pa. He pioneered in methods of electrochemical analysis, made atomic weight determinations for eight elements, and studied complex acids of tungsten, molybdenum, and niobium. Smith published several books on inorganic and analytical chemistry and several biographies of early American chemists. His large collection of early chemistry books forms the basis of the Smith Collection at the Univ. of Pennsylvania. He was a member of the National Academy of Sciences.—*A. I.*

William Smith
(Bettmann Archive)

SMITH, WILLIAM, 1769–1839, English geologist; b. Churchill, Oxfordshire. His recognition and elaboration of the sequence of rocks and fossils in W England earned him the title of "Father of English Geology." He was the first to demonstrate clearly that the chronological sequence of rock strata can often be determined by the fossils they contain, and his publication of this discovery (*Strata Identified by Organized Fossils,* 1816) is a landmark in the history of science.—*A. L. McA.*

SMITHSON, JAMES, 1765–1829, English scientist, founder of the Smithsonian Institution, b. France. An analytical chemist of considerable fame, Smithson bequeathed his property to the United States for the founding of the Smithsonian Institution, Washington, D. C., for the "increase and diffusion of knowledge among men."—*A. P. E.*

SMOG: see ATMOSPHERIC POLLUTION; FOG.

SNELL (or **SNELLIUS**) **WILLEBRORD,** 1591–1626, Dutch mathematician and physicist; b. Leyden. He is best known for his discovery of a simple relationship between the angle of incidence and the angle of refraction for a ray of light crossing a boundary between two media (Snell's law), although he never published this discovery, but merely lectured on it. Snell was a pioneer in the use of triangulation in determining (1817) the size of a degree of longitude and, hence, the size of Earth. Professor of mathematics at the Univ. of Leyden, he published a number of books on mathematics and physics. —*D. H. D. R.*

SNELL'S LAW: see REFRACTION.

SNOW: see PRECIPITATION.

SOAP: the best-known cleanser, made by the action of alkali on fats by the process of saponification (see FATS AND OILS). Although there are many soaps, the word *soap* commonly applies to the sodium or potassium salts of the fat acids,

$$\left[R{-}\overset{\displaystyle O}{\underset{\displaystyle \|}{C}}{-}O \right]^{-} Na^+ \quad \text{or} \quad \left[R{-}\overset{\displaystyle O}{\underset{\displaystyle \|}{C}}{-}O \right]^{-} K^+$$

where R in the negative ion represents a hydrocarbon chain of 10 to 18 carbon atoms. Potassium soap tends not to have a firm consistency and is therefore used in shaving creams or in "soluble" soap; sodium soap is the usual hard, bar soap. The detergent action of these soaps is caused by the long hydrocarbon chains in their molecules; these chains are oil-soluble and have at one end the carboxylic acid group, which is water-soluble. This combination enables soap and water to emulsify oily particles of dust and dirt and float them away from skin or clothing. Sodium and potassium soaps are said to be the best detergents in water that is *soft, i.e.* water free from dissolved salts containing ions such as calcium and magnesium; such ions in *hard* water convert soluble soap into insoluble calcium and magnesium soaps that form curdy precipitates. (See DETERGENT; EMULSION.)

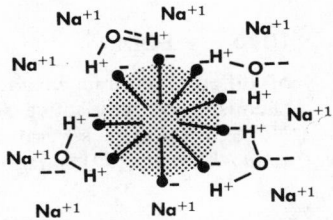

Sodium soap film around oil droplet: Carbon chains of soap molecules (not shown) are attracted to and absorbed by droplet, but salt groups at ends of chains are attracted to water and thus protrude from droplet, forming film. This double attraction enables soap to carry away oily particles in water. *(From Wood)*

The salts that fat acids form with metals other than sodium and potassium are also called soaps, though they are not water-soluble and are not detergents. They dissolve in gasoline, enabling it to be used in flame-throwers. They are also used to thicken lubricating greases, and as dusting powders for infants. (See STEARIC ACID AND STEARATES.)—*Ru. M.*

SOCIOLOGY OF SCIENCE: a specialized branch of general sociology, built on the premise that science is as much a social activity as any other human enterprise is. Science is neither entirely apart from society nor yet merely a set of ideas and applications which have consequences for society. Not only does science affect society; it is itself in part the consequence of social events. Questions important to the sociology of science include why there is some science in all societies; why science is much more developed in some societies than in others; and why its rate of development within a given society varies from time to time as internal conditions change—*e.g.* politics, economics, religion, ideology, class relationships, communications systems, technology, and education. The effects of science on social structures and cultural patterns are also investigated. The sociology of science aspires to make informed predictions about the social consequences of science. Predictions have often been too crude to be of much use, but are becoming more accurate as our knowledge of both society and science improves.—*B. B.*

SODA ASH: anhydrous sodium carbonate, Na_2CO_3. Soda ash occurs naturally in underground beds, and may be obtained from brine of salty lakes such as Owens Lake in California (see EVAPORITES); but most commercial soda ash is produced by the Solvay process, in which a mixture of carbon dioxide and ammonia gases is passed into sodium-chloride solution at a definite concentration and temperature to yield sodium bicarbonate. The solid sodium bicarbonate is then heated, giving soda ash, water, and carbon dioxide. Hydrated soda ash ($Na_2CO_3 \cdot 10H_2O$) is known as *washing soda* or *sal soda*, as opposed to baking soda (sodium bicarbonate, $NaHCO_3$). Soda ash is used as a flux in the manufacture of glass; in the manufacture of soap, wood pulp, and other chemicals and textiles; as a cleansing and water-softening agent; and in the refining of petroleum.—*G. W. M.*

SODDY, FREDERICK, 1877–1956, English chemist; b. Eastbourne, Sussex. After investigating radioactive decay and the structure of the atom, he concluded that certain of the elements produced in radioactive decay have the same place in the periodic system as corresponding normal elements. He gave the name "isotopes" to such chemically identical elements of different atomic weights. For his contributions to the chemistry of radioactive substances he received the 1921 Nobel prize. His several books include *Chemistry of the Radio-Elements* (1911). He was a fellow of the Royal Society. —*E. F.*

SODIUM: an alkali-metal element (Na); at. no. 11; at. wt 22.991; mp 97.5°C; bp 880°C; sp gr 0.971; valence 1. The 6th most abundant element in Earth's crust, it is found in combined state in a number of salts; the most important source is *rock salt* (sodium chloride, NaCl), deposits of which are widely distributed (see SALT, common). Sodium chloride also constitutes somewhat over 2% of ocean water, but is difficult to obtain in pure form from this source because of the numerous other salts present. Elemental sodium, a soft, silvery metal that oxidizes rapidly in air, was first isolated by Sir Humphry Davy in 1807. It reacts violently with water, forming sodium hydroxide and liberating gaseous hydrogen, which usually ignites because of the high heat of reaction. Metallic sodium is manufactured in large tonnages by the electrolysis of either fused sodium hydroxide (Castner process) or fused sodium chloride (Downs process). It is a very powerful reducing agent, standing near the positive end of the ELECTROMOTIVE SERIES, and is used extensively for converting hard-to-reduce metallic oxides or halides, *e.g.* those of titanium, to the corresponding free metals. It is the preferred reducing agent for converting esters to alcohols, and for many other organic reduction reactions. Sodium is used on a large scale in preparing sodium-lead alloy, which is an intermediate in the making of tetraethyl lead, an anti-knock agent. Sodium hydroxide, NaOH, is one of the strongest and most widely used alkalies; it is prepared by the electrolysis of aqueous sodium chloride, or by the reaction of sodium carbonate with calcium hydroxide. Sodium also forms a peroxide, Na_2O_2, widely used as an oxidizing agent. Sodium salts are, with few exceptions, soluble in water, reluctant to form complexes with other soluble cations, and relatively inexpensive. For these reasons sodium salts are more frequently encountered in chemical technology than the salts of any other metal.—*A. M. S.*

SODIUM HYDROXIDE: a white, hygroscopic, solid compound (NaOH). It is a typical strong BASE, and is prepared by the electrolysis of sodium-chloride brine or by the action of calcium hydroxide on sodium carbonate. It is one of the most important industrial chemicals, some of its major uses being in the making of soap, rayon, paper, and textiles, and in the refining of petroleum and extraction of chemicals from coal tar.—*G. W. M.*

SOIL: naturally occurring material synthesized in profile form from a variable mixture of broken and weathered minerals (see EROSION; WEATHERING) and decaying organic matter. It covers the land surface of the globe (except for steep mountain peaks and lands of perpetual ice and snow) with a thin layer of variable thickness. When it contains the proper amounts of air and water, it supplies mechanical support and, in part, sustenance for plants. Soil is also the "link" between the rock core of Earth and the living things on its surface, and is differentiated from the regolith below by physical, chemical, and biological activities that combine to produce layers called *soil horizons*. Physically, soil consists of a framework of solid organic and mineral components, with reciprocally varying amounts of water and air (see SOIL PHYSICS AND MECHANICS).

Modern soil scientists of W Europe developed the concept that soil productivity depends upon a balance of mineral elements in the soil; this led to the use of fertilizers and

management practices that have greatly increased production. Russian scientists, trying to discover why marked regional differences occur in soil, realized that soil is born of parent rock and slowly develops under the influence of climate, vegetation, and topography. American scientists investigated additional problems connected with irrigation, drainage, salinity, tillage, and plant growth; these problems require a combination of physical, chemical, and biological approaches.

Sediment basin with sampler tanks in foreground is type of installation (modified Parshall flume) used to study runoff and sediment production from cultivated fields. (*USDA*)

Most soil reactions take place in a thin layer of ion-containing liquids adsorbed tightly on solid soil particles. The quantity of organic and inorganic colloid present controls the amount of this solution. The ions are exchangeable for others brought near the colloid by moving water or produced there by biological activity. Thus, respiring organisms and decaying organic matter produce carbon dioxide that hydrolyzes in water to produce hydrogen ions, which may exchange with calcium, potassium, or other ions in the soil solution. The latter ions may, in turn, be absorbed and removed by the plant or drainage water. Hydrogen ions may thus increase and the soil become more acid (see PH).

In cool, humid, forested regions with abundant rainfall, iron and aluminum compounds are dissolved from the surface soil (A-horizon) and accumulate, along with clays, in the lower B-horizon, which grades gradually into unaltered parent material called the C-horizon. Soils of this kind, called *podzolic*, are usually acidic. In warmer climates, the iron and aluminum compounds remain in the A-horizon, and silica is leached. Such soils are red or yellow, and are called *lateritic*. With low rainfall and sparse grass and shrubs, the leaching is less severe. The soils that develop, called *pedocals* because calcium carbonate accumulates at some depth, contain little organic matter and may have soluble salts that cause salinity and alkalinity (high pH). *Prairie* and *chernozem* soils develop under intermediate rainfall with grass cover. They are fertile, deep, black soils, rich in organic matter, nearly neutral in pH, non-saline, and highly productive. Hundreds of soil types have been classified according to recognizable physical and chemical properties.

When vegetation that protects soil from wind and water is destroyed by misuse, erosion can begin. The fertile topsoil, which can be replaced only by many years of soil formation, is lost first. Erosion can be best controlled by a perpetual vegetative cover; it can be reduced by contour cultivation, strip-cropping, grassed waterways, and other means that decrease wind and water velocities at the soil surface (see CONSERVATION OF NATURAL RESOURCES). Such measures also conserve water by encouraging infiltration, thus recharging the ground water, which is gradually used or released to streams and lakes (see WATER SUPPLY).—*S. A. T.*

SOIL PHYSICS AND MECHANICS: sciences concerned with the physical nature of soils. By conventional usage, soil physics relates primarily to agricultural soils; soil mechanics, to soil as an engineering material.

In *soil physics,* soil is regarded as a complex system of particles, liquids, and gases strongly influenced by interacting surface phenomena. The interrelationship of the various soil elements is seldom static. Ability to supply water and nutrients to a plant, tilth, and tillability are closely related to the balance between the various physical elements. Particles are ordinarily classed by size as: clay (<0.002 mm), silt (0.05–0.002 mm), sand (1.0–0.05 mm), and gravel (>1.0 mm). Because of its relatively great surface area, clay exhibits ION EXCHANGE and other colloidal phenomena which influence the transfer of both moisture and nutrients and the formation of secondary agglomerations of particles (aggregates) of various stability. *Texture* refers to size of the primary particles; *structure* to size, nature, and stability of the aggregates. A. Atterberg (1913) delineated the effect of moisture on soil plasticity. For soil moisture, surface tension is the significant factor, and the concept of the capillary potential (W. Gardner, 1922) has led to a widening understanding of the dynamics of soil moisture; studies of the thermodynamics of surface phenomena have also proved helpful, as well as investigations of the transfer of moisture under various energy gradients including gravity, surface energy, and temperature. Transfer of moisture in the vapor phase or between liquid and vapor phases has been observed. Molecular-surface adsorption of gas, liquid, and dissolved ions by the plate-like lattice crystal structures of various clays is responsible for many of soil's physical properties. Predominating H ions cause acidity, and Na and K, alkalinity; Ca neutralizes. (See pH VALUE.) Moisture content also has a profound effect on soil properties; *e.g.* if moisture content is low, surface-tension forces tend to produce stability. Hydraulic transmissivity rapidly decreases with decreasing moisture; dissolved salts decrease the osmotic energy gradient to the roots, and displacement of air by waterlogging leads to drowning of roots. See also HYDROLOGIC CYCLE; WATER TABLE.

Soil mechanics treats the entire soil mantle as a construction material. Soil may be used in place, as for foundations, or may be replaced, as for dams. Prior to about 1920 theories of passive earth thrust, soil friction, soil cohesion, and empirical foundation-bearing values had been developed, but modern soil mechanics began with the work of Karl (Charles) Terzaghi (1925) on consolidation and settlement of clays under load. Terzaghi also studied the relation between strain, frictional resistance, and the stress state of a soil mass. Classification based on textural analysis and Atterberg limits (for the effect of moisture on soil plasticity) led to semi-quantitative evaluation systems useful in construction of embankments, subgrades, and foundations. Capability of soils for artificial compaction has been shown to depend on their moisture content. The relationships between shearing strength, strain, density, pore pressure, and surface phenomena have been extensively studied. Water plays an important role in soil stability as the result of buoyancy and seepage drag. Soil mechanics relies heavily on field-drilling sampling, testing, and engineering evaluation. Many modern earth dams, highways, airports, subways, and other structures owe their successful construction to soil mechanics.—*D. F. P.*

SOLAR CELL: the working element of a solar battery which converts sunlight directly to electric power. It operates on the principle that photons of light energy striking atoms of certain materials will dislodge electrons from the atoms. If these electrons are segregated before they can return to their former locations, they can be drawn off as electric current. The vacancies or "holes" left by the electrons constitute positive charges and will also conduct a current. The cell consists of a thin silicon wafer containing an admixture of a material such as arsenic. The surface layer of the wafer contains an additional admixture of boron or a similar material. The junction between the surface layer and the rest of the wafer forms a barrier in the nature of an electric field. As light passes through both layers, it creates pairs of electrons and holes in each, and the field at the junction drives the positive charges to the boron side of the junction and the electrons to the arsenic side. When conducting leads are attached to both layers, electrons flow from the arsenic side through the circuitry to recombine with "holes" on the boron side, and this current provides electric power.—*K. A.*

SOLAR CONSTANT: the total incoming SOLAR RADIATION received per unit of time on a surface of unit area at right angles to the Sun's rays in the absence of an atmosphere when Earth is at mean distance from the Sun. The value that is most generally accepted for the solar constant is 2.00 gm-cal/cm^2/min (see also HEAT BALANCE OF EARTH).—*J. L.*

SOLAR ENERGY: energy liberated by thermonuclear reactions inside the SUN and radiated out into space as (1) radio waves; (2) light in the infrared, visible, and ultraviolet spectra; and (3)

Shear resistance of silty soil is determined by exerting axial pressure on cylindrical sample in chamber at left. Sample is saturated, covered by rubber membrane, with ends open and bearing on porous stone. Volume change is measured by water drained off through rubber tubing. (*U. S. Army*)

x-rays. The Sun also discharges electrons, protons, and the nuclei of some elements (see COSMIC RAYS). Earth intercepts less than one-billionth of the Sun's radiant energy, of which about 25% is absorbed or reflected by Earth's atmosphere. Yet with the exception of man-made nuclear energy, all available energy on Earth comes directly or indirectly from the Sun. Uneven heating of land and sea, and of the air masses covering them, creates powerful convection currents in the atmosphere, and winds are born. Sea water evaporated into the air by solar heat is carried by winds over the land and there released as rain or snow, keeping the processes of erosion going, and supplying mechanical energy for man's water wheels and hydroelectric generators. Sunlight operates the immense chemical factory of green plants that produces oxygen to sustain animal life. Green plants also convert and store solar energy in the form of chemical energy, releasing it directly to man when he consumes food and indirectly as heat energy when he burns coal, peat, oil, and natural gas—the remains of plants that stored this energy long ago. Focusing the Sun's heat with the mirror of a solar furnace will produce temperatures almost as high as those on the surface of the Sun, about 10,000°F. In warm climates with little cloudy weather, solar heat stored during the day is used to heat buildings at night. With a SOLAR CELL, incident sunlight can be converted directly into electric power to meet small, special power requirements, *e.g.* space-vehicle instrumentation and some telephone lines. See ATMOSPHERIC RADIATION; SOLAR CONSTANT.—*K. A.*

SOLAR RADIATION: electromagnetic energy emitted by the SUN. Although most of this comes from regions close to the apparent surface of the Sun (the photosphere), the source of the far-ultraviolet and x-ray radiation as well as the radio emission lies in the upper solar atmosphere, or corona. The total emitted solar radiation is equivalent to that of a BLACK BODY radiator at a temperature of about 5900°K, and 97% of this energy is contained within the wavelength limits 0.3 to 3μ. In this spectral region the distribution of solar energy approximates that of a black body.

The so-called color temperature of the Sun (*i.e.* that temperature which follows from Wien's Displacement Law) is 6080°K, corresponding to a wavelength of maximum solar-radiation intensity in the blue-green part of the spectrum (0.475μ). The insolation (incoming solar radiation) received on a horizontal surface at the top of the atmosphere depends on the SOLAR CONSTANT, the distance between Earth and Sun, and the angle the Sun's rays make with the vertical (zenith angle). Thus insolation on a horizontal surface is a maximum at low latitudes and at noon (when the Sun is high in the sky); at high latitudes, average insolation is quite small. Solar radiation is depleted as it penetrates to Earth's surface, by scattering (by air molecules, water vapor and dust particles, and clouds) and by absorption (principally by ozone, water vapor, clouds, and dust). Because of strong absorption in the upper atmosphere, no solar radiation short of 0.3μ is received at Earth's surface. Of the total solar radiation which reaches Earth and its atmosphere, on the average approximately 35% is reflected back to space, 18% is absorbed in the atmosphere, and 47% is absorbed at Earth's surface.—*J. L.*

SOLAR SYSTEM: the Sun and those astronomical bodies temporarily or permanently moving in orbits around it. Besides the Sun, the system consists of the planets and their satellites, comets, meteorites, and interplanetary gas and dust. The SUN is an average star, 865,000 mi in diameter, with a surface temperature of 11,000°F. It is the only star whose surface can be studied; all other stars are essentially points

of light in the largest telescopes. The nine principal planets, ranging from 3,000 to 86,000 mi in diameter, are, in order from the Sun, MERCURY, VENUS, EARTH, MARS, JUPITER, SATURN, URANUS, NEPTUNE, and PLUTO. There are also thousands of minor planets, or ASTEROIDS, almost 2,000 of which have been catalogued; these are objects ranging down to a mile or two in diameter, with orbits typically between Mars and Jupiter. The planets revolve around the Sun, all in the same direction, in closed orbits, for the most part nearly circular, and almost in the same plane. Their surfaces possess such temperatures as solar heating produces; those at great distances from the Sun are very cold. Some planets are surrounded by gaseous atmospheres. Tables of physical data for elements of the solar system appear in the articles ASTEROID, METEOR, PLANET, and SATELLITE (NATURAL).

There are 32 known natural satellites; they accompany six of the principal planets. In addition, since Oct. 4, 1957, man has given Earth some dozens of artificial satellites. The MOON is a natural satellite, which we can study in great detail and which may be typical of others. Satellites vary from about 3,000 mi in diameter for the few largest down to 5 or 10 mi for the smallest yet discovered. Satellites possess no appreciable atmospheres, Titan (Saturn's largest satellite) being the only proved exception. Some are known always to keep the same face toward their primary, and probably all satellites behave in this way. Rough surfaces and extremes of temperature may further characterize them. Some satellites have highly eccentric or greatly inclined orbits, or revolve backward relative to the direction of planetary orbital revolutions; and it is probable that a planet's system of satellites is subject to very occasional losses or gains.

COMETS are occasionally spectacular to the eye, with heads as large as the Moon and tails stretching from horizon to zenith. Far more common is the telescopic comet showing only a small, faint, hazy coma. The orbits of comets are usually extremely eccentric ellipses, frequently highly inclined to the plane of the ecliptic; their orbital revolution is often retrograde. Nevertheless, comets are permanent members of the solar system. Briefly visible while near Earth and Sun, most comets most of the time are far beyond the orbit of the most remote planet, and are too faint to detect. The total number of comets is very large, perhaps 100 billion.

METEORITES are bodies which enter Earth's atmosphere from outer space at great velocities and are briefly visible as glowing METEORS plunging through the atmosphere. Some fragments reach the ground, there to be recovered as iron or stone meteorites.

Meteorites are permanent members of the solar system, not visitors from outside. They are of scientific interest as the only

Relative Sizes of Bodies in Solar System.

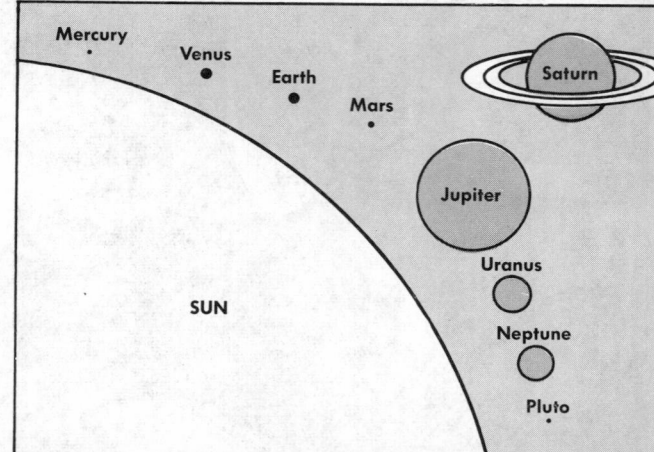

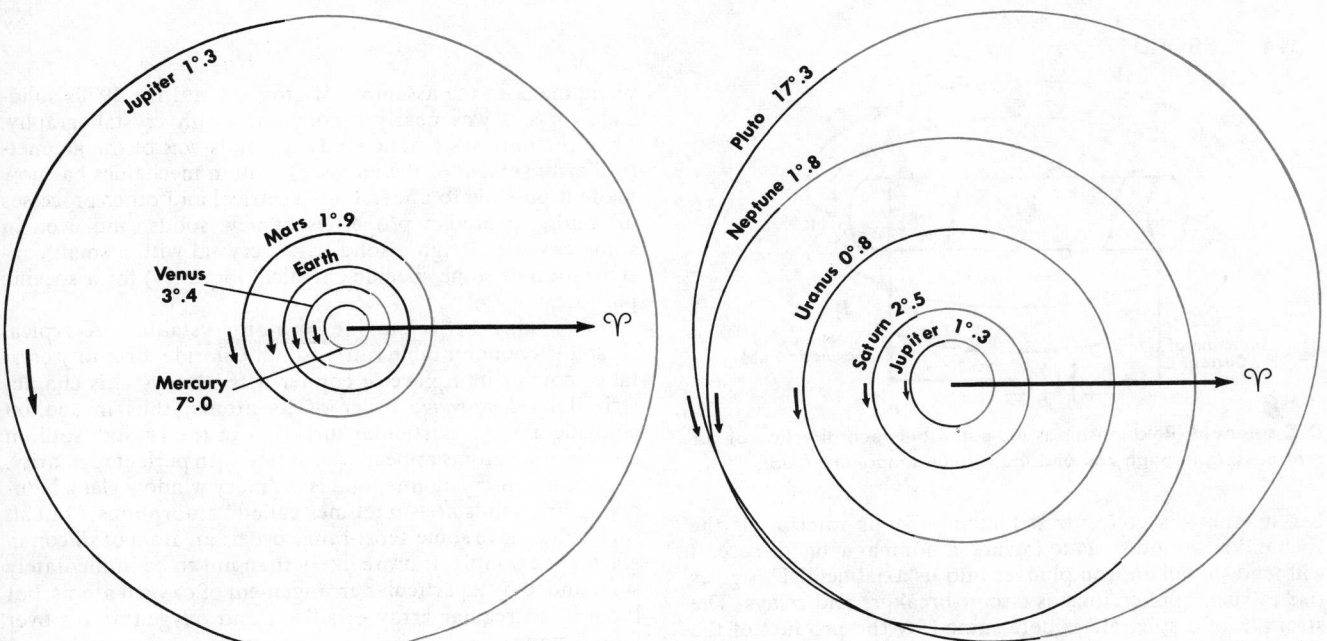

"Inner" (*left*) **and outer solar system** (*right*): Planets revolve in same direction, in nearly circular elliptical orbits, in nearly the same plane, except for Pluto, which is inclined at a rakish 17°. With name of each planet is given the inclination of its orbital plane to that of Earth. Portion of orbital plane that lies below Earth's is indicated in blue. Orbits of asteroids (not shown) are often much more eccentric; they lie mostly between orbits of Mars and Jupiter. Long arrow indicates orientation of system with regard to vernal equinox (♈). Inner system is shown at approximately 7½ times scale of the outer system.

bodies from outer space that are subject to direct laboratory analysis. Such analysis has revealed no new elements, but some new minerals have been found.

The space between the planets is a much better vacuum than we have yet been able to produce in the laboratory. Even so, there must be some gas and dust between the planets from such sources as the escape of gases from planetary atmospheres, the ejection of matter in high-velocity solar prominences, and the progressive diffusion of material in old comets of short periods. Interplanetary dust is directly visible in the ZODIACAL LIGHT, a cone of light near the plane of the ecliptic, and the GEGENSCHEIN, a very faint patch of light opposite the Sun. The dust particles responsible are estimated to have diameters of ½₅ to ½₅,₀₀₀ in.—*W. H.*

SOLAR WIND: a thin, ionized gas flowing continuously outward in all directions from the Sun. It is actually an extension of the Sun's corona, which expands at an increasing rate as distance from the Sun increases. The charged particles of the gas are mainly protons (nuclei of hydrogen atoms), with some heavier nuclei as well as electrons stripped from atoms. In the vicinity of Earth, the solar wind normally travels at a speed of 350 to 700 km/sec (about 800,000 to 1,500,000 mi/hr) and consists of 1 to 5 protons/cm³.

Following solar flares or sunspot activity, the solar wind increases in density and velocity. Carrying with it part of the Sun's magnetic field, it sweeps low-energy cosmic rays from the skies, accounting for their decrease during heightened solar activity. The intensified solar wind, by causing fluctuations in Earth's magnetic field, produces magnetic storms and accompanying disruption of radio communications. The solar wind supplies particles to the outer VAN ALLEN RADIATION belt and produces the AURORA. It apparently causes the tails of comets to stream out in a direction always away from the Sun and stretches out the Earth's magnetic field in a similar tail. The solar wind's existence and effects have been verified by spacecraft observations.—*R. G. M.*

SOLDER: any relatively low-melting, low-strength alloy used to bond higher-melting, dissimilar metals. Typical solder com-

positions are lead-tin EUTECTICS, often containing antimony, bismuth, cadmium, and other relatively low-melting metals. The lead-tin solders have melting points in the 350°F to 400°F range, and most solders melt at 800°F or below. Higher-melting alloys—in the 1000°F to 1300°F range—are properly classed as brazing materials and are stronger than low-melting solders. These "hard solders" are generally silver-copper-zinc combinations. Solders are commonly supplied in coil form and applied with the aid of a soldering iron; they may, however, be made in paste form. For large-scale industrial applications, solder preforms—thin foils stamped in the shape of the joint to be made—are available. In some cases solders (particularly hard solders) may be applied with the aid of a gas torch instead of a soldering iron. Since the bonding action of solders depends on their ability to "wet" and adhere to the metals being joined, fluxes are usually provided to aid the wetting action. These fluxes are chemical compounds that remove oxides and other substances and keep the joint surfaces chemically clean. The flux may be applied separately, in advance of soldering, or it may be built into the soldering material itself, as in "acid core" solders and soldering pastes.—*A. R. G.*

SOLENOID: a wire-wound helical coil, electrically energized by direct or alternating current. The magnetic field of a solenoid—which, for objects outside it, resembles that of a

Current-carrying loop, one element of a solenoid, shows how magnetic fields centered about wire combine to yield a field through the axis of the loop. (*Berenice Abbott*)

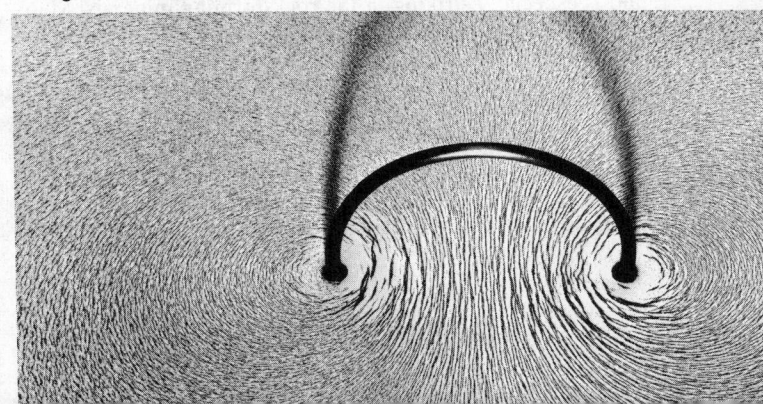

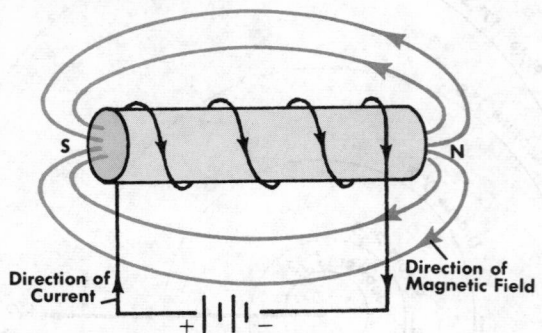

D-C solenoid: Relationship is indicated between direction of current passing through coil and the resulting magnetic field.

bar magnet—is concentrated mainly in its interior. If the solenoid is wound so as to include a nonmagnetic air core, it will tend to pull an iron plunger into its axial field. This gives rise to such applications as circuit-breakers and relays. The strength of a solenoid is determined by the product of the number of turns composing its winding and the exciting current, as well as by the permeability of its core. The figure shows the magnetic field of a d-c solenoid.—*A. E.*

SOLID: one of the three states of matter, distinguished from the liquid and gaseous phases in that a solid tends to retain shape and volume. Solids exhibit a crystalline structure in which the individual atoms, ions, or molecules are arranged in a repeated pattern, at least over small volumes. True solids have definite melting points. On the boundary between true solids and liquids there exists classification of noncrystalline materials, examples of which are glass and tar. These substances do not have a definite melting point but, rather, grow increasingly soft and less viscous as they are heated. Even at temperatures (say, room temperature for glass) low enough for these materials to exhibit the properties normally associated with solids, they tend to creep under the influence of small sustained forces. A length of glass rod supported only at its ends will in a matter of weeks acquire a permanent bend from its own weight, although it normally acts like an elastic solid and cannot be permanently deformed without breaking. See CRYSTALLOGRAPHY; PHASE; SOLID-STATE PHYSICS. —*E. M. R.*

SOLID SOLUTION: the common phenomenon in which crystalline species exhibit ranges in chemical composition. The ranges are generally due to substitution of individual atoms or even groups of atoms in a given kind of structure; on the other hand, some are the result of atomic omission and others are the result of occupancy of interstitial structural sites. Compositional variations may range from slight to complete. The ability of different elements to occupy one kind of structural site is referred to as *diadochy*. Two or more elements may be diadochic in a given structure.

Solid solution is dependent upon environment of formation, and extensive solid solution is particularly favored by higher temperatures. Solid solution is a common feature in minerals and is especially striking in the rock-forming minerals. Many metals and alloys exhibit solid solution, and their properties depend upon the extent and type. Another term, which is essentially synonymous, is *crystalline solution*. Crystals exhibiting solid solution are sometimes referred to as mix-crystals or mixed crystals.—*A. Ha. and D. H.*

SOLID-STATE PHYSICS: the science of the arrangement of atoms in rigid structures and the relations among the properties of the atoms, the structures, and the properties of and

phenomena in the assembly of atoms. Until the 1920s solid-state physics was nearly synonymous with crystallography, since the only systematic study of solids was of the geometrical arrangement of the atoms. Quantum mechanics has now made it possible to understand electrical and other processes in solids, to predict properties of new solids, and even in some cases to design a solid (*e.g.* a crystal with a small concentration of some specific chemical impurity) for a specific purpose.

Solids may be crystalline or non-crystalline. A typical crystal is common table salt, sodium chloride, or a tiny crystal of copper in a piece of copper wire. A crystal is characterized by *long-range* order of its atoms; thus in sodium chloride along a particular direction in the crystal, sodium and chlorine atoms appear alternately with perfect regularity. A typical non-crystalline solid is ordinary window glass. Noncrystalline solids are sometimes called "amorphous," but all such solids have some short-range order; an atom of silicon in glass, for example, is more likely than not to be immediately surrounded by a particular arrangement of oxygen atoms, but there is no regular array of silicon and oxygen atoms over long distances.

The properties of solids are of two kinds: "structure-insensitive" and "structure-sensitive." The former are properties, like density or melting point, that do not depend sensitively on impurities or other imperfections. The density is, of course, related to the spacing between atoms. This interatomic spacing is determined by the balance between attractive forces and repulsive forces. Attractive forces arise from the electrostatic interactions among point charges (electrons, nuclei) when these charges are distributed in space as predicted by quantum mechanics. The repulsive forces arise almost completely from the EXCLUSION PRINCIPLE. Quantum theory has been highly successful in dealing quantitatively with the binding of atoms together to form solids.

The most varied, intriguing, and technologically important properties of solids are structure-sensitive. Thus a tiny concentration (a few parts per million) of copper in a zinc sulfide crystal makes such a crystal luminesce when it is bombarded by electrons or irradiated by ultraviolet light. Another example is the increase in electrical conductivity of a non-metallic crystal, *e.g.* silicon or magnesium oxide, by factors of thousands or millions when small concentrations of chemical impurities are incorporated into the crystals.

Metals are solids containing large concentrations (of the order of one to five per atom) of electrons which are free to move throughout the crystal. These electrons are good conductors of electricity and heat, and produce the typical metallic reflection of light from a surface. Perhaps the most striking feature of a highly purified solid is the fact that an electron can travel long distances (millions of interatomic spacings) without being scattered by the medium of electrons and nuclei through which it moves. This feature is a strictly quantum mechanical phenomenon originating in the wave nature of the electron and the regularity of the array of atoms. At low temperature, vibrations of the crystal atoms about their equilibrium positions are not serious, and the electrons in a metal conduct electricity with a very small resistance. Some solids show an additional phenomenon: below a critical temperature (different for each solid) they exhibit an exact vanishing of resistance, or "superconductivity."

Non-metals at sufficiently low temperatures (usually room temperature is low enough) are excellent electrical insulators. These solids when pure have no free electrons to conduct electricity, and a good insulator can have an electrical resistivity larger by as much as a factor of 10^{25} than that of a good metal! By raising the temperature or incorporating chemical impurities into such crystals, electrical conduction can be made to occur (see CONDUCTOR AND SEMICONDUCTOR). Furthermore, by adding different chemical impurities to different parts of a single crystal, solid-state amplifiers (transistors) or rectifiers can be constructed. Not only are such devices of practical importance, but they are versatile systems for studying a host of solid-state phenomena that are more varied and sophisticated than mere electrical conduction.

Solid-state physics encompasses the study of properties such as the electrical properties already described and such as compressibility, dielectric constant, refractive index, elastic constants, plasticity, magnetic susceptibility, and many more. But the study of *processes* in solids is even more characteristic of this field, processes such as the alignment of electron spins to make a large intrinsic magnetization (ferromagnetism); alignment of groups of atoms to make a large intrinsic electrical polarization (ferroelectricity); the motion of atoms (diffusion, ionic conductivity); the interactions among temperature differences, electric fields, and magnetic fields (thermoelectric and thermomagnetic effects); the emission of electrons from the surfaces of solids (thermionic, photoelectric, and field emission); internal field emission (Zener effect); the enhancement of electrical conductivity by light (photoconductivity); change of a given solid from one crystal structure to another (phase transformations); resonant absorption of radio frequency energy by nuclear or electronic spins (magnetic resonance); ultrasonic attenuation; x-ray and neutron diffraction; and many others.—*R. Sp.*

SOLSTICE: either of two positions on the CELESTIAL SPHERE occupied by the Sun when it is farthest from the celestial equator. When the Sun is farthest *north* of the equator it is at the *summer* (or northern) *solstice* and summer begins in the northern hemisphere; when farthest south, it is at the *winter* (or southern) *solstice.* The term solstice is also applied to the moments in time when the Sun is farthest north or south, about June 21 and Dec. 22, respectively. The plane of the Sun's apparent orbit, the ecliptic, is inclined to the equator by about 23½°, so that at the summer solstice the Sun is 23½° north of the equator, and is overhead at noon at a place on Earth in north latitude 23½°. The circle of latitude 23½°N is called the Tropic of Cancer. The Tropic of Capricorn, the circle of latitude 23½°S, is similarly related to the winter solstice.—*M. W. O.*

SOLUBILITY: the capacity of one substance (the *solute*) to form a uniform or homogeneous mixture with another substance (the *solvent*). Since both solute and solvent may be solid, liquid, or gaseous, the resulting SOLUTIONS (or single phases) may be of manifold types. For example, gases (as solvents) can dissolve other gases, also vaporized liquids, or sublimed solids (*e.g.* iodine); solids can dissolve gases (palladium and hydrogen), also liquids, or other solids (various alloys and glasses); and liquids can dissolve other liquids (water and alcohol), also gases (water or alcohol and ammonia), or solids. While water is the commonest liquid solvent, there are countless other liquids with different solvent powers, boiling points, etc. Some of them (alcohol, acetone, acetic acid) mix with water in all proportions; others (ether, ethyl acetate) are only slightly soluble; and still others (chloroform, benzene, nitrobenzene) are practically immiscible with water. For solids insoluble in water, organic solvents are commonly used; most of these are inflammable and must be handled with care. The solubility of solids in liquids usually, but not always, increases with rise of temperature, while gases become less soluble with rise of temperature.—*J. R.*

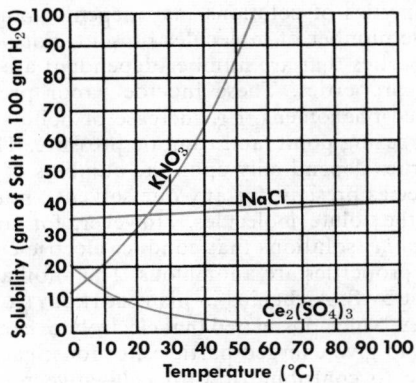

Effect of temperature on solubility of solids: Solubility of potassium nitrate (KNO_3) rises sharply with increasing temperature, and common salt ($NaCl$) becomes only very slightly more soluble with increasing temperature; but cerium sulfate ($Ce_2(SO_4)_3$), an exception to the general rule, becomes less soluble with rising temperature. (*After Wood*)

In *biological systems,* the solvent is always water. Since a compound is most soluble in that solvent to which it is most closely related in structure, certain substances, *e.g.* lipids or steroids, are poorly soluble in aqueous media. Organisms overcome this difficulty to some degree by combining these substances with water-soluble ones or by forming water-soluble salts. Compounds of very high molecular weight frequently exhibit decreased solubility in water. Thus, while glucose is readily soluble, the polymers starch, cellulose, and glycogen are insoluble in this solvent.—*F. F.*

SOLUTION: in chemistry, a homogeneous mixture of two or more components, whose percentages may be varied. A solution may be gaseous, liquid, or solid. The atmosphere is a solution of gases; grease in carbon tetrachloride and carbon dioxide in water are examples of liquid solutions. A solution in which water is the SOLVENT is an aqueous solution. Sterling silver, an alloy of copper and silver, is an example of a SOLID SOLUTION. However, not all alloys are solid solutions; in some cases the alloy may be a true metallic compound with definite composition, and in other cases the alloy may not be homogeneous.

In a solution, the natural attraction between the solute molecules of the dissolved substances has been overcome. If the attraction between molecules was slight to begin with (*i.e.* if the molecules are nonpolar), the energy required to overcome this attraction is likewise slight. However, a polar solvent will not dissolve a non-polar solute, because the solvent molecules have great attraction for each other; in this case a non-polar solvent is necessary and the process of solution is one of dilution, with little energy involved. For a polar solute, a polar solvent is needed. The polar solvent molecules both orient themselves around the polar solute species and "solvate" them, and also tend to insulate the solute molecules or charged particles (ions) from each other. The energy in this process is sufficient to overcome both solute-solute and solvent-solvent attractions. A polar solute will not dissolve in a non-polar solvent, because the solvent molecules exert less attractive force upon the solute particles than solute-solute attraction does. Because energy changes are involved in these solution phenomena, each process of solution is accompanied by a characteristic "heat of solution"; this heat may be either positive or negative, depending upon whether the solvation energy or lattice energy of the solute crystal is greater.

The properties of solutions may depend upon the kind and relative number of molecules present. For liquid solutions, properties that are number-dependent are known as colligative properties. These include vapor pressure and closely allied phenomena, *e.g.* increase of boiling point, decrease in freezing point, and osmotic pressure. The colligative properties depend only upon the numbers of molecules of each species present (for any one solvent), not upon the nature of the solute molecules. However, for solutions of electrolytes, *i.e.* solutions that conduct electric current, the colligative properties are anomalous. The anomaly was explained first by S. Arrhenius in his ELECTROLYTIC DISSOCIATION THEORY, which postulated that electrolytes can dissociate in solution to give charged particles, or ions; each of these ions is able to contribute toward colligative properties as if it were a molecule. See also SUPERSATURATED SOLUTION.— *L. Sc.*

SOLVAY, ERNEST, 1838–1922, Belgian chemist and industrialist; b. Rebecq. In 1861 he devised the Solvay process for making sodium carbonate by way of sodium bicarbonate from a purified brine of common salt, ammonia, and carbon dioxide. The process gave him and his brother Alfred practically a world monopoly in the manufacture of soda.—*E. F.*

SOLVENT: in general, that substance in a SOLUTION which is present in the larger amount, the other substance being called the *solute.* When liquids are dissolved in liquids (*e.g.* alcohol and water) it matters little which liquid is considered as the solvent because there is no change in state, though if water is one of the liquids it is usually (though not always logically) regarded as the solvent. In dissolving gases or solids in liquids, the liquid is regarded as the solvent because it does not undergo a change in state. Each of the states of matter (solid, liquid, or gas) may serve as the solvent for each of the other states of matter. A solvent tends to dissolve a solute of like nature: a polar solvent such as water ("polar" because the water molecule is asymmetrical, *i.e.* the two hydrogens and the one oxygen are not arranged in a straight line) will tend to dissolve polar substances such as salt or sugar; a non-polar solvent such as carbon tetrachloride (non-polar because the molecule is symmetrical) will tend to dissolve non-polar solutes such as grease.—*L. Sc.*

SOLVENT EXTRACTION: a very old technological process in which a solvent is used to extract the substance desired from a solid or liquid base material. In the oldest techniques water was used to extract constituents of herbs and plants for medicines and dyes, sugar from cane and beets, or tannin from bark. In certain cases lye or acids were added to the water, and extraction and chemical conversion were combined (*e.g.* lixiviation of minerals). Later wine or strong alcohol was used as a solvent. A century ago tar-oils, petroleum naphtha, and organic solvents came into use for extracting oils from seeds (*e.g.* rape oil, soybean oil), fat from bones, resin from wood-pulp, and quinine from bark. The choice of solvent depends primarily upon its selectivity for the type of component to be removed. It must be cheap and readily available, resistant to chemical change during use, and safe to handle. The desired product should be easily obtained from the extract by simple distillation or evaporation. Extraction formerly took place in a percolator in which the solid material was packed and through which the solvent was led. The process is now seldom used in large-scale operation; instead, crushed and prepared base material continuously meets solvent in counter-current flow, and the solvent is continuously removed from the extract to be reused. In modern industry solvent extraction of liquids has become a very important means of removing cer-

tain less desirable compounds rather than isolating a valuable one. Thus in the petroleum industry, one of the largest users, an undesirable group of components, *e.g.* aromatics, asphalt, or wax, can be removed from a petroleum fraction by using a solvent by which the components are preferentially dissolved. Mixing results in two layers, the lower "extract" phase containing the dissolved components, the upper "raffinate" phase the undissolved bulk of the basic oil. Mixing and separating are combined in a tower filled with suitable packing material to break up the flow of liquid. Oil and solvent enter near the bottom and top respectively, mixing as they flow through the packing. Raffinate is withdrawn from the top and extract from the bottom; the solvent is distilled from both. Solvents such as liquid sulfur dioxide, nitrobenzene, propane, phenol, or furfural are used. A series of such extractions may be combined in one extraction plant. A similar refining of fatty oils (*Solexol process*) uses propane, liquefied under pressure, to separate the desired components.—*R. J. F.*

SOMMERFELD, ARNOLD JOHANNES WILHELM, 1868–1951, German physicist; b. Königsberg. His early field of research was electromagnetic theory, including studies of the dynamics of the electron, wave propagation under a great variety of circumstances, and x-rays. From 1911 on, his research was principally on atomic theory. His theoretical work brought order to the vast quantity of experimental research in spectroscopy, and his *Atombau und Spektrallinien* (1919) became the standard work on theoretical spectroscopy. He was the author or coauthor of nearly 300 scientific papers and a dozen books, including one on the theory of the gyroscope, *Theorie des Kreisels* (with F. Klein, 1897–1916). He was a fellow of the Royal Society and an associate of the U. S. National Academy of Sciences.—*D. H. D. R.*

SONAR: a device for "seeing" under water. The name is from RADAR, which it resembles in principle, though as "underwater sound echo ranging" it preceded radar by many years. Like radar, it locates remote objects by sending out high-power short pulses of radiant energy in a known direction, receiving the reflected pulses, and measuring the time of travel of energy to the target and back. Unlike radar, it uses acoustic radiation instead of electromagnetic radiation. This is dictated by the propagation medium: electromagnetic waves can travel

Sonar operators watch oscilloscope screen. Sonar signals sent in all directions are reflected and picked up by rotating receiver. Received signal, transduced into electrical signal, is displayed on screen. Strength of signal is indicated by intensity of spot on screen. Thus both direction and distance of detected object are determined. (*U. S. Navy*)

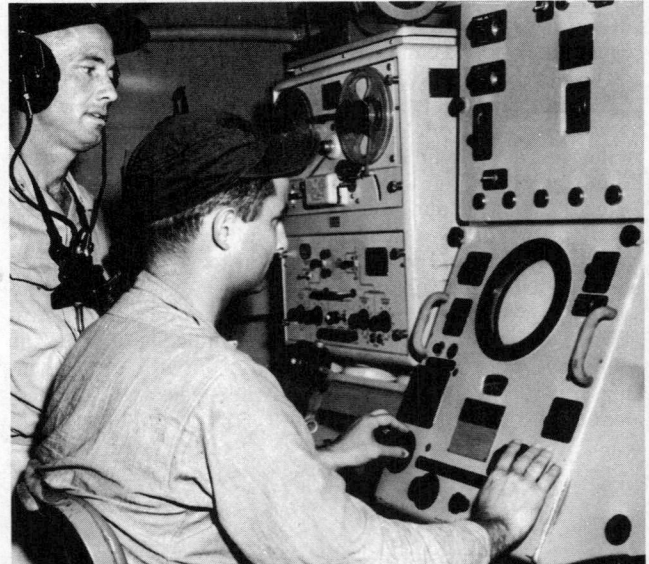

only very short distances in water, while acoustic waves travel faster and farther in water than in air.

Acoustic energy is radiated into water and received from water by a TRANSDUCER, corresponding to the radar antenna. The active element in a sonar transducer is usually a mechanically resonant device, corresponding to a loud-speaker, that is made to oscillate by oscillating electric or magnetic fields; or conversely, when driven by acoustic energy, it will generate electrical voltages, as a microphone does. Such materials as piezoelectric crystals, magnetostrictive rods, ferromagnetic ceramics, and, at lower frequencies, electromagnetically driven diaphragms are used as active elements.

The attenuation of acoustic radiation in water varies greatly with frequency. High-frequency sonar, excellent for seeing small targets or for observing large targets in great detail, is good for only a few hundred yards' range; low-frequency sonar may be good for hundreds of miles. The velocity of sound propagation in water, moreover, about 5,000 ft/sec, varies with water temperature and pressure. Since warm surface layers cause bending upward, the energy near the surface tends to stay near the surface. Denser layers below cause bending downward, so energy directed downward at too steep an angle tends to disappear in the deep.

Developed as a military instrument for locating submerged submarines, sonar is extensively used in peacetime for locating fish, measuring water depth, and, in arctic regions, measuring ice thickness. See ECHO AND ECHO RANGING; SOUND; ANIMAL SONAR.—R. M. P.

SONIC BOOM: a noise caused by a shock wave that emanates from an aircraft or other object traveling at or above the speed of sound (see AERODYNAMICS, *Transonic and Supersonic Flight*). Since a shock wave is a sharp pressure disturbance, it is received by the ear as a noise or clap of "thunder."—D. B.

SONIC REGIMES: ranges of flight speed or fluid-flow speed distinguished by their relation to the speed of sound. Speeds less than that of sound are termed *subsonic;* speed equal to sound speed, *sonic;* and speeds higher than sound speed, *supersonic.* Motion at very high supersonic speeds is called *hypersonic.* The division between the supersonic and hyper-sonic regimes has been commonly taken to occur at Mach 5.00. At high subsonic speeds, say at Mach 0.7 or 0.8 and higher, acceleration of the flow over the surface of an aircraft can produce a local region of supersonic flow; this is the *transonic* regime. The term "sonic barrier" has been applied to this regime because of the large increase in drag that acts upon an aircraft approaching sonic speed. (See AERODYNAM-ICS, *Transonic and Supersonic Flight.*) Similarly the term "thermal barrier" (or "thermal thicket") has been applied to

hypersonic motion because of the high aerodynamic heating at such speeds. (See THERMAL STRESS AND SHOCK.)—D. B.

SOSIGENES, fl. 1st cent. B. C.; Egyptian astronomer of Alexandria. Most of his works have been lost. He is best remembered for his reformation of the calendar under Julius Caesar, introduced in 46 B. C. Sosigenes fixed the mean length of the year as 365¼ days; every fourth year of his calendar (the "Julian" Calendar) had 366 days, all others 365 days. See CALENDAR.—R. N. M.

SOUND: popularly, any disturbance of air, ground, or water that can be heard; technically, any continuous or pulsing mechanical vibration of a material medium that, whether audible or not, carries energy outward from its source with a speed characteristic of the medium carrying it. If the pulse is so short as to be only a single vibration, the sound is a "shock wave." Although a body may vibrate in a vacuum, no sound can be radiated, since there is no medium to carry the vibration. The basic mechanical properties of elasticity and density together determine the velocity of sound in any medium; viscosity, heat conductivity, and molecular constitution determine the rate of absorption of sound energy. Formally, the velocity of sound is given by $(B/\rho)^{1/2}$, where B is the appropriate elastic modulus, and ρ is the density. For gases this becomes $(\gamma P/\rho)^{1/2}$, where P is the static pressure and γ is the ratio of the two specific heats, C_P/C_v, a basic thermodynamic property. By the use of the perfect gas law this may be rewritten $(\gamma RT/M)^{1/2}$, where R is the gas constant, T the absolute temperature, and M the molecular weight. Accordingly, the velocity of sound in gases increases as the square root of the absolute temperature. As a consequence, layers of hot and cold air can refract sound waves passing through them and cause curious focusing and channeling effects at long distances. In air at 70°F the velocity is about 1,129 ft/sec.

Sound travels faster in liquids than in gases, and faster still in solids: *e.g.* about 4,800 ft/sec in sea water, 16,000 ft/sec in steel, and fastest of all in quartz—18,000 ft/sec. Although these materials are much denser than gases, their rigidity is even higher. Air is, in fact, very ill-adapted to carry sound. Under favorable conditions the explosion of a pound or two of TNT has been heard underwater for several thousand miles, whereas a mile or two is maximum in air. Formal expression of this fact is that the "acoustic impedance" (*i.e.* the product of density and velocity) of solids and liquids is thousands of times larger than for gases; dense, stiff media carry more energy than tenuous, soft ones.

The attenuation of sound as it diverges from its source through an infinite, uniform medium is formally governed by the usual "law of inverse squares," but there is in addition an

At subsonic speed (Mach 0.96), shock waves begin to appear at local regions of supersonic flow around missile (*left*). At supersonic speed (Mach 1.07), a fully developed shock wave appears well in advance of missile's nose (*middle*). At higher supersonic speed (Mach 1.27), missile produces a more bowlike shock wave (*right*). In photos below, blurred images are missile models, clear black images are shadows. Shock waves are invisible, but visible representation is done by transmitting light through varying density of air flow surrounding missile onto a screen. (*U. S. Army*)

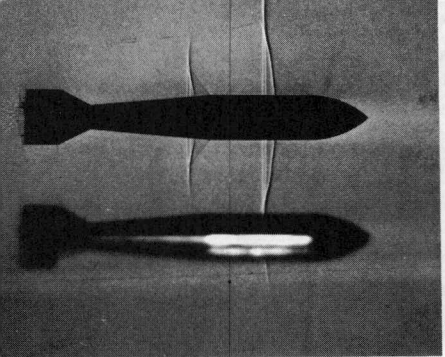

inherent exponential absorption in the medium itself that ultimately predominates. The energy received at a distance of r meters, compared to the energy received at one meter, is given by $E_r = E_1/(r^2 e^{\alpha r})$. The coefficient α is, in general, proportional to the square of the frequency, but varies enormously from subtance to substance. In air the absorption is complicated because the oxygen does most of the absorbing, and it does so most efficiently at a frequency determined by the humidity; dampness shifts the absorption peak to higher frequency. The fact that α is a function of frequency accounts for the change in quality of a concert when heard from a distance outdoors: the higher frequencies are absorbed first. Moreover, sounds are so rarely produced in an "infinite, uniform medium," and are so much affected by reflection and reverberation that the formal law is of limited usefulness in practice.

Sound exhibits nearly all possible properties of wave motion: frequency, wavelength, velocity, dispersion, refraction, reflection, diffraction, interference, absorption. However, in gases and liquids the actual vibrational motion of the individual particles of the medium as it carries the sound is back and forth along the direction of sound travel—unlike the corresponding motion in light waves, surface water waves, or waves on a string—and hence there is no possibility of polarization. Grossly, the motion of the medium consists of a series of alternate rarefactions and condensations, spaced respectively a "wavelength" apart and all traveling outward together with characteristic velocity. In air at 70°F, with velocity of 1,129 ft/sec and frequency 440 cycles/sec (tuning "A" for the orchestra), the wavelength is about 2.57 ft. The number of waves/sec that pass a given point is the frequency.

An important and fortunate characteristic of air and most fluids is that they carry audible sounds of any frequency with substantially the same velocity, *i.e.* without dispersion. Another fundamental feature of sound transmission is that at all ordinary loudness levels the response of most media is "linear," with the result that each wave of each frequency present is without effect upon any other; there is no "cross-modulation," and each component can be treated as if it alone were present. However, this is by no means true of the ear itself.

Audible sounds range in quality or timbre all the way from the "pure tone" given by tuning fork and test oscillator, which emit a single frequency only, to the complex combination of pure tones related harmonically that is characteristic of most musical instruments. Less musical is the screech of bluejay or peacock, and still less are noises such as the roar of traffic or heavy surf, or the multiple random shock waves of applause. In general, in a given sound the fewer the tones and the simpler their harmonic relationship and the less random noise, the sweeter is the musical effect—but the cymbals and drums have their place nevertheless.

In addition to quality there are two other measures of a sound: its intensity, or loudness; and its frequency, or pitch. Intensity and frequency are unique physical specifications, but loudness and pitch, though closely related to them, are subjective measures and depend upon the physiological and psychological nature of hearing. Intensity is defined as the number of watts per square centimeter falling on a surface perpendicular to the sound beam. It is usually measured on a logarithmic scale relative to a level considered to be the threshold of hearing at 1,000 cycles/sec; *i.e.* an increase in intensity of a factor of 10 raises the level 10 db (decibels); by a factor of 100, 20 db; etc. The threshold is taken to be that corresponding to a sound pressure (*RMS*) of 0.0002 dynes/cm², which in air is equivalent to 10^{-16} watts/cm². The static pressure of the atmosphere is 10^6 dynes/cm². The range of hearing from threshold up to sounds so loud as to be painful is about 120 db, or a million-millionfold increase in intensity, but even at $+$ 120 db, the intensity is only 10^{-4} watts/cm². These figures illustrate the minuteness of the pressures and powers involved in ordinary sound phenomena. A trained voice singing fortissimo radiates about 0.03 watts, and the intensity level at 3 ft is about 70 db.

Loudness, in effect a subjective estimate of intensity, depends upon the way in which the ear's sensitivity alters with the frequency structure of the sound being estimated. High frequencies and low frequencies require more intensity before they seem to have the same loudness as tones in the middle range. The average human ear is most sensitive from 3,000 to 4,000 cycles/sec, though there is not much difference from 500 to 5,000. The full range of audibility is about 20 to 20,000 cycles/sec, but deafness to the higher frequencies usually sets in as an individual gets older, and any degree of deafness may affect any portion or all of the spectrum at any age.

The frequencies present in a musical sound are exactly verifiable quantities physically, but the apparent pitch, which is the ear's judgment of "highness or lowness," depends also upon loudness and quality. A very loud sound in the middle range seems lower in pitch than a soft sound of the same frequency. This is a subjective phenomenon whose explana-

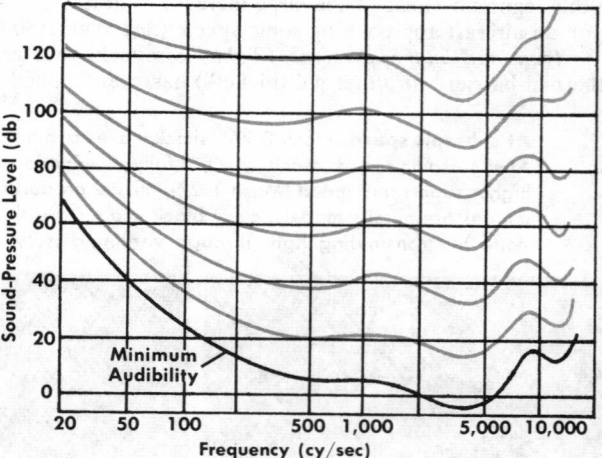

Equal-loudness curves: Sounds of equal energy (sound-pressure level) do not seem equally loud at all frequencies. Curves show that ear is most sensitive in the region of 3,000 cy/sec.

tion depends upon what physiological theory of hearing is accepted. The ability to perceive pitch is a highly variable one; many persons are "tone deaf," while others possess "absolute pitch" and are able to name a note or frequency with remarkable precision. Absolute pitch is not needed for tuning musical instruments, because tuning is readily done by the method of "beats," which are the more or less rapid fluctuations in intensity when two notes within 25 cycles of each other are sounded together. At "zero beat" (no fluctuation) the two are exactly "in tune." The beat phenomenon is a form of interference in which the intensity varies in time at one place. Since sound is a wave motion, analogous *spatial* interference exists also, and advantage is taken of this fact in the design of directional loudspeakers and microphones.

The ear, because of its nonlinear nature, possesses the remarkable capacity of hearing low frequencies when only high frequencies are physically present. If the A string of a violin (440 cycles/sec) is sounded before an amplifier system, and the amplifier is arranged so that no sound whatever of frequency less than 1,000 cycles is reproduced, the ear will still hear the "pitch" of the note as A (440). The higher harmonics of the violin tone are all multiples of 440, so their successive differences are 440, and the ear recreates, by cross-modulation, the original pitch, even though the corresponding frequency is physically absent. The small loudspeaker, woefully deficient in ability to reproduce bass notes, depends upon the ear to replace them.

If the source of sound and the observer are moving toward or away from each other, the source will seem to the observer to have a pitch different from the actual one: higher if they are approaching, lower if receding. This is the well-known DOPPLER EFFECT, readily observable in a train or automobile when passing a stationary bell. See ACOUSTICS.—*M. C. H.*

SOUND REPRODUCTION: the process whereby a sound, as it is being generated, may be stored in some material medium and be re-created at some later time as desired. Modern sound-reproducing systems are commonly of three types: sound on film, disk recordings, and magnetic-tape recordings. Sound is stored on film as a variation in density, or darkness, along a narrow strip (sound track) running the length of the film. Two types of recording are in common use: variable-width and variable-density. The variable-width track consists of a transparent and an opaque portion, with the ratio of the portions varying from position to position along the track. The variable-density type varies in density from position to position along the track, although the density of the blackening is the same across the track. The sound is reproduced by placing a photoelectric cell behind the track with a light source of constant intensity on the opposite side. As the film is moved along at constant speed, the amount of light striking the cell varies in accordance with the sound stored. This variation is converted to a varying voltage, which is then amplified and converted back to a sound by means of a LOUDSPEAKER.

Disk recordings constitute the most widely known method of storing sounds. The recording consists of a groove cut with a diamond stylus on a hard plastic material. The stylus is made to vibrate slightly in consonance with the sound being recorded; thus the groove is not smooth but contains many wiggles, which become apparent if viewed through a reading glass. The sound is reproduced by placing a stylus in the groove and moving the storage medium at constant speed. Thus the stylus is set into vibration, and this motion is converted to a voltage by use of a piezoelectric, an electrodynamic, or a variable-reluctance principle.

A magnetic tape consists of a plastic strip with a coating of powdered magnetic iron oxide on one side. Sound is stored in this medium in the form of variations in the magnetization of the oxide coating. Both recording and reproducing are accomplished through the use of a magnet with a very small spacing between the poles. The tape is moved at constant speed across the poles of the magnet. For recording, the magnetic field of the magnet is varied in consonance with the sound being recorded; for reproduction, a fluctuating voltage is induced in a coil wound on the magnet.— *H. M. T.*

SOUTHERN LIGHTS: see AURORA.

SPACE: broadly, the entire universe with all objects removed. Every object—Earth, atmosphere, celestial bodies—occupies a portion of space. Where no substances are thought to exist, the space is empty, although physicists sometimes imagine it filled with ETHER, a fiction invented to accommodate physical theories. In a more restricted sense, physical space may refer to a part of this empty universe. We speak of the space in a room, for example. Geometry has often been described as the science of space, meaning physical space. In its beginnings it had this nature, and was conceived as a physical science. In making geometry abstract, the Greek geometers were idealizing physical space, and continued to believe that the abstract science actually described the physical universe. Superficially, the three-dimensional geometry of Euclid appears to do so. In fact, the choice of the Euclidean postulates seemed to be dictated by physical appearances. This belief persisted until early in the 19th cent., when the creation of NON-EUCLIDEAN GEOMETRY demonstrated that this long-held view was not justified. In the modern theory of RELATIVITY, physical space is more closely approximated by a non-Euclidean geometry. The discovery of non-Euclidean geometry had the further effect that geometry was freed from the necessity of fitting the physical world. Geometrical space is today an abstract construction that is not required to conform to physical facts.

Geometrical spaces are often classified according to dimension. The physical space in which we live is intuitively conceived as three-dimensional. A plane is two-dimensional, and a straight line is one-dimensional. Spaces of more than three dimensions cannot be visualized, but they can be abstractly conceived and studied mathematically in ways that are analogous to the mathematics of two and three dimensions. A great deal of modern analysis of a highly practical kind utilizes spaces of n dimensions, where n can be any positive integer, and even of infinitely many dimensions.

COORDINATE GEOMETRY provides a convenient way of describing spaces. Thus, the two-dimensional space of a plane is defined as the set of all ordered pairs of real numbers, (x, y), and three-dimensional space as the set of all ordered triples of real numbers, (x, y, z). Even though we cannot visualize four-dimensional space, we may define it as the set of all ordered quadruples of real numbers, (x_1, x_2, x_3, x_4), and n-dimensional space as the set of all ordered n-tuples of real numbers, $(x_1, x_2, \ldots, x_n)$. A vector space is one in which the points are given by vectors. In three dimensions it differs from the space defined by coordinates of points only in the point of view. The three coordinates (x, y, z) are equivalent to the vector from the origin to this point.

The abstract mathematical conception of space has extremely broad connotations, and is not capable of an explicit definition that is suitable for all purposes. In the broadest sense it differs little from "set," which is a basic undefined term of mathematics. A space is a set of elements which are made to conform to certain postulates. Euclidean space consists of points, themselves undefined, which are subjected to the Euclidean postulates. Two examples of spaces of a more abstract nature are (1) metric space, characterized by a distance measure associated with each pair of elements, and (2) topological space, in which each element possesses a neighborhood, and limit points play a dominating role. (See also SPACE-TIME.)—*H. C.*

SPACE BIOLOGY: the study of the vital functions of living organisms beyond the atmospheric limits and terrestrial influences of Earth. Its domain includes not only organisms propelled from Earth, but also any living forms of their organic precursors existing freely in space or as inhabitants of cosmic materials and bodies. The function of space biology is the evaluation of biological changes occurring in living forms, from single cells to higher mammals, as a result of the various physical stresses in space. From these studies, environmental systems capable of maintaining man safely in space are developed. Such systems maintain the atmosphere in a spaceship, control the temperature, shield against cosmic radiations, compensate for weightless conditions, and protect against the effects of acceleration. As man penetrates deeper into space, these protective systems will undoubtedly be improved.

Observations of living organisms placed in space for the purpose of collecting biological data are secured by telemetering to a laboratory on Earth those changes measured by specific instrumentation of the specimen. In simple cell specimens or cell colonies, analysis of gaseous changes or acid-base variations can signify important metabolic changes that are related to the biologic stresses. Changes in life cycle dominated by cell division and genetics are directly observed by televised microscopy. In the biological study of more complex animal life in space, more direct physiological instrumentation, with telemetering of information, is used. Electrocardiographic pickups show heart action, pulse rate, and blood pressure; the electroencephalograph indicates changes in brain waves; the oximeter or direct blood sampling measures the oxygen content of the blood. The effectiveness of environmental systems in space craft is measured by the adequacy of performance of animals placed in the systems. The animal performs a primary task, such as pushing a lever in response to an auditory or visual cue. Proper performance results in the elimination of a disagreeable stimulus, such as a mild electric shock, or a reward in the form of a pleasing tidbit. Crewmen are fitted with instruments which record biological data in experimental space vehicles. Thus the crewman is monitored from Earth by checking his physical state through telemetered or televised biological information. If dangerous conditions arise as manifested in changes from the normal, control of the vehicle can be taken over by an Earth monitor and the vehicle can be safely returned to Earth.

The study of living organisms existing freely in space or on cosmic bodies involves such methods as collecting microscopic particles with satellites capable of "sweeping" space, and sending probes to collect samples on or under the surface of space bodies. These samples are then analyzed and the information as to their identity telemetered back to Earth; or the samples themselves may be returned to Earth for analysis. See LIFE, EXTRATERRESTRIAL; SPACE TRAVEL; WEIGHTLESSNESS.—*C. G.*

SPACE CHARGE: a cloud of charged particles, surrounding a charged body, that inhibits the emission of additional charged particles. In a vacuum tube, unless the anode (plate) is at a very high potential with respect to the cathode, some of the

electrons emitted fail to travel from cathode to plate. These electrons tend to repel other emitted electrons back to the cathode, thereby limiting the current through the tube.—*E. M. R.*

SPACE-TIME: the four-dimensional blend of space and time that resulted from the theory of RELATIVITY. To specify where and when an event occurs, one needs three spatial coordinates for the "where" and a time coordinate for the "when"; in this sense the world is four-dimensional. Before relativity, the time coordinate was believed unaffected by relative motion, so that the time dimension stood apart from the three spatial dimensions, and the world was rather three-plus-one-dimensional than four-dimensional.

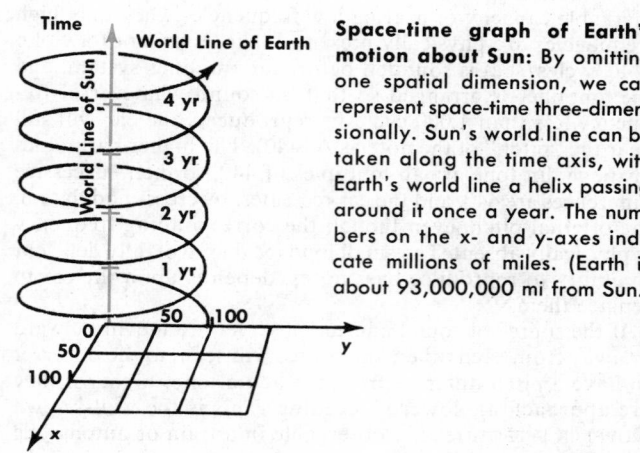

Space-time graph of Earth's motion about Sun: By omitting one spatial dimension, we can represent space-time three-dimensionally. Sun's world line can be taken along the time axis, with Earth's world line a helix passing around it once a year. The numbers on the x- and y-axes indicate millions of miles. (Earth is about 93,000,000 mi from Sun.)

In 1907, H. Minkowski noted that the basic equations of Einstein's *special* theory of relativity belong to a "flat" four-dimensional space-time in which time intermingles with space. The Lorentz transformation between observers in uniform relative motion is a type of rotation of time and space coordinate axes in space-time. It leaves unaltered the "interval" ds between neighboring events, where $ds^2 = c^2dt^2 - (dx^2 + dy^2 + dz^2)$, c being the speed of light, dt the difference of the time coordinates of the events, and dx, dy, dz the differences of their space coordinates. Except for effects associated with the different signs, time and space coordinates enter on an equal footing. A point moving in space is a "world line" in space-time, much as a changing stock average becomes a fixed jagged line on a graph. Since light moves so that $ds = 0$, a burst of light sent from the origin traces out a (three-dimensional) "light cone" in space-time. Only events within this cone can occur definitely earlier than or definitely later than the event represented by the origin. An event outside the light cone can appear earlier than the event at the origin to one observer but later to another; therefore it can neither cause nor be caused by the event at the origin, for causality cannot depend on which observer is looking.

In the *general* theory of relativity, space-time is no longer flat but curved, and its curvature represents gravitation. —*Ba. H.*

SPACE TRAVEL: navigation of a manned spacecraft in a region beyond Earth's atmosphere—a region generally considered to begin at an altitude of about 100 mi. Until recently, knowledge of outer space was derived solely from light and other radiations that penetrate the atmosphere from the vastness of the universe. Today jet propulsion, computers, and miniaturized electronic components make it possible to reach outer space from Earth and return safely, as first demonstrated by Yuri Gagarin, who circled Earth in 89 min at an altitude of 188 mi on Apr. 12, 1961, in the spaceship Vostok I (see SATELLITE, ARTIFICIAL). But the historical development of the theory and technology which culminated in space travel in 1961 began when astronomers such as Hipparchus and Ptolemaeus abandoned the flat Earth concept. Plutarch speculated that the Moon is much like Earth, but smaller, and *c.* A. D. 160 the Greek writer Lucian wrote about a voyage to the Moon. After the decline of Greek civilization, interest in space travel disappeared for nearly fourteen centuries, during which the church authorities, following Aristotle, opposed belief in the existence of life on other worlds. But new, revolutionary ideas in astronomy proposed in the 16th and 17th cent. by Copernicus, Kepler, and Galileo, among others, combined with the invention of the telescope, revived interest and speculation about space travel to other planets, and Kepler himself, toward the end of his life, wrote a fantasy about travel to the Moon. In 1687 Sir Isaac Newton showed in his famous *Principia* that a projectile with a velocity of 7 mi/sec can escape into space from the gravitational pull of Earth. But in those days actual space travel seemed impossible, and serious interest in it disappeared again until the beginning of the present century, when advances in rocketry made it feasible.

Pioneer Efforts: At the beginning of the 19th cent., solid-propellant ROCKETS were being used extensively for military purposes. A working model of a liquid-propellant rocket was built in 1895 by P. E. Paulet, a South American engineer. In 1903 the first sound theoretical treatise on space travel, by the Russian mathematics teacher K. E. Tsiolkovsky, was published; it carried the title "Probing Space by Means of Jet Devices." Tsiolkovsky discussed the most important theoretical points related to space travel and even suggested the use of liquid oxygen and hydrogen as propellants. But his efforts, like those of the great American physicist Dr. Robert H. Goddard, who pioneered the development of rocketry between 1914 and World War II in the U. S. A., went largely unheeded. Interest in rocketry and space travel took hold only after Herman Oberth published, in 1923, a detailed mathematical theory of rockets, which included a number of striking practical ideas on space travel. Like Goddard, he conceived the step rocket (Fig. 1), and also proposed the first self-cooled rocket motor—two very important principles which have been used in all space vehicles. Oberth also showed that it is possible to place a large rocket-powered spaceship into an orbit around Earth as a space station, and that passengers could reach it or leave it by means of smaller "landing rockets."

Interest in rocketry was particularly keen in Germany because the rocket was one of the few weapons not forbidden to the German army under the Versailles Treaty. In 1929, the German army began the development of the large rockets which eventually resulted in the V-2, fired successfully for the first time Oct. 3, 1942. From then on the realization of man's age-old dream of space travel was only a matter of time. In 1949 the United States sent the second stage of a two-step rocket with a V-2 as the first stage to a height of 250 mi, and on Oct. 4, 1957, the U. S. S. R. launched Sputnik I, the first artificial satellite to orbit Earth.

Vehicle Design: The design of a space vehicle is governed by its mission. The dominating design factor is the combina-

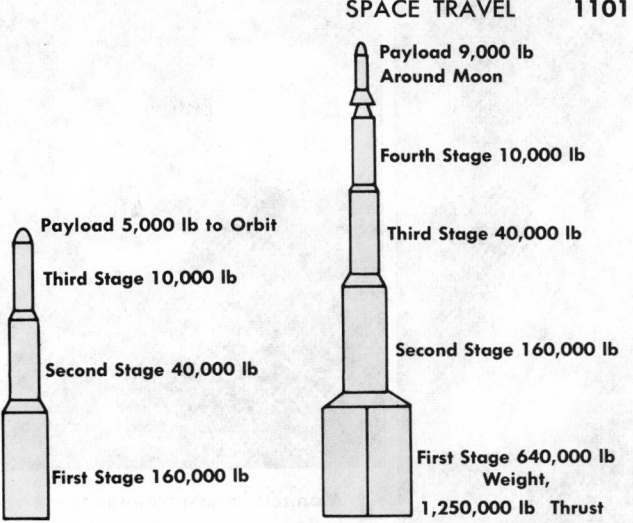

Fig. 1—Step-rocket configuration for orbit mission around Earth (*left*) is compared to configuration for circumlunar mission (*right*).

tion of space dynamics and propulsion system which determines the feasibility of a given mission. The concept of a space station is an intermediate step in space travel necessitated by the limitation of propulsion devices. The development of space-flight systems goes hand in hand with the growth of propulsion capability. The first step, exemplified by the U. S. Project Mercury, which sent a man over a 300-mi flight May 5, 1961, is a ballistic vehicle. Such a vehicle is boosted to some predetermined set of conditions (altitude, velocity, and attitude) and then coasts under the influence of gravity, through a ballistic path, to its preset destination with minor auxiliary power for guidance and control. Such a vehicle, while capable of manned space flight, has no means

Spacecraft Aurora 7: NASA space-capsule technicians look on as Astronaut Scott Carpenter inspects Aurora 7 prior to his programmed three-orbit mission. (*NASA*)

Manned lunar-reconnaissance vehicle could be assembled at space-station satellite and launched from orbit. Forward section (*top*) is crew's gondola. (*General Dynamics*)

Lunar capsule (*above left*) may be designed to separate from parent spacecraft about 25 mi from Moon. After crash landing, it will telemeter data to Earth for over one month. (*NASA*) **Moon landing** (*right*) will be accomplished in vehicle probably similar to this. (*North Amer. Aviation*)

for landing on and taking off from another planet. The next step in space-flight technology is the manned satellite, a vehicle boosted to approximately 90% of orbital velocity, followed by a coast to orbital altitude and final propulsive force injection into a circular or elliptical orbit around Earth. Such a launch program was exemplified by the flight of Vostok I and Friendship VII. A vehicle of this type would be capable of landing on the Moon from a highly eccentric orbit and could, if capable of carrying a payload which includes a satisfactory lunar launching system, return to Earth. The third and final step is the true space craft, capable of carrying man to another planet and back. One basic flight plan consists of building an orbiting space station with vehicles designed for shuttle service to and from the Earth. Another vehicle, designed strictly for space travel, would then provide the means of reaching another planet and return to the space station.

Most concepts of space travel are based on step-type flights (Fig. 1). The reason for using more than one vehicle is that the space-flight capability of a rocket ship is greatly dependent on the ratio of the weight of the vehicle to the weight of the propellant it carries. The velocity at the end of powered flight V is given by

$$V = I_{sp}\, g\, (\log_e M) - \text{(drag and gravity losses)}$$

where I_{sp} is the pounds of thrust developed per propellant consumption rate in lb/sec, called the specific impulse; g is the gravitational acceleration; and M is the mass ratio, *i.e.* weight of structure and propellant (the take-off weight) to weight of structure alone (the weight at burn-out). This equation shows that to achieve high velocities a large specific impulse and a light vehicle with a large fuel storage capacity are necessary. A single space vehicle with a specific propellant impulse of 300 lb/sec, capable of landing on the Moon and taking off again (requiring an additional velocity increment of 14,000 fps), would have to be designed with a mass ratio of more than 150—a technical impossibility. To partially overcome the need to carry useless weight, *i.e.* empty propellant tanks, spaceships are staged. A series of them are joined in tandem; the first stage, or booster, carries the remaining stages to its terminal velocity and is then discarded, thereby reducing the over-all mass of the combination. And this operation can be repeated. Each subsequent stage commences powered flight at the terminal velocity of the preceding stage,

and the effective mass ratio of a two-step rocket, each step of which has a mass ratio of 5, increases, therefore, to the order of 25. Take-off from a space station in orbit further increases space-flight capabilities.

Vehicle Limitations: Although the step-vehicle concept has made space travel possible, there are practical limitations to its usefulness. The larger the number of stages, the more complicated and expensive the vehicle becomes, and the chance of malfunction of one of the components increases. In addition, of course, the payload capability is limited. The realization of extended space travel depends, therefore, on the development of propulsion systems with high specific im-

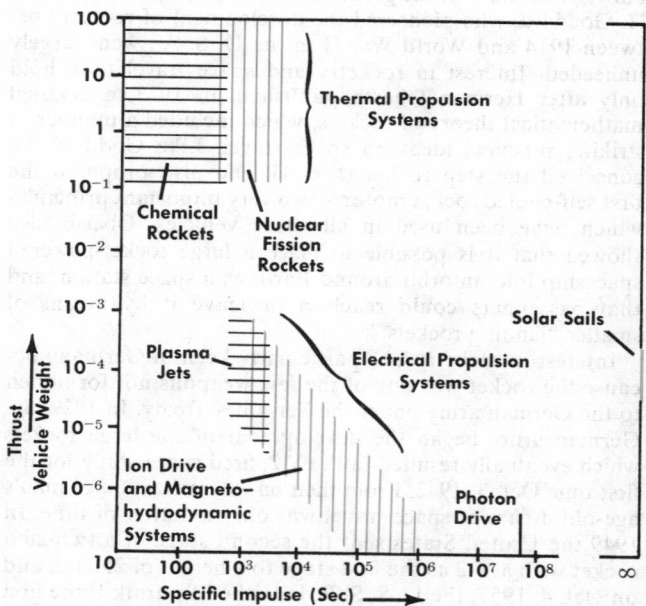

Fig. 2—Performance capabilities of various propulsion systems: This graph of thrust-to-weight ratio (a measure of vehicle acceleration capability) vs. specific impulse (ratio of pounds of thrust per pound of fuel burned per second, a measure of fuel economy) compares the various propulsion systems now envisioned. (The specific impulse of solar-sail systems is infinite because they require no propellant at all.)

pulse. Fig. 2 illustrates the performance capabilities of various types of space propulsion systems in terms of their thrust-to-gross-weight ratios and specific impulses. A specific mission requires certain values of thrust-to-weight ratios and I_{sp}. Chemical rockets are limited to I_{sp} of about 400, but nuclear rockets can be expected to reach an I_{sp} of 600, and electrical propulsion systems are theoretically capable of 1,000 I_{sp} or better. Ion propulsion systems, for example, despite their small thrust-to-weight ratios, which limit their acceleration capabilities to the order of 0.01 g, are capable of propelling spacecraft on extended missions with appreciable payloads. A typical ion-propelled vehicle for traveling to Mars and back could carry a payload of 150 tons. The round trip, taking about 400 days, would require about 365 tons of propellants, with an electrical propulsion system capable of delivering about 23,000 kw. The take-off weight would be about 730 tons.

Human Factors: Although the specific impulse and the thrust-to-weight ratio are the most important parameters for space travel, the system reliability, guidance, control, and human factors cannot be ignored. Also, the problem of landing on a planet requires careful consideration; the deceleration from the tremendous flight velocities necessary for space travel must be kept within limits tolerable to a human being, and the actual velocities must be kept low enough to prevent the vehicle from being destroyed by the high rates of heat transfer caused by the frictional drag of an atmosphere. These problems have, however, been essentially solved by the use of retro-rockets and parachutes for deceleration, and by ABLATION-cooled heat shields for thermal protection of the vehicle and its occupant.

Extended space travel will require further development and research not only in the propulsion and guidance fields, but also in the area of human engineering. Crews of space vehicles will have to function in an environment which is drastically different from that encountered in ordinary life. Their normal pattern of living will be altered by the confinement and isolation in a space capsule, and psychological, physiological, and biochemical adaptations will have to be made if the crew is to perform its functions in the artificial habitat of a space cabin for protracted periods such as will be necessary for trips to other planets. The space cabin will have to be designed to protect the crew against harmful radiation, meteors, and space debris. It will also have to be provided with mechanisms which can control the internal environment to meet human requirements, *e.g.* comfortable temperature and pressure, adequate light and oxygen, and food. Advanced space vehicles will also need a system by which the crew can exercise control during flight.

Among the absolute necessities for any prolonged space trip is a supply of food and oxygen. Whereas for relatively short trips adequate supplies can be taken along, for trips requiring months or years the habitable area of the space vehicle will have to be a completely balanced, self-sustaining, closed ecological system. A balanced regenerative system will require the development of microscopic plant organisms which, when exposed to solar or stellar radiation, can effect photosynthesis or gas exchange between man and plant, re-utilization of wastes from all sources, and production of food from materials within the system.

The power required for propulsion and for the internal operation of the craft, including crew needs, will have to be supplied either from energy sources taken along as payload or from conversion of solar or stellar radiation into useful power. Although nuclear energy sources might yield a large amount of power per unit weight, radiant conversion types of power supplies will probably be preferable for long trips. Recent advances in solar-battery design and other types of

Assembled space station (*left*): Whole station rotates at high speed, creating artificial gravity. Interior artificial atmosphere is preserved by air lock, which allows space voyagers to enter and leave station. **Space-station sections** (*right*): Each "pod" is one half of a space station, in readiness to be launched into space to point where station will be assembled. (*General Electric*)

direct-energy conversion systems suggest that efficient radiation-driven generators will be available soon. The possibility of using photons to propel space craft, *e.g.* by means of solar "sails" (surfaces to be acted upon by light pressure), has been suggested, and navigation in space without continuous expenditure of mass for propulsion and control appears feasible.—*F. K.*

Assuming that space travelers are adequately protected by their craft from meteorite impacts, the cold of space, and lethal radiation, they will still face problems of survival on any extraterrestrial bodies on which they can make landings. On the Moon and the planets, extremes of temperature, gravity, atmospheric conditions, topography, and radiation would be encountered (see articles on these celestial bodies). Exploration and life on extraterrestrial bodies, none of which offers a naturally friendly environment to man, will require techniques and equipment unprecedented on Earth.

An apparently absolute limitation on space travel is suggested by the magnitude of interstellar distances. Although journeys of hundreds of millions of miles within the solar system are now conceivable, the fact that the star nearest to our Sun, Proxima Centauri, is some 26 million million miles away makes clear that interstellar travel would be of an entirely different order. A round trip between Proxima Centauri and Earth at the speed of light (which actually is unattainable) would take nearly 10 yr. A one-way voyage across our Milky Way galaxy would take 100,000 yr, and to reach our nearest neighbor-galaxies, the Magellanic Clouds, another 150,000 yr would be required. The informed science-fiction writer knows that for interstellar travel we must learn how to circumvent "time."

The most modest achievements in interplanetary travel will require the combined efforts of workers in practically every phase of biological and physical science. Many obstacles will have to be overcome, but there is no doubt that man's ingenuity and ambition, with his innate desire to explore the unknown, will eventually succeed in conquering at least the nearer reaches of outer space.—*J. W.*

SPACE VELOCITY OF A STAR: the velocity of the star measured on the assumption that the Sun is fixed in space. The space velocity of a star cannot be observed directly, but must be calculated from observations of PROPER MOTION, distance, and RADIAL VELOCITY of the star; these cannot always be obtained. The component of the space velocity in the direction of the line joining the Sun to the star is the radial velocity; it can be measured directly in mi/sec from the star's spectrum by the Doppler effect. The component at right angle to this is

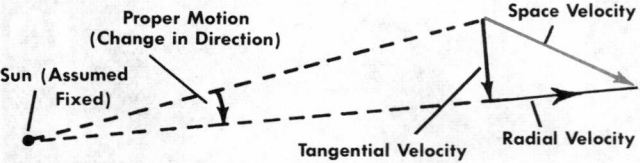

Space velocity of star with respect to Sun can be calculated from star's tangential and radial velocities.

called the *tangential velocity*. It cannot be measured directly, but if the star is near enough its proper motion can be measured by its angular displacement, as it would appear to an observer on the Sun. Proper motion can be converted into tangential velocity if the distance of the star from the Sun is known, since the same tangential velocity will cause a larger proper motion for a nearby star than for a more distant one.—*M. W. O.*

SPALLANZANI, LAZZARO, 1729–99, Italian physiologist and anatomist; b. Scandiano. Outstanding for his studies of the circulation of the blood, digestion, and respiration, he engaged in a celebrated controversy with J. T. Needham (1713–81) over the idea of spontaneous generation. Needham, on finding an abundance of microorganisms in an infusion of meat broth after it had been thoroughly boiled to destroy all organisms, believed he had proved that life was spontaneously produced. By repeating Needham's experiment but keeping the boiled infusion in sealed containers, Spallanzani showed that no growth could be found as long as the broth was not exposed to the air. However, after the containers were left unsealed, organisms were found growing in the infusion, and thus it was shown that the microorganisms were not spontaneously produced but were carried by the air. Spallanzani also experimentally studied regeneration in amphibians. His *Dissertazioni de fisica animale e vegetabile* was published in 1780. He was a fellow of the Royal Society.—*D. H. D. R.*

SPARK: the almost instantaneous phenomenon that occurs when the voltage across a region of poorly conducting matter is increased to a level that causes the matter to become suddenly highly conductive. The voltage then drops rapidly, a brilliant flash of light is emitted that is rich in ultraviolet, a sharp noise is created, and the entire phenomenon ends in a time much less than 1 microsecond. If the light does not go out, the spark is said to have gone over into an arc. Despite lay usage, all electrically produced flashes of light are by no means sparks, but are frequently arcs (see ARCS AND DISCHARGES). LIGHTNING is a form of spark. The spark plays an important role in the ignition system of the INTERNAL COMBUSTION engine.—*R. N. V.*

SPAWNING: production by AQUATIC ANIMALS of a large number of small eggs. When an oyster spawns, it produces 100 million to 500 million eggs. The spawn of a sturgeon, known as caviar, may include three million eggs and weigh nearly a third as much as the parent. At spawning time, a toad commonly produces 15,000 eggs, and a bullfrog 50,000.—*L. and M. M.*

SPECIAL FUNCTIONS: a growing class of functions in mathematical physics. The first of these were introduced in the 18th cent. when mathematicians found that the previously known elementary functions were inadequate to describe physical phenomena. Many special functions occur in problems concerning such physical phenomena as wave motion, heat flow, diffusion processes, and gravitational and electrostatic potential. Generally these problems lead to partial differential equations which can, under rather general conditions, be reduced to systems of ordinary differential equations. The solutions of these ordinary differential equations belong to the family of special functions. As a rule these equations are second-order linear ones of the hypergeometric or confluent hypergeometric type. The general hypergeometric equation is

$$z(1 - z)\,d^2u/dz^2 + [c - (a + b + 1)\,z]\,du/dz - abu = 0$$

and the general confluent hypergeometric equation is

$$z\,d^2u/dz^2 + (c - z)\,du/dz - au = 0$$

In both cases *a, b, c* are arbitrary parameters.

Among the most important of the special functions are the Bessel, Hankel, Legendre, and Mathieu functions; also others belonging to the general class of orthogonal polynomials. Another major class is the elliptic functions. They are generalizations of the periodic trigonometric functions. For example, the sine function is periodic with period 2π; *i.e.* $\sin(x + 2\pi)$ $= \sin x$. Elliptic functions are doubly periodic: they have two periods whereas ordinary trigonometric functions have only one. This can be shown symbolically by stating that the elliptic function $f(x)$ has the property that

$$f(x + p_1) = f(x); \qquad f(x + p_2) = f(x)$$

where p_1 and p_2 denote the two periods. It is necessary that the ratio p_1/p_2 be a complex number. Elliptic functions are important in the theory of the motion of the pendulum, and also arise in many potential problems.

Although the special functions were first studied in connection with various physical phenomena, they also are of intrinsic interest from a mathematical viewpoint, their study having led to significant mathematical advances.—*H. Ho.*

SPECIES: the lowest and most important of the primary groupings used in classifying plants and animals. There is no clear-cut definition of species that applies equally well to all organisms. For animals and plants that reproduce sexually, with cross fertilization, a species is defined as a group of individuals capable of breeding with one another but not with members of other species. Organisms that do not reproduce in this manner, *e.g.* most bacteria and some plants, are classified into species on the basis of structural similarities and

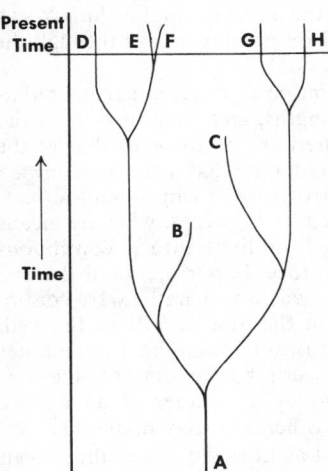

Development of new species: In this diagram of a phylogenetic tree, a single ancestral species (*A*) has given rise to several new species. Two of these species (*B* and *C*) have become extinct. Three distinct species (*D*, *G*, and *H*) derived from the common ancestor are extant. Two additional derivatives (*E* and *F*) are, at present, so close in time to point at which they began to diverge that they might properly be considered subspecies rather than distinct species. (*After Manter*)

differences. The same is true for fossil organisms separated in time. Many species that occupy large geographic areas show marked differences in structure from one region to another; the differing local groups, which interbreed freely where they come into contact, are called *subspecies* (or *races, varieties,* or *breeds*). When closely related plants or animals are separated by geographic barriers, their classification either as

Distinction between species is usually sharp, as between snails at extreme left of Group I and extreme right of Group II. But some species, like these snails, seem to be connected by living intermediate forms that are progressively more alike (snails toward center). This suggests that all the forms evolved from a common ancestor. (*From Young; after Neumayr*)

subspecies of a single species or as separate species depends on whether they are judged to be so similar that they would interbreed freely if their habitats overlapped. For the naming of species, see BIOLOGICAL NAME. See also CLASSIFICATION OF LIVING THINGS; EVOLUTION; ISOLATION; VARIATION.—*G. R. P.*

SPECIFIC GRAVITY: the ratio of the DENSITY of a material to the density of water. Since the latter is 1 gm/cm^3 (at 4°C and under a pressure of one atmosphere) the specific gravity of any material (under similar conditions) is numerically equal to its density expressed in gm/cm^3.—*S. K.*

SPECIFIC HEAT (or **heat capacity**): the amount of heat required to produce a unit rise in temperature in a unit mass of a substance. The specific heat of different substances varies. To produce the same temperature rise in equal masses of several different materials, each must be given different amounts of heat. Specific heat is expressed as a number indicating the ratio of heat absorbed to consequent temperature rise for a substance in comparison with a similar ratio for some standard, usually water, which has a higher specific heat than other common substances. For example, it takes about half as much heat to produce a given temperature rise in acetone as it does in an equal mass of water. Accordingly the specific heat of acetone is one-half that of water, or 0.50.

The specific heats of most solids and liquids remain approximately constant over a considerable range of temperature. For gases, however, specific heats change, not only with the temperature at which they are measured, but also with the conditions of measurement. If, for example, the gas is confined in a rigid vessel, the heat requirement for a given temperature rise is less than the amount needed if the container expands during the heating, as in the case of a balloon. This is to be expected, since the expanding vessel must do work against the atmospheric pressure in order to become larger, and the amount of heat absorbed is necessarily greater than is needed merely to increase the gas temperature.

The fact that water has a larger specific heat than almost any other substance accounts in part for the well-known moderating influence exercised by large bodies of water on climate. As solar radiation pours down upon adjacent land and water masses, the water temperature rises more slowly than that of the land, and the energy acquired is therefore conserved longer, for the heated matter loses energy at a rate which depends on its temperature. After nightfall the water still has a large part of the energy ration which it absorbed during the day, and, as the environmental temperature falls, the water becomes a source of heat for its cooler surroundings.—*J. E. W.*

SPECIFIC IMPULSE: thrust produced by a rocket engine when a unit weight of propellant is burned per unit time; or, ratio of thrust to propellant mass flow. Specific impulse indicates efficiency of the propulsion system rather than its ability to supply a desired thrust. (See THRUST LOADING.) Specific-impulse values for chemical solid propellants range up to about 250 sec. For ION PROPULSION, specific impulse may be 100 times greater; *i.e.* a unit weight of ion fuel may last 100 times longer than an identical weight of chemical fuel.—*D. B.*

Group I

Group II

SPECTROHELIOGRAPH: an instrument used to observe the Sun in monochromatic light; basically, a spectroscope with a second slit placed in the plane in which the spectrum is formed. An image of the Sun is focused by the objective of a telescope upon the entrance slit. The light is dispersed, forming a spectrum, and a small wavelength interval passes through the second slit. The image of the Sun is scanned by moving the first slit perpendicular to its length. The second slit is moved in synchronism with the first, and a photographic emulsion receives the light from the second slit. Thus, a composite picture of the Sun in the selected spectral region is built up, consisting of a series of images of the regions on the Sun as defined by the first slit, placed side by side to form a complete picture.

The second slit of the spectroheliograph is usually set along the spectrum at the wavelength of one of the strong spectral lines (see SUN), so that a picture of the Sun will be formed, *e.g.* in the light of hydrogen, calcium, or sodium. Thus the spectroheliograph may be used to identify bright plages or flares in the solar atmosphere from which the light emitted by hydrogen is particularly strong, or dark filaments in which hydrogen strongly absorbs light. The instrument may also be used with a CORONAGRAPH to observe prominences on the limb of the Sun. A slight variation in operating procedure allows measurement of the line-of-sight velocity of the emitting or absorbing gas by the Doppler shift of the line.

Another device which performs the same function as the spectroheliograph is the birefringent filter. It consists of a stack of elements cut from crystals of quartz or calcite with pieces of polaroid separating the elements. This stack combined with a suitably colored glass filter will transmit only the light from a selected wavelength region, and the solar images photographed through it show the same phenomena that appear on spectroheliograms.—*D. E. B. and L. H.*

SPECTROMETER: see SPECTROSCOPE AND SPECTROSCOPY.

SPECTROSCOPE AND SPECTROSCOPY: The spectroscope is an instrument that disperses electromagnetic radiation into a SPECTRUM consisting of one or more single wavelengths. The simplest form of spectroscope is a glass prism of the type used by Isaac Newton in 1666. The dispersion by a prism of sunlight into its component colors, or wavelengths, is possible because each wavelength passes through a material medium at a different velocity. As a result each wavelength passing through a prism has a different index of refraction; the shorter wavelengths in the violet region bend more sharply than the longer red waves, and thus colors are separated. The prism spectroscope (see figure) utilizes the same principle. Light from a source passes through an adjustable narrow slit, which is placed at the principal focus of a collimating lens. The parallel rays from the lens are refracted and dispersed by the prism, then focused by the telescope

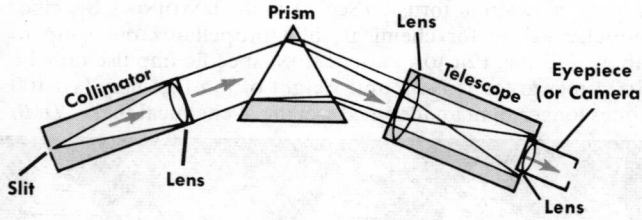

Collimator lens of spectroscope takes diverging light entering slit at left and refracts it so that emerging rays are parallel. These are refracted and dispersed by prism into a spectrum which is viewed through telescope and eyepiece at right.

lens. The image of the spectrum can be viewed directly or can be recorded on a photographic plate, a fluorescent screen, or a thermopile (see THERMOCOUPLE).

A spectroscope with a wavelength scale for measuring the position and determining the wavelengths of the dispersed waves is a *spectrometer;* a spectroscope equipped with a camera for securing a photographic record of the spectrum is a *spectrograph.* The most powerful and precise spectrographs use DIFFRACTION GRATINGS. Grating spectrographs have these advantages over the prism-type instruments: greater resolution, more freedom from optical aberration, less absorption of light, greater uniformity (distances along the spectrum are approximately proportional to the range of wavelengths), and greater latitude in the wavelengths utilized. Since wavelengths beyond the visible spectrum, *e.g.* ultraviolet and infrared radiation, are transmitted but slightly by glass, prisms of other materials must be used to produce spectra in these regions. Halides, such as rock salt, transmit infrared radiation; quartz and fluorite transmit ultraviolet radiation. But neither can transmit radiation of the extreme ultraviolet and infrared ends of the optical region; for extremely-long-wave infrared radiation and for ultraviolet radiation of wavelength shorter than 2,000 Å (angstroms), gratings must be used. However, for X-RAYS, whose wavelengths are of the order of 1 Å, it is not possible to use diffraction gratings (except at the grazing angle), and X-RAY DIFFRACTION is accomplished by passing x-rays through the regularly spaced atoms of a crystal.

Spectroscopy involves separation of electromagnetic radiation into its individual wavelengths, and analysis of both the character of the electromagnetic radiation and that of the material through which the radiation has been transmitted comprises the science of spectroscopy. It can be said to have been started by Newton in the late 17th cent. when by means of a glass prism he dispersed sunlight into a continuous spectrum of its component colors. Experiments in the dispersion of light into its component wavelengths were continued by Joseph Frauenhofer in the first decade of the 19th cent. While examining a spectrum of sunlight, Frauenhofer observed, as had William Wollaston before him, that the continuous spectrum was crossed by a number of dark lines. Turning his spectroscope to other celestial bodies, he observed additional lines as well as lines similar to those seen in the Sun's spectrum. With the aid of diffraction gratings of his own construction, he succeeded in measuring the wavelengths of many of the lines. In 1859, Gustav Kirchhoff published the results of his work in spectrum analysis (done in collaboration with Robert Bunsen) and fully identified the character of these lines, now known as *Frauenhofer lines.* He also explained the general character of *dark-line* or *absorption-line spectra* as well as the character of *bright-line* or *emission-line spectra.* He thus established spectroscopy as one of the most powerful tools in physical science.

The Sun or a hot incandescent body such as a tungsten lamp filament produces a continuous spectrum. An element vaporized by being placed in a flame produces a discontinuous spectrum, *i.e.* a series of bright lines called a *bright-line* or an *emission-line spectrum.* Those elements that remain in a molecular state rather than in an atomic state when volatilized produce *band spectra.* Each element, whether alone or in combination, when vaporized by flame, electric spark, or one of the many tubes designed to contain volatilized elements at reduced pressures, produces an easily recognized, characteristic series of bright lines. The identification of an element is further simplified by the fact that elements diluted in mixtures show progressively simplified spectra until the limit of one line remains to represent its trace presence. As

Spectrum of atomic hydrogen shows lines of Balmer series, so called after Balmer equation, which yields wavelengths of hydrogen. (*By courtesy of Professor Sir Harrie Massey*)

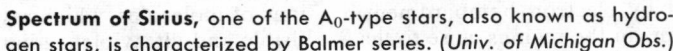

Spectrum of atomic sodium is characterized by three regular series of spectral lines, although third line in each group may be extremely faint. (*Sir Harrie Massey*)

Spectrum of Sirius, one of the A_0-type stars, also known as hydrogen stars, is characterized by Balmer series. (*Univ. of Michigan Obs.*)

Kirchhoff discovered, when the continuous range of wavelengths, as in the continuous spectrum produced by the Sun, travels through a gas, such as the gaseous atmosphere surrounding the Sun, any wavelength in the continuous spectrum equal to the wavelength of the emission lines produced by the gas is absorbed and shows up as a dark line against the brighter background of the continuous spectrum. For example, sodium, either pure or in combination, when placed in a flame produces a series of lines, the most prominent of which are two closely spaced lines in the yellow region. If light from an incandescent source, which includes the wavelengths of sodium's spectral lines, is passed through sodium vapor, precisely those lines which ordinarily appear as bright lines when the sodium is placed in a flame will now appear as black lines against a bright background. Thus with the discovery, identification, and explanation of dark-line and bright-line spectra, chemical analysis of the Sun and other celestial bodies became possible. Applying these principles, ASTROPHYSICS uses the spectrograph—a spectroscope able to make a permanent record of the transmitted light, usually by means of a photographic plate attached to the eyepiece of an astronomical telescope. Spectrographic analysis determines the surface composition, temperature, pressure, radial motion, and surrounding electrical and magnetic fields of the celestial bodies observed. Spectrographic analysis is also used to establish the presence of binary stars, *i.e.* stars so close to each other as to be undetectable by any other means.

The visible spectrum comprises only a part of the complete spectrum of electromagnetic radiation. The infrared spectrum extends from the red boundary of the visible spectrum (7,800 Å) on one side to the beginning of the microwave spectrum (10^7 Å) on the other. It was first detected by Sir William Herschel in 1800, who accidentally found while measuring the temperature of various regions of the visual spectrum that the highest temperature was recorded in the zone just beyond the red part of the spectrum. From this he inferred the existence of radiation similar to light but invisible to the eye. At present, it is known that all matter at temperatures above absolute zero emits infrared radiation. Glass is largely opaque to infrared, and although halides, such as rock salt, transmit INFRARED RAYS in the wavelengths nearer the visible spectrum, diffraction gratings must be used to disperse the longer infrared wavelengths. Spectrographic analysis of the infrared

spectrum was advanced when in 1880 S. P. Langley invented the BOLOMETER, an instrument which utilizes the principle that the resistance of a strip of wire changes with changes in its temperature. Sensitive to changes of less than 0.0001°C, bolometers measure the energy of electromagnetic radiation and are especially useful in charting the infrared portion of the spectrum. Absorption spectroscopy, which utilizes the infrared spectrum to a great extent, makes use of the fact that matter absorbs radiation selectively, so that of a range of wavelengths passed through a compound in sequence, only specific wavelengths will be absorbed. This is because the atoms constituting a particular molecule vibrate at a frequency unique to the molecule; radiation at that frequency will be absorbed, increasing the natural vibration of the molecule, while radiation of other frequencies will be transmitted unchanged. Since infrared radiation is in the range of molecular frequencies, it is widely used in the analysis of organic compounds, whose infrared absorption pattern is their most characteristic property. The amount of energy absorbed is a measure of the concentration of molecules present.

The ultraviolet spectrum extends from the violet boundary of the visible spectrum (4,000 Å) on one side to the beginning of the x-ray spectrum (400 Å) on the other. Its existence was first discovered in 1801 by J. Ritter, who observed the blackening of silver chloride placed beyond the violet end of the visible spectrum. In 1842, Edmund Becquerel produced a picture of the ultraviolet spectrum by means of a photographic plate, for although the eye is not sensitive to ultraviolet, a photographic plate is highly sensitive to ultraviolet radiation greater than 2,000 Å in wavelength. As with infrared rays, glass generally is opaque to ultraviolet radiation. Quartz and fluorite prisms can transmit and disperse rays in the near ultraviolet regions, but to disperse radiation in the more extreme ultraviolet region (and to produce a more *normal* spectrum, *i.e.* a spectrum whose length is proportional to the difference in wavelengths) a diffraction grating must be used. The use of ultraviolet radiation in chemical analysis is accomplished in much the same manner as infrared absorption spectroscopy. Although ultraviolet spectroscopy is more sensitive than infrared, it is not as specific in its identification. Also widely used in chemical identification is the analysis of the fluorescent light emitted by a substance while exposed to ULTRAVIOLET RADIATION.

Starting at approximately 1,000 Å and extending to 10^{-5} Å, x-rays occupy the electromagnetic spectrum between ultraviolet and gamma ray radiation. X-ray spectroscopy has proved to be one of the most informative techniques in modern physics; generally, it falls into the following categories: (1) the analysis of x-ray spectra emitted when a metallic target is bombarded by electrons or cathode rays, and (2) the analysis of diffraction patterns resulting from the passage of x-rays through both crystalline and noncrystalline material. When metallic targets are subjected to bombardment by a stream of ELECTRONS, x-rays are emitted. These electromagnetic radiations result in part from the deceleration of the electrons themselves and in part from bombarded atoms returning from excited states (high energy levels), produced by collisions with the bombarding electrons, to their normal states (lower energy level). In the visible region, spectral lines are caused by the return to a normal energy level of electrons in the regions most distant from the nucleus; X-RAY SPECTRA are caused by the return to a normal energy level of electrons close to the nucleus. The exciting of these electrons close to the nucleus requires the absorption of great amounts of energy, such as that supplied by electron bombardment. Because there are fewer electrons in the regions close to the nucleus (in contrast to the relatively greater number on the boundary of the atom), x-ray spectral lines are less complex than emission-line spectra in the visible spectrum. As a result, x-ray spectra are more easily interpreted and have been increasingly useful in suggesting present-day models of atomic structure.

The use of the atomic structure of a crystal to diffract x-rays was suggested by Max von Laue in 1912. Since then, x-rays in the range of 1 angstrom have been used to produce diffraction patterns for chemical identification as well as to establish much of the data used in SOLID-STATE PHYSICS, *e.g.* the crystalline or noncrystalline structure of a substance, the determination of the limits of solid-solubility, and the amount of strain to which a substance has been subjected. X-ray diffraction, as originally suggested by Laue and subsequently undertaken by Friedrich and Knipping, involved the passing of x-rays of various wavelengths (polychromatic) through a thin crystal and then recording the pattern of maxima and minima intensities on a photographic plate. This has been largely superseded by the method in which x-rays of about a single wavelength (monochromatic) are reflected from the surface of a crystal or a powder and the pattern of diffraction is recorded by a Geiger counter or a scintillation counter. See ATOMIC SPECTRA; COUNTER; ELECTROMAGNETIC WAVES; FLUORESCENCE; ULTRAVIOLET RADIATION.—*A. L.*

SPECTRUM: a set of quantities or intensities arranged in order of some property. There are many types of spectra in physics, chemistry, and mathematics. For example, the number of

particles of each mass in a mixed gas, arranged in the order of their masses, constitutes a *mass spectrum*. The intensity of sound as a function of frequency is an *acoustic spectrum*. The part of this spectrum that is heard by the human ear ranges from 16 to 20,000 cycles/sec; lower frequencies are called infrasonic, higher ones ultrasonic. Dogs, bats, and other creatures can hear sounds well up in the ultrasonic range.

Electromagnetic Spectrum: The type of spectrum most commonly considered is that of the intensity of electromagnetic radiation, as a function of frequency or wavelength. This spectrum may be divided into three major regions: electronic, optical, and high-energy. The electronic spectrum ranges from zero frequency up to 3×10^{11} cycles/sec. It includes direct current, power frequencies, audio frequencies, radio frequencies, and microwaves. These frequencies may be produced by batteries, rotating machinery, vacuum tubes, and transistors. The optical region of the electromagnetic spectrum ranges from 3×10^{11} to about 10^{17} cycles/sec, or from 1 mm to 30 Å (angstroms) in wavelength (an angstrom is 10^{-10} meters). The optical region comprises the infrared, visible, and ultraviolet sections. Infrared radiation is produced by the vibrations of molecules, which result from their thermal energy. Visible and ultraviolet radiation is produced by the transitions of electrons in atoms from one energy level to another, which may be caused by heat energy, electrical forces, or collision of particles. The visible spectrum, as seen by the average human eye, ranges from violet (3,800 Å) through indigo, blue, green, yellow, orange, and red (7,800 Å). The eye is most sensitive to 5,550 Å, which is a yellow-green color. The analysis of optical spectra has explained the structure of atoms and molecules and was the basis for producing the quantum theory, which is the keystone of modern physics. At still higher frequencies is the high-energy spectrum, comprising x-rays and gamma rays. These are highly penetrating and are used to examine opaque objects, such as the human body and metal structures. X-rays have a wavelength of the order of one angstrom, which is roughly the spacing of atoms in a crystal. Hence, diffraction of x-rays has led to an understanding of the structure of crystals and their molecules, and has been basic to the growth of solid-state physics. Gamma rays are produced in nuclear reactions. See ABSORPTION SPECTRUM, SPECTROSCOPE AND SPECTROSCOPY.—*I. R.*

SPEED: SEE VELOCITY AND SPEED.

SPEMANN, HANS, 1869–1941, German anatomist and cell physiologist; b. Stuttgart. For discovering the organizer effect in embryonic development, he received the 1935 Nobel prize. He was an associate of the U. S. National Academy of Sciences. —*D. H. D. R.*

SPENCER, HERBERT, 1820–1903, English philosopher; b. Derby. Evolution, he held, is a universal rather than a local character-

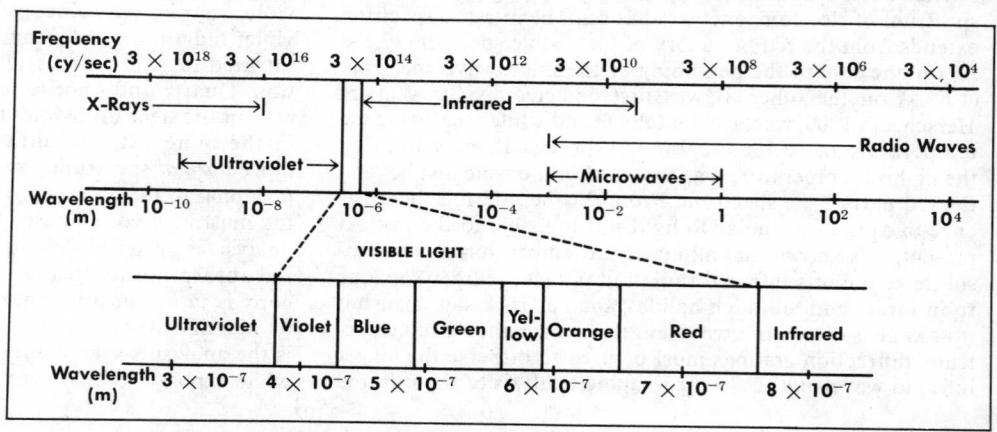

Electromagnetic spectrum encompasses about 47 octaves of frequencies. Here the single octave of frequencies that covers the visible spectrum is expanded.

1. Layers of sediments, now rock, are apparent in eroded peaks in Jasper National Park, Canada. Many mountain ranges consist of folded sedimentary strata. *(Canadian National Travel Bureau)*

Plate 76   SEDIMENTS

Sediments—mud, sand, gravel, precipitates, and organic materials—are characteristically deposited in layers, and constitute the source material for sedimentary rocks. Mud, under pressure, is compacted to form shale, and sand and gravel particles are cemented together to form sandstone and conglomerate, respectively.

2. Badlands of South Dakota are remnants of deep, soft sedimentary strata, mostly clays, carved and almost entirely eroded away by action of running water aided by wind. Lack of vegetation in dry region hastens erosion. *(Jerome Wyckoff)*

3. Chalk in Wind Cave National Park, S. Dak., is a form of limestone consisting of microscopic shells of marine organisms, primarily foraminifera. Famous chalk cliffs of Dover, England, have same origin. *(Jack E. Boucher/National Park Service)*

1   2   3

4   5

Plate 77   SEDIMENTARY ROCK

Sedimentary rocks, characterized by their layered structure, are composed of consolidated mineral and rock particles. They may form from the debris of erosion, from precipitates (as from sea water), and from organic matter.

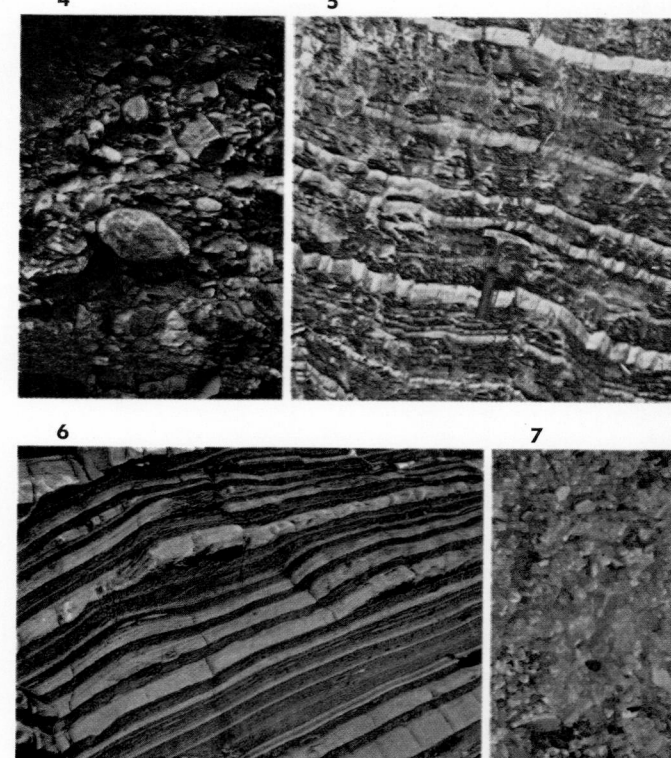

6   7

1. Interbedded layers exposed on Colorado highway include arkose (a variety of sandstone), siltstone, and some limestone. *(Joan E. Gordon)* **2. Breccia** is a conglomerate. In this rock, formed from erosion debris, the pebbles are angular. *(Amer. Mus. of Nat. Hist.)* **3. Shale,** eastern New York, was once mud in a delta of Devonian Period. *(Jerome Wyckoff)* **4. Conglomerate,** near Suffern, N. Y., was formed by debris from erosion of mountains in Triassic Period. *(Jerome Wyckoff)* **5. Cyclic bedding,** Waverly, New South Wales, shows a repetition of similar types of beds. *(Harold Wanless)* **6. Mudstones,** Aberystwyth, Wales, are essentially shales. *(Harold Wanless)* **7. Quartz and shell fragments.** *(Russ Kinne)* **8. Limestone** is exposed under overlying beds at West Franklin, Ind. *(Harold Wanless)* **9. Sandstone** in southern Utah is cross-bedded. *(Harold Wanless)* **10. Limestone** in Kereford Quarry, Atchison, Kans. *(Harold Wanless)*

8   9   10

1

Plate 78 SEEDS

Most seeds have special attachments or coverings that facilitate their wide distribution by wind, water, animals, or other means. Seeds of all plants shown here are enclosed in dry fruits rather than in fleshy ones—the type popularly called "fruit."

Seed dispersal: 1. Thistle burrs with enclosed seeds hook onto fur of passing animals. *(Russ Kinne)* **2.** Ripened capsule of **turtlehead** explodes and ejects seeds inside. *(Rutherford Platt)* **3. Buttercup seeds** ripen in individual nutlets, often buried by mice and chipmunks. *(Rutherford Platt)*

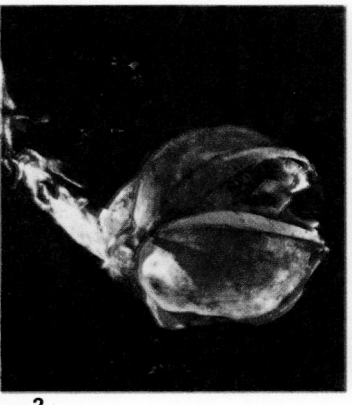

4

2   3

Splitting milkweed pod (4) exposes satiny tufted seeds to wind, which bears them for great distances. *(Rutherford Platt)*

Plate 79 SPONGES

After a brief stage as a free-swimming embryo, each young sponge becomes permanently attached to the bottom of the body of water in which it lives. Through minute pores, the sponge propels streams of water through its body—water which furnishes it oxygen and particles of food. Sponges are unusual among multicellular animals in that any cell appears to take over the duties of any other cell. In the sea, some sponges grow into enormous masses (1) as much as 2 ft in diameter. Yet they retain an amazingly simple colonial organization. In sunlit tropical waters, sponges grow amid a profusion of branching corals (2). Many sponges of shallow waters display brilliant colors of yellow, red, green, and even purple (3). *(All from Russ Kinne)*

1

2   3

Plate 80   SUN

Total solar eclipse at St. Paul, Minn., on June 30, 1954, is shown on multiple-exposure photograph. Sun, partially covered by Moon, rises as a crescent. Gradually Moon covers more and more of Sun until, for a minute or more, it completely hides Sun from observer on Earth. During this period of totality, solar corona is visible. It disappears as a thin crescent of Sun reappears and grows to full size, which marks end of eclipse. See ECLIPSE for information on past and future solar eclipses. *(Mel Tinklenberg, St. Paul)*

istic of nature, and all things, human societies included, evolve from simple "homogeneous" structures through various stages to complex, differentiated structures. The expression "survival of the fittest" is his, and *Social Statics* (1850) is his most influential book.—*A. D.*

SPERM: see GAMETE.

SPERMATOPHYTE: see SEED PLANT.

SPHERE: a solid figure all points of whose bounding surface are equidistant from a fixed point. The fixed point is the center, and the common distance the radius. A straight line through the center is a diameter. A part of the sphere cut off by one plane, or lying between parallel cutting planes, is a segment. Every intersecting plane cuts out a circular cross section. If the plane passes through the center, the circle is called a great circle; otherwise, it is a small circle. The part

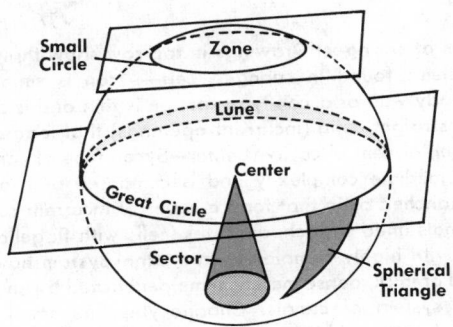

Parts of a Sphere

of the surface of a sphere cut off by a plane, or lying between two parallel planes, is a zone. The part of the surface bounded by halves of two great circles is a lune. The part of the sphere cut out by a circular conical surface, with vertex at the center of the sphere, is a spherical sector. If *r* denotes the radius, then the area of the surface is $4\pi r^2$ and the volume is $\frac{4}{3}\pi r^3$. A spherical triangle is a part of a spherical surface bounded by arcs of three great circles meeting in three points. Spherical TRIGONOMETRY is concerned with spherical triangles, and is important in navigation because Earth's surface is approximately spherical. The CELESTIAL SPHERE is an imaginary sphere of indefinite radius on which are located points corresponding to the positions of the heavenly bodies.—*H. C.*

SPIDER: see ARACHNID.

SPINAL CORD: that portion of the central NERVOUS SYSTEM behind or below the BRAIN and beyond the confines of the skull. Usually it is protected by the bony structure of the VERTEBRAL COLUMN; always it is surrounded by one or more sheaths

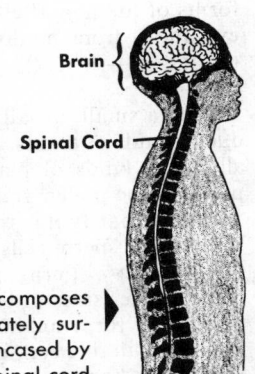

Spinal cord, which together with brain composes the central nervous system, is immediately surrounded by cerebrospinal fluid and is encased by membranous sheaths, the meninges. Spinal cord passes through neural arches of the vertebrae; the vertebral column thus forms a bony protective covering about the cord. (*From Young*)

of connective tissue, the meninges (singular, meninx). From the sides of the spinal cord, paired *spinal nerves* arise, each by two roots, a more posterior *dorsal root* and a more anterior *ventral root.*

The dorsal root of each spinal nerve is enlarged at a *dorsal root ganglion,* which contains the cell bodies of sensory neurons whose dendrites serve sensory cells in the skin; their axons communicate with neurons in the upper extension of the gray H on that side. These, in turn, communicate both with the brain by way of *sensory tracts* in the adjacent white matter and also with motor neurons in the lower extension of the gray H on that side. The motor neurons have axons extending out from the cord by way of the ventral root of the spinal nerve to associated muscles and glands. Additional motor fibers from neurons in the brain compose the *motor tracts* in the white matter of the cord; these emerge from the cord at one spinal nerve after another and provide the basis for voluntary movements and some REFLEXES.

The innermost meninx ensheathing the spinal cord is the *pia mater.* It is richly supplied with blood vessels that bring oxygen and food to the spinal cord. Between the pia mater and the cord, and between the successive sheaths (meninges) outside of the pia, is *cerebrospinal fluid,* which is a special kind of lymph. Cerebrospinal fluid also fills the small central canal that extends lengthwise through the spinal cord and connects with the fourth ventricle in the medulla region of the brain. Samples of cerebrospinal fluid, withdrawn through a long, sterile, hollow needle inserted between the vertebrae into the spaces between the meninges, are helpful in diagnosing some abnormal conditions of the spinal cord. Special anesthetics ("spinal anesthetics") may be injected into these same spaces.—*L. and M. M.*

SPIRACLES: breathing pores on the bodies of insects, centipedes, and millipedes. These openings lead into a system of internal tubes (tracheae), which form the respiratory system. Sharks and rays have a pair of spiracles, used in breathing, that are the external openings of short passageways leading from the throat to the surrounding water.—*C. J. H.*

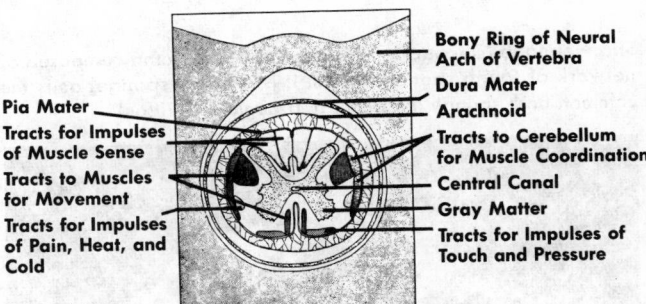

Spinal cord in cross-section: Dura mater, arachnoid, and pia mater are the three layers of protective membranes (meninges) that surround the spinal cord. The white matter (the part of the spinal cord surrounding the H-shaped gray matter) is composed of longitudinal bundles of nerve fibers called tracts, or fasciculi. These tracts carry nerve impulses in either an upward or a downward direction, depending on whether their fibers arise from lower or higher levels of the spinal cord, respectively. The gray matter contains the nuclei of motor neurons, and associative neurons which act as links between sensory and motor neurons. The central canal within the gray matter is a hollow tube filled with cerebrospinal fluid. It communicates with the ventricles (cavities) within the brain. (*From Villee*)

SPIRAL NEBULA: see GALAXY.

SPLEEN: a distinct organ, lying in the body cavity of most vertebrate animals, with important functions in the circulatory system. In birds and mammals, the spleen contains two well-defined tissues: one lymphoid, with the typical functions of lymph nodes; the other filled with large spaces packed with red blood cells and in direct communication with the circulatory system. The latter tissue serves as a storage place for red cells, which on suitable stimulation can be added to the circulating blood; this normally happens in violent exercise or at other times when the oxygen requirement is increased, and the splenic contraction is responsible for the "stitch in the side" felt at such times. In lower vertebrates and in human embryos the spleen is the site of formation of both red and white blood cells.—*B. T. S.*

SPONGE: the simplest of multicellular animals, without a differentiated mouth, organs, or tissues. Most sponges are found in the sea, ranging from shallow coastal waters to depths of more than 3½ mi. One family occurs in fresh water and is frequently found in streams and lakes in most parts of the U. S. A. The body of some sponges has a definite form—vaselike, cylindrical, branched, or globular—but other sponges grow irregularly as round, flat, or branching encrustations on submerged rocks, shells, or other objects. Adult sponges are incapable of moving about; this is one reason why they were once thought to be plants. Sponges are permeated with a system of canals through which water currents flow, the water being pumped through by the waving motion of whiplike projections called flagella. The water currents bring oxygen and food into the body and aid in the removal of metabolic waste products. Internally most sponges are supported by a skeleton of characteristic spicules (hard, sharp-pointed structures) made of calcium carbonate or silicic acid; the shape of these spicules is used in sponge classification. One group also has a skeleton made partly or wholly of "spongin," a sulfur-containing protein peculiar to these sponges and chemically similar to the scleroproteins found in the hair and nails of man. The commercial sponge is the flexible skeleton of a marine sponge (*Euspongia*) with all the living protoplasm re-

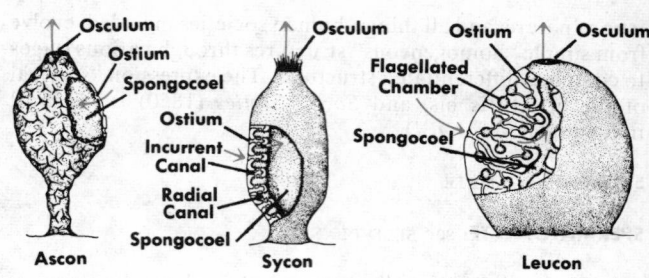

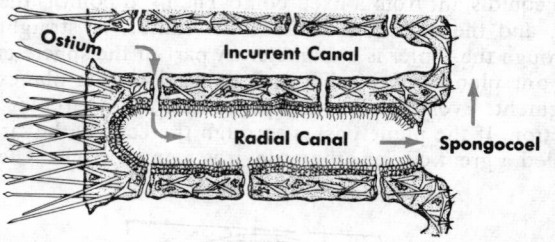

Structures of sponges: Drawings in top row show three types of canal systems found in sponges. *Left*—Ascon is simplest canal system. Body wall of ascon-type sponge is thin and is perforated by short, straight ostia (incurrent openings) that lead directly to spongocoel, or central cavity. *Center*—Sycon type of canal system is of intermediate complexity and is composed of two types of canals: branched ostia that form a series of incurrent canals, and radial canals lined with choanocytes (cells with flagella). *Right*—Sponges with highly complex leucon canal system have a body composed of thick, dense mesenchyme penetrated by an intricately branched system of canals. Choanocytes line small spherical chambers. Spongocoel is greatly reduced. Drawing in second row is enlarged view of section of body wall from sponge with sycon-type canal system. Arrows indicate paths of water flow. (*From Manter*)

moved. All sponges are members of the phylum Porifera, which includes three classes: the calcareous sponges (Calcarea); the glass sponges (Hexactinellida); and the Demospongiae.—*C. F. L.*

SPONTANEOUS GENERATION: a belief, held universally in ancient times, that inanimate objects can give rise to living beings, *e.g.* maggots develop from decaying meat, worms from horse hair soaked in water. This notion, as applied to most living things, was disproved by the experiments of Francesco Redi in 1668 and Louis Pasteur in 1862 (see BACTERIOLOGY). But the possibility remains that very simple forms of life (*e.g.* the VIRUS) may originate (or did in early evolution) from nonliving materials. See BIOGENESIS; LIFE, ORIGIN OF.—*A. R. D.*

SPORE: a small, usually unicellular and microscopic reproductive unit of plants. Spores of some type are produced by all major kinds of plants. The conspicuous spore of seed plants is the pollen grain, which serves in sexual REPRODUCTION. Ultimately it is responsible for the production of male gametes, or sperm cells, which are formed in the pollen tube (see POLLEN). Ferns produce spores which are usually on the under sides of their leaves. One spore-producing fern plant may form millions of these microscopic spores each year; on suitable soil, each spore grows into a small, sexual fern plant known as a prothallus or a gametophyte. The spores of mosses are produced in a case called a sporangium. The sexual spores of mosses, ferns, and seed plants are called meiospores, because they are produced by the special proc-

Slimy sponge (*Desmacidon fruticosum*) has skeleton composed of network of tough spongin fibers. It is a horny sponge, as is the common bath sponge (*Euspongia*). (*Douglas P. Wilson*)

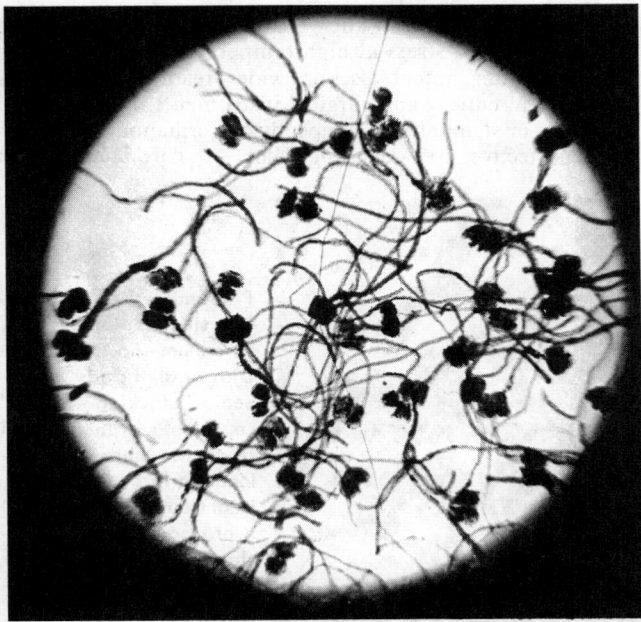

Spores of horsetail plant (*Equisetum*) are seen (*above*) under microscope to have ribbonlike strips (elaters) that probably aid in spore dispersal. (*Leonard L. Rue/Monkmeyer*) *Right:* **Spores of fungus** *Pilobolus crystallinus* develop in black sporangium at end of stalk (X 85). Adjacent part of stalk swells and bursts, shooting sporangium up to 6 ft toward light. (*Eric V. Grave*)

ess of nuclear division that is known as MEIOSIS or reduction division.

Fungi and algae produce not only meiospores, but many other kinds of spores. Some of these spores serve primarily for withstanding harsh environmental conditions, especially drought. Such spores owe their resistance both to low water content and to a protective spore wall. Examples that might be cited include the zygospores of water molds and certain pond-scum algae. The drought-resistant spores of black bread mold and of most other molds, where the spore is called a conidium, are asexual reproductive structures that accomplish multiplication on a massive scale. The conidium of some fungi is made of several cells. The asexual spores of many aquatic fungi and algae can swim by means of flagella or cilia. Sometimes these planospores or zoospores also serve as gametes or sex cells.—*W. Ko.*

SPRENGEL, CHRISTIAN KONRAD, 1750–1816, German botanist; b. Brandenburg. His discoveries in plant fertilization were published in his *Das entdeckte Geheimnis der Natur im Bau und in der Befruchtung der Blumen* (1793), but remained largely unnoticed in his own lifetime. Charles R. Darwin, who read the book in 1841, utilized Sprengel's ideas and made them known.—*D. H. D. R.*

SPRING (in geology): an opening in the ground through which GROUND WATER flows to become surface water. Springs are more numerous in mountainous or dissected areas than in relatively flat terrain. As a rule the location of a spring depends on local rock structure. Where an aquifer (water-bearing rock stratum) outcrops on the side of a hill, or in a deeply incised valley, there will be a spring. If the aquifer lies on a formation that is impervious to water and prevents loss of water by downward percolation, there may be copious flow. The presence of fractures, as the result of faulting, and the presence of jointing will allow water that is under pressure to flow from depth, seeking its level as it travels to the surface (see ARTESIAN WELL). Springs with permanent flow are called *perennial;* those that flow only at certain periods are called *intermittent. Thermal springs* are those whose mean annual temperature exceeds that of the locality where they flow; they discharge warm water. Their heat is derived from hot rocks at depth, and varies from a few degrees above air temperature to boiling. Hot springs that eject water at intervals are GEYSERS. Springs, chiefly hot springs, deposit minerals around their orifices; travertine, siliceous sinter, and sulfur are among the most common deposits. Some hot springs will build a series of basins to form terraces, *e.g.* Mammoth Hot Springs in Yellowstone National Park. Because of the mineral content even in cold springs, their water is often bottled and sold for its good taste or claimed medicinal value. Health resorts (spas) have grown up around many such springs.—*R. E. M.*

SPRING (in physics): an elastic body that alters its shape (undergoes a displacement) under a force. The displacement produced bears a definite relation to the force applied, a fact that is utilized in calibrating spring balances. According to HOOKE'S LAW, the tension in the spring is directly proportional to displacement produced, provided the elastic limit of the spring has not been exceeded. The factor of proportionality between elongation and tension is known as the *spring constant.* Springs are of many types and have many different uses, *e.g.* as sources of mechanical power (watch springs, door-closing springs), as shock absorbers (rubber-block springs), and as vibration-control devices (see VIBRATION).—*A. E.*

SQUARE: a plane figure bounded by four straight sides of equal length meeting to form four right angles; one of the most basic figures in geometry. Because of the ease of fitting squares together, the square provides the most natural kind of unit for measuring areas. A unit of area is merely an arbitrarily chosen square. The area of any figure in terms of this unit is the number of times it can be fitted to the figure without overlapping. The areas of figures to which squares cannot be fitted exactly may be found indirectly. The square area unit has each of its sides one unit long. Consequently, the area of a square x units on a side is $x \times x$, written x^2. This second power of x is called its square, and we read it "x squared."

The word square is applied to objects in which the right angle is all important. In everyday language we refer to square corners. The *carpenter's square* and the draftsman's *T-square* are instruments for constructing right angles. Because right-angled objects fit together readily, it is common practice to "square" individual parts of a structure in order to obtain a good fit.

The diagonals of a square are equal and bisect each other perpendicularly. But the diagonal is incommensurable with a side. This follows from the Pythagorean theorem: $(\text{diagonal})^2 = (\text{side})^2 + (\text{side})^2$, whence $(\text{diagonal})^2 = 2(\text{side})^2$, and diagonal $= \sqrt{2}\,(\text{side})$.—*H. C.*

SQUARE ROOT: a number whose square is a given number. Thus 2 is a square root of 4; -2 is also a square root of 4. The operation of extracting a square root is customarily expressed by the radical sign: $\sqrt{4} = 2$. It was the necessity of having a square root of every positive integer that first brought out the need for irrational numbers, *e.g.* $\sqrt{2}$. In order that negative numbers might have square roots, imaginary numbers were invented. $\sqrt{-1}$ is the unit of imaginary numbers, usually denoted by i, and $\sqrt{-4} = \sqrt{4} \cdot \sqrt{-1} = 2i$. Imaginary and complex numbers have square roots within the complex number system, each number having two square roots, one the negative of the other. For example, $\sqrt{2i} = 1 + i$ or $-1 - i$.

Calculation of an approximate square root of a number in several digits is illustrated by the following example: $\sqrt{595.21}$. Starting at the decimal point, block out the digits in groups of two.

$$
\begin{array}{r}
5'95'.21 \quad \underline{|24.4} \\
4 \\
40 + 4 \quad \overline{|195} \\
\underline{|176} \\
480 + 4 \quad \overline{|1921} \\
\underline{|1936}
\end{array}
$$

Take the square root of the first group on the left, which may have one or two digits. The largest number whose square is less than or equal to 5 is 2. Square 2 and subtract, bringing down the next group. Double 2, annex 0, and divide into 195, obtaining 4. Add to 40 and multiply $44 \times 4 = 176$. Subtract and bring down the next group. Double 24, annex 0, and divide into 1921, obtaining 4. Add to 480 and multiply $484 \times 4 = 1936$. If the process were to be continued further, 4 would have to be replaced by 3, and the step repeated, since 1936 is greater than 1921.—*H. C.*

SQUARING THE CIRCLE: see CONSTRUCTION PROBLEMS.

STAHL, GEORG ERNST, 1660–1734, German physician and chemist; b. Ansbach, Bavaria. He publicized and extended the phlogiston theory of combustion which had been proposed by J. J. Becher and experimented on oxidation and reduction processes. His *Theoria medica vera* (1707) expounded an animistic theory associating the soul with the control of physiological processes.—*A. I.*

STAINLESS STEEL: a steel alloy that has a marked resistance to corrosion and stress at high temperatures because of its high chromium content. Uses are widespread: from structural members to cutlery and surgical instruments. Resistance to corrosion in stainless steels depends on formation of a rather thin protective, self-renewing film of chromium oxide.

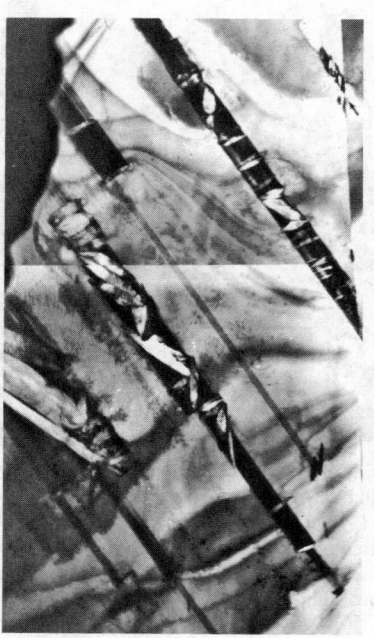

Photomicrograph of stainless steel containing 18% chromium and 12% nickel: Diagonal bands represent "stacking faults," *i.e.* planes within crystal structure where atom dislocation has taken place. Heat treatment (tempering) is not possible with high-chromium steels (over 17%), but if a high percentage of nickel is added, as in alloy shown, the alloy can be heat-treated as if it were an ordinary carbon steel. (*RIAS*)

Adequate resistance to corrosion demands at least 10 to 11% chromium; up to 14% is present in steels used for cutlery and medical instruments. The most useful stainless steels have 16 to 18% chromium and are widely used for kitchen equipment, dairy equipment, and chemical equipment capable of resisting acid and alkali attack. See STEEL.—*A. L.*

STALACTITES AND STALAGMITES: Stalactites are normally carrot- or icicle-shaped pendants hanging from the roofs of limestone CAVES; stalagmites are corresponding forms rising from the cave floor. In many cases the two join, forming a continuous column. Most such deposits, which were made after the cave formed, are composed of grains of the mineral calcite (calcium carbonate), though some are of other minerals. Collectively, stalagmites and stalactites are called drip-

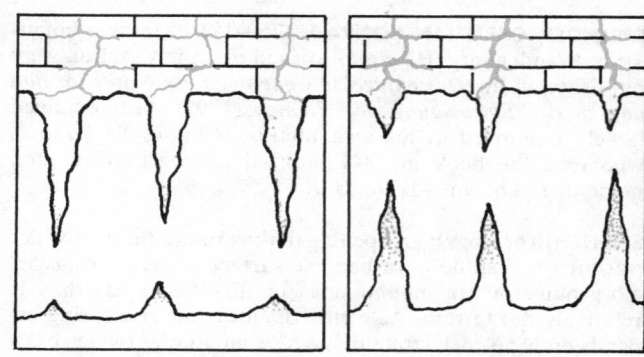

Formation of dripstone: Deposits of calcium carbonate left by evaporation of dripping water at cave ceiling form stalactites. Some water may travel down through a channel within the stalactite, then evaporate as it emerges at the tip. Water that drips to floor of cave forms stalagmites. More rapid dripping (*right*) may result in smaller stalactites and larger stalagmites.

STANDARD DEVIATION: in statistics, a measure of the variability of a distribution around the arithmetic mean: the square root of the arithmetic mean of the squares of the deviations from the arithmetic mean. If there are n items of data, $X_1, X_2, X_3, \ldots, X_n$, of which the arithmetic mean is $\overline{X}$, the quantity

$$\sigma^2 = \frac{1}{n} \sum_{i=1}^{n} (X_i - \overline{X})^2$$

is called the variance; its square root, σ, is the standard deviation. Because of the nature of the definition, it is often called the root-mean-square. In practice, the formula for the variance is written

$$\sigma^2 = \frac{1}{n} (\Sigma_i X_i^2 - n\overline{X}^2)$$

The mean, $\overline{X}$, is first found by adding the individual values and dividing the total by n. Each individual value is squared; from the sum of these squares is subtracted n times the square of the mean. The result is divided by n, the square root of the quotient being the standard deviation. If the individual values form a sample from a larger population and the mean of the population is not known, the sample mean is used for $\overline{X}$ in the formula, but the divisor is replaced by $(n - 1)$.

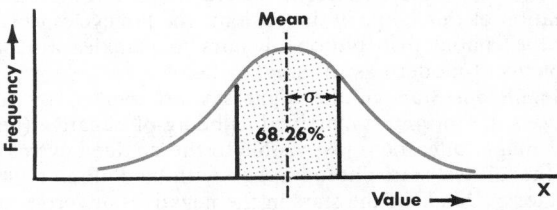

Gaussian, or normal, distribution: The values of 68.26% of the population are within one standard deviation of the mean.

The variability of a gaussian, or normal, frequency distribution is expressed in terms of the standard deviation. In such a distribution, 68.26% of the entire distribution is within one standard deviation of the mean, 95.44% is within two standard deviations, and 99.74% is within three standard deviations. The normal distribution is very useful both in the theory and in the applications of STATISTICS. For example, if a production line in a manufacturing plant is operating satisfactorily, the dimensions of a product will be normally distributed. If the mean and the standard deviation of a certain dimension are 3 in. and 0.02 in., then approximately 68% of the production is between 2.98 and 3.02 in., 95% is between 2.96 and 3.04 in., and practically the entire production is between 2.94 and 3.06 in.—*H. E. W.*

STANDARD TEMPERATURE AND PRESSURE (STP): the conditions under which the physical properties of gases and liquids are usually measured or tabulated. These conditions are a temperature of 0°C and normal atmospheric pressure (corresponding to a barometric pressure of 760 mm of mercury). If not actually measured under these conditions, the measurements can be converted to STP by application of such formulas as the GAS law.—*I. R.*

STANLEY, WENDELL MEREDITH, 1904–   , U. S. biochemist; b. Ridgeville, Ind. He isolated and crystallized tobacco mosaic virus, a significant finding in that it demonstrated that a living entity (the virus) could be crystallized like a chemical compound. For their preparation of enzymes and virus proteins in a pure form, Stanley and J. H. Northrop shared the 1946 Nobel prize in chemistry with J. B. Sumner.—*D. H. D. R.*

Limestone caves with their displays of dripstone are the work of ground water. Their interest for tourists is increased by use of colored lighting and fanciful names. Time required for formation of stalactites and stalagmites is often exaggerated; depending upon local conditions, it may amount to decades or millennia. Scene here is Queen's Chamber, Carlsbad Caverns, N. Mex. (*Josef Muench*)

stone, since they are formed by deposition of their component minerals from water dripping from roof to floor. When the water table stands below a cave floor, much of the moisture which does penetrate the cave seeps along the roof, accumulating in places until there are drops large enough to fall. During this process, the loss of some carbon dioxide from the mineralized water results in decomposition of soluble calcium bicarbonate carried in the water and deposition of a small amount of calcium carbonate. In this slow manner dripstones grow. In some caves, like Carlsbad Caverns in SE New Mexico and Luray Caverns in Virginia, there are magnificent displays of dripstones.—*N. E. A. H.*

STANDARD ATMOSPHERE: a hypothetical distribution of ATMOSPHERIC PRESSURE, temperature, and density in relation to height above the ground, based upon meteorological observations and designed to define, by international agreement, a representative normal atmosphere. Standard-atmosphere tables are used for calibrating pressure altimeters, calculating estimates of aircraft performance, and for other similar tasks for which an agreed average state of the atmosphere is required.—*D. H. L.*

STAR: a self-luminous, roughly spherical, gaseous celestial body. The universe as a whole is composed of galaxies, the largest containing billions of stars. The stars seen in the night sky are all in our own Milky Way Galaxy. They appear to be fixed in the flat patterns of the CONSTELLATIONS, but actually move within and around the Galaxy with velocities that are very high by terrestrial standards, and their distances from each other are so great as to be measured in light-years (the distance light travels in a year at 186,000 mi/sec, about 6 trillion mi) and parsecs (about 3.3 lt-yr). Many stars occur in pairs, triples, and other multiples, separated by much shorter distances and moving about a common center; others occur in larger associations and clusters. See STAR CLUSTER.

Basic Properties: The fundamental properties of a star are its radius, mass (amount of matter contained), luminosity (output of light energy), surface temperature, and chemical composition. Our SUN is the nearest star, and a typical one. There are, however, extremely hot stars with 100 times the mass, 5,000 times the luminosity, and 50 times the radius of the Sun; and—vastly more numerous per unit volume of space—there are feeble stars with $\frac{1}{10,000}$ the luminosity, $\frac{1}{10}$ the mass, and $\frac{1}{10}$ the radius of the Sun. In addition, some stars are so tenuous that their density is that of a laboratory vacuum, while others are so dense that a cubic inch of their material, if weighed on Earth, would weigh 5 tons. The explanation of this range in dimensions, the life cycles of stars, and the spatial distribution of stars in galaxies are basic problems of modern astronomy.

Magnitude: Stars of the night sky are ranked by MAGNITUDES, the brightest classified as being of negative (below zero) magnitude, those just visible to the unaided eye as 6th, and the faintest stars photographed with the Palomar 200-in. reflector as 22nd. Of the stars in the negative- or zero-magnitude category, a few appear bright because they are comparatively close, e.g. Sirius at 8.7 lt-yr; others, though more distant, shine brilliantly because of their great intrinsic brightness. Even though the star Deneb is about 1,400 lt-yr away, it looks relatively very bright; its intrinsic brightness or luminosity is 6,000 times the Sun's.

Luminosity: The luminosity of a star is a measure of its rate of total energy output. For most stars this energy is furnished by thermonuclear reactions deep in the interior. The luminosity can be calculated from the observed apparent brightness if a star's distance is known (for a method of obtaining the distance to a star, see PARALLAX, STELLAR). Stellar luminosities range from about 500,000 times that of the Sun to $\frac{1}{500,000}$. The mass of a star can be determined if it is a member of a binary system (see BINARY STAR). The more massive a star, the greater will be its luminosity (Fig. 1): this so-called *mass-luminosity law* holds for all normal stars.

Spectra: The spectra of stars provide the key to knowledge of their physical and chemical structure. When a star's light is passed through a spectroscope, usually it becomes a continuous band of colored light crossed by numerous dark absorption, or Fraunhofer, lines (see SPECTROSCOPE AND SPECTROSCOPY). The strength of the generally conspicuous dark hydrogen lines formed the basis for the Harvard system of spectral classification. The Harvard astronomers soon realized that an arrangement of the star types in the order O,B,A,F, G,K, and M furnishes a continuous sequence of spectra related to the colors and therefore the surface temperatures of the stars. The types have been further subdivided by numbers representing a tenth of a spectral class, e.g. A9, F0, F1.

The *color index,* or difference between the magnitudes of a star when measured in blue and in red light, expresses the color of a star quantitatively. The blue stars typically have high temperatures, 25,000°K (45,000°F) for spectral type B0, whereas the reddish stars have surface temperatures of 3000°K (5400°F) or less. The O-type spectra include lines of ionized helium (see Fig. 2), these lines being indicative of the high temperature of extremely luminous blue stars. The A-type spectra have comparatively few lines, the only strong ones arising from hydrogen and ionized metals. A G-type spectrum, like that of the Sun, displays numerous lines of iron, titanium, magnesium, and other metals, as well as a few strong lines of hydrogen, sodium, and ionized calcium. At the red end of the sequence, the M-type spectra contain conspicuous bands of titanium oxide, which remains intact as a molecule at the comparatively low temperatures around 3000°K.

A redward displacement of the stellar spectrum lines compared with laboratory standards is interpreted according to the Doppler effect as a motion of the star away from the observer; similarly a blue shift indicates a velocity toward the observer (see SPACE VELOCITY). Some stars showing cyclic changes in the positions of their spectrum lines prove to be members of spectroscopic binary systems.

A small but exceedingly interesting minority of stars cannot be classified among the normal spectral types. Such spectra exhibit a variety of abnormalities ranging from emission lines to no lines at all. Studies of these cases have disclosed unusual binary systems, stars with extended atmospheres or gaseous shells, stars with strong magnetic fields, white dwarfs, VARIABLE STARS, and stars in rapid evolution. Exploration of these abnormal spectra is an active area of research in contemporary astronomy.

H-R Diagram: A plot of luminosity against spectral type (or surface temperature or color index) is known as the Hertzsprung-Russell diagram (Fig. 3), after E. Hertzsprung and H. N. Russell, who independently derived it early in this century. The majority of stars, including the Sun, fall across the H-R diagram in a diagonal line called the *main sequence.*

Capella, a G-type star like the Sun, lies directly above the Sun on the H-R diagram because of its greater luminosity. The amount of energy radiated per surface area depends on its temperature, and since the Sun and Capella have equal temperatures, equal areas of their surfaces must radiate equally. The total surface area of Capella must therefore be greater than the Sun's, and in fact, Capella is 16 times larger in diameter. Stars near Capella on the H-R diagram are called *giants.* A few even larger and more luminous stars,

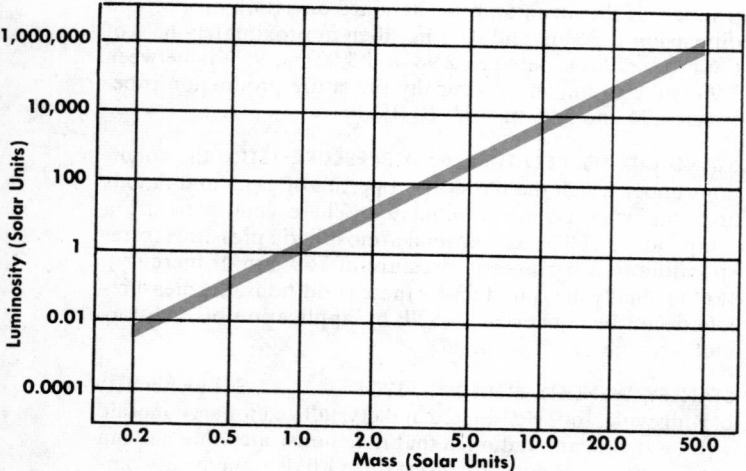

Fig. 1—Empirical mass-luminosity law for main-sequence stars: Masses of stars are determined from observation of their motions as members of binary systems.

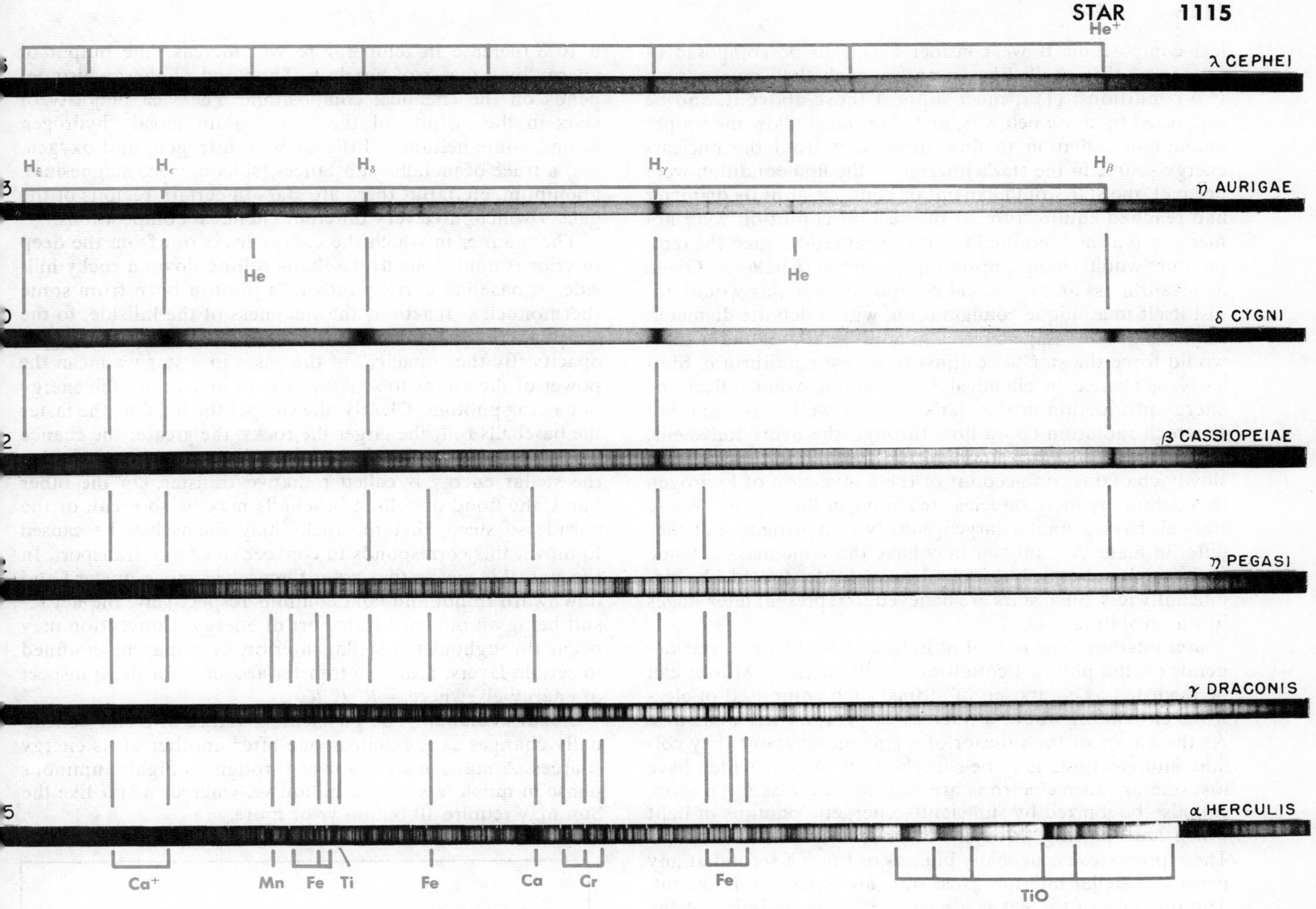

He⁺ → He^+

λ CEPHEI

H_ζ H_ϵ H_δ H_γ H_β

η AURIGAE

He   He

δ CYGNI

β CASSIOPEIAE

η PEGASI

γ DRACONIS

α HERCULIS

Ca⁺   Mn Fe Ti   Fe   Ca Cr   Fe   TiO

Fig. 2—Principal types of stellar spectra: Adapted from photos made at Mt Wilson and Palomar Observatories.

intrinsically rare, are called *supergiants*. In contrast, stars located along the main sequence directly below the giants are *dwarfs*. Direct information on sizes of about 200 stars has been provided by analysis of the light curves of eclipsing binaries.

Chemical Composition: A stellar spectrum can be analyzed for the chemical composition of a star's atmosphere. The principal differences between the types of spectra indicate physical rather than chemical variations, and stars of the main sequence are notable for their chemical similarity. Investigations show variations between certain groups of stars in regard to abundances of elements. In particular, some of the oldest stars reveal a deficiency of metal atoms, presumably because the interstellar material from which the stars formed was almost pure hydrogen. Nearly 90% of the atoms in main-sequence stars are hydrogen. Helium constitutes the remainder, except for a small residue of the other elements. A few exceptional stars may have widely different chemical compositions, however.

H. N. Russell and H. Vogt derived a theorem which states that the size, luminosity, and temperature of any star in equilibrium depend on two basic quantities: mass and chem-

Fig. 3—Schematic Hertzsprung-Russell diagram: The main sequence is the mass-locus of stars of uniform chemical composition. When the hydrogen in a star becomes depleted, the star moves quickly into the "giant" and "supergiant" regions of the diagram, and eventually ends its life as a white dwarf of low luminosity.

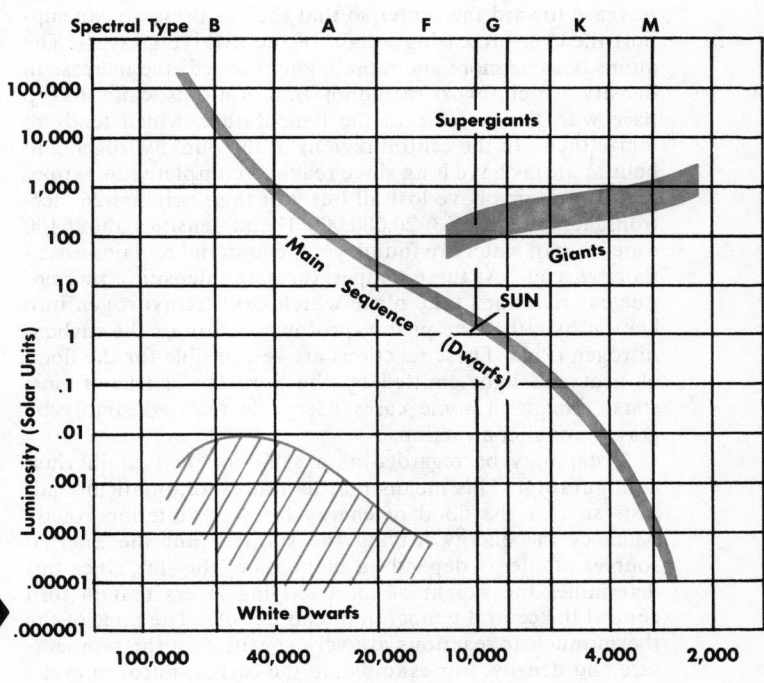

Spectral Type   B   A   F   G   K   M

Supergiants

Giants

SUN

Main Sequence (Dwarfs)

Luminosity (Solar Units)
100,000
10,000
1,000
100
10
1
.1
.01
.001
.0001
.00001
.000001

White Dwarfs

100,000   40,000   20,000   10,000   4,000   2,000

Surface Temperature (°F)

ical composition. If we consider a star to be composed of numerous thin shells like an onion, each shell must satisfy two conditions: (1) it must support those above it, and be supported by those below it; and (2) it must allow the proper amount of radiation to flow through it from the nuclear-energy source in the star's interior. If the first condition were not met, the star would expand or contract until its diameter had reached equilibrium. If the second condition were not met, *e.g.* if a shell retained too much radiation, then the temperature would change, upsetting the pressure balance. Given a certain mass and chemical composition, a star would adjust itself to a unique configuration, with a definite diameter, luminosity, and temperature. An additional amount of mass would force the star to readjust to a new equilibrium. Similarly, a change in chemical composition would affect the energy production in the star's core, as well as the manner in which radiation could flow through the overlying shells.

The chemical composition of main-sequence stars must be slowly changing, on account of the conversion of hydrogen into helium by thermonuclear reactions in the interior. These stars all have a similar large quantity of hydrogen, but they differ in mass. A giant star may have the same mass as some main-sequence star, but its hydrogen content would be significantly less. Such stars are believed to represent later stages in star evolution.—*O. G.*

Star Interiors: The output of light and heat from a star depends on the physical conditions in its interior. Matter can be regarded as composed of atoms, each composed of electrons circulating about a nucleus of protons and neutrons. As the atoms of the interior of a star move about they collide, and electrons may be sloughed off. Atoms which have lost one or more electrons are said to be *ionized*. An atom can also be ionized by sufficiently energetic photons of light which are "passing through" on their way out of the star. These processes occur many billions of times a second at any point in a stellar interior. Most stars are gaseous throughout. The pressure of the gas is a measure of the buffeting of the atoms, and is proportional to its temperature and density. At any point in the interior, this gas pressure supports the weight of the overlying layers. Thus the temperature and density must increase toward the center so that the gas pressure can support the ever-increasing weight of the overlying layers. The atoms become more and more highly ionized; the increase in density, which favors recombination of atoms, cannot keep pace with the increase in the temperature, which tends to ionize them. In the central regions of the Sun, hydrogen and helium atoms have long since reached complete ionization, and iron atoms have lost all but 9 of their original 26 electrons; temperatures of 20,000,000°F and densities about 100 times that of water are found, yet the material remains essentially gaseous. At these temperatures and densities, thermonuclear reactions take place which convert hydrogen into helium by either the proton-proton reaction or the carbon-nitrogen cycle. These reactions are responsible for the flood of heat and light emitted by the Sun. This is true of most stars, though in some cases energy is released simply by gravitational contraction.

A star may be regarded as a self-contained equilibrium configuration. This means that its radius automatically adjusts so that the flood of energy from the interior exactly balances the energy leaving the surface. But the internal sources of energy depend on the mass of the star, since this determines the weight of the overlying layers that in turn control the central temperature and density. The rates of the thermonuclear reactions are very sensitive to the temperature and density. For example, in the carbon-nitrogen cycle, the rate depends on the 18th power of the temperature;

a 10% increase in temperature will increase the output of energy by a factor of nearly 6. The flood of energy also depends on the chemical composition. The vast majority of stars in the vicinity of the Sun contain mostly hydrogen atoms, some helium, a little carbon, nitrogen, and oxygen, and a trace of metallic substances (silicon, iron, magnesium, aluminum, etc.). But there are stars in certain regions of the galaxy which have very different chemical compositions.

The manner in which the energy leaks out from the deep interior is analogous to baseballs rolling down a rocky hillside. A baseball corresponds to a photon born from some thermonuclear reaction; the steepness of the hillside, to the temperature gradient; and the rocks, to what is called the opacity. By the "opacity" of the gases in a star we mean the power of the atoms to soak up, *e.g.* in ionization, the energy of passing photons. Clearly, the steeper the hillside, the faster the baseballs roll; the larger the rocks, the greater the chance that a baseball will get blocked. This way of transporting the stellar energy is called radiative transfer. On the other hand, the flood of rolling baseballs may be so great, or the hillside so steep, that the rocks may themselves be caused to move; this corresponds to convective energy transport. In the star, this means that gases themselves move upward and downward in hot and cold columns respectively, the net result being an outward transport of energy. Convection may occur throughout the stellar interior, or it may be confined to certain layers; radiative transfer accounts for the transport of energy elsewhere.—*R. P. K.*

Stellar Evolution: The physical structure of a star continually changes as it exhausts one after another of its energy sources. A massive star evolves through its highly luminous phase in much less than a billion yr, whereas a star like the Sun may require 10 billion yr or more.

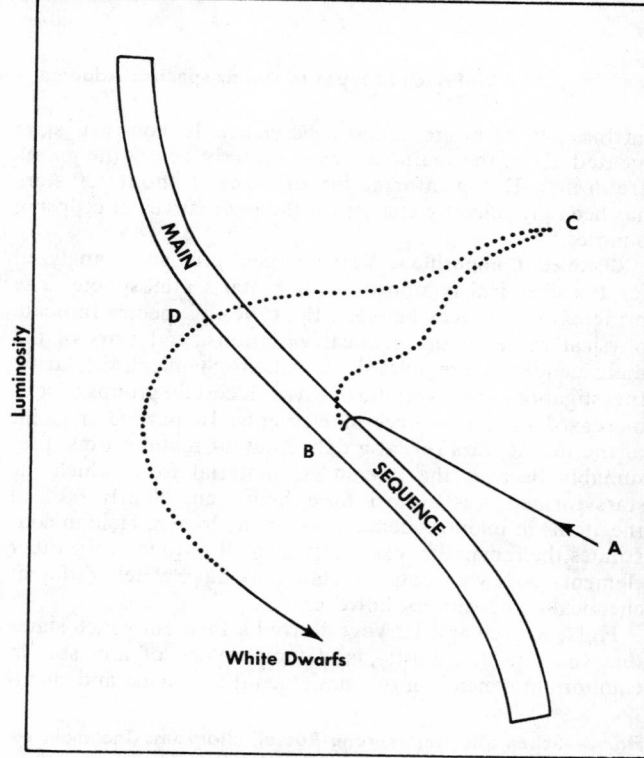

Fig. 4—Evolutionary path of the Sun: Solid line indicates its probable past evolution; dotted line, its future. Compare with Fig. 3.

THE 30 NEAREST STARS

Note: If star is a multiple system, data are given for primary component only.

Name	Color	Visual Magnitude	Visual Luminosity (Sun = 1)	Radial Velocity (km/sec)	Proper Motion (sec/yr)	Distance (lt-yr)
Sun....................	Yellow	−26.73	1.0	—	—	—
α Centauri..............	Yellow	− 0.01	1.50	−23	3.68	4.3
Barnard's Star..........	Red	+ 9.54	0.00045	−108	10.30	6.0
Wolf 359..............	Red	+13.66	0.00003	+13	4.84	7.7
Lalande 21185.........	Red	+ 7.47	0.0055	−86	4.78	8.1
Sirius.................	Blue	− 1.43	23.	−8	1.32	8.7
Luyten 726-8..........	Red	+12.5	0.00006	+29	3.32	8.7
Ross 154..............	Red	+10.6	0.00041	−4	0.67	9.6
Ross 248..............	Red	+12.24	0.00011	−81	1.58	10.3
ε Eridani..............	Orange	+ 3.73	0.30	+15	0.97	10.8
Ross 128..............	Red	+11.13	0.00054	−13	1.36	11.0
Luyten 789-6..........	Red	+12.58	0.00009	−60	3.27	11.0
61 Cygni.............	Orange	+ 5.19	0.084	−64	5.22	11.1
Procyon..............	Yellow	+ 0.38	7.3	−3	1.25	11.3
ε Indi................	Orange	+ 4.73	0.14	−40	4.67	11.4
Σ 2398................	Red	+ 8.90	0.0031	+8	2.29	11.7
BD + 43° 44..........	Red	+ 8.07	0.0066	+18	2.91	11.7
τ Ceti................	Yellow	+ 3.50	0.45	−16	1.92	11.8
CD −36° 15693........	Red	+ 7.39	0.013	+10	6.87	11.9
BD +5° 1668..........	Red	+ 9.82	0.0014	+26	3.73	12.2
CD −39° 14192........	Red	+ 6.72	0.027	+21	3.46	12.8
Kruger 60.............	Red	+ 9.77	0.0017	+26	0.87	12.9
Kapteyn's Star..........	Red	+ 8.81	0.0041	+242	8.79	13.0
Ross 614.............	Red	+11.13	0.00050	+24	0.97	13.1
BD −12° 4523.........	Red	+10.13	0.0013	−13	1.24	13.4
v. Maanen's Star........	Yellow	+12.36	0.00018	+30	2.98	13.8
Wolf 424..............	Red	+12.7	0.00014	−5	1.87	14.5
BD +50° 1725..........	Red	+ 6.59	0.041	−27	1.45	14.7
CD −37° 15492........	Red	+ 8.59	0.0066	+24	6.09	14.9
CD −46° 11540.........	Red	+ 9.34	0.0035	—	1.15	15.3

Adapted with permission from G. H. Herbig and C. E. Worley, "Some Basic Astronomical Data" (rev. 1960), in Leaflet No. 325, Astronomical Society of the Pacific, San Francisco, Calif.

The birth of the Sun probably took place by the contraction of an enormous whirling tenuous mass of gas and dust; such an idea was proposed in 1755 by the philosopher Immanuel Kant. As such a mass of diffuse gas and dust contracts, it becomes warmer and ultimately begins to glow. During the 19th cent., Lord Kelvin showed that energy from gravitational contraction could maintain solar luminosity for a few tens of millions of years. In this phase a star would gradually increase its temperature, and its position in the H-R diagram would change from right to left (A to B in Fig. 4).

The Kelvin contraction in the Sun temporarily ceased about 5 billion yr ago. By that time the internal temperature had become sufficiently high to sustain thermonuclear reactions, which provide energy by conversion of hydrogen into helium. A star stays on the main sequence throughout the long period of hydrogen burning; because the contraction stage occurs relatively rapidly in comparison, stars undergoing contraction (to the right of the main sequence) are rarely observed.

For several billion years, as the reservoir of hydrogen has been slowly expended, no significant changes have occurred in the Sun's structure. Astronomers believe that although much of the hydrogen in the solar core has already disappeared, the Sun is only partly through its long stable period. After the hydrogen in the central core has been exhausted, gravitational contraction will recommence, and the physical structures will change relatively rapidly. The temperature will increase not only in the central core (now made primarily of helium), but also in the surrounding regions. Thus, in a shell surrounding the core, hydrogen fusion can take place. As the core further contracts, the hydrogen burning will take place in shells farther and farther out in the Sun. In spite of the contraction of the core, however, the outer layers will swell up because of the increased interior temperatures. The Sun will be on its way to the giant stage (B to C in Fig. 4), expanding out to swallow up Mercury, Venus, and possibly even Earth. When the interior temperature reaches 100 million °K, the helium nuclei, inert at lower temperatures, will themselves be able to undergo nuclear reactions. As a result, the Sun will become hotter at the surface, and smaller, moving from C to D in Fig. 4.

For stars more massive than the Sun, the core may reach such high temperatures that still further nuclear reactions occur. A gigantic explosion will take place if the reactions become sufficiently violent; supernovas may be just such spectacular cataclysms. Ultimately all available nuclear fuel will be exhausted, leaving the star to contract slowly into a ball of incredible density. Such stars, with densities averaging 5 tons/in.³, are called "white dwarfs."

The theory of a star's life cycle is supported by studies of star clusters. The more luminous a star, the more rapidly it spends its nuclear fuels, and hence the more quickly it evolves. In a stellar group with a common origin in the dis-

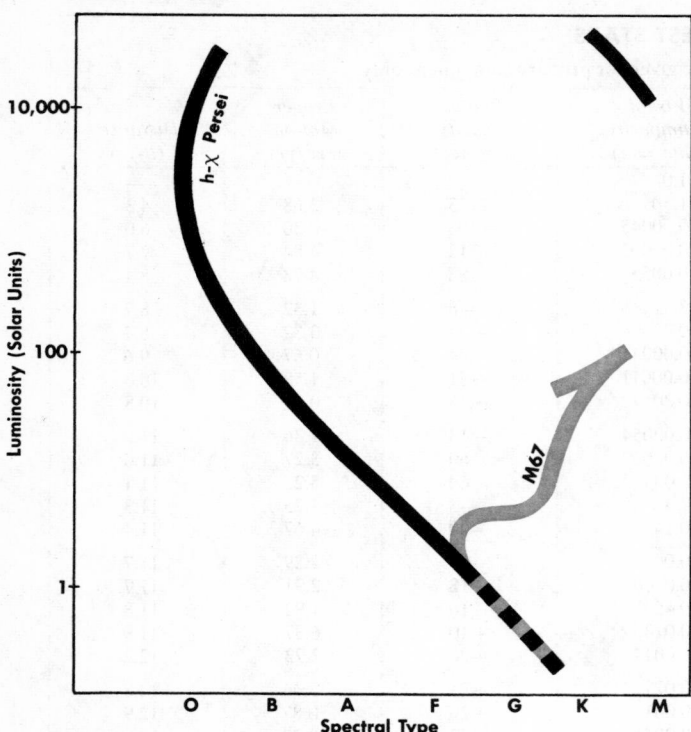

Fig. 5—Schematic H-R diagram for a very young galactic star cluster (h-χ Persei) and a very old one (M67).

tant past, the most luminous stars have already exhausted their nuclear fuels. The H-R diagram for an old galactic star cluster such as M67 (Fig. 5) shows that the luminous, rapidly evolving stars have left the main sequence and become red giants. The most luminous stars, which remain on the main sequence less than 100 million yr, have presumably become white dwarfs.

Star Populations: In 1944, Walter Baade divided stars into groups according to their ages and habitats. Population I includes younger stars associated with gas and dust, *e.g.* those found in galactic clusters or the spiral arms of galaxies. Population II includes older stars found in regions essentially devoid of gas and dust, *e.g.* globular clusters or the nuclei of spiral galaxies, or elliptical galaxies.

The spiral arms of galaxies contain clouds of interstellar material, with bright Population I stars outlining the arms like frosting on a cake. From a study of star evolution, we know that the most luminous stars exhaust their nuclear energy sources in a few hundred million years, a short time compared to the age of our several-billion-year-old galaxy. Thus the high-luminosity stars of Population I must be comparatively young, having condensed from the interstellar matter long after the earliest stars were formed. The clouds of gas and dust are remnants of the material from which these stars were born. In the old, stable, dust-free globular

THE 30 BRIGHTEST STARS

Note: If star is a multiple system, data are given for primary component only.

Name	Constellation	Color	Visual Magnitude	Visual Luminosity (Sun = 1)	Proper Motion (sec/yr)	Radial Velocity (km/sec)	Distance (lt-yr)
Sirius	Canis Major	Blue	−1.42	23	1.32	− 7.6	8.7
Canopus	Carina	Yellow	−0.72	1,500	0.02	+20.5	100
—	Centaurus	Yellow	−0.01	1.5	3.68	−22.7	4.3
Arcturus	Boötes	Orange	−0.06	110	2.28	− 5.2	36
Vega	Lyra	Blue	+0.04	55	0.34	−13.9	26
Capella	Auriga	Yellow	+0.05	170	0.44	+30.2	47
Rigel	Orion	Violet	+0.14	40,000	0.00	+20.7	800
Procyon	Canis Minor	Yellow	+0.38	7.3	1.25	− 3.2	11.3
Betelgeuse	Orion	Red	+0.41	17,000	0.03	+21.0	500
Achernar	Eridanus	Violet	+0.51	200	0.10	+19	65?
—	Centaurus	Violet	+0.63	5,000	0.04	−12	300
Altair	Aquila	Blue	+0.77	11	0.66	−26.3	16.5
—	Crux	Violet	+1.39	4,000	0.04	− 6	400
Aldebaran	Taurus	Orange	+0.86	100	0.20	+54.1	53
Spica	Virgo	Violet	+0.91	2,800	0.05	+ 1.0	260
Antares	Scorpius	Red	+0.92	5,000	0.03	− 3.2	400
Pollux	Gemini	Orange	+1.16	45	0.62	+ 3.3	40
Fomalhaut	Piscis Aust.	Blue	+1.19	14	0.37	+ 6.5	23
Deneb	Cygnus	Blue	+1.26	60,000	0.00	− 4.6	1400
—	Crux	Violet	+1.28	6,000	0.05	+20	500
Regulus	Leo	Violet	+1.36	120	0.25	+ 3.5	75
Adhara	Canis Major	Violet	+1.48	8,000	0.00	+27.4	600
Shaula	Scorpius	Violet	+1.60	1,700	0.03	0	300
Castor	Gemini	Blue	+1.97	27	0.20	+ 4	45
Bellatrix	Orion	Violet	+1.64	2,300	0.02	+18.2	360
El Nath	Taurus	Violet	+1.65	360	0.18	+ 8.0	150
—	Carina	Blue	+1.67	45	0.18	− 5	50
—	Crux	Red	+1.69	800	0.27	+21.3	200
Alnilam	Orion	Violet	+1.70	40,000	0.00	+26	1400
Al Na'ir	Grus	Violet	+1.76	70	0.19	+11	64

Adapted with permission from G. H. Herbig and C. E. Worley, "Some Basic Astronomical Data" (rev. 1960), in Leaflet No. 325, Astronomical Society of the Pacific, San Francisco, Calif.

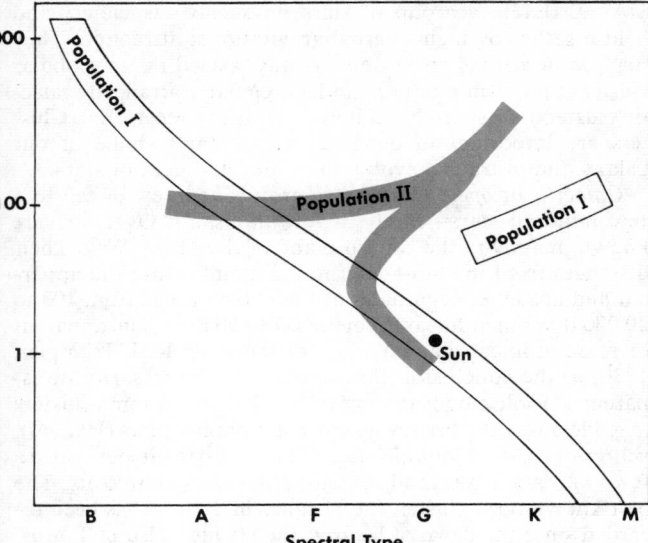

Fig. 6—The H-R diagram for the two stellar populations.

clusters that contain stars of Population II, the brightest stars have evolved into red giants. Consequently the H-R diagram shows a marked contrast between the two populations (Fig. 6).

Development of the concept of stellar populations led to the recognition that the cepheid variable stars also are of two basic types, each having its own period-luminosity relation. This discovery, in 1951, forced astronomers to double their distance scale for remote galaxies.—*O. G.*

Space Motions: Determinations of the real motions of stars are made from observations of RADIAL VELOCITY, PROPER MOTION, and distance, after allowing for the effects of the motion of the Sun through space. The Sun's motion can be determined from an analysis of the systematic tendencies apparent in stellar motions. Thus, the radial velocities of stars in the direction toward which the Sun is moving tend, on the average, to be negative (indicating relative approach), and in the opposite direction to be positive (indicating relative recession). An analogous systematic behavior is shown by proper motions.

The real motions can be interpreted in terms of orbits about the center of the Galaxy. If all orbits were circular, and stars nearer to the center of the Galaxy moved faster, then (see Fig. 7) stars in the shaded quadrants of the sky

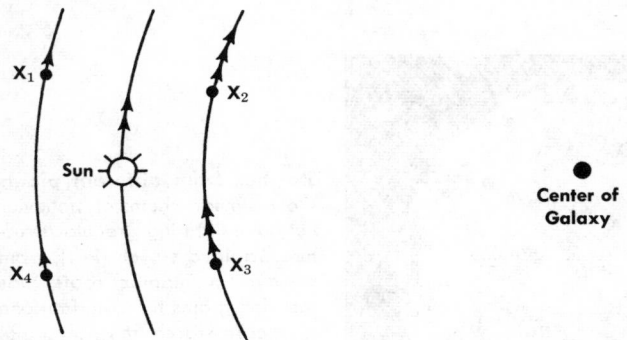

Fig. 7—The Sun is catching up to star X₁, which thus has a velocity of *approach*. The Sun is lagging behind star X₂, which thus has a velocity of *recession*. The star X₃ is catching up to the Sun, and thus has a velocity of *approach*. The star X₄ is lagging behind the Sun, and thus has a velocity of *recession*.

should have velocities of recession (with respect to the Sun), while stars in the unshaded quadrants should have velocities of approach. Statistically, this is found to be so, but the real motions show a spread because stellar orbits may be elliptical as well as circular. In general, a star would be just as likely to have a velocity greater than the circular velocity by a given amount as one less than the circular velocity by the same amount. However, the circular velocity of the Sun is about 43 mi/sec less than the escape velocity from the Galaxy (in the solar neighborhood). Nearby stars whose velocity of rotation exceeded the Sun's by 43 mi/sec have escaped from the Galaxy. On the other hand, stars whose velocity is less by 43 mi/sec than that of the Sun remain, and are called "high-velocity stars." Relative to the velocity of the Sun, their velocities are greater than 43 mi/sec, but their velocities about the center of the Galaxy are less than that of the Sun. Stars that are "high-velocity" with respect to the Sun are thus "low-velocity" as regards their motion about the center of the Galaxy.—*M. W. O.*

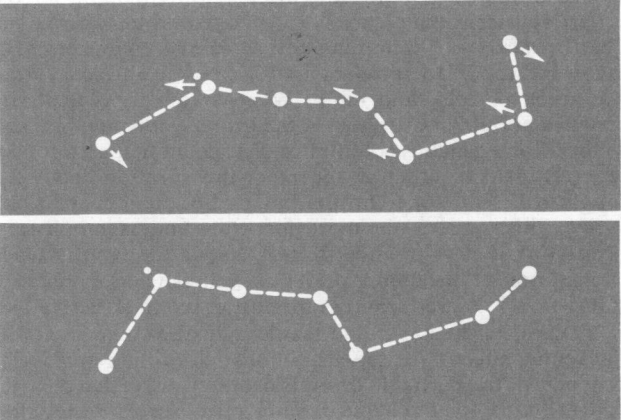

Motions of stars in Big Dipper, with respect to our line of sight, are indicated by arrows in upper drawing. After 100,000 yr these motions will have produced the new pattern shown in lower drawing.

STAR ASSOCIATIONS: scattered groupings of physically related stars. There are two types: "O," referring to the hottest stars of the spectral sequence (see STAR, *spectra*, page 1114); and "T," referring to a kind of irregular variable star (T Tauri) frequently found in association with nebulosity (see VARIABLE STAR). "O" associations generally consist of about 100 massive, hot stars confined to a volume of space with a radius of 100 to 600 lt-yr. In such regions the number of stars with surface temperatures over 50,000°F and masses greater than 10 suns is much greater per unit volume of space than in the general galactic field. "O" associations have been found to be unstable and are disintegrating under the action of the galactic gravitational field. The ages of their stars are evidently not more than 10 million yr, much less than the age of Earth; they therefore provide evidence for the continual formation of stars from the interstellar material. "T" associations consist of young stars, recently formed, which by gravitational contraction become the fainter stars of the main sequence (see STAR). These groupings of fainter stars are usually found in connection with dark or bright nebulosity, and seem to be generically associated with nebulosity.— *R. P. K.*

STAR ATLASES AND CATALOGS: see ASTRONOMICAL CATALOGS, MAPS, AND ATLASES.

STARCH: a high-polymeric carbohydrate, $(C_6H_{10}O_5)_n$, the polymer chain of which is composed of glucopyranose units joined together by alpha glucosidic linkages. One component of the starch polymer, *amylose,* has a straight chain in which all the linkages are in the 1-4 position and the value of n averages about 1,000. The second component, *amylopectin,* has a branched chain containing some 1-6 linkages, as well as the 1-4, and an average n value of about 1,500. Starch occurs in plant cells in the form of white granules, each of which is an intimate mixture of amylose and amylopectin (in varying proportions depending on the species) so arranged as to be insoluble in cold water and comparatively resistant to hydrolysis. The most common raw materials for the commercial preparation of starch are the cereal grains corn, rice, and wheat and the tuberous roots potato and tapioca. The starches from these different sources vary somewhat in physical and chemical properties, corresponding to variations in the degree of polymerization (value of n in the chemical formula), the ratio of straight- to branched-chain material, and the granule structure. Starch is obtained in pure form by crushing and grinding the dried grain; steeping in cold water; and separating from the associated protein, germ, and fiber by a series of skimming and screening operations. The recovered modified starch is sold in several physical forms, *e.g.* pearl, powder, and lump. When starch is treated with water at about 70°C or above, the granules disintegrate and a thick homogeneous solution of characteristic pasty consistency is formed. When evaporated, this solution deposits a tough, adherent, coherent film having little tendency to pulverize. This is one of the most important and useful physical properties of starch. Aside from its use in foodstuffs, which stems from its thickening power as well as from its nutrient value, starch is used in great quantities as an adhesive and as a SIZING in the paper and textile industries. Because of its thickening effect it is used also in oil-well drilling muds. The products of the partial hydrolysis of starch are called dextrins and are used for the same general purposes as unmodified starch. Complete hydrolysis of starch yields glucose, usually isolated in the form of the aqueous solution called *corn syrup.* The conversion of starch (unisolated, in the form of crushed grain) to glucose by means of enzymes is an essential step in the production of grain alcohol, the alcohol being formed by further action of other enzymes on the glucose. Starch can be esterified and etherified to form a variety of POLYMER derivatives, some of which have found use as plastics and coatings. In general, however, the starch-based polymers have not been so widely accepted as the closely related CELLULOSE-based polymers. See SUGAR.—*A. M. S.*

STAR CLUSTER: a group of stars physically associated, and held together by their internal gravitational attraction. They may be numerous and symmetrically spaced (as in globular clusters), fewer in number and less regularly arranged (galactic clusters), or sparsely scattered (STAR ASSOCIATIONS). Clusters are important in defining the size and shape of our galaxy and in tracing evolutionary development of stars.

Galactic, or *open, clusters* are groups of a few dozen to a few hundred stars—rarely, a few thousand. Over 600 are known, mainly in the central plane of the Milky Way. Their distances from the Sun, determined mainly from the apparent and absolute magnitudes of their stars, range from 100 to 20,000 lt-yr; their linear diameters, 7 to 50 lt-yr. The apparent increase of linear diameter with distance led R. J. Trumpler, 1930, to the conclusion that space is not necessarily transparent; cosmic clouds in it may absorb light. In some clusters (*e.g.* Pleiades), the brightest stars are blue; in others (Hyades), yellow-red. Many double stars occur in open clusters; also a few VARIABLE STARS, and sometimes gaseous nebulosity. The best-known open cluster, the Pleiades in Taurus, has been recorded since the dawn of history; the Hyades, also in Taurus, is another conspicuous naked-eye group. Praesepe and the Double Cluster in Perseus are fine objects for binoculars. A *moving cluster* is an open cluster in which the common motion of the individual stars is relatively large; although the space motions of these stars are essentially parallel, an effect of perspective makes them appear to converge. The Hyades is the best example; another is the Ursa Major cluster which includes many stars of the Big Dipper.

Globular clusters are spherical groups of thousands or hundreds of thousands of stars. About 120 are known, associated with our galaxy. Showing rotational symmetry, they contain material amounting to as much as several hundred thousand solar masses. Their distances from the Sun range from 7,000 to 175,000 lt-yr, the linear diameters from 60 to 500 lt-yr. Despite their remoteness, M13 in Hercules and Omega Centauri in the southern sky are visible to the naked eye as small hazy patches. The brightest stars in globular clusters are yellow giants; variable stars are commonly present and may be used to derive distances. Though found in all regions of the sky, globulars are strongly concentrated in the Scorpius-Sagittarius region and hence gave Harlow Shapley, *c.* 1918, a clue that the center of our galaxy is located there. The globular clusters are satellite systems of our galaxy, moving in and around it on extended orbits whose radii are in tens of thousands of light years. Intergalactic globular clusters have been found in recent years at distances up to several hundred thousand light years from our Sun—well be-

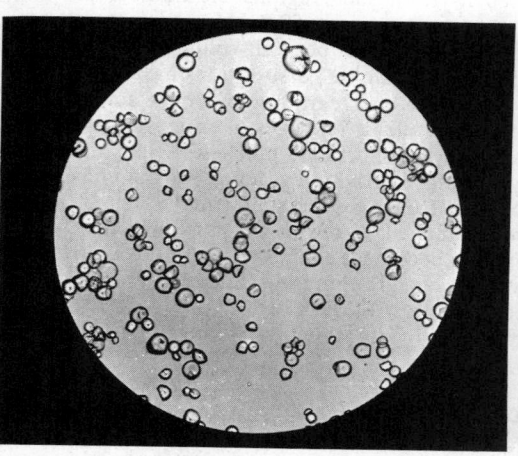
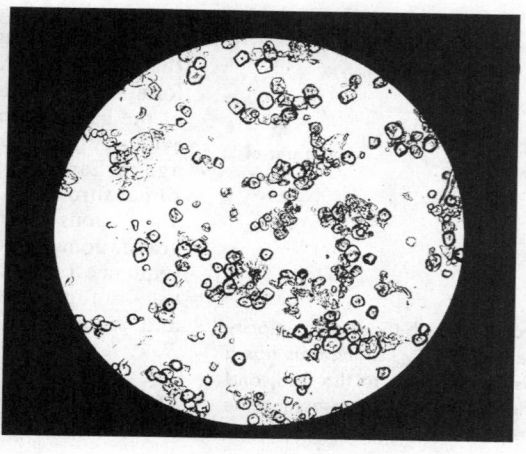

Starches from different plants show similar chemical behavior but have differing granular structure. Tapioca starch (*left*), from cassava or manioc roots, has rounded grains truncated on one side; corn starch has polygonal grain. (Both $\times$ 135.) (*U. S. Food and Drug Adm.*)

Star counts in cluster: Before photography, use of telescopes of greater and greater light-gathering power brought a whole new magnitude within reach every time quantity of light received was multiplied by 2.5. Today a similar advantage is achieved by increasing exposure time on photographic plates. These photos of globular cluster M13 in Hercules (*above*) represent exposures of 6, 15, 37, and 94 sec—an increase of one magnitude for each exposure. Aggregation of stars toward center of cluster becomes so dense that, with increasing exposure, the central part looks solid. (*Mt Wilson*)

yond the borders of our galaxy. Extragalactic star clusters, both open and globular, have been identified around the nearer of the external galaxies, *e.g.* the Magellanic Clouds and the Andromeda galaxy. About a thousand globulars have been distinguished around the massive galaxy M87.

On the theory that the stars of a given cluster are coeval, their distribution according to color and absolute magnitude is used to determine the age of the cluster. This is done by comparison with a standardized distribution ("standard main sequence") to determine the time interval necessary for the observed evolutionary development to have occurred. For a certain period after a star condenses out of a primordial cosmic mass of gas, it gives off energy from its own contraction. Then atomic sources of power provide the energy; this involves transmutation of elements, *e.g.* hydrogen building into helium. Computed from such theories, the ages of galactic clusters range from less than a million years for the very young

(*e.g.* Orion cluster) to as great as 5,000 million for several very old ones (M67). Stars in globular clusters are abnormally weak in metals: an indication of their formation at an early stage of our galaxy before the heavier elements were built up. All globulars seem to be very old systems, 6,000 to 12,000 million yr old. Distances within a globular cluster are more nearly comparable to those between planets in the solar system than to distances customarily associated with stars.—*H. S. H.*

STARK, JOHANNES, 1874–1957, German physicist; b. Schickenhof. In 1905 he verified with experiments his hypothesis that the light produced by canal rays in a cathode-ray tube shows the Doppler effect. In 1913, by passing canal rays through a region in which a strong electric field was produced, he showed that the usual spectral lines were split into several discrete lines (STARK EFFECT). For these two achievements, he received the 1919 Nobel prize.—*D. H. D. R.*

Open star clusters are represented by "Beehive" (Praesepe) cluster in Cancer. A mere hazy patch to the naked eye, it was first recorded by Hipparchus about 150 B.C. Some 500 lt-yr away, it contains 358 stars brighter than 19th magnitude. (*Yerkes Obs.*)

Globular clusters are represented by Omega Centauri, the brightest and one of the nearest—22,000 lt-yr away. To the eye a hazy patch of 4th or 5th magnitude, in large telescopes it resolves into innumerable 12th-magnitude stars. (*Harvard Obs.*)

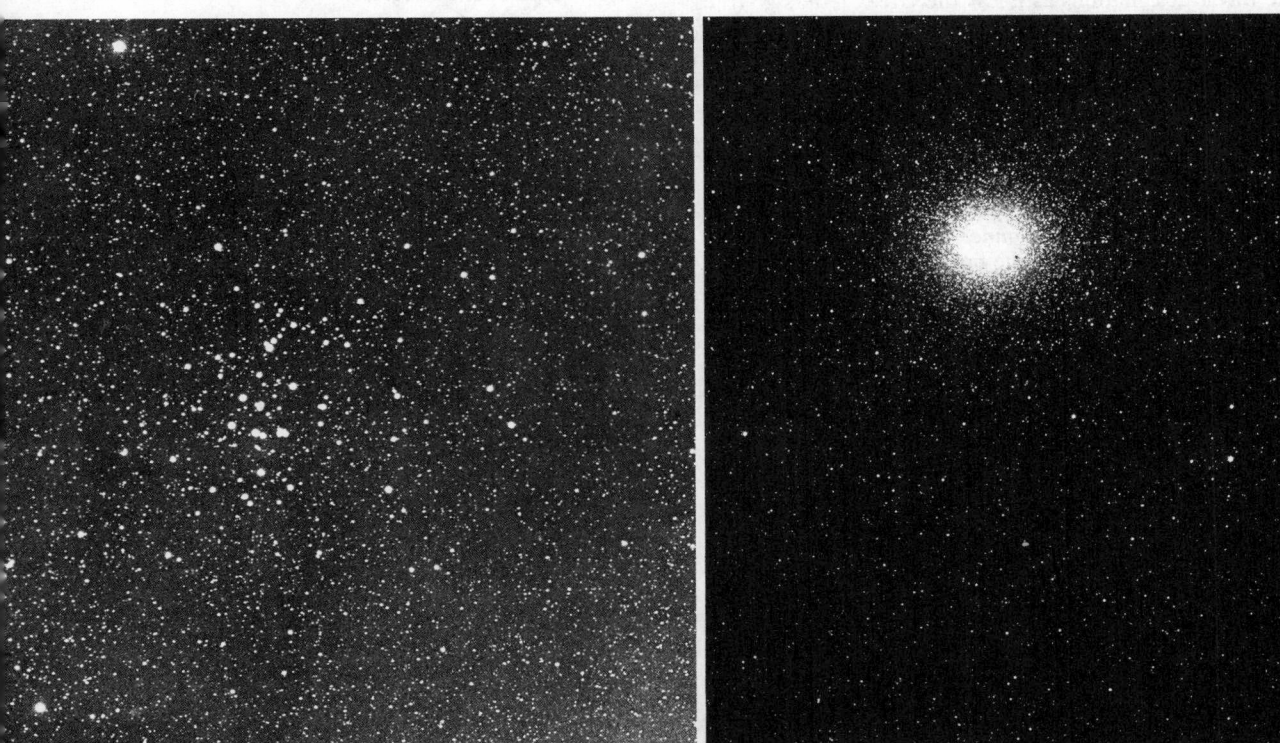

STARK EFFECT: a small shift in the frequency of the light emitted by an atom when placed in an electric field. An externally applied electric field causes the electron cloud surrounding the atomic nucleus to be moved "off-center" with respect to the nucleus, because the two are oppositely charged. This results in distortions of the electron orbits, and changes in the energies associated with them. Since the frequency of the light emitted by an atom is directly proportional to the energy lost by an electron in falling from one orbit into another, it follows that there will be a slight shift in the frequency of the light emitted in transitions between the altered ENERGY LEVELS. The effect was discovered by Johannes Stark (1913).—*S. K.*

STAR NAMES AND DESIGNATIONS have their origin in antiquity. Distinctive star groups were given the names of mythological or legendary figures. The majority of the individual stars in each group were given names, sometimes relating to their position in the mythological figures. Most of the names retained today are of Greek, Latin, and Arabic origin, such as Sirius, Aldebaran, Spica, Polaris, Altair, Betelgeuse. Since all early works on astronomy were confined to the visual stars, relatively few stars were identified by name. But shortly after the invention of the telescope, the astronomer Bayer (1572–1625), in his *Uranometria* (1603), introduced a new method of designating the stars. The stars in each constellation were identified by small letters of the Greek alphabet, for the most part beginning with alpha (α) as the brightest star, beta (β) as the next brightest, and so on. If more letters were required than the Greek alphabet afforded, the Roman alphabet was used to continue the system. Bayer identified a star further by putting after its Greek letter the genitive case of the Latin name of the constellation; thus, α Tauri, the brightest star in Taurus. If several stars in the same constellation were of about the same brightness, they were lettered in order of position, beginning at the head of the mythological figure.

With the advent of the telescope it became necessary to seek other methods of identification. Flamsteed (1646–1719) developed a plan of numbering the stars consecutively from west to east across each constellation. Today most star maps use the Bayer designations as far as the Greek letters go (the Roman letters are seldom used), together with the ancient names of most of the brightest stars. Additional stars bear the Flamsteed numbers. Examples: α Cygni, Deneb; and 61 Cygni. This is the manner of designating and naming many thousands of stars visible to the unaided eye. These methods fail, however, in regard to telescopic stars, referred to by number in an astronomical catalog, *e.g.* HD 235861 (referring to a star so numbered in the *Henry Draper Catalog* of 359,083 stars).

Argelander's (1799–1875) *Bonner Durchmusterung* (1863), containing 324,000 stars from the north pole to −2° declination, and Schönfeld's (1828–91) supplement of 134,000 stars to −23°, are still used as standard references. The stars are numbered in order of increasing right ascension in zones of 1° declination, and references are given in this manner: BD + 10° 2652. The same system is used in the *Cordoba Durchmusterung* (CD) of 570,000 stars for the southern sky.

Many other systems of names are used for special objects. Variable stars are named in each constellation by Roman capital letters beginning with R and continuing through the alphabet; then by RR to RZ, SS to SZ, to ZZ, then AA to AZ, and so on until the combinations are used up, ending with QZ, the 334th variable star. Additional variables are designated V335, V336, and so on. Novae are given names in the variable-star sequence. A variable star is sometimes designated by six digits, thus: 213843, for SS Cygni, where the first two figures represent the hours of right ascension, the middle two figures the minutes of right ascension,

and the last two the degrees of declination of the star, for epoch 1900. A southern star is indicated by underlining or by italicizing the last two figures.

Galaxies, nebulae, and clusters are given NGC numbers that represent the numbers in Dreyer's (1852–1926) *New General Catalog* (1888). The brighter objects, about 100, are listed also in Messier's (1730–1817) *Catalog of Nebulae and Clusters,* and are designated on most star maps by numbers preceded by M, as M42 for the Great Nebula in Orion. Special catalogs designate double stars by a number preceded by Σ for the stars in F. G. W. Struve's *Catalog of Double Stars,* β for those in S. W. Burnham's catalog, etc. Some doubles are indicated by superscripts, *e.g.* $\varepsilon^{1,2}$ Lyrae. The brightest component in a multiple-star system is designated by A, the fainter by B, C, etc., as δ Andromedae A. Where data are given for combined brightness, the stars are designated thus: ε Hydrae ABC.—*R. N. M.*

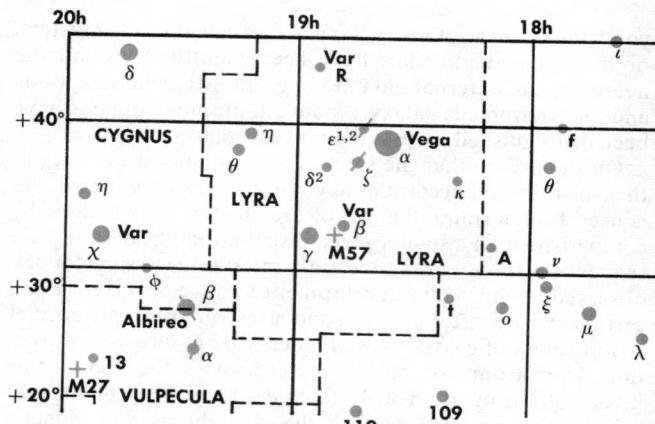

Designations of celestial objects are exemplified on this section of a star map. In the constellation Lyra, α (Vega) is the brightest star; stars labeled "Var" are variables. M27 and M57 are gaseous nebulas. Double stars are indicated by a line through the dot. Size of dot indicates relative magnitude. Right ascension is given in hours, declination in degrees.

STAS, JEAN SERVAIS, 1813–91, Belgian chemist; b. Louvain. He became famous for his careful determination of the atomic weights of many elements, showing, contrary to William Prout's hypothesis, that they are integers as multiples of hydrogen. Together with Saint-Claire Deville (Henri Etienne), he investigated platinum and iridium alloys for their suitability as international standards. He also discovered a method for the detection of vegetable alkaloids; it is still known as the Stas-Otto method. He was a fellow of the Royal Society and an associate of the U. S. National Academy of Sciences.—*R. J. F.*

STATE OF SYSTEM (in physics): a term which usually refers to a specification of the assumed momentary values of all independent variables in a given system (*e.g.* coordinates and velocities) required to predict its future behavior. The form of the specification depends on the assumed structure of the system and on the theoretical basis of the calculation. To deal with the solar system, for example, in terms of classical mechanics, it may suffice to define the state of the system at any instant by the corresponding values of the coordinates of the mass centers of the members of the system and the conjugate moments. The state of a thermodynamic system is described in terms of such gross observable quantities as temperature, pressure, and chemical concentration. In quantum mechanics the disturbance of atomic systems by observation and the impossibility of simultaneous exact measurements of position and velocity lead to the specification of the state of the system in terms of continuous functions of coordinates and time from which the statistical behavior of assemblages of similarly prepared systems can be evaluated.—*G. Ho.*

STATIC: a hissing or crackling noise heard in RADIO receivers. It is most severe in the low-frequency and broadcast bands. Static is usually produced by electrical storms in the atmosphere or by sparking in electrical apparatus. Both electrical storms and sparking radiate ELECTROMAGNETIC WAVES that are random in character but are indistinguishable to radio receivers from the signals to which the receivers are tuned. Accordingly, the random "signals" are processed by the receiver and emerge as noise from the loudspeaker. The frequency components of such signals are limited at the high-frequency end, and it is for this reason that the static signals are not strongly picked up by receivers tuned to the short-wave band. Because static signals act to increase the amplitude of the received signal, they do not appear in the output of FM receivers, which are sensitive only to frequency variations.—*I. R.*

STATICS: the branch of MECHANICS that treats of bodies at rest. A body is at rest (or in uniform motion), according to Newton's first law of motion, when the resultant of the external forces on the body is zero. The identification, evaluation, location, and orientation of the external forces acting on a body at rest are the proper domain of statics. Newton's first law, elaborated, states that (1) the vertical components of all external forces on a body at rest are equal to zero; (2) the horizontal components of all external forces on such a body are equal to zero; and (3) the torque, or moment, of the external forces acting on the body is equal to zero. The application of these relationships is a fundamental part of the design of much engineering construction; the same relationships determine the forces on any structure, from the smallest machine part to the largest masonry dam. Given the forces acting on a body, the scientist can determine mathematically the magnitude and direction of the unknown forces keeping the body at rest, provided the number of unknowns does not exceed the number of relationships (usually three) appropriate to the situation. When the number of unknowns does exceed the number of relationships derived from statics, other considerations, such as the material character of the body and the internal forces, must be used to resolve this *statically indeterminate* situation. See FORCE; NEWTON'S LAWS OF MOTION.—*A. L.*

STATISTICAL DESIGN OF EXPERIMENTS: The main body of mid-20th-cent. mathematical STATISTICS is concerned with two natural questions as to the numerical data that characterize a class of phenomena: how best to collect such data, and how best to use them.

Collecting Data: The first question is basic to a subdiscipline of mathematical statistics known as the *theory of experimentation*. Here are two examples illustrating the problems of this theory:

1. A governmental agency contemplating a particular piece of legislation L is interested in the proportion P of the population favoring L. To estimate P, a sum of money is assigned for a sampling survey in which a number of citizens are to be asked: "Do you favor the proposed legislation L?" The easiest way to conduct such a poll is to get all of the individuals of a large group, *e.g.* an army corps, to answer the question. However, even if a relatively large number of answers are collected in this manner, it is obvious that the results of the poll are likely to be biased. Opinions on any important question vary from one group of citizens to the next and, within a single group, from one part

of the country to another. To obtain unbiased results reflecting the opinions of the entire population, it is necessary to take a number of precautions. One precaution—*stratification*—ensures that the persons polled are divided into age groups, socio-economic backgrounds, places of birth, and so on, in the same proportion as the population at large. Another precaution—*randomization*—seeks to eliminate other sources of bias.

2. An agronomer wants to select out of four available varieties of wheat, *A, B, C,* and *D,* the one promising the

Fig. 1: Primitive design of an experiment with four variables.

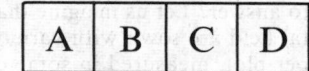

highest yields if grown on a given type of soil in a given locality. For this purpose the four varieties are to be grown on an apparently uniform field, and the observed yields are to be used for the decision. The question arises: How should the four varieties be distributed over the field; or, in technical terms, how should the experiment be designed?

One possibility is to cut the field into four consecutive plots, as indicated in Fig. 1, and to assign each of the four varieties to a particular plot. However, intuition and experience suggest that this design is not very efficient. Even though the field selected for the experiment appears uniform, a certain amount of fertility variation over the field is unavoidable. Furthermore, ordinarily the fertility variation is patchy, and quite frequently there is a systematic change from one end of the field to the other. In these circumstances, the design exhibited in Fig. 1 is bound to "favor" some of the varieties compared and may easily lead to wrong conclusions. A number of experimental layouts designed to avoid such dangers have been introduced by R. A. Fisher, a notable statistician, and by his school. The simplest of these

Fig. 2: The randomized block experiment with four varieties and five replicates.

designs, called the *randomized block design,* is illustrated in Fig. 2. It consists in dividing the field into a convenient number n, say five, equal "blocks" and in dividing each block into as many equal "plots" as there are varieties, or treatments, to compare (four in this example). Then each of the four varieties is assigned randomly one plot in each of the blocks. As a result of this randomization, the danger of bias in the yields, caused by the possible fertility gradient, is reduced. Also, the randomized block design provides data (which the primitive design of Fig. 1 does not) for calculating how safe it is to assert, for example, that variety A is superior to variety B.

The theory of experimentation has a very extensive literature, which may be classified under two headings. The first is *experimental tactics,* which is concerned with the details of single experiments, taking into account particularities of conditions in each specific domain, *e.g.* field experiments in agriculture, laboratory experiments, experimentation in industry, medicine. The second heading, *experimental strategy,* includes literature involving refined mathematics, but as yet having little practical application. Here, the object of study is not a single experiment but a chain of successive experiments, all related to the same broad question under investigation. The main problem of experimental strategy is to determine the best way to use the results of completed experiments of a chain to design the next experiment of the chain.

Using Data: Once data have been collected, the next question is: what is the best way to use the data? This question occupies the main body of modern mathematical statistics. It is very relevant to the theory of experimentation on both tactical and strategic levels and plays an increasing role in many domains of scientific research. Besides, the question of how to use data involves a most interesting mathematical discipline. The main subdisciplines are the *theory of testing statistical hypotheses* and the *theory of estimation*. To illustrate, let us return to the randomized block experiment with four varieties and five replications.

First, exactly what question do we want the experiment to answer? Let us imagine that all 20 plots of the experimental field are sown with variety A. Suppose the average yield per plot, measured in some convenient units, is $Y_A = 1.53$. Now imagine that, rather than variety A, it is variety B that is grown on all plots of the experimental field, and assume that the average yield is, say, $Y_B = 1.21$. One possible interpretation of the purposes of the experiment is that we want to compare the numbers Y_A and Y_B, to determine the potential average yields that varieties A and B are able to produce if grown in identical conditions on the same field. If these yields were known, then we could say with certainty that variety A produces, in the indicated condition, $Y_A - Y_B = 1.53 - 1.21 = 0.32$ units more per plot than variety B. This increase is slightly more than 26% of the potential yield of variety B and represents a considerable advantage. Unfortunately, if one plants a given plot with variety A, it is impossible to use the same plot for variety B, and therefore a direct comparison of the numbers Y_A and Y_B is impractical. It is this circumstance that creates the problem of experimentation.

TABLE I
POTENTIAL YIELDS OF VARIETIES A AND B ON PLOTS OF THE FIRST BLOCK

$Y_{A1} = 1.60,$	$Y_{A2} = 1.63,$	$Y_{A3} = 1.50,$	$Y_{A4} = 1.43$
$Y_{B1} = 1.61,$	$Y_{B2} = 1.00,$	$Y_{B3} = 0.95,$	$Y_{B4} = 0.80$

Consider just one block of the field, say the first, and imagine that the potential yields of the two varieties A and B are as those given in Table I. If the first plot of the first block were sown with variety A, the resulting yield would have been $Y_{A1} = 1.60$ units of weight. The variety B sown on the same plot would yield $Y_{B1} = 1.61$, a little more. However, on the second plot of the block, the yields of the same varieties would have been 1.63 and 1.00 units, respectively. The variation in the potential yields reflects the usual slight changes in soil occurring from plot to plot and the different reactions to these changes of the two biologically distinct varieties A and B.

TABLE II
OBSERVABLE DIFFERENCES OF POTENTIAL YIELDS OF THE TWO VARIETIES ON BLOCK 1

$Y_{A1} - Y_{B2} = 0.60,$	$Y_{A1} - Y_{B3} = 0.65,$	$Y_{A1} - Y_{B4} = 0.80$
$Y_{A2} - Y_{B1} = 0.02,$	$Y_{A2} - Y_{B3} = 0.68,$	$Y_{A2} - Y_{B4} = 0.83$
$Y_{A3} - Y_{B1} = -0.11,$	$Y_{A3} - Y_{B2} = 0.50,$	$Y_{A3} - Y_{B4} = 0.70$
$Y_{A4} - Y_{B1} = -0.18,$	$Y_{A4} - Y_{B2} = 0.43,$	$Y_{A4} - Y_{B3} = 0.48$

The contribution of the first block to the comparison of varieties A and B may be one of 12 possible combinations of numbers, or perhaps one of 12 differences, as in Table II. If the randomization of the experiment resulted in assigning plots 1 and 2 to varieties A and B, respectively, then the yields of the two varieties harvested from plots in the first block would have been 1.60 and 1.00 units, respectively, and the difference between the two would have been 0.60 units. To calculate the true average yields Y_A and Y_B over the whole field, the total of 40 numbers must be available. Instead, the experiment will yield only a sample of 10 numbers, two from each block, or a sample of five differences of potential yields, one from each block. Table II exhibits the totality of such differences for the first block, of which only one can be observed in the given experiment. For example, the actually observed difference in this block may be $Y_{A4} - Y_{B1} = -0.18$, and this may be combined with four other numbers observed in the remaining four blocks, which may well be negative also. This result of the experiment would, then, suggest a wrong conclusion, namely that variety A is inferior to B. The possibility of such occurrence illustrates that, once the experiment has been performed, no definitive statement about the entities compared is possible, and the quantities Y_A and Y_B must remain unknown. In these circumstances one may wonder what exactly the methods of mathematical statistics can provide and how they can be useful in any problem of experimentation or other scientific research. The answer is of considerable conceptual delicacy: While an already performed experiment of the kind described cannot yield any precise information about the varieties compared (or, in statistical parlance, "about the state of the universe"), if the design of the experiment (or some other source) provides at least some information about the chance mechanism governing the variability of the results, then it is possible to devise methods of dealing with experimental data that will permit the calculation of the long-range frequency of errors in the assertions made on the basis of the experiments. Furthermore, among all such methods available, it is possible to select those that will guarantee a smaller long-range frequency of certain errors than any alternative methods. The determination of these optimal methods of handling statistical data is the typical problem of mathematical statistics.

Returning again to the experiment with four varieties A, B, C, and D, we notice that the complete set of potential yields illustrated in Table I, or the somewhat incomplete set of differences in Table II (12 rather than 16), must remain unknown. However, the experiment contemplated is not the only one that will be performed. There will be many such experiments, with the same varieties A, B, C, D or with different varieties. In fact, many similar experiments will be performed with entirely different subjects of study, *e.g.* machines in factories, medicines, methods of controlling weather. Suppose a large number of such experiments can be arranged in randomized blocks (which need not be blocks of plots in a field, but could be, say, a set of litters of four mice each used to study four drugs). As a result of this randomization, the first block will show the combination of "yields" (Y_{A1}, Y_{B2}) just as frequently as the combination (Y_{A3}, Y_{B1}). This is the chance mechanism behind the variability of the experimental results. Combined with certain other information, this chance mechanism can be used to deduce methods of handling experimental data so that, for example, the long-range relative frequency of assertions that variety A is inferior to B—when, in actual fact, the opposite is true—will not exceed a preassigned limit, say once in a hundred.

The technical terms used to designate mathematical statistics with particular reference to problems just described include *statistical inference, theory of statistical decisions,* and *mathematical theory of inductive behavior.—J. Ne.*

STATISTICAL MECHANICS: the branch of physics that seeks to describe by statistical methods the average properties of complicated physical systems. If one knows the nature of the forces acting between component particles of any system and knows the state of motion of the particles at one instant of time, one should be able—in principle—to describe the condition of that system at all other times, using the techniques of QUANTUM MECHANICS. However, this can be done only for simple systems containing a few particles. A gram of matter contains roughly 10^{22} (1 followed by 22 zeros) atoms. Obviously, it is impossible to observe the state of motion of every atom in such a system, let alone to solve and interpret the resulting equations. Nevertheless, we know from experience that such systems exhibit some well-defined over-all properties, and it is the task of statistical mechanics to relate the observed macroscopic (large-scale) properties to appropriate averages of the allowable internal microscopic motions. Essentially, then, statistical mechanics gives partial, but experimentally useful, descriptions of complicated systems on the basis of incomplete knowledge of the intricacies of the system. Roughly analogous is the task of the insurance-company actuary, who must predict the number of policyholders who will die within the year, without having moment-to-moment or detailed information about the health of each of the insured persons and without being able to predict which ones in a given group will actually die.

To illustrate, consider the simplest statistical-mechanical system—a perfect GAS, which consists of a large number of essentially free molecules moving in all directions at a great variety of speeds. When the gas is in equilibrium with its surroundings, it has a well-defined volume, temperature, and pressure, which are interrelated by a simple equation. The pressure is the average force exerted on the walls of the container by the molecules which collide with it, and the temperature is proportional to the average kinetic energy of the moving molecules. Statistical mechanics makes the fundamental assumption that at any instant of time all of the many conceivable internal states of motion compatible with a given temperature and volume of the gas, and allowed by the laws of mechanics, are equally probable. On this assumption it can be shown that an overwhelming majority of the allowed internal conditions correspond to a single value of the pressure. Although the pressure may deviate somewhat from this expected value, the probability is so infinitesimally small that the deviation is essentially never observed experimentally. Thus, the relation between pressure, volume, and temperature, which had long ago been formulated empirically, can be derived by the methods of statistical mechanics, as can the two fundamental laws on which the science of THERMODYNAMICS is based. More complicated systems, in which the forces of interactions between the component atoms play an important role, can also be described. Also, there has been progress in relating macroscopic properties of systems not in equilibrium.

In enumerating the possible microscopic states of a system, it is important to consider the types of elementary PARTICLES making up the system. If they are electrons or protons, for example, no two of the particles can be in the same state simultaneously, so the number of possible states is limited (see EXCLUSION PRINCIPLE). If the constituent particles are helium atoms or mesons, no such restriction applies. The statistical mechanics appropriate for the former types of particles is called Fermi-Dirac statistics, and for the latter, Einstein-Bose statistics (see QUANTUM STATISTICS).—*S. K.*

STATISTICS: In recent years, statistics and statistical methods have made themselves felt in practically every major phase of human activity. Statistics no longer consists merely of the collection of data and their presentation in charts and tables, but it is now considered to encompass the entire science of decision making in the face of uncertainty. It is virtually impossible, even on the elementary level, to read books or possible, even on the elementary level, to read books or

articles in the natural as well as the social sciences without having at least a speaking acquaintance with the subject. Even those who have little or no knowledge of statistics find that it has an immediate effect on their lives—the wages of millions of workers go up or down automatically depending on the *Consumer Price Index* of the Bureau of Labor Statistics, and subsidies paid to farmers are, similarly, determined by the *Parity Index* of the federal government. Numerical data derived from surveys, experiments, and other sources form the raw material on which interpretations, analyses, and decisions are based. Hence, not only is it essential to know how to "squeeze" usable information from such data, but it is equally important to conduct surveys and experiments in such a way that intelligent inferences are possible. In fact, these are the questions which are of major concern in statistics.

Historically, the origin of statistics may be found partly in mid-18th-cent. studies of the political arrangement of populations ("political arithmetic") and partly in the development of PROBABILITY THEORY a few decades earlier. As a result of the discovery that the theory developed for "heads or tails" or "red or black" in games of chance applied also to situations where the outcomes are "life or death" or "boy or girl," probability theory was soon used in actuarial mathematics and some other phases of social science. Later, statistical concepts were introduced into physics by Ludwig Boltzmann, J. Willard Gibbs, and James Clerk Maxwell, and in this century the methods of statistics have found applications in most phases of human activity. The names most prominently connected with the 20th-cent. growth of statistics are those of R. A. Fisher, J. Neyman, E. S. Pearson, and A. Wald.

In addition to its uses in the natural and social sciences, statistics has recently found many important applications in industry and business management. The development of statistical quality control has had a pronounced effect on industry since its inception during World War II. The growth of *operations research*, which is essentially the application of mathematics and statistics to problems of management and production, is beginning to have an equally pronounced effect on business management.

Traditionally, the methods of statistics have been divided into *descriptive* methods and the *inductive* methods of statistical inference. Descriptive methods include the presentation of data in tables and charts as well as their summarization by means of a few well-chosen descriptions; statistical inference concerns generalizations based on sample data, predictions, estimations, and tests of hypotheses. Although emphasis is shifting more and more to problems of statistical inference, purely descriptive methods are still widely used and are important in everyday life—*e.g.* the numerous statistical charts and tables in newspapers, magazines, and books.

There are numerous ways in which information that is contained in large sets of data can be summarized by means of appropriate statistical measures. Most widely used are the *measures of location,* also called measures of central tendencies or simply averages. Foremost among these is the *mean,* which for a given set of values $x_1, x_2, \ldots, x_n$ is given by their sum divided by n. The mean is also referred to as the *arithmetic mean* to distinguish it from the *geometric mean* and the *harmonic mean,* two other measures used for "averaging" a set of data. Since the mean can give a somewhat distorted picture when there are some very large or very small values, it is sometimes preferable to "average" a set of data by giving their *median,* their middle value when they are arranged according to size. For instance, it might be very misleading to say that the average income of five persons is $24,000 if four of them have incomes of $5,000 while the fifth has an income of $100,000. The median of $5,000 will give a description which is for most purposes more suitable. Two other common measures for averaging a set of data are the *mode* (the value which occurs most often) and the *mid-range* (the mean of the largest and the smallest). When averaging relative changes—measures of growth—one can also use one of the many *index number* formulas which have been devised primarily for the measurement of economic growth. They play a vital role in the appraisal of data relating to problems of business and economics.

Although the information contained in a measure of location may be sufficient in some instances, there are many problems in which it is necessary to describe additional features of the data, notably their *variability,* spread, or dispersion. The variability of repeated measurements of a certain quantity is indicative of the intrinsic accuracy of these measurements. Also, the variability of a set of sample values provides an indication of chance variation, or random fluctuations. Foremost among the measures of variability is the STANDARD DEVIATION or its square, the *variance.* The variance of a given set of data $x_1, x_2, \ldots, x_n$ is given by the sum of the squares of their deviations from the mean, divided by $n - 1$. Other measures of variability that are sometimes used are the *average deviation* and the *range* (the largest value minus the smallest). Because of its computational simplicity, the range is frequently used in industrial quality control.

There is literally no limit to the number of ways in which a set of data can be described. When dealing with grouped data, *i.e.* data that have been tallied into a table showing how many of the values fall into successive intervals or classes, it is sometimes of interest to give further descriptions of the shape of such *frequency distributions.* Most commonly, the symmetry or skewness of a distribution or its peakedness (kurtosis) are expressed in terms of *moments.* The kth moment of a set of values is given by the sum of their kth powers divided by n.

When dealing with paired data, *e.g.* the heights and weights of n individuals or the ages and prices of n secondhand cars, it is common to measure the degree of association between the two variables under consideration (height and weight, age and price) by means of the *correlation coefficient r.* Actually, a correlation coefficient is indicative only of the *linear* relationship between the two variables: if r is $+1$ or -1, then all the points representing the paired data fall on a straight line. For r lying between -1 and $+1$, the value of the correlation coefficient is indicative of the extent to which the points are scattered about the line which provides the best possible fit (see LEAST SQUARES). If the relationship between the two variables is clearly nonlinear, one can use one of the many statistical techniques which have been developed for fitting various kinds of curves to paired data.

Many problems of statistics deal with the estimation of unknown quantities such as means, standard deviations, and percentages, called the *parameters* of the populations from which the respective data are obtained. Thus, an engineer may wish to estimate the true average lifetime of a certain kind of tube, a TV producer may wish to estimate what percentage of the total viewing audience is dialed to his show, and a manufacturer of missile components may wish to estimate how much variability there is in his product. In each case the inference (the generalization) is to be made on the basis of a sample. If an estimate consists of a single number, *e.g.* if the true average lifetime of certain tubes is estimated as being 6,000 hr, the estimate is referred to as a *point estimate;* if an estimate consists of an interval, *e.g.* if it is claimed that the interval from 112 to 124 covers the true average I.Q. of all college students in the U. S. A., the estimate is referred to as an *interval estimate.*

When using a point estimate, *i.e.* when estimating an unknown quantity (parameter) by means of a single number, it is always desirable to accompany such an estimate with some statement concerning the possible size of the error or concerning the relative merits of the method of estimation being used. This may be done by giving the *standard error* or *probable error,* a quantity for which one can assert that there is a 50-50 chance that it will not be exceeded by the error of the estimate. Similarly, when giving an interval estimate, it is desirable to accompany the interval with some statement concerning the degree of confidence with which one can assert that it actually covers the quantity it is intended to estimate. To handle problems of this kind, it is necessary to assume an underlying mathematical model, *i.e.* to make some assumptions concerning the distributions of the random variables whose values constitute the sample. The methods of mathematical statistics, based on the theory of probability, can then be used to evaluate the relative merits of a method of point estimation and to assign a degree of confidence to an interval estimate. Although an interval estimate either does or does not cover the quantity it is intended to estimate, it is possible to determine the probability that intervals obtained by a certain method will do so in general, and it is customary to refer to this probability as the *degree of confidence* and to the corresponding interval as a *confidence interval.*

If an agronomist has to decide on the basis of experiments whether one variety of corn has a higher yield than another, if a medical research worker has to decide whether 90% of all patients given a new drug will recover from a certain disease, or if a sociologist has to decide if there is a greater variability in the I.Q.'s of one ethnic group than of another, these problems can all be translated into the language of statistical tests of hypotheses. Using the methods of mathematical statistics it is then possible to put such decisions on a scientific basis. With appropriate models—assumptions about the distributions of underlying random variables—it is possible to construct decision criteria for which one knows the probabilities of making wrong decisions, a wrong decision being the acceptance of a hypothesis that should be rejected or the rejection of a hypothesis that should be accepted.

A kind of test that is very widely used is the *test of significance,* which consists of deciding whether differences between practice and theory (differences between values obtained from samples and the corresponding theoretical expectations) can reasonably be attributed to chance. For example, if 100 flips of a coin yielded 53 heads and 47 tails, a significance test might be used to decide whether the difference between the 53 heads obtained and the 50 heads expected (under the assumption that the coin is balanced) may reasonably be attributed to chance.

The examples of the preceding paragraphs illustrate some of the simpler problems of statistical inference. A vast body of statistical methods has been developed to handle increasingly complicated experimental situations; these methods include such powerful techniques as the analysis of variance, the analysis of covariance, regression analysis, and response surface analysis. Since none of these methods can be applied unless the experiments, surveys, or other research are carefully and appropriately planned, questions of experimental design have become an integral part of statistics.

The whole problem of statistical inference, including estimation as well as tests of hypotheses, may be looked upon within the general unified framework of decision theory (see DYNAMIC PROGRAMMING) and game theory. In this unified approach it is necessary to consider gains, losses, and risks accounting for the consequences of various possible actions leading to correct as well as incorrect decisions. This generalized approach to statistical inference, though still in its infancy, has already found important applications.—*J. E. F.*

STAUDINGER, HERMANN, 1881–1965, German chemist; b. Worms. His research was centered primarily in the area of macromolecular chemistry, and he published hundreds of papers on that subject. For his work in high-polymer chemistry, which has helped to lay the foundation for industrial developments in plastics and synthetic fibers, he received the 1953 Nobel prize.—*D. H. D. R.*

STAUDT, KARL GEORG CHRISTIAN VON, 1798–1867, German mathematician; b. Rothenburg. He was educated at Ansbach and Göttingen, being one of the few pupils of Gauss who were close personal friends of the master. He is known mainly for his *Geometrie der Lage* (1847), in which he developed geometry entirely independently of numbers, and even succeeded in defining numbers in a purely geometric way. His work contains the first complete general theory of imaginary points, lines, and planes in projective geometry.—*H. C.*

STEADY-STATE THEORY: a theory of the universe that assumes it to be, on the large scale, not only uniform in space (as other theories assume) but also unchanging in time. It argues that if the universe were changing in time, then, since local conditions (inertia, radiation balance) are likely to be determined by the state of the universe, physics itself might be changing in time. Our knowledge of physics having been derived in a cosmically very brief period, such changes would be virtually unknowable, so that little could be said about the universe with any confidence. If, however, the universe is in a steady state, then present conditions are typical, and so knowledge acquired *now* can be applied throughout space and time. Thus a particularly clear and definite picture of the universe emerges that can be tested by comparison with observation. The steady-state universe is expanding, as required both by thermodynamics and by the RED SHIFT. The consequent denudation of matter is avoided by supposing matter (hydrogen) to be created continually (and reasonably uniformly), not only keeping the density of matter constant, but perpetually rejuvenating the universe. New galaxies form out of newly created matter, while the distances between old galaxies increase because of the expansion. The theory is expressed geometrically as the DE SITTER UNIVERSE. Continual creation is far too rare for direct observation, and is hard to incorporate into current physical theories based on conservation of matter. The theory, however, makes many predictions testable by observation. Example: the travel time of light means that distant galaxies are seen as they were billions of years ago; hence their average properties should be the same as those of near ones if and only if the universe is in a steady state. The steady-state theory also denies any different earlier state (BIG BANG) and thus stimulated the modern theory of the origin of the elements.—*H. B.*

STEAM: the gaseous PHASE of water. Steam is a colorless, odorless gas. (The cloudy material seen when water boils is not properly called steam, since it consists of fine droplets of water rather than being a true gas.) Steam has a high thermal capacity. This ability to absorb and give off heat makes steam ideal for heating and for use as the working substance in heat engines. Although STEAM ENGINES are becoming obsolete in land transport, steam TURBINES still retain their pre-eminence in water transport and as the prime movers in electric generating plants. Nuclear power installations may be

used to provide heat for the generation of steam, which is used to drive conventional turbines. See NUCLEAR REACTOR; SUPERHEATING.—*E. M. R.*

STEAM ENGINE: a machine that uses the expansion of steam to convert heat energy into mechanical energy.

Early Steam Engines; Watt's Engine: Efforts to use steam for production of mechanical energy date back to ancient times. Hero of Alexandria built a steam-jet turbine as early as 120 B. C., but its efficiency was low. The first practical engine, designed by Thomas Savery in 1698, was used to lift water from a well. In Savery's engine, two closed vessels worked alternately. Steam from the boiler entered the first vessel and expanded, displacing the water through a check valve into a tank placed at a higher level. The vessel was then water-

Newcomen's atmospheric steam engine: Steam from boiler (*bottom*) enters cylinder (*middle*), lifting piston. After steam has forced out all air and water, pipe at lower left of cylinder sprays cold water into cylinder, condensing steam and leaving partial vacuum. Atmospheric pressure pushes piston down, and cycle starts over again. (*British Crown Copyright, Science Museum, London*)

cooled on the outside and the steam condensed, producing a vacuum in the vessel. As a result, water from the well was forced into the vessel by atmospheric pressure. While the first vessel was being filled, the second vessel became connected with the boiler, and the cycle was repeated. A modified version of this machine (Hall's pulsometer) is now used for pumping water from mines. Although its efficiency is low, it is more adaptable to certain working conditions than reciprocating steam-driven pumps are. The cylinder-and-piston (atmospheric) engine invented by Denis Papin in 1690 had no separate boiler. Water was converted to steam in the cylinder. The expanding steam raised the piston nearly out

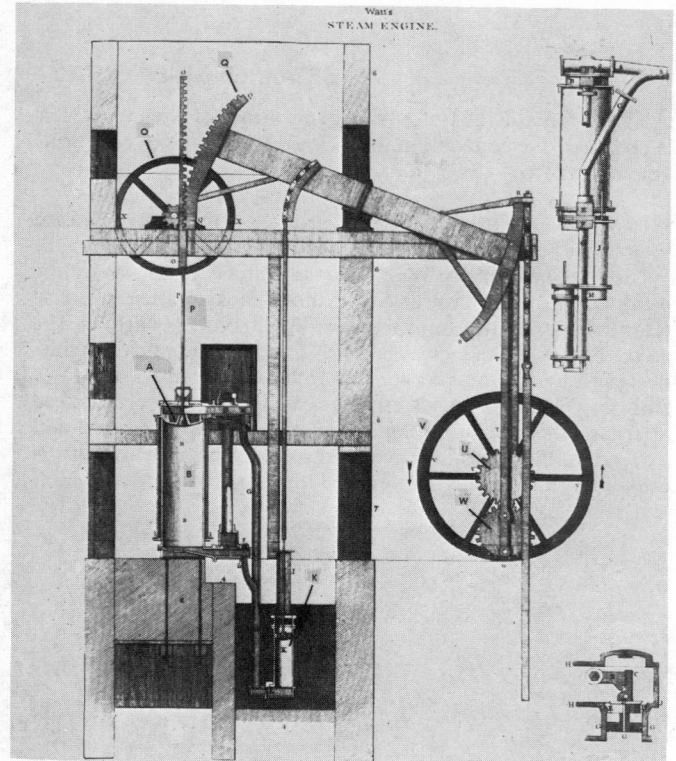

Watt's
STEAM ENGINE.

degree of wear of the cylinder metal due to alternate heating (by fresh steam) and cooling (by the condensate).

To overcome these defects James Watt (1763) modified the beam engine. The cylinder was kept uniformly hot by means of a steam jacket. The exhaust steam, after full expansion, entered a separate condensing chamber. An air pump was installed to improve the vacuum inside the cylinder; and as a safety measure a throttle valve inserted in the boiler controlled the rate of steam admission to the cylinder. The speed of the piston's upward and downward strokes was regulated by a governor, in this case a double conical pendulum actuated by centrifugal force which partially opened or closed a throttle valve in the pipe connecting the boiler to the cylinder. The initial steam pressure and therefore the speed of the piston were thus adjusted to achieve greater uniformity. Later patents by Watt included a *reciprocating engine,* in which steam replaced atmospheric pressure to push the piston back into the cylinder. Watt's principal innovation was replacing the beam by a connecting rod coupled with a crank that turned a flywheel. The reciprocating piston action was thus converted to rotation, which meant that Watt's steam engine could operate high-efficiency machines in factories and shops.

of the cylinder, cooling in the process. A partial vacuum resulted and the atmospheric pressure pushed the piston far back into the cylinder, driving out the cool, used steam. Water was again admitted into the cylinder, and the cycle was repeated. Papin later modified his machine, but a better model (a beam atmospheric engine) was designed by Thomas Newcomen and John Cawley in 1705. The piston was fastened to a rocking beam and the latter linked to the rod of a pump. A separate boiler eliminated the inconvenience of boiling the water inside the cylinder. The steam in the cylinder was condensed by a jet of cold water, a high vacuum resulted, and the piston was pushed back to the very bottom of the cylinder by atmospheric pressure. The vigorous piston work was used to operate a powerful pump, which could lift water from a great depth, *e.g.* in mine drainage. The Newcomen engine was thus the first used to operate a mechanical device. The disadvantages of the Newcomen engine included (1) excessive cooling of the cylinder during condensation, which led to undercooling of fresh steam coming in from the boiler and consequent waste of steam; and (2) a high

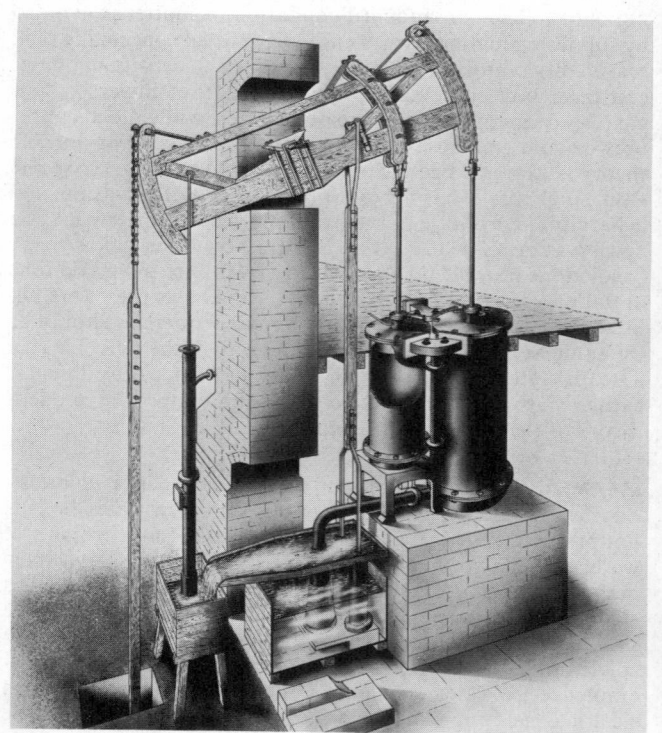

The engine's drawback was low initial pressure of fresh steam (slightly over one atmosphere), providing a relatively low expansion power.

Reciprocating Steam Engines After 1800: Richard Trevithick (England) and Oliver Evans (U. S. A.) were the first (1800) to use a *high-pressure boiler* for generating fresh steam. And attempts were made to adapt these engines for larger passenger carriages. The *compound steam engine* marked another outstanding development of the reciprocating steam engine. First patented by Jonathan Hornblower (1781) and later improved by Arthur Woolf (1804) and William MacNaught (1845), this engine replaced the system of a single expansion of high-pressure steam down to one atmosphere in one large pressure drop, by several successive expansions, each representing a small pressure drop. Steam initially under high pressure entered the first cylinder and was expanded but not discharged into a condenser. Instead, it was passed on to the second cylinder under lower pressure, where it expanded to a still lower pressure level. The modern compound engines have three and even four cylinders. This arrangement offers several important advantages: (1) the combined action of all the pistons on the flywheel mechanism produces a more uniform rotation at higher speed; (2) fuel consumption is greatly reduced, since steam can be used more efficiently when its initial pressure is increased; (3) the wear of the metal walls is decreased, since a small pressure drop produces a reduced fall of temperature during expansion; and (4) waste of fresh steam (partial condensation) caused by the large pressure and temperature drop is practically eliminated. Two-cylinder engines are still used today (*e.g.* in LOCOMOTIVES). Three-cylinder (triple-expansion) engines are widely used in cargo steamships (see SHIP). But two serious drawbacks limited the efficiency of these engines. First, the method of discharging used steam was inadequate. In the best designs separate admission and discharge valves were provided, but both were placed at the end of the cylinder where the temperature was close to the boiler temperature. As a result, the cool, used steam was heated as it entered the condenser, while fresh steam became overcooled by the discharged steam and underwent partial condensation. Secondly, in a single-cylinder, steam-jacketed engine, the initial pressure and temperature of fresh steam could not be high enough to meet modern requirements. The *uniflow* (reciprocating) engine developed by J. Stumpf (1908) eliminates both these defects. Only admission openings are placed at the ends of the cylinder, while the discharge openings are placed along the middle circumference of the wall. Also, only the ends of the cylinder are kept hot by steam jackets, while the middle section remains sufficiently cool to permit safe expansion and prevents overheating of discharge steam. At the same time fresh steam is isolated from the used steam, and hence does not undergo partial condensation. A new feature is the control of discharge openings by the piston. On the upward stroke the piston first closes these openings in the middle of the cylinder, then opens them as it clears the mid-section. On the down-ward stroke the piston again covers the discharge openings. In this brief interval, however, only a fraction of the steam has been discharged. Most of it still remains in the cylinder and is compressed by the piston nearly to the initial pressure of fresh steam. The temperature is raised by compression nearly to the boiler temperature. A large portion of the steam can therefore be used over and over again, which reduces the work of the boiler and saves both water and fuel. Also, the heat of compression prevents excessive cooling of the mid-section of the cylinder by discharge steam; this increases the life span of the metal walls and eliminates any undercooling of the fresh expanding steam. Thus, with steam waste and heat losses kept at a minimum, the uniflow engine compares favorably with multi-cylinder models and with steam turbines.

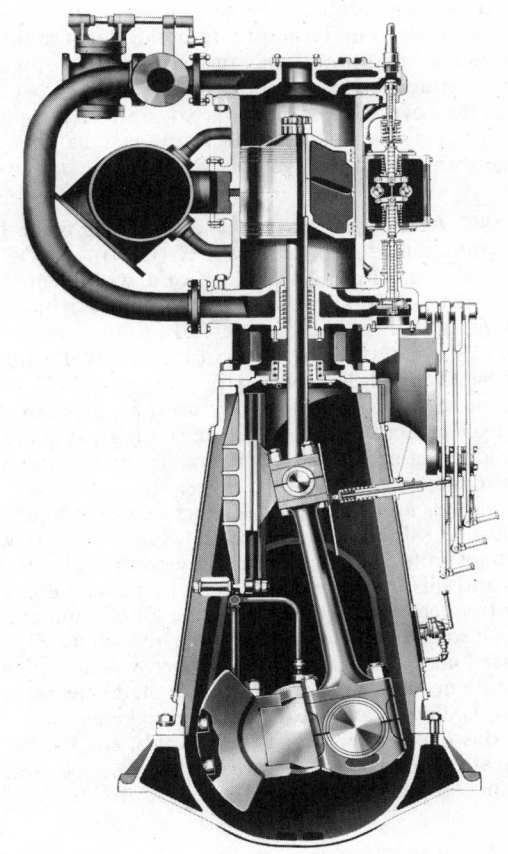

Marine uniflow steam engine is similar in principle to horizontal engine. Although more rugged in construction than stationary engines, like all uniflow engines it has a low rate of steam consumption per horsepower and operates at a high efficiency over a wide range of loads. (*Skinner Engine Co.*)

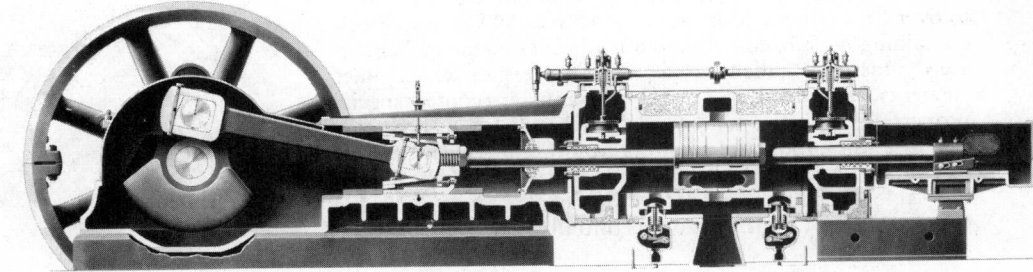

Uniflow steam engine has advantage of exhaust port in center of cylinder; piston is used as exhaust valve. This maintains temperature of cylinder walls and piston head, materially reducing initial steam condensation. (*Skinner Engine* Co.)

Steam Turbines: Although modern reciprocating steam engines achieve a relatively high degree of operating efficiency, they are inferior, especially for large-capacity installations, to the steam turbine. In general there are two types of turbines: (1) impulse turbines, in which a high-velocity steam jet from a stationary nozzle is directed against the blade of a rotor; and (2) reaction turbines, where steam flows through moving blades which are themselves shaped like nozzles. When the steam expands while passing through the nozzle, a reactive force is produced, opposite in direction to the steam flow, which turns the rotor. Many turbines are combinations of both types and both types use multiple stages, *i.e.* a number of rotors on the same shaft, each using as inlet steam the exhaust steam of the preceding rotor. In this way full expansion is achieved and efficiency is improved. Large reaction turbines may have 50 or more stages. Compared to reciprocating engines, steam turbines are lighter, more compact, and less costly to build. Because they need no internal lubrication they can use steam at higher intake temperatures, and since they can exhaust at lower temperatures, their over-all efficiency is greater. Steam turbines are used in all major steam-electric generating installations and for all large ship-propulsion systems. See ENGINE; TURBINE.—*C. S.*

STEARIC ACID AND STEARATES: Stearic acid is the 18-carbon, straight-chain, saturated acid $CH_3(CH_2)_{16}$—COOH. When pure it is a white, crystalline solid with a melting point of 69.9°C, only slightly soluble in water, but soluble in organic solvents. The commercial product, made from fats and oils, is contaminated with other acids. Distilled grades can be obtained, however, with more than 90% stearic-acid content. Stearic acid has many uses, *e.g.* in manufacture of emulsifiers, cosmetics, and textile coatings. It is the principal ingredient of so-called stearin candles, and in small amounts it is added to paraffin-wax candles.

Stearates are the salts and esters of stearic acid. The most important salt is sodium stearate (ordinary soap), which also contains salts (soaps) of the other acid radicals present in the fats and oils from which the soap is made. Salts of divalent and trivalent metals (calcium, zinc, aluminum, etc.) are also called soaps, but are not soluble in water. Zinc stearate is used in large quantity in rubber vulcanization; copper stearate in fungus prevention; other metal stearates in grinding aids, flatting agents for paints, thickeners for lubricating oils, dusting powders for sticking molds, etc. Esters, *e.g.* butyl stearate, find use in vanishing cream, lipstick, and polishes, and in compounding lubricating oils.—*Ru. M.*

STEARIN: a solid fat which melts at 71°C. It is the triglyceride of stearic acid, and is a "simple" glyceride. Commercial stearin from an animal fat (tallow) is generally "mixed" (see FATS AND OILS).—*Ru. M.*

STEEL: a commercial form of IRON containing up to 1.7% carbon and minor amounts of other elements, some of which are unavoidably present. The term "iron and steel" covers a very wide range of iron-carbon alloys containing from 0.01% to over 5% carbon and from about 65% to 99.9% iron. Steels containing no substantial amounts of other elements deliberately added are called *carbon steels.* Steels to which other elements are added in sizable amounts, to confer special properties, are called *alloy steels.* Steel is distinguished from cast iron, the product of smelting iron ore in a blast furnace, in containing much less carbon and in being malleable or forgeable when first formed. Cast iron can be made malleable by suitable heat treatment but is initially brittle. Steel is dis-

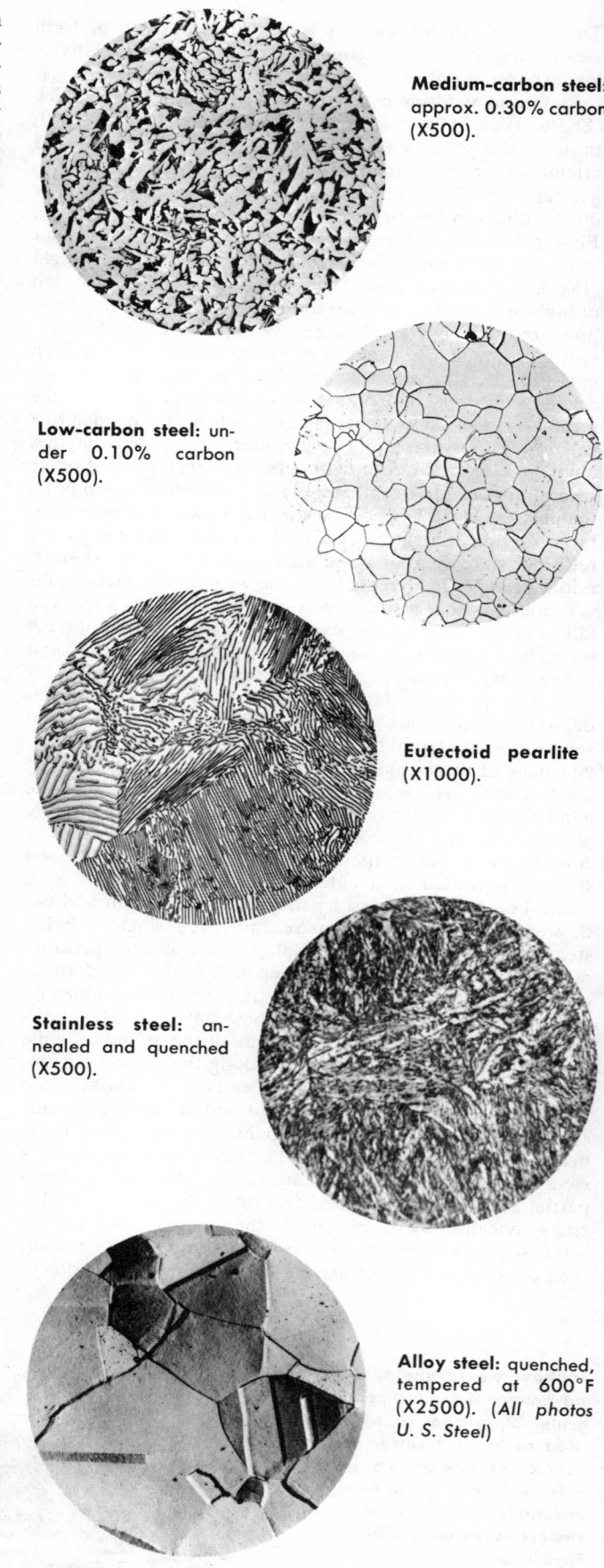

Medium-carbon steel: approx. 0.30% carbon (X500).

Low-carbon steel: under 0.10% carbon (X500).

Eutectoid pearlite (X1000).

Stainless steel: annealed and quenched (X500).

Alloy steel: quenched, tempered at 600°F (X2500). (*All photos U. S. Steel*)

tinguished from WROUGHT IRON, the low-carbon product of the puddling furnace, in not containing slag inclusions and in being hardenable (although it should be noted that steels of very low carbon content are likewise not hardenable). In modern practice steel is always produced in the fluid, molten state, whereas wrought iron at the hottest stage in its production cycle is a pasty, plastic mass from which the slag is expressed by squeezing and hammering.

The numerous useful properties that can be imparted to steel have made it today's most widely used metal and the most characteristic material of our present civilization. These properties include high ultimate strength and high yield point; hardenability by heat treatment; toughness; malleability and ductility when either hot or cold; resistance to corrosion; resistance to fatigue and shock; hardness; resistance to abrasive wear; machinability; weldability; and good magnetic and electrical properties. One or more of these properties can be made to predominate in a particular steel by varying the chemical composition of the steel and its heat treatment after fabrication. Before the era of close chemical control, steelmaking was largely an art; processes varied greatly from area to area depending on local tradition and on the quality of available raw materials (*i.e.* the local type of iron ore as well as the type of charcoal or coke). Steels are still classified broadly by the process of manufacture, and these processes are still to a large extent adapted to the most available raw materials; but the requested specifications of the finished product are also, today, an important factor in the choice of a process.

Steelmaking Processes: The starting material for modern steelmaking is iron from the blast furnace. This may be solidified in the form of pig iron or iron castings, or it may be used directly in the molten state, in which case it is called "hot metal." This material (which can generally be referred to as cast iron) typically contains about 3 to 5% carbon, 1% silicon, 1% manganese, 0.03 to 0.5% sulfur, and 0.1 to 0.8% phosphorus. Aside from cast iron, the other important raw material for steelmaking is steel or iron scrap. This usually enters the furnace cold, although it can be pre-melted separately in a cupola or electric furnace. The composition of scrap is quite variable, but in good practice it is well controlled by chemical analysis. The steelmaking process consists essentially in lowering the carbon content of the iron by oxidation, and lowering or adjusting the content of the other elements, while holding the metal in the molten state. To aid in this purifying operation a certain amount of slag or nonmetallic flux is usually added. Depending on the relative proportions of silica and lime in this flux, and in the refractory lining of the furnace, the process is classed as "acid" or "basic." It is desirable during the process to have all nonmetallic material separate cleanly from the molten steel and be eliminated with the slag layer. If this does not occur, the steel is referred to as "dirty," and is likely to be weaker and more brittle than it should be. The three major processes used in modern steelmaking are carried out, respectively, in the Bessemer, the open-hearth, or the electric furnace. Each furnace can be used with either acid or basic fluxes and furnace linings; and the electric furnace can be run with a neutral refractory lining when appropriate. Steel may sometimes be started in one type of furnace or converter and transferred to another for finishing. This is called duplex processing. See FURNACE.

In the BESSEMER PROCESS, invented independently by William Kelly (1852), an American, and Henry Bessemer 1855), an Englishman, molten iron is charged into a conical vessel called a converter, and air is blown through it. The silicon and manganese are converted to their oxides, which float to the top as slag, and the carbon is converted to carbon monoxide, which burns at the mouth of the converter with a

Air blast through molten pig iron in Bessemer converter oxidizes sulfur, silicon, and manganese—all impurities. Similarly carbon content is reduced, and steel results. Color of burning gases streaming from top of converter indicates to operator how far process has gone. (*Amer. Iron and Steel Inst.*)

Molten steel from open-hearth furnace runs into ingot mold. Man in foreground holds stopper rod, which is used to control flow of steel into mold. (*U. S. Steel*)

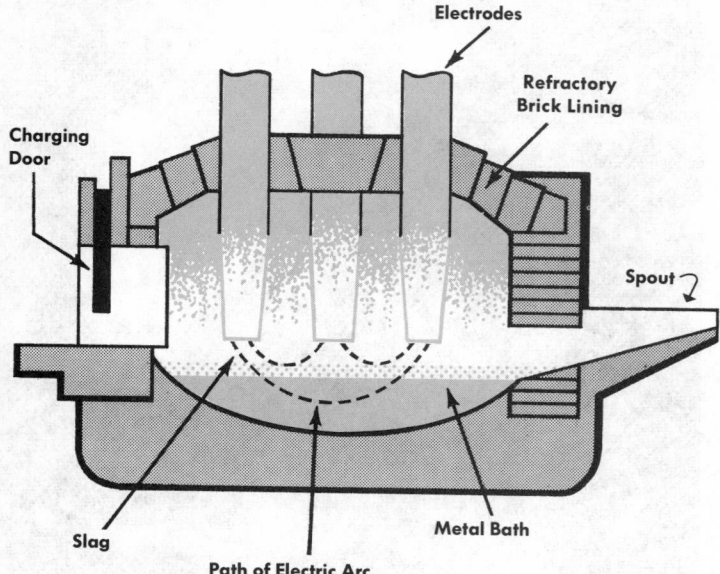

Electrodes

Refractory Brick Lining

Charging Door

Spout

Slag

Path of Electric Arc

Metal Bath

Electric-furnace capacity ranges from several hundred pounds to 200 tons. Preserving high degree of cleanliness and close control of temperature, electric furnaces are used to produce the bulk of stainless and high-alloy steels. (Bethlehem Steel)

successfully established in its modern form about 1890, avoids these difficulties. The charge of pig iron and scrap is melted in a reverberatory furnace under a layer of slag to which a pure grade of hematite (iron-oxide ore) is added. This acts as an oxidizing agent for both the carbon and the minor element impurities. The oxidation or "heat" is completed in about 8 hr, after which the required amount of recarburizing and deoxidizing alloy is added; the steel is then ready to be poured. Periodic chemical analysis during the heat affords good control of quality and uniformity. The open hearth is almost invariably run as a basic process and therefore is very effective in removing sulfur and phosphorus. Because the charge is not in direct contact with the heating fuel, and is not stirred violently, the finished steel tends to be clean and free of inclusions. At present the basic open-hearth process produces the major portion of the world's steel.

Most new steelmaking facilities use the recently developed, highly successful basic oxygen process. The furnace carries a basic refractory and is charged with hot metal, scrap, ore, and lime. A water-cooled lance blows pure oxygen down onto the molten charge. When the desired carbon content has been reached, the steel is poured and final adjustments are made in the ladle. High-quality steel is thus produced rapidly, the average blow taking less than 60 min. Tonnage produced per furnace per year is much greater than in the open-hearth process. Furnaces now being installed have rated capacities of about 300 tons. In 1966 the total basic oxygen steelmaking capacity in the U. S. A. was reportedly over 35 million tons per year.

The ELECTRIC-FURNACE process utilizes either a resistance or an induction furnace to melt and heat the charge (either scrap or pig iron). It has the great advantage of providing heat while avoiding contact with any unwanted combustion products in the flame, and since both the temperature and the

spectacular flame. When this flame subsides, indicating that the impurities are oxidized, the blow is stopped and the desired amount of carbon and deoxidizer is added in the form of a high-carbon alloy. The steel is then ready to be poured into ingot molds. In the U. S. A. the Bessemer process is invariably run with an acid-lined converter, which does not substantially reduce the phosphorus or sulfur content of the steel. These two elements can be eliminated by using a basic lining and adding lime to the slag. This basic Bessemer process, better known as the Thomas-Gilchrist process after its inventors, is widely used in Europe, where many of the ores are high in phosphorus.

The Bessemer process is rapid and inexpensive but has the inherent limitations of poor control and lack of flexibility. The OPEN-HEARTH PROCESS, invented in France in 1864 and

Pipe-mill control station: Operator in control pulpit oversees operation of continuous butt-weld pipe mill. Mills such as this can produce pipe of ½ to 4 in. diameter. (*U. S. Steel*)

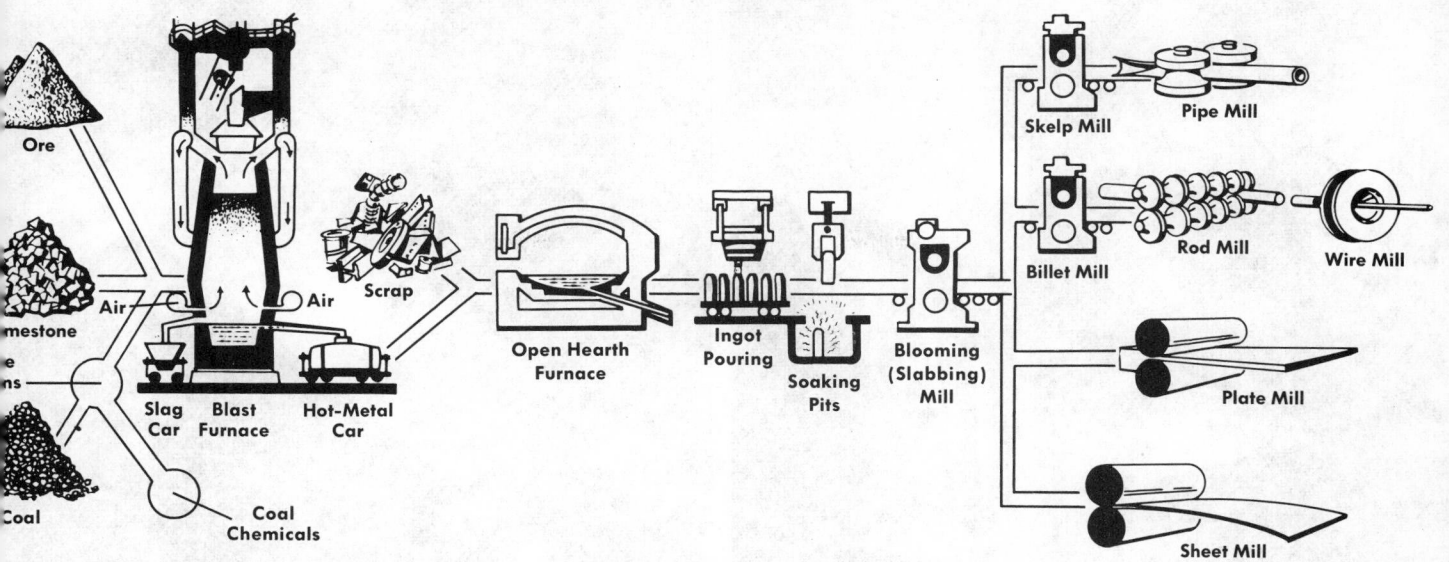

Ore

Air

Air

Scrap

Slag
Car

Blast
Furnace

Hot-Metal
Car

Coal
Chemicals

Coal

mestone

ns

Open Hearth
Furnace

Ingot
Pouring

Soaking
Pits

Blooming
(Slabbing)
Mill

Skelp Mill

Pipe Mill

Billet Mill

Rod Mill

Wire Mill

Plate Mill

Sheet Mill

Steel manufacture flow chart: Iron ore, coke, and limestone are successively fed into blast furnace to form alternate layers of each material. As blast furnace is continuously charged and operated, and alternate layers of material continuously descend shaft of furnace into combustion zone, "hot metal" or "hot iron" collects at bottom. Ordinarily, blast furnaces operate continuously for periods of 4 to 5 yr, being stopped only for repairs required by deterioration of furnace lining. The hot metal is collected in hot-metal cars or cast into ingots (pig iron) for further refinement into steel. Next, the open-hearth furnace is charged with lime-stone, iron ore, and steel scrap, and this charge is melted and the hot metal or pig iron added. By oxidation of the impurities of silicon, phosphorus, and manganese present in the hot metal, and by reducing percentage of carbon present (usually 4%) to desired level (usually less than 1%), steel is produced. It is then cast into ingots, which are reheated in soaking pits until a uniform temperature is achieved. At this point, steel in form of hot ingots is delivered to blooming mill, where ingots are elongated in readiness for further rolling into pipe, rod, or sheet form. Other finishing mills (not shown) produce rails and structural members.

composition of the contained atmosphere can be adjusted, it affords the highest degree of control. Most high-alloy steels and tool steels are made in the electric furnace.

Chemical Composition of Steel: Other than iron, the most important element in steel is carbon. In general, the higher the carbon content, up to about 0.83%, the greater is the ultimate tensile and yield strength of the steel. The ductility and weldability, however, decrease with increasing carbon content. Steels containing more than about 0.2% carbon can be greatly hardened by heat treatment. The relationship between carbon content and strength for typical steels, before heat hardening, is shown in the accompanying table.

RELATIONSHIP BETWEEN CARBON CONTENT
AND STRENGTH FOR TYPICAL STEELS

(before heat hardenings)

Type of Steel	Percent Carbon	Ultimate Tensile Strength in 1,000 lb/in.² (1,000 psi)	Yield Strength in 1,000 lb/in.² (1,000 psi)
Soft steel	0.03 to 0.10	45 to 50	25 to 30
Structural steel	0.25	60	37
Machinery steel	0.40	80	50
Spring steel	0.75	100	60
Tool steel	1.0	130	75
Cast iron	2.8 to 3.5	30 to 50	25 to 40

Each of the other elements commonly present in carbon steel has its typical effect on the processing characteristics and properties. Sulfur tends to prevent the slag from settling during the heat. It also causes the finished steel to be brittle when hot and therefore unsuitable for hot-rolling or forging. It does, however, make the steel free-cutting and easily machinable. Phosphorus increases the fluidity when molten, but makes the finished steel more brittle. Silicon decreases the incidence of blowholes (formed by the release of dissolved gas) in the finished ingots, and increases hardness. Manganese is an oxygen scavenger, and also overcomes the bad effects of sulfur by combining with it to form manganese sulfide. Oxygen, in the form of metallic oxides, has a harmful weakening effect. Nitrogen, in the form of nitrides, increases surface hardness and is sometimes added in a special heat treatment for this purpose.

The behavior and properties of steel are greatly dependent on the heat treatment it receives after fabrication, and are best understood in terms of phase relationships in the iron-carbon system. The thermodynamically stable phases of this system at room temperature are *cementite,* a hard brittle iron carbide (Fe_3C) containing approximately 6.7% carbon, and *ferrite,* which is pure alpha iron. Pure ferrite, on heating to 1,670°F, changes to gamma iron, a nonmagnetic allotropic form that remains stable to nearly 2,800°F, the melting point. Gamma iron and cementite form a eutectic mixture that melts at 2,066°F and contains 4.2% carbon. It is noteworthy that commercial cast irons melt in the range of 2,000 to 2,100°F, while steels melt in the range of 2,600 to 2,800°F. The solid phase which separates when a molten steel is cooled below the melting point is a solid solution of carbon in gamma iron called *austenite,* a name also applicable to pure gamma iron with no dissolved carbon. Austenite can hold up to 2% carbon in solid solution at 2,066°F, but if an austenite of this composition is cooled slowly it will separate out cementite. Dissolved carbon lowers the point at which gamma iron of the austenite phase transforms to alpha iron, and the eutectoid of this transformation occurs at 1,334°F and 0.83% carbon. The eutectoid forms a characteristic structure called *pearlite,* which consists of an intimate striated mixture of ferrite and cementite. Thus steels of less than 0.83% carbon, which have been cooled slowly or annealed so that the transformations are completed, consist of a mixture of ferrite and pearlite. Similarly, equilibrated steels of higher carbon content consist of a mixture of pearlite and cementite. If steels of moderate or high carbon content are cooled rapidly through the phase transformation temperatures, *e.g.* by quenching in water, the austenite changes to ferrite but the cementite is retained in supersaturated solution. The resulting

Removal of molds from red-hot steel ingots is being done by 150-ton stripper crane. Following this operation, ingots which have cooled on the outside are placed in soaking pits to be brought up to uniform temperature for rolling.

Steel slabbing mill "breaks down" ingot into a slab—the first step in the rolling of plates, sheets, and strip. Glowing ingot here is going through horizontal and vertical rolls of 45-in. mill. (*Both photos U. S. Steel*)

metastable phase has a characteristic needle-like structure and is called *martensite.* It is very hard and strong and is the desired component in cutting tools. The amount of martensite formed can be controlled by the rate of cooling. Oil quenching provides slower cooling than water quenching, and can produce *troostite,* another metastable phase, less brittle but almost as hard as martensite. Rapid quenching sets up internal strains in the metal. These can be relieved by tempering, which is heating to a temperature high enough to allow strain relief but too low to allow the cementite to precipitate. Tempering temperatures range from 400 to 1,200°F, depending on the steel's composition and the degree of hardness desired. Hardening by heat treatment can easily double the strength of steel and in many instances can increase it threefold or more; thus strengths of over 300,000 psi can be obtained by heat hardening. The strength of steel can also be increased by cold-working, *i.e.* forging, drawing, or rolling. This decreases the grain size rather than bringing about any phase changes, and is called "work-hardening." See METALLURGY.

Alloy Steels: Alloying metals used in moderate amounts form solid solutions and have relatively little effect on the critical points (phase-transformation points) of steel, but they can greatly decrease the *rate* of transformation. Thus austenite and other phases normally stable only at high temperatures can be retained intact in the finished steel. When present in higher percentages, an alloying metal may form its own carbides or other separate phases to contribute the desired special properties. Three major groups of alloy steels are the low-alloy structural steels, corrosion-resistant stainless steels, and high-speed tool steels.

In the low-alloy group the metals commonly used are nickel, manganese, silicon, chromium, molybdenum, and vanadium. NICKEL (about 3.5%) and MANGANESE (about 1.75%) produce smaller grain size and greater strength, with no loss of ductility. Steels of this type are used in bridges. Steels containing 12 to 25% nickel or 10 to 12% manganese remain austenitic on cooling and therefore cannot be heat-hardened. The manganese alloy known as Hadfield steel is extremely tough and abrasion resistant, and is used for bank vaults. Spring steel is made with 0.5 to 1.0% SILICON and 0.7 to 0.9%

manganese. Minor proportions of CHROMIUM and MOLYBDENUM, in the range of 1%, increase the tensile strength and hardness of steel. VANADIUM (up to 1%) is frequently used as an alloying element to improve hardenability; it is also one of the most powerful deoxidizers.

The stainless steels fall into three major groups—austenitic, martensitic, and ferritic. The austenitic steels, which are non-hardenable and nonmagnetic, contain 0.08 to 0.2% carbon, 16 to 24% chromium, and 6 to 20% nickel. The martensitic group, hardenable and magnetic, contain 0.1 to 1.2% carbon, 11 to 18% chromium, and 0 to 2.5% nickel. Ferritic stainless steels contain 0.08 to 0.35% carbon and 11 to 27% chromium.

High-speed cutting tools are made from a special class of alloy steels capable of maintaining a hard, sharp edge even when running at red heat (1,000 to 1,100°F). The principal alloying elements, present in quantities ranging from 10 to 30%, are TUNGSTEN, molybdenum, and COBALT. Tungsten may be used alone or with either of the other two elements. Cobalt and molybdenum are used only in combination. The basic steel to which these carbide-forming elements are added contains 0.7 to 1.5% carbon, about 4% chromium, and 1 to 5% vanadium.—*A. M. S.*

STEFAN-BOLTZMANN LAW: a statement of the way in which the temperature of a body influences the rate at which heat is radiated from it. The rate of radiation varies with the fourth power of the absolute temperature of a body; thus a body at 373° Kelvin (the boiling point of water) radiates $(373/273)^4$ or 3½ times as fast as one at 273° K (the freezing point of water).—*E. M. R.*

STEINER, JAKOB, 1796–1863, Swiss mathematician; b. Utzendorf. Although completely illiterate until the age of 14, he was taken at the age of 17 by Johann Heinrich Pestalozzi to the latter's school in Yverdon. Here he gained a love of mathematics and laid the foundation for a career as one of the world's greatest geometers. His work in the development of synthetic geometry was of the highest importance. He wrote several notable treatises dealing with the complete quadrilateral, projective ranges, and the theory of curves and surfaces of the second degree.—*H. C.*

STEINMAN, DAVID BARNARD, 1886–1960, American engineer; b. New York City. He was a specialist in the design and construction of long-span bridges. His study of bridge aerodynamics (effects of high winds on bridges) led to his being chosen as designer of the Mackinac Bridge, which connects upper and lower Michigan across the Straits of Mackinac. This 5-mi-long bridge, in its design and method of construction, is an engineering landmark. He was co-author of *Bridges and Their Builders* (1941).—*H. I. S.*

STELLAR PARALLAX: see PARALLAX, STELLAR.

STELLUTI, FRANCESCO, 1577–1653, Italian microscopist; b. Fabriano. He was perhaps the first to use a compound microscope. His pamphlet "Stellutus Lynceus Fabrianensis microscopio observavit" (1625) contained remarkable drawings of the bee as viewed through a microscope. Stelluti was a member of a group of scientists who formed the first regularized scientific society, the *Accademia dei Lincei* (1609).—*D. H. D. R.*

STEM: normally, the aerial organ of VASCULAR PLANTS, bearing leaves, buds, and sometimes flowers. It is organized into regions called *nodes* and *internodes,* a node being the point of leaf attachment and an internode the distance between adjacent leaves. In most plants the leaves are separated by internodes of varying lengths, but in some plants, *e.g.* dandelion, the internodes are so compressed that the adjacent leaves are in contact with one another and form leaf rosettes.

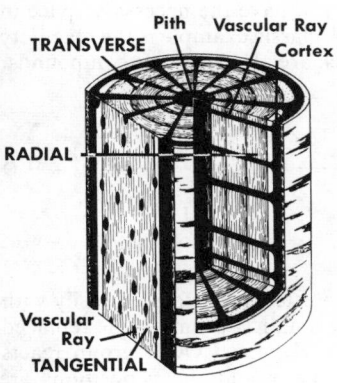

Woody stem: Cuts made in transverse, radial, and tangential planes show course of vascular rays. These bands, which radiate out from central pith, are composed of parenchyma, or food-storage tissue. (*From Whaley*)

The forward growth of the stem occurs at the *apical meristem.* This is a dome-shaped region of cells that undergo rapid cell division. The leaves originate as leaf primordia on the flanks of the apical meristem. The *terminal bud* of the stem includes these structures. The *lateral,* or *axillary, buds* develop in the angle between the leaf and the stem and may grow into branches. Buds that develop anywhere else on the stem are called *adventitious buds.*

The stem functions to support the leaves in the most favorable orientation in relation to the light. Raw materials, *e.g.* water and mineral elements, are transported by the vascular tissues of the stem to the leaves, and the manufactured foods, as sugars (see PHOTOSYNTHESIS), are conducted from the leaves to the rest of the plant.

Perennial vascular plants that have soft, herbaceous aerial parts commonly develop underground stems known as *rhizomes.* Rhizomes serve to help the plant survive unfavorable climatic conditions. Many grasses, sedges, and ferns live through the winter as rhizomes. Underground stems are differentiated from roots by the presence of nodes, internodes, and usually scale-like leaves. In some plants, *e.g.* iris, canna, and Solomon's seal, the rhizome is a fleshy storage organ. Horizontal, short, thick rhizomes, as in the white

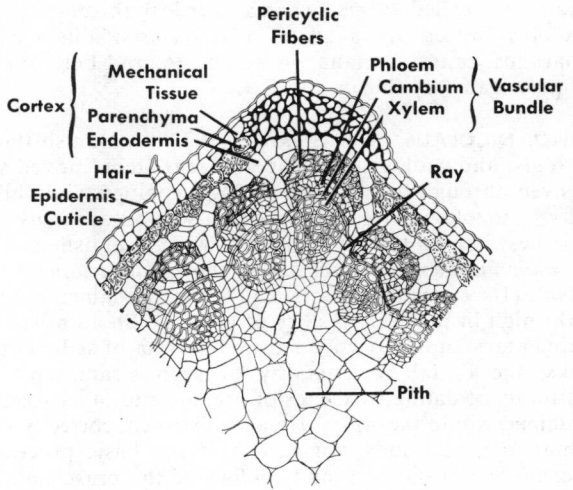

Portion of cross-section through stem of a herbaceous dicotyledon, alfalfa: Vascular bundles, arranged in definite circle, are composed of phloem (food-conducting tissue), cambium (growth tissue), and xylem (water- and mineral-conducting tissue). Pericycle fibers above vascular bundle serve to strengthen stem. Cells of cortex and of pith function as food-storage and supporting tissue. Cuticle and epidermis surround and protect functional tissues of stem. (*From Villee*)

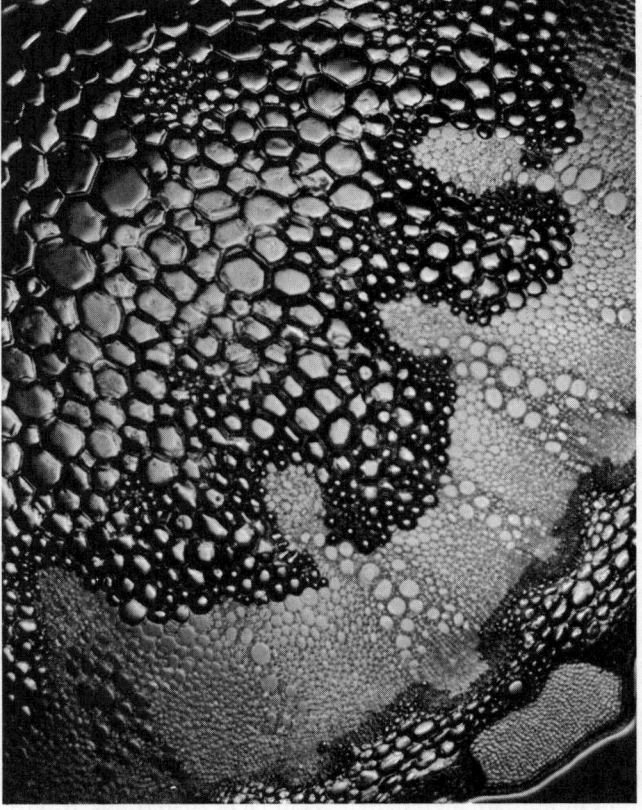

Stem of carrot—photomicrograph of portion of cross-section: Cells of cortex and pith appear as dark, glistening structures. Vascular bundles may be identified by the large, nearly rounded, very light-colored cells of the xylem tissue. Pericycle fibers form narrow, periodically arched band near periphery of stem, immediately beneath cortex. (*Carl Strüwe/from Monkmeyer*)

potato, are called *tubers,* whereas vertical rhizomes, as in gladiolus and crocus, are known as *corms.* Plants such as asparagus, canna, banana, white potato, and bent grasses are propagated by rhizomes.—*F. L.*

STENO, NICOLAUS (Niels Stensen), 1638–86, Danish-Italian zoologist and geologist; b. Copenhagen. Steno moved successively through the fields of zoology, geology, and philosophy to theology. His early research was on anatomy, but he is best known for his geological work, published in his *De solido intra solidum naturaliter contento dissertationis prodromus* (1669), which with its many new, fundamental ideas ranks high in the early history of geology. Steno noted the sedimentary and successive nature of strata of sedimentary rocks, the initial horizontality of such strata, and the possibility of dating by means of organic and other remains contained within the strata. He also observed, correctly, that mountain ranges may originate by three basic processes: volcanic action, faulting and folding of the crust, and the erosion of highlands.—*D. H. D. R.*

STEPHENSON, GEORGE, 1781–1848, English inventor; b. Wylam. An engineer for mine engines who investigated the possibility of using steam engines for moving loaded coal cars, he moved 30 tons at 4 mi/hr in 1814. After deciding that the gradients of the common roads precluded using steam-driven vehicles there, he concluded that railways of nearly level roadbeds must be built. An 8-mi railroad designed by him (1822) was put in use at the Hetton colliery. His Stockton line, which used an 8-ton locomotive that reached a speed of 16 mi/hr, was opened in 1825. His "Rocket" locomotive, which won an open competition (1829), was the type used on the Liverpool and Manchester Railway when it opened (1830). Stephenson devoted the rest of his life to the development of the English railway system.—*D. H. D. R.*

STEREOCHEMISTRY (or space-chemistry): a branch of chemistry that deals with the spatial arrangement of the constituent atoms of a molecule. The four valency bonds of the carbon atom were tacitly assumed by August Kekulé (1858) to lie in one plane; hence a flat, or two-dimensional, model for the molecule, as for example in the structural formulas of

$$\text{methane: } H—\overset{\displaystyle H}{\underset{\displaystyle H}{C}}—H; \text{ and lactic acid: } CH_3—\overset{\displaystyle H}{\underset{\displaystyle OH}{C}}—COOH.$$

Pasteur's work on tartaric acid (1848 onward) had shown, however, that this substance exists in two different, "stereoisomeric" forms, related as a right hand and a left hand. Solutions of these two forms of tartaric acid rotate polarized light to the right (dextro-rotatory) or left (levo-rotatory) respectively. See OPTICAL ACTIVITY.

Very many similar examples are known, including lactic acid. Molecules showing this peculiarity must necessarily be three-dimensional, as recognized in J. A. Le Bel and J. H. van 't Hoff's theory of molecular configuration (1874), according to which the carbon atom lies at the center of a tetrahedron with its four combined atoms or groups occupying the four vertices (see ASYMMETRIC CARBON ATOM). If the four groups are all different, as in lactic acid (CH₃, H, OH, and COOH), the molecule becomes asymmetrical and can exist in right- and left-handed forms. All organic molecules, whether symmetric (like methane) or asymmetric (like lactic acid), must therefore be pictured as tridimensional. Many consequences flow from this conception, which is of fundamental importance in understanding the reactions of organic

chemistry and in determining the geometric structure of complex (inorganic) ions. See ORGANIC CHEMISTRY.—*J. R.*

STEREOSCOPE AND STEREOVISION: a device and a process for perceiving objects in depth, *i.e.* in three dimensions. The two eyes, whose axes form an angle known as the *ocular parallax,* perceive slightly different images. In a manner not yet fully understood, the brain "compares" and "combines" the two separate sets of sensations, achieving a three-dimensional or stereoscopic perception of the object. In the stereoscope or stereoscopic camera, two lenses are employed, separated by 6.5 cm, which is the mean interoculary distance. The viewing device concentrates simultaneously on two dissimilar two-dimensional scenes, with the result that the observer achieves (and the camera registers) an additional dimension. In stereoscopic motion-picture photography, the separate pictures recorded with a two-lens camera are projected on the same screen but are polarized differently by a pair of Polaroid disks covering the projector lenses and arranged with their axes perpendicular to one another. The viewer wears glasses fitted with another set of Polaroid disks, also placed with their axes at right angles. The simultaneous perception of two different "flat" pictures yields the desired stereoscopic effect. Stereoscopic aerial photographs are of great importance in reconnaissance in making contour maps of inaccessible areas.—*A. E.*

STERIC HINDRANCE: in chemistry, a term which describes the situation in a molecule when its component atoms or groups are so arranged that they do not have the necessary space in which to function normally. A classic example is the reactivity of those carboxylic acids which are also aromatic compounds:

$$\underset{\text{Benzoic acid}}{C_6H_4(X)(Y)\text{C}=\text{O}—OH} + \underset{\text{Ethyl alcohol}}{C_2H_5OH} \longrightarrow \underset{\text{Ethyl benzoate}}{C_6H_4\text{C}=\text{O}—OC_2H_5} + \underset{\text{Water}}{H_2O}$$

This reaction (formation of an ester) is performed easily with benzoic acid. However, if the small H atom at x is replaced by the larger methyl group CH_3, the COOH group reacts with difficulty; and if both the x and the y positions are occupied by CH_3 groups, the reaction does not take place at all.—*Ru. M.*

STERN, OTTO, 1888–   , German-U. S. physicist; b. Sohrau, Ger. For his contributions to the development of the molecular-ray method and for his discovery of the magnetic moment of the proton, he received the 1943 Nobel prize. His work was extended by I. I. Rabi. Stern left Nazi Germany for the U. S. A. in 1933. He is a member of the National Academy of Sciences.—*D. H. D. R.*

STERNBERG, GEORGE MILLER, 1838–1915, U. S. bacteriologist; b. Otsego County, N. Y. His studies on the bacteriology of yellow fever, malaria, tuberculosis, and typhoid fever led him into research on disinfection. He was one of the originators of scientific disinfection. Sternberg was U. S. Surgeon General 1893–1902. —*D. H. D. R.*

George Miller Sternberg
(Culver Service)

STERN-GERLACH EXPERIMENT: see MOLECULAR BEAM.

STEROLS: a class of naturally occurring, solid, higher secondary alcohols widely distributed in plants and animals. They are in general colorless crystalline compounds, non-saponifiable, and soluble in certain organic solvents. Their molecules contain four hydrogenated carbon rings: three fused six-membered rings and one five-membered. With this basic structure, sterols are related to the naturally occurring animal bile acids, plant saponins and sapogenins, and some animal sex hormones. A large number of related, chemically modified compounds have been produced, some of which are effective chemotherapeutic agents. All sterols have this skeletal structure:

Cholesterol

The many related animal sterols are generically called *zoosterols,* and those occurring in plants, *phytosterols.* Cholesterol, $C_{27}H_{45}OH$ (a monounsaturated sterol), is the most thoroughly investigated animal sterol. It occurs in almost all normal body tissue, blood, and bile; it is particularly abundant in the adrenal glands and in brain and nerve cells, and is the major constituent of gallstones. It occurs both as the free alcohol and as the ester of higher fatty acids. Excessive deposits of cholesterol in the walls of the blood vessels are believed to produce a common form of "hardening of arteries," known as atherosclerosis. How this occurs is not well understood, but diets high in animal fats have been implicated. Cholesterol's eight asymmetric carbon atoms give rise to numerous isomers. The dihydro derivatives exist in the *cis-trans* isomeric forms, and some are known as dihydrocholesterol, epidihydrocholesterol, coprosterol, and epicoprosterol. Most of the simple related sterols may contain one, two, or three double bonds and additional methyl or ethyl groups. Intestinal bacterial action will also result in modified cholesterols in the body. In fact, microbiological reactions are frequently employed in the manufacture of sterol-based products. 7-Dehydrocholesterol lacks two hydrogen atoms and is found mainly in the skin layers.

The major plant sterols include sitosterol, which is isolated from wheat germ oil, cottonseed oil, tall oil, and soy bean oil; stigmasterol, also present in soy oil and other plants, which has the same skeleton as cholesterol with an additional ethyl group in the side chain; ergosterol, found in ergot of rye and yeast, which differs from cholesterol in having two additional double bonds and a methyl group in the side chain. Many other minor plant sterols exist. Both sitosterol and stigmasterol are useful in the manufacture of cortisone, hydrocortisone, and other steroid and adrenal hormones. Ergosterol and 7-dehydrocholesterol, on irradiation by ultra-violet light, yield products with vitamin D activity. A variety of other related sterols are present in yeasts, algae, and marine invertebrates.

The sterol nucleus is combined with certain sugar glycoside units forming two classes of plant saponins: the digitalis glycosides and certain other saponins have a powerful action on the heart; many non-cardiac-active saponins are isolated from plant sources. Partial hydrolysis yields the sapogenins, some of which also have an effect on the heart. These materials, many of which are isolated from the yam, yucca, and similar plants, are employed in the commercial manufacture of the corticoid and sex hormones. The bile acids of higher animals, *e.g.* cholic acid, are closely related members of the sterol family and are usually combined with specific amino acids. Only a few are sufficiently abundant for use in synthesis of therapeutic substances. Male and female sex hormones, produced by the testes and ovaries, belong to the class of sterol derivatives known as *steroids,* as do the adrenal cortex hormones, *e.g.* corticosterone. The structural similarity among these compounds is very striking:

Pregnenolone
(a sex hormone)

Corticosterone
(a corticoid hormone)

The liver is largely responsible for the synthesis of cholesterol. In a series of reactions, acetyl coenzyme A is converted to a 6-carbon compound, mevalonic acid. This compound loses one carbon atom to form an unsaturated 5-carbon isoprene unit. Six of these units condense together to form the unsaturated straight-chain hydrocarbon squalene. Squalene is then partially reduced and cyclized to form the basic 4-membered ring system of the sterols. Squalene is also the starting material for the synthesis of the β-carotenes and of the natural rubbers.—*R. W. F.*

STEVENS, JOHN, 1749–1838, U. S. engineer and inventor; b. New York City. He secured establishment of the Federal patent system (1790). In 1808 he constructed a paddle-wheel steamboat which operated on the Delaware River, and he operated the world's first steam ferry (1811), between Hoboken and N. Y. City. In 1825 he constructed the first U. S.-built steam locomotive, which attained 12 mi/hr. Stevens' son **Robert Stevens** (1787–1856) was the inventor of the universally used T-rail, the hook-headed spike, the balance valve, and the fishtail for rail joints.—*S. B.*

STEVIN (STEVINUS), SIMON, 1548–1620, Dutch engineer, mathematician, and physicist; b. Bruges, Belg. He wrote on military science, hydraulic engineering, navigation, geography, logic, astronomy, mechanics, and mathematics, as well as several nontechnical subjects. He discovered the hydrostatic paradox ("the pressure in a liquid depends only on depth and not on shape or size of the container"), introduced decimal fractions into arithmetic, and demonstrated the mathematical equivalence of the Ptolemaic and Copernican theories of astronomy. He also invented a carriage propelled by sails. His most famous work, *De Beghinselen der Weeghconst* (1586), is concerned with statics, and on its title page is a famous drawing representing Stevin's proof of the law of the inclined plane.—*D. H. D. R.*

STOCK: a mass of igneous rock formed from MAGMA intruded into overlying rock. Stocks are identical with BATHOLITHS except for being smaller in size, *i.e.* not over 40 mi² in area. The Henry Mts. of Utah were carved from a stock.—*J. Si.*

STOMACH: typically, in vertebrates, an enlarged saclike portion of the digestive tube. The mucous membrane that lines its walls contains glands which secrete hydrochloric acid (HCl) and the proteolytic enzyme pepsin. These substances are formed only in the vertebrates. The structures called stomachs in the invertebrates are not strictly comparable to the vertebrate stomach.

The stomach commonly has two regions: the *fundus,* which the food enters first, and the *pylorus,* which opens into the intestine. Walls of the fundus contain the glands that secrete a fluid containing HCl and pepsinogen, the latter being the inactive form in which pepsin is secreted. Pepsinogen is converted to pepsin by the action of HCl. In lower vertebrates, HCl and pepsin are secreted by the same cells, but in mammals the large parietal cells form HCl, while smaller "chief" cells form pepsinogen. Glands of the pylorus secrete a mildly alkaline fluid that contains no enzymes. Both parts of the stomach secrete mucus. The gastric juice is the composite fluid formed by the mixing of all of these secretions in the stomach. The HCl serves not only to activate pepsin, but also to provide the acidity necessary for its activity, to soften some types of fibers in food, and to restrain bacterial action. Pepsin initiates protein digestion, attacking certain specific peptide bonds in the protein molecules.

Gastric secretion is under control of a nervous network in the wall of the stomach. This network may be stimulated either indirectly by the vagus nerve from the brain or directly by the stretching of stomach walls. When the network is stimulated, its nerve endings liberate acetylcholine, which

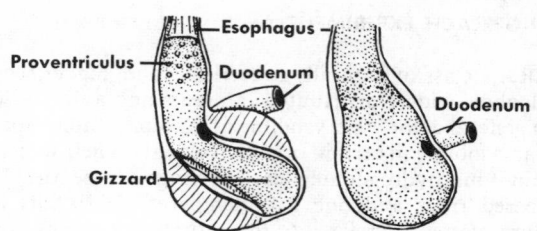

Stomachs of herbivorous and carnivorous birds compared: *Left*—Stomach of seed-eating bird, the turkey, has a distinct lower portion (gizzard or ventriculus) in which food is ground up by action of the thickly muscled walls, aided by grit which bird has swallowed. *Right*—Stomach of flesh-eating bird, the buzzard, is a single, thin-walled chamber. (*From Eaton, after Kingsley*)

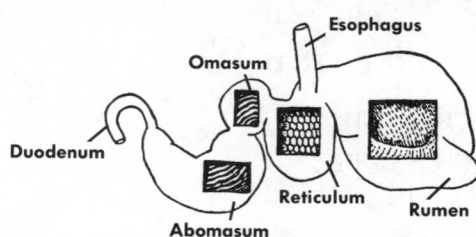

Stomach of ruminant, or cud-chewing, animal (in this case a cow) consists of several chambers. Swallowed food passes through esophagus into large rumen, where it is temporarily stored. Later, food mass is regurgitated in small portions, rechewed, reswallowed, and enters first the reticulum and then the omasum. In both these chambers, food mass is subjected to abrasive action. Finally, food passes to abomasum, where actual digestion takes place. (*From Eaton, after Flower and Lydekker*)

stimulates parietal, chief, and pyloric cells to secrete. The action on parietal and pyloric cells may be direct, but the action on the chief cells probably involves formation in the stomach walls of a polypeptide known as gastrin, which in turn stimulates the chief cells. In normal digestion, the nervous network is stimulated first from the brain; a stimulus may be the sight or smell of food, or anything else that has become associated with food by "conditioning." (The discovery of the CONDITIONED RESPONSE was made by Pavlov in the course of studies of gastric secretion in dogs.) The first, or cephalic, phase of secretion is reinforced when food enters the stomach and stimulates the nerve net directly (gastric phase). Finally, as the partly digested food is passed from stomach to intestine, a reflex stimulation through the brain and vagus nerve causes gastric secretion to continue (intestinal phase). Gastric secretion is inhibited by a polypeptide hormone called enterogastrone, which is formed in the walls of the intestine in the presence of certain foods and is carried by the blood stream to the stomach; this inhibition of secretion probably causes the sensation of fullness.

Regular peristaltic contractions of the stomach occur most of the time and are greatly enhanced during digestion. These contractions serve to mix the stomach contents and to break up the food by mechanical action. The pyloric sphincter is

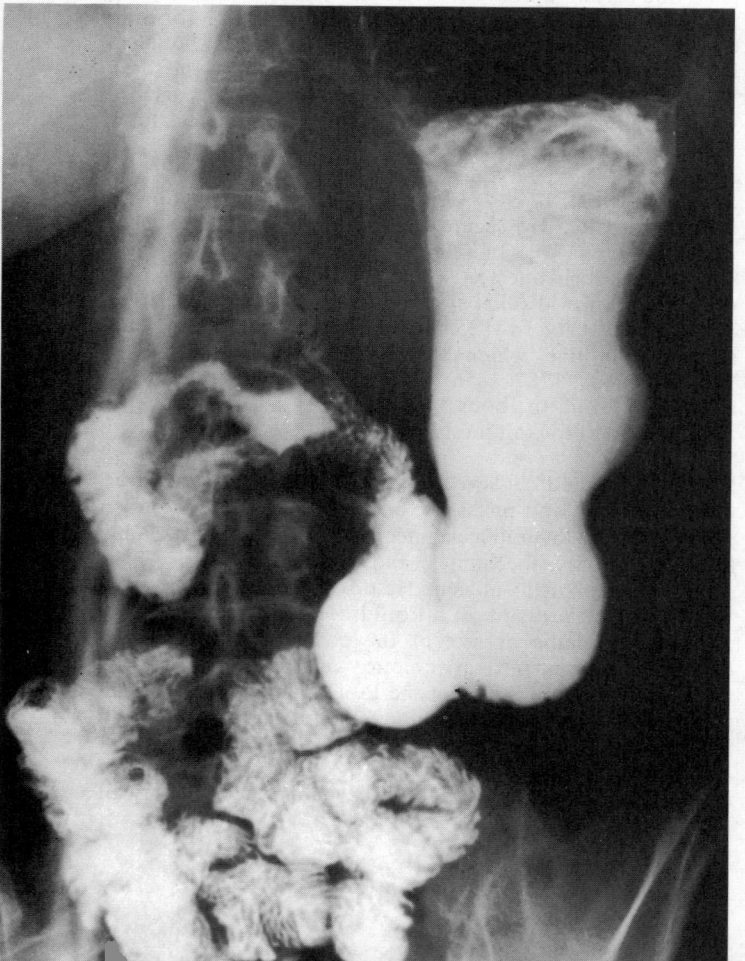

X-ray of stomach (large white mass) and portion of small intestine (coiled structure, *lower left*): Patient has ingested barium sulfate, a radio-opaque substance, which makes soft tissues within the body visible on the x-ray plate. When this photo was made, the stomach had begun to empty. The fundus (uppermost portion) appears in faint outline just above body of stomach. J-shaped lower part is pyloric region; it leads to pylorus which, in turn, opens into first portion of small intestine, the duodenum. (*A. John Geraci from Nancy Palmer*)

normally closed, but when the stomach contents reach the consistency of a thin paste, the sphincter opens as each contraction wave reaches it, allowing part of the contents to pass into the small intestine. The sensation of hunger arises when vigorous contractions occur in an empty stomach; the contractions probably occur in response to a decrease in sugar content of the blood, and to stimuli from the brain.

In crocodiles and birds, the pyloric region of the stomach is modified into a gizzard by a great increase in musculature and replacement of the mucous membrane by a tough covering; the gizzard holds small pebbles that serve as grinding tools. In ruminant mammals such as the cow, the stomach has four chambers. Newly eaten food first enters the large *rumen,* or paunch, where the food is stored and subjected to vigorous bacterial action. At intervals, some of the food is passed to the reticulum, whence the solid portions are returned to the mouth as the cud for further chewing. The fluid portion moves into the *omasum* with its many partitions, and thence into the *abomasum,* which contains the glands secreting HCl and pepsin and hence corresponds to the fundus of other stomachs. See DIGESTION.—*B. T. S.*

STORM: (1) In meteorology, a transient local disturbance of the atmosphere, severe enough to cause damage or threaten life. The word is generally used with prefixes such as snow, hail, thunder. (2) In geomagnetism, a world-wide disturbance of Earth's magnetic field, attributable to solar disturbances, *e.g.* flares. Magnetic storms cannot be detected by the senses, but often affect long-distance radio communications. (3) In hydrology, the space and time distribution of rainfall.—*O. G. S.*

STÖRMER, CARL FREDRIK, 1874–1957, Norwegian mathematician and geophysicist; b. Skien. His research included work in mathematics, the theory of the auroras, mother-of-pearl clouds (1948), noctilucent clouds (1933), and cosmic rays. Störmer's studies of the motion of charged particles in magnetic fields showed the feasibility of explaining the polar auroras as caused by such particles, and magnetic storms as caused by a "ring current" of charged particles circling Earth. He was a fellow of the Royal Society.—*D. H. D. R.*

STRAIN: see STRENGTH OF MATERIALS.

STRATIGRAPHY: in geology, the study of layered rocks or strata (see SEDIMENTARY ROCK). Stratigraphy deals with the description and naming of rock units, determination of relative age by means of position in the sequence, correlation with rocks of other areas, and the deciphering of Earth's history.

The earliest stratigraphic observations were made by Nicolaus Steno in 17th-cent. Italy. He noted that in a given series of rocks, the layers at the base must be oldest (*law of superposition*). He also observed that sediments are usually deposited as horizontal layers (*law of horizontality*). We know now, in addition, that sheets of sediment are continuous over more or less extensive areas, but wedge out against the sides of the depositional basin (*law of original continuity*). Superposition establishes the relative age of strata, while lateral continuity permits correlation by rock type (lithology) over broad areas.

Early in the 19th cent. an English canal engineer, William Smith, discovered that fossils could be used to correlate strata where differences in lithology were slight. It was soon learned that a definite sequence of fossil assemblages existed, and that parts of this sequence could be found repeated in many places (*law of faunal succession*). Previously rocks could

be correlated only in a single depositional basin, where the beds were continuous, but the use of fossils permits correlation between separate basins without physical continuity of the strata. Stratigraphic *zones* based on fossils were established, each zone being characterized by a distinctive assemblage distinguishing it from the underlying and overlying zones.

The first job of the stratigrapher in a new area is to construct a geologic map showing the various kinds of rocks exposed in the area, and their distribution. He studies the rocks in the field, notes their lithology, determines their order, and observes their structure. The rocks are classified, usually on the basis of gross lithology. The basic lithologic unit is the *formation,* defined as a mappable body of rock. Formations may be lumped together to form a *group,* or subdivided into *members*. In a given area, the record preserved by the rocks is either continuous (see CONFORMITY) or discontinuous and incomplete (see UNCONFORMITY).

From the completed map, cross sections are constructed to determine the structure of the area. From the cross sections and map, the geologic history of the area can be reconstructed. The rocks of the mapped area may be correlated with those of adjacent areas by means of lithology and stratigraphic position (lithostratigraphic correlation).

Study of the fossils collected in the area permits correlation with more distant areas, and with the standard of the geologic column (see GEOCHRONOLOGY). For purposes of correlation, index FOSSILS, which are often restricted to a single zone, are most useful. Stratigraphic units based on fossils are called biostratigraphic units, and a correlation based on index fossils is a biostratigraphic correlation. Such a correlation indicates that the deposits were laid down at the same time, although their lithology may be quite different (see FACIES). A biostratigraphic correlation is, then, essentially a time-stratigraphic correlation. The basic biostratigraphic unit is the *zone*. One or more zones constitute a *stage,* several stages make a *series,* and two or more series form a *system*. These terms all refer to rocks of specific age. For geologic time itself, another set of terms is used. The length of time represented by a stage is an *age;* that represented by a series, an *epoch;* that represented by a system, a *period.* Periods are grouped into *eras* (see GEOLOGICAL TIME CHART).

The modern stratigrapher uses many tools. In addition to the geologist's hammer, there are instruments which provide detailed information about the rocks encountered in drilling a well, methods for detecting slight differences in lithology, and techniques for the study of fossils too small to be seen with the naked eye. Stratigraphy provides important clues in the search for petroleum, uranium, and other natural resources as well as useful information to engineering geologists selecting construction sites.—*W. Ha.*

STRATOSPHERE: the lower part of the outer region of Earth's atmosphere, characterized by relatively little change of temperature with height. Originally, the name was given to the whole of the atmosphere above the TROPOSPHERE, the lowest part of the atmosphere in which temperature, on the average, decreases with height. The depth of the stratosphere is between 12 and 15 mi and its lower boundary (the TROPOPAUSE) varies from about 13 mi above sea level at the equator to about 6 mi at the poles. The stratosphere is very cold (between −45° and −75°C) and dry, and often has strong winds that form circulation patterns more regular and persistent than those in the troposphere. Clouds and precipitation are rare, and these features, together with the decreased air resistance resulting from the lower density, make the stratosphere suitable for high-speed flying.—*O. G. S.*

STREAMLINE: see AERODYNAMICS; FLUID FLOW.

STRENGTH OF MATERIALS: an engineering discipline concerned with stress analysis, which determines internal stresses caused by external forces, and strain analysis, which determines internal strains and over-all deformations. Study of stress, strain, and material properties results in the ability to analyze members or complete structures for strength, deformation, and stability. The loading (total stress and strain) may be either static or dynamic, the member may be either "determinate" or "indeterminate," and the material may be either elastic or inelastic.

Stress is the intensity of force on a unit area. For example, if a rod is put into tension by pulling at each end with a force P, the stress at any cross-section will be uniformly distributed over the cross-sectional area and will have magnitude $\sigma = P/A$. (See Fig. 1.) Since stress is force divided by area, its units may be lb/in.^{2}, tons/ft^2, and so on.

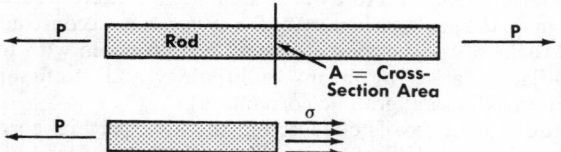

Fig. 1: Rod in tension: Normal stress (σ) on rod is determined by the intensity of the applied force divided by unit cross-sectional area (A).

Normal stress, σ, refers to stress which acts in a direction perpendicular to the area involved, *e.g.* tension or compression. *Shear stress*, τ, denotes a stress which acts in a direction tangent to the area in question. (See Fig. 2.)

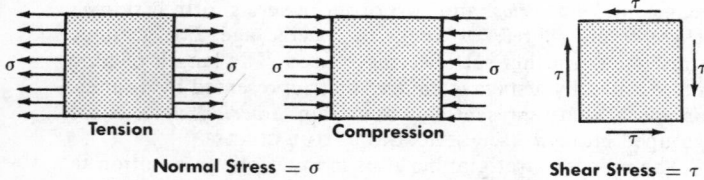

Normal Stress $= \sigma$ Shear Stress $= \tau$

Fig. 2: Normal and shear stresses.

Strain is a measure of the amount of deformation a body undergoes when it experiences stress or temperature change (see THERMAL STRESS AND SHOCK). In the previous example of the rod under tension, the material will stretch a certain amount, and the change in length divided by the original length is called the strain (ε): $\varepsilon = \Delta L/L$. (See Fig. 3.) Since

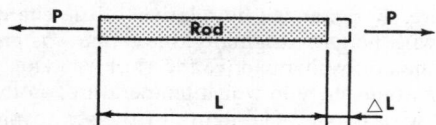

Fig. 3: Elongation of a rod under tension is an example of normal strain, which is calculated by dividing the original length of the rod (L) by its elongated length ($\triangle L$).

strain is length divided by length, it is dimensionless, but it is usually expressed in inches per inch. *Normal strain* corresponds to tension or compression stresses, and *shear strain* (γ) accompanies shear stress (Fig. 4).

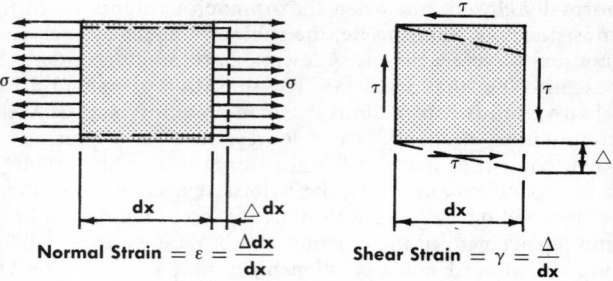

Normal Strain $= \varepsilon = \dfrac{\Delta dx}{dx}$ Shear Strain $= \gamma = \dfrac{\Delta}{dx}$

Fig. 4: Normal and shear strains.

For elastic materials an experimental plot of stress versus strain is practically a straight line; therefore, strain is proportional to stress (HOOKE'S LAW). The proportionality factors between stress and strain are called the *modulus of elasticity, E,* for normal stress and the *modulus of rigidity, G,* for shear stress. These moduli are useful for computing de-

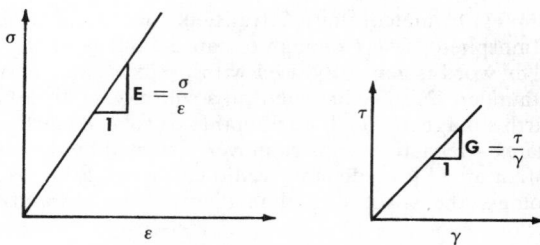

$E = \dfrac{\sigma}{\varepsilon}$ $G = \dfrac{\tau}{\gamma}$

Fig. 5: Stress-strain graphs: for an elastic material under normal stress (*left*) and under shear stress (*right*).

formations in strain analysis. With the rod under tension (Fig. 1), the elongation may be computed from the force, the dimensions, and the elastic property E. Thus, $\Delta L = \varepsilon \cdot L = \sigma/E \cdot L = PL/AE$.

The influence of temperature variation and the concept of *statical indeterminacy* may both be explained in a single example. With the rod contained between two unyielding restraints at each end, let the temperature rise an amount T. The rod tends to lengthen because of the temperature change, but it is restrained from doing so. This tendency to expand gives rise to an unknown compression force in the rod. (See Fig. 6.) If it is imagined that the restraint at one end is removed temporarily, the rod will expand freely and

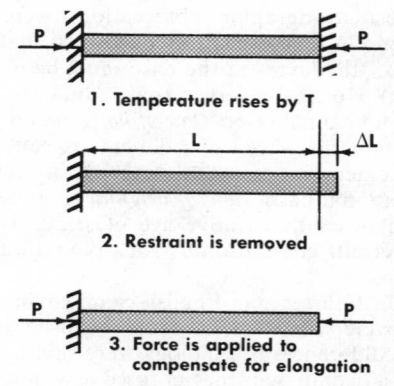

1. Temperature rises by T

2. Restraint is removed

3. Force is applied to compensate for elongation

Fig. 6: Stages in calculation of an indeterminable force arising from a change in temperature.

the elongation can be computed by use of another property of the material, called the *coefficient of thermal expansion, α.* This coefficient is the proportionality factor expressing the fact that for most engineering materials the free temperature strain is proportional to the temperature change (Fig. 7).

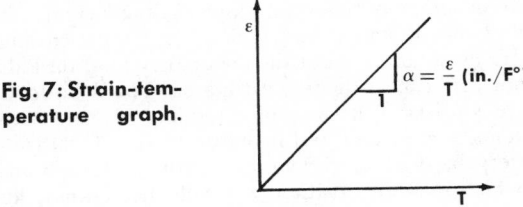

Fig. 7: Strain-temperature graph.

$$\alpha = \frac{\varepsilon}{T} \text{ (in./F°)}$$

Using the coefficient of thermal expansion, the free elongation of the rod may be computed: $\Delta L = \varepsilon \cdot L = \alpha TL$. To return the rod to its original restrained length, a compressive force P must be applied, straining the rod in compression an amount equal to the free thermal expansion: $P = \sigma \cdot A = \varepsilon EA = \alpha TEA$. The important idea here is that a force has been solved which is indeterminable, or "statically indeterminate" (unless, that is, the properties of the material are precisely known).

Flexure theory deals with laterally loaded members (beams). If the rod used in previous examples is placed upon two end supports and a load is applied laterally, internal normal (flexure) stresses and shear stresses arise. For a typical loading the internal stresses vary in intensity. The accumulative effect of all the flexure stresses on a particular cross-section is called the *bending moment* at that location, and the total effect of the shear stresses is called simply the *shear*. (See Fig. 8.) Since the top of the beam is stressed in compression

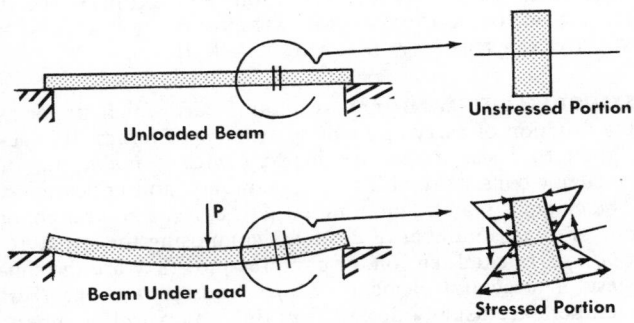

Fig. 8: Flexure of a beam.

and the bottom in tension, the upper region shortens and the lower region elongates, producing an over-all deflected shape. Internal stresses and deflections of determinate or indeterminate beams can be found by the methods of strength of materials.

Torsion theory involves the analysis of shear stresses in members which are subjected to twist, or torque. Torque applied to a rod causes internal shear stresses (τ), and adjacent cross sections rotate slightly with respect to each other. The cumulative effect of the shear stresses on a cross section equals the torque, and the additive effect of relative rotations

along the length of the rod equals the total angle of twist, or torsional deformation. (See Fig. 9.)

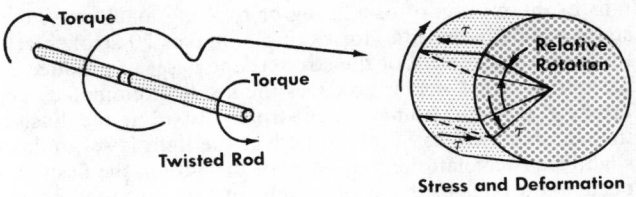

Fig. 9: Torsion in a rod.

Column theory is devoted to the study of the stability of long members subjected to compression forces. A compression force applied to a short rod may be increased in magnitude until the material is squashed or crushed. But a compression force applied to a long rod may only be increased to a limiting ("critical") load, at which time the member will buckle sidewise. This phenomenon may be observed by pressing on the ends of a flexible plastic ruler or similar object. (See Fig. 10.)

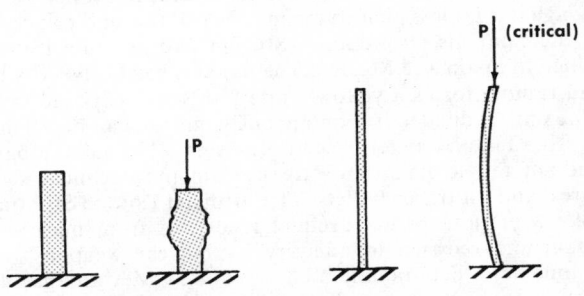

Fig. 10: Effects of compression: on a short rod (*left*) and on a long rod (*right*).

Experimental stress analysis is the determination of stresses, *e.g.* in structural members and machine parts, by means of precise measurements of unit strain at one or more points on a model or prototype. Strains to be measured may be produced by application of stresses, temperature changes, or other influences. They may be elastic or inelastic, static (constant), or dynamic (varying) in nature. The technique of measuring strain in a body consists basically of the accurate measurement of the distance between two closely spaced points at a specific location before, after, or during a particular test. The change in distance between the two points, divided by the original distance between them, is the unit strain at that location.

Strain may be measured with mechanical, optical, and electrical instruments. Electrical strain gages make use of the principle that resistance, capacitance, and inductance vary with change of length or location of a probe. The optical phenomenon of PHOTOELASTICITY is often used in experimental stress analysis, particularly with models of irregularly shaped machinery or of objects with irregular stress patterns, *e.g.* airfoils or turbine blades. Optically isotropic transparent solids, *e.g.* glass or celluloid, will exhibit visual internal patterns of deformation when subjected to stress. The degree of deformation is proportional to the stress, and may be measured. Transparent models may be subjected to loads and the resulting stress distribution thus analyzed.—*W. W.*

STRESS: see STRENGTH OF MATERIALS.

STRIKE: see DIP AND STRIKE.

STROBOSCOPE: a lamp that produces brief pulses of light at a controllable frequency, or a shutter that permits only brief pulses to be seen. Stroboscopes are used to observe the details of the motion of oscillating or rotating machinery. If a sewing-machine needle, for example, makes 20 strokes/sec, the frequency control of the stroboscope is set to produce 20 flashes/sec. An observer now sees the needle illuminated very briefly at the same point in each stroke, providing the illusion that the motion has been stopped. If the light is set to flash slightly slower than the frequency of the action, the flash will occur a bit later in the stroke each time, giving the impression of very slow motion. In this way, the detailed behavior of the sewing-machine thread, for example, can be studied and photographed.—*D. H. L.*

STRÖMGREN SPHERE: see H II REGION.

STRONTIUM: an alkaline-earth metallic element (Sr); at. no. 38; at. wt 87.62; valence 2. The existence of strontium was reported by several researchers in the late 18th and early years of the 19th cent. but final confirmation did not come until 1808, when Sir Humphry Davy isolated the metal by electrolysis of fused strontium chloride. Strontium very much resembles calcium and barium in chemical properties, although it is far less plentiful than either; it is found principally in the minerals strontianite ($SrCO_3$) and celestite ($SrSO_4$), mined in Spain and Mexico. The metal is hard, silvery-white, and rapidly forms a yellow oxide film when exposed to air. When finely divided it spontaneously ignites, and hence must be stored in an oxygen-free liquid or gas. The salts impart a brilliant red to flame and are used in pyrotechnics, signal flares, and on tracer bullets. The artificial isotope Sr^{90} (half-life, 28 yr) is a fission product recovered from nuclear reactors and released in quantity by nuclear weapons. This isotope has a beta-radiation energy of 0.54 Mev and has thus been employed as a radiation source for thickness gages and as a tracer for calcium in chemical processes. Because it can virtually replace calcium, Sr^{90} is extremely dangerous in fallout from nuclear explosions. Long-term exposure results in substantial substitution of Sr^{90} for calcium in the human body and destruction of the blood-cell-forming bone marrow (99% of the calcium in the human body is found in the bones). —*R. B. T.*

STRUCTURAL DESIGN: the process of laying out, proportioning, selecting materials for, and devising joining methods for the parts of a total structure so that it can efficiently, safely, and economically perform its function of bearing loads or enclosing space. Civil engineers are primarily concerned with design of fixed structures, *e.g.* buildings, bridges, dams, hydraulic structures, piers, towers, roadways, and storage tanks. Other branches of engineering deal with structural design of aircraft, missiles, ships, pressure vessels, machines, and electrical equipment. Typical procedure in structural design consists of (1) determination of design criteria—the intended function of the structure and the loads to be resisted; (2) establishment of the general layout of the structure as dictated by the functional requirements; (3) proposal of several possible solutions which conform to the general layout; (4) preliminary design of the several possible solutions; (5) selection of the most desirable alternative after comparison of the preliminary designs with respect to strength, rigidity, function, economy, and appearance; (6) detailed structural design of the best alternative.

The designer combines experience with judgment to proportion the parts of a structure; then he makes an approximate analysis of the structure under the required loads in order to check his initial estimate. In the preliminary design stage the loads acting on the structure, including its own estimated weight, are determined as accurately as possible. Next the preliminary design is subjected to detailed structural analysis, and finally the dimensions of its members and details of connections are determined. If the weights and properties of the members so determined differ significantly from the preliminary design, the detailed design procedure must be repeated until they agree.

Loads for which structures are designed vary greatly as to type and accuracy of determination; *e.g.* the weight of water to be contained in an elevated tank of certain dimensions can be precisely calculated, but the occupancy load on a dance-hall floor can at best be only estimated. The dead load of a structure consists of the weight of roofing, flooring, architectural items (*e.g.* plaster and insulation), structural framing, machinery, and other permanent fixtures. Live loads are those which vary in position, *e.g.* vehicles, cranes, human beings, furniture, files, book stacks, merchandise, and industrial equipment. If live loads are applied suddenly (impact), the stresses in a structure are higher than if the same loads are applied statically. Many other varying and irregular loads may have to be considered. Snow load is the weight of snow accumulated on roofs or decks. Wind load is the pressure acting perpendicular to external surfaces exposed to the force of the wind. Pressure is normally positive (greater than atmospheric) on the windward side and negative (below atmospheric pressure) on the leeward side of a structure. Earthquake loads are inertia forces which interact between a structure and the surface of the earth when the ground shakes during an earthquake; the magnitude of the force depends upon the dead weight of the structure, its rigidity, and the severity of the earthquake. Blast loads are the result of a shock wave impinging upon a structure, causing transient air pressures of high intensities. Vibration loads are inertia forces which build up in a structure when it resonates with some cyclic disturbance, *e.g.* a motor with an eccentric rotor. Fluid pressures exert hydrostatic and hydrodynamic forces on structures, and soils impose active, passive, and friction forces. Other forces are those due to CREEP, temperature change (see THERMAL STRESS AND SHOCK), shrinkage, settlement, and various types of motion. See ARCHITECTURAL ENGINEERING; ARCHITECTURE; STRENGTH OF MATERIALS; STRUCTURAL THEORY AND ANALYSIS.—*W. W.*

STRUCTURAL ELEMENT: any structural part which performs the function of carrying loads or systems of forces. It is designed to resist its service loading with a maximum of efficiency consistent with safety, economy, and appearance. The element may be the total structure, *e.g.* a solid arch, or one of a large number of elements composing the structure. *Links* carry axial tension, or compression; they are the simplest of structural elements. *Shafts* transmit torsion. *Truss* members are usually designed as links. Flexural members, on the other hand, support lateral loads and are called *planks, joists, stringers, beams,* or *girders,* according to their relative strengths. *Columns* are subjected primarily to longitudinal compression, which makes them susceptible to lateral buckling. Flexible *cables* are stressed in pure tension only, but their geometric curves are determined by the loads. *Arches* resist applied loads chiefly in compression with a minimum of bending. Structural *diaphragms* transmit shearing forces in their own planes by virtue of their two-dimensional stiffness. *Plates* having general supports bend in two directions and have strength which is greater than that for one-way flexure. *Shells* are curved surfaces of small thickness and great strength due to their geometric efficiency; they resist distributed forces through tension, compression, and shearing stresses, with some secondary flexure.— *W. W.*

LINKS

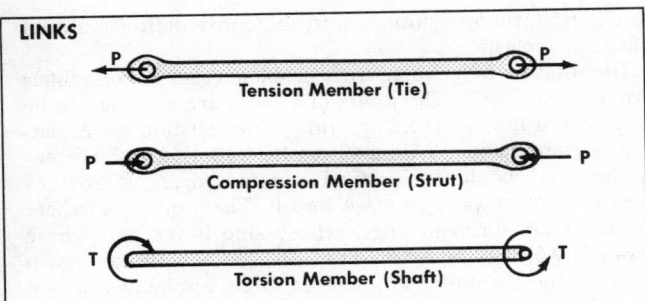

Tension Member (Tie)

Compression Member (Strut)

Torsion Member (Shaft)

TRUSS MEMBERS

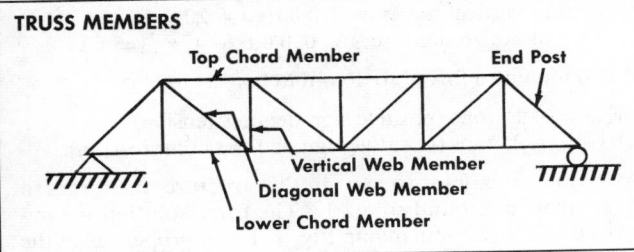

Top Chord Member

End Post

Vertical Web Member

Diagonal Web Member

Lower Chord Member

FLEXURAL MEMBERS

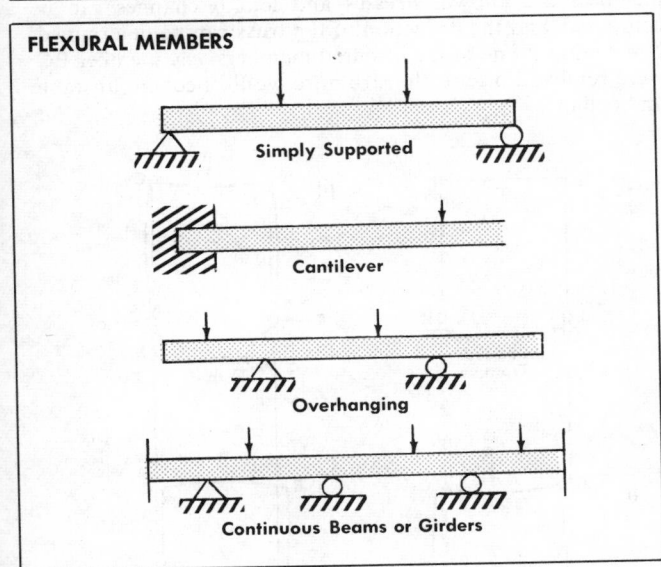

Simply Supported

Cantilever

Overhanging

Continuous Beams or Girders

COLUMN

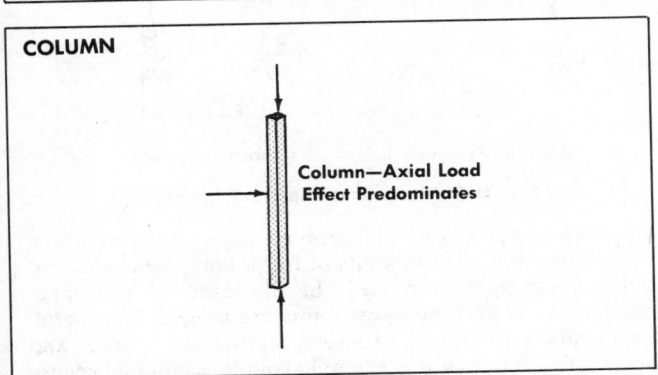

Column—Axial Load Effect Predominates

CABLES

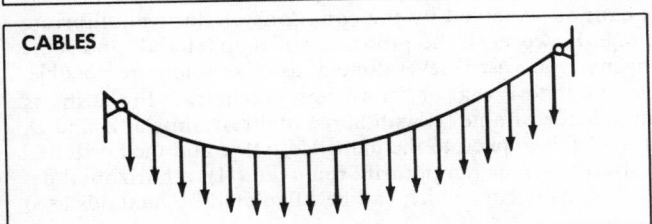

ARCHES

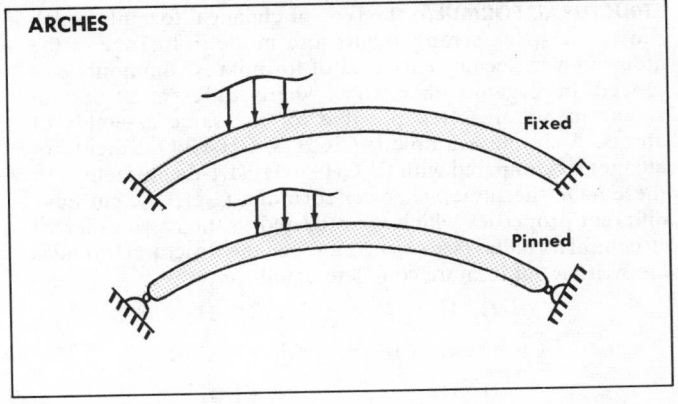

Fixed

Pinned

DIAPHRAGMS

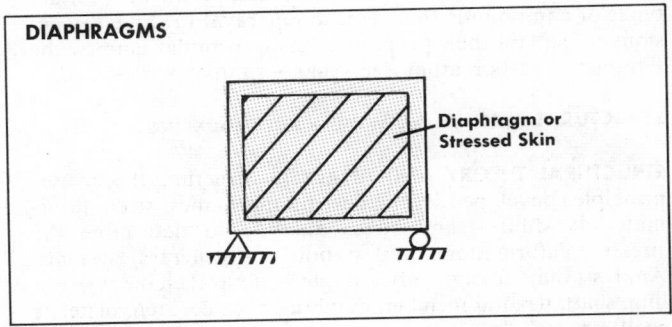

Diaphragm or Stressed Skin

PLATES AND SLABS

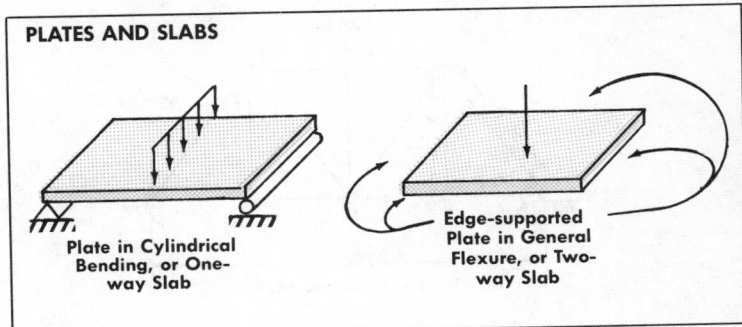

Plate in Cylindrical Bending, or One-way Slab

Edge-supported Plate in General Flexure, or Two-way Slab

SHELLS

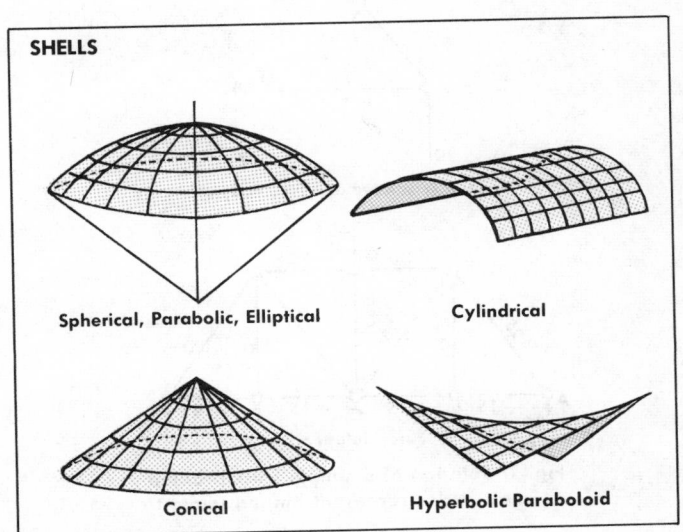

Spherical, Parabolic, Elliptical

Cylindrical

Conical

Hyperbolic Paraboloid

STRUCTURAL FORMULA: the type of chemical formula which shows the space arrangements and mode of linkage of the atoms in a molecule. This kind of formula is commonly employed in organic chemistry, where different structural arrangements are often possible for the same assembly of atoms. A simple example is $ClCH_2—CH_2Cl$ (1,2-dichloroethane), as compared with $Cl_2CH—CH_3$ (1,1-dichloroethane); these have the same *molecular* formula, $C_2H_4Cl_2$, but have different properties which are reflected in their two different structural formulas (see ISOMERS). When the structural formulas are written out in more complete detail—

$$Cl-\overset{\overset{\displaystyle H}{|}}{\underset{\underset{\displaystyle H}{|}}{C}}-\overset{\overset{\displaystyle H}{|}}{\underset{\underset{\displaystyle H}{|}}{C}}-Cl \qquad Cl-\overset{\overset{\displaystyle H}{|}}{\underset{\underset{\displaystyle Cl}{|}}{C}}-\overset{\overset{\displaystyle H}{|}}{\underset{\underset{\displaystyle H}{|}}{C}}-H$$

—they are sometimes referred to as *graphic* formulas. The use of the structural formula is especially important with certain types of compounds that require portrayal in three dimensions to explain their properties. Such formulas employ the tetrahedral carbon atom (see STEREOCHEMISTRY).—*Ru. M.*

STRUCTURAL MODELS: see MODELS AND MODELING.

STRUCTURAL THEORY AND ANALYSIS: Structural theory uses principles developed in engineering mechanics, strength-of-materials studies, and stress analysis to determine the stresses, deformations, and stability of structural systems. Analysis may involve only a single structural element (*e.g.* a link, shaft, flexural member, diaphragm, cable, arch, plate, or shell) or a whole system of structural elements (*e.g.* a truss, frame, floor system, or roof system). The type of loading may be either static or dynamic, and the construction material elastic or inelastic.

The solution of a simple truss problem (Fig. 1) exemplifies structural analysis. The joints of a truss are assumed to be hinged, and the members are links which sustain either tension or compression. With a 40-ton load applied at the center of the truss as shown, vertical reaction forces of 20 tons must exist at support points A and E. The joint at A (where the members form an angle whose sine is 0.8 and whose cosine is 0.6) may be isolated as a free body with the known reaction and the unknown member forces applied as shown. By writing two equations of static equilibrium,

Sum of vertical forces $= 0 : 0.8\,F_{AF} + 20 = 0$
Sum of horizontal forces $= 0 : 0.6\,F_{AF} + F_{AB} = 0$,

the two unknown forces are found to be:

$F_{AB} = +15$ tons (positive sign denotes tension)
$F_{AF} = -25$ tons (negative sign denotes compression).

Proceeding from joint to joint in the structure, the forces in all members are found similarly. The force solution is summarized in the accompanying Fig. 1. If the properties of the members are known, stresses and length changes can be computed, and the deflection of the truss can be determined. Notice that if one of the essential members, *e.g.* member BC, were removed or cut, the structure would become unstable and collapse.

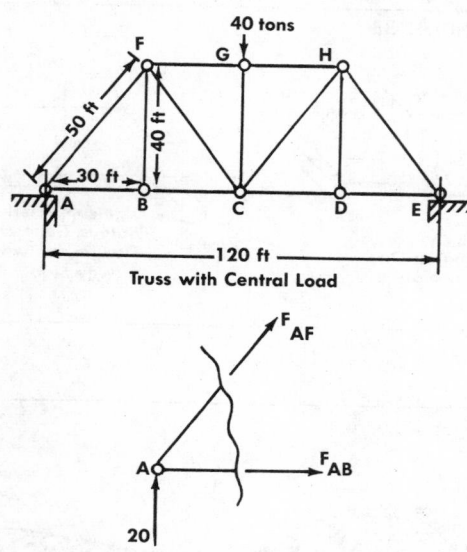

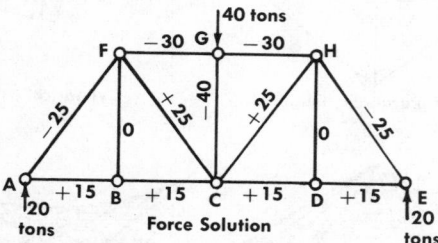

Fig. 1: Solution of a simple truss problem.
(Small circles represent hinged joints.)

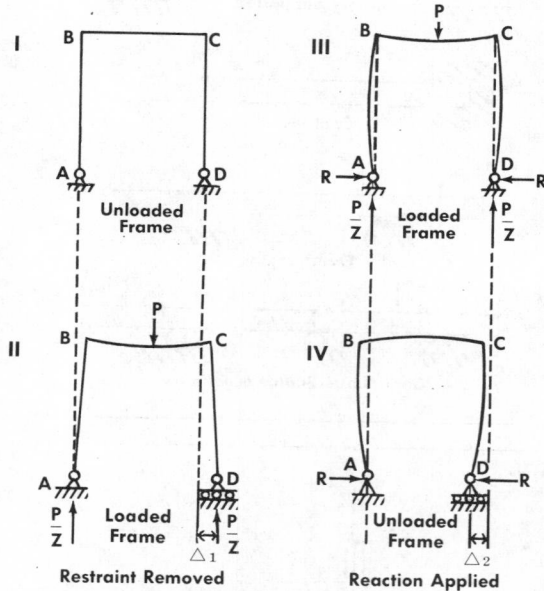

Fig. 2: Analysis of a one-story frame.

A more complex structural problem is presented by a one-story frame (Fig. 2). The joints of frames may be considered to be either rigid or hinged. In this example the upper joints are rigid and the lower joints are hinged. In general, the members of frames experience both axial forces and flexure. The frame in this example is indeterminate because it cannot be solved by the equations of static equilibrium alone. However, if the properties of the materials and some ingenuity are used, several methods of solution are possible. One method is that of "consistent geometry." Fig. 2 shows an unloaded frame (I) with horizontal restraints at *A* and *D*. If load *P* is applied to the unloaded frame and the horizontal restraint at *D* is temporarily removed (II), a horizontal deflection Δ_1 occurs which can be calculated by methods used in analysis of STRENGTH OF MATERIALS. If the horizontal restraint is reapplied to the loaded frame (III) and the load then is removed from the frame (IV), then—on the hypothesis that the horizontal reaction force is applied to the unloaded modified structure (IV)—a deflection Δ_2 may be computed in terms of R. For the geometry to be consistent, the two deflections must be equal: $\Delta_1 = \Delta_2$. This equation can be solved for R, and the remainder of the structure is then determinate.—*W. W.*

STRUVE, FRIEDRICH GEORG WILHELM VON, 1793–1864, German-Russian astronomer; b. Altona, Ger. He observed double stars at the Dorpat Observatory and published the results of his work in his *Catalogus 795 stellarum duplicium* (1822) and *Catalogus novus generalis stellarum duplicium et multiplicium* (1827), which recorded a large number of doubles. Later he participated in longitude determinations. He founded and directed the Central Observatory of the Russian Empire at Pulkovo (1839), and was succeeded there by his son, **Otto Wilhelm von Struve** (1819–1905; b. Dorpat, Latvia). Otto was director of the Pulkovo Observatory 1862–89. For his determination of the constant of precession, he was awarded the gold medal of the Royal Astronomical Society of England. He continued his father's cataloguing of double stars and published a number of studies of the motion of comets. He was a fellow of the Royal Society and an associate of the U. S. National Academy of Sciences.—*D. H. D. R.*

STYRENE: a compound made in large quantity for the manufacture of polystyrene plastics. It is a VINYL COMPOUND,

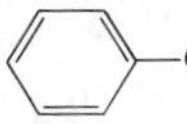

$$\text{\Large \phenyl}-CH\!=\!CH_2.$$

Its other chemical names, based on its structure are phenylethylene and vinylbenzene. Styrene, a liquid, is present in coal tar, but is made commercially in a process of several steps from benzene and ethylene.—*Ru. M.*

SUBLIMATION: see CHANGE OF STATE.

SUBMARINE CANYON: a conspicuous valley extending across a continental shelf from near shore to deep water, becoming broader and deeper at the off-shore end, and often having tributary valleys. So great are the scale and ruggedness of these valleys (they resemble river valleys) that they are called "submarine canyons." An example is Monterey Canyon off central California, which starts almost in the surf zone and 50 mi offshore reaches a depth of 9,000 ft. Explanations of these huge features as based on erosion by submarine water currents in present times, or by streams operating on exposed areas when the sea level was somewhat lower during the great glaciations, have not proved satisfactory. Possibly they were formed by subaerial erosion in pre-Miocene times when the continental margins stood much higher, and have been kept open by "turbidity currents" of suspended sand moving downslope.—*M. S.*

SUBMISSION: see DOMINANCE-SUBORDINATION.

SUBSIDENCE: see ISOSTASY.

SUBSTITUTION REACTION: see HYDROCARBON.

SUBTRACTION: see ARITHMETIC.

SUCCESSION: in biology, the gradual replacement of plant and animal species by others on a given site, during the course of invasion and settlement of vegetation. The principal cause of succession is that species suited to invade the original site are unable to continue when the habitat becomes more densely settled. Thus a COMMUNITY "spoils" its own habitat, preparing the way for new settlers. The soil improves, humus is formed, root systems use minerals from deeper layers; thus the habitat is progressively better utilized. Successions are classified according to the original substrate: water (successions in marshes, bogs), rock (colonized by lichens and mosses), sand (pioneered by dune grasses). Pioneer communities are followed by a consolidation stage such as meadow. Where climate permits, woodland and forest then become established, first with trees able to invade unforested habitats (subclimax), later replaced by shade-loving species as a *climax community* (see FOREST). Succession may at first progress from year to year, then slow up as the community becomes more complex and integrated. Many areas take several centuries to reach climax condition. In others, succession is set back or blocked by fires, grazing, poor drainage, and other factors.

Succession should not be confused with the change in vegetation following climatic changes, *e.g.* following Pleistocene glaciation.—*K. L.*

SUESS, EDUARD, 1831–1914, Austrian geologist, b. London, Eng. He stressed the importance of world-wide crustal movements in geological history, representing the crust as a pattern of stable blocks between which weaker portions are crumpled into mountains by horizontal forces. His writings about Earth's surface, *Das Antlitz der Erde* (1885–1907) and other books, have dominated subsequent work on tectonics. Professor at the Univ. of Vienna (1857–1901), he was a recipient of the Copley medal (1903) of the Royal Society, of which he was a fellow.—*D. H. D. R.*

SUGAR: in everyday parlance, *sucrose,* the common table sweetening; among physicians and biological scientists, *glucose,* the sugar of the blood; among chemists, any of a group of chemically related compounds (including glucose and sucrose) which belong to the larger class of carbohydrates. In the last sense, sugars are present in every living organism and as a group are the most abundant of organic materials on earth. When pure, sugars are white crystalline solids, readily soluble in water. Many have a sweet taste.

Simple sugars (*monosaccharides*) are classified according to structure as polyhydroxy aldehydes (*aldoses*) or polyhydroxy ketones (*ketoses*):

HCO	CH$_2$OH
HCOH	CO
HOCH	HOCH
HCOH	HCOH
HCOH	HCOH
CH$_2$OH	CH$_2$OH
Aldose	Ketose
(glucose)	(fructose)

They may be further classified according to the number of carbon atoms in their molecules, *e.g.* trioses (three carbon atoms), tetroses (four), pentoses (five), hexoses (six), etc. Glucose and fructose, shown above, are hexoses. The bulk of sugar in nature occurs in combined form. Thus sucrose (see structure, Fig. 3, page 1147) is a *disaccharide* with one molecule each of the simple sugars glucose and fructose; cellulose is a large polymer containing as many as 2,000 to 3,000 glucose units joined to form a single molecule. Small polymers (with up to 10 monosaccharide units per molecule) are termed *oligosaccharides;* larger polymers are termed *polysaccharides.*

Glyceraldehyde, $CH_2OH \cdot CHOH \cdot CHO$, is the smallest molecule which exhibits all the common properties of the sugars and is considered to be the simplest true sugar. Glyceraldehyde possesses (1) an aldehyde group, —CHO, which is responsible for the characteristic ability of sugars to reduce certain reagents such as Benedict's alkaline copper sulfate solution (used in urine tests for diabetes mellitus), (2) a secondary alcohol group, =CHOH, which has four different substituents on the carbon atom (see ASYMMETRIC CARBON ATOM) and thus confers on solutions of glyceraldehyde the ability to rotate a beam of plane polarized light (see OPTICAL ACTIVITY), and (3) a primary alcohol group, —CH_2OH, to terminate the chain. Glyceraldehyde is the prototype or parent compound of the aldoses. An isomer of glyceraldehyde, dihydroxyacetone, $CH_2OH \cdot CO \cdot CH_2OH$, is similarly the parent of the ketoses, in which the ketone group, =CO, is the reducing group. Glyceraldehyde and dihydroxyacetone are the only possible trioses.

Compounds like glyceraldehyde that have an asymmetric carbon atom exist in two isomeric forms which are usually identical in chemical reactivity and in other physical properties but which rotate a beam of polarized light in opposite directions. The two forms of glyceraldehyde are depicted below:

```
      CHO              CHO
     HOCH             HCOH
     CH2OH            CH2OH
  L-glyceraldehyde  D-glyceraldehyde
```

Historically, the designations L- and D- were made solely on the basis of optical activity, L- referring to the form rotating polarized light to the left (*laevo*), and D- to the right (*dextro*). However, the configurations or relative positions of the hydroxyl groups in these two forms of glyceraldehyde have lately been established in an absolute way, and the designations L- and D- have structural meaning irrespective of optical activity: all sugars with terminal groups which may be written

```
|
HCOH
CH2OH
```
, as in the case of D-glyceraldehyde, are D-sugars;

and those which may be written
```
      |
    HOCH
    CH2OH
```
, as in L-glyceraldehyde, are L-sugars. The great majority of naturally occurring sugars belong to the D- series; the enzymes of living organisms usually act on only this one isomer.

Dihydroxyacetone, the parent ketose, does not have an asymmetric carbon atom and thus does not exhibit optical activity. However, the next larger ketose, the four-carbon erythrulose, $CH_2OH \cdot CHOH \cdot CO \cdot CH_2OH$, has D- and L- forms with terminal groups arranged like those of the respective glyceraldehydes. Because each of the secondary alcohol groups, =CHOH, can have two configurations, the number of possible sugars becomes very great as chain length is increased. The table lists the sugars having up to six carbon atoms in the chain. Points to note are: (1) ketoses and aldoses of the same number of carbon atoms are isomers; (2) each listed compound, except dihydroxyacetone, has both a D- and an L- form; and (3) compounds are arranged horizontally according to their structural relationships. There is no theoretical limit to the chain length of sugars (heptoses, octoses, and nonoses have been synthesized in the laboratory), but above six carbon atoms only one compound, the seven-carbon ketose, D-sedoheptulose, is known to be of great biological significance (see PENTOSE PHOSPHATE PATHWAY). Sugars with a chain length of five or more carbon atoms ordinarily do not exist to any great extent in a linear structure like that shown for aldoses and ketoses. Instead they

SUGARS HAVING UP TO SIX CARBON ATOMS IN CHAIN

Aldoses

Aldotriose	Aldotetroses	Aldopentoses	Aldohexoses
glyceraldehyde	threose	xylose	glucose
	erythrose	lyxose	mannose
		ribose	allose
		arabinose	altrose
			gulose
			idose
			galactose
			talose

Ketoses

Ketotriose	Ketotetrose	Ketopentoses	Ketohexoses
dihydroxyacetone	erythrulose	xylulose	fructose (gluculose)
		ribulose	psicose (allulose)
			sorbose (idulose)
			tagatose (galactulose)

form rings as a result of interaction and chemical union of their reducing group, —CHO or =CO, with one of the hydroxyl groups on another carbon atom of the same molecule. Among organic compounds in general the most stable rings are those containing five or six atoms, and sugars form rings of this size. Sugars with five-membered rings are called *furanoses;* those with six-membered rings, *pyranoses.* Fructose in the furanose form and glucose in the pyranose form are represented in Fig. 1. Both compounds are depicted in two

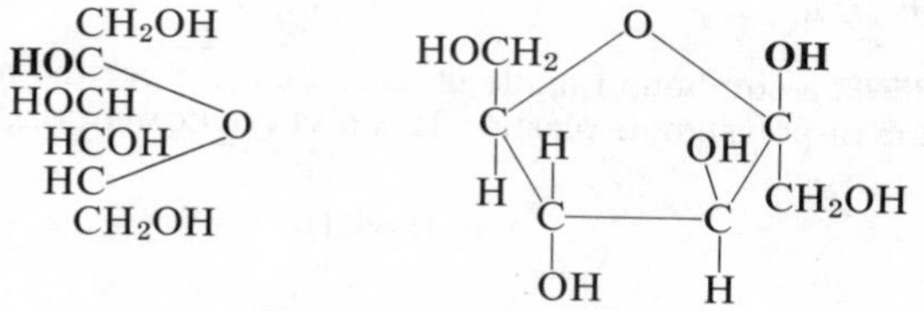

Fructose (furanose form)

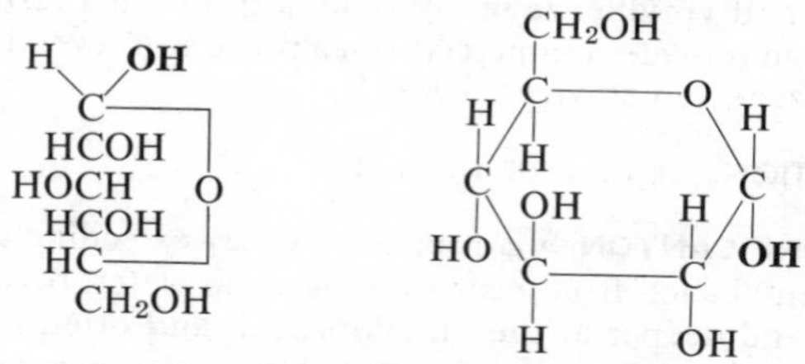

Glucose (pyranose form)

Fig. 1

ways. The structure to the left more clearly shows the relationship between the ring structure and the linear form of the same molecule; the one to the right more accurately shows the three-dimensional relationships among all the groups in the molecule. All sugars that can form stable rings exist in solution as an equilibrium mixture of a small proportion of the linear form and a large proportion of the ring form; they may undergo chemical reaction in either form.

With the closure of the ring, a further possibility for isomers is introduced into the sugar structure. The reducing carbon atom of the linear form becomes, in the ring form, an asymmetric carbon atom—it now has four different substituents—and the two isomers corresponding to the two positions of the hydroxyl group (OH) relative to the ring are possible. These positions are designated α and β. The great significance of the α and β forms of glucose and other sugars is best illustrated by a comparison of the structures of starch and cellulose. Starch—the principal carbohydrate foodstuff of man—is a polymer of α-glucopyranose units; cellulose, which is useless to man as a foodstuff, is a polymer of β-glucopyranose. See Fig 2.

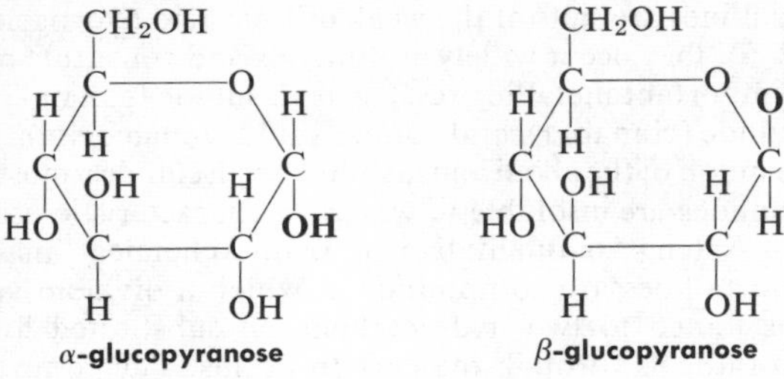

α-glucopyranose   β-glucopyranose

Fig. 2

The reactions which sugars undergo in the laboratory and in living organisms are characteristic of their functional groups: they react either as aldehydes (aldoses), ketones (ketoses), or alcohols (all sugars). Sugar aldehyde or ketone groups are relatively easily oxidized or reduced, giving rise respectively to acids or alcohols:

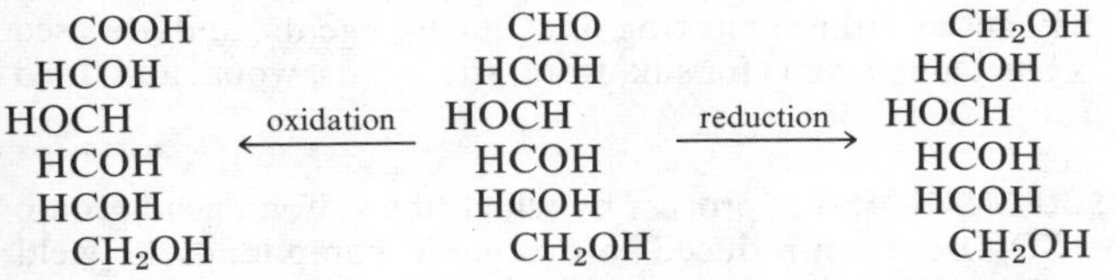

Gluconic Acid   Glucose   Sorbitol (Glucitol)

Enzymes present in many cells and tissues may also oxidize the terminal —CH_2OH group without concomitant oxidation of the reducing group. The reaction is illustrated for glucose in the pyranose ring form:

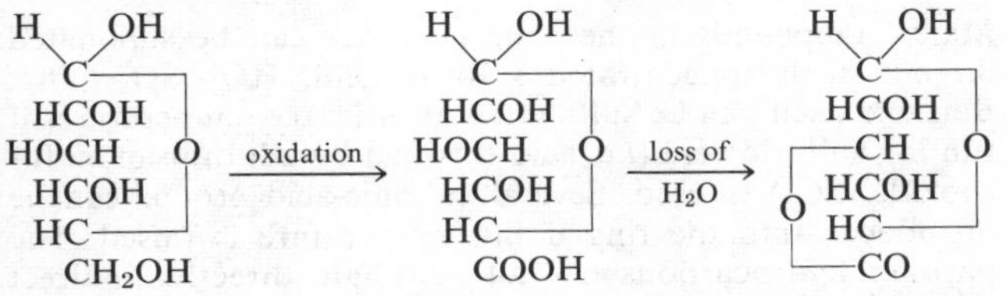

Glucose   Glucuronic Acid   Glucuronolactone

Uronic acids may form a second ring in the same molecule as indicated. This is a type of ester formation (see below). The most important reactions of the sugar alcohol groups, aside from their participation in ring formation, are (1) reactions with acids to form esters and (2) reaction between two sugars to form glycosides.

Sugar esters of phosphoric acid are present in every living cell; phosphate esters of glucose and its derivatives are intermediates in the cellular conversion of glucose to lactic acid in GLYCOLYSIS, while phosphate esters of ribose and deoxyribose are structural components of nucleic acids.

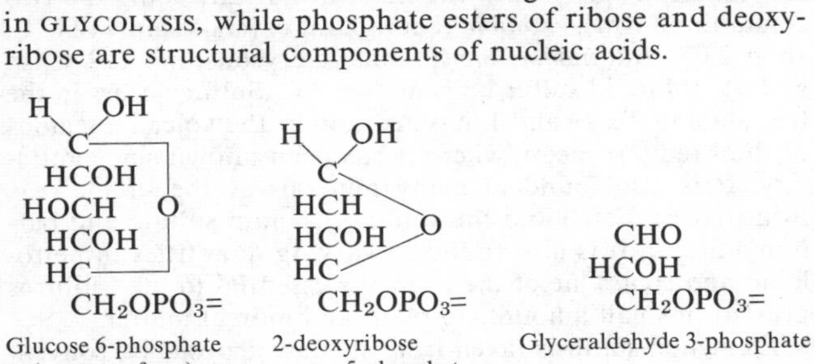

Glucose 6-phosphate (pyranose form)   2-deoxyribose 5-phosphate (furanose form)   Glyceraldehyde 3-phosphate

Glycosides are the most plentiful variety of combined sugar to be found in nature; the glycosidic bond is the means by which the monosaccharide sub-units of such compounds as lactose (milk sugar), sucrose (cane sugar), starch, glycogen, and cellulose are held together. In essence, the glycosidic bond occurs between two sugar hydroxyl groups by the elimination

of water (R'—OH + R—OH → R'—O—R + HOH). However, one of the two hydroxyl groups is always the group produced on the reducing carbon atom of a linear sugar when it closes into a furanose or pyranose ring. Fig. 3 illustrates typical glycosidic bonds. Particular points to be noted are (1) the two different positions of the glycosidic bond indicated by α or β; (2) that both hydroxyl groups used to form the bond in sucrose were on reducing carbon atoms; and (3) that maltose and isomaltose differ solely as to which carbon atom of the sugar molecule on the right is used in the glycosidic bond.

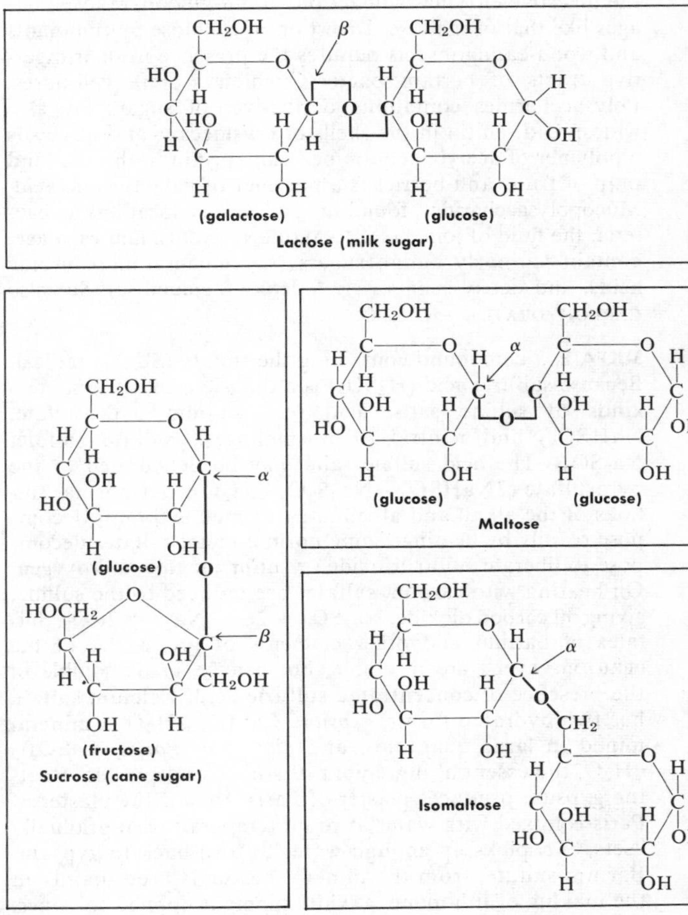

Fig. 3

The pathways for synthesis of glycosidic bonds in the cell involve many enzymatic steps and the phosphate esters of the sugars as intermediates. Degradation is simpler. A variety of specific enzymes found in plant and animal tissues and in microorganisms catalyze the addition of water to the glycosidic bond (hydrolysis) with the formation of free monosaccharides.

Digestion of starch and glycogen involves hydrolysis by amylases, enzymes secreted by the salivary glands and pancreas, to yield maltose, which is then hydrolyzed to glucose by an intestinal glucosidase. Intracellular metabolism of glycogen involves a phosphorylase and a debranching glycosidase.

Polysaccharides are found nearly everywhere and in many varieties in nature. The storage carbohydrates of plants (starch) and animals (glycogen) are polymers of α-glucopyranose units. Starch is a mixture of two polymers: *amylose,* in which 200 to 300 glucose units are joined by bonds like that of maltose into a linear chain; and *amylopectin*, in which short amylose-like chains are held together by bonds like that of isomaltose to form a highly branched structure. Animal glycogen resembles amylopectin and is even more highly branched.

Cellulose, the single most abundant organic substance in the world, is a polymer of β-glucopyranose units. Dextran, which is produced by bacteria and has found some use as an emergency substitute for blood plasma, is a polymer of α-glucopyranose units joined by bonds like that of isomaltose. Neither of these substances can be digested by man because the digestive enzymes will act only on α-glucopyranose linkages like that of maltose. Digestion of cellulose by ruminants and wood-eating insects requires the presence in their digestive tracts of certain bacteria which secrete cellulases. Polysaccharides containing derivatives of sugars are also widespread; chitin in the shells of crustaceans and insects is a polymer of acetylglucosamine, while pectin in the skin and pulp of fruits and berries is a polymer of galacturonic acid. Mucopolysaccharides, found in such diverse locations as bacteria, the fluid of joints (see HYALURONIC ACID), and cartilage, contain variously amino sugars (*e.g.* glucosamine), uronic acids, and deoxy sugars (*e.g.* 6-deoxy-L-galactose). See also CARBOHYDRATES.—*R. K. C.*

SULFATE: a compound containing the sulfate $(SO_4)^{-2}$ radical. Because sulfuric acid (H_2SO_4) is a dibasic acid, it forms two kinds of sulfate salts, acid (*e.g.* sodium hydrosulfate, $NaHSO_4$) and neutral or normal (*e.g.* sodium sulfate, Na_2SO_4). The acid sulfate salts may be dehydrated to the pyrosulfate $(2NaHSO_4 \rightarrow Na_2S_2O_7 + H_2O)$; but normal sulfates of the alkali and alkaline-earth metals do not decompose readily by heating. Some normal metal sulfates decompose to liberate sulfur trioxide or sulfur dioxide and oxygen. On heating with carbon, sulfates are reduced to the sulfide, giving off carbon dioxide: $Na_2SO_4 + 2C \rightarrow Na_2S + 2CO_2$. Sulfates of barium and other elements of group IIA of the PERIODIC TABLE are insoluble, but can be made soluble in the presence of concentrated sulfuric acid. Calcium sulfate has two hydrated forms, *gypsum*, $CaSO_4 \cdot 2H_2O$, a mineral mined in large quantities, and *plaster of Paris*, $(CaSO_4)_2 \cdot H_2O$, the essential ingredient of stucco and plaster. Heating gypsum produces plaster of Paris; then if the plaster of Paris is mixed with water at room temperature, it gradually "sets," *i.e.* picks up enough water to turn back to gypsum. Barium sulfate, from the mineral barite, is used mainly in the making of lithopone, a white pigment applied to paper, linoleum, rubber, paint, plastics, and cloth.

Many ALUMS contain two $(SO_4)^{-2}$ radicals as anions and 12 molecules of hydration. Aluminum is commonly a constituent (thence the name *alum*), as in $KAl(SO_4)_2 \cdot 12H_2O$, used for water purification and in fire extinguishers, and $NaAl(SO_4)_2 \cdot 12H_2O$, an ingredient of some baking powders. —*D. P. B.*

SULFHYDRYL COMPOUNDS: biochemical compounds containing one or more free —SH groups, which are readily oxidized to disulfides (—S—S—). These include enzymes, hormones, and coenzymes such as COENZYME A, glutathione, and lipoic acid. Proteins and polypeptides owe their —SH groups to the presence of cysteine. Inactivation by oxidation and by sulfhydryl inhibitors like p-chloromercuribenzoate (PCMB), iodoacetate (IAA), and heavy metals is evidence for participation of the —SH groups of cysteine in the function of some enzymes.—*E. S.*

SULFIDE: a chemical compound containing as the essential radical, ion, or combining group a divalent sulfur atom. The metal sulfides are salts of the weak dibasic acid hydrogen sulfide (H_2S); they occur widely as minerals and constitute many of the important metallic ores, *e.g.* lead sulfide (galena), mercury sulfide (cinnabar), and copper sulfide (chalcocite). With the exception of the alkali and alkaline-earth sulfides, most metallic sulfides are insoluble in water—a characteristic used in various systems of qualitative inorganic chemical analysis. Organic sulfides are compounds in which a divalent sulfur atom is joined to two hydrocarbons on substituted hydrocarbon radicals through the carbon atoms. The compound carbon bisulfide (CS_2) is used in making rayon.—*A. M. S.*

SULFITE: any salt of sulfurous acid, H_2SO_3. Typical is sodium sulfite, Na_2SO_3, but a series of *acid sulfites* containing hydrogen, *e.g.* potassium acid sulfite, $KHSO_3$, also occurs. A solution of calcium bisulfite, $Ca(HSO_3)_2$, is extremely important in making wood pulp, the raw material for paper and rayon, since it dissolves lignin, leaving purified cellulose. Sulfites may act as either oxidizing or reducing agents, and are used as bleaching agents for silk, wool, straw hats, wood, and dried fruit.—*G. W. M.*

SULFONATION: the process by which the sulfonic acid group, $-SO_2OH$, is introduced into organic compounds to yield compounds with a direct link between carbon and sulfur. Examples:

$$H_3C{-}SO_2OH \qquad \bigcirc{-}SO_2OH$$

Methanesulfonic acid   Benzenesulfonic acid

Many compounds in the benzene series can be sulfonated directly with concentrated sulfuric acid, $HO{-}SO_2{-}OH$. Benzene itself can be sulfonated at ordinary temperatures if fuming sulfuric acid (*i.e.* acid fortified by addition of sulfur trioxide, SO_3) is used. Several sulfonic-acid groups can be introduced into the ring if the temperature is raised. The paraffin hydrocarbons do not sulfonate directly; indirect methods can be used, *e.g.* oxidation of mercaptans:

$$2\,R{-}SH + 3\,O_2 \longrightarrow 2\,R{-}SO_2OH$$

The sulfonic acids are strong acids in water solution, in contrast with carboxylic acids, which are generally weak. —*Ru. M.*

SULFUR: a nonmetallic element (S) belonging to group VIA of the periodic table; at. no. 16; at. wt 32.066; valence 2, 4, or 6; one of the most active of all elements. It occurs in several allotropic forms, the most important being the two crystalline forms, *rhombic* (octahedral crystals, mp 112.8°C, sp gr 2.07) and *monoclinic* (prismatic crystals, mp 119°C, sp gr 1.957). Liquid sulfur boils at 444.6°C. Sulfur occurs in the free state in Texas and Louisiana and in the volcanic regions of the Mediterranean, where it has been known since antiquity. It is also found in many minerals as the sulfide (*e.g.* iron pyrites, FeS_2) and the sulfate (calcium sulfate and barium sulfate). It is also found in varying quantities in petroleum and coal. One of the elements essential to life, sulfur is present in small amounts in plant and animal matter.

Elemental sulfur is taken from shallow deposits by conventional mining methods. However, the deep deposits of the U. S. Gulf Coast region are mined by the Frasch process (invented by Herman Frasch in 1891), which involves sinking a set of three concentric pipes into the deposit, then pumping hot water down through the outer pipe to melt the sulfur, and compressed air through the inner pipe to force the molten sulfur to the surface. Iron pyrites is also an important commercial source of sulfur; this mineral can be burned in air to

World's first offshore sulfur mine, which began operations in 1960, is 7 mi off coast of Louisiana in Gulf of Mexico. In foreground is heating plant with boilers, air compressors, pumps, and generators. Other units (in order toward rear) are housing facilities, heliport, and drilling and production platform. (*Laurence Lowry/ Freeport Sulphur Co.*)

form sulfur dioxide. Sulfur reacts with chlorine, bromine, and fluorine to produce mono-, di-, and trihalides. It reacts with most metals except gold and the platinum metals; with many metals sulfur vapor reacts rapidly enough to give a flame. With hydrogen the principal product of reaction is hydrogen sulfide (H_2S), and with carbon at high temperatures carbon disulfide (CS_2) is formed. Sulfur is a constituent of many organic compounds, in which it is bonded directly to a carbon atom. Sulfur forms two oxides—the dioxide (SO_2) and the trioxide (SO_3), both of which are acid anhydrides. Burning sulfur in air produces sulfur dioxide, which forms sulfurous acid in water and reacts with bases to form sulfites. Sulfur trioxide and its hydrate, SULFURIC ACID (one of the most important and widely used of all chemicals), are formed by the catalytic oxidation of sulfur dioxide.—*A. M. S.*

SULFUR DIOXIDE: a colorless, pungent, and irritating gas (SO_2) that can be liquefied with moderate pressure at room temperatures (4 atm liquefies the gas at 25°C). The liquid is a good solvent for many organic compounds. It unites with water reversibly to form sulfurous acid (H_2SO_3). It is used either in gaseous form or, after conversion to sulfurous acid or its salts, as a bleaching and reducing agent. Large tonnages of sulfur dioxide are converted by catalytic oxidation to SULFUR TRIOXIDE, which is the anhydride of SULFURIC ACID. —*D. P. B.*

SULFURIC ACID: the compound H_2SO_4. It can be described chemically as the monohydrate of sulfur trioxide (*i.e.* sulfur trioxide, SO_3, to which one molecule of water, H_2O, has been added), or as an aqueous solution of sulfur trioxide. Sulfuric acid is a colorless, viscous, highly reactive, and corrosive liquid of density 1.85 and freezing point 10.5°C. Sulfur trioxide is made by the catalytic oxidation of sulfur dioxide, the primary product of burning elemental sulfur in air. The sulfur trioxide is then reacted with water, usually in the form of pre-diluted sulfuric acid, to produce sulfuric acid of the desired strength. Sulfuric acid is marketed in various concentrations, the most common being 93.5% (66 degrees Baumé density), 95%, and 100%. Solutions of excess sulfur trioxide in 100% sulfuric acid are called "oleum" or "fuming sulfuric acid." Because it can enter into a wide variety of chemical reactions, sulfuric acid is used in

large tonnages in many industries. Particularly extensive is its use in making fertilizer from phosphate rock, in descaling steel, in making inorganic salts and acids such as hydrochloric acid, as a condensing and sulfonating agent in organic-chemicals manufacture, and in the refining of petroleum.—*A. M. S.*

SULFUR TRIOXIDE: a chemical compound (SO_3) existing as either solid or liquid. As a solid, it occurs in three forms: alpha, beta, gamma. The stable form, alpha, melts at 62°C. Liquid SO_3 is colorless. Sulfur trioxide combines with water to form sulfuric acid. When dissolved in concentrated sulfuric acid, the product is known as *fuming sulfuric acid.* Like sulfuric acid, the trioxide is highly corrosive, a strong dehydrating agent, and very reactive chemically.—*D. P. B.*

SUMNER, JAMES BATCHELLER, 1887–1955, U. S. biochemist; b. Canton, Mass. In 1926 he extracted and crystallized the enzyme urease from the jack bean, the first such finding. For his discovery that enzymes can be crystallized, he shared the 1946 Nobel prize with J. H. Northrop and W. M. Stanley. He was a fellow of the Royal Society and a member of the National Academy of Sciences.—*D. H. D. R.*

SUN: the STAR around which Earth revolves. Since the dawn of history the Sun has been recognized, often worshiped, as the source of life-giving heat and light. It is the only star near enough to us to be examined in detail, being about 93 million mi away from Earth, 1/270,000 the distance of the next nearest star. It is quite an ordinary star, about average in size, mass, and brightness, and is thought to be in a stable stage of evolution: it has changed little during the past 2 to 4 billion yr, and is not expected to change much during the next 2 to 4 billion yr. (See STAR.) For the relationships of the Sun with other members of the solar system, see SOLAR SYSTEM and the separate articles on members of the system (EARTH, MARS, COMET, ETC.). Apparent movements of the Sun in the sky are described in DAY AND NIGHT, MIDNIGHT SUN, SEASONS, and TIME.

Gross features of the Sun are determined by fairly direct observations. Its mass of 2.2×10^{27} tons (334,000 Earth masses) is obtained by applying the theory of gravitation to the motion of the planets (see BINARY STAR). Its diameter,

THE SUN

SOLAR FLARE

N P

CHROMOSPHERE

JETS OR
SPICULES

DISORDERED
MAGNETIC
FIELD

BIPOLAR
SUNSPOT

CORONA

FILAMENT

ARCH
PROMINENCE

PHOTOSPHERE

SUNSPOT
GROUP

(Above) **Parts of Sun:** Spectroheliogram taken May 10, 1959, shows great solar flare. Prominences (see other photos) were added by artist. NP indicates Sun's north pole. (*Lockheed Solar Obs.*)

(Below) **Solar prominences,** examples of which appear in this spectroheliogram, may reach heights of hundreds of thousands of miles. (*High Altitude Obs., Univ. of Colorado*)

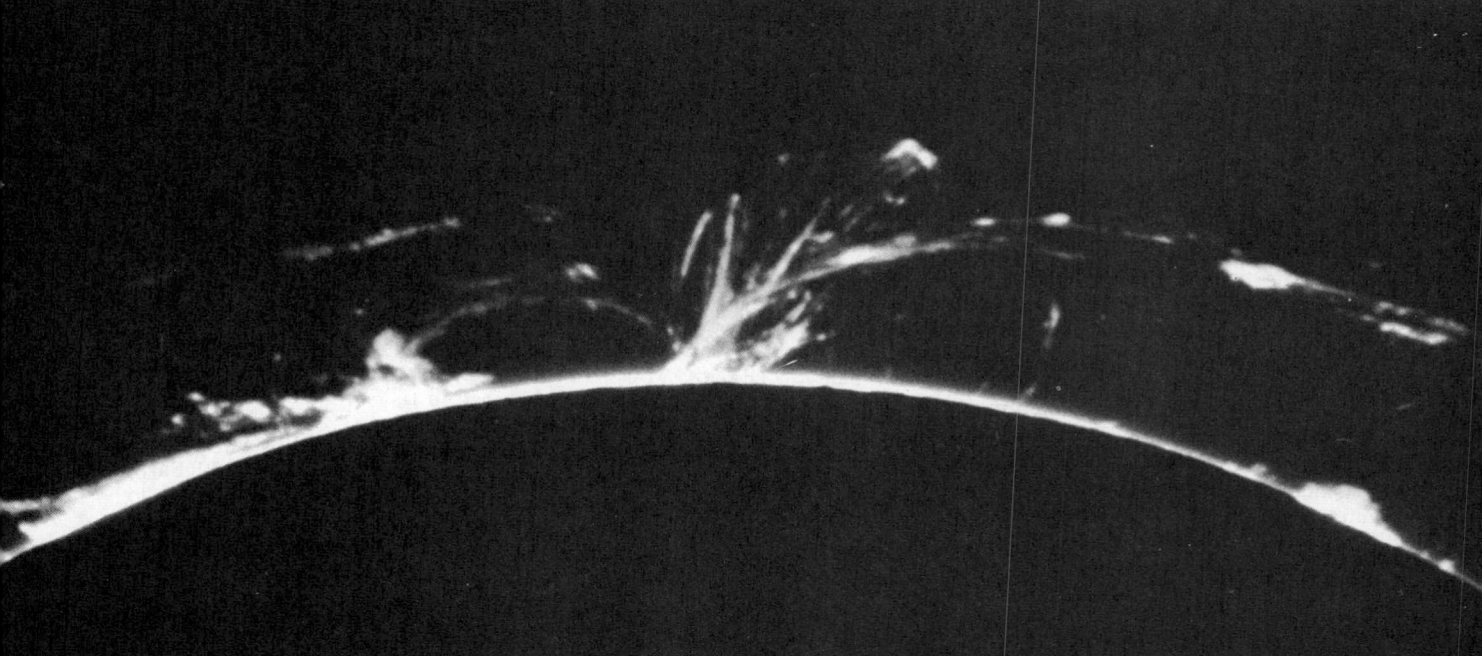

864,400 mi, is computed directly from its apparent size and its distance from Earth (see PARALLAX, SOLAR). Its energy output in the form of light and thermal radiation, 5×10^{23} hp, is determined by measuring the SOLAR CONSTANT. The energy given off in corpuscular, ultraviolet, and x-radiation is more difficult to measure because of absorption by Earth's atmosphere, and is now being estimated by rocket and satellite observations. Finally, the peculiar rotation of the Sun, with the equator rotating in 25 days and the polar regions in about 30 days, is determined by direct day-by-day observations of positions of sunspots and other surface features.

The Sun is a gas throughout, but certain layers have distinctive physical characteristics. Most familiar is the *photosphere*, the bright surface seen through an ordinary telescope. It is opaque to almost all wavelengths of light because it contains a considerable number of hydrogen ions, which absorb light strongly. Hence, to the eye, it appears as a clear-cut surface with a sharply defined outer edge, but a closer look reveals that it is not smooth. Most of the time it is marked by at least a few SUNSPOTS. In the vicinity of sunspots near the limb, coarse bright features called *faculae* are usually visible. Also, the photosphere is completely covered by a mosaic of small, bright, polygonal cells called *granules*.

The spectrum of photospheric light reveals the photosphere's temperature, 11,000°F, by the distribution of color. The spectrum is intersected by several thousand dark lines; each line is caused by the absorption of a fraction of the sunlight by a particular chemical element in the vapor through which the light has passed. The wavelengths of the lines indicate which elements are present; the blackness of the line, coupled with a theoretical calculation of the absorbing ability of the atom involved, provides information on how abundant that particular kind of atom is. Such analysis reveals that almost all elements found in Earth are also present in the Sun, and that a great many are in about the same ratio as on the surface of Earth. The most notable exception is hydrogen, which on Earth is less abundant than several other elements but on the Sun is many thousand times more abundant than any other element. On the Sun there is also more helium, about ⅒ as much as hydrogen.

Since the photosphere is opaque, that portion of the Sun inside it must be studied by inference, based on the following necessary conditions: The temperature of the interior must everywhere be sufficiently great for the gas pressure to equal the weight of the overlying gas; the total mass of gas contained under these various conditions of pressure and temperature must equal the known mass of the Sun and must be contained within the known volume of the Sun; the Sun must be able to generate, presumably by thermonuclear reactions, the energy it actually releases; this energy, in turn, must be transmitted outward to the photosphere and in such a manner that the temperature may decrease outward from the high values needed for thermonuclear reactions to the known temperature of the photosphere. Astrophysicists have devised models of the solar interior to fit known data. In all models, the major thermonuclear reaction is the direct conversion of hydrogen into helium; this reaction takes place in a core of very high density (about 100 times that of water) and temperatures of about 25,000,000°F; and the energy is transmitted outward by radiation for some distance from the core, but nearer the photosphere the gas becomes more opaque and convection takes place. There is disagreement on whether convection also takes place near the core, and as to the thickness of the outer convective layer. Many scientists believe granules result from convective cells impinging on the photosphere. The photosphere is a thin layer not more than 100 or 200 mi deep. Going outward through this layer, the tempera-

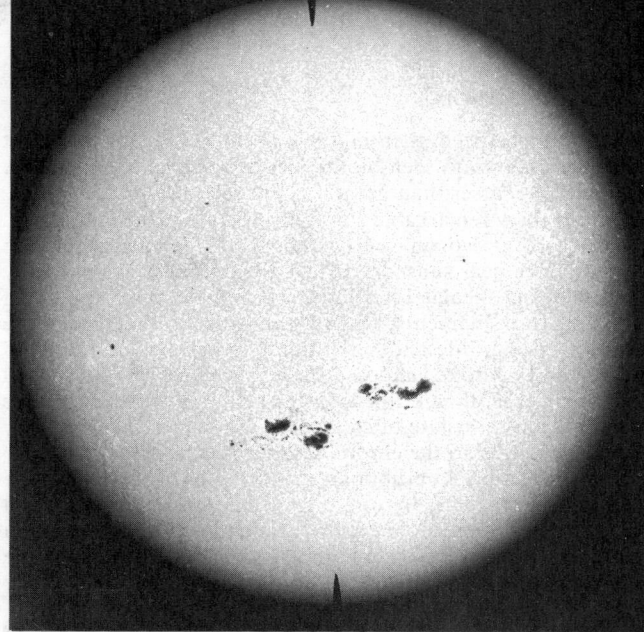

Face of Sun, or photosphere, is shown above in direct photograph taken July 31, 1949. Visible here are granulation of surface, darkening of outer edge or "limb," scattered luminous areas (faculae) near E and W limbs, and several sunspots, the largest forming bridged pairs. *(Mt Wilson)*

ture drops from 11,000 to 8,000°F. It is this decreasing temperature that causes absorption lines in the spectrum of sunlight. (A decade or two ago these were attributed to a distinct cooler layer, called the reversing layer, overlying the photosphere.)

Just above the photosphere in the next layer of the Sun, the *chromosphere,* the temperature rises abruptly. At the base of the chromosphere, the temperature is about 10,000°F; 10,000 mi further up, in the upper chromosphere, it is about 40,000°. The density of the chromosphere is only about ¹⁄₁₀₀,₀₀₀ that of the photosphere, and under these circumstances it emits light almost entirely in distinct colors, giving a bright-line spectrum. The chromosphere is generally studied with a spectrograph during a total eclipse, just at the moment the photosphere is covered by the Moon, or with a SPECTROHELIOGRAPH or birefringent filter. The outer chromosphere is made up of a system of small jets (*spicules*), which constantly shoot out-

Details of sunspots and granulations are remarkably clear in photograph made with balloon-borne telescope at 80,000 ft—above much of the atmospheric dust and turbulence that handicap earthbound astronomical photography. *(Project Stratoscope)*

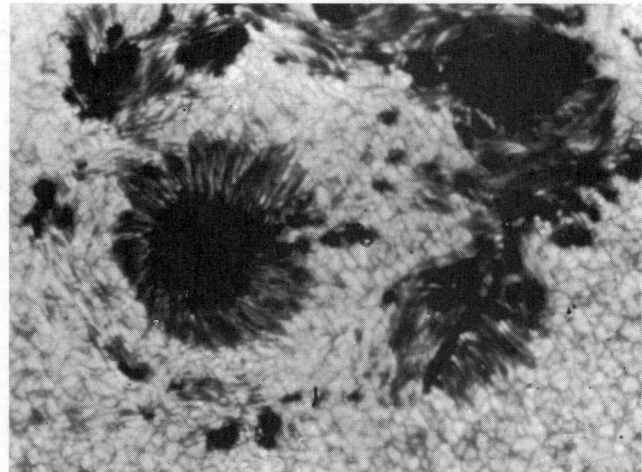

ward at high speed, then in a few minutes fade away. Bright and dark markings seen on the disk in spectroheliograms are somewhat coarser than granules, and may be spicules. These features show remarkable spiral configurations near sunspots.

Appearing also on spectroheliograms or filtergrams are bright areas near sunspots, called *plages*. These are probably extensions of faculae into the chromosphere. Also appearing are long dark filaments; when these rotate to the edge of the Sun, they protrude above the limb, sometimes hundreds of thousands of miles, and are called *prominences*. Some will last for weeks, then erupt and disappear in minutes; others are in a constant state of change. In temperature and density they are similar to the chromosphere. Spectroheliograms also show sudden bright eruptions appearing in or just above the chromosphere. These eruptions, called *flares*, brighten for a few minutes, then decline more gradually. While they are in progress, short-wave communication on Earth is likely to be disrupted.

Late 18th-cent. sundial of French manufacture, made of silver, has hinged gnomon, so that instrument can be carried flat in pocket. (*Sheila La Farge/C. H. Johnson Collection*)

Solar corona is revealed in total eclipse of June 8, 1918. Minor irregularities at edge of Moon's disk are due to lunar topography. Opposite areas of weakened corona correspond to solar poles; this corona effect appears during sunspot minima. (*Mt. Wilson*)

Outside the chromosphere and engulfing the prominences is a very hot, very tenuous body of gas called the *corona*. Its density is about 1/10,000 that of the chromosphere; its temperature near the Sun, 3,000,000°F. The corona extends millions of miles into the solar system, possibly engulfing Earth. The very faint light from the corona arises in part from photospheric light scattered by free electrons in the corona and in part from atoms that have been mostly stripped of electrons by the high-temperature gas. This faint light can be observed only during a total eclipse, or by means of a coronagraph; additional information about the corona can also be obtained by radio telescopes receiving electromagnetic waves from 10 to 200 cm in length.—*D. E. B. and L. H.*

SUNDIAL: an instrument for telling time by measuring the Sun's hour angle, altitude, or azimuth. In ancient times the sundial was the principal timekeeper; stationary dials served as clocks, portable dials as watches. The essential parts are the gnomon, to cast a shadow, and a dial plate, upon which hours may be inscribed, to receive the shadow. The sundial indicates local apparent solar time. Since the apparent day

varies in length throughout the year, clocks are set to give mean time, which is based on the regular movement of a fictitious body called the *mean sun*. The difference between apparent and mean time is called the *equation of time*, and is often incorporated in the construction of a sundial so that it will tell mean time. A correction for longitude may also be included so that standard time can be read directly. Heliochronometers are modern sundials that directly indicate either local mean time or standard time, without use of tables of correction.—*R. N. M.*

SUN PILLAR: a vertical streak or "column" of light seen fairly often above the rising or setting Sun. It is seen most easily when the Sun is just below the horizon; it is scarcely ever observed when the Sun is high. The sun pillar is caused by reflection of sunlight from the flat surfaces of the tiny plate-like ice crystals which form cirrus clouds.—*D. H. L.*

SUNSHINE RECORDER: an instrument for recording the duration (but not the intensity) of sunshine. A common type has an electric timer which operates as long as sunshine is falling upon (and thus warming) a blackened thermometer bulb. In another type, sunshine is passed through a glass sphere and focused on a sheet of paper. As the Sun moves across the sky, the heat burns a line on the paper, and the length of the line gives the duration of sunshine.—*D. H. L.*

SUNSPOT: a transient dark feature observed on the face of the Sun. It is dark only by contrast, being 1,800–3,600°F cooler than the 11,400°F photosphere which surrounds it. This cooling may be caused by strong magnetic fields, always present in a sunspot. There are two regions visible in a sunspot: the umbra, a dark central region; and the penumbra, a brighter filamentary region surrounding the umbra. The size of sunspots varies from small pores 200–300 mi in diameter, at the limit of resolution of telescopes, to spots 30,000 mi across. Spots frequently occur in complex groups, which may be 100,000 mi long and consist of 50 or more distinct areas. A group generally consists of a large spot followed (in the Sun's east-to-west rotation) by one or more smaller ones. Leading and following spots are always of opposite magnetic polarity, and the order of polarity is reversed between leading and following spots in the Sun's northern and southern hemispheres. Groups typically evolve over a period of a few weeks from a collection of many small spots, through a stage in which leading and following spots are better defined, into a single large spot which then grows smaller and disappears. A maximum number of sunspots is observed about every 11 yr. At the beginning of such a cycle, new spots appear near latitudes 40° N and S of the equator; later, spots form progressively nearer the equator. Throughout each cycle the

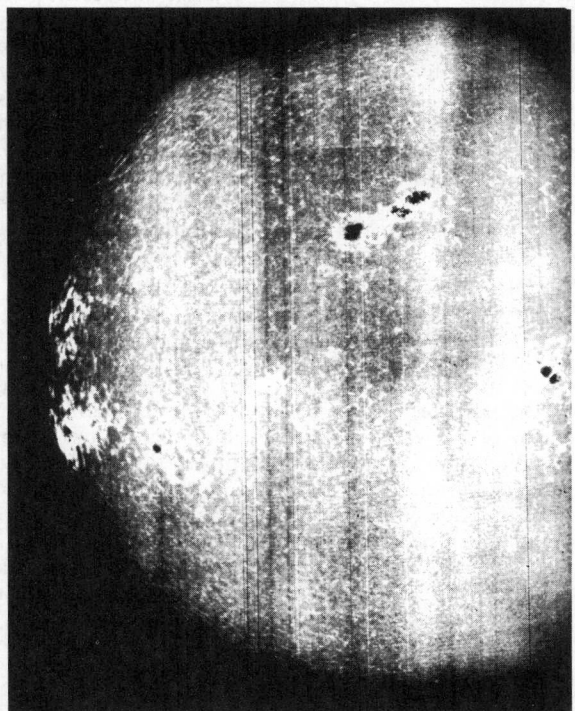

An eruption of sunspots during the period of July 17–28, 1928, was recorded on this spectroheliogram. Note concentration of spots in equatorial zone. (*Yerkes Obs.*)

order of magnetic polarity of the spots in each hemisphere is opposite to what it was in the preceding cycle. In the vicinity of sunspots, a number of phenomena in the solar atmosphere occur, notably flares, faculae, and loop prominences. Disturbances in short-wave radio communications, auroral activity, and fluctuations in Earth's magnetic field are more frequent at the maximum phase of the sunspot cycle than at other times. As to the origin of sunspots, there is no generally accepted theory, but most hypotheses point to circulation phenomena below the photosphere and imply some relationship to the different rotation periods of areas at different latitudes on the Sun's surface.—*D. E. B. and L. H.*

SUPERCONDUCTIVITY: disappearance of electrical resistance and magnetic permeability in certain metals and alloys at temperatures near absolute zero. The phenomenon was discovered in 1911 by the Dutch physicist Heike Kamerlingh Onnes, who observed that at 4.1°K (about −269°C) the resistance of a sample of (solid) mercury vanished quite suddenly as the metal was cooled. Twenty-four pure metals and many alloys and intermetallic compounds are superconductors, but occurrence of superconductivity seems confined to the lowest 20° of the absolute temperature scale. The lowest transition temperature is that of ruthenium (0.47°K), the highest that of Nb_3Sn (18°K). The fact that a compound (Au_2Bi) of two

non-superconductive parent metals can become superconductive shows that the phenomenon is not a property of the atom but of the free electrons in the metal. Zero electrical resistance can be demonstrated by inducing a current in a closed ring of superconductive metal: the deflection of a compass needle then shows that this current will run in the ring as long as the metal is kept cold. Such "persistent currents" have been maintained for more than a year without diminishing in strength. When a substance is in the superconducting state, it expels all magnetic fields; a bar magnet, dropped over a superconductive dish, will hover above it, repelled by its own magnetic image. Normal resistance of a superconductive metal can be restored by application of a magnetic field or by passing through it a current which exceeds a certain "critical" value. The strength of the critical magnetic field or current varies with temperature and differs from metal to metal. Thus, when two insulated wires of different superconductive metals are crossed, it is possible to quench superconductivity in one of them through the magnetic field produced by a current in the other (which, however, retains its superconductivity). This device, called a cryotron, is becoming important as a computer element.

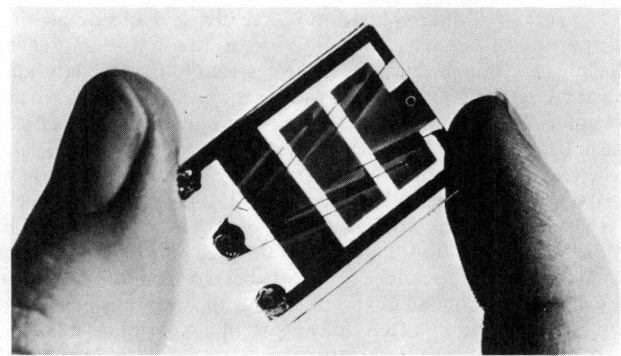

Electronic switch consisting of a six-cryotron circuit of tin and lead vaporized and deposited as thin films on glass employs principle of superconductivity. Switch was developed for use in computers. (*Lead Industries Assn.*)

The most important application of superconductivity is based on the recent discovery that suitably treated wires of some alloys, such as niobium-tin, retain zero resistance up to very high fields and considerable current densities. With these loss-free solenoids, operating in liquid helium, fields in excess of 100,000 oersted have been produced. Modern theory explains superconductivity by the formation of electron pairs of opposite spin and momentum.—*K. Me.*

SUPERCOOLING: the cooling of a liquid to a temperature below the usual freezing point without its freezing. Small quantities of pure water, for example, may often be cooled down to −10°F (−25°C) before freezing, *e.g.* in the laboratory or the upper atmosphere. The mechanism of supercooling in water may be taken as typical of the phenomenon in other substances as well. As water is cooled, the thermal motion of the molecules lessens, and forces of intermolecular attraction begin to pull adjacent molecules together into "pseudonuclei," or tightly packed clumps of a few tens of members. The tight packing means that the clumps contain little stored internal energy, but also that they cannot join one another in an orderly crystal lattice (see CRYSTALLOGRAPHY) to form a solid (ice). The relatively high energy content of the unattached molecules between clumps more than overbalances the low energy of the clumps and causes the mass of supercooled water to have a higher net internal energy than that of an equal mass of ice.

Before the mass can crystallize, or freeze, the clumps must be broken up, leaving the molecules free to enter the minimum-energy lattice array. This may be effected by physical agitation; or if the water is cooled to below −40°, boundary stresses destroy the clumps, and the water freezes spontaneously. At higher temperatures, freezing may be triggered by the addition of a particle of ice or of a freezing nucleus—some substance whose crystallographic structure is close to that of ice (see NUCLEI). The surface of the ice or of the nucleus acts as a pattern to which some of the molecules of the supercooled water quickly become attached in the lattice spacing proper for ice formation. This process of organization spreads, and the mass freezes. The surplus energy of the free molecules over the lattice-bound molecules appears as latent heat (see HEAT, LATENT).—*D. H. L.*

SUPERFLUIDITY: the property of liquid helium of being able to pass through fine channels without friction. Liquid helium undergoes a profound change in physical properties at a temperature of 2.18° Kelvin, called the "lambda-point," which is marked by a maximum in the specific heat. There is also a corresponding maximum in the density, and below this temperature the heat conductivity of the liquid increases sharply, attaining values of 10^6 times that above the lambda-point. A striking example of the lambda-phenomenon is the complete loss of resistance to flow through capillaries of less than 10^{-4} cm (0.0001 cm) diameter. In wider channels the flow resistance is small but finite above a certain critical velocity. When a test tube filled with liquid helium is freely suspended, helium will escape by superflow through a thin invisible film of liquid covering the glass wall and collect in drops at the outside of the tube. In general the flow phenomena of mass and heat below the lambda-point are complex, depending often on the specific experimental conditions. At the same temperature and pressure, the values of viscosity may differ by a factor of 10^6, depending on whether they have been obtained from flow through a tube or by observations of the damping of an oscillating disk or cylinder. Closely connected with superfluidity are mechano-caloric and thermomechanical effects. The first produces a drop in temperature of liquid helium passing in superflow through a fine channel. The second is observed when two volumes of liquid helium are connected by a fine channel and heat is supplied to one of them: a flow of liquid then takes place through the channel and toward the heat supply.—*K. Me.*

SUPERHEATING: the heating of a vapor to a temperature above that at which it is in equilibrium with its liquid PHASE. Superheating of water vapor yields dry steam at temperatures far above the boiling temperature of water. This is of importance in a STEAM ENGINE, since the heating ability, or energy content, of a given quantity of steam increases directly with increasing temperature.—*E. M. R.*

SUPERNOVA: see NOVA.

SUPERPOSITION: see EUCLIDEAN GEOMETRY; STRATIGRAPHY.

SUPERSATURATED SOLUTION: a solution that has a higher concentration of solute than a saturated solution. A saturated solution is one in which the amount of solute is equal to its maximum equilibrium solution in a solvent. A supersaturated solution is accordingly in a non-equilibrium state, and readily reverts to the saturated (equilibrium) state by precipi-

tating the excess solute. Supersaturated solutions may be prepared from saturated solutions by cooling the latter carefully. —*G. W. M.*

SUPERSONICS: see SONIC REGIMES; ULTRASONICS.

SURFACE-ACTIVE AGENT: any of a class of substances which tend to concentrate at surfaces or at other boundaries such as those between solids and liquids or between two liquids which do not ordinarily mix; in so doing the surface-active agent changes the surface or boundary properties significantly, chiefly by reducing the surface or boundary tension. Common surface-active agents are soaps, detergents, emulsifying and dispersing agents, certain classes of chemical corrosion inhibitors, flotation agents, and wetting agents. Typically they are composed of chemical compounds in which each molecule exhibits an affinity for both oil and water. Thus, common soap is made up of molecules each of which contains an oil-like (nonpolar) part and a salt-like (polar) part. Although ability to reduce surface or boundary tension is a general characteristic of surface-active agents, the mode of action varies with the agent and the conditions of use. The action of soap and detergents, for example, is thought to depend upon their ability to attach themselves to oily or greasy dirt particles through the nonpolar part of the molecule and to carry the particles into suspension in the surrounding water by virtue of the water solubility of the polar part of the molecule. Oil additives for improving lubrication act by becoming attached to the metal surface to be protected by the polar ends of the molecules, the nonpolar ends forming a strong, oily film which prevents metal-to-metal contact between the rubbing surfaces and is slippery. The major uses of surface-active agents are as washing and cleaning compounds in textile, leather, and metal treatment; as flotation agents in ore recovery; as disinfectants; as emulsifying and wetting agents in insecticide sprays; as emulsifying agents in food and cosmetics; as foaming agents in fire-fighting; as emulsifying and spreading agents in water-based paints and floor waxes. —*H. W. F.*

SURFACES: Although the geometrical concept of a surface is familiar, it has no definition that is universally satisfactory. Probably the most familiar intuitive conception of a surface is that of the boundary of a solid object or a boundary separating two solids. Thus the boundary of a sphere is a spherical surface; two hemispheres are separated by a bounding plane surface. A surface is itself two-dimensional, although it is often embedded in three-dimensional space. It has no volume; the measure of a surface is its area. Most surfaces are conceived as two-sided. Thus a spherical surface has an outside and an inside. Some surfaces, however, cannot be so considered and really have only one side. The best-known example is the Möbius band. This can be constructed physically by cutting a long strip of paper, twisting it 180°, and then sealing the ends together. It is possible to pass from any mark on the paper to any other without passing through the paper or over the edge. This is not the case with a two-sided surface.

In solid analytic geometry a surface is defined as the locus of points satisfying an equation in the three coordinates. More generally, it may consist of several parts that satisfy different equations in different sections. Surfaces are classified according to the types of equations that represent them. For example, equations of the second degree represent QUADRIC SURFACES—ellipsoids, paraboloids, and hyperboloids.

Some surfaces can be generated, or cut out of space, by a moving line or curve. This is analogous to a curve being generated by a moving point. A plane can be generated by a straight line moving in various ways: it may remain parallel to some fixed line and move along an intersecting line; or it may pass through the center of a circle and swing around on the circumference. Cylindrical and conical surfaces are generated by lines moving in specified ways. Such surfaces are called ruled surfaces—they are made up of infinitely many lines or rulings. A surface of revolution is generated by a plane curve rotating about an axis. For example, a spherical surface is obtained by rotating a circle about a diameter.—*H. C.*

SURFACE TENSION: the tendency of the surface of a liquid to contract in area and thus behave like a stretched rubber membrane. The contractile force is a manifestation of the LEAST ENERGY PRINCIPLE, whereby the potential energy of the surface configuration "seeks" to attain a minimum value.

Because of surface tension, a greased needle or a dry razor blade can be made to float *on top* of water without penetrating its surface. The objects rest in little hollows or depressions, supported by the force of elasticity exerted by the surface. For the same reason, raindrops and soap bubbles assume a spherical shape, the sphere exhibiting the smallest possible surface for a given volume. Larger drops, of course, are pear-shaped because of the additional effect of gravity.

Surface tension decreases with rising temperature and the addition of detergents. Because of such a decrease in surface tension, bits of camphor, pointed at one end, will dart about in all directions when placed on top of water. As the camphor dissolves, particularly at the pointed ends, the surface tension near those ends diminishes, with the result that an unbalanced pull acts on the bits of camphor, causing them to move about.

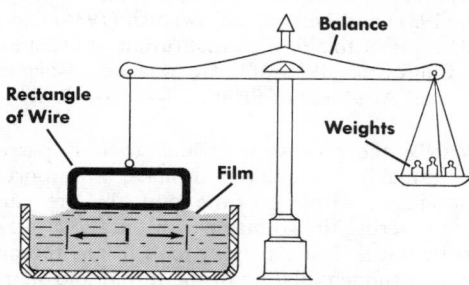

Measurement of surface tension: Weights are added to pan (*right*) of balance to determine the force required to break the film of liquid that clings to the rectangle of wire (*left*).

The figure shows a method of measuring surface tension with an open rectangle of wire. Weights are added to the right side of the balance, establishing the force F required to break the film which clings to the wire. The surface tension, expressed as the force per unit length of the film, is thereupon given by $T = F/2l$, where l is the length of the film. (The factor 2 accounts for the *two* surfaces of the film in question.)—*A. E.*

SURVEYING: the science of determining the positions of points on Earth's surface. Surveying is believed to have begun in ancient Egypt as a method of imposing proportional taxation on owners of farmland. In the 19th cent., with the expansion of technology and commerce, and the increase in population pressures, surveys of entire nations were accomplished. Significant recent improvements have included the use of aerial photography and electronic devices.

The surveying method chosen depends upon the magnitude of the area to be surveyed and the purpose of the survey; all surveying is based on direct linear measurement and the measurement of angles, from which distances, directions, and heights are computed. The principal instruments for surveying are those for measuring lengths (chain, tape, or metal rods), a transit (theodolite) for measuring both horizontal and vertical angles, and a prismatic ASTROLABE for determining latitudes. The type of transit generally used for field work consists of a telescope on a tripod, fitted with a pair of bubble-type levels and graduated circles which allow the surveyor to measure both vertical and horizontal angles. By means of triangulation, vertical distances (elevations) as

Surveying crew at work: Instrument man (*foreground*) has located surveyor's level over point whose altitude is known. Rod man holds graduated leveling rod vertically over point whose altitude is to be calculated. Instrument man, keeping telescope level, views leveling rod through it, noting at what height above ground the telescope's line of sight intersects the rod. This height is difference between known and unknown altitudes. (*Union Carbide*)

well as horizontal distances can be determined. Elevations can be determined with reference to known elevations which are represented by BENCH MARKS; elevations also may be obtained by means of an altimeter. In *geodetic surveying*, the purpose is to determine the configuration of Earth's surface over a large area, taking into account its curvature (see GEODESY), whereas small areas are mapped by *plane surveying*, which treats an area as a horizontal plane. For a large geodetic survey, observations are made of points 30 to 40 mi apart. With one measured line and angles carefully observed, the survey is accomplished by triangulation, a systematic solution of a chain or network of triangles. Accuracy of the order of 1 sec in the sum of the angles of a triangle is achieved. Second and third triangulations based on points closer together produce information in greater detail.

A *topographical survey* determines relative positions of surface features, shown on a contour map. A *hydrographic survey* produces the information for navigational charts. *Land surveying* (*cadastral surveying*) is used to locate parcels of land to determine their dimensions and area, the usual method being to travel along the boundaries of the property, using a transit and a steel tape, measuring direction and distance along each side. *Mine* or *underground surveying* determines the relation of mine shafts and tunnels to surface boundaries. *Engineering surveys* entail such activities as designating grades of land in a construction site, and are made for railroads, highways, transmission lines, and other purposes.

Aerial surveying, which requires a minimum of contacts with the ground, is being used increasingly for reconnaissance work, highway location, preparation of assessment maps, mapping of large, remote tracts, and hydrographic and shoreline maps. As early as the mid-19th cent., aerial surveys were made from balloons, and a few balloon reconnaissance surveys were carried out during the Civil War. The advent of the airplane brought a rapid expansion of this type of survey, particularly with the use of aerial photographs, which are the basis of modern aerial surveys. The photographs are taken in strips, with each picture overlapping the next. (Compilation of maps from these photographs is a part of PHOTOGRAMMETRY.) Some field surveying for control purposes is usually required with aerial surveying; but occasionally the ground control is omitted, and the location of selected photographs in a flight line is determined by radar from distant stations. Modern developments in aerial photography have made aerial surveys increasingly effective. With color photography, hydrographic surveys can be made accurately to a depth of 70 ft. Infrared photography has made possible high-contrast, accurate shoreline surveys, since infrared rays do not penetrate water.—*H. C. and A. J. W.*

SUSPENSION: a dispersion of solid particles, of larger than molecular size, in a fluid medium. In this two-phase system there is a definite surface of separation between each particle and the liquid medium. The particles of a suspension are of microscopic size or larger, whereas those in the colloidal state are submicroscopic but larger than molecular size. However, no distinct line can be drawn between a suspension and a colloidal system. Because of its small dimensions, a particle in suspension never settles, but undergoes haphazard movement in all directions. This erratic motion, known as BROWNIAN MOTION, is observed with all types of suspended particles, and is found to be independent of the nature of the substance suspended or the dispersing medium, whether gaseous or liquid. Abundant use of suspensions is made in medicinal preparations so that they can be dispensed readily and exactly.—*G. W. M.*

SUTTON, SIR OLIVER GRAHAM, 1903– , British mathematician and meteorologist; b. Cwmcarn, Monmouthshire. He has worked mainly in the field of micrometeorology, especially in relation to diffusion and convection. He is now the Director-General of the Meteorological Office, the British national weather service. He is a fellow of the Royal Society. —*O. G. S.*

SUTTON, WILLIAM S., 1876–1916, U. S. geneticist. His research included studies of chromosome sizes and shapes and of the accessory chromosome which assumes a place for itself at the time of nuclear division of a cell. His major contribution is the theory that Mendel's formula of inheritance of characters could be applied to chromosomes.—*D. H. D. R.*

SVEDBERG, THEODOR, 1884– , Swedish chemist; b. Valbro. He designed and developed centrifuges in which solutions of organic substances could be rotated at very high speeds and simultaneously photographed. The centrifugal separation of a material in solution is partially counterbalanced by the material's diffusion through the solvent, and observations of the equilibrium between these two effects make possible the computation of the molecular weight of the material in solution. For these researches on disperse systems, he received the 1926 Nobel prize. He is a fellow of the Royal Society and an associate of the U. S. National Academy of Sciences.—*D. H. D. R.*

SVERDRUP, HARALD ULRIK, 1888–1957, Norwegian oceanographer and meteorologist; b. Sogndal. His research has been on the meteorology of the Arctic, turbulence of the air near the ground, ocean currents, tides, and surface waves. He was in charge of the scientific work of the expeditions of the *Maud* (1917–25) and the *Nautilus* (1931), and of the Wilkins-Ellsworth (1931) and Norwegian-Swedish (1934) expeditions. He was director of the Scripps Institution of Oceanography, Univ. of California (1936–48). He was an associate of the U. S. National Academy of Sciences.—*D. H. D. R.*

SWALLOWING: the process by which food is passed from mouth to stomach. For aquatic animals, an important part is the squeezing or wringing of the food; this prevents excess water from entering the stomach with the food and diluting the digestive juices. For a frog or toad in air, the process is often merely a sudden dilation of the throat and short esophagus as the insect prey is flicked by the sticky tongue directly into the stomach; closure of the esophagus and mouth follows. For a snake, swallowing may be a lengthy operation in which the two sides of the lower jaw alternate in pulling the prey into the mouth and down the throat. In amphibians, many reptiles, birds, and mammals, the whole animal may undergo gulping movements to help shift food of large size into the stomach. In mammals, swallowing involves three stages. First, the masticated food, mixed with saliva, is formed into a compact bolus by the tongue acting against the hard palate, and the bolus is forced by the tongue into the pharynx. Second, while the bolus moves rapidly through the pharynx under the impetus given it by the tongue, the entry to the nasal passage is closed by elevation of the soft palate, and the opening into the larynx and trachea is closed by elevation of the larynx against the epiglottis. Third, the bolus moves through the esophagus, either under its initial impetus or propelled by PERISTALSIS, to the stomach.—*B. T. S.*

SWAMMERDAM, JAN, 1637–80, Dutch physician and naturalist; b. Amsterdam. The founder of the theory of preformation, he also devised the method of injections for studying the circulatory system and was one of the earliest users of the compound microscope. His excellent descriptions and illustrations of the minute anatomy of insects, with particular regard to metamorphosis, were published posthumously in his *Biblia naturae* (1737–38).—*D. H. D. R.*

SWAMP: an area of poorly drained land where there is an abundant supply of water. Some swamps are lakes that have been largely filled with sediment and organic debris; others are margins of rivers where active sedimentation and growth of vegetation prevent continuous flow of water. Swamps are developed in other environments also. Coastal swamps, or *marshes* as they are often called, are lands once covered by tidewater, but now showing abundant islands of sediment and vegetation.—*N. E. A. H.*

SWEAT GLAND: a tiny, coiled, tubular gland embedded in the skin of most mammals. Guinea pigs and rabbits have none; in the domestic cat and most rodents, sweat glands occur only on the soles and pads of the feet. In man, there are 500 to 3,000 sweat glands per square inch of skin surface, depending on the part of the body. These glands commonly secrete their watery liquid when the environmental temperature rises beyond about 85°F. They also secrete when a person is feverish (particularly evident when body temperature is restored, hence "breaking" the fever) or in certain emotional states. Even under normal conditions when the body is cool, the skin loses fluid at the rate of about a pint a day (called

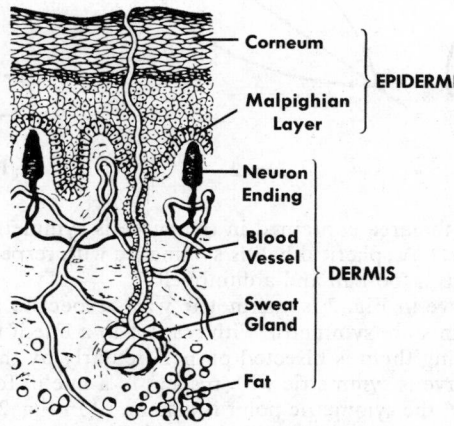

Sweat gland in man lies coiled in deep layer (dermis) of skin. When gland receives nerve impulses from brain, it secretes sweat through duct opening at skin's surface. (*After Buchanan*)

"insensible water loss"). The main function of the sweat glands is regulation of body temperature. As each droplet of sweat evaporates from the skin surface, heat is carried off, which tends to keep body temperature from rising. In sweat the body loses ordinary salt (which must be replaced after excessive sweating), as well as carbonates, water, and urea.—*A. R. D.*

SWEETENING AGENTS: substances that give a "sweet" taste; they are found among a wide variety of compounds. No correlation between sweetness and chemical structure has been discovered: some SUGARS are not sweet. Many sweet compounds have appreciable toxicity; one of these has about 4,000 times the sweetening power of sucrose (ordinary sugar),

but its use in food is prohibited. Only two synthetic sweetening agents have at present writing government approval for use in foods. They are saccharin and Sucaryl (a trade-mark

Saccharin   Sucaryl (sodium salt)

name). Sucaryl is stable in cookery at baking temperatures. It is estimated to have about 30 times the sweetening power of sucrose, and saccharin is about 300 times as sweet as sucrose. Neither has food value.—*Ru. M.*

SWIM-BLADDER: in fishes, a thin-walled sac located along the dorsal wall of the body cavity, just under the vertebral column. The swim-bladder is filled with gas, and the degree of inflation regulates the specific gravity of the fish, permitting it to swim at varying depths without rising or sinking. In most fresh-water fishes, the swim-bladder opens into the mouth, and the gas it contains is replenished when the fish swallows air. This ability to exchange the gas content of the swim-bladder for air is used by some fishes to supplement respiration through the gills, and in the lungfishes the swim-bladder serves as a lung during estivation. Lungs of all higher vertebrates are considered to have evolved from the swim-bladder of an ancestral fishlike form. In most marine fishes, the swim-bladder has no external opening; gas is secreted into the bladder from the blood, or removed from the bladder and returned to the blood through an extensive bed of capillaries. The swim-bladder gas may include nitrogen, oxygen, and carbon dioxide. Composition and pressure of these gases vary. It is uncertain whether the oxygen in the swim-bladder can be used as a reserve store. Bottom-dwelling fish, and those that live in very deep water, generally do not have swim-bladders.—*B. T. S.*

SYLLOGISM: in logic, a form of argument based ultimately on the principle that "if p then q" and "if q then r" leads to "if p then r," where p, q, and r are either statements or statement forms (see SENTENTIAL FUNCTION). The traditional syllogism can be reduced to the above form by the use of free variables and the methods of the sentential calculus. This is also true of syllogisms containing a particular premise and can be shown by use of the *antilogism*, which states that if two premises imply a third, then either of the two premises together with the contradictory of the conclusion imply the contradictory of the other premise. The contradictory of a particular is a *universal*. Syllogistic reasoning occurs whenever rules are applied to particular cases and is of much more frequent occurrence in daily life than is realized by those untaught in logic, because such syllogisms are apt to be enthymemes (arguments in which one of the propositions is implicit, not stated), *e.g.* "Since bridges are built to benefit the public, they are subject to government regulation."—*H. T.*

SYLVESTER, JAMES JOSEPH, 1814–97, English mathematician; b. London. His principal work was in algebra and the theory of numbers. With ARTHUR CAYLEY he founded the theory of algebraic invariants (the theory governing those expressions in the coefficients of algebraic forms which remain unchanged as the variables undergo specified transformations). His collected mathematical papers were published 1904–12. He was a fellow of the Royal Society and an associate of the U. S. National Academy of Sciences.—*H. C.*

SYMBIOSIS: associations between unlike kinds of organisms, other than associations in which an animal eats plants or preys upon other animals. (The term is from the Greek for "living together.") Several types of symbiotic associations can be recognized. Where both partners benefit, the association is termed mutualism. This is evident in such partnerships as cellulose-digesting bacteria in the stomach of cud-chewing animals and also cellulose-digesting protozoans in the intestines of wood-eating cockroaches and termites. As another example, the roots of leguminous plants enclose and nourish special bacteria that can synthesize nitrogenous compounds from nitrogen in soil (see NITROGEN CYCLE).

Where only one partner gains and the other is unharmed, the association is called COMMENSALISM. If one partner gains at the expense of the other, the association represents PARASITISM; the partner benefiting is the parasite, and the other the host. Of course, it must be recognized that it is often difficult or impossible to ascertain the exact relation between partners.

Some symbiotic relationships seem on the border line between mutualism and parasitism. The algal partner in each LICHEN is able to grow independently in ponds, whereas the fungal partner is dependent upon associating with the correct alga. The algae in a lichen seem to benefit by being supplied with water and being protected from intense sun; they may also derive useful nutrients from the fungus. Together the partners build a distinctive plant, unlike either alone.—*L. and M. M.*

SYMBOLIC LOGIC: see FORMAL LOGIC.

SYMMETRY: in mathematics, a characteristic possessed by many geometrical figures and algebraic expressions, and by some mathematical processes. In general, symmetry implies the possibility of interchanging parts without altering the whole.

Geometrical Symmetry: A figure may be symmetric with respect to a point, a line, or a plane. Two points are symmetric with respect to a third point if the line connecting them passes through the third point and is bisected by it. A curve is symmetric with respect to a point if, for every point on the curve, the symmetric point is also on it. The curve in Fig. 1 is symmetric with respect to *O;* on it the points *P* and *P'* are symmetric points. The definitions of symmetry of a plane area and of three-dimensional figures are essentially the same.

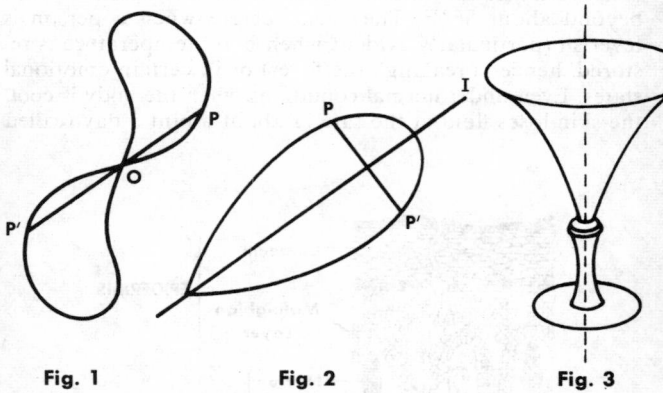

Fig. 1   Fig. 2   Fig. 3

In Fig. 1, the area contained in the curve is symmetric with respect to *O*. A spherical ball is symmetric with respect to its center, as is a football and a dumbbell.

The curve in Fig. 2 is symmetric with respect to the line *l*. Two points are symmetric with respect to a line if the segment joining them is bisected perpendicularly by the given line. A curve is symmetric with respect to a line if, for every point on it, the symmetric point is also on it. In Fig. 2, *P* and *P'* are symmetric points. Symmetry of an area with respect to a line is defined in the same way, as is the symmetry of volume of any three-dimensional figure. A circle is symmetric with respect to any diameter; an ellipse with respect to both the major axis and the minor axis, but not with respect to any other diameter. A wine glass is symmetric with respect to its central axis (Fig. 3), not with respect to any other line.

Symmetry with respect to a plane is defined in much the same way as symmetry with respect to a line. A sphere is symmetric with respect to every plane through its center. The wine glass in Fig. 3 is symmetric with respect to every plane that includes its axis. A person's head is approximately symmetric with respect to a vertical plane through the middle of the nose. An object and its image in a plane mirror are symmetric with respect to the surface of the mirror.

The symmetry of geometrical figures is a valuable aid in drawing them. If, for example, a curve is known to be symmetric with respect to both coordinate axes, one need plot only that part in the first quadrant and the remainder of the curve is immediately known.

Symbiotic relationship between animal and plant: This animal, *Lithocircus*, a marine protozoan, has skeleton of silica forming an elliptic ring. Main body mass is the large, roughly spherical portion within skeletal ring. Small spherical cells scattered among antlerlike pseudopodia and within skeletal ring are individual plants—algae of genus *Xanthella*. In their mutualistic relationship the protozoan gives off carbon dioxide which is used by algae in photosynthesis. Algae, in turn, give off oxygen which is utilized by the animal. (L. Magdeburg/Monkmeyer)

Algebraic Symmetry: Geometrical symmetry refers to an interchangeable arrangement of points. Symmetry in an algebraic expression involves an interchangeability of algebraic symbols—in particular, of letters denoting numbers. For example, $x^2 + 2xy + y^2$ is symmetric in x and y. This means that x and y can be interchanged without altering the meaning of the expression. The expression $x^2 + y^2 - z^2$ is symmetric in x and y, but not in x, y, and z, whereas $xy + yz + zx$ is symmetric in the three letters. In the study of the theory of equations the symmetric functions of the roots of an equation play a role. Thus, if the roots of the cubic equation, $x^3 + ax^2 + bx + c = 0$, are r_1, r_2, and r_3, a symmetric expression of the first degree is equal to a: $-(r_1 + r_2 + r_3) = a$; a symmetric function of the second degree is equal to b: $r_1r_2 + r_2r_3 + r_1r_3 = b$; and a symmetric function of the third degree is equal to c: $-(r_1r_2r_3) = c$.

Other Forms of Symmetry: Many mathematical processes contain a reciprocity of terms and concepts that has the main attribute of symmetry, *i.e.* interchangeability. In coordinate geometry, equations and their graphs are so closely identified that what is said about one has an interpretation for the other. A more perfect example is provided by the principle of duality in projective geometry. In the application of this principle a theorem proved about points and lines in a plane carries with it a second theorem in which "line" is replaced by "point," and "point" by "line."—*H. C.*

SYMMETRY PRINCIPLES: Three kinds of symmetry interest physicists: symmetry in space, in time, and in electric charge. In the ordinary world, where the motion of macroscopic bodies is considered, these symmetries unquestionably exist, but in the atomic domain, where the behavior of a system has to be described in terms of quantum mechanics, experiments in recent years have indicated certain violations of the symmetry principles.

Space: The idea of spatial symmetry arises because the motion of a system is most conveniently described in terms of a set of three mutually perpendicular coordinate axes. By convention the system is set up using the thumb of the right hand as the x axis, the forefinger as the y axis, and the middle finger as the z axis, but one could just as well define a system by using the left hand, though in that case one of the axes (the x axis) would be reversed in direction relative to the right-handed axes. Since there is no reason for choosing the right hand in preference to the left, the laws of physics should be independent of which one is chosen, as is the case in classical physics.

It can be seen that the two coordinate frames are merely mirror images of each other, and one can go from one frame to the other either by a straightforward reflection or by reversing the direction of all three of the axes. In QUANTUM MECHANICS this concept of spatial inversion is used to define a quantity called *parity,* which is a property of the wave function describing the system. If a wave function changes in algebraic sign under inversion, it is said to have "odd" parity, whereas if it is unchanged its parity is described as "even." One of the consequences of the theory is that parity is conserved, remaining constant even if the system changes its state, *e.g.* by decaying (see PARITY).

Time: The second kind of symmetry has to do with the behavior of a system in time. Customarily one thinks of time progressing always forward, with no possibility of halting or reversing, but, mathematically, time occurs in the equations governing physical phenomena in a symmetric manner, and it could just as well go backward as forward. This invariance under time inversion corresponds, for classical systems, merely to a reversal of the direction of motion, and it is

evident that here it holds rigorously. On the atomic scale the situation is not so clear-cut, but a detailed examination of QUANTUM THEORY shows that time reversal should not yield any new results. Experimental tests have been devised to demonstrate this, and so far no breakdown of the principle has been found.

Charge: Symmetry with respect to charge also arises because there is no absolute way of defining positive and negative, for the existing convention could just as easily be reversed without changing any of the consequences of electromagnetic theory. For atomic systems, charge symmetry appears as an integral part of quantum theory when the subject is treated relativistically. Then, for every solution for a PARTICLE with positive charge, there is a corresponding one for a negative particle. This situation calls for the existence of an ANTIPARTICLE as a counterpart to every particle. When observed, these antiparticles are found to behave exactly as predicted, except, once again, in situations where weak interactions are important. As mentioned above, parity is not conserved under such circumstances, and a complete analysis of the results of certain experiments shows that charge invariance does not always hold, either.

That two of the symmetry principles are violated is expected, for it can be shown that if all three symmetry operations are performed on a system, the system should be unchanged as far as physical behavior is concerned. This is the so-called C. P. T. (charge-parity-time) theorem.

Even though parity conservation and charge independence are separately violated in weak interactions, in most cases their product is conserved, and a mirror image of a system behaves in exactly the same manner as the original, provided that particle is replaced by antiparticle. This is called CP invariance, and the only known exception occurs in the decays of long-lived neutral K mesons (see PARTICLE, ELEMENTARY), where there is a small violation. This was discovered in 1964 by J. Cronin and V. Fitch of Princeton, who found that the decay $K_2^0 \rightarrow \pi^+ + \pi^-$ occurs 0.2% as often as $K_1^0 \rightarrow \pi^+ + \pi^-$, whereas it should not occur at all if CP conservation holds. The effect is not understood, and none of the theories put forward to account for it have been verified by experiment, but the violation is so small that it may not be detectable in any process except K decay.—*D. C. C.*

SYNCHROTRON: see PARTICLE ACCELERATORS.

SYNCLINE: a downfold in layered rocks. In such a fold the two limbs dip inward towards the FOLD axis. Most commonly synclines alternate with anticlines in areas where the crustal rocks have been crumpled by compression.—*J. Sh.*

SYNERESIS: The spontaneous exudation of liquid from a GEL, accompanied by contraction and shrinkage of the gel. Syneresis is the opposite of swelling, the chemical process undergone by a gel-forming substance when placed in an appropriate solvent.—*H. W. F.*

SYNERGISM: interaction between components of a mixture so that the mixture is more efficacious than any of the individual components would be if used alone. Frequently, one of the synergists (participating components) may be ineffective itself. For instance, sesame oil exhibits no insecticidal properties against houseflies, but when added to a solution of pyrethrum in kerosene it greatly enhances the insecticidal effects.—*D. P. B.*

SYNGE, RICHARD LAWRENCE MILLINGTON, 1914– , English biochemist; b. Liverpool. With A. J. P. Martin, he developed partition chromatography, a method of separating biochemical compounds, and for this they shared the Nobel prize, 1952. Their work led to major advances in the study of the sterols, and to the discovery of new antibiotics and amino acids in bacteria. Synge is a fellow of the Royal Society.— *D. H. D. R.*

SYNODIC PERIOD: the interval of time between two consecutive conjunctions of a planet or the Moon with the Sun. For the Moon, conjunction time coincides with New Moon; thus the synodic period is equal to one lunation and averages 29½ days; it is the basis of the lunar month in ancient calendars. In the case of Mercury and Venus, which have alternating inferior and superior conjunctions, the synodic period refers to the time elapsed between two conjunctions of the same kind—both inferior or both superior. If a planet were to remain fixed in its orbit, its synodic period would be exactly 1 yr, or the time required by Earth to return to the same position with respect to that planet and the Sun. Since, however, planets revolve around the Sun with speeds different from Earth's, one lap must be gained by those which are faster than Earth—Mercury and Venus—whereas Earth must gain one lap over the remaining, slower ones. Venus and Mars have the largest synodic periods (584 and 780 days, respectively) because their angular speeds are closest to Earth's. On the other hand, Neptune and Pluto move so slowly that their synodic period (367 days) barely exceeds 1 yr. Corresponding values for the other planets are: 116 days for Mercury, 399 for Jupiter, 378 for Saturn, and 370 for Uranus.—*S. D. G.*

SYNTAX, LOGICAL: the study of those properties of a formalized language which depend not upon any particular interpretation or use of the language but rather upon mutual relations among the signs and sequences of signs of the language. Logical syntax is to be distinguished from *semantics,* which is the study of those properties of a language which have to do with the concepts of meaning, denotation, and truth, relative to some interpretation of the language. A *formalized language* (or formal deductive system) must have a well-determined and fixed class of symbols. Furthermore, without reference to anything but the symbols themselves, there must be an effective characterization of: (1) a collection of sequences of symbols called *well-formed formulas;* (2) the well-formed formulas which are to be taken as *axioms;* (3) *rules of inference,* which specify that from certain collections of well-formed formulas certain others may be drawn as consequences. The theorems are those well-formed formulas which may be obtained by starting with axioms and successively applying the rules of inference. More precisely, a *proof* is a sequence of well-formed formulas such that each formula in the sequence is either an axiom or is a consequence, by some rule of inference, of preceding formulas in the sequence. The last well-formed formula in a proof is called a *theorem.* The most important syntactical properties are consistency and completeness. A formalized language is said to be *absolutely consistent* if not all well-formed formulas are theorems. In the most common formalized languages containing a symbol for negation, this is equivalent to ordinary consistency, *i.e.* the assertion that there is no formula A such that both A and not-A are theorems. In languages containing variables, a formula is called a *sentence* if all variables occurring in it are subject to some "bounding" condition, such as "for all x" or "there is an x such that." For instance, in formalized number theory, the formula "$x + 2 = 4$" is not a sentence, but "for all x, $x + 2 = 4$" and "there is an x such that $x + 2 = 4$" are sentences. Given any interpretation of the formalized language, it is only the sentences which express assertions that are true or false. A formalized language is *complete* if, for any sentence A, either A is a theorem or not-A is a theorem. (See METAMATHEMATICS; UNDECIDABLE PROPOSITION; GÖDEL'S PROOF.)—*El. M.*

SYSTEMA NATURAE, sive Regna tria Naturae systematice proposita per classes, ordines, genera, et species (System of Nature), by Carolus Linnaeus (1735): Published originally as a set of charts with explanatory notes and covering 11 large folio pages, this work of Linnaeus' grew in later editions into a multi-volume classificatory system for the whole of the mineral, vegetable, and animal worlds. The species was adopted as the starting point for classification; various species were grouped into genera, and the genera into classes. After 1753 Linnaeus introduced the famous binary nomenclature, by which every plant or animal could be identified and given its place in the system by means of two words, *e.g.* Homo sapiens. Plants were classified by the number and type of reproductive organs, while animals were recognized by purely external characteristics. Linnaeus was aware of the weakness of this wholly formal classificatory scheme and attempted in later life to develop a natural method for recognizing affinities between closely related groups.—*E. Me.*

SZENT-GYÖRGYI VON NAGYRAPOLT, ALBERT, 1893– , Hungarian-U. S. biochemist; b. Budapest. In 1928 he isolated "hexuronic acid" from the adrenal cortex. ("Hexuronic acid" was later shown to be vitamin C, ascorbic acid, by W. A. Waugh and C. G. King.) For his discoveries in connection with the biological combustion processes, with especial reference to vitamin C and the catalysis of fumaric acid, he received the Nobel prize, 1937. He is a leading investigator of the biochemical mechanisms of muscle contraction. He is an associate of the U. S. National Academy of Sciences.— *D. H. D. R.*

I. PETRÆ	sunt Lapides SIMPLICES, qui Metallurgis dicuntur *Bergarter.* constant particulis tantummodo similaribus.			II.
Asbestus.	Constat Fibr. papposis intertextis.	Asbestus natans, solido-flexilis. A natans fibroso-coriaceus. A ponderosus fissilis.	Suber montanum. Aluta montana. Caro fossilis.	Berghaber. Berghleber. Berghrot.
Amiantus.	Fibris parallelis.	A fibris capillaceis flexilibus tenacibus. A fibris capillaceis flexilibus fragilis. A fibris setosis rigidis. A fibris angulosis rigidis.	Linum incombustibile. Alumen plumos. offic. Amiantus immaturus. Pseudo-amiantus.	Berglin. Bergstun. Galthaae. Unegen Amiant.
Ollaris.	Fibris sparsis.	O fibris accrosis friabilibus. O fibris acerosis rigidis. O fibris e centro radiatis. O fibris fasciculatim inflexis.	Lebetum Lapis. Acerosus Lapis. Radians Lapis. Torosus Lapis.	Tälgsten. Acktag. Stiernslag. Fels.
Talcum.	Membranis carnosis, inaequalis superficiei.	T durum crassum, cortice nitido. T durum coriaceum. T friabile molliusculum. T friabile fragile membranaceum.	Corneus Lapis. Tunicatus Lapis. Talcum offic. Talcum aureum.	Hornsten. Sinslag. Hvit Talk. Guld-talk.
Mica.	Membranis squamosis, aequalis superficiei.	M particulis impalpabilibus. M particulis squamosis. M particulis membranaceis fissilibus. M particulis squamosis & membr. mixtis. M particulis prismaticis immixtis.	Sterile nigrum. Mica vulgaris. Vitrum Moscoviticum.	Glimmer. Sattsmid. Qimta.

Portion of page from Linnaeus' Systema naturae includes part of his first group of rocks—the fire-resistant kinds—with notes on their properties and with Latin names (genus and species) and the German names. (*N. Y. Public Library*)

T

TAIT, PETER GUTHRIE, 1831–1901, Scottish mathematician and physicist; b. Dalkeith. He did research in mathematics on the quaternions of Sir W. R. Hamilton and in physics on electric discharges through gases. He also published research on thermodynamics, thermoelectricity, and the mathematics of knots, and his published papers on the foundations of the kinetic theory of gases are of particular importance. He was the author of numerous books, including some highly influential textbooks.—*D. H. D. R.*

TALUS: a pile or scattering of boulders broken from steep slopes or cliffs above, and transported down by the direct force of gravity. Such rock has become detached by weathering. Freezing of water in joints pries rock masses apart until some of them fall. Also, expansion of rock minerals by addition of water (*hydration*) during chemical weathering causes

Fallen weathered rock fragments, called "talus," litter the eroded rock terraces of Lone Butte in SE Utah. Talus often lies thick at the foot of cliffs in desert country (see page 189). (*Josef Muench*)

fragmentation of rock masses. Generally the boulders pile up at the base of slope or cliff in cone-shaped deposits called *talus cones*. Where production of boulders is very active, the cones unite to form *talus slopes* or *talus aprons;* these may extend for miles, with the apexes of the cones rising many hundreds of feet above their bases. The most striking development of talus is above the tree line in rugged mountains. —*N. E. A. H.*

TANGENT: in geometry, a line that touches a curve. The attempt to express the concept precisely, and to find reliable methods of determining tangents to large classes of curves, occupied mathematicians for 2,000 yr, and eventually led to the invention of differential calculus. The idea of a tangent as a line that "touches" a curve at one point suffices to determine tangents to circles. This idea, however, is quite inadequate to determine tangents in a general way. The relation of tangency to a curve at a point P involves more points of the curve than P—in fact, all the points of the curve in an interval including P. The method of differential calculus recognizes this fact. It starts by approximating the intuitive image of a tangent by a chord through P and a second point of the curve, Q, as shown in the figure. The point Q is conceived as free to move along the curve, and if the chord PQ approaches a limiting position as Q approaches P, the line in this position is defined to be the tangent at P. This process is made more precise by fixing attention upon the slope of the chord, which is a numerical concept, and defining the slope of the tangent to be the limit approached by the slope of PQ as Q approaches P. If the slope of PQ does not tend to a unique limit as Q approaches P, there is no tangent at P. This occurs at certain special points such as cusps, double points, and isolated points. Because of the way the tangent is defined, a curve having an equation $y = f(x)$ has a tangent at a point only if $f(x)$ has a derivative there. A tangent approximates a curve in the neighborhood of the point of tangency more closely than any other straight line.

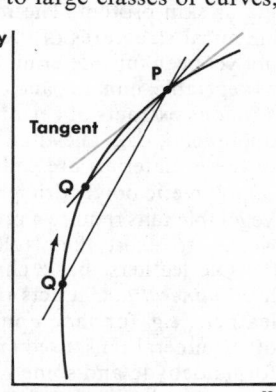

Development of a Tangent to a Curve at Point P

Tangent planes to surfaces are defined similarly to tangent lines to curves. Because a surface lies in three dimensions it is expressed by a function of two variables, and partial derivatives with respect to both are essential to the determination of a tangent plane. The tangent plane at a point approximates the surface in the neighborhood of the point more closely than any other plane.—*H. C.*

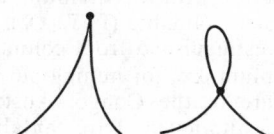

No tangent exists at the points shown on these curves: a cusp (*left*) and a double point (*right*).

TANGENTIAL VELOCITY: in astronomy, the velocity of a star across the line of sight; a component of SPACE VELOCITY.

TANNING: the process of converting suitably prepared hides or skins into leather or fur pieces. Leather differs from rawhide in being resistant to putrefaction and attack by microorganisms; it has greatly improved dimensional stability under changing conditions of temperature and humidity, and has greater toughness and flexibility and lower permeability. Leather retains, however, the original morphological structure of the skin. Tanning has been practiced since prehistoric times. Vegetable, alum, and oil tanning, all used today, were apparently well known to the ancient Egyptians. Although all tanning processes accomplish a generally similar result, and all involve prolonged soaking of the skin in a solution of the tanning agent, the tanning agents differ widely in chemical composition and speed of action. Each has advantages and limitations; each produces its own characteristic type of leather. The agents combine chemically with collagen, the major skin protein. The mechanism of the reaction and the chemical structures of the resulting leather substances have not yet been fully determined. The tanning agents are grouped as vegetable, mineral, and organic. The *vegetable tans* comprise aqueous extracts of certain barks and plant tissues, notably quebracho, oak, chestnut, and wattle. The active substances in these materials are called tannins and have the structure of polymeric polyhydric phenols and phenol carboxylic acids. Vegetable tans require a prolonged soaking period, sometimes weeks, to exert their full effect; they are used primarily for sole leathers. Basic chromium sulfate is the most widely used *mineral tan;* it acts rapidly and is used to prepare thin leathers, *e.g.* for shoe uppers. Alum and zirconium tans are other mineral tans, used largely on furs. Among *organic tans,* formaldehyde and some of its condensates with urea constitute one subgroup, and are used for special leathers. Naphthalene formaldehyde sulfonates are widely used as auxiliary tanning agents. The easily oxidized fish oils, also classed as organic tans, are used as tanning agents in producing the special type of water-absorbent, spongy-textured leather called chamois.

Technically, tanning is only one step in leather manufacture. Before undergoing the tanning operation, hides are normally washed, dehaired, and bated. Bating is a treatment with a proteolytic enzyme that loosens and removes skin proteins other than collagen, allowing faster and more uniform penetration of tanning agents. After tanning, leather goes through several finishing operations, which may include drying, oiling, filling, lacquering, polishing, and calendering.—*A. M. S.*

TANTALUM: a metallic element (Ta); at. no. 73; at. wt 180.88; density 16.6; mp 2996°C; bp above 4100°C; valence usually 5, but also 2, 3, and 4. It was discovered (1802) by A. G. Ekeberg in fossils found in Finland. Tantalum is almost always intermingled in its ores with NIOBIUM (Nb) and often with tin, titanium, manganese, germanium, and tungsten; tantalite ($FeTa_2O_6$), the principal mineral, often is not distinguished from columbite ($FeNb_2O_6$), the principal niobium ore, for mining purposes. The main tantalum deposits are in the Congo, Australia, South Dakota, Brazil, and Scandinavia. Pure tantalum is prepared by the reduction of its alkali fluoride complex with hydrogen.

Tantalum is one of the most acid-resistant metals, and is widely used in chemical and industrial equipment where resistance to corrosion, acids, and highly reactive compounds (*e.g.* halogens) is important. It is not easily alloyed, because of its high melting point, but tantalum-silicon alloys are made which are almost as hard as diamond. Tantalum electric-light bulb filaments, because they are incandescent at lower temperatures than the common tungsten filaments, are used where cooler and more vibration-free filaments are desired. Tantalum also finds use as a catalyst in synthetic-rubber manufacture, surgical instruments, pen points, lenses of aerial cameras, radio and radar tubes operating at high temperatures, vacuum tubes (to absorb gases), and in rectifiers because tantalum passes a-c current in only one direction. A special medical application is in nerve and bone surgery for repair of bone segments (*e.g.* by a tantalum skull plate), since living tissues adhere to rather than recede from

tantalum. The compound tantalum carbide (TaC) is extremely hard, and is employed as an alloy in the manufacture of high-speed cutting tools.—*G. W. M.*

TAR: a dark-colored, viscous liquid mixture consisting mainly of hydrocarbons. A residue from crude oil distillation, it is also produced by coking coal or by dry distillation of wood. Further distilled, it becomes asphalt or pitch. Principal uses are as fuel and as a binder in roofing and road construction, briquette manufacture, etc. Coal tar also yields many useful chemicals. (See COAL and COAL PRODUCTS.)—*W. B. P.*

TARSKI, ALFRED, 1902– , Polish-American mathematical logician; b. Warsaw. He is best known for his investigation of the conditions under which the semantic conception of truth can be adequately defined syntactically (1931), and for his studies on various DECISION PROBLEMS in mathematics.—*I. L.*

TARTAGLIA, NICCOLÒ (Nicola Fontana), *c.* 1506–59, Italian mathematician; b. Brescia. Self-taught, he reached a degree of proficiency which permitted him to earn a living as a teacher of mathematics at Verona, Vicenza, Brescia, and Venice. He completed the solution of the cubic equation and gave the secret to Cardan under a pledge of secrecy. Cardan published the solution in 1545. Tartaglia was the first to apply mathematics to the science of artillery; he wrote the best book on arithmetic of the 16th cent. and edited works of Euclid and Archimedes.—*H. C.*

TARTARIC ACID: an acid found in nature, dihydroxysuccinic acid, $HOOC—(CHOH)_2—COOH$. A salt in which *one* of the terminal acidic H atoms is replaced by potassium is obtained from the juice of grapes. This is the *cream of tartar* (a mild acid) used in baking powder. When the remaining acidic H atom in cream of tartar is neutralized with sodium hydroxide to give sodium potassium tartrate, the product is the purgative Rochelle salt. Because of its pronounced PIEZOELECTRIC EFFECT, crystalline Rochelle salt is used in phonograph pickup cartridges and in microphones. Tartaric acid had an important role in the history of stereoisomerism.—*Ru. M.*

TASTE AND SMELL: in animals, the senses responding most readily to chemical stimuli. Of the two, taste (or gustation) is much more limited and depends upon more intense stimuli. In most animals taste allows discrimination only among the four qualities (sweet, sour, salty, and bitter) to which the taste buds on the human tongue respond. Ordinarily a solution containing the substance to be tasted must be brought in contact with some part of the animal, making taste strictly a contact sense. Smell (or olfaction) shows a far wider repertoire in most animals, and permits a response to far fewer molecules than does taste; generally the sense of smell enables an animal to detect food, mates, or sources of danger at a distance. At its best, taste requires at least 25,000 times as many molecules to elicit a sensation as will serve to provide a distinctive odor. A small amount of diluted musk from which 800,000 molecules are escaping per second will yield

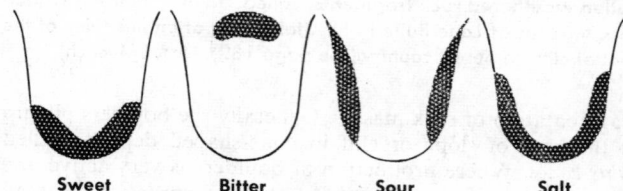

Sweet   Bitter   Sour   Salt

Taste buds for four basic taste sensations are embedded in different parts of human tongue. Flavor depends not only on the way these sensations are blended, but also on such other sensations as smell, touch, and temperature. (*From Villee*)

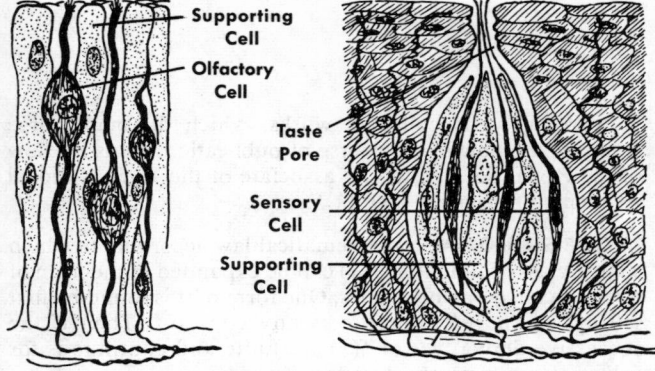

Odor and taste receptors of human body: *Left*—Olfactory cells lie embedded in mucous membrane of uppermost interior part of nose. *Right*—Taste buds like this one are embedded in covering of the papillae on surface of tongue. (*From Whaley, after Woodruff*)

enough molecules in two seconds to permit discovery and identification by the human nose. Most people require a much higher concentration of ethanethiol (ethyl mercaptan) to recognize the odor of skunk: the inhalation of about 19,400,000,000 molecules, which is about 0.000,000,000,000,000,071 oz.

Flavor is a blend of taste and smell. It is sharpened if volatile components of food can reach the olfactory cells in the mammalian nose both via the nostrils and via the throat and nasal passages above the palate.

Probably, olfaction is the most ancient of all senses used in detecting things at a distance. It permits most aquatic animals to be alert to a great variety of concealed events in their surroundings. Among simpler animals, responses to chemical substances reaching them from the surrounding medium are often described as "chemokinetic" rather than as taste or smell; presumably the mechanism is comparable. Coelenterates discharge their nematocysts, in capturing prey and in defending themselves, when the distinctive chemical glutathione comes to them from live animals close by. Many marine worms, mollusks, and echinoderms discharge their reproductive cells into the sea when they detect the chemical substances liberated during this process by other members of their own species.

Terrestrial insects have chemoreceptors on their antennae, mouthparts, and legs, with which they locate and recognize food, mates, egg-laying sites, and members of their own and other species. Many flies are able to discriminate among substances in solution more readily when the solution wets their front feet than when it reaches their mouthparts; the feet allow a response to perhaps a tenth as many molecules of the stimulating substance. In many moths, the antennae excel in detecting odors and serve to direct the males in flying as much as seven miles upwind to a female releasing the attractive substance.

Among vertebrate animals, the distribution and number of sense organs for taste and smell vary greatly. In sharks and many other fishes, these organs are located both within and around the mouth and on more remote parts of the body surface. In amphibians, reptiles, and warm-blooded vertebrates, these sense organs are restricted to the mouth and nasal areas. Most birds have little or no sense of smell, and their sense of taste seems much reduced; parrots have more taste buds (about 400) than other birds, some of which get along with from 20 to 60. Probably most mammals suffer a progressive loss of taste buds as they age. In children, taste buds stud the hard palate, soft palate, walls of the throat, and the central upper surface of the tongue, but these are lost as the individual ages. Taste buds on the tip, edges, and back of the tongue remain until old age. The sense of taste fades at a comparable rate: young adults can identify as sweet a solution containing a third as much sugar as that re-

quired to give a similar sense of taste to an elderly person. The sense of smell does not deteriorate at a corresponding rate, but is no better understood. Despite many attempts to classify odor qualities (*e.g.* fruity, spicy, burnt), no satisfactory scheme has been found. See HUNGER AND THIRST; NOSE; SENSES; TONGUE.—*L. and M. M.*

TATUM, EDWARD LAWRIE, 1909– , U. S. geneticist; b. Boulder, Colo. His research has included work in nutrition, biochemistry, and the nutrition and genetics of microorganisms. For the discovery, through experiments with bread mold, that genes transmit hereditary characters by controlling single enzyme chemical reactions, he and G. W. Beadle shared the 1958 Nobel prize with Joshua Lederberg. He is a member of the National Academy of Sciences.—*D. H. D. R.*

TAUTOLOGY: in common speech, any redundant or unnecessary utterance; in contemporary logic, roughly and picturesquely speaking (following Leibniz's account of logical necessity), a sentence which is "true in all possible worlds." A clearer definition must await a few preliminary considerations.

Propositions may be either true or false—a fact which we state equivalently by saying that a proposition may have one of two *truth-values:* namely, *truth* and *falsehood.* Interest in truth-values stems from the fact that we can consider FUNCTIONS of ordered *n*-tuples of truth-values, which take truth-values as values. For example, the *negation function* (or simply "negation") takes truth into falsehood, and conversely. We express this in the following truth-table (where *p* is an arbitrary proposition):

p	not-*p*
true	*false*
false	*true*

The sense of the table is that if we choose a proposition *p* which has the truth-value *true,* then the denial "not-*p*" ("it is not the case that *p*") will be false (*i.e.* have the truth-value *false*). And if *p* is false, then not-*p* is true.

Similarly, we can define the *conjunction* ("and") of two propositions *p* and *q* as a truth-function of *p* and *q* which is true when both *p* and *q* are true, and false otherwise; and the *disjunction* ("or") of *p* and *q* is true if at least one of *p* and *q* is true, and false otherwise. These connectives have the following tables:

p	*q*	*p* and *q*	*p* or *q*
true	*true*	*true*	*true*
true	*false*	*false*	*true*
false	*true*	*false*	*true*
false	*false*	*false*	*false*

(The second row, for example, means that if *p* has the value *true,* and *q* has the value *false,* then their conjunction "*p* and *q*" has the value *false,* and their disjunction "*p* or *q*" has the value *true.*)

Now it happens that some truth-functional compounds are true *regardless* of the truth-values of the propositions of which they are compounds—such compounds being called *tautologies* (after Wittgenstein, *Tractatus Logico-Philosophicus,* 1919). Example:

p	*q*	not-*p*	or	(not-*q*	or	*p*)
true	*true*	*false*	*true*	*false*	*true*	*true*
true	*false*	*false*	*true*	*true*	*true*	*true*
false	*true*	*true*	*true*	*false*	*false*	*false*
false	*false*	*true*	*true*	*true*	*false*	*false*

Notice that we have assigned (on the left) all possible combinations of *true* and *false* to *p* and *q,* and then computed the truth-value of "not-*p* or (not-*q* or *p*)" (between the heavy bars) for each assignment. Thus in the third row, p is false and q is true; hence not-p is true and not-q is false; (not-q or p) is then false (as we see by consulting the table for "or"); but since not-p is true, the whole disjunction is true. A similar computation for each row shows that in every case the expression assumes the value *true;* hence "not-p or (not-q or p)" is a tautology—it is true, so to speak, *whatever* p and q may be.

Many-valued logics are a natural generalization of the two-valued logic. Instead of confining attention to the two truth-values *truth* and *falsehood,* we can instead consider an arbitrary number of "truth-values," and define "truth"-functions in an analogous way. Then some of the many truth-values are taken as *designated* ("true-ish," so to speak), and tautologies in many-valued systems are by definition those expressions which take designated values for every assignment of values to the propositional variables.

Two-valued (*true* and *false*) truth-tables are treated in any contemporary elementary text on logic. The first many-valued logic was a three-valued system studied by Łukasiewicz in 1920. *N*-valued logics have been investigated extensively in Rosser and Turquette, *Many-valued Logics* (1952). See also LOGIC; SEMANTICS; SYNTAX, LOGICAL.—*A. R. A.*

TAUTOMERISM: the phenomenon, exhibited by certain compounds, of behaving as if they possessed two different structures. Such compounds, *e.g.* ethyl acetoacetate, do in fact consist of a mixture of the two different types of molecules, convertible spontaneously into each other and existing in dynamic equilibrium.—*A. M. S.*

TAXONOMY: the science of classification of plants and animals. As begun by Aristotle (384–322 B. C.) and developed by Carolus Linnaeus (1707–78) and others, taxonomy involved little more than a simple grouping of plants and animals on the basis of structure. Following publication of Darwin's *Origin of Species,* 1859, classification became based on evolutionary relations. The aim of the taxonomist was to group together living forms having common ancestors. During this period, emphasis was placed on the higher categories of classification: phylum, class, and order. Today emphasis is on species and subspecies. The taxonomist studies EVOLUTION within species and the relation of subspecies to their environment (ECOLOGY). The term taxonomy is often used in a limited sense to cover solely the naming and grouping of living forms, whereas *systematics* is used in a broader sense to include not only naming and grouping, but also the study of ecological and evolutionary relationships of biological groups. See CLASSIFICATION OF LIVING THINGS.—*H. M. S.*

TAYLOR, BROOK, 1685–1731, English mathematician; b. Edmonton, Middlesex. He is best known for TAYLOR'S THEOREM, which gives a means of approximating more or less arbitrary functions by polynomials. Lagrange termed this theorem the fundamental principle of differential calculus. Taylor's *Methodus incrementorum directa et inversa* (1715) added the subject of calculus of finite differences to mathematics. He published works on perspective, giving the first general treatment of vanishing points. He also wrote works on physics, logarithms, and series. He was a fellow of the Royal Society.—*H. C.*

TAYLOR, SIR GEOFFREY INGRAM, 1886– , British mathematical physicist; b. St. John's Wood, London. His wide range has covered fluid dynamics, meteorology, and the mechanics of the solid state. His outstanding achievements are in the field of turbulent motion, in which he created the statistical theory of turbulence, and in aerodynamics and

meteorology. His collected works, which fill many large volumes, are now in the course of publication. He is a fellow of the Royal Society and an associate of the U. S. National Academy of Sciences.—*O. G. S.*

TAYLOR'S THEOREM: a mathematical law according to which a large class of functions $f(x)$ can be expanded in the form of a series, called Taylor's series. One form of it is found by first setting $x = a + h$, where a is any constant. Then if the successive derivatives of $f(x)$ are finite and continuous for values of x sufficiently close to a,

$$f(x) = f(a + h) = f(a) + f'(a)h + \frac{1}{2!}f''(a)h^2 + \cdots$$
$$+ \frac{1}{n!}f^{(n)}(a)h^n + \cdots$$

Since $h = x - a$, the series may also be written:

$$f(x) = f(a) + f'(a)(x - a) + \frac{1}{2!}f''(a)(x - a)^2 + \cdots$$
$$+ \frac{1}{n!}f^{(n)}(a)(x - a)^n + \cdots$$

If $a = 0$ in this expansion, we obtain Maclaurin's series:

$$f(x) = f(0) + xf'(0) + \frac{x^2}{2!}f''(0) + \cdots + \frac{x^n}{n!}f^{(n)}(0) + \cdots$$

(Here $f'(0)$ is the result of differentiating $f(x)$ and then equating x to 0; and similarly for higher derivatives.) Maclaurin's form yields what is called a power series, *i.e.* a series of the form $c_0 + c_1x + c_2x^2 + \cdots$, wherein the c's are constants. Such series are useful for many functions, including the trigonometric and exponential ones. To expand $\sin x$ we first note that if $f(x) = \sin x$, then $f'(x) = \cos x$, $f''(x) = -\sin x$, $f'''(x) = -\cos x$, and so on. Thus $f(0) = 0$, $f'(0) = 1$, $f''(0) = 0$, $f'''(0) = -1$, and so on. Hence,

$$\sin x = x - \frac{x^3}{3!} + \frac{x^5}{5!} - \frac{x^7}{7!} + \cdots$$

To expand e^x, we note that all its derivatives are equal to e^x. Equating x to 0, we obtain e^0, or 1, so that

$$e^x = 1 + x + \frac{x^2}{2!} + \frac{x^3}{3!} + \cdots$$

Setting $x = 1$ yields one of the definitions of e:

$$e = 1 + 1 + \frac{1}{2!} + \frac{1}{3!} + \cdots$$

See CALCULUS, DIFFERENTIAL AND INTEGRAL; SERIES; *e.*— *B. P. S.*

TEAR GAS: any substance designed to cause a blinding flow of tears (lacrimation) and thus incapacitate the victim. Compounds used can be in the form of gas, liquid droplets, or finely divided solids. The lacrimator best known to the layman is onion juice. Chloroacetophenone, a crystalline solid, is used by military and police.—*Ru. M.*

TEAR GLANDS (or **lacrimal glands**): in higher vertebrates, organs that secrete the watery, slightly salty fluid known as tears. In man each of the two tear glands is the size and shape of an almond and is located in the upper, outer corner of the EYE socket. Tears keep the inner surface of the eyelids and, especially, the exposed part of the eyeball from drying (which would make clear vision impossible). Except when the eyes are closed, water continuously evaporates from the cornea, whose dryness then acts as a stimulus for evoking the winking reflex. By this momentary closure of the eye, a thin layer of tears is spread over the eye's surface. An increase in the flow of tears may be caused by emotional upset or by anything that irritates the surface of the eye, *e.g.* small particles, inflammation, or volatile substances given off by freshly cut onions.—*A. P. E.*

TECHNETIUM: a synthetic metallic element (Tc); at. no. 43; at. wt 99 (most stable isotope). The first artificially made element, it was produced (1937) by E. Segrè and C. Perrier, who bombarded molybdenum with deuterons in the 37-in. cyclotron at the Univ. of Calif. Before 1937, researchers had searched for technetium in natural ores, since the PERIODIC TABLE indicated that a "missing element" of atomic number 43 should exist. Technetium has since been isolated in quantity from the fission products of uranium.—*G. W. M.*

TECTONICS: the study of rock deformation produced by forces generated within the earth. Rocks studied under laboratory conditions exhibit considerable departure from the ideal elastic response described by HOOKE'S LAW of proportionality between stress and strain. Rocks exhibit elastic *after-working*, a phenomenon in which appreciable time is required for a stressed material to reach its full elastic deformation. The measured breaking strength of rocks depends on loading conditions, temperature, and rate of application of stress. Crushing strengths range from 60 kg/cm² for certain limestones to 5,000 kg/cm² for certain igneous rocks, *e.g.* gabbro and diabase. Shearing strengths are of the same order of magnitude. Temperature decreases these values, while hydrostatic confining pressure and high strain rates increase them. Under natural conditions of elevated temperature and pressure, rocks often do not fail in the sense of fracture, but exhibit the phenomenon of *creep*, a permanent nonelastic change in shape akin to the flow of viscous fluids. The

Tectonic forces folded these shale strata in SE New York. Strata were deposited originally as horizontal layers of mud on a delta. Only a small part of one limb of a fold is exposed here; upper portions have been removed by erosion. (*Jerome Wyckoff*)

strength of rocks can be estimated from maximum heights of mountains and depths of ocean trenches, which give values of the order of 1,000 kg/cm² for forces exerted. The viscosity of rocks can be estimated from the isostatic rebound (see ISOSTASY) of regions recently freed of glacial load, such rebound yielding values of 10²² poise (value for water at 20°C: 0.010 poise).

Several sources of energy are available for producing tectonic forces, but there is no general agreement on their relative importance in producing observed surface features. Such sources include Earth's rotation and the variation in rotation time due to tidal friction and planetary air and sea movements; shifts in Earth's axis of rotation with respect to the axis of figure, such shifts being produced possibly by subcrustal plastic flow; lunar and solar tidal forces (see TIDE); thermal stresses caused by solar radiation, and by secular cooling or heating; and mechanical stresses from convection currents (see CONVECTION THEORY) produced by lateral thermal gradients. The effects of these tectonic forces are evident in the structure and geographical distribution of MOUNTAINS and oceanic DEEPS AND TRENCHES, both ancient ones and those still forming; in volcanic activity, and in the pattern of seismicity of Earth (see VOLCANO; EARTHQUAKE). The principal mountain belts, centers of volcanic activity, and oceanic trenches largely parallel the geographic distribution of earthquakes. The close connection among these features suggests a fundamental and underlying system of tectonic forces. —*Sa. K.*

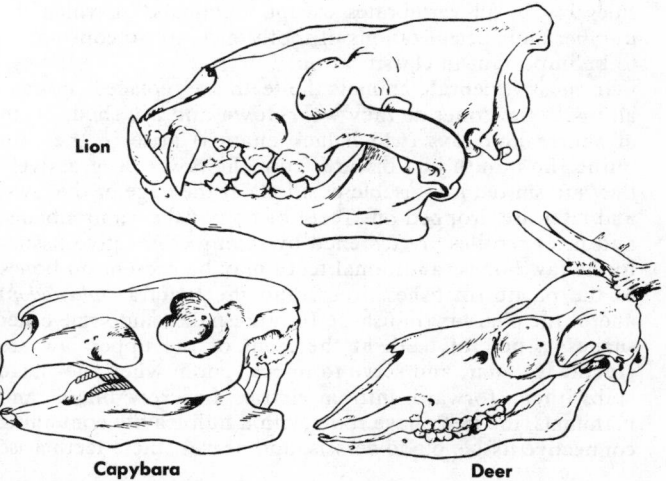

Characteristic teeth of a carnivore, a rodent, and an herbivore are shown in drawings of skulls. Lion has teeth especially suited for tearing flesh. Last cheek tooth is modified into a large, sharp-edged, three-cusped ("canine") tooth. Capybara has chisel-like incisor teeth suited for gnawing. These incisors continue to grow throughout rodent's life. Deer lacks incisor teeth, but has modified cheek teeth (premolars and molars) suited for crushing and grinding coarse herbage. (*From Guyer*)

TEETH: angular or rounded hard parts in the mouth and associated regions of the digestive tract, used in seizing and masticating food, in offense and defense; also, structures of similar form that provide alignment of the two-part shell in hinged brachiopods and clams. Among invertebrates, calcareous teeth are found in the masticatory apparatus (Aristotle's lantern) of sea urchins (as a cluster of five) and in the gastric mill of many crustaceans; chitinous teeth occur on the walls of the eversible pharynx of some marine worms (*e.g.* the polychaete *Nereis*) and in the gastric mill (mastax)

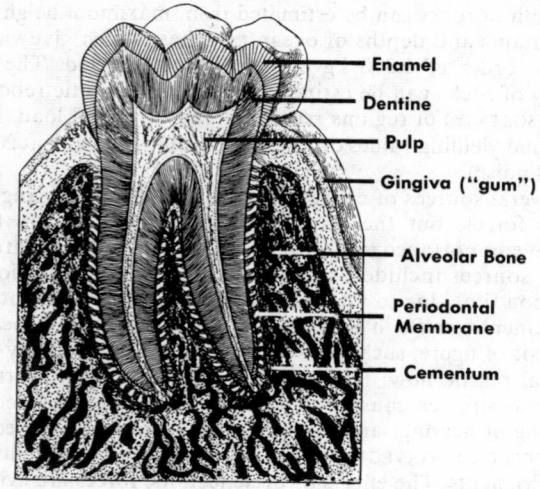

- Enamel
- Dentine
- Pulp
- Gingiva ("gum")
- Alveolar Bone
- Periodontal Membrane
- Cementum

Section through human molar shows internal structure and attachment of tooth in bone. (*From Villee*)

of wheel animalcules (rotifers). Among vertebrate animals without jaws (cyclostomes), teeth studding the mouth cavity and borne on the tongue are sharp, horny caps over conical projections of the skin. In all other vertebrates, the teeth are calcareous. A bonelike mass of *dentine* (ivory) arises from the dermis; it is usually capped by a harder coat of *enamel* secreted by the epidermis. The number of teeth varies considerably in all vertebrates except mammals, in which the number and specializations of tooth form are so constant as to be important in classification.

In most vertebrate animals the teeth are replaced continually with new ones as they wear down and are shed. Teeth of sharks and rays (which lack enamel) arise in the skin lining the mouth just inward from the jaws; progressively they are shifted into usable positions at the edge of the jaws, and later are dropped off. Teeth of bony fishes, amphibians, and most reptiles are fastened by strong connective tissues to the jaw bones; additional teeth may be present on bones of the palate (in fishes, frogs, and the tuatara *Sphenodon*) and of the pharynx (in fishes). In rattlesnakes and some other snakes, a pair of teeth at the front of the upper jaw are erectile, tubular, and serve to inject venom when the snake stabs them forward into a victim. In crocodilians and mammals, the teeth have roots with a pulp cavity containing connective tissue, blood vessels, and nerves; these teeth arise

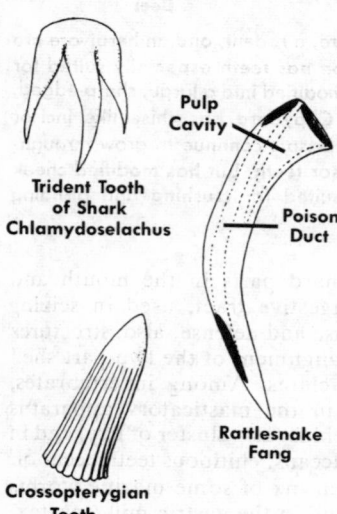

Pulp Cavity

Poison Duct

Trident Tooth of Shark Chlamydoselachus

Rattlesnake Fang

Crossopterygian Tooth

Modifications of teeth: Primitive frilled shark, *Chlamydoselachus,* has three-pronged teeth used for tearing flesh from prey. These teeth are unlike single-pronged, roughly triangular teeth of modern sharks. Extinct crossopterygian fishes had sharp, pointed teeth that frequently had external longitudinal grooves. Rattlesnake fang is a highly specialized tooth used as a weapon rather than for masticating food. Poison glands, located above fang, produce toxic venom that passes through hollow poison duct and into victim via an opening near tip of fang. (*From Eaton*)

in definite sockets, held firmly by a *cementum* between the roots and the bony sockets. Marsupials, toothed whales, and some rodents have only one set of teeth. Other mammals with teeth ordinarily develop two sets: a *milk dentition* and its replacement, an *adult dentition.* In man, there are 20 milk teeth (2 pairs of incisors, 1 pair of canines, and 2 pairs of premolars, both above and below), all of which are in use by age 3; the adult set totals 32 teeth (2 pairs of incisors, 1 pair of canines or eyeteeth, 2 pairs of premolars or bicuspids, and 3 pairs of molars, both above and below), which replace and extend the earlier set, beginning about age 7 and continuing until age 25 (when third molars, or wisdom teeth, develop).

It is customary to represent the number of teeth in mammals by a *dental formula,* which shows the number of each type in one side of the upper jaw by numbers above a horizontal line, and those in one side of the lower jaw below the line. Thus the adult dentition of man would be shown as $\frac{2,1,2,3}{2,1,2,3}$, of the cat as $\frac{3,1,3,1}{3,1,2,1}$, of the pig as $\frac{3,1,4,3}{3,1,4,3}$, of the rat as $\frac{1,0,0,3}{1,0,0,3}$, and of the sheep as $\frac{0,0,3,3}{3,1,3,3}$.

The tusks of elephants are incisors and have almost no enamel; those of pigs, hippopotamuses, and walruses are canines. The slender twisted tusk of the narwhal, which may be the unicorn's horn of European fables, is one of the upper incisors in the male of this Arctic whale. In rabbits and hares (lagomorphs) and rodents, the incisors are particularly well developed and used in gnawing; they grow continuously from persistent roots and are coated with enamel only on front surfaces, with the result that the rear surfaces wear away faster than front surfaces, making the teeth self-sharpening. These animals and the larger herbivores (odd-toed horses and their kin, even-toed cud-chewing mammals, and elephants) lack canine teeth; they have a gap where canines would normally be. An elephant has only one or two grinding teeth functional at a time in each side of the mouth, above and below, and these are replaced from behind as they become worn; each tooth is enormous, and during its development becomes folded, so that many transverse rows of enamel are evident on its grinding surfaces.

Vertebrate teeth are probably homologous with the placoid scales of sharks and rays. But they show extreme specialization. In some kinds of animals, the teeth are lost during embryonic growth and the adults are toothless. Modern birds are completely toothless, whereas fossil birds include many with teeth like those of lizards. Egg-laying mammals have teeth only while young. The scaly anteater (order Pholidota) and the American anteaters and armadillos (order Edentata) lack teeth, but the arboreal sloths (also Edentata) possess a number of molars (without enamel) toward the front of the mouth. Aardvarks, which are insectivorous, have many teeth in the milk dentition, but only a few grinding teeth (without enamel or roots) in the permanent set. Whalebone whales lack teeth; the teeth of toothed whales lack enamel.—*L. and M. M.*

TEISSERENC DE BORT, LÉON PHILIPPE, 1855–1913, French meteorologist; b. Paris. An authority on the upper atmosphere, he explored it extensively, using balloons. He discovered the stratosphere, distinguishing it from the troposphere below. He directed the Central Meteorological Bureau, Paris, 1892–96, and in 1896 established at Trappes an observatory that bears his name.—*D. H. D. R.*

TEKTITE: one of the small, glassy stones that are believed to consist of rock shattered and fused by the impact of a meteorite, and fused again by rapid passage through the atmosphere. Tektites are found in but few localities; *e.g.* the moldavites of

Tektites: Two samples from Libyan desert show smooth and bubbly surfaces, both of which are common. Smaller specimens were cut as gemstones. (*Amer. Mus. of Nat. Hist.*)

Bohemia, the bediasites of Texas, and the australites of Asia. The best-preserved specimens are usually spheroidal or drop-shaped, and greenish brown to gray or black. Because tektites differ in composition from other kinds of natural glass, it has been suggested that they were blasted out of the Moon's crust and drawn to Earth by gravity. However, since they are not widely distributed (as would be expected had they come to Earth all the way from the Moon), and since some tektite fields can be related both geographically and chronologically to specific terrestrial meteorite craters, a terrestrial origin is indicated. Apparently the tektites were projected into the atmosphere by the impacts.—*J. W.*

TELECOMMUNICATION: communication at a distance (Gr. *tele,* "far off"), especially telephony and telegraphy. Telephony is the transmission of speech or sound, as in everyday radio. More strictly, it is the direct modulation of the communication carrier wave by a signal source, *e.g.* the human voice or musical instruments. Telegraphy is transmission by interruption of the communication carrier wave; the simplest example is Morse code, with its dots and dashes. Television is a more complicated form of telecommunication. Today telephone, radio, and television communication is aided by the use of artificial satellites that serve as relay stations.—*G. S.*

TELEGRAPHY: a system of communication that utilizes pre-arranged signals; at present the term is wholly reserved for systems utilizing electrical impulses. The electrical telegraph stems from Joseph Henry's successful use (1831) of an ELECTROMAGNET to transmit a signal by means of a wire over a distance of 1 mi. In 1844, Samuel F. B. Morse, after much experimentation, sent a message between Washington and Baltimore, a distance of over 40 mi. Morse's sending apparatus was a crude form of the familiar telegraph key. The receiver was an electromagnet that attracted an iron armature mounting a pen or stylus. A clockwork motor drew a paper tape under the pen or stylus, which marked it in accordance with the pulses of current in the circuit (see ELECTRIC CIRCUIT). Subsequently it was found that the operator could easily "read" the message by merely listening to the clicks emitted by the apparatus, and the familiar telegraph sounder

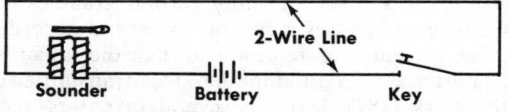

Fig. 1: Basic telegraphic circuit.

(Fig. 1) was substituted for the stylus-tape device. At present, commercial telegraph traffic is processed manually at an average speed of about 25 to 30 wd/min.

The simplest telegraph transmission path is the two-wire line with conductors on poles or cables. Since the strength of the signals diminishes with distance, the signals often have to be regenerated enroute with repeaters (relays), which raise the level of the weak signals by synchronously connecting a strong local battery to the next stretch of line. Messages can also be transmitted simultaneously in both directions (duplex operation) over a single metallic path (wire): the current pulses sent on the line by the local transmitter being known, the local receiver "subtracts" these from the total current pulses being received on the line; the balance are those from the distant transmitter. Where the length is great, as in submarine transoceanic cables, the cable circuit has an enormous CAPACITANCE (*i.e.* a capacity to store enormous quantities of electricity), and a great amount of electricity must be poured into the cable to "fill it up" before a perceptible voltage appears at the far end; for this reason transoceanic telegraphy has always been slow. However, recent success in increasing the INDUCTANCE of the cable to compensate for large capacitance has partly corrected this condition and has allowed more rapid transmission. Nevertheless, receivers must be extremely sensitive, and submerged vacuum-tube-amplifier repeaters are used to strengthen the signal.

Fast and efficient *record communication* (communication in which a graphic record is received after transmission) requires that the transmitting operator be able to cause a character to be printed automatically at the receiver by simply pressing the appropriate key on his transmitter. Transmission by such a method at first appeared uneconomical, since it seemed that a separate wire would be required for each character sent. However, Morse's concept of transmission by applying sequential electrical impulses to one pair of wires was extended to semiautomatic transmission, and this has resulted in the *teleprinter.* The characters of a tele-

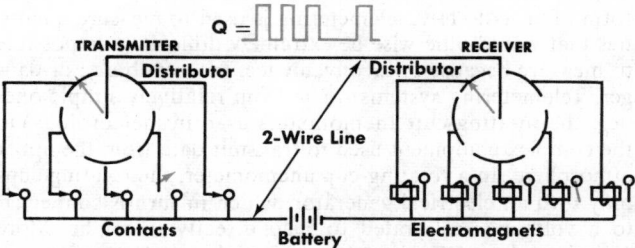

Fig. 2: Teleprinter (here shown transmitting the letter Q) uses the synchronous rotation of two 5-contact distributors to cause the 5-unit code set up at the transmitting contacts to be set up at the receiving electromagnets, whereupon receiver prints character.

printer code are represented by sets of five pulses occurring in specific combinations. This is a binary code (see NUMBER SYSTEMS), since there are two states; either a pulse occurs during an interval or it does not. The number of possible combinations is $2 \times 2 \times 2 \times 2 \times 2 = 32$; but there are 31 usable codes, since one combination has no pulses. The code can also be transmitted by a paper tape in which are punched a set of holes out of a possible five; the tape is fed through a reading device in which five "fingers" sense the presence or absence of holes and set five electrical contacts accordingly. In both cases, the contacts are scanned by a distributor that connects them sequentially to the line. A simple teleprinter circuit is shown in Fig. 2. The distributors in the transmitting and receiving teleprinters are synchronized, the transmitter contacts being connected in sequence through the line to the corresponding receiver electromagnets. After rotation of the distributors, according to the code combination, certain among the five receiver magnets will be operated and latched; the corresponding character is thereupon printed out and the magnets are unlatched preparatory to reception of the next character. When energized, the electromagnets push or turn five bars or cams and thereby mechanically cause the proper character to be printed. Actually, in present-day machines, mechanical linkages enable a single electromagnet to set successively five arms. In circuits such as that in Fig. 2, it is possible to "multiplex" teleprinter circuits (operate simultaneously more than one circuit over a single pair of wires). Transmitting and receiving distributors are used that have five segments for each circuit in the multiplex. When the distributor arm sweeps the first five segments, the first character for the first circuit is sent. The next five segments send the first character for the second circuit, and so on, until the arm arrives back at the first five segments, at which time the second character for the first circuit is sent.

A major transmission path for telegraphic signals is high-frequency radio (2 to 30 megacycles), in which a radio transmitter is either turned on and off or shifted back and forth in frequency, thus transmitting the message impulses; both microwave line-of-sight and ionospheric and tropospheric scatter paths are used in a similar manner (see MICROWAVES; RADIO). For most paths, carrier transmission can be used. The telegraph pulses are converted to an electrical tone of a super-audio alternating-current burst of signal. With the use of a series of receivers sensitive only to the frequencies of their corresponding transmitters (see FILTER), hundreds of telegraph signals can be simultaneously sent on one path. Currently about 20 telegraph channels, each carrying 60 wd/min, are packed into the frequency band occupied by one voice-frequency (telephone) channel.—*A. L.; J. E. S.*

TELEMETERING: transmission of physical data and presentation of the data at a distance from their source. Basically a form of TELEGRAPHY, telemetering is used to measure quantities that would otherwise be extremely difficult or impossible to measure because of inconvenience, inaccessibility, or danger. Telemetering systems range from relatively simple ones (*e.g.* the rotating-cup anemometers used in meteorology) to the complex equipment used to transmit data from the upper atmosphere. In a rotating-cup anemometer, the rotating cups may turn an electrical generator, which in turn is connected to a voltmeter calibrated to read directly in mi/hr. More complex telemetering systems are used in space satellites to sense environmental data (*e.g.* temperature, pressure, and radiation), to transmit the data by radio to an observational point, and to decode and record the data. The sensing element may be a TRANSDUCER, which converts one form of energy into another. Transducers have been developed that can measure almost every conceivable quantity, *e.g.* weight, angle, interval, electric or magnetic fields, light, temperature, motion, flow of liquids, pressure, biological activities, and atomic radiation. In telemetry, transducers and sensing elements generally have an electrical output, since most transmission is either by wires or by radio. The simplest signal transmission path is a pair of wires, but where motion or distance makes these impractical, radio transmission is used. The signal from the transducer is applied to a simple radio transmitter to alter either the amplitude or the frequency of the radio wave.

It is often unnecessary that the measurement be transmitted continuously; the quantity can be sampled and the measurement transmitted at intervals. The sampling rate must be sufficiently rapid, however, to include all significant transient variations in the quantity measured. Using the above sampling system for each measurement, samples for all measurements are interleaved and transmitted in sequential rotation, and pulse coding schemes (see MODULATION) indicate which sample corresponds to which measurement.—*J. E. S.*

TELEOLOGY AND TELEOLOGICAL EXPLANATIONS: Teleology, most broadly, refers to the view that some processes—*e.g.* embryological development, organic self-regulation, adaptive behavior, motivated goal seeking—are objectively goal-directed. Some teleologists maintain the stronger thesis that the form of such processes is in some sense determined by the end or goal in which they normally terminate. The first thesis is not controversial; everyone agrees there are teleological processes, although there is considerable disagreement as to how they may be defined. The majority of contemporary scientists, however, deny the stronger thesis, holding that teleology consists in nothing more than complex patterns of non-teleological processes which dovetail in such a way that their joint outcome, under normal conditions, is the achievement of a specified goal. Such a pattern is exhibited, for example, by the mutually compensating activities of a voltage-regulating circuit. Since teleological processes are reducible in this way to non-teleological ones, most scientists hold that teleological explanations—explanations in terms of the goal or function served—may be eliminated in favor of the patterns of explanation employed in dealing with non-teleological phenomena. Accordingly, such activities as physiological self-maintenance and adaptive behavior can be dealt with by means of the theory of feedback mechanisms. It is, however, generally admitted that a teleological point of view is sometimes of value: it may facilitate the formation of appropriate concepts for scientific analysis of teleological processes; and it may suggest useful non-teleological hypotheses. But the point of view, unless assumed with great caution, does entail danger of interpreting too much after the model of human purposive actions.—*M. Be.*

TELEPHONE: an electric apparatus for conversing at a distance. Telephony involves the *transmission* of electric signals representing the voice and the *switching* necessary to connect one telephone instrument to another.

Transmission: Following other work dating from as early as 1837 on the transmission of the pitch of sounds by making and breaking an electric current, Philip Reis (Germany, 1860) tried to transmit speech by means of a make-and-break contact. Then, in 1874, Alexander Graham Bell realized from his work in phonetics that a smoothly changing current was needed to transmit accurately pressure variations of sound waves. At first he doubted that current generated by a voice would be strong enough. We now know we can understand speech when its average power is a ten-millionth of a millionth of a watt per square centimeter. Modern telephone receivers supply to the listener from a hundred-millionth to a billionth of a watt of acoustic power. Bell demonstrated transmission of speech and filed an application for a patent, 1876. In Bell's telephone receivers (as in today's) the increasing and decreasing attraction of an electromagnet moved a diaphragm in accord with an electric current. In present-day telephone transmitters (or microphones) motion of a diaphragm against a pinch of shiny carbon granules changes the resistance and causes a current to vary in accord with a sound. The current is more powerful than the sound, so that the transmitter acts as an amplifier. This transmitter derives from the work (1877–1890) of several inventors, including Thomas A. Edison.

Alexander Bell's original workshop: It was in this Boston workshop that Bell first built in 1875 an apparatus capable of transmitting sound. The reconstructed workshop, exhibiting early telephone models and Bell's original patent, now stands in the lobby of the headquarters of the New England Telephone and Telegraph Co. (*AT&T*)

In modern transmission, lead- or plastic-covered cables are used; these contain hundreds to thousands of twisted pairs of paper- or plastic-covered wires. The loss or attenuation of long circuits can be reduced by the periodic insertion of inductors or *loading coils* (originated by Michael I. Pupin and George A. Campbell, 1899). Transmission over greater distances was made possible by placing amplifiers called *repeaters* along the route, using the triode vacuum tube (Lee de Forest, 1906). Transcontinental telephony was first achieved in 1915; however, economical long-distance transmission was not possible until the development of carrier telephony, demonstrated 1908–11 and employed commercially in 1918. Different conversations are carried over the same wires by different bands of frequencies, much as in radio and TV broadcasting. In *single sideband* carrier transmission a particular constant frequency is added to each frequency of a signal at the transmitting end and is subtracted at the receiving end. Carrier telephony was made possible by the *filter* (G. A. Campbell, 1915), used to select a band of frequencies, and the *negative feedback amplifier* (H. S. Black, 1927), which can amplify many signals simultaneously without their interacting. (See FILTER, ELECTRIC; FEEDBACK). As an alternative to this *frequency-division* technique of carrier transmission, different signals can be transmitted over the same circuit as sequences of very short electric pulses occurring at different times; this is called *time-division* transmission. In pulse-code modulation (PCM) signals are transmitted as sequences of off-or-on pulses; different sequences of off and on represent different amplitudes. Carrier telephony allows the transmission of as many as 24 telephone signals over one pair of wires in a cable and the transmission of several thousand signals over a wire surrounded by a metal tube, called a coaxial cable. Carrier telephony has been used since 1951 in sending thousands of telephone signals across the country in a series of horizon-to-horizon hops via microwave radio.

Speech transmission from Washington, D. C., to Hawaii and Paris by means of long-wave radio (a frequency of 60,000 cy/sec) was demonstrated in 1915 and commercial transatlantic service was inaugurated in 1927. Short-wave radio (10 to 30 Mc/sec) has been used for transoceanic telephony since 1929. The radio frequencies useful for transoceanic telephony are limited and transmission is somewhat erratic at times. In 1956 a submarine telephone cable system linking the U. S. A. and Great Britain went into operation. The underwater amplifiers used must withstand high pressures, must last decades without failing, and must be supplied with power over the cable itself. In 1960 cables connected continental U. S. A. with Great Britain, France, Hawaii, Alaska, Puerto Rico, and Cuba. Such cable systems provide up to forty-eight 3,000 cy/sec voice channels. The capacity of two systems was increased during 1960 by TASI (Time Assignment Speech Interpolation) in which voice channels are shared by more than one conversation. Also in 1960 experimental transmission of telephone conversations over thousands of miles was achieved by means of the Echo I satellite. In 1962, a number of simultaneous two-way voice conversations were transmitted across the Atlantic by the Bell System's Telstar satellite, which also transmitted television programs across the Atlantic.

Switching: Following crude initial switching systems, the plug-and-jack manual switchboard was devised. In 1889 Almon B. Strowger invented the *step-by-step* automatic telephone switching system, which was first used in 1892. In step-by-step switching the customer is connected to an idle switch which he operates by means of a dialed digit; this connects him to another idle switch which he then operates, and so on, until he is able to reach his party. In *common-control* switching systems (first used in England, 1914) various pieces of equipment such as *translators* (to convert one number into another), *senders* (to send out the digits of the

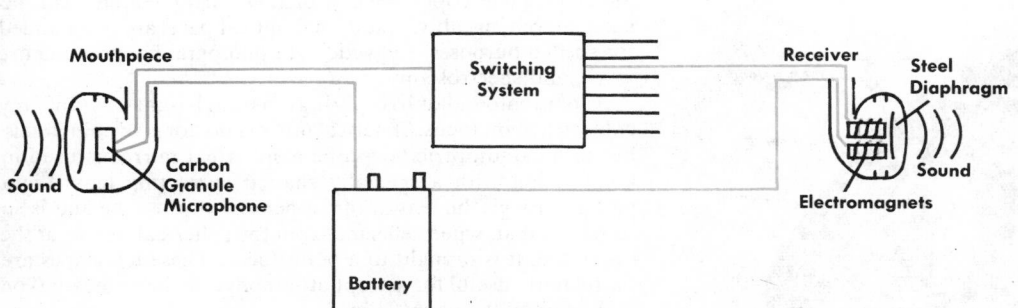

A basic telephone circuit: Sound impulses striking the mouthpiece diaphragm compress carbon granules so as to vary their electrical resistance and hence the current in the wire. These current fluctuations produce varying magnetic field around electromagnets in receiver. Changing field moves springy receiver diaphragm to re-create original sound.

Bell's first telephone: On an instrument similar to this, called a "gallows frame" transmitter, Bell transmitted the first sentence ever carried by a telephone circuit. (AT&T)

new number), and *markers* (which locate and select an idle talking path and establish a connection) are used by the customer only while the connection is being set up. A common control switching system uses an electric computer to operate switches, usually of a type called *crossbar* switches. By 1962 various electronic switching systems using diodes, transistors, and magnetic memories rather than relays and contacts were available.

A switching system would be impractically expensive if it were to provide a guaranteed path between each pair of subscribers. Instead, *multistage switching* is used. For example, in a typical system one of about 50 subscribers can be connected to any of 10 wires, each of these to any of another 10 wires, and so on. Mathematical studies of multistage switching have been made in order to minimize *blocking* (one connection preventing another). Modern automatic switching systems choose among available routes to distant parts of the country; provide ringing, "busy," and other tones; record the length and charges for calls; and perform other complicated functions. Also, telephone companies provide teletype-

Modern telephone: Although the telephone in principle has changed little since the latter part of the 19th cent., there have been improvements in the instrument's durability as well as progress in the efficiency of transmission, signaling, and switching, as exemplified by the complexity of this cutaway view of a present-day telephone. (*Bell Telephone Labs.*)

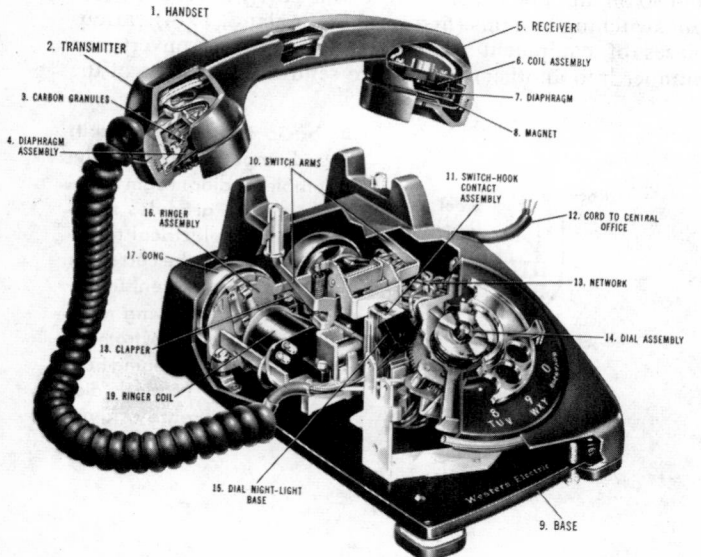

1. HANDSET
2. TRANSMITTER
3. CARBON GRANULES
4. DIAPHRAGM ASSEMBLY
5. RECEIVER
6. COIL ASSEMBLY
7. DIAPHRAGM
8. MAGNET
10. SWITCH ARMS
11. SWITCH-HOOK CONTACT ASSEMBLY
12. CORD TO CENTRAL OFFICE
13. NETWORK
14. DIAL ASSEMBLY
16. RINGER ASSEMBLY
17. GONG
18. CLAPPER
19. RINGER COIL
15. DIAL NIGHT-LIGHT BASE
9. BASE

writer and data service, and supply circuits for telegraph and television transmission. In 1961, there were 74 million telephones in the U. S. A. and 141 million in the world.

In the past 50 yr, research stemming from the desire to develop better telephone systems has been chiefly responsible for present knowledge of psychoacoustics. Telephone research has also led to many discoveries, insights, and inventions in other areas, *e.g.* single-sideband transmission, vocoders, thermal noise, negative feedback amplifiers, electron diffraction, radio astronomy, waveguides, electronic computers, transistors, blocking and queueing theory, the application of Boolean algebra to switching theory, and information theory.—*J. R. P.*

TELESCOPE, OPTICAL: an arrangement of lenses, mirrors, or both, that gathers light, enables the observer to distinguish close objects, and makes distant objects appear closer than they are. Telescopes for terrestrial observation give an erect image; for astronomical work this is not required. The three types of optical telescopes are: the refractor, in which light is brought to a focus by passing through a lens; the reflector, in which light is focused by reflection from a mirror; and the catadioptric type, which uses both a lens and a mirror.

Reflecting telescopes tend to be favored over refractors for photography because a mirror, as an objective, produces less chromatic aberration than a lens does. Reflectors also may be favored for detection and study of very faint objects because reflectors can be built larger. Whereas the mirror of a reflector can be supported at the back, the lens of a refractor cannot. Reflectors of over 200 in. aperture are practicable, but the limit for refractors at present is 40 in.—the aperture of the Yerkes Observatory instrument.

Principal Designs: The main lens, or objective, of a refracting telescope is a combination of two or more simple lenses. A simple lens focuses each color in a different point, causing chromatic aberration (see LENS); hence suitably chosen lenses are combined to form an achromatic, nearly color-free objective. Parallel rays of light enter through the objective of the telescope and are refracted (bent) to a focus at the other end (Fig. 1). The focal image may then be photographed, studied visually through an eyepiece (ocular) which is a magnifying set of lenses, or measured photoelectrically.

The principal component of a reflecting telescope is a concave glass mirror ground to the shape of a paraboloid (nearly spherical) and coated with a reflecting layer of aluminum (formerly silver). Starlight passes down the tube to the concave primary mirror at the lower end and is reflected back to the *prime focus* at the upper end (Fig. 2). A secondary flat mirror is often placed in the converging beam of light at a 45° tilt to bring the light to the *Newtonian focus* at the side of the tube. There it may be magnified by an eyepiece. Greater magnification is obtained if the secondary mirror is convex, reflecting the light through a central hole in the primary and bringing it to the *Cassegrain focus*. A concave *Gregorian* secondary may also be used. A further arrangement of two secondary flat mirrors brings the light to the *coudé focus,* which remains stationary even when the telescope is rotated. With the largest telescopes, several of these arrangements can be used interchangeably. Additional optical parts are often added for special purposes, *e.g.* wide-field photography, photometric work, and spectroscopy.

A paraboloidal mirror brings parallel light rays of any color to a point focus. Spherical mirrors do not give point focus, but in a catadioptric telescope a spherical mirror is used in conjunction with a specially shaped correcting lens. Light passes through the lens at the upper end of the tube and is so refracted that, when reflected from the spherical mirror at the lower end, it is brought to a point focus. These telescopes are particularly useful for astrophotography; the best-known type is the Schmidt camera (Fig. 3).

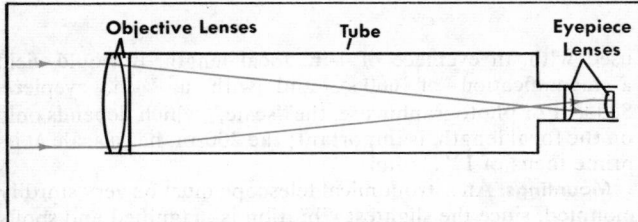

Fig. 1: Refracting Telescope

Labels: Objective Lenses, Tube, Eyepiece Lenses

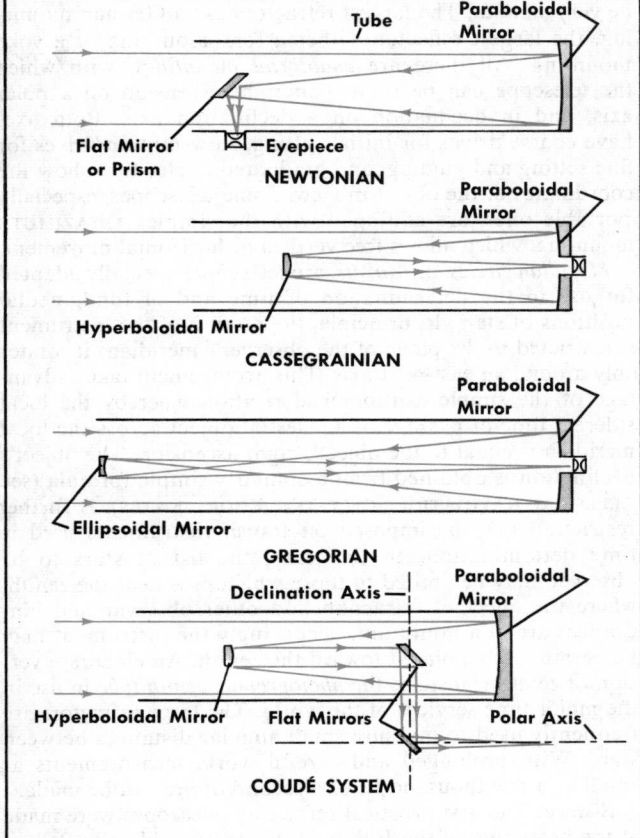

Labels: Tube, Paraboloidal Mirror, Flat Mirror or Prism, Eyepiece — **NEWTONIAN**

Paraboloidal Mirror, Hyperboloidal Mirror — **CASSEGRAINIAN**

Paraboloidal Mirror, Ellipsoidal Mirror — **GREGORIAN**

Declination Axis, Paraboloidal Mirror, Hyperboloidal Mirror, Flat Mirrors, Polar Axis — **COUDÉ SYSTEM**

Fig. 2: Reflecting Telescopes

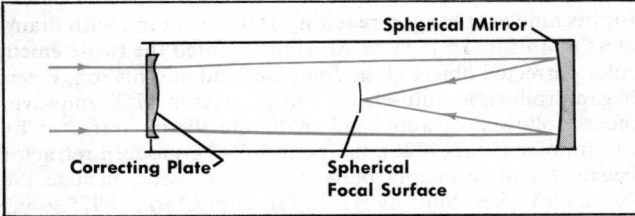

Labels: Spherical Mirror, Correcting Plate, Spherical Focal Surface

Fig. 3: Schmidt Camera

Functions: The primary function of an optical telescope is to collect light. A measure of the light-gathering power is the ratio of the area of the mirror or objective to the area of the pupil of the dark-adapted eye. A 200-in. diameter mirror collects 360,000 times more light than the eye. In addition, a telescope can collect invisible radiant energy; photographic emulsions, the photoelectric photometer, and the image-tube detect ultraviolet and infrared radiation as well as visible light.

Through even a small telescope, properly constructed, an observer can in many instances see both components of a double star that appears to the naked eye as a single point. A

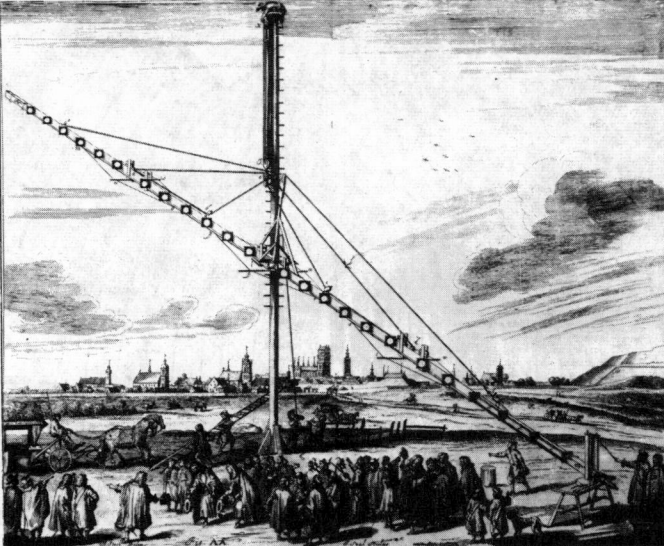

Telescopes of long focal length were favored in second half of 17th cent. as means of reducing effect of chromatic dispersion. A 150-ft system featuring lensless "stops" against stray light is seen above in engraving from first part (1673) of Hevelius' *Machina coelestis*. Hevelius, an accomplished instrument maker, was a brewer in city of Danzig, seen in distance. (*U. S. Navy*)

telescope's resolving power—optimum angular separation—increases with the diameter of the objective or mirror. In practice, the resolving power of large instruments is limited by disturbances in the atmosphere (SEEING).

A telescope's eyepiece magnifies the focal image of the objective or mirror and makes distant objects appear closer. All medium and large telescopes show the planets as discs. Stars are so far away that they appear as points in all telescopes (but the larger the telescope, the greater its ability to show faint stars, because of its light-gathering power). The distance from a lens or mirror to its prime focus is called its focal length; the ratio of the focal length of the objective or mirror to that of the eyepiece is the magnifying power of the arrangement. The 200-in. telescope has a focal length of 660 in.; if

Herschel's great reflector had focal length of 40 ft, aperture of 48 in. Sheet-iron tube was supported by tentlike structure of poles and ladders set on roller-borne octagonal platform. Erected at Slough, 18 mi west of London, structure was completed Aug. 27, 1789. Within three weeks Herschel had discovered Mimas, innermost satellite of Saturn. (*U. S. Navy*)

Largest lens (40 in.) is the one ground by Alvan Graham Clark and mounted at Yerkes Observatory, Williams Bay, Wis., in 1897. Long (62-ft) focal length minimizes aberrations. (*Yerkes Obs.*)

Equatorial mounting of fork type supports 48-in. Schmidt telescope on Palomar Mountain, Calif. (*Mt Wilson*)

used with an eyepiece of 1-in. focal length, it would yield a magnification of $660\times$, and with a ¾-in. eyepiece, $880\times$. For photographic use, the "scale," which depends only on the focal length, is important; the 200-in. has a scale at its prime focus of 12″.3/mm.

Mountings: An astronomical telescope must be very sturdily mounted, since the slightest vibration is magnified and spoils the image. It must be so mounted that it can be pointed in any direction above the horizon, and the steering drive must be very smooth. The largest refractors use a German mounting, the largest reflectors either a fork mounting or a yoke mounting. All these are *equatorial mountings,* with which the telescope can be rotated in right ascension on a polar axis, and in declination on a declination axis. Both axes have coarse drives for initial setting, slow-motion drives for fine setting and guiding, and graduated circles that show the coordinates of the object in view. Some telescopes, especially portable ones, are equipped with the simpler ALTAZIMUTH mounting, which allows free vertical or horizontal movement.

Meridian circles, or *transits,* are telescopes specially adapted for use in the determination of time and of fundamental positions of stars. In principle, the motion of the instrument is restricted to the plane of the observer's meridian; it rotates only around an east-west axis. This arrangement takes advantage of the simple astronomical relation whereby the local sidereal time of passage of a celestial object across the local meridian is equal to the object's right ascension. The object's declination is obtained from a similarly simple formula (see CELESTIAL NAVIGATION; CELESTIAL COORDINATES). A further restriction may be imposed on transit instruments used in time determination. In this case, the list of stars to be observed may be limited to those which pass near the zenith, where the effect of refraction and other observational hindrances are at a minimum; accordingly the instrument may be permanently pointed toward the zenith. An elaborate version of zenith transits is the *photographic zenith tube* in use in the major time services of the world. The large refractors are frequently used to measure small angular distances between stars. With prolonged and careful work, measurements as small as a few thousandths of a second of arc can be made.

History: The first practical refracting telescopes were made at the beginning of the 17th cent. By 1610 Galileo, in Padua, had made several small telescopes and turned them toward the sky. Throughout the 17th cent. the single-element refractor became ever longer, reaching 150 ft or more, with diameters up to 8 in. In 1733, C. M. Hall invented the two-element color-corrected object glass. John Dollond and his son, Peter, began producing multi-element achromats in 1758. Improvements followed steadily and, with the 9½-in. refractor by Fraunhofer (1787–1826), the period of the modern refractor began. Giant refractors built in the 19th cent. include the 40-in. at Yerkes, built by Alvan Graham Clark, 1897; 36-in., Lick, Clark, 1888; 32.7-in., Paris-Meudon, Henry Bros., 1889; 31.5-in., Potsdam, C. A. Von Steinheil, 1899; and dozens of others almost as large.

The reflecting telescope of speculum metal (an alloy of copper and tin) was first shown to the Royal Society in 1672 by Newton. The first effective reflector, however, a 6-in., was made in 1721 by John Hadley. Further improvements were made by James Short (1710–68) with reflectors up to 18 in. Sir William Herschel, an acknowledged master of both telescope making and observational astronomy, completed a 48-in. in 1789. The largest speculum of all, a 72-in., was made in Ireland in 1845 by Lord Rosse.

In 1856 Steinheil and Foucault, following the discovery by Liebig of a chemical method for silvering, independently introduced the first silver-on-glass reflectors. By 1864, a 31.5-in.

1

Plate 81   SYMBIOSIS

2

The close association of two unlike kinds of organisms is called symbiosis. Four examples are shown. **1. Three-toed sloth** (*Bradypus*) of American tropics has microscopic green algae growing in longitudinal grooves along its stiff brown hairs. Sloth may gain a little camouflage from the algae's greenish color, but the plants are the principal gainers. Sloth feeds on foliage high in trees, where algae receive plenty of light. (*Carl W. Rettenmeyer*) **2. Tropical clownfish** (*Amphiprion percula*) takes refuge near spreading tentacles of large sea anemone *Stoichactis*. The anemone grows to maximum size only when it has a clownfish partner. Clownfish reputedly lures other fishes within reach of anemone's tentacles. (*Walter Dawn*) **3. Moth-pollinated flower** *Melandrium album* opens only after sunset, and lures hawkmoths (e.g. *Choerocampa elpenor*) with strong scent and free nectar. (*Hermann Eisenbeiss*) **4. Cattle egret** (*Bubulcus ibis*) of Africa and parts of Europe has spread recently to Americas. It lives in close association with large grazing animals, catching insects which they flush from grass. (*Norval R. Barger, Jr.*)

3

4

Plate 82   TREES

Plants are known as "herbs," "shrubs," and "trees" in accordance with the character of their stems. In general, herbs have soft stems, whereas shrubs and trees have woody stems. Shrubs branch near the ground and are not as tall as trees, although the distinction between a shrub and a tree is not always clear-cut. A tree must invest many years of growth in building its massive trunk and many branches. It succeeds in reaching maturity where land and climate are relatively stable and where moisture is available throughout the growing season. In such regions, trees tend to increase in number until they cover the land in an unbroken forest, except where they are destroyed by man, fire, wind, or other agencies.

1

2

1. Weeping willow (*Salix babylonica*) is an Asiatic tree, now cultivated all over the world for its graceful form. (*Russ Kinne*) **2. Red mangrove** (*Rhizophora*) "walks" into shallow brackish and salt water on its branching roots. Mangrove swamps collect debris, extending shore until it becomes tropical forest. (*Robert C. Hermes*)

3

4

3. Forest of conifers—pines, spruces, firs—extends across northern Canada and down mountain chains of U.S.A. Most conifers are evergreens. (*Alfred O. Holz*) **4. Date palm** (*Phoenix dactylifera*) originated in Middle East, where its sugary, oblong fruits are dried, forming staple food for millions. (*Russ Kinne*)

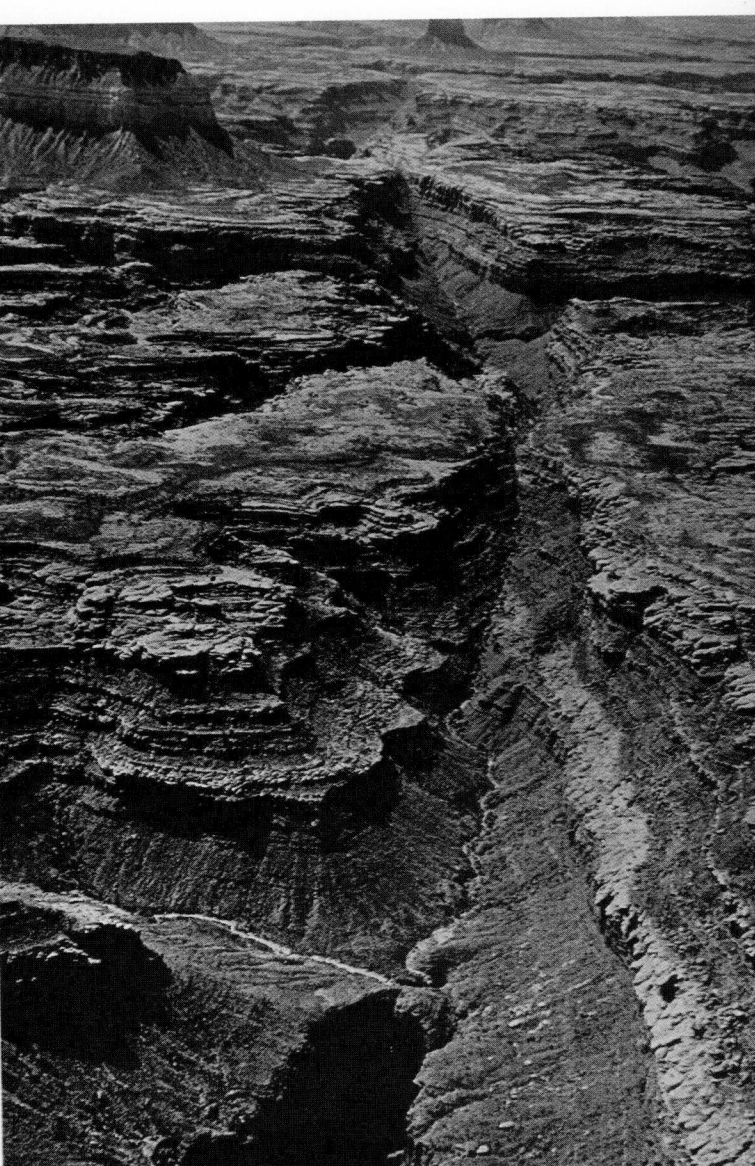

Plate 83   VALLEYS

Most valleys have been excavated largely by rivers. Flowing water picks up loose material from the river bed, and this moving load in turn abrades any rock over which the river may flow. A valley is widened by the weathering of the rock walls into fragments, which then slide or fall down to the river and are washed away.

1. Glaciated valley, Switzerland: A glacier flowing down a previous river-cut valley modified the shape to form the rounded, U-shaped valley profile shown. *(Manfred d'Elia)*

2

2. Fault-line valley in the Colorado Plateau near Havasu Creek: The Sinyala fault formed a weak zone in the rock layers and thus determined the path for a stream to erode a valley. *(Ruth Pieroth)*

3. Zion Canyon, Utah: A steep-walled valley with a flat floor cut by river action into the horizontal rock layers of the Colorado Plateau. *(Harold Wanless)*

1

Plate 84 WATERFALLS

Waterfalls and rapids, characteristic of "youthful" rivers where downcutting is prominent, often occur where a stream moves from relatively resistant rock to softer material downstream. Falls and rapids tend to disappear rather quickly, by geological standards, because of the rapid erosion occurring at such sites.

2

1. Kaieteur Falls on Potaro River, British Guiana. *(George Hunter/ Shostal)* **2. Latourell Falls** on Columbia River Highway, Oreg. *(Chuck Abbott/Rapho-Guillumette)* **3. Cascades** below Rifle Falls Fish Hatchery, Rifle, Colo. *(Merton W. Jones/Shostal)*

3

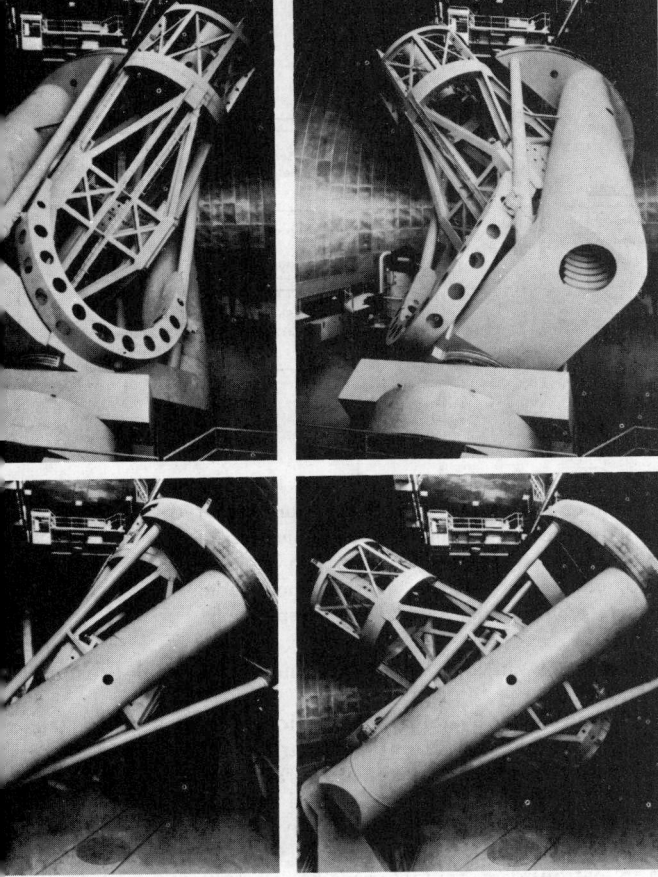

Easy movement of 500-ton weight of 200-in. yoke-mounted reflector at Mt Palomar is assured by film of pressurized oil forced through five bearing pads—two under the 48-in. horseshoe and three under the hemispherical south bearing. A torque of 50 lb-ft will turn the entire structure; mirror-bearing tube is here seen pivoting westward (*above*) and northward (*below*). (*Mt Wilson*)

had been installed at Marseilles. In 1895, the 36-in. Crossley reflector, the first truly modern instrument, was put into operation at Lick Observatory in California. The 20th cent. is the age of the giant reflector. At Mt Wilson in 1908 a 60-in. was completed that incorporated the many advanced ideas of George W. Ritchey (1864–1945). In 1917 Ritchey completed the 100-in. Hooker reflector after 7 yr of work. In 1939 the McDonald 82-in. was put into operation in Texas.

The saga of the building of the 200-in. Palomar Mt telescope in California extends over the period 1927–1948 and is largely the story of the inspiration of George Ellery Hale (1868–1938). The Hale telescope weighs 500 tons, yet moves freely on oil-pad bearings; the observer rides in a cage at the prime focus. The world's second largest reflector, the 120-in. at Lick, was placed in operation in 1959. The Russians completed (1961) a 102-in. for use in the Crimea. A large Schmidt with 98-in. spherical mirror is under way in England. In addition, an 84-in. is being built for use in S Arizona. Other large reflectors have been in use or are being installed in Canada, S Africa, Argentina, Egypt, Australia, Japan, Russia, and other locations in the U. S. A. —J. G. Ba.

TELESCOPE, RADIO: see RADIO TELESCOPE.

TELEVISION: the transmission of moving scenes or pictures by radio or over wires. The word itself means "seeing at a distance." The process of television requires three steps: (1) analysis of a light image and its transformation into electrical

signals; (2) transmission of the signals; and (3) reconversion of the received signals back to the original image.

Basic Principles: Inventors long dreamed of projecting images from locations or over distances beyond the reach of the human eye or of conventional optical devices. Many ingenious schemes were proposed years before the development of the necessary tools. The first logical solution came with the invention of the scanning disc (P. G. Nipkow, 1884), a rapidly rotating metallic disc perforated with a number of small apertures arranged in a spiral pattern. The purpose of the scanning disc was to dissect the original light image into a number of parallel lines. A photoelectric device was placed behind the disc to produce electrical impulses corresponding to the variation of light at each point of the image. The scanning disc was abandoned after a short time because of the difficulty of transmitting images in sufficient detail. However, the principle of scanning has been retained in today's electronic systems.

The modern all-electronic television system, used throughout the world, was made possible by the invention of the cathode-ray scanning tube (see CATHODE-RAY TUBE), and iconoscope (V. K. Zworykin, 1923). This contained two principal working parts: a 4-by-5-in. plate holding millions of tiny PHOTOELECTRIC CELLS, and a narrow beam of electrons shot at high velocity from an electron gun within the tube. An image of the scene being televised was focused through a lens onto the sensitive plate, where each of the tiny cells generated a voltage proportional to the amount of light falling upon it, creating an over-all pattern of voltage corresponding to the image. The electron beam was then scanned back and forth in successive lines from top to bottom of the plate, collecting the voltage from the tiny cells and conducting it out through amplifiers. The amplifiers conveyed the information in the form of stronger signals to the transmitter. These operating principles, in which the image is "stored" on a sensitive target, have been employed in many modifications since the original iconoscope made its appearance. They are used today in the image orthicon and vidicon television pick-up tubes, which are in service around the world. The scanning method used in television produces a train of electrical signals representing the value of light at every point of the image. The signals are transmitted by radio or wire systems adapted for transmission of high-frequency pulses up to 4.5 megacycles/sec. The present standard in the U. S. A. is 525 interlaced lines/picture frame transmitted at 30 double frames/sec, in synchronization with our 60-cycle power system. These standards vary in other countries.

The iconoscope, an early television camera tube: The image of the scene is projected by a lens on the light-sensitive mosaic, forming an electrical charge pattern. An electron beam scanning the mosaic neutralizes the charge and generates the picture signal across a resistance connected to the signal plate. (*From Zworykin*)

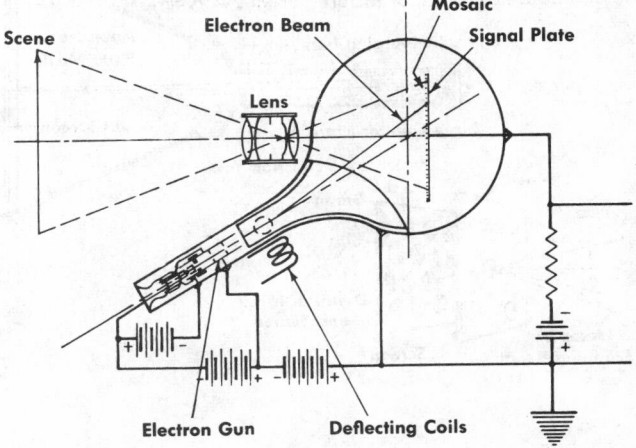

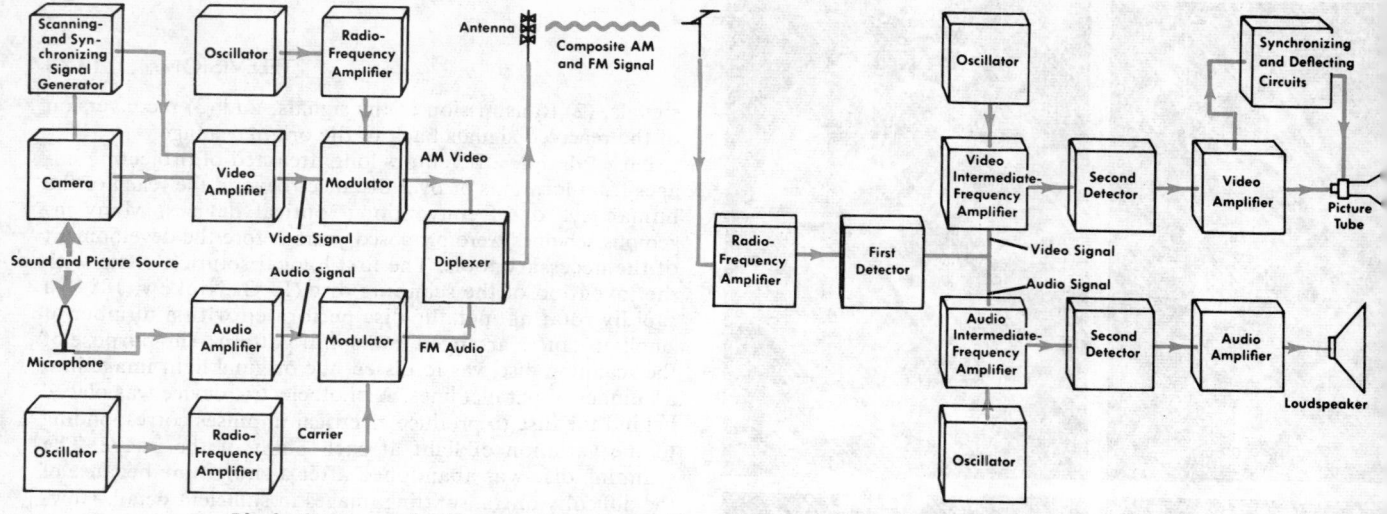

Block diagram of television system: At the transmitting station the amplified picture signal generated by the television camera and the sound signal generated by the microphone are impressed on suitable carriers and combined into a composite signal which is radiated by the station antenna. At the receiver the signal is amplified, demodulated, and separated into the video and audio signal components. The latter are applied to the picture tube and the loudspeaker, respectively.

Broadcasting: Transmission is of two kinds: (1) broadcast transmission, used predominantly for mass communication and entertainment; and (2) point-to-point transmission for specific purposes, often called "industrial television." Reception is accomplished with high-frequency radio receivers, which modulate the intensity of the electron beam in a reproducing cathode-ray tube, the kinescope. The kinescope is practically identical with the iconoscope in all basic respects, except that it has a fluorescent screen rather than the mosaic plate of tiny photoelectric cells. In the reproducing tube, the fluorescent screen reproduces the original image in light of one color as a result of bombardment by the scanning electron beam, whose intensity corresponds to the variation of the light in every point of the transmitted image. Although the reproduced picture is composed of a great number of discrete points, the persistence of human vision fixes it in a continuous image. In order to reproduce a steady picture, the receiver must be synchronized with the transmitter. To accomplish this, synchronizing signals are transmitted with the picture signals. One such synchronizing signal is sent at the end of each scanned line, and a slightly different one is transmitted at the end of each frame.

Few countries today are without television systems. In the U. S. A. alone, there are more than 60 million television receivers now in use, served by more than 500 broadcast transmitters.

Closed-circuit Systems: In addition to broadcasting, television has other important uses, particularly in closed-circuit systems, in which images are transmitted, usually over wires, to one or a few individual receivers. Although the use of such systems today is relatively small in comparison to broadcasting, this technique is finding many important applications, *e.g.* in factories, hospitals, laboratories, and military and space projects.

Color: Color television was introduced when black-and-white television was already widespread; hence the color system was designed to operate within the broadcast standards already adopted for the monochrome service. Since additional information must be transmitted to reproduce pictures in color, however, a somewhat more complicated circuit is required. Color television, as now operated in the U. S. A., is entirely compatible with black-and-white television, *i.e.* standard receivers can receive color pictures in black-and-white without alteration, while all color receivers can reproduce pictures that are broadcast only in black-and-white. For color transmission, present systems use three standard-type pick-up tubes, *e.g.* image orthicons, in combination with an optical system that divides the original image into three separate color images of red, green, and blue. For reproduction, a special color kinescope is used, employing a screen composed of red, green, and blue phosphors.—*V. Z.*

Principle of color kinescope: Three electron beams, generated by a triple gun, scan a perforated mask in front of the viewing screen. Behind every mask aperture there is a trio of red, blue, and green phosphor dots so located that every beam strikes dots of only one color. The red, blue, and green component pictures formed by the three beams coalesce into a natural-color picture. (*From Zworykin*)

TELLER, EDWARD, 1908– , Hungarian-U. S. physicist; b. Budapest. He worked on the Manhattan project, first with Enrico Fermi at Columbia and Chicago Univs. and then with R. J. Oppenheimer at the Univ. of California and Los Alamos. He also worked with a group (1949–51) that showed the hydrogen bomb to be feasible. In 1952 he became director of the Livermore Laboratory of the Atomic Energy Commission. He is a member of the National Academy of Sciences.—*D. H. D. R.*

TELLURIUM: a metalloid element (Te) of the sulfur group (VIA) of the periodic table; at. no. 52; at. wt 127.60; valence 2, 4, or 6; some 20 isotopes have been recognized. The element was discovered in 1782 by F. J. Muller von Reichenstein, a mining inspector in Transylvania, who distinguished it from antimony in auriferous ore; this discovery was confirmed by the chemical analysis of M. H. Klaproth in Berlin, 1798. Tellurium is produced either as a grayish-white, brittle, crystalline solid or as a dark gray to brown amorphous powder with metallic characteristics. Although tellurium is not toxic, inhalation causes "tellurium breath," which resembles garlic breath. The high percentages in tellurium of the heavy isotopes Te[128] (31.75%) and Te[130] (34.27%) make tellurium's atomic weight more than that of iodine (at. wt 126.91), although tellurium precedes iodine (at. no. 53) in the periodic table; thus tellurium is one of the four naturally occurring elements whose atomic weight exceeds the atomic weight of the element directly following it in the periodic table (see ELEMENT). Until 1913, when H. G. J. Moseley showed that the properties of the elements are periodic on the basis of their atomic numbers (rather than on the basis of their atomic weights), this circumstance led many chemists to believe that tellurium was an exception to the PERIODIC LAW. Use of 0.1% tellurium with lead improves resistance to fatigue and vibration and increases tensile strength; as a vulcanizing agent with sulfur in rubber manufacture, tellurium serves to make the rubber tougher and longer-lasting. Like selenium, tellurium degasses and increases the machinability of stainless steel and copper; in small amounts it increases the abrasion resistance of steel. Lead telluride and bismuth telluride are important thermoelectric materials, used either as sources of electricity or as cooling devices. Tellurium is also used as a catalyst in hydrocarbon processing, and as a coloring agent for blue, brown, red, or black glass and porcelain.—*R. B. T.*

TEMPERATURE: the degree or intensity of hotness, as measured on a suitable scale. Heat intensity depends on the kinetic energy (energy of motion) of the molecules or atoms of a substance. Thus anything that increases the kinetic energy of a substance (*e.g.* agitation of a liquid, or hammering of a piece of metal) raises its temperature. A number of observable effects are dependent on temperature, including electrical resistance, the color of a glowing material, the length of metal bars, the volume of liquids, and the volume or pressure of gases. Any of these phenomena may be used to measure temperature, provided that the measuring device is suitably calibrated (see TEMPERATURE SCALES; THERMOMETER).—*E. M. R.*

TEMPERATURE SCALES: scales, used in the calibration of thermometers, consisting of two fixed reference temperatures, with the temperature interval between them divided into an arbitrary number of degrees. The three scales extensively used in the U. S. A. and Europe all employ the same reference points—the freezing and boiling temperatures of pure water—but differ in the number of degrees between these points. All three were devised by and named after Europeans in the 18th cent.

The Fahrenheit scale designates the freezing point of water as 32°F and the boiling point under normal atmospheric pressure as 212°F. The Celsius scale (the official name of the commonly known centigrade scale) marks these temperatures as 0°C and 100°C, respectively. The interval of 100° on the Celsius scale is thus equivalent to 180° on the Fahrenheit scale, and the Fahrenheit degree therefore represents only 5/9 as great a temperature range as does the Celsius degree. On the Réaumur scale the freezing point is also 0°, but the boiling point is 80°. The Celsius scale is preferred everywhere for scientific measurement of temperature, whereas the Fahrenheit scale is the popular one in English-speaking countries.

Having established the length of the degree by dividing the same temperature range into 180 parts (F), 100 parts (C), or 80 parts (R), the thermometer maker extends the scale on either side of the reference points by marking off degrees of the same length over as great a range as he chooses, numbering the degrees below zero by increasing negative numbers. A mercury-in-glass thermometer is therefore a direct-reading instrument, whatever temperature scale it may carry. Electrical thermometers, because the relationship between temperature input and voltage output is not linear, in general require the use of a calibration chart to translate the observed reading into a temperature reading.

One more temperature scale is derived from the Celsius scale by merely shifting the zero downward about 273°. There are cogent reasons for believing that a minimum temperature exists at −273.16°C. It is logical to designate such a temperature as absolute zero, and a scale starting at this point will exclude negative readings. This scale, in Celsius degrees, is called the Kelvin scale (K) and is important in thermodynamic calculations. A similar absolute scale based on the Fahrenheit degree is called the Rankine scale. Absolute zero corresponds to −460°F. The following formulas summarize the relationships between the five temperature scales and permit conversion of readings on one scale to readings on another:

$$F = 9/5C + 32°$$
$$C = 5/9 (F - 32°)$$
$$\text{Réaumur} = 4/5C = 4/9 (F - 32°)$$
$$K = C + 273°$$
$$\text{Rankine} = F + 460°$$

—*J. E. W.*

TENSILE STRENGTH: the resistance of a body to being pulled apart. It is due to cohesion between the molecules or atoms of which the body is composed. Generally, the forces applied to a body can be resolved into either compressive forces (pushing together) or tensile forces (pulling apart). Materials vary in their ability to resist these forces; those with good tensile strength tend to have good compressive strength also, but often materials with high compressive strength have poor tensile strength, *e.g.* concrete and rock. Steel, perhaps the most widely applied of industrial metals, is outstanding in its capacity to develop compressive and tensile strength almost equally well. When properly alloyed, it can develop a tensile strength close to 200,000 lb/in.²—*A. L.*

TENSION: a force that causes or tends to cause an elongation of a body. See ELASTICITY; STRENGTH OF MATERIALS; SURFACE TENSION.—*A. E.*

TENSOR ANALYSIS: a generalization of VECTOR ANALYSIS due mainly to M. M. G. Ricci. Consider a force in a two-dimensional space. Being a vector, it can be represented there by two components with respect to, for example, the pair of x- and y-axes of a rectangular Cartesian coordinate system. But there are important quantities that have more components than vectors do. For example, an ellipse with its center at the origin would here be represented by an equation of the form $ax^2 + bxy + cy^2 = 0$, or, in the notation that paves the way for the study of tensors, $a_{11}x^2 + (a_{12} + a_{21}) xy + a_{22}y^2 = 0$. The ellipse is thus determined by the four quantities a_{11}, a_{12}, a_{21}, a_{22}, and these are components of what is called a tensor of the second order. If the coordinate system is changed the components of the force change, but they have to change in such a way that they still represent a force having the same magnitude and direction as before. Similarly, when the coordinates x, y are changed to new coordinates x', y', the components a_{11}, a_{12}, etc., of the tensor must transform in such a way that the new equation $a'_{11}x'^2 + (a'_{12} + a'_{21})\,x'y' + a'_{22}y'^2 = 0$ represents the same ellipse as before.

These ideas can be carried over to the representation of physical or geometrical entities in n-dimensional space and expressed in more effective mathematical notation. Label the coordinates x^1, x^2, . . . , x^n (these are not powers of x) and denote them collectively by x^i, where i (like other indices used later) runs through the values 1, 2, . . . , n. In this coordinate system a vector **V** has n components, V^i, and when the coordinates are changed to x'^i the components of **V** change to V'^i where

$$V'^i = \sum_{j=1}^{n} \frac{\partial x'^i}{\partial x^j}\,V^j \qquad (1)$$

Since vectors are objective entities, this transformation formula has valuable properties: (a) a succession of coordinate transformations ending with the original coordinates brings the V^i back to their original values; (b) if $U^i = V^i$, then $U'^i = V'^i$, so that $U^i = V^i$ is an objective relationship independent of the coordinate system.

A tensor is an entity having n to the power r components $T^{ij\cdots}_{hl\cdots}$ in each coordinate system (r being the number of indices), these components transforming according to a generalization of (1) that retains the crucial properties (a), (b). Tensors are therefore important objective entities, though generally they cannot be pictured. A tensor with no indices is a scalar. With one index it is a vector, there being two types, T^i (contravariant) and T_i (covariant).

In an n-dimensional space, the square of the distance between two points having coordinates x^i and $x^i + dx^i$, respectively, is given by $g_{ij}\,dx^i\,dx^j$, where g_{ij} are the components of the *metrical tensor,* and, by Einstein's *summation convention,* there is summation over the repeated indices i, j. Similarly, the square of the magnitude of a vector T^i is given by $g_{ij}\,T^iT^j$. The components g_{ij} transform in such a way that the expressions for the above distance and magnitude yield the same numerical values after the change of coordinates as before. From g_{ij} and its derivatives are formed non-tensorial *Christoffel symbols* measuring the curvature of the coordinate system; also Riemann's *curvature tensor* measuring the objective curvature of the space. In covariant differentiation Christoffel symbols cancel the masking effects of coordinate curvature, thus yielding objective derivatives.

Because they deal with objective relations, tensors are extremely important in geometry and physics. Their use became widespread when Einstein found them crucial for his general theory of relativity, wherein the g_{ij} of space-time represents both metric and gravitation.—*Ba. H.*

TEPHIGRAM: a thermodynamic diagram used by meteorologists to calculate the stability of a column of air and to identify and compare the properties of air masses. The coordinates of the diagram are temperature (T) and the logarithm of the potential temperature (φ). The energy released or absorbed by a parcel of air rising or sinking in the atmosphere is easily measured by plotting its changing properties in tephigram coordinates.—*D. H. L.*

TERBIUM: a lanthanide (rare-earth metal) element (Tb); at. no. 65; at. wt 158.93; valence 3. It is found in monazite sand as the metal phosphate and was discovered (1843) in the mineral gadolinite by Carl Gustav Mosander at the same time he discovered ERBIUM. The pure metal has not been isolated, although fairly pure terbium has been obtained beginning with the work of Georges Urbain (1905). Today, ion-exchange methods produce measurable quantities of high-purity terbium. No use is known for it. (See LANTHANIDES; RARE EARTHS.)—*E. H. H.*

TERPENES: a large family of chemical compounds of the open-chain and alicyclic types, including such compounds as pinene and camphor. Both chain and ring structures in terpenes have skeletons built up from one or more units of the C_5H_8 hydrocarbon called isoprene. The chains or rings may have oxygen atoms attached as carbonyl or hydroxyl groups. —*Ru. M.*

TERRACE: a level surface, generally long and narrow, bounded on one side by a cliff or scarp face and on the other by rising land. The term *bench* is sometimes used synonymously, but to some authors implies a surface underlain by bedrock, whereas *terrace* implies a surface underlain by unconsolidated material, *e.g.* layers of sand or gravel. A wave-cut (marine) bench may be found along a coast which is being eroded by action of the sea. Such a bench, with perhaps a sea stack rising above it, is cut in bedrock and terminates against the land in a wave-cut cliff. Following a relative drop in sea level, such a surface appears as an elevated bench on the seaward side of a land mass. Such features are easily noted at places along the Pacific Coast of the U. S. A. A wave-built submarine terrace composed of material eroded from the land may be built seaward from the outer margin of the wave-cut bench. Terraces associated with rivers may result when a stream lowers its bed by cutting into a former floodplain deposit, leaving remnants of it as flat areas bordering its newly eroded level. In regions of horizontal rock layers where deep valleys have been cut, *e.g.* the Grand Canyon in the Colorado Plateau, the walls consist of a series of steps or benches one above the other; each bench with the associated cliff is formed by a layer of rock more resistant to erosion than those above or below it.—*J. Sh.*

TERRESTRIAL MAGNETISM (or *geomagnetism*): Earth's magnetism, and its variations. Its existence was first proved by the English scientist William Gilbert in *De magnete* (1600). The main geomagnetic field originates deep within the planet, and it extends outside Earth to the magnetosphere at a distance of several Earth radii. The north and south magnetic poles, to which a compass needle points, are located about 1,200 mi, respectively, from the north and south geographic poles. Compared with fields used in industry and in the laboratory, Earth's magnetic field is weak (0.3 oersted at the equator and 0.6 oersted at each pole); everywhere on Earth a compass needle can easily be deflected by a small magnet. During the last century, the distribution of the planet's magnetic field was determined by special expeditions, by routine observations from ships, and by a network of magnetic observatories; at present this knowledge is being much expanded by measurements from airplanes and spacecraft. See INTERNATIONAL GEOPHYSICAL YEAR.

Three components must be used in defining the magnetic field at any locality. The *angle of declination* (D) is the deflection from true north of a compass needle or other magnet free to move horizontally. It is measured by sighting with a telescope along a magnet suspended by a torsionless fiber and then measuring the angle through which the telescope must be rotated to bring it to due north. The *angle of dip,* or inclination (I), is the angle with the horizontal assumed by a magnetized needle in the magnetic meridian, pivoted about its center of gravity. The needle, setting along the magnetic lines of force, is horizontal at the magnetic equator and vertical at the poles. Both declination and dip have been measured with magnetic needles for some centuries. Dip was measured also by a dip inductor, in which a coil is rotated about an axis lying in the magnetic meridian and the position of the axis, in which there is no induced electromotive force, is determined. The third component is the *total intensity* (F) of the magnetic field, or its horizontal (H) or vertical (Z) component (Fig. 1). Abso-

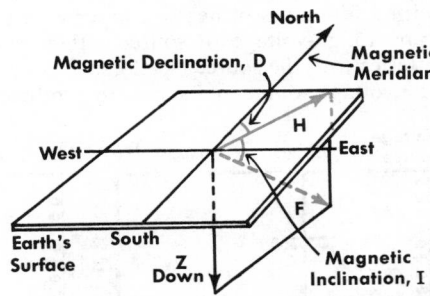

Fig. 1: Components of the geomagnetic field, F.

lute measurements of F, H, and Z have been possible only since the 19th cent., when K. F. Gauss showed how H could be measured with vibration and deflection MAGNETOMETERS. Later, absolute instruments for the measurement of H and Z and for the recording of their variations were installed in a world network of observatories. Between the two world wars, portable variometers were produced that could detect differences in field values of 10^{-5} oersted, or 1 γ (gamma). Since small deviations of Earth's field occur over mineral deposits and, to a lesser extent, over all geological structures, these variometers were much used in GEOPHYSICAL PROSPECTING. Recently, methods of measuring the total field to 1 γ from an airplane have been developed. The fluxgate magnetometer, employing a highly permeable magnetic alloy, can be made into an instrument for measuring all three field components, though not to the high accuracy of observatory instruments. Such an aerial magnetometer provides a very effective method of survey over the oceans. A second device for aerial measurement of the total

field to 1 γ, the nuclear resonance magnetometer, uses the moments of the hydrogen nuclei in a container of water.

The magnetic field of Earth, as measured at the surface, is quite similar to the field of a dipole, or small magnet, appropriately oriented and placed at the center of the planet. At the present time the field is better represented by that of a dipole inclined to the axis of rotation by 11° than by one along the axis of rotation (often called the axial dipole field). The magnetic poles, points on Earth's surface where the dip angle is 90°, are near but do not coincide with the position of the axis of the inclined dipole. This is because the field is not exactly that of a dipole, and the residual (Fig. 2) is highly complicated.

The gradual change of the geomagnetic field with time, called secular variation, is often recorded on survey maps. This is a complicated field which has many local centers, called isoporic foci, where the changes are most rapid.

The geomagnetic field is thought to be produced by the flow of electric currents in Earth's core, which has been found by the study of SEISMOLOGY to be a dense fluid, probably molten iron with a solid center (see EARTH). Since the solid mantle surrounding the core is not metallic, being composed of silicates or oxides, it has a much smaller electrical conductivity than the core. This conductivity is not negligible, however, for at temperatures of thousands of degrees SEMICONDUCTION becomes important. On the geophysical scale, the power required to produce the electrical and magnetic energy is small, and it appears to come from the kinetic energy of motions within the core. These motions are the result of convection, probably due to heat generated by small quantities of radioactive elements in the deep interior (see CONVECTION THEORY). The fluid currents are thought to generate electric currents by electromagnetic induction, as in a dynamo, except that the generated currents produce the generating magnetic field, so that the dynamo is self-excited. Such a dynamo in a fluid sphere has yet to be demonstrated in the laboratory.

Studies of the natural remanent magnetization of rocks of different geological ages (*paleomagnetism*) yield knowledge of the behavior of Earth's field during the past 1,500 million

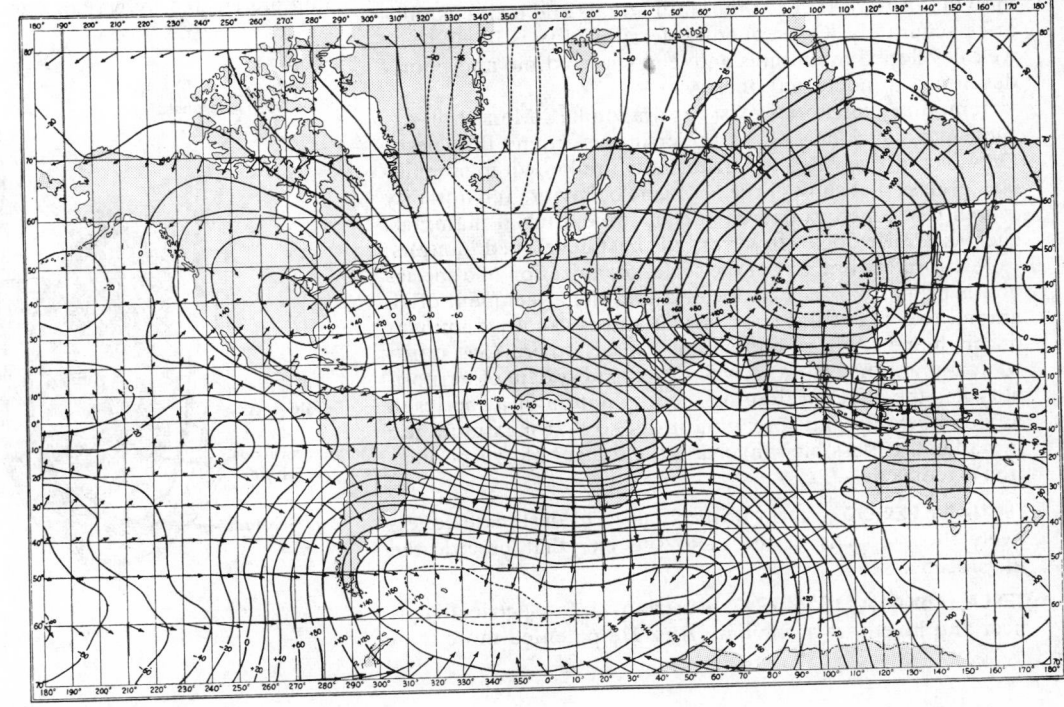

Fig. 2: Map of non-dipole, or residual, geomagnetic field for 1945: Contours show where the vertical components of the difference between the geomagnetic field and that dipole field which best fits are equal. Interval between contours is 0.02 gauss. Arrows give corresponding difference between horizontal components; an arrow 5.8 mm long represents 0.1 gauss.

yr. It has been shown that although the field at any one time deviated some 10° to 20° from that of a dipole along the axis of rotation, the ever-present secular variation caused the mean field, averaged over some thousands of years, to be very exactly that of an axial dipole. However, the polarity of the field appears to reverse at irregular intervals through geological time, though not more often than once in about 1 million yr. Such studies of rock magnetism show that in rocks older than 100 million yr there are significant differences between the present magnetic field and the ancient one in all continents. The results are difficult to reconcile without supposing that the geographical pole was not always in its present position and the distances between continents are not constant. In fact there is much evidence to support Wegener's theory of CONTINENTAL DRIFT.

Earth's magnetic field also shows daily variations of the order of 20 γ. Since these variations have periods of a solar day and a lunar day, they have been shown to arise from the atmospheric tides raised by Sun and Moon. These move the electrically conducting layers that form the part of the atmosphere known as the ionosphere, and the geomagnetic field induces in them varying currents. The fields resulting from these currents and those induced in Earth's mantle account for the daily variation, which is also modified by induced currents in Earth. It is possible to show that the electrical conductivity of the planet begins to rise rapidly at a level about 1,000 km deep.

Occasionally, during sunspot activity and in connection with auroras and radio fadeouts, large transient geomagnetic storms occur, sometimes of 1,000 γ, lasting about two days. These result as streams of conducting gas from the Sun interact with the geomagnetic field. See MAGNETISM; MAGNETIC COMPASS; SOLAR WIND.—*S. K. R.*

TERRITORIALITY: the tendency of an animal or a group of animals to defend a particular area. A territory is thus different from a "range," the area over which an animal habitually wanders, although the two may coincide. For example, wolves defend the immediate area around their den as a territory, but have a much wider hunting range. Territoriality can exist only in those species having the capacity for developing the agonistic (combative) behavior needed for defense. It also depends upon sense organs (particularly sight) that enable individuals to recognize other individuals and locate boundaries accurately. Consequently, territoriality is likely to be well developed in animals active in the daytime and poorly developed in nocturnal ones.

Temporary territories exist for dragonflies. Many fish, *e.g.* sunfish and sticklebacks, set up territories around their nests. Only one or two cases of territoriality are known in amphibians, a class that shows little agonistic behavior. Territoriality is well developed in lizards and in some diurnal mammals such as prairie dogs. However, it is best developed in BIRDS.

Territoriality is a part of the social organization of a species and is primarily based on localization, the attachment of an animal to a particular spot. An animal is usually dominant on his home territory and submissive elsewhere. (See DOMINANCE-SUBORDINATION.) A well-developed system of territoriality has the effect of limiting the population of a species in any one locality and spreading it out so that maximum use is made of its possible range, and the danger of overpopulation is reduced.—*J. P. S.*

TERTIARY PERIOD: a term formerly used to designate collectively those epochs of the CENOZOIC ERA that precede the Pleistocene.

TESLA, NIKOLA, 1856–1943, Austrian-U. S. electrical engineer and inventor; b. Smiljan, Aus. He patented more than 100 inventions, most of them concerned with electric-power transmission systems, dynamos and motors, high-frequency currents, and radio. His polyphase alternating system made long-distance transmission of electrical power possible. He is the inventor of the Tesla high-voltage induction coil. See ELECTRIC MOTOR.—*D. H. D. R.*

TESLA COIL: a form of induction coil whose air-core primary, wound with a few turns of heavy copper wire or tubing, is energized by a high-voltage a-c source with a spark gap connected in series with the source (see figure). A condenser, C_1, bridges the voltage source and serves to produce an oscilla-

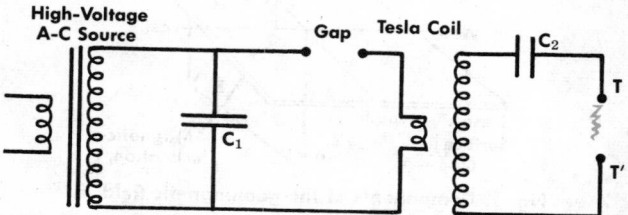

High-voltage a-c source (e.g. auto spark coil) is diagramed with Tesla coil and its additional tuning capacitor.

tory discharge across the gap. The secondary of the Tesla consists of many turns of fine insulated wire and is tuned by another condenser, C_2. When resonance is established, a powerful high-frequency discharge is produced between the terminals, T-T′. The coil is suitable for exciting x-ray and Crookes (vacuum) tubes.—*A. E.*

TESTIS (or **testicle**): the male gonad; the organ that produces sperm. In vertebrate animals the testes are paired structures, usually located in the lower body cavity region. In many mammals, however, the testes descend into a pouch, called the scrotum, outside the body cavity. In some species, including man, the descent of the testes occurs during early fetal life and is permanent; in other species, the descent is seasonal, corresponding to the breeding season.

A mature testis contains many *seminiferous tubules* lined with cells ready to undergo MEIOSIS. Meiotic divisions of these cells produce millions of sperm, which during copulation are ejected by way of ducts from the body. In addition

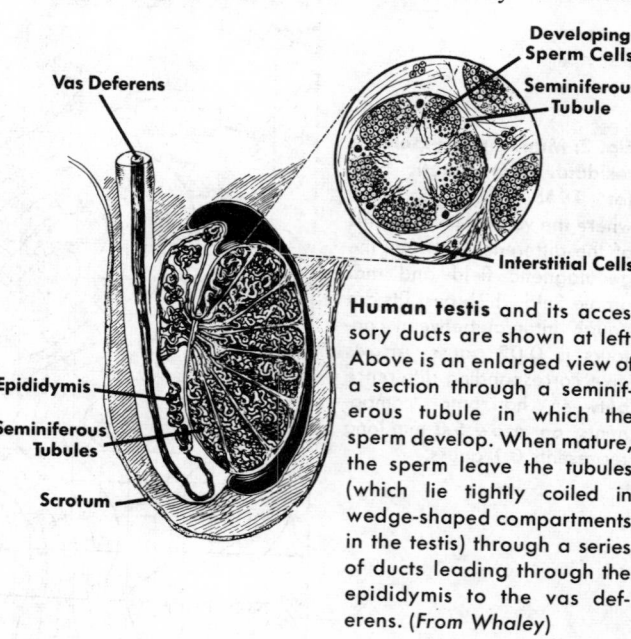

Human testis and its accessory ducts are shown at left. Above is an enlarged view of a section through a seminiferous tubule in which the sperm develop. When mature, the sperm leave the tubules (which lie tightly coiled in wedge-shaped compartments in the testis) through a series of ducts leading through the epididymis to the vas deferens. (*From Whaley*)

to producing sperm, the testes secrete male hormones, or androgens (*e.g.* testosterone), which are important in developing male secondary sexual characteristics, *e.g.* hair on face, deepening of voice.—*A. R. D.*

TESTOSTERONE: the principal steroid hormone produced by the interstitial (Leydig) cells of the testis. It is the most potent of the naturally occurring ANDROGENS and is responsible for the maintenance of (1) spermatogenesis, (2) the accessory genital organs, and (3) the secondary male sex characteristics.—*F. U.*

testosterone

TETRODE: see ELECTRON TUBE.

TEXTILE: originally, a woven fabric, now a broad term applied to fibers, filaments, yarns, and their products made by spinning, weaving, knitting, knotting, felting, and other twisting and interlacing processes. In the textile industry, fibers are divided into the natural (*e.g.* cotton, wool, silk, jute, and flax) and the man-made; the latter are subdivided into cellulosics (*e.g.* rayon) and synthetics (*e.g.* nylon, polyesters, and polyacrylics). A given textile fiber usually belongs to one of three chemical classes: CELLULOSE (cotton, jute, flax, rayon), PROTEIN (wool, silk), and RESIN (most man-made fibers other than rayon). Before World War I, wool, cotton, flax, jute, silk, and other natural fibers and filaments constituted the basic textile materials. The first man-made fiber, RAYON, became a major textile material in the 1930s. Many other man-made fibers have been introduced in recent years, most of them manufactured from synthetic organic compounds. These fibers are often called synthetic, to distinguish them from the cellulose-based rayon and acetate. However, it is preferable to classify fibers as either natural or man-made (manufactured) and to depend on their botanical name or chemical composition for further differentiation within each group. (In the U. S. A. law requires that the fiber content of textile-fiber products be indicated on appropriate labels.) Man-made fibers can be manufactured for many specific end-uses, and their production has been growing rapidly. However, the natural fibers still account for over ¾ of the total world textile market.

History: Textile-making is one of man's oldest occupations. Remains of spinning and weaving tools, and of wool and linen fabrics, have been found in several prehistoric sites, and there is evidence that textiles were invented by Neolithic man. Linen fabrics dating back to 5000 B. C. have been found in Egypt; silk was woven in China in 2500 B. C., and cotton in India in 2000 B. C. Ancient Rome brought cotton cloth from India and from Egypt, and much silk was brought to Europe from China. In the 5th cent. silk culture spread westward, and textile-making developed rapidly. In the 14th cent. the Mediterranean peoples were producing beautiful silk, linen, and wool fabrics in practically all the basic weaves known today. The art of weaving, however, remained a handicraft until the mechanization of textile manufacturing in England in the early 19th cent., an event that ushered in a new era in the history of man. (See AUTOMATION.)

The basic processes and equipment used in textile manufacturing for converting fibers into yarns and fabrics were developed in the 18th and 19th cent. In general, they consist of separating, cleaning, blending, and parallelizing of fibers; forming fibers into rope-like strands, attenuating or drawing the strands and twisting them into yarns; interlacing yarns to make fabrics; and finishing the fabrics. Historically, two

major systems developed, and all textile fibers, natural and manufactured, are processed on either the "cotton" or the "woolen" system, depending on the length and the mechanical and chemical properties of the fiber.

Cotton System: Cotton is delivered to the spinning mill in highly compressed 500-lb bales. The bales are opened, and pickers, breakers, intermediates, and finishers loosen up lumps and remove dirt, leaves, and other foreign particles from the lint fibers. These machines form the cotton into "laps" of fairly uniform density, resembling the absorbent cotton sold in drug stores. The laps are fed to carding machines, where they are drawn on revolving cylinders covered with fine hooks or wire brushes. These pull all the fibers in one direction, partially straightening and parallelizing the tangled mass. The thin sheet formed in this manner is then drawn through a funnel-like apparatus from which it emerges as a rope-like sliver. In the production of high-quality goods the card sliver is subjected to a combing process, in which the fibers are parallelized further and the shorter fibers removed. The card or comb slivers pass on to drawing frames, in which they are doubled and then drawn out again to approximately the original diameter. In the roving frames, which follow next, the sliver is drawn further and is given, for the first time, a slight twist. The strand is then fed to spinning frames, on which it is again drawn out; finally the strand is twisted into a yarn. Single yarns are often twisted together into plied yarns when high strengths are required, as for example in the manufacture of sewing thread. Plied yarns can be twisted together into cable yarns, *e.g.* for use in making automobile-tire cord.

Fabrics can be manufactured from yarns by several methods, of which weaving and knitting are most important. Weaving consists, in principle, of interlacing at right angles two systems of yarns, warp and filling. The *warp*—yarns which run the length of the fabric—is prepared by rewinding yarns from several hundred cheeses, cones, or other yarn packages onto warper beams, which resemble giant spools. The yarns are given a SIZING, usually a thin coating of starch, to protect them from chafing in the loom, and are rewound on loom beams. They are then drawn through the eyes of "needles," fine steel wires suspended from frames on the loom called harnesses. In the making of plain-weave fabrics, only two harnesses are required, and the first, third, fifth, and all other odd warp yarns are threaded through the needles of one harness, while the second, fourth, sixth, and all other even yarns go through the needles of the second harness. In weaving, one harness is raised and the other is depressed; this raises half the yarns and lowers the other half, thus creating a "shed" between them. The shuttle, a small, boat-like device containing the *filling* yarn, is driven through this shed, leaving the filling thread in its wake. The position of the harnesses is then reversed, and the shuttle is driven back, again depositing a filling yarn. This process is repeated continuously and rapidly; many types of looms are capable of weaving in 180 filling yarns/min, or of producing 5 yd/hr of a fabric having 60 picks (filling yarns) to the in.; even higher weaving speeds are attainable on the new looms, in which the filling yarn is deposited across the warp by compressed air or other shuttleless means.

In the plain-weave fabrics each warp yarn passes over one filling yarn, under the second, over the third, and so on. Similarly, each filling yarn passes under one warp yarn, over the second, under the next, and so on. In such fabrics the lengths of each yarn appearing on each side of the fabric are the same, and the face and the back side of the fabric are alike. By using more than two harnesses it is possible to produce fabrics with weaves giving the effect of diagonal lines (twills); the use of more than two harnesses also permits concentration

TABLE OF GENERIC NAMES, TRADE NAMES, AND COMPOSITIONS OF MAN-MADE FIBERS

(Based in Part on Information Supplied by *Federal Trade Commission*)

Generic	Trade	The fiber-forming substance is—	Generic	Trade	The fiber-forming substance is—
Acrylic	Orlon Acrilan Creslan Zefran	Any long-chain synthetic polymer composed of at least 85% by weight of acrylonitrile units ($-CH_2-CH-$). $\mid$ CN	Nylon	DuPont Nylon Chemstrand Nylon Caprolan	Any long-chain synthetic polyamide in which amide groups ($-\overset{\displaystyle O}{\overset{\|}{C}}-NH-$) recur as an integral part of the chain.
Modacrylic	Dynel Verel	Any long-chain synthetic polymer composed of less than 85% but at least 35% by weight of acrylonitrile units ($-CH_2-CH-$). $\mid$ CN	Rubber	Lastex Contro Darleen	Natural or synthetic rubber.
Polyester	Dacron Kodel Fortrel Vycron	Any long-chain synthetic polymer composed of at least 85% by weight of an ester of a dihydric alcohol and terephthalic acid (p$-HOOC-C_6H_4-COOH$).	Spandex	Lycra Vyrene	A long-chain synthetic polymer composed of at least 85% by weight of a segmented polyurethane.
Rayon	Topel Avron Bemberg Avril Tyrex Fortisan Zantrel	Regenerated cellulose, or regenerated cellulose in which substituents have replaced not more than 15% of the hydrogens of the hydroxyl groups.	Vinal	Vinylan Kuralon	Any long-chain synthetic polymer composed of at least 50% by weight of vinyl alcohol units ($-CH_2-CHOH-$), and in which the total of the vinyl alcohol units and any one or more of the various acetal units is at least 85% by weight of the fiber.
Acetate	Arnel Tricel	Cellulose acetate; when not less than 92% of the hydroxyl groups are acetylated, the term *triacetate* may be used as a generic description of the fiber.	Olefin	Prolene Reevan Meraclon Royalene	Any long-chain synthetic polymer composed of at least 85% by weight of ethylene, propylene, or other olefin units.
Saran	Velon Rovana Dawbarn	Any long-chain synthetic polymer composed of at least 80% by weight of vinylidene chloride units ($-CH_2-CCl_2-$).	Vinyon	Rhovyl Bexan	Any long-chain synthetic polymer composed of at least 85% by weight of vinyl chloride units ($-CH_2-CHCl-$).
Azlon	Vicara Zycon	Any regenerated, naturally occurring proteins.	Metallic	Lurex Lame	Metal, plastic-coated metal, metal-coated plastic, or core completely covered by metal.
Nytril	Darvan	A substance containing at least 85% by weight of a long-chain polymer of vinylidene dinitrile ($-CH_2-C(CN)_2-$), where the vinylidene dinitrile content is no less than every other unit in the polymer chain.	Glass	Fiberglas Garan	Glass.
			Fluoro-carbon	Teflon	Long-chain carbon molecules with fluorine-saturated available bonds.

of either filling or warp on the face of the fabric (filling or warp satin weaves). More intricate designs and large patterns can be woven on Jacquard looms, in which warp yarns are individually controlled.

Woven fabrics are inspected, graded, and shipped to a finishing plant. Preparatory finishing processes to which cotton greige goods are generally subjected are singeing, desizing, kiering, bleaching, tentering, shearing, and drying. The fabric is first passed rapidly through a gas flame to burn off loose threads and lint on its surface. It is then quenched, and piled in a bin or a J-shaped box, where it is steeped for some time to permit enzymes added to the water to solubilize sizing materials. The next cleaning operation, kiering, in which the fabric is subjected to hot caustic solution, is now often combined with bleaching, in which the natural yellowish color of cotton is changed to white by the action of hydrogen peroxide or sodium hypochlorite. Subsequent finishing operations depend on the intended use of the fabrics: mercerizing, a strength, absorbency, and luster-improving treatment, dyeing, and printing are common procedures. In recent years chemical treatments which impart desirable functional properties have become popular; *e.g.* in 1960 about 1.9 billion linear yd of cotton cloth were treated to give wash-and-wear properties.

Woolen System: Wool fibers are woven into two types of fabrics, worsteds and woolens. Yarns for worsteds are spun from parallelized long fibers, while yarns for woolens are made from more randomly arranged shorter hairs. The basic steps of the woolen system are scouring, spooling, dressing, and weaving. Because of the differences between the various wools, the first step is fiber sorting. The stock is then opened and scoured in a series of large tanks. It is then freed from dust and dirt, spray-oiled, and blended. The blended stock is carded to remove foreign matter and to disentangle and separate the fibers. The carded fibers are formed into a strand, or roving, which is then attenuated, twisted, and wound on bobbins. In making yarns for worsteds the roving is subjected to further parallelizing and combing operations before twisting. Finishing of wool fabrics utilizes moisture, heat, and pressure, which are used in crabbing to release the strains introduced into the fabric by previous manufacturing operations and to set the fabric in the flat, smooth state. In the fulling finishing process, pressure is applied intermittently (*e.g.* by beating), causing the wool fibers to migrate and become entangled; this produces a more compact and dense structure which permits napping. Worsteds are generally not fulled, but instead are permitted to shrink in scouring and in this way gain in density. Subsequent brushing and shear-

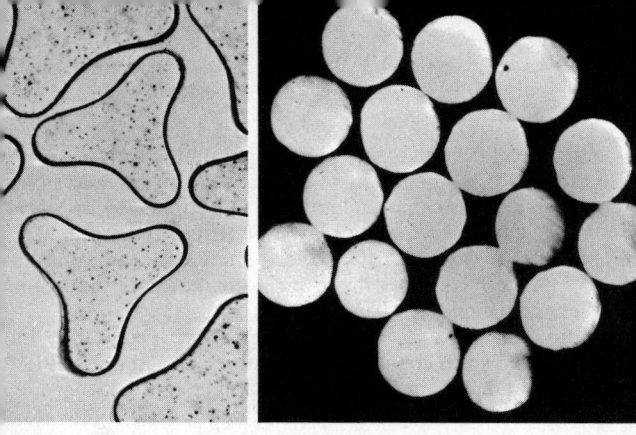

"Antron" tri-lobal multifilament nylon yarn (*left*) in cross section is magnified here 1,000 times. This yarn contains 1½ to 3 deniers per filament. **Typical nylon thread** (*right*) in cross section (X660) has remarkably round and smooth filaments. This thread is used in sheer stockings and fine knit goods. (*DuPont*)

ing (in which projecting hairs are first raised and then cut), followed by pressing, give the smooth surface with apparent weave patterns characteristic of worsteds. Thermoplastic fiber fabrics are generally heat-set in finishing to improve their shape-holding and dimensional-stability characteristics.

Knitting consists of interconnecting loops of yarns. The vertical loop chains are called wales; the horizontal ones are called courses. There are five major knitting systems: plain or jersey, rib, purl, interlock, and warp knitting. Rib knitting, in which some wales are linked differently from others, produces a fabric showing a ribbed structure and capable of considerably more stretch than a plain knit. The interlock knit is essentially a double-rib fabric and is generally stronger, heavier, and more durable than a rib knit; it is also less subject to curling at the edges, so that it is more easily cut and sewn. Purl knitting (links and links) produces soft, lofty fabrics closely resembling hand knits. Warp knitting can be done largely on tricot machines and is used in high-speed production of comparatively dimensionally stable fabrics. Knits traditionally conform better than woven fabrics, but lack the latter's dimensional stability. However, this disadvantage can be overcome with recently developed mechanical compacting and chemical- and heat-setting treatments for knits.—*W. P. C.*

THALES, *c.* 640–546 B. C., the earliest known Greek philosopher of nature; b. Miletus. Rejecting supernatural interpretations of natural events, he held that all things are formed out of a single element, which he identified as water. In mathematics he proved several geometric propositions and thus introduced the idea of logical demonstration. He is credited with predicting the solar eclipse of May 28, 585 B. C. —*A. P. E.*

THALLIUM: a metallic element (Tl); at. no. 81; at. wt 204.37; valence 1 or 3. The element was discovered in 1861 by Sir William Crookes and independently in the same year by the Belgian chemist Claude August Lamy while both were studying the spectrum of tellurium. Closely resembling lead in many properties, thallium is a bluish-white, very soft, heavy, and malleable metal with low tensile strength; unlike lead, it forms a heavy oxide crust. The metal occurs in zinc ores and pyrites and is primarily obtained from flue dusts associated either with the smelting of sphalerite (ZnS) ores or with the manufacture of sulfuric acid. Thallium salts (*e.g.* the sulfate and sulfide) are poisonous and are used for rodent poisons and insecticides. Various thallium compounds find use in infrared detectors and infrared (military) signaling systems. A mercury-thallium alloy freezes at $-60°$C and is used in place of mercury in certain thermometers, relays, and switches designed for arctic and stratospheric conditions.—*R. B. T.*

THALLOPHYTES: the FLOWERLESS PLANTS.

THEOPHRASTUS, *c.* 372–288 B. C., Greek botanist; b. Eresus. He was a pupil of Plato and Aristotle and succeeded Aristotle as head of the Lyceum. Two of his books, one on plants and one on stones, were important sources of knowledge to European scientists in late medieval times. He identified the brain as the seat of intelligence and did research in many areas of natural history.—*D. H. D. R.*

THEORELL, AXEL HUGO TEODOR, 1903– , Swedish biochemist; b. Linköping. His research has been principally the study of enzymes, particularly the oxidative enzymes. He was the first to extract and purify myoglobin, the red coloring substance of the muscles. For his discoveries on the nature and action of oxidative enzymes, he received the Nobel prize, 1955. He is a fellow of the Royal Society and an associate of the U. S. National Academy of Sciences.—*D. H. D. R.*

THEORIE ANALYTIQUE DE LA CHALEUR (Analytic Theory of Heat), by Joseph Fourier (1822): This book introduced for the first time, in systematic form, the methods used in the integration of linear partial differential equations under given boundary conditions; it was an introduction to the methods of mathematical physics. After deriving the differential equation of heat

$$\frac{\partial V}{\partial t} = k \left(\frac{\partial^2 V}{\partial x^2} + \frac{\partial^2 V}{\partial y^2} + \frac{\partial^2 V}{\partial z^2} \right)$$

the author solves it for a rectangular solid, a ring, a sphere, a cylinder, and other figures, under specially given boundary conditions. This leads to the expansion of functions in series, among which the trigonometric series stand out (therefore called FOURIER SERIES). Also, more complicated series are used, as well as the so-called *Fourier integral*. There is an English translation by A. Freeman (1878).—*D. J. S.*

THÉORIE DES PROPORTIONS CHEMIQUES (Theory of Chemical Proportions), by Jöns Jakob Berzelius (1819): This classic of chemical literature was published in a French translation from the Swedish in 1819. Its full title is *Essai sur la théorie des proportions chimiques et sur l'influence chimique de l'electricité.* A German translation appeared in 1820 and a second French edition in 1835; it was never translated into English. Dealing with the implications of atomic theory in explaining chemical combination, the book developed the "dualistic theory," which viewed all chemical compounds as essentially made up of two parts, and explained chemical combination in terms of electrical attractions between atoms or atomic groups carrying characteristic and opposite polarities, *e.g.* metal oxide-nonmetal oxide. The discussion of atomic weight proved of great importance in the development of chemical thought, but the dualistic theory, based on studies of inorganic compounds, was not serviceable when applied to organic compounds, and fell out of use.—*A. I.*

THEORY OF PARALLELS, GEOMETRICAL RESEARCHES ON, by Nicholas Lobachevski (1840): This was the sixth and most influential of Lobachevski's publications on NON-EUCLIDEAN GEOMETRY, or the geometry that follows from the assumption that through a given point there is more than one parallel to a given line. This geometry, independently developed by Lobachevski and then J. Bolyai (but partly anticipated, without their knowledge, by Gauss) was destined to affect profoundly the subsequent development of geometry, physics, and epistemology.—*G. G.*

THEORY OF THE EARTH WITH PROOFS AND ILLUSTRATIONS, by James Hutton (1795): Published first in much abbreviated form in the Transactions of the Royal Society of Edinburgh (1785), the *Theory of the Earth* was based upon long observation of geologic phenomena. This work contained the revolutionary conception that the past history of Earth's surface is explainable only by those forces observed in operation now or in the recent past. In his theory Hutton recognized both great heat and water as powerful agencies, thus avoiding the contemporary battle between the Vulcanists, who held that basalt and granite are of igneous origin, and the Neptunists, who believed these substances originated as sediments in water. The Huttonian ideas became known as *uniformitarianism* and were important to the development of theories of organic EVOLUTION as well as to GEOLOGY.—*E. Me.*

THERMAL STRESS AND SHOCK: effects of heat on a material body, usually serving to weaken it. When a material or structure is subjected to a temperature gradient, or when a composite structure consisting of two or more materials is heated, the various fibers tend to expand according to their individual temperatures and coefficients of expansion. Since the structure is continuous, the individual fibers are not free to expand on their own, and constrain each other. These constraints give rise to thermal and associated *stresses* whose magnitude depends upon the temperature levels and the mechanical and physical properties of the materials of construction. When the effect occurs with extreme rapidity, it may be called thermal *shock*. See STRENGTH OF MATERIALS.—*W. Ho.*

THERMIONIC EMISSION: the emission of electrons from a hot body. It was first discovered, though not explained, by Thomas A. Edison, 1883. Edison found that when he sealed an extra electrode into an evacuated filament-type lamp, a current was established between the filament and this extra electrode if the electrode was maintained at a positive potential with respect to the filament. Since the electron had not yet been discovered, this *Edison effect* remained a laboratory curiosity for 20 yr, until J. A. Fleming provided the proper explanation of it. The number of electrons emitted by a hot metal increases rapidly with its temperature and depends on the particular metal being heated. Metals differ in the value of their WORK function, or energy required to separate electrons from the metallic surface.—*A. E.*

THERMISTOR: see BOLOMETER.

THERMOCHEMISTRY: the branch of physical chemistry that deals with the heat changes accompanying chemical reactions. Reactions that evolve heat are called *exothermic;* those that absorb heat are called *endothermic.* Certain physical changes, *e.g.* solution, absorption, and change of phase, are accompanied by the absorption or evolution of heat, and come within the realm of thermochemistry. Thermochemistry is largely experimental and is more restricted in scope than the field of THERMODYNAMICS, which encompasses transformations of all forms of energy and is noted for its role in the development of new scientific theory. The relatively few broad laws of thermochemistry are essentially specialized expressions of the first law of thermodynamics, *i.e.* the law of the conservation of energy; the two best-known and most widely applicable laws are attributed respectively to A. L. Lavoisier and P. S. de Laplace (1780) and Germain Henri Hess (1840). The Lavoisier-Laplace rule states that the heat required to decompose a compound into its elements is equal to the heat evolved when the same compound is formed from its elements. More generally, the heat effects in reversible reactions are identical in magnitude but opposite in sign. Hess's law, also known as the law of constant heat summation, states that the heat change in a chemical reaction that can take place by two or more different paths is the same regardless of which path is followed.

Thermochemical data are of the greatest importance in designing large-scale chemical preparations and in most other phases of chemical engineering. An efficient endothermic reaction requires the right amount of heat at the right rate; similarly, exothermic reactions must be controlled by adequate heat-absorbing devices to prevent a potentially dangerous acceleration of the reaction. The heat of combustion of various fuels, *i.e.* the heat evolved when a given weight of the fuel is completely burned by elemental oxygen, is of fundamental importance in the design of practically all types of heat engines, including boilers, automotive and aircraft engines, and rocket engines. The heat of formation of chemical compounds, *i.e.* the amount of heat evolved or absorbed when the compound is formed from its elements, is an important thermodynamic constant of the compound, useful in predicting the reactions it can undergo. This quantity frequently must be determined indirectly, applying Hess's law, since most compounds cannot be formed directly from their elements.

Heat effects are usually measured experimentally by carrying out the desired reaction in a CALORIMETER; this is essentially a well-insulated vessel fitted with sensitive thermometers, which may contain two or more chambers, one within the other. The reaction between carefully weighed quantities of the reactants is made to take place in the inner chamber. The outer chamber is filled with water or other liquid of known specific heat, and the total temperature rise during the reaction is measured. From this value and the weights and specific heat of the reactants, the water, and the vessel, the heat of reaction is calculated. Heats of reaction are usually expressed as calories (cal) or kilocalories (kcal) and are stated in equation form. In such equations the physical state of both reactants and products should be specified, *e.g.*

$$H_2(g) + \tfrac{1}{2} O_2(g) = H_2O(g), \quad \Delta H_{298°K} = -57.81 \text{ kcal}$$

clearly states that when 1 mole of gaseous hydrogen combines with ½ mole of gaseous oxygen to form 1 mole of water (the mole of water being measured in the vapor state at 298°K or 25°C), 57.81 kcal is given off by the reaction.—*A. M. S.*

THERMOCOUPLE: a temperature-measuring device, composed of two dissimilar metals, metallic alloys, or semiconductors, and based on the Seebeck effect discovered in 1821. Thermocouples, though primarily intended for use as *pyrometers* (for temperatures ranging to 3000°F), may also be used for measuring temperatures as low as −300°F. Special thermocouples attain an accuracy of ¼%. If two wires of different metals are joined at their ends, a temperature difference between these junctions will produce a thermal electromotive force in the circuit, which in turn will cause a weak current to flow through the wires (see THERMOELECTRIC EFFECT). This current may be passed through a series-connected milliammeter, previously calibrated so that its readings can be translated into temperature differences. If one junction is maintained at a fixed known temperature, these readings yield temperatures directly. Typical low-temperature thermocouples use combinations of copper and iron, iron and constantan (a copper-nickel alloy), copper and constantan, antimony and bismuth, and chromel-alumel (chromium-nickel and nickel-aluminum alloys). For measuring high temperatures, the wires are usually made of platinum and a platinum-rhodium alloy. Iron-constantan couples are adversely affected by the presence of oxygen or water vapor, chromel-alumel couples by reducing agents such as hydrogen or carbon monoxide. Platinum thermocouples are subject to contamination at high temperatures by hydrogen, phosphorus, silicon, and some metallic vapors. They must therefore be enclosed in a gas-tight thermal well. A number of thermocouples may be joined in series to form a *thermopile,* alternate junctions being mounted close together. This affords multiplication of the weak currents that flow through a single couple, so that even greater sensitivity is achieved. Thermopiles make use of bismuth-silver, bismuth-cadmium, and certain p-n type semiconductors. Such devices can be made so sensitive that they can detect a candle flame 40 mi away and can be used to measure the radiation from distant stars. —*A. E.*

THERMODYNAMICS: basically, the science of heat and work and the conversion of one into the other. In modern times the scope of the subject has broadened to embrace all phenomena in which temperature plays an important part. The foundations of thermodynamics rest upon two natural laws discovered in the 19th century. The first law asserts that when heat is transformed into other kinds of energy, the total energy remains constant. This principle is known as the law of conservation of energy. The second law describes the limitations in the conversion of heat into work, and leads to criteria for predicting the direction of natural processes.

Thermodynamics dispenses with all assumptions about the internal structure of matter; it derives relations among the various physical properties of bodies in terms of directly measurable quantities such as volume, pressure, temperature, and amount of material. Consequently, any changes in the theoretical picture of matter which may be demanded by fresh evidence leave thermodynamics largely unaffected. Its findings therefore serve as standards to which all hypothetical estimates of nature must conform.

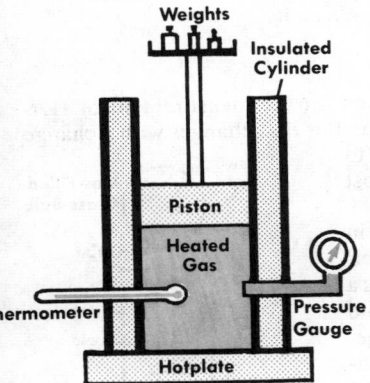

Basic heat engine: Hotplate heats gas, which expands against piston and thus raises weights. Heat is in this way converted into work.

Thermodynamic States: In thermodynamics, any unique set of values for the variables used to describe a body (volume, mass, pressure, temperature, etc.) defines a separate "state." For example, if a gas is enclosed in a vessel at a given pressure, it is said to be in one thermodynamic state, and if the temperature, volume, or pressure is altered the gas is said to be in another thermodynamic state. Clearly the number of states, in this sense, that any specimen can occupy is infinite.

First Law of Thermodynamics: This formulation of the law of conservation of energy may be conveniently illustrated by

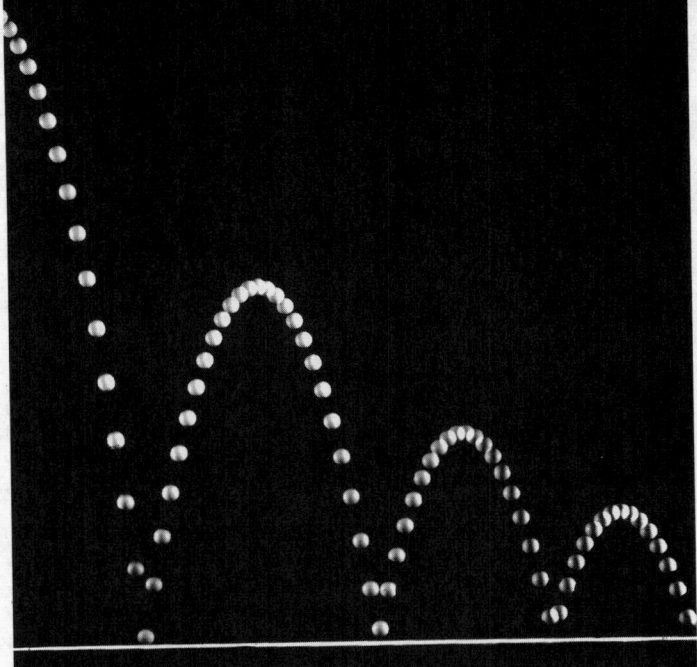

Energy becoming unavailable for conversion to work: With each bounce, ball rises less, since part of its kinetic energy is spent in heating the ball, the surface on which the ball bounces, and the air. (*Berenice Abbott*)

a simple example. Imagine a gas-filled cylinder fitted with a piston that can slide up or down without friction. The cylinder is surrounded by insulating material to prevent the escape of heat, except for the bottom, which rests upon a hot plate. A certain amount of heat passes into the gas, which consequently expands and also increases in temperature. In rising, the piston lifts a weight, thereby doing mechanical work. Measurements show that, for any definite final temperature of the gas, the difference between the heat added to the gas (Q) and the work it does against gravity (W) is always the same. This difference is described as the gain in internal energy and is symbolized by $\triangle U$ (many chemists prefer the symbol $\triangle E$). This experimental truth is the first law of thermodynamics, which is concisely represented by the equation

$$\triangle U = Q - W$$

Note that it is the difference between Q and W that is constant. Whether the process is fast or slow, the load heavy or light, the expansion large or small, the difference remains the same, provided the gas undergoes the same increase in temperature. If the weight is raised to a greater height, more work is done, but a correspondingly larger amount of heat is taken from the heat source. Even if the piston does not fit smoothly, and friction with the walls contributes to heating the gas, the change in internal energy is still the same, for then less heat is taken from the plate and the piston rises less, doing less work.

The internal energy is thus dependent only on the initial and final thermodynamic states of the gas and not upon the steps by which the transition occurred. If a certain mass of substance has a particular volume, temperature, and pressure, its internal energy is a fixed amount, irrespective of the way in which its state was achieved. (It is assumed in this simple example that the specimen has no electrical, magnetic, or other form of additional energy.) For this reason, internal energy is known as a property of the state of the system under consideration. Work and heat, on the other hand, are not determined by the thermodynamic state, nor by the difference between states, but by the way in which the change occurred.

Second Law of Thermodynamics: Heat is unique among the various forms of energy in that heat can never be transformed completely into work in any continuous process. An axle rotating without friction could convert its kinetic energy entirely into work, say, by lifting a load. An electric cell could perform mechanical work as long as its electrical energy lasted. But the internal energy in, for example, a hot gas could never be entirely transformed into work unless the temperature of the gas eventually fell to absolute zero.

Heat engines convert heat into work by a cyclical process. Heat is absorbed by a working substance, usually a vapor or a gas, either from an outside source or by the burning of fuel within the apparatus. When the working substance has expanded to a predetermined value, it must then be restored to its original state for the next cycle, and this restoration is accompanied by the rejection of some energy—as heat, not as work. The lower the temperature at this stage, the less heat will be rejected, but in all cases much of the heat absorbed is never converted into work at all, however ideally the engine may operate. Expressed more concisely, the second law asserts that no actual heat engine, operating in cycles, can convert heat energy completely into work; some of the heat supplied must always be discarded. In any heat engine, the work involved is just the difference between the heat Q_1 which is transferred at the higher temperature and the heat Q_2 which is exchanged at the lower temperature, if we except any losses due to heat leakage and friction in the moving parts. At the end of every cycle the working substance is back in its initial state; hence, its internal energy is unchanged ($\triangle U = 0$) and the net heat $Q_1 - Q_2$ equals the work W. Only in the event that Q_2 could be made zero, which would require a temperature of absolute zero, would the heat Q_1 equal the work W (see CARNOT CYCLE). An alternative statement of the second law, first propounded by Rudolf Clausius, is that heat cannot be transferred continuously from a cold body to a hot one without the performance of work.

Similarly, we may state that heat does not spontaneously flow from a cold body to a hot one. In this form, the principle is sometimes called the zeroth law of thermodynamics.

The engine that we have just considered was a theoretical ideal capable of perfect reversibility. All natural processes, however, are irreversible, for, although it may be possible to run them backwards, this can never be accomplished without making some energy less useful than it was before. As a very simple example, consider a steel ball which is dropped from a certain height to a steel plate beneath it. Since no body is perfectly elastic, the rebounding ball will not quite reach the height from which it fell. Thus, the potential energy it had at the start is not entirely regained. If we arrange to have the ball lifted through the small distance which it failed to recover, additional work must be done at the expense of some other energy source, such as the potential energy of another descending weight. Clearly such spontaneous, natural processes are always accompanied by a debasement of energy, some part of the initial energy becoming less capable of performing work than it was before the process took place. The energy in a hot body can be converted partly into motion or other useful forms, as happens in a steam engine, but that fraction of the energy which inevitably flows into a colder body thereby becomes less convertible than it was before—less available for translation into work—even though its amount is unchanged. A measure of the degree of irreversibility of a thermodynamic process is known as ENTROPY.—*J. E. W.*

THERMOELECTRIC EFFECT: the production of electricity by the application of heat to the junction of dissimilar materials. When two wires made of different metals are joined at their

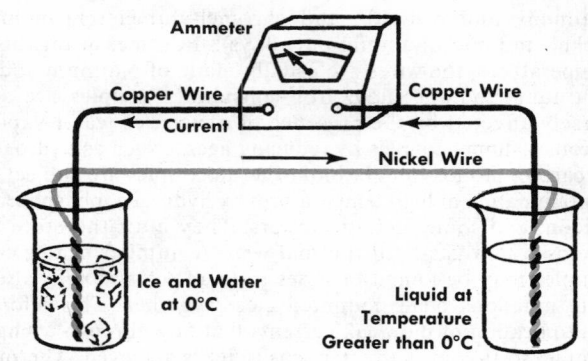

Thermoelectric effect: Since each junction of two metals is at a different temperature, a current, as indicated in the ammeter, flows in the circuit.

ends and the junctions are kept at different temperatures, a small electric current flows around the circuit. This phenomenon, first observed by T. J. Seebeck, 1821, is called the *Seebeck effect.* It is assumed that free electrons are present in both metals, but in different concentrations and average speeds. In consequence, some electrons drift across each boundary to produce a difference of potential between the two metals. At the hot junction the potential difference is greater than at the cold junction; hence, a small but steady current flows. Conversely, if an electric current is sent around the circuit when both junctions have the same temperature, heat is evolved at one and absorbed at the other. This phenomenon, discovered in 1834 by J. C. A. Peltier, is called the *Peltier effect.* Both transformations are manifestations of the thermoelectric effect.

If semiconductors are used instead of metals, much larger currents are produced for a given temperature difference, and this type of THERMOCOUPLE can serve as a low-voltage electric generator; operated in reverse, it functions as a practical refrigerator or heater.

The usefulness of the thermoelectric effect for thermometry arises from the fact that the magnitudes of the potential and the resulting current vary with the difference in temperature between the two junctions.—*J. E. W.*

THERMOMETER: a device used for the measurement of TEMPERATURE. Any property of matter that changes with a change of temperature may be used to measure temperature; most commonly the property is size. As a rule, bodies increase in size fairly regularly when their temperature increases. Thus a metal rod or a column of liquid becomes progressively longer as it becomes hotter; gases expand to larger volumes or exert greater pressure with increasing temperature. Any device that registers such changes on a suitable scale is a thermometer. The type in widest use is a long glass tube whose small bore terminates at the bottom in a bulb containing liquid. The liquid is usually mercury, although alcohol colored to make it more visible is used in

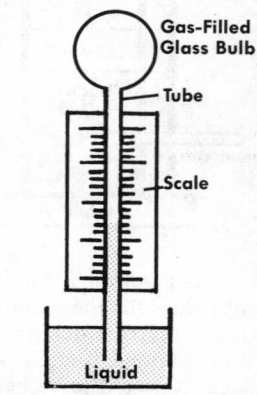

Gas thermometer: The higher the temperature, the greater is the pressure of the gas in the bulb and the lower the column of liquid in the tube.

household thermometers. The glass tube, or the frame on which it may be mounted, is engraved with a scale so that the level of liquid in the tube can be designated by the corresponding number on the scale. Gases are much more expansible with changing temperature than liquids are. Accordingly, a gas thermometer is much more sensitive than the liquid type, although more cumbersome and more fragile. Galileo designed what may have been the earliest thermometer of this kind—the thermoscope.

Other properties used for temperature measurement are the electrical resistance of metals and the small voltage produced between two metallic junctions when their temperatures differ (see THERMOCOUPLE).—*J. E. W.*

THIAMINE: see VITAMIN.

THIOCYANATES: salts or esters of thiocyanic acid, H—S—C≡N. The alkali-metal salts are prepared by heating alkali-metal cyanides with sulfur. They are used as laboratory reagents in chemical analysis and in pyrotechnics. The ammonium salt is isomeric with thiourea and can be converted into thiourea by heating to 140°C. Ferric thiocyanate is deep red, and serves as an identifying compound for detecting ferric ion. The alkyl thiocyanates, made by reacting an alkyl halide with sodium or potassium thiocyanate, are widely used as insecticides. They are isomeric with the corresponding isothiocyanates or *mustard oils,* which occur naturally in a variety of plant species. Allyl isothiocyanate is responsible for the characteristic flavor and irritancy of mustard. (See ISOMERS.)—*A. M. S.*

THOMPSON, PHILIP DUNCAN, 1922–   , U. S. meteorologist; b. Rossville, Ind. His research has been on the mathematical and physical basis of weather prediction and the theory of large-scale disturbances in atmospheric and oceanic currents. He has been head of the Research and Development Section of the Joint Numerical Prediction Center since 1954.—*D. H. D. R.*

THOMSON, SIR CHARLES WYVILLE, 1830–82, Scottish naturalist; b. Bonsyde. He directed the six-man civilian scientific staff of the voyage of the *Challenger* (1872–76), a 70,000-mi exploring expedition which laid the basis for the study of OCEANOGRAPHY. Thomson published *The Voyage of the Challenger in the Atlantic* (1877), but illness and his death prevented his participation in the expedition's main report, which required 13 yr to complete. Thomson was a member of the Royal Society and was professor of natural history at the Univ. of Edinburgh from 1870.—*D. H. D. R.*

THOMSON, GEORGE PAGET, 1892–   , English physicist; b. Cambridge. Late in World War I he worked on aerodynamical research for the Royal Flying Corps. For the experimental discovery of the wave nature of electrons, he and C. J. Davisson shared the 1937 Nobel prize. Thomson is a fellow of the Royal Society.—*D. H. D. R.*

THOMSON, SIR JOHN ARTHUR, 1861–1933, Scottish biologist; b. East Lothian. His research in zoology was principally on alcyonarians. Much of Thomson's effort was devoted to popularizing biology and to correlating science and religion, through both lectures and his many well-written books, which included *Progress of Science in the 19th Century* (1904), *Heredity* (1908), *The Bible of Nature* (1909), *Darwinianism and Human Life* (1910), *What Is Man?* (1923), and *The New Natural History* (1925–26). From 1899 he was professor of natural history at Aberdeen Univ.—*D. H. D. R.*

THOMSON, SIR JOSEPH JOHN, 1856–1940, English physicist; b. near Manchester. In 1895 Thomson, along with E. Rutherford, investigated the conductivity of gases exposed to x-rays. Two years later, he succeeded in measuring the ratio of mass to charge of cathode rays. With the aid of the Wilson cloud chamber he determined the value of such charges and thus was able to determine the mass of cathode-ray particles; from this he inferred that there were smaller

Sir Joseph John Thomson
(*Brown Bros.*)

particles than the atom. Using methods of positive ray analysis, he was the first to confirm the existence of nonradioactive isotopes. Thomson was head of the Cavendish Laboratory of Cambridge Univ. (1884–1918), and in 1906 received the Nobel prize in physics for his theoretical and experimental investigations on the transmission of electricity through gases. He was knighted in 1908, and in 1918 became master of Trinity College, Cambridge. Thomson was a fellow of the Royal Society and an associate of the U. S. National Academy of Sciences.—*A. L.*

THORAX: the body region of an animal between its head (or neck, if present) and abdomen. In land-dwelling vertebrates, the thorax (literally "chest") contains the heart and lungs. In insects the thorax commonly bears three pairs of legs and may bear wings; within it are the muscles for moving these appendages, as well as parts of the digestive, nervous, and circulatory systems.—*R. G. M.*

THORIUM: a radioactive metal element (Th) of the ACTINIDE series; at. no. 90; at. wt 232.04; mp 1845°C; bp above 4500°C; sp gr 11.3; valence 4. The element was discovered, 1828, by J. J. Berzelius in a mineral from Norway he named thorite (chiefly thorium silicate, $ThSiO_4$); thorium's radioactivity was discovered in 1898 by Marie Curie (and independently by the German physicist Gerhardt Carl Schmidt). It is a grayish-white, lustrous, reactive metal that combines readily with oxygen and burns brilliantly in air. Its most abundant source is the monazite sands of Brazil, E Africa, India, and the Carolinas and Idaho in the U. S. A., in which it is found (as the nitrate, oxide, and phosphate) in association with RARE-EARTH compounds. The use of thorium as a fuel for nuclear power plants has gained increasing attention, since it is estimated that there is more energy available from the Earth's thorium than from both uranium and fossil fuels combined. The following sequence of reactions is utilized in nuclear reactors: thorium[232] is made to capture a neutron, forming thorium[233]; Th[233] then decays, emitting a beta particle, to protactinium[233]; in a second decay Pa[233] emits a beta particle, yielding fissionable uranium[233]. Besides its use as a nuclear fuel, thorium (as thorium nitrate, $Th(NO_3)_4$) has long been of use as the principal constituent of the incandescent Welsbach mantle for gas lights. This mantle, invented by Carl Auer, Baron von Welsbach, in 1886, is composed of 98 to 99% thorium nitrate and 1 to 2% ceria (cerium oxide, CeO_2); it emits a brilliant white light when heated to a high temperature by a nonluminous flame (*e.g.* the flame of a Bunsen burner). The presence of ceria in the mixture acts as a catalyst, giving a more intense light than if the mantle were composed solely of thorium nitrate. Monazite sands were extensively sought and worked in the late 19th and early 20th cent., until electric LIGHTING began to replace the gas light on a large scale and the demand for thorium compounds diminished. Thorium is used in small amounts in several nonferrous alloys, *e.g.* in nickel-chromium alloys to increase life; it also finds use in luminous paints.—*R. B. T.*

THREE-BODY PROBLEM: the problem of finding the orbits in space of three bodies moving under their mutual gravitational attractions. With only two bodies, if at any time the position and velocity (in size and direction) of one body relative to the other is known, then the relative positions and velocities of the two bodies can be calculated by formulas for any time in the future. These formulas are expressible in terms of known functions (*e.g.* the sine of a known angle). It is known that the relative positions and velocities at any particular time of three bodies completely determine the subsequent behavior of the system. However, it has not been possible to find any practical solutions in terms of known functions that permit the direct calculation of the positions and velocities of the bodies at some later time. (This is true even if one of the bodies has an infinitesimally small mass, in which case we have the "restricted three-body problem.") The three-body problem is one of the most celebrated of mathematical problems, and it has been estimated that upward of 1,000 memoirs and papers have been written about it since Newton's time. (See ORBIT.)—*M. W. O.*

THROAT: externally, the front part of the neck; internally, the cavity from the arch of the palate to the upper openings of the trachea and the esophagus. See PHARYNX.—*A. P. E.*

THROWING POWER: the ability of an electrolytic solution to deposit a uniform metal coating on an electrode of irregular shape. Addition of colloidal matter generally increases the throwing power of a solution; increasing the temperature or disturbing the solution decreases throwing power. High conductance and cathode potential produce good throwing power. —*G. W. M.*

THRUST LOADING (or THRUST-WEIGHT RATIO): ratio of the gross weight of a jet or rocket-propelled aircraft or other vehicle to its thrust, expressed as the gross weight in pounds divided by the thrust in pounds. Thrust is the forward-directed force on the vehicle developed by its engine. Within limits, the higher the thrust-loading value, the greater a vehicle's initial boost.—*D. B.*

THULIUM: a lanthanide (rare-earth metal) element (Tm); at. no. 69; at. wt 168.94; valence 3; other physical constants not determined (1962). One of the rarest of the LANTHANIDES, thulium occurs combined with other rare earths in the minerals

xenotime, gadolinite, and euxenite. It was discovered in 1879 by the Swedish chemist Per Theodor Cleve in an impure sample of erbium oxide; the American Charles James prepared the first fairly pure oxide (1911) by repeated fractional crystallization and by 1933 the pure metal had been isolated. Thulium is a component with other rare earths (largely CERIUM) of the alloy *misch metal,* used in making aluminum, steel, and iron alloys; the isotope Tm^{170}, produced in nuclear reactors, is used in nuclear research.—*E. H. H.*

THUNDERSTORM: a severe weather disturbance producing thunder and lightning. Typically of local extent and short duration, these storms are usually accompanied by rain and strong gusty surface winds, and occasionally by hail and tornadoes. According to U. S. weather-reporting procedures, lightning must be seen or thunder heard before a local storm can be called a thunderstorm. Conditions in nature suitable for development of strong electric charge centers (with their accompanying lightning discharges and thunder) are limited to interiors of cumulus and cumulonimbus CLOUDS; hence the terms thundercloud, thunderstorm, thunderhead, and thundersquall through popular usage refer to any large cumulonimbus cloud having the appearance and the severe local weather usually associated with thunderstorms, even though distance may prevent hearing the thunder or daylight may restrict the observation of lightning. The ability of cumulonimbus clouds to develop large regions of intense electrical charge makes them unique among atmospheric phenomena (see ATMOSPHERIC ELECTRICITY).

Thunderstorms occur in a variety of forms and in numbers that vary with season and locality. They may occur singly as an isolated summer afternoon storm rising majestically against a clear blue sky; in early spring months, in the Great Plains of the U. S. A. they may group into long lines known as "squall lines," the progenitors of tornadoes; or they may occur as complex groups embedded in the general rain areas of winter and spring weather systems (cyclonic disturbances). The largest of all thunderstorms occur in the tropics, where tops frequently extend above 60,000 ft; the most violent probably occur over mid-latitude continental areas in early spring months. According to a study of C. E. P. Brooks, thunderstorms are infrequent in the polar regions. Regions of maximum thunderstorm occurrence are Java (average, 225 thunderstorm days per year), central Africa (150), Central America (140), central Brazil (100). Areas of maximum thunderstorm activity in the U. S. A. are the Florida peninsula and the coastal plains along the Gulf of Mexico (70 to 80) and the mountains of New Mexico (50 to 60). Brooks estimated about 1,800 thunderstorms are in progress at any one moment throughout the world.

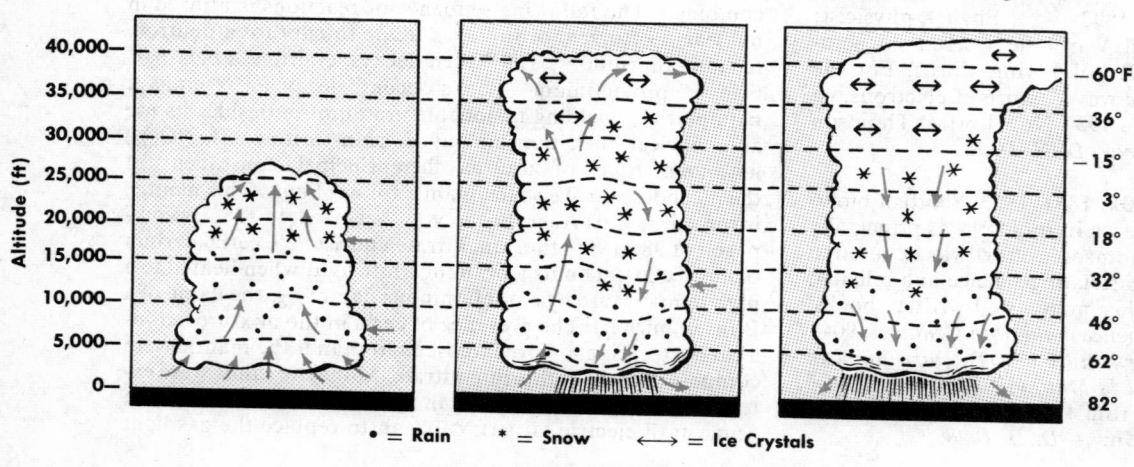

Development of thunderstorm: When air currents reach about 25,000 ft, cumulus clouds form (*left*). As air ascends higher and is cooled further, precipitation occurs, and the falling rain and ice crystals cool the air so as to produce downdrafts (*middle*). Final stage comes when entire cloud is sinking and becoming adiabatically warmed, so that precipitation ceases (*right*). Meanwhile high-altitude winds may blow top of cloud into anvil form. (*After Braham*)

• = Rain   * = Snow   ⟷ = Ice Crystals

- - - - = Levels of Equal Temperature

Lightning, the most dramatic feature of thunderstorms, is produced by electrical discharges between positive and negative centers within clouds and between clouds and the ground. (*Science Service*)

Despite outward differences and apparent complexities, thunderstorms are basically rather simple heat engines, using water vapor as the working substance. Most such storms consist of a cluster (3 to 10) of several smaller storm units called cells, each being a nearly circular, quasi-vertical cloud column 3 to 5 mi in diameter and extending from the base to the top of the thundercloud. All important thunderstorm processes occur in thunderstorm cells; hence a ground observer may note several periods of heavy rain, thunder and lightning, and hail as a single thunderstorm passes overhead. Each cell has a three-stage life cycle, characterized principally by changes of air within the cell. In no other weather phenomenon do the vertical air currents (updrafts and downdrafts) reach the size and vigor of those in thunderstorms.

The initial stage is characterized by an updraft throughout most of the cell. At first this current may be irregular and disconnected, like a series of warm air-bubbles rising through water. On reaching the top of the cloud, these "bubbles" give rise to the cauliflower appearance typical of cumulus clouds in early stages of development. If there is an inadequate supply of warm, moist, unstable air from below, the series of bubbles will weaken and the cloud dissipate; but given an ample supply, the bubbles will finally amalgamate into a continuous core of rising air capable of pushing the cloud top to heights where copious amounts of precipitation (rain and snow) can be formed. Then comes the second stage of development, one of the most interesting of all atmospheric phenomena. Intense electrical charges develop, hail forms, and internal motions become most violent. In place of the continuous updraft which filled the entire cell in the late building stage, both a strong updraft and a strong downdraft, side by side, extend from the cloud base to heights of at least 30,000 ft. Just how the downdraft forms is not well understood, but appears related to the fact that the air of the updraft, as it rises, entrains or enfolds air from the clear air surrounding the cloud. Part of the moisture of the cloud is evaporated by the enfolding air; the evaporation causes cooling; the updraft thus becomes progressively colder until finally a point is reached where the slightest downward push (*e.g.* by the falling rain) can cause the air to come cascading to earth as a current of cold air heavier than its surroundings. At the ground, the onset of heavy rain, accompanied by the cold, gusty, downdraft air, signifies the transition of the cell from the building to the mature stage. As the downdraft nears the ground, it spreads out to form a wind squall blowing outward from the rain area. In the final or dissipating stage, the entire cell is filled with descending air motions, but by this time, perhaps an hour after it began, the cell has lost most of its vigor. The large amounts of rain initially supported within the updraft have fallen to the earth, leaving only a period of lingering light rain which may last a few minutes or several hours, depending upon conditions of the air mass in which the storm originally formed. See also ATMOSPHERIC ELECTRICITY; LIGHTNING.—*R. R. B.*

THYMUS GLAND: a ductless gland that occurs in fishes, amphibians, reptiles, birds, and mammals. It attains full size by the time the individual has reached sexual maturity, after which it ceases to grow and gradually dwindles until it almost disappears. In man, the gland lies partly in the neck, below the thyroid gland. Until 1962 the function of the thymus was unknown. Evidence now supports the view that the thymus lays down the foundation for the body's natural immunity mechanism. This acts against foreign proteins such as invading bacteria and viruses as well as tissues and organs transplanted from one person to another except in the case of identical twins. The thymus apparently produces or stimulates production of master lymphocyte cells in early infancy. These cells spread to various sites—spleen, bone marrow, lymph nodes—where they form plasma cells, which produce antibodies in the presence of antigens (*i.e.* foreign proteins). In birds the bursa of Fabricius appears to share with the thymus the role of creating the mechanism of immunity.—*R. G. M.*

THYROID GLAND: an ENDOCRINE GLAND of vertebrate animals that secretes the iodine-containing hormone thyroxine into the blood stream when stimulated to do so by the thyrotropic hormone from the PITUITARY GLAND. An inadequate supply of iodine in the diet can lead to a deficiency of thyroxine (known as hypothyroidism), which becomes evident in a general lowering of the metabolic rate; in amphibians, hypothyroidism blocks METAMORPHOSIS. In mammals, continued hypothyroidism commonly induces the pituitary to release thyrotropic hormone at a consistently high rate, which in turn induces the thyroid gland to enlarge; an excessively large thyroid gland bulges in the neck, and the condition is called simple *goiter*. In man, this condition is commonest in glaciated and mountainous parts of the world from which the iodine compounds of the soil have been leached away and carried to the sea. A dietary deficiency of iodine can be corrected through use of iodized table salt or the eating of sea foods. An excessive output of thyroxine induces almost all cells of the body to increase their metabolic rate, with a consequent increase in hunger and decrease in weight. In man, this condition (*hyperthyroidism*) is accompanied by deposition of a pad of fat in the eye sockets, pushing the eyes into greater prominence; such *exophthalmia* is sometimes described as exophthalmic goiter

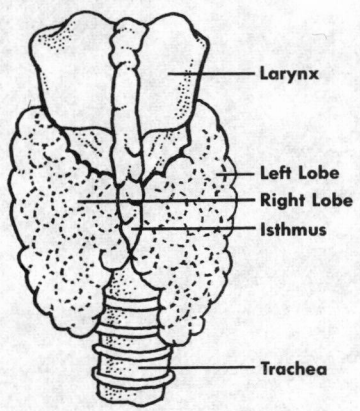

Human thyroid gland, front view: Lying immediately below larynx, thyroid gland consists of two lobes, one on each side of trachea, connected by an isthmus. Gland is composed of masses of spherical, closed sacs, or alveoli, lined with a single layer of epithelial cells. Cavities of the alveoli are filled with a colloid that contains the thyroid hormone thyroxine, secreted by the epithelial lining cells. (From Whaley)

and treated by surgical removal of a part of the overactive thyroid gland. Since the thyroid gland captures about 99% of the iodine in the body, hyperthyroidism may also be treated by injection of radioactive iodine, which becomes concentrated in the thyroid and destroys some of the abnormal tissue without surgery.

A recognizable thyroid is present in the adult lamprey; it is a derivative of the endostyle, which is a ciliated food-handling groove in the floor of the pharynx in the larval lamprey. At metamorphosis, the endostyle becomes detached from the pharynx and develops into typical thyroid tissue, consisting of epithelial follicles filled with the colloidal secretion, located between the capillaries of an exceptionally rich vascular network. In fishes, the thyroid sometimes consists of clustered cells in scattered groups, or a single lobe (in sharks and rays) or double lobe (in many bony fishes) at the anterior end of the ventral aorta. In amphibians, the thyroid consists of two separate lobes, whereas in all reptiles except lizards, it is single. In lizards, birds, and mammals the gland is bilobed, with one lobe on each side of the neck.—*L. and M. M.*

THYROXINE: a hormone produced by the thyroid gland. Congenital deficiency of this hormone causes infantile myxedema or cretinism characterized by dwarfism. In adults, thyroxine deficiency may cause lower basal metabolic rate with lowered body temperature, slow pulse, and reduction in blood pressure. In thyroid hyperfunction (hyperthyroidism) the opposite symptoms occur: increased pulse rate, pulse pressure, and blood flow. The patient shows nervousness, emotional instability, and often protruding eyes. Thyroxine is relatively inactive when given orally, probably because of insolubility in water, but desiccated thyroid and the related hormone triiodothyronine are effective by mouth. It is not known exactly how thyroxine acts in the body.—*F. F.*

TIDAL BORE: a rushing wave of tidewater moving like a wall upstream into the tributary river at the head of a large converging estuary. A bore may develop, especially at spring tide, where the channel rapidly shoals and narrows in the upstream direction. The bores in the Severn River at the head of the Bristol Channel in England, and those of the Petitcodiac River at the northern end of the Bay of Fundy, New Brunswick, Canada, are well known. The bore on the Amazon River reaches a height of 16 ft and moves upriver with a speed of over 12 mi/hr.—*J. Sh.*

TIDAL THEORY: a hypothesis, now obsolete, proposed *c.* 1920 by J. H. Jeans to explain the origin of the solar system. It assumes that the tidal forces created by the close approach of a passing star caused the ejection of a hot gaseous filament from the Sun. The outermost part of the filament dissipated into space, whereas the innermost fell back into the Sun. Rapidly cooling gases in the central section condensed into liquid planets, which later acquired solid crusts. The shape of the filament governed the size of the planets, small at the ends (Mercury, Venus, Earth, Mars, Pluto), large near the center (Jupiter, Saturn, Uranus, Neptune). This theory, a modification of the PLANETESIMAL HYPOTHESIS, fails to account for several observed phenomena. Furthermore, it has been shown that the direct condensation of planets from material ejected from the Sun is a physical impossibility.—*S. D. G.*

TIDAL WAVE: see TSUNAMI.

TIDE: the twice-, or sometimes once-, daily rise and fall of water level at a seashore. On some coasts, as around the Mediterranean, the tide is so small as to attract little attention. On others, as around the Bay of Fundy, high water is at times as much as 50 ft higher than low water. In narrow estuaries or straits where there are large tides, swift currents are observed which alternately ebb and flow with the same period as the tide. Even in the open sea, refined observations demonstrate the existence of small tidal currents. Although the connection is not simple, tides are caused fundamentally by horizontal motions of the water due to the gravitational action of Sun and Moon. The general relationship is demonstrated by a good set of tide records such as that for New York. Thus the interval between a high tide and the second (occasionally the first) one following it has the same length (24 hr 50 min) as the lunar day. The highest tide of the lunar month, the *spring tide,* is always the same number of days after the new or full moon. The highest tide of the year is generally the spring tide occurring closest to the solstice. The two *high tides* of a given day, or the two *low tides,* are usually not the same, and the inequality can be predicted from the declinations of Moon and Sun. The Sun is less than half as effective as the Moon in raising tides. Fundamental principles of tidal dynamics (as worked out especially by Newton, Laplace, Kelvin, and, recently, J. Proudman and A. Defant) make prediction of tides possible. Tide machines are analog computers which generate the tidal curves for a given place from constants derived by harmonic analysis of an extended tide record for that place. The predicted tides are subject to distortion by wind, barometric pressure, and other circumstances.

Besides the tides of the water in the sea, tides of the atmosphere (see ATMOSPHERIC TIDES) and of the solid earth have been recognized. The semidiurnal component of earth tides, which is the major one, has been calculated as 20 in.—*M. S.*

◄ **Bore ascending Severn River** carries surge of tidal water funneled successively through Bristol Channel and mouth of Severn; it is here viewed upstream from Gloucester Bridge. (*British Info. Services*)

TILE: a shaped structural member made of fired clay (ceramic tile); also, a flat, rectangular composition sheet used for flooring (asphalt or plastic tile). One major type of *ceramic tile* is whiteware, *e.g.* the floor tile and wall tile used in bathrooms. Floor tile is usually vitreous, of very low water-absorbing capacity, composed of a relatively low proportion of clay and relatively high proportion of feldspar or flint; it is made by the one-fire or porcelain process. Wall tile is usually semi-vitreous, highly glazed, and made by a two-fire china process. Structural ceramic tile, which resembles brick more than it does whiteware, is made in various shapes for various applications, *e.g.* as conduit, drainage tile, pipe, hollow block, roofing shingle, and facing. Structural ceramic tile is made from shale or fireclay rather than from the surface clays used for common brick; it is frequently glazed. *Asphalt and plastic tiles* typically consist of about 30% organic resinous binder and about 70% inorganic filler. The filler material is usually a mixture of asbestos fines (powdery material too short to be used as fiber) and ground limestone or other similar soft granular material. Among the binders that may be used are asphalts and bituminous substances, hydrocarbon resins, coumarone-indene resins, rosin derivatives, polystyrene, and vinyl resins. Plasticizers and coloring materials are normally included in the mixture.—*A. M. S.*

TILL AND TILLITE: see GLACIAL DRIFT.

TIMAEUS, by Plato (*c.* 375 B. C.): Since Plato believed that the search for truth must be directed to the eternal and ideal rather than the ephemeral and imperfect, his one dialogue devoted to scientific philosophy has little respect for specific phenomena. Its importance is rather in the doctrine of the Pythagorean, Timaeus, that nature is pervaded by a mathematical harmony (as in the relative sizes of planetary orbits) and a mathematical architecture (as in the composition of the four elements). The *Timaeus,* for centuries a source of inspiration for esoteric speculation about the universe, gave rise to much absurdity and mysticism, but also it stimulated the idea—realized scientifically by Kepler, Galileo, and Newton—that scientific truth is expressed in mathematical relationships.—*A. R. H.*

TIME: the instant at which an event occurs; or, the dimension of the universe represented by the succession of events. Time may be measured by the recurrence of any periodic phenomenon, *e.g.* the swing of a pendulum, the vibrations of atoms in a crystal, or the daily rotation or annual revolution of Earth. Ordinary timekeeping is based on Earth's rotation as determined from an average value of the apparent daily revolution of the Sun. Sidereal time, used for astronomical observations, is measured by the apparent daily revolution of the stars; and ephemeris time, used for fundamental astronomical work, is measured by Earth's orbital motion.

Solar Time—*Apparent Solar Time:* The moment when the Sun reaches its highest point in the sky is *local apparent noon;* the moment when it reaches its lowest point is *local apparent midnight;* and the interval between two successive midnights is one *apparent solar day.* This is the time measured by a sundial. Since the Sun moves once around the sky per day, or 360° in 24 hr, the time increases by 1 hr for each 15° of motion, 4 min for 1° of motion, and 4 sec for 1′ of motion.

Mean Time: Time measured by the Sun is not uniform. During December and January, Earth is closest to the Sun and moves more rapidly than it does in June and July, when it is farthest. Therefore, the Sun's eastward motion against the stars is faster in December and January, and the length of the day is longer. Furthermore, the Sun's motion is along the ecliptic, at an angle to the celestial equator; this tends to

lengthen the day when the Sun is near the solstices and moving parallel to the equator, and to shorten it when the Sun is at the equinoxes and moving at an angle to the celestial equator, so that the eastward component of its motion is least. To obtain a uniform system, *mean time* was introduced. This is measured by a fictitious body, the *mean sun,* which is imagined to move eastward around the celestial equator at a uniform rate once per year. Its diurnal rate is regular and equal to the average rate of diurnal motion of the real Sun. The moment when the mean sun crosses the lower branch of the observer's meridian is 0 hr *local mean time;* when the mean sun crosses the upper branch it is 12 hr local mean time, or local mean noon.

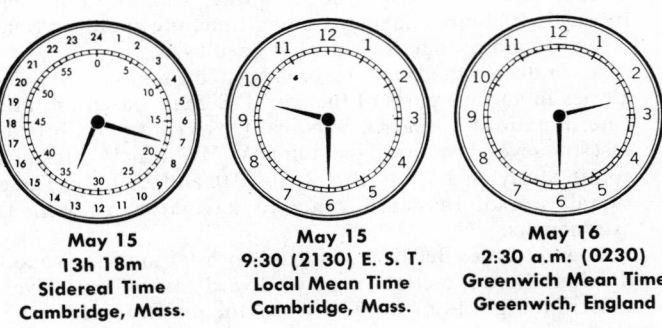

May 15
13h 18m
Sidereal Time
Cambridge, Mass.

May 15
9:30 (2130) E. S. T.
Local Mean Time
Cambridge, Mass.

May 16
2:30 a.m. (0230)
Greenwich Mean Time
Greenwich, England

Time on observatory clocks: Sidereal clock gains 24 hr a year, or about 4 min a day, on other two clocks, which show local mean time at the 75°W and 0° meridians, respectively. Greenwich Mean Time is also known as Universal Time.

The difference between mean time and apparent time is the angular distance between the hour circles of the mean sun and the real Sun; it is called the *equation of time.* Four times a year the hour circles of the two bodies coincide; at all other times they differ. The maximum difference is reached in early December—about 16½ min of time. This should not be confused with the difference between the lengths of the mean and apparent solar days, which is some seconds at most.

Standard Time: If local time were commonly used, nearly all communities on Earth would have different times; even in cities as close as Dallas and Fort Worth, clocks would differ by some minutes. To obtain some degree of uniformity, *standard time* or, in ocean areas, *zone time* is adopted: this is the mean time of some reference meridian that is accepted as standard throughout a given geographical area. Thus, Eastern Standard Time is the local mean time of the 75° meridian.

The reference meridians are spaced 15° apart in longitude, beginning with the meridian through Greenwich, England. Time zones extend 7½° in longitude on each side, with considerable modification of boundaries to conform to political, geographic, or economic boundaries. Since the standard meridians are 15° apart, the time difference between two adjacent zones is exactly 1 hr. The difference between the standard times of any two zones is a whole number of hours: the minutes and seconds are the same. As will be seen from the map, some regions, *e.g.* Newfoundland, are outside the time-zone system.

Greenwich mean time, or Universal time, is the local mean time of the Greenwich meridian, longitude 0°. The difference between the standard time in any zone and Greenwich mean time is equal to the longitude of the standard meridian of the zone expressed in hours (1 hr for each 15°). For stations in west longitude, Greenwich time is later; for stations in east longitude, Greenwich time is earlier. At longitude 180°, the difference is 12 hr. For the half of the zone that is west of Greenwich, Greenwich time is 12 hr later; for the half east of Greenwich, 12 hr earlier. Thus, though the time is numerically the same in the two halves of the zone, it actually differs by 24 hr when reckoned from Greenwich. When it is Thursday in the half east of Greenwich, it is Wednesday in the half west of Greenwich. Longitude 180° is therefore the basis for the *International Date Line.*

To extend the span of daylight into the evening hours, many countries and cities adopt *daylight saving time,* which is the standard time of the next zone to the east; the Sun then rises and sets 1 hr later by the clock. In places that adopt daylight saving time during the summer months only, clocks are set forward 1 hr in spring, back 1 hr in fall. In wartime, double daylight saving time, the standard time of the second zone to the east, has been used.

Accurate *time signals* are broadcast by national observatories in various parts of the world. Signals based on time determinations by the U. S. Naval Observatory are broadcast by several stations including WWV, which transmits continuously on 2.5, 5.0, 10.0, 15.0, 20.0, and 25.0 Mc. These signals are of immense value to navigators as well as astronomers.

Sidereal Time: Because of Earth's orbital motion around the Sun, there is a continuous westward shift of each given star from night to night. Therefore, the duration of Earth's rotation *with respect to the stars* or to any chosen fixed reference point is slightly shorter (by about 3 min 56 sec) than the mean solar day. By convention, time reckoned by this sidereal rotation of Earth uses the vernal equinox as reference point, and *sidereal time* is the angular distance from the vernal equinox eastward to the celestial meridian of the observer, *i.e.* the local hour angle of the vernal equinox. The same distance can also be expressed as the right ascension of the local meridian. Zero hours sidereal time occurs at upper transit of the vernal equinox; 12:00, at lower transit. Sidereal time coincides with solar time once per year, when the Sun arrives at the autumnal equinox. The relation between sidereal time and mean time is a calculated value, and is tabulated for every day in *The American Ephemeris and Nautical Almanac.* The sidereal time at local meridian of an observer is called *local sidereal time;* at the Greenwich meridian, *Greenwich sidereal time.* The difference between the sidereal times at any two stations is equal to the difference in longitude of the stations.

Slight variations in the length of the sidereal day are averaged out to produce *mean sidereal time* and the *mean sidereal day.* One mean sidereal day of 24 hr mean sidereal time is $23^h 56^m 04^s.091$ mean solar time; one mean solar day of 24 hr mean solar time is $24^h 03^m 56^s.555$ mean sidereal time.

In practice, the transit of the vernal equinox across the local meridian cannot be observed directly by instruments, because it does not coincide with any star. The astronomical determination of time uses the fact that the sidereal time is precisely equal to the right ascension of a star when the latter crosses the meridian. The sidereal time thus obtained may be converted into Universal Time from tabulated values. The principal instrument used for this purpose is the photographic zenith tube (see TELESCOPE).

Ephemeris Time: The speed of Earth's rotation is subject to occasional changes of an irregular and unpredictable kind, possibly due to some random activity inside the planet. Within the past few decades, astronomical observations have become sufficiently precise to show that these changes cause variations in mean solar and sidereal time, and that these time systems are no longer satisfactory for the most refined astronomical work. A more precise, uniform measure of time—ephemeris time—is based on Earth's revolution around the Sun. It is obtained from observations of the revolution of Moon around Earth, and although the motions of Earth and Moon are not uniform, their variations can be calculated and a very accurate time system obtained. The ephemeris second, the fundamental unit of time, is defined as $1/31,556,925.9747$ of the tropical year in progress at noon on Dec. 31, 1899; one ephemeris second is very nearly equal to 1 sec of mean solar time. Accurate predictions of astronomical events are made in ephemeris time, but observations are recorded in Universal Time and the corresponding ephemeris time is calculated some months later, when sufficient observations of the Moon for the corresponding period are available.—*B. P. S.*

TIN: a silver-white metal element (Sn); at. no. 50; at. wt 118.70; mp 232°C; bp 2260°C; valence 2 or 4. One of the seven metals known to the ancients, tin occurs in two well-defined allotropic forms: *gray tin* (diamond lattice, density 5.765 g/ml) which changes at 13.20°C into *white tin* (tetragonal, density 7.285 g/ml). The gray form, because of its lower density, is characterized by crumbling, called "tin pest." The chief ore is cassiterite or tinstone, SnO_2. Boliva and Malaya have the richest ore deposits; U. S. A. has almost none. The metal is won from the ore by reacting (reducing) the ore with charcoal in a reverberating or blast furnace; tin's low melting point makes a simple purification process possible. The metal is malleable at about 100°C and can be rolled into tinfoil. The so-called "tin can" is made by dipping a steel can into molten tin. Tin loses two electrons when treated with acids such as hydrochloric or dilute nitric to form stannous salts; it loses four electrons when treated with concentrated nitric or sulfuric acids to form stannic compounds. Tin ALLOYS include BRONZE, PEWTER, and soft SOLDERS.—*L. Sc.*

TINCTURE: a solution of a substance, usually a medicinal, in alcohol. It is often prepared by direct extraction from a plant material. An alcohol-ether solution is an "ethereal tincture." —*Ru. M.*

TISELIUS, ARNE WILHELM KAURIN, 1902– , Swedish chemist; b. Stockholm. He developed the moving-boundary method of studying ELECTROPHORESIS in proteins (1930), and then began the study of adsorption chromatography. In 1937 Tiselius began to use electrophoretic methods for the separation of proteins in the blood serum. For his research on electrophoresis and adsorption analysis, especially for his discoveries concerning the complex nature of the serum proteins, Tiselius received the 1948 Nobel prize. He is a fellow of the Royal Society and an associate of the U. S. National Academy of Sciences.—*D. H. D. R.*

TISSUE: a group of cells of similar structure that perform an identical or closely related function. The study of tissues is known as *histology.* The differentiation of the body into tissues, each specialized for a particular function, developed early in the evolution of plants and animals, and made possible the increased efficiency resulting from division of labor in a large multicellular organism. There are two main types of tissues: reproductive and somatic. Reproductive tissues are concerned with the perpetuation of the race. In higher animals they are the ova and sperm; in higher plants they may be sex cells, in the form of male and female gametes, or asexual reproductive bodies in the form of spores. Somatic tissues have as their function the survival of the individual.

Somatic tissues in animals are of five main types. (1) *Epithelial tissue* covers the surface of the body and lines its cavities; this tissue has protective, absorptive, secretive, and excretive functions. (2) *Connective tissue* holds the body to-

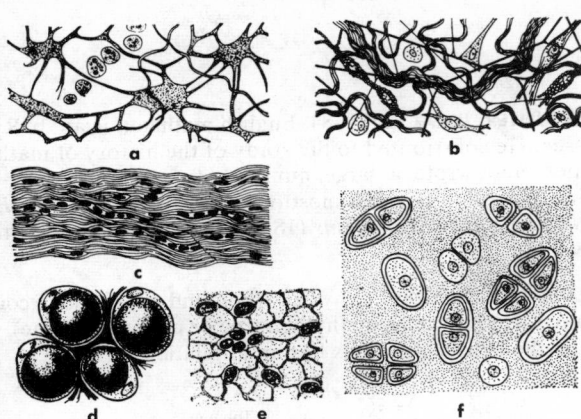

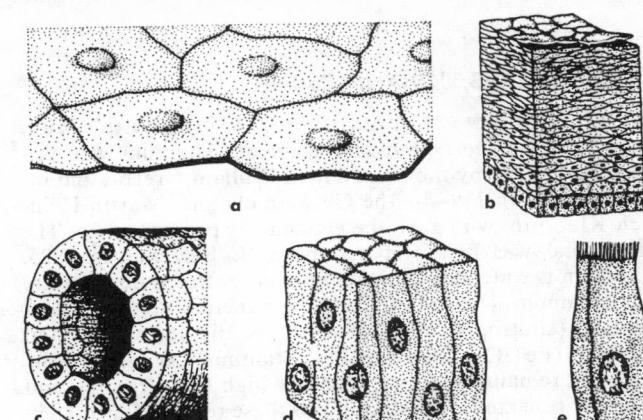

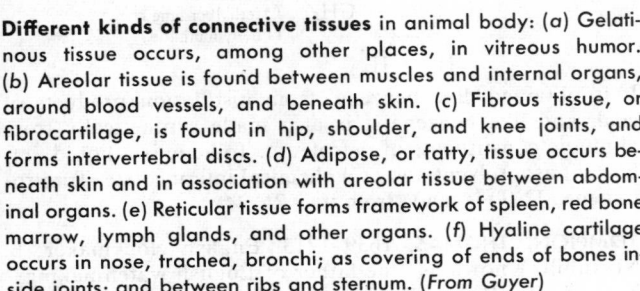

Different kinds of connective tissues in animal body: (*a*) Gelatinous tissue occurs, among other places, in vitreous humor. (*b*) Areolar tissue is found between muscles and internal organs, around blood vessels, and beneath skin. (*c*) Fibrous tissue, or fibrocartilage, is found in hip, shoulder, and knee joints, and forms intervertebral discs. (*d*) Adipose, or fatty, tissue occurs beneath skin and in association with areolar tissue between abdominal organs. (*e*) Reticular tissue forms framework of spleen, red bone marrow, lymph glands, and other organs. (*f*) Hyaline cartilage occurs in nose, trachea, bronchi; as covering of ends of bones inside joints; and between ribs and sternum. (*From Guyer*)

Different kinds of epithelial tissues in animal body: (*a*) Squamous epithelium forms peritoneal lining of body cavity and lining of mouth and nasal cavities. (*b*) Stratified epithelium, found in skin and cornea, is composed of several layers (strata) of the same or different kinds of epithelial cells. Here, upper layers are squamous, lowermost layer is cuboidal. (*c*) Cuboidal epithelium occurs in salivary and thyroid glands and in kidney tubules. (*d*) Columnar epithelium is found in lining of stomach and intestines. (*e*) Ciliated columnar epithelium occurs in linings of the air passages. (*From Manter*)

gether and furnishes support; familiar examples are fibers, cartilage, and bone. (3) *Contractile tissue* specializes in movement and includes skeletal, cardiac, and smooth muscle. (4) *Nervous tissue* receives, transmits, and coordinates stimuli, and initiates many body activities; the basic unit is the nerve cell, or neuron. (5) *Vascular tissue* is a fluid serving as a circulating and transporting medium; it is composed of plasma, red corpuscles, and white corpuscles.

Somatic, or vegetative, tissues in plants are of seven main types. (1) *Meristematic tissue* is capable of continuous growth and is able to produce new permanent tissues. Terminal meristems form the growing points of roots and stems; meristem between wood and bark, known as cambium, causes growth in diameter; a special meristem in stems and roots, known as cork cambium, produces bark. The remaining tissues are permanently differentiated. (2) *Epidermis* forms the outer protective layer of leaves, flowers, young stems, and roots. (3) *Parenchyma* is a relatively unspecialized tissue with storage functions, as the pith of stems and roots, and with photosynthetic functions in leaves. (4) *Sclerenchyma* cells, with thick walls, serve in skeletal structure, as in the fibers of flax stems. (5) *Cork* is found in the bark of old stems and

roots, where it protects against injury and desiccation. (6) *Phloem* is a complex tissue found in roots, stems, veins of leaves, and flowers; its chief function is transport of foods. (7) *Xylem* is another complex tissue found also in roots, stems, and veins; its chief function is transport of water. See BARK; BLOOD; BONE; CARTILAGE; CONNECTIVE TISSUE; LEAF; MEMBRANE; MUSCLE; NERVOUS SYSTEM; PLANT ORGANS AND TISSUES; SKIN; WOOD.—*C. J. H.*

TITAN: largest and first-known satellite of the planet Saturn, discovered by Huygens in 1655. This satellite, about 3,000 mi in diameter, is the 6th in order of distance from Saturn, at a mean distance of about 760,000 mi. It requires nearly 16 days to complete a sidereal revolution in its orbit. Though the velocity of escape for a particle from Titan is not much greater than in the case of the Moon, the satellite is always much colder than the Moon, and therefore the velocities of gas molecules there are much smaller. Thus it can have an atmosphere, which has actually been observed and found to contain methane and possibly ammonia.—*M. W. O.*

TITANIUM: a silvery-white metallic element (Ti); at. no. 22; at. wt 47.90; mp 1795°C; bp above 3000°C; sp gr 4.5; va-

Titanium's low thermal conductivity and low (4.5) specific gravity, along with its retention of structural properties up to 1000°F, make it a key material in aeronautics. Welded trapezoidal sections of titanium are seen here as they are assembled to form inner skin of Mercury capsule. (*Titanium Metals Corp. of America*)

lence 2, 3, or 4. It constitutes about 0.63% of Earth's crust, being the 9th most abundant element. Titanium was discovered in 1791 by the Englishman William Gregor, and independently in 1794 by the German chemist Martin Heinrich Klaproth, who gave the element its present name. The free metal was first prepared by J. J. Berzelius in 1825. Titanium is widely distributed, but concentrated deposits are not common. The major titanium minerals are rutile and anatase (allotropic forms of titanium dioxide, TiO_2) and ilmenite ($FeTiO_3$). Pure metallic titanium has high tensile strength, remains tough at relatively high temperatures, and is highly resistant to corrosion. For these reasons it is used in chemical processing equipment, and in aircraft and missiles where high strength-to-weight ratio is important. Metallic titanium, alloyed with iron, is used as a scavenger to remove oxygen and nitrogen in steel making. Titanium forms three series of halides; those in which its valence is 2 or 3 are powerful reducing agents. Titanium tetrachloride, $TiCl_4$, is very easily hydrolyzed to titanic acid, $Ti(OH)_4$, which is weakly acidic and forms salts with alkalis. The anhydride of titanic acid, titanium dioxide (TiO_2), has a very high refractive index. When finely ground it forms a pure white powder of great opacity, very extensively used as a PIGMENT in paints, lacquers, and enamels.—*A. M. S.*

TITIUS, JOHANN DANIEL, 1729–1796, German mathematician and astronomer; b. Konitz, W Prussia. He tried to determine whether the distances of the planets from the Sun conformed to some regular law, and pointed out in 1772 a remarkable symmetry in their disposition, which became known as BODE'S LAW (after J. E. Bode, who publicized it).—*R. N. M.*

TITRATION: the process of determining the quantity of a solution of known concentration that will react completely with a certain amount of a sample being analyzed. For solutions that can react with each other, titration involves the addition of a solution of known concentration (*standard solution*) to a solution of *unknown* concentration, until by some means, either visual or instrumental, the stoichiometric or equivalence point is reached, *i.e.* the substances are completely reacted. The best-known example is the titration of an acid of unknown concentration with a standard solution of a base, or the reverse; in this case, the stoichiometric point may be determined through the use of a dye (INDICATOR) which changes color when either the acid or the base is in very slight excess, or by an instrument such as the pH meter. The stoichiometric point may be specifically defined as that volume of standard solution which contains the exact number of MOLES necessary to react with the number of moles of the unknown, as described by the balanced equation for the reaction. The end point refers to that volume of standard solution added which causes the marked change in properties (*e.g.* change in indicator color, pH, or electromotive force) which signals the stoichiometric or equivalence point. The end point may or may not coincide with the equivalence point; any lack of coincidence introduces a titration error. Titrations may be performed on the basis of different types of reactions: NEUTRALIZATION, oxidation-reduction, precipitation, and complex formation.—*L. Sc.*

TODD, SIR ALEXANDER ROBERTUS, 1907– , British organic chemist; b. Glasgow, Scotland. His research has been concerned with determination of the chemical structure of nucleotides and nucleic acids. For his work on nucleotides and nucleotide coenzymes, he received the Nobel prize, 1957. He is a fellow of the Royal Society and an associate of the U. S. National Academy of Sciences.—*D. H. D. R.*

TODHUNTER, ISAAC, 1820–84, English mathematician; b. Rye, Sussex. He contributed to the study of the history of mathematics, and wrote a large number of textbooks, some of which are still in use. His most original work was *Researches in the Calculus of Variations* (1871). He was a fellow of the Royal Society.—*H. C.*

TOLUENE: in chemistry, a hydrocarbon and an aromatic compound (also known as methylbenzene or phenylmethane), in which the benzene nucleus has an aliphatic side chain.

Toluene
(Methylbenzene)
(Phenylmethane)

It is obtained, like benzene, from distillation products of coal, and like benzene it is also made synthetically from aliphatic constituents of petroleum. Toluene is a liquid, important as a solvent and as a chemical intermediate. Trinitrotoluene (TNT) is made from it.—*Ru. M.*

TOMPION, THOMAS, 1639–1713, English clockmaker; b. Northhill. Known as "the father of English watchmaking," he made (for Robert Hooke) one of the first English watches with a spring balance (1675) and (for Edward Barlow) one of the first repeating watches. In 1676 he built the first clocks for the Royal Observatory. He collaborated with Barlow and John Houghton (1695) in the invention of the cylinder escapement.—*C. J. S.*

TONGUE: a structure in the buccal cavity (mouth) of vertebrates, often muscular and normally attached only at one end, which may aid in the capture or swallowing of food and may have an important sensory function. In fishes, the tongue is made up of a small bone (*hyoid*) covered with the

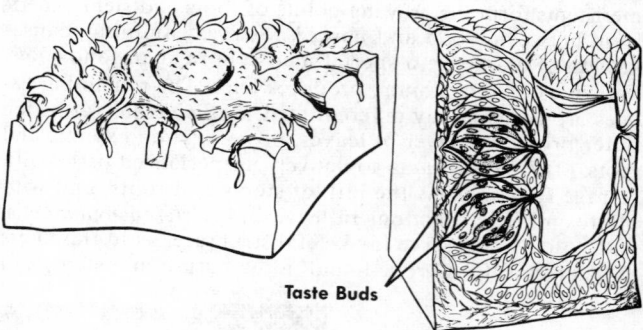

Taste Buds

Human tongue: *Left*—Enlarged portion of tongue's surface reveals varying shapes of projections, or papillae, some of which contain taste buds. *Right*—Cross section of tongue shows two taste buds.

Protrusible tongue of frog, attached far forward on floor of mouth cavity, flips out to catch insect, then folds back into mouth, its tip pointing throatward. (*From Guyer*)

same epithelial lining found in the rest of the mouth. In insect-eating amphibians and reptiles, the tongue usually is sticky with adhesive secretion and can be extended suddenly from the mouth as a means for capturing prey. The mammalian tongue is muscular and used in SWALLOWING. The tongue is usually provided with mucous glands and papillae, or projections, that give it a rough surface. In lower vertebrates, the organs of taste (taste buds) stud the walls, roof, and floor of the mouth, but in mammals they are concentrated in the tongue and soft palate.—*B. T. S.*

TONSILS: clumps of lymphoid tissue projecting into the mouth cavity or pharynx of higher vertebrates. In mammals, the tonsils form a ring of tissue around the border between the mouth and nasal cavities and the pharynx. The part of the ring near the nasal cavity is called the pharyngeal tonsils, or adenoids. When infected, the tonsils may become enlarged and interfere with breathing; they are frequently removed by surgery. The tonsils may serve as part of the defense against bacteria entering the mouth and nose. See LYMPH SYSTEM.—*B. T. S.*

TOOLS: see HAND TOOLS; MACHINE TOOLS.

TOPOGRAPHY: the appearance of Earth's surface with respect to relief. Topographers are concerned with land forms—their recognition, description, and mapping—but not with their origins, erosional age, or structure. Every land surface has at least one of three land forms: plains, mountains, plateaus. Plains are the lowlands of Earth—low with respect to adjoining highlands, height above sea level being irrelevant. The plains of E Colorado lie 5,000 ft above tide, but are several thousand feet lower than the adjoining Front Range of the Rocky Mts to the west. Plains are characterized by relatively flat or gently rolling surfaces. Streams have seldom cut into them deeper than a few hundred feet; usually stream dissection is well under 100 ft. Mountains, which are the highlands of Earth with small summit area, are high with respect to adjoining lowlands. They are characterized by steep slopes and maximum relief, and have many non-concordant summit points. Low mountain land forms are hills: the relief of mountains is over 500 ft, that of hills under 500 ft. Plateaus also are highlands, but differ from mountains in possessing vast summit areas of concordant elevation, usually within 200 ft. Some plateaus have been dissected by erosion to form mountains—*e.g.* the Catskill plateau. There are many types of plains, mountains, and plateaus, but the physiographer rather than the topographer establishes these classifications. Topography is concerned only with the recognition of the basic land forms.

Topography is commonly shown by means of topographic or contour maps on which the configuration of the earth's surface is indicated by means of lines (contours) connecting all points of equal elevations at selected intervals. Also useful in showing topography are relief models. Other methods include shading, coloring, hachuring, and even aerial photographs, but for engineering purposes contour lines are by far the most useful.—*R. E. M.*

TOPOLOGY: the branch of mathematics that studies spatial pattern, or structure, without regard to size. Topology began as a branch of geometry during the latter part of the 19th and the beginning of the 20th cent. But unlike classical geometry, in which two figures are considered equivalent if they are congruent, in topology they are equivalent in a much more general way denoted by the word *homeomorphic*. This relation may be intuitively (though not precisely) described by physical notions. Thus, we say that two figures are congruent if one can be moved into coincidence with the other by a rigid motion, and they are homeomorphic if one can be deformed continuously into coincidence with the other without either tearing or attaching two points together (called folding). Because of this, topology has been called "rubber-sheet geometry." A circle and a square are homeomorphic, two circles of different sizes are homeomorphic, but a circle and a figure eight are not homeomorphic. In three dimensions, a sphere and a cube are homeomorphic, but a sphere and a torus (the shape of a doughnut) are not.

A basic notion in topology is that of *limit point*. If *p* is a point and *M* a collection of points, then *p* is called a limit point of *M* if there are points of *M* (different from *p*) arbitrarily near to *p*. Thus, if *p* is a point of a line segment *S*, then *p* is a limit point of the set of points all on *S;* similarly, every point of a plane *P* is a limit point of the set of all points of *P*. This concept is used in the definition of "homeomorphic." To obtain it, let us first analyze the meaning of "congruent." Two figures *A* and *B* are congruent if all points of *A* can be paired to all points of *B* so as to preserve distances; that is, if a_1 and a_2 are points of *A* which are paired respectively to points b_1 and b_2 of *B*, then the distances a_1a_2 and b_1b_2 must be equal. In topology, two figures *A* and *B* are homeomorphic if the points of *A* can be paired to the points of *B* so as to preserve limit points; that is, if *a* is a point of *A* which is a limit point of a set of points *A'* in *A*, then the corresponding point *b* in *B* must be a limit point of the set of points *B'* corresponding to *A'*; and conversely. Thus, not only are congruent figures homeomorphic, but all simple polygons, circles, ellipses, etc., without regard to size, are homeomorphic and are called *simple closed curves* (Fig. 1).

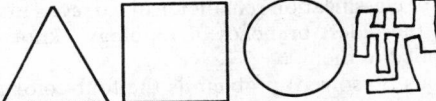

Fig. 1: Homeomorphic figures: simple closed curves.

Fig. 2: Moebius strip: a one-sided surface.

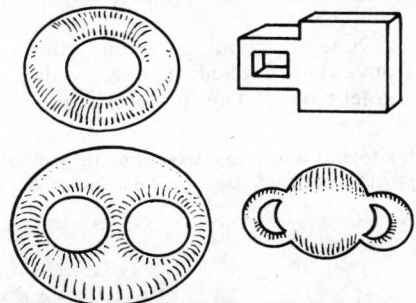

Fig. 3: Homeomorphic surfaces of genus 1 (*above*) and genus 2 (*below*).

In classical geometries the configurations are considered as lying in some space, as for instance a plane ("plane geometry") or 3-space ("solid geometry"); similarly in topology certain spaces are studied. These may be much more general than the spaces of the classical geometries; indeed, any collection of things in which the limit points of the various collections of points are specified can be considered a *topological space*. It is largely to this generality that topology owes its importance in modern mathematics and its applications. It has been found that every part of mathematics can be studied topologically, due to the fact that the elements with which it deals—*e.g.* numbers—can be called "points," and the notion of "limit point" suitably interpreted so as to yield some kind of topological space. As a result, topology appears no longer to be subject to precise definition; in only certain of its aspects is it considered a geometry, and it is growing rapidly in both scope and method. Classical geometry was found to be susceptible to algebraic and analytic treatment ("analytic geometry"), and algebraic methods, especially GROUP THEORY, have also been introduced into topology.

In such a general subject, what kinds of properties can be studied? Of central interest are *topological invariants; i.e.* properties of a figure *F* which hold for all figures homeomorphic to *F*. An example is DIMENSION, a concept first successfully defined by topological methods. The simplest definition is based on an idea that goes back to Euclid; the dimension of a space *S* at a point *p* is the number *n* if arbitrarily small "pieces" of *S* containing *p* (*neighborhoods* of *p*) are detachable by "cutting" along an $(n - 1)$-dimensional border, and this is not possible for a smaller *n*. This idea leads to a MATHEMATICAL-INDUCTION definition, starting with the dimension of empty space as -1.

Surfaces may be classified by means of topological invariants. A sphere and its homeomorphs are two-sided, but a closed surface containing a Moebius strip (Fig. 2) is one-sided. Two-dimensional closed surfaces have been classified by their "connectivity" (related to the number of "holes," as shown in Fig. 3) and by whether or not they are two-sided; if two-sided they are representable in Euclidean 3-space (surfaces like the Klein Bottle are not representable in 3-space). Many of the problems of classification remain unsolved, even in dimension 3; one of the oldest branches of topology—knot theory—is being applied to them.

A famous (unsolved) problem is the four-color map problem: can every planar map be colored with at most four colors so that no two countries with a common boundary have the same color? (A state like Michigan that is in two parts is considered to be two countries.) The size of the map is of no consequence; what matters is the arrangement of the countries. Because the sizes and precise shapes of the individual countries are of no concern, the map problem belongs to the domain of topology.—*R. L. W.*

TORNADO: a violently rotating column of air extending downward from a thundercloud. It is nearly always recognizable as a "funnel cloud." The funnel is composed of small water droplets formed in the whirl as low pressure near the center leads to cooling and condensation. The tornado, or "twister," does not always reach the ground; sometimes it oscillates upward and downward before finally making contact with the earth. A tornado over water is called a "waterspout."

Tornadoes usually have diameters of several hundred yards, usually rotate counterclockwise, and have wind speeds estimated to reach more than 300 mi/hr. Most tornadoes produce a loud roaring noise, compared by observers to the buzzing of countless bees or the roar of flights of jet airplanes. Such a whirling air column commonly lasts no more than a few minutes, but in that time may cause great destruction. Since the pressure at its center is usually considerably lower than in the surroundings, as the tornado moves over buildings the sudden reduction of external pressure may cause them to explode from the pressure of the air trapped inside. The extremely high associated winds complete the devastation by tearing apart and carrying away almost anything in their path.

Tornadoes have been observed on all continents and are very common in the U. S. A., being most frequent during spring over the Central Plains. Tornadoes in the U. S. A. have averaged about 150 per yr and have caused an annual average of 230 casualties and 14 million dollars' worth of damage. In areas of high tornado frequency, people resort to underground cellars and caves—the only sure refuges, though some protection is afforded by basements and interior walls. Since flying debris is a serious hazard, it is essential to get under cover.—*L. J. B.*

TORQUE (or MOMENT): a measure of the effectiveness of a force in producing rotation about a particular reference axis. Torque (τ) is a vector quantity, numerically equal to the product of the force (F) and its distance, measured perpendicular to the direction of the force, from the reference axis. Thus a weight of 10 lb (a downward force), applied to a lever at a perpendicular distance of 5 ft from the fulcrum, produces a torque about this fulcrum of 10×5, or 50 lb-ft. If the fulcrum is moved to a point only 2 ft from the applied force, the resulting torque is reduced to 20 lb-ft. For a condition of rotational equilibrium, the net torque on a body must be equal to zero.—*A. E.*

Funnel of this tornado in Kansas reaches to ground, and much dust is being sucked up. (*U. S. Dept. of Commerce/Weather Bureau*)

Tornado at Meriden, Kans., May 19, 1960, shows on Weather Bureau radarscope. The range markers are 5 nautical mi apart.

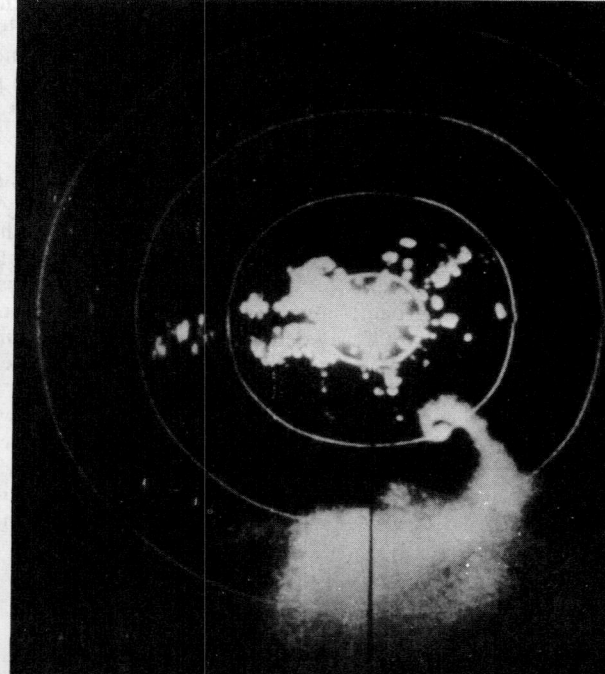

TORREY, JOHN, 1796–1873, U. S. botanist and chemist; b. N. Y. City. A pioneer botanical taxonomist, he classified many plants, at first mainly from the eastern U. S. A., later more from the West, brought back by expeditions such as those of Frémont, Marcy, and Whipple. Among his books are *Flora of the State of New York* (1843) and, with Asa Gray, *Flora of North America* (1838–43, not completed). He was a member of the National Academy of Sciences.—*D. J. S.*

TORRICELLI, EVANGELISTA, 1608–47, Italian physicist and mathematician; b. Faenza; ed. Collegio di Sapienza, Rome. A disciple of Galileo, he did mathematical research on conic sections, the acute hyperbolic solid, and the cycloid. Torricelli's theorem is concerned with the velocity of flow of fluids from orifices. He proposed the concept that we live in a sea of air which exerts a continual pressure on us and on everything around us. He devised an instrument (the mercury barometer) to measure this pressure (1643), and was the first to produce evacuated spaces (near-vacuums), by means of his barometer. His *Opere* were published, 1919–44.—*D. H. D. R.*

TORSION: the twisting of structural elements such as shafts in response to a *torsional moment*. Such moments cause shear stresses which can be calculated by considerations of equilibrium and by the geometry of deformations of the member. The classical analysis of prismatic members subject to torsion was by B. De St. Venant (1797–1886). The strength of plates loaded normal to their plane is largely dependent on their capacity to resist torsion. Deformations caused by torsion are measured in terms of the *unit angle of twist*, or *angle of detrusion, i.e.* the angle (in radians) through which two transverse planes, a unit distance apart, will twist with respect to each other. See STRENGTH OF MATERIALS.—*K. G.*

TORSION BALANCE: an instrument designed to measure weak forces, *e.g.* the force of gravitational attraction between two small masses (see GRAVITATION) or the force of attraction or repulsion between two feebly magnetized or electrified bodies (see COULOMB'S LAW). The classical version of the instrument consists of an elastic fiber on which is suspended a light horizontal bar. Any force exerted on the ends of the bar imparts a twist or torque to the fiber, which acts to resist the applied torque. The amount of deflection produced may be measured by means of the shift in the direction of a pencil of light reflected from a mirror attached to the fiber.—*A. E.*

TOUCH: a sensation provoked by deformation or vibration of the skin. Around each follicle from which a hair or a feather arises is a special plexus of nerve fibers that are easily excited by deformation. The receptors for skin deformation have not been certainly identified, but the existence of specific touch receptors is shown by the fact that touch activates the largest and fastest-conducting fibers of the cutaneous nerves. The tactile receptors adapt rapidly, so that a constant stimulus goes unnoticed after deformation of the skin is completed. See SENSES; SKIN.—*W. P. C.*

TOWING TANKS AND WATER TUNNELS: the principal facilities for ship-model testing and research. Towing tanks are employed primarily for research on hull form and powering and (in conjunction with a highly developed procedure of preliminary design, testing, and extrapolation) for the prediction of performance of specific ship designs. The size of existing tanks (or "model basins") varies greatly; the world's major towing tanks are several hundred feet long (the largest in the U. S. A. is about 3,000 ft long) and as much as 50 ft wide and 20 ft deep. In such tanks, the usual ship model is about 20 ft long, and made of either wood or special wax.

Hull model of a sailing yacht undergoes testing in the Davidson Laboratory Towing Tank. (*Stevens Inst. of Tech.*)

Only the exterior shape of the hull is modeled accurately, the desired weight or displacement being achieved by ballasting internally. Models are towed (to determine basic hull resistance) or controlled (in a self-propulsion test) from a carriage which spans the tank and is driven along carefully leveled rails. The carriages contain balances and dynamometers to measure towing resistance and powering requirements. For self-propulsion tests, dynamometers are normally installed in the model itself. For ship or planing boat-model work, carriage speeds usually do not exceed 15 to 20 knots; for research on seaplane hulls, special tanks have been constructed with carriage speeds as high as 60 to 100 knots. Many tanks are now also equipped with machines to simulate conditions in a seaway.

Water tunnels ("cavitation tunnels") are experimental facilities used for tests in which CAVITATION phenomena are to be observed. When operating at high speeds, marine propellers and other hydraulic machines may cause pressures low enough in the surrounding liquid to produce cavitation (boiling). Consequently, a special feature of water tunnels, which are otherwise similar in principle to the familiar WIND TUNNEL, is their capacity to operate under reduced pressure

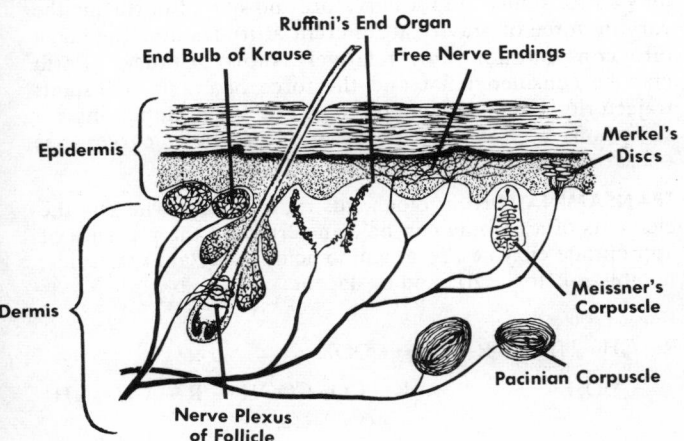

▶ **Receptor organs of touch** and other cutaneous sensations are shown in this diagram through section of human skin. Stimulation of Meissner's corpuscle and Merkel's discs elicits the sensation of touch. End bulb of Krause responds to cold; Ruffini's end organ, to heat; Pacinian corpuscle, to deep pressure. Sensation of pain results from stimulation of free nerve endings. (*From Villee*)

as well as high water velocities. Originally conceived for experiments on marine propeller models, cavitation tunnels are now used extensively for model tests of underwater missiles, hydraulic structures which may cavitate, and (with suitable test-section modifications) hydraulic pumps and turbines. By far the largest number of tunnels are of the closed-circuit type, comprising test-section equipment for suspending and measuring various forces on the model, an impeller for pumping the tunnel water through the circuit, and suitable flow-straightening and control sections. Although many special-purpose tunnels with very small test sections exist, the majority of tunnels have test-section diameters ranging from about 1 ft to as much as 4 ft. Maximum test-section velocities range from 50 to 100 ft/sec.—*P. E.*

TRACER: see RADIOISOTOPE.

TRACHEA: in vertebrates, the windpipe. This is a single tube leading from the larynx, or glottis, to the LUNGS. At the entrance to the lungs, the tube branches into two smaller tubes, the bronchi. The walls of the trachea are stiffened by incom-

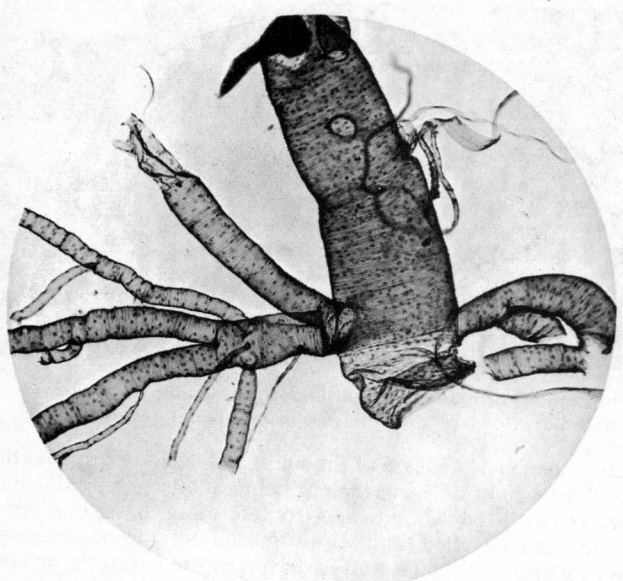

Part of grasshopper trachea with its branches is shown in this microphotograph. Dark lines are chitinous rings that reinforce tube; dark spots are cell nuclei. (*General Biological Supply House*)

plete rings of cartilage, which serve to keep the tube open at all times. In insects and certain other arthropods, a trachea is any one of the tubes that pipe air from the body surface directly into the tissues. In vascular plants, a trachea is a conducting tube in the XYLEM. Commonly called a vessel, it arises by the consolidation of many cells aligned end to end into a single continuous tube. See PHARYNX.—*B. T. S.*

TRACHEOPHYTE: see VASCULAR PLANT.

TRADE WINDS: the belt of steady low-latitude easterly surface winds that blow from the equatorward sides of the subtropical highs toward the DOLDRUMS. In the southern hemisphere these winds are known as the southeast trades; north of the equator, as the northeast trades. The northeast trades over the Atlantic extend from 30°N (in winter) or 35°N (in summer) southward to about 5°N latitude. It is in this belt of winds that hurricanes are formed. The trade-wind belts of both the N Pacific and the S Pacific are the breeding grounds

of the N Pacific typhoons and the hurricanes of the southern hemisphere. See ATMOSPHERE, GENERAL CIRCULATION OF.—*P. L.*

TRAITÉ DE LA LUMIÈRE (Treatise on Light), by Christiaan Huygens (1690): The wave theory of light, proposed qualitatively by Grimaldi and Hooke in 1665, received its first mathematical expression in this little book, written in 1678. Huygens showed how wave-trains could be both reflected and refracted, and endeavored to surmount Newton's objection that light-waves would bend into the shadow (as sound-waves do). He also attacked the difficult problem of double refraction (polarization), but he did not try to explain color. Long neglected by Newtonian theorists, Huygens' work received fresh attention with the revival of the wave theory soon after 1800, and it is now recognized as the pioneering venture in this branch of mathematical physics.—*A. R. H.*

TRAITÉ ÉLÉMENTAIRE DE CHIMIE (Elementary Treatise on Chemistry), by Antoine Laurent de Lavoisier (1789): Lavoisier's experimental and theoretical onslaught upon the phlogiston theory (see STAHL, GEORG ERNST) and his formulation of a new theory of chemical combination, laying the foundations of modern chemistry, were carried out in a series of great papers in scientific journals. The *Traité Élémentaire,* appearing when the majority of chemists were still not converted to Lavoisier's views, was a general synthesis of the new chemistry, presenting, for instance, a table of the elements as he defined them (substances experimentally resisting analysis), the oxygen theory of combustion and formation of acids, and the "caloric" theory. Although soon outmoded in matters of detail, in its rationality Lavoisier's textbook for a new science reflects the greatness of the revolution in ideas he effected.—*A. R. H.*

TRAJECTORY: the path described by a body moving in space. In accord with NEWTON'S LAWS OF MOTION the trajectory of any body in motion through space depends on (1) its initial velocity and direction; (2) other forces, if any, which are applied to it while in the powered phase of flight, as is the case with rockets; and (3) gravitational forces arising from the proximity of other bodies. Thus the trajectory of a celestial body, *e.g.* a meteor, comet, or planet, is affected by its velocity and the mass of other celestial bodies and the distance between it and them. For bodies moving in any medium other than a vacuum, the frictional drag, as well as any other aerodynamic effects, must be taken into account; thus the shape of a body will affect its trajectory in terms of the ratio of weight to drag coefficient. For those bodies projected from Earth to great heights for the purpose of striking a target at a distance, not only air resistance but the curvature and spin of Earth and the varying force of gravity at different altitudes must be taken into consideration. For relatively short distances, Earth may be considered flat and the force of gravity constant; trajectories computed on the basis of such simplifying assumptions approximate portions of parabolic curves. See CELESTIAL MECHANICS; DYNAMICS.—*A. L.*

TRANSAMINATION: in biochemistry, a process whereby the elements of ammonia can be transferred, in the presence of appropriate enzymes, from amino acids to certain keto acids, notably α-ketoglutaric and oxalacetic:

Amino acid #1   Keto acid

$$R-CH-NH_2 + R^2-CO\cdot COOH \rightleftharpoons$$
$$\underset{COOH}{|}$$

$$R^1\cdot CO\cdot COOH + R^2-CH-NH_2$$
$$\underset{Amino\ acid\ \#2}{} \qquad \underset{COOH}{|}$$

Reaction with α-ketoglutaric acid produces glutamic acid; oxalacetic acid yields aspartic acid (see AMINO ACIDS). These reactions aid in the elimination of ammonia from the oxidation of amino acids (see UREA CYCLE).—*K. H.*

TRANSCENDENTAL NUMBER: a number that is not a root of any equation whose coefficients are integers (positive or negative whole numbers or zero). This amounts to saying that a transcendental number is one which is not an ALGEBRAIC NUMBER. It is not apparent from the definition that transcendental numbers exist. Their existence was established in 1851 by J. Liouville, who proved the transcendence of certain numbers constructed for the purpose, *e.g.* the number $10^{-1} + 10^{-2} + 10^{-6} + 10^{-24} + \ldots$; the exponents here, apart from the minus signs, are products of positive integers, $1, 1 \cdot 2, 1 \cdot 2 \cdot 3, 1 \cdot 2 \cdot 3 \cdot 4$, etc.

About 30 yr after Liouville proved that transcendental numbers exist, it was established that the fundamental mathematical constants π and e are transcendental. The knowledge of the transcendental character of π settled an outstanding classical construction problem in Euclidean geometry. Known as "squaring the circle," the problem is to construct a square of the same area as a given circle by the use of straight edge and compass. If the radius of the given circle is 1 unit of length, the area of the circle is π square units, so the square would have sides of length $\sqrt{\pi}$ units. Thus the problem is to construct a line of length $\sqrt{\pi}$ from a given unit length. The transcendence of π implies that this construction is impossible, because any line segment that can be constructed from a unit length by the straight edge and compass methods has a length which is an algebraic number. Thus a length $\sqrt{\pi}$, which like π is transcendental, cannot be constructed.

Other examples of transcendental numbers are the common logarithms—logarithms to base ten, apart from a few obvious exceptions like log 100, which equals 2. This result is part of a more comprehensive theorem proved in 1934. Other parts of the theorem state that numbers like $2^{\sqrt{2}}$ and $3^{\sqrt{5}}$ are transcendental; more generally, if n is an integer greater than 1, and k is irrational but algebraic, then n^k is transcendental. See also COMPLEX NUMBER; CONSTRUCTION PROBLEMS; IRRATIONAL NUMBER.—*I. N.*

TRANSDUCER: a device that transforms energy from one form into another. A phonograph pick-up is a transducer whose input is the physical motion of the needle and whose output is electrical oscillations; the phonograph's loudspeaker is a transducer whose input is the electrical oscillations and whose output is the mechanical vibrations that transmit sound energy to the air. For transducers to be effective the output must be proportional to the input, so that the output is a meaningful, measurable indication of the input. A generator, which transforms mechanical energy into electrical energy, is a transducer, as are a photoelectric cell, which transforms light energy into electrical energy, and a piezoelectric crystal, which transforms mechanical stress into electricity. Transducers have been developed to sense and measure almost any desired quantity. Consequently, they are widely used in TELEMETERING, especially in satellites and other space vehicles, to measure and transmit data; they are also used in ultrasonic submarine detection. Commonly used are transducers whose output is electrical, because of the ease with which electrical signals can be transmitted and translated into precise quantitative readings.—*M. C. H.*

TRANSFINITE NUMBERS: numbers used to compare infinite sets, *e.g.* the set of whole numbers or the set of points on a line. Georg Cantor (1845–1918) defined transfinite cardinal numbers by using the principle fundamental to counting, that of one-to-one correspondence. Two sets are said to be in one-to-one correspondence if, to every element in one set, there is one and only one corresponding element in the second set and, to every element in the second set, there is one and only one corresponding element in the first set. We use this idea frequently: the set of chairs and the set of people in a room are in one-to-one correspondence if each person is seated in a chair, and if each chair has one person seated in it.

The transfinite cardinal number $\aleph_0$, aleph null, is assigned to the set of integers (whole numbers) and to any set that can be put in one-to-one correspondence with this set. Thus $\aleph_0$ is also the cardinal number of many other sets, *e.g.* the set of even numbers, the set of odd numbers, the set of numbers that are multiples of five, the set of positive and negative whole numbers, and the set of all integers and fractions (the rational numbers). We notice that the set of even numbers, although it is a part of the set of integers, can be put into one-to-one correspondence with the set of integers. This is a characteristic property of sets that have transfinite cardinal numbers.

The set of all points on a line *cannot* be put into one-to-one correspondence with the positive integers. To prove this we first note that the set of points is in one-to-one correspondence with the set of all real numbers, since any point on a line can be represented by one and only one real number, and conversely. If, then, the set of all real numbers is in one-to-one correspondence with the positive integers, then so is the set of points on a line. Let us suppose that the real numbers from 0 to 1 (expressed as infinite decimals) are in one-to-one correspondence with the positive integers; that is:

$$1 \longleftrightarrow 0.a_1b_1c_1d_1 \cdots$$
$$2 \longleftrightarrow 0.a_2b_2c_2d_2 \cdots$$
$$3 \longleftrightarrow 0.a_3b_3c_3d_3 \cdots$$
$$\cdot \qquad \cdots\cdots\cdots$$

where all the letters represent digits from 0 to 9. But consider the number formed by increasing by 1 each digit of $0.a_1b_2c_3d_4 \ldots$ (increasing 9 by 1 changes it to 0). The new number differs in (at least) the first digit from $0.a_1b_1c_1d_1 \ldots$, in the second digit from $0.a_2b_2c_2d_2 \ldots$, and so on throughout the list. Therefore there are real numbers not on the list, and therefore the set of real numbers (and the set of points on a line) cannot be put into one-to-one correspondence with the positive integers. The transfinite number, C, which is the cardinal number of the set of points on a line, is thus larger than that of the positive integers, $\aleph_0$. The cardinal C is also the cardinal number of all points in the plane, of all points in three- or higher-dimensional spaces, and of all real and of all complex numbers.

Transfinite ordinal numbers are assigned to infinite sets to represent the order of the elements in the set. The ordinal number of the set of positive integers in natural order 1, 2, 3, 4, 5, . . . is ω. The ordinal number of the set 2, 3, 4, 5, . . . , 1 is $\omega + 1$, etc. Both sets have the same transfinite cardinal number $\aleph_0$. The properties of these transfinite ordinal numbers are different from those of the transfinite cardinal numbers.—*H. E. W.*

TRANSFORMATIONS: in mathematics, changes in algebraic expressions or in geometrical relationships among points. In algebra and analysis, expressions involving variables are transformed by the introduction of new variables related to the old by stated equations, the usual purpose being to simplify forms or change them to other forms with known properties. In geometry, transformations result in new configurations. An important part of the study of transformations is the discovery of *invariants*—forms or geometrical relations which do not change as a result of the transformations.

One type of algebraic transformation yields an important step in solution of quadratic and cubic equations. By putting $x = u - b/a$, the quadratic equation $ax^2 + 2bx + c = 0$ becomes $a^2u^2 - k^2 = 0$, whence $u = \pm k/a$, where $k^2 = b^2 - ac$. The same transformation reduces the general cubic $ax^3 + 3bx^2 + 3cx + d = 0$ to a readily solvable form.

The most important algebraic transformations are homogeneous linear ones, generally called simply *linear transformations*. As applied to two variables this transformation has the form $x = mu + nv$, $y = ru + tv$. The applications of transformations of this kind to homogeneous algebraic forms play a major role in algebra. The determinant, Δ, of the transformation is

$$\Delta = \begin{vmatrix} m & n \\ r & t \end{vmatrix}$$

its value being defined as $mt - rn$. If $\Delta = 0$, the transformation is *singular;* otherwise, it is *nonsingular*. A nonsingular transformation has an inverse transformation, by which u and v are replaced by linear expressions in x and y. A transformation followed by its inverse leaves the variables unchanged. Suppose a second transformation is applied, with determinant

$$D = \begin{vmatrix} h & k \\ j & l \end{vmatrix}$$

The effect of both transformations is that of a single transformation with determinant equal to

$$\Delta \cdot D = \begin{vmatrix} mh + nj & mk + nl \\ rh + tj & rk + tl \end{vmatrix}$$

This determinant is obtained by multiplying Δ times D by the rule for multiplying matrices. (See MATRIX.)

By the application of the first linear transformation above, the quadratic form $ax^2 + 2bxy + cy^2$ becomes $Au^2 + 2Buv + Cv^2$, where $A = am^2 + 2bmr + cr^2$, $B = amn + bmt + bnr + crt$, and $C = an^2 + 2bnt + ct^2$. It can be shown that the *discriminant*, $B^2 - AC$, of the transformed quadratic is equal to that of the original, multiplied by a number determined by the transformation and independent of the coefficients of the quadratic, namely, the square of the determinant of the transformation. That is, $B^2 - AC = \Delta^2(b^2 - ac)$. The discriminant is an *invariant of index 2* with respect to the transformation. If $\Delta = 1$, as in the case of rotation of axes, the discriminant is an absolute invariant (index 0), for the equations of rotation are

$$x = \cos \theta \cdot u - \sin \theta \cdot v$$
$$y = \sin \theta \cdot u + \cos \theta \cdot v$$

with

$$\Delta = \begin{vmatrix} \cos \theta & -\sin \theta \\ \sin \theta & \cos \theta \end{vmatrix} = 1$$

Let $f(x, y)$ denote a homogeneous polynomial in (x, y) of any degree. The *Hessian* (named after Otto Hesse) of f is the determinant

$$\begin{vmatrix} \dfrac{\partial^2 f}{\partial x^2} & \dfrac{\partial^2 f}{\partial x \partial y} \\ \dfrac{\partial^2 f}{\partial y \partial x} & \dfrac{\partial^2 f}{\partial y^2} \end{vmatrix}$$

If F is the function obtained from f by a linear transformation of determinant Δ, the Hessian of F is equal to the product of the Hessian of f and Δ^2. The Hessian of a quadratic is constant, and therefore invariant (of index 2); that of a polynomial of higher degree contains the variables, and is a *covariant*. For the general cubic, $ax^3 + 3bx^2y + 3cxy^2 + dy^3$, the Hessian is $36[(ac - b^2)x + (ad - bc)xy + (db - c^2)y]$. The Hessian of this quadratic is free of x and y, and is an invariant of the original cubic, of index 6. Except for the constant factor, 36, it is $(ad - bc)^3 - 4(ac - b^2)(bd - c^2)$, which is called the discriminant of the cubic. The important fact about a discriminant is that its vanishing is the condition for the existence of multiple factors of the polynomial, or multiple roots of the corresponding equation. (See EQUATIONS, THEORY OF.)

A quadratic form can be reduced to X^2 or XY, where X and Y are linear expressions, according as the discriminant is, or is not, equal to 0. A cubic form can be reduced to X^2Y or X^3 if its discriminant is equal to 0, and, if not, to $X^3 + Y^3$.

Transformations are essential at many points in the study of calculus and its applications. The simplest example is that of a compound function $y = f(u)$, $u = \phi(x)$. Here the variable u is replaced by a function of x, and it is important to know how the derivative is affected. This is answered by the chain rule, which states that $dy/dx = dy/du \cdot du/dx$. The transformation $u = \phi(x)$ has an inverse which restores u as the independent variable, if $du/dx \neq 0$. By the same transformation an integral is affected as follows:

$$\int f(u) \, du = \int f[\phi(x)] \, du/dx \, dx, \text{ since } du = du/dx \, dx$$

If $u = \phi(x, y)$ and $v = \psi(x, y)$, a function $f(u, v)$ becomes $f[\phi(x, y), \psi(x, y)]$. An expression in the partial derivatives known as the *Jacobian*, or *functional determinant*, plays a role analogous to that of the derivative in the case of one variable. The Jacobian is

$$J = \begin{vmatrix} \dfrac{\partial u}{\partial x} & \dfrac{\partial u}{\partial y} \\ \dfrac{\partial v}{\partial x} & \dfrac{\partial v}{\partial y} \end{vmatrix}$$

The transformation can be inverted to restore u and v as the independent variables if $J \neq 0$. Now if x and y are transformed by $x = g(r, s)$, $y = h(r, s)$, u and v are related in a compound way to r and s. The Jacobian of this relation is the product of the Jacobians of the two transformations, in analogy to the chain rule for a single variable. Thus

$$\begin{vmatrix} \dfrac{\partial u}{\partial r} & \dfrac{\partial u}{\partial s} \\ \dfrac{\partial v}{\partial r} & \dfrac{\partial v}{\partial s} \end{vmatrix} = \begin{vmatrix} \dfrac{\partial u}{\partial x} & \dfrac{\partial u}{\partial y} \\ \dfrac{\partial v}{\partial x} & \dfrac{\partial v}{\partial y} \end{vmatrix} \cdot \begin{vmatrix} \dfrac{\partial x}{\partial r} & \dfrac{\partial x}{\partial s} \\ \dfrac{\partial y}{\partial r} & \dfrac{\partial y}{\partial s} \end{vmatrix}$$

A double integral of $f(u, v)$ is transformed to an integral relative to x and y by the formula

$$\iint f(u, v) du dv = \iint f[\phi(x, y), \psi(x, y)] J \, dx \, dy.$$

Transformations in analysis have important geometrical interpretations because of the representation of functions on coordinate systems. Other geometrical transformations are illustrated by those of projective geometry. The object of the study of projective geometry is to find and analyze properties of figures which are invariant under projective transformations. As an example of a projective transformation, consider two planes π and π', not necessarily parallel, and a point O exterior to both (Fig. 1). A point P of π is projected onto π' by a line from O through P intersecting π' in the projection P'. By this projection, configurations on π are transformed

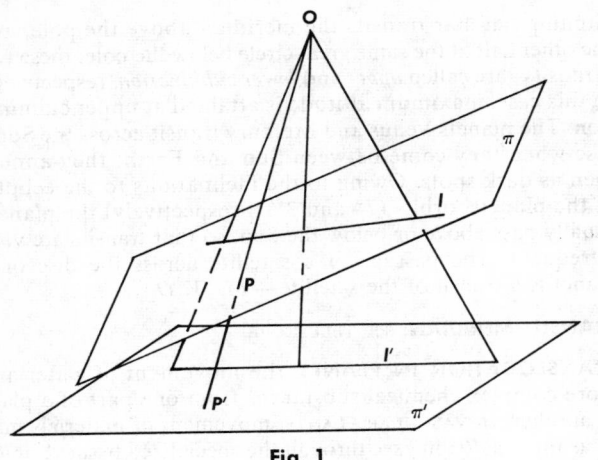

Fig. 1

into configurations on π'. Clearly, an invariant of this transformation is collinearity: all points on line l of π project into points on a single line l' of π'. One of the most important of the invariants which are found in the study of projective geometry is the *cross-ratio* of four points on a straight line.

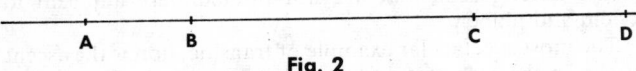

Fig. 2

The cross-ratio of points A,B,C,D of Fig. 2 is

$$(AC/BC)/(AD/BD)$$

a ratio of two ratios. If these points are subjected to any number of projective transformations, this double ratio remains invariant.

Another large class of geometrical transformations is the principal concern of the subject of TOPOLOGY.—*H. C.*

TRANSFORMER: an alternating-current device which transfers electric power from one circuit to another by means of a magnetic circuit. Its usual though not exclusive purpose is to change the magnitude of the voltage. The transformer makes possible economical transmission of electrical power over great distances. Michael Faraday (1831) discovered the principle of induction, which is the basis for the transformer. He found that when a conductor is placed in a changing magnetic field, a voltage is induced in the conductor.

A transformer consists of two coils of wire, the primary and the secondary, looped around a core made of layers of steel sheet bolted together. The alternating current in the primary produces a changing magnetic field which induces an alternating-current voltage in the secondary. If the secondary has more turns of wire than the primary, the transformer is said to be step-up, *i.e.* the voltage of the secondary will be higher than the primary; a step-down transformer decreases voltage. An ELECTRIC-POWER TRANSMISSION system has at the generator end step-up transformers which increase the voltage (and reduce the current). The higher the voltage on the line, the smaller the losses. The voltage is stepped down to a usable level by transformers at the consumer end. Besides the conventional-type transformers there are several specialized types used to step up or step down current for special applications, *e.g.* the auto-transformer, constant-current transformer, and instrument transformer. The Scott connection for transformers is used for changing two-phase to three-phase voltage or *vice versa*.—*H. I. S.*

TRANSISTOR: an amplifier of electrical power. Like the vacuum tube, it accomplishes amplification by having available

a source of external power, an input circuit into which the control signal is introduced, and an output circuit into which the transistor delivers power from the supply in accordance with the input signal. The transistor was first announced in 1948 by Bell Telephone Laboratories, where the principal forms of transistor were invented by J. Bardeen, W. H. Brattain, and W. Shockley, who shared the 1956 Nobel prize in physics for their contributions to semiconductor research and discovery of the transistor effect. The transistor is the first serious competitor of the vacuum tube to appear in about four decades. At present it is displacing the vacuum tube in many applications. Its advantages over the vacuum tube are its small size, the fact that it does not need a hot cathode (which consumes power and requires a warm-up time when the equipment is first turned on), its lower level of operation (which makes it particularly suitable for computers), its mechanical ruggedness, and its longer life in service. Many of these advantages were only potential when the transistor was first announced, but after almost a decade of development are being realized economically.

The transistor is made of a semiconductor, and its electri-

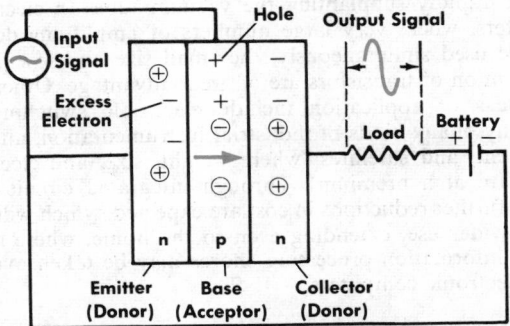

Junction transistor: Emitter (n) region becomes more negative with increased input signal. Excess electrons diffuse across base (p) region and are drawn by battery voltage across collector junction, allowing current to flow through load. ("Hole" indicates positive charge produced by missing electron.) Low-power input signal controls pattern of high-power output signal, and thus amplification is achieved. Circled plus signs indicate "donor atoms," which give up electrons; circled minus signs indicate "acceptor atoms," which receive the free electrons.

cal action can be understood in terms of the two mobile electronic imperfections, the hole and the excess electron, and the stationary chemical imperfections, the donor and acceptor (see CONDUCTOR AND SEMICONDUCTOR). The simplest form of transistor, and the type in largest production, is the junction transistor. It is made of a single crystal of silicon or germanium, and the chemical impurities are differently distributed in three layers like a sandwich, as in the diagram. The dividing surfaces between the different conductivity types are called *p-n* junctions. It is after them that the junction transistor is named. Separate metal connections are made to the three regions. Under operating conditions, the collector junction is biased by the power supply (represented by a battery in the diagram) with the *n*-side positive and the *p*-side negative. In this "reverse" direction the excess electrons are pulled into the *n*-region and the holes into the *p*-region. If a forward bias voltage is applied across the other (emitter) junction, the electrical positive current flows into the base region in the form of holes which attract excess electrons into the *p*-region. These excess electrons diffuse or migrate, as a result of their thermal agitation, through the base *p*-region to the collector junction, where they are collected by the positively charged collector region; they then flow as an output current through the load resistor R. Small input voltages and currents applied across the emitter junction by the signal generator can produce large voltages and currents at the collector junction and power gain in the load resistor R, which may actually be a loudspeaker coil or input to another amplifier circuit. In this way the flow of holes under the influence of the input signal controls the flow of excess electrons, so that amplified power is delivered from the power source to the load.

Field-effect transistors and metal-oxide-semiconductor (MOS) transistors use only one kind of carrier, electrons or holes, and alter their number by neutralizing their charge with external electric fields applied from metal conductors outside the semiconductor. Integrated circuits consist of many junction transistors or MOS transistors on a single tiny plate of silicon. These are connected with metal wiring to form transistor circuits suitable for computers and many other uses.

Originally, transistors were used for special purposes, as in hearing aids, where small size and low power drain are important. Another early use was in pocket-size radios. Now, however, transistors find application in every field of electronics and are rapidly supplanting the vacuum tube. In electronic computers, where very large numbers of amplifying devices must be used simultaneously, the small size and low power consumption of transistors are of great advantage. Other current areas of application include electronic switching for telephony, many kinds of industrial instrumentation, military equipment, and satellites (where weight, size, and electrical power are at a premium). Through integrated circuit technology, further reductions in cost are expected, which will lead to still wider use, extending even to the home, where many routine information processing chores may be taken over by small electronic computers.—*W. S.*

TRANSIT: in astronomy, the passage of one celestial body across the disc of another, or across a chosen great circle of the celestial sphere. The most common use of the word refers to passage across the observer's MERIDIAN, the celestial object having then its maximum altitude for that observer. A circumpolar star transits the meridian above the pole, and the other half of the same great circle below the pole; these two "transits" are called *upper* and *lower culmination,* respectively; in this case, maximum altitude is attained at upper culmination. The planets Venus and Mercury transit across the Sun's disc when they come between Sun and Earth; they appear then as dark spots. Owing to the inclinations to the ecliptic of the planets' orbits (7° and 3½°, respectively) the planets usually pass above or below the Sun, so that transits are very infrequent. The passage of a satellite across the disc of a planet is a transit of the satellite.—*M. W. O.*

TRANSIT, MERIDIAN: see TELESCOPE.

TRANSLOCATION IN PLANTS: the movement of water and more complex chemical substances from one part of a plant to another. In VASCULAR PLANTS, movement of materials may be as rapid as 7½ in./sec through the specialized tissues known as xylem and phloem. In non-vascular plants (*e.g.* algae, fungi, liverworts, and mosses), translocation is much slower and probably occurs through a combination of secretory activity on the part of the cell providing the substance and absorptive activity on the part of the cell receiving the substance. This slower method of translocation is found also in vascular plants among cells that are not immediately adjacent to xylem and phloem.

The most spectacular example of translocation is the ascent of sap in the xylem of ROOTS and STEMS, particularly in tall trees. Water is the principal material transported. It enters the root hairs or the fungus threads (mycorrhizae) that serve in place of root hairs (*e.g.* in pine, heaths, and orchids); it is translocated from one living cell to another through the cortex parenchyma of the root, through the sheath of pericycle cells, and is secreted into the dead tubular cells of the xylem. Until the leaves expand and begin losing moisture to the air (see TRANSPIRATION), the plant pushes the water upward by root pressure. After the leaves open, the upward movement is probably achieved passively through transpiration pull. The water passes from one xylem tube to another through the root, the stem, and finally out the xylem strands in the petiole of a LEAF into the veins and to tissues capable of carrying on PHOTOSYNTHESIS. About a tenth of the water translocated is used in photosynthesis, the rest disposed of by transpiration.

Dissolved inorganic compounds are transported in the xylem tubes at their own characteristic speeds, at a pace that is rarely as rapid as the transport of water molecules. Yet the movement of water is important in their translocation, if only to carry them from one end of a xylem tube to the other.

Elaborated organic compounds, including sugars and hormones, are conducted chiefly in the sieve tubes of the phloem, and distributed throughout the plant. It is the sugar-rich sap descending toward the roots in the inner bark of a tree that is "tapped" in a maple orchard and dehydrated to make syrup. Both food substances and water are transported in radial directions within a woody plant from one parenchyma cell to the next by way of the medullary rays through the xylem and phloem.

The phloem appears able to carry inorganic compounds in solution, but at slower rates than these travel in the xylem. Such compounds, bearing tagged atoms of radioactive isotopes, have been followed as they progress downward and throughout a plant after the compounds have been painted on the leaves. For most of the major inorganic nutrients required by plants (salts containing calcium, phosphorus, sulfur, nitrogen, magnesium, iron, and potassium), the rate of translocation through the phloem is too slow to permit an agriculturalist to fertilize his crop through the leaves rather than through the soil.—*L. and M. M.*

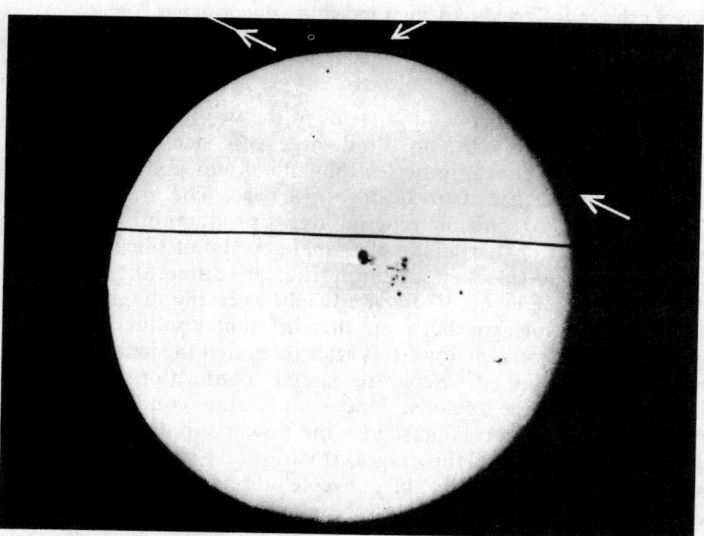

Transit of Mercury occurs at intervals of 3 to 13 yr when Mercury comes directly between Earth and Sun. On this photograph of transit of Nov. 14, 1907, arrows point to Mercury and direction of its movement. Transits always occur in May or November; next ones will be in 1970, 1973, 1986, and 1999. (*Yerkes Obs.*)

TRANSMETHYLATION: in biochemistry, the process by which the body transfers methyl (—CH₃) groups, a step in the synthesis of some essential compounds. Mammals can synthesize only a limited amount of methyl groups; most are derived from dietary sources, *e.g.* methionine, or from choline. Choline acts as a methyl-group donor, giving a methyl group to homocysteine to form methionine. Methionine can then act as a methyl donor to form creatine. By means of these reversible transfer reactions, catalyzed by methyltransferase enzymes, the body cells can get by with limited supplies of methyl groups. See also AMINO ACIDS.—*J. F. S.*

TRANSMITTER: an emitter of signals which bear information or other intelligence; more generally, a device which applies an appropriate transformation upon a signal input which will in turn permit it to be transmitted over some other medium. A radio transmitter is a familiar example, in which the transmitter equipment accepts the voice, music, or other input and transforms it into a radio signal which is then broadcast. The term transmitter can also be applied to the mechanical device, usually called the "key," used to send Morse code over telegraph wires. One can also speak of sound transmitters; *e.g.* a public-address system or undersea sonar. A transmitter is employed at the input of a TELECOMMUNICATION system the output of which is a RECEIVER of some sort.—*G. S.*

TRANSMUTATION OF ELEMENTS: the changing of one element to another. The desire to transform base metals into gold was an avowed goal of ALCHEMY and contributed greatly to the modern concept of a chemical ELEMENT. It was the discovery of radioactivity, however, that led ultimately to a realization of the tremendous energy fluxes needed for transmutation. (Radioactivity was recognized as a naturally occurring transmutation rather soon after its discovery by A. H. Becquerel in 1896.) Lord Ernest Rutherford was the first to succeed in transmuting elements artificially when he converted nitrogen into oxygen atoms (1919) by bombarding nitrogen gas with the high-speed alpha particles given off by radium. A large number of transmutations, or NUCLEAR REACTIONS as they are now called, were subsequently accomplished by the use of naturally occurring products of radioactivity. The development of the cyclotron and other devices for producing very-high-energy particles greatly facilitated the study of nuclear reactions. The four particles that have been most extensively used to bombard atomic nuclei and bring about elemental transmutations are alpha particles, protons, deuterons, and neutrons.

Disintegration of an element by bombardment with an alpha particle (*i.e.* a helium nucleus) occurs with the emission of a proton or neutron. Emission of a proton is observed with many of the lighter elements, *e.g.* the reaction of an alpha particle with B^{10} to give a proton and the element C^{13}. An example of emission of a neutron is the reaction of an alpha particle with Na^{23} to give Al^{26} and a neutron. A proton or deuteron can penetrate the potential barrier of a nucleus more easily than an alpha particle because of its smaller charge. The proton bombardment of N^{14} gives C^{11} and an alpha particle. Bombardment of B^{10} with a deuteron gives C^{11} and a neutron. Both of these reactions lead to further transmutation by reaction of the neutron or alpha-particle product with another element. The reaction is then a *consecutive transmutation*. Neutrons, obtained most easily by bombardment of beryllium with alpha particles or deuterons, have no charge and can readily penetrate a nucleus. For example, neutron bombardment of Al^{27} gives either Na^{24} and an alpha particle or Mg^{27} and a proton. The most important neutron reaction is the bombardment of U^{235} causing nuclear fission, in which several nuclear reactions occur. The uranium nucleus breaks into large fragments and emits an excess of new neutrons, which further accelerate the reaction. This effect is called a *chain reaction*.—*A. M. S.*

Parabolic dish (*right*) at Holmdel, N. J., receives UHF radiation from tripod-borne waveguide at focus and reflects this radiation outward to space, there to be picked up by passing Echo satellite. (*Bell Telephone Labs.*)

Complete tunnel-diode transmitter (*below*) is compared in size with 50-cent piece. Transmitter consists of one variable and two fixed ceramic capacitors, a coil that tunes to the operating frequency (which may be higher than 1 kilomegacycle/sec), and the tunnel diode itself, located inside "can" in center of device. (*General Electric*)

TRANSPEPTIDATION: the synthesis of peptides by PROTEOLYTIC ENZYMES such as chymotrypsin. Normally these enzymes hydrolyze peptides by adding the elements of water, giving a free amino acid and a peptide with one less amino acid. However, under certain conditions, when another peptide is present, the amino acid which is broken off is attached to this other peptide, giving two new peptides. It is not known whether these reactions are involved in specific PROTEIN SYNTHESIS in the cell. See also PEPTIDE.—*P. S.*

TRANSPIRATION: the escape of water vapor from the above-ground parts of plants, chiefly via the stomates of leaves. Such water loss is unavoidable, because the intercellular spaces of the leaf have a high vapor pressure (caused by a water film covering every exposed cell wall). As a result, water diffuses into the external air with its lower vapor pressure. Transpiration can be demonstrated by a *potometer,* which consists of a water-filled glass tube with one end inserted into a sealed jar of water, the other attached to the cut end of a leafy stem; as transpiration takes place, an air bubble located in the tube can be seen to move toward the stem at a rate commensurate with the water loss of the plant. Transpiration rates vary with type of plant and its environment. Transpiration loss for an acre of corn during the growing season has been estimated at 400,000 gal, but an acre of cactus has an annual transpiration loss of only 275 gal. Transpiration is greater with an increase in leaf surface; thus plants with broad, flat leaves have a higher water loss than plants with narrow, thick leaves. Transpiration is reduced in plants whose leaves have depressed stomates or thickly cutinized epidermis, both of which are characteristics of conifer needles (see EVERGREEN). Environmental factors play an important role in determining transpiration rate. Bright sunlight, high temperature, low atmospheric humidity, or strong wind increases transpiration; conversely, shade, low temperature, considerable humidity, or calm reduces transpiration loss. See LEAF.—*C. J. H.*

TRANSURANIUM ELEMENTS: the chemical elements beyond uranium in the periodic table; the ten that have now been produced are neptunium (element 93), plutonium (94), americium (95), curium (96), berkelium (97), californium (98), einsteinium (99), fermium (100), mendelevium (101), nobelium (102), and lawrencium (103). All these are ARTIFICIAL ELEMENTS; none exists in nature. They are made by bombarding the nuclei of lighter elements with neutrons and protons. In most cases, rather complex nuclear reactions are involved; *e.g.* neptunium was first made by bombarding uranium[238] with neutrons to form the unstable isotope uranium[239], which quickly decays (disintegrates), losing a nuclear electron, to become neptunium[239]. Transuranium elements so far discovered are all ACTINIDES ("heavy rare earths") and are highly electropositive metals. The elements beyond 103 will not be actinides but, rather, will fall back in line in the periodic table, element 104 taking its place under hafnium, element 105 under tantalum, and element 106 under tungsten. (See periodic table, accompanying article PERIODIC LAW.) It is not expected that any of these—if they can be made at all—will have forms that are stable or even very long-lived. However, long-lived isotopes of the first four transuranium elements are available; *e.g.* neptunium[237], with a half life of 2 million yr; plutonium[239], 24,000 yr; and plutonium, americium, and curium, which have isotopes with half lives of 400 yr or more. For the elements above curium, no long-lived isotopes have been found and none is expected.—*A. R. G.*

TRAPEZIUM: in mathematics, a four-sided plane figure in which no side is parallel to any other side. In astronomy the term "trapezium" is applied to a trapezium-shaped group of four close, hot stars (of which two are spectroscopic binary stars) that illuminate the Great Nebula (M42) in the constellation Orion. Trapezium-type systems are similar groups of young stars often found as the nucleus of "O"-type STAR ASSOCIATIONS.—*R. P. K.*

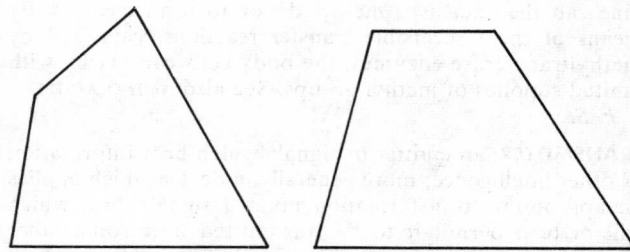

Trapezium and trapezoid: In trapezium (*left*), no two sides are parallel. In trapezoid (*right*), two sides only are parallel.

TRAPEZOID: a plane figure bounded by four straight line segments, or sides, meeting in four points, two sides being parallel and the other two non-parallel. If the two non-parallel sides are equal, the trapezoid is isosceles. The parallel sides are called the bases of the trapezoid, and the perpendicular distance between them is its altitude. The area of the trapezoid is equal to one-half the sum of the bases multiplied by the altitude: $A = \frac{1}{2}(b_1 + b_2)h$. A number of theorems of geometry concern trapezoids, but this figure does not play as important a role as do the triangle and the parallelogram. —*H. C.*

TREATISE ON ELECTRICITY AND MAGNETISM, by James Clerk Maxwell (1873): In this monumental work Maxwell presents his mathematical elaboration of Faraday's findings and conceptions which constitutes classical electromagnetic theory. Most striking is his introduction (suggested to him solely by a sense of symmetry) of an additional term into one of the equations; the term enabled him to deduce the existence of electromagnetic waves having the velocity of light before their experimental detection, and thence to infer the electromagnetic nature of light.—*G. G.*

TREE: generally, a large woody plant with a single stem or trunk, bearing a definite crown of leaves and branches, and growing to a height of 10 ft or more. There are two large groups of trees on Earth today: the cone-bearing trees and the broad-leaved, dicotyledonous trees. The cone-bearing trees

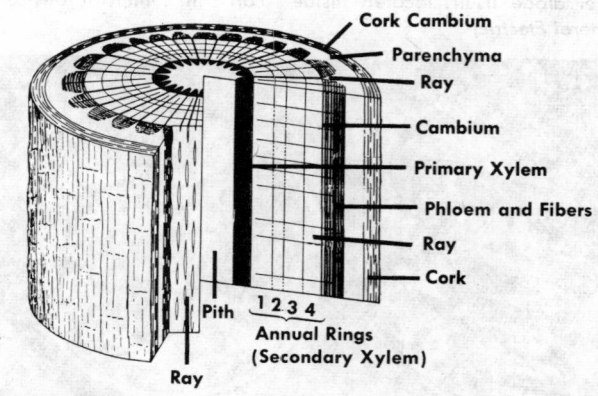

Cork Cambium
Parenchyma
Ray
Cambium
Primary Xylem
Phloem and Fibers
Ray
Cork
Pith
1 2 3 4
Annual Rings
(Secondary Xylem)
Ray

Trunk of 4-yr-old tree is cut to show internal structures. Note four annual rings. (*From Villee, after Weatherwax*)

include the pines, spruces, firs, larches, hemlocks, cedars, and junipers (see GYMNOSPERM). These trees furnish the soft woods of commerce, used extensively for construction, furniture, and pulpwood. Important broad-leaved trees are the oaks, maples, hickories, ashes, birches, poplars, and willows, furnishing the economically important hardwoods, used chiefly for flooring, furniture, and small-boat construction. Trees are the tallest and oldest living organisms. The redwood (*Sequoia semper-virens*) of the Pacific Coast forest reaches an authenticated 364 ft, and a species of the eucalyptus tree of Australia grows more than 300 ft tall. The oldest-known living organisms are the bristlecone pine trees (*Pinus aristata*), which have reached an age of over 4,600 yr. These trees are found in the Inyo National Forest in the White Mts of east central California at an altitude of nearly 10,000 ft. See ANNUAL RINGS; BARK; DECIDUOUS PLANT; EVERGREEN; FLOWERING PLANT; LEAF; WOOD.—*F. L.*

TREMBLEY, ABRAHAM, 1700–84, Swiss zoologist and microscopist; b. Geneva. He showed by experiment the asexual nature of the reproduction of animals by budding, demonstrated that protozoa reproduce by division, found that certain animals can be made to multiply by artificial division, observed cell division (in the multiplication of single-celled algae), and recognized the animal nature of Bryozoa and the sessile coelenterates. His *Mémoires* (on fresh-water polyps, 1744) have been regarded as a model of biological investigation. He was a fellow of the Royal Society.—*D. H. D. R.*

TRENCH: see DEEPS AND TRENCHES.

TRIAL AND ERROR: see ANIMAL BEHAVIOR.

TRIANGLE: a plane figure bounded by three straight line segments, or sides, meeting in three distinct points, or *vertices*. A triangle is the polygon with the least possible number of

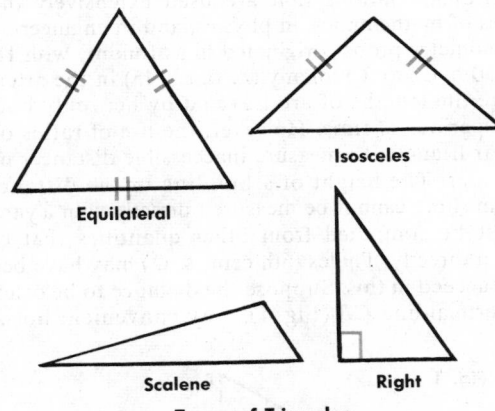

Isosceles

Equilateral

Scalene   Right

Types of Triangles

sides. It is the basic figure in geometry, facts about other rectilinear figures being discovered by decomposing them into triangles. The triangle is of fundamental importance in architecture and engineering. If three bars are bolted together into a triangle the figure is rigid, unlike a quadrilateral or other polygon; a framework composed of a system of triangles is therefore completely rigid. The triangle is also highly important in astronomy, navigation, and surveying. After measuring three parts, one of which must be a side, it is possible to compute all other parts; the techniques for doing this are developed in TRIGONOMETRY. By "triangulation," a large area can be surveyed from one measured base line and subsequently measured angles.

Triangles are classified into *equilateral* triangles, which have all three sides equal; *isosceles* triangles, in which just

two sides are equal; and *scalene* triangles, in which all three sides are different. Any side of a triangle can be considered its base, the corresponding altitude being the perpendicular distance of the opposite vertex from this side. The area of a triangle can be found by multiplying one-half of a base by the corresponding altitude. A basic fact about triangles is that the sum of two sides is always greater than the third. This follows from the still more fundamental theorem that the shortest path between two points is the straight line joining them. In Euclidean geometry the sum of the angles of a triangle is 180°. One angle may be a right angle (90°), in which case the triangle is a right triangle. The side opposite the right angle is called the hypotenuse, and the perpendicular sides are the legs. Perhaps the most familiar theorem of geometry is the PYTHAGOREAN THEOREM, according to which the area of the square formed on the hypotenuse of a right triangle is equal to the sum of the areas of squares formed on the other two sides.—*H. C.*

TRIASSIC PERIOD: see GEOLOGICAL TIME CHART; MESOZOIC ERA.

TRIGONOMETRIC FUNCTIONS: functions derived from the trigonometric ratios; also called *circular functions* because of their intimate connection with a circle. The trigonometric ratios associated with an angle are defined by placing the angle θ on a rectangular coordinate system (Fig. 1) with vertex at O and initial side on the positive x axis; choosing a point P on the terminal side, with coordinates denoted by (a, b), and distance from O equal to r; and naming the ratios of a, b, and r as follows:

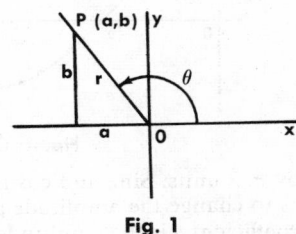

Fig. 1

sine θ = sin θ = b/r,
cosine θ = cos θ = a/r,
tangent θ = tan θ = b/a,
cosecant θ = csc θ = r/b
secant θ = sec θ = r/a
cotangent θ = cot θ = a/b

Since these ratios are independent of the position of P on OP, as long as it is not at O, we can select it with r always 1 unit. That is, we can place P on a unit circle (Fig. 2). Then the ordinate MP is the value of the sine. The sine is clearly a function of the angle θ. The equation $y = \sin \theta$ becomes a functional relation between numerical variables, once we have agreed upon a unit of angular measure. The most convenient unit is the *radian*, the central angle that intercepts an arc equal to the radius (π radians = 180°). In the unit circle the arc AP is θ units long. It is therefore immaterial whether we think of θ as referring to the angle or to the arc.

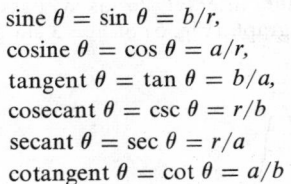

Fig. 2

In order to graph this function we replace θ by x and lay off its values on the x axis. The graph can be formed geometrically as indicated in Fig. 3: make $OQ_1 = AP_1$ and erect $Q_1P'_1 = MP_1$; repeat for as many points of the circle as appear necessary. Passing around the circle a second time produces a repetition of the cycle of values obtained the first time. That is, the function is periodic, with period equal to the length of the circumference, 2π. This fact is expressed by the identity $\sin (x + 2\pi) = \sin x$. The graph oscillates between $+1$ and -1: its amplitude is 1. The curve is known as a sinusoid.

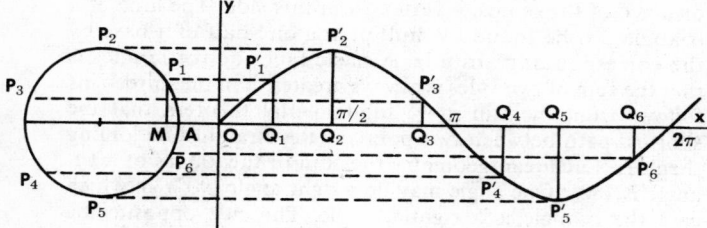

Fig. 3: Development of a sine curve.

A fundamental identity of trigonometry is $\cos x = \sin (x + \pi/2)$. Hence the cosine function is similar to the sine function. The height of its graph for a given value of x is the same as that of the sine function for a value $\pi/2$ units greater. If we move the origin (and y axis) $\pi/2$ units to the right in the graph of $\sin x$, we have (Fig. 4) the graph of $y = \cos x$. These two functions are said to differ in phase

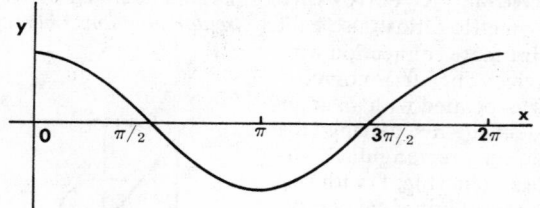

Fig. 4: Cosine curve.

by $\pi/2$ units. Sine and cosine functions can be modified so as to change the amplitude and period. In $y = a \sin bx$, the coefficient a is the amplitude, since the maximum value of a $\sin bx$ is a. The period of this function is $2\pi/b$, since the quantity bx passes through the interval 2π as x passes through the interval $2\pi/b$. The graph (Fig. 5) of $y = 3 \sin 2x$ illustrates these facts.

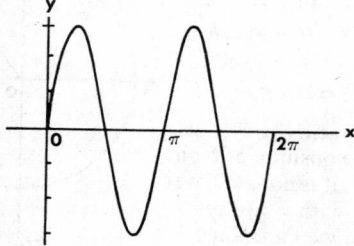

Fig. 5: Graph of $y = 3 \sin 2x$.

The importance of sine and cosine functions in modern science arises from their suitability to represent oscillatory motion. For this reason they are central in the study of sound, light, electromagnetic phenomena, and other vibratory motions. The motion which is the key to understanding many of these phenomena is simple harmonic motion. This can be defined as follows. If a point P moves around a circle at a constant speed, the motion of its projection P' on any diameter is called simple harmonic motion. The sine and cosine functions give the precise relationship between the movements of P and P'. The other four trigonometric functions—tangent, cotangent, secant, and cosecant—stem from the corresponding trigonometric ratios in the same manner as the sine and cosine functions, but are far less important.

By changing the point of view to consider x as a function of y in the relation $y = \sin x$, we arrive at the notion of an

inverse trigonometric function. We write $x = \text{arc sin } y$, or $x = \sin^{-1} y$. This produces a single value of x for each y numerically less than or equal to 1 only if a restriction is placed upon it. The usual restriction is to the principal value of arc sin y, written Arc sin y. This is the value of x having the smallest numerical value for a given value of y. For example, Arc sin $.5 = \pi/6$, and Arc sin $(-.5) = -\pi/6$. The value of Arc sin y ranges (Fig. 6) from $-\pi/2$ to $\pi/2$. If x and y are interchanged by writing $y = \text{Arc sin } x$, then x ranges

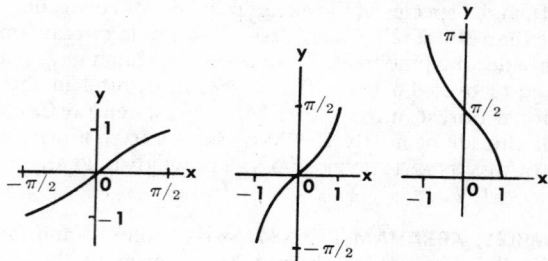

Fig. 6: Graphs of $x = \text{Arc sin } y$ (*left*), $y = \text{Arc sin } x$ (*center*), and $y = \text{Arc cos } x$ (*right*).

from -1 to 1 and y from $-\pi/2$ to $\pi/2$. The principal value of arc cos x, written Arc cos x, is the smallest positive value of y having its cosine equal to x.—*H. C.*

TRIGONOMETRY: originally, a specialized area of geometry concerned with relations among the parts of a triangle, the word trigonometry meaning "triangle measurement." Relations among the parts of a triangle are used in computing the values of some parts from the known values of the others. In its primitive form, trigonometry is little more than a systematic use of the equality of the ratios of the sides of similar figures. This simple beginning, however, gives rise to functional relations that are used extensively in other branches of mathematics, in physics, and in engineering.

Trigonometry proper originated in astronomy with Hipparchus (150 B. C.) and Ptolemy (A. D. *c.* 145) in the attempt to calculate the lengths of arc traveled by heavenly bodies in definite periods of time. However, the use of ratios of sides of similar triangles to measure inaccessible distances may be much older. The height of a building or the distance of a ship from shore cannot be measured directly with a yardstick, but must be computed from other quantities that can be measured directly. Thales (6th cent. B. C.) may have been the first to succeed in this. Suppose the distance to be calculated is the vertical line CB (Fig. 1). Any convenient horizontal

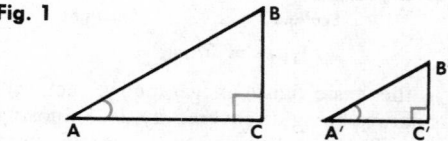

Fig. 1

distance AC can be measured, and the angle BAC can be found with a transit or sextant. We now have a right triangle with right angle at C, and side AC and angle BAC known. If we draw a right triangle $A'B'C'$ with angle $A' = $ angle BAC, its sides are proportional to triangle ABC. In particular, $BC/B'C' = AC/A'C'$ and $BC/AC = B'C'/A'C'$. If $AC = 150$, and, in triangle $A'B'C'$, $A'C' = 2$ and $B'C' = 1$, then $BC/150 = \frac{1}{2}$, whence $BC = 75$.

The Trigonometric Ratios of an Acute Angle: Since the size of an acute angle determines the shape of the right triangle containing it, the acute angle determines the ratios of the sides. Thus, for each acute angle there are definite values of the ratios. For convenience they are given names:

sine of angle $A = \sin A = CB/AB =$ side opposite $A \div$ hypotenuse

cosine of angle $A = \cos A = AC/AB =$ side adjacent to $A \div$ hypotenuse

tangent of angle $A = \tan A = CB/AC =$ side opposite $A \div$ side adjacent to A

cosecant of angle $A = \csc A = AB/CB =$ hypotenuse $\div$ side opposite A

secant of angle $A = \sec A = AB/AC =$ hypotenuse $\div$ side adjacent to A

cotangent of angle $A = \cot A = AC/CB =$ side adjacent to $A \div$ side opposite A

If the values of these trigonometric ratios were tabulated for all acute angles, a problem like the example given could be solved without constructing a similar triangle. Instead, we would write $\tan A = CB/AC$, whence $CB = AC \tan A$. In this case $\tan A = \frac{1}{2}$, $AC = 150$, and therefore $CB = 75$. By means of these ratios, if we know one side and one other part, in addition to the right angle of a right triangle, we can find the unknown parts. Values of the ratios have been tabulated for all acute angles.

Angles of Any Size: The trigonometric ratios are extended to angles of any size as follows. First, place the angle θ on a coordinate system with its vertex at the origin O and one side on the positive horizontal axis, as in Fig. 2. We think of this side as the initial side, and the terminal side is reached by a rotation about O, considered positive if it is counter-

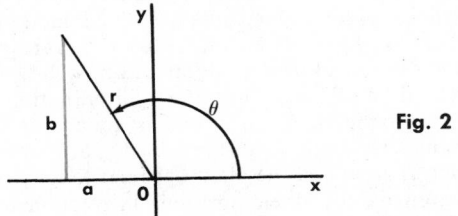

Fig. 2

clockwise and negative if it is clockwise. Any point P on the terminal side other than O is a distance a from the vertical axis, a distance b from the horizontal, and lies at a distance r from O. We now define: $\sin \theta = b/r$, $\cos \theta = a/r$, $\tan \theta = b/a$, $\csc \theta = r/b$, $\sec \theta = r/a$, $\cot \theta = a/b$. Here a is positive if it is measured from O to the right, negative if to the left; b is positive if it is measured from O upward, negative if downward; and r is always positive. Exceptions must be made for any ratio having a zero denominator; e.g. there is no tangent of $90°$. It is clear that these definitions extend, but do not conflict with, the right triangle definitions. The extended definitions are useful for dealing with oblique triangles, i.e. triangles containing no right angle, and for the creation of the trigonometric functions. For solving oblique triangles, two formulas are of special importance: the law of sines and the law of cosines. If the side opposite the angle A is a, the side opposite angle B is b, and that opposite angle C is c, the law of sines states that $a/\sin A = b/\sin B = c/\sin C$. The law of cosines is $a^2 = b^2 + c^2 - 2bc \cos A$. These two formulas are sufficient for the solution of all oblique triangles.

Trigonometric Functions: The trigonometric ratios are clearly functions of an angle; i.e. for each angle the six ratios are determined, with exceptions as noted. If the angle is measured in terms of an agreed unit, they become functions of a numerical

variable. For most purposes it is convenient to let the angle be measured in radians, a radian being the angle at the center of a circle which intercepts an arc equal in length to the radius. Since one revolution of $360°$ contains 2π radians, or $360°$, one radian is equivalent to $180/\pi$ degrees. To write $y = \sin \theta$ is to give a rule for determining a value of y for each numerical value of θ, and therefore this equation is a functional relation. The six geometric ratios thus yield six numerical functions. These functions constitute the chief contributions of trigonometry to modern mathematics. (See TRIGONOMETRIC FUNCTIONS.)

Identities: It is at once apparent that the six functions are not independent. There are several fundamental identities which connect them. In particular, $\tan \theta = (\sin \theta)/(\cos \theta)$; $\csc \theta = 1/\sin \theta$; $\sec \theta = 1/\cos \theta$; $\cot \theta = 1/\tan \theta$; $\sin^2\theta + \cos^2\theta = 1$; $\tan^2\theta + 1 = \sec^2\theta$; $\cot^2\theta + 1 = \csc^2\theta$ (where $\sin^2\theta$ is written for $(\sin \theta)^2$, etc.). Other identities connect functions of θ, $\theta \pm \pi/2$, $\theta \pm \pi$, etc. For example, $\sin (\theta + \pi/2) = \cos \theta$; $\sin(\theta + \pi) = -\sin \theta$. A particularly important set of relations result from the fact that the values of the functions repeat as the angle rotates beyond 2π radians. Each of them has the same value for $x + 2\pi$ as for x. The tangent and cotangent repeat even oftener, since $\tan (x + \pi) = \tan x$, and $\cot (x + \pi) = \cot x$. Because of this repetition the functions are said to be periodic. The period of sine, cosine, cosecant, and secant is 2π, and that of tangent and cotangent is π. A further set of identities govern the combination of two or more independent variables. These grow out of the addition formulas:

$$\sin (\theta + \phi) = \sin \theta \cos \phi + \cos \theta \sin \phi$$
$$\cos (\theta + \phi) = \cos \theta \cos \phi - \sin \theta \sin \phi.$$

Trigonometric Equations: There are usually two steps in solving an equation whose terms are trigonometric—to find the values of some trigonometric function of x, and then to determine x. For example, if $2 \sin^2 x + \sin x - 1 = 0$, we first solve the quadratic equation for $\sin x$. This can be done by factoring, $(2 \sin x - 1) \cdot (\sin x + 1) = 0$. Hence $\sin x = \frac{1}{2}$, or $\sin x = -1$. Now $\sin x = \frac{1}{2}$ is satisfied by $x = \pi/6$ (or $30°$), and $\sin x = -1$ by $x = \pi$ (or $180°$). Hence $\pi/6$ and π are solutions of the given equation. But they are not the only solutions. Because of the periodicity of the sine, $(\pi/6 + 2\pi)$ and $(\pi + 2\pi)$ are also solutions, as are many other values. A trigonometric equation therefore has many solutions if it has any. We often, although not always, restrict the solution to the principal values.

Spherical Trigonometry: A specialized branch of trigonometry is concerned with solving spherical triangles. The curves on a sphere which correspond to straight lines in a plane are the great circles, i.e. circles whose center is the center of the sphere. On Earth the equator and the meridian circles are great circles, whereas the circles of latitude other than the equator are small circles. A spherical triangle is a figure on the surface of a sphere which is bounded by arcs of three great circles. In such a triangle both angles and sides are measured in angular units. Each of the sides is an arc of a circle whose radius is that of the sphere. With the radius as the unit of measure of length, the number of units in the arc is the same as the number of radians in the corresponding central angle. If a side of a spherical triangle is given as a number of degrees, then the angle at the center of the sphere which intercepts this arc has the same measure.

The sum of the angles of a spherical triangle can be any number of degrees between $180°$ and $540°$. If one of them is a right angle, we have a spherical right triangle. Two, or even three, angles may be right angles, but in any such case the solution of the triangle is almost trivial. Formulas for solving spherical right triangles are summarized by two statements, known as Napier's rules, devised by John Napier who invented logarithms. Let C denote the right angle. Now arrange in a circle the five quantities, a, b, A', c', B', where $A' = 90° - A$, $c' = 90° - c$, and $B' = 90° - B$, following the same order as a b A c B in the triangle (Fig. 3). Napier's rules state that, in this arrangement, (1) the sine of any part is equal to the

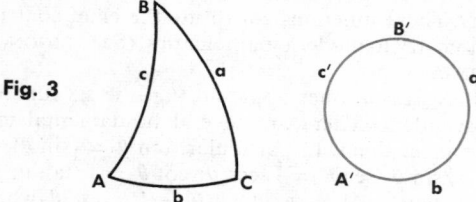

Fig. 3

product of the cosines of the two opposite (non-adjacent) parts, and (2) the sine of any part is equal to the product of the tangents of the two adjacent parts. For example,

$$\sin a = \cos A' \cos c' = \cos (90° - A) \cos (90° - c)$$
$$= \sin A \sin c$$

and

$$\sin a = \tan b \tan B' = \tan b \tan (90° - B) = \tan b \cot B$$

With these rules it is possible to solve any spherical right triangle if two of the five parts are given.

For spherical oblique triangles we have the law of sines: $(\sin a)/(\sin A) = (\sin b)/(\sin B) = (\sin c)/(\sin C)$; and the law of cosines: $\cos a = \cos b \cos c + \sin b \sin c \cos A$. In these formulas a small letter denotes the side opposite the angle labeled by the same letter capitalized. Spherical trigonometry has applications in astronomy and navigation, although in modern navigation, practical results are obtained from tables. —*H. C.*

TRIPLE POINT: the conditions of temperature and pressure at which solid, liquid, and gaseous phases of a pure crystalline substance are in equilibrium with one another. Since boiling is a manifestation of an equilibrium between the liquid and gaseous phases, and the beginning of freezing a manifestation of an equilibrium between the liquid and solid phases, at the triple point a substance is theoretically capable of either freezing, boiling, or condensing completely. In actuality, to supply

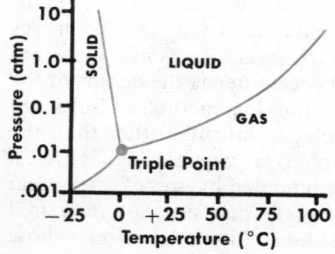

Pressure-temperature graph (phase diagram) for water shows triple point at 0.01°C and 0.006 atm pressure.

the energy necessary for these phase changes the temperature and/or pressure must be adjusted slightly away from the triple point in the appropriate direction. —*E. M. R.*

TRITIUM: the heaviest isotope of HYDROGEN (symbol T or H^3). It has 2 neutrons and 1 proton, its mass number (atomic weight) being 3. Tritium is found in infinitesimal quantities naturally and can be produced by irradiating lithium. It is radioactive, decaying by beta-particle emission, and has a half-life of 12.5 yr.—*D. P. B.*

TROJAN GROUP: asteroids moving in the same orbit as the planet Jupiter, with mean positions either 60° ahead or 60° behind Jupiter; *i.e.* they occupy one of the vertices of an equilateral triangle with the Sun and Jupiter at the other two. Trojans correspond to a special solution of the THREE-BODY PROBLEM: the equilateral triangle thus formed is a stable configuration. Actually, a Trojan may oscillate as much as 40° from its mean position, and PERTURBATIONS by Saturn may cause its ejection from the group, whereas others may be captured. To distinguish them from ordinary asteroids, they are named for Homeric heroes. The first, Achilles, was discovered in 1906. At present, nine are known in the position ahead of Jupiter and five behind.—*S. D. G.*

TROPISM and TAXIS: oriented movements of organisms in response to external stimuli. Present usage seems to favor confining the meaning of tropism to growth and turgor movements, while using the term taxis for movement involving locomotor structures of animals. A tropism (literally "a turning") is achieved through differences in the rate of growth or in the turgor of special cells. The roots and stem tips of plants respond to gravity, roots growing toward the earth (positive *geotropism*), stem tips away (negative geotropism). Both stems and roots show growth responses to light (*phototropism*). Response to wind is *anemotropism;* to electric currents, *galvanotropism;* and to contact with surfaces, *thigmotropism* or *stereotropism*. The turning of a sunflower to face the light is another example of a phototropic response, although it may be achieved in part through changes in the turgor of cells rather than growth in the stalk.

Many tropisms are caused by differences in the concentration of plant growth hormones (auxins). When light strikes a growing stem tip only on one side, leaving the other shaded, auxins in the shadowed side stimulate stem elongation, whereas those on the lighted side are inactivated and enlongation there is slight. These differences in rate of growth around the stem bend it until illumination of the growing regions is equal on all sides. In uniform illumination, the light intensity may be high enough to inactivate auxins all around the stem and keep a plant short and bushy, or may be so faint that growth is great and the plant becomes long and straggly.

Many animals alter their positions in relation to definite stimuli, and are said to show tactic responses in this orientation. Those that face toward or away from a light source, or at some definite angle to it, show phototaxis. Orientation with respect to gravity is geotaxis; to a current of water or air, rheotaxis; to a current of electricity, galvanotaxis. To show a tactic response, the animal need not move in any direction; a mere turning is enough. But often a tactic orientation is followed by movement elicited by a continuation of the same stimulus. See PLANT MOVEMENTS.—*L. and M. M.*

TROPOPAUSE: in meteorology, the boundary between troposphere and STRATOSPHERE. It is defined as the lowest point in the atmosphere at which the average decrease of temperature with height, or LAPSE RATE, becomes less than 2°C (3.6°F) per km. The tropopause consists of several discrete, overlapping "leaves" rather than a single, continuous layer and is about 11 mi above sea level at the equator and 5 mi at the poles. See also JET STREAM.—*D. H. L.*

TROPOSPHERE: see ATMOSPHERE.

TRUTH, THEORIES OF: Most philosophical theories of truth attempt to specify the meaning of the term "is true" when it is applied to statements or propositions. Others attempt to stipulate the conditions that must obtain before we can apply the term "is true" in that manner. The best-known traditional theories of truth are the *correspondence* and the *coherence* theories. In rough-and-ready terms, defenders of the correspondence theory maintain that a statement is true if it corresponds to the state of affairs it purports to describe. Unfortunately, some champion the dubious theory that our sensations are copies of reality—but the latter, then, is not essential to the correspondence theory. Many philosophers object to the correspondence theory on the grounds that it suggests that statements can be tested in isolation from others, and insist that scientific statements are always tested as parts of a system; hence one should discuss the truth of theories taken as units and conclude that a theory as a whole is true if it is consistent and makes possible a coherent account of experience. Against the latter viewpoint (the coherence approach), proponents of the *pragmatic* theory of truth insist that the only way of knowing that a system is coherent is to employ it predictively and see if it works successfully.

Another approach is the semantic theory of truth developed by Alfred Tarski. Its supporters object that most other theories do not carefully specify the properties of the language and the rules that must be satisfied by statements in that language before they can be considered true or false. Tarski has shown that, unless such rules are carefully stipulated, contradictions arise. It is one of the aims of the semantic theory of truth to stipulate the nature and rules of the language in which truth assertions can be made.

Two points remain to be mentioned. Truth is to be distinguished from *falsehood,* not from probability or the evidence for it; hence it is misleading to say that scientific statements are merely probable and hence not true. Finally, some philosophers insist that "is true" is not a descriptive predicate and that we add nothing by saying about a statement that it is true; all we do is reiterate it with force.—*S. M.*

TSIOLKOVSKY, KONSTANTIN EDUARDOVICH, 1857–1935, Russian schoolteacher and pioneer in rocket propulsion; b. Kaluga. Entirely self-taught in physics, mathematics, and engineering, he anticipated many of the problems and possibilities of rocket research, artificial satellites, and space travel. His most famous scientific paper, *Probing of Space by means of Jet Devices* (1903), outlines the theoretical basis on which a jet-propelled space craft could be constructed. He is also the author of *Fantasies of Earth and Sky* (1895) and *Beyond the Earth* (1920), both science fiction, and *Space Rocket Trains* (1929), outlining the principles of multistage rockets.—*S. D. G.*

TSUNAMI: one of a series of oceanic water waves (popularly called *tidal waves*) usually originating at or near the epicenter of an earthquake, located beneath or at the margins of an ocean. The maximum height of the waves in various tsunamis has ranged from a few inches to over 100 ft. There are often six or more waves, with periods of 5 to 30 min. Some tsunamis last many hours and even days. Large displacements of the ocean floor, caused by faulting, submarine slides, submarine volcanic activity, and landslides, have been suggested as causes of tsunamis. A few tsunamis are known to have been started by gigantic oceanic volcanic explosions (Krakatoa, 1883); others have accompanied great storms and typhoons. Whatever the mechanism, the surface configuration of the ocean is abruptly changed; the inertia of the water returning toward a level surface carries it beyond equilibrium and sets the surface into oscillation. The resulting waves travel with a velocity $\sqrt{gh}$, where g is the gravitational acceleration and h is the ocean depth. Typical velocities in the deep oceans are 450–500 mi/hr. The amplitude of these waves decreases with distance from the source. At large distances their wavelengths are in the range of hundreds of miles, while their amplitudes are several feet; as a result they are not usually detected by ships at sea. When such waves strike coastal areas, even after propagating many thousands of miles, great destruction may result. Their effect is most severe in long V-shaped bays, which magnify the waves as they sweep into the bay. On a shallow coast, the observed sequence of events is often a recession of the water outward, often a mile or more, followed within several minutes by a wave advance which can inundate large areas.

Among the most destructive tsunamis was that of June 15, 1896, which devastated the Sanriku district of Japan, taking 27,000 lives. The epicenter of the associated earthquake was located some 200 km offshore; waves attained a height of 60 ft. This tsunami was recorded on the San Francisco tide gage 4,780 mi away, having traversed the Pacific Ocean in 10 hr 34 min, with a mean speed of 450 mi/hr. An earthquake in the same area, Mar. 2, 1933, produced an even more devastating tsunami, with wave heights of 75 ft recorded in Japan and 11 ft near San Francisco, Calif. On Aug. 8, 1868, a series of waves reaching a height of 47 ft devastated the harbor of Arica, Chile; this tsunami accompanied a large earthquake in the same region, and extensive damage resulted in Hawaii. On Apr. 1, 1946, an earthquake in the Aleutian Is. produced a large tsunami, with waves of over 100 ft near the epicenter and 55 ft on Hawaii, causing extensive loss of life and destruction of property.—*Sa. K.*

TUNDRA: treeless country beyond the northernmost limits of the forests. Tundra is much more developed in the northern hemisphere, in N America and Eurasia, because this hemisphere has more subpolar land area than the

Mound of earth raised and split by frost action reveals permafrost underlying the vegetation. Such mounds, called pingoes, are common in tundra. (*U. S. Geological Survey*)

southern hemisphere. The winters on the tundra are long and very cold; summers are cool. Average temperature of the warmer months is less than 50°F, but more than 32°F. During some of the warmer days, temperatures slightly over 70° have been measured. Because of the intense cold, which has endured for tens of thousands of years, water in the ground is frozen to depths of a few score to more than 1,500 ft. During warmer months, this *permafrost* melts for a very few feet below the surface, allowing growth of sedges, grasses, and shrubs. Upon this vegetation feed a host of Arctic animals—reindeer, caribou, muskox, and many others. Most of the tundra in very recent time was covered by ice sheets like those now present on Antarctica and Greenland.—*N. E. A. H.*

TUNGSTEN: a metallic element (W) at. no. 74; at. wt 183.86; density 19.3; mp 3370°C; bp 5900°C; valences 2,4,5, and 6. Tungsten occurs principally in the ores wolframite, (Fe, Mn) WO_4, and scheelite, $CaWO_4$. It is obtained by fusing the ores with sodium carbonate to form sodium tungstate and precipitating the tungstic acid by digestion with hydrochloric acid. Intense heating of tungstic acid with carbon or hydrogen produces the pure metal. In 1781 the Swedish chemist Carl Wilhelm Scheele showed that the mineral then known as "tungsten" (now called scheelite), and thought to be a tin compound, really contains a new acid, which he called tungstic acid. The oxide of tungsten was soon recognized, and the element itself was isolated in 1783 by the Spanish brothers J. J. and Don Fausto d'Elhuyar. Tungsten is used in filaments of light bulbs, in electrical contact points, and in targets in x-ray tubes. But

its greatest use is in alloys. Tungsten steels have the property of maintaining their hardness even when red hot, and thus can be used for high-speed cutting tools. Tungsten carbide is used as a refactory material and in cutting tools. Tungstic acid (H_2WO_4) and its addition complexes are used in chemical processing as catalysts and precipitants.—*A. M. S.*

TUNNEL: an enclosed underground passage, usually horizontal or nearly so. Most tunnels are for transportation—for pedestrian use and to accommodate canals, railroads, and highways. Tunnels are also used in mining to approach and remove subsurface mineral deposits, as water mains, as sewers, as culverts for drainage, and as conduits for electric and other utility lines. Highways and railroads, along with the increased need of water for all purposes, *e.g.* hydroelectric power production, irrigation, and general use, have provided most of the reasons for modern tunnel construction. Modern tunneling techniques were initiated in the 19th cent., but many ancient peoples built tunnels, *e.g.* the water-supply tunnel built in Samos in 687 B. C.; the highway tunnel built at Furlo by the Roman Emperor Vespasian in A. D. 78; and various other tunnels built through solid rock by the Egyptians and the Aztecs.

Tunnels through Solid Rock: Tunneling through solid rock entails breaking and removing (mucking) the rock, constructing interior structural supports, and, for tunnels of any size, providing a means of ventilation. The Romans and their predecessors shattered rock by heating its face with open fires and then pouring cold water on it; this practice pre-

Subaqueous tunneling: Longitudinal cross-section (*below*) of third tube of Lincoln Tunnel, and exterior view of concrete bulkhead (*right*), show how construction of a subaqueous tunnel progresses. As shield is pushed ahead into unexcavated material (*far left of longitudinal cross-section*), workmen dig out silt; at right of shield, cast-iron sections are bolted together to form the circular tube, then sealed with grout (equal parts of Portland cement and sand) to resist external pressure of silt and river. Beyond concrete bulkhead are air locks designed (1) to preserve the greater-than-atmospheric pressure in working end of tunnel when silt is removed or construction materials brought in, (2) to prepare workmen by slow compression for entrance into high-pressure zone of tunnel, and (3) to decompress workmen at the end of their working day at a rate slow enough so that they will not get caisson disease. (*Port of N. Y. Authority*)

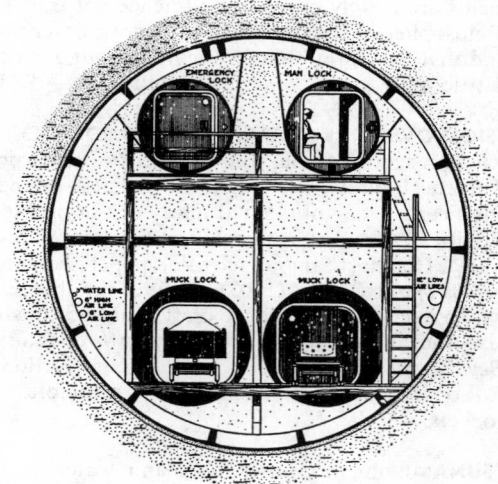

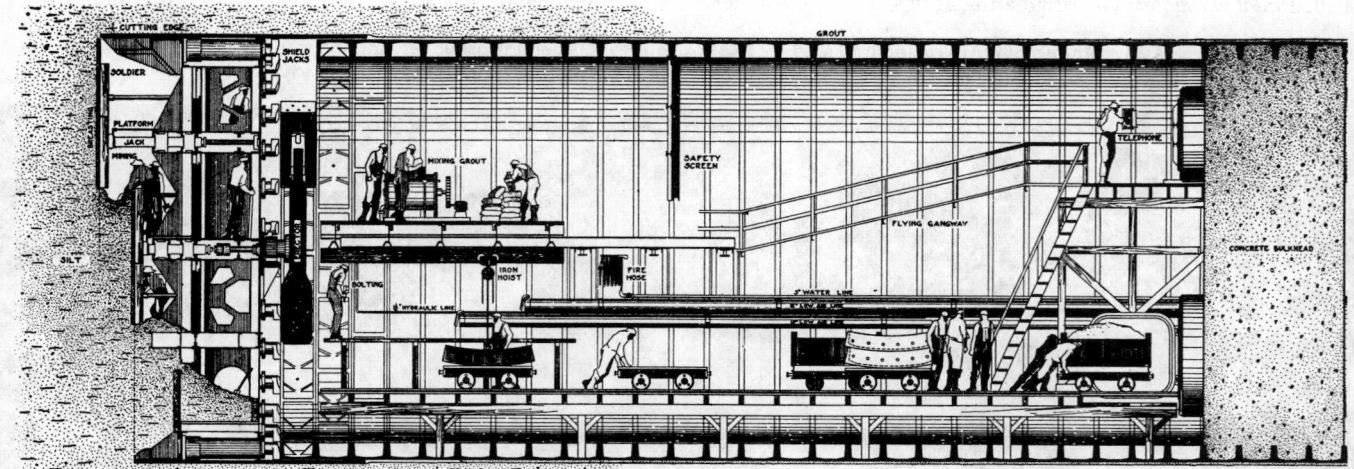

Tunnel shield: Workmen are assembling nine-section, 240-ton shield that was used to drive the third tube of Lincoln Tunnel. (*Port of N. Y. Authority*)

vailed up through the medieval era. The process of drilling holes in rock, filling the holes with explosives, and detonating these was utilized for the first time in the construction (1857–71) of the Mt Cenis tunnel connecting Italy and France through the Alps. Hand drilling was used in the early work at Mt Cenis, but this tunnel's construction was markedly accelerated by the introduction of the compressed-air drill developed by G. Sommeiller in 1861. (GUNPOWDER, used for blasting at Mt Cenis, was superseded in subsequent Alpine tunneling by nitroglycerin and, later, by DYNAMITE. See also EXPLOSIVE.) The Mt Cenis tunnel introduced engineers to many of the problems associated with all deep rock tunnel construction, *e.g.* the high temperatures encountered in mountains and the high stresses transmitted to the mass of surrounding rock by the weight of the overlying material. Extensive geological explorations of a tunnel's proposed route became mandatory as engineers became aware of the danger of encountering rock faults which would weaken the tunnel excavation. In the late 19th cent., *headings* were commonly used. These are small tunnels excavated along the entire proposed path of the large tunnel for the purpose of inspecting the tunnel's route; their small dimensions allow them to be built rapidly, with minimum interior bracing. Headings that precede the full excavation by only one day have also been common and are occasionally still used; they allow the more convenient removal of the full cross-section of the tunnel. Present-day practice, however, favors the removal of the whole cross-section at once whenever this is practicable; it is faster and therefore more economical. Where complex geological conditions are expected, pioneer or pilot headings are still drilled the complete length of the tunnel. Because of higher labor costs, U. S. engineers make greater use than do European engineers of highly mechanized drilling and mucking equipment. Batteries of compressed-air drills using interchangeable carbide bits are mounted on movable platforms; these *jumbo rigs* drill the holes in which the blasting formulations are inserted.

Tunnels through Dry Earth: In dry earth, even the small headings (*drifts*) commonly used in mining operations must be protected from cave-ins; timber polings and braces have been used for this purpose since medieval times. Dry-earth tunneling on a larger scale, however, did not become possible until the introduction of the *shield*, invented by Marc I. Brunel in 1818 and further developed by James Henry Greathead (1844–96), whose Greathead shield was used in the construction of the first underground railway in London (1886–90). The shield is a cylinder of cast iron or cast steel, 3 to 6 ft in length, with a diameter slightly less than the diameter of the tunnel. Its action can be compared to driving a tin can, both of whose ends have been removed, horizontally through sand. As the tunnel is dug, the interior surface behind the shield is lined with circular cast-iron ribs to prevent cave-ins. Hydraulic jacks between the last-placed cast-iron ring and the rear of the shield are used to push the cutting rim of the shield into the soil to be excavated. If the earth is solid enough, it can be excavated the length of the shield before the shield's next advance. After the shield is advanced, the jacks are removed temporarily and a cast-iron ring is added to the others making up the lining. The jacks are then replaced and the shield is advanced again. The shield has a circular cross-section because (1) as the shield advances it tends to rotate, and (2) the circle is the smallest perimeter for any given cross-section and best resists the stresses of the surrounding earth.

Subaqueous Tunneling: For tunnels built beneath bodies of water, the shield must have a solid diaphragm over the face pushing against the unexcavated soil. The diaphragm is so constructed that one part at a time can be removed. Usually a plank of the diaphragm is removed, the earth behind it excavated for a specified depth, the plank replaced, another plank removed, and the process repeated until the whole area behind the diaphragm is excavated. The shield is then advanced. In tunneling through very plastic silts, such as those underlying the Hudson River, the shield is advanced, allowing the silt to extrude through an opening in the diaphragm into the tunnel, whence it is removed. In the construction of the Queens-Midtown Tunnel in New York City, the hand excavation of the material behind the diaphragm of the shield was made necessary because of the varying character of the soils under the East River. To prevent water, under great hydrostatic pressure, from seeping in, subaqueous excavations are filled with compressed air at the same pressure as the water at that depth. This technique, patented by Lord Cochrane in 1830, was not put into use until 1879. The depth of tunnels using compressed air in their construction is limited to 110 ft, since men are usually not allowed to work under pressures greater than 50 lb/in.^{2}. The method of constructing sections of a subaqueous tunnel on land, transporting them to their location, and sinking them in position in a trench previously dredged has been increasingly used, although there are many situations where this method is not practicable, *e.g.* where underwater currents are particularly strong. A method of building a tunnel under a body of shallow water is to use sheetpiling to construct a COFFERDAM, *i.e.* a vertical surface of interlocking steel sections which acts to separate a chosen area from surrounding waters; water is pumped out of the area behind the cofferdam, the resulting dry area is excavated and the tunnel constructed. The area is then overlayed with earth and the water permitted to recover the site.

Cut and Cover: This is the simplest and cheapest method of tunneling through dry earth, and is used wherever a tunnel is placed no deeper than 30 ft from the surface. A trench is dug, the tunnel lining (usually concrete) is constructed, and then the ditch is refilled. Such open-trench methods have been used in the construction of various New York subways.

NOTABLE TUNNELS OF THE WORLD

Name	Length	Year Completed
Lebanon, Pa., Tunnel (*Railroad*)	720 ft	1827
Thames Tunnel, England (*Pedestrian*)	1,200 ft	1843
Mt Cenis Tunnel, Switzerland (*Railroad*)	7½ mi	1871
Hoosac Tunnel, Mass. (*Railroad*)	4¾ mi	1876
Rothschonberger Tunnel, Germany (*Mining*)	31½ mi	1877
St. Gotthard Tunnel, Switzerland (*Railroad*)	9¼ mi	1882
Pennsylvania R. R. Tunnel, Pa. (*Railroad*)	900 ft	1883
Mersey River Tunnel, England (*Highway*)	2½ mi	1886
Severn River Tunnel, England (*Railroad*)	4⅓ mi	1886
Croton Aqueduct, N. Y. (*Water Supply*)	31 mi	1890
Sarnia Tunnel, Michigan (*Railroad*)	6,000 ft	1891
Twin McAdoo Tunnels, N. Y. (*Railroad*)	1 mi	1904
Delaware Aqueduct, N. Y. (*Water Supply*)	85 mi	1942
Kammon Highway Tunnel, Japan (*Highway*)	2 mi	1958
Mt Blanc Tunnel, France (*Highway*)	7.3 mi	1962

The Problem of Ventilation: With the successful construction of longer tunnels, ventilation has become a major problem. During the trial runs made after the opening of the Mt Cenis tunnel, two locomotive engineers died of suffocation. Steam locomotives ascending a grade to an exit portal of a tunnel so filled the tunnel with smoke that engineers and passengers were threatened. The use of engines with reduced exhaust smoke somewhat alleviated the situation, and vertical shafts with exhaust fans have also been fairly successful. However, in the Alps, such shafts are unfeasible, and alpine tunnels have come to rely on the Saccardo system, which utilizes a fan that blows air through a portal chamber into the tunnel; this air then serves to draw in with it outside air on a path coaxial with the tunnel. Electric-powered locomotives have helped reduce the danger resulting from smoke, and, at present, ventilation is accomplished in a number of mountain tunnels by closing the entrance portal after the train enters the tunnel and then creating a forced draft by the use of fans. The highway tunnel has the added problem of a high concentration of carbon monoxide from the exhaust of motor-vehicle engines. In the Holland Tunnel, the first (1927) automotive tunnel long enough to raise the problem of carbon-monoxide poisoning, effective ventilation was achieved by fans located above ground which force air into a conduit running the full length of the tunnel. Air from the conduit is forced from vents at floor level at approximately 10-ft intervals; the air travels transversely across the roadway and returns to an exhaust conduit on the other side of the tunnel. A similar system has been designed for the Mt Blanc Tunnel, which is the longest (7.3 mi) highway tunnel in the world.—*A. L.*

TUNNEL EFFECT: Quantum theory states that even if an electron does not have enough energy to surmount a POTENTIAL BARRIER, it has a finite probability of penetrating or "tunneling" through the barrier. The probability increases if the barrier is thin and low. Examples are FIELD EMISSION from cold cathodes and the emission of particles from radioactive nuclei (see RADIOACTIVITY).—*I. R.*

TURBINE: a wheel or cylinder with buckets, paddles, or blades arranged on its circumference so that an impinging flow of liquid or gas will apply a torque or rotational force to set the wheel or cylinder in motion. It converts some of the energy of the fluid's motion to mechanical energy, which is then conducted by the drive shaft to supply mechanical power to drive a machine. A *waterwheel* or a *hydraulic turbine* utilizes water that has been given kinetic energy by the constant force of gravity, *e.g.* a rapidly flowing waterway or water falling from a dammed reservoir. In both the *steam turbine* and the *gas turbine,* heat and pressure are employed to move a gas, thus giving the gas kinetic energy. The turbine's ancestor, the overshot waterwheel, moved only under the weight of water loaded into buckets at the top of the wheel, pulling them down on one side while empty buckets came up on the other side. In the undershot wheel—dipping into the water like the paddlewheel of an old river boat—the impact (or impulse) of swiftly moving water against the wheel's paddles moves the wheel, which can move only as rapidly as the stream flows. In the breast wheel, water was impacted at the middle of the wheel and turned the wheel both by weight and by impact. In modern *hydraulic turbines,* the moving part may be a wheel with shallow dish-like blades (Pelton wheel) which take the impact of water jetted from a nozzle behind which there is great pressure from a higher body of water. Or, if less pressure is available, the turbine may be shaped like a marine propeller. In another configuration, the blades are set at an angle to the wheel's radius; water comes in simultaneously around the circumference, strikes the blades a glancing blow, and is discharged through the center of the wheel.

Impulse and Reaction Principles: Force supplied to the turbine is of two general types: *impulse,* by which the turbine rotor blades are moved in the same direction as the flowing fluid; and *reaction,* by which the turbine rotor blades are

Hydraulic turbine propeller, being installed at Fort Loudon Dam, is of type used where the head (*i.e.* difference between upstream and downstream levels) is low. Tilt of blade is adjustable in order to maintain operating efficiency as head varies. (*TVA*)

moved in one direction while the fluid flow impacting upon them is deflected in another direction. Blading is thus described as either impulse or reaction, depending on which kind of force it is designed to utilize; advanced turbines often combine the two types of blading. The velocity of a fluid has two components, speed and direction; if there is a change in either of these components, a force results. In the operation of the firehose, water ejected under pressure from a NOZZLE is capable of exerting a high impact (impulse) force; but a reactive force is also evident, pushing back on the hose and requiring the firemen to lean heavily against the hose. This reactive force results from an increase of speed (and drop in pressure) of the water as it flows out the nozzle into an area of lower pressure. These principles are utilized in steam turbines where steam escaping from a stationary nozzle to an area of lower pressure expands and picks up speed before hitting the turbine blading. In some steam and gas turbines, fluid flows down the length of a cylinder, passing through several series of helically arranged blades. At each stage, the casing around the turbine is enlarged slightly; this enlargement produces a decrease in pressure with an attendant increase in the velocity of the steam or gas. Such an arrangement imparts a reaction force (owing to the acceleration of the steam or gas) to the blade just passed, and an increased impulse force to the blade that is upcoming. See ENGINE; GAS TURBINE; STEAM ENGINE.—K. A.

TURBOJET: see AIRCRAFT PROPULSION.

TURBULENCE: a disordered motion of air or other fluid generally characterized by random fluctuations in the fluid velocity. Turbulence often looks like a superposition of irregular swirls or eddies constantly changing in form and size. Turbulent motion is a common occurrence, and can be seen in a ship's wake, pipe flow, rising cigarette smoke, engine exhaust gases, or the atmosphere on a windy day. Turbulence is not well understood, but is thought to have its origins in the viscous nature of fluids. The energy in a turbulent fluid is continually being transferred from the larger-scale motions to smaller motions and is eventually dissipated as random motion of the molecules. This is exemplified by the wake far behind a ship or airplane.—D. B.

In meteorology, the term turbulence is applied to irregular, apparently random, short-period fluctuations in the speed of the wind. The speed fluctuations are both horizontal and vertical. Turbulence occurs at low levels over rough terrain, in the rising air beneath cumuliform clouds and in the clouds themselves, and at high levels (20,000 ft and over) both in clouds and in clear air. Clear-air turbulence, sometimes found associated with the JET STREAM, is caused by the strong speed differences between winds at different levels (vertical wind-shear) and by the rapid changes in wind speed across short distances at the same level (horizontal wind-shear) that are typical of the jet-stream region; it is also found in the giant eddies on the lee side of mountains (mountain waves). Turbulence (often called "rough air") causes discomfort to fliers and air passengers; heavy turbulence often causes temporary difficulty in controlling aircraft and, in extreme cases, structural damage. Turbulence is one of the least understood of meteorological phenomena; thus it is very difficult or impossible to forecast.—P. L.

TURGOR: the normal state of tension of the wall of a cell, especially a plant cell. The cell becomes swollen and the cell wall rigid because there is a greater tendency for water to enter the cell by OSMOSIS than to escape. When plant cells lose their turgor as the result of certain environmental conditions (e.g. when rate of evaporation from leaves is more rapid than rate of absorption of water through roots), the plant wilts—a condition known on the cellular level as *plasmolysis.* Some plant cells alternate between periods of turgidity and plas-

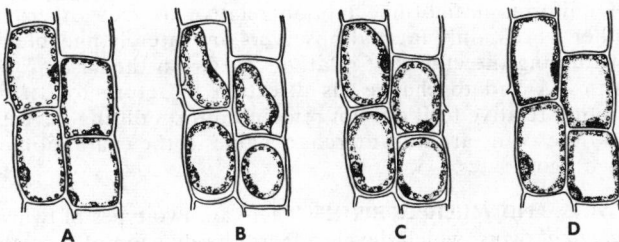

Loss and recovery of turgor: Leaf cells of *Elodea*, an aquatic plant, (A) show normal turgor when in water, (B) become plasmolyzed 2 min after being placed in salt solution, (C) partially recover shortly after being put back in water, and (D) fully recover after ½ hr in water. (*From Kenoyer*)

molysis, but if the plasmolysis is severe, the cells may die. Variations in turgor are responsible for certain PLANT MOVEMENTS.—R. G. M.

TURPENTINE (or **oil of turpentine**): an essential oil obtained by distillation from resinous exudates of certain trees. Chiefly a mixture of TERPENES, it is a colorless or slightly yellow liquid with important uses as a solvent in paints and varnishes. —*Ru. M.*

TWILIGHT: the period of time after sunset, or before sunrise, when the Sun is below the horizon but its light, scattered by Earth's atmosphere, illuminates the sky. After sunset, civil twilight lasts until the Sun's center is 6° below the horizon; astronomical twilight lasts until the Sun's center is 18° below the horizon, after which the faintest visible stars can be seen. The same phenomena recur in reverse order before sunrise. The duration of twilight depends upon latitude and time of year. Astronomical twilight is shortest at the equator (about $1^h 10^m$) because the Sun's diurnal path is perpendicular to the horizon there. At the summer solstice, astronomical twilight persists all night north of latitude $48\frac{1}{2}°$, and civil twilight north of $60\frac{1}{2}°$. North of $66\frac{1}{2}°$, the Sun at the summer solstice remains above the horizon all night (see MIDNIGHT SUN).—M. W. O.

TWIN PARADOX (or **clock paradox**): a consequence of the theory of RELATIVITY, often quoted in support of the contention that this theory is self-contradictory. According to Einstein, a clock in motion runs more slowly than a clock at rest; he believed also that biological processes are similarly slowed—*e.g.* heartbeat may be likened to a clock—hence physiological aging would also be retarded in a man moving at high speeds. The slowing-up of a clock in motion, called *time dilatation,* was verified indirectly by the laboratory observation that the lifetime of mu mesons increases with their speed.

Let it be assumed that a man A takes a rocket trip while his twin B stays at home. A's watch runs more slowly than B's, and on his return A is younger than B. At foreseeable rocket speeds the age differences are extremely small, but at speeds approaching the speed of light (186,000 mi/sec) A could age only by hours while B aged by years or centuries.

This is considered a disproof of relativity by those who claim that, since B's speed relative to A is the same as A's speed relative to B, one may view the whole trip just as well from A's point of view. In this case B appears to be in motion and A to be at rest; thus B should be the younger of the two on their reunion. This apparent paradox—*i.e.* that A and B should be simultaneously younger than each other—stems from a misinterpretation of relativity. Actually, Einstein stated the equivalence of *inertial observers, i.e.* of observers in uniform, straight-line motion relative to each other; in other words, only inertial observers are interchangeable in evaluating the effects of relative speeds. In the case of the twins, A had to change his direction to return to B; his motion relative to B did not remain uniform during his trip, and the twins are not interchangeable in the evaluation of their aging rates.—*S. D. G.*

TWINS AND MULTIPLE BIRTHS: There are two types of twins: *identical twins,* which develop from the division of a single fertilized egg; and *fraternal twins,* which develop from two separate eggs. Identical twins, having identical sets of hereditary factors (genes), are always of the same sex and are so nearly alike that they are often practically indistinguishable. Fraternal twins may or may not be of the same sex, and resemble each other to about the same degree as do brothers and sisters born at different times.

In triplets, and in other multiple births, all possible combinations of one-egg, two-egg, and multiple-egg arrangements are found. There seem to be no reliable records of more than six human babies in a single birth. Many cases of quintuplets are on record, but only in a few instances have all five lived. The incidence of twins is one in 87 births; triplets, one in 7,000; quadruplets, one in 550,000; and quintuplets, one in 57,000,000.

Studies of twins are particularly useful for the analysis of the roles of heredity and environment in the development of human characteristics. Fraternal twins of the same sex reared together provide good evidence of the influence of heredity, since their environment is perhaps as nearly identical as can be found for human beings. Identical twins who have been separated soon after birth and reared in different environments furnish the best available control on the force of environmental differences in the production of characteristic differences. Identical twins often differ considerably at birth in such characteristics as size and vitality. These differences appear to be due to prenatal environmental differences, especially inequality of blood exchange between the twin embryos.—*A. P. E.*

TYNDALL, JOHN, 1820–93, British scientist; b. Leighlin Bridge, Ireland. His main scientific work consisted of research on the transparency and opacity of gases and vapors for radiant heat (1859–71). He showed the dispersion of a light beam by particles in colloids and gases (TYNDALL EFFECT). He was noted for his teaching skills, becoming professor of natural philosophy at the Royal Institution (1853). Among his many works are *Heat Considered as a Mode of Motion* (1863), *Six Lectures on Light* (1873), and *Essays on the Floating Matter of the Air* (1881), an important study of air pollution, as well as essays on sound, heat, and magnetism. He was a fellow of the Royal Society.—*R. J. F.*

TYNDALL EFFECT: the scattering of light by suspended particles in the colloidal size range. When a beam of light is passed through a suspension of particles that are submicroscopic but much larger than single molecules, some light will be scattered from each particle. This effect was first discovered by Michael Faraday (1857) and later studied in detail by John Tyndall (1869). When viewed through a microscope from a direction perpendicular to a light beam (*i.e.* in the apparatus called an *ultramicroscope*) each particle appears as a luminous point, usually scintillating because of BROWNIAN MOTION; suspended

Beam of light, projected through colloidal solution, is scattered (Tyndall effect) and polarized. In upper photo, polarization is visible through polarizing filter, orientation of filter being indicated by white arrow at bottom. When filter is rotated 90° (*lower photo*), polarized light is extinguished. (*Robert F. Waldeck/FLO*)

particles too small to be seen in the conventional microscope are thus easily detected. The ultramicroscope was first described by Richard Zsigmondy (1903).—*A. M. S.*

TYPES, THEORY OF: a theory developed by Bertrand Russell for eliminating the logical PARADOXES. The basic idea is Russell's Vicious Circle Principle, that "whatever involves *all* of a collection must not be one of that collection." To take a familiar example, the catalog of *all* books not mentioning themselves must not be treated as a book on a par with those it lists, because it is defined in terms of *all* those books. Books *about* books, like the imaginary catalog, should be distinguished as *second-order* books. Books about second-order books will be third-order books, and so on without end. No completely general statement about books, ignoring their differences in "orders," is regarded as legitimate.

A similar separation of classes results in an endless series of *types.* Classes are counted as belonging to a higher type than the types of any of their members. Every legitimate class must be of a definite type, and no comprehensive statement about all classes, ignoring differences of types, is permitted. It is easily seen that the "class of all classes not containing themselves as members" violates this restriction. Although this theory does appear to eliminate the logical paradoxes and has the merit of arising from a clear and plausible principle, it cripples mathematical reasoning. Contemporary logicians usually accept only as much of it as concerns "types," ignoring the supplementary distinctions of "orders."—*M. B.*

TYPHOON: see HURRICANE.

TYROCINIUM CHYMICUM (Chemistry for Beginners), by Jean Beguin (1610): This small volume marked the emergence of chemistry as an empirical science. In no sense a work of genius, it is the first attempt to make chemistry straightforward and practical, in the service of medicine. Beguin was equally uninterested in the mysticism of Paracelsus and the fabulous beliefs of the alchemists; his subject was chemical technique and its products. His book furnished the model for the later, trustworthy experimental chemists, though these came to far surpass him in theoretical insight.—*A. R. H.*

U

ÜBER DEN ANSCHAULICHEN INHALT DER QUANTENTHEO-RETISCHEN KINEMATIK UND MECHANIK, by Werner Heisenberg, *Zeitschrift für Physik*, Vol. 43 (1927): This paper is the first expression by Heisenberg of his UNCERTAINTY PRINCIPLE. Because light and electrons have both wave and particle properties, there are in principle limitations in the accuracy of the simultaneous measurements of quantities such as co-ordinates and momenta. The greater the accuracy with which one measures the first, the less the accuracy in the simultaneous determination of the others, and vice versa. The product of the minimum inaccuracies is a constant. These inaccuracies do not result from technological difficulties but (according to the prevailing though by no means unanimous view) constitute a fundamental attribute of nature. This principle enables one to gain an intuitive grasp of the fundamentals of wave mechanics and has also had important philosophical consequences.—*S. Bo.*

ÜBER EINEN DIE ERZEUGUNG UND VERWANDLUNG DES LICHTES BETREFFENDEN HEURISTISCHEN GESICHTSPUNKT, by Albert Einstein, *Annalen der Physik*, Vol. 17 (1904): In 1900, Philipp Lenard showed that the maximum energy of electrons emitted photoelectrically depended on the frequency and not the intensity of the light used in the experiment. In this paper Einstein shows that this puzzling result can be explained by the hypothesis that the photoelectric effect is the result of the collision of a photon and an electron in the emitter. The importance of this paper lies in its demonstration that Planck's quantum hypothesis has wide applicability and is to be used whenever light interacts with matter. In a subsequent paper, on the specific heat of solids, Einstein showed that the quantum concept is valid not only for light waves but also for acoustic waves in solids.—*S. Bo.*

UHLENBECK, GEORGE EUGENE, 1900– , Dutch-U. S. physicist; b. Batavia, Java. His fields of research have been nuclear physics, quantum mechanics, theory of atomic structure, statistical mechanics, and kinetic theory. His name is associated with that of S. A. Goudsmit for the theory of electron spin in the classical model of the atom proposed by them in 1925. He is a member of the National Academy of Sciences.—*D. H. D. R.*

ULTRASONICS: sounds that have frequencies too high for the human ear to hear—*i.e.* above 15,000 or 20,000 cycles/sec; also, the study of such sounds. The upper limit of ultrasonics, originally a few hundred kilocycles per second (kc/sec), is continually being raised, and soundlike phenomena are now observable in solids and liquids at frequencies of many thousands of megacycles per second. In this region wave-lengths become so small as to approach molecular dimensions. In less extreme regions—tens or hundreds of kc/sec—ultrasonics of high intensity are used to homogenize milk or other emulsions, clean castings and cooking ware, test for flaws in materials, and even degrade high polymers into simpler molecules. At sea, underwater ultrasonics has important uses in measuring depth (echo-sounding); detecting schools of fish, hostile submarines, or mines; and signaling over long distances (see SONAR). Some transducers for high-power ultrasonic radiation use magnetostrictive effect in nickel, but for the highest frequencies the piezoelectric effect in quartz is more convenient—even essential. Recently synthetic ceramics, *e.g.* barium titanate, which also show this effect and are less fragile and costly than quartz, have been introduced. It has recently been established that light of high intensity from a LASER will produce ultrasonic vibrations, and the interaction of these with the light itself is of great interest to researchers. See also ANIMAL SONAR; ECHO AND ECHO RANGING.—*M. C. H.*

ULTRAVIOLET RADIATION: the range of electromagnetic radiations extending from the violet (short-wavelength) end of the spectrum to the beginning of the x-ray spectrum. Near-ultraviolet covers a range of wavelengths from 380 to 320 millimicrons (mμ), middle-ultraviolet extends from 320 to 280 mμ, and far-ultraviolet extends from 280 to about 10 mμ. Ultraviolet radiation, often called "black light," may be detected by its photographic and ionizing effects as well as by its ability to cause FLUORESCENCE or PHOSPHORESCENCE—both involving the emission of visible light—in many materials.

About 5% of the Sun's radiation lies in the ultraviolet zone; however, because solar ultraviolet radiation is absorbed by oxygen and ozone as well as by window glass, relatively little of this radiation reaches Earth. Artificial sources of ultraviolet radiation include the iron arc, carbon arc, and

"Fishfinder" (*right*) enables commercial fishermen to make use of ultrasonic techniques. Instrument provides permanent record on paper of contour of sea bottom as well as locations of schools of fish. A typical record, with interpretation of the information recorded, is reproduced below. (RCA)

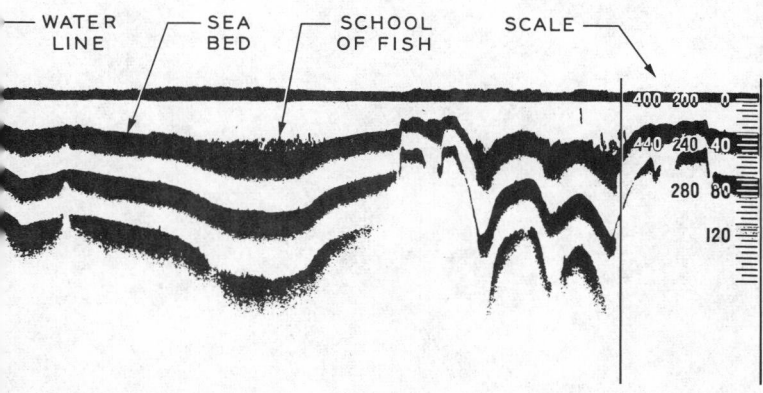

mercury-vapor arc. For maximum transmission, quartz or fluorite envelopes, which are transparent to ultraviolet radiation, must be used in place of glass. Lenses and prisms designed for work in the ultraviolet region must likewise be made of quartz or fluorite, or of certain synthetic halides. Ultraviolet radiation is used in medicine for the treatment of rickets and certain skin conditions. Foods exposed to ultraviolet radiation, *e.g.* milk, become activated with vitamin D. The ability of ultraviolet radiation to cause fluorescence and phosphorescence is used in such diverse applications as lighting, display signs, the identification of minerals, and the detection of "invisible" writing.—*A. E.*

ULUGH BEG, 1394–1449, Tatar astronomer. A grandson of Tamerlane, he founded (*c.* 1420) an observatory at Samarkand; its ruins are still to be seen. The star tables he published held primacy until those of Tycho and Kepler became available. A modern edition, based on Persian manuscripts in England, was published by F. B. Knobel: *Ulugh Beg's Catalog of Stars* (1917).—*O. G.*

UNCERTAINTY PRINCIPLE: a theorem, formulated by Werner Heisenberg in 1927, that defines the ultimate accuracy of measurement. It shows that it is basically impossible to fix the coordinates of a particle or to determine a physical event with higher accuracy than is given by the magnitude of Planck's quantum constant h, which is of the order of 6.5×10^{-27} metric units (see PLANCK'S LAW; QUANTUM THEORY).

Any rigorous interpretation of the concept of physical reality has to rely on observation. Nothing which in principle is unobservable may be considered as real. Heisenberg showed that, since observation must always necessarily affect the event being observed, this interference will lead to a fundamental limit in the accuracy of the observation. For instance, it may be desired to record the motion of an elementary particle, say an electron. To know where the electron is, we must use some sort of probe, such as a light wave, with which we can "see" the electron. If we want to fix the position of the electron very accurately, the wavelength of light used in the experiment must be short. However, a short wavelength corresponds to a large quantum of energy, and the electron's state of motion will be changed in an unknown manner at the collision with the light quantum. If, on the other hand, a long wavelength, corresponding to a small quantum of energy, is used, the change in the electron's state of motion will be

small, but the determination of its position will become less accurate.

This dilemma is of a quite general nature and is not confined to any particular type of experiment. Since the limit of uncertainty is very small when viewed from the dimensions of our everyday world, it does not affect observations except on the atomic or molecular scale. There, however, the detailed mechanism of events, as in the transition of an electron from one orbit to another inside an atom, must remain always beyond our knowledge. Thus, statements concerning any individual event that occurs within the confines of this basic uncertainty are devoid of meaning and not admissible in physics.

This fundamental indeterminacy of quantum physics has given rise to much philosophical speculation on questions of causality and free will. However, while the discovery of the uncertainty principle has given physicists a deeper insight into the meaning of the laws of nature, it has not altered the general pattern of physical concepts. Most observations are carried out on entities comprising a great number of particles and individual events, and are therefore statistical in nature. Although we must remain uncertain about each individual event, the laws of probability see to it that their sum total is fully determined. Having all possible measurements at our disposal, we cannot, for instance, say whether one particular radium atom will break up in the next second or remain intact for another 100,000 yr. However, we can predict with perfect certainty that in any lump of radium metal half the atoms will have disintegrated in 1,600 yr.—*K. Me.*

UNCONFORMITY: in geology, the physical evidence of a break or interruption in the record of geologic history as a result of the cessation of deposition. Ordinarily, an unconformity implies uplift, erosion, and resumption of deposition. The missing part of the geologic record is said to be represented by a *hiatus.* Four major types of structural evidence for unconformity are recognized. The first, called a *nonconformity,* consists of sedimentary deposits (see SEDIMENTARY ROCK) that rest on igneous or metamorphic rocks (Fig. 1). "Nonconformity" implies a complex sequence of events. Older rocks were metamorphosed or intruded by igneous rocks, and then subjected to subaerial erosion. Following this, new deposits were laid down over the old land surface. In the second case, termed *angular unconformity,* two sedimentary deposits have discordant dip; *i.e.* the beds of the younger deposit rest on the truncated edges of the beds of the lower deposit (Fig. 2). An angular unconformity may be strikingly developed in a

Angular unconformity is clearly visible where basal Wasatch conglomerate lies on the so-called Laramie Sandstone, in Park County, Wyo. (*U. S. Geological Survey*)

single outcrop, or the difference in dip may be so slight that it can be detected only through study of a large area (*regional angular unconformity*). The angular unconformity implies deformation or tilting of the older beds, erosion, and resumption of deposition. The third kind, called a *disconformity,* consists of an erosion surface separating the younger deposits from the older ones. The bedding planes of the younger and older deposits are parallel (Fig. 3). Usually the result of subaerial erosion, a disconformity might also be produced by strong currents causing submarine erosion. The fourth sort of unconformity, termed *paraconformity* or *parallel unconformity,* is distinguishable only through the use of index FOSSILS. The strata above and below the paraconformity are parallel and apparently conformable. No visible erosion surface separates the

Fig. 1: Nonconformity.

Fig. 2: Angular unconformity.

Fig. 3: Disconformity.

Fig. 4: Paraconformity (parallel unconformity).

younger and older deposits. However, study of the fossils occurring above and below the paraconformity reveals that a measurable hiatus is present (Fig. 4). The hiatus may represent a period of subaerial or submarine erosion, or it may merely represent a period of nondeposition. Unconformities play a major role in interpretation of the geologic history of a given area. See STRATIGRAPHY.—*W. Ha.*

UNDECIDABLE PROPOSITION: a proposition such that neither it nor its negation is provable, in some formal deductive system. Of course, a proposition may be undecidable in one formal system, but not in another. It should be emphasized that a proposition which, at the present time, we do not know how to prove or disprove is not necessarily an undecidable proposition. K. Gödel showed in 1931 that, given a certain consistency assumption, any sufficiently strong formal system has undecidable propositions (GÖDEL'S PROOF). It has been suggested that there are propositions, appropriately called absolutely undecidable, the truth or falsity of which it is theoretically impossible for human beings to discover. However, this notion, which is independent of a specific formal system, has never been precisely defined.—*El. M.*

UNGULATES AND SUBUNGULATES: chiefly herbivorous mammals, usually of large size, that walk or run swiftly on the tips of the toes or hoofs, or whose ancestors moved in

this way. The *unguligrade* foot posture (Lat. *unguis,* a nail, claw, or hoof) represents an extreme adaptation in that the leg is extremely elongated for greater speed. This increases the chances of escape from predators. The unguligrade foot posture contrasts with *digitigrade* foot posture, in which the animal's leg is lengthened, in effect, by the standing on the toes though not on their tips (as among cats and other terrestrial mammalian carnivores), and with *plantigrade* posture, in which the entire foot is supported by the substratum (as among insectivores and primates).

The true ungulates, which rest only upon their hoofs while walking or running, include members of the orders Perissodactyla (*e.g.* horses, zebras, tapirs, rhinoceroses) and Artiodactyla (*e.g.* pigs, deer, giraffe, camel, antelope, cattle, sheep, goats). Perissodactyls are "odd-toed," with the axis of the foot passing through the third toe. Horses have almost lost all but the third, or middle, toe on each foot, and they stand upon the hoof (the thickened, modified nail) at its tip. Tapirs and rhinoceroses use the three middle digits as functional toes. Artiodactyls are "even-toed," with the axis of the foot passing between the third and fourth digits. Pigs and their kin bear most of their weight on the third and fourth toe tips, but on soft ground gain additional support from the second and fifth digits, which also end in small hoofs. Deer and domesticated cattle, like most other artiodactyls, have only two functional toes, the hoofs being on the third and fourth toes of each foot.

The subungulates rest part of their weight on the toe tips, supplementing these with a firm pad behind the toes. Subungulates include members of orders Proboscidea (elephants, mastodons, and mammoths), Hyracoidea (dassies), and the ancestors from which contemporary aquatic members of the order Sirenia (sea cows) presumably evolved. Elephants have five toes on each foot, four of the toes on the front feet and three on the back feet usually bearing nails. Dassies (*Hyrax*), which are rabbit-sized, short-eared, and almost tailless animals of the Middle East and Africa, have four toes on the front feet and three on the back feet, all with little hoofs; behind these toes are pads somewhat like the pads that bear so much of the weight of elephants. Modern sea cows, found from Florida to Brazil and in Africa, India, and Australia, are exclusively aquatic vegetarians, living most of their lives barely submerged in shallow bays and rivers, where they find edible plants. These animals have lost their hind legs and propel themselves with a broad flattened tail aided by forelegs modified as flippers. Features of the skull and teeth, as well as foot posture, suggest a relationship between the subungulate orders and the ungulates.—*L. and M. M.*

UNIFIED FIELD THEORY: the mathematical theory, as yet unattained, that would reconcile and unify the RELATIVITY theory of the universe, the electromagnetic theory of wave phenomena (see ELECTROMAGNETIC WAVE), and the QUANTUM THEORY of atomic and subatomic particles. Believing in the fundamental unity of nature, Albert Einstein worked on this problem continuously, reporting his tentative conclusions in an appendix to the 4th edition of his *Meaning of Relativity* (1953). His death in 1955 interrupted these labors.

The equations of general relativity relate the fundamental mechanical quantities—mass, energy, momentum, and gravitation—that govern the motions of celestial bodies. Einstein showed, in particular, that a four-dimensional universe (of which three dimensions are those of Euclidean space and the fourth is time) is distorted by the presence of matter, and that this distortion accounts for the observed motions. Thus the solution offered by relativity is purely geometrical in character.

The first step in achieving a unified field theory would be to discover similar geometric properties that could account for electromagnetic forces, preferably in terms of another distortion of the space-time universe. Electromagnetic phenomena, however, are described by Maxwell's equations, which are nongeometric. The complex problem of handling these equations in terms of relativity made Einstein's task so difficult that he was unable to complete it in his lifetime.

The final step in completing the theory—*i.e.* to account geometrically for the statistical behavior of the atom—has not yet been undertaken.—*S. D. G.*

UNIFORMITARIANISM: see GEOLOGY.

UNIFORMITY OF NATURE: It has frequently been maintained, *e.g.* by John Stuart Mill in *A System of Logic,* that every event in nature is related by universal laws to certain antecedent events, that the course of nature is uniform. Mill held that this principle of uniformity "is our warrant for all inferences from experience." He called it "an assumption involved in every case of induction," "a principle implied in the very statement of what induction is." But unlike Kant, who regarded this principle as *a priori,* Mill maintained that the principle of uniformity is itself an induction from experience. That Mill is inconsistent when he claims the principle is both empirical and our sole warrant of the validity of inductive inference has been a major complaint of his critics. But even if this difficulty be put aside, it has never been clearly explained, in a detailed way, by Mill or by anyone else how the principle may logically serve the purpose of a premiss in any inductive argument. In fact, contemporary analysts no longer construe inductive argument as a deduction from the principle of uniformity. Accordingly, the principle of the uniformity of nature, in recent thought, serves as an idealized expression of the scientific aspiration to learn to view nature as a highly lawful system.—*A. Sm.*

UNIVERSE: see COSMOLOGY; GALAXY.

UNSATURATED COMPOUNDS: chemical compounds which can add elements or groups of elements by simple addition, without losing any of their own components. Thus ethylene, $CH_2{=}CH_2$, can add a molecule of hydrogen, H—H, to yield ethane, $CH_3{-}CH_3$. Ethylene is an unsaturated hydrocarbon, in contrast with ethane, which is saturated. Aldehydes and ketones are similarly unsaturated:

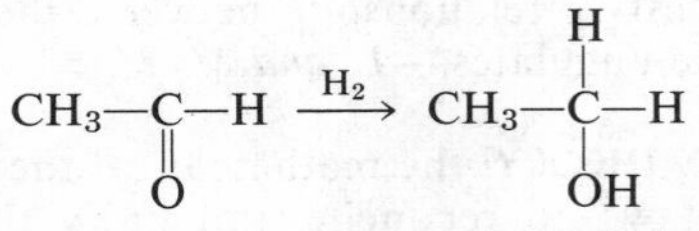

$$CH_3{-}\underset{O}{\overset{H}{C}}{-}H \xrightarrow{H_2} CH_3{-}\underset{OH}{\overset{H}{C}}{-}H$$

Acetaldehyde　　　　　Ethyl alcohol

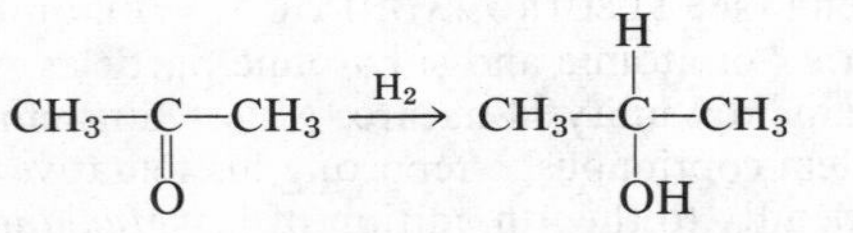

$$CH_3{-}\underset{O}{C}{-}CH_3 \xrightarrow{H_2} CH_3{-}\underset{OH}{\overset{H}{C}}{-}CH_3$$

Acetone　　　　　　Isopropyl alcohol

Addition need not be restricted to hydrogen; *e.g.* the following reaction is catalyzed by sulfuric acid:

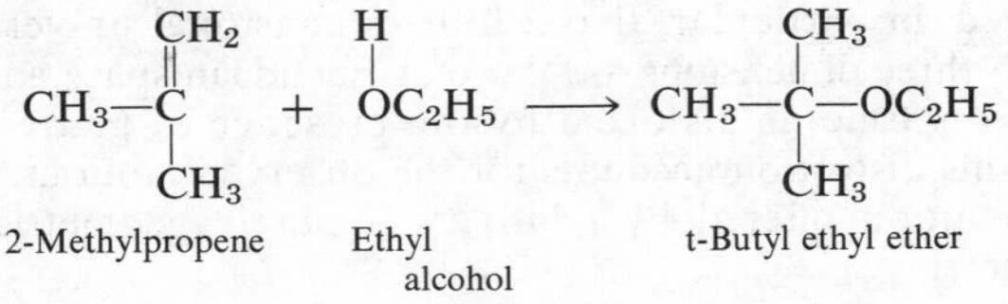

$$CH_3{-}\underset{CH_3}{\overset{CH_2}{C}} + \underset{\text{}}{\overset{H}{OC_2H_5}} \longrightarrow CH_3{-}\underset{CH_3}{\overset{CH_3}{C}}{-}OC_2H_5$$

2-Methylpropene　　Ethyl　　　t-Butyl ethyl ether
　　　　　　　　alcohol

From these examples it is obvious that unsaturation is a useful property in synthesis of more complex compounds.—*Ru. M.*

URANIUM: an actinide element (U); at. no. 92; at. wt 238.07; sp gr 18.68; mp 1150°C; bp about 3500°C; valences 3, 4, 5, and 6. In 1789 M. H. Klaproth, working with the mineral pitchblende, which was thought to be an ore of zinc, iron, and tungsten, discovered the presence of a new element, which he named in honor of F. W. Herschel's discovery of the planet Uranus. The material isolated by Klaproth was really an oxide of uranium; the metal itself was isolated by E. M. Péligot in 1842. Because of their beautiful yellow fluorescence, uranium salts were used during the 19th cent. to color glass and ceramics, and uranium was employed in ferrous metallurgy; but it was not until the discovery of RADIOACTIVITY in 1896 that the element became highly valued and the object of intensive study as the parent substance of radium. With the advent of nuclear fission, uranium became still more widely sought and investigated. The major ores of uranium are carnotite ($K_2O \cdot 2UO_3 \cdot V_2O_5 \cdot 3H_2O$), autunite [$(UO_2)_2Ca(PO_4)_4 \cdot 8H_2O$], uraninite ($UO_2$ and U_3O_8), and pitchblende (UO_2 and U_3O_8). The latter two minerals have essentially the same composition, but pitchblende is amorphous, whereas uraninite is crystalline and generally occurs with minor amounts of thorium and lead. It is usually found in pegmatites or high-temperature deposits, while pitchblende is more common in veins deposited at moderate temperatures. The age of uraninite crystals can be estimated from the proportions of radioactive isotopes; this is an important method of dating geological formations (see RADIOACTIVE DATING). The richest deposits of uranium occur in central Europe, the Congo, Colorado, Utah, and Canada. They contain, on an average, somewhat less than 1 part of the fissionable U^{235} isotope for every 100 parts of U^{238}. Uranium forms no less than five oxides, of which the best known are UO_2 and UO_3, corresponding to the tetravalent and hexavalent states of uranium, respectively. The hexavalent uranic salts are derivatives of uranic acid $UO_2(OH)_2$; they contain the uranyl group, UO_2, which acts as a divalent cation, forming compounds such as uranyl chloride UO_2Cl_2 and uranyl nitrate $UO_2(NO_3)_2 \cdot 6H_2O$. Uranium forms a volatile hexafluoride, UF_6, which is used in one of the processes by which the different uranium isotopes are separated from one another.—*A. M. S.*

URANUS: the 7th principal planet in order from the Sun; it is one of the giant planets. Though faintly visible to the eye as a 6th-mag "star" under favorable conditions, Uranus went unrecognized until accidentally discovered by William Herschel in 1781. In telescopes it exhibits a greenish disc 3 to 4″ in diameter. Uranus revolves around the Sun with a period of 84 yr, at an average distance of 1,780 million mi. The eccentricity of the orbit is 0.047, and the inclination to the ecliptic 0°46′. Its mean diameter is about 29,000 mi, the polar diameter being 7% less than the equatorial. Its mass is 14.5 times that of Earth. The surface temperature is probably near −270°F. Methane and hydrogen have been identified above the reflecting surface of the very deep atmosphere. A large increase in density toward the center, the low average density (1.56 times that of water), and the high reflecting power of about 63% further identify Uranus as one of the group of giant planets (the others being Jupiter, Saturn, and Neptune). Surface features are difficult to observe, and some of those recorded are optical effects; but there are cloud belts resembling Jupiter's. The period of rotation has been determined to be near 10 hr 45 min. The equator has the remarkable inclination of 98° to the plane of the orbit; or, we may say 82° if we consider Uranus to rotate backward. On this planet the tropics would extend to latitude 82° and overlap with arctic and antarctic zones, which reach to within 8° of the equator.

Uranus has five known satellites, ranging in distance from 81,000 mi to 364,000 mi, with periods from 1 day 10 hr to 13 day 11 hr. Miranda, the closest, is much the smallest; the others are estimated to be roughly 200 to 700 mi in diameter. The satellite orbits lie in the plane of the planet's equator. They are seen sometimes on edge (as in 1966) and sometimes almost at right angles (as in 1945).—*W. H.*

UREA CYCLE (ornithine cycle): In the higher animals the chief end-product of nitrogen metabolism is urea, $CO(NH_2)_2$, formed in the liver and excreted by the kidney. The method whereby ammonia (from amino acids) is converted to urea was first outlined by H. A. Krebs, 1932, and can with present knowledge be represented as follows:

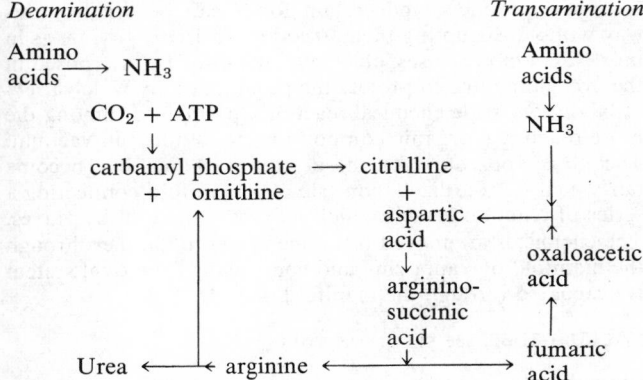

When ammonia is formed by DEAMINATION it can be made to react with CO_2, in the presence of ATP, to form carbamyl phosphate, $NH_2 \cdot CO \cdot O \cdot H_2 \cdot PO_3$, which now reacts with ornithine to form citrulline. This latter compound reacts with aspartic acid to form arginino-succinic acid. At this stage of the cycle another molecule of ammonia has been brought in, derived from amino acids by transamination. Arginino-succinic acid is then split to fumaric acid and arginine; the former may be converted through the CITRIC-ACID CYCLE to oxaloacetic acid, and thence by transamination back to aspartic acid; the latter is hydrolyzed by the enzyme arginase to ornithine and urea. The over-all process is represented by $CO_2 + 2NH_3 \longrightarrow CO(NH_2)_2 + H_2O$.—*K. H.*

UREY, HAROLD CLAYTON, 1893–   , U. S. chemist; b. Walkerton, Ind. For his discovery (1931) of deuterium, an isotope of hydrogen known as heavy hydrogen, he received the 1934 Nobel prize in chemistry. In further work on the separation of isotopes, Urey contributed to the procedures used in separating fissionable uranium[235] from the more available uranium[238] and thus to the development of the atom bomb. After World War II he worked on chemical and thermodynamic means for determining the origin and age of the solar system, reaching the conclusion that Earth and the Moon were formed by the gravitational aggregation of pre-existing solid particles, and were not originally molten as many scientists have believed. Urey is a fellow of the Royal Society and a member of the National Academy of Sciences. —*A. L.*

URIC ACID: a rather insoluble weak acid and purine derivative. It is the excretory product of purine metabolism in man and other primates, as well as in birds and most reptiles. In birds and reptiles it is the main nitrogen excretory product (they make no urea). In gout, too much uric acid is produced, and deposits of it are found in the joints. It also forms kidney stones. See also ALLANTOIN.—*J. F. S.*

URIDINE DIPHOSPHATE GLUCOSE (UDPG): in biochemistry, a NUCLEOTIDE which takes part in the synthesis of starch in plants and glycogen in animals, as

$$\text{UDPG} + \text{(n) glucose} \rightarrow \text{UDP} + \text{(n + 1) glucose}$$
$$\text{(glycogen)} \qquad\qquad\qquad \text{(glycogen)}$$

—*K. H.*

URINARY BLADDER: a thin sac of muscle and connective tissue that serves as a reservoir for urine in most vertebrates. In mammals, urine is delivered to the bladder from the ureters. The bladder fills progressively with urine without any great change in pressure, but the stretching of the walls beyond a certain point sets up a reflex contraction of the muscles, which opens the muscular valve in the orifice of the urethra; the urine then flows through the urethra to the outside. The reflex is subject to voluntary control from the brain.—*B. T. S.*

UROGENITAL SYSTEM: the organs of the vertebrate body that function in EXCRETION and REPRODUCTION. The mesonephros is the functional kidney of adult fishes and amphibians (*A* in diagram). In the male it is connected by tubules to the gonad (testis) and carries sperm to the segmental duct, which transports both sperm and urine to the cloaca. In the female, an oviduct collects eggs shed by the gonad (ovary) and carries them to the cloaca. The metanephros is the functional kidney of reptiles, birds, and mammals. In males (*B*) the mesonephros and segmental duct develop, respectively, into the epididymis and the vas deferens, which carry sperm from the testis. In females (*C*) the oviduct is well developed, but the mesonephros and segmental duct are vestigial. In both male and female mammals, urinary and intestinal wastes leave the body through separate ducts (not shown).—*W. P. C.*

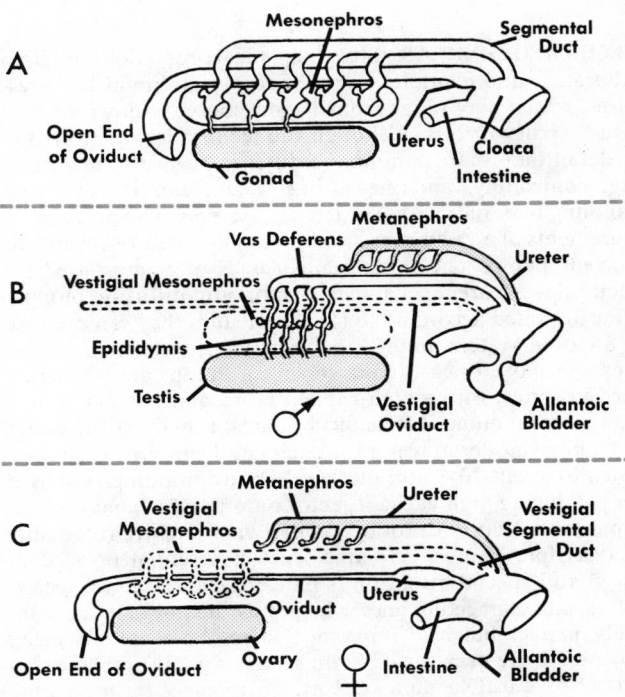

Urogenital systems of vertebrates (*From Guyer*)

V

VACUUM: space that is empty of matter; more commonly, any enclosed space in which the gas pressure is reduced to below atmospheric pressure. The first successful attempt to obtain a vacuum was made by Otto von Guericke (c. 1650). In 1660 Robert Boyle built a piston-operated vacuum pump, which permitted him to perform the first physics experiments under controlled vacuum conditions. Today there are many different types of pumps and gages for obtaining and measuring vacuum (see PUMP; VACUUM TECHNIQUES). The applications of vacuum technology have made possible devices ranging from the incandescent light bulb to giant accelerators. The industrial utilization of various vacuum techniques has grown tremendously in the last 20 yr (see DISTILLATION; DRYING). Today the physics of vacuum is vital not only to the science laboratory but to almost all modern industry.

The pressure in a vacuum system is normally measured relative to atmospheric pressure, which is the pressure required to support a column of mercury 760 mm high at a temperature of 0°C. The most widely used unit in measuring vacuum is the micron (μ), which is the pressure of a column of mercury $1/1,000$ mm high. The vacuum of a system whose pressure is reduced slightly below atmospheric pressure is sometimes called a *partial vacuum*. The term *high vacuum* is usually applied to the range of pressures from one millionth to one billionth mm of mercury. Pressures of one ten-billionth mm of mercury and below are often called ultra-high vacuum. A perfect or absolute vacuum, which would be the complete absence of any matter, is never attained in the laboratory; the highest vacuum still contains many gas molecules. For example, the lowest practically attained pressures are of the order of one 100-billionth mm of mercury. At this pressure there are still roughly 300,000 molecules/cm^3 of evacuated space.—*E. E.*

VACUUM TECHNIQUES: Many chemical operations in both laboratory and plant are best carried out at diminished pressures, which may range from 10 mm mercury down to 10^{-4} mm mercury or less. Although the techniques differ greatly in detail they share common features in regard to maintaining, controlling, and measuring vacua, and in regard to handling materials within evacuated systems. The primary requirements of a vacuum system are a well-sealed vessel and an efficient pump. The three main classes of pumps used for vacuum work are mechanical, ejector, and diffusion pumps; these are rated according to (1) the vacuum they can produce in a closed system and (2) their capacity, or amount of gas they can move (measured in ft^3/min). Pumps are frequently used in series, with a high-capacity fore pump backing up a high-vacuum pump. Mechanical pumps, usually of the rotary type, have moderately high capacity and can produce vacua down to about 10^{-2} mm mercury. Diffusion pumps are used for producing high vacua. Ejector pumps, which have a high capacity but do not produce a high vacuum, are frequently used as fore pumps. Avoiding leaks is essential in vacuum work, and special attention is paid to gaskets, joints, seals, valves, and connecting lines, which must be not only mechanically perfect but also impermeable to the materials being processed. Devices for detecting leaks are also an essential part of practical vacuum systems, as are gages for measuring the low pressures. (See PRESSURE MEASUREMENTS.)

Chemical processing in vacuum is complicated by the very high vapor volumes per unit mass that must be handled, and by the difficulty of heat transfer through the rarefied vapor; thus the vacuum stills used in *vacuum distillation* (possibly the most widely used vacuum process) must be specially designed to overcome these two difficulties. Certain metallurgical processes, *e.g.* those for making uranium, zirconium, calcium, and magnesium, are carried out in vacuum. Ingenious design of equipment is necessary to avoid leaks at the high operating temperatures. At the other end of the temperature scale is *freeze-drying* or lyophilization (see DRYING). In this process wet material to be dried is first frozen, and the water is then removed by vacuum sublimation. Antibiotics, plasma, other biological products, and certain foods can be dried in this way without disrupting their structure. In freeze-drying, as in most vacuum processes, efficient traps must be interposed in the evacuating line to protect the pumps. A very wide variety of laboratory-scale chemical reactions, particularly among the more reactive inorganic compounds, are studied in vacuum. The glass apparatus for these studies, which has become fairly well standardized, consists of a manifold connecting a series of reaction vessels which may be sealed off by valves. The chemicals are moved from one vessel to another through the manifold by vaporizing and condensing. The total system is evacuated through the manifold.—*A. M. S.*

VACUUM TUBE: see ELECTRON TUBE.

VALENCE: the combining power of a chemical element when it unites with others to form molecules. The meaning of "combining power" can be understood from the formulas of these simple molecules:

$$\begin{array}{ccc} \text{H—H} & \text{H—O—H} & \text{H—N—H} \\ \text{Hydrogen} & \text{Water} & \overset{|}{\underset{}{\text{Ammonia}}} \end{array}$$

In hydrogen compounds, only one line (valence bond) is needed to indicate the union of the H atom with another H atom or with other atoms. The H atom is assigned a valence of *one*, and is the standard for assignment of valence powers to other elements. Valence, then, is defined as the number of hydrogen atoms with which an element can combine. It will be seen that the valence of the oxygen atom in water is *two*, and the valence of the nitrogen atom in ammonia is *three*. It is possible, however, for an element to exhibit several valences; there are compounds in which oxygen has a valence of *three*, and nitrogen *four*.

Its ability to explain valence is one of the triumphs of the modern conception of atomic structure. The atom has a positively charged nucleus, surrounded by electrons rotating in specific orbits in concentric shells. The outermost shell is called the valence shell, because electrons in that shell take part in valence bond formation. Certain atoms in their normal, uncombined state have 8 electrons in the valence shell, and are chemically inert; these are the inert gases in group O of the PERIODIC TABLE. All atoms seek a similar stable state. This they do by combining with other atoms so as either to build up the electron quota in the valence shell to the magic number 8, or to lose electrons from that shell to uncover an inner shell with its 8 electrons. Valence bond formation, on this basis, can be illustrated with atoms of sodium and chlorine:

$$Na\cdot \quad + \quad \cdot\ddot{\underset{..}{Cl}}: \quad \longrightarrow \quad Na^+ \; :\ddot{\underset{..}{Cl}}:^-$$

Sodium atom   Chlorine atom   Sodium chloride molecule

$$:\ddot{\underset{..}{Cl}}\cdot \quad + \quad \cdot\ddot{\underset{..}{Cl}}: \quad \longrightarrow \quad :\ddot{\underset{..}{Cl}}:\ddot{\underset{..}{Cl}}:$$

Chlorine atom   Chlorine atom   Chlorine molecule

Here the dots represent the number of electrons in the valence shell as determined from the periodic table; sodium is in group I (1 electron) and chlorine is in group VII (7 electrons). The chlorine atom fills its valence shell and becomes a chloride ion by acquiring the lone electron from the valence shell of the sodium atom, which in turn has been reduced to a lower electron shell and becomes a positive ion because of loss of the electron. The sodium chloride molecule consists of ions held together by electrostatic forces; this linkage is an *electrovalence bond*. The chlorine molecule, on the other hand, consists of atoms which share a pair of electrons in such a way that each atom fills its quota of 8 in the valence shell. This tight linkage is called a *covalence bond*.

Variable valence can be illustrated with compounds of nitrogen, which has 5 electrons in its valence shell (group V in the periodic table). In the ammonia molecule the N atom has a valence of 3 (three covalence bonds), but it still has a

$$\cdot\ddot{N}\cdot \quad + \quad 3H\cdot \quad \longrightarrow \quad H:\overset{..}{\underset{H}{N}}:H$$

Nitrogen   Hydrogen   Ammonia
atom   atom   molecule

$$+ \quad H:\overset{..}{O}:H \quad \longrightarrow \quad \left[H:\overset{H}{\underset{H}{N}}:H \right]^+ \left[:\overset{..}{O}:H \right]^-$$

Water
molecule   Ammonium hydroxide molecule

free electron pair it can furnish for bond formation. It forms the bond by extracting from a water molecule a hydrogen ion, which has no electrons. In the ammonium ion, nitrogen has a valence of 4. The fourth bond is called a *co-ordinate covalence bond*, but it is probably more often referred to as a *dative bond* (Lat. *dare*, to give); here the N atom has given the electron pair. The dative bond is important in the formation of several types of molecules, *e.g.* ring structures (see CHELATES). The *hydrogen bond*, perhaps better called the *hydrogen bridge*, is also due to dative bonds, *e.g.* the polymerization of ordinary water, H—O → H—O → H—O → ...,

where the arrow denotes the donated electron pair bond. The electron pair bond, which is so universal in molecule formation, is regarded as *the* CHEMICAL BOND.—*Ru. M.*

VALENCE ELECTRON: any of the electrons in the outermost shell of an atom. These are the electrons that take part in chemical reactions and in electrical conduction. Valence electrons determine the characteristic properties of atoms.—*I. R.*

VALLEY: a long hollow, depression, or trench in the land, cut by a RIVER and associated agents of erosion. Valleys vary greatly in size, shape, and age, and are occupied by water temporarily or perennially. Many features called valleys are not truly such; *e.g.* the Great Central Valley and Death Valley, Calif., and the Jordan-Dead Sea basin in Asia Minor were developed not by river erosion but by deformation of Earth's crust—they are GRABEN. True valleys are evolved by deepening, widening, and lengthening due to the action of running water, weathering, and mass wasting, and their evolution is cyclic. In the *young* stage the river's gradient is steep, the emphasis is thus on valley deepening, and a roughly V-shaped canyon develops which may have nearly vertical or widely flaring walls. The Grand Canyon of the Colorado River in Arizona and the Grand Canyon of the Yellowstone River in Yellowstone National Park are examples. But with continued downcutting the river loses gradient and its downcutting ability wanes; then the emphasis shifts to valley widening by weathering, slopewash, and mass wasting on the valley sides. The valley bottom tends to become flat, widening downstream, though abutting against slopes that may still be high and steep. Thus is evolved the *mature* valley. Finally, if there is long-continued stability in the region, erosion may greatly reduce the divides between streams. Then the mature valley becomes still wider and shallower, and mostly covered with flood-plain sediments. In this stage it is called *old*.—*N. E. A. H.*

Erosion by valley glaciers produces U-shaped valley profiles. The view is eastward from Alpine Park in Glacier National Park, Montana. (*Great Northern Railway*)

VALVE: a mechanical device installed in pipes, chutes, boilers, pressure tanks, and similar apparatus to check or control the flow of gases, liquids, or powdered solids. Valves vary in size from very small (as in the automobile tire) to enormous (locks of the Panama Canal). *Rigid valves* made of brass, bronze, or cast iron are used to control fluids such as air, steam, oil, or water at temperatures up to 500°F and pressures up to 300 lb/in.². Stainless, cast, or forged steel (for ammonia) and various alloys are used for corrosive fluids. For pressures up to 1,350 lb/in.² forged steel proves durable, and for steam at high temperatures and pressures, nickel-chromium steel is best. *Flexible* and *tight-fitting valves* are manufactured from hard rubber, alone or in combination with metal. Asbestos and other soft materials are used in special instances.

Valve Operation and Types: Valves can be operated manually, mechanically, or by the flowing material itself. All valves have a *seat* with an opening for admitting the flowing material, and a *lid* which opens or closes the orifice. The designs are of two types: (1) a valve which cannot be regulated but is fully opened or closed in order to start or stop the flow; (2) a valve which opens or closes by degrees in order to control the flow. In a *gate valve,* an example of the first type, the lid consists of two movable gates (right and left) and two wedges (upper and lower) placed between the gates. The upper wedge is provided with a threaded stem. As the stem turns to close the valve, the gates descend until the upper wedge moves across the lower wedge, exerting pressure on the gates. The gates contact their seats, closing the orifice. When the stem turns in the opposite direction, the upper wedge moves away from the lower one, forcing the gates to rise until the valve is completely open. Advantages of this mechanism are a relatively low pressure drop and a full, undisturbed flow. This type of valve is used in boilers and turbines. The *butterfly valve* has a modified gate lid. The gate is hinged to the seat and in closing the orifice swings rather than comes down. Its advantages are low pressure drop and absence of turbulence; a disadvantage is the fact that the closing is not completely tight. This valve is used where the material flows under low pressure, as in water pipes. In the *diaphragm valve* the seat is a transverse weir

damming the flow. A pressure-operated lid closes the opening tightly; the pressure drop is very low and the passage clear. This valve is used in the food-processing and beverage industries.

Valves that open and close by degrees include globe, needle, check, safety, poppet, and gridiron valves. The *globe valve* has a globe-shaped lid with a threaded stem and a round, raised seat (to prevent accumulation of sediment). The disadvantage of this seat is partial obstruction of the flow. These valves are installed in the throttles of turbines and other engines. *Needle valves* are used for spraying or atomizing fluids. The tight-fitting, long lid tapers at the bottom and is closed and opened by a stem. The flow is controlled by varying the angle of the needle point. The needle valve is used in diesel engines to admit fuel into the combustion chamber. *Check valves* (back-pressure valves) stop the reversal of flow in pumps and pipelines. The lid is either flat (closing by gravity) or ball-shaped. The ball lid revolves continuously under the action of flow, producing a circuitous movement of the fluid. *Safety valves* for letting out excess steam have spring- or lever-operated conical lids fitting tightly a seat of the same shape; they are used in boilers, pressure tanks, and similar apparatus. The valve opens when the steam pressure reaches the danger limit. Adjustment to desired pressure level is made by changing the spring or the weight of the lever. The *poppet* (or puppet) *valve* has a spring-operated, tall, heavy lid that fits tightly into a ring-shaped seat. The lid is lifted to open the valve. Flexible, resilient, or rigid poppet valves are installed in steam engines and compressors to admit or discharge steam or gas. *Gridiron* (*multiported*) *valves* have flat lids with stems, and seats with several openings, which pass the flowing material simultaneously in many directions. These valves serve as automobile exhaust valves.—*C. S.*

VANADIUM: a metallic element (V); at. no. 23; at. wt 50.94; mp 1710°C; bp 3000°C; sp gr 5.96; valence 2, 3, 4, or 5. Credit for discovery of vanadium is generally given to the Swedish chemist Nils Gabriel Sefström (1830), who was alerted by the atypical properties of a sample of wrought iron in his possession. However, some 30 yr before, in 1801, the Spanish mineralogist Andres Manuel del Rio had claimed, then disclaimed, discovery of the metal in "brown lead" (now known as vanadinite, $9PbO \cdot 3V_2O_5 \cdot PbCl_2$), believing that the metals present in the mineral were simply lead and chromium. In 1831, Friedrich Wöhler again analyzed brown lead, and showed that del Rio's original suspicions had been correct. Vanadium is a light-gray, lustrous, nonductile, very hard metal; it does not tarnish (oxidize) in air and is resistant to the attack of some acids. The element is found in the minerals patronite (Peru), vanadinite (Arizona, Mexico, and Spain), carnotite (Colorado and Utah), and roscoelite (Colorado); other vanadium-bearing minerals are found in Rhodesia, SW Africa, and the U. S. S. R. World production is about 3,000 tons/yr, of which over 90% is initially converted into ferrovanadium, a master alloy containing 30 to 40% vanadium (with up to 6% carbon, up to 15% silicon, and the balance iron). Ferrovanadium is used to add vanadium to alloy steels—principally high-speed tool steels—to which fractional percentages of vanadium (up to 1.5%) impart increased tensile strength, elasticity, toughness, and hardness. These so-called "vanadium steels" (0.1 to 1.5% vanadium) may also contain small percentages of tungsten, molybdenum, and chromium, and, in

Gate valve of 48-in. diameter: The valve stands 217 in. high and weighs more than 10 tons. It will be used as a positive shutoff on hydrocarbons at temperatures up to 1,000°F in a petroleum refinery. (Crane Co.)

Vanadium is extracted from a variety of ores, notably the yellow carnotite of the Colorado Plateau, which is processed to form "red cake." Red cake, or sodium hexavanadate ($Na_2H_2V_6O_{17}$), is further processed to yield its rich (85%) content of vanadium pentoxide in purified form. (*Vanadium Corp. of America*)

VAN ALLEN RADIATION: an accumulation of electrically charged atomic particles (electrons and protons) confined to the vicinity of Earth by its magnetic field. The trapped radiation is named for J. A. Van Allen, who suggested its existence from the data gathered by the U. S. satellite Explorer I in 1958. Many measurements of the radiation's composition, energy spectrum, and intensity as a function of position and time have been made with detectors aboard spacecraft. Observations indicate the electrons are confined primarily to two shells having peak intensities at 1.35 and 5 Earth radii, respectively. The number of electrons in the outer shell fluctuates widely, showing some correlation with fluctuations in the magnetic field. The inner shell, which seemed more stable, is now masked by electrons from high-altitude hydrogen-bomb explosions by the U. S. and the U. S. S. R. in 1962. Measurements of the gradual decrease in intensity of these electrons over a period of years should provide clues as to mechanisms of loss. The protons seem distributed in many merging shells, with proton energy increasing from outer to inner shells. There is still no quantitatively successful explanation of the observed particle distributions; qualitatively it appears that a principal source of electrons and protons for the outer layers must be the SOLAR WIND—a continuous stream of electrons and protons emanating from the Sun. Many high-energy particles in the inner zones probably arise from decay of neutrons produced by bombardment of oxygen and nitrogen atoms in the upper atmosphere by cosmic rays. (Within about 12 minutes after being knocked out of a nucleus, a neutron decays into a proton plus an electron and an anti-neutrino.)

For space travelers Van Allen radiation constitutes a varying hazard. Detectors aboard Mariner IV demonstrated that Mars has neither trapped radiation nor a measurable magnetic field, but radio astronomical evidence indicates Jupiter does have trapped radiation belts.—*S. K.*

addition to their application in high-speed cutting tools, are used in engine and transmission parts of automobiles and aircraft and in many other applications requiring a hard, tough, corrosion-resistant steel. Vanadium is also used occasionally in nonferrous alloys, *e.g.* with titanium and columbium, to impart corrosion resistance and improve strength-to-weight ratio; titanium-vanadium alloys, for example, are used for missile cases, jet-engine housings, and nuclear reactor components. Various vanadium compounds are used in the glass, ceramics, and dye industries, *e.g.* the pigment vanadium-tin yellow. Vanadium pentoxide is a catalyst in the manufacture of sulfuric acid.—*R. B. T.*

VAN ALLEN, JAMES ALFRED, 1914– , U. S. physicist; b. Mount Pleasant, Iowa. His research has been concerned with nuclear physics, cosmic rays, atmospheric physics, and the use of rockets in physical research. He was a part of the research team that developed the proximity fuse during World War II, and later became heavily involved in work on rockets, satellites and their instruments, and the technical

James Alfred Van Allen
(*Wide World*)

and scientific information obtained from satellites. A region around Earth found to possess a high density of fast-moving charged particles is named the "Van Allen belt" after him. He is a member of the National Academy of Sciences. See VAN ALLEN RADIATION.—*D. H. D. R.*

VAN DE GRAAFF, ROBERT JEMISON, 1901–67, U. S. physicist; b. Tuscaloosa, Ala. He is best known for his invention of the Van de Graaff electrostatic generator.—*D. H. D. R.*

VAN DE GRAAFF GENERATOR (or Van de Graaff Accelerator): a device invented by R. J. Van de Graaff, 1931, that provides high electrostatic potentials and may be used to accelerate electrons or ions to high energies. Used as an electron accelerator, it operates as shown in the figure. Electrons from a separately powered source are sprayed onto the moving belt, which carries them up to the high-voltage terminal—a large, hollow conducting sphere—and deposits them there. In accordance with the laws of ELECTROSTATICS, the belt can continue to deposit charge on the high-voltage terminal regardless of how much has been previously collected there. The accumulated electrons produce an electric field that is most intense in the space between the high-voltage and grounded terminals. An electron gun—a source of relatively low-energy electrons—injects these electrons into the high-intensity field region, where they are accelerated through an evacuated tube toward the grounded terminal. The resulting beam comes out through a thin window in this terminal.

The instrument can be converted to an ion accelerator by replacing the electron gun with an ion source and by replacing the electron source at the bottom of the belt with a device that removes electrons from the belt rather than adding electrons to it, thus building up a net positive charge on the high-voltage terminal. The ion source is a device that removes electrons from the atoms of a gas and ejects the resulting ions.

The electrostatic accelerator is an extremely important tool in nuclear physics research, because it provides a continuous

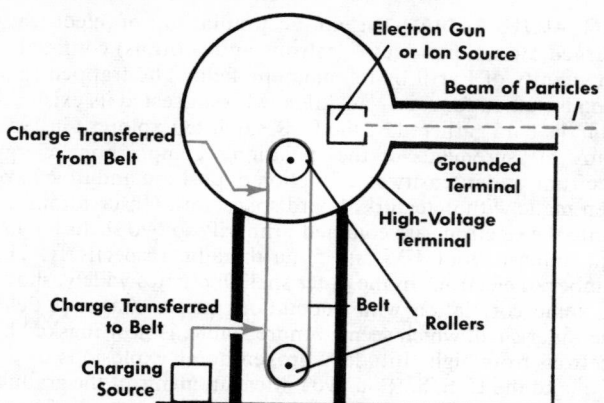

Electron Gun or Ion Source

Beam of Particles

Charge Transferred from Belt

Grounded Terminal

High-Voltage Terminal

Charge Transferred to Belt

Belt

Rollers

Charging Source

Van de Graaff generator: Electrons from charging source are carried by moving belt to inside of hollow sphere. Hollow sphere accumulates any amount of charge brought into *internal* contact with it, subject to leakage. Resulting high-intensity electric field accelerates electrons toward grounded terminal.

beam of projectiles with precisely known energy for probing atomic nuclei. Beams from these accelerators are also used in studies of the effects of radiation on crystals and on living tissues, and in the treatment of cancer. Electron beams are used in industry for sterilization of foods, vulcanization of rubber, and polymerization of plastics. If the beam is allowed to strike a metal target, it produces a penetrating beam of X-RAYS, which are used in industrial radiography. Beams of some light atomic nuclei striking special targets produce intense beams of neutrons, which are used in nuclear physics experiments, production of radioactive isotopes, and analysis of materials for trace impurities. See also ELECTROSTATIC GENERATOR.—*S. K.*

VAN HISE, CHARLES RICHARD, 1857–1918, U. S. geologist; b. Fulton, Wis. A pioneer in the application of quantitative methods to problems of metamorphism and diastrophism, he was also one of the leading authorities on the Precambrian geology of N America. His *Treatise on Metamorphism* (1904) was significant for its use of physics and chemistry. He was professor of geology (1879–1903) at the Univ. of Wisconsin and its president (1903–18). He was a member of the National Academy of Sciences.—*D. H. D. R.*

VAN'T HOFF, JACOBUS HENDRICUS, 1852–1911, Dutch physical chemist; b. Rotterdam. STEREOCHEMISTRY, the science of the spatial arrangement of the atoms in the molecule, grew out of his concept that the four valences of the carbon atom are directed toward the vertices of a tetrahedron. For the discovery of the laws of chemical dynamics and of osmotic pressure, he received the first Nobel prize in chemistry (1901). He later applied his discoveries to the problem of natural salt deposits. He was a fellow of the Royal Society.—*E. F.*

VAPOR PRESSURE: the pressure due to colliding molecules of a vapor in a confined space. Molecules escaping from the free surface of a liquid collect as vapor above the surface when confined. Vapor pressure increases with temperature, and at any given temperature each substance has a characteristic maximum vapor pressure. In mixtures the vapor pressures of the ingredients exist independently.—*C. E. B.*

VARIABLE: in mathematics, a symbol to which can be assigned any number of a set of two or more numbers. The set may consist of discrete numbers, like the first 10 integers; or of all numbers in an interval, such as all numbers (including frac-

tions and irrationals) between 0 and 10. In many practical instances it is all positive numbers. A symbol associated with a single number is a constant. A variable is "varied" merely by exchanging one number in the set for another. Any number assigned to the variable cannot itself change. The set of numbers from which the values of a variable are drawn is its *domain.*

The term variable is often applied to the letter representing an unknown in an equation to be solved, since, in our ignorance of its value at the outset, we assume only that it is one of the set of all numbers. Variables play a central role in the study of relations between quantities, which are called functional relations. Mathematically, the quantities are variables, and the relation associates values of one variable with those of another. For example, in the relation $y = x^2$, it is assumed that x can vary over all numbers, while for each value of x, the value of y is x^2. Here, x is called the independent variable, y the dependent variable.

The notion of a variable is carried over into geometry in such terms as *variable point* and *variable line.* A curve is often said to be generated by a moving point. This is a physical concept which has considerable heuristic value, but it would be incorrect to think that the coordinates of a variable point are moving, or changing numbers. Numbers do not change. To say that a curve is described by a variable point is merely to say that it is made up of a set of points. In coordinate geometry the variable point has variable coordinates. Different numerical coordinates belong to different points. Similarly, a set of lines, *e.g.* all the lines through a particular point, may be termed a variable line. The different lines correspond to the different values of the variable slope.—*H. C.*

VARIABLE STAR: a star that varies in brightness, the variation ranging from a few thousandths of a MAGNITUDE to 20 mag. or more. Variable stars are keys to understanding of the universe, and are used to determine distances and dimensions of our galaxy and of others. There are two types: *intrinsic,* in which variation is caused by physical change within the star itself or in its surrounding atmosphere; and *extrinsic,* in which variation is due to an eclipsing effect in a system of

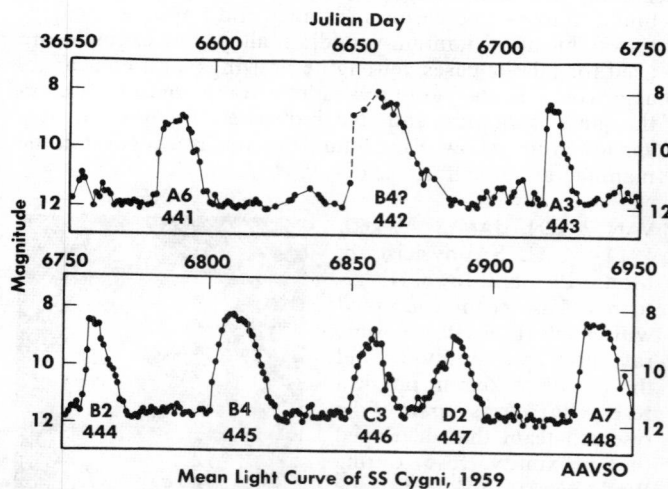

Julian Day

Magnitude

Mean Light Curve of SS Cygni, 1959

AAVSO

Variable star of nova type: Apparent magnitudes of the much-observed intrinsic variable SS Cygni are plotted against elapsed time (50-day intervals, in Julian days). The somewhat irregular pattern features novalike bursts every few weeks; these are marked by an explosive rise in brightness, with declines showing similar slopes from one burst to next. Range of brightness is about 4 magnitudes. Identifying notations appear beneath curve. (*AAVSO*)

PRINCIPAL CHARACTERISTICS OF PULSATING VARIABLE STARS

Type of Variable	Period (hours or days)	Amplitude	Spectrum	Absolute Magnitude	Distribution
β Canis Majoris.................	3^h–6^h	0.1	B	−3	Spiral arms—Population I
Dwarf Cepheids.................	1^h–4^h	1	A–F	+2	Spiral arms—Population I
RR Lyrae or Cluster..............	12^h	1–2	A	0	Halo—Population II
Classical Cepheids..............	2^d–50^d	0.1–2	F–G	−3	Spiral arms—Population I
W Virginis.....................	2^d–75^d	1	F–G	−2	Halo—Population II
RV Tauri......................	30^d–150^d	1–3	G–K	−2	Halo—Population II
Semi-regular...................	30^d–1000^d	1–2	M,N,S	−2	Halo and spiral arms—Populations I & II
Long-period...................	175^d	5	M	−1	Halo—Population II
Long-period...................	350^d	6	M	0	Spiral arms—Population I

two or more bodies (see BINARY STAR). Intrinsic types include pulsating stars, red variables, irregular rapidly changing stars, and explosive stars. Some have regular periods, some semi-regular, and others irregular periods. Some do not fit into any class, and others seem to be combinations of classes. Variable stars within a given constellation are designated by a single or double capital letter, or by the letter V followed by a number.

When observed magnitudes of a variable are plotted against a time scale, a "light curve" results, showing times of maximum and minimum brightness. Inspection of a light curve may indicate whether a star varies periodically or undergoes a recurring pattern of variations; the shape of the curve may give a clue to type of variability. Points to notice in a light curve are: (1) the period or interval between successive maxima or minima; (2) the range in brightness, or amplitude; (3) the curve's shape and symmetry; and (4) the regularity or irregularity of occurrence of maxima and minima.

Pulsating stars vary in brightness because they are continually contracting and expanding, becoming hotter and cooler in turn. Typical are the classical Cepheid variables, which are among the most luminous stars known, visible at great distances. There is in these Cepheids a definite correlation between period and luminosity; hence, since period can be directly observed, luminosity can be estimated, and by comparing luminosity (true brightness) with apparent magnitude (brightness as seen from Earth), the Cepheid's distance from Earth can be calculated. Cepheids have been identified in other galaxies, and thus have become yardsticks for the universe. The relations between period and spectra (indicating temperature), period and radial velocity, and period and form of light curve are other useful correlations in Cepheids. The RR Lyrae or cluster-type Cepheids have periods of about half a day and light curves which resemble those of the classical Cepheids, but unlike the classical Cepheids, show no correlation between period and luminosity.

In *red variables,* including many giants and supergiants, variability involves temperature variations. Among these stars are long-period variables having a cycle of 3 months to 2 or more yr, with fairly regular periods, and amplitudes of 2½ to 5 or more magnitudes. MIRA (O Ceti) is typical. Its period averages about 331 days, and its maximum brightness varies between mags. 2 and 5; at minimum, it drops to between 8 and 10. Irregular red variables have no defined period, and the amount of variability is small—not more than 2 mag. Flare stars are red dwarfs, and often show intense outbursts of short duration. These outbursts, unlike those in pulsating stars, are believed to be confined to small surface areas, but are so bright they increase the total light by as much as six magnitudes.

Explosive stars are the novas, or new stars, characterized by sudden outbursts of brightness of 7 to 16 mag., then a long, slow return to the original magnitude. The most spectacular explosions occur in the supernovas, where the outbursts often amount to more than 20 mag. A few novas have had two or more maxima, showing similar developments, a number of years apart; they are called recurrent novas. Some variables, *e.g.* SS Cygni, have a variation of nova-like character; their maxima occur at irregular intervals, but each star of the type has a mean cycle which remains fairly constant over the years. Their outbursts are much less violent than those of novas and average about 2 to 6 mag. Spectrum variables have a very small range of light variation, but the intensity of groups of lines in their spectra varies with the brightness. They also have magnetic fields which vary with the same period as the light and spectral lines. Another group of variables, the T Tauri class, are always associated with dark nebulosity. They are unstable stars which vary erratically and are thought to be very young stars which are still undergoing gravitational contraction.

The *General Catalogue of Variable Stars* (1958) by B. V. Kukarkin and P. P. Parenago contains all basic information on about 14,711 variables. There are doubtless many thousands more in our galaxy waiting to be discovered. Thousands have been discovered photographically by examination of photographic plates of the same region of the sky taken at different times; a few have been discovered visually. Because of peculiarities in their variations over long periods of time, long-range programs for continued observation are necessary.—*M. W. M.*

VARIATION: in biology, a difference among individuals of the same interbreeding population, or SPECIES. Variations may be transitory, but the majority persist in spite of age and season, and some are transmitted in reproduction. Adjustment to altitude demonstrates the types and sources of variation. A man living at sea level and transported to the mountains increases his respiration rate immediately and his red blood cell count more slowly. These are momentary, reversible modifications for a lower oxygen concentration. If identical twins are separated at birth, however, and one is brought to the mountains, the highland brother develops greater lung capacity than his lowland twin. The variation, though induced by environment, is permanent even if the boy returns to live by the sea. In contrast, of a hundred men living at the same elevation, no two have identical lung capacity, even though they perform similar exercise. The reason is that lung capacity is, in part, inherited. On the average, parents with relatively large lungs have children with relatively large lungs. Sexual reproduction recombines the hereditary material from the two parents (see HEREDITY) in a variety of ways. In man the hereditary material is borne on 23 pairs of chromosomes. These split into unpaired sets of 23 chromosomes, for which there are more than 8 million possible combinations, and are combined with 23 chromosomes from the other parent, so that a child represents one of more than 70 trillion possible combinations (see MEIOSIS). Also, the hereditary material itself changes (see MUTATION). Since children of the same parents have only an infinitesimal chance of the same hereditary complement, and since each complement produces unique development, no two individuals (except identical twins) will be identical. Because different individuals survive better in some environments (*e.g.* a large-lunged man in the mountains), hereditary variations are selected by the environment and furnish the raw material for EVOLUTION.—*J. B.*

VARNISH: a liquid protective coating which "dries," or hardens, by air oxidation after being applied in the same manner as a PAINT. In this respect it differs from a LACQUER, which is a solution of a solid resin that dries by simple evaporation of the solvent. Varnishes differ from paints and enamels in being clear coatings containing no pigment; they are prepared by heating a mixture of a drying oil and an oil-soluble resin which may be natural or synthetic. During the heating, or "cooking" as it is referred to by varnish makers, the two components react to form a material that dries more rapidly and forms a harder, more durable film than straight drying oil does. Because they lack pigment to protect them from the deteriorating effects of sunlight, most varnishes are limited to indoor use. Those made from specially resistant oils and resins, however, can stand considerable outdoor weathering without deterioration and are called *spar varnishes.* Varnish is used primarily on wood, but it can also be used on ceramic surfaces to retard penetration of water without changing the ceramic's appearance.—*A. M. S.*

VARVE: in geology, a layer of fine-grained sediments deposited during one year or during one season. The formation of varves in glacial lakes is typical. During the summer, streams bearing coarse debris deposit it along the lake margins while the finer sediment spreads out over the bottom. When winter comes the lake is frozen over, large streams are materially reduced in volume for the same reason, and small streams

Sequence of varves in organic marlstone from Garfield Co., W Colorado: Thick, light-colored bands represent summer seasons, during which glacial melting and consequent sedimentation were rapid. (*U. S. Geological Survey*)

are largely converted into ice. Below the ice of the lake the finest sediment, which has remained in suspension during the summer months, and much fine organic debris settle to the lake floor. These sediments are thinner and finer-grained than those of summer, because they do not contain the coarser sediments brought to the lake by the streams in summer. This double band which represents a year's deposit is generally but a fraction of an inch thick, but may vary in thickness and coarseness from one year to the next because of seasonal changes (an especially warm summer will be represented by a thicker and coarser pair than usual). By counting the number of pairs it is possible to determine the time represented by any varved deposit. Furthermore, it is possible to time the rate of retreat of the last glacier after matching the varve sequence from the top layers of a southern lake with the bottom layers of a younger, more northerly lake uncovered by the retreating ice sheet at a later date.—*N. E. A. H.*

VASCULAR PLANTS (or **tracheophytes**): plants having specialized fluid-conducting vessels. The simplest known vascular plant was *Rhynia,* which lived early in the Devonian Period, about 300,000,000 yr ago. The plant body was a slender forked axis only a few inches long, and with no leaves or differentiation into stem and roots. Reproduction was by spores produced in capsules at the ends of some forks of the axis. From *Rhynia* a fairly plausible evolutionary series may be traced through a near relative to each of four major lines of vascular plant development, as follows: (1) fern line, beginning with *Protopteridium;* (2) horsetail line, beginning with *Psilophyton;* (3) club moss line, beginning with *Asteroxylon;* (4) Psilotum line, the only one with living near-relatives of *Rhynia. Psilotum* is a whisk-broomlike plant growing in the tropics. The fern line of development is thought to have given rise not only to the FERNS, but also to the cone-bearing trees, such as the pine (see GYMNOSPERM), and the FLOWERING PLANTS. See PHLOEM; PLANT; SEED PLANT; XYLEM.—*L. B.*

VASOMOTOR SYSTEM: the system that controls blood pressure and blood flow within the vertebrate circulatory system. It depends on the state of contraction or relaxation of muscles in the walls of the arterioles and muscles encircling the capillaries at the points where these branch off from the arterioles. These muscles are under nervous control through a system of reflexes constituting a feedback mechanism, and under local control through products of tissue activity, as shown in the diagram.

The arteriolar muscles are caused to contract by impulses which reach them along the vasoconstrictor nerves. Contraction of muscles constricts blood vessels and thus increases resistance of these vessels to blood flow. This in turn tends to increase blood pressure and to decrease flow of blood through the constricted vessels. The muscles may be caused to relax by nervous impulses reaching them along the vasodilator nerves or by the effects of products of local tissue activity (*e.g.* carbon dioxide or lactic acid). Relaxation causes dilation, decreases resistance to blood flow, and hence tends to decrease blood pressure and increase flow through the dilated vessels.

The vasodilator and vasoconstrictor nerve impulses originate in the spinal cord and in a vasomotor nerve center in the medulla oblongata of the brain. The brain center is responsible for excitation of the spinal centers. The activities of the vasomotor center may be described as pressor, tending to increase blood pressure, and depressor, tending to decrease blood pressure. Pressor activities include vasoconstriction and acceleration of the heart beat; depressor activities include vasodilation and inhibition of the heart beat. The vasomotor center, at normal levels of blood pressure, continuously sends

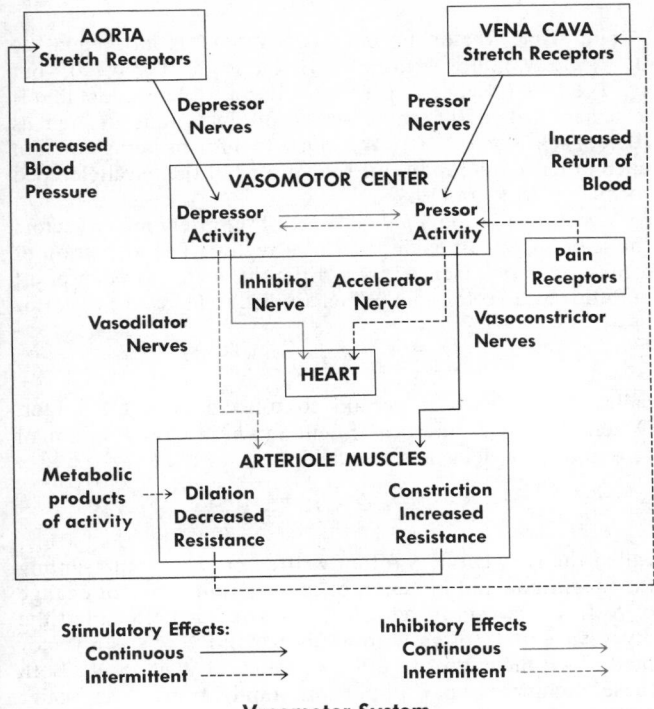

Stimulatory Effects:
Continuous ——————→
Intermittent ‑‑‑‑‑‑‑‑‑→

Inhibitory Effects
Continuous ——————→
Intermittent ‑‑‑‑‑‑‑‑‑→

Vasomotor System

out impulses along the vasoconstrictor nerves and along the inhibitor nerves to the heart.

Activities of the vasomotor center are influenced by impulses conducted to it by three sets of sensory nerves. Depressor nerves originate in sense organs located in the walls of the aorta and carotid arteries. When these sense organs are stimulated by stretch of the arterial walls, they send impulses along the depressor nerves to the vasomotor center. The sense organs are active at all normal levels of blood pressure and are probably stimulated by each pulse; the intensity of their activity increases if the blood pressure increases. In the vasomotor center, they have two actions. First, they stimulate the center to send out inhibitory impulses to the heart, so that the heart is always under some restraint. Second, they inhibit to some extent the vasoconstrictor activity of the center. This part of the system operates as a "feedback," since any increase in blood pressure sets in motion inhibition of constrictor activity and thus brings about a return to normal levels, while a decrease in pressure releases constrictor activity from inhibition and also results in return to normal levels.

Two other sets of nerves have pressor effects. Stimulation of pain receptors, located throughout the body, stimulates the vasomotor center to send out constrictor impulses and impulses along the accelerator nerve to the heart. The same effects can be produced by emotional centers located higher in the brain. A set of pressor nerves has its origin in stretch receptors located in walls of the great veins. When increased tissue activity dilates the arterioles, more blood flows through tissues and into veins. This stimulates the stretch receptors and hence the pressor nerve, leading to vasoconstriction and acceleration of the heart. In general, the pressor effects of vasoconstriction appear first in the splanchnic region (intestines), and in exercise, pain, or emotion blood is diverted from this region to the skin and muscles, without any great change in blood pressure but with an increase in heart rate.—*B. T. S.*

VAVILOV, NICOLAI IVANOVITCH, 1885–1942, Russian geneticist. He set up a nationwide network of more than 400 agricultural research institutes and experimental stations in the Soviet Union. He undertook a number of expeditions.

abroad for the collection of varieties of plants of economic value, both for use by Soviet plant breeders and for research on the origin of cultivated plants. His theories on the latter laid the groundwork for the systematic and cytogenetical study of variation within species of cultivated plants. About 1940 he fell into political disfavor because of his position in genetics. His publications include *The Centers of Cultivated Plants* (1926) and *The New Systematics* (1940).—*D. H. D. R.*

VEBLEN, OSWALD, 1880–1960, U. S. mathematician; b. Decorah, Iowa. As professor at Princeton, 1910–32, he did much to establish Princeton as a great mathematics center. In 1932 he became first professor of mathematics at the Institute for Advanced Study at Princeton. Primarily a geometer, Veblen made noteworthy contributions in that field. His colloquium lectures at Cambridge were devoted to analysis situs (topology) and were published in 1922. His books include *Infinitesimal Analysis* (with N. J. Lennes, 1907), *Projective Geometry* (with J. W. Young, 2 vol., 1910–18), *Invariants of Quadratic Differential Forms* (1927), and *Foundations of Differential Geometry* (with J. H. C. Whitehead, 1932).—*H. C.*

VECTOR ANALYSIS: a branch of mathematics that deals with vectors, *i.e.* quantities that have magnitude and direction and combine according to the parallelogram law described below. Forces, displacements, velocities (velocity is speed in a particular direction), accelerations, angular momenta, and many other important quantities behave like vectors. But not all quantities that have magnitude and direction do; for example, archers' arrows do not. A quantity without direction but with a magnitude that is the same in all reference systems is called a scalar. Examples of scalars are the magnitude of a vector, and mass, volume, and energy.

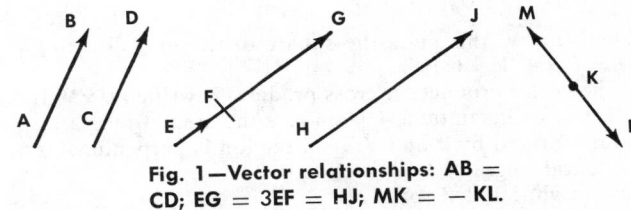

Fig. 1—Vector relationships: $AB = CD$; $EG = 3EF = HJ$; $MK = -KL$.

A vector can be represented by drawing an arrow, such as **AB** in Fig. 1, whose length and direction represent the magnitude and direction of the vector. In Fig. 1, vectors **AB** and **CD** have the same magnitude and the same direction. Sometimes such vectors are counted as equal, the vectors then being called free vectors. If vector **EG** in Fig. 1 has, say, three times the magnitude of vector **EF** there, we say it is three times the vector **EF** and write $EG = 3EF$; if we are dealing with free vectors, we can also write $HJ = 3EF$. Vectors **KL** and **KM** in Fig. 1 have equal magnitudes but opposite directions; we say that **KM** is the negative of **KL** and write $KM = -KL$.

Vectors combine according to the parallelogram law. This states that two vectors such as **U** and **V** in Fig. 2 are together equivalent to the single vector **W** given by the diagonal of the parallelogram formed by **U** and **V**. One writes $U + V = W$, and

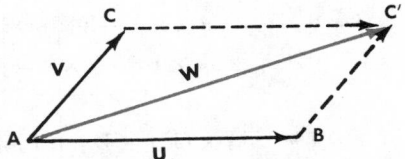

Fig. 2—Vector addition: The sum or resultant of **U** and **V**, **W** is found by the parallelogram rule.

calls **W** the resultant, or sum, of **U** and **V**. To subtract **V** from **U**, one adds − **V** to **U**.

Given a vector **W**, we can form a parallelogram, with sides in any directions, as in Fig. 2, and resolve **W** into two vectors **U** and **V** that are equivalent to it. In Fig. 3, **i** and **j** are per-

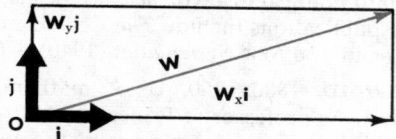

Fig. 3—Resolution of vector W into perpendicular components.

pendicular vectors of unit magnitude. If the lengths of the sides of the rectangle are W_x and W_y, we have $\mathbf{W} = W_x\mathbf{i} + W_y\mathbf{j}$. In three dimensions, similarly, if unit vectors **i**, **j**, and **k** are taken along mutually perpendicular directions,

$$\mathbf{W} = W_x\mathbf{i} + W_y\mathbf{j} + W_z\mathbf{k}$$

The numbers W_x, W_y, and W_z are called the components of **W**.

If θ is the angle between two vectors **U** and **V**, of magnitudes U and V, the scalar $UV \cos \theta$ is called the scalar product (or dot product) of **U** and **V**, and one writes: $\mathbf{U} \cdot \mathbf{V} = \mathbf{V} \cdot \mathbf{U} = UV \cos \theta$. The work done by a constant force **F** in giving a body a displacement **D** is **F · D**. Since the angles between **i**, **j**, and **k** are all 90°, we have

$$\mathbf{i} \cdot \mathbf{i} = 1 \qquad \mathbf{i} \cdot \mathbf{j} = \mathbf{j} \cdot \mathbf{i} = 0$$
$$\mathbf{j} \cdot \mathbf{j} = 1 \qquad \mathbf{j} \cdot \mathbf{k} = \mathbf{k} \cdot \mathbf{j} = 0$$
$$\mathbf{k} \cdot \mathbf{k} = 1 \qquad \mathbf{k} \cdot \mathbf{i} = \mathbf{i} \cdot \mathbf{k} = 0$$

Therefore,

$$\mathbf{U} \cdot \mathbf{V} = (U_x\mathbf{i} + U_y\mathbf{j} + U_z\mathbf{k}) \cdot (V_x\mathbf{i} + V_y\mathbf{j} + V_z\mathbf{k})$$
$$= U_xV_x + U_yV_y + U_zV_z \qquad (1)$$

When **U** = **V**, this gives the square of the magnitude of **V**: $V^2 = V_x{}^2 + V_y{}^2 + V_z{}^2$.

The vector product (or cross product) is written **U**×**V**. It is a vector. Its magnitude, $UV \sin \theta$, is the area of the parallelogram formed by **U** and **V**; its direction is perpendicular to the parallelogram, and such that a right-handed corkscrew twisted from **U** to **V** would move forward in the direction of **U** × **V**. Since rotating in the opposite direction would move the corkscrew backward, **U** × **V** = − **V** × **U** (Fig. 4). If a vector **r** reaches from a point O to the line of action of a force **F**, then **r** × **F** represents the moment of **F** about O. If **i**, **j**, and **k** form a right-handed reference system (one in which twisting from **i** to **j** moves the corkscrew in the positive direction of **k**), then

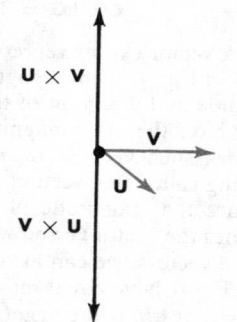

Fig. 4—Vector multiplication yielding cross products (other vectors).

$$\mathbf{i} \times \mathbf{i} = 0 \qquad \mathbf{i} \times \mathbf{j} = -\mathbf{j} \times \mathbf{i} = \mathbf{k}$$
$$\mathbf{j} \times \mathbf{j} = 0 \qquad \mathbf{j} \times \mathbf{k} = -\mathbf{k} \times \mathbf{j} = \mathbf{i}$$
$$\mathbf{k} \times \mathbf{k} = 0 \qquad \mathbf{k} \times \mathbf{i} = -\mathbf{i} \times \mathbf{k} = \mathbf{j}$$

Therefore,

$$\mathbf{U} \times \mathbf{V} = (U_x\mathbf{i} + U_y\mathbf{j} + U_z\mathbf{k}) \times (V_x\mathbf{i} + V_y\mathbf{j} + V_z\mathbf{k})$$
$$= (U_yV_z − U_zV_y)\mathbf{i} + (U_zV_x − U_xV_z)\mathbf{j}$$
$$+ (U_xV_y − U_yV_x)\mathbf{k} \qquad (2)$$

The triple vector product $(\mathbf{U} \times \mathbf{V}) \times \mathbf{W}$ is not equal to $\mathbf{U} \times (\mathbf{V} \times \mathbf{W})$; for example, $(\mathbf{i} \times \mathbf{i} \times \mathbf{j} = 0 \times \mathbf{j} = 0$, but $\mathbf{i} \times \mathbf{i} \times \mathbf{j}) = \mathbf{i} \times \mathbf{k} = − \mathbf{j}$. There is also a triple product that is a scalar. Called the triple scalar product, it is defined as $(\mathbf{U} \times \mathbf{V}) \cdot \mathbf{W}$, or $\mathbf{U} \cdot (\mathbf{V} \times \mathbf{W})$, these two forms being equal to each other. Each represents the volume of the parallelepiped formed by **U**, **V**, and **W**.

A vector (or scalar) *field* is a set of infinitely many vectors (or scalars), one at each point of a region. The attraction of a magnet is represented by a different vector at each point and thus by a vector field. When applied to fields, the operator

$$\nabla \equiv \mathbf{i}\frac{\partial}{\partial x} + \mathbf{j}\frac{\partial}{\partial y} + \mathbf{k}\frac{\partial}{\partial z}$$

called *del*, behaves, in certain circumstances, like a vector. When ∇ operates on a scalar field S (where S is a function of x, y, and z), it yields a vector field,

$$\nabla S \equiv \mathbf{i}\frac{\partial S}{\partial x} + \mathbf{j}\frac{\partial S}{\partial y} + \mathbf{k}\frac{\partial S}{\partial z}$$

called the *gradient* of S (often written grad S), representing the magnitude and direction of the maximum rate of change of S. If **V** is a vector field, $\nabla \cdot \mathbf{V}$ is a scalar field called the divergence of V (often written div **V**), and $\nabla \times \mathbf{V}$ is a vector field called the curl of **V** (often written curl **V**, or rot **V**). Both these quantities have important applications. The scalar product $\nabla \cdot \nabla$, written ∇^2 and called the *Laplacian*, can be applied to scalar and vector fields; Laplace's equation, $\nabla^2 S = 0$, represents the inverse square law of force (see POTENTIAL THEORY). Expressions for $\nabla \cdot \mathbf{V}$, $\nabla \times \mathbf{V}$ are obtainable from (1) and (2) by replacing U_x by $\partial/\partial x$, etc. See also TENSOR ANALYSIS.—*Ba. H.*

VEGETABLE: popularly, any edible part of a plant—whether root, stem, leaf, flower, or fruit—that is not sweet and is usually salted, or flavored with other condiments, before it is eaten. Although the word vegetable has no precise botanical significance at present, it used to be a synonym for plant. Until late in the 19th cent., one spoke of vegetable anatomy or vegetable physiology or the vegetable kingdom, whereas today one would say plant anatomy, plant physiology, and the plant kingdom.—*H. Cr.*

VEGETATIVE REPRODUCTION: in plants, any asexual method of REPRODUCTION. The rooting of stem or leaf cuttings, grafting and budding, the growing of plants from bulbs, corms, tubers, tuberous roots, and portions of rhizomes, grafts, or division are all methods of vegetative reproduction, in contrast to reproduction by SEEDS.—*H. Cr.*

VEIN (in anatomy): any of the vessels that carry blood toward the heart. The smallest branches, or venules, receive blood from capillaries. In vertebrate animals, the venules unite to form larger veins, which continue to join together to form eventually the two great venae cavae (caval veins), which unite at the entrance to the heart. In lower vertebrates this junction forms a definite cavity, the sinus venosus; in higher vertebrates the venae cavae drain directly into the right auricle of the heart.

Veins are tubes with relatively thin walls. The inner surface of the walls is lined with endothelium, continuous with the walls of capillaries and the endothelial lining of arteries, and like these made of thin, flat cells. Surrounding the endothelium is a layer of connective tissue which may have circular and in some cases longitudinal muscle fibers. Veins serve to conduct blood from tissues to heart and act as important reservoirs of blood. Their highly extensible walls enable them to expand and to hold large amounts of blood when there is a sudden increase in blood flow through the tissues. Distribution of blood through the venous system depends on flow through the arterioles and capillaries, and varies with posture

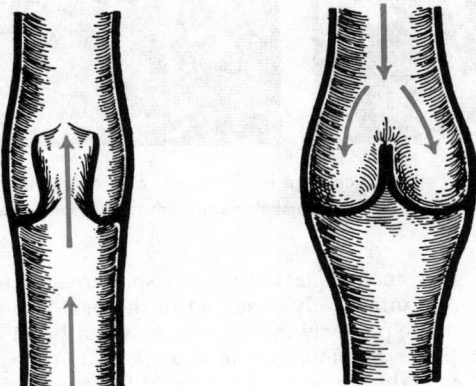

Valves in larger veins help maintain flow of blood to heart by preventing backflow. These diagrammatic sections through a vein show operation of a valve, which is formed from leaflike extensions of the vein walls. First drawing shows valve open as blood flows toward heart, and second drawing shows how valve closes to stop reverse flow. (*From Young*)

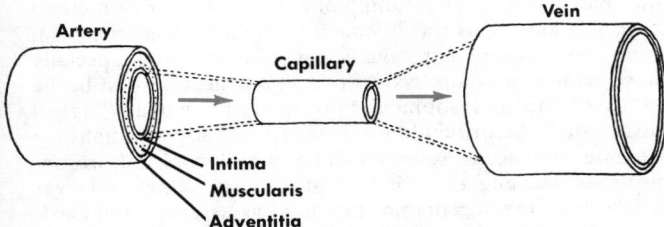

Comparison of artery, capillary, and vein: Structure of blood vessels shows continuity of endothelial lining (intima) from artery to capillary to vein. Walls of most veins have same three layers that walls of arteries have. Veins are usually larger than corresponding arteries, but have thinner, less muscular walls; they are thus adapted for transport of large volume of slow-moving blood under low pressure. (*From Eaton*)

and bodily activity. Change from a recumbent to an erect posture greatly increases the work required to move blood from the extremities to the heart and tends to cause accumulation of blood in the veins of extremities. Movements of body muscles, by compressing the veins, tend to force blood out of the active region. This effect is aided by the presence, in the larger veins, of valves which prevent back flow. Return of blood to the heart is also aided by respiratory movements which alternately enlarge and constrict the thoracic cavity and thus draw blood into the large thoracic veins. Veins in the skin and intestines have constrictor nerve fibers, but the fibers' roles are uncertain.—*B. T. S.*

VEIN (in mining): a "lode," or any deposit of ORE which is generally of slight thickness as compared to its length and breadth. To the geologist, a "vein" is any crack or fissure filled more or less solidly by minerals introduced by water solutions, vapors, or gases, whether or not the resultant filling has any economic value. Most veins are irregular tabular or sheetlike bodies, frequently branched or divided into swarms of veinlets or stringers, and characterized by a banded or

zoned structure corresponding to successive waves of mineralization. Veins emplaced along fault fissures often contain brecciated portions. Common vein minerals are quartz and calcite, with or without accessory minerals; veins containing appreciable amounts of sulfide ore minerals are relatively rare, yet it is from such infrequent deposits that enormous quantities of lead, zinc, silver, and copper have been mined. Gold is most commonly associated with iron and copper sulfides, particularly in quartz veins cutting across schists and gneisses.—*J. Si.*

VELOCITY AND SPEED: A sharp technical distinction exists between velocity and speed. Speed, as here used, refers to the rate at which distance is covered in relation to time, as "50 mi/hr," and not, for example, to the speed of a chemical reaction. Velocity involves direction as well as speed, as "50 mi/hr due east." A point can move in a circle with constant speed, but not with constant velocity; for the velocity changes when the direction changes. Velocity is a *vector* quantity; its magnitude, the speed, is a *scalar* quantity. Dictionaries usually ignore this distinction and accept velocity as a synonym for speed. Scientists themselves are not meticulous in their usage; in relativity they often say the velocity of light is the same for all observers, using "velocity" where they mean "speed."—*Ba. H.*

VELOCITY CURVE: the plot, against time, of the line-of-sight velocity of one component of a spectroscopic BINARY STAR. (The line-of-sight velocity is determined by the Doppler effect, and the observations are corrected for Earth's rotation and orbital motion.) If the orbit of the star (about the center of gravity of the binary system) is a circle, the velocity curve is a simple sine wave; if the orbit is an ellipse, the velocity curve shows asymmetry. If both spectra are visible, two velocity curves may be drawn. Information about the physical characteristics of the binary system may be drawn from an analysis of the velocity curves.—*M. W. O.*

VELOCITY OF ESCAPE: see ESCAPE VELOCITY.

VENING-MEINESZ, FELIX ANDRIES, 1887–1966, Dutch geophysicist; b. The Hague. He was a specialist in mapping the gravity field of Earth and interpreting its variations. After a pioneering gravity survey of the Netherlands (1911–20), he developed a 3-pendulum apparatus capable of accurate gravity measurements from the relatively steady base of a submerged submarine. From 1923 to 1938 he investigated deep marine trenches, finding that most have less gravitational attraction than balanced conditions would suggest (see ISOSTASY). These are areas of negative isostatic anomaly, which Vening-Meinesz believed to be related to slow convection currents (see CONVECTION THEORY) in the mantle. He wrote (with W. Heiskanen) *The Earth and Its Gravity Field* (1958). He was a fellow of the Royal Society and an associate of the U. S. National Academy of Sciences.—*R. W. D.*

VENUS: the second principal planet outward from the Sun, and one of the four terrestrial planets. Usually between −3.4 and −4.3 in stellar magnitude, Venus is the brightest planet and is frequently visible in the daytime to the unaided eye. The orbit lies inside Earth's, so that this planet is never seen more than 48° away from the Sun; it is normally seen either as an "evening star" in the west or as a "morning star" in the east. Telescopic studies are often made in the daytime, chiefly to reduce glare.

Orbit: The average distance from the Sun is 67,200,000 mi. The eccentricity of the orbit is 0.007, the least for all prin-

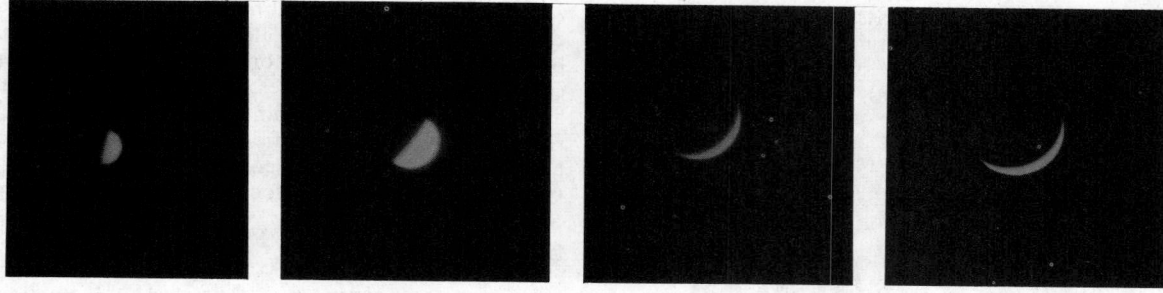

Phases of Venus in the course of two months: Full cycle (584 days) would show six-fold change in diameter, and crescents facing both ways. "Lunar" regimen of phases was seized upon by Galileo in 1610 as evidence against Ptolemaic model. *(Hans Pfleumer)*

cipal planets, and the inclination to the ecliptic is 3° 24′. Venus comes closer to Earth than any other principal planet, its minimum distance being about 26,000,000 mi. The period of revolution around the Sun is 224.70 days. Venus shows the same phases as the Moon, and the interval between consecutive "full" or "new" phases is 583.92 days. These phases, observed by Galileo, were early evidence of the correctness of the Copernican system.

Physical Data and Atmosphere: In some respects Venus is Earth's twin: diameter 7,600 mi, mass 81% of Earth's, and density about five times that of water. The reflecting surface is the top of a heavy layer of clouds; about 76% of sunlight received is reflected—a value possible only for clouds. The temperature of the sunlit visible surface is given by J. Strong and W. M. Sinton as −40° F; the night parts have a similar temperature, as in Earth's stratosphere. The underlying solid surface must be very much warmer. Radio emission suggests a temperature of around 800° F.—perhaps even higher—beneath the clouds, but some astronomers have argued that this could be due to electrical phenomena within the clouds. The planet's changes in brightness according to phase show the reflecting surface to be smooth. The spectroscope has revealed carbon dioxide above the cloud layer; N. Kozyrev reported nitrogen, and, in a spectrum obtained by a balloon flight, M. Ross and C. B. Moore found evidence of water vapor. No direct evidence is available as to gases present below the cloud layer. The non-sunlit hemisphere is often reported to be very faintly visible, perhaps owing to an atmospheric aurora or airglow. Venus has no known satellite.

As to whether life could exist on Venus, the high surface temperatures would raise serious doubts. Apparently the terrain in a desert, swept by violent winds.

Rotation and Markings: All detail on Venus is extremely difficult to perceive, and visual observers often disagree completely. Probably all the visible features are clouds. Photographs in violet and ultra-violet light by F. E. Ross, G. Kuiper, B. Smith, and others reveal bandlike markings curiously suggestive of the belts of Jupiter and Saturn. Little or nothing is present on photographs at longer wavelengths. Rotation periods determined chiefly by visual observers from these elusive markings either were near 24 hr or were extremely long, approaching the 225-day period of revolution. Failure to detect a Doppler effect (see RADIAL VELOCITY) at the edge of the disc implied a period of rotation longer than 10 days. Radar data give a rotation period of about 249 days, the direction of the rotation being retrograde.

Solar Transits: Venus usually passes north or south of the Sun when between it and Earth. Very near to June 7 and Dec. 8, when crossing the plane of Earth's orbit, Venus can transit the solar disc. The last two transits occurred Dec. 9, 1874, and Dec. 6, 1882; the next ones will be June 8, 2004, and June 6, 2012. Venus in transit is visible to the unaided

eye through a smoked glass as a black spot crossing the Sun. Transits were intensively observed in the past in efforts to determine more precisely the distance between Earth and the Sun, but better methods are now available. A bright rim around Venus during transits presumably demonstrates refraction of light in the planet's atmosphere.—*W. H.*

VERIFIABILITY PRINCIPLE (or Principle of Verifiability): a modern formulation of the conditions to be satisfied by a meaningful statement. It may be regarded as a sophisticated revision of the guiding principle of the philosophical tendency known as "empiricism": that all scientific knowledge is derived from the senses. The principle was stated by Friedrich Waismann thus: "The meaning of a proposition is its method of verification." This was intended to exclude from science all statements having no observable consequences, and especially those belonging to any system of *a priori* metaphysics. In the hands of the philosophical movement known as "logical positivism," the principle was a sharp weapon in a fight for the independence of science from any philosophical presuppositions. The effect of this earliest form of the principle was to interpret any acceptable statement as asserting the existence of the relevant verifying situations. Since a statement about another person's thoughts or feelings is tested by observing his behavior, the principle led some of its advocates to identify consciousness with behavior (a form of behaviorism). Again, since statements about the past are tested by examining documents and archeological remains in the future, the principle was sometimes held to require that statements seemingly about the past are "really" about the future. It soon became clear that scientific statements containing theoretical terms failed to satisfy the principle, because they could not be completely translated into logical functions of statements about direct observations. So the principle has had to be modified, lest respectable scientific statements be branded as "nonsensical." A plausible modification consists in counting the principle as defining *directly verifiable* statements. Other statements may then be accepted as meaningful if they allow directly verifiable statements to be obtained, within some scientific theory, that would not be obtainable otherwise. Such a shift to meaning *within a theory* answers better to actual scientific practice than did the original principle.—*M. B.*

VERNAL EQUINOX: see EQUINOX.

VERNE, JULES, 1828–1905, French author; b. Nantes. After studying law and working briefly as a playwright, he began writing highly imaginative adventure stories involving science and invention. Verne foretold with amazing accuracy and dramatic style the submarine, the airplane, television, rockets, and space travel. He is regarded by many as the originator of science fiction. His first success, *Cinq semaines en ballon*

(1863), was followed by book after book. Among his most popular novels are *Voyage au centre de la terre* (1864), *De la terre à la lune* (1865), *Le tour du monde en quatre-vingts jours* (1873), and *Michael Strogoff* (1876). Some of his works were later made into plays and motion pictures.—*C. S. V.*

VERSUCHE ÜBER PFLANZEN-HYBRIDEN (Experiments in Plant-Hybridization), by Gregor Mendel, *Verhandlungen des Naturforscher Vereins zu Brünn*, Vol. 4 (1865): This seminal paper in the study of heredity, although published in 1866, remained almost unknown until its results were independently resubstantiated by three botanists, K. E. Correns, E. von Tschermak-Seysenegg, and H. de Vries, in 1900. Mendel's resulting fame rests solely upon the studies reported in this and one other paper. Experimenting with certain easily observable characteristics of the pea plant, Mendel derived several fundamental laws of inheritance. Upon crossing two lines of peas, he found that all the seedlings resembled one parent. This type he termed "dominant," and its latent alternative, "recessive." Each parent contains two factors controlling the inheritance of a given character, and these factors separate or *segregate* when passed to the sex cells. When observing the inheritance of several characteristics, Mendel found that during reproduction they separated and *independently recombined*. Although much has been added since the turn of the century, Mendel's work provided the basis of modern genetics and an important factor in the understanding of organic evolution. See HEREDITY.—*E. Me.*

VERTEBRAL COLUMN: the backbone; a series of ringlike bones called vertebrae, which enclose the spinal cord in most VERTEBRATES. The 26 vertebrae in man, from the head down, are: a bone just under the skull (the atlas), a pivoted vertebra (the axis), five neck (cervical) vertebrae, 12 upper back (thoracic) vertebrae (ribs attach to the vertebral joints on each side of the thoracic vertebrae), five lower back (lumbar) vertebrae, one fused large bone (sacrum) between the hip bones, one small rudimentary tail bone (the coccyx).—*A. R. D.*

VERTEBRATE: any animal having a backbone consisting of cartilaginous or bony vertebrae. About 40,000 living kinds of vertebrates are recognized, including fishes, amphibians, reptiles, birds, and mammals. They include all the largest, fastest, and most intelligent of marine animals, all the large land animals, and many small ones, too. Vertebrates were once regarded as constituting a separate phylum, but now they are classed as the subphylum Vertebrata within the phylum Chordata. They are so classed because, like a few invertebrate chordates, they possess an internal stiffening rod (the notochord) at least during embryonic development. Vertebrae replace the notochord to form a spinal column in all advanced vertebrates; it extends from the skull to the tip of the tail. In the most primitive fishes, however, the vertebrae remain as slender separate pieces of cartilage arranged in a segmental pattern. The form and location of the skull and spinal column allow them to cover and protect the brain and spinal cord. They also provide excellent anchorage for muscles important in moving the body, and give support to vertebrates that run or jump or fly. Growth of the vertebrate skeleton is achieved without periodic molting. Other unique or almost unique characteristics of the vertebrates include: a true skin, consisting of both epidermis and dermis; a brain, consisting of from three to five hollow lobes; a pair of camera-style eyes capable of forming good optical images; a closed circulatory system with a ventral heart, arteries, capillaries, and veins; red blood cells; and a tail posterior to the anus.—*H. M. S.*

VESALIUS, ANDREAS, 1514–64, Belgian-Italian anatomist; b. Brussels. He migrated to Italy and established himself at Padua, first as a tutor and then as professor of anatomy. Although Vesalius published a number of works, his fame rests upon the *De humani corporis fabrica* (1543), a major anatomical work that provided a great modern compendium of anatomical knowledge to replace the older sources. The book is known principally for its remarkable drawings of the human body, attributed to a pupil of Titian, Stephen van Calcar.—*D. H. D. R.*

VESTIGE: a structure or part of a plant or animal that, through degeneration or failure to develop fully, is smaller than is usual among related plants or animals. In man, the third eyelid (nictitating membrane) of each eye, the muscles that might move the ears, the hair on the body, and some whole organs are regarded as vestigial. So are mammary glands in the male mammal. In man, the tail is a vestigial organ that grows into a conspicuous part of the embryo during the embryo's first month of uterine life; although tail bones and muscles develop, the organ itself rarely enlarges enough to remain evident outside the body, and man consequently is described as tail-less. The human vermiform appendix similarly represents a side branch (cecum) at the junction of the small and large intestines; in a rabbit, the corresponding structure may be as long as the entire body and may serve the animal as a place in which additional bacterial action can proceed, aiding in the digestion of plant food.

Vestigial organs often provide evidence important in discovering the ancestral relationships between animals or between plants. In pythons, a pelvic girdle with attached bones ending in little claws projecting through the skin beside the cloacal opening is regarded as a reliable indication that the ancestors of all snakes once had hind legs—and probably forelegs too. Whales also have the remains of hind-leg bones and hip girdles. In a South American bird (the hoactzin), the nestlings are hatched with workable fingers with claws on the featherless wings; they use these in clambering in the trees near the nest, until feathers develop. Thereafter the skeletal elements and muscles remain as vestiges, but they correspond exactly to structures in the human hand.

Many cacti, as they grow and extend new parts, produce vestigial leaves in the center of clusters of spines. Usually the leaves drop off in the first few weeks of dry weather, and the stem takes over the work of photosynthesis. Similarly, some flowers (*e.g.* a buttercup of swampy ground) have vestigial petals.—*L. and M. M.*

VIBRATION: the periodic displacement, usually relatively small, of a body from a reference position. Vibration implies that when the body is displaced there is a restorative force; and by virtue of the body's mass and the restorative force, the body accelerates (see NEWTON'S LAWS OF MOTION). A simple example is the PENDULUM, which when displaced by an external force is then acted on by the restorative force of gravity. A similar instance is a body at the end of a SPRING. When the body is displaced, the elastic force of the spring accelerates it in a direction opposite to its displacement. In both cases the energy imparted to the body is more than enough to return it to its original position, and when the body overshoots its rest position the process repeats itself. Energy losses due to friction eventually bring the body to rest. Since any force produces some displacement, any force applied to any body (especially to a body of high ELASTICITY) tends to cause vibration. If a portion of the body's energy (the sum of the kinetic energy and potential energy of the body) is transmitted to another medium, waves are set up. Thus, a reed vibrating at an audible frequency (approximately 20 to 20,000 cycles/sec) sets up audible sound waves. In practice, most vibrations are of a complex character extending in all three dimensions. For analysis, certain of the outstanding vibrations are reduced to their simple components (see FOURIER SERIES). A desired vibration may be maintained by the application of an exterior force whose period is the same as that of the vibrating body. All bodies have a natural frequency, *i.e.* the frequency of the body if allowed to oscillate freely. If an external force is applied whose frequency is equal to the body's natural frequency, the displacement increases rapidly. Ordinary vibration can be damaging because it causes wear, fatigue failure, and noise; and if a body is acted on by a force whose frequency is equal to its natural frequency, *i.e.* if there is resonance, with large amplitudes, vibration can be destructive. This is the reason why soldiers are ordered to break step when crossing a bridge, lest the rhythm of their steps coincide with the natural frequency of the bridge. A notorious example of destruction by resonance was the Tacoma Narrows bridge disaster (1940). The wind in the Tacoma Narrows happened to blow in gusts at intervals whose frequency coincided with the natural frequency of the bridge—a completely unforeseen circumstance. As it was struck by the wind, the bridge tended to vibrate up and down like a vibrating string, until the displacement became so great as to completely wrench the bridge from its foundations.

Vibration Control: Vibration is controlled by damping and by isolation. *Damping* is the process of converting the mechanical energy of vibration into heat energy, and is generally accomplished by placing some element of the vibrating body in frictional contact with another body. *Viscous damping* involves putting some portion of the vibrating body into intimate contact with a viscous liquid. The automobile shock absorber and the artillery dashpot are examples of viscous damping. *Isolation* is achieved by interposing between the vibrating body and its surroundings a resilient (*i.e.* non-elastic) material, which absorbs vibrational energy. In some cases an unbalanced periodic force can be exactly canceled by an equal and opposite force. This is accomplished by attaching a tuned *dynamic absorber,* which often is simply a spring and a mass. The tuning is crucial; hence such absorbers can be used only with truly constant-speed machines. Today more efficient torsional dampers of the dynamic-absorber type are used; they have a carefully controlled amount of internal friction, so that when suitably tuned for a particular frequency of vibration they are effective over a range of machine speeds. (See PERIODICITY.) —*A. L.; E. E. W.*

VIERORDT, KARL VON, 1818–84, German physiologist; b. Lahr. A pioneer in the quantitative study of the circulation of the blood, Vierordt measured the pressure of human blood, invented a hemotachometer (1858) for measuring blood speed, made accurate counts of red blood corpuscles, and was the first to engage in quantitative spectrophotometry upon hemoglobin derivatives (1876).—*D. H. D. R.*

VIETA (VIÈTE), FRANÇOIS, 1540–1603, French mathematician; b. Fontenay-le-Comte. A member of the king's privy council, he was able to devote much leisure time to mathematics, and the results of his amateur mathematical studies gave him high rank in the field. His works were printed at his own expense and communicated to scholars throughout Europe. They were chiefly on algebra, but he had an interest in geometry, trigonometry, and other subjects also. Vieta discovered general methods for solving equations of 2nd, 3rd, and 4th degree, and how to alter an equation so as to increase, decrease, multiply, or divide the roots by a given quantity. His *Opera mathematica* appeared in 1646.—*H. C.*

VINCI: see LEONARDO DA VINCI.

VINYL COMPOUNDS: a large family of organic compounds that underlie much of the plastics and fibers industry. The vinyl group ($CH_2=CH-$) is the ETHYLENE molecule minus one H atom; it has a valence of one. One method for producing vinyl compounds starts with acetylene:

$$HC\equiv CH \quad + \quad HCl \quad \longrightarrow \quad H_2C=CH$$
$$|$$
$$Cl$$

Hydrogen chloride   Vinyl chloride

Acetic acid can also be added to acetylene, to make vinyl acetate:

$$H_2C=CH$$
$$|$$
$$OOC-CH_3$$

These two vinyl compounds can be polymerized into a copolymer making the commercially important plastic, vinylite, and the textile fiber, vinyon. Representative vinyl compounds and plastics into which they are manufactured, as well as the mechanisms by which vinyl compounds join end-to-end, are described in the article POLYMERS.—*Ru. M.*

VIRTANEN, ARTTURI ILMARI, 1895–   , Finnish chemist and biologist; b. Helsinki. He introduced improvements in the conservation of green fodder in silos and studied the nitrogen metabolism of plants, particularly in connection with nitrifying bacteria. For his researches and inventions in agricultural and nutritive chemistry, especially for his method of fodder preservation, he received the 1945 Nobel prize in chemistry.—*E. F.*

VIRUS: a nucleoprotein particle capable of multiplication in certain living cells. The term virus was originally applied to an agent that would pass through a filter able to hold back bacteria and that would produce symptoms of sickness in humans, animals, and plants. Diseases caused by viruses include smallpox, influenza, poliomyelitis, measles, mosaic disease in tobacco, and bushy stunt disease in tomato plants. Viruses were subsequently identified as *nucleoprotein* particles. The active agent is a form of NUCLEIC ACID, a long-chain compound of four bases, sugar, and phosphate. For many viruses the nucleic acid is ribonucleic acid, in which the sugar is ribose and the four bases are adenine, guanine, cytosine, and uracil. The nucleic acid is contained in a capsule, or coat, of protein, which is quite simple for poliomyelitis virus and bushy stunt virus, but more elaborate for viruses of influenza and measles.

The life history of a virus starts as it leaves the cell in which it was made. The virus remains stable so long as the temperature is moderate, and awaits the time when it will encounter a new cell that is suitable for its growth. Upon such encounter it must attach itself, and such attachment is *specific,* in that only certain cells will hold on to a specific virus. After the virus becomes attached, the protein coating acts to open a hole in the cell and at the same time releases the nucleic acid, which is a long, threadlike molecule, through the coat and into the cell. Once in the cell the nucleic acid makes changes in the way the cell behaves, which is a necessary prelude to the process of making more virus. Shortly after, the cell and the virus together begin to make nucleic acid, up to hundreds of times the original amount that came in. When the nucleic acid is made, the manufacture of protein for the coat begins. Hundreds of completed virus particles appear, emerging from the cells one at a time or escaping en masse by wholly disrupting the cell. The life cycle then starts over again.

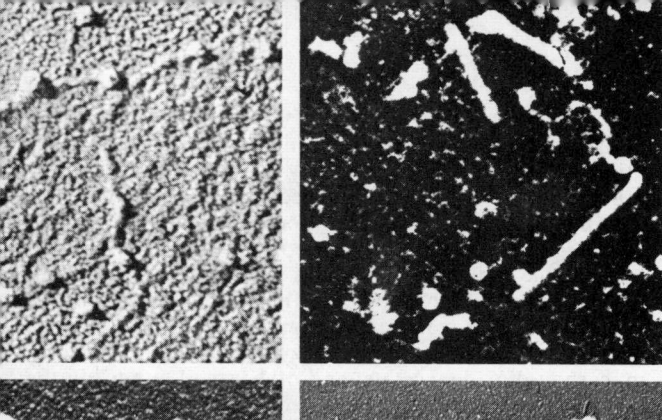

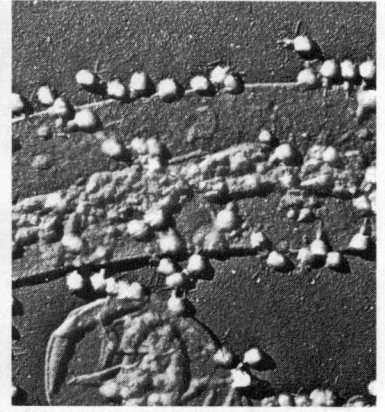

Electron micrographs of viruses: *Upper left*—Hepatitis viruses; *right*—Asian influenza viruses ($\times$13,000). *Lower left*—Four vaccinia, or cowpox, viruses ($\times$28,000), solutions of which are used in smallpox immunizing vaccinations; *right*—T$_2$ bacterial viruses, or bacteriophages ($\times$25,000), attacking wall of the intestinal bacterium *Escherichia coli*. (*Science Service; Walter Reed Institute; Virus Lab., Univ. of Calif., Berkeley; Edouard Kellenberger/Univ. of Geneva*)

Very important advances have been made in virus knowledge by the discovery that bacteria are susceptible to viruses known as *bacteriophages*. These bacterial viruses differ from other viruses in their nucleic acid content, in which the sugar is deoxyribose and the base thymine is substituted for uracil.

Viruses are very good *antigens,* which means that they can stimulate lymphatic cells to grow and release *antibodies*, which combine rather firmly with the virus coat. A virus particle in combination with an antibody is very ineffective at becoming attached to a cell; so an individual who is producing virus antibodies is relatively immune to the virus disease. On occasion scientists have found viruses with a different kind of nucleic acid that does not cause great cell damage and hence disease; but the coats of these viruses are the same as those of *virulent* viruses. An example is *vaccinia*, or cowpox virus, which produces no more than a local action, yet generates effective antibodies against *variola*, or smallpox. Such IMMUNIZATION is very desirable and, in addition to the process of vaccination just described, is available for several diseases, notably yellow fever. A "killed-virus vaccine" can be made by inactivating the nucleic acid without damaging severely the protein coat. The process demands skill, but it can be done, notably in the Salk vaccine against polio.

The origin of viruses is not really known. One class of bacterial virus is a detached piece of the genetic thread, or chromosome, of a bacterium. Whether such a detachment is general for all viruses cannot be said and is doubtful, for the nucleic acid of most viruses is not the same as that in the chromosome (see CHROMOSOMES AND GENES). Viruses can show MUTATION, which is a permanent change found in the progeny. It has recently been shown that viruses in which one of the bases is changed are mutated. Thus a very great ac-

curacy of molecular structure is required for the nucleic acid. Some forms of cancer and leukemia can be produced by viruses. Most workers expect that many new forms of virus yet remain to be discovered.—*E. C. P.*

VISCOSE: see RAYON.

VISCOSITY: the resistance to flow exhibited by fluids (liquids and gases). A fluid in motion undergoes a progressive displacement of its layers, the resulting shearing stress being balanced, under conditions of equilibrium, by the viscosity, or internal friction. Viscosity bears an inverse relationship to mobility. Thus oil, which is less mobile than alcohol, is more viscous. The coefficient of viscosity, usually stated in *poise*, is the force in dynes required to move a square centimeter of a surface across the top of a liquid layer 1 cm thick, the motion taking place at the rate of 1 cm/sec. In engineering practice, the time required for a liquid to flow through a standard orifice of a viscosimeter serves as a measure of the viscosity of the liquid.—*A. E.*

VISCOUS FLOW: the flow of a fluid as influenced by the fluid's viscosity, or resistance to flow. As a result of viscosity, fluids adhere to the walls of pipes; the boundary layer of a fluid has no velocity in relation to these walls. Viscous flow is numerically determined by the *kinematic coefficient of viscosity,* or the ratio of viscous resistance to gravitational inertia. A so-called "Newtonian" fluid is characterized by a constancy of the coefficient of viscosity. An orderly flow of a viscous fluid is described as *laminar* or sheet-like, a disorderly one as *turbulent.* Flow in a straight pipe remains laminar if the REYNOLDS NUMBER (R)—the ratio of inertial force to viscous force—is below 2,200. Transition to turbulent flow occurs when the value of R exceeds 2,200. See FLUID FLOW; SKIN FRICTION.—*A. E.*

VISION: the sense in animals that is stimulated by patterns of light. To possess this sense an animal needs some means for detecting the intensity of light coming to it from each small area of the surroundings. Usually the detector takes the form of an *eye.* Some animals, such as horses, flounders, and dragonflies, have panoramic vision and can keep alert to events in a visual field that extends almost all around and above them. Others are more like man, monkeys, and owls in having the eyes so far forward that at least two-fifths of the environment is behind the head and invisible.

The advantage in having eyes with large overlapping visual fields is that the distance to objects can be estimated more accurately when the brain compares the slightly unlike pictures reported by the two eyes. This stereoscopic vision is most conspicuous in animals with predatory habits, such as cats and praying mantises, or in those jumping habitually from tree to tree and in danger of falling to the ground. Most vertebrate animals, and possibly the octopus as well, learn something of the distance to objects by the amount of exertion the eye muscles require to bring the lens into best possible focus. This is especially important in examining objects close to the eyes.

Animals differ greatly in their visual acuity, the ability to see fine details. At 500 yd, a black spot on a white background would have to be 45 ft in diameter for a honeybee to see it. Our own eyes can find a 5-in. spot at this distance, whereas a hawk can locate a dot ½ in. in diameter. Human vision excels in detecting contrasts between shades of gray. Under good illumination, two adjacent areas need differ only by 0.6% in the amount of light they send to our eyes for us to distinguish the darker from the brighter. This gives us a scale of about 500 shades of gray between black and white. A honeybee detects no boundary unless the difference in light output exceeds 25%. As a result, it sees only about a dozen different shades of gray, plus black and white.

The honeybee is like many other insects in its ability to see the ultraviolet portion of the solar spectrum, to which our eyes are blind. For the bee, ultraviolet is both the brightest part of the spectrum and also a distinct color. Two areas of white paint, one reflecting ultraviolet and the other absorbing it, appear identical to our eyes but not to the insect. At the other end of the spectrum, however, the honeybee detects nothing where our eyes report red light. When a bee visits a red flower, it is because the blossom reflects attractive ultraviolet; otherwise it would appear as black as a shadow to the insect. Our inability to see ultraviolet is due to the filtering action of the yellowish lens in the eye. It prevents these short-wave radiations from reaching the light-sensitive cells of the retina. Sensitivity to radiant energy of all types depends upon the absorption of the energy by special pigments within the sensitive cells. In each case, the pigment is bleached when light is absorbed. A chemical train of events set off by this change leads to the discharge of messages along the optic nerve to the brain.

After about 45 minutes in the dark, the visual pigments in a human eye attain full concentration, and vision becomes most sensitive. The bleaching process is much more rapid: within two minutes we can become fully adapted to bright sunlight after being in the dark. In a moderately illuminated place, a large part of the visual pigment in the eye becomes bleached, with reduced sensitivity. An approximate equilibrium is reached between the rate of bleaching of the remaining pigment and the rate of formation of new pigment. Upon slight variation in these rates, depending upon the patterns of light energy entering the eye, the entire sense of vision depends. See COLOR VISION; EYE.—*L. and M. M.*

VITAMIN: any of the organic chemical substances that are present in natural foods and are needed in small amounts by man and other animals. A diet may contain enough carbohydrates, fats, proteins, and minerals, but unless vitamins are also present, the animal will develop nutritional deficiency diseases. For example, the disease called scurvy was common 200 yr ago among sailors who lived for many weeks without fresh meat, vegetables, or fruit. It was found that these foods, especially the juices of citrus fruits, cured the disease rapidly. Early in this century, guinea pigs, but not other experimental animals such as rats, were shown to develop scurvy on special diets. In the 1930s the curative substance was obtained in the pure crystalline state from lemon juice and other foods: this substance, vitamin C or ascorbic acid, is related to glucose and can be made artificially in a form identical in all respects with the natural vitamin. Its presence in foods can be measured quantitatively by chemical tests; hence diets can be planned that will contain good sources of the vitamin, and the conditions that cause destruction of the vitamin, *e.g.* exposure to air, can be studied.

The history of the other vitamins is similar: first the deficiency disease due to a lack of the vitamin in question was discovered. The disease was then produced in experimental animals, and the substance that would prevent or cure it was isolated from foods, and identified. The vitamins could then be manufactured commercially by large-scale organic chemical synthetic processes or by industrial fermentation; now they are cheap and plentiful. Vitamins are used as food additives, in pharmaceutical preparations, and in feeding farm animals, especially poultry. Synthetic vitamins are identical in all respects with natural vitamins and have an equal nutritional value. This makes it possible to eliminate the vitamin-deficiency diseases even when there is a shortage of the "protective" foods. In many countries these diseases are now controlled by adding the necessary vitamins to foods.

Vitamin C is needed in the food of human beings and guinea pigs because their bodies do not contain enzymes that transform the simple carbohydrates glucose and galactose into the vitamin. Green plants and most animals do possess these enzymes. In many cases enzymes act in conjunction with smaller molecules called coenzymes that transfer hydrogen, carbon dioxide, acetate, and other small "units" in the chemical processes of life. Some of the vitamins (B_1, B_2, nicotinide) are coenzymes, and this is the way they function in the biochemical processes of the body. However, the other vitamins must be obtained, by most animals, from their diets, because during evolution these animals have lost the ability to produce enzymes responsible for the synthesis of these vitamins. Many animals, especially ruminants, obtain part of their supply of certain B-complex vitamins and vitamin K from bacteria that normally inhabit the digestive tract.

Most vitamins are substances of very low toxicity, and overdoses are rapidly excreted in the urine. The exceptions are vitamins A and D, which have produced toxic effects when given at levels corresponding to 100 or more times the normal daily requirement. Vitamins are conventionally classified as water-soluble or fat-soluble.

Vitamin A: a yellow substance formed by animals from carotene, which is a red plant pigment present in green leaves, tomatoes, and carrots. Vitamin A is present in fish-liver oils and in some animal fats. A deficiency causes xerophthalmia, a disease in which the surface of the eyes becomes dry and infected. Vitamin A forms a substance which is present in the retina and makes possible vision in dim light. Green and yellow vegetables are good food sources.

Vitamin B₁: thiamine, or "cocarboxylase," a colorless, highly soluble nitrogen compound that contains sulfur. It is

Vitamin B-12 crystals are shown in a photomicrograph. This vitamin, synthesized on a large scale in drug laboratories, is used to treat pernicious anemia. (*Merck & Co.*)

present in the germ and outer layers of cereal grains. These parts are removed by milling, so that refined products, *e.g.* white flour and white rice, are deficient in thiamine. This deficiency led to widespread occurrence of the disease beriberi in the Orient. Thiamine is now added to wheat flour, rice, and other cereal products. It acts in the body as a coenzyme to an enzyme that oxidizes carbohydrates.

Vitamin B₂: riboflavin, an orange pigment, present in green leaves, milk, and eggs. It is needed in the body as a biological catalyst for the combustion of food substances to produce energy (cf. FLAVIN NUCLEOTIDES). Riboflavin deficiency produces sores at the corners of the mouth and at the nostrils.

Vitamin B₆: a colorless nitrogenous substance present in cereals, meat products, and yeast. It is important in the diet of infants; cases of convulsions have sometimes been traced to a deficiency of vitamin B₆. It is involved in the utilization of amino acids by the body (*cf.* TRANSAMINATION; AMINO ACIDS).

Vitamin B₁₂ (cobalamin): a dark red substance present in liver and other animal products but more commonly manufactured by a fermentation process. Certain human beings are unable to absorb vitamin B₁₂ from food into the blood. This disturbance of metabolism leads to pernicious anemia, formerly fatal but now easily treated with injections of vitamin B₁₂.

Vitamin C: ascorbic acid, the "fresh fruit and vegetable vitamin," discussed above. Scurvy is very rare today because of improved food habits and the ready availability of ascorbic acid.

Vitamin D: the "sunshine vitamin," formed in the skin when exposed to ultraviolet rays, as in direct sunlight. Essential for the formation of normal bones and teeth, it is manufactured cheaply by treating certain sterols with ultraviolet light. One form, vitamin D₂, is also called "calciferol." The form produced in the skin is vitamin D₃.

Vitamin E (tocopherol): the "anti-sterility vitamin," found in vegetable oils. Experimental animals develop muscular weakness if given diets deficient in vitamin E, and female rats are unable to produce living young. Vitamin E has the property of protecting liquid fats from oxidation.

Vitamin K: the "antihemorrhagic vitamin," present in green leaves. Another form is produced by bacteria in the intestines and elsewhere. It is too insoluble to be absorbed from the digestive tract unless bile is present; thus vitamin K deficiency may develop if the bile duct is obstructed. In this deficiency, the blood fails to clot and hemorrhages occur.

Folic Acid: a yellow substance chemically related to the pigments in the wings of butterflies. Folic acid is essential for the formation of new cells. It acts as a coenzyme in the metabolism of "one-carbon" groups. A deficiency, especially in pregnant women and infants, may prevent red and white blood cells from being produced, causing anemia. It is present in green leaves, liver, legumes, and other "protective" foods.

Nicotinamide: one form of the anti-pellagra vitamin. Nicotinic acid (niacin) is another commonly used form. A deficiency causes pellagra, formerly common in the South and other regions where corn is a principal food. Pellagra is marked by emaciation, diarrhea, skin eruptions, and mental symptoms. The disease has almost entirely disappeared as a result of improved nutrition, including the addition of niacin to foods. The amino acid tryptophane can give rise to niacin in the body; thus meat, milk, and other good protein foods help to prevent pellagra. The nicotinamide molecule is part of the structure of the PYRIDINE NUCLEOTIDES (the coenzymes DPN and TPN), which are necessary to the oxidation of many substances. (See CITRIC-ACID CYCLE; HYDROGEN TRANSPORT; OXIDATIVE PHOSPHORYLATION.)

Biotin: a water-soluble vitamin and universal cell constituent needed for growth by microorganisms, green plants, and animals, including man. Biotin deficiency does not occur naturally in animals; adequate amounts are produced by intestinal microorganisms. Biotin is required in enzymatic reactions in which carbon dioxide is removed from or added to various chemical compounds, *e.g.* in the reversible carboxylation of pyruvic acid to aspartic acid or in a carboxylation step required in the biosynthesis of long-chain fatty acids.—*T. J.*

VITRIOL: a term designating either a sulfate salt (usually containing water of hydration) or sulfuric acid (H_2SO_4). Blue vitriol is hydrated copper sulfate ($CuSO_4 \cdot 5H_2O$); white vitriol, zinc sulfate ($ZnSO_4 \cdot 7H_2O$); and green vitriol (copperas), ferrous sulfate ($FeSO_4 \cdot 7H_2O$). Concentrated sulfuric acid is also called *oil of vitriol.*—*G. W. M.*

VITRUVIUS POLLIO, MARCUS, 1st cent. B. C., Roman architect and engineer; b. Verona, Italy. Practically nothing is known about his life. His book *De architectura* was a comprehensive treatise on architecture and building techniques. A manuscript of it, discovered in the 15th cent., exerted enormous influence on building design from that time on.—*D. H. D. R.*

VOLCANIC NECK: solidified material in the upper part of the pipe of an inactive volcano. The eroding away of the cone, which usually consists partly of fragmentary material, commonly leaves the neck (or "plug") standing as a towerlike mass aboveground because of its superior resistance. Some necks show remarkable development of vertical shrinkage cracks and radiating dikes. In the U. S. A. necks are numerous on the Colorado Plateau and western High Plains.—*J. W.*

Ship Rock, New Mexico, is spectacular example of volcanic necks that dot regions of former volcanic activity. It rises 1,400 ft above plain. Dikes radiate from neck. (*N. Mex. State Tourist Bureau*)

VOLCANISM (or **vulcanism**): any of the natural processes that are associated with VOLCANOES, LAVA flows, hot SPRINGS, GEYSERS, and FUMAROLES. Strictly speaking, volcanism (or "volcanic activity") refers to the eruption of MAGMA at Earth's surface through the vents of volcanoes or through fissures in the crust. It includes the processes by which EXTRUSIVE ROCKS (such as basalt and rhyolite) and PYROCLASTICS are formed. Volcanism is related to processes of igneous intrusion (sometimes called "plutonism") and to distortions and breaks in the planet's crust (see DIASTROPHISM and EARTHQUAKE).—*J. W.*

VOLCANO: a vent in Earth's crust through which molten and solid rock and/or hot gases are erupted to the surface. More commonly a volcano is thought of as the mountain or hill built up around the vent by erupted materials. Its shape depends upon the nature of the materials and the severity of the eruptions. Some volcanoes are cone-shaped and range up to thousands of feet high with a conspicuous pit or crater near the summit (Mt Vesuvius); others are broad, gently sloping features (Mauna Loa in Hawaii).

Molten rock below the surface is called MAGMA; after issuing from the volcano it is known as LAVA. Initially at high temperature (approximately 600–1200°C), the lava cools rapidly at the surface and solidifies to form the IGNEOUS ROCK also called lava. Gases (principally steam, carbon dioxide, chlorine), contained in the melt under high pressure, may issue from the volcano in great volume. These vapors develop huge, dense clouds above the vent during eruptions, or escape less conspicuously from small vents (FUMAROLES) or from the lava surfaces.

Two types of solid products are formed by eruption: lava flows and PYROCLASTIC rocks. Silica-poor flows (BASALT) are comparatively fluid and may flow for miles down gentle gradients. They develop chilled crusts in contact with the air above and the ground below, but the liquid within continues to move, thereby permitting the mass to extend itself downslope. Such flows are characterized by smooth or minutely wrinkled surfaces (*pahoehoe* lava). Perhaps because of change in viscosity and turbulence in the flow downslope, pahoehoe lava may change to a type (*aa* lava) characterized by an extremely rough surface composed of a layer of sharp irregular fragments resembling clinkers. Flows richer in silica (ANDESITE) typically develop block lavas in which the rubble is composed of rather regular polygonal blocks. Silica-rich lavas (RHYOLITE) tend to be more thoroughly fragmented and form what are called brecciated flows. The BRECCIA probably forms because of movement of the highly viscous lava and the explosive action of escaping gases.

Pyroclastic rocks owe their existence to explosive activity. As magma approaches the surface, pressure on it is greatly reduced, thereby permitting contained gases to expand and escape into the atmosphere. Gas-escape from highly fluid lava is readily accomplished, but escape from viscous lava is impeded and violent explosion may result. Violent eruptions shatter highly viscous lava to form angular fragments. The smallest of these fragments (*volcanic dust* and *ash*) may be spread widely over the surface. Coarser fragments (*lapilli*) fall closer to the vent to build up thick layers of volcanic *tuff*. The coarsest material accumulates about the vent as *agglomerate* and *volcanic breccia*.

One type of volcanic structure is the *cinder cone* (Paricutín), formed of coarse frothy fragments called *cinders*, which pile up around the vent during explosive eruption. Such cones show a cup-shaped depression or crater near their summits and commonly breaches in their sides through which lava flows may escape. A contrasting type, the shield volcano (Mauna Loa), is formed by eruption not from a single vent but from openings and fissures within a restricted area. The fluid nature of the basaltic lava permits it to spread widely and to build up a broad, slightly dome-shaped form resembling a warrior's shield. Pyroclastic rocks are insignificant

Hot springs are among the features often produced by volcanism. This view of Mammoth Hot Springs, Yellowstone Park, Wyo., shows terraces of minerals deposited by the springs. In background is Liberty Cap, built up by a fumarole. (*B. L. Brown/Northern Pacific Railway*)

Steam produced by volcanism is conveyed ¼ mi through pipe from wells to power plant, where it drives 12,500-kw generator. This project, in California, represents first use of geothermal steam for electric-power generation in U. S. A. (*Pacific Gas and Elec. Co.*)

Paricutín in Michoacan, Mexico, is a typical cinder-cone volcano. It formed in a farmer's field in 1943, and is unique among volcanoes in having been closely studied by volcanologists since its birth. (*Amer. Mus. of Nat. Hist.*)

components of shield volcanoes. A third type, the composite volcano (Mt Fuji, Mt Shasta), is the most common and is composed of more or less alternating layers of flows and pyroclastic material. Collapse of a volcanic cone may follow withdrawal of magma from beneath, thus forming a pronounced depression or *caldera* (Crater Lake, Oregon).

Special types of eruptive materials are the flood basalts, which spill out on the surface from great fissures and build up thick accumulations covering many thousands of square

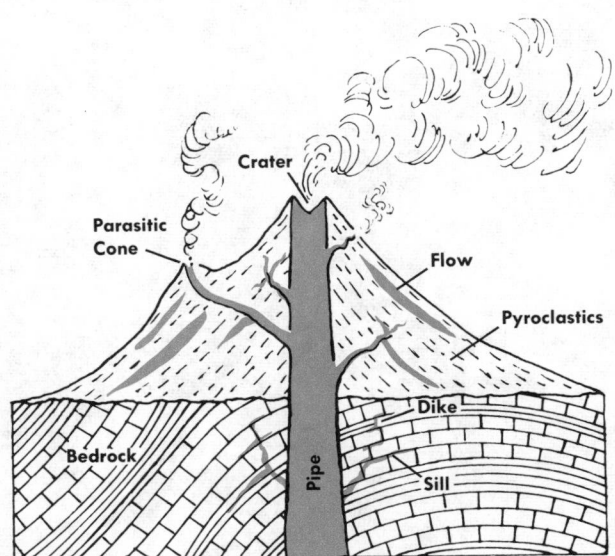

Anatomy of a volcano: This is a cinder-cone type (vertical scale exaggerated). Cone has been built up of successive flows of lava and deposits of pyroclastics. Shield-type volcanoes, with low profile, have cones built up mainly by flows.

miles. These enormous deposits are composed of hundreds of horizontal flows, each 100 to 200 ft thick, arranged in layered fashion one above another. The Deccan region of India and the Columbia River plain of Idaho, Oregon, and Washington are two such flooded areas.

Recent and relatively recent volcanoes appear to be concentrated in two great belts, one circling the Pacific Ocean, the other extending from the Solomon Is. through New Guinea and Indonesia to the Mediterranean. Many others are scattered over Earth's surface, *e.g.* Iceland, Canary Is., E Africa, Antarctica, Galápagos Is., and Hawaiian Is. The two great belts more or less coincide with the young mountain chains of the world and the most active belts of earthquakes.—*C. C.*

VOLT: see ELECTRICAL AND MAGNETIC UNITS.

VOLTA, COUNT ALESSANDRO, 1745–1827, Italian physicist; b. Como. He was the inventor of the electrophorus, a device for producing electric charge, and of a condensing electroscope. Immediately after the announcement (1791) of Luigi Galvani's theory of animal electricity, Volta began to publish objections to it. Volta's theory was that the effects of "animal electricity," reported by Galvani, are actually due to "metallic electricity" produced by the contact of two dissimilar metals. Research on this subject led Volta to the discovery of the Voltaic cell and the Voltaic pile or battery. He described this new device, of enormous significance as a producer of electric current, in his "On the Electricity Excited by the Mere Contact of Conducting Substances of Different Kinds" (1800). He was a fellow of the Royal Society.—*D. H. D. R.*

VOLTAGE: a measure of potential difference, which is the work required to bring a unit charge from one point to another in space or in an electrical circuit. The common unit of potential difference is the volt, defined as the potential difference when one joule of work is required to bring one coulomb of charge from the point of lower potential to the point of higher potential.—*W. P. C.*

VOLTAIC CELL: see CELL, VOLTAIC.

VOLTMETER: a device used for direct measurement of the potential drop between two points in an electric circuit. Portable voltmeters consist of a sensitive galvanometer in series with a high resistance. The higher the resistance of the voltmeter, the less current it will draw and the more nearly it will measure the potential drop that existed before the voltmeter was inserted in the circuit.—*W. P. C.*

VON BRAUN, WERNHER, 1912– , German-U. S. engineer; b. Wirsitz, Germany. A specialist in rocket design, he was director of the German Rocket Research Center, Peenemünde, during World War II. He began to work for the U. S. A. as a technical adviser (1945) and supervised development of the Army Redstone missile. He is director of NASA's Marshall Space Flight Center at Huntsville, Ala.—*D. H. D. R.*

VON NEUMANN, JOHN, 1903–57, Hungarian-U. S. mathematician; b. Budapest. His researches were of a high order in a diversity of fields, including mathematical logic, set theory, quantum theory, theory of continuous groups, ergodic theory, theory of operations, and high-speed computers. During World War II he was a consultant to the army, the navy, and the Atomic Energy Commission. He was a member of the National Academy of Sciences.—*H. C.*

John Von Neumann
(*Wide World*)

VORTEX: in HYDRODYNAMICS and AERODYNAMICS, a more or less circular or cylindrical eddy formed in the course of turbulent or rotational flow. Such flow results when, for example, a flat plate is interposed in the path of original, normally directed lines of flow. Vortex formation characterizes the region of "underpressure" in the wake of turbulent flow and is responsible for the phenomenon of CAVITATION in liquids and gases. Vortices and the laws governing their behavior were investigated by H. Helmholtz in 1858. See FLUID FLOW.—*A. E.*

VRIES, HUGO DE, 1848–1935, Dutch botanist; b. Haarlem. Famous for his studies on osmosis and variability of plants, he stated in his *Intracellular Pangenesis* (1889) that hereditary characteristics reside in all cells. He was one of three botanists who rediscovered Mendel's work independently, and presented it with comments for publication to Deutsche Botanische Gesellschaft (1900). He showed that some of the Linnaean species are not homogeneous in hereditary constitution but are composed of a number of "elementary species" arising by sudden discontinuous change (MUTATION). In his *Die Mutationstheorie* (1901–03) he reported his experiments with the plant *Oenothera.*—*R. J. F.*

VTOL: see AIRCRAFT.

VULCANISM: see VOLCANISM.

VULCANIZATION: a process used to make raw rubber useful; it decreases sensitivity to extremes of temperature, confers resistance to flow under stress, and stabilizes rubber's valuable properties, *e.g.* abrasion resistance, resilience, and impermeability to fluids. Chemically, vulcanization creates strong bonds between the long linear molecules of the rubbery polymer, effectively fixing the molecules' positions with respect to one another and preventing their slippage under stress. Solid rubber (natural crude, reclaimed, or synthetic) is prepared for vulcanization by a process known as compounding, *i.e.* mixing with other ingredients either on two-roll mills or in internal (Banbury) mixers, which uniformly blend the rubber and the added ingredients. Sulfur is the most-used vulcanizing agent. Other materials commonly added before vulcanization include: accelerators to speed vulcanization, zinc oxide and fatty acid to improve properties, processing aids to make mixing and forming easier, carbon black or other fillers to strengthen the final product, and antioxidants to protect against effects of light, heat, and oxygen. The fully compounded rubber is extruded or calendered (depending on the properties wanted) to nearly the final form, and then vulcanized or "cured." This usually is done in a mold with the aid of heat, although some mixtures permit cure at room temperature. (The name vulcanization derives from Charles Goodyear's discovery, 1839, of the effect of heat on a mixture of rubber, white lead, and sulfur—Vulcan being the Roman god of fire.) Vulcanizing agents other than sulfur are often used, particularly for some heat- and solvent-resistant rubbers, including peroxides, modified phenols (for butyl rubber), and metallic oxides (for neoprene). In urethane rubbers, water or amines initiate vulcanization. Some types of rubber have been vulcanized experimentally by high-energy radiation. See POLYMERS; RUBBER.—*E. M. B.*

Vulcanization of tire inner tube: After addition of vulcanizing agent, "raw" rubber tube is heated to about 300°F in a mold held closed by hydraulic presses; resulting vulcanized tube (*above*) has durability and other desirable properties. (*Standard Oil, N. J.*)

WAALS, JOHANNES DIDERIK VAN DER, 1837–1923, Dutch physicist; b. Leiden. He developed an extended kinetic theory of fluid state and the continuity of liquid and gaseous states, expressed in the Van der Waals equation. As professor of physics at the Univ. of Amsterdam, 1877–1907, he was influenced by the work of J. W. Gibbs. With H. Kamerlingh Onnes and J. Dewar he worked out the *law of corresponding states*, which yielded valuable data for the liquefaction of the permanent gases. In 1910 he was awarded the Nobel prize for physics for his work concerning the equation of state of gases and liquids. His studies of the forces of the electrons gyrating around the nucleus were linked to the quantum theory by E. London, 1926, and these inter-molecular attractions are still known as the Van der Waals forces.—*R. J. F.*

WAKE: the disturbed fluid left behind a body moving through that fluid. The wake is usually wedge-shaped, with highly turbulent motion. Its size can be reduced by streamlining the body; this usually also reduces drag. Wakes are sometimes deliberately generated to mix or stir fluid.—*Wm. R.*

WAKSMAN, SELMAN ABRAHAM, 1888–   , U. S. biologist; b. Priluka, Kiev, Russia. His research has included many areas of microbiology, and he is particularly known for the isolation of many new antibiotics. For discovering streptomycin, he received the 1952 Nobel prize. Director of Institute of Microbiology, Rutgers Univ., 1949–58, he is a member of the National Academy of Sciences.—*D. H. D. R.*

WALCOTT, CHARLES DOOLITTLE, 1850–1927, U. S. geologist; b. New York Mills, N. Y. As both scientist and administrator, he was pivotal in the growth of American geology. His prolific research on Cambrian rocks and fossils (*Cambrian Geology and Paleontology,* 1910–28) made him the leading authority. Walcott was director of the U. S. Geological Survey (1894–1907) and secretary of the Smithsonian Institution (1907–27). He was a member of the National Academy of Sciences.—*A. L. McA.*

WALLACE, ALFRED RUSSEL, 1823–1913, English naturalist; b. Usk. His research on the geographical distribution of animals was of major importance. In 1858 he wrote an essay on evolution through natural selection and sent it to Charles R. Darwin. Confronted with this ready-to-be-published statement, Darwin was spurred to publish his similar conclusions in his *Origin of Species* (1859). Among Wallace's many books are *Contributions to the Theory of Natural Selection* (1870), *The Malay Archipelago* (1869), and *Geographical Distribution of Animals* (1876). His achievements won for him honorary degrees from Dublin and Oxford univs., the first Darwin Medal, and the Royal Medal of the Royal Society, of which he was a fellow.—*D. H. D. R.*

WALLACH, OTTO, 1847–1931, German chemist; b. Königsberg. His pioneer research in chemistry of terpenes and alicyclic combinations is described in his *Terpene und Campher* (1909). He was awarded the 1910 Nobel prize in chemistry for his pioneering in the field of alicyclic substances. His work provided a solid chemical basis for the growth of the perfume and essential-oil industry.—*E. F.*

WALLIS, JOHN, 1616–1703, English mathematician; b. Ashford, Kent; ed. Cambridge. Professor of geometry at Oxford, 1649–1703, he was one of the founders of the Royal Society (1663), and his work in physics and mathematics might have attracted greater attention had he not been overshadowed by the great Newton. In *Arithmetica infinitorum* he used the method of indivisibles of Cavalieri to obtain areas under many curves. He also connected the problem of finding the length of a curve with that of area. His *De algebra tractatis, historicus & practicus* (1685) represented the first serious attempt in England to write on the history of mathematics. This work contains the first graphical representation of imaginary numbers. He was a fellow of the Royal Society. —*H. C.*

WALTON, ERNEST THOMAS SINTON, 1903–   , Irish physicist; b. Belfast. In 1932, working with Sir J. D. Cockcroft, he built the first high-energy particle accelerator, which was used to bombard lithium atoms with protons, producing helium atoms from the lithium. The results of this research offered experimental support for Einstein's theory of the equivalence of mass and energy. For their pioneer work

Ernest Thomas Sinton Walton
(*Wide World*)

on the transmutation of atomic nuclei by artificially accelerated atomic particles, Walton and Cockcroft shared the 1951 Nobel prize and the 1938 Hughes Medal of the Royal Society. (See COCKCROFT-WALTON EXPERIMENT.)—*D. H. D. R.*

WARBURG, OTTO HEINRICH, 1883–   , German biochemist; b. Freiburg-in-Baden. His research has been on intracellular enzymes and the metabolism of tumors. For his discovery of the nature and mode of action of the respiratory enzymes, particularly cytochromes and cytochrome oxidase, he received the 1931 Nobel prize. He was a fellow of the Royal Society. —*D. H. D. R.*

WARM-BLOODEDNESS: see BODY TEMPERATURE.

WARM LAYER: see MESOSPHERE.

WASSERMANN, AUGUST VON, 1866–1925, German bacteriologist; b. Bamberg. He is best known for his work on the diagnosis of syphilis and for the complement fixation test for that disease, known as the *Wassermann test* (1906). He also developed a differentiation classification for blood groups, inoculations against tetanus, typhoid, and cholera, and an antitoxin treatment for diphtheria. Wassermann was director of the Institute for Experimental Therapy, Berlin.—*D. H. D. R.*

WATER: the most plentiful, and probably the most important, of molecular compounds; *symbol* H_2O. Water covers almost three-quarters of Earth's surface and makes up 50 to 90% of the weight of plants and animals. Many standard measurements are defined in terms of water. The freezing and boiling points of water at atmospheric pressure determine respectively

0° and 100° on the centigrade scale. A liter is the volume occupied by a kilogram of water. A calorie is the average amount of heat required to raise the temperature of 1gm of water 1°C anywhere between 0° and 100°C; or, put another way, the specific heat of water is 1 cal. This specific heat is relatively high (*e.g.* the specific heat of limestone is 0.2 cal) and explains why large bodies of water heat and cool more slowly than surrounding land masses and so exert a tempering effect on the climate. Most substances expand when heated and contract when cooled. Water, however, reaches its maximum density at 4°C and so expands when heated or cooled from that point. The boiling point of water is considerably higher than that of related hydrogen compounds such as hydrogen sulfide, H_2S, and ammonia, NH_3. Moreover, its heat of vaporization (heat needed to form a gram of steam from a gram of water at 100°C) is high—539.6 cal. These properties indicate that water in the liquid state does not exist as the simple molecule indicated by its formula, but probably comprises dimers (*i.e.* POLYMERS formed from two molecules of a monomer), trimers (polymers of three molecules of the monomer), and other polymers of H_2O, held together by strong inter-molecular forces. Pure water is a poor conductor of electricity, but conductivity improves if trace impurities are present, as in common tap water. Water is an excellent solvent for a wide range of compounds including gases; even rainwater, the purest form found naturally, contains dissolved gases from the atmosphere. Although it is a stable compound that does not decompose readily, water does take part in a wide variety of reactions: it reacts by addition with most inorganic OXIDES to form acids or bases. It also adds to certain salts, forming HYDRATES, which are stable in the solid or dissolved state. Water can react with the metallic elements more electropositive than hydrogen, *e.g.* sodium, to form the metal HYDROXIDES and hydrogen. It undergoes a similar reaction with carbon at high temperatures, forming carbon monoxide and hydrogen. Possibly the most important reaction of water is HYDROLYSIS, in which the water reacts with a salt to form an acid and a base. Analogous hydrolysis reactions occur with organic esters (to form an alcohol and an acid) and with organic amides (to form an amine and an acid). Hydrolysis of carbohydrates, fats, and proteins is an essential step in the digestion and assimilation of food. Thus the chemical reactivity of water, as well as its solvent properties, plays an essential role in the life processes.—*A. M. S; D. P. B.*

WATER CYCLE: see HYDROLOGIC CYCLE.

WATERFALLS AND RAPIDS: Where a stream plunges down a very steep slope or over a cliff, it forms a waterfall; where the slope is gentler but still pitched enough to cause fast and turbulent flow, a rapid is formed. Rapids are much more common than waterfalls, but there is no sharp distinction between the two. If the volume of water flowing over a cliff is great, the term *cataract* is sometimes used; thus, the magnificent falls of the upper Nile River in equatorial Africa are known as the Cataracts of that river. Waterfalls are common in young canyons (see RIVER AND RIVER VALLEY), especially in the tributaries, where the slopes have a higher gradient than along the main stream. Also, waterfalls occur where there are cliff faces of resistant rock underlain by gentler slopes eroded in weaker rocks; this is true of Niagara Falls. If the canyon has been wholly or partly glaciated, the mouths of tributary canyons in the glaciated section may have been trimmed off by vigorous ice action, leaving them perched above steep slopes or cliffs which are hundreds of feet high. When the glaciers disappear, streams flowing through the tributary gorges (often called "hanging valleys") plunge over the cliffs below their mouths. Yosemite Falls in Yosemite National Park, Calif., drops in three stages—a sheer plunge of 1,400 ft, followed by 800 ft of wildly turbulent rapids, then a 300-ft drop to the floor of Yosemite Valley. Many waterfalls are found along sea cliffs, where the shoreline is being cut back by the waves, and along FAULT scarps, where movement of Earth's crust has lowered the river bed. In the normal course of a river's evolution, a waterfall tends to become a rapid as the stream works to level its bed, and the rapid itself eventually disappears.—*N. E. A. H.*

Left: **Angel Fall,** in SE Venezuela, is reportedly the highest uninterrupted waterfall in the world. The drop, from a lofty plateau, is estimated to be over 3,200 ft. (*Karl Weidmann/Nat. Audubon Soc.*) *Right:* Waterfalls and rapids in the gorge of the Genesee River, Letchworth State Park, New York, are characteristic of "young" river of steep gradient. (*Arthur W. Ambler/Nat. Audubon Soc.*)

Delaware Water Gap: Delaware River, flowing across peneplain, gradually cut through folded sedimentary rock strata previously buried in erosion detritus. After removal of this less-resistant material by erosion, the folded rock strata remained as a highland (now known as Kittatinny Mt) bisected by the river. Gap separates Pennsylvania from New Jersey near Stroudsburg, Pa. (*U.S. Geological Survey*)

WATER GAP: in geology, a gap in a ridge eroded by the river which flows through the gap. Such a narrows is formed by a stream as it cuts across tilted or folded strata, and develops where the stream valley crosses the more resistant beds. Water gaps are common in the Appalachian Mts and serve as important passes. Examples are the Delaware Water Gap, where the Delaware River cuts across a ridge of resistant sedimentary rock, and the gaps formed by the Susquehanna River near Harrisburg, Pa.—*J. Sh.*

WATER GAS: a gaseous fuel made by passing steam through a bed of incandescent fuel, usually coke. In manufacture it differs from PRODUCER GAS in that air (with its high nitrogen content) is not introduced simultaneously with the steam, and the gas is collected only at the time the steam is being decomposed. This procedure accounts for the fact that the composition of water gas is hydrogen (H_2) and carbon monoxide (CO) in approximately equal volumes, with only relatively small amounts of hydrocarbons, carbon dioxide (CO_2), and nitrogen (N_2). Water gas has a much higher heating value and a higher flame temperature than producer gas, and is used both domestically and in industry. The heating value of water gas can be further raised by fortifying it with volatile carbon compounds obtained from the cracking of petroleum; this is called *carbureted water gas*. The carbureting process also makes water gas more satisfactory for illumination purposes, although the high carbon-monoxide content of the gas makes it dangerously toxic.—*Ru. M.*

WATER OF CRYSTALLIZATION: the water molecules present in a true HYDRATE, which is a compound that contains discrete water molecules in a definite proportion. Examples of compounds (hydrates) containing water of crystallization are copper sulfate pentahydrate, $CuSO_4 \cdot 5H_2O$; magnesium sulfate heptahydrate, $MgSO_4 \cdot 7H_2O$; beryllium sulfate tetrahydrate, $BeSO_4 \cdot 4H_2O$; and sodium sulfate decahydrate, $Na_2SO_4 \cdot 10H_2O$. In all these compounds the water molecules retain their identity as water molecules but are integral parts of the crystal. Thus in the case of $BeSO_4 \cdot 4H_2O$, every Be^{2+} ion is at the center of a tetrahedral group of four water molecules, and each water molecule is so oriented or polarized that its negative end (the oxygen atom) points toward the positive beryllium ion. Materials that have an indefinite number of molecules, *e.g.* certain clay minerals and proteins, are not considered to contain water of crystallization.—*L. Sc.*

WATER POLLUTION: contamination of surface or ground-water supplies by sewage, industrial wastes, or garbage and other refuse. Water pollution arises from the activities of man in his cities, industries, and agricultural pursuits. It has become not only a health hazard but also a critical economic problem—a threat to industries, agriculture, and metropolitan areas. It destroys fish and wildlife and spoils the potential recreational areas so much needed for man's increased leisure hours.

Sources of Pollution: From 1900 to 1960 the volume of municipal and industrial waste waters discharged into streams, lakes, and other watercourses in the U. S. A. increased about 600%, and by 1980 the present volume should double. In 1960 municipalities were using 22 billion gal/day (B. G. D.) of water, while industries were using 160 B. G. D. The average city required 150 gal/day for each person; *e.g.* New York City used 1.2 B. G. D. for about 8 million people. This water is for domestic, commercial, industrial, and municipal uses. About 90% is discharged as waste waters to the sewers.

These combined waste waters contain about 0.1% of contaminating materials (household sewage is 99.9% water), of which an average of 70% is organic, the remainder being mineral matter. All waste waters contain suspended, colloidal, and dissolved substances in varying proportions depending on the city. From the standpoint of stream pollution, the detrimental components are the organic substances which will be decomposed by bacteria and other microorganisms, which in turn will consume the oxygen of the stream below the level required for fish life. Streams will accomplish self-purification without detrimental effects when small amounts of organic contaminants are present (10 parts per million). Ground water may also be polluted by seepage from, *e.g.*,

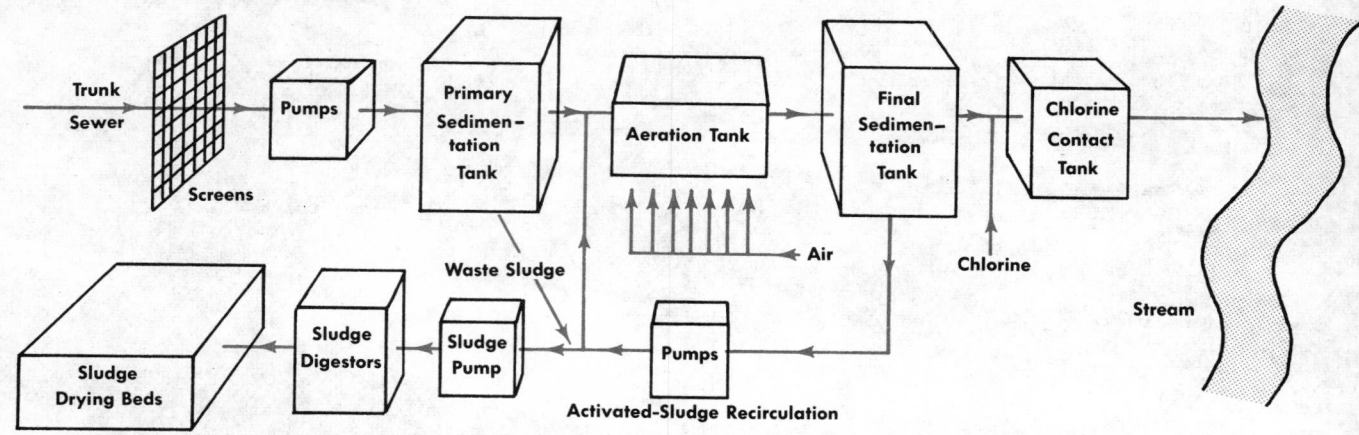

Waste-water treatment: Flow diagram shows stages
of treatment by means of activated-sludge process.

privies and garbage dumps. This was formerly a serious source
of infection for water-borne diseases.

Effects of Pollution: Before 1900 serious outbreaks of typhoid
fever, now almost eliminated by strict water-treatment programs, were caused by polluted water. Other, more subtle
health and nuisance effects may result from the presence in
streams of minute quantities (parts per billion) of many new
chemical compounds used in homes, industrial processes, and
agriculture. Some of the insecticides and weed-killers that
drain off the ground into streams during rainstorms are toxic
to fish. Damage to property and lowering of property values
also result from pollution. Rising populations, increasing
urbanization, and longer leisure hours increase the magnitude
of the problem.

Pollution Control: An over-all reduction in the quantities of
contaminants discharged to watercourses is necessary. The
users of public waters have a responsibility for returning
them as clean as possible, commensurate with economy and
technical practicability. Adoption of better industrial and
agricultural practices will be necessary to prevent the more
toxic wastes from being discharged into lake, stream, or
ocean. For the majority of wastes from cities and industries,
the solution lies in treatment by physical, chemical, and biological processes which will remove suspended, colloidal, and
dissolved solids. Sedimentation, coagulation, and filtration
will remove up to 50% of the organic matter. For more
thorough removals it is necessary to use biological processes
in which large masses of bacteria and other microorganisms
are brought into intimate contact with, and use as food, the
soluble and colloidal organic matter in the waste waters. "Biological filters" and "activated sludge" are the agencies used
in most of the biological processes. The key to the activated-
sludge process (see diagram) is the aeration tank, into which
compressed air is blown through air diffusers in the bottom
of the tank, supplying the oxygen which microorganisms
need to metabolize the food in this aerobic process. The
organisms coagulate to form floc particles about 1 mm in
diameter (containing millions of bacteria), which adsorb
organic matter from the waste. As additional organisms grow
in the presence of dissolved oxygen, the surfaces of the particles become more active adsorbers of organic matter; hence
the term "activated sludge." This settles out in the final sedimentation tank, then is pumped back to the aeration tank to
feed on waste matter again. Clear liquid overflows the weirs
and passes to a disinfection tank, where chlorine is added in a
dosage ranging from 1 to 5 p.p.m. to kill many of the bacteria during the 20-min retention period. The effluent then
passes to the stream, with 90% of the organic matter and

99.9% of the bacteria removed. The heavy organic solids
which settle out in the primary sedimentation tanks are
pumped to the sludge digestion tank, where anaerobic fermentation takes place. Microorganisms consume the organic
matter in the absence of air and reduce it to an innocuous
humus and gases, principally methane and carbon monoxide.
The gas yield averages about 7 million B. T. U. per day per
1,000 population. This gas (sewage gas) is often used as a
fuel to meet the power needs of the sewage-disposal plant;
some cities use it to fuel large gas engines that drive generators and pumps. See SANITARY ENGINEERING; WATER SUPPLY;
WATER TREATMENT.—*R. E.*

WATERPROOFING: any process by which materials are caused
to resist penetration by water. Waterproofing of textiles by
coating them with wax, asphalt, or pitch is an old expedient,
and is still practiced with products such as awnings; but the
treating formulations now used are generally based on RUB-
BER, oxidized oils, or synthetic RESINS, are transparent and
odorless, and retain their toughness and elasticity over a
wide temperature range. Completely moisture-impervious
coatings do not allow textiles to "breathe," and textiles so
treated lack comfort and other properties desirable for
apparel. However, products impervious to water in the liquid
form (*i.e.* to rain), but permeable to water vapor, can be prepared from textiles whose component fibers are not wetted
by water (hydrophobic fibers), and which are so constructed
that the spaces between fibers are smaller than the smallest
raindrop. The construction requirement is satisfied by densely
woven (high-count) fabrics made with loosely spun
(low-twist) yarns; and the fibers can be made hydrophobic
by treatments with formulations based on any of a host of
compounds, *e.g.* aluminum, lead, or zirconium soaps; stear-
amidomethyl pyridinium chloride or other quaternary
ammonium compounds; thermosetting silicone resins; or
fluorinated hydrocarbons. Waterproofing treatments are
classified as renewable, semidurable, and durable, depending
on the nature of both the treating agent and the fibers and
their resistance to laundering.—*W. P. C.*

WATERSHED: a drainage divide or a DRAINAGE BASIN.—*E. A.*

WATER SOFTENING: see WATER TREATMENT.

WATERSPOUT: a column of water raised by a TORNADO occurring over a body of water, especially a tropical or subtropical
sea. Except for small-scale waterspouts, akin to dust devils
over land, waterspouts are found only in association with

heavy cumulus or cumulonimbus clouds. As many as ten spouts have been sighted simultaneously by observers flying in the tropics.—*P. L.*

WATER SUPPLY: water resources used for domestic, municipal, and industrial purposes. These supplies may come from surface water or ground water; thus the 17 U. S. states west of the Mississippi River get about a quarter of their supplies from ground water, while the other states obtain only about an eighth from this source. Water supplies were a functional part of the history of ancient cities. Still standing are some of Rome's great aqueducts, which in A. D. 97 were nine in number, with lengths from 10 to 50 mi and with cross-sectional diameters as great as 8 ft. The course of civilizations, from ancient China, Egypt, and Mesopotamia to modern times, follows the course of fresh-water streams and lakes from which water could be drawn to support life and commerce. As more people congregated along rivers, more elaborate water systems were developed. Re-use of water downstream necessitated purification to prevent the spread of water-borne diseases such as cholera and typhoid fever. Water is the lifeblood of civilization, and on the wise use of water rest the future development and growth of metropolitan areas.

Water Use: Rainfall in the U. S. A. averages 30 in. per year, but it is unevenly distributed; much is lost by evaporation, is used by plants, or runs off into the oceans. The ultimate available U. S. supply is estimated to be 650 billion gal/day (B. G. D.) from all sources. Presently a little over 300 B. G. D. is available and in use. Industries are the largest users of water in production processes and steam-power generation; in 1960 they used 160 B. G. D., and reliable estimates forecast a demand of 400 B. G. D. by 1980. IRRIGATION of the nation's farms consumed 141 B. G. D. in 1960, and 166 B. G. D. has been forecast for 1980. Municipalities used 22 B. G. D. in 1960, an average of 150 gallons/day per capita; the "population explosion" in cities will raise this to 37 B. G. D. by 1980. The additional supply can be obtained only by construction of many new reservoirs and by extensive water re-use through a program of WATER-POLLUTION control.

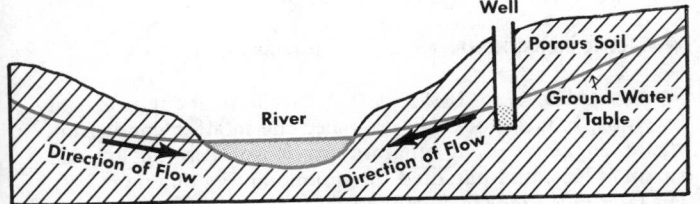

Level of water table, here represented in simplified form, determines water supply available from wells.

Surface and Ground Water: Few rivers flow at rates adequate for municipal and industrial WATER TREATMENT plant capacities. Most surface water therefore must be held in reservoirs (often made by the construction of dams); these provide storage, retain peak flows, and release flows at the desired rates. Aqueducts serve to transport water from the dam sites to water-treatment plants or distribution reservoirs in cities. (See DAM; RESERVOIRS AND AQUEDUCTS.) The principal source of GROUND WATER is rain that has percolated into the ground, either directly or from surface waters—ponds, recharge basins, and streams. Ground-water recharge takes place only at times of high-intensity rainfall; it is an intermittent process dependent on the geology, topography, and soil permeability in the region. Geologic strata or formations through which ground water flows are known as aquifers. Springs may occur where ground water leaves the aquifer, which in turn becomes exposed, usually at a hillside. Springs may be excel-

lent sources of water, depending on the storage capacity and rate of replenishment in the aquifers. The capacities of aquifers as natural storage reservoirs depend on porosity of the formation (ratio of pore volume to total volume). Water may be withdrawn as desired, but must be replaced during the course of the year, so that the average water level in the ground will not vary greatly (see diagram). This level, the ground WATER TABLE, is the free surface subjected to atmospheric pressure (hydraulic grade line). The water table slopes in the direction of the ground-water flow—usually toward a stream. Wells must be dug or drilled below the minimum ground-water table. ARTESIAN WELLS yield ground water which is under a pressure greater than atmospheric, such pressure occurring when ground-water flows through impermeable lenses of clay in a downward-sloping course.

Water Quality: Surface and ground waters vary in quality. Frequently surface waters are high in color and turbidity, due to presence of clays and organic debris. They may be contaminated from the discharge of municipal or industrial wastes upstream and thus contain colloidal and dissolved organic matter in addition to high bacterial counts. Most surface waters must be subjected to treatment, although some large cities, *e.g.* Boston, New York, Seattle, San Francisco, and Los Angeles, have such long storage times (6 mo to 3 yr) in their reservoirs that the water achieves excellent quality by natural purification processes. Potable water should be low in color and turbidity, have a salt content less than 500 parts/million (0.05%), and yield a bacterial count of less than 4 coliform organisms/100 milliliters (10/cupful).

Ground waters are usually clean because of their long passage through the soil. They may, however, dissolve some mineral material, particularly where there are bedrocks of limestone. "Hard" waters, familiar in many parts of the U. S. A., contain salts (bicarbonates, sulfates, chlorides) whose associated cations (mostly calcium and magnesium) will react with common sodium soaps to produce a curd or precipitate. Since many synthetic detergents do not exhibit this reaction, they are preferred in hard-water areas. Water softening (see WATER TREATMENT) is desirable to improve the quality of many ground waters.

Distribution Systems: From the distribution reservoir or treatment plant the water must be distributed to industries, commercial establishments, and households. If gravity is not sufficient, a pumping station may be needed to furnish adequate pressure for all users at the highest rate of demand, which usually occurs during firefighting. These determine the pressures and control the sizes of the pipes constituting the distribution network. Depending on the type of fire risk, the maximum quantity of water in any area of the city will be determined by the number of fire pumpers to be assigned to fight the fire.— *R. E.*

WATER TABLE: in geology, the upper surface of the zone of saturation (see GROUND WATER). The water table does not lie at a permanent level, for it will rise and fall with the quantity of infiltrating water reaching it. Its position depends upon the rate of recharge of ground water from rainfall. See also WATER SUPPLY.—*R. E. M.*

WATER TREATMENT: application of physical and chemical processes to a WATER SUPPLY to remove tastes, odors, dirt, and debris, to reduce "hard" elements and salts, and to destroy harmful organisms. Water is treated to improve its quality not only for human but for industrial consumption.

Debris removal, required for surface-water supplies, is accomplished by adding coagulation chemicals, *e.g.* aluminum sulfate (alum) or iron sulfate (copperas), and lime in a mixing chamber (see diagram, next page). Coagulation is effected by

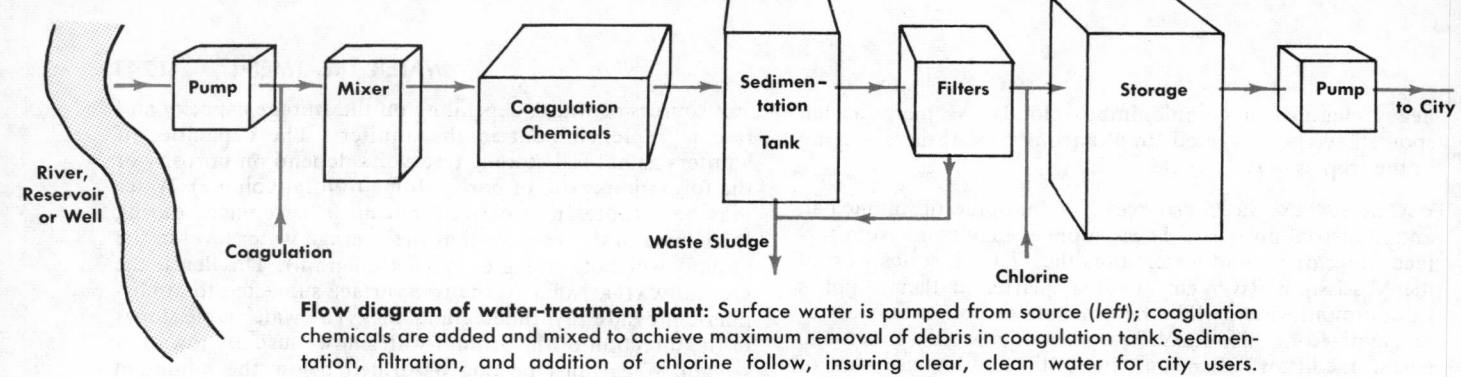

Flow diagram of water-treatment plant: Surface water is pumped from source (*left*); coagulation chemicals are added and mixed to achieve maximum removal of debris in coagulation tank. Sedimentation, filtration, and addition of chlorine follow, insuring clear, clean water for city users.

slow and thorough mechanical agitation for about ½ hr, during which coagulant particles about snowflake size are formed; these are aluminum or iron hydroxides. Particles of dirt and organic debris (turbidity and color) adhere to the coagulant. Sedimentation then takes place for several hours, clarifying the water of debris and coagulant particles. For a sparkling water, sand filtration follows.

Water softening may be practiced in a treatment plant using the same equipment. The principal chemical added is lime $(Ca(OH)_2)$, which will react with the bicarbonates of calcium to form calcium carbonate. This substance may be coagulated and precipitated, following which the water should be filtered. If there is high magnesium hardness, an excess of lime may be added to precipitate magnesium hydroxide. Ion exchange may also be used to exchange sodium (a non-hardness element) for calcium and magnesium in a column or bed containing natural or synthetic zeolites—a method familiar to millions of homeowners who have household softening tanks. Regeneration of these softeners consists of replacing sodium on the zeolites by passage of salt (sodium chloride) through the bed and flushing the resulting calcium and magnesium chlorides to the sewers.

In brackish-water areas, where water is too salty for human consumption, *demineralization* can be done by ELECTRODIALYSIS. An electric current pulls the cations (sodium, magnesium, calcium) and anions (chlorides, sulfates, bicarbonates) through semi-permeable membranes, leaving fresh water in alternate spaces between membranes. For sea water, distillation is employed. See DEMINERALIZATION OF SALINE WATER.

Additives also are used. Chlorine is added as a disinfectant to all municipal water supplies to protect against enteric diseases such as typhoid fever. Chlorination usually takes place before water is pumped into the distribution system; it follows filtration or open reservoir storage. The amount added is very small, about one part per million (8.3 lb/million gal of water). Activated carbon may be added in filtration plants to remove taste- and odor-producing substances. Lime, sodium silicate, and metaphosphates are frequently added to waters which are slightly acid or low in alkalinity to control corrosion in pipelines. Fluoride ions (*e.g.* from sodium fluoride) may be added to water in amounts up to 1.5 parts per million for prevention of dental caries in children, since FLUORINE has been proved to interfere with the chemical reactions leading to the production of tooth-decaying acids in the mouth. Thousands of communities, large and small, are practicing fluoridation under supervision of public health authorities.—*R. E.*

WATER VAPOR: in meteorology, water particles dispersed as a gas in the atmosphere. The water is evaporated by solar energy from the surfaces of oceans, lakes, rivers, and moist soil and is carried aloft by winds. The quantity of water vapor contained in a given volume is rather variable but rarely exceeds 1% by weight. At any one time the *total* water vapor content of the atmosphere is only about 1/100,000th of that in the oceans and is equivalent to a global rainfall of about 2.5 cm. Water vapor is continually being condensed during cloud formation and returned to the earth as precipitation, the atmospheric stock of water vapor being replaced, on average, every 10 days. Since the condensation of 1 gm of water vapor liberates 600 cal of heat, this is an important source of energy for atmospheric motion. Also, because water vapor absorbs some of the incoming solar radiation and the infrared radiation sent back by the earth, it plays an important role in the radiative transfer of heat in the atmosphere. Virtually all the water vapor in the atmosphere is found in the troposphere.—*B. J. M.*

WATT: see MEASUREMENT SYSTEMS; POWER.

WATT, JAMES, 1736–1819, Scottish mechanical engineer and inventor; b. Greenock. He produced the modern condensing steam engine, with a separate condenser for the exhaust steam (1765), and patented the double-acting engine (1782). His later inventions included the centrifugal governor for controlling the speed of rotative engines, and the steam indicator. A patent he obtained in 1784 described a steam locomotive. The *watt*, a unit of power, was named in his honor.—*S. B.*

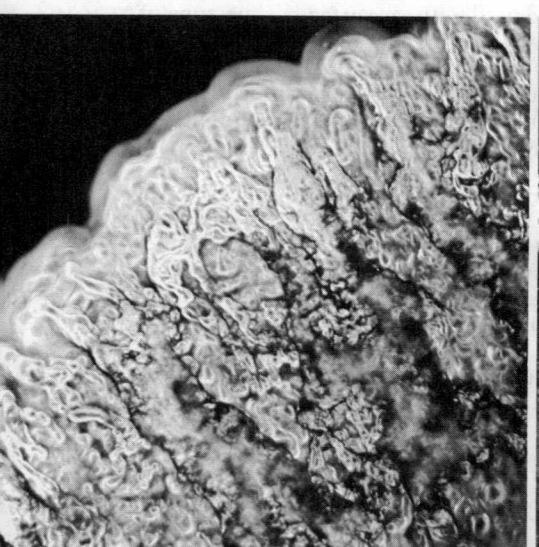

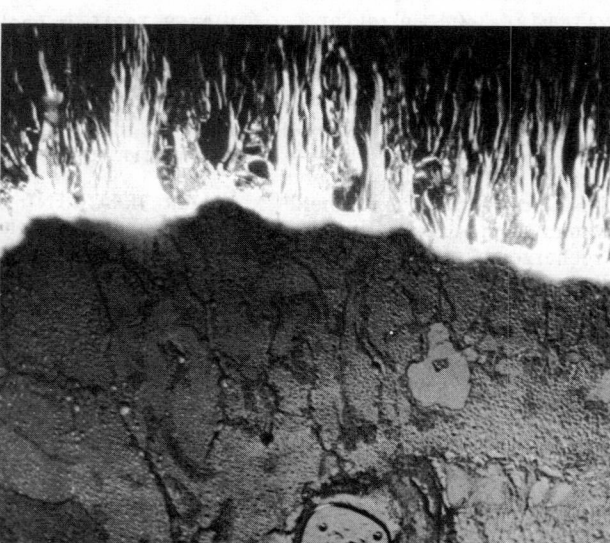

Hard water vs. soft water: Photomicrographs show how presence of calcium ions in hard water prevents soap from dissolving in water (*left*); this inhibits soap's cleansing action, since undissolved soap cannot emulsify oily particles of dust and dirt. If, however, calcium ions are removed by the addition of lime, the resulting soft water readily dissolves soap (*right*). (Permutit Co.)

WAVE, OCEAN: see OCEAN WAVES.

WAVE, STANDING: a form of vibratory motion which has a definite frequency, amplitude, and wavelength, but in which no net energy transport occurs. Two waves of equal frequency, amplitude, and speed, traveling in opposite directions, produce standing waves as their resultant motion. For example, when a wave in a string is reflected from one end, the reflected wave and the direct wave can combine to produce a standing wave. The cord's motion breaks up into equal segments, separated by stationary points called *nodes*. Between the nodes, the string forms loops that open and shut with the frequency of the wave. All the motion in the cord is transverse; hence no energy is transferred. See WAVES AND WAVE MOTION.—*S. Br.*

WAVE, TRAVELING: the propagation of a disturbance in a medium, with finite speed. If one part of a medium is disturbed or displaced in any way, the displacement will not immediately manifest itself in all the rest of the medium, but will take time to spread. Thus, if one end of a string is made to vibrate, a continuous *train* of disturbances will result, traveling with a speed depending on the physical properties of the string. This traveling disturbance constitutes the wave. See WAVES AND WAVE MOTION.—*S. Br.*

WAVE GUIDE: a hollow, metallic, cylindrical conductor, usually in the form of a rectangular or circular pipe, for the propagation of high-frequency electromagnetic energy (1,000 to 30,000 megacycles/sec). Transmission occurs through constructive INTERFERENCE of the electromagnetic waves as they reflect repeatedly from and along the interior surface of the guide. Two "modes" of propagation are characteristic of the cylindrical shape, both involving three mutually perpendicular components of the electromagnetic field: two components, one electric and one magnetic, lie at right angles to the wave-guide axis; the third component, pointing along the axis, is electric for one mode ("transverse magnetic" or "TM" mode) and magnetic for the other ("transverse electric" or "TE" mode). Each wave-guide shape and size has (1) a "cut-off" frequency (f_c) of the electromagnetic radiation below which propagation will not take place; (2) a characteristic IMPEDANCE (Z_o) relating the magnitudes of the magnetic and electric fields; (3) a characteristic velocity for the propagation of the electromagnetic waves (PHASE VELOCITY) and for the energy carried by the waves (GROUP VELOCITY); (4) a unique relationship between the cut-off frequency, the frequency of the propagated radiation, and the periodicity (or guide wavelength) of the electromagnetic field in the wave guide.—*P. D. and F. J. E.*

WAVE NUMBER: in optics, the number of wavelengths in 1 centimeter. Wave number is therefore the reciprocal of the wavelength.—*S. Br.*

WAVES AND WAVE MOTION: Waves are progressive transmissions of local oscillations from point to point in a material medium or in space. If a stone is dropped into a quiet pool of water, waves will travel outward in expanding circles whose centers are at the source of the disturbance. Similarly, a vibrating string or tuning fork will set up a motion among the neighboring air molecules, and this motion will, in turn, be transmitted to air molecules farther out, so that *sound waves* travel outward in expanding spheres whose centers are at the source of the vibration. X-rays, light (visible and invisible), radio, and radar fall into a large class called ELECTROMAGNETIC WAVES.

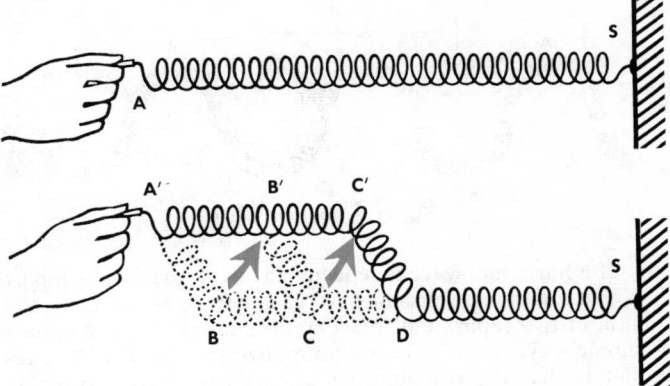

Fig. 1: Transmission of pulse along a spring.

To understand how waves are generated, consider the effect of disturbing a long elastic spring *AS* (Fig. 1). Suppose the end *A* is suddenly moved up to *A'* by the hand. The neighboring parts of the spring, having inertia, cannot immediately change to new positions, and so the spring stretches in the region from *A'* to *B*. In time, however, this stretching force will cause part *B* to move up to *B'*, resulting in a stretching force between *B'* and *C*. Part *C*, like the other parts, resists movement but eventually is pulled up to *C'*, causing a tension in the spring from *C'* to *D*. Thus a pulse, whose shape is *A' C' D*, travels from the hand toward *S*. Similar reasoning makes it clear that when the pulse reaches *S*, which is fixed, a pulse will be reflected back toward the hand. The speed with which the pulse travels will depend principally on two factors: the stiffness of the spring, which determines the stretching force, and the mass per unit length of the spring, which determines the inertial resistance to motion. If the hand is moved up and down with simple

Wave guides: Guides for transmission of microwaves are usually rectangular or circular in cross section. They are made of highly conductive material such as copper or aluminum. Shapes shown above are used to make junctions between wave guides or to impart special effects to the transmitted waves.

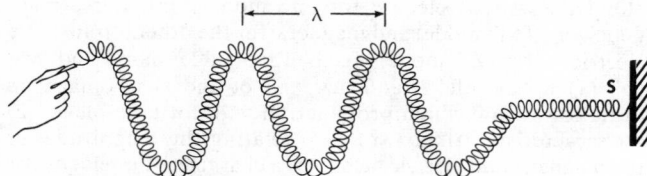

Fig. 2: Transmission of transverse wave along spring.

HARMONIC MOTION (Fig. 2), each part of the spring will be set into harmonic oscillation, but the parts will not be in step, or *phase*, with each other. The inertial resistance to motion causes the parts farther away from the hand to lag behind those closer to the hand. However, over a sufficient length of spring, some parts will become out of phase with each other by a whole period, so that they will be in similar phases at the same time. The least distance between such points is said to be one *wavelength,* usually represented by the Greek letter λ.

What we have so far described is a *harmonic wave* of a *transverse* nature. The motion of each part of the spring is a harmonic oscillation perpendicular to the direction in which the wave travels. No part of the spring moves in the same direction as the propagation of the wave. This point is easily verified for waves on a water surface: floating objects simply bob up and down as a wave passes, and show no tendency to move in the direction of the wave. The frequency f of the harmonic oscillations in a wave is related to the velocity V and the wavelength λ by the relation $V = f\lambda$.

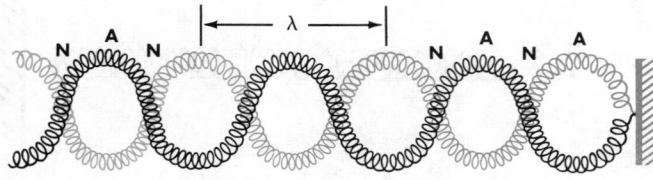

Fig. 3: A standing wave.

If a harmonic wave is reflected, as from the fixed support S, the resulting displacement of each part of the spring is the sum of two separate displacements caused by the two harmonic waves moving in opposite directions (Fig. 3). The result is that the two motions always cancel each other at certain points N, called *nodes*, which are ½ wavelength apart. Between the nodes the parts of the spring oscillate with varying amplitudes, reaching maxima at points A, called *antinodes*, halfway between the nodes. Such wave patterns are called *standing waves*. The strings of musical instruments normally vibrate so that several transverse standing waves are set up simultaneously.

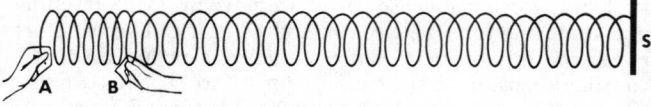

Fig. 4: A compressional wave is started along spring.

Compressional, or *longitudinal*, *waves* are generated in the spring by grasping neighboring parts of it, as in Fig. 4, so that the spring is compressed in the space between A and B. If the hand at B now suddenly releases the spring, the compressional force will start a pulse moving to the right, the

velocity of the pulse again being determined by the stiffness of the spring and the mass per unit length. The parts of the spring again oscillate harmonically, but, in contrast with transverse waves, the oscillations are in the same direction as the propagation of the wave. Such waves may also be reflected back on themselves, producing standing waves with nodes and antinodes as before. Wave patterns of this nature are set up in the air columns in organ pipes and in instruments such as woodwinds and brasses.

Solids can transmit either longitudinal or transverse waves, because their rigidity makes possible restoring forces in all directions, whereas liquids and gases can transmit only compressional waves, as a result of their lack of internal transverse restoring forces.

Diffraction: If a water surface is disturbed in one spot at regular intervals of time, waves will travel outward in expanding circles, all of which have the source of disturbance as a center. Along an advancing wave, the particles that are in phase form a *wave front,* which becomes less and less curved as the distance from the source increases until a segment of the wave may be considered practically straight. Fig. 5 pictures such a series of waves striking a small aperture A.

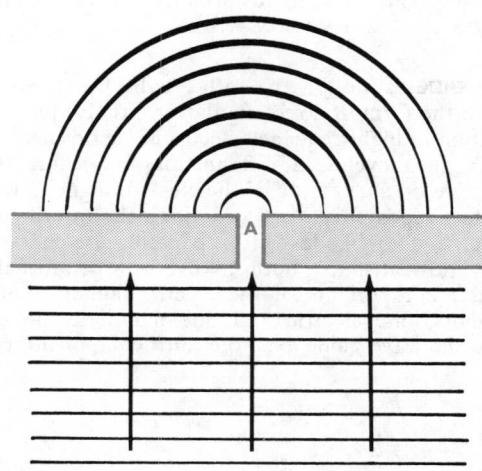

Fig. 5: Straight waves striking a small aperture A.

Instead of the waves being cut into small segments that are transmitted without change of curvature, the transmitted waves bend into the shadow and assume new shapes, which are circles with a common center at A. This effect, called *diffraction,* was recorded first by Francesco Grimaldi (1618–63), who observed that an illuminated aperture produced a larger bright region on a white surface than was expected on purely geometrical grounds. The effect was known to Isaac Newton (1642–1727), but was first explained by Christian Huygens (1629–95). The famous *Huygens' principle* may be stated as follows: Every point on a wave front behaves as if it were a source of new wavelets, each of the same nature as the periodic disturbance that brought the wave into being, and if the wavelets emanating from such points are joined by a continuous tangential surface, this surface is also a wave front. To illustrate Huygens' principle in two dimensions, consider a small vibrating source of water waves at A in Fig. 6. Circular waves move outward from A, and BC and DE are segments of such waves. Now, according to Huygens' principle, the wave front BC may be thought to consist of a very large number of sources A', each of which emits new

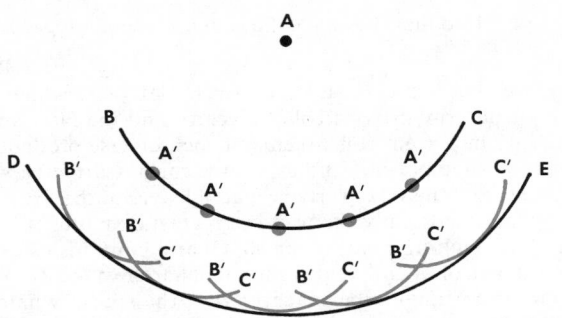

Fig. 6: Spread of circular wave front by Huygens' principle.

circular wavelets $B'C'$. If the water particles along BC vibrate like the source A, why should they not emit similar waves? It can be shown geometrically that all these wavelets $B'C'$ cancel each other out except along their common tangent DE, which is the new wave front. Thus, in Fig. 5, the waves that emerge from A are roughly circular; those wavelets that would have added themselves to the emerging circular wave to produce a plane wave front, if they had been allowed to pass through the barrier, have been eliminated. A simple experiment with waves on a water surface will establish that (1) the amplitudes of the circular waves emerging from A are greatest in the forward direction and decrease steadily as they get farther into the shadow until they can scarcely be seen at right angles to the forward direction; (2) as the water surface is interrupted more and more frequently, making the wavelength shorter and shorter, the effect in (1) is increased, and the emerging waves tend more and more to lose their circular character and to assume the shape of short segments of relatively straight wave fronts. It was this fact, completely consistent with Huygens' principle, that made diffraction so difficult to discover for the very short waves that constitute visible LIGHT.

Reflection: Huygens' principle explains the *reflection* of waves. Consider plane waves incident on a reflecting surface AD (Fig. 7). Point A, where the incident wave first strikes

the reflector, becomes a source of waves proceeding to the left. By the time a wavelet from A has reached position A', another point B of the reflector has been struck, and this also becomes a source of reflected waves. When the lower edge of the advancing wave has struck the point D, the wavelets reflected from A, B, and C have reached positions A''', B'', and C' respectively, and a tangent drawn to these wavelets determines the location of the reflected wave front. In actuality, the points A, B, C, and D lie extremely close to each other, so that the reflected wave front is quite smooth. Reflected waves move away from the reflector in a direction such that the angle of reflection equals the angle of incidence. This relation can be established by simple geometry from the diagram and has been experimentally verified for sound, light, and radio waves.

Refraction: Huygens' principle also explains what happens to a wave when it moves from one medium to another in which the velocity is different. Consider the passage of a light wave from air to water (Fig. 8). On the wave advancing through air we choose points A, B, C, and D, consider them as point sources of waves, and draw arcs of equal radii, using each of the points as a center. The common tangent to these arcs marks the new wave front in air an instant later.

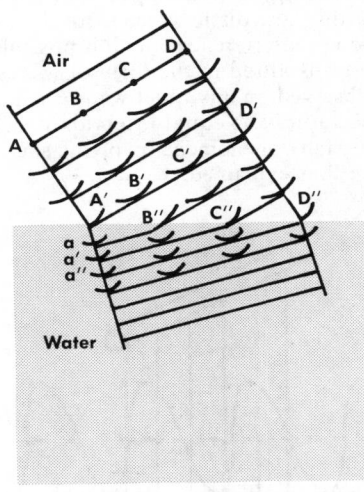

Fig. 8: Refraction explained by Huygens' principle.

The process is continued for subsequent instants of like duration until one edge of the beam has reached the water surface at A'. During the next equal time interval, a wavelet constructed about B' in the air will extend to B'', but a wavelet constructed in the water with A' as a center will extend only to a, where $A'a$ is ¾ the length of $B'B''$. This is true because, as is shown by actual measurement, speed of light in water is ¾ the speed in air. As successive points on the original wave front reach the boundary at C'' and D'', these points become centers of shorter wavelets in the water. The tangents drawn to the wavelets in water mark the new wave front of the light beam as it proceeds through the water. This explanation is in quantitative agreement with the observed facts.

Interference: Huygens' wave principle explains *interference*, too. Suppose a barrier has two small openings close together (Fig. 9). As a plane water wave reaches the barrier, each opening transmits a small portion of the wave front. The two trains of transmitted waves are diffracted into the shadow of the barrier and must therefore overlap each other. The continuous lines in the figure represent wave crests, and

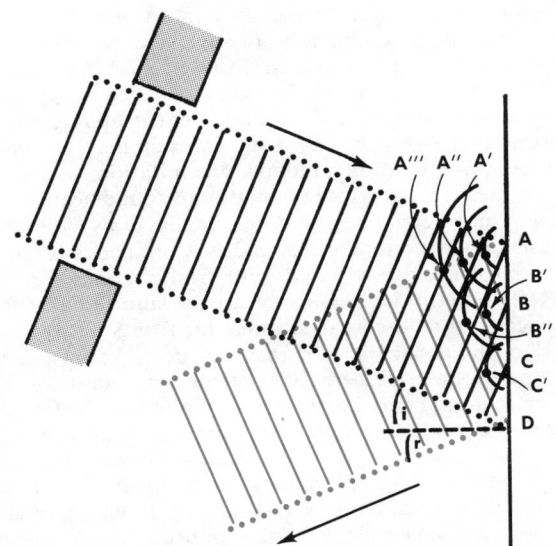

Fig. 7: Reflection of plane wave according to Huygens' principle.

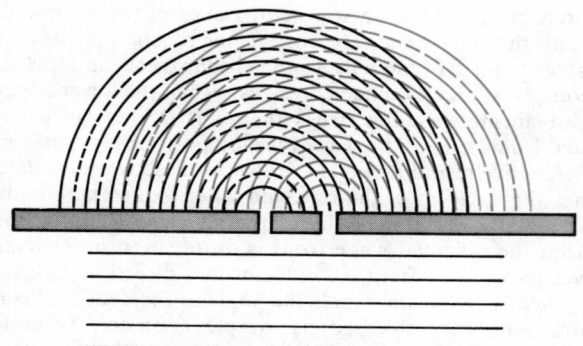

Fig. 9: Interference of waves from two apertures.

the broken lines represent wave troughs. Wherever the wave crests of one train cross those of the other, there forms a crest larger than the normal height. Similarly, wherever the troughs of each train intersect, there is a deeper trough than before. But at those points where a crest of one train meets a trough of the other train, there is no agitation of the water at all. The water, which is being urged upward by the disturbance advancing from one opening, is simultaneously urged downward by the disturbance from the other. This is the phenomenon of interference, and it is possible only in the case of energy transmitted in the form of waves. The effect can easily be observed on any quiet water surface if the surface is touched rapidly at equal intervals with two fingers simultaneously. Many phenomena involving sound, light, and radio waves are thus explained.

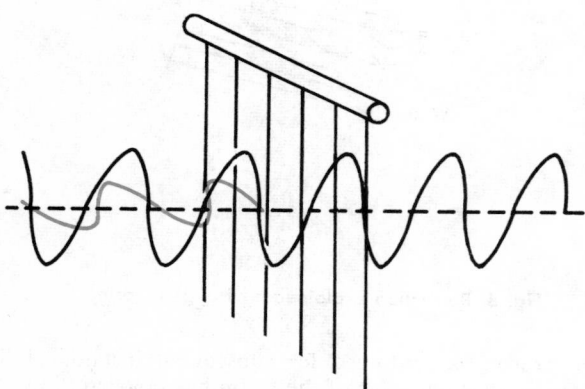

Fig. 10: Polarization of transverse waves.

Polarization: This can be explained by the wave theory as follows: Fig. 10 represents two transverse wave trains with the displacements of one wave at right angles to those of the other. A grating of vertical bars set astride this combination would permit only the vertical vibrations to pass through. The transmitted waves are said to be *polarized.* This effect, explained first for light by Augustin Fresnel (1788–1827) and later observed also for radio waves, can be explained only on the assumption of transverse waves and cannot occur for compressional, or longitudinal, waves.—*H. Sw.*

WAVE THEORY: see LIGHT.

WAX: a solid substance that has the characteristics everyone knows as "waxy." Chemically, waxes are defined as esters of monohydroxy alcohols, R—OH, and the higher fatty acids,

R′—COOH, so that they have the general formula $R'—C=O$.
$$\overset{|}{OR}$$
They are thus close relatives of FATS AND OILS, which are esters of the trihydroxy alcohol glycerin and the fatty acids. Waxes are important constituents of such diverse products as floor wax, shoe polish, candles, and varnish. Carnauba wax, obtained from the waxy surface coat of leaves of the Brazilian wax palm, is probably the wax in greatest demand. It has a fairly high melting point (over 80°C) and contains esters in which the alcohol and acid components are in the 32- to 34-carbon atom range. Spermaceti (from the sperm whale) is mostly the ester cetyl palmitate, $C_{15}H_{31}COOC_{16}H_{33}$, from the 16-carbon alcohol, cetyl alcohol, and the 16-carbon acid, palmitic acid; it melts at slightly over 40°C. Beeswax has an intermediate melting point.

Waxes having the structure just defined are built up from acids and alcohols with even numbers of carbon atoms. Certain waxy substances in plants are simply saturated hydrocarbons (see PARAFFINS). From carnauba wax can be obtained hydrocarbons from $C_{25}H_{52}$ to $C_{31}H_{64}$. These have odd numbers of carbon atoms. It is believed that certain chemical processes in the plant lead to removal of the COOH group from the acids (a process called *decarboxylation*), so that the odd numbers result. The paraffin wax from petroleum consists of saturated hydrocarbons in the range $C_{22}H_{46}$ to $C_{30}H_{62}$. Paraffin wax is widely used to impregnate paper and other fibrous materials to make them water- and moisture-proof.—*Ru. M.*

WEATHER: the state of the ATMOSPHERE at a given time. Weather conditions include pressure, temperature, humidity, winds, clouds, visibility, hydrometeors, precipitation, etc. Weather is distinguished from climate as the current, or short-term, state of the atmosphere rather than the average state of the atmosphere over long periods of time.—*P. L.*

WEATHER ANALYSIS: identification of dynamic and physical processes that produce weather; it is done by study of observations made simultaneously over large areas. Such information is usually displayed on *synoptic charts.* The most common synoptic chart is the surface WEATHER MAP. Data, collected four times daily, are sent by teletypewriters or radio to central collection points and retransmitted to weather stations and centrals, where they are plotted on charts. The basic elements of the surface-chart analysis are isobars and fronts. The isobars define the pressure field, which consists of highs, lows, troughs, and ridges. Closely spaced isobars are found in areas of strong winds; isobars spaced far apart define areas of light winds. Fronts are located by reference to the previous charts (continuity) and by examining the reports of temperature, humidity, clouds, precipitation, winds, and 3-hourly pressure change; they are usually found near stations reporting much cloudiness and between stations with strong contrasts in temperature and humidity. Continuous precipitation is most often associated with frontal zones. Pressure tends to rise with the passage of a front and fall as a front approaches; thus the analyst looks for fronts between stations showing either sharp increases or decreases of pressure in the past 3 hr. Isallobars (lines connecting points of equal pressure change) may be drawn to help locate the fronts. A nephanalysis (analysis of cloud patterns) is usually drawn at weather stations serving aviation interests; it may show areas of high, middle, and low clouds; areas of clear, scattered, broken, or overcast conditions; or any combination of cloud conditions the meteorologist wishes to use. The surface chart shows the weather patterns that existed at the time of the observations, and is used as a basis for forecasting.

Data collected from radiosondes, dropsondes, rawinsondes, pilot reports, and weather reconnaissance aircraft are plotted on upper-air charts. Separate charts are plotted for each of the standard pressure levels agreed upon by the World Meteorological Organization; these, with their average heights above mean sea level, are: 1,000 millibars, near sea level; 850 mb, 5,000 ft; 700 mb, 10,000 ft; 500 mb, 18,000 ft; 300 mb, 30,000 ft; 250 mb, 35,000 ft; 200 mb, 39,000 ft; 150 mb, 45,000 ft; 100 mb, 53,000 ft; 50 mb, 68,000 ft. The reported height, temperature, wind, and humidity from each upper-air observation are plotted on charts for each standard pressure level. A preliminary analysis is made by drawing the height contours and the isotherms. The preliminary analysis is compared with the previous analysis to see if normal developments have taken place. If a report appears abnormal, the analyst checks it against the original reports to see that it was plotted as transmitted. If it was plotted properly and still appears abnormal, a hydrostatic check is made to see that the reported height (or temperature) is physically possible. After all checking has been completed, the preliminary analysis is corrected and completed. Isotachs, which outline areas of equal wind speeds, and sometimes the jet streams, are drawn on the chart. At the lower levels, 850 mb (and sometimes 700 mb), humidity lines called isodrosotherms are drawn. Isodrosotherms are seldom drawn on higher-level charts, because humidity measurements tend to be unreliable at the very cold temperatures found at these heights. The upper-level charts and the surface chart are then "stacked," or placed on top of each other, to assure that the three-dimensional picture of the atmosphere that these charts represent is consistent with proved theories of hydrodynamics.

Today, much analysis of upper-air charts is done by high-speed electronic computers which accept coded data from the teletype lines, convert them to machine language, check them hydrostatically, compare them with previous data and the previous analysis, and print out a final analysis.

Meteorologists analyze many other kinds of charts better to understand atmospheric processes. Since the atmosphere has depth as well as horizontal extent, vertical cross-sections can be analyzed to help the weather man get a picture of the state of the atmosphere. A vertical cross-section may extend from Los Angeles to New York, from the pole to the equator, or any distance desired, and from the surface of Earth to 50,000 ft or more above the ground. The usual cross-section includes ground and upper-air observations of winds, clouds, temperatures and dew-point temperatures, precipitation, pressure, and pressure heights. For special purposes, air temperature may be converted to potential temperature, and such parameters as vorticity and angular momentum may be computed for entry on the chart and eventual analysis.

All the charts mentioned so far can be used for research purposes as well as for current analyses and forecasts (see WEATHER FORECASTING). Mean charts of temperature, pressure, humidity, clouds, sunshine, and many other elements of weather are used to describe average, or climatological, conditions. Monthly, seasonal, annual, and cumulative mean charts are used for various purposes. For example, mean charts based on the weather today and of the past two days, and extrapolated two days into the future, are the basis of extended five-day forecasts. Meteorological satellites are now furnishing cloud pictures and data on infrared radiation from Earth.—*P. L.*

WEATHER BUREAU: a government agency organized to observe the weather and to collect and disseminate information about it. Besides the general benefit to the public, farmers, aviators, mariners and fishermen, truckers, and distributors of electricity and fuel receive valuable specialized services. It

was the invention of the telegraph that made organized weather services practicable. Development of rapid communications systems in the mid-1800s allowed meteorologists to bring together observations from a wide network of stations into a *synoptic* analysis of the weather, *i.e.* a chart which portrays weather conditions over a wide area at some particular moment in time (see WEATHER ANALYSIS). Such charts have become the foundation of modern weather forecasting practice, and much of the work of weather bureaus is concerned with handling the vast amount of data necessary to support the preparation of accurate forecasts by their meteorologists. In addition to forecasts, weather bureaus provide data about climate, *e.g.* for architects and for heating and air-conditioning engineers. The hydrology division of a weather bureau studies the flow of water in the nation's rivers to advise those responsible for water supply and hydroelectric projects. Weather forecasters and hydrologists work together to provide flood warnings, which save thousands of lives and millions of dollars. Weather bureaus of many countries have special sections to study hurricanes, tornadoes, hailstorms, and other locally severe weather problems. The demands of air-transport agencies, particularly, for specialized weather service have been responsible for much of the expansion of weather bureaus during the past two decades. Nearly every airport in the world has its weather station to make local observations and forecasts and to receive reports and forecasts from other stations. Many airlines have their own staff of meteorologists to prepare flight plans and monitor the company's routes for unexpected weather dangers; these meteorologists receive their data from the national weather bureaus. National weather services cooperate in the international exchange of weather data through the World Meteorological Organization, an agency of the United Nations. This agency's technical committees decide upon standard weather instruments and methods of observation so that weather data gathered anywhere in the world will represent the true state of the atmosphere. Its

Up-to-the-minute weather information is essential to operations of U. S. Air Force. Weather officer here is checking incoming reports against weather map. Air Force maintains its own weather stations besides using U. S. Weather Bureau data. (*USAF*)

communications experts arrange for rapid dissemination of weather information so that meteorologists working anywhere in the world may have an up-to-date picture of the weather pattern over the entire globe. Its technical assistance units help underdeveloped nations to set up local weather services.

The U. S. Weather Bureau traces its origin to the meteorological observing system set up during the War of 1812 to study the effects of climate upon the health of soldiers. Beginning in the early 1860s, after the Army's telegraph lines made systematic collection of weather data possible, occasional semi-official forecasts were issued. In 1870 the Signal Corps was put in charge of the newly formed Weather Bureau, combining the Army's communications with the meteorological knowledge of a scattering of municipal forecasting services, notably that of the *Cincinnati Weather Bulletin,* headed by the astronomer and pioneer meteorologist Cleveland Abbe. The Weather Bureau was placed under the civil authority of the Dept. of Agriculture in 1891, where it remained until the requirements of the aviation industry for weather service resulted in its transfer to the Dept. of Commerce in 1940.—*D. H. L.*

WEATHER CONTROL: see WEATHER MODIFICATION.

WEATHER FORECASTING: the application of meteorology to prediction of the state of the atmosphere for any desired areas or levels. Prediction may refer to winds, temperatures, pressures, clouds, precipitation, particulate matter (*e.g.* dust or atomic fallout), or other elements of especial concern. Although the astute layman can formulate some reasonably successful rules based on wind direction and appearance of the sky, accurate forecasting is highly technical, requiring not only extensive and specialized training but the collection and assimilation of prodigious amounts of weather information gathered over much of a hemisphere. These weather observations, taken not only at Earth's surface but also by radio-transmitting and radar-tracked balloons, and now by satellites and rockets, provide the basis for analysis of winds and weather conditions almost on a global basis. The purpose of this analysis is to delineate WEATHER SYSTEMS, which give broader meaning to each of the individual observations by affording a larger perspective. These atmospheric weather systems are of many different dimensions or scales; depending upon what he is asked to predict, the weather forecaster usually concentrates on phenomena of a certain scale. The meteorologist who must predict the weather for the next 3 to 6 hr may be concerned with individual thunderstorms (say 20 mi across) which begin to show up in his radar, or with winds in his immediate vicinity which may shift from off a nearby body of water and, under certain conditions, bring fog in summer or perhaps snow flurries in winter. The forecaster who wishes to predict tomorrow's weather must be concerned largely with broad-scale aspects of weather often covering hundreds or even thousands of miles—*e.g.* the CYCLONES and ANTICYCLONES (low- and high-pressure areas) shown on the WEATHER MAP which may move into his area. Similarly, the extended or long-range forecaster studies not only the above systems but entire families of cyclones and anticyclones, their life histories, their tendency to recur in certain areas, and in general their complex interactions and statistical properties.

Basic Procedure: The mass of information necessary for scientific forecasting would be overwhelming but for modern high-speed electronic methods of communication, data processing, and computation. In the U. S. A. coded meteorological observations gathered through international collaboration by radio and teletype four times a day over the northern

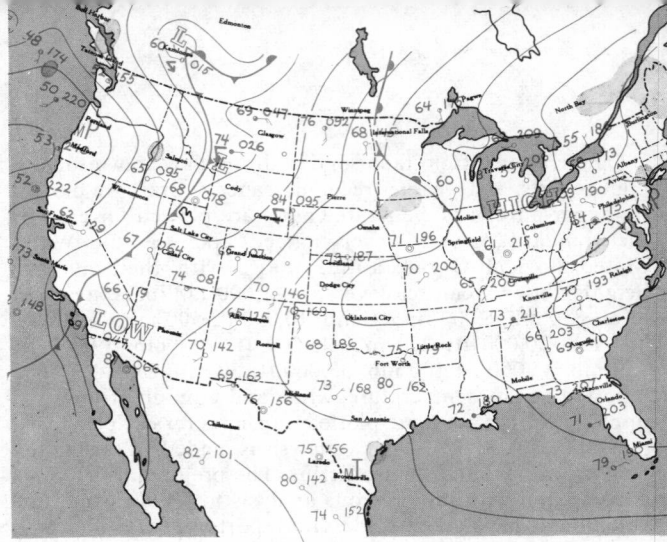

Amateur short-range forecasting (6 to 12 hr ahead) can be done from daily weather maps (as above) by the principle of "persistence," which assumes, for example, that a front moving at 20 mi/hr will continue at that rate with the same weather accompanying it, and that a stationary high will remain stationary. Position of fronts can be determined from location of "lows"; other information given on weather maps includes wind speed and direction, temperature, visibility, amount and type of clouds, various pressure readings, changes, and tendencies, and also inches of precipitation.

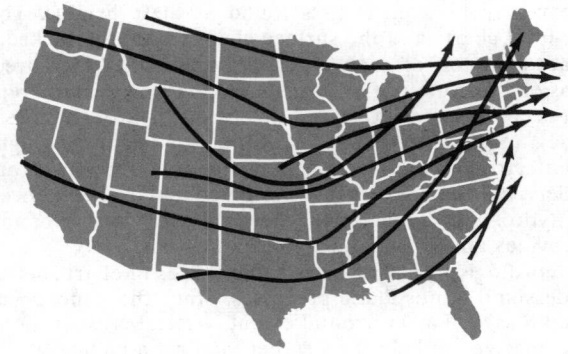

Storm tracks are the paths usually followed by surface lows. Tracks such as those over U. S. A. (*above*) are plotted through the low-pressure area occurring at the apex of cyclone wave as it moves over the land (see diagram, p. 1252). However, patterns of **air flow in the upper air** (as indicated by the 500-millibar constant-pressure chart, *below*) frequently cause surface lows (storms) to depart from their normal tracks. Solid lines show the height above sea level at which air pressure is 500 millibars. The standard height of the 500-millibar level is 18,280 ft; but it can vary from 15,800 to 19,400 on a single chart. Two upper-air lows exist in the far north and northwest; a high lies over the SW U. S. A. The path and development of a surface low would be greatly affected by these upper-air currents.

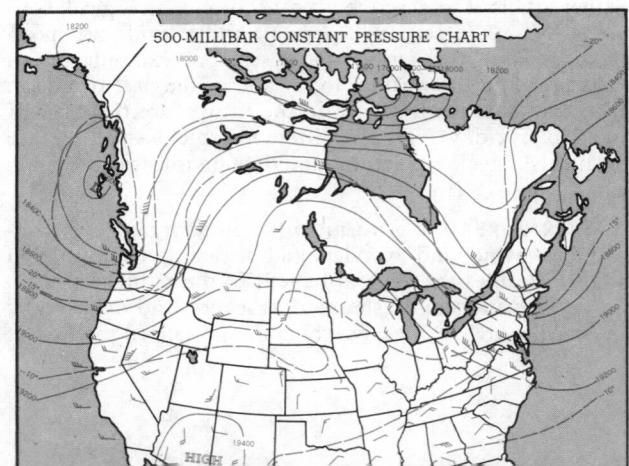

500-MILLIBAR CONSTANT PRESSURE CHART

hemisphere are assembled at a large National Weather Central, fed into electronic computers, and in part analyzed into pressure, wind, and temperature patterns. Other observations, especially those relating to character of the sky, clouds, precipitation, and the like, are plotted in abbreviated symbols on maps and are analyzed by teams of meteorologists—a task presently too complex for automation. The prognosis is made by first examining the analyzed information and attempting to explain what has been happening in a weather domain perhaps the size of N America, and then projecting the weather systems into the future. Projection once consisted largely of an extrapolation of past movement and behavior, and methods of "transporting" weather systems and their associated wind systems still occupy a place in the forecaster's methodology. He may, for example, track the center of a cyclone on maps 6 hr apart, connect the sequence of positions with a curved line, and attempt to project this to a future position. He may similarly track and extrapolate the edge of a cloud or precipitation area, or a cold front. Special computations enable him to estimate the positions of certain features of the isobaric (surface pressure) pattern by considering the field of pressure itself and the field of rate of change of pressure (BAROMETRIC TENDENCY) as reported by all observing stations having a barometer.

Numerical Prediction: But preparation of prognostic charts today depends more upon dynamic considerations, especially the strong tendency of atmospheric columns to conserve their total absolute vorticity, or spin about a vertical axis with reference to an observer in space. This modern method, called "numerical prediction," capitalizes on the inertia of atmospheric wind systems; it requires the use of high-speed electronic computing machines to deal with millions of computations from thousands of observations. The computation is made especially for the wind patterns at about 20,000 ft. At desired advance time intervals, usually 12, 24, 36, and 48 hr, the machine is instructed to print out a prognostic wind map. Such maps contain the essence of the forecast because they suggest the deployment of air masses, storm paths, and rate of growth or decay of cyclones. However, since numerical prediction does not yet include many factors which are known to influence wind patterns, the machine products must be interpreted, modified, and expanded by an experienced meteorologist. Using the numerical product as a base, he prepares additional and modified prognostic charts until he arrives at a consistent solution representing the weather-producing atmospheric layers. One of the most important of these prognostic charts is a surface weather map. Initially this chart contains only the expected positions of weather fronts, air masses, and isobars, but gradually it is filled out to include cloud and precipitation forms and may be interpreted in terms of other weather elements as well.

Local Forecasts: "Translation" of these elementary prognostic charts into probable weather for selected areas is done mainly by experienced meteorologists usually stationed at or near cities. They receive all the above-described analysis and charts by facsimile and thus get the "big picture," both as observed and as predicted at the National Center; then they tailor this material to their particular areas. At this point the smaller-scale phenomena mentioned earlier must be considered. For example, an early winter-time cold north wind over the central plains of the U. S. A. will generally be characterized by clear or partly cloudy skies, but the same wind on the leeward shores of the Great Lakes (say at Buffalo, N. Y.), having picked up moisture and heat in the lower layers from the underlying water, may deposit a foot of snow. Naturally, each area has important local problems which vary with time of year, so that the big picture in itself

does not suffice to make a weather forecast, though without it the forecaster cannot begin to estimate the local effects. A similar pattern is followed in aviation forecasting, upper-air wind information being furnished from the National Center, but predictions of ceilings, visibility, and other conditions at the airport being left to the airways meteorologist.

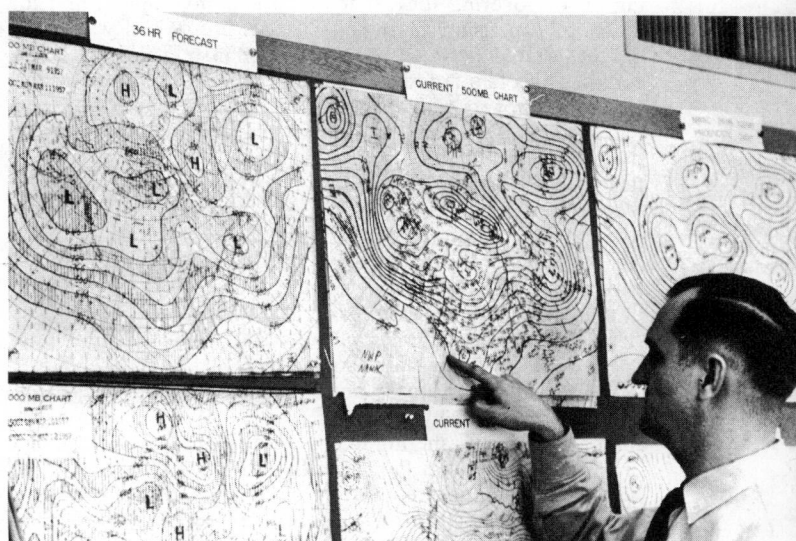

Surface and upper air charts are checked by a forecaster at U. S. Weather Bureau's National Meteorological Center at Suitland, Md. *(United Press)*

Long-range Forecasting: A relatively new branch of extended and long-range forecasting has been developed since the 1940s. Predictions are much less detailed than airway or day-to-day forecasts but have proved of considerable economic value. Such prognostications indicate the general or prevailing conditions expected over the following 5 days and the broad trends anticipated during the 5-day period, with special emphasis on temperature and precipitation. The hard core of these forecasts also is produced by electronic computer, and the big picture of winds, temperature, and precipitation is furnished by facsimile to regional forecasters, who again adapt the predictions to their specific areas. In this case, the picture consists of average surface and upper-air wind patterns for the 5-day period, temperature and precipitation departures from normal, and a series of estimated day-to-day weather maps which serve as guides for the weather activity anticipated.

A still longer-range prediction is the 30-day forecast. Here no detailed breakdown of weather in either time or space is attempted, but only average or prevailing conditions expressed in terms of departures from normal. The stress is on temperature, precipitation, principal storm tracks, and prevailing upper-air winds. In this case, the methods deal with "ensembles" of weather systems and with maps averaged for varying periods and for the entire northern hemisphere. Projection of these average maps into the future involves a larger input of climatological statistics than the daily or 5-day predictions, about which more of the physics is known. Forecasts for still longer periods are usually based on climatological records. An almanac's forecasts for spells of anomalous weather are apt to be merely a restatement of climatological statistics.—*J. N.*

WEATHERING: any of the processes by which rock exposed to the atmosphere decomposes or breaks into fragments, which are then removed by MASS WASTING and EROSION. The unconsolidated material—clay, sand, gravel, and boulders—that litters Earth's surface consists of rock that has been broken up or altered by weathering. The processes involved are both mechanical and chemical.

As rock that was deep underground is exposed by the eroding off of covering rock, it tends to expand slightly, and the forces of expansion cause some fracturing. When water that has penetrated between rock grains or into cracks freezes, it expands by a tenth of its volume, and further fracturing occurs. Growing plant roots, by prying, widen cracks that they invade. Alternate warming and cooling of rock surfaces, especially in the presence of moisture, weakens them and causes grains or flakes to fall off.

Chemical weathering involves the chemical change of rock to form new combinations of minerals. The carbon dioxide, oxygen, and moisture of the air, moving through joints, along bedding planes, and between grains, penetrate rock to depths of many feet. The rock is thus altered by carbonization, oxidation, and hydration. Breaking down chemically, the minerals in the rock may recrystallize or crumble.

Weathering is an important agent in the sculpturing of all landscapes, especially in humid regions. Many landforms are the product of weathering mainly. Domes such as Half Dome in Yosemite National Park, Calif., and Stone Mountain, Ga., were formed by the EXFOLIATION, or "peeling off," of successive layers of weakened material from exposed surfaces of even-textured granitic rock. Profile rocks on the faces of cliffs result ordinarily from uneven weathering of rock outcrops of unequal resistance, known as differential weathering. Large individual boulders such as Balanced Rock in the Black Hills, S. D., and some great boulder aggregations like that in Hickory Run State Park, Pa., are due largely to weathering of rock in place. The freak rock formations called hoodoos or goblins, which are common especially in arid regions such as SE Utah, have been sculptured by weathering, with the aid of rainwash and wind erosion, on rock formations of varying resistance. At the foot of steep rocky slopes there are usually cone- or apron-shaped accumulations of rock fragments, called TALUS, which have tumbled down after having been detached by weathering.—*R. E. M.*

WEATHER LORE: the body of traditional observations, sayings, and superstitions that "explain" weather phenomena, interpret weather events as portents, or give rules for foretelling weather. Weather lore is passed on by word of mouth from generation to generation, the false and misleading statements perversely enduring along with the considerable number of true and useful ones. Many folk explanations are connected in some way with traditional myths which connect the weather with activities of traditional culture-heroes, gods, demons, and the like; thus the ancient Greeks saw the rainbow as the path of Iris, a goddess of the elements and messenger of the major gods. The idea that the weather portends events to come illustrates the widespread ancient belief that the weather shows the moods of the gods. (This, the so-called "pathetic fallacy," appears in drama when the action reaches its climax to the accompaniment of a crashing thunderstorm or a hurricane at sea.)

Some folk ideas have a basis in reality. One typical old rhyme states:

> Rainbow in the morning, sailors take warning;
> Rainbow at night, sailor's delight.
> Rainbow to windward, foul fall the day;
> Rainbow to leeward, damp runs away.

As a rough-and-ready guide, this verse is fairly reliable, reflecting generations of seagoing weather experience. Because both sunshine and rain must be present for a rainbow to form, rainbows are generally seen only at the edges of sharply defined rain areas. If a rainbow is seen in the morning, when the Sun is in the east, the rain area must lie to the west of the observer. Since weather in mid-latitudes moves generally from west to east, the rain will probably move in within an hour or two. On the other hand, if the rainbow is seen in the evening, *i.e.* when the Sun is in the west and the rain in the east, the rain has likely already passed and the clear area where the Sun is shining will reach the observer soon. Because a bright red sky when the Sun is slightly below the horizon also indicates a nearby clear area, the same rule is often repeated with "Red sky" replacing "Rainbow." The last two lines of the rhyme give essentially the same rule, but generalize it to apply also to the tropics, for example, where weather usually moves with the local winds rather than from west to east.

A HALO, or thin ring of light, around Sun or Moon also is a popular herald of an approaching storm. "The moon with a circle brings water in her beak" is typical of sayings common in most northern countries. Since halos are often formed when sunlight or moonlight shines through a layer of ice crystals such as a thin cirrus cloud, and since cirrrus clouds are frequently the first sign of an approaching cold front, the halo is a fairly reliable precursor of rain or snow. If a halo appears with freshening southwesterly winds and a falling barometer, rain or snow occurs within 48 hr in about three quarters of the cases.

Although these two examples of weather lore are essentially valid, if not complete, forecasting rules, many equally popular ones are worthless. The notion that the weather on a certain day or during a certain period indicates the weather of the coming season or year, for example, is completely without foundation. Checks of weather records in dozens of places have shown that whether or not the Sun shines on Groundhog Day (in Europe, Candlemas) has no effect at all on the weather for the next 6 weeks. Equally mistaken is the belief that the weather of the 12 days between Christmas and Epiphany foretells the weather of the 12 months of the new year. Other superstitious approaches to year-long weather prediction are based on positions of Moon and planets, on behavior or appearance of animals (*e.g.* stripes on the woolly-bear caterpillar), and on the belief that weather repeats itself in certain cycles. Most almanac-makers claim their predictions are drawn from weather records of some past year, the choice of which is made by analysis of the "natural rhythms" of the weather. Meteorologists who have studied such long-range forecasting are generally agreed that beyond about 30 days, no valid estimate of even the broad character of the coming weather is yet possible, and beyond 5 to 7 days in the future, detailed forecasts such as those usually given in almanacs are worthless.—*D. H. L.*

WEATHER MAP: the popular term for a surface or sea-level chart of weather conditions. Weather maps are based on simultaneous surface WEATHER OBSERVATIONS made at specified times of the day by weather stations all around the world. Data collected include pressure, temperature, humidity, clouds, precipitation, visibility, wind direction and speed, and pressure tendency. See WEATHER FORECASTING.—*P. L.*

WEATHER MODIFICATION: any alteration of weather by artificial means. (The term *weather control* implies much greater domination of weather than science can presently achieve.) Scientific efforts to influence weather date from the early 19th cent., when the observation that heavy rains followed certain great battles led several early meteorologists to the conclusion (although the rain was almost surely coincidental) that sound waves from gunfire had jostled cloud droplets into coalescing to form raindrops. Soon a swarm of charlatans, especially in the midwestern U. S. A., were bombarding the skies with mortars and rockets carrying explosives and secret chemical mixtures; many of them were good practical weather forecasters who timed their operations to occur just as a natural rain situation was developing. Modern attempts are mostly based on the observation that many natural clouds are composed of supercooled droplets which remain liquid although their temperature is below 32°F (0°C). This condition occurs when the droplets do not contain the impurities needed to initiate the growth of ice crystals. Although exceptions do occur, most clouds will not yield rain unless both liquid water and ice crystals are present. By "seeding" the supercooled clouds with dry-ice pellets, which freeze some of the droplets on contact, or with smoke containing freezing nuclei, *e.g.* silver iodide particles, to promote spontaneous freezing of the droplets, modern rainmakers seek to produce conditions like those found in natural rainclouds. How successful these efforts are is still unsettled, but the available evidence suggests that expert seeding can achieve a significant increase in rainfall in mountainous areas, where supercooled clouds are common. Cloud seeding has also been employed to make cumulus clouds dissipate their moisture as rain before they grow to thunder- or hail-storm size; some success has resulted, but evidence is still too limited for a final evaluation. Another form of weather modification is that of dissipating fog from airports. If the fog is composed of supercooled droplets, seeding with freezing nuclei is often successful; but most fogs are formed at temperatures above freezing and can be dissipated only by heating the air until the fog droplets evaporate. During World War II, some airfields in foggy locations were furnished with gasoline burners which could clear away even dense fogs over a limited area. This method is too expensive for common use, and an effective, practical means of fog control remains a serious problem.— *D. H. L.*

WEATHER OBSERVATIONS: A primary purpose of weather observations is to provide a quantitative description of the atmosphere for weather forecasting. Weather observations are supplied to the public generally and to other users, *e.g.* industrial firms and agricultural operators, who require regular information about both local and distant weather conditions. Tables of up-to-date information on temperatures, rainfall, wind, and other conditions are published daily.

Many long-range planning activities require information about the climate of various regions. Such data may be used to establish whether or not a given crop can be grown successfully, a certain industry operated profitably, or a proposed vacation area developed. The data are obtained by summarizing weather observations taken over long periods. Detailed measurements of the atmosphere and its properties also provide basic data for meteorological research. Observations collected for other purposes, *e.g.* short-term forecasting, may constitute useful research information, but more often specialized measurements are needed to confirm or reject a particular scientific hypothesis. Observations for research purposes are generally made with laboratory-type equipment over limited time periods and/or geographical areas.

The global nature of the atmosphere has required the development of a system of measurements made simultaneously over large areas of Earth. Such measurements, called *synoptic observations,* are made on an international schedule at 6-hr intervals by land stations and by ships at sea. Similar measurements, usually at 12-hr intervals, are made at balloon sounding stations; they provide a synoptic description of the upper atmosphere. In the continental U. S. A. (excluding Alaska), land-station synoptic observations are made by the Weather Bureau at about 230 stations, and upper-air observations at about 65 locations. This network is supplemented by observations from military stations and ships, from merchant vessels of all nationalities, and from foreign countries. To facilitate exchange of data between countries, observations are transmitted in a weather code which serves as an "international language" between meteorologists. It is based upon agreements reached through the World Meteorological Organization, which maintains a permanent secretariat in Geneva, Switzerland.

Observations made by stations at the earth's surface which are regularly exchanged through international channels include measurements of temperature, humidity, wind direction and speed, precipitation (rain, snow, etc.), barometric pressure, and cloudiness. Certain specialized phenomena, *e.g.* thunderstorms, lightning, and restrictions of visibility, are al-

"Racetrack in clouds," with 20-mi-long straightaways and 5-mi-long end turns, was formed by seeding a stratus cloud with dry ice. The dry ice caused supercooled water droplets of cloud to change into snow or ice crystals, which then evaporated or fell. (*U. S. Army*)

so included. Ships report most of the same elements as well as information on sea conditions (waves and swell).

Measurements of the high atmosphere are obtained primarily through sounding balloons (see METEOROLOGICAL INSTRUMENTS). These enable temperature, humidity, barometric pressure, and wind direction and speed to be measured. Sounding balloons are capable of obtaining measurements to levels slightly over 100,000 ft; above that level the use of sounding rockets is being initiated. Data on high-level temperatures and winds are obtained also from aircraft flights.

Recent developments in electronic equipment have provided new observational tools. In aviation, electronic instruments now measure the height of cloudiness (ceiling) and the atmospheric transmissivity (visibility) at airports. Transmissivity measurements, combined with observations of background brightness, provide calculations of the runway visual range (a derived measurement which tells the pilot how far he will be able to see down the runway as he comes in for a landing). Weather radar, developed in World War II, provides information on locations of hurricanes, tornadoes, and other storms. An extensive network of weather-search radars now covers most of eastern U. S. A. In the Antarctic and other remote places, unmanned weather stations powered by atomic generators have been set up. METEOROLOGICAL SATELLITES also are valuable aids in weather observation.—*J. C. T.*

WEATHER SYSTEM: a meteorological entity that can be observed as an organized phenomenon of nature. Such systems range in size from the small but terrifying tornado, perhaps 100 yd across, through the 1,000-mi-diameter cyclones or low-pressure areas of the weather map, to the great planetary pressure waves of temperate latitudes which influence weather over entire continents. Systems are interrelated.

Planetary Waves: The largest-scale systems, known as planetary waves, are great horizontal, wavelike undulations in the temperate-latitude winds of the middle troposphere and lower stratosphere, occurring in the layers from 10,000 to 60,000 ft and having horizontal dimensions of the order of 5,000 mi from crest to crest. Under general conditions four to six of these waves can be observed in middle latitudes on an upper-air wind map of the northern hemisphere. They appear to be the main agents by which air masses are transported from the arctic and the tropics into the temperate latitudes. Within one such air mass, which may measure 1,500 mi across, weather may be fairly uniform. It is uniform partly because the air mass was formed under roughly uniform conditions (*e.g.* over snow and with little sunlight over the Canadian arctic) and travels as a unit; but it is also subject to weather conditioning by air motions within it, particularly the gentle up-and-down motions associated with the planetary wave. These are usually of a descending or subsiding nature behind the troughs of the waves, and ascending in advance of them; their vertical velocity is of the order of less than 1 cm/sec. Such vertical motions are important weather-manufacturing devices, since air parcels become compressed while descending and expand during ascent. Compression leads to heating and thus drying (in terms of relative humidity), while ascending air is cooled by expansion, generally with the consequence of higher relative humidities and, eventually, condensation with cloud formation and subsequent precipitation (see ADIABATIC PROCESS). Therefore, especially over continents, the rear portions of planetary waves are usually relatively free of cloud and precipitation, while the advance portions are frequently cloudy and rainy (or, if cold enough, snowy).

Cyclone Waves: But the above account is greatly oversimplified. The contrasting air masses from the arctic and tropics, when driven into temperate latitudes by the planetary waves,

Hurricanes are weather systems with characteristic birth, development, and decline. Photograph was taken from above a hurricane's "eye," looking outward from the central area of partly clear sky and gentle winds toward the zone of deep rain clouds and spiraling strong winds. (*Science Service*)

develop another type of wave, this time along the interface of the polar and tropical air masses, which have quite different densities. These waves are called cyclone waves, and the interface is called the polar front. The cyclone waves, perhaps 500 to 1,000 mi across, soon become low-pressure areas ("lows"), and in so doing induce concentrated regional vertical motions (subsidence and ascent) which initiate or inhibit cloud formation and precipitation. The most extensive

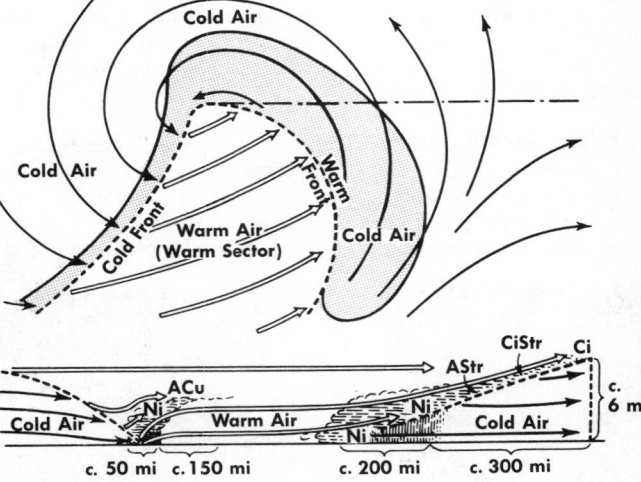

Typical cyclone wave of northern latitudes forms at interface (*dotted line, left, lower figure*) of adjacent air streams arising, respectively, from polar and tropical air masses. At apex of wave (*upper figure*) a low-pressure area (a "low") forms, while warm air soon develops a large bulge (warm sector). Surface of separation (polar front) between cold air and warm air (*dotted line, upper figure*) is divided into a "cold front" (behind warm air) and a "warm front" (ahead of warm air). As whole system moves in west-to-east direction (*lower figure*), the wedgelike cold front lifts the warm air, while at the warm front the warm air ascends the colder, denser receding wedge of air. Characteristic conditions (*e.g.* rain) along this cross section south of the center of the cyclone are depicted in the figure; cloud types are designated by abbreviations (*i.e.* ACu, altocumulus; AStr, altostratus; Ci, cirrus; CiStr, cirrostratus; and Ni, nimbus). This concept of the cyclone wave originated with the BJERKNES and H. Solberg about 1920.

and gradual ascent occurs near the warm front of the cyclone wave, where warm air is forced to ascend a colder and denser receding wedge of air (see FRONT). Here, then, one is likely to find steady rain or, if temperatures are low enough, snow. A narrow band of heavy rain, sometimes with intense showers or thundershowers, is frequently observed along the cold front, where cold air undercuts the warm air, forcing it to rise.

Between the warm and the cold front lies the *warm sector,* where the air has come from the warmer south, often the tropics, and may be associated with fog or low cloud because it is being cooled by the underlying surface. Behind and west of the cyclone waves the air is likely to be cold and relatively cloudless, having arrived from the north and descended en route. Sometimes the air in the warm sector may be completely lifted off the ground by the fronts as they collide to form an OCCLUSION.

Squall Lines: Under special conditions, particularly in spring, a separate weather system called a squall line (see LINE SQUALL) may develop in the warm sector a couple of hundred miles ahead of the cold front. This is an elongated area where violent upward motions are concentrated and where the thermodynamic properties of the tropical air mass favor ascent. In these squall lines, severe thunderstorms are spawned, often ascending to 50,000–60,000 ft; they are often observed by the transcontinental jet passenger as beautiful cloud towers. Individual thunderstorms may be about 15 to 20 mi in diameter, but many appear to be linked together in the squall line, which may extend a few hundred miles. The squall line is so named because when it passes an observer on the ground, the wind shifts and picks up very abruptly, often to destructive force. Squall lines are now detectable by radar, through reflection of the radar beam from raindrops; thus timely warnings are possible.

Tornadoes and Hurricanes: Occasionally, when an individual thunderstorm cloud rises to great heights (*e.g.* 60,000 ft), nature's most destructive weather system, the tornado, develops. Air in this powerful vortex, which is usually only a few hundred feet in diameter, rotates around the vertical axis at speeds often exceeding 300 mi/hr, but moves over ground at speeds usually around 20 mi/hr. The hurricane, too, is a rotating vortex of wind, but with a diameter of the order of a few hundred miles. Such storms, of tropical origin, are characterized by destructive winds of 75 to 150 mi/hr and torrential rains, and by an "eye" or center where winds are light and the sky partly clear. Radar pictures, and most recently pictures from meteorological satellites, reveal bands of deep rain clouds spiraling into the eye (see photo).

Recognition of Systems: Until the era of rocket and satellite, man had a worm's-eye view of the atmosphere. Rocket and satellite photos combined with other aerial surveys now reveal organized rows of clouds (cloud streets), doughnut-like clouds in groupings covering thousands of square miles, and cloud patterns associated with the high-speed cores of planetary waves known as JET STREAMS. Thus systems, previously unknown, are now accepted by meteorologists as normal features of the atmosphere.—*J. N.*

WEBER, ERNST HEINRICH, 1795–1878, German anatomist and physiologist; b. Wittenberg. With his brother E. F. Weber he discovered the inhibitory influence of the vagus nerve on heart action (1845), and he did work in physics with another brother, W. E. WEBER. His name is preserved in *Weber's law,* which states that the smallest detectable change in a stimulus varies with strength of the stimulus. His *Annotationes anatomicae et physiologicae* was published in 1834.—*D. H. D. R.*

WEBER, WILHELM EDUARD, 1804–91, German physicist; b. Wittenberg. Founder of the modern system of electrical measurements, he improved upon the tangent galvanometer and used it to define a unit of electric current in terms of the effect of a current on a magnet. An electrodynamometer was invented by him to measure forces exerted by one electric current on another. He defined a unit of electromotive force, and from the units of current and electromotive force and Ohm's law he was was able to define a unit of electrical resistance. The system of units proposed by Weber and Gauss was adopted internationally in 1881. Weber was a fellow of the Royal Society.—*D. H. D. R.*

WEED, WALTER HARVEY, 1862–1944, U. S. geologist; b. St. Louis, Mo. He worked for the U. S. Geological Survey (1883–1906) and participated in the mapping and study of Yellowstone Park and Montana. He discovered that the coloring of hot springs and geysers in the Yellowstone area is due to living algae. His theory of secondary enrichments of ore deposits was published in 1899. Weed wrote a number of books on mining and mineral deposits.—*D. H. D. R.*

WEED: any undesirable or unwanted kind of plant. Weeds also have been defined as "overly successful plants." Usually they are introduced kinds that are Sun-tolerating, rapid-growing, profuse-flowering, many-seeded, easily dispersed, and hence ready to colonize areas man has bared around his home. Seldom is a weed successful far from human habitations or cultivated land, where shrubs and trees shade the ground. Sometimes an overly successful animal is described as a "weed species." Recently this term has been applied to rabbits in Australia and deer in America. See BALANCE OF NATURE; ECOLOGY.—*L. and M. M.*

WEEK: in its present use, an arbitrary subdivision of the CALENDAR, consisting of seven consecutive days. There is no astronomical period corresponding to the week. The custom of resting every seventh day is of unknown origin, but was practiced by Assyrians of the 10th cent. B. C. The week became a part of the Roman calendar in the 1st or 2nd cent. B. C.; the Gregorian calendar reform made special provision to insure that there be no break in the sequence of weekdays. Shortly before the Christian era, astrologers introduced the practice of naming each day for an astronomical body (Sun, Moon, Mars, Mercury, Jupiter, Venus, Saturn); the names of Teutonic gods (Tiu, Wotan, Thor, Freya) eventually replaced some of these in Germanic and Anglo-Saxon languages.—*S. D. G.*

WEGENER, ALFRED LOTHAR, 1880–1930, German meteorologist and geophysicist; b. Berlin. The preponderance of his scientific work was in meteorology, and he wrote a treatise on *Thermodynamics of the Atmosphere* (1911). Wegener is best remembered, however, for the startling theory of CONTINENTAL DRIFT set forth in his *The Origins of Continents and Oceans* (1915).—*R. W. D.*

WEIERSTRASS, KARL WILHELM THEODOR, 1815–97, German mathematician; b. Ostenfelde, Münster. While a teacher in secondary schools, in his spare time he did brilliant research in mathematics. Some of his papers were published in *Crelle's Journal* and created a sensation. Later he was appointed professor at the Royal Polytechnic School in Berlin, held a position in the Univ. of Berlin, and was elected to the Berlin Academy. Many of the most able young mathematicians were attracted to him and did much to propagate his ideas. Weierstrass was a great analyst, perhaps the greatest in the 19th cent., and, more than anyone else, he was responsible for the arithmetization of analysis. He was a fellow of the Royal Society.—*H. C.*

WEIGHT: the gravitational pull or force exerted by Earth on a physical body; similarly the gravitational force exerted by the Moon, a planet, or other celestial body on a nearby object. Weight is often identified with the net downward force on an object as measured, for example, by a spring balance, which includes the effect of centrifugal force caused by the Earth's rotation as well as the effect of gravitational attraction. The weight of a body at sea level on Earth is smallest at the equator and largest at the poles (a body weighing 299 lb at the equator would weigh 300 lb at either pole), because the surface of Earth is nearest its center at the poles and because of the greater centrifugal force at the equator. Weight diminishes both with increased altitude and with depth below the surface, as in deep mines. The diminution is about 0.1% when an object is 2 mi above the Earth's surface or 4 mi below it.

In contrast to weight, *mass* is a quantity of matter or, more exactly, a numerical measure of a body's inertia or its gravitational effect. Since weight is proportional to mass at any given point, weight may be measured in mass units in static situations (in commerce and in bridge stresses), but in dynamical problems weight must be expressed in force units. Thus we assign the *gram* and the *kilogram* as the fundamental units of mass in the cgs and mks systems respectively, and derive the *dyne* and the *newton* as the forces which impart to these unit masses accelerations of 1 cm/sec^2 and 1 m/sec^2 respectively. One gram of mass, subjected to a gravitational acceleration (g) of 980 cm/sec^2, therefore weighs 980 dynes, and a kilogram of mass, experiencing an acceleration of 9.8 m/sec^2, weighs 9.8 newtons. Thus W (weight) = M (mass) $\times$ g (acceleration of gravity).

In the English gravitational (fps) system, the fundamental unit is a pound of weight and the derived unit of mass is the slug, defined as a mass which, when acted upon by a force of one pound, accelerates at 1 ft/sec^2. If a slug of mass were to fall freely, it would accelerate at about 32 ft/sec^2; hence it would be acted upon by a force (or weight) of 32 lb. Thus one slug weighs 32 lb. Another English system takes the pound as a unit of mass and derives the *poundal* as a force unit.—*A. E.*

WEIGHT, MOLECULAR: see MOLECULAR WEIGHT.

WEIGHTLESSNESS: in space science, the state experienced by a physical body in the absence of any gravitational force or when falling freely under the pull of a gravitational field (see FREE FALL). In interplanetary space the gravitational forces of Earth and other celestial bodies can be virtually zero; in a space ship moving with constant velocity, there would be no "up" and "down," and bodies would tend to float. A satel-lite in orbit around the Earth does not move in a straight line, but constantly falls. Thus it and its contents also experience weightlessness (see SATELLITE, ARTIFICIAL). Weightlessness in a satellite is often explained as the result of a balance between "centrifugal" and gravitational forces; but this "centrifugal force" is fictitious, the real factor being acceleration of the satellite (see CENTRIPETAL AND CENTRIFUGAL FORCE).

An astronaut in the weightless state cannot drink from a cup, since the liquid will not pour, but he can drink through a straw. Experiments both in satellites and in simulated conditions in aircraft and the laboratory have suggested that, in spite of losing his sense of position, a weightless person can adjust to the environment.—*B. P. S.*

WEISMANN, AUGUST, 1834–1914, German biologist; b. Frankfurt-am-Main. He is best known for his neo-Darwinistic attempt to account for the facts of heredity by the continuity of the germ plasm and the omnipotence of natural selection. The "germ plasm" postulated by Weismann is transmitted from parent to child but is not all used up in forming the child, some of it being transmitted to the third generation, and so on. Thus the germ plasm serves as the mechanism of heredity, and the "natural selection" of Darwin operates on variations in the germ plasm. The latter is in Weismann's theory unaffected by environment; he denies Lamarckianism. His many publications include *Studien zur Deszendenztheorie* (1875) and *Die Kontinuität des Keimplasmas als Grundlage einer Theorie der Vererbung* (1885). Weismann was a fellow of the Royal Society and an associate of the U. S. National Academy of Sciences.—*D. H. D. R.*

WEIZMANN, CHAIM, 1874–1952, German-English-Israeli chemist and statesman; b. Motol, Russia. After moving to England (1904), he became director of the laboratories of the British Admiralty (1916–19). He discovered a process of making butanol and acetone by fermentation; both these chemicals are important intermediates for explosives. He also played a major role in the establishment of a Jewish homeland in Palestine and in the creation of Israel. At the Daniel Sieff Institute, Rehovoth, Israel, he engaged in research on agronomics, particularly concerning the castor bean.—*D. H. D. R.*

WEIZSÄCKER, KARL FRIEDRICH VON, 1912– , German astronomer and cosmologist; b. Kiel. His research has been in atomic physics, astrophysics, and natural philosophy. He independently proposed the carbon, or Bethe, cycle for generation of energy in the Sun and offered a NEBULAR HYPOTHESIS (see also DUST-CLOUD THEORY) of the solar system (1945). He is the author of *Zum Weltbild der Physik* (1943; trans. *The World View of Physics,* 1952); *Die Geschichte der Natur* (1948; trans. *The History of Nature,* 1949); and *Atomenergie und Atomzeitalter* (1957).—*D. H. D. R.*

WELDING: any of a group of related processes for joining metals at high temperature. Any metal or alloy can be successfully welded, but each involves special techniques. High temperatures required may be produced by an electric arc (arc welding), by resistance to electric current flow (resistance welding), by induced electric current (induction welding), by combustion of a fuel gas in oxygen (gas or flame welding), by chemical reaction between a metal oxide and finely divided aluminum (thermit welding), or by heating

Men in a test chamber experience brief period of weightlessness. Success of man-carrying artificial satellites has made possible the study of effects of weightlessness prolonged for hours and days. (U. S. Air Force)

Upper left: **Wheelbarrow stamping die** is rebuilt by arc-welding, using electrode designed to weld tool steel. *Lower left:* Low-hydrogen electrode is used to correct machining errors made in tire-curing mold. *Above:* Welder deposits long-life chromium carbide hard-surfacing on large die ring worn from severe abrasion and moderate impact. (*Lincoln Electric* Co.)

in a forge or furnace (forge welding). Welding usually occurs by superficial liquefaction of the parts to be joined, coalescence of the liquid layers, and solidification to a continuous, joined mass on cooling. Welding can occur without liquefaction in cases where heating renders the surfaces amenable to coalescence, *e.g.* in the "sintering" of powders or small grains, or the hand-forging of chain links. Newest developments include electron-beam vacuum welding; the high-temperature, high-velocity plasma jet; electroslag welding; and high-frequency welding. In electron-beam welding, spot areas are bombarded with high-energy electrons inside an evacuated welding chamber. The plasma arc torch ejects a stream of ionized atoms at a temperature of up to 30,000°F, so far the highest controlled temperature used in industry. The ionic jet or "plasma" is considered to be a fourth state of matter—neither gas, solid, nor liquid. Electroslag welding, an arc process without an arc, utilizes the electrical resistance of a pool of molten slag to melt the parent and filler metals. The new high-frequency process employs a current of around half a million cycles per second to weld thin-wall tubing at speeds up to 1,000 ft/min.

Welding may be done with or without pressure and with or without filler metal. Some cast irons and steels are joined by means of a brass or bronze filler metal having a melting point well below that of the parent metal. This process, called braze welding, is similar to BRAZING.

For centuries the forge-heating and hammering of the village blacksmith was the only known welding method. Today there are some 40 variations of welding processes, but the three major ones are the arc, gas, and resistance types. *Resistance welding* came first. In 1856 James Joule welded a bundle of charcoal-buried wires by heating them electrically. In 1877 Elihu Thomson invented a small, low-pressure resistance welder. A patent for carbon-arc welding was filed by N. V. Bernardos in 1885, shortly after the introduction of arc lights, but the arc method did not fully come into its own until after the invention of the coated electrode in the 1920s. The

oxyacetylene torch was invented 1900–01 by Edmund Fouche. Like the present welding torch, the pioneer model was connected with cylinders of compressed acetylene and oxygen. Oxyacetylene welding was the dominant process for many decades, but today the most popular process is arc welding. Currently, 85% of U. S. industrial plants are using some form of welding for production and/or maintenance.

Arc welding may be done with either alternating or direct current. The usual arc is from a single electrode to a grounded workpiece. If the arc is between two carbon or two tungsten electrodes, the electrode holder is called an arc torch. Welding electrodes are classified as consumable and nonconsumable. A consumable electrode is generally the same as the base metal and serves as the source of the filler metal. Nonconsumable electrodes, tungsten and carbon, may require auxiliary welding rods, as in gas welding. Tungsten electrodes are often employed in connection with inert-gas-shielded arc welding. Carbon-arc welding continues to be used for copper, a hard-to-weld metal. Whereas arc temperature with a consumable metal electrode is approximately 6,000°F, a carbon arc may have a temperature of from 6,850 to 9,550°F.

About 85% of all arc welding is done manually with coated consumable electrodes. The coating ingredients burn to produce a smoke that eliminates oxygen from the area of the arc and a slag that shields the molten weld metal from atmos-

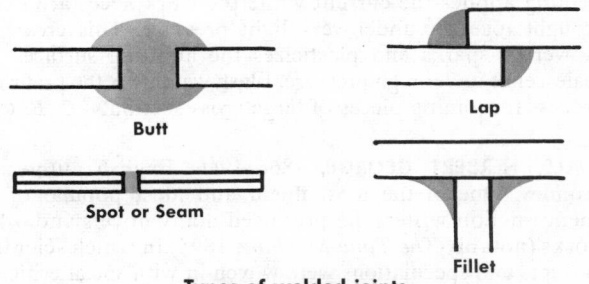

Types of welded joints

pheric oxygen. With automatic and semiautomatic arc welding, shielding is a matter of equal importance, but coated stick electrodes are seldom employed. Instead a coil of bare welding wire is fed to the arc, which is shielded by (1) an automatically fed granular flux, or (2) one of the so-called "inert" gases. *Submerged-arc welding,* which blankets the weld with flux, is adaptable to either semiautomatic or automatic set-ups. Semiautomatic equipment feeds the welding wire and flux; the fully automatic welding head additionally maintains arc travel at a preset speed.

Inert-gas-shielded arc welding has grown enormously since 1942. Combinations of a tungsten electrode with inert gas, and of a consumable metal electrode with inert gas, are known respectively as "tig" and "mig" welding. The tungsten-electrode process is the older and more extensively used. Tig may be employed for manual, semiautomatic, or fully automatic welding; the mig process is generally automatic. The first shielding gases were helium and argon, both truly inert but likewise high-cost gases. The search for cheaper substitutes has led to nitrogen and carbon dioxide: nitrogen for welding copper and its alloys, carbon dioxide for steel. The general trend is toward carbon dioxide.

For most *flame welding,* a mixture of equal parts of oxygen and acetylene is used. This produces a "neutral" flame with a temperature of 5,850°F. Excess oxygen will yield as high a temperature as 6,300°F, but the oxidizing flame may be very harmful to metals. The hydrogen-fluorine flame likewise has metal-arc temperature, but the high cost and extreme chemical activity of fluorine are decided drawbacks. The gentler oxyhydrogen flame, around 4,300°F, is used for braze welding, BRAZING, and to weld such low-melting-point metals as aluminum, magnesium, and lead. Still lower flame temperatures result from combining oxygen with natural gas, city gas, methane, butane, propane, etc.

Resistance welding usually combines heat with pressure and operates on electronically controlled weld cycles. Machines, controls, and electrodes are currently totaling about 6% of the annual welding dollar. The processes are fast, quality is readily controllable, and the equipment can be operated by unskilled workers. Chief types of machines are spot, seam, upset, and flash welders.

Spot welding presses overlapped sheets of metal between upper and lower copper-alloy electrodes. In seam welding, the upper and lower electrodes are copper-alloy wheels that roll to weld a continuous seam. Spot welders are sometimes equipped with multiple pairs of electrodes, permitting many spots to be welded in a single cycle. Such a welder may cost as much as one million dollars if sufficiently large and complex. Portable spot welders operated by compressed air or hydraulic pressure are called welding guns. Small hand-operated spot welders are called welding tongs.

Upset and flash welding are both employed to butt-weld adjacent ends of wires, rods, bars, plates, tubes, etc. Both require heavy pressure and high-amperage current. Upset welding applies the full pressure before heating starts. Flash welding applies the current while the workpieces are being brought together under very light pressure. This creates a shower of sparks and plasticizes the abutting surfaces for coalescence under high pressure. Flash welding is the preferred process for joining pieces of large cross section.—*C. B. C.*

WELLS, HERBERT GEORGE, 1866–1946, English author; b. Bromley. One of the most fluent and most popular of all science-fiction writers, he produced many novels and other works (notably *The Time Machine,* 1895) in which scientific concepts and speculations were woven in with social criticism and forecasts concerning the future of civilization. Wells's

most notable nonfictional works are *The Outline of History* (1920) and *The Science of Life* (1931).—*J. W.*

WELSBACH, BARON VON: see AUER, CARL.

WERNER, ABRAHAM GOTTLOB, 1749–1817, German geologist; b. Wehrau. He did much to shape the academic discipline of geology from unorganized principles and data, and taught it to an influential and international generation of students at the *Bergakademie* (Mining Academy) at Freiberg, Saxony. His own theories placed too much emphasis on the role of water in the formation of Earth's crust (Neptunism) and were soon superseded (see GEOLOGY), but his influence on geology, exerted through his students, was enormous.—*D. H. D. R.*

WERNER, ALFRED, 1866–1919, Swiss chemist; b. Muhlhausen, Alsace. His first important scientific work was in stereochemistry of nitrogenous compounds. In 1893 he announced the coordination theory of valency: an extension of the classical views to complex compounds between simpler molecules, including those of metal salts with water or ammonia, and their various three-dimensional forms. In recognition of his work on the linkage of atoms in molecules, by which he threw fresh light on old problems and opened up new fields of research, particularly in inorganic chemistry, Werner was awarded the 1913 Nobel prize in chemistry. He wrote *A Manual of Stereo-Chemistry* (1904) and *New Opinons in the Field of Inorganic Chemistry* (1905).—*E. F.*

WETTING AGENT: any of a class of SURFACE-ACTIVE AGENTS that cause a liquid to which they have been added to spread readily over a solid, thus "wetting" it. In paint manufacture, for example, some substances used as pigments are not easily wet by the vehicle in which the pigment particles are to be dispersed; the addition of butyl stearate or zinc naphthenate gives an improved dispersion. This property is a consequence of the wetting agent's tendency to concentrate at liquid/air and liquid/solid boundaries, thereby reducing the SURFACE TENSION between the two phases. Wetting agents are widely used in many fields, especially textile finishing, mineral flotation, and washing compounds. Like all surface-active substances, wetting agents are composed of molecules with an affinity for both oil and water, but their particular chemical composition will generally depend on intended use.—*H. W. F.*

WEXLER, HARRY, 1911–62, U. S. meteorologist; b. Fall River, Mass. Responsible over many years for the direction of research in the U. S. Weather Bureau, he made contributions in radiation, hurricane structure, and the climatology of the polar regions, especially the Antarctic. In recent years he devoted much attention to organizing weather observations from artificial satellites.—*O. G. S.*

WEYL, HERMANN, 1885–1955, German-U. S. mathematician; b. Elmshorn, Germany. He made major contributions in a large number of fields, including differential equations, function theory, group theory, quantum mechanics, relativity, topology, and the philosophy of mathematics. His books include *Space-Time-Matter* (1921), *Mind and Nature* (1934), *The Classical Groups* (1939), *Algebraic Theory of Numbers* (1940), and *Philosophy of Mathematics and Natural Science*

Hermann Weyl
(Wide World Photos)

(1949). He was a fellow of the Royal Society and a member of the National Academy of Sciences.—*H. C.*

WHEATSTONE, SIR CHARLES, 1802–75, English scientist and inventor; b. Gloucester. A musical-instrument maker by profession, he studied E. F. F. CHLADNI's figures and invented the kaleidophon for combining harmonic motions. Wheatstone worked with Sir W. F. Cooke (1806–79) on the development of electric telegraphy, made contributions to the development of the dynamo, and created the stereoscope. His name survives in the term "Wheatstone bridge," an important device in electrical measurement, although the device was not one of his inventions. His *Scientific Papers* appeared in 1879. He was a fellow of the Royal Society.—*D. H. D. R.*

WHEATSTONE BRIDGE: an electric circuit used for the accurate measurement of electrical resistance independently of any fluctuations of a voltage source. The bridge circuit, named in honor of Sir Charles Wheatstone, was first suggested by Samuel Hunter Christie several years before Wheatstone published its description in 1843. It consists of four resistances (any one of which may be unknown), a voltage source, and a galvanometer. The bridge is balanced

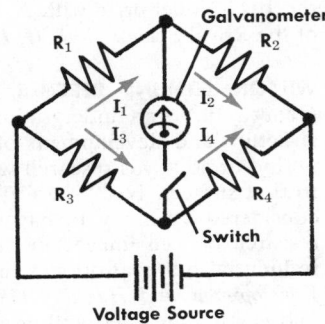

Wheatstone bridge: If, when the switch is closed, the galvanometer shows no reading, the ratio of the resistances is $R_1/R_2 = R_3/R_4$. Thus, if three are known, the fourth can be calculated.

by adjusting the known resistances so that the galvanometer shows no deflection, the potential drop across its terminals then being zero. The voltage drop I_1R_1 across an unknown resistance, say R_1, must then be equal to I_3R_3, the drop across R_3; similarly $I_1R_2 = I_3R_4$. From these two relations $R_1/R_2 = R_3/R_4$.—*H. Sw.*

WHEEL: The invention of the wheel in ancient times provided the major basis for mechanization. Countless mechanical devices rest on its principle, from vehicles and gears to turbines and propellers. Derived forms, *e.g.* rotating shafts, trains of gears, and belted wheels, permit the transmission of power. A wheel operates as an infinite series of levers (as in the spokes of a wagon wheel). When power is applied to the rim or axle, the opposite point is the fulcrum. A train of gears of varied sizes increases or diminishes power as through a series of levers.

As in all inventions, that of the wheel involved a new combination of earlier experiences. It originated as a cart wheel in the Near East in the Bronze Age, about 6,000 yr. ago, where rollers were placed under the dragging ends of burden-laden shafts pulled by draft animals. The oldest known carts (Sumeria, 3,500 B. C.) are developed forms having free-moving disc wheels; somewhat later chariots had spoke-wheels. Diffusion of the idea accounts for similar vehicles in China by 1,500 B. C. and in Europe by 500 B. C. Adaptations as water-wheels came early in Mesopotamia. Pulleys were in use in the pre-Christian Mediterranean area. The spinning-wheel, an early adaptation in India, had spread to Europe by the Middle Ages. Gearing was conceived by Greeks in the 2nd cent. B. C. but may have had no practical form beyond pairs

of toothed wheels. The wheel was not known in the Americas until brought by the Europeans.

Rotary devices probably had rudimentary beginnings apart from the wheel. The potter's wheel on a vertical pivot came into use in Sumeria, a development from a clay-supporting plate shifted by hand. Grindstones, turned by crank, are known from China about 2,000 B. C. and in Europe in the 5th cent. A. D. The rotary hand-mill of two horizontal stone discs was extensively used in Greece by the 2nd cent. B. C. Rotating shafts in the form of windlasses are equally old; the lathe was known to the Etruscans (7th–4th cent. B. C.).—*L. Sp.*

WHITEHEAD, ALFRED NORTH, 1861–1947, British mathematician and philosopher; b. Ramsgate, England. His work before 1914 was mainly in logic and foundations of mathematics; his later studies were in philosophical cosmology. His first book, *A Treatise on Universal Algebra* (1898), was an attempt at a generalization of algebra. *Principia Mathematica* (3 vols., 1910–13), co-authored with Bertrand Russell, originally Whitehead's pupil, showed that mathematics is deducible from the principles of logic. "Mathematical Concepts of the Material World" (*Phil. Trans. Royal Soc.,* 1906) foreshadowed his later interests. Whitehead became convinced that the conceptual framework with which philosophers have traditionally attempted to describe nature was inadequate for a proper account of change. *An Enquiry Concerning the Principles of Natural Knowledge* (1919) and *The Concept of Nature* (1920) presented a new philosophy of natural science. *The Principle of Relativity* (1922) articulated within the framework of Whitehead's new philosophy a physical theory of relativity alternative to Einstein's. His most popular work, *Science and the Modern World* (1925), written after his appointment as professor of philosophy at Harvard, criticized the "bifurcation of nature" inherited from Galileo, Descartes, and Locke, in accordance with which the properties to which experience testifies (*e.g.* colors, sounds) are not, strictly speaking, features of the world we inhabit. His last major works were *Process and Reality* (1929) and *Adventures of Ideas* (1933). He was a fellow of the Royal Society.—*F. Sc.*

WHITNEY, ELI, 1765–1825, U. S. inventor; b. Westboro, Mass. He invented and patented a hand-operated cotton gin to separate short-staple upland cotton from its seeds (1794). In partnership with Phineas Miller, Whitney manufactured the gins at New Haven, Conn. After a struggle to protect his invention from infringement, he abandoned its manufacture and unsuccessfully undertook mass production of firearms, 1798.—*S. B.*

Eli Whitney
(Yale University Art Gallery from Bettmann)

WHITTAKER, SIR EDMUND TAYLOR, 1873–1956, English mathematician; b. Lancashire. He wrote five major treatises which made available, in English, the most up-to-date thinking in analysis and dynamics: *A Course of Modern Analysis* (1902; rev. with G. N. Watson, 1915), *Analytic Dynamics* (1904), *Theory of Optical Instruments* (1907), *Calculus of Observations* with G. Robinson (1924), and his famous *A History of the Theories of Aether and Electricity* (1910; rewritten 1941, rev. 1951). His researches included automorphic functions, partial differential equations, Lamé and Mathieu functions, and the theory of relativity. He was a fellow of the Royal Society.—*H. C.*

WIEDEMANN-FRANZ-LORENZ LAW: see CONDUCTIVITY (electrical).

WIELAND, HEINRICH OTTO, 1877–1957, German chemist; b. Pforzheim, Baden. He was awarded the 1927 Nobel prize in chemistry for his work on the bile acids and analogous substances. He also conducted research on the organic nitrogen compounds, *e.g.* hydrazines and alkaloids. He was a fellow of the Royal Society and an associate of the U. S. National Academy of Sciences.—*E. F.*

WIEN, WILHELM, 1864–1928, German physicist; b. Gaffken. His research on electromagnetic radiation led him to studies of heat radiation. For his displacement law and his distribution law for heat radiation, he received the 1911 Nobel prize. His studies laid the foundation for Max Planck's development of the quantum theory of radiation. Wien also did research on canal rays and x-rays.—*D. H. D. R.*

WIENER, NORBERT, 1894–1964, U. S. mathematician; b. Columbia, Mo. His early training was in philosophy and logic, but a major part of his work was done in applied mathematics, including probability, potential theory, relativity, quantum theory, electrical networks, trigonometric expansions, Fourier integrals, Fourier transforms, and the field of CYBERNETICS, which he founded. His publications include *Cybernetics* (1953).—*H. C.*

WIEN'S RADIATION LAWS: equations that describe the radiant energy SPECTRUM emitted by a hot body at different temperatures. An incandescent solid emits a continuous (white) spectrum of light. The distribution of energy in this spectrum is not uniform, but has a peak whose position is given by Wien's displacement law: $\lambda_m T = b$, where λ_m is the wavelength at which the greatest amount of energy is radiated, T the absolute temperature of the body in question, and b a constant whose value is 0.288 cm°C. This law states that the peak energy moves toward the short-wavelength, or ULTRAVIOLET, end of the spectrum as the temperature of the body goes up.

Wien's radiation law, valid only in the short-wavelength region of the spectrum, expresses the energy density per unit frequency range of the spectrum (u_ν) in terms of the absolute temperature (T) of the body and atomic constants. The law is

$$u_\nu = \frac{8\pi h \nu^3}{c^3} e^{-h\nu/kT}$$

where h is Planck's constant, ν the frequency, c the velocity of light, and k Boltzmann's constant. The laws were formulated by Wilhelm Wien in 1896. See BLACK-BODY RADIATION; RADIATION.—*S. Br.*

WILLIAMSON, ALEXANDER WILLIAM, 1824–1904, English chemist; b. London. He developed a reaction for the preparation of ethers, and his work led to a new level of theoretical understanding which associated water, alcohols, and ethers. He synthesized ethylene glycol and introduced the intermediate-compound theory of catalysis. He was a fellow of the Royal Society.—*A. I.*

WILLIS, THOMAS, 1621–75, English anatomist and physician; b. Great Bedwin. He described the nervous system in great detail (1664) and accurately gave for the first time the anatomical relations of the main cerebral arteries. His name is preserved in "the circle of Willis," the term for the anastomosis at the base of the brain between the branches of the vertebral and internal carotid arteries. He was a fellow of the Royal Society.—*D. H. D. R.*

WILLSTÄTTER, RICHARD, 1872–1942, German chemist; b. Karlsruhe. He was a pioneer in the study of the chemistry of plant coloring matter (anthocyanins and chlorophyll) and of enzymes. For research on coloring matter in the vegetable kingdom, principally on chlorophyll, he received the 1915 Nobel prize in chemistry. He was director of the Kaiser Wilhelm Inst. for Chemistry 1912–16. A fellow of the Royal Society, Willstätter was also an associate of the U. S. National Academy of Sciences.—*E. F.*

WILSON, CHARLES THOMSON REES, 1869–1959, Scottish physicist; b. Glencorse. He did research on atmospheric phenomena, particularly cloud formation and atmospheric electricity, and in 1895 he began the production of artificial clouds within the laboratory. In 1910 he proposed the theory that under certain circumstances drops of water would condense along the path traversed by an α or β particle, leaving a streak of cloud that marked the path and that could be observed and photographed. By 1911 he had constructed the first Wilson CLOUD CHAMBER and observed the predicted tracks of subatomic particles. For the development of this apparatus and the vapor-condensation method of rendering visible the paths of electrically charged particles, he shared the 1927 Nobel prize with A. H. Compton. He was a fellow of the Royal Society.—*D. H. D. R.*

WILSON, EDMUND BEECHER, 1856–1939, U. S. biologist; b. Geneva, Ill. As an undergraduate he became interested in the structure and development of the animal cell, and over a period of 40 yr his research was devoted almost exclusively to that subject. His "The Cell Lineage of *Nereis*" (1892) is considered by many to have inaugurated the long line of research on cell lineage in the U. S. A. Probably his most influential publication was the third edition of *The Cell in Development and Heredity* (1925), which remains a classic and is still consulted with great profit today. He was a fellow of the Royal Society and a member of the National Academy of Sciences.—*D. H. D. R.*

WILSON, JOHN TUZO, 1908– , Canadian geophysicist; b. Ottawa. He has been a major theorist on mountain building from a mathematical and physical viewpoint, and has urged the concept that continents have grown throughout geologic time by successive additions of mountain belts along their margins. Reorganization of the Precambrian geological time scale on the basis of radioactive age measurements has had his strong support. A leader in seeking more quantitative approaches to geology, Wilson wrote (with Jacobs and Russell) *Physics and Geology* (1959).—*R. W. D.*

WINCHELL, ALEXANDER, 1824–91, U. S. geologist; b. Northeast, N. Y. Well known as a lecturer and writer, he also directed state geological surveys (notably Michigan, 1869–71). He was professor of geology and paleontology at the Univ. of Michigan (1879–91). Among his many publications are *Sketches of Creation* (1870), *The Doctrine of Evolution* (1874), and *Geological Studies* (1886).—*C. S. V.*

WIND: air in motion over the Earth. This motion results primarily from the unequal heating of the Earth by the Sun, which causes changes in pressure over the globe. On the global scale, winds transfer heat and momentum from the tropics to the polar regions. The highest winds are the 300-mph whirls of tornadoes and the 100- to 150-mph winds of tropical hurricanes and high-atmosphere jet streams.

Causes: Winds result from several forces acting upon the atmosphere, chiefly the barometric-pressure gradient force, the deflection due to the earth's rotation (Coriolis force), and friction. Of these, the pressure-gradient force is generally most important. If the only force acting on the air arose from the pressure gradient, the wind would blow directly *across* the isobars (the lines of equal barometric pressure that are a feature of every WEATHER MAP) from high toward low pressure. However, winds usually blow *along* the isobars, be-

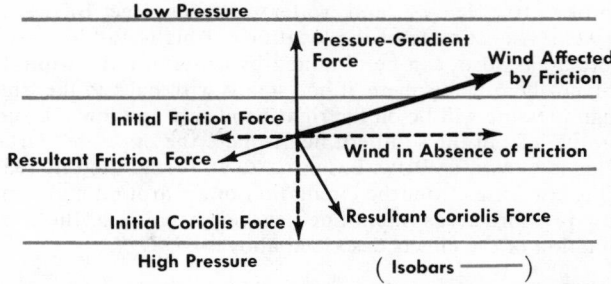

Fig. 3—The effect of friction with the ground is to lower wind speed and to lower Coriolis force. Thus the balance characteristic of the geostrophic or gradient wind is upset, and the wind blows across the isobars at an oblique angle.

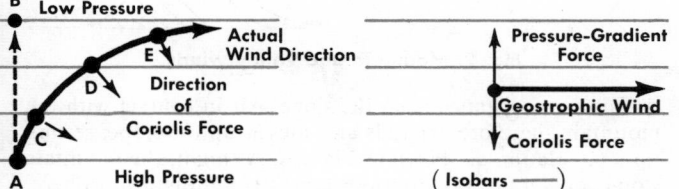

Fig. 1—Geostrophic wind: If Earth were not rotating, winds would blow directly across isobars (path AB in diagram at left), since the only force exerted on the air would be that arising from the pressure gradient. Because of Earth's rotation, the path (in the northern hemisphere) is bent to the right as if a second force were acting perpendicular to the pressure-gradient force. This "Coriolis force" alters the path from AB to AC, bending it progressively farther at D and E. Eventually the actual wind path is maintained at right angles to the pressure-gradient force by an exactly equal and opposite Coriolis force. This is the geostrophic wind.

cause of the Coriolis force, which outside the equatorial regions causes objects in motion to be deflected toward the right of an observer in the northern hemisphere facing south, to the left of an observer in the southern hemisphere facing north. When the pressure-gradient force exactly balances the Coriolis force, the winds blow along the isobars: if the isobars are straight, the winds are *geostrophic* (Fig. 1), but if the isobars are significantly curved, the centrifugal effect of the curvature becomes important and the wind is called *gradient* (Fig. 2).

The effect of friction is to slow down the air motion near the earth's surface. The balance between the pressure-gradient and Coriolis forces is then disturbed and the wind tends to turn again across the isobars toward lower pressure (Fig. 3). This is the wind actually observed in nature. An inspection of a typical weather map shows the winds generally along the isobars, but inclined about 20° to 30° to-

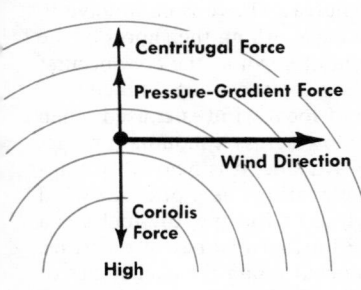

Fig. 2—Gradient wind: When isobars (blue lines) are curved, a third force—the centrifugal force of the air—is added to the forces involved in the geostrophic wind. This gives rise to the anticyclonic gradient wind (wind about a barometric high) and the cyclonic gradient wind (wind about a barometric low). The former is always greater than the geostrophic wind or the cyclonic gradient wind for the same pressure gradient.

ward lower pressure in the surface layers. Winds blow clockwise around highs and counterclockwise around lows in the northern hemisphere, and vice versa in the southern hemisphere. Sudden shifts in wind direction are usually associated with the passage of FRONTS and hence with changes in weather.

Variation with Height: The frictional effect of the surface of the earth decreases with elevation. Accordingly, with height the wind usually increases in speed and its direction becomes more nearly along the isobars. The level at which the effect of friction ceases is usually between 2,000 and 3,000 ft; it is generally lower over water and smooth ground, where frictional drag is small, and higher over rough terrain, where drag is large. Above the level where friction ceases, winds generally continue to increase in speed. In middle latitudes this increase often continues throughout the troposphere (see ATMOSPHERE). These differences in speeds are due to variations in the pressure-gradient force with elevation, caused by changes in the air temperatures at different levels. For this reason the difference between the geostrophic winds at different levels is called the *thermal wind.*

Local Winds: Movements of air which do not depend markedly upon the large-scale pressure distribution, but rather upon the topography and other features of the restricted regions over which they are found, are called local winds. (See WIND, LOCAL.)

Gustiness: On most days, wind is characterized by gusty, turbulent motions, resulting from surface obstructions, *e.g.* rough terrain, trees, or buildings, and from convection currents due to local heating. In addition, a form of gustiness called "clear-air" turbulence has been discovered in the upper atmosphere in regions where large variations in wind speed occur over short distances. Such variations are frequently associated with JET STREAMS—narrow ribbons of high-speed winds which blow from the west in middle latitudes at heights of 20,000 to 40,000 ft.

Measurements: Measurement of wind direction began as early as A. D. 900, when wind vanes were first installed on tall buildings and church steeples. In 1667 a crude anemometer, for measuring wind speed, was invented by Robert Hooke in England. By the end of the 18th cent., knowledge of oceanic winds was well established, and in 1846 a classic study of wind and ocean currents by Matthew Maury, an American naval officer, provided the basis for modern knowledge of the global wind systems. Observations began in the early 19th cent. with use of tethered balloons and kites, and soon after small free balloons were used for wind measurements. When such a balloon is released, it drifts with the wind as it rises; and by observation with a theodolite, an instrument similar to a surveyor's transit, wind speed and direction aloft can be found by triangulation. Today a radar beam is substituted for visual observation, permitting measurements even though clouds may make the balloon invisible. Although accurate measurements of wind speed require instruments, the method of estimating speed invented in 1804 by Adm. Beaufort of the British Navy is still useful: speed is judged by observing wind effect on such commonplace objects as smoke, tree leaves, and water surfaces (see BEAUFORT SCALE). An estimate of the locations of high- and low-pressure areas, also, can be obtained by observing the wind. In the northern hemisphere, if one stands with back to the wind high pressure will be on the right-hand side and low pressure on the left; in the southern hemisphere the opposite is true. This is known as BUYS BALLOT'S LAW, formulated in 1857. This law arises from the circulation of air around high- and low-pressure areas (mentioned earlier) because of the combination of the effects described above.—*J. C. T.*

WIND, LOCAL: a motion of the air which affects a limited geographical area. Such areas may range in size from the greater part of a continent to a few square miles. For the most part, local winds are related to three general meteorological processes: (1) unequal absorption of solar heating by land and sea, (2) periodic heating and cooling of dissimilar topographic features, and (3) modification of larger-scale wind currents by mountains and other terrain forms. Combinations of these processes are also observed. Many local winds are known by special names peculiar to the locality in which they occur. Usually they are singled out in this way because of some unpleasant or dangerous characteristic with which they are associated; *e.g.* extreme heat or cold, excessive dryness, or destructive velocity.

Land and Sea Breezes: Perhaps the best known and most universal of the local winds, at least to coastal inhabitants, are the land and sea breezes. They are caused by daily heating and cooling of land and sea surfaces. In the absence of any large-scale wind, there is usually little or no motion of air across the coast during early morning hours. During the day, however, the surface of the land becomes warmer than that of the sea. The heated air next to the ground expands and rises, allowing cooler and denser air over the ocean to blow inland across the coast, hence the sea breeze. At the same time, a return circulation is set up at higher levels (Fig. 1A). At night the ground cools more rapidly than the ocean and therefore, a few hours after sunset, the wind circulation is reversed: the wind blows back across the coast from the land, causing the land breeze (Fig. 1B).

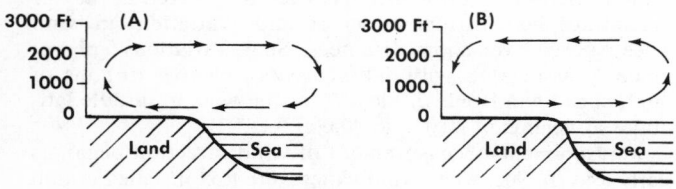

Fig. 1: (A) Daytime sea breeze. (B) Nighttime land breeze.

These processes are often modified by effects of topography, especially along rugged coast lines, and by prevailing large-scale winds. Furthermore, the deflecting influence of Earth's rotation, *i.e.* the CORIOLIS FORCE (see also ATMOSPHERE), tends to make the winds turn parallel to the coast line as the breeze becomes stronger. In the northern hemisphere, the afternoon sea breeze will turn so that the coast line is on the left side as one faces forward with the wind; in the southern hemisphere, the coast line will be on the right. Practical use is made of land and sea breezes by yachtsmen and fishermen, who frequently set out to sea during the land-breeze regime and return to shore with the sea breeze.

Mountain and Valley Winds: In almost the same fashion as variable absorption of solar heat produces land and sea breezes, daily heating and cooling of mountain slopes cause mountain and valley winds. During the daytime, the side of the mountain facing the Sun warms up more quickly than

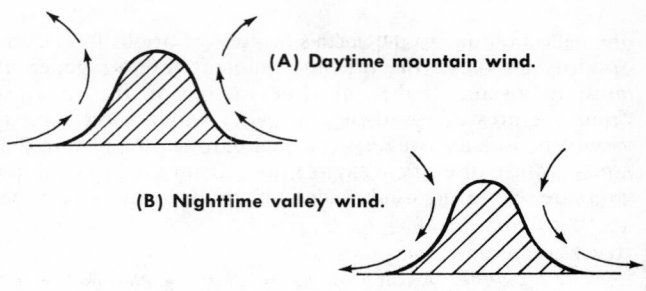

Fig. 2: Mountain and valley winds.

the air some distance from the slope. Air in contact with the mountain therefore expands and moves up the slope, setting up a circulation as shown in Fig. 2A. At night, the mountain slope cools more rapidly than the surrounding atmosphere, and the air flows downward into the valley (Fig. 2B). Because this nighttime flow is usually forced by the narrowing of the valley sides into a smaller volume than the expanding daytime circulation, the night wind in the valley is frequently stronger than the daytime breeze.

Drainage Winds: Another type of local wind occurs in areas where large amounts of cold air have accumulated over a high plateau or elevated mountain region. Occasionally the migration of a large-scale disturbance, such as a storm system, will displace the cold air, which then flows down the mountain slopes and produces strong winds in the valleys below (Fig. 3). Such winds are called *drainage, katabatic,* or *fall* winds. Because of their frequently destructive character they are also known by special names in the localities where they occur.

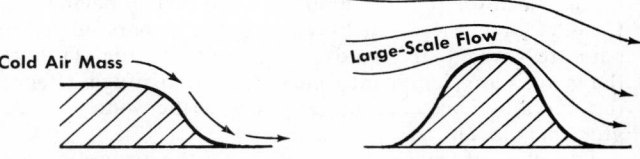

Fig. 3: Drainage wind.   **Fig. 4: Foehn wind.**

One such local wind is the *Santa Ana* of S California. It originates in the high desert plateau of the interior and flows through the mountain passes (including the Santa Ana Canyon; hence its name). It then spreads out into the coastal area as a dry, dusty, sand-carrying gale, which may cause damage to homes, crops, and even coastal shipping. Similar drainage winds occur along the coast of Greenland, where the perpetual ice field on the plateau above is conducive to the establishment of a cold air mass. Along the shores of the Adriatic Sea a cold drainage wind known as the *bora* occurs; the *mistral* is a similar wind along the coast of S France.

Foehn Winds: Another type of local wind is caused when large-scale atmospheric winds blow across a mountain range. As the air flows down the leeward side, it is heated by compression and arrives at lower elevations as a hot, dry wind known generally as a foehn wind. In Europe, the foehn is a common occurrence along the northern slopes of the Alps. In North America such winds occur along the east slopes of the Rocky Mts, where they are called *chinooks*. Because of their dryness and warmth, a thick blanket of snow may disappear in a few hours when a chinook is blowing. Some features of the Santa Ana winds of S California, particularly during the fall and spring months, also exhibit foehn characteristics.

Other Local Winds: Other local winds include the *blizzard*, a term originally used to describe the driving snow and cold gales of the Great Plains of the U. S. A. It is now more generally used to describe any strong wind accompanied by snow or sleet. Similar cold winds are the *buran* of Siberia, the *burga* of Alaska, the Texas *norther,* and the *boulbie* of S France. Cooling winds of the tropics are the *levanter* of S Spain and *el norte* of the east coast of Mexico. The *harmattan* is a cool dry wind which brings welcome relief to the summer heat of the west coast of Africa, and the *sumatra* is a squall-like wind which blows along the Sumatra and Malay coasts during the monsoon season (Apr.–Nov.). Warm winds include the *sirocco,* which blows northward across the coast of Africa and the Mediterranean toward the south coast of Europe. A similar wind is the *khamsin,* a hot dry gale which blows from the Libyan Desert across Egypt and out into the E Mediterranean. In the desert areas of Africa and SW Asia, the *simoom* is an extremely hot dry wind which results in unpleasant and dangerous sandstorms.—*J. C. T.*

WINDAUS, ADOLF, 1876–1959, German biochemist; b. Berlin. For his studies on the constitution of the sterols and their connection with the vitamins, he received the Nobel prize, 1928. His work on cholesterol laid the foundation for the study of sex hormones, and his method for the conversion of ergosterol into vitamin D by means of ultraviolet light was applied to the production of vitamin D in milk. He also did research on digitalis.—*D. H. D. R.*

WIND GAP: in geology, a low point or pass in a ridge, initially cut as a WATER GAP by a stream which has abandoned this part of its path subsequent to the lowering of the general level of the land. Such gaps are common in the ridges of the folded Appalachian Mts, and in places they serve as passes across the mountains.—*J. Sh.*

WIND TUNNEL: a tube-like structure or passage, together with its adjuncts, in which airflow is produced by one of various means, *e.g.* fan, exhaust nozzle from a high-pressure storage vessel, or a traveling shock wave. Within this airflow are placed airfoils, engines, or other components of aircraft, rockets or other flight vehicles, or models thereof, for purposes of investigating the airflow about them and the aerodynamic forces or heating effects acting upon them.

 Evolution: The first wind tunnel was designed (1871) by F. H. Wenham in England. The Wright brothers set up (1901) a small wind tunnel in their bicycle shop in Dayton and measured forces on airfoils, as well as the center of pressure on cambered surfaces at various angles of attack. A larger wind tunnel, made of wood and having a cross section 6-ft square,

Testing in 1915: Biplane model was tested in early U. S. Navy wind tunnel. *(Inst. of Aerospace Sciences)*

was used (1902–03) by A. F. Zahm in Washington, D. C., to study air velocity and aerodynamic pressure and friction. Other early tunnels were those of Sir Thomas Stanton in England (1903) and D. Riabouchinsky in Russia (1906). Today, the wind tunnel continues to be the chief laboratory facility for aerodynamic study. However, aerodynamics is now so complex and diversified that no single tunnel design could possibly be used for all problems of current interest. One classification of tunnels is based on the Mach number regime in which they operate; *i.e.* a tunnel may be classed as subsonic, transonic, supersonic, or hypersonic. Another classification is by mode of operation, the two major categories being *continuous* and *intermittent.* In the former, airflow is maintained continuously by blowers, compressors, or pumps. Continuous tunnels may be of the closed-circuit type in which the working fluid is continuously recirculated, or they may employ an air-intake and exhaust system. The intermittent tunnel uses either air exhausted from high-pressure tanks, or atmospheric air drawn through the test section into vacuum tanks. Duration of flow in such tunnels

Hypersonic wind tunnel at Ames Research Center, Moffett Field, Calif., is cylindrical, 3½ ft in diameter, 10 ft long. Through it a stream of heated air is driven at high speeds past test model. Four interchangeable nozzles permit tests at Mach numbers 5, 7½, 10, and 15. (NASA)

may vary from a fraction of a minute to several minutes. Tunnels are also classified by specific technical functions: smoke tunnels enable visualization of streamlines; variable-density tunnels enable measurements to be made at varying Reynolds numbers; the shock tunnel successfully simulates, and permits measurement of, the very high heating rates associated with ballistic-missile re-entry. A *hot-shot tunnel* is one in which a small volume of air under high pressure, before expanding through a nozzle into the test section, is further compressed and heated by the spark discharge of stored electrical energy. Test-section flow is usually in the range Mach 15–20, and lasts about 0.02 sec. The tunnel is adapted to tests simulating altitudes above 150,000 ft.

Aerodynamic Physical Measurements: Laboratory measurements to test performance of airplane components are usually made in conjunction with scaled models in a wind tunnel. Suitable measurements can yield information on lift, drag, heating effects, stall conditions, or landing and take-off characteristics. Techniques may be divided into two broad classes. In one class, measuring elements, *e.g.* pressure tubes, may be installed directly on the model itself and the resulting measurements recorded during wind-tunnel operation. In the other, airflow around the model is investigated; for this purpose, there exist special techniques of flow visualization. Studies of the over-all dynamic behavior of the model itself are concerned with three force components—drag, lift, lateral force—and with three moment or torque components—pitch, yaw, roll. Special wind-tunnel balances of many types have been devised in which a force or torque on the model is transmitted by suspension wires or struts so as to allow comparison with a standard force or torque, *e.g.* a calibrated chemical balance. In flow visualization, one of the most useful techniques at lower speeds is to inject smoke into the air so as to observe the streamlines around a model. At speeds approaching sonic and higher, the airflow becomes noticeably refractive, suggesting a weak lens. Special photographic techniques then become possible. Two of these, *Schlieren* and shadow, are especially useful in locating shock waves and in the study of boundary layers, wakes, and turbulence. Another, called interferometry, uses the interference of two beams of light to analyze the flow. Photographs of the interference patterns give information on density, pressure, temperature, and Mach number distribution. (See PHOTOGRAPHY.) Then, by using proper scaling factors (see REYNOLDS NUMBER), these data elucidate the flight characteristics of the full-scale vehicle under study.—*D. B.*

WING: that part of an animal or of a flying machine which generates lifting forces due to aerodynamic reaction with the air. It may be fixed relative to the body, as in a gliding animal or a conventional airplane, and rely for its action on the forward motion of the body through the air, or it may move in relation to the body, as in flapping flight or in a helicopter, so that hovering is possible. The aerodynamic performance

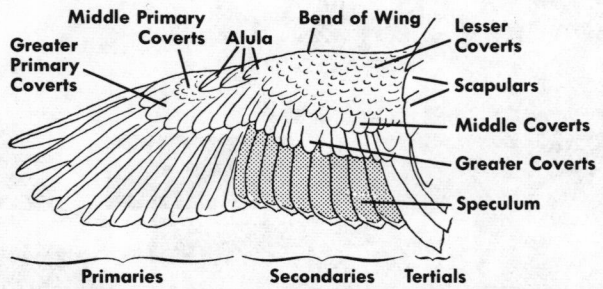

Wing of a bird: Diagram identifies different feathers that make up the upper surface of bird's wing. (*After Palmer*)

of a wing depends on its *span* (dimension transverse to the line of air flow), its *chord* (dimension parallel to the air flow), the *wing section* at various positions along the span, and the degree of *twisting* from wing base to wing tip. Other things being equal, the performance is better with a high *aspect ratio* (the ratio of span to chord). The construction of man-made and animal wings is similar. It relies on one or more spars to bear the bending moments, and accessory members or a stressed surface material to take drag and twisting loads. Bird and bat wings have a single bony spar, with ligaments for torsional and drag bracing; most modern sailplane and many airplane wings are similar, but have a rigid surface for withstanding drag and torsion. Insect wings have more than one spar, formed by thickenings of the surface, which also resist drag and torsion. High-speed airplanes must have a very smooth surface to ensure laminar (non-turbulent) flow, and birds probably achieve this by means of feathers. The small auxiliary, or bastard, wing of birds is analogous to the slot of an airplane, preserving lift at low airspeeds; the spreading of tip feathers in soaring birds has a similar function. See AERODYNAMICS; AIRFOIL.—*J. W. S. P.*

Wings of extinct reptile, bat, and bird show how structure of forelimb has been modified for flight. (*From Guyer*)

WINKLER, CLEMENS ALEXANDER, 1838–1904, German chemist; b. Freiberg. Probably the leading inorganic chemist of the last quarter of the 19th cent., he made notable advances in technical gas analysis, and was the founder of the modern contact sulfuric-acid industry. Most important was his discovery (1886) of the element GERMANIUM in argyrodite.—*R. E. O.*

WINTER: see SEASONS.

WISLICENUS, JOHANNES ADOLF, 1835–1902, German chemist; b. Klein-Eichstädt. His work on lactic acids led J. H. van't Hoff and J. A. Le Bel to the concept of the asymmetric carbon atom as an explanation of optical activity. Wislicenus clarified the structural character of numerous optical and geometric isomers. He was a fellow of the Royal Society.—*A. I.*

WITHERING, WILLIAM, 1741–99, English physician and naturalist; b. Wellington. He discovered the mineral witherite, describing it in his "Experiments and Observations on the Terra Ponderosa" (1748). His *Account of the Fox-Glove* (1785) reported the use of foxglove (digitalis) in curing dropsy and showed that dropsy could be cardiac in origin. His most important publication was *A Botanical Arrangement of All the Vegetables Naturally Growing in Great Britain According to the System of the Celebrated Linnaeus* (1776). He was a fellow of the Royal Society.—*D. H. D. R.*

WÖHLER, FRIEDRICH, 1800–82, German chemist; b. Eschersheim. In 1828 he made urea, until then known only as a product of kidney activity in animals, from inorganic substances in the laboratory. Wöhler isolated beryllium and yttrium (1828); he also prepared an impure form of aluminum (1827), isolating the pure metal in 1845, and was the first to describe its properties (1827). He was a fellow of the

Royal Society and an associate of the U. S. National Academy of Sciences.—*E. F.*

WOLFF, KASPAR FRIEDRICH, 1733–94, German naturalist and embryologist; b. Berlin. His doctoral dissertation, *Theoria generationis* (1759), rejected the doctrine of preformation and opened the field of embryology. His attempts to find common factors in animal and plant anatomy influenced the development of the cell theory.—*D. H. D. R.*

WOLLASTON, WILLIAM HYDE, 1766–1828, English physiologist, chemist, and physicist; b. East Dereham. His discovery of a process for making platinum malleable provided him with an adequate income and enabled him to spend the remainder of his life in scientific research. He discovered the elements palladium (1803) and rhodium (1804), invented a form of the camera lucida (1807) for use in drawing objects under the microscope, and invented the reflecting goniometer (1809) used in determining angles of crystals. His work in medicine was concerned with the metabolic problems of diabetes. A firm advocate of the atomic theory of matter and the wave theory of light, he did research that contributed to the acceptance of those theories. He was a fellow of the Royal Society.—*D. H. D. R.*

WOOD, ROBERT WILLIAMS, 1868–1955, U. S. physicist; b. Concord, Mass. His fields of research were ultrasonics and optics, and light in all its aspects. He is particularly known for the production of diffraction gratings for astrophysical research. His *Physical Optics* (1905) became a classic. He was professor of experimental physics at Johns Hopkins Univ. (1901–38), a fellow of the Royal Society, and a recipient of the Society's Rumford Gold Medal. He was also a member of the National Academy of Sciences.—*D. H. D. R.*

WOOD (or **xylem**): the hard, fibrous tissue found in the roots, stems, and branches of many plants; its chief functions are conduction of materials throughout the plant and the imparting of mechanical strength. With the nutrients supplied by the roots and from the substances synthesized in the leaves, plants condense many molecules of simple sugar (saccharides) into complex polysaccharides and lignin to form wood. The polysaccharides, comprising highly condensed celluloses and the less condensed hemicelluloses, are deposited in regular patterns to form the cellwalls. The lignin, combined with a smaller proportion of polysaccharides, is inserted between adjacent cells. The cambium layer between bark and wood is the site of the plant's greatest chemical activity: here, cells are formed and then combined into fibrils which knit together into fibers of various shapes and functions. In the dicotyledonous (broad-leaved) angiosperms (*e.g.* oak, maple, beech, and birch) and the gymnosperms or conifers (*e.g.* the "evergreens" pine, spruce, and cedar), which together provide most of the commercially utilized wood, an envelope of new fiber systems is built each year, exhibiting slight differences between its earlier (spring) and later (summer) growth section; these differences are noticeable in the somewhat greater lightness and higher lignin content of the earlier spring wood. Such *annual rings* are absent in monocotyledonous plants, *e.g.* palms and yuccas. As the fiber bundles in the center of the plant get older, they cease to participate in the growth processes and become *heartwood,* in which substances from the cell sap are deposited, making the heartwood darker and less permeable than the surrounding younger *sapwood.* Radial rays, which carry food materials from the outer cambium, are visible in many woods without magnification. There are important differences among woods in chemical composition, density, and strength, according to the species and the growth conditions. Non-porous woods, *e.g.* the conifers, are those in which the conducting elements are tapering cells of small diameter called tracheids; porous woods, *e.g.* the broad-leaved dicotyledons, have long, tubelike conducting elements called vessels.

The wood substance of the conifers or *softwoods* contains about 26 to 30% lignin, 55 to 60% celluloses, and 8% pentosans, *i.e.* polysaccharides of the 5-carbon pentoses, mostly xylose. Broadleaf plants, usually called *hardwoods,* contain much higher proportions of pentosans, 20–24% on an average; and the lignin varies from about 23% in red maple and beech to 30% in some members of the oak family.

Lumber Production, Treatment, and Use: About five times more softwood lumber (in board feet) is produced in the U. S. A. than hardwood. Principal softwoods cut in the U. S. A., in order of greatest use, are Douglas fir, southern yellow pine, ponderosa pine, white fir, hemlock, redwood, and western red cedar. Principal hardwoods are oak, yellow poplar, maple, sweet gum, black gum, beech, and birch. In many of the larger lumber mills, logs are debarked before sawing; this is always done before the cutting and slicing operations required to produce thin veneers. In the living tree, wood has a high water content. Usually the greater part of this water must be removed by drying with heated air. Drying is carried out according to specific schedules of temperature and moisture to avoid any warping or splitting that might occur because of the contraction of the water-swollen fibers. The exposed surface of wood used in construction or for furniture is treated with various chemical compounds for protection and color. Natural resins and synthetic polymers are used for durable coatings and paints. Protection against insects and molds is obtained by impregnation with toxic inorganic salts containing zinc, copper, or arsenic in various combinations, or with phenolic substances such as creosote or pentachlorophenol. With such treatment the service life of telephone poles and railroad crossties is considerably extended. For protection against fire, wood is coated with incombustible materials that expand, under heat, to form a porous, heat-insulating layer. Impregnation with compounds containing phosphates, chlorine, or bromine retards combustion.

Nails, screws, and glues have long been used in building with wood, but the recent development of synthetic RESINS as bases for adhesives has provided bonds as strong and durable as the wood itself. Laminated structures of any desired length and thickness, and in many forms, can thus be manufactured. New types of mechanical connectors have also been designed (see JOINING METHODS). *Particle boards* of several kinds are made by gluing small pieces of wood together under pressure. The particles for this purpose are chips or flakes produced in specified dimensions. The adhesives are selected according to anticipated end-use of the board. For example, flakes to which solutions of intermediate-stage urea-formaldehyde resins have been applied by spraying are distributed to form mats. They are hot-pressed into boards of uniform thickness. Water-repellent paraffin and other modifying ingredients can be added. *Fiber boards* are made by first separating chips into fibers and then combining them under heat and pressure. Low-density fiber boards are manufactured for insulation; the stronger high-density boards, for construction purposes. Minerals for flame-retarding, asphalt for waterproofing, and other special materials can be added.

Pulp Manufacture: In the manufacture of wood pulp for PAPER, separation into fibers is accomplished either by mechanical grinding (groundwood) or with partial removal of the lignin (chemical pulp). Only a little of the lignin is removed by treating with soda at low temperatures, much more by cooking at high temperatures with caustic soda or with acid sulfite salts. Complete removal for the production of high-grade CELLULOSE is achieved with chlorine and chlorine dioxide. The water-soluble lignin derivatives are washed out of the insoluble cellulose.

Wood Hydrolysis (saccharification): Acids attack celluloses in wood and leave the lignin essentially unchanged. The celluloses are split and water is molecularly introduced so that water-soluble sugars are formed. The process is, therefore, called wood-hydrolysis or saccharification. It is carried out in two different ways. Either dilute acids are used at high temperatures (*e.g.* 0.5% sulfuric acid at 160 to 180°C); or concentrated acids are used at lower temperatures (*e.g.* 72% sulfuric acid or 41% hydrochloric acid at about 20°C). Thus, solutions can be obtained which contain pentoses (mainly xylose) and hexoses (glucose with some mannose). After purification, they can be subjected to fermentations for alcohol, yeast, and other products, or the pure sugars can be produced by crystallization. Saccharification of wood is carried out extensively in Europe; in the U. S. A. saccharification of STARCH is favored.

Other Wood-derived Products: The soluble lignin derivatives from pulping processes and the insoluble lignin from hydrolysis are used for *synthetic resins, tanning materials,* and in further chemical conversions. For example, gentle oxidation of the lignin derivatives yields a certain proportion of vanillin. When wood is heated without added chemicals, decomposition slowly begins above 100°C and becomes very strong at about 275°C. A series of exothermic reactions produces large volumes of gases, mainly carbon dioxide and monoxide with some hydrogen and methane, water, acetic acid, methanol, and tars. After heating to 400 to 500°C, about one-third of the wood substance is left as charcoal. Formerly, all the *methanol* and most *acetic acid* came from wood distillation. The tars were mainly regarded as nuisance. Now that synthesis supplies methanol and acetic acid, more attention is given to products obtainable by refining the tars. *Charcoal* is valued as an almost flameless fuel of high heat and low ash content. For convenience in handling, it is pressed into briquets by the aid of binders. By removing residual tar with superheated steam (up to 1,000°C) the surface of charcoal is "activated" so that it acquires specific adsorptive actions on gases or high-molecular materials in solutions. Therefore, *activated charcoal* is used in gas masks and in various chemical purification processes.

Pine trees are the source of turpentine and ROSIN ("naval stores"). These products are obtained from living trees by tapping, *i.e.* cutting through the cambium layer and collecting the liquid flowing out of the resin ducts. They are extracted from stumps with organic solvents and by steam-distillation. About 600,000 tons of rosin were produced in 1960. *Talloil* is a by-product of the manufacture of cellulose by cooking with solutions containing caustic soda. It consists of a mixture of rosin and fatty acids. One of its uses is in ore flotation to separate valuable mineral substances from the gangue. A corresponding by-product from sulfite-cooking is *cymol*. The bark of certain species has long been used for its effectiveness in tanning substances. Cinchona bark is famous as the source of quinine. Many other barks contain potentially valuable, extractable substances, but at present the chemical utilization of bark is insufficiently developed. A start has been made in producing bark extractives for addition to oil-well drilling muds and other purposes. For use as mulch, bark is compounded with plant nutrients. An increasing tendency in the lumber industry to regard wood as an annual crop has contributed much to the care and maintenance of our forests.

More efficient utilization of wood, *e.g.* the use of "residues" from the manufacture of lumber, veneer, and pulp, is also an encouraging trend; but much remains to be done to achieve full and efficient utilization of wood.—*E. F.*

WOOD ALCOHOL: see METHYL ALCOHOL.

WOODWARD, JOHN, 1665–1728, English geologist and physician; b. Derbyshire; ed. Cambridge Univ. He is best known for his *An Essay Toward a Natural History of the Earth* (1695), in which he recognized that fossils were once living animals but attributed their burial in sediments to the Biblical flood. His fossil collection formed the nucleus of the Woodwardian Museum at Cambridge Univ. He was a fellow of the Royal Society.—*D. H. D. R.*

WOOL: strictly speaking, the hair of sheep, but in the U. S. A. the legal definition of wool covers hair—never previously used—of sheep, Angora goats, camels, alpacas, llamas, and vicuñas. (Wool reclaimed from both unused and used wool products in the U. S. A. must be called reprocessed and re-used, respectively.) Wool is largely keratin, a protein composed of chains of some 17 amino acids connected through peptide linkages and cross-linked laterally through disulfide —S—S— cystine groups. The arrangement of these chains in the fiber is not known with certainty, but it is generally accepted that keratin can exist both in alpha (folded) and beta (extended) configurations. This ability of keratin to extend and contract accounts for the well-known resilience and warmth of wool products. On the outside of the fiber is the so-called cuticle, a layer of flat, minute, overlapping scales, which can interlock and are largely responsible for wool's felting ability. The inner portion of the fiber is called the cortex.

Sheep are generally shorn in the spring, when the fleece is heaviest. Because machine clippers speed up the operation considerably, their use has become widespread in recent years. There are detectable differences between the fleece shorn from living animals and the pulled fibers from sheepskins; between fibers from animals of different ages; and even between fibers from the various parts of the sheep's body. Classification and selection of wools for specific uses requires much skill: among the important factors are fineness, color, luster, staple length, crimp, and softness. The clipped wool is dirty and greasy, so that 40 to 60% of the weight delivered to the mill door is removed on first scouring. The grease is recovered because it contains LANOLIN, a fat which can be absorbed through the human skin and is therefore used widely in pharmacological and cosmetic preparations. The 1960 world wool production was 5,541,000,-000 lb on grease basis, and 3,184,000,000 lb clean; the corresponding figures for 1960 U. S. production were 300,163,000 and 145,153,000 lb.

WORK: the product of a force F and the displacement d in the direction of the force applied. If the force is exerted on a body at an angle θ to the observed displacement of the body, the work done is expressed by $F \cos \theta\, d$, where $F \cos \theta$ is the component of the force along the displacement. In a broad sense, work is energy "in transit." The units of work are therefore identical with those of energy.

In the foot-pound-second system, a force of 1 lb, producing a displacement of 1 ft in the direction of the force, performs 1 ft-lb of work. In the centimeter-gram-second system, a force of 1 dyne, with a corresponding displacement of 1 cm, accounts for 1 erg of work. In the meter-kilogram-second system, a force of 1 newton (10^5 dynes) multiplied by a displacement of 1 meter (100 cm) yields 1 joule of work (10^7 ergs). The time rate of doing work is POWER.—*A. E.*

WORK FUNCTION: see ELECTRON EMISSION.

WORMS: animals with elongated bodies, which progress by wriggling, gliding, creeping, walking (on many legs), or swimming (by means other than a few fins and a propulsive tail). An elongated body is advantageous to animals living in crannies under stones or in burrows in mud or sand, or to parasites holding to the inner surface of the alimentary canal of the host animal or traveling about in its blood vessels (see PARASITISM). Many worms are found in streams and tide pools, others in the bottom sediments of ponds and seas, and still others in terrestrial situations. Almost every phylum of animals from Platyhelminthes to Chordata has representatives referred to as worms or wormlike. The roundworms (NEMATODES), which are sometimes classified as a separate phylum (Nematoda) and sometimes as a class in phylum Aschelminthes, probably outnumber all other worms together. The term worm is used for many representatives of phylum Arthropoda, such as the velvet worms (*e.g. Peripatus*), the hundred-legged worms (centipedes), the thousand-legged worms (millipedes), and the wireworms (beetle larvae), cutworms (moth larvae), and caddisworms (caddisfly larvae) among insects. Burrowing lizards, which are legless, are often called "worm lizards" or "worm snakes." More commonly, however, the word worm refers to any member of these phyla: Platyhelminthes (flatworms), Nematomorpha (horsehair worms), Nemertinea (ribbon worms), Acanthocephala (spiny-headed worms), Chaetognatha (arrow worms), Sipunculoidea (peanut worms), Priapuloidea (priapuloids), Echiuroidea (echiuroids), Pogonophora (beard worms), Annelida (segmented worms), and Hemichordata (acorn worms or tongue worms).

Platyhelminthes: Of the approximately 9,000 species of flatworms, about 3,200 are free-living turbellarians (often called planarians, in reference to the genus *Planaria*). Most turbellarians have a blind digestive cavity with a protrusible pharynx opening at the middle of the under surface; with it they pull into the cavity bits of decaying meat they find while scavenging, or smaller animals (*e.g.* crustaceans, hydroid coelenterates) on which they prey. Turbellarians (Class Turbellaria) are mostly aquatic, occurring in marine or freshwater situations; a few live on land in regions of high humidity. About

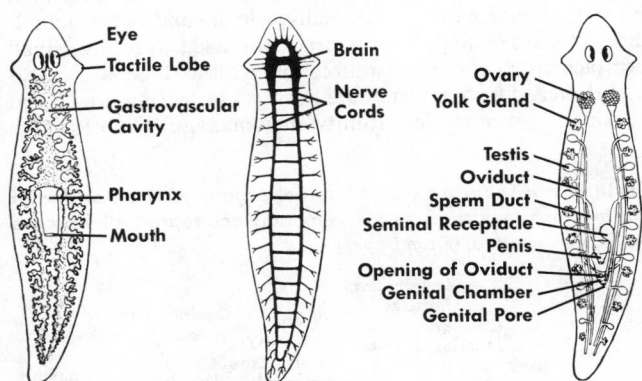

Flatworm *Planaria* lives in fresh water and is about ½ in. long. Its mouth, located in middle of under surface, leads to blind digestive cavity (*left*). Simple nervous system (*center*) is of ladder type—so called because it resembles ladder. Tactile lobes are sensitive to touch, possibly to other stimuli. Reproductive system (*right*) features organs of both sexes in a single individual. (*After Kenoyer*)

3,700 species of flatworms are flukes (Class Trematoda), all of them parasitic, mostly on vertebrate animals. As adults, flukes live in the alimentary canal of their host, or in its lungs, its urinary bladder, or its blood stream. Usually the fluke holds to the host with one or more suckers while taking tissues or body fluids into its blind digestive tract. The life history of many kinds of flukes is complex, with a series of larval forms transferring from one host to another until the final host is reached. The remaining flatworms, about 1,500 species, are parasitic tapeworms, which have no digestive tract but depend upon absorbing digested foodstuffs from the alimentary canal in which they live. Ordinarily one portion of the worm (the scolex) is specialized as an anchoring individual, with hooks or suckers; from its posterior end the worm produces asexually a series of new individuals (proglottids), which mature first as males and then as females. Mature proglottids with fertilized eggs already well along in embryonic development separate from the younger portions of the tapeworm and are carried out with the feces of the host. If the embryo-containing eggs are swallowed by a new host, they develop further into tapeworms within the host's small intestine.

Nematomorpha: Approximately 80 species of horsehair worms spend a larval stage in insects, particularly ground beetles and orthopterans such as crickets, before emerging full grown at a length of from ½ to 12 in. The digestive tract of the larval stage extends from a mouth at one end to an anus at the other, but often the adults feed no more and have a degenerate digestive tract. They mate and lay eggs, which insects eat, and the eggs hatch into larvae in the insects. Usually the horsehair worms emerge only when an adult insect, carrying a mature worm, falls into a pond or puddle. The adult worms cannot withstand drought, but the eggs are resistant to desiccation and to frost.

Nemertinea (Nemertea or Rhynchocoela): About 570 species of ribbon worms are known, ranging from ¼ in. to 80 ft long; most of them are free-living in coastal marine situations. The unsegmented body is soft, flattened, and slender, but is equipped with external cilia and muscles in the body wall, which enable the ribbon worm to glide or swim about. With an extensible proboscis, the worm manipulates small animals (living or dead) into its mouth; they are digested in an alimentary canal extending to an anus at the opposite end of the body. The body cavity is filled with large loose cells.

Acanthocephala: Spiny-headed worms, of which about 400 species are known, range in length from 1½ to 26 in. long. All are parasites, the larval stages living in arthropods and the adults in vertebrate hosts. Neither larva nor adult has a digestive tract; instead, products of digestion are absorbed through the body wall of the worm, particularly in the region of its spiny head, which holds the parasite to the lining of the alimentary canal of the host or enables the parasite to burrow through the canal into the body cavity. A common spiny-headed worm reaches maturity in the domestic pig; eggs passed with the feces of the host are eaten by the white grubs of May beetles, which serve as the arthropod host for the larval stage; pigs eat the white grubs and become infected with the worm.

Chaetognatha: About 30 species of arrow worms have been found, all of them voracious predators among the minute plankton animals in the open sea. Although the slender body, which may be from ¾ to 3 in. long, bears lateral fins and a tail fin, arrow worms dart after prey merely by flexing the body. They capture and hold victims with sickle-shaped hooks or heavy bristles borne on a pair of lobes beside the mouth; usually the prey is swallowed whole and becomes the most conspicuous feature in the body of the extremely transparent arrow worm. The principal genus is *Sagitta* (Lat. "arrow").

Peacock worms, *Sabella* (*left*), are tube-dwelling marine annelids of class Polychaeta. Crown of ciliated tentacles collects microscopic food particles and serves a gill-like respiratory function. **A peculiar terrestrial worm** of tropics and subtropics, *Peripatus* (*right*), is generally classified in a subphylum (Onychophora) of phylum Arthropoda. *Peripatus* has structural features of both annelids and arthropods, a fact suggesting that the latter may have been derived from an annelid-like ancestor. (*Douglas P. Wilson; Ward's Nat. Science Establishment, Inc.*)

Sipunculoidea: All the 250 known species of peanut worms are marine; some reach a length of 18 in. The unsegmented body is subdivided into an anterior "introvert" bearing the mouth and covered with chitinous papillae, and a larger trunk region into which the introvert can be retracted. Peanut worms feed on microorganisms caught in mucus secreted from ciliated tentacles surrounding the mouth; or they engulf bottom sediments and digest the organic matter from these, much as an earthworm might. The digestive tract extends almost to the posterior end of the trunk, then spirals back upon itself to open at the anus near the junction between trunk and introvert.

Priapuloidea: The six known species are all marine; some reach a length of 3 in. They plow through bottom sediments by muscular movements of the forward end of the body, which has fine encircling grooves and lengthwise lines of rough warts or teeth. Food passes through a straight digestive tract to the anus at the opposite end of the body, where the animal bears a large number of hollow, gill-like outgrowths of uncertain function.

Echiuroidea: Most of the 60 known species of echiuroids live in U-shaped burrows in the sea bottom; all are marine. The body is unsegmented, soft, sausage-shaped, and bears a flexible proboscis in front of the mouth. Usually the worm uses its proboscis to place a secreted thimble of mucus inside the opening of the burrow. The mucous thimble serves as a trap for microorganisms in water pumped through the burrow by movements of the worm's body. At intervals the loaded mucous thimble is swallowed and a new one put in position. The European echiuroid worm *Bonellia* has become famous because of its extreme sexual dimorphism. The female has a green egg-shaped body a few inches in length, with a threadlike proboscis as much as 3 ft long, forked at the tip. The minute male lacks proboscis, mouth, and gut; as a larva swimming by means of cilia, he finds a female, enters her digestive tract, and attaches himself as a parasite; later he moves to her excretory organ (nephridium), where he can provide sperm to fertilize eggs as they pass him in reaching the ocean water outside his host and mate.

Pogonophora: The 22 known species of beard worms are all marine. They are extremely slender, from ½ to nearly 8 in.

long, and live in secreted tubes on pilings or firm objects on the sea bottom. The food and method of feeding are not known, for neither the larval stage (which is ciliated and free-swimming) nor the sedentary adults have any digestive tract. The anterior end of the body bears a complex series of ciliated tentacles that are held in a tightly parallel group extended from the tube; each has a loop of blood vessels and may serve as a gill; they are the "beard" of the beard worm.

Annelida: The distinguishing feature of the 6,500 species of segmented worms is the organization of the body into a series of similar segments from anterior to posterior, each segment with a ganglion of the nerve cord, a pair of excretory organs (nephridia), and a set of branches of the longitudinal blood vessels. Partitions (septa) separate the segments. The digestive tract, nerve cord, and blood vessels extend from one end of the worm to the other; the circulatory system is like that of a vertebrate animal in having capillaries linking arteries to veins throughout the body. About 3,500 species are marine worms with a distinct head end and lateral paddles on at least some of the body segments; some of these polychaetes (Class Polychaeta) are active scavengers and predators that swim or creep about on the bottom; others are sedentary, living in burrows or tubes of their own secretion while gathering plankton as food from the water. Another 2,700 species of segmented worms have no distinct head, and live primarily in fresh water or in burrows in soil. The earthworms used by freshwater fishermen belong to this group (Class Oligochaeta), whereas the clamworms used by saltwater fishermen are polychaetes. In earthworms, each segment bears four pairs of bristles, which are used in locomotion; in clamworms, somewhat comparable bristles give support and provide movement for paddlelike extensions of the body wall used in swimming or in creating a current of water in the burrow. Earthworms possess both male and female reproductive organs; mated pairs exchange sperm cells, insuring cross-fertilization; development is direct, the small worms emerging from small lemon-shaped cocoons into the soil. Marine segmented worms, unlike earthworms, usually are male or female; fertilization ordinarily occurs in the sea, and the young develop through a top-shaped larval stage that swims by means of an encircling band of cilia.

Some 300 additional species of segmented worms consist of leeches (Class Hirudinea), with a large posterior sucker and exactly 34 segments. They are found in fresh and salt water and on land in humid jungles from SE Asia to Tasmania. All have transverse wrinkles externally, which conceal the boundaries of the segments, and a large crop used to receive small crustaceans and other captured prey or to hold a meal of blood sucked from a vertebrate host. While leeches are "blood suckers" if given an opportunity, they manage to subsist quite

Earthworm: Diagram shows internal organs of anterior end of earthworm, *Lumbricus terrestris*. Nephridia and reproductive organs have been omitted. (*From Guyer*)

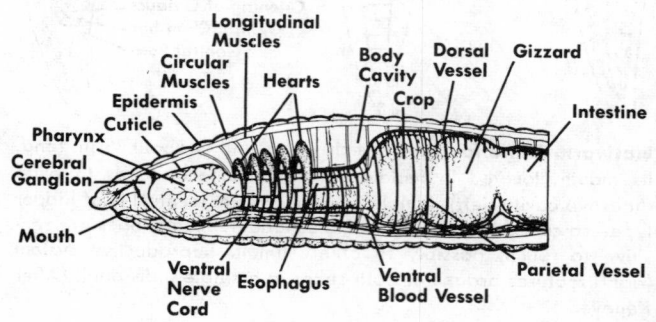

1266

well on smaller worms, insect larvae, and crustaceans. Most leeches capture food with an anterior sucker surrounding the mouth, and cut into the prey (or the skin of a vertebrate animal) with three horny teeth. The saliva contains an anticoagulant.

Hemichordata: Approximately 100 species of acorn worms and tongue worms are known, all of them marine. They are soft-bodied denizens of sandy or muddy bottoms, where they burrow shallowly by movements of a hollow proboscis that extends forward from a narrow collar. Although the greater part of the body (which may be from 1 to 100 in. long) is the trunk region behind the collar, the name acorn worm refers to the appearance of the proboscis and collar, and tongue worm to the proboscis itself. Debris from the bottom, together with water, is pushed into the mouth between proboscis and collar. The water escapes through paired slits in the pharyngeal region, while food and much of the undigestible sedimentary material passes along the digestive tract toward the anus at the posterior end. For many years, the Hemichordata was placed among the lower chordates, because these animals have pharyngeal slits, a dorsal nerve cord (which is hollow in some species), and notochordlike tissue in the proboscis. Today they are usually separated into a distinct phylum, because they have a ventral nerve cord as well as a dorsal one, because their blood travels anteriorly in the dorsal blood vessel (as in annelid worms) instead of posteriorly (as in chordates), and because they have no post-anal tail.—*L. and M. M.*

WREN, SIR CHRISTOPHER, 1632–1723, English architect; b. East Knoyle; ed. Wadham College, Oxford. Wren designed many buildings in London, Oxford, and Cambridge, the most famous of which was St. Paul's Cathedral, which he rebuilt after the Great Fire of 1666. Also involved in the scientific work of his day, he was one of the founders of the Royal Society and was engaged in scientific research in many areas, including air pressure, experimental anatomy, astronomical theory and observation, gunpowder explosions, and mechanics. He also made drawings for books on microscopy and published original mathematical work.—*D. H. D. R.*

WRIGHT, FRANK LLOYD, 1869–1959, U. S. architect; b. Richland Center, Wis. He was a pioneer in functional architecture and in designing houses with an organic growth from interior to exterior. His more notable designs include the Prairie Houses; the Imperial Hotel, Tokyo; the Kaufmann or Falling Water House, Bear Run, Pa.; and the Solomon R. Guggenheim Museum, New York. His many books included *An Autobiography* (1932).—*D. H. D. R.*

WRIGHT, ORVILLE, 1871–1948, U. S. inventor; b. Dayton, Ohio. About 1895 he became impressed by accounts of Otto Lilienthal's gliding experiments, and in 1899 he and his brother Wilbur constructed a biplane kite, which they controlled by warping the wings. In 1900 they built their first glider, testing it at Kitty Hawk, N. C. Between 1900 and 1902 they constructed a series of successful gliders, based partly on information from wind-tunnel tests. These gliders led to the first successful powered man-carrying airplane, which flew at Kitty Hawk Dec. 17, 1903. Between 1903 and 1915 Orville Wright devoted himself to the construction and demonstration of various models of the Wright biplane. From 1915 until his death he served as a member of the National Advisory Board for Aeronautics. His *How We Invented the Airplane* (1953) is a deposition (1920) in a lawsuit. He was a member of the National Academy of Sciences.—*D. H. D. R.*

WRIGHT, SEWALL, 1889–   , U. S. biologist; b. Melrose, Mass. He received recognition as an outstanding geneticist

for his early work on the genetics of the guinea pig. Later he worked on the mathematical foundations of population genetics. His recognition of the possibility of the random fixation of heredity factors in small populations was a contribution of major importance to evolutionary theory. He is a member of the National Academy of Sciences.—*D. H. D. R.*

WRIGHT, THOMAS, 1711–86, English astronomer; b. Durham. In *An Original Theory or New Hypothesis of the Universe* (1750), Wright became the first to propose that numerous stars distributed in a plane account for the appearance of the Milky Way.—*O. G.*

WRIGHT, WILBUR, 1867–1912, U. S. inventor; b. near Millville, Ind. Interested in the sport of gliding, Wilbur and his brother Orville constructed gliders controlled in flight by adjusting the wing angles (*i.e.* by wing warping); this method was subsequently developed into aileron control. They studied airflow over airfoils by means of a wind tunnel which they built in Dayton, Ohio, in 1901. On Dec. 17, 1903, at Kitty Hawk, N. C., Orville achieved the first sustained free flight by a heavier-than-air machine. In 1905, Wilbur flew for 38 min over a distance of 24 mi and later made flights in France and Italy. He served as president of the Wright Company, formed to manufacture the Wright biplane, until his death.—*A. L.*

WROUGHT IRON: iron containing about 0.2% carbon and total impurities amounting to less than 0.5%. It is made by melting pig iron on a ferric-oxide bed. A strong metal, it can

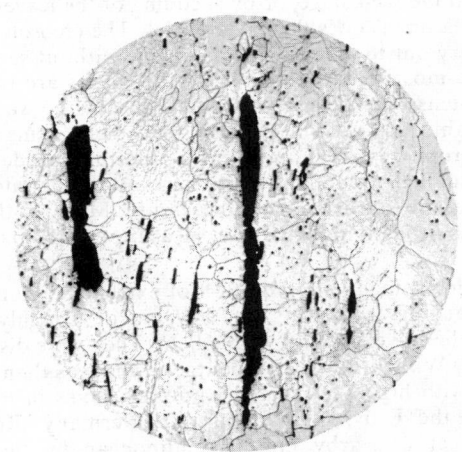

In photograph of wrought iron (×70) slag filaments are seen oriented along direction of rolling. (*U. S. Steel Corp.*)

be easily welded or forged and has been used in past years for making chains and wire. It has been largely replaced, except for a few special purposes, by various forms of very low-carbon (mild) STEEL.—*G. W. M.*

WURTZ, CHARLES ADOLPHE, 1817–84, French physician and organic chemist; b. Wolfisheim, near Strasbourg. Following early research on acids of phosphorus, alkyl isocyanates, amines, and compound ureas, in 1855 he demonstrated that two hydrocarbon radicals could be combined by the action of sodium on alkyl iodides (*Wurtz synthesis*). He unraveled the constitution of glycerine and glycols (1856) and hydroxy- and amino-acids, synthesized neurine (1867), and discovered aldol (1872). He explained abnormal vapor densities by dissociation (1865). Author of *La théorie atomique* (1879), he was a fellow of the Royal Society and an associate of the U. S. National Academy of Sciences.—*R. J. F.*

X Y Z

XENON: a gaseous element (Xe); at. no. 54; at. wt 131.3; mp −112°C; bp −107.1°C; density of the gas approx. 5.9 gm/liter at 0°C and 1 atm. It is extremely rare, being found in the atmosphere in about one part per 20 million. Discovered by Sir William Ramsay and M. W. Travers (1898) in the residue left after evaporation of other fractions of liquid air, xenon is the rarest and heaviest of the INERT GASES (excluding the radioactive trace element RADON). Produced in small quantities by fractional distillation of air, it is used in thyratron and rectifier tubes and high-speed photographic lamps, and has anesthetic properties. In 1962, workers in Canadian and U. S. laboratories produced the first known xenon compounds (*e.g.* xenon difluoride) by reacting the gas with fluorine under special conditions.—*T. M.*

XEROPHYTES: plants adapted to dry situations, mostly in deserts. Through specialized physiological and structural features, they thrive in climates in which most plants could not live. Adaptations include deep root systems reaching water far below the surface, reduction in area of leaf surface exposed to drying, and covering of the surfaces of stems and leaves with substances retarding evaporation. Many of these plants grow rapidly during the brief rainy season and later evade the effects of drought by death of the parts above ground, by survival in the seed stage, or by shedding of the leaves during the dry season, as does the palos verdes. The creosote bush is able to dry out to a considerable extent without serious injury. The most remarkable xerophytic plants are the cacti, whose extensive shallow root systems absorb the water from even a light rain and whose leafless succulent stems store it. Other xerophytes occur in areas bordering the deserts or on ridges of high mountains where the evaporation rate is high because of the low atmospheric pressure. Many of these are adapted to drought in the same ways as DESERT plants.—*L. B.*

X-RAY: electromagnetic radiation of extremely short wavelength, ranging from 10^{-7} to 10^{-11} cm or, roughly, about $\frac{1}{10,000}$ of the wavelength of visible light. They were discovered in 1895 by Wilhelm Conrad Roentgen, who was then experimenting with highly evacuated CROOKES TUBES in his laboratory at the Univ. of Würzburg in Germany. Roentgen noticed that a nearby barium platinocyanide fluorescent screen glowed when cathode rays, or electrons, traversing his Crookes tube struck the walls of the tube. He observed the same effect when the tube was completely encased in a cardboard box, and he concluded from this that, whatever the nature of the new "emanation" produced, it could not possibly be that of visible light or even ULTRAVIOLET. Roentgen announced his discovery of the so-called x-rays a month later, pointing to their ability to darken a photographic plate, ionize gases, and penetrate many materials opaque to ordinary light. The new rays could not, for the moment, be reflected or refracted, but their application to making shadow pictures, or shadowgraphs, of the human body excited immediate interest. Roentgen received the Rumford medal for his discovery and was awarded in 1901 the first Nobel Prize in physics. The wave nature of x-rays was established as early as 1911 by Max von Laue, who sent a beam of rays through a crystal and observed an interference pattern on a photographic plate. The so-called *Laue spots,* like dark and bright spots in an optical interference pattern, suggest unmistakably that the lattice structure of the crystal acts as a diffraction grating for x-ray waves. Additional experiments in the field of x-ray crystallography, carried out by Friedrich and Knipping, as well as by W. H. Bragg and W. L. Bragg, confirmed the undulatory or wave character of x-rays.

X-rays are generated whenever high-speed electrons, traversing an evacuated tube, strike a target, usually made of metal. The energy lost by the decelerating electrons may be radiated directly as high-frequency (short-wavelength) "light," which produces a continuous SPECTRUM, or may be absorbed and then re-emitted by the atoms, producing x-ray line spectra that are characteristic of the target substance. The early x-ray tubes (Fig. 1) operated at 30,000 to 40,000 volts and consisted of

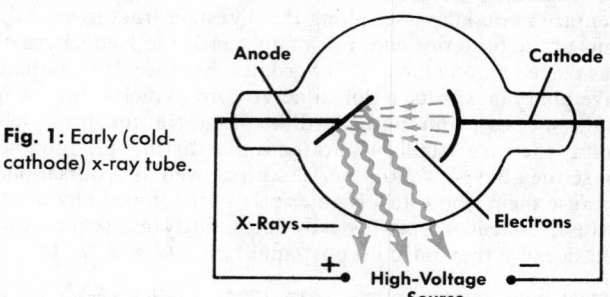

Fig. 1: Early (cold-cathode) x-ray tube.

two principal elements, a flat or concave cathode and a light-metal anode that received the impact of the electrons and emitted x-rays. Such tubes grew "harder" or more penetrating with use, because of the progressive reduction of residual gas that was adsorbed on the walls of the tube. To correct this, means were provided for the admission of a measured amount of gas by diffusion through a thin sheet of metal. In the modern x-ray tube, devised by W. D. Coolidge of the General Electric Laboratories (Fig. 2), electrons are supplied by

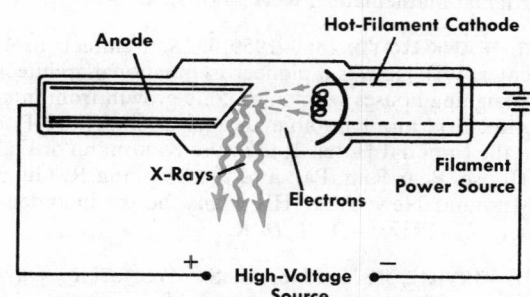

Fig. 2: Coolidge (heated-cathode) x-ray tube.

THERMIONIC EMISSION from a hot wire, the number of electrons released depending on the filament temperature. The indirectly heated concave cathode and a massive tungsten or molybdenum anode are enclosed in a highly evacuated tube maintained at a potential reaching one million volts or higher. To withstand the kinetic energy of the impinging electrons, the anode must be made of a metal that will not melt under this bombardment. In addition, anodes may be water-cooled or air-cooled by special radiators attached to the end of the target arm. In the Coolidge tube, two separate controls over x-rays are possible: filament temperature, governing the number of electrons delivered to the anode; and tube voltage, determining the speed imparted to the electrons.

X-rays may be detected by ionization chambers, the Geiger-Müller and scintillation counters, photographic plates, or a fluorescent screen coated with barium platinocyanide, cadmium tungstate, or zinc-cadmium sulfate. Physicians use a fluoroscope for examining the internal organs of the human body where continuous observation is important. For greater contrast of detail the photographic plate provides a clearer picture. The making of x-ray photographs is known as radiography. X-ray tubes operating at extremely high potentials have been employed both for diagnosis and for treatment of otherwise inaccessible cancerous growths. The use of powerful x-ray tubes, if uncontrolled, can cause serious damage to healthy tissue both in a patient and the technician administering x-rays. To guard against this, such precautionary measures as lead shielding, the use of special film badges, radiation-detecting dosimeters, and general "survey" instruments are employed.—A. E.

X-RAY DIFFRACTION: the scattering of a beam of x-rays into many beams, at definite angles to the original beam, by atoms in regular orderly arrangement in a crystal. The phenomenon was discovered by Von Laue, Friedrich, and Knipping in 1912, who thus confirmed that x-rays are a kind of light with very short wavelengths and that a crystal is an array of atoms in repetitive order. Following up their discovery and analysis, Sir William Bragg gave simplified expression to the principal law governing x-ray diffraction; and he and his son applied it to determine the atomic arrangements in many crystals, establishing it as the central tool of modern CRYSTALLOGRAPHY.

This tool can be most simply understood by thinking of successive similar planes of atoms, evenly spaced in a crystal (Fig. 1A), as if they were a succession of incompletely reflecting mirrors (Fig. 1B). When the x-rays are all of one wavelength, the fraction of the beam reflected by the top plane will be reinforced by the fractions reflected by the others only when the additional distance that those other fractions must travel is an exact multiple of the wavelength of the x-rays. This requirement can be put mathematically as *Bragg's law*, $n\lambda = 2d \sin \theta$, where n is an integer, λ is the wavelength, d is the spacing of the planes, and θ is the angle made by the beam to the planes. Hence a strongly diffracted beam will be observed only when λ, d, and θ satisfy this relation. The same crystal can be regarded as made of many differently chosen "planes of atoms" (*e.g.* Fig. 1C), at different angles, with different spacings. The atomic arrangement is inferred by determining, with the aid of Bragg's law, what families of planes give strongly diffracted beams.

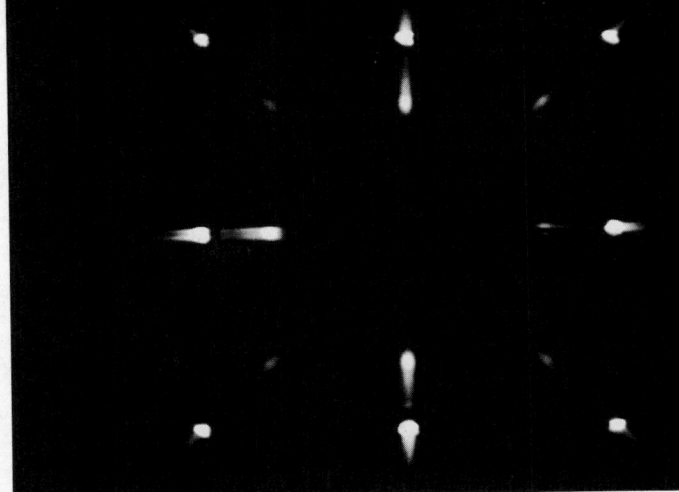

A complete experimental determination of atomic arrangement usually requires a single crystal, but some information can be had from a crystalline powder. Today this information forms a file of "fingerprints" of many substances, useful to the analyst in identifying unknown materials.

Bragg's law is obeyed by a beam of anything having wavelike properties, so long as its wavelength is comparable with the interatomic spacings in crystals. Hence it applies to ELECTRON DIFFRACTION and to NEUTRON DIFFRACTION, which have become valuable supplementary tools for the study of crystals.—A. H.

X-RAY SPECTRA: the patterns of emission from matter bombarded by high-velocity electrons. X-ray spectra comprise continuous spectra (sometimes called *Bremsstrahlung*), which are electromagnetic radiations arising from the deflections of charged particles as they come close to the nucleus of an atom; and line spectra, which are electromagnetic radiations given off by an atom as a result of the direct interaction of the bombarding electrons with those in the matter under bombardment. The line spectra are also known as "characteristic" spectra, because individual groups of x-ray lines are characteristic of the atoms of different elements. See SPECTRUM; X-RAY DIFFRACTION; X-RAY.—E. E.

X-RAY TUBE: a device used to generate X-RAYS. The common commercial x-ray tube, invented in 1913 by W. D. Coolidge, has a hot tungsten filament, as a source of electrons (see THERMIONIC EMISSION), and a target of tungsten or another metal, both enclosed in an evacuated glass envelope. A potential difference of several thousand volts is applied between the target and the filament. This accelerates the electrons, which strike the target at high speed. When the electrons are slowed down in the metal, x-rays called *Bremsstrahlung* are produced. Since the energy lost in slowing down varies from one electron to another, and since the x-rays have the energies lost by the electrons, the x-rays display a continuous range of energies and of wavelengths; this is called *white* radiation. In addition, there are collisions between electrons and atoms in which an electron gives up just exactly the right amount of energy to an atom for a quantum jump to take place; this produces *characteristic* radiation. See ENERGY LEVEL; X-RAY SPECTRA.—S. Br.

XYLEM: tissue that conducts water and mineral salts through VASCULAR PLANTS, and also provides support for the plants. The WOOD of trees and shrubs is xylem. A second conducting tissue is PHLOEM. See PLANT ORGANS AND TISSUES.—R. G. M.

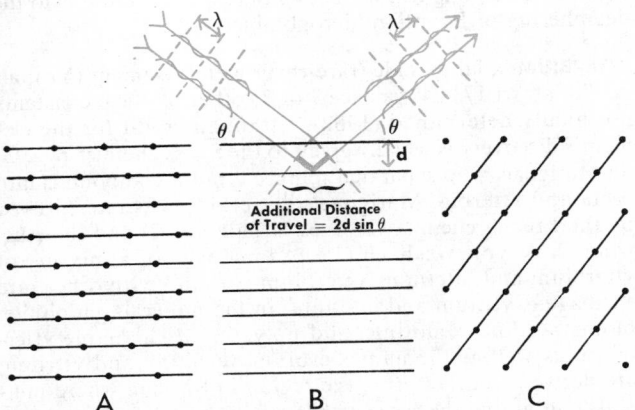

Fig. 1: Arrangement of atoms within crystal can be thought of as successive, evenly spaced similar planes (A) and (C). X-rays striking crystal (B) are reflected from successive planes (atoms are not shown), producing characteristic diffraction pattern.

YANG, CHEN NING, 1922– , Chinese-U. S. physicist; b. Hofei, Anhwei. His research has been in statistical mechanics, field theory, and meson physics. In 1956 Yang and T. D. Lee proposed that the principle of conservation of parity is not valid in what are called weak interactions, and they specified certain experimental tests of their theory. Experimental verification was quickly obtained by others. For their research, Yang and Lee shared the 1957 Nobel prize. Yang became a member of the Institute for Advanced Study, Princeton, in 1949.—*D. H. D. R.*

YEAR: one of the principal subdivisions of the CALENDAR; an astronomical period equal to the time interval between consecutive passages of the Sun at a chosen point on the celestial sphere or of Earth at a given point in its orbit. The principal kinds of year used in astronomy are the following:

The *tropical year* is measured by consecutive passages of the Sun at the vernal EQUINOX. Thus it coincides with the course of the seasons, and is used as the basis for the calendar year. Its length (currently 365.2422 days) decreases by 0.53 sec/century because of a slow acceleration in the motion of the Sun and in the PRECESSION OF THE EQUINOXES. Since the tropical year is nearly 365¼ days, leap years are included in the calendar.

The *sidereal year* is defined with respect to a fixed star instead of the vernal equinox. It is somewhat longer than the tropical year (365.2564 days) because it is not subject to the shortening effect of precession.

The *anomalistic year* is measured by consecutive passages of Earth at perihelion, *i.e.* at the point in its orbit nearest the Sun. Its length, 365.2596 days, slightly exceeds that of the sidereal year, because the gradual displacement of Earth's perihelion is in direction of Earth's motion.—*S. D. G.*

YEAST: any member of a group of single-celled plants regarded as primitive or degenerate members of the sac FUNGI (Ascomycetes). The cells may be spherical, ellipsoidal, or somewhat elongate. Most yeasts are free-living saprophytes, but a few are parasites of terrestrial vertebrate animals, causing diseases of the skin, mucous membranes, and lungs. The best-known yeast is *Saccharomyces cerevisiae,* brewer's or wine yeast, which (as Pasteur discovered) produces alcohol and carbon dioxide by fermentation when growing in a sugar solution with little or no oxygen. (In the presence of oxygen, Brewer's yeast derives energy from sugar while converting it into carbon dioxide and water.) Since prehistoric times man has used yeasts to make alcoholic beverages

Budding yeast: Photomicrographs show Brewer's yeast (*Saccharomyces cerevisiae*) reproducing asexually by budding. Single cell first develops small bud, which enlarges into daughter cell. Both cells then develop buds, and so on. Cells soon separate. (*Fleischmann Labs., Standard Brands, Inc.*)

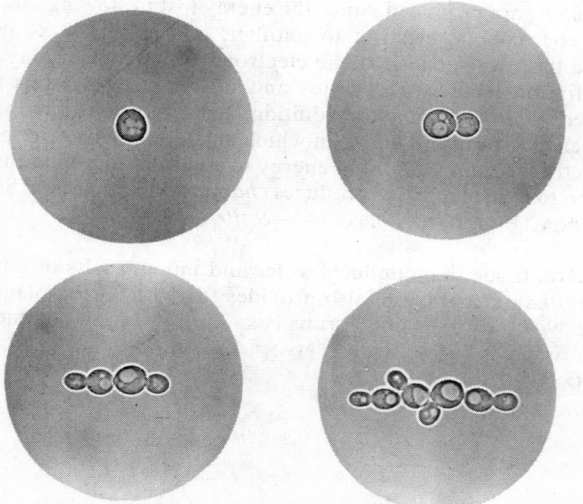

and to lighten the texture of bread by filling it with small bubbles prior to and during the first stage of baking. More recently he has discovered that yeast can be raised in large quantities as a source of proteins and vitamins.

Although some yeasts reproduce asexually by simple fission, brewer's yeast undergoes a slightly different type of cell division called budding. Division of the cell is asymmetrical, but the small "buds" soon grow to become full-sized cells and usually separate from the parent cell. Brewer's yeast undergoes conjugation, followed after a time by reduction division and formation of an ascus with four spores; both the haploid and the diploid cells of this yeast reproduce asexually by budding. Ascospores of cultivated brewer's yeast and also of wild yeasts are distributed widely by the wind as dust particles, which settle from the air on overripe fruits and assist in their decay.—*L. and M. M.*

YIELD POINT: the stress (lb/in.²) at which a body will materially elongate without an appreciable increase in stress. For metals, especially steel, an increase in stress produces a proportional increase in strain (elongation/in.). At one point, however, the elongation is no longer proportional to the stress. As further tension is applied, the body continues to elongate while the stress remains constant; this stress is the *yield point.*—*A. L.*

YOUNG, JAMES, 1811–83, Scottish technologist; b. Glasgow. After successfully refining natural petroleum (1848), he produced illuminating oil, lubricating oils, and naphtha by dry distillation of cannel coal (obtaining his English patent in 1850), and he originated the Scottish shale-oil industry. His U. S. patent (1852) preceded Drake's drilling of the first oil well in the U. S. A. (1859). From 1856 he produced paraffin wax, and later (1865), ammonium sulfate from cannel coal and shale distillates.—*R. J. F.*

YOUNG, THOMAS, 1773–1829, English physician and physicist; b. Milverton, Somersetshire. He became professor of natural philosophy at the Royal Institution in 1801 and was foreign secretary of the Royal Society 1802–29. He discovered the interference of light, and made the first rough measurements of the wavelengths of various colors. His many other contributions to physics included the introduction of the concept of energy in its present meaning, and the study of sound and elasticity (*Young's modulus*). He also discovered astigmatism (in himself), explained accommodation, and initiated a theory of color vision later developed by Helmholtz. A gifted linguist, he made notable contributions to the deciphering of Egyptian hieroglyphics.—*M. P.*

YTTERBIUM: a lanthanide (rare-earth metal) element (Yb); at. no. 70; at. wt 173.04; valence 2 or 3; other physical constants not finally determined (1962). Although credit for the element's discovery is usually given to the Swiss chemist J. C. G. de Marignac, who separated impure erbium compounds into erbia and ytterbia, Marignac's "ytterbia" was later proved by the French chemist Georges Urbain (1907) and the Austrian C. A. von Wesbach (1908) to consist of a mixture of ytterbium and lutetium. Ytterbium is found with other rare earths (*e.g.* yttrium and lutetium) in the minerals gadolinite, blomstrandine, xenotime, and polycrase. (The name ytterbium, as well as the names erbium, terbium, and yttrium, are derived from Ytterby, the region in Sweden where minerals containing the rare earths were first found.) Ytterbium and many of its pure compounds have been prepared by distillation and ion-exchange methods. The element is present in misch-metal lighter flints in mixture with other RARE EARTHS (see also LANTHANIDES).—*E. H. H.*

YTTRIUM: a metallic element (Y); at. no. 39; at. wt 88.91; it is often classed as a RARE-EARTH element, though it is not a member of the LANTHANIDE series. Discovery of yttrium is usually credited to Johan Gadolin, who, on analyzing (1794) a black, hard mineral from a quarry in Sweden, announced that the mineral contained a new "elemental earth." It was subsequently named yttrium after the place (Ytterby) of its discovery. However, C. G. Mosander showed in 1843 that Gadolin's yttrium was a mixture of three elements: the name yttrium was kept by Mosander for the one of these that was the strongest base, while the other two were named by him ERBIUM and TERBIUM. Yttrium is found always in association with two or more rare-earth elements in gadolinite, fergusonite, and nuevite, as well as in many other minerals; also, radioactive isotopes of yttrium and other rare earths are produced as fission products of uranium in atomic piles. Very pure yttrium is now obtained by ion-exchange CHROMATOGRAPHY. It is produced commercially in small quantities from yttrium fluoride (YF_3) and is used as an alloying material to drive out undesired impurities from metals. Because of its low CROSS SECTION for neutron capture, yttrium is of interest in nuclear chemistry.—*E. H. H.*

YUKAWA, HIDEKI, 1907–   , Japanese physicist; b. Tokyo. In 1935 Yukawa postulated the existence of a new type of field of force, attempting thereby to explain the holding together of the particles that compose an atomic nucleus. To account for the field he showed that there should be a hitherto-unknown kind of particle having a mass about 200 times the mass of the electron and hence about ⅑ the mass of the proton. The existence of this particle, called the MESON, was subsequently confirmed experimentally. For having predicted, as a result of his theoretical work on nuclear forces, the existence of mesons, Yukawa received the Nobel prize for 1949. He is an associate of the U. S. National Academy of Sciences.—*D. H. D. R.*

ZEEMAN, PIETER, 1865–1943, Dutch physicist; b. Zonnemaire. In 1896 he noticed the splitting up of spectral lines in a magnetic field (*Zeeman effect*); this was soon explained theoretically by H. A. Lorentz. For their investigations concerning the influence of magnetism upon the phenomena of radiation, Zeeman and Lorentz shared the Nobel prize in physics for 1902. Zeeman also studied the propagation of light in moving media (1927), finding that the results agreed with Lorentz' formula rather than with Fresnel's earlier one. Zeeman was a member of the Royal Netherlands Academy of Sciences and a fellow of the Royal Society.—*R. J. F.*

ZEEMAN EFFECT: the splitting of spectroscopic lines of a source of radiation when it is placed in a magnetic field. The effect was first observed by Pieter Zeeman in 1896. Analysis of the Zeeman effect led to one of the first determinations of the ratio of electronic charge to mass. It constitutes an important experimental means for analyzing angular-momentum properties of atoms. More recently, it has been used to measure the magnetic field near stars.

The Zeeman effect is the result of the energy change associated with the interaction of the spin and orbital magnetic moment of the atom with the magnetic field in which it is placed. The classic Zeeman pattern, sometimes called the Paschen Back effect, occurs at very high fields. A single spectroscopic line, when viewed perpendicular to the field, is split into three groups, each group polarized with its electric vector either parallel or perpendicular to the field. A longitudinal view shows two circularly polarized groups. The Zeeman pattern at lower field strength (less than about 10,000 oersted) is usually more complicated.—*S. Bo.*

ZENITH: in astronomy, the point on the CELESTIAL SPHERE directly above an observer. The direction of the astronomical zenith is opposite that of gravity. The distance from any point or body in the sky to the zenith is called its *zenith distance* or coaltitude.—*T. N.*

ZENO OF ELEA, fl. early 5th cent. B. C., Greek natural philosopher; birthplace unknown. A pupil of Parmenides, Zeno attacked the idea of plurality in order to support his teacher's monism, and he is thus credited with having invented *dialectic,* or argument that aims not at victory but at discovering or transmitting knowledge. He is best known for the examples (Zeno's PARADOXES) he used to demonstrate the absurdity of assuming a plurality of things in time and space. —*D. H. D. R.*

ZEOLITE: any of a group of hydrous alumino-silicates of sodium, calcium, etc., occurring as minerals and also produced synthetically for use as ion-exchange agents and "molecular sieves." Important species include:

Isometric	$NaAlSi_2O_6 \cdot H_2O$	Analcite
Trigonal	$(Ca,Na,K)_2Al_2Si_4O_{12} \cdot 6H_2O$	Chabazite
Orthorhombic	$Na_2Al_2Si_3O_{10} \cdot 2H_2O$	Natrolite
	$Ca_2Na_2Al_6Si_9O_{30} \cdot 8H_2O$	Mesolite
	$CaAl_2Si_3O_{10} \cdot 3H_2O$	Scolecite
	$Ca_2NaAl_5Si_5O_{20} \cdot 6H_2O$	Thomsonite
Monoclinic	$(Ca,Na,K)_2Al_2Si_7O_{18} \cdot 6H_2O$	Heulandite
	$(Ca,Na,K)_2Al_2Si_7O_{18} \cdot 7H_2O$	Stilbite
	$(Ba>Ca,Na,K)_2Al_2Si_7O_{18} \cdot 7H_2O$	Harmotome
	$CaAl_2Si_4O_{12} \cdot 4H_2O$	Laumontite (metastable)

As in the chemically related feldspars and feldspathoids, zeolite structures are based on a continuous network of SiO_4 and AlO_4 tetrahedra, interlocked through the sharing of oxygen ions, with cations including sodium, potassium, calcium, and barium filling the interstices and balancing the charges. Zeolite structures, however, are of relatively wide mesh, with channelways in which water and other molecules can be loosely held. On moderate heating, zeolites lose their water evenly, without collapse of the crystal structure. The resulting openings can selectively absorb various molecules from liquids or gases, depending on the size of the molecules and the structure of the zeolite. Thus, specific zeolites are selected or manufactured for use as "molecular sieves" for various concentration and purification processes (see WATER TREATMENT). Within a limited range in each structure, cation replacement is also readily accomplished, accounting for the value of the zeolites as ion-exchange agents, particularly in water softening.

Because of their open structures and water content, zeolites form only at relatively low temperatures and pressures. Most zeolites occur as deuteric or hydrothermal alteration products in IGNEOUS and METAMORPHIC ROCKS and in mineral veins. Good crystals line vugs in extrusive rocks, and joint openings in intrusives. Some zeolites occur as reaction products in alumina-rich sediments, *e.g.* clays and volcanic ash that have been soaked by alkali-rich brines in marine or playa-lake basins. Thomsonite and natrolite in the form of varicolored, radial, fibrous aggregates are cut as semi-precious stones. See MINERAL (table).—*L. M.*

ZERNIKE, FRITZ, 1888–1966, Dutch physicist; b. Amsterdam. From work on statistics and galvanometers he turned to optics and (from 1931) developed the phase-contrast method: by inserting a glass plate with a groove about 1 mm wide and half of a wavelength deep in the focal plane of a microscope objective, he greatly increased the contrast in the image of a transparent object. For this method, which is also used for locating smallest surface irregularities of lenses and mirrors, he received the Nobel prize in 1953. He was a fellow of the Royal Society.—*E. F.*

ZERO: a number occupying a unique place in the number system; denoted by 0 in modern symbols, it is frequently taken as designating a void, or nothing. For example, zero length is no distance at all. Similar interpretations apply to zero area, zero force, zero time. Other usages are closer to its mathematical meaning; thus, zero temperature is simply a point on the temperature scale, with other temperatures above and below it. In the real number system, 0 occupies a place midway between -1 and $+1$, and is generally classed among the integers. It has the property that it annihilates all numbers in multiplication, every product with 0 as a factor being itself equal to 0. As a consequence it is the one number which cannot be used as a divisor. The rules of operation with 0 are the following, in which a is not equal to 0: (1) $a + 0 = 0 + a = a$; (2) $a - 0 = -(0 - a) = a$; (3) $a \cdot 0 = 0 \cdot a = 0$; (4) $0 \div a = 0$; (5) $a \div 0$ cannot be performed.

Zero probably originated in the effort to make POSITIONAL NOTATION unambiguous. Without a symbol for 0, positional notation for three hundred and five could be confused with that for thirty-five or that for three thousand and five. The zero symbol makes it possible to distinguish clearly among these numbers by writing 305, 35, and 3005. This use of zero, alone, makes its invention one of the most valuable and far-reaching in all mathematics.—*H. C.*

ZERO-POINT ENERGY: the energy remaining in kinetic form at the temperature of absolute zero. Under this condition, there is still a finite amount of kinetic energy left, manifesting itself in the lattice vibrations of a solid or as a constituent of the binding energy of a crystal. Thus, at absolute zero, molecular energy is a minimum, but is not quite zero.—*A. E.*

ZINC: a bluish-white metallic element (Zn); at. no. 30; at. wt 65.38; density 7.14; mp 419°C; bp 907°C; valence 2. Zinc was apparently known to the ancients, but knowledge of the metal appears to have been spotty in the middle ages; it received its modern name in the 17th cent. The principal ores of zinc are sphalerite (zinc sulfide), calamine (zinc silicate), and smithsonite (zinc carbonate); these are converted to the metal either by thermal metallurgical processes (roasting and smelting with carbon) or by leaching and electrolysis of the soluble salts. Zinc is oxidized by strong aqueous acids or alkalies, to form the zinc ion Zn^{++} or the zincate ion $Zn\,OOH^-$. Zinc is relatively resistant to atmospheric corrosion and is used as a protective coating on iron and steel, the product so coated being known as galvanized iron. Zinc is also used in dry-cell batteries and in a variety of alloys, notably brass and die-casting alloy. Zinc salts are toxic to microorganisms and are used as wood preservatives and disinfectants. Zinc oxide is used in medical ointments and as a pigment; the carbonate and sulfide, as white pigments in paints and enamels. Zinc sulfide is widely used as a PHOSPHOR for television screens and fluorescent coatings.—*A. M. S.*

ZIRCONIUM: a metallic element (Zr) of the titanium family; at. no. 40; at. wt 91.22; sp gr 6.4; mp approx. 1850°C; valence 4. The 19th most abundant element in Earth's crust, zirconium occurs principally in baddeleyite (also called zirkite), ZrO_2, in association with 1.5 to 2% HAFNIUM. Some beach sands (*e.g.* those of the Oregon coast) are rich in zirconium compounds in percentages up to 70%. The orange-

red gemstone zircon, valued since prehistoric times, is a form of zirconium silicate, $ZrSiO_4$; careful analysis of a Ceylon zircon led the German chemist Martin Heinrich Klaproth to discover the new "earth" element zirconium in 1789. (Formerly, zircons had been thought to consist of aluminum silicate.) In 1808, Davy attempted to isolate pure zirconium by electrolysis, but failed. Berzelius (1824) tried heating potassium hexafluorozirconate (K_2ZrF_6) with metallic potassium, but could not obtain pure zirconium; not until 1914 was the pure metal finally prepared. Very pure zirconium is now produced commercially by heating its tetrachloride with magnesium or sodium in a helium atmosphere (Kroll process) or by heating crude zirconium and iodine in a vacuum at approx. 1300°C (Van Arkel process). The metal is resistant to a wide variety of corrosive media. In dry, powdered form, it is highly flammable and reacts violently with oxidizing agents. Zirconium forms stable tetrahalides (ZrX_4) with chlorine, bromine, and iodine, and unstable lower halides such as $ZrCl_3$ and $ZrCl_2$ (see HALOGEN). It forms a carbide (ZrC) and a hydride (ZrH_2), but does not appear to form a true hydroxide, "zirconium hydroxide" being probably a hydrated zirconia ($ZrO_2 \cdot xH_2O$). The element is present in a number of organic compounds through a linkage with oxygen or nitrogen.

Uses: Zirconium metal can be drawn into wire, pressed into rods, rolled into thin foil, and burnished to a brilliant surface. Although more abundant than nickel, zirconium is more expensive because of the difficulty of obtaining the pure metal. It is used as a "getter" to remove residual traces of gases in electric bulbs and vacuum tubes and for making vacuum-tube grids. In nuclear reactors, zirconium is employed to inhibit the passage of neutrons because of its relatively low cross section for absorption of neutrons. Molten zirconium, which gives a brilliant white light at high temperatures, is used in special arc

Oxidation of zinc: The two electrons in outer shell of zinc atom are loosely held. Strip of zinc held in beaker of hydrochloric acid promptly releases hydrogen bubbles as hydrogen of acid is displaced. (*International Nickel* Co.)

lights. Among several nonferrous zirconium alloys are *zirconium bronze,* which has high tensile strength and virtually the same electrical conductivity as pure copper, used for electrical parts; and *nickel-zirconium,* used for high-speed cutting tools and as a master alloy for adding zirconium to nonferrous alloys, as well as for deoxidation of alloys and degasification of nickel. *Zirconium ferrosilicon* is used for deoxidizing, denitrogenizing, and desulfurizing steel and iron, and for adding zirconium to ferrous alloys. *Zirconium steel* has a highly uniform grain, and is ductile and shock- and fatigue-resistant. Among the useful zirconium compounds are zirconia (zirconium oxide, ZrO_2), used principally as a refractory material and in other applications requiring resistance to heat, and as an opacifier in ceramics. Zircon, capable of withstanding repeated heat shocks and having good electrical-insulation properties, is used in electric heaters. Zirconium sulfate ($Zr(SO_4)_2 \cdot 4H_2O$) has a wide range of applications, from use in high-temperature lubricants to uses in tanning, waterproofing, and flameproofing. Zirconium compounds also find use as abrasive powders (*e.g.* zirconium carbide).—*E. H. H.*

ZODIAC: a belt on the CELESTIAL SPHERE, about 16° wide, which represents the pathway of Sun, Moon, and major planets. (Pluto and many asteroids are not confined to the pathway.) The midline of this pathway is the ecliptic pathway. The zodiac has 12 divisions, each 30° long, called the "signs." These are laid off toward the east, beginning at the vernal equinox. Their names are those of the constellations corresponding to the divisions 2,000 yr ago; but because of PRECESSION OF EQUINOXES, the vernal equinox has since moved westward about 30°, and the signs have moved the same amount. The signs and the constellations having the same names therefore no longer correspond. Thus when the Sun enters the sign of Aries, Mar. 21, it is actually in the constellation Pisces; it will not be in Aries until a month later. The zodiac (Greek *zodiakos,* "circle of animals") is of ancient origin, and early maps show the outlines of many constellations as they are today. Symbols and names of the signs arranged according to season are:

SPRING	AUTUMN
1. ♈ Aries (The Ram)	7. ♎ Libra (The Scales)
2. ♉ Taurus (The Bull)	8. ♏ Scorpius (The Scorpion)
3. ♊ Gemini (The Twins)	9. ♐ Sagittarius (The Archer)
SUMMER	WINTER
4. ♋ Cancer (The Crab)	10. ♑ Capricornus (The Goat)
5. ♌ Leo (The Lion)	11. ♒ Aquarius (The Water Carrier)
6. ♍ Virgo (The Virgin)	12. ♓ Pisces (The Fishes)

—*R. N. M.*

ZODIACAL LIGHT: a faint, hazy cone of light visible in the western sky after sunset or in the east before sunrise. The cone extends along the ecliptic, and the glow is confined mainly to the constellations of the zodiac. In the tropics the ecliptic is nearly perpendicular to the horizon, so that the zodiacal light can be seen on any clear moonless night. In northern latitudes it is conspicuous from February to April after evening twilight, when the cone is tilted about 30° from the vertical. It is best seen in mid-ocean, or in the countryside away from city glare. The length of the cone is ill-defined, depending on the darkness of the sky and the eyesight of the observer. Zodiacal light is sunlight reflected from billions of meteoritic dust particles which move around the Sun, forming a lens-shaped disc in the plane of the solar system, with the Sun at the center. See GEGENSCHEIN.—*G. S. H.*

ZOOGEOGRAPHY: the geographic distribution of animals, as it can be marked on a map and investigated for similarities and differences. Usually distribution can be correlated with geological information to show changes in the existence of land bridges between continents and seaways connecting major bodies of water. Isolation, whether on a land mass or in a semipermanent lake or ocean, leads through evolution to specialization and uniqueness. Connections, over or through which plants and animals can spread from one region to another, permit aggressive species to extend their range and encounter new habitats, which pose new barriers and test adaptations and mutations.

Land bridges are believed to account for the similarities in animal life in northern N America, Asia, and Europe. This, the Holarctic Realm, is the home of musk ox, caribou, polar bear, walrus, lemmings, varying hares, and ptarmigans. Farther south it contains almost all the known bears, foxes, lynxes, marmots, squirrels, deer, sheep, loons, and tailed amphibians. Long periods of comparative isolation are believed to explain the differences between the animals of the Holarctic Realm in the New World and the Old. Greenland and America north of Mexico constitute a Nearctic Region, with skunks, raccoons, porcupines, and rattlesnakes. A corresponding Palearctic Region, consisting of Africa north of the great deserts, Europe and neighboring islands, and Asia north of the Himalayas, has native horses, sheep and goats, hedgehogs, wild boars, a profusion of mice and rats, and the viper as the most widely distributed venomous snake.

Seas, deserts, and high mountains appear to have isolated a Paleotropical Realm south of the Palearctic Region. In it are found almost all of the big cats (lions, tigers, leopards), the anthropoid apes, rhinoceroses, and elephants, with cobras as the most common poisonous snakes. The realm is divided by the Indian Ocean into an Ethiopian Region (Arabia plus Africa south of the great deserts, and the unique island of

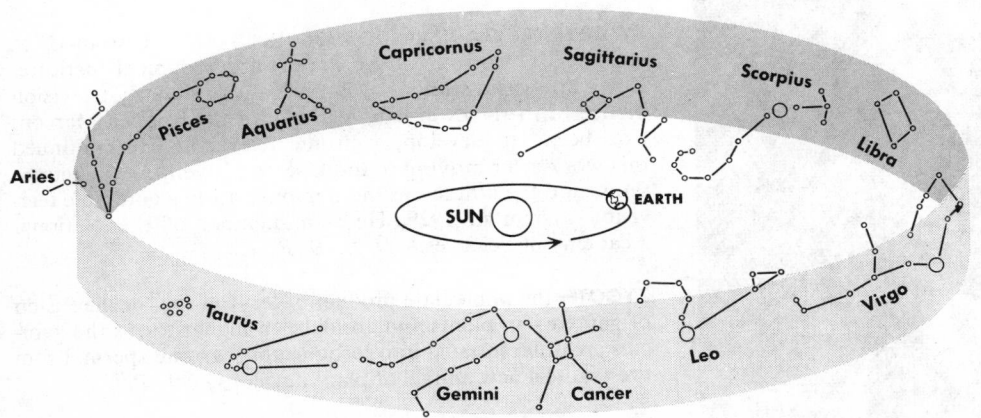

The Zodiac: Zodiac is visualized here as a band circling Earth and Sun, and lying in plane of Earth's orbit around Sun. As seen from Earth, band is pathway followed by Sun, Moon, and planets in their apparent motions, which occur against the background of "fixed" stars that form the constellations shown here. Constellations on near side of band are reversed, as they would be if seen from outside the band.

Madagascar) and an Oriental Region (Asia south of the Himalayas, including the E Indian islands as far as Bali, Borneo, and the Philippines). The extensive grasslands of the Ethiopian Region have become the home of baboons, zebras, hippopotamuses, a great variety of sociable antelopes, giraffes, ostriches, and secretary birds. Forested areas shelter gorillas, chimpanzees, and the okapi. Malagasy Republic (Madagascar) has many lemurs and chameleons. The Oriental Region, by contrast, is more extensively forested. In it roam gibbons, the orangutan, the tarsier, and the peafowl.

An ancient barrier of deep water, known as "Wallace's Line" after its discoverer Alfred Russell Wallace, separates the Paleotropical Realm from the highly distinctive Australasian Realm. Australia, together with its neighboring islands as far as Lombok and Celebes, have all of the world's egg-laying mammals, most of its pouched mammals (marsupials), and such bird oddities as kiwis, birds of paradise, mound-builders, lyre birds, and cockatoos. More than any other realm, the Australasian has been isolated until recent geological times, permitting these unusual animals to evolve with little pressure from aggressive species that otherwise would have migrated in from other continents. See ADAPTATIONS IN ANIMALS AND PLANTS; ECOLOGY; LIFE ZONES.—*L. and M. M.*

ZOOLOGY: the science concerned with the study of animals now living on Earth. Vertebrate zoology is the study of animals with backbones; invertebrate zoology, of animals without backbones. With many scientists contributing to different branches, zoology has necessarily become divided into numerous subdivisions.

Aristotle (384–322 B. C.), father of natural history, was the first zoologist worthy of that name. His book *The Parts of Animals* formed the basis for modern work in morphology and anatomy. Aristotle was interested also in classification of animals, but it was Linnaeus who, in 1758, laid the foundation for modern taxonomy by giving each species of animal two Latin names (binomial nomenclature). Harvey in 1616 discovered the function of the heart and the circulation of the blood through arteries and veins, thereby laying the foundation for modern work in physiology. The development and improvement of the compound microscope made pos-

Zoologist in field attaches band to leg of duck. This and other methods of identification (e.g. dyes) are used in studying longevity, migration patterns, and breeding habits of birds and other wildlife. (*U. S. Dept. of Interior, Fish and Wildlife Service*)

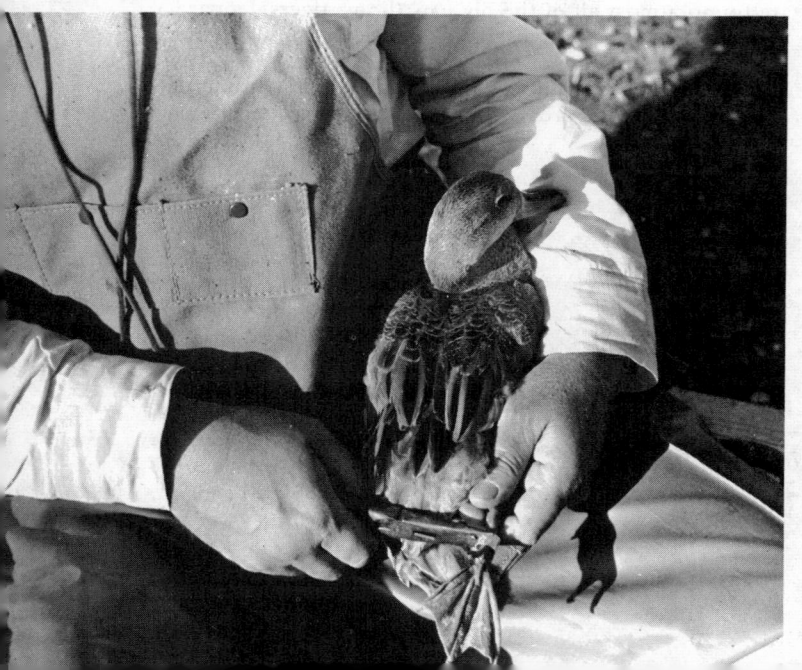

sible the discovery (*c.* 1840) by Theodor Schwann that all animals are composed of cells and that the living material of cells, *i.e.* protoplasm, is the basis of life. It also made possible work of the early histologists and embryologists, which led to modern research in cytology. The work of August Weismann (1892) and others who followed led to the discovery that genes found in the chromosomes of cells are the bearers of heredity. Although the idea of organic evolution was in the minds of early zoologists, it was not until *The Origin of Species* (1859) by Charles Darwin that a satisfactory explanation of how evolution might have occurred was given to the world: natural selection of animals possessing favorable variations. However, not until the development of genetics was there a real explanation of the nature of organic evolution, *i.e.* that it has occurred by natural selection of favorable mutations. Since the late 19th cent., interest in the experimental as distinguished from the observational approach to zoology has grown; hence many new fields have been investigated, often in cooperation with scholars in other sciences. To learn more about living activities, the zoologist has joined hands with the biochemist; for better understanding of radiation as applied to animal life, zoologists are working with physicists; and for better understanding of embryonic development the embryologist has joined with the geneticist to ascertain how genes operate in bringing about transformation of the fertilized egg into a functional animal. See BIOLOGY.—*W. He.*

ZSIGMONDY, RICHARD ADOLPH, 1865–1929, Austrian chemist; b. Vienna. Together with H. F. W. Siedentopf, he developed an ultra-microscope, through which colloidal particles as small as one millionth of a centimeter in diameter could be measured. For his elucidation of the heterogeneous nature of colloid solutions he received the 1925 Nobel prize in chemistry. His book *Zur Erkenntnis der Kolloide* appeared in 1905. —*E. F.*

ZUR THEORIE DES GESETZES DER ENERGIEVERTEILUNG IM NORMALSPEKTRUM, by Max Planck, *Verhandlungen der Deutschen Physik. Gesell.,* Vol. 2, 1900: Here Planck formulated a theory to explain the distribution of energy in the spectrum of BLACK-BODY RADIATION (see PLANCK'S LAW). To make the theory conform to experimental observations, he had to assume that the radiation at any frequency is emitted and absorbed by the body in multiples of a fundamental indivisible unit of light energy, which was subsequently called the *photon.* The photon energy is proportional to its frequency. This view was in contrast to the classical one, which held light energy to be infinitely divisible. The energy of the photon is very small (of the order of 3×10^{-30} ergs for visible light), so that at the macroscopic level the photon hypothesis and classical theory do not in general lead to conflicting results.—*S. Bo.*

ZWORYKIN, VLADIMIR KOSMA, 1889–   , Russian-U. S. engineer; b. Murom. At St. Petersburg Technical Institute, Zworykin was a student of Boris Rosing, an early television pioneer. In 1917 Zworykin, working for the Russian Marconi Co., began to develop electronic television. He continued this work after moving to the U. S. A., inventing the iconoscope and the kinescope and demonstrating a complete television system in 1929. He is a member of the National Academy of Sciences.—*D. H. D. R.*

ZYGOTE: the immediate product of fertilization, or the fusion of gametes, in plants and animals. In higher forms the gametes are differentiated into recognizable egg and sperm. From the zygote a new animal or plant develops.—*W. P. C.*

CONSULTANTS AND AUTHORS

BOARD OF CONSULTANTS

J. Bazer, Associate Professor of Mathematics, Washington Square College, New York University *J.Ba.*

Morton O. Beckner, Associate Professor of Philosophy, Pomona College *M.Be.*

Benjamin Bederson, Professor of Physics, New York University *B.Be.*

Silvio A. Bedini, U.S. National Museum *S.B.*

James Richard Beerbower, Professor of Geology, McMaster University *J.B.*

Richard Bellman, Mathematician, The RAND Corporation *R.B.*

Clarence E. Bennett, Professor and Head, Department of Physics, University of Maine *C.E.B.*

Lyman Benson, Professor and Head, Department of Botany, Pomona College *L.B.*

Edmund C. Berkeley, President, Berkeley Enterprises, Incorporated *E.C.B.*

Daniel Bershader, Professor of Aerophysics, Stanford University, and Consulting Scientist, Lockheed Missiles and Space Company *D.B.*

Edward M. Bevilacqua, Senior Research Scientist, United States Rubber Company *E.M.B.*

Rupert E. Billingham, Professor of Zoology, University of Pennsylvania *R.E.B.*

Donald E. Billings, Research Staff, High Altitude Observatory, Boulder, Colo. *D.E.B.*

A. Alvin Bishop, Head, Dept. of Agricultural and Irrigation Engineering, Utah State University *A.A.B.*

Francis Bitter, Professor of Geophysics, Massachusetts Institute of Technology *F.B.*

Max Black, Professor of Philosophy, Cornell University *M.B.*

Stephen W. Blodgett, Secretary, The Conservation Foundation *S.W.B.*

Ina Bohrer, Editor and Author *I.B.*

Bart Jan Bok, Director, Steward Observatory, University of Arizona *B.J.B.*

John G. Bolton, Officer-in-charge, Australian National Radio Astronomy Observatory *J.G.Bo.*

Hermann Bondi, Professor of Applied Mathematics, King's College, University of London *H.B.*

John Tyler Bonner, Professor of Biology, Princeton University *J.T.B.*

Alfred M. Bork, Professor of Physics, University of Alaska *A.M.B.*

Sidney Borowitz, Professor of Physics, New York University *S.Bo.*

Carl B. Boyer, Professor of Mathematics, Brooklyn College *C.B.B.*

Hervey Brackbill, Elective Member, American Ornithologists' Union; Member, Wilson Ornithological Society, Cooper Ornithological Society *H.Br.*

Roscoe Riley Braham, Jr., Associate Professor of Meteorology, University of Chicago *R.R.B.*

Percy W. Bridgman, late Professor of Physics, Harvard University *P.W.B.*

Selma Blazer Brody, Professor of Physics, Saint John's University *S.Br.*

Frank A. Brown, Professor of Biology, Northwestern University *F.A.B.*

Walter Franklin Buehr, Artist and Author *W.B.*

Donald P. Burke, *Chemical Week* *D.P.B.*

Alastair G. W. Cameron, Institute for Space Studies *A.G.W.C.*

Carleton A. Chapman, Professor of Geology, University of Illinois *C.C.*

Vernon H. Cheldelin, Director, Science Research Institute, Oregon State University *V.H.C.*

Colin Cherry, Imperial College of Science and Technology, University of London *E.C.C.*

Austin H. Church, Professor of Mechanical Engineering, New York University *A.C.*

Clyde B. Clason, Technical Writer *C.B.C.*

Leonard A. Cohen, Head, Dept. of Physiology, Albert Einstein Medical Center *L.A.C.*

Waldo E. Cohn, Biology Division, Oak Ridge National Laboratory *W.E.C.*

Larry S. Cole, Head, Electrical Engineering Department, Utah State University *L.S.C.*

Derek C. Colley, Department of Physics, Birmingham University, England *D.C.C.*

Carl W. Condit, Professor of Humanities, Northwestern University *C.W.C.*

Edward Uhler Condon, Professor of Physics, Washington University, St. Louis *E.U.C.*

Esther M. Conwell, Physicist, General Telephone and Electronics Laboratories *E.M.C.*

Hollis R. Cooley, Professor of Mathematics, New York University *H.C.*

Irving M. Copi, Professor of Philosophy, University of Michigan *I.C.*

Robert K. Crane, Chairman, Department of Biochemistry, The Chicago Medical School *R.K.C.*

Harriet Baldwin Creighton, Professor of Botany, Wellesley College *H.Cr.*

Forest Crossen, Author *F.C.*

Arthur C. Danto, Associate Professor of Philosophy, Columbia University *A.D.*

Albert Rolke Dawe, Chief Scientist, Office of Naval Research, Chicago *A.R.D.*

L. Sprague de Camp, Author *L.S.de C.*

ROBERT W. DECKER, Associate Professor of Geology, Dartmouth College *R.W.D.*

ROBERT L. DeHAAN, Staff Embryologist, Carnegie Institution *R.L.D.*

PETER T. DEMOS, Professor of Physics, Massachusetts Institute of Technology *P.D.; P.T.D.*

ROBERT SINCLAIR DIETZ, Marine Geologist, United States Navy Electronics Laboratory, San Diego, Calif. *R.S.D.*

American Peoples Encyclopedia *A.P.E.*

EDGAR ALLEN EDELSACK, Physicist, Office of Naval Research, San Francisco *E.E.*

SIDNEY MILTON EDELSTEIN, President, Dexter Chemical Corporation *S.M.E.*

ALEXANDER EFRON, Chairman, Department of Physics, Stuyvesant High School, New York, N. Y. *A.E.*

PHILLIP EISENBERG, President, Hydronautics, Incorporated *P.E.*

ROLF ELIASSEN, Professor of Sanitary Engineering, Stanford University *R.E.*

FREDERIC J. EPPLING, Lecturer in Physics, Massachusetts Institute of Technology *F.J.E.*

DAVID R. EVANS, Assistant Professor of Biology, The Johns Hopkins University *D.R.E.*

RALPH M. EVANS, Physicist, Eastman Kodak Co. *R.M.E.*

GORDON MASKEW FAIR, Professor of Sanitary Engineering, Harvard University *G.M.F.*

EDUARD FARBER, Research Professor, American University, Washington *E.F.*

DONALD S. FARNER, Professor of Zoophysiology, Washington State University *D.S.F.*

NORMAN FEATHER, Professor of Natural Philosophy, University of Edinburgh *N.F.*

PHILIP FEIGELSON, Assistant Professor of Biochemistry, Columbia University College of Physicians and Surgeons *Ph.F.*

JOSEPH M. FELD, Professor of Mathematics, Queens College of the City University of New York *J.M.F.*

G. J. FERGUSSON, Isotope Laboratory, Institute of Geophysics, University of California *G.J.F.*

PAUL K. FEYERABEND, Professor of Philosophy, University of California, Berkeley *P.K.F.*

JEAN FITZPATRICK, Medical Author and Editor *J.F.*

J. ERNEST FLACK, Associate Professor of Civil Engineering, University of Colorado *J.E.Fl.*

RICHARD FOSTER FLINT, Professor of Geology, Yale University *R.F.*

JOHN E. FLYNN, Biologist, Office of Naval Research, New York, N. Y. *J.Fl.*

ROBERT JAMES FORBES, Professor of History of Science and Technology, University of Amsterdam *R.J.F.*

DANIEL MARTIN FORSYTH, Assistant Professor of Psychology, Goucher College *D.M.F.*

H. W. FOX, Supervisor, Physical Chemistry Program, Office of Naval Research, Washington, D.C. *H.W.F.*

HERBERT C. FREEMAN, JR., E. I. du Pont de Nemours and Company *H.C.F.*

JOHN E. FREUND, Professor of Mathematics, Arizona State University *J.E.F.*

FELIX FRIEDBERG, Professor of Biochemistry, Howard University *F.F.*

HUBERT W. FRINGS, Professor of Zoology, University of Hawaii *H.W.Fr.*

RICHARD W. FULMER, Chemist, Central Research Laboratory, General Mills, Inc. *R.W.F.*

HELEN B. FUNK, Professor of Biological Sciences, Goucher College *H.B.F.*

JOSEPH G. GALL, Associate Professor of Zoology, University of Minnesota *J.G.G.*

ANNESTA R. GARDNER, Senior Associate Editor, *Product Engineering* *A.R.G.*

CARL W. GARTLEIN, IGY World Data Center, Cornell University *C.W.G.*

CHARLES FREDRIC GELL, Scientific Director, Submarine Medical Research Laboratory *C.G.*

KURT H. GERSTLE, Professor of Civil Engineering, University of Colorado *K.G.*

OWEN JAY GINGERICH, Lecturer, Harvard University *O.G.*

GEORGE GOE, Associate Professor of Philosophy, Rensselaer Polytechnic Institute *G.G.*

BETTY GOLDSTEIN, Technical Editor *E.G.*

JOSEPH L. GOSSNER, Astronomer and Editor *J.L.G.*

SIMONE DARO GOSSNER, Astronomer and Editor *S.D.G.*

R. W. GRAHAM, Research Laboratories, Eastman Kodak Company *R.W.G.*

S. GRANICK, Associate Professor of Biochemistry, The Rockefeller Institute for Medical Research *S.G.*

PAUL E. GREEN, JR., Lincoln Laboratory, Massachusetts Institute of Technology *P.E.G.*

RUSSELL S. GREENBAUM, Deputy Technical Information Officer, Office of Naval Research, Washington, D.C. *R.G.*

WALTER H. HAAS, Physical Science Laboratory, New Mexico State University *W.H.*

HELEN HABERMAN, Assistant Professor of Biological Sciences, Goucher College *H.H.*

ARTHUR F. HAGNER, Professor of Geology, University of Illinois *A.Ha.*

A. RUPERT HALL, Professor of History of Science, Indiana University *A.R.H.*

HOWARD L. HAMILTON, Department of Zoology and Entomology, Iowa State University *H.L.H.*

WILLIAM J. HAMILTON, Department of Conservation, Cornell University; Zoology Editor, *Ecological Monographs* *W.J.H.*

EUGENE H. HANDLER, Aerospace Engineer, Bureau of Naval Weapons *E.H.Ha.*

KENNETH P. HARRISON, Professor of Biochemistry, University of Teheran *K.H.*

EDMUND H. HARVEY, JR., Editor and Author *E.H.H.*

JULIUS J. HARWOOD, Manager, Metallurgy Department, Scientific Laboratory, Ford Motor Company *J.J.H.*

M. D. HASSIALIS, Executive Officer and Krumb Professor of Mining, The Henry Krumb School of Mines, Columbia University *M.D.H.*

GERALD S. HAWKINS, Professor of Astronomy and Director, Boston University Observatory *G.S.H.*

WILLIAM W. HAY, Assistant Professor of Geology, University of Illinois *W.Ha.*

BRUCE C. HEEZEN, Assistant Professor of Geology, Columbia University *B.H.*

CLIFFORD L. HELBERT, Associate Professor, College of Journalism, Marquette University *C.L.H.*

DONALD HENDERSON, Department of Geology, University of Illinois *D.H.*

MALCOLM C. HENDERSON, Research Professor, Catholic University of America *M.C.H.*

WALTER N. HESS, Professor of Biology, Winthrop College *W.He.*

NORMAN E. A. HINDS, late Professor of Geology, University of California *N.E.A.H.*

CHRISTOPHE H. W. HIRS, Biochemist, Brookhaven National Laboratory *C.H.W.H.*

ERICH HIRSCHBERG, Assistant Professor of Biochemistry, Columbia University *E.H.*

HARRY HOCHSTADT, Professor of Mathematics, Polytechnic Institute of Brooklyn *H.Ho.*

KLAUS HOFFMAN, Department of Biology, Princeton University *K.Ho.*

BANESH HOFFMANN, Professor of Mathematics, Queens College of the City University of New York *Ba.H.*

HELEN SAWYER HOGG, Professor of Astronomy, The David Dunlap Observatory *H.S.H.*

ALAN HOLDEN, Bell Telephone Laboratories *A.H.*

LAWRENCE J. HOLLANDER, Director Undergraduate Evening Division, School of Engineering and Science, New York University *L.J.H.*

GERALD HOLTON, Professor of Physics, Harvard University *G.Ho.*

B. L. HORECKER, Professor of Molecular Biology, Albert Einstein College of Medicine *B.Ho.*

WILFRED H. HORTON, Associate Professor of Aeronautics, Stanford University *W.Ho.*

CLARENCE F. HOTCHKISS, JR., Vice President, Stow Manufacturing Company, Inc. *C.F.H.*

LEWIS L. HOUSE, Research Staff, High Altitude Observatory, Boulder, Colorado *L.H.*

ROSS E. HUTCHINS, Entomologist, Mississippi State University *R.E.H.*

CLARENCE J. HYLANDER, Consultant in the Biological Sciences *C.J.H.*

AARON IHDE, Professor of Chemistry and History of Science, University of Wisconsin *A.I.*

WOODROW C. JACOBS, Director, National Oceanographic Data Center, Washington, D.C. *W.C.J.*

ELIZABETH JAFFE, Research Geologist *E.J.*

HOWARD W. JAFFE, Dept. of Geology, University of Massachusetts *H.J.*

BERNARD J. JANDORF, Chief, Biochemical Research Div., U.S. Army Chemical Research and Development Laboratories, Army Chemical Center, Md. *B.J.J.*

HERBERT E. JOHNSON, Associate Professor of Mechanical Engineering, University of Colorado *H.E.J.*

REGINALD VICTOR JONES, Professor of Natural Philosophy, The University, Aberdeen, Scotland, *R.V.J.*

CHARLES L. JORDAN, Associate Professor, Department of Meteorology, Florida State University *C.L.J.*

ALEXANDER JOSEPH, Professor of Physics and Head, Department of Mathematics and Physics, Bronx Community College, City University of New York *A.J.*

THOMAS HUGHES JUKES, Director of Biochemistry, Agricultural Division, American Cyanamid Company *T.J.*

RUSSELL KAHL, Associate Professor of Philosophy, San Francisco State College *R.K.*

DONALD KALISH, Associate Professor of Philosophy, University of California *D.K.*

KRISHNAMURTI KARAMCHETI, Department of Aeronautical Engineering, Stanford University *K.K.*

SAMUEL KATZ, Professor of Geophysics, Rensselaer Polytechnic Institute *Sa.K.*

WILLIAM WARREN KELLOGG, Chief Scientist's Staff, Lockheed Missiles and Space Company *W.K.*

JOHN S. KELLY, Editor and Author *J.S.K.*

MILTON KERKER, Chairman, Department of Chemistry, Clarkson College of Technology *M.K.*

MORRIS KLINE, Chairman, Department of Mathematics, Washington Square College, New York University *M.Kl.*

WILLIAM J. KOCH, Associate Professor of Botany, University of North Carolina   *W.Ko.*

DANIEL E. KOSHLAND, JR., Senior Biochemist, Brookhaven National Laboratory   *D.Ko.*

ARNOLD KOSLOW, Department of Philosophy, Columbia University   *A.K.*

ROBERT P. KRAFT, Staff Member, Mount Wilson and Palomar Observatories   *R.P.K.*

MILDRED BROOKS KRAINOCK, Information Services, Eastman Kodak Company   *M.B.K.*

SOL KRASNER, Dept. of Physics, University of Chicago
S.K.

FRANK KREITH, Professor of Mechanical Engineering and Chairman of the Superior Student Program in Engineering, University of Colorado   *F.K.*

EDMUND A. LAPORT, Director of Communications Engineering, Radio Corporation of America   *E.A.L.*

RALPH E. LAPP, Member of the Board, Quadri-Science, Incorporated   *R.La.*

P. R. LEACH, JR., Product Information Service, E. I. du Pont de Nemours   *P.R.Le.*

PHILIPPE LE CORBEILLER, Professor Emeritus, Harvard University   *P. le C.*

PAUL E. LEHR, Meteorologist, United States Weather Bureau   *P.L.*

MORRIS C. LEIKIND, National Institutes of Health
M.C.L.

KORNELIUS LEMS, Assistant Professor of Biological Sciences, Goucher College   *K.L.*

ISAAC LEVI, Assistant Professor of Philosophy, The City College, New York   *I.L.*

LILLIAN LEVY, Senior Science Writer, NASA, Washington, D.C.   *L.L.*

HAROLD LIEBOWITZ, Head, Structural Mechanics Branch, Office of Naval Research, Washington, D.C.
H.L.

FRANK G. LIER, Associate Professor of Botany, Columbia University   *F.L.*

PETER RICHARD LIMBURG, Editor and Author   *P.R.L.*

M. STANLEY LIVINGSTON, Professor of Physics, Massachusetts Institute of Technology; Director, Cambridge Electron Accelerator, Harvard University
M.S.L.

JOHN H. LOCHHEAD, Professor of Zoology, University of Vermont   *J.H.L.*

JULIUS LONDON, Professor, Department of Astro-Geophysics, University of Colorado   *J.L.*

DANIEL HARLOW LUFKIN, Meteorological Officer, United States Air Force   *D.H.L.*

ALVIN LUKASHOK, Editor and Author   *A.L.*

CHARLES F. LYTLE, Department of Zoology, Tulane University   *C.F.L.*

RAYMOND A. LYTTLETON, Fellow of St. John's College, Cambridge   *R.A.L.*

RUDOLPH MACY, Chemist and Author   *Ru.M.*

EDWARD H. MADDEN, Department of Philosophy, San Jose State College   *E.H.M.*

FRANCIS ROMERIL MADDISON, Assistant Curator, Museum of the History of Science, University of Oxford
F.R.M.

HENRY R. MAHLER, Professor of Chemistry, Indiana University   *H.M.*

L. MARTON, International Relations, National Bureau of Standards   *L.L.M.*

BASIL JOHN MASON, Professor of Cloud Physics, Imperial College, London   *B.J.M.*

MARGARET W. MAYALL, Director, American Association of Variable Star Observers   *M.W.M.*

R. NEWTON MAYALL, Consulting Engineer   *R.N.M.*

A. LEE MCALESTER, Assistant Professor of Geology, Yale University   *A.L.McA.*

JAMES E. MCCLELLAN, Associate Professor of Education, Teachers College, Columbia University   *J.E.M.*

ALTON MEISTER, Professor of Biochemistry, Tufts University School of Medicine   *A.M.*

THEODORE MELNECHUK, Associate Editor, *International Science and Technology*   *T.M.*

EVERETT MENDELSOHN, Assistant Professor of the History of Science, Harvard University   *E.Me.*

ELLIOTT MENDELSON, Associate Professor of Mathematics, Queens College   *El.M.*

K. MENDELSSOHN, Reader in Physics, University of Oxford   *K.Me.*

KARL MENGER, Department of Mathematics, Illinois Institute of Technology   *K.M.*

ROGER G. MENGES, Editor and Author   *R.G.M.*

PAUL W. MERRILL, late Staff Member, Mount Wilson & Palomar Observatories   *P.Me.*

EDWIN THEODORE MERTZ, Professor of Biochemistry, Purdue University   *E.M.*

GERALD WILLIAM MILLER, Chemist, Glass Research Center, Pittsburgh Plate Glass Co.   *G.W.M.*

STANLEY L. MILLER, Assistant Professor of Chemistry, University of California   *S.L.M.*

PETER M. MILLMAN, Astrophysicist, National Research Council, Ottawa, Canada   *P.M.*

LORUS AND MARGERY MILNE, Department of Biology, University of New Hampshire   *L. and M.M.*

GAIRDNER BOSTWICK MOMENT, Professor of Biology, Goucher College   *G.B.M.*

ERNEST A. MOODY, Professor of Philosophy and Chairman of Department, University of California at Los Angeles   *E.A.M.*

FLORENCE MOOG, Professor of Zoology, Washington University, St. Louis   *F.M.*

SIDNEY MORGENBESSER, Professor of Philosophy, Columbia University   *S.M.*

LOUIS MOYD, Exploration Geologist   *L.M.*

MILTON K. MUNITZ, Professor of Philosophy, New York University   *M.K.M.*

RICHMOND E. MYERS, Professor of Geology, Moravian College   *R.E.M.*

ERNEST NAGEL, Professor of Philosophy, Columbia University   *E.N.*

JEROME NAMIAS, Chief, Extended Forecast Branch, United States Weather Bureau   *J.N.*

JAMES R. NEWMAN, Editor and Author   *J.R.N.*

JERZY NEYMAN, Department of Statistics, Statistical Laboratory, University of California   *J.Ne.*

THOMAS D. NICHOLSON, Astronomer, American Museum—Hayden Planetarium   *T.N.*

IVAN NIVEN, Professor of Mathematics, University of Oregon   *I.N.*

RALPH EDWARD OESPER, Professor Emeritus of Analytical Chemistry, University of Cincinnati   *R.E.O.*

JOHN J. O'NEILL, Associate Professor of Pharmacology, University of Maryland, School of Medicine   *J.J.O'N.*

OYSTEIN ORE, Professor of Mathematics, Yale University   *O.O.*

MICHAEL WILLIAM OVENDEN, Lecturer in Astronomy, University of Glasgow   *M.W.O.*

ROBERT MORRIS PAGE, Director of Research, United States Naval Research Laboratory, Washington, D.C.   *R.M.P.*

ROBERT WILLIAM PENNAK, Professor of Biology, University of Colorado   *R.P.*

HARLAN J. PERLIS, Associate Professor of Electrical Engineering, Rutgers University   *H.J.P.*

JAMES WHITNEY PERRY, Numerical Analysis Laboratory, University of Arizona   *J.W.P.*

DEAN FREEMAN PETERSON, JR., Dean, College of Engineering, Utah State University   *D.F.P.*

SVERRE PETTERSSEN, Professor of Meteorology, and Chairman, Department of Geophysical Sciences, University of Chicago   *S.P.*

MELBA PHILLIPS, Professor of Physics, University of Chicago   *M.P.*

OWEN MARTIN PHILLIPS, Professor of Fluid Mechanics, The Johns Hopkins University   *O.M.P.*

JAMES S. PICKERING, Assistant Astronomer, American Museum—Hayden Planetarium   *J.P.*

JOHN R. PIERCE, Executive Director, Research Communications Principles Division, Bell Telephone Laboratories   *J.R.P.*

WILLIAM B. PLUMMER, Technical Consultant   *W.B.P.*

JEROME M. POLLACK, Division of Science & Mathematics, State University of New York, Harpur College   *J.M.P.*

ERNEST C. POLLARD, Professor of Biophysics, Pennsylvania State University   *E.C.P.*

FRED HENRY P. E. POSSER, Manager, Quality Assurance   *F.P.*

GEORGE R. PRICE, Advanced Systems Division, International Business Machines Corporation   *G.R.P.*

JOHN W. S. PRINGLE, Professor of Zoology, Oxford University   *J.W.S.P.*

MAYNARD E. PULLMAN, Associate Member, The Public Health Research Institute, New York   *M.E.P.*

WAYNE D. RASMUSSEN, Secretary-Treasurer, Agricultural History Society; Chief of Agricultural History Branch, United States Department of Agriculture   *W.R.*

JOHN READ, Professor of Chemistry, The University, St. Andrews, Scotland   *J.R.*

GIBSON REAVES, Department of Astronomy, University of Southern California   *G.R.*

SCOTT H. REINIGER, Bendix Corporation   *S.R.*

WILLIAM C. REYNOLDS, Associate Professor of Mechanical Engineering, Stanford University   *Wm.R.*

EDWIN M. RIPIN, Editor and Author   *E.M.R.*

DUANE H. D. ROLLER, Associate Professor History of Science, University of Oklahoma; Curator of the DeGolyer Collection in the History of Science and Technology   *D.H.D.R.*

HAROLD J. ROSENBERG, General Precision, Inc.   *H.J.R.*

HUNTER ROUSE, Director, Iowa Institute of Hydraulic Research   *H.R.*

IRVING ROWE, Physicist, Office of Naval Research   *I.R.*

DOROTHEA RUDNICK, Professor of Biology, Albertus Magnus College   *D.R.*

STANLEY KEITH RUNCORN, Professor and Director of Department of Physics, King's College, Newcastle upon Tyne   *S.K.R.*

FRANK B. SALISBURY, Head, Plant Science Dept., College of Agriculture, Utah State University   *F.S.*

MARSTON C. SARGENT, Oceanographer, Office of Naval Research   *M.S.*

WILLIAM L. SCHAAF, Professor of Education, Brooklyn College, City University of New York   *W.L.S.*

BRADLEY T. SCHEER, Professor of Biology, University of Oregon   *B.T.S.*

FREDERIC SCHICK, Assistant Professor of Philosophy, Rutgers University   *F.Sc.*

Jes Erich Schlaikjer, Technical Press, International Telephone and Telegraph Corporation *J.E.S.*

Cecil J. Schneer, Associate Professor of Geology, University of New Hampshire *C.J.S.*

Leo Schubert, Chairman, Chemistry Department, The American University, Washington, D.C. *L.Sc.*

Anthony M. Schwartz, Assistant Director of Research, Harris Research Laboratories, Inc. *A.M.S.*

John Paul Scott, Senior Staff Scientist, Roscoe B. Jackson Memorial Laboratory *J.P.S.*

Glenn T. Seaborg, Chairman, U.S. Atomic Energy Commission, Washington, D.C. *G.T.S.*

Raymond J. Seeger, Physicist, National Science Foundation *R.J.S.*

Clara S. Shapiro, Chemist *C.S.*

Harold I. Sharlin, Associate Professor of Economics and History, Polytechnic Institute of Brooklyn *H.I.S.*

Barbara Sheridan, Technical Editor *B.P.S.*

John A. Shimer, Department of Geology, Brooklyn College *J.Sh.*

William B. Shockley, Director, Shockley Transistor, Unit of Clevite Transistor *W.S.*

Arnold Shostak, Head, Electronics Branch, Office of Naval Research, Washington, D.C. *A.S.*

Philip Siekevitz, Professor of Biochemistry, Rockefeller University *P.S.*

Shirleigh Silverman, Associate Director, National Bureau of Standards, Washington, D.C. *S.S.*

Eric J. Simon, Department of Medicine, New York University School of Medicine *E.S.*

John Sinkankas, Captain, U.S.N. (Ret.), Mineralogist and Author *J.Si.*

Hobart M. Smith, Professor of Zoology, University of Illinois *H.M.S.*

Arthur F. Smullyan, Professor and Chairman of the Department of Philosophy, University of Washington *A.Sm.*

R. E. Snodgrass, late Honorary Research Associate, Smithsonian Institution *R.E.S.*

Joseph H. Speyer, Cold Spring Harbor Biological Laboratories *J.F.S.*

Leslie Spier, late Professor Emeritus of Anthropology, University of New Mexico *L.Sp.*

George C. Sponsler, Chief Scientist, United States Navy Bureau of Ships *G.S.*

Michael A. Spronck, *Construction Equipment Magazine* *M.A.S.*

Robert L. Sproull, Professor of Physics, Cornell University *R.Sp.*

Grace Marmor Spruch, Associate Research Scientist, New York University *G.M.S.*

Larry Spruch, Professor of Physics, New York University *L.S.*

S. S. Stevens, Director, Psycho-acoustical Laboratory, Harvard University *S.S.S.*

Harold Strain, Argonne National Laboratories *H.H.S.*

Dirk J. Struik, Professor Emeritus, Massachusetts Institute of Technology *D.J.S.*

Jay Eli Strum, Instructor in Mathematics, Washington Square College, New York University *J.S.*

Sir (Oliver) Graham Sutton, Director-General of the Meteorological Office, United Kingdom *O.G.S.*

Hugo M. Swenson, Professor of Physics, Queens College *H.Sw.*

Harry Tarter, Dept. of Philosophy, City College, University of the City of New York *H.T.*

Sterling A. Taylor, Professor of Soil Physics, Utah State University *S.A.T.*

H. S. Thayer, Dept. of Philosophy, City College, University of the City of New York *H.S.T.*

Jack C. Thompson, Meteorologist, United States Weather Bureau *J.C.T.*

Klaus D. Timmerhaus, Professor of Chemical Engineering, University of Colorado *K.T.*

Robert B. Travis, Lead Industries Association, Incorporated *R.B.T.*

Joseph M. Trefethen, Professor of Geology, University of Maine *J.T.*

Horace M. Trent, Head, Applied Mathematics Staff, Naval Research Lab., Washington, D.C. *H.M.T.*

Joseph Turner, Associate Editor, *Science* magazine *J.Tu.*

Frank Ungar, Dept. of Physiological Chemistry, University of Minnesota Medical School *F.U.*

Wilbur G. Valentine, Professor of Geology, Brooklyn College *W.G.V.*

Arlo M. Vance, Entomology Research Division, Agricultural Research Service, U.S. Dept. of Agriculture *A.M.V.*

John van Heijenoort, Associate Professor of Mathematics, New York University *J.H.*

Robert N. Varney, Professor of Physics, Washington University, St. Louis *R.N.V.*

Charles Spain Verral, Author and Editor *C.S.V.*

Howard E. Wahlert, Professor of Mathematics, New York University *H.E.W.*

Salih J. Wakil, Department of Biochemistry, Duke University Medical Center *S.J.W.*

Andrew H. Wallace, Department of Mathematics, Indiana University *A.H.W.*

Bruce O. Watkins, Professor, Department of Electrical Engineering, Utah State University *B.O.W.*

SARA RUTH WATSON, Professor of Civil Engineering, Fenn College
S.R.W.

WILLIAM WEAVER, JR., Assistant Professor of Civil Engineering, Stanford University
W.W.

E. E. WEIBEL, late Professor of Mechanical Engineering, University of Colorado
E.E.W.

ALVIN M. WEINBERG, Oak Ridge National Laboratory
A.M.W.

G. W. WHARTON, Chairman, Dept. of Zoology and Entomology, The Ohio State University and the Ohio Agricultural Experiment Station
G.W.

CHARLES GRADY WILBER, Dean, Graduate School and Professor of Biological Sciences, Kent State University
C.G.W.

RAYMOND LOUIS WILDER, Research Professor, University of Michigan
R.L.W.

J. TUZO WILSON, Director, Institute of Earth Sciences, University of Toronto
J.T.W.

ROBERT A. WOLFFE, Chemical Engineering Department, Lehigh University
R.W.

J. EDMUND WOODS, late Professor of Physics, Queens College
J.E.W.

A. JOSEPH WRAIGHT, Professor of Physical Geography, Edinboro State College
A.J.W.

RAY J. WU, Associate Member, Public Health Research Institute of New York
R.Wu

JEROME WYCKOFF, Editor and Author
J.W.

DONALD B. ZILVERSMIT, Professor of Physiology, University of Tennessee
D.B.Z.

VLADIMIR KOSMA ZWORYKIN, Vice President, Radio Corporation of America Laboratories
V.Z.

BIBLIOGRAPHY

This bibliography offers a reading list for each of the major scientific disciplines covered in the Encyclopedia:

ASTRONOMY	CHEMISTRY	MATHEMATICS
BIOCHEMISTRY AND	GEOLOGY	METEOROLOGY
BIOPHYSICS	HISTORY AND PHILOSOPHY	PHYSICS
BIOLOGY	OF SCIENCE	TECHNOLOGY

A GENERAL SCIENCE category also is included.

Most categories have a *General* division followed by citations grouped under specific headings. Some of the works cited require previous knowledge or, at least, a willingness to confront unfamiliar concepts and a technical vocabulary; but many contain information, especially in introductory chapters, that the layman will find readable and instructive. Texts especially suitable for the general reader are marked with an asterisk (*). All but a few of the books listed are in print; those available in paperback form are so designated. Out-of-print books listed because of their importance can be located in libraries and in the old-books trade.

The bibliography cites some articles that have appeared in periodicals. These articles are in some instances the only satisfactory available treatment of the particular topic; in other cases they are more suitable than the existing books for general reading. But no attempt is made here to cover the large amount of periodical literature on science that exists. Such literature is well indexed in such established publications as the *Reader's Guide to Periodical Literature, Applied Science and Technology Index, Agricultural Index, Engineering Index, Mathematical Reviews, Chemical Abstracts,* and *Biological Abstracts.*

Bibliographical references for the biographies are not given here, because biographical information is readily available in reference libraries. Biographical information on scientists now living in the United States can be found in the very comprehensive and current *American Men of Science,* in the current *Who's Who in America,* in the *McGraw-Hill Modern Men of Science,* and in various specialized current biographical directories. For American scientists no longer living, there are such publications as the *Dictionary of American Biography* and the older editions of *American Men of Science* and *Who's Who in America.* For living British scientists there is the current *Who's Who,* and for those not living, the *Dictionary of National Biography.* .

The best general source for ancient scientists is Sarton's *Introduction to the History of Science,* listed again in this bibliography under HISTORY AND PHILOSOPHY OF SCIENCE. Poggendorff's *Biographisch-Literarisches Handwörterbuch,* although written mostly in German, is international in scope and covers the period from ancient times to our own; it is often the best source of information on a scientist's published works. Libraries regularly index biographical material, including books and periodicals, under individual names in their catalogs; hence the catalogs of large libraries, such as the New York Public Library, are mines of biographical information about scientists—including not only the most eminent but also those less renowned.

Paperbound editions are listed if available. When both a hardbound edition and a paperback are offered by the same publisher, the latter is indicated by "(also pap.)." When hardbound and paperbound editions are published by different publishers, the hardbound is listed first and the paperbound second in order, thus: "Harper, 1949 (Dover, pap.)." If the only edition in print is paperbound, "(pap.)" appears after the publisher's name and year of publication.

In the citations, publishers' names are abbreviated. Following is a list of abbreviations in alphabetical order, with the publishers' full names and their locations:

Abelard—Abelard-Schuman, Ltd., New York, N. Y.
Academic—Academic Press, Inc., New York, N. Y.
Addison—Addison Wesley Publishing Co., Inc., Reading, Mass.
Aero—Aero Publishers, Inc., Fallbrook, Calif.
Aldine—Aldine Publishing Co., Chicago, Ill.
Allyn—Allyn & Bacon, Inc., Boston, Mass.
A.A.A.S.—American Association for the Advancement of Science, Washington, D. C.
American—American Book Co., New York, N. Y.
American Chemical Soc.—American Chemical Society, New York, N. Y.
A.G.I.—American Geological Institute, Washington, D. C.
A.M.S.—American Meteorological Society, Boston, Mass.
A.O.U.—American Ornithologists Union, Washington, D. C.
Amer. Sci.—The American Scientist, Princeton, N. J.
A.S.M.—American Soc. for Metals, Cleveland, Ohio
American Tech. Soc.—American Technical Society, Chicago, Ill.
Anchor—Anchor Books (imprint of Doubleday & Co., Inc., Garden City, N. Y.)
Apollo—Apollo Editions, Inc. (co-imprint of T. Y. Crowell, Dodd, Mead & Wm. Morrow, New York, N. Y.)
Appleton—Appleton-Century-Crofts, New York, N. Y.
Atheneum—Atheneum Publishers, New York, N. Y.
Audel—Theodore Audel & Co., Indianapolis, Ind.
Ballantine—Ballantine Books, Inc., New York, N. Y.
Bantam—Bantam Books, Inc., New York, N. Y.
Barnes—Barnes & Noble, Inc., New York, N. Y. .
Basic—Basic Books, Inc. New York, N. Y.
Batchworth—Paul Hamlyn, Ltd., London, England
Batsford—B. T. Batsford, Ltd., London, England
Beacon—Beacon Press, Boston, Mass.
Benjamin—W. A. Benjamin, Inc., New York, N. Y.
Bennett—Chas. A. Bennett Co., Inc., Peoria, Ill.
Bison—Bison Books (imprint of Univ. of Nebraska Press, Lincoln, Neb.)
Blaisdell—Blaisdell Publishing Co., Waltham, Mass.
Boston Tech.—Boston Technical Publishers, Cambridge, Mass.
Bowker—R. R. Bowker Co., New York, N. Y.

Boxwood—Boxwood Press, Pittsburgh, Penn.
Braziller—George Braziller, Inc., New York, N. Y.
Britannica—Encyclopaedia Britannica, Inc., Chicago, Ill.
Burgess—Burgess Publishing Co., Minneapolis, Minn.
Butterworth—Butterworth, Inc., Washington, D. C.
California—Univ. of California Press, Berkeley, Calif.
Cambridge—Cambridge Univ. Press, New York, N. Y.
Central—Central Book Co., Inc., Brooklyn, N. Y.
Chelsea—Chelsea Publishing Co., Bronx, N. Y.
Chemical Rubber—Chemical Rubber Publishing Co., Cleveland, Ohio
Chicago—Univ. of Chicago Press, Chicago, Ill.
Chilton—Chilton Books, Philadelphia, Penn.
Collier—Collier Books (imprint of Crowell Collier & Macmillan, Inc., New York, N. Y.)
Columbia—Columbia Univ. Press, New York, N. Y.
Comstock—Comstock Publishing Associates, Ithaca, N. Y.
Cornell—Cornell Univ. Press, Ithaca, N. Y.
Coward—Coward McCann, Inc., New York, N. Y.
Crowell—Thomas Y. Crowell Co., New York, N. Y.
Day—John Day Company, Inc., New York, N. Y.
DeGraff—John DeGraff, Inc., Tuckahoe, N. Y.
Dell—Dell Publishing Co., Inc., New York, N. Y.
Devin—Devin-Adair Co., New York, N. Y.
Dial—Dial Press, Inc., New York, N. Y.
Dodd—Dodd, Mead & Co., New York, N. Y.
Doubleday—Doubleday & Co., Inc., Garden City, N. Y.
Dover—Dover Publications, New York, N. Y.
Duckworth—Gerald Duckworth & Co. Ltd., London, England
Dutton—E. P. Dutton & Co., Inc., New York, N. Y.
Elsevier—American Elsevier Publishing Co., New York, N. Y.
Emerson—Emerson Books, Inc., New York, N. Y.
Fawcett—Fawcett World Library, New York, N. Y.
Fell—Frederick Fell, Inc., New York, N. Y.
Field—Field Enterprises Educational Corp., Chicago, Ill.
Franklin—Franklin Book Programs, Inc., New York, N. Y.
Free Press—The Free Press, New York, N. Y.
Freeman—W. H. Freeman & Co., Publishers, San Francisco, Calif.
Funk—Funk & Wagnalls, New York, N. Y.
George Allen—George Allen and Unwin, Ltd., London, England
Gernsback—Gernsback Library, Inc., New York, N. Y.
Golden—Golden Press, Inc., New York, N. Y.
Grolier—Grolier Incorporated, New York, N. Y.
Grosset—Grosset & Dunlap, Inc., New York, N. Y.
Grove—Grove Press, Inc., New York, N. Y.
Gun Digest—Follet Publishing Co., Chicago, Ill.
Hafner—Hafner Publishing Co., Inc., New York, N. Y.
Harcourt—Harcourt, Brace & World, Inc., New York, N. Y.
Harper—Harper & Row Publishers, New York, N. Y.
Harrap—George G. Harrap & Co., Ltd., London, England
Harvard—Harvard Univ. Press, Cambridge, Mass.
Hayden—Hayden Book Companies, New York, N. Y.
Heath—D. C. Heath & Co., Boston, Mass.
H. M. Stationery Office—Her Majesty's Stationery Office, London, England
Herbert Jenkins—Herbert Jenkins, Ltd., London, England
Hillary—Hillary House Publishers, Ltd., (an affiliate of Humanities Press, Inc., New York, N. Y.)
Holden—Holden-Day, Inc., San Francisco, Calif.
Holt—Holt, Rinehart & Winston, Inc., New York, N. Y.
Houghton—Houghton Mifflin Co., Boston, Mass.
Humanities—Humanities Press, Inc., New York, N. Y.
Hutchinson—Hutchinson & Co., Ltd., London, England
Illinois—Univ. of Illinois Press, Urbana, Ill.
Industrial—Industrial Press, New York, N. Y.
International—International Textbook Co., Scranton, Penn.
Interscience—Interscience Publishers, Inc. (imprint of John Wiley & Sons, Inc., New York, N. Y.)
Johns Hopkins—Johns Hopkins Press, Baltimore, Md.
Jour. of Chem. Ed.—Journal of Chemical Education, New York, N. Y.
Knopf—Alfred A. Knopf, Inc., New York, N. Y.
Lea—Lea & Febiger, Philadelphia, Penn.
Lippincott—J. B. Lippincott Co., Philadelphia, Penn.
Littlefield—Littlefield, Adams & Co., Totowa, N. J.
Longmans—Longmans, Green & Co. Ltd., London, England
Louisiana—Louisiana State Univ. Press, Baton Rouge, La.
Macmillan—Crowell Collier & Macmillan, Inc., New York, N. Y.
M.I.T.—M.I.T. Press, Cambridge, Mass.

McGraw—McGraw-Hill Book Co., New York, N. Y.
McKnight—McKnight & McKnight Pub. Co., Bloomington, Ill.
Mentor—Mentor Books (imprint of New American Library, Inc., New York, N. Y.)
Meridian—Meridian Books (imprint of World Publishing Co., Cleveland, Ohio)
Messner—Julian Messner, New York, N. Y.
Methuen—Methuen & Co. Ltd., London, England
Michigan—Univ. of Michigan Press, Ann Arbor, Mich.
Minnesota—Univ. of Minnesota Press, Minneapolis, Minn.
Momentum—Momentum Books (imprint of D. Van Nostrand Co., Inc., Princeton, N. J.)
Muller—Frederick Muller Ltd., London, England
Murray—John Murray Ltd., London, England
N.A.S.—National Academy of Sciences, National Research Council, Washington, D. C.
NASA—National Aeronautics and Space Administration, Washington, D. C.
Natural History—Natural History Press, New York, N. Y.
Nat. Sci. Teachers Assn.—National Science Teachers Association, Washington, D. C.
Nelson—Thomas Nelson & Sons, Camden, N. J.
N.A.L.—The New American Library, Inc., New York, N. Y.
Newnes—George Newnes Ltd., London, England
New York—New York Univ. Press, New York, N. Y.
North Carolina—Univ. of North Carolina Press, Chapel Hill, N. C.
Northwestern—Northwestern Univ. Press, Evanston, Ill.
Norton—W. W. Norton & Co., Inc., New York, N. Y.
Odyssey—Odyssey Press, Inc., New York, N. Y.
Ohio—Ohio State Univ. Press, Columbus, Ohio
Oklahoma—Univ. of Oklahoma Press, Norman, Okla.
Open Court—Open Court Publishing Co., LaSalle, Ill.
Orion—Orion Press, Inc., New York, N. Y.
Oxford—Oxford Univ. Press, Inc., New York, N. Y.
Pelican—Pelican Books (imprint of Penguin Books, Inc.)
Penguin—Penguin Books, Inc., Baltimore, Md.
Pergamon—Pergamon Press, Inc., New York, N. Y.
Peter Smith—Peter Smith, Gloucester, Mass.
Philosophical Lib.—Philosophical Library, Inc., New York, N. Y.
Pitman—Pitman Publishing Corp., New York, N. Y.
Pocket Books—Pocket Books, New York, N. Y.
Premier—Premier Books (imprint of Fawcett World Library, New York, N. Y.)
Prentice—Prentice-Hall, Inc., Englewood Cliffs, N. J.
Princeton—Princeton Univ. Press, Princeton, N. J.
Putnam—G. P. Putnam's Sons, New York, N. Y.
Random—Random House, Inc., New York, N. Y.
Reinhold—Reinhold Publishing Corp., New York, N. Y.
Rider—John F. Rider Publisher, Inc., New York, N. Y.
Rockefeller—Rockefeller Univ. Press, New York, N. Y.
Ronald—Ronald Press Co., New York, N. Y.
Routledge—Routledge & Kegan Paul, Ltd., London, England
Rutgers—Rutgers Univ. Press, New Brunswick, N. J.
St. Martin's—St. Martin's Press, Inc., New York, N. Y.
Sams—Howard W. Sams & Co., Inc., Indianapolis, Ind.
Saunders—W. B. Saunders Co., Philadelphia, Penn.
Science Eds.—Science Editions, Inc. (imprint of John Wiley & Sons, Inc., New York, N. Y.)
Sci. Amer.—Scientific American, Inc., New York, N. Y.
Scott—Scott, Foresman & Co., Glenview, Ill.
Scribner's—Charles Scribner's Sons, New York, N. Y.
Signet—Signet Science (imprint of New American Library, Inc., New York, N. Y.)
Simmons—Simmons-Boardman Publishing Corp., New York, N. Y.
Simon—Simon and Schuster, Inc., New York, N. Y.
Sky—Sky Publishing Co., Cambridge, Mass.
Smithsonian—Smithsonian Institution, Washington, D. C.
Soc. of N.A.M.E.—Society of Naval Architects and Marine Engineers, New York, N. Y.
Southern Illinois—Southern Illinois Univ. Press, Carbondale, Ill.
Spartan—Spartan Books, Inc., New York, N. Y.
SportShelf—imprint of Soccer Associates, New Rochelle, N. Y.
Springer—Springer Publishing Co., Inc., New York, N. Y.
Stackpole—Stackpole Books, Harrisburg, Penn.
Stanford—Stanford Univ. Press, Stanford, Calif.
Stechert—Stechert-Hafner, New York, N. Y.
Swallow—Alan Swallow, Publisher, Denver, Colo.

Technical—Technical Press, Ltd., London, England
Texas—Univ. of Texas Press, Austin, Texas
Textile—Textile Book Service, New York, N. Y.
Thames—Thames and Hudson, London, England
Thomas—Charles C. Thomas, Publisher, Springfield, Ill.
Time—Time-Life Books (a Division of Time, Inc.), New York, N. Y.
Toronto—Univ. of Toronto Press, Toronto, Ontario, Canada
Transatlantic—Transatlantic Arts, Inc., New York, N. Y.
Tudor—Tudor Publishing Co., New York, N. Y.
Twayne—Twayne Publishers, Inc., New York, N. Y.
Ungar—Frederick Ungar Publishing Co., Inc., New York, N. Y.
U. S. Dept. of Agriculture, Washington, D. C.
U. S. Dept. of the Army—U. S. Dept. of Defense, Washington, D. C.
U. S. Hydrographic Office—U. S. Government Printing Office, Washington, D. C.

U. S. Soil Conservation Service—U. S. Dept. of Agriculture
U. S. Steel Corp., New York, N. Y.
Van Nostrand—D. Van Nostrand Co., Inc., Princeton, N. J.
Viking—Viking Press, Inc., New York, N. Y.
Vintage—Vintage Books (imprint of Random House, Inc.)
Wadsworth—Wadsworth Publishing Co., Inc., Belmont, Calif.
Warne—Frederick Warne & Co., Inc., New York, N. Y.
Washington—Univ. of Washington Press, Seattle, Wash.
Watts—Franklin Watts, Inc., New York, N. Y.
Wiley—John Wiley & Sons, Inc., New York, N. Y.
William-Frederick—William-Frederick Press, New York, N. Y.
Williams—Williams & Wilkins Co., Baltimore, Md.
Wisconsin—Univ. of Wisconsin Press, Madison, Wisc.
World—World Publishing Co., Cleveland, Ohio
Yale—Yale Univ. Press, New Haven, Conn.

GENERAL SCIENCE

BIBLIOGRAPHIES

British Scientific and Technical Books; a Select List of Recommended Books Published in Great Britain and the Commonwealth in the Years 1935–53, Supplement 1953–57, Hafner, 1956–60.
Deason, H. J., ed., *A Guide to Science Reading,* N.A.L., 1966 (pap.)*
Deason, H. J., ed., *Science Books, A Quarterly Review,* A.A.A.S. (pap.)*
McGraw-Hill Basic Bibliography of Science and Technology, McGraw-Hill, 1966*
Martin, R. C., and W. Jett, *Guide to Scientific and Technical Periodicals,* Swallow, 1963 (also pap.)*
Steckler, P. B., ed., *American Scientific Books, 1960–1962,* supplements every two years; Bowker

ENCYCLOPEDIAS AND DICTIONARIES

Book of Popular Science, Grolier, 10 vol., 1967*
Compton's Illustrated Science Dictionary, Britannica, 1963*
Encyclopedia Science Supplement, Grolier, annually*

Flood, W. E., and M. West, *Elementary Scientific and Technical Dictionary,* 3d ed., Humanities*
Hechtlinger, A., *A Modern Science Dictionary,* Franklin, 1959
McGraw-Hill Encyclopedia of Science and Technology, McGraw-Hill, 15 vol., 1966
Science Year, The World Book Science Annual, Field, annually*
Uvarov, E. B., and D. R. Chapman, *Dictionary of Science,* 4th ed., Penguin (pap.)*
Van Nostrand's Scientific Encyclopedia, 3rd ed., Van Nostrand, 1958

GENERAL DISCUSSIONS
(See also books cited under PHILOSOPHY AND HISTORY OF SCIENCE)

Asimov, I., *Intelligent Man's Guide to the Physical Sciences,* Pocket Books, 1960 (pap.)*
Beveridge, W. I. B., *The Art of Scientific Investigation,* Vintage, 1960
Bronowski, J., *Science and Human Values,* rev. ed., Messner, 1956 (Harper, pap.)*
Campbell, N., *What is Science?* Dover, 1952
Edelson, E., *Parents' Guide to Science,* Crowell, 1966*
Gray, D. E., and J. W. Coutts, *Man and His Physical World,* 3d ed., Van Nostrand, 1958

Harrison, G. R., *The Role of Science in Our Modern World,* Apollo, 1961 (pap.)*
Hogben, L., *Science for the Citizen,* rev. ed., Norton, 1957*
Hutchings, E. M., Jr., and others, eds., *Frontiers in Science,* Basic Books, 1958*
Jaffe, B., *Men of Science in America,* rev. ed., Simon and Schuster, 1958*
Jones, W. T., *The Sciences and the Humanities; Conflict and Reconciliation,* California, 1965*
Keenan, B. R., ed., *Science and the University,* Columbia, 1966*
Laurence, W. L., *New Frontiers of Science,* Bantam, 1964*
Moulton, F. R., and J. J. Schifferes, eds., *Autobiography of Science,* rev. ed., Doubleday, 1960
Newman, J. R., ed., *What is Science?,* Simon and Schuster, 1955 (also pap.)*
Piel, G. *Science in the Cause of Man,* Knopf, 1961 (Vintage, pap.)*
Platt, John R., *The Excitement of Science,* Houghton, 1962 (pap.)*
Sullivan, W., *Assault on the Unknown: The International Geophysical Year,* McGraw-Hill, 1961
Thomson, G., *The Foreseeable Future,* Viking, 1960 (pap.)*
Wright, H., and S. Rapport, eds., *Great Adventures in Science,* Harper, 1956*

ASTRONOMY

GENERAL

Abetti, G., *The History of Astronomy,* Abelard-Schuman, 1952
Baker, R. H., *Astronomy,* 8th ed., Van Nostrand, 1964
Bergamini, D., and others, *The Universe,* Time-Life, 1962
Bondi, H., *Universe at Large,* Doubleday, 1960 (pap.)
Chamberlain, Joseph, *Time and the Stars,* Doubleday, 1964*
Danby, J. M. A., *Fundamentals of Celestial Mechanics,* Macmillan, 1962
Hoyle, F., *Astronomy,* Doubleday, 1962*
Hoyle, F., *Frontiers of Astronomy,* Harper, 1955 (also pap.)*
Hoyle, F., *Of Men and Galaxies,* Washington, 1964*

Inglis, S. J., *Planets, Stars and Galaxies,* Wiley, 1961
Jones, H. S., *General Astronomy,* 4th ed., St. Martin's, 1962
Kuhn, T. S., *Copernican Revolution,* Harvard, 1957 (Random House, pap.)
Moore, P., *The Picture History of Astronomy,* Grosset, 1964*
Neugebauer, Otto, *The Exact Sciences in Antiquity,* Harper, 1962
Pannekoek, A., *A History of Astronomy,* Interscience, 1961
Rudaux, L., and G. De Vaucouleurs, eds., *Larousse Encyclopedia of Astronomy,* Putnam, 1959
Shapley, H., ed., *Source Book in Astronomy, 1900–1950,* Harvard, 1960
Sidgwick, J. B., *Amateur Astronomer's Handbook,* 2d ed., Macmillan, 1961

Struve, Otto, Beverly Lynds and Helen Pillans, *Elementary Astronomy,* Oxford, 1959
Struve, Otto, *The Universe,* M.I.T., 1962
Wallenquist, A., *Dictionary of Astronomical Terms,* Natural History, 1966

SOLAR SYSTEM

Alexander, A. F. O'D., *Planet Saturn,* Macmillan, 1962
Alter, Dinsmore, ed., *Lunar Atlas,* Dover, 1966
Baldwin, Ralph B., *The Measure of the Moon,* Chicago, 1963
Blackwell, D. E., "Zodiacal Light," *Sci. Amer.,* Jul. 1960*
Blanco, V. M., and S. W. McCuskey, *Basic Physics of the Solar System,* Addison-Wesley, 1961

Chamberlain, J. W., *Physics of the Aurora and Airglow,* Academic, 1961

Hawkins, G. S., *Meteors, Comets, and Meteorites,* McGraw-Hill, 1964*

Jackson, Joseph H., *Pictorial Guide to the Planets,* Crowell, 1965*

Kaiser, T. R., ed., *Meteors,* Pergamon, 1955

Kopal, Zdeněk, *The Moon: Our Nearest Celestial Neighbor,* 2d ed., Academic, 1963

Kuiper, G. P., ed., *Solar System: vol. I, The Sun,* 1953; vol. II, *Earth as a Planet,* 1954; vol. III, *Planets and Satellites,* 1961 (B. M. Middlehurst also ed.); vol. IV, *Moon, Meteorites, and Comets,* 1963, Chicago

Mason, B., *Meteorites,* Wiley, 1962

Menzel, D. H., *Our Sun,* rev. ed., Harvard, 1959

Moore, P., *Planets,* Norton, 1962*

Moore, P., *Survey of the Moon,* Norton, 1962*

Nininger, H. H., *Out of the Sky,* Dover, 1959 (pap.)*

Sagan, D., and others: *Planets,* Time-Life, 1966*

Stumpff, K., *Planet Earth,* Michigan, 1959* (also pap.)

Whipple, Fred L., *Earth, Moon and Planets* (rev. ed.), Harvard, 1963

Zirin, Harold, *The Solar Atmosphere,* Blaisdell, 1966

STARS, GALAXIES, NEBULAE, AND COSMOLOGY

Alfvén, Hannes, *Worlds-Antiworlds: Antimatter in Cosmology,* Freeman, 1966

Aller, L. H., *Gaseous Nebulae,* Wiley, 1956

Bok, B. J., and P. F. Bok, *The Milky Way,* 3d ed., Harvard, 1957*

Bondi, H., and others, *Rival Theories of Cosmology,* Oxford, 1960*

Hoyle, Fred, *Galaxies, Nuclei, and Quasars,* Harper, 1965*

Kopal, Z., *Close Binary Systems,* Wiley, 1959

McVittie, G. C., *General Relativity and Cosmology,* 2d ed., Illinois, 1965

Morrison, P., "Neutrino Astronomy," *Sci. Amer.,* Aug. 1961*

Munitz, M. K., ed., *Theories of the Universe,* Macmillan, 1957 (also pap.)

Schwarzschild, M., *Structure and Evolution of the Stars,* Princeton, 1958 (Dover, pap.)

Shapley, H., *Galaxies,* rev. ed., Harvard, 1961

OBSERVATION: EQUIPMENT AND TECHNIQUES

Hawkins, Gerald S., *Stonehenge Decoded,* Doubleday, 1965*

Ingalls, A. G., *Amateur Telescope Making,* 4th ed., *Sci. Amer.,* 1943

King, H. C., *The History of the Telescope,* Sky, 1955*

Kuiper, G. P., and B. Middlehurst, eds., *Telescopes,* Chicago, 1960

Mayall, N., and others, *The Sky Observer's Guide,* Golden, 1965 (pap.)*

Miczaika, G. R., and W. M. Sinton, *Tools of the Astronomer,* Harvard, 1961*

Texereau, J., *How to Make a Telescope,* Wiley, 1957* (Doubleday, pap.)

Zim, H., and R. H. Baker, *Stars,* Golden, 1956 (also pap.)*

RADIO ASTRONOMY

Kraus, John, *Radio Astronomy,* McGraw-Hill, 1966

Piddington, J. H., *Radio Astronomy,* Harper, 1962*

Smith, Alexander G., and Carr, Thomas D., *Radio Exploration of the Planetary System,* Van Nostrand, 1964 (pap.)

Vaucouleurs, G. de, *Astronomical Photography,* Macmillan, 1962*

SPACE EXPLORATION

(See also "Space" listings on Technology list and "General" listings on Biology list)

Berman, A. I., *Physical Principles of Astronautics,* Wiley, 1961

Clarke, A. C., *Exploration of Space,* rev. ed., Harper, 1959 (Fawcett, pap.)*

Clarke, A. C., and others, *Man and Space,* Time-Life, 1964*

EXTRATERRESTRIAL LIFE

Dole, Stephen, and Isaac Asimov, *Planets for Man,* Random, 1964*

Jones, H. S., *Life on Other Worlds,* 2d ed., Macmillan, 1954 (N.A.L., pap.)*

Shklovsky, I. S., and Carl Sagan, *Intelligent Life in the Universe,* Holden-Day, 1966*

Young, R. S., *Extraterrestrial Biology,* Holt, 1966 (pap.)

BIOCHEMISTRY AND BIOPHYSICS

GENERAL

Ackerman, E., *Biophysical Science,* Prentice-Hall, 1962

Asimov, I., *Life and Energy,* Doubleday, 1962

Baldwin, E., *The Nature of Biochemistry,* Cambridge, 1962 (also pap.)

Bonner, J., and J. Varner, eds., *Plant Biochemistry,* Academic, 1965

Borek, E., *Man, the Chemical Machine,* Columbia, 1952

Bourne, G. H., *Division of Labor in Cells,* Academic, 1962 (pap.)

Brachet, J., *Biochemical Cytology,* Academic, 1957

Chambers, R. W., and A. S. Payne, *From Cell to Test Tube: The Science of Biochemistry,* Scribner's, 1960 (also pap.)

Florkin, M., *Unity and Diversity in Biochemistry: An Introduction to Chemical Biology,* Pergamon, 1960

Fox, S. W., and J. F. Foster, *Introduction to Protein Chemistry,* Wiley, 1957

Harrison, K., *Guide-Book to Biochemistry,* 2d ed., Cambridge, 1965 (also pap.)

Harrow, B., and A. Mazur, *Textbook of Biochemistry,* 9th ed., Saunders, 1966

Hawk, P. B., *Physiological Chemistry,* 14th ed., McGraw-Hill, 1965

Loewy, A., and P. Siekevitz, *Cell Structure and Function,* Holt, 1963

Long, C., and others, eds., *Biochemists' Handbook,* Van Nostrand, 1961

Lotka, A. J., *Elements of Mathematical Biology,* Dover, 1957 (pap.)

McElroy, W. D., *Cell Physiology and Biochemistry,* 2d ed., Prentice-Hall, 1964 (also pap.)

Moore, R., *The Coil of Life,* Knopf, 1961

Neilands, J. B., and P. K. Stumpf, *Outlines of Enzyme Chemistry,* 2d ed., Wiley, 1958

Oncley, J. R., ed., *Biophysical Science,* Wiley, 1959

Stanley, W. M., and E. G. Valens, *Viruses and the Nature of Life,* Dutton, 1961 (also pap.)

Wald, G., "Innovation in Biology," *Sci. Amer.,* Sep. 1958

CELLULAR BIOCHEMISTRY

Albanese, A. A., ed., *Protein and Amino Acid Nutrition,* Academic, 1959

Brachet, J., "The Living Cell," *Sci. Amer.,* Sep. 1961*

Calvin, M., and J. A. Bassham, *Photosynthesis of Carbon Compounds,* Benjamin, 1962 (pap.)

Changeux, J. P., "The Control of Biochemical Reactions," *Sci. Amer.,* April 1965

Comar, C. L., and F. Bronner, eds., *Mineral Metabolism,* Academic, 2 vol., 1960–1963

de Duve, C., "The Lysosome," *Sci. Amer.,* May 1963

Fieser, L. F., "Steroids," *Sci. Amer.,* Jan. 1955*

Gross, J., "Collagen," *Sci. Amer.,* May 1961*

Hanahan, D. J., *Lipide Chemistry,* Wiley, 1960

Hokin, L. & M., "Chemistry of Cell Membranes," *Sci. Amer.,* Oct. 1965

Huxley, H. E., "Mechanism of Muscle Contraction," *Sci. Amer.,* Dec. 1965

Kamen, M. D., *Primary Processes in Photosynthesis,* Academic, 1963 (pap.)

Lehringer, A. L., *The Mitochondrion,* Benjamin, 1964 (pap.)

Meister, A., *Biochemistry of the Amino Acids,* 2d ed., 2 vol., Academic, 1965

Perutz, M. F., "The Hemoglobin Molecule," *Sci. Amer.,* Nov. 1964

Phillips, D. C., "Three-Dimensional Structure of an Enzyme Molecule," *Sci. Amer.,* Nov. 1966

Porter, K. R., and C. Franzini-Armstrong, "The Sarcoplasmic Reticulum," *Sci. Amer,* Mar. 1965

Racker, E., *Mechanisms in Bioenergetics,* Academic, 1965 (pap.)

Schmitt, F. O., "Giant Molecules in Cells and Tissues," *Sci. Amer.,* Sep. 1957*

Stein, W. H., and S. Moore, "The Chemical Structure of Proteins," *Sci. Amer.,* Feb. 1961*

Stumpf, P. K., "ATP," *Sci. Amer.,* Apr. 1953*

Thompson, E. O. P., "The Insulin Molecule," *Sci. Amer.,* May 1955*

Wald, G., "Life and Light," *Sci. Amer.,* Oct. 1959*

Zamecnik, P. C., "The Microsome," *Sci. Amer.,* Mar. 1958*

CHEMISTRY OF REPRODUCTION

Cairns, J., "The Bacterial Chromosome," *Sci. Amer.,* Jan. 1966

Crick, F. H. C., "The Genetic Code," *Sci. Amer.,* Oct. 1966

Davidson, J. N., *Biochemistry of the Nucleic Acids,* 4th ed., Wiley, 1960

Fraenkel-Conrat, H., *Design and Function at the Threshold of Life; The Viruses,* Academic, 1962 (also pap.)

Fraenkel-Conrat, H., "Genetic Code of a Virus," *Sci. Amer.,* Oct. 1964

Holley, R. W., "Nucleotide Sequence of a Nucleic Acid," *Sci. Amer.,* Feb. 1966

Rich, A., "Polyribosomes," *Sci. Amer.,* Dec. 1963

Spiegelman, S., "Hybrid Nucleic Acids," *Sci. Amer.,* May 1964

Taylor, J. H., "The Duplication of Chromosomes," *Sci. Amer.,* Jun. 1958*

Zuckerkandl, E., "The Evolution of Hemoglobin," *Sci. Amer.,* May 1965

Gray, G. W., "Electrophoresis," *Sci. Amer.,* Dec., 1951*

Gray, G. W., "The Ultracentrifuge," *Sci. Amer.,* Jun. 1961*

Kamen, M. D., "Tracers," *Sci. Amer.,* Feb. 1949*

Shedlovsky, T., ed., *Electrochemistry in Biology and Medicine,* Wiley, 1955

Stein, W. H., and S. Moore, "Chromatography," *Sci. Amer.,* Mar. 1951*

LABORATORY TECHNIQUES

Broda, E., *Radioactive Isotopes in Biochemistry,* Elsevier, 1960

BIOLOGY (See also BIOCHEMISTRY and BIOPHYSICS)

GENERAL

Abercrombie, M., and others, *Dictionary of Biology,* Aldine, 1951 (Penguin, pap.)

Asimov, Isaac, *Short History of Biology,* Doubleday, 1964*

Darwin, C., *The Voyage of the Beagle,* ed., abridged with commentary by M. E. Selsam, Harper, 1959

Frisch, Karl von, *Man and the Living World,* Harcourt, 1963*

Gabriel, M., and S. Fogel, eds., *Great Experiments in Biology,* Prentice-Hall, 1955

Hanrahan, J. S., and D. Bushnell, *Space Biology,* Basic Books, 1960

Hardin, Garrett, *Biology: Its Principles and Implications,* 2d ed., Freeman, 1966

Henderson, I. F., and W. D., *Dictionary of Biological Terms,* 8th ed. by J. H. Kenneth, Van Nostrand, 1963

Jaeger, E. C., *Source-Book of Biological Names and Terms,* 3d ed., Thomas, 1959

Moore, J. A., ed., *Ideas in Modern Biology,* Doubleday, 1965

Nordenskiold, E., *History of Biology,* Tudor, 1960

Otto, J. H. and A. Towle, *Modern Biology,* Holt, 1966*

Savory, Theodore, *Naming the Living World,* Wiley, 1963*

Simpson, G. G., and others, *Life: An Introduction to Biology,* 2d ed., Harcourt, 1965 (also pap.)

Singer, C., *A History of Biology,* rev. ed., Abelard-Schuman, 1959

Slager, U. T., *Space Medicine,* Prentice-Hall, 1962

Telfer, William, and Donald Kennedy, *The Biology of Organisms,* Wiley, 1965

Zim, H. S., and others, Golden Nature Guide series, Golden, New York*

ANIMALS

Allen, G. M., *Bats* (1939), Dover, (pap.)*

American Ornithologists' Union, *Check-list of North American Birds,* 5th ed., A.O.U., 1957

Austin, O. L., *Birds of the World,* Golden, 1961*

Bent, Arthur C., *Life Histories of North American Birds,* Dover, 1961–1965, 23 vol. (pap.)*

Blackwelder, Richard E., *Classification of the Animal Kingdom,* Southern Illinois, 1963 (pap.)

Borror, D. J., and D. M. DeLong, *Introduction to the Study of Insects,* rev. ed., Holt, 1964

Bouliére, F., *The Natural History of Mammals,* Knopf, 1954*

Buchsbaum, R., *Animals Without Backbones:*

An Introduction to the Invertebrates, rev. ed., Chicago, 1948*

Buchsbaum, R. and M., and L. and M. Milne, *Lower Animals; Living Invertebrates of the World,* Doubleday, 1960*

Cloudsley-Thompson, J. L., *Spiders, Scorpions, Centipedes, and Mites,* Pergamon, 1958*

Cochran, D. M., *Living Amphibians of the World,* Doubleday, 1961*

Cockrum, E. L., *Introduction to Mammalogy,* Ronald, 1962

Comstock, J. H., *The Spider Book,* rev. by W. J. Gertsch, Comstock, 1948*

Conant, R., *Field Guide to Amphibians and Reptiles,* Harcourt, 1958*

Curtis, B., *The Life Story of the Fish,* 2d ed., Harcourt, 1949 (Dover, pap.)*

Engel, Fritz-Martin, *Life Around Us: The Strange Planet Earth and the Stranger Creatures That Live on It,* Crowell, 1966*

Herald, E., *Living Fishes of the World,* Doubleday, 1961*

Lanham, U., *Fishes,* Columbia, 1962*

Laycock, G., *The Alien Animals,* Nat. Hist., 1966*

Marshall, A. J., ed., *Biology and Comparative Physiology of Birds,* Academic, 2 vol., 1960–1961

Marshall, N. B., *The Life of Fishes,* World, 1966*

Michener, C. D., *American Social Insects,* Van Nostrand, 1951*

Moment, G. B., *General Zoology,* 2d ed., Houghton, 1967

Morris, D., *The Mammals: A Guide to the Living Species,* Harper, 1965*

Ommanney, F. D., *A Draught of Fishes,* Crowell, 1966*

Palmer, R. S., *Mammal Guide; Mammals of North America North of Mexico,* Doubleday, 1954*

Pennak, R. W., *Freshwater Invertebrates of the United States,* Ronald, 1953*

Peterson, R. T., *Field Guide to the Birds,* rev. ed., Houghton, 1947*

Peterson, R. T., *Field Guide to Western Birds,* rev. ed., Houghton, 1961*

Pope, C. H., *Reptile World: a Natural History of the Snakes, Lizards, Turtles and Crocodilians,* Knopf, 1955*

Romer, A. S., *Man and the Vertebrates,* Penguin, 2 vol., 1954 (pap.)

Sanderson, I., *Living Mammals of the World,* Doubleday, 1955*

Saunders, A. A., *Guide to Bird Songs,* Doubleday, 1951*

Schmidt, K. P., and R. F. Inger, *Living Reptiles of the World,* Doubleday, 1957*

Scientific American, eds. of, *Twentieth Century Bestiary,* Simon & Schuster, 1956 (pap.)

Snodgrass, R. E., *Textbook of Arthropod Anatomy,* Hafner, 1952

Storer, T. I., and R. L. Usinger, *General Zoology,* 4th ed., McGraw-Hill, 1965

Swain, R. B., *Insect Guide: Orders and Major Families of North American Insects,* Doubleday, 1948*

Thomson, A. L., ed., *A New Dictionary of Birds,* McGraw-Hill, 1964*

Van Tyne, J., and A. J. Berger, *Fundamentals of Ornithology,* Wiley, 1959

Walker, Ernest P., *Mammals of the World,* Johns Hopkins, 3 vol., 1964

Wilbur, K. M., and C. M. Yonge, eds., *Physiology of Mollusca,* vol. 1, Academic, 1964

Wolfson, A., ed., *Recent Studies in Avian Biology,* Illinois, 1955

ANATOMY AND PHYSIOLOGY

Asimov, Isaac, *The Human Body: Its Structure and Operation,* Houghton, 1963*

Bartley, S. H., *Fatigue,* Thomas, 1965

Bloom, W., and D. W. Fawcett, *Textbook of Histology,* 8th ed., Saunders, 1963

Boyd, W. C., *Fundamentals of Immunology,* 3d ed., Wiley, 1956

Brown, F. A., Jr., *Biological Clocks,* Heath, 1962*

Burnet, F. M., *The Integrity of the Body,* Harvard, 1962*

Carlson, A. J., and V. E. Johnson, *Machinery of the Body,* 5th ed., Chicago, 1961*

Comfort, A., *The Biology of Senescence,* Holt, 1964*

Comfort, A., "The Life Span of Animals," *Sci. Amer.,* Jul. 1961*

Cowdry, E. V., *A Textbook of Histology,* 4th ed., Saunders, 1952

Fenn, W. O., "Mechanism of Breathing," *Sci. Amer.,* Jan. 1960*

Fox, H. H., and G. Vevers, *The Nature of Animal Colors,* Macmillan, 1960*

Galambos, Robert, *Nerves and Muscles,* Anchor, 1962 (pap.)*

Geldard, F. A., *Human Senses,* Wiley, 1953

Gray, H., *Anatomy of the Human Body,* 27th ed., Lea, 1966

Gray, J., *How Animals Move,* rev. ed., Cambridge, 1959 (pap.)*

Harvey, E. N., *Bioluminescence,* Academic, 1952

Hoar, W. S., *General and Comparative Physiology,* Prentice-Hall, 1966

Horrobin, David F., *The Communication Systems of the Body,* Basic Books, 1964

Houssay, B. A., and others, *Human Physiology,* 2d ed., McGraw-Hill, 1955

Kare, M., and B. P. Halpern, eds., *Physiological and Behavioral Aspects of Taste,* Chicago, 1961

Luce, G. G., and J. Segal, *Sleep*, Coward-McCann, 1966*

McElroy, W. D., and H. H. Seliger, "Biological Luminescence," *Sci. Amer.*, Dec. 1962*

McLean, F. C., and M. R. Urist, *Bone: An Introduction to the Physiology of Skeletal Tissue*, rev. ed., Chicago, 1961

Mendelsohn, Everett, *Heat and Life: The Development of the Theory of Animal Heat*, Harvard, 1964

Milne, L. and M., *Senses of Animals and Men*, Atheneum, 1962*

Montagna, W., *Structure and Function of Skin*, Academic, 1961

Prosser, C. L., and F. A. Brown, Jr., *Comparative Animal Physiology*, 2d ed., Saunders, 1961

Ranson, S. W., *Anatomy of the Nervous System*, 10th ed., Saunders, 1959

Rubinstein, Max R., *You and Your Hormones*, Twayne, 1960*

Ruth, T. C., and H. D. Patton, ed., *Howell and Fulton, Physiology and Biophysics*, 19th ed., Saunders, 1965

Scheer, Bradley T., *Animal Physiology*, Wiley, 1963

Smith, H. W., *Principles of Renal Physiology*, Oxford, 1956

Sollberger, A., *Biological Rhythm Research*, Elsevier, 1965

Suckling, E. E., *Bioelectricity*, McGraw-Hill, 1961

Williams, R. H., ed., *Textbook of Endocrinology*, 3d ed., Saunders, 1962

Wright, R. H., *The Science of Smell*, Basic Books, 1964

Young, J. Z., *A Model of the Brain*, Oxford, 1964

BEHAVIOR AND LEARNING

Armstrong, Edward A., *Bird Display and Behavior: An Introduction to the Study of Bird Psychology*, Dover, 1965 (pap.)

Beck, S. D., *Animal Photoperiodism*, Holt, 1963 (also pap.)

Carthy, J. D., *Animal Navigation*, Scribner's, 1956 (also pap.)*

Carthy, J. D., *The Behavior of Arthropods*, Freeman, 1965 (pap.)

Carthy, J. D., and F. J. Ebling, eds., *The Natural History of Aggression*, Academic, 1964

Fraenkel, G. S., and D. L. Gunn, *The Orientation of Animals*, Dover, 1960 (pap.)

Frings, H. and M., *Animal Communication*, Blaisdell, 1964 (pap.)

Griffin, Donald R., *Listening in the Dark: The Acoustic Orientation of Bats and Men*, Yale, 1958*

Howard, E., *Territory in Bird Life*, reissue of 1920 ed. with foreword summarizing recent work, Atheneum, 1965

Kare, M., and B. P. Halpern, eds., *Physiological and Behavioral Aspects of Taste*, Chicago, 1961

Kellogg, W. N., *Porpoises and Sonar*, Chicago, 1961 (also pap.)*

Lorenz, K. Z., *King Solomon's Ring*, Crowell, 1952*

Ribbands, C. R., *Behavior and Social Life of Honeybees*, Dover, 1953

Roe, A., and G. G. Simpson, *Behavior and Evolution*, Yale, 1958

Schaller, G. B., *The Year of the Gorilla*, Chicago, 1964 (also pap.)*

Scott, J. P., *Animal Behavior*, Chicago, 1958

Thorpe, W. H., *Learning and Instinct in Animals*, Harvard, 1963

Tinbergen, N., *Social Behavior in Animals*, Wiley, 1965

Tinbergen, N., *The Study of Instinct*, Oxford, 1951

Viand, G., *Intelligence, Its Evolution and Forms*, Harper, 1960*

Von Frisch, K., *The Dancing Bees*, Harcourt, 1955*

Wheeler, W. M., *Social Life Among the Insects*, Harcourt, 1923

Williams, Carrington B., *Insect Migration*, Macmillan, 1958*

REPRODUCTION, DEVELOPMENT, GROWTH

Asdell, S. A., *Patterns of Mammalian Reproduction*, 2d ed., Cornell

Austin, C. R., *Fertilization*, Prentice-Hall, 1965

Balinsky, B. I., *Introduction to Embryology*, Saunders, 1960

Berrill, N. J., *Growth, Development, and Pattern*, Freeman, 1961

Berrill, N. J., *Sex and the Nature of Things*, Dodd, 1953 (Pocket Books, pap.)*

Bonner, J. T., *Morphogenesis*, Princeton, 1952 (Atheneum, pap.)*

Goodrich, E. S., *Studies on the Structure and Development of Vertebrates*, Dover, 1958 (pap.)

Snodgrass, R. E., *Insect Metamorphosis*, Smithsonian Institution, 1954 (Its Miscellaneous Collections, vol. 122, no. 9)*

Sussman, M., *Animal Growth and Development*, Prentice-Hall, 1960 (also pap.)

Thompson, D. W., *Growth and Form*, abr. ed., Cambridge, 1961

Wigglesworth, V. B., *Control of Growth and Form*, Cornell, 1954

PLANTS

Alexopoulos, G., *Introductory Mycology*, 2d ed., Wiley, 1962*

Beale, J. H., *Evergreens*, Doubleday, 1960*

Bold, Harold C., *The Plant Kingdom*, 2d ed., Prentice-Hall, 1964

Chapman, Valentine J., *The Algae*, St. Martin's, 1962

Christensen, Clyde M., *The Molds and Man: An Introduction to the Fungi*, 3rd ed., Minnesota, 1965

Cobb, B., *A Field Guide to the Ferns*, Houghton, 1956*

Cochrane, V. W., *Physiology of the Fungi*, Wiley, 1958

Core, E., *Plant Taxonomy*, Prentice-Hall, 1955

Crocker, W., and L. V. Barton, *Physiology of Seeds*, Ronald, 1953

Dawson, E. Y., *Marine Botany: An Introduction*, Holt, 1966

Dittmar, H. J., *Phylogeny and Form in the Plant Kingdom*, Van Nostrand, 1964

Galston, A. W., *Life of the Green Plant*, 2d ed., Prentice-Hall, 1964 (also pap.)*

Gray, Asa, *Gray's Manual of Botany*, 8th ed., American, 1950

Hylander, C. J., *World of Plant Life*, 2d ed., Macmillan, 1956*

Johansen, D. A., *Plant Embryology*, Ronald, 1950

Kingsbury, John M., *Poisonous Plants of the United States and Canada*, Prentice-Hall, 1964

Leopold, A. C., *Auxins and Plant Growth*, California, 1955

Lloyd, F. E., *Carnivorous Plants*, Ronald, 1942*

Meyer, B. S., and others, *Introduction to Plant Physiology*, Van Nostrand, 1960*

Petrides, G. A., *Field Guide to the Trees and Shrubs*, Houghton, 1958*

Quer, F. P., *Anatomy of Plants*, Harper, 1960

Ramsbottom, J., *Mushrooms and Toadstools*, Collins, 1954*

Rickett, H. W., *Wild Flowers of the United States, Vol. I, in Two Parts: The Northeastern States*, McGraw-Hill, 1966*

Rosenberg, Jerome L., *Photosynthesis: The Basic Process of Food-Making in Green Plants*, Holt, 1965

Scientific American, eds. of, *Plant Life*, Simon & Schuster, 1957 (pap.)

Scott, B. I. H., "Electricity in Plants," *Sci. Amer.*, Oct. 1962*

Sinnott, E. W., *Plant Morphogenesis*, McGraw-Hill, 1960

Sinnott, E. W., and K. S. Wilson, *Botany*, 6th ed., McGraw-Hill, 1962*

Smith, G. M., *Fresh-Water Algae of the United States*, 2d ed., McGraw-Hill, 1950

Sterling, Dorothy, *Story of Mosses, Ferns and Mushrooms*, Doubleday, 1955*

U. S. Dept. of Agriculture, *Grass; the Yearbook of Agriculture, 1948*, U. S. Gov. Printing Office, 1948*

U. S. Dept. of Agriculture, *Trees; the Yearbook of Agriculture, 1949*, U. S. Gov. Printing Office, 1949*

Van Overbeek, Johannes, and Harry K. Wong, *The Lore of Living Plants*, Nat. Sci. Teachers Assn., 1964 (pap.)*

Winthrow, Robert B., ed., *Photoperiodism and Related Phenomena in Plants and Animals*, A.A.A.S., 1959

CELLS AND MICROORGANISMS

Bell, Thomas M., *An Introduction to General Virology*, Lippincott, 1965

Bonner, J. T., *Cells and Societies*, Princeton, 1955 (Atheneum, pap.)

Brachet, J., and A. E. Mirsky, eds., *Cells: Biochemistry, Physiology, Morphology*, Academic, 5 vol., 1959–64

Burnet, F. M., and W. M. Stanley, eds., *The Viruses*, Academic, 3 vol., 1959

Dubos, Rene, *The Unseen World*, Rockefeller, 1962*

Frobisher, M., *Fundamentals of Microbiology*, 7th ed., Saunders, 1963*

Hall, Richard P., *Protozoa: The Simplest of all Animals*, Holt, 1964*

Pfeiffer, John, and Eds. of Life, *The Cell*, Time-Life, 1964*

Picken, L. E. R., *The Organization of Cells and Other Organisms*, Oxford, 1960

Roman, W., ed., *Yeasts*, Academic, 1957

Salle, A. J., *Fundamental Principles of Bacteriology*, 5th ed., McGraw-Hill, 1961

Scientific American, eds. of, *The Living Cell*, Freeman, 1965

Swanson, C. P., *The Cell*, Prentice-Hall, 1960 (also pap.)

Weidel, Wolfhard, *Virus*, Michigan, 1959 (pap.)*

ECOLOGY, BIOGEOGRAPHY, CONSERVATION

Allen, D., *Our Wildlife Legacy*, 2d ed., Funk, 1962*

Andrewartha, H. G., *Study of Animal Populations*, Chicago, 1961

Baer, J. G., *Ecology of Animal Parasites,* Illinois, 1951

Bates, M., *The Forest and the Sea,* Random, 1960 (also pap.)*

Buchsbaum, R. and M., *Basic Ecology,* Boxwood, 1957 (pap.)

Cameron, T. W. M., *Parasites and Parasitism,* Wiley, 1956

Carson, R. L., *Silent Spring,* Houghton, 1962*

Carson, R. L., *The Sea Around Us,* rev. ed., Oxford, 1961 (N.A.L., pap.)*

Daubenmire, R. F., *Plants and Environment,* 2d ed., Wiley, 1959*

Dowdeswell, W. H., *Animal Ecology,* 2d ed., Methuen, 1959 (Harper, pap.)*

Edmondson, W. T., H. B. Ward, and G. C. Whipple, *Fresh-Water Biology,* 2nd ed., Wiley, 1959

Ekman, S., *Zoogeography of the Sea,* Macmillan, 1953

Elton, C. S., *The Ecology of Invasions by Animals and Plants,* Methuen, 1958*

Farb, Peter, *Ecology,* Time-Life, 1963*

Gleason, Henry A., and Arthur Cronquist, *The Natural Geography of Plants,* Ohio, 1964

Good, R., *Geography of Flowering Plants,* 2d ed., Longmans, 1953

Gunther, K., and K. Decker, *Creatures of the Deep Sea,* George Allen, 1956*

Hardy, A., *The Open Sea,* Houghton, 1956*

Hubbs, C., ed., *Zoogeography,* A.A.A.S., 1958

Jaeger, E. C., *Desert Wildlife,* Stanford, 1961

Klots, E. B., *New Field Book of Freshwater Life,* Putnam, 1966*

Lack, D., *Natural Regulation of Animal Numbers,* Oxford, 1954

Moore, H. B., *Marine Ecology,* Wiley, 1958

Odum, E. P., *Ecology,* Holt, 1963

Oosting, H. J., *Study of Plant Communities,* 2d ed., Freeman, 1956

Polunin, N. V., *Introduction to Plant Geography,* McGraw-Hill, 1960

Portmann, A., *Animal Camouflage,* Michigan, 1959 (also pap.)*

EVOLUTION AND GENETICS

(See also "Chemistry of Reproduction" under BIOCHEMISTRY AND BIOPHYSICS)

Asimov, Isaac, *The Genetic Code,* New American, 1962 (pap.)*

Auerbach, C., *The Science of Genetics,* Harper, 1961 (also pap.)*

Beadle, G., and M. Beadle, *The Language of Life,* Doubleday, 1966*

Clark, W. E. L., *History of the Primates,* Chicago, (pap.), 1966*

Colbert, E. H., *Dinosaurs,* Dutton, 1961*

Colbert, E. H., *Evolution of the Vertebrates,* Wiley, 1955*

Darwin, C., *Origin of Species,* 1859 (many subsequent editions available)

de Beer, G., *Atlas of Evolution,* Nelson, 1965

Dobzhansky, T., *Evolution, Genetics, and Man,* Wiley, 1955 (also pap.)

Dobzhansky, T., *Genetics and the Origin of Species,* 3d ed., Columbia, 1951

Dobzhansky, T., *Mankind Evolving,* Yale, 1962 (also pap.)

Eiseley, L., *Darwin's Century: Evolution and the Men Who Discovered It,* Doubleday, 1958 (also pap.)*

Eiseley, L., *The Firmament of Time,* Atheneum, 1960 (also pap.)*

Eiseley, L., *The Immense Journey,* Random, 1957 (also pap.)*

Fisher, R. A., *Genetical Theory of Natural Selection,* Dover, 1958 (pap.)

Grant, Verne, *The Origin of Adaptations,* Columbia, 1963

Huxley, J. S., *Evolution: The Modern Synthesis,* Harper, 1942

International Symposium on the Origin of Life, *Proceedings:* ed. A. I. Oparin and others, Pergamon, 1957

Mayr, Ernst, *Animal Species and Evolution,* Harvard, 1963

Moody, P., *Introduction to Evolution,* 2d ed., Harper, 1962*

Moore, Ruth, *Man, Time and Fossils: the Story of Evolution,* 2d ed., Knopf, 1961*

Oparin, A. I., *Life, Its Nature, Origin and Development,* Academic, 1961

Oparin, A. I., *Origin of Life on the Earth,* 3d ed., Academic, 1957 (Dover, 2d ed., pap.)

Rensch, B., *Evolution Above the Species Level,* Columbia, 1960

Ryan, F., and R. Sager, *Cell Heredity,* Wiley, 1961

Scheinfeld, A., *Your Heredity and Environment,* Lippincott, 1965*

Simpson, G. G., *Life of the Past,* Yale, 1953 (also pap.)

Simpson, G. G., *Meaning of Evolution,* Yale, 1949 (also pap.)

Srb, A. M., and B. Wallace, *Adaptation,* Prentice-Hall, 1964 (also pap.)

Stebbins, G. L., *Processes of Organic Evolution,* Prentice-Hall, 1966

Stebbins, L., *Variation and Evolution in Plants,* Columbia, 1950

Stern, C., *Principles of Human Genetics,* 2nd ed., Freeman, 1960

Tax, S., ed., *Evolution After Darwin,* Chicago, 3 vol., 1960

Wallace, B., and T. Dobzhansky, *Radiation, Genes and Man,* Holt, 1959*

Whitehouse, H. L. K., *Towards an Understanding of the Mechanism of Heredity,* St. Martin's, 1965

CHEMISTRY

GENERAL

Alexander, W., and A. Street, *Metals in the Service of Man,* Penguin, 1952 (pap.)*

American Chemical Society, *Chemical Nomenclature,* American Chemical Soc., 1953

Berry, A. J., *From Classic to Modern Chemistry,* Cambridge, 1954

Brady, G. S., *Materials Handbook,* 9th ed., McGraw-Hill, 1963

Caron, M., and S. Hutin, *Alchemists,* Grove, 1961

Clark, G. L., and G. G. Hawley, eds., *Encyclopedia of Chemistry,* 2d ed., Reinhold, 1966

Clow, A., and N. L., *The Chemical Revolution,* Batchworth, 1948

Crane, E. J., *Guide to the Literature of Chemistry,* 2d ed., Wiley, 1957

Davis, H. M., *The Chemical Elements,* 3d ed., rev. Glenn Seaborg, Ballantine, 1961 (pap.)

Ewing, G. W., *Instrumental Methods For Chemical Analysis,* 2d ed., McGraw-Hill, 1960

Friend, J. N., *Man and the Chemical Elements,* rev. ed., Scribner's, 1961

Hodgman, C. D., and others, eds., *Handbook of Chemistry and Physics,* Chemical Rubber (Revised frequently)

Holmyard, E. J., *Alchemy,* Penguin, 1957 (pap.)

Jaffe, B., *Crucibles; the Story of Chemistry*
from Ancient Alchemy to Nuclear Fission, rev. ed., Fawcett, 1960 (pap.)

Kent, J. A., ed., *Riegel's Industrial Chemistry,* 6th ed., Reinhold, 1962

Kirk, R. E., and D. F. Othmer, eds., *Encyclopedia of Chemical Technology,* Interscience, 18 vol. Vol. 1 & 2, 1963; vol. 3–5, 1964; vol. 6–8, 1965; 2d ed., vol. 9–18 in prep.

Leicester, H. M., and H. S. Klickstein, *A Source Book in Chemistry 1400–1900,* Harvard, 1952

Lessing, L. P., *Understanding Chemistry,* Wiley, 1959 (N.A.L., pap.)*

Palmer, W. G., *Valency, Classical and Modern,* 2d ed., Cambridge, 1959

Partington, J. R., *A History of Chemistry,* St. Martin's, 4 vol.; 1962–1964

Partington, J. R., *A Short History of Chemistry,* Harper, 1960 (pap.)

Pauling, Linus, *College Chemistry,* 3d ed., Freeman, 1964

Pauling, L., *Nature of the Chemical Bond and the Structure of Molecules and Crystals; an Introduction to Modern Structural Chemistry,* 3d ed., Cornell, 1960

Potter, E. C., *Electrochemistry; Principles and Applications,* St. Martin's, 1961

Read, J., *Through Alchemy to Chemistry,* Harper (pap.)*

Rosin, J., *Reagent Chemicals and Standards,* 5th ed., Van Nostrand, 1961

Seaborg, G. T., and E. G. Valens, *Elements of the Universe,* Dutton, 1958 (pap.)*

Snell and Hilton, *Encyclopedia of Industrial Chemical Analysis,* Wiley, 3 vol., 1966

Watt, G. W., *Basic Concepts in Chemistry,* McGraw-Hill, 1958

Weeks, M. E., *Discovery of the Elements,* 6th ed., Journal of Chemical Education, 1956

Wood, J. H., and C. W. Keenan, *General College Chemistry,* 3d ed., Harper, 1966

INORGANIC CHEMISTRY AND CHEMICAL TECHNOLOGY

Emeleus, H. J., and J. S. Anderson, *Modern Aspects of Inorganic Chemistry,* 3d ed., Van Nostrand, 1960

Ephraim, Fritz, *Inorganic Chemistry,* 6th English ed., Wiley, 1954

Gilreath, E. S., *Fundamental Concepts of Inorganic Chemistry,* McGraw-Hill, 1958

Hildebrand, J. H., and R. E. Powell, *Principles of Chemistry,* 7th ed., Macmillan, 1964

Kaufmann, D. W., *Sodium Chloride; the Production and Properties of Salt and Brine,* Reinhold, 1960

Kingery, W. D., *Introduction to Ceramics,* Wiley, 1960

Martell, A. E., and M. Calvin, *Chemistry of the Metal Chelate Compounds,* Prentice-Hall, 1952

Parkes, G. D., *Mellor's Modern Inorganic Chemistry,* 5th ed., Wiley, 1961

Sauchelli, V., ed., *Chemistry and Technology of Fertilizers*, Reinhold, 1960

Sconce, J. S., ed., *Chlorine; Its Manufacture, Properties and Uses*, Reinhold, 1962

Vinal, G. W., *Storage Batteries*, 4th ed., Wiley, 1955

ORGANIC CHEMISTRY AND CHEMICAL TECHNOLOGY

Astle, M. J., and J. R. Shelton, *Organic Chemistry*, 2d ed., Harper, 1959

Burger, A., *Medicinal Chemistry*, Interscience, 1960

Casey, J. P., *Pulp and Paper*, 2d ed., Wiley, 3 vol., 1960

Fieser, L. F., and M. Fieser, *Advanced Organic Chemistry*, Reinhold, 1961

Frear, D. E. H., *Chemistry of the Pesticides*, 3d ed., Van Nostrand, 1955

Golding, B., *Polymers and Resins; Their Chemistry and Chemical Engineering*, Van Nostrand, 1959

Gowan, J. E., and T. S. Wheeler, *Name Index of Organic Reactions*, 2d ed., Wiley, 1961

Gunther, F. A., and L. R. Jeppson, *Modern Insecticides and World Food Production*, Wiley, 1960

Guthrie, V. B., *Petroleum Products Handbook*, McGraw-Hill, 1960

Hammett, L. P., *Physical Organic Chemistry*, McGraw-Hill, 1940

Heilbron, I., and others, *Dictionary of Organic Compounds*, 4th ed., 5 vol., Oxford

Kirschenbauer, H. G., *Fats and Oils; an Outline of Their Chemistry and Technology*, 2d ed., Reinhold, 1960

Mark, H., and others, *Encyclopedia of Polymer Science and Technology*, 5 vol., Wiley, 1964

Mauersberger, H. R., ed., *Matthews' Textile Fibers; Their Physical, Microscopic and Chemical Properties*, 6th ed., Wiley, 1954

Morton, M., ed., *Introduction to Rubber Technology*, Reinhold, 1959

Natta, G., "Precisely Constructed Polymers," *Sci. Amer.*, Aug. 1961*

Newman, M. S., *Steric Effects in Organic Chemistry*, Wiley, 1956

Noller, C. R., *Chemistry of Organic Compounds*, 3d ed., Saunders, 1965

Pigman, W. W., ed., *Carbohydrates; Chemistry, Biochemistry, Physiology*, Academic, 1957

Pinder, A. R., *Chemistry of the Terpenes*, Wiley, 1960

Press, J. J., ed., *Man-Made Textile Encyclopedia*, Wiley, 1959

Read, J., *Direct Entry to Organic Chemistry*, Harper, 1960 (pap.)

Roberts, J. D., and M. C. Caserio, *Basic Principles of Organic Chemistry*, Benjamin, 1964 (pap.)

Schildknecht, C. E., *Polymer Processes*, Interscience, 1960

Schwartz, A. M., and J. W. Perry, *Surface Active Agents*, Wiley, 2 vol., 1949–1958

Simonds, H. R., and J. M. Church, *Concise Guide to Plastics*, 2d ed., Reinhold, 1963

Venkataraman, K., *Chemistry of Synthetic Dyes*, Academic, 2 vol., 1952

Warth, A. H., *Chemistry and Technology of the Waxes*, 2d ed., Reinhold, 1956

Wilberg, K. B., *Physical Organic Chemistry*, Wiley, 1964

Zeiss, H., *Organometallic Chemistry*, Reinhold, 1960

PHYSICAL AND COLLOID CHEMISTRY

Daniels, F., and R. A. Alberty, *Physical Chemistry*, 2d ed., Wiley, 1961

Durham, K., ed., *Surface Activity and Detergency*, St. Martin's, 1962

Dushman, S., and J. M. Lafferty, *Scientific Foundations of Vacuum Techniques*, 2d ed., Wiley, 1962

Glasstone, Laidler and Eyring, *Theory of Rate Processes*, McGraw-Hill, 1941

Glasstone, S., *Textbook of Physical Chemistry*, 2d ed., Van Nostrand, 1946

Hirschfelder, Curtiss and Bird, *Molecular Theory of Gases and Liquids*, Wiley, 1964

Lewis, G. N. and M. Randall, *Thermodynamics*, 2d ed., by Pitzer and Brewer, McGraw-Hill, 1961

Mysels, K. J., *Introduction to Colloid Chemistry*, Wiley, 1959

Osipow, L. I., *Surface Chemistry; Theory and Industrial Application*, Reinhold, 1962

Partington, J. R., *An Advanced Treatise on Physical Chemistry*, Wiley, 5 vol., 1960

Rideal, E., and J. T. Davies, *Interfacial Phenomena*, 2d ed., Academic, 1963

Van Hook, A., *Crystallization; Theory and Practice*, Reinhold, 1961

METALLURGY

A.S.M., *Metals Handbook*, 8th ed., 5 vol.

Birchenall, C. E., *Physical Metallurgy*, McGraw-Hill, 1959

Bray, J. L., *Non-Ferrous Production Metallurgy*, 2d ed., Wiley, 1947

Camp, J. M., and C. B. Francis, *Making, Shaping, and Treating of Steel*, 6th ed., U. S. Steel Corp., 1951

Committee on Metallurgy, *Engineering Metallurgy*, Pitman, 1957

Evans, U. R., *Corrosion and Oxidation of Metals*, St. Martin's, 1960

Grosvenor, A. W., and G. W. Zuspan, ed., *Basic Metallurgy*, A.S.M., 2 vol., 1957

Hampel, C. A., ed., *Rare Metals Handbook*, 2d ed., Reinhold, 1961

Low, A. H., *Technical Methods of Ore Analysis*, 11th ed., Wiley, 1939

Newton, J., *Extractive Metallurgy*, Wiley, 1959

Williams, R. S., and V. O. Homenberg, *Principles of Metallography*, 5th ed., McGraw-Hill, 1948

Zapffe, C. A., *Stainless Steels*, A.S.M., 1949

CHEMICAL ENGINEERING

Coulson, J. M., and J. F. Richardson, *Chemical Engineering*, Pergamon, 2 vol., 1964

Cremer, H. W., *Chemical Engineering Practice*, Butterworth, 12 vol., 1966

Drew, T. B. and J. W. Hoopes, Jr., *Advances in Chemical Engineering*, Academic, to date 6 vol., 1956

Griswold, J., *Fuels, Combustion and Furnaces*, McGraw-Hill, 1946

Larian, M. G., *Fundamentals of Chemical Engineering Operations*, Prentice-Hall, 1958

Lewis, B., and others, eds., *Combustion Processes*, Princeton, 1956

McCabe, W. L., and J. Smith, *Unit Operations of Chemical Engineering*, McGraw-Hill, 1956

Zenz, F. A., and D. F. Othmer, *Fluidization and Fluid-Particle Systems*, Reinhold, 1960

GEOLOGY, GEOPHYSICS, AND PALEONTOLOGY

GENERAL

Adams, F. D., *Birth and Development of the Geological Sciences* (1938), Dover, 1954 (pap.)

Cloos, Hans, *Conversations with the Earth*, Knopf, 1953*

Fenton, C. L., and M. A. Fenton, *Giants of Geology*, Doubleday, 1952 (also pap.)*

Geikie, Archibald, *Founders of Geology*, 2d ed., 1905, Dover (pap.)

Howell, J. V., ed., *Glossary of Geology*, 2d ed., A.G.I., 1960

Lyell, C., *The Principles of Geology*, 12th ed., Murray, 2 vol., 1875

Mather, K. F., and S. L. Mason, *A Source Book in Geology*, McGraw-Hill, 1939

Moore, R., *The Earth We Live On*, 1956*

White, J. F., *Study of the Earth*, Prentice-Hall, 1962

PHYSICAL GEOLOGY

Billings, M. P., *Structural Geology*, 2d ed., Prentice-Hall, 1954

Bullard, F. M., *Volcanoes in History, in Theory, in Eruption*, Texas, 1962*

Dyson, James, *The World of Ice*, Knopf, 1962*

Emmons, W. H., and others, *Geology: Principles and Processes*, McGraw-Hill, 1960

Flint, R. F., *Glacial and Pleistocene Geology*, Wiley, 1957

Holmes, Arthur, *Principles of Physical Geology*, 2d ed., Ronald, 1965*

Leet, L. Don, and Sheldon Judson, *Physical Geology*, 3d ed., Prentice-Hall

Longwell, C. R., and R. F. Flint, *Introduction to Physical Geology*, 2d ed., Wiley, 1962

Mather, Kirtley G., *The Earth Beneath Us*, Random, 1964*

Shelton, John, *Geology Illustrated*, Freeman, 1966

Sitter, L. U., de, *Structural Geology*, 2d ed., McGraw-Hill, 1963

Strahler, Arthur N., *The Earth Sciences*, Harper, 1963

Trefethen, J. M., *Geology for Engineers*, 2d ed., Van Nostrand, 1958

Wyckoff, Jerome, *Geology*, rev. ed., Golden, 1967 (pap.)*

HISTORICAL GEOLOGY

Beerbower, J. R., *Search for the Past; an Introduction to Paleontology*, Prentice-Hall, 1960

Colbert, E. H., *Dinosaurs*, Dutton, 1961*

Colbert, E. H., *Evolution of the Vertebrates*, Science Eds., 1955 (pap.)*

Dunbar, C. O., *Historical Geology*, 2nd ed., Wiley, 1960

Dunbar, C. O., and J. Rodgers, *Principles of Stratigraphy*, Wiley, 1957

Erdtmann, G., *Introduction to Palynology*, Ronald, 2 vol., 1952–1958

Fenton, C. L., and M. A. Fenton, *The Fossil Book*, Doubleday, 1959*

Kay, Marshall, and Colbert, E. H., *Stratigraphy and Life History*, Wiley, 1964

Krumbein, W. C., and L. L. Sloss, *Stratigraphy and Sedimentation*, 2d ed., Freeman, 1961

Kummel, B., *History of the Earth,* Freeman, 1961

Matthews, W. H., *Fossils: An Introduction to Prehistoric Life,* Barnes, 1962

Shimer, H. W., and R. R. Shrock, *Index Fossils of North America,* M.I.T., 1944

Shrock, R. R., and W. H. Twenhofel, *Principles of Invertebrate Paleontology,* McGraw-Hill, 1953

Simpson, G. G., *Life of the Past,* Yale, 1953* (also pap.)*

Weller, J. M., *Stratigraphic Principles and Practice,* Harper, 1960

MINERALOGY, PETROLOGY, AND GEOCHEMISTRY

Barth, T. F. W., *Theoretical Petrology,* 2nd ed., Wiley, 1962

Bateman, A. M., *Economic Mineral Deposits,* 2d ed., Wiley, 1950

Berry, L. G., and B. Mason, *Mineralogy,* Freeman, 1959

Cameron, E. N., *Ore Microscopy,* Wiley, 1961

Dana, E. S., and C. S. Hurlbut, *Manual of Mineralogy,* 17th rev. ed., Wiley, 1959

Dana, E. S., *System of Mineralogy,* 7th ed., Wiley, 3 vol., 1944–1962

Faul, H., ed., *Nuclear Geology,* Wiley, 1954

Fenton, C. L., and M. A. Fenton, *The Rock Book,* Doubleday, 1940*

Mason, B., *Principles of Geochemistry,* 2d ed., Wiley, 1958

Moorhouse, W. W., *The Study of Rocks in Thin Section,* Harper, 1959

Sinkankas, J., *Gemstones of North America,* Van Nostrand, 1959

Smith, O. C., *Identification and Qualitative Chemical Analysis of Minerals,* 2d ed., Van Nostrand, 1953

Wahlstrom, E. E., *Optical Crystallography,* 3d ed., Wiley, 1960

Winchell, A. N., *Elements of Optical Mineralogy,* Wiley, 3 vol., 1937–1951

Young, G. J., *Elements of Mining,* 4th ed., McGraw-Hill, 1946

GEOCHRONOLOGY

Faul, Henry, *Ages of Rocks, Planets, and Stars,* McGraw-Hill, 1966

Hurley, P. M., *How Old Is the Earth?* Doubleday, 1959 (pap.)*

Libby, W. F., *Radiocarbon Dating,* 2nd ed., Chicago, 1955 (also pap.)

Zeuner, F. E., *Dating the Past,* 4th ed., Hafner, 1964

GEOMORPHOLOGY

Cotton, C. A., *Volcanoes as Landscape Forms,* Wiley, 1952

Fenneman, Nevin, *Physiography of Eastern United States,* McGraw-Hill, 1948

Fenneman, Nevin, *Physiography of the Western United States,* McGraw-Hill, 1931

Guilcher, A., *Coastal and Submarine Morphology,* Wiley, 1958

King, C. A. M., *Beaches and Coasts,* St. Martin's, 1959

Leopold, Luna B., and others, *Fluvial Processes in Geomorphology,* Freeman, 1964

Lobeck, A. K., *Things Maps Don't Tell Us,* Macmillan, 1956*

Miller, V. C., and C. F. Miller, *Photogeology,* McGraw-Hill, 1961

Shimer, J. A., *This Sculptured Earth, The Landscape of America,* Columbia, 1959*

Thornbury, W. D., *Principles of Geomorphology,* Wiley, 1954

Thornbury, W. D., *Regional Geomorphology of the U. S.,* Wiley, 1965

Wyckoff, Jerome, *Rock, Time, and Landforms,* Harper, 1966*

OCEANOGRAPHY AND HYDROLOGY

Bascom, Willard, *Hole in the Bottom of the Sea,* Doubleday*

Bascom, Willard, *Waves and Beaches,* Doubleday, 1964 (pap.)*

Bigelow, H. B., and W. T. Edmondson, *Wind Waves at Sea* (U. S. Hydrographic Office Publ. no. 602), U. S. Government Printing Office, Washington, D. C., 1947

Meinzer, O. E., ed., *Hydrology* (1949), Dover, 1957 (pap.)

Menard, H. W., *Marine Geology of the Pacific,* McGraw-Hill, 1964

Sears, Mary, *Oceanography,* A.A.A.S., 1961

Shepard, F. P., *Submarine Geology,* 2d ed., Harper, 1963

Sverdrup, H. A., and others, *Oceans; Their Physics, Chemistry and General Biology,* Prentice-Hall, 1942

Todd, D. K., *Ground Water Hydrology,* Wiley, 1959

Von Arx, W. S., *Introduction to Physical Oceanography,* Addison-Wesley, 1962

GEOPHYSICS

Bucher, Walter H., *Deformation of the Earth's Crust,* Hafner, 1963

Bullen, Keith E., *Introduction to the Theory of Seismology,* 3d ed., Cambridge, 1963

Dobrin, M. B., *Introduction to Geophysical Prospecting,* 2d ed., McGraw-Hill, 1960

Gutenberg, B., *Physics of the Earth's Interior,* Academic, 1959

Howell, B. F., *Introduction to Geophysics,* McGraw-Hill, 1959

Jacobs, J. A., and others, *Physics and Geology,* McGraw-Hill, 1959

Jeffreys, H., *Earth,* 4th ed., Cambridge, 1959

Richter, C. F., *Elementary Seismology,* Freeman, 1958

U. S. Air Force, *Handbook of Geophysics,* rev. ed., Macmillan, 1960

FIELD GUIDES

Lahee, F. H., *Field Geology,* 6th ed., McGraw-Hill, 1961

Pough, F. H., *Field Guide to Rocks and Minerals,* Houghton, 1955*

Rhodes, F. H. T.; H. S. Zim, and P. R. Shaffer, *Fossils,* Golden, 1962*

Zim, H. S., and P. R. Shaffer, *Rocks and Minerals,* Golden, 1957 (also pap.)*

HISTORY AND PHILOSOPHY OF SCIENCE

GENERAL

Beveridge, W. I. B., *The Art of Scientific Investigation,* Vintage, 1960 (pap.)

Boas, Marie, *The Scientific Renaissance, 1450–1630,* Harper, 1966

Bohr, N., *Atomic Physics and Human Knowledge,* Wiley, 1958 (also pap.)

Bridgman, P. W., *The Logic of Modern Physics,* Macmillan, 1946 (also pap.)

Butterfield, H., *The Origins of Modern Science, 1300–1800,* rev. ed., Macmillan, 1957 (also pap.)

Campbell, N. R., *Foundations of Science,* Dover, 1957 (pap.)

Carnap, Rudolf, *Philosophical Foundations of Physics,* Martin Gardner, ed., Basic Books, 1966

Clagett, M., *Science of Mechanics in the Middle Ages,* Wisconsin, 1959

Cohen, M. R., and I. E. Drabkin, *Source Book in Greek Science,* Harvard, 1959

Cohen, M. R., and E. Nagel, *Introduction to Logic and Scientific Method,* Harcourt, New York, 1934

Clifford, W. K., *The Common Sense of the Exact Sciences* (1885), ed. J. R. Newman, Knopf, 1946 (Dover, pap.)

Crombie, A. C., *Augustine to Galileo, the History of Science,* 2d ed., Harvard, 2 vol., 1961

Dampier, W., *A History of Science and Its Relations with Philosophy and Religion,* 4th ed., Cambridge, 1948

Danto, Arthur, and Sidney Morgenbesser, *Philosophy of Science,* Meridian, 1960 (pap.)

Dijksterhuis, E. J., *The Mechanization of the World Picture,* Oxford, 1961

Dugas, R., *History of Mechanics,* Central, 1955

Duhem, R., *The Aim and Structure of Physical Theory* (1906), Princeton, 1954

Farrington, B., *Greek Science: Its Meaning for Us,* Penguin, (pap.)

Feigl, H., and M. Brodbeck, eds., *Readings in the Philosophy of Science,* Appleton, 1953

Feigl, H., and W. Sellars, eds., *Readings in Philosophical Analysis,* Appleton, 1949

Frank, Philipp, *Modern Science and Its Philosophy,* Collier, 1961 (pap.)

Fuller, B. A. G., and S. M. McMurrin, *History of Philosophy,* 3d ed., Holt, 1955

Galilei, G., *Dialogue on the Two Great World Systems* (1632), G. de Santillana, ed., Chicago, 1953

Galilei, G., *Dialogues Concerning Two New Sciences* (1638), Northwestern (Dover, pap.)

Glass, Bentley, *Science and Ethical Values,* North Carolina, 1965*

Hall, A. R., *The Scientific Revolution 1500–1800,* rev. ed., Longmans, 1966 (Beacon, pap.)

Hall, A. R., and Marie Boas Hall, *A Brief History of Science,* Signet, 1964 (pap.)*

Holton, Gerald, *Science and Culture,* Houghton, 1965*

Huxley, Aldous, *Literature and Science,* Harper, 1963*

Jammer, M., *Concepts of Force: A Study in the Foundations of Dynamics,* Harvard, 1957 (Harper, pap.)

Jammer, M., *Concepts of Mass in Classical and Modern Physics,* Harvard, 1961 (Harper, pap.)

Jammer, M., *Concepts of Space; The History of Theories of Space in Physics,* Harvard, 1954 (Harper, pap.)

Jevons, W. S., *The Principles of Science* (1874), Dover, 1958 (pap.)

Mach, E., *History of the Science of Mechanics* (1883), Open Court, 1960 (also pap.)

Merz, J. T., *A History of European Thought in the 19th Century,* Dover (pap.)

Meyerson, E., *Identity and Reality* (1907), Dover, 1962 (pap.)

Nagel, E., *Structure of Science, Problems in the Logic of Scientific Explanation,* Harcourt, 1961

Nagel, E., and J. R. Newman, *Gödel's Proof,* New York, 1958

Neurath, O., and others, *International Encyclopedia of Unified Science,* Chicago, 1955

Ornstein, M., *Role of Scientific Societies in Seventeenth Century,* 3d ed., Chicago, 1938

Pap, A., *Introduction to the Philosophy of Science,* Free Press, 1962

Passmore, J., *A Hundred Years of Philosophy,* 3d ed., Basic, 1966

Pearson, K., *Grammar of Science* (1892, 1899), rev. ed., Dutton, 1937 (World, pap.)

Pledge, H. T., *Science Since 1500,* Peter Smith (Harper, pap.)

Poincaré, J. H., *Science and Hypothesis* (1902), Dover (pap.)

Popper, K. R., *Logic of Scientific Discovery,* Basic, 1959 (Harper, pap.)

Pyke, Magnus, *The Boundaries of Science,* Pelican, 1963 (pap.)

Randall, J. H. Jr., *The Career of Philosophy from the Middle Ages to the Enlightenment,* Columbia, 1962

Ritchie, A. D., *Scientific Method,* Littlefield, 1960 (pap.)

Russell, B., *Introduction to Mathematical Philosophy,* Humanities

Russell, Bertrand, *The Scientific Outlook,* Norton, 1962 (pap.)*

Sarton, G., *A History of Science,* Harvard, 2 vol., 1952, 1959 (Science Eds., pap.)

Sarton, G., *Introduction to the History of Science,* Williams, 5 vol., 1927–47

Schück, H., and others, *Nobel, the Man and His Prizes,* Elsevier, 1962

GENERAL

Cooley, H. R., and others, *Introduction to Mathematics,* 3d ed., Houghton, 1967*

Courant, R., and H. Robbins, *What is Mathematics?,* Oxford, 1941*

Friedman, B., *Principles and Techniques of Applied Mathematics,* Wiley, 1956

Grazda, E. E., and M. E. Jansson, *Handbook of Applied Mathematics,* 4th ed., Van Nostrand

Hogben, L., *Mathematics for the Million,* 3rd ed., Norton, 1951*

James, G., and R. C., eds., *Mathematics Dictionary,* 2d ed., Van Nostrand, 1959

Kasner, E., and J. R. Newman, *Mathematics and the Imagination,* Simon and Schuster, 1940*

Klein, F., *Elementary Mathematics from an Advanced Standpoint,* 3d ed., Dover, 2 vol., 1924, 1939 (pap.)

Kline, M., *Mathematics: A Cultural Approach,* Addison-Wesley, 1962*

Littlewood, D. E., *Skeleton Key of Mathematics,* Harper, 1960 (pap.)

Newman, J. R., ed., *World of Mathematics,* Simon and Schuster, 4 vol., 1956 (also pap.)*

Polya, G., *Mathematical Discovery on Understanding, Learning, and Teaching Problem Solving,* Wiley, 2 vol., 1962, 1965*

Rademacher, H., and O. Toeplitz, *The Enjoyment of Mathematics,* Princeton, 1957 (also pap.)*

Sedgwick, W. T., and H. W. Tyler, *A Short History of Science,* rev. ed., Macmillan, 1939

Singer, C., and others, eds., *A History of Technology,* Oxford, 5 vol., 1954–58

Snow, C. P., *The Two Cultures and a Second Look,* Mentor, 1964 (pap.)*

Tarski, A., *Introduction to Logic and to the Methodology of Deductive Sciences,* 3d ed., Oxford, 1965 (Galaxy, pap.)

Thorndike, L., *History of Magic and Experimental Science,* Columbia, 8 vol., 1923–1958

Toulmin, S., *Foresight and Understanding,* Premier, 1962 (pap.)

Toulmin, S., *The Philosophy of Science,* Hutchinson, 1953 (Harper, pap.)

Whitehead, A. N., *Concept of Nature,* Cambridge, 1919 (also pap.)

Whitehead, A. N., *Science and the Modern World,* Macmillan, 1926 (N.A.L., pap.)

Whitehead, A. N., and B. Russell, *Principia Mathematica* (1910–1913), 2d ed., Cambridge, 3 vol., 1925–1927 (also pap.)

Wightman, W. P. D., *The Growth of Scientific Ideas,* Yale, 1951 (also pap.)

SPECIAL TOPICS

Amis, K., *New Maps of Hell; a Survey of Science Fiction,* Harcourt, 1960

Ayer, A. J. (ed.), *Logical Positivism,* Free Press, 1966 (pap.)

Bates, R. S., *Scientific Societies in the United States,* 2d ed., Columbia, 1958*

Beckner, M., *Biological Way of Thought,* Columbia, 1959

MATHEMATICS

Rosenthal, E. B., *Understanding the New Mathematics,* Fawcett, 1965 (pap.)*

Sawyer, W. W., *Mathematician's Delight,* Penguin, 1943 (pap.)*

Sawyer, W. W., *Prelude to Mathematics,* Penguin, 1955 (pap.)*

Schaaf, W. L., *Basic Concepts of Elementary Mathematics,* 2d ed., Wiley, 1965*

Singh, J., *Great Ideas of Modern Mathematics,* Dover, 1959 (pap.)*

Smith, David E., *Source Book in Mathematics,* Dover, 2 vol., 1929 (pap.)

Sutton, O. G., *Mathematics in Action,* Dover, 1959

Van Der Waerden, B. L., *Science Awakening,* Oxford, 1961

Weyl, H., *Symmetry,* Princeton, 1952

Whitehead, A. N., *An Introduction to Mathematics,* Oxford, 1948 (also pap.)

HISTORY

Aaboe, A., *Episodes from the Early History of Mathematics,* Random, 1964 (also pap.)

Bell, E. T., *Development of Mathematics,* 2d ed., McGraw-Hill, 1945

Bell, E. T., *Men of Mathematics,* Simon and Schuster, 1937 (also pap.)*

Cajori, F., *History of Mathematics,* rev. ed., Macmillan, 1919

Dickson, L. E., *History of the Theory of Numbers,* Chelsea, 3 vol., 1952

Eves, H., *Introduction to the History of Mathematics,* rev. ed., Holt, 1964

Heath, T. L., *A History of Greek Mathematics,* Oxford, 2 vol., 1921

Berkeley, E. C., *Symbolic Logic and Intelligent Machines,* Reinhold, 1959

Beth, E. W., *Foundations of Mathematics,* 2d rev. ed., Humanities, 1965 (Harper, pap.)

Braithwaite, R. B., *Scientific Explanation,* Cambridge, 1953 (Harper, pap.)

Bunge, Mario, *Causality: The Place of the Causal Principle in Modern Science,* Meridian, 1963 (pap.)

Cassirer, E., *Determinism and Indeterminism in Modern Physics,* Yale, 1956*

Church, A., *Introduction to Mathematical Logic,* Princeton, 1956

Industrial Research Laboratories of the United States, 11th ed., National Academy of Sciences, 1960*

Kleene, S. C., *Introduction to Metamathematics,* Van Nostrand, 1952

Kneale, W. C. and M., *The Development of Logic,* Oxford, 1962

Lewis, C. I., and C. H. Langford, *Symbolic Logic,* 2nd ed., Peter Smith, (Dover, pap.)

Meier, Richard L., *Science and Economic Development,* 2d ed., M.I.T., 1966 (also pap.)

Mises, R. von, *Positivism: A Study in Human Understanding,* Braziller, 1956*

Price, Don K., *Government and Science,* Galaxy, 1962 (pap.)*

Quine, W. V. O., *Methods of Logic,* rev. ed., Holt, 1959

Scientific and Technical Societies of the United States and Canada, 7th ed., National Academy of Sciences, 1961*

Wolfle, Dael, *Science and Public Policy,* Bison, 1959 (pap.)*

Woodger, J. H., *Biological Principles,* Humanities, 1966

Heath, T. L., ed., *The Works of Archimedes,* Dover, (pap.)

Kline, M., *Mathematics in Western Culture,* Oxford, 1953 (also pap.)*

Reid, Constance, *A Long Way from Euclid,* Crowell, 1963*

Smith, D. E., *History of Mathematics,* Dover, 2 vol., 1925 (pap.)

Struik, D. J., *A Concise History of Mathematics,* 2d ed., Dover, 1948 (pap.)

Turnbull, H. W., *The Great Mathematicians,* New York Univ., 1961 (Simon and Schuster, pap.)

ALGEBRA

Asimov, I., *Realm of Algebra,* Houghton, 1961*

Benner, C. P., and others, *Topics in Modern Algebra,* Harper, 1962

Birkhoff, G., *Survey of Modern Algebra,* 3d ed., Macmillan, 1965

Bocher, M., *Introduction to Higher Algebra,* Dover, 1935

Cullen, C., *Matrices and Linear Transformations,* Addison-Wesley, 1966

MacDuffee, C. C., *Theory of Equations,* Wiley, 1954

Nering, Evar D., *Linear Algebra and Matrix Theory,* Wiley, 1963

Rogers, C. A., *Elements of Algebra,* Wiley, 1962

Whitesitt, J. E., *Principles of Modern Algebra,* Addison-Wesley, 1964

Yefimov, N. V., *Quadratic Forms and Matrices,* Academic, 1964 (also pap.)

CALCULUS AND ANALYSIS

Agnew, R. P., *Differential Equations,* 2d ed., McGraw-Hill, 1960

Akhiezer, N. I., *Theory of Approximation,* Ungar, 1956

Bliss, G. A., *Calculus of Variations,* Open Court, 1935

Bowman, F., *Introduction to Elliptic Functions with Applications,* Dover, 1953 (pap.)

Brand, L., *Vector Analysis,* Wiley, 1957

Buck, R. C., *Advanced Calculus,* 2d ed., McGraw-Hill, 1965

Carslaw, H. S., *Introduction to the Theory of Fourier's Series and Integrals,* 3d ed., Dover, 1952 (pap.)

Courant, R., *Differential and Integral Calculus,* Wiley, 2 vol., 1936–1937

Dettman, John W., *Applied Complex Variables,* Macmillan, 1965

Franklin, P., *Functions of Complex Variables,* Prentice-Hall, 1958

Halmos, P., *Introduction to Hilbert Space,* Chelsea, 1957

Hardy, G. H., *Pure Mathematics,* Cambridge, 1959 (also pap.)

Kline, M., *Calculus: An Intuitive and Physical Approach,* Wiley, 1967

Knopp, K., *Theory and Applications of Infinite Series,* 2d ed., Hafner, 1948

Milne-Thomson, L. M., *Calculus of Finite Differences,* St. Martin's, 1933

Sokolnikoff, I. S., *Tensor Analysis,* 2d ed., Wiley, 1964

Tricomi, F. G., *Integral Equations,* Wiley, 1958

COMPUTING MACHINES AND LINEAR PROGRAMMING

Adler, I., *Thinking Machines,* Day, 1961

Berkeley, E. C., *The Computer Revolution,* Scott, 1963*

Fink, D. G., *Computers and the Human Mind,* Doubleday, 1966 (pap.)

Glicksman, A. M., *Linear Programming and the Theory of Games,* Wiley, 1963 (also pap.)

Murray, F. J., *Mathematical Machines,* Columbia, 2 vol., 1961

Pfeiffer, J., *The Thinking Machine,* Lippincott, 1962

Vajda, S., *Introduction to Linear Programming and the Theory of Games,* Wiley, 1960

FOUNDATIONS OF MATHEMATICS

Beth, E. W., *Foundations of Mathematics: A Study in the Philosophy of Science,* 2d ed., Humanities, 1965

Church, A., *Introduction to Mathematical Logic,* Princeton, 1956

Eves, H., and C. V. Newsom, *An Introduction to the Foundations and Fundamental Concepts of Mathematics,* rev. ed., Holt, 1965*

Fraenkel, A. A., *Abstract Set Theory,* 3d ed., Humanities, 1965

Fraenkel, A. A., and Y. Bar-Hillel, *Foundations of Set Theory,* Humanities

Goodstein, R. L., *Essays in the Philosophy of Mathematics,* Ungar, 1965

Kleene, S. C., *Introduction to Metamathematics,* Van Nostrand, 1952

Suppes, P., *Axiomatic Set Theory,* Van Nostrand, 1960

Wilder, R. L., *Introduction to the Foundations of Mathematics,* 2d ed., Wiley, 1965

GAME THEORY

Blackwell, D., and M. S. Girschick, *Theory of Games and Statistical Decisions,* Wiley, 1954

Dresher, M., *Games of Strategy; Theory and Applications,* Prentice-Hall, 1961

Luce, R. D., and H. Raiffa, *Games and Decisions,* Wiley, 1957

McKinsey, J. C. C., *Introduction to the Theory of Games,* McGraw-Hill, 1952

Rapoport, A., "The Use and Misuse of Game Theory," *Sci. Amer.,* Dec. 1962*

Vajda, S., *An Introduction to Linear Programming and the Theory of Games,* Wiley, 1960

Von Neumann, J., and O. Morgenstern, *Theory of Games and Economic Behavior,* 3d ed., Wiley, 1964 (pap.)

GEOMETRY AND TRIGONOMETRY

Bonola, R., *Non-Euclidean Geometry,* Dover, 1955 (pap.)

Cell, J. W., *Analytic Geometry,* 3d ed., Wiley, 1960

Chin, M. G., and N. Steenrod, *First Concepts of Topology,* Random, 1966

Corliss, J., and W. V. Berglund, *Plane Trigonometry,* 2d ed., Houghton, 1958

Coxeter, H. S. M., *Introduction to Geometry,* Wiley, 1961

Euclid, *Elements,* ed. T. L. Heath, Dover, 3 vol., 1926 (pap.)

Eves, H., *A Survey of Geometry,* Allyn, 2 vol., 1963 and 1965

Forder, H. G., *Geometry: An Introduction,* Harper, 1962 (pap.)*

Hall, D. W., and G. L. Spencer, *Elementary Topology,* Wiley, 1955

Hausner, M., *A Vector Space Approach to Geometry,* Prentice-Hall, 1965

Hilbert, D., and S. Cohn-Vossen, *Geometry and the Imagination,* Chelsea, 1952*

Hodge, W. V. D., and D. Pedoe, *Methods of Algebraic Geometry,* Cambridge, 3 vol., 1947–1954

Lehmann, C. H., *Analytic Geometry,* Wiley, 1942

Levy, H., *Projective and Related Geometries,* Macmillan, 1964

Lietzmann, W., *Visual Topology,* Elsevier, 1965

Meschkowski, H., *Noneuclidean Geometry,* Academic, 1964 (also pap.)

Schacht, J., and R. C. McLennan, *Plane Geometry,* Holt, 1957

Semple, H. G., and L. Roth, *Introduction to Algebraic Geometry,* Oxford, 1949

Springer, C. E., *Geometry and Analysis of Projective Spaces,* Freeman, 1964

Struik, D. J., *Analytic and Projective Geometry,* Addison-Wesley, 1953

Willmore, T. J., *Introduction to Differential Geometry,* Oxford, 1959

Young, J. W., *Projective Geometry,* Open Court, 1930

INFORMATION THEORY

Abramson, N., *Information Theory and Coding,* McGraw-Hill, 1963

Ashby, W., *Introduction to Cybernetics,* Wiley, 1956 (pap.)

Brillouin, L., *Science and Information Theory,* 2d ed., Academic, 1962

Fano, R. M., *Transmission of Information,* M.I.T., 1961

Pierce, J. R., *Symbols, Signals, and Noise,* Harper, 1961 (pap.)*

Shannon, C. E., and W. Weaver, *Mathematical Theory of Communication,* Illinois, 1949 (also pap.)

Singh, J. M., *Information Theory, Language and Cybernetics,* Dover, 1967 (pap.)

Wiener, N., *Cybernetics; or Control and Communication in the Animal and the Machine,* 2d ed., M.I.T., 1961 (also pap.)

NOMOGRAPHY

Levens, A. S., *Nomography,* 2d ed., Wiley, 1959

NUMBER THEORY

Davenport, H., *The Higher Arithmetic: An Introduction to the Theory of Numbers,* Hillary, 1952

Griffin, Harriet, *Elementary Theory of Numbers,* McGraw-Hill, 1963 (pap.)

LeVeque, W. J., *Elementary Theory of Numbers,* Addison-Wesley, 1962

Niven, I., *Numbers, Rational and Irrational,* Random, 1961 (pap.)*

Pollard, H., *Theory of Algebraic Numbers,* Wiley, 1959

Shanks, Daniel, *Solved and Unsolved Problems in Number Theory,* Spartan, vol. 1, 1963

Weyl, H., *Algebraic Theory of Numbers,* rev. ed., Princeton, 1954

PROBABILITY

Alder, H. L., and E. B. Roessler, *Introduction to Probability and Statistics,* 3d ed., Freeman, 1964

Borel, E., *Probabilities and Life,* Dover, 1962 (pap.)*

Feller, W., *An Introduction to Probability Theory and Its Applications,* 2d ed., Wiley, 2 vol., 1957, 1966

Gnedenko, B. V., and A. Y. Khinchin, *An Elementary Introduction to the Theory of Probability,* Freeman, 1961 (pap.)

Keynes, J. M., *A Treatise on Probability,* St. Martin's, 1952 (Harper, pap.)

Neyman, J., *First Course in Probability and Statistics,* Holt, 1950

Niven, Ivan, *Mathematics of Choice,* Random, 1965 (pap.)

Weaver, Warren, *Lady Luck: The Theory of Probability,* Doubleday, 1963 (pap.)*

RECREATIONS, PUZZLES, GAMES, AND CODES

Ball, W. W. R., *Mathematical Recreations and Essays,* Macmillan (pap.)

D'Agapeyeff, A., *Codes and Ciphers,* Oxford, 1949*

Gardner, M., ed., *Scientific American Book of Mathematical Puzzles and Diversions,* Simon and Schuster, 2 bks, 1961, 1964 (pap.)

Graham, L. A., *Ingenious Mathematical Problems and Methods,* Dover, 1959 (pap.)*

Kraitchik, M., *Mathematical Recreations,* 2d ed., Dover, 1953* (pap.)

Maxwell, A. E., *Fallacies in Mathematics,* Cambridge, 1959*

Smith, L. D., *Cryptography; The Science of Secret Writing,* Dover, 1955 (pap.)*

STATISTICS

Cochran, W. G., and G. M. Cox, *Experimental Designs,* 2d ed., Wiley, 1957

Fisher, R. A., *Design of Experiments,* 8th ed., Hafner, 1966

Fisher, R. A., *Statistical Methods for Research Workers,* 13th ed., Hafner, 1958

Hoel, P. G., *Introduction to Mathematical Statistics,* 3d ed., Wiley, 1962

Kendall, M. G., and A. Stuart, *The Advanced Theory of Statistics,* vol. 1, rev. ed., 1958; vol. 2, rev. ed., 1961; vol. 3 in prep., Hafner

Moroney, M. J., *Facts from Figures,* Penguin, 1956 (pap.)*

Tippett, L. H. C., *Statistics,* 2d ed., Oxford, 1956

METEOROLOGY

GENERAL

Berry, F. A., and others, *Handbook of Meteorology,* McGraw-Hill, 1945

Blair, T. A., and R. C. Fite, *Weather Elements,* 5th ed., Prentice-Hall, 1965

Blumenstock, D. I., *The Ocean of Air,* Rutgers, 1959

Byers, H. R., *General Meteorology,* 3d ed., McGraw-Hill, 1959

Day, John A., *The Science of Weather,* Addison-Wesley, 1966

Huschke, R. E., *Glossary of Meteorology,* A.M.S., 1959

Johnson, J. C., *Physical Meteorology,* Wiley, 1954

Kendrew, W. G., *Climatology,* 2d ed., Oxford, 1957

Kendrew, W. G., *The Climate of the Continents,* 5th ed., Oxford, 1961

Lehr, Paul E., R. Will Burnett, and H. S. Zim, *Weather,* Golden, 1965 (also pap.)*

Malone, T. F., ed., *Compendium of Meteorology,* A.M.S., 1951

Petterssen, S., *Introduction to Meteorology,* 2d ed., McGraw-Hill, 1958

Shapley, H., ed., *Climatic Change,* Harvard, 1954*

Sutcliffe, R. C., *Weather and Climate,* Norton, 1966

Sutton, O. G., *The Challenge of the Atmosphere,* Harper, 1961*

Thompson, P. D., and R. O'Brien, *Weather,* Time-Life, 1965 (Silver Burdett)

Trewartha, G. T., *Earth's Problem Climates,* Wisconsin, 1961

Visher, S. S., *Climatic Atlas of the United States,* Harvard, 1954

SPECIAL TOPICS

Battan, L. J., *Radar Meteorology,* Chicago, 1959

Battan, L. J., *The Unclean Sky,* Anchor, Doubleday, 1966 (pap.)*

Byers, H. R., *Elements of Cloud Physics,* Chicago, 1965

Byers, H. R., ed., *Thunderstorm Electricity,* Chicago, 1953

Chalmers, J. A., *Atmospheric Electricity,* Pergamon, 1957

Dunn, G. E., and B. I. Miller, *Atlantic Hurricanes,* Louisiana, 1964

Fleagle, R. G., and J. A. Businger, *An Introduction to Atmospheric Physics,* Academic, 1963

Flora, S. D., *Tornadoes of the United States,* rev. ed., Oklahoma, 1958*

Geiger, R., *The Climate Near the Ground,* Harvard, 1957

Haltiner, G. J., and F. L. Martin, *Dynamical and Physical Meteorology,* McGraw-Hill, 1957

Hess, S. L., *Introduction to Theoretical Meteorology,* Holt, 1959

Mason, B. J., *The Physics of Clouds,* Oxford, 1957

Meetham, A. R., *Atmospheric Pollution,* 2d ed., Pergamon, 1956

Middleton, W. E. K., and A. F. Spilhaus, *Meteorological Instruments,* 3d ed., Toronto, 1953

Nakaya, U., *Snow Crystals,* Harvard, 1954

Pasquill, F., *Atmospheric Diffusion,* Van Nostrand, 1962

Petterssen, S., *Weather Analysis and Forecasting,* 2d ed., McGraw-Hill, 2 vol., 1956

Spilhaus, A. F., *Weathercraft,* Viking, 1957

Sutton, O. G., *Micrometeorology,* McGraw-Hill, 1953

Thompson, P. D., *Numerical Weather Analysis and Prediction,* Macmillan, 1961

PHYSICS

GENERAL

Adler, I., *The Wonders of Physics,* Golden, 1966*

American Institute of Physics, *Handbook,* 2d ed., McGraw-Hill, 1963

Andrade, E. N. daC., *An Approach to Modern Physics,* Peter Smith, 1956 (Doubleday, pap.)*

Andrade, E. N. daC., *Physics for the Modern World,* Barnes, 1963 (also pap.)*

Blackwood, O. H., and others, *General Physics,* 3d ed., Wiley, 1963

Blass, G. A., *Theoretical Physics,* Appleton, 1962

Bonner, F. T., and M. Phillips, *Principles of Physical Science,* Addison-Wesley, 1957*

Born, M., *Physics in My Generation,* Pergamon, 1956*

Born, M., *The Restless Universe,* 2d ed., Dover, 1957 (pap.)*

Bridgman, P. W., *The Logic of Modern Physics,* Macmillan, 1946 (pap.)*

Cajori, F., *A History of Physics,* Peter Smith, 1929 (Dover, pap.)

Condon, E. U., and Odishaw, H., *Handbook of Physics,* McGraw-Hill, 1958

Crew, H., *The Rise of Modern Physics,* Williams and Wilkins, 1935

De Broglie, L., *Physics and Microphysics,* Grosset (pap.)*

De Broglie, L., *The Revolution in Physics,* Routledge, 1954

Einstein, A., and Infeld, L., *The Evolution of Physics,* Simon and Schuster, 1938 (also pap.)

Galilei, G., *Dialogues Concerning Two New Sciences* (1638), Dover, 1914 (pap.)

Hix, C. F., Jr., and R. F. Alley, *Physical Laws and Effects,* Wiley, 1958

Holton, G., and D. H. D. Roller, *Foundations of Modern Physical Science,* Addison-Wesley, 1958

International Dictionary of Physics and Electronics, 2d ed., Van Nostrand, 1961

Lemon, H. B., *From Galileo to the Nuclear Age,* rev. ed., Chicago, 1946 (also pap.)*

Lindsay, R. B., and H. Margenau, *Foundations of Physics* (1936), Dover, 1955 (pap.)*

Magie, W. F., *A Source Book in Physics,* Harvard, 1963

Newton, Isaac, *Mathematical Principles,* F. Cajori, ed., California, 1934 (also pap.)

Page, L., *Introduction to Theoretical Physics,* 3d ed., Van Nostrand, 1952

Park, David, *Contemporary Physics,* Harcourt, 1964 (also pap.)

Peierls, R. E., *Laws of Nature,* Scribner's, 1956 (also pap.)

Physical Science Study Committee, *Physics,* 2d ed., Heath, 1965

Ridenour, L. N., *Modern Physics for the Engineer,* McGraw-Hill, 1961

Rogers, E. M., *Physics for the Inquiring Mind,* Princeton, 1960

Schrödinger, E., *Science, Theory and Man,* Dover, 1957 (pap.) (Originally published as *Science and the Human Temperament,* 1935)*

Sears, F. W., and M. W. Zemansky, *University Physics,* 3d ed., Addison-Wesley, 1964

Shamos, M. H., *Great Experiments in Physics,* Holt, 1959 (also pap.)

Swenson, H. N., and J. E. Woods, *Physical Science for Liberal Arts Students,* Wiley, 1957*

Thewlis, J., and others, eds., *Encyclopaedic Dictionary of Physics,* Pergamon, 9 vol., 1962

Weast, R. C., ed., *Handbook of Chemistry and Physics,* 46th ed., Chemical Rubber, 1965

White, H. E., *Modern College Physics,* 5th ed., Van Nostrand, 1966

Whittaker, E. T., *History of the Theories of Aether and Electricity,* Harper, 2 vol., 1951, 1953 (pap.)

Wilson, W., *A Hundred Years of Physics,* Duckworth, 1950

ATOMIC AND NUCLEAR PHYSICS

Adler, I., *Inside the Nucleus,* Day, 1963 (N.A.L., pap.)*

Adler, I., *The Elementary Mathematics of the Atom,* Day, 1965*

Anderson, D. L., *The Discovery of the Electron,* Van Nostrand, 1964 (pap.)

Andrade, E. N. daC., *Rutherford and the Nature of the Atom,* Doubleday, 1964 (pap.)*

Berthelot, A., *Radiations and Matter,* Macmillan, 1960

Bilaniuk, O. M., "Semiconductor Particle-Detectors," *Sci. Amer.,* Oct. 1962*

Bohr, N., *Essays 1958/1962 on Atomic Physics*

and Human Knowledge, Wiley, 1964 (Vintage, pap.)

Calder, R., *Living With the Atom,* Chicago, 1962

Carroll, J. M., *The Story of the Laser,* Dutton, 1964

Cook, C. S., *Structure of Atomic Nuclei,* Van Nostrand, 1964 (pap.)

de Benedetti, S., "Mössbauer Effect," *Sci. Amer.,* Apr. 1960*

Friedman, F., and L. Sartori, *The Classical Atom,* Addison-Wesley, 1965

Ford, K. W., *World of Elementary Particles,* Blaisdell, 1963

Frisch, D. H., and A. M. Thorndike, *Elementary Particles,* Van Nostrand, 1964 (pap.)

Frisch, O. R., *Atomic Physics Today,* Basic Books, 1961 (Fawcett, pap.)*

Halliday, D., *Introductory Nuclear Physics,* 2d ed., Wiley, 1955

Heavens, O. S., *Optical Masers,* Wiley, 1964

Hecht, S., *Explaining the Atom,* rev. ed., Viking, 1954 (also pap.)*

Hill, R. D., *Tracking Down Particles,* Benjamin, 1963 (also pap.)

Latham, O., *Nuclear Physics,* Addison-Wesley, 1955

Leinwoll, S., *Understanding Lasers and Masers,* Hayden, 1964 (Rider, pap.)

Lyons, H., "Atomic Clock," *Sci. Amer.,* Feb. 1957*

Millikan, R. A., *The Electron,* Chicago, 1963 (also pap.)

Morrison, P., "The Overthrow of Parity," *Sci. Amer.,* Apr. 1957*

Ratner, B. S., *Accelerators of Charged Particles,* Pergamon, 1964

Swartz, C. E., *The Fundamental Particles,* Addison-Wesley, 1965 (pap.)

Thomson, G. P., *The Atom,* 6th ed., Oxford, 1962 (pap.)*

Troup, G. J. F., *Masers and Lasers,* 2d ed., Wiley, 1963

Wilson, R. R., and R. Littauer, *Accelerators: Machines of Nuclear Physics,* Doubleday, 1960 (pap.)*

ELECTRICITY AND MAGNETISM

Bitter, F., *Magnets: the Education of a Physicist,* Doubleday, 1959 (pap.)*

Bozorth, R. M., *Ferromagnetism,* Van Nostrand, 1951

Duckworth, H. E., *Electricity and Magnetism,* rev. ed., Holt, 1966

Egli, P. H., "Direct Energy Conversion," *Amer. Sci.,* Sep. 1960*

Faraday, M., *Experimental Researches in Electricity* (1839–45), Dover, 2 vol., 1962

Goldsmid, H. J., *Applications of Thermoelectricity,* Wiley, 1960

Heikes, R. R., and R. W. Ure, *Thermoelectricity: Science and Engineering,* Wiley, 1961

Maxwell, J. C., *Electricity and Magnetism,* 3d ed., (1891), Dover, 2 vol., 1904 (pap.)

Purcell, E. M., *Electricity and Magnetism,* McGraw-Hill, 1965

ELECTROMAGNETIC WAVES AND RADIATION

Andrews, C. L., *Optics of the Electromagnetic Spectrum,* Prentice-Hall, 1960

Corson, D. R., and P. Lorrain, *Introduction to Electromagnetic Fields and Waves,* Freeman, 1962

Hackforth, H. L., *Infrared Radiation,* McGraw-Hill, 1960

Koller, L. R., *Ultraviolet Radiation,* 2d ed., Wiley, 1965

Laver, F. J. M., *Waves,* Oxford, 1960*

Reich, H. J., and others, *Microwave Principles,* Van Nostrand, 1957

Squires, T. L., *Introduction to Microwave Spectroscopy,* Newnes, 1963

HEAT AND THERMODYNAMICS

Bosworth, R. C. L., *Heat Transfer Phenomena,* Wiley, 1952

Brown, W. H., *Thermodynamics and Heat Engines,* Pitman, 1964

Davidson, N. R., *Statistical Mechanics,* McGraw-Hill, 1962

Knight, C. A., *The Freezing of Supercooled Liquids,* Momentum, 1967

Lee, J. F., and F. W. Sears, *Thermodynamics,* 2d ed., Addison-Wesley, 1963

McAdams, W. H., *Heat Transmission,* 3rd ed., McGraw-Hill, 1954

McClintock, M., *Cryogenics,* Reinhold, 1964

Mendelssohn, K., *Cryophysics,* Wiley, 1960 (also pap.)

Sears, F. W., *Thermodynamics, the Kinetic Theory of Gases, and Statistical Mechanics,* 2d ed., Addison-Wesley, 1953

Sittig, M., and S. Kidd, *Cryogenics; Research and Applications,* Van Nostrand, 1963

Zemansky, M. W., *Heat and Thermodynamics,* 4th ed., McGraw-Hill, 1957

Zemansky, M. W., *Temperatures Very Low and Very High,* Van Nostrand, 1964 (also pap.)

LIGHT, OPTICS, AND SPECTROSCOPY

Birren, F., *Color, Form, and Space,* Reinhold, 1961

Bragg, W. H., *The Universe of Light,* Peter Smith, 1933 (Dover, pap.)*

Candler, C., *Atomic Spectra,* 2d ed., Van Nostrand, 1964

Clark, G. L., ed., *Encyclopedia of Microscopy,* Reinhold, 1961

Clark, G. L., ed., *Encyclopedia of Spectroscopy,* Reinhold, 1960

Conrady, A. E., *Applied Optics and Optical Design,* Dover, 2 vol., 1959–1960 (pap.)

Ditchburn, R. W., *Light,* 2d ed., Wiley, 2 vol., 1963 (pap.)

Jenkins, F. A., and H. E. White, *Fundamentals of Optics,* 3d ed., McGraw-Hill, 1957

Minnaert, M., *The Nature of Light and Colour in the Open Air,* Dover, 1954 (pap.)*

Optical Society of America, *Science of Color,* T. Y. Crowell, 1953*

Sears, F. W., *Optics,* 3d ed., Addison-Wesley, 1949

Strong, J., *Concepts of Classical Optics,* Freeman, 1958

Waldron, R. A., *Waves and Oscillations,* Van Nostrand, 1964 (pap.)

Wolf, T. H., *The Magic of Color,* Golden, 1964

MECHANICS AND FLUID MECHANICS

Arnold, R. N., and L. Maunder, *Gyrodynamics and Its Engineering Applications,* Academic, 1962

Bridgman, P. W., *Physics of High Pressure,* Macmillan, 1949

Constant, F. W., *Theoretical Physics; Mechanics,* Addison-Wesley, 1954

Corben, H. C., and P. Stehle, *Classical Mechanics,* 2d ed., Wiley, 1960

Gamow, G., *Gravity,* Doubleday, 1962 (pap.)*

Goodier, J. N., and P. G. Hodge, *Elasticity and Plasticity,* Wiley, 1958

Guggenheim, E. A., *Elements of the Kinetic Theory of Gases,* Pergamon, 1960

Mach, E., *The Science of Mechanics,* 6th ed., Open Court, 1960 (also pap.)

Maxwell, J. C., *Matter and Motion* (1877), Dover, 1952 (pap.)

Reif, F., "Superfluidity and 'Quasi-particles,'" *Sci. Amer.,* Nov. 1960*

Sears, F. W., *Mechanics, Heat, and Sound,* 2d ed., Addison-Wesley, 1950

Steinherz, H. A., and P. A. Redhead, "Ultrahigh Vacuum," *Sci. Amer.,* Mar. 1962*

Symon, K. R., *Mechanics,* 2nd ed., Addison-Wesley, 1960

Vennard, J. K., *Elementary Fluid Mechanics,* 4th ed., Wiley, 1961

PLASMA PHYSICS AND MAGNETOHYDRODYNAMICS

Francis, G., *Ionization Phenomena in Gases,* Academic, 1960

Linhart, J. G., *Plasma Physics,* Wiley, 1960

Loeb, L. B., *Basic Processes of Gaseous Electronics,* 2d ed., California, 1955

Rose, D. J., and M. Clark, *Plasmas and Controlled Fusion,* M.I.T., 1961

QUANTUM PHYSICS

Bohm, D., *Causality and Chance in Modern Physics,* Van Nostrand, 1957

Bohm, D., *Quantum Theory,* Prentice-Hall, 1951

Dicke, R. H., and J. P. Wittke, *Introduction to Quantum Mechanics,* Addison-Wesley, 1960

Dirac, P. A. M., *The Principles of Quantum Mechanics,* 4th ed., Oxford, 1958

Gardner, M., *The Ambidextrous Universe,* Basic Books, 1964

Heisenberg, W., *Physical Principles of the Quantum Theory,* Dover, 1930 (pap.)

Heitler, W., *Elementary Wave Mechanics,* 2d ed., Oxford, 1956

RELATIVITY

Bergmann, P. G., *Introduction to the Theory of Relativity,* Prentice-Hall, 1942

Bohm, D., *The Special Theory of Relativity,* Benjamin, 1965 (also pap.)

Born, M., *Einstein's Theory of Relativity,* rev. ed., Dover, 1962 (pap.)

Coleman, J. A., *Relativity for the Layman,* William-Frederick, 1958 (N.A.L., pap.)*

Einstein, A., *The Meaning of Relativity,* 5th ed., Princeton, 1956 (pap.)

Gardner, M., *Relativity for the Millions,* Macmillan, 1962 (Pocket Books, pap.)*

Katz, R., *An Introduction to the Special Theory of Relativity,* Van Nostrand, 1964 (pap.)

SOLID STATE PHYSICS

Azaroff, L. V., *Introduction to Solids,* McGraw-Hill, 1960

Bragg, L., ed., *Crystalline State,* Cornell, 4 vol.

Buerger, M. J., *Crystal-Structure Analysis,* Wiley, 1960

Bunn, E. S., *Chemical Crystallography; An Introduction to Optical and X-ray Methods,* 2d ed., Oxford, 1961

Cullity, B. D., *Elements of X-Ray Diffraction,* Addison-Wesley, 1956

Dash, W. C., and A. G. Tweet, "Observing Dislocations in Crystals," *Sci. Amer.,* Oct. 1961*

Holden, A., and P. Singer, *Crystals and Crystal Growing,* Doubleday, 1960 (pap.)*

Kittel, C., *Introduction to Solid State Physics,* 2d ed., Wiley, 1956

Mason, W. P., *Piezoelectric Crystals and Their Applications to Ultrasonics,* Van Nostrand, 1950

Stewart, A. T., *Perpetual Motion; Electrons and Atoms in Crystals,* Doubleday, 1965 (pap.)

Wahlstrom, E. E., *Optical Crystallography,* 3d ed., Wiley, 1960

Wannier, G. H., *Elements of Solid State Theory,* Cambridge, 1963 (pap.)

Wood, E. A., *Crystals and Light,* Van Nostrand, 1964 (pap.)

Wooster, W. A., *Experimental Crystal Physics,* Oxford, 1957

SOUND

Benade, A. H., *Horns, Strings and Harmony,* Doubleday, 1960 (pap.)

Carlin, B., *Ultrasonics,* 2nd ed., McGraw-Hill, 1960

Hueter, T. F., and R. H. Bolt, *Sonics,* Wiley, 1955

Hunt, F. V., *Electracoustics,* Harvard, 1954

Josephs, J. J., *The Physics of Musical Sounds,* Van Nostrand, 1967

Kock, W. E., *Sound Waves and Light Waves,* Doubleday, 1965 (pap.)

Officer, C. B., *Introduction to the Theory of Sound Transmission,* McGraw-Hill, 1958

Randall, R. H., *Introduction to Acoustics,* Addison-Wesley, 1961

Rayleigh, J. W. S., *Theory of Sound* (1877–1878), 2d ed., Dover, 2 vol., 1945 (pap.)

Stevens, S. S., F. Warshofsky, and Life eds., *Sound and Hearing,* Time-Life, 1965*

TECHNOLOGY

(See also books cited under CHEMISTRY and PHYSICS)

GENERAL

Gillispie, C., ed., *Diderot Pictorial Encyclopedia of Trades and Industry,* 2 vol., Dover, 1959

Krick, Edward, *An Introduction to Engineering and Engineering Design,* Wiley, 1965 (also pap.)*

Ley, Willy, *Engineer's Dreams,* rev. ed., Viking, 1964 (also pap.)*

Meyer, Jerome S., *Great Inventions,* Pocket Books, 1962 (pap.)*

Mumford, L., *Technics and Civilization,* Harcourt, 1963 (pap.)

Polon, D. D., ed., *Encyclopedia of Engineering Signs and Symbols,* Odyssey, 1965

Tweney, C. F., and L. E. C. Hughes, *Chambers' Technical Dictionary,* 3d rev. ed. with suppl., Macmillan, 1958

Walker, A. P., ed., *NAB Engineering Handbook,* 5th ed., McGraw-Hill, 1960

Walker, C. R., *Modern Technology and Civilization,* McGraw-Hill, 1962* (also pap.)

HISTORY

Armytage, W. H. G., *A Social History of Engineering,* 2d ed., M.I.T., 1966*

Derry, T. K., and T. I. Williams, *A Short History of Technology,* Oxford, 1961

Finch, J. K., *The Story of Engineering,* Doubleday, 1960 (pap.)*

Forbes, R. J., *Man the Maker,* rev. ed., Abelard-Schuman, 1958

Klemm, F., *A History of Western Technology,* M.I.T., 1964 (also pap.)

Singer, C., and others, eds., *A History of Technology,* Oxford, 5 vol., 1954–1959

Thirring, H., *Energy for Man; Windmills to Nuclear Power,* Indiana, 1958 (Harper, pap.)*

Wolf, A., *History of Science, Technology and Philosophy in the 16th and 17th Centuries,* Peter Smith, 2 vol., 1959

Wolf, A., *History of Science, Technology and Philosophy in the 18th Century,* Peter Smith, 2 vol., 1961 (Harper, pap.)

AERONAUTICS

Adams, F. D., *Aeronautical Dictionary,* National Aeronautics and Space Administration, 1959

Allen, J. E., *Aerodynamics: A Space Age Survey,* Harper, 1963 (also pap.)*

Bridgman, L., *Jane's All the World's Aircraft, 1961–1962,* McGraw-Hill, 1966*

Caidin, Martin, *Wings Into Space,* Holt, 1964, (also pap.)*

Clarke, B., *History of Airships,* Herbert Jenkins, 1961

Gibbs-Smith, C. H., *Aeroplane, an Historical Survey of Its Origins and Development,* H. M. Stationery Office, 1960*

Gibbs-Smith, C. H., *History of Flying,* Cambridge, 1957 (pap.)*

Martynov, A. K., *Practical Aerodynamics,* Pergamon, 1964

Pope, A., *Wind-Tunnel Testing,* 2d ed., Wiley, 1954

GUIDANCE AND NAVIGATION

Arnold, R. N., and L. Maunder, *Gyrodynamics and Its Engineering Applications,* Academic, 1962

Hymoff, E., *Guidance and Control of Spacecraft,* Holt, 1965 (also pap.)*

McClure, C. L., *Theory of Inertial Guidance,* Prentice-Hall, 1960

Mixter, George W., *Primer of Navigation,* 4th ed., Van Nostrand, 1960

Povejsil, D. J., and others, *Airborne Radar,* Boston Tech., 1961

Sonnenburg, G. J., *Radar and Electronic Navigation,* 3d ed., Van Nostrand, 1963

U. S. Navy Hydrographic Office, *Air Navigation* (H. O. Publ. 216), U. S. Government Printing Office, Washington, D. C., 1955

AGRICULTURE

American Chemical Soc., *New Approaches to Pest Control and Eradication,* American Chemical Soc., 1963 (pap.)

Donahue, Roy L., *Soils: An Introduction to Soils and Plant Growth,* 2d ed., Prentice-Hall, 1965

Gunther, F. A., and L. R. Jeppson, *Modern Insecticides and World Food Production,* Wiley, 1960

Pyke, M., *Food Science and Technology,* Transatlantic, 1964

Raper, A. F. and others, *Guide to Agriculture, U. S. A.,* U. S. Dept. of Agriculture, 1955*

Sauchelli, V., ed., *Chemistry and Technology of Fertilizers,* Reinhold, 1960

Smith, H. P., *Farm Machinery and Equipment,* 5th ed., McGraw-Hill, 1964

U. S. Department of Agriculture, *Yearbooks* (series), U. S. Government Printing Office, Washington, D. C., published annually

Yeates, N. T. M., *Modern Aspects of Animal Production,* Butterworth, 1965

ARCHITECTURE, ARCHITECTURAL ENGINEERING, AND BUILDING CRAFTS

Beranek, Leo L., *Music, Acoustics, and Architecture,* Wiley, 1962

Burris-Meyer, Harold and Lewis S. Goodfriend, *Acoustics for the Architect,* Reinhold, 1957

Carson, A. B., *Foundation Construction,* McGraw-Hill, 1965

Condit, C. W., *American Building Art,* Oxford, 2 vol., *The Nineteenth Century,* 1960; *The Twentieth Century,* 1961

Durbahn, W. E., *Fundamentals of Carpentry,* 3d ed., American Technical Society, 2 vol., 1961

Fischer, Robert E., *Architectural Engineering; Environmental Control,* McGraw-Hill, 1964

Fischer, Robert E., *Architectural Engineering; New Structures,* McGraw-Hill, 1964

Fleming, J., H. Honour, and N. Pevsner, *The Penguin Dictionary of Architecture,* Penguin, 1966 (pap.)*

Giedion, S., *Space, Time and Architecture,* 4th ed., Harvard, 1962*

Hall, Edward T., *The Silent Language,* Doubleday, 1959 (Fawcett, pap.)*

Hornung, W. J., *Architectural Drafting,* 4th ed., Prentice-Hall, 1966

Huntington, Whitney C., *Building Construction,* 3d ed., Wiley, 1963

Merritt, Frederick S., *Building Construction Handbook,* 2d ed., McGraw-Hill, 1965

AUTOMATION AND INSTRUMENTATION

Amber, George H. and Paul S., *Anatomy of Automation,* Prentice-Hall, 1962*

Baker, H. D., and others, *Temperature Measurement in Engineering,* Wiley, 2 vol., 1953–1961

Buckingham, Walter, *Automation: Its Impact On Business and People,* Harper, 1961 (N.A.L., pap.)

Considine, D. M., ed., *Process Instruments and Controls Handbook,* McGraw-Hill, 1957

Considine, D. M., and S. D. Ross, eds., *Handbook of Applied Instrumentation,* McGraw-Hill, 1964

Elliott, A., and J. H. Dickson, *Laboratory Instruments,* 2d ed., Tudor, 1960

Foster, David, *Modern Automation,* Pitman, 1963*

Holzbock, Werner G., *Instruments for Measurement and Control,* 2d ed., Reinhold, 1962

Lossiyevskii, V. L., ed., *The Automation of Production Processes,* Pergamon, 1963

Prensky, Sol D., *Electronic Instrumentation,* Prentice-Hall, 1963

Weeks, R. P., *Machine and the Man: A Sourcebook on Automation,* Appleton, 1961*

Wiener, N., *Cybernetics,* 2d ed., M.I.T., 1961* (also pap.)

CIVIL ENGINEERING

Abbett, Robert W., Ed., *American Civil Engineering Practice,* 3 vol., Wiley, 1956–1957

Breed, C. B., and G. L. Hosmer, *Principles and Practice of Surveying,* vol. 1, *Elementary Surveying,* 10th ed.; vol. 2, *Higher Surveying,* 8th ed., Wiley, 1962

Davis, Raymond E., and Francis S. Foote, *Surveying: Theory and Practice,* 5th ed., McGraw-Hill, 1963

Hammond, R., *Dictionary of Civil Engineering,* Philosophical Lib., 1965

Legault, A. R., *Highway and Airport Engineering,* Prentice-Hall, 1960

Sandstrom, Gosta E., *Tunnels,* Holt, 1963

Steinman, D. B., *Famous Bridges of the World,* Dover, 1953 (pap.)*

Steinman, D. B., and S. R. Watson, *Bridges and Their Builders,* 2d ed., Dover, 1957 (pap.)*

Straub, Hans, *A History of Civil Engineering,* M.I.T., 1964 (pap.)*

Urquhart, Leonard C., ed., *Civil Engineering Handbook,* 4th ed., McGraw-Hill, 1959

CLOCKS AND WATCHES

Asimov, Isaac, *The Clock We Live On,* Abelard, 1965 (Collier, pap.)*

Cowan, Harrison J., *Time and Its Measurement,* World, 1958*

Gordon, G. F. C., *Clockmaking Past and Present,* rev. ed., The Technical Press, 1949*

Harris, Henry G., *Handbook of Watch and Clock Repairs,* Emerson, 1962

Milham, W. I., *Time and Timekeepers, The Construction, Care and Accuracy of Clocks and Watches,* Macmillan, 1941*

ELECTRONICS AND ELECTRONIC COMMUNICATIONS

Black, H. S., *Modulation Theory,* Van Nostrand, 1953

Borden, P. A., and W. J. Mayo-Wells, *Telemetering Systems,* Reinhold, 1959

Buckwalter, Len, *ABC's of Television,* Sams, 1964 (pap.)*

Caceres, Cesar A., Ed., *Biomedical Telemetry,* Academic, 1965

Chirlian, P. M., and A. H. Zemanian, *Electronics,* McGraw-Hill, 1961

Chute, George M., *Electronics in Industry,* 3d ed., McGraw-Hill, 1965

Cook, J. Gordon, *Electrons Go To Work,* Dial, 1957 (pap.)*

Evans, J., *Fundamental Principles of Transistors,* 2d ed., Van Nostrand, 1962

Fink, D. G., and D. Lutyens, *Physics of Television,* Doubleday, 1960 (pap.)*

Frye, John T., *Basic Radio Course,* rev. ed., Gernsback, 1962 (pap.)*

Garner, Louis E., *Getting Started With Transistors,* Gernsback, 1963 (pap.)*

Handel, S., *A Dictionary of Electronics,* Penguin, 1962 (pap.)*

Kiver, Milton S., *Color Television Fundamentals,* 2d ed., McGraw-Hill, 1964

Page, Robert M., *The Origin of Radar,* Doubleday, 1962 (pap.)*

Parr, G., and O. H. Davie, *Cathode Ray Tube and Its Applications,* 3d ed., Reinhold, 1959

Pierce, John R., *Electrons and Waves: An Introduction to the Science of Electronics and Communication,* Doubleday, 1964 (pap.)*

Rider, J. F., and H. Jacobowitz, *Basic Vacuum Tubes and Their Uses,* Hayden, 1955 (pap.)

Sands, Leo G., *ABC's of Radiotelephony,* Sams, 1962 (pap.)*

Slurzberg, M., and W. Osterheld, *Essentials of Radio Electronics,* McGraw-Hill, 2d ed., 1961

Stiltz, H. L., ed., *Aerospace Telemetry,* Prentice-Hall, 2 vol., 1961, 1966

Susskind, C., ed., *Encyclopedia of Electronics,* Reinhold, 1962

Talley, D., *Basic Carrier Telephony,* Rider, 1960 (pap.)

Upton, M., *Electronics for Everyone,* 2d ed., Devin-Adair, 1959 (N.A.L., pap.)*

Upton, Monroe, *Inside Electronics,* Devin-Adair, 1964 (N.A.L., pap.)*

Villchur, Edgar, *Reproduction of Sound,* Dover, 1966 (pap.)*

Zworykin, V. K., and others, *Television in Science and Industry,* Wiley, 1958*

CONSERVATION AND SANITARY ENGINEERING

Coyle, D. C., *Conservation: An American Story of Conflict and Accomplishment,* Rutgers, 1957*

Ehlers, Victor M., and E. W. Steel, *Municipal and Rural Sanitation,* 6th ed., McGraw-Hill, 1965

Hamm, Russell L., and L. G. Nason, *An Ecological Approach to Conservation,* Burgess, 1964*

Hardenbergh, W. A., and E. B. Rodie, *Water Supply and Waste Disposal,* International Textbook, 1961

Hays, S., *Conservation and the Gospel of Efficiency,* Harvard, 1959*

Nordell, E., *Water Treatment for Industrial and Other Uses,* 2d ed., Reinhold, 1961

Smith, G. H., *Conservation of Natural Resources,* 3d ed., Wiley, 1965

Stern, A. C., ed., *Air Pollution,* Academic Press, 2 vol., 1962

United States Soil Conservation Service, *Manual on Conservation of Soil and Water,* U. S. Government Printing Office, 1954

ELECTRICAL ENGINEERING

Carter, R. C., *Introduction to Electrical Circuit Analysis,* Holt, 1966 (also pap.)

Dunsheath, P., *A History of Electrical Engineering,* Pitman, 1962

Fitzgerald, A. E., and D. E. Higginbotham, *Electrical and Electronic Engineering Fundamentals,* McGraw-Hill, 1964

Gray, Alexander, and G. A. Wallace, *Principles and Practice of Electrical Engineering,* 8th ed., McGraw-Hill, 1962

Kerchner, R. M., and G. F. Corcoran, *Alternating Current Circuits,* 4th ed., Wiley, 1960

Kholodovskii, G. Y., *The Principles of Power Generation,* Pergamon, 1964

Oppenheimer, S. L., and J. P. Borchers, *Direct and Alternating Currents,* McGraw-Hill, 1963

Skrotzki, B. G. A., *Electric Transmission and Distribution,* McGraw-Hill, 1954

Vinal, G. W., *Storage Batteries,* 4th ed., Wiley, 1955

Walsh, J. B., and K. S. Miller, *Introductory Electric Circuits,* McGraw-Hill, 1960

ENGINEERING MATERIALS AND PROCESSES

Brady, G. S., *Materials Handbook,* 9th ed., McGraw-Hill, 1963

Brick, R. M., R. B. Gordon, and A. Phillips, *Structure and Properties of Alloys,* 3d ed., McGraw-Hill, 1965

Casey, J. P., *Pulp and Paper,* 2d ed., Wiley, 3 vol., 1960–61

Dean, Frederick E., *Steel,* Muller, 1960

Diamond, Freda, *Story of Glass,* Harcourt, 1953*

Golding, B., *Polymers and Resins; Their Chemistry and Chemical Engineering,* Van Nostrand, 1959

Greene, C. H., "Glass," *Sci. Amer.,* Jan. 1961

Guthrie, V. B., *Petroleum Products Handbook,* McGraw-Hill, 1960

Huntington, Whitney C., *Building Construction: Materials and Types of Construction,* 3d ed., Wiley, 1963

Lee, P. W., *Ceramics,* Reinhold, 1961

Miner, D. F., and J. B. Seastone, *Handbook of Engineering Materials,* Wiley, 1955

Morton, M., ed., *Introduction to Rubber Technology,* Reinhold, 1959

Nissan, A. H., ed., *Textile Engineering Processes,* Textile Book, 1959

Panshin, A. J., and others, *Forest Products,* 2d ed., McGraw-Hill, 1962

Payne, H. F., *Organic Coating Technology,* Wiley, 2 vol., 1961

Rusinoff, Samuel E., *Manufacturing Processes: Materials and Production,* 3d ed., American Technical Soc., 1962

Shand, E. B., *Glass Engineering Handbook,* 2nd ed., McGraw-Hill, 1958

Sharp, H. J., *Engineering Materials,* Elsevier, 1966

Simonds, H. R., *Concise Guide to Plastics,* 2nd ed., Reinhold, 1963

Skeist, I., ed., *Handbook of Adhesives,* Reinhold, 1962

Trinks, W., *Industrial Furnaces,* Wiley, vol. I, 5th ed., 1961; vol. II, 3d ed., 1955

ENGINEERING MECHANICS, STRENGTH OF MATERIALS, STRUCTURAL ANALYSIS

Biggs, John M., *Introduction to Structural Dynamics,* McGraw-Hill, 1964

Douglas, R. A., *Introduction to Solid Mechanics,* Wadsworth, 1963

Frederickson, Arnold G., *Principles and Applications of Rheology,* Prentice-Hall, 1964

Jessop, H. T., and F. C. Harris, *Photoelasticity: Principles and Methods,* Dover, 1949 (pap.)

Morgan, W., and D. T. Williams, *Structural Mechanics,* 2d ed., Pitman, 1963

Panlilio, Filadelfo, *Elementary Theory of Structural Strength,* Wiley, 1963
Parker, H., *Simplified Mechanics and Strength of Materials,* 2d ed., Wiley, 1961
Timoshenko, S., and D. H. Young, *Elements of Strength of Materials,* 4th ed., Van Nostrand, 1962
Timoshenko, S., and D. H. Young, *Theory of Structures,* 2d ed., McGraw-Hill, 1965

ENGINES AND ENGINEERING THERMODYNAMICS

Anderson, Edwin P., *Audel's Gas Engine Manual,* Audel, 1963
Carrier, W. H., and others, *Modern Air Conditioning, Heating and Ventilating,* 3d ed., Pitman, 1959
El-Saden, Munir, *Engineering Thermodynamics,* Van Nostrand, 1965
Emerick, Robert H., *Heating Handbook: A Manual of Standards, Codes and Methods,* McGraw-Hill, 1964
Gerard, Geoffrey, *The Book of Water Power,* Warne, 1963*
Kates, Edgar J., *Diesel and High-compression Gas Engines,* 2d ed., American Technical Soc., 1965
Laub, Julian M., *Air Conditioning and Heating Practice,* Holt, 1963
Morse, F. T., *Power Plant Engineering,* 3rd ed., Van Nostrand, 1953
Rogers, Tyler S., *Thermal Design of Buildings,* Wiley, 1964
Sandfort, John F., *Heat Engines,* Doubleday, 1962 (pap.)*
Severns, W. H., and others, *Steam, Air and Gas Power,* 5th ed., Wiley, 1954
Shepherd, D. G., *Introduction to the Gas Turbine,* 2d ed., Van Nostrand, 1960
Shields, C., *Boilers,* McGraw-Hill, 1961
Solberg, H. L., and others, *Thermal Engineering,* Wiley, 1960

FIREARMS

Amber, J. T., ed., *Gun Digest,* rev. annually, Gun Digest (also pap.)
Brodie, Bernard, and Fawn, *From Crossbow to H-Bomb,* Dell, 1962 (pap.)*
Smith, W. H. B., *Small Arms of the World; the Basic Manual of Military Small Arms,* 8th ed., Stackpole, 1966
Stephens, Phillip N., *Artillery Through the Ages,* Watts, 1965

FLUID MECHANICS AND HYDRAULICS

Bradshaw, P., *Experimental Fluid Mechanics,* Pergamon, 1964 (Macmillan, pap.)
Carlson, C. W., and B. W., *Water Fit to Use,* Day, 1966*
Crocker, S., *Piping Handbook,* 5th ed., McGraw-Hill
Davis, C. V., ed., *Handbook of Applied Hydraulics,* 2d ed., McGraw-Hill, 1952
Kristal, F., and F. A. Annett, *Pumps,* 2nd ed., McGraw-Hill, 1953
Morris, H. M., *Applied Hydraulics in Engineering,* Ronald, 1963
Pai, S., *Viscous Flow Theory,* Van Nostrand, 2 vol., 1956–1957
Robinson, J. Lister, *Basic Fluid Mechanics,* McGraw-Hill, 1963
Schlichting, H., *Boundary Layer Theory,* 4th ed., McGraw-Hill, 1960

MACHINERY AND TOOLS

American Society of Tool and Manufacturing Engineers, *Tool Engineers' Handbook,* 2d ed., McGraw-Hill, 1959
Dudley, Darle W., *Gear Handbook: the Design, Manufacture and Application of Gears,* McGraw-Hill, 1962
Habicht, Frank H., *Modern Machine Tools,* Van Nostrand, 1963
Hallett, Frederick H., *Machine Shop Theory and Practice,* St. Martin's, 1961*
Ham, C. W., and others, *Mechanics of Machinery,* 4th ed., McGraw-Hill, 1958
Oberg, Erik, and Franklin D. Jones, *Machinery's Handbook,* 17th ed., Industrial, 1964

MAPS

Bomford, Guy, *Geodesy,* 2d ed., Oxford, 1962
Greenhood, David, *Mapping,* rev. ed., Chicago, 1963 (also pap.)
Hallert, B., *Photogrammetry,* McGraw-Hill, 1960
Raisz, Erwin J., *Principles of Cartography,* McGraw-Hill, 1962
U. S. Dept. of the Army, *Map Reading,* U. S. Government Printing Office, 1956*

MECHANICAL ENGINEERING

Baumeister, T., ed., *Marks' Mechanical Engineers' Handbook,* 7th ed., McGraw-Hill
Burstall, Aubrey F., *A History of Mechanical Engineering,* M.I.T., 1965 (pap.)*
Naparstek, Marvin I., *Mechanical Engineering,* Macmillan, 1964
Shigley, Joseph E., *Mechanical Engineering Design,* McGraw-Hill, 1963

MOTOR VEHICLES

Crouse, W. H., *Automotive Mechanics,* 5th ed., McGraw-Hill Book Co., New York, 1965
Weinstein, William, *The Automobile Engine,* Chilton, 1961*
Yerkow, C., *Automobiles: How They Work,* Putnam, 1966*

NUCLEAR ENGINEERING

Dietz, David, *Atomic Science, Bombs and Power,* rev. ed., Collier, 1962 (pap.)*
Mann, Martin, *Peacetime Uses of Atomic Energy,* rev. ed., Viking, 1961 (pap.)*
Redman, Lister A., *Nuclear Energy,* Oxford, 1963*
Salmon, Alan, *The Nuclear Reactor,* Wiley, 1964
U. S. Atomic Energy Commission, *Reactor Handbook,* 2d ed., Wiley, 4 vol., 1960–1964
Weinstein, Roy, and others, *Nuclear Engineering Fundamentals,* McGraw-Hill, 1964

PHOTOGRAPHY

Boucher, Paul E., *Fundamentals of Photography,* 4th ed., Van Nostrand, 1963
Dunn, J. F., *Exposure Manual,* 2d ed., Wiley, 1959
Mees, C. E. K., and T. H. James, *The Theory of the Photographic Process,* 3d ed., Macmillan, 1966
Sauvenier, H., ed., *Scientific Photography,* Macmillan, 1962
Zim, H. S., and R. W. Burnett, *Photography,* Golden, 1964 (also pap.)

PRINTING

Cogoli, John E., *Photo-offset Fundamentals,* McKnight, 1960
Jackson, H. E., *Printing: a Practical Introduction to the Graphic Arts,* McGraw-Hill, 1957
Updike, D. B., *Printing Types: Their History, Forms and Use,* 3d ed., Harvard, 2 vol., 1951

RAILROADS AND SHIPS

Allen, C. J., *Modern Railways,* Macmillan, 1960*
Barnaby, K. C., *Basic Naval Architecture,* 5th ed., DeGraff, 1967
Hardy, A. C., and E. Tyrrell, *Shipbuilding: Background to a Great Industry,* Pitman, 1964
Hay, W. W., *Railroad Engineering,* Wiley, 1953
Landström, Björn, *The Ship: An Illustrated History,* Doubleday, 1961*
Lewis, E. V., R. O'Brien, and Life eds, *Ships,* Time, 1965*
Sampson, H., ed., *Jane's World Railways,* McGraw-Hill, 1966*

SOIL PHYSICS

Baver, L. D., *Soil Physics,* 3d ed., Wiley, 1956
Cook, James G., *Our Living Soil,* Dial, 1960*
Marshall, C. Edmund, *The Physical Chemistry and Mineralogy of Soils, vol. 1., Soil Materials,* Wiley, 1964

SPACE

Baar, J., and W. E. Howard, *Spacecraft and Missiles of the World,* Harcourt, 1966
Clarke, Arthur C., *Interplanetary Flight: An Introduction to Astronautics,* 2d ed., Harper, 1960*
Ehricke, K. A., *Space Flight,* 3 vol., Van Nostrand, vol. 1, *Environment and Celestial Mechanics,* 1960; vol. 2, *Dynamics,* 1962; vol. 3, *Operations,* in prep.
Emme, Eugene M., *A History of Space Flight,* Holt, 1965 (also pap.)*
Faget, M., *Manned Space Flight,* Holt, 1965 (also pap.)*
Feodosiev, V. I., and G. B. Siniarev, *Introduction to Rocket Technology,* Academic, 1959
Gatland, K. W., ed., *Spaceflight Today,* Aero, 1964*
Giannini, G., "Electrical Propulsion in Space," *Sci. Amer.,* Mar. 1961*
Hobbs, Marvin, *Fundamentals of Rockets, Missiles and Spacecraft,* 2d ed., Rider, 1962*
Jaffe, Leonard, *Communications in Space,* Holt, 1965 (also pap.)*
Koelle, H. H., ed., *Handbook of Astronautical Engineering,* McGraw-Hill, 1961
Ley, Willy, ed., *Harnessing Space,* Macmillan, 1963*
Ley, Willy, *Missiles, Moonprobes and Megaparsecs,* N.A.L., 1964 (pap.)
Ley, W., *Rockets, Missiles, and Space Travel,* rev. ed., Viking, 1961*
Massey, Harrie S., *Space Physics,* Cambridge, 1964 (also pap.)
Newell, Homer E., *Express to the Stars,* McGraw-Hill, 1961*
Newman, D., *Space Vehicle Electronics,* Van Nostrand, 1963
Turcotte, Donald L., *Space Propulsion,* Blaisdell, 1965 (pap.)
Van Allen, J. A., ed., *Scientific Uses of Earth Satellites,* 2d ed., Michigan, 1958

SPECIAL ACKNOWLEDGMENTS

The editors thank the many institutions and persons—too numerous to list here—who supplied photographs, prints, and other illustrative material for this work. For their patience in searching out material on particular topics, and for their courtesy in making it available, special gratitude is due the following: American Cancer Society; Photographic and Slide Libraries, American Museum of Natural History; Bausch & Lomb, Inc., Rochester; Bendix Radio; Bethlehem Steel Company; Brookhaven National Laboratory; The Burndy Library; California Institute of Technology Bookstore; The Chase Manhattan Bank; Peter David; Paul Desautels; Dorr-Oliver, Inc.; E. I. du Pont de Nemours, Co., Inc.; George Eastman House; General Biological Supply House; General Electric Research Laboratory; Simone Gossner, formerly of U. S. Naval Observatory; Institute of Aerospace Sciences; International Business Machines; Dr. Herbert Jaffe, The Rockefeller Institute; Jane and Russ Kinne; Arlene Longwell; The Metropolitan Museum of Art; Mt. Wilson and Palomar Observatories; National Academy of Sciences; National Aeronautics and Space Administration; National Audubon Society Photo and Film Department; National Bureau of Standards; New York Public Library Picture Collection; New York Zoological Society; Chas. Pfizer and Co.; Dr. Keith R. Porter, Harvard University—Biological Laboratories; Royal Canadian Air Force; Smithsonian Institution; U. S. Department of Agriculture, Photograph Section of Information; U. S. Geological Survey; Magazine and Book Branch, U. S. Navy Office of Information; U. S. Weather Bureau; Harold Wanless; Westinghouse Electric Corp.; Douglas P. Wilson; Yerkes Observatory.

Space was lacking in the body of the encyclopedia for full credit lines in all instances. Credit lines that were abbreviated are indicated below, followed by credits in complete form. Numbers of pages are cited only when necessary.

AAVSO—American Association of Variable Star Observers. **Alaska RR**—Steve McCutcheon/ Mac's Foto Service. **Amer. Mus. of Nat. Hist.**—American Museum of Natural History; *(plate 7)* Robert C. Murphy/American Museum of Natural History. **American Museum of Photography**—Ansco Historical Collection, American Museum of Photography. **Amer. Petroleum Inst.**—Standard Oil Co. of New Jersey, from archives of American Petroleum Institute. **A.T.&T.**—American Telephone and Telegraph Co. **Avco**—*(page 1)* Avco Corporation; *(page 19)* New Idea Division, Avco Corporation. **Ballistic Research Lab., Aberdeen**—Ballistic Research Labs., Aberdeen Proving Grounds. **Bausch and Lomb**—Bausch and Lomb, Inc., Rochester. **Bendix Corp.**—Bendix Radio Division, Bendix Corp. **Berenice Abbott**—Berenice Abbott for Physical Science Study Committee. **Bert S. Gittins**—from Bert S. Gittins, for the Farm Equipment Institute. **Best**—V. H. Best and N. B. Taylor, *The Human Body*, 4th ed., Henry Holt and Co., New York, 1956. **Bonner**—J. T. Bonner, *The Ideas of Biology*, Harper & Row, New York, 1962. **Braham**—R. B. Braham and H. R. Byers, *Journal of Meteorology* (1948), 5 (3): 71-86. **Buffalo Chamber of Commerce**—Textron's Bell Aerosystems Co., from Buffalo Chamber of Commerce. **Carlson**—A. J. Carlson and V. Johnson, *The Machinery of the Body*, 3rd ed., Univ. of Chicago Press, Chicago, 1948. **C. B. Bridges**—After Bridges, *Jour. Hered.*, 29:11, 1938. **Clay-Adams, Inc.**—Medichrome slide, Clay Adams, Inc. **Cox**—J. T. Bonner, *The Ideas of Biology*, Harper & Row, New York, 1962. **Cronquist**—A. Cronquist, *Introductory Botany*, Harper & Row, New York, 1961. **Densmore**—Densmore, *General Botany*, Ginn & Co., Boston. **Dover Publications**—Sadi Carnot, *Reflections on the Motive Power of Fire*, E. Mendoza, ed., reprinted through permission of Dover Publications, Inc. **Downes**—H. R. Downes, *The Chemistry of Living Cells*, 2nd ed., Harper & Row, New York, 1962. **Du Pont**—E. I. du Pont de Nemours & Co. **Eaton**—T. H. Eaton, *Comparative Anatomy of the Vertebrates*, 2nd ed., Harper & Row, New York, 1960. **Franklin Photo Agency**—Fogg/Franklin Photo. **Garrels**—R. M. Garrels, *A Textbook of Geology*, Harper & Row, New York, 1951. **General Biological Supply House**—General Biological Supply House, Inc., Chicago. **General Electric**—General Electric Research Laboratory. **Guyer**—M. F. Guyer, *Animal Biology*, 4th ed., Harper & Row, New York, 1948; *(page 1192 bot.)* Guyer from the Cambridge Natural History. **Haneda**—Haneda, Yokosuka Museum, Japan. **Harry C. Knode & Co.**—Jack Dutton Collection, courtesy Harry C. Knode & Co. **Harvard News Bureau** *(page 182)*—P. Donaldson, Croft Lab., Harvard. **Harvard Obs.**—Harvard College Observatory. **Hoover**—Adapted from W. H. Hoover, *Smithsonian Inst. Misc. Coll.*, 95 (21):11, 1937. **Hylander**—C. J. Hylander and O. B. Stanley, *College Botany*, Macmillan Co., New York, 1949. **IBM**—International Business Machines, Inc. **J. O.**

Almquist—J. O. Almquist, Pennsylvania State University. **Kenoyer**—L. A. Kenoyer and others, *General Biology*, Harper & Row, New York, 1953; *(pages 451 and 452 top)* Kenoyer, modified from Buchanan, *Elements of Biology*, Harper & Row. **L. and M. Milne**—Lorus and Margery Milne, Durham, N. H. **Larousse**—*Larousse Encyclopedia of Astronomy*, Prometheus Press, New York, 1959. **Lawrence Radiation Lab., Univ. of Calif.**—University of California, Lawrence Radiation Laboratory, Berkeley. **Lee**—A. E. Lee and O. T. Breland, *Laboratory Studies in Biology*, Harper & Row, New York, 1954. **Lehr et al.**—P. E. Lehr and others, *Weather*, Golden Press, New York, 1959. **Leonard Lee Rue/Monkmeyer**—Leonard Lee Rue III/Monkmeyer. **Lick**—Lick Observatory. **Lull**—R. S. Lull, *Organic Evolution*, rev. ed., Macmillan Co., New York, 1929. **Manter**—H. W. Manter and D. D. Miller, *Introduction to Zoology*, Harper & Row, New York, 1959. **Massey**—Courtesy of Professor Sir Harrie Massey, from *The New Age in Physics*, Harper & Row, New York, 1960. **Moment**—G. B. Moment, *General Zoology*, Houghton Mifflin Co., Cambridge, Mass., 1958. **Mt. Wilson**—Mount Wilson and Palomar Observatories. **NASA**—National Aeronautics and Space Administration. **Nat. Gallery of Art**—National Gallery of Art, Washington, D.C. /Rosenwald Collection. **National Park Service**—U. S. Department of the Interior, National Park Service; *(plate 3)* Yellowstone National Park, Wyoming/etc. **North American Aviation**—Rocketdyne, a Division of North American Aviation, Inc. **N. Y. Public Library**—*(page 541)* Graphic Color Plate Co., from the N. Y. Public Library Picture Collection; *(page 995)* L. H. Stracke, *Radium, a Magic Mineral*, Harper & Row, New York, 1941, from the N. Y. Public Library. **Oneida Ltd.**—Oneida Silversmiths. **Palmer**—R. S. Palmer, ed., *Handbook of North American Birds*, vol. I, Yale Univ. Press, New Haven, 1962. **Permutit Co.**—Permutit Water Conditioning, Inc. **Pettingill**—O. S. Pettingill, Jr., *A Laboratory and Field Manual of Ornithology*, Burgess Publ. Co., Minneapolis, 1956. **Pfizer**—Chas. Pfizer & Co., Inc. **Pratt & Whitney**—Pratt & Whitney Co., Inc., industrial component of Fairbanks Whitney Corp. **Project Stratoscope**—Project Stratoscope of Princeton University, sponsored by ONR, NSF, and NASA. **RIAS**—Research Institute of Advanced Study. **Rocketdyne**—Rocketdyne, division of North American Aviation, Inc. **Rock of Ages Corp.**—Rock of Ages Corp., Barre, Vt. **R. S. Longhurst**—R. S. Longhurst, *Geometrical and Physical Optics*, Longmans Green & Co., New York, 1957. **Russ Kinne & Met. Mus. of Art** *(plate 24)*—(7) gift of Admiral F. R. Harris, in memory of his wife, Dena Sperry Harris, 1946; *(8, 9, 11-16)* gifts of J. Pierpont Morgan, 1917; *(10)* gift of George Coe Graves, 1930, the Sylmaris Collection; *(18)* bequest of Laura Frances Hearn, 1917; *(19)* purchase 1942, Joseph Pulitzer bequest; *(7, 9-19)* by Russ Kinne. **Shepard**—F. Shepard, *The Earth Beneath the Sea*, Johns Hopkins Press, Baltimore, 1959. **Sikorsky**—Sikorsky from National Air Museum, Smithsonian Institution, U. S. Air Force Collection. **Smallwood**—Smallwood and others, *Elements of Biology*, rev. by Ruth A. Dodge, Allyn & Bacon, Boston, 1959. **Standard Oil**—Standard Oil Co. of New Jersey. **Storer**—T. I. Storer, *General Zoology*, 2nd ed.,

McGraw-Hill Book Co., New York, 1951. **Stow Mfg.**—Stow Manufacturing Co., Binghamton, N.Y. **Strüwe/Monkmeyer**—Carl Strüwe/Monkmeyer. **Texas Co.**—Texas Co., from archives of American Petroleum Institute. **N. Tinbergen**—J. T. Bonner, *The Ideas of Biology*, Harper & Row, New York, 1962. **Transeau**—E. N. Transeau and others, *Textbook of Botany*, rev. ed., Harper & Row, New York, 1953. **Trude Fleischmann**—Trude Fleischmann, New York. **Turner**—C. D. Turner, *General Endocrinology*, W. B. Saunders Co., Philadelphia, 1948. **TVA**—Tennessee Valley Authority. **United Press; UPI**—United Press International. **USAF**—U. S. Air Force. **U. S. Army**—*(page 459)* National Aeronautics and Space Administration; *(pages 880, 917, 1097)* Ballistic Research Labs., Aberdeen Proving Grounds. **USDA**—U. S. Department of Agriculture. **U.S.D.C.**—U. S. Department of Commerce, National Bureau of Standards. **U. S. Geological Survey**—*(pages 346-7)* G. K. Gilbert/U. S. Geological Survey; *(page 429)* Calkins/etc.; *(page 473)* W. B. Lang/ etc.; *(page 672)* I. C. Russell/etc.; *(page 679)* E. W. Shaw/etc.; *(page 869)* Balsley/etc.; *(page 1207)* R. E. Fellows/etc.; *(page 1214)* Fisher/etc.; *(page 1224)* W. H. Bradley/etc.; *(page 1239)* G. W. Stose/etc. **U. S. Navy** *(pages 99, 221, 290, 454, 493, 558, 922, 1072, 1171)*—U. S. Naval Observatory from S. D. Gossner. **Victoreen Inst. Co.**—The Victoreen Instrument Co., Cleveland, Ohio. **Villee**—C. A. Villee, *Biology*, 3rd ed., W. B. Saunders Co., Philadelphia, 1957; *(page 1166)* C. A. Villee, *Biology: The Human Approach*, W. B. Saunders Co., Philadelphia, 1950 (courtesy I. Schour) (Maximow and Bloom). **Villee after Jasper**—C. A. Villee, *Biology*, etc. (From Jasper; in *Epilepsy and Cerebral Localization*, by Penfield and Erickson). **Villee after Weatherwax**—C. A. Villee, *Biology*, etc., after Weatherwax, *Botany* (see below). **Waldeck from FLO** *(pages 175 and 539)*—Waldeck and James/Frances L. Orkin. **Weatherwax**—P. Weatherwax, *Botany*, 3rd ed., W. B. Saunders Co., Philadelphia, 1956. **Westinghouse**—Westinghouse Electric Corporation. **Whaley**—W. G. Whaley and others, *Principles of Biology*, 2nd ed., Harper & Row, New York, 1958. **Wilson Hole/Mt. Wilson**—Mount Wilson and Palomar Observatories, copyright 1958, California Institute of Technology. **Wolcott**—R. H. Wolcott, *Animal Biology*, McGraw-Hill Book Co., New York, 1946. **Wood**—J. H. Wood and C. W. Keenan, *General College Chemistry*, Harper & Row, New York, 1961. **Yale University**—Yale University News Bureau. **Young; Young after Neumayr; Young and Stebbins**—C. W. Young and G. L. Stebbins, *The Human Organism and the World of Life*, rev. ed., Harper & Row, New York, 1951. **Zeiss Ikon**—Carl Zeiss, 444 Fifth Ave., New York. **Zworykin**—*(page 1173)* V. K. Zworykin, "The Inconoscope: A Modern Version of the Electric Eye," *Proc. IRE*, vol. 22, pp. 16-22, 1934; *(page 1174)* V. K. Zworykin and G. A. Morton, *Television*, 2nd ed., John Wiley & Sons, New York, 1954.

Acknowledgment is due also for the following illustrations, which carry no credit line: *Page 173*, New York Public Library. *Page 361*, Burndy Library. *Page 394 (bot.)*, Berenice Abbott. *Plate 73*, Dr. Roman Vishniac.

INDEX

ALL ARTICLES appearing in the body of the encyclopedia are listed in this index with their exact titles or close equivalents. Thousands of additional specific topics also are listed. All entries have been phrased in the form in which they are most likely to be sought, and the many multiple listings increase the reader's chance of finding his information on the first try. Where space permits, the information to which an index entry refers is suggested (if desirable) by means of parentheses or subentries.

Each article title or its equivalent, when given as a main index entry, is identified by means of a boldface page number. Such a number signifies "main coverage." Lightface page numbers indicate where further information is to be found. Asterisks designate pages on which relevant illustrations appear. "Pl." indicates a color plate, and "*f*" indicates the page following which the color plate will be found.

The listing of all substantial items as separate main entries has made it unnecessary for the reader to look under broad topics for specific items (*e.g.* under "Rodent" for "mouse"). The specific item should generally be looked for as a separate main entry; this entry will be found to carry all the necessary page citations.

The policy of providing separate main entries for all substantial items has made it possible to keep subentries to a minimum. Generally, subentries are limited to items covered on pages not indicated with the main entry. When following up a subentry, the reader should consult not only the page cited with the subentry but also pages cited with the main entry.

Cross-referencing has been limited to what is really necessary and practicable. All cross references are to other index listings, not to the body of the encyclopedia. Cross references in the index are amply supplemented by those in the text.